D1510651

CONGRESSIONAL QUARTERLY

ALMANAC

VOL. XLVI

1990

CONGRESSIONAL QUARTERLY

ALMANAC

101st CONGRESS
2nd SESSION 1990

VOLUME XLVI

Congressional Quarterly Inc.

1414 22nd St. N.W.
Washington, D.C. 20037

1990 ALMANAC

Congressional Quarterly Inc.

Congressional Quarterly Inc. is a publishing and information services company and a recognized leader in political journalism. For almost half a century, CQ has served clients in the fields of news, education, business and government with timely, complete, unbiased and accurate information on Congress, politics and national issues.

At the heart of CQ is its acclaimed publication, the Weekly Report, a weekly magazine offering news and analyses on Congress and legislation. The CQ Researcher (formerly Editorial Research Reports), with its focus on current issues, provides weekly balanced summaries on topics of widespread interest.

Congressional Quarterly Inc. publishes the Congressional Monitor, a daily report on Congress and current and future activities of congressional committees, and several newsletters, including Congressional Insight, a weekly analysis of congressional action, and Campaign Practices Reports, a semimonthly update on campaign laws.

Congressional Quarterly Inc. also publishes a variety of books including political science textbooks under the CQ Press imprint and public affairs paperbacks to keep journalists, scholars and the public abreast of developing issues and events. CQ Books publishes highly regarded information directories and reference books on the federal government, national elections and politics, including the Guide to the Presidency, the Guide to Congress, the Guide to the U.S. Supreme Court, the Guide to U.S. Elections, Politics in America, the Federal Regulatory Directory and Washington Information Directory. The CQ Almanac, a compendium of legislation for one session of Congress, is published each year. Congress and the Nation, a record of government for a presidential term, is published every four years.

Washington Alert, Congressional Quarterly's online congressional and regulatory tracking service, provides immediate access to both proprietary and public databases of legislative action, votes, schedules, profiles and analyses.

Printed in the United States of America

Library of Congress Catalog Number 47-41081
ISBN: 0-87187-655-8 ISSN: 0095-6007

"By providing a link between the local newspaper and Capitol Hill we hope Congressional Quarterly can help to make public opinion the only effective pressure group in the country. Since many citizens other than editors are also interested in Congress, we hope that they too will find Congressional Quarterly an aid to a better understanding of their government.

"Congressional Quarterly presents the facts in as complete, concise and unbiased form as we know how. The editorial comment on the acts and votes of Congress, we leave to our subscribers."

Foreword, Congressional Quarterly, Vol. I, 1945
Henrietta Poynter, 1901-1968
Nelson Poynter, 1903-1978

How To Use This Book

The Congressional Quarterly Almanac chronicles the course of major legislation during each session of Congress. Drawing on the reporting and writing done throughout the year by the staffs of the Congressional Quarterly Weekly Report and the Congressional Monitor, the Almanac distills, reorganizes and cross-indexes the full year in Congress and politics for permanent reference.

Here is a description of the major elements of the volume:

Table of Contents. The **Summary Table of Contents** *(p. vii)* lists the names of chapters and appendixes. The detailed **Table of Contents** *(p. viii)* is a complete listing of stories by chapter. A detailed Table of Contents for each chapter also appears on the title page at the beginning of each chapter.

Errata. Corrections of errors noted in previous volumes appear on page vi.

Members List. A list of the members of the 101st Congress as of adjournment appears on pages xiv-xv. A list of the members elected to the 102nd Congress appears in Chapter 13 — Political Report *(Senate, p. 912; House, pp. 920-21).*

LEGISLATIVE CHAPTERS

Session Overview. The opening chapter, "The 101st Congress," presents an overview of what Congress did and did not do during the second session. It also includes statistical information on the session, such as the length of the session, number of bills introduced, number of laws enacted and presidential vetoes. In addition, the chapter contains four special CQ vote studies: Presidential Support, Party Unity, Conservative Coalition and Voting Participation.

Supreme Court. A final section of the opening chapter gives an overview of the Supreme Court's term as its decisions affected Congress. An accompanying box lists some of the court's major decisions of the term; stories on individual rulings that had a particular impact on issues being considered in Congress appear in the appropriate legislative chapter.

Legislative Chapters. Stories on individual bills outline the background of the legislation and trace the course of the bill from initial committee consideration through any floor debate and any conference or other final action. For major legislative measures, a Boxscore at the beginning of the story highlights the major legislative action and cites the committee reports for further reference. For some major legislative measures, a detailed listing of final provisions appears separately along with the main story for greater accessibility and readability.

Stories within each chapter are grouped by common subject matter.

Appropriations. Stories on appropriations bills include individual charts showing overall amounts by agency and program from the president's budget request and the House, Senate and final versions of the measure.

Political Report. This chapter provides overviews of the 1990 Senate, House and gubernatorial elections along with official final results in those races. Charts show the members elected to the 102nd Congress and the occupants of statehouses. Special CQ analyses also examine political trends suggested by the results.

APPENDIXES

Public Laws. This appendix contains a complete listing of public laws enacted during the session in the order they were signed by the president.

Voting Studies. CQ's Key Votes record members' voting on issues selected by CQ editors as the most controversial or important during the past session. This appendix also contains 1990 ratings of members of Congress by four interest groups: Americans for Democratic Action, the AFL-CIO, the U.S. Chamber of Commerce and the American Conservative Union.

Four CQ voting studies that previously appeared in the appendix — Presidential Support, Party Unity, Conservative Coalition and Voting Participation — now appear in the opening chapter.

The Legislative Process. This appendix provides an overview of the legislative process along with a diagram, "How a Bill Becomes Law," depicting the typical course of a bill through the legislative process.

Glossary. The Glossary provides definitions of 150 parliamentary terms important to understanding legislative procedure in Congress.

Roll Call Charts. This appendix contains a complete set of roll call vote charts for the House and Senate during the session.

Indexes. The **General Index** *(p. 3-I)* indexes the Almanac's contents by name and subject matter. The **Roll Call Vote Index** *(p. 58-I)* helps locate votes on a particular topic, and the **Bill Number Index** *(p. 62-I)* indexes floor votes by the number of the measure being acted on.

Errata

1976 Almanac, p. 519, Indian Claims Commission, 5th paragraph: Both chambers' versions of the bill authorized $1.65 million (not $1.65 billion) for the commission in fiscal 1977.

1980 Almanac, p. 525, Sen. Talmadge, 2nd paragraph: Talmadge was defeated in his bid for re-election.

1984 Almanac, p. 287, Cable deregulation, 1st paragraph under Provisions: The cited popular name for the law is the Cable Telecommunications Policy Act.

1986 Almanac, p. 589, Banking legislation, col. 2, 2nd paragraph: The correct number for the administration's bill on the Federal Savings and Loan Insurance Corporation (FSLIC) was HR 4907 (not HR 4709).

1989 Almanac, General Index, "Regulation and deregulation: federal regulatory agencies, 1989 (chart)": The chart appears on p. 332 (not p. 322).

SUMMARY TABLE OF CONTENTS

Chapter 1 — 101st Congress ... 3
Chapter 2 — Inside Congress ... 59
Chapter 3 — Economic Policy ... 111
Chapter 4 — Environment & Energy ... 229
Chapter 5 — Commerce ... 323
Chapter 6 — General Government ... 405
Chapter 7 — Law & Judiciary ... 447
Chapter 8 — Health & Human Services/Education ... 547
Chapter 9 — Housing & Community Development ... 631
Chapter 10 — Defense ... 671
Chapter 11 — Foreign Policy ... 717
Chapter 12 — Appropriations ... 811
Chapter 13 — Political Report ... 901

Appendixes
- Public Laws ... 3-A
- Voting Studies ... 3-B
- Congress and Its Members ... 3-C
- Roll Call Votes
  - House ... 2-H
  - Senate ... 2-S
- Indexes
  - General Index ... 3-I
  - Roll Call Vote Index ... 58-I
  - Bill Number Index ... 62-I

TABLE OF CONTENTS

Chapter 1 — 101st Congress

Second Session Highlights ... 3
- The Second Session at a Glance ... 4
- Congress' Approval Rating ... 5
- Public Laws ... 6
- Senate Cloture Votes in 1990 ... 7

Capitol Bombing Case ... 7
Leadership ... 8
- 101st Congress Leaders ... 9
- Chairmanship Changes ... 11
- Sergeant-at-Arms ... 12

Term Limitations ... 13
Membership Changes ... 14
The President and Congress ... 16
- Vetoes Cast by President Bush ... 17
- State of the Union Address ... 18
- Pocket-Veto Limitation Measures ... 21

CQ Voting Studies ... 22
- Presidential Support ... 22
- Party Unity ... 32
- Conservative Coalition ... 40
- Voting Participation ... 48

Supreme Court ... 52
- Major Court Decisions, 1989-90 ... 53
- Legislative Intent ... 55

Chapter 2 — Inside Congress

Campaign Financing ... 59
- Corporate Spending Limitations ... 61
- House/Senate Bills ... 64
- State Reform Efforts ... 67
- Broadcasting Rates ... 68

'Motor Voter' Registration ... 71
Pay, Honoraria ... 73
- Federal Workers' Honoraria Ban ... 74

Franking Privilege ... 75
Keating Five Ethics Hearings ... 78
- Key Players ... 79
- Special Counsel Bennett ... 81
- Overview of Case ... 83
- The 'Appearance Standard' ... 87
- Senators' Statements ... 89

Sen. D'Amato Case Pending ... 97
Sen. Durenberger Denounced ... 98
- 20th-Century Cases ... 99
- Terms of Opprobrium ... 100

Rep. Frank Reprimanded ... 103
Rep. Gingrich Case Dismissed ... 104
Rep. Savage Inquiry Concluded ... 105
Rep. Lukens Resigns ... 106
Rep. Flake Charges Dropped ... 106
Rep. Ford Case Ends in Mistrial ... 107
Ex-Rep. Garcia's Conviction Upset ... 107
Del. Fauntroy Case Dropped ... 107
No Action on Rep. Stangeland ... 107
Rep. Dyson Case Dismissed ... 108
Rep. Sikorski Case Dismissed ... 108

Chapter 3 — Economic Policy

Fiscal 1991 Budget ... 111
- Deficit-Reduction Plan ... 112
- Chronology ... 114

Bush's Budget ... 116
- Economic Report ... 116
- Budget Authority, Outlays by Agency ... 118
- Economic Assumptions ... 119
- Budget by Function ... 120
- Major Provisions ... 122

Budget Resolution I ... 127
Budget Summit ... 129
- Summit Participants ... 130
- Bush Statement on Taxes ... 131
- Bush Address to Congress ... 133
- Bush Television Address ... 135

Budget Resolution II ... 136
- Veto of Continuing Resolution ... 137

Reconciliation Bill ... 138
- House Reconciliation Instructions ... 138
- Senate Reconciliation Instructions ... 139
- Spending Allocations ... 140
- Reconciliation Provisions ... 141
- Debt Limit Extension ... 165
- Bush Signing Statement ... 166

New Taxes ... 167
- Capital Gains Tax Cut ... 168
- Social Security Tax ... 170
- Major Tax Provisions ... 171

New Budget Process 173
- Balanced-Budget Amendment 174
- Discretionary Spending Caps 176
- Key Dates 177
- Credit Reforms 178

Thrift Bailout Bill 179
- Ryan Confirmed as Thrift Regulator 180
- Bank Fraud Penalties 182

Deposit Insurance Premiums 184
Money-Laundering Bills 187
Foreign Banks Bill 189
SEC Market Control Authority 190
- Market Reform Provisions 191
- SEC Enforcement Bills 193
- Stock-Index Futures 194

Coin Redesign 196
Export Administration Act 198
- Veto Message 200

Defense Production Act 202
Trade With Former East Bloc 204
- Czechoslovak President's Visit 204
- U.S.-Soviet Trade Accord 205
- European Development Bank 206

U.S.-Japan Trade 208
GATT Talks 209
Caribbean Trade Bill 211
- Customs and Trade Act Provisions 212

Latin America Aid 217
Mexico Trade Pact 218
Textile Quota Bill 219
- Veto Message 221

Foreign Investments 222

Chapter 4 — Environment & Energy

Clean Air Act Amendments 229
- Clean Air Deadlines 231
- Motor Vehicles 233
- Urban Smog 235
- Acid Rain 237
- Alternative Fuels 240
- Clean Air Provisions 248
- Assistance for Displaced Workers 277

Fuel Economy Standards 279
Octane-Labeling Bill 282
Oil Spill Liability 283
- Environmental Crimes 285

Pipeline Inspection 286
Coastal Zone Management 288
Coastal, Great Lakes Cleanup 289
Beach Pollution Bill 290
EPA Cabinet Status 291
- EPA Investigators 292
- Office of Environmental Education 293

Tongass National Forest 294
Timber, Northern Spotted Owl 296
Water Resources Act 297
- New Projects 299

Grand Canyon Erosion Control 300
Great Lakes Cleanup 301
Barrier Islands Protection 302
Florida Keys Protection 303
Zebra Mussels Control Program 303
Arizona Wilderness Protection 304
Antarctica Mining Ban 305
Global Warming 307
Waste Laws Compliance 308
Stello Energy Nomination 309
Uranium Enrichment Spinoff 310
NRC Operating Costs 311
Energy Issues in 1990 312
- Energy-Related Tax Proposals 313

Strategic Petroleum Reserve 314
Arctic National Wildlife Refuge 315
Oil-Shale Lands Bill 316
Alternative Power 317
Hydrogen Fuel Research Program 318
Energy Conservation, Efficiency 319

Chapter 5 — Commerce

1990 Farm Bill 323
- Great Lakes Ports 338
- Farm Bill Provisions 342
- Rural Development Aid 352
- Food Stamp Program 354

Nutrition-Monitoring Bill 355
Screwworm Bill 355
Irrigation Subsidies 356
Low-Cost Timber Sales 358
Pesticide-Residue Regulation 358
Mandated Family Leave Bill 359
- Veto Message 361

Age Protection Bill 362
Whistleblower Bill 364
Job-Training Bill 365
- Displaced Homemakers Bill 366

Pension Reversions 367
Pension Benefit Guaranty Corporation 368
Unemployment Benefits 368
Eastern Airlines Strike Veto 369
Martin Named to Labor Department 369
Cable Reregulation 370
FCC Authorization 372
Ads During Children's TV 373

Chapter 5 — Commerce (continued)

TV Violence ... 374
Closed-Captioning Bill ... 375
Radio Frequencies Shift ... 376
Business Curbs on 'Baby Bells' ... 377
Operator Services Rates ... 378
'Junk Fax' Curbs ... 379
FCC Minority Preference Policies ... 379
Transporting Hazardous Materials ... 380
'Backhauling' Limits ... 382
Aviation Package ... 384
Coast Guard Fees ... 386
Airline Leveraged Buyouts ... 388
Aviation Security Bills ... 389
Airline Rights Bill ... 389
Amtrak Reauthorization ... 390
Veto Message ... 391
Amtrak Waste Disposal ... 392
Consumer Product Safety Commission ... 393
Fastener Standards ... 395
SBA Bill ... 395
Fish Inspection Bill ... 396
'Dolphin-Safe' Tuna Labeling ... 399
Product Liability ... 400
Insurance Antitrust Bill ... 401
Hotel Fire Safety ... 402
'Fire-Safe' Cigarettes ... 402
Telemarketing Fraud ... 402

Chapter 6 — General Government

Federal Workers' Pay Overhaul ... 405
Lump-Sum Retirement Benefits ... 406
Hatch Act Revisions ... 408
Veto Message ... 410
Paperwork Reduction Act ... 411
OMB's Review Powers Curbed ... 412
Regulatory Negotiation Guidelines ... 413
Pacts on Fund Transfers ... 414
Census Undercount Claimed ... 415
Federal Financial Centralization ... 416
Deceptive Mailings ... 417
Anti-Pornographic Mail Bill ... 417
Child-Proof Packaging ... 417
Veterans Affairs ... 418
Federal Indian Policy ... 421
Bush Indian Preference Act Veto ... 423
Puerto Rico's Status ... 424
D.C. Mayor, 'Shadow' Delegation ... 428
Aid to D.C. Metro Rail ... 429
Acid-Free Paper ... 429
National Endowment for the Arts ... 430
NASA ... 434
Space Station Design Overhaul ... 436
Space Patent Law ... 437
Superconducting Super Collider ... 438
Technology Programs ... 440
Animal Rights Protests ... 441
Earthquake Research and Preparedness Act ... 442
Mining Research ... 442

Chapter 7 — Law & Judiciary

Americans With Disabilities Act ... 447
ADA Provisions ... 452
Civil Rights Bill ... 462
Civil Rights Division Head ... 465
Veto Message ... 472
Immigration Act of 1990 ... 474
AIDS Exclusion Policy ... 480
Immigration Act Provisions ... 482
Crime Control Act of 1990 ... 486
Death Row Appeals ... 488
Crime Act: Major Provisions ... 499
Gun Control ... 500
Antidrug Measures ... 502
Martinez Named to 'Drug Czar' Post ... 503
Juvenile Justice Agency Head ... 506
'Hate Crime' Statistics ... 506
Biological Weapons Ban ... 507
Violence Against Women ... 507
Souter Supreme Court Confirmation ... 508
Bush Nomination Announcement ... 509
Brennan's Judicial Legacy ... 510
Souter's Statement at Hearings ... 512
Bush's Nominations to U.S. Courts ... 515
Imprints on the Bench ... 517
Thomas Confirmed to D.C. Circuit ... 518
New Judgeships ... 520
Judicial Improvements Act of 1990 ... 522
Administrative Law Judges Corps ... 523
Flag Protection Amendment ... 524
Abortion Issue in 1990 ... 528
Legal Services Corporation ... 531
North's Iran-Contra Convictions Set Aside ... 534
RICO Limitations ... 536
Vertical Price-Fixing ... 539
Antitrust Penalties Raised ... 540
Copyright Bills ... 541
Disaster Litigation ... 543

Chapter 8 — Health & Human Services/Education

Child-Care Assistance ... 547
Head Start Expansion ... 552
WIC Program Emergency Funding ... 554
Children's Aid Bill ... 556
Social Security Earnings Test ... 557
Community Service Bill ... 559
Medicare Costs ... 563
 Medicare Mammogram Coverage ... 564
 'Living Will' Rights ... 566
Medicaid Help for Poor Children ... 569
 Prescription Drug Discounts ... 570
 Reimbursement Rates ... 571
Regulation of Medigap Plans ... 572
Nutrition Labeling ... 575
Orphan Drug Bill ... 577
 Veto Message ... 578
Medical Devices Regulation ... 579
FDA Automation, Consolidation ... 581
AIDS Assistance ... 582
 AIDS Resources Act Provisions ... 584
Disabilities Prevention ... 589
Nursing Home Regulations ... 589
Radiation Victims' Compensation ... 590
Childhood Vaccine Programs ... 591
Antismoking Bills ... 592
TB Prevention Program ... 594
National Health Service Corps ... 595
Health Programs for Minorities ... 596
Organ and Bone Marrow Programs ... 596
Emergency Services, Trauma Care ... 597
Injuries Research Grants ... 598
Elderly, Alzheimer's Programs ... 598
Mental Health Projects ... 599
National Institutes of Health ... 600
 NIH Director ... 602
Family Planning Program ... 604
Cancer-Screening Grants ... 606
Pepper Commission Report ... 607
Health Planning Grants ... 609
Developmental Disabilities ... 609
Educational Excellence Act ... 610
 Math, Science Education ... 612
Alexander Named to Education Department ... 614
Compensatory Education ... 615
Education for Disabled ... 616
Library Programs ... 617
Student Religious Groups Ruling ... 618
Dropout Prevention Program ... 618
Vocational Education Aid ... 619
 Vocational Education Act Provisions ... 620
EEOC Probe of University Tenure ... 623
Student 'Right-to-Know' Act ... 624
Student Loan Defaults ... 626
Taft Institute Funding ... 628

Chapter 9 — Housing & Community Development

National Affordable Housing Act ... 631
 Housing Act Provisions ... 644
FHA Insurance Fund ... 657
Housing Benefit Plans ... 659
Mortgage 'Prepayment' Compromise ... 661
Homeless Assistance Act ... 665
HUD Scandal Investigation ... 666

Chapter 10 — Defense

National Defense Authorization Act ... 671
 Cheney Defense Programs ... 673
 Pentagon Pay Deadlock ... 676
 Staten Island Home Port ... 681
 Defense Act Provisions ... 684
B-2 'Stealth' Bomber ... 687
Strategic Defense Initiative ... 691
Base Closings Commission ... 693
National Guard Ruling ... 694
Reserves Call-Up for Persian Gulf Crisis ... 695
Conventional Forces in Europe Treaty ... 696
 CFE Limits ... 697
Strategic Arms Reduction Treaty ... 704
 Bush-Gorbachev Statement on START ... 708
U.S.-Soviet Chemical Weapons ... 709
Nuclear Testing Limits Treaties ... 711

Chapter 11 — Foreign Policy

Persian Gulf Crisis ... 717
 Map of Mideast Region ... 718
 Chronology ... 719
 Map of Kuwait ... 725
Operation Desert Shield ... 726
 Bush Aug. 8 Address ... 726
 Bush Aug. 28 Briefing ... 729
 Bush Address to Congress ... 731
 U.S. Arms Sales to Allies ... 734
The Offensive Option ... 737
 U.N. Resolution 678 ... 737
 War Powers Suit ... 739

Chapter 11 — Foreign Policy (continued)

Choice of Allies Questioned ... 740
Bush News Conference ... 741
Rationales, Objectives ... 744
Operation Desert Storm ... 747
Bush Letter to Congress ... 747
Use of Force Resolution ... 748
Senate Vote on Use of Force ... 749
House Vote on Use of Force ... 750
Congressional Debate ... 752
Bush Jan. 16 Address ... 754
U.S.-Soviet Relations ... 757
Moscow Embassy ... 760
German Unification ... 762
U.S.-China Relations ... 764
Chinese Students Veto Sustained ... 767
Pakistan Aid ... 768
U.S.-Nicaragua Relations ... 770
Credit-Taking for Chamorro's Win ... 772
Panama Aid ... 774
El Salvador Aid ... 779
U.S. South Africa Policy ... 787
Kenya Aid ... 790
Zaire Aid ... 790
Intelligence Bill ... 791
Veto Message ... 798
State Department Authorization ... 799
State Department Nominations ... 801
United Nations Funding ... 802
Food for Peace Program ... 803
Andean Initiative Drug Strategy ... 805
Torture Treaty Ratification ... 806
'Armenian Genocide' Resolution ... 807
Palau 'Compact of Free Association' ... 808

Chapter 12 — Appropriations

Fiscal 1991 Appropriations ... 811
Fiscal 1991 Spending ... 811
Defense ... 812
Defense Appropriations ... 813
Funding for Major Weapons ... 815
Major Provisions ... 824
Military Construction ... 826
Military Construction Appropriations ... 828
Foreign Aid ... 830
Foreign Aid Appropriations ... 832
U.N. Family Planning Agency ... 838
Fiscal 1990 Supplemental ... 844
Labor/HHS/Education ... 847
Labor/HHS/Education Appropriations ... 848
VA/HUD/Independent Agencies ... 854
VA/HUD Appropriations ... 855
The Archenemy of Pork ... 857
Energy, Water ... 861
Energy/Water Appropriations ... 862
Agriculture ... 867
Agriculture Appropriations ... 869
Interior ... 870
Interior Appropriations ... 873
Transportation ... 876
Transportation Appropriations ... 879
Commerce/Justice/State ... 881
Commerce/Justice/State Appropriations ... 882
Treasury/Postal Service ... 886
Treasury/Postal Service Appropriations ... 887
District of Columbia ... 891
D.C. Appropriations ... 892
Legislative Branch ... 894
Legislative Branch Appropriations ... 895
Continuing Resolutions ... 896

Chapter 13 — Political Report

1990 Elections Overview ... 901
Voter Turnout ... 901
Personal Characteristics, New Members, 101st Congress ... 902
Incumbents' Performance ... 903
Incumbent Re-Election Rates, 1946-90 ... 903
Incumbents' Falloff ... 904
Close Calls in House ... 905
Personal Lows ... 906
1990 Vote Totals by Party ... 907
Congressional Election Spending ... 908
Yeutter Selected To Head RNC ... 909
Senate Races ... 911
Senate Membership — 102nd Congress ... 912
Senate Membership Changes ... 913
Seymour Appointed To Succeed Wilson ... 913
Years of Expiration of Senate Terms ... 914
House Races ... 916
House Members Defeated ... 917
House Membership Changes ... 918
Party Gains and Losses ... 919
House Membership — 102nd Congress ... 920
Independent Bernard Sanders ... 922
Characteristics of 102nd Congress ... 923
Minorities in Congress ... 924
Occupations, Religion ... 925
Gubernatorial Races ... 926

1991 Statehouse Occupants 927
Reapportionment and Redistricting 930
Key Redistricting States 931
Patronage Ruling 933
1990 Special Elections 934
1990 Election Results 935

Appendixes

Public Laws 3-A

Voting Studies

CQ Key Votes 3-B
Interest Group Ratings 22-B

Congress and Its Members

Legislative Process in Brief 3-C
How a Bill Becomes Law 4-C
Glossary 7-C

Roll Call Votes

House 2-H
Senate 2-S

Indexes

General Index 3-I
Roll Call Votes Index 58-I
Bill Number Index 62-I

Members of the 101st Congress, Second Session . . .

As of Oct. 28, 1990

Representatives

D 258; R 175

(2 Vacancies†)

A

Ackerman, Gary L., D-N.Y. (7)
Alexander, Bill, D-Ark. (1)
Anderson, Glenn M., D-Calif. (32)
Andrews, Michael A., D-Texas (25)
Annunzio, Frank, D-Ill. (11)
Anthony, Beryl Jr., D-Ark. (4)
Applegate, Doug, D-Ohio (18)
Archer, Bill, R-Texas (7)
Armey, Dick, R-Texas (26)
Aspin, Les, D-Wis. (1)
Atkins, Chester G., D-Mass. (5)
AuCoin, Les, D-Ore. (1)

B

Baker, Richard H., R-La. (6)
Ballenger, Cass, R-N.C. (10)
Barnard, Doug Jr., D-Ga. (10)
Bartlett, Steve, R-Texas (3)
Barton, Joe L., R-Texas (6)
Bateman, Herbert H., R-Va. (1)
Bates, Jim, D-Calif. (44)
Beilenson, Anthony C., D-Calif. (23)
Bennett, Charles E., D-Fla. (3)
Bentley, Helen Delich, R-Md. (2)
Bereuter, Doug, R-Neb. (1)
Berman, Howard L., D-Calif. (26)
Bevill, Tom, D-Ala. (4)
Bilbray, James, D-Nev. (1)
Bilirakis, Michael, R-Fla. (9)
Bliley, Thomas J. Jr., R-Va. (3)
Boehlert, Sherwood, R-N.Y. (25)
Boggs, Lindy (Mrs. Hale), D-La. (2)
Bonior, David E., D-Mich. (12)
Borski, Robert A., D-Pa. (3)
Bosco, Douglas H., D-Calif. (1)
Boucher, Rick, D-Va. (9)
Boxer, Barbara, D-Calif. (6)
Brennan, Joseph E., D-Maine (1)
Brooks, Jack, D-Texas (9)
Broomfield, William S., R-Mich. (18)
Browder, Glen, D-Ala. (3)
Brown, George E. Jr., D-Calif. (36)
Brown, Hank, R-Colo. (4)
Bruce, Terry L., D-Ill. (19)
Bryant, John, D-Texas (5)
Buechner, Jack, R-Mo. (2)
Bunning, Jim, R-Ky. (4)
Burton, Dan, R-Ind. (6)
Bustamante, Albert G., D-Texas (23)
Byron, Beverly B., D-Md. (6)

C

Callahan, Sonny, R-Ala. (1)
Campbell, Ben Nighthorse, D-Colo. (3)
Campbell, Tom, R-Calif. (12)
Cardin, Benjamin L., D-Md. (3)
Carper, Thomas R., D-Del. (AL)
Carr, Bob, D-Mich. (6)
Chandler, Rod, R-Wash. (8)
Chapman, Jim, D-Texas (1)
Clarke, James McClure, D-N.C. (11)
Clay, William L., D-Mo. (1)
Clement, Bob, D-Tenn (5)
Clinger, William F. Jr., R-Pa. (23)
Coble, Howard, R-N.C. (6)
Coleman, E. Thomas, R-Mo. (6)
Coleman, Ronald D., D-Texas (16)
Collins, Cardiss, D-Ill. (7)
Combest, Larry, R-Texas (19)
Condit, Gary, D-Calif (15)
Conte, Silvio O., R-Mass. (1)
Conyers, John Jr., D-Mich. (1)
Cooper, Jim, D-Tenn. (4)
Costello, Jerry F. D-Ill. (21)
Coughlin, Lawrence, R-Pa. (13)
Courter, Jim, R-N.J. (12)
Cox, C. Christopher, R-Calif. (40)
Coyne, William J., D-Pa. (14)
Craig, Larry E., R-Idaho (1)
Crane, Philip M., R-Ill. (12)
Crockett, George W. Jr., D-Mich. (13)

D

Dannemeyer, William E., R-Calif. (39)
Darden, George "Buddy," D-Ga. (7)
Davis, Robert W., R-Mich. (11)
DeFazio, Peter A., D-Ore. (4)
de la Garza, E. "Kika," D-Texas (15)
DeLay, Tom, R-Texas (22)
Dellums, Ronald V., D-Calif. (8)
Derrick, Butler, D-S.C. (3)
DeWine, Mike, R-Ohio (7)
Dickinson, Bill, R-Ala. (2)
Dicks, Norm, D-Wash. (6)
Dingell, John D., D-Mich. (16)
Dixon, Julian C., D-Calif. (28)
Donnelly, Brian, D-Mass. (11)
Dorgan, Byron L., D-N.D. (AL)
Dornan, Robert K., R-Calif. (38)
Douglas, Chuck, R-N.H. (2)
Downey, Thomas J., D-N.Y. (2)
Dreier, David, R-Calif. (33)
Duncan, John J. "Jimmy" Jr., R-Tenn. (2)
Durbin, Richard J., D-Ill. (20)
Dwyer, Bernard J., D-N.J. (6)
Dymally, Mervyn M., D-Calif. (31)
Dyson, Roy, D-Md. (1)

E

Early, Joseph D., D-Mass. (3)
Eckart, Dennis E., D-Ohio (11)
Edwards, Don, D-Calif. (10)
Edwards, Mickey, R-Okla. (5)
Emerson, Bill, R-Mo. (8)
Engel, Eliot L., D-N.Y. (19)
English, Glenn, D-Okla. (6)
Erdreich, Ben, D-Ala. (6)
Espy, Mike, D-Miss. (2)
Evans, Lane, D-Ill. (17)

F

Fascell, Dante B., D-Fla. (19)
Fawell, Harris W., R-Ill. (13)
Fazio, Vic, D-Calif. (4)
Feighan, Edward F., D-Ohio (19)
Fields, Jack, R-Texas (8)
Fish, Hamilton Jr., R-N.Y. (21)
Flake, Floyd H., D-N.Y. (6)
Flippo, Ronnie G., D-Ala. (5)
Foglietta, Thomas M., D-Pa. (1)
Foley, Thomas S., D-Wash. (5)
Ford, Harold E., D-Tenn. (9)
Ford, William D., D-Mich. (15)
Frank, Barney, D-Mass. (4)
Frenzel, Bill, R-Minn. (3)
Frost, Martin, D-Texas (24)

G

Gallegly, Elton, R-Calif. (21)
Gallo, Dean A., R-N.J. (11)
Gaydos, Joseph M., D-Pa. (20)
Gejdenson, Sam, D-Conn. (2)
Gekas, George W., R-Pa. (17)
Gephardt, Richard A., D-Mo. (3)
Geren, Pete, D-Texas (12)
Gibbons, Sam M., D-Fla. (7)
Gillmor, Paul E., R-Ohio (5)
Gilman, Benjamin A., R-N.Y. (22)
Gingrich, Newt, R-Ga. (6)
Glickman, Dan, D-Kan. (4)
Gonzalez, Henry B., D-Texas (20)
Goodling, Bill, R-Pa. (19)
Gordon, Bart, D-Tenn. (6)
Goss, Porter J., R-Fla. (13)
Gradison, Bill, R-Ohio (2)
Grandy, Fred, R-Iowa (6)
Grant, Bill, R-Fla. (2)
Gray, William H. III, D-Pa. (2)
Green, Bill, R-N.Y. (15)
Guarini, Frank J., D-N.J. (14)
Gunderson, Steve, R-Wis. (3)

H

Hall, Ralph M., D-Texas (4)
Hall, Tony P., D-Ohio (3)
Hamilton, Lee H., D-Ind. (9)
Hammerschmidt, John Paul, R-Ark. (3)
Hancock, Mel, R-Mo. (7)
Hansen, James V., R-Utah (1)
Harris, Claude, D-Ala. (7)
Hastert, Dennis, R-Ill. (14)
Hatcher, Charles, D-Ga. (2)
Hawkins, Augustus F., D-Calif. (29)
Hayes, Charles A., D-Ill. (1)
Hayes, Jimmy, D-La. (7)
Hefley, Joel, R-Colo. (5)
Hefner, W. G. "Bill," D-N.C. (8)
Henry, Paul B., R-Mich. (5)
Herger, Wally, R-Calif. (2)
Hertel, Dennis M., D-Mich. (14)
Hiler, John, R-Ind. (3)
Hoagland, Peter, D-Neb. (2)
Hochbrueckner, George J., D-N.Y. (1)
Holloway, Clyde C., R-La. (8)
Hopkins, Larry J., R-Ky. (6)
Horton, Frank, R-N.Y. (29)
Houghton, Amo, R-N.Y. (34)
Hoyer, Steny H., D-Md. (5)
Hubbard, Carroll Jr., D-Ky. (1)
Huckaby, Jerry, D-La. (5)
Hughes, William J., D-N.J. (2)
Hunter, Duncan, R-Calif. (45)
Hutto, Earl, D-Fla. (1)
Hyde, Henry J., R-Ill. (6)

I, J

Inhofe, James M., R-Okla. (1)
Ireland, Andy, R-Fla. (10)
Jacobs, Andrew Jr., D-Ind. (10)
James, Craig T., R-Fla. (4)
Jenkins, Ed, D-Ga. (9)
Johnson, Nancy L., R-Conn. (6)
Johnson, Tim, D-S.D. (AL)
Johnston, Harry A., D-Fla., (14)
Jones, Ben, D-Ga. (4)
Jones, Walter B., D-N.C. (1)
Jontz, Jim, D-Ind. (5)

K

Kanjorski, Paul E., D-Pa. (11)
Kaptur, Marcy, D-Ohio (9)
Kasich, John R., R-Ohio (12)
Kastenmeier, Robert W., D-Wis. (2)
Kennedy, Joseph P. II, D-Mass. (8)
Kennelly, Barbara B., D-Conn. (1)
Kildee, Dale E., D-Mich. (7)
Kleczka, Gerald D., D-Wis. (4)
Kolbe, Jim, R-Ariz. (5)
Kolter, Joe, D-Pa. (4)
Kostmayer, Peter H., D-Pa. (8)
Kyl, Jon, R-Ariz. (4)

L

LaFalce, John J., D-N.Y. (32)
Lagomarsino, Robert J., R-Calif. (19)
Lancaster, H. Martin, D-N.C. (3)
Lantos, Tom, D-Calif. (11)
Laughlin, Greg, D-Texas (14)
Leach, Jim, R-Iowa (1)
Leath, Marvin, D-Texas (11)
Lehman, Richard H., D-Calif. (18)
Lehman, William, D-Fla. (17)
Lent, Norman F., R-N.Y. (4)
Levin, Sander M., D-Mich. (17)
Levine, Mel, D-Calif. (27)
Lewis, Jerry, R-Calif. (35)
Lewis, John, D-Ga. (5)
Lewis, Tom, R-Fla. (12)
Lightfoot, Jim Ross, R-Iowa (5)
Lipinski, William O., D-Ill. (5)
Livingston, Bob, R-La. (1)
Lloyd, Marilyn, D-Tenn. (3)
Long, Jill, D-Ind. (4)
Lowery, Bill, R-Calif. (41)
Lowey, Nita M., D-N.Y. (20)
Luken, Thomas A., D-Ohio (1)

M

Machtley, Ronald K., R-R.I. (1)
Madigan, Edward, R-Ill. (15)
Manton, Thomas J., D-N.Y. (9)
Markey, Edward J., D-Mass. (7)
Marlenee, Ron, R-Mont. (2)
Martin, David O'B., R-N.Y. (26)
Martin, Lynn, R-Ill. (16)
Martinez, Matthew G., D-Calif. (30)
Matsui, Robert T., D-Calif. (3)
Mavroules, Nicholas, D-Mass. (6)
Mazzoli, Romano L., D-Ky. (3)
McCandless, Al, R-Calif. (37)
McCloskey, Frank, D-Ind. (8)
McCollum, Bill, R-Fla. (5)
McCrery, Jim, R-La. (4)
McCurdy, Dave, D-Okla. (4)
McDade, Joseph M., R-Pa. (10)
McDermott, Jim, D-Wash. (7)
McEwen, Bob, R-Ohio (6)
McGrath, Raymond J., R-N.Y. (5)
McHugh, Matthew F., D-N.Y. (28)
McMillan, Alex, R-N.C. (9)
McMillen, Tom, D-Md. (4)
McNulty, Michael R., D-N.Y. (23)
Meyers, Jan, R-Kan. (3)
Mfume, Kweisi, D-Md. (7)
Michel, Robert H., R-Ill. (18)
Miller, Clarence E., R-Ohio (10)
Miller, George, D-Calif. (7)
Miller, John, R-Wash. (1)
Mineta, Norman Y., D-Calif. (13)
Mink, Patsy T., D-Hawaii (2)
Moakley, Joe, D-Mass. (9)
Molinari, Susan, R-N.Y. (14)
Mollohan, Alan B., D-W.Va. (1)
Montgomery, G. V. "Sonny," D-Miss. (3)
Moody, Jim, D-Wis. (5)
Moorhead, Carlos J., R-Calif. (22)
Morella, Constance A., R-Md. (8)
Morrison, Bruce A., D-Conn. (3)
Morrison, Sid, R-Wash. (4)
Mrazek, Robert J., D-N.Y. (3)
Murphy, Austin J., D-Pa. (22)
Murtha, John P., D-Pa. (12)
Myers, John T., R-Ind. (7)

N

Nagle, Dave, D-Iowa (3)
Natcher, William H., D-Ky. (2)
Neal, Richard E., D-Mass. (2)
Neal, Stephen L., D-N.C. (5)
Nelson, Bill, D-Fla. (11)
Nielson, Howard C., R-Utah (3)
Nowak, Henry J., D-N.Y. (33)

O

Oakar, Mary Rose, D-Ohio (20)
Oberstar, James L., D-Minn. (8)
Obey, David R., D-Wis. (7)
Olin, Jim, D-Va. (6)
Ortiz, Solomon P., D-Texas (27)
Owens, Major R., D-N.Y. (12)
Owens, Wayne, D-Utah (2)
Oxley, Michael G., R-Ohio (4)

P

Packard, Ron, R-Calif. (43)
Pallone, Frank Jr., D-N.J. (3)
Panetta, Leon E., D-Calif. (16)
Parker, Mike, D-Miss. (4)
Parris, Stan, R-Va. (8)
Pashayan, Charles "Chip" Jr., R-Calif. (17)
Patterson, Liz J., D-S.C. (4)
Paxon, Bill, R-N.Y. (31)
Payne, Donald M., D-N.J. (10)
Payne, Lewis F. Jr., D-Va. (5)
Pease, Don J., D-Ohio (13)
Pelosi, Nancy, D-Calif. (5)
Penny, Timothy J., D-Minn. (1)
Perkins, Carl C., D-Ky. (7)
Petri, Thomas E., R-Wis. (6)
Pickett, Owen B., D-Va. (2)
Pickle, J. J. "Jake", D-Texas (10)
Porter, John, R-Ill. (10)
Poshard, Glenn, D-Ill. (22)
Price, David E., D-N.C. (4)
Pursell, Carl D., R-Mich. (2)

Q, R

Quillen, James H., R-Tenn. (1)
Rahall, Nick J. II, D-W.Va. (4)
Rangel, Charles B., D-N.Y. (16)
Ravenel, Arthur Jr., R-S.C. (1)
Ray, Richard, D-Ga. (3)
Regula, Ralph, R-Ohio (16)
Rhodes, John J. III, R-Ariz. (1)
Richardson, Bill, D-N.M. (3)
Ridge, Tom, R-Pa. (21)
Rinaldo, Matthew J., R-N.J. (7)
Ritter, Don, R-Pa. (15)
Roberts, Pat, R-Kan. (1)
Robinson, Tommy F., R-Ark. (2)
Roe, Robert A., D-N.J. (8)

. . . Governors, Supreme Court, Cabinet-Rank Officers

Rogers, Harold, R-Ky. (5)
Rohrabacher, Dana, R-Calif. (42)
Ros-Lehtinen, Ileana, R-Fla. (18)
Rose, Charlie, D-N.C. (7)
Rostenkowski, Dan, D-Ill. (8)
Roth, Toby, R-Wis. (8)
Roukema, Marge, R-N.J. (5)
Rowland, J. Roy, D-Ga. (8)
Rowland, John G., R-Conn. (5)
Roybal, Edward R., D-Calif. (25)
Russo, Marty, D-Ill. (3)

S

Sabo, Martin Olav, D-Minn. (5)
Saiki, Patricia, R-Hawaii (1)
Sangmeister, George E., D-Ill. (4)
Sarpalius, Bill, D-Texas (13)
Savage, Gus, D-Ill. (2)
Sawyer, Thomas C., D-Ohio (14)
Saxton, H. James, R-N.J. (13)
Schaefer, Dan, R-Colo. (6)
Scheuer, James H., D-N.Y. (8)
Schiff, Steven H., R-N.M. (1)
Schneider, Claudine, R-R.I. (2)
Schroeder, Patricia, D-Colo. (1)
Schuette, Bill, R-Mich. (10)
Schulze, Richard T., R-Pa. (5)
Schumer, Charles E., D-N.Y. (10)
Sensenbrenner, F. James Jr., R-Wis. (9)
Serrano, Jose E., D-N.Y. (18)
Sharp, Philip R., D-Ind. (2)
Shaw, E. Clay Jr., R-Fla. (15)
Shays, Christopher, R-Conn. (4)
Shumway, Norman D., R-Calif. (14)
Shuster, Bud, R-Pa. (9)
Sikorski, Gerry, D-Minn. (6)
Sisisky, Norman, D-Va. (4)
Skaggs, David E., D-Colo. (2)
Skeen, Joe, R-N.M. (2)
Skelton, Ike, D-Mo. (4)
Slattery, Jim, D-Kan. (2)
Slaughter, D. French Jr., R-Va. (7)
Slaughter, Louise M., D-N.Y. (30)
Smith, Bob, R-Ore. (2)
Smith, Christopher H., R-N.J. (4)
Smith, Denny, R-Ore. (5)
Smith, Lamar, R-Texas (21)
Smith, Lawrence J., D-Fla. (16)
Smith, Neal, D-Iowa (4)
Smith, Peter, R-Vt. (AL)
Smith, Robert C., R-N.H. (1)††
Smith, Virginia, R-Neb. (3)
Snowe, Olympia J., R-Maine (2)
Solarz, Stephen J., D-N.Y. (13)
Solomon, Gerald B. H., R-N.Y. (24)
Spence, Floyd D., R-S.C. (2)
Spratt, John M. Jr., D-S.C. (5)
Staggers, Harley O. Jr., D-W.Va. (2)
Stallings, Richard, D-Idaho (2)
Stangeland, Arlan, R-Minn. (7)
Stark, Pete, D-Calif. (9)
Stearns, Cliff, R-Fla. (6)
Stenholm, Charles W., D-Texas (17)
Stokes, Louis, D-Ohio (21)
Studds, Gerry E., D-Mass. (10)
Stump, Bob, R-Ariz. (3)
Sundquist, Don, R-Tenn. (7)
Swift, Al, D-Wash. (2)
Synar, Mike, D-Okla. (2)

T

Tallon, Robin, D-S.C. (6)
Tanner, John, D-Tenn. (8)
Tauke, Tom, R-Iowa (2)
Tauzin, W. J. "Billy," D-La. (3)
Taylor, Gene, D-Miss. (5)
Thomas, Bill, R-Calif. (20)
Thomas, Craig, R-Wyo. (AL)
Thomas, Lindsay, D-Ga. (1)
Torres, Esteban E., D-Calif. (34)
Torricelli, Robert G., D-N.J. (9)
Towns, Ed, D-N.Y. (11)
Traficant, James A. Jr., D-Ohio (17)
Traxler, Bob, D-Mich. (8)

U, V

Udall, Morris K., D-Ariz. (2)
Unsoeld, Jolene, D-Wash. (3)
Upton, Fred, R-Mich. (4)
Valentine, Tim, D-N.C. (2)
Vander Jagt, Guy, R-Mich. (9)
Vento, Bruce F., D-Minn. (4)
Visclosky, Peter J., D-Ind. (1)
Volkmer, Harold L., D-Mo. (9)
Vucanovich, Barbara F., R-Nev. (2)

W

Walgren, Doug, D-Pa. (18)
Walker, Robert S., R-Pa. (16)
Walsh, James T., R-N.Y. (27)
Washington, Craig, D-Texas (18)
Watkins, Wes, D-Okla (3)
Waxman, Henry A., D-Calif. (24)
Weber, Vin, R-Minn. (2)
Weiss, Ted, D-N.Y. (17)
Weldon, Curt, R-Pa. (7)
Wheat, Alan, D-Mo. (5)
Whittaker, Bob, R-Kan. (5)
Whitten, Jamie L., D-Miss. (1)
Williams, Pat, D-Mont. (1)
Wilson, Charles, D-Texas (2)
Wise, Bob, D-W.Va. (3)
Wolf, Frank R., R-Va. (10)
Wolpe, Howard, D-Mich. (3)
Wyden, Ron, D-Ore. (3)
Wylie, Chalmers P., R-Ohio (15)

X, Y, Z

Yates, Sidney R., D-Ill. (9)
Yatron, Gus, D-Pa. (6)
Young, C. W. Bill, R-Fla. (8)
Young, Don, R-Alaska (AL)

Delegates

Blaz, Ben, R-Guam
de Lugo, Ron, D-Virgin Islands
Faleomavaega, Eni F.H., D-Am. Samoa
Fauntroy, Walter E., D-D.C.

Resident Commissioner

Fuster, Jaime B., Pop. Dem.-Puerto Rico

Senators

D 55; R 45

Adams, Brock, D-Wash.
Akaka, Daniel K., D-Hawaii
Armstrong, William L., R-Colo.
Baucus, Max, D-Mont.
Bentsen, Lloyd, D-Texas
Biden, Joseph R. Jr., D-Del.
Bingaman, Jeff, D-N.M.
Bond, Christopher S., R-Mo.
Boren, David L., D-Okla.
Boschwitz, Rudy, R-Minn.
Bradley, Bill, D-N.J.
Breaux, John B., D-La.
Bryan, Richard H., D-Nev.
Bumpers, Dale, D-Ark.
Burdick, Quentin N., D-N.D.
Burns, Conrad, R-Mont.
Byrd, Robert C., D-W.Va.
Chafee, John H., R-R.I.
Coats, Daniel R., R-Ind.
Cochran, Thad, R-Miss.
Cohen, William S., R-Maine
Conrad, Kent, D-N.D.
Cranston, Alan, D-Calif.
D'Amato, Alfonse M., R-N.Y.
Danforth, John C., R-Mo.
Daschle, Tom, D-S.D.
DeConcini, Dennis, D-Ariz.
Dixon, Alan J., D-Ill.
Dodd, Christopher J., D-Conn.
Dole, Bob, R-Kan.
Domenici, Pete V., R-N.M.
Durenberger, Dave, R-Minn.
Exon, Jim, D-Neb.
Ford, Wendell H., D-Ky.
Fowler, Wyche Jr., D-Ga.
Garn, Jake, R-Utah
Glenn, John, D-Ohio
Gore, Al, D-Tenn.
Gorton, Slade, R-Wash.
Graham, Bob, D-Fla.
Gramm, Phil, R-Texas
Grassley, Charles E., R-Iowa
Harkin, Tom, D-Iowa
Hatch, Orrin G., R-Utah
Hatfield, Mark O., R-Ore.
Heflin, Howell, D-Ala.
Heinz, John, R-Pa.
Helms, Jesse, R-N.C.
Hollings, Ernest F., D-S.C.
Humphrey, Gordon J., R-N.H.*
Inouye, Daniel K., D-Hawaii
Jeffords, James M., R-Vt.
Johnston, J. Bennett, D-La.
Kassebaum, Nancy Landon, R-Kan.
Kasten, Bob, R-Wis.
Kennedy, Edward M., D-Mass.
Kerrey, Bob, D-Neb.
Kerry, John, D-Mass.
Kohl, Herb, D-Wis.
Lautenberg, Frank R., D-N.J.
Leahy, Patrick J., D-Vt.
Levin, Carl, D-Mich.
Lieberman, Joseph I., D-Conn.
Lott, Trent, R-Miss.
Lugar, Richard G., R-Ind.
Mack, Connie, R-Fla.
McCain, John, R-Ariz.
McClure, James A., R-Idaho
McConnell, Mitch, R-Ky.
Metzenbaum, Howard M., D-Ohio
Mikulski, Barbara A., D-Md.
Mitchell, George J., D-Maine
Moynihan, Daniel Patrick, D-N.Y.
Murkowski, Frank H., R-Alaska
Nickles, Don, R-Okla.
Nunn, Sam, D-Ga.
Packwood, Bob, R-Ore.
Pell, Claiborne, D-R.I.
Pressler, Larry, R-S.D.
Pryor, David, D-Ark.
Reid, Harry, D-Nev.
Riegle, Donald W. Jr., D-Mich.
Robb, Charles S., D-Va.
Rockefeller, John D. IV, D-W.Va.
Roth, William V. Jr., R-Del.
Rudman, Warren B., R-N.H.
Sanford, Terry, D-N.C.
Sarbanes, Paul S., D-Md.
Sasser, Jim, D-Tenn.
Shelby, Richard C., D-Ala.
Simon, Paul, D-Ill.
Simpson, Alan K., R-Wyo.
Specter, Arlen, R-Pa.
Stevens, Ted, R-Alaska
Symms, Steve, R-Idaho
Thurmond, Strom, R-S.C.
Wallop, Malcolm, R-Wyo.
Warner, John W., R-Va.
Wilson, Pete, R-Calif.
Wirth, Tim, D-Colo.

Governors

D 28; R 22

Ala.—Guy Hunt, R
Alaska—Steve Cowper, D
Ariz.—Rose Mofford, D
Ark.—Bill Clinton, D
Calif.—George Deukmejian, R
Colo.—Roy Romer, D
Conn.—William A. O'Neill, D
Del.—Michael N. Castle, R
Fla.—Bob Martinez, R
Ga.—Joe Frank Harris, D
Hawaii—John Waihee III, D
Idaho—Cecil D. Andrus, D
Ill.—James R. Thompson, R
Ind.—Evan Bayh, D
Iowa—Terry E. Branstad, R
Kan.—Mike Hayden, R
Ky.—Wallace G. Wilkinson, D
La.—Buddy Roemer, D
Maine—John R. McKernan Jr., R
Md.—William Donald Schaefer, D
Mass.—Michael S. Dukakis, D
Mich.—James J. Blanchard, D
Minn.—Rudy Perpich, D
Miss.—Ray Mabus, D
Mo.—John Ashcroft, R
Mont.—Stan Stephens, R
Neb.—Kay A. Orr, R
Nev.—Bob Miller, D
N.H.—Judd Gregg, R
N.J.—James J. Florio, R
N.M.—Garrey Carruthers, R
N.Y.—Mario M. Cuomo, D
N.C.—James G. Martin, R
N.D.—George Sinner, D
Ohio—Richard F. Celeste, D
Okla.—Henry Bellmon, R
Ore.—Neil Goldschmidt, D
Pa.—Robert P. Casey, D
R.I.—Edward D. DiPrete, R
S.C.—Carroll A. Campbell Jr., R
S.D.—George S. Mickelson, R
Tenn.—Ned McWherter, D
Texas—William P. Clements Jr., R
Utah—Norman H. Bangerter, R
Vt.—Madeleine M. Kunin, D
Va.—L. Douglas Wilder, D
Wash.—Booth Gardner, D
W.Va.—Gaston Caperton, D
Wis.—Tommy G. Thompson, R
Wyo.—Mike Sullivan, D

Supreme Court

Rehnquist, William H.—Va., Chief Justice
Blackmun, Harry A.—Minn.
Kennedy, Anthony M. Calif.
Marshall, Thurgood—N.Y.
O'Connor, Sandra Day—Ariz.
Scalia, Antonin—Va.
Souter, David H.—N.H.★
Stevens, John Paul—Ill.
White, Byron R.—Colo.

Cabinet

Baker, James A. III—State
Brady, Nicholas F.—Treasury
Cavazos, Lauro F.—Education★★
Cheney, Dick—Defense
Derwinski, Edward J.—Veterans Affairs
Dole, Elizabeth H.—Labor‡
Kemp, Jack F.—HUD
Lujan, Manuel Jr.—Interior
Mosbacher, Robert A.—Commerce
Skinner, Samuel K.—Transportation
Sullivan, Louis W.—HHS
Thornburgh, Dick—Attorney General
Watkins, James D.—Energy
Yeutter, Clayton—Agriculture

Executive Branch Officers

Quayle, Dan—Vice President
Bennett, William J.—Director, Drug Policy‡‡
Darman, Richard G.—OMB Director
Hills, Carla A.—U.S. Trade Representative
Sununu, John H.—Chief of Staff

---

† James J. Florio, D-N.J., was elected governor of New Jersey on Nov. 7, 1989. He resigned his seat Jan. 16, 1990. Donald E. "Buz" Lukens, R-Ohio, resigned Oct. 24.

†† Robert C. Smith was sworn in to the Senate on Dec. 7 after winning election for a six-year term Nov. 6. He succeeded Gordon J. Humphrey, who did not seek reelection. Humphrey resigned Dec. 4 to assume a seat in the New Hampshire state Senate.

★ David H. Souter was sworn in Oct. 9; he succeeded William J. Brennan Jr., who retired July 20.

★★ Lauro F. Cavazos resigned effective Dec. 15; on Dec. 17, President Bush announced his intention to nominate Lamar Alexander to the post.

‡ Elizabeth H. Dole resigned effective Nov. 23; on Dec. 17, President Bush announced his intention to nominate Lynn Martin to the post.

‡‡ William J. Bennett resigned effective Nov. 31; on Nov. 30, President Bush announced his intention to nominate Bob Martinez to the post.

Chapter 1

101st CONGRESS

Second Session Highlights 3
- The Second Session at a Glance 4
- Congress' Approval Rating 5
- Public Laws 6
- Senate Cloture Votes in 1990 7

Capitol Bombing Case 7
Leadership 8
- 101st Congress Leaders 9
- Chairmanship Changes 11
- Sergeant-at-Arms 12

Term Limitations 13
Membership Changes 14
The President and Congress 16
- Vetoes Cast by President Bush 17
- State of the Union Address 18
- Pocket-Veto Limitation Measures 21

CQ Voting Studies 22
- Presidential Support 22
- Party Unity 32
- Conservative Coalition 40
- Voting Participation 48

Supreme Court 52
- Major Court Decisions, 1989-90 53
- Legislative Intent 55

Achievements Obscured by Criticism

Members survived late campaign, unfinished agenda

Exhausted from a year of partisan battles, public recriminations and a final month of marathon floor sessions, the 101st Congress adjourned at 1:17 a.m. EST on Oct. 28, giving lawmakers just nine days to campaign in a midterm election widely seen as a test of voters' anti-incumbent sentiment.

Congress managed to grind out an impressive stack of laws in its final month, including a $495 billion budget deficit-reduction plan, a massive overhaul of the Clean Air Act, a child-care assistance plan and broad revisions of federal housing and farm programs.

Those achievements were overshadowed in the minds of many people, however, by Congress' unfinished agenda — notably, campaign financing legislation — and by the yearlong drone of ethics inquiries, partisan caviling and congressional irresolution.

"We are the laughingstock of the nation," said Rep. Silvio O. Conte, R-Mass., as the Congress was struggling to adjourn for good. When members finished their work on Oct. 28, it was 23 days past the scheduled adjournment. Not since 1942, when it did not take an official recess, was Congress in session as close to an election as it was in 1990.

To some members, staying in Washington was preferable to facing the wrath of the disgruntled voters in their districts. Public opinion polls in late October registered Congress' popular approval rating at 23 percent — the lowest figure since 1979. *(Chart, p. 5)*

Despite signs of discontent, only 15 House members were defeated in the November elections — the fourth-straight election that House incumbents had a 95 percent-plus re-election rate. That high rate suggested to some that the anti-incumbent mood may have been exaggerated.

Closer scrutiny of the election statistics, however, showed that the average vote for House incumbents with major-party opposition in 1990 dropped noticeably. Such incumbents averaged 63.5 percent — nearly 5 percentage points below the incumbent average in 1986 and 1988, and barely 2 points above the incumbent average in the volatile Watergate election of 1974.

More than two-thirds of the House incumbents who had major-party competition in both 1988 and 1990 saw their vote percentage fall in 1990. And roughly 50 House incumbents suffered a decline of at least 10 percentage points from their showing in 1988. Altogether, about 85 House incumbents were re-elected with less than 60 percent of the vote, roughly twice the number in that category in 1988.

New Dynamics

U.S. policy, and Congress, hardly seemed to keep up with the kaleidoscopic changes in world affairs in 1990: Nelson Mandela of the African National Congress was released from prison in South Africa; the Sandinistas were voted out of office in Nicaragua; the two Germanys were reunified; and Soviet President Mikhail S. Gorbachev won the Nobel Peace Prize.

Iraq's invasion of Kuwait on Aug. 2 provoked a huge deployment of U.S. troops in the region, threatened the economy with higher energy prices and unsettled debate over defense policy in the post-Cold War era.

Immediately after Iraq's invasion of Kuwait, both chambers passed resolutions supporting President Bush's decision to send U.S. troops to the Persian Gulf. Congress also approved, and the president signed, a $1.9 billion supplemental appropriation to pay for the deployment in fiscal 1990.

Backing for Operation Desert Shield remained strong, but lawmakers aimed increasingly sharp and skeptical questions at the administration concerning its ultimate goals in the gulf. The White House and many Democrats also were at odds over whether the administration was required to seek advance congressional approval for a military strike against Iraq.

Despite such suggestions, the 101st Congress never formally debated U.S. policies in the gulf and refused to hold a special session after the November elections. Members opted to take up the issue when the 102nd Congress convened.

While both chambers had been scheduled to recess in 1991 from Jan. 5 to Jan. 23, leaders announced by the end of 1990 that members would remain in Washington during that period because of the situation in the gulf. Congressional leaders did not specify when debate would begin or what form it would take, until just before it started.

A sharply divided Congress voted Jan. 12 to authorize the president to go to war against Iraq if it did not end its occupation of Kuwait. The vote came just three days before the expiration of a U.N. deadline, after which member nations could "use all necessary means" to force Iraq to withdraw from Kuwait. The joint resolution authorized the president "to use United States Armed Forces" to enforce the ultimatum set by the U.N. Security Council in its Resolution 678.

Budget Fiasco

It was the ugly and public battle over the budget, though, that transformed domestic political dynamics.

The year began with Bush riding high in public approval after commanding a quick military victory in Panama. Democrats did not know whether to deal with Bush or defy him.

In April, it looked like an old-fashioned brand of leadership was coming back in style when Bush asked a handful of congressional leaders to join him in a budget summit to craft a bipartisan solution to the burgeoning deficit. But Congress' rejection of their product Oct. 5 was a vivid reminder that the days when major decisions could easily be made in such close quarters were long gone.

"Eight men met in secret for several weeks to prepare this budget," Rep. Dan Glickman, D-Kan., said of the summit agreement. "That is not the democratic way to do business."

In the end, the public seemed to be asking the most damaging question about Congress as a whole: Was it incompetent? Public fury in 1989 over the ethical behavior of former Speaker Jim Wright, D-Texas, for example, paled in comparison with the blast that arose from the government's handling of the savings and loan crisis.

That was matched by the ridicule heaped on the government during the year-end fiscal fracas that featured the humiliating defeat of the leadership-backed budget and a three-day shutdown of the government. It ended with the White House and Congress haggling over relatively small differences that had been imbued with enormous political importance.

The congressional year ended with an acknowledged recession, Bush undercut by defections within his own party and Democrats flexing their muscles.

Exuberant Democrats reveled in their newfound tactical advantage, but their credibility waned with that of the rest of the government.

WHAT CONGRESS DID

Defenders of the 101st Congress pointed to many of the major legislative programs and packages that emerged from the session. Issues and challenges that had confronted lawmakers for years were resolved — at least temporarily and satisfactorily for most involved parties.

Following are some of the major legislative measures passed during 1990, the second session of the 101st Congress:

- **Budget package.** A clearly exhausted Congress cleared the budget-reconciliation bill during its final session before adjournment. The bill achieved $28 billion in deficit reduction in fiscal 1991 and $236 billion over five years through tax increases, user fees and savings in entitlements and other mandatory programs. It also included significant changes in the Gramm-Rudman deficit-reduction process.
- **Clean air.** After three months of agonizing conference negotiations, conferees ratified the first rewrite of clean air legislation in 13 years. The bill set up an ambitious program to reduce smog and toxic emissions from industry, including pollutants that caused acid rain, to clean up motor vehicles and fuels and to phase out chemicals, particularly chlorofluorocarbons, that harmed the Earth's protective ozone layer.
- **Farm programs.** After a year of wrangling, Congress passed legislation reauthorizing most farm and nutrition programs until 1995. The centerpiece of the new program was a plan to reduce by 15 percent the amount of cropland eligible for government income-support payments. Price- and income-support levels were also frozen at their existing levels. The budget-reconciliation bill reduced subsidy levels and made cuts of $13.6 billion in farm programs.
- **Housing programs.** After lengthy negotiations with the Bush administration, Congress cleared the first major overhaul of federal housing programs since 1974. Convinced that the Reagan administration had cut the federal commitment to housing too deeply, Congress moved to increase the nation's stock of affordable housing and to help public housing tenants become homeowners.
- **Child care.** As part of the deficit-reduction bill, Congress approved $18.3 billion in tax credits and $4.25 billion for new grant programs over five years to help low- and moderate-income families cope with the costs of child care and to help states improve the quality and availability of such care. In the end, the White House backed off its threats to veto any major new grant program that kept child-care measures from becoming law in 1989.

The Second Session at a Glance *

The second session of the 101st Congress ended Oct. 28, when the Senate adjourned sine die at 1:17 a.m. EST. The House adjourned at 1:02 a.m. EST. Convened on Jan. 23, the session lasted 279 days — 45 days less than the first session of the 101st Congress.

The second session was the 34th longest in history, the 11th longest for an election year. *(CQ Guide to Congress Third Edition, p. 410)*

Each chamber met for 138 days in 1990.

There were 6,963 bills and resolutions introduced during the session, compared with 7,390 in 1989 and 3,740 in 1988. A total of 410 bills cleared by Congress in 1990 became public law.

President Bush vetoed 10 public bills and one private bill during the year. None were overridden.

During 1990, the House took 536 recorded votes and quorum calls, 157 more than in 1989. The Senate took 326 recorded votes and quorum calls, 14 more than in 1989.

Year	House	Senate	Total
1990	536	326	862
1989	379	312	691
1988	465	379	844
1987	511	420	931
1986	488	359	847
1985	482	381	863
1984	463	292	755
1983	533	381	914
1982	488	469	957
1981	371	497	868
1980	681	546	1,227
1979	758	509	1,267
1978	942	520	1,462
1977	782	636	1,418
1976	864	700	1,564
1975	828	611	1,439
1974	727	578	1,305
1973	726	594	1,320

* *Figures are for recorded votes and quorum calls in each chamber. In previous Almanacs (through 1987), tabulations were for recorded votes only.*

• **Rights for the disabled.** The Americans with Disabilities Act (ADA) prohibited discrimination on the basis of disability in employment, public services and public accommodations. It also went well beyond that, requiring employers to make "reasonable accommodations" for disabled workers, and stores, restaurants, doctors' offices and other facilities to make "readily achievable" modifications to accommodate the disabled.

• **Defense spending.** As part of the fiscal 1991 budget package, Congress and the White House agreed to reduce spending for the Defense Department and defense-related programs to $288 billion from President Bush's initial budget request of $307 billion. Bush's fiscal 1991 defense budget request amounted to a 2 percent decline in purchasing power, after allowing for inflation. But the apparent collapse of the Soviet conventional military threat to Western Europe fueled congressional demands for larger cuts.

• **Central America aid.** In dealing with Central American nations, partisanship in Congress often yielded to bipartisan compromise in 1990. Congress and the administration agreed on $462 million in emergency aid to the new government of Panama following the U.S. invasion that toppled dictator Manuel Antonio Noriega and $300 million in assistance to the new government in Nicaragua headed by the U.S.-backed anti-Sandinista leader Violeta Chamorro. The administration more grudgingly accepted Congress' decision to withhold half of the $85 million military assistance package for El Salvador — and in early 1991 determined it could release the aid, triggered by the killing of two U.S. servicemen and continued rebel activities against the pro-U.S. government.

• **Medicare/Medicaid.** Congress agreed to trim $44.2 billion over five years from the fast-growing Medicare program, slashing payments to providers and raising out-of-pocket costs to beneficiaries by an estimated $10.1 billion. Congress also brushed aside protests from the states and mandated $1.1 billion over five years in child-related program expansions for Medicaid — the joint federal-state health program for the poor — to cover all children in families at or below the federal poverty level.

• **Head Start expansion.** Brushing aside administration objections, Congress on Oct. 18 cleared for the president the biggest expansion of Head Start since the program's inception in 1965. The bill authorized $2.39 billion for Head Start for fiscal 1991, $4.27 billion in fiscal 1992, $5.92 billion for 1993 and $7.66 billion for 1994.

• **Emergency AIDS relief.** Congress on Aug. 4 cleared for President Bush fast-track legislation aimed at bolstering aid to areas hit by the AIDS epidemic, mainly through a series of grant programs. The bill authorized $875 million in fiscal 1991 for programs aimed at helping health and social service organizations cope with the mounting costs of the AIDS epidemic.

• **Immigration.** Congress cleared the most sweeping revision of legal-immigration laws in a quarter century, moving to admit more immigrants — especially those with education and skills needed in the United States. Under the new bill, legal immigration would climb from about 500,000 annually to about 700,000 during each of the first three years of the act. After that, a permanent level of 675,000 would be set.

• **Vocational education.** In the most significant education legislation cleared in 1990, Congress revised vocational education programs and authorized an infusion of funds with fewer federal strings attached. The bill authorized $1.6 billion in fiscal 1991 for programs designed to serve students unlikely to pursue a traditional college education.

• **Community service.** Congress responded to President Bush's "A Thousand Points of Light" campaign by passing legislation to spur community service by the young and old. The bill authorized grants to establish national, community- and school-based volunteer service programs — $62 million in fiscal 1991, $105 million in fiscal 1992 and $120 million in fiscal 1993. Conferees dropped the most contentious provision, a student-loan forgiveness proposal.

• **Securities market regulation.** Congress cleared three bills making sweeping changes in the regulation of the nation's securities markets. The first gave the Securities and Exchange Commission (SEC) authority to halt trading, to collect data on large traders and the health of investment houses, and to restrict so-called program trading where it was shown to contribute to wide price swings. The others increased civil penalties for securities law violations and gave the SEC authority to cooperate more closely with foreign governments in security fraud investigations.

• **Oil-spill liability.** Congress ended 16 years of deadlock over oil pollution by passing a bill meant to prevent oil spills and punish spillers. The bill increased spillers' liability many times over existing federal limits and imposed stiffer civil and criminal penalties. Liability could top $200 million for big tankers.

• **'Superfund' reauthorization.** Congress on Oct. 27 cleared a three-year reauthorization of the 1986 "superfund" hazardous waste cleanup law and a four-year extension of the taxes that supported the superfund hazardous waste cleanup program. The provisions were tucked into the fiscal 1991 budget-reconciliation bill.

• **Tongass forest protection.** Compromise legislation

Congress' Approval Rating

Do you approve or disapprove of the way Congress is handling its job?

Date	Approve	Disapprove	Don't Know/ No Answer
April 1974[1]	30	47	23
August 1974[1]	48	35	17
March 1975[1]	32	50	18
November 1975[1]	28	54	18
July 1977[2]	31	49	20
October 1977[2]	31	50	19
January 1978[2]	29	50	20
April 1978[2]	31	50	19
June 1978[2]	30	53	17
September 1978[2]	29	51	20
June 1979[1]	19	61	20
August 1980[2]	32	51	18
October 1982[2]	33	50	17
April 1983[1]	33	43	24
September 1987[1]	42	49	9
January 1990[2]	42	47	11
August 1990[2]	40	44	16
Oct. 8-10, 1990[2]	27	60	13
Oct. 18-21, 1990[1]	23	64	13
Oct. 25-28, 1990[1]	24	68	8
Oct. 28-31, 1990[2]	23	69	8

Sources: [1] Gallup Poll; [2] New York Times/CBS News Poll

Public Laws

A total of 410 bills cleared by Congress in 1990 became public laws. Following is a list of the number of public laws enacted since 1971:

Year	Public Laws	Year	Public Laws
1990	410	1980	426
1989	240	1979	187
1988	471	1978	410
1987	242	1977	223
1986	424	1976	383
1985	240	1975	205
1984	408	1974	402
1983	215	1973	247
1982	328	1972	383
1981	145	1971	224

that withheld more than 1 million additional acres of the Alaskan Tongass National Forest from timber-cutting cleared late in the 101st Congress. The measure designated 296,000 acres of the forest as wilderness (meaning no logging, mining or road-building) and another 722,000 acres on which some mining and road-building could occur.

• **Antarctica protection.** Seeking to avert environmental despoliation of Antarctica, Congress enacted legislation to bar U.S. exploration or development of minerals there and called on Bush to begin negotiations aimed at tighter international guardianship of the ice-covered continent.

• **Aviation package.** President Bush achieved some of his administration's major transportation policy objectives when both chambers passed an aviation package as part of the final budget package. Congress approved new airline ticket fees of up to $3 per flight and new guidelines on aviation noise. The bill also contained further restrictions on noisy jets and required the Transportation Department to adopt a noise policy by July 1991.

• **Federal judgeships.** With relatively little controversy, Congress passed legislation giving President Bush 85 new federal judgeships to fill — the first increase in the federal judiciary since 1984. The legislation added 74 new district court judgeships and 11 appellate positions.

WHAT CONGRESS DIDN'T DO

On the other hand, many issues expected to be dealt with during the 101st Congress were left untouched or unresolved. Major policy initiatives, revisions and reforms failed because of partisan bickering, presidential veto, institutional turf battles, lack of time, lack of support — or some combination of those factors. Following are some of the major issues that held up the 101st Congress in 1990 or stalled during the session:

• **Campaign finance.** Both chambers passed bills to rework the campaign finance system, but the measures died in a conference committee that never met. The Senate voted to forswear speaking fees known as honoraria, which House members had already agreed to give up in 1991, but the Senate ban died without becoming law.

Both campaign finance bills would have introduced public financing and spending limits; the Senate bill also would have dismantled political action committees.

• **Ethics investigations.** The Senate took its first disciplinary action in more than a decade when it denounced Dave Durenberger, R-Minn., for financial improprieties that the Ethics Committee said had been reprehensible.

As the year drew to a close, the Senate was still conducting hearings on the Keating Five, a group of senators (Alan Cranston, D-Calif.; Dennis DeConcini, D-Ariz.; John Glenn, D-Ohio; John McCain, R-Ariz.; and Donald W. Riegle Jr., D-Mich.) accused of improperly intervening with federal regulators in behalf of Charles H. Keating Jr., who headed the failing Lincoln Savings and Loan. A special counsel submitted his report to the Ethics Committee on Sept. 10; public hearings began Nov. 15 and extended into 1991.

House members voted to reprimand Barney Frank, D-Mass., for misusing his official position to help a male prostitute.

Just before adjournment, Donald E. "Buz" Lukens, an Ohio Republican who was convicted on a sexual misconduct charge in 1989, resigned from Congress in the face of new allegations that he sexually harassed a Capitol Hill elevator operator. Rep. Robert Garcia, D-N.Y., had also resigned earlier in the year, after being convicted in 1989 on federal charges of extortion.

• **Family and medical leave.** The House failed by a wide margin to override President Bush's veto of a bill that would have required employers to grant unpaid leave to workers caring for newborn children or ill relatives. Bush, in vetoing the bill, said such matters were the domain of labor-management relations.

• **Civil rights bill.** Civil rights activists suffered their first major defeat in more than a quarter century when they were unable to override President Bush's veto of the 1990 civil rights measure.

The legislation sought to reverse or modify six 1989 Supreme Court decisions that narrowed the scope and reach of laws prohibiting employment discrimination. Bush argued that the bill would lead employers to adopt hiring and promotion quotas to avoid litigation.

• **Anticrime proposals.** As cleared, the anticrime bill was a bare-bones measure that bore little resemblance to versions passed by both chambers. Controversial provisions to expand the federal death penalty, limit appeals by condemned prisoners and enact new gun controls were dumped, leaving a stripped-down bill that set new penalties for bank fraud, certain drug offenses and child abuse, and authorized funding increases for law enforcement and prison alternatives.

• **Hatch Act revisions.** After intense lobbying by the White House, the Senate on June 21 fell two votes short of overriding President Bush's veto of a bipartisan bill to amend the so-called Hatch Act, which prohibited the nation's 3 million federal employees from taking part in partisan politics. The House had voted the day before to override the veto, 327-93.

• **Thrift bailout.** The House failed to consider a measure to provide additional financing for the Resolution Trust Corporation, the thrift salvage agency, in the final hours of the 101st Congress. The RTC was expected to tap $18.8 billion in borrowing authority to stay in business through the first few months of 1991. If Congress did not reconsider the issue soon after reconvening in January, the RTC would be forced to stop closing down failed thrifts.

• **Flag burning.** Supporters of a constitutional amendment aimed at preventing flag burning failed for the second year in a row to get the measure through Congress, falling well short of the two-thirds majority needed in the House

Senate Cloture Votes in 1990

The Senate invoked cloture five times in 1990, out of the 15 times it voted on such debate-limiting motions. Cloture motions required a three-fifths majority of the total Senate to be adopted.

The 15 cloture votes brought to 297 the number taken since 1917, when the Senate's filibuster rule was adopted; the five successful votes brought to 103 the number of successful cloture votes.

Following is a list of all 1990 cloture votes. Successful cloture votes are indicated in **boldface** type.

Bill	Date	Vote	Story
Armenian Genocide Day of Remembrance (S J Res 212)	Feb. 22	49-49	p. 807
Armenian Genocide Day of Remembrance (S J Res 212)	Feb. 27	48-51	p. 807
Hatch Act Revisions (S 135)	**May 1**	**70-28**	**p. 408**
AIDS Emergency Relief (S 2240)	**May 15**	**95-3**	**p. 582**
Chemical Weapons Sanctions (S 195)	**May 17**	**87-4**	**p. 198**
Omnibus Crime Package (S 1970)	June 5	54-37	p. 486
Omnibus Crime Package (S 1970)	June 7	57-37	p. 486
Air Travel Rights for the Blind (S 341)	June 12	56-44	p. 389
Civil Rights Act of 1990 (S 2104)	**July 17**	**62-38**	**p. 462**
Fiscal 1991 Defense Authorization (S 2884)	Aug. 3	58-41	p. 671
Motor Vehicle Fuel Efficiency Act (S 1224)	**Sept. 14**	**68-28**	**p. 279**
Motor Vehicle Fuel Efficiency Act (S 1224)	Sept. 25	57-42	p. 279
Title X Family Planning Amendments (S 110)	Sept. 26	50-46	p. 604
National Motor-Voter Registration (S 874)	Sept. 26	55-42	p. 71
Fiscal 1991 Foreign Operations Appropriations (HR 5114)	Oct. 12	51-38	p. 830

and Senate. The June 21 House vote fell 34 votes short of the two-thirds necessary for passage of an amendment. In a vote that was moot, the Senate also defeated a resolution for such an amendment, falling nine votes short of the required two-thirds.

• **Abortion.** Anti-abortion forces suffered some electoral setbacks but — backed by veto threats from Bush — won re-enactment of existing bans on federal funding of abortions except in cases in which the woman's life would be endangered by carrying the pregnancy to term. For the District of Columbia, Congress extended an existing ban on the use of either federal or local funds to pay for abortions.

• **Fuel-efficiency standards.** Heavy lobbying by the auto industry and the Bush administration stalled a Senate attempt to raise automobile fuel-efficiency standards, killing the issue for the 101st Congress. The bill would have forced automakers to increase standards by 20 percent by 1995 and 40 percent by 2001.

• **Cable reregulation.** Legislation to reregulate the cable television industry died on the Senate floor Sept. 28 despite strong backing fueled by consumer complaints about price increases during nearly four years of deregulation. A similar bill, somewhat more to the liking of the cable industry, had cleared the House by voice vote Sept. 10. Both bills would have allowed the Federal Communications Commission to regulate rates for basic cable service.

• **RICO curtailment.** Differing bills aimed at cutting back private suits under the federal antiracketeering law known as RICO won approval from the Senate and House Judiciary committees, but the industry-dominated coalition behind the bills failed for the third consecutive Congress to push a measure to enactment.

• **Product liability.** A scaled-back bill to establish federal standards for product-liability suits cleared the Senate Commerce Committee on May 22 but never reached the floor for debate. It was the fifth time since 1980 that the industry coalition, pushing measures aimed at reducing payments to consumers injured by dangerous or defective products, had won committee approval of its legislation but had failed to get a floor vote.

• **Education initiatives.** Senate Republicans refused to lift objections to the bill that contained President Bush's education initiatives, killing it near the end of the session. Among other things, the bill included Bush's proposals to provide cash awards for excellent schools and teachers, math and science scholarships and alternative methods for certifying teachers. ■

Capitol Bombing Case

Three women pleaded guilty in U.S. District Court in Washington on Sept. 7 to bombing the U.S. Capitol in 1983 as a political protest and were sentenced Nov. 28 to prison terms ranging from five years to 20 years.

Marilyn J. Buck, Linda S. Evans and Laura J. Whitehorn also admitted participating in a conspiracy to bomb several other buildings in Washington and New York from 1983 to 1985.

Whitehorn and Buck received 10-year sentences in the Capitol bombing case, Evans a five-year term. Buck and Evans drew five-year terms on the conspiracy count, to run concurrently with the other sentence; Whitehorn drew five-year terms on the broader charges, to run consecutively.

The Capitol explosion occurred Nov. 7, 1983, just outside the Senate chamber. The blast caused minor damage but no injuries. A telephoned message said the bombing was a protest against U.S. military actions in Grenada and Lebanon. *(1983 Almanac, p. 592)*

Seven people were charged with the bombings in May 1988, but one remained a fugitive, and charges against three others were to be dropped because of legal problems. ■

Congressional Leadership Tested

Congressional leaders in 1990 found it even more difficult than usual to prod, cajole, plead and threaten the rank-and-file membership to do their bidding.

The year was replete with countless reminders to the elected leaders of the House and Senate that their powers were largely symbolic and that leading a group of 535 independent and strong-willed individuals was much more an art than a science.

The limits of leadership power — always tenuous in a democratic body of so many strong-willed individuals — were further reduced by members' own uncertainties, buttressed by scorn and ridicule from constituents, about Congress' ability to deal with the pressing issues of the day.

As was the case in past years, Congress was unable to meet statutory or self-imposed deadlines for action on important legislation. The session dragged on until late October — just nine days before Election Day and a full three weeks later than leaders had originally hoped.

But the problems facing the leadership in the second session of the 101st Congress went beyond their inability to get Congress to do its work on time.

The most dramatic example of the congressional leadership's troubles was the humiliating, bipartisan repudiation by the House of a budget agreement negotiated by a handful of congressional leaders and White House officials.

"I have been in the Senate for 16 years, and I have never seen a time that I thought was more ominous for the future of the country than now," said Dale Bumpers, D-Ark.

The budget spectacle sent the government lurching from one crisis to the next. With the economy teetering and the federal budget deficit growing to record levels, Congress and the White House were unable for several agonizing weeks to reach an agreement to resolve the budget impasse.

At one point, the government shut down for three days when President Bush vetoed a stopgap spending bill.

Another budget agreement was finally hammered out — this time with input from a much larger group of members — and Congress adjourned, but the standing of Congress and its leaders had taken a battering.

BACKGROUND

The year began with stable leadership teams on both sides of Capitol Hill, a welcomed change from 1989, when ethics scandals led to the resignations of House Speaker Jim Wright, D-Texas, and House Democratic Whip Tony Coelho of California and poisoned relationships between the parties. *(1989 Almanac, pp. 36, 41)*

The leaders' top legislative priorities when 1990 began were dealing with the budget deficit, responding to the political upheaval in Eastern Europe, overhauling campaign finance laws, expanding federal aid for child care, revamping the Clean Air Act and putting a stop to discrimination against minority and female job-seekers and the handicapped.

The scorecard at year's end was mixed, at best, reflecting not only problems with the budget but also the Democratic leadership's inability to develop a consensus on campaign finance or to override a presidential veto of the job discrimination bill. *(101st Congress overview, p. 3)*

In the last weeks of the session, however, Congress cleared a five-year deficit-reduction measure, a rewrite of the Clean Air Act, a child-care bill, a major immigration measure and a five-year renewal of federal farm programs, permitting congressional leaders to declare the 101st Congress a success.

Leaders conceded, however, that critics had a point. "Much of [the criticism] is valid," Senate Majority Leader George J. Mitchell, D-Maine, acknowledged. "Much of it is well-taken."

Budget Mess Tarnishes Leadership Image

Prospects for timely action to address the budget deficit appeared favorable in May, when congressional leaders and Bush agreed to conduct high-level negotiations to develop a deficit-reduction plan, and again in June, when Bush abandoned his 1988 campaign pledge of "no new taxes."

Unlike previous White House-congressional budget summits that were called only after the normal budget process had failed to produce an agreement, the 1990 summit was started much earlier in the process, before the entire membership of Congress could grapple with the problems posed by the deficit and begin to understand that a summit was needed.

Also, only 21 members of Congress were involved in the initial negotiations, excluding dozens of influential members, including most committee chairmen, and grating on the sensibilities of hundreds of members who felt ignored.

The final details of the budget compromise were worked out by an even smaller group, further irritating the membership: "Eight men met in secret for several weeks to prepare this budget. That is not the democratic way to do business," complained Rep. Dan Glickman, D-Kan.

The leaders realized they had a tough task in selling the budget plan to the membership. The chore became impossible in the face of opposition led by Minority Whip Newt Gingrich, R-Ga. Gingrich was a party to the budget summit. By many accounts, however, he did not participate actively, and he distanced himself from the final agreement.

Gingrich, who rose to the whip position in 1989, had made his reputation as something of a backbench bomb-thrower. It was Gingrich who pressed hard for the ethics probe that led to Wright's downfall in 1989.

But in 1990, Gingrich's fight against the administration-backed budget deal made him persona non grata at the White House, and he became the target of some disgruntled Republicans who talked openly of dumping him from his job as No. 2 House Republican.

Fundamental Problems Revealed

Problems of political leadership went beyond partisan differences over budget priorities and government's role in shaping society. The budget fracas laid bare forces in Congress and the country that had been gathering for years to make the government seem rudderless. They included:

- The decentralization of power in Congress. A generation before, leaders could run Congress in consultation with a handful of its titans because power was concentrated and junior members did not expect to share it.

By the mid-1970s, however, all that had changed. Post-Watergate reforms weakened committee chairmen, making them more accountable to their colleagues and forcing them to share power with subcommittee chairmen. Habits of deference all but evaporated. Leadership became the art of building consensus across a much broader spectrum.

- The erosion of party identity. Both parties lacked a firm sense of direction in the post-Reagan, post-Cold War era and were riven by divisions over policy and political strategy. Members of Congress were not beholden to the party for their election success to anywhere near the same degree as their predecessors.
- The erosion of public confidence in the government. Politicians themselves fueled hostility toward government by running against Washington, and a groundswell of anti-incumbent sentiment among the American electorate made members of Congress more fearful than ever about enacting policies that demanded sacrifice.

An exasperated Mitchell asked his colleagues near the end of the year: "Do we have the minimum level of courage necessary to do something that is difficult, unpleasant, unpopular? Or must we forever say that this institution is incapable of taking any action that meets any of that description?"

101st Congress Leaders

SENATE

President Pro Tempore — Robert C. Byrd, D-W.Va.
Majority Leader — George J. Mitchell, D-Maine
Majority Whip — Alan Cranston, D-Calif.
Secretary of the Democratic Conference — David Pryor, D-Ark.

Minority Leader — Bob Dole, R-Kan.
Assistant Minority Leader — Alan K. Simpson, R-Wyo.
Chairman of the Republican Conference — John H. Chafee, R-R.I.
Secretary of the Republican Conference — Thad Cochran, R-Miss.

HOUSE

Speaker — Thomas S. Foley, D-Wash.
Majority Leader — Richard A. Gephardt, D-Mo.
Majority Whip — William H. Gray III, D-Pa.
Chairman of the Democratic Caucus — Steny H. Hoyer, D-Md.

Minority Leader — Robert H. Michel, R-Ill.
Minority Whip — Newt Gingrich, R-Ga.
Chairman of the Republican Conference — Jerry Lewis, R-Calif.
Chairman of the Republican Policy Committee — Mickey Edwards, R-Okla.

THE SENATE

According to a study of party unity — based on votes on which a majority of Democrats opposed a majority of Republicans — 1990 was the most partisan year in the Senate in nearly 30 years. *(Party unity, p. 32)*

The growing partisanship reflected many of the controversial issues before the chamber — civil rights, campaign finance, child care, the budget — and posed challenges and opportunities to the leaders of both parties.

Democrats

Settling into his second year as majority leader, Mitchell was determined to deal with legislation in a pragmatic manner. The other top leaders had been in place for several years.

Mitchell earned generally good marks from colleagues for his fairness and serious intent. Despite his devoted partisanship, he shunned excessive partisan politics when it threatened legislative goals he was determined to achieve. And he was careful in using his power, mindful that in many ways he owed his election as leader to reform-minded Democrats who had opposed power-hungry autocratic leaders in the past.

On being elected majority leader late in 1988, for example, Mitchell immediately gave away some of the positions traditionally held by the No. 1 Democrat.

Mitchell tried his best to accommodate the needs of all of his 99 colleagues, scheduling few votes on Mondays or Fridays, and alternately pleaded for cooperation and threatened to hold late-night or weekend sessions. But Mitchell found himself singing an old, sad refrain as he tried and failed to coax the Senate into something a bit quicker than its glacial pace of action on important legislation. "What should take an hour takes a day. What should take a day takes a week, and as a result the progress is painfully slow," he complained.

Mitchell devoted much of his effort in 1990 toward producing (eventually successfully) an extension of the Clean Air Act.

The most serious test of Mitchell's leadership came during the debate on clean air. Robert C. Byrd, D-W.Va., the powerful chairman of the Appropriations Committee and Mitchell's predecessor as majority leader, sought passage of an amendment to grant relief to coal miners hurt by some of the bill's controls on acid rain.

Bush had promised to veto the bill if the Byrd amendment was adopted; Mitchell, determined to see a clean air bill passed in 1990, decided to fight Byrd. "Sen. Mitchell is fighting for what he believes in," Byrd said the day before the vote. "And I'm fighting for what I believe in."

When the vote occurred, Mitchell won; the amendment fell by one vote with just 70 percent of the Democrats (38 of 54) sticking with Mitchell.

"It was one of the classic struggles of the Senate," said Tom Korologos, a high-powered Republican-leaning lobbyist and longtime Congress-watcher. "There was more high drama in that thing than I've seen in a long time."

Republicans

Minority Leader Bob Dole, R-Kan., meanwhile, had put to rest concerns that he might retain or exploit the bitterness between Bush and himself — any remnants of a nasty presidential primary season in 1988. Dole emerged in 1989 as one of Bush's staunchest allies on Capitol Hill and had answered nearly all questions about his loyalty by 1990.

Some Republicans attributed the increased partisanship in 1990 to election-year politicking by Mitchell; Democrats said it was their ability to stick together and the nature of the issues.

Norman J. Ornstein of the American Enterprise Institute said that Mitchell "began to frame things in ways that were uncomfortable for the Republicans and George Bush." Ornstein said Mitchell clearly pressed for votes that Republicans did not want to take. That, he said, brought out the partisanship in Dole. "Both sides were trying mightily to frame the debate, and you get votes set to make a point," Ornstein said.

The Senate voted in July to cut off debate and vote on the civil rights bill, although negotiations over the content were ongoing. The move sparked a bitterly angry reaction from Dole, who said Mitchell was treating the Republicans like "a bunch of bums." Dole accused the Democrats of forcing action on the bill "to put the Republicans on record as being against civil rights."

"What we lack is coherence, working together in support of a political agenda or strategy," said Thad Cochran, R-Miss., before Senate leadership elections at the end of 1990.

Yet when Republicans met to choose their leaders for the 102nd Congress, no challenge was mounted to Dole or Assistant Minority Leader Alan K. Simpson, Wyo. Conservatives had chafed when GOP leaders cut deals with Mitchell that precluded clear votes on Republican alternatives — such as when Dole joined with Mitchell during debate on the budget to block an amendment to eliminate proposed increases in the gas tax. But when it came to fielding leadership candidates, conservatives regarded Dole as unbeatable, and year-end talk of mounting a challenge to Simpson went nowhere.

THE HOUSE

In the House, Democrats were seeking to restore some stability to a chamber still reeling from the resignations in 1989 of their two top leaders. Republicans, meanwhile, were struggling to avoid an ideological rift that threatened to keep the party more preoccupied with intraparty struggles rather than interparty debate.

Democrats

Leaders in the House in 1990 were more cautious about using their power. Thomas S. Foley, D-Wash., began his first full year as Speaker of the House, and his low-key, non-confrontational style gave members reason to believe that the House could put the memories of 1989 behind them.

Foley received a great deal of credit for restoring stability to the House after the 1989 resignations of Wright and Coelho. Even Republicans who were extremely critical of Wright praised Foley for his civil ways and attempts at bipartisanship.

But within his own party, Foley sometimes received criticism from both ideological wings. Conservatives and moderates criticized him for being an old-fashioned liberal still championing policies they said most voters had rejected. Liberals, though, occasionally found Foley too accommodating and lacking the aggression they saw necessary to push their agenda.

Foley did not seem so determined that he played hardball with colleagues and was reluctant to use his influence over committee assignments to reward people who stuck with the leadership and to punish those who did not. Foley much preferred to let the legislative process work, however slowly, rather than imposing his own views or pushing specific legislation. "There is a degree to which you can sort of push, encourage, support, direct," Foley said. "But the speakership isn't a dictatorship."

And arm-twisting could backfire, as Wright learned. His heavy-handed use of power alienated even fellow Democrats, whose shallow loyalty helped doom his speakership when ethics problems arose in 1989.

Unlike the cautious Foley, Majority Leader Richard A. Gephardt, D-Mo., loudly trumpeted issues of concern to him throughout 1990 — just as he had done throughout his political career, including his 1988 bid for the Democratic presidential nomination. His ability to attract attention led Gephardt to become a common target for Republicans within both chambers on Capitol Hill as well as in the White House.

In March, one of Gephardt's attacks on Bush so angered Simpson that he took to the Senate floor to assail Gephardt for excessive partisanship. Gephardt, though, seemed to relish the role of combatant as he sought to fill the political void created by the resignation of his predecessor, Coelho.

Republicans

Bitter divisions among Republicans were most apparent in the House, where GOP conservative partisans and the party's more pragmatic members openly clashed over budget strategy and policy in 1990; even their leaders were divided into two camps.

Michel was back for his 10th year as Republican leader, mindful of the split in the House GOP membership between pragmatists such as himself and the mostly younger generation of ideologically conservative and combative Republicans led by Gingrich.

Michel, of all Republican leaders, was regarded by the White House as its most stalwart soldier. Working with a Republican White House ever since he became leader in 1981, Michel had referred to himself as a "handmaiden to the president."

Gingrich, on the other hand, alienated dozens of Republican colleagues by helping scuttle the budget deal backed by Bush. By the time the 101st Congress ended in October, even some of his erstwhile supporters were calling for his head. And he barely won re-election in November to his congressional seat in Georgia's 6th District, finishing fewer than 1,000 votes ahead of his challenger.

Gingrich in 1990 began his first full year in the No. 2 House Republican post, which required him to occasionally moderate his strident partisan tone that he had employed effectively since his election to the House in 1978.

The biggest test of how Gingrich would juggle his roles as ideological guru and congressional leader came when Michel named him a member of the budget summit.

That made it harder for Gingrich to lambaste a process he feared — correctly — would scuttle the GOP's no-tax stand.

But he played the outsider even in one of Washington's most exclusive back rooms. At some summit meetings, Gingrich kept his distance from the proceedings by reading novels, skimming magazines and clipping newspapers.

Although some of his conservative allies feared that the budget talks would lead Gingrich to betray the principles he was elected to defend, those fears were put to rest when he came out of the summit swinging, ready to fight the deal Bush had endorsed.

But while his opposition to the budget helped him shore up his base among conservatives, he irritated some of the moderate Republicans who had helped to elect him whip.

THE 102ND CONGRESS

Partisan events at the end of 1990 set the tone for the 102nd Congress. While the top leaders in both chambers, and from both parties, would be the same

Continued on p. 12

House Democrats Oust Two Chairmen

Setting a boisterous tone for the 102nd Congress, the Democratic Caucus on Dec. 5 unexpectedly ousted two committee barons: Public Works Chairman Glenn M. Anderson of California and House Administration Chairman Frank Annunzio of Illinois.

Although only two chairmen were toppled, many others were nudged. Banking Chairman Henry B. Gonzalez of Texas was challenged, unsuccessfully, by a junior member of his committee. Several other veterans faced unusually broad opposition to their re-election as chairmen, typically a routine matter.

The agitation reflected a desire by many Democrats to make their caucus more assertive legislatively and politically in the run-up to the 1992 elections. Both Anderson and Annunzio were regarded as weak, ineffective leaders and were replaced by younger, more aggressive Democrats: Robert A. Roe of New Jersey and Charlie Rose of North Carolina, respectively.

"It sends a message to all chairmen that they have to be more responsive," said David R. Obey, D-Wis. "What this demonstrates is that people don't want to have to work around chairmen. They want to be able to work through them."

Some insurgents hoped this episode would increase pressure on the House's Old Guard to retire in 1992, when a great deal of turnover already was expected.

"This House is going to change dramatically in 1992," said Rep. Byron L. Dorgan, D-N.D.

After the Dec. 5 dust-up, five committees had new chairmen. In addition to Roe on Public Works and Rose on House Administration, William D. Ford, D-Mich., replaced the retiring Augustus F. Hawkins, D-Calif., on Education and Labor; William L. Clay, D-Mo., replaced Ford on Post Office and Civil Service; and George E. Brown Jr. replaced Roe on Science. That represented the biggest turnover in House committee leadership since 1981, when 11 committees got new chairmen.

The last time a chairman had been ousted was January 1985, when the enfeebled Democrat Melvin Price of Illinois (1945-88) was usurped as Armed Services chairman by the committee's seventh-ranking Democrat, Les Aspin of Wisconsin. *(1985 Almanac, p. 5)*

Rumblings of discontent with committee leadership had long been standard fare among junior members. But there had been recent signs of growing tension between the younger generation of media-oriented, outward-looking politicians and the old-school, inside players who still dominated the leadership of House committees. (In the 101st Congress, six of the 22 chairmen of standing committees were 70 or older; 15 were over 60.)

"There was a mandate, a clear message that the American public felt there should be change and Congress should be more responsible," said Dave McCurdy, an Oklahoma Democrat who was active in the 1985 revolt against Price. "We need strong leadership to address those concerns."

Anderson, Annunzio Fall

Dissatisfaction with Anderson's leadership had been brewing for some time among Democrats on his committee. Critics said Anderson, 77, relied too heavily on aides and seemed to lack command of the national issues before the committee. Members of the panel began to feel they were paying for his weak leadership in the currency of their own power, as Public Works suffered repeated losses in turf wars with other committees.

Anderson tried to salvage his position by promising that this would be his last term as chairman, but the caucus voted against him, 100-152.

Norman Y. Mineta, D-Calif., had hoped to succeed Anderson. Mineta had some formidable advantages — such as a large base of support in California's 26 Democrats — but his biggest obstacle was the continued power of seniority. Some who voted to oust Anderson did not see any equivalent rationale for skipping over Roe to elect the No. 3 Democrat.

"Where other factors are basically equal, the seniority system should predominate," said Rick Boucher, D-Va.

California got a consolation prize in the wake of Mineta's defeat with Brown's election to succeed Roe as chairman of the Science Committee. Brown defeated Marilyn Lloyd, D-Tenn., 166-33.

Annunzio, unlike Anderson, faced a discontent that reached outside the committee he chaired. House Administration was the one committee with direct bearing on all members' daily lives: It oversaw their office accounts, computer equipment and other administrative matters. Many members complained that the committee was being run not by Annunzio but by an unresponsive and arrogant staff.

Annunzio was only narrowly rejected by the caucus, 125-127. But Democrats then voted overwhelmingly to dip down into the committee ranks to elect Rose, the No. 3 Democrat, who had openly challenged Annunzio. Rose defeated Joseph M. Gaydos of Pennsylvania, who ranked immediately behind Annunzio, by a 158-64 vote. While Gaydos was regarded as an old-school politician, Rose was portrayed as a force for change: He had been instrumental in modernizing the House's computers and office equipment.

The Message to Others

The challenge to Gonzalez focused on complaints about his handling of the Banking Committee and on allegations that he had recorded a campaign endorsement for a Republican member of Congress.

Concerns about the committee's leadership had taken on new urgency because Gonzalez and Annunzio would be in charge of a daunting legislative job in 1991: restructuring the financial services industry.

But those concerns did not crystallize into an opposing candidacy until the day of the balloting, when Bruce F. Vento of Minnesota, No. 7 Democrat on Banking, announced that he was challenging Gonzalez. The last-minute effort fell short, 163-89.

No other committee chairmen were openly challenged, but many faced significant opposition. Eleven chairmen received more than 20 votes opposing their re-election; in 1988, none did.

Continued from p. 10
(Mitchell and Dole, Foley and Michel), changes at lower leadership tiers appeared to presage a sharpening of the political edges in the new Congress.

Democrats vented their frustration somewhat in selecting their leaders for the 102nd Congress. House members unexpectedly ousted two senior committee chairmen and registered negative votes on others who were retained. In the Senate, a conservative Southerner — Wendell H. Ford of Kentucky — advanced to the leadership team.

Republicans, meanwhile, sent mixed messages from each chamber. In the Senate, conservatives took or held on to nearly all the contested leadership posts. Their counterparts in the House, though, kept their leadership team intact, rejecting challenges by conservative stalwarts to more moderate incumbents.

Democrats

House Democrats, who met during the week of Dec. 3, deposed two aging committee chairmen — Glenn M. Anderson of California, who headed the Public Works and Transportation Committee, and Frank Annunzio, Ill., who chaired the Committee on House Administration.

"It sends a message to all chairmen that they have to be more responsive," said David R. Obey, D-Wis. "What this demonstrates is that people don't want to have to work around chairmen. They want to be able to work through them." *(Democratic chairmen ousted, p. 11)*

Earlier during their meetings, the Democrats re-elected their party leadership with no change. That left Foley as Speaker, Gephardt as majority leader, William H. Gray III of Pennsylvania as majority whip, and Hoyer as chairman of the Democratic Caucus.

The complexion of Democratic leadership in the Senate, though, had changed by year's end. While Mitchell was unchallenged for another term as majority leader, the second-highest post went to the much more conservative Ford. He was chosen to replace Alan Cranston of California, who relinquished the post after revealing that he had been diagnosed as having prostate cancer. A more moderate Southerner, David Pryor of Arkansas, explored but backed away from a challenge to Ford, who had been campaigning for the post for two years and had carefully accumulated political debts in his 16 years in the Senate.

Cranston announced Nov. 8 that he would step down immediately as whip and not seek re-election to the Senate in 1992. Cranston's political standing, both within the Senate and in California, had diminished throughout 1990 by a protracted ethics investigation of his relationship with thrift executive Charles H. Keating Jr. *(Keating investigation, p. 78)*

Republicans

Both Michel and Gingrich were unopposed in their bids for re-election to the leadership when the House Republican Conference met on Dec. 3. In a more surprisingly strong endorsement of the status quo in troubled times for the party, House Republicans turned back aggressive efforts to dump two of their other leaders for the 102nd Congress.

Jerry Lewis of California was re-elected chairman of the conference, defeating Carl D. Pursell of Michigan for the No. 3 leadership post despite strong support for the challenger from Gingrich.

And Guy Vander Jagt of Michigan held on as chairman of the National Republican Congressional Committee (NRCC), the House GOP campaign and fundraising arm, despite criticism of his stewardship from challenger Don Sundquist of Tennessee.

The rivalry between Lewis and Gingrich was highlighted by Pursell's challenge because he was backed by Gingrich and his allies in the leadership, including Vin Weber of Minnesota and Duncan Hunter of California. But despite the conservative firepower behind Pursell's call for more aggressive leadership, Lewis triumphed by a surprisingly wide margin of 98-64.

Vander Jagt was re-elected over Sundquist on a 98-66 vote — a margin many considered extraordinary in light of the barrage of criticism leveled by Sundquist about the committee's management and electoral record.

Senate Republicans, by contrast, gave conservatives a decisively louder voice in their party hierarchy for the 102nd Congress through leadership elections that reflected GOP divisions opened earlier in 1990 by the budget battle.

The Senate Republican Conference took the unusual step of ousting an incumbent leader when it voted Nov. 13 to replace its politically moderate chairman, John H. Chafee of Rhode Island, with the more conservative Thad Cochran of Mississippi.

Those changes were thought to foreshadow a more confrontational, partisan GOP strategy in the Senate heading toward the crucial 1992 elections — when Republicans hoped to recapture some of the seats lost in 1986 when Democrats regained control of the chamber.

Chafee was the most serious target of conservatives' ire because he was one of the most liberal Republicans in the Senate. Cochran was more conservative than Chafee to draw support from the disaffected, and he won by the narrowest of margins, 22-21.

The conference elected Bob Kasten of Wisconsin to replace Cochran as conference secretary. Kasten beat Christopher S. Bond of Missouri, 26-17.

The conservative favorite won the post of chairman of the Policy Committee when Don Nickles of Oklahoma defeated Pete V. Domenici of New Mexico 23-20.

Another contest that saw the triumph of a hard-line conservative was the election of Phil Gramm of Texas as chairman of the campaign committee. Gramm beat Mitch McConnell of Kentucky, 26-17. ■

New Sergeant-at-Arms

Martha S. Pope won designation from the Senate's Democratic majority on Nov. 14 to become the Senate's sergeant-at-arms — the first woman to be chosen for the chamber's second-ranking position. She was formally elected to the post at the opening of the 102nd Congress.

Pope had served since 1989 as chief of staff to Senate Majority Leader George S. Mitchell, of Maine, who named her to succeed retiring Sergeant-at-Arms Henry K. Giugni. The Senate Democratic Caucus ratified the selection at its organizational meeting Nov. 14.

As sergeant-at-arms, Pope would preside over the Senate's chief administrative office, overseeing payroll, Capitol security, computer services, the radio and television recording studio, post office, printing facility and other housekeeping functions.

Term Limitations Gain Public Support

The issue of legislative term limitations attracted serious attention in 1990 and by year's end had garnered enough momentum for some observers to predict that it would be a prominent issue for years. Indeed, voters in Colorado approved a ballot initiative in November to apply a 12-year limit to U.S. senators and House members, though the constitutionality of such a limit on federal lawmakers was widely questioned.

Voters in both California and Oklahoma (as well as Colorado) approved ballot measures in 1990 limiting the terms of state legislators.

Whether enforced by constitutional mandate or political practice, term limits would profoundly alter Congress. They would not only change the cast but also revise the hierarchical systems by which Congress had long been organized and operated.

The public, meanwhile, started to warm to the idea of limiting members' tenures — even as the voters were returning to office nearly all incumbents who sought reelection.

A Gallup Poll released Jan. 11, 1990, found strong nationwide support for limits: 70 percent of those surveyed were in favor of limiting congressional tenure. A New York Times/CBS News poll in October found nearly 60 percent of the respondents favoring limits.

Some saw the drive as a bipartisan expression of voters' low esteem for Congress, as the idea gave concrete focus to inchoate dissatisfaction with politicians. Others viewed the process as one of sour grapes by a Republican Party unable to break the seeming permanence of Democratic control of Congress and many state legislatures.

Debate about congressional tenure tended to center on the virtues of legislative experience vs. "new blood" in politics. But it was, at bottom, a debate about what was wrong with Congress and what to do about it.

Proponents of limiting congressional terms saw Congress' problems as rooted in the high rate of re-election of House incumbents — four straight elections over 95 percent — and warned that Congress was becoming an ossified ruling class.

Others countered that Congress had many problems but that lack of turnover was not one of them. They also sought to refute the notion of a permanent Congress by noting that two-thirds of all House members in the 101st Congress had served less than 12 years.

BACKGROUND

The question of whether members should be allowed unlimited terms first arose at the founding.

In 1777, the Continental Congress included a three-year limit on delegates under the Articles of Confederation. But when the Constitution was drafted 12 years later, no cap was imposed either on congressional or presidential tenure. The Constitutional Convention laid aside a proposal to limit congressional service, one of several issues it characterized as "entering too much into detail."

Proposals to limit congressional service were introduced in the First Congress but died, as did similar proposals that followed.

Presidents eventually were limited to two four-year terms under the 22nd Amendment to the Constitution, a reaction to Franklin D. Roosevelt's 12-year tenure as president.

Congress approved the amendment in 1947, and ratification by the states was completed in 1951. *(Congress and the Nation Vol. 1, p. 1434; 1947 Almanac, p. 69)*

Because congressional tenure was not also limited, some have argued that the 22nd Amendment tipped the balance of power against the White House.

Endorsing limits on congressional terms three years after he left the White House, Dwight D. Eisenhower said, "What's good for the president might very well be good for Congress."

In the late 1980s, proposals to limit congressional terms dovetailed with increasing GOP attacks on the powers of congressional incumbency.

In an unprecedented move, the GOP endorsed congressional tenure limits in its 1988 platform. The platform committee adopted unspecified term limits as part of a package of provisions on congressional reform. The provision was introduced by former Republican Rep. Thomas F. Hartnett of South Carolina (1981-87).

"We favor a constitutional amendment," the platform read, "which would place some restriction on the number of consecutive terms a man or woman may serve in the U.S. House of Representatives or the U.S. Senate."

Historical Analogy

Terry Considine, a Republican state senator who led the drive for term limits in Colorado, liked to compare his cause to the direct election of senators.

"We expect the 'Colorado idea' to do for 21st-century politics what the 'Wisconsin idea' did for 20th-century politics," said Considine.

At the beginning of the 20th century, U.S. senators were still being chosen by state legislatures, as the Constitution had specified.

Progressives wanted to make Congress more directly accountable by requiring senators to be chosen by direct popular election, just like House members.

But a constitutional amendment needed approval by the Senate itself, so the reformers crafted an ingenious alternative.

Using the freshly minted procedures for state ballot initiatives, they enacted state laws that laid the groundwork for a new system.

These initiative-generated laws established direct party primaries for Senate candidates. In some cases, they even bound state legislators to vote for Senate candidates who won popular ballot contests similar to the non-binding "beauty contests" more recently familiar in the presidential primary process.

The plan worked.

By 1912 senatorial primaries were in use in 29 states. In that year, the Senate bowed to popular will and approved what became the 17th Amendment, establishing direct election of senators nationwide.

The parallel was far from perfect, of course, especially because the term-limit idea was opposed by many incumbents and also by other elements of the political system at all levels — including academics and much of the press.

In Considine's scenario, a popular movement favoring limits could change Congress long before final victory. In

Membership Changes, 101st Congress, 2nd Session

SENATE

Member	Party	Died	Resigned	Successor	Party	Appointed	Sworn In
Spark M. Matsunaga, Hawaii	D	4/15/90		Daniel K. Akaka	D	4/28/90	5/16/90
Gordon J. Humphrey, N.H. [1]	R		12/4/90	Robert C. Smith	R	12/7/90	12/7/90

HOUSE

Member	Party	Died	Resigned	Successor	Party	Elected	Sworn In
Guy V. Molinari, N.Y. [2]	R		1/1/90	Susan Molinari	R	3/20/90	3/27/90
Robert Garcia, N.Y. [3]	D		1/7/90	Jose E. Serrano	D	3/20/90	3/28/90
James J. Florio, N.J. [4]	D		1/16/90	Robert E. Andrews	D	11/6/90	1/3/91
Daniel K. Akaka, Hawaii [5]	D		5/16/90	Patsy T. Mink	D	9/22/90	9/27/90
Donald E. "Buz" Lukens, Ohio [6]	R		10/24/90	Vacant	—	—	—
Robert C. Smith, N.H. [1]	R		12/7/90	Vacant	—	—	—

[1] *Gordon J. Humphrey, who was elected Nov. 6 to the New Hampshire state Senate, resigned from the U.S. Senate on Dec. 4. Robert C. Smith, who was elected to a six-year term in the Senate on Nov. 6, resigned from the House on Dec. 7 to be appointed to the Senate for the remainder of Humphrey's term.*

[2] *Guy V. Molinari was sworn in as Staten Island borough president on Jan. 14.*

[3] *Robert Garcia was convicted of extortion Oct. 20, 1989. A federal appeals court overturned the conviction June 29.*

[4] *James J. Florio was sworn in as governor of New Jersey on Jan. 16. Robert E. Andrews was elected to fill Florio's seat in a special election Nov. 6, after the 101st Congress had adjourned, and sworn in with the 102nd Congress on Jan. 3, 1991.*

[5] *Daniel K. Akaka was appointed successor to Sen. Spark M. Matsunaga. Akaka was elected to complete the remaining four years of Matsunaga's term in a special election Nov. 6, 1990. Patsy T. Mink won a special election to fill Akaka's House seat.*

[6] *Donald E. "Buz" Lukens resigned amid further allegations of sexual misconduct. Lukens was convicted in May 1989 of a misdemeanor for having sex with a 16-year-old girl. Lukens lost his re-election bid in the primary.*

states where term limits were favored, incumbents might find them hard to ignore.

THE DEBATE

The term-limits movement won its first electoral successes in 1990. The California measure passed only narrowly, with 52 percent of the vote, but the Colorado and Oklahoma measures were approved by more than two out of three voters.

The Colorado measure set a limit of eight consecutive years for any single state office while also trying to apply a 12-year limit to U.S. senators and House members. It was not retroactive.

Under the California measure, state Assembly members were limited to six years (three two-year terms) and state senators to eight years (two four-year terms). The Oklahoma measure limited lifetime service in the state Legislature to 12 years.

Both supporters and opponents of term limits vowed to gear up for impending battles throughout the country. Some observers predicted that voters in as many as 20 states would have the chance by 1992 to vote on restricting the length of service of their congressional representatives and state legislators.

Constitutional Questions

Ardent supporters of term limits aimed to pass a constitutional amendment limiting congressional tenure to six terms in the House and two six-year terms in the Senate or get states to impose the limits themselves.

Lawyers for Congress and academic experts, however, insisted that a constitutional amendment was the only legal way to limit terms and that state statutes such as Colorado's were unconstitutional. They said the U.S. Constitution explicitly gave Congress power to determine the qualifications of its members and to control substantive aspects of congressional elections.

Stephen Glazier, a Washington lawyer and sometime critic of Congress, disagreed and argued that state initiatives enacting congressional term limits would be constitutional. He contended that states received the power to limit re-election of members of Congress straight from the Constitution, Article 1, Section 4, Clause 1: "The times, places and manner of holding elections for Senators and Representatives shall be prescribed in each State by the Legislature thereof; but the Congress may at any time by law make or alter such regulations."

The Supreme Court and lower federal courts had used this clause, Glazier said, to uphold two types of state election laws affecting who could run for Congress — laws barring a candidate from seeking office as an independent after being defeated in a party primary for the same office and so-called resign-to-run statutes, which required officials to quit one office to run for another.

Glazier saw no legal difference between these restrictions and a term limit. He acknowledged that the Constitution gave Congress the right to override state provisions affecting congressional elections. But he believed it was unlikely that Congress would defy voters by doing so.

House legal counsel Steven Ross, though, noted that the Constitution set only three qualifications for members of Congress: age, U.S. citizenship and state residency. A separate provision (Article 1, Section 5, Clause 1) stated: "Each House shall be the judge of the elections, returns and qualifications of its own members."

Together, Ross said, the two provisions made clear that a state could not add a substantive qualification for election to Congress. As for Glazier's analogy to state election procedures, Ross said, "It's an exercise in the constitutional 'theory of the absurd' to pretend that [a term limit] is the same as requiring all candidates to get 100 signatures to be on the ballot."

Proponents

"Entrenchment has turned senators into sovereigns and representatives into royalty," said Trudy Pearce, senior policy analyst for Citizens for Congressional Reform, summarizing much of the sentiment for term limits.

Proponents also argued that limiting tenure would make members more bold about dealing with thorny, long-term policy questions — such as reducing the federal deficit — and less preoccupied with running for re-election.

Promoting the idea nationally in 1990 was Americans to Limit Congressional Terms (ALCT), a group that made its public debut with a Feb. 13 news conference.

The group was headed by former Rep. Jim Coyne, a Pennsylvania Republican who lost his re-election bid in 1982 after only one term in office; it was set up by executives of the Eddie Mahe Co., a GOP consulting firm.

Although the majority of members of its advisory board — state legislators and former members of Congress — were Republican, the group said its mission was nonpartisan. The issue continued to attract prominent GOP support throughout the year. Less than two weeks before Election Day, both President Bush and Vice President Dan Quayle endorsed the idea.

Bush called term limits for members of Congress "an idea whose time has come" and Quayle, referring to the 22nd Amendment, said that "what is good for the president is good for the Congress."

Despite the heavy GOP flavor of the political leaders who urged term limits, supporters said the issue was not partisan. "This is not a Republican issue," said Cleta Mitchell, a Democrat on the group's board of directors and former member of the Oklahoma Legislature. She said the Democratic Party had to show it had "more to offer the American people than the simple powers of incumbency."

The group's aim was to pass a constitutional amendment and they were urging state legislatures to pass resolutions calling on Congress to enact such an amendment.

Unless lawmakers were pressured, Considine said, asking them to pass a term limit "is like asking the chickens to vote for Colonel Sanders."

Elsewhere, the term-limit concept had a smattering of supporters among Democrats. In California, one of the term-limit measures was sponsored by Democratic state Attorney General John Van de Kamp. In Colorado, the term-limit initiative was supported by Democratic Rep. Ben Nighthorse Campbell.

Term-limit activists also counted among their number Ralph Nader, the consumer advocate and co-founder of Public Citizen.

Outside the Republican Party, term limits enjoyed support from the Free Congress Federation, Citizens for Congressional Reform, the National Taxpayers Union and several conservative think tanks.

Opponents

Critics of the term-limit proposals contended that most of the consequences, foreseen or unforeseen, would be bad.

"It seems clear that reducing incumbents' advantages will not significantly improve how Congress works, and it could well make matters worse," wrote Gary S. Becker, an economist and sociologist at the University of Chicago.

Political scientists generally warned that term limits would banish veteran members regardless of their ability or popularity, disenfranchise voters wishing to re-elect such incumbents and ultimately empower those in non-elective jobs: bureaucrats, lobbyists and congressional staff.

"These proposals are the easy way out," said Catherine E. Rudder, executive director of the American Political Science Association. "They abdicate responsibility for dealing with more serious issues like the undue influence of money in politics and the fact that citizens don't pay adequate attention to what members are doing."

Indeed, some argued that limiting terms would make Congress worse, depriving it of members with historical perspective and established expertise in complex areas of modern government.

"When you have to deal with these enormous institutions, it does take quite a while to become proficient at it," said Rep. Don Edwards, a California Democrat who was elected in November to his 15th term in Congress.

Moreover, experts argued, the limits could have unforeseen effects. A 12-year limit might become, in practice, a 12-year guarantee — as prospective challengers waited for open seats. In the Senate, 12-year limits would make senators lame ducks for half their service.

Rudder, of the political science association, said, "It's much better to throw the rascals out if they are not doing a good job than to have to throw them out if they are doing a good job."

Some conservatives argued that term limits would actually restrict voters' rights.

"The basic issue is freedom," said Rep. Joel Hefley, R-Colo., "It's un-American. I came here to give Americans more freedom, not less."

In the House, Hefley was joined in opposition to the initiative by Colorado Democrat Patricia Schroeder.

"The image of a House top-heavy with long-term incumbents is false," Schroeder told constituents who wrote her. "Since 1980, more than half the House has turned over due to defeat, resignation, retirement or death. The average length of service is five terms."

Question of Motive

Although many Republicans as well as Democrats have opposed limiting congressional tenure, Arkansas Democratic Rep. Beryl Anthony Jr. said the idea's promotion was a GOP stratagem.

"One should see this movement for what it is: An attempt by the Republican Party to attempt to legislate congressional victories," said Anthony, who headed his party's House campaign committee. "The GOP can't win at the polls, and now they are trying to circumvent the ballot box."

But officials at the National Republican Congressional Committee said they were not pushing the idea. And it was not clear how much it would help Republicans.

"Republicans are not well-placed to take advantage of many of these seats," said Steve Hofman, a former House GOP leadership aide. But he said that limiting terms could make it easier for the GOP to recruit candidates.

"Republicans are more likely to field as good candidates people who accept the culture of the House as a transitory one; Democrats tend to accept the culture of the House as a career." ■

Bush: Mixed Results but Veto-Proof

In George Bush, lawmakers encountered a president who appeared to relish taking on, threatening, cajoling, even baiting, the Congress while achieving very little overall success after having done so. On the major issues of 1990, though, Bush fared considerably better.

Bush used various events throughout the year to test the limits of the executive branch and to emerge as a determined champion of presidential power. Often, Bush set out not only to protect the executive branch from congressional intrusion but also to reclaim lost ground.

On congressional votes during 1990 on which Bush announced a position, however, he prevailed only 46.8 percent of the time — the second-lowest score since Congressional Quarterly began compiling such ratings in 1953. *(Presidential support, p. 23)*

Democrats saw Bush's low rating as confirmation of their view of Bush as a president with weak legislative skills and a frequent indifference to domestic issues.

Conversely, 11 more successful vetoes stretched Bush's record to 21 without being overridden and made him the first Republican president to make it through a Democratic Congress without an override since Dwight D. Eisenhower survived the 85th Congress in 1957-58.

Republicans argued that CQ's numerical rating misrepresented Bush's actual successes, among which the president's defenders included passage of the five-year budget deal and the far-reaching clean air bill, as well as his successful vetoes. "I think it was a good year for the president," said Rep. Bill Gradison, R-Ohio. "On the big ones, the president came out just fine."

An Imperial Presidency?

During his tenure, Bush tried, among other things, to extend his pocket-veto power, launch a search for a legal rationale on which to assert line-item veto power, maintain control over federal agencies and regulations, and dominate foreign policy and defense issues.

"The president genuinely respects the role of Congress, but he also has decided to stand up forthrightly to preserve the powers of his own office," said Defense Secretary Dick Cheney, in explaining Bush's assertion of authority.

Meanwhile, the Justice Department advanced a legal theory for ignoring or reinterpreting laws the president considered unconstitutional. And the president routinely issued his constitutional interpretation of bills as he signed them, in effect laying out legal buoy markers to guide agencies and departments and challenging congressional efforts to circumscribe his powers.

The events of the year were an interesting contrast to Bush's maiden State of the Union address on Jan. 31. Bush unveiled no bold legislative ventures he would undertake from the commanding heights he had scaled in public-approval polls. Rather, he identified goals for the year — such as school improvement and environmental cleanup — about which no politician would dare quibble. His speech, unlike his actions throughout 1990, sounded few partisan or confrontational notes at the outset of the election year. *(State of the Union address, p. 18)*

Vetoes: Regular, Pocket

Tapping a traditional wellspring of presidential power, Bush and his lieutenants threatened vetoes on almost every major bill that had a chance of becoming law in the closing weeks of the 101st Congress.

"Every time we go to the bathroom around here somebody says, 'Check on the White House. They are going to veto,' " House Science Committee Chairman Robert A. Roe, D-N.J., complained.

Bush's success was so consistent that just the threat of a veto carried considerable weight. "He's had an extraordinary batting average," said Sen. Richard G. Lugar, R-Ind. "His threats have credibility."

Bush used the veto threat not only to kill legislation but also to stimulate serious bargaining, thereby serving his penchant for negotiation rather than confrontation.

"We have a lot of veto threats out there, but we don't take any of them lightly," said E. Boyd Hollingsworth Jr., the White House's chief lobbyist in the Senate, late in the session. "They are all there for a reason."

The president's veto successes were built squarely on the backs of his GOP troops. When the Senate sustained Bush's vetoes of bills to allow Chinese students to stay in the United States, to liberalize the Hatch Act's restrictions on the political activities of federal employees and to enact a broad new civil rights bill, every vote to sustain was cast by Republicans. Only one Democrat joined the Republicans in sustaining his veto of a bill setting conditions on the joint development of the FS-X fighter plane with Japan.

None of these veto fights were won with more than two votes to spare, and the White House worked hard to keep Republicans in line. Some GOP lawmakers did not share the president's opposition to the content of the bills but voted with him to preserve his (and their) political power.

Through it all, Bush's record of never having a veto overridden became a burden to maintain for some in the administration. Said an administration official, "I hate the idea of never having lost a veto."

Bush was not content, however, in using his regular veto powers. He sought to expand the use of the pocket veto — and led Congress to counter his attempts.

Two House committees approved legislation in 1990 designed to limit the president's use of the pocket veto to adjournment after a two-year session of Congress. But the legislation stalled, leaving the issue unresolved. *(Pocket-veto limitations, p. 21)*

Vetoes: Line-Item

Even when Bush signed bills, he still insisted on challenging the same Congress that passed the legislation. In his signing statements, Bush sometimes pronounced certain provisions of legislation unconstitutional and said he would not enforce them.

During 1990, Bush expanded the practice, routinely expressing concern over provisions in a wide range of measures. He cited sections of nearly all the appropriations measures — including those for the Treasury, defense, interior, foreign operations, energy and water, and military construction.

Most of the line-item concerns dealt with presidential powers and what Bush viewed as congressional overreaching in the appropriations (and other) measures. Other objections, though, dealt with foreign policy encroachments, the area Bush guarded most closely.

In the Antarctic Protection Act, Bush objected to a

Vetoes Cast by President Bush

President Bush vetoed 10 public bills and one private bill in his second year in office. In 1990, Congress tried to override eight of Bush's vetoes, six from 1990 and two from 1989, including the veto of the Chinese immigrant status bill (HR 2712), which Bush claimed was a pocket veto. *(Pocket veto, p. 21)*

All override attempts were unsuccessful. Although the House was able to achieve the two-thirds necessary to override three times, the Senate always sustained, preserving all of Bush's vetoes for the second year in a row. *(Previous vetoes, 1989 Almanac, p. 6)*

Under Article I, Section 7, of the Constitution, the president had 10 days (Sundays excepted) after receiving a bill passed by Congress to sign the measure into law or veto it, returning it to Congress with his objections. Congress could override a veto by a two-thirds vote of each chamber.

Any bill neither signed nor vetoed within those 10 days "shall be a law ... unless the Congress by their adjournment prevent its return, in which case it shall not be a law."

Bush's 11 vetoes in 1990 brought his total to 21. The greatest number of vetoes, 635, was cast by Franklin D. Roosevelt. Seven presidents vetoed no bills during their tenures. The total number cast by the first six presidents in the 40 years from 1789 to 1829 was 10. More recently, Ronald Reagan vetoed 78 during his term; Jimmy Carter vetoed 31; Gerald R. Ford, 66; Richard M. Nixon, 43; Lyndon B. Johnson, 30; and John F. Kennedy, 21.

Bill	Veto Date	Outcome	Story
Eastern Airlines Strike Resolution (HR 1231)	Nov. 21, 1989	House sustained 261-160, Mar. 7*	p. 369
Chinese Immigrant Status (HR 2712)	Nov. 30, 1989	House overrode 390-25, Jan. 24; Senate sustained 62-37, Jan. 25*	p. 767
Amtrak Reauthorization (HR 2364)	May 24, 1990	House overrode 294-123, June 7; Senate sustained 64-36, June 12*	p. 390
Hatch Act Revisions (HR 20)	June 15, 1990	House overrode 327-93, June 20; Senate sustained 65-35, June 21*	p. 408
Family and Medical Leave (HR 770)	June 29, 1990	House sustained 232-195, July 25*	p. 359
Textile Trade Act (HR 4328)	Oct. 5, 1990	House sustained 275-152, Oct. 10*	p. 219
Continuing Appropriations (H J Res 660)	Oct. 6, 1990	House sustained 260-138, Oct. 6*	p. 136
Civil Rights Act of 1990 (S 2104)	Oct. 22, 1990	Senate sustained 66-34, Oct. 24*	p. 462
Orphan Drug Act (HR 4638)	Nov. 8, 1990	Pocket-vetoed †	p. 577
Private Bill (HR 3134)	Nov. 16, 1990	Pocket-vetoed †	—
Indian Preference Act (S 321)	Nov. 16, 1990	Pocket-vetoed †	p. 421
Omnibus Export Amendments (HR 4653)	Nov. 16, 1990	Pocket-vetoed †	p. 198
Intelligence Authorization (S 2834)	Nov. 30, 1990	Pocket-vetoed †	p. 791

** Veto overrides required a two-thirds majority vote of both houses*   *† President's memorandum of disapproval issued on this date*

provision dealing with international agreements. The aviation security bill contained provisions on international terrorism and negotiations that bothered Bush. And Bush excised portions of the defense authorization bill that "impinge[d] on the president's authority as Commander in Chief and as head of the executive branch."

By the end of 1990, though, Bush had yet to assert the line-item objections to provisions that he viewed as merely too costly, not unconstitutional.

Such an assertion most certainly would have led to a legislative uproar and serious challenge — in Congress, if not in the courts.

Foreign Policy Focus

In a January 1987 speech to the Federalist Society, Bush bemoaned the "erosion of presidential authority" and urged a limited role for Congress in foreign affairs. As president, Bush pressed, if not for monopoly, then for preeminence in foreign affairs.

White House Counsel C. Boyden Gray contended that Bush was not trying to exclude Congress entirely from foreign affairs. "As a matter of constitutional law and political reality you don't ignore the Congress of the United States. But his trade is: I will consult with you, but in return I expect you not to micromanage. Get your say in a coordinated way."

Bush's actions in the Persian Gulf — deploying 400,000 troops to the area and maintaining that he could, without formal congressional approval, order an offensive attack against Iraqi forces — clearly demonstrated the degree to which he saw a president's power extending.

Continued on p. 20

State of Union Strikes Broad Themes

On Jan. 31, President Bush delivered his first State of the Union address to a joint session of Congress. Following is the Reuter transcript of the speech as delivered:

PRESIDENT BUSH: Mr. President, Mr. Speaker, members of the United States Congress: I return as a former president of the Senate and a former member of this great House. And now, as president, it is my privilege to report to you on the State of the Union.

Tonight, I come not to speak about the "state of the government," not to detail every new initiative we plan for the coming year, nor describe every line in the budget. I'm here to speak to you and to the American people about the State of the Union, about our world, the changes we've seen, the challenges we face — and what that means for America.

There are singular moments in history, dates that divide all that goes before from all that comes after. Many of us in this chamber have lived much of our lives in a world whose fundamental features were defined in 1945. And the events of that year decreed the shape of nations, the pace of progress, freedom or oppression for millions of people around the world.

1945 provided the common frame of reference — the compass points of the postwar era we've relied upon to understand ourselves. And that was our world — until now. The events of the year just ended — the revolution of '89 — have been a chain reaction, change so striking that it marks the beginning of a new era in the world's affairs.

Think back — think back just 12 short months ago to the world we knew as 1989 began.

One year ago, the people of Panama lived in fear, under the thumb of a dictator. Today democracy is restored — Panama is free. Operation "Just Cause" has achieved its objective. The number of military personnel in Panama is now very close to what it was before the operation began. And tonight, I am announcing that well before the end of February the additional numbers of American troops, the brave men and women of our armed forces who made this mission a success, will be back home.

A year ago in Poland, Lech Walesa declared that he was ready to open a dialogue with the communist rulers of that country. And today, with the future of a free Poland in their own hands, members of Solidarity lead the Polish government.

A year ago, freedom's playwright, Vaclav Havel, languished as a prisoner in Prague. And today, it's Vaclav Havel — president of Czechoslovakia.

And one year ago, Erich Honecker of East Germany claimed history as his guide. He predicted the Berlin Wall would last another hundred years. Today, less than one year later, it's the wall that's history.

Remarkable events, events that fulfill the long-held hopes of the American people — events that validate the longstanding goals of American policy, a policy based on a single, shining principle: the cause of freedom. America — not just the nation, but an idea, alive in the minds of people everywhere. As this new world takes shape, America stands at the center of a widening circle of freedom — today, tomorrow and into the next century.

Our nation is the enduring dream of every immigrant who ever set foot on these shores and the millions still struggling to be free. This nation, this idea called America, was and always will be a new world. Our new world.

At a workers' rally — in a place called Branik on the outskirts of Prague — the idea called America is alive. A worker, dressed in grimy overalls, rises to speak at the factory gates. He begins his speech to his fellow citizens with these words, words of a distant revolution: "We hold these truths to be self-evident: that all men are created equal, that they are endowed by their Creator with certain unalienable rights, that among these are life, liberty and the pursuit of happiness."

Goals for America

It's no secret that, here at home, freedom's door opened long ago. The cornerstones of this free society have already been set in place: Democracy. Competition. Opportunity. Private investment. Stewardship. And, of course, leadership.

And our challenge today is to take this democratic system of ours — a system second to none — and make it better — a better America.

Where there's a job for everyone who wants one.

Where women working outside the home can be confident their children are in safe and loving care, and where government works to expand child-care alternatives for parents.

Where we reconcile the needs of a clean environment and a strong economy.

Where "Made in the U.S.A." is recognized around the world as the symbol of quality and progress. And where every one of us enjoys the same opportunities to live, to work and to contribute to society. And where, for the first time, the American mainstream includes all of our disabled citizens.

Where everyone has a roof over his head — and where the homeless get the help they need to live in dignity.

Where our schools challenge and support our kids and our teachers — and where all of them make the grade.

Where every street, every city, every school and every child is drug-free.

And, finally, where no American is forgotten. Our hearts go out to our hostages, our hostages who are ceaselessly on our minds and in our efforts.

That's part of the future we want to see, the future we can make for ourselves. But dreams alone won't get us there. We need to extend our horizon, commit to the long view. Our plans for the future start today.

In the tough competitive markets around, America faces great challenges and great opportunities. We know that we can succeed in the global economic arena of the '90s, but to meet that challenge we must make some fundamental changes — some crucial investment in ourselves.

'Invest in America'

Yes, we are going to invest in America. This administration is determined to encourage the creation of capital — capital of all kinds.

Physical capital — everything, from our farms and factories to our workshops and production lines, all that is needed to produce and deliver quality goods and quality services.

Intellectual capital — the source of ideas that spark tomorrow's products. And, of course, our human capital — the talented work force we'll need to compete in the global market. And let me tell you: If we ignore human capital, we lose the spirit of American ingenuity, the spirit that is the hallmark of the American worker. That would be bad. The American worker is the most productive worker in the world.

We need to save more. We need to expand the pool of capital for the new investments that mean more jobs and more growth. And that's the idea behind a new initiative I call the Family Savings Plan, which I will send to Congress tomorrow.

We need to cut the tax on capital gains. Encourage risk-takers — especially those in our small businesses — to take those steps that translate into economic reward, jobs and a better life for all of us.

We'll do what it takes to invest in America's future. The budget commitment is there. The money is there. It's there for Research and Development, R&D — a record high. It's there for our housing initiative — HOPE — to help everyone from first-time home buyers to the homeless.

The money's there to keep our kids drug-free: 70 percent more than when I took office in 1989. It's there for space exploration. And it's there for education — another record high.

And one more thing. Last fall at the education summit, the governors and I agreed to look for ways to help make sure kids are ready to learn — the very first day they walk into that classroom. And I've made good on that commitment — by proposing a record increase in funds, an extra half a billion dollars, for something near and dear to all of us: Head Start.

America's Education Goals

Education is the one investment that means more for our future because it means the most for our children. Real improvement in our schools is not simply a matter of spending more. It is a matter of asking more — expecting more — of our schools, our teachers, of our kids and our parents and ourselves. That's why tonight I am announcing America's education goals — goals developed with the nation's governors. And, if I might, I'd like to say I'm very pleased that Governor [Booth] Gardner [D-Wash.] and Governor [Bill] Clinton [D-Ark.], Governor [Terry E.] Branstad [R-Iowa], Governor [Carroll A.] Campbell [Jr., R-S.C.], all of whom were very key in these discussions, these deliberations, are with us here tonight.

- By the year 2000, every child must start school ready to learn.
- The United States must increase the high school graduation rate to no less than 90 percent.
- And we're going to make sure our schools' diplomas mean something. In critical subjects — at the fourth, eighth and 12th grades — we must assess our students' performance.
- By the year 2000, U.S. students must be first in the world in math and science achievement.
- Every American adult must be a skilled, literate worker and citizen.
- Every school must offer the kind of disciplined environment that makes it possible for our kids to learn — and every school in America must be drug-free.

Ambitious aims? Of course. Easy to do? Far from it. But the future's at stake. This nation will not accept anything less than excellence in education.

These investments will keep America competitive. And I know this about the American people: We welcome competition. We'll match our ingenuity and energy, our experience and technology, our spirit and enterprise, against anyone. Let the competition be free — but let it also be fair. America is ready.

Controlling the Deficit

Since we really mean it, and since we are serious about being ready to meet that challenge, we're getting our own house in order. We've made real progress. Seven years ago, the federal deficit was 6 percent of our gross national product — 6 percent. In the new budget I sent up two days ago, the deficit is down to 1 percent of gross national product.

That budget brings federal spending under control. It meets the Gramm-Rudman target, brings that deficit down further, and balances the budget by 1993 — with no new taxes.

And let me tell you, there's still more than enough federal spending. For most of us, $1.2 trillion is still a lot of money. And once the budget is balanced, we can operate the way every family must when it has bills to pay. We won't leave it to our children and our grandchildren. Once it's balanced, we will start paying off the national debt.

Protecting the Environment

And there's something more. There's something more we owe the generations of the future: stewardship, the safekeeping of America's precious environmental inheritance. As just one sign of how serious we are, we will elevate the Environmental Protection Agency to Cabinet rank. Not more bureaucracy, not more red tape — but the certainty that here at home, and especially in our dealings with other nations, environmental issues have the status they deserve.

This year's budget provides over $2 billion in new spending to protect our environment, with over $1 billion for global change research. And a new initiative I call "America the Beautiful," to expand our national parks and wildlife preserves and improve recreational facilities on public lands. And something else — something that will help keep this country clean, from our forest land to the inner cities, and keep America beautiful for generations to come: the money to plant a billion trees a year.

And tonight — tonight, let me say again to all the members of the Congress: The American people did not send us here to bicker. There is work to do, and they sent us here to get it done. And once again, in a spirit of cooperation, I offer my hand to all of you, and let's work together to do the will of the people. Clean air. Child care. The Educational Excellence Act. Crime and drugs. It's time to act. The farm bill. Transportation policy. Product-liability reform. Enterprise zones. It's time to act together.

Social Security, Health Care

And there's one thing I hope we will be able to agree on. It's about our commitments. And I'm talking about Social Security. To every American out there on Social Security, to every American supporting that system today and to everyone counting on it when they retire: We made a promise to you, and we are going to keep it.

We rescued the system in 1983 — and it's sound again. Bipartisan arrangement. Our budget fully funds today's benefits, and it assures that future benefits will be funded as well. And the last thing we need to do is mess around with Social Security.

There's one more problem we need to address. We must give careful consideration to the recommendations of the health care studies under way now, and that's why tonight, I am asking Dr. Sullivan, Lou Sullivan, secretary of health and human services, to lead a Domestic Policy Council review of recommendations on the quality, accessibility and cost of our nation's health care system. I am committed to bring the staggering costs of health care under control.

The "state of the government" — the "state of the government" does indeed depend on many of us in this very chamber. But the State of the Union depends on all Americans. We must maintain the democratic decency that makes a nation out of millions of individuals. And I have been appalled at the recent mail bombings across this country. Every one of us must confront and condemn racism, anti-Semitism, bigotry and hate. Not next week, not tomorrow, but right now. Every single one of us.

'The Idea We Call America'

The State of the Union depends on whether we help our neighbor — claim the problems of our community as our own. We've got to step forward when there's trouble, lend a hand, be what I call a point of light to a stranger in need. We've got to take the time after a busy day to sit down and read with our kids, help them with their homework, pass along the values we learned as children. And that's how we sustain the State of the Union.

Every effort is important. It all adds up — it's doing the things that give democracy meaning. It all adds up to who we are — and who we will be.

And let me say that so long as we remember the American idea, so long as we live up to the American ideal, the State of the Union will remain sound and strong.

And to those who worry that we've lost our way, well, I want you to listen to parts of a letter written by James Markwell, Private First Class James Markwell, a 20-year-old Army medic of the 1st Battalion, 75th Rangers. It's dated December 18th, the night before our Armed Forces went into action in Panama. It's a letter servicemen write — and hope will never be sent. And sadly, Private Markwell's mother did receive this letter. She passed it along to me out there in Cincinnati.

And here is some of what he wrote: "I have never been afraid of death, but I know he is waiting at the corner. I have been trained to kill and to save, and so has everyone else. I am frightened of what lays beyond the fog, and yet, do not mourn for me — revel in the life that I have died to give you. But most of all, don't forget the Army was my choice — something that I wanted to do. Remember I joined the Army to serve my country and insure that you are free to do what you want and live your lives freely."

Let me add that Private Markwell was among the first to see battle in Panama and one of the first to fall. But he knew what he believed in. He carried the idea we call America in his heart.

I began tonight speaking about the changes we've seen this past year. There is a new world of challenges and opportunities before us. And there is a need for leadership that only America can provide.

Nearly 40 years ago, in his last address to the Congress, President Harry Truman predicted such a time would come. He said: "As our world grows stronger, more united, more attractive to men on both sides of the Iron Curtain, then inevitably there will come a time of change within the communist world."

Today, that change is taking place.

For more than 40 years, America and its allies held communism in check and ensured that democracy would continue to exist. Today, with communism crumbling, our aim must be to ensure democracy's advance, to take the lead in forging peace and freedom's best hope, a great and growing commonwealth of free nations.

And to the Congress and to all Americans, I say it is time to acclaim a new consensus at home and abroad, a common vision of the peaceful world we want to see.

Here in our own hemisphere, it's time for all the people of the Americas, North and South, to live in freedom.

In the Far East and Africa, it is time for the full flowering of free governments and free markets that have served as the engine of progress.

It is time to offer our hand to the emerging democracies of Eastern Europe, so that continent, for too long a continent divided, can see a future whole and free.

It's time to build on our new relationship with the Soviet Union, to endorse and encourage a peaceful process of internal change toward democracy and economic opportunity.

Troop Reduction in Europe

We are in a period of great transition, great hope, yet great uncertainty. We recognize that the Soviet military threat in Europe is diminishing, but we see little change in Soviet strategic modernization.

Therefore, we must sustain our own strategic offense modernization and the strategic defense initiative. But the time is right to move forward on a conventional arms control agreement to move us to more appropriate levels of military forces in Europe, a coherent defense program that ensures the U.S. will continue to be a catalyst for peaceful change in Europe. I've consulted with leaders of NATO — and in fact I spoke by phone with [Soviet] President [Mikhail S.] Gorbachev just today.

And I agree with our European allies that an American military presence in Europe is essential — and that it should not be tied solely to the Soviet military presence in Eastern Europe. But our troop levels can still be lower.

So tonight I am announcing a major new step, for a further reduction in U.S. and Soviet manpower in Central and Eastern Europe to 195,000 on each side. This number — this number, this level — reflects the advice of our senior military advisers. It is designed to protect American and European interests and sustain NATO's defense strategy. A swift conclusion to our arms control talks — conventional, chemical and strategic — must now be our goal. And that time has come.

Still, we must recognize an unfortunate fact: In many regions of the world tonight, the reality is conflict, not peace. Enduring animosities and opposing interests remain. Thus the cause of peace must be served by an America strong enough and sure enough to defend our interests and our ideals. It's this American idea that for the past four decades helped inspire this Revolution of '89.

And here at home and in the world, there is history in the making and history to be made.

Six months ago, early in this season of change, I stood at the gates of the Gdansk Shipyard in Poland at the monument to the fallen workers of Solidarity. It's a monument of simple majesty. Three tall crosses rise up from the stones. And atop each cross, an anchor, an ancient symbol of hope. The anchor in our world today is freedom — holding us steady in times of change, a symbol of hope to all the world. And freedom is at the very heart of the idea that is America.

Giving life to that idea depends on every one of us. Our anchor has always been faith and family. In the last few days of this past momentous year, our family was blessed once more, celebrating the joy of life when a little boy became our 12th grandchild. When I held the little guy for the first time, the troubles at home and abroad seemed manageable and totally in perspective.

Now, I know you're thinking: That's a grandfather talking. Well, maybe you're right. But I've met a lot of children this past year, across this country and everywhere from the Far East to Eastern Europe. All kids are unique. Yet all kids are alike: the budding young environmentalists I met this month, who joined me exploring the Florida Everglades; the Little Leaguers I played catch with in Poland, ready to go from Warsaw to the World Series. Even the kids who are ill or alone — and God bless those boarder babies, born addicted to drugs, coping with problems no child should have to face.

But, you know, when it comes to hope and the future, every kid is the same — full of dreams, ready to take on the world, all special because they are the very future of freedom. To them belongs this new world I've been speaking about.

And so tonight I'm going to ask something of every one of you. Let me start with my generation, with the grandparents out there. You are our living link to the past. Tell your grandchildren the story of struggles waged at home and abroad, of sacrifices freely made for freedom's sake. And tell them your own story as well — because every American has a story to tell.

Parents, your children look to you for direction and guidance. Tell them of faith and family. Tell them we are one nation under God. Teach them that of all the many gifts they can receive, liberty is their most precious legacy. And of all the gifts they can give, the greatest — the greatest — is helping others.

And to the children and young people out there tonight: With you rests our hope, all that America will mean in the years and decades ahead. Fix your vision on a new century, your century. On dreams we cannot see. On the destiny that is yours — and yours alone.

And, finally, let all Americans — all of us together here in this chamber, the symbolic center of democracy — affirm our allegiance to this idea we call America. And let us all remember that the State of the Union depends on each and every one of us.

God bless all of you, and may God bless this great nation, the United States of America. ■

Continued from p. 17

In one of his most sweeping challenges to congressional intervention in foreign policy-making, Bush said he would consider ignoring at least nine provisions of an otherwise routine State Department authorization bill that he signed Feb. 16.

While Bush had in the past challenged the constitutionality of individual legislative provisions that he insisted infringed on his powers, he had never before raised such complaints about as many items in one bill. One administration official said the broad attack on the bill amounted to a White House move to "reassert dominance" over foreign affairs. *(State Department authorization, p. 799)*

Other Areas of Contention

In a variety of other areas during Bush's first two years in office, the president challenged and tested the legislative branch. Among those were the following:

- **Defense deferrals.** The administration in February proposed a controversial plan to defer almost $2.2 billion in defense spending previously approved by Congress. It justified the bulk of the deferrals on the basis of global change, a rationale many members considered suspect and possibly in violation of the law.

"I am concerned that the spirit of mutual respect and cooperation may be breaking down," Sen. Daniel K. Inouye, D-Hawaii, told Deputy Defense Secretary Donald J. Atwood.

Under the 1974 budget act, the administration was allowed to defer previously appropriated spending for management, not policy, reasons. It was required to present Congress with a detailed description and justification for any deferral proposals, which then must be reviewed by

Congress' auditing arm, the General Accounting Office (GAO) for their legitimacy.

The administration sent such a proposal to Congress on Feb. 6, outlining 19 deferrals.

Said Department of Defense Comptroller Sean O'Keefe, "We ain't going to spend the money" for the purposes Congress intended.

"If they get away with it, it's tantamount to a line-item veto," said one Senate Appropriations Committee aide.

• **Agency control.** There had long been struggles to control the form and content of regulations issued by federal departments and agencies; 1990's battle was fought over reauthorization of the 1980 Paperwork Reduction Act. *(Paperwork reduction, p. 411)*

The act's main goal was to reduce the public's paperwork burden on such tasks as federal employment guidelines for small businesses, defense procurement contracts and even individual income tax forms. But its effect was to give the White House — specifically, the Office of Management and Budget (OMB) — growing control over the form and content of regulations issued by federal departments and agencies.

Members of Congress, arguing that the Constitution empowered them to oversee the agencies, answered with legislative efforts to regain a measure of control. Various congressional committees had in the past used their legislative and appropriations power to control agency decisions, often in ways contrary to White House directives.

Even some members of Congress, though, opposed legislation before the 101st Congress to restrict OMB's authority to review government regulations. Sen. Sam Nunn, D-Ga., said he was concerned that Congress might be stepping over the line into executive branch powers.

"It gets to be a matter of great constitutional concern in terms of separation of powers," Nunn said.

• **U.S. food aid.** A 1954 law, known as Food for Peace or by its public law number, PL 480, was drastically changed by the 1990 farm bill. To the Bush administration, though, the effort to restructure PL 480 — the U.S. food aid program that provided for commodity sales and donations— was a naked power play by Congress.

"We think it's really inappropriate for the legislative branch to dictate to the administration to quite such a degree," said Christopher E. Goldthwait, the Agriculture Department administrator who oversaw PL 480.

The Bush administration perceived the congressional effort to revamp PL 480 as an assault on its foreign policy prerogatives. Publicly, officials in both the Agriculture Department and the Agency for International Development argued against the changes, and said they would diminish the president's flexibility and exclude important viewpoints from deliberations over food aid.

• **Secrecy agreements.** Bush's efforts to assert control over national security policy renewed a clash with Congress over secrecy agreements. He expressed "profound constitutional concerns" about a congressional effort, in the fiscal 1990 Treasury appropriations bill, to forbid the administration from making its employees sign secrecy agreements.

In signing the bill, Bush indicated that he would ignore Congress. His role as commander in chief included the duty "to ensure the secrecy of information whose disclosure would threaten our national security," he wrote.

"This is something that can only be described as presidential lawlessness," argued Steven Ross, counsel to the House. "The president has no authority whatsoever to determine what duly enacted statutes shall constitute the law of the land."

The Justice Department thought differently. In a January 1989 brief, Justice argued that the Constitution's requirement that the president "shall take care that the laws be faithfully executed" included authority to disregard acts of Congress. "The president has the authority to decline, in the absence of a judicial resolution of the matter, to implement a statute that is patently unconstitutional or that he reasonably believes undermines his powers under the Constitution." ■

Pocket-Veto Measures Fail To Survive

Two House committees — Rules and Judiciary — approved legislation designed to limit the president's use of the pocket veto to adjournment after a two-year session of Congress. The measure, though, stalled before it reached the House floor or the Senate.

Under the Constitution, the president could prevent a bill from becoming law by withholding his signature if Congress, by adjourning, prevented him from returning the bill. The House and Senate designated agents to receive veto messages when they adjourned. The 1990 legislation (HR 849) sought to resolve a dispute between Congress and the White House over when the president could use this power.

President Bush had argued that he could exercise his pocket veto whenever Congress adjourned for more than three days. Twice in 1989, he pocket-vetoed bills under circumstances objected to by congressional leaders.

Many members of Congress contended, with the backing of a federal appeals court, that a president could pocket-veto a bill only after the final adjournment. HR 849 sought to codify that position.

The issue was important to the relationship between the two branches because a pocket veto was absolute, whereas a regular veto could be overridden by two-thirds votes of each chamber.

Background

After Presidents Jimmy Carter and Gerald R. Ford had agreed to pocket-veto bills only after the adjournment to end a Congress, Presidents Ronald Reagan and Bush reversed course.

Reagan broke the pattern twice to pocket-veto bills between the first and second sessions of Congresses. His second such veto — to block legislation barring aid to El Salvador — prompted a lawsuit. The administration lost in the federal appeals court in 1984, and the Supreme Court declined to rule on the merits of the case, saying the underlying issue was moot. *(1984 Almanac, p. 204)*

The appeals court said that the president could exercise his pocket veto only after the sine die adjournment that ended a Congress. The Bush administration, relying on Supreme Court rulings from 1929 and 1938, contended that it could exercise this power any time Congress adjourned for more than three days.

Bush quietly flexed his muscle in August 1989. While Congress was in its summer recess, he pocket-vetoed a minor measure (H J Res 390) to expedite signing of the savings and loan bailout bill. He thus became the first president since Richard M. Nixon to use a pocket veto within a legislative session.

Lawmakers regarded Bush's action as an attempt to set a precedent, because the legislation was otherwise inconsequential. Rep. Butler Derrick, D-S.C., chairman of the House Rules Subcommittee on the Legislative Process, said members considered suing Bush but backed off because the resolution was moot.

Derrick's subcommittee on Nov. 15 approved an early version of HR 849; it would also have written into law House and Senate rules designating legislative agents to receive presidential vetoes during lesser adjournments.

Two weeks later, on Nov. 30, 1989, Bush declared that he had pocket-vetoed a bill granting special immigration relief to Chinese students. He nonetheless returned the bill to Congress and proceeded to defeat an override attempt in the Senate, which prevented the issue from coming to another court test. *(1989 Almanac, p. 62)*

Legislative Action

The House Rules Committee on March 7 approved HR 849 (H Rept 101-417, Part I) by a party-line vote of 7-2. Derrick told the committee the measure was not aimed at Bush so much as it was an attempt to clear muddy waters.

"We're not trying to make a confrontation," he said. "All we're trying to do is codify what the courts have said over the last 20 years."

Nonetheless, Republicans characterized the bill as inviting a needless fight. The House GOP leader, Robert H. Michel of Illinois, who generally supported the congressional position in the past, said in a letter to Rules Committee Chairman Joe Moakley, D-Mass., that he would oppose this effort.

"Codification means confrontation with the president, and what is worse, useless confrontation," Michel wrote. "Any bill that neatly summarizes this view of the pocket veto will accomplish just that, and nothing more."

Despite Michel's warning, the bill proceeded to the House Judiciary Committee, where it was approved on a near party-line vote, 23-13, on May 22 (H Rept 101-417, Part II). The committee's Economic and Commercial Law Subcommittee had approved the bill by voice vote May 17.

Tom Campbell, R-Calif., a former Stanford University law professor who once clerked at the Supreme Court, voted for the bill. He was the only committee member to cross party lines.

Carlos J. Moorhead, R-Calif., argued the Republican position that nothing would be accomplished by sending a bill to the president that he would likely veto. "We don't need a new law; we need a final, definitive ruling from the Supreme Court," he said. ■

Bush's Success Rate Drops 16 Points

George Bush did not have a very good year in 1990, at least according to Congressional Quarterly's annual study of voting patterns in Congress.

On those congressional votes on which the president staked out a position, he prevailed only 46.8 percent of the time, the second lowest score since 1953, when CQ began its vote studies.

The lowest (43.5 percent) was compiled by Ronald Reagan in the second to last year of his presidency.

Bush's 1990 success rate was 16 percentage points below his 1989 score, a decline made all the more serious because he started his term so poorly: His first-year score of 62.6 percent was the lowest first-year rating of any elected president. The 1990 decline gave him the worst two-year record in the 38-year history of the CQ presidential support vote study. *(Background, 1989 Almanac, p. 22-B)*

Bush was hurt most in the House, where he lost nearly seven of every 10 contested votes.

He did much better in the Senate, scoring 63 percent, although even the Senate score was almost 10 percentage points lower than 1989's.

The president lost ground in both chambers and among both Democrats and Republicans.

Democrats saw Bush's low rating as confirmation of their view of Bush as a president with weak legislative skills, a frequent indifference to domestic issues and an ambiguous agenda that failed to make a clear choice between extending the Reagan legacy and moving beyond it.

"The administration has sought to 'stay the course' on the one hand while articulating new directions on the other," said House Majority Whip William H. Gray III, D-Pa., referring to a slogan made popular during Reagan's presidency.

"When they have to take a stand," Gray added, "they elect to 'stay the course.' "

Some Democrats suggested a more nuts-and-bolts ex-

Continued on p. 30

CQ Vote Analyses

Congressional Quarterly has since 1945 done various analyses of the voting behavior of members of Congress. The studies have become references for academics, journalists, politicians and students of how Congress behaves as an institution and how individual members vote.

CQ changed the methodology of several of these studies in 1987; other changes were made in individual studies in previous years. In the charts of individual members' scores that follow, for instance, a member's score was calculated two ways: once based on all votes, whether or not the member voted; another time based only on the votes the member actually cast. For consistency with previous years, graphs and the lists of individual leaders were based on the first set of scores. *(Discussion of methodology changes, 1987 Almanac, p. 22-C)*

Leading Scorers: Presidential Support

Highest Scorers — Support

Those who in 1990 voted most often for President Bush's position:

Senate Democrats		Senate Republicans		House Democrats		House Republicans	
Heflin, Ala.	60%	Mack, Fla.	88%	Montgomery, Miss.	56%	Walker, Pa.	85%
Boren, Okla.	58	Lugar, Ind.	86	Parker, Miss.	56	Archer, Texas	84
Breaux, La.	57	Cochran, Miss.	85	Stenholm, Texas	56	Crane, Ill.	84
Nunn, Ga.	57	Nickles, Okla.	83	Hutto, Fla.	54	DeLay, Texas	83
Ford, Ky.	55	Bond, Mo.	82	Ray, Ga.	53	Hansen, Utah	83
Robb, Va.	55	Burns, Mont.	81	Hall, Texas	51	Armey, Texas	81
Shelby, Ala.	55	Dole, Kan.	80	Huckaby, La.	50	Gekas, Pa.	81
Exon, Neb.	54	Simpson, Wyo.	80	Skelton, Mo.	50	Shumway, Calif.	81
				Barnard, Ga.	49		
				Taylor, Miss.	49		

Highest Scorers — Opposition

Those who voted most often against President Bush's position:

Senate Democrats		Senate Republicans		House Democrats		House Republicans	
Simon, Ill.	80%	Cohen, Maine	56%	Dymally, Calif.	87%	Morella, Md.	70%
Harkin, Iowa	78	Hatfield, Ore.	51	Hayes, Ill.	86	Conte, Mass.	69
Akaka, Hawaii	75	Jeffords, Vt.	46	Vento, Minn.	86	Schneider, R.I.	69
Kohl, Wis.	75	Heinz, Pa.	43	Wheat, Mo.	86	Gilman, N.Y.	66
Lautenberg, N.J.	75	Specter, Pa.	42	Dellums, Calif.	85	Shays, Conn.	66
Burdick, N.D.	73	Chafee, R.I.	41	Gonzalez, Texas	85	Horton, N.Y.	65
Cranston, Calif.	73	Packwood, Ore.	41	Jontz, Ind.	85	Machtley, R.I.	62
Mikulski, Md.	73	Pressler, S.D.	39	Kastenmeier, Wis.	85	Boehlert, N.Y.	60
Rockefeller, W.Va.	73	Durenberger, Minn.	35	Weiss, N.Y.	85	Leach, Iowa	59

How Often Presidents Won

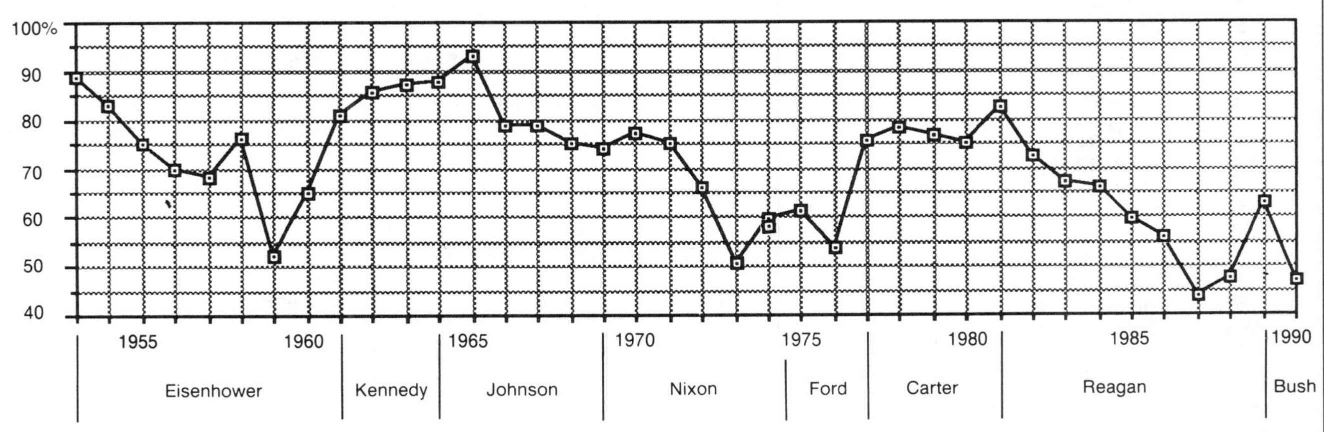

1990 Senate Presidential Position Votes . . .

The following is a list of Senate and House votes in 1990 on which there was a clear presidential position, listed by roll call number with a brief description and categorized by topic.

Senate

Vote # **Description**

Domestic Policy

31 Victories

Vote #	Description
10	Education Programs
13	Hate Crimes Statistics
32	Clean Air Bill
34	Clean Air Bill
35	Clean Air Bill
37	Clean Air Bill
40	Clean Air Bill
41	Clean Air Bill
43	Clean Air Bill
47	Clean Air Bill
49	Clean Air Bill
51	Clean Air Bill
52	Clean Air Bill
55	Clean Air Bill
108	Crime Bill
115	Amtrak Reauthorization
121	Hatch Act
132	Housing Programs
140	Crime Bill
143	Crime Bill
152	Americans with Disabilities Act
168	Farm Programs
170	Farm Programs
172	Farm Programs
248	CAFE Standards
282	OSHA Penalties
304	Civil Rights Bill — Veto
317	Farm Programs
323	Immigration
324	Clean Air Bill
325	Housing Programs

23 Defeats

Vote #	Description
6	Teacher Certification
30	Clean Air Bill
44	Clean Air Bill
48	Clean Air Bill
53	Clean Air Bill
69	D.C. Abortion Funds
90	Hatch Act
103	Crime Bill
128	Flag Constitutional Amendment
133	Crime Bill
136	Crime Bill
137	Crime Bill
139	Crime Bill
141	Crime Bill
161	Civil Rights Bill
187	Farm Bill
188	Campaign Finance
204	Campaign Finance
252	Family Planning
253	Family Planning
275	Civil Rights Bill
276	Civil Rights Bill
303	Spotted Owl

Defense/Foreign Policy

24 Victories

Vote #	Description
1	Chinese Students — Veto
16	Armenian Genocide
17	Armenian Genocide
39	Recognition of Lithuania
64	Aid to Panama
208	Stealth Bomber
209	Stealth Bomber
210	Base in Italy
212	Military Abortions Overseas
213	Forces in Europe
214	Military Pay
215	*Iowa*-class Battleships
216	Defense Spending
219	Antisatellite Program
221	Military Base Closings
225	SDI Funding
226	SDI Funding
249	Test Ban Treaty
263	German Unification Treaty
270	U.N. Population Fund
271	Troops in Europe
272	Stealth Bomber
295	El Salvador Aid
297	Egyptian Debt Forgiveness

7 Defeats

Vote #	Description
101	Chemical Weapons
181	Iraq Sanctions
220	Military Base Closings
223	SDI Funding
293	El Salvador Aid
296	Egyptian Debt Forgiveness
298	AID Family Planning

Nominations

2 Victories

Vote #	Description
56	T. Timothy Ryan Jr. (OTS)
259	David H. Souter (Supreme Court)

Economic Affairs/Trade

2 Victories

Vote #	Description
63	Caribbean Basin Initiative
326	Budget Package

2 Defeats

Vote #	Description
61	Footwear Tariffs
157	Textile Bill

Appropriations

2 Defeats

Vote #	Description
231	Treasury/Postal Appropriations
260	VA/HUD Appropriations

. . . And House Position Votes, by Category

House

Vote # **Description**

Domestic Policy

22 Victories

22 Eastern Airlines Strike
66 Hate Crimes Statistics
82 Money Laundering
93 Superconducting Super Collider
94 Superconducting Super Collider
123 Americans with Disabilities Act
182 Washington Center Funds
228 Americans with Disabilities Act
262 Parental and Medical Leave — Veto
342 Military Abortions Overseas
403 Immigration
410 Crime Bill
412 Crime Bill
413 Crime Bill
417 Crime Bill
418 Crime Bill
424 Crime Bill
494 D.C. Appropriations/Abortion
508 Farm Programs
523 D.C. Appropriations/Abortion
525 Clean Air Bill
530 Immigration

50 Defeats

7 Fisheries Bill
11 Voter Registration
40 Rural Economic Development Bill
45 Garbage Backhauling
49 EPA Cabinet Status
50 EPA Cabinet Status
52 D.C. Subway Funding
57 Child Care
58 Child Care
60 Child Care
68 Economic Development
74 Vertical Price Fixing
103 Amtrak Reauthorization
107 Parental and Medical Leave
111 Head Start
121 Americans with Disabilities Act
132 Clean Air Bill
137 Clean Air Bill
162 Amtrak Reauthorization — Veto
163 Hatch Act
168 AIDS Programs
184 Hatch Act — Veto
192 Flag Constitutional Amendment
214 Drug-Abuse Programs
221 High Technology Programs
234 Education Programs
256 Education Programs
258 Farm Programs
266 Farm Programs
274 D.C. Appropriations/Abortion
290 Housing Programs
294 Housing Programs
299 Farm Programs
309 Civil Rights Bill
310 Civil Rights Bill
318 Campaign Finance
330 National Service Programs
364 Indian Environmental Programs
365 Great Lakes Water Quality
369 Earthquake Program
380 Small Business Loans
386 Coastal Zone Management
387 Water Projects
399 Immigration
406 Immigration
422 Crime Bill
423 Crime Bill
425 Crime Bill
426 Crime Bill
478 Civil Rights Bill

Defense and Foreign Policy

10 Victories

99 Biological Weapons
128 Aid to Panama and Nicaragua
337 SDI Funding
345 ICBM Funding
347 Defense Spending
395 Antarctica Protection
453 Defense Spending
454 Defense Spending
479 Aid to UNITA
481 Covert Action

15 Defeats

4 Chinese Students — Veto
126 El Salvador Aid
127 El Salvador Aid
324 Base in Italy
327 Military Base Closings
339 SDI Funding
343 Nuclear Test Ban
351 Defense Spending
352 Defense Spending
480 Aid to UNITA
482 Aid to UNITA
483 Trade With China
484 Trade With China
485 Trade With China
486 Trade With China

Economic Affairs/Trade

2 Victories

440 Textile Imports — Veto
528 Budget Package

7 Defeats

89 Budget Resolution
238 Balanced Budget Amendment
286 Social Security — Deficit
335 Textile Imports
421 Budget Summit Package
474 Budget Package
475 Budget Package

Appropriations

1 Victory

433 Continuing Appropriations — Veto

1 Defeat

46 Federal Agency Appropriations

Presidential Support Definitions

Congressional Quarterly determines presidential positions on congressional votes by examining the statements made by President Bush or his authorized spokesmen. *Support* measures the percentage of the time members voted in accord with the position of the president. *Opposition* measures the percentage of the time members voted against the president's position. *Success* measures the percentage of the contested votes on which the president prevailed. Absences lower members' scores.

National Security vs. Domestic Issues

1990 presidential success scores broken down into domestic and national security issues, with national security including foreign policy and defense. Scores for 1989 are in parentheses:

	National Security	Domestic	Total
Senate	78% (79)	56% (69)	63% (73)
House	39 (58)	31 (47)	32 (50)
Total	60 (71)	41 (57)	47 (63)

Average Scores

Scores for 1989 are in parentheses:

Support

	Democrats	Republicans
Senate	38% (55)	70% (82)
House	25 (36)	63 (69)

Opposition

	Democrats	Republicans
Senate	60% (43)	27% (16)
House	70 (58)	34 (27)

Regional Averages

Scores for 1989 are in parentheses:

Support

	East	West	South	Midwest
Democrats				
Senate	31% (50)	38% (55)	49% (65)	33% (51)
House	21 (32)	21 (30)	34 (47)	22 (32)
Republicans				
Senate	61% (75)	69% (83)	79% (85)	73% (83)
House	52 (58)	67 (72)	68 (75)	65 (71)

Opposition

	East	West	South	Midwest
Democrats				
Senate	68% (49)	58% (42)	50% (34)	65% (48)
House	73 (61)	76 (65)	62 (49)	75 (64)
Republicans				
Senate	37% (23)	26% (14)	20% (14)	25% (15)
House	45 (36)	29 (25)	29 (22)	31 (26)

(CQ defines regions of the United States as follows: ***East:*** *Conn., Del., Maine, Md., Mass., N.H., N.J., N.Y., Pa., R.I., Vt., W.Va.* ***West:*** *Alaska, Ariz., Calif., Colo., Hawaii, Idaho, Mont., Nev., N.M., Ore., Utah, Wash., Wyo.* ***South:*** *Ala., Ark., Fla., Ga., Ky., La., Miss., N.C., Okla., S.C., Tenn., Texas, Va.* ***Midwest:*** *Ill., Ind., Iowa, Kan., Mich., Minn., Mo., Neb., N.D., Ohio, S.D., Wis.)*

Success Rate History

Eisenhower	
1953	89.0%
1954	82.8
1955	75.0
1956	70.0
1957	68.0
1958	76.0
1959	52.0
1960	65.0

Kennedy	
1961	81.0%
1962	85.4
1963	87.1

Johnson	
1964	88.0%
1965	93.0
1966	79.0
1967	79.0
1968	75.0

Nixon	
1969	74.0%
1970	77.0
1971	75.0
1972	66.0
1973	50.6
1974	59.6

Ford	
1974	58.2%
1975	61.0
1976	53.8

Carter	
1977	75.4%
1978	78.3
1979	76.8
1980	75.1

Reagan	
1981	82.4%
1982	72.4
1983	67.1
1984	65.8
1985	59.9
1986	56.1
1987	43.5
1988	47.4

Bush	
1989	62.6%
1990	46.8

	1	2	3
Alabama			
Heflin	60	39	61
Shelby	55	45	55
Alaska			
Murkowski	75	22	78
Stevens	72	23	76
Arizona			
DeConcini	40	57	41
McCain	74	25	75
Arkansas			
Bumpers	35	62	36
Pryor	34	62	36
California			
Cranston	27	73	27
Wilson	49	33	60
Colorado			
Wirth	37	60	38
Armstrong	62	18	77
Connecticut			
Dodd	39	58	40
Lieberman	37	62	37
Delaware			
Biden	33	67	33
Roth	72	28	72
Florida			
Graham	53	47	53
Mack	88	12	88
Georgia			
Fowler	43	55	44
Nunn	57	43	57
Hawaii			
Akaka [1]	23	75	24
Inouye	45	53	46
Idaho			
McClure	69	26	73
Symms	74	24	76
Illinois			
Dixon	53	47	53
Simon	20	80	20
Indiana			
Coats	77	18	81
Lugar	86	11	89

	1	2	3
Iowa			
Harkin	22	78	22
Grassley	70	30	70
Kansas			
Dole	80	20	80
Kassebaum	68	29	70
Kentucky			
Ford	55	45	55
McConnell	78	22	78
Louisiana			
Breaux	57	41	58
Johnston	53	41	56
Maine			
Mitchell	34	66	34
Cohen	44	56	44
Maryland			
Mikulski	26	73	26
Sarbanes	31	69	31
Massachusetts			
Kennedy	25	70	26
Kerry	25	70	26
Michigan			
Levin	33	66	34
Riegle	30	63	32
Minnesota			
Boschwitz	72	24	75
Durenberger	62	35	64
Mississippi			
Cochran	85	15	85
Lott	76	24	76
Missouri			
Bond	82	16	84
Danforth	74	25	75
Montana			
Baucus	51	49	51
Burns	81	19	81
Nebraska			
Exon	54	42	56
Kerrey	40	60	40
Nevada			
Bryan	44	55	45
Reid	44	55	45

	1	2	3
New Hampshire			
Humphrey	70	28	71
Rudman	74	20	78
New Jersey			
Bradley	32	66	33
Lautenberg	25	75	25
New Mexico			
Bingaman	35	54	40
Domenici	67	29	70
New York			
Moynihan	31	69	31
D'Amato	68	31	68
North Carolina			
Sanford	41	54	43
Helms	68	32	68
North Dakota			
Burdick	27	73	27
Conrad	34	66	34
Ohio			
Glenn	39	61	39
Metzenbaum	27	68	28
Oklahoma			
Boren	58	39	60
Nickles	83	16	84
Oregon			
Hatfield	38	51	43
Packwood	56	41	58
Pennsylvania			
Heinz	57	43	57
Specter	58	42	58
Rhode Island			
Pell	25	72	26
Chafee	58	41	59
South Carolina			
Hollings	52	48	52
Thurmond	78	22	78
South Dakota			
Daschle	31	66	32
Pressler	58	39	60
Tennessee			
Gore	38	62	38
Sasser	33	67	33

Democrats ***Republicans***

	1	2	3
Texas			
Bentsen	52	47	52
Gramm	78	14	85
Utah			
Garn	73	24	76
Hatch	77	22	78
Vermont			
Leahy	32	68	32
Jeffords	51	46	52
Virginia			
Robb	55	45	55
Warner	78	22	78
Washington			
Adams	34	65	35
Gorton	76	24	76
West Virginia			
Byrd	42	58	42
Rockefeller	26	73	26
Wisconsin			
Kohl	25	75	25
Kasten	71	29	71
Wyoming			
Simpson	80	17	82
Wallop	76	17	82

Presidential Support and Opposition: Senate

1. Bush Support Score, 1990. Percentage of 93 recorded votes in 1990 on which President Bush took a position and on which a senator voted "yea" or "nay" *in agreement* with the president's position. Failures to vote lower both support and opposition scores.

2. Bush Opposition Score, 1990. Percentage of 93 recorded votes in 1990 on which President Bush took a position and on which a senator voted "yea" or "nay" *in disagreement* with the president's position. Failures to vote lower both support and opposition scores.

3. Bush Support Score, 1990. Percentage of 93 recorded votes in 1990 on which President Bush took a position and on which a senator was present and voted "yea" or "nay" *in agreement* with the president's position. In this version of the study, absences are not counted; therefore, failures to vote do not lower support or opposition scores. Opposition scores, not listed here, are the inverse of the support score; i.e., the opposition score is equal to 100 percent minus the individual's support score.

[1] *Sen. Daniel K. Akaka, D-Hawaii, was sworn in May 16, 1990, to succeed Spark M. Matsunaga, D, who died April 15, 1990. Matsunaga was eligible for 24 of 93 presidential support votes in 1990. His presidential support score was 17 percent; opposition score was 21 percent; presidential support score, adjusted for absences, was 44 percent. Akaka was eligible for 64 of 93 presidential support votes in 1990.*

Presidential Support, Presidential Opposition: House

1. Bush Support Score, 1990. Percentage of 108 recorded votes in 1990 on which President Bush took a position and on which a representative voted "yea" or "nay" *in agreement* with the president's position. Failures to vote lower both support and opposition scores.

2. Bush Opposition Score, 1990. Percentage of 108 recorded votes in 1990 on which President Bush took a position and on which a representative voted "yea" or "nay" *in disagreement* with the president's position. Failures to vote lower both support and opposition scores.

3. Bush Support Score, 1990. Percentage of 108 recorded votes in 1990 on which President Bush took a position and on which a representative was present and voted "yea" or "nay" *in agreement* with the president's position. In this version of the study, absences are not counted; therefore, failures to vote do not lower support or opposition scores. Opposition scores, not listed here, are the inverse of the support score; i.e., the opposition score is equal to 100 percent minus the individual's support score.

[1] *Rep. Pasty T. Mink, D-Hawaii, was sworn in Sept. 27, 1990, to succeed Daniel K. Akaka, D, who was appointed to replace the late Democratic Sen. Spark M. Matsunaga. Akaka was eligible for 23 of the 108 presidential support votes in 1990. His presidential support score was 17 percent; his opposition score was 74 percent; and his presidential support score, adjusted for absences, was 19 percent in 1990. Mink was eligible for 36 of the 108 presidential support votes in 1990.*

[2] *Rep. James J. Florio, D-N.J., resigned Jan. 16, 1990, to become governor of New Jersey.*

[3] *Rep. Susan Molinari, R-N.Y., was sworn in March 27, 1990, to succeed her father, Guy V. Molinari, R, who resigned Jan. 1, 1990. Susan Molinari was eligible for 103 of the 108 presidential support votes in 1990.*

[4] *Rep. Jose E. Serrano, D-N.Y., was sworn in March 28, 1990, to succeed Robert Garcia, D, who resigned Jan. 7, 1990. Serrano was eligible for 101 of the 108 presidential support votes in 1990.*

[5] *Rep. Donald E. "Buz" Lukens, R-Ohio, resigned Oct. 24, 1990. Lukens was eligible for 104 of the 108 presidential support votes in 1990.*

[6] *Rep. Thomas S. Foley, D-Wash., as Speaker of the House, voted at his discretion. He voted on five of the 108 presidential support votes in 1990.*

KEY

† Not eligible for all presidential-support votes in 1990 or voted "present" to avoid possible conflict of interest.

Democrats ***Republicans***

	1	2	3
Alabama			
1 ***Callahan***	63	32	66
2 ***Dickinson***	66	31	68
3 Browder	41	59	41
4 Bevill	42	56	42
5 Flippo	29	41	41
6 Erdreich	37	63	37
7 Harris	39	59	40
Alaska			
AL ***Young***	56	38	60
Arizona			
1 ***Rhodes***	77	22	78
2 Udall	22	73	23
3 ***Stump*** †	73	12	86
4 ***Kyl***	79	19	81
5 ***Kolbe***	64	31	68
Arkansas			
1 Alexander	27	62	30
2 ***Robinson***	47	29	62
3 ***Hammerschmidt***	59	36	62
4 Anthony	27	71	27
California			
1 Bosco	25	73	25
2 ***Herger***	69	30	70
3 Matsui	21	75	22
4 Fazio	19	81	19
5 Pelosi	15	84	15
6 Boxer	14	81	15
7 Miller	16	81	16
8 Dellums	15	85	15
9 Stark	16	82	16
10 Edwards	17	82	17
11 Lantos	26	74	26
12 ***Campbell*** †	50	47	51
13 Mineta	16	83	16
14 ***Shumway***	81	19	81
15 Condit	25	70	26
16 Panetta	20	78	21
17 ***Pashayan***	57	40	59
18 Lehman	19	81	19
19 ***Lagomarsino***	70	30	70
20 ***Thomas***	54	35	60
21 ***Gallegly***	70	29	71
22 ***Moorhead***	74	26	74
23 Beilenson	26	71	27
24 Waxman	20	75	21
25 Roybal	16	81	16
26 Berman	20	77	21
27 Levine	19	78	20
28 Dixon	20	78	21
29 Hawkins	11	54	17
30 Martinez	18	79	18
31 Dymally	11	87	11
32 Anderson	18	82	18
33 ***Dreier***	73	27	73
34 Torres	17	81	17
35 ***Lewis***	65	26	71
36 Brown	19	76	20
37 ***McCandless***	71	29	71
38 ***Dornan***	68	27	72
39 ***Dannemeyer***	75	21	78
40 ***Cox***	75	24	76
41 ***Lowery***	67	29	70
42 ***Rohrabacher***	74	25	75
43 ***Packard***	71	26	73
44 Bates	16	80	17
45 ***Hunter***	69	28	71
Colorado			
1 Schroeder	18	81	18
2 Skaggs	21	79	21
3 Campbell	35	64	36
4 ***Brown***	70	29	71
5 ***Hefley***	71	29	71
6 ***Schaefer***	64	36	64
Connecticut			
1 Kennelly	22	78	22
2 Gejdenson	19	81	19
3 Morrison	13	61	18
4 ***Shays***	34	66	34
5 ***Rowland***	31	42	43
6 ***Johnson***	52	46	53
Delaware			
AL Carper	23	77	23
Florida			
1 Hutto	54	45	54
2 ***Grant***	56	44	56
3 Bennett	33	67	33
4 ***James***	58	41	59
5 ***McCollum***	74	23	76
6 ***Stearns***	71	29	71
7 Gibbons	32	66	33
8 ***Young***	68	30	70
9 ***Bilirakis***	51	29	64
10 ***Ireland***	75	20	79
11 Nelson	24	36	40
12 ***Lewis***	68	31	68
13 ***Goss***	72	28	72
14 Johnston	23	72	24
15 ***Shaw***	75	24	76
16 Smith	18	76	19
17 Lehman	19	81	19
18 ***Ros-Lehtinen***	50	45	52
19 Fascell	24	73	25
Georgia			
1 Thomas	43	56	43
2 Hatcher	37	59	38
3 Ray	53	44	54
4 Jones	34	63	35
5 Lewis	16	84	16
6 ***Gingrich***	66	29	70
7 Darden	43	57	43
8 Rowland	42	58	42
9 Jenkins	44	51	47
10 Barnard	49	40	55
Hawaii			
1 ***Saiki***	42	55	43
2 Mink † [1]	22	78	22
Idaho			
1 ***Craig***	59	25	70
2 Stallings	42	56	42
Illinois			
1 Hayes	13	86	13
2 Savage	19	80	20
3 Russo	29	70	29
4 Sangmeister	32	67	33
5 Lipinski	41	57	42
6 ***Hyde***	68	31	68
7 Collins	10	82	11
8 Rostenkowski	33	59	36
9 Yates	17	79	17
10 ***Porter***	65	33	66
11 Annunzio	35	65	35
12 ***Crane***	84	12	88
13 ***Fawell***	70	30	70
14 ***Hastert***	67	31	68
15 ***Madigan***	69	27	72
16 ***Martin***	45	35	56
17 Evans	16	84	16
18 ***Michel***	75	18	81
19 Bruce	20	80	20
20 Durbin	16	83	16
21 Costello	26	73	26
22 Poshard	23	77	23
Indiana			
1 Visclosky	22	76	23
2 Sharp	20	74	22
3 ***Hiler***	72	26	74

	1	2	3
4 Long	29	71	29
5 Jontz	14	85	14
6 ***Burton***	77	22	78
7 ***Myers***	69	29	71
8 McCloskey	20	78	21
9 Hamilton	27	73	27
10 Jacobs	23	76	23
Iowa			
1 ***Leach***	38	59	39
2 ***Tauke***	48	49	50
3 Nagle	20	78	21
4 Smith	27	72	27
5 ***Lightfoot***	68	30	70
6 ***Grandy***	63	37	63
Kansas			
1 ***Roberts***	71	27	73
2 Slattery	32	67	33
3 ***Meyers***	65	35	65
4 Glickman	27	72	27
5 ***Whittaker***	71	29	71
Kentucky			
1 Hubbard	42	57	42
2 Natcher	29	71	29
3 Mazzoli	31	68	32
4 ***Bunning***	71	28	72
5 ***Rogers***	69	31	69
6 ***Hopkins***	66	33	66
7 Perkins	24	76	24
Louisiana			
1 ***Livingston***	75	23	76
2 Boggs	19	70	21
3 Tauzin	46	49	49
4 ***McCrery***	68	25	73
5 Huckaby	50	44	53
6 ***Baker***	69	27	72
7 Hayes	38	49	44
8 ***Holloway***	67	29	70
Maine			
1 Brennan	19	68	22
2 ***Snowe***	48	51	49
Maryland			
1 Dyson	33	65	34
2 ***Bentley***	61	36	63
3 Cardin	21	79	21
4 McMillen	27	73	27
5 Hoyer	19	79	20
6 Byron	48	49	50
7 Mfume	15	81	15
8 ***Morella***	26	70	27
Massachusetts			
1 ***Conte***	31	69	31
2 Neal	19	72	21
3 Early	28	67	29
4 Frank	19	76	20
5 Atkins	20	80	20
6 Mavroules	23	76	23
7 Markey	15	82	15
8 Kennedy	21	73	23
9 Moakley	24	75	24
10 Studds	18	82	18
11 Donnelly	26	71	27
Michigan			
1 Conyers	16	81	16
2 ***Pursell***	53	38	58
3 Wolpe	15	82	15
4 ***Upton***	61	39	61
5 ***Henry***	58	40	59
6 Carr	29	69	29
7 Kildee	19	81	19
8 Traxler	25	66	28
9 ***Vander Jagt***	66	29	70
10 ***Schuette***	47	30	61
11 ***Davis***	44	52	46
12 Bonior	18	81	18
13 Crockett	13	47	22
14 Hertel	18	82	18
15 Ford	12	65	16
16 Dingell	20	78	21
17 Levin	19	81	19
18 ***Broomfield***	72	26	74
Minnesota			
1 Penny	34	66	34
2 ***Weber***	63	33	65
3 ***Frenzel***	74	14	84
4 Vento	13	86	13
5 Sabo	19	81	19
6 Sikorski	15	82	15
7 ***Stangeland***	59	40	60
8 Oberstar	17	82	17
Mississippi			
1 Whitten	34	62	36
2 Espy	20	75	21
3 Montgomery	56	44	56
4 Parker	56	44	56
5 Taylor	49	51	49
Missouri			
1 Clay	16	80	17
2 ***Buechner***	65	35	65
3 Gephardt	14	74	16
4 Skelton	50	48	51
5 Wheat	13	86	13
6 ***Coleman***	64	33	66
7 ***Hancock***	80	20	80
8 ***Emerson***	57	41	58
9 Volkmer	35	65	35
Montana			
1 Williams	24	72	25
2 ***Marlenee***	69	24	74
Nebraska			
1 ***Bereuter***	62	38	62
2 Hoagland	27	73	27
3 ***Smith***	73	23	76
Nevada			
1 Bilbray	33	67	33
2 ***Vucanovich***	72	23	76
New Hampshire			
1 ***Smith***	73	27	73
2 ***Douglas***	70	27	72
New Jersey			
1 Vacancy [2]			
2 Hughes	26	73	26
3 Pallone	29	71	29
4 ***Smith***	43	56	43
5 ***Roukema***	45	45	50
6 Dwyer	19	73	20
7 ***Rinaldo***	47	51	48
8 Roe	27	71	27
9 Torricelli	20	65	24
10 Payne	16	81	16
11 ***Gallo***	60	37	62
12 ***Courter***	60	32	65
13 ***Saxton***	57	42	58
14 Guarini	33	64	34
New Mexico			
1 ***Schiff***	55	44	55
2 ***Skeen***	68	32	68
3 Richardson	29	69	30
New York			
1 Hochbrueckner	23	77	23
2 Downey	19	81	19
3 Mrazek	16	81	16
4 ***Lent***	67	28	71
5 ***McGrath***	49	46	51
6 Flake	14	81	15
7 Ackerman	14	79	15
8 Scheuer	16	81	16
9 Manton	26	72	26
10 Schumer	19	78	19
11 Towns	11	82	12
12 Owens	12	80	13
13 Solarz	22	75	23
14 ***Molinari*** † [3]	56	44	56
15 ***Green***	41	58	41
16 Rangel	13	81	14
17 Weiss	14	85	14
18 Serrano † [4]	17	77	18
19 Engel	18	75	19
20 Lowey	14	83	14
21 ***Fish***	42	51	45
22 ***Gilman***	33	66	34
23 McNulty	27	72	27
24 ***Solomon***	67	32	67
25 ***Boehlert***	40	60	40
26 ***Martin***	60	39	61
27 ***Walsh***	44	54	45
28 McHugh	23	77	23
29 ***Horton***	32	65	33
30 Slaughter	16	84	16
31 ***Paxon***	69	30	70
32 LaFalce	30	67	31
33 Nowak	17	82	17
34 ***Houghton***	57	39	60
North Carolina			
1 Jones	28	66	30
2 Valentine	42	58	42
3 Lancaster	38	61	38
4 Price	24	75	24
5 Neal	36	59	38
6 ***Coble***	68	32	68
7 Rose	19	75	21
8 Hefner	33	67	33
9 ***McMillan***	66	33	66
10 ***Ballenger***	73	26	74
11 Clarke	33	66	34
North Dakota			
AL Dorgan	17	82	17
Ohio			
1 Luken	25	69	26
2 ***Gradison***	76	24	76
3 Hall	22	72	24
4 ***Oxley***	73	27	73
5 ***Gillmor***	69	29	71
6 ***McEwen***	69	29	70
7 ***DeWine***	65	33	66
8 ***Lukens*** † [5]	64	19	77
9 Kaptur	23	76	23
10 ***Miller***	68	29	70
11 Eckart	20	79	21
12 ***Kasich***	69	30	70
13 Pease	30	69	30
14 Sawyer	21	79	21
15 ***Wylie***	69	25	74
16 ***Regula***	56	44	56
17 Traficant	19	81	19
18 Applegate	30	69	30
19 Feighan	18	71	20
20 Oakar	17	80	17
21 Stokes	14	81	15
Oklahoma			
1 ***Inhofe***	69	31	69
2 Synar	17	82	17
3 Watkins	36	40	48
4 McCurdy	44	56	44
5 ***Edwards***	69	25	74
6 English	47	53	47
Oregon			
1 AuCoin	20	66	24
2 ***Smith, B.***	66	34	66
3 Wyden	24	76	24
4 DeFazio	19	75	21
5 ***Smith, D.***	59	21	74
Pennsylvania			
1 Foglietta	24	76	24
2 Gray	16	76	17
3 Borski	27	71	27
4 Kolter	24	69	26
5 ***Schulze***	61	37	62
6 Yatron	34	66	34
7 ***Weldon***	50	44	53
8 Kostmayer	20	80	20
9 ***Shuster***	63	36	64
10 ***McDade***	47	41	54
11 Kanjorski	25	74	25
12 Murtha	33	64	34
13 ***Coughlin***	58	36	62
14 Coyne	17	81	17
15 ***Ritter***	66	32	67
16 ***Walker***	85	15	85
17 ***Gekas***	81	19	81
18 Walgren	20	76	21
19 ***Goodling***	54	39	58
20 Gaydos	32	65	33
21 ***Ridge***	49	51	49
22 Murphy	29	69	30
23 ***Clinger***	66	32	67
Rhode Island			
1 ***Machtley***	38	62	38
2 ***Schneider***	30	69	30
South Carolina			
1 ***Ravenel***	54	46	54
2 ***Spence***	62	36	63
3 Derrick	31	68	31
4 Patterson	37	62	37
5 Spratt	29	69	30
6 Tallon	43	57	43
South Dakota			
AL Johnson	25	75	25
Tennessee			
1 ***Quillen***	65	29	69
2 ***Duncan***	74	26	74
3 Lloyd	43	56	43
4 Cooper †	37	62	38
5 Clement	25	74	25
6 Gordon	25	73	25
7 ***Sundquist***	74	25	75
8 Tanner	31	67	32
9 Ford	8	53	14
Texas			
1 Chapman	34	62	36
2 Wilson	35	50	41
3 ***Bartlett***	78	22	78
4 Hall	51	38	57
5 Bryant	13	84	13
6 ***Barton***	68	29	70
7 ***Archer***	84	15	85
8 ***Fields***	79	19	80
9 Brooks	18	71	20
10 Pickle	33	66	34
11 Leath	36	38	49
12 Geren	44	56	44
13 Sarpalius	48	48	50
14 Laughlin	47	48	50
15 de la Garza	24	73	25
16 Coleman	20	76	21
17 Stenholm	56	44	56
18 Washington	12	81	13
19 ***Combest***	78	22	78
20 Gonzalez	15	85	15
21 ***Smith***	68	31	69
22 ***DeLay***	83	16	84
23 Bustamante	25	69	26
24 Frost	22	77	22
25 Andrews	32	68	32
26 ***Armey***	81	18	82
27 Ortiz	30	69	30
Utah			
1 ***Hansen***	83	15	85
2 Owens	21	74	22
3 ***Nielson***	80	19	81
Vermont			
AL ***Smith***	33	56	37
Virginia			
1 ***Bateman***	69	31	69
2 Pickett	47	52	48
3 ***Bliley***	66	34	66
4 Sisisky †	43	57	43
5 Payne	42	58	42
6 Olin	35	63	36
7 ***Slaughter***	68	30	70
8 ***Parris***	60	37	62
9 Boucher	20	79	21
10 ***Wolf***	71	29	71
Washington			
1 ***Miller***	55	43	56
2 Swift	19	80	19
3 Unsoeld	15	76	16
4 ***Morrison***	51	46	52
5 Foley [6]	40	60	40
6 Dicks	28	70	28
7 McDermott	20	79	21
8 ***Chandler***	59	37	62
West Virginia			
1 Mollohan	31	66	32
2 Staggers	17	80	17
3 Wise	19	81	19
4 Rahall	14	81	15
Wisconsin			
1 Aspin	24	70	25
2 Kastenmeier	15	85	15
3 ***Gunderson***	60	40	60
4 Kleczka	21	78	21
5 Moody	17	78	18
6 ***Petri***	69	31	69
7 Obey	15	83	15
8 ***Roth***	63	35	64
9 ***Sensenbrenner***	75	25	75
Wyoming			
AL ***Thomas***	70	28	72

Continued from p. 22
planation for Bush's low rating, saying he had not devoted as much energy and attention to pushing his domestic agenda as he had to foreign policy issues.

Republicans contended that the rating misrepresented Bush's actual successes, citing passage of a five-year budget deal and a far-reaching clean air bill, plus six more successful vetoes, which stretched his 1989-90 record to 16 vetoes without being overridden.

"The numbers are misleading," said Nick Calio, the White House's chief lobbyist for the House. "You can't judge George Bush's success simply by the numbers of total bills and how many are passed over presidential objections."

One of Bush's chief jobs, he said, was to stop unsound legislation. "As long as we maintain our vetoes, that's one sign we're doing our job."

Poor House Showing

Bush suffered his biggest setback in the House, where his success rate fell from 50 percent in 1989 to 32.4 percent in 1990. His Senate score dropped from 73 percent to 63.4 percent. Democrats held a 258-175 advantage in the House and a 55-45 advantage in the Senate.

Bush was able to do better in the Senate, in part because it took fewer Democratic votes to lift the GOP to victory, and because on some votes — such as a veto override —there were enough Republicans to give him a victory even without Democratic support.

In addition, Senate rules gave Republicans much more freedom than their House colleagues to manipulate floor proceedings, which forced the majority to accommodate them more often than in the House. GOP senators could also force votes that Democrats could block in the House.

Support for Bush's positions — as measured by the frequency with which individual members supported presidentially declared positions — slipped across the board from 1989 to 1990, among Republicans as well as Democrats. Republican support for Bush in the Senate dropped from 82 percent in 1989 to 70 percent in 1990. In the House, GOP backing for the president declined from 69 percent to 63 percent.

The slippage among Democrats was more profound in the Senate, where Bush dropped from 55 percent to 38 percent support. In the House, Bush's Democratic support was already an abysmal 36 percent in 1989; it dropped to 25 percent in 1990.

As the antagonism between Bush and House Democrats increased in 1990, divisions between House Democrats and House Republicans decreased — a typical election-year pattern.

According to a CQ study of party unity (the number of votes on which a majority of Democrats opposed a majority of Republicans), partisanship in the House fell from 55 percent in 1989 to 49 percent in 1990.

Most analysts doubted that the president's poor track record would have much bearing on the success of his Persian Gulf policy, an issue that many said transcended the rumble of day-to-day politics. But they did say it augured even more trouble for his next two years in office, when there would be even fewer Republicans in Congress.

Too Few Republicans

The generic explanation for Bush's low success rate in 1990 was the same as it was for the first year of his presidency. Unlike Reagan before him, Bush came to the White House saddled with a Congress in which his party controlled neither body. Worse, Bush had fewer Republicans to work with in the House than any other newly elected GOP president in the 20th century.

Reagan entered office with a broad mandate for change, the Senate newly in the hands of the GOP, and a working majority of Republicans and conservative Democrats in the House. Bush had none of that.

Thomas E. Mann, director of governmental studies at the Brookings Institution, said Bush's first year found him confronting a House distracted by turmoil over the resignation of Speaker Jim Wright, D-Texas, and the uproar over the pay raise issue. In the second year, Mann said, the new House leadership finally found its footing and presented much more solid opposition to the White House.

Analysts said Senate Majority Leader George J. Mitchell, D-Maine, also appeared to have hit his stride in 1990.

Win-Loss Record

CQ's vote study was built on an analysis of all the roll call votes on the House and Senate floors in which the president staked out a clear position. The two-part study measured two indices:

- Presidential success: How often did the president win votes on which he took an unambiguous position?
- Members' support: How often did each member support the president, without regard to whether that position prevailed?

The study was based on all votes with a clear presidential position — a wide net that caught major, turning-point votes along with less important tests, such as multiple roll calls on the same issue.

Of the 862 recorded votes in both chambers of Congress in 1990, CQ's analysis identified 201 with clear presidential positions — 93 in the Senate and 108 in the House. *(List of votes with presidential positions, p. 24)*

One statistical explanation for Bush's poorer showing in 1990 lay in a big increase in the number of votes taken in the House (511, up from 368 in 1989) and a corresponding increase in the number of presidential positions taken (108, up from 86 in 1989).

Though Bush's success rate in the House stayed about the same, the additional House votes had the effect of giving the lower House rating added weight in determining Bush's overall score.

Overall, Bush had much better success with national security issues, on which he won 60 percent of the time when House and Senate votes were combined. National security votes included foreign policy and defense, issues that Bush said engaged him more than domestic policy. Nonetheless, Bush still did much better on national security votes in the Senate (78 percent) than in the House (39 percent), mirroring his overall success rate.

Bush's national security victories in the Senate came on a variety of issues, from Chinese students' visas — a veto the Senate failed to override — to the B-2 stealth bomber and NATO troop cuts, among others. Bush lost critical Senate votes on aid to El Salvador and the strategic defense initiative.

In the House, Bush fended off across-the-board cuts in defense authorization and appropriations bills, but he lost key tests on military aid to El Salvador, most-favored-nation status for China and Chinese students' visas — on which the House voted to override his veto (which was immaterial, because the Senate sustained it).

Domestic policy votes, on which Democrats tended to

unite more readily against the White House, proved significantly tougher for Bush. Overall, he won 41 percent of the domestic policy votes on which he staked out a clear position. Again, he did much better in the Senate (56 percent) than in the House (31 percent).

Bush pumped up his domestic average in the Senate with a series of votes on amendments to the clean air bill, on which the Democratic leadership had promised to back the White House position as part of a deal to get the legislation passed. Of the 17 votes on clean air, Bush's position prevailed 13 times. *(Clean Air Act, p. 229)*

The president won a major victory as well when the Senate failed to override his veto of the civil rights bill, which Bush insisted promoted racial hiring quotas. *(Civil rights, p. 462)*

Among Bush's Senate losses on domestic policy were teacher certification, campaign finance and the constitutional amendment to ban flag desecration.

House domestic policy votes were Bush's single worst category. He had at least one high-profile victory on a key test of wills when the House failed by 54 votes to override his veto of the family and medical leave bill. But his losses outnumbered his wins by more than 2-to-1.

Bush's most significant defeat came Oct. 5 when the House — including a majority of Republicans — slapped down the budget resolution (H Con Res 310) produced by the bipartisan budget summit and endorsed by Bush at a Rose Garden ceremony just days before the vote.

Bush made a rare prime-time TV appearance to rally public support for the budget agreement and called in House members for face-to-face sessions at the White House. When the vote was taken, however, the president could not hold a majority even of his own party.

"The House is clearly his big problem," said political scientist Jones. "The Republicans are so damn frustrated, for obvious reasons. They're the ones who get stuck all the time supporting him on veto overrides, yet they haven't experienced any of the rewards of majority status."

Michael S. Johnson, who until early 1990 worked for House Minority Leader Robert H. Michel, R-Ill., was not surprised by the low success rate in the House. "It suggests that the administration has some work to do in terms of whom it listens to on matters of strategy and how it deals with the legislative branch."

But Johnson saw little prospect for good vote scores as 1992 approached. "Democrats are addicted to regaining the White House and turning Congress into a partisan political playground; that's just going to get worse."

Surprise From GOP Leaders

While Bush suffered erosion in his congressional support across the board, perhaps the big surprise was the falloff in the support he enjoyed from leaders in his own party.

In 1989, House Minority Leader Michel and Minority Whip Newt Gingrich, R-Ga., were Bush's top two supporters when it came time to vote, rolling up support ratings of 88 percent and 87 percent, respectively.

In 1990, however, they were way back in the pack. Michel's 75 percent support rating tied him for 18th among House Republicans, while Gingrich's 66 percent tied him at 88th out of the House's 175 Republicans.

Gingrich, who parted ways with the president over Bush's abandonment of the no-new-taxes pledge, led the opposition to the Bush-approved budget deal that developed into an embarrassing rout for the president when a majority of the House GOP turned against the deal.

Bush's top two GOP supporters in the House in 1990 were Robert S. Walker, Pa. (85 percent), and Bill Archer, Texas (84 percent), who took diametrically opposed positions on the budget deal.

Walker, a Gingrich lieutenant, helped galvanize opposition to the deal, while Archer, a member of the Ways and Means Committee and one of the original budget-summit negotiators, backed the pact.

Bush suffered a less serious loss of support at the top of the GOP hierarchy in the Senate. Minority Leader Bob Dole, Kan., who led the Senate in 1989 with a 94 percent support rating, dropped to 80 percent in 1990.

Among the Senate Democrats who supported Bush most consistently in 1990 were two potential presidential candidates, whose voting records helped burnish their centrist credentials. Sam Nunn, Ga. (57 percent), and Charles S. Robb, Va. (55 percent), scored among Bush's top five Democratic supporters. So did John B. Breaux, La. (57 percent), outgoing chairman of the Democratic Senatorial Campaign Committee (Robb was incoming chairman), and Wendell H. Ford, Ky., newly elected majority whip for the 102nd Congress, (55 percent).

Majority Leader Mitchell, however, ran counter to the middle-of-the-road trend among Democratic leaders. His 34 percent support rating would have been even lower had he not agreed to stand with Bush to defeat deal-busting amendments to the clean air bill. *(Individual scores, p. 27)*

Some Caveats

The CQ analysis of presidential success in Congress gave a rough view of the president's ability to have his way on Capitol Hill. Since it measured only those issues that came to recorded votes on the House or Senate floor, however, it excluded some of the important ways in which a president influences the legislative process. For that reason, its results must be interpreted with care.

The study did not measure the way in which a president affected legislation before it reaches the floor, sometimes by threat of a veto. For instance, Bush played a major role in shaping child-care legislation, forcing the addition of a tax credit component to a bill that House Democrats had originally wanted to center on a grant program. *(Child-care bill, p. 547)*

Further, the president sometimes declined to take a position on major issues, with the result that some important votes did not become part of the CQ study. For instance, Bush allowed the controversy over restrictions on arts funding by the National Endowment for the Arts (NEA) to come to floor tests in the House and Senate without signaling a clear position.

Results of the study were also strongly affected by issues on which legislators took repeated roll call votes. For example, Bush's Senate success rating was significantly increased when the Senate voted 17 times on the clean air bill and 14 times on the fiscal 1991 defense authorization bill, with Bush's position prevailing 25 times against six losses.

Finally, as long as the president staked out a clear position, the CQ study did not discriminate between key tests of political strength and routine votes whose outcome was all but foreordained. For example, the study gave equal weight to the Senate vote to override the veto of the civil rights bill — which Bush won by a single vote — and a bill requiring the Justice Department to collect data on hate crimes. ■

Partisan Votes at 30-Year-High in Senate

After a year of low-intensity heat in 1989, partisan fires were rekindled in the Senate in 1990, with Democrats facing off against Republicans more frequently than in any year since 1961.

According to Congressional Quarterly's annual study of party unity — based on votes on which a majority of Democrats opposed a majority of Republicans — the Senate cast 54 percent of its roll call votes along partisan lines, up from 35 percent in 1989.

While partisanship rose in the Senate, however, it fell in the House. That was a typical pattern in that chamber during an election year, when lawmakers often voted their districts' interests before their parties'. In 1990, party-unity votes fell to 49 percent, from 55 percent in 1989.

Why partisanship took such a leap in the Senate was open to dispute. Some Republicans attributed it to election-year politicking by Majority Leader George J. Mitchell, D-Maine, while Democrats said it was their ability to stick together and the nature of the issues.

"In his second year, Mitchell really came into his own as a leader," said Norman J. Ornstein of the American Enterprise Institute. "He began to frame things in ways that were uncomfortable for the Republicans and George Bush."

Ornstein said Mitchell clearly pressed for votes that Republicans did not want to take. That, he said, brought out the partisanship in Minority Leader Bob Dole, R-Kan. "Both sides were trying mightily to frame the debate, and you get votes set to make a point," Ornstein said.

Tom Daschle, D-S.D., who worked closely with Mitchell on the Democratic Policy Committee, agreed that the jump in partisan numbers could be attributed to the majority leader's style. But he said it was a style that built consensus among Democrats.

"I honestly don't believe that George Mitchell called for one vote where the intent was to embarrass or put the Republicans on the defensive," Daschle said. "He doesn't work that way; he's a lot more interested in showing Democratic cohesion than Republican disarray."

Thomas E. Mann, director of governmental studies at the Brookings Institution, said it was more significant that Democrats and Republicans continued to vote with their party at about the same rate as the year before.

Mann suggested the party-unity statistics could be misleading, illustrating his point by noting that 13 votes on the clean air bill (S 1630 — PL 101-549) counted as party-unity votes actually reflected regional, not partisan, interests. He pointed out that the only reason senators were voting on the bill in the first place was because of a bipartisan agreement to move the legislation. *(Clean Air Act, p. 229)*

"The irony is that you impugn a more partisan environment, and yet it's all built on a string of votes whose essential core is made possible by a bipartisan agreement," Mann said.

Removing clean air votes from the calculation of party unity would have pushed the Senate score back to 50 percent, roughly what it was in 1985-86.

Still, many party-unity votes seemed to reflect an attempt by Democrats to pin down or embarrass Republicans. *(Vote list, p. 35)*

For example, debate over the Civil Rights Act painted Republicans as hostile to women and minorities — groups the GOP had assiduously courted under President Bush. The bill (S 2104) would have made it easier to prove job discrimination, nullifying six 1989 Supreme Court rulings.

In July, the Senate voted 62-38 to cut off debate and vote on the measure, although negotiations over the content were ongoing. The move sparked a bitterly angry reaction from Dole, who said Mitchell was treating the Republicans like "a bunch of bums."

Dole accused the Democrats of forcing action on the bill "to put the Republicans on record as being against civil rights." Mitchell, however, said he would not have called the vote if he had believed an agreement was near or if Republicans had agreed to a timetable to finish negotiations.

When the civil rights conference report reached the floor in October, the Senate rejected, 35-61, a motion by Dole to send it back to conference to make it more palatable to Bush. Despite repeated veto threats and charges from the administration that it was really a quota bill, the Senate approved the conference report 62-34, with the help of nine liberal Republicans.

As expected, Bush vetoed the legislation, providing another opportunity for Democrats to point up their differences with Senate Republicans. On Oct. 24, the Senate fell one vote short in its effort to override Bush's veto. *(Civil rights bill, p. 462)*

"They clearly saw a partisan advantage," said Sheila Burke, Dole's chief of staff. "A lot of our guys have a strong history of support of civil rights legislation, and they are never comfortable voting against it."

Rudy Boschwitz, R-Minn., was obviously uneasy. He voted against the legislation initially but in the midst of a heated campaign for re-election voted for the conference report on the bill. The switch opened him up to ridicule by his Democratic opponent, Paul Wellstone, who won.

Playing Politics?

In an election year, Republicans often used crime to beat up on Democrats. Having shown themselves to be vulnerable on crime issues in recent national elections, Democrats attempted to wrest the issue away and pin the "weak on crime" tag on the GOP.

As the omnibus anticrime package (S 1970) was being debated, Republicans failed in their attempts to take out stringent language banning semiautomatic weapons. That surprise threw the legislation off track and prompted Republicans to stall.

Twice, Mitchell tried to invoke cloture and limit debate in order to bring the bill to a final vote. Both times the effort failed, 54-37 on June 5 and 57-37 on June 7. (A three-fifths majority of the Senate, or 60 votes, was required to limit debate.) *(Anticrime package, p. 486)*

Two weeks before the cloture votes, Judiciary Committee Chairman Joseph R. Biden Jr., D-Del., told reporters that if amendments were not stopped and debate cut off, "you just declare that Republicans killed the crime bill."

After the second cloture vote, Mitchell played the partisan: "If there is one thing that is clear, Democrats want a crime bill. We did not just talk about wanting a crime bill. We voted for a crime bill, just this morning."

Legislation to revise campaign finance rules also brought out partisanship in lawmakers in both parties, in

Continued on p. 39

Leading Scorers: Party Unity

Highest Scorers — Support

Those who in 1990 most often voted with their party's majority against the majority of the other party:

Senate

Democrats		Republicans	
Adams, Wash.	93%	Symms, Idaho	93%
Gore, Tenn.	93	Burns, Mont.	92
Leahy, Vt.	93	Nickles, Okla.	91
Sarbanes, Md.	93	Hatch, Utah	89
Cranston, Calif.	90	Thurmond, S.C.	89
Sasser, Tenn.	90	Garn, Utah	88
Simon, Ill.	90	Gramm, Texas	88
Dodd, Conn.	89	Helms, N.C.	88
Kennedy, Mass.	89	Wallop, Wyo.	88
Mikulski, Md.	89	Coats, Ind.	87
Mitchell, Maine	89		
Moynihan, N.Y.	89		

House

Democrats		Republicans	
Evans, Ill.	97%	Hancock, Mo.	98%
Levin, Mich.	97	Armey, Texas	95
Hoyer, Md.	96	Burton, Ind.	95
Bonior, Mich.	95	Walker, Pa.	95
Cardin, Md.	95	Bunning, Ky.	94
Gejdenson, Conn.	95	Dreier, Calif.	94
Hayes, Ill.	95	Herger, Calif.	94
Kildee, Mich.	95	Kyl, Ariz.	94
Lewis, Ga.	95	Dannemeyer, Calif.	93
Moakley, Mass.	95	Moorhead, Calif.	93
Sabo, Minn.	95	Paxon, N.Y.	93
Studds, Mass.	95	Sensenbrenner, Wis.	93
Vento, Minn.	95		
Wheat, Mo.	95		

Highest Scorers — Opposition

Those who in 1990 most often voted against their party's majority:

Senate

Democrats		Republicans	
Heflin, Ala.	46%	Jeffords, Vt.	61%
Shelby, Ala.	41	Hatfield, Ore.	58
Boren, Okla.	34	Cohen, Maine	53
Exon, Neb.	34	Packwood, Ore.	53
Breaux, La.	31	Heinz, Pa.	47
Dixon, Ill.	30	Specter, Pa.	46
Ford, Ky.	30	Durenberger, Minn.	40
Johnston, La.	29	Chafee, R.I.	36
Baucus, Mont.	28		

House

Democrats		Republicans	
Stenholm, Texas	47%	Conte, Mass.	71%
Parker, Miss.	46	Horton, N.Y.	66
Hutto, Fla.	44	Morella, Md.	65
Taylor, Miss.	43	Gilman, N.Y.	63
Hall, Texas	41	Green, N.Y.	60
Jacobs, Ind.	41	Schneider, R.I.	57
		Smith, N.J.	54
		Boehlert, N.Y.	52

Proportion of Partisan Roll Calls

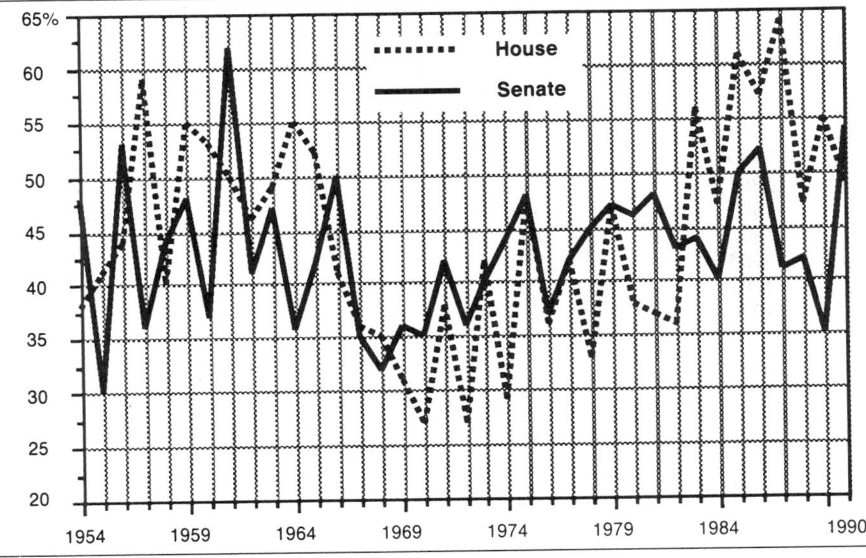

Party-Unity Definitions

Party-unity votes. Recorded votes in the Senate or the House that split the parties, with a majority of voting Democrats opposing a majority of voting Republicans.

Party-unity scores. Percentage of party-unity votes on which a member voted "yea" or "nay" *in agreement* with a majority of his party. Failures to vote, even if a member announced his stand, lower his score.

Opposition-to-party scores. Percentage of party-unity votes on which a member voted "yea" or "nay" *in disagreement* with a majority of his party. A member's party-unity and opposition-to-party scores add up to 100 percent only if he voted on all party-unity votes.

Average Scores by Party

	1990		1989	
	Dem.	Rep.	Dem.	Rep.
Party Unity	81%	74%	81%	73%
Senate	80	75	78	78
House	81	74	81	72

	1990		1989	
	Dem.	Rep.	Dem.	Rep.
Opposition	13%	21%	14%	23%
Senate	18	22	20	20
House	13	21	13	24

Sectional Support, Opposition

SENATE	Support	Opposition
Northern Democrats	83%	15%
Southern Democrats	74	24
Northern Republicans	73	24
Southern Republicans	84	14

HOUSE	Support	Opposition
Northern Democrats	84%	9%
Southern Democrats	73	20
Northern Republicans	72	23
Southern Republicans	80	15

1990 Victories, Defeats

	Senate	House	Total
Democrats won, Republicans lost	113	220	333
Republicans won, Democrats lost	64	43	107

Unanimous Voting by Parties

The number of times each party voted unanimously on 1990 party-unity votes. Scores for 1989 are in parentheses:

	Senate	House	Total
Democrats voted unanimously	28 (5)	13 (5)	41 (10)
Republicans voted unanimously	5 (7)	17 (9)	22 (16)

Party-Unity Average Scores

Year	Democrats	Republicans	Year	Democrats	Republicans
1990	81%	74%	1975	69	70
1989	81	73	1974	63	62
1988	79	73	1973	68	68
1987	81	74	1972	57	64
1986	78	71	1971	62	66
1985	79	75	1970	57	59
1984	74	72	1969	62	62
1983	76	74	1968	57	63
1982	72	71	1967	66	71
1981	69	76	1966	61	67
1980	68	70	1965	69	70
1979	69	72	1964	67	69
1978	64	67	1963	71	72
1977	67	70	1962	69	68
1976	65	66	1961	71	72

Breakdown of Party-Unity Votes

Following are the votes, listed by roll call number, on which a majority of Democrats voted against a majority of Republicans.

House

(263 of 536 votes)

2, 3, 5, 6, 9, 10, 11, 19, 22, 24, 25, 27, 28, 35, 37, 38, 47, 49, 52, 53, 54, 55, 57, 58, 59, 60, 69, 71, 72, 73, 74, 80, 89, 93, 95, 97, 100, 101

104, 105, 106, 107, 109, 112, 113, 114, 117, 118, 119, 120, 121, 122, 125, 126, 127, 128, 132, 133, 139, 140, 143, 144, 145, 146, 147, 148, 153, 158, 159, 161, 162, 164, 165, 166, 172, 173

174, 177, 178, 179, 180, 183, 184, 189, 190, 191, 192, 193, 197, 200, 201, 203, 209, 216, 217, 218, 219, 220, 221, 222, 224, 227, 231, 232, 236, 237, 238, 239, 240, 241, 242, 244, 245

246, 247, 248, 250, 251, 254, 261, 262, 264, 270, 273, 274, 275, 277, 278, 279, 280, 281, 282, 284, 287, 291, 297, 300, 301, 304, 305, 307, 308, 309, 310, 311, 312, 313, 314, 315, 316

317, 318, 319, 322, 324, 326, 327, 328, 330, 333, 334, 335, 337, 338, 339, 340, 341, 342, 343, 345, 346, 348, 351, 352, 353, 354, 355, 364, 369, 371, 372, 373, 374, 375, 376, 378, 384, 385

388, 392, 398, 399, 400, 402, 404, 405, 406, 408, 411, 413, 416, 417, 418, 419, 422, 423, 424, 425, 431, 432, 433, 434, 436, 437, 438, 440, 442, 443, 447, 450, 454, 456, 458, 459, 460

461, 463, 466, 467, 468, 470, 471, 472, 474, 475, 476, 478, 479, 480, 482, 483, 488, 490, 491, 493, 494, 496, 499, 500, 501, 502, 512, 513, 516, 517, 519, 523, 526, 527, 528, 529, 531, 536

Senate

(177 of 326 votes)

1, 6, 7, 8, 9, 16, 17, 19, 20, 22, 23, 25, 30, 37, 39, 40, 43, 44, 46, 47, 49, 50, 51, 53, 54

56, 61, 64, 65, 68, 69, 72, 73, 74, 76, 77, 78, 79, 80, 81, 82, 83, 84, 85, 86, 87, 90, 92, 93, 95

99, 103, 104, 105, 106, 107, 108, 109, 110, 111, 112, 114, 115, 120, 121, 122, 123, 125, 128, 129, 130, 131, 133, 136, 137

138, 139, 141, 148, 150, 151, 155, 156, 157, 158, 159, 160, 161, 163, 164, 166, 167, 168, 169, 171, 173, 176, 177, 178, 180

182, 183, 186, 188, 189, 190, 191, 192, 194, 195, 197, 198, 199, 200, 201, 202, 204, 208, 209, 210, 212, 213, 215, 216, 219

220, 221, 223, 225, 226, 228, 229, 234, 244, 246, 247, 248, 252, 253, 255, 256, 257, 262, 266, 267, 268, 270, 271, 272, 275, 276

278, 279, 280, 281, 285, 286, 287, 289, 293, 295, 297, 298, 301, 302, 303, 304, 305, 307, 310, 311, 312, 313, 316, 321, 322, 326

Party Unity and Party Opposition: House

1. Party Unity, 1990. Percentage of 263 party-unity recorded votes in 1990 on which a representative voted "yea" or "nay" *in agreement* with a majority of his or her party. (Party-unity roll calls are those on which a majority of voting Democrats opposed a majority of voting Republicans.) Failures to vote lower both party-unity and party-opposition scores.

2. Party Opposition, 1990. Percentage of 263 party-unity recorded votes in 1990 on which a representative voted "yea" or "nay" *in disagreement* with a majority of his or her party. Failures to vote lower both party-unity and party-opposition scores.

3. Party Unity, 1990. Percentage of 263 party-unity recorded votes in 1990 on which a representative was present and voted "yea" or "nay" *in agreement* with a majority of his or her party. In this version of the study, absences are not counted; therefore, failures to vote do not lower unity or opposition scores. Opposition scores, not listed here, are the inverse of the unity score; i.e., the opposition score is equal to 100 percent minus the individual's unity score.

[1] *Rep. Pasty T. Mink, D-Hawaii, was sworn in Sept. 27, 1990, to succeed Daniel K. Akaka, D, who was appointed to replace the late Democratic Sen. Spark M. Matsunaga. Akaka was eligible for 42 of the 263 party-unity votes in 1990. His party-unity score was 86 percent; opposition score was 0 percent; unity score, adjusted for absences, was 100 percent in 1990. Mink was eligible for 74 of the 263 party-unity votes in 1990.*

[2] *Rep. James J. Florio, D-N.J., resigned Jan. 16, 1990, to become governor of New Jersey.*

[3] *Rep. Susan Molinari, R-N.Y., was sworn in March 27, 1990, to succeed her father, Guy V. Molinari, R, who resigned Jan. 1. Susan Molinari was eligible for 247 of the 263 party-unity votes in 1990.*

[4] *Rep. Jose E. Serrano, D-N.Y., was sworn in March 28, 1990, to succeed Robert Garcia, D, who resigned Jan. 7. Serrano was eligible for 246 of the 263 party-unity votes in 1990.*

[5] *Rep. Donald E. "Buz" Lukens, R-Ohio, resigned Oct. 24, 1990. Lukens was eligible for 252 of the 263 party-unity votes in 1990.*

[6] *Rep. Thomas S. Foley, D-Wash., as Speaker of the House, voted at his discretion. He voted on nine of 263 party-unity votes.*

KEY

† Not eligible for all party-unity votes in 1990 or voted "present" to avoid possible conflict of interest.

Democrats *Republicans*

	1	2	3
Alabama			
1 ***Callahan*** †	73	20	79
2 ***Dickinson***	82	12	87
3 Browder	74	25	75
4 Bevill	71	23	76
5 Flippo	50	17	75
6 Erdreich	73	27	73
7 Harris	73	26	74
Alaska			
AL ***Young***	60	25	70
Arizona			
1 ***Rhodes***	90	9	91
2 Udall	76	7	92
3 ***Stump***	79	3	96
4 ***Kyl***	94	4	96
5 ***Kolbe***	82	14	86
Arkansas			
1 Alexander	72	10	88
2 ***Robinson***	52	18	75
3 ***Hammerschmidt***	72	21	77
4 Anthony	85	11	89
California			
1 Bosco	84	11	88
2 ***Herger***	94	4	96
3 Matsui	89	5	95
4 Fazio	91	5	95
5 Pelosi	92	3	96
6 Boxer	86	4	95
7 Miller	89	6	94
8 Dellums	87	5	94
9 Stark	88	5	95
10 Edwards	92	3	97
11 Lantos	89	6	93
12 ***Campbell*** †	69	28	71
13 Mineta	92	2	98
14 ***Shumway***	84	13	87
15 Condit	70	24	75
16 Panetta	89	7	93
17 ***Pashayan***	66	29	69
18 Lehman	89	6	94
19 ***Lagomarsino***	89	11	89
20 ***Thomas***	74	11	87
21 ***Gallegly***	91	6	94
22 ***Moorhead***	93	6	94
23 Beilenson	89	8	92
24 Waxman	90	4	96
25 Roybal	92	4	96
26 Berman	93	3	97
27 Levine	93	3	96
28 Dixon	89	3	97
29 Hawkins	63	4	94
30 Martinez	81	6	93
31 Dymally	87	3	97
32 Anderson	93	7	93
33 ***Dreier***	94	6	94
34 Torres	94	2	98
35 ***Lewis***	70	19	78
36 Brown	79	5	94
37 ***McCandless***	92	7	93
38 ***Dornan***	83	6	93
39 ***Dannemeyer***	93	2	98
40 ***Cox***	86	8	92
41 ***Lowery***	68	19	78
42 ***Rohrabacher***	90	10	90
43 ***Packard***	82	13	86
44 Bates	80	14	85
45 ***Hunter***	84	11	89
Colorado			
1 Schroeder	72	27	73
2 Skaggs	93	6	94
3 Campbell	72	23	76
4 ***Brown***	87	11	88
5 ***Hefley***	90	6	93
6 ***Schaefer***	88	11	89
Connecticut			
1 Kennelly	92	6	93
2 Gejdenson	95	4	96
3 Morrison	59	4	94
4 ***Shays***	60	40	60
5 ***Rowland***	37	35	51
6 ***Johnson***	54	43	56
Delaware			
AL Carper	88	11	89
Florida			
1 Hutto	51	44	54
2 ***Grant***	64	33	66
3 Bennett	68	31	69
4 ***James***	83	16	84
5 ***McCollum***	83	15	85
6 ***Stearns***	89	10	90
7 Gibbons	82	14	86
8 ***Young***	74	21	78
9 ***Bilirakis***	70	13	85
10 ***Ireland***	83	8	92
11 Nelson	35	10	77
12 ***Lewis***	86	8	91
13 ***Goss***	88	11	89
14 Johnston	81	11	88
15 ***Shaw***	75	21	78
16 Smith	87	4	95
17 Lehman	94	4	96
18 ***Ros-Lehtinen***	70	26	73
19 Fascell	88	7	92
Georgia			
1 Thomas	76	23	77
2 Hatcher	76	19	80
3 Ray	56	37	61
4 Jones	84	14	85
5 Lewis	95	5	95
6 ***Gingrich***	83	8	91
7 Darden	75	24	76
8 Rowland	73	22	77
9 Jenkins	62	30	67
10 Barnard	52	37	58
Hawaii			
1 ***Saiki***	41	51	45
2 Mink † [1]	81	5	94
Idaho			
1 ***Craig***	75	8	91
2 Stallings	67	29	70
Illinois			
1 Hayes	95	4	96
2 Savage	79	10	89
3 Russo	82	16	83
4 Sangmeister	77	19	80
5 Lipinski	76	20	79
6 ***Hyde***	78	18	81
7 Collins	87	3	96
8 Rostenkowski	76	12	87
9 Yates	88	4	96
10 ***Porter***	69	29	71
11 Annunzio	83	14	85
12 ***Crane***	89	2	98
13 ***Fawell***	88	11	89
14 ***Hastert***	91	6	94
15 ***Madigan***	73	19	79
16 ***Martin***	65	15	81
17 Evans	97	3	97
18 ***Michel***	78	15	84
19 Bruce	90	9	91
20 Durbin	91	6	94
21 Costello	86	14	86
22 Poshard	85	14	85
Indiana			
1 Visclosky	90	8	92
2 Sharp	79	17	82
3 ***Hiler***	91	8	92

	1	2	3
4 Long	78	22	78
5 Jontz	90	10	90
6 ***Burton***	95	2	98
7 ***Myers***	65	33	66
8 McCloskey	93	6	94
9 Hamilton	78	22	78
10 Jacobs	55	41	57
Iowa			
1 ***Leach***	62	37	63
2 ***Tauke***	75	21	79
3 Nagle	88	7	93
4 Smith	88	10	90
5 ***Lightfoot***	90	7	93
6 ***Grandy***	81	17	83
Kansas			
1 ***Roberts***	87	11	88
2 Slattery	73	25	75
3 ***Meyers***	70	29	70
4 Glickman	81	17	82
5 ***Whittaker***	83	15	84
Kentucky			
1 Hubbard	59	40	59
2 Natcher	86	14	86
3 Mazzoli	87	12	88
4 ***Bunning***	94	2	98
5 ***Rogers***	85	14	86
6 ***Hopkins***	90	9	91
7 Perkins	88	12	88
Louisiana			
1 ***Livingston***	71	23	75
2 Boggs	78	8	90
3 Tauzin	56	40	59
4 ***McCrery***	62	23	73
5 Huckaby	54	40	57
6 ***Baker***	81	7	92
7 Hayes	63	24	73
8 ***Holloway***	84	8	91
Maine			
1 Brennan	81	6	93
2 ***Snowe***	57	43	57
Maryland			
1 Dyson	73	22	77
2 ***Bentley***	76	17	82
3 Cardin	95	4	96
4 McMillen	92	8	92
5 Hoyer	96	2	98
6 Byron	59	35	63
7 Mfume	86	7	92
8 ***Morella***	32	65	33
Massachusetts			
1 ***Conte***	27	71	28
2 Neal	85	6	93
3 Early	78	14	85
4 Frank †	90	5	95
5 Atkins	93	4	96
6 Mavroules	88	5	94
7 Markey	92	2	98
8 Kennedy	90	4	96
9 Moakley	95	4	96
10 Studds	95	4	96
11 Donnelly	82	10	89
Michigan			
1 Conyers	86	3	97
2 ***Pursell***	57	30	66
3 Wolpe	90	7	93
4 ***Upton***	89	11	89
5 ***Henry***	75	21	78
6 Carr	81	15	84
7 Kildee	95	5	95
8 Traxler	81	11	88
9 ***Vander Jagt***	73	20	79
10 ***Schuette***	58	12	83
11 ***Davis***	46	49	48
12 Bonior	95	4	96
13 Crockett	42	2	95
14 Hertel	93	6	94
15 Ford	67	3	96
16 Dingell	87	5	95
17 Levin	97	3	97
18 ***Broomfield***	76	19	80
Minnesota			
1 Penny	66	33	67
2 ***Weber***	80	15	84
3 ***Frenzel***	74	11	87
4 Vento	95	4	96

	1	2	3
5 Sabo	95	3	97
6 Sikorski	79	17	83
7 ***Stangeland***	80	17	82
8 Oberstar	92	4	96
Mississippi			
1 Whitten	79	16	83
2 Espy	82	9	90
3 Montgomery	60	37	62
4 Parker	52	46	53
5 Taylor	57	43	57
Missouri			
1 Clay	75	12	86
2 ***Buechner***	79	19	81
3 Gephardt	89	2	97
4 Skelton	68	29	70
5 Wheat	95	3	97
6 ***Coleman***	75	23	77
7 ***Hancock***	98	2	98
8 ***Emerson***	65	31	68
9 Volkmer	73	25	75
Montana			
1 Williams	77	12	87
2 ***Marlenee***	83	12	88
Nebraska			
1 ***Bereuter***	73	25	74
2 Hoagland	84	16	84
3 ***Smith***	67	28	70
Nevada			
1 Bilbray	83	15	84
2 ***Vucanovich***	84	8	92
New Hampshire			
1 ***Smith***	91	8	92
2 ***Douglas***	89	8	92
New Jersey			
1 Vacancy [2]			
2 Hughes	79	19	80
3 Pallone	79	20	80
4 ***Smith***	44	54	45
5 ***Roukema***	58	32	65
6 Dwyer	87	5	95
7 ***Rinaldo***	46	51	48
8 Roe	86	9	91
9 Torricelli	83	8	92
10 Payne	92	5	95
11 ***Gallo***	65	29	69
12 ***Courter***	71	21	77
13 ***Saxton***	68	29	70
14 Guarini	78	16	83
New Mexico			
1 ***Schiff***	56	41	57
2 ***Skeen***	63	35	64
3 Richardson	84	10	89
New York			
1 Hochbrueckner	94	6	94
2 Downey	93	4	96
3 Mrazek	92	2	98
4 ***Lent***	60	33	64
5 ***McGrath***	56	37	60
6 Flake	85	5	95
7 Ackerman	92	2	98
8 Scheuer	93	3	96
9 Manton	89	6	94
10 Schumer	89	6	94
11 Towns	88	4	96
12 Owens	86	3	96
13 Solarz	89	5	95
14 ***Molinari*** † [3]	70	28	72
15 ***Green***	37	60	38
16 Rangel	85	3	97
17 Weiss	92	6	93
18 Serrano † [4]	93	2	98
19 Engel	83	2	98
20 Lowey	94	4	96
21 ***Fish***	44	47	49
22 ***Gilman***	35	63	36
23 McNulty	92	7	93
24 ***Solomon***	84	13	87
25 ***Boehlert***	47	52	48
26 ***Martin***	72	22	76
27 ***Walsh***	54	41	57
28 McHugh	92	7	93
29 ***Horton***	27	66	29
30 Slaughter	94	5	95
31 ***Paxon***	93	5	95

	1	2	3
32 LaFalce	80	14	85
33 Nowak	90	7	93
34 ***Houghton***	58	36	62
North Carolina			
1 Jones	80	12	87
2 Valentine	66	30	69
3 Lancaster	76	22	77
4 Price	92	8	92
5 Neal	66	25	72
6 ***Coble***	92	7	93
7 Rose	88	7	92
8 Hefner	79	19	81
9 ***McMillan***	79	19	81
10 ***Ballenger***	90	6	93
11 Clarke	79	19	80
North Dakota			
AL Dorgan	82	16	84
Ohio			
1 Luken	83	8	92
2 ***Gradison***	74	24	76
3 Hall	78	12	87
4 ***Oxley***	82	14	86
5 ***Gillmor***	66	32	68
6 ***McEwen***	77	16	83
7 ***DeWine***	83	15	85
8 ***Lukens*** † [5]	74	7	91
9 Kaptur	86	8	92
10 ***Miller***	87	10	89
11 Eckart	83	15	85
12 ***Kasich***	78	19	80
13 Pease	87	10	89
14 Sawyer	92	8	92
15 ***Wylie***	69	22	76
16 ***Regula***	75	24	76
17 Traficant	86	14	86
18 Applegate	73	24	75
19 Feighan	86	5	95
20 Oakar	87	6	94
21 Stokes	88	5	95
Oklahoma			
1 ***Inhofe***	92	6	94
2 Synar	93	4	96
3 Watkins	49	23	68
4 McCurdy	73	25	74
5 ***Edwards***	79	10	89
6 English	60	38	61
Oregon			
1 AuCoin	81	5	94
2 ***Smith, B.***	91	9	91
3 Wyden	94	6	94
4 DeFazio	86	8	92
5 ***Smith, D.***	75	6	92
Pennsylvania			
1 Foglietta	92	5	95
2 Gray	90	2	98
3 Borski	90	7	93
4 Kolter	83	13	87
5 ***Schulze***	67	23	74
6 Yatron	73	26	73
7 ***Weldon***	67	29	70
8 Kostmayer	89	8	92
9 ***Shuster***	78	19	81
10 ***McDade***	43	40	52
11 Kanjorski	87	13	87
12 Murtha	85	13	87
13 ***Coughlin***	68	28	71
14 Coyne	93	2	98
15 ***Ritter***	73	22	76
16 ***Walker***	95	4	96
17 ***Gekas***	92	7	93
18 Walgren	84	12	87
19 ***Goodling***	71	20	78
20 Gaydos	78	17	82
21 ***Ridge***	68	27	72
22 Murphy	61	33	65
23 ***Clinger***	65	29	69
Rhode Island			
1 ***Machtley***	50	48	51
2 ***Schneider***	40	57	41
South Carolina			
1 ***Ravenel***	59	39	60
2 ***Spence***	75	24	76
3 Derrick	81	17	83
4 Patterson	66	33	67
5 Spratt	86	14	86
6 Tallon	67	31	68

	1	2	3
South Dakota			
AL Johnson	82	17	82
Tennessee			
1 ***Quillen***	60	31	66
2 ***Duncan***	87	13	87
3 Lloyd	71	25	74
4 Cooper	74	25	75
5 Clement	85	14	86
6 Gordon	93	6	94
7 ***Sundquist***	90	9	91
8 Tanner	73	21	78
9 Ford	62	3	96
Texas			
1 Chapman	71	19	79
2 Wilson	64	18	78
3 ***Bartlett***	79	19	81
4 Hall	39	41	48
5 Bryant	89	9	91
6 ***Barton***	86	7	92
7 ***Archer***	86	13	87
8 ***Fields***	92	3	97
9 Brooks	87	5	94
10 Pickle	81	17	83
11 Leath	43	21	67
12 Geren	69	30	70
13 Sarpalius	58	38	60
14 Laughlin	58	33	64
15 de la Garza	84	10	90
16 Coleman	90	7	93
17 Stenholm	52	47	52
18 Washington	73	4	95
19 ***Combest***	82	16	84
20 Gonzalez	93	7	93
21 ***Smith***	82	13	87
22 ***DeLay***	91	5	94
23 Bustamante	85	7	93
24 Frost	91	5	95
25 Andrews	79	20	80
26 ***Armey***	95	4	96
27 Ortiz	86	13	87
Utah			
1 ***Hansen***	85	10	90
2 Owens †	84	10	89
3 ***Nielson***	81	17	83
Vermont			
AL ***Smith***	46	46	50
Virginia			
1 ***Bateman***	63	33	66
2 Pickett	72	27	72
3 ***Bliley***	84	13	87
4 Sisisky	77	22	77
5 Payne	75	25	75
6 Olin	76	22	77
7 ***Slaughter***	87	12	88
8 ***Parris***	78	18	81
9 Boucher	90	5	95
10 ***Wolf***	78	21	79
Washington			
1 ***Miller***	68	28	71
2 Swift	92	6	94
3 Unsoeld	90	4	96
4 ***Morrison***	49	46	52
5 Foley [6]	100	0	100
6 Dicks	91	8	92
7 McDermott	92	5	95
8 ***Chandler***	71	25	74
West Virginia			
1 Mollohan	84	11	88
2 Staggers	88	10	90
3 Wise	92	6	94
4 Rahall	79	16	83
Wisconsin			
1 Aspin	83	10	90
2 Kastenmeier	92	7	93
3 ***Gunderson***	67	31	68
4 Kleczka	91	6	94
5 Moody	79	11	88
6 ***Petri***	78	20	80
7 Obey	92	6	94
8 ***Roth***	77	20	80
9 ***Sensenbrenner***	93	6	94
Wyoming			
AL ***Thomas***	86	13	87

Democrats *Republicans*

	1	2	3
Alabama			
Heflin	53	46	54
Shelby	59	41	59
Alaska			
Murkowski	85	14	86
Stevens	66	31	68
Arizona			
DeConcini	74	21	78
McCain	78	19	81
Arkansas			
Bumpers	84	14	86
Pryor	85	13	87
California			
Cranston	90	8	92
Wilson	54	23	70
Colorado			
Wirth	88	10	90
Armstrong	79	2	98
Connecticut			
Dodd	89	8	92
Lieberman	86	13	87
Delaware			
Biden	83	16	84
Roth	80	20	80
Florida			
Graham	76	23	77
Mack	86	14	86
Georgia			
Fowler	84	14	86
Nunn	70	27	73
Hawaii			
Akaka [1]	88	10	90
Inouye	84	15	85
Idaho			
McClure	85	13	87
Symms	93	5	95
Illinois			
Dixon	70	30	70
Simon	90	8	91
Indiana			
Coats	87	11	89
Lugar	86	12	88
Iowa			
Harkin	85	15	85
Grassley	85	15	85
Kansas			
Dole	86	14	86
Kassebaum	67	31	69
Kentucky			
Ford	69	30	70
McConnell	84	15	85
Louisiana			
Breaux	68	31	69
Johnston	65	29	69
Maine			
Mitchell	89	11	89
Cohen	47	53	47
Maryland			
Mikulski	89	6	94
Sarbanes	93	7	93
Massachusetts			
Kennedy	89	7	92
Kerry	85	11	89
Michigan			
Levin	82	18	82
Riegle	85	12	88
Minnesota			
Boschwitz	79	15	84
Durenberger	55	40	58
Mississippi			
Cochran	83	15	84
Lott	82	16	84
Missouri			
Bond	86	12	87
Danforth	71	29	71
Montana			
Baucus	70	28	72
Burns	92	7	93
Nebraska			
Exon	63	34	65
Kerrey	84	16	84
Nevada			
Bryan	81	19	81
Reid	79	20	80
New Hampshire			
Humphrey	82	16	83
Rudman	73	23	76
New Jersey			
Bradley	80	19	81
Lautenberg	88	12	88
New Mexico			
Bingaman	76	18	81
Domenici	69	24	74
New York			
Moynihan	89	9	91
D'Amato	68	32	68
North Carolina			
Sanford	81	16	83
Helms	88	11	89
North Dakota			
Burdick	86	14	86
Conrad	75	24	76
Ohio			
Glenn	79	21	79
Metzenbaum	85	10	89
Oklahoma			
Boren	58	34	63
Nickles	91	7	93
Oregon			
Hatfield	31	58	34
Packwood	45	53	46
Pennsylvania			
Heinz	52	47	53
Specter	53	46	53
Rhode Island			
Pell	86	9	91
Chafee	58	36	62
South Carolina			
Hollings	73	27	73
Thurmond	89	10	90
South Dakota			
Daschle	87	12	88
Pressler	74	22	77
Tennessee			
Gore	93	7	93
Sasser	90	9	91
Texas			
Bentsen	75	23	76
Gramm	88	8	91
Utah			
Garn	88	6	94
Hatch	89	11	89
Vermont			
Leahy	93	7	93
Jeffords	36	61	37
Virginia			
Robb	73	27	73
Warner	69	31	69
Washington			
Adams	93	7	93
Gorton	81	19	81
West Virginia			
Byrd	74	26	74
Rockefeller	86	13	87
Wisconsin			
Kohl	86	12	88
Kasten	80	20	80
Wyoming			
Simpson	86	11	88
Wallop	88	6	94

Party Unity and Party Opposition: Senate

1. Party Unity, 1990. Percentage of 177 party-unity recorded votes in 1990 on which a senator voted "yea" or "nay" *in agreement* with a majority of his or her party. (Party-unity roll calls are those on which a majority of voting Democrats opposed a majority of voting Republicans.) Failures to vote lower both party-unity and party-opposition scores.

2. Party Opposition, 1990. Percentage of 177 party-unity recorded votes in 1990 on which a senator voted "yea" or "nay" *in disagreement* with a majority of his or her party. Failures to vote lower both party-unity and party-opposition scores.

3. Party Unity, 1990. Percentage of 177 party-unity recorded votes in 1990 on which a senator was present and voted "yea" or "nay" *in agreement* with a majority of his or her party. In this version of the study, absences are not counted; therefore, failures to vote do not lower unity or opposition scores. Opposition scores, not listed here, are the inverse of the unity score; i.e., the opposition score is equal to 100 percent minus the individual's unity score.

[1] *Sen. Daniel K. Akaka, D-Hawaii, was sworn in May 16, 1990, to succeed Spark M. Matsunaga, D, who died April 15, 1990. Matsunaga was eligible for 26 party-unity votes in 1990. His party-unity score was 27 percent; opposition score was 4 percent; unity score adjusted for absences, was 88 percent. Akaka was eligible for 129 of 177 party-unity votes in 1990.*

Continued from p. 32

part because few expected the bill to be enacted. Out of 17 votes cast on the Democratic-crafted bill, 14 were party-unity votes, with a majority of Democrats voting against a majority of Republicans. *(Campaign financing, p. 59)*

Many Republican staff members said it seemed that the number of party-unity votes intensified during the two months leading up to the November elections.

Michael Tongour, chief counsel to Minority Whip Alan K. Simpson, R-Wyo., said the Democrats were more interested in playing politics than in moving legislation.

"Toward the end of the year, the Democrats had an agenda they wanted to complete," Tongour said. "The strategy was definitely a partisan one, primarily for the purpose of election politics and not necessarily for the purposes to achieve bipartisan support on legislation."

An aide to Mitchell denied that votes were taken simply to score political points.

The GOP suggestion that partisanship increased as the election got closer was not supported by the numbers in the CQ study. In September and October, 46 of the 98 roll call votes taken in the Senate were partisan, a rate of 47 percent. That was 10 percentage points lower than the previous months of the session.

Party Cohesion

The CQ study also examined how often Democrats and Republicans stuck with their own party when called upon for partisan votes.

In the Senate, Democrats voted with their party 80 percent of the time on unity votes in 1990, compared with 78 percent the year before. Republicans voted together 75 percent of the time in 1990, compared with 78 percent in 1989. *(Average scores, p. 34)*

In the House, Democrats continued to vote together at the rate of 81 percent in 1990, the same as in 1989.

Somewhat more surprising was the composite House Republican score of 74 percent, up from 72 percent in 1989, despite the visible end-of-session infighting.

Political analysts said the Republicans split loudly on one issue — the budget — while sticking together on most other party-unity votes.

The one vote that shattered Republican unity came in the early morning hours of Oct. 5, when conservative Republicans and liberal Democrats joined together to kill the budget package that had been negotiated behind closed doors over the previous five months. The vote was 179-254. *(Budget summit, p. 129)*

The vote exposed serious differences in the Republican Party and among its House leaders: House Minority Leader Robert H. Michel of Illinois, a centrist, was opposed by his top deputy, conservative Minority Whip Newt Gingrich of Georgia. (Because a majority of each party voted against the bill, it was not included in the CQ list of party-unity votes.)

Other than that very public rift, however, most votes "reflect an extraordinarily high homogeneity among House Republicans," Ornstein said.

For House Democrats, the battle over the budget provided an issue that played well with the public — fairness. Democrats planned to capitalize on the theme again in 1991, which some observers said could lead to a much higher partisanship score.

"Democrats like the taste of partisan warfare with the president," Mann said. In the last few weeks, Democratic members were saying, "God, that felt so good," he added.

Partisanship was also likely to increase in 1991, a non-election year. Since 1965, partisan roll call votes dropped every election year and rose the year after.

In addition, House Speaker Thomas S. Foley, D-Wash., made a conscious effort in 1990 to lower the volume of partisan dissonance after his predecessor, Jim Wright, D-Texas, resigned halfway through 1989.

"I think there was a feeling when Foley took over that things had become pretty polarized, and there was just a general desire to fight less," said Jack Dooling, staff director of the House Rules Committee, which determined the amendments that could be offered and in what order when a bill went to the floor.

On the other side of the aisle, Republicans said that while Democrats may have seemed more polite, political maneuvering on rules did not stop.

"I will say that we have had a much more cordial working relationship with the new Speaker and Rules Committee chairman [Joe Moakley, D-Mass.], but that has not yet translated into greater procedural fairness," said Gerald B. H. Solomon, R-N.Y., who was taking over as ranking minority member on the Rules Committee.

Republicans frequently expressed their frustration at Democratic control of the rules by voting against the House Journal, which contained the minutes from the previous day.

In 1990, Republicans turned routine approval of the Journal into partisan votes 31 times. Excluding those from the list of party-unity votes, the percentage of partisan votes in the House dropped six points, to 43 percent.

Settled Without a Vote

Occasionally, some issues that were expected to provoke a fight over the rule or substantive amendments simmered down before they could reach the floor.

As the House prepared to reauthorize the National Endowment for the Arts (NEA), conservatives were offended by the possibility that federal grants might be used to produce pornography or obscenity. Arts supporters and mostly liberal Democrats vowed to protect the agency from censorship.

By the time the bill went to the floor, however, both sides agreed there was little political capital to gain from a fight. Members worked out a compromise, and the rule governing debate was approved by voice vote. The rule was structured so that members could first vote to restrict the endowment but then vote for the compromise, which would eliminate those restrictions.

Two of the four amendments broke down into a party-unity vote. One was by Dana Rohrabacher, R-Calif., to prohibit the NEA from funding child pornography, obscenity, or works denigrating a religion or individual, among other things. It was rejected, 175-249. The other was by Pat Williams, D-Mont., substituting the compromise language to leave questions of obscenity up to the courts. It was adopted, 234-171. *(NEA reauthorization, p. 430)*

Party Mavericks

Among the individual members in both chambers were mavericks who did not always go along with the party line.

Sen. Wendell H. Ford, D-Ky., a Southern conservative elected to majority whip late in 1990, strayed from the Democrats 30 percent of the time in 1990 and 36 percent of the time the year before, not counting absences.

Also in the leadership ranks, Chief Deputy Whip Alan J. Dixon, D-Ill., voted with the Democrats on partisan tests only 70 percent of the time — up from 62 percent in 1989.

Of the senators facing competitive elections in 1990, Pete Wilson had one of the hottest. Running for governor of California against former San Francisco Mayor Dianne Feinstein, he voted with the Republican Party 54 percent of the time. The year before, the GOP counted on him for 79 percent of his votes.

Sen. Tom Harkin, D-Iowa, on the other hand, voted more frequently with the Democrats during 1990, as he faced a challenge from Rep. Tom Tauke, R-Iowa.

Harkin voted with the Democrats 85 percent of the time, compared with 78 percent in 1989.

Tauke, however, turned away from the Republicans. On party-unity votes, he voted with the GOP 75 percent in 1990, compared with 85 percent the year before.

Rep. Lynn Martin, R-Ill., also strayed from her party during a year in which she challenged Sen. Paul Simon, D-Ill. Martin voted with the Republicans on 65 percent of all partisan votes, compared with 81 percent in 1989.

While many House members tended to vote with their party less often during an election year, there were exceptions — among them, freshman Rep. Peter Smith, R-Vt., whose party-unity rating rose from 40 percent in 1989 to 42 percent in 1990. He lost his bid for re-election. ■

Conservative Coalition Rarely Seen in 1990

The conservative coalition, once a political force in Congress that influenced the legislative fortunes of presidents from Franklin D. Roosevelt to Ronald Reagan, appeared barely alive under President Bush.

In 1990, the teaming of Southern Democrats and Republicans in opposition to Northern Democrats was a rare event. As in the first half of the 101st Congress in 1989, the coalition emerged in 1990 on only one of every 10 votes. And while it usually won when it did appear — supporting defense programs and voting against social spending and pornography — the occasions usually arose on peripheral amendments that had little bearing on the overall character of the legislation.

The coalition "is out there," said Walter J. Oleszek, political analyst at the Congressional Research Service and author of many studies on Congress. "But it's simply not as powerful as it once was."

The conservative coalition — defined by Congressional Quarterly as a bloc consisting of a majority of Republicans and a majority of Southern Democrats voting against a majority of Northern Democrats — emerged on 10 percent of votes taken in the House in 1990 and 11 percent of votes taken in the Senate, for a combined rate of 11 percent.

In 1989, the appearance rate was also 11 percent. In 1987 and 1988, the rates were 8 percent and 9 percent, respectively, the lowest since CQ began compiling the index in 1957. During the 1960s, the conservative coalition regularly emerged on more than one-fifth of the votes in Congress. *(Chart, p. 41)*

Despite its low number of showings in recent years, the coalition continued to win when it did appear. It won 82 percent of the time in 1990; in the Senate, the coalition was successful on 95 percent of its votes, while in the House, where it was not as strong, the coalition was still successful on 74 percent of its votes.

The fact that the coalition usually won when it appeared was evidence, experts said, that while its forces were sluggish, they were still at work in Congress.

But while the coalition continued to make appearances, its clout was diminishing as a result of ever-changing voting patterns and political alliances, especially in the South, where the "Boll Weevils," conservative Democrats, were no longer as active.

On the 32 "key votes" identified by CQ in 1990 — 16 in each chamber — the conservative coalition appeared five times in the House and four times in the Senate. *(Key votes, p. 3-B)*

In the House, the coalition won two key votes — on the unsuccessful effort to override Bush's veto of parental leave legislation and on an amendment to the farm bill to limit crop subsidies.

The coalition was defeated, however, on three key votes, including a constitutional amendment allowing Congress and the states to prohibit physical desecration of the American flag.

In the Senate, the coalition won three of its four key votes, including two defense authorization amendments and a clean air bill amendment. The bloc helped Majority Leader George J. Mitchell, D-Maine, succeed on a tabling motion to kill an effort by Tim Wirth, D-Colo., to strengthen motor vehicle emissions standards.

On other key votes on which the conservative coalition might traditionally have been expected to emerge — civil rights, fiscal policy and abortion — the bloc never materialized in 1990.

Win Some . . .

In the House, the coalition appeared on 12 votes dealing with a major crime bill (HR 5269) and was defeated only once. The victories included an amendment by Bill McCollum, R-Fla., to authorize the death penalty for people found guilty of trafficking in large amounts of drugs; an amendment by George W. Gekas, R-Pa., to authorize the death penalty for 10 additional federal offenses; and an amendment by Jolene Unsoeld, D-Wash., to allow semi-automatic weapons to be assembled from domestic parts. *(Anticrime package, p. 486)*

However, most of the crime bill amendments the coalition won on the House floor were later scrapped in conference with the Senate.

One area in which the coalition showed no signs of weakening was defense, and on this issue, at least, the Senate remained a conservative stronghold. Southern Democrats, including Armed Services Committee Chairman Sam Nunn of Georgia, were more likely to side with Republicans on defense than were their Northern counterparts.

"In the Senate, the Southern Democratic-Republican coalition has been more effective [than in the House] and has carried the day," said John Isaacs, president of the Council for a Livable World.

The coalition appeared five times on defense-related votes in the House and nine times in the Senate, winning on each vote.

Continued on p. 47

Leading Scorers: Conservative Coalition

Highest Scorers — Support

Those who in 1990 voted most often with the "conservative coalition." This term refers to a bloc consisting of a majority of Southern Democrats and a majority of Republicans voting against a majority of Northern Democrats.

Senate

Southern Democrats		Republicans	
Shelby, Ala.	95%	Bond, Mo.	100%
Heflin, Ala.	95	Cochran, Miss.	100
Breaux, La.	95	Gramm, Texas	100
Bentsen, Texas	89	Thurmond, S.C.	100
Ford, Ky.	86	Hatch, Utah	97
Johnston, La.	84	Lott, Miss.	97
Nunn, Ga.	78	Lugar, Ind.	97
		Simpson, Wyo.	97
		Warner, Va.	97

Northern Democrats

Dixon, Ill.	73%	Byrd, W.Va.	62%
Exon, Neb.	68	Inouye, Hawaii	59

House

Southern Democrats		Republicans	
Tauzin, La.	100%	Combest, Texas	100%
Parker, Miss.	96	Fields, Texas	100
Huckaby, La.	94	Hiler, Ind.	100
Hutto, Fla.	94	Shumway, Calif.	100
Lloyd, Tenn.	94	Archer, Texas	98
Montgomery, Miss.	94	DeLay, Texas	98
Ray, Ga.	94	Lightfoot, Iowa	98
Sarpalius, Texas	94	McCandless, Calif.	98
Thomas, Ga.	94	Moorhead, Calif.	98
		Packard, Calif.	98

Northern Democrats

Skelton, Mo.	94%	Volkmer, Mo.	81%
Byron, Md.	87	Stallings, Idaho	81

Highest Scorers — Opposition

Those who voted most often against the conservative coalition:

Senate

Southern Democrats		Republicans	
Gore, Tenn.	59%	Cohen, Maine	70%
Sasser, Tenn.	59	Hatfield, Ore.	59
Fowler, Ga.	57	Jeffords, Vt.	46
Sanford, N.C.	49	Packwood, Ore.	46
		Pressler, S.D.	46

Northern Democrats

Harkin, Iowa	92%	Simon, Ill.	92%
Lautenberg, N.J.	92		

House

Southern Democrats		Republicans	
Lewis, Ga.	94%	Morella, Md.	72%
Lehman, Fla.	85	Conte, Mass.	65
Synar, Okla.	85	Schneider, R.I.	63
Washington, Texas	80	Shays, Conn.	59
Gonzalez, Texas	78	Green, N.Y.	56

Northern Democrats

Weiss, N.Y.	100%	Pelosi, Calif.	96%
Dellums, Calif.	96	Studds, Mass.	96

Conservative Coalition History

Appearances (Percentage of all votes)

Victories (Percentage of appearances)

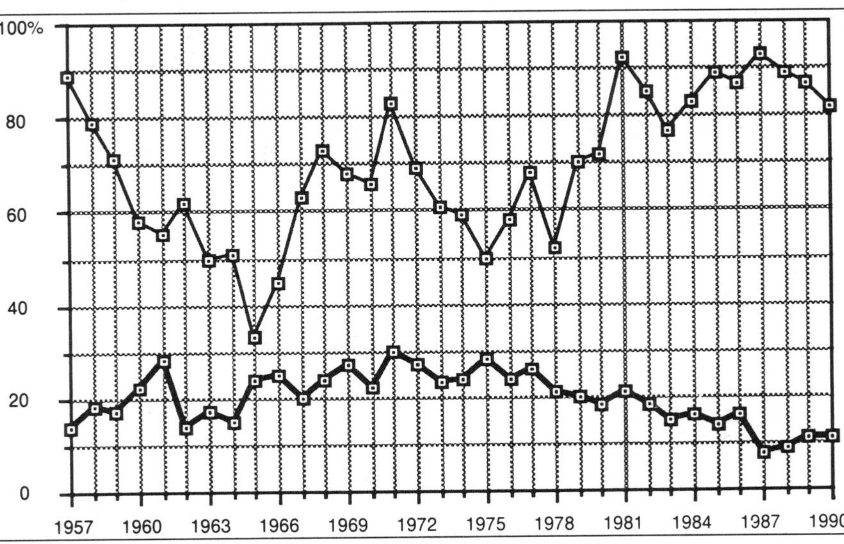

Conservative Coalition Definitions

Conservative coalition. As used in this study, "conservative coalition" means a voting alliance of Republicans and Southern Democrats against the Northern Democrats in Congress. This meaning, rather than any philosophic definition of the "conservative coalition" position, provides the basis for CQ's selection of coalition votes.

Conservative coalition support score. Percentage of conservative coalition votes on which a member voted "yea" or "nay" *in agreement* with the position of the conservative coalition. Failures to vote, even if a member announced a stand, lower the score.

Conservative coalition vote. Any vote in the Senate or the House on which a majority of voting Southern Democrats and a majority of voting Republicans opposed the stand taken by a majority of voting Northern Democrats. Votes on which there was an even division within the ranks of voting Northern Democrats, Southern Democrats or Republicans are not included.

Conservative coalition opposition score. Percentage of conservative coalition votes on which a member voted "yea" or "nay" *in disagreement* with the position of the conservative coalition. Failures to vote, even if a member announced a stand, lower the score.

Average Scores

Scores for 1989 are in parentheses:

Coalition Support	Southern Democrats		Republicans		Northern Democrats	
Senate	69%	(68)	80%	(82)	28%	(31)
House	66	(65)	82	(84)	26	(26)

Coalition Opposition	Southern Democrats		Republicans		Northern Democrats	
Senate	29%	(31)	16%	(15)	70%	(67)
House	30	(31)	14	(13)	70	(69)

Regional Scores

Scores for 1989 are in parentheses:

Regional Support

	East		West		South		Midwest	
Democrats								
Senate	20%	(25)	32%	(38)	69%	(68)	34%	(33)
House	25	(28)	23	(19)	66	(65)	29	(28)
Republicans								
Senate	63%	(72)	80%	(84)	95%	(92)	81%	(81)
House	68	(71)	87	(86)	91	(93)	83	(86)

Regional Opposition

	East		West		South		Midwest	
Democrats								
Senate	78%	(73)	64%	(59)	29%	(31)	65%	(66)
House	69	(66)	74	(77)	30	(31)	67	(68)
Republicans								
Senate	35%	(26)	13%	(13)	4%	(7)	16%	(18)
House	28	(24)	10	(12)	6	(5)	13	(11)

(CQ defines regions of the United States as follows: ***East:*** *Conn., Del., Maine, Md., Mass., N.H., N.J., N.Y., Pa., R.I., Vt., W.Va.* ***West:*** *Alaska, Ariz., Calif., Colo., Hawaii, Idaho, Mont., Nev., N.M., Ore., Utah, Wash., Wyo.* ***South:*** *Ala., Ark., Fla., Ga., Ky., La., Miss., N.C., Okla., S.C., Tenn., Texas, Va.* ***Midwest:*** *Ill., Ind., Iowa, Kan., Mich., Minn., Mo., Neb., N.D., Ohio, S.D., Wis.)*

Conservative Coalition History

Following is the percentage of the recorded votes for both chambers of Congress on which the coalition appeared and its percentage of victories:

Year	Appearances	Victories	Year	Appearances	Victories
1990	11%	82%	1979	20%	70%
1989	11	87	1978	21	52
1988	9	89	1977	26	68
1987	8	93	1976	24	58
1986	16	87	1975	28	50
1985	14	89	1974	24	59
1984	16	83	1973	23	61
1983	15	77	1972	27	69
1982	18	85	1971	30	83
1981	21	92	1970	22	66
1980	18	72	1969	27	68

Conservative Coalition Vote Breakdown

Following is a list of votes, by roll call number, cast in 1990 on which a majority of Southern Democrats and a majority of Republicans voted against a majority of all other Democrats.

House

40 Victories

Vote #	Vote Captions
38	Supreme Court Brief on Flag Desecration
39	Supreme Court Brief on Flag Desecration
56	Child Care
81	Money Laundering
118	Americans With Disabilities Act
128	Foreign Aid/El Salvador
142	Supplemental Appropriations
175	Rocky Flats Plant
188	TV Marti
203	Aid to Cambodia
237	Balanced Budget Amendment
262	Parental and Medical Leave — Veto
266	Farm Programs
272	D.C. Appropriations
277	Farm Programs
291	Housing Programs
301	Airport User Fees
326	Troops in Korea
333	Persian Gulf Mail/Franking
337	SDI Funding
345	ICBM Funding
347	Defense Spending
376	Crime Bill
400	Immigration
408	Crime Bill
410	Crime Bill
413	Crime Bill
414	Crime Bill
415	Crime Bill
416	Crime Bill
417	Crime Bill
418	Crime Bill
424	Crime Bill
450	Farm Programs
454	Defense Spending
479	Aid to UNITA
498	Legislative Branch Funding
500	Legislative Branch Funding
522	Crime Bill
526	Immigration

14 Defeats

Vote #	Vote Captions
80	Money Laundering
107	Parental and Medical Leave
117	Americans With Disabilities Act
192	Flag Constitutional Amendment
227	Americans With Disabilities Act
238	Balanced Budget Amendment
297	Farm Programs
404	Immigration
406	Immigration
419	Crime Bill
447	NEA Funding Restrictions
480	Aid to UNITA
482	Aid to UNITA
531	Foreign Aid

Senate

35 Victories

Vote #	Vote Captions
34	Clean Air Bill
35	Clean Air Bill
37	Clean Air Bill
43	Clean Air Bill
54	Clean Air Bill
56	T. Timothy Ryan Jr. Nomination
71	Supplemental Appropriations/Death Penalty
108	Crime Bill
110	Americans With Disabilities Act
130	Housing Programs
140	Crime Bill
165	Farm Programs
170	Farm Programs
178	Farm Programs/Soviet Lending
194	Campaign Finance
208	Stealth Bomber
209	Stealth Bomber
213	Forces in Europe
216	Defense Spending/Drug Treatment
222	Land-Sale Revenues
225	SDI Funding
226	SDI Funding
228	Treasury/Postal Funding
234	D.C. Appropriations
244	Garbage Dumping
247	CAFE Standards
255	Strategic Petroleum Reserve
271	Troops in Europe
272	Stealth Bomber
279	Budget Package
280	Budget Package
282	OSHA Penalties/Budget Package
285	Budget Package
288	Budget Package
317	Farm Programs

2 Defeats

Vote #	Vote Captions
128	Flag Constitutional Amendment
177	Farm Programs

Conservative Coalition Support and Opposition: House

1. Conservative Coalition Support, 1990. Percentage of 54 recorded votes in 1990 on which the conservative coalition appeared and on which a representative voted "yea" or "nay" *in agreement* with the position of the conservative coalition. Failures to vote lower both support and opposition scores.

2. Conservative Coalition Opposition, 1990. Percentage of 54 recorded votes in 1990 on which the conservative coalition appeared and on which a representative voted "yea" or "nay" *in disagreement* with the position of the conservative coalition. Failures to vote lower both support and opposition scores.

3. Conservative Coalition Support, 1990. Percentage of 54 recorded votes in 1990 on which the conservative coalition appeared and on which a representative was present and voted "yea" or "nay" *in agreement* with the position of the conservative coalition. In this version of the study, absences are not counted; therefore, failures to vote do not lower support or opposition scores. Opposition scores, not listed here, are the inverse of the support score; i.e., the opposition score is equal to 100 percent minus the individual's support score.

[1] *Rep. Pasty T. Mink, D-Hawaii, was sworn in Sept. 27, 1990, to succeed Daniel K. Akaka, D, who was appointed to replace the late Democratic Sen. Spark M. Matsunaga. Akaka was eligible for six of the 54 conservative coalition votes in 1990. His conservative coalition support score was 17 percent; opposition score was 83 percent; support score, adjusted for absences, was 17 percent in 1990. Mink was eligible for 24 of the 54 conservative coalition votes in 1990.*

[2] *Rep. James J. Florio, D-N.J., resigned Jan. 16, 1990, to become governor of New Jersey.*

[3] *Rep. Susan Molinari, R-N.Y., was sworn in March 27, 1990, to succeed her father, Guy V. Molinari, R, who resigned Jan. 1. Susan Molinari was eligible for 52 of the 54 conservative coalition votes in 1990.*

[4] *Rep. Jose E. Serrano, D-N.Y., was sworn in March 28, 1990, to succeed Robert Garcia, D, who resigned Jan. 7. Serrano was eligible for 52 of the 54 conservative coalition votes in 1990.*

[5] *Rep. Donald E. "Buz" Lukens, R-Ohio, resigned Oct. 24, 1990. Lukens was eligible for 51 of the 54 conservative coalition votes in 1990.*

[6] *Rep. Thomas S. Foley, D-Wash., as Speaker of the House, voted at his discretion on two of the 54 conservative coalition votes — roll call votes 192 and 482 — for a support score of 0 percent.*

NOTE: Southern states — Ala., Ark., Fla., Ga., Ky., La., Miss., N.C., Okla., S.C., Tenn., Texas and Va.

KEY

† Not eligible for all conservative coalition votes in 1990 or voted "present" to avoid possible conflict of interest.

Democrats *Republicans*

	1	2	3
Alabama			
1 ***Callahan***	96	0	100
2 ***Dickinson***	94	4	96
3 Browder	93	7	93
4 Bevill	85	11	88
5 Flippo	63	9	87
6 Erdreich	83	17	83
7 Harris	93	7	93
Alaska			
AL ***Young***	78	15	84
Arizona			
1 ***Rhodes***	93	7	93
2 Udall	24	69	26
3 ***Stump*** †	85	2	98
4 ***Kyl***	96	4	96
5 ***Kolbe***	87	11	89
Arkansas			
1 Alexander	44	43	51
2 ***Robinson***	78	2	98
3 ***Hammerschmidt***	93	2	98
4 Anthony	56	43	57
California			
1 Bosco	37	57	39
2 ***Herger***	94	6	94
3 Matsui	17	76	18
4 Fazio	26	72	26
5 Pelosi	4	96	4
6 Boxer	11	83	12
7 Miller	6	93	6
8 Dellums	4	96	4
9 Stark	6	89	6
10 Edwards	7	89	8
11 Lantos	30	70	30
12 ***Campbell***	48	43	53
13 Mineta	11	89	11
14 ***Shumway***	100	0	100
15 Condit	54	44	55
16 Panetta	17	80	17
17 ***Pashayan***	87	7	92
18 Lehman	31	65	33
19 ***Lagomarsino***	93	7	93
20 ***Thomas***	83	7	92
21 ***Gallegly***	96	4	96
22 ***Moorhead***	98	2	98
23 Beilenson	15	81	15
24 Waxman	6	93	6
25 Roybal	15	81	15
26 Berman	7	93	7
27 Levine	6	94	6
28 Dixon	17	83	17
29 Hawkins	6	57	9
30 Martinez	31	63	33
31 Dymally	11	87	11
32 Anderson	26	72	26
33 ***Dreier***	94	6	94
34 Torres	20	78	21
35 ***Lewis***	89	7	92
36 Brown	31	61	34
37 ***McCandless***	98	2	98
38 ***Dornan***	87	7	92
39 ***Dannemeyer***	93	7	93
40 ***Cox***	83	13	87
41 ***Lowery***	89	4	96
42 ***Rohrabacher***	80	20	80
43 ***Packard***	98	2	98
44 Bates	24	72	25
45 ***Hunter***	87	9	90
Colorado			
1 Schroeder	13	83	13
2 Skaggs	19	81	19
3 Campbell	67	31	68
4 ***Brown***	87	13	87
5 ***Hefley***	91	9	91
6 ***Schaefer***	89	9	91
Connecticut			
1 Kennelly	17	83	17
2 Gejdenson	7	89	8
3 Morrison	6	61	8
4 ***Shays***	41	59	41
5 ***Rowland***	52	20	72
6 ***Johnson***	65	31	67
Delaware			
AL Carper	35	65	35
Florida			
1 Hutto	94	4	96
2 ***Grant***	93	7	93
3 Bennett	61	39	61
4 ***James***	94	4	96
5 ***McCollum***	91	9	91
6 ***Stearns***	91	7	92
7 Gibbons	48	52	48
8 ***Young***	93	6	94
9 ***Bilirakis***	81	4	96
10 ***Ireland***	87	6	94
11 Nelson	37	20	65
12 ***Lewis***	93	2	98
13 ***Goss***	85	15	85
14 Johnston	30	69	30
15 ***Shaw***	91	7	92
16 Smith	24	69	26
17 Lehman	15	85	15
18 ***Ros-Lehtinen***	70	24	75
19 Fascell	39	52	43
Georgia			
1 Thomas	94	4	96
2 Hatcher	85	13	87
3 Ray	94	6	94
4 Jones	67	30	69
5 Lewis	6	94	6
6 ***Gingrich***	94	4	96
7 Darden	87	13	87
8 Rowland	91	9	91
9 Jenkins	87	9	90
10 Barnard	89	6	94
Hawaii			
1 ***Saiki***	72	24	75
2 Mink † [1]	21	75	22
Idaho			
1 ***Craig***	89	2	98
2 Stallings	81	19	81
Illinois			
1 Hayes	11	87	11
2 Savage	17	80	17
3 Russo	24	74	25
4 Sangmeister	50	46	52
5 Lipinski	56	43	57
6 ***Hyde***	81	15	85
7 Collins	9	81	10
8 Rostenkowski	33	56	38
9 Yates	6	89	6
10 ***Porter***	70	30	70
11 Annunzio	52	48	52
12 ***Crane***	87	7	92
13 ***Fawell***	81	19	81
14 ***Hastert***	91	9	91
15 ***Madigan***	87	11	89
16 ***Martin***	67	19	78
17 Evans	9	91	9
18 ***Michel***	91	6	94
19 Bruce	33	67	33
20 Durbin	26	74	26
21 Costello	48	52	48
22 Poshard	43	57	43
Indiana			
1 Visclosky	30	69	30
2 Sharp	41	56	42
3 ***Hiler***	100	0	100

	1	2	3
4 Long	67	33	67
5 Jontz	28	72	28
6 ***Burton***	94	2	98
7 ***Myers***	94	6	94
8 McCloskey	26	72	26
9 Hamilton	43	57	43
10 Jacobs	30	67	31
Iowa			
1 ***Leach***	52	48	52
2 ***Tauke***	63	35	64
3 Nagle	22	76	23
4 Smith	41	59	41
5 ***Lightfoot***	98	2	98
6 ***Grandy***	76	22	77
Kansas			
1 ***Roberts***	87	9	90
2 Slattery	48	48	50
3 ***Meyers***	78	22	78
4 Glickman	37	61	38
5 ***Whittaker***	85	13	87
Kentucky			
1 Hubbard	83	13	87
2 Natcher	67	33	67
3 Mazzoli	44	52	46
4 ***Bunning***	96	2	98
5 ***Rogers***	94	2	98
6 ***Hopkins***	94	2	98
7 Perkins	41	59	41
Louisiana			
1 ***Livingston***	87	7	92
2 Boggs	35	44	44
3 Tauzin	100	0	100
4 ***McCrery***	87	7	92
5 Huckaby	94	0	100
6 ***Baker***	85	7	92
7 Hayes	85	6	94
8 ***Holloway***	91	6	94
Maine			
1 Brennan	19	69	21
2 ***Snowe***	67	33	67
Maryland			
1 Dyson	76	24	76
2 ***Bentley***	87	11	89
3 Cardin	13	87	13
4 McMillen	44	56	44
5 Hoyer	22	76	23
6 Byron	87	13	87
7 Mfume	9	91	9
8 ***Morella***	24	72	25
Massachusetts			
1 ***Conte***	33	65	34
2 Neal	19	72	20
3 Early	35	56	39
4 Frank	11	85	12
5 Atkins	17	83	17
6 Mavroules	20	80	20
7 Markey	7	89	8
8 Kennedy	13	80	14
9 Moakley	28	69	29
10 Studds	4	96	4
11 Donnelly	35	56	39
Michigan			
1 Conyers	7	85	8
2 ***Pursell***	65	19	78
3 Wolpe	15	85	15
4 ***Upton***	85	15	85
5 ***Henry***	70	30	70
6 Carr	46	52	47
7 Kildee	9	91	9
8 Traxler	39	57	40
9 ***Vander Jagt***	91	9	91
10 ***Schuette***	65	6	92
11 ***Davis***	74	22	77
12 Bonior	6	94	6
13 Crockett	0	50	0
14 Hertel	7	91	8
15 Ford	9	65	13
16 Dingell	37	61	38
17 Levin	19	81	19
18 ***Broomfield***	80	19	81
Minnesota			
1 Penny	56	44	56
2 ***Weber***	80	17	83
3 ***Frenzel***	70	19	79
4 Vento	7	91	8

	1	2	3
5 Sabo	15	83	15
6 Sikorski	15	81	15
7 ***Stangeland***	89	11	89
8 Oberstar	13	83	13
Mississippi			
1 Whitten	69	30	70
2 Espy	50	48	51
3 Montgomery	94	6	94
4 Parker	96	4	96
5 Taylor	93	7	93
Missouri			
1 Clay	7	89	8
2 ***Buechner***	80	19	81
3 Gephardt	17	74	18
4 Skelton	94	4	96
5 Wheat	11	87	11
6 ***Coleman***	89	7	92
7 ***Hancock***	94	6	94
8 ***Emerson***	96	2	98
9 Volkmer	81	19	81
Montana			
1 Williams	20	72	22
2 ***Marlenee***	81	9	90
Nebraska			
1 ***Bereuter***	87	13	87
2 Hoagland	50	50	50
3 ***Smith***	93	6	94
Nevada			
1 Bilbray	63	37	63
2 ***Vucanovich***	89	2	98
New Hampshire			
1 ***Smith***	87	13	87
2 ***Douglas***	83	17	83
New Jersey			
1 Vacancy [2]			
2 Hughes	39	59	40
3 Pallone	54	46	54
4 ***Smith***	56	44	56
5 ***Roukema***	63	24	72
6 Dwyer	24	69	26
7 ***Rinaldo***	63	37	63
8 Roe	41	50	45
9 Torricelli	35	57	38
10 Payne	9	89	9
11 ***Gallo***	85	13	87
12 ***Courter***	74	17	82
13 ***Saxton***	78	22	78
14 Guarini	41	56	42
New Mexico			
1 ***Schiff***	78	22	78
2 ***Skeen***	91	9	91
3 Richardson	54	44	55
New York			
1 Hochbrueckner	22	78	22
2 Downey	6	94	6
3 Mrazek	4	91	4
4 ***Lent***	78	19	81
5 ***McGrath***	54	39	58
6 Flake	9	80	10
7 Ackerman	7	85	8
8 Scheuer	6	91	6
9 Manton	35	61	37
10 Schumer	6	89	6
11 Towns	6	93	6
12 Owens	2	93	2
13 Solarz	15	76	16
14 ***Molinari*** † [3]	79	19	80
15 ***Green***	41	56	42
16 Rangel	6	87	6
17 Weiss	0	100	0
18 Serrano † [4]	6	90	6
19 Engel	13	80	14
20 Lowey	15	81	15
21 ***Fish***	56	41	58
22 ***Gilman***	52	48	52
23 McNulty	35	65	35
24 ***Solomon***	87	13	87
25 ***Boehlert***	61	39	61
26 ***Martin***	85	13	87
27 ***Walsh***	74	24	75
28 McHugh	26	74	26
29 ***Horton***	56	39	59
30 Slaughter	11	89	11
31 ***Paxon***	94	6	94

	1	2	3
32 LaFalce	35	61	37
33 Nowak	31	67	32
34 ***Houghton***	72	22	76
North Carolina			
1 Jones	57	41	58
2 Valentine	89	11	89
3 Lancaster	83	17	83
4 Price	48	52	48
5 Neal	74	24	75
6 ***Coble***	93	7	93
7 Rose	48	44	52
8 Hefner	89	11	89
9 ***McMillan***	85	13	87
10 ***Ballenger***	91	6	94
11 Clarke	67	33	67
North Dakota			
AL Dorgan	35	61	37
Ohio			
1 Luken	37	56	40
2 ***Gradison***	81	15	85
3 Hall	28	63	31
4 ***Oxley***	94	2	98
5 ***Gillmor***	91	9	91
6 ***McEwen***	94	2	98
7 ***DeWine***	83	13	87
8 ***Lukens*** † [5]	82	6	93
9 Kaptur	41	56	42
10 ***Miller***	89	9	91
11 Eckart	46	52	47
12 ***Kasich***	94	6	94
13 Pease	19	81	19
14 Sawyer	30	70	30
15 ***Wylie***	80	9	90
16 ***Regula***	81	19	81
17 Traficant	37	63	37
18 Applegate	52	46	53
19 Feighan	17	78	18
20 Oakar	15	85	15
21 Stokes	7	89	8
Oklahoma			
1 ***Inhofe***	96	4	96
2 Synar	13	85	13
3 Watkins	74	6	93
4 McCurdy	78	17	82
5 ***Edwards***	87	4	96
6 English	93	7	93
Oregon			
1 AuCoin	13	76	15
2 ***Smith, B.***	96	4	96
3 Wyden	22	78	22
4 DeFazio	19	80	19
5 ***Smith, D.***	87	2	98
Pennsylvania			
1 Foglietta	17	80	17
2 Gray	11	81	12
3 Borski	33	67	33
4 Kolter	52	44	54
5 ***Schulze***	74	13	85
6 Yatron	65	35	65
7 ***Weldon***	80	15	84
8 Kostmayer	13	85	13
9 ***Shuster***	85	9	90
10 ***McDade***	65	20	76
11 Kanjorski	44	54	45
12 Murtha	61	39	61
13 ***Coughlin***	76	22	77
14 Coyne	7	91	8
15 ***Ritter***	78	19	81
16 ***Walker***	85	15	85
17 ***Gekas***	94	6	94
18 Walgren	33	65	34
19 ***Goodling***	72	17	81
20 Gaydos	59	41	59
21 ***Ridge***	70	28	72
22 Murphy	44	54	45
23 ***Clinger***	89	9	91
Rhode Island			
1 ***Machtley***	50	48	51
2 ***Schneider***	35	63	36
South Carolina			
1 ***Ravenel***	83	17	83
2 ***Spence***	94	4	96
3 Derrick	70	28	72
4 Patterson	81	19	81
5 Spratt	72	28	72
6 Tallon	85	11	88

	1	2	3
South Dakota			
AL Johnson	54	46	54
Tennessee			
1 ***Quillen***	85	7	92
2 ***Duncan***	87	13	87
3 Lloyd	94	6	94
4 Cooper †	62	34	65
5 Clement	59	41	59
6 Gordon	46	52	47
7 ***Sundquist***	94	2	98
8 Tanner	85	9	90
9 Ford	6	67	8
Texas			
1 Chapman	78	19	81
2 Wilson	61	26	70
3 ***Bartlett***	94	6	94
4 Hall	78	7	91
5 Bryant	33	67	33
6 ***Barton***	94	2	98
7 ***Archer***	98	2	98
8 ***Fields***	100	0	100
9 Brooks	39	52	43
10 Pickle	67	33	67
11 Leath	69	7	90
12 Geren	91	9	91
13 Sarpalius	94	4	96
14 Laughlin	85	7	92
15 de la Garza	56	43	57
16 Coleman	44	52	46
17 Stenholm	91	9	91
18 Washington	7	80	9
19 ***Combest***	100	0	100
20 Gonzalez	22	78	22
21 ***Smith***	91	6	94
22 ***DeLay***	98	2	98
23 Bustamante	39	48	45
24 Frost	43	57	43
25 Andrews	69	31	69
26 ***Armey***	94	6	94
27 Ortiz	52	46	53
Utah			
1 ***Hansen***	93	4	96
2 Owens	30	69	30
3 ***Nielson***	93	7	93
Vermont			
AL ***Smith***	50	39	56
Virginia			
1 ***Bateman***	96	4	96
2 Pickett	78	22	78
3 ***Bliley***	91	7	92
4 Sisisky	91	9	91
5 Payne	83	17	83
6 Olin	67	30	69
7 ***Slaughter***	94	6	94
8 ***Parris***	91	4	96
9 Boucher	35	57	38
10 ***Wolf***	83	15	85
Washington			
1 ***Miller***	57	39	60
2 Swift	15	85	15
3 Unsoeld	13	80	14
4 ***Morrison***	76	24	76
5 Foley [6]	0	100	0
6 Dicks	37	63	37
7 McDermott	7	93	7
8 ***Chandler***	74	20	78
West Virginia			
1 Mollohan	50	50	50
2 Staggers	28	72	28
3 Wise	28	72	28
4 Rahall	37	63	37
Wisconsin			
1 Aspin	48	46	51
2 Kastenmeier	9	91	9
3 ***Gunderson***	80	19	81
4 Kleczka	17	78	18
5 Moody	15	85	15
6 ***Petri***	80	19	81
7 Obey	15	83	15
8 ***Roth***	89	7	92
9 ***Sensenbrenner***	80	20	80
Wyoming			
AL ***Thomas***	89	9	91

Democrats ***Republicans***

	1	2	3
Alabama			
Heflin	95	5	95
Shelby	95	5	95
Alaska			
Murkowski	92	0	100
Stevens	84	5	94
Arizona			
DeConcini	35	59	37
McCain	76	22	78
Arkansas			
Bumpers	57	43	57
Pryor	65	32	67
California			
Cranston	11	86	11
Wilson	51	19	73
Colorado			
Wirth	14	81	14
Armstrong	78	3	97
Connecticut			
Dodd	30	65	31
Lieberman	22	78	22
Delaware			
Biden	16	84	16
Roth	76	24	76
Florida			
Graham	59	41	59
Mack	95	5	95
Georgia			
Fowler	43	57	43
Nunn	78	19	81
Hawaii			
Akaka [1]	23	73	24
Inouye	59	38	61
Idaho			
McClure	92	5	94
Symms	95	5	95
Illinois			
Dixon	73	27	73
Simon	8	92	8
Indiana			
Coats	92	8	92
Lugar	97	3	97
Iowa			
Harkin	8	92	8
Grassley	70	30	70
Kansas			
Dole	95	5	95
Kassebaum	76	16	82
Kentucky			
Ford	86	14	86
McConnell	92	5	94
Louisiana			
Breaux	95	5	95
Johnston	84	11	89
Maine			
Mitchell	22	78	22
Cohen	30	70	30
Maryland			
Mikulski	16	81	17
Sarbanes	11	89	11
Massachusetts			
Kennedy	14	81	14
Kerry	5	86	6
Michigan			
Levin	35	65	35
Riegle	27	70	28
Minnesota			
Boschwitz	78	14	85
Durenberger	76	19	80
Mississippi			
Cochran	100	0	100
Lott	97	0	100
Missouri			
Bond	100	0	100
Danforth	81	19	81
Montana			
Baucus	51	46	53
Burns	95	5	95
Nebraska			
Exon	68	30	69
Kerrey	49	51	49
Nevada			
Bryan	51	49	51
Reid	32	68	32
New Hampshire			
Humphrey	70	27	72
Rudman	81	14	86
New Jersey			
Bradley	14	86	14
Lautenberg	8	92	8
New Mexico			
Bingaman	32	57	36
Domenici	84	8	91
New York			
Moynihan	11	89	11
D'Amato	65	32	67
North Carolina			
Sanford	43	49	47
Helms	84	14	86
North Dakota			
Burdick	32	68	32
Conrad	38	62	38
Ohio			
Glenn	41	59	41
Metzenbaum	8	89	8
Oklahoma			
Boren	76	22	78
Nickles	89	11	89
Oregon			
Hatfield	32	59	35
Packwood	51	46	53
Pennsylvania			
Heinz	73	27	73
Specter	59	41	59
Rhode Island			
Pell	11	81	12
Chafee	65	30	69
South Carolina			
Hollings	57	43	57
Thurmond	100	0	100
South Dakota			
Daschle	41	59	41
Pressler	49	46	51
Tennessee			
Gore	41	59	41
Sasser	41	59	41
Texas			
Bentsen	89	11	89
Gramm	100	0	100
Utah			
Garn	86	3	97
Hatch	97	3	97
Vermont			
Leahy	22	78	22
Jeffords	49	46	51
Virginia			
Robb	76	24	76
Warner	97	3	97
Washington			
Adams	11	89	11
Gorton	86	14	86
West Virginia			
Byrd	62	38	62
Rockefeller	41	59	41
Wisconsin			
Kohl	19	81	19
Kasten	81	19	81
Wyoming			
Simpson	97	0	100
Wallop	89	5	94

Southern states - Ala., Ark., Fla., Ga., Ky., La., Miss., N.C., Okla., S.C., Tenn., Texas, Va.

Conservative Coalition Support and Opposition: Senate

1. Conservative Coalition Support, 1990. Percentage of 37 recorded votes in 1990 on which the conservative coalition appeared and on which a senator voted "yea" or "nay" *in agreement* with the position of the conservative coalition. Failures to vote lower both support and opposition scores.

2. Conservative Coalition Opposition, 1990. Percentage of 37 recorded votes in 1990 on which the conservative coalition appeared and on which a senator voted "yea" or "nay" *in disagreement* with the position of the conservative coalition. Failures to vote lower both support and opposition scores.

3. Conservative Coalition Support, 1990. Percentage of 37 recorded votes in 1990 on which the conservative coalition appeared and on which a senator was present and voted "yea" or "nay" *in agreement* with the position of the conservative coalition. In this version of the study, absences are not counted; therefore, failures to vote do not lower support or opposition scores. Opposition scores, not listed here, are the inverse of the support score; i.e., the opposition score is equal to 100 percent minus the individual's support score.

[1] *Sen. Daniel K. Akaka, D-Hawaii, was sworn in May 16, 1990, to succeed Spark M. Matsunaga, D, who died April 15, 1990. Matsunaga was eligible for six conservative coalition votes in 1990. His conservative coalition support score was 17 percent; opposition score was 17 percent; coalition support score, adjusted for absences, was 50 percent. Akaka was eligible for 30 of 37 conservative coalition votes in 1990.*

Continued from p. 40

Isaacs attributed the success of the coalition to Nunn, who, as a Southern Democrat and powerful committee chairman, was in a unique position to lead his Southern colleagues and bring along Democrats from other regions as well. For example, Democrats Alan J. Dixon of Illinois, Jeff Bingaman of New Mexico and Jim Exon of Nebraska generally voted with Nunn on defense spending. In addition, about 12 Southern Democratic senators consistently voted with Nunn in support of higher military spending.

Without Nunn, Isaacs said, the coalition would have been considerably weakened. Instead, that core of support helped to secure a 56-41 win for Nunn on a motion to table an amendment by Dale Bumpers, D-Ark., to cut $594 million from the amount authorized for the strategic defense initiative in the defense authorization bill. The coalition also helped to defeat (45-53) an amendment by William S. Cohen, R-Maine, to cut $1.8 billion for two B-2 bombers in fiscal 1991. *(Defense authorization, p. 671)*

... Lose Some More

The coalition continued to emerge on fiscal matters that had long divided it from Northern Democrats. In the House, the coalition emerged on two votes on legislation to propose a constitutional amendment to require a balanced budget. The coalition's support was not enough, however, to muster the two-thirds majority needed to pass the amendment.

In the Senate, the coalition appeared five times on a variety of amendments to legislation dealing with fiscal 1991 budget reconciliation (S 3209). Most of the votes were on unsuccessful amendments to increase spending or change revenue levels, which required waivers from budget law restrictions.

Aside from these bedrock conservative issues, the coalition appeared most often on issues that "reflect the politics of values" and on symbolic issues such as flag desecration, Oleszek said.

The coalition helped gain House approval on July 26 for an amendment by Stan Parris, R-Va., on the District of Columbia appropriations bill to eliminate $1.6 million in funding for the University of the District of Columbia. The university planned to use the money to renovate a building to house the sculpture "Dinner Party" by Judy Chicago. Parris and his supporters said the sculpture was obscene. *(D.C. appropriations, p. 891)*

The coalition also emerged, this time unsuccessfully, on a vote on the fiscal 1991-95 authorization for the National Endowment for the Arts (NEA).

An amendment by Dana Rohrabacher, R-Calif., would have prohibited the NEA from funding child pornography, works that contained any part of the human fetus or embryo, and works that denigrated persons on the basis of race, sex or handicap. The House rejected the amendment, 175-249, on Oct. 11. Although a 114-58 majority of Republicans backed Rohrabacher, Southern Democrats were divided on the vote, with a slim 43-37 majority voting in favor of the amendment. *(NEA reauthorization, p. 430)*

The coalition was also defeated in the House on a big labor vote — the passage of parental leave legislation to require employers to give unpaid leave to employees to care for an infant, or a child, parent or spouse who was seriously ill. The House passed the bill May 10, 237-187, despite the opposition of a majority of Republicans and Southern Democrats.

However, the coalition did succeed on parental leave when the House voted July 25 to sustain Bush's veto of the bill. The 232-195 vote was not enough to achieve the two-thirds majority needed to override. Republicans voted 38-138 and Southern Democrats voted 38-43 to oppose the bill — and therefore to support the president's veto. *(Parental leave, p. 359)*

Civil Rights Scenario

One piece of legislation on which the conservative coalition notably failed to emerge was the civil rights bill. For decades, Southern Democrats and Republicans had joined forces to defeat many initiatives to expand civil rights for blacks and other minorities.

Ten years earlier, the coalition was a big winner on votes to limit federal remedies for school segregation. With coalition support, both the House and Senate in 1980 voted to prevent the Justice Department from seeking court-ordered busing and to prevent the Internal Revenue Service from seeking to deprive segregated schools of their tax-exempt status. *(1980 Almanac, p. 34-C)*

In 1990, however, the coalition did not appear on even one vote on the civil rights bill of 1990.

Some observers said the coalition's absence resulted from a changing attitude on the part of Southern Democrats, many of whom were not only trying to shed the South's reputation for bigotry and racism but were actively courting black voters. The civil rights bill thus was not able to draw the coalition partners together.

"It was such a politically volatile issue that members were not willing to take the political heat for opposing a bill called civil rights," said an aide to Rep. Charles W. Stenholm, D-Texas, chairman of the Conservative Democratic Forum.

In the House, the bill passed 272-154 on Aug. 3 with Southern Democrats voting for the bill 70-10. Those who voted against the bill included Stenholm and three out of five members of the Mississippi delegation: Mike Parker, G. V. "Sonny" Montgomery and Gene Taylor. But in every Southern state besides Mississippi, a majority of Democratic lawmakers voted for the bill.

In the Senate, Southern Democrats on Oct. 24 voted 17-0 to override the president's veto of the bill. *(Civil rights bill, p. 462)*

Oleszek said the votes on the civil rights bill were further evidence that the coalition had been weakened by "the Northernization of the South." There was more party identification among Northern and Southern Democrats, he said, and less of a regional focus except on defense and foreign policy issues.

The Democrats elected from the South by 1990 were "more like their Northern brethren," he said.

Loyal Supporters

The coalition still had a number of loyal supporters among Democrats. In the House, Democrat W. J. "Billy" Tauzin of Louisiana supported the coalition 100 percent of the time. He was followed by Parker with 96 percent and seven others with 94 percent.

Four House Republicans tied for the highest score for their party with 100 percent: John Hiler of Indiana, Jack Fields of Texas, Norman D. Shumway of California and Larry Combest of Texas.

Some Northern Democrats also joined forces with the conservative coalition. Ike Skelton of Missouri had the highest score of any Northern Democrat with 94 percent.

In the Senate, three Democrats — Richard C. Shelby

and Howell Heflin of Alabama, and John B. Breaux of Louisiana — had conservative coalition scores of 95 percent. Republicans Strom Thurmond of South Carolina, Thad Cochran of Mississippi, Phil Gramm of Texas and Christopher S. Bond of Missouri had perfect 100 percent scores.

A Changing Congress

The declining clout of the conservative coalition was not a recent phenomenon. Its appearance in congressional voting had dropped steadily since the late 1970s with only a brief upsurge in activity during the early years of the Reagan administration.

Changing dynamics among Southern Democrats was not the only reason, Oleszek said. Republicans had their own troubles. During the recent budget battle, for example, intraparty squabbling escalated in the House with Minority Whip Newt Gingrich of Georgia openly disagreeing with Bush and other party leaders.

The moderation of Southern Democrats and the splintering of Republicans made it more difficult for conservatives to strategize. "The job of being a minority leader like Bob Michel is truly made more difficult," Oleszek said, referring to the Illinois Republican leader of the House.

Despite signs that the coalition's strength had waned, some saw evidence that the ranks of conservative Southern Democrats was growing. According to Stenholm's aide, the freshman class was more fiscally conservative, and the Conservative Democratic Forum, which had 51 House members, expected to pick up eight or nine more. However, the coalition would need a lot more to be successful more often, the aide said, because Republican numbers in the House were so small, requiring even more conservative Democrats to win.

Experts said that while reviving the coalition was not a hopeless task, it could not be done without issues that sparked a rallying cry. Such issues as flag desecration might raise some emotion and more rhetoric, but they would not sustain momentum. "They don't rate with the peace and prosperity of the Great Society," Oleszek said. ■

Attendance Record Sets Election-Year High

Despite pressures to return home in an election year, members of Congress turned out in record numbers for roll call votes.

Members on average voted on 95 percent of recorded votes, since Congressional Quarterly began studying attendance in 1953. That matched 1989's record high voting rate and set a new record for participation in an election year. *(Chart, p. 3-B)*

House freshmen averaged 96 percent; two first-termers — John J. "Jimmy" Duncan Jr., R-Tenn., and Gene Taylor, D-Miss. — showed up for every vote.

Higher scores stemmed from changes in the way votes were scheduled and from election challengers making an issue of incumbents' missing votes, observers said.

Senators on average voted 97 percent, down 1 percentage point from 1989. House members on average voted 94 percent, equaling 1989's tally.

Pressure to return home to campaign usually lowered voting participation scores in election years. The average in 1988, the last year with a general election, was 92 percent. The previous record for voting participation in an election year was 93 percent in 1986.

Voting participation scores were often used as an indication of a legislator's dedication.

But legislative experts warned that this could be misleading. Members may have missed minor votes because they were busy with other duties — such as committee meetings in which bills were crafted.

"The scores are distortive and ignore the fact that some votes are more important than others," argued Roger H. Davidson, a specialist on Congress at the University of Maryland.

However, Davidson added that they provided one of the few objective measures to compare members.

Even voting participation champion Rep. William H. Natcher, D-Ky., questioned the value of a perfect record.

"I have my doubts that it means that much anymore," Natcher said. "I don't advise new members to start a record like this. I have my doubts that I'd even try it again."

Natcher extended his perfect voting record to 37 years— 12,627 votes, excluding quorum calls.

Congress' average had not slipped below 90 percent since 1980, and in recent years perfect or near-perfect scores were not unusual. In 1990, 12 House members received a perfect score while 77 scored 99 percent. Senators did even better: Roughly half scored 99 percent or better, including 15 who scored 100 percent.

The rise stemmed from two developments. Both chambers' leaders "have made the scheduling of votes a lot more predictable," says Bruce I. Oppenheimer of the University of Houston.

Most roll call votes were in the middle of the week, allowing members to visit their districts over long weekends with little fear of missing a vote. Perhaps more important, however, was incumbents' growing fear that they would suffer at the polls if they missed votes. Ten years ago, Davidson noted, "records weren't sweated over so much. They didn't have the main parties and interest groups poring over them."

Sen. Lowell P. Weicker Jr., R-Conn., was defeated in 1988 after attacks by Democratic challenger Joseph I. Lieberman, who said Weicker had received more than $200,000 in honoraria while missing important votes.

In the 1990 California gubernatorial race, Dianne Feinstein needled Republican Sen. Pete Wilson for his failure to cast key votes, but he won anyway.

Only 52 House members scored under 90 percent. Bill Nelson, D-Fla., scored the lowest with 44 percent, missing votes while campaigning unsuccessfully for the gubernatorial nomination. Of the 10 lowest House scorers, five were seeking higher office, three were retiring, and one, Harold E. Ford, D-Tenn., was fighting charges of bank and tax fraud. William D. Ford, D-Mich., was ill.

Three members of the Senate dipped below 90 percent. Wilson came in last with 78 percent. William L. Armstrong, R-Colo., with 81 percent, retired with adjournment. And Mark O. Hatfield, R-Ore. — at 88 percent — made last-minute trips home to fend off a tough challenge. ■

	1	2
Alabama		
Heflin	99	99
Shelby	100	100
Alaska		
Murkowski	98	98
Stevens	96	96
Arizona		
DeConcini	97	97
McCain	98	98
Arkansas		
Bumpers	98	98
Pryor	97	97
California		
Cranston	98	98
Wilson	78	77
Colorado		
Wirth	98	98
Armstrong #	81	81
Connecticut		
Dodd	97	97
Lieberman	99	99
Delaware		
Biden	98	98
Roth	99	99
Florida		
Graham	99	99
Mack	99	99
Georgia		
Fowler	98	98
Nunn	98	98
Hawaii		
Akaka [1]	99	99
Inouye	97	97
Idaho		
McClure	97	97
Symms	97	97
Illinois		
Dixon	100	100
Simon	99	99
Indiana		
Coats	98	98
Lugar	99	99
Iowa		
Harkin	100	100
Grassley #	99	99
Kansas		
Dole	100	100
Kassebaum	98	98
Kentucky		
Ford	99	99
McConnell	99	99
Louisiana		
Breaux #	99	99
Johnston	94	94
Maine		
Mitchell	100	100
Cohen	100	100
Maryland		
Mikulski #	97	97
Sarbanes	100	100
Massachusetts		
Kennedy	96	96
Kerry	96	96
Michigan		
Levin	99	99
Riegle #	95	95
Minnesota		
Boschwitz	93	93
Durenberger	95	95
Mississippi		
Cochran	99	99
Lott	98	98
Missouri		
Bond	98	98
Danforth	99	99
Montana		
Baucus	98	99
Burns	99	99
Nebraska		
Exon	97	97
Kerrey	99	99
Nevada		
Bryan	99	99
Reid	99	99
New Hampshire		
Humphrey	97	97
Rudman #	94	94
New Jersey		
Bradley	99	99
Lautenberg	100	100
New Mexico		
Bingaman #	94	94
Domenici	94	94
New York		
Moynihan	98	98
D'Amato	99	99
North Carolina		
Sanford	97	97
Helms	99	99
North Dakota		
Burdick	99	99
Conrad	99	99
Ohio		
Glenn	100	100
Metzenbaum	97	97
Oklahoma		
Boren #	92	92
Nickles	98	98
Oregon		
Hatfield	88	88
Packwood	95	95
Pennsylvania		
Heinz	98	98
Specter	99	99
Rhode Island		
Pell	96	96
Chafee	96	96
South Carolina		
Hollings	100	100
Thurmond #	99	99
South Dakota		
Daschle	99	99
Pressler #	96	97
Tennessee		
Gore	99	99
Sasser	99	99
Texas		
Bentsen	98	98
Gramm	96	96
Utah		
Garn	94	95
Hatch	99	99
Vermont		
Leahy	100	100
Jeffords	97	97
Virginia		
Robb	100	100
Warner	99	99
Washington		
Adams	99	99
Gorton	100	100
West Virginia		
Byrd	100	100
Rockefeller	99	99
Wisconsin		
Kohl	99	99
Kasten	100	100
Wyoming		
Simpson	95	95
Wallop	90	91

KEY

\# Member absent a day or more in 1990 due to illness or illness or death in family.

Democrats ***Republicans***

Voting Participation: Senate

1. Voting Participation, 1990. Percentage of 326 recorded votes in 1990 on which a senator voted "yea" or "nay."

2. Voting Participation, 1990. Percentage of 324 recorded votes in 1990 on which a senator voted "yea" or "nay." In this version of the study, votes to instruct the sergeant-at-arms to request the attendance of absent senators were not included.

[1] *Sen. Daniel K. Akaka, D-Hawaii, was sworn in May 16, 1990, to succeed Spark M. Matsunaga, D, who died April 15, 1990. Matsunaga was eligible for 57 of 326 votes in 1990. Akaka was eligible for 234 of 326 votes in 1990.*

NOTE: Scores are rounded to nearest percentage, except that no scores are rounded up to 100 percent.

Voting Participation: House

1. Voting Participation, 1990. Percentage of 511 recorded votes in 1990 on which a representative voted "yea" or "nay."

2. Voting Participation, 1990. Percentage of 481 recorded votes in 1990 on which a representative voted "yea" or "nay." In this version of the study, votes of approval of the House Journal were not included.

[1] *Rep. Pasty T. Mink, D-Hawaii, was sworn in Sept. 27, 1990, to succeed Daniel K. Akaka, D, who was appointed to replace the late Democratic Sen. Spark M. Matsunaga. Akaka was eligible for 99 votes in 1990, 89 not including votes to approve the Journal. Mink was eligible for 141 of 511 votes in 1990, 136 not including votes to approve the Journal.*

[2] *Rep. James J. Florio, D-N.J., resigned Jan. 16, 1990, to become governor of New Jersey.*

[3] *Rep. Susan Molinari, R-N.Y., was sworn in March 27, 1990, to succeed her father, Guy V. Molinari, R, who resigned Jan. 1. Molinari was eligible for 474 of 511 votes, 450 not including votes to approve the Journal.*

[4] *Rep. Jose E. Serrano, D-N.Y., was sworn in March 28, 1990, to succeed Robert Garcia, D, who resigned Jan. 7. Serrano was eligible for 468 of 511 votes, 445 not including votes to approve the Journal.*

[5] *Rep. Donald E. "Buz" Lukens, R-Ohio, resigned Oct. 24, 1990. Lukens was eligible for 487 votes in 1990, 457 not including votes to approve the Journal.*

[6] *Rep. Craig Washington, D-Texas, was sworn in Jan. 23, 1990, to succeed Mickey Leland, D, who died Aug. 7, 1989. He was ineligible for the first roll call vote in 1990. However, because the first vote was a quorum call, it did not affect Washington's voting participation score.*

[7] *Rep. Thomas S. Foley, D-Wash., as Speaker of the House voted at his discretion.*

NOTE: Scores are rounded to nearest percentage, except that no scores are rounded up to 100 percent.

KEY

† Not eligible for all recorded votes in 1990 or voted "present" to avoid possible conflict of interest.

Member absent a day or more in 1990 due to illness or illness or death in family.

Democrats ***Republicans***

	1	2
Alabama		
1 ***Callahan*** †	94	95
2 ***Dickinson***	94	94
3 Browder	99	99
4 Bevill	96	95
5 Flippo	64	64
6 Erdreich	100	100
7 Harris	98	98
Alaska		
AL ***Young***	91	93
Arizona		
1 ***Rhodes***	99	99
2 Udall	85	88
3 ***Stump*** # †	82	82
4 ***Kyl***	98	98
5 ***Kolbe***	97	97
Arkansas		
1 Alexander	85	86
2 ***Robinson***	75	75
3 ***Hammerschmidt***	95	95
4 Anthony	96	98
California		
1 Bosco	96	96
2 ***Herger***	98	99
3 Matsui #	95	95
4 Fazio	95	95
5 Pelosi	96	97
6 Boxer	89	89
7 Miller	95	95
8 Dellums	95	95
9 Stark	94	94
10 Edwards	96	96
11 Lantos	96	96
12 ***Campbell*** †	97	97
13 Mineta	96	96
14 ***Shumway***	97	98
15 Condit	95	96
16 Panetta	97	97
17 ***Pashayan***	96	96
18 Lehman	93	94
19 ***Lagomarsino***	99	99
20 ***Thomas*** #	87	87
21 ***Gallegly***	98	98
22 ***Moorhead***	99	99
23 Beilenson	97	97
24 Waxman	94	95
25 Roybal	97	98
26 Berman	96	97
27 Levine	95	96
28 Dixon	94	97
29 Hawkins	67	66
30 Martinez	87	88
31 Dymally	92	93
32 Anderson	99	99
33 ***Dreier***	99	99
34 Torres	97	97
35 ***Lewis***	88	88
36 Brown	87	87
37 ***McCandless***	99	99
38 ***Dornan***	93	93
39 ***Dannemeyer***	96	96
40 ***Cox***	95	95
41 ***Lowery***	89	92
42 ***Rohrabacher***	99	99
43 ***Packard***	96	96
44 Bates	92	93
45 ***Hunter***	95	96
Colorado		
1 Schroeder	98	98
2 Skaggs	99	99
3 Campbell	95	95
4 ***Brown***	99	99
5 ***Hefley***	98	98
6 ***Schaefer***	98	98
Connecticut		
1 Kennelly	99	99
2 Gejdenson	99	99
3 Morrison	59	59
4 ***Shays***	100	100
5 ***Rowland***	70	70
6 ***Johnson***	98	98
Delaware		
AL Carper	99	99
Florida		
1 Hutto #	96	96
2 ***Grant***	97	97
3 Bennett	99	100
4 ***James***	99	99
5 ***McCollum***	96	97
6 ***Stearns***	99	99
7 Gibbons	95	95
8 ***Young*** #	94	95
9 ***Bilirakis*** #	84	84
10 ***Ireland*** #	90	91
11 Nelson	44	45
12 ***Lewis***	95	95
13 ***Goss***	99	99
14 Johnston	91	91
15 ***Shaw***	96	97
16 Smith #	90	91
17 Lehman	97	98
18 ***Ros-Lehtinen***	97	98
19 Fascell	96	97
Georgia		
1 Thomas	98	98
2 Hatcher	93	93
3 Ray	94	94
4 Jones	98	98
5 Lewis	100	100
6 ***Gingrich***	90	91
7 Darden #	99	99
8 Rowland	96	96
9 Jenkins	92	92
10 Barnard	87	88
Hawaii		
1 ***Saiki***	93	93
2 Mink † [1]	88	88
Idaho		
1 ***Craig***	82	83
2 Stallings	97	97
Illinois		
1 Hayes	97	98
2 Savage	89	91
3 Russo	97	97
4 Sangmeister	96	96
5 Lipinski	95	95
6 ***Hyde***	96	96
7 Collins #	88	90
8 Rostenkowski	89	90
9 Yates #	90	91
10 ***Porter***	97	97
11 Annunzio	97	97
12 ***Crane***	91	93
13 ***Fawell***	99	99
14 ***Hastert***	97	98
15 ***Madigan***	93	93
16 ***Martin***	78	78
17 Evans	100	100
18 ***Michel***	92	92
19 Bruce	99	99
20 Durbin	97	98
21 Costello	99	99
22 Poshard	99	100
Indiana		
1 Visclosky	98	98
2 Sharp	95	95
3 ***Hiler***	98	99

	1	2
4 Long	99	99
5 Jontz	99	99
6 ***Burton***	97	97
7 ***Myers***	98	98
8 McCloskey	98	98
9 Hamilton	99	100
10 Jacobs	97	97
Iowa		
1 ***Leach***	98	98
2 ***Tauke***	96	96
3 Nagle	96	97
4 Smith	98	99
5 ***Lightfoot***	97	98
6 ***Grandy*** #	99	99
Kansas		
1 ***Roberts***	98	99
2 Slattery	96	96
3 ***Meyers***	99	99
4 Glickman	97	97
5 ***Whittaker***	97	97
Kentucky		
1 Hubbard	99	99
2 Natcher	100	100
3 Mazzoli	99	99
4 ***Bunning***	97	97
5 ***Rogers***	99	99
6 ***Hopkins***	98	98
7 Perkins	100	100
Louisiana		
1 ***Livingston***	96	96
2 Boggs	88	88
3 Tauzin #	96	97
4 ***McCrery***	87	89
5 Huckaby	94	94
6 ***Baker***	91	91
7 Hayes	88	88
8 ***Holloway***	93	93
Maine		
1 Brennan	86	86
2 ***Snowe***	99	99
Maryland		
1 Dyson	96	98
2 ***Bentley***	95	96
3 Cardin	99	99
4 McMillen	100	100
5 Hoyer #	98	98
6 Byron #	94	94
7 Mfume	96	98
8 ***Morella***	96	96
Massachusetts		
1 ***Conte***	97	97
2 Neal	93	93
3 Early	90	90
4 Frank †	95	95
5 Atkins	97	98
6 Mavroules	94	95
7 Markey	95	96
8 Kennedy	94	94
9 Moakley	99	99
10 Studds	99	99
11 Donnelly	93	93
Michigan		
1 Conyers	89	91
2 ***Pursell***	89	90
3 Wolpe	95	95
4 ***Upton***	99	99
5 ***Henry*** #	97	97
6 Carr	96	96
7 Kildee	100	100
8 Traxler	92	92
9 ***Vander Jagt***	94	95
10 ***Schuette***	69	69
11 ***Davis***	95	95
12 Bonior #	98	99
13 Crockett	48	48
14 Hertel	99	99
15 Ford #	74	75
16 Dingell	93	95
17 Levin	99	99
18 ***Broomfield***	95	95
Minnesota		
1 Penny	99	99
2 ***Weber***	94	94
3 ***Frenzel***	87	88
4 Vento	98	98
5 Sabo	99	99
6 Sikorski	97	97
7 ***Stangeland***	98	99
8 Oberstar	98	98
Mississippi		
1 Whitten	94	94
2 Espy	89	89
3 Montgomery	97	97
4 Parker	98	99
5 Taylor	100	100
Missouri		
1 Clay	89	90
2 ***Buechner***	98	98
3 Gephardt	90	91
4 Skelton #	96	96
5 Wheat	98	98
6 ***Coleman***	98	98
7 ***Hancock***	99	99
8 ***Emerson*** #	97	98
9 Volkmer	98	99
Montana		
1 Williams	90	93
2 ***Marlenee***	93	93
Nebraska		
1 ***Bereuter***	99	99
2 Hoagland	99	99
3 ***Smith***	95	95
Nevada		
1 Bilbray	98	99
2 ***Vucanovich***	94	94
New Hampshire		
1 ***Smith***	98	98
2 ***Douglas***	96	96
New Jersey		
1 Vacancy [2]		
2 Hughes	98	99
3 Pallone	99	100
4 ***Smith***	98	98
5 ***Roukema***	90	90
6 Dwyer	93	93
7 ***Rinaldo***	98	99
8 Roe	96	97
9 Torricelli	89	88
10 Payne	95	95
11 ***Gallo***	96	96
12 ***Courter***	93	93
13 ***Saxton***	98	99
14 Guarini	94	94
New Mexico		
1 ***Schiff***	98	99
2 ***Skeen***	99	99
3 Richardson	97	98
New York		
1 Hochbrueckner	99	99
2 Downey	98	98
3 Mrazek	93	93
4 ***Lent***	92	92
5 ***McGrath***	94	94
6 Flake	89	90
7 Ackerman	92	92
8 Scheuer	96	96
9 Manton #	94	94
10 Schumer	96	96
11 Towns	91	92
12 Owens	88	88
13 Solarz	95	95
14 ***Molinari*** † [3]	98	99
15 ***Green***	98	98
16 Rangel	89	91
17 Weiss	99	99
18 Serrano † [4]	94	94
19 Engel	86	88
20 Lowey	97	97
21 ***Fish***	93	94
22 ***Gilman***	99	99
23 McNulty	99	99
24 ***Solomon***	97	98
25 ***Boehlert***	99	99
26 ***Martin***	95	95
27 ***Walsh***	96	97
28 McHugh	99	99
29 ***Horton***	95	95
30 Slaughter	99	99
31 ***Paxon***	97	97
32 LaFalce	94	94
33 Nowak	97	98
34 ***Houghton***	94	94
North Carolina		
1 Jones	94	94
2 Valentine	97	98
3 Lancaster	99	99
4 Price	99	99
5 Neal	94	96
6 ***Coble***	99	99
7 Rose	95	95
8 Hefner	98	99
9 ***McMillan***	98	99
10 ***Ballenger***	97	97
11 Clarke	98	98
North Dakota		
AL Dorgan #	97	97
Ohio		
1 Luken	90	90
2 ***Gradison***	97	96
3 Hall	90	91
4 ***Oxley***	97	97
5 ***Gillmor***	97	98
6 ***McEwen***	94	95
7 ***DeWine***	98	99
8 ***Lukens*** † [5]	82	81
9 Kaptur	95	95
10 ***Miller*** #	98	98
11 Eckart	98	99
12 ***Kasich***	97	98
13 Pease	98	98
14 Sawyer	99	99
15 ***Wylie***	91	91
16 ***Regula***	98	98
17 Traficant	100	100
18 Applegate	98	99
19 Feighan	90	90
20 Oakar	92	93
21 Stokes	95	96
Oklahoma		
1 ***Inhofe***	98	98
2 Synar	97	98
3 Watkins	76	77
4 McCurdy	97	98
5 ***Edwards***	89	90
6 English #	99	99
Oregon		
1 AuCoin #	88	89
2 ***Smith, B.***	99	99
3 Wyden	100	100
4 DeFazio	95	95
5 ***Smith, D.*** #	81	80
Pennsylvania		
1 Foglietta	97	97
2 Gray	89	90
3 Borski	98	98
4 Kolter	94	94
5 ***Schulze***	90	90
6 Yatron	98	98
7 ***Weldon***	96	96
8 Kostmayer	97	97
9 ***Shuster***	96	96
10 ***McDade*** #	84	85
11 Kanjorski	99	99
12 Murtha	97	97
13 ***Coughlin***	96	96
14 Coyne	95	96
15 ***Ritter***	96	97
16 ***Walker***	99	99
17 ***Gekas***	99	99
18 Walgren	96	97
19 ***Goodling***	93	93
20 Gaydos	96	97
21 ***Ridge***	95	95
22 Murphy	94	95
23 ***Clinger***	95	94
Rhode Island		
1 ***Machtley***	98	98
2 ***Schneider***	97	97
South Carolina		
1 ***Ravenel***	98	98
2 ***Spence***	98	98
3 Derrick	97	96
4 Patterson #	99	99
5 Spratt	98	98
6 Tallon	98	98
South Dakota		
AL Johnson	99	99
Tennessee		
1 ***Quillen***	92	92
2 ***Duncan***	100	100
3 Lloyd	97	98
4 Cooper †	99	99
5 Clement	98	98
6 Gordon	98	98
7 ***Sundquist***	98	98
8 Tanner #	95	95
9 Ford	62	64
Texas		
1 Chapman	92	93
2 Wilson	82	84
3 ***Bartlett***	99	99
4 Hall	81	81
5 Bryant	98	98
6 ***Barton*** #	94	95
7 ***Archer***	98	98
8 ***Fields*** #	95	96
9 Brooks	92	92
10 Pickle	97	98
11 Leath	69	70
12 Geren	99	99
13 Sarpalius	96	97
14 Laughlin	93	93
15 de la Garza	92	93
16 Coleman #	97	97
17 Stenholm	99	99
18 Washington † [6]	78	79
19 ***Combest***	98	99
20 Gonzalez	99	99
21 ***Smith***	95	96
22 ***DeLay***	98	98
23 Bustamante	91	91
24 Frost	95	96
25 Andrews	99	99
26 ***Armey***	99	99
27 Ortiz	98	98
Utah		
1 ***Hansen***	96	96
2 Owens †	96	97
3 ***Nielson***	96	97
Vermont		
AL ***Smith***	90	89
Virginia		
1 ***Bateman***	98	98
2 Pickett	99	99
3 ***Bliley***	98	98
4 Sisisky †	99	99
5 Payne	99	99
6 Olin	98	98
7 ***Slaughter***	99	99
8 ***Parris***	94	94
9 Boucher	95	95
10 ***Wolf***	99	99
Washington		
1 ***Miller***	95	95
2 Swift #	97	97
3 Unsoeld	95	96
4 ***Morrison***	95	95
5 Foley [7]		
6 Dicks	98	98
7 McDermott	99	99
8 ***Chandler***	95	95
West Virginia		
1 Mollohan	93	93
2 Staggers	98	98
3 Wise	97	98
4 Rahall #	95	96
Wisconsin		
1 Aspin	91	91
2 Kastenmeier	99	99
3 ***Gunderson***	98	98
4 Kleczka	96	96
5 Moody	91	91
6 ***Petri***	97	97
7 Obey	97	97
8 ***Roth***	98	98
9 ***Sensenbrenner***	99	99
Wyoming		
AL ***Thomas***	97	97

Justices Left Many Issues to Lawmakers

The Supreme Court continued in its 1989-90 term to make more and more clear its desire to leave policy-making to Congress and the states.

This was a "take-your-problems-elsewhere" court, said Walter F. Murphy, a constitutional interpretation professor at Princeton University.

Sen. Orrin G. Hatch, R-Utah, agreed, saying, "This is definitely not an activist court."

Legal scholars predicted that social issues increasingly would be played out in legislatures, rather than in the Supreme Court. The vestiges of the activist Earl Warren era (1953-69) lingered through the 1980s, particularly because of the persuasive ability of liberal William J. Brennan Jr. But Brennan retired in July, after nearly 34 years on the court.

"Those who are interested in social reform on the liberal side should stay away from the court," said Cass Sunstein, a constitutional law professor at the University of Chicago. "They should go to Congress. The liberal orthodoxy of the last generation of justices no longer makes sense."

While the court continued to show a clear conservative bent, both the circumspect tone of its rulings and a decrease in the number of cases the court accepted showed a resistance to enter the fray.

The court declined to forge a consensus on an individual's "right to die" — stemming from a tragic Missouri case — or to broadly rule on abortion rights in two cases involving teenagers' access to abortion. The justices showed that they were more inclined to refine the decisions of the "activist" era of the 1960s and '70s than to overrule, for example, a landmark like the 1973 *Roe v. Wade* decision, which legalized abortion nationwide.

House legal counsel Steven R. Ross said, "The court has been asked to deal with a number of very difficult issues, and there is a recognition among many of the justices that these types of issues are best dealt with legislatively."

Part of the resistance to chart a dramatic course likely stemmed from the court's polarization along a 5-4 conservative-liberal divide. One-third of the court's decisions were 5-4 rulings.

On the right were Chief Justice William H. Rehnquist and Justices Byron R. White, Sandra Day O'Connor, Antonin Scalia and Anthony M. Kennedy. On the left were Brennan, Thurgood Marshall, Harry A. Blackmun and — most of the time — John Paul Stevens.

While White and O'Connor usually lined up on the conservative side, each occasionally swung to the liberal column, giving the liberals an occasional victory. More often than not the conservative side prevailed.

In its 1990-91 term, the court was expected to have an even more conservative bent with Brennan succeeded by Justice David H. Souter.

Though Souter did not say during his confirmation hearings how he would vote on many of the major issues before the court, it was clear that he would offer a more conservative voice and vote than his predecessor. *(Souter confirmation, p. 508)*

Looking to Congress

The court in 1990 continued to cut back on defendants' rights, upholding state laws on executions and allowing law enforcement authorities more power in the detection and prosecution of drunken drivers.

Among the rulings was a decision in *Michigan v. Sitz* that the Constitution permitted the police to stop drivers at roadside checkpoints to determine whether they were intoxicated.

In one notable victory for liberals, the court declined to further narrow civil rights law, as it had in 1989. In *Metro Broadcasting Inc. v. Federal Communications Commission*, the court voted 5-4 to uphold policies forced on the Federal Communications Commission (FCC) by Congress to give preferential treatment to minority group applicants seeking broadcast licenses.

Although the court continued to pass on authority for social issues such as abortion to legislators, the term did not rattle politicians as much as the previous one.

In 1989, state and federal lawmakers struggled with how to respond to court decisions on flag burning, job discrimination and abortion.

The court considered those issues in 1990, but the rulings were incremental or, in the rejection of a flag-protection statute, more predictable.

The June 11 decision in *United States v. Eichman* was a repeat of the court's 1989 ruling in *Texas v. Johnson*, in which a state law against flag burning was struck down.

To counter *Texas v. Johnson*, Congress had enacted a statute that tried to make flag burning illegal. But that law was struck down in *Eichman*, with the court ruling that the statute infringed on First Amendment guarantees of free expression.

While the flag-statute ruling vexed Congress, the court upheld several federal statutes during its term.

The court tied its decision in *Metro Broadcasting* directly to Congress' authority. "It is of overriding significance in these cases that the FCC's minority ownership programs have been specifically approved — indeed, mandated — by Congress," Brennan wrote for the majority.

In *Board of Education of Westside Community Schools v. Mergens*, the court by 8-1 upheld a federal statute that allowed student religious groups to meet in public high schools on the same basis as other extracurricular clubs.

Additionally, in *Perpich v. Department of Defense*, the justices unanimously upheld a federal statute giving the president the power to order National Guard units to training missions in Central America and other places outside the United States without the approval of state governors.

The court also said elected officials should decide regulations on corporate involvement in political campaigns. In *Austin v. Michigan State Chamber of Commerce*, the court by 6-3 upheld the power of both the federal government and states to bar corporations from running independent political campaigns.

The court did not, however, defer to the political process in its 5-4 ruling on patronage laws in *Rutan v. Republican Party of Illinois*.

The court ruled on First Amendment grounds that a state government could not use party affiliation as a basis for hiring, promoting or transferring employees. But it stressed that it was not breaking new ground. "Political parties have already survived the substantial decline in patronage employment practices in this century," Brennan wrote.

Continued on p. 54

Major Supreme Court Decisions of 1989-90

Following are some of the most important rulings of the Supreme Court's 1989-90 term in the chronological order in which they were announced:

University of Pennsylvania v. Equal Employment Opportunity Commission, 9-0, ruled that colleges and universities enjoyed no academic freedom privilege against disclosure of faculty peer review materials in course of EEOC investigation of alleged discrimination in tenure decisions. Opinion by Blackmun; Jan. 9. *(Story, p. 623)*

Spallone v. United States, 5-4, ruled that a federal district judge abused his discretion when he imposed a contempt fine on four Yonkers, N.Y., council members for their refusal to vote for legislation needed to carry out public housing plans. Opinion by Rehnquist; dissenting: Brennan, Marshall, Blackmun, Stevens; Jan. 10.

Dole v. United Steelworkers of America, 7-2, barred the Office of Management and Budget from using the Paperwork Reduction Act to nullify an agency's health and safety disclosure regulations. Opinion by Brennan; dissenting: Rehnquist, White; Feb. 21. *(Story, p. 412)*

Washington v. Harper, 6-3, upheld involuntary treatment of mentally ill state prison inmate with anti-psychotic medication if the inmate was dangerous to himself or others and treatment was in the inmate's medical interest. Opinion by Kennedy; dissenting: Brennan, Marshall, Stevens; Feb. 27.

Boeing Co. v. United States, 9-0, ruled that a federal conflict-of-interest statute did not bar a private contractor from giving lump-sum severance payments to employees about to enter government service. Opinion by Stevens; Feb. 27.

Austin v. Michigan State Chamber of Commerce, 6-3, ruled that states could require corporations to make their political expenditures through separate political action committees. Opinion by Marshall; dissenting: O'Connor, Scalia, Kennedy; March 27. *(Story, p. 61)*

Osborne v. Ohio, 6-3, upheld an Ohio statute prohibiting the possession or viewing of child pornography in one's home. Opinion by White; dissenting: Brennan, Marshall, Stevens; April 18.

Missouri v. Jenkins, 5-4, ruled that a federal judge could order local authorities to raise property taxes to pay for school desegregation. Opinion by White; dissenting: Rehnquist, O'Connor, Scalia, Kennedy; April 18.

Board of Education of Westside Community Schools v. Mergens, 8-1, upheld a federal law requiring public high schools to allow student religious groups to meet on the same basis as other extracurricular activity groups. Plurality opinion by O'Connor; dissenting: Stevens; June 4. *(Story, p. 618)*

United States v. Eichman, 5-4, ruled that the 1989 Flag Protection Act outlawing flag desecration was an impermissible infringement on First Amendment rights. Opinion by Brennan; dissenting: Rehnquist, White, Stevens, O'Connor; June 11. *(Story, p. 524)*

Perpich v. Department of Defense, 9-0, upheld a federal statute that gave the president the authority to order National Guard units to train outside the United States without the approval of state governors. Opinion by Stevens; June 11. *(Story, p. 694)*

Michigan v. Sitz, 6-3, ruled that police could stop drivers at roadside checkpoints and examine them for signs of intoxication, despite the absence of individual suspicion. Opinion by Rehnquist; dissenting: Brennan, Marshall and Stevens; June 14.

Wilder v. Virginia Hospital Association, 5-4, allowed health-care providers to challenge adequacy of Medicaid reimbursement rates by the states. Opinion by Brennan; dissenting: Rehnquist, O'Connor, Scalia, Kennedy; June 14. *(Story, p. 571)*

Pension Benefit Guaranty Corp. v. LTV Corp., 8-1, upheld Pension Benefit Guaranty Corporation's authority to make financially ailing companies take back responsibility for pension plans. Opinion by Blackmun; dissenting: Stevens; June 18. *(Story, p. 368)*

Milkovich v. Lorain Journal Co., 7-2, rejected news organization's assertion of a separate "opinion" privilege limiting application of state libel laws. Opinion by Rehnquist; dissenting: Brennan, Marshall; June 21.

Rutan v. Republican Party of Illinois, 5-4, ruled that the First Amendment barred public employers from hiring, promoting or transferring most public employees based on party affiliation. Opinion by Brennan; dissenting: Rehnquist, O'Connor, Scalia, Kennedy; June 21. *(Story, p. 933)*

Cruzan v. Director, Missouri Department of Health, 5-4, ruled that a state could require clear and convincing evidence of an incompetent patient's wish to die before allowing life-support systems discontinued. Opinion by Rehnquist; dissenting: Brennan, Marshall, Blackmun, Stevens; June 25. *(Story, p. 566)*

Hodgson v. Minnesota, 5-4, upheld a Minnesota law requiring a minor to tell both parents before obtaining an abortion as long as she had the alternative of seeking permission from a judge. Plurality opinion by Kennedy; separate opinion by O'Connor; dissenting: Brennan, Marshall, Blackmun, Stevens; June 25. *(Story, p. 529)*

Ohio v. Akron Center for Reproductive Health, 6-3, upheld an Ohio statute that required teenagers to tell one parent before obtaining an abortion. Opinion by Kennedy; dissenting: Brennan, Marshall, Blackmun; June 25. *(Story, p. 529)*

Idaho v. Wright, 5-4, barred use in criminal trial of hearsay statements made by suspected child victim of sex abuse to her treating pediatrician. Opinion by O'Connor; dissenting: Rehnquist, White, Blackmun, Kennedy; June 27.

Maryland v. Craig, 5-4, upheld state procedure allowing child victim of alleged sexual abuse to testify in criminal trial by one-way closed circuit television outside the defendant's presence. Opinion by O'Connor; dissenting: Brennan, Marshall, Stevens, Scalia; June 27.

Metro Broadcasting Inc. v. Federal Communications Commission, 5-4, ruled that Congress could require preferential treatment of minorities to increase their ownership of broadcast licenses. Opinion by Brennan; dissenting: Rehnquist, O'Connor, Scalia, Kennedy; June 27. *(Story, p. 379)*

Continued from p. 52

In dissent, Scalia, the court's most vocal advocate of deference to the political branches of government, complained that the court-ordered "constitutional civil-service reform ... may well have disastrous consequences for our political system."

Scalia also voiced sharp criticism of the court's abortion rulings, in which a tenuous majority ambivalently clung to the holding of *Roe v. Wade*, if not its spirit.

Scalia complained about the hodgepodge of opinions in two decisions upholding laws that prohibited teenagers from obtaining abortions without first notifying one or both of their parents or getting a judge's permission.

Scalia, who would have preferred that legislators take over all abortion regulations, said, "The random and unpredictable results of our consequently unchanneled individual views make it increasingly evident, term after term, that the tools for this job are not to be found in the lawyer's — and hence not in the judge's — workbox."

Legislative Intent

From Congress, the court demonstrated its preference for more explicit statutes. The court appeared to be saying it was the letter of a statute, not inferred congressional intent or a social agenda, that would be its guide. *(Views on legislative intent, p. 55)*

It was Scalia again who raised the issue most pointedly, criticizing the court's reliance on legislative history, mocking the staff-written committee reports cited as proof of legislative intent and calling on Congress to say what it meant in statutes.

"That the court should refer to ... a document issued by a single committee of a single house as the action of Congress displays the level of unreality that our unrestrained use of legislative history has attained," he wrote in a concurring opinion in a 1989 case, *Blanchard v. Bergeron*.

Unless the court turned to extrastatutory materials, it either had to rely on its own interpretation of what an ambiguous statute meant or adopt an executive branch construction. U.S. Appeals Court Judge Patricia M. Wald, chief judge for the District of Columbia Circuit, was among those who said that a disregard for legislative history necessarily gave the executive branch the upper hand.

"For, if the clarity of Congress' will must be discerned solely from the text [of a statute], without access to legislative history, there will be fewer cases where judges can confidently decide what that is, and more cases will be decided by the executive under the ... principle that where Congress has not spoken precisely to the issue, the executive's interpretation trumps the court's," Wald said in an article that appeared in the winter 1989 issue of The American University Law Review.

Lawmakers in both parties also challenged Scalia's views.

"The courts are supposed to allow the laws to evolve," said Rep. Don Edwards, D-Calif., chairman of the House Judiciary Subcommittee on Constitutional Law. "We expect judges and our colleagues and the regulators to learn more about what our intentions are."

Some critics of the Scalia approach suggested that because Republicans had held the presidency for 18 of the past 22 years, and GOP appointees made up more than half the federal bench, the judiciary was inclined to favor the executive branch at the expense of the Democratic-controlled Congress. But Scalia justified his stance with strongly held philosophical and constitutional views, not partisan or practical considerations.

Scalia's approach was supported in a 123-page document produced by the Justice Department's Office of Legal Policy in January 1989. The report noted that when the president signed a bill, he was approving the language of the bill, not the entire congressional record.

Scalia suggested in opinions and said publicly that members were not aware of what went into a committee report and that lobbyists often drafted the language.

But members and their aides insisted that reports were written under scrutiny from committee chairmen.

Scalia suggested that when the judiciary gave weight to committee reports, it allowed Congress to unconstitutionally delegate its responsibility to staff.

But defenders of Congress, such as Sen. Arlen Specter, R-Pa., said the enormousness of government required elected officials to delegate responsibility. Specter, respected for his command of constitutional law, also said members of Congress were more likely to read a committee report than the bill itself.

"I think when justices disregard that kind of material [legislative history], it is just another way to write their own law," he said.

Congressional Reaction

The Supreme Court, though, did not necessarily have the final say. If Congress objected to the way a court interpreted a federal statute, it could enact legislation reversing the decision.

Congress waged efforts in 1990 — some successful, others not — to counter several rulings from the 1988-89 court term. In contrast to the situation during the Warren Court era, it was often liberals, not conservatives, who sought to overturn Supreme Court decisions.

- **Civil rights.** With bipartisan support, Congress passed a major civil rights bill that would have modified or overturned six 1989 Supreme Court decisions. But President Bush vetoed the bill, and the veto was narrowly sustained in the Senate.

The measure targeted decisions that narrowed the reach and remedies of laws prohibiting employment discrimination and made it harder to prove job discrimination and easier to challenge affirmative-action programs. Some of the rulings also reduced the remedies available to victims of job discrimination. *(Civil rights bill, p. 462)*

- **Age-based discrimination.** Compromise legislation was enacted, however, to reverse a 1989 ruling that allowed age-based discrimination in employee benefits. The bill cleared Congress late in the session and, despite previous reservations from the administration, was signed by Bush.

The court's 7-2 ruling had held that the strict antibias provisions of the 1967 Age Discrimination in Employment Act did not extend to retirement benefits. The complex compromise that Congress passed overturned that holding but sought to neutralize opposition from employers by exempting most early-retirement incentive plans. *(Age discrimination, p. 362)*

- **Disabled education.** Congress acted to reassert that states were liable for failing to meet the needs of students under the handicapped education act.

The moves responded to *Dellmuth v. Muth*, a 1989 decision in which the court held that Congress had failed to state clearly that it intended states to be liable for failing to provide to disabled students the "free, appropriate" education guaranteed by the federal law.

The court had held that the state was immune, under

the 11th Amendment, from suits in federal court arising out of the act. But a provision included in a reauthorization of the handicapped education law clarified that it was the intention of Congress to allow litigants the right to sue in federal court to enforce their rights under the act. *(Education for the disabled, p. 616)*

• **Right to die.** Congress responded quickly, if narrowly, to the court's decision in *Cruzan v. Missouri* that a state could require strict proof of a comatose patient's previously expressed wish to die before allowing life-support systems to be disconnected.

Congress ordered health-care providers paid by Medicare and Medicaid to inform patients about their rights under state law to execute "living wills" or other advance directives about their care should they become unable to communicate. The action came in the Medicare section of the budget-reconciliation bill. *(Medicare, p. 563)*

• **Abortion.** Abortion rights forces, chastened by the court's 1989 ruling giving states more discretion to regulate abortion procedures, sought to take the offensive in 1990 with a bill to prohibit states from restricting abortion rights.

Sponsors said the bill would have codified the *Roe* ruling. Opponents insisted that the measure would have gone beyond *Roe* by forbidding certain restrictions on abortion that the Supreme Court expressly allowed in subsequent rulings.

The bill won approval from Edwards' Constitutional Law Subcommittee on Oct. 4, but went no further. Edwards said he would reintroduce the bill on the first day of the 102nd Congress. *(Abortion, p. 528)*

• **Flag burning.** Members of Congress, in response to *Eichman*, pushed for a constitutional amendment to protect the flag.

Supporters of the amendment failed for the second year in a row to get the measure through Congress, falling well short of the two-thirds majority needed in the House and Senate.

Predictions that the vote would be an issue in the November elections proved wrong. *(Flag burning, p. 524)*

In one instance, however, Congress acted to take advantage of a Supreme Court ruling — its decision upholding criminal laws against possession of child pornography. A provision in the omnibus crime bill cleared by Congress on its last day made possession of child pornography a federal offense and required producers to keep a record of the age

Justices' Views on Legislative Intent

"... As anyone familiar with modern-day drafting of congressional committee reports is well aware," the references in a committee report "were inserted, at best by a committee staff member on his or her own initiative, and at worst by a committee staff member at the suggestion of a lawyer-lobbyist; and the purpose of those references was not primarily to inform the members of Congress what the bill meant ... but rather to influence judicial construction."

—**Justice Antonin Scalia,** concurring opinion, *Blanchard v. Bergeron* (February 1989)

"It is our task, as I see it, not to enter the minds of members of Congress — who need have nothing in mind in order for their votes to be both lawful and effective — but rather to give fair and reasonable meaning to the text of the United States Code, adopted by various Congresses at various times."

—**Scalia,** partial dissent, *Pennsylvania v. Union Gas Co.* (June 1989)

"Even though, as Judge Learned Hand said, 'the words used, even in their literal sense, are the primary, and ordinarily the most reliable, source of interpreting the meaning of any writing,' nevertheless 'it is one of the surest indexes of a mature and developed jurisprudence not to make a fortress out of the dictionary; but to remember that statutes always have purpose or object to accomplish, whose sympathetic and imaginative discovery is the surest guide to their meaning.'"

—**Justice William J. Brennan Jr.,** for the majority, *Public Citizen v. Department of Justice* (June 1989)

"There is a ready starting point, which ought to serve also as a sufficient stopping point, for this kind of analysis: the plain language of the statute.... Reluctance to working with the basic meaning of words in a normal manner undermines the legal process. This case demonstrates that reluctance of this sort leads instead to woolly judicial construction that mars the plain face of legislative enactments."

—**Justice Anthony M. Kennedy,** concurring opinion, *Public Citizen*

"Our mode of reviewing challenges to an agency's interpretation of its governing statute is well established: We first ask whether Congress has directly spoken to the precise question at issue. If the intent of Congress is clear, that is the end of the matter.... But if the statute is silent or ambiguous with respect to the specific issue, the question for the court is whether the agency's answer is based on a permissible construction of the statute, that is, whether the agency's construction is rational and consistent with the statute."

—**Scalia,** for the majority *Sullivan v. Everhart* (February 1990)

"The kingly power to rewrite history has not been delegated to the Secretary of Health and Human Services. Nevertheless, the secretary now claims authority to determine that no underpayment has been made to a beneficiary who concededly received a deficient monthly payment.

"... The net effect of these distortions of statutory language is to defeat clear congressional intent.... Just as we do not sit to supply statutory directives where Congress gave none, we likewise do not sit to insist that Congress express its intent as precisely as would be possible. Our duty is to ask what Congress intended, and not to assay whether Congress might have stated that intent more naturally, more artfully, or more pithily."

—**Justice John Paul Stevens,** dissenting, *Sullivan*

of people appearing in hard-core pornography. *(Anticrime package, p. 486)*

Less Active Court

While issuing its fair share of notable and controversial decisions, overall in 1990, the court chose to hear fewer cases.

The court issued 129 opinions during the term, down slightly from the 133 of the 1988-89 term and the 139 of the term before that — and sharply down from the 151 cases decided in each of the terms ending in 1982 and in 1983. During the 1970s, the court averaged 130 signed opinions a term.

The number of cases accepted for the next term, beginning the first Monday in October, also was sharply lower.

As the court concluded its 1989-90 term, only 56 cases awaited the court for its next term, a 10-year low for that time of year. At the close of the term in 1989, 81 cases had awaited the justices; in 1988, 105 cases.

The court received about 5,000 requests for review during the past year. Four votes were required to accept a case for review.

There were several theories of why the court was hearing fewer cases. One was that the older justices (including Brennan, three were in their 80s and two in their 70s) had a sense of historical perspective that caused them to be nonchalant to certain legal disputes. Another was that the liberal justices did not want the court to take up issues on which the conservative majority might be able to set precedent, so they voted defensively not to review the case.

Another factor might have been the decline in requests for lower-court review by the U.S. solicitor general. President Ronald Reagan's solicitors general pushed for review of a record number of rulings. Bush's solicitor general, Kenneth W. Starr, pursued far fewer appeals.

Hatch said another reason for the small number of cases might have been that the conservative-leaning Supreme Court was more willing to accept decisions of lower-court judges, about half of whom were Reagan appointees.

Whatever the reason, the trend frustrated at least one justice. White dissented nearly 70 times from court decisions not to review cases.

By sitting on the sidelines in some disputes, White wrote in a dissent June 28, the Supreme Court was subjecting residents of different states to different rules.

"In some of these cases it is perhaps arguable that the alleged conflict was not 'real' or 'square,'" White wrote. "In most of these cases, however, it is very difficult to deny the conflict, especially where ... the court of appeals expressly differs with another court, yet *certiorari* is denied because the conflict is 'tolerable' or 'narrow,' or because other courts of appeals should have the opportunity to weigh in on one side or another of the unsettled issue, or for some other unstated reason.

"In any event, denial [of *certiorari*] underlines the fact that the federal law is being administered in different ways in different parts of the country; citizens in some circuits are subject to liabilities or entitlements that citizens in other circuits are not burdened with or entitled to."

The Next Term

The new Supreme Court term began Oct. 1 with observers wondering whether the conservatives would strike out in bold new directions on politically divisive social issues or continue to peel slowly away at the legacy of the liberal activist years.

"There are some fundamental choices to be made," said Senate Judiciary Committee Chairman Joseph R. Biden Jr., D-Del., noting that the court was narrowly divided on standards for freedom of religion, protections for civil liberties, equal protection of minorities and privacy rights.

Specter said, "There has been overriding concern about the abortion question, and while it is of great moment, there are many other matters of tremendous importance to this country."

The court in 1991 would have to rule again, for example, on the reach and interpretation of antidiscrimination law. One case — viewed by women's rights groups as the most important sex discrimination issue in years — challenged a common practice among manufacturers of excluding women from jobs that might lead to birth defects through exposure to dangerous chemicals.

Labor and civil rights groups contended that the policy was unjustifiable sex discrimination under Title VII of the 1964 Civil Rights Act. The company insisted the practice protected the unborn and was required for industrial safety.

Another key dispute over a congressional enactment was a challenge to rules issued by the Reagan administration and defended by the Bush administration barring public family planning funds from being used for abortion counseling. The regulations by the Department of Health and Human Services were designed to implement Title X of the Public Health Service Act, which prohibited federal funds for abortion but did not specifically address whether public money could be spent for abortion counseling.

More than 100 members of Congress argued in an amicus brief that the legislative silence showed unambiguously that Congress did not mean to bar funds for abortion counseling or referral. But an opposing brief signed by more than 50 lawmakers asked the justices to construe the law to bar Title X funds to "any entity which would present abortion as a means to plan the number and spacing of one's children." *(Family planning, p. 604)* ■

Chapter 2

INSIDE CONGRESS

Campaign Financing 59
Corporate Spending Limitations 61
House/Senate Bills 64
State Reform Efforts 67
Broadcasting Rates 68
'Motor Voter' Registration 71
Pay, Honoraria 73
Federal Workers' Honoraria Ban 74
Franking Privilege 75
Keating Five Ethics Hearings 78
Key Players 79
Special Counsel Bennett 81
Overview of Case 83
The 'Appearance Standard' 87
Senators' Statements 90
Sen. D'Amato Case Pending 97
Sen. Durenberger Denounced 98
20th-Century Cases 99
Terms of Opprobrium 100
Rep. Frank Reprimanded 103
Rep. Gingrich Case Dismissed 104
Rep. Savage Inquiry Concluded 105
Rep. Lukens Resigns 106
Rep. Flake Charges Dropped 106
Rep. Ford Case Ends in Mistrial 107
Ex-Rep. Garcia's Conviction Upset 107
Del. Fauntroy Case Dropped 107
No Action on Rep. Stangeland 107
Rep. Dyson Case Dismissed 108
Rep. Sikorski Case Dismissed 108

Partisanship Dooms Campaign Bills

Impasse reached on bills to limit spending, curb PACs

Despite the professed support of both political parties for the idea, legislation to revise the widely unpopular system of financing congressional campaigns died in 1990, the victim of sharp differences between Republicans and Democrats over the best approach to take and divisions within the majority Democrats as well.

The House and Senate passed separate bills (HR 5400, S 137) — both generally backed by Democrats and strongly opposed by Republicans — aimed at reducing campaign spending and limiting the influence of political action committees (PACs). But President Bush threatened to veto any bill with campaign spending limits, and with ideological and political differences too wide to bridge so late in the session, conferees on the two bills never met.

Both the Senate and House were poised, at the beginning of 1990, to begin the first major overhaul of the campaign finance system since the Watergate era. Senate Majority Leader George J. Mitchell of Maine had vowed to move a bill early in the year, but partisan bickering and intraparty disagreement prevented either the House or Senate versions from reaching the floor until the last days before the August recess.

Public attention was riveted on the flaws of the campaign finance system for much of the year by the ongoing investigation into the so-called Keating Five — five senators suspected of doing favors for a wealthy campaign contributor, Charles H. Keating Jr. And a CBS News/New York Times poll conducted a month before the November elections found 71 percent of those surveyed agreeing that "most members of Congress are more interested in serving special interest groups than the people they represent." *(Keating Five case, p. 78)*

The Senate bill would have dismantled PACs and created a system of voluntary spending limits for Senate elections with incentives such as discounted broadcast rates and reduced postage for campaign mailings, in addition to other major changes.

The House bill would also have created voluntary spending limits, but, unlike the Senate bill, would have imposed a flat cap instead of establishing limits on a state-by-state basis. Rather than eliminate PACs, the House measure would have divided them into two categories, dependent upon the size of contributions they raised, and would have placed aggregate limits on the money candidates could accept from them. *(Provisions, House and Senate bills, p. 64)*

When the effort to go to conference on the two bills stalled, lawmakers tried in late September and into October to push through a measure to force broadcasters to lower advertising rates for candidates. But the late effort to win House approval of a bill (HR 5756) comparable to a measure (S 1009) approved by the Senate Commerce Committee in 1989 met opposition from the main citizens' group pushing campaign financing legislation, Common Cause, and from the broadcasting industry. Neither chamber voted on either bill. *(Campaign ad costs, p. 68; 1989 Almanac, p. 386)*

BOXSCORE

Legislation: Campaign financing (HR 5400, S 137).

Major action: House conferees named, Sept. 26; Senate conferees named, Sept. 18.
HR 5400 passed by House, 255-155, Aug. 3; S 137 passed by Senate, 59-40, Aug. 1.

Reports: Rules and Administration (S Rept 101-253).

BACKGROUND

Congress tried for most of the 20th century to devise a system to limit the influence of money in politics. The underlying rationale was consistent: to curb the ability of interest groups to dominate the flow of campaign money and to try to establish level playing fields for challengers as well as incumbents, and for politicians of modest means as well as wealthier campaigners.

Congress had argued the issues since the first law regulating campaigns was enacted during the administration of Theodore Roosevelt. Major new laws, however, came only after scandals: Teapot Dome in the 1920s, Watergate in the 1970s.

In 1925, the Teapot Dome scandal yielded the Federal Corrupt Practices Act, an extensive statute governing the conduct of federal campaigns. That act codified earlier laws limiting campaign expenditures, but the figures were considered so unrealistically low and the law was so riddled with loopholes that it was ineffectual.

Almost 40 years later, less than six months before the Watergate break-in, Congress adopted two pieces of legislation containing some of the ground rules under which elections were conducted into the 1990s.

First, President Richard M. Nixon signed the Revenue Act of 1971 (PL 92-178), allowing the $1 tax checkoff for presidential campaign financing to take effect after almost five years of debate. As a condition for his signature, however, Nixon insisted on postponing the measure until after the 1972 election. *(1971 Almanac, p. 430)*

During his re-election campaign, Nixon signed the Federal Election Campaign Act (FECA) on Feb. 7, 1972 (PL 92-225). The law required comprehensive disclosure of contributions and expenditures by candidates for federal office.

FECA repealed the ineffective Corrupt Practices Act and required meaningful disclosure for the first time. Political committees with receipts of more than $1,000 had to file regular reports. Expenditures and contributions of more than $100 to candidates and political committees had to be disclosed, including names and addresses of contributors. (The threshold was raised to the existing $200 in 1979.) *(1972 Almanac, p. 161; 1971 Almanac, p. 875)*

But FECA ultimately had a limited impact on controlling campaign spending. In the wake of the Watergate scandal, Congress passed the FECA Amendments of 1974 (PL 93-443), which President Gerald R. Ford signed on Oct. 15, 1974. The law set limits on contributions and expenditures for congressional and presidential elections, established an independent Federal Election Commission to oversee federal elections laws, and created a specific framework for providing presidential candidates with public financing. *(1974 Almanac, p. 611)*

The two years of debate that preceded passage of this law was, until 1990, the closest Congress had ever come to enacting public financing of congressional campaigns.

Supreme Court Involvement

In 1976, the Supreme Court ruled on a constitutional challenge to FECA in the case of *Buckley v. Valeo*. The court upheld FECA's disclosure requirements, contribution limitations and public financing of presidential elections. But it struck down spending limits for congressional and presidential races, including restraints on the use of a candidate's personal assets, except for presidential candidates who accepted public financing. It also struck down limits on independent expenditures.

The justices weighed First Amendment rights against the 1974 act's underlying purpose: prevention of the abuses that occurred during Watergate. In the case of contributions, the court concluded that First Amendment considerations were outweighed because "the quantity of communication by the contributor does not increase perceptibly with the size of his contribution." But it found limiting expenditures to be a "substantial" restraint on free speech that could preclude "significant use of the most effective modes of communication." *(1976 Almanac, p. 459)*

Many subsequent congressional efforts to change the campaign finance system were driven by the desire to find a way to limit congressional campaign spending without violating the mandates of the *Buckley* decision. With the ceilings on expenditures removed, campaign costs grew apace during the next decade, and candidates became increasingly dependent on raising money from PACs.

In striking down restraints on independent expenditures, the Supreme Court also spurred the rise of another type of PAC; the non-connected, or ideological, PAC. Sharply negative ads often underwritten by such groups gained the enmity of both parties.

In 1979, Congress passed a package of FECA amendments (PL 96-187) that included a section allowing state and local parties to underwrite voter-registration and get-out-the-vote drives in behalf of presidential tickets without regard to financial limits. This provision generated the practice of raising "soft money," funds normally prohibited under federal election law — excess individual contributions, direct corporate or labor union treasury money. *(1979 Almanac, p. 558)*

Critics said that while national parties nominally used soft money to bolster state parties, the money effectively went to aid federal candidates. Such funds played an important role in the 1988 elections, and they became significant targets of proposed legislation by both parties in 1990.

Recent Legislative Maneuvers

Although both parties during the Reagan era debated public financing for congressional campaigns, no significant legislation was passed. In 1987, with Democrats back in control of the Senate, Majority Leader Robert C. Byrd of West Virginia decided to make campaign financing a major issue. Democrats brought a public financing bill (S 2) to the floor in June, but it was shelved in February 1988 after a record eight cloture votes failed to break a GOP filibuster. *(1987 Almanac, p. 33; 1988 Almanac, p. 41)*

As the 101st Congress convened in January 1989, charges of ethical violations involving Speaker Jim Wright, D-Texas, intensified pressures on House Democrats to act on campaign finance legislation. Two bills embracing variations on the public financing theme (HR 13, HR 14) were filed. Wright, facing charges that would lead to his resignation from Congress, embraced campaign finance reform and created a bipartisan Task Force on Campaign Reform.

In the Senate, Minority Leader Bob Dole of Kansas and GOP campaign finance point man Mitch McConnell of Kentucky introduced S 7 to increase limits on individual contributions and reduce PAC donations. Senate Democrats revived S 2 in the form of S 137, which was introduced by David L. Boren of Oklahoma and Mitchell, the newly elected majority leader Mitchell, along with 24 other Democrats as sponsors. *(1989 Almanac, p. 48)*

Momentum continued to build throughout 1989 as the leaders of both parties in both chambers vowed to press for campaign finance measures. Packages of proposals were offered by Bush and by House Republicans. A House task force could not bridge the yawning partisan gulf on major issues, but it agreed in principle on several lesser changes in federal election law.

Bush on June 29, 1989, proposed what he called a "sweeping system of reform" for raising and spending money in congressional elections. Saying he would "free our electoral system from the grips of special interests," Bush outlined a plan that sought to eliminate most PACs, enhance the role of political parties and grind down the electoral advantages enjoyed by incumbents.

But no sooner had the president announced his package than its political problems became clear — and not only from Democrats who assailed it as baldly partisan. Even within the GOP, there was no consensus on major items such as curbing the frank and eliminating certain PACs.

House Republicans pulled together their own 25-point plan to rewrite election laws. Adopted Sept. 21 by the GOP Conference, the package represented a compromise between the party's senior members and its young turks. Broadly speaking, the older faction had advocated the financial protection of the status quo while the latter had sought to overthrow a system they thought protected the House's Democratic majority.

The 21 members of the bipartisan House task force were not able to compromise on central issues such as the cost of campaigns and the role of special-interest money. They did agree to call for:

- Eliminating the "bundling" of individual contributions by intermediaries who often filled in the candidate payee on contributors' checks.
- A bar to members converting their campaign funds to personal use after leaving office under the so-called grandfather clause.
- Heightened disclosure requirements to better identify sponsors of independent campaigns run by private groups for or against candidates.
- A prohibition against "leadership PACs," political action committees run by politicians to further their own ambitions by distributing contributions to colleagues.
- Restoration of a tax credit to encourage small individual donations.

EARLY HOUSE ACTION

House task force leaders, Democrat Al Swift of Washington and Republican Guy Vander Jagt of Michigan, announced in early 1990 that they had advanced as far as

Corporate Campaign Spending Limits OK'd

In a victory for advocates of limiting corporate campaign spending, the Supreme Court on March 27 upheld the authority of the states or the federal government to bar private corporations from using their funds to run independent political campaigns.

The court said in its 6-3 decision in *Austin v. Michigan State Chamber of Commerce* that a Michigan law requiring corporations to make their political expenditures through separate political action committees did not violate the First Amendment's protection of free speech. The case grew out of a newspaper advertisement, purchased by the chamber with treasury funds, that endorsed a candidate for the Michigan House of Representatives.

Federal election law and the laws of 20 other states had similar prohibitions on direct corporate campaign spending.

Writing for the majority, Justice Thurgood Marshall said, "Michigan identified as a serious danger that corporate political expenditures will undermine the integrity of the political process.... By requiring corporations to make all independent political expenditures through a separate fund made up of money solicited expressly for political purposes, [the act] reduces the threat that huge corporate treasuries amassed with the aid of favorable state laws will be used to influence unfairly the outcome of elections."

Three justices — Sandra Day O'Connor, Antonin Scalia and Anthony M. Kennedy — dissented from the court's ruling, which came while Congress and several state legislatures were considering measures to tighten the rules on campaign financing.

In his dissent, Kennedy said, "The Court's hostility to the corporate form used by the speaker in this case and its assertion that corporate wealth is the evil to be regulated is far too imprecise to justify the most severe restriction on political speech ever sanctioned by this Court."

O'Connor and Scalia joined Kennedy's opinion. Scalia also wrote a more sharply worded opinion and read portions of it from the bench — an out-of-the-ordinary step dissenting justices used to call special attention to their disagreement.

"The fact that corporations amass large treasuries," Scalia wrote, was "not sufficient justification for the suppression of political speech unless one thinks it would be lawful to prohibit men and women whose net worth is above a certain figure from endorsing political candidates."

The ruling limited the Supreme Court's 1986 decision, *Federal Election Commission v. Massachusetts Citizens for Life Inc.*, that certain small nonprofit corporations could spend directly from their treasuries because they would have difficulty establishing separate funds, creating a disincentive to political speech.

The court in the *MCFL* case established a three-part test for nonprofit corporations that it said the Michigan chamber failed to meet. One of these tests was its independence from the influence of business corporations.

The federal ban on direct corporate expenditures in political campaigns dated to the 1907 Tillman Act. Besides Michigan, the 20 other states that prohibited direct corporate campaign spending were Alabama, Connecticut, Iowa, Kentucky, Minnesota, Mississippi, Montana, New Hampshire, New York, North Carolina, North Dakota, Ohio, Oklahoma, Pennsylvania, South Dakota, Tennessee, Texas, West Virginia, Wisconsin and Wyoming.

they could without intervention by House leaders. This step led to meetings in early March between Wright's successor, Democrat Thomas S. Foley of Washington, and Minority Leader Robert H. Michel of Illinois.

Michel had heightened expectations of a compromise in December 1989 when he said he would consider spending limits for House races if they were set high enough, perhaps at $1 million. Few GOP colleagues rushed to embrace Michel's suggestion, and many expressed concern that he had opened a door they had considered firmly shut.

Though the Democratic leadership had planned to put the legislation on the floor by the summer of 1990, partisan differences and intraparty wrangling delayed the process. Democrats feared Republican proposals to enhance the financial role of political parties, a GOP strength. Republicans, in contrast, sought to curb PACs and to regulate political activity by labor unions, two sources of Democratic strength.

Foley's commitment to seek campaign finance reform also spurred some in traditionally Democratic ranks to voice their own opposition. Organized labor expressed concern about measures to regulate political activity within unions, which had contributed an estimated $45 million to candidates in the 1988 elections, according to University of Southern California political scientist Herbert E. Alexander, an authority on campaign spending. And just as National Republican Congressional Committee (NRCC) Executive Director Ed Rogers had criticized spending limits, Jim Ruvolo, Ohio Democratic Party chairman and president of the Association of State Democratic Chairs, complained about measures to curb soft money.

Finger-pointing soon began in the House. Talks between Foley and Michel produced nothing but Republican discontent, and the list of reforms agreed on in 1989 by the bipartisan task force began to shrink.

In April 1990, for example, Democrats began asserting that they had agreed to give up leadership PACs only if Republicans agreed to prohibit state parties from contributing to candidates across state lines — a trade-off the joint statement never mentioned. Swift, attempting to avoid a partisan fight for fear of losing agreement on smaller points, nevertheless insisted that the Democrats stood by their interpretation of the agreement. "I don't want to get into a partisan fight at this point," said Swift. "It could wipe out what small points of agreement are left."

EARLY SENATE ACTION

The atmosphere for change was thickest in the Senate in 1990, which was facing pressure in the wake of the ethics investigation of Dave Durenberger, R-Minn. The probe focused on, among other things, the accusation that Durenberger improperly converted campaign funds to personal use by transferring to a Minnesota publisher, Piranha Press, a $5,000 check written to his campaign in December 1986 from the Pathology Practice Association Federal PAC. *(Durenberger investigation, p. 98)*

Senators were also feeling added pressure from all sides because of the Keating Five controversy. This offshoot of the savings and loan scandal added fuel to a fire that Common Cause, a public interest lobby, lit under Congress to revise the way members financed their campaigns.

The Keating Five had raised $1.5 million for various political causes through their relationship with Keating, the chairman of the parent corporation of a California thrift institution, Lincoln Savings and Loan. The episode had proved far more effective at raising questions about the relationship between elected officials and major contributors than the flood of statistics about PACs that were issued by good-government groups.

Senate leaders early in 1990 decided to set up a bipartisan advisory panel of six outsiders — including academics, lawyers and party operatives — to review proposals and to issue recommendations to the Senate leaders by March 6. They hoped the panel would jump-start bipartisan negotiations, and it did just that.

On March 7, the panel weighed in with a plan that produced an unusual turn of events in the long-running campaign finance debate. The panel embraced what it called "flexible spending limits" — voluntary, state-by-state limits that would be "reasonably high" and allow exemptions for party funds and instate contributions. Candidates who accepted the limits would get lower postal and advertising rates, and their in-state contributors would receive tax credits for modest contributions.

Instead of targeting specific caps, the panel chose to focus on ways to encourage candidates to raise "good money" and discourage their pursuit of "bad money." The panel also called upon Congress to give political parties free broadcast time and more freedom to spend; reduce contributions from PACs once they exceeded an unspecified percentage of a candidate's funds; forbid bundling for corporate, union and trade-association PACs; forbid independent expenditures by corporate, union and trade association PACs; and disclose soft-money donations.

Even Republicans, who traditionally viewed spending limits as anathema, spoke kind words about the plan. Dole and Mitchell said in a joint statement that the report "shows the issue is capable of being resolved despite the differences between Republicans and Democrats." At the time, Mitchell said he would put campaign finance on the Senate agenda after clean air and omnibus crime legislation. He predicted it could reach the floor by early April.

Committee Action

The Senate Rules and Administration Committee on March 8 approved, on a 7-3 party-line vote, a Democratic bill (S 137) to reward candidates who obeyed firm state-by-state spending limits with discounted advertising and punish those who did not by compensating their opponents' campaigns with tax dollars.

Despite the partisan vote, Senate leaders were optimistic that negotiations would produce a compromise before the bill reached the floor. "I am for the first time optimistic that there can be a truly bipartisan campaign finance reform bill," said McConnell, a leader on the issue.

Boren, who sponsored S 137 along with Mitchell, was unwilling March 8 to back away from direct public financing. But senators including Ted Stevens, R-Alaska, offered fewer objections to indirect forms of public financing or shifting the costs elsewhere.

A tax credit along the lines suggested by the panel of experts — for example, covering contributions up to $250 — would cost tens of millions of dollars at a minimum. For its part, the Postal Service estimated that proposals to reduce the cost of mail could cost more than $100 million if used in all congressional campaigns, costs that would run higher under free-mail proposals.

Broadcasters could also take a hit if they were forced to require stations to sell candidates guaranteed time slots at their lowest cost for any ad, as proposed by a bill (S 1009) approved in 1989 by the Senate Commerce Committee. Proposals for free time would, of course, cost even more.

As the committee met, Sen. John C. Danforth offered a striking example of the difficulty McConnell, Dole and the White House faced as they sought to hold Republicans in line. "This senator, frankly, is up for grabs," the Missouri Republican said in a statement that rejected spending limits as the central issue.

Instead, he said the modern television campaign drove up costs while turning voters' stomachs. He called for discounting broadcast advertising and suggested that the government could help finance campaigns by buying two- and five-minute slots of TV time — long enough for discussions of substance — and turning them over to candidates.

Danforth in 1988 backed the GOP filibuster of Democratic legislation. He thus became the latest in a string of Republicans to name his own price for campaign reform. And he noted that he was not alone.

Republicans Regroup

Republicans huddled at a weekend retreat March 24-25 and, bolstered by advice from GOP consultants, came away renewed in their opposition to spending limits. White House Chief of Staff John H. Sununu reiterated Bush's pledge to veto a bill that included spending limits or that otherwise appeared harmful to the GOP.

"I think it's safe to say we are coming behind a measure," McConnell said. "If you were summing up Republicans at the moment, there is a growing sense of unity to ax PACs and do something about non-party soft money."

One of the chief concerns senators expressed at their West Virginia retreat was the way the public viewed the GOP on the issue. They complained that Republicans often came off as the impediment to reform because they opposed Democratic initiatives that they believed would tilt the playing field.

"We need to stand on the positive side rather than just be against what the Democrats do," said Stevens.

McConnell said the Republican measure would be introduced within weeks and he hoped it would help put them back on the offensive by the time Mitchell brought Democratic campaign finance finance legislation to the floor.

While Bush had proposed eliminating all business and labor PACs, McConnell indicated that the Senate GOP conference was unwilling to go that far. He said the bill likely would seek a limit of $1,000.

Outsiders invited to address Senate Republicans on the issues showered criticism on spending limits. GOP consultants Eddie Mahe and Charlie Black both advised against them. Black said he heard little dissent about the package McConnell proposed.

Mahe said there was considerable debate on the "flexible spending limits" proposed to the Senate by a panel of outside advisers chosen by Mitchell and Dole. The advisers said that money raised from people living outside a senator's home state or from PACs should be subject to spending limits but that money raised from individuals within a state should not.

McConnell gave colleagues a partisan pep talk of his own, cautioning that they should not be considering an ethics bill. "We passed the ethics bill last year," McConnell told them. "This is a bill about partisan advantage, and it's safe to say Republicans are not going to get rolled and let the Democrats write the rules for our democracy."

Democrats Caucus

In April, Senate Democrats spent the weeks leading up to the floor debate negotiating within their 54-member caucus rather than across the aisle.

The Democratic bill (S 137), approved by committee in March, was substantially rewritten in caucus. But voluntary, state-by-state limits on spending remained its centerpiece. The limits would have cut millions of dollars in election spending in large states such as California while placing modest restrictions on the amount of money candidates could take from PACs.

Under the Democratic plan, participating candidates would get reduced mail rates, the lowest rate for the broadcast ads they purchased and free television time that would cost the government tens of millions of dollars. Some Democratic strategists said they believed that tax-paid elections could be sold to the public as a way certain to take special interests out of politics — from the Democratic perspective, a needed answer to the GOP's plan to kill PACs.

During intraparty negotiations, the Democrats found themselves bickering over several issues. And none was more nettlesome than how to make the transition to 1992, when the first election would be waged under new rules. The election would be particularly important for Democrats, who would be seeking to maintain control of the Senate. Some senators expressed concern that the changes being touted would prevent them from having enough money to gain re-election.

Boren said the issue would be resolved by grandfathering all money raised by candidates as of the law's effective date. Other technical problems nagging Democrats stemmed from the increasing use of campaign accounts by senators for catchall political expenses, such as flying their spouses to campaign events. Senators did not want these expenses to count against the amount they could spend on television ads or the like.

As a result of the meetings, Boren added several twists to his bill, including:

- Tax-paid television advertisements. The government would provide candidates with vouchers equal to 20 percent of their general election spending limit to be used to purchase longer blocks of television time, in hope of moving campaigns away from reliance on 30-second spots.
- Exemption for in-state fundraising. Candidates could raise and spend an additional amount equal to 25 percent of their spending limit so long as they raised it in small, instate contributions. The size of a qualifying contribution was not set.

GOP Senators Respond

Fearful that spending limits would reduce their chances of regaining the majority in Congress, Senate Republicans challenged the Democrats' drive by trying to refocus the debate on the sources of money.

Republican senators agreed during their own conference April 24 on legislation to eliminate PACs. The measure would also halve to $500 the size of contributions candidates could accept from out-of-state donors, a step designed to slow down fundraising treks to Hollywood and New York City. The measure also would would have placed new restrictions on unions and other tax-exempt groups.

By April 27, McConnell said more than 31 senators, including Dole, had agreed to sign the bill. The McConnell bill as drafted also contained several new approaches:

- A total ban on PACs. This was the first attempt for a complete ban on PACs, a step that even McConnell conceded could flunk the First Amendment's free-speech test.
- Regulation of campaign activity by tax-exempt organizations. Certain but not all tax-exempt organizations would have been prohibited from engaging in political activity that benefited a particular candidate. The bill would have extended the prohibition to all tax-exempt organizations, including unions.
- Parties would have been allowed to buy their candidates large blocks of advertising time in addition to the money they could already spend in behalf of candidates.
- Out-of-state contributions would have been limited to $500, down from $1,000 under existing law. This would restrict out-of-state fundraising without shutting down direct-mail operations that relied on out-of-state donors.

Competing Proposals

In dueling news conferences held May 1 and May 3, Republicans and Democrats both suggested that they were preparing for legislative failure, with each party bidding for the reformist label in the event that agreement proved impossible.

Eleven senators turned out to announce the GOP proposal endorsed by 34 Republicans. Their plan sought to ban PACs; curtail out-of-state fundraising; sharply restrict the political activities of tax-exempt organizations, including unions and trade associations; and substantially increase spending by, and contributions to, political parties.

McConnell said Republicans wanted to shift the focus from how much money was spent to where it was raised. Dole several times during the period portrayed the media as obsessed with spending limits as the only solution to the money chase.

The Republican proposal to "ax the PACs" sent Democrats, accustomed to the offensive on this issue, scrambling. The Democrats' attempt to write a substitute for the Boren-Mitchell bill had been held up by squabbling over transition rules for 1992 candidates, exemptions from spending limits for activities such as flying spouses to political events and use of tax dollars to supplement private efforts.

The Democrats shifted ground substantially and announced their new plan May 3. The party's leaders on the issue — Boren, Mitchell and Senate Rules and Administration Committee Chairman Wendell H. Ford of Kentucky — hammered out an agreement to take PAC contributions out of Senate campaigns. Under pressure to replace the money, they added public financing to their plan for general election spending limits.

Democrats had abandoned this very position two years earlier. And just weeks before, Ford's committee, in the report accompanying S 137, had "concluded that sufficient support was not there at this time for public financing."

Mitchell said increased public attention and a "sense of

House/Senate Campaign Finance Bills

Following are major provisions of campaign financing bills passed by the House and Senate in 1990: HR 5400 and S 137, respectively:

Spending Limits

House. Voluntary spending limits of $550,000 would be established for a House candidate's primary and general election combined, with no more than $300,000 to be spent for the primary and $100,000 for a runoff. The bill included the following exceptions:

1) A $400,000 primary limit in states where a candidate who won a majority in the primary was elected to office without a general election. Louisiana was the only state affected.

2) An additional $165,000 added to the limit of a candidate who won a primary with less than 66.7 percent of the vote.

3) A candidate under all circumstances would be limited to spending no more than $550,000 in the general election.

Senate. Voluntary limits would be established that would vary from state to state and rise in part with a candidate's ability to raise money from residents of his state. The limit for primaries would be set at 67 percent of the general election limit for a state or $2.75 million, whichever was less. Only California candidates would run up against the $2.75 million cap. The limit for a runoff election would be 20 percent of the general election limit.

The general election limit would be set by the following formula: $400,000, plus 30 cents multiplied by the state's voting-age population beyond 4 million. The limit would not be less than $950,000, or more than $5.5 million.

Exceptions included:

1) In states with no more than one VHF transmitter, such as New Jersey, the limit would be set by the following formula: $400,00, plus 80 cents multiplied by the voting-age population up to 4 million, plus 70 cents multiplied by the voting-age population beyond 4 million.

2) A candidate could exceed the general election spending limit by as much as 25 percent — but only with money raised in contributions of $250 or less from residents of the state.

3) If $10,000 or more were spent by an independent campaign against or for his opponent, the eligible candidate's spending limit would increase by an amount equal to the independent expenditure.

4) If a non-complying candidate spent more than 133.33 percent of the limit, an eligible candidate would be allowed to ignore the spending limit, while still receiving other incentives.

5) Candidates would be allowed to spend campaign funds up to 15 percent in excess of the spending limit for legal and accounting costs related to the campaign committee, expenses related to holding office, and their official office accounts.

Incentives

House. Qualifying candidates would receive one free television or radio spot from broadcasters for every two purchased. They would also pay only half the rate for first-class postage and the same rate as nonprofits for third-class bulk mail. They would also be eligible, in tax years beginning in 1991, to solicit contributions eligible for a tax credit. A 100 percent tax credit would be given for contributions made by residents of the same state as the candidate, up to $50 for an individual return, $100 for a couple.

Senate. Television and radio broadcasters would be required to sell ads to candidates during the general election on the most favorable terms, in effect allowing candidates to buy airtime that could not be pre-empted at the lowest unit rate charged for any advertising by the station. Stations would have to make five minutes per week of prime time available for sale during the last five weeks of the campaign.

Candidates could send first-class mail at one-fourth the normal rate and third-class mail at 2 cents less than the normal charge, up to an amount equal to 5 percent of the general election limit.

An eligible candidate would receive up to 100 percent of the spending limit from the government if his opponent broke the spending limit. Once an opponent broke the limit, the eligible candidate would get an amount equal to two-thirds of the general election spending limit. Once an opponent spent 133.3 percent of the limit, the eligible candidate would get the remaining third.

The government would give eligible candidates a voucher equal to 20 percent of the spending limit, to be used to purchase television time in one- to five-minute chunks.

The vouchers and contingency fund would be paid from a Senate Election Campaign Fund, which, according to a sense of the Senate resolution, would be raised from fines, fees and contributions by taxpayers from tax refunds.

Political Action Committees

House. Divided political action committees into two categories, called political committees and newly defined small donor committees, which would be limited to accepting contributions from individuals of $240 or less per year. Political committees could give a candidate up to $1,000 per year; small donor committees could give up to $5,000 per year.

All candidates would be prohibited from taking PAC contributions that, in the aggregate, amounted to more than 50 percent of the applicable spending limit.

Leadership PACs would be banned.

Senate. PACs were banned, but restrictions on contributions were included if the ban was declared unconstitutional.

Bundling

House. Contributions made through a political committee acting as an intermediary or conduit would count against the contribution limit of the original donor and the committee.

Senate. Contributions by an individual, if made through or arranged by an intermediary or conduit, would count against the intermediary's contribution limit if the intermediary was a political committee, an official of a political committee, a registered lobbyist, or an officer of a union, corporation or trade association

---

urgency" had made bolder steps necessary. And the Democrats took one step that would not play well with their larger state parties, particularly in California, Ohio and Texas. The new proposal maintained a ban against soft-money operations used by state parties to pay for voter registration and get-out-the-vote drives.

Democrats narrowed some of the gap between the parties, as the PAC proposal illustrated. The Democratic proposal also emphasized in-state fundraising. And Boren left open the possibility that Democrats would abandon public financing as quickly as they had re-embraced it, given the right set of compromises.

One of the most curious aspects of the new proposals was the Republican decision to let the Democrats outbid them for one of their own. A plan by Danforth to require broadcasters to let the government or parties purchase large blocks of television time for candidates — an attempt to raise the level of political dialogue — was embraced by the Democrats. Danforth declined to endorse the GOP bill and was rebuffed by McConnell, even though McConnell had talked up the idea only a week before.

The Republican measure, S 2595, was introduced on May 9 by McConnell and 33 cosponsors. The Democratic substitute, with 43 cosponsors, was taken up by the Senate May 11.

SENATE NEGOTIATIONS/FLOOR ACTION

Senate leaders set up two tracks for campaign finance legislation the week of May 14 — one for airing partisan

acting on behalf of the organization.

Broadcast Provisions

House. Broadcasters were barred from setting special rates for political ads, required to give candidates priority over other political users in buying airtime and released from "equal time" requirements.

Senate. Candidates would have to appear in television ads and state their approval of the ad. Candidates who did not comply with the spending limit would have to say so in their ads.

Soft Money

House. Voter registration and get-out-the-vote activities conducted on behalf of a presidential ticket that used the candidates' names would have to be paid for with funds raised and spent under federal rules. State law would continue to apply to such activities that did not specifically name a federal candidate even if they benefited federal candidates.

Coordinated expenditures made on behalf of House and Senate candidates by state party committees would have to come from funds raised under federal law.

Presidential candidates would be prohibited from raising money, directly or indirectly, for any account other than those subject to federal law. Receipt of public financing for a presidential campaign was conditioned on obeying this provision. Other federal candidates and certain party officials could continue to solicit funds for state party activities.

Candidates for federal office would be prohibited from soliciting funds on behalf of their campaign committee and depositing the money in separate accounts not subject to federal law.

Senate. In general, the bill would limit spending by state and federal parties for generic campaign activities when federal candidates were on the ballot. Further, new rules would subject this money to federal rules for spending, contributions and reporting.

A state party's spending to elect the presidential ticket, including get-out-the-vote and voter registration activities, would be limited to 4 cents multiplied by the voting-age population of the state.

Any money raised or spent for get-out-the-vote or voter registration activity, beginning 60 days before the first federal primary, would be brought under federal limits and reporting rules.

All generic campaign activities conducted by federal or state party committees — that is, even those that did not mention federal candidates specifically — would be subject to a maximum spending limit of 30 cents multiplied by the voting-age population.

A national committee could not solicit contributions that were not subject to the limits and reporting requirements of federal law in behalf of state parties.

The bill provided for one exception: Money contributed for a party's building fund would not be subject to limits, only to reporting requirements.

Contribution Limits

House. A candidate could take only $5,000 from all state party committees combined. This provision was designed to stop the use of state party committees as conduits for contributions to congressional candidates in other states, a practice that became widespread in 1989 special elections.

Senate. Campaign committees would be barred from accepting contributions of more than $250 from residents of other states.

Individuals would be permitted to contribute $20,000 to state party committees, up from $5,000. The aggregate limit on an individual's contributions to all federal committees would be increased beyond the existing $25,000 limit to the amount an individual contributed to a state party committee, not to exceed a maximum of $5,000.

If the PAC ban in the bill was declared unconstitutional, PACs could contribute $15,000 to a state party committee, up from $5,000.

Union Dues

House. No provision.

Senate. The bill in general would modify the Supreme Court's decision in *Beck v. Communications Workers of America* by writing into law the following provisions:

A union operating under a closed-shop contract would have to annually give non-union members required to pay agency fees to the union an opportunity to object to the payment of fees going for political activities. The court had ruled that workers could object to payment of fees for any activity, not just political, that were not related to contract bargaining. The union would have to state what political activities the union was engaged in, reduce the fees paid by the objecting worker by an amount reflecting the cost of political activities and use an allocation formula to determine the cost of these political activities.

Independent Expenditures

House. The bill would tighten the definition of an independent political expenditure to prohibit "any arrangement, coordination or direction" between the candidate and the person making the expenditure, with respect to the expenditure.

Political committees run by corporations, trade associations and unions could not use treasury funds to underwrite the administration and solicitation costs associated with any independent political expenditure. The entire cost of the campaign would have to be borne by contributions.

The bill would require any television ad not authorized by a candidate's committee to run a continuous statement "of sufficient size to be clearly visible to the viewer" stating the name of the person and connected organization paying for the ad.

Senate. The definition of "independent expenditure" would be tightened to preclude virtually all contact between a candidate involved in a campaign and an organization or individuals running an independent expenditure campaign for or against the candidate's campaign.

The independent campaigner could not maintain a relationship with any political consultant who had a relationship with any of the candidates the independent campaigner was supporting or opposing. An independent campaigner would have to inform a broadcaster of an intent to purchase broadcast time. The station in turn would have to inform the other candidate, who would be sold time to respond immediately afterward. ■

---

differences, and the other for resolving them.

When no progress was made on the floor, both sides agreed that the floor was not the place to work out the differences.

Instead, Mitchell and Dole, playing down expectations, each named four-member squads May 16 to conduct off-the-floor negotiations.

Mitchell named Boren, the Democratic floor manager for the issue, as his lead negotiator. Other members were John Kerry of Massachusetts, a strong backer of public financing; Tom Daschle of South Dakota, one of 20 Democrats up in the crucial 1992 elections; and John B. Breaux of Louisiana, chairman of the Democratic Senatorial Campaign Committee and one of only eight Democrats not to sign on to the Democrats' proposal. Mitchell and Ford, chairman of the Rules and Administration Committee, were advisers.

Dole named McConnell, the chief author of the GOP bill; Bob Packwood of Oregon, a strong opponent of spending limits; and Don Nickles of Oklahoma, chairman of the Republican National Senatorial Committee. The GOP leader picked Warren B. Rudman of New Hampshire and Stevens of Alaska, ranking Republican on the Rules and Administration Committee, as advisers.

With the off-the-floor negotiations set for the week of May 21, the two sides used the floor debate on May 18 to shine light through the loopholes in each other's plans. Nickles noted that the Democrats would eliminate PAC contributions to candidates but not to parties.

"The Democratic bill is a laundering bill. That's worse

than the present situation," said Nickles.

Boren, for his part, deplored a GOP provision that would have allowed individuals to give 1,260 percent more to federal election committees than they could under existing law. "This is reform?" Boren asked. "That's a loophole — one of the biggest loopholes I've seen in my career."

Common Cause clarified the stakes in the debate by issuing a study that calculated how S 137 would have influenced elections. The public interest lobby said that had every candidate in the 1988 Senate elections participated in the system, in the 27 races involving incumbents, challengers would have gained $21.7 million in resources and incumbents would have lost $23.6 million.

Initial Negotiations

During the week of May 21, Senate negotiators began the tedious process of feeling their way through the contentious issues. They found common ground where it was most expected — issues that hit both parties equally — and agreed that they should tackle the following problems:

- **The cost of television advertising.** Both sides wanted broadcasters to grant candidates better rates.
- **Independent expenditures.** A wild-card campaign operating outside the aegis of formal candidate committees could intervene decisively in an election by spending a lot of money at the last minute. The Democrats proposed public assistance to candidates attacked by independent groups; the GOP wanted wider disclosure of their activities.
- **Personal funds.** Democrats would have barred a candidate from lending his campaign money and then repaying himself from contributions collected later. They also would have prohibited a candidate who spent more than $250,000 of his own money from receiving public funds. Under the Republican proposal, if a candidate spent more than $250,000 of his own funds, an opponent could have collected individual contributions of $5,000, up from $1,000.
- **Bundling.** Both sides would have barred bundling of contributions by PACs, corporations, unions, trade associations or their representatives. Republicans, however, wanted to allow bundling by party committees.

Even as campaign finance legislation headed for the floor in both chambers, the maneuvering looked more like a warm-up for swapping blame than a prelude to a bill-signing ceremony. After failing to break a deadlock over how to limit spending in Senate campaigns, negotiators kicked S 137 upstairs to their leaders, Mitchell and Dole late in the week of June 11.

Preparing for Failure

Leading where many GOP senators did not want to follow, Dole on July 25 tested the Democrats' resolve on the contentious issue of spending limits.

Dole told Mitchell that the GOP for the first time was willing to limit spending from money raised through out-of-state contributions, but only those of more than $250. Republicans had previously said they also would eliminate all contributions from PACs and limit out-of-state contributions to $500.

Calling the proposal "a major step," Dole managed to bring along McConnell and Packwood, both of whom said they disliked the proposal but agreed to go along with it. McConnell nevertheless said he doubted Dole's proposal had the support of half the GOP conference.

The Republican move apparently was designed to force the Democrats into the position of eschewing compromise on the eve of the debate. But with Republicans refusing any limits on money raised in a senator's state, the proposal fell short of the standard Democrats had set. Spending limits had been the heart of every Democratic proposal, and Mitchell indicated that there would be no way to resolve the difference short of fighting it out on the floor.

Floor Debate, Votes

The Senate on Aug. 1 finally passed the Democrats' version of S 137, 59-40, with five of 45 Republicans voting yes and only one Democrat voting no. The measure would have eliminated PACs, limited out-of-state contributions to $250, established voluntary state-by-state spending limits and, to lure participation by candidates, offered campaigns low-cost mail, free television time and extra funds to fight opponents who pierced the limits. *(Vote 204, p. 43-S)*

Spurred by election-year ethics turmoil, senators did not stop at campaign finance. They voted 77-23 to prohibit members from taking speaking fees from lobbying groups and 51-49 to cap all other forms of outside income, a measure that would have hit the Senate's many millionaires hard had it survived. *(Pay and honoraria, p. 73; votes 196, 197, p. 42-S)*

The Senate debate, which stretched over three days and required 16 roll call votes on amendments, was striking for its lack of rancor, compared with the 100th Congress, when the Senate struggled through eight cloture votes as Republicans filibustered a Democratic campaign finance package.

Each party came to the floor to fight over the merits, not procedure. To this end, Mitchell and Dole cut a deal: The Democrats would not try to cut off debate as long as the Republicans did not delay in presenting amendments.

From the outset, the parties drew the line at spending limits. "That is the central issue; that is the point dividing the two parties," Mitchell said.

As the debate opened, Democrats incorporated the GOP ban on PAC contributions. Democrats had previously favored either an aggregate limit on PAC contributions or a ban that excepted gifts to party committees.

This compromise steered the Senate debate toward four key issues: spending limits; the public funding used to make spending limits possible; the role tax-exempt organizations, in particular labor unions, played in elections; and the advantages enjoyed by incumbents.

Boren, the Democrats' floor manager, argued that "real reform must include some kind of overall restraint on runaway campaign spending." Otherwise, he said, senators would continue to be "full-time fundraisers and part-time senators."

McConnell, the GOP floor manager, countered that because the U.S. election system equated campaign spending with free speech — the *Buckley v. Valeo* decision — the Democratic bill "punishes the candidate who exercises his First Amendment freedom" by giving public money to his opponent.

The Senate legislation offered candidates incentives to observe spending limits: a voucher equal to 20 percent of the general election spending limit, to be used to purchase television time in blocks of one minute or more; reduced mail costs; and contingent public financing if an opposing candidate exceeded the spending limit.

The Congressional Budget Office estimated that the contingency funds would cost $30 million per election. The TV vouchers would add another $21 million and reduced mail costs $5 million, according to McConnell. This added up to $56 million every two years for Senate elections alone.

McConnell sought to strike all such public funds. The amendment failed, 46-49 — on a near party-line vote that saw just two Democrats break ranks to vote with a solid bloc of 44 Republicans. *(Vote 188, p. 41-S)*

But Democrat Kerry's effort to increase public funding by giving candidates, in addition to the TV vouchers, public funds equal to 70 percent of the general election spending limits, failed, 38-60 — with 17 Democrats joining 43 Republicans in opposition. *(Vote 194, p. 42-S)*

Democrats from the South and those up for re-election in particular, wanted to make it clear that the TV vouchers and contingency funds would not be diverted from general tax revenues as were public funds in presidential campaigns. Boren soothed these fears with a sense of the Senate resolution stating that the money should be raised from voluntary contributions as opposed to a diversion from tax payments. The Boren amendment passed 55-44 on a near party-line vote. *(Vote 200, p. 42-S)*

Republicans called this a back door to tax funding sometime later. They noted that only 20 percent of taxpayers were checking off funds for the presidential system, which was projected to run out of money in the 1990s. *(Presidential checkoff, 1989 Almanac, p. 49)*

GOP Amendments

Republicans made two runs at reducing the role labor unions played in elections. The first, an amendment by Orrin G. Hatch, R-Utah, sought to let all workers covered by union contracts, including union members, opt out of paying dues or other fees that went for any activity other than bargaining contracts. The second, an amendment offered by McConnell, sought to prohibit tax-exempt status for any organization that supported or opposed candidates. Both measures were vigorously opposed by union lobbyists and defeated on virtually identical, near party-line votes: 41-59 and 41-58. *(Votes 189, 192, p. 41-S)*

Not every Republican amendment met defeat. Nickles won a move to impose tighter restrictions on the franking privilege, which allowed members of Congress to sign their name to mail in lieu of postage. The Nickles amendment, which carried 98-1, would have barred using the frank for mass mailings in election years. Further, it would have barred senators from assigning their franking budget to other senators. This would prevent senators up for re-election from borrowing from their colleagues and repaying them in subsequent years. The measure also took aim at the House, which had routinely exceeded its mail budget; it would have prohibited franking once the annual appropriation was depleted. It would also have required House members to join senators in disclosing their spending for mail. *(Vote 193, p. 41-S)*

An amendment by Pete V. Domenici, R-N.M., to limit contributions from individuals who did not live in a candidate's state to $250 per election, passed by voice vote. Republicans were surprised when the Democrats embraced the measure. Some Democrats were surprised, too, and expressed concern to Boren. Boren later said that there was room to appease the upset Democrats and not every amendment would make it out of conference.

Other Provisions

The Senate also:

- Approved 73-27 an amendment by Lloyd Bentsen D-Texas., to bar companies with majority foreign ownership from operating a PAC. *(Vote 191, p. 41-S)*

Continued on p. 68

State Reform Efforts

A public financing law for congressional campaigns was enacted in 1990 — but not by Congress.

In a year when the Hill once again failed to put its campaign finance house in order, one state decided to begin some housekeeping through the back door.

In the final hours of its annual session, the Minnesota Legislature on April 25 overwhelmingly adopted partial public financing with voluntary spending limits for congressional campaigns. The law, the first of its kind, applied to congressional candidates running in general or special elections, beginning in 1991.

In 1989, New Hampshire first delved into the arena of federal campaigns by passing a law that created voluntary spending limits for U.S. Senate and House races. Candidates choosing not to abide by the limits would incur the added burden of paying a $5,000 filing fee and submitting notarized signatures to appear on the ballot. The Federal Election Commission in 1989 partially voided the law as it applied to parties, arguing that states were preempted by federal statutes from regulating federal candidates. Although some 1990 New Hampshire congressional candidates grumbled about the law, none mounted a legal challenge to finish it off.

Minnesota lawmakers went beyond their New Hampshire counterparts by using public financing as an incentive for the spending limits of $3.4 million for U.S. Senate candidates and $425,000 for House candidates in each election cycle. If both candidates agreed to limit spending, neither would receive public funds. If one candidate agreed to abide by the limits but another did not, the participating candidate not only would receive matching public funds, but also would have the spending limits waived.

The public grants could equal 25 percent of the candidate's spending limits. They would be financed with general appropriations rather than by the state's voluntary income-tax checkoff that was used to finance state races.

Candidates who waged a tough primary battle would be permitted to spend a slightly higher amount of money in the general election.

Political observers predicted that the Minnesota law would come under legal challenge as soon as congressional candidates began announcing for the 1992 campaign.

Meanwhile, New Hampshire lawmakers in 1990 backed away from plans to regulate another area of federal elections — independent spending. Although both chambers of the Legislature passed measures that would have limited independent expenditures by political action committees (PACs) in elections for congressional seats, conferees could not agree on a method for enforcing the law before their April 20 adjournment. Supporters of the measures had wanted to create a three-member commission that would rule on whether a candidate should be released from a pledge to abide by spending limits if his opponent enjoyed the benefit of independent PAC spending in excess of $1,000.

Attempts To Lower Broadcasting Rates

With campaign finance overhaul presumed dead for the year, lawmakers in late September peeled off the one part of the effort that every politician could agree on: getting broadcasters to lower advertising rates for candidates.

But the effort encountered opposition from broadcasters and from the citizens' group Common Cause, and neither chamber acted on the proposal.

John D. Dingell, D-Mich., chairman of the House Energy and Commerce Committee, introduced a bill Sept. 30 that would redefine how broadcasters set the lowest rates offered to those running for public office.

Dingell and Telecommunications Subcommittee Chairman Edward J. Markey, D-Mass., then rushed the bill (HR 5756) through a hearing and markup Oct. 2 and sent it to the floor (H Rept 101-871).

The Senate Commerce Committee approved a similar measure (S 1009) on Oct. 5, 1989 (S Rept 101-225). A substitute draft closer to Dingell's bill was ready for Senate floor action. *(1989 Almanac, p. 386)*

The Dingell effort drew immediate fire from Common Cause, a lobbying group that had been fighting for the campaign finance reform legislation (S 137, HR 5400) stalled in conference committee after having passed the House and Senate in early August. Both of those bills included provisions dealing with advertising rates for candidates. *(Campaign financing legislation, p. 59)*

In an Oct. 2 letter to lawmakers, Common Cause President Fred Wertheimer said the Dingell bill "would provide incumbent members of the House with a major benefit in the form of reduced broadcast advertising, without taking any steps to deal with the fundamental problems that have made the congressional campaign finance system a national scandal."

Congress since 1972 had required broadcasters, as part of their public trust obligation, to offer political candidates the lowest advertising rate available. When the law (PL 92-225) was written, finding a lowest rate often was simply a matter of checking a broadcaster's rate card. *(1972 Almanac, p. 161)*

By 1990, however, the broadcast advertising marketplace had become far more sophisticated, and many considered the "lowest unit charge" concept obsolete. Rate cards were somewhat a thing of the past. Instead, negotiations often were based on the season, time of day or night, and ratings points of a particular show.

Worse yet for candidates, most buyers agreed up front that their ads could be pre-empted and moved to another day or time if another buyer was willing to pay more. With timing critical in a campaign, candidates usually would not risk having their ads pre-empted. So they bought "non-pre-emptible" time — usually during prime time — at premium rates.

A study released Sept. 7 by the Federal Communications Commission (FCC) of 30 radio and television stations in five metropolitan areas — Cincinnati, Dallas-

Continued from p. 67

- Rejected 44-55 an amendment by John McCain, R-Ariz., to close loopholes in the bill written for incumbents. One would have created a special add-on fund for travel and other incidental political expenses not directly involved in a campaign. A second would have exempted money already spent by incumbents facing re-election in 1992 from the new limit. *(Vote 201, p. 42-S)*
- Rejected 49-49 a McCain amendment to restrict the use of campaign money to bona fide election activities and to require all surplus funds at the end of a campaign to be turned over to the Treasury to reduce the deficit. A disparate group of 11 Democrats voted with Republicans in favor of the amendment, but five GOP senators opposed it — producing the tie. *(Vote 195, p. 42-S)*
- Rejected 44-55 a Dole amendment to substitute a GOP package for the Democratic bill. This sought to ban PACs; cut the limit on individual contributions from $1,000 to $500; limit the amount of money a candidate could spend from his own funds; and limit the amount of money raised from individuals living outside a candidate's state, with an exception for money raised in amounts of $250 or less. *(Vote 202, p. 43-S)*

The Senate finally passed its package 59-40. Democrats lost only the vote of Ernest F. Hollings, S.C., and picked up Republicans McCain; Durenberger; James M. Jeffords, Vt.; William S. Cohen, Maine; and Larry Pressler, S.D.

The Bush administration threatened a veto, citing its opposition to spending limits and public financing at a time of significant fiscal constraints. Democrats, though, warned Bush about a veto. Said Boren, "If I were the president of the United States, I don't think I'd want to veto a bill with so many basic reforms."

HOUSE NEGOTIATIONS/FLOOR ACTION

By mid-June, House Democrats and Republicans, who long before had given up bridging their differences, began to prepare for floor action. Speaker Foley described the disagreements as "very stark" and did not dispute the notion that the lack of consensus probably doomed the issue. "On the other hand, I think if we just throw up our hands and say we haven't a consensus, and therefore we are not going to bring the bill to the floor, we wouldn't advance it at all," he told reporters June 19.

House members had not cast votes on how they raised and spent money for their own elections since 1979. Doing so was a prospect not everyone welcomed. Illustrative of this was the difficulty Washington's Swift, chairman of a House Democratic task force on the issue, had forging a Democratic package.

Swift tried two different approaches to PACs. In one, a member could take up to $275,000 in the aggregate from the PACs, an amount pegged at half the $550,000 spending limit Swift would set for races.

In the other, members could take all the PAC money they wanted, but the PACs themselves would change. "We are, in effect, making PACs small-donor committees, which is what they ought to be," Swift said.

Some Democrats began to worry how the issue would play if they were left defending PACs even if Republicans refused to go along with spending limits. Mike Synar of

Stall After Measures Meet Opposition

Fort Worth, Philadelphia, San Francisco, and Portland, Ore. — found that candidates were paying higher prices than commercial advertisers at a majority of stations.

In one case, the FCC reported, candidates paid $5,500 for a 30-second spot that was offered to commercial advertisers for no more than $3,000.

In most cases, candidates were encouraged by broadcasters to buy non-pre-emptible fixed rates, the study said. And broadcasters rarely negotiated with candidates as they did with commercial advertisers.

Calculating Rates

Dingell's bill and the substitute measure for S 1009 by Sens. John C. Danforth, R-Mo.; Daniel K. Inouye, D-Hawaii; and Ernest F. Hollings, D-S.C., chairman of the Commerce Committee, spelled out how the lowest charge should be calculated.

Both measures would have prohibited pre-emption of any class of ads bought by candidates, although they would have allowed for "circumstances beyond the control of the broadcasting station."

The lowest charge available to candidates would have to be set on a per-show basis. And the length of time during which candidates could use the lower rates would be shortened from 45 days to 30 days for a primary and from 60 days to 45 days for a general or special election — a provision designed to give broadcasters a break.

However, under the Dingell bill, the lowest rate would be calculated over a 90-day period before a general or special election and a 60-day period before a primary. Broadcasters complained that this would unfairly force them to set rates during the summer rerun season when rates were lowest, even though most candidates would be buying time for October, when the new fall television lineup and football season sent rates soaring.

Edward O. Fritts, president of the National Association of Broadcasters, said at the Oct. 2 hearing that his group would work with Congress on the legislation. He blamed any rate-setting problems on the lack of FCC guidance since the 1972 law.

Rep. Al Swift, D-Wash., a former broadcaster, expressed concern that broadcasters might be forced to base lowest rates on "fire sale" prices often offered at the last minute, during slow sales periods.

He got an agreement from Dingell to work on problems with the bill before floor action.

Swift rejected complaints by Common Cause that separating the broadcast rate issue would further damage the already dim prospects for campaign finance legislation in 1990.

"Candidates who accept limits will still get the better broadcast benefits," Swift said, referring to his proposal in the campaign finance bill (HR 5400) to allow such candidates three ads for the price of two.

"I don't see this as in conflict with what we're trying to do there."

Oklahoma was at the forefront of a group including Dan Glickman, Kan., and Dennis E. Eckart, Ohio, that was pushing to phase in deeper cuts over a period of years and replace PAC cash with tax-funded vouchers to be spent on mail, television or other campaign devices.

But Charles W. Stenholm, Texas, the leader of a group of conservative Southern Democrats, warned that public financing was the "absolute fault line" that, if crossed, would cost their votes.

A month later, House Democrats were still readying their own proposal for floor action. Leading Democrats on the issue met July 26 with Foley to resolve such issues as how to structure the party's basic package and how to write an amendment that would offer deeper reform.

The Democratic package would, as expected, have limited spending to $550,000 for House races and limited the PAC contributions a member could accept to 50 percent of that, or $275,000. It would also have permitted only PACs that accepted contributions of $240 a year or less from their members to continue contributing up to $5,000 annually to federal candidates. All other PACs would be limited to $1,000.

An amendment offered by Democrats David R. Obey of Wisconsin and Synar would have cut the PAC limit to 40 percent, cut the individual contribution limit to $500 from $1,000 and granted up to $100,000 in public funds to candidates who qualified.

Floor Debate

On Aug. 3, two days after the Senate passed its bill, the House voted on legislation to cap spending in House races. House Democrats had been locked in a fierce intraparty battle that nearly prevented their leaders from bringing HR 5400 to the floor before the August recess. The leadership was forced to water down the measure just days before its consideration.

The Democratic measure to impose spending limits on House campaigns and modest limits on PAC contributions (HR 5400) passed the House 255-155 on Aug. 3. Republicans contributed only 15 "yes" votes and briefly imperiled the bill with parliamentary maneuvering that yielded a byzantine voting pattern. *(Vote 318, p. 104-H)*

Swift, the Democratic floor manager, called the final bill "good for the country, good for the House, good for all of us." Noting that campaigns had increased in costs almost twofold since 1980, he added, "Without spending limits, the cost of an election has gone wild.... It's absurd, and we all know it."

Despite their losses, Republicans argued that voters would hesitate to assign Democrats the reformist label once they learned the cost, estimated at hundreds of millions of dollars.

Swift, and through him Foley and the Democratic leadership, came under pressure from all sides.

Outside groups such as Common Cause criticized the package for not going far enough on public financing or the reduction in PAC limits. Many insiders questioned the need for action at all, arguing that there was no public cry for new election laws.

And a trio of pragmatic liberals who had quarreled with Foley over legislative strategy in the past — George Miller of California, Charles E. Schumer of New York and Marty

Russo of Illinois — was at the center of a rebellion that forced late changes in the package.

"Everyone wants to vote for it, but no one likes what's in it," Robert T. Matsui, D-Calif., said Aug. 1, as the arguments raged.

In closed-door meetings, Democrats yelled about the "what ifs" of their particular circumstances. Democrats from urban areas feared that the $550,000 spending limit would prove too little once depleted by a tough primary fight. Swift responded by writing a $165,000 exception to the spending limit for candidates who won their primaries with less than 66.7 percent of the vote and faced general election opposition. Exceptions were also written to permit lobbyists to continue serving on members' fundraising committees and to exempt legal and accounting fees from the spending limit.

The House bill also created a two-tiered system of PACs that would have diminished the clout of PACs that relied on large contributions from their members. PACs that took donations of more than $240 a year from members would be barred from giving candidates more than $1,000 per election. PACs that took contributions of $240 or less from members would be able to give up to $5,000 — a standard that preserved the clout of labor and trade association PACs that favored Democratic incumbents. Democratic incumbents relied on PACs for 51 percent of their donations in the 1988 election cycle.

Last-Minute Action

The Democrats did not finish drafting the bill until late in the night of Aug. 2. When it came to the floor the next day, Republicans complained it was being run through the House in a hurried fashion at a time when members were itching to go home. Republicans lost efforts to keep the bill off the floor, including an attempt to adjourn the House.

The GOP pushed an alternative that would have limited contributions from PACs to $1,000 and required candidates to raise at least half their funds within their congressional district. It would have imposed no overall spending limits. "Let the people who actually vote in your campaign determine how much you spend," said Bill Thomas, Calif., the GOP floor manager.

Illinois Democrat Dan Rostenkowski, chairman of the Ways and Means Committee, joined Republicans in complaining that the Democratic task force that wrote the bill had short-circuited the committee process. His was one of four committees that otherwise would have claimed jurisdiction.

Democrats favoring the Obey-Synar amendment depicted its plan to cut individual contributions and introduce public finance as an influence-redistribution mechanism. "It takes from the high rollers" and gives to "average Americans," Obey said.

Republican Bill Frenzel, Minn., led the charge against public financing, criticizing not only the cost of the programs, but also the establishment of a new bureaucracy.

Many Southern Democrats did not support Obey-Synar because of its public spending, but were willing to support the Swift bill. Democratic freshman Glen Browder of Alabama summed up many lawmakers' feelings when he said, "It's not perfect, and anybody can find a reason or excuse to say no. But it's clearly better than what we have now."

Obey-Synar Amendment

The Democratic leadership, meanwhile, had committed to support the Obey-Synar amendment to sharpen the lines on campaign reform. The amendment, cast as an attack on "fat cats," sought to commit up to $100,000 in public financing for House campaigns, cut PAC contributions deeper than the underlying bill and reduce the amount an individual could give to House candidates.

But Republicans turned the tables on the vote. They knew the Democrats were counting on GOP votes to kill the amendment; after all, the Democratic leadership's vote tally showed that the amendment's taxpayer financing, unpopular with Southerners and conservatives, would bring down the entire bill.

To make the point clear, the Republicans forced the Democrats to ask for the roll call vote needed to kill the amendment and then, with a handful of exceptions, voted present. The result was that even Obey and Synar worked against passage of their amendment. It failed, 122-128, with 153 members voting present.

Three Democrats who had spoken in favor of the amendment on the floor and one member of the party's leadership, Steny H. Hoyer of Maryland, the Democratic Caucus chairman, also voted present. Four Democrats who spoke in favor of the amendment voted "no." *(Vote 317, p. 104-H)*

CONFERENCE/FINAL ACTION

Conferees faced the prospect of bridging the huge gulf separating House and Senate Democrats.

Dole warned that "there should be no illusions." Unless Democrats removed taxpayer financing and reduced the influence of union money, Dole said Aug. 4, there would be no deal.

The differences between the House and Senate bills showed up most starkly in their treatment of PACs and public financing. The Senate, for example, would ban PACs, but the House would set a limit on PAC contributions that, by 1988 election standards, would hit only 99 members.

A similar gap existed in their treatment of soft money — the tens of millions of dollars raised off the books to influence federal elections. The Senate would take a big step toward imposing federal rules on state election activities; the House limited itself primarily to abuses that cropped up in the 1988 presidential campaigns.

The House and Senate by Sept. 26 were set to meet in conference on the differences over their versions of campaign finance legislation (HR 5400, S 137). But time and the preoccupation of key players with budget matters had made it clear that the legislation would not advance.

The House on Sept. 26 named 28 members as conferees. This followed the Senate's Sept. 18 decision also to move to conference.

A Republican effort on Sept. 26 to instruct House conferees to accept Senate provisions on franked mail and PACs failed 225-194. Both were issues on which the GOP had failed to gain recorded votes during the floor debate on the bill. *(Vote 385, p. 122-H)*

The makeup of the House Democratic conferees reflected an effort by Foley to give representation to party members who voiced objections to both the bill and the task force process by which it was written. Among those named, for instance, were three Californians: Miller, Howard L. Berman and Vic Fazio. California Democrats had expressed concern on the eve of House floor action that the bill could damage activities conducted by the state party in behalf of its nominees.

Foley addressed objections from chairmen of committees with jurisdiction over the bill — Ways and Means, Post Office and Civil Service, Energy and Commerce — that they lacked adequate representation on the task force that wrote the bill. He named the Energy and Commerce and Post Office chairmen to the conference and gave Ways and Means representation.

Despite the moves toward conference, negotiators never met.

The rush to adjournment and the need to handle other must-pass legislation left the campaign finance measure unfinished.

"I see no point in our trying to convene a conference at this time," said Senate sponsor Boren in mid-October, less than two weeks before the 101st Congress adjourned. "It's over," he added, referring to the chance of reaching a compromise to suit both parties, both chambers and President Bush. ■

Senate Republicans Kill 'Motor Voter' Bill

Senate Republicans on Sept. 26 effectively killed chances for passage of a bill aimed at increasing voter registration.

With only two exceptions, Republicans voted solidly against cutting off debate on a motion to take up S 874 (S Rept 101-140), known as the "motor voter" bill because it would have tied voter registration to obtaining a driver's license. Two Democrats crossed party lines to vote against cloture.

The bill would have established uniform, nationwide voter registration procedures. An application, renewal or change of address on a driver's license would have served as an automatic application to register to vote.

The vote to cut off debate, 55-42, fell five votes short of the number required. *(Vote 257, p. 51-S)*

Republicans said they opposed the bill because of the potential for fraud and abuse and the costs it would have imposed on states. They also said that elections were state matters and the federal government should not impose uniform regulations.

Because of the lengthy list of business that still faced the Senate and the impending close of the session, staff members said the measure was finished for the 101st Congress.

Wendell H. Ford, D-Ky., sponsor of the bill, said he would push it again in the 102nd Congress. The House passed a similar version of the bill (HR 2190) on Feb. 6.

The Bush administration had threatened to veto the measure. Administration officials said the bill would have increased the potential for voter fraud and imposed a financial burden on the states.

BACKGROUND

The motor-voter bill began its journey through Congress in 1989. The House Administration Committee approved HR 2190 on May 3, 1989 (H Rept 101-243). The Senate Rules and Administration Committee reported S 874 on Sept. 26, 1989 (S Rept 101-140).

What the Bills Would Have Done

The motor-voter bills in the House and Senate would have:

- Established uniform, nationwide voter registration procedures. An application, renewal or change of address on a driver's license would have served as an automatic application to register to vote.
- Made applications available at libraries, unemployment and public assistance offices, schools, and offices that sold hunting and fishing licenses.
- Required states to establish procedures to register voters by mail. Under penalty of perjury, applicants would have had to sign an application form stating that they met each voter-eligibility requirement.

Voters would have been required to sign an oath of citizenship under penalty of perjury, but Republicans argued unsuccessfully that notarization should also have been required.

- Required that registration be completed 30 days prior to a federal election unless state law specified a shorter period of time. The bill would have prohibited changes to the registration list 60 days prior to a federal election.
- Included an address-verification procedure designed to prevent fraud and clear "deadwood" from the rolls by checking the whereabouts of voters. In addition, the bill would have made voter fraud a federal crime.
- Required that states, to prevent fraud, clean their voter roles by periodically verifying addresses. Voters whose addresses could not be verified would have been placed on an inactive list.

Those on the inactive list could have been removed completely from the voter rolls at their own request, if the voter died, or if state law required removal because of a criminal conviction, mental incompetence or change of address.

Those placed on an inactive list who later wished to vote would have had to either present proof that they were wrongly taken off the active rolls or vote under a special procedure defined by state law.

- Applied to all states except North Dakota, which did not require voter registration.

The bill's provisions were in addition to the Voting Rights Act of 1965 and would not have affected that law.

Lauded as an example of true bipartisanship, the success of the bill hinged on the idea that it could be all things to all people. Democrats crafted the motor-voter sections of the bill, while Republicans wrote the antifraud portions.

To Republicans such as Minority Whip Newt Gingrich, Ga., who supported the bill despite last-minute Republican efforts to kill it, it represented a chance to bring potential GOP voters into the fold.

Gingrich tried to ease the concerns of Republicans who feared that the bill could somehow aid the Democrats, saying studies showed that half of the Americans eligible to vote were Democrats and half were Republicans.

"We're at parity in this country," he said. "I say to my Republican colleagues, I don't think we have anything to fear by encouraging registration."

But the bill was closer to the hearts of Democrats. Key party leaders, including Ronald H. Brown, chairman of the Democratic National Committee, held a news conference

Feb. 6 to call attention to the bill.

The Democrats described HR 2190 as a bill of "inclusion." Al Swift, D-Wash., who cosponsored the bill with Bill Thomas, R-Calif., said a large number of Americans did not vote because too many obstacles still existed.

They cited U.S. voter turnout statistics, which they said were the lowest of any democracy in the world.

Majority Leader Richard A. Gephardt, D-Mo., said part of the problem lay in a cumbersome system of voter registration, in which "bureaucracy can get in the way of democracy."

Black House members, including Majority Whip William H. Gray III, D-Pa., John Conyers Jr., D-Mich., and John Lewis, D-Ga., called the bill an extension of the Voting Rights Act passed 25 years earlier. On the floor, they recalled the days of the civil rights movement in asking members to support the legislation.

"Eliminating the registration barrier is particularly significant for African-Americans for whom registration, along with poll taxes and literacy tests, has historically served as an obstacle to exercising their constitutional right," Conyers said.

Gray said that 25 years earlier, supporters of the Voting Rights Act heard the same arguments being used against HR 2190. The bill was a continuation of the struggle for inclusion of all voters, he said.

"Each generation has widened the circle of participation," Gray said. "With this bill 60 to 70 million unregistered voters will have an easier time getting inside that circle."

Although civil rights groups had questioned portions of the bill, Gray said all had come on board, including the NAACP and the National Urban League.

Jesse Jackson also endorsed the measure, although he had supported same-day-as-the-election registration — as had a number of House Democrats — rather than the bill's requirement that registration come at least 30 days before an election.

The measure was also supported by the League of Women Voters and the AFL-CIO.

FLOOR ACTION

Though motor-voter legislation made its way into both chambers as expected, the fate that befell the measure was not predicted.

After the House approved HR 2190 in February, supporters expressed confidence that the Senate would pass its bill sometime before the end of the 101st Congress. But growing Republican misgivings about the bills, the constant threat of a Bush veto and the increasing pressure on Congress to complete its business and adjourn for the year led to the death of the legislation.

House Action

The House on Feb. 6 ignored the president's veto threat, overcame a Republican challenge and passed HR 2190 by a vote of 289-132. *(Vote 11, p. 6-H)*

Before passage, Republicans, led by Minority Leader Robert H. Michel, Ill., offered a substitute amendment.

It would have strengthened the bill's antifraud provisions and would have made the voter-registration procedures voluntary. The amendment also would have provided $120 million in block grants to fund state programs that were designed to encourage voter registration.

Members voted 129-291 to reject the amendment and then voted 156-265 against a motion by Paul E. Gillmor, R-Ohio, to recommit the bill to the Committee on House Administration for further study. *(Votes 9, 10, p. 6-H)*

In the final days before the vote on the bill, Michel and other Republicans angered Swift by criticizing the bill as too costly and asking for more debate. The White House followed suit.

The controversy over HR 2190 was aired Jan. 31, when members took up the rule (H Res 309) for floor consideration of the bill.

Republicans objected because the rule would allow only two amendments when the bill reached the floor Feb. 7. The rule was eventually approved on an almost straight party-line vote of 254-166, but not before a heated debate that went far beyond the rule. *(Vote 6, p. 4-H)*

Michel charged that the bill, although backed by key Republicans, was not bipartisan because changes had been made without the knowledge of GOP members.

Michel said he had concerns about how the bill was drafted. The bill should have been handled in the same way that campaign-reform legislation was handled, he argued. Leadership on both sides should have had an opportunity to look at the bill and negotiate its contents.

An irate Swift said prime sponsors for the bill included "half the Republican Party," and he warned that Michel's opposition threatened bipartisanship in the future.

Swift said both sides were ready to vote on the agreement that had taken months to hammer out when Michel decided "to unilaterally and single-handedly trash that agreement."

Michel, who also voiced the objections of Illinois Republican Gov. James R. Thompson, argued that states would face high costs to comply with the law. Illinois officials estimated that it would cost $38 million to put the law into effect in that state.

But Conyers told House members that the motor-voter procedure was already in effect in Michigan without computers at a cost of $100,000 annually.

The bill would have provided $50 million nationwide to help the states implement the procedures.

Some states also warned that their constitutions would have to be changed to accommodate the bill. Opponents also argued that voter registration was the purview of the states, not the federal government.

Critics in the House also said the bill was inviting voter fraud by not requiring notarization of mail-in applications.

"If you come from Illinois, you have got to be sensitive to that issue of fraud," Michel said.

The antifraud sections of the bill were drafted primarily by Thomas, who was the ranking Republican on the House Administration Committee's Subcommittee on Elections.

Senate Inaction

S 874 made its way to the Senate floor in late September, as Congress was dealing with the budget impasse and a host of other issues that postponed its scheduled adjournment. The Senate debated the issue briefly before voting on the cloture motion on Sept. 26.

Democrats could persuade just two Republicans — Oregon's Mark O. Hatfield and Bob Packwood — to join in voting to cut off debate on the bill. Meanwhile, two Democrats — Howell Heflin, Ala., and Max Baucus, Mont. — defected and joined Republicans in voting against cloture.

When the cloture vote fell five votes short, supporters recognized that there was little hope of victory in 1990. They did vow to revive the issue in 1991. ■

Lawmakers' Pay Raised, Fees Curbed

Members of Congress were set to receive fatter salaries in 1991, with House members receiving about 23 percent more than senators under a two-tier compensation system set up in 1989.

As of Jan. 1, 1991, House members' salary increased from $96,600 to $125,100; at the same time, House members were prohibited from keeping speaking fees known as honoraria. Senators' salaries increased from $98,400 to about $101,900. They were still able to accept honoraria but were allowed to keep only a lower overall amount, because the ceiling went down as their pay went up. That meant that the $27,337 maximum that senators could keep in 1990 fell to $23,837 in 1991. Between pay and honoraria, a senator could earn roughly the same amount as a House member.

Fearful of political fallout, senators in 1989 had denied themselves the second stage of the scheduled pay hike, accepting only a cost of living increase (COLA) and continuing to allow honoraria. An amendment by Christopher J. Dodd, D-Conn., to ban senators from keeping honoraria was approved Aug. 1 as part of the Senate's campaign finance bill, but that measure died in conference. *(Campaign financing bill, p. 59)*

While only House members received the 25 percent increase on Jan. 1, 1991, both chambers did get a 3.6 percent COLA on that date. The size of the COLA was determined under a formula set in the 1989 law that linked congressional COLAs to private-sector salaries rather than, as in the past, to federal workers' pay increases. Federal workers were getting a 4.1 percent increase Jan. 1, 1991, under the terms of the fiscal 1991 Treasury-Postal Service appropriations bill. *(Federal pay revision, p. 405)*

Legislation to return congressional salaries to their 1989 level of $89,500 — repealing both the pay raise that took effect in early 1990 and the one scheduled to start in January 1991 — was introduced during the year by Reps. Hank Brown, R-Colo., and Andrew Jacobs Jr., D-Ind., but it was never brought to a vote in the House or Senate.

BACKGROUND

After foundering in public embarrassment early in 1989 when it attempted to raise its own pay by 51 percent, Congress enacted in November 1989 a more modest pay hike. Success brought along with it the two-tiered pay system, with different salaries for senators and representatives.

The legislation (HR 3660 — PL 101-194) increased senators' pay 10 percent in 1990, with COLAs in later years. The package banned honoraria payments for House members in 1991, when the largest pay raise was set to kick in, and set up a process for gradually scaling back honoraria levels in the Senate. *(1989 Almanac, p. 51)*

Pay Raise Opposition

Buoyed by the defeat of the 51-percent pay hike in 1989, opponents of congressional pay increases stayed active in 1990. Consumer activist Ralph Nader on Aug. 2 announced a stepped-up campaign to repeal the smaller pay raise Congress approved for itself.

Nader and a coalition of self-described citizens' groups were joined at a news conference by Brown, who July 31 introduced HR 5416 to roll congressional salaries back to the 1989 level.

The 1989 law, which linked House and Senate pay raises to new ethics rules, increased congressional salaries in 1990 from $89,500 for both chambers to $96,600 in the House and $98,400 in the Senate. Later in the year, both the House and the Senate received another COLA.

Brown acknowledged that it would be difficult to bring the bill to a vote on the House floor over expected leadership opposition. He said action would likely have to begin in the Senate, where amendments could be brought more easily to the floor.

Hoping to rekindle the passion that helped defeat the pay raise in early 1989, Nader and the other activists hoped to build on growing public disaffection with Washington and pressure members of Congress in the final months of their re-election campaign.

Jacobs, who cosponsored the bill with Brown, said it might be difficult to get the House to repeal the raise because it was approved by a roll call vote in the first place. Having already taken the political risk of going on record supporting the raise, Jacobs said, "it might be easier for members to vote against repeal."

SENATE ACTION

Forced to examine special-interest influence in their personal finances as well as political campaigns, senators Aug. 1 overwhelmingly voted to stop accepting speaking fees and to curb other outside income. The vote came on an amendment to the campaign finance bill (S 137).

The 77-23 vote to ban honoraria was the first time the Senate so clearly repudiated the speaking fees that critics said were tantamount to legalized bribery. *(Vote 196, p. 42-S)*

"We now know how the Senate stands on this question," Dodd, the amendment's sponsor, said afterward.

In a surprise move, the Senate also narrowly approved an amendment to cap all other forms of outside income — apparently including the dividends, interest and other investment income that made many senators millionaires.

But some members viewed the amendment more as an expression of resentment by the less-wealthy senators than a serious vote to make law. Asked what the vote signified, Texas Democrat Lloyd Bentsen said, "Class warfare." That laid bare some of the divisions within the Senate that typically underlay debate on the subject of compensation.

Although many senators said they would like to abolish the honoraria system, few wanted to do so without a compensatory pay raise. But there were many wealthy senators who did not need the raise and did not want the political hassle of supporting one, so the Senate was always even more reluctant than the House to vote for raises.

Many members assumed that the only forum in which the Senate would raise its pay in an election year would be a lame-duck session.

The wide margin of Dodd's victory belied the heavy pressure he was under from colleagues not to offer an amendment that could, if enacted, have meant a substantial loss of income for some senators. That was because it would have banned honoraria as of January 1991, without a pay raise to make up for it.

Federal Workers Hit With Honoraria Ban

Federal employees mounted a campaign on Capitol Hill and in the courts late in 1990 to nullify a little-noticed provision in the 1989 congressional pay and ethics package that prohibited even the lowest-grade civil servant from being paid for outside speeches or non-fiction writings. They failed to block the ban, but proposals to modify or repeal it began advancing through congressional committees in early 1991.

The 1989 Ethics Reform Act (PL 101-194) had packaged a congressional pay raise with new restrictions on honoraria — a ban on such speaking fees for House members and a reduced limit for senators. The act, which was to take effect Jan. 1, 1991, also included a ban on honoraria for federal officials. *(Pay and honoraria, p. 73; 1989 Almanac, p. 51)*

The extent of the government-wide honoraria ban, however, had gone largely unrecognized during congressional consideration of the bill in 1989.

Only as the law was about to go into effect was it widely publicized that the act banned all federal employees in the three branches, except senators and Senate staff, from accepting writing or speaking fees, even if the topic was unrelated to their work and presented to audiences with no knowledge of the employees' official duties. Violators of the law were subject to fines of $10,000 or the amount of the honorarium, whichever was greater.

Previously, federal regulations had prohibited receiving payment for speaking or writing if the subject specifically dealt with an employee's agency's "responsibilites, policies and programs" and had limited any other honorarium to $2,000 per appearance or speech.

Many members of Congress said they were unaware of the ban on rank-and-file federal workers until they heard from outraged constituents. A U.S. Forest Service office manager in Arizona complained to Rep. John J. Rhodes III, R-Ariz., that she could no longer pursue an outside interest in archaeology and genealogy. An Army Corps of Engineers employee in Arkansas told her senator, Democrat David Pryor, that she would have to stop writing romance novels.

"This is wacky," said Rep. Barney Frank, D-Mass., who chaired the Judiciary Subcommittee on Administrative Law and Governmental Relations. But Frank said lawmakers became aware of the controversy too late in 1990 to block the ban.

Interim regulations issued by the Office of Government Ethics on Nov. 28 exempted a number of outside activities from the pay ban, including writing fiction or poetry, teaching a course, or performing a comedy routine at a dinner theater. Accepting payment for non-fiction articles, however, was expressly forbidden, as was payment for any outside speech or appearance.

The American Federation of Government Employees and the National Treasury Employees Union filed suit in U.S. District Court in Washington in December, seeking a preliminary injunction to block enforcement of the law. The court rejected their plea.

Several bills were introduced to modify or repeal the ban early in 1991. Sponsors included Frank in the House and the two leaders of the Senate Governmental Affairs Committee — Chairman John Glenn, D-Ohio, and ranking Republican William V. Roth Jr. of Delaware.

But action on the legislation was complicated by two issues: whether to retain the honoraria ban for high-ranking executive branch officials and whether to use any bill on the issue as a vehicle for a renewed effort to ban honoraria for senators and their staffs.

"Absent the political will to vote a pay raise, however, the integrity of this institution remains threatened by the continued receipt of honoraria," said Dodd.

No one dared speak against Dodd's amendment. Minority Leader Bob Dole of Kansas said he had considered offering an amendment to make the honoraria ban contingent on enactment of a pay hike, but did not have enough votes to pass it. "The honoraria ban is coming, nobody quarrels with that," Dole said. "The larger question is whether this bill is going anywhere."

The Dodd amendment also would have barred members from keeping legal fees and other professional income, codifying curbs that had been in Senate rules for years. It would have limited any other form of outside earned income to an amount equal to 15 percent of a senator's salary, which would then have been a cap of about $15,000.

Moynihan's Plan

Even as Dodd was speaking to reporters after his victory, Daniel Patrick Moynihan, D-N.Y., was making mischief with the finances of the Senate's millionaires.

Neither the House nor Senate rules imposed any limit on unearned income, allowing members to continue drawing great wealth from family businesses, stock investments and other sources.

Moynihan's amendment would have extended the 15 percent cap on earned income to cover unearned income as well. "In order that there be a level playing field, let everybody be a little equal in the Senate," said Moynihan, who would have felt the pinch of his own amendment. He reported unearned income on his 1989 financial-disclosure form in excess of the $15,000 cap he proposed.

Moynihan introduced his handwritten amendment at a time when few other senators were on the floor. As his colleagues came to the floor for the vote, jocular senators teased each other as they all seemed to vote according to financial need: the wealthiest voted against the amendment and the less wealthy voted for it.

As opponents nearly defeated the amendment on a 50-50 tie, Moynihan stood in the center aisle of the chamber, hands outstretched. "One more vote!" he pleaded.

Laughing, Alaska Republican Frank H. Murkowski switched his vote to support Moynihan, bringing the final tally to 51-49. *(Vote 197, p. 42-S)*

"Turnabout is fair play," Murkowski said in a statement explaining his vote.

"Some of our well-to-do brethren have never quite understood the predicament of the less well-off members. They have taken strong positions against honoraria and pay raises. . . ."

Although the Senate did not enact the 1989 House plan to bar members from earning honoraria after 1990, more than one-third of all senators voluntarily refused to supplement their income with speaking fees by mid-1990. A 1989 survey by the independent citizens' lobbying group Common Cause found that 19 senators had refused to keep honoraria in 1988.

Many developments built pressure on members to forgo honoraria.

In 1988, one of the few incumbents to be defeated in his bid for re-election was Sen. Lowell P. Weicker Jr., R-Conn., who was heavily criticized by his Democratic opponent, Joseph I. Lieberman, for making honoraria speeches — and missing key Senate votes in the process. The message was not lost on his Connecticut colleagues: All eight members of the state's congressional delegation by 1990 refused to keep honoraria. (However, Rep. Sam Gejdenson, D-Conn., did not establish a no-honoraria policy until mid-1989, by which time he had already earned the maximum he was allowed to keep for that year.)

Dodd said Weicker's defeat did not inspire his drive to ban honoraria.

But Rep. Barbara B. Kennelly, D-Conn., said it gave her a big push to direct all 1989 speaking fees to charity. "We all knew it was over with that election," she said. "It was a very clear message." ■

Congress Adopts New Franking Restrictions

The franking privilege, constantly under criticism as a weapon used unfairly by incumbents to protect their positions, once again was the centerpiece of dispute and change in 1990.

Congress imposed new restrictions on the use of congressional mailing privileges in both the House and the Senate, adding another chapter to an interchamber dispute played out mainly on the legislative branch appropriations measure for Congress.

Though the fiscal 1991 appropriations bill for the legislative branch totaled 11 percent more than the amount provided the previous year, it also imposed new restrictions on the frank.

The bill (HR 5399 — PL 101-520), cleared by Congress on Oct. 27, still provided $122 million to pay for the franking privilege: $59 million for the House, $30 million for the Senate and $33 million to make up for a shortfall in fiscal 1990 appropriations. The shortfall resulted from the House's spending almost double its $44 million fiscal 1990 appropriation. *(Legislative branch appropriations, p. 894)*

The provisions restricting House mail, for the first time, required each representative to disclose the amount spent on franked mailings, gave each member an individual mailing budget and required all mass mailings to be approved by the House Franking Commission.

The bill also limited senators' use of the frank by, among other things, barring them from transferring mail funds from one senator to another.

BACKGROUND

The first Continental Congress in 1775 adopted the 17th-century British practice of granting free use of the public mail system to legislators for official business.

The franking privilege, allowing senators and representatives to send virtually unlimited amounts of mail with the stroke of a pen, evolved into a cherished perquisite that helped members keep their names and faces before the voters — and keep themselves in office.

Each chamber revised its own rules from time to time and tried to crack down on overuse. Both, for instance, had guidelines limiting photographs and the number of references to the member on each page of a newsletter.

But attempts to rein in use of the frank were always hotly contested by members who said they needed to retain the ability to communicate freely with their constituents.

Mailing costs increased nearly fourfold from 1972 to 1988; even adjusted for inflation, that represented an 86 percent increase.

Costs were higher still for 1990 because of the elections. Since 1976, mail volume in election years averaged 51.4 percent more than in preceding off years. The House mail budget, for example, exceeded $113 million in 1988.

This trend had continued despite periodic attempts by Congress to control incumbents' self-promotion, such as a prohibition since 1978 on mass mailings within 60 days of an election.

The fiscal 1990 appropriations bill for the first time divided mail funds between the two chambers.

The House agreed to limit members to using their franking privilege no more than three times a year for newsletters sent to every postal patron. But the House in 1989 refused to join the Senate in making each member publicly accountable for a mail budget.

In the Senate, the annual mail appropriation was divided into accounts for individual senators based on state populations. However, senators could pay for additional postage with money from office expense accounts, campaign committees, personal savings and honoraria.

The Senate resolution also reinstated allocation and disclosure rules that had been suspended for part of the year — rules that demonstrated how effective open disclosure could be as a cost-cutter.

Senators, tired of taking equal blame for a deficit mostly of the House's making in their joint mail account, in midyear dropped the disclosure requirement they had imposed in 1986. The Senate spent $6 million on official mail during the first five months of 1989, when each member was required to account publicly for a specific allotment. The system was lifted for the next seven months, and spending shot up to $29 million, according to the Senate Rules Committee.

HOUSE ACTION

The House came under criticism early in 1990 after the U.S. Postal Service projected that the chamber would overspend its $44 million mail budget by more than $38 million for the year while the Senate would spend $6 million less than the $24 million allotted for its mail in 1990.

The National Taxpayers Union had been combing the

files of the House Franking Commission to calculate how much each member mailed. Faced with the likelihood that the group's estimates, for technical reasons, could overstate their mailing, about 200 House members agreed to disclose voluntarily how much they mailed in 1989, according to a spokesman for the taxpayers' group.

Facing the large overrun, House members on an appropriations conference committee May 17 — led by Democratic leaders — won approval of a provision to let the chamber use $25 million left over from past years to help cover the deficit in the fiscal 1990 franking budget.

The conference committee accepted the provision over the objection of Sen. Don Nickles, R-Okla., who denounced the House for overspending its mail appropriation.

The provision added to the supplemental appropriations bill would give the House broad authority to transfer unspent money appropriated for congressional operations from prior fiscal years to other purposes, including mail costs.

The amendment was proposed in the conference by Vic Fazio, D-Calif., chairman of the House Appropriations Subcommittee on the Legislative Branch. He said that even with the transfer authority, more money would have to be appropriated for House mail later in the year.

Nickles, ranking Republican on the Senate Legislative Branch Subcommittee, called the proposal "further evidence of the need for reform" of franking rules. He called on the House to officially adopt the Senate requirement that members disclose how much they spend on mail.

The leadership lost the provision, though, on the House floor a week later when Congress cleared a $4.3 billion supplemental spending bill (HR 4404) for fiscal 1990. While Democratic leaders had led the effort to use the leftover money, Republicans successfully fought against it.

The Republicans' victory came in a show of election-year skittishness about congressional perks. Despite intense arm-twisting by Speaker Thomas S. Foley, D-Wash., and other leaders, 60 Democrats joined 148 Republicans in rejecting the provision, 161-208 on May 25. *(Vote 146, p. 50-H)*

The vote was mostly symbolic. The Postal Service was required to deliver congressional mail whether or not enough money had been appropriated.

Pressure for Change

Stung by the rebuff on the supplemental appropriations bill, under pressure from critics and frustrated by colleagues who would not publicly support the mailing privileges they enjoyed, Fazio floated a proposal in July to impose sharp new restrictions on the use of the frank as part of the legislative branch appropriations bill.

Fazio started circulating a plan to give each House member a mailing budget for the first time. Under Fazio's plan, each member would be allotted the cost of three mailings to each household in their district — on average, $160,000 a year, although that figure was a point of contention. Members would be allowed to use money from office and staff accounts for additional mail.

The move by Fazio mobilized members adamantly opposed to blunting that tool for keeping incumbents' names before their constituents.

"There is real concern that we should not retreat on that," said Chief Deputy Whip David E. Bonior, D-Mich., after hearing from colleagues at a July 12 meeting of Democratic whips.

Said one House Democrat, "Going into a critical national campaign in 1992 after redistricting, this is a poor time to start undermining the advantages of incumbency."

After the July 12 whip meeting, several Democrats volunteered to see whether there was more support for the existing franking system than the May roll call indicated. "Such a fundamental change in how members relate to their constituents should not be made based on that vote," said Robert G. Torricelli, D-N.J. "We asked for a chance to make the argument again."

But others said the House would at least have to disclose how much each member mailed. Such changes were "not only necessary but politically inevitable," said Pat Williams, D-Mont.

A spokeswoman for Minority Leader Robert H. Michel of Illinois acknowledged that it would be hard to sell tough mailing restrictions to Republicans as well. "It's a difficult issue on both sides of the aisle," she said.

Bipartisan Compromise

When the fiscal 1991 spending bill for the legislative branch was approved July 30 by the Appropriations Committee (H Rept 101-648), however, the issue of franking curbs was noticeably absent. Democratic leaders said they hoped to bring the bill before the full chamber later that week and offer the new franking curbs.

The leaders, though, changed their minds and kept the issue of legislators' mailing privileges off the floor in the face of divisions among Democrats and between the two parties. Republicans generally backed the proposed limits, but many Democrats opposed any curbs on their mail.

To allow the House to avert a repeat of 1989's floor fight over franking, some members pushed a bipartisan compromise when the legislative appropriations bill finally made its way to the chambers' floors in October. The compromise would make House members individually accountable for the money they spent on official mail.

The deal struck by House leaders was an acknowledgment by the Democratic leadership that the cost of fighting the battle to preserve the frank as it existed was not worth the gain, if it could be won at all.

Fazio and Rep. Bill Frenzel, R-Minn., worked out the details and offered it as an amendment during House consideration of the legislative appropriations bill on Oct. 21.

The amendment, adopted by voice vote, called for assigning each member a mail budget and halting mailings when the budget was depleted. The member's budget would be determined by multiplying the number of non-business addresses in each House district by three and then multiplying the product by the first-class postage rate. This was expected to amount to about $180,000 per member. Members could supplement the account with up to $25,000 a year from other office accounts.

The amount spent by a member on mail would be disclosed quarterly in the report of members' expenses compiled by the House clerk.

Gulf Politics

The franking controversy also emerged during a September debate over mail service to members of the armed services stationed in the Persian Gulf.

The House on Sept. 17 cast a symbolic vote to give preference to free mail for members of the armed services over free mail for members of Congress. Members voted 227-142 for a motion to pay for postage of military mail from the Persian Gulf with funds appropriated for congressional franked mailings. *(Vote 333, p. 110-H)*

The fast-moving proposal snagged on the House floor

Sept. 13 on the issue of the franking privilege when Tom Ridge, R-Pa., demanded a roll call on a proposal to fund the mailings from appropriations for congressional franked mailings. The vote was put off until Sept. 17.

By that time, the bill on which the vote occurred, HR 5611, already had become moot when the House, earlier on Sept. 17, cleared by voice vote a measure (S 3033) authorizing free postage without a franking provision.

SENATE ACTION

The Senate, meanwhile, dealt with a variety of other issues and proposals. The Rules and Administration Committee acted first on June 13 when it approved by a 9-0 vote a resolution on mass mailings to take from the small states and give to the big.

The resolution provided a 50 percent increase in the Senate's mail budget in fiscal 1991. The resolution was expected to run into trouble on the Senate floor from critics of the franking privilege. Some critics pointed out that the Senate had previously boasted of staying within its fiscal 1990 mail budget while the House had overspent its allocation.

The proposal, worked out by Rules Committee Chairman Wendell H. Ford, D-Ky., and ranking Republican Ted Stevens of Alaska, would have allotted every senator an amount based upon the cost of one mass mailing to each constituent address. Senators from the six states with only one congressional district would be allocated the cost of two mailings, a move designed to seek parity with House members from such districts who were also allowed more than one mailing.

The resolution, however, did not guarantee mass mailings to all constituents, because all office postage expenses were to be paid from the allocation, committee aides said.

Under existing rules, the Senate provided at least $100,000 for all states, which allowed members from lightly populated states to send as many as three mailings. Although larger states got larger allotments, they often allowed less than one mailing per constituent address.

For example, under the existing formula, senators from Alaska, Delaware, North Dakota, South Dakota, Vermont and Wyoming were all allowed more than 2.2 mailings per constituent address, according to committee aides. Thirty-four states were allowed less than one mailing per address.

The proposal also would have allowed senators to stockpile mailings in non-election years and send out up to three mailings in an election year.

The new plan proposed a budget for Senate mail of $35.5 million for fiscal 1991, up from the $24 million allocated for this year.

Having previously criticized the House for failing to follow the Senate's lead in staying within amounts allocated for mailings, Ford defended the proposed increase in allocations as necessary to remedy the advantage enjoyed by senators from small states.

Campaign Finance, Legislative Appropriations

On July 31, the Senate added mail curbs to its campaign finance bill (S 137). The curbs, adopted 98-1, would have barred using the frank for mass mailings in election years and would have also barred senators from assigning their franking budget to other senators. *(Campaign financing, p. 59; vote 193, p. 41-S)*

The ban on assigning mail budgets was designed to prevent senators up for re-election from borrowing from their colleagues and repaying them in subsequent years.

The measure also took aim at the House's routinely exceeding its mail budget by prohibiting franking once the annual appropriation was depleted. It would also have required House members to join senators in disclosing their spending for mail.

But the campaign finance package eventually died and the mailing curbs, as in the House, made their way into the legislative operations appropriations bill.

The Senate Appropriations Committee approved its appropriations bill (S 3207) on Oct. 16, allocating $35.5 million for Senate mail, the amount proposed by the Rules Committee — although members expected that amount to be cut during floor action.

Oklahoma's Nickles tried in committee to offer amendments to bar senators from transferring mail funds among one another and from carrying forward unspent funds from one year to the next. He also sought to limit the amount a senator could transfer into the mail account from other office accounts or from his mail account into his office accounts. At the request of Appropriations Committee Chairman Robert C. Byrd, D-W.Va., Nickles agreed to hold his amendments for floor action. Byrd said he did not want to trespass on matters in the purview of the Senate Rules Committee.

FINAL ACTION

Before final passage of the appropriations bill, the Senate also adopted, by voice vote, an amendment to reduce the amount included for Senate mail from the $35.5 million recommended by the Appropriations Committee to $30 million. Amendment sponsor Nickles initially sought a deeper cut — to $24 million, the amount appropriated for fiscal 1990 — but compromised in the face of vigorous objections from Stevens.

Other amendments adopted during the Senate debate would:

- Allow senators to retain unused mail funds for future use, but only until the next fiscal year. Existing carryover authority had no time limit.
- Allow senators to transfer money from their mail accounts to other accounts in amounts up to $100,000 or 50 percent of their mass mail budget, whichever was less. The Appropriations Committee proposed allowing that new transfer authority with no limit on the amount.
- Bar the transfer of mail funds from one senator to another, as had been allowed without restriction.

The conference committee accepted both the Senate amendments and the House compromise crafted by Fazio and Frenzel (H Rept 101-965).

For House members, the provisions would:

- Give each member an individual mail budget equal to the amount needed to make three first-class mailings to every non-business address in his district.
- Allow members to supplement their mail budget by transferring up to $25,000 a year from other accounts for other office expenses.
- Require the amount each member spends to be reported quarterly.
- Require all mailings to more than 500 recipients to be approved by the House Franking Commission.

The House acted first on the conference report, adopting it by a vote of 259-129 on Oct. 27. The Senate cleared the measure by voice vote the same day, and President Bush signed it Nov. 5. *(Vote 529, p. 166-H)* ■

Panel Probes Senators' Aid to Keating

The Senate Ethics Committee opened to public view in the last months of 1990 a sweeping investigation of possible wrongdoing as it conducted hearings into five senators' actions to help a troubled savings and loan institution.

For two grueling months — 26 days of public testimony and argument that stretched into the 102nd Congress — the Senate aired its dirty laundry in front of a national television audience. Never before had the Senate investigated so many of its own members at one time. The senators — Alan Cranston, D-Calif.; Dennis DeConcini, D-Ariz.; John Glenn, D-Ohio; John McCain, R-Ariz.; and Donald W. Riegle Jr., D-Mich. — were suspected of doing favors between 1987 and 1989 for a wealthy campaign contributor, Charles H. Keating Jr. *(Senators' links to Keating, p. 79)*

Keating was the head of a California-based thrift, Lincoln Savings and Loan Association, whose failure in 1989 cost taxpayers an estimated $2 billion and became a symbol of one of the largest financial debacles ever to hit the nation, the near collapse of the savings and loan industry. *(Chronology, 1989 Almanac, p. 135)*

Keating gave a total of $1.5 million to the campaigns and political causes of the senators, and their actions in his behalf — in particular their participation in two 1987 meetings with federal regulators who were closing in on Keating's thrift — won for them the unwelcome moniker of the Keating Five. The name stuck even though each senator strove mightily to differentiate his actions from the others, and even though the man who conducted the investigation for the committee, special counsel Robert S. Bennett, declared on the opening day that Glenn and McCain had done nothing wrong.

The hearings, which began Nov. 15, 1990, and concluded Jan. 16, 1991, were called to examine whether any of the five violated Senate rules against exerting improper influence in return for compensation. Technically, the hearings were only a preliminary inquiry aimed at determining whether the Ethics Committee should proceed to a formal investigation and hearing; formal disciplinary action — censure or expulsion — would have to be voted by the full Senate.

All five senators denied wrongdoing, saying their efforts in behalf of Keating were no more than any member of Congress would do to help a constituent having problems with a federal agency. They denied that they helped Keating because of his fundraising and maintained that their actions did not influence the decisions of government regulators with regard to Lincoln.

Like previous hearings into the Watergate, Koreagate and Abscam scandals, the inquiry gave the public an opportunity to look deeply into the inner workings of politics — in this instance, the possible connection between campaign contributions and government favoritism.

The Keating hearings raised a delicate question for all members of Congress: How far can a politician go to aid a supporter?

Establishing the facts in the case turned out to be substantially easier than deciding at what point a senator's conduct crossed ethical boundaries.

Committee leaders vowed when the hearings opened that they would conclude the case by the end of 1990, but the meticulousness of the special counsel's presentation, the combativeness of the senators' attorneys and the sudden scheduling of a surprise witness carried the matter into the new year. As the hearings ended, it was apparent that the committee was divided over the outcome and would not reach a decision quickly.

After more than 33 hours of closed-door deliberations spread over six weeks, the Ethics Committee announced its findings on Feb. 27, 1991. It decided to proceed against Cranston, finding evidence that some of his official actions were "substantially linked" with his fundraising. The other four senators were criticized in written statements for poor judgment, with DeConcini and Riegle also chided for giving the appearance of acting improperly. But the panel decided that existing rules did not warrant further action.

Cranston protested that he had been "unfairly singled out." The others generally expressed relief at the end of a long ordeal.

BACKGROUND

Charles Keating grew to be a rich and influential figure in the thrift industry as chairman of American Continental Corp., an Ohio-chartered corporation based in Phoenix, and deeply involved in home construction and land development. In 1984, American Continental purchased Lincoln Savings and Loan Association despite Keating's 1979 brush with the Securities and Exchange Commission (SEC) over insider loans.

Lincoln took aggressive advantage of permissive California state and federal rules to become a high-flying institution that boomed on the strength of relatively risky investments. After 1985, Lincoln became the subject of increasing scrutiny from federal regulators. Keating fought back; after long delays, American Continental [Lincoln] filed for bankruptcy in April 1989 and Lincoln was seized by federal regulators.

Keating was generous with his money, especially to the less privileged: Mother Teresa got $1 million; New York's Covenant House for runaway children and all manner of Arizona charities got assistance. And he dabbled in politics, for a time heading John B. Connally Jr.'s unsuccessful 1980 presidential bid.

In 1989 Keating boasted to reporters of the clout his political contributions had given him with Congress. "One question among the many raised in recent weeks had to do with whether my financial support in any way influenced several political figures to take up my cause," Keating said. "I want to say in the most forceful way I can, I certainly hope so." Keating later said his remark was misinterpreted.

Not every politician Keating approached took up his cause. Sen. Jake Garn, R-Utah, who chaired the Banking Committee through the first half of the 1980s, disliked his attitude and after 1981 would have nothing to to do with him. Then-Sen. Pete Wilson, R-Calif., collected about $16,000 for his campaign from Keating in 1985 but never questioned regulators about Lincoln and said he approved of the Federal Home Loan Bank Board's efforts to curb thrift industry abuses. Former Arizona Gov. Bruce Babbitt disliked Keating's financial dealings and told Cranston in March 1989 that he considered Keating a "crook."

A California grand jury indicted Keating in September 1990 on securities fraud charges, and he was jailed for more

Continued on p. 80

Key Players in the Keating Five Case

ALAN CRANSTON
Democrat — California

Connection to Keating: Lincoln Savings and Loan based in Irvine, Calif.

- Met privately with Edwin J. Gray, chairman of the Federal Home Loan Bank Board, on April 2, 1987, in behalf of Lincoln Savings and Loan.
- Met with bank board examiners April 9, 1987, in behalf of Lincoln. Cranston's appearance at this two-hour-long meeting was brief.
- Called M. Danny Wall, Gray's replacement as bank board chairman, in August or September 1987 to urge a speedy conclusion of Lincoln examination.
- Intervened with California state and federal thrift regulators in late 1988 and until April 1989 to urge sale rather than seizure of Lincoln.
- Received $49,000 from Charles H. Keating Jr. and associates for his 1984 presidential campaign.
- Solicited and received $850,000 from Keating for three voter-education projects tied to Cranston and his son, Kim.
- Solicited and received $85,000 for a 1986 California Democratic Party get-out-the-vote drive.
- Solicited and received $300,000 line of credit from Lincoln in final days of 1986 campaign but never drew upon it.

Main Senate post: Stepped down as majority whip in November; chairman of Veterans' Affairs Committee.

Next election: Did not seek re-election.

DENNIS DECONCINI
Democrat — Arizona

Connection to Keating: American Continental Corp. — Lincoln's parent — headquartered in Arizona.

- Hosted both April 1987 meetings, which were held in DeConcini's office. Gray testified that DeConcini offered the government a deal in Keating's behalf. DeConcini disputed this.
- Intervened with California state and federal thrift regulators in late 1988 and until April 1989 to urge sale rather than seizure of Lincoln.
- Received $54,000 from Keating and associates for his 1988 re-election campaign, and $31,000 for his 1982 campaign. DeConcini returned the contributions in September and October 1989, after allegations that money might have been siphoned from Lincoln.
- Associated with two aides, campaign manager Ron Ober and fundraiser Earl Katz, who received together about $50 million in real estate loans from Lincoln in 1986-88. DeConcini said he was unaware of their connection to Lincoln at the time of the April 1987 meetings.

Main Senate post: Chairman of the Appropriations Treasury, Postal Service and General Government Subcommittee.

Next election: 1994.

JOHN GLENN
Democrat — Ohio

Connection to Keating: American Continental chartered in Ohio.

- Attended both meetings in April 1987 with Gray and regulators.
- Received $24,000 in campaign contributions for re-election campaigns from Keating and associates and $18,200 for his 1984 presidential campaign. A defunct political action committee associated with Glenn received $200,000 from Keating's companies in 1985-86.

Main Senate post: Chairman of Governmental Affairs Committee.

Next election: 1992.

JOHN McCAIN
Republican — Arizona

Connection to Keating: Personal friend; American Continental headquartered in Arizona.

- Attended both meetings in April 1987 with Gray and regulators.
- Received $110,000 in campaign contributions from Keating and associates for his 1982 and 1984 House campaigns and his 1986 Senate race. (McCain announced in February 1991 that he would give the funds to the Treasury.)
- In May and June 1989 McCain reimbursed American Continental for $13,433 for nine plane trips to the Bahamas for himself and his family in 1984-86; on three of those trips, McCain and his family stayed at Keating's residence on Cat Cay. The Ethics Committee indicated that since McCain was not in the Senate at the time, the trips would not play a role in the deliberations.

Main Senate posts: Member of Armed Services and Commerce committees.

Next election: 1992.

DONALD W. RIEGLE JR.
Democrat — Michigan

Connection to Keating: A major Detroit hotel owned by American Continental.

- Met with Lincoln's auditor in February 1987, to discuss its problems with regulators. In a March 1987 meeting with Gray on other matters, Riegle suggested he meet with the four other senators and the next day took a tour of Keating's Phoenix headquarters.
- Attended April 9, 1987, meeting with regulators.
- Received $78,250 from Keating and associates for his 1988 re-election; returned that money in March 1988. In July 1990, Riegle announced he would return all thrift industry individual and political action committee (PAC) contributions received since 1983 — about $120,000 — and no longer accept money from PACs and officers of companies under purview of committees he chaired.

Main Senate post: Chairman of Banking Committee.

Next election: 1994.

Continued from p. 78
than a month until his $5 million bail was reduced. The federal government sought $1.1 billion from Keating and some of his associates in civil penalties on racketeering charges and $40.9 million in restitution for money that allegedly was siphoned improperly from Lincoln.

Lincoln's failure was the subject of six intense days of hearings in 1989 by the House Banking Committee. Its chairman, Henry B. Gonzalez, D-Texas, looked broadly at Keating's business practices and the regulatory failures that allowed Lincoln to collapse so spectacularly. He called the scandal a mini-Watergate.

Keating appeared at those hearings but refused to testify, citing his constitutional protection against self-incrimination. (He later claimed the same privilege when subpoenaed to testify by the Senate Ethics Committee, as did six other American Continental employees.) *(Lincoln hearings, 1989 Almanac p. 133)*

Ethics Complaint

The Keating case first came to the attention of the Ethics Committee when Ohio Republicans filed a complaint against Glenn on Sept. 26, 1989. Common Cause, an independent citizens' group that filed the charges leading to the resignation of House Speaker Jim Wright, D-Texas, in 1989, sent a letter Oct. 13 seeking an investigation of all five senators.

On Nov. 17, 1989, the committee named Robert S. Bennett as special counsel for the matter. Bennett was handling the committee's investigation into the finances of Sen. Dave Durenberger, R-Minn., which resulted in discipline for Durenberger in July 1990. A preliminary inquiry into the Keating case was announced Dec. 22, 1989. *(Durenberger, p. 98)*

The committee was evenly divided between the two parties. The chairman, Howell Heflin, D-Ala., was a former chief justice of the Alabama Supreme Court known for his caution and deliberative pace. Almost as important a player was the Republican vice chairman, Warren B. Rudman of New Hampshire, a hard-charging former state attorney general. The other members were Democrats David Pryor, Ark., and Terry Sanford, N.C., and Republicans Jesse Helms, N.C., and Trent Lott, Miss.

The investigation remained out of the public eye for the first part of 1990 as Bennett's staff quietly collected documents and interviewed witnesses, including the senators under investigation.

Contributions Under Scrutiny

Although none of the senators was up for re-election in 1990, the publicity accorded the Keating case cast a shadow over their future electoral prospects and spilled over into other races.

On Nov. 8, 1990, shortly before the hearings commenced, Cranston announced he would not run again in 1992 because of health problems. The terms of McCain and Glenn lasted through 1992; DeConcini and Riegle would not be up again until 1994.

There were ominous warning signs, however, in the 1990 elections. Two House members with direct thrift connections lost their re-election bids — Charles "Chip" Pashayan Jr., R-Calif., who had ties to Keating, and Denny Smith, R-Ore., who was personally involved with another failed thrift.

Public opinion polls conducted on Election Day reported that by margins of 60 percent or higher, voters in Arizona and Michigan believed that DeConcini and Riegle should either resign or not run again when their terms expired.

Political contributions from the savings and loan industry, whether tied to Keating or not, became controversial. Common Cause released a study June 29 identifying more than $11.6 million in contributions from S&L interests to members of Congress and political parties in the 1980s.

Four of the Keating Five senators — Riegle ($200,900), Cranston ($143,700), DeConcini ($84,200) and McCain ($80,393) — ranked among the top 10 senators. (Glenn, with $32,600, was 30th.)

Tops among all members was Cranston's Republican colleague from California, Wilson, with $243,334. California politicians were seven of the top 10 S&L fundraisers in the House, led by Republican Bill Lowery, with $85,088. Many of the nation's largest and most profitable thrifts were located in California.

To compile the study, Common Cause sifted through Federal Election Commission (FEC) records of contributors from January 1981 to April 1990. It identified money given by 157 PACs operated by thrifts and their trade associations and by 1,074 individuals affiliated with S&Ls, including family members.

Riegle announced July 19 that he would turn over to the Treasury all campaign contributions he had received since 1983 from political action committees (PACs) and individuals tied to the thrift industry.

At the same time, Riegle said that he would no longer accept contributions from PACs or officers of companies whose principal business was under the jurisdiction of the Banking Committee or the Finance Subcommittee on Health, both of which he chaired.

Riegle said the amount in question, up to $120,000, was about 2 percent of his total contributions — "a tiny amount, chicken feed." He cast the decision as a personal effort at campaign finance reform. Riegle was a cosponsor of a bill (S 137) to limit campaign spending. *(Campaign finance legislation, p. 59)*

Preliminary Skirmishes

Bennett was preoccupied with the Durenberger investigation until July 25, when the Senate voted to denounce the Minnesota senator. But Bennett's staff had kept working on the Keating case, and on Sept. 10, he gave the Ethics Committee a 350-page report and thousands of pages of supporting evidence. It was widely reported that he recommended dismissing the cases of Glenn and McCain and proceeding with charges against the other three, but the committee kept silent about the contents of the report.

After studying the report, the committee took testimony from the five senators in early October. In the middle of October, leaks began to spring that increased the heat on Cranston, DeConcini and Riegle, and the other senators protested that they should be separated from the case.

Reports by The New York Times, The Washington Post and The Associated Press, among other media organizations, indicated that the three senators were more deeply involved with Keating than previously had been disclosed.

McCain took the Senate floor Oct. 22 to ask for Bennett's report to be released and its recommendation to be acted on quickly. "Justice delayed is justice denied," McCain said. Other senators joined his cause. Senate Democratic leaders denounced the leaks and suggested that Republicans wanted to hurry the case in order to leave only Democrats under suspicion as the elections approached.

Special Counsel Bennett: No Shrinking Violet

The Keating Five case was the third celebrated investigation Washington lawyer Robert S. Bennett had handled for the Senate Ethics Committee.

A partner in the Washington office of the New York law firm of Skadden, Arps, Slate, Meagher & Flom, Bennett was hired in 1989 to lead the committee's investigation into allegations that Sen. Dave Durenberger, R-Minn., breached ethics rules. That case concluded in July with the Senate denouncing Durenberger. *(Durenberger case, p. 98)*

Bennett also led the Senate inquiry into the actions of Sen. Harrison A. Williams Jr. in 1981, growing out of the Abscam scandal, which resulted in Williams' resignation in 1982. *(1982 Almanac, p. 509)*

In the Durenberger case, Bennett's tough manner, even sarcastic at times, had set some senators on edge.

During floor proceedings in the Durenberger case July 25, former prosecutor Dale Bumpers, D-Ark., questioned Bennett's role as finder of both facts and law for the committee. "Is that not the prerogative and the duty of the committee and the U.S. Senate and not the special counsel?" he asked.

And Don Nickles, R-Okla., went further in his criticism. "I did not really see a special counsel; I saw a prosecutor. And it bothered me," he said.

Ethics Committee members defended Bennett on the floor then, and the panel's leaders — Chairman Howell Heflin, D-Ala., and Vice Chairman Warren B. Rudman, R-N.H. — frequently came to his defense during the Keating hearings.

Heflin cautioned early in the proceedings that Bennett's role "must be carried out impartially," but added: "It is inevitable that at times he may appear to be prosecutorial."

That was definitely the opinion of some of the other key players in the case. Bennett was despised by some of the senators in the dock, and some committee members complained about the relevance and breadth of evidence he marshaled.

On the first day of the hearings, Pryor questioned Bennett's presentation. "In my opinion, you're beginning to reach personal conclusions, and also, you are deciding for us what is relevant and not relevant. I think that is our decision to make," Pryor said.

Bennett, known as an attorney who reveled in a courtroom brawl, was hobbled by the rules of the Keating proceeding. Because the hearing took place before any official charges were filed, he was not supposed to act as a prosecutor but — in the words of committee Chairman Heflin — as an impartial fact-finder "to re-create the past events that are at the center of this controversy, in a manner which is not prejudicial to any party." Bennett was clearly unhappy in that corset of impartiality.

Bennett was accused in the first days of tilting the facts. "The facts tilt," he replied. He was accused of creating a new "appearance standard" against which the senators should be judged. "These are not my standards; these are your standards," he told the committee repeatedly. He was accused throughout the hearings of relying upon hearsay rather than hard evidence of impropriety. But Heflin and Rudman allowed hearsay to be admitted by all parties.

More than any of the other senators under inquiry, Dennis DeConcini, D-Ariz., himself a former prosecutor, bristled at Bennett's performance, repeatedly calling him a special prosecutor, not a special counsel.

On the next to last day of the hearings, James Hamilton, DeConcini's attorney, stung Bennett with affidavits from two former U.S. attorneys accusing him of unfairness.

"Mr. Bennett's conduct is going to be an issue," Hamilton said, if the committee should recommend that the full Senate discipline DeConcini. "I think it is fair to say that on the floor of the Senate there are many issues that may affect a senator's judgment."

Bennett fired back: "Sen. DeConcini and his counsel would like me to be a flower girl distributing the flowers at a wedding in equal shares to each senator without regard to the evidence. I will not do that.

"I think the not-so-subtle threat to this committee is an outrage and you should be offended by it," he said.

On Oct. 23, the committee voted unanimously to open a fact-finding hearing including all five soon after the November elections. The committee reportedly had split in a vote to follow Bennett's recommendation and dismiss McCain and Glenn. Those two senators objected strongly to the decision.

By receiving a report from Bennett at the outset and by scheduling public hearings without making preliminary judgments, the committee departed from the typical steps taken in other recent ethics cases, which would have led to a public hearing only after official charges were filed. The committee's resolution said that the committee would, barring "extraordinary circumstances," conclude the case by Dec. 31. But the hearings continued beyond that date.

Throughout the Senate hearings, Keating remained a shadow on the hearing-room wall. His broad-ranging legal troubles kept him far from the Hart Senate Office Building, where the hearings took place. Committee members said that no thought was given to forcing Keating to testify by granting limited immunity from prosecution — largely because of the chance that doing so would make it difficult to prosecute him in court. Bennett remarked in his opening statement, "One could ask the question: If Mr. Keating was here, would you believe what he said anyway?"

Cranston announced, a week before the hearings were scheduled to begin, that he had prostate cancer and would be unable to attend the hearings while he was undergoing treatment in California beginning in late November. He anounced at the same time that he would not seek another term as Democratic whip and would not run for re-election in 1992.

TESTIMONY AT HEARINGS

The hearings opened Nov. 15 to the glare of television lights in a large wood- and marble-paneled hearing room in the Hart Building. Eight long tables were reserved for the press. Each senator was given his own desk, next to one for his attorney.

In his opening remarks, Heflin provided an evenhanded view of the problem that gave little insight into his own idea of the standard to which the senators would have to be held. Rudman offered an equally oblique view, noting only that "the committee cannot act on the basis of laws, rules and standards that some people might like to see."

Pryor and Helms did not address the issue of standards at all.

But Lott and Sanford, the two most junior members of the committee, each offered detailed views of what might constitute an ethical violation.

Sanford seemed to challenge the tough standards Bennett had laid down for the committee to consider.

"In rulemaking and administrative matters, the member may ... specifically or indirectly ask for favorable action," Sanford said. "The member may ... complain about the treatment of citizens by investigators or other staff members of the agency." And, he said, "the member may call for reconsideration of a decision."

And, Sanford argued, "if indeed there is an appearance of wrongdoing when in fact no wrongdoing is found, the problem is not that of the individual, but of the institution." It would be unfair, he said, "to impose penalties for this appearance on individual senators."

Lott said he could identify a specific point at which intervention with regulators became improper. "The line is crossed, and the action is improper," he said, "if a senator requests that the regulator break the law, if he demands the regulator take a specific action or if he threatens the regulator with reprisal."

On the second day of the hearings, Cranston's attorney, William W. Taylor III, asked Helms to step aside from the deliberations because of remarks Helms had made in an early November campaign appearance drawing connections between Cranston and Keating. Helms refused, and the committee did not press the point.

Bennett's Opening

Committee special counsel Bennett laid out in broad strokes the case he would make over the next two months. Much of what Bennett cited had long been known. But he offered some new information — including affidavits and memorandums — that suggested the possibility of specific connections between Keating's fundraising and some actions by the senators. *(Bennett opening statement, p. 83; profile, p. 81)*

Bennett was in an unusual position. Unlike in the Durenberger case, he was not presenting a set of formal charges. Instead, he had to present all relevant facts and gently suggest to the committee members how they might view them.

"I'm not suggesting that there is wrongdoing at this stage," he told the committee at the start of his presentation. Nevertheless, he repeatedly said the evidence would show actions that could be interpreted by the committee as violations.

Bennett noted that he and his staff interviewed 140 people, took affidavits from 44 of them and deposed 16 witnesses. That did not count the seven — among them Keating — who refused to testify, citing their constitutional prerogatives.

Bennett said his most important witness would not be a person. "The most important witnesses are the product of the examination of the pieces of paper," he said. "Ernest Hemingway once said that paper doesn't bleed, and what I think he meant by that is that paper isn't subject to the normal human frailty." The paper he would introduce, Bennett said, had special credibility because it "never thought it would be here."

Bennett said the evidence pointed to a strategy by Keating to pressure regulators by seeking assistance from members of Congress. And to do so, Bennett said, Keating engineered "substantial sums for political contributions."

"It is clear," Bennett said, "that Sens. Cranston and DeConcini were important players in Mr. Keating's strategy." He added, "I must reluctantly state that there is substantial evidence that Sen. Riegle played a much greater role than he now recalls.... The evidence shows that Sen. Riegle played an important role at the early stages."

Bennett confirmed that he had found little evidence that Glenn or McCain had stepped across the line of propriety. "Was there anything improper about Sen. McCain's conduct? The evidence discovered by special counsel suggests not," Bennett told the committee. Later, he said, "We know of no evidence linking [political] contributions to any action on the part of Sen. Glenn."

Keating began to seek help from members of both chambers in 1984-86, when he and other thrift executives from around the country were seeking help from Congress to stop the Federal Home Loan Bank Board from putting in force a regulation limiting direct ownership by thrifts of real estate and other assets.

More than 200 House members cosponsored legislation in 1985 to delay the direct investment rule, and numerous senators denounced it. But efforts to nullify the rule went nowhere. Bennett said he looked for but could not find any evidence to suggest that the five senators lobbied on the rule as a result of Keating's contributions.

"Throughout the period that these four senators [all but Riegle] were responding to Mr. Keating's request for assistance in derailing the direct investment rule, they did receive political contributions from Mr. Keating and his associates." Bennett said. "There is insufficient evidence that any of the senators, any of them, asked for or expected that he would receive such contributions contemporaneously with Lincoln's request for assistance in opposing the rule. I looked for it, can't read it. It wasn't there."

Where Bennett Saw Problems

The key events of the investigation were two meetings held in April 1987. In the first, on April 2, four of the senators (but not Riegle) met privately in DeConcini's office with Edwin J. Gray, then chairman of the Federal Home Loan Bank Board, which was responsible for regulating the thrift industry. Gray contended after the meeting that the senators pressured him to withdraw the direct investment rule, which would rein in Lincoln's ability to pursue its high-flying investment strategy.

At the second meeting, held April 9 in DeConcini's office, all five of the senators met with bank board employees who were examining Lincoln's books. Bennett contended that notes taken at the meeting by one of the regulators showed that at least some senators were trying to ease the pressure on Lincoln. The meeting broke up shortly after the examiners revealed confidential information that they were going to make criminal referrals to the Justice Department about some Lincoln practices. Bennett said a key reason for differentiating Glenn and McCain

Continued on p. 86

Overview of Case Against 'Keating Five'

Following are excerpts from the opening statement of Robert S. Bennett, special counsel to the Senate Ethics Committee, at the beginning Nov. 15 of hearings into the Keating Five — Sens. Alan Cranston, D-Calif.; Dennis DeConcini, D-Ariz.; John Glenn, D-Ohio; John McCain, R-Ariz.; and Donald W. Riegle Jr., D-Mich.:

Because there is a great deal of misunderstanding about such subjects as constituent service and political contributions, it is essential — absolutely essential — if we are to be fair to these five senators and to the Senate as an institution, to articulate the applicable standards and principles on which you must judge the evidence....

What are the applicable standards? Senate Resolution 338, Section 2(a) as amended makes it the duty of this committee to investigate and recommend discipline for members who engage in improper conduct which may reflect upon the Senate.... In determining what is improper conduct the committee must ... consider the totality of the circumstances surrounding the conduct under inquiry.

What are the standards and the principles in this case that exist now?

One, a senator should not take contributions from an individual he knows or should know is attempting to procure his services to intervene in a specific matter pending before a federal agency....

Two, a senator should not take unusual or aggressive action with regard to a specific matter before a federal agency on behalf of a contributor when he knows or has reason to know the contributor has sought to procure his services.

Three, a senator should not conduct his fundraising efforts or engage in office practices which lead contributors to conclude that they can buy access to him.

Four, in addition to these, what are commonly called more objective standards, there is a well-recognized and established appearance standard.... And that standard is this. A senator should not engage in conduct which would appear to be improper to a reasonable, nonpartisan, fully informed person. Such conduct undermines the public's confidence in the integrity of the government and is an abuse of one's official position. Such conduct is wrong in addition to appearing to be wrong....

* * *

We are not talking about appearances to uninformed persons who do not understand the legal and ethical aspects of constituent service or political contributions, or who do not understand the legitimate realities of American political life, namely, that there should be to some extent, for the health of our democracy, a rough-and-tumble play between this body and the executive branches of government....

Let's talk just a little bit about constituent service. Even though it is not mentioned in the Constitution, there can be little doubt that constituent service is a valuable part of our system of government. Its absolutely chief function is to provide a check on the abuse of power by executive agencies in individual cases....

Now, simply because constituent service is generally a good thing, it does not mean, members of the committee, by merely asserting that "what I did was constituent service," that by simply that, that a senator can erect an impenetrable shield barring ethical inquiry.

While important, constituent service cannot be elevated to the status of a religion....

* * *

Now in this regard, let me make a point that is of absolute importance: Let me state that it would be grossly unfair to conclude that these senators were responsible for the collapse of the Lincoln Savings and Loan, or that they urged or condoned the sale of ACC [American Continental Corp., Lincoln's parent] bonds at Lincoln branches which has caused such hardship to so many people.

But ... there is another side. While it is unfair to blame these particular senators, or any of them, for the very heavy burden to be borne by the taxpayers of this country for Lincoln's losses, it is not unfair to ask them whether or not — or at least some of them — before acting on Mr. Keating's behalf, carefully analyzed what the impact would be if Mr. Keating's goals, which were the objectives of senatorial intervention, were achieved?...

This case also presents the issue of the propriety of performing constituent service for someone who is a political contributor. Under our system of government, there is absolutely nothing wrong, and this is where there is a lot of public misperception, if a senator provides constituent services for a political contributor. A judge cannot take money from a litigant. A member of the executive branch cannot take money from a contractor. An honorable and an ethical U.S. senator can and indeed must take money from his political contributors. That is a part of our system. It would be absolutely absurd to say that you can help those who do not support you, as Sen. [Terry] Sanford [D-N.C.] says, but you cannot help those who do.

* * *

Now before we start looking at all the trees ... let's talk about the forest a little bit. Charles Keating was the chairman and the controlling shareholder of ACC, the American Continental Corp., an Ohio-chartered company. In February of 1984, ACC acquired Lincoln. Lincoln was a federally insured California-chartered S&L. Lincoln operated in California, but its executives and most of its employees were in Arizona. And there is simply no doubt that Mr. Keating personally controlled Lincoln insofar as all of the events relevant to this proceeding. And even though it was state-chartered, it had to comply with certain regulations of the Federal Home Loan Bank Board, or the FHLBB, to enjoy the significant benefit of having its accountants protected by federal insurance, and that's why you are receiving all these letters and all these calls, because there was federal insurance.

In May of 1984, three months after ACC acquired Lincoln, the bank board proposed a regulation to limit severely the amount of direct investments. Specifically, the so-called direct investment rule sought to restrict the kinds and amounts of investments that S&Ls could make. Now for many years S&Ls made almost all of their investments in long-term home mortgages, 30-year mortgages, at fixed rates. And there is simply no question that because of inflation and the high cost of borrowing, many S&Ls were caught in a squeeze. As a result, in the early '80s, regulators permitted S&Ls to make so-called direct investments, which by nature were riskier but more profitable than home mortgage loans.

After some experience with the more liberal investment policy, the Federal Home Loan Bank Board perceived that S&Ls were engaged in speculative and sometimes, not always, but sometimes risky investments. And this was of major concern to Ed Gray [Edwin J. Gray, former chairman of the Federal Home Loan Bank Board]. The direct investment rule was proposed to restrict these riskier investments and after a very lengthy notice and comment period, a modified proposal was published in 1984.

Consultants that were hired by Lincoln's law firm submitted various reports and comments to the board concerning the rule. And this included a 108-page report ... that was authored by two economists, George Benson and Alan Greenspan, who is now chairman of the Federal Reserve....

The final rule was promulgated in January 1985. The direct investments which were made before Dec. 10 or which were in the works before Dec. 10, 1984, were grandfathered. In other words, they were allowed to stand. Now although Mr. Keating controlled Lincoln only for a very short period of time before implementation of the rule, Lincoln made substantial direct investments. Indeed, one of the major disputes that developed between the bank board and Lincoln was whether $600 million in direct investments made by Lincoln qualified for grandfather....

The day after the rule was promulgated, Lincoln applied for an exemption to permit it to make up to $900 million in direct investments, and this was denied.

Now throughout this period of time that I've just been talking about that this rule was pending, Lincoln and Mr. Keating aggressively lobbied members of Congress to oppose implementation of the rule. For our purposes, this included Sens. Cranston and DeConcini, Sens. Glenn and John McCain, who was at that time a congressman. Sen. Riegle has no recollection and we have found no evidence to indicate that he was asked to take any action on Mr. Keating or Lincoln regarding the direct investment program. Sens. Cranston, DeConcini and Glenn, and Rep. McCain wrote letters to Chairman Gray and these letters urged [him] to postpone implementation of the rule to give Congress time to consider the matter.

Sens. DeConcini and Glenn additionally wrote letters to the Banking Committee members.... Sen. DeConcini also drafted and circulated legislation to delay implementation of the rule for one year....

Now Charles Keating was by no means, and this is important, the exclusive opponent of this direct investment rule. And it must be said that these four senators were part of a very large group of lawmakers who questioned its wisdom. The lobbying by Mr. Keating and others garnered the support of numerous lawmakers, and at one point Rep. [Frank] Annunzio [D-Ill.] introduced a resolution to delay implementation of the regulation for six months. This resolution had more than 200 sponsors, including then-Rep. McCain.

Now it's very important that what I am about to say is listened to, particularly by the members of the press, carefully. Throughout the period that these four senators were responding to Mr. Keating's request for assistance in derailing the direct investment rule, they did receive political contributions from Mr. Keating and his associates. The contemporaneousness of some of these contributions with the senators' conduct in opposition to limitations on direct investments was of initial concern. However, there is insufficient evidence that any of the senators, any of them, asked for or expected that he would receive such contributions contemporaneously with Lincoln's request for assistance in opposing the rule. I looked for it, can't read it. It wasn't there. Couldn't find it, and I don't think it exists....

Now, when Mr. Keating failed to delay promulgation of the direct investment rule, his tactics became much more aggressive. In short, Mr. Keating made the decision — it is very clear from the paper — to engage in an all-out war with Gray and the board.

Mr. Keating tried, and with the help of Sen. DeConcini, briefly succeeded, to place Keating's man, Lee [H.] Henkel [Jr.], on the bank board. In addition, Mr. Keating took legal action against the board and Chairman Gray, and engaged in a media campaign attacking the chairman, and perhaps some of the attacks were justified — not particularly relevant to our ethical issue here.

For our purposes, an essential key to Mr. Keating's strategy was to put as much political pressure on Chairman Gray and the board as possible, and to do this, the paper clearly shows that he sought the assistance of many members of Congress, and he also raised substantial sums for political contributions to members of Congress, including the ... senators who sit before you today....

The high-water mark of Mr. Keating's strategy came when he, Mr. Keating, engineered a meeting on April 2, 1987, between Chairman Gray and Sens. Cranston, DeConcini, Glenn and McCain. This meeting led to another one April 9, 1987, between four officials of the Federal Home Loan Bank Board's San Francisco office, and those senators plus Sen. Riegle, but Mr. Keating continued to bring political pressure to bear on the board even after those meetings, and even after Mr. Gray was no longer chairman. Mr. Wall — Mr. M. Danny Wall, who was chairman of the board from 1987 to 1989 — Sens. DeConcini and Cranston contacted him on behalf of Lincoln on Mr. Keating's request....

It is clear from the paper and it will be clear from the testimony — that Sens. Cranston and DeConcini were important players in Mr. Keating's strategy. While Sens. Glenn and McCain were active participants in opposing the direct investment rule and attended the meetings on April 2 and 9, they were not the organizers of the meeting, nor did they play any meaningful role on Mr. Keating's behalf after the meetings.

Sen. Riegle has advised this committee that he has little recollection of relevant past events regarding the Keating matter, but that based on his reconstruction of events, he firmly believes that he did nothing wrong. He has told the committee that, based upon his reconstruction of events, he is certain that his role was minor and largely passive.

However, members of the committee, I must reluctantly state that there is substantial evidence that Sen. Riegle played a much greater role than he now recalls. While Sens. Cranston and DeConcini were by far the most active on Mr. Keating's behalf, the evidence shows that Sen. Riegle played an important role at the early stages. On the other hand, it is to be said for Sen. Riegle that, like Sens. Glenn and McCain, his efforts on behalf of Lincoln appear to have ended as of April 9, 1987....

* * *

On March 6, 1987, Sen. Riegle set into motion plans for the meeting with Chairman Gray. When he told Chairman Gray that he should meet with several other senators who were concerned about Lincoln — this occurred March 6 — Chairman Gray claims that he protested but that Sen. Riegle told him that he would be getting a call from several senators.

The very next day, Sen. Riegle left on a trip to Phoenix that included, according to documents, a fundraising visit to ACC and at least a brief meeting with Mr. Keating.

Sen. Riegle has testified that he was unaware of the fundraising aspects of this trip. However, there are several documents which I'll present in evidence, which, I respectfully submit, rebut Sen. Riegle's claim.

After some time after Sen. Riegle, according to the evidence, returned from his trip to Phoenix sometime in March — we believe it was either the 16th or the 17th of March — Sen. DeConcini approached Sen. Riegle, asking Sen. Riegle what he, Sen. Riegle, thought would be the best way to deal with Lincoln's problems with the bank board.

Sen. Riegle told Sen. DeConcini that meeting with Mr. Gray would be a good way of handling Mr. Keating's complaints. Sen. Riegle did not tell Sen. DeConcini that he already had spoken to Chairman Gray about this on March 6, 1987.

Three, Sen. DeConcini took the lead role in setting up the meeting. He made the arrangements, and he contacted Sen. McCain, Sen. Cranston, Sen. Glenn, with both a time and a place. And he also contacted Chairman Gray.

There is no question by the evidence that a decision was made that no aides would be present. While in fairness to the senator, Sen. DeConcini, he denies that it was his instruction, the overwhelming evidence suggests that the no-aides instruction came from Sen. DeConcini's office....

Under all of the circumstances, including the articulated purpose of the meeting, it is at best strange that there was a purposeful effort made to exclude staff. The most troubling aspect, according to the evidence, of the no-aides policy is not that the senators did not have aides, but that Chairman Gray was given a clear instruction from someone in Sen. DeConcini's office to come alone. This troubled Chairman Gray and he complained to his staff about it before the meeting. ...

The senators who attended the meeting each had different agendas in mind. The evidence shows that the purpose of the meeting, at least in the mind of Sen. DeConcini, was to put substantial pressure on Mr. Gray so as to get the board to adopt certain goals of Mr. Keating, goals that were memorialized in the paper, memorialized in correspondence and staff memoranda.... The other senators were there with varying degrees of intensity to pressure the board to end promptly the link in examination.

... [T]he mere fact that a senator puts pressure on a regulator, even substantial pressure, is not, under existing standards, not in and of itself improper. However, the application of pressure is an important fact in our totality of circumstances analysis.

Chairman Gray — this is point seven — Chairman Gray says that Sen. DeConcini proposed at that April 2 meeting that the direct investment rule, which was duly promulgated, all the rules were followed, be withdrawn, and in return Lincoln would make more home loans. Mr. Gray characterized it as a quid pro quo....

Eight, Sen. DeConcini denies Chairman Gray's description of what occurred April 2. On the other hand, several other senators refused to say flatly that Chairman Gray's version is false....

Moreover, Sen. DeConcini's undisputed comments of April 9 to the San Francisco regulators strongly suggest the accuracy of Mr. Gray's position.

* * *

The memo of the April 9 meeting ... speaks for itself. It was written by William Black, one of the bank board officials who attended the meeting. ... Everyone who has seen that memo says that this transcript-like memo is accurate in all essential respects.

Now, that is important, not only because it is a reliable report of April 9, but also because it largely corroborates Chairman Gray's version, absent the gloss, of what occurred on April 2. ...

A fair reading of that memo, ... I suggest, reveals clearly that Sen. DeConcini was negotiating or trying to strike a deal for Lincoln. ...

As I will make clear shortly, all senators were not present when Sen. DeConcini made his statement on page four of the Black memo. Let me read that statement to you. ... This is Sen. DeConcini: "We wanted to meet with you because we have determined that potential actions of yours could injure a constituent. This is a particular concern to us, because Lincoln is willing to take substantial actions to deal with what we understand to be your concerns. Lincoln is prepared to go into a major home loan program, up to 55 percent of its assets. We understand that that's what the bank board wants S&Ls to do. It's prepared to limit its high risk bondholdings in real estate investments. It's even willing to phase out of the insurance process if you wish.

"They have two major disagreements with you. First with regard to direct investment. Second on your reappraisal. They're suing against your direct investment regulation. I can't make a judgment on the grandfathering issue. We suggest that the lawsuit be accelerated, and that you grant them forbearance while the suit is pending."

I ask you, is this appropriate constituent service?

It is also clear from the memo that the senators were told that a criminal referral would be made, and, more importantly, that that criminal conduct to some extent was described, such as file stuffing. Serious regulations, serious violations of regulations, were described.

And in fact, a criminal referral was made a few weeks later. ...

In fairness to Sen. McCain, ... immediately after this statement was made, Sen. McCain was troubled, injected himself, and raised questions as to certain things. ...

There is no question that there is substantial evidence that the meeting was tense, and that in the view of the regulators, it was extraordinary. The regulators concluded that Mr. Keating and Lincoln had unusual and substantial political muscle.

In fairness to all senators, Chairman Gray and the San Francisco regulators say that they were not intimidated by either meeting, and they were not threatened by the senators. They further say that the meetings had no effect on either the timing or the findings contained in San Francisco's Lincoln examination report, which was issued just three weeks later.

But as I will show, the senatorial intervention made itself well-known throughout the system, that Mr. Keating was a pretty special person who could bring together four senators one week and five senators seven days later.

* * *

Let's talk just for a few minutes about contacts through fundraisers. There are many examples of Mr. Keating using fundraisers as a conduit for obtaining a senator's assistance on an issue.

Earl Katz was Sen. DeConcini's campaign finance manager and chief fundraiser. In 1985, Mr. Keating went through fundraiser Earl Katz to get Sen. DeConcini to call Sen. [Jake] Garn [R-Utah] about holding Banking Committee hearings on the direct investment rule. ... It lays it out, and at the bottom is a note from Sen. DeConcini that he made the call, and that Mr. Keating was told, or words to the effect, that the call was made. ...

It should be noted that Mr. Katz, who was a good friend of Sen. DeConcini's, was indebted to Lincoln for millions of dollars.

Two, Joy Jacobson was Sen. Cranston's campaign finance chairman, and a chief fundraiser for his voter registration groups. Mr. Keating and his staff repeatedly dealt with Ms. Jacobson, to get on the senator's schedule, or to make requests of the senator, to meet with or call the chairman of the bank board. ...

What message is a senator sending to constituents who need his help when he allows his fundraiser to be seen as holding the keys to access to both his time and his attention? I ask you, why should fundraisers like Joy Jacobson and Earl Katz, who are not even employees of the U.S. Senate, play such a role in the nation's business? ...

Another approach of Mr. Keating was the use of senators who were on the Banking Committee. The Senate Banking Committee, it must be emphasized, had oversight responsibilities for the Federal Home Loan Bank Board. ...

Mr. Keating made numerous requests that Sen. Cranston contact the bank board on his behalf. Sen. Cranston, at the time, was the second-ranking member of the Banking Committee, and he had approximately one dozen contacts with bank board Chairman Danny Wall from 1987 to 1989. And he also called other board members on behalf of Lincoln.

As I will show in a little while, Mr. [Bruce] Babbitt, Gov. Babbitt, the distinguished governor of Arizona, Democratic presidential candidate, a man who was devoted to his constituents, a man who follows all the things we're talking about, about the importance of constituent service, told Sen. Alan Cranston in a meeting, when asked, that Charles Keating was, quote, a crook. ...

Finally, the timing and circumstances of Mr. Keating's contributions. It is evident from a chronology of contributions and conduct in this case that Mr. Keating more often than not coupled his requests for assistance with a marshaling of campaign contributions. ... One, within a few days — a few weeks of the date that Sen. Glenn wrote letters at Lincoln's request seeking to delay the direct investment rule, Mr. Keating sent checks from ACC employees for Sen. Glenn's presidential and Senate campaigns.

This happened twice. In July 1984, $10,000, and in December 1984, $8,200. ... Sen. Glenn denies that he was aware of this.

Two, there is evidence that at the same time Mr. Keating brought his complaints about the bank board to Sen. Riegle in early 1987, he also offered to organize a fundraiser for Sen. Riegle. In February to March 1987, as the meeting with Chairman Gray was being implemented, Mr. Keating and his associates contributed more than $70,000 to Sen. Riegle's campaign. Now, we have been unable to find any evidence of Sen. Riegle ever receiving any monies from Mr. Keating prior to the time that he was on the board, on the Banking Committee.

Now, in July of 1985, Sen. DeConcini called White House officials at Mr. Keating's request, and he asked that Ed Gray be removed from office.

That same month, Mr. Keating raised $20,000 for his campaign. Likewise, in the summer of '86, Sen. DeConcini lobbied heavily, at Mr. Keating's request, for the appointment to the bank board of Lee Henkel, a man that we understand that the senator had never met. Mr. Keating raised $11,000 for Sen. DeConcini's campaign that summer.

In Sen. Cranston's case there's evidence that on a number of occasions Mr. Keating's company gave hundreds of thousands of dollars, and we'll get into the details shortly, to Sen. Cranston's voter registration groups at or about the same time he asked for and received the senator's help.

Now, there is a question that I want to raise and I want to make this very, very clear. I don't think that there is any question that raising monies for minority groups so they can increase voter registration is a very important thing for our democracy. But one is forced to ask, didn't the thought ever occur to Sen. Cranston — and I suppose I can say this — he's known as a liberal Democrat — why would Mr. Keating, the anti-pornographer, the well-known Republican — why would he be giving hundreds and hundreds of thousands of dollars to someone so that more black citizens and more Hispanic citizens could vote? ...

Now Mr. Keating himself said at a press conference in April, quote — and I think you can put very little stock in what he says — "One question among the many raised in recent weeks had to do with whether my financial support in any way influenced several political figures to take up my cause. I want to say in the most forceful way I can, I certainly hope so." ■

Continued from p. 82
from the other senators was that the first two saw the need to back away from Keating after they learned there might be a criminal investigation into Keating and Lincoln. (Riegle backed away as well.)

In his opening, Bennett homed in on an unusual aspect of the first meeting: that Gray was told to bring no aides with him. "While in fairness to the senator, Sen. DeConcini, he denies that it was his instruction, the overwhelming evidence suggests that the no-aides instruction came from Sen. DeConcini's office.... Under all of the circumstances, including the articulated purpose of the meeting, it is at best strange that there was a purposeful effort made to exclude staff."

Detailed notes of the second meeting taken by one of the regulators seemed to be unusually accurate, Bennett said, and they indicated that DeConcini seemed to be negotiating in behalf of Lincoln.

Bennett made clear that he viewed Cranston's efforts in Keating's behalf to be the most questionable. He received the most money from Keating, he allowed his fundraisers to serve as an important link with Keating, he remained active in helping Keating into 1989, and he seemed the most ideologically incompatible with Keating.

"The evidence will show," Bennett said, "that on approximately four separate occasions Sen. Cranston accepted or solicited several hundred thousand dollars from Mr. Keating for Sen. Cranston's voting registration groups and that each of these four occasions was linked by time and circumstance to a request by Mr. Keating for assistance with the bank board."

Those events, from early 1987 to early 1989, were documented by extensive memorandums from Cranston's fundraiser, Joy Jacobson, Bennett said.

"One is forced to ask, didn't the thought ever occur to Sen. Cranston — and I suppose I can say this — he's known as a liberal Democrat — why would Mr. Keating, the anti-pornographer, the well-known Republican — why would he be giving hundreds and hundreds of thousands of dollars" to Cranston's pet political causes, Bennett asked.

Bennett's Standards

Establishing the facts of the case was substantially easier than deciding at what point a senator's conduct crossed ethical boundaries.

The senators maintained to a man that they had been intervening in behalf of their constituents (depositors, American Continental and Lincoln employees, and so forth), and that they had only questioned regulators to ascertain whether an important economic entity was being treated fairly.

Bennett spent much of his opening statement, delivered Nov. 15 and 16, laying out the standards by which he thought a senator should be judged.

Bennett said there was no doubt that intervention was proper, but he set several "objective" standards for when such intervention might be appropriate. These were:

- A senator should not take contributions from an individual he knows or should know is attempting to procure his services to intervene in a specific matter pending before a federal agency.
- A senator should not take unusual or aggressive action with regard to a specific matter before a federal agency on behalf of a contributor when he knows or has reason to know the contributor has sought to procure his services.
- A senator should not conduct his fundraising efforts or engage in office practices that lead contributors to conclude that they can buy access to him.
- A senator should not engage in conduct which would appear to be improper to a reasonable, nonpartisan, fully informed person.

Most controversial was Bennett's contention that the senators should also be judged by a broader "appearance standard," under which a senator should not do anything "which would appear to be improper to a reasonable, nonpartisan, fully informed person." He argued that a senator could be disciplined for violating that standard even if his specific actions did not, in themselves, directly violate a Senate rule. *(Appearance standard, p. 87)*

Senators' Presentations

After Bennett finished his overview of the case, the senators responded in person — some claiming that Bennett's presentation exonerated them, others protesting that Bennett gave a one-sided case that ignored exculpatory evidence and drew too-neat connections between Keating's fundraising efforts and their actions. Four of the senators gave their statements on Nov. 16, immediately after Bennett had finished his; DeConcini waited until the hearing resumed on Nov. 19 after a weekend break. *(Senators' opening statements, p. 89)*

For Riegle, it was his first detailed comment on the Keating affair, and he held forth for an hour, focusing particularly on Bennett's suspicion that Keating's fundraising might have influenced the senator's actions.

"I would never dishonor my family name or the public trust for any reason or purpose. You couldn't make me do it," Riegle said. "The idea that I would do it for a campaign fundraiser is sheer nonsense."

Glenn emphasized that he had received no contributions from Keating since a year before the 1987 meetings and that he stopped helping Lincoln after learning of its legal troubles. He went on to defend the practice of questioning regulators about their actions. "I believe that a crucial part of my job as a U.S. senator is to ensure that federal regulators and bureaucrats are treating people fairly and carrying out their regulatory activities responsibly," he said.

McCain said he, too, ended his involvement with Lincoln once he heard the federal regulators' side of the story on April 9, 1987. He acknowledged that he and Keating had been friends when he was in the House, taking his family on several vacations at Keating's private resort in the Bahamas, but insisted he had exerted no improper pressure in Keating's behalf.

"When he came to see me in March of 1987 and asked me to do something I thought was improper, I said no," McCain told the committee. "When he asked me to get Ed Gray off his back, I said no. When he asked me to negotiate for him, I said no. The only thing I said I could do was to inquire whether American Continental Corp. and Lincoln Savings were being treated fairly."

Cranston made his only appearance during the hearings a dramatic one Nov. 16 as he displayed a long list of aides, including some in every senator's office, who were designated under Senate rules to accept campaign donations. "It is absurd to suggest that fundraising and substantive issues are separated in Senate offices by some kind of wall," Cranston said. "The notion that it violates Senate rules and established ethical standards if the fundraiser participated in a meeting in which substantive issues are dis-

Continued on p. 88

Violating the 'Appearance Standard'

Can a senator's conduct be improper merely because it looks bad?

In the "Keating Five" case, Special Counsel Robert S. Bennett urged the Senate Ethics Committee to conclude that, even absent a finding of actual improper conduct, members could be disciplined just for looking as though they behaved improperly — for violating what he called the "appearance standard." *(Keating Five, p. 78)*

"Legislators who appear to reasonable persons to do wrong actually do wrong by eroding the trust between citizens and their representatives," Bennett told the panel. He argued that longstanding traditions, Senate and House precedents, previous Ethics Committee pronouncements and common sense supported his position.

Such a finding could be precedent-setting. Although Bennett cited several past ethics cases in which appearances came into play, he offered no example of a lawmaker having been punished merely because his behavior looked improper.

The senators under investigation for their ties to savings and loan executive Charles H. Keating Jr. — Alan Cranston, D-Calif.; Dennis DeConcini, D-Ariz.; John Glenn, D-Ohio; John McCain, R-Ariz.; and Donald W. Riegle Jr., D-Mich. — maintained that their actions were in accord with accepted standards and that it should not matter how they could be interpreted by others.

Said Cranston: "We must do what we think is right, not just what appears to be right."

What Is 'Improper Conduct?'

Senate rules prohibited members from engaging in "improper conduct which may reflect upon the Senate" — the catchall phrase included in the 1964 resolution that created the Ethics Committee. *(Congress & the Nation Vol. I, p. 1773)*

Bennett did not build his whole case around the appearance standard; he argued that some of the senators' fundraising activities and actions to help Keating were clear examples of improper conduct. But if the committee decided that none of the senators' actions by themselves violated Senate rules, Bennett said, it still could hold some of them them accountable.

The circumstances, as reflected in many media reports, indeed could look bad. Ethics Committee Chairman Howell Heflin, D-Ala., said that many voters thought the senators were bribed with huge political contributions to come to Keating's aid during his bitter fight with thrift regulators.

Bennett's Standard

Bennett presented his conclusion about the appearance standard in a lengthy legal brief analyzing the history of government ethics. He formulated the suggested standard this way: "A senator should not engage in conduct which would appear to be improper to a reasonable, nonpartisan, fully informed person."

Bennett's first principle was not contested: Senators were required to follow not just written rules and laws; they also had to adhere to certain unwritten standards of conduct. He cited numerous precedents going back to the late 1700s to show that senators could be punished, even expelled, for violating unwritten standards.

When the Select Committee on Standards and Conduct first proposed a code of conduct in 1968, it stated in a report that "the Senate must not only be free of improper influence but must also be ... free from the appearance of impropriety." *(Congress & the Nation Vol. II, p. 921)*

In 1964, the committee's report on its investigation of a top Senate employee (Bobby Baker, who was found to have used his office to promote outside business interests) said that "officials have an obligation ... to refrain not only from actual wrongdoing but from conduct leaving the appearance of wrongdoing."

In its 1978 report on the Korean influence scandal, the Ethics Committee said "a key element" of previous conduct-related Senate resolutions "is that a senator must avoid the appearance of impropriety, as well as impropriety itself." *(1978 Almanac, p. 803)*

Durenberger, House Cases

Bennett said that the standard had been invoked most recently in the 1989-90 case against Dave Durenberger, R-Minn. Before the Senate unanimously voted to denounce Durenberger for unethical financial dealings, Warren B. Rudman, R-N.H., vice chairman of the Ethics Committee, said his colleague "failed his obligation of protecting both the appearance and reality of propriety." *(Durenberger case, p. 98)*

Bennett cited three House cases as well, those of Robert L. F. Sikes, D-Fla., in 1976; Raymond F. Lederer, D-Pa., in 1981; and Mario Biaggi, D-N.Y., in 1988. *(Sikes, 1976 Almanac, p. 30; Lederer, 1981 Almanac, p. 386; Biaggi, 1988 Almanac, p. 34)*

All four of Bennett's precedents involved more than just appearances, however. The committee found that Durenberger violated rules on speech fees, financial disclosure, gifts and campaign contributions. Lederer and Biaggi were charged with violating criminal bribery statutes, while Sikes was found to have violated House disclosure requirements.

Senators' Arguments

The Keating senators urged the committee to focus on whether their behavior itself violated any rules, laws or standards of conduct.

DeConcini's attorney, James Hamilton, contended that the standard set in S Res 338 — prohibiting "improper conduct which may reflect upon the Senate" — was a "twofold test."

Its appearance standard, he said, could not be imposed independently. First, the conduct in question must be found to be improper, then it must be shown to reflect badly on the Senate.

William W. Taylor III, Cranston's attorney, said that any appearance problems that did arise should be left to the voters: "That is a matter for which the American electorate is uniquely equipped to decide."

Continued from p. 86
cussed is sheer hypocrisy. . . . I submit that if you decide that it's improper to take a lawful and proper action at any time in behalf of someone who has contributed legally and properly, then every senator, including every member of this committee, had better run for cover — because every senator has done it; every senator must do it."

Cranston, known as a master fundraiser among Democrats, said that laws and rules governing campaign finance should be reformed. "But they haven't been changed yet," he concluded. "Until they are, the Senate and every senator and candidate will be in dire jeopardy."

DeConcini made his rebuttal Nov. 19, after a weekend's recess. He was particularly aggressive toward the special counsel's tactics, accusing Bennett of behaving like a prosecutor bent on improving his courtroom record. "Bennett says that the facts tilt," DeConcini said. "No, the facts don't tilt. He tilts them, and why does he do that? . . . He wants the victory. He wants to nail somebody."

DeConcini insisted that Keating's complaints of harassment by federal regulators seemed to have merit in 1987. Moreover, he said that he did not always do Keating's bidding. When Keating asked him to push through a sale of Lincoln in early 1989, the senator said, "I said no. . . . I did not push for the approval of that sale." DeConcini acknowledged, however, that he asked regulators about the sale and asked them to give it close consideration.

Witnesses Begin

The first witnesses were aides to the senators. They sought to differentiate the actions of their bosses from the other senators, with much testimony focusing on who had taken the initiative in setting up the first meeting with bank board Chairman Gray.

Gwendolyn van Paasschen, McCain's legislative assistant appeared Nov. 19-20 and testified that she called an independent auditor to check out Keating's claims of unfair treatment by regulators, and was convinced that they had merit. But, she said, she had an uneasy feeling about Keating and warned McCain not to do too much for him.

Van Paasschen said it was her recollection that Riegle had initiated the meeting, even though he did not attend, and that DeConcini had kept staff away. She also said she heard DeConcini tell McCain in March 1987 that he "wanted to get the regulators off of Mr. Keating's back."

Laurie Sedlmayr, an aide to DeConcini, testified Nov. 26 that she believed that the April 2 meeting had been the "brainchild" of Riegle. But under cross-examination by Riegle attorney Thomas C. Green, she said that she had no facts to support her belief.

McCain's attorney, John M. Dowd, endeavored to show that McCain had nothing to do with a letter written by Sedlmayr and signed by DeConcini, inviting Riegle to the April 9 meeting. The letter said the invitation was from DeConcini and McCain; Sedlmayr said that had been her belief, but she had mistakenly forgotten to send a copy to McCain's office.

Sedlmayr also testified that she advised DeConcini to avoid helping Keating. "She let me know she didn't think it was a good idea," DeConcini said Nov. 26.

The Meeting With Gray

For the equivalent of three days in the week of Nov. 26, the panel heard from the best-known accuser of the Keating senators, Edwin Gray. The meeting that four of the senators — all but Riegle — attended with the nation's top savings and loan regulator on April 2, 1987, was in many ways the beginning of the case against them.

Gray had testified at length before the House Banking Committee a year earlier that the four senators present at the meeting had acted improperly.

Gray had been upset by the session and had complained to his aides about it immediately afterward. Gray testified that he had first publicly mentioned the meeting when a reporter called him in May 1989.

He told the committee that he was improperly pressured at the meeting to withdraw a bank board regulation adopted Feb. 27, 1987, limiting certain thrift investments in real estate and other enterprises that was being strongly opposed by Lincoln. And he alleged that DeConcini offered him a "quid pro quo" that Lincoln would change some of its controversial practices if the rule was abandoned. While Riegle did not attend the meeting, Gray testified that the senator had told him to "expect a call" to set it up.

Bennett had told the committee in his opening statement Nov. 15 that Gray could be "emotional," and he said he did not intend to rely heavily upon Gray's version of events. Gray's testimony indeed gave heartburn to many involved in the hearings. He leveled broadside upon broadside not only at the Keating Five but also at Congress in general, charging that the system of campaign contributions was little more than bribery. "It's a case of too much money chasing too many politicians," he said on more than one occasion.

Attorneys for the senators homed in on the former regulator, challenging his suitability for the job of bank board chairman, his memory of dates and other facts, and, most of all, his broad assertions that the senators had acted improperly.

Some members of the Ethics panel had trouble with Gray's assertions. Lott acknowledged "shaking my head in disgust" at some statements, and Sanford said to Gray: "I think probably your explanation of all of this as being politicians chasing money is perhaps not quite accurate."

Gray conceded that he had been the one to suggest that the senators hold a second meeting, on April 9, with the regulators who were in charge of the Lincoln case. He said he had been shocked that Riegle had attended that meeting. But he told Green that he had no recollection of meeting with Riegle on April 21, 1987, less than two weeks later, to ask for help in getting a job on Wall Street. His term as bank board chairman was about to expire.

Meeting With Regulators

All five senators attended the meeting a week later in DeConcini's office with examiners from the San Francisco Federal Home Loan Bank and the Washington office of the bank board. Two of the regulators who attended the April 9, 1987, meeting testified at the hearings: William Black, then-deputy director of the Federal Savings and Loan Insurance Corporation (FSLIC), and Michael Patriarca, head of the San Francisco regional office.

A memorandum summarizing notes that Black took during the meeting was submitted by Bennett as a reliable account of what went on. "It is a fairly remarkable document," Bennett said. "Everyone who has seen that memo says that this transcript-like memo is accurate in all essential respects."

"A fair reading of that memo," Bennett went on, "reveals clearly that Sen. DeConcini was negotiating or trying to strike a deal for Lincoln."

Continued on p. 93

'Keating Five' Appear Before Ethics Panel

On Nov. 16, four of the five senators being investigated for their ties to Charles H. Keating Jr. defended their actions at hearings before the Senate Ethics Committee. The fifth senator, Dennis DeConcini, D-Ariz., spoke Nov. 19. Following are excerpts of their statements:

SEN. JOHN McCAIN, R-ARIZ.: ... Once again, I'm glad to have the opportunity to fully and publicly account for my relationship with Charles Keating and my conduct in connection with April 1987 meetings with Chairman Ed Gray and regulators at the Federal Home Loan Bank Board.

Mr. Chairman, and members of the committee — Charlie Keating was a political friend and supporter from 1981 to 1987. When he came to see me in March of 1987 and asked me to do something I thought was improper, I said no. When he asked me to get Ed Gray off his back, I said no. When he asked me to negotiate for him, I said no. The only thing I said I could do was to inquire whether American Continental Corporation and Lincoln Savings were being treated fairly.

On April 2, I attended a meeting in Senator DeConcini's office with Chairman Ed Gray to ask those questions about whether Lincoln was being treated fairly. I asked Mr. Gray if it was proper to meet and ask questions. He said it was proper. Chairman Gray said he didn't know the facts of the Lincoln investigation, and he suggested that we meet the following week with the Bank Board regulators from San Francisco, who could answer my questions. I again asked if that would be proper. Mr. Gray said it would be proper.

On April 9, I joined other senators in Senator DeConcini's office to meet with these San Francisco regulators as Mr. Gray had suggested. There's a transcript of that meeting, which has been referred to several times already during this hearing. I'd like to excerpt again what I said at the beginning of that meeting. And I quote — and remember, this is from Mr. [William] Black, who was one of the members of the meeting, and this transcript was taken unbeknownst to me, at least:

"One of our jobs as elected officials is to help constituents in a proper fashion. American Continental is a big employer and important to the local economy. I would not want any special favors for them." And I went on to say, "I do not want any part of our conversation to be improper."

I was able at this April 9 meeting to make my inquiries. I learned at this meeting that Lincoln's complaints of bad treatment from the regulators were unfounded and that there would be a criminal referral to the Justice Department against Lincoln.

That, Mr. Chairman, was the end of any involvement I had with American Continental or Lincoln Savings. From then on, I had no further dealings at all with the Federal Home Loan Bank Board. I had no further contact on this issue with other government officials. I had no contact with Danny Wall or others to support the sale of Lincoln Savings in 1989.

I had no further contact with Mr. Keating or any American Continental representatives. I neither solicited nor accepted any campaign contributions from Mr. Keating or American Continental employers. My relationship with Mr. Keating was ended, over. There's nothing more.

* * *

I went to the meeting because I felt that was the way that I could get answers to legitimate — what I believed were legitimate — questions, and I might add that Mr. Gray had said that it was proper to attend both that meeting and the one before to ask questions — to ask questions — to be very clear.

And so, I hope that that answers the question that I think the special counsel legitimately raised, as to why I would attend the meeting on April 2 and April 9, after basically terminating the relationship that I had had with Mr. Keating. I know I acted ethically and properly and in compliance with all applicable standards of conduct, including my own.

* * *

SEN. JOHN GLENN, D-OHIO: This committee and your very able special counsel have already spent a year investigating this matter. And each of you has come to know all there is to know about my conduct as it relates to Charles Keating and Lincoln Savings and Loan. There are no facts, as yet unrevealed, and no surprises in store for you. Nothing will emerge in these hearings about John Glenn that has not already been established and reviewed by the thorough and professional inquiry of special counsel Bennett.

... The truth is that at no time did I pare my principles or compromise my convictions. At no time did I ask for special treatment for anyone. And at no time did I trade favors or perform actions in return for money.

I acted honorably, I behaved honestly, and I have neither tainted my own reputation nor tarnished the reputation of this body. ...

* * *

As for my own conduct, the facts are very clear, were fairly and accurately laid out for you yesterday by the special counsel. On April 2, 1987, I attended a meeting with three other senators on behalf of Lincoln Savings, a financial institution headed by a former Ohioan, and whose parent company was an Ohio chartered corporation. A former employee of mine, Jim Grogan, had told my staff that Lincoln was being harassed, was receiving unfair treatment by federal banking regulators. But my staff knew that before I would agree to go to such a meeting, I would have to be persuaded that Lincoln's complaints had merit. They knew that because it was and is my normal office procedure and they knew these procedures would have to be adhered to, even though they knew and trusted Jim Grogan.

As a result, I received detailed assurance from a senior partner at one of the nation's largest independent accounting firms that the still ongoing audit of Lincoln was longer and more intrusive than he had ever seen. In addition, I was given a copy of a 1985 letter written by Alan Greenspan, one of America's most respected economists, vouching for Lincoln's financial stability. And with this evidence in hand, I decided to attend the April 2 meeting with bank board Chairman Ed Gray. I did not talk with any other senators before the meeting, discuss any aspect of it afterwards. And at the meeting itself, no one spoke for me, I spoke for myself and only for myself.

In fact, I went to the meeting with only one purpose and that was to ask why the audit of Lincoln had gone on so long and to urge that the bank board reach some kind of a decision: either bring charges against Lincoln if they're warranted or close the audit if they were not.

Chairman Gray could not answer my questions and in fact claimed to know very little about the Lincoln situation. So Chairman Gray himself proposed that a second meeting be held with some of his supervisory staff on April 9, and I agreed to go to that meeting as well.

As the transcript of that second meeting attests, I asked the very same questions I asked at the first meeting, but this time I got some answers. What I learned was the government had a very, very different view of Lincoln from the one I'd received from Lincoln, the Arthur Young accounting firm and Dr. Greenspan. Specifically, the regulators told me that Lincoln had very serious problems and there would be a criminal referral to the Justice Department.

Well, that was all I needed to hear. Having received the explanation I sought, I closed my file, told my staff I could not disclose what happened at the meeting. I instructed them to tell any of Lincoln's representatives who asked that we could say nothing about the meeting, and I had absolutely no contacts whatsoever with the bank board about Lincoln's problems thereafter.

Nevertheless I know there are some who argue that I should not have attended either of the April meetings. They say it's improper for senators or congressmen to question regulators about their actions. Others argue that what made those meetings appear improper was the fact that five senators, five senators were in attendance. And having five senators in the room was intimidating to Mr. Gray and his staff.

Mr. Chairman, I just respectfully disagree. I believe that a crucial part of my job as a U.S. senator is to ensure that federal regulators and bureaucrats are treating people fairly and carrying out their regulatory activities responsibly. I submit that every senator on this panel has office files full of cases where regulatory mistakes have been made and injustices against individuals and businesses have occurred.

* * *

And if, as I have said, my decision to go to that meeting was proper, was it made improper because of Charles Keating's political contribution? The answer is no. In the first place, from the day I walked into the U.S. Senate in 1975 I have never accepted contributions from anyone who so much as implies even indirectly that their contribution is linked to a request for my assistance.

I have also made it my policy not to even respond to requests for assistance if they're linked in any way whatsoever, even to offers of contributions.

I can summarize it in a phrase: John Glenn does not peddle influence, period. So let me make several points with respect to the contributions Mr. Keating made to me. In 1984 Mr. Keating apparently arranged for contributions to help retire my presidential campaign debt. And in that same year I sent letters to the bank board asking that it delay implementation of the so-called direct investment rule until Congress could fully consider the issue. When I signed those letters neither I nor my assistant who staffed this issue knew of Mr. Keating's contributions. And even more importantly, as the text of the letters themselves indicates, they were sent only after my staff had studied the direct investment issue and determined that the proposed rule might well have an adverse effect on Ohio thrift institutions.

That was because Ohio thrifts were at that time under a state insurance system. It was highly sensitive to changes in federal regulation.

In short, Mr. Keating's contributions to a losing political campaign of mine that was already over had nothing whatsoever to do with those letters. But what about those substantial contributions Mr. Keating's company made in 1985 and 1986 to a political action committee for which I was the spokesman? Here again, I want to emphasize several points.

First, those contributions were made more than a year before the meeting I attended with Mr. Gray — this is important — and before the federal audit of Lincoln had even started. And second, not one cent of those contributions was used either for my personal benefit or to support my Senate election campaign.

And third, if Mr. Keating ever thought his money would influence any of my actions or decisions, he was surely disabused of that thought when he saw how I responded to the two requests he made of me in the months immediately following those contributions.

In the spring of 1986, Mr. Keating's staff asked that I support the nomination of Mr. Lee Henkel to the bank board. Special counsel indicated yesterday [that] Mr. Keating apparently went to considerable lengths to secure that appointment. When I was asked to support that nomination, I did not believe I had enough knowledge about Mr. Henkel's qualifications, and so I refused.

Then in the summer of 1986, Mr. Keating himself strongly urged, strongly urged me to support the nomination of Daniel Manion to the United States Court of Appeals. But because I disagreed with Judge Manion on a number of critical issues and did not believe that his confirmation would be in the best interests of Ohio or the nation, I again turned down Mr. Keating's request and voted against Mr. Manion.

Finally, let me mention one last point. In the 15 years I have been in the Senate, I have made it my policy not to accept contributions from anyone whom I know to be under investigation. That's why in the summer of 1987 I instructed my staff to turn down Mr. Keating's offer to help raise a substantial amount of money to retire my presidential debt.

The bottom line, Mr. Chairman, is this: To my knowledge, I have received no contributions from Mr. Keating or his associates since February of 1986, more than a year before the bank board meetings in 1987. And I have had no contact with the bank board or any other agency on behalf of Lincoln since I learned of Lincoln's legal troubles on April 9, 1987.

* * *

SEN. ALAN CRANSTON, D-CALIF.: ... With all my heart and soul, I want to make very clear certain facts that the evidence presented to you subsequently will substantiate.

One, I engaged in no unethical conduct. Two, you know that I broke no law. Three, you know that I broke no Senate rule.

Four, you know that I pocketed no money, that there was no personal gain for me or any member of my family.

Most of the money now in question was in the form of charitable deductible contributions for nonpartisan registration drives in California and in approximately 20 other states, all conducted by organizations I did not control, all of this after I was re-elected in 1986.

Five, I never recommended, much less demanded, that any government official do anything improper or grant any constituent any special favor.

There is absolutely no evidence to the contrary.

Six, I did nothing that affected or delayed any government action in any way. There is absolutely no evidence to the contrary.

Seven, at the now-famous 1987 meetings of senators and regulators, on April 2, I asked only why an audit was going on endlessly.

And on April 9, I attended for only a few seconds and said nothing of consequence. There is absolutely no evidence to the contrary.

Eight, I had good reason to believe that a business which employed almost 1,000 of my constituents in my state of California, and thus benefitted their families and the communities where they lived, was being dealt with improperly by a huge bureaucracy which couldn't make a decision and had a reputation for incompetence. There is abundant supporting evidence.

For example, the Los Angeles Times had called on the chief regulator to resign in 1986, after he was compelled to refund $27,000 of public funds which he had misused.

The Washington Post had reported in 1986 that this chief regulator was feuding with the head of the business in my state. The chief of staff in Ronald Reagan's White House, Donald T. Regan, decided that the chief regulator was a liability. A federal judge accused the regulators' bank board in January 1987 of being, "high-handed, arbitrary, bureaucratic."

I had personally received numerous complaints from a variety of sources about the unresponsive and uncooperative behavior of the bank board.

I was told that an employee of the bank board's San Francisco office had complained that the regulators were harassing the business in my state.

A new chief regulator was installed. He told me that the bank board shared responsibility for the problems with the business. It takes two to tango, he said.

[L. William] Seidman, head of Federal Deposit and Insurance Corporation, expressed concern to me about the performance of the regulators.

The Enforcement Review Committee, an internal management organ within the bank board, concluded that the regulators were dealing with the business in an inappropriate and arbitrary way.

Nine, when I first received complaints regarding the way bureaucrats were mishandling this business, and for a long, long time thereafter, there was abundant substantiating evidence that this business was solvent, sound, and well-managed.

Among those who gave me confidence in the business, in one way or another, were Alan Greenspan, now chairman of the Federal Reserve Board; two of the nation's leading accounting firms, Arthur Young and Arthur Andersen; The Arizona Gazette; The Los Angeles Times; and Thrift News.

Yes, yes, Mr. Chairman, I was persistent in expressing my concerns about the way bureaucrats were dealing with this large business in my state.

I believe that its failure, if it came to that, and it finally did, would be a catastrophe for countless constituents of mine, as it finally was. But I repeat: There is absolutely no evidence, none at all, that I ever sought to persuade any government official to do anything improper.

* * *

Mr. Bennett complained on April 30: "There have to be some rules."

Mr. Bennett, you don't write the rules. I don't write the rules. This committee doesn't write the rules. The Senate writes the rules. The fact is that the Senate does not have any rules like those Mr. Bennett seems to want. If it did, senators would be afraid to act on behalf of any constituents who have contributed or who may contribute in the future, no matter how legitimate the problems of these constituents might be.

Yesterday, Mr. Bennett shifted his stance. He now proposes a new standard of ethical conduct for the Senate.

He declares that senators must not engage in activities that, although otherwise entirely proper, might appear to be improper to some mythical but reasonable person.

But what he is really saying is that that mythical person is reviewing the entire matter in hindsight, as is Mr. Bennett himself.

He was not there. You were not there. I was there. And I know that what I knew at the time about this business, about the bank board and about the industry generally, convinced me that my inquiries — and that's all they were — were appropriate at that time.

You, the members of this committee, have been counseled by Mr. Bennett to judge me and all our colleagues, all of them, 99 others beyond myself, henceforth on the basis of Mr. Bennett's unwritten rules that define unethical behavior in accordance with some notion of ethics never adopted by this body.

* * *

Sen. Rudman and Mr. Bennett, when I was deposed on April 1, you both asked me if it was normal practice to have someone with fundraising responsibilities present in a meeting with a constituent, who also was a contributor, when a substantive matter was discussed. You asked me that question because a fundraiser of mine attended a few such meetings in my office. That fundraiser was not a member of my Senate staff. What your question suggests is that this violated some Senate rule. It clearly does not.

I now want to present some charts. My name is on the charts. Your names, all six of you, will find your names on the charts. Every senator's name is on them. Senate Rule 41 permits every senator to appoint three members of his or her Senate staff who may solicit and receive campaign contributions. These charts show the Senate staffers who have been authorized by their senators and by Rule 41 to raise funds.

Some of these staffers and their senator's principal fundraisers, some have enormous power to schedule, to expedite, to slow down, to draft and amend legislation, and also to deal with the executive branch. More than 90 of them are administrative assistants, the chiefs of staff who run their senator's office, work on legislation, deal with the executive, and can raise and receive campaign money. More than 35 are executive assistants, legislative directors and legislative assistants, who have direct responsibility for legislation and can raise money from people who are interested in legislation. At least a dozen are personal secretaries who screen telephone calls and grant requests for appointments. To use some words Mr. Bennett uttered yesterday, these are people who "hold the keys to access." About 30 are state directors in charge of their senator's work back home, and about 40 more are also on their senator's staff back home, right where the most contributors are.

Let me ask you this, members of the committee: How many of these Senate staffers who are legally empowered to raise money do you think have sat in meetings with their senator and contributors, potential or proven, when substantive issues were discussed, like problems with bureaucrats and legislation? How many of you — how many of you — could testify that some member of your Senate staff who you have authorized to raise money has never ever said to you something like: John Doe is coming in and about to meet with you, and I'll sit in; here's what I think you ought to do, and, remember, he's been a big help to you.

I say that it's absurd to suggest that fundraising and substantive issues are separated in Senate offices by some kind of wall. The notion that it violates Senate rules and established ethical standards if a fundraiser participates in a meeting in which substantive issues are discussed is sheer hypocrisy. Plainly, the Senate in its wisdom has decided that there is no appearance of impropriety in this situation, and therefore there was no appearance of impropriety in mine. . . .

Let me now close by saying this. We all take an oath to uphold the Constitution. One of the most fundamental precepts of that Constitution is that our liberties clearly imply that the rules citizens are to follow must be stated so they can be understood before citizens can be charged with breaking those rules.

Stated another way, we can't change the rules in midstream.

It may be that after this experience the Senate will decide to adopt new rules governing how and when senators may receive contributions. But that reform, if it comes, must not be seen as reflecting on the integrity of honorable people, including myself, who have conducted our public lives always in compliance with the present law and rules as we understand them.

I have made justice, fairness and moral behavior the guiding stars of my life. I do not waver from those principles. This experience has been a shattering one for me and for my family. But I am confident that this hearing will end with no blemish on my cherished reputation.

* * *

SEN. DONALD W. RIEGLE JR., D-MICH.: There are very important institutional issues that are being raised here about how we finance our campaigns for public office and how constituent service activities in the future are to be viewed in relationship to campaign contributions.

. . . I think it's right to say that our campaigns cost too much, that too many good people lack the resources to run for office, and special interest money is coming to dominate the electoral process.

I think Bob Bennett yesterday was right on this point. In my view, it doesn't look right and it isn't right. And as independent as any of us may be — and I think I'm as independent as anybody here, and I think my career shows that — the present campaign financing system is cutting against our democracy, and it must be changed.

If this inquiry — as miserably unpleasant as it has been for all of us — helps bring about the change that we need, then our country will be the better for it. . . .

Let me move directly to this case now, and say, first, that I am fully responsible for my official conduct as a senator, and I believe my conduct was absolutely proper in this matter. And as for any judgments or misjudgments I made some years ago in this matter, I'm fully responsible for those as well. . . .

Yesterday, Mr. Bennett's personal characterizations on my part in this matter were inaccurate in some important respects. . . .

What we have out of this case is not all of the pieces of this puzzle, but we just have some of the pieces. . . . You're never going to be sure because you don't have all the pieces. . . .

Let me go straight to the bottom line on my conduct. There are two events here with respect to me. One is what did I do with respect to the regulatory process? And the other is: What's the story on the fundraiser that Charles Keating hosted in Detroit? And that's a central question for each one of the senators here. What did each one of us do? What official actions did we take as a senator? And was my official conduct proper and ethical? And you're going to see, day by day, witness by witness — and I think you've already seen most of that because you've been through this before, you've been through it before in closed session — that my conduct was normal, it was proper, and it was ethical in every respect. Now, here's what the record shows — this is what's in those documents over there with respect to me on conduct:

First, the record of facts here shows that at no time did I ever ask any regulator to take any action or not take any action with respect to the regulatory oversight of Lincoln. No one contests that.

Second, the facts also show that any actions taken by the regulators or not taken by the regulators regarding the regulatory treatment of Lincoln was not caused or influenced by me in any way whatsoever. And the regulators themselves have confirmed that with sworn testimony. It's been hard to get that in the press — it's only a year old in terms of it having been said over on the House side, but it's all been said here in your documents.

Third, this — the record will also show that I had no part whatsoever in keeping Lincoln open a single day. The regulators will testify to that fact as they have testified before, and they're going to testify to it right here in this room. Now, the false charge which has helped make this story a lot bigger than it really is, that senators kept Lincoln open two and a half years at great cost to the taxpayers, that everybody in this country has heard probably a million times — that's just not true, never been true, not a shred of truth to that. But it gets printed and reprinted, and I'm not talking about in The National Enquirer; I read it in an editorial in The New York Times two or three weeks ago. They're still saying that, despite the record. I don't know why. It's not the truth.

Fourth, with respect to my conduct. The record shows that I only had two contacts with the regulators where the subject of Lincoln arose. One was on March 6 of 1987, and the other was a month later on April 9, and I'm going to talk about both.

I think both contacts were entirely proper and ethical and well within the appropriate standards of official conduct. And, frankly, if there were not an unrelated fundraising event in the proximity of these two proper contacts, I wouldn't be here today — I wouldn't be in this room —I wouldn't be here. That's what this issue is about with respect to me. I'm going to come back to those two.

You heard John Glenn say, and you've heard John McCain say, and you're going to hear me say, when I left the April 9 meeting, there's no guesswork about what went on in the meeting because we've got a transcript — we know what went on in that meeting. It's like there was a tape recorder under the couch, so, you know, we know what was said there. When I walked out the door of that meeting, I didn't have any other contact with any regulator on Lincoln ever, period. And that's been confirmed as well by this evidence over here. . . .

* * *

The totality of my conduct with respect to the regulators on this matter is those two events that I've mentioned to you. As I understand it, special counsel — and I'm not speaking for him, so this is my interpretation — has not found either of these events, by themselves, to be improper or unethical.

That's my impression; it may not be correct, but that's the impression that I have. . . .

* * *

SEN. DENNIS DECONCINI, D-ARIZ.: . . . We are here, and we have heard the special prosecutor, Mr. Bennett, present his case on behalf of what he has done for over one year now. We are here because a complaint has been filed by Common Cause, an organization that has legitimate legislative interests before the Congress and has decided to file a complaint against five senators, based on press reports, if you read their complaint.

Common Cause has not been subject to an interrogation that I know, not that they are on trial or any charges have been filed against them, but I would submit that a good investigation would indeed ask a question or two of who filed the complaint.

What was their motive? Did they have a board of directors meeting or an executive committee meeting deciding, let us file some complaints here, and what are we going to achieve by it?

I do not know the answers because nobody has asked them, but I can tell you what they are trying to achieve. They are trying to raise money. They are trying to damage the reputation of a number of senators, and they are trying to pass certain legislation, and I think it is a travesty in and of itself. . . .

So Mr. Bennett very skillfully — and he has been skillful I must say, and he has a long reputation as a prosecutor — very skillfully brought up some very, very interesting items in his presentation. He used the word bribery twice. Now he qualified it, he said, now, in all fairness to the senators, we do not want any inference that they are involved in bribery here.

He used the bondholders losses that occurred by Lincoln Savings selling and American Continental, and then he qualified it, and then he qualified it, oh, no, we are not going to make any inference or anything that would tie the senators to that, the elderlies who were invested, the taxpayer who has to pick up the bill for the savings and loan crisis and the failure of Lincoln.

But then he carefully says, no, we are not suggesting that they had anything to do with that.

That is a technique of a very skilled prosecutor because what do you do? You plant the seed, some of you have been farmers and you know farmers, they plant a seed and they water it carefully and they pull the roots out, but that seed grows, does it not, if it has been carefully done, even though you pull other things out and you qualify it. . . .

Bennett says that the facts tilt. No, the facts don't tilt. He tilts them, and why does he do that? Because he's like all of us. He's got something at stake here. And it's not just representing this committee, gentlemen. He wants the victory. He wants to nail somebody. He wants to get somebody, I'm sorry to say. He wants another trophy on the wall as someone who's represented the committee and been able to nail up another senator for ethical misconduct, another trial.

* * *

The special prosecutor goes into the fundraising aspects. I have raised funds for more than 20 senators. I have given some of the names and the amounts even, and a guy named Katz is my fundraiser and the head of my finance committee. When you raise money around here, something else that maybe Mr. Bennett is just finding out, it is a darn big job to raise $3 million or $4 million.

You do not just get that real easy, particularly in a small state like Arizona, or say, Vermont, or New Hampshire, or Maine. You have got to go outside the state if you have got to have $1 million, or in my case, $3 million.

Mr. Bennett has never had to go through that. How can he suggest what is proper and improper when you do not have to go through that burning fire of trying to raise that kind of money so you can win an election? Some of you just went through it. I think you will agree it is an awesome thing, and you probably did not enjoy it any more than I did.

Have you ever received checks from a fellow senator or collected from his state? Well, I have. Have I ever given checks to a senator that were collected in my state for that senator? Yes, I have, and Sen. Riegle was one of them, and Sen. Riegle helped me, as did about 10 or 12 other senators. There is nothing wrong with that. Proximity or reciprocity or whatever.

There are no standards that say one senator cannot raise money for another senator, and ask him, will you help me, too? But he wants to paint a picture. The special prosecutor wants to paint a picture that there is something wrong here, because one guy had promised to raise money for the other guy when he raised money for him. That is nonsense, and you know it. [That's] how this place runs; there is nothing wrong with it.

Now, I am not saying it should not be changed, gentlemen, because it should. It looks like hell. I do not like it, and I have supported campaign reform every year that I have been here. I have been part and parcel of trying to change it. I support public financing, and I support limits on how much you can give and how much you can spend, because I want to see it changed.

* * *

Now, Mr. Katz was the chairman of my finance committee. We had more than 100 people on it. We had 12 or 15 — I cannot remember the number — that would raise substantial funds, close to $100,000, and Mr. Keating was one of them. . . .

Mr. Keating raised $48,000, less than 1.5 percent of the entire amount of money. We did not ask him to raise the full $100,000 that he had suggested that he would raise, because we ended up with a surplus of half a million dollars.

You know, what is so discouraging, gentlemen, for this senator — maybe for everybody — is the public has a perception, as Chairman [Howell] Heflin, [D-Ala.] said, that maybe you have been bought. That is the most discouraging thing in this whole process, and I realize some people think that, Sen. Heflin. The tragedy for this senator, or any senator, the tragedy for this whole institution, is that I have never been bought. . . . ■

Continued from p. 88

Black, who at the time of the hearings was chief counsel of the Western region of the Office of Thrift Supervision (OTS), testified that he and other regulators were improperly pressured by the senators in the controversial meeting. But, he said, he and his colleagues did nothing in response to the meeting.

Black provided the committee with a picture of Lincoln's deep financial problems and the "scam," as he termed it, that the thrift used to stay solvent.

He testified that the thrift was basically a Ponzi scheme that used fraudulent accounting of prohibited ownership investments in real estate to generate income that could be paid to the parent corporation, American Continental. When the bank board began in 1986 to crack down on Lincoln's real estate investments, the thrift was put in the position of potential insolvency, Black said.

As had Gray before him, Black drew few distinctions on his own among the senators who met with him on April 9. He noted repeatedly that DeConcini at the meeting had used the word "we" to refer to the senators' concerns about Lincoln, and said he assumed DeConcini was speaking for everyone.

Black asserted that by poisoning the atmosphere involving Lincoln, the actions of the senators may have led to a two-year delay in closing the thrift at tremendous additional cost to the taxpayers. Regulators first formally recommended in May 1987 that Lincoln be closed. It finally happened in April 1989. There was no corroborating evidence for Black's assertion, however, and it seemed not to be accepted by members of the Ethics Committee or even Bennett.

None of the regulators present at the April meetings, nor any who came later, testified that they were prevented from doing their jobs because of political pressure from the senators.

Patriarca, the head of the San Francisco regional office of the OTS, confirmed details of Black's memo and agreed with Gray and Black that DeConcini had made the most strenuous efforts in Keating's behalf. He testified that DeConcini had "negotiated" with him for special treatment for Lincoln during the April 9 meeting, which he considered improper.

Patriarca described Glenn as "blunt," McCain as "uncomfortable" and Riegle as having conducted a "cross-examination" of the regulators. Cranston made a "cameo appearance," he said.

The senators' tone changed markedly, Patriarca said, after the regulators informed them that there would be a criminal referral to the Justice Department because of some of Lincoln's practices.

M. Danny Wall, who succeeded Gray as chairman of the Federal Home Loan Bank Board in July 1987, testified Dec. 4 that he had been approached by both DeConcini and Cranston in Lincoln's behalf and that neither had done anything wrong. Wall took sharp issue with Black's testimony that political pressure had led to a delay in closing Lincoln.

Cranston Fundraising

The committee focused in the week of Dec. 3 largely on the possibility of a connection between Cranston's fundraising and his concern for Lincoln.

In his opening remarks, Bennett had used Cranston's candor against him, particularly his admission that campaign contributions result in favored treatment. Bennett cited Cranston's sworn deposition: "A person who makes a contribution has a better chance to get access than someone who does not."

Memorandums to Cranston from a key aide, Joy Jacobson, released by the committee Dec. 3, showed the possibility that Keating expected help in return for his financial contributions.

Jacobson was chief fundraiser for Cranston's 1986 re-election campaign. She testified that after 1986 she worked regularly out of Cranston's majority whip office to raise money for a variety of voter-registration and get-out-the-vote drives and for the Democratic Senatorial Campaign Committee.

In those efforts, she said, she helped collect hundreds of thousands of dollars from Lincoln and American Continental.

Jacobson's strongest testimony was contained in a series of memos to Cranston in 1987 and 1988.

A Jan. 2, 1987, summary of her fundraising plans noted that, because the Democrats again had a majority in the Senate, "there are a number of individuals who have been very helpful to you who have cases or legislative matters pending with our office who will rightfully expect some kind of resolution."

Among them she listed Keating, who, she said, "is continuing to have problems with the Bank Board and Ed Gray."

In a Sept. 6, 1987, memo, Jacobson noted that Keating should be pleased with the appointment of Wall to succeed Gray at the bank board. Noting that Cranston had an upcoming Sept. 24 meeting with Keating, Jacobson said he should ask for $250,000 for one of the voter-registration committees Cranston supported.

And in a Jan. 18, 1988, memo, she noted that Cranston and Keating had recently had dinner and reminded him that Keating wanted him to call Wall about Lincoln's continuing troubles with the bank board.

Less than a month later, Keating gave $500,000 to two of Cranston's voter drives during a trip to Keating's headquarters in Phoenix.

Jacobson testified under questioning by Cranston's attorney, Taylor, that the senator never said he was taking action because of the money. But she conceded to Bennett that "in retrospect" there was probably a link in Keating's mind.

As evidence of Cranston's continuing help for Keating and the degree to which Keating apparently counted on the California Democrat, Bennett cited an urgent message to the senator from Keating in April 1989. The message asked for Cranston's help to persuade Wall to approve the sale of Lincoln to a group of employees and other investors. Such a sale would have preserved some or all of Keating's investment in the thrift.

"The consequences of not doing the above are a political disaster for anybody and everybody connected with Lincoln's past," Keating wrote.

Defending Cranston

Testimony Dec. 11 from another Cranston aide, Carolyn Jordan, appeared to provide some cover for her boss. She testified that although she regularly inquired about Lincoln with regulators, she had no knowledge that Keating had contributed large sums to Cranston or to his various political causes.

Although Jordan said she had no knowledge of Keating's contributions at the time she and Cranston were meeting with Lincoln officials, she conceded that Cranston fundraiser Jacobson was also sometimes present.

Jordan testified that on her own, or with the cooperation of others in Cranston's office — but without Cranston's knowledge — she regularly inserted statements into the Congressional Record that passed for comments seemingly made during floor debates by Cranston himself.

On one such occasion in 1987, she inserted comments contradicting a floor statement by then-Banking Committee Chairman William Proxmire, D-Wis., on a subject of direct interest to Lincoln. The thrift later cited those comments, attributed to Cranston, as "legislative history" in a lawsuit against federal regulators.

Jordan testified that Lincoln officials had not asked for the action. "It may have inadvertently assisted them, but it was certainly not the purpose of the statement," she said.

Jordan's testimony was replete with instances in which she said she could not recollect details of conversations and meetings. For instance, on April 13, 1987, Jordan flew to Phoenix and spent three days at American Continental's headquarters; she had dinner with Keating and made a speech to American Continental officials. This was only four days after the April 9, 1987, meeting that the Keating Five senators held with federal regulators to complain about the treatment of Lincoln. Jordan testified that she had known in advance of the April 9 meeting. But, she said, she had no recollection that that meeting had been discussed while she was in Phoenix. Nor did she recall any specific conversations with Keating, or anyone else, during the Phoenix visit about Lincoln's general complaints against the regulators.

DeConcini Fights Back

Of the five senators, DeConcini tried hardest to mount a vigorous defense — largely by calling a phalanx of character witnesses. He called Sen. Daniel K. Inouye, D-Hawaii, and Arizona's governor, Democrat Rose Mofford, to testify in his behalf.

Inouye had experience in dealing with politically sensitive inquiries: He served on the Senate Watergate Committee investigating the Nixon administration in 1973; in 1987 he was chairman of the Senate special committee probing the Iran-contra affair.

Linking DeConcini's actions to the normal duties of a senator, Inouye reminded the Ethics Committee members that they all went to bat for constituents who had battles with government agencies. "I think Sen. DeConcini's conduct was spotless," Inouye said. By implication, the same was true of the rest. If what DeConcini did was improper, "I think all of us at one time or another have done that," he said.

"I believe that what is on trial here are not the five colleagues of mine but the United States Senate."

On Dec. 10, DeConcini called former U.S. Customs Commissioner William Von Raab and three Arizona residents, the head of a drug rehabilitation center, a sheriff and a disabled World War II veteran, all of whom had sought and received assistance from DeConcini.

DeConcini also introduced statements and affidavits from three colleagues and one former senator, all attesting to his character and taking issue with the contention that his actions in the Lincoln case were out of the ordinary. The statements and affidavits were provided by Ernest F. Hollings, D-S.C.; Paul Simon, D-Ill.; Strom Thurmond, R-S.C.; and former Sen. Robert Morgan, D-N.C. (1975-81).

Von Raab testified that during the eight years he ran the Customs Service, beginning in 1981, DeConcini intervened with him repeatedly, particularly in behalf of importers when the senator believed the agency had overreacted. He said that DeConcini was "always firm, resolute, but always fair." And he said DeConcini's behavior was no different from that of any other member of Congress.

DeConcini's aggressive defense backfired somewhat on Dec. 10, when former American Continental tax accountant David Stevens testified that DeConcini had tried to use him to discredit McCain.

Stevens had written to the Ethics Committee in October, saying that he believed that McCain had never intended to repay American Continental for travel provided members of McCain's family in 1984-86.

Failing to receive a response from the Ethics Committee, Stevens wrote to DeConcini and sent him a copy of the original letter. Stevens testified that DeConcini then called him and asked him to sign an affidavit for use in the hearings. He testified that DeConcini also asked if he could release the letter to the news media.

The letter was leaked to several newspapers in late November. Under examination by McCain attorney John M. Dowd, Stevens retracted his assertion that McCain had not intended to reimburse American Continental for the trips.

The issue of DeConcini's request to release the Stevens letter to the media raised a sore point because numerous documents in the case had been leaked and Lincoln had previously complained that federal regulators leaked damaging information about the institution. Committee member Pryor had gone so far in his opening remarks at the hearings to say that staff caught leaking information should be fired, senators who were caught expelled and lawyers who were caught disbarred.

DeConcini's office asserted that the letter from Stevens was not Ethics Committee property. But Stevens' appearance was plainly damaging to DeConcini.

Surprise Witness: Keating Lobbyist

The hearings got a surprise in December when the committee announced that it would make a grant of immunity from future criminal prosecution to obtain the testimony of a new witness.

James J. Grogan was vice president and chief counsel of Lincoln, corporate counsel for American Continental and Keating's point man on Capitol Hill. When Keating came to visit a member, Grogan usually came along; when members visited American Continental's Phoenix headquarters, Grogan went too. He talked to all five senators about Lincoln's problems with regulators, and he delivered some of the $1.5 million in contributions made by Keating and his associates to the senators' campaigns and political causes.

Grogan had previously cited constitutional protections against self-incrimination in declining to testify. Although he faced no criminal charges at the time, a federal grand jury in Los Angeles was looking broadly into the Lincoln affair.

In a carefully worded statement Dec. 5, the committee said "it cannot fulfill its obligations to these members [the five senators] and to the Senate without obtaining [Grogan's] testimony."

To obtain the testimony, the committee had to grant Grogan limited immunity from prosecution — meaning that he could not be prosecuted for what he told the committee and that prosecutors could not use what he told the committee to develop new evidence against him. He would be subject to prosecution for perjury, however, if he lied under oath.

The committee first questioned Grogan in closed sessions and then put him on the stand publicly on Dec. 14-15.

Grogan raised serious questions about the depth of Riegle's involvement with Keating, and he made a direct link between legislative actions that Keating sought from Cranston and financial assistance that Cranston sought from Keating.

He testified that in early 1987 he and Riegle had discussed Lincoln's problems with the Federal Home Loan Bank Board, which Keating thought was harassing Lincoln. Grogan testified that Riegle told him he knew the bank board chairman, Gray.

"He had done favors for Ed Gray. He thought that he could set up a meeting," Grogan testified. He said Riegle further suggested that Grogan ask DeConcini and McCain to set up the meeting and have them invite Riegle, apparently to provide Riegle with cover.

"It was apparent to me that Sen. Riegle knew, as a shrewd politician, that this was a potentially politically explosive situation," Grogan said.

As evidence that Riegle had arranged the April 2 meeting, Grogan testified that the senator had mentioned the idea of a meeting to him in early March 1987 when Riegle was visiting Keating and American Continental headquarters in Phoenix. A few days later, Grogan said, Keating told him that Riegle had called and had spoken with Gray.

Other evidence that appeared to corroborate Grogan's testimony was a page from Cranston's calendar for April 2, which noted a meeting in DeConcini's office with Gray, Riegle and McCain. It did not mention Glenn.

Grogan said the other senators were "miffed" because they had expected Riegle to attend the April 2 meeting.

Grogan said the first meeting had gone so badly that he was unsure the second meeting would come off. So, he said, he flew to Washington during the interim "to keep the team together."

He also testified that the original purpose of the meetings — as he had promoted them — was to inquire about the status of a long-running examination of Lincoln by the regulators.

Keating wanted more, he said. According to notes of the second meeting, talking points for the meetings drafted by Lincoln employees and memorandums prepared by DeConcini's staff, the subject expanded to a request that the regulators grant "forbearance" to Lincoln on some of its investments that regulators said violated bank board regulations. And the regulators were asked to reappraise Lincoln's real estate holdings that the thrift said were being undervalued.

'The Mutual Aid Society'

Grogan also testified extensively about Cranston's fundraising. He said that within days of meeting Cranston in 1984 at a Democratic Party event, he was called by Cranston fundraiser Jacobson, who asked him to help raise money for the senator. At that time, Grogan said, Cranston said to him: "I've been very good to savings and loans. I worked hard for California savings and loans. You all should really support me."

In late 1986, Grogan testified, he asked Jacobson for help in killing a Senate floor amendment that would have hurt Lincoln's business. According to Grogan, Jacobson called him back to report that she had tried just that.

In that same conversation, Grogan testified, Jacobson said she had another matter to discuss. Grogan quoted Jacobson as saying, "I want to switch gears, and I want you to know this is totally unrelated."

Grogan testified that Jacobson then asked for help in securing a personal loan for Cranston's re-election campaign. A short time later, Lincoln granted Cranston a personal line of credit for $300,000, though the senator never used it.

Grogan recalled that Cranston greeted Keating at a dinner in Los Angeles in January 1988 by saying, "Ah, the mutual aid society."

Grogan said he had few contacts with DeConcini, Glenn and McCain, despite the fact that he had once worked for Glenn. DeConcini, Grogan testified, had a personal relationship with Keating. He said the two men had repeated contacts to which Grogan was not a party.

He said he was not always privy to Keating's thinking. And, he said, on numerous times he misread Keating's intentions.

Ultimately, he said, the two had a falling out over Grogan's handling of bankruptcy proceedings involving American Continental. They had not spoken since June 1990, he said, when Grogan left the company.

Grogan testified that Keating had decided after the April 1987 meetings not to continue to use the senators to pressure the regulators further.

Keating believed the meetings were a "horrible disaster," Grogan said. "It was a mistake. It intensified the wrath of San Francisco."

Grogan was a cooperative witness, answering questions directly. He cast his, Keating's and Lincoln's actions in the most positive light, insisting — as Keating did — that Lincoln was a profitable firm hounded out of business by zealous regulators. Soliciting help from members of Congress to counter those regulators, he said, was only proper.

According to Grogan, there was never a hint that Keating used political contributions as a means to enlist the senators' help. "It never bothered me because I never, either from the senators — any of them — or from Mr. Keating, I never got even a hint that the money was being given in exchange for anything," Grogan said.

As evidence that contributions do not buy influence, Grogan testified that Cranston, DeConcini and Glenn had not always done Keating's bidding. And he said that when Riegle announced in early 1988 that he was returning more than $75,000 that Keating had raised for him a year earlier, Keating was angry and offended.

Nevertheless, Grogan said he believed contributions helped open congressional doors. He also acknowledged the appearance of a conflict of interest when members acted in behalf of large contributors.

Grogan also contradicted Jordan's recollections of the genesis of the statement she inserted in the Congressional Record to offset comments by Sen. Proxmire. Grogan said that he had specifically alerted her to problems in the Proxmire statement and had asked her to insert a statement to neutralize it.

Other Witnesses

The committee on Dec. 2 heard another side to the story of why federal regulators moved slowly to close down Lincoln. According to Rosemary Stewart, former head of enforcement at the Federal Home Loan Bank Board and its successor agency, the Office of Thrift Supervision, the delay had nothing to do with the senators.

Stewart had participated in the 1988 decision to remove the San Francisco regulators from their role in supervising Lincoln, a year after they had recommended that the thrift be seized. Stewart said she believed that the San Francisco regulators had a vendetta against the thrift, as Lincoln was charging at the time. And, she said, the San Francisco regulators had not made their case.

"It would have been unprecedented" to have taken control of an institution that had not yet failed, as the San Francisco regulators were urging, Stewart testified.

Stewart was called as a witness by Cranston's attorney, Taylor. Although her testimony was a strong counterpoint to that of the San Francisco regulators, questioning from Ethics Committee Vice Chairman Rudman showed that he was not convinced that Stewart had acted in the government's best interests.

The panel heard Jan. 10, 1991, from a Keating lobbyist, Washington lawyer Margery Waxman, who had written to Keating in May 1988 that he had the regulators "right where you want them." Waxman testified that Keating had hired another attorney and that she had used hyperbole to get Keating to notice her letter. She said she had no contacts with the five senators.

Rebuttal: Glenn, McCain

The senators and their attorneys got a chance to make their cases after the committee took a Christmas and New Year's recess.

Glenn and McCain took a low-key approach as they made their cases on Jan. 4, 1991, reflecting the fact that little had appeared in the hearings to damage them.

During a day of testimony, the committee heard Glenn and McCain argue that they did nothing inappropriate by attending two April 1987 meetings with federal regulators.

Glenn's attorney, Charles F. C. Ruff, urged the committee to "judge him by the sternest ethical standard that you can apply to the conduct of all of your colleagues in the Senate." Even in that light, he said, Glenn emerged unscathed.

Glenn emphasized that he ended virtually all contacts with Keating after the second April 1987 meeting, at which regulators informed the senators that criminal charges might be filed. "I came to the conclusion that Lincoln was in deep trouble," Glenn said.

Glenn's only action after that time was to set up a lunch meeting in January 1988 between Keating and then-House Speaker Wright. In the summer of 1987, Glenn testified, he turned down Keating's offer to raise campaign contributions because of Keating's battles with the regulators.

McCain testified that he broke off his friendship with Keating just before the April meetings, when Keating asked him to negotiate.

"I told him that he was trying to do something that was inappropriate," he said. "I would not do it."

Committee Chairman Heflin questioned McCain closely about vacations he took with Keating between 1983 and 1986, while McCain was still a member of the House. McCain reimbursed American Continental for some of the flights at the time they were taken.

In 1989, however, American Continental accountants informed McCain that about $13,400 in flights had not been reimbursed. In May and June of that year, McCain paid the company.

The matter was raised before the House ethics committee, which ruled that his repayment ended the matter. The Senate panel had previously concluded that the matter was one for the House to decide, because McCain had been a representative at the time.

McCain, who became somewhat defensive during the questioning, insisted that he would have paid for the flights if American Continental had told him sooner that the payments had not been made.

There was little suggestion that McCain had done anything wrong beyond not checking on the payments. "You owe John McCain something," argued his attorney, Dowd. "You owe him a straight, crisp, clear finding, based on the overwhelming, undisputed evidence in the record that his actions, at all times, were honest and ethical."

At the conclusion of McCain's testimony, committee member Lott said, "I am compelled to say that you have shown repeatedly that you did nothing improper."

Rebuttal: Riegle, DeConcini

The appearances of Riegle on Jan. 7-8 and DeConcini on Jan. 9-10 concluded the major testimony.

Riegle's attorney blamed "whimsical circumstances" for the close scheduling between a March 23, 1987, Keating-sponsored fundraiser that netted $78,250 and the controversial April 9 meeting that Riegle attended. And he denied that Riegle had had any intention of misleading the committee, particularly with reference to setting up the April 2 meeting with Gray.

Riegle took pains to say that more than $10,000 collected for his campaign from American Continental employees days before the trip to Phoenix was unrelated to his discussions with Keating. In fact, Riegle testified, the money was intended to be given as part of a Keating-sponsored fundraiser scheduled for Riegle in Detroit a few weeks later.

And Riegle insisted that he had not discussed fundraising during the trip.

Rudman zeroed in on Riegle's inability to recall events and conversations. Rudman said he found Riegle's testimony "remarkably inconsistent."

In particular, he seemed incredulous at Riegle's description of the trip to Phoenix, when Riegle met with Keating, toured American Continental Corp., and — according to other testimony — discussed Keating's problems with federal regulators and proposed a meeting with the senators and Gray.

Rudman said he was confused about why Riegle had visited American Continental but told his aides not to deal with issues involving Lincoln. Riegle said he kept his aides out of the issue because the California-based thrift was not a direct constituent. But he said he visited American Continental because the firm was investing in Detroit.

Bennett made clear in his cross-examination of Riegle that he did not believe the protests of several of the senators that they were concerned in the meetings not just about Lincoln but about the entire thrift industry.

"I don't see . . . in a year and a half of investigation," Bennett said, "a single piece of paper that suggests you or any of the other senators in connection with this matter were concerned or had an issue about a systematic problem that might be affecting the industry."

DeConcini argued in his own defense that a senator could not be punished for the appearance of improper conduct unless there was improper conduct. And his attorney, James Hamilton, argued that DeConcini had not tried to negotiate for Keating, and even if he had, there would be nothing wrong with it.

Hamilton contested Bennett's contention that senators

could be punished merely for violating an "appearance standard." But he also argued that adopting such a standard should not condemn DeConcini because he was only doing what many senators did. "Even under special counsel's standard, Sen. DeConcini's conduct is wholly proper. ... No appearance standard can be used to condemn conduct that is commonplace and generally accepted."

The committee voted Jan. 8 not to call Cranston, who was undergoing treatment for prostate cancer in California. Members decided that the record on Cranston was complete enough to make a decision, and the senator did not ask to speak further.

Speaking on Cranston's behalf, his attorney, Taylor, said senators had a duty to act to help constituents — whether or not they were big contributors. "This duty may create an appearance of mutual dependence," he said. But "there is nothing improper, nor is there an appearance that there is anything improper, about that mutuality."

Bennett Closes

Bennett took more than three hours on Jan. 15-16 to sum up his view of the facts and the standards that should apply to the case.

He distinguished carefully among the five and, without actually making recommendations, in essence urged the committee to find that Cranston, DeConcini and Riegle had acted improperly. Bennett again called upon the committee to find that Glenn and McCain had acted properly at all times. Bennett distinguished them from the others by arguing that their acceptance of contributions was far removed in time from their actions, eliminating any taint from their fundraising.

Bennett argued that DeConcini had gone beyond the bounds of proper behavior to negotiate for Keating with the regulators in 1987, and he noted that DeConcini weighed in with them again in 1989 on the pending sale of Lincoln, despite knowledge that the regulators had referred evidence of possible criminal conduct at Lincoln to the Justice Department.

Bennett argued that Cranston's case provided the closest connections between money and action. He cited four separate occasions in which Cranston took actions for Keating after soliciting or receiving large amounts of cash for his own campaign or for voter registration groups with which he was affiliated.

Of Riegle, Bennett also drew a connection between fundraising and action, all of which occurred in a three-month period in 1987. And he made a damning accusation that Riegle had misled the committee, perhaps intentionally, about his role in the Keating affair.

As for the senators' contention that their meetings with and repeated phone calls to regulators were merely "status inquiries" to find out whether the Lincoln case was being handled properly, Bennett was derisive. "If I'm sitting on a park bench, and an 800-pound gorilla comes along and says, 'Excuse me, I'm just making a status inquiry if there are any seats available,' you say, 'You're damn right, there's a seat available.' And there's a lot of 800-pound gorillas around this place."

Bennett reiterated his position that the senators' actions had been wrong, and that they should have known how wrong they would appear to the public. "For this body to conclude ... that there is no appearance standard requires you to disregard what you have written before, what you have said before, what you have decided before."

Reactions of Committee

The comments of Ethics Committee members made it clear that the panel was not going to reach a ruling quickly in the case.

"I would dare say ... that there are six visions — six visions — of this case and what it means or what it doesn't mean, what is relevant, what is not relevant," Pryor said in his closing comments on Jan. 16.

A few days earlier, Helms referred to the senators as "Keystone Cops" and to Keating as "Daddy Warbucks." He told Riegle, "I don't believe you would have gone out to Phoenix — I don't believe anybody would have been involved with Mr. Keating, if he didn't have the ability to give away other people's money," Helms said.

Helms added that he was unhappy with the way the senators under investigation seemed to feel there was nothing in the slightest wrong with anything they did. "If I'm disturbed about one thing — and I'm disturbed about many things — It's that not once have I heard anything remotely resembling a mea culpa about this," he said.

Lott, who seemed uncomfortable with the image problems the whole proceeding was creating for the Senate, told reporters on Jan. 8 that he expected the committee to find some significant violations. "I would be amazed if in at least one case it did not go to the Senate floor" for punishment, he said. ■

D'Amato Inquiry Pending

A Senate Ethics Committee inquiry into allegations that New York Republican Alfonse M. D'Amato improperly exerted pressure on the Department of Housing and Urban Development (HUD) to support projects developed by relatives and political allies remained pending at the end of 1990.

An outside counsel had been appointed and a preliminary inquiry opened in late 1989, but the case dropped out of public sight in 1990, with details of the investigation closely guarded by special counsel Henry F. Schuelke III and his staff.

The case was initiated by D'Amato's unsuccessful 1986 opponent, Democrat Mark Green, who asked the Ethics Committee to look into a variety of newspaper reports concerning D'Amato. *(1989 Almanac, p. 47)*

The most publicized allegations suggested that D'Amato had improperly pressured HUD officials to finance housing projects in New York and Puerto Rico that benefited his relatives and political contributors. He was also accused of taking illegal campaign contributions from New York-based defense contractors.

D'Amato denied wrongdoing. He said he supported housing projects that benefited his constituents based on need. As for the campaign contributions, D'Amato said he did not know of either of the contribution schemes at issue.

After the Ethics Committee issued its report on the Keating hearings on Feb. 27, 1991, committee Chairman Howell Heflin, D-Ala., said a decision on moving to a more formal investigation against D'Amato was still a while away. "There's lots of investigation completed — and there's still lots to go," Heflin said. ■

Durenberger Denounced Over Finances

The Senate on July 25, by a vote of 96-0, denounced Dave Durenberger, R-Minn., for conduct it called "clearly and unequivocally unethical." The charges against Durenberger focused mainly on a 1985-86 book deal the senator had with a Minnesota publishing company and on Senate reimbursement Durenberger received for rent he paid on a Minnesota condominium from August 1983 to November 1989.

The denouncement (S Res 311 — S Rept 101-382) — one of several terms the body had used to rebuke members without expelling them — also said that Durenberger's conduct "has been reprehensible and has brought the Senate into dishonor and disrepute."

The action marked the first disciplinary action the Senate had voted against a member since 1979, although Harrison A. Williams Jr., D-N.J., resigned in 1982 just hours before the Senate was due to vote on an Ethics Committee recommendation that he be expelled. *(Discipline cases, p. 99; terms of opprobrium, p. 100)*

Along with the denouncement, the Senate ordered Durenberger to pay more than $124,000 in restitution for the housing reimbursements and speaking fees he improperly accepted.

In recommending restitution, the Senate directed Durenberger to pay back the Senate $29,050 plus interest for reimbursements he received for the cost of staying in his Minneapolis condominium. That sum was owed on top of the $11,005 Durenberger had already repaid the Senate in early 1990, based on an incomplete calculation by the Rules Committee of the wrongful reimbursements he had received.

The Senate also required Durenberger to pay approximately $95,000 to charities with which he had no affiliation — the amount of honoraria he allegedly obtained improperly. The Senate also referred the case to the Republican Party Conference, though it did not recommend a particular action and the conference did not take any action.

Though Durenberger had previously called denouncement too harsh a penalty, he did not challenge the sanction or the version of events Ethics Committee Chairman Howell Heflin, D-Ala., presented to the Senate.

"Today is an ending, and it is a beginning," Durenberger said. "For past mistakes, I ask your forgiveness. For future challenges, I need your friendship."

The only senator to rise in Durenberger's defense was Rudy Boschwitz, a fellow Minnesota Republican. Boschwitz contended, as Durenberger had in committee hearings, that the senator had relied on lawyers' advice before going ahead with the questionable book and real estate deals.

Boschwitz and Durenberger voted present when the roll was called. Two senators were absent. *(Vote 175, p. 38-S)*

Durenberger did receive some solace from the debate. Several colleagues, including Republican leader Bob Dole of Kansas, offered paeans to the legislative style that had made him one of the Senate's rising stars. Many who voted to denounce him gave him a verbal lift during the proceedings and an emotional embrace when they ended. "There isn't a senator in this chamber who could stand up today and say Dave Durenberger didn't do his homework, didn't know the issues and didn't vote his conscience," Dole said.

After the vote, Durenberger pledged to bring new vigor to his work. He said in a news conference that he had never considered resigning and had not decided whether to seek re-election in 1994.

The resolution passed by the Senate cited Durenberger for the following:

- Having a book deal with Piranha Press, a Minnesota company, that the committee's special counsel, Robert S. Bennett, said amounted to a gimmick to "sanitize" speaking fees that Durenberger otherwise could not have accepted under Senate limits on honoraria.
- Failing to report expense-paid trips he took in connection with the book deal.
- Accepting Senate reimbursement for rent paid on a Minneapolis condominium in which he shared ownership.
- Having improper communications with the blind trust that held his interest in the condominium.
- Accepting free limousine services for personal use.
- Converting campaign funds to personal use when he signed over a $5,000 political donation to Piranha Press.

BACKGROUND

The Ethics Committee initiated a preliminary inquiry into Durenberger's book-publishing deal in March 1989. Based on its findings, the committee voted in August to proceed to an "initial review" and in December expanded the review to include allegations about his condominium deal. In January 1990, the Rules Committee, responding to a request by Durenberger, told the senator that he had improperly sought reimbursement from the Senate for renting the Minneapolis condominium he partially owned.

After receiving the ruling Jan. 25, Durenberger announced that he would repay the Senate $11,005 for reimbursements he collected in 1983-87. He said he would also pay interest when the amount due was calculated. *(1989 Almanac, p. 43)*

Durenberger's case marked the first time the full Senate debated disciplining one of its members since 1982, when it considered expelling Williams for the New Jersey Democrat's role in the Abscam scandal. Williams resigned before the Senate voted. *(1982 Almanac, p. 509)*

The last time the Senate actually voted on a disciplinary resolution was in the 1979 case of Herman E. Talmadge, a Georgia Democrat also accused of financial improprieties. Talmadge, who lost his 1980 bid for re-election, was the only previous senator to whom the term "denouncement" was applied. *(1979 Almanac, p. 566)*

The case also marked Durenberger's second brush with the Ethics Committee in two years. In 1987-88 the panel investigated allegations that Durenberger, chairman of the Intelligence Committee in 1985-86, improperly disclosed classified information. Though the panel did not recommend any punishment, it did criticize Durenberger for appearing to disclose "sensitive national security information." *(1988 Almanac, p. 39)*

ETHICS COMMITTEE ACTION

The Ethics Committee on July 18 unanimously called for Durenberger to be formally denounced for his financial dealings. The panel went beyond the recommendation of special counsel Bennett — who also handled the committee's investigation of Williams — by calling for Durenber-

Senators Disciplined in the 20th Century

1990 — Dave Durenberger, R-Minn.: Denounced. Accused of financial misconduct in connection with a book deal and Senate reimbursement received for rent he paid on a Minnesota condominium. Denounced on recommendation of the Ethics Committee. *(p. 98)*

1982 — Harrison A. Williams Jr., D-N.J.: Resigned. Accused of corruption in connection with Abscam scandal. Williams had been convicted in federal court in 1981 of accepting stock in a mining company in return for government contracts. Resigned after it became clear he would be expelled. *(1982 Almanac, p. 509)*

1979 — Herman E. Talmadge, D-Ga.: Denounced. Accused of financial misconduct for improperly collecting $43,436 in reimbursements between 1973 and 1978 by submitting false expense vouchers. He also failed to report more than $10,000 in campaign contributions. Denounced upon recommendation of the Ethics Committee, which rejected a censure proposal. *(1979 Almanac, p. 566)*

1967 — Thomas J. Dodd, D-Conn.: Censured. Accused of financial misconduct for spending campaign funds for personal purposes, double-billing for travel expenses and exchanging favors with a West German public relations representative. Censured for campaign-fund violations only. *(1967 Almanac, p. 239)*

1954 — Joseph R. McCarthy, R-Wis.: Condemned. Accused of obstruction of legislative process, especially refusal to testify before the Rules Committee in 1952; insulting senators, especially the defamation of Millard E. Tydings, D-Md.; habitual contempt for people. The original 40,000-word report from a Select Committee to Study Censure Charges recommended McCarthy be censured, but the Senate substituted the word "condemned" for "censured." *(1954 Almanac, p. 456)*

1929 — Hiram Bingham, R-Conn.: Censured. Accused of bringing the Senate into disrepute for hiring a secretary to the president of the Connecticut Manufacturers' Association to assist him with tariff legislation. *(CQ Guide to Congress Third Edition, p. 832)*

1902 — John L. McLaurin, D-S.C., and Benjamin R. Tillman, D-S.C.: Censured. Accused of assault. During a debate on the Philippines, the two engaged in a brief fistfight on the Senate floor. *(CQ Guide to Congress Third Edition, p. 832)*

ger to pay more than $124,000 in restitution for housing reimbursements and speaking fees.

The recommendation came more than five months after the committee met with Durenberger for the first time after officially opening its investigation.

Durenberger had appeared before the committee Feb. 8 to defend himself against the allegations that he improperly enriched himself through his financial dealings. Durenberger said he told the panel that he had gotten approval from "appropriate, official bodies" before opening the book and real estate deals.

But he added, "I have acknowledged that, had I to do it over again, some decisions would be made differently."

The day before the committee meeting, one of his hometown newspapers raised new questions about whether Durenberger got preferential terms on nearly $1 million in loans from a St. Paul bank.

The Minneapolis Star Tribune reported Feb. 7 that the Commercial State Bank in St. Paul gave Durenberger $927,078 in loans over 10 years, most without collateral and some at low interest rates.

Durenberger said the loans were part of a "normal, longstanding relationship with a bank" and accused the paper of "blatant distortion of facts."

The bank's president said the terms of the loans to Durenberger were in line with what the bank gave to others with comparable accounts who, like the senator, were long-time customers.

Little more was made of the bank-loan allegation during the rest of the inquiry, and the Senate did not mention the issue in its resolution of denouncement.

The Ethics Committee on Feb. 22 found "substantial credible evidence" that Durenberger broke federal law and Senate rules and set in motion the next phase of the formal trial-like investigation. The committee said there was evidence that Durenberger's book arrangement violated limits on outside income and other rules governing senators' finances. The committee also said limousine service provided Durenberger during trips to Concord, Mass., in 1985 and 1986 might have violated conflict of interest rules.

The committee said it found no evidence to continue examining allegations that Durenberger improperly solicited speeches in Boston during 1985 and 1986 or that he improperly used his staff to help write his books.

The committee said, however, that it was continuing a preliminary inquiry — the first step of the committee's consideration of an ethics case — of the condo arrangement.

"It was never my intent to circumvent Senate rules for my own benefit," Durenberger said in a Feb. 22 statement. "I made every effort to seek opinion from the appropriate bodies and from legal counsel."

He acknowledged, "I made mistakes and had lapses in judgment on these matters, and I take full responsibility for them."

An investigation — the committee's term for a trial-like hearing — followed the new findings.

Committee leaders emphasized that the panel's action did not mean Durenberger violated any rules. The official investigation would be the third and final stage of the committee's action and would follow the initial review, just completed.

The committee said it would examine five subjects in the hearing:

- Whether the financial arrangement between Durenberger and Piranha Press improperly circumvented limits on a senator's honoraria income. Interest groups that invited Durenberger to speak during the two years were asked to write checks to the company rather than pay the senator an honorarium, even though books were not always available at the senator's appearances. Senate rules capped honoraria at $22,500 in 1985 and $30,000 in 1986.

- Whether Durenberger's failure to report the travel expenses paid by Piranha Press on his yearly financial statements violated disclosure rules.
- Whether he turned campaign money to personal use in violation of federal law when he transferred to Piranha Press a $5,000 check written to his Senate campaign committee.
- Whether his use of Senate-controlled space for six appearances to promote his book violated rules barring commercial uses of such space.
- Whether limousine service provided by businesses and lobbying groups during his trips to Boston in 1985 and 1986 violated conflict-of-interest provisions against accepting certain gifts.

Public Hearing

On June 12-13, the Ethics Committee conducted the formal public hearings on the Durenberger case. It was the first time in the committee's 26-year history that it had conducted business before television cameras.

Bennett presented the special counsel's findings on the first day of the hearing, and Durenberger offered his defense on the second day. Though the hearings were originally expected to last at least two weeks, they abruptly ended after just two days. In his address to the committee, Durenberger petitioned to halt the proceedings to avoid the political cost and financial burden of weeks of trial-like hearings.

Bennett's investigation produced 23 volumes of evidence, the result of 198 subpoenas for internal documents, 240 interviews with witnesses, numerous depositions and at least 75 affidavits.

When the hearings ended, the committee was left to decide not what to believe, but what to make of it. "There is not a great deal of dispute about the facts," said Warren B. Rudman, R-N.H., the vice chairman. "There's obviously a great deal of dispute about what those facts mean." The dispute boiled down to Bennett's June 12 attack on Durenberger and the senator's June 13 defense of his actions.

Bennett's attack: A senator on the financial brink set out to increase his income and cut his living expenses — deliberately skirting Senate rules along the way. He set up a book promotion deal to launder honoraria and converted a personal residence into a business property so he could charge the government for its use. That was unethical.

Durenberger's defense: He did set out to increase his income, but did so in good faith, with a bevy of lawyers advising him. Personal trials and tribulations haunted him at every turn. "I recognize that real damage has been done by what has been perceived as my desire to push the limits and take advantage of the Senate, and for that I am sorry," he said.

In presenting his case, Bennett focused on what he said were the two most salient matters: the book deal with Piranha Press and the Minneapolis condominium. He devoted little time to two other allegations against Durenberger: his use of Capitol facilities for commercial purposes and his acceptance of free limousine service.

The Book Deal

Piranha Press was a company owned by Gary L. Diamond, a friend of Durenberger who also published trade

Terms of Opprobrium

Under the Constitution, each chamber had the power to "punish its members for disorderly behavior and, with the concurrence of two thirds, expel a member."

Throughout its history the Senate has imposed punishments short of expulsion, usually by adopting resolutions on the floor. *(CQ Guide to Congress Third Edition, p. 828)*

While on occasion much energy has been expended on the semantics of these resolutions, there was no formal or agreed-upon hierarchy of punishment, according to a historical review by Jack Maskell of the Congressional Research Service.

The situation was clearer in the House, where precedents and rules of the ethics committee had established "censure" as the most severe punishment short of expulsion, and "reprimand" as a milder rebuke.

Some of the terms the Senate has used, based largely on Maskell's paper:

Expulsion — Removing a member from his seat was traditionally reserved for cases involving disloyalty or a crime involving abuse of office. Fifteen senators have been expelled, and in 1982 Harrison A. Williams Jr., D-N.J., resigned to avoid a vote to expel him.

Censure — This term was not officially used until 1902, but Maskell said historians and parliamentarians were generally using it to describe any punishment short of expulsion that was voted on by the full Senate. In 1967, Thomas J. Dodd, D-Conn., was censured for spending campaign funds for personal purposes.

The two following terms were considered instances of censure, according to Maskell, even though the Senate chose to use other words.

Condemnation — The Senate has "condemned" two members — Joseph R. McCarthy, R-Wis., in 1954 and Hiram Bingham, R-Conn., in 1929.

Denouncement — Dave Durenberger, R-Minn., was "denounced" in 1990 for financial misconduct. The term was used previously only in the 1979 case of Herman E. Talmadge, D-Ga. The committee chose the term to distinguish Talmadge's case from others; Talmadge claimed "a personal victory," but he lost the next election.

The House but not the Senate has imposed these disciplines:

Reprimand — The Senate rejected a proposal to substitute the term for "censure" in Dodd's case.

Loss of chairmanship or seniority — While not used in the Senate, the Ethics Committee's rules of procedure included among possible punishments the recommendation to a party's conference that it strip a member of positions of responsibility.

journals for the restaurant and hospitality industries. He published two books by Durenberger: "Neither Madmen Nor Messiahs," a collection of white papers on defense policy, in 1984; and "Prescription for Change," a collection of speeches about health care, in 1986. The only other book Diamond had published, Bennett said, was about wrestling holds.

Piranha Press paid Durenberger $100,000 in quarterly installments of $12,500 that began in 1985 and ended in early 1987 in return for his making 113 appearances to promote the books. Bennett contended that there was never a real intent to promote books. The arrangement "was little more than a pretext to sanitize what were honestly honoraria payments."

Bennett traced the deal to Durenberger's need to replace lost honoraria income. The senator reported $92,750 in honoraria in 1983, the last year the Senate permitted members to collect unlimited speech fees. New Senate rules capped Durenberger's honoraria income at $22,530 in 1985 and $30,040 in 1986, the years of the book deal.

In those two years, Durenberger made traditional honoraria speeches until he reached the limit. At that point, speeches would be designated as "Piranha Press events," Bennett said.

The senator's attorney, Michael C. Mahoney of Minneapolis, in 1983 asked the Federal Election Commission (FEC) to rule on the nature of the publishing agreement. The FEC ruled that Durenberger's stipend from Piranha was acceptable — a ruling Durenberger would repeatedly use as a shield. The request for the opinion, however, never mentioned what Bennett said were three crucial facts: Durenberger's contract called for the groups he addressed to pay the publisher a fee; the appearances stemmed from requests for speeches, not book promotions; and the promotional events were identical to traditional honorarium events.

Here's the way it usually worked:

Groups wanting to hear Durenberger were referred by his staff to Mahoney, the agent for Piranha Press. With a call or a letter, Mahoney would tell the organizations that Durenberger's appearance was a book promotion.

"What were honoraria events one day magically became book promotion events the next," Bennett said.

Never in the 113 times Durenberger appeared for Piranha did an organization actually ask Durenberger to promote his book, Bennett said.

Some organizations and constituencies important to the senator objected to the arrangement. James F. Doherty, president of the Group Health Association of America, a trade association of health maintenance organizations, in an affidavit characterized the letter he got from Diamond regarding a Piranha promotion as "abrupt, harsh and heavy-handed." Saying he believed the association was "being hustled," he canceled Durenberger's June 1986 appearance.

William C. Mattox, director of federal relations for The Equitable Life Assurance Society of the United States, in 1986 invited Durenberger to address a breakfast meeting on health issues.

When Durenberger's aide informed Mattox that the appearance would be regarded as a book promotion, Mattox said in an affidavit that he told the aide, "I did not have any interest in any agreement between the senator and his publisher."

A representative of Piranha later called Mattox and asked him to write the check to the publisher. "I refused to do so," Mattox said. "He then informed me that the senator might not appear."

Durenberger did appear on July 29, 1986, and the discussion centered on long-term health care. His books were never mentioned. Still, when Durenberger got Equitable's $2,000 check, he endorsed it to Piranha.

It was the exception, not the rule, for Durenberger to promote the books, Bennett said. And Durenberger made light of the book in one appearance, saying he was trying to write a "real book" on health policy. As for the health book he was promoting, "Prescription for Change," Durenberger once said, "I don't know where it's available, except in my office."

"This is some promotion, senators," Bennett told the committee.

The special counsel depicted the genesis of "Prescription for Change," the second book, as "some of the most troubling evidence." At the time, Durenberger was getting paid to promote the defense book even though he addressed mostly health groups. Jon Schroeder, an aide on the senator's Minnesota staff, discussed the second book's origin in a November 1985 memo.

"I understand and agree with the necessity of doing this, because of the desirability of broadening the audience of the senator's health speeches and enhancing his role and perception as the 'Health Senator,' and to make sure that we have a sound justification for the compensation which he is receiving from Piranha for delivering health speeches around the country," Schroeder wrote. The memo said the book could be "quick and dirty" but must not embarrass the senator.

In all, the arrangement generated $248,360 in revenue for Piranha. Of this, $15,562, or about 6 percent, came from the book sales, mostly through B. Dalton bookstores in Minnesota and Washington, D.C. The remainder came from Durenberger's speaking appearances. In turn, Piranha paid Durenberger $100,000 and Mahoney $24,502.

"This very hungry fish, Piranha Press, was allowed to engage in a feeding frenzy on responsible organizations who thought they were sponsoring traditional honorarium events," Bennett said. "And unfortunately, the evidence shows that Sen. Durenberger ... allowed himself and the stature of his office to be used as the bait, and he got $100,000 for his trouble."

Durenberger said he wrote the books because he had something to say, not to make money. His friend Diamond was interested in breaking into public policy publishing.

Only after "Neither Madmen Nor Messiahs" was published, he said, did the promotion deal arise. "I relied on paid professional counsel, the FEC and the Ethics Committee to guide me," Durenberger said June 13. He later said he should have known that the appearance, if not the actual substance, of the deal raised questions.

"Giving speeches to organizations that usually pay honoraria, but in this case pay sponsor fees to a publisher who pays me in a quarterly stipend, sure as heck looks like a way to get around the law limiting honoraria. Take away the legal opinions, take away the assurances, I should have known it, and I should have avoided it. And I'm sorry I didn't."

The Condominium Deal

Bennett depicted Durenberger's handling of his Minneapolis condominium as a "search for loopholes." It began in 1983, when Durenberger decided he could not afford two residences — a house in McLean, Va., and the one-bedroom condominium. Owning the Minneapolis condo where he stayed also prevented the Senate from reimbursing him for living expenses on his frequent trips to Minnesota.

Durenberger took two steps in 1983 to change this situation. First, he changed his legal residence to his parents' address in Avon, Minn. Second, he sought to change the ownership of the condo. Initially, he and Roger Scherer, a friend and political backer who owned another condo in the same building, considered swapping condos. After discovering the swap had unfavorable tax implications, they instead settled on a partnership, Bennett said.

The partnership's assets were the two condos — Durenberger's 603, Scherer's 703. Durenberger stayed in the same condo on his trips home but began billing the Senate for his expenses, paying rent to the partnership.

The partnership documents were not completed until 1984, but they were backdated to July 1983 and notarized by Durenberger's friend and campaign attorney, Randall E. Johnson of Bloomington, Minn. That enabled Durenberger to justify vouchers submitted to the Senate for his expenses during the August 1983 recess.

In March 1984, the name of the partnership was changed from the Durenberger/Scherer Partnership to the 703/603 Association. Bennett contended the change was designed to obscure the ownership. He pointed to a memo written by Durenberger's bookkeeper saying it did not look good to have Durenberger's name on invoices submitted to the Senate.

The 1986 tax overhaul removed the partnership's tax advantages, so Scherer decided to dissolve it. Durenberger sold his condo for $52,804 in 1987 to the Independent Service Co., a company owned by a political associate, Paul Overgaard, a 15-year state senator and a candidate for governor in 1982.

For reasons never fully explained in the proceeding or documents, Durenberger's attorney, Mahoney, did not forward the sale documents to Overgaard until late in 1989. By then, Overgaard had grown upset with Durenberger. In a letter, he questioned why the senator and Mahoney were stalling.

"Whatever the reason, I want out," Overgaard wrote Durenberger in September 1989. "The last thing I need is to get involved in your ethics investigation and be accused of participating in a sham transaction by which you collect per diem from the Senate on a residence you actually own."

In a later affidavit, Overgaard said the sale was real, "not a sham." Although there was "an embarrassing looseness in the procedure," he said, "most certainly there was no scheme or conspiracy to mislead the Senate."

From August 1983 until mid-November 1989, Durenberger collected $40,055 from the U.S. Treasury for per diem expenses while staying at the condo. After receiving the ruling from the Senate Rules Committee in January 1990, Durenberger reimbursed the Treasury for $11,005 in expenses paid. The committee ruled that Durenberger's resident city for the purposes of reimbursement was Minneapolis, not Avon, during these periods.

Before seeking reimbursement for staying in the condo, Durenberger said, his staff consulted with the Rules and Ethics committees, which raised no objections at the time.

In documents submitted for the December 1989 review that Durenberger requested, the only evidence he offered of earlier approval from Rules and Ethics was an interoffice memo from one Durenberger aide to another. "No one has a problem with the partnership situation," it said, without specifying who had been consulted.

In his defense, Durenberger contended that the first transaction, the partnership, dated to July 28, 1983, was the date he and Scherer agreed orally to the deal. The paperwork, he said, was a mere formality.

"Every decision was on the basis of legal advice," Durenberger said.

What's more, he noted, the Senate disbursing office never questioned the arrangement, even when the nature of the partnership was clear. Finally, he said, the condo was a matter of convenience and a relatively inexpensive way to live on his frequent trips home, compared with staying in a hotel. "It was not a financial windfall," he said.

Durenberger's Response

In perhaps the most important speech of his public career, a speech carried live on Minnesota Public Radio, Durenberger on June 13 had his chance to rebut the case presented by Bennett the day before.

Durenberger recounted his story once more in his hourlong address to the committee. He told how his first wife died at age 31; how he remarried, to a woman widowed by the Vietnam War; and how their lives together faltered.

"With a mother lost to Charlie, David, Mike and Danny, a husband lost to Penny and a wife lost to me, sadness made bonding difficult in our family," he said. "Some of that sadness was acknowledged, and some was never dealt with. My grief counseling was to throw myself into my work."

He walked the committee through his version of the charges. He talked about his ideal of public service, his cloudy judgment and his reliance on others. In the end, though, he took responsibility for it all and asked for a judgment tempered by consideration of the "whole person of Dave Durenberger, what I did wrong and what I've done right for this institution."

Even Bennett was touched. "There is a big part of me that wants to say 'enough.' Here are the books. Let's go home. No human being in this room could feel good right now. I sure don't."

But Bennett did not let go, and he admonished the committee, "Let's keep our eye on the ball here."

Durenberger acknowledged that some punishment was appropriate, but did not say what. His counsel, James Hamilton — a Washington lawyer who defended Herman Talmadge — called denouncement draconian and unwarranted by the evidence.

A month after the hearing, Bennett completed his final report on the case and submitted it to the Ethics Committee. On July 18, the committee unanimously approved the resolution of denouncement.

The report on the Durenberger inquiry was released July 20 and included the full report filed with the panel by Bennett.

The committee found no criminal wrongdoing but referred Durenberger's case to the Justice Department and the FEC for further investigation.

During the committee's closed deliberations, Ethics Chairman Heflin said, one senator proposed changing the sanction from denouncement to censure — apparently intended as a stronger sanction — but the proposal was rejected.

FLOOR ACTION

The case reached the Senate floor on July 25 when the chamber conducted a three-hour proceeding and then, without a fight from Durenberger, voted 96-0 to denounce him.

Despite the unanimity of the verdict, some members questioned the process that led to the year and a half investigation of Durenberger, particularly Bennett's role as special counsel.

Dale Bumpers, D-Ark., expressed concern about "the prosecutorial nature" of Bennett's work and asked, "By what authority does the special counsel who is hired by the committee ... find that there are violations of the ethics of the Senate?" That task belongs to senators, Bumpers argued.

Heflin said of the special counsel, "I thought he was a little bit too prosecutorial but clearly he was acting within the scope of his responsibility to the committee."

The term of opprobrium recommended by the committee also came in for scrutiny. Ethics Committee member Trent Lott, R-Miss., said the committee considered censure the harsher punishment when voting. "The committee chose denouncement instead of censure largely because, I think, of the mitigation that was present and because, as the defense counsel emphasized in our hearings, there was no venal intent."

William L. Armstrong, R-Colo., described the difficult task senators faced in policing their ranks: "When this is all over and after we have voted to denounce him, we will still want him to be our friend. We will still want to go down to the dining room and have lunch with him." ■

Frank Reprimanded for Ties to Prostitute

The House of Representatives on July 26 formally reprimanded Barney Frank for improperly using his office to help a male prostitute. The House voted 408-18 to reprimand the Massachusetts Democrat after a roiling, unusually partisan debate about how harshly to punish Frank. *(Vote 271, p. 90-H)*

Despite the reprimand (H Res 440 — H Rept 101-610) from his colleagues, Frank had little trouble winning reelection to a sixth term in November. Frank's most serious GOP opponent dropped out of the race in June, indicative of the trouble the GOP has had fielding credible challengers.

Despite politicians' election-year jitters about ethics issues — heightened in a case involving homosexuality — the House turned back efforts to overturn the recommendation of its ethics committee, the Committee on Standards of Official Conduct, and punish Frank more severely.

That came in the wake of a passionate appeal by House ethics committee Chairman Julian C. Dixon, D-Calif., for his colleagues to stand by the panel as their bulwark against political attacks. "We will throw no one to the wolves," Dixon said.

The House rejected, 138-390, a resolution to expel Frank (H Res 442), the ultimate sanction. The intermediate penalty of censure was turned down largely along party lines, 141-287. *(Votes 268, 270, p. 90-H)*

Frank did not contest the ethics committee's finding that he "reflected discredit upon the House" by using his status as a congressman to fix improperly 33 parking tickets and by writing a misleading memorandum in behalf of Steve Gobie, a male prostitute with whom he associated in 1985-87.

Frank, who publicly acknowledged his homosexuality in 1987, went to the well of the House near the end of debate to apologize to his colleagues. Attributing his misconduct to the strain of concealing his homosexuality at the time, Frank said, "I should have known better. I do now."

In the eyes of other participants in the debate, more was at stake than just one member's conduct.

"We are here to repair the integrity of the United States House of Representatives," said GOP Whip Newt Gingrich of Georgia, who proposed upping the sanction to censure.

Democrats saw GOP efforts to force votes on increased sanctions as an election-year ploy to stockpile political ammunition against Democrats.

Dixon, indignant at challenges to his committee's unanimous verdict, cast the debate as a referendum on the ethics panel itself. "This case boils down to, really, who do you trust?" said Dixon.

BACKGROUND

The reprimand of Frank was the first time in almost three years, and only the 33rd time in history, that the House voted to punish one of its members. The last time was in 1987, when Austin J. Murphy, D-Pa., was reprimanded for "ghost" voting, payroll padding and misuse of government resources. *(1987 Almanac, p. 29)*

The political crosscurrents in the Frank investigation were strong from the day the committee opened its investigation in September 1989. *(1989 Almanac, p. 43)*

The Washington Times a few weeks earlier had disclosed Frank's relationship with Gobie, a felon on probation. After buying sex from Gobie in 1985, Frank befriended him and paid him to help with household chores.

ETHICS COMMITTEE ACTION

In its report on the inquiry filed July 20, the panel said it found no conclusive evidence that Frank knew Gobie was running a prostitution service out of his apartment until his landlady told him that she had seen suspicious activity in his absence.

But the panel criticized Frank for a misleading memo written in support of ending Gobie's probation. The memo included assertions that Gobie had met Frank through "mutual friends" — when in fact Frank had responded to Gobie's escort-service ad in a gay newspaper — and that Gobie was adhering to his probation requirements, when Frank knew Gobie was engaged in prostitution. Frank said candor on those two points would have revealed his own homosexuality.

Although the panel concluded that Frank had not improperly pressured probation officials, it said that the memo "could be perceived as an attempt to use political influence."

The panel also ordered Frank to pay the parking tickets improperly waived because it was not clear whether they were incurred on official business. Having agreed on those two areas of impropriety, many Democrats on the ethics committee had sought a light sanction that would have avoided action by the House — a letter of reproval.

That was the punishment meted out in two of the most recent cases before the committee: Jim Bates, D-Calif., and Gus Savage, D-Ill., in 1989 both received mild rebukes for sexual harassment of women in connection with official duties. *(1989 Almanac, p. 43)*

But members on and off the committee were concerned that Frank might get off lightly. George "Buddy" Darden, D-Ga., said a letter of rebuke would have been too mild. The publicity surrounding Frank's case, he said, had "held the House up to a certain amount of public embarrassment. There's no other way to look at it."

On July 19 the House ethics committee went further than some members had anticipated when it unanimously agreed to the somewhat harsher punishment of reprimand for Frank after it became clear that the committee would be overturned by the House if it did not send something stronger to the floor.

FLOOR ACTION

From the beginning, it was all but certain that the effort to expel Frank would be rejected. Expulsion, the most extreme punishment, had been reserved in the past for more serious transgressions such as treason. Its proponent in the Frank case, California Republican William E. Dannemeyer, was not considered an influential advocate because even some of his own Republican colleagues regarded him as an anti-gay zealot.

Dannemeyer questioned the committee's conclusion that Frank did not know his apartment was being used for prostitution. He said the panel too lightly dismissed damning evidence, such as testimony from one of Gobie's associates, who said a man she believed to be Frank had called to ask if there were any "clients" in the house before he came home.

Only two Democrats voted to expel Frank — conservative Texans Bill Sarpalius and Ralph M. Hall.

Anticipating the effort to censure Frank, a task force of Democrats sympathetic to him had worked for months to drum up support among his colleagues.

Censure was considered harsher than a reprimand because, under House rules, the chastised member had to stand in the well of the House when the charges were read and could not hold a chairmanship for the rest of that Congress. Frank was chairman of a Judiciary subcommittee.

Although the ethics committee voted unanimously to recommend reprimand, three Republican panel members voted for censure on the floor. One of them, Thomas E. Petri, Wis., said he favored a harsher sanction because, he said, there was inadequate evidence that Frank had legitimately employed Gobie. The other two ethics members supporting censure were Larry E. Craig of Idaho and James V. Hansen of Utah.

Dixon closed the debate with an institutional, not political, appeal. He depicted the vote as a choice between a unanimous, bipartisan committee that had studied the case for almost a year and GOP demagogues who would throw their colleagues to the wolves.

The committee's position was strengthened among Democrats by Gingrich's role in opposing it. Many Democrats still resented Gingrich's part in the 1989 resignation of Jim Wright, D-Texas (1955-89). Wright, the former House Speaker, was forced by scandal to resign after a yearlong inquiry into his financial dealings. *(1989 Almanac, p. 36)*

Democrats were also annoyed that Gingrich was criticizing the same committee that he once praised for clearing his own name. The ethics committee in March dismissed formal complaints against Gingrich over his own financial dealings. *(Gingrich case, this page)*

Republicans had tried but failed to persuade someone other than Gingrich to offer the censure motion. GOP leader Robert H. Michel of Illinois voted for censure but did not speak on the floor. In the end, only 12 Democrats, most of them Southerners, joined 129 Republicans in supporting censure. ■

Gingrich Case Dismissed

The House ethics committee on March 7 dropped its investigation of House Republican Whip Newt Gingrich of Georgia after a yearlong review of a torrent of allegations.

Dismissing two formal complaints filed by Rep. Bill Alexander, D-Ark., the panel said in its report, "The committee is of the firm view that no adequate basis exists for initiating a preliminary inquiry....

"The facts alleged in the complaints, even if true, have been generally deemed not to state violations" of House rules or law, said the Committee on Standards of Official Conduct.

The panel did, however, scold Gingrich for relatively minor violations: an omission from his financial disclosure form and misuse of congressional stationery by an aide.

But the committee found no impropriety in the central focus of the complaint: a partnership, financed largely by his political backers, set up to promote a 1984 book coauthored by Gingrich.

Interest in the case was high because Gingrich instigated the 1988-89 investigation that led to the resignation of Speaker Jim Wright of Texas. *(1989 Almanac, p. 36)*

At a news conference March 8, Gingrich dismissed the accusations as a "political smear.... I am glad the committee was thorough, and I am happy the charges have been exposed as politically inspired nonsense."

The committee's decision to drop its investigation also defused a potential campaign issue against Gingrich. In November, Gingrich defeated Democrat David Worley, his 1988 opponent, by 974 votes, or less than 1 percent.

Background

The controversy surrounding Gingrich's book deal began two days before his election as whip when The Washington Post on March 20, 1989, published an article detailing the formation of a partnership to promote Gingrich's book, "A Window of Opportunity."

The partnership, which was managed by Gingrich's wife, Marianne, raised $105,000 to supplement the publisher's meager promotional budget. The enterprise had 22 partners, including 14 who had also made political contributions to Gingrich.

Alexander filed a complaint with the committee on April 11, 1989, raising questions about whether the arrangement was a means of circumventing House rules on outside income, acceptance of gifts and conversion of campaign funds or government resources to personal use. Alexander amended his complaint in July and again in October, when he added a long list of allegations unrelated to the book deal. *(1989 Almanac, p. 43)*

Among them, the complaint cited Gingrich's failure to mention on his annual financial disclosure report a mortgage he cosigned with his daughter when she bought a house.

The complaint also alleged that Gingrich improperly used official stationery to help recruit cruise participants for a Florida travel company. An aide sent a letter providing information about a cruise for senior citizens sponsored by a Florida travel agency.

Alexander's initial complaint was reviewed by the ethics committee staff, which concluded that many of the allegations were conjectural and that others were not supported by facts, were based on unusual legal arguments or were accompanied by no facts that amounted to House rule violations.

The staff concluded in a June 1989 memo that the reams of paper provided by Alexander did not meet the threshold required for opening a preliminary investigation: that the allegations "merit further inquiry."

The same conclusion was reached by the committee's outside counsel in the case, the Chicago law firm of Phelan, Pope & John, which also handled the Wright investigation. In October, the firm presented the committee with its conclusion that there was no basis for opening a formal investigation.

After further questioning of Gingrich, the committee concurred and voted 11-0 on March 7, 1990, to dismiss all of Alexander's allegations.

"Rep. Alexander's complaint asserts that the partnership was, in fact, a scheme whereby influential friends of the Gingriches sought to funnel to them either gifts, campaign contributions or both," the committee report said. "In the committee's view, there is no support for this proposition."

The committee did conclude, however, that Gingrich should have reported his participation in his daughter's home purchase. In its letter to him, the committee directed Gingrich to amend his financial disclosure forms to include the real estate transaction.

The panel also concluded that a Gingrich aide violated House rules in sending out the cruise promotion on official stationery under the congressional frank.

Gingrich said that he had not known of the mailing and that neither he nor the aide profited from it. But the committee told Gingrich he had been "remiss in your oversight and administration of your congressional office" and directed him to guard against future abuse of mail and office resources. ■

Savage Denies Impropriety

In a report released Feb. 2, the House Committee on Standards of Official Conduct concluded that Rep. Gus Savage, D-Ill., made improper sexual advances to a young woman while on an official trip to Africa. But the committee did not propose disciplinary action because Savage had apologized to the woman. *(1989 Almanac, p. 43)*

The committee concluded the inquiry without a formal disciplinary hearing. The panel based its conclusion on interviews with Savage and others on the tour, and on a sworn deposition from the woman, a Peace Corps worker who was not further identified.

In his interview with the committee, Savage denied any impropriety — including the woman's allegations that he kissed her and asked her to spend the night with him.

But Savage wrote a letter to the woman Nov. 20, 1989, saying: "I never intended to offend and was not aware that you felt offended at the time."

The committee concluded in its report (H Rept 101-397), approved Jan. 31, that "Rep. Savage did, in fact, make sexual advances to the Peace Corps volunteer."

The report stated that his actions were contrary to the House rule requiring members' behavior to "reflect creditably" on the House. "The committee clearly disapproves of Rep. Savage's conduct," the report said.

Accusations of impropriety by Savage surfaced in The Washington Post on July 19, 1989, when it reported the allegations.

Savage stirred a new controversy with a floor speech criticizing the ethics inquiry.

Furor Over Floor Remarks

The House on Feb. 7 overwhelmingly approved a resolution calling for a review of rules that allowed members to change the text of what they said during floor debate when it was reprinted in the Congressional Record.

The resolution (H Res 330) was approved 373-30 in the wake of a Feb. 1 speech in which Savage criticized three colleagues who had asked the House ethics committee to investigate the sexual allegations against him. *(Vote 13, p. 414)*

Those critical remarks were not included in the Record's account of the speech, which Savage made just after the ethics committee filed its report saying it disapproved of his conduct.

Savage contended that he was a victim of racism in politics and the media.

The resolution asked the Committee on House Administration to make recommendations about congressional rules that allowed such deletions. It was introduced by Pennsylvania Republican Robert S. Walker, who said the review was needed to maintain the "integrity of the proceedings" of the House.

Savage deleted his criticisms from the text he submitted for the record at the suggestion of the House parliamentarian, William H. Brown, who said the presiding officer should have ruled the personal criticism out of order because it impugned the motives of colleagues.

The three members who had asked for the investigation of Savage were Democrats Barney Frank of Massachusetts, Matthew F. McHugh of New York and Patricia Schroeder of Colorado.

In his floor speech, Savage referred to Frank, who had acknowledged having a relationship with a male prostitute, when he said, "Believe it or not, among these self-appointed guardians of personal morality was one who since has admitted keeping and prostituting a homosexual." *(Frank case, p. 103)*

Savage also said, "As for the other two so-called liberals, I urge them to review their sensitivity to racism and their respect for fairness."

Most members of Congress have routinely edited their

remarks before submitting them for the record, but they typically made minor changes, such as corrections of grammar, rather than wholesale omissions.

Campaign Remarks Come Under Fire

Savage also faced growing criticism over a campaign speech he made at a rally in his Chicago district March 17, three days before his narrow primary victory. Savage rejected allegations that his remarks were anti-Semitic or racist.

At the rally, Savage listed what he called "pro-Israel, Jewish" contributors to the campaign of his strongest challenger, Mel Reynolds.

Federal Election Commission reports, he said, showed that 96 percent of Reynolds' receipts from political action committees in early 1990 came from pro-Israel PACs. "He who pays the piper plays the tune," Savage said.

The speech put in an awkward position two powerful black members — Majority Whip William H. Gray III of Pennsylvania and Charles B. Rangel of New York, a senior Democrat on the Ways and Means Committee — who endorsed Savage at the Chicago rally. Gray and Rangel said they left before Savage made his remarks.

Six days after the rally, Rangel released a statement saying, "If I had known that such foul statements would be made, in my presence or out of it, I would not have gone to Chicago."

On March 26, Gray said: "I find much of his language and remarks unacceptable, divisive and bigoted."

Savage invited colleagues and reporters to view a videotape of the speech on March 29. In a news conference afterward, Savage said his speech was not anti-Semitic but was distorted by news organizations that he contended were controlled by racist whites. ■

Lame Duck Lukens Resigns

Rep. Donald E. "Buz" Lukens, R-Ohio, confronted with new allegations of sexual misconduct, resigned from Congress on Oct. 24 rather than face ethics sanctions in his final days in the House.

The Ohio Republican, who lost his bid for re-election in a May primary, announced his resignation two days after the House ethics committee Oct. 22 passed a resolution revealing new charges that he made "unwanted and unsolicited sexual advances to a congressional employee."

The panel said it was expanding its long-dormant investigation of Lukens on other sexual misconduct charges to look into the new allegations. They centered on reports that he had fondled and propositioned an elevator operator in the Capitol.

Lukens did not comment on the allegations but said in his resignation letter to Ohio Democratic Gov. Richard F. Celeste that he was leaving "for the good of the Congress and the integrity of the institution."

The ethics committee, officially the Committee on Standards of Official Conduct, first began investigating Lukens in August 1989, after his conviction in May of that year of contributing to the delinquency of a minor for having sex with a 16-year-old girl in Columbus, Ohio. He was sentenced to 30 days in jail and given a $500 fine.

Lukens appealed the decision but a state appeals court on June 12 upheld the conviction. Lukens then appealed his case to the state Supreme Court.

The congressional investigation went dormant after Lukens lost in the primary.

After the committee revealed the new charges Oct. 22, Lukens came under heavy pressure from fellow Republicans, including Minority Leader Robert H. Michel of Illinois, to resign.

Lukens was the fourth member to resign from the House under an ethics cloud during the 101st Congress. The others were House Speaker Jim Wright, D-Texas and Democratic Whip Tony Coelho, Calif., in 1989; and Robert Garcia, D-N.Y., on Jan. 7, 1990. *(1989 Almanac: Wright, p. 36; Coelho, p. 41; Garcia, p. 45)* ■

Flake Indicted Over Funds

The 101st Congress took yet another ethics jolt on Aug. 2 with the indictment of New York Democratic Rep. Floyd H. Flake and his wife, Margarett, on charges of conspiracy, fraud and tax evasion.

Announcing the indictment at a New York City news conference, U.S. Attorney Andrew Maloney said the Flakes allegedly embezzled funds from a senior citizens' housing project run by a church that the congressman headed and failed to report the income on their tax returns. Maloney alleged that Flake siphoned off $75,000 in transportation funds from the Allen Senior Citizens Apartments and used $66,000 in other church funds for personal purposes.

Flake, who was in his second House term, denied the charges and said he had cooperated with the investigation. "The prosecutor has decided to charge me, basically, with tax violations which he has attempted to bolster with allegations of misapplying a portion of the transportation expenses," Flake said.

With the indictment, Flake found his career potentially threatened by a project that initially helped make him a popular figure in New York's 6th Congressional District, a majority-black district in southern Queens. As pastor of the Allen African Methodist Episcopal church, Flake organized efforts to obtain projects to assist local low-income residents. One of his successes was a $10 million federal grant to the church to build the 300-unit seniors' housing project that became the focus of Flake's legal troubles.

Flake did not face immediate political danger, however. No one filed to run against him in the Sept. 11 Democratic primary. William Sampol, a Republican-Conservative, and John Cronin, a Right-to-Life Party candidate, were his opponents in November.

The district had a strong Democratic orientation — Michael S. Dukakis got 71 percent of the vote there in 1988 — and Flake won re-election with 72 percent of the vote.

The Flakes' trial got under way on March 11, 1991. But three weeks into the trial, prosecutors dropped all criminal charges on April 3 because of unfavorable testimony and restrictive rulings by the judge. ■

Ford Case Ends in Mistrial

Almost four years after he was indicted, Rep. Harold E. Ford, D-Tenn., faced the prospect of a second trial after the first ended April 27 with a hung jury in Memphis.

Government prosecutors said they planned to seek another trial of the Tennessee Democrat and filed a motion to move a second trial away from Memphis or to sequester the jurors. Ford's attorneys filed motions to dismiss the case.

No new trial date had been set as of early 1991.

Neither Ford nor any of his three co-defendants testified during seven weeks of arguments. The four were indicted April 24, 1987, on 19 counts of bank, mail and tax fraud, based on accusations that they participated in an influence-buying scheme. *(1987 Almanac, p. 32)*

The trial had been delayed because of a change in venue from Knoxville to Memphis, Ford's hometown.

While under indictment, Ford, first elected to the House in 1974, had to give up his chairmanship of the Ways and Means Subcommittee on Human Resources.

In November, Ford defeated Republican Aaron C. Davis, although his 65 percent showing was his worst since 1976. Earlier, he won 69 percent of the vote in the Aug. 2 Democratic primary in beating state Rep. Pam Gaia, who promised "honesty and integrity" in her campaign.

Ford sought to turn his trial to political advantage, repeatedly accusing federal prosecutors of waging a "personal racial vendetta" against him. Shortly after he was indicted, he told a cheering crowd at Memphis' airport that the federal prosecutor "wants to destroy the black political power in Tennessee." ■

Garcia Conviction Upset

A federal appeals court June 29 overturned the extortion convictions of former Rep. Robert Garcia (D-N.Y., 1978-90) and his wife.

U.S. District Judge Leonard Sand refused, however, on Dec. 3 to block a new trial for Garcia, who had resigned from Congress on Jan. 7. *(1989 Almanac, p. 43)*

The Garcias argued that a new trial would violate the Double Jeopardy clause of the Constitution since they would be tried twice for the same offense. Sand ruled, however, that the Constitution did not bar the retrial of a defendant who won a reversal of a conviction on appeal.

The Garcias were convicted Oct. 20, 1989, of extorting more than $170,000 from the Wedtech Corp., a Bronx machine shop that became an active defense contractor. The jury acquitted them of four counts of bribery and of receipt of illegal gratuities.

In overturning the convictions, the appellate court said the Garcias' actions fell short of extortion.

"Garcia never even hinted that he was prepared to use his power to harm Wedtech," a three-judge panel of the 2nd U.S. Circuit Court of Appeals wrote.

"In making the payments, the company was motivated by desire, not fear." ■

Fauntroy Case Dropped

The Justice Department, after deciding not to prosecute Del. Walter E. Fauntroy, D-D.C., on allegations of payroll padding, referred the case to the House ethics committee, a department spokesman said May 9.

The ethics committee, officially the Committee on Standards of Official Conduct, took no action on the case and let the case die with Fauntroy leaving office at the end of the 101st Congress.

Fauntroy, the non-voting delegate from the District of Columbia, had been the subject of a 15-month federal investigation, which concluded in late April, concerning allegations that he improperly kept Thomas John Savage, son of Illinois Democratic Rep. Gus Savage, on his payroll at the same time the younger Savage was living in Chicago and running for the Illinois Legislature.

House rules required staff members to work in Washington, D.C., or in the representative's district.

Fauntroy said he hired the younger Savage to help coordinate the drive for D.C. statehood.

When told that the Justice Department had decided not to prosecute the case, Fauntroy said in a statement, "I am pleased that this matter has been closed and that this will no longer have to divert attention from the real issues" of the campaign.

Fauntroy gave up his congressional seat to be a candidate for D.C. mayor during the investigation, but he finished fifth in the Democratic primary on Sept. 8. ■

No Action on Stangeland

The Minnesota Democratic Farmer-Labor Party the week of April 2 filed a complaint with the House Committee on Standards of Official Conduct against Minnesota Republican Rep. Arlan Stangeland over a series of telephone calls Stangeland charged to his House credit card.

The House ethics committee took no action in 1990 and let the matter drop after Stangeland lost his re-election bid.

In a January story, the St. Cloud Times reported that Stangeland made 341 long-distance calls, at a cost of $762, to or from phones of a Virginia woman who Stangeland said was a friend and lobbyist. Although he initially said that some of the calls might have been personal, Stangeland later said that all were made for business reasons. A former staff aide, he said, stole phone records from his office to try to smear him.

Stangeland lost his bid for re-election to Democrat Colin C. Peterson, who was making his fifth try for the seat — his third as the Democratic nominee. Peterson made the issue a focus of his campaign.

Peterson, who had not planned to seek the seat in 1990, jumped into the race a week after the first news report. He defeated Stangeland with 54 percent of the vote. ■

Dyson Case Dismissed

The House Committee on Standards of Official Conduct dismissed an investigation against Roy Dyson, D-Md., on Feb. 2, the same day the panel concluded its cases against Gus Savage, D-Ill., and Gerry Sikorski, D-Minn.

The complaint against Dyson, filed by a GOP official just before Election Day 1988, alleged that Dyson misused official funds for campaign purposes and discriminated against women in hiring. Dyson's office practices had been thrust into the public eye in mid-1988 when his administrative aide, Tom Pappas, committed suicide after a Washington Post article reported on his unorthodox personnel practices. *(1989 Almanac, p. 43; 1988 Almanac, p. 54)*

Despite the dismissal of the charges, ethics remained a major issue in Dyson's campaign for re-election. He lost to his 1988 opponent, Republican Wayne T. Gilchrest. ■

Sikorski Case Closed

The House Committee on Standards of Official Conduct Feb. 2 dismissed its investigation of Gerry Sikorski, D-Minn., the same day the panel concluded its case against Gus Savage, D-Ill., and dismissed an investigation against Roy Dyson, D-Md.

The case against Sikorski was filed after articles in several newspapers reported allegations that the congressman had misused staffers by requiring them to do personal chores and campaign work. *(1989 Almanac, p. 43)* ■

Chapter 3

ECONOMIC POLICY

Fiscal 1991 Budget.... 111
  Deficit-Reduction Plan.... 112
  Chronology.... 114
Bush's Budget.... 116
  Economic Report.... 116
  Budget Authority, Outlays by Agency.... 118
  Economic Assumptions.... 119
  Budget by Function.... 120
  Major Provisions.... 122
Budget Resolution I.... 127
Budget Summit.... 129
  Summit Participants.... 130
  Bush Statement on Taxes.... 131
  Bush Address to Congress.... 133
  Bush Television Address.... 135
Budget Resolution II.... 136
  Veto of Continuing Resolution.... 137
Reconciliation Bill.... 138
  House Reconciliation Instructions.... 138
  Senate Reconciliation Instructions.... 139
  Spending Allocations.... 140
  Reconciliation Provisions.... 141
  Debt Limit Extension.... 165
  Bush Signing Statement.... 166
New Taxes.... 167
  Capital Gains Tax Cut.... 168
  Social Security Tax.... 170
  Major Tax Provisions.... 171
New Budget Process.... 173
  Balanced-Budget Amendment.... 174
  Discretionary Spending Caps.... 176
  Key Dates.... 177
  Credit Reforms.... 178
Thrift Bailout Bill.... 179
  Ryan Confirmed as Thrift Regulator.... 180
  Bank Fraud Penalties.... 182
Deposit Insurance Premiums.... 184
Money-Laundering Bills.... 187
Foreign Banks Bill.... 189
SEC Market Control Authority.... 190
  Market Reform Provisions.... 191
  SEC Enforcement Bills.... 193
  Stock-Index Futures.... 194
Coin Redesign.... 196
Export Administration Act.... 198
  Veto Message.... 200
Defense Production Act.... 202
Trade With Former East Bloc.... 204
  Czechoslovak President's Visit.... 204
  U.S.-Soviet Trade Accord.... 205
  European Development Bank.... 206
U.S.-Japan Trade.... 208
GATT Talks.... 209
Caribbean Trade Bill.... 211
  Customs and Trade Act Provisions.... 212
Latin America Aid.... 217
Mexico Trade Pact.... 218
Textile Quota Bill.... 219
  Veto Message.... 221
Foreign Investments.... 222

Budget Adopted After Long Battle

Five-year plan promises $496 billion deficit reduction

The battle over the fiscal 1991 budget — which pitted Democrats against Republicans and sometimes the GOP against itself — took the entire session, locked the leadership into endless meetings, periodically exploded into nasty partisan name-calling and delayed work on other pressing legislation. In the end, frustrated and angry lawmakers were forced to stay in session closer to the fall elections than at any time since World War II before putting the finishing touches on a budget-reconciliation bill, the centerpiece of the year's fiscal work.

The result of their efforts was a budget package that promised to cut $42.5 billion from the deficit in fiscal 1991 and $496.2 billion over five years. The biggest cuts over five years came from discretionary spending, especially defense. The next largest portion was from tax increases totaling $146.3 billion. Entitlement cuts and user fee increases yielded $99 billion over five years. And net interest on the federal debt was expected to drop $68.4 billion because of the other budget savings. In a bid to establish budget peace for the next few years, members also revised the budget calendar and process. *(Budget calendar, p. 177)*

The year began in a traditional manner, with the submission of President Bush's fiscal 1991 budget on Jan. 29.

Normally, the next step would have been the development and adoption of a congressional budget resolution, Congress' own blueprint for tax and spending bills for the coming fiscal year. But Democrats were divided over how much money to shift from defense to domestic programs in the wake of the Cold War and leery of calling for tax increases while Bush maintained his 1988 campaign pledge of "no new taxes." *(Bush pledge, 1988 Almanac, p. 41-A)*

Republicans concentrated on a call for a congressional-White House budget summit as a way to resolve the tax and spending differences, but Democrats were suspicious. As a result, Congress failed in its first attempt to pass a budget resolution, settling temporarily for an ad hoc arrangement that allowed the House to begin working on appropriations bills.

Attention Shifts to Budget Summit

Then on May 6, Bush, who was reportedly worried about a worsening economy and rising deficit projections, invited top congressional leaders to the White House for a rare Sunday meeting to discuss the possibility of high-level budget talks. Based on the assurance that there would be "no preconditions," Democrats and their GOP counterparts accepted the invitation.

The congressional and White House negotiators rather quickly agreed on a deficit-reduction goal: cutting $50 billion in the first year and $500 billion over five years. But for months they were unable even to begin detailed bargaining.

The summer doldrums were broken briefly when Bush agreed June 26 that tax increases would have to be part of any deficit-reduction package. The shift, which enraged some Republicans, gave new life to the talks. But negotiators retreated into partisan bickering in late July. By the August recess, no concrete progress had been made.

Meanwhile, the problem kept growing. By mid-July, the Office of Management and Budget (OMB) was predicting that the 1991 deficit would be $159 billion rather than the $100.5 billion it had projected in January.

The real bargaining began in September — first at Andrews Air Force Base, just outside Washington, and then among a small, core group of negotiators back on Capitol Hill. By then, Congress and Bush were facing the possibility of crippling spending cuts under the Gramm-Rudman antideficit law. Under Gramm-Rudman, the fiscal 1991 deficit could not exceed $74 billion — $64 billion plus a $10 billion margin for error. If it climbed above that ceiling, automatic cuts, known as a sequester, would take effect Oct. 1 — half from defense and half from domestic spending.

With the clock ticking, the summit negotiators finally announced a budget deal on Sept. 30 — only to see it turned into failure five days later when the House voted overwhelmingly to dump the summit package, the fruit of five months of work. The defeat was administered by a coalition of conservative Republicans, outraged at the plan's new taxes, and liberal Democrats, furious over cuts in safety net programs and additional taxes on low- and middle-income taxpayers.

Finally, a Package of Fiscal Legislation

Within hours, Budget committee leaders from the two chambers began crafting a new budget resolution, this one reflecting the bottom line of the budget-summit package but leaving the details to House and Senate committees. The resolution, adopted Oct. 9, provided a total pool of money for the appropriations bills — freeing the appropriators at last to finish the 13 regular spending measures — and deficit-reduction instructions to 12 House and 10 Senate committees responsible for drafting a budget-reconciliation bill.

Although the budget standoff had stalled work on the appropriations bills, in the end the budget forced few changes in the discretionary accounts funded by the annual spending measures. Defense still took a relatively big cut,

FISCAL 1991 BUDGET

Summary .... p. 111
Deficit reduction plan...... p. 112
Chronology............... p. 114
Bush's budget............. p. 116
Economic Report .... p. 116
Budget by agency......... p. 118
Economic assumptions .... p. 119
Budget by function........ p. 120
Major provisions.......... p. 122
Budget resolution I......... p. 127
Budget summit .... p. 129
Summit participants....... p. 130
Bush statement on taxes... p. 131
Bush address to Congress . p. 133
Bush television address.... p. 135
Budget resolution II .... p. 136
Veto of continuing resolution p. 137
Reconciliation bill .... p. 138
Reconciliation instructions.. p. 138
Spending allocations ...... p. 140
Reconciliation provisions... p. 141
Debt limit extension .... p. 165
Bush signing statement.... p. 166

The Deficit-Reduction Pie

Fiscal 1991 Total Savings $42.5 Billion

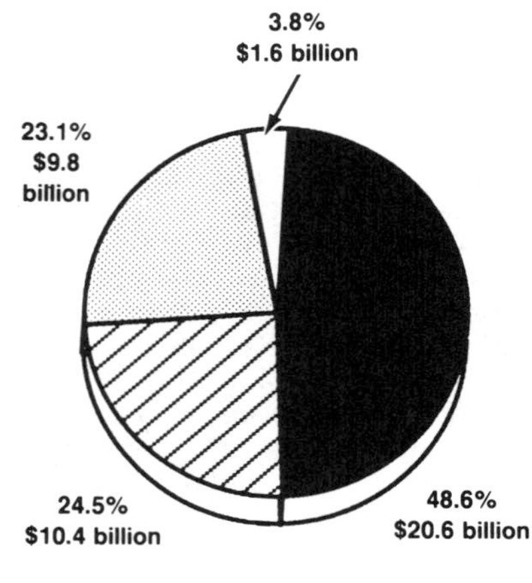

Fiscal 1991-95 Total Savings $496.2 Billion

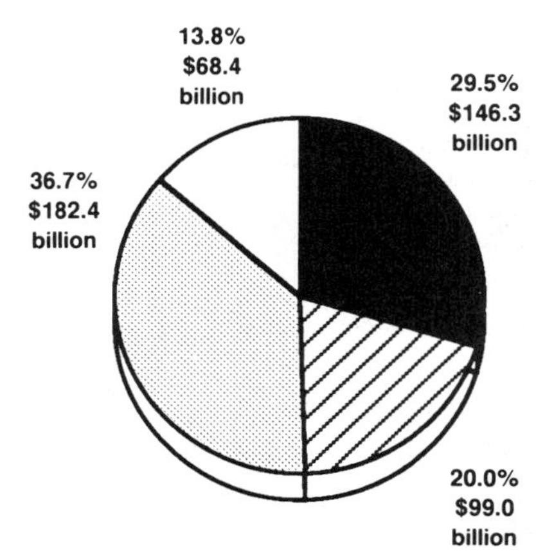

- Taxes and Other Revenues
- Entitlement Cuts, Other Mandatory Spending Cuts and User Fees
- Discretionary Spending Cuts
- Interest on the Federal Debt

By any measure, the deficit-reduction bill was the most ambitious effort ever to turn the tide of federal spending.

Projected tax increases and spending cuts totaling $42.5 billion in fiscal 1991 and $496.2 billion over five years far exceeded the two-year $75 billion deficit-reduction package that came out of the 1987 budget summit or the $121 billion three-year package of tax increases and domestic and defense spending cuts enacted in 1984. *(1987 Almanac, p. 609; 1984 Almanac, p. 143)*

The five-year savings projection anticipated that the biggest cuts would come in discretionary spending: $182.4 billion.

The first-year discretionary cut of $9.8 billion was to come entirely from defense, as were cuts in the second and third years. Although some in Congress — particularly House Democrats — assumed the entire five-year discretionary savings would come from defense, that was not certain. Mechanisms to enforce the cuts left sizable leeway in 1994 and 1995 to cut domestic spending and foreign aid.

Overall, discretionary spending, which yielded 23 percent of the cuts in 1991 and 37 percent over five years, made up about two-fifths of all outlays. Virtually all defense and foreign aid spending was discretionary, but domestic discretionary spending was little more than 25 percent of all domestic outlays.

The next biggest chunk of the savings was to come from tax increases totaling $20.6 billion the first year and $146.3 billion over five years. Those numbers included $3 billion for fiscal 1991 and $9.4 billion over five years due to enhanced Internal Revenue Service tax-collection efforts.

Entitlement cuts — Medicare and farm price- and income-support payments, especially — and user fee increases were slated to yield one-fifth of the total deficit reduction, $99 billion over five years. Entitlements remained the largest and fastest-growing part of the federal budget.

Finally, net interest on the federal debt, expected to top $1 trillion over the next five years, would be $68.4 billion more if the other savings evaporated and the government had to borrow more to offset the difference or if interest rates did not fall in response to the budget-cutting effort.

SOURCE: House Budget Committee

and foreign aid was nicked for several million dollars. But many domestic programs were given modest increases. With the path cleared, Congress finished all 13 bills in the last eight days of the session.

Along the way, members approved six stopgap "continuing resolutions" to keep spending flowing until the regular bills were enacted. (Five were enacted; one was vetoed.) *(Continuing resolutions, p. 896)*

The more difficult piece of the puzzle was the reconciliation bill, which was expected to provide about half the deficit reduction called for in the budget resolution through tax increases and cuts in entitlements and other mandatory programs. House Democrats on Oct. 16 passed a highly partisan version touted as a soak-the-rich plan. The Senate, reflecting that chamber's much closer partisan split, produced a more moderate package.

It took eight more days for conferees to wrestle with the differences in the bills and for the two chambers to approve the results. With the fall elections drawing near, the struggle over taxes remained bitter and partisan. Democrats campaigned for "tax fairness" and charged that the GOP tax policies benefited the rich. Republicans countered by depicting Democrats as addicted to high-tax, high-spending policies that burdened taxpayers and threatened economic growth.

The final bill (HR 5835 — PL 101-508) provided $28 billion in deficit reduction in fiscal 1991 and $236 billion over five years. And it included a new budget process that changed the budget calendar and the scheme of automatic spending cuts under Gramm-Rudman. *(Budget process, p. 173)*

The White House — including Bush, Chief of Staff John H. Sununu and budget director Richard G. Darman — pronounced itself satisfied with the sprawling budget deal. On Capitol Hill leaders of both parties simultaneously called it a historic achievement and the best compromise under the circumstances.

In many ways the outcome appeared as a major political victory for Democrats, who managed to paint Bush and the Republicans into a corner, forcing them to explain why they did not want to tax millionaires.

Having retreated from his 1988 campaign pledge of no new taxes, Bush had tried to keep the battle on familiar GOP turf by insisting that any new taxes be balanced by what he said were growth-inducing tax cuts such as a reduction in the capital gains rate. The Democrats made him swallow that demand as well.

In the end, the package boosted the top marginal tax rate for the richest taxpayers from 28 percent to 31 percent. And the deal included virtually no incentives for growth. Save for a largely cosmetic change that set a top tax rate of 28 percent for capital gains and the addition of some energy incentives at the insistence of Senate Finance Chairman Lloyd Bentsen, D-Texas, Republicans had little to brag about.

"Our group was out-negotiated by the other side," conceded Rep. Bill Frenzel, Minn., ranking Republican of the House Budget Committee and a budget-summit negotiator who had carried the party's flag in the unsuccessful struggle to significantly cut capital gains or get substantial growth incentives. The few shreds that Republicans came away with were "not my idea of a great national stimulus," Frenzel said resignedly.

No sooner had Congress finished the bill than opening shots in the next tax battle were sounded. Bush immediately lashed out at the Democratic-controlled Congress, saying he had been forced to accept large tax increases as "ransom" to get spending cuts.

"The president has made it clear he was forced to pay the tax ransom once in order to save the economy. He will not be forced to pay [it] again," Sununu said in a Dec. 11 speech to the National Press Club.

For their part, Democrats, riding high on what they saw as a political victory in the year's campaign to restore more fairness to the tax system, made it clear that they planned to pick up the fight early in the new year.

BACKGROUND

When Bush's fiscal 1991 budget arrived on Capitol Hill, the scars of the previous year's budget war were still fresh, adding to the leftover bitterness of eight years of partisan clashes between the White House and congressional Democrats under President Ronald Reagan. *(Background, 1989 Almanac, p. 92)*

The first year of the 101st Congress had begun with high hopes for a modest bipartisan agreement on the fiscal 1990 budget, paving the way for a big budget deal that would slash the red ink for 1991 and beyond. The first step was taken in April 1989, when congressional leaders and the White House sealed a one-year, $28 billion deficit-reduction package that was filled with gimmicks but seemed to satisfy both parties. The agreement was designed to bring the 1990 deficit, projected at $126.9 billion by the administration in January, to $99.4 billion, or slightly below the $100 billion Gramm-Rudman limit for that year.

Instead of moving quickly to deal with the longer-term problem of the deficit, however, the two parties fell into bitter wrangling that delayed completion of the annual budget until Thanksgiving and killed any hope for a head start on a big 1991 deal.

What happened? The short answer was capital gains. The summit negotiators in 1989 agreed to come up with $5.3 billion in new revenues, but left the details to the tax-writing committees. Filling in the blanks was tricky, because Bush had vowed to stick with his 1988 campaign pledge of "no new taxes" — a pledge that budget director Darman translated into a "duck test" for flunking revenue proposals.

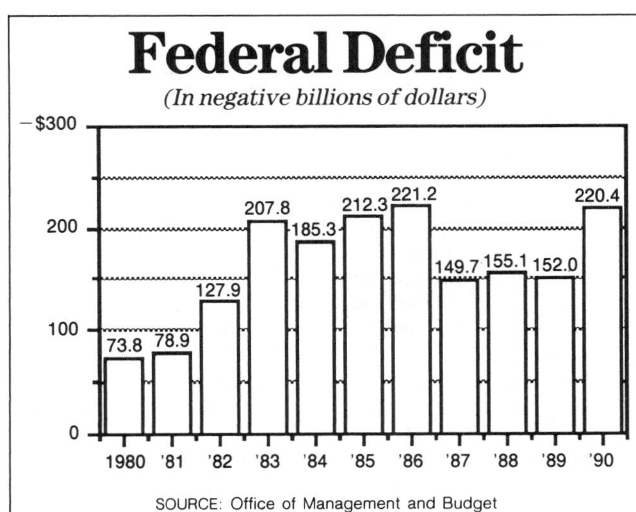

"If it looks like a duck, walks like a duck and quacks like a duck, then it's a duck," he told Congress.

Republicans insisted that a capital gains tax cut was the best way to get $4.8 billion of the needed money. Democrats acknowledged that the summit pact did not specifically rule out a capital gains cut. But it did hold that any revenues be acceptable to both sides.

Senate Majority Leader George J. Mitchell, D-Maine, later said: "From their standpoint, it meant we would raise the revenues in a way that the president could credibly say did not violate his campaign pledge of no new taxes. From our standpoint, it meant no capital gains this year."

Initially, the agreement seemed to be on track. But trouble arose when the Ways and Means Committee tried to fill in the details on taxes. Following some mixed signals on capital gains from Chairman Dan Rostenkowski, D-Ill., conservative Democrats on the committee joined with Republicans to push through a capital gains rate cut — over Rostenkowski's opposition, as it turned out.

Bush, who had proposed a capital gains cut but had not given the issue high visibility during the year, seized on the opening and soon made capital gains an issue of principle.

The House included the capital gains cut in its version of the fiscal 1990 reconciliation bill, but Democrats were able to block a similar move in the Senate by requiring Republicans to come up with 60 votes to overcome a budgetary point of order.

The administration, with Darman carrying the president's water, tried to hold out, insisting that capital gains be included. After a week of futile maneuvering, Senate Minority Leader Bob Dole, R-Kan., and Pete V. Domenici, N.M., senior Republican on the Senate Budget Committee, broke with the administration and reached a face-saving compromise with Democrats that stripped hundreds of items, including capital gains and several Democratic priorities, from the reconciliation bill. For another bitter week, the White House held out, trying to come up with a way to force the Democrats to accede on capital gains. Finally, on Nov. 2, 1989, Bush acknowledged defeat, saying capital gains would not be part of the bill but vowing not to sign the measure unless Congress removed allegedly phony savings, including some that had been approved by the bipartisan budget summit.

The final bill (PL 101-239) — cleared by Congress on

Continued on p. 116

Recapping the Budget Negotiations . . .

Jan. 29 — President Bush released his $1.2 trillion fiscal 1991 budget, which claimed a deficit of $64.7 billion. Democrats immediately criticized the plan for relying on overly optimistic economic projections and for cutting too much from domestic spending and not enough from defense. Despite Bush's pledge not to raise taxes, his plan called for $13.9 billion in new tax revenues and $5.3 billion from increased user fees.

March 5 — In its annual re-estimate of the president's budget, the Congressional Budget Office (CBO) projected a deficit of $131 billion, nearly $70 billion more than the administration's estimate. About $26 billion of the difference came from CBO's use of less optimistic economic assumptions. Another $29 billion resulted from CBO's estimate of additional funds needed for the thrift bailout.

April 19 — The House Budget Committee approved a $1.2 trillion plan calling for less defense spending and more for domestic programs than proposed by Bush. The package, which used the administration's optimistic assumptions, was approved along party lines.

May 1 — The House passed its budget resolutions (H Con Res 310) by a party-line vote of 218-208, with Republicans arguing that high-level talks were required to resolve tax and spending differences. Democrats resisted, saying they needed to be convinced that such talks were necessary and that the administration was willing to consider additional taxes.

May 2 — The Senate Budget Committee approved a $1.2 trillion budget calling for steeper defense cuts than those sought by either Bush or the House. With bipartisan budget talks now almost a certainty, Democrats acknowledged that the package was more a bargaining chip than a serious fiscal blueprint.

May 6 — Bush, apparently concerned about a worsening economy and rising deficit projections, called top congressional leaders to the White House for a rare Sunday meeting to discuss the possibility of high-level budget talks. House and Senate leaders said they would consider the proposal as long as there were "no preconditions."

May 9 — Congressional leaders accepted Bush's invitation. Twenty administration and congressional representatives were appointed to participate in the talks along with Bush and top House and Senate leaders.

May 15 — Administration and congressional negotiators began a series of closed-door sessions. They aimed for an early agreement, but the talks got off to a slow start with seminarlike discussions of deficit projections and the economy. Each side remained wary of the other's intentions; Democratic leaders said they would continue to pursue the regular congressional budget process while the talks proceeded.

June 26 — After more than a month of going in circles, the negotiations appeared headed for collapse. Under pressure from congressional leaders, Bush released a surprise statement that "tax revenue increases" needed to be a part of any deficit-reduction plan. Democrats said they were now willing to discuss deep cuts in entitlements, and the mood turned optimistic. But rank-and-file Republicans expressed outrage over Bush's concession on the no-new-taxes issue, which they considered the strongest plank in their party's platform.

July 11 — The spurt of optimism before the July Fourth recess gave way to rising partisan tensions over taxes. Republicans bristled at comments by Senate Majority Leader George J. Mitchell, D-Maine, that he would not accept a cut in capital gains taxes without an increase in the top marginal income tax rate.

July 16 — The administration projected a fiscal 1991 deficit of $231.4 billion. Budget director Richard G. Darman said that across-the-board cuts of about $100 billion in government programs were a real possibility on Oct. 1 if no action was taken to reduce the deficit.

July 18 — Despite Darman's dire warnings, differences came to a full boil. Over the protests of House GOP leaders and the administration, rank-and-file Republicans in the House approved a non-binding resolution opposing any new taxes to reduce the deficit. A heated summit meeting was held the following day, but Republican leaders and White House officials assured Democrats they would continue to bargain on all issues.

July 26 — Plans to exchange serious offers by week's end were dropped as Democrats and Republicans failed in private caucuses to produce opening bids. Details leaked of a tentative Republican proposal, which included new taxes on alcoholic beverages and limits on state and local tax deductions. A number of GOP negotiators immediately distanced themselves from the plan. Democrats started laying the groundwork for intense negotiations after the monthlong August recess, arguing that the sides were too far apart to complete a deal before then.

Aug. 4 — Congress left town after negotiators agreed to meet in early September with the goal of hammering out a quick budget deal and enacting it by the start of the fiscal year. Members hoped that the impending threat of across-the-board cuts in October would force both sides to make concessions.

Sept. 7 — Negotiators returned from the August recess and went into seclusion at Andrews Air Force Base, outside Washington, where they began what they hoped would be the final round of budget talks. But the bargaining quickly stalled over the capital gains dispute, with Democrats insisting that a cut be paired with an increase in the top tax rate and Republicans and the White House resisting.

. . . An Arduous Year of Give and Take

Sept. 17 — After 10 days of intensive but inconclusive talks, summit negotiators ended the Andrews sessions and turned the problem over to a core group consisting of five congressional leaders and three White House negotiators.

Sept. 30 — Just hours before automatic spending cuts were set to take effect under the Gramm-Rudman antideficit law, Bush and congressional negotiators announced agreement on a budget-summit package.

The House then voted 382-41 to approve a continuing resolution (H J Res 655 — PL 101-403) to continue government funding and suspend the Gramm-Rudman cuts until midnight Oct. 5.

The Senate approved the continuing resolution on a voice vote.

Oct. 1 — The new fiscal year began.

Oct. 6 (session of Oct. 5) — In a rebuff to Bush and party leaders, the House rejected, 179-254, a budget resolution (H J Res 310) that would have codified the budget-summit agreement. Opposition from liberal Democrats and conservative Republicans left the agreement with no majority support in either party.

After the early morning vote, the House voted 300-113 to pass another continuing resolution (H J Res 660) that would continue government funding, extend the debt limit and suspend Gramm-Rudman cuts to midnight Oct. 12; the Senate followed suit by voice vote.

Oct. 6 — Bush vetoed the continuing resolution, insisting Congress first pass a budget resolution. The federal government began to shut down non-essential services. Late in the afternoon, the House failed to override Bush's veto, 260-138, six votes short of the necessary two-thirds. Meanwhile, House and Senate negotiators, minus the angrily divided House Republicans, worked on a new budget resolution.

Oct. 8 (session of Oct. 7) — About 2:30 a.m., the House voted 250-164 to approve the conference report on a new, broad-brush budget resolution (H Con Res 310).

Shortly before 4 a.m., the House voted 305-105 to approve a new continuing resolution (H J Res 666 — PL 101-412) to continue government funding, extend the debt ceiling, and suspend Gramm-Rudman cuts until midnight Oct. 19.

That evening, at 10:30 p.m., the Senate amended and then approved the continuing resolution by voice vote.

Oct. 9 (session of Oct. 8) — Shortly before 1 a.m., the Senate passed the budget resolution on a 66-33 vote. At nearly 2 a.m., the House voted 362-3 to approve the Senate-amended continuing resolution. Bush signed the continuing resolution in time for federal employees to return to work after the Columbus Day holiday weekend.

Oct. 10 — The House Ways and Means Committee gave voice-vote approval to a "bare-bones" reconciliation package that followed much of the budget-summit agreement but altered unpopular items, reducing the cuts in Medicare, dropping small-business tax incentives and increasing tax credits to the working poor.

Oct. 12 — Ways and Means Democrats approved an alternative reconciliation package to be offered on the floor that would raise taxes on wealthiest Americans while easing the burden on low- and middle-income taxpayers.

Oct. 13 — Senate Finance voted 15-5 to approve a bipartisan reconciliation package that moderated cuts in Medicare and made some tax changes but generally stuck close to the budget-summit agreement.

Oct. 16 — The House approved the reconciliation bill, 227-203, after amending it, 238-192, with the Democratic alternative.

Oct. 18 — The House voted 379-37 to approve another continuing resolution (H J Res 677 — PL 101-444) to continue government spending, extend the debt limit and suspend Gramm-Rudman spending cuts through midnight Oct. 24. Bush indicated he would sign the bill if there was "satisfactory progress" on reconciliation.

Oct. 19 (session of Oct. 18) — About 1:30 a.m., the Senate approved the reconciliation bill, 54-46. Later in the morning, House and Senate conferees began trying to resolve differences between the two chambers on the bill.

The Senate cleared the continuing resolution, by unanimous consent; Bush signed it.

Oct. 20 — Conferees began meeting, with high hopes of cutting a quick deal. But discussions broke down over how to increase taxes on the rich. In the end, the negotiations were saved by a agreement to phase out the personal exemption for wealthy taxpayers.

Oct. 24 — The House voted 380-45 to pass yet another continuing resolution (H J Res 681 — PL 101-461), lasting through Oct. 27.

Oct. 27 (session of Oct. 26) — After an all-night session, the House voted 228-200 near dawn to approve the conference report on the reconciliation bill (HR 5835 — PL 101-508). Near dusk the same day, the Senate cleared the measure.

Oct. 27 — The House voted 283-49 to pass a sixth continuing resolution (HJ Res 687 — PL 101-467) that was good through Nov. 5 to give time for regular appropriations bills to be enrolled and signed. The Senate cleared the bill by voice vote.

Oct. 28 (session of Oct. 27) — Congress adjourned, shortly after 1 a.m. EST.

Nov. 5 — Bush signed the reconciliation bill.

Bush's Economic Report to Congress

Following are excerpts from President Bush's Feb. 6 economic report to Congress; subtitles were part of the text:

Goals and Principles

... The primary economic goal of my administration is to achieve the highest possible rate of sustainable economic growth. Achieving this goal will require action on many fronts — but it will permit progress on many more.

Growth is the key to raising living standards, to leaving a legacy of prosperity for our children, to uplifting those most in need and to maintaining America's leadership in the world.

To achieve this goal, we must both enhance our economy's ability to grow and ensure that its potential is more often fully utilized than in previous decades. To these ends, ... my administration will:

- Reduce government borrowing by slowing the growth of federal spending while economic growth raises revenue until the budget is balanced, and reduce the national debt thereafter.
- Support a credible, systematic monetary policy program that sustains maximum economic growth while controlling and reducing inflation.
- Remove barriers to innovation, investment, work and saving in the tax, legal and regulatory systems;
- Avoid unnecessary regulation and design necessary regulatory programs to harness market forces effectively to serve the nation's interest.
- Continue to lead the world to freer trade and more open markets, and to support market-oriented reforms around the world. ...

Macroeconomic Prospects And Policies

The economy's performance during 1989, the seventh year of economic expansion, has set the stage for healthy growth in the 1990s. Growth in national output was more moderate in 1989 than the very rapid pace in 1988 and 1987.

But, in sharp contrast to most past periods of low unemployment and high capacity utilization, inflation was kept firmly in check. Measured broadly, the price level rose 4.1 percent during 1989, down from 4.5 percent during 1988.

If my budget proposals are adopted, and if the Federal Reserve maintains a credible policy program to support strong noninflationary growth, the economy is projected to expand in 1990 at a slightly faster pace than in 1989.

Growth is projected to pick up in the second half of the year and to continue at a strong pace as the level of output rises to the economy's full potential. Fiscal and monetary policies should establish credible commitments to policy plans aimed at maximizing sustainable growth over the long run. A steady hand at the helm is necessary to produce rapid and continuous increases in employment and living standards.

My budget proposals reflect a strong commitment to the principles of the Gramm-Rudman-Hollings law, which has helped reduce the federal deficit from 5.3 percent of GNP in fiscal 1986 to 2.9 percent in fiscal 1989.

My budget proposals reflect a strong commitment to the principles of the Gramm-Rudman-Hollings law, which has helped reduce the federal deficit from 5.3 percent of GNP in fiscal 1986 to 2.9 percent in fiscal 1989.

That is why I insisted last fall that the Congress pass a clean reconciliation bill and stood by the sequestration order that resulted from my strict adherence to the Gramm-Rudman-Hollings law.

I have also proposed a fundamental new rule for fiscal policy that would ensure that projected future Social Security surpluses are not spent for other purposes but are used to build the reserves necessary to guarantee the soundness of Social Security.

Moreover, it would transform the federal government from a chronic borrower, draining savings away from private investment, to a saver, providing funds for capital formation and economic growth by reducing the national debt.

I remain strongly committed to the principles of low marginal tax rates and a broad tax base developed in the Economic Recovery Tax Act of 1981 and the Tax Reform Act of 1986. Steady adherence to these principles reduces government's distorting effect on the market forces that drive economic growth.

I strongly support the Federal Reserve's goal of noninflationary growth and share with them the conviction that inflation must be controlled and reduced in a predictable fashion. Accelerating inflation not only erodes the value of families' savings, it produces economic imbalances and policy responses that often lead to recessions.

The United States is part of an increasingly integrated global economy, in which domestic fiscal and monetary policies affect the economies of other nations, though the main impacts are on the domestic economy. My administration remains committed to participating actively in the valuable process of coordinating macroeconomic policies internationally.

Encouraging Economic Growth

As we begin the 1990s, a central focus of my economic policies will be to build on the successes of the 1980s by creating an environment in which the private sector can serve as the engine that powers strong, noninflationary economic growth.

America's continued economic progress depends on the innovation and entrepreneurship of our people. I will therefore continue to press for a permanent research and experimentation tax credit, for increased Federal support of research with widespread societal benefits and that private firms would not have adequate incentives to undertake, for removal of regulatory and legal barriers to innovation, and for a lower tax rate on capital gains.

Continued from p. 113

Nov. 23, 1989, and signed by Bush on Dec. 19 — promised $14.7 billion in savings. But because many committees had failed to contribute the program reductions assigned them, negotiators had to retain a portion of the sequester that had gone into effect when Congress failed to complete its work by Oct. 1.

The reliance on those arbitrary cuts illustrated the continuing deadlock between Republicans opposed to any major tax hikes and Democrats opposed to significant cuts in social programs that would dog budget negotiators in 1990.

As for the deficit, the $126.9 billion estimate from April proved highly optimistic.

In October 1990 — as another year of budget wrangling was coming to an end — the administration found that the fiscal 1990 deficit actually had been the second largest in the nation's history, reaching $220.4 billion. The major cause of the increase was spending for the savings and loan salvage operation. *(Chart, p. 113)*

THE BUSH BUDGET

Bush sent his fiscal 1991 budget request to Capitol Hill Jan. 29, kicking off a fierce battle over deficit reduction that would last until the final hours of the 101st Congress. *(Budget figures by agency, p. 118; by function, p. 120; details, p. 122)*

Bush's $1.2 trillion budget got predictably bad reviews from Democrats, who attacked it as filled with gimmicks and based on excessively rosy economic assumptions.

"This is not a serious effort at trying to achieve deficit reduction," warned House Budget Committee Chairman Leon E. Panetta, D- Calif.

At the same time, House Speaker Thomas S. Foley,

We must remove impediments to saving and investment in order to enhance the economy's growth potential. The fiscal policy I described earlier will raise national saving.

In addition, I have asked the Congress to enact the Savings and Economic Growth Act of 1990, which contains a comprehensive program to raise household saving across the entire income spectrum.

This program would help American families plan for the future and, in the process, make more funds available to finance investment and spur productivity, thus raising living standards, enhancing competitiveness and expanding employment opportunities.

One of my highest legislative priorities this year is to reduce the capital gains tax rate.

This tax reform would promote risk-taking and entrepreneurship by lowering the cost of capital, thereby encouraging new business formation and creating new jobs. A capital gains tax cut would stimulate savings and investment throughout the economy.

Government can encourage economic growth but cannot manage it. I remain strongly opposed to any sort of industrial policy, in which the government, not the market, would pick winners and losers. Second-guessing the market is the way to raise government spending and taxes, not living standards.

The growth of our Nation's labor force is projected to slow in the 1990s, and demands for skilled workers are expected to continue to increase.

These developments will shift attention away from worries about the supply of jobs that have haunted us since the 1930s and toward new concerns about the supply of workers and skills.

We cannot maintain our position of world leadership or sustain rapid economic growth if our workers lack the skills of their foreign competitors.

As I demonstrated last fall at the Education Summit, the Federal Government can lead in improving the inadequate performance of our elementary and secondary schools. Because school systems must be held accountable for their students' performance, the nation's governors and I have developed ambitious national education goals.

To meet these goals, we must give students and parents the freedom to choose their schools, and we must give schools the flexibility to meet their students' needs.

More disadvantaged Americans must be brought into the economic mainstream, not just to enhance our nation's economic growth, but as a matter of simple decency.

To this end, I have supported legislation to open new opportunities for the disabled, increased assistance to the homeless, helped implement welfare reform, proposed more effective job training programs, and introduced initiatives that will bring jobs and better housing to depressed inner cities.

I have proposed substantial increases in spending for Head Start to prepare children from disadvantaged families for effective learning.

Those who cannot read and write cannot participate fully in the economy. Mrs. Bush and I will continue to support the difficult but important struggle to eliminate adult functional illiteracy.

Regulatory Reform

The improved performance of U.S. markets that were deregulated during the 1980s showed clearly that government interference with competitive private markets inflates prices, retards innovation, slows growth and eliminates jobs. But in some cases, well-designed regulation can serve the public interest.

My proposals for reform of food safety regulation and the Clean Air Act follow the two key principles that apply in these cases: the goals of regulation must balance costs and benefits; and the methods of regulation must be flexible and cost-effective.

One of my top legislative priorities is to improve the Clean Air Act in a way that preserves both a healthy environment and a sound economy.

When confronted with a threat to the solvency of our thrift institutions, my administration moved swiftly to resolve the crisis. We must continue to reform the regulation of financial institutions and markets to preserve the soundness of the U.S. financial sector while encouraging innovation and competition.

The Global Economy

The 1980s have underscored the increased importance of global economic events in shaping our lives. We have all been touched by the movements toward political and economic freedom in Eastern Europe. We have been impressed by the rapid growth of market-oriented Asian economies. And we have great expectations for the movement in the European Community toward a single, open market by 1992.

Reductions in trade barriers between nations have raised living standards around the world.

Investment has become more globally integrated, as citizens of other countries recognize the great strength and potential of our economy, and as Americans continue to invest abroad.

My administration is strongly committed to supporting the historic efforts of the governments and people of Eastern Europe to move toward market-based economies.

Similarly, under the Brady Plan we will continue to support heavily indebted nations that adopt sound economic policies to revive economic growth. In both cases, reform must be comprehensive to succeed, but the rewards of success will be great.

America will continue to lead the way to a world of free, competitive markets. Increased global competition is an opportunity for the United States and the world, not a threat. But we cannot remain competitive by avoiding competition.

My administration will therefore continue to resist calls for protection and managed trade. To serve the interests of all Americans, we must open markets here and abroad, not close them.

I will strongly resist any attempts to hinder the free international flows of investment capital, which have benefited workers and consumers here and abroad. And my Administration will work to reduce existing barriers to international investment throughout the world. . . . ■

D-Wash., and Senate Majority Leader George J. Mitchell, D-Maine, led a partywide effort to depict Bush's budget as an effort to get credit for popular programs without putting real money into them.

"You can't become the education president . . . by proposing a meager 2 percent increase in the education budget," Foley said.

Bush seemed to have extra leverage at the outset, however, because he was better positioned than Democrats to risk automatic Gramm-Rudman spending cuts if he could not get agreement on a budget plan that he favored. The reason: It appeared that Gramm-Rudman, which struck equally at defense and domestic programs, would mean deeper cuts in domestic spending than Congress was likely to approve and defense cuts in the range of what many on Capitol Hill were espousing anyway.

That would have been a reversal of previous years, when Democrats had used the threat of defense cuts under Gramm-Rudman to win cooperation on fiscal policy from a Republican White House.

However, Bush's leverage was to fade quickly, as deficit projections for fiscal 1991 ballooned, making the threat of across-the-board cuts politically unthinkable for either Republicans or Democrats.

Meanwhile, as Bush presented his budget, the seeds of much of the year's conflicts could already be seen. A fight was brewing over defense spending, with liberal Democrats looking for a "peace dividend" in the wake of the Cold War that was much larger than anything Bush was proposing. And, despite Bush's oft-repeated promise of "no new taxes," more than half the deficit reduction in his budget came from added taxes, user fees and other receipts. While Democrats rejected important items on Bush's list, the

Continued on p. 126

Budget Authority, Outlays By Agency

(Fiscal years; in millions of dollars †)

	BUDGET AUTHORITY			OUTLAYS		
AGENCY	**1989 actual**	**1990 estimate**	**1991 estimate**	**1989 actual**	**1990 estimate**	**1991 estimate**
Legislative Branch	$ 2,276	$ 2,240	$ 2,671	$ 2,095	$ 2,317	$ 2,678
The Judiciary	1,476	1,734	2,075	1,492	1,701	2,028
Executive Office of the President	129	287	355	124	174	319
Funds Appropriated to the President	10,953	12,393	12,377	4,280	9,162	12,188
Agriculture	55,733	55,141	55,310	48,316	48,246	48,715
Commerce	2,807	3,558	2,544	2,571	3,861	2,771
Defense — Military	290,837	291,369	295,131	294,880	286,791	292,145
Defense — Civil	37,234	36,656	38,386	23,450	24,751	25,517
Education	22,956	24,111	24,618	21,608	22,316	23,711
Energy	11,697	14,296	14,761	11,387	12,290	13,438
Health and Human Services, except Social Security	196,638	212,349	232,442	172,301	191,174	204,082
Health and Human Services, Social Security	279,918	306,625	340,393	227,473	244,587	260,089
Housing and Urban Development	14,347	18,368	23,700	19,680	22,802	23,023
Interior	5,482	6,248	5,590	5,213	5,832	5,698
Justice	6,732	8,587	8,943	6,232	6,898	8,990
Labor	29,923	32,475	32,104	22,654	24,935	26,274
State	4,093	4,211	5,457	3,722	3,777	4,094
Transportation	28,455	30,177	29,336	26,607	28,281	28,764
Treasury	232,080	248,501	256,054	230,571	247,239	254,928
Veterans Affairs	29,893	29,907	30,869	30,041	28,733	30,143
Environmental Protection Agency	5,081	5,400	5,402	4,906	5,492	5,824
General Services Administration	187	119	40	−463	253	47
National Aeronautics and Space Administration	10,969	12,324	15,240	11,036	12,026	14,137
Office of Personnel Management	51,248	55,602	58,197	29,073	33,211	33,628
Small Business Administration	421	928	350	85	1,056	280
Other Agencies	67,501	21,321	17,835	32,463	26,637	23,523
Allowances	—	—	−1,070	—	—	−1,070
Undistributed offsetting receipts	−89,155	−97,305	−112,634	−89,155	−97,305	−112,634
(On budget)	(−72,903)	(−76,114)	(−86,782)	(−72,903)	(−76,114)	(−86,782)
(Off budget)	(−16,252)	(−21,191)	(−25,852)	(−16,252)	(−21,191)	(−25,852)
TOTAL	**$ 1,309,913**	**$ 1,337,621**	**$ 1,396,476**	**$ 1,142,643**	**$ 1,197,236**	**$ 1,233,331**
(On budget)	(1,044,638)	(1,048,100)	(1,078,980)	(931,732)	(971,452)	(997,374)
(Off budget)	(265,275)	(289,521)	(317,496)	(210,911)	(225,784)	(235,957)

† *Figures may not add to totals due to rounding.*

SOURCE: Fiscal 1991 Budget

Administration Economic Assumptions

(Calendar years; dollar amounts in billions)

	Actual 1988	FORECAST 1989 *	1990	1991	ASSUMPTIONS 1992	1993	1994	1995
MAJOR ECONOMIC INDICATORS								
Gross national product (percent change, fourth quarter over fourth quarter):								
Current dollars	7.5	6.7	7.0	7.6	7.1	6.7	6.3	6.0
Constant (1982) dollars	3.4	2.7	2.6	3.3	3.2	3.1	3.0	3.0
GNP deflator (percent change, fourth quarter over fourth quarter)	4.0	4.0	4.2	4.1	3.8	3.5	3.2	2.9
Consumer Price Index (percent change, fourth quarter over fourth quarter) [1]	4.2	4.4	4.1	4.0	3.8	3.5	3.2	2.9
Unemployment rate (percent, fourth quarter) [2]	5.3	5.3	5.4	5.2	5.2	5.1	5.0	5.0
ANNUAL ECONOMIC ASSUMPTIONS								
Gross national product:								
Current dollars:								
Amount	4,881	5,236	5,583	6,002	6,439	6,881	7,324	7,771
Percent change, year over year	7.9	7.3	6.6	7.5	7.3	6.9	6.4	6.1
Constant (1982) dollars:								
Amount	4,024	4,144	4,244	4,379	4,521	4,662	4,804	4,948
Percent change, year over year	4.4	3.0	2.4	3.2	3.2	3.1	3.0	3.0
Incomes:								
Personal income	4,064	4,424	4,701	5,039	5,384	5,730	6,079	6,429
Wages and salaries	2,429	2,626	2,805	3,022	3,246	3,469	3,686	3,904
Corporate profits before tax	307	303	360	421	472	515	548	579
Price level:								
GNP deflator:								
Level (1982 = 100), annual average	121.3	126.4	131.6	137.1	142.4	147.6	152.5	157.1
Percent change, year over year	3.3	4.2	4.1	4.2	3.9	3.6	3.3	3.0
Consumer Price Index: [1]								
Level (1982-84 = 100), annual average	117.0	122.6	127.3	132.5	137.6	142.6	147.3	151.7
Percent change, year over year	4.0	4.8	3.9	4.0	3.9	3.6	3.3	3.0
Unemployment rates:								
Total, annual average [2]	5.4	5.2	5.4	5.3	5.2	5.1	5.0	5.0
Insured, annual average [3]	2.1	2.1	2.2	2.1	2.0	1.9	1.9	1.8
Federal pay raise, January (percent)	2.0	4.1	3.6	3.5	4.0	3.7	3.4	3.1
Interest rate, 91-day Treasury bills (percent) [4]	6.7	8.1	6.7	5.4	5.3	5.0	4.7	4.4
Interest rate, 10-year Treasury notes (percent)	8.8	8.5	7.7	6.8	6.3	6.0	5.7	5.4

** Based on data available as of mid-November 1989.*

[1] *CPI for urban wage earners and clerical workers. Two versions of the CPI are now published. The index shown here is that currently used, as required by law, in calculating automatic cost-of-living increases for indexed federal programs. The manner in which this index measures housing costs changed significantly in January 1985.*

[2] *Percent of total labor force, including armed forces residing in the United States.*

[3] *This indicator measures unemployment under state regular unemployment insurance as a percentage of covered employment under that program. It does not include recipients of extended benefits under that program.*

[4] *Average rate on new issues within period, on a bank discount basis. These projections assume, by convention, that interest rates decline with the rate of inflation.*

SOURCE: Fiscal 1991 Budget

Fiscal 1991 Budget by Function

(Figures for 1990 and 1991 are estimates; in millions of dollars †)

	BUDGET AUTHORITY			OUTLAYS		
	1989	1990	1991	1989	1990	1991
NATIONAL DEFENSE						
Military Defense	$290,837	$291,369	$295,131	$294,880	$286,791	$292,145
Atomic Energy Defense Activities	8,100	9,653	10,966	8,119	8,903	10,401
Defense-Related Activities	630	609	760	560	648	705
TOTAL	299,567	301,631	306,857	303,559	296,342	303,251
INTERNATIONAL AFFAIRS						
International Security Assistance	7,666	8,464	8,833	1,467	6,288	8,812
International Development/Humanitarian Assistance	5,296	5,517	6,111	4,837	4,873	5,383
Conduct of Foreign Affairs	2,775	2,932	4,055	2,886	2,962	3,206
Foreign Information and Exchange Activities	1,126	1,323	1,232	1,106	1,153	1,319
International Financial Programs	390	373	−232	−722	−722	−548
TOTAL	17,252	18,608	19,998	9,574	14,554	18,172
GENERAL SCIENCE, SPACE AND TECHNOLOGY						
General Science and Basic Research	2,851	3,202	3,678	2,642	3,033	3,465
Space Research and Technology	10,097	11,393	14,182	10,196	11,112	13,145
TOTAL	12,949	14,596	17,860	12,838	14,145	16,609
ENERGY						
Energy Supply	2,789	4,058	2,280	2,226	1,813	1,760
Energy Conservation	314	368	183	333	341	326
Emergency Energy Preparedness	422	635	430	621	472	593
Energy Information, Policy and Regulation	538	550	359	521	568	349
TOTAL	4,062	5,611	3,252	3,702	3,194	3,029
NATURAL RESOURCES AND ENVIRONMENT						
Pollution Control and Abatement	5,068	5,402	5,442	4,878	5,478	5,847
Water Resources	4,312	4,186	4,321	4,271	4,273	4,343
Conservation and Land Management	3,706	3,201	4,107	3,324	3,809	4,003
Recreational Resources	1,895	2,112	1,608	1,817	1,871	1,793
Other Natural Resources	2,005	2,054	2,167	1,890	2,069	2,181
TOTAL	16,987	16,955	17,645	16,182	17,499	18,168
AGRICULTURE						
Farm Income Stabilization	19,223	15,753	17,848	14,846	12,342	12,726
Agricultural Research and Services	2,112	2,221	2,223	2,102	2,229	2,212
TOTAL	21,335	17,973	20,071	16,948	14,571	14,938
COMMERCE AND HOUSING CREDIT						
Mortgage Credit and Deposit Insurance	57,634	11,861	8,829	25,504	16,556	12,988
Postal Service	2,046	4,577	3,366	127	2,878	2,132
(On budget)	(436)	(490)	(411)	(436)	(490)	(411)
(Off budget)	(1,610)	(4,087)	(2,955)	(−310)	(2,388)	(1,721)
Other Advancement of Commerce	2,246	3,115	2,090	2,088	3,254	2,064
TOTAL	61,926	19,553	14,285	27,719	22,688	17,184
(On budget)	(60,317)	(15,466)	(11,330)	(28,029)	(20,300)	(15,463)
(Off budget)	(1,610)	(4,087)	(2,955)	(−310)	(2,388)	(1,721)
TRANSPORTATION						
Ground Transportation	18,605	19,501	17,152	17,946	18,377	17,882
Air Transportation	7,494	8,326	9,658	6,622	7,412	8,234
Water Transportation	3,112	3,196	3,322	2,916	3,321	3,484
Other Transportation	132	143	160	124	140	159
TOTAL	29,342	31,167	30,293	27,608	29,250	29,758
COMMUNITY AND REGIONAL DEVELOPMENT						
Community Development	3,061	3,281	3,277	3,693	3,822	3,833
Area and Regional Development	3,512	3,795	3,305	1,894	2,936	2,791
Disaster Relief and Insurance	1,308	1,935	380	−226	2,017	1,201
TOTAL	7,881	9,011	6,961	5,361	8,776	7,825
EDUCATION, TRAINING, EMPLOYMENT, SOCIAL SERVICES						
Elementary, Secondary and Vocational Education	10,164	11,290	12,165	9,193	9,768	11,296
Higher Education	11,008	10,899	10,481	10,649	10,506	10,433
Research and General Education Aids	1,426	1,489	1,641	1,391	1,510	1,656
Training and Employment	5,392	5,553	5,612	5,292	5,457	5,660
Other Labor Services	802	815	877	786	800	852
Social Services	9,962	9,583	11,188	9,374	9,611	11,107
TOTAL	38,754	39,630	41,964	36,684	37,652	41,005

Fiscal 1991 Budget by Function

(Figures for 1990 and 1991 are estimates; in millions of dollars †)

	BUDGET AUTHORITY			OUTLAYS		
	1989	1990	1991	1989	1990	1991
HEALTH						
Health Care Services	$ 42,017	$ 49,873	$ 54,054	$ 39,164	$ 47,910	$ 53,318
Health Research	7,706	8,316	8,744	7,325	7,867	8,341
Education, Training of Health Care Work Force	575	669	500	545	590	558
Consumer and Occupational Health and Safety	1,397	1,485	1,476	1,356	1,451	1,481
TOTAL	51,694	60,341	64,775	48,390	57,819	63,698
MEDICARE	107,339	116,933	125,224	84,964	96,616	98,615
INCOME SECURITY						
General Retirement and Disability Insurance	6,618	6,632	6,410	5,650	5,202	5,492
Federal Employee Retirement and Disability	83,777	86,239	91,698	49,151	52,520	53,864
Unemployment Compensation	22,548	24,818	24,054	15,616	18,098	18,601
Housing Assistance	9,568	11,076	17,977	14,715	16,295	17,663
Food and Nutrition Assistance	21,262	23,828	23,200	21,192	23,396	23,350
Other Income Security	29,584	30,626	35,553	29,706	31,090	34,769
TOTAL	173,357	183,218	198,894	136,031	146,601	153,738
SOCIAL SECURITY	284,987	310,500	345,115	232,542	248,462	264,811
(On budget)	(5,069)	(3,875)	(4,722)	(5,069)	(3,875)	(4,722)
(Off budget)	(279,918)	(306,625)	(340,393)	(227,473)	(244,587)	(260,089)
VETERANS' BENEFITS AND SERVICES						
Income Security	16,384	16,416	16,396	16,544	15,108	16,200
Education, Training and Rehabilitation	421	325	322	459	429	427
Housing	778	314	484	878	350	167
Hospital and Medical Care	11,523	12,037	12,744	11,343	11,997	12,469
Other Benefits and Services	919	940	1,045	843	1,003	1,045
TOTAL	30,025	30,030	30,990	30,066	28,888	30,308
ADMINISTRATION OF JUSTICE						
Federal Law Enforcement Activities	4,697	5,089	5,633	4,667	4,942	5,404
Federal Litigative and Judicial Activities	3,288	3,827	4,432	3,255	3,591	4,325
Federal Correctional Activities	1,553	2,536	1,746	1,044	1,417	2,230
Criminal Justice Assistance	424	774	749	455	540	648
TOTAL	9,963	12,225	12,560	9,422	10,489	12,608
GENERAL GOVERNMENT						
Legislative Functions	1,807	1,779	2,147	1,651	1,827	2,161
Executive Direction and Management	137	290	357	129	178	321
Central Fiscal Operations	5,900	5,863	6,092	5,570	5,660	5,882
General Property and Records Management	605	242	166	−341	450	276
Central Personnel Management	146	156	164	134	168	161
General Purpose Fiscal Assistance	2,043	2,068	2,114	2,061	2,166	2,136
Other General Government	822	835	1,324	813	836	1,307
Deductions for Offsetting Receipts	−893	−725	−962	−893	−725	−962
TOTAL	10,568	10,508	11,402	9,124	10,560	11,282
NET INTEREST						
Interest on the Public Debt	240,863	254,850	259,763	240,863	254,850	259,763
Interest Received by On-Budget Trust Funds	−40,547	−45,233	−49,167	−40,547	−45,233	−49,167
Interest Received by Off-Budget Trust Funds	−11,395	−15,610	−19,890	−11,395	−15,610	−19,890
Other Interest	−19,784	−18,416	−17,728	−19,784	−18,416	−17,728
TOTAL	169,137	175,591	172,979	169,137	175,591	172,979
(On budget)	(180,532)	(191,201)	(192,869)	(180,532)	(191,201)	(192,869)
(Off budget)	(−11,395)	(−15,610)	(−19,890)	(−11,395)	(−15,610)	(−19,890)
ALLOWANCES	—	—	−1,070	—	—	−1,070
UNDISTRIBUTED OFFSETTING RECEIPTS	−37,212	−36,462	−43,578	−37,212	−36,462	−43,578
(On budget)	(−32,354)	(−30,881)	(−37,615)	(−32,354)	(−30,881)	(−37,615)
(Off budget)	(−4,858)	(−5,581)	(−5,962)	(−4,858)	(−5,581)	(−5,962)
TOTAL	**$1,309,913**	**$1,337,621**	**$1,396,476**	**$1,142,643**	**$1,197,236**	**$1,233,331**
(On budget)	(1,044,638)	(1,048,100)	(1,078,980)	(931,732)	(971,452)	(997,374)
(Off budget)	(265,275)	(289,521)	(317,496)	(210,911)	(225,784)	(235,957)

† Figures may not add due to rounding.

SOURCE: Fiscal 1991 Budget

President Bush's Fiscal 1991 Budget

President Bush's budget proposal, submitted Jan. 29, included increases for the president's priorities — including space, science, research, foreign aid and drug-fighting programs.

Spending on education and the environment also were slated for increases, but not enough to match inflation except for select programs such as Head Start and the "superfund" for toxic-waste cleanups.

The budget provided for nominal spending increases in most government functions. In many cases, however, the increases did not keep up with the expected inflation rate of 4 percent for the fiscal year.

The budget was presented in terms of budget authority, the money that a program could obligate, and outlays, the amount the program was actually expected to spend during the fiscal year.

The following are highlights:

Defense

Bush proposed to cut real defense spending authority by 2.1 percent in fiscal 1991. The defense budget included $306.9 billion in new budget authority, compared with $301.6 billion in 1990.

The total covered $295.1 billion for the Defense Department and $11.7 billion for defense-related activities of the Energy Department, the Federal Emergency Management Agency and other agencies. That translated into $303.3 billion in outlays for fiscal 1991, a nominal 2.3 percent increase over 1990.

Outlays for the Pentagon were set at $292.1 billion. Over the next five years, the Pentagon projected a 2 percent real annual decline in spending authority, resulting in a $325.7 billion defense budget in fiscal 1995. For the most part, the defense savings were to come from management initiatives, reductions in military manpower and the termination of a number of conventional weapons. Bush wanted to proceed with the development of strategic weapons programs and the strategic defense initiative (SDI).

Submitted with the budget was a plan to close 35 domestic military bases and 12 U.S. bases overseas.

The administration asked for a $900 million increase in funding for the SDI program to $4.7 billion (including $192 million in the Energy Department budget), with continued development of the so-called brilliant pebbles technology. This approach was based on thousands of interceptor missiles orbiting Earth that could each destroy a Soviet intercontinental ballistic missile (ICBM) shortly after launch.

Bush called for $2.5 billion to produce five B-2 "stealth" bombers and components for future production, as well as $1.6 billion for continued research and development of the radar-evading aircraft. He requested $2.8 billion for the MX program, including funding for the purchase of rail-mobile launchers and 12 of the big multi-warhead ICBMs. Another $202 million was requested for continued development of the Midgetman, a smaller ICBM. The administration sought to fund procurement of the 18th Trident submarine at a fiscal 1991 cost of $1.2 billion, and 52 Trident II missiles at a cost of $1.3 billion.

To continue these programs while keeping the overall defense budget down, the Pentagon proposed to terminate 20 major weapons programs, for an estimated savings of almost $3 billion.

Cheney also wanted to transfer or defer spending of nearly $2.3 billion in previously appropriated funds.

Among the programs proposed for termination was the Army's M-1 tank, after the production of 225 additional tanks in fiscal 1991. Also on the list was the Apache attack helicopter, for an estimated fiscal 1991 savings of $682 million. But the Pentagon wanted to go ahead with the development of a smaller "new generation" attack helicopter, the LHX, at a cost of $465 million. The budget provided no new funds for the Army's AHIP scout helicopter modification program.

The Navy's F-14D fighter jet and the long-range Phoenix missile, carried by the F-14, were also slated for termination. The budget included $780 million to convert 12 older aircraft models into the F-14D.

Defense Secretary Dick Cheney also resubmitted proposals to terminate the Marine Corps' V-22 Osprey, a hybrid airplane/helicopter, and the Air Force's F-15E. The previous year, Congress rejected Cheney's plan to cancel the V-22.

The Pentagon also expected savings from reductions in military personnel and changes in force structure. The fiscal 1991 plan envisioned a drop of almost 38,000 in military personnel, for an active force of slightly more than 2 million. The level of selected reserves was to remain relatively unchanged at 1.2 million.

Bush also sought to eliminate two active Army divisions — the 9th Infantry Division at Fort Lewis, Wash., and the 2nd Armored Division at Fort Hood, Texas. And he proposed to retire two battleships, deactivate eight nuclear-powered attack submarines and begin planning to deactivate two nuclear cruisers. Deactivation of the two Army divisions was expected to save about $1.2 billion in fiscal 1991, although deactivating the nuclear cruisers would initially cost money, about $99 million in fiscal 1991.

The budget also provided for a 3.5 percent military pay raise, the same as was being considered for the entire federal work force.

The defense request also included:

- $1.2 billion, up from $800 million in fiscal 1990, for Defense Department drug-fighting efforts. This included money to expand the campaign to detect and monitor airborne and maritime drug-smuggling activities and to increase the role of the National Guard in counternarcotics efforts.
- $2.4 billion for the Energy Department's program to clean up nuclear waste from aging defense plants, and $817 million for the Pentagon's environmental restoration fund, used to clean up toxic waste and debris at current and former military facilities.
- No funds for construction of the Energy Department's Special Isotope Separation (SIS) project, which was to be used to process plutonium, a key ingredient for nuclear weapons. Energy Secretary James D. Watkins cited budget problems and the availability of plutonium from other sources as a reason to kill the SIS plant.

Agriculture

The Bush budget charted a course for agriculture programs that extended beyond fiscal 1991 and positioned the administration for the coming debate over retooling federal farm programs, most of which had to be reauthorized before the year's end.

For fiscal 1991, Bush proposed a modest $300 million increase in outlays for federal agriculture programs from the estimated $14.6 billion provided for fiscal 1990. Bush dropped the federal crop insurance program from the budget and called for a $1.5 billion cut in price- and income-support payments to farmers.

The overall Agriculture Department budget came to $48.7 billion in outlays, an increase of $500 million over fiscal 1990. Even if Congress approved a full $1.5 billion in subsidy-payment cuts, spending by the Commodity Credit Corporation, the federal entity that funded the support programs, was expected to increase about $2 billion in fiscal 1991 to $10.4 billion.

The Bush budget baseline — the projected level of future spending from which cuts would be made — also assumed a freeze on target prices, the so-called ideal commodity prices that Congress set to guarantee farmers a minimum income. Target prices had been declining since 1985 — as a result of the 1985 farm bill and subsequent deficit-reduction acts — and government support payments also had been shrinking. The five-year farm bill was due to expire in 1990.

The assumption of a target-price freeze into fiscal 1991 meant that spending trends for commodity programs were no longer shown on a downward path. In fact, administration projections showed commodity programs becoming more expensive in coming years — from $11.8 billion in fiscal 1991 to $14.4 billion in fiscal 1993 — if no action were taken to reduce them.

That would allow the Budget and Agriculture committees to start from a higher projected spending level before starting to cut.

Moreover, the Bush assumption of frozen target prices would allow Congress and the administration to claim savings in the agriculture budget that would have occurred anyway if a continuing downward trend in target prices had been assumed.

As a result, congressional budget experts predicted that $1.5 billion in annual cuts would be required from commodity programs over the life of the next farm bill. This was the same amount proposed in Bush's fiscal 1991 budget and was expected to be politically palatable among farm-state lawmakers.

But the administration also called for better enforcement of limits on federal subsidy payments to farmers. At the time, farmers could receive no more than $50,000 in income-support payments and no more than $250,000 in total subsidy payments. But farmers and large agribusiness operations engaged in complicated schemes to evade the limits.

Also, the budget tried to force Congress to settle on a way to compensate farmers battered by bad weather. At the time, Congress provided both subsidized crop insurance and periodic, multimillion-dollar disaster relief aid. The administration said it would no longer pay for both. And it insisted that the crop insurance program had to be overhauled or thrown out.

The budget included deep cuts in the Farmers Home Administration (FmHA) and the Rural Electrification Administration (REA), continuing the Reagan-era policy of shifting from direct to guaranteed loans for farm lending. But it proposed some cuts in guaranteed loan programs as well.

The FmHA farm-credit budget called for an overall level of $3.4 billion in outlays in 1991, down from $4.2 billion provided in fiscal 1990. Direct farm-operating loans were to be cut from an estimated level of $932 million in fiscal 1990 to $500 million in fiscal 1991. Even guaranteed loans were cut back slightly to $2.3 billion. For farm ownership lending, the budget included $100 million for guarantees, down from $719 million, and $38 million for direct loans, down from $80 million.

To encourage the shift to guaranteed loans, the budget included $50 million to subsidize the interest rates offered by private lenders to borrowers.

At REA, roughly $2 billion in direct loan programs were to be slashed to $325 million. Another $1.3 billion in guaranteed loans were to be substituted to finance electric and telephone service.

Commerce

Overall, federal spending on the promotion and regulation of trade and commerce, including grants for community development, remained fairly stable under Bush's request.

But the hefty costs of handling failed savings and loan institutions in recent years boosted outlays in fiscal 1989 and 1990 above those slated for 1991. As a result, total outlays in these functions of $25 billion showed a 20.5 percent cut from fiscal 1990.

• **Financial institutions.** Deposit-insurance costs associated with salvaging the thrift industry dominated this category. Net deposit-insurance spending for 1991 was put at $8.9 billion, compared with $10.9 billion in 1990 and $20.5 billion in 1989.

That included interest payments of $1.7 billion on bonds to finance closing failed thrifts, and net spending by the Resolution Trust Corporation, charged with handling the thrift bailout, of $7.3 billion. The total for deposit insurance, however, included an expected surplus of $1.7 billion in the Bank Insurance Fund administered by the Federal Deposit Insurance Corporation. In the previous two years, record bank failures had resulted in net losses in that fund.

• **SEC.** The budget included a 15 percent increase in outlays by the Securities and Exchange Commission (SEC) to $186.6 million.

The administration intended to ask Congress to make permanent a temporary fee increase on securities registrations and also to increase fees on securities transactions, an idea that had some support in Congress as a means of providing additional budget increases to the SEC in future years.

• **Housing credit.** Bush also proposed a fee increase for the issuers of securities backed by federally insured mortgages, for which principal and interest payments were guaranteed by the Government National Mortgage Corporation (Ginnie Mae). This fee increase, expected to raise $10 million in 1991, was designed to boost Ginnie Mae reserves against losses from default.

Bonds and securities of the Federal National Mortgage Association (Fannie Mae) and Federal Home Loan Mortgage Corporation, were expected to raise $52 million in 1991.

• **Community development.** Bush requested $2.8 billion in new budget authority for Community Development Block Grants, $100 million less than was provided in 1990, and he sought changes in the program's emphasis. The Department of Housing and Urban Development (HUD) planned to target the block grant funds for low- and moderate-income programs and to fight poverty.

• **Postal service.** Bush wanted to bar nonprofit corporations from taking advantage of reduced postal rates to promote commercial activities. A similar initiative by President Ronald Reagan had failed. Unlike the fiscal 1990 Reagan budget, however, Bush's budget did not do away with the subsidy; it proposed a $32 million increase over the estimated $453 million provided in fiscal 1990.

• **Small business.** Bush proposed to convert all Small Business Administration (SBA) direct lending to guaranteed lending, except for direct loans to firms participating in the Section 8(a) program, which gave aid to minority businesses seeking government contracts. He also proposed higher guarantee fees to help offset SBA losses, with a lower increase for minority investment companies.

Education and Training

For education, training, employment and social services, Bush sought $41 billion in outlays in 1991, compared with $37.7 billion in 1990. The budget included $23.4 billion in outlays for elementary, secondary, vocational and higher education, a reduction in real spending from 1990's $21.8 billion.

The budget boosted spending for elementary and secondary education, while maintaining level funding for vocational education and reducing spending for higher education.

The administration requested $3.1 billion in new budget authority for guaranteed student loans, less than the $3.9 billion provided in 1990, mostly due to administration predictions of lower interest rates. Outlays for guaranteed student loans were put at $3.2 billion. Budget authority for work-study grants and supplemental grants remained the same as in 1990 — $601.8 million and $458.7 million, respectively.

Chapter 1, a compensatory education program for disadvantaged children, was to get $5.6 billion in budget authority, up from $5.1 billion. The program, never fully funded, helped about 50 percent of the children who qualified.

The administration also sought to boost funds for the Chapter 2 program, which provided block grants to states to improve the quality of elementary and secondary education. Budget authority for Chapter 2 was $457 million in 1990; Bush sought $475 million.

The budget included an additional $500 million for the popular Head Start program, which provided education, nutrition, health and social services for low-income preschoolers. The increase would boost funding to $1.9 billion from $1.4 billion — enough, officials said, to enroll another 180,000 children.

Like Reagan, Bush proposed virtual elimination of the Community Services Block Grant, which provided funds for a variety of poverty-fighting programs at the local level.

For employment and training programs, Bush asked $5.6 billion in budget authority, a $60 million increase over 1990's level.

Most of the request was for programs under the Job Training and Partnership Act (JTPA). The budget included $4.2 billion for JTPA in fiscal 1991, $300 million more than the 1990 level. Of those funds, $1.7 billion was for youth job-training grants, a $200 million increase over fiscal 1990.

Bush also proposed $50 million in new budget authority for a multi-year grant program, Youth Opportunities Unlimited (YOU), that would target high-poverty inner cities and rural areas and require grantees to provide matching finds.

Bush wanted Congress to save $230.5 million by eliminating the Trade Adjustment Assistance program, which was created in 1988 to train workers who lost their jobs because of foreign competition. Following Reagan's lead, Bush instead proposed $400 million in budget authority — $20 million in fiscal 1991 outlays — for an Economic Dislocation and Worker Adjustment Assistance program, which was not tied solely to trade. Congress provided no funds for that proposal in fiscal 1990.

Energy

In one important respect, Bush's energy budget — down 5.2 percent to $3 billion in outlays — was a stark contrast to his predecessor's: Bush did not propose to cut research and development for conservation and solar and renewable energy.

The Bush budget allotted about $177 million in budget authority to renewable energy (solar, wind and biofuels, among others) and $183 million to conservation research. The $359 million total represented a modest increase over 1990 spending of $333 million, but it was far ahead of the $201 million level requested for fiscal 1990 under Reagan.

That total included $54 million toward a six-year, $336 million proposal for new initiatives aimed at cutting U.S. energy needs by $32 billion over the next decade.

Despite these increases, Bush asked Congress to cut state and local conservation grants from $217 million to $30 million.

The administration proposed to increase Nuclear Regulatory Commission fees by $296 million and impose a 1 percent fee on loan guarantees by the Rural Electrification Administration (REA). The REA's electrification budget was to be cut to $33 million from $1.2 billion; Congress resisted such efforts during the Reagan years.

Environment

Despite a new environmental initiative and several spending increases, Bush proposed a comparatively modest 3.8 percent boost in outlays for the environment and natural resources — from $17.5 billion in fiscal 1990 to $18.2 billion in fiscal 1991.

On its face, the increase was a dramatic reversal of the final Reagan budget proposal, which would have cut total spending by 13 percent in fiscal 1990. But much of the proposed Reagan reduction would have come with the help of offsetting revenues from oil and gas leasing, which never materialized.

Reagan actually proposed increases in some of the same key environmental spending priorities Bush sought to beef up, such as the Environmental Protection Agency (EPA), and the "superfund" hazardous-waste cleanup program. In fiscal 1989, Reagan had proposed a 6 percent increase in environmental spending.

The flagship of the Bush environmental budget was a new program called "America the Beautiful," which combined a tree-planting initiative with a repackaging of existing land acquisition, natural resources and recreational facilities programs. Bush requested a total of $630 million in new budget authority for the program, $175 million for tree planting and $455 million for the existing programs — $94 million more than in fiscal 1990.

Bush requested a 6 percent boost in funds for the EPA, from $5.5 billion in fiscal 1990 to $5.8 billion in fiscal 1991. That included requests for $230 million in new budget authority for the agency's operating budget, an 11.9 percent increase, and $209.8 million in new budget authority for superfund, a 13.7 percent increase.

Bush sought to cut grants for the construction of sewage-treatment plants by more than $300 million, to $1.6 billion in new budget authority. This was a program Congress had vigorously defended in the past.

Outlays for the Interior Department dropped 2.3 percent in the Bush budget, from $5.8 billion in fiscal 1990 to $5.7 billion in 1991.

Notably absent were projected revenues from controversial oil and gas lease sales that the Bush administration had postponed.

Several of the Bush budget's spending increases for environmental programs were spread across a variety of departments and agencies. These included a 56.9 percent increase for research on global climate change, from $659 million to $1.03 billion in new budget authority, and an 23.7 percent increase for wetlands protection, up $88 million to $460 million in new budget authority.

Foreign Affairs

Bush sought total budget authority for international affairs of $20 billion, an increase of $1.4 billion over fiscal 1990. That translated into an increase of $3.6 billion in outlays, to $18.2 billion in fiscal 1991.

The outlay figure was misleading, though. Of the nominal increase, nearly half ($1.7 billion) was due to a technicality of the budgeting process. As a result, the actual outlay increase for international affairs programs was closer to $1.9 billion, or 13 percent.

In any event, the budget authority figure more accurately represented program levels for international affairs.

Most big components of the international affairs budget — covering all U.S. foreign aid programs and operations of the State Department, the United States Information Agency and related agencies — were slated for increases in fiscal 1991. Spending authority for foreign aid programs was to increase to $14.9 billion from $14 billion in fiscal 1990.

The broad category called "diplomacy" (such as State Department operations and U.S. support for the United Nations) was to grow by $1 billion to $5.3 billion.

Bush proposed only two major new programs in fiscal 1991.

One was a $300 million request for a new package of aid to countries in Eastern Europe. The administration offered no details about how this money would be spent, however.

The other was a $270 million allocation to rebuild the U.S. Embassy office building in Moscow. The United States started work on a new embassy there in 1979, only to halt construction in 1985 when listening devices were found embedded in the building's walls, ceilings and floors.

Nearly $1 billion of Bush's foreign affairs request was to pay obligations that the United States had incurred to international agencies. The biggest chunk — $620 million — was to clear up past-due obligations to the United Nations and its specialized agencies. Throughout most of the 1980s, Congress and the Reagan administration withheld millions of dollars that the United States was supposed to pay to U.N. agencies.

Those payments were in addition to $794 million in regularly scheduled U.S. payments to those agencies in fiscal 1991.

The budget also included $279 million for past-due U.S. contributions to the World Bank and other multilateral development banks. In addition, the United States would make its regular contributions to those banks, including the first $1 billion payment to a replenishment of resources for the International Development Association, an arm of the World Bank.

Bush asked for increases — some of them substantial — for other international affairs programs, including:

- **'Security aid.'** Bush proposed to increase military aid to help foreign countries buy U.S. weapons by $189 million to $5 billion in fiscal 1991. Direct economic aid would rise to $3.4 billion, a $179 million increase over fiscal 1990.
- **Philippines.** Bush sought a second annual donation to an international economic aid program for the Philippines. Congress approved $160 million in fiscal 1990 (a cut of $40 million from the request). Bush again asked for the full $200 million for fiscal 1991. This money was in addition to more than $450 million for bilateral U.S. aid programs for the Philippines.
- **Narcotics control.** The budget included $528 million for various overseas programs to combat drug trafficking.

One new element, fulfilling a promise Bush made in 1989, was $175 million in economic aid to Bolivia, Colombia and Peru, the centers of the cocaine trade. The State Department's overseas antinarcotics program was slated to grow to $150 million in fiscal 1991, a boost of about $35 million.

Health

For health and Medicare combined, Bush assumed $162.3 billion in outlays in fiscal 1991, compared with $154.4 billion in 1990.

With only a few exceptions, Bush's health budget bore a striking resemblance to the Reagan budgets that preceded it. Like Reagan, Bush sought to curb the fast-growing Medicare program for the elderly and disabled, and, like their predecessors, Bush administration officials denied that the proposed $5.5 billion in outlay reductions were "cuts."

The changes were described as necessary to prevent Medicare from eating the rest of the budget. In fiscal 1991, the insurance program was expected to cost nearly $99 billion and pay for health care for about 33.5 million elderly and disabled people.

Some of the proposals had been made in the past but rejected by Congress. One was to raise about $1.87 billion by requiring all state and local employees to pay the Medicare portion of the Social Security payroll tax (1.45 percent of wages each for worker and employer). Under current law, only workers hired after March 31, 1986, were required to participate. Another oft-rejected proposal was to cut payments to teaching hospitals by about $1.2 billion to help offset training costs.

Other proposals had won support in Congress in the past. They included holding Medicare payments to hospitals below the projected inflation rate ($640 million in savings), reducing payments for capital improvements ($1.5 billion), freezing most physician fees at fiscal 1990 levels ($450 million) and reducing payments for services deemed overpriced ($510 million in savings).

Despite the urging of Health and Human Services Secretary Louis W. Sullivan, the budget did not propose major expansions of Medicaid, the federal-state health-care program for the poor. In fiscal 1991 the budget estimated that Medicaid would serve 26.6 million people at a cost to the federal government of $44.9 billion. (The federal government paid about 55 percent of Medicaid's costs.)

The budget outlined a major initiative to curb health-care costs by encouraging the use of "managed care" in both Medicare and Medicaid. Such care involved fixed per-enrollee payments to health maintenance organizations (HMOs) and reduced-rate payments to preferred provider organizations.

The administration hoped to entice more HMOs to participate in Medicare by increasing payment rates. To encourage beneficiaries to enroll in such group plans, it planned to create a "Medicare plus" program combining regular Medicare coverage with services that were available only through private supplemental insurance, known as Medigap.

In Medicaid, the administration proposal featured a stick as well as a carrot. The federal government would pay states higher matching rates for three years to encourage them to enroll Medicaid recipients in managed-care plans. After that, reduced rates would be paid for Medicaid beneficiaries *not* so enrolled.

In another major proposal, Bush sought to shift costs borne by the federal government to the states, drug companies and health-care providers. Bush wanted drug companies to pay the Food and Drug Administration fees to cover the costs of the drug-approval process, a Reagan proposal repeatedly rejected by Congress.

The budget also called for user fees to cover the costs of inspecting and certifying hospitals, nursing homes and home-health agencies for participation in Medicare and Medicaid.

The remainder of the health budget contained only minor changes, and most increases were offset by decreases elsewhere.

For AIDS prevention and research, the budget included $1.7 billion, an increase of $109 million from fiscal 1990. AIDS groups, however, decried the amount as inadequate.

Income Security

For income security, which included housing assistance, food and nutrition, and low-income energy programs, Bush's budget would have resulted in outlays of $418.5 billion in fiscal 1991, compared with $395.1 billion in 1990.

The budget did not touch Social Security. The administration estimated fiscal 1991 benefits for the old-age and disability programs would cost $265.03 billion, which assumed a 3.9 percent cost-of-living adjustment (COLA) beginning Jan. 1, 1991.

No such COLA was allowed, however, for federal retirees in 1991. Bush also proposed eliminating a popular option for federal retirees to take their contributions to their pensions in a lump sum upon retirement.

The administration proposed requiring state and local government employees who did not participate in a public-employee retirement system to join the Social Security system. Budget officials estimated that about 3.8 million workers would be affected yielding an estimated $2.3 billion in payroll taxes in fiscal 1991.

Bush's housing budget emphasized home ownership, while other forms of housing assistance for the poor suffered cuts more drastic than in Reagan's last housing request to Congress. Altogether, Bush wanted to add 82,049 units to the assisted-housing rolls in 1991. The previous year, Reagan proposed adding 109,000 units. During the Carter administration, assisted housing increased by more than 300,000 units per year.

Officials at the Department of Housing and Urban Development (HUD) said the $23.7 billion in budget authority they were seeking in 1991 was a 29 percent increase over 1990's $18.4 billion.

But when renewals for Section 8 rental-assistance programs that were scheduled to expire were taken out, and two other programs preapproved by Congress subtracted, HUD showed only a slight increase of $50 million in its total budget request.

The Bush budget cut new housing construction for elderly, handicapped and chronically mentally ill people from 2,096 units in 1990 to 870 in 1991. Section 8 rental-assistance certificates were to drop from 30,523 in 1990 to 6,889 in 1991.

Moderate rehabilitation, a program plagued by scandal in the Reagan era, was to be eliminated.

No new public or Indian housing was proposed for 1991; 8,115 units were funded in 1990. Rural housing programs under the Farmers Home Administration were to be cut from $5 billion to $3.9 billion. Instead, the Bush administration requested $1.2 billion in new spending in fiscal 1991 for its HOPE program — Home ownership and Opportunity for People Everywhere. The program would require states and local governments to come up with $1 for every $2 of federal funds spent. The budget also called for $187 million in tax benefits for first-time home buyers and others.

Of the $1.2 billion in new program funding, $250 million would go toward HOPE grants to help low-income families and tenants become homeowners. Another $251 million was earmarked for rent assistance; and $412 million would go toward helping groups of residents buy their buildings if current owners prepaid their HUD-subsidized mortgages.

The budget shifted money within nutrition programs, cutting some while increasing others. Overall outlays were to drop slightly, from $23.4 billion in fiscal 1990 to $23.35 billion in fiscal 1991.

Critics complained loudest about the administration's failure to seek funding increases in the WIC program for nursing mothers, infants and children deemed at nutritional risk. In his 1988 campaign, Bush often singled out the $2.2 billion program for praise.

The most controversial proposal in this area would have eliminated subsidies for school lunches for students from families with incomes over 350 percent of the federal poverty threshold.

Although Bush proposed to increase subsidies for poorer children, program supporters had long complained that unless subsidies were available for all children, school districts would not find it cost-effective to participate in the program.

Another controversial proposal would have cut $293 million in the popular Low Income Home Energy Assistance Program, known as LIHEAP. The Reagan administration had tried, with some success, to pare the program, which helped low-income households weatherize their homes and pay fuel bills.

Law

For law enforcement and administration of justice activities, Bush proposed $12.6 billion in outlays, an increase of $2.1 billion over the 1990 estimated level. Much of the money was earmarked for the fight against drug trafficking. Bush assumed a total of $9.7 billion in anti-drug outlays, a 41 percent increase over the 1990 level. Of that amount, $6.8 billion was for law enforcement programs; the rest was for drug treatment and prevention activities.

The Justice Department was to get $9 billion of the total administration of justice outlay, a 4.2 percent increase over 1990. If a multi-year prison construction program that was launched in the 1990 budget was excluded, the department budget was 19 percent higher, according to Attorney General Dick Thornburgh.

Highlights included:

- $700 million in budget authority for the Drug Enforcement Administration, the government's lead investigator of drug trafficking. The Justice Department said the $151 million, or 28 percent, increase over 1990 was one of the largest annual increases in the agency's history and would mean the addition of more than 500 agents and other specialists.
- $1.64 billion for the FBI, an increase of $141 million, or 9.4 percent. While the number of agents assigned to drug and organized-crime units was slated to climb, the number of agents in white-collar crime units was expected to decrease.
- 16 new positions and a 21 percent increase in budget authority for the Civil Rights Division, to $39 million, in anticipation of redistricting challenges stemming from the 1990 census.

Science and Space

Funding for science and space programs were slated to grow dramatically, with NASA getting what amounted to a bigger percentage increase than any other major agency and a slew of so-called "big science" projects getting huge increases.

Overall, outlays for science — including all of the National Science Foundation (NSF), most of NASA and a chunk of the Energy Department — were expected to increase by $2.5 billion, to $16.6 billion, in fiscal 1991 under Bush's proposals.

Budget authority for NASA, set at $15.2 billion, represented a 24 percent increase over fiscal 1990.

The NSF also did well, with a proposed 14 percent increase, to $2.4 billion. Several "big science" projects scattered throughout the government also were slated to receive healthy increases:

- $318 million for the Energy Department's superconducting supercollider, nearly $100 million more than the fiscal 1990 appropriation of $225 million.
- $154 million for a human gene-mapping project run by the National Institutes of Health and the Energy Department, a 56 percent increase.
- $1.3 billion for space exploration, bolstering NASA's plan to send humans to the moon and Mars. The proposed space station, the driving force in NASA's budget in recent years, would have its funding increased by 36 percent, to $2.6 billion.
- $1 billion for multiagency efforts to study worldwide climate change, a 57 percent increase over fiscal 1990. Most of that was earmarked for NASA's space-based observatory system, Mission to Planet Earth. Another multiagency effort, science-related education, was to increase 26 percent to $1.1 billion.

Overall, Bush sought to increase research and development (R&D) spending — which cut across many agencies and functions — to $71 billion, a 7 percent jump.

Bush propsed to spend $20 million of the NSF budget for a new program to build university research facilities, through a peer-review process. The NSF had resisted the program in the past, but Congress carved almost $20 million for it from the rest of the 1990 NSF budget.

Transportation

In step with Reagan administration proposals for transportation programs, Bush requested new user fees and greater state and local involvement in funding the nation's infrastructure.

Overall, Bush's budget assumed $29.8 billion in fiscal 1991 outlays, slightly above the 1990 level of $29.3 billion. Most of the money was for programs within the Transportation Department, although the overall request for that agency was 4.2 percent below fiscal 1990 outlays of $28.1 billion.

Bush's asked for increased spending on aviation safety and capacity, resulting in $2.5 billion in outlays to modernize Federal Aviation Administration facilities and equipment, a $700 million increase over the fiscal 1990 level.

The budget also included large cuts in mass transit grants and elimination of subsidies for the Amtrak national passenger railroad, proposals Congress had rejected in the past. Mass transit outlays were cut from $3.6 billion in fiscal 1990 to $3.4 billion. A large portion of the decrease came from the propsed elimination of Urban Mass Transit Administration grants to the 30 largest cities with populations of more than 1 million.

Among the proposed new user fees was an increase from 8 percent to 10 percent in the airline passenger ticket tax, and commensurate increases in aviation fuel and air freight fees, for an increase of $623 million in new revenues in fiscal 1991.

Bush also proposed $200 million in Coast Guard user fees, derived in part from an annual charge of $25 per boat.

Besides increasing passenger ticket fees and other aviation fees that finance the Airport and Airway Trust Fund, the budget called for spending the trust fund balance faster than it was accumulated to help reduce expenditures from general funds. Under this proposal, the trust fund balance would decline from an estimated $7.6 billion at the end of 1990 to $3 billion by the end of 1995.

Bush also proposed eliminating restrictions that prevented airports from raising revenue through charges levied on departing passengers. Those funds could be used by airports in lieu of a portion of their federal airport grant funds for improvements in airport capacity and security, the budget said.

The president proposed $1.5 billion for fiscal 1991 budget authority for such grants to airports; savings from new departure charges were to go to other capacity-expansion projects and to smaller airports that would not benefit from such a tax.

Veterans' Affairs

Bush assumed a modest increase for veterans' programs — $30.3 billion in outlays compared with $28.9 billion in fiscal 1990.

The budget requested an increase over fiscal 1990 of nearly $1 billion in new budget authority for health care funding, including pay increases for physicians, nurses and dentists, which Veterans Affairs Department (VA) officials hoped would enable VA hospitals to compete for qualified staff.

Bush also proposed to collect an additional $364 million in fees and revenues, including $112 million by expanding the liability of insurance companies for non-service-connected medical treatment, and $30 million by requiring user fees for outpatient care and prescriptions.

The budget sought to limit to $25,000 the benefits accumulated by legally incompetent veterans with no dependents, producing an estimated savings of $170 million in fiscal 1990 outlays.

And for the first time, veterans would have to pay a minimum 4 percent down payment for home loans of more than $25,000. Down payments were not required under existing law.

Under a bill (HR 901, PL 101-237) passed at the close of the 1989 session, the VA had just begun charging a 1.25 percent mortgage fee as foreclosure insurance.

Bush proposed to raise the fee to 1.75 percent, although veterans rated at least 30 percent disabled would be exempt from paying the fee. ■

Continued from p. 117

concept that half of the deficit reduction should come from revenues took hold. Who would pay — and who would take the political blame — would become the biggest fight of all.

Dueling Over the Deficit

When Bush submitted his budget in January, the administration predicted that, without any further action by Congress, the fiscal 1991 deficit would be $100.5 billion. That was an estimate of the "baseline" budget, which assumed no changes in law but did allow for inflation and for demographic changes, such as the number of people eligible for mandatory programs like Medicare.

Bush predicted that his budget would bring the deficit, as calculated under Gramm-Rudman, to $64.7 billion, coming in below the law's $74 billion ceiling.

The bipartisan Congressional Budget Office (CBO) took a less sanguine view. When CBO released its annual re-estimate of the president's budget March 5, it projected a $161 billion baseline deficit and a $131 billion deficit under Bush's proposal. The difference was due largely to different economic assumptions and to costs of the savings and loan bailout that were not included in Bush's budget.

Of the $35.8 billion Bush promised to cut from the Gramm-Rudman deficit, more than half, or $19.5 billion, was slated to come from new revenue sources. The top money-raiser was a plan to lower the tax rate on capital gains, which the administration projected to raise $4.9 billion in fiscal 1991.

Other projected revenues included $5.6 billion from user fees, which were routinely proposed but mostly went unrealized; $3.8 billion from mandating that all state and local government employees pay Medicare payroll taxes, a proposal that Congress repeatedly had rejected; $2.5 billion from unspecified Internal Revenue Service "management reforms;" and $1 billion from expedited collections of telephone and payroll taxes.

Although Democrats derided many of these as gimmicks and retreads of previously rejected ideas, they included a number of them in an early House budget plan.

About a third of Bush's proposed deficit reduction, or $12 billion, came from cuts in entitlement programs, notably Medicare, farm price supports and federal employees' health and retirement benefits. Medicare took the brunt, $5.5 billion, though Bush stressed that the cuts would affect payments to doctors and hospitals, not patient's benefits. *(Farm programs, p. 323; Medicare, p. 563)*

Bush also proposed killing a number of domestic programs, including several that had been targeted unsuccessfully throughout the Reagan years. Among them were Amtrak, the Economic Development Administration, Small Business Administration disaster loans and mass transit operating subsidies.

Less than 10 percent of Bush's proposed cut in the deficit came from defense programs. The administration sought $303.3 billion in fiscal 1991 spending for defense, a cut of 2.1 percent after inflation was taken into account. Bush kept major increases for strategic weaponry, including the B-2 stealth bomber, the MX missile and the strategic defense initiative. Many Democrats were talking about cutting deeper, even below the $288 billion that would be left if Congress failed to cut the deficit and Gramm-Rudman took effect. *(Defense appropriations, p. 812)*

Rosy Redux

The administration's budget was hitched to highly optimistic economic assumptions. White House economists projected much stronger growth and far lower interest rates in both 1990 and 1991 than did CBO or many private economists. *(Economic assumptions, p. 119)*

Even some Republicans attacked the forecast. "I can't find any economist who agrees with that," Sen. Warren B. Rudman, R-N.H., told OMB Director Darman. "How do we deal in good faith with that kind of projection?"

White House economists presumed big changes in the prevailing economic trends. For instance, despite initial calculations that the economy grew by a spare 0.5 percent in the last quarter of 1989, the administration predicted a strong rebound in the latter part of 1991 and in 1992. In fact, it predicted that real growth in 1990 would reach 3.3 percent. And despite a recent rise in interest rates, administration economists projected that short-term rates would fall by more than a full percentage point in each of the following two years and that long-term rates would fall by almost as much.

Few private economists were as hopeful as the administration. The Blue Chip Economic Indicators, a monthly forecast that reflected the consensus views of about 50 private economists, showed growth improving steadily in 1990 at a rate of 1.8 percent, well below administration forecasts. CBO, which had a growth forecast similar to Blue Chip's, and the participants in the Blue Chip survey doubted that interest rates would fall as much in 1990, much less in 1991.

The differing projections had significantly different implications for the deficit. A fractional change in economic growth could send revenues soaring or plummeting; interest rate changes could greatly increase the cost of payments on the $3.1 trillion national debt.

BUDGET RESOLUTION: FIRST TRY FAILS

Congress' first try at completing a fiscal 1991 budget resolution — lawmakers' own guideline for spending bills and deficit reduction — failed as Democrats disagreed over priorities, and deficit projections escalated.

Democrats had derided President Bush's budget, but they found it next to impossible to come up with one of their own. When they began trying in February, Bush was ruling out a budget summit, leaving them with the prospect of calling for painful spending cuts and revenue increases on their own, without the political cover that had been offered in recent years by bipartisan summit accords. Passing a budget on their own would have required strong party unity, but Democrats were sharply divided over defense.

The House did pass its own version, but the Senate managed to pass only a skeleton resolution, which the House was unwilling to consider in conference. In the end, the two chambers passed stopgap measures that allowed appropriations bills to move forward while congressional leaders and the White House tried to reach a deficit-reduction deal.

House Budget Committee Action

Led by Chairman Panetta, Democrats on the House Budget Committee set out gamely in February to draft a budget that would match Bush's bottom line of $36.5 billion in deficit reduction but reflect party priorities.

Generally, that goal was thought to mean cutting more from defense and making room for several billion dollars extra for favored domestic initiatives, including programs for low-income children, housing and transportation. But negotiations broke down as liberals looked for larger defense cuts and heftier domestic hikes than conservatives could stomach.

Weeks went by with Budget Committee Democrats meeting informally but failing to reach agreement. When Congress returned from its spring break on April 18, the committee still had not produced a resolution. By then, however, projections of the deficit were rising and the exercise was beginning to seem somewhat academic. A midterm budget review, due from OMB in July, was expected to show the baseline deficit not at $100.5 billion, as in January, but at $140 billion. That would mean over $60 billion in deficit cuts, a far more drastic undertaking.

The increasingly bad news on the deficit sparked predictions from Panetta, ranking Budget Committee Republican Frenzel and others that a congressional-White House budget summit would be necessary after all.

Darman began meeting with junior members to build pressure in the ranks for high-level talks. But many Democrats remained skeptical, insisting that Bush take the lead in endorsing major deficit-cutting steps, including taxes.

"The first action has to be taken by the president," said House Speaker Foley. "First with the president, then with us."

In the meantime, committee Democrats stuck to their aim of crafting a budget resolution that would meet the minimum deficit savings set in Bush's budget. But increasingly, they saw a Democratic budget as a platform from which to enter eventual negotiations rather than as a congressional blueprint for the year.

On April 19, the committee finally approved a $1.24 trillion budget resolution (H Con Res 310 — H Rpt 101-455). The 21-14 vote was strictly on party lines, with all Republicans opposed.

The resolution provided less for defense and more for domestic programs than did Bush's budget and the same amount in higher revenues. Like the Bush plan, it claimed to cut about $36 billion from the deficit.

It called for $11.5 billion in defense spending cuts, $13.9 billion in new revenues, $3.8 billion in entitlement savings and $9.3 billion in "other savings and adjustments" in fiscal 1991. It also included about $6.4 billion in new spending initiatives.

The budget contained instructions to authorizing committees to come up with about $19 billion in entitlement savings and tax increases by July 16 to be incorporated into an omnibus deficit-reduction bill. Details on taxes were left to the Ways and Means Committee. However, at the request of Ways and Means Chairman Dan Rostenkowski, D-Ill., the accompanying report stated that the House would not act on proposed tax increases "unless and until such time as there is bipartisan agreement with the President of the United States on specific legislation to meet or exceed such reconciliation requirements."

The resolution called for another $5.6 billion in revenues from various user fees and $1.6 billion from federal asset sales. And it included $3 billion to be gained through increased tax collections and unspecified management changes at the IRS.

Such provisions, particularly the IRS savings, had drawn sharp Democratic criticisms in January. Now, the Democrats not only recommended some of the same fiscal gimmicks, but also adopted the White House's economic assumptions for 1991.

The Democrats' show of unanimity in passing the resolution was marred by persistent divisions over the depth of the proposed defense cuts that nearly jeopardized committee action.

Panetta's draft prepared for committee consideration included $286 billion in budget authority for defense, the amount that could be obligated for multi-year expenses such as weapons systems. Committee liberals were irate. In a last-minute change designed to save the budget resolution from failing its first test in committee, the leadership agreed to lower the figure to $283 billion. That in turn, drew protests from conservatives. "It gives a lot of us conservatives real heartburn," said committee member Jerry Huckaby, D-La.

Another last-minute change in the budget before committee consideration was a softening of proposed Medicare cuts from $2.1 billion to $1.7 billion, made at Rostenkowski's request. Bush's budget called for cuts of more than $5 billion, a proposal that attracted bipartisan opposition in Congress.

Another $800 million in entitlement savings was to come from reductions in farm program expenditures.

The $6.2 billion added for domestic spending initiatives was for education programs, Head Start, child care, drug fighting, job training, health, nutrition, housing, environmental protection, transportation, science and research. Some of the domestic initiatives carried relatively modest first-year costs but ballooned in subsequent years. For example, a package of Medicaid proposals included at the urging of Henry A. Waxman, D-Calif., to address infant mortality, children's health, hospice care and the needs of the mentally retarded and AIDS patients was slated to cost an estimated $280 million in 1991, covering fourth-quarter costs only. Through 1995, however, costs grew to a cumulative $7.2 billion.

House Floor Action

The House approved the budget resolution May 1 by a vote of 218-208. No Republicans supported the plan; 34 Democrats voted against it — including both conservatives dissatisfied with the defense spending figure and liberals opposed to the domestic spending cuts. *(Vote 89, p. 32-H)*

Democratic leaders sold the package primarily as a negotiating position in any future talks with the Senate and the White House. "Obviously, it is not the last word on the budget. It is the beginning of a process," Foley said.

Republicans had initially planned to offer the president's budget as a substitute, but decided at the last minute not to do so, much to the glee of the Democrats. Illinois Democrat Marty Russo said Republicans would not offer the GOP plan because "they raised defense spending $7 billion, and they cut Medicare programs $5.5 billion, and they cannot take the heat of the vote in clear daylight."

Publicly, Republicans, who had been pushing for summit talks since early in the year, said they decided not to offer it because even the administration agreed that its economic estimates were obsolete.

Before approving the budget, the House rejected three substitutes.

Two GOP proposals were defeated on April 26. The first, offered by Budget Committee member John R. Kasich of Ohio, called for a freeze of both defense and domestic discretionary budget authority at existing levels. The result would have been higher defense and lower domestic spending than called for in the committee resolution. The plan was defeated 106-305. *(Vote 84, p. 30-H)*

The House also rejected, 48-354, a substitute offered by William E. Dannemeyer, Calif., that called for the issuance of gold-backed bonds to refinance the federal debt *(Vote 85, p. 30-H)*

A proposal by the Congressional Black Caucus, offered on May 1, would have reduced the deficit to $63.8 billion in fiscal 1991 through greater defense cuts and larger revenue increases than called for in the committee plan. It was rejected by a vote of 90-334 *(Vote 88, p. 32-H)*

Senate Budget Committee Action

Democrats on the Senate Budget Committee began meeting privately in March, but they were even more sharply divided than their House counterparts. Unable to count on Republican votes, Chairman Jim Sasser, D-Tenn., had no choice but to try to bridge their difference over defense spending and the size of overall budget cuts.

In late April, still short of the votes needed to approve a budget, Sasser — who opposed the idea of a budget summit before Democrats had a firm position — decided to go ahead with formal committee meetings. In an unusual procedure, he tried to forge agreement on an overall budget framework before working out details. In three days of open sessions — which Sasser described as "a way of letting members express their views" — members considered and rejected a series of plans.

On May 2, the committee finally agreed to a $1.23 trillion budget plan (S Con Res 129) that promised to bring the deficit to $58.6 billion, but only after Sasser had made a number of concessions that threatened to prove troublesome on the floor. The resolution was approved 14-9, with the panel's 13 Democrats and one Republican, Charles E. Grassley of Iowa, voting for it.

To win approval, Sasser assembled a plan that incorporated the diverse demands of committee Democrats. He reduced earlier proposed defense cuts, shielded farm programs from large reductions and substantially increased the amount of unspecified domestic spending cuts needed to meet his deficit-reduction target.

To reach his deficit figure, Sasser proposed $293.9 billion in defense outlays — compared with $303.3 billion requested by Bush and $295.5 billion proposed by the House.

The package also instructed authorizing committees to raise $25.5 billion in fiscal 1991 through revenues, user fees and entitlement cuts, and set an overall domestic discretionary spending ceiling for appropriators that was $3.6 billion below the existing inflation-adjusted level.

The plan did not specify how those domestic cuts would be made or how an additional $5 billion increase assumed for a variety of science, space, environmental, transportation, housing, education, health and antidrug programs would be paid for.

While the committee distributed spending increases throughout the budget's functional categories, it lumped most of the required domestic spending cuts under the vague category of "offsetting receipts."

Committee aides said that the panel had decided not to make any assumptions about how the Appropriations committees should make the cuts.

But the arrangement prompted the panel's ranking Republican, Pete V. Domenici of New Mexico, to complain that now "everyone can go home and say they voted to increase everything."

The plan required the Finance Committee to come up with $13.9 billion in unspecified tax increases and $5.8 billion of a total $6.2 billion in user fees. The amounts were identical to those requested by Bush.

In addition, the resolution required about $5.6 billion in unspecified entitlement savings. It allowed Bush's proposed $5.5 billion cut in Medicare to be substantially trimmed, probably to no more than $2 billion.

The committee also effectively rejected Bush's proposals for large reductions in farm-subsidy programs by not requiring the Agriculture Committee to make any reconciliation cuts.

Sasser said he agreed to the unusual arrangement at the request of farm-state senators who argued that agriculture spending cuts should not be made until after work was completed on the 1990 farm bill, which was to set farm program policy for the next five years.

Sasser conceded that the change was also made to firm up support for his deficit-reduction package.

Senate Floor Action

Once out of committee, the resolution looked as if it were headed for serious trouble on the Senate floor. Republicans were arguing that it should be dumped in favor of a White House-congressional budget summit. And Democrats remained sharply divided over the defense number.

Senate Armed Services Committee Chairman Sam Nunn, D-Ga., warned that the proposed $13 billion cut in spending would do "some very severe damage, particularly to personnel." But other Democrats were expected to push for even bigger reductions in Pentagon spending to help offset the cuts proposed for domestic programs.

Prospects for bringing the measure to the floor were weakened further when Bush and congressional leaders agreed May 9 to begin top-level budget talks. Republicans in particular insisted that considering the measure would undercut the summit negotiations by bringing into the open many thorny spending and tax debates the summit negotiators were trying to settle behind closed doors.

However, there was pressure to move ahead from another corner. House and Senate Appropriations committees were eager to get to work on annual spending bills and were urging Budget leaders to move forward with the budget resolution, which would set overall totals for the appropriations bills. Concern was particularly great in the Senate; unlike the House, Senate appropriations measures were subject to a point of order if brought to the floor before both houses agreed on a congressional budget plan.

In a compromise, the Senate on June 14 approved a separate budget resolution (S Con Res 110) by voice vote. Leaders described it as a "policy-neutral" measure aimed at allowing the appropriations process to go forward.

The measure called for a discretionary spending pot of $482.5 billion in budget authority and $503.4 billion in outlays, compared with $492.8 billion and $513.7 billion in the House-passed resolution.

Senate leaders hoped to have a quick conference with the House that would focus on the overall discretionary spending figure.

Final Action: An Ad Hoc Solution

Despite Senate hopes, House Budget leaders resisted going to conference on the skeletal Senate measure. Many Democrats wanted to keep the regular congressional budget process going as a way of pressing the administration to take the first step in proposing a deficit-reduction plan in the summit. Democrats, in control of both chambers, also worried that if they did not begin work on appropriations bills and the talks failed, they would be stuck with too much unfinished business by the Oct. 1 start of the new fiscal year.

So, in the absence of a conference agreement, each chamber passed a so-called deeming resolution, under which its own budget was considered final for purposes of bringing spending bills to the floor.

The House held off for two weeks because Republicans were so unhappy with the idea. But on June 19, members in that chamber agreed on a near party-line vote of 276-136 to a rule deeming H Con Res 310 to be final for appropriations bills. *(Vote 174, p. 62-H)*

On July 12, the Senate approved by voice vote its own deeming resolution (S Res 308), enabling appropriations bills to move forward. The measure limited overall appropriated spending authority to $680.5 billion, with an outlay limit of $690.6 billion. The figures, lower than the House-imposed limits of $686.3 billion in budget authority and $694.4 billion in outlays, were reached in informal negotiations between leaders of the Senate Appropriations and Budget committees.

The resolution was approved by voice vote, despite some Republican concerns that a budget-summit agreement would probably set lower spending levels.

However, Appropriations leaders said they were worried that the committee would be unable to complete its work on time if it did not begin soon.

THE BUDGET SUMMIT

With deficit projections soaring and administration fears that a continuing slowdown in the economy could turn into a recession, Bush and Democratic leaders bowed to the inevitable in May and began top-level negotiations aimed at reaching a bipartisan deficit-reduction deal.

The talks began with no clear agenda or direction. One participant characterized the task as one of building a house without a blueprint. Virtually no decisions were made until members returned in September from the fall recess. Then, after months of talks — with late-night ses-

Budget Summit Players

White House negotiators: Chief of Staff John H. Sununu, Office of Management and Budget Director Richard G. Darman, Treasury Secretary Nicholas F. Brady.

House negotiators: Majority Leader Richard A. Gephardt, D-Mo.; Democratic Whip William H. Gray III, Pa.; Appropriations Chairman Jamie L. Whitten, D-Miss.; Budget Committee Chairman Leon E. Panetta, D-Calif.; Ways and Means Chairman Dan Rostenkowski, D-Ill.; GOP Whip Newt Gingrich, Ga.; Ranking Appropriations Committee Republican Silvio O. Conte, Mass.; Ranking Budget Committee Republican Bill Frenzel, Minn.; Ranking Ways and Means Republican Rep. Bill Archer, Texas.

Senate negotiators: Appropriations Chairman Robert C. Byrd, D-W.Va.; Budget Chairman Jim Sasser, D-Tenn.; Finance Chairman Lloyd Bentsen, D-Texas; Wyche Fowler Jr., D-Ga.; Ranking Appropriations Committee Republican Mark O. Hatfield, Ore.; Ranking Budget Republican Pete V. Domenici, N.M.; Ranking Finance Republican Bob Packwood, Ore.; Phil Gramm, R-Texas.

sions and the threat of enormous across-the-board cuts under the Gramm-Rudman antideficit law looming — they finally produced a plan — only to have it meet with resounding, bipartisan defeat in the House. The deep partisan differences over taxing and spending policy that had made it so difficult to reach a summit agreement resurfaced as soon as the rank and file were asked to endorse the effort.

Early Signs of Trouble

After weeks of speculation about a budget summit, Bush broke the ice by inviting congressional leaders to the White House for preliminary talks on May 6. Out of that session — attended by Speaker Foley, House Minority Leader Robert H. Michel, R-Ill.; Senate Majority Leader Mitchell; and Senate Minority Leader Bob Dole, R-Kan. — came agreement to hold a full-scale congressional-White House budget summit.

Democrats, who had been fearful that a summit would be a political trap in which they would be forced to take the blame for tax increases, accepted on the basis that there be "no preconditions." Both Democrats and Republicans interpreted that to mean that taxes would be on the table. What taxes if any would actually go into the final package would become the most divisive issue in the summit.

Conservative Republicans immediately sounded the alarm. Connie Mack of Florida and 17 other Senate Republicans sent Bush a letter stating that they "unequivocally" opposed new taxes. House Republicans took to the floor with the same message. The fear that Bush was abandoning his "no new taxes" pledge was particularly acute among conservatives facing tough races in the fall elections.

Although Democrats were initially reassured by the pledge that everything would be on the agenda, they quickly became disenchanted when a White House official, later identified as Chief of Staff Sununu, told The Washington Post that Democrats could propose taxes, but the administration would oppose them. "It is their prerogative to put them on the table, and it's our prerogative to say no. And I emphasize the 'no'," Sununu was quoted as saying.

Democrats were leery of the talks after that and determined to force Bush to take the lead publicly before they would offer anything. Indeed, at the start at least some Democrats felt that an agreement would be more advantageous to Bush and the GOP and that they should exact a high price for their cooperation.

The initial skirmishing set the stage for five months of meetings and negotiations, during which efforts at bipartisan good will were repeatedly interrupted by nasty bouts of name-calling, reflecting deep disagreement over fundamentals. Finding the right combination of spending cuts and tax increases that would allow negotiators to paper over their differences was the challenge.

Besides Bush and the four top congressional leaders — Foley and Michel from the House and Mitchell and Dole from the Senate — the talks involved 17 congressional leaders and three White House negotiations. Bush himself played little direct role, and the four main Hill leaders also stayed away except at crucial moments. House Majority Leader Richard A. Gephardt, D-Mo., chaired the meetings. *(Budget-summit participants, this page)*

Weeks of Seminars

The early phase of the summit, which lasted from May 15 to the August recess, resembled a seminar, with detailed briefings from the OMB, CBO, and subcommittee and committee chairmen with jurisdiction over specific spending areas.

The first task was to agree on a fiscal 1991 deficit-reduction target. After weeks of debate, they settled on $50 billion the first year and $500 billion overall. But they had yet to decide how to meet those targets.

Meanwhile, the magnitude of the problem was growing. On June 20, CBO Director Robert D. Reischauer and OMB Director Darman provided new deficit projections. Reischauer said his office now expected the fiscal 1991 deficit to be $162 billion without the growing costs of the savings and loan crisis and $232 billion if they were included. The CBO was now projecting a fiscal 1995 deficit of $157 billion without savings and loan costs, compared with an earlier estimate of $119 billion.

Darman surprised negotiators by announcing that his earlier deficit estimates had also risen. He said he now expected the fiscal 1991 deficit to be $159 billion, rather than the $138 billion he had projected in late May. He said this figure could rise to anywhere from $200 billion to $227 billion if the savings and loan costs were included.

The new deficit numbers made it virtually certain that Congress would have to revise the Gramm-Rudman deficit targets as part of any budget deal. Making the cuts necessary to meet the current targets would have been politically impossible and, many argued, damaging to the economy.

Democrats, reluctant participants in the sessions, insisted that the administration go first in proposing a budget package that would get real negotiations going. Just hours after releasing OMB's new projections, Darman presented the administration's opening bid: a $51 billion deficit-reduction plan that relied on the president's January budget augmented by deep domestic spending cuts. Democrats denounced the proposal but made no move to come up with a plan of their own, insisting that Bush had yet to make a serious offer. In a series of meetings late in the week of June 18, they warned Bush and his advisers that the president would have to make a stronger statement on taxes if the negotiations were to have a chance of success.

Bush's Shift on Taxes

With the summit on the brink of collapse, Bush took the plunge, issuing a statement effectively endorsing higher taxes. The move provided a tonic for the talks, at least briefly. Negotiators suddenly stopped dancing around the issue of deficit reduction and began to broach even the most sensitive topics, from limiting Social Security to raising taxes.

"There is not any of the paranoia that was there before the president's statement," said an optimistic House Budget Chairman Panetta.

Bush's abrupt shift on taxes came June 26 in a two-hour breakfast meeting with the bipartisan congressional leadership and his own negotiators, Darman, Sununu and Treasury Secretary Nicholas F. Brady. After the session, the White House released a statement that "tax revenue increases" would have to be part of any deficit-reduction plan. *(Text, this page)*

The White House apparently underestimated the impact of the decision. Sununu went up to the Hill to claim to Republicans that it represented no change in the president's position that everything was on the table, but many Republicans were furious. And while the Democratic leadership avoided gloating, it did not take long for the party's jubilation to bubble to the surface. After three days, Bush tried to limit the political damage, holding a news conference to explain his decision.

He argued that "getting this deficit down, continuing economic expansion and employment in this country" were more important than his earlier campaign pledges not to raise taxes. "I knew I'd catch some flak on this decision," he said, "but I've got to do what I think is right."

In what they described as a goodwill gesture in response to Bush's concession, Democratic negotiators initiated summit discussion of their least favorite topic: finding more savings in entitlement programs, such as Medicare, farm subsidies and Social Security. "We're trying to be evenhanded about this — tit for tat," said Senate Budget Chairman Sasser.

But Democrats also made clear that they would not accept just any new taxes and that they planned to make "tax equity" an issue in the upcoming budget debate. In a letter to Foley, 134 House Democrats said that any new taxes should be levied against those families with incomes of more than $200,000 a year, "those who have gotten the biggest tax cuts in recent years and have enjoyed the lion's share of income growth."

The sense of forward motion generated by Bush's move was quickly interupted by the July Fourth recess, however. When members returned, partisan tensions began to mount over taxes. The Democratic Leadership Council, a group of moderate to conservative Democrats, held a news conference July 11 to say they would not support an agreement that did not make the tax system more progressive, raising the burden on the wealthy.

The same day, in a move that House Minority Whip Newt Gingrich, R-Ga., called "arrogant and outrageous," Mitchell threw down what would turn out to be an important marker. He said he could not support Bush's proposed cut in capital gains taxes without an increase in the top marginal rate for the wealthiest taxpayers from 28 percent to at least 33 percent. While Mitchell's position was not new, he had previously been reluctant to draw any limits on the scope of the negotiations.

'Tax Revenue Increases'

Following is the written statement President Bush issued on the budget June 26:

I met this morning with the Bipartisan leadership — the Speaker, the Senate Majority Leader, the Senate Republican Leader, the House Majority Leader and the House Republican Leader — to review the status of the deficit-reduction negotiations.

It is clear to me that both the size of the deficit problem and the need for a package that can be enacted require all of the following: entitlement and mandatory program reform; tax revenue increases; growth incentives; discretionary spending reductions; orderly reductions in defense expenditures; and budget process reform — to assure that any Bipartisan agreement is enforceable and that the deficit problem is brought under responsible control. The Bipartisan leadership agree with me on these points.

The budget negotiations will resume promptly with a view toward reaching substantive agreement as quickly as possible. ■

On July 18, the House Republican Conference, which represented that chamber's 176 GOP members, passed a non-binding resolution opposing new taxes as a means of reducing the deficit.

Democrats, a few with apparent glee, jumped on the measure as evidence of GOP fractiousness. "Which Republican Party are we supposed to be negotiating with?" asked Sen. Wyche Fowler Jr., D-Ga., who was serving as Mitchell's point man for the negotiations.

The prospects for reaching agreement in the short time remaining before the August recess were now extremely slim, even as news on the deficit was getting worse.

In its midsession budget review, released July 16, OMB projected a deficit high of $231 billion. If the costs of the federal savings and loan rescue effort were excluded, the number would be $149 billion — and it would jump another $18 billion if Congress reauthorized the food stamp program as expected. Without congressional action, that would have resulted in roughly a $100 billion sequester.

Panetta had told reporters ahead of time that the numbers "should hit the White House, the Congress and the summit like a fire alarm in the middle of the night." But the news seemed to fall on deaf ears. For many, the sheer size of the impending sequester made it unthinkable.

Toward the end of the month, Bush began a series of almost daily meetings with the bipartisan leadership, and the two parties talked about at least exchanging proposals before August. The White House even suggested delaying the recess, but Democrats argued that this would only anger members, making agreement even more difficult.

Republicans did put together a package, which was quickly leaked and denounced for its inclusion of tax increases on alcohol and limits on deductions for state and local tax payments. The experience seemed to prove that anything left out on the table over the recess would be demolished by public criticism. In any case, the Democrats were unable to agree on a counter plan of their own.

So, hoping that the threat of automatic cuts in October would force both sides to reach an agreement in September, negotiators broke Aug. 3 for a monthlong recess. Before leaving, they set an ambitious schedule for the fall. They agreed to resume talks Sept. 6, a few days before the end of the recess, perhaps in a secluded place; reach agreement within five days; win passage of a new budget resolution based on that agreement; and clear a budget-reconciliation measure putting much of the agreement into effect — all by Oct. 2. In addition, they had to clear 13 appropriations bills and raise the federal debt ceiling. It was a tall order, because up to then nothing substantial had been accomplished. *(Debt limit, p. 165; appropriations, p. 811)*

Although the budget summit was stymied, the appropriations process did get under way. Democrats saw progress on the spending bills as a way of making sure they would not get blamed at the end of the fiscal year for failing to do their part to fund the government. And they saw it as a way of keeping up the pressure on the summit negotiations.

Republicans feared, however, that spending levels would be set in concrete, making them difficult to cut after a budget agreement was reached.

By the start of the recess, the House had passed 10 of the 13 regular spending bills, the Senate just one.

Moving Into High Gear

By the time the talks resumed on Sept. 7 — at Andrews Air Force Base, outside Washington, to seclude them from the press and other distractions — a major new factor had entered the equation: the Iraqi invasion of Kuwait.

The Iraqis' Aug. 2 invasion came two days before Congress began their monthlong recess. While lawmakers were back home, Bush had begun a massive deployment of U.S. troops to Saudi Arabia.

Now the talk was of higher oil prices, escalating defense needs, even war, and possible recession. Rumors abounded that the negotiators would seize on the Persian Gulf crisis as a reason to give in a bit on their deficit-reduction targets.

As they prepared to go to Andrews, however, Hill leaders and White House officials recommitted themselves to their original goal of a $50 billion cut in the deficit the first year and $500 billion over five years. The atmosphere suddenly grew optimistic.

"For the first time in months, I think this is going to be a [productive] meeting," said Stephen Bell, an investment banker who had been a top aide to ranking Senate Budget Committee Republican Domenici.

"They're concerned they're going to look like worse fools than they already do in the public's mind if they don't do something," Bell said. "People are saying, 'Let's get this thing done.' "

Dole told reporters: "If we don't get a budget agreement, we're in real trouble. I mean everybody — Congress, the president. We just have to get it done."

But Dole also expressed a very real fear among leaders of both parties, noting that reaching an agreement inside the summit was only part of the problem. "The bottom line around here is you've got to have the votes," he said, "so you've got to be fairly careful what goes into the package, or it'll all blow up on the floor."

Cloistered in the Officers Club at Andrews, the negotiators finally got down to serious bargaining. The schedule laid out before the break proved too optimistic; self-imposed deadlines came and went. But with the specter of a mammoth sequester hanging over the talks, the outlines of a budget deal began to emerge.

However, the key dispute dogging negotiators — Republican calls for a capital gains cut and Democratic insistence that it be paired with an increase in taxes on the richest — remained unresolved. The longer it took to work out a deal, the more details leaked out, and the more time members had to rally opposition.

Proposed Medicare changes drew angry criticism from California Democrat Waxman, who called possible increased costs to beneficiaries "absolutely outrageous." Waxman was joined in the Senate by Bob Graham, D-Fla., and John McCain, R-Ariz., both of whom vowed not to vote for any plan that loaded spending cuts disproportionately onto the Medicare program.

And all 34 members of the New York House delegation signed a letter vowing not to support any package that eliminated the deductibility of state and local taxes.

Addressing a joint session of Congress on the Persian Gulf crisis Sept. 11, Bush sought to turn up the heat. With or without a summit agreement, he called for a "straight, up-or-down vote" by Sept. 28 on a five-year, $500 billion deficit-reduction package. "If the Congress cannot get me a budget," he said, "then Americans will have to face a tough, mandated sequester." *(Excerpts, p. 133)*

But the negotiations remained stuck. On Sept. 17, the participants pulled the plug on 10 days of intensive talks at Andrews and turned the bargaining over to a core group, consisting of Mitchell, Foley, Gephardt, Dole, Michel, Darman, Sununu and Brady.

The bipartisan truce that had prevailed during the Andrews talks broke down, with Democrats returning to Capitol Hill to hammer away at the "fairness" issue, charging that Republicans were holding the talks hostage to favors for the rich, notably the capital gains cut, while proposing tax increases for low- and middle-income taxpayers.

Dole tried to break the stalemate by suggesting that Republicans drop capital gains as part of a deficit-reduction deal, packaging it separately with Democratic spending initiatives, plus some combination of tax increases or spending cuts that could make the measure deficit-neutral. But Darman and Sununu rejected that approach.

With the leadership foundering, restless rank-and-file members began talking of taking matters into their own hands. Worried that the drastic Gramm-Rudman spending cuts could mean political disaster for anyone perceived as responsible, rebellious House Democrats talked openly of putting together their own budget deal and seeking a vote for it on the floor if the summit remained deadlocked.

"I think we have to break off these negotiations and prepare an alternative that we can send to the president to either veto or sign," said Thomas J. Downey, D-N.Y.

At the same time, a group of conservative House Republicans sporting bright yellow "Junk the Summit" buttons summoned the media to charge that Democratic posturing had sabotaged the talks and to call for the full Congress to take over the job instead. Tom DeLay, Texas, said the group already had its own no-new-taxes budget package ready for a floor vote.

Threat of Sequester

As frustration mounted over the summit's inability to reach an agreement, the Gramm-Rudman cuts — once all but unthinkable because of the crippling blow they would deal to the federal government — seemed to become a real possibility.

Republicans and Democrats alike positioned themselves to point the finger if summit talks failed to produce a deal that would avert the automatic cuts. Members also began talking as if it might take at least a taste of the cuts to force negotiators to come to an agreement.

The across-the-board federal spending cuts were to take

Bush Discusses Budget, Economic Issues

Following are excerpts from the closing passages of an address by President Bush to a joint session of Congress on Sept. 11. Although the address dealt primarily with the U.S. response to Iraq's invasion of Kuwait, Bush concluded with a discussion of budget and economic issues:

Our ability to function effectively as a great power abroad depends on how we conduct ourselves at home. Our economy, our armed forces, our energy dependence and our cohesion all determine whether we can help our friends and stand up to our foes. For America to lead, America must remain strong and vital. Our world leadership and domestic strength are mutual and reinforcing; a woven piece, strongly bound as Old Glory. To revitalize our leadership capacity, we must address our budget deficit — not after Election Day or next year, but now.

Higher oil prices slow our growth, and higher defense costs would only make our fiscal deficit problem worse. That deficit was already greater than it should have been — a projected $232 billion for the coming year. It must — it will — be reduced. To my friends in Congress: Together we must act this very month, before the next fiscal year begins on Oct. 1, to get America's economic house in order. The gulf situation helps us realize we are more economically vulnerable than we ever should be. Americans must never again enter any crisis, economic or military, with an excessive dependence on foreign oil and an excessive burden of federal debt.

Most Americans are sick and tired of endless battles in the Congress and between the branches over budget matters. It is high time we pulled together — and get the job done right. It is up to us to straighten this out.

And the job has four basic parts. First, the Congress should this month, within a budget agreement, enact growth-oriented tax measures to help avoid recession in the short term and to increase savings, investment, productivity and competitiveness for the longer term.

These measures include extending incentives for research and experimentation; expanding the use of IRAs [Individual Retirement Accounts] for new homeowners; establishing tax-deferred family savings accounts; creating incentives for the creation of enterprise zones and initiatives to encourage more domestic drilling; and, yes, reducing the tax rate on capital gains.

Second, the Congress should this month enact a prudent multiyear defense program, one that reflects not only the improvement in East-West relations, but our broader responsibilities to deal with the continuing risks of outlaw action and regional conflict.

Even with our obligations in the gulf, a sound defense budget can have some reduction in real terms, and we are prepared to accept that. But to go beyond — to go beyond such levels, where cutting defense would threaten our vital margin of safety, is something I will never accept.

The world is still dangerous. Surely that is now clear. Stability is not secure. American interests are far-reaching. Interdependence has increased. The consequences of regional instability can be global. This is no time to risk America's capacity to protect her vital interests.

And third, the Congress should this month enact measures to increase domestic energy production and energy conservation in order to reduce dependence on foreign oil.

These measures should include my proposals to increase incentives for domestic oil and gas exploration, fuel-switching, and to accelerate the development of the Alaskan energy resources — without damage to wildlife.

As you know, when the oil embargo was imposed in the early 1970s, the United States imported almost 6 million barrels of oil a day. This year, before the Iraqi invasion, U.S. imports had risen to nearly 8 million barrels per day. We had moved in the wrong direction. And now we must act to correct that trend.

And, fourth, the Congress should this month enact a five-year program to reduce the projected debt and deficits by $500 billion — that is, by half a trillion dollars. And if, with the Congress, we can develop a satisfactory program by the end of the month, we can avoid the ax of sequester — deep across-the-board cuts that would threaten our military capacity and risk substantial domestic disruption.

I want to be able to tell the American people that we have truly solved the deficit problem. And for me to do that, a budget agreement must meet these tests:

- It must include the measures I've recommended to increase economic growth and reduce dependence on foreign oil.
- It must be fair. All should contribute, but the burden should not be excessive for any one group of programs or people.
- It must address the growth of government's hidden liabilities.
- It must reform the budget process, and, further, it must be real.

I urge Congress to provide a comprehensive five-year deficit-reduction program to me as a complete legislative package — with measures to assure that it can be fully enforced. America is tired of phony deficit reduction, or promise-now save-later plans.

Enough is enough. It is time for a program that is credible and real.

- And, finally, to the extent that the deficit-reduction program includes new revenue measures, it must avoid any measure that would threaten economic growth or turn us back towards the days of punishing income tax rates.

That is one path we should not head down again.

I have been pleased with recent progress, although it has not always seemed so smooth. But now it's time to produce. I hope we can work out a responsible plan. But with or without agreement from the budget summit, I ask both houses of the Congress to allow a straight up-or-down vote on a complete $500 billion deficit-reduction package — not later than Sept. 28.

And if the Congress cannot get me a budget, then Americans will have to face a tough, mandated sequester.

I am hopeful — in fact I am confident — the Congress will do what it should. And I can assure you that we in the executive branch will do our part. . . . ■

---

effect if Congress and the president did not agree to waive the Gramm-Rudman deficit target by Oct. 1. Otherwise, the law's $74 billion deficit ceiling — $64 billion plus a near-miss factor of $10 billion — would trigger a sequester. OMB's official projection now showed a Gramm-Rudman deficit of at least $149.4 billion, which would require $85.4 billion in budget cuts.

Updating the deficit estimate to reflect congressional action expected by mid-October was projected to add another $20.3 billion to the total, boosting the cuts to $105.7 billion when the sequester became final Oct. 15.

At that level, the cuts would slash 43.6 percent out of non-personnel defense spending and 40.7 percent from non-defense accounts — amounts far larger than those mandated by the biggest sequester ever allowed to stay in effect, which trimmed outlays by less than 5 percent in 1986.

No one expected the budget summit to bring the 1991 deficit below $74 billion. But there had long been agreement that if negotiators produced an acceptable bipartisan deal, the Gramm-Rudman targets could be changed and a sequester avoided.

But there was barely a week left to strike a deal and move it through the complex and time-consuming procedure required to approve a budget resolution, craft and pass a budget-reconciliation bill and pass a continuing resolution to keep the government going until the appropriations bills were enacted.

"The problem is we have to see some event to push the parties together," said Budget Committee Republican

Frenzel. "No one wants to concede anything until the last minute. We have to declare a last minute."

Finally, a Deal

Just hours from a sequester — and a government shutdown in the absence of a continuing resolution — budget negotiators who had missed every deadline since talks began bargained right up to the only deadline that ever really mattered: the start of the new fiscal year on Oct. 1.

Emerging periodically from the tiny private dining room in the Capitol where they met throughout the week of Sept. 24, the core negotiating group indicated they still believed they would have an agreement in time to stave off fiscal chaos.

By week's end, congressional leaders began to brief members on agreed-to items in an attempt to calm the troops and begin the hard-sell job necessary to get any package through Congress. But the capital gains/top tax rate conundrum remained.

The bargaining went through much of the weekend. Congress remained in session, waiting for news of a deal, which would enable them to pass a continuing resolution in time to avoid fiscal chaos. Democrats had readied a stopgap spending bill, which included a controversial provision to temporarily suspend the Gramm-Rudman cuts, but Bush had warned he would veto the measure in the absence of a deal.

Finally, the afternoon of Sept. 30, Bush appeared in the Rose Garden flanked by summit participants to announce that agreement had been reached.

The deal met two of the three requirements established by its authors early on: It claimed to reduce expected government spending by $500 billion over five years, and it contained numerous changes to the congressional budget process designed to prevent the agreement's key provisions from being breached in later years.

Negotiators had failed to reach their third goal: cutting $50 billion from the fiscal 1991 deficit. In the end they settled for savings of $40 billion.

In the final days of their talks, the summit negotiators had dropped the idea of a capital gains cut. The White House apparently decided that the cost being exacted by Democrats was too high. Without the capital gains cut and the Democrats' proposed top-rate increase, the negotiators fell $10 billion short in the first year.

Also dropped in the final days were competing proposals to tax Social Security benefits or delay Social Security cost of living increases, both of which were seen as too politically dangerous.

Briefing reporters shortly after the agreement was completed, Darman said, "This is all real. You will find that to be true when you examine it closely and see every detail."

Many longtime critics of budget shenanigans agreed. "For the most part the spending cuts and revenue increases are real," said Carol Cox, president of the Committee for a Responsible Federal Budget.

But the agreement contained important elements that were highly distasteful to rank-and-file majorities of both parties: an enormous increase in cost to Medicare beneficiaries, higher taxes that socked the middle class especially hard, and new tax breaks that critics claimed would "riddle" the tax code with loopholes. Regional and partisan interests also were inflamed by a new tax on home heating oil, opposed by Northeastern members, and the overall size of the tax increase, which put off conservative Republicans.

Also, the savings presumed in the deal were probably not as real as its authors claimed. Optimistic economic assumptions — a frequent bugaboo of budget forecasts — accounting gimmicks, and other illusory savings were likely to conspire to prevent it from achieving its ambitious aims.

The pain of the five-year, $500 billion in savings was spread broadly among the parts of the budget. Under the plan:

- Defense and domestic discretionary spending, an ever-shrinking slice of the budget pie, were cut $182.4 billion.
- Entitlements such as Medicare and farm subsidies were cut $106.3 billion.
- New taxes and user fees for government services added $147.7 billion to the government's coffers.
- Interest payments on the huge federal debt, which was expected to top $4 trillion during the life of the agreement, were reduced by $64.8 billion.

In many cases, the agreement assumed specific program changes, but there was an ongoing debate over how much flexibility Congress would have to make adjustments.

The agreement also incorporated significant budget process changes, including stretching out the Gramm-Rudman deficit targets. It appeared to yield a balanced budget by 1996, not 1993 as under existing law, but members said this point was in dispute. The changes included provisions intended to hold the line against appropriations and entitlement spending increases not envisioned in the agreement.

In addition, it included so-called credit reform measures. Long sought by Darman and some in Congress, these changes were designed to account better for the subsidies inherent in government loans and loan guarantees and to reduce the threat of untold liabilities on the government — such as those imposed by the savings and loan debacle. *(Credit reform, p. 178)*

The agreement assumed federal government spending would actually decline by a total of $49.1 billion in fiscal 1993 and 1994 — measured in absolute, not inflation-adjusted, terms. The last time government outlays had fallen was in 1965 — by a mere $300 million. Drops of the magnitude anticipated had occurred in the 20th century only at the conclusion of the two world wars and the Korean War.

There were many holes through which the agreement could plummet, making it unlikely that a balanced budget would be achieved according to schedule.

For example, it was based on economic assumptions that appeared relatively realistic for the first two years, but less so in the latter three. In particular, the expected savings in interest payments depended heavily on projected declines in interest rates.

In many places the agreement did not identify the source of savings but assumed that congressional committees would find specific program cuts — in veterans' programs, farm price and income supports, and payments to providers of health care to the elderly through the Medicare program. In one notable case, the agreement presumed $3 billion over five years from entirely unspecified entitlement savings.

The plan also included what some considered imaginary savings. It presumed savings of $3 billion in fiscal 1991 and $9.4 billion over five years through improved tax collection activities of the IRS.

Certain accounting gimmicks also served to make the deficit appear smaller than it might otherwise be calculated. While deposit-insurance premiums paid by banks and savings and loans were counted as revenue to reduce

Bush Appeals for Public Support

Following are excerpts from President Bush's remarks Oct. 2 in a broadcast speech urging support for the budget agreement:

... This budget agreement is the result of eight months of blood, sweat and fears — fears of the economic chaos that would follow if we fail to reduce the deficit.

Of course, I cannot claim it's the best deficit-reduction plan possible; it's not. Any one of us alone might have written a better plan. But it is the best agreement that can be legislated now.

It is the biggest deficit-reduction agreement ever: half a trillion dollars. It's the toughest deficit-reduction package ever, with new enforcement rules to make sure that what we fix now stays fixed.

And it has the largest spending savings ever, more than $300 billion.

For the first time, a Republican president and leaders of a Democratic Congress have agreed to real cuts that will be enforced by law — not promises. No smoke, no mirrors, no magic act, but real and lasting spending cuts.

This agreement will also raise revenue. I'm not, and I know you're not, a fan of tax increases. But if there have to be tax measures, they should allow the economy to grow. They should not turn us back to higher income tax rates, and they should be fair.

Everyone who can should contribute something, and no one should have to contribute beyond their fair share.

Our bipartisan agreement meets these tests, and through specific new incentives, it will help create more jobs. It's a little-known fact, but America's best job creators and greatest innovators tend to be our smaller companies.

So our budget plan will give small and medium-size companies a needed shot in the arm.

Just as important, I am convinced that this agreement will help lower interest rates, and lower interest rates mean savings for consumers, lower mortgage payments for new homeowners, and more investment to produce more jobs. And that's what this agreement will do.

And now let me tell you what this agreement will not do. It will not raise income tax rates, personal or corporate. It will not mess with Social Security in any way. It will not put America's national security at risk, and most of all, it will not let our economy slip out of control.

Clearly, each and every one of us can find fault with something in this agreement. In fact, that is a burden that any truly fair solution must carry. Any workable solution must be judged as a whole, not piece by piece. Those who dislike one part or another may pick our agreement apart, but if they do, believe me, the political reality is, no one can put a better one back together again.

Everyone will bear à small burden. But if we succeed, every American will have a large burden lifted.

If we fail to enact this agreement, our economy will falter; markets may tumble; and recession will follow. In just a moment, the Democratic majority leader, Senator [George J.] Mitchell [of Maine], will offer what is known as the Democratic response: often, a rebuttal.

But not tonight.

Tonight, the Democratic and Republican leadership and I all speak with one voice, in support of this agreement. Tonight we ask you to help us move this agreement forward.

The congressional leadership and I both have a job to do in getting it enacted. And tonight, I ask for your help.

First, I ask you to understand how important, and for some, how difficult this vote is for your congressmen and senators. Many worry about your reaction to one part or another. But I know you know the importance of the whole.

And so second, I ask you to take this initiative, tell your congressmen and senators you support this deficit-reduction agreement. If they are Republicans, urge them to stand with the president. Urge them to do what the bipartisan leadership has done: come together in the spirit of compromise to solve this national problem.

If they're Democrats, urge them to stand with their congressional leaders. Ask them to fight for the future of your kids by supporting this budget agreement.

Now is the time for you, the American people, to have a real impact. Your senators and congressmen need to know that you want this deficit brought down; that the time for politics and posturing is over, and the time to come together is now.

This deficit-reduction agreement is tough, and so are the times. The agreement is fair, and so is the American spirit. The agreement is bipartisan, and so is the vote.

The agreement is real, and so is this crisis.

This is the first time in my presidency that I've made an appeal like this to you, the American people. With your help we can at last put this budget crisis behind us and face the other challenges that lie ahead.

If we do, the long-term result will be a healthier nation. And something more: We will have once again put ourselves on the path of economic growth, and we will have demonstrated that no challenge is greater than the determination of the American people. ■

---

the deficit, spending on the thrift bailout and losses accrued in closing failed banks were not added to the deficit for Gramm-Rudman purposes.

The agreement completely ignored some costs. Spending on the Desert Shield operations in the Persian Gulf — estimated at $15 billion over three years if there were no hostilities — was not counted in the agreement's cap on defense outlays and budget authority. Nor did it count for Gramm-Rudman purposes.

Big-Ticket Items

About 80 percent of the deficit reduction in the deal came from five broad items:

- **Defense spending.** During the first three years, the Pentagon was slated to contribute all of the cuts in discretionary spending, totaling $67.2 billion. Domestic discretionary spending, by contrast, appeared to have been spared any significant cuts.
- **Medicare.** Cuts in payments to doctors and other providers and increases in deductibles, premiums and copayments by beneficiaries were expected to save $60 billion over five years. Roughly half the savings were to come from the providers and half from the beneficiaries.
- **Energy taxes.** A 10-cents-per-gallon increase in the excise tax on gasoline, diesel fuels and other specialty motor fuels and a new 2-cents-per-gallon tax on all refined petroleum products were expected to raise $56.8 billion over five years.
- **Taxes on upper-income individuals.** The agreement assumed $31 billion in new revenue over five years from two tax changes that would affect upper-income individuals exclusively: limits on deductions for mortgage interest payments, charitable contributions and the like, and an increase in the amount of income that was taxed for the Medicare trust fund.

The agreement called for a floor under the total amount of itemized deductions available to taxpayers with incomes above $100,000. The complex calculation would require taxpayers to reduce their itemized deductions by $3 for every $100 earned in excess of $100,000. The earnings limit would apply to single taxpayers as well as married couples.

Payroll taxes for Medicare would be increased for people earning more than $51,300; at the time, the 1.45 percent Medicare tax did not apply to wages above that amount. Under the agreement, wages up to $73,000 would be subject to the tax.

- **Interest savings.** Reduced interest payments, resulting from a smaller deficit and reduced interest rates, would save $64.8 billion.

A variety of deficit-reduction proposals in the agreement had been on the table before but were dropped because of strong opposition. This time, with little else available, they survived.

Chief among them were:

- **State and local government workers.** Social Security and Medicare coverage was to be extended to state and local government employees not covered by another pension plan. The change was expected to raise $16.9 billion over five years and to have little effect on future outlays, since many covered workers would have earned Social Security or Medicare coverage in other jobs.
- **Nuclear Regulatory Commission (NRC) fees.** Long-running efforts to have the NRC charge fees equal to 100 percent of the costs of its inspections and licensing of nuclear-powered electric plants were finally successful. The fee increase was expected to raise $1.7 billion over five years. *(NRC fees, p. 311)*
- **Coast Guard fees.** The agreement adopted a long-sought proposal to require owners of all boats that traveled in Coast Guard-patrolled waters to purchase an annual $25 decal. And fees would be charged for Coast Guard licensing and inspections. The change would yield $1.1 billion over five years. *(Coast Guard fees, p. 386)*

With the deal in place, the House voted 382-41 to approve a stopgap spending bill (H J Res 655 — PL 101-403) to continue government funding and suspend the sequester. The Senate approved the bill by voice vote. In what would become a pattern over the next month, the measure was good only until midnight Oct. 5, thus keeping the threat of a government shutdown as a way to keep members moving toward agreement. *(Vote 393, p. 128-H)*

BUDGET RESOLUTION

The five months of budget-summit talks were agonizingly difficult, but the next step proved impossible: A new budget resolution adopting the summit agreement went down to disastrous defeat in the House. In its place, Congress passed a broad fiscal blueprint, adopting the overall goals of the budget summit, but leaving much of the detail to the committees that were responsible for crafting an omnibus reconciliation bill.

Conservative Republicans and liberal Democrats who had seethed in frustration for months as mostly moderate negotiators drew up a budget deal finally got their chance to join the process, combining forces to kill the package (H Con Res 310 — H Rept 101-802) in a decisive 179-254 vote in the early hours of Oct. 5. *(Vote 421, p. 136-H)*

BOXSCORE

Legislation: Fiscal 1991 budget resolution (H Con Res 310).

Major action: Approved by Senate, 66-33, Oct. 9 (session of Oct. 8); by House, 250-164, Oct. 8 (session of Oct. 7). Budget summit version defeated by House, 179-254, Oct. 5 (session of Oct. 4); pre-summit version approved by House, 218-208, May 1.

Reports: Conference reports (H Rept 101-820, H Rept 101-802); Budget Committee (H Rept 101-455).

Opposition to Summit Mounts

Opposition in the House surfaced as soon as the budget agreement was announced Sept. 30, and it grew louder as the week progressed. The leadership finally brought the measure to a vote without a solid whip count and with trepidation over the outcome. But it was clear that every day of delay was bringing more defections.

Republicans were outraged at the plan's new taxes, and many were unswayed by arguments that the package was the only alternative to budget chaos.

Given the choice between Gramm-Rudman cuts and the budget package, Dick Armey, R-Texas, said, "I'll take sequestration.... "Sequestration hurts the government, and this package hurts the American people and their economy."

For their part, Democrats were furious over cuts in safety net programs, especially Medicare, and the added burden on low- and middle-income taxpayers.

"Overall, I think it stinks," said David R. Obey, D-Wis. "I will do everything in my power to defeat it."

President Bush tried to save the package with one-on-one persuasion of reluctant Republicans and a direct appeal to the public on prime-time television. The TV pitch flopped, and Bush failed to hold even half his party in the House vote. *(Bush text, p. 135)*

House Debate

On the House floor, Michel and Foley both made impassioned pleas for their members to vote for the package.

"I wish there were a better way of doing it," Michel said.

"Suffice it to say that the strong point of our agreement can be found only in its totality. We have to accept it as a whole, as it provides the only bipartisan basis for attacking the deficit problem."

Foley sought to allay members' concerns that they had been shut out of policy decisions by stressing that legislative committees would have a chance over the next two weeks to design alternative ways of making the spending cuts called for in the package.

Then, like Michel, Foley closed with an appeal for members to "stand together ... to make this process work for ourselves, for the president, for the parties and for the American people.

"We must ask ourselves this question: if not now, when; if not us, who?"

But the disaffection among House members was too deep.

Democratic opponents attacked not just the cuts, but the process. Oregon's Peter A. DeFazio stressed the package's extended lifetime, saying it would leave the country "locked in for five more years with the cruel and discredited policies of Reaganomics."

Republicans called the package the biggest tax increase in U.S. history and predicted that the promised spending cuts would never materialize.

"The American people want a lid put on spending," said

Bush Vetoes Continuing Resolution

Following is the text of President Bush's Oct. 6 message to Congress vetoing a continuing resolution (H J Res 660) to extend funding for the federal government through Oct. 12:

To the House of Representatives:

I am returning herewith without my approval H J Res 660 — a resolution making continuing appropriations — which would extend funding for the Federal Government through Oct. 12, 1990. In providing for such funding, H J Res 660 would also suspend the sequester that is required by the Gramm-Rudman-Hollings law. The sequester would be suspended even though the Congress has failed repeatedly to act in any meaningful way to reduce the Federal deficit. Under these circumstances, I simply cannot approve H J Res 660.

When the Budget Summit Agreement was announced by the Bipartisan Leadership on Sept. 30, I indicated that I would not sign a continuing resolution until a satisfactory budget resolution was passed. The Congress failed to pass such a budget resolution during the past week. I have made the difficult political decisions that are required to achieve a meaningful reduction in the Federal deficit.

Responsible congressional action to reduce the deficit can be delayed no longer. It is time for the Congress to act responsibly on a budget resolution — not time for business as usual.

I urge the Congress to concentrate its energies on passing a satisfactory budget resolution to clear the way for approval of another short-term continuing resolution, and the enactment of meaningful deficit reduction legislation no later than Oct. 19.

I note that H J Res 660 would also increase the Federal debt limit until Oct. 12. If it becomes clear that the Congress cannot pass a satisfactory budget resolution by Oct. 9, I urge that it enact a clean bill extending the debt limit so that the U.S. Government will not default on its obligations on Oct. 11. The latest date by which action on a debt limit extension is needed to avoid default is Oct. 9, so that the Treasury can auction securities on Oct. 10 and settle them on Oct. 11. ■

Indiana's Dan Burton. "They do not want new taxes."

Assessing the Vote

It had long been agreed that for the budget package to pass, both parties would have to deliver a majority of their members. Though supporters jumped to an early lead, it was clear 10 minutes into the vote that the package would fail. In the end, Republicans rejected it 71-105, and Democrats voted against it 108-149.

Foley and Gephardt were able to sell the package to only 14 of the House's 27 Democratic committee chairmen. Michel saw his top deputy, Minority Whip Gingrich, defect along with most of the party's whip organization.

Still, the outcome — announced just after 1 a.m. — left even the members who had wrought it a little stunned. And in the aftermath, blame was assessed widely.

Many on Capitol Hill placed responsibility for the debacle squarely on the White House, complaining in particular of heavy-handed lobbying by White House aides Darman and Sununu. Observers outside Congress viewed the defeat as a failure of will — a refusal by Democratic lawmakers to accept responsibility for painful budget cuts or Republican lawmakers to acknowledge the need for unpopular tax hikes. Still others saw the gridlock as the all too foreseeable product of the divided government that the voters had sent to Washington for the past decade.

Back to Basics

To give themselves time to regroup, House leaders assembled a second stopgap spending bill to provide funding for the federal government while efforts went on to resuscitate the budget plan. The first continuing resolution, passed on Sept. 30, was set to run out at midnight Oct. 5. After a day of negotiations, the House on the evening of Oct. 5 voted 300-113 in favor of a bill (H J Res 660) to keep funds flowing through midnight Oct. 12. The bill would also have extended the debt limit and continued a suspension of Gramm-Rudman cuts for the same period. The Senate cleared it by voice vote later that evening. *(Vote 431, p. 140-H)*

But an angry Bush vetoed the bill on Saturday morning, Oct. 6, insisting that Congress must first pass an acceptable budget resolution. As the three-day Columbus Day weekend began, the government began to shut down non-essential services — most visibly, museums and other tourist attractions in WAshington. *(Veto message, this page)*

Congress remained in session, trying to find a way out of the impasse — with many of the disappointed tourists in the galleries. On Saturday afternoon, the House tried but failed to override the veto. The vote was 260-138, six votes short of the necessary two-thirds. *(Vote 433, p. 140-H)*

Meanwhile, House and Senate Budget leaders — minus the deeply divided House Republicans — began trying to patch together a new budget resolution that could win approval. The result was a measure (H Con Res 310 — H Rept 820) that contained a set of broad guidelines, leaving much of the detail to be filled in by the committees. Suddenly, the traditional congressional process — which had been supplanted by the budget summit — was back.

The measure set binding limits for fiscal 1991 — $1.5 trillion in budget authority and $1.2 trillion in outlays. It called for $1.2 trillion in revenues. While the overall spending targets were the same as those in the budget-summit agreement, the resolution called for smaller cuts in Medicare and left open the possibility for changes in the capital gains tax rate.

The House debated past midnight on Sunday, Oct. 7, approving the measure 250-164 at about 2:30 the following morning. An hour and a half later, the House voted 305-105 to approve yet another continuing resolution (H J Res 666), this one good through Oct. 19. *(Votes 436, 438, p. 140-H)*

In the early hours of Oct. 9, the Senate passed the budget resolution 66-33, and the House cleared the continuing resolution, 362-3. *(Senate vote 261, p. 53-S; House vote 439, p. 140-H)*

This time, Bush signed the continuing resolution (PL 101-412) — around 7 a.m., just in time for federal employees to return to their jobs after the holiday weekend. Bush pronounced himself "not fully satisfied" with the measure but said it provided "a framework" for fulfilling the spirit of the rejected budget-summit agreement. Then, repeating his vow not to accept "business as usual," the president said a final reconciliation bill had to include "real" savings, growth-oriented tax incentives, budget-process reforms and enforcement mechanisms.

With a budget resolution finally in place, the appropriators had the spending limits they needed to complete their bills. And Congress turned to the next task: crafting and

House Reconciliation Instructions

The following are deficit-reduction instructions to House committees. The summit package would have specified the source of savings; the budget resolution (H Con Res 310 — H Rept 101-820) adopted Oct. 8 provided only committee totals. *(Savings in outlays; in millions of dollars; by fiscal year)*

Committee	Summit Package		Budget Resolution	
	1991	1991-95	1991	1991-95
Agriculture	1,409	13,627	1,022	13,627
Agriculture fees	79	433	—	—
Forest Service fees *	8	40	—	—
EPA fees *	22	154	—	—
Agriculture programs	1,300	13,000	—	—
Banking	1,507	13,528	1,507	13,258
Flood, crime insurance	14	833	—	—
FHA assignment waivers	193	925	—	—
Other FHA reforms	200	2,500	—	—
Bank Insurance Fund	1,100	9,000	—	—
Education and Labor	215	3,770	215	3,770
OSHA, MSHA penalties	95	1,130	—	—
Stafford Loans	0	2,000	—	—
Pension Benefit Guaranty Corporation *	120	640	—	—
Energy and Commerce	4,731	62,221	3,731	43,721
Medicare *	4,700	60,000	—	—
Medicaid savings	195	2,380	—	—
Medicaid package	-500	-2,100	—	—
NRC fees *	287	1,554	—	—
EPA fees *	22	154	—	—
Railroad safety fees	20	170	—	—
Travel, tourism fees	7	63	—	—
Interior	343	2,018	343	2,018
NRC fees *	287	1,554	—	—
Corps of Engineers fees *	20	100	—	—
Forest Service fees *	8	40	—	—
Hardrock mining claims	0	120	—	—
Tongass timber fund	28	204	—	—
Judiciary	91	495	91	495
Patent/trademark fees	91	495	—	—
Merchant Marine	222	1,231	222	1,231
Coast Guard fees	200	1,077	—	—
EPA fees *	22	154	—	—

Committee	Summit Package		Budget Resolution	
	1991	1991-95	1991	1991-95
Post Office	2,165	14,350	2,165	14,350
Civil Service retirement	1,230	8,050	—	—
Other savings	935	6,300	—	—
Public Works and Transportation	42	254	42	254
EPA fees *	22	154	—	—
Corps of Engineers fees *	20	100	—	—
Science, Space and Technology	5	25	5	25
NOAA weather service fees	5	25	—	—
Veterans' Affairs	620	3,350	620	3,350
Veterans Affairs fees	120	650	—	—
Unspecified savings	500	2,700	—	—
Ways and Means	18,545	194,403		
Mandatory savings/fees	—	—	3,320	55,603
Customs fees	0	2,292	—	—
Medicare *				
Provider payments	3,100	30,000	—	—
Beneficiary payments	1,600	28,000	—	—
Miscellaneous	0	2,000	—	—
Social Security package	-500	-2,000	—	—
Railroad pension fund	25	200	—	—
Pension Benefit Guaranty Corporation *	120	640	—	—
Unemployment insurance	0	4,600	—	—
Social Security overpayments	0	71	—	—
Unspecified	—	—	2,000	20,000
Tax package	14,200	128,600	13,225	118,800
Total reconciliation	24,694	246,206	24,307	246,206
Other deficit reduction				
IRS enforcement	3,037	9,376	3,037	9,376
Miscellaneous	600	3,000	600	3,000
Total deficit reduction	28,331	258,582	27,944	258,582

* *Joint committee jurisdiction; savings counted only once in totals*

SOURCE: Conference reports on H Con Res 310 (H Rept 101-802, H Rept 101-820)

passing a budget-reconciliation bill. *(Spending allocations, p. 140)*

BUDGET RECONCILIATION

It took Congress less than three weeks to clear a budget-reconciliation bill — a task that in previous years had often required months of work. After an all-night session, the House voted 228-200 near dawn on Oct. 27 to approve the bill. Eleven hours later, near dusk, the Senate cleared it, 54-45. The 101st Congress adjourned for good only hours later — at 1:17 a.m. EST on Oct. 28. *(House vote 528, p. 166-H; Senate vote 326, p. 63-S)*

The reconciliation measure (HR 5835 — PL 101-508), which Bush signed into law Nov. 5, provided $28 billion in deficit reduction in fiscal 1991 and $236 billion over five years — roughly half of that called for in the budget resolution. The rest was achieved through $184 billion in cuts from appropriations bills, with the biggest hit coming from defense, and lower interest payments on the national debt. More than half of the deficit reduction in the bill — $137 billion over five years — came from revenue increases, the remainder from savings in entitlements and other mandatory programs. *(Provisions, p. 141)*

Senate Reconciliation Instructions

The following are deficit-reduction instructions to Senate committees. The summit package would have specified the source of savings; the budget resolution (H Con Res 310 — H Rept 101-820) adopted Oct. 8 provided only committee totals. *(Savings in outlays; in millions of dollars; by fiscal year)*

Committee	Summit Package		Budget Resolution	
	1991	1991-95	1991	1991-95
Agriculture	1,387	13,473	1,000	13,473
Animal and Plant Health Inspection Service	79	433	—	—
Forest Service fee *	8	40	—	—
Agriculture programs	1,300	13,000	—	—
Banking	1,507	13,258	1,507	13,258
Flood, crime insurance	14	833	—	—
FHA assignment	193	925	—	—
Other FHA reforms	200	2,500	—	—
Bank Insurance Fund	1,100	9,000	—	—
Commerce	232	1,335	232	1,335
Coast Guard	200	1,077	—	—
NOAA weather service	5	25	—	—
Railroad safety inspections	20	170	—	—
Travel, tourism fees	7	63	—	—
Energy	36	364	36	364
Forest Service fees *	8	40	—	—
Hardrock mining claims	0	120	—	—
Tongass timber fund *	28	204	—	—
Environment	329	1,808	329	1,808
Corps of Engineers fees	20	100	—	—
EPA	22	154	—	—
NRC	287	1,554	—	—
Finance	18,240	194,683	18,240	194,683
Mandatory savings/ fees	—	—	3,015	55,883
Customs	0	2,292	—	—
Medicare	4,700	60,000	—	—
Medicaid	195	2,380	—	—

Committee	Summit Package		Budget Resolution	
	1991	1991-95	1991	1991-95
Unemployment insurance	0	4,600	—	—
Railroad Pension Fund	25	200	—	—
Social Security overpayments	0	71	—	—
Pension Benefit Guaranty Corporation *	120	640	—	—
Medicaid package	-500	-2,100	—	—
Social Security package	-500	-2,000	—	—
Tax package	14,200	128,600	13,225	118,800
Unspecified	—	—	2,000	20,000
Government Affairs	2,165	14,350	2,165	14,350
Civil Service retirement	1,230	8,050	—	—
Postal FEHB	689	4,200	—	—
Postal COLA	0	1,187	—	—
Other	246	913	—	—
Judiciary	91	495	91	495
Labor	165	3,480	165	3,480
Revenues	—	—	45	840
OSHA/MSHA penalties	95	1,130	—	—
Pension asset reversion *	-50	-290	—	—
Mandatory savings	—	—	120	2,640
Stafford loans	0	2,000	—	—
Pension Benefit Guaranty Corporation *	120	640	—	—
Veterans	620	3,350	620	3,350
Total Reconciliation	24,694	246,206	—	—
Other deficit reduction				
IRS enforcement	3,037	9,376	3,037	9,376
Miscellaneous	600	3,000	600	3,000
Total Deficit Reduction	28,331	258,582	27,944	258,582

** Joint committee jurisdiction; savings counted only once in totals*

SOURCE: Conference reports on H Con Res 310 (H Rept 101-802, H Rept 101-820)

The bill also included significant changes in the Gramm-Rudman deficit-reduction process. *(New budget process, p. 173)*

Gone was the heating oil tax increase that had raised the ire of Northeasterners during the budget summit; it had been dropped by both the House and Senate. The measure did include a gas tax increase, but it was smaller than envisioned in the summit, raising $25 billion over five years, compared with $45 billion in the summit plan. To make up the difference, the top income tax rate was raised to 31 percent from 28 percent and the value of personal exemptions was gradually reduced for upper-income taxpayers, yielding $22 billion over five years. The change in personal exemptions — a last-minute idea that had not been part of the summit plan or the House or Senate bills — was an alternative to a surtax on millionaires sought by the House but strongly opposed by the administration. *(Taxes, p. 167)*

The reconciliation bill cut $44.2 billion over five years from the fast-growing Medicare program.

While the amount was significant, it was smaller than that envisioned at the summit and required only modest increases in the costs borne by Medicare beneficiaries. And it included a child-care package, estimated to cost

Spending Allocations

The following are Appropriations subcommittee allocations for fiscal 1991 in millions of dollars.

	House [1]	Senate [2]	Final [3]
Agriculture			
Budget Authority	$ 51,169	$ 50,874	$ 51,712
Outlays	34,941	34,563	35,675
Commerce, Justice, State, Judiciary			
Budget Authority	20,195	20,185	19,335
Outlays	19,597	19,133	19,660
Defense			
Budget Authority	262,969	263,489	268,242
Outlays	276,219	276,243	277,759
District of Columbia			
Budget Authority	570	570	570
Outlays	580	580	570
Energy and Water Development			
Budget Authority	20,900	20,900	21,050
Outlays	19,900	19,900	20,160
Foreign Operations			
Budget Authority	15,775	15,353	15,370
Outlays	13,875	13,301	13,607
Interior			
Budget Authority	12,871	12,871	12,771
Outlays	12,071	11,997	12,022
Labor, Health and Human Services, and Education			
Budget Authority	$ 176,696	$ 173,477	$ 174,323
Outlays	177,597	176,108	176,921
Legislative Branch			
Budget Authority	2,340	2,340	2,302
Outlays	2,322	2,227	2,297
Military Construction			
Budget Authority	8,500	7,980	8,500
Outlays	8,700	8,666	8,700
Transportation			
Budget Authority	13,079	13,179	12,979
Outlays	29,677	29,477	29,677
Treasury, Postal Service, General Government			
Budget Authority	20,432	20,432	20,629
Outlays	19,521	19,521	19,793
VA-HUD-Independent Agencies (NASA)			
Budget Authority	80,846	78,861	77,831
Outlays	79,424	78,890	79,808
Total			
Budget Authority	$ 686,342	$ 680,512	$ 685,615
Outlays	694,424	690,606	696,649

[1] *Approved June 13 by House Appropriations based on the original House-passed budget resolution (H Con Res 310 — H Rept 101-455).*

[2] *Approved July 17 by Senate Appropriations based on an overall spending target set by the Senate July 12 in the absence of an approved budget resolution.*

[3] *Approved Oct. 10 by Senate Appropriations based on the final budget resolution (H Con Res 310 — H Rept 101-820).*

SOURCES: House and Senate Appropriations committees

$22.5 billion over five years. *(Medicare, p. 563; child care, p. 547)*

With the budget resolution in place, the House and Senate Budget committees quickly assembled separate versions of the reconciliation bill from provisions submitted by the authorizing committees. *(Reconciliation instructions, p. 138)*

The stricture that had governed the budget-summit package — that an agreement win majority approval from both sides of the aisle — was no longer in effect. Instead, House Democrats, convinced that the fairness issue was winning them support among voters, pushed through a tough bill that stressed taxes on the rich, including a surtax on millionaires.

The process was driven by the size of the partisan majorities in the two chambers. With a crushing 258-176 advantage in the House, Democrats were able to do pretty much what they wanted. With a much narrower 55-45 edge in the Senate, Democrats in that chamber had to bring along Republicans if they wanted a deal.

House and Senate conferees at first bogged down as House Democrats demanded a bill closer to their version and Senate negotiators resisted. In the end, however, House resolve wavered as members clamored to finish and go home for the congressional elections. Conferees resolved a major dispute by dropping a surtax on millionaires contained in the House bill and substituting a phaseout of the personal exemption for wealthy taxpayers.

BOXSCORE

Legislation: Omnibus Budget Reconciliation Act, PL 101-508 (HR 5835).

Major action: Signed, Nov. 5. Conference report adopted by Senate, 54-45, Oct. 27; by House, 228-200, Oct. 27 (session of Oct. 26). Passed by Senate, amended, 54-46, Oct. 18; by House, 227-203, Oct. 16.

Reports: Conference report (H Rept 101-964); Budget Committee (H Rept 101-881).

House Floor Action

Working from provisions submitted by 12 committees, the House Budget Committee on Oct. 15 reported a bud-

Continued on p. 164

Budget Reconciliation Act Provisions

Following are provisions of the Omnibus Budget Reconciliation Act of 1990 (HR 5835 — PL 101-508) as signed by President Bush on Nov. 5:

Title I — Agriculture

• **Triple base.** Reduced by 15 percent the amount of program crop acreage on which the government would make subsidy payments from 1991 through 1995.

Under this so-called triple-base plan, farms receiving subsidies had three categories of land: the annually announced acreage-reduction percentage, which took land out of production; the permitted acreage on which the program crop was planted and which was eligible for deficiency payments; and the 15 percent of their land that was not eligible for payments.

On land in the third category, producers could plant any program crop (wheat, corn, cotton or rice), oilseeds (such as soybeans, canola and sunflower) and all non-program crops except fruits and vegetables. Crops planted on this land were eligible for marketing and other loans.

For the 1991 crop of winter wheat, producers had the option of participating in the 15 percent triple-base plan or having their deficiency payments calculated on a 12-month average.

For other crops of wheat, feed grains and rice, the deficiency payment would be calculated on a 12-month basis, rather than the existing five-month basis, in 1994 and 1995, reducing government outlays.

• **Acreage reduction.** Established maximum acreage-reduction levels of 20 percent for wheat and feed grains, 25 percent for cotton and 35 percent for rice, based on certain surplus levels.

Set a minimum acreage-reduction program (ARP) level for wheat of 6 percent in 1992, 5 percent in 1993, 7 percent in 1994 and 5 percent in 1995.

Set a minimum ARP level of 7.5 percent for feed grains.

• **Other commodities.** Authorized loan-origination fees and other assessments on other commodities. Dairy producers were required to pay a 5-cent fee in fiscal 1991 and an 11-cent fee from 1992 through 1995. The Agriculture secretary had authority to refund this fee if a producer could prove that his milk production had not increased from the previous year's level.

Producers of oilseeds were required to pay a 2 percent loan-origination fee. Peanuts, honey and tobacco were subject to a 1 percent loan fee. Wool and mohair producers would have 1 percent deducted from their incentive payments.

• **Loan authorizations.** Established loan levels for the Rural Electrification and Telephone Revolving Fund, then reduced the levels in order to claim the savings, as follows: an $896 million authorization in fiscal 1991 reduced by $224 million, a $932 million authorization in fiscal 1992 reduced by $234 million, a $969 million authorization in fiscal 1993 reduced by $244 million, a $1.01 billion authorization in fiscal 1994 reduced by $256 million and a $1.05 billion authorization for fiscal 1995 reduced by $267 million.

Established loan levels for the FmHA Agricultural Credit Insurance Fund, then reduced the levels in order to be able to claim the savings, as follows: a $4.2 billion authorization in fiscal 1991 and a reduction in direct loans of $482 million; a $4.3 billion authorization for fiscal 1992 and a reduction in direct loans of $614 million; a $4.5 billion authorization for fiscal 1993 and a reduction in direct loans of $760 million; a $4.7 billion authorization in fiscal 1994 and a reduction in direct loans of $859 million; and a $4.9 billion authorization for fiscal 1995 and a reduction in direct loans of $907 million.

• **GATT.** Required that if the United States did not enter into an agreement under the General Agreement on Tariffs and Trade (GATT) by June 30, 1992, the Agriculture secretary would have to increase by $1 billion the level of spending in fiscal years 1994 and 1995 on export promotion programs for agricultural goods. The secretary was also authorized to waive minimum levels of acreage that would have to be retired by producers of program crops in 1993, 1994 and 1995. And the secretary could allow producers to repay their crop loans for wheat and feed grains at levels established in the Agricultural Act of 1949.

If there were no GATT agreement by June 30, 1993, the Agriculture secretary could waive all cuts required in agriculture spending to meet the deficit-reduction targets, in addition to the other measures.

Title II — Banking, Housing

Banking

• **Deposit insurance premiums.** Authorized the Federal Deposit Insurance Corporation (FDIC) to set deposit insurance premiums for banks (covered by the Bank Insurance Fund) and savings and loan institutions (covered by the Savings Association Insurance Fund) at whatever level was necessary to maintain a minimum reserve in each of the insurance funds to cover potential losses.

In addition, the FDIC was authorized to adjust insurance premiums twice a year, instead of annually, as under current law. And the law repealed a provision enacted in 1989 as part of the thrift industry salvage bill (PL 101-73) that required the FDIC to rebate excess bank or thrift premiums once the insurance funds achieved a ratio of 1.25 percent of total liabilities (or 1.5 percent if the FDIC board chose to seek a higher ratio).

• **FDIC borrowing.** Authorized the FDIC to borrow working capital from the Federal Financing Bank, a Treasury Department entity, instead of from more expensive private sources. Existing legal limits on FDIC borrowing from private sources would apply to Federal Financing Bank borrowing.

Housing

• **Increase in mortgage limit.** Removed the termination date of fiscal 1990 from the $124,875 Federal Housing Authority (FHA) mortgage limit.

• **Mortgagor equity.** Prevented homeowners from borrowing more than the value of their home when other fees were financed into the mortgage. Limited the insured principal to 98.75 percent of the appraised value of the property, plus the amount of the mortgage insurance premium paid at the time the mortgage was insured. For properties with an appraised value of more than $50,000, the insured principal obligation was limited to 97.75 percent.

• **Mortgage insurance premiums.** Required the secretary of Housing and Urban Development (HUD) to institute a new premium structure to shore up the financially shaky FHA insurance fund for single-family homes. The plan, which used a risk-based premium based on how much money a buyer put into the down payment, was designed to prevent people who were likely to default on loans from receiving them.

For mortgages on single- to four-family homes executed on or after Oct. 1, 1994, required the secretary, at the time of insurance, to collect a single payment equal to 2.25 percent of the amount of the original insured principal of the mortgage.

Required the secretary to refund a portion of the initial premium charge paid on payment in full of the principal obligation before the maturity date of the mortgage. Allowed HUD to devise a refund schedule laying out how long HUD had to handle the insurance on a loan before the homeowner no longer qualified for the return on the initial premium. The purpose of this was to allow homeowners to recoup some of their initial costs when HUD did not insure the loan for a long period.

Authorized the secretary to collect annual premium payments equal to 0.5 percent of the remaining insured principal balance. For any mortgage involving an original principal obligation that was less than 90 percent of the appraised value of the property, the premium had to be paid for the first 11 years of the 30-year loan. For mortgages greater than or equal to 90 percent of the value, premiums had to be paid for the entire 30-year life of the loan.

For mortgages involving an original principal obligation that was greater than 95 percent of the appraised value of the property, the secretary was authorized to collect an annual premium of 0.55 percent of the remaining insured principal balance during the 30-year loan.

• **Transition premiums.** Until Oct. 1, 1994, when the new risk-based insurance program was to be instituted, the act provided for a transition period to change the premium structure. For mortgages executed during fiscal 1991 and 1992, the secretary was authorized to collect at the time of insurance a single premium payment equal to 3.8 percent, which was the current upfront premium.

In addition, the secretary was authorized to collect annual premium payments equal to 0.5 percent of the remaining insured principal balance. For any mortgage involving an original principal obligation of less than 90 percent of the appraised value of the property, the annual premium had to be paid for the first five years of the loan. For any mortgage that was originally from 90 percent to 95 percent of the value of the property, the annual premium had to be paid for the first eight years of the loan. And for mortgages greater than 95 percent of the value, annual premiums had to be paid for 10 years.

For mortgages executed during fiscal 1993 and 1994, the secretary was authorized to collect at the time of insurance a single premium payment equal to 3 percent of the amount of the original insured principal obligation.

In addition, the secretary was authorized to collect annual premium payments equal to 0.5 percent of the remaining insured principal balance. For mortgages involving an original principal obligation of less than 90 percent of the appraised value of the property, the premium had to be paid for the first seven years of the loan. For mortgages from 90 percent to 95 percent of the value, premiums had to be paid for the first 12 years. And for mortgages in which the principal obligation was more than 95 percent of the value, premiums had to be paid for the full 30 years of the loan.

Required the secretary to refund all of the unearned premium charges paid during fiscal 1991-1994 on payment in full of the principal obligation of the mortgage before maturity.

Required the secretary to issue regulations to carry out this section no later than 90 days after enactment.

• **Mutual Mortgage Insurance Fund distributions.** Required the secretary to consider the actuarial status of the fund in determining whether there was a surplus of funds to distribute to mortgagors.

• **Actuarial soundness of Mutual Mortgage Insurance Fund.** Required the secretary to ensure that the fund attained a capital ratio of no less than 1.25 percent within 24 months after enactment. The capital ratio was the percentage of the amount of cash on hand out of the total amount of outstanding mortgages. [During a 10-year period, the capital ratio had steadily declined, with cash on hand dropping from $3.4 billion in 1979 to $2.6 billion in 1989. Had it been sound, the fund would have grown to $8 billion during that decade, according to a report by the accounting firm of Price Waterhouse.]

Required the secretary to ensure that the fund attained a capital ratio of no less than 2 percent within 10 years of the date of enactment and to ensure that the fund maintained that ratio at all times thereafter.

Required the secretary to submit a report to Congress 24 months after enactment describing the actions that would be taken to ensure that the fund attained the required capital ratio.

Required the secretary to conduct an annual independent actuarial study of the fund and to report annually to Congress on its financial status.

Prohibited the secretary from sending mortgagors distributive shares, or excess premiums, if the insurance fund was not meeting operational goals. For example, during the 1970s, FHA-insured loans had a low default rate and HUD returned some premiums when owners paid off their loans. Operational goals included:

• Maintaining the required capital ratio.

• Meeting the needs of home buyers with low down payments and first-time home buyers by providing access to mortgage credit.

• Minimizing the risk to the fund and to homeowners from defaults.

• Avoiding policies that caused low-risk borrowers to go instead to commercial lenders, a phenomenon called "adverse selection."

Also authorized the secretary to adjust the insurance premiums if the fund was not meeting its operational goals. Required the secretary to notify Congress of the proposed change and the reasons for the change. Changes in premiums would take effect no earlier than 90 days after Congress was notified unless Congress acted during that time to increase, prevent or modify the change.

• **Home equity conversion mortgage insurance demonstration.** Extended the termination date to Sept. 30, 1995, from Sept. 30, 1991. Limited the total number of mortgages insured under the program to no more than 25,000.

• **Auction of federally insured mortgages.** Required HUD to arrange for the sale of interests in mortgage loans through an auction rather than accepting the multifamily mortgages from the original holders and giving a 10-year market-rate bond. To entice people to invest in multifamily housing during the late 1960s and early '70s, HUD offered to take over mortgages after 20 years in exchange for an interest-bearing bond. HUD now wanted to buy out these mortgage agreements in order to save money.

Required HUD to arrange the auction at a price, to be paid to the mortgagee, of the base amount plus accrued interest to the date of sale. Provided that the sale price also include the right to a subsidy payment to the mortgagee that would make up for any improvements on the property.

Required HUD to conduct a public auction to determine the lowest interest rate necessary to accomplish a sale of the mortgage and any benefits accrued to it on the property and insurance.

Required a mortgagee, who decided to assign a mortgage to HUD, to provide the department and bidders at auction a description of the property and mortgage, including the principal mortgage balance, original stated interest rate, service fees, real estate and tenant characteristics, level and duration of federal subsidies and any other information HUD said was appropriate.

Required HUD to provide information regarding the status of the property relating to the Emergency Low-Income Housing Preservation Act of 1989 that had to do with prepayment provisions. (This was to ensure that affordable housing for low-income people was not lost to the market as owners paid off their federally subsidized mortgages.)

Required HUD, after receiving the description of the property, to advertise for auction and publish mortgage descriptions in advance of the auction. Authorized HUD to wait up to six months to conduct the auction but prohibited HUD from holding the auction sooner than two months after receiving the mortgagee's written notice of intent to assign its mortgage to HUD.

Required HUD to accept the interest rate bid for purchase that HUD determined to be acceptable and required HUD to publish the accepted bid in the Federal Register.

Required settlement to occur no later than 30 business days after the winning bidders were selected in the auction, unless HUD determined that extraordinary circumstances required an extension.

Authorized mortgagees to retain all rights to assign the mortgage loan to HUD if there were no acceptable bids received or settlement did not occur within the required time period.

Required HUD, as part of the auction, to agree to provide a monthly interest subsidy payment from the General Insurance Fund to the purchaser of the original property and mortgage securing that property. This was part of the buyout of the mortgagee's right to an interest-bearing bond.

Required HUD to encourage state housing finance agencies, nonprofit organizations, tenant organizations and mortgagees participating under an Emergency Low-Income Housing Preservation plan of action to participate in the auction.

Required HUD to put the requirements under this section into effect within 30 days from enactment and not subject them to the requirement of prior issuance of regulations in the Federal Register. Required HUD to issue implementing regulations within six months of enactment.

Prohibited any of these provisions from diminishing or impairing the low-income use restrictions applicable to the project under the original regulatory agreement or the revised agreement entered into under the Emergency Low-Income Housing Preservation Act or other agreements to provide federal assistance to the housing or its tenants.

Specified that these provisions would not apply after Sept. 30, 1995, and required HUD to report to Congress on these provisions no later than Jan. 31 of each year beginning in 1992.

Crime, Flood Insurance

• **Crime insurance.** Reauthorized the federal crime insurance program for four years through Sept. 30, 1995. The law also allowed policyholders to keep their coverage through Sept. 30, 1996, should the program be terminated, and it continued an existing 15 percent limit on premium increases through Sept. 30, 1995.

• **Flood insurance.** Reauthorized the federal flood insurance program for four years through Sept. 30, 1995. The law also continued an existing 10 percent limit on premium increases through Sept. 30, 1995. But beginning in fiscal 1991, insurance premiums would be increased to include administrative and flood-plain mapping costs. The limit on increases would not apply to fiscal 1991 administrative costs.

Title III — Student Loans, Labor

Student Loans

• **Payments for supplemental preclaims assistance.** Reversed the incentive system provided by the government for collection of delinquent student loans by paying collection agencies for their work in getting students to repay loans. Under existing law, guaranty agencies trying to collect on loans for banks were paid by the government for their work only after the loans went into default. The fiscal 1991 reconciliation provision required the secretary of Education to pay the guaranty agency $50 for each loan on which students did not default.

• **First-year students.** Prohibited schools from giving first-year students the first installment of any loan until 30 days after the student enrolled in the institution. The loans, however, could be delivered to the school before the end of that 30-day period. This was effective for loans made on or after the date of enactment to cover the cost of instruction beginning on or after Jan. 1, 1991.

• **Ineligibility based on high default rates.** Prohibited institutions whose default rate was equal to or greater than 35 percent in fiscal 1991 and 1992 and 30 percent for fiscal 1993 through 1996 from participating in the student loan program. The default rate had to equal or exceed those rates for each of the three most recent fiscal years in which data was available. The school would be ineligible in the fiscal year in which the determination was made and for the next two fiscal years.

Schools could appeal the ineligibility ruling within 30 days of notification from the secretary of Education. The secretary was required to rule on the appeal within 45 days of receiving it.

The school could continue to participate in the student loan program if the secretary decided that the calculation of the default rate was not accurate and recalculation would reduce it for any of the three fiscal years. Or the school could continue to participate in the student loan program if the secretary decided there were exceptional mitigating circumstances. During the appeal, the secretary could permit the institution to continue to participate in the program.

• **Exceptions.** Until July 1, 1994, historically black colleges and universities, tribally controlled community colleges, and the Navajo Community College in Tsaile, Ariz., would remain eligible for student loans even though they had high default rates.

• **Refusal to provide statement to lender.** Authorized schools' financial aid administrators to certify students for loans. Even if a student was eligible for a loan, according to the bank, schools could determine whether the student's expenses could be met more appropriately from other sources, such as the institution or the student. Schools wanted a say in determining eligibility because they were held accountable for their students' defaults.

• **Effective date.** Required default rate cutoffs and exceptions to begin July 1, 1991.

• **Ability to benefit.** Required that people without high school diplomas, who were admitted to schools based on the ability to benefit from the education and offered any grant, loan or work assistance, to pass an independently administered examination approved by the secretary. The exam had to be taken before enrollment. This took effect Jan. 1, 1991.

• **Maximum supplemental loans to students.** Extended existing provisions through fiscal 1996. Authorized $4,000 for full-time students; $2,500 for students attending school two-thirds of full time; $1,500 for less than two-thirds but at least one-third of full-time attendance.

• **Bankruptcy laws.** Prohibited accreditation, state licensure and student aid from being considered protected assets during bankruptcy proceedings of a school.

• **Sunset.** Terminated the student loan provisions on Oct. 1, 1996.

Labor

• **Occupational Safety and Health Act penalties.** Increased maximum civil penalties sevenfold, bringing fines for each willful or repeated violation to $70,000. The bill also imposed a new minimum mandatory penalty of $5,000 for willful violations of OSHA laws. The new fines were expected to produce nearly $900 million in new revenue over five years.

• **Mine Safety and Health Act penalties.** Increased maximum civil penalties fivefold to $50,000 for violations of mine safety and health laws. The new fines were expected to produce $247 million over five years.

• **Fair Labor Standards Act penalties.** Imposed a maximum civil penalty of $10,000 for violations of child labor laws. The increase would produce $15 million over five years.

Title IV — Medicare

Medicare — Part A

• **Medicare hospital payments/capital costs.** Continued through fiscal 1991 the 15 percent reduction in payments to hospitals under Medicare's Prospective Payment System (PPS) for capital-related costs (including depreciation, interest and rent). Exempted from the reductions were facilities designated as Rural Primary Care hospitals, Essential Access Community Hospitals and sole community hospitals. Capital costs still had to be folded into the Prospective Payment System by Oct. 1, 1991.

• **Medicare hospital payments/payment update.** Provided for payment rate increases, beginning Jan. 1, 1991, for hospitals (other than rural hospitals, listed below) under PPS as follows:

For the remainder of fiscal 1991, hospitals would receive increases equal to the increase in the "market basket" (a measure of goods and services bought by hospitals) less 2 percentage points. (The fiscal 1991 market basket increase was estimated at 5.2 percent, meaning the increase would be 3.2 percent.)

For fiscal 1992, the payment update would be market basket less 1.6 percentage points.

For fiscal 1993, market basket less 1.55 percentage points.

In fiscal 1994 and 1995, hospitals would receive the full market basket increase.

• **Medicare hospital payments/disproportionate share.** Increased and made permanent the so-called disproportionate share adjustment, a special add-on payment for hospitals that served a disproportionately large share (15 percent or more) of poor patients, whose ailments tended to be more expensive to treat.

• **Medicare hospital payments/rural hospitals.** Provided for payment rate increases for rural hospitals under PPS as follows:

For fiscal 1991, market basket (5.2 percent) less 0.7 percentage points (yielding an increase of 4.5 percent).

For fiscal 1992, market basket less 0.6 percentage points.

For fiscal 1993, market basket.

For fiscal 1994, market basket plus 1.5 percentage points.

For fiscal 1995, market basket plus whatever percentage increase was needed to close the gap between rates paid to rural hospitals and those paid to urban hospitals.

• **Medicare hospital payments/area wage index.** Delayed until Jan. 1, 1991, the requirement that the Department of Health and Human Services (HHS) use a new wage index based on 1988 data. [Under Medicare's PPS, hospital payments were adjusted for labor costs using an index that compared hospital wages in a particular geographic area with those paid nationwide. The existing wage index was based on a 1984 survey of wages and wage-related costs, after adjustments for inflation].

• **Medicare hospital payments/regional floor.** Extended through fiscal 1993 a special payment adjustment, known as the regional floor, for hospitals in areas of the country with costs higher than the national average. Required the HHS secretary to collect data on non-labor costs in order to create a geographic index for non-labor costs.

• **Prospective Payment Assessment Commission.** Expanded the responsibilities of the Prospective Payment Assessment Commission (ProPAC), a 17-member board charged with making recommendations concerning hospital payments under PPS. Charged ProPAC with recommending the development or modification of policies to promote the delivery of efficient, accessible, high-quality health care.

Continued to require ProPAC to recommend the hospital update factor under PPS annually by March 1. In addition, though, every June 1, ProPAC would have to report on trends in health-care costs, payment of institutional providers (including hospitals, outpatient departments, nursing homes and ambulatory surgery centers) and new methods of health-care cost containment.

[In their report, conferees noted that they intended that ProPAC include in its analysis and recommendations proposals for changes in policies regarding: 1) payment of inner-city hospitals, taking into account the costs of charity care and bad debts; 2) payment of rural hospitals, taking into account appropriate responses to issues affecting access to health-care services in rural areas; and 3) ways to help constrain the costs of health care to employers, including the ways in which Medicare payment policies affect other payers.]

Further required ProPAC, by Oct. 1, 1991, to analyze Medicaid payment to hospitals and recommend any changes in federal law relating to Medicaid hospital reimbursement.

• **DRG payment window.** Under PPS, Medicare payments were made on the basis of a patient's diagnosis, according to what was called a diagnosis-related group, or DRG. The DRG payment was intended to cover all hospital services provided to a Medicare beneficiary during his or her stay. In recent years, however, many hospitals had begun having patients scheduled for a hospital stay come in two or three days in advance for routine tests and then billing them separately for those tests under Medicare's Part B, which covered outpatient costs.

Beginning Jan. 1, 1991, the new rule provided that services related to the admission rendered up to 72 hours before the day of hospital admission were to be considered part of the hospital stay and could not be separately billed to Part B.

• **Hospitals exempt from PPS.** Required the HHS secretary to develop a prospective payment methodology for hospitals exempt from PPS (including children's hospitals, cancer hospitals, psychiatric hospitals, rehabilitation hospitals and long-term care hospitals) by April 1, 1992.

Further provided that PPS-exempt hospitals, which were paid based on their costs up to a specific target amount, be allowed to receive 50 percent of their costs in excess of that target, up to a limit of 120 percent (thereby making them eligible to receive 110 percent of their target amount).

• **Hospice care.** Beginning Jan. 1, 1990, allowed Medicare beneficiaries to receive hospice-care services in excess of the existing 210-day limit if the beneficiary was recertified as terminally ill by a physician or hospice medical director. [This provision was part of the 1988 Medicare Catastrophic Coverage Act and was repealed along with most of the remainder of the law in 1989.]

• **Partial sequester.** Froze all payments under Medicare Part A at their fiscal 1990 levels through Dec. 31, 1990.

• **Waiver of liability for skilled nursing facilities and hospices.** Extended through Dec. 31, 1995, the so-called waiver of liability for skilled nursing homes and hospices, which allowed them to receive Medicare payment for patients not technically eligible for the services if the agencies involved reasonably thought they were providing covered services.

• **Hospital antidumping provisions.** Further clarified provisions of past deficit-reduction bills that required hospitals that participated in Medicare to treat any patients with health emergencies, particularly women in "active" labor, regardless of whether they were covered by Medicare or any other health insurance.

The provisions reduced to $25,000 (from $50,000) the maximum penalty that could be assessed against small hospitals (those with fewer than 100 beds). It also changed the standard for what could be considered "patient dumping" to make it easier to assess civil penalties against hospitals and doctors and clarified standards for excluding providers from the program.

Medicare — Part B

• **Part B premium.** Set the Part B premium as follows: For calendar year 1991, the monthly premium would be $29.90. For calendar year 1992, $31.80; for 1993, $36.60; for 1994, $41.10; and for 1995, $46.10. [The calendar year 1990 monthly premium was $28.60.]

• **Part B deductible.** Increased the annual Part B deductible from $75 to $100 for calendar year 1991 and thereafter.

• **Overpriced procedures.** Beginning Jan. 1, 1991, cut Medicare payments for 244 procedures that analysts had determined to be overpaid by Medicare. The procedures would be cut by the same amount for which payments were reduced in 1990. Also reduced by 6.5 percent payment for certain other procedures that had been identified as overvalued.

• **Radiology services.** For 1991, reduced, by up to 9.5 percent, fees for radiology services under Medicare. Exact reductions would vary by the area of the country in which they were performed.

• **Anesthesiology services.** Beginning Jan., 1, 1991, reduced fees for anesthesiology services by up to 15 percent. Reductions would average about 7 percent and would vary by locality. Also extended, through Dec. 31, 1995, payment reductions imposed in the 1987 deficit-reduction bill [PL 100-203] for anesthesiologists who supervised multiple procedures in which anesthesia was delivered by certified registered nurse anesthetists.

• **Pathology services.** Beginning Jan. 1, 1991, reduced most fees for pathology services by 7 percent and provided that pathology services be paid according to a fee schedule beginning Jan. 1, 1992, instead of Jan. 1, 1991.

• **Physician payment update.** For calendar 1991, froze Medicare fees for all physician services except primary care, which would increase by 2 percent. Reduced fees for 1992 by 0.4 percent below inflation projections [which would produce an estimated fee increase of 2 percent]. Set minimum payment for primary care services at 60 percent of the national average. Also, for calendar 1991, increased from 125 percent of the Medicare-approved amount to 140 percent the total amount a physician could charge for so-called evaluation and management services, such as most routine office visits.

• **Medicare volume performance standards.** Required the HHS secretary to set separate volume targets for surgery and all other medical procedures. The volume target, known as the MVPS, in conjunction with the fee schedule, was intended to control increases in both the price and volume of Medicare physician services.

• **New physicians.** Made permanent the policy of setting fees for physicians in their first year of practice at 80 percent of the amount otherwise payable, and at 85 percent in their second year.

Also provided that fees for physicians in their third year be set at 90 percent, and those in their fourth year 95 percent.

Beginning Jan. 1, 1991, set similar limits for non-physician health practitioners (including physician assistants, psychologists and nurse midwives).

• **Assistants at surgery.** Limited payments for doctors who served as assistants during surgical procedures to no more than 16 percent of the primary surgeon's fee. Eliminated payments for assistants at surgery for procedures in which a physician served as an assistant less than 5 percent of the time.

• **Diagnostic tests.** Limited payments for the technical component of certain diagnostic tests to the national median charge. Also, beginning Jan. 1, 1992, eliminated separate payments for the interpretation of a routine electrocardiogram (EKG) ordered or performed in conjunction with an office visit or consultation.

• **Reciprocal billing arrangements.** Specifically allowed payment to a physician who arranged for services to be provided by another physician when the first physician was unavailable on an occasional, reciprocal basis.

• **Practicing Physicians Advisory Council.** Established a 15-member Practicing Physicians Advisory Council whose role would be to consult with the HHS secretary on proposed changes in Medicare's physician payment policies.

• **Study of regional variations in the impact of Medicare physician payment reform.** Required the HHS secretary to conduct a study of regional variations in impact of Medicare's physician payment reform law [included in the fiscal 1990 reconciliation bill, PL 101-239]. The study would examine:

1) factors contributing to variations in charges not attributable

to variations in practice costs;

2) the impact on access to care in areas that would experience disproportionately large payment reductions under the new fee schedule (set to begin Jan. 1, 1992); and

3) appropriate adjustments or modifications in the transition to or determining payments under the fee schedule.

• **Hospital outpatient services.** Reduced capital payments for hospital outpatient services by 15 percent in fiscal 1991 and by an additional 10 percent in each of the following four fiscal years.

The same hospitals that were exempt from the Part A capital reductions (see above) would be exempt from the outpatient capital reductions.

In addition, payments for hospital outpatient services would be cut by 5.8 percent from fiscal 1991 through 1995, except for hospitals exempt, as noted above.

Directed the HHS secretary to develop, by Sept. 1, 1991, a proposal for paying for hospital outpatient services under a prospective payment system, as was the existing case for most inpatient hospital care.

• **Overpriced Durable Medical Equipment (DME).** Reduced by 15 percent fees paid for transcutaneous electrical nerve stimulation (TENS) devices (used primarily to treat chronic pain). This was in addition to the 15 percent reduction ordered for 1990.

Coverage and payment for seatlift chairs furnished in 1991 and thereafter would be limited to the lift mechanism only and would not include the chair and upholstery.

• **National limits on DME fees.** Eliminated the system in which fees were determined on a regional basis in favor of one instituting upper and lower national fee limits for various items of durable medical equipment. Limits for all items except customized equipment would be phased in over a three-year period.

• **Rental items.** Allowed patients the option to purchase certain rented items of DME (including wheelchairs and hospital beds) following nine months of continuous rental. If the patient exercised the option, rental payments would continue through the 13th month of continuous use, after which ownership of the item would transfer to the patient. Medicare would continue to make payments for servicing and maintenance at rates to be determined by the secretary.

• **Oxygen retesting.** Required patients who qualified for oxygen therapy to be retested after three months to confirm their continued need for such use.

• **DME payment update.** Reduced the inflation increase for DME by 1 percentage point in each of 1991 and 1992. Stipulated that no increases be granted for enteral and parenteral (largely intravenous) nutrients, equipment and supplies, and that payments for orthotics and prosthetics (orthopedic items) be frozen at 1990 levels for calendar year 1991.

• **Medical necessity forms.** Before Medicare would pay for certain items of DME, a physician had to certify that the equipment was medically necessary. Beginning Jan. 1, 1991, the provision prohibited DME suppliers from distributing completed or partially completed Medicare medical-necessity forms to physicians or beneficiaries in order to facilitate purchase of a particular item. Violators would be subject to civil penalties of up to $1,000 for each form distributed.

• **Clinical laboratory services.** Limited the annual payment update for clinical laboratory services to 2 percent for each of 1991, 1992 and 1993. Also, beginning Jan. 1, 1991, limited payment for clinical laboratory services to no more than the amount that represented 88 percent of the median fee paid for such services nationwide. The previous national limit was 93 percent.

• **Partial sequester.** Reduced all payments to Part B providers (except health maintenance organizations) by 2 percent for services furnished between Nov. 1, 1990 and Dec. 31, 1990.

• **Alzheimer's disease demonstration projects.** Reauthorized for one additional year, at $15 million, demonstration projects to provide comprehensive services to Medicare beneficiaries with Alzheimer's disease.

• **Coverage of nurse practitioners and clinical nurse specialists in rural areas.** Allowed direct reimbursement for services provided by nurse practitioners and clinical nurse specialists in rural areas. Under existing law, reimbursement for both categories of health professionals was generally limited to the physician for whom the service-provider worked.

Payments would be limited to 85 percent of the amount that could be paid to a physician providing the same service, and services would be required to be provided only on an assignment basis (under which the provider agreed to accept the Medicare-approved fee as payment in full).

• **Coverage of injectable drugs for treatment of osteoporosis.** Beginning Jan. 1, 1991, and ending Dec. 31, 1995, provided for Medicare coverage of injectable drugs used to treat bone fractures related to post-menopausal osteoporosis.

Coverage would include only patients who were otherwise eligible for Medicare home-care coverage and whose physicians certified that they were unable to learn the skills needed to administer the drug themselves or were otherwise physically or mentally incapable of self-administration. Also required the secretary to study the impact of such coverage and report any findings and recommendations to Congress by Oct. 1, 1994.

• **Partial hospitalization services provided by community mental health centers.** Partial hospitalization services included individual and group therapy, occupational therapy, administration of certain drugs and other services provided by a hospital or hospital-affiliated institution on a less than 24-hour basis. Beginning April 1, 1991, the provision allowed Medicare payment for partial hospitalization services provided by community mental health centers, as well.

• **Certified registered nurse anesthetists.** Altered the payment system for certified registered nurse anesthetists (CRNAs) over six years to conform them to the manner in which physicians who performed anesthesia services would be paid under the new Medicare fee schedule.

By 1995, payments for CRNAs working under the direct supervision of a physician would be approximately 70 percent of the amount that would be paid to a physician performing the same service.

• **Mammography screening.** Beginning Jan. 1, 1991, provided coverage for mammograms used to screen for breast cancer. (Medicare already paid for diagnostic mammography, used after breast cancer was suspected.)

For Medicare beneficiaries over age 65, Medicare would pay for a screening mammogram every two years.

For those under age 65:

1) No coverage would be provided for women under age 35.

2) A baseline screening would be covered for those between age 35 and 40.

3) Biennial coverage would be provided for women between age 40 and 49 who were not determined to be at high risk for breast cancer.

4) Annual coverage would be provided for all female beneficiaries between ages 50 and 64, as well as for high-risk women between 40 and 49.

Payment would be limited to $55 in 1991, with that amount to be increased for inflation in future years. Providers would be prohibited from charging more than 125 percent of the Medicare-approved price in 1991, 120 percent in 1992 and 115 percent in 1993.

Medicare — Parts A and B

• **End stage renal disease facility payments.** For the remainder of 1990, required that the rate of payment to free-standing and hospital-based kidney dialysis facilities be maintained at the rates in effect on Sept. 30, 1990. Beginning Jan. 1, 1991, increased the per-patient rate by $1.

• **Coverage of erythropoietin (EPO).** Beginning July 1, 1991, allowed coverage of EPO, an anti-anemia drug used by kidney dialysis patients. Under existing rules, EPO was covered when administered in a dialysis facility, but only in home-dialysis settings if administered directly by a physician. Also restructured the way Medicare paid for the drug.

• **Demonstration for staff-assisted home dialysis.** Required establishment of a three-year demonstration to evaluate the safety and cost-effectiveness of providing professional assistance to up to 800 Medicare End Stage Renal Disease beneficiaries who used dialysis at home and met other conditions. The final report on the demonstration would be due no later than Dec. 31, 1995.

• **Secondary payer provisions.** Extended, through Sept. 30, 1995, authority for Medicare to gain access to records of the Social Security Administration and Internal Revenue Service in order to identify Medicare beneficiaries who had other forms of health insurance. (Medicare was supposed to be the "secondary" payer for many beneficiaries with other forms of insurance, covering only costs not paid by the primary insurer.)

Also extended, through Oct. 1, 1995, a provision making Medicare the secondary payer for disabled Medicare beneficiaries covered by an employer health plan in a business with more than 100 employees.

Extended from 12 to 18 months the period during which employer-provided insurance was the primary payer for Medicare End Stage Renal Disease patients. Made it illegal to offer incentives to an individual not to enroll in (or to terminate enrollment from) a health plan that would be a primary payer under Medicare rules unless the same incentives were offered to all individuals covered under the plan, regardless of their Medicare status.

• **Patient self-determination/living wills.** Beginning one year after enactment, required hospitals, nursing homes, home health agencies, hospice programs and health maintenance organizations that participated in Medicare or Medicaid to provide written information to all adult patients with respect to their rights under state law to make decisions concerning their medical care, including the right to accept or refuse medical or surgical treatment and the right to formulate advance directives.

[Such advance directives included so-called living wills, in which individuals could state in advance whether they wanted life-sustaining treatment continued should they become unable to communicate their wishes, or "durable powers of attorney," in which a patient delegated to another person the right to make decisions regarding medical care if the patient became incapacitated.]

Providers would be required to maintain written policies detailing how those rights would be protected, including documenting in the patient's medical record whether the patient had executed an advance directive. They would also be required to provide education for staff and the community regarding advance directives but could not condition the provision of services or otherwise discriminate against a patient based on whether he or she had executed an advance directive.

This provision left room for states to allow health-care providers to object, as a matter of conscience, and refuse to carry out a patient's advance directive.

• **Health Maintenance Organizations (HMOs).** Watered down previous efforts to prevent HMOs from cutting costs by offering incentives to doctors not to provide patient care.

Repealed a provision of the fiscal 1987 budget-reconciliation legislation (PL 99-509) that would have prohibited HMOs and Competitive Medical Plans (CMPs) from paying physicians incentives designed to directly or indirectly encourage needed care to be withheld from patients. Replaced that requirement with a provision that physician-incentive plans operated by HMOs and CMPs be operated with certain protections for both physicians and patients.

• **Payment cycles.** Made permanent a provision barring the HHS secretary from making policy changes whose primary effect was to slow down or speed up the rate at which Medicare claims were paid.

• **Waiver of liability for home health agencies.** Extended through Dec. 31, 1995, the so-called waiver of liability for home health agencies, which allowed them to receive Medicare payment for patients not technically eligible for the services if the agencies involved reasonably thought they were providing covered services.

• **Social health maintenance organizations.** Extended through Sept. 30, 1995, authority for a series of social health maintenance organizations (SHMOs), which provided not only traditional HMO health care services but also long-term care and other social services. Required the creation of up to four additional SHMOs.

• **Case-management demonstrations.** Required the secretary to reinstate three demonstration projects to test the cost-effectiveness of providing case-management services to Medicare beneficiaries with high-cost illnesses. (Case management involved designating a single person to oversee and coordinate all health services for particular individuals.)

The demonstrations were originally authorized as part of the 1988 Medicare Catastrophic Coverage Act, but the authority was repealed along with most of the rest of that law in 1989. Authorized $2 million for each of fiscal 1991 and 1992 to cover administrative costs.

• **Prospective payment for home health agencies.** Required the secretary to develop a prospective payment system for home health agencies and submit it to Congress by Sept. 1, 1993.

• **User fees for survey and certification.** Specifically prohibited HHS from imposing, or from requiring states to impose, on hospitals, nursing homes, hospices, kidney dialysis facilities or other health institutions, fees to offset the costs of inspections to certify compliance with Medicare rules and regulations. (The prohibition was in response to a similar user-fee proposal included in President Bush's fiscal 1990 budget.)

• **Peer Review Organizations.** Made several alterations in the requirements for Medicare Peer Review Organizations (PROs), which reviewed the appropriateness, reasonableness, medical necessity and quality of care provided to Medicare beneficaries. Among the changes were:

1) Requiring PROs to notify state licensing boards when a physician was excluded from Medicare.

2) Requiring coordination in review activities between PROs and insurance company "carriers" that paid Medicare claims.

3) Allowing podiatrists and optometrists to participate in decisions about payment denials for services provided by those specialists.

Title IV — Medicaid

Prescription Drug Discounts for State Medicaid Programs

• **Required rebate agreements.** Beginning Jan. 1, 1991, generally prohibited federal Medicaid funds from being spent for prescription drugs made by any drug manufacturer that did not enter into an agreement to provide specified rebates to states on a quarterly basis.

States that elected to offer prescription drug coverage under Medicaid [although such coverage was optional, all 50 states offered it] would be required to cover all drugs sold by a manufacturer who had entered into a rebate agreement, except for vaccines and classes of drugs specifically excluded by statute. To assist states with start-up administrative costs, the federal government would pay 75 cents of each dollar spent on the program in fiscal 1991.

• **Excluded drugs.** Drugs whose coverage was not required included drugs to treat anorexia or weight gain; fertility drugs; drugs used for cosmetic purposes or hair growth; smoking cessation drugs; cough and cold remedies; prescription vitamins and minerals, except for vitamins and fluoride preparations prescribed for pregnant women; non-prescription drugs; drugs for which the manufacturer required, as a condition of sale, that associated tests or monitoring services be purchased exclusively from the manufacturer or its designee; and barbiturates and minor tranquilizers.

Required the HHS secretary to update the list periodically to add or strike classes of drugs determined to be subject to clinical abuse or inappropriate use.

• **Prior authorization.** Permitted states to impose "prior authorization" requirements for certain drugs, under which a state official would have to grant specific permission before a prescribed drug could be dispensed to the patient.

However, beginning July 1, 1991, states were required to have an official available to grant such permission 24 hours per day, and had to ensure that patients had access to a 72-hour emergency supply of a prescribed drug. New drugs could not be subject to prior authorization requirements until after they had been available for six months.

• **Amount of rebates.** In calendar 1991 and 1992, required rebates to be the difference between the average manufacturer price (AMP) and the lower of 12.5 percent or the "best price" at which the manufacturer sold the drug to any other customer except the Department of Veterans Affairs.

The average manufacturer price was defined as the average price paid to the manufacturer in the United States by wholesalers for drugs distributed to retail pharmacies. Rebates did not have to be higher than 25 percent of the AMP in calendar 1991 and

50 percent of the AMP in 1992. In calendar 1993 and thereafter, the rebate was the difference between the AMP and lower of 15 percent of the AMP or the manufacturer's "best price."

• **Single-source drugs.** Rebates for drugs available from only a single source and the original of a drug for which generic copies were available would include an inflation adjustment.

Prior to 1994, the adjustment would be made on a drug-by-drug basis; in 1994 and thereafter, the inflation adjustment would be made on an aggregate basis for each manufacturer's entire product line, weighted for the volume of sales in the state.

• **Multiple-source drugs.** Rebates for generic and over-the-counter drugs would be 10 percent of the AMP in each of calendar 1991 through 1993, and 11 percent of the AMP thereafter.

• **Pricing information.** Required manufacturers, wholesalers, and direct sellers of drugs to provide pricing information, subject to confidentiality restrictions. Violators were subject to fines of up to $100,000 for failure to provide information or for providing false information, and up to $10,000 per day for every day required information was late in being provided.

• **Electronic point-of-sale systems.** Provided for a federal match of 90 percent for each of fiscal 1991 and 1992 to help states create mechanisms to electronically document and manage claims at the point-of-sale.

• **Generics required.** Beginning July 1, 1991, prohibited federal matching payments for the original version of a drug available in generic form if a less expensive copy could have been dispensed.

• **Pharmacy reimbursements.** Prohibited states from reducing payments to pharmacists for dispensing drugs to Medicaid patients for four years.

• **Prospective drug review.** Before any covered drug was dispensed to the patient, required that a review be performed to screen for potential problems caused by drug interactions, contra-indications, potentially serious interactions with non-prescription medications, incorrect dosage or duration of treatment, allergies, and potential misuse or abuse.

• **Retrospective drug review.** Required ongoing review, through a mechanized drug claims processing and information retrieval system, of claims data and other records in order to identify patterns of fraud, abuse, gross overuse, or inappropriate or medically unnecessary care among physicians, pharmacists and patients or associated with specific drugs or classes of drugs.

• **Education programs.** Required states to operate outreach programs to educate physicians and pharmacists on common drug therapy problems with the aim of improving prescribing or dispensing practices.

Child Health

• **Phased-in coverage of children in families with incomes below poverty level.** Beginning July 1, 1991, required states to begin to provide Medicaid coverage to all children born after Sept. 30, 1983, in families with incomes up to 100 percent of the federal poverty level. Thus, by 2002, all children up to age 19 would be covered.

• **Outreach.** Beginning July 1, 1991, required states to receive and process applications from children and pregnant women for Medicaid at locations other than welfare offices. Such alternate locations would have to include hospitals that served large numbers of low-income patients and community and migrant health centers.

• **Continuation of benefits throughout pregnancy and first year of life.** Required states to continue to provide Medicaid coverage for low-income women for at least 60 days after they gave birth, even if they would otherwise lose eligibility because of a change in income. States would also have to continue Medicaid coverage for an infant born to a Medicaid-eligible woman throughout the first year of its life, so long as the infant remained in the mother's household and she would remain eligible if she was still pregnant.

Home- and Community-Based Elderly Care

• **Option to provide services.** Allowed states, at their option, to use Medicaid funds to provide home- and community-care services to Medicaid beneficiaries over age 65 who were "functionally disabled." Defined functionally disabled as meeting one of the following requirements:

1) the person was unable to perform without substantial assistance two of the three daily-living activities of eating, moving about or going to the bathroom;

2) the person had been diagnosed with Alzheimer's disease; and

a) was unable to perform without assistance or supervision at least two of the five activities of bathing, dressing, going to the bathroom, moving about or eating; or

b) required supervision because he or she engaged in inappropriate behavior that posed serious health or safety hazards to himself or herself or others.

• **Types of services.** Services provided could include homemaker/home health aide; chores; personal care; nursing care provided by or under the supervision of a registered nurse; respite care to allow family or other unpaid caregivers time off; training for family members in caring for the patient; adult day health, or certain mental health services.

• **Assessments, care plans.** Before a person could receive services, states would have to perform a comprehensive assessment to determine if the person was functionally disabled. The assessment would have to reviewed and revised at least once a year. Care would have to be provided according to an individualized care plan.

• **Spending limits.** Limited the amount of federal Medicaid funds that could be spent for such services to $40 million in fiscal 1991, $70 million in fiscal 1992, $130 million in fiscal 1993, $160 million in fiscal 1994 and $180 million in fiscal 1995.

Community Living Arrangements for the Mentally Retarded

• **Option to provide services.** Allowed up to eight states, at their option, to use Medicaid funds to provide "community supported living arrangements services" to individuals with mental retardation or a related condition that would permit them to live in the community rather than in an institution.

Eligible states would be selected by the HHS secretary. To be eligible, individuals would have to be otherwise eligible for Medicaid and living with no more than three other individuals receiving services.

• **Types of services.** Specific services provided could include personal assistance, training and rehabilitation needed to help the individual attain increased independence and productivity, 24-hour emergency assistance, assistive technology or adaptive equipment.

• **Spending limits.** Limited the amount of federal Medicaid funds that could be spent for such services to $5 million in fiscal 1991, $10 million in fiscal 1992, $20 million in fiscal 1993, $30 million in fiscal 1994 and $35 million in fiscal 1995.

Miscellaneous

• **Required payment of premiums for group health plans.** Beginning Jan. 1, 1991, required states to pay premiums and other cost-sharing for group health plans for which Medicaid beneficiaries could be eligible if enrollment in the group plan could save Medicaid money.

Required the HHS secretary to issue guidelines to determine cost-effectiveness. Beneficiaries could not be required to pay more for group coverage than if they were receiving only regular Medicaid benefits, and states would have to provide "wraparound" coverage to ensure that beneficiaries remained eligible for the full range of Medicaid-required services.

• **State matching payments.** Extended through Dec. 31, 1991, the moratorium on HHS regulations limiting states' ability to use donated funds to meet their matching requirement under Medicaid. Also provided that states would be able to use provider-specific taxes to help pay the state share of Medicaid costs, with certain restrictions.

• **Minimum qualifications for physicians.** Beginning Jan. 1, 1992, prohibited Medicaid payment to physicians for services provided to pregnant women and children under age 21 unless the physician was board-certified in family practice, pediatrics or obstetrics, had admitting privileges at a Medicaid-participating hospital, was a member of the National Health Service Corps, or had a documented consulting relationship with a certified family practitioner, pediatrician or obstetrician for purposes of providing specialized treatment or hospital admission. Physicians not meeting any of the above requirements could apply to the secretary for special certification.

• **Notice to state medical boards.** Required state Medicaid agencies to notify state licensing boards when a physician was terminated, suspended or sanctioned by Medicaid.

• **Required continuation of health insurance coverage.** The fiscal 1986 budget-reconciliation bill, COBRA (PL 99-272), required that employers with 20 or more workers who provided group health insurance offer continued coverage for up to 18 months for certain former employees as long as the former employee paid the full premium plus 2 percent in administrative costs.

The fiscal 1990 reconciliation bill (PL 101-239) extended coverage to 29 months in certain cases, with the former employee to pay a premium of up to 150 percent of the employer's cost. The provision allowed state Medicaid programs to pay COBRA continuation premiums for people with incomes below 100 percent of the federal poverty level and assets less than twice the limit to qualify for benefits under the Supplemental Security Income program. The provision would apply only to people employed by firms with 75 or more workers, and states would have to determine that anticipated Medicaid savings would be larger than the cost of the premiums.

• **German reparations.** Excluded payments to Holocaust victims made by the Federal Republic of Germany from being counted as income in determining how much income an institutionalized Medicaid beneficiary had to contribute to the cost of his care.

• **Personal care services.** Allowed Minnesota, for fiscal 1991 through 1994, to use Medicaid funds to pay for the provision of personal care services (including helping with basic personal hygiene and administering medications) at home or elsewhere as long as they were prescribed by a physician, provided by a qualified person, and supervised by a registered nurse. Beginning in fiscal 1995, all states were to be given the option of providing such personal care services.

• **Alcohol and drug treatment.** Clarified when states might use Medicaid funds to pay for substance-abuse treatment.

• **Reciprocal billing arrangements.** Specifically allowed payment to a physician who arranged for services to be provided by another physician when the first physician was unavailable on an occasional, reciprocal basis. [This was essentially identical to the Medicare provision, above.]

• **Demonstration projects for low-income families.** Authorized $40 million over three years for up to four states to conduct three-year demonstration projects to test the effect on access to and costs of health care for uninsured families with incomes below 150 percent of poverty who were not otherwise eligible for Medicaid.

• **New Jersey respite care demonstration.** Extended through Sept. 30, 1992, authority for a project in New Jersey that provided "respite" care for people who cared for Medicaid-eligible and other elderly and disabled people.

• **HIV demonstration.** Authorized up to $30 million for three-year demonstration projects in two states to provide regular Medicaid coverage as well as additional services to people who tested positive for HIV, the AIDS virus.

Services in addition to those normally provided by Medicaid would include general and preventive medical care, prescription drugs, counseling and social services, substance abuse treatment, home care, case management, health education, respite care and dental services.

Nursing Home Reform Amendments

[As part of the fiscal 1988 budget-reconciliation bill (PL 100-203), Congress overhauled the way the federal government regulated nursing homes that participated in Medicare and Medicaid. Among other things, the new law required facilities to significantly beef up staffing, to ensure that nurses' aides had been adequately trained, and barred people with mental illnesses or mental retardation from being kept inappropriately in nursing homes. The fiscal 1990 reconciliation bill (PL 101-239) pushed back the deadline for states and facilities to come into compliance with nurse's aide training rules.] The fiscal 1991 reconciliation bill:

• Prohibited the HHS secretary from taking punitive actions against states that had made a good-faith effort to comply with the nurse's aide training requirements before May 12, 1989, the effective date of the HHS guidelines. The secretary was also prohibited from taking action against states that made good-faith efforts to comply with rules relating to preadmission screening of patients and annual resident reviews before May 26, 1989.

• Prohibited from operating their own nurse's aide training programs nursing homes that, within the previous two years, had been subject to certain sanctions, including civil fines of $5,000 or more or having had payment denied by Medicare or Medicaid or residents transferred because of substandard care.

Also prohibited from operating their own training programs were facilities that had operated under a waiver permitting them to have a licensed nurse on duty less often than 24 hours per day, five days per week.

• Extended until Oct. 1, 1990, authority for enhanced federal matching rates (up to 90 percent) to help states pay the cost of training nurses' aides or assessing the competency of those already working in the field. The authority had expired July 1, 1990, when the federal payment was to revert to a flat 50 percent.

• Modified the definition of mental illness to target pre-admission screening rules on patients with serious disorders.

• Extended from four to 14 days the period during which a nursing home would have to complete the initial assessment of a newly admitted resident.

• Clarified conditions under which states could grant nursing homes waivers of the nurse staffing rules, which generally required facilities to have on duty a licensed nurse 24 hours per day, seven days per week. Allowed waivers only to the extent that a facility could not recruit adequate staff and required that notice of any nurse staffing waiver be given to residents, their families and appropriate state agencies.

• Required that results of inspections be made available to the public within 14 days of the time they were made available to the nursing home and that approved plans to correct any deficiencies found would also have to be made available.

• Required the secretary to establish requirements for social workers, dieticians and other "activities" professionals that were at least as strict as those applicable to such professionals before enactment of the nursing home reform law.

Title IV — Medigap

(Congress in 1980 and again in 1988 imposed federal standards for the promotion and sale of so-called Medigap plans; private insurance policies that supplemented Medicare coverage. These provisions built on and expanded those earlier efforts.)

• **Simplification.** Required all Medigap insurers to offer in their policies a core group of benefits. The specific benefits would be determined by the National Association of Insurance Commissioners (NAIC) or, if the association failed to develop such standards within nine months, by the secretary of Health and Human Services (HHS).

Insurers could also sell policies including up to nine other packages of commonly offered benefits in addition to the core package (for a total of 10 different policies) but would have to offer to all individuals purchasing policies the option of buying a policy containing only the core benefits.

New or innovative benefits in addition to the approved packages could be offered but only if they were first approved by the state or the secretary. The secretary would have to review the simplification standards every three years to determine if changes were needed to accommodate new benefits.

The simplification standards would generally apply to new policies (not renewals) sold after the standards had been adopted by the state.

The secretary could waive the simplification requirements for states already operating simplification programs as of the date of enactment (Massachusetts, Minnesota and Wisconsin already had such programs in effect). Violators would be subject to fines of up to $25,000 for each violation.

Required the General Accounting Office to study the effectiveness of the simplification program on consumer protection, health benefit innovation, consumer choice and health-care costs.

• **Uniform policy description.** Required that insurers provide to prospective customers a summary information sheet describing the policy's benefits and premium. To facilitate comparison of policies, the summary information had to be printed on a standardized form. Violators would be subject to fines of up to $25,000 for each violation.

• **Preventing duplication.** Made it illegal to sell any Medigap policy without obtaining a written statement from the prospective purchaser detailing other Medigap policies the person owned and whether he or she was eligible for Medicaid. The form including the statement had to include:

1) a statement to the effect that a Medicare beneficiary did not need more than one Medigap policy;

2) a statement that individuals age 65 or older could be eligible for Medicaid and that Medicaid beneficiaries usually did not need Medigap policies at all, (because Medicaid paid all health costs covered by Medigap policies);

3) the telephone numbers of the state Medicaid office, a new toll-free number to be established by HHS that would provide information regarding Medicare, Medicaid and Medigap insurance;

4) the address and any local telephone number of any state agency providing counseling services for health insurance or the telephone number of the state agency on aging.

Made it illegal to sell or issue a policy to any individual whose statement indicated that they already owned another Medigap policy or were entitled to Medicaid coverage.

It would also be illegal to sell a Medigap policy to a person who already owned another Medigap policy unless the buyer indicated in writing that the new policy would replace the old policy or the seller certified that, to the best of his or her knowledge, the new policy did not duplicate other coverage. In general, it made it illegal to sell Medigap policies to Medicaid beneficiaries. The law included an exception in cases in which the state Medicaid program paid the premium on the policy for the beneficiary.

Sellers of policies who violated the duplication rules would be liable for fines of up to $15,000 per violation, and companies who issued such policies would be liable for fines of up to $25,000 per violation.

• **Suspension of policies while eligible for Medicaid.** Required that at the request of the policyholder, Medigap benefits and premiums be suspended for up to 24 months if the policyholder became eligible for Medicaid. Should Medicaid eligibility be lost, the policy would have to be automatically reinstated.

• **Loss ratios and refund of premium.** Increased to 65 percent from 60 percent the required projected loss ratio (the percentage of each premium dollar returned in benefits) for individual policies, including those sold through the mail or by mass media advertising. The required loss ratio for group policies would remain at 75 percent. Allowed states to require higher loss ratios.

Required companies to submit annually to state regulators (or HHS, in the case of states without an approved program) information on actual loss ratios. To facilitate comparison, the information would have to be compiled using a standardized methodology and be submitted on a standardized form developed by the NAIC.

Companies whose policies failed to meet the required loss ratios would have to provide a proportional refund or a credit against future premiums, including interest, to policyholders to make up the difference between the required and actual loss ratio. Violators would be subject to fines of up to $25,000 for each violation.

Required states to report to HHS annually on Medigap loss ratios of policies sold in the state and the use of sanctions to enforce the requirements. Beginning in 1993, the secretary would have to report to Congress annually regarding loss ratios, use of sanctions and provide a list of policies that failed to meet the loss-ratio requirements.

• **Guaranteed renewability.** Required that Medigap policies be guaranteed renewable and not be canceled solely for reasons of health status or for any other reason except non-payment of premiums or material misrepresentation.

If group policies were canceled by the group and not replaced, required that policyholders be offered individual policies offering equivalent benefits. If a group policy was canceled and replaced by a different group policy, required that the new policy not exclude coverage based on any pre-existing condition that would have been covered under the old policy.

Violators would be subject to fines of up to $25,000 for each violation.

• **Pre-existing condition limitations and limitations on medical underwriting.** Required an "open enrollment" period of six months after a person age 65 or older became eligible for Medicare Part B, during which he or she could purchase any individual Medigap policy sold in the state and could not be turned down or be charged higher premiums because of medical or health status.

Such policies could exclude benefits for the first six months based on pre-existing conditions for which the policyholder was diagnosed or received treatment during the six months immediately before the policy became effective. However, policies that replaced similar policies in effect for at least six months could not impose pre-existing condition restrictions, or waiting, elimination or probationary periods. Violators would be subject to fines of up to $25,000 for each violation.

• **Prior approval of policies/enforcement of standards.** Beginning July 1, 1991, required all Medigap policies to be approved in advance either by the state, if the state had in place a regulatory program approved by HHS, or by HHS in states with no such program. Required the secretary to review periodically state regulatory programs to ensure that they remained in compliance with the required standards.

In order to be approved by HHS, required states to have in place a process to review proposed premium increases, including the holding of public hearings before approval of premium increases.

• **Medicare 'select' policies.** Authorized a three-year demonstration program in up to 15 states in which policies could be sold that otherwise met the requirements except that certain benefits and services would only be available through selected health-care providers.

• **Health insurance information, counseling and assistance grants.** Required HHS to establish a health insurance advisory service program to assist Medicare beneficiaries with the receipt of services related to Medicare, Medicaid and other health insurance programs.

The program would provide information regarding eligibility, benefits, payment processes, rights and appeals processes, linkages between Medicare and Medicaid, and other information.

The program would have to provide information on private insurance plans regarding federal standards, ways to make informed decisions about purchasing such plans and any other information deemed appropriate by the secretary.

Authorized $10 million for each of fiscal 1991, 1992 and 1993 (to be paid from the Medicare Hospital Insurance Trust Fund) for a series of grant programs to help states create and operate information, counseling and assistance programs to help Medicare beneficiaries obtain appropriate health insurance coverage.

• **Medicare and Medigap information by telephone.** Required the secretary to make the program known to those eligible to use it, as well as to set up a toll-free telephone number to provide information and counseling. Also authorized a five-state demonstration project in which statewide toll-free numbers would be set up to provide information regarding Medicare, Medicaid and Medigap policies available in that state.

Title V — Income Security

Child Support Enforcement

• **Extension of IRS intercept.** Bolstered the Internal Revenue Service's (IRS) authority to help custodial parents recover overdue child support payments. Previous law gave the IRS permanent authority to deduct from non-custodial parents' federal tax refunds past-due support for children receiving benefits under the Aid to Families with Dependent Children (AFDC) program. The fiscal 1991 reconciliation bill:

• Made permanent the IRS' authority to intercept tax refunds for children not getting AFDC benefits; and

• Permitted the IRS to intercept refunds to collect overdue payments for non-minor disabled children and payments due to spouses when spousal and child support were included in the same support order.

• **Extension of Interstate Child Support Commission.** Extended through 1992 authority for the Interstate Child Support Commission. The 15-member commission, established under the 1988 Family Support Act (PL 100-485), was to hold one or more national conferences on interstate child support enforcement reform and to submit to Congress recommendations for improving the interstate child support system by May 1, 1991. Because the commission was appointed late, the provision extended that deadline for one year.

• **Texas waiver.** Waived for Texas certain child support enforcement requirements so Bexar County, including San Antonio, could continue an ongoing demonstration project to monitor child support payments. Required the state to study the cost-effectiveness of the project and report to the federal government.

Unemployment Compensation

• **Unemployment compensation — the Reed Act of 1954.** Made permanent the Reed Act, which allowed excess federal unemployment tax revenues in the Unemployment Trust Fund to be used for administrative purposes or benefits by the states. The law was to expire over a three-year period beginning July 1, 1991. Overflows occurred only in 1956, 1957 and 1958. Another surplus was not expected until 1997. The formula by which states would get any overflow funds also was modified so that each state would receive the extra cash based on its share of wages subject to federal unemployment taxes paid in the prior calendar year, instead of the state's total taxable wages.

Supplemental Security Income (SSI)

• **Treatment of victims' compensation payments.** Exempted amounts paid to crime victims from state victim compensation funds from being counted as income in determining SSI eligibility or benefit amounts. Also excluded from estimation of resources for nine months amounts received for expenses incurred or losses suffered as a result of the crime. [Eligibility and benefit amounts for SSI, the federal welfare program for the aged, blind and disabled, were determined by requirements based on both income and resources (savings and other assets).]

• **Treatment of state relocation assistance.** Exempted amounts paid for relocation assistance from being counted as income in determining SSI eligibility or benefit amounts. Such payments would not count toward the resource limit for nine months after being received.

• **Work incentives.** Eliminated several minor disincentives for disabled SSI recipients who wished to work without losing benefits. Permitted disabled SSI recipients to continue to participate in a special work incentive program after they reached age 65 (the existing limit). Expanded situations under which earnings needed to pay for work expenses related to a person's disability were not counted for purposes of reducing benefits. Also treated certain royalties and honoraria as earned income rather than unearned income. Unearned income resulted in a dollar-for-dollar reduction in benefits, while earned income amounts were partly disregarded.

• **Evaluation of child's disability by pediatrician.** Beginning six months after enactment, required the secretary of Health and Human Services (HHS) to make "reasonable efforts" to ensure that a pediatrician or other specialist in a field of medicine appropriate to the disability in question evaluated a child's disability to determine eligibility for SSI.

• **Reimbursement for vocational rehabilitation.** Authorized the secretary to pay for the vocational rehabilitation of SSI recipients in months that they were not actually receiving SSI benefits because they were involved in special programs or were eligible only for state benefits. [Previously, vocational rehabilitation costs could be paid by the federal government only in months in which a person received SSI benefits.]

• **Presumptive eligibility.** Expanded from three to six months the time during which the Social Security Administration could presume eligibility and pay benefits while a blind or disabled prospective SSI beneficiary's application was being processed.

• **Continuing disability and blindness reviews.** Permitted the Social Security Administration to review no more often than once every 12 months whether certain SSI beneficiaries were still blind or disabled

Aid to Families with Dependent Children

• **Treatment of foster care maintenance and adoption assistance payments.** Excluded amounts paid by states or localities for foster care from determination of AFDC eligibility or payments. Also excluded federal, state or local adoption assistance payments.

• **Temporary assistance.** Repealed, for fiscal 1990 and 1991 only, the $1 million limit on the amount of emergency assistance HHS could provide to U.S. citizens and their dependents who had returned or been returned to the United States because of destitution, illness, war, threat of war, invasion or similar crisis. Also permitted HHS to receive gifts from private entities to assist with repatriation costs.

• **National Commission on Children.** Clarified that the final reporting date for the National Commission on Children was March 31, 1991.

• **Moratorium on emergency assistance regulations.** Prohibited HHS, through Oct. 1, 1991, from issuing final regulations altering the AFDC emergency assistance program. Emergency assistance was an optional state program that permitted payments to needy families with children (who might or might not otherwise be eligible for AFDC) to prevent a child from becoming destitute or to provide living arrangements.

Child Welfare and Foster Care

• **Administrative costs.** Specifically included "child placement" activities among those for which states were entitled to receive federal reimbursement.

• **Bar on payment reductions.** Continued, through Oct. 1, 1991, the ban on HHS reducing payments to states or seeking repayments from states because they failed to meet certain standards regarding child welfare provisions included in the Adoption Assistance and Child Welfare Amendments of 1980 (PL 96-272).

• **Independent Living Program changes.** Permitted states, at their option, to provide services under the Foster Care Independent Living program to youths up to age 21, instead of the existing cutoff of 18. The program sought to help youths in foster care, beginning at age 16, make the transition to living independently.

Title V — Social Security

• **Continuation of disability benefits during appeal.** Made permanent the option of recipients of Disability Insurance benefits who were found to be no longer disabled to continue to receive benefits during the appeals process. In certain cases in which the appeal failed, the money might have to be returned.

• **Definition of disability for disabled widows or widowers.** Made the definition of disability the same for widows or widowers of workers covered by Social Security as for workers and applicants for benefits under the Supplemental Security Income program (SSI). Previously, widows or widowers of a worker covered by Social Security were subject to a definition of disability stricter than that for covered workers or SSI applicants.

• **Survivors' benefits for adopted children.** Beginning with applications filed on or after Jan. 1, 1991, made eligible for Social Security survivors' benefits a child adopted by the surviving spouse of a deceased worker so long as the child had either lived with the worker or received one-half support from the worker in the year preceding the worker's death.

• **Representative payee reforms.** Made several alterations in the program under which Social Security or SSI checks were paid to a relative or other person, known as a "representative payee," in cases in which the beneficiary was unable to handle his or her finances. The new provisions:

• Required a more extensive investigation of representative payee applicants, including requiring applicants to submit documented proof of identity.

• Required the compilation of a list of payees found to have misused benefit payments.

• Restricted categories of persons who could serve as representative payees.

• Provided for appeals processes for persons for whom the Department of Health and Human Services (HHS) determined a representative payee was needed.

• Permitted, for three years only, certain community-based social service agencies that served as representative payees for five or more beneficiaries to collect monthly fees for such services. The fee, deducted from the beneficiary's Social Security or SSI check, could not exceed 10 percent of the check or $25.

• **Attorneys' fees.** Streamlined the system under which attorneys representing Social Security beneficiaries in Social Security Administration (SSA) proceedings were paid. For cases in which an application for past-due benefits was approved, the agency would generally approve any petition, signed by both the attorney and client, for an agreed-upon fee not to exceed the lower of 25 percent of the back payments or $4,000. The HHS secretary would be permitted to adjust the maximum figure periodically for inflation. The administrative law judge who decided the case could protest the agreed-upon fee if he or she determined that it was excessive in light of the services rendered.

• **Beneficiary protections based on faulty information provided by the SSA.** Provided that, if a person who was denied benefits reapplied rather than appealed the denial based on incorrect, incomplete, or misleading information provided by the SSA, the failure to appeal would not constitute a basis for denial of the second application. [Information provided by SSA prior to May 1989 neglected to inform those whose applications for benefits were denied that reapplying rather than appealing the adverse ruling could result in the denial of the claim without further review of the evidence.]

• **SSA telephone service.** Required the secretary to re-establish as soon as possible but at the latest within 180 days telephone service to local SSA offices, which was cut off in October 1989, when all calls made to the agency's 800 number began to be routed to one of 37 SSA teleservice centers around the country. The General Accounting Office would have to report within 120 days on the level of telephone access to local offices. Also required the secretary to carry out demonstration projects to test the accountability procedures in three of the teleservice centers. Under the projects, certain callers would have to be provided with written documentation of their phone call, including the name of the SSA employee, a description of any action that the employee said would be taken and of any advice that was given.

• **Earnings and benefit statements.** Required, beginning Oct. 1, 1999, that all workers covered by Social Security be sent an annual statement of earnings credited to their account as well as potential benefits payable upon retirement. The fiscal 1990 reconciliation bill required such statements to be sent only once every two years.

• **Trial work period for disabled beneficiaries.** Made it easier for disabled beneficiaries to test their ability to return to work without threat of losing their disability benefits. Previously, beneficiaries were permitted only a single nine-month trial work period in which earnings were not counted toward elimination or reduction of benefits. The bill required that beneficiaries be allowed to work on a trial basis until a total of nine months had been worked over any five-year period.

• **Elimination of advance tax transfer.** Repealed a provision of the 1983 Social Security overhaul bill (PL 98-21) requiring that estimated Social Security payroll tax receipts be credited to the Social Security trust fund in advance each month based on the estimated amount of taxes due that month. The provision returned to the method under which tax funds were credited to the trust fund only as they were received, although it retained authority for the secretary of the Treasury to use the advance tax transfer mechanism if he determined it was needed for Social Security to meet its payment obligations to beneficiaries.

• **Repeal of retroactive benefits for certain beneficiaries.** Eliminated eligibility for six months of retroactive benefits for certain categories of beneficiaries under age 65. [The provision, which would save an estimated $700 million over five years, would also relieve significant administrative burdens on the SSA.]

• **Dependent benefits for disabled workers.** Codified the SSA practice of suspending payment of benefits to dependents of disabled workers in months when the worker was still eligible but did not receive benefits because earnings were too high.

• **Payment of benefits to 'deemed' spouses.** Beginning Jan. 1, 1991, permitted benefits to be paid to both a legal spouse and a "deemed" spouse. "Deemed" partners were those later found not to have been legally married because of some defect in the marriage ceremony or because the spouse was not legally divorced from a previous spouse.

Previously, deemed spouses could not receive benefits at the same time benefits were paid to a legal spouse.

• **Vocational rehabilitation demonstrations.** Required the HHS secretary to establish demonstration programs permitting disabled beneficiaries to select their own vocational rehabilitation programs. Previously, disabled beneficiaries were automatically referred to state-run rehabilitation agencies.

• **Use of Social Security number by illegal aliens granted amnesty.** Exempted from prosecution for fraudulent use of Social Security numbers or cards illegal aliens granted amnesty under the 1986 Immigration Reform and Control Act. The exemption did not apply to individuals who sold Social Security cards, possessed cards with intent to sell them, or counterfeited or possessed counterfeit cards with intent to sell.

• **Special minimum benefit.** Reduced the amount of wages needed to earn a year of coverage toward Social Security's special minimum benefit paid to those who worked many years at low wages.

Instead of having earnings equal to 25 percent of the "old law" contribution and benefit base [$9,900 in 1991], workers would have to earn 15 percent of that amount [$5,940 in 1991].

• **Collection of employee Social Security tax on group life insurance.** Beginning Jan. 1, 1991, required former employees who continued to receive taxable group-life insurance benefits from their former employers to pay with their personal taxes the amount of Social Security tax due on the life insurance benefits they received.

• **Waiver of waiting period for certain divorced spouses.** Beginning Jan. 1, 1991, waived the two-year waiting period during which a divorced spouse was ineligible for spousal benefits if the worker in question was already receiving benefits before the divorce. [The purpose of the two-year waiting period was to prevent couples from divorcing to allow the worker's spouse to obtain benefits even though the worker would not be eligible because he or she was still working.]

• **Social Security Administration review of favorable disability determinations.** Lowered from 65 to 50 the percentage of cases that SSA had to review after a state agency judged a person to be disabled and thus eligible for disability benefits. SSA would also have to review as many cases in which a state agency certified that a beneficiary was still disabled as were necessary to maintain a high level of accuracy in such decisions. Formerly the agency was required to review 65 percent of those cases, as well.

• **Recovery of overpayments from former Social Security beneficiaries.** Beginning Jan. 1, 1991, permitted SSA to recover overpayments of benefits from former beneficiaries by arranging with the Internal Revenue Service to deduct any amount owed from any federal tax refund due.

• **Railroad retirement Tier 2 fund.** Required that proceeds from income taxes on railroad retiree Tier 2 benefits continue to go into the Railroad Retirement Account for two more years, rather than into the general fund as previously scheduled for Oct. 1, 1990. The extension was estimated to give an additional $385 million to the railroad account.

Title V — Child Care

Tax Credits

The following changes in tax law were the compromise version of changes included in omnibus child-care bills (HR 3, S 5) passed by the House and the Senate in the 101st Congress. The tax credit increases for low-income working families, along with other unrelated tax changes included to offset the cost of the new benefits, were included both here and under the revenue section.

• **Earned-Income Tax Credit (EITC).** Increased the refundable credit allowed low-income working families with children, from what had been a projected maximum of $994 in 1991 to $1,186 for those with one qualifying child and $1,228 for those with two or more qualifying children. For 1990, the credit was 14 percent of the first $6,810 of earned income, and was phased out at a rate of 10 percent of the amount of adjusted gross income or earned income, whichever was greater, that exceeded $10,730. The base income amount and the point at which the phaseout began were adjusted annually for inflation.

The law increased the credit for taxpayers with one qualifying child to 16.7 percent in 1991, 17.6 percent in 1992, 18.5 percent in

1993 and 23 percent in 1994 and after. The phaseout rate for such families was 11.93 percent in 1991, 12.57 percent in 1992, 13.21 percent in 1993 and 16.43 percent in 1994 and after.

The credit for those with two or more qualifying children was 17.3 percent in 1991, 18.4 percent in 1992, 19.5 percent in 1993 and 25 percent in 1994 and after. The phaseout rate for such families was 12.36 percent in 1991, 13.14 percent in 1992, 13.93 percent in 1993 and 17.86 percent in 1994 and after.

The law also stiffened and clarified eligibility requirements for the EITC.

- **Supplemental young child credit.** Provided an additional 5 percent credit, with an increase in the phaseout rate of 3.57 percent, for those with qualifying children under the age of 1. The maximum supplemental credit was expected to be $355 in 1991. Any child for whom the credit was claimed was not considered a qualifying child for the separate dependent-care tax credit.
- **Supplemental EITC for health insurance.** Allowed an additional credit for premiums paid on health insurance coverage for one or more qualified children. The credit was calculated in a way similar to that used for the EITC, except that the credit percentage was 6 percent and the phaseout rate was 4.285 percent. The maximum credit for 1991 was projected to be $426, although the credit could not exceed the amount paid in health insurance premiums. A taxpayer's medical expenses deduction would also be limited by the amount of any credit claimed.
- **EITC and means-tested programs.** Provided that the EITC and supplemental credits not be considered income or a resource (in the month of receipt or the following month) in determining eligibility for Aid to Families with Dependent Children (AFDC), Supplemental Security Income, Medicaid, food stamps and certain housing programs.
- **Study of advance payments.** Required the comptroller general, with the secretary of the Treasury, to conduct a study of the existing system that allowed those eligible for the EITC to request advance payment of the credit. The study was aimed at finding ways to improve the administration of the advance payment system and learning why participation was low. The study had to be submitted to the House Ways and Means and Senate Finance committees within a year of enactment.
- **Public awareness program.** Required the secretary of the Treasury to establish a program in 1991 to increase taxpayer awareness of the earned income, dependent care and health insurance credits.
- **Taxpayer identification number.** Required taxpayers to provide a taxpayer identification number for any dependent age 1 or older.

Grants to States Under Title IV of Social Security Act

- **Expansion of Title IV child-care program.** The 1988 Family Support Act (PL 100-485) created an open-ended entitlement to help states pay the cost of child care for children of welfare recipients participating in education or training activities aimed at getting them off the welfare rolls. Under the program created in the 1988 act, states were required to "match" child-care funds at the same rate they were required to match costs for Medicaid, the joint federal-state health plan for the poor (ranging from about 20 percent up to 50 percent).

The new provision authorized an additional $300 million for each of fiscal 1991 through 1995 that states could use to help pay child-care costs for low-income families not receiving welfare who needed such care in order to work or who would otherwise be at risk of becoming dependent on welfare.

The new funding would be a "capped entitlement," meaning that the amount would not be subject to the annual appropriations process, but states would be able to claim only their allotted share of the $300 million, which would be based on the number of eligible children in each state.

- **Provision of services.** Permitted states to provide child-care services directly, by paying providers directly, by providing cash or vouchers to the family in advance, by reimbursing the family, or any other arrangement the state agency deemed appropriate.
- **Family contribution.** Required families to contribute to the cost of the child care according to a sliding fee schedule to be established by the state based on ability to pay. Stipulated that the value of the care received by the family not be treated as income for purposes of determining eligibility for other federal or federally assisted needs-based programs. However, the family may not claim costs paid by the state as work-related expenses for the purpose of claiming the dependent-care tax credit.
- **Provider requirements.** To be eligible for federal funds, child-care providers (except for those providing care exclusively to members of their own family) had to be licensed, regulated or registered with the state, and permit parents unlimited access to their children.
- **State reports.** Beginning with fiscal 1993, required states to submit to the federal government an annual report on activities carried out with the federal funds. The report would have to detail how much was spent for various types of child care (center-based care, group-home, family care, and relative care), the number of children who received care, as well as the average cost of such care. Reports could also have to provide the criteria used to determine eligibility or priority, the state's child-care regulation requirements, and any enforcement policies in effect.
- **Grants to states to improve child-care standards.** Reauthorized, at $50 million for each of fiscal 1992 through 1994, a provision of the Family Support Act authorizing grants to states to improve child-care licensing and registration requirements for child care and to monitor care provided to AFDC children. Required that half the funds be used only for training child-care providers, with the remainder to be used for improving licensing and registration requirements and procedures, and for enforcement. Stipulated that activities applied to all children receiving services under Title IV-A of the Social Security Act, not just children receiving welfare. (Non-welfare children receiving Title IV-A services could include those for whom the state agency was pursuing collection of child support or who were receiving child-care grants, above).

Child-Care and Development Block Grant

- **Authorization.** Authorized $750 million in fiscal 1991, $825 million in fiscal 1992, $925 million in fiscal 1993 and "such sums as may be necessary" in fiscal 1994 and 1995 for new grants to states to help improve the quality, availability and affordability of child-care services.
- **State application and plan.** In order to receive funds, required states to designate a lead agency whose job it would be to coordinate the program with other federal, state and local child-care programs and to develop a plan to carry out the requirements of the act.
- **Use of funds.** Permitted states to use grants funds to provide child-care services as well as for activities designed to improve the availability and quality of child care.

Funds would be distributed according to a formula based on the number of children in the state under age 5 and the number of children eligible for free or reduced-price school lunches. One-half of 1 percent of appropriated funds would be reserved for payments to Guam, American Samoa, the Virgin Islands of the United States, the Commonwealth of the Northern Mariana Islands and the Trust Territory of the Pacific Islands. Another 3 percent of funds would be reserved for payments to Indian tribes and tribal organizations.

States could use up to 75 percent of grant funds to pay for care for eligible children, defined as those under age 13 in families in which a parent or parents worked or attended school or job training activities, and with a family income that did not exceed 75 percent of the state median income for a family of that size. In providing services, states would have to give priority to children with special needs or who came from families with very low incomes, and costs for such services would have to be shared by families according to a sliding scale based on ability to pay.

States would be required to reserve at least 25 percent of their grant funds for activities designed to improve the quality of child care and increase the availability of early childhood development and before- and after-school child-care programs.

- **Parental choice of providers.** Required states to assure that the parents of children receiving assistance under the act, to the maximum extent practicable, be able to use the child-care provider of their choice. That included the ability of parents to receive aid in the form of a child-care certificate, or voucher, that could be used to purchase sectarian (religious) child-care services. States, however, would not have to put child-care certificate programs into effect until Oct. 1, 1992.

• **Unlimited parental access.** Required states to assure that all child-care providers receiving aid under the act afford parents unlimited access to their children while the children were in the care of the providers.

• **Parental complaints.** Required states to maintain a record of substantiated parental complaints and make such information available to the public upon request.

• **Consumer education.** Required states to make available to parents and the general public information regarding licensing and regulatory requirements, complaint procedures, and other policies and practices related to child-care services in the states.

• **Compliance with state and local requirements.** Required that all child-care providers receiving grant funds comply with all applicable state and local licensing or regulatory requirements (including registration requirements). Further required that providers who were not bound by state or local law to be licensed or regulated nevertheless would have to be registered with the state before receiving payment. Stipulated that the language not be construed to bar a state from imposing more stringent standards.

• **Health and safety requirements.** Required, at the state or local level, standards to protect the health and safety of children in care provided with funds under the act. Such standards had to cover: prevention and control of infectious diseases (including immunization requirements); safety of buildings and physical premises; and minimum health and safety training appropriate to the type of provider setting (i.e., child-care centers, group-care homes). States had to have in effect procedures to enforce such standards and could only reduce existing standards after informing the secretary of Health and Human Services (HHS) of the need for a reduction.

• **Bar on substitution.** Required that states use federal grant funds only to supplement, not supplant, other federal, state and local child-care funds.

• **Payment rates.** Required states to pay rates sufficient to ensure that families receiving assistance have equal access to child-care services comparable to those available to families in the same area not receiving federal or state aid. Stipulated that the language not create a private right of action to sue on grounds that payments were not adequate.

• **Construction of facilities.** Prohibited the use of federal funds to purchase or improve land or to purchase, construct or permanently improve (except for minor remodeling) any building or facility. The same prohibitions applied to sectarian organizations, except that they could use funds for renovations or repairs only to the extent that such changes were needed to bring the facility into compliance with state or local health and safety requirements.

• **Quality improvement activities.** Of the 25 percent of funds that states were required to reserve for quality improvement and program expansion, required that states spend at least 20 percent on one or more of the following activities:

1) supporting the creation or operation of resource and referral programs to help parents locate appropriate child care;

2) making grants or loans to child-care providers to help them make improvements needed to comply with state or local child-care standards;

3) improving enforcement of applicable standards;

4) providing training or technical assistance for child-care providers in areas such as health and safety, nutrition, first aid, recognizing communicable diseases, preventing and detecting child abuse, and caring for children with special needs; and

5) improving salaries and/or benefits for full- and part-time staff members who provided child care with federal funds.

• **Early childhood development and before- and after-school programs.** Of the 25 percent of funds that states had to reserve for quality improvement and program expansion, required that states spend at least 75 percent to establish or operate early childhood development or before- and after-school child-care programs. Funds had to be provided through grants or contracts rather than by use of vouchers.

Early childhood-development programs would have to consist of services to provide "an environment that enhances the educational, social, cultural, emotional and recreational development of children."

Before- and after-school programs had to be provided Monday through Friday, including school (but not public) holidays and would have to provide services that were not intended to replace any regular academic program. States had to give priority for such programs to areas of the state eligible for "concentration grants" under the Chapter 1 program (which provided compensatory education services for educationally disadvantaged children), areas with concentrations of poverty, and areas with very high or very low population densities.

• **HHS activities.** Required the secretary to coordinate child-care activities both within HHS and, to the maximum extent practicable, between HHS and other federal agencies. The secretary was required also to collect, publish and make available to the public, at least once every three years, a listing of state child-care standards, and would have to provide states with technical assistance to help carry out requirements of the act.

The secretary was also charged with monitoring compliance by the states with the requirements and was authorized to terminate payments to any state found to have failed to "comply substantially" with any of the requirements. The secretary was also authorized to impose additional sanctions, including seeking repayment of funds found to have been used in violation of the act.

• **State annual reports.** Beginning Dec. 31, 1992, and annually thereafter, required states to submit to HHS an annual report detailing how the grant funds were being spent. The report had to provide available data on how the state's child-care needs were being filled, including:

1) the number of children receiving federal assistance;

2) the types and numbers of child-care programs in the state;

3) salaries and other compensation paid to child-care providers;

4) activities to encourage public-private partnerships to promote business involvement in meeting child-care needs.

The report also had to detail:

1) the extent to which affordability and availability of child-care services in the state had increased;

2) if applicable, the findings of the review of state licensing and regulatory requirements and policies or any reduction of those requirements; and

3) a description of the standards and health and safety requirements applicable to child-care providers in the state, including any state efforts to improve the quality of child care.

• **Federal annual reports.** Beginning July 31, 1993, and annually thereafter, required the secretary to submit to the House Education and Labor and Senate Labor and Human Resources committees a report summarizing and analyzing the state reports. The secretary's report also had to include an assessment of, and any recommendations concerning, efforts needed to improve the public's access to quality, affordable child-care services.

• **Limitations on use of federal funds for religious child-care programs.** Stipulated that funds provided under the act not be used "for any sectarian purpose or activity, including sectarian worship and instruction," except for care paid through use of a voucher or certificate.

• **Limitations on use of federal funds for tuition.** Stipulated that funds provided under the act could not be used to provide:

1) any service to students in grades 1 through 12 provided during the regular school day;

2) any service for which students received academic credit toward graduation; or

3) any instructional services that supplanted or duplicated the academic program of any public or private school.

• **Religious discrimination.** Provided that nothing in the act be construed to modify or affect the provisions of any other federal law or regulation relating to discrimination in employment on the basis of religion, "except that a sectarian organization may require that employees adhere to the religious tenets and teachings of such organization . . . and may require that employees adhere to rules forbidding the use of drugs or alcohol."

Generally barred discrimination in hiring on the basis of religion for workers whose primary responsibility would be working directly with children in the provision of care services but permitted preference between two or more qualified applicants to a person already participating on a regular basis in other activities of the organization.

Generally prohibited discrimination against children on the basis of religion in providing child-care services, except permitted preference in admitting children for slots not funded under the act to those whose family members participated on a regular basis in other activities of the organization.

Notwithstanding the provisions of the two paragraphs above, generally prohibited discrimination in hiring or admissions in any child-care program whose operating budget was 80 percent or more funded with federal or state money.

Further stipulated that none of the requirements were intended to modify or supersede any provision of a state constitution or state law barring use of public funds in or by sectarian institutions, "except that no provision of a state constitution or state law shall be construed to prohibit the expenditure in or by sectarian institutions of any federal funds provided" under the act. (This provision was intended to preserve the ability to use federal funds to pay for sectarian care even if state law barred it.)

• **Severability.** Provided that if any provision of the act was held invalid, other provisions would not be affected.

• **Parental rights and responsibilities.** Stipulated that nothing in the act "be construed or applied in any manner to infringe on or usurp the moral and legal rights and responsibilities of parents or legal guardians."

Title VI — Energy, Environment

Abandoned-Mine Reclamation Fund

• **Reauthorization.** Extended the collection of fees from the coal industry through fiscal 1995. First imposed under a 1977 law (PL 95-87) to finance the restoration and cleanup — or "reclamation" — of abandoned coal mining lands, the fees had been scheduled to expire in August 1992. Extending them would raise an additional $832 million, bringing the total collected under the 1977 law to more than $4 billion.

• **Abandoned mines — grant formula.** Revamped the grant formula under which money from the fund was allocated to coal-producing states to run cleanup programs. The new formula would continue sending states with federally approved reclamation programs 50 percent of the funds collected within their borders (not counting some Indian lands, which were dealt with separately).

The distribution of the remaining money, however, was no longer left completely up to the Interior secretary. Twenty percent had to go to the Agriculture Department to fund an existing rural abandoned-mine program. Forty percent had to be set aside for supplemental grants for high-priority health and safety projects in a way that assured that much of that money go to heavily damaged areas in Appalachian and Midwestern states.

The rest of the money would continue to be used by the secretary for emergencies, for cleanup activities in states that did not have approved programs and for administrative costs.

• **High-priority mines.** Allowed money from the fund to be used to clean up high-priority mines that were active after 1977 if there were not enough reclamation funds available from other sources. The 1977 law prohibited the use of funds to clean up mines abandoned after enactment, but some mining operations and their bonding companies had gone bankrupt, creating a new generation of abandoned mines.

• **Acidic water seepage.** Authorized states to set up programs, financed by money from the fund, to halt and mitigate damage caused by acidic water seeping from abandoned mines. Such deposits harmed water quality and other biological resources.

• **Water treatment facilities.** Allowed states to use money to protect, repair, replace, construct or enhance water supply and treatment facilities to replace water supplies adversely affected by past coal mining.

• **Other cleanup projects.** Continued to allow states that had completed all priority coal mine reclamation projects to use money from the fund to clean up after other mineral mining operations, and to protect, repair, replace, construct or improve water-supply utilities, roads and other facilities adversely affected by mining operations.

• **Reclamation fund surpluses.** Required the Treasury to invest surplus money from the fund in public-debt securities and credit the earned interest back to the fund.

• **Coal producer audits.** Gave the Interior secretary expanded authority to audit coal producers to ensure full payment of fees.

Coastal Zone Management Act (CZMA)

• **General.** Expanded, revamped and reauthorized for five years the 1972 law (PL 92-583) providing federal grants to states to encourage them to draft plans for protecting their shore areas from the adverse impacts of development.

• **CZMA program authorization.** Authorized appropriations for five years at continually increased levels, totaling $58.75 million in fiscal 1991 and $119.24 million in fiscal 1995.

• **Consistency provision.** Bolstered the so-called consistency provision by overturning a 1984 Supreme Court decision in *Secretary of the Interior v. California*. The original provision was meant to assure states that federal coastline activities would be consistent with federally approved plans. But the court ruled that federal outer continental shelf oil and gas-drilling lease sales were not covered by the provision because they had no "direct" affect on state-controlled coastal zones, which did not extend into shelf areas.

The new provision declared that all federal agency activities, whether in or outside of the coastal zone, were subject to the consistency requirement. The president could grant a waiver if he found that a specific activity was "in the paramount interest of the United States."

• **Coastal cleanup loans.** Repealed the Coastal Energy Impact Program, which until 1983 gave states loans to help them mitigate the impact of offshore oil and gas drilling and other energy-related activities. Loan repayments (averaging more than $6 million a year) would now go to a new, more limited Coastal Zone Management Fund, from which the Commerce secretary would fund the program's administrative costs, special projects, emergency assistance, grants to help states develop plans and other discretionary activities.

• **Coastal enhancement grants.** Enticed states with new Coastal Zone Enhancement Grants to improve their plans in one or more of eight areas: coastal wetlands protection; natural hazards management (including potential sea and Great Lakes level rise); public access improvements; reduction of marine debris; coastal growth and development impact assessments; special area management planning for important coastal areas; ocean resource planning; and siting of coastal energy and government facilities.

• **Achievement awards.** Authorized the Commerce secretary to make annual "Walter B. Jones" achievement awards of up to $5,000 each to recognize individuals and local governments for outstanding accomplishments in the field of coastal zone management. Rep. Jones, D-N.C., was the chairman of the House Merchant Marine and Fisheries Committee.

• **Coastal pollution control.** Established a Coastal Non-Point Pollution Control program, requiring shoreline states to develop plans for protecting their waters from non-point-source pollution from nearby land uses. States would get new grants to help them develop their programs, but the government would withhold parts of their CZMA and Water Pollution Control Act grants starting in 1996 if they failed to submit "approvable" non-point-pollution plans.

• **Coastal non-point-pollution guidelines.** Required the Environmental Protection Agency to establish uniform national guidelines for controlling non-point-source pollution to coastal waters. States were required to follow these guidelines in developing their plans.

Environmental Protection Agency

• **Agency fees.** Imposed additional fees totaling $28 million in fiscal 1991 and $38 million a year in fiscal 1992-95 on entities regulated or serviced by the Environmental Protection Agency (EPA).

The provision left most of the specifics to the EPA, but it limited new fees charged under the Water Pollution Control Act to $10 million a year.

It also prohibited the EPA from increasing fees for programs under the jurisdiction of the House Energy and Commerce Committee with two exceptions — fees specifically authorized by the 1990 Clean Air Act amendments and fees collected under the Toxic Substances Control Act that were in effect on the date of enactment of the reconciliation bill.

Revenues from the new fees had to be deposited in a special account in the Treasury and, subject to appropriations bills, used for the services for which they were charged.

• **Pollution prevention.** Created a new $16 million-a-year EPA program aimed at preventing pollution "at the source" by changing production methods in ways that reduced waste.

Called the Pollution Prevention Act of 1990 and authorized in fiscal 1991-93, the provisions were similar to those in three other bills that had been working their way toward enactment (S 585 — S Rept 101-526, approved by voice vote Oct. 4 by the Senate Environment Committee; HR 5931, approved by voice vote by the House on Oct. 27; and HR 1457 — H Rept 101-555, approved by voice vote by the House on June 25).

The law required the EPA to develop and implement a strategy to promote pollution source reduction; set up a new office to carry out the program; and make matching grants to states to encourage them to create their own source-reduction programs.

The EPA was also required to offer technical assistance to businesses on the subject, including funding for experts; improve public access to source-reduction data collected by the federal government and open a computerized Source Reduction Clearinghouse for that purpose; establish a technical advisory panel on pollution source reduction; create a training program and publish guidance documents on the subject; and give annual awards to companies with outstanding pollution source-reduction programs.

In addition, certain businesses that used toxic chemicals were required to file reports with the government disclosing the level of chemicals they released into the environment; the level recycled; the type of source-reduction techniques they used; and where they learned of such practices.

The EPA was required to issue reports on the new program and detailed analyses of the newly collected data every two years, including an assessment of whether the program was effective and whether the data was useful and valid.

Other

• **Superfund extension.** Extended superfund program authorization for three years, from Sept. 30, 1991, when it was set to expire, to Sept. 30, 1994.

• **Nuclear Regulatory Commission.** Increased NRC user fees to raise an extra $287 million in fiscal 1991 and $1.554 billion through fiscal 1995. The bill accomplished this by requiring the agency to impose fees on its licensees to recover 100 percent of its budget, up from 45 percent in fiscal 1988-90. Without congressional action, the percentage requirement would have reverted to 33 percent, the floor established by the 1985 reconciliation bill (PL 99-272). The same held true for fiscal 1996: Without further action, the 100 percent figure would have reverted to 33 percent.

Title VII — Civil Service, Post Office

• **Lump-sum benefits.** Suspended lump-sum benefits for retirees for five years. Workers retiring on or before Nov. 30, 1990, or after Sept. 30, 1995, were not affected. Employees "involuntarily separated" from their jobs continued to receive a 50/50 lump-sum benefit. Critically ill employees continued to be eligible for lump-sum benefits. Federal workers employed because of Operation Desert Shield would be required to wait an additional year to be eligible for the lump-sum payment. Workers entitled to the 50/50 lump-sum payments would receive payments in two calendar years.

• **Federal employees health benefits.** Required carriers of the Federal Employees Health Benefits Program (FEHBP) to implement cost-containment measures. It exempted the FEHBP from state premium taxes. It required better coordination between the Office of Personnel Management and the Department of Health and Human Services to ensure correct Medicare payments and limits. The bill also required cash-management controls in administering payments from the Employees Health Benefits Fund.

• **Postal Service Federal Employees Health Benefits Program liability.** Required the Postal Service to pay premiums for postal employees and survivors of postal workers who retired after June 30, 1971.

• **Cost of living adjustments.** Required the Postal Service to fund Civil Service Retirement Systems cost of living adjustments (prorated) for postal retirees and survivors of retirees who retired after reorganization of the Postal Service in 1971. Before fiscal 1991, the adjustments were funded by the federal government.

• **Non-appropriated fund employees.** Contained text of a bill (HR 3139) that passed the House on Oct. 1. It allowed nearly 200,000 non-appropriated fund (NAF) employees at the Defense Department to change work classifications (for example, from NAF to civil service positions) without a loss in pay, benefits, sick leave, etc.

Title VIII — Veterans' Programs

• **Compensation benefits for incompetent veterans.** Suspended compensation for incompetent veterans with no dependents (spouse, child or parent), whose estate (excluding their home) exceeded $25,000, until the estate was reduced to $10,000. If the veteran regained competence for more than 90 days, he or she would receive the money withheld in a lump-sum payment. The measure was expected to save $125 million in fiscal year 1991 and a total savings of $291 million through fiscal 1995.

• **Elimination of presumption of total disability.** Eliminated the presumption of total and permanent disability for veterans 65 or older, and references to age on the presumption for veterans who became unemployable. Under existing law, after age 65, veterans who became unemployable were considered permanently and totally disabled. A veteran who became unemployable at any age as a result of a disability expected to continue throughout his or her life would be considered permanently disabled for purposes of pension eligibility. The provision was expected to save $17 million in fiscal 1991 and $313 million in fiscal years 1991-95.

• **Reduced pensions for veterans receiving Medicaid-covered nursing home care.** Limited monthly pension payments to $90 for some Medicaid-eligible recipients of a Veterans Affairs (VA) pension and prohibited any portion of the $90 from being spent on a veteran's nursing home care. Those in state veterans' homes were exempt. The provision was set to take effect the month after enactment and expire Sept. 30, 1992. Veterans would not be liable for overpayment unless they "willfully concealed" information that would lead to a pension reduction.

• **Ineligibility of remarried spouses and married children for reinstatement.** Stipulated that remarried spouses of veterans would no longer be able to reinstate their veterans' benefits if the marriage ended in annulment, divorce or death. Under existing law, veterans' spouses who remarried could reinstate veterans' benefits from their spouses if the marriage ended. The provision also applied to married children of veterans.

• **Policy on cost of living adjustment (COLA) increases.** Set at 5.4 percent the fiscal 1991 COLA for compensation of veterans with service-connected disabilities and the survivors of veterans who died as a result of such injuries. The figure was based on the COLA for Social Security benefits. The increase that would have been received during December 1990 would be paid at the same time as compensation and DIC payments for January.

However, because Congress did not pass a bill authorizing the payment of a COLA, a COLA bill had to be enacted before the percentage policy could take effect.

• **Health-care benefits (third-party insurers).** Authorized the VA to collect from a third-party payer under a health-plan contract the "reasonable" cost of a non-service-connected injury to a veteran with a service-connected disability. The authority to make these collections was to expire Oct. 1, 1993.

• **Establishment of** Medical Recoveries Fund. Required that funds collected from third-party insurers be credited to a new Medical Recoveries Fund. Existing law required the money to be deposited into the Treasury as miscellaneous receipts. The VA secretary could use the money for expenses for the identification, billing and collection from third-party insurers.

• **Medication copayments.** Required a veteran to pay $2 for each 30-day supply of a medication provided on an outpatient basis. (Veterans with a service-connected disability rated 50 percent or more would be exempt.) The money collected would be credited to the new Medical Recoveries Fund. The provision applied to medications received from Oct. 31, 1990 through Sept. 30, 1991. Copayments were not required for medical supplies.

• **Health-care categories.** Changed health-care categories for determining a veteran's eligibility for hospital and nursing home care. The three existing categories (A, B and C according to income) were decreased to two: veterans who were required to pay a copayment and those who were not.

• **Copayment requirements.** Required all veterans not entitled to care to pay the copayments for inpatient and nursing home care. Copayments would be: $10 per day for hospital care, $5 per day for nursing home care and the existing copayment for outpatient visits, which was an amount equal to 20 percent of the estimated cost of a VA outpatient visit. Copayments would also be linked to Consumer Price Index increases.

• **Annual copayment caps.** Deleted existing caps on the amount veterans could pay in copayments. Required existing copayments for hospital care and other health care to be paid by non-entitled veterans in addition to the copayments for care per day.

• **Education and employment.** Limited the vocational rehabilitation eligibility to veterans with service-connected disabilities rated at 20 percent or more. This applied only to veterans originally applying for benefits on or after Nov. 1, 1990.

• **Housing and loan guaranty assistance.** Allowed the lender to choose between the claim procedure under the current law and submitting the lender's claim when the VA notified the lender of VA's estimated value of the home. The lender would bear any loss or profit on the actual resale.

• **Burial and grave marker benefits.** Eliminated the headstone allowance for veterans who died after Nov. 1, 1990, and whose families chose to purchase a private marker. Existing law allowed for reimbursement of no more than an $87 stipend. The marker would still be provided for those who chose a veteran's marker. The provision would save $3 million in outlays in fiscal 1991 and $19 million through fiscal 1991-95.

• **Plot Allowance.** Also limited the $150 plot allowance for those veterans who were in receipt of veterans' benefits at the time of death or were eligible for compensation. Effective Nov. 1, 1990. The provision would result in savings of $27 million in outlays in 1991 and total savings of $147 million in outlays in fiscal 1991-95.

• **Line-of-duty compensation.** Provided that injuries and diseases occurring during service as "a result of the veteran's own willful misconduct or abuse of alcohol and drugs" would not be compensated by a disability pension. The provision covered illnesses, such as cirrhosis of the liver, found to be the secondary effects of alcohol and drug abuse. Under existing law, veterans received no compensation for such illnesses but did receive disability pensions. The VA estimated that each year 28,000 veterans suffered from such illnesses. The provision covered claims filed after Oct. 31, 1990. The Congressional Budget Office estimated that it would save $10 million in outlays in fiscal 1991 and $334 million in outlays in fiscal 1991-95.

• **Requirements to provide Social Security numbers.** Required, upon the VA secretary's request, that compensation and pension claimants disclose their Social Security numbers as well as those of their dependents to receive claims. Benefits would not be paid to those who refused to provide a number, but claimants who did not have a number would not be required to provide one. Also required the VA to verify that recipients of these benefits were not deceased. The measure was expected to save $4 million in fiscal 1991 and $47 million in fiscal 1991-95.

Title IX — Transportation

• **Passenger facility charges.** Allowed airports to impose ticket fees of $1, $2 or $3 on passengers to pay for facility improvements. The charges were limited to two boardings per one-way trip and could not be levied on passengers traveling to or from cities receiving subsidized essential air service.

The fees could be used for any project normally eligible for federal airport improvement funds, noise-abatement projects or airport gates. The charges could be assessed at one airport and used for another airport controlled by the same authority. Proceeds also could be used to pay interest on bonds for eligible projects. The Transportation Department had to approve all passenger facility charges and make a decision within 120 days of application. Before submitting an application to levy the charges, airports were required to give notice and provide an opportunity for consultation by air carriers.

No new fees could be put into effect after Sept. 30, 1992, if trust fund spending for airport improvement programs was less than $3.7 billion for fiscal 1991 or 1992, or if essential air service funding was less than $26.6 million in fiscal 1991 or $38.6 million in fiscal 1992. Existing passenger fees were not affected by this provision.

Also, no passenger charges could be imposed until the Transportation secretary issued a rulemaking notice on allocation of landing and takeoff slots, as well as a final rule establishing procedures for airports to submit proposed noise restrictions on newer, quieter Stage 3 aircraft.

State and local governments could not regulate the collection of the passenger charges or the use of the revenues, nor could contracts between carriers and airports limit an airport's ability to collect the fees or spend fee revenues.

Large and medium hub airports imposing the passenger fees had their federal airport improvement entitlements reduced by half. Of the half forfeited, 25 percent would go into the trust fund's discretionary program account. The remaining 75 percent would go into a new small airport fund for general aviation and small commercial airports.

• **Federal aviation noise policy.** Required the secretary, by July 1, 1991, to issue regulations establishing a national aviation noise policy that included the phaseout of older, Stage 2 aircraft by Dec. 31, 1999. Carriers that had 85 percent of their fleets complying with Stage 3 noise levels by Jan. 1, 2000, could apply for waivers that would extend the date by which all their aircraft had to comply with the higher standards by 2003.

The noise guidelines did not apply to aircraft flying solely outside the continental United States.

• **Authorization of Airport Improvement Program:** Authorized $1.8 billion for fiscal 1991 and $1.9 billion for fiscal 1992.

• **Authorization of Federal Aviation Administration (FAA) facilities and equipment program:** Authorized $2.5 billion for fiscal 1991 and $3 billion for fiscal 1992.

• **Elimination of the 'penalty clause.'** Repealed a law that reduced authorizations for FAA operations from the Airport and Airways Trust Fund if amounts for capital programs were not fully funded.

• **Funding of FAA operations from the trust fund.** Allowed 75 percent of the FAA budget to come from the trust fund.

• **Military airport program.** Earmarked 1.5 percent of airport improvement funds for conversion of up to eight military airports for civilian commercial service by September 1992.

• **Expanded East Coast plan.** Required an environmental impact statement and safety studies for the FAA's expanded East Coast plan for air-traffic routings.

• **Buy American and related provisions.** Required the FAA to use products made in the United States, with exceptions; provided that persons using fraudulent made-in-America labels be ineligible for FAA contracts for three to five years; banned the FAA from contracting with foreign firms whose governments were found by the president to engage in procurement practices that discriminated against U.S. companies.

• **Allocation of existing capacity at certain airports.** Required the secretary by July 1, 1991, to initiate a rulemaking proceeding to consider more efficient methods of allocating existing capacity at high-traffic airports, in order to provide improved opportunities for operations by new entrant air carriers (defined as a carrier having less than 12 operating rights at such airports).

Title X — Miscellaneous User Fees

• **Customs fee.** Extended merchandise processing fees and other user fees through Sept. 30, 1995.

• **Customs adjustment authority.** Authorized the secretary of the Treasury to adjust the merchandise processing fee on formal entries to take into account changes in economic conditions or trade flows, to avoid unintended under- or over-collections, and to help ensure that the user fee would continue to conform to the requirements of the General Agreement on Tariffs and Trade (GATT). The provision established a formula for adjusting the fee and set out requirements for the secretary to provide notification, allow for public comment and consult with Congress before adjusting the fee.

● **Small user-fee airports.** Provided that user-fee airports that processed fewer than 25,000 informal entries (generally, those valued at less than $1,250) a year would be required to collect an entry-by-entry fee and make a specified reimbursement to the Customs Service but would not have to reimburse Customs in an amount double their current assessment for Customs processing services, as was the existing case. User-fee airports processing 25,000 or more informal entries a year would continue to be exempt from the entry-by-entry fees but would be subject to the double reimbursement requirement. Conferees added a technical amendment that reflected the fact that the double reimbursement requirement worked an unintended hardship on user-fee airports that processed a low volume of informal entries.

● **Technical corrections.** Corrected technical and drafting errors in the Customs and Trade Act of 1990 (PL 101-382) and reinstated two statutory provisions of the Customs Forfeiture Fund that were inadvertently deleted from existing law.

● **Patent and Trademark Office.** Placed all receipts raised by the surcharge on patent user fees in fiscal 1991 in a special fund in the Treasury and credited them as offsetting receipts. The special fund was solely for the use of the Patent and Trademark Office. Of this money, $91 million would be available to the Patent and Trademark Office to the extent provided in appropriations acts, and $18.8 million would be available directly to the patent office. In fiscal 1992-95, all receipts would be placed in this fund in the Treasury and credited as offsetting receipts, to be available to the patent office only to the extent provided in appropriations acts. The conferees agreed to raise user fees 13 percent above the House and Senate reconciliation bills, and expected to generate $109.8 million in surcharges.

● **National Oceanic and Atmospheric Administration (NOAA).** Increased fees for services provided by NOAA, a division of the Commerce Department that included the National Weather Service. The increases totaled $2 million a year in fiscal 1991-93 and $3 million a year in fiscal 1994-95. The Commerce secretary was required to waive the fees if necessary to continue providing emergency weather services, such as warnings and watches.

● **Radon proficiency program.** Required the Environmental Protection Agency (EPA) to research radon measurement methods. Required that EPA charge a fee sufficient to cover the costs of an existing radon proficiency program, plus an additional $1.5 million a year for the new research. The EPA was required to conduct a study on the feasibility of establishing a mandatory proficiency program, which could require that any measuring device meet minimum performance criteria and any person conducting such measurements meet minimum proficiency criteria. The EPA had to report to Congress by March 1, 1991.

● **Department of Energy study.** Directed the secretary of Energy to study the department's user-fee assessment and collection practices and make recommendations on ways to improve those practices.

● **Department of Transportation.** Required the Transportation Department to report on the assessment and collection of licensing fees under the Commercial Space Launch Act.

● **Travel and tourism fee.** Required the Commerce secretary to collect a fee from each commercial airline and passenger cruise ship line bringing passengers to the United States. The fee was to be $1 for each alien arriving at any U.S. port via that airline or cruise line during calendar 1991, with fees for later years calculated by the number of alien passengers during the previous year.

● **Coast Guard fees.** Directed the Coast Guard to set up a system for the collection of $200 million from payments by users of direct and indirect services provided by the Coast Guard. The fee system went into effect immediately and continued through fiscal 1995.

The Coast Guard's authority to collect fees was extended to include direct user fees for inspection and examination of certain vessels and licensing, certification and documentation of personnel.

Indirect fees also were to be collected annually from owners or operators of recreational boats over 16 feet in length. Boats longer than 16 feet but less than 20 feet could be assessed a fee of not more than $25. Fees for boats longer than 20 feet but less than 27 feet could be no more than $50. For vessels 40 feet in length and more, the fee could not exceed $100.

The assessment was limited to vessels operating in navigable waters of the United States where the Coast Guard had a presence. Failure to pay the fees could result in a fine of up to $5,000.

● **Tonnage duties.** Imposed increased tonnage duty for all vessels entering a port of the United States from any foreign port or place in the Western Hemisphere to 9 cents per ton, not to exceed 45 cents per ton per year, up from 2 cents per ton, not to exceed 10 cents per ton per year.

Duties on vessels entering U.S. ports from other foreign ports were to increase to 27 cents per ton, not to exceed $1.35 per ton per year. The current rate for these vessels was 6 cents, not to exceed $1.35 per ton per year.

After fiscal 1995, the tonnage fees would return to the amount imposed under existing law.

Vessels departing a U.S. port and returning to the same port, without going to another port or place, excepting vessels of the United States, recreational vessels or some barges, would pay 9 cents per ton, not to exceed 45 cents per ton per year for the next five fiscal years. In 1996 the rate for these vessels would be lowered to 2 cents per ton, not to exceed 10 cents per ton per year.

Vessels in distress, and fishing boats or vessels not engaged in trade were not required to pay the duties.

● **Railroad user fees.** Required the Transportation secretary to establish a schedule of fees to be assessed to railroads. Fees could be collected by any federal, state or local agency chosen by the secretary and would be used to offset administrative costs incurred to carry out provisions of the Federal Railroad Safety Act of 1970. At no time could the aggregate of fees received for any fiscal year exceed 105 percent of the amount appropriated for activities to be funded by the fees.

The secretary was required to report to Congress within 90 days after the end of each fiscal year the impact of the fees on the financial health of the railroad industry and its competitive position relative to each competing mode of transportation — including the total cost of federal safety activities for each such other mode of transportation, and the portion of that total cost, if any, defrayed by federal user fees. If any significant difference in costs and fees existed, the secretary, within 90 days of submitting the report, had to submit recommendations for legislation to correct any such difference.

Title XI: Revenues

● **Effective date.** Provisions went into effect for the 1991 tax year unless otherwise noted.

Individual Income Taxes

● **Tax rates.** Replaced the previous rate structure with three rates: 15 percent, 28 percent and 31 percent. The new 31 percent rate affected single individuals with taxable incomes of $49,200 or more; joint filers with taxable incomes of $82,050 or more; single heads of households with incomes of $70,350 or more; and married individuals filing separately with incomes of $41,025 or more.

The 31 percent marginal rate replaced the 33 percent paid by those in the "bubble," an anomaly created by the 1986 Tax Reform Act as the benefits of the lower 15 percent rate and the personal exemption for upper-income taxpayers were phased out. Those in the bubble — couples with taxable incomes of between roughly $80,000 and $200,000 and single filers with incomes of between $50,000 and $110,000 — paid a 33 percent marginal rate while those with higher incomes paid a flat 28 percent rate. The new 31 percent rate applied to those in and above the bubble range. The 15 percent and 28 percent marginal rates remained in effect for those with lower incomes.

● **Capital gains.** Set a maximum tax rate of 28 percent on profits from the sale of appreciated assets, such as real estate, stocks or timber.

● **Alternative minimum tax.** Increased from 21 percent to 24 percent the alternative minimum tax rate paid by high-income taxpayers who would otherwise be able to reduce their liability substantially through the use of numerous deductions and other tax breaks.

● **Personal exemption phaseout.** Phased out the value of the personal exemption, the deduction allowed each taxpayer and dependent, as a taxpayer's adjusted gross income exceeded a certain level. The phaseout began at $150,000 for joint returns, $125,000 for heads of households, $100,000 for single filers and $75,000 for married individuals filing separately. The phaseout ended at $122,500 above each of these amounts. The figures would be adjusted each year to offset the effects of inflation. The value of the deduction, $2,050 in 1989, would also be adjusted each year for inflation.

Under the law, the value of the exemption would be reduced by 2 percent (4 percent for married individuals filing separately) for each $2,500 or fraction thereof that a taxpayer's adjusted gross income exceeded the threshold amount. Thus, a single taxpayer with $162,500 in adjusted gross income (halfway through the phaseout range) could deduct half of his or her personal exemption.

The change would expire after the 1995 tax year.

• **Limit on itemized deductions.** Limited the value of itemized deductions, other than medical expenses, casualty and theft losses and investment interest, by 3 percent of the amount a taxpayer's adjusted gross income exceeded $100,000. For example, a taxpayer with income of $140,000 would have his or her itemized deductions lowered by $1,200, or 3 percent of $40,000. In no case would a taxpayer's deductions be reduced by more than 80 percent.

The $100,000 threshold amount, which applied to both single and joint filers, was indexed for inflation. The provision was set to expire at the end of 1995.

• **Appreciated tangible personal property.** Repealed for the 1991 tax year a provision requiring the appreciated value of certain property donated to charitable organizations to be included in income subject to the alternative minimum tax. The change generally provided a one-year tax break to upper-income individuals who donated artwork and manuscripts to libraries, universities and museums.

• **Cosmetic surgery.** Prohibited deductions for expenses paid for unnecessary cosmetic surgery.

• **Earned Income Tax Credit (EITC).** Increased the refundable credit allowed working poor families, from what had been a projected maximum of $994 in 1991 to $1,186 for those with one qualifying child and $1,228 for those with two or more qualifying children. For 1990, the credit was 14 percent of the first $6,810 of earned income and was phased out at a rate of 10 percent of the amount of adjusted gross income or earned income, whichever was greater, that exceeded $10,730. The base income amount and the point at which the phaseout began was adjusted annually for inflation.

The law increased the credit for taxpayers with one qualifying child to 16.7 percent in 1991, 17.6 percent in 1992, 18.5 percent in 1993 and 23 percent in 1994 and after. The phaseout rate for such families was 11.93 percent in 1991, 12.57 percent in 1992, 13.21 percent in 1993 and 16.43 percent in 1994 and after.

The credit for those with two or more qualifying children was 17.3 percent in 1991, 18.4 percent in 1992, 19.5 percent in 1993 and 25 percent in 1994 and after. The phaseout rate was 12.36 percent in 1991, 13.14 percent in 1992, 13.93 percent in 1993 and 17.86 percent in 1994 and after.

The law also stiffened and clarified eligibility requirements for the EITC.

• **Supplemental young child credit.** Provided an additional 5 percent credit, with an increase in the phaseout rate of 3.57 percent, for those with qualifying children under the age of 1. The maximum supplemental credit was expected to be $355 in 1991. Any child for whom the credit was claimed was not considered a qualifying child for the separate dependent care tax credit.

• **Supplemental EITC for health insurance.** Allowed an additional credit for premiums paid on health insurance coverage for one or more qualified children. The credit was calculated in a way similar to that used for the EITC, except that the credit percentage was 6 percent and the phaseout rate was 4.285 percent. The maximum credit for 1991 was projected to be $426, although the credit could not exceed the amount paid in health insurance premiums. A taxpayer's medical expenses deduction would also be limited by the amount of any credit claimed.

• **EITC and means-tested programs.** Provided that the EITC and supplemental credits not be considered income or a resource in determining eligibility for Aid to Families with Dependent Children, Supplemental Security Income, Medicaid, food stamps and certain housing programs.

• **Study of advance payments.** Required the comptroller general, with the secretary of the Treasury, to conduct a study of the existing system that allowed those eligible for the EITC to request advance payment of the credit. The study was aimed at finding ways to simplify the advance payment system and learning why participation was low. The study had to be submitted to the House Ways and Means and Senate Finance committees within a year of enactment.

• **Public awareness program.** Required the secretary of the Treasury to establish a program in 1991 to increase taxpayer awareness of the earned income, dependent care and health insurance credits.

• **Taxpayer identification number.** Required taxpayers to provide a taxpayer identification number for any dependent age 1 or older.

Excise Taxes

• **Alcoholic beverages.** Increased excise taxes on distilled spirits, beer and wine. The tax on distilled spirits was increased from $12.50 per proof gallon to $13.50 per proof gallon. This translated into an increase of 16 cents in the $2 tax on a fifth of 80-proof liquor.

The tax on beer was doubled from $9 per barrel to $18 per barrel. This meant the tax on a six-pack of beer went from 16 cents to 32 cents. The law continued the previous $7 per barrel tax on the first 60,000 barrels of beer produced by domestic breweries with total production of 2 million barrels or less a year.

The tax on still wines with up to 14 percent alcohol content rose from 17 cents per wine gallon to $1.07 per wine gallon; with 14 percent to 21 percent alcohol from 67 cents to $1.57 per wine gallon; and for wine with 21 percent to 24 percent alcohol the tax rose from $2.25 per wine gallon to $3.15 per wine gallon. The tax on artificially carbonated wines increased from $2.40 per wine gallon to $3.30 per wine gallon. The increase translated into an 18-cent increase in the 3-cent tax on a bottle of table wine.

The law provided a credit of 90 cents per wine gallon on the first 100,000 gallons of wine produced annually for wineries that produced 150,000 gallons or less during the year. The credit was phased out for wineries with total production of between 150,000 and 250,000 gallons during the year. Champagne and sparkling wines were not included in determining the first 100,000 gallons eligible for the credit; however, they were included when determining a winery's total production for phasing out the credit.

• **Tobacco.** Increased excise taxes on tobacco products by 25 percent on Jan. 1, 1991, and the identical dollar amount on Jan. 1, 1993. Thus, the tax on a pack of 20 small cigarettes went from 16 cents to 20 cents in 1991 and to 24 cents two years later.

The tax for small cigars rose from 75 cents per thousand to $0.9375 per thousand in 1991 and $1.125 per thousand in 1993. For large cigars, it rose in 1991 from 8.5 percent of the suggested wholesale price, with a cap of $20 per thousand, to 10.625 percent of the manufacturer's price, with a cap of $25 per thousand. In 1993, it would increase to 12.75 percent of the manufacturer's price, up to $30 per thousand.

The existing tax for small cigarettes, $8 per thousand, went to $10 per thousand in 1991 and $12 per thousand in 1993. For larger cigarettes, $16.80 per thousand, the tax increased to $21 per thousand in 1991 and $25.20 per thousand in 1993. The 25 percent tax increase also applied to cigarette papers, cigarette tubes, chewing tobacco, snuff and pipe tobacco.

• **Ozone-depleting chemicals.** Expanded the list of ozone-depleting chemicals subject to tax by including carbon tetrachloride, methyl chloroform, CFC-13, CFC-111, CFC-112, CFC-211, CFC-212, CFC-213, CFC-214, CFC-215, CFC-216 and CFC-217. The base tax rate, multiplied by an ozone-depleting factor assigned to each chemical, was $1.37 per pound for 1991 and 1992, $1.67 per pound for 1993, $3.00 per pound for 1994, $3.10 per pound for 1995 and an additional 45 cents per pound each year after 1995.

• **Motor fuels.** Raised the excise taxes on highway and motorboat fuels by 5 cents per gallon, effective Dec. 1, 1990. The increase resulted in a 14-cents per gallon tax on gasoline and a 20-cents per gallon tax on diesel fuel. The law also imposed a 2.5-cents per gallon tax on fuel used in rail transportation.

Half of the revenue from the highway fuels tax increase was dedicated to the Highway Trust Fund, and half of the motorboat fuels increase was dedicated to the Aquatic Resources Trust Fund. The other half in each case, as well as all revenue from the tax on fuels used in rail transportation, would be kept in the general fund.

The law also established a wetlands restoration program, generally benefiting Louisiana, within the Sports Fish Restoration Account of the Aquatic Resources Trust Fund and financed it through the taxes on gasoline used in small-engine outdoor power equipment.

• **Aviation.** Increased and extended through 1995 a number of aviation excise taxes, effective Dec. 1, 1990. The law increased the tax on air passenger transportation from 8 percent to 10 percent, the tax on air freight from 5 percent to 6.25 percent, the tax on non-commercial aviation gasoline from 12 cents per gallon to 15 cents per gallon, and the tax on non-commercial aviation jet fuel from 14 cents per gallon to 17.5 cents per gallon.

Revenues from the tax increases would go to the general fund through 1992 and to the Airport and Airway Trust Fund for 1993-95. All revenue from the extension of existing taxes would go to the trust fund.

• **Harbor maintenance.** Increased from 0.04 percent to 0.125 percent the tax used to fund the Harbor Maintenance Trust Fund. The tax was generally imposed on the commercial value of cargo loaded and unloaded at U.S. ports and on commercial ship passenger fares. The provision limiting expenditures from the trust fund to 40 percent of eligible harbor maintenance and related costs was changed to allow expenditures on up to 100 percent of eligible costs.

• **Leaking underground storage tanks.** Reimposed and extended through 1995 a 0.1-cent per gallon tax on gasoline, diesel fuel, special motor fuels, aviation fuel and fuels used on inland waterways to be deposited in the Leaking Underground Storage Tank Trust Fund. A $500 million revenue ceiling for the trust fund was eliminated.

• **Gas guzzlers.** Doubled the tax on automobiles that did not meet statutory fuel economy standards. The tax began at $1,000 for vehicles that did not meet the 22.5 miles per gallon standard and rose to $7,700 for those with fuel economy ratings of less than 12.5 miles per gallon. Exemptions for stretch limousines and small manufacturers were repealed.

• **Telephones.** Permanently extended the 3 percent tax on local and toll telephone service.

• **Luxuries.** Imposed a 10 percent excise tax on the portion of the retail price of certain items that exceeded the following: $30,000 for automobiles, $100,000 for boats and yachts, $250,000 for aircraft and $10,000 for jewelry and furs. The tax generally did not apply to boats or automobiles used exclusively in a trade or business. Also exempted were aircraft used at least 80 percent of the time in a trade or business.

The tax was set to expire at the end of 1999 and did not apply to articles purchased pursuant to a contract binding as of Sept. 30, 1990.

Superfund Tax Extension

• **General.** Extended superfund taxes and trust fund for four years, from Dec. 31, 1991, to Dec. 31, 1995. Trust funds were generally available for expenditures incurred in connection with releases or threats of releases of hazardous substances into the environment.

• **Cap.** Increased cap on the aggregate amount of superfund tax revenue that could be collected from $6.65 billion to $11.97 billion.

• **Petroleum tax.** Extended a tax on petroleum, imposed at a rate of 9.7 cents per barrel, on domestic or imported crude oil or refined products.

• **Hazardous chemicals tax.** Extended a tax on listed hazardous chemicals, imposed at a rate that varied from 24 cents to $10.13 per ton.

• **Imported substances tax.** Extended a tax on imported substances that contained or used chemical derivatives of one or more of listed hazardous chemicals.

• **Environmental tax.** Extended an environmental tax equal to 0.12 percent of the amount of modified alternative taxable income of a corporation that exceeded $2 million.

Miscellaneous

• **Life insurance.** Required insurance companies to amortize over a 120-month period certain policy acquisition costs that firms had previously been allowed to deduct in one year. These costs were determined as a set percentage of the net premiums on three categories of insurance contracts: annuities (1.75 percent), group life (2.05 percent) and other life (7.70 percent).

To help small companies, a shorter amortization period of 60 months was allowed for the first $5 million of amortizable policy acquisition expenses for the taxable year. This provision was phased out as the total of such expenses for the year increased from $10 million to $15 million. Small firms, those with assets of less than $500 million at the close of the year, were also exempted from certain amortization requirements for acquisition expenses under the corporate alternative minimum tax.

The provision was generally effective Sept. 30, 1990.

• **Property and casualty insurance.** Clarified the treatment of salvage and subrogation claims in limiting the deduction firms could take for losses.

• **Compliance.** Made a number of changes to improve tax collections. They included: new penalties on multinational firms that overstated the value of certain property or services resulting in tax underpayments; tighter information reporting requirements and record maintenance rules for foreign corporations that carried on a trade or business in the United States; suspension of the three-year statute of limitations on a tax return while the taxpayer and the Internal Revenue Service (IRS) were in court litigating over whether the taxpayer had to comply with an IRS summons; an extension from six to 10 years in the statute of limitations for collection of taxes after an IRS assessment; extension for five years of IRS fees to supply written rulings or determinations in response to taxpayer requests; increased penalties for failure to report cash transactions involving more than $10,000.

• **Corporate taxes.** Included a number of provisions covering corporate transactions. The law required corporations restructuring their debt to pay taxes on the difference between the face value of the original debt instrument and the fair market value of the new debt. The law also attempted to prohibit the use of certain tax-free distributions of subsidiary stock to disguise what was in effect a sale of the subsidiary, a transaction subject to tax. Both provisions generally were effective for transactions after Oct. 9, 1990.

• **Corporate tax underpayments.** Increased the interest rate corporations were required to pay on tax underpayments from 3 percentage points above the short-term federal rate to 5 percentage points above, after the corporation had been notified of the deficiency by the IRS. The increased rate did not apply to underpayments of $100,000 or less for any one kind of tax during any one taxable period.

• **Hospital insurance payroll tax.** Increased from $51,300 to $125,000 the amount of employee wages and self-employment income subject to the Medicare hospital insurance payroll tax. The 1.45 percent tax was paid by both the employer and employee; self-employed individuals paid both portions of the tax for a total of 2.9 percent. The wage base would be indexed each year after 1991 to reflect increases in average wages.

• **State and local employees.** Extended Social Security and Medicare coverage, and the payroll taxes used to fund the programs, to state and local government employees who did not otherwise participate in a retirement plan. An exception was provided for students employed in public schools, colleges and universities, who could be covered at the option of the state.

The change was effective for services performed after June 30, 1991.

• **Unemployment taxes.** Extended through 1995 a 0.2 percent surtax included in the 6.2 percent federal unemployment insurance tax employers paid each year on the first $7,000 of wages paid to an employee. Employers in states with no overdue federal loans and that met certain other requirements were still eligible for a 5.4 percentage point credit on the tax.

• **Tax deposits.** Required employers to deposit income taxes withheld from employee wages and payroll taxes on the first banking day after the business accumulated an amount to be deposited of $100,000 or more.

• **Grantor trusts.** Provided that a U.S. citizen who was a beneficiary of a trust be treated as the grantor, or owner, of the trust for income tax purposes to the extent the beneficiary transferred property as a gift to a foreign person who otherwise would have been treated as the owner of the trust.

Extension of Expiring Provisions

• **Allocation of research expenditures.** Extended through 1991 rules governing allocation of research and experimental expenditures to U.S. and foreign source income.

• **Research and experimentation credit.** Extended through 1991 a 20 percent tax credit allowed for new research expenditures and certain payments to universities for basic research.

• **Employer-provided educational assistance.** Extended through 1991 the exclusion allowed an employee for up to $5,250 a year of certain employer-provided educational assistance. A prohibition against use of the assistance for graduate-level courses was repealed.

• **Group legal services.** Extended through 1991 the exclusion for certain employer-provided group legal services. The law also extended the tax-exempt status of organizations that had the exclusive function of providing qualified group legal services.

• **Targeted jobs.** Extended through 1991 the tax credit available to employers of certain hard-to-place workers, including those who were economically or physically disadvantaged. The credit was generally equal to 40 percent of the first $6,000 of qualified first-year wages and 40 percent of up to $3,000 of wages for a disadvantaged summer youth employee.

• **Business energy investments.** Extended through 1991 a 10 percent credit allowed for business investment in solar and geothermal energy. A 15 percent credit allowed for investment in ocean thermal energy was allowed to expire Sept. 30, 1990.

• **Low-income rental housing.** Extended through 1991 a tax credit, allowed in installments over a 10-year period, for certain construction or rehabilitation of existing property to produce low-income rental housing. The bill increased the annual state limit on the credit from $.9375 per resident in 1990 to $1.25 per resident.

• **Mortgage revenue bonds.** Extended through 1991 authority for state and local government entities to issue tax-exempt mortgage revenue bonds or mortgage credit certificates to help certain qualified individuals with the purchase, improvement or rehabilitation of single-family, owner-occupied homes.

• **Small-issue bonds.** Extended through 1991 authority for small issues of tax-exempt private-activity bonds if at least 95 percent of the net proceeds was used to finance manufacturing facilities or certain land or property for first-time farmers.

• **Health insurance for self-employed.** Extended through 1991 a deduction for 25 percent of the cost of health insurance for a self-employed individual and the individual's spouse and dependents.

• **Orphan drugs.** Extended through 1991 a 50 percent credit allowed for the costs of human clinical testing of drugs for certain rare diseases and conditions.

Other Tax Incentives

• **Non-conventional fuels.** Extended a credit allowed for production of certain non-conventional fuels. The credit, equal to $3 per barrel or Btu oil barrel equivalent, had been available for fuels produced from a well drilled, or a facility placed in service, before Jan. 1, 1991, if the fuel was sold before Jan. 1, 2001. The law extended each of these dates by two years. It also liberalized eligibility requirements for the credit for gas produced from tight formations.

• **Alcohol fuels.** Allowed a new 10-cent per gallon credit for production of up to 15 million gallons a year of ethanol by a small producer, defined as one with a productive capacity not in excess of 30 million gallons of alcohol per year.

The law also reduced from 60 cents per gallon to 54 cents per gallon the credit ethanol blenders were allowed for 190 or greater proof ethanol. The credit for 150 proof to 190 proof ethanol was cut from 45 cents to 40 cents per gallon. The 6-cent per gallon exemption from federal motor fuels excise taxes for alcohol fuel mixtures was reduced to 5.4 cents per gallon. Corresponding reductions were made in tariffs on ethanol and ETBE (ethyl tertiary butyl ether), an ethanol blend.

The credit and excise tax exemption generally expired Jan. 1, 2001, and Oct. 1, 2000, respectively.

• **Enhanced oil recovery.** Created a new domestic energy tax credit equal to 15 percent of costs for qualified enhanced oil recovery projects, also referred to as tertiary recovery projects. The credit would be reduced when the average price of crude oil exceeded $28 per barrel (adjusted annually for inflation) and would be completely phased out when the price exceeded this amount by $6 or more.

• **Percentage depletion.** Liberalized the allowance oil and gas producers received for depletion. The deduction had previously been limited to no more than 50 percent of the taxpayer's net taxable income from the property, computed without the deduction. The law increased the limit to 100 percent of net income from the property. A prohibition against claiming the deduction on certain transferred oil and gas properties was repealed, and the percentage depletion rate was increased for certain marginally producing properties when the domestic wellhead price of crude oil dropped.

• **Alternative minimum tax relief.** Reduced the value of certain oil- and gas-related tax preferences used in calculating income subject to the alternative minimum tax. The reductions applied to deductions taken for certain intangible drilling costs and the percentage depletion allowance on marginally producing properties. The tax break would be phased out in taxable years following years in which the price of crude exceeded $28 per barrel (adjusted annually for inflation). It would be completely phased out when the average price of oil exceeded this amount by $6 or more.

• **Estate freezes.** Revised estate-tax rules governing the transfer of small, family-run businesses from one generation to the next. The law repealed complex and controversial provisions enacted in 1987 that were designed to prevent tax avoidance through the use of so-called estate freezes, which allowed owners to transfer a business to their heirs and avoid estate taxes on any appreciation in the value of the business from the time of the transfer until the original owner's death. The new provisions, effective for transfers of property after Oct. 8, 1990, shifted the focus back onto the value of the stock at the time of the transfer. They included requirements aimed at setting a more accurate value on the property and to prevent transactions designed to avoid transfer taxes.

• **Barrier removal.** Allowed small businesses a 50 percent income tax credit for expenditures of between $250 and $10,250 in any taxable year to make their businesses more accessible to the disabled. Such expenditures could include amounts spent to remove physical barriers and to provide interpreters, readers or equipment that make materials more available to the hearing or visually impaired, and others. To be eligible, a business had to have gross receipts for the preceding taxable year of $1 million or less or have no more than 30 full-time employees in the preceding year. The credit was available for expenditures paid or incurred after the date of enactment.

• **IRS regulations.** Required the IRS to consider comments by the Small Business Administration on proposed regulations and to discuss them in the preamble of the final regulations.

• **Pie charts.** Required the IRS to include in individual tax-form instruction booklets two pie charts, one showing where the government gets its revenues and the other showing how they are spent.

• **Technical corrections.** Included numerous technical corrections (as reported by the House Ways and Means Committee in HR 5822) to the Revenue Reconciliation Act of 1989, the Technical and Miscellaneous Revenue Act of 1988 and other recent tax bills. The law also repealed numerous obsolete provisions in the Internal Revenue Code.

• **Tax information.** Allowed the release of certain third-party and self-employment tax information to the Department of Veterans Affairs to help the department determine eligibility for certain needs-based pension and other programs. The General Accounting Office was required to do a detailed report on the impact of the provision, which was effective upon enactment and expireed after two years.

Title XI: Public Debt

• **Permanent limit.** Increased from $3,122,700,000,000 to

$4,145,000,000,000 the permanent limit on the public debt, effective upon enactment. The change was expected to accommodate government borrowing needs until sometime in 1993.

• **Federal funds.** Instructed the secretary of Treasury to credit federal funds, excluding the Civil Service Retirement and Disability Trust Fund and the Thrift Savings Fund of the Federal Employees' Retirement System, for interest income lost due to any disruptions in debt issuance between Oct. 15 and Dec. 31, 1990.

Title XII — Pensions

• **Treatment of employer reversions.** Increased the rate of tax imposed on employers who terminated employee pension plans and reverted excess pension assets to the employer.

The rate, formerly 15 percent, jumped to 20 percent or 50 percent, depending on the circumstances.

The excise tax rate was to be 20 percent if the employer set up a replacement plan and left a "cushion" equal to 25 percent of the surplus, or gave cash payments equaling 20 percent of the surplus to retirees and workers.

Otherwise, the reversion tax would be 50 percent if the company did not maintain a qualified replacement plan or offer the lump-sum payments.

All qualified participants who had a right to an accrued benefit under the terminated plan as of the termination date had to be provided the benefit increases. Those who terminated employment before the termination date and received a lump-sum distribution of their benefits would not be qualified participants.

• **Transfers to retiree health accounts.** Permitted, on a temporary basis, qualified transfers of excess assets from the pension assets in a defined benefit pension plan to the 401(h) retiree health benefit account that was part of such a plan. The assets transferred were not includable in the gross income of the employer and not subject to the excise tax on reversions. Such transfers could only occur once in a taxable year between Dec. 31, 1990, and Jan. 1, 1996.

• **Increase in pension-benefit guarantee premiums.** Raised the flat-rate Pension Benefit Guarantee Corporation (PBGC) premium to $19 from $16, and increased an additional premium of $6 per $1,000 of unfunded vested benefits to $9. Also, the per-participant cap on the additional premium (calculated by dividing the total additional premium by the number of plan participants) was raised from $34 to $53.

The increases were effective for plan years beginning after Dec. 31, 1990.

Title XIII — Enforcement

Discretionary Spending Limits

• **Categories of discretionary spending.** Divided discretionary spending in fiscal 1991-93 into three categories: defense, international and domestic. For fiscal 1994-95, all discretionary spending was lumped together in a single category.

• **Discretionary spending caps.** Mandated the following 1991-93 and 1994-95 caps for discretionary budget authority and outlays (amounts in billions of dollars):

Fiscal Years

	1991	1992	1993	1994	1995
Defense					
Budget authority	$ 288.9	$ 291.6	$ 291.8		
Outlays	297.7	295.7	292.7		
International					
Budget authority	20.1	20.5	21.4		
Outlays	18.6	19.1	19.6		
Domestic					
Budget authority	182.7	191.3	198.3		
Outlays	198.1	210.1	221.7		
Total discretionary					
Budget authority				510.8	517.7
Outlays				534.8	540.8

• **CBO, OMB responsibilities.** Required that, as soon as practicable after Congress completed action on a discretionary appropriation (any of the 13 appropriations bills, a supplemental appropriations bill or a continuing resolution), the Congressional Budget Office (CBO) had to give the Office of Management and Budget (OMB) an estimate of the bill's new discretionary spending authority and outlays for the current year (if any) and for the budget year covered by the bill.

Within five calendar days of enactment of any such bill, OMB was required to send the House and the Senate a report containing the CBO and OMB estimates of budget authority and outlays for the bill, along with an explanation of any differences between the two.

OMB estimates had to be made using existing economic and technical assumptions. OMB and CBO were required to use scorekeeping guidelines agreed to after consultation among CBO, OMB and House and Senate Budget committees.

Under the new law, OMB's role shifted from looking primarily at the overall budget deficit (chiefly through the Oct. 15 sequestration provisions under previous law) to a bill-by-bill evaluation process.

This had the effect of involving the agency even more directly than it already was in congressional lawmaking.

• **General sequestration.** Required that, if discretionary spending in any category exceeded the annual cap, there had to be an across-the-board spending cut — known as sequestration — within that category to reduce spending in all non-exempt accounts by a pro-rata share of the excess.

Such a sequestration had to take place within 15 days of the end of a session of Congress, except for certain circumstances (see below).

• **Look-back sequestration.** Required that, if a supplemental appropriations bill enacted after June 30 for the fiscal year in progress broke a spending cap in any category, the cap for that category for the next fiscal year had to be reduced by the amount of the excess.

• **Within-session sequestration.** Required that, if a supplemental appropriations bill that broke the cap in any category was enacted between the time Congress adjourned at the end of one session but before July 1 of the following year, there be a sequestration 15 days after enactment to reduce the excess in that category.

• **Desert Shield.** Stated that any contributions from other nations to defray the cost of Operation Desert Shield not be counted under any discretionary spending category (and therefore not be used to offset any spending increase). At the same time, any U.S. spending for Desert Shield was to be treated as emergency spending not subject to the defense spending cap.

• **Adjustments to discretionary spending caps.** Required that when the president submitted the budget for fiscal 1992-95, OMB adjust discretionary spending caps to reflect: 1) changes in concepts and definitions; 2) changes in inflation; 3) re-estimates of the costs of federal credit programs; 4) funding for Internal Revenue Service compliance initiatives, within specified limits; 5) debt forgiveness in calendar 1990-91 for Egypt and Poland; 6) International Monetary Fund funding; and 7) presidentially designated emergency supplemental appropriations.

• **Special allowances for new discretionary budget authority and outlays.** Required the president to increase discretionary budget authority caps in fiscal 1992-93 by a specified formula that varied according to category and fiscal year. Outlay caps could also be increased by specified dollar amounts as long as the budget authority cap for an applicable category was not exceeded.

The special budget authority allowance was designed to add roughly $3 billion a year to discretionary spending in fiscal 1992-93. The special outlay allowance was designed to insulate the legislative process from differences between OMB and CBO cost estimates.

Pay-As-You-Go Limits

• **Sequestration.** Required that any legislation to decrease revenues or increase direct spending (defined as spending for entitlement programs, food stamps and any spending programs not subject to appropriations) that caused a net increase in the deficit trigger an offsetting, across-the-board sequestration in non-exempt entitlement programs.

The sequestration would occur 15 days after Congress adjourned at the end of a session.

• **Exemptions.** Stated that sequestration could not be ordered on the basis of any legislation that continued full funding and the continuation of the deposit insurance commitment, or because of presidentially designated emergency spending.

• **Sequestration procedure.** Required that the amount to be sequestered come from non-exempt direct spending accounts in the following order: 1) reductions in automatic spending increases for the National Wool Act, the special milk program and vocational rehabilitation basic state grants; 2) the maximum reductions permissible in guaranteed student loans and foster care and adoption assistance; 3) reductions in each remaining non-exempt account.

• **Medicare.** Stated that Medicare could not be reduced by more than 4 percent as part of any sequestration to enforce pay as you go.

• **CBO, OMB responsibilities.** Required that as soon as practicable after Congress completed action on any direct spending or revenue legislation, CBO provide OMB with an estimate of the change the legislation would make in outlays or revenues. Within five days of enactment of any such legislation, OMB was required to report to Congress on OMB and CBO estimates of the deficit impact of such legislation, along with an explanation of any difference.

Deficit Targets

• **New deficit targets.** Established new "maximum deficit amounts" (by fiscal year, in billions of dollars) as follows:

1991	1992	1993	1994	1995
$ 327.0	$ 317.0	$ 236.0	$ 102.0	$ 83.0

• **Margins.** Stated that the margin — the amount by which the deficit could exceed the maximum deficit amount in any given year without triggering a sequestration — was zero in fiscal 1992-93. The margin for fiscal 1994-95 was $15 billion.

• **Sequestration.** Required that within 15 days after Congress adjourned at the end of a session, but after any sequestration to enforce discretionary spending caps or pay as you go, a sequestration would be required to eliminate any deficit that still exceeded the margin.

• **Excess deficit.** Stated that the excess deficit was the amount by which the estimated deficit exceeded the maximum deficit amount, minus: 1) emergency direct spending or revenue legislation; and 2) the re-estimate of deposit insurance costs, if there was not a full adjustment for technical and economic re-estimates in 1994-95.

• **Dividing the sequestration.** Required that, in implementing a sequestration, half the outlay reductions come from non-exempt defense accounts and half from non-exempt non-defense accounts.

• **Medicare.** Stated that Medicare could not be reduced by more than 2 percent under any sequestration to enforce maximum deficit limits. If Medicare already had been reduced by 2 percent or more under a pay-as-you-go sequestration, it could not be further reduced under a sequestration to enforce the maximum deficit amount.

• **Adjustments to maximum deficit amounts.** Required that when submitting the budget for fiscal 1992-93, the president adjust the maximum deficit amounts for that year and the remaining fiscal years through 1995 to reflect up-to-date re-estimates of economic and technical assumptions and any changes in concepts and definitions. The president could make similar adjustments for the fiscal 1994 and 1995 budgets.

For the purposes of a sequestration to enforce a maximum deficit, OMB would have to continue to use the economic and technical assumptions submitted with the president's budget.

This meant that, at least through fiscal 1993 (and in fiscal 1994-95 if the president so chose), a sequestration would cover only excess spending legislated by Congress — excesses already subject to sequestration under the procedures to enforce the discretionary caps and pay as you go. It was unlikely there would be a sequestration to enforce a maximum deficit target until fiscal 1994 — and not in fiscal 1994-95 if the president opted to continue adjusting the maximum deficit amounts.

Sequestration Reports and Orders

• **Timetable.** Created a timetable for sequestration reports and orders as follows:

Jan. 21	President must notify Congress (in 1993 and 1994) whether he will exercise the option to adjust the maximum deficit amounts for fiscal 1994-95.
5 days before president submits budget	CBO sequestration preview report
First Monday in February	President's budget is due; at the same time OMB must provide sequestration preview report.
Aug. 10	President must notify Congress if he intends to exempt military personnel from sequestration or sequester such accounts at a lower percentage rate.
Aug. 20	OMB sequestration update report
10 days after end of session	CBO final sequestration report
15 days after end of session	OMB final sequestration report; presidential order
30 days later	GAO compliance report

• **Low-growth report.** Provided that CBO had to notify Congress if CBO or OMB determined that real economic growth was projected or estimated to be less than zero in any two consecutive quarters within the six-quarter period beginning with the preceding quarter. CBO was also required to notify Congress if the Commerce Department's advance, preliminary or final report of actual real economic growth for each of the most recently reported quarters and the immediately preceding quarter was less than 1 percent.

• **Economic and technical assumptions.** Required that in all reports under this section, OMB use the same economic and technical assumptions used in the most recent budget submitted by the president.

• **Exemptions for Social Security and Railroad Retirement.** Exempted from sequestration Social Security benefits and Tier 1 Railroad Retirement benefits.

• **Non-defense unobligated balances.** Prohibited sequestration of unobligated balances of non-defense budget authority carried over from prior fiscal years.

• **JOBS portion of AFDC.** Required that any sequestration order achieve the fully required reduction in the Job Opportunities and Basic Skills (JOBS) program under the Aid to Families with Dependent Children (AFDC) program without reducing any federal matching rate. The provision set out formulas for determining amounts available to states in the event of a sequestration.

Budget Agreement Enforcement

• **General.** Set out maximum deficit amounts and discretionary spending caps (see figures above). Provided that it not be in order in the Senate to consider any budget resolution or related legislation for fiscal 1992-95 or any appropriations bill for fiscal 1992-93 that would exceed the caps or the suballocations made under the caps. The point of order would not apply if war had been declared or if the low-growth provision had been triggered. The law provided for allocations of the total budget amount to committees and suballocations of discretionary amounts among Appropriations subcommittees.

• **Adoption of president's budget.** Provided that, if Congress did not adopt a budget resolution by April 15, the chairman of the House Budget Committee would have to make an allocation to the House Appropriations Committee based on the most recent budget submitted by the president. As soon as practicable after that, the Appropriations Committee was required to make suballocations to its subcommittees.

• **Implementing pay as you go in the House.** Provided that, if legislation were enacted that provided for a net reduction in revenues in any fiscal year (not offset in the same measure by cuts in direct spending), the House Budget Committee could report, within 15 legislative days during a Congress, a reconciliation directive in the form of a concurrent resolution that would specify the amount of revenues needed to make up the gap and direct the appropriate committees to make the necessary changes in law.

• **Five-year budget resolutions.** Made temporary changes in the Budget Act to create five-year budget resolutions that would be enforced by points of order against exceeding committee allocations for both the first year and the five years covered by the budget resolution.

• **Additional changes in budget process.** Allowed for display in the budget resolution of the increase in the national debt as an alternative measure of the deficit, display of federal retirement trust fund balances and the creation in budget resolutions of pay-as-you-go provisions similar to reserve funds established in budget resolutions since 1987. Made a variety of other procedural changes, including codifying the so-called Byrd rule against extraneous matter in reconciliation bills.

• **Clarification of presidential authority absent appropriations.** Made clear that sequestered funds could no be spent, and that ongoing, regular operations of the federal government could not be sustained in the absence of appropriations. This provision was adopted to guard against what the conferees believed might be an overly broad interpretation of a 1981 opinion by the attorney general that addressed the president's authority to continue government operations during a lapse in appropriations.

Credit Reform

• **General.** Recognized that federal credit programs were displayed in the budget on a cash accounting basis, which overstated the real economic cost of direct loans but understated the real costs of loan guarantee programs in the year loans were made. This section in effect reversed that status, so that the real costs of both types of credit would be more accurately reflected in the budget.

• **OMB and CBO roles.** Provided that the OMB director be responsible for coordinating credit cost estimates for the executive branch. OMB was required to consult with CBO in developing guidelines for credit cost estimates and in reviewing and improving those estimates.

• **Budgetary treatment.** Required that, beginning with fiscal 1992, the budget cost of credit programs be the net present value of the long-term costs to the government, excluding administrative costs and incidental effects. All other cash flows resulting from credit programs were to be treated as means of financing and included in a non-budgetary financing account.

• **Appropriations required.** Required the appropriation of new budget authority for new direct loans or loan guarantees for fiscal 1992 and thereafter. The law provided an exception for entitlement credit programs (such as the guaranteed student loan program and the veterans' home loan guaranty program) and for the credit programs of the Commodity Credit Corporation.

Also provided that budget authority must be available for the cost of modifying any outstanding direct loan or loan guarantee. Administrative expenses for credit programs were to continue to be counted on a cash flow basis, but they had to be displayed in a separate subaccount within the account for the credit program.

• **Point of order.** Provided, as part of the transition provisions, that new credit authority be subject to a point of order (based on violation of allocations) in the Senate during fiscal 1991. This provision was good only until the beginning of fiscal 1992.

• **Exemptions for deposit insurance and other insurance programs.** Provided that these credit reforms not apply to the credit or insurance activities of the Federal Deposit Insurance Corporation, the National Credit Union Administration, the Resolution Trust Corporation, the Pension Benefit Guaranty Corporation, national flood insurance, the National Insurance Development Fund, crop insurance or the Tennessee Valley Authority. OMB and CBO were required to study whether the accounting for federal deposit-insurance programs should be on a cash basis, on the same basis as loan guarantees or on a different basis.

Each agency was told to report to the president and Congress by May 31, 1991.

President's Budget Submission

• **Date change.** Provided that the president could delay submitting his budget to Congress from the date required under current law — on or before the first Monday after Jan. 3 of each year — to no later than the first Monday in February.

Status of Social Security Trust Funds

• **Exclusion from all budgets.** Prohibited counting the receipts or the disbursements of the Old Age and Survivors Insurance trust fund and the Disability Insurance trust fund (collectively: OASDI) in the budget submitted by the president, the congressional budget or for the purposes of the Gramm-Rudman antideficit law.

• **'Fire wall' protection in the House.** Prohibited consideration in the House of any legislation that would expand Social Security benefits without providing offsetting Social Security tax increases or cut Social Security taxes without providing offsetting cuts in benefits or a corresponding increase in Medicare taxes. The legislation expressed these prohibitions in a complex formula that would bar changes in the actuarial balance of the Social Security trust funds over five years or 75 years.

• **'Fire wall' protection in the Senate.** Barred Social Security benefit increases or tax cuts that were not offset with corresponding tax increases or benefit cuts, much as the House fire wall did, but achieved this by expanding certain Budget Act enforcement procedures, rather than through creating restrictions, as the House did. The Senate provision was confined to changes that would alter the actuarial balance of the Social Security trust funds over five years.

Restoration of Sequestered Funds

• **Undoing fiscal 1991 sequestration.** Rescinded the sequestration ordered by the president Aug. 25, 1990, and Oct. 15, 1990, which had been postponed by a series of continuing resolutions while Congress debated the budget issue.

The law required that any sequesterable resource that was reduced or sequestered be restored and that any federal employees who were furloughed during the lapse of appropriations from midnight Oct. 5 until the enactment of a continuing resolution further postponing the sequestration had be paid for that period.

Government-Sponsored Enterprises

• **Definition.** Defined government-sponsored enterprises (GSEs) as the Farm Credit System (including the Farm Credit Banks, Banks for Cooperatives and the Federal Agricultural Mortgage Corporation), the Federal Home Loan Bank system, the Federal Home Loan Mortgage Corporation, the Federal National Mortgage Association and the Student Loan Marketing Association.

• **Treasury Department study and proposed legislation.** Required the Treasury Department to submit to Congress by April 30, 1991, a study of GSEs and recommended legislation. The study had to include an objective assessment of the financial soundness of GSEs, the adequacy of existing regulations, the financial exposure to the federal government and the effects of GSEs on Treasury borrowing.

• **CBO study.** Required CBO to submit to Congress by April 30, 1991, a study of GSEs that included an analysis of the financial risks assumed by each GSE, the supervision and regulation of risk management, the financial exposure GSEs posed for the federal government and the effects of GSEs on Treasury borrowing. The study also was to include alternatives for GSE oversight, and the costs and benefits of those alternatives.

• **Requirement to report legislation.** Required the committees of jurisdiction in the House to report to the House no later than Sept. 15, 1991, legislation to ensure the financial soundness of GSEs and to minimize the possibility that a GSE might require future assistance from the government. The provision expressed the sense of the Senate that the relevant Senate committees must also report such legislation.

• **President's budget.** Required that the president's annual budget include an analysis of the financial condition of GSEs and the financial exposure, if any, that they posed to the government. ■

Continued from p. 140
get-reconciliation bill that in many ways resembled the budget-summit package. With that good-housekeeping task done, Democrats abandoned any attempt to compromise with the GOP. When the measure came to the floor Oct. 16, they pushed through a block of floor amendments heavily touted as a soak-the-rich approach.

The plan — drawn up by Democrats on the Ways and Means Committee — was designed to emphasize charges that Republicans were the party of the wealthy, while Democrats were looking out for low- and middle-income taxpayers. The Democratic leadership used its heavy majority to control floor action and muscle the package through without allowing Republicans to present an alternative of their own.

The Democratic alternative passed on a virtual party-line vote of 238-192. The amended reconciliation bill then passed on a closer 227-203 vote. *(Votes 474, 475, p. 150-H)*

The Democratic plan targeted wealthy taxpayers with a 10 percent surcharge on individuals with taxable income above $1 million, a boost in the top marginal income tax rate to 33 percent from 28 percent and a jump in the alternative minimum tax rate paid by wealthy taxpayers who took advantage of a large number of deductions from 21 percent to 25 percent. It increased the wage cap for Medicare payroll taxes to $100,000 from $51,300; it increased premiums and deductibles for Medicare Part B, but at a lower rate than in the summit agreement.

The Democratic alternative included a capital gains tax cut specifically targeted at the middle class, allowing individuals $1,000 in capital gains tax-free each year and a lifetime exclusion of $100,000.

In a bid to ease the burden on low- and middle-income taxpayers, the package did away with the budget summit's proposal to increase the gasoline tax and add a 2-cents-a-gallon tax on refined petroleum products, including heating oil. It made up for the resulting revenue shortfall — nearly $57 billion over five years — by forgoing for one year the indexing of tax brackets and personal exemptions to account for inflation, a change that was expected to yield $36 billion over five years.

That opened the way for Republicans to charge the Democrats with aiming at the rich but hitting the middle class.

Bush warned before the measure passed that it would be dead on arrival if it ever got to the White House.

In fact, it was widely believed that the House Democratic plan would never get that far, because it first had to make its way through the Senate, where a much more muscular GOP minority and moderate Democrats had already combined to press for a bipartisan reconciliation bill. But the House floor debate was less about probability than about scoring political points that would serve candidates' interests in the elections now only three weeks away.

The Republicans came up with their own alternative budget package that promised $400 billion to $410 billion in savings over five years, mostly by freezing spending. But the Democratic-controlled Rules Committee refused to let them offer the plan on the floor.

Senate Floor Action

The Senate bill, unlike its House counterpart, was kept intact by a united bipartisan leadership front.

Mitchell and Dole were able to keep reluctant troops in line long enough to block all substantive amendments. They argued repeatedly, and sometimes emotionally, that the fragile deficit-reduction plan could easily unravel. The bill, approved 54-46 on Oct. 18, was largely the same as the measure reported by the Budget Committee two days earlier by a vote of 15-7. *(Vote 292, p. 58-S)*

The leadership had little choice but to stick together, in large part because of the Democrats' narrow majority. Mitchell and other Democratic leaders had promised to protect the package against potentially fatal amendments to help win passage of a major component of the plan in the Finance Committee, where Democrats held only a two-member majority. Still, Mitchell and others said it pained them to have to oppose a number of amendments they found attractive, especially proposals to shift more of the tax burden onto wealthy taxpayers.

The bill, which incorporated the recommendations of 10 committees, called for $253 billion in mandatory spending cuts and new revenues over five years, slightly higher than the amount required by the budget resolution.

The largest amount came from the Finance Committee, which approved $142 billion in net new revenues and $53 billion in spending cuts. The biggest piece of that came from Medicare, with a $49.3 billion reduction over five years. About $32 billion of the savings came from reductions in payments to health-care providers.

The bill increased motor fuels taxes by 9.5 cents a gallon, a provision not in the House bill, and raised alcohol and cigarette taxes in line with the House measure. It included a 10 percent luxury tax on expensive cars, boats, yachts, jewelry, furs and airplanes, similar to a provision in the House bill.

Unlike the House measure, it limited itemized deductions by 5 percent of the amount a taxpayer's adjusted gross income exceeded $100,000. It raised the amount of wages subject to a Medicare payroll tax to $89,000, as compared with $100,000 in the House bill.

It extended Medicare to all state and local government employees and Social Security's retirement and disability program to state and local employees who did not participate in a public retirement plan. The House had included the latter but not the former.

The Senate measure called for increasing the earned-income tax credit for poor families by $16.9 billion over five years, although $11.9 billion of that amount was to pay for separate child-care legislation.

The Senate bill also included a number of tax incentives that were not in the House-approved version. These included a one-year extension of 11 expiring tax breaks, including tax credits for business research and development and for low-income housing, at a five-year cost of $5.6 billion.

It also called for $6.6 billion in tax breaks for small businesses and the energy industry, including new oil and gas exploration incentives if the price of oil dropped below $34 per barrel. It called for a $15.1 billion cut in farm program spending over the five years and a $14.1 billion cut in banking and insurance activities, including a provision to allow federal regulators to increase deposit insurance premiums paid by banks and thrift institutions.

The first crucial test for the package came at the start of debate Oct. 17 when Steve Symms, R-Idaho, tried to eliminate the proposed increase in federal gasoline taxes.

Symms argued that the change would hurt low- and middle-income taxpayers the most and further damage a shaky economy. But Republican and Democratic leaders quickly painted the vote on his plan — which would have left the bill $43 billion short of its five-year $253 billion deficit-reduction goal — as a referendum on the entire package. Eventually the proposal was defeated by a procedural move.

In action Oct. 17-19, the Senate also:

- Refused, 45-55, to waive the budget act to allow an amendment by Al Gore, D-Tenn., and Barbara A. Mikulski, D-Md., to increase taxes on the wealthy so that proposed increases in payments by Medicare beneficiaries could be eliminated and a proposed 9.5 cents-per-gallon increase in gasoline taxes cut to 6 cents. They would have increased the top marginal tax rate to 33 percent, imposed a 10 percent surtax on millionaires and increased the alternative minimum tax to 25 percent. *(Vote 280, p. 56-S)*
- Agreed by voice vote to an amendment by Orrin G. Hatch, R-Utah, to remove provisions setting minimum civil penalties for violations of job safety and health standards set by the Occupational Safety and Health Administration.
- Rejected, 44-56, a sense of the Senate amendment by David L. Boren, D-Okla., and Sam Nunn, D-Ga., that conferees raise taxes on the very rich and use the funds to lower the proposed gasoline tax hike, cut capital gains taxes and provide for more generous Individual Retirement Accounts. *(Vote 281, p. 56-S)*
- Agreed, 98-2, to an Ernest F. Hollings, D-S.C., and John Heinz, R-Pa., amendment to remove Social Security from deficit calculations under Gramm-Rudman. *(Vote 283, p. 56-S)*
- Agreed by voice vote to a Don Nickles, R-Okla., amendment to reduce the federal debt limit increase in the bill to $321 billion, which was expected to be enough to meet government borrowing needs through fiscal 1991. The bill had provided for a $1.9 trillion extension, enough to meet needs through fiscal 1995. A motion to table the amendment failed 0-100. *(Vote 284, p. 56-S)*
- Refused, 39-61, to waive the budget act to allow a Bob Kasten, R-Wis., amendment to remove deductions for charitable contributions from a proposed 5 percent limit on deductions for the wealthy. *(Vote 286, p. 57-S)*
- Failed, 48-52, to waive the budget act to allow a Symms amendment to require all revenues from the motor fuels tax increase, except those paid by railroads, to be dedicated to the Highway Trust Fund. *(Vote 287, p. 57-S)*
- Adopted, by voice vote, a leadership amendment to overhaul the budget process.

House-Senate Conference

Buoyed by quick House and Senate passage of the bill the previous week, conferees met during the Oct. 20-21 weekend with high hopes of cutting a deal that would at last send everyone home. But they quickly fell into partisan wrangling over how to tax the super-rich.

The White House and Senate Republicans rejected the House Democrats' plan to slap a highly visible surtax on millionaires.

As an alternative, negotiators tried substituting a beefed-up version of a plan crafted by Rep. Don J. Pease, D-Ohio, to reduce deductions by 3 percent to 4 percent for taxpayers with incomes over $100,000, and by as much as 8 percent for those with incomes over $1 million.

A meeting of the House Democratic Caucus on Oct. 23, however, indicated that approach would not fly. Members were unhappy about a 5-cents-a-gallon tax increase, Medicare cuts they still considered too high and a host of other problems. But their chief complaint was the Pease proposal, and the chief critics were members from big states like New York, California and New Jersey, whose high state taxes would no longer be fully deductible under the plan.

Leaders tried to explain that it was impossible to get anything like the House-passed surtax through the Senate, but rank-and-file Democrats expressed frustration that their Senate counterparts were not trying hard enough.

With the fall elections less than two weeks away, prospects for a deal seemed bleak. Then Dole and fellow Senate Finance Committee member Bob Packwood, R-Ore., produced a compromise that resuscitated the agreement.

Packwood suggested relaxing the Pease plan deduction limits and adding instead a provision phasing out the $2,050 personal exemption for wealthy taxpayers above certain income levels.

The effect would be to raise the top marginal tax rate on the richest taxpayers, but the mechanism was not nearly so explicit as a surtax on millionaires.

Packwood bitterly opposed the surtax on the grounds that it would bring back what he felt were the bad old days of higher and higher tax rates that spawned bigger and bigger tax breaks for wealthy taxpayers — a thicket Packwood thought he had helped clear with the Tax Reform Act of 1986.

Late on Oct. 23, Dole and House Minority Leader Michel had a lengthy meeting at the White House, trying to convince Bush that they had to agree on an alternative to higher limits on deductions under the Pease plan.

The next day, Rostenkowski presented the idea to Ways

Debt Limit Raised

Legislation raising the federal debt limit to a level expected to last until spring 1993 cleared Congress on Oct. 27 as part of the budget-reconciliation bill.

The bill (HR 5835 — PL 101-508) increased the permanent debt ceiling to $4.145 trillion. Congressional staff estimated that the $950 billion increase could last until May or April 1993.

Raising the debt limit was a simple fiscal housekeeping task that allowed the Treasury Department to borrow money to pay for spending that Congress had already approved. But, as in previous years, the must-pass legislation became tied up with the fate of controversial budget negotiations.

Unwilling to approve a long-term extension in the absence of a budget deal, and with Treasury warning that the federal debt would exceed its statutory limit by mid-August, Congress passed a short-term extension (HR 5350 — PL 101-350) on Aug. 4.

The temporary new ceiling, approved just before the August recess, was good through Oct. 2. A second short-term extension (HR 5755 — PL 101-405) was cleared Sept. 30. Further short-term extensions were included in the continuing resolutions that carried the government through until the appropriations bills were enacted.

The agreement announced by budget summit negotiators Sept. 30 assumed a $1.9 trillion increase that was projected to be enough to accommodate government borrowing needs through fiscal 1995. But that was scaled back to $950 billion by conferees as part of the final reconciliation bill. *(Budget summit, p. 129; reconciliation bill, p. 138)*

Bush Signs Budget Reconciliation Act

Following is the statement President Bush made on the budget provisions of the Omnibus Budget Reconciliation Act of 1990 (HR 5835 — PL 101-508) when he signed it into law Nov. 5:

Today, I am signing HR 5835, the Omnibus Budget Reconciliation Act of 1990, the centerpiece of the largest deficit reduction package in history and an important measure for ensuring America's long-term economic growth. This act is the result of long, hard work by the administration and the Congress. No one got everything he or she wanted, but the end product is a compromise that merits enactment.

HR 5835, and the discretionary spending caps associated with it, will achieve nearly $500 billion — almost half a trillion dollars — in deficit reduction over the next five years. Over 70 percent of that deficit reduction derives from outlay reductions; less than 30 percent from revenue increases. In addition, the act enacts significant budget process reforms to ensure that the agreement is fulfilled and that budgetary discipline is extended and strengthened.

Entitlement reforms. The act provides for the most comprehensive and substantial reform of mandatory "entitlement" programs ever — about $100 billion in savings from restructuring and reforms in the following major programs:

- Farm programs;
- Federal housing programs;
- Student loan programs;
- Veterans programs;
- Postal subsidies;
- Federal employee benefits; and
- Medicare.

Discretionary program caps. The act establishes five-year caps on overall discretionary spending that will result in savings of over $180 billion. To keep domestic and international spending from growing any faster than inflation, the act creates new automatic "mini-sequesters." The act also provides for an orderly defense reduction without threatening national security.

Energy security. The act provides incentives for energy conservation and for exploratioan and development of domestic energy resources.

Social Security. Social Security is fully protected and taken off-budget.

Enforcement and process reform. The act contains the toughest enforcement system ever. The Gramm-Rudman-Hollings sequester process is extended and strengthened with caps, mini-sequesters, and a new "pay-as-you-go" system.

Credit reform. The act implements a new federal accounting and budgeting system to expose and limit previously hidden (and rapidly growing) liabilities.

Tax changes. The act includes a tax rate cut from 33 percent to 31 percent for about 3.5 million middle- and upper-middle-income taxpayers and an overall decrease in taxes paid by those with incomes under $20,000. There are higher excise taxes on luxury items and limitations on itemized deductions and the personal exemption for higher-income taxpayers. The total net tax changes comprise 28 percent of the deficit reduction package.

This act creates the conditions that should allow future interest rates to be lower than they would be otherwise. Lower interest rates can benefit the entire economy. They can mean more housing starts; more Americans driving new cars; reductions in mortgage payments for homeowners; more long-term investment; greater productivity; and increased numbers of jobs.

In signing this landmark act, I pledge the continuing best efforts of my administration to maintain not only the letter, but the spirit of the new fiscal order for the federal government that is embodied in this agreement. . . . ■

---

and Means Democrats in a private briefing, but members came out scowling.

Downey called the idea "screwy," arguing that it penalized people for having children, since the phaseout would raise tax rates by limiting personal exemptions claimed by taxpayers for themselves and for their dependent children.

Leaders then convened the House Democratic Caucus again to try out the idea. When members emerged, the desire to cut a deal and go home seemed to have overwhelmed their reservations about the plan.

"It ain't perfect, but life ain't perfect," said James H. Scheuer, D-N.Y. "We ought to do it and get out."

Conferees also agreed to impose a new top marginal tax rate of 31 percent, with a 28 percent top rate on capital gains. They agreed to limit a taxpayer's itemized deductions by 3 percent of the amount his or her income exceeded $100,000.

Along the way, with none of the 13 regular appropriations bills enacted, lawmakers had cleared two more stopgap spending bill, keeping the government funded through Oct. 24 and then Oct. 27 (H J Res 677 — PL 101-444 and H J Res 681 — PL 101-461).

POSTSCRIPT

As he signed the budget-reconciliation bill Nov. 5, Bush called it "a compromise that merits enactment." Terming it "the centerpiece of the largest deficit-reduction package in history," Bush stressed that over 70 percent of the deficit reduction was to come from spending cuts and only 28 percent from "tax changes." *(Signing statement, this page)*

Just two days later, in a post-election news conference, he told reporters Nov. 7 he had "serious regrets" about "being forced" to abandon his pledge and promised that he would "absolutely" refuse to accept any further increases in income tax rates.

Public discontent with the budget wrangling was viewed by many observers as a major factor in a dropoff of incumbents' re-election margins in the midterm balloting. And the influence of budget politics was hinted in some of the 15 races where House incumbents were defeated. Republican freshman Peter Smith of Vermont, who had been one of the first GOP lawmakers to embrace the budget-summit agreement, was narrowly defeated. And GOP challenger Scott L. Klug scored an upset victory over veteran Democrat Robert W. Kastenmeier in Wisconsin after a campaign in which Klug criticized Congress for excessive spending and promised to support a balanced-budget amendment and a line-item veto.

As the new Congress began, the fragility of the budget accord was manifested in an important procedural clash between House Democrats and the White House. On Jan. 3 — the first day of the 102nd Congress — the House Democratic leadership muscled through a rules change to give CBO rather than OMB the power to decide whether a new tax cut or entitlement bill met the new "pay-as-you-go" budget limits.

The rules change was approved on a party-line, 242-160 vote over the objections of outraged Republicans, who claimed Democrats were reneging on a key provision of the 1990 budget agreement. Democrats, however, contended the issue had not been resolved. Before the vote, Bush had threatened to veto any bill that included the cost-estimate language mandated by the new House rule. ■

Deficit-Reduction Bill Has 'New Taxes'

Few could have predicted at the start of 1990 how much the tax debate would shift to the Democrats' terrain.

The year began with President Bush reiterating his "no new taxes" campaign pledge and, in fact, promoting a tax break for capital gains — the gains on sale of stock, real estate, timber or other assets.

The session ended, however, with passage of a deficit-reduction bill (HR 5835 — PL 101-508) that promised to raise a net of $137 billion in new taxes over five years and increase the top rate on the very wealthiest taxpayers from 28 percent to 31 percent. Congress approved only a cosmetic change in the capital gains rate, and the GOP took a drubbing from Democrats on the issue of "tax fairness."

As they scrambled for a compromise that would make the tax system more progressive without imposing a highly visible surcharge on the rich, Congress and the administration added new complexity to a tax system that was supposed to have been simplified once and for all by the 1986 tax overhaul. They agreed to pop one tax-rate "bubble" only to create another. Instead of eliminating deductions, lawmakers made it more difficult for the wealthy to calculate them. And the final tax package included a complicated, last-minute plan to phase out personal exemptions for high-income taxpayers.

BACKGROUND

The dispute over taxes had deep ideological underpinnings — and major political implications — that made compromise extremely difficult.

Republicans stressed tax policies that did not take dollars away from savings and investment, arguing that U.S. capital pools were too shallow already and that spurring investment was crucial to sustaining growth and maintaining a competitive position in the world economy.

Thus, Republicans preferred tax cuts — particularly for capital gains. When they discussed tax increases at all, they generally wanted to tax the sale of consumer goods such as gasoline, alcohol and tobacco. Those sorts of taxes, they argued, did less to hinder economic growth, investment or productivity. But they were also regressive, meaning they would be levied without regard to one's ability to pay and so hit the poor harder than they would the wealthy.

For their part, many Democrats resisted talking about specific taxes until Bush endorsed some himself — acutely aware that Bush and President Ronald Reagan before him had painted Democrats into a corner on tax issues in the past three presidential campaigns. Seeking to find a better message, Democrats stressed their preference for more progressive revenue measures that would place a greater burden on business and upper-income taxpayers.

Democrats argued the tax policies of the 1980s — beginning with the 1981 tax cut — already had done yeoman's work for the investing class, tilting the system too far toward regressive taxes, including the Social Security levy. Now, Democrats maintained, it was time to reverse the trend. *(Reagan policies, 1988 Almanac, p. 187; tax cut, 1981 Almanac, p. 91)*

In February, House Speaker Thomas S. Foley of Washington and Senate Majority Leader George J. Mitchell of Maine made a joint pitch for a higher top rate on the income tax. And Sen. Daniel Patrick Moynihan, D-N.Y., risked his reputation as a defender of Social Security by calling for a rollback in the payroll taxes that supported it. *(Social Security tax, p. 170)*

Democrats argued that any taxes that emerged from the budget summit should redress the growing inequity in both pretax and after-tax incomes.

Republicans Lose Control of Debate

A number of factors accounted for the way in which Republicans gradually lost control of the tax issue as the parties debated and maneuvered throughout 1990.

Administration officials, concerned that a soaring deficit could severely damage the economy and hurt Bush's re-election chances in 1992, sought Democrats' help in May to work out a bipartisan deficit-reduction deal. Democrats entered budget-summit talks May 15, but they shrank from talking about taxes and refused to negotiate on reducing the deficit until Bush abandoned his no-new-taxes campaign pledge. On June 26, Bush issued a statement that "tax revenue increases" would have to be part of any package. *(Bush statement, p. 131; budget summit, p. 129)*

With Republicans deeply split over Bush's tax shift and polls revealing a growing public perception that GOP tax policies had favored the rich, Democrats seized on the issue of tax equity and made it the focus of the year's debate. They argued that tax changes made during the 1980s had largely benefited the wealthy and that this trend needed to be reversed.

Toward the end of the budget-summit negotiations, a trade seemed possible between the capital gains tax cut, which many Democrats privately favored, and an increase in tax rates on the rich. But strong opposition from rank-and-file members on both sides blocked such an agreement. When party leaders unveiled the final summit package Sept. 30, both ideas had been dropped. *(Capital gains, p. 168)*

This did not halt the partisan debate, however. Rank-and-file Democrats criticized the package as doing nothing to address their concerns that the tax system was unfair. They said it imposed too much of the burden on low- and middle-income taxpayers and not enough on the rich. Republicans complained that the deal would impede economic growth by calling for too many new taxes and too few breaks for investors. Others said that a limit on deductions for upper-income taxpayers was a thinly disguised attempt to raise the top income tax rate.

Gas, tobacco, alcohol and luxury tax proposals produced partisan and regional splits.

And just about everyone thumbed their noses at a last-minute goodie, inserted to attract conservative support, that would have provided generous tax breaks for investors in small business.

The package of benefits for investors in small corporations would have cost $12.1 billion over five years. Among the incentives proposed were a tax deduction for individuals of 25 percent of the value of stock purchases in qualifying small corporations; indexing to the rate of inflation of the "basis" or purchase price of stock in a small corporation to provide protection against large capital gains taxes on the sale of such stock; and an extra research and development credit for small corporations.

"It's just mucking up the code again," complained House Ways and Means Committee Chairman Dan Ros-

Bush Bid for Capital Gains Tax Cut Fails

For the second year in a row, capital gains taxes threatened to be the spoiler in high-level deficit-reduction negotiations. While many questions divided Republican and Democratic budget negotiators, it was the dispute over President Bush's proposal to cut capital gains taxes that brought those differences to a head.

When the issue appeared to lose momentum, Bush himself brought it back to the fore, leaving no doubt that it remained his top tax priority. *(Background, 1989 Almanac, p. 113)*

Bush called for a cut in the taxes on capital gains — the profits from the sale of real estate, corporate stock, timber and other assets — in his January budget. He proposed that taxpayers who held assets a year or more be allowed a 10 percent exclusion for each year (up to 30 percent). In effect, the cap on the tax rate would have been 25.2 percent after one year, 22.4 percent after two and 19.6 percent after three. The rate would have applied only to individuals, not corporations, and would not have been available for collectibles, such as artwork.

At the time, capital gains were taxed at the same rates as ordinary income, which went as high as 33 percent.

Bush's plan would have applied to existing assets. The phase-in rules would have allowed investors to take the full 30 percent exclusion through the remainder of 1990 on assets held for one year. In calendar 1991, gains could have received the 30 percent exclusion after being held for two years.

The administration projected that the rate cut would actually yield a $4.9 billion revenue increase in the first year. Beyond that, according to the Treasury Department, the tax cut would continue to contribute net revenue, not only during the five-year period of official estimates but thereafter. The estimate through fiscal year 1995 was $12.5 billion.

In February, the Joint Committee on Taxation released its own sharply different estimates, showing that Bush's plan would bring in $3.2 billion in the first year, but lose $11.4 billion over five years.

A Yearlong Dispute

With Bush's strong backing, it was assumed from the outset that a capital gains cut would be an important component of any budget negotiations. "Capital gains won't make the big budget deal happen," Sen. Bob Packwood, Ore., the ranking Republican on the Finance Committee, said in April. "The budget deal will make capital gains happen."

Democrats, however, made clear that they would accept a cut, which would largely benefit the rich, only if it were offset by new taxes on the wealthy. Senate Majority Leader George J. Mitchell, D-Maine, infuriated Republicans when he told reporters in the midst of budget-summit negotiations July 11 that he would not support Bush's plan without an increase in the top marginal rate for the wealthiest taxpayers from 28 percent to at least 33 percent. *(Budget summit, p. 129)*

By the time budget negotiators recessed for the August break, the impasse seemed so great that some predicted capital gains would fade as an issue. But Bush strongly endorsed it again Sept. 11 in a speech before a joint session of Congress, and the political costs of concession by either side soared. *(Bush address, p. 133)*

During 10 days of closed-door deliberations at Andrews Air Force Base outside Washington following the August recess, budget negotiators for the two sides were unable to break the deadlock. Republicans proposed offsetting the five-year cost of a capital gains cut with limits on deductions for upper-income taxpayers. These included a final offer of a cap on state and local income tax deductions for those with adjusted gross incomes above $200,000.

Democrats offered to lower the capital gains rate to 23 percent and offset it with an income tax surcharge on high-income taxpayers. But Republicans countered that the surcharge would amount to an increase in the top marginal tax rate, something they vowed to oppose as a disincentive to economic growth.

In an effort to break the renewed impasse, Senate Minority Leader Bob Dole, R-Kan., proposed Sept. 19 that capital gains be dealt with in separate legislation that would also include new spending proposals sought by the Democrats. But White House officials and conservative Republican negotiators were unreceptive.

Finally, the negotiators gave up, producing a summit package Sept. 30 that included neither a capital gains cut nor a marginal rate increase. The plan went down to defeat in the early hours of Oct. 5, in part because of fierce disputes over other tax provisions.

By then, Democrats had turned GOP support for a capital gains cut into the cornerstone of their argument that Republicans were out to help the rich at the expense of the lower- and middle-class taxpayer. And Republicans were deeply divided, with GOP House members pushing for some trade between a capital gains tax cut and a marginal rate increase in the reconciliation bill, Senate Republicans trying to keep the two contentious issues off the negotiating table, and the White House waffling in a highly public manner that contributed to a portrait of a presidency in disarray.

With pressure mounting to finish the reconciliation bill, it became clear that a capital gains cut was simply undoable. Republicans were willing to accede to Democratic demands to push up the top rate — but only to 31 percent — in exchange for a capital gains cut. Democrats wanted to take the top rate up to 33 percent.

House Speaker Thomas S. Foley, D-Wash., said during the week that Democrats could live with 32 percent, but that was where the negotiating appeared to stop. Republicans said going higher than 31 percent violated their insistence that the top-rate change be revenue-neutral; Democrats said going much below 33 percent would constitute a cut for those now paying at that level.

In the end, conferees included a House provision that lowered the top rate on capital gains to 28 percent. With the top marginal rate for ordinary income set at 31 percent in the bill, the change was dismissed as negligible by many who had campaigned for a cut.

tenkowski, D-Ill., a prime sponsor of the 1986 bill that eliminated numerous special-interest tax breaks in exchange for lower rates.

The summit package also included:

- **Enterprise zones.** Tax benefits to businesses that located in economically depressed urban and rural areas, which would have added $1 billion to the deficit over five years.
- **Energy production incentives.** Tax breaks to oil producers for new drilling activities and development of improved extraction methods, as well as benefits for ethanol producers, which would have added $4 billion all told to the deficit over five years.

Budget Summit Rejected

Differences over the tax provisions were a major factor in the Oct. 5 defeat of the summit deal in the House. That defeat in turn gave Democrats, who controlled both chambers, an opening to fashion a new plan more to their own liking.

With time running out and no better alternative in sight, the administration had little choice but to negotiate. The result was a set of tax provisions in the reconciliation bill that not only raised the top rate but also imposed other changes designed to shift the tax burden to the wealthy.

Taxpayers with adjusted gross incomes of $200,000 or more were expected to see their tax bills go up 6.3 percent, compared with a 2 percent increase for most other income groups and a tax cut for those with incomes under $20,000, according to the Joint Committee on Taxation.

The distribution was dramatically different than that projected for the budget-summit package, which would have given the smallest increase, 1.7 percent, to those with the highest incomes.

The package phased out the personal exemption and limited itemized deductions for upper-income taxpayers. It expanded incentives for oil and gas exploration; levied a new "luxury" tax on expensive cars, furs, jewelry and boats; raised taxes on gasoline, alcoholic beverage and tobacco; and made a host of other changes.

Critics said the revisions not only would complicate tax law but also could lead to further unraveling of the 1986 overhaul. "What we're seeing is that support for tax reform is about this thick," said Rep. Bill Gradison, R-Ohio, holding his fingers less than an inch apart.

The alternative, however, was stalemate.

Democrats in the conference on the reconciliation bill proposed an increase in the top rate of 33 percent for upper-income taxpayers and 28 percent for the very richest. Republicans were opposed, arguing that such a change would be damaging both to the economy and to the principles of tax reform. White House officials and their Republican supporters argued that higher marginal rates provided a disincentive for taxpayers to earn more money.

Congressional Democrats insisted that a rate increase would be the most direct way to make the wealthiest bear a larger share of the tax burden.

Privately, they acknowledged that a rate hike would also be the most direct way to remind voters that Bush had to renege on his "no-new-taxes" campaign pledge to deal with the federal deficit.

In the end, however, as the fall elections drew near, negotiators were not all that picky about how they resolved the impasse.

"People are ready to vote for bad tax policy just to go home," said Rep. Beryl Anthony Jr., D-Ark., shortly after House Democrats signaled their support Oct. 24 for the outlines of the final deal.

TAX HIGHLIGHTS

The reconciliation bill called for $164.6 billion in new taxes over five years, offset by $27.4 billion in tax breaks. The following were major provisions:

Individual Tax Changes

- **Tax rates.** The most notable change in the package was the increase from 28 percent to 31 percent in the marginal rate paid by the wealthiest taxpayers.

Before the law took effect, taxpayers generally paid either a 15 percent or a 28 percent marginal rate. However, certain taxpayers were subject to what was in effect a 33 percent rate as the benefits of the 15 percent rate and personal exemptions were phased out. Once those benefits were eliminated, a taxpayer paid a flat 28 percent rate.

The legislation repealed this so-called bubble. Instead, those paying the 33 percent or flat 28 percent rate were subject to a new 31 percent rate. The 15 percent and 28 percent rates paid by lower-income taxpayers remained.

The change was expected to result in a slight tax cut for the almost 4 million taxpayers in the bubble and a tax increase for the 600,000 highest-income taxpayers. The new rate affected single taxpayers with taxable incomes of $49,200 or more and married couples with combined taxable incomes of $82,050 or more.

Ironically, another change in the bill created a new tax bubble by phasing out the value of the personal exemption for upper-income taxpayers.

- **Exemptions.** Under the bill, the value of the personal exemption — then $2,050 for each taxpayer and dependent — was to be gradually reduced as a taxpayer's adjusted gross income rose above a certain amount. The phaseout began at $100,000 of adjusted gross income for single filers, $150,000 for joint filers, $125,000 for single heads of households and $75,000 for married individuals filing separate returns. The phaseout ended at $122,500 above the threshold amount.

A key piece of the final compromise, the limit on exemptions, was embraced primarily as a way to break an impasse over Democrats' insistence that a 10 percent surtax be imposed on millionaires, a change the administration found too close to a rate hike for comfort.

The phaseout worked as follows: The value of the exemption was reduced by 2 percent (4 percent for married individuals filing separately) for each $2,500 or fraction thereof that a taxpayer's income exceeded the threshold amount. For example, a married couple with an adjusted gross income of $212,500 would be able to claim half their personal exemptions.

The thresholds were to be indexed annually to reflect inflation; the provision was set to expire at the end of 1995.

Indirectly, the phaseout had the effect of increasing a taxpayer's marginal rate by as much as 0.5 of a percentage point for each personal exemption claimed.

Thus, a married couple with two children could have their 31 percent marginal rate hiked to as much as 33 percent.

- **Itemized deductions.** Another provision in the measure effectively raised high-income taxpayers' rate by an additional percentage point by limiting itemized deductions. Taxpayers with adjusted gross incomes of $100,000 or more would have their itemized deductions reduced by

Effort to Shift Social Security Taxes Fails

Sen. Daniel Patrick Moynihan, D-N.Y., failed Oct. 10 in a largely symbolic quest to cut Social Security taxes for low- and middle-income workers and increase them for better-paid workers.

For two days the Senate debated a bill (S 3167) that would have fundamentally changed the Social Security financing system for the second time in less than a decade. But the bill failed on a 54-44 vote, six votes short of the 60 needed. The vote was on a parliamentary motion that did not require senators to go on record for or against Moynihan's proposal. *(Vote 262, p. 53-S)*

BACKGROUND

Moynihan captured widespread attention at the start of the year when he proposed to reduce the Social Security payroll tax and stop building surpluses in the Social Security trust funds. He said a rate increase in the payroll tax effective Jan. 1, 1990, should be repealed and refunded. In 1991, he said, the rate should be cut again.

Moynihan wanted to cut the payroll tax rate of 6.2 percent gradually to 5.1 percent in 1996 (an additional 1.45 percent tax was imposed to pay part of Medicare costs). And he wanted to increase the amount of income subject to the tax from $51,300 in 1990 to $85,500 in 1996. The effect would have been to stop the rate of growth of the trust fund surpluses, provide a tax cut for those at the lower end of the income scale and a tax increase for those at the upper end, and preserve a small reserve cushion.

The aim was to return Social Security to the pay-as-you-go scheme that had been used from the program's inception until 1983. Then, with the trust funds running dry, Congress voted to increase present taxes to pay for future benefits. Otherwise, taxes would have had to rise sharply in the next century to cover the retiring baby boom generation. *(1983 Almanac, p. 219)*

Although Moynihan served on the 1983 Social Security Commission that proposed building the surplus, he said he no longer supported high payroll taxes because "the Social Security trust fund surpluses are being used to finance the deficit in the operating budget." This, he said, "masks the true size of the budget deficit and perverts the original purpose of the surpluses."

Moynihan, chairman of the Senate Finance Subcommittee on Social Security, said the inclusion of the Social Security surplus disguised the actual size of the 1989 deficit by $52 billion: The deficit was not the official $152 billion but rather $204 billion.

Allowing the Social Security surplus to ameliorate the deficit was particularly distressing to liberals such as Moynihan because the revenue flowed from a flat-rate tax. "The United States almost certainly now has the most regressive tax structure of any Western nation," said Moynihan.

The problem was not that Social Security taxes were being channeled directly to government operations. Rather, the surplus was being invested — but, by law, only in securities issued by the federal government. That meant the Social Security surplus was invested in Treasury securities, a form of federal debt.

This might have been well and good if there had been no operating deficit. But under existing circumstances, it had the effect of narrowing the apparent gap between federal income and outlays (the annual deficit), while doing nothing to reduce the true difference between the government's resources and its obligations.

Moreover, it meant that the accumulating surplus was in the form not of cash but of IOUs from the government that would have to be redeemed for cash somehow before benefits could be paid to retiring baby boomers.

SENATE ACTION

Moynihan and other senators with similar views, such as Ernest F. Hollings, D-S.C., and Terry Sanford, D-N.C., forced the Senate to consider the measure by threatening to amend a continuing appropriations bill (H J Res 666) that contained a temporary increase in the government's borrowing authority, necessary to prevent a default on government bonds.

During the debate, other proposals were discussed, including one by Bob Graham, D-Fla., that would have allowed the Social Security trust funds to be invested in something other than Treasury securities — namely high-grade state and local bonds used to finance roads, schools, water-treatment plants and the like.

And knowing that the bill was going nowhere, the Senate was free to adopt other controversial changes to Social Security, including eliminating the outside earnings cap for recipients and providing increased benefits to so-called notch babies, those born between 1917 and 1926. *(Earnings test, p. 557)*

In the end, the bill was effectively killed when Ted Stevens, R-Alaska, asked to have it ruled out of order because it would have violated the statutory requirement that bills not be considered if they would increase the federal deficit above the limit set in the Gramm-Rudman antideficit law. Moynihan's motion to waive the Gramm-Rudman requirement got only 54 of the 60 votes needed to pass.

A sizable majority of Democrats supported Moynihan, and an equally large number of Republicans opposed him. But some key members of both parties found themselves in odd camps. The chairmen of the Senate Finance and Budget committees — Lloyd Bentsen, D-Texas, and Jim Sasser, D-Tenn., respectively — joined Majority Leader George J. Mitchell, D-Maine, to vote against Moynihan. But ranking Finance Republican Bob Packwood of Oregon voted with the New York senator.

Afterward, Moynihan claimed a victory of sorts, noting that he had a majority on his side in the flesh and many more in spirit. "The day has only begun," he said. "Next year, we will be here, and the year after that. Every year I am here — and I am here for another four. We are going to vote on this measure, not once but more than once; not a few times, but many times."

Major Tax Provisions Compared

(Amounts are in billions of dollars for fiscal years 1991 and 1991-95)

	Summit		House		Senate		Final	
	'91	'91-95	'91	'91-95	'91	'91-95	'91	'91-95
Revenue Raisers								
Income tax rate structure	$0	$0	$4.5	$50	$0	$0	$0.8	$11.2
Personal exemption phaseout	0	0	0	0	0	0	1.0	10.8
Limit on itemized deductions	0.5	18.0	0	0	0.9	29.5	0.5	17.9
Fuel tax increase	5.4	45.0	0	0	4.6	42.6	4.4	25.0
25% increase in tobacco taxes	0.6	5.9	0.5	5.8	0.5	5.8	0.5	5.9
Alcohol tax increase	1.5	10	1.4	9.3	1.4	9.1	1.3	8.8
10% luxury tax	0.2	1.9	0.3	2.8	0.2	2.1	*	1.5
Environment taxes [1]	0.2	1.1	0.3	1.6	0.2	1.1	0.3	1.5
Airport Trust Fund tax	1.3	11.8	1.4	11.9	1.3	11.8	1.4	11.9
Harbor maintenance tax	0.3	1.8	0.3	1.8	0.3	1.8	0.3	1.8
Telephone excise tax	0	0	0	0	1.6	13.1	1.6	13.1
Amortize insurance costs	1.5	8.0	1.5	8.0	1.5	8.0	1.4	8.0
Corporate tax underpayments	1.4	3.9	0	0	3.5	4.1	1.6	1.8
Social Security for state and local employees	2	11.7	1.3	10.0	0	8.1	0.4	9.2
Federal Unemployment surtax	0	0	0.8	5.4	0.8	5.4	0.8	5.4
Medicare wage cap	0.9	13	1.5	22.0	1.3	19.0	1.8	26.9
Revenue Losers								
Expiring provisions	−0.8	−2.9	0	0	−2.1	−5.6	−2.2	−5.9
Energy incentives	−0.4	−4.0	0	0	−0.2	−3.5	−0.2	−2.5
Small business incentives	−3.8	−18.1	0	0	−0.4	−3.2	*	−0.8
Earned-income tax credit	−0.1	−5.0	−0.1	−11.0	−0.1	−16.9	0.1	−13.1
Child health insurance credit	0	0	0	0	0	0	*	−5.2

** Less than $100 million* [1] *Ozone-depleting chemicals tax; Leaking Underground Storage Tank trust fund. House and final bills also included tax on low mpg cars.*

3 percent of the amount their income exceeded $100,000. The provision did not apply to deductions for medical expenses, casualty and theft losses, or investment interest.

For example, a taxpayer with income of $140,000 would have itemized deductions lowered by $1,200, or 3 percent of $40,000. In no case, however, would a taxpayer's deductions be reduced by more than 80 percent. The $100,000 threshold amount was to be indexed for inflation, and the provision was set to expire at the end of 1995.

House Ways and Means Committee Democrat Don J. Pease, Ohio, who proposed the idea, said raising the top rate or imposing a surtax on the rich would be "the cleanest way to make the tax system more progressive." But, recognizing the impending political logjam, he came up with a plan that allowed both sides to claim some victory.

At the last minute, Senate Republican negotiators proposed to raise the limit to 4 percent of income over $125,000, arguing that those earning between $100,000 and $125,000 would be hit twice under the deal. They would be subject to the reduction in itemized deductions plus the provision raising the wage base for the 1.45 percent Medicare payroll levy from $51,300 to $125,000.

But Democratic leaders rejected the proposal, in part because they feared a 4 percent deduction limit would generate opposition on the floor from big-state members.

• **Capital gains.** Although Democrats vehemently rejected Bush's demand for a capital gains tax cut, the final package did include a small cut in the tax on capital gains (profits from the sale of assets, such as stocks, real estate or lumber) for those taxpayers who were currently in the 33 percent bubble.

Before the law took effect, taxpayers paid the same tax rate on capital gains income as they did on ordinary income. The bill set a nominal maximum capital gains tax rate of 28 percent. Thus, those who paid the 33 percent rate would get a reduction.

Business groups that had been pushing a capital gains tax cut, however, dismissed the change as too insignificant to have much effect on investment. Bush had proposed that the rate be reduced to as low as 15 percent.

In fact, some high-income taxpayers with high capital gains could have a slight increase in their capital gains taxes because of the backdoor rate impact of the deductions limit and the phaseout of the personal exemption.

• **Alternative minimum tax.** The legislation also increased to 24 percent from 21 percent the alternative minimum tax rate on taxpayers who otherwise would have been able to reduce their liability substantially by using numerous deductions and other tax breaks.

However, the bill repealed for one year, 1991, a provision that applied the alternative minimum tax to the appreciated value of tangible personal property such as artworks and manuscripts that were donated to museums, libraries and universities.

• **Help for low-income taxpayers.** As part of child-care legislation folded into the reconciliation bill, a number of tax changes were made to help lower-income families. *(Child care, p. 547)*

The measure called for an increase in the earned-income tax credit (EITC) for working poor families with children. At the time, the credit was equal to 14 percent of the first $6,810 of earned income and began to phase out after $10,730 of income. The maximum credit in 1991 was projected to be $994 under existing law.

The new measure increased the credit in 1991 to a maximum of $1,186 for taxpayers with one child and $1,228 for those with two or more.

Taxpayers receiving the EITC were eligible for an additional tax credit for each child under the age of 1. The maximum supplemental credit was expected to be $355 in 1991.

An additional refundable credit was allowed for those who purchased health insurance for qualifying children under the EITC. The maximum credit for 1991 was expected to be $426.

New Excise Taxes

The package raised almost half of its revenues through new or increased excise taxes.

The largest increase came from a 5-cents-per-gallon increase in motor fuels taxes, beginning Dec. 1. This brought the total federal excise tax on gasoline to 14 cents per gallon and on diesel fuel to 20 cents per gallon.

Fuel used in rail transportation was subject to a 2.5-cent-per-gallon tax. Previously, railroads were not subject to the fuels tax, and the trucking industry fought hard to have their competitors pay.

Half of the increased tax revenue was dedicated to reducing the deficit; the remainder was to go to the Highway Trust Fund, with 20 percent of that amount allocated to mass transit, as under existing law.

The bill doubled the existing tax — ranging from $500 to $3,850, depending on a vehicle's fuel efficiency — on automobiles that did not meet legal fuel economy standards. Limousines were also subjected to the so-called gas-guzzler tax.

Excise taxes on wine, beer and distilled spirits also went up under the bill. The result was a doubling of the beer tax from 16 cents to 32 cents per six-pack; an increase from 3 cents to 21 cents in the tax on a bottle of table wine; and a distilled spirits tax hike that translated into an increase of 16 cents in the existing $2 tax on a fifth of 80-proof liquor.

A reduced tax was allowed for small breweries and domestic wineries.

Taxes on tobacco products were to go up 25 percent Jan. 1, 1991, and a like amount on Jan. 1, 1993. For example, the 16-cent tax on a pack of cigarettes was to increase 4 cents in 1991 and an additional 4 cents two years later.

As part of the effort to hit the wealthiest taxpayer, the bill imposed a new "luxury" tax on expensive automobiles, boats and yachts, private airplanes, jewelry and furs. The tax equaled 10 percent of the price over a certain threshold amount: $30,000 for automobiles, $100,000 for boats and yachts, $250,000 for aircraft, and $10,000 for jewelry and furs. The tax was set to expire in nine years.

Taxes that funded the Airport and Airway Trust Fund, due to expire Dec. 31, were extended for five years and increased 25 percent.

That meant an increase from 8 percent to 10 percent in the airline ticket tax and increased levies on air freight and fuels used in non-commercial aviation. Increased revenues would go toward deficit reduction in 1991 and 1992 and to the Airport and Airway Trust Fund for the three years after that. *(Aviation package, p. 384)*

The existing 3 percent excise tax on local and toll telephone service, set to expire at the end of 1990, was permanently extended.

The bill also expanded the list of ozone-depleting chemicals subject to federal excise taxes; more than tripled the harbor maintenance tax on the value of cargo loaded and unloaded at U.S. ports; and continued a special 0.1-cent-per-gallon fuels tax to be deposited in a trust fund to pay for cleaning up leaking underground storage tanks.

Another provision inserted to shift more of the tax burden onto upper-income taxpayers was an increase from $51,300 to $125,000 in the wage base subject to the 1.45 percent Medicare payroll tax. The tax was paid by both employer and employee for a total of 2.9 percent. *(Medicare, p. 563)*

The bill also extended Social Security retirement, disability and hospital insurance coverage to state and local workers not covered by a public employee retirement system. The provision was effective after June 30, 1991.

A 0.2 percent surtax on federal unemployment insurance taxes paid by employers was extended through 1995. The tax had been set to expire after 1990.

Taxes also went up for employers wanting to use excess funds in overfunded pension plans. The bill raised from 15 percent to 20 percent the excise tax on assets that reverted to an employer upon a plan's termination. If an employer failed to meet certain requirements, the excise tax was raised to 50 percent. Those who used excess pension funds to pay premiums on retiree health plans were subject to the tax. *(Pension reversions, p. 367)*

The bill also raised the premiums that employers with defined benefit pension plans had to pay the Pension Benefit Guaranty Corporation. It increased from $16 to $19 the flat rate, per-participant premium, and increased from $6 to $9 the additional premium that had to be paid for each $1,000 of unfunded vested benefits.

The bill made few changes in corporate taxes, although the life insurance industry got an $8 billion hit over five years because of a lengthening in the period over which firms were required to write off certain acquisition costs.

The bill also increased by 2 percentage points the interest rate paid by corporations on tax underpayments following notification by the Internal Revenue Service. The increase did not apply to underpayments of $100,000 or less. The provision was expected to raise $1.8 billion over five years, far less than the $4.1 billion that would have been raised by the Senate-passed provision it replaced. The Senate would have denied corporations a deduction for interest on such tax underpayments.

Tax Breaks

Not everyone's taxes were increased by the bill. It provided $2.5 billion in energy-related tax breaks, primarily to benefit oil and gas operations, over five years. It also allowed $773 million in tax breaks for small businesses.

The bill extended tax credits for the production of non-conventional and alcohol fuels; provided new credits for ethanol production and costs associated with certain difficult oil-recovery projects; expanded percentage depletion deductions allowed independent oil and gas producers; and provided alternative minimum tax relief for oil and gas producers.

Small businesses benefited from revised rules governing taxation of estates and a new tax credit for costs associated with making a facility more accessible to the disabled. The bill, however, lowered from $35,000 to $15,000 the amount that a business could deduct for such expenses.

The bill also extended, through the end of 1991, 11 popular tax breaks that were set to expire. The cost for these so-called extenders was projected to be $5.9 billion. over the five-year period. Some critics noted, however, that these provisions were usually extended each year and that the five-year cost could be much higher.

The extensions were:

- A 20 percent tax credit for new business research expenditures.
- Continuation of rules governing the allocation of research expenditures between foreign and domestic sources.
- Exclusion from income of certain employer-provided education assistance, not to exceed $5,250 per year.
- Exclusion from income of employer-provided group legal services and the tax exemption for qualified group legal services organizations.
- A targeted jobs tax credit, available to employers who hired hard-to-place workers.
- Tax credits for businesses that invested in solar or geothermal energy. A credit for ocean thermal energy was allowed to expire.
- A credit for construction or rehabilitation of low-income rental housing.
- Tax-exempt mortgage revenue bonds and mortgage credit certificates, which could be issued by state and local entities to help people purchase, rehabilitate or improve single-family, owner-occupied homes.
- Tax-exempt "small-issue" bonds issued to finance certain manufacturing or farming operations.
- A 25 percent deduction for the health insurance costs of self-employed people.
- A 50 percent credit for the costs of testing drugs for certain rare diseases or conditions. ■

New Budget Process for Congress, President

One of the biggest selling points of the 1990 deficit-reduction package — for Congress and the White House alike — was a package of procedural changes designed to make the budget savings stick.

Included within the budget-reconciliation bill (HR 5835 — PL 101-508) were changes that drastically altered the budget process that Congress had followed since passage of the Gramm-Rudman antideficit law (PL 99-177) in 1985. *(Provisions: Title XIII, Enforcement, p. 161)*

Gramm-Rudman — or Gramm-Rudman-Hollings to include its third congressional author — set a goal of a balanced budget by 1991, later pushed back to 1993. It mandated specific deficit targets each year and established a procedure for automatic spending cuts — called a sequester — if Congress and the president could not agree on a budget that met the targets.

By 1990, however, the goal of a balanced budget was dismissed as impossible and the law was being criticized by budget experts and lawmakers as leading to accounting gimmickry rather than true deficit reduction.

President Bush and his budget officials supported Gramm-Rudman but backed other ways of revising the budget process. Bush endorsed two constitutional changes — a balanced-budget amendment and a line-item veto — and called on Congress repeatedly to include tightened procedures changes in any budget agreement.

At the same time, the Democratic chairmen of the House and Senate Budget committees developed their own plans for overhauling Gramm-Rudman, focusing on longer-range budgeting and greater flexibility on spending. Many features of their plans, including a "pay-as-you-go" provision for entitlements or revenue-reducing measures, were eventually adopted.

To some, the final product seemed the end of Gramm-Rudman as it had been known. But in hailing the process reforms as he signed them into law Nov. 5, Bush said they "extended" and "strengthened" the law and its enforcement mechanisms. *(Bush statement, p. 166)*

Key Changes

The process reforms changed the budget calendar in Congress and altered the roles of the Appropriations and Budget committees. They replaced the scheme of automatic spending cuts under Gramm-Rudman with three discrete sequesters that worked in significantly different ways.

- **Calendar changes.** The president's budget request to Congress was now due the first Monday in February, not the first Monday after Jan. 3. If a budget resolution was not adopted by April 15, the Budget committees would have to report spending limits for the Appropriations committees based on discretionary spending in the president's budget. And while the fiscal year still began Oct. 1, automatic spending cuts would not be triggered until 15 days after Congress adjourned.
- **Five-year budgeting.** Budget resolutions and necessary reconciliation bills had to project spending, revenues and deficits for five years.
- **Automatic spending cuts.** The Gramm-Rudman procedure — an initial automatic spending cut or sequester that was calculated in mid-August and took effect Oct. 1, followed by a final sequester Oct. 15 — was gone.

Instead, the bill created a set of three sequesters, each of which would kick in 15 days after Congress adjourned: The first would offset discretionary appropriations for the coming fiscal year that exceeded statutory limits; it only affected discretionary spending. The second would be triggered if Congress enacted entitlement spending increases or revenue decreases during the year and would only affect "non-exempt" entitlements. The third would offset an increase in the deficit above the limit set in the law, if the first two sequesters had not eliminated the excess deficit; it would cover all non-exempt spending. The discretionary and entitlement sequesters would also "look back" to offset spending increases or revenue cuts that affected the prior fiscal year.

- **Discretionary spending caps.** Appropriations bills had to stay within specific caps for defense, foreign aid and domestic discretionary spending for fiscal 1991-93; for fiscal 1994-95, the law set overall discretionary spending caps. Bills exceeding the caps would be out of order for floor consideration. Each year these caps were to be adjusted upward to account for inflation.
- **Deficit targets.** The law set new, higher deficit targets

Balanced-Budget Amendment Fails . . .

After a six-hour debate filled with sharp rhetoric and anguished complaints about Congress' inability to balance the federal budget on its own, the House fell seven votes short July 17 of approving a balanced-budget constitutional amendment (H J Res 268). The vote was 279-150, less than the two-thirds majority needed in both chambers to submit the amendment to the states for ratification. *(Vote 238, p. 82-H)*

The next day, the House passed a Democratic-backed balanced-budget statute (HR 5258 — H Rept 101-603) that Republicans denounced as a joke. The Senate never acted on the measure.

The House vote was the third time in eight years that a balanced-budget amendment had been defeated on the floor of either the House or the Senate.

As voted on by the House, H J Res 268 would have:

- Required that the president submit a balanced budget and that Congress and the president agree on an estimate for receipts for the coming year.
- Required, except during a declared war, a three-fifths vote of Congress for spending in excess of that estimate or for any increase in the national debt limit.
- Required a majority vote of the total membership of each chamber by roll call vote for any tax increase.
- Taken effect beginning in fiscal 1995 or two years after ratification, whichever was later.

Republicans, who solidly backed the measure along with many conservative and moderate Democrats, said the amendment was needed because Congress had lost the ability to be fiscally responsible.

But Democratic leaders said the measure would be ineffective, invite court intervention in budget issues and give control of the budget to a minority of the House.

The Senate Judiciary Committee approved a similar measure (S J Res 183 — S Rept 101-391) on June 14, but after the House vote it was not brought to the floor for debate.

BACKGROUND

Efforts to amend the Constitution to control federal budget deficits dated from 1936, when Rep. Harold Knutson, R-Minn., proposed to set a per capita limit on the public debt.

By the mid-1970s, pressure for a balanced-budget amendment forced the issue in Congress.

In 1979, a Senate Judiciary subcommittee approved a balanced-budget amendment offered with bipartisan sponsorship. But the full committee rejected the measure, 9-8, on March 15, 1980. *(1980 Almanac, p. 304)*

Presidential candidate Ronald Reagan promised in his 1980 campaign to balance the federal budget by 1982 or 1983. By 1982, however, with the deficit headed toward $110 billion, President Reagan threw his weight behind the constitutional amendment. The Republican-controlled Senate debated a proposal by Orrin G. Hatch, R-Utah, for two weeks and, with last-minute lobbying by Reagan, approved the amendment 69-31 on Aug. 4, 1982. The Democratic-controlled House, however, rejected a similar amendment, 236-187 — 46 votes short of the two-thirds majority required. *(1982 Almanac, p. 391)*

In 1986, a balanced-budget amendment again reached the floor of the Senate, but failed, 66-34, one vote short of a two-thirds majority. *(1989 Almanac, p. 578)*

In 1988, the Republican Party platform endorsed a balanced-budget amendment, and presidential candidate George Bush echoed the call in campaign appearances. As president, Bush took up the issue in his first budget message to Congress in 1989, urging lawmakers to "honor the public's wishes" by approving a balanced-budget amendment.

"Such an amendment, once phased in, will discipline both Congress and the Executive branch," he said.

Proposals Introduced

The basic mechanism of balanced-budget amendment proposals remained unchanged throughout the 1980s: a three-fifths majority requirement in each house of Congress for approving a budget deficit except in time of war.

Two slightly different versions were introduced in the House and the Senate in mid-1989.

Rep. Charles W. Stenholm, a conservative Texas Democrat, introduced H J Res 268 on May 11, 1989, with more than 230 cosponsors.

In the Senate, a softer proposal was introduced on July 27, 1989, by liberal Paul Simon, D-Ill., and the conservative Hatch. Unlike Stenholm's proposal, the Simon-Hatch measure did not call for a three-fifths majority to increase the national debt or a majority of total membership to approve a tax hike.

Simon's Judiciary Subcommittee on Constitutional Law approved his measure the same day it was introduced, 4-2.

In the House, the Judiciary Committee did not schedule hearings on Stenholm's amendment, forcing him to

---

for fiscal 1991-95. These targets were to be automatically adjusted in fiscal 1992-93 to account for changes in the economy and technical estimates of the cost of entitlements. The president had the option of adjusting the deficit caps for economic or technical changes in fiscal 1994-95.

- **Pay-as-you go entitlements and revenues.** Bills containing increases in entitlement or other mandatory spending or reducing revenues had to be deficit-neutral. They would be out of order for floor consideration unless accompanied by offsetting entitlement cuts or revenue increases.
- **Supplemental appropriations and emergencies.** Supplemental appropriations enacted before July 1 that exceeded spending caps would trigger sequesters 15 days after their enactment; the automatic cuts would offset the excess within the spending category in which the excess occurred. If requested to do so by the president, Congress could enact emergency appropriations, entitlement increases or revenue cuts without triggering sequesters.
- **Social Security and deposit insurance.** Social Security receipts and expenditures were no longer included in budget calculations. Increased spending for deposit in-

. . . House Backers Seven Votes Short

begin gathering signatures on a discharge petition to bring the matter onto the House floor.

SENATE COMMITTEE ACTION

Simon's proposal — amended to include the total-majority requirement for tax increases — was approved by the Senate Judiciary Committee, 11-3, on June 14.

Democrats voting for the measure included committee Chairman Joseph R. Biden Jr., Del.; Dennis DeConcini, Ariz.; Howell Heflin, Ala.; and Herb Kohl, Wis. All six committee Republicans supported it.

Biden and Kohl, however, said the amendment was too inflexible and should be revised on the floor.

Voting against the measure were three liberal Democrats: Edward M. Kennedy, Mass.; Howard M. Metzenbaum, Ohio; and Patrick J. Leahy, Vt.

HOUSE ACTION

On June 19, Stenholm announced he had received enough signatures — 218 — on the discharge petition to remove H J Res 268 from the Judiciary Committee and bring it to the House floor.

Forced into action, the Judiciary Subcommittee on Economic and Commercial Law held two days of hearings July 10-11. White House budget director Richard G. Darman endorsed the amendment, but most other witnesses opposed it.

On July 13, the Rules Committee scheduled the amendment for floor debate July 17.

Floor Debate

During six hours of floor debate, Stenholm and other backers argued the amendment was the only way to force budget discipline in Congress. "Courage and guts," said Stenholm, "we do not have it and we have not shown it. We need some help and an extra tool."

"Legislation has not worked," said Rep. Hamilton Fish Jr., R-N.Y. "Huge budget deficits have proved intractable," he said, despite passage of the Gramm-Rudman antideficit law.

Judiciary Chairman Jack Brooks, D-Texas, leading the opposition, argued the amendment would not "magically create a balanced budget," and could instead "produce a host of dangerous and unintended consequences."

The amendment's ambiguity would invite endless intervention by an "activist judiciary," Brooks said, and its requirement for a three-fifths vote would empower a minority of the House to control the budget process.

Opponents also complained that while Bush and Reagan had both endorsed a balanced-budget amendment, neither ever submitted a balanced budget to Congress.

Joe L. Barton, R-Texas, tried to tighten the proposal by amending it to require a three-fifths vote for any tax increase. But his amendment gained only 35 Democratic votes and failed, 184-244. *(Vote 236, p. 80-H)*

On the main amendment, Democrats were more evenly divided: 110 voted for the amendment, including several who changed their stance from earlier years, while 145 stuck with the party leadership. Among Republicans, only five members voted against it.

Speaker Thomas S. Foley, D-Wash., said the narrow vote reflected "frustration" on the part of Democrats who wanted to "send a message to the administration, and to the Congress as well, that they wanted . . . to see something more dramatically done." But Foley ruled out another vote on the issue, something backers said they might seek if the Senate approved the amendment.

Statutory Alternative

Instead, the Democratic leadership sped onto the floor July 18 a bill to require the president and the House and Senate Budget committees to offer a balanced budget every year.

Under the proposal, the president or either committee could also submit a budget out of balance, but only with a written explanation why a balanced budget was "infeasible." Votes would have been in order on all versions. The measure would take effect in fiscal 1992.

Budget Committee Chairman Leon E. Panetta, D-Calif., speaking for the bill, said the requirement for alternative proposals would force "a vote on the specific approach to balancing the budget."

He and other Democrats noted pointedly that the bill was to take effect sooner than the proposed balanced-budget amendment.

GOP opponents, such as Lynn Martin, Ill., countered that the bill had no teeth and was designed for political cover. "Do you think for a minute the American people don't see through this ploy for what it is?" Martin asked.

After surviving a Republican motion to recommit, the measure rolled to an easy 282-144 approval, largely along party lines. But despite the strong vote, the Democratic-controlled Senate never brought the measure up. *(Votes 245, 246, p. 84-H)*

---

surance activities — chiefly the savings and loan salvage operation — would not be allowed to trigger sequesters.

- **War and recession.** A declaration of war would still cancel the sequester process. Congress could still vote to cancel the sequester process in the event of a projected recession or measured economic growth below 1 percent for two consecutive quarters.

BACKGROUND

Congress and the White House had been battling over budget procedures since President Richard M. Nixon asserted a right to impound congressional appropriations in order to control federal spending.

The Nixon administration was forced to yield on its broadest assertions of presidential prerogatives, but the dispute contributed to a congressional overhaul of budget procedures in 1974.

The 1974 Congressional Budget and Impoundment Control Act (PL 93-344) established new Budget committees in each chamber.

It also changed the beginning of the fiscal year from

Discretionary Spending Caps

(In billions of dollars, by fiscal year)

	1991	1992	1993	1994	1995
Defense					
Budget authority	$ 288.9	$ 291.6	$ 291.8		
Outlays	297.7	295.7	292.7		
International					
Budget authority	20.1	20.5	21.4		
Outlays	18.6	19.1	19.6		
Domestic					
Budget authority	182.7	191.3	198.3		
Outlays	198.1	210.1	221.7		
Total discretionary					
Budget authority *	(491.7)	(503.4)	(511.5)	510.8	517.7
Outlays *	(514.4)	(524.9)	(534.0)	534.8	540.8

* *Budget authority and outlay numbers for the first three years are informational; the law specified only the defense, international and domestic caps for those years.*

SOURCE: 1990 Omnibus Budget Reconciliation Act

July 1 to Oct. 1 to allow more time to fix overall spending and set priorities.

And it limited the president's power to defer or rescind appropriations without first notifying Congress. *(1974 Almanac, p. 145)*

Budget battles intensified under President Ronald Reagan as he and congressional Democrats repeatedly blamed each other for the growing deficits of the 1980s. Reagan called on Congress to pass a balanced-budget amendment and a line-item veto, but neither was enacted.

In 1985, however, Republican Sens. Phil Gramm of Texas and Warren B. Rudman of New Hampshire, along with Democratic Sen. Ernest F. Hollings of South Carolina, crafted a new approach to controlling federal spending: mandated deficit reductions to be enforced by automatic spending cuts if Congress and the president did not agree on a budget that met the target. The measure won approval as a rider on a must-pass bill increasing the national debt limit but only after Democratic modifications that exempted Social Security from the sequester procedure and required that automatic cuts be split equally between defense and domestic spending. *(1985 Almanac, p. 459)*

In 1986, the Supreme Court invalidated the automatic spending cut procedures on separation of powers grounds because of the role played by the General Accounting Office (GAO), an arm of Congress, in ordering the cuts. Congress and the White House followed the law in enacting the budget for fiscal 1987, however, and the next year Congress fixed the defect by putting enforcement of the sequester in the hands of the Office of Management and Budget (OMB). At the same time, the goal of a balanced budget was pushed back to 1993. *(1987 Almanac, p. 604)*

Gramm-Rudman Under Scrutiny

The Gramm-Rudman sequester procedure had been viewed as such a draconian threat that Congress and the White House were expected to settle any differences in order to avert it. But in 1989, the across-the-board cuts were triggered when Bush and the Democratic-controlled Congress failed to reach agreement by Oct. 1 on a budget to stay within the law's stated deficit target of $110 billion.

Bush signed a sequester order on Oct. 16. It remained in effect until a $14.7 billion deficit-reduction plan that relied on some of the automatic cuts to achieve its goal cleared Congress a month later and was signed into law on Dec. 19. *(1989 Almanac, p. 94)*

Bush reiterated his support for Gramm-Rudman in 1990 in his State of the Union address Jan. 31 and his economic report to Congress Feb. 6. He said the law had helped reduce the deficit and recalled how he had "stood by the sequestration order that resulted from my strict adherence to the Gramm-Rudman-Hollings law." *(Economic report, p. 116)*

Democrats in Congress, however, were stepping up their criticism of the law and drafting plans to overhaul or scrap it. Two principal proposals came early in the year from the House and Senate Budget chairmen — Rep. Leon E. Panetta, D-Calif., and Sen. Jim Sasser, D-Tenn. Both wanted to replace Gramm-Rudman and its threatened automatic cuts with procedures requiring about $30 billion in annual deficit reduction, enforced with new parliamentary rules and — in Sasser's case — with the reward of payroll tax cuts for compliance.

OMB Director Richard G. Darman responded by issuing veto threats against any repeal of Gramm-Rudman and charging that Democrats wanted to escape the law's discipline. But proponents of repeal countered that, far from enforcing budget discipline, the law prompted the president and Congress alike to use increasingly creative gimmickry to evade its penalties.

The critics noted, for example, that every deficit projection since Gramm-Rudman became law had significantly understated the actual deficit because of erroneous economic assumptions and false savings claims. When Congress and the president annually discovered the gap between the actual deficit and the next year's target, both resorted to bookkeeping ploys — such as moving expenditures from one fiscal year to the next — and rosy economic assumptions to reach the goal.

LEGISLATIVE ACTION

Lawmakers in both chambers talked about budget-process changes through much of the year and held some formal legislative proceedings toward that goal. Once the White House-congressional budget summit got under way, however, it became the real forum for making any decisions about procedural changes.

Panetta, Sasser Plans

Both Sasser's and Panetta's plans took the approach of specifying annual spending cuts — about $30 billion — without mandating what the resulting deficit must be.

Many fiscal experts had sought that change, considering it more realistic and less conducive to fiscal chicanery.

Both plans also called for removing Social Security surpluses from deficit calculations, an idea with support among lawmakers of both parties. Including the surpluses, it was said, understated the true extent of the deficit.

Panetta included in his bill (HR 3929) a "pay as you go" provision mandating that any spending increases or tax cuts be offset by other spending cuts or tax hikes. The bill would also have mandated that the budget meet deficit-reduction targets not just for the coming fiscal year but also for the four successive years.

Finally, in response to chronic complaints that OMB's economic projections were overly favorable, Panetta would have required Congress to use data from the nonpartisan CBO. For fiscal 1991, for example, CBO was forecasting a deficit of $138 billion early in the year while OMB's projection was $100.5 billion.

Sasser's plan was unveiled Jan. 25 but not put into legislative language immediately. Its key distinguishing feature was a plan to permit $17 billion in payroll tax cuts annually contingent on Congress' and the president's achievement of at least $30 billion in deficit reduction.

House Budget Hearing

A House Budget Committee hearing on March 7 gave critics of Gramm-Rudman a public forum for rehearsing their arguments against the law. The witnesses were three budget experts — economist Henry Aaron of the Brookings Institution and two former CBO directors, Alice M. Rivlin of Brookings and Rudolph G. Penner of the Urban Institute — who all had previously called for repealing the law.

Under the law, Rivlin said, "the obsession with appearing to meet next year's [deficit] target intensified incentives to use rosy forecasts of economic growth and interest rates, to move activities off budget, and to engage in gimmickry that reduced next year's deficit at the expense of future years."

Aaron, noting that the law's automatic cuts no longer posed an equal threat to all sides, said, "The political equilibrium that made agreement on some package better than sequestration has been upset."

Penner said the law had "led to extremely disorderly and dishonest results with only modest improvements in the deficit outlook — most of which, I would argue, occurred despite the budget process and not because of it."

Senate Budget Committee

Although the budget summit got under way in May, Democratic leaders decided to keep the regular congressional budget process going while the talks proceeded. Process reforms were a secondary issue in the talks, but during much of June and July the summit seemed as likely as not to end in an impasse.

In that atmosphere, the Senate Budget Committee scheduled a markup on a number of budget process changes. Before it acted, though, the House took up — and rejected on July 17 — the most prominent of budget process changes: a balanced-budget constitutional amendment. *(Balanced-budget amendment, p. 174)*

On July 26, the Senate Budget Committee reported out nine measures to revise the budget process.

Aides acknowledged that the markup was held largely because of pressure from members who wanted some action on budget-process plans they had authored even if none reached the floor.

Key Dates

Jan. 21	Notice of optional adjustment of deficit target for fiscal 1994-95.
First Monday in February	President submits budget request and economic forecast that will control budget activity for the following year; budget also includes OMB sequester preview (CBO sequester preview due five days earlier).
April 15	Congress completes action on budget resolution.
May 15	Appropriations bills may be considered in the House.
June 30	Congress completes action on appropriations bills.
July 1	Supplemental appropriations for the current fiscal year that exceed discretionary spending targets and are enacted before this date trigger 15-day post-enactment sequester.
Aug. 10	Notice of optional sequester exemption for military personnel.
Aug. 15	CBO updates sequester preview.
Aug. 20	OMB updates sequester preview.
Oct. 1	Start of the new fiscal year.
10 days after adjournment	CBO final sequester report.
15 days after adjournment	OMB final sequester report; president issues sequester order.
30 days later	GAO sequester compliance report.

Among the plans approved by the committee were the following:

- A proposal by Frank R. Lautenberg, D-N.J., approved 13-9, to set an annual ratio of defense to domestic spending cuts under the Gramm-Rudman law rather than the fixed 50-50 split.
- A measure by Kent Conrad, D-N.D., approved 15-5, to require automatic spending cuts if the preceding year's deficit was more than $10 billion above the deficit target for that year.
- A measure, approved 13-6, by Hollings, to give the president the power to veto individual items in appropriations bills.
- A measure by Rudy Boschwitz, R-Minn., approved 13-8, that would require Congress to use existing spending levels, without inflation adjustments, in preparing the annual budget.

Summit Negotiations

The budget summit resumed in September after the August congressional recess still with no assurance that an accord would be reached. While spending cuts and tax measures dominated public speculation, Republican negotiators were also maintaining pressure to include process changes to tighten the fiscal reins on Congress.

The agreement reached Sept. 30 included proposals that did not go quite so far as Republicans wanted in giving the president more authority to limit federal spending but were generally viewed as likely to impose at least some additional fiscal restraint on Capitol Hill.

Among the most important proposals was an extension

Darman Scores Win With Credit Reforms

In a victory for White House budget director Richard G. Darman, reforms aimed at disclosing and controlling the cost of government loans, loan guarantees and insurance were included in the 1990 budget-reconciliation bill.

Credit reform provisions in the bill (HR 5835 — PL 101-508) required that beginning in fiscal 1992, the net long-term costs of loan and loan guarantee programs be included in the current fiscal year's budget.

Also beginning in fiscal 1992, specific congressional appropriations were to be required for new direct loans or loan guarantees and specific budget authority required for modifications to loan or loan guarantee programs. Exempted from the requirements were entitlement loan programs such as the guaranteed student loan and veterans' home loan guarantee programs and the credit programs of the Commodity Credit Corporation.

The credit and insurance activities of several agencies were exempted for the time being from both the budgeting and appropriations requirements, including the agencies protecting the nation's financial institutions: the Federal Deposit Insurance Corporation, the Resolution Trust Corporation and National Credit Union Administration.

But the Office of Management and Budget (OMB) and Congressional Budget Office (CBO) were to report to the president and Congress by May 31, 1991, on what accounting system should be used for the deposit insurance programs. *(Provisions: Title XIII, Credit Reform, p. 163)*

OMB Director Darman had raised the credit reform issue with a provocative warning in sending President Bush's budget to Congress on Jan. 29. With the thrift bailout fresh in the minds of the public and officials alike, Darman said the government faced a largely undisclosed $5.7 trillion in contingent liabilities under various loan, loan guarantee and insurance programs.

Darman called these future liabilities "hidden Pac-men," a reference to the devouring creature in a popular video arcade game. He said that even though the liabilities would not all fall due at the same time, likely losses on loans and loan guarantees alone were "virtually certain" to total tens of billions of dollars.

An April 11 hearing by the House Budget Committee Task Force on Urgent Fiscal Issues found Darman's warnings seconded by Comptroller General Charles A. Bowsher, head of the General Accounting Office, and CBO Director Robert D. Reischauer. All three officials criticized the growth in loan guarantees, which were not included in calculating the deficit and which had spiraled upward while direct loans were decreasing.

"Our perverse budgetary accounting procedures have led us to dish out credit as if it were cost-free," said Charles E. Schumer, D-N.Y., chairman of the task force. "If we do not apply the brakes now, we will speed off a trillion-dollar cliff."

The credit reforms were rolled into the budget reconciliation bill cleared by Congress on Oct. 27 with little public discussion.

But Bush noted them in signing the bill Nov. 5, saying they would "expose and limit previously hidden (and rapidly growing) liabilities."

---

through fiscal 1995 of the Gramm-Rudman antideficit law, which was set to expire at the end of fiscal 1993. It was to be reinforced with a new layer of caps and so-called mini-sequesters designed to prevent spending and tax breaks from getting out of control before it was too late. Deficit targets were revised, and separate caps were to be set for fiscal 1991-93 in three budget categories: defense, international and domestic programs.

The House vote Oct. 6 rejecting the summit agreement forced negotiators to try again, but the budget-process reforms changed little between that setback and the final budget-reconciliation bill cleared on Oct. 27.

Lawmakers and administration officials alike stressed the spending controls in the bill. But the final plan also included features that would allow the deficit to grow as long as Congress did nothing explicit to cause the increase. Specifically:

- Discretionary spending would be allowed to grow at the rate of inflation.
- Entitlement spending programs such as Medicare could grow without penalty as more people became eligible for benefits.
- And there would be no penalties for increases in spending or reductions in revenues that resulted from a deterioration in the economy or a mistake in technical forecasts, such as the estimated rate of tax revenue growth.

Moreover, spending for some special things — debt forgiveness for foreign countries, additional Internal Revenue Service agents and the military operations in the Persian Gulf crisis — were exempted from the spending caps.

Lawmakers got several things from the new procedures. The Appropriations committees gained by virtue of the inflation-based increases in domestic spending along with an additional $20 billion in budget authority spread over fiscal 1991-93. As long as spending stayed within those caps, appropriators could raise domestic spending without facing the threat of automatic cuts.

Congress would also be spared the political pain of voting on entitlement cuts to get the deficit down. Any spending authorized by existing entitlement law would be tolerated without penalty.

The White House and congressional Republicans did win some concessions, too. Through fiscal 1993, appropriators would not be able to raid international or defense accounts to boost domestic spending without facing a point of order on the floor, which would require 60 votes to overcome in the Senate. In addition, only the president was given authority to determine that a particular supplemental spending bill could qualify as an emergency measure exempt from automatic spending cuts.

White House clout on budget matters was also increased by a provision giving OMB the power to determine the net budget impact of new entitlement legislation. On the other hand, use of CBO rather than OMB economic forecasts would shift power toward the Hill and away from the White House. ■

Bill To Add Thrift Bailout Funds Dies

A year of partisan debate, financial uncertainty and political maneuvering over the spiraling cost of bailing out failed thrift institutions ended in Congress' final hours when a single lawmaker blocked a last-gasp effort to add needed funds to the bailout operation.

When the thrift bailout law (PL 101-73) was enacted in August 1989, the Bush administration said there were about 500 failed or failing thrifts and projected the cost of closing them at no more than $73 billion. By early 1990, however, the number of failed thrifts had grown, and it was clear to almost everyone that far more money would be needed.

Congress began talking about the problem in January, but the scent of scandal and the political costs of asking taxpayers to shoulder a higher burden created an atmosphere in which no one — in Congress or in the administration — wanted to take responsibility for seeking more money.

The bickering turned into public squabbling over the summer and reached a high point in October. The House and Senate Banking committees approved legislation that would have provided a short-term infusion of cash, but it died on the House floor. Members blamed Treasury Secretary Nicholas F. Brady, saying he lacked the political courage to make a forthright request for more money. Democrats in Congress refused to act without an administration request as a cover.

Even when the House leadership finally agreed to let a bill (HR 5891) for more money come to the floor, the effort was thwarted by Frank Annunzio, D-Ill. The senior Banking Committee member objected to a unanimous-consent request to act on the measure in the early hours of Oct. 28, as Congress was struggling to adjourn; several other lawmakers, however, were also said to have been ready to make the parliamentary objection if necessary.

With Congress gone and the bailout coffers nearly empty, the administration decided Nov. 1 to exploit a loophole in the 1989 thrift salvage law that raised the limit on temporary borrowing for the bailout by $18.8 billion — enough, it was estimated, to keep the salvage operation in business until March 1991.

Congress and the administration went back to work on the problem in January 1991, after the Bush administration requested an additional $30 billion to keep the bailout going. At a Senate Banking Committee meeting Jan. 23, 1991, Brady said Congress' failure to act in 1990 had added as much $300 million to the cost of the salvage operation.

The cost of the salvage operation was one of several fronts in the frequently partisan sniping between Congress and the administration stemming from the crisis in the thrift industry in the late 1980s. *(Background, 1988 Almanac, p. 242; 1987 Almanac, p. 628)*

T. Timothy Ryan, the administration's choice to head the new Office of Thrift Supervision (OTS), won Senate confirmation April 4 only after overcoming criticism about his lack of experience in the field. *(Ryan confirmation, p. 180)*

And throughout the year, lawmakers charged the administration with inadequate efforts to bring criminal prosecutions or other enforcement actions against thrift executives. The charges hit especially close to President Bush when Hill Democrats criticized the handling of a regulatory investigation of the collapse of the Denver-based Silverado Banking, Savings and Loan Association and the role of his son, Neil, a former director of the thrift. *(Thrift fraud, penalties, p. 182)*

BACKGROUND

When enacted in 1989, the Financial Institutions Reform, Recovery and Enforcement Act was described as the most sweeping overhaul of laws governing savings and loan institutions in half a century. Its aim was to dramatically restructure federal thrift regulations and to clean up the mess in the thrift industry. *(1989 Almanac, p. 117)*

The cleanup was to be handled by the Resolution Trust Corporation (RTC), which was created to take possession of insolvent thrifts and to dispose of their assets.

With the 1989 law, Congress gave the RTC $50 billion to cover net losses from failed thrifts. The money was provided through a combination of appropriations and off-budget borrowing — to be repaid by the thrift industry — for thrift closures between 1989 and 1992.

An additional sum — assumed to be about $23 billion, but not specified in the law — was to be parceled out from the Treasury to cover losses after 1992 until the end of the century. The $73 billion total did not include costs incurred by the government to close about 200 failed thrifts in 1988 — before the bailout bill was enacted. Nor did it include interest costs over as much as 40 years on government bonds sold to raise the money for the bailout.

In addition, the RTC was given the authority to borrow funds to be used for "working capital," essentially bridge loans that the RTC floated as it worked to close insolvent thrifts. The money would be used to purchase and hold the assets of failed thrifts — mortgage loans, shopping centers, office buildings and undeveloped land. The RTC was to repay those loans when the assets were sold — possibly as long as 10 years in the case of some real estate.

The cost of the bailout turned out to be far higher than the administration's 1989 estimate for a number of reasons. There were far more than 500 failed thrifts to deal with, interest rates paid on borrowed money were higher than forecast, and the economy went into a recession, pushing down the value of assets owned by failed thrifts and making their disposal by the RTC far more difficult than had been anticipated. There were also problems with management of the RTC, particularly in its early months.

While it was clear from the start of 1990 that more money was needed, the Bush administration did not try to deal with the issue in its fiscal 1991 budget proposal, waiting instead until the summer to make a specific request.

Congress, which had thought the issue was resolved in the 1989 bailout bill, was angry and embarrassed to be dealing with it again in 1990. Both political parties had trouble finding a solution to the problem because both were afraid of being blamed for it.

COMMITTEE HEARINGS

Warnings about a shortage of funds came early in 1990 and persisted throughout the year.

On Jan. 24, L. William Seidman, chairman of both the RTC and the Federal Deposit Insurance Corporation (FDIC), which insured deposits in banks and thrifts, told

Ryan Confirmed as Top Thrift Regulator

Despite questions about his experience and background, T. Timothy Ryan Jr. won Senate confirmation April 4 to be the nation's top thrift regulator.

The Senate's 62-37 vote to confirm Ryan to become director of the Office of Thrift Supervision (OTS) came despite objections from Democrats that he was ill-suited for the job, as well as reservations from many Republicans that someone with experience in financial regulation might have been preferable. *(Vote 56, p. 14-S)*

The Senate Banking Committee had recommended Ryan for confirmation on a virtually party-line, 11-10 vote on March 30. Two Democrats, Richard C. Shelby of Alabama and Terry Sanford of North Carolina, crossed party lines to give Ryan's nomination the votes needed to get out of committee.

In the final vote, 17 Democrats, including eight committee chairmen, voted with all 45 Republicans to give Ryan a comfortable margin of victory. Supporters and opponents alike credited lobbying by Treasury Secretary Nicholas F. Brady; Sen. John W. Warner, R-Va., Ryan's longtime friend; and Ryan himself, who met with dozens of senators over the week leading up to the vote.

The administration was eager to have Ryan confirmed swiftly because of a challenge to the legality of OTS actions.

A federal district court had ruled that the 1989 thrift-bailout bill (PL 101-73) unconstitutionally put former Federal Home Loan Bank Board Chairman M. Danny Wall in the OTS job and that the agency's actions were therefore improper. Wall, a target of Democratic attacks for his handling of the thrift crisis, announced Dec. 4, 1989, that he would resign, although he stayed in office until March 8. *(1989 Almanac, p. 132)*

Once in office, Ryan reissued all the agency's orders made while Wall was head of the OTS.

Ryan was an experienced Washington labor and pension lawyer who had been solicitor of the Labor Department in 1981-83.

His critics said they had no concerns about his integrity or his intellectual capacity.

But the nomination ran into trouble because of Ryan's lack of experience in financial services.

"At the minimum, you want somebody who has a well-established reputation as an expert in finance," said Banking Committee Chairman Donald W. Riegle Jr., D-Mich. "Timothy Ryan does not bring those kinds of qualifications."

Riegle noted repeatedly that Ryan not only would supervise all the nation's remaining healthy thrifts as director of the OTS, but also would serve on the boards of the Federal Deposit Insurance Corporation, which insured deposits in banks and savings and loans, and the Resolution Trust Corporation, which was charged with closing down failed thrifts.

On the floor, Democrats did not make the vote on Ryan an issue of party discipline. Majority Leader George J. Mitchell, D-Maine, did not speak against Ryan's nomination, though he voted no.

Wyche Fowler Jr. of Georgia was one of the 17 Democrats who supported Ryan. He said he was not contacted by Brady but had spent an hour and a half with Ryan.

"I think you ought to give the president the benefit of the doubt," Fowler said. "It was certainly a leap of faith. I hope he's up to the task."

Ryan's confirmation had one effect unrelated to the thrift industry that was widely seen as salutary. He admitted to administration officials that, while he was a law student in the early 1970s, he had twice tried cocaine and had also smoked marijuana.

Lawmakers such as Warner and Utah Republican Jake Garn expressed a hope that Ryan's willingness to disclose his previous drug use and the Senate's willingness to ignore it would mean that incidental drug use would never again be a factor in rejecting someone for government service.

---

the House Banking Committee that the $50 billion approved by Congress in August 1989 almost certainly would not be enough to cover losses in what were then more than 600 failed or failing thrifts.

Seidman declined to put a dollar amount on the shortfall, but RTC figures suggested that a minimum of $20 billion more might be needed before the end of 1990.

At the same time Seidman warned that another $40 billion to $100 billion would have to be borrowed during 1991 by the RTC for short-term working capital.

By May the news had grown much worse. Treasury Secretary Brady told the Senate Banking Committee on May 23 that between 722 and 1,037 thrifts were facing closure, with expected losses to the government of $89 billion to $132 billion.

That was an increase of $16 billion to $59 billion above the 1989 administration cost estimate of $73 billion. The new money had to come entirely from taxpayers, Brady said, because the industry was not in a position to contribute any more than it was already to solving the problem.

Although Brady insisted that the new estimates were reasonable, he said costs could rise further as circumstances changed. "No one should assume that the estimates presented today will not change," he said. "They will."

Public Anger

Brady's testimony seemed to strike a raw nerve with the public, which had been reading months of press coverage of fraud and abuse in the thrift industry and the government's failure to stop it. Within weeks partisan knives had been drawn, and members of Congress and the administration were at each other's throats.

Hearings in the House Banking Committee, followed by federal court actions, generated high-intensity publicity about the costly failure of Lincoln Savings and Loan in California and the roles played by its owner, Charles H. Keating Jr., and five senators to get federal regulators to leave the thrift alone. *(Keating investigation, p. 78)*

The Banking Committee had also turned its attention to Neil Bush, who had been an outside director of the Silverado Banking, Savings and Loan Association in Denver before it collapsed in 1988 at high cost to the taxpayer.

There were also persistent news accounts of disarray in the agencies charged with the bailout, including squabbling among officials and the apparent decision of the White House to try to force out Seidman.

Sensing public outrage, congressional Democrats stepped up their rhetoric in early June, charging Bush personally with failing to take charge of what Charles E. Schumer, D-N.Y., dubbed "the second S&L crisis."

At the same time, the House Democratic Caucus was encouraging its membership to attack Bush in a nine-page list of "talking points" about his administration's "mishandling" of the salvage operation.

The White House responded with a assault on the Democrats, saying they had been in the pockets of the thrift industry and should not be pointing fingers. "I'm saying the Democrats had a big role" in the thrift debacle, White House spokesman Marlin Fitzwater said June 19. "If they want to make this a political issue, we'd be glad to do it."

Fitzwater read off the names of a half-dozen Democrats embroiled in the thrift crisis, among them former House Speaker Jim Wright of Texas and former House Majority Whip Tony Coelho of California. Both men had close ties to the thrift industry and resigned from Congress in 1989 under ethics questions. *(Wright resignation, 1989 Almanac, p. 36; Coelho resignation, 1989 Almanac, p. 41)*

Members of both parties, meanwhile, were feeling the heat from voters angry at the rising cost of the bailout. "Constituents are starting to fix blame, and they're looking at Congress," said Rep. Constance A. Morella, R-Md.

Rep. Jim Leach, R-Iowa, called the thrift crisis "a congressional Watergate" and said all members were on the line for having allowed it to happen.

One response was to demand increased Justice Department prosecution of former thrift owners and managers who were alleged to have stolen or defrauded their institutions into bankruptcy. Members of both parties in both chambers called for special prosecutors or for devoting whole units of the Justice Department to thrift fraud.

On June 20, the House voted 420-1, over administration objections, to earmark $75 million for thrift investigation and prosecutions in fiscal 1991 as part of the appropriations bill for the Departments of Commerce, Justice and State (HR 5021). *(Vote 187, p. 64-H; Commerce, Justice, State appropriations, p. 881)*

Bush then changed his position June 22 and asked for another $25 million on top of what the House approved. Congress complied.

The most visible sign of member concern about voters' reaction to the thrift scandal was the rush to pass new penalties for bank fraud and provide the Justice Department with more resources to investigate thrift crimes. In a long amendment to the omnibus anticrime bill (S 1970), the Senate voted on July 11 to set mandatory minimum sentences for certain crimes and a term of life in prison for so-called S&L kingpins, people who acted with three or more other people and derived more than $5 million from their crimes. The maximum sentence for a single case of bank fraud would increase from 20 years to 30 years. *(Crime bill, p. 486)*

The amendment passed 99-1, with only William L. Armstrong, R-Colo., opposed. *(Vote 146, p. 33-S)*

Administration Warning

On July 30, the administration came back to Congress to clarify its need for more money, stressing that if Congress failed to act promptly, the thrift bailout would run out of money and have to shut down before the end of 1990.

The news, delivered by Treasury Under Secretary Robert R. Glauber to the House Banking Committee, came as no surprise. But Glauber offered several proposals for how to pay for the higher losses.

Brady previously had suggested that Congress enact a permanent, indefinite appropriation for the RTC, and Glauber again suggested that option. That would have allowed the RTC to pay whatever was required, and Congress would not have had to vote again on the subject.

But Stan Parris, R-Va., and others unhappy with the proposal likened it to giving the RTC a blank check. In part, members seemed wary of giving the administration unlimited spending authority lest Congress lose control over the way the thrift bailout was being managed.

"I don't think that a permanent, indefinite appropriation would be a blank check," Glauber said, disputing the notion that Congress would give up any control. "This committee has, in fact, heard testimony from the oversight board, from the RTC on numerous occasions, and I'm sure will continue very carefully to scrutinize the process of the resolution program, whatever the appropriation."

As an alternative to that approach, however, Glauber suggested that Congress could appropriate $5 billion to get the RTC through January 1991 or $10 billion to get the agency through February. That would have allowed Congress and the administration to get past the elections and then decide later how to finance the rest of the bailout.

A third option, Glauber said, was to appropriate enough for all of fiscal 1991. That idea got little attention.

Glauber and Seidman were plainly concerned about the limit on working capital borrowing. But they offered no specifics for solving the problem except to hint that the limit might need to be eliminated.

By this time, financing the thrift bailout had been put on the agenda of the budget-summit negotiations, which were aimed at finding a long-term solution to the federal budget deficit and getting Congress and the White House through the fall elections without appearing to paper over the budget and thrift problems. *(Budget summit, p. 129)*

As a result of the higher cost estimates as well as a planned accelerated pace of thrift closings, the administration had also greatly increased its estimate of the budgetary impact of the bailout.

Even though a large part of the bailout cost was off budget, interest expenses and short-term borrowing for working capital were not. As a result, by summer, administration officials were estimating that the bailout would add as much as $61 billion to the fiscal 1991 deficit.

The summit negotiators already had problems on the thrift bailout, however, because they did not believe the public would take kindly to paying more of the bill. So they ignored the question other than to recommend a provision — included in the final budget-reconciliation bill — that the bailout costs be counted as part of the federal budget but not in Gramm-Rudman deficit calculations.

Asked Oct. 10 why money for the RTC was not included in the package, House Budget Chairman Leon E. Panetta, D-Calif., said: "We opposed it. There's enough garbage to carry in this thing."

COMMITTEE ACTION

By the fall, the political tensions between Congress and the administration had turned into a public deadlock.

Continued on p. 184

Under Pressure of Savings and Loan Crisis,

Congress, under political pressure from the growing savings and loan crisis, cleared provisions to step up penalties against individuals and financial institutions convicted of fraud and other crimes as part of the omnibus anticrime bill (S 3266 — PL 101-647).

Public anger turned the savings and loan crisis into a political nightmare for lawmakers and the Bush administration in 1990. Democratic lawmakers claimed the administration had been slow in pursuing criminal prosecutions of thrift executives. And members of Congress discovered that the S&L crisis was a major topic in many of their re-election campaigns.

For those reasons, both Democrats and Republicans backed new bank fraud penalties, much as politicians had jumped on the antidrug bandwagon two years earlier.

Tougher thrift fraud penalties were added in the Senate to a broad crime bill (S 1970) that dealt with such hot-button issues as capital punishment, death row appeals and gun control. Similar provisions made their way onto the House's anticrime bill (HR 5269) too.

Ironically, conferees on the two bills hit an impasse on those major issues, and the thrift fraud provisions ended as the centerpiece of the stripped-down bill that cleared Congress on Oct. 27 and was signed into law Nov. 29. *(Crime bill, p. 486)*

As enacted, the measure increased — in future cases — the civil and criminal penalties for financial fraud, including the maximum sentence of life in prison for defendants who received $5 million or more in gross receipts from a continuing financial enterprise during any two-year period. Those defendants could also face a fine of $10 million — $20 million for organizations.

Federal banking agencies and the Justice Department were also given enhanced authority to seize assets fraudulently obtained from banks and savings and loans. A new office of special counsel for financial institutions fraud was established at the Justice Department; and new prosecutors, FBI agents and Secret Service agents were authorized to focus on financial crimes.

BACKGROUND

Congress and the administration were caught in a firestorm of criticism over the costs and handling of the S&L bailout.

Lawmakers approved $50 billion in 1989 to address the losses caused by the crisis, but those funds proved inadequate. The administration projected in 1990 that as much as $130 billion in taxpayer funds might be needed to cover thrift losses. *(Thrift bailout, 1989 Almanac, p. 117)*

As the partisan bickering heated up, lawmakers were critical of the administration for what they called a lack of aggressiveness in going after savings and loans crooks.

In particular, Democrats took aim at the president's son Neil, who had been accused of conflict of interest during his tenure as an outside director of a Denver-based thrift. A federal investigation into the 1988 collapse of Silverado Banking, Savings and Loan Association in Denver led to a regulatory complaint by the federal Office of Thrift Supervision (OTS) that cited Neil Bush's ties to businessmen who had sizable loans from the thrift while he served as a Silverado director.

The OTS held a public hearing on the complaint Sept. 25. And the Federal Deposit Insurance Corporation said it was considering filing a $200 million federal civil suit against Silverado's former directors, including Bush.

On July 13, 11 members of the House Judiciary Committee had sent a petition calling on Attorney General Dick Thornburgh to seek appointment of a special prosecutor to investigate the Silverado case.

The case drew the White House more closely into the political brouhaha over the thrift crisis, and in a speech on June 22 President Bush defended his administration's record of prosecutions in thrift cases.

Bush said the Justice Department had one "simple, uncompromising position: Throw the crooks in jail." Bush said the investigation of thrift fraud had paid off with more than 150 convictions and $100 million ordered in restitution.

In January 1991, the Justice Department reported that 403 S&L convictions had been obtained since 1989.

SENATE ACTION

Thrift fraud provisions were added as an amendment to the Senate's anticrime bill on July 11 by a 99-1 vote. *(Vote 147, p. 33-S)*

Only William L. Armstrong, R-Colo., voted against the amendment, which was sponsored by his Democratic colleague from Colorado, Tim Wirth, and Pennsylvania Republican John Heinz.

"It is high time that Congress declares savings and loan crooks public enemy No. 1," Heinz said.

Armstrong did not speak on the floor, but later termed the amendment a "knee-jerk response."

"Perhaps the amendment will provide senators a smoke screen to shift the culpability for the S&L mess from the Congress and on to a few unscrupulous businessmen," Armstrong said. "But the fact is the S&L mess, which the American taxpayer has been called upon to clean up, was not primarily the result of the wrongdoing of a few thrift executives, but of a collapse of a thrift system established by and overseen by the Congress."

The provisions would have stepped up civil and criminal penalties, including tough sentences up to life imprisonment for so-called financial kingpins. The measure also would have given the government new authority to use wiretaps in the investigation of financial fraud and related offenses. A financial institutions crime unit would have been established along with a special counsel for financial crimes.

Financial executives convicted of offenses would not have been allowed to use bankruptcy as a protection against civil or criminal liability or to maintain the capital in an institution. Concealment of assets from banking agencies would also have been considered a federal offense. Regulators would also have been given the authority to seize assets or property that was secured through illegal acts.

Congress Raises Penalties for Bank Fraud

The bill authorized $162.5 million for investigation and prosecution of financial crimes, more than double existing Justice Department resources for combating bank and thrift fraud. The 1989 thrift-bailout bill (PL 101-73) had authorized $75 million annually for criminal investigations and prosecution.

In addition, $16 million was to be earmarked for the Internal Revenue Service (IRS) for tax issues related to financial fraud and $25 million for the judicial system to process additional cases.

Enforcement authorities estimated in 1990 that the Federal Bureau of Investigation (FBI) had more than 20,000 referrals and complaints involving fraud in the financial services industry and that 7,000 cases were ongoing.

HOUSE ACTION

Following the Senate's lead, the House Judiciary Committee added financial fraud provisions to the anticrime bill (HR 5269) that it began marking up July 17.

Similar to the Senate language, the measure would have authorized $153 million annually for three years for the Justice Department to investigate and prosecute fraud in the thrift industry.

The bank fraud section was a compromise between Charles H. Schumer, D-N.Y., and Hamilton Fish Jr., R-N.Y. Many of the provisions were taken from a Republican-sponsored bill (HR 5050) that the House Banking Subcommittee on Financial Institutions had approved June 28.

The thrift section would have made it illegal to conceal the assets of a failed thrift and would have established procedures for the government to seize U.S. and overseas assets of thrift officials convicted of fraud.

A 12-member bipartisan commission would also have been created to probe the causes of the thrift crisis and recommend strategies for law enforcement.

Despite agreement on the need to spend more to investigate and penalize thrift fraud, the deliberations took on partisan overtones after the provisions were laid out before the committee.

The bill would have authorized the Justice Department to set up a special counsel to investigate bank fraud. An acrimonious debate ensued over an amendment offered by Chuck Douglas, R-N.H., to authorize the special counsel to investigate past and current members of Congress.

Douglas linked the amendment to Democrats' call for an independent counsel to investigate Neil Bush.

"We get 11 letters from Democrats [asking] to investigate Neil Bush, but they won't get a roll call vote to investigate their buddies," Douglas said.

Almost unanimously, the Democrats denounced Douglas for painting with a broad brush the relations of members of Congress with thrift officials tainted by the existing crisis. Some suggested that such a probe include inquiries into financial affairs of the president, the vice president, Cabinet members and their families.

Douglas' amendment was narrowly defeated, 17-19. Joining Republicans in voting with Douglas were Democrats John Bryant, Texas; George E. Sangmeister, Ill.; and Craig Washington, Texas.

Dan Glickman, D-Kan., then offered a different amendment, to give the special counsel authority to investigate executive branch officials and their families for involvement in bank and thrift irregularities. That amendment carried, 35-1.

House Floor Action

Fearful that the anticrime bill might not clear Congress, lawmakers decided to include the thrift and bank fraud provisions in a stand-alone bill (HR 5401).

Just days before heading home for the August recess — and intensive campaigning — lawmakers on July 31 voted 424-4 to pass S&L and bank fraud penalties and to beef up the Justice Department's financial fraud resources. Language in the measure was identical to fraud provisions included in HR 5269. *(Vote 288, p. 94-H)*

The anticrime bill did make it to the House floor in October. Members spent most of the time debating issues other than the financial crimes provisions. The House passed HR 5269 by a vote of 368-55 on Oct. 5. *(Vote 427, p. 138-H)*

FINAL ACTION

With time running out on the 101st Congress, House and Senate conferees on the anticrime bill abandoned attempts to pass a broad measure and agreed on a stripped-down version (S 3266), which included the S&L fraud provisions.

Both chambers passed the bill Oct. 27 — the House by 313-1, the Senate by voice vote. *(Vote 534, p. 168-H)*

Besides the stepped-up penalties, the measure placed a lifetime ban on convicted felons from controlling or participating in the management of a financial institution. Obstructing a bank examination was made a federal offense with a five-year maximum prison sentence.

The measure prohibited failing institutions from offering so-called golden parachutes — lucrative buyouts or bonuses — to bank executives.

Funding for bank and thrift investigations was increased. In fiscal 1991, $162.5 million was authorized for investigating and prosecuting financial crime. Of those funds, $78 million was earmarked for the FBI; $65 million for U.S. district attorneys; and $7 million and $3.4 million for the Justice Department's criminal and tax divisions, respectively.

In addition, the bill authorized $16 million for the IRS to pursue tax-related violations dealing with financial crime and $25 million for the federal court system to help process the extra load of cases.

Although the bill was praised by Democrats and Republicans alike, the criminal provisions could not be applied retroactively to any previous crimes.

"These provisions are touted as addressing the thrift crisis, yet they will not apply to those who brought the thrifts to insolvency," noted House Banking Committee Chairman Henry B. Gonzalez, D-Texas.

Continued from p. 181

Although the administration had conceded the need for more bailout money — and had sent Glauber and Seidman to ask for it — members wanted Brady to appear personally and answer questions.

In September and October, Brady declined repeated requests to appear, while his aides sought to portray congressional pique as petty. Brady did send a sheaf of letters, spelling out his request and answering some direct questions. But the letters did not placate members.

In a joint missive dated Oct. 9, Donald W. Riegle Jr., D-Mich., and Henry B. Gonzalez, D-Texas, chairmen of the Senate and House Banking committees, respectively, wrote: "We have still not received a specific request from the administration. We are now just 10 days away from the end of this session."

"They're being ridiculous, don't you think," said one Treasury lobbyist Oct. 10. "We gave them a couple options months ago. It's up to Congress to decide what to do about it."

House Democrats, however, accused Brady of hiding so that Congress would have to take the lead in spending more money on the thrift debacle.

"He wants us to take all the heat for this," said Schumer.

"In addition to failing to provide answers to a number of nagging questions about the RTC, the secretary's refusal fueled a feeling among members that the administration was attempting to dodge any responsibility for the operation of the bailout and its massive costs," Gonzalez said.

Late Oct. 10, Brady wrote the committees that Treasury still preferred that Congress give the RTC unlimited spending authority, but $57 billion would be fine for a specific appropriation for fiscal 1991.

The Senate Banking Committee acted Oct. 12 in direct response to Brady's letter and essentially in line with its recommendations. It went even further on one point, giving the RTC an unlimited appropriation to cover costs of renegotiating the controversial December 1988 thrift deals.

By voice vote, it approved a bill (S 3222 — S Rept 101-549) on Oct. 12, providing a $57 billion cash infusion that would have given the RTC $40 billion more to cover losses and effectively provided a $17 billion increase in an existing law cap on borrowing for working capital.

The House panel voted Oct. 23 for a bill (HR 5891 — H Rept 101-974) that would have provided an additional $10 billion for losses. It would also have clarified the bailout law loophole and allowed the borrowing cap to rise by $18.8 billion. That action would have freed $7 billion to $10 billion of the original $50 billion, which the RTC was holding in reserve to meet the convoluted terms of the lower borrowing cap. And it would have given the administration the go-ahead to take the action it did Nov. 1.

FINAL ACTION

Opposition to both measures was sufficient, as the session ground to a close, to make House and Senate leaders wary of bringing up the bills.

Congressional aides said there was silence from the administration in the final days of the session. Other than last-minute letters from Seidman and the Congressional Budget Office, pointing out that a delay in approving additional money for losses would add to the overall cost as sick thrifts continued to operate, there was no external pressure on Congress to act.

Moreover, White House and congressional negotiators had already decided not to include the money in a must-pass bill, such as the deficit-reducing budget-reconciliation measure, fearing political opposition to such a maneuver.

Treasury officials had proposed using a bill to increase penalties for bank fraud as a vehicle for the RTC money. But there seemed little inclination to take that route.

So, after the Oct. 27 session went past midnight and Congress was less than two hours from adjournment, Gonzalez asked for unanimous consent for the House to take up HR 5891.

The motion was necessary, because ordinary procedures at that hour — known in House parlance as "suspension of the rules" — required a two-thirds majority for passage. House leaders did not believe they had the necessary votes. In fact, aides said, they were unsure whether they had a majority and were certain there would have been a roll call vote.

But with the two words "I object," Annunzio prevented the House from considering the bill, and there it died.

An aide said later that Annunzio was unwilling to give the RTC more money. "It was an open and shut deal," the aide, Curt Prins, told The Washington Post. "Open your wallet and shut your mouth."

Moments after Annunzio's action on the House floor, the Senate, knowing the House had spiked the bill, did call up S 3222, amended it to incorporate the House bill language and passed the measure by voice vote.

That bill never came to a floor vote in the House. Congressional aides said that even if Annunzio had been placated, other members — Democrats and Republicans — were ready to object to its consideration. ■

Higher Deposit Insurance Premiums OK'd

Reports of a looming crisis in the banking industry sent lawmakers scurrying to approve legislation to give the Federal Deposit Insurance Corporation (FDIC) the authority to increase the premiums banks and savings and loans paid to insure their deposits.

Provisions included in the omnibus reconciliation bill (HR 5835 — PL 101-508), which cleared Congress on Oct. 27, removed the restrictions placed on the FDIC to raise insurance premiums. Under existing law, the premiums could only be raised to 19.5 cents per $100 of deposits. Before passage of the law, the FDIC had announced plans to increase the premiums for 1991 to the highest amount allowed by law.

The proposal achieved the double aim of reducing the federal deficit and shoring up the insurance funds.

L. William Seidman, chairman of the FDIC, had been pleading with Congress to remove a cap on premium increases. He warned that continued bank failures could bleed the fund dry.

Action taken in 1990 served as a precursor to major

action expected in the 102nd Congress. Congress had required the Treasury to produce by early 1991 a deposit insurance reform plan under the 1989 thrift-industry salvage law (PL 101-73).

The Bush administration, on Feb. 5, 1991, unveiled the long-awaited plan to overhaul the nation's financial system by reducing risks to the federal deposit insurance funds and providing new business opportunities for banks.

Treasury Secretary Nicholas F. Brady had told Congress the previous summer that the nation's banking laws and deposit insurance system desperately needed an overhaul. "The result is overcapacity and layers of regulation, concentration in the riskier parts of commercial lending, uneven product diversification with rules and exceptions that sometimes make little sense, and inefficient limitations on geographical distribution," he told the Senate Banking Committee on July 25.

Few had expected Congress to tackle deposit insurance head-on in 1990, however. Election-year jitters and weariness from 1989's savings and loan battle left members without much appetite for such a potentially momentous change. *(1989 Almanac, p. 117)*

BACKGROUND

In 1933, the nation's banking system collapsed, bankrupted by devastating "runs" that sucked out what little cash was held in vaults, forcing President Franklin D. Roosevelt to order a "bank holiday" on March 6, two days after he was sworn into office.

Cash and gold withdrawals were prohibited for days, and in some cases weeks or months, as the banking industry struggled. Before the year was over, 4,004 banks had closed, costing depositors $540 million.

Three months after Roosevelt's action, Congress passed a sweeping reform of banking laws that included a system of federal deposit insurance that took effect Jan. 1, 1934. The FDIC was created to insure accounts to $2,500, raised within months to $5,000 — a sizable sum in the midst of the Depression. Banks had to pay premiums to finance the fund.

Roosevelt signed the deposit insurance bill into law reluctantly. He and the American Bankers Association strongly opposed insurance. Roosevelt was concerned that the government would be on the hook for losses, despite assertions that the insurance program would be privately financed. The banks were upset for the opposite reason. They would have to pay for insurance, and they had no promise of government aid.

The Federal Savings and Loan Insurance Corporation (FSLIC) was created in 1934 with a $5,000 insurance limit for thrifts, the same as that for banks, and a similar but somewhat more costly premium system. Banks had moved quickly into the insurance system; thrifts did not. The number of insured thrifts did not surpass that of uninsured savings institutions until 1951.

Recent Changes

Over the years, Congress made few changes in the growing system of deposit insurance other than to increase the insurance limits periodically. In 1950 the limit was raised to $10,000, in 1966 to $15,000, in 1969 to $20,000, and in 1974 to $40,000.

Then in 1980, with little debate, Congress approved a provision to more than double the limit to $100,000 as part of a broad bank and thrift deregulation law (PL 96-221). At the end of the decade, many observers said change contributed to the thrift-industry collapse in the late 1980s. *(Depository institutions deregulation, 1980 Almanac, p. 275)*

In 1988, the FDIC closed 200 banks and gave financial assistance to 21 more to keep them open. It was a post-Depression record that declined only slightly to 206 failed and assisted banks in 1989. As a consequence, FDIC reserves fell by $4 billion over the two years, as the bank insurance fund suffered its first losses.

For thrifts, the situation was more devastating, with 205 failures in 1988 and about 600 insolvent or potentially insolvent institutions likely to be shut down over the next three years. *(Failed banks, thrifts, 1988 Almanac, p. 243)*

As part of the 1989 thrift bailout (PL 101-73), the FSLIC, which became technically bankrupt in 1986, was abolished. Two new insurance funds — one for banks and one for thrifts — were created under the FDIC.

Premiums for banks and thrifts were increased. Not only was the thrift fund out of cash, but the bank insurance fund also suffered its first-ever losses in fiscal 1988 and 1989, and Congress wanted to shore it up. And for the first time Congress appropriated taxpayer money for deposit insurance, a decision that was projected to possibly cost taxpayers as much as $500 billion over the next 40 years.

Bank Insurance Fund

The bank insurance fund, which covered about $2 trillion in deposits, had lost $6.1 billion since January 1988 because of record failures, with another $4 billion loss expected before the end of 1990. Those losses were expected to decrease the fund's reserves to little more than $9 billion by the end of 1990, which would have been their lowest level as a percentage of total insured deposits since the FDIC was created in 1934.

In reports to Congress on Sept. 11 and 12, the General Accounting Office (GAO) and the Congressional Budget Office (CBO) warned that the bank insurance fund was being drawn to dangerously low levels by repeated years of 200-plus bank failures. The GAO and CBO reports were the first official confirmations that the fund faced a real threat. The GAO and CBO also warned that a recession could wipe out the fund.

CBO Director Robert D. Reischauer told the Senate Banking Committee that as many as 700 banks could fail in the following three years, continuing a trend of nearly 200 annual failures since 1987.

That could cost the insurance fund a net loss of $21 billion, Reischauer said, and cash outlays of as much as $40 billion, part of which would be repaid to the fund as failed bank assets were sold back to the public.

The GAO took a narrower look, finding 35 banks out of a sample of 300 that required recapitalization or regulatory assistance — or that were likely to fail. The cost to the fund could be as much as $6 billion, the GAO reported.

The immediate cash needs of the insurance fund also accelerated the debate over how best to overhaul the entire deposit insurance system to avoid another crisis like that in the thrift industry. Lawmakers were expected to address that issue in 1991 after the Treasury Department completed its study of deposit insurance and the financial services industry in general.

COMMITTEE ACTION

As part of its contribution to deficit reduction, the Senate Banking Committee approved Oct. 12 legislative proposals that included new authority for the FDIC to increase insurance premiums for banks and thrifts.

The 1991 premium for banks was raised from 12 cents to 19.5 cents per $100 of deposits — adopted by the FDIC within the existing statutory cap. In addition, the FDIC was expected to increase premiums in 1992 to 23 cents.

Thrift institutions paid 23 cents per $100 in deposits and no further premium increase for them was expected.

Lawmakers added the premium increase to the budget-reconciliation bill because, aside from supporting the bank insurance fund, it had the salutary effect of reducing the deficit.

The panel did not take action on a proposal by Alan J. Dixon, D-Ill., to require the Federal Reserve System to pay interest on bank reserves directly to the insurance fund.

Under existing law, these reserves held by the Fed were invested in Treasury securities, and the earnings were paid into the Treasury's general fund for government expenses. Dixon and others had long wanted the Fed to pay interest on these reserves directly to banks.

On the House side, the GAO and CBO reports prompted Banking Committee members to introduce a variety of bills to address the crisis.

Legislation Proposed

In anticipation of action on bank premium and deposit insurance issues coming before the 102nd Congress, some members in 1990 offered legislative proposals and ideas late in the year as a precursor to action in 1991.

Among the legislative proposals were the following:

- Rep. Frank Annunzio, D-Ill., proposed that banks be required to pay 1 percent of their deposits — about $25 billion — into the insurance fund. Both the fund and the banks could count the money on their books as an asset until it was used to close failed banks. Thus, the plan would not immediately reduce bank capital. Annunzio incorporated the idea into a bill (HR 5590) that he introduced Sept. 12.

An identical approach was used by the National Credit Union Administration in the mid-1980s to shore up the deposit insurance fund for credit unions.

Annunzio never offered the proposal in committee after many panel members said the plan should be considered when a broader review of deposit insurance was considered in 1991. FDIC chief Seidman said the Annunzio plan "appears to merit consideration."

- Reps. Gerald D. Kleczka, D-Wis., and Richard H. Lehman, D-Calif., introduced a bill (HR 5599) on Sept. 12 to limit insurance coverage to 100 percent of the first $50,000 put on deposit by an individual and 90 percent of the next $50,000.

Their bill would have required risk-based premiums and prohibited insurance coverage for deposits placed by third-party brokers. It would also also have prohibited so-called pass-through insurance where large deposits such as those from pension funds were presumed to be insured up to $100,000 for each beneficiary.

- Sen. Dixon offered a proposal Sept. 12, to require the Federal Reserve System to pay interest on bank reserves directly to the insurance fund. Under existing law, these reserves held by the Fed were invested in Treasury securities, and the earnings were paid into the Treasury's general fund for government expenses.

Dixon and others long wanted the Fed to pay interest on these reserves directly to banks. Dixon saw this proposal as a logical extension of that idea.

- Dixon introduced a bill (S 3040) on Sept. 13 to establish a system of private deposit insurance that would assume 10 percent of the government's risk.

Insurance premiums would be allowed to fluctuate within a range to reward those banks that invested in less risky assets and provided additional premium income from those with more risky investments.

Dixon's bill would not have altered the existing scheme of $100,000 in insurance per account, but it would not have allowed the FDIC to cover 100 percent of deposits above $100,000, as it did already in some cases.

- Senate Banking Committee Chairman Donald W. Riegle Jr., D-Mich., introduced another measure (S 3045) on Sept. 13 to allow the FDIC to set insurance premiums for banks and thrifts at whatever level was necessary to shore up the fund.
- Riegle introduced S 3103 on Sept. 25, calling for increasing minimum requirements for investor capital in depository institutions and requiring regulators to close institutions before all their owners' money was exhausted as a means to protect the insurance funds. The bill also sought to restrict all but the healthiest state-chartered and regulated banks from engaging in activities not permitted for federally chartered banks.

FLOOR ACTION

The House passed a bill (HR 5610) in September to eliminate the premium cap. The two panels included similar language in their recommendations to the House and Senate Budget committees, which later rolled them into the budget-reconciliation bill.

The House passed HR 5835, the budget-reconciliation bill, on Oct. 16, by a 227-203 vote. The deposit premium increase drew no special attention. *(Vote 475, p. 150-H)*

The Senate passed HR 5835 on Oct. 18 by a 54-46 vote, after rejecting amendments by Bob Graham, D-Fla., to revise the deposit insurance system. *(Vote 292, p. 58-S)*

Graham wanted to prescribe tougher standards for the FDIC to use when determining whether to provide deposit insurance to an institution.

Graham said that the amendment was important to fill a gap left by existing law that mandated the FDIC to insure nationally chartered banks. Under existing law, the FDIC could withhold insurance for a state-chartered bank but not for an institution nationally chartered by the Office of the Comptroller of the Currency.

Another amendment offered by Graham would have authorized the FDIC to establish a risk-based premium system for bank deposits. Under the proposal, a bank's deposit premiums would have been linked to the riskiness of its financial activities.

Existing law only allowed the FDIC to assess banks at a standard rate that was not affected by the type of investments the institution made.

Graham said that both amendments dealt "with the fundamental question of the solidity of financial institutions as part of our overall desire for a more rational national financial house."

But many lawmakers, while acknowledging the merit of the proposals, argued that the amendments were not germane to the deficit-reduction bill and should be taken up in 1991 when Congress was expected to consider the broader issue of deposit insurance reform.

"Federal insurance reform, however, is too important to be hastily debated on the Senate floor in the closing hours of the 101st Congress," said John H. Chafee, R-R.I.

Ultimately, Graham was unable to convince a majority of senators of the merit of the proposals, and the amendments were rejected on a procedural vote.

FINAL ACTION

Action on the reconciliation bill was held up by issues unrelated to the proposal to remove caps on deposit insurance premiums, which were not altered after being approved by the two chambers.

On Oct. 27, the conference report to HR 5835 was approved by a 54-45 vote in the Senate and a 228-200 vote in the House. *(Senate vote 326, p. 63-S; House vote 528, p. 166-H)*

Bad news continued to come from the banking industry after Congress adjourned.

FDIC Chairman Seidman told the House Banking Subcommittee on Financial Institutions on Dec. 17 that the bank insurance fund expected to lose $4 billion in 1990.

He said the fund would be in need of a major recapitalization.

Besides increasing premiums, Seidman suggested as one option for raising capital requiring banks to place 1 percent of their deposits into the insurance fund.

Premiums and the 1 percent deposit requirement would provide the FDIC with $53 billion to handle bank failures in years 1991 through 1993, Seidman said. He predicted that the FDIC would spend $10 billion in 1991 closing failed institutions. ■

Money-Laundering Schemes Bills Falter

Armed with data showing that the nation's financial institutions were often used by narcotics traffickers to store their drug profits, lawmakers crafted legislation to crack down on banks and bank officers that aided drug dealers in hiding or "laundering" their profits. But the three similar measures, burdened by the weight of election politics and unrelated initiatives, failed to clear Congress in 1990.

Under the legislation, banks, thrifts and credit unions could have received the financial equivalent of the death penalty — revocation of their charters or termination of their federal deposit insurance — if found guilty of laundering money. Bank officials caught engaging in money-laundering schemes could have been permanently barred from working in a financial institution. Reporting requirements for cash transactions would also have been stiffened.

The House passed HR 3848 by a 406-0 vote on April 25, and the Senate passed S 3037 by voice vote Oct. 5. *(House vote 82, p. 30-H)*

Neither chamber, however, took up the other's bill. When it appeared the issue would die with adjournment, the House passed a new bill (HR 5889) by voice vote on Oct. 26, but the Senate never considered the measure.

Despite the overwhelming support for a money-laundering bill, the weight of the add-ons was too much for lawmakers to bear.

In addition to money-laundering provisions, for example, the Senate-passed S 3037 included language from many other bills. Among the other provisions were ones to require a redesign of the back of the nation's circulating coins; to require banks, other depository institutions and mutual funds to use a standardized method of computing the annual yield on savings and investments; and to require mortgage lenders to provide copies of house appraisals to applicants. *(Coin redesign, p. 196)*

BACKGROUND

Money laundering was the practice, common among narcotics traffickers, of using financial institutions to hide illegal proceeds, making them appear as if they came from legitimate business transactions. Law enforcement officials estimated that the laundering of illegal drug money in the United States was a $100 billion-a-year business.

Drug dealers and other illegal enterprises first converted the currency to deposits in a financial institution through the cooperation of corrupt employees or under the guise of a front company.

To get around a requirement that institutions notify the government of every cash transaction over $10,000, traffickers used couriers to deposit cash just under the limit in numerous accounts — a tactic known as "smurfing."

The money was then transferred to other accounts to disguise its origin. At that point, it had been effectively "cleansed" and could be shifted to legitimate businesses or investments maintained by the traffickers.

To detect laundering schemes in the United States, Congress in 1970 passed the Bank Secrecy Act, which required banks to file a currency transaction report (CTR) for every large cash transaction. *(1970 Almanac, p. 884)*

Major antidrug legislation cleared in 1986 and 1988 strengthened the statute by making money laundering a felony, authorizing "sting" operations and requiring the government to negotiate anti-money-laundering agreements with other countries. *(1988 Almanac, p. 85; 1986 Almanac, p. 92)*

The rate of CTR filings shot up in the early 1980s as the government began aggressively enforcing bank secrecy laws and penalizing banks and their officers for non-compliance. "We put an awful lot of bankers in jail in the early 1980s, and we got their attention," said Justice Department official Charles S. Saphos. Eight times as many CTRs were filed in 1988 as in 1984.

HOUSE ACTION

The House Banking Subcommittee on Financial Institutions approved HR 3848 on March 8. The panel approved the bill by voice vote after agreeing to give regulators discretion in determining whether to take control of an institution convicted of money laundering. As originally written, the bill would have made the sanctions mandatory.

The new language was a compromise between subcommittee chairman and bill sponsor Frank Annunzio, D-Ill., who wanted the penalty automatic in the cases of conviction, and other lawmakers, who felt that an automatic revocation with no review would have been too harsh.

While regulators would not have been required to levy punishment, they would have had to hold an enforcement hearing each time an institution or its officers were found guilty of money laundering.

After considering the underlying circumstances — including whether senior management had been extensively involved and whether the institution had cooperated with law enforcement authorities — regulators would have then decided whether the case merited the tough sanctions.

In the case of state-chartered institutions convicted of laundering money, the Federal Deposit Insurance Corporation could have terminated federal deposit insurance after holding a hearing and considering the same factors.

Other provisions of the bill would have:

- Permanently barred any person convicted of money laundering or structuring transactions to evade reporting requirements from working in a financial institution.
- Provided "safe harbor" civil action protection to people who in good faith reported suspicious transactions.
- Provided state financial institution regulators with access to currency transaction reports, maintained by the Treasury Department on cash transactions of $10,000 or more.
- Required Treasury to report annually to Congress for the following three years on the use of the reports.

Full Committee

When the House Banking Committee considered the measure March 22, debate centered on how to stop narcotics traffickers from using the wire-transfer system to funnel billions of dollars of drug profits in and out of the country.

Rep. Esteban E. Torres, D-Calif., introduced an amendment to require institutions to maintain records — much like the CTR a bank had to maintain for cash transactions of at least $10,000 — on non-currency wire transfers of more than a set dollar amount.

Torres' proposal ran into opposition from several lawmakers who argued that such extensive recordkeeping would be too cumbersome and costly for banks.

The requirement would have entailed "hundreds of millions of dollars in compliance costs without any guarantee that the information would be used," said ranking Republican Chalmers P. Wylie, Ohio.

In addition, the Federal Reserve and the Treasury Department were concerned that the requirement would discourage foreign bank activity in the United States.

Torres tried unsuccessfully to garner support by scaling his amendment back to include only international wire transfers.

With several Democrats and all Republicans in support, Bill McCollum, R-Fla., and Doug Barnard Jr., D-Ga., pushed through by a vote of 32-17 a substitute that would have given the Treasury Department discretion over wire-transfer requirements.

By Jan. 1, 1991, Treasury would have had to adopt regulations to ensure that banks, thrifts and credit unions maintained international wire-transfer records. The department would have been given latitude to decide what records should be kept.

Rep. Steve Bartlett, R-Texas, tried to strike the wire-transfer provision, objecting that it was included in the committee print without having first been considered by the subcommittee. But he was soundly defeated, 5-43.

Wire transfers were a central part of drug trafficking. The Federal Reserve estimated that every day $1 trillion was moved through international wire transfers, making it easy for drug profits to be overlooked in the shuffle.

Once drug money had been placed in an institution, it could be wired around the world, effectively concealing its origin. Much of the money could eventually be wired back to the United States.

Floor Action

The House passed HR 3848 on April 25 after rejecting another attempt by Torres to require banks to keep records on wire transfers.

Supporters of the Torres amendment argued that the failure to include wire-transfer requirements left a "gaping loophole" in the law that would continue to allow narcotics traffickers to use the international banking system to hide drug profits. "We're telling the drug lords to transfer this way because, if you do it by wire, you won't be affected," said Charles E. Schumer, D-N.Y.

The bill, approved 406-0, would have authorized federal regulators to revoke the charter, appoint a conservator or terminate deposit insurance for an institution convicted of money laundering. Bank officers convicted of engaging in laundering schemes could be permanently barred from working in a financial institution.

Torres' amendment would have required Treasury to conduct a one-year pilot program to determine the usefulness of recordkeeping for international wire transfers.

Treasury would have been left to determine which banks and which categories of wire transfers to study. Customers at selected banks would have been required to supply basic information, such as names, addresses and account numbers used on wire-transfer transactions.

Torres' amendment was a significantly watered-down version of one he had offered in committee. His earlier proposal would have established permanent requirements for banks to keep records of all wire transfers.

Critics of Torres' floor amendment argued that the volume of wire transfers — 100 million per year worldwide — would jam the regulatory process while imposing undue costs on financial institutions. Barnard called the amendment well-meaning but said it amounted to regulatory "overkill" that would cost institutions $360 million a year.

But Schumer said the additional paperwork that banks might have to do would be justified if it helped stop the flow of drugs into the country. "Where the heck are our priorities?" he asked. "If we can't vote for this, then we're not serious about the war on drugs."

Members remained unconvinced, and about half of all Democrats present joined almost all Republicans in rejecting the amendment 127-283. *(Vote 81, p. 30-H)*

By a thin 207-200 vote, lawmakers approved an amendment offered by Thomas M. Foglietta, D-Pa., designed to encourage states to oversee check-cashing companies. The provision would have established model regulations to limit the fee for cashing a check to 1.5 percent of the value of the check or $8, whichever was less. *(Vote 80, p. 30-H)*

SENATE ACTION

The Senate Banking, Housing and Urban Affairs Committee on July 17 approved S 3037, its version of money-laundering legislation. In many ways, the bill resembled the House measure. It would have given federal regulators the authority to revoke the charter of, or appoint a conservator for, a bank convicted of laundering money. Bank officers would face a lifetime ban on working in a financial institution. Non-bank financial institutions — such as urban check-cashing centers and money exchange businesses along the U.S.-Mexican border — would receive much more scrutiny by federal regulators.

To detect illegal check-cashing and money exchange activities, depository institutions would have been required to notify the Treasury Department of non-bank financial institutions that they served. Officials of institutions that did not have the appropriate state licenses would be subject to felony charges.

Panel members also agreed to lump other legislative initiatives into the bill to improve the chances that all the measures would be considered by the Senate.

The other measures included:

- Truth-in-savings requirements that would have stipulated that institutions use a standardized method to calculate the yield on savings accounts and investments (S 307).
- A phased-in redesign of coins in general circulation (S 428).
- Steps to further deter the counterfeiting of U.S. currency (S 2748).
- New requirements on how long an institution could put a hold on deposits from automated teller machines (ATMs).

FINAL ACTION

Although the Senate passed S 3037 by voice vote on Oct. 5, progress toward clearing a money-laundering bill came to a halt. John Kerry, D-Mass., spent four days trying to get the Senate to act on it, but several Republicans — most notably, Steve Symms of Idaho — objected.

Symms ticked off a list of new reporting requirements for banks and said that the only thing that Congress "never wants to slow down is the ever-growing size and scope and interference of the U.S. government."

But some Democrats said the real reason for Republican objections was politics. They charged that Republicans were blocking the bill because it might have helped Kerry in his re-election bid.

Kerry alluded to the tactic on the Senate floor. "We seem to be delayed as people want to raise the ugly head of politics," he said.

Republicans countered that it was Kerry who was playing politics by bringing up the bill at the "11th hour" from "legislative left field."

Despite House attempts to resurrect the measure, the Senate never named conferees to hammer out the differences between the two chambers' versions. Democrats claimed that Minority Leader Bob Dole, R-Kan., blocked the appointment of GOP conferees.

The unrelated bills added on by the Senate Banking Committee also created obstacles for the measure; the coin redesign legislation, for example, was opposed by key members of the House Banking Committee. ■

Foreign Banks Bill Dies

Legislation designed to pressure foreign governments to open up their financial services markets to U.S. firms died under the weight of administration opposition.

The language inserted into a bill to reauthorize the Defense Production Act (HR 486) would have given U.S. banking and securities regulators broad discretion to retaliate in cases where U.S. firms were prevented from expanding abroad. *(Defense Production Act, p. 202)*

The language was pushed hard by Senate Banking Chairman Donald W. Riegle Jr., D-Mich., and the panel's ranking Republican, Jake Garn of Utah.

Under existing law dating to 1978, foreign banks and financial firms in the United States were given the same rights to expand, open branches and engage in restricted practices as domestic banks and securities firms.

This standard, which was known as "unilateral national treatment," was extended even though some other countries imposed tighter controls on U.S. firms than they did on their own nationals.

The provisions would have created a new standard of "reciprocal national treatment," which would have allowed the United States to give free rein only to those foreign banks whose home countries granted national treatment to U.S. banks.

Early in the year, the Bush administration signaled some receptiveness toward a change in policy. During a Feb. 28 Senate Banking Committee hearing, David C. Mulford, under secretary of the Treasury, said that a change in policy was under review. "The issue is whether we need to look at a more sophisticated version of national treatment," Mulford said. "That's an open question to the administration at this time."

In April, Mulford returned to the panel, but this time against a change in policy. He told lawmakers that a reversal in policy could have an adverse effect if countries retaliated and restricted U.S. banks' access to their markets. That did not sit well with Garn, who called Mulford's testimony the "same old garbage from the Treasury." Garn said he was tired of Treasury's preaching patience while "our markets are being gutted" by the Japanese.

The committee approved by voice vote legislation (S 2028 — S Rept 101-367) to revise U.S. national treatment policy on May 24. The bill — sponsored by Riegle and Garn — had strong bipartisan support on the panel.

Although the measure would have revised policy, it would not have allowed for existing operations to be curtailed, nor would it have required true "reciprocity," where a foreign country would have been required to allow U.S. firms to operate with the same freedoms they enjoyed in the United States.

The committee turned aside an amendment by Phil Gramm, R-Texas, that would have prohibited sanctions against foreign banking and securities firms, unless it was shown that there would be no adverse consequences for U.S. consumers.

The committee accepted an amendment by Christopher J. Dodd, D-Conn., that would have focused the bill even more sharply on Japan. Dodd's amendment clarified that a country's past practice of extending national treatment to U.S. financial firms would be a mitigating factor in determining whether a particular action constituted a denial of national treatment.

The Banking Committee had originally included the foreign banks provisions in the Defense Production Act, which it also handled and which the Senate passed Oct. 3. During negotiations on the bill, Senate conferees persuaded their House counterparts to accept the sections.

The House adopted the conference report on HR 486 on Oct. 25. But when Congress adjourned Oct. 28, the Senate had not taken up the conference report and the measure died. ■

SEC Market Control Authority Increased

Lawmakers took what they hoped would be a significant step toward stabilizing securities trading by passing legislation to give regulators more authority over the stock markets.

The bill (HR 3657), cleared by Congress on Sept. 28, sought to improve the ability of securities regulators to limit major market disruptions, such as the shock that struck the market in October 1987. President Bush signed the legislation Oct. 16.

Passage of the bill was part of a broader congressional effort to rewrite securities laws. Lawmakers also sent to the president a measure (S 647 — PL 101-429) to establish new civil penalties for securities law violations and a bill (HR 1396 — PL 101-550) to give the Securities and Exchange Commission (SEC) more authority to cooperate with foreign governments in securities fraud investigations. *(Securities enforcement, p. 193)*

> **BOXSCORE**
>
> **Legislation:** Securities Market Reform Act, PL 101-432 (HR 3657).
>
> **Major action:** Signed, Oct. 15. Cleared by House, Sept. 28; passed by Senate, Sept. 25. S 648 passed by Senate, Aug. 4; HR 3657 passed by House, June 5; HR 3656 passed by House, May 8.
>
> **Reports:** Energy and Commerce (HR 3657: H Rpt 101-524; HR 3656: H Rpt 101-477); Finance (S 648: S Rpt 101-300).

Congress failed, however, to pass a bill to shift regulatory control over stock-index futures from the Commodity Futures Trading Commission (CFTC) to the SEC, as urged by the Bush administration. That impasse also killed the CFTC's reauthorization measure, which contained some enforcement-enhancement provisions. *(Stock-index futures, p. 194)*

The provisions of the market stabilization bill, largely drawn from requests to Congress submitted by the SEC, required improved clearance and settlement procedures for stock and related options and futures transactions. The objective was to make all financial markets more liquid.

The SEC was also granted the authority to close the nation's stock exchanges in an emergency. Previously, presidential action was required to halt trading.

Lawmakers also gave regulators authority to restrict so-called program trading — a computer-driven trading technique — if it was shown to contribute to wild price swings.

And the SEC was also given new tools to track transactions by large traders — to better guard against market manipulation — and to monitor the financial strength of brokerage houses. *(Provisions, p. 191)*

BACKGROUND

The drive to pass stock-market reform legislation was largely spurred by the 508-point drop in the Dow Jones Industrial Average — a closely watched market indicator — on Oct. 19, 1987. In all, over $1 trillion in paper wealth was wiped out in one week that October.

The wild swings led lawmakers and regulators to look for ways to tighten regulations and provide traders more information on the market.

The market disturbance — and the interplay between stocks and their "derivative" instruments traded in the futures markets — were the subject of several government studies and many examinations by the markets themselves.

Most studies warned that without regulatory restructuring, the markets would continue to be volatile. "We are looking down the barrel, and the gun is still loaded," said Nicholas F. Brady in 1988. Brady was chairman of the Presidential Task Force on Market Mechanisms, which was formed by President Ronald Reagan to study the 1987 disruption. In 1990, he was serving in the Bush administration as secretary of the Treasury when the stock market reform legislation cleared.

The Brady report, released in 1988, recommended that one agency, preferably the Federal Reserve Board, oversee regulation of activities cutting across traditional market divisions and that the clearance process for settling futures and stock transactions be unified to reduce financial risk. In addition, the report recommended that margins for stock and futures purchases be similar to control speculation and leverage and that trading be halted during wild market swings.

In 1988 Senate Banking Committee Chairman William Proxmire, D-Wis., introduced legislation based loosely on the Brady report to create an "intermarket coordinating committee" composed of the chairmen of the Federal Reserve, the SEC and the CFTC. The committee would have been charged with coordinating clearance systems and "harmonizing" margin requirements for stocks and futures contracts. *(1988 Almanac, p. 253)*

But the bill stalled after Promxire met resistance from heads of the three main market regulatory bodies. "Specific legislative proposals mandating a new regulatory structure appear premature," Fed Chairman Alan Greenspan said.

Stock-Index Futures

In the House, Energy and Commerce Finance Subcommittee Chairman Edward J. Markey, D-Mass., introduced a measure that would have gone further than Proxmire's bill by shifting jurisdiction over stock-index futures from the CFTC to the SEC.

Stock-index futures were a hybrid instrument, neither a commodity nor a security. But an agreement between the SEC and CFTC enacted into law in 1982 gave the CFTC jurisdiction over index futures.

Markey immediately ran into opposition from rural lawmakers and representatives from Chicago, where the futures markets were located. House Agriculture Committee member Dan Glickman, D-Kan., called the debate a "turf battle. . . . Right now, if there was a battle between Energy and Commerce and Agriculture on this issue," he said, "Energy and Commerce would lose."

Faced with opposition even within his own subcommittee, Markey never pushed action on the bill.

Conflicting Advice

One of the reasons Congress took three years to act on legislation was differing views on what caused market volatility and what changes should be considered to counter them. Most observers believed that economic factors —

Securities Market Reform Act Provisions

Here are major provisions of the Securities Market Reform Act, PL 101-432 (HR 3657), as signed by President Bush Oct. 15:

Trading halts. Provided the Securities and Exchange Commission (SEC) with additional authority to suspend trading in any specific security for up to 10 business days and a national securities exchange for a period not to exceed 90 calendar days. Before taking the action, the SEC was required to notify the president of its decision. The president could block the action by not approving the SEC decision.

Before taking action to halt trading, the SEC was charged with consulting with the Commodity Futures Trading Commission (CFTC) to consider the impact of emergency action on the futures markets.

Emergency powers. Gave the SEC the authority, in the event of a major market disturbance or excessive fluctuation of securities prices, to take steps to maintain or restore order to the securities markets and ensure prompt and accurate settlement of transactions.

Among the options open to the SEC were the authority to alter, supplement, suspend or impose requirements or restrictions with respect to hours of trading, position limits, and clearance and settlement.

The SEC could keep the emergency orders in effect for 10 business days, including extensions. The president could rescind an order at any time.

Large trader reporting. Required brokerage houses to provide information to the SEC when engaging in securities transactions involving a substantial volume. After the Oct. 19, 1987, market crash, the SEC was unable to easily reconstruct trading. To help the SEC monitor the impact of large transactions on the markets, brokers were required to identify the trader and accounts used for the transactions. The requirement applied to large transactions, as identified by the SEC, in publicly traded securities. The SEC was given the authority to issue regulations on the manner in which the transactions and accounts would be reported.

Financial institutions that offered customers trust services, which included the buying and selling of securities for the account of the trustees, would be subject to SEC reporting requirements on large transactions.

Recordkeeping requirements. Required brokers and dealers to keep records on large securities transactions. The figures used to determine a substantial volume or large transaction would be set by the SEC. The records had to be available for reporting to the SEC on the morning of the day following the transaction. The records could also be examined by the SEC or other regulatory bodies at any time. The SEC was given the authority to exempt persons or transactions from reporting requirements.

Risk assessment requirements. Required brokers and dealers to keep records on policies, procedures and systems for monitoring and controlling financial and operational risks. The records were designed to provide information to the SEC regarding the overall financial condition of a firm. The provisions were included to address a growing occurrence of brokers forming holding companies and moving potentially risky activities outside of the broker-dealer and away from direct regulatory supervision.

Firms were required to maintain records on securities activities, sources of capial and funding and the business activities of any person likely to have an impact on the financial or operational condition of the organization. The SEC was authorized to require the brokers and dealers to provide additional information if needed. The SEC was given the authority to exempt certain individuals and businesses.

Financial institutions that offered trust services would be subject to SEC requirements on risk assessment.

Settlement of transactions. Provided the SEC with authority to establish a national system for settlement and clearance of securities transactions. The intent of establishing the system was to improve the clearance and settlement process, which had been overloaded during times of extraordinary market volatility. The SEC was granted the authority to establish linked or coordinated facilities for clearance and settlement of transactions in securities options, futures contracts and commodity options.

Program trading. Authorized the SEC to adopt rules or regulations concerning acts or practices that affected or contributed to market volatility. In order to do this, the SEC would first have to make a finding that a specific practice had contributed to instances of wild price swings.

The language was directed at program trading, which involved large blocks of stocks and related instruments, such as options of futures, and often involved use of a computerized order system to cope with the volume of stocks involved.

The SEC was authorized to seek civil penalties and issue cease-and-desist orders against individuals or firms that continued to employ a practice banned by the SEC.

The SEC was given the authority to take steps to prevent manipulation of stock prices that were reasonably likely to affect market volatility.

Securities subsidiaries. Required federal banking agencies to report to the SEC any concerns regarding a significant financial or operational risk to a broker or dealer resulting from the activities of a financial institution.

Congressional reports. Required the secretary of the Treasury, the Federal Reserve Board chairman and chairmen of the SEC and CFTC to report to Congress no later than May 31, 1991, and annually thereafter on efforts to coordinate securities, futures and banking regulatory activities. The reports were to cover agency views on the adequacy of margin levels and efforts to create a mechanism for clearance and settlement. The agencies were to file the reports separately. ■

such as the trade deficit, interest rates and fear of inflation — had an effect on market stability.

Free-market advocates put almost all the blame on the "speculative bubble" that oversold the worth of the stock investments. Market swings were just the stock market at work, they argued, adjusting market prices to reality.

Others believed that the volatility was caused by a breakdown in market mechanisms — led by the futures market — and that those mechanisms had to be adjusted.

With conflicting advice, lawmakers were reluctant to make quick decisions on the best medicine for the markets, although a market disturbance in October 1989 put more pressure on them to do so.

Members were also divided on restrictions on program trading — a collection of strategies involving the buying or selling of large blocks of stock. Program trading relied on computers to execute mammoth buy or sell orders and to tell investors when to take advantage of market conditions. It was blamed as a contributing cause of severe price fluctuations, including the October 1987 and October 1989 market disruptions.

In 1989, both chambers began to focus on specific proposals on market regulation. In the Senate, Christopher J. Dodd, D-Conn., introduced a bill to give the SEC authority to shut down markets for up to 90 days if necessary in an emergency to protect investors and the public interest.

Markey introduced similar legislation in the House, with one major difference. Markey's bill would have authorized the SEC to adopt rules to prevent stock price "manipulation" or "any practice" that had previously resulted in excessive stock swings.

The language was intended to allow the SEC to restrict

program trading. The Senate bill only called for the SEC to study the issue.

COMMITTEE ACTION

Bills began moving through House and Senate committees in November 1989. The Senate Banking Committee completed work on its legislation Nov. 16; a House subcommittee markup Nov. 14 was followed by full committee approval of companion bills on March 13, 1990.

House Action

The House Energy and Commerce Subcommittee on Finance approved two market stabilization bills (HR 3656, HR 3657) by voice vote Nov. 14, 1989. Final congressional action combined the provisions of HR 3656 into HR 3657.

Debate in the markup centered on a section unique to the House bills to give the SEC new authority to attack trading practices resulting in "high levels of volatility."

Finance Subcommittee Chairman Markey had been pushing to give the SEC some limited authority to restrict program trading.

The 190-point fall on Oct. 13, 1989, of the Dow Jones Industrial Average and the Dow's 88-point rise the next trading day renewed interest in curbing wide price swings.

Markey's bill would have allowed the SEC to write regulations to constrain "manipulative, abusive or disruptive practices" likely to unsettle the market excessively. The SEC would be able to impose stiff civil fines on firms or individuals that violated its rules.

The administration agreed with everything but the word "disruptive." In a letter to Markey, Treasury Under Secretary Robert Glauber said the word "appears unusually vague" but signaled an intent to ban program trading altogether. After a large contingent of Finance Subcommittee members from both sides of the aisle banded to oppose the language, Markey agreed to drop it.

The full Energy and Commerce Committee took up the measures March 13 and approved both bills by voice vote.

The most controversial provision gave the SEC authority to stop certain securities trading strategies that involved buying or selling large blocks of stock in a single order. For many market critics, program trading — the catchall term for these strategies — had become synonymous with price instability.

Other elements of the bills were less controversial but still generated problems for Markey and the committee.

The bills gave the SEC enhanced authority to suspend trading in emergencies, to require reporting by large traders about their activities, to collect data on the financial condition of some companies affiliated with brokerages and to negotiate expedited clearance and settlement of securities and related transactions.

The clearance and settlement provision was aimed at closing transactions much more quickly than the five days previously required, so investors would have quicker access to their money and the markets would stay "liquid."

Provisions of Committee Bills

As approved by the Commerce Committee on March 13, HR 3656:

- Directed the SEC to work with other market regulators, including the Federal Reserve Board and the CFTC, to devise a linked or coordinated process to settle transactions across all markets. The SEC was required to report to Congress within two years on its progress.
- Authorized the SEC to develop uniform national regulations on transferring securities to allow for faster clearance and settlement of securities transactions.

The SEC was authorized to write such rules even if they overrode state law on establishing liens and security interests in property. But to override state law, the SEC had to consult with the Treasury secretary and the Fed. It also had to find that the proposed regulation was necessary to protect investors or the public interest and that, without the regulation, efforts for a coordinating clearance and settlement system would be "substantially impeded."

As approved by the panel, HR 3657:

- Authorized the SEC to issue regulations restricting certain trading practices that it believed could manipulate prices or that had led to excessive price swings in the past and were likely to do so again.

After determining which trading practices — chiefly presumed to be program-trading — were likely to destabilize market prices, the SEC could restrict such practices during periods of "extraordinary market volatility."

The SEC was authorized to issue cease-and-desist orders against traders that it believed were violating such rules or were likely to do so. Failing to comply with cease-and-desist orders could lead to fines of up to $100,000 per person and $500,000 per securities firm for each violation.

- Amended existing law slightly to give the SEC authority to suspend trading on the securities markets for up to 90 days, provided that the president notified the SEC that he did not disapprove. (Existing law required the president to approve a trading suspension.) The president was authorized to reverse an order suspending trading.

The SEC was also given blanket emergency authority to suspend its own regulations or impose new rules for up to 10 days if necessary to protect or restore orderly markets or ensure safe clearance and settlement of transactions.

- Required large traders, as defined by the SEC, to identify themselves and their accounts to the SEC and to brokerages used by the trader.

Brokerages were required to maintain records on large-trader transactions that exceed SEC-specified levels and to provide that information to the SEC when requested, including the day after a transaction. Information collected under this provision would be confidential, although the SEC could provide it to Congress or other federal agencies.

- Required securities brokerages and dealers to maintain records on financial risks of the brokerage's parent holding company or any affiliated firm whose business activities might have a "material impact" on the financial condition of the brokerage.

Records kept under this provision were to be available to the SEC, and the agency would be authorized to require quarterly reports about the financial condition of affiliates that had significant financial dealings with the brokerage.

In cases of adverse market conditions or when the SEC believed a firm might have a financial problem, the SEC would be authorized to request more detailed information on the financial condition of broker affiliates. The information collected would be confidential, although the SEC could provide it to Congress or other federal agencies.

Senate Action

The Senate Banking Committee voted 20-1 on Nov. 16, 1989, to report its version of the legislation (S 648).

Members agreed to language that:

- Allowed the SEC to order trading halts in "major market disturbances."

• Allowed the SEC to collect new information on securities firms making very large trades.

• Required the SEC and the CFTC, along with the Federal Reserve and the Treasury, to develop coordinated and expedited methods to settle stock and futures transactions to ease cash-flow problems.

Lawmakers were unsure how to address program trading. The panel accepted an amendment by Alfonse M. D'Amato, R-N.Y., that asked the SEC to report within three months of the bill's enactment on the need for more authority to restrain "any practices that are inconsistent with the statutory mission of the SEC to protect shareholders and investors."

Committee members also battled over a provision to require the SEC and other agencies to formulate uniform settlement procedures. The provision authorized the SEC to craft rules that might contravene state law — for instance, in establishing liens or security interests in stock by banks or brokers that loaned to investors. That troubled many committee members, but an amendment by Phil Gramm, R-Texas, to strike the language overruling state law was defeated 10-11.

FLOOR ACTION

Although the two House bills traveled together through the committee process, they were considered separately on the House floor.

On May 8, the House passed by voice vote HR 3656, which required the SEC to develop coordinated and expedited methods for settling securities transactions.

The House passed the broader bill (HR 3657) to give the SEC new authority to control wide market swings on June 5, also by voice vote and with no amendments.

The Senate passed S 648 on Aug. 4 voice vote after approving an amendment that required the SEC to use existing financial reports made to bank regulatory agencies, where such reports parallel SEC requests.

Senate floor action on S 648 had been delayed by a fight over the regulation of stock-index futures contracts, which some analysts contended added to wild stock price swings. The administration wanted jurisdiction over index futures transferred to the SEC from the CFTC, but resistance to the proposal bogged down the securities bill.

FINAL ACTION

The breakthrough on market legislation came in September, when House, Senate and administration negotiators agreed on compromise legislation to enhance regulatory authority over the markets. On Sept. 25, the Senate passed HR 3657 by voice vote after agreeing to a substitute amendment that included the provisions of HR 3656.

The agreement centered on revised language on program trading. Provisions to increase the SEC's authority to halt trading and to collect information on large trades and the financial health of brokerage houses were kept intact.

The program trading compromise gave the SEC the authority to determine what specific individual program trading practices that had caused wide price swings and were likely to do so in the future. In those cases, the SEC could order the practices suspended.

The House placed its seal of approval on the compromise Sept. 28, clearing HR 3657 on a voice vote. ■

Congress Passes Bills Strengthening SEC

Lawmakers in 1990 cleared two bills that gave the Securities and Exchange Commission (SEC) broad new powers to crack down on securities violations abroad and at home. By passing the bills, Congress addressed two concerns: Poor international cooperation and lack of SEC enforcement tools to keep up with an increasing workload of cases.

The measures moved through Congress as part of a broader plan to overhaul the nation's securities laws. *(Market regulation, p. 190)*

To counter international scams, the House on Oct. 26 cleared a measure (HR 1396 — PL 101-550) to give the SEC additional authority to cooperate more closely with foreign governments in securities fraud investigations.

The House on Oct. 1 had cleared legislation (S 647 — PL 101-429) to establish new civil penalties for securities law violations and new disclosure and trading requirements for issuers and traders in so-called penny stocks, inexpensive securities not traded on national exchanges.

According to the SEC, requests for cooperation by foreign countries had more than doubled in recent years. But the governments were said to be concerned that documents they shared might be released to the public in the United States.

HR 1396, requested by the administration, explicitly exempted foreign confidential information from disclosure under the Freedom of Information Act and allowed the SEC and U.S. stock exchanges to ban individuals from domestic trading if they had been convicted of securities fraud overseas.

The measure also reauthorized the SEC at a level of $178 million for fiscal 1990 and $212.6 million for fiscal 1991.

S 647 allowed the SEC to impose an array of civil fines for securities violations. Under existing law, the SEC was allowed to pursue only criminal penalties in many cases involving violations.

The SEC had requested the bill to gain more flexibility to prosecute fraud, since the standard of proof in civil cases was substantially easier to meet.

International Enforcement

After nearly a year of inaction on the measure, the House on Oct. 1 agreed to a conference with the Senate on HR 1396. Both chambers had passed versions of the bill in 1989. *(1989 Almanac, p. 141)*

Conferees were left to resolve a difference over a Senate provision to remove the pay cap for SEC employees. The SEC had complained that the rigid federal pay scale had made it difficult for the agency to attract and retain personnel, particularly lawyers. Despite SEC complaints, the Senate accepted the House position keeping the SEC within the federal pay structure.

The Senate finally agreed to the conference report

Oct. 25. The House agreed to the report Oct. 26, clearing the measure for President Bush.

Sponsored by Edward J. Markey, D-Mass., the measure allowed the SEC to exchange information on securities investigations with foreign enforcement agencies. The measure also insulated the SEC from Freedom of Information requests for information obtained through foreign sources.

The SEC and exchanges were also given the authority to bar individuals who were convicted of securities violations from trading in the United States.

Senators also included in the bill provisions to overhaul the Trust Indenture Act, which governed registration of corporate bonds, and to require that mutual funds pass along to their shareholders information from firms in which the funds invested.

The House had passed HR 1396 (H Rept 101-240) on Sept. 25, 1989, with no amendments. The Senate had passed the bill Nov. 16, 1989, after substituting the text of S 1712, a two-year SEC reauthorization.

Securities Civil Penalties

Congress also passed S 647, giving regulators and the courts more enforcement tools when dealing with violators of securities law.

The measure substantially increased the range of civil penalties that the SEC and courts could impose in securities fraud cases. Fines ranged from $5,000 for individuals and $50,000 for businesses for basic violations of securities laws. Fines for violations involving fraudulent actions and substantial financial loss would be higher. Lesser penalties would apply to securities cases not involving fraud.

In addition, the SEC was given the authority to issue cease and desist orders against people or businesses found to be violating securities laws.

The Senate on July 18 passed the measure by voice vote. The Banking Committee had approved the bill May 24, after agreeing to a substitute that instituted a three-tier system for the dollar amounts of civil penalties and clarifying who was subject to SEC cease and desist orders.

The House approved S 647 on July 23 after striking its text and inserting the provisions of HR 5325, its version of securities penalties.

While the two measures were similar, a key difference was a Senate provision allowing the SEC access to grand jury materials. Such information could be used by the SEC to develop civil fraud cases, even if the grand jury investigation did not result in a criminal prosecution.

The House bill also included provisions to bring the penny-stock industry under tighter SEC regulation. The House bill would have required penny-stock dealers to provide buyers with a risk-disclosure document explaining that these stocks were often difficult to trade because the market for them was small and less liquid.

Negotiators spent the next month hammering out the differences. The compromise included the House-passed language on the tighter SEC regulation of penny stocks and removed the Senate-passed language giving the SEC access to grand jury information.

The full Senate agreed to the changes Sept. 27, and the House followed suit Oct. 1. ■

Futures Bill Fails Over Agency Control

Despite a two-year effort, the 101st Congress failed to clear legislation reauthorizing and strengthening the Commodity Futures Trading Commission (CFTC).

Although legislation was approved in 1989 by the House (HR 2869) and by one Senate committee (S 1729), lawmakers could never resolve a fight over which agency, the CFTC or the Securities and Exchange Commission (SEC), was to control stock-index futures contracts — financial instruments used in complicated trading strategies by big institutional investors, brokerage houses and speculators.

Besides reauthorizing the agency, the measures would have provided the agency, which regulated futures trading, with new authority to crack down on trading violations. The legislation would have:

- Required the CFTC to restrict dual trading — a broker trading for his own account as well as that of a customer.
- Required the exchanges to establish a system of reconstructing trading.

The system would have been designed to deter trading abuses and provide regulators with an audit trail to investigate abuse.

- Given the CFTC expanded authority to impose fees on the industry to defray its operating expenses.

BACKGROUND

Congressional action on the CFTC bill broke down into two issues: enforcement and futures trading.

In 1989, lawmakers had a heated debate on whether the CFTC should be forced to better monitor the scandal-ridden futures exchanges. *(1989 Almanac, p. 393)*

In 1990, lawmakers argued over which agency should have control over stock-index futures — a dispute that halted progress on the bills. The battle over the jurisdiction of futures pitted the New York-based stock markets and their regulator, the SEC, against the Chicago-based futures markets and their regulator, the CFTC.

Stock-index futures were contracts used by speculators to bet on the market's direction and by holders of larger stock portfolios to "hedge" or buy insurance against declines in the value of their holdings.

Since the October 1987 market crash, stock-index futures had been at the center of a debate about whether the stock market was a safe place for investors, especially small investors, to put their money.

Some analysts argued that speculative trading in stock-index futures, which were closely tied to stock prices, could be blamed for large swings in stock prices.

Part of the problem, critics argued, was the low level set for futures margins, the amount of money an investor pays upfront for stock or futures contracts. Stock margins were set at 50 percent of the purchase price; futures margins varied but were generally much lower.

The issue amounted to a battle among the New York-based stock markets and retail stock brokerage firms and the Chicago-based futures industry. The brokerage firms were concerned about small investors fleeing the market and were searching for a "fix" that would stabilize trading. The futures industry was motivated in large part by agriculture interests, which feared harm to the futures markets that helped stabilize farm prices.

Neither side in the conflict had the strength to prevail over the other.

HOUSE ACTION

The House Agriculture Committee approved legislation (HR 2869 — H Rept 101-236) to reauthorize the CFTC on Aug. 2, 1989.

Sponsors of the bill were aided by an announcement the day of the markup that 46 futures traders in Chicago had been indicted on charges of illegal floor trading.

Like the Senate bill, the measure would have required the CFTC to improve its audit functions, restrict dual trading and increase user fees for traders.

The bill also would have:

- Made insider trading of non-public information a felony for futures trading. Existing CFTC regulations prohibited insider trading; the amendment would have made it a crime that would carry a maximum fine of $500,000, five years in jail, or both.
- Required exchanges to "make every effort" to notify the CFTC before taking an emergency action, such as a suspension of trading.
- Required each exchange to "monitor closely" traders who were granted hedging exemptions that allowed them to exceed regular limits.

Floor Action

The House voted 420-0 to pass HR 2869 on Sept. 13, 1989. The measure sailed through the floor with few changes to the bill approved by the House Agriculture Committee.

One amendment agreed to by the House would have required the CFTC to monitor the margin levels for stock-index futures to ensure that they were sufficient to maintain the integrity of the markets.

The exhanges would also have been barred from lowering margin requirements as part of an emergency action unless the CFTC approved.

Other amendments approved by the House would have:

- Required that CFTC commissioners have a "demonstrated knowledge" of futures trading, regulation of the markets or the industry in general. Existing law merely stated that the president should appoint commissioners with such qualifications.
- Required that any exceptions issued by the CFTC to the bill's dual trading standards be "in the public interest."

SENATE ACTION

The Senate Agriculture Committee approved its version of the legislation (S 1729 — S Rept 101-191) by voice vote on Nov. 2, 1989.

Committee action on the measure came over the objections of the futures industry, which vehemently opposed the proposals. In particular, the industry was opposed to a provision that would have given the CFTC authority to impose $68 million in new fees. The fees were to be used by the agency to help defray its operating expenses.

The panel turned back an amendment by David L. Boren, D-Okla., and Rudy Boschwitz, R-Minn., to lower the fees. The panel voted 12-7 in favor of a substitute amendment to set yearly caps on CFTC user fees.

Lawmakers kept intact the bulk of the measure, which would have required the exchanges to establish an audit system to reconstruct trading. The system would have been designed to deter trading abuses and provide regulators with an audit trail to investigate abuse.

The bill also would have required the CFTC to restrict dual trading, which occurred when a broker traded for his own account and that of a customer.

Lawmakers accepted by voice vote an amendment to allow the CFTC to suspend traders who had been indicted for crimes "that would reflect on the honesty or fitness of the person to act as a fiduciary."

Jurisdictional Dispute Kills Bill

When the focus of the bill shifted in 1990 to jurisdiction over stock-index futures, progress on the measure came to a grinding halt. Lawmakers spent most of the year searching for a compromise that would appease both the securities and futures markets.

At the center of the battle were the four members of a White House working group on market regulation who studied the issue. Of those members, the SEC and Treasury Department favored transferring regulation of futures contracts from the CFTC to the SEC. The CFTC was firmly against the proposal; the Federal Reserve Board was on the fence.

During the long debate, lawmakers advanced a compromise that would have allowed the Federal Reserve to set the margins and kept jurisdiction over futures trading with the CFTC. But no deal was agreed to.

William J. Brodsky, president of the Chicago Mercantile Exchange, said he believed the futures industry had the votes to hold off the administration without a compromise. "I don't think we need to consider that," he said.

In March, Fed Chairman Alan Greenspan joined the SEC and the Treasury in calling for closer federal regulation of futures contracts. He advocated transferring jurisdiction of futures contracts to the SEC.

In an effort to end the jurisdictional struggle, House Agriculture Committee member Dan Glickman, D-Kan., and Dennis E. Eckart, D-Ohio, introduced in April legislation (HR 4477) to merge the SEC and CFTC. But the measure never moved.

In October, Alan J. Dixon, D-Ill., and others blocked an effort by Senate Agriculture Committee Chairman Patrick J. Leahy, D-Vt., and ranking Republican Richard G. Lugar, Ind., to move S 1729 to the floor.

The Leahy-Lugar proposal would have allowed for votes on two amendments. The first amendment would have given the Fed authority to set futures margins and the CFTC to retain jurisdiction over futures contracts. The second would have shifted jurisdiction of futures contracts from the CFTC to the SEC.

Dixon was one of several senators who objected to bringing the bill to the floor. Another attempt was made to bring the bill to the floor with an agreement to shelve the turf battle for one year, but senators who advocated shifting jurisdiction blocked that attempt.

Leahy summed up the dilemma in a floor speech Oct. 23. "Opponents of jurisdictional change refuse to debate S 1729 with amendments," he said. "Supporters of jurisdictional change refuse to debate the bill without amendments. The public sits in the middle and gasps at the absurdity of important reforms being killed in the cross-fire." ■

Coin-Redesign Lobbying Efforts Fail

Despite efforts that extended into the waning hours of the 101st Congress, proponents of coin redesign failed to pass their proposals or attach them to any last-minute legislation. The prime sponsors of the legislation, Sen. Alan Cranston, D-Calif., and Rep. Henry B. Gonzalez, D-Texas, championed bills to require the federal Mint to redesign the backs of the five major circulating coins — the penny, nickel, dime, quarter and half dollar. The redesigns were to reflect themes embodied in the Constitution.

When the stand-alone bills (S 428, HR 505) failed to move in 1990, the provisions of S 428 were attached to several other measures, including several bills that died, among them a money-laundering bill (HR 3848) and a bill naming a Postal Service building in Cleveland for former Olympic track star Jesse Owens (HR 5235). Coin-redesign provisions were also stricken from the omnibus housing programs reauthorization bill (S 566) and the budget-reconciliation bill (HR 5835), both of which cleared Oct. 27, the last full day of the session. It was on the housing bill that redesign proponents placed their greatest efforts and came closest to achieving their goals. *(Housing, p. 631; reconciliation, p. 138; money laundering, p. 187)*

Cranston lobbied members on the House floor repeatedly in the final days of the session with Gonzalez as they continued to look for vehicles that might carry the coin measure to enactment. "They've stuck it on everything but the Pledge of Allegiance," complained House Rules Committee Chairman Joe Moakley, D-Mass.

Despite their ranks as Senate Democratic whip and chairman of the House Banking Committee, respectively, Cranston and Gonzalez were unable to get their way.

The Bush administration mounted strong opposition to the redesign idea in the closing days of the Congress.

Cranston and Gonzalez were not expected to give up the idea of requiring a redesign of the nation's coins and planned to renew their efforts in the 102nd Congress. And despite the failure of the Susan B. Anthony dollar coin to gain popular approval in the late 1970s, other members were considered likely to press for introduction of a new dollar coin, which had long been sought by the vending machine industry.

BACKGROUND

Except for the years 1976-77, when the reverse sides of the quarter and half dollar were temporarily changed to commemorate the bicentennial of the Declaration of Independence, the last major coin redesign had been in 1964, when the John F. Kennedy half dollar was first minted. Proponents said it was time for another redesign.

The prime mover behind the effort was Diane Wolf, a prominent Upper East Side New York socialite. A contributor to Republican campaigns, Wolf was appointed to the U.S. Commission on Fine Arts by President Ronald Reagan in 1985. The main task of the seven-member fine arts commission was to oversee the architectural appearance of government buildings in the District of Columbia.

But since the term of President Warren G. Harding (1921-23), the commission was also authorized to review coin designs. So, starting in 1987, Wolf used her seat on the commission to press her case. Improbably, given her Republican background, Wolf picked up powerful Democratic friends, most notably Cranston and Gonzalez.

Through constant visits to members, Wolf signed up a majority of the Senate and nearly half the House on coin redesign bills in 1987. Though a bill passed the Senate twice in 1988, it died in the 100th Congress. Bills were quickly reintroduced in both chambers in 1989. The Senate passed S 428 on June 23, 1989, but it saw no action in the House. *(1989 Almanac, p. 141; 1988 Almanac, p. 248)*

Wolf was aided in her efforts by the nation's numismatists, who wanted new coins to collect and promoted the idea of new designs in their publications. Wolf called the old designs "ordinary and boring" and said the public would be happy to see them replaced.

For his part, Gonzalez argued that U.S. coin designs were stodgy and that the U.S. engraving industry had lost its international competitive edge. "Have you ever seen Italian coins? They're fantastic," Gonzalez said.

Critics, though, pointed out that the Mint was authorized to redesign the reverse sides of all coins after they had been in circulation 25 years. Its reluctance to do so before these efforts, they said, reflected doubt that there was a public demand for a change. All five major coins had long passed their 25th anniversaries; the oldest extant design, on the quarter, dated to 1932.

And, while Wolf made some influential allies during her fight, she also made some powerful enemies. Among them was Rep. Frank Annunzio, D-Ill., who got into some pointed altercations over her motives for the coin redesign.

At one point in a hearing in September 1988, Annunzio's chief aide, Curtis Prins, demanded to know whether it was true that Wolf had tried to get the words "In God We Trust" stricken from a commemorative coin. Wolf said she had not, but engaged in a war of words with Annunzio that continued even through the 1990 debate.

Annunzio effectively blocked the bill in 1988, when he chaired the House Coinage Subcommittee. During the next two years, Annunzio's successor as head of the panel, Richard H. Lehman, D-Calif., also held up the bill. Lehman wanted to strike a compromise with Gonzalez to allow the redesign of a single coin and vote on additional redesigns later if the public supported the change.

What the Bill Would Have Done

Supporters of the redesign said it would renew interest in coin collecting, give coins a more "modern" look, stimulate civic pride through the portrayal of constitutional themes and make money for the Treasury.

The bill would have:

- Authorized a change of design on the reverse side of the half dollar, quarter, dime, nickel and penny.
- Allowed one or more coins to be redesigned at the same time, but the first redesigned coin would have a design commemorating the 200th anniversary of the U.S. Constitution for a period of two years after it was issued. The measure would have allowed the coin with the commemoration design to be changed to a new design after the two-year period.
- Allowed the faces on the coins to be changed, though the five presidents depicted could not be replaced.
- Required the secretary of the Treasury to select new designs, to be phased in over six years. New designs would be authorized to contain themes such as freedom of speech

and assembly, freedom of the press, right to due process of law, right to a trial by jury, right to equal protection under the law, right to vote, themes from the Bill of Rights, separation of powers and the independence of the judiciary.

- Required the Treasury secretary to consult with the U.S. Commission on Fine Arts in selecting new designs.
- Required that any profits received from the sale of uncirculated and proof sets of coins be deposited by the secretary in the general fund of the Treasury and used to reduce the national debt.

Wolf argued that a design change would bring the Treasury money in two ways.

First, it would reawaken coin collectors who would buy fancy sets of specially polished, uncirculated coins at a premium. That could yield $18 million in profits over six years, the Treasury had estimated.

Second, people would hold onto the old coins for sentimental reasons, requiring the Treasury to put more coins into circulation than it had before. The resulting seigniorage — essentially the difference in price between the cost of minting a coin and its face value — would be $250 million over six years, according to the Treasury.

While the booked income would reduce the total amount of money borrowed by the government it would technically be off budget and thus it would not reduce the budget deficit.

Early in the debate in 1987, Wolf contended that minting newly designed coins could raise as much as $2.3 billion, but Treasury Department officials shot that down.

CHAMBER ACTION

While a majority in both chambers had cosponsored redesign bills (HR 505, S 428), backing was soft and there was some strong opposition.

Conferees on the omnibus housing bill, though, did agree to a coin-redesign provision — offering redesign proponents their best shot at enacting their plan.

Subcommittee Chairman Lehman opposed a full-scale redesign of the nation's circulating coins, and the bill remained bottled up in subcommittee.

Gonzalez protested that Lehman refused to mark up the bill. Lehman said that he would have allowed a markup, but the measure would not have been the one Gonzalez wanted.

"It doesn't have support in committee," Lehman said. "Clearly, the only way to get it passed is to jam it into a non-related conference report at the last minute."

But after the Senate attached the language to the housing bill (S 566), Gonzalez said he thought that he could accomplish his aims by accepting the Senate provision.

Lehman tried to get on the housing conference committee to fight the coin provision, but he was rebuffed by Gonzalez.

And, although Lehman apparently had promises from enough House Democratic conferees to kill the provision, he did not hold them to it.

The House conferees voted 7-5 on Oct. 15 — with only Democrats in favor and Republicans opposed — to accept the Senate coin language.

Conferee Jim McDermott, D-Wash., a freshman Gonzalez put on the conference as a housing ally, said he voted with the chairman at his request. "We're about to put the first housing bill into law in 10 years," McDermott said. "It seems immaterial."

And Barney Frank, D-Mass., who worked closely with Gonzalez on the housing reauthorization, said Lehman had released him to support the chairman. "I got a deal out of it," Frank said. "We're putting [White House Chief of Staff John H.] Sununu on the $3 bill."

The Republicans on the conference were less jovial.

Coinage Subcommittee ranking Republican John Hiler of Indiana cited a Colorado poll showing almost 90 percent of the respondents opposed to redesigning coins. And he disputed the importance of the number of House cosponsors, noting that he had cosponsored the bill at one time.

"People sign onto coin bills in easy fashion," Hiler said. "I tell members that they're going to authorize new coinage on the housing bill, and they say, 'What?' "

Despite their obvious reluctance to redesign coins on their own, Treasury and Mint officials had testified that they did not oppose Congress telling them to do so. But they also said they did not believe the general public was seeking a redesign. And, they said, a full-blown redesign could backfire, as it did when the Susan B. Anthony dollar coin was issued in 1978.

"The design of Monticello on the nickel or the Lincoln Memorial on the penny can hardly be viewed as dated," said Mint Director Donna Pope.

Final Efforts Stalled

Despite the success of coin-redesign proponents in attaching their plan to the housing bill in conference, their efforts stalled. A rank-and-file revolt against redesign caused an uproar on two major bills the week of Oct. 22.

First, conferees on the housing bill were forced to call the measure back and issue a new conference report that did not include the coin provision. Housing bill supporters were afraid that antagonism to the coin language could sink the first major housing bill in 10 years.

"I went through the Susan B. Anthony fiasco, and I don't want to go on record for changing the design," said Rep. Chalmers P. Wylie, R-Ohio, the ranking minority member of the Banking Committee.

Members threatened to excise the coin language from the conference report on the House floor. But that would have left the bill open to unfriendly amendments in the Senate — probably killing it.

Despite persistent lobbying on the floor of the House by Cranston to retain the coin provisions, Gonzalez finally told him that the bill would die unless the offending language was dropped. Conferees agreed to refile the conference report without the coin language.

Though most of the fighting over the coin bill occurred out of sight, it spilled into public view during a House Rules Committee hearing on the housing bill on Oct. 24.

"Changing the nation's coins is not to be taken lightly," said Doug Barnard Jr., D-Ga., a prime opponent. "It's a very emotional issue for most Americans."

As conferees concluded their work on the massive deficit-reducing reconciliation bill, there were repeated moves to place and keep the coin language on that measure. Those efforts had failed as well as conferees finally stripped the redesign provision from the bill.

Cranston's final lobbying effort came about 30 minutes before the 101st Congress adjourned early Oct. 28. He was seen on the House floor, where redesign language was still alive on a Christopher Columbus commemorative coin bill. That last-ditch effort failed, too.

Rules Chairman Moakley observed of Cranston's continued efforts on behalf of Wolf's redesign idea, "That's an awfully insistent lobbyist." ■

Bush Pocket-Vetoes Export Control Law

> **BOXSCORE**
>
> **Legislation:** Export Administration Act authorization (HR 4653).
>
> **Major action:** Pocket-vetoed, Nov. 16. Conference report adopted by Senate, Oct. 26; by House, Oct. 26. Senate passed S 2927, Sept. 13; House passed HR 4653, 312-85, June 6.
>
> **Reports:** Conference report (H Rept 101-944); Banking, Housing and Urban Affairs (S Rept 101-399); Foreign Affairs Committee (H Rept 101-482).

Lawmakers cleared legislation on Oct. 26 to overhaul U.S. export controls, but President Bush pocket-vetoed the bill (HR 4653) over restrictions on foreign aid to countries that used chemical weapons or aided others in manufacturing chemical weapons. Administration officials said the restraints would have given the president too little discretion.

Although the sanctions drew wide bipartisan backing — 79 senators signed a letter to the president on Oct. 27, urging him to sign the bill — Bush said the provisions "unduly interfere with the president's responsibility for carrying out foreign policy." *(Veto text, p. 200)*

The sanctions provisions would have punished foreign companies that helped countries "use, develop, produce, stockpile or otherwise acquire chemical or biological weapons." A company could have faced the loss of U.S. government contracts and been prevented from selling its products in the United States. Governments found to be using chemical weapons would have been subject to a host of penalties, including a cutoff of aid.

The sanctions were added to a bill to reauthorize through 1992 the Export Administration Act of 1979, which established the federal government's licensing program for sales of high-technology goods to foreign countries. U.S. licensing of militarily sensitive sales — such as high-grade metal-milling equipment and computers — had been a subject of dispute for years between those who wanted to promote U.S. trade and those who regarded export of some high-tech items as a threat to U.S. national security.

HR 4653 would have sharply reduced the number of items on the Commerce Department's list of controlled exports and eased restrictions on exports to certain Eastern European nations in line with actions taken in June by the 17-nation Coordinating Committee on Multilateral Export Controls (Cocom).

Concern about Iraq's chemical weapons capacity and aid that Iraq reportedly received from other countries prompted inclusion of the contentious sanctions provisions. The provisions, added during Senate floor consideration, contained the text of a measure that had passed both chambers in various forms but had stalled in conference.

Although the president vetoed the bill, he had authority under other laws, chiefly the International Emergency Economic Powers Act of 1976, to continue export controls, and, before announcing the veto, Bush issued an executive order implementing portions of the bill.

BACKGROUND

The 1979 Export Administration Act was a continuation of legislative initiatives in place since 1949 to control the flow of U.S. exports to communist countries.

In 1969, the law was rewritten to ease restrictions on the sale of items to communist countries if they were freely available from such areas as Japan and Western Europe. It was reworked again in 1979 to limit shipments of militarily sensitive goods, such as sophisticated computer technology, to the Soviet Union, its allies, non-NATO countries and even close U.S. allies.

Congress reauthorized the act in 1985 (PL 99-64), but only after 2½ years of negotiations. The act was extended through Sept. 30, 1990, and its procedures eased somewhat, as part of the 1988 Omnibus Trade and Competitiveness Act (PL 100-418). *(1988 Almanac, p. 212; 1985 Almanac, p. 259)*

The push to reauthorize the act was driven by concerns on the effects export controls had on U.S. companies' ability to build or hold worldwide markets in the face of stiff competition. In addition, bill sponsors said that simplified licensing procedures would allow enforcement to be focused on the most sensitive high-tech exports.

In June, Cocom (which included most NATO countries, plus Japan and Australia) moved to greatly relax restraints on exports to the former East bloc. HR 4653 embodied in major part the principles of relaxed controls it had adopted. Pressure from Japan and Western Europe to ease international export controls paralleled efforts by pro-export forces in Congress to make it easier to ship previously controlled goods to many countries.

At the same time, the bill would have tightened controls on a limited number of militarily important items in order to better guard against shipment to the Soviet Union and other countries, notably Iraq, which the United States was on the verge of hostilities with in 1990 over the Iraqi invasion of Kuwait on Aug. 2. *(Persian Gulf crisis, p. 717)*

Chemical Weapons Legislation

Last-minute disputes in the Senate in 1988 and 1989 held up sanctions against countries that used chemical weapons.

At the end of the 1988 session, Sen. Jesse Helms, R-N.C., blocked action on an omnibus foreign relations bill that included sanctions against Iraq for its use of chemical weapons against its Kurdish minority. Helms' action was over an unrelated foreign policy issue. *(1988 Almanac, p. 510)*

In 1989, a jurisdictional dispute between the Banking and Foreign Relations committees prevented the Senate from taking up a broader measure (S 195) to impose sanctions against any country that used chemical or biological weapons in violation of international law. The bill also would have required sanctions against foreign companies that helped those nations develop such weapons.

The Foreign Relations Committee on Oct. 6, 1989, approved S 195, but the Banking Committee insisted that parts of the bill belonged in its jurisdiction and demanded changes.

The House had passed its version (HR 3033) Nov. 13, 1989. The Bush administration supported the House bill because it would have given the president greater discretion in imposing sanctions than would the Senate version. *(1989 Almanac, p. 501)*

HOUSE ACTION

The House Foreign Affairs Committee on May 3 approved HR 4653 by voice vote. Its Subcommittee on International Economic Policy and Trade had approved the bill on April 24. The subcommittee adopted two technical amendments, but members agreed to withhold substantial amendments for full committee consideration.

Unlike previous versions that did not make it out of the committee, the panel's 1990 reauthorization focused on shortening the list of restricted items and clarifying the classifications.

The bill also sought to resolve struggles between executive branch departments, particularly the Commerce and Defense departments, and to otherwise ease the process by which U.S. businesses obtained licenses to export such products to the Soviet Union and its former satellites.

The committee's action was overshadowed by an announcement May 2 that the Bush administration was willing to ease restrictions on exports to the Soviet Union and Eastern Europe. The plan would immediately trim the list of restricted product categories from 120 to 90 and narrow the scope of another 13.

White House spokesman Marlin Fitzwater said that by the end of 1990 Bush wanted a "complete overhaul of the control list" leading to a "new core list of goods and technologies that is far shorter and less restrictive." Fitzwater stressed that reducing the list would allow more careful enforcement of the remaining barriers to highly sensitive military technology.

Sam Gejdenson, D-Conn., chairman of the subcommittee and author of the reauthorization bill, called the administration move an improvement but said it "falls short." Gejdenson sought to streamline the system so that businesses interested in exporting would not have to wait for months or years while license applications languished or got caught in interagency conflicts.

Committee action was made easy by the support of panel Republicans, many of whom had, in the past, sought to keep the fences around technology insuperable.

Floor Action

Despite strong administration opposition to many of the key provisions, the House passed HR 4643 on June 6 by a vote of 312-86, with bipartisan majorities in favor. The bill was designed to do what many in Congress had sought for years — end restrictions on exports that were widely available or of little or no consequence to foreign military aims. *(Vote 160, p. 54-H)*

"This bill's major focus is to limit the bureaucratic wrangling, infighting and the inefficiencies which leave American workers and corporations at a disadvantage," said Gejdenson.

Gejdenson estimated that between $10 billion and $50 billion a year in export sales was lost because of delays and other difficulties in getting licenses for high-tech exports that other countries were willing to supply.

But critics, such as Bill Dickinson, R-Ala., argued that the measure would go too far in making sensitive technologies available to the Soviet Union and other countries. "I share the view of one writer who recently termed HR 4653 the 'Soviet Military Relief Act,' " Dickinson said.

The bill would have eliminated what Gejdenson called a "three-headed monster" composed of the Commerce, Defense and State departments, all of which had a say in export licenses under existing law. Instead, the bill would have made the Commerce Department responsible for all controlled items, except those specifically intended for military use.

Moreover, the lengthy list of restrictions on high-tech exports to countries other than the Soviet Union and its allies would have been wiped out in October 1992. Commerce would have to offer justification for any items put back on the list.

Unlike committee action on the bill, which was swift and relatively uncontroversial, floor debate consumed an entire day and resulted in a dozen roll call votes on substantive amendments.

Three adopted amendments were designed to remove benefits that would have been accorded by the bill to the Soviet Union and China, based on unrelated human rights concerns. Many were turned aside under complaints from sponsors that they were "killers" designed to undo the very reforms envisioned in the bill.

One such amendment, by Duncan Hunter, R-Calif., would have prohibited the sale to the Soviet Union of advanced telecommunications equipment that would be made available to emerging democracies in Czechoslovakia, Hungary and Poland.

Noting that the United States and Great Britain had turned down applications for the sale of fiber-optics telecommunications transmission systems to the Soviets, Hunter said the bill should be tough on telecommunications. "We do not have to give them carte blanche to sell everything to the Soviet Union," Hunter argued. The amendment was defeated, 78-315. *(Vote 156, p. 54-H)*

SENATE ACTION

The Senate passed HR 4653 on Sept. 13. Before passage, lawmakers added the text of S 195 to require the president to impose economic sanctions on countries that used chemical weapons and on companies that helped produce them.

Bush opposed the provisions, claiming that they would mandate the sanctions and would not provide presidential discretion in decision-making. He threatened to veto the measure if it cleared Congress in that form.

Chemical Weapons Provisions

After resolving a turf battle between committees and allaying some concerns expressed by the administration, the Senate on May 17 without dissent approved HR 3033 to require the president to impose trade and aid sanctions on countries that used chemical or biological weapons.

The Senate version of HR 3033 contained most of the provisions of S 195 approved by the Foreign Relations Committee Oct. 6, 1989.

The bill would have imposed trade sanctions on companies — U.S. or foreign — that supplied equipment or materials to countries that used such weapons. The vote was 92-0. *(Vote 101, p. 23-S)*

Among the sanctions the president could impose were an arms-sale ban, export and import restrictions, and bans on foreign aid and financial assistance.

The Bush administration had opposed the Senate bill and threatened to veto it, insisting that the measure reduced the president's flexibility in conducting foreign affairs. The Senate sought to reduce some of the administra-

Export Amendments Act Veto Message

Following is the memorandum of disapproval President Bush issued Nov. 16 announcing that he would not sign the Omnibus Export Amendments Act of 1990 (HR 4653):

I am withholding my approval of HR 4653, the Omnibus Export Amendments Act of 1990. Although this legislation contains constructive provisions, it would severely constrain presidential authority in carrying out foreign policy.

I agree with the principal goals of this bill, which include improved export controls for and sanctions against the use of chemical and biological weapons; sanctions on Iraq; missile technology sanctions; and reauthorization of the Export Administration Act. Indeed, I have recently signed into law provisions on missile technology sanctions and sanctions against Iraq comparable to those contained in this bill.

HR 4653, however, contains elements that I believe would undermine these objectives and our ability to act quickly, decisively and multilaterally at a time when we must be able to do so. These provisions unduly interfere with the president's constitutional responsibilities for carrying out foreign policy. Rather than signing the bill, I am directing action under existing authorities to accomplish the bill's principal goals.

I am pleased that the Congress endorses my goals of stemming the dangerous proliferation of chemical and biological weapons. The administration has worked closely with the Congress to design appropriate and effective legislation to improve our ability to impose sanctions on the nations that use such weapons and any companies that contribute to their spread. Indeed, the administration supported the House version of the sanctions provision.

Throughout discussions with the Congress, my administration insisted that any such legislation should not harm cooperation with our partners and should respect the president's constitutional responsibilities. Unfortunately, as reported from conference, HR 4653 does not safeguard those responsibilities, nor does it meet our broader foreign policy goals.

The major flaw in HR 4653 is not the requirement of sanctions but the rigid way in which they are imposed. The mandatory imposition of unilateral sanctions as provided in this bill would harm U.S. economic interests and provoke friendly countries who are essential to our efforts to resist Iraqi aggression. If there is one lesson we have all learned in Operation Desert Shield, it is that multilateral support enhances the effectiveness of sanctions.

Because of my deep concern about the serious threat posed by chemical and biological weapons, I have signed an executive order directing the imposition of the sanctions contained in this bill and implementing new chemical and biological weapon export controls. This executive order goes beyond HR 4653 in some respects. It sets forth a clear set of stringent sanctions while encouraging negotiations with our friends and allies. It imposes an economic penalty on companies that contribute to the spread of these weapons and on countries that actually use such weapons or are making preparations to do so. At the same time, it allows the president necessary flexibility in implementing these sanctions and penalties. Furthermore, the executive order reaffirms my determination to achieve early conclusion of a verifiable global convention to prevent the production and use of chemical weapons.

The executive order also directs the establishment of enhanced proliferation controls, carefully targeted on exports, projects and

tion's objections by adopting an amendment by Bob Dole, R-Kan., allowing the president to waive the sanctions against foreign countries for up to one year. As drafted by the Foreign Relations Committee in 1989, the bill allowed the president to waive the sanctions only for nine months.

Even with the Dole amendment, the Senate bill remained unacceptable to Bush, according to a State Department official, who said Bush favored the House version.

In addition to administration opposition, the bill faced objections from the Banking Committee, which said that its jurisdiction over several provisions was violated. Those objections were resolved while the Senate debated the bill. By a 96-0 vote, the Senate adopted an amendment by John Heinz, R-Pa., calling for stronger international efforts to restrain trade in supplies and equipment needed to make chemical weapons. *(Vote 98, p. 23-S)*

Meanwhile, even after the provisions of S 195 were attached to the export-control bill, Congress continued to act on HR 3033.

The House on Oct. 22 again passed HR 3033 by voice vote. As the Senate bill languished under the veto threat, the House opted to send back to the Senate its version of the sanctions legislation, which House members said the administration preferred.

Committee Action

The Senate Banking Committee approved its version of the export-control legislation (S 2927) by voice vote on July 17. The bill differed in many respects from the House measure, which was drafted and voted on before Cocom voted to relax controls on exports to Eastern Europe.

While both the House and Senate bills would have made it easier to export high-tech goods to the former East bloc, the Senate bill earned administration support because it closely followed the Cocom agreement. For example, unlike the House bill, the measure did not alter the relationship between the Commerce, Defense and State departments, all of which had a say in whether export licenses of high-tech goods were granted.

The House bill drew strong administration fire for limiting the Defense Department's role to goods that had strictly military applications.

Most committee action on the measure was not contentious, with the exception of an amendment to open the Export-Import Bank's coffers to finance military sales abroad.

The Ex-Im Bank had been prohibited for more than 20 years from financing military sales to Third World countries and by policy had refused to finance military sales to developed countries.

The amendment was sponsored by Missouri Republican Christopher S. Bond and Connecticut Democrat Christopher J. Dodd, who argued that defense-based companies in the United States needed to find new outlets for products and that other developed countries provided government financing to military sales.

The committee adopted the amendment on a 16-5 vote after rejecting on an 8-9 vote a substitute offered by Heinz that would have allowed the Ex-Im Bank to use only its "excess" loan guarantee authority to help finance military sales.

Floor Action

The Senate passed HR 4653 on Sept. 13, after substituting the text of S 2927 and adding several amendments. Senators left intact the provisions allowing the Ex-Im Bank to finance military sales.

Lawmakers agreed by voice vote to add the text of

countries of concern. On this issue, as with other important export control matters, my goal is to pursue effective, multilateral export controls that send the clear message that the United States will not tolerate violations of international law.

I am also concerned that other features of HR 4653 would hamper our efforts to improve the effectiveness of export controls. In the rapidly changing situation in Eastern Europe and in bilateral relationships with the Soviet Union, we have demonstrated the ability to adjust, in cooperation with our allies, export controls on high technology to reflect the new strategic relationships. Last May, I asked our allies to liberalize dramatically our multilateral export controls. Negotiations designed to liberalize trade to encourage democratic institutions and open market economies will continue. Our multilateral export controls have contributed significantly to the positive changes brought about in West-East relations. The micromanagement of export controls mandated by HR 4653 can only damage these ongoing efforts.

In other areas, HR 4653 would be harmful to closely linked U.S. economic and foreign policy interests. For example, under Section 128 of the bill, there would be extraterritorial application of U.S. law that could force foreign subsidiaries of U.S. firms to choose between violating U.S. or host country laws.

Other sections of HR 4653 contain useful provisions that will be implemented as soon as possible. However, additional legal authority is not required to make our export control system reflect the economic and national security realities of today's world. In response to recent world events, I am directing executive departments and agencies to implement the following changes:

- By June 1, 1991, the United States will eliminate all dual-use export licenses under Section 5 of the Export Administration Act to members of the export control group known as CoCom, consistent with multilateral arrangements. In addition, all re-export licenses under Section 5 to and from CoCom will be eliminated, consistent with multilateral arrangements.
- By June 1, 1991, the United States will remove from the U.S. munitions list all items contained on the CoCom dual-use list unless significant U.S. national security interests would be jeopardized.
- By Jan. 1, 1991, U.S. review of export licenses subject to CoCom Favorable Consideration and National Discretion procedures will be reduced to 30 and 15 days, respectively.
- By Jan. 1, 1991, new interagency procedures will be instituted to make dual-use export license decisions more predictable and timely.
- By Jan. 1, 1991, the secretary of State will initiate negotiations to ensure that supercomputer export controls are multilateral in nature and not undermined by the policies of other supplier countries. By June 1, 1991, in consultation with industry, we will devise and publish a method to index supercomputer license conditions to reflect rapid advances in the industry and changes in strategic concerns.
- By Jan. 1, 1991, we will significantly increase the threshold for distribution licenses to free-world destinations and ensure that, at least annually, these thresholds are adjusted to reflect changes in technology and are consistent with international relationships, including changing requirements to stem the proliferation of missile technology and nuclear, chemical and biological weapons.

In summary, HR 4653 contains serious and unacceptable flaws that would hamper our efforts to prevent the proliferation of weapons of mass destruction and to ease restrictions on the legitimate sale of dual-use goods to acceptable users. Rather than sign this bill, I have chosen to take a series of steps under existing authorities to ensure that mutually shared objectives are met in a timely and effective manner. I will work with the Congress, upon its return, to enact an appropriate extension of the Export Administration Act. ■

S 195 dealing with chemical weapons sanctions. Bush again voiced his opposition to the provisions, claiming that they would mandate the sanctions and would not provide presidential discretion in decision-making.

Other amendments, all approved by voice vote, would have:

- Increased civil and criminal penalties for businesses and individuals who violated the United Nations trade embargo against Iraq and Kuwait.
- Clarified that the Defense Department could block sales of goods that could be used for chemical, biological or nuclear weapons or missile technology to Iran, Iraq, Libya or Syria.
- Reinstated sanctions against sales to Cuba by foreign subsidiaries of U.S. firms.

VETO, AFTERMATH

When the Senate voted to tack on the text of S 195 to the measure, it did so over the Bush administration's objections. Using the Export Administration Act reauthorization as a vehicle was more or less a last-ditch effort to move the chemical weapons bill.

Using the conference on HR 4653, House and Senate negotiators spent the month of October trying to hammer out agreements on the chemical weapons provisions and other outstanding issues.

In informal meetings, conferees were able to craft a compromise; the chemical weapons provisions were left in the bill.

Conferees also resolved differences with the Export Administration Act language, agreeing to retain House-passed language to allow the Defense Department to maintain a role in licensing the sale of high-tech goods abroad. Senate-passed language that would have allowed the Ex-Im Bank to offer loans for military sales was removed. It was replaced by language that called on the 102nd Congress to examine the issue.

Both chambers then adopted the conference report on Oct. 26, during the second to last session of the 101st Congress. The Senate's action cleared the bill for Bush.

Bush decided to stick by his position that the chemical weapons sanctions language was too restrictive and pocket-vetoed HR 4653.

"The major flaw with HR 4653 is not the requirement of sanctions, but the rigid way in which they are imposed," Bush said in announcing the veto.

The veto meant that the Commerce and Defense departments were left waiting until the 102nd Congress for a legislative mandate to change export-licensing controls. Under the International Emergency Economic Powers Act of 1976, however, the president had the authority to impose controls on militarily sensitive goods.

In an attempt to address a number of congressional concerns, Bush signed an executive order on the day before the veto was to take effect that included many of the provisions of HR 4653.

The order included approving the sale of high-tech goods to U.S. allies and deterring the sale of chemical weapons to certain countries. Unlike the legislation's required sanctions, however, Bush said the executive order "allows the president necessary flexibility in implementing these sanctions and penalties."

Bush also ordered a series of steps to liberalize trade. His actions included eliminating, by June 1991, the licenses that had been required for the export to NATO allies and Japan of products that had both civilian and military uses. ■

Defense Preparedness Measure Falls . . .

Congress failed to clear long-term legislation to extend the government's emergency defense preparedness and procurement authority for three years. The bill (HR 486) died when the Senate, faced with administration opposition, failed to act on a House-passed conference agreement before adjourning.

The Defense Production Act, the government's basic emergency preparedness and special military procurement law dating to 1950, had been extended temporarily through Oct. 20. With the bill's demise, though most provisions of the law expired. Under the 1950 act, the president had the authority to ensure defense-related production in times of a national emergency.

The administration also had the authority to ration certain materials and provide loans and purchase guarantees to ensure production of products the Defense Department deemed vital.

The law further allowed the president to promote the development of strategic materials and technologies, to stockpile critical materials not readily available from domestic sources and to give the military first claim on strategic goods during emergencies.

Measures considered by the House and Senate in 1990 represented substantial rewrites of the law. The House passed its bill Sept. 24; the Senate approved its version (S 1379) on Oct. 3.

The conference agreement (H Rept 101-933) would have expanded presidential and Defense Department authority to promote development of domestic suppliers of strategic goods and technologies and also to require that certain goods be purchased from U.S. companies. Those provisions drew strong administration fire and an implied veto threat from Defense Secretary Dick Cheney, despite bipartisan support in Congress. The administration complained that the bill would have constituted unnecessary interference in the marketplace and come close to creating an industrial policy for the United States, which was anathema to free-marketeers.

The compromise agreed to by House and Senate negotiators was unacceptable to the administration. It particularly objected to an unrelated provision that would have given federal banking regulators discretionary authority to restrict the expansion of foreign-based banks in the United States. The new authority would have been tied to the treatment of U.S. banks and securities firms received abroad. *(Foreign banks, p. 189)*

The House adopted the conference report Oct. 25, but the Senate did not act on the measure in the waning days of the 101st Congress.

Despite Congress' failure to extend the act, the president retained authority under other laws to continue some emergency preparedness activities and expedited military procurement.

BACKGROUND

The Defense Production Act was first authorized in 1950 to increase the flow of goods to the Korean War front. Although the economy was running close to capacity in 1950, it was clear that defense needs could not be met without some restriction on consumer claims.

Upon the request of President Harry S Truman, Congress cleared the Defense Production Act to give the administration the power to set price controls and ration food; prevent hoarding; offer loans and loan guarantees; and establish priorities for defense contracts and allocation of materials. The measure also gave the Federal Reserve Board the power to curb consumer lending, but that authority expired in 1953.

In general, the act gave the president the power to offer loans and loan guarantees for materials considered vital to national security that otherwise would not be produced. By establishing priorities on defense contracts, the president could also ensure that domestic firms were given preference for contracts to produce defense-related materials.

After the Korean War, Congress continued to extend the law to keep the United States prepared for a military emergency. The act was revised to address what lawmakers saw as new threats to national security.

For example, in the 1950s lawmakers were concerned that important U.S. industries were too concentrated and susceptible to attack. In 1956, lawmakers amended the act to promote geographic dispersal of key U.S. industries. The oil crises of the 1970s spurred lawmakers to amend the act to require the Defense Department to purchase synthetic fuels as an alternative to oil to meet national security needs.

As action on legislation progressed in 1990, lawmakers cleared three bills (HR 5432 — PL 101-351; HR 5725 — PL 101-407; S 3155 — PL 101-411) temporarily extending the act until Sept. 30, Oct. 5 and Oct. 20, respectively.

COMMITTEE ACTION

Both chambers' Banking committees approved extensions of the Defense Production Act. The House panel reported a bill authorizing the act through late 1995 while the Senate committee measure only extended the act through 1993.

Senate Action

The Senate Banking Committee approved S 1379 on May 24. The measure would have given the president $250 million to promote private-sector development of key technologies and reauthorized the act through 1993.

The panel approved the bill over the objections of some Republicans, who complained that it was a step toward legislating an industrial policy for the United States.

But the bill's sponsors, such as committee Chairman Donald W. Riegle Jr., D-Mich., countered that other governments — in particular, Japan's — spent billions of dollars to promote private industrial activities.

"This bill requires the government to identify [technological] gaps and provides the means to encourage private industry to fill them," said Riegle. "Companies helping to build a strong America deserve our government's cooperation."

. . . To Strong Administration Opposition

The bill would have made several changes in the existing law. One key change would have provided a new $250 million revolving fund, not subject to annual appropriations, for grants, loans and loan guarantees to develop strategic materials. Initial capital for the revolving fund would come from uncommitted surpluses in a fund used to buy stockpiles of strategic materials, such as aluminum, lead and rubber.

Another change would have limited so-called offsets in foreign military sales contracts, whereby U.S. companies selling overseas agreed to either make purchases from a foreign country or to subcontract parts of the work on the main purchase contract to firms in the purchasing country. Bill sponsors Alan J. Dixon, D-Ill., and John Heinz, R-Pa., complained that such offsets harmed U.S. competitiveness.

Texas Republican Phil Gramm opposed the idea of providing a $250 million revolving fund not subject to the appropriations process. "I'm not opposing setting up the fund, [although] it's a crazy idea," he said, but "it ought to be appropriated."

A Gramm amendment to require annual appropriations was defeated by voice vote.

House Action

The House Banking Subcommittee on Economic Stabilization approved HR 486 on July 19. The measure was designed to reduce U.S. dependence on foreign sources for strategic military materials. The act would have been authorized though 1992.

To reduce reliance on foreign production of key materials, the bill would have authorized the president to exempt from competitive bids certain goods that the administration deemed should be produced by a domestic company.

Members adopted an amendment offered by Norman D. Shumway, R-Calif., to treat Canadian companies as domestic.

Shumway said excluding Canada could have violated the U.S.-Canada free-trade agreement. Democrats reluctantly accepted the amendment. "I'm not crazy about putting Canada in there, but I will do it in the spirit of compromise," said subcommittee Chairwoman Mary Rose Oakar, D-Ohio.

The measure would have increased the authorization level of the act from $50 million to $130 million. To ensure the production of essential military goods, companies would have been offered purchase and loan guarantees.

When the full Banking Committee took up the measure Sept. 11, panel members approved HR 486 by a 39-8 vote. They amended the measure to authorize the act through September 1995.

During the markup, lawmakers turned back several amendments by Shumway to strike or water down the section of the bill that would create new authority for the president to give domestic suppliers exclusive rights to sell the government certain critical materials.

The new language was intended to support the continued existence of domestic industries faced with stiff overseas competition. It was opposed by virtually all committee Republicans, and its inclusion in the bill caused eight members to vote against reporting the measure to the House floor.

FLOOR/FINAL ACTION

The House voted 295-119 on Sept. 24 to approve HR 486 as reported by committee. *(Vote 371, p. 120-H)*

The administration objected to the provisions that would have authorized the president to give exclusive contracts to U.S. manufacturers of goods that were essential to the national defense, were designed to preserve domestic industries that were threatened by overseas competition and that might be needed in a national emergency.

The Senate passed S 1379 on Oct. 3. Before passing the measure, lawmakers dropped a controversial provision — strongly opposed by the administration — that would have have transferred $250 million from a Defense Department strategic materials stockpile fund to create a separate revolving fund for grants, loans and loan guarantees for businesses seeking to develop strategic materials.

The bill would have retained authorization for the fund but provided no money from the stockpile fund to pay for it.

Final Action

Prospects for passage of a long-term reauthorization bill became muddled when House negotiators agreed to a Senate provision designed to pressure foreign governments to open up their financial services markets to U.S. firms.

The language inserted into the measure would have given U.S. banking and securities regulators broad discretion to retaliate in cases where U.S. firms were prevented from expanding abroad.

During hearings in 1990 on the issue, the administration had opposed a change in policy. David C. Mulford, under secretary of the Treasury, told lawmakers that a change in policy could cause countries to retaliate and restrict U.S. banks' access to their markets.

Besides a change in policy on foreign bank treatment, several features of the Defense Production Act package agreed to by House and Senate conferees came under administration fire. The chief administration criticism was that the measure would have gone too far in promoting U.S. companies.

In particular, the administration opposed a section that would have granted the president the authority to limit government procurement of critical components to domestic sources. The administration also objected to the authorization level of $130 million and language that would have required the president to develop policies to ensure that a minimum amount of critical technologies were acquired from domestic suppliers.

The House adopted the conference report on Oct. 25. But faced with administration objections, the Senate did not take up the measure.

U.S. Acts To Ease Trade With East Bloc

With the ramparts of the Cold War appearing to crumble in Eastern Europe and even the Soviet Union, the United States began taking the first steps in 1990 to revise its trade policy with Moscow and the former East bloc.

President Bush and Soviet President Mikhail S. Gorbachev signed a trade agreement June 1 granting the Soviets normal trade status. But Bush said he would not send the pact to Congress for approval until the Soviet parliament had codified more open Soviet emigration policies. Although Soviet leaders said many times that an emigration law was about to be completed, the Soviet parliament did not act on it in 1990.

Shortly before it adjourned, Congress approved a trade agreement reached in April granting temporary normalized trade relations with Czechoslovakia. Lawmakers also approved a business and economic treaty with Poland intended to aid trade and investment between the two countries. The measures were the first post-Cold War economic agreements with former East bloc countries.

The House in 1989 had passed a bill (HR 1594 — H Rept 101-99) to authorize a three-year extension of most-favored-nation (MFN) trade status for Hungary. But the Senate used the bill in 1990 as a vehicle for a miscellany of customs and trade provisions, including an extension of the Caribbean Basin Initiative, and stripped the measure of the Hungary provisions. *(1989 Almanac, p. 503)*

In a largely symbolic act, the House also passed two bills on MFN status for China; the Senate did not act on either measure. H J Res 647 would have disapproved a Jackson-Vanik waiver for China; HR 4939 would have set new human rights conditions for renewal of MFN status in 1991. *(U.S.-China relations, p. 764)*

Havel's Plea for 'Aid'

In a dramatic appearance before a joint session of Congress on Feb. 21, Czechoslovakia's President Vaclav Havel, the dissident playwright turned politician, said the United States could best aid the newly freed countries of Eastern Europe by encouraging the Soviet Union's slow march away from communism.

"You can help us most of all if you help the Soviet Union on its irreversible but immensely complicated road to democracy," Havel told the lawmakers.

The sooner the Soviet Union begins down the road toward "genuine political pluralism," he said, "the better it will be, not just for Czechs and Slovaks, but for the whole world."

In his address to Congress, Havel made no specific request for monetary aid. Later, he said Czechoslovakia needed limited technical help in specific areas rather than large amounts of direct U.S. aid.

At the White House, President Bush told Havel he was lifting one major barrier to U.S.-Czechoslovak trade: the 1974 Jackson-Vanik restriction setting higher tariffs on goods entering the United States from most communist countries.

Havel was the second major political figure from Eastern Europe to address Congress since the region's political upheavals began in 1989. The first was Lech Walesa, the leader of Poland's Solidarity labor union, in November 1989. *(1989 Almanac, p. 517)*

Most-Favored-Nation Status

Despite its name, MFN trading status was not a special preference for favored nations; it was virtually synonymous with normal or non-discriminatory treatment.

Under the General Agreement on Tariffs and Trade, the United States provided MFN treatment to nearly every country in the world. For those countries that did not have it, however, MFN was an important prize that meant they could pay lower, often much lower, tariffs on goods imported into the United States.

Under the 1974 Trade Act (PL 93-618), the president could grant MFN to communist countries, but only as part of a congressionally approved commercial trade agreement. However, the 1974 law also erected a major new roadblock: the so-called Jackson-Vanik amendment barring MFN — as well as the extension of government credits — to countries with "non-market economies" that denied their citizens free emigration. The measure was aimed at improving the ability of Jews to emigrate from the Soviet Union and was strongly backed by U.S. Jewish organizations. Jackson-Vanik specifically did not apply to Poland, which had gained MFN status in 1960. *(1974 Almanac, p. 553; 1973 Almanac, p. 833;)*

To grant MFN status to a communist country, the president was required to certify that the nation allowed free emigration. Alternatively, he could waive the Jackson-Vanik requirement for a year at a time. Congress could reject a presidential certification or a Jackson-Vanik waiver by a joint resolution.

U.S.-SOVIET TRADE RELATIONS

The signing of the U.S.-Soviet trade agreement June 1 came as a surprise at the end of a dramatic summit meeting in Washington.

In the days before the summit, administration aides had played down the likelihood of a trade deal because of concerns over a Soviet crackdown in the Baltic State of Lithuania. *(U.S.-Soviet relations, p. 757)*

But Gorbachev himself reportedly appealed to Bush to sign the agreement, if only as a symbol of further Soviet integration into the world economy. Gorbachev also reportedly tied Soviet approval of a long-term wheat deal to the signing of the trade accord.

According to White House spokesman Marlin Fitzwater, Bush decided to go forward with the trade agreement a half-hour before the two leaders sat down to sign it. *(Highlights of agreement, p. 205)*

In a news conference at the end of the summit, Bush stressed that his approval was tied to the issue of emigration, nothing more.

Congress made it clear, however, that there would be no trade agreement until the Kremlin also negotiated in good faith with the Lithuanian government and lifted an economic embargo against the breakaway republic.

The Senate took that position, 73-24, on May 1 in a sense of the Senate amendment to a supplemental appropriations bill; the House followed suit June 6, voting 390-24

U.S.-Soviet Trade Accord: Highlights

Following are key provisions of the trade agreement signed June 1 by President Bush and Soviet President Mikhail S. Gorbachev.

• **Most-favored-nation treatment:** Each country agreed to grant unconditional most-favored-nation (MFN) treatment to goods produced by the other and imported for domestic consumption. The agreement covered customs duties, rules concerning shipment, warehousing and customs clearance, and payment for imports with hard currency. Generally MFN meant treatment no less favorable than that accorded other countries.

• **Market access:** Each country agreed to base purchase decisions on customary commercial considerations, such as price, quality and terms of delivery, and not to require or encourage barter or countertrade, where imports were conditioned on reciprocal purchases. Each country agreed not to apply technical standards or rules to protect domestic production or imports from a third country (although a side letter to the agreement exempted textile imports into the United States). The Soviet Union agreed, as it moved toward membership in the General Agreement on Tariffs and Trade (GATT) — the organization that governed world commerce — to allow increased "national treatment" for U.S. goods and services.

• **Business promotion and development:** Each country agreed to allow companies (including government-owned enterprises) to maintain ordinary business operations in the other. This included the ability to acquire living and office quarters whether or not they were intended for foreigners, to hire nationals of either country and pay them in agreed-upon currency, to advertise in publications designed for that purpose and through the mails, to conduct market studies and to import goods duty-free for trade shows. The Soviet Union agreed to expedite accreditation of U.S. businesses and to pay particular attention to the needs of small businesses.

• **Financial conditions:** Each country agreed that transactions would be paid for in dollars or other freely convertible currencies, unless otherwise agreed between the parties. (The Soviet ruble was not convertible on world markets and could not be exported.) The Soviet Union agreed that U.S. businesses would be treated as favorably as those of any other country on the question of maintaining bank accounts in rubles and having access to convertible currencies. The Soviet Union agreed to consider requests from U.S. businesses to use rubles to pay for local expenses.

• **Intellectual property protection:** Each country agreed to adhere to broad international copyright and patent protection conventions, including the Berne Convention on artistic and literary works, to protect copyrights on sound recordings produced domestically and in the other country, to protect copyrights on computer programs and data bases, and to protect patents on industrial processes, except those used solely in production of nuclear weapons.

• **Market disruption:** Each country agreed to consult when imports threatened to disrupt domestic markets and to allow for unilateral protections of domestic industries (as allowed under the GATT). In such cases, the other country would be free to deny equivalent benefits granted by the trade agreement so as not to be unfairly disadvantaged.

• **Dispute settlement:** Each country agreed to seek arbitrated settlement of commercial disagreements and to treat businesses from either country alike in its judicial and administrative proceedings.

• **General:** Once approved by Congress, the agreement was to be in effect for three years, renewable for successive three-year periods. The agreement in no way restricted actions deemed necessary for national security reasons, and it permitted adoption of laws and rules, such as those governing health and antitrust, that were otherwise consistent with it. The Soviets also agreed in a side letter to resume repayments on $674 million in World War II lend-lease assistance, conditioned on repeal of U.S. laws that restricted credit to the Soviet Union. ■

---

to add similar language to an export control bill. *(Senate vote 75, p. 18-S; House vote 149, p. 52-H)*

Jackson-Vanik Waiver

A legal barrier to completing the trade agreement was temporarily removed Dec. 12, when Bush announced that he was waiving Jackson-Vanik restrictions against the Soviet Union until June 1991.

While emigration, particularly of Soviet Jews, had increased dramatically, Bush had expected to await enactment of the new Soviet law before lifting Jackson-Vanik. However, growing instability in the Soviet Union and the prospects of severe winter food shortages led him to grant a short-term waiver, thereby allowing the extension of agricultural credits.

Bush suspended the 15-year-old Jackson-Vanik ban on extending commercial credits to the Soviets, enabling them to buy up to $1 billion worth of U.S. agricultural goods. Bush said he was acting "to help the Soviet Union stay the course of democratization and to undertake market reforms."

The Jackson-Vanik waiver also qualified the Soviets to receive credit from the Export-Import Bank. (However, a separate amendment to the 1974 Ex-Im Bank reauthorization that set a $300 million limit for Ex-Im Bank credits to the Soviets, remained in place.)

In addition to providing agricultural credits, Bush approved sending technical experts to the Soviet Union to help improve the country's troubled food distribution network. The administration also said that it would give financial aid to private groups sending medical equipment and pharmaceutical supplies to Moscow.

During the year, Congress also amended language in the Jackson-Vanik provision to overcome a possible constitutional challenge based on a 1983 Supreme Court decision *(Immigration and Naturalization Service v. Chadha).*

Jackson-Vanik originally provided that Congress could reject a presidential waiver or a presidential certification through a simple resolution in either chamber. *Chadha,* however, ruled that such legislative vetoes were unconstitutional and that in order to reject an administration action, Congress had to pass a bill that was signed by the president or enacted over his veto. *(1983 Almanac, p. 565)*

Provisions included in a customs and trade bill signed Aug. 20 (HR 1594 — PL 101-382) changed the 1974 trade law to require enactment of joint resolutions to disapprove Jackson-Vanik waivers and certifications.

Prior law also allowed Congress to approve trade agreements granting MFN status by adopting concurrent resolutions. Though *Chadha* did not explicitly apply to concurrent resolutions, Congress played it safe and required enactment of joint resolutions for approval of trade agreements as well. *(Customs and Trade Act, p. 211)*

CZECHOSLOVAKIA

A trade agreement granting normalized trade relations with Czechoslovakia was approved by Congress on Oct. 24.

The Senate by voice vote cleared for the president a joint resolution (H J Res 649) approving the trade agreement and extending MFN status to Czechoslovakia for one year.

The House passed the bill Oct. 17 by voice vote.

The president signed it into law (PL 101-541) on Nov. 8.

The trade agreement, signed by Czechoslovak and U.S. trade officials April 12, was intended to eliminate or reduce tariffs and other trade barriers, to provide better patent and copyright protections for U.S. companies, to allow immediate repatriation of profits and otherwise to improve economic relations between the two countries.

The agreement also called for the two countries to apply international trading rules established under GATT to their transactions, though Czechoslovakia was not a party to GATT. Czechoslovakia agreed to improve currency exchange provisions for U.S. businesses and legal protections for U.S. patents and other intellectual property rights.

Congress' action had the effect of approving the trade agreement and granting MFN status to Czechoslovak goods sold in the United States.

The House Ways and Means Committee approved H J Res 649 (H Rept 101-773) on Sept. 25. The Senate Finance Committee favorably reported S J Res 361 (S Rept 101-537) on Oct. 18.

POLAND

The Senate on Oct. 28 (Oct. 27 session) approved ratification of a limited business and economic treaty with Poland that had been signed by Bush and Polish Prime Minister Tadeusz Mazowiecki on March 21.

Among its provisions, the treaty allowed for favorable treatment of U.S. investors in Poland and gave U.S. companies free access to the Polish market. "We can now take this treaty to the U.S. business community and say, 'This is why you should invest in Poland,' " Bush said.

Bush and Mazowiecki met twice at the White House during a three-day visit to Washington by the Polish leader, who took office in August 1989 after Solidarity-led forces swept Polish national elections.

In 1989, Bush called for several aid packages for Poland in response to its break from the Soviet bloc. Congress went even further than the administration proposed in passing more ambitious and costly economic aid packages that included $125 million in food aid in fiscal 1990 and an off-budget $200 million trade credit insurance program. ■

Lawmakers Divided on Development Bank

Fights over a new bank to aid the emerging democracies of Eastern and Central Europe, debt relief for Poland and Latin America and restrictions on World Bank loans to post-Tiananmen Square China dominated debate in 1990 over U.S. contributions to multilateral lending institutions.

Following a pattern that had become almost routine, Congress was unable to move needed free-standing authorization bills for the multilateral banks in 1990. Instead, provisions approving U.S. participation in a handful of lending institutions were added to the fiscal 1991 foreign aid appropriations bill (HR 5114 — PL 101-513). *(Foreign aid appropriations, p. 830)*

A broad authorization bill (HR 5153) died in the House without being considered on the floor. The measure would have authorized U.S. contributions totaling $1.17 billion over five years to the European Bank for Reconstruction and Development (EBRD). Only about $350 million of that was to be paid directly to the bank.

The bill also would have authorized U.S. payments to the so-called 9th Replenishment of the International Development Association (IDA), the concessional lending arm of the World Bank.

Payments to IDA would have totaled $3.18 billion over three years, all of it paid directly to the bank. And it would have permanently authorized U.S. contributions to the African Development Fund, the concessional arm of the African Development Bank, which aided the poorest African countries.

In the Senate, a bill (S 2944) that would have authorized $535 million in bilateral aid for Eastern and Central European countries was also the vehicle for multilateral bank authorizations. Strong GOP opposition to the bilateral aid package kept it off the Senate floor.

The foreign aid appropriations bill, however, as enacted, contained language adapted from HR 5153 that authorized U.S. participation in the multilateral banks.

European Development Bank

To aid Eastern and Central European countries in moving toward market-based economies, representatives from 42 nations, including the United States, agreed in principle April 9 to form a new development bank for those countries. Final terms were adopted May 29, and the bank was to begin its London-based operations in early 1991.

The EBRD was to be capitalized at about $12 billion; the United States was to contribute 10 percent of that amount. Britain, France, Italy, Japan and West Germany were to contribute 8.5 percent apiece. Only 30 percent of the capital was to be paid in. The remainder was to be pledged as collateral for the new bank's borrowing from world financial markets. It would have been "callable" only in case of default.

The U.S. paid-in share was to be $70 million a year over five years. U.S. participation had to be approved by Congress, which would also have to appropriate the money.

The Soviet Union was to contribute 6 percent and was entitled to borrow during the first three years only as much as it had paid in. After that, additional Soviet borrowing would have to be approved by 85 percent of the bank's members. The size of the U.S. vote was seen as virtually ensuring that expanded borrowing by the Soviet Union could be blocked, if the White House so desired.

Bank loans were to be concentrated on private companies trying to expand or begin operations in Europe's newly democratic countries, or on the privatization of state-owned enterprises. But 40 percent of the loans could go to government-sponsored activities, including road-building and other infrastructure development.

Approval from Congress, however, was uncertain for much of the year. Some lawmakers were wary of the Soviet role and others wanted a higher percentage of loans earmarked for private enterprise.

House Action

The House Banking Committee on June 26 approved HR 5153 by voice vote. The measure would have authorized spending for international development activities and U.S. export financing. Committee members fought only over two elements of the bill: provisions promoting debt relief for Third World countries and criticizing China's human rights practices. The China provisions were intended to pressure the administration to hold firm on a policy severely restricting World Bank loans to Beijing.

In the end, most substantive amendments to those sections were rejected, and the measure was little changed from a version that had been approved June 20 by the International Development Subcommittee.

The bill would have authorized full participation in the EBRD and IDA, and permanently authorized the African Fund. But in cases where IDA made loans to China that were not for "basic human needs," the secretary of the Treasury would have been required — with some exceptions — to withhold U.S. contributions equal to the U.S. share of those loans.

Committee members disagreed little over the desirability of the IDA restrictions. But several Republicans tried to blunt the provisions by extending the restrictions to other countries that denied their citizens internationally accepted human rights.

Jim Bunning, R-Ky., offered an amendment to add Ethiopia, Laos, Vietnam, Cambodia and South Yemen as countries for which the U.S. should discourage IDA loans. Democrats opposed Bunning's language, at least in part because of the inclusion of Ethiopia. They also argued that China was a special case because of its size and the likelihood that resumed World Bank lending to Beijing — limited after the June 1989 crackdown on the country's pro-democracy movement — would spark a flood of new commercial bank loans. Bunning's amendment was defeated 17-24 on a near-party-line vote.

The bill also would have authorized the Export-Import Bank to make loans for purchases by certain Eastern and Central European countries not then eligible for Ex-Im Bank credits. And it would have increased the Ex-Im Bank's "tied-aid" war chest to combat the practices of countries that combined foreign aid grants with conventional export loans to promote purchases of their products. The war chest would have been authorized through fiscal 1992, and its existing $300 million authorization would have been increased to $500 million in fiscal 1991 and again in 1992.

The bill called on the secretary of the Treasury to negotiate with other industrialized countries to reduce the government-to-government debt of the poorest Third World nations. It would have directed the Treasury to urge other members of the so-called Paris Club of creditor nations to write off on a case-by-case basis loans that they had made to very poor countries. It would also have authorized the president to write off U.S. loans to poor countries if such write-offs were in the national interest and were used to implement an international debt-relief agreement.

The committee made one key change in the debt-relief language by extending the provision to Latin American countries and others that met specific poverty-level criteria. Previously, the bill focused only on Eastern Europe and sub-Saharan Africa.

An amendment by Joseph P. Kennedy II, D-Mass., to require the Treasury to submit detailed evaluations of debt-reduction efforts involving commercial bank loans was defeated. Kennedy and others had long complained that commercial banks were being subsidized by multilateral lending to Third World countries. Treasury Secretary Nicholas F. Brady in March 1989 announced a plan for reducing commercial bank debt that involved negotiations and subsidies paid by the World Bank and the International Monetary Fund (IMF).

Kennedy's amendment would have required the Treasury to evaluate and report to Congress on Brady plan negotiations a year after their completion. The Treasury would have been required to assess the changed economic conditions of a country resulting from debt-reduction negotiations and its ability to repay the World Bank and the IMF. The amendment was defeated 14-23.

Senate Action

The Senate Foreign Relations Committee approved S 2944 on July 19. The bill was a follow-on to a 1989 bilateral aid measure for Eastern European countries, principally Poland and Hungary, called the Support for Eastern European Democracies Act of 1989 (SEED) (PL 101-179). The 1990 measure — S 2944, known as SEED II — would have expanded the provisions of the 1989 bill in an effort to boost the business opportunities of U.S. companies in the region. *(SEED I, 1989 Almanac, p. 503)*

Like the House measure, S 2944 would have fully authorized EBRD, IDA and the African Fund.

Senate Republicans were so opposed to the bilateral measure, however, that they boycotted the Foreign Relations Committee markup of the measure. With GOP members absent, the panel approved the bill, 10-0. But the measure never made it to the Senate floor.

Final Action

Provisions from HR 5153 authorizing contributions to the EBRD and IDA, permanently authorizing the African Fund, and increasing and extending the Ex-Im Bank's "tied-aid" program were added in conference to HR 5114, the foreign aid appropriations bill.

Most of the language was adapted from HR 5153, the House Banking Committee-approved multilateral authorizations bill. Not included, however, were provisions from HR 5153 imposing sanctions against World Bank loans to China and creating Third World and Eastern European debt-relief incentives.

However, the House version of the foreign aid bill had all along contained very similar language to that in HR 5153 regarding loans to China. The original foreign aid bill language on China loans was retained in the final version. The House foreign aid bill also had tied the U.S. appropriation for the EBRD to U.S. government action to reduce Poland's debt. Similar debt-relief language was retained in the final version.

The House passed HR 5114 by 308-117, on June 27. The Senate passed the bill Oct. 24 by a 76-23 vote. *(House vote 204, p. 70-H; Senate vote 306, p. 60-S)*

With adjournment nearing, lawmakers settled differences over the appropriations bill largely unrelated to the multilateral authorizations language. The House agreed to the conference report, 188-162, on Oct. 27. The Senate cleared the measure the same day by voice vote. President Bush signed the bill Nov. 5 (PL 101-513). *(Vote 531, p. 168-H)* ■

Japan Makes Some Concessions on Trade

Despite early, sometimes heated, complaints in Congress about the persistent U.S. trade deficit with Japan, lawmakers ended 1990 without taking any substantive action. But the Bush administration did manage to get Japan to agree to make a number of long-term changes that seemed to defuse congressional concerns.

With no trade bill moving through Congress, there was no easy vehicle for legislative action. So lawmakers had to fall back on tongue-lashing the administration for failing to use the main tool created by Congress for punishing nations that ran consistent surpluses with the United States.

In addition, as the year went on, other trade matters — China's trade status and later the global trade talks under the General Agreement on Tariffs and Trade (GATT) — further deflected Congress' attention.

BACKGROUND

The U.S. trade deficit, which soared in the mid-1980s, had begun to decline somewhat in 1987. In the case of the 12-nation European Community, the picture had improved considerably. In 1989, U.S. merchandise trade with Europe showed a slight surplus.

But the change with Japan had been far less dramatic. The merchandise deficit had fallen only slightly, from $52.1 billion to $49.1 billion. And it accounted for nearly half the total U.S. trade deficit of $109.4 billion, re-enforcing the conviction of many in Congress that tougher policies would be required to change Japan's trading practices.

'Super 301'

Congress had tried in 1988 to stiffen U.S. policy by including a set of provisions known as "Super 301" in the omnibus trade bill (PL 100-418). Super 301 — a strengthened version of Section 301 of the 1974 Trade Act — was designed to identify, cajole, and, ultimately, punish trade partners that inhibited access to their markets. *(1988 Almanac, p. 209)*

Under Super 301, the U.S. trade representative (USTR) was required in 1989 and 1990 to identify specific "priority countries" engaged in "priority practices" that limited market access. The cases were selected from the National Trade Estimate, a catalog of unfair foreign trade practices prepared annually by the USTR. The law gave the administration one year to negotiate removal of the barriers, with an option for a six-month extension. If the talks failed after that, the administration was authorized to raise tariffs on the goods of a priority country by as much as 100 percent.

The threat that a country would be placed on the Super 301 "hit list" aided the administration in persuading several countries, including South Korea, to modify their trade policies in 1989. But, while the law's existence proved a useful tool, the administration was not eager to actually name countries for potential retaliation.

In May 1989, the Bush administration had named three countries: Japan, Brazil and India. Japan was cited for barriers to government and university purchases of supercomputers, to government purchases of satellites and to imports of wood products. Brazil was cited for banning and limiting imports through a complex government licensing system and for failing to provide patent or copyright protection. India was put on the list for imposing detailed conditions on foreign investment and prohibiting private companies from selling insurance in India.

From Super 301 to SII

At the same time, the Bush administration initiated a separate set of high-level talks with Japan that became known as the Structural Impediments Initiative (SII).

The SII talks were conceived to address deep-seated structural practices in Japan that had the effect of excluding imports. These included laws that allowed Japanese corporations to collude in setting prices and allocating sales territory, practices that were forbidden in the United States under antitrust laws.

Other SII targets included *keiretsu*, the interlocking relationships among Japanese companies; land-use policies; low spending on public works; legal restrictions that forced big retailers to get approval from smaller local competitors before opening an outlet; and pricing mechanisms that forced Japanese consumers to pay as much as 70 percent more than U.S. consumers for the same goods.

The administration said that SII was a way of addressing long-term issues that were not appropriate subjects for Super 301 cases. Many lawmakers saw the initiative, which was not mandated by Congress and had no provision for retaliation, as a way to finesse Super 301. "I've never had a lot of faith in the idea of those talks," said Senate Finance Committee Chairman Lloyd Bentsen, D-Texas.

When the talks began, Japan succeeded in having them redefined to include U.S. practices that it said hurt U.S. competitiveness. Japan said the United States should cut its budget deficit, increase its savings rate and train its workers to produce better goods at lower cost.

ADMINISTRATION ACTIONS

In the spring of 1990, a series of impending trade deadlines focused congressional attention on the trade deficit in general and on Japan in particular.

On March 31, the USTR was to submit the new National Trade Estimate filled with lists of countries and practices that were potential targets for new Super 301 cases. On April 30, the USTR was to submit the new Super 301 list and report on progress made on the first round of cases announced in 1989. And by June 16, the administration had to announce the results of the three 1989 cases. In addition, the administration had set July 18 as a deadline for a final report on the SII talks.

But the administration successfully sidestepped pressure to cite Japan again under Super 301 and was able to announce enough progress in the SII talks to blunt congressional criticism.

Beginning in early March, the administration turned up the heat in the SII talks, culminating with President Bush meeting personally with Prime Minister Toshiki Kaifu and other high-ranking Japanese political figures in Washington on April 2-5. Following four days of intensive negotiations, the administration on April 5 declared a tentative victory in the talks, citing progress on large retail stores, exclusionary business practices and public works spending.

At the same time, U.S. Trade Representative Carla A. Hills was proclaiming success in negotiations with Japan on the 1989 Super 301 cases on satellites and supercomputers.

Hills urged lawmakers not to focus solely on Super 301. "Our objectives are all the same," she said in testimony before the Senate Finance Committee on April 25. "I'm asking you to work with me. I must be allowed some discretion to say which tools should be used."

Hills got a vote of confidence from Finance Committee free-traders Bill Bradley, D-N.J., and Bob Packwood of Oregon, the committee's ranking Republican.

But others were firm that Japan should be cited under Super 301. "By definition, Japan has to be on that list," said Donald W. Riegle Jr., D-Mich.

Hills came to that meeting with an ace: She was able to announce that, earlier that day in Japan, agreement had been reached on the third and last target issue from the 1989 Super 301 process, the import of forest products such as plywood from the United States.

Hills said the agreement would result in a flow of U.S. products to Japan worth "in the range of $1 billion a year." That was good news for Max Baucus, D-Mont., chairman of the Finance Subcommittee on International Trade, whose home state stood to benefit. Baucus had been one of the strongest Senate voices on the need to strengthen the 301 process if Japan were not named.

Hills argued that trade relations with Japan were improving because the Japanese wanted the lower consumer prices that would follow if trade barriers came down. Such domestic political pressure, she said, was better mobilized by SII-style talks because the average Japanese resented the punitive tone of the Super 301 process.

"That's certainly not my position," said John C. Danforth, R -Mo., who considered the 1988 act "the cornerstone of U.S. trade policy."

Hills said she would use a 301 complaint procedure when it would achieve the desired results. "Commercial objectives and results are what I'm after," she told Danforth, "but you have got to give me just a little more leeway."

Two days later, on April 27, the administration issued its new Super 301 list naming a single country: India. Hills stressed progress with Japan, both in the past Super 301 cases and in SII. Danforth called the decision "deeply disappointing" and said it was "sure to result in an extremely adverse reaction from the Congress."

There was talk of legislating further proscrptions on the president's discretion in enforcing the trade laws, but no action materialized. Members on the key trade committees instead turned their attention to the question of extending normal trade status of China and later to the fate of the faltering GATT talks. *(GATT, this page; China, p. 764)*

On June 14, the administration announced that it would not impose sanctions against India, even though that country had failed to negotiate an end to practices that had put them on the Super 301 list in 1989. Hills said retaliation was inappropriate given the continuing negotiations on some of the same issues at GATT. The decision drew little congressional response. ■

GATT Talks Stall Over Farm Subsidies

By not backing down from its demands for liberalization of agricultural trade, the Bush administration rewrote the script that had guided global trade negotiations for three decades and, for the first time, isolated the European Community (EC) behind its fortress of farm subsidies.

Negotiations in Brussels, aimed at broadening and strengthening international trading rules to cover agriculture and other non-manufacturing industries, broke off Dec. 7 over the Europeans' unwillingness to consider deep cuts in the export subsidies and other measures that had helped them become major exporters of food to the developing world.

The breakdown had been predicted for some time. The United States and the 12-nation EC had been divided over how to treat farm subsidies since the latest round of negotiations on the General Agreement on Tariffs and Trade (GATT) — the multilateral accord governing most world trade — began four years earlier in Uruguay.

The EC and the United States heavily subsidized farmers and, much the way the farm bloc wielded clout in the U.S. Congress, farmers had strong political influence in European countries, particularly France and Germany.

Although the EC had agreed to put agriculture on the table in the GATT talks, European negotiators were hoping that what they described as unrealistic U.S. demands for phasing out farm subsidies would be abandoned in Brussels. Then a deal could be struck in less disputatious areas, such as intellectual property, services and investment, in which the EC's interests coincided more often with its industrialized ally, the United States.

"The [Europeans] made a major miscalculation," said Dale E. Hathaway, an agricultural trade consultant who served as under secretary of Agriculture in the Carter administration. "They assumed that when the chips were down the U.S. would cave [on agriculture] and together they could roll everybody else. They clearly were wrong."

The United States and the Europeans agreed on many of the other issues being negotiated at GATT — for example, adding new protections for intellectual property, such as copyrighted material and software, which was often pirated abroad. But when the Latin American delegates walked out of the talks because of European and Japanese intransigence on agriculture, the United States followed.

Before the talks were scheduled to resume in early 1991, U.S. Trade Representative Carla A. Hills, who was assisted in Brussels by Agriculture Secretary Clayton Yeutter, put the likelihood of getting an agreement at 25 percent.

GATT: Past and Present

In 1955, the United States joined with the Europeans in carving agriculture out of the original GATT accord. Along with textiles, agriculture had remained outside of the world trading rules ever since — usually at the insistence of industrialized countries.

Beginning in 1986, the Reagan administration — led by Yeutter, who was then the U.S. trade representative — embarked on what seemed a quixotic effort to eradicate agriculture subsidies worldwide by the year 2000. The Bush administration had since pulled back from that goal, although U.S. officials were still calling for deep cuts in "trade-distorting" subsidies in coming years.

For the Bush administration, liberalizing agriculture

trade offered tremendous potential gain — and several pitfalls. It offered the chance to compete on a level playing field with the Europeans, who had transformed themselves from food importers to major exporters in two decades, using subsidies a good deal more generous than those offered to U.S. farmers.

But with the growth in world trade of agriculture slowing, exporting countries were finding stiffer competition for markets overseas. And given the U.S. budget crunch, the Bush administration was afraid it would be too expensive to try to outsubsidize the Europeans.

At GATT, the United States formed an alliance with the so-called Cairns Group of 14 agricultural nations even more desperate to secure open export markets for their products — and even more vulnerable to a subsidy war. Together, these countries refused to negotiate on issues such as services and intellectual property without a prior agreement for imposing strong "disciplines" on European export subsidies.

When the talks stalled, the standoff was over which agriculture subsidies should be reduced and by how much. The Europeans were restricting their offer to internal subsidies, those that countries worldwide used to prop up the domestic price of farm goods or the payments governments made to farmers to ensure them a minimum income.

Europe's offer was to reduce domestic support levels by 30 percent over 10 years, retroactive to 1986. It was widely criticized by U.S. officials and others as insufficient.

The United States proposed a 75 percent cut in internal subsidies. More important, the Bush administration proposed a 90 percent cut in export subsidies, the array of measures governments used to make their farm products attractive in international markets. It was also seeking the removal of barriers that restricted the flow of farm goods across national borders.

Led by France and Germany, the EC's largest agricultural producers, European negotiators refused to consider making specific commitments to reduce export subsidies; U.S. negotiators insisted that such reductions were crucial to any deal.

EC officials maintained that Washington's expectations were too high. "Unless and until they reduce the expectations they have had for quite some time now, there will not be an agreement on agriculture," Raymond MacSharry, the community's agriculture commissioner, said at a news conference Dec. 7.

Congress' Role

Congress was likely to have a twofold role in determining the success of the negotiations. If the talks continued past March 1, 1991, as expected, Congress would have to extend special procedures, known as the fast-track, to provide expedited consideration of legislation implementing a GATT agreement. Second, Congress would have to approve the implementing legislation.

The president could request a two-year extension of the fast-track authority, as long as he certified the negotiations were making "significant" progress. But it would be easy for Congress to block the extension; a vote against it in either the House or the Senate was sufficient.

In the Senate, a coalition of farm- and textile-state members were intent on blocking the fast track already formed. Ernest F. Hollings, D-S.C., introduced a resolution in late 1990 that would have barred fast-track approval of the GATT. It attracted 34 cosponsors but faced GOP opposition and was not considered before adjournment.

Most trade experts said that the GATT talks would be doomed if Congress blocked extension of the fast track. The Bush administration could no longer assure other nations that it could shepherd an agreement through Congress without its being picked apart.

Farm Bill Impact

Some of the pain of the fiscal 1991 deficit-cutting budget-reconciliation bill for U.S. agriculture — it called for approximately $14 billion in cuts — was lessened when the Bush administration failed to reach the agreement it sought to reduce agriculture subsidies in the GATT talks.

Under a provision that lawmakers included in reconciliation, if there were no GATT agreement by 1992, the Agriculture secretary would be required to take steps designed to put the United States on more aggressive footing to counter the EC and boost exports of U.S. grain.

The secretary would have to offer $1 billion in additional export subsidies and adopt a marketing loan — a subsidy to allow U.S. farmers to sell their crops at lower world prices — for wheat and feed grains. In addition, the secretary could waive requirements that wheat and corn farmers receiving subsidies idle a portion of their land.

Lawmakers had won the support of the administration for the provision after altering language that would have automatically exempted agriculture from budget cuts in the event of a GATT breakdown. Under the final bill, the secretary could waive such cuts only if no GATT agreement were reached by June 1993. *(Farm bill, p. 323)*

Textile Issue

Supporters of the textile industry, who had failed for the third time to override a presidential veto of an import quota bill (HR 4328), also had an eye on the GATT talks. *(Textile bill, p. 219)*

Negotiators at GATT were discussing proposals to replace the existing international regime that governed much of the world's trade in textiles. That regime, known as the Multi-Fiber Arrangement (MFA), provided the framework under which the United States had negotiated 38 bilateral and multilateral agreements limiting textile imports.

U.S. negotiators at GATT proposed phasing out the MFA over 10 years, a change favored by developing countries that were eager for additional exports. In return, the United States was seeking other concessions from them.

The U.S textile industry did not like the MFA, arguing that it had not worked and that imports exceeded agreed-upon limits because multiple quotas for individual countries were difficult to enforce.

But U.S. textile interests also did not want a world in which all restraints had been phased out. So they opposed the GATT agreement, threatening to fight extension of the fast track and the implementing legislation itself.

The textile industry and its supporters on Capitol Hill argued that textiles formed the original heart of U.S. manufacturing and that the industry had lost 500,000 jobs in the past decade to foreign competition.

Opponents countered that the job-loss figures were inflated, that unemployment in textile-producing states was lower than the national average and that wrecking the GATT talks could disrupt the entire international trade regime to the detriment of the United States.

The textile industry's position was complicated, however. Without a GATT agreement, the MFA was set to expire in 1991. In that case, they would have to renew their drive for U.S. quotas. ■

Congress Passes Caribbean Trade Bill

After months of public bargaining and behind-the-scenes negotiations, Congress on Aug. 4 cleared and sent to the president a trade bill that included permanent trade breaks for the Caribbean Basin. The measure also contained a permanent ban on unprocessed-timber exports from public lands and new rules governing congressional approval of trade relations with communist countries.

President Bush signed the legislation on Aug. 20.

The Senate had approved the conference report by voice vote late on the night of July 31. The House followed suit, also by voice vote, shortly after midnight on Aug. 4 (session of Aug. 3), just before beginning a month-long congressional recess.

House and Senate conferees had completed work the previous week and signed off on a written compromise on the last issues in dispute, including duties and taxes on ethanol, customs user fees, and a ban on imports from Burma (renamed Myanmar).

> **BOXSCORE**
>
> **Legislation:** Customs and Trade Act, PL 101-382 (HR 1594, incorporating S 504, HR 1233).
>
> **Major action:** Signed, Aug. 20. Conference report adopted by House, Aug. 4 (session of Aug. 3); by Senate, July 31. HR 1594, amended to include S 504, passed by Senate, 92-0, April 24; HR 1233 passed by House in omnibus budget-reconciliation act (HR 3299), 333-91, Oct. 5, 1989; HR 1594 passed by House, 221-169, Sept. 7, 1989.
>
> **Reports:** Conference report (H Rept 101-650). HR 1594: Finance (S Rept 101-252); Ways and Means (H Rept 101-99). HR 1233: Ways and Means (H Rept 101-136).

At first glance, the final legislation seemed to contain as much disappointment as achievement for its original sponsors. Florida Democrats Rep. Sam M. Gibbons and Sen. Bob Graham had sought not only to extend the 1983 Caribbean Basin Initiative (CBI) beyond its 1995 expiration date but also to expand its duty-free treatment to goods not included in the original law.

The 1983 act did not include textiles, apparel, petroleum, "flat goods" such as gloves and luggage, or canned tuna.

Gibbons and Graham were especially interested in providing a higher quota for Caribbean sugar. The region's sugar imports had dropped by more than 70 percent after quotas were imposed in the early 1980s.

But nearly all the expansions of the CBI were lost as the bill moved through Congress.

At one point, after the conferees dropped his sugar provision, Gibbons said the measure was scarcely worth fighting for in its diluted state. In the end, however, both sponsors indicated they were glad to support the watered-down bill.

Virtually all the House-Senate conflicts over the bill were resolved in the first weeks of the conference, which began May 11. Even the potentially troublesome differences over log exports, a 50 percent cut in the duty on certain goods and a minimum sugar quota had been cleared by both sides by June 19.

But the conference then nearly foundered in a dispute over ethanol imports, which included tax issues that had not even been part of the bill as passed by either chamber.

Ultimately, a new compromise was devised extending the existing arrangement for CBI ethanol through Dec. 31, 1992.

Two other late-starting issues that held up the conference for a time — one relating to a tax break for investors in Puerto Rico instituted in the 1986 tax overhaul and another that would have lowered the tariff for an imported ingredient in an ulcer drug manufactured in North Carolina — were dropped in exchange for a promise of later consideration.

While the CBI expansions shrank in scope as the bill weaved its way through Congress, the rest of the bill snowballed in size and attracted a variety of add-ons.

Chief among these was a ban on log exports from public lands aimed at keeping more of the harvest at home and therefore more domestic mills operating in the Pacific Northwest and upper Rocky Mountain states.

The Senate added an amendment renewing authorizations for the Customs Service, the Office of the U.S. Trade Representative and the International Trade Commission.

Also added were provisions, negotiated with the administration, to cure a constitutional defect in the 1974 Trade Act relating to normal trade relations with non-market economy (communist) nations.

The Jackson-Vanik amendment in the 1974 act had barred most-favored-nation (MFN) status to such a country unless the president certified that the nation allowed its citizens free emigration rights or waived the requirement. Congress could disapprove of the certification or waiver by the vote of a single chamber, a procedure that was declared unconstitutional in a 1983 Supreme Court decision.

HR 1594 changed the procedure to require enactment of a joint resolution to disapprove a certification or waiver. It also changed procedures for approving trade agreements with communist countries.

BACKGROUND

The CBI — first approved in 1983 for 12 years as the Caribbean Basin Economic Recovery Act (PL 98-67) — allowed duty-free access to the U.S. market for a variety of Caribbean imports. *(1983 Almanac, p. 852)*

Although the act was not due until 1995, advocates pressed for an early extension to encourage and support investment in the region. They also sought to extend duty-free or low-tariff treatment to products such as leather goods, textiles, apparel, petroleum and other items important to the Caribbean economies.

These goods were left out of the original law because of objections from domestic producers and labor unions. They were also omitted from the version of the bill that Lloyd Bentsen, D-Texas, brought to the Senate Finance Committee in 1990. Bentsen said from the outset he wanted a virtually non-controversial trade bill, with a clean CBI, so that it would clear the Senate floor almost without a vote.

The beneficiary countries of the CBI were Antigua and Barbuda, Aruba, the Bahamas, Barbados, Belize, the Brit-

Customs and Trade Act Provisions

Here are provisions of the Customs and Trade Act (PL 101-382 — HR 1594) (omitting detailed tariff provisions of Title III):

Title I: Authorizations, Customs Fees

• **ITC.** Authorized the International Trade Commission to spend $41,170,000 in fiscal 1991 and $44,052,000 in fiscal 1992.

• **Customs Service.** Authorized the U.S. Customs Service to spend $516,217,000 in fiscal 1991 and $542,091,000 in fiscal 1992 for salaries and expenses incurred in non-commercial operations; no less than $672,021,000 in fiscal 1991 and $705,793,000 in fiscal 1992 for salaries and expenses incurred in commercial operations; and $143,047,000 in fiscal 1991 and $150,199,000 in fiscal 1992 for its air interdiction program.

• **USTR.** Authorized the Office of the U.S. Trade Representative (USTR) to spend $23,250,000 in fiscal 1991 and $21,077,000 in fiscal 1992.

• **Customs fees.** Replaced the existing across-the-board ad valorem customs fee with a new cost-based fee structure intended to bring the United States into conformance with the General Agreement on Tariffs and Trade (GATT).

The new schedule limited fees to the approximate cost of the services rendered and to customs operations related to the processing of imports covered by the fee. It provided for an ad valorem fee, but set a minimum of $21 and a maximum of $400. The purpose was to ensure that imports of very high or very low value, which might not have differed substantially in the cost of import processing, did not pay unduly different import fees. The new structure eliminated excess collections on high-value imports and avoided the subsidization of low-value entries.

The bill also set fees for informal entries by air courier facilities and others not covered under the current merchandise processing fee. It declared that operations identified by GATT as inappropriate (activities associated with passenger processing, export controls and international affairs) were not funded out of the merchandise processing fee.

• **Israel.** Exempted Israeli products from customs user fees if the USTR determined that the government of Israel had made reciprocal concessions.

• **Customs Forfeiture Fund.** Required the Customs Forfeiture Fund to provide annually a complete set of audited financial statements for the previous fiscal year. The bill also required Customs to deposit all forfeited cash into the fund, and it authorized $20 million for discretionary purposes of the fund, of which $14,855,000 was available in fiscal 1991 and $15,598,000 in fiscal 1992 for spending by the Customs Service.

• **Czechoslovakia, East Germany.** Made Czechoslovakia and East Germany eligible for preferential duty rates under the Generalized System of Preferences (GSP).

Because East and West Germany achieved economic and monetary union on July 1, the president was authorized to provide tariff treatment for East German products comparable to that of West German products, pending complete political unification.

• **Jackson-Vanik.** Revised the Jackson-Vanik provisions of the 1974 Trade Act to cure a constitutional defect.

Under Jackson-Vanik, the president could extend most-favored-nation (MFN) (non-discriminatory) trade status to a communist country as part of a commercial trade agreement, but only if he certified that the country allowed free emigration, or waived the requirement.

The bill provided that adoption of a joint (rather than concurrent) resolution, under fast-track procecdures, was required for approval of such a bilateral trade agreement or for congressional disapproval of a presidential waiver of Jackson-Vanik or a presidential determination that a country met the freedom-of-emigration criteria.

The changes were intended to protect the congressional procedures from challenge under a 1983 Supreme Court decision *(Immigration and Naturalization Service v. Chadha)* that held legislative vetoes unconstitutional.

The bill also clarified that the fast track was triggered by the introduction of a resolution of disapproval on or after the date that the president recommended that the waiver authority be extended.

---

ish Virgin Islands, Costa Rica, Dominica, the Dominican Republic, El Salvador, Grenada, Guatemala, Guyana, Haiti, Honduras, Jamaica, Montserrat, the Netherlands Antilles, Panama (reinstated after the overthrow of Gen. Manuel Antonio Noriega), St. Christopher and Nevis, St. Lucia, St. Vincent and the Grenadines, and Trinidad and Tobago.

A House bill to expand the CBI and make it permanent moved in the House in 1989, sponsored by Gibbons. It was the companion to Graham's original CBI bill (S 504).

Gibbons, a leading free-trader, saw his bill (HR 1233) through committee in June 1989, holding off colleagues whose districts relied on textiles and apparel. The bill would have expanded duty-free treatment for Caribbean textiles and apparel while reducing duties on non-leather shoes and on leather and non-leather luggage and handbags.

To expedite floor consideration of his bill in the fall, however, Gibbons agreed to delete the extension of duty-free treatment to leather footwear and to weaken provisions that would have eased access for textile and apparel imports. By doing so, Gibbons avoided a showdown with Rules Committee Chairman Joe Moakley, D-Mass., over footwear and with the powerful Congressional Textile Caucus on the House floor.

The remainder of the bill was then wrapped into the House version of the omnibus budget deficit-reduction bill (HR 3299). But even these provisions were dropped when HR 3299 was pared to a minimum in conference with the Senate. *(1989 Almanac, p. 142)*

COMMITTEE ACTION

The Senate Finance Committee on March 1 approved the permanent extension of duty-free status for Caribbean imports without resolving disagreements over sugar and certain other goods not covered under the 1983 CBI.

S 504 was sent to the floor by voice vote, but only after the committee rejected several potentially controversial amendments.

Finance Chairman Bentsen repeatedly resisted efforts to load the bill with provisions — such as an overall floor for sugar imports — that could have prevented its reaching the floor under a unanimous-consent agreement.

"The key is to try to avoid crippling controversy," Bentsen said. "Without question the worst thing for the Caribbean Basin would be to not pass this extension of CBI. Then the region's problems would surely multiply."

Dropped from the bill for this reason was a provision guaranteeing exporters in the Caribbean a fixed share of the sugar imports allowed into the United States annually.

At a brief Finance Subcommittee on International Trade hearing Feb. 9, U.S. Trade Representative Carla A. Hills expressed the Bush administration's objection to the sugar-share guarantee. She said such special consideration would violate agreements being negotiated under the Gen-

A presidential recommendation would have to be made at least 30 calendar days before the previous year's waiver authority expired; Congress had up to 60 calendar days following the expiration to pass a resolution. So, in effect, Congress had 90 calendar days to pass a resolution disapproving a Jackson-Vanik waiver.

If the president vetoed the joint resolution, Congress would have to act within 15 days of receiving the veto message to override. MFN status would terminate 60 calendar days after a resolution disapproving a presidential waiver or compliance report. Senate consideration of a veto message was limited to 10 hours.

The bill made the Jackson-Vanik changes applicable to presidential recommendations made after May 23, 1990. The result was to cover President Bush's May 24 announcement of a one-year renewal of MFN for China. A "transition rule" in effect provided that the fast-track procedures for a resolution of disapproval on China applied for 60 calendar days, beginning on the date of the bill's enactment.

- **Burma (Myanmar).** Required economic sanctions on Burma (renamed Myanmar), unless the president certified it had met human rights conditions, including the reinstatement of civilian government, the lifting of martial law and the release of political prisoners.
- **Census employees.** Stipulated that services performed after April 20, 1990, by temporary employees of the Bureau of the Census relating to the 1990 census constituted "federal service" under the unemployment compensation program. As a result, wages earned by these temporary census workers would be credited to them in determining their eligibility for unemployment compensation.

Title II: Caribbean Basin

- **Permanent status.** Repealed the Sept. 30, 1995, termination date for duty-free treatment of eligible imports from beneficiary countries under the 1983 Caribbean Basin Economic Recovery Act.
- **Leather goods.** Authorized the president to reduce tariff rates applicable to leather products — handbags, luggage, flat goods, work gloves and leather wearing apparel — from CBI beneficiary countries by 20 percent, but not more than 2.5 percent ad valorem for any item, to be phased in in five equal annual stages beginning on Jan. 1, 1992. The provision applied to goods that were not eligible for duty-free treatment under GSP.
- **Workers' rights.** Prohibited the president from designating as a CBI beneficiary any country that was not taking steps to afford internationally recognized workers' rights to workers in the country.
- **Report.** Required the president to submit a complete report on CBI operations to the Congress by Oct. 1, 1993, and every three years thereafter. The report would have to review CBI countries based on all the beneficiary criteria, including that on workers' rights.
- **Puerto Rico.** Provided that any article grown, produced or manufactured in Puerto Rico qualified for duty-free treatment otherwise available under the CBI if (1) the article was imported directly from a CBI beneficiary country into the United States, (2) its value was increased in a CBI beneficiary country, and (3) any materials added in a CBI country were products of a beneficiary country or the United States.
- **Duty-free allowance.** Increased the duty-free allowance for U.S. residents returning directly or indirectly from a CBI beneficiary country from $400 to $600 and allowed them to bring one additional liter of alcoholic beverages duty and excise-tax free if it was produced in a CBI country. The bill increased the duty-free allowance for U.S. residents returning from U.S. insular possessions from $800 to $1,200.
- **U.S. components.** Granted duty-free and quota-free treatment for articles (other than textiles and apparel and petroleum and petroleum products) that were assembled wholly from U.S. fabricated components or processed wholly from U.S. ingredients in a CBI beneficiary country. The components and ingredients and the final article could not enter the commerce of a third country.
- **Rules of origin.** Authorized the president to proclaim, effective Jan. 1, 1991, new rules-of-origin requirements for articles eligible for duty-free treatment under the CBI. Under previous law, the article had to be imported directly from a CBI country, at least 35 percent of its value had to be added in a CBI country, and it had to be wholly grown, produced or manufactured — or substantially transformed — in a CBI country. The president would have to first consult with the private sector and report to congressional committees on the new rules.

eral Agreement on Tariffs and Trade (GATT).

Among the amendments considered but rejected on March 1 was an increase in the quota for all sugar imports regardless of source. Sponsor Bill Bradley, D-N.J., said an increased overall quota would surely benefit Caribbean countries.

But increased imports raised the ire of the domestic sugar industry, and Bentsen opposed Bradley's amendment as a probable stumbling block for the overall bill. The amendment was defeated 5-9.

Also defeated, 6-11, was an amendment by Bob Packwood, R-Ore., to ease the entry of rubber-soled footwear from Caribbean assembly plants.

The amendment was supported by Bernard W. Aronson, assistant secretary of State for inter-American affairs. Aronson said the committee's action would be a signal to the new democratic governments in Panama and Nicaragua and to other economically desperate countries in the region.

But the amendment was opposed by John Heinz, R-Pa., who said it would cost the jobs of 300 people doing such work in Wilkes-Barre, Pa.

The committee also passed by voice vote the changes in the 1974 Jackson-Vanik amendment. Jackson-Vanik denied MFN trade status to non-market economy countries that did not permit free emigration of their citizens. The president could grant such status, but only if he certified that the country no longer restrained emigration or waived the requirement. Congress could disapprove of the action by a simple resolution in either chamber. A trade agreement granting MFN status had to be approved by a concurrent resolution; such a resolution had to be adopted in identical form by both chambers, but did not require presidential signature.

The amendments were intended to protect Congress' Jackson-Vanik prerogatives from challenge under a 1983 Supreme Court decision, *Immigration and Naturalization Service v. Chadha*, which held "legislative vetoes" unconstitutional and said that Congress instead had to pass a bill that was signed by the president or enacted over his veto.

Though *Chadha* did not explicitly apply to concurrent resolutions, Congress played it safe and required enactment into law of joint resolutions to approve trade agreements as well as to disapprove presidential waivers and certifications of Jackson-Vanik.

By maintaining the constitutionality of Jackson-Vanik, the changes preserved provisions in that law for expedited consideration of resolutions of approval and disapproval. Such procedures were extremely important, especially in the filibuster-prone Senate. The Bush administration supported efforts to preserve the procedure.

FLOOR ACTION

After four days of off-the-floor discussion and intermittent floor debate, the Senate on April 24 approved the CBI

• **Cumulation.** Allowed CBI imports to be counted separately — not aggregated with non-CBI imports — in antidumping or countervailing duty cases for the purpose of determining whether the CBI imports were causing material injury to a U.S. industry.

Such imports could still be aggregated with imports from other CBI countries under investigation. And imports from CBI countries would continue to be aggregated with those of non-CBI countries under investigation for purposes of determining whether the non-CBI imports were causing injury.

• **Ethanol.** Extended through Dec. 31, 1992, a provision (enacted as part of the 1989 Steel Trade Liberalization Act) easing local feedstock requirements imposed on Caribbean ethanol producers by the 1986 Tax Reform Act.

The 1989 provision granted duty-free treatment for ethanol (and any mixture thereof) that was only dehydrated within a CBI beneficiary country or an insular possession if it met the following annual criteria: 1) no feedstock requirement was imposed on imports up to 60 million gallons or 7 percent of the domestic ethanol market, whichever was greater, 2) a local feedstock requirement of 30 percent by volume applied to the next 35 million gallons of imports, and 3) a local feedstock requirement of 50 percent by volume applied to any additional imports.

The conferees expressed their intent to consider later in 1990 the extension of tax preferences enjoyed by the domestic ethanol industry, including a tax credit for blenders of gasohol (gasoline and ethanol), and a partial exemption from the motor-fuel excise tax for sellers of gasohol. The expiration date for the CBI ethanol provision was linked to the expiration of the blenders' tax credit. It was the conferees' intent that this provision would continue in effect in the future as long as this additional tariff or other similar restrictions applied to imports of ethanol.

Ethyl alcohol (or a mixture thereof) that was produced by a process of full fermentation in an insular possession or beneficiary country remained eligible for duty-free treatment in unlimited quantities without regard to feedstock requirements.

These provisions were effective for calendar years 1990 and 1991.

• **Puerto Rico investment.** Required the government of Puerto Rico to ensure that at least $100 million in new investments that qualified for tax-free treatment under Section 936 of the Internal Revenue Code be made each year in eligible Caribbean Basin countries. Refinancings of existing investments could not constitute "new investments" for this purpose.

• **Scholarships.** Required the Agency for International Development to establish and administer a program of scholarship assistance to enable students from CBI beneficiary countries that also received U.S. foreign assistance to study in the United States.

• **Tourism.** Required the secretary of Commerce to complete a study begun in 1986 on tourism development strategies for the Caribbean region. The commissioner of Customs was required to carry out a pilot preclearance program during fiscal years 1991 and 1992 at a U.S. Customs Service facility in a Caribbean Basin country to test how such procedures could contribute to increased tourism and to submit a report to Congress.

• **Nicaragua.** Authorized the president to designate Nicaragua as a beneficiary country under the CBI and GSP programs, effective through 1990.

• **Andean region.** Urged the president to consider the merits of extending CBI benefits to the Andean region, explore additional mechanisms to expand trade opportunities for the Andean region, and report to Congress on the results of this review.

Title IV: Unprocessed Timber

• **Permanent ban.** Prohibited any person who acquired unprocessed timber originating from federal lands west of the 100th meridian in the contiguous 48 states from exporting, selling, trading, exchanging or otherwise conveying that timber to anyone for the purpose of export.

The bill excepted specific quantities and species of unprocessed timber from federal lands that the secretary of Agriculture or the secretary of the Interior determined to be in surplus to domestic processing needs.

• **Direct substitution.** Prohibited any person from purchasing directly from any department or agency of the United States unprocessed timber if such timber was to be substituted for exported timber originating from private lands or the person had during the preceding 24 months exported unprocessed timber originating from private lands.

Contracts for the purchase of federal timber in effect at the time of enactment would be honored.

---

extension. Final passage came on a vote of 92-0, approving an underlying bill on trade with Hungary (HR 1594) as amended to include reauthorization of the 1983 CBI and the other elements of the package. *(Vote 63, p. 16-S)*

But the Senate firmly rejected efforts to expand the CBI program where doing so might have meant lost sales for U.S. manufacturers or lost jobs for American workers.

Though the provisions to make CBI permanent had been approved by the Finance Committee, their journey to the floor — where they were appended to the underlying Hungary trade bill — was delayed by debate over clean air legislation.

Bentsen resisted efforts on the floor, as he had in committee, to broaden the Caribbean trade preferences. He argued that it was better to pass a narrow bill than to see a more ambitious version defeated.

Most of the early floor time was spent on non-controversial amendments or unrelated matters.

The Bush administration and some senators had also urged expansion of the CBI to more countries — such as the Andean nations wracked by drug-war violence.

But that move was opposed by several industries concerned about low-cost imports from those countries.

Another amendment accepted without a vote, sponsored by Sen. Christopher J. Dodd, D-Conn., included Nicaragua in CBI benefits that were denied during the reign of the Sandinista government.

A key attempt by Graham to extend the bill to cover inexpensive footwear from the Caribbean region was killed 63-33 despite support from the Bush administration and a small, bipartisan bloc of free-traders. *(Vote 61, p. 16-S)*

Graham's largely symbolic effort would have reduced by half the duty on imported Caribbean rubber-soled shoes with fabric uppers. Graham said 97 percent of the shoes in this category sold in the U.S. market were produced in Pacific Rim countries, with the preponderance coming from China.

With a lower duty, Graham said, such shoes could be economically produced closer to home. Holding aloft a pair of children's shoes, Graham said jobs could be created at the United States' doorstep at a cost to no one in this hemisphere.

For the next two hours, practically every senator who spoke had a pair of shoes to gesture with and describe.

Heinz brandished two pairs of athletic shoes — one an import and the other made at a Wilkes-Barre plant employing several hundred of his constituents.

Democrat George J. Mitchell, D-Maine, though without a footwear prop, told of how soaring imports had cost jobs in Maine. "If this amendment is adopted, American companies would suddenly face competition whose duties have been cut in half," he said. "The choice they will face is either to concede even more market share, close down still more plants in the United States or shift their operations to the Caribbean."

Packwood, supporting Graham, introduced letters from

• **Indirect substitution.** Prohibited, within 21 days of enactment, indirect substitution of unprocessed timber from federal lands for exported unprocessed timber from private lands. The bill exempted a small number of companies in Oregon and Washington state that were permitted to continue indirectly purchasing western red cedar from federal lands while exporting private logs.

• **24-month rule.** Exempted from substitution prohibitions the acquisition of unprocessed timber from federal lands from an area designated by the secretary of the Interior or the secretary of Agriculture if the acquirer, in the previous 24 months, had not exported such timber from private lands within the designated area. The acquirer could not, during the period of this approval, export unprocessed timber from private lands within the designated area. The 24-month test would not apply to any person who had legally substituted federal timber for exported unprocessed timber originating from private lands under a historical export quota approved by the secretary of Agriculture or the secretary of the Interior.

• **Denied applicants.** Set rules for people whose sourcing area boundary application was denied. In the event of such a denial, this section provided an opportunity to phase out federal timber purchases over 15 months and maintain such export operations, or to terminate export of private logs from the area within 15 months and maintain eligibility for federal timber purchases.

• **Export ban from state lands.** Prohibited the export from the United States of unprocessed timber harvested from lands owned or administered by a state or any political subdivision of a state, subject to certain conditions.

The effective date was 21 days after enactment for states with annual sales of 400 million board feet or less. For states with annual sales greater than that, the bill set a schedule for the issuance of orders by the secretary of Commerce.

• **Exceptions.** Permitted the secretary of Commerce to increase the amount of unprocessed state timber barred from export (in states with sales greater than 400 million board feet) if the domestic log supply was insufficient to meet the demand of domestic mills.

• **Equitable allocations.** Required each state to consider the species, grade and geographic origin of its public timber so that restrictions were allocated in a representative and equitable manner — especially with a view to existing state laws. Much of the timber in question was held by states in trust for counties or schools.

• **State rules.** Provided that each state should develop its own regulations for restricting state exports of unprocessed timber.

• **GATT conformity.** Authorized the president, after suitable notice and a public comment period, to suspend the provisions of this section if a GATT panel, or a ruling issued under the formal dispute settlement proceeding under any other trade agreement, found that the state export restrictions were in violation of, or inconsistent with, U.S. international obligations.

• **Presidential exceptions.** Authorized the president to remove or modify any state export restrictions if a state petitioned to do so and the president determined it was in the national economic interests to remove or modify such restrictions.

• **Previous commitments.** Clarified that no provision of previously enacted federal law that imposed requirements related to the generation of revenue from state timberlands was to affect any action of a state taken pursuant to this act. The state of Washington held a substantial portion of its lands in trust for the benefit of its educational institutions under the 1889 act granting statehood.

• **Surplus marketing.** Established that the prohibitions on state timber exports should not apply to specific grades and species of unprocessed timber from federal lands that the secretaries of Agriculture and the Interior determined to be surplus to domestic processing needs.

• **Review of restrictions.** Provided that, beginning in 1997, the president could suspend the restrictions on the export of unprocessed timber from state lands if they were determined to no longer meet the intent of the bill. The bill did not limit the authority of the president or the USTR to respond to any measure taken by a foreign government in connection with this act.

• **Enforcement.** Anyone who directly or indirectly acquired unprocessed federal timber had to report the receipt and disposition of such timber to the secretaries of Agriculture and the Interior. The bill provided for civil penalties against violators and provided that they could be barred from entering a contract for the purchase of unprocessed timber from federal lands.

• **Effective date.** Provided that, except as otherwise specified, the effective date was the date of enactment. ■

U.S. shoe companies saying they would move production to the Caribbean from Asia, not the United States, if Graham's amendment passed. He also read a letter from U.S. Trade Representative Hills praising the amendment and noting that duties on shoes from the Caribbean were as high as 67 percent. Hills supported the argument that the amendment would not cost U.S. jobs.

The only major item added in floor action was an amendment by Packwood to ban the export of unprocessed timber taken from federally owned lands. Packwood, ranking Republican on the Finance Committee, was co-manager of the bill. After several hours of discussion, primarily among senators from the Pacific Northwest, the log amendment was agreed to 81-17. *(Vote 59, p. 16-S)*

Besides making permanent an existing ban on selling federal timber abroad, Packwood's proposal tightened restrictions to prevent both direct substitution of federal logs for private logs exported and indirect substitution through third-party arrangements.

The amendment was designed to alleviate the shortage of cut timber for mills in the Northwest. After the eruption of Mount St. Helens in 1980, timber surpluses led to increased log exports. With the surplus gone and forest cutting under pressure, domestic mills found themselves competing with foreign buyers for logs.

To expedite passage, Packwood did not attempt to extend his amendment to timber taken from state lands or private lands (where three-fourths of the logging was done), as many in his home state had urged. He also exempted his neighboring state of Washington, where some logging revenues from public lands were used to support public schools.

The bill also included the changes in the 1974 Jackson-Vanik amendment. The changes, negotiated with the Bush administration, were intended to preserve Congress' power to reject trade agreements, within certain constitutional boundaries.

Though most of the tariff changes and temporary suspensions in the bill had been brought to committee and approved there without objection, senators continued to bring individual tariff concerns to the floor throughout the protracted process, usually winning inclusion by voice vote after clearing the fresh concessions with the administration and with Bentsen and Packwood.

Only two such amendments were put to roll call votes.

In one case, the senators from North Carolina, Republican Jesse Helms and Democrat Terry Sanford, went to bat for a state company that produced a popular medicine for treating ulcers.

A key ingredient, ranitidine hydrochloride, was produced in Singapore and elsewhere and imported. The company, Glaxo Inc., wanted a temporary duty suspension, but its prime competitor in the anti-ulcer field, SmithKline Beecham of Pennsylvania, objected.

On hand in behalf of the latter company were Heinz and his fellow Pennsylvania Republican Arlen Specter.

After a spirited debate among the four senators, the Senate voted to allow Glaxo its temporary suspension 68-30. *(Vote 60, p. 16-S)*

Just before passing the bill, the Senate took up an amendment by Dennis DeConcini, D-Ariz., to donate a turboprop aircraft seized by federal agents in a drug case to the University Medical Center in Tucson for transferring emergency cases from remote areas.

Bentsen objected to this procedure for disposing of seized property. And for several minutes DeConcini was unable to obtain a second despite the presence of dozens of senators.

Continuing to hold the floor, DeConcini eventually attracted a second for his motion. But Bentsen won the roll call vote and tabled the amendment, killing it 62-31. *(Vote 62, p. 16-S)*

The final vote on passage ended a night session that might have gone into the morning hours if several senators had not agreed to withhold controversial amendments.

Chief among them was the sugar-quota increase that Bradley had failed to push through the committee.

And when the trade package came to the floor, Ernest F. Hollings, D-S.C., agreed not to add his textile-import quota bill as long as no one else offered anything like it. Bentsen also assured Hollings he would have his day in committee. Although widely supported in the Senate, Hollings' bill (S 2411) would have subjected its vehicle to a presidential veto — the fate that befell textile bills regularly in past years *(Textile bill, p. 219)*.

CONFERENCE ACTION

The conference on the bill began May 11, and negotiators were able to settle most of the House-Senate disagreements within the first few weeks. By the June 19 public session, conferees had even hammered out an agreement over the more controversial issues such as the log exports and sugar-import quotas.

After resolving the differences on logs and sugar, though, the conference nearly foundered in a dispute over ethanol imports, which included tax issues that had not been part of the bill as passed by either chamber.

Gibbons and Ways and Means Chairman Dan Rostenkowski, D-Ill., indicated to senators that they were willing to lose the bill rather than make further concessions on issues added in conference.

But both sides relented the week of July 23 — and the conference report was eventually completed and filed July 30 — in an exchange of letters between Rostenkowski and Senate Republican leader Bob Dole of Kansas.

Ethanol Debate

Dole, who rarely played a major role in trade conferences, had joined this one in part to plead the case of Midwestern farmers who grew corn and other grains for distillation into ethanol, an alcohol used as a gasoline additive.

The domestic ethanol industry objected to competition from Caribbean plants that made cheap ethanol from surplus European wine. In 1986, the domestic industry won new requirements forcing Caribbean operators to rely on local feedstock materials if they wanted duty-free access to U.S. markets. But late in 1989, Gibbons won at least a temporary reprieve from the high local-content requirement through a provision added to a steel quota bill (HR 3275 — PL 101-221). *(1989 Almanac, p. 144)*

That deal allowed the Caribbean plants 7 percent of the U.S. ethanol market (or 60 million gallons annually) if as much as 35 percent of the product's value had been added in the Caribbean.

The threshold for the next 35 million gallons was 30 percent and the threshold for additional amounts was 50 percent. This arrangement was to last through Dec. 31, 1991.

Gibbons' original bill would have made the arrangement permanent.

Dole opposed any extension of the 1989 compromise unless Gibbons and Rostenkowski promised to support two tax breaks for the domestic ethanol industry that were soon to expire.

One was a tax credit for blenders of gasohol (gasoline with ethanol); the other was a partial exemption from the motor-fuel excise tax for sellers of gasohol, who collected 3 cents instead of 9 cents tax per gallon.

The blenders' credit was scheduled to expire Dec. 31, 1992; the excise exemption was scheduled to expire Sept. 30, 1993.

Rostenkowski balked at committing himself to a tax change that would be highly controversial within his committee, where some members had eyed the ethanol credit as a source of revenue in the past.

At the same time, representatives of the domestic ethanol industry backed off, concerned that holding the trade bill hostage then could haunt them in their dealings with the tax-writing committees later.

Ultimately, a new compromise was devised extending the existing arrangement for CBI ethanol through Dec. 31, 1992 — the expiration date for the blenders' tax credit. By matching the expiration dates of the two provisions, the deal effectively linked their respective fates.

CBI supporters viewed this as a positive development, as they generally also supported the domestic tax breaks that helped create a market for ethanol regardless of its origin.

Log Exports

In June, conferees also finally agreed on the permanent ban on log exports from public lands. Senate conferees accepted House provisions to coordinate state and federal policy under the ban and to set rules against switching logs from private and public lands.

The Senate's original timber amendment would have banned the export of logs from federal and state lands. It would have exempted logs from the "public trust" lands in Washington state, where logging revenue helped support the public schools.

The House language went further in trying to prevent circumvention of the public-land ban through the substitution of logs taken from private lands.

But the House's initial offer in conference "came 80 percent of the way," according to one Senate aide, raising hopes of an easier-than-expected resolution to the issue.

Progress was slowed early in conference by the number of conferees — nearly three dozen on the House side alone — on the log export provisions. Four House committees had addressed the issue in the spring. Concern over foreign purchase of unprocessed logs was especially acute in the Pacific Northwest, where several factors combined to idle local mills.

Complicating the timber issue further was an administration-backed amendment added in the House Foreign

Affairs Committee that would have set aside any language found in conflict with an international trade agreement.

Sugar, Leather, Other Issues

The dispute over sugar imports created some major debate early in conference, although conferees eventually dropped the provision.

While the Senate bill had no sugar provision, the House bill would have set a minimum quota for Caribbean sugar at the 1989 level of 371,449 metric tons. This guaranteed market share would have applied even if the global quota were lowered in the future, a clear advantage for Caribbean producers.

Gibbons was upset that no sugar provision made it into the final bill.

"We thought we'd get about enough Brownie points to just about cover everything else [at issue] in the bill," Gibbons said. "We want something for that sugar provision, Mr. Chairman."

On leather goods, Gibbons had pressed for a House provision that would have cut by half the existing duties imposed on handbags, luggage, work gloves and leather clothing imported from CBI countries.

The leather provision, backed by the Bush administration, was a vestige of the long list of tariff reductions Gibbons had sought in his original bill.

Negotiators compromised on a 20 percent reduction.

Conferees also wrestled with a tax break for companies investing in Puerto Rico, an item not covered in either the House or the Senate bill.

The Puerto Rico issue was raised in conference by Rep. J. J. "Jake" Pickle, D-Texas, chairman of the Ways and Means Subcommittee on Oversight.

Pickle had been disturbed that companies receiving tax advantages under the 1986 tax act for investing $14 billion in Puerto Rico had not generated $100 million for local development as promised in a 1986 memorandum of agreement.

Pickle's proposed solution would have made the $100 million mandatory by statute. But several senators objected to injecting this matter without a hearing on the Senate side, suggesting that it might also interfere with impending votes on statehood for the island territory.

Pickle agreed to drop the matter in return for a guarantee of future consideration.

One other late-starting issue that held up the conference for a time was the amendment added on the Senate floor by Helms and Sanford.

It would have lowered the tariff for the imported ingredient in the ulcer drug manufactured in North Carolina.

In the end, the Senate conferees dropped that fight also in exchange for a promise of future hearings on the House side.

FINAL ACTION

Once negotiators had hammered out an agreement after resolving the myriad issues, final passage became a formality. The conference report was filed the night of July 30 without another formal meeting of conferees, who had last met publicly on June 19.

House members whose districts were affected by the bill, especially by the ban on log exports, were eager to clear it before going home for the August recess.

Both chambers gave their approval to the conference report by voice vote.

"From an investment security and promotion standpoint, it was important to do it," said Ben Marsh, legislative director for Caribbean/Central American Action, an industry-financed trade promotion group.

"We have to make it amenable for U.S. exporters to take the first step toward Caribbean operations," Marsh added, noting that the bill contained many small provisions that might grow in significance with time — such as an allowance of duty-free treatment for assembly of fabricated components of U.S. origin. ■

Latin America Aid Plan Fails To Advance

A plan to boost economic development in Latin America and the Caribbean, unveiled by President Bush on June 27, won praise from Congress in 1990, but no legislation was passed to put its proposals into law. The administration indicated it would push the initiative again in 1991.

The plan, introduced as the Enterprise for the Americas Initiative (HR 5855), aimed to boost economic development as a way to support fledgling democratic and market-based governments in the region.

The three-part program included an offer of trade negotiations designed to lead to a Western Hemisphere free-trade zone; new private investment incentives, including a $300 million program of annual grants; and forgiveness of some loans owed to the U.S. government to bolster an effort to reduce commercial bank debt.

In all cases, the proposal required Latin American countries to continue their march toward market-oriented economies in order to qualify for aid.

Bush's plan moved too slowly through Congress to clear in 1990.

The House passed the measure on Oct. 22; just five days before the 101st Congress adjourned. The measure was never considered in the Senate.

BACKGROUND

The Bush plan was designed to address several concerns. One was that unless Latin America's debt problem was resolved, the region's newly established democracies would be in danger of falling victim to civil strife and military coups.

Another was that the United States might lose control of the process of reducing Latin America's debt to U.S. banks. The Latin debt burden stood at about $400 billion, a large part of which was considered uncollectable because the region's economies were weak.

Parts of the plan, such as official debt relief, already had congressional proponents. Other ideas — particularly a hemispheric free-trade zone — faced skepticism and some immediate opposition.

Because free-trade negotiations appeared far down the road and the $300 million investment incentive was so modest, the plan's centerpiece was the proposal to relieve part of the Latin American debt to the U.S. government.

That proposal was a companion to the so-called Brady plan announced in March 1989 by Treasury Secretary Nicholas F. Brady to encourage commercial banks to reduce the Third World's debt. *(1989 Almanac, p. 139)*

The Brady plan relied on negotiations by individual countries with their creditor banks to reduce debt principal or interest owed or to provide new money at better rates. As an incentive, the World Bank and the International Monetary Fund guaranteed repayment of reduced principal or interest.

Many critics said that the Brady plan was flawed because it did not deal with debt owed to governments, particularly the United States. Smaller countries were more burdened by government loans than by debts to commercial banks. And commercial banks had been unwilling to reduce their debt while the U.S. and other governments demanded full repayment.

Brady said that the new plan was designed to address Latin American debt owed to the United States. The proposal would have partly reduced $7 billion in Latin American loans from the Agency for International Development (AID) and the Food for Peace (PL 480) program.

Much of that money was lent on concessional terms that probably did not anticipate full repayment. The United States had an additional $5.3 billion in outstanding loans to Latin America that were not covered under the proposal.

Members of Congress who had been eager for government debt relief had also been pushing for more pressure on commercial banks. But that was not a part of Bush's proposal. "It doesn't look like the administration is ready to cross that bridge yet," Barry Hager, a Washington consultant for some Third World countries, remarked. "That is going to be the fault line between the administration and Congress."

LEGISLATIVE ACTION

The House Foreign Affairs Committee gave voice vote approval to HR 5855 on Oct. 18. The measure was not amended.

The bill would have authorized the president to begin negotiating reductions in some nations' long-term, low-interest debt owed to the AID. As of the end of fiscal 1989, AID had $5.3 billion in outstanding concessional, or below market-rate, loans.

The measure would have authorized long-term talks on a hemisphere free-trade zone and short-term bilateral negotiations on free-trade agreement "frameworks." It would also have unilaterally cut U.S. tariffs for Latin American countries as part of global trade talks.

A new, five-year $300 million annual multilateral grant program would have been established tied to specific market reforms. Some U.S. development loans would have been written off on a case-by-case basis.

Under the bill, eligible countries could pay the interest on their debts in local currency and put it into a yet-to-be created Environment Fund, which would fund local environmental protection and cleanup activities.

With just days remaining in the 101st Congress, the House passed HR 5855 by voice vote on Oct. 22.

Referred to the Senate, the measure died there. The Senate Foreign Relations Committee held hearings on a companion measure (S 3064), but never acted on it.

In his State of the Union address in 1991, Bush reaffirmed his support for the Enterprise for Americas Initiative and pushed for its passage. ■

Mexico Trade Pact Sought

President Bush notified Congress on Sept. 26 that he planned to move forward with talks aimed at achieving a U.S.-Mexico free-trade agreement that would eventually remove most trade barriers between the countries.

Noting that Mexico was the third-largest trading partner of the United States, Bush wrote, "We see substantial opportunities for mutual benefit in further lowering impediments to bilateral trade in goods and services and to investment." He called ongoing changes in Mexico aimed at returning some previously nationalized businesses to the private sector and a reduced reliance on government subsidies "dynamic, market-oriented reforms."

Key congressional leaders were cautiously supportive. Senate Finance Chairman Lloyd Bentsen, D-Texas, said he favored the talks, but was apprehensive about economic consequences for the United States. "Never before have we negotiated a free-trade agreement with a country so different from us economically," Bentsen said.

Bentsen noted that Mexican wages remained below those in the United States, resulting in stiff competition for U.S. businesses. He also said parts of the Mexican market were still closed to U.S. exporters and investors.

Some House members considered preparing a "sense of the Congress" resolution to show the administration just how deep the ambivalent feelings on Capitol Hill ran — both on an agreement with Mexico and on a free-trade zone that might encompass all of North America.

An additional problem in the talks was Canada's interest in participating. The United States already had a free-trade pact with Canada. Bush said he would not discourage a broadening of the talks, although Bentsen and others said it troubled them.

Administration plans to seek a free-trade agreement had drawn opposing reactions in June hearings before the House Ways and Means Trade Subcommittee.

U.S. Trade Representative Carla A. Hills told the subcommittee June 14 that the Mexican government had "undergone a sea change since 1988" in its approach to trade and the economy. She said that Mexico had reduced its tariff rates from 100 percent to 20 percent or less and that goods representing only about 7 percent of the total value of U.S. exports to Mexico were still subject to the previous import license requirements.

But Mark A. Anderson, an economist for the AFL-CIO, testified June 28 that a free-trade agreement would fatten profits for big corporations, help "a narrow elite" in Mexico and invite "disaster" for U.S. workers.

Mexican President Carlos Salinas de Gortari emphasized his desire for wider trade with the United States in a June visit to Washington. At the White House on June 10, Salinas and Bush endorsed the goal of a "comprehensive free-trade agreement" to be negotiated "in a timely manner." Little headway was made in 1990, but in early 1991 the Bush administration renewed its support for the pact and said Canada would be included in the talks. ■

Textile Quota Bill Falls to Veto Again

Textile interests failed, in the face of the third presidential veto in five years, to enact legislation sharply restricting imports of fabrics, clothing and shoes.

By wide majorities in both chambers, Congress passed a textile quota bill (HR 4328) that would have limited textile and apparel import growth to 1 percent per year and permanently frozen imports of most shoes at 1989 levels.

But President Bush vetoed the measure Oct. 5, calling it "highly protectionist." And the House on Oct. 10 fell 10 votes short, 275-152, of the two-thirds majority needed to override the veto. *(Veto message, p. 221; House vote 440, p. 142-H)*

President Ronald Reagan had vetoed textile quota bills in 1985 and 1988; both vetoes were sustained. *(1988 Almanac, p. 228; 1986 Almanac, p. 347; 1985 Almanac, p. 255)*

U.S. textile manufacturers claimed the quotas were needed to blunt the effects of low-wage competition from abroad on a vital domestic industry that had lost 500,000 jobs since 1980. Opponents countered that the textile industry was actually prospering and that quotas would drive up the cost of consumer goods, violate international trade agreements and invite retaliation by U.S. trading partners.

Supporters of the 1990 bill improved on previous votes in the Senate, gaining 68-32 approval July 17 in part by winning over some farm-state senators with a provision designed to encourage agricultural exports. In the House, however, the 271-149 vote in favor of the bill Sept. 18 fell slightly short of the number reached in the previous unsuccessful veto-override attempts, presaging the final outcome after Bush delivered his anticipated veto. *(Senate vote 157, p. 35-S; House vote 335, p. 110-H)*

BOXSCORE

Legislation: Textile, Apparel and Footwear Trade Act (HR 4328).

Major action: Veto sustained by House, 275-152, Oct. 10. Vetoed, Oct. 5. Passed by House, 271-149, Sept. 18; by Senate, 68-32, July 17.

Reports: Ways and Means (H Rept 101-649).

BACKGROUND

The textile industry was the nation's largest manufacturing sector, employing 2 million people. But during the 1970s and '80s it came under increasing pressure from competition from foreign manufacturers.

According to textile industry supporters, imports of textiles and textile products tripled from 1980 to 1989, contributing to a textile and clothing trade deficit of $26 billion in 1989.

Even more so, imports came to dominate the U.S. footwear market. In 1980, imports had claimed 50 percent of the domestic market; in 1989, 80 percent.

Plant closings in the traditional textile centers of the Southeast and Northeast created for many the impression of an industry facing extinction at the hands of low-wage competitors in Third World countries. Always a powerful force on Capitol Hill, the industry began in the mid-1980s to push a stringent quota bill as a way of protecting it from foreign competition.

Opponents, however, maintained that the quotas were unnecessary because the industry was adapting to competition from abroad through plant modernization. They also said the industry was adequately protected by existing tariffs and bilateral trade agreements.

Textile imports were governed by the 1973 Multi-Fiber Arrangement (MFA), which was aimed at helping fledgling textile and apparel industries in developing countries while providing protection to their domestic competitors. The MFA was enforced through separate bilateral trade agreements with a total of 38 countries.

Textile industry supporters argued that under the MFA imports had increased at 10 times the rate of growth of the U.S. market. So in 1985, they won congressional approval of a bill to set country-by-country quotas on textile, apparel and footwear imports that would have called for rollbacks in imports from some countries. Hit hardest by the bill would have been Pacific Rim nations and Asian countries that had become major sources of U.S. textile and apparel imports.

Reagan vetoed the bill in October 1985. Supporters delayed an override attempt in hope of maintaining leverage on negotiations to renew the MFA. In August 1986, the override attempt failed, 276-149, eight votes short of the needed two-thirds majority.

In 1988, textile industry supporters modified their proposal to provide overall quotas rather than country-by-country allotments. They also sought to pick up farm-state support by adding a provision that would have allowed for countries to increase their textile quotas by increasing their imports of U.S. agricultural products.

After the bill cleared Congress, however, Reagan vetoed that measure, too, and the override attempt again failed in the House, 272-152.

After those reversals, textile-state senators and members spent the first 15 months of the Bush administration trying to negotiate a compromise. Sen. Jesse Helms, R-N.C., said the administration showed interest in a global quota system but refused to commit itself to one in the ongoing talks under the General Agreement on Tariffs and Trade (GATT).

Bill's Provisions

In the end, supporters of import quotas decided instead to take another run at enacting a 1 percent growth cap. So in April 1990, a new quota bill (HR 4496, S 2411) was introduced, with a majority of members in both chambers signed on as cosponsors: 54 in the Senate, including Majority Leader George J. Mitchell, D-Maine, and Minority Leader Bob Dole, R-Kan.; and 249 in the House.

The administration opposed the bill, saying it would raise consumer prices and hobble U.S. negotiators just as the four-year Uruguay Round of talks under GATT were nearing their scheduled completion in December.

As introduced, the bill would have:

- Imposed global quotas on textile and apparel with 1 percent growth annually.
- Frozen non-rubber footwear at 1989 levels.
- Directed the secretary of Commerce to set regulations to put the quotas into effect.
- Allowed the president to negotiate reductions in textile

and apparel tariffs of 5 percent to 10 percent over five years to compensate other countries adversely affected.

- Required the secretary of Treasury to implement a one-year pilot program for the issuance and sale to U.S. companies at public auction of import licenses on textiles and apparel.
- Given increases in quotas to countries that increased their purchases of U.S. agricultural products.
- Exempted products of Canada and Israel because of free-trade agreements between those two nations and the United States.
- Guaranteed Caribbean Basin Initiative countries their 1989 market share.

SENATE ACTION

Textile state senators opened the push for passage of the 1990 bill with testimony before the Senate Finance Committee on June 7 filled with dire warnings about the industry's health.

Hollings said the bill was intended to "prevent the outright extinction of the U.S. textile, apparel and non-rubber footwear industry."

Two weeks later, the Finance Committee allowed proponents to advance the bill to the floor, agreeing by voice vote to report it without recommendation. About half the 20 members had indicated support for the bill, but several had opposed it vigorously.

"I can't think of a single justifiable smidgen of comment to say in favor of this bill," said Bob Packwood of Oregon, the committee's ranking Republican, who offered the motion to report it. He said the bill violated both the MFA and GATT.

The action discharged the committee's responsibility without a bruising confrontation. Finance Chairman Lloyd Bentsen, D-Texas, noted that the measure could, in any event, be brought up as a floor amendment at any time.

Floor Debate

The Senate took up the bill July 12, attaching the Senate measure (S 2411) to a minor House-passed trade bill (HR 4328) on the floor.

The same day, the White House warned that the president's senior advisers would recommend a veto because "the quotas set by the bill would cause harm to consumers and the economy, violate our international obligations and virtually destroy any chance of a successful conclusion of the Uruguay Round of international trade negotiations."

Senators' arguments paralleled those made during more than a decade of textile bill debates in Congress.

Hollings, Thurmond and Helms dominated the floor debate, insisting that the U.S. textile industry, and its 2 million jobs, would soon disappear unless import growth was restrained.

"If we don't do anything, it's safe to say the demise of the industry is at hand," said Helms.

Thurmond noted that a disproportionate percentage of the industry's jobs were held by minorities and women. He also argued that the U.S. military would have to rely on foreign sources of footwear, uniforms and other textile products if the U.S. sources of these products disappeared.

Packwood spearheaded the opposition, joined by a colleague from the free trade-minded Pacific Northwest: Slade Gorton, R-Wash.

They argued that the legislation would lead to higher costs and to retaliation against U.S. interests in trade talks and against U.S. products in the marketplace.

But Hollings argued that the bill would help the U.S. position in the Uruguay Round of negotiations under GATT. "This strengthens our negotiators' hand in the Uruguay Round," he said. "They can say: 'Watch out for what they're doing up there in Congress.' By cracky, this'll show 'em."

Opponents' Amendments

Opponents of the bill brought six amendments to roll-call votes. All were easily defeated as the bill's sponsors rallied 65 to 70 votes for tabling motions.

On the first day of debate, Packwood offered two amendments. One, tabled by a vote of 68-32, would have exempted non-rubber footwear from the bill. The other, tabled by a vote of 69-30, would have made the bill's provisions subject to existing U.S. obligations under international agreements. *(Votes 150, 151, p. 34-S)*

The next day, July 13, Gorton proposed an amendment to strip the bill and substitute a sense of the Senate resolution relying on international trade negotiators. It was killed 69-29. *(Vote 153, p. 35-S)*

Phil Gramm, R-Texas, another longtime foe of import quotas, prepared a series of amendments but pushed only one to a roll-call vote. It would have suspended the limits under the bill if the president found they had raised the cost of textiles and textile products by 5 percent or more. It was tabled 69-24. *(Vote 154, p. 35-S)*

The last two amendments, both debated on July 16 and voted down on July 17, were offered by Gorton and Pete Wilson, R-Calif.

Gorton's amendment sought to undercut the textile-agricultural coalition by providing an alternative method of encouraging U.S. agricultural exports.

It would have allowed any country increasing its imports of U.S. farm goods to increase its quota of textile exports to the United States by 50 percent of the increased value of its U.S. farm imports. It was tabled 65-35. *(Vote 156, p. 35-S)*

Wilson also proposed that the bill's limits be suspended if the president could not certify that they would cost consumers less than $1 billion in any given year. The amendment was killed, 70-29. *(Vote 155, p. 35-S)*

Final Vote

On final passage, the bill's sponsors scored their best showing ever in the Senate: 68-32, eight votes more than they won for the 1985 bill and 11 more than in 1988. The majority was sufficient to override a veto if all the votes held firm. *(Vote 157, p. 35-S)*

The big difference for the bill's sponsors came in the Farm Belt. Seven senators voted for the 1990 bill who had voted against textile-import limits before the farm products provision was added. Most were from farm states.

A bare 23-22 majority of Republicans stood with Bush in opposing the bill. Some who voted for the measure had big textile industries in their states (Thurmond and Helms); others had factories that made shoes or clothing (William S. Cohen of Maine and John Heinz and Arlen Specter of Pennsylvania).

Southern Democrats, traditional defenders of the textile industry, backed the bill by a score of 16-1. The one exception was Bob Graham of Florida, a major promoter of free trade for the Caribbean Basin, where textile and footwear exporters would have been hobbled by any limit on U.S. import growth.

Bush Veto Message on Textile Quota Bill

Following is the statement issued by President Bush on Oct. 5 when he vetoed HR 4328, the textile bill:

I am returning herewith without my approval HR 4328, the "Textile, Apparel, and Footwear Trade Act of 1990," which imposes import quotas on textiles, textile products, and nonrubber footwear. This highly protectionist bill would damage the national economy, increase already artificially high costs to consumers of several basic goods, and abrogate our international agreements. It would also reverse the tremendous progress we are making to generate a global economic renaissance.

Economic indicators illustrate that the problems this bill is intended to address do not exist. Despite assertions to the contrary, the textile industry has done well. Domestic production has been up slightly since 1987. Unemployment in major textile-producing States is currently lower than the national average. Since 1989, the textile industry has continued to operate at a higher rate of capacity than the average for all U.S. manufacturing industries.

All consumers, particularly those at lower income levels, would be adversely affected if this legislation were to become law. The consumer costs of all restrictions on textile and apparel imports are conservatively estimated to increase to a total of $160 billion over the next five years: That amounts to an onerous $2,600 for a family of four over that same period. These costs would continue to rise annually. In essence, this legislation picks the pockets of U.S. consumers in order to subsidize the textile industry at a cost of $70,000 annually per job saved.

Furthermore, U.S. merchandise exports, which have increased by more than 9 percent in the first half of this year, would be jeopardized. We could anticipate swift retaliation by countries exporting textiles and footwear if this bill became law. These countries have large and rapidly growing markets for U.S. exports, which would be placed at risk by the new restrictions required under HR 4328. They would retaliate against our most competitive exports, such as agriculture, aerospace, high technology, capital goods, and services, to the detriment of domestic employment in these industries.

All of these economic costs to consumers and American industry would be incurred without eliminating a single "unfair" trade practice or opening even one closed market abroad. Rather than address the industry's competitive problems constructively, this legislation merely closes our markets and insulates the textile, apparel, and footwear industries from international competition.

We already have very effective laws that provide remedies to unfair competition from abroad, which various sectors of the textile and apparel industries have used when necessary. Our best hope for opening new markets overseas and for sustaining our textile and apparel industries is not this legislation, but the Uruguay Round of global trade talks, now in its critical final weeks.

We are working in the Uruguay Round to negotiate a means for the textile and apparel industries to:

- Enhance their international competitiveness in the long term and to open foreign markets to our exports.
- Ensure that the current special quota protection for the industry is not terminated abruptly, but is phased in over a reasonable period of time to protect those parts of the industry that require more time to adjust to import competition.
- Provide sufficient stability so that our textile and apparel industries, as well as our importers and retailers, have a smooth, gradual path of adjustment to the regular rules of the General Agreement on Tariffs and Trade (GATT), as they are strengthened in the [Uruguay] Round.

HR 4328 would eliminate any hope we have of achieving a successful Uruguay Round agreement in December that accomplishes these objectives. The bill would do this by taking a sector of considerable importance in international trade off the negotiating table. Furthermore, it would be an egregious violation of GATT rules, our commitments under the Multi-Fiber Arrangement (MFA), and the numerous bilateral agreements we have negotiated under the MFA's auspices. This protectionist bill unquestionably would result in a mass exodus of perhaps half the 100 nations participating in the [Uruguay] Round. All we hope to achieve for the textile and apparel industries would be lost, as would all of our efforts for American businesses, consumers, and workers.

Beyond this economic calamity, HR 4328 is reprehensible at a time when the United States' highest international priority is to strengthen international cooperation. Many of the countries whose interests would be damaged by HR 4328, such as Turkey and Egypt, are ones that have cooperated effectively in resisting Iraqi aggression in the Persian Gulf.

In addition, this bill would undercut our attempts to rebuild economies on free-market principles and to build a strengthened global trading system that will permit trade to expand and thereby increase world prosperity and stability. Additionally, while the Congress holds the authority to regulate commerce with foreign nations, several provisions of HR 4328 interfere with the President's constitutional prerogatives in conducting international negotiations and in proposing legislation.

The Textile, Apparel, and Footwear Trade Act of 1990 is simply not the panacea advertised by its proponents. Instead, it is blatantly protectionist, unwarranted, economically harmful, and internationally unviable.

Accordingly, I am disapproving HR 4328. ■

Northern Democrats split 30-8 in favor of the bill. Five of the no votes came from senators representing Western states, where open trade benefited many industries with significant foreign sales.

The vote heartened supporters who hoped to persuade the House to act and the president to withhold his veto. Thurmond said that if Bush "wants this country's textile industry to survive, he'll sign this bill."

HOUSE ACTION

House action on the legislation had been considered uncertain before the Senate vote. Ways and Means Committee Chairman Dan Rostenkowski, D-Ill., whose committee had jurisdiction over the measure, showed little interest in the bill. And Trade Subcommittee Chairman Sam M. Gibbons, D-Fla., an active opponent of textile quotas, had scheduled no hearings on it.

But after the Senate action, the House leadership asked Rostenkowski to expedite a floor vote, and he obliged.

On July 25, the Ways and Means Committee sent the Senate-passed bill to the House floor by voice vote without recommendation and virtually without debate.

Rostenkowski opened the meeting by saying that he would rather the committee not approve the textile bill and would prefer to avoid a roll-call vote. Ed Jenkins, D-Ga., a cosponsor of the original House bill, then moved that the bill be reported without recommendation. He did not deliver a speech in its behalf.

Bill Frenzel, R-Minn., a veteran opponent of trade restraints, reciprocated by saying he, too, would defer comment on the bill — which he referred to in passing as "simply awful."

The one committee member who did speak on the merits of the bill was Gibbons.

"If this bill is passed, it will tie the hands of the executive branch so that nothing more can be negotiated in this area," he said.

"If we want to stop the world and get off," Gibbons continued, "this is the legislation we pass."

Floor Vote

Approval by the full House came quickly when it was brought to the floor Sept. 18. The House voted 271-149 to accept the bill as passed by the Senate, sending it on to Bush.

The brief debate covered familiar ground. Supporters of the bill spoke of plant closings and rising imports to depict the domestic textile industry as in jeopardy. Opponents countered that the industry was healthy, that its factories were being modernized and running at 90 percent capacity, and that textile states enjoyed a lower average unemployment rate than the nation as a whole.

"It's a healthy, prosperous industry. Like any other industry, it has its ups and downs," Gibbons said. "Old plants are going to close; they've got to close."

Replied Jenkins, "My people are working. They're getting $4.50 an hour working at McDonald's."

Opponents also said quotas would invite retaliation against U.S. exports and drive up the price of clothing — tantamount to imposing a clothing tax that would be especially harmful to poor people. "This comes to a tax of $250 a year for every family," argued John Miller, R-Wash.

Supporters scoffed at the claims. "We're always afraid of a little retaliation," Jenkins said. "Because of that fear, we are giving away little by little our manufacturing base. Every nation except us stands up for its people."

Support for the bill was strongest among Democrats. Southern Democrats showed near unanimity, voting 71-9 for the bill, while Northern Democrats supported it 129-39. A majority of Republicans, however, opposed it (71-101).

Effect on Trade Talks

Recognizing the likelihood of a veto, supporters of the bill had a secondary reason for pushing it. They wanted to pressure U.S. negotiators at the GATT talks in Geneva to provide ample protection for the U.S. textile industry.

U.S. negotiators in the talks had proposed phasing out the bilateral agreements under the MFA over a 10-year period. Developing countries participating in the talks had set removal of the MFA import restrictions as a major goal, and the United States wanted other important concessions from these countries.

"The mood of negotiations ... is to sacrifice away the textile industry," said Marilyn Lloyd, D-Tenn., chief sponsor of the House textile bill.

A strong vote for the textile bill, supporters reasoned, would warn the negotiating team about the difficulty of winning congressional approval for legislation needed to put a trade barrier reduction agreement into effect.

"We've established an overwhelming majority against ending quotas," said Jenkins. "They'll have a hard time getting implementing legislation through here."

Using the textile bill as a lever on international trade talks was not a new idea. In 1986, the House vote to override Reagan's veto of a similar textile import-quota bill was delayed and timed to coincide with negotiations to extend the MFA.

Opponents of the textile bill complained that its enactment would jeopardize the GATT talks. "There's a cheaper way to send a signal than this bill," said Gibbons.

PRESIDENT'S VETO

Bush's anticipated veto came Oct. 5 with a strongly worded message saying the bill "would damage the national economy, increase already artificially high costs to consumers ... and abrogate our international agreements." He also said it would "eliminate any hope" of a successful completion of the trade talks in Geneva and added that the measure would particularly hurt two countries, Turkey and Egypt, that were providing important support for U.S. policy in the Persian Gulf crisis. *(Gulf crisis, p. 717)*

When the House debated overriding the veto Oct. 10, the arguments again pitted the interests of textile workers against consumers at large.

"These people don't care about economic indicators," said quota supporter Beverly B. Byron, D-Md., of her constituent workers. "They care about whether they can put food on the table."

"Those who object to paying a penny more a gallon for gasoline don't mind paying hundreds of billions of dollars to protect an industry that's doing just fine by itself," complained Frenzel.

Quota supporters picked up four more votes than they had when the House originally passed the bill, but that was not enough. Solid Democratic support for the bill (206-49) was offset by relatively strong Republican backing for Bush (103-49), leaving quota supporters 10 votes short of the two-thirds majority they needed to override the veto. ■

Better Data on Foreign Investment Sought

After years of fighting over the notion of collecting information from foreign owners of U.S. businesses and broadly disclosing that data, Congress in 1990 took a new tack, focusing on legislation seeking to better analyze existing data collected by a variety of federal agencies.

With broad bipartisan support, the House cleared the bill by voice vote Oct. 23. The Senate passed the bill, incorporating negotiated amendments, by voice vote in the early hours of Oct. 19 (session of Oct. 18).

President Bush signed the bill (S 2516 — PL 101-533) on Nov. 7.

The measure required the Commerce Department to report on the extent of foreign ownership of U.S. businesses and to compare those companies' employment, investment and other activities with their U.S.-owned counterparts.

It did not require foreign-owned companies to file any new data, nor would it allow any proprietary information that was confidential to be disclosed publicly. And the bill increased the fines and jail terms that could be imposed for disclosure of confidential information or for failure to provide accurate data to the Bureau of Economic Analysis (BEA).

The effort was aided by an administration shift away from opposition to any foreign investment bill to support for the idea of data sharing between the Census Bureau, which maintained confidential plant-by-plant information, and the BEA, charged with analyzing foreign investment in the United States. The two Commerce Department bureaus would have access to each other's information and would use the shared data to compile detailed annual reports of foreign-owned U.S. businesses.

In addition, employment data from the Labor Department's Bureau of Labor Statistics (BLS) would be incorporated, and the General Accounting Office (GAO) would have access to Census Bureau and BEA data so that it could critique the annual Commerce Department report and make recommendations for improvements in data collection and analysis.

Versions of the bill were reported by the Senate Commerce Committee and the House Energy and Commerce and Foreign Affairs committees. At each step, members and aides said, the measure was adjusted in consultation with the administration.

The version approved by House Foreign Affairs was substituted on the Senate floor for the text of S 2516, and it was that bill that passed.

BACKGROUND

The demand for more and better data on foreign ownership stemmed from the rapid rise in overseas capital flowing into the United States in the 1980s. Foreign direct investment — defined as a 10 percent or greater ownership interest in a U.S. business — doubled between 1984 and 1988, according to the BEA.

From 1980 through 1989, total foreign ownership of U.S. assets quadrupled — from $501 billion to just under $2 trillion. Of that, foreign controlling interest in U.S. businesses and real estate increased to $390 billion from $83 billion.

"It matters a great deal who owns businesses, assets and technologies," said Jim Exon, D-Neb., sponsor of the Senate bill and a leading critic of foreign investment. "American economic policy must be concerned about the creation of American wealth and international economic leadership, as well as the creation of American jobs."

With controlling-interest holdings worth $102 billion in 1988, Britain remained the largest single investor, according to the Commerce Department. But it was Japanese investments that seized public attention.

The rate of increase in Japanese investments was almost twice that of Britain's. And in 1988 Japan moved into second place among all countries, with more than $53 billion invested in control of U.S. assets.

Japan's economic might frightened many in the United States, at a time when international economic competition appeared to be overtaking national security concerns.

"You can't confuse the meaning of the sale of Rockefeller Center or Columbia Pictures, or today, Southland Corp. . . . to the Japanese," said Rep. John Bryant, D-Texas, who was among the most outspoken congressional critics of U.S. policy toward foreign investors. "Everybody knows what that means and everybody's immediately uncomfortable about it."

Public opinion polls seemed to reinforce Bryant's views. A Wall Street Journal/NBC News poll in January 1990 showed that 58 percent of those surveyed would favor laws restricting foreign investment. A February 1989 Gallup Poll for the Los Angeles Times found that 70 percent believed foreign investment was bad for the U.S. economy. And the same month, eight out of 10 respondents to a Washington Post/ABC News poll said limits should be placed on Japanese ownership of U.S. businesses.

Strong public sentiment was not necessarily enough, however. Similar support in 1987 and 1988 was sufficient to push foreign investment data-collection bills through the House, but not the Senate, where the measures died.

Although the House twice supported bills sponsored by Bryant in 1987 and 1988, the only foreign investment provisions to become law in that period was language in the 1988 omnibus trade bill granting the president authority to restrict takeovers on narrow national security grounds. *(Foreign investment, 1988 Almanac, p. 218)*

Pros and Cons

Bryant continued his effort in the 101st Congress. But, in 1990, the Bush administration and a bipartisan coalition of House members and senators maneuvered around him. Together, they promoted bills aimed at refining and better analyzing existing data, collected by 16 government agencies. S 2516 was designed to improve the coordination of the data-collection effort.

Many labor unions, which complained that foreign investors stifled efforts to organize workers in their plants, supported disclosure bills as a minimum step. And some industries — particularly auto-parts makers — favored increased disclosure.

Rep. Nancy L. Johnson, R-Conn., a cosponsor of a House bill, said that Commerce Department data lumped automakers and parts manufacturers together in one investment category.

"It's ludicrous for the nation not to distinguish between automobiles and auto parts," she said, noting that the parts industry relied on Japanese data to know the extent of Japanese imports and U.S. investment in that industry.

Other industries that had a greater international base, such as chemical manufacturers, strongly resisted any restraint on foreign investment.

Among the most compelling arguments made by economists — notably Federal Reserve Chairman Alan Greenspan — in favor of investment was that foreigners owned but a small fraction of total U.S. assets, that they provided jobs and that they supplied capital to cover the federal budget deficit.

That view was important because it was the one espoused by the White House.

"I welcome Japanese investment in this country. You know why? Jobs. American jobs," Bush told a March 3 news conference.

Opponents of foreign investment bills, including two successive Republican administrations, argued that they would drive away capital needed both for domestic economic growth and for financing the budget deficit. That, in turn, would push up interest rates.

Even collecting data cost money, and the threat of disclosure of confidential information would have a chilling effect, critics said.

During the Reagan administration, the government flatly opposed Bryant's efforts to require more collection and dissemination of data on foreign control of U.S. companies.

Bush administration officials, however, finally agreed that policy-makers could use better information on foreign ownership.

"As extensive as the U.S. foreign investment data-collection efforts already are, it has generally been conceded that room exists for improvement, principally with regard to the level of industrial detail," Commerce Under Secretary Michael R. Darby told the House Energy and Commerce Subcommittee on Competitiveness on June 13.

Provisions

As cleared, S 2516:

• **Commerce Department reports.** Required the Commerce Department to report to Congress within six months of enactment and annually thereafter on the scope, history, economic impact and trends in foreign ownership of U.S. businesses.

The Commerce Department was required to analyze existing data by industry classification and region and to compare foreign businesses with their U.S.-owned counterparts in terms of their employment, market share, productivity, exports and imports, profitability, taxes paid, and investment incentives and services provided by state and local governments.

• **Data sharing.** Required that information for the annual reports be drawn from existing sources of foreign investment data, including the Commerce Department's BEA and Census Bureau, the BLS, the Agriculture Department, the Internal Revenue Service (IRS), the Energy Department, foreign governments and private sources.

The bill specifically authorized the BEA and the Census Bureau to exchange their individually collected confidential information; such sharing was previously prohibited by law.

• **Confidentiality.** Required generally that data shared among agencies be protected so as not to disclose facts about specific foreign or domestic persons or businesses.

Unlawful disclosure of confidential information was subject to fines of between $2,500 and $25,000 and prison terms of up to five years. The same penalties could be imposed on persons who used fraud to obtain confidential data.

The bill also imposed fines of between $2,500 and $25,000 on foreign-owned businesses that failed to file timely or accurate disclosure reports.

• **GAO reports.** Required the GAO to assess the annual Commerce Department report and to suggest improvements to its data collection and analysis.

The bill allowed the GAO access to the same data that was used in preparing the report.

• **Foreign government ownership.** Required that the BEA's data collection and analysis under existing law be expanded to include information on U.S. businesses and real estate in which foreign governments owned at least a 50 percent share. Existing practices did not require specific data collection or analysis of foreign government ownership — as distinct from ownership by any foreign interest.

• **Foreign ownership controls.** Authorized the interagency Committee on Foreign Investment in the United States (CFIUS) to request aggregate foreign ownership data from the BEA, including data on foreign government ownership. The requested data had to be provided within 14 days when the CFIUS was investigating a particular foreign purchase. Under existing law, the CFIUS recommended to the president whether the foreign purchase of a U.S. business should be stopped on national security grounds.

LEGISLATIVE ACTION

A number of approaches were tried in 1990 on Capitol Hill to get a handle on the growth of foreign investment.

The narrowest approach was embodied in an administration-drafted bill, introduced in April in the House by Norman F. Lent, R-N.Y., and in the Senate by Exon (HR 4608, S 2516). It sought only to improve the analysis of existing data and was the measure eventually enacted.

Bryant and Sen. Tom Harkin, D-Iowa, sponsored somewhat broader measures (HR 5, S 289) to impose a new regimen of data collection on foreign ownership. They argued that existing information was insufficient and too scattered.

Rep. Philip R. Sharp, D-Ind., and Sen. Frank H. Murkowski, R-Alaska, argued that existing data in the hands of the BEA and the Census Bureau was more than adequate, except that existing law forbade the two Commerce Department agencies to share their files. Their bills (HR 4060, S 856) would have ended that ban.

Sharp, joined by Lee H. Hamilton, D-Ind., and Connecticut Republican Johnson, also had a bill (HR 4520) to allow broader disclosure of data on foreign investment.

Another bill (HR 4308) sponsored by House Ways and Means Chairman Dan Rostenkowski, D-Ill., would have given the IRS additional data-collection tools to capture what many believed to be billions of dollars in unpaid taxes by U.S. branches and subsidiaries of foreign firms.

Rep. Tom Campbell, R-Calif., introduced HR 3699 to require the United States to treat a foreign investor in the same way that U.S. investors were treated in the foreigner's home country. According to the Office of the U.S. Trade Representative, most industrialized countries restricted foreign investment to some degree.

Bryant also advocated reciprocity in foreign investment rules, but he dropped such a provision from an earlier version of his bill to make it more palatable.

Senate Committee Action

The Senate Commerce Committee on July 31 by voice vote approved S 2516, the administration-backed bill intended to improve federal data collection on foreign investments. The bill had become a less-sweeping alternative to the measures (S 856, HR 4520) being pushed by Murkowski and Sharp.

Before approving Exon's bill (S Rept 101-443), the Commerce Committee adopted language adapted from Murkowski's measure to allow some further use of foreign investment data.

The Murkowski language, which was watered down from S 856, would have allowed the CFIUS to request information from the Bureau of Economic Analysis on the extent of foreign government purchases of U.S. businesses.

The interagency committee CFIUS was charged under a provision of the 1988 omnibus trade bill with recommending to the president whether foreign acquisitions of U.S. businesses were a threat to national security. The president was authorized to halt such investments but rarely did so.

Supporters of a stronger federal posture on foreign investments considered the Senate committee action modest at best.

Sharp's bill would have gone further than the Exon measure as approved by the Senate committee in allowing the Census Bureau and BEA to share data with each other and with the CFIUS. Sharp would also have given the GAO access to foreign investment data and required some reporting to Congress about investment trends.

House Energy and Commerce Committee

The Energy and Commerce Subcommittee on Commerce by voice vote on Sept. 18 approved a bipartisan compromise intended to improve the collection of data on foreign investment in the United States. The subcommittee sent HR 4520 on for full committee consideration.

HR 4520 would have required annual reports by the Commerce Department to Congress detailing the extent and effects of foreign investment in the United States, broken down by industry and region. It would also have given the GAO some access to the department's data. The GAO would be charged with recommending improvements to the department's data-collection and analysis efforts.

During the subcommittee markup, Sharp and Norman F. Lent, R-N.Y., offered a comprehensive substitute to the bill that dropped one of its most contentious provisions.

Sharp had wanted to allow the Census Bureau and the BEA to share data with the CFIUS. This Treasury-led interagency committee recommended to the president whether particular foreign takeovers of U.S. businesses should be blocked on national security grounds. The Sharp-Lent compromise dropped that section from the bill, and supporters said that removed administration opposition.

The companion Senate bill did not allow such broad sharing of data with the CFIUS, but it did allow the interagency committee to request data from the BEA, a provision to which the administration reportedly did not object.

The full House Energy and Commerce Committee approved the subcommittee's version of HR 4520 on Oct. 2 (H Rept 101-855, Part II).

House Foreign Affairs Committee

HR 4520, calling on the Commerce Department to gather information and make annual reports on foreign investment in the United States won voice vote approval from a House Foreign Affairs subcommittee on Oct. 3.

The bill, approved by the International Economic Policy and Trade Subcommittee, would have required the publication of detailed statistics on foreign firms with operations in the United States and called for a more coordinated process for gathering the information.

The secretary of Commerce would have been required to issue an annual report comparing the employment, wages, research and development, and capital investments of U.S. firms and foreign firms based in the United States.

Commerce would have better access to the foreign investment data needed for the report. The measure would have authorized an information exchange between the BEA and other agencies, notably, the Census Bureau.

The full committee approved HR 4520 on Oct. 11 by voice vote (H Rept 101-855, Part I).

Final Action

Action by the two House committees set the stage for final negotiations on a measure acceptable to both the House and Senate and to the administration.

An agreed on bill went first to the Senate, which approved it by voice vote in the early morning hours of Oct. 19 (session of Oct. 18). The House cleared the measure for the president, also by voice vote, on Oct. 23.

"This is a tough bill that will give us exactly what members of Congress and their constituents have been seeking for years: accurate, timely and useful information," said House sponsor Johnson.

But in signing the bill Nov. 7, Bush was more cautious. He stressed that it imposed no additional reporting requirements on businesses and contained "significant safeguards to protect the confidentiality of sensitive business information." ■

CQ

Chapter 4

ENVIRONMENT & ENERGY

Clean Air Act Amendments ... 229
Clean Air Deadlines ... 231
Motor Vehicles ... 233
Urban Smog ... 235
Acid Rain ... 237
Alternative Fuels ... 240
Clean Air Provisions ... 248
Assistance for Displaced Workers ... 277
Fuel Economy Standards ... 279
Octane-Labeling Bill ... 282
Oil Spill Liability ... 283
Environmental Crimes ... 285
Pipeline Inspection ... 286
Coastal Zone Management ... 288
Coastal, Great Lakes Cleanup ... 289
Beach Pollution Bill ... 290
EPA Cabinet Status ... 291
EPA Investigators ... 292
Office of Environmental Education ... 293
Tongass National Forest ... 294
Timber, Northern Spotted Owl ... 296
Water Resources Act ... 297
New Projects ... 299
Grand Canyon Erosion Control ... 300
Great Lakes Cleanup ... 301
Barrier Islands Protection ... 302
Florida Keys Protection ... 303
Zebra Mussels Control Program ... 303
Arizona Wilderness Protection ... 304
Antarctica Mining Ban ... 305
Global Warming ... 307
Waste Laws Compliance ... 308
Stello Energy Nomination ... 309
Uranium Enrichment Spinoff ... 310
NRC Operating Costs ... 311
Energy Issues in 1990 ... 312
Energy-Related Tax Proposals ... 313
Strategic Petroleum Reserve ... 314
Arctic National Wildlife Refuge ... 315
Oil-Shale Lands Bill ... 316
Alternative Power ... 317
Hydrogen Fuel Research Program ... 318
Energy Conservation, Efficiency ... 319

Clean Air Act Rewritten, Tightened

Stricter controls enacted on smog, cars, acid rain

After more than a decade of political stalemate over the nation's clean air laws, the Senate on Oct. 27 cleared sweeping legislation to impose stricter federal standards on urban smog, automobile exhaust, toxic air pollution and acid rain.

The overwhelming approval in the Senate, one day after passage by an even stronger vote in the House, capped nearly two full years of work by the 101st Congress and the Bush administration to strengthen the main federal law aimed at reducing air pollution.

Previous efforts to revise and extend the 1977 Clean Air Act (PL 95-95) had been bottled up since at least 1981. But President Bush spurred the legislation forward by proposing a clean air package on June 12, 1989 — a marked shift from his predecessor, Ronald Reagan, who had opposed efforts to strengthen the law. *(1989 Almanac, p. 665)*

BOXSCORE

Legislation: Clean Air Act Amendments, PL 101-549 (S 1630).

Major action: Signed, Nov. 15. Conference report adopted by Senate, 89-10, Oct. 27; by House, 401-25, Oct. 26. HR 3030 passed by House, 401-21, May 23; S 1630 passed by Senate, 89-11, April 3.

Reports: Conference report (H Rept 101-952); Energy and Commerce (H Rept 101-490, Part I); Ways and Means (Part II); Public Works and Transportation (Part III); Environment and Public Works (S Rept 101-228).

The Senate Environment and Public Works Committee had originally approved its bill (S 1630) on Nov. 16, 1989, but that version was substantially rewritten on the Senate floor after extensive negotiations with the administration. Senate passage of the modified bill — less pleasing to environmental groups than the original — came on April 3.

House Energy and Commerce subcommittees had begun work in 1989 on the administration's proposal — introduced as HR 3030 by Energy Committee Chairman John D. Dingell, D-Mich. — but progress stalled at the end of the year because of interregional disputes over how to reduce acid rain and who should pay for doing so.

When work resumed in 1990, marathon markup sessions ended with a committee-approved bill on April 5 that went on to win House approval May 23.

House and Senate conferees spent the summer and early fall working out a compromise version. Most of the negotiations were conducted in private at the staff level, with conferees convening formally only to ratify agreements on individual titles of the bill. Conferees completed action on Oct. 22 after yet another in a series of all-night bargaining sessions.

Four Main Titles

Like the original Senate and House bills, the final version was divided into four main titles, dealing with attainment and maintenance of air quality standards (smog); motor vehicles and alternative fuels; toxic air pollutants; and acid deposition (acid rain). Other titles outlined permit and enforcement requirements and provisions for phasing out chemicals that contributed to the depletion of the ozone layer. *(Deadlines, p. 231; provisions, p. 248)*

As enacted, the bill included the following agreements:

- **Motor vehicles and fuels.** The agreement to tighten controls on automobiles and gasoline required automakers to install new pollution controls to reduce emissions of hydrocarbons and nitrogen oxides. The equipment had to last 10 years or 100,000 miles, twice as long as under existing law. The Environmental Protection Agency (EPA) could impose stricter tailpipe standards beginning in 2003.

In cities where high carbon monoxide levels were due to car exhaust, controls had to be installed to cut the increased carbon monoxide emitted by automobiles in cold weather. In a last-minute concession for the administration and auto lobbyists, conferees knocked the cold-start requirement back one year, to 2001. *(Motor vehicles summary, p. 233)*

To reduce ozone-forming emissions, only reformulated fuel could be sold in the nine smoggiest cities. Areas with high levels of carbon monoxide had to offer fuel blended with the oxygenators methanol, which was made from natural gas, or ethanol, which came from corn. The California pilot program would eventually require auto companies to produce 300,000 clean-fueled vehicles a year. Taxis and other centrally fueled vehicles had to use that new California technology to cut their emissions by 80 percent. *(Alternative fuels, p. 240)*

- **Urban smog.** Language to clean up polluted cities and suburbs established five categories of so-called "ozone nonattainment" areas and set deadlines for them to meet federal air quality standards. That required new antismog equipment for a slew of industries ranging from large industrial facilities to gas stations. *(Smog summary, p. 235)*
- **Air toxics.** Plants that emitted any of 189 toxic substances had to cut those emissions to the average level of the 12 cleanest similar facilities. Plants would have to shut down if they still posed more than a 1-in-10,000 risk of cancer to nearby residents by 2003, after the best available technology was installed. An extension until 2020 was granted to steel industry coke ovens if they met certain interim conditions. *(Air toxics table, p. 255)*
- **Acid rain.** This agreement overcame years of stalemate between regions where acid rain-causing pollutants rose from towering smokestacks and where acid rain fell on trees, mountains and streams. Coal-burning utilities were the main sources of sulfur dioxide and nitrogen oxide emissions, which caused acid rain. Those pollutants reacted in the atmosphere to form tiny acidic particles that could remain airborne for hundreds of miles before being washed out of the atmosphere by rains.

In Congress, compromise had been elusive because any control strategy had to balance the needs of two broad camps. On one side were "clean states" — those with utilities that burned less polluting, low-sulfur coal, or that had installed "scrubbers" or other pollution control devices. On the other side were "dirty states," mostly in the Midwest, that mined and burned high-sulfur coal.

The "cleans" wanted to be given credit for earlier emissions reductions and be able to expand their electric utility capacity, if needed, without busting tight emissions caps. They also did not want to pay for the Midwest's cleanup. The "dirties" wanted to preserve jobs for high-sulfur coal miners in the Midwest and Appalachian states. They also wanted cost-sharing among states to keep the cleanup from further depressing Midwest economies.

Acid rain legislation in previous years had involved such a cost-sharing component, but Bush opposed that approach, calling it a form of taxation. Instead, his bill put forth a market-based system of pollution "allowances" that could be granted to utilities that limited sulfur dioxide emissions. That proposal became the key ingredient in political trade-offs that eventually cemented an acid rain agreement. *(Acid rain summary, p. 237)*

- **Chlorofluorocarbons.** Chemicals that harmed the Earth's protective ozone layer had to be phased out more rapidly than under the Montreal protocol, an international agreement signed by the United States.

BACKGROUND

A comprehensive reauthorization and overhaul of the Clean Air Act, the nation's most complex and far-reaching pollution-control law, had been overdue since 1982. The law was enacted in 1970 (PL 91-604) and amended significantly in 1977 (PL 95-95). *(Congress and the Nation Vol. III, p. 757; 1977 Almanac, p. 627)*

The law required that states enact pollution controls sufficient to meet federal air-quality standards and protect public health. But by 1990, most urban areas still violated air-quality standards for ozone — which was caused largely by pollutants from industrial facilities, chemical plants and motor vehicles — and carbon monoxide, which came primarily from automobiles.

The EPA had authority to impose sanctions on states, such as bans on the construction of large new pollution sources or cutoffs in federal highway funds, but it rarely used that power.

The Clean Air Act had also largely failed to limit industrial emissions of air toxics — hazardous pollutants such as benzene that caused cancer, neurological disorders or other serious ailments, even when emitted at relatively low concentrations. Since 1970, EPA had brought only seven of some 275 industrial air toxics under federal regulation.

Few argued against the value of clean air, but the potential price in lost jobs and increased costs to industry and consumers left Congress intractably divided for a decade. Although environmentalists had insisted they had the needed votes on the floor, the Reagan administration's lack of interest in new regulation strengthened the hand of key obstructionists in the House and Senate.

Chief among them was auto industry ally Dingell, who used his House Energy and Commerce Committee chairmanship to stall any bills that would impose tough new standards on Detroit automakers.

In the Senate, Robert C. Byrd of West Virginia, who served as Democratic leader from 1977 to 1989, discouraged action because of fear that acid rain proposals would throw coal miners out of work by destroying the market for high-sulfur coal mined in his home state.

Underlying their opposition were seemingly endless parochial divisions: Midwesterners, for example, opposed acid rain bills year after year because of the heavy cost to coal-burning utilities in their states. California and other states sought controls on emissions from offshore oil drilling, but states bordering the Gulf of Mexico would have none of such proposals. (In fact, the conference agreement on the 1990 act exempted Texas, Louisiana, Mississippi and Alabama from such controls.)

The Clean Air Act required the EPA to establish safe concentrations for seven major air pollutants and set a 1975 deadline for states to meet those standards. When it appeared most states would not meet the deadline, Congress extended it to 1982, or, for areas with severe auto-related pollution, to 1987. *(Clean Air Act summary, 1981 Almanac, p. 425)*

After legislation again failed to clear in 1987, Congress decided to address the issue in the middle of the 1988 election campaign by extending the deadline when cities would face penalties for failing to meet existing air-quality standards. But even with an election-year deadline, various clean air measures proposed during 1988 failed to make it to the floor of either the House or the Senate. Finally, Sen. George J. Mitchell, D-Maine, the leader of a months-long search for a compromise bill, conceded defeat in October in a charged Senate floor speech. *(1988 Almanac, p. 142)*

Mitchell's bill was blocked for almost a year by then-Majority Leader Byrd, who controlled the Senate's floor schedule. In the House, clean air legislation in the Energy and Commerce Committee had been slowed by various members, most notably Chairman Dingell. But even Henry A. Waxman, D-Calif., a longtime advocate for tougher clean air laws, played a role in delaying legislation when it appeared he might get a stricter bill in the next Congress.

New Dynamic in 1989

Clean air legislation got a boost in 1989 when President Bush not only supported the rewrite, but also offered his own comprehensive proposal.

For most of the eight previous years, proponents of clean air legislation had faced off with President Reagan over toughening federal controls on air pollution. His opposition, combined with regional divisions over acid rain regulation and disputes between industry and environmentalist forces, had effectively blocked clean air bills.

In 1989, new concerns about the environment, fed by reports of a hole in the protective ozone layer and global warming, added urgency to the drive for legislation.

Bush's introduction of a clean air bill in June 1989 changed that political dynamic almost overnight. It did not resolve regional conflicts, but it forced key players to sit down and deal. Within a year after he presented his clean air bill, members of the House and Senate had struggled through often bitter and prolonged fights to produce bills that had far more similarities than differences.

Another important change was Mitchell's ascension as Senate majority leader, succeeding Byrd, who retired from the leadership post but remained powerful as chairman of the Appropriations Committee.

Under pressure from Mitchell, the Senate Environment and Public Works Committee agreed to a package (S 1630) of measures to reduce smog, acid rain and toxic air pollution. Mitchell and his generally pro-environment allies on the panel brushed aside complaints about excessive speed and on Nov. 16, 1989, pushed a massive anti-pollution package through the committee in a single day's markup.

Mitchell then vowed to make S 1630 the Senate's first

order of business when Congress reconvened in 1990.

Meanwhile, the House Energy Subcommittee on Health and the Environment on Oct. 11, 1989, approved HR 3030 after markup sessions that included adoption of a dramatic agreement on provisions governing auto emissions between Dingell and subcommittee Chairman Waxman, longtime adversaries on the issue.

But the House bill then stalled in the Energy Subcommittee on Energy and Power, which had jurisdiction over provisions on acid rain and alternative fuels. At year's end the bill remained in subcommittee with pressure building for the full Energy Committee to act.

The session ended with the Senate poised to take up a bill and pressure building in the House for action. *(1989 Almanac, p. 665)*

SENATE FLOOR ACTION

The bill that won overwhelming 89-11 approval on the Senate floor April 3 was a far cry from the measure that Mitchell had made the first order of Senate business in 1990. The bill was changed markedly, mostly away from environmentalists' positions. But the environmentalist coalition lobbying for the bill pronounced the Senate's action a major step forward and hoped to recover some of the lost ground in the House. *(Senate vote 324, p. 63-S)*

Initial Floor Action

As promised, Mitchell had brought S 1630 to the floor when the Senate reconvened Jan. 23. But the hope that the bill might clear Congress in time for Bush to sign it by Earth Day in April evaporated quickly.

The bill reported on Nov. 16, 1989, by the Senate Environment Committee was the most stringent measure in play — far more restrictive in many respects than the corresponding House bill (HR 3030) or the original White House proposal.

Moreover, the speedy, one-day markup and 15-1 approval by the Environment Committee prompted complaints that important issues had been left unresolved and many viewpoints left unconsidered. Lobbyists worked the Senate office corridors during the Christmas recess to try to make sure floor action was more deliberate.

Early skirmishing on the bill centered on disagreements about how much it would cost. Critics insisted it was too expensive; advocates countered that its costs would be more than offset by savings in the costs of health care and other expenses people incurred because of pollution.

Mitchell had vowed to keep the bill on the floor until it was finished. Yet debate abruptly ended by the second week, as key senators and Bush administration officials vanished behind closed doors to seek out compromises on the most contentious sections of the legislation.

The sudden disappearance of the debate's key players from the Senate floor came after several days of sporadic speechmaking that yielded only a single roll call vote on a relatively minor provision. The big issues that threatened to split the Senate — acid rain cost-sharing, motor vehicle emissions controls and health standards for toxic air pollutants — seemed to be little closer to resolution than they were when the Senate took up the measure Jan. 23.

The bill's managers appeared to be unsure of where the votes lay on those critical provisions, and they also appeared to be fearful of what environmental lobbyists asserted was a filibuster threat orchestrated by the Bush administration. After a day of no substantive floor action Feb. 1, Mitchell emerged from the talks to pronounce them "productive and reassuring of the good faith of all parties to reach agreement." Mitchell then pulled the bill off the floor to allow time for the negotiations.

The White House, along with industry and Senate critics, had mounted a heavy assault on the Senate bill, which was much stricter in several important areas than the one proposed by Bush (S 1490). The EPA had charged that the Senate bill would be more than twice as costly as the Bush bill ($41.9 billion vs. $18.9 billion a year), and Bush had threatened to veto any bill with a cost more than 10 percent higher than his. The bill's backers said that the EPA cost estimate was wildly exaggerated.

The unexpected shutdown of debate prompted environmentalists to sharply criticize Bush and his Senate allies

Clean Air Deadlines

Cities and Towns

1993: "Marginal" areas to reach ozone standard (39 cities).
1996: Deadline for "moderate" non-attainment areas (32 cities).
1999: Deadline for "serious" areas (16 cities).
2005-07: Deadline for "severe" areas (8 cities).
2010: Deadline for "extreme" areas (Los Angeles).

Cars, Trucks and Buses

Model Year 1994: 60% less nitrogen oxide; 35% less hydrocarbons.
MY 1998: Cars to be equipped with emission control systems with "useful life" of 10 years or 100,000 miles.
MY 2003: Stage Two tailpipe standards to go into effect subject to EPA veto.

Motor Fuels

1992: Cities with CO_2 non-attainment to use gasoline with 2.7% oxygen, unless EPA delayed standard.
1995: Nine smoggiest cities to sell only reformulated gasoline. Volatile organic compounds (VOCs) and toxic emissions to be cut 15%.
1996: 150,000 "clean fueled" vehicles to be sold in California.
1998: Fleet program required 80% emissions cut for cars and 50% cut for trucks.

Utilities

1995: 111 dirtiest coal-fired plants to cut SO_2 emissions.
2000: Annual SO_2 emissions limited to 10 million tons.

Other Industries

1995: EPA to regulate 90% of 30 most serious toxic pollutants emitted by dry cleaners, gas stations and other "area" sources. Cancer risks to be reduced 75%.
2003: Major sources (chemical plants, oil refineries, etc.) to apply best available technology to reduce emissions of 189 toxic chemicals by the average of the 12 cleanest similar plants. "Residual" cancer risk to most exposed persons to be reduced to 1-in-10,000.
2020: Extended "residual risk" deadline for coke ovens, which had to meet tougher interim standards.

for what they viewed as an attempt to weaken the bill by holding the chamber hostage to a filibuster threat.

"This is a pivotal point in this administration's role in this legislation," said Richard Ayres, chairman of the National Clean Air Coalition, the umbrella environmentalist group lobbying the bill. "Sadly, when the need for leadership is greatest, Mr. Bush has abandoned his commitment to clean air for all Americans."

Ayres said environmentalists' tallies showed that backers of the Senate bill would prevail on floor fights, but might be short of the 60 votes needed to thwart a filibuster.

Negotiated Agreement

Senate and White House negotiators emerged from a month of backroom talks March 1 with a clean air agreement that disappointed environmentalists, heartened industry and appeared to have pacified enough filibuster-prone senators to ensure passage.

The proposed substitute, which substantially moderated the Environment Committee bill, was unveiled at a lunch-hour news conference attended by more than a dozen senators and top Bush administration officials. Senate leaders and White House officials presented a united front in support of the measure, saying it was an aggressive improvement over existing law that also met White House objections to the projected cost of the committee bill.

"The president is extraordinarily pleased with this agreement," said Roger B. Porter, White House assistant for domestic and economic affairs and leader of the Bush negotiating team.

Mitchell said the measure "dramatically expands and strengthens" current clean air law. Minority Leader Bob Dole, R-Kan., called the package "the single most important piece of legislation we'll deal with this year" and pledged to join Mitchell and other backers of the deal in efforts to fight off any significant amendments.

The marathon closed-door talks between a bipartisan "Group of 15" and White House officials resulted in major changes to bill provisions on toxic air pollutants, motor vehicle emissions, acid rain and urban smog.

In some cases, negotiators compromised by retaining strict second-round emissions standards but at the same time providing less stringent alternatives or making imposition of the standards conditional on progress under other sections of the bill. Second-round auto emissions standards, for example, would go into effect nationwide only if a minimum number of smoggy cities remained unacceptably polluted after 10 years of cleanup under the bill's urban-smog provisions.

The resulting compromise steered something of a middle course between the committee measure, which was favored by environmentalists, and the original Bush proposal, which business and industry found more tolerable. With backing from the Senate leadership, the White House and an apparent majority of the Environment Committee, the substitute was expected to be very difficult to amend in any significant way on the floor.

Details of Substitute Bill

Key changes to S 1630:

- **Motor vehicles.** The substitute moderated the first and second phases of the bill's motor vehicle emissions limits. Instead of imposing first-round limits all at once in 1993, the substitute phased them in, beginning with 40 percent of vehicles sold in 1993, rising to 100 percent of vehicles sold in 1995.

Even stricter second-round restrictions, which were to be imposed unconditionally in 2003, would instead be imposed nationwide (after Oct. 1, 2003) only if at least 12 of the nation's 27 most polluted urban areas continued to violate health standards at the end of 2001.

- **Air toxics.** The substitute mandated a study of the best way to assess the health risk remaining after first-round, maximum achievable control technology was installed on major sources of toxics such as refineries, chemical plants and coke ovens. A new panel could recommend a different health-risk policy, but Congress would have to vote to agree.

Otherwise, the substitute retained the committee bill's second-round limit on cancer risks posed by emissions from major pollution sources — no more than one additional cancer case per 10,000 population. But the substitute provided a new alternative: Instead of meeting a risk test for a hypothetical "most-exposed individual," a pollution source could subject itself to a site-specific, "actual man" test to assess risk to public health in the vicinity. In addition, coke ovens that installed maximum achievable control technology before 1995 would be given an extension to 2020 to begin meeting the 1-in-10,000 risk test.

- **Acid rain.** The substitute retained most major features of the committee bill, which focused sulfur dioxide (SO_2) cleanup requirements on the 107 largest coal-fired utilities. The substitute increased the number to 111 but added provisions encouraging them to use scrubbers so they could continue burning high-sulfur coal.

Coal-fired utility plants that used technology such as scrubbers to reduce SO_2 emissions by the Phase I deadline (1995) could either get an extra two years to meet the restrictions or receive bonus pollution allowances for reductions made between 1995 and 1997. As in the committee bill, utilities could sell those allowances to generate cash to defray the cost of installing scrubbers.

Plants using scrubbers would receive 2-ton pollution allowances for every ton of SO_2 reduced during Phase I that went beyond their Phase II (2000) target. Bonus allowances would be given to "clean states" that had already reduced SO_2 emissions, thus allowing some utility growth.

- **Alternative fuels.** The substitute added a section to require use of alternative fuels in the nation's nine most polluted urban areas. Phase I required all new cars in those areas to meet tight new emissions standards beginning in model year 1995 — most likely by burning reformulated gasoline, rather than methanol, ethanol or other alternatives. Phase II further tightened the emissions standard beginning in model year 1999 and was expected to require changes in the design of the cars themselves.

In addition, a fleet program targeted federally owned fleet vehicles (beginning in 1995) and then privately owned fleets (1997) for even stricter reductions.

- **Global warming.** The substitute dropped the committee bill's plan to enlist motor vehicles in the fight against global warming. The bill would have set carbon dioxide limits roughly equal to 33 miles per gallon (mpg) for the 1996-99 model years and 40 mpg in the year 2000.

Reaction to Substitute

Senate clean air negotiators also came away with a vital no-filibuster pledge from Byrd, long a bitter foe of any acid rain provisions that might force utilities to quit burning the high-sulfur coal mined in his state.

Byrd persuaded other members of the negotiating group to give Midwestern utilities extra compliance time and additional, salable pollution "allowances" for installing scrubbers or other technological controls that helped them meet acid rain restrictions. The Byrd formula would make it more likely that utilities would continue to burn high-sulfur coal rather than switch to low-sulfur coal to meet SO_2 limits.

Though not happy enough with the substitute to back it formally, the Senate's senior Democrat uttered the words Mitchell and others long wanted to hear: "I'm not going to be engaged in any filibuster."

Environmentalists, whose expectations had been raised by the comparatively tough bill produced by the Environment Committee, were troubled when the measure disappeared behind closed doors early in February and angry about what emerged March 1. "The backroom dealing has generated bad deals for the American people," said Ayres of the National Clean Air Coalition.

Industry representatives, in contrast, were relieved to see the bill go into closed-door talks and happier with what came out than what went in. "The movement's in the right direction," said Bill Fay of the industry-funded Clean Air Working Group.

The substitute's Senate defenders preferred not to compare it with the committee bill, but rather with existing clean air law, which had remained unchanged since 1977.

"This bill is a very major improvement over current law," said Max Baucus, D-Mont., chairman of the Environment Subcommittee on Environmental Protection and the Democratic floor manager of the clean air debate.

John H. Chafee of Rhode Island, ranking Republican on Environment and a key player in the agreement, noted that he, like Baucus, would be "in the awkward situation of voting against" amendments to put back provisions that he helped put in the committee bill in the first place — but which he also helped strip out in the backroom talks.

Several senators immediately signaled they would try to amend the compromise on the floor. Tim Wirth, D-Colo., planned to offer one amendment to toughen the bill's motor-vehicle provisions, but he conceded that he faced an uphill fight. "They put us in a box," Wirth said of Mitchell's and other Senate environmentalists' agreement to oppose amendments. "It would have been hard to get 51 votes for these [types of amendments] anyway."

Floor Debate Resumes

When the bill finally returned to the Senate floor the week of March 5, Mitchell and others successfully defended the compromise against a series of "deal-buster" amendments that they said would have unraveled the Senate-White House coalition, either by strengthening or weakening the deal worked out with the White House.

Environmentalist senators tried in vain to restore some of the tough restrictions that were stripped out of the bill, while conservative senators were just as unsuccessful in their attempts to weaken provisions of the measure they said were too tough on business and industry.

Mitchell repeated an earlier promise that the Senate would "stay on this bill until we finish it."

The compromise survived two deal-buster challenges by senators trying to toughen environmental provisions.

First, Richard H. Bryan, D-Nev., agreed to withdraw an amendment to restore a modified version of a carbon dioxide (CO_2) emissions-limits provision stripped out in the negotiations. Bryan's amendment would have set corporate average fuel economy (CAFE) standards of 34 miles per gallon (mpg) by 1995 and 40 mpg by 2001.

Motor Vehicles

Following are highlights of the motor vehicle provisions of the Clean Air Act amendments:

First-round tailpipe standards. Required cut of 35 percent in hydrocarbon tailpipe emissions and 60 percent in nitrogen oxide emissions, beginning in 1994. By 1998, cars had to contain emission control equipment that would last 10 years or 100,000 miles.

Second-round tailpipe standards. Imposed a second round of tailpipe emissions standards — cutting the first-round standards by half — beginning in MY 2003, subject to veto by the Environmental Protection Agency (EPA) administrator if they were not technologically feasible, cost-effective or necessary.

Alternative fuels. Beginning in 1996, 150,000 clean-fueled vehicles had to be sold in California, rising to 300,000 in later years. Also set up a clean-fuel fleet program in polluted cities requiring an 80 percent cut in emissions for cars and a 50 percent reduction for trucks beginning in 1998. The requirement could be delayed for three years, depending on vehicle availability. Fleet cars parked at private homes at night were not covered.

Reformulated gasoline. Reformulated gasoline required in nine smoggiest cities by 1995.

Cities with carbon-dioxide non-attainment had to use gasoline containing 2.7 percent oxygen, starting in 1992. The EPA administrator could grant up to a two-year delay if an area's supply and distribution capacity was lacking.

Volatile organic compounds and toxic emissions had to decrease by 15 percent by 1995; in 2000, emissions had to decrease by 20 percent or more, up to a technologically feasible amount, taking cost into account.

Non-road vehicles. EPA required to regulate emissions within 30 months if study determined it was warranted. Railroad locomotives were not to be included in the study, and states and local governments were pre-empted from regulating new non-road engines smaller than 175 horsepower used in construction or farm equipment.

Automakers insisted the standards were wildly unrealistic and exorbitantly expensive. But Bryan and backers said the proposal was important both for fuel savings and as a first step toward controlling global warming. Mitchell persuaded Bryan to withdraw the amendment by promising that the Senate would revisit the issue later in the year. *(Fuel economy standards, p. 279)*

Later, Frank R. Lautenberg, D-N.J., sought to restore a motor-vehicles provision to a section of the bill that sought to cut cancer deaths by controlling so-called area sources of toxic air pollutants. Lautenberg said motor vehicles had been exempted from controls under this section of the bill at the insistence of White House cost-cutters, who, he said, ignored the fact that motor vehicles were responsible for more than half of all air toxics.

Baucus, a party to the White House deal, countered that there were ample controls on motor vehicles in other sections of the bill.

And he added: "The deal will be off, the deal will be

busted, and there could very well be no Clean Air Act."

The Senate agreed March 8 to table (kill) Lautenberg's amendment on a 65-33 vote. *(Vote 34, p. 9-S)*

Environmental lobbyists said the Lautenberg amendment was not a true test of their strength and predicted they would do better on other amendments their Senate allies planned to offer on other motor-vehicle, urban smog and air-toxics provisions. "No doubt [the Lautenberg amendment] was our low-water mark," said Daniel Weiss, a lobbyist for the Sierra Club. Even so, Weiss said, "Mitchell had to twist arms to keep us from breaking 40 votes."

Others were also trying to amend the compromise. Steve Symms, R-Idaho, who had emerged as the Senate's most dogged critic of what he saw as the measure's dangerously high cost to business and industry, circled around the air-toxics section of the bill throughout the week.

First, Symms offered an amendment to require a community referendum before any plant emitting air toxics could be closed down for health reasons. He withdrew that proposal for lack of votes, substituting instead a proposed prohibition on imports from any nation that did not adhere to air-toxics regulations as stringent as those the bill proposed for the United States.

GOP floor manager Chafee argued that Symms' measure would violate the deal with the White House. The amendment was killed March 8 on a tabling motion, 81-16. *(Vote 32, p. 9-S)*

Two New Proposals Accepted

Although Senate leaders agreed to no amendments that expressly violated the White House deal, the Senate did accept two new proposals in action on March 8:

- **Hydrochlorofluorocarbons (HCFCs).** Al Gore, D-Tenn., won 80-16 approval on March 8 of an amendment to phase out use of HCFCs, chemicals that would take over if, as called for in the bill, chlorofluorocarbons (CFCs) were phased out of production. Chlorine from CFCs was widely blamed for progressive destruction of the stratospheric ozone layer, which shielded life on Earth from damaging ultraviolet rays from the sun. Gore argued that HCFCs could cause almost as much damage as CFCs; his amendment proposed to freeze production levels in 2015 and end production in 2030. *(Vote 33, p. 9-S)*
- **Radionuclide emissions.** John Glenn, D-Ohio, and John Heinz, R-Pa., won approval of an amendment to delete a provision in the bill giving sole regulatory jurisdiction over air-toxics emissions from commercial nuclear facilities to the Nuclear Regulatory Commission. Glenn argued that by ending the EPA's concurrent jurisdiction, the bill also ended state authority to regulate such facilities, which he said was an unacceptable infringement on states' rights. The Senate agreed to the Glenn-Heinz amendment by voice vote after refusing to kill it on a tabling motion, 36-61. *(Vote 30, p. 9-S)*

Holding the Compromise Together

Senate environmentalists tried to toughen the Senate clean air compromise the week of March 19, but failed on two close votes to overcome leadership muscle or dispel their colleagues' fears that tinkering with the White House-approved deal might kill clean air legislation for years.

Senate leaders Mitchell and Dole, who together had pledged to defend the bipartisan substitute version of the clean air bill, managed to hold enough of their colleagues behind the deal to kill the two amendments.

Mitchell had warned senators that adoption of any of the so-called deal-breaker amendments could destroy the agreement with the White House, with dire consequences. "If we do not get a clean air bill this year, we are not going to get a clean air bill in this century," Mitchell said.

The rejected proposals would have added back some of the strict provisions on motor-vehicle emissions and urban smog that Senate negotiators had modified or dropped as part of the February deal with the White House.

The motor-vehicles amendment, which was backed by Tim Wirth, D-Colo., and Pete Wilson, R-Calif., was the first and most critical test for environmentalists; it was tabled, 52-46, on March 20. *(Vote 35, p. 10-S)*

The smog amendment, introduced by John Kerry, D-Mass., was killed, 53-46, on March 21. *(Vote 37, p. 10-S)*

When it was over, EPA Administrator William K. Reilly acknowledged relief at having dodged the political bullet. "This was very important, one of the key votes, one that we were not 100 percent confident of going in, and we're happy to have it behind us," he said.

Defeat of the two amendments was an important victory for the administration, which had taken a hard line against any provisions that would have pushed up the bill's cost. Administration officials argued that extra restrictions would add little pollution cleanup but would inflate costs enormously for business and consumers.

Mitchell and other traditional Senate environmentalists who defended the compromise contended that it was much tougher than existing clean air law and that trying to perfect it could kill it altogether.

But Wirth, Wilson, Kerry and other backers of the amendments argued the opposite — that the substitute retreated from existing law and that threats to pull down the whole bill were hollow and politically unthinkable.

Wirth-Wilson Amendment Defeated

For the environment lobby, the vote on Wirth-Wilson was a long-awaited showdown — yes or no on a get-tough amendment to the most important antipollution bill in a decade. "Key Environmental Vote of 1990!" screamed a flier from the Sierra Club, which was among those environmental groups promoting the March 20 showdown as the "Super Tuesday" of the clean air debate.

Wirth and Wilson wanted to make the bill's auto-emissions controls and clean-fuel provisions substantially tougher than the White House-Senate compromise. They wanted to require an automatic, second round of tailpipe emissions reductions in 2002 — not a conditional review as called for in the White House compromise. They also wanted to require the use of cleaner burning gasoline mixes by 1993 in all smog-heavy areas — 60 to 70 in all — not just the nine worst cities, as the compromise stipulated.

For all the frantic lobbying beforehand, however, the defeat of Wirth-Wilson appeared to be less a measure of environmentalist vs. industry muscle than of the cross-winds of clean air politics.

Farm-state members liked the Wirth-Wilson amendment because they believed it favored grain-based ethanol as an alternative clean fuel. Others went for it thinking it would help small businesses by shifting more of the pain of cleaning the air to big oil companies and automakers.

Meanwhile, normally pro-environment senators voted against the amendment, fearing that it would scuttle the still-tenuous compromise with the Bush administration.

Then again, some normally pro-industry senators voted for the Wirth-Wilson amendment — at least one hoping that it would indeed become a deal-buster.

Advocates on both sides were left shaking their heads. A lobbyist following the vote jotted down about two dozen names of members who deviated from the expected norm.

Voting for Wirth-Wilson were Republicans who rarely toed the environment lobby's line: Jesse Helms of North Carolina, James A. McClure and Symms of Idaho, Jake Garn and Orrin G. Hatch of Utah, and Malcolm Wallop of Wyoming.

Conversely, voting to table were senators who usually voted the environmentalist position, including Democrats Christopher J. Dodd of Connecticut, Paul S. Sarbanes of Maryland and Howard M. Metzenbaum of Ohio, and Republican Gordon J. Humphrey of New Hampshire.

There was speculation that some of the conservatives were engaging in a conspiracy to kill the bill. In fact, much of the debate over Wirth-Wilson focused on whether it would indeed doom the bill's chances for yet another year.

Environmental groups fought hard to counter that argument, but many of their traditional allies were swayed by it and sided with Mitchell in voting to table the amendment. "I made the commitment to go with the leader to hold the package together," said Dodd.

Advocates of Wirth-Wilson believed some conservatives used the same reasoning in voting the opposite way. "They bought this bogus argument that it's a deal-breaker," said Blake Early of the Sierra Club. Even Republican leader Dole, who voted to preserve the leadership compromise, acknowledged the possibility. "I know Symms is troubled by the whole bill," Dole said. "But I don't think there was much of that."

Senators themselves denied having any such disingenuous intentions. "Not in my case," said Helms, saying he was convinced by the populist argument that Wirth-Wilson would help small businesses. McClure recalled that he once drove an electric car for a whole year to show his commitment to gasoline alternatives. Garn simply pointed to the problems of his hometown: "Salt Lake City's major pollution problem is the automobile."

As for Symms, spokesman Dave Pearson said the senator was not trying to kill the bill itself, though he freely admitted that Symms' primary intention was to bust up the White House compromise. Symms was a vocal critic of most clean air proposals under consideration — he was the only Environment Committee member to vote against reporting the bill to the floor. If the deal were dealt a serious blow, Pearson said, Symms would have a better shot with his own amendments — measures that environmentalists said would drastically weaken the bill, but which Symms maintained would make it more flexible and workable.

Kerry Amendment Fails

Kerry's amendment had three main elements. It sought to restore the mandatory duty of the EPA under existing law to propose a "federal implementation plan" when a state produced a "state implementation plan" inadequate to clean up a smoggy area. It also would have restored what Kerry said was existing EPA authority to require reasonable, cost-effective cleanup of stationary sources that emitted as little as 3 tons of pollutants a year in the smoggiest cities, instead of forbidding cleanup of sources below 50 tons. And it would have deleted a provision in the substitute that allowed cities to get waivers from some cleanup requirements after six years if they could show that costs were too high or that technology was unachievable.

Kerry argued that the substitute badly weakened existing law, making it unlikely that cities would meet the cleanup goals. He insisted that federal plans — or merely the threat of them — were a vital tool to force states to produce tough cleanup plans of their own. He said putting small and mid-sized pollution sources off-limits would take nearly half of all smog-causing pollution emissions out of the cleanup equation. And he argued that allowing a cost and technology waiver would turn the cleanup process into a political struggle at the state level, with well-connected polluters besieging governors for waivers.

Baucus countered that Kerry wanted a "theoretical, pie-in-the-sky" cleanup plan that was too expensive and cumbersome. He argued that federal cleanup plans had never worked. Further, he said, leaving small sources open to pollution controls was "a small-business buster."

Kerry responded that the EPA should retain the authority to require "reasonable" cleanup of small sources and insisted that regulators had not extended onerous controls to small business. "This is a scare tactic," he said.

But Mitchell, Baucus and Dole were able to hold a majority behind the substitute.

Floor Amendments

The Senate approved, mostly on voice votes, amendments by:

- Wirth and William L. Armstrong, R-Colo., to require

Urban Smog

Following are highlights of the urban smog provisions of the Clean Air Act amentments:

Deadlines for attainment. Established five classes, beginning with "marginal." Graduated deadlines and minimum control requirements — three years for marginal areas, six years for moderate, nine years for serious, 15-17 years for severe and 20 years for extreme.

Boundaries of non-attainment areas. Set by states with EPA approval, except that boundaries of serious, severe and extreme ozone and carbon monoxide areas were to be expanded to include the entire metropolitan statistical area or consolidated metropolitan statistical area.

Size of sources subject to controls. Lowered definition of major source to 50 tons a year of volatile organic compounds (VOCs) in serious ozone areas, 25 tons in severe areas and 10 tons in extreme areas. Thus, states were to be allowed to impose pollution controls and permit requirements on smaller sources such as dry cleaners and auto paint shops.

Yearly reduction requirements/waiver. All except marginal ozone areas required to achieve a 15 percent reduction in VOC emissions within six years and 3 percent a year thereafter. (Motor vehicle emissions could not be counted.) Annual reductions of VOCs and nitrogen oxides were also required.

The EPA's authority to waive the 3 percent requirement was limited to when all technologically feasible control measures had been used.

Federal implementation plans. EPA required to issue a federal implementation plan two years after a state failed to submit an adequate state plan. The federal plan could be partial or complete but had to provide for attainment of the air quality standard.

the EPA to continue testing auto emissions in at least one high-altitude site until fiscal 1995 to make sure that vehicles there met federal regulations similar to those in lower altitudes. Another Wirth-Armstrong amendment required the agency to fund a high-altitude emissions research center for heavy-duty vehicles because high altitudes exacerbated vehicle-related pollution.

- Rudy Boschwitz, R-Minn., and David L. Boren, D-Okla., to require states and the EPA to establish technical-assistance programs to help small businesses comply with the Clean Air Act. The amendment also allowed states to establish a special-permit program for small businesses to make it easier for them to comply. As originally proposed, the measure would have required states to set up the special-permit program, but the sponsors modified it in the face of leadership opposition, and it was approved 98-0. *(Vote 36, p. 10-S)*
- Dole, to require the EPA to assess the impact of provisions on small communities before implementing them.
- Edward M. Kennedy, D-Mass., to require the National Institute of Environmental Health Sciences to establish grant programs to research the health effects of air pollution and to train doctors in treating pollution-related ailments.

The measure originally would have authorized more than $140 million over five years, but Kennedy removed specific funding levels at the behest of the leadership.

- Symms, to strike a requirement that would have forced the EPA and other agencies to study methane emissions from farm animals — a provision that had prompted a flurry of mocking comments from senators about targeting bovine flatulence as an air pollution problem.
- Lloyd Bentsen, D-Texas, to strike several provisions related to fees that would be levied by the EPA and to convert other fees to penalties.

Tax-policy writers in the House, which under the Constitution had sole authority to initiate revenue proposals, objected to the provisions, so Bentsen, chairman of the Finance Committee, offered the amendment to mollify his counterparts.

- Dennis DeConcini, D-Ariz., to authorize the EPA to negotiate with Mexico to undertake joint clean air efforts for the border area.

Amendments Defeated

The Senate rejected amendments by:

- Helms, urging Bush to recognize and establish relations with the Baltic republic of Lithuania, which had just declared its independence in defiance of the Soviet government. It was defeated 36-59. *(Vote 39, p. 11-S)*
- Slade Gorton, R-Wash., and Alan J. Dixon, D-Ill., asking the House to attach provisions to the bill that would impose import fees on foreign products made in ways that did not comply with the Clean Air Act. The fees, aimed at making sure that domestic businesses could continue to compete with foreign businesses, were to be based on the cost to U.S. businesses of complying with the act and on expenditures by foreign businesses aimed at reducing air pollution.

It was killed, 52-47, on a tabling motion. *(Vote 40, p. 11-S)*

- Symms, to require the EPA to waive vehicle-emissions standards if they were found to increase U.S. dependence on strategic minerals from South Africa by more than 150 percent. Emission-reduction systems in cars used platinum-group metals, many of them imported from South Africa. The amendment was killed on a tabling motion, 91-5. *(Vote 41, p. 11-S)*

Byrd Amendment

Even while Mitchell and Dole were beating back potential clean air deal-busters, a more ominous showdown loomed in the form of an amendment by Byrd that had little to do with environmental issues.

Byrd, who had long blocked clean air legislation from coming to the floor, had offered an amendment early in the Senate floor debate to provide financial support and job-training benefits for the estimated 3,000 to 5,000 coal miners who were expected to lose their jobs as a result of the bill's acid rain control provisions. Those provisions made it far more difficult and expensive for utilities to continue burning the high-sulfur coal mined in West Virginia and other Appalachian and Midwestern states.

In an often emotional debate that kept the Senate in session until almost 1 a.m. on March 9, Byrd argued that there was ample precedent for helping workers who were thrown out of their jobs by congressional legislation. "I'm asking for fairness and justice, and every senator in here knows in his heart that it's right to help people," Byrd said.

The original Byrd plan would have given miners from 50 percent to 100 percent of their average $50,000-a-year package of salary and benefits over a six-year period, at a total cost to taxpayers of as much as $1.4 billion. Under pressure to economize, Byrd modified the proposal to scale back its maximum cost to $700 million.

But even that was far too much for Minority Leader Dole, who warned that the White House was adamantly opposed to the amendment on the ground that it would push the bill through Bush's self-imposed cost ceiling. Dole said he was warned by the administration that "this bill is dead if this amendment's adopted."

GOP Assistant Minority Leader Alan K. Simpson of Wyoming joined the chorus against the Byrd amendment, but he summed up the difficulty of voting against the powerful Appropriations Committee chairman. "I don't want to take on Robert Byrd of West Virginia," Simpson said. "I write him letters all the time, saying, 'How about a little fence around the elk refuge?' "

Nonetheless, Simpson warned, "If you vote for this you're going to lose this bill."

Mitchell delayed action on the Byrd amendment, a move that some took as a sign that Byrd probably had the votes to prevail. Senate leaders were believed to be using the Easter recess either to pry senators off the proposal or to come up with a counteroffer for Byrd.

Byrd subsequently modified his amendment a second time to reduce its maximum potential cost to $500 million.

Byrd Loses in Cliffhanger

Finally, the week of March 26 produced a nail-biting confrontation. In the end, Byrd's bid to provide generous job-loss benefits to coal miners displaced by the clean air bill fell one vote short — the victim of inclement weather, a last-minute veto threat and three broken promises.

The 49-50 vote on the amendment on March 29 proved to be the most dramatic moment during debate on the far-reaching bill. The administration had promised to veto the legislation if the Byrd plan were approved. For Mitchell, the vote was his biggest test of mettle since succeeding Byrd at the helm of the Senate. *(Vote 47, p. 12-S)*

Mitchell was matched with the chamber's master of debate and not-so-subtle persuasion. With nothing to gain politically after five easy re-elections, Byrd was fighting a passionate crusade in behalf of what he said was the very survival of West Virginia's coal-miner towns.

"Sen. Mitchell is fighting for what he believes in," Byrd said the day before the vote, his arm around a coal miner's son at a photo session in his office. "And I'm fighting for what I believe in."

Ever since Byrd's amendment surfaced in early March, key players on the clean air bill had drawn firm lines.

The bill's acid rain provisions were expected to cut deeply into the Ohio Valley and Appalachian high-sulfur coal industry because they would severely limit sulfur emissions from coal-burning power plants. Many utilities were expected to switch to low-sulfur coal and other fuels, and thousands of miners would probably lose their jobs as a result, devastating many rural towns in nine or so states that relied heavily on high-sulfur coal mines.

Byrd's amendment would have authorized $500 million to provide three years of job-loss and retraining benefits to coal miners, giving them cash payments of up to 90 percent of their pay and benefits the first year, 80 percent the second year and 70 percent the third year.

As for displaced workers from other industries hurt by the clean air bill, Byrd would have provided them with much less.

Opponents called the proposal too generous to coal miners, unfair to other workers and a deficit-aggravating budget-buster. Other senators threatened to offer amendments to add other classes of workers into the more generous category. Fretting about the potential for unemployment in the oil industry, Phil Gramm, R-Texas, said with characteristic bravado, "People in other states are not going to be treated better than the people in Texas."

Mitchell, pleading with senators to oppose the amendment, used examples showing that the average displaced coal miner could receive more than $41,000 the first year, while an out-of-work chemical worker would receive $8,500.

Grim-faced as he finished debating the man who in the past had blocked clean air legislation as majority leader, Mitchell said, "None of us like the choice we now face."

Byrd, a man with 32 years' worth of IOUs in one vest pocket and countless future chits to hand out in the other, had gone door to door in the past several weeks to meet with Republicans and Democrats alike and had penned and typed them many notes.

Republican leader Dole was himself daunted by the challenge. Going into the day, he said later, Mitchell had promised he could deliver votes from only 16 Democrats, which meant Dole had to secure votes from 34 Republicans. Bush was enlisted to call eight or nine GOP senators to request their support.

Byrd said he had 50 yeas lined up, including the cancer-stricken Spark M. Matsunaga, D-Hawaii, who had to be transported to the Capitol in a special van and rolled into the chamber on a wheelchair to vote.

On the day of the vote, however, Democrat J. Bennett Johnston of Louisiana had to fly home to attend the funeral of the mother of an aide. He had planned to return in time for the scheduled 3 p.m. roll call to cast his vote for Byrd, but bad weather delayed his plane, Byrd said.

Through Byrd's eyes, though, things still looked hopeful as the vote began before a nearly full, completely silent gallery.

As Byrd made the rounds, his confident smile was a stark contrast to Mitchell's pained expression. The former majority leader offered Mitchell his outstretched hand and then ambled up to the clerk's desk to request a vote-counting chart.

The final tally did not match Byrd's expectations, said the Senate's undisputed champion of nose-counting. "Two or three who were uncertain went with me," Byrd said later. But then, "three of my votes took wings," he added, flapping his arms, "with the help of the boys downtown" in the White House.

Byrd refused to name names, but circumstantial evidence pointed to two senators as possible defectors: Democrat Joseph R. Biden Jr. of Delaware and Idaho Republican Symms, both of whom switched at the last minute.

Biden, under heavy pressure from both sides, had waited until near the end of the roll call to cast his vote. Byrd had his arm around Biden when things went awry. On the floor, Biden was heard telling Byrd, "I'm with you, as long as I know this is not going to be vetoed."

Dole had issued veto threats on behalf of the White House, but he appeared to back off in the days leading up to the vote, saying on the floor only that the amendment would "probably lead" to a veto.

Byrd's opponents quickly arranged a call from the White House. Biden was hustled into the Democratic cloakroom by assistant GOP leader Simpson, where a call was waiting from John H. Sununu, Bush's chief of staff. "He guaranteed me the president would veto the bill," Biden said on the floor after the vote. "On merits alone, I would have been for it."

Acid Rain

Following are highlights of the acid rain provisions of the Clean Air Act Amendments:

Sulfur Dioxide, Phase I. Mandated controls to begin Jan. 1, 1995, for 111 plants emitting at a rate above 2.5 pounds per million British thermal units (lbs./mmBtu). Two-year extension available for 90 percent scrubbing.

Sulfur Dioxide, Phase II. To begin Jan. 1, 2000. Total emissions cap of 8.9 million tons nationwide. Plants to reduce emission to 1.2 lbs./mmBtu unless they were under 75 megawatts and part of systems with total capacity under 250 megawatts. Small plants under 25 megawatts exempted.

Allowance System. Granted sources one "allowance" for each ton of SO_2 within one year. Incentive allowances offered in Phase I to high-sulfur coal plants that made reductions below 1.2 lbs./mmBtu, up to 3.5 million allowances. Allowances could be traded to any unit in the country. Trading for NOx not permitted.

Bonus allowances offered to "clean" and "growth" states in Phase II, under either a federal or state-option formula.

Allocated an additional 200,000 annual SO_2 allowances to plants in Ohio, Illinois and Indiana during Phase I, and an additional 50,000 allowances to 10 Midwestern plants during Phase II.

Nitrogen Oxides (NOx). Mandated controls to begin Jan. 1, 1995, for 111 plants, with limits of 0.45 lbs./mmBtu for tangentially fired boilers or 0.5 lbs./mmBtu for dry-bottom wall-fired boilers and cell burners.

Symms, who had voted for Byrd's amendment, also came under heavy pressure from Dole and others. A strong opponent of the bill, Symms had been trying to derail it. As pressure was applied, Symms made his motives known. "He said, 'I don't like this bill,'" Simpson said later.

But Symms made the mistake of hanging out in front of the vote-counter too long. "By standing there, you become prey to the pleas of your colleagues," Simpson said. Symms switched.

That put the vote at 49-49, with Alfonse M. D'Amato, R-N.Y., the one vote uncounted. D'Amato, an Appropriations Committee member with a penchant for bringing home pork-barrel projects, had a political interest in pleasing his chairman.

But D'Amato voted against the amendment and thus killed it. He was among only nine of 29 Appropriations Committee members to oppose the chairman.

Winding Down Debate

The Senate thus disposed of the last, and perhaps biggest, threat to a tenuous White House-approved compromise, capping a week of intense action in both chambers on the far-reaching measure:

- On March 27, Mitchell persuaded the Senate to schedule an up-or-down vote on the bill for April 3. When GOP senators had rejected a similar request the week before, Mitchell had threatened his colleagues with weekend sessions and all-nighters until they finished work on his top priority of the year, if not his entire Senate career.
- For the first time during floor debate, the Senate also broke with the Bush administration and narrowly rejected, 47-50, an industry-backed amendment by Don Nickles, R-Okla., and Howell Heflin, D-Ala., to soften the measure's enforcement provisions. Mitchell and his pro-environment allies said the plan would have gutted the entire bill. The vote followed an initial roll call and hours of arm-twisting, during which several lawmakers switched sides after the Senate refused to kill the amendment on a 47-50 tabling motion. *(Votes 43, 44, p. 12-S)*
- Also on March 27, the Mitchell-White House alliance easily tabled, 71-26, another major amendment by Arlen Specter, R-Pa., and Metzenbaum, one to provide big tax breaks to high-pollution Midwestern utilities for installing anti-pollution devices called scrubbers. But the alliance later failed by a big margin, 30-69, to kill a farm-state-backed amendment by Tom Daschle, D-S.D., to promote the use of grain-based ethanol as a clean alternative fuel. *(Votes 45, 48, p. 12-S)*

Finally, on April 3, the Senate passed its version of the legislation, 89-11, the first time the chamber had moved clean air legislation since revision efforts began in 1981.

Voting against the measure were six conservative Republicans — Garn, Helms, McClure, Nickles, Symms and Wallop — and five Midwestern Democrats: Byrd and his West Virginia colleague John D. Rockefeller IV; Ohio's Glenn; and Illinois' Dixon and Paul Simon.

HOUSE COMMITTEE ACTION

At the same time the Senate was preparing to move its clean air bill back to the floor, long-stalled House legislation (HR 3030) showed signs of life.

Cost-Sharing Issue

Philip R. Sharp, D-Ind., chairman of the Energy Subcommittee on Energy and Power, had held up the bill since October 1989 in hope of obtaining a cost-sharing compromise for Indiana and other Midwestern states that would be hard hit by the measure's acid rain provisions.

On Feb. 28, Sharp announced his long-awaited acid rain compromise proposal. Stripped to its essentials, Sharp's complex proposal would have levied a fee on industrial emitters of large amounts of sulfur dioxide (SO_2), a principal acid rain precursor, and funnel the money to Midwestern utilities to help defray the costs of adding scrubbers to remove SO_2.

Sharp insisted the proposal was not "cost sharing" in the traditional sense of a nationwide utility tax. But it was not immediately clear whether his new formulation would appeal to the heavy majority of his colleagues who opposed cost sharing in virtually any form.

Indeed, earlier in February, Sharp had held a short subcommittee session that only confirmed what the participants already knew. Despite mounting pressure to move, Midwesterners were holding fast for some sort of national cost-sharing plan to help pay the substantial expenses involved in cleaning up their coal-fired utility plants; members from most other states did not want to give it to them.

Judging from members' opening statements Feb. 7, positions had not changed appreciably over the winter adjournment. Vote counters could count on one hand the hard votes for cost sharing among the panel's 23 members.

Sharp said he hoped to overcome that problem by forging an alliance between Midwesterners who wanted cost-sharing and members from the so-called clean states who were worried that the bill's acid rain emissions cap would hobble their plans to expand utility capacity in the future.

But members on and off the subcommittee signaled they would fight linkage between cost-sharing and cap fixing. Health Subcommittee Chairman Waxman, whose panel completed the last public markup of the bill Oct. 11, 1989, was annoyed that Midwesterners on his panel voted against him on key issues in what they later said publicly was a tit-for-tat deal to get support for cost-sharing. He insisted that issues be considered separately.

Power Subcommittee member Jim Cooper, D-Tenn., another no-linkage advocate, put together a stand-alone amendment to solve "clean" states' growth problems by giving them access to extra pollution allowances without having to go hat in hand to Midwestern utilities. Under the bill, "dirty" utilities could generate pollution allowances by cleaning beyond what was required and sell those allowances to utilities that wanted to grow. But clean states feared that the Midwest might hoard allowances or charge exorbitant prices for them, and that the trading system would break down.

Cooper was also part of a small group of members called together by Energy Committee Chairman Dingell to try to work out a compromise on cost-sharing. Cooper maintained that existing clean-coal-technology funding and the bill's allowance-trading system already constituted subsidies to the Midwest. "Since no one's objecting to those subsidies, perhaps they can be enhanced" to satisfy the Midwesterners, he said. "Most people I know feel pretty good if they've got two subsidies."

But the Midwesterners did not feel good. They said the bill would cause their utility rates to rise, their coal-mining jobs to disappear and their economies to suffer. Sharp and Terry L. Bruce, D-Ill., another pro-cost-sharing subcommittee member, tried to remind their colleagues that Congress usually helped regions or localities that faced heavy costs. Both cited the savings and loan bailout, which they argued channeled disproportionate benefits to Texas and other Southwestern states.

At the end of the markup, Sharp said he was at least happy that his colleagues had at least begun to focus on the subject after the winter break. "That process of getting up to the edge of decision has clearly been started," he said. "These issues are not yet resolved.... I don't think anybody knows what the outcome will be."

Sharp said March 8 that he had won endorsement from the National Clean Air Coalition, the umbrella group of environmental organizations involved in the clean air debate. "We're absolutely thrilled about this development," said Sharp, who said he hoped the environmentalists' imprimatur would help his proposal attract more votes.

However, David Hawkins, a senior attorney with the Natural Resources Defense Council, a member of the coalition, said the umbrella group had told Sharp that it would endorse the environmental aspects of his proposal but not its emissions-fee or cost-sharing elements. Hawkins added that the coalition had already given its approval to the acid rain component of the Senate substitute, and to a House bill sponsored by Gerry Sikorski, D-Minn. "We're not offering support for Sharp over any other bill," Hawkins said. "It's not a position on cost sharing."

Sharp tried for two more weeks to pull together enough votes for a politically acceptable plan to help Midwestern utilities pay for acid rain controls. Finally, Dingell called a halt to those negotiations and brought the bill before the full committee on March 14.

Compromise on Antismog Provisions

Although the committee got no further than opening statements March 14-15, Dingell put the clean air bill on something of a fast track, saying he wanted the measure reported before the Easter recess began on April 6. He added that he was under instructions from the House leadership to have the legislation ready to go to the House floor by early May, if not sooner.

Almost from the start, however, committee members and their staffs withdrew behind closed doors to work out the more nettlesome provisions of the wide-ranging bill. On March 22, members emerged to reveal a surprise compromise that incorporated some of the same antismog provisions the Senate had just rejected. The agreement took a bitterly divisive issue off the table for the committee and seemed likely to help the panel meet its April 6 deadline to finish work on the bill, which would allow floor action in late April or early May.

The Energy Committee's compromise made an important element of the legislation much clearer. The compromise not only incorporated key parts of the defeated Senate smog amendment, but it also adopted what committee members depicted as strengthening provisions throughout the entire title of the bill that would set standards to control urban and rural air pollution.

The committee voted 38-2 on March 22 to approve the substitute for the bill's Title I, which divided the smoggiest cities and nearby rural areas into categories depending on the severity of their pollution and established methods to bring them into compliance with health standards.

The compromise defined the methods for controlling air pollution from stationary sources ranging from large factories and power plants to small emitters, such as gas stations and dry cleaners. The Health and the Environment Subcommittee had reached a similar compromise in October on pollution from mobile sources, such as cars, trucks and buses. Together, the two agreements neutralized disputes over some of the bill's most controversial sections, making floor fights on those provisions unlikely.

The Title I deal had the support of the committee's traditional adversaries, Dingell and Waxman. Joining them in an agreement to back the deal all the way through conference with the Senate were ranking Republican Norman F. Lent, N.Y., and two key members of the committee's "Group of 9" moderate and conservative Democrats — Al Swift, Wash., and Dennis E. Eckart, Ohio.

Noticeably absent from the closed-door negotiations that produced the arrangement was the White House. An administration official who attended the March 22 markup had no comment except to say the administration still preferred Bush's bill and would immediately start running cost estimates of the committee agreement to see whether it violated the president's limits.

Eckart said he was worried that the administration might try to stir up "weekend White House mischief" against the deal, but he cautioned the White House to note that the chief House sponsors of the Bush bill, Dingell and Lent, had backed the committee compromise.

Swift said the committee's 38-2 vote had been impressive and suggested that the White House risked becoming the "odd man out" if its officials worked to undo the deal.

Details of Compromise

The House agreement kept the EPA's mandatory duty to implement a federal cleanup plan if states did not come up with adequate plans, but it also gave federal regulators more time to develop such plans. It allowed planners to target sources as small as 10 tons in Los Angeles, the nation's most polluted city, and as small as 25 tons in other badly polluted cities. And it did not provide for the cost waivers offered by the Senate substitute.

The agreement would also:

- Set cleanup "milestones" for targeted cities, requiring them to periodically assess their progress toward attaining health standards and to implement contingency plans if it looked as though they would not meet their goals on time.
- Put Los Angeles in a cleanup category by itself, giving it 20 years to comply with health standards. Several other cities were placed in a "severe" category with a 15-year deadline. Houston, Chicago and New York fell into that category but could be given two years more than other severely polluted cities to clean up.
- Required progressively tougher cleanup methods in targeted cities depending on the severity of their air pollution problems. In addition to lowering the size of sources subject to controls in the smoggiest cities to 25 tons or even 10 tons, the compromise called for increased offsets for construction of new pollution sources.
- Set mandatory sanctions for areas that did not comply with their obligations under clean air law. While areas that tried in good faith to comply with the law but failed to meet health standards would simply be required to carry out more cleanup, areas that declined to comply faced mandatory cutoffs of highway construction funding or mandatory two-for-one offsets for construction of new pollution sources, or possibly both.
- Strengthened provisions in the original House bill that encouraged manufacturers to develop lower-polluting consumer and commercial products. Such products as paints and solvents were estimated to cause as much as 27 percent of smog-creating pollution in many cities.

The compromise drew quick but qualified support from

Alternative Fuels

Use of motor fuels other than gasoline had been looked to in the 1970s and '80s as a way to reduce U.S. dependence on foreign oil. In 1990, faced with diminishing returns from traditional air pollution controls, lawmakers and the administration turned to proposals to mandate a partial shift to alternative-fueled vehicles in order to ease severe ozone and toxic-air pollution in major cities.

Following are the main alternative fuels that could be used as substitutes for traditional, liquid, oil-derived motor vehicle fuels, such as gasoline or diesel fuels:

Methanol — An alcohol fuel derived from natural gas, coal, wood or municipal wastes and used as a pure fuel (M-100) or as an 85 percent additive to gasoline (M-85). Its potential to reduce air pollutants — particularly the emissions of ozone-forming hydrocarbons — was hotly debated. The Environmental Protection Agency (EPA) said M-85 and M-100 could dramatically reduce hydrocarbons, but the oil industry and Sierra Research, a California consulting company, disputed that contention.

Ethanol — Also an alcohol fuel, derived from fermented agricultural commodities such as corn, wheat and barley; usually blended with gasoline to form gasohol. From 5 percent to 10 percent of motor fuel was sold as gasohol in 1990. Emissions resulted in less ozone-forming hydrocarbons than gasoline.

Compressed Natural Gas — Considered one of the cleanest alternatives because of low hydrocarbon emissions that were relatively non-ozone producing. The EPA also expected a 50 percent reduction in tailpipe emissions of carbon monoxide. However, it did emit a significant quantity of nitrogen oxides, and it required refitting gasoline-powered cars.

Propane and Butane — Components of liquefied petroleum gas, derived by processing natural gas and refining crude oil. It had similar air-quality benefits to natural gas vehicles — that is, less ozone-forming hydrocarbons than gasoline.

Electricity — Electric vehicles powered by rechargeable batteries. They still required considerable research and development — particularly in developing small, long-range battery power — before they could be commercially available.

Hydrogen — Produced from natural gas, petroleum, coal or water. It had low exhaust emissions and, because hydrogen reacts with oxygen to produce water, virtually no hydrocarbon emissions. But hydrogen could not be compressed effectively, creating the problem of finding room to store it on cars.

Reformulated Gasoline — Gasoline whose composition had been changed to achieve more benign emission characteristics, both from the tailpipe and from evaporative emissions. Though some versions were sold in Detroit and Southern California, reformulated gasoline was still in development. It was the favored alternative of the oil and auto industries. The Energy Department expected it to have less reactive hydrocarbon emissions and less benzene emissions than existing gasoline.

groups that represented state and local air pollution control officials. Bill Becker, executive director of the State and Territorial Air Pollution Program Administrators and the Association of Local Air Pollution Control Officials, said the committee agreement was a "good" and "courageous" compromise that met many of the groups' concerns, though he added that air officials planned to seek to strengthen various provisions.

Becker said it was "a very perverse irony" that the House Energy Committee, which had long been viewed as less environmentally aggressive than the Senate, "now has a stronger clean air bill, at least a non-attainment bill, than the Senate — probably for the first time in 10 years."

Fay, administrator of the business- and industry-funded Clean Air Working Group, had no immediate evaluation of the proposal, though he said it would probably need some amendments. "We are stunned. We're taking a close look at it," he said.

Alternative Fuels

While the compromise reduced the number of divisive issues left for the committee to work out, the strife was far from over. A week later, the full committee refought one of the battles of the 1989 markup in the Health and the Environment Subcommittee. Once again, members disagreed sharply over how aggressive and costly to make alternative-fuels programs for cars, trucks and buses.

The full committee wound up late March 29 by voting narrowly to keep in place a modified version of an alternative-fuels plan that industry officials said they could live with but that environmentalists found unacceptably weak. Both sides indicated that they would keep trying to negotiate a compromise to head off yet another showdown on the issue on the House floor.

In October, the subcommittee had decided to throw out the administration's much-touted alternative-fuels program, which would have mandated production of up to 1 million clean-fuel cars a year in the nation's smoggiest cities by 1997. Instead, with implicit support from some quarters of the White House, the subcommittee had voted 12-10 to substitute a less aggressive program with no production mandate and a less stringent clean-fuel standard.

The sponsors of that substitute, Ralph M. Hall, D-Texas, and Jack Fields, R-Texas, said it was a more realistic and workable approach that would achieve virtually the same emissions reductions.

Critics, led by subcommittee Chairman Waxman, had argued that it would gut Bush's program. They threatened to take the issue to the floor, where they were widely believed to have the upper hand in any struggle to reimpose tougher alternative-fuels requirements.

Lingering discomfort over Hall-Fields sent members behind closed doors once again the week of March 26 in search of a compromise. Just the week before, the committee had concluded a surprise backroom deal on the bill's urban and rural smog provisions; that followed a similar and even more dramatic subcommittee deal in the fall of 1989 on motor-vehicle tailpipe emissions.

Hopes were high that the same magic would affect talks on alternative fuels, but it was not to be.

Frantic, closed-door negotiations that began in earnest early March 29 produced concessions on both sides, according to later accounts, but they failed to bring committee factions together. When the committee finally convened a public markup late in the afternoon, it was not to announce a compromise but to debate controversial amendments that divided the panel into pro-industry and pro-environmental blocs, which were split over how and how much to change the original Hall-Fields program.

Members on both sides of the debate traded complaints that they had had little time to study the hastily cobbled-together proposals, often insisting that the committee clerk read the text of long amendments while they twisted arms to line up last-minute votes. The committee's cavernous Rayburn House Office Building meeting room and the hallway outside were packed with lobbyists from the oil and auto industries, which could have been significantly affected by some of the more far-reaching proposals.

The first test came on an amendment by Bill Richardson, D-N.M., to require that reformulated gasoline replace conventional gasoline in more than 30 of the nation's smoggiest cities. The amendment also sought to mandate specific guidelines for making reformulated gasoline, a cleaner, reblended form of conventional gasoline still being perfected by the oil industry.

Some analysts viewed reformulated gasoline as the lowest common denominator of alternative fuels. It would cut emissions by far less than more exotic alternatives such as compressed natural gas, but, unlike most of the exotics, reformulated gasoline could be distributed through the same system that provided conventional gasoline. There was general agreement that if it were used widely enough, reformulated gasoline could provide important air pollution reductions.

Richardson said the blending dictates would help reduce toxic and smog-causing emissions, while forcing the industry to use alcohol additives such as ethanol. That would give farmers a much bigger market for corn and other crops (from which ethanol was derived), saving as much as $1.4 billion a year in farm subsidies.

But the oil industry and the Bush administration adamantly opposed Richardson's blending dictates, contending that the guidelines would raise costs to consumers by $100 billion, adding anywhere from 5 cents to 25 cents a gallon to the price of reformulated gasoline. Further, said Joe L. Barton, R-Texas, Richardson's proposal would have skewed the playing field for alternative fuels, establishing ethanol as the heavy favorite.

The committee rejected Richardson's amendment on a 21-22 vote. It went on to adopt a less stringent alternative-fuels provision that required that reformulated gasoline be offered for sale in the nine most polluted cities, but not that it completely displace conventional gasoline.

That provision was included in a much larger package that Hall and Fields offered to replace their original amendment. Fields said that, to accommodate such committee members as W. J. "Billy" Tauzin, D-La., he and Hall had given substantial ground, beefing up their urban mass transit bus program, strengthening their motor vehicle fleet requirements and setting tighter standards for passenger cars in the nine smoggiest cities.

The debate over the new proposal became the key vote of the markup, which had stretched into the evening. In a complicated parliamentary maneuver, Hall-Fields was offered as a weakening amendment to a stricter Tauzin proposal; Tauzin in turn offered a slightly modified version of his proposal again as an amendment to Hall-Fields.

Tauzin argued that Hall and Fields had produced a promising proposal but had left it "riddled with loopholes" that were "big enough to drive a whole fleet of dirty cars and dirty buses through." He complained that the bus, fleet and clean-car provisions all had trapdoors that would allow targeted entities to opt out of the restrictions relatively easily.

Dingell weighed in for Hall-Fields, saying the dispute was in part a question over whether to extend tough alternative-fuels requirements to eight or nine polluted cities or to 40 of them, as he said Tauzin would do. "I think it's important that we approach this thing with moderation," Dingell said.

The committee went along with its chairman, voting 19-24 to reject Tauzin's amendment. The new Hall-Fields plan was then adopted by voice vote.

That did not end the debate, however. Fields said he hoped that the committee would be able to continue to negotiate and "come forward with an even better piece of legislation" before the bill reached the floor. Tauzin had earlier warned that adopting Hall-Fields would mean that "we're going to have one heck of a floor fight over it," but he said after the markup that he would continue to work with his adversaries to craft a compromise.

Richardson warned that he planned to offer a much stronger proposal for clean and extremely clean cars on the House floor, including a much-debated production mandate that would require automakers to build and offer to sell new-generation clean-fuel cars.

Warranty Requirements

In one final showdown, Waxman and Dingell sparred over proposed warranty requirements for motor-vehicle emissions systems. To extend the life span of emissions systems, while at the same time protecting independent garage mechanics whose livelihoods depended on the need to repair them, Waxman proposed to modify the bill's five-year/50,000-mile minimum warranty by splitting it into two parts. Big-ticket emission-control items, such as catalytic converters and electronic emission-control systems, would have to be warranted for eight years or 80,000 miles. Less expensive items would be covered for only two years or 24,000 miles.

Waxman said the shorter warranty for less expensive parts would keep car owners from going to auto dealers for all their repairs, a practice that he said robbed business from independent garages.

On March 27, the committee gave voice vote approval to a package of "technical amendments" by ranking Republican Lent to modify an urban-smog deal the committee had reached the week before. The amendments, which Lent conceded were more than merely technical, were designed to partly mollify the White House, which was caught off guard by the committee's smog deal.

Dingell agreed with part of Waxman's rationale, proposing an amendment of his own that would establish a two-year/24,000-mile warranty for most parts and keeping the five-year/50,000-mile warranty for big-ticket items.

Dingell prevailed easily on a 29-14 vote.

Air Toxics

The committee began its final week of negotiations with a third compromise, this one on air toxics, the poisonous and often carcinogenic emissions of sources that ranged from huge oil refineries and chemical plants to small "area" sources such as neighborhood gas stations and dry cleaners.

This had been expected to be a bitterly contested issue, with environmentalists insisting on tough second-round health standards and industry resisting on the ground that those health standards could force plants or even entire industries to shut down.

But in a move that caught many observers off guard, the committee's environmentalist bloc agreed to significantly moderate the second-round health standards. In exchange, they got much more comprehensive first-round technology requirements that covered virtually all major toxics sources and extended controls to many smaller ones, such as gas stations, dry cleaners, print shops and electroplating shops. Motor vehicles, a main toxics source, were specifically exempted because they were covered in a separate section of the bill.

Industry lobbyists were surprised and gratified that one of their biggest problems had suddenly all but disappeared, at least in the House bill. Fay, lobbyist for the industry-funded Clean Air Working Group, said the House compromise recognized what business and industry had said all along — that the first-round technology standards would cut toxics by 70 percent to 90 percent, making the far more costly second-round "residual risk" standards unnecessary.

Key environmentalists said they were also happy with the compromise. David Doniger, a senior attorney for the Natural Resources Defense Council and a widely recognized expert on air-toxics issues, said the agreement guaranteed "a pretty good program for the first 10 years."

Doniger originally favored "bright line" health standards that would have forced plants to pose less than a 1-in-1 million cancer risk or shut down. That language had been so diluted in the Senate bill that environmentalists could no longer support it, he said.

Doniger noted that the House bill would reinstate tough existing toxics standards unless Congress acted to set a different risk level within 10 years. Although those existing standards had proved difficult or impossible for the EPA to enforce, he said they were preferable to the "bad or mushy bright line" in the Senate bill.

The Energy Committee adopted the toxics compromise, 43-0, on April 3, leaving only one big issue to be resolved. But that issue was acid rain, which had already paralyzed the committee for months.

Acid Rain

The acid rain dispute pitted a small group of Midwesterners, who wanted some form of cost-sharing to help their utilities defray the costs of meeting acid rain controls, against a much larger group of "clean state" members who did not want to pay.

But the clean-state members had a problem of their own — the bill's tough cap on emissions meant they would have to buy pollution "allowances," most likely from Midwestern utilities, if they wanted to increase coal-burning utility capacity in the future. The Midwesterners sensed the possibility of a deal.

Midwesterners Sharp of Indiana and Bruce and Republican Edward Madigan, both from Illinois, all pursued such a deal for months, but could not persuade their colleagues to budge. Part of the problem was that Sharp and the others wanted cash cost-sharing from an emissions fee on industrial sulfur dioxide (SO_2) emitters, a concept that violated Bush's no-new-taxes pledge and that many members found unacceptable.

Some committee members suggested enhancing the bill's existing allowance trading system, which Cooper said was already a form of cost-sharing, since dirty, coal-fired utilities in the Midwest would be selling allowances to the rest of the country for cash. But Sharp distrusted the allowance scheme and worried about what the allowances would actually be worth.

As with many clean air issues on both sides of Capitol Hill, resolution was possible only after staff and members had worked themselves to exhaustion. Dingell scheduled a meeting for 10 a.m. on April 4 to mark up an acid rain compromise. The committee, as it later turned out, would miss that deadline by 34 hours.

Staff and members horse-traded throughout the day and into the night. At 2 a.m. on April 5, according to some accounts, 30 to 35 of the committee's 43 members were still on hand. Dingell had extended the committee meeting time, but only a little bit at a time, to keep members negotiating. Scores of lobbyists milled in the hallway outside the closed doors of the committee room, where a hand-lettered sign was intermittently updated by crossing out the previous meeting time and writing in a new one.

Offers and counteroffers were made as late as 4:30 a.m. before members went home for a few hours, only to return to begin negotiating again.

Negotiators finally reached a deal sometime in the afternoon of April 5. Markup convened about 8 p.m., and Sharp and others revealed that they had abandoned cash cost sharing in favor of a system that manipulated the allowance trading scheme to give both the Midwest and the clean states extra allowances.

Sharp lamented the loss of true cost sharing, calling the compromise only "a modest victory." The committee approved it 39-4, with four Texans (Democrats Fields, Hall and John Bryant and Republican Joe L. Barton) opposing it on the ground that it did not do right by their state.

Finally, the committee voted 42-1 to report the clean air bill, with William E. Dannemeyer, R-Calif., voting "no" because he said the bill would be too costly.

HOUSE FLOOR ACTION

Driven by compromises that cut most of the controversy out of the bill before it reached the floor, the House dispatched a sweeping rewrite of the nation's clean air laws in only two days of floor debate, approving the bill (HR 3030) May 23 on a 401-21 vote. *(Vote 137, p. 48-H)*

Job-Loss Benefits

The Energy and Commerce Committee earlier produced so many agreements on so many divisive issues that the rest of the House was given only a handful of choices to make before final passage. The long-awaited floor showdown evolved at times into a bipartisan love-in, with members clamoring to take credit for a series of compromise amendments that passed largely on overwhelming votes.

House passage added to the growing momentum behind a measure that most observers assumed was certain to go to Bush before the end of the year; it also locked in virtually all of the legislation's major components. The House bill was broadly similar to one (S 1630) the Senate passed April 3. Both set out new programs to clean up smoggy cities, cut motor-vehicle pollution, reduce acid rain and slash emissions of toxic air pollutants.

Although there were hundreds of differences between the 507-page House measure and its 698-page Senate counterpart, many of them significant, the two bills were so alike in general philosophy and overall structure that participants expected no intractable disputes when negotiators met in conference.

In one of its most controversial votes, the House shrugged off White House veto warnings and agreed 274-146 to approve a $250 million five-year program for unemployment and retraining benefits to workers who lost their jobs because of the new law. *(Vote 132, p. 46-H)*

The Senate just barely rejected a similar but more expensive program on a 49-50 vote March 29. The large House margin and the narrow Senate defeat combined to make it seem likely that the conferees would ultimately approve some form of job-loss compensation.

But the wild card was the White House, which had opposed the Senate proposal and issued veto warnings over the House amendment. White House Chief of Staff Sununu and EPA Administrator Reilly warned in a letter to House Speaker Thomas S. Foley, D-Wash., that the president's senior advisers would recommend a veto unless administration concerns were addressed. Sununu and Reilly argued that the amendment would become an open-ended entitlement that would cost far more than $250 million and set a dangerous precedent.

Bush said the day after the vote that he remained opposed to the amendment and hoped it would be stripped from the bill in conference. But Bush did not issue an explicit veto threat, and his aides' veto warnings were widely discounted during the House debate. Said amendment sponsor Bob Wise, D-W.Va., "I can't believe the president's going to veto the environmental bill of the decade over $50 million a year."

The Dingell-Waxman Axis

The House made several additions to its core bill during floor debate to bring it closer to the Senate measure. In addition to the sections on smog, motor vehicles, acid rain and air toxics, whose outlines were similar in both bills, the House added key amendments to complement similar Senate provisions on clean-fueled vehicles, reformulated gasoline, substances that depleted Earth's stratospheric ozone layer, offshore drilling, visibility in national parks and automotive pollution-control equipment warranties.

Environmentalists said they liked bits and pieces of both bills. "There are better parts in each," said Ayres, chairman of the National Clean Air Coalition. "If the conferees choose the best parts of the two bills, they can fashion a good law and the nation will benefit."

Business and industry representatives celebrated a bill they feared could have been worse, but promised to keep fighting to change provisions they still found obnoxious.

Fay, of the Clean Air Working Group, said environmentalists' "most extreme demands" had been headed off by last-minute compromises, but he complained that other compromises had boosted the cost of the bill. The American Petroleum Institute, which had mounted an advertising campaign costing more than $1 million to defeat a strict reformulated-gasoline amendment, said the amendment the House finally agreed to was so tough the industry might not be able to meet its requirements.

But if industry and environmentalists were not entirely pleased, the bill's chief House architects — and chief House antagonists — pronounced themselves satisfied with what they had wrought. Energy Committee Chairman Dingell and Health and the Environment Subcommittee Chairman Waxman came a little warily to the same table for a joint late-night news conference and called the bill "very strong" (Waxman) and "a good piece of legislation" (Dingell).

That the bill came to the floor at all was due in part to the two men's willingness to compromise on critical issues after years of stalemate. Long the respective leaders of the committee's industry and environmentalist blocs, Dingell and Waxman began agreeing to agree in the fall of 1989 with a surprise deal on automobile tailpipe emissions. With help from other key members, the committee went on to reach several more compromises that resolved arguments on smog, acid rain, air toxics and other matters.

Dingell was said to have given ground because he thought a bill was inevitable this time and because he calculated that a somewhat pro-environmental House floor would be an unfriendly place for him to try to hold the line on issues dear to him. Observers described Waxman's motivation as uncertainty over just how far he could push tough environmental positions on the floor and a willingness to accommodate members who begged him not to force them to choose between him and Dingell, or between environmental lobbyists and industry or autoworkers.

Mandating Clean-Fueled Cars

Despite all the agreements Dingell and Waxman wound up making, the process was never easy or automatic. Even in the final hours of the House debate, the two were still sparring over one last deal.

As usual, the subject was cars. Dingell, the auto industry's staunchest congressional ally, was taking a tough line against requiring automakers to produce and sell as many as 1 million clean-fueled cars a year. Waxman, whose Los Angeles district suffered some of the nation's worst smog — much of it caused by auto emissions — wanted the requirement but was willing to deal.

That "production mandate" had been a part of the original Bush proposal, but it drove automakers crazy, and the administration had long since backed down from it. Even environmentalists who liked the idea conceded that there was widespread concern about it on the floor, where members shared automakers' fears that no one would buy the new-generation cars. A vote might have been close, but few members wanted to have to vote.

It took Speaker Foley's intercession to force the final deal. While other members bought time by calling for roll call votes on non-controversial amendments, Foley sat calmly as Dingell and Waxman and their staffs stood around him, haggling. Foley did not bully or cajole, said a House staff member who was there. "The closest he came was he rolled his eyes once. It looked like he wasn't going to leave until there was a deal. That's a powerful influence. It's like when someone's sitting on your throat."

In the end, the broad production mandate was jettisoned in favor of a California-only pilot program that would require 150,000 clean-fueled vehicles a year from 1994 through 1996 and 300,000 cars a year beginning in 1997. Waxman got what he described as tough urban bus and commercial fleet programs that would require use of clean fuels.

The bottom line for House members was that they were spared an agonizingly tough vote. When Dingell announced the compromise, members rushed to pass it in a breeze, 405-15. *(Vote 136, p. 48-H)*

Floor Amendments

The Energy Committee's eight months of on-again, off-again public markups and private bargaining sessions from October 1989 to approval of the last deal in late May were a dramatic contrast to the Senate Environment Committee's quick markup, which produced a bill in five comparatively brief sessions spaced out over a month in the fall of 1989.

The floor action in the two chambers differed just as radically.

The Senate bill underwent about a month of backroom negotiations with the White House and six weeks of floor debate before Senate leaders could finally bring it to final passage. The House bill came to the floor with an ironclad rule governing debate and amendments and the House leadership's insistence that it be done in short order. It took only two days to finish the mammoth bill.

Among the major floor amendments considered during House debate were the following:

- **Reformulated gasoline.** Adopted by voice vote as part of a package of Energy Committee amendments, this compromise required the sale of nothing but specially blended ("reformulated") gasoline in the nation's nine smoggiest cities beginning in 1994. In addition, gasoline with a minimum oxygen content had to be sold in 44 cities that had high carbon monoxide levels. The amendment established a "recipe" for the gasoline that was widely interpreted to require increased use of ethanol or ethanol-based additives, but the proposal allowed refiners to use alternative formulas as long as emissions reductions were equal to or greater than those produced by the recipe. This was similar to the Senate provision.
- **Chlorofluorocarbons (CFCs).** Approved 416-0, this compromise called for phasing out CFCs and other substances that depleted the Earth's stratospheric ozone layer on a timetable that would end CFC production in 2000 and phase out other substances between 2005 and 2035. This was similar to the Senate provision. *(Vote 134, p. 46-H)*
- **Warranties.** Approved 239-180, this proposal extended warranty requirements for the most expensive auto emissions control equipment — the catalytic converter and electronic control unit — from the existing five years/50,000 miles to eight years/80,000 miles. Warranties for other pollution control parts were dropped to two years/24,000 miles to help shift repair business from dealers to independent garages. This was also similar to the Senate provision. *(Vote 133, p. 46-H)*
- **Ways and Means amendment.** The House rejected, 170-253, the Ways and Means Committee's plea that its jurisdiction over taxes be strictly observed. Ways and Means Chairman Dan Rostenkowski, D-Ill., argued that the Energy Committee had written several taxes and a tariff into its bill in the guise of fees. Leaving the "fees" in the bill would invite the Senate to ignore the House's right to initiate revenue measures, Rostenkowski said.

Dingell countered that the fees were, in fact, fees, and were essential for enforcement. *(Vote 131, p. 46-H)*

- **Offshore drilling.** The House voted 411-5 to adopt a proposal to require the EPA to place strict air pollution controls on oil and gas drilling and production platforms in federal waters offshore most of the United States. Units offshore of Texas, Louisiana, Mississippi and Alabama remained under the control of the Interior Department. *(Vote 135, p. 48-H)*
- **Parks visibility.** Adopted by voice vote as part of the Energy Committee package, this proposal was to require the EPA to promulgate regulations to prevent man-made sources of regional haze from reducing visibility in national parks and wilderness areas. It was to require states to make reasonable progress toward controlling such haze. The Senate provision required a study.

CONFERENCE ACTION

It was universally accepted that the House-Senate conference on clean air legislation would produce a bill to send to the White House, but just when that would happen remained murky throughout the summer.

One view was that the two sides were so close on so many major issues that conferees could produce a compromise by the August recess. Pessimists said it would take longer, however, and they were in the majority.

"My guess is we won't finish until October," said House Energy Committee member Cooper, a key player in some of the negotiations that produced the House bill's section on acid rain.

One Senate aide likened the process of marrying the two broadly similar bills to being halfway through a heart transplant, with the old heart out and the new one already in. All the conferees had to do was sew up a million tiny blood vessels. "It's going to be a slow, agonizing, tedious process," he said.

Although artificially imposed deadlines had proven indispensable in forcing members in both chambers to make final decisions on clean air, no one appeared in a hurry to set time limits for the conference. "I don't think it's wise to impose deadlines," said Senate Majority Leader Mitchell.

When would conferees finish, then? "As soon as possible," Mitchell said.

However, it was more than a month before Speaker Foley, on June 28, named the 140 House conferees. The House delegation included 26 of 43 members of the Energy Committee, which had written the bulk of the bill. In addition, the House contingent included other members from committees with limited jurisdiction over pieces of the bill: 26 members each from Public Works, Ways and Means, Education and Labor, and Science; five members each from Interior and Merchant Marine; plus two other members who weighed in on specific amendments.

Energy Committee Chairman Dingell intended to begin the conference July 12. The delay in appointing conferees centered, sources said, on a prickly battle involving Foley, Dingell and Health Subcommittee Chairman Waxman.

At issue was the exclusion of various Energy Committee Democrats who had worked hard on the bill but had alienated Dingell. This group reportedly included, among others, Minnesota's Sikorski and Oklahoma's Mike Synar, who were named to the conference only after Foley intervened.

An aide to Dingell said personalities were not the issue; rather, Dingell wanted the conferees to be a balanced group that was not unwieldy.

The conference convened on July 13, but Senate efforts to quickly accelerate the negotiations ran into a speed bump in the form of Dingell, who declined to be rushed into responding to two early offers from Senate conferees.

Senate conferees produced two offers to close the gap between House and Senate bills on sections dealing with stratospheric ozone depletion and with permits and enforcement — areas in which the two bills already were very close. The offers appeared to be intended as much to set a brisk early pace for the conference as to make clean air law.

Senate Environmental Protection Subcommittee Chairman Baucus prefaced the proposals by noting that there were only 40 legislative days left before Congress' target adjournment date, Oct. 5.

"There are those who will try to weaken this legislation" by delay and by emphasizing differences, Baucus said, urging conferees to move rapidly by focusing on the broad similarities of the two massive bills.

Once he and the Senate GOP floor manager for the bill, Chafee, had made the Senate offers, Baucus tried to nail down a date in the following week for a response from the

House, noting that "it's human nature to procrastinate."

"I've not found that to be the case in the House," Dingell replied.

He declined to set a date for a response, but said he would refer the offers to the House staff and try to work with Baucus "to try to arrange for a meeting sometime early next week."

Dingell, a veteran of huge, high-stakes conferences, became the figure to watch. Environmentalists worried that the dwindling time before adjournment would put them at a disadvantage by empowering those who wanted to force concessions by holding the bill hostage to the calendar.

Ayres, chairman of the National Clean Air Coalition, called a news conference the day before the conference began to discuss the time factor. "At this point there is a real question about whether we can finish this legislation and get a good bill out of it at the end," he said.

Dingell, long the leader of the pro-industry faction in the clean air debate, had also been a focus of environmentalists' fears that the bill could be delayed and weakened in conference.

However, at the opening session, Dingell said, "It is my hope we'll write the best possible bill in the shortest possible time."

Another critical role at the conference was to be played by the White House, which sent domestic policy adviser Porter to lead a large contingent of administration aides at the opening session.

The White House had set tough criteria for the cost of clean air legislation, insisting the president would veto a bill that put too costly a burden on industry. Talking with reporters, Porter repeated the administration's opposition to the House-approved job-loss protection package, which he said could bring a veto if it was kept in the final bill.

CFCs

The conference ground to a halt during its first full week, as House staff spent five days poring over an opening Senate offer on what had seemed to be a comparatively non-controversial section of the bill.

Chafee said Senate conferees had hoped to build momentum and get the conference off to a speedy start, but the hope was dashed.

House staff spent the week of July 16 working their way through the Senate offer on chlorofluorocarbons (CFCs). Both the Senate and House versions of the bill proposed to phase out production and use of CFCs, related substances and interim substitute substances called partially halogenated chlorofluorocarbons (HCFCs). The phaseout schedules and other details differed, but the gaps between the House and Senate were not wide.

Some House staff said one reason for the delay was that the House CFC provisions, which passed on a 416-0 vote during floor consideration May 23, had not gone through the Energy Committee markup process.

Instead, the CFC section was crafted in last-minute, backroom negotiations as the bill came to the floor and was only recently getting a thorough going-over by all interested parties.

Another "big part of what was going on was a huge array of industry lobbyists looking at their last shot at the CFC provisions," said a House aide.

Some saw the delay as confirmation of their fears that Dingell had gone into a stall mode. But others familiar with the proceedings said the process was only a deliberate approach to legislating. "I don't think anyone wants the House to look slow or like they're delaying," said one participant.

Smog Deal

After weeks of slow progress on relatively minor differences between House and Senate clean air bills, conferees the week of Sept. 10 sprinted to agreement on the largest portion of the bill: urban smog.

Compared with the time spent over minor differences on CFCs, conferees reached the agreement in lightning speed. There were few details to discuss; the Senate went along with virtually all the House-passed language.

That left a bill that imposed pollution limits further out into suburbs and rural areas and that covered far more industries than the version approved by the Senate — requiring even small emitters such as dry cleaners and bakeries to install antismog equipment.

The agreement was a defeat for the administration, which fought to weaken smog controls in the Senate bill, arguing that the cost could cripple small businesses.

But the administration declined to commit senators to the deal through conference, leaving conferees free to opt for stricter new controls on industrial pollutants. "It was the White House that gave the Senate conferees the right to vote their conscience," said Becker, lobbyist for state and local pollution officials.

Dingell said he expected no backlash from the administration. "My feelings are they will be content with what we have done," he said.

But Senate conservatives said the action did not bode well for getting a final bill that would impose costs on industry acceptable to the administration. Bush had said in January that he would not accept legislation that exceeded by more than 10 percent the compliance cost of his own clean air bill, estimated at $20 billion.

"I don't know what the motivations were of my colleagues in receding so quickly," said Idaho's Symms, who was not a conferee. "If they recede on every stricter, costlier provision in the House and Senate bills, we'll have a bill that will surely trigger a presidential veto."

Industry lobbyists immediately sent the word out to senators that the conference was forging ahead on its own. "I want the senators that are not on the conference to understand what the senators who are on the conference are doing to the bill," said Fay of the Clean Air Working Group. "The Senate Environment Committee is going to abrogate every single deal and walk away from the Senate bill whenever they want to."

As a result, Fay said, conferees "may have to pay the piper down the road."

Others predicted no revolt in the Senate over an agreement that was negotiated with the White House but that many members had little allegiance to. "Most folks two weeks before the election would like to vote for the clean air bill," said House conferee Cooper.

Senators had far more at stake, for example, in ensuring that their states were not the losers in the delicate political balance on acid rain. Offers by the Senate conferees indicated they were sticking closer to agreements reached with other senators than with the administration.

Indeed, Senate conferees reminded their House counterparts of their generosity on urban smog; Chafee said he was hoping for a "mood of reciprocity."

Meanwhile, environmentalists and state pollution officials were exuberant that the tougher smog controls had prevailed. In addition to its greater reach, the House bill required the EPA to issue a federal plan within two years after a state failed to submit an acceptable pollution-reduction strategy. Both groups had pushed hard for that language.

Becker said this "hammer" provision was critical to giving state pollution officials leverage to resist outside pressures from regulated industries. The Senate bill would have rolled back existing law by giving the EPA discretion to issue a federal plan.

Conferees did part from the House provisions by reducing controls on nitrogen oxides in areas that had not attained federal air quality standards for ozone, a change pushed primarily by the natural gas industry.

They also chose to leave until the end of conference negotiations those parts of the smog title that had overlapping jurisdictions with other committees, including controversial provisions to protect visibility in national parks and to provide $250 million over five years to compensate and retrain workers who lost their jobs because of the bill.

Permits

Conferees also completed work on relatively minor differences over permit requirements for individual plants and businesses. Permits essentially translated the Clean Air Act into enforceable requirements.

The staff agreement left industry groups grumbling about excessive paperwork and state regulators about federal intrusion, but conferees made no changes in staff recommendations.

A snag in negotiations over permit requirements for small businesses forced conference leaders to cancel a meeting scheduled for Sept. 13, however, while Ron Wyden, D-Ore., and Rick Boucher, D-Va., finished work on a proposal to mandate a state assistance program and broaden its eligibility criteria for small businesses.

The final agreement required states to set up an office to help small sources of pollution — those that emitted no more than 50 tons of any regulated pollutant or 75 tons of all regulated pollutants and employed 100 or fewer workers — to comply with Clean Air Act requirements. Sources emitting up to 100 tons of pollutants could petition to enter the program.

Motor Vehicles, Fuels

Working furiously against a leadership deadline of midnight, Oct. 14, to wrap up a deal on the bill, exhausted House and Senate aides churned out an agreement the week of Oct. 8 to clamp down on dirty gas and cars.

Late in the day Oct. 12, staff members were working to complete a second agreement to limit factory emissions of cancer-causing toxic pollutants. But negotiators still faced the Herculean task of finishing the rest of the bill over the weekend, including acid rain controls, enforcement, provisions to improve visibility in national parks and a proposal to allocate $250 million over five years to aid displaced workers, particularly coal miners.

The Sunday night deadline was set during a meeting Oct. 10 among key House and Senate conferees and House Speaker Foley.

After months of painfully slow negotiations, lobbyists late in the week of Oct. 8 found themselves struggling to influence agreements that could be reached in a matter of hours, if conferees and staff members adhered to the new deadline. "It's sausage and legislation all over again," said Fay of the industry's Clean Air Working Group. "This is a time when some of the worst bills come out of Congress. There are a lot of weary people drafting bills up there."

Industry lobbyists questioned whether auto and oil companies would be able to meet the new regulations, which they characterized as stringent. "Some of these standards are extremely technology-forcing," said Ron Hamm of the Motor Vehicle Manufacturers Association. "They've deliberately been written beyond the capabilities of companies today."

Negotiators hewed largely to the House-passed language on tailpipe emissions, requiring a 60 percent cut in nitrogen oxides and a 40 percent reduction in hydrocarbons, two primary components of smog, by 1994. More stringent standards would go into effect in 2003, unless the EPA blocked them as not technologically feasible, cost-effective or necessary.

Industry lobbyists and staff members said the second phase of emissions standards would probably go into effect.

Cars designed to meet those requirements were expected to be developed in the meantime under a more stringent California pilot program.

The agreement on motor vehicles and fuels indicated, however, that the auto and oil industries had managed to win some important concessions. Negotiators, for example, stretched out the deadlines for when the nine most polluted cities would be required to sell only gasoline that was mixed with cleaner-burning fuels.

They also linked clean-fueled vehicle programs in California and the rest of the country to ensure that automakers would not have to meet separate standards. And they delayed deadlines for when equipment would have to be installed in cars to capture fuel vapors at the gas pump.

Industry lobbyists said the changes made sense. "It's all been rationalized considerably over even what the House bill was," Hamm said.

Environmentalists could claim some victories as well. By 1996, automobiles had to be built to meet new tailpipe emissions standards for 10 years or 100,000 miles, meaning that equipment installed in cars had to be twice as durable as required under existing law.

In addition, in cities where high carbon monoxide levels were due to car exhaust, negotiators took the more stringent Senate language to control the larger amounts of carbon monoxide emitted from automobiles in cold weather — a requirement that automakers argued would shoot up the cost of cars.

But Sierra Club lobbyist Weiss said the overall result of the agreement was that significantly cleaner cars would not make it on to the nation's highways for almost a decade.

"It's an ambitious program that won't have any real-world effect until the late 1990s," he said. "In the past we have talked about a more modest program that would take effect right away."

That had implications for whether smoggy cities would be able to come into compliance with federal standards for clean air. "It is a program that has a half tank of gas," said Becker of the state pollution administrators group. "It's enough to get us started, but it's not enough to get us to finish the journey."

Becker said many of the control measures would not be implemented until well past the bill's statutory deadlines for states to comply with federal air quality standards.

Waxman, however, said he was confident the bill would bring states into compliance. "This is the most aggressive air pollution control package for cars and trucks anywhere in the world, including California," he said. "We are going to make tremendous advances, especially in California, which will benefit the rest of the country after these goals are technologically met."

The fact that negotiators reached agreement on motor-vehicle controls and air toxics left observers far more optimistic that action would be completed on legislation by the end of the session. When conferees had last met on Sept. 28, they appeared deadlocked on the issue.

Led by Dingell, House conferees were refusing to budge from their proposed controls on auto emissions and had developed a plan for clean fuels and clean-fueled vehicles that diverged from both bills in key ways.

House conferees were also still haggling over standards for reformulated gasoline. Oil-state conferees wanted House negotiators to relax their position before talks even began with the Senate.

That roadblock was cleared Oct. 6-7, when Dingell, Waxman and Energy Committee ranking Republican Lent met through that Saturday night with Republican Fields and Democrat Hall, both from Texas, to work out a new proposal on reformulated gas.

Their plan, which was part of the motor vehicles agreement, required that reformulated gasoline be the only gasoline sold in the nine smoggiest cities. Instead of being phased in beginning in 1992, however, fuel-makers had until 1995 to come up with a mixture that would cut ozone-forming and toxic emissions by 15 percent.

Industry also got a long-sought "feasibility" exemption for a second stage of emissions standards: If the EPA determined that the standard for the year 2000 — a 25 percent reduction in emissions — was not technologically feasible, taking into account cost, that requirement could drop to 20 percent.

Reformulated gas including 2.7 percent oxygen content had to be sold in the 40 cities that did not meet federal air quality standards for carbon monoxide beginning in 1992. The EPA could delay that requirement for as long as two years if insufficient fuel was available.

Another breakthrough in conference negotiations came when Dingell backed down on his insistence that states lose the authority they had under existing law to enforce California tailpipe emissions standards, if they chose to adopt them, by testing and recalling vehicles. That authority instead would have gone to the EPA.

Environmentalists and state pollution officials said the EPA would not have the resources to adequately enforce the program.

New York on Sept. 27 became the first state to opt in to the California program, which called for tailpipe controls that were stricter than federal laws.

Dingell's proposal first surfaced in September and had not been included in either the House or Senate bills. Automakers, who at the time were building separate cars to meet California and federal standards, were concerned they would have to build still another "third car" if New York or other states enforced the California standards differently.

Waxman also supported the proposal, arguing that shifting enforcement authority to the EPA made it easier for states to opt in to the California program. "There are a lot of small states that would like to have the advantage of the tougher California standards but cannot afford to go forward with it," he said.

Under heat from New York Democrat Daniel Patrick Moynihan and other senators, as well as from state governors and pollution control officials, Dingell dropped that proposal in exchange for assurances that automakers would be required to design only two types of cars.

Becker of the state pollution administrators group said retaining state authority to enforce the program was critical not only for states that adopted the existing California tailpipe emissions standards, but also for polluted cities that opted in to the California clean-fueled-vehicle pilot program proposed in the bill. The agreement required automakers to produce 150,000 ultra-clean cars for Southern California beginning in 1996 and 300,000 in later years.

Becker said states dissatisfied with the bill's program for tailpipe emissions reductions nationwide might be eager to adopt the stronger California standards. "Don't be surprised if there is a flurry of activity over the next several years as states opt in to the program," he said.

Clean-fuel requirements also were imposed in polluted cities for fleets of 10 or more vehicles, such as taxicabs, that were fueled at central locations and not driven to private homes at night. Environmentalists said the new exemption for fleet cars that were driven home opened a large loophole in the fleet program.

The fleet program was to be phased in beginning in 1998 and by 2003 would require the same emissions reductions as the California pilot program. The EPA was not required to mandate the sale of clean fuels for fleets or cars sold in states other than California.

The idea behind the clean-fueled-vehicle programs was to force development of cars that ran on clean, non-gasoline fuels such as natural gas, methanol or electricity.

Environmentalists, however, said that those new cars might not be built until the 21st century because the bill's emissions standards until then could be met with reformulated gasoline.

Air Toxics

In a last-gasp effort to bring a clean air bill to the floor before Congress adjourned, conferees reached a tentative compromise Oct. 17 on the third of four major sections of the bill, agreeing to tough new controls to reduce industrial emissions of airborne toxics.

The new proposal, which affected industries ranging from oil refineries to dry cleaners, covered 189 different air toxics, pollutants that posed especially serious health risks such as cancer and birth defects to people who lived near the emissions sources. Most of those toxic emissions had never been regulated by the federal government.

Conferees were clearly relieved that an agreement had been reached. A leadership deadline of Oct. 14 for completion of the entire bill passed with staff still deadlocked on that one issue, forcing conferees to meet until 3:00 a.m. the morning of Oct. 17 to break the impasse.

Much of the delay resulted from a standoff between Waxman and fellow House conferees from Ohio and other states who wanted to weaken emissions reduction standards for the steel industry.

Although Waxman was forced to abandon the House position and grant an extension for steelmakers, he said he was "pleased with the overall agreement."

"I've felt strongly for a long time that we had to do something about ... the harm being done to people who live near industrial facilities in this country," he said. "They are still being killed slowly."

Dave Durenberger, R-Minn., the chief Senate sponsor of the air toxics proposal, said it included "realistic requirements which, if funded, will get the job done."

The air toxics agreement was aimed at jump-starting

Continued on p. 275

Clean Air Act Amendments

Following are provisions of the Clean Air Act Amendments (S 1630 — PL 101-549) as cleared by Congress on Oct. 27 and signed into law by President Bush on Nov. 15:

Title I — Ambient Air Quality (Smog)

General Planning Requirements

• **Designations.** Required each state, after new or revised National Ambient Air Quality Standards (NAAQS) had been promulgated by the administrator of the Environmental Protection Agency (EPA), to designate each area within the state as non-attainment, attainment or unclassifiable (due to inadequate information) for the new or revised standard. The EPA administrator then had to promulgate the designations with any appropriate modifications.

• **Timetable.** Required that after promulgating a new or revised standard, the administrator had to designate all areas of the country as quickly as practicable but within two years, although a one-year extension was available.

• **Current designations.** Provided that areas designated under the existing Clean Air Act at a minimum retain their designation.

• **Redesignation to attainment.** Allowed the administrator to redesignate a non-attainment area to attainment only if: the area had attained the NAAQS; 2) the area had a fully approved plan; 3) the improvement in the air quality was due to permanent and enforceable reductions in emissions; 4) the state had submitted, and the administrator had approved, a maintenance plan for the area; and 5) the area had met all applicable requirements under the Clean Air Act.

• **Size of areas.** Required that serious, severe or extreme ozone or carbon monoxide (CO) non-attainment areas be expanded to include the entire metropolitan statistical area (MSA) or consolidated metropolitan statistical area (CMSA). All or a part of a metropolitan area could be excluded from that designation at the request of the governor, provided that the administrator found that sources in that area did not contribute significantly to a violation of the ozone or CO NAAQS.

• **Designations for PM-10.** Provided specific requirements for particulate matter (PM-10) designations: Areas identified in the Aug. 7, 1987, Federal Register as Group I areas (except as modified by EPA before enactment) and areas that had recorded air quality monitoring data exceedances of the PM-10 NAAQS before Jan. 1, 1989, would be designated non-attainment.

All other areas would be designated unclassifiable until redesignation.

• **Designations for lead.** Allowed the EPA administrator at any time to require a state to designate any area as non-attainment for lead.

State Implementation Plans

• **Plan requirements.** Required that each state implementation plan include, among other things: enforceable emissions limits; provisions for developing air quality data; provisions to control interstate air pollution; adequate personnel, funding and authority; requirements that stationary sources monitor emissions and that states report such data; and provisions for revision of the plan to adapt to revisions in the NAAQS or to findings by the EPA that the plan was substantially inadequate to attain the NAAQS.

• **State implementation plan disapproval; federal implementation plan.** Required that, if the EPA found that a state has failed to include the required elements in its state implementation plan, the administrator had to disapprove the plan.

If the state failed to correct the deficiency within two years, the administrator had to promulgate a federal implementation plan correcting the deficiency.

• **Sanctions — when to apply.** Allowed the administrator to apply sanctions against states if: 1) the administrator found that the state had failed to submit one or more of the elements required for a non-attainment area; the administrator disapproved such an element submitted by the state; 3) the state failed to make any other required submission (including a maintenance plan) or the EPA had disapproved such other required submission; or any requirement of an approved plan was not being implemented.

• **Federal facilities.** Made federal facilities subject to any state or local agency requirement to pay a fee or charge to defray the costs of the agency's air pollution regulatory program.

Non-Attainment Areas

• **Attainment dates.** Required that for a primary NAAQS, a non-attainment area had to reach attainment as expeditiously as practicable but no later than five years from the date of designation to non-attainment.

The EPA could grant an extension of up to 10 years, depending on the severity of the problem and the feasibility of control measures.

• **Extensions.** Permitted the administrator to grant up to two one-year extensions of the attainment date, upon request by the state, if the state complied with all plan requirements and no more than a minimal number of exceedances of the standard had occurred in the preceding year.

• **Non-attainment plan provisions.** Established requirements for all non-attainment-area plans, including those for ozone, CO and PM-10. Among the required provisions were: use of reasonably available control technology (RACT) on existing stationary sources; requirements for new or modified major sources; enforceable emissions limits; and automatic implementation of contingency measures when an area failed to meet any applicable milestone, make reasonable further progress or attain the NAAQS by the deadline date.

• **New source requirements.** Retained, revised and expanded existing requirements for new and modified major stationary sources.

The bill retained the requirement that new sources or modifications in non-attainment areas obtain offsets for their emissions.

The bill also retained the requirement that states analyze possible alternative sites in issuing new source permits. Major sources had to obtain offsets, with certain exceptions in zones targeted by federal agencies for economic development.

• **Offsets.** Clarified that a new or modified major stationary source had to obtain enforceable emissions reductions — at least equal to the increased emissions from the new or modified source — from the same source or other sources in the same non-attainment area. However, a state could allow a source to obtain emissions reductions in a second area (or other additional areas) if the second area had an equal or greater classification and emissions from that second area contributed to a violation of the NAAQS in the first area.

• **Sanctions.** Specified mandatory sanctions for a state's failure to submit or implement an approvable state implementation plan. If a state had not corrected a deficiency within 18 months from the administrator's finding, one of two sanctions (a cutoff of federal highway funding for other than safety or mass transit, or a 2-to-1 offset requirement for new sources or modifications) would apply immediately upon expiration of the 18-month period.

If the deficiency was not corrected within six more months, the second sanction also applied immediately. Both sanctions would apply at the expiration of the original 18-month period if the administrator found that the state was not making a good-faith effort to rectify the deficiency.

The sanctions would remain in place until the administrator found that the deficiency had been corrected and that the state had come into compliance. In addition to any other applicable sanction, the administrator could withhold all or part of state air quality grants.

• **Failure to attain.** Provided that states that submitted and properly implemented a plan but failed to attain would not be sanctioned. Instead, they would be required to comply with additional pollution control measures and other requirements.

Ozone Non-Attainment Areas

• **Classification and attainment dates.** Classified ozone non-attainment areas as marginal, moderate, serious, severe or extreme based on ozone design values. Areas were required to reach attainment as expeditiously as practicable but no later than the relevant attainment date, subject to other provisions for extension.

Classifications, design values and attainment deadlines were as follows:

Area Classification	Ozone design value (parts per million)	Deadline
Marginal	.121 up to .138	3 years after enactment
Moderate	.138 up to .160	6 years after enactment
Serious	.160 up to .180	9 years after enactment
Severe	.180 up to .280	15 years after enactment
Extreme	.280 and above	20 years after enactment

• **Extensions.** Permitted the administrator to allow up to two one-year extensions of the attainment date if the state met all state implementation plan commitments and did not record more than one exceedance of the ambient air quality standard in the year preceding the extension year.

• **Extension for certain severe areas.** Provided that severe areas with a design value between 0.190 and 0.280 parts per million (ppm) be allowed an attainment date 17 years after enactment (instead of 15).

• **Reclassification upon failure to attain ('bump-up').** Required that in the case of marginal, moderate or serious areas, EPA had to reclassify ("bump-up") each such area to the next higher classification (or to whichever classification had become applicable to the area's design value). There was no bump-up for severe or extreme areas.

• **Voluntary bump-up.** Required the administrator to allow a state to reclassify a non-attainment area to a higher classification.

• **Failure of severe areas to attain.** Required that severe areas that failed to attain by the applicable attainment date were subject to emissions-fee provisions and percentage-reduction requirements necessary to achieve reasonable further progress at successive three-year intervals after the attainment date. Areas that failed to make the required emissions reductions would be subject to mandatory sanctions.

In addition, severe areas that failed to attain and that still had a design value of greater than 0.14 ppm in the attainment year, or that failed to meet the most recent applicable milestone, would also be subject to the new source review and RACT requirements applicable to extreme areas but not to other extreme area requirements. Such areas would also be required to regulate existing sources with emissions of 10 tons or more per year as "major sources," which meant that such sources would have to obtain permits and implement RACT.

Marginal Areas

• **General.** Required that for marginal areas, states submit a comprehensive emissions inventory within two years after enactment. States also had to submit various state implementation plan revisions, including 1) reasonably available control technology (RACT) requirements; 2) corrections to any previously required motor vehicle emissions-control inspection and maintenance program to ensure that the program complied with EPA regulations; and 3) requirements that new or modified sources obtain permits and undergo new source review.

• **Offsets.** Required marginal areas to have an offset ratio of total required emissions offsets to total increased emissions from a new or modified facility of at least 1.1 to 1.

Moderate Areas

• **General.** Required that moderate ozone non-attainment areas meet all the requirements applicable to marginal areas, plus these additional requirements:

• **Emissions reductions.** Required states to submit state implementation plans within three years of enactment providing for a 15 percent or greater reduction from baseline emissions of volatile organic compounds (VOCs) in the year of enactment, to be achieved within six years after enactment. The state plan had to provide for specific annual reductions in emissions of VOCs and nitrogen oxides (NOx) as necessary to attain the primary ozone standard by the attainment deadline.

• **Reasonably available control technology.** Required the implementation of RACT on all major stationary sources.

• **Motor vehicle inspection and maintenance.** Required all moderate areas to establish an inspection and maintenance program meeting EPA specifications.

• **Stage II.** Required states to submit revised state implementation plans within two years of enactment to require gasoline dealers and other refueling facilities selling more than 10,000 gallons a month (or 50,000 gallons a month for certain independent dealers) to install and operate gasoline refueling vapor recovery systems ("Stage II controls"). This requirement was to take effect within six months to two years of state adoption of the state implementation plan revision.

• **Moderate area offsets.** Required moderate areas to have an offset ratio of total required emissions offsets to total increased emissions from a new or modified facility of at least 1.15 to 1.

Serious Areas

• **General.** Required that serious ozone non-attainment areas meet all the requirements applicable to moderate areas, plus these additional requirements:

• **'Major sources.'** Defined "major source" or "major stationary source" to include any stationary source or group of sources within a contiguous area and under common control that emitted or had the potential to emit at least 50 tons per year of VOCs. Thus, new or modified sources of 50 tons or more were subject to new source review requirements; existing sources of 50 tons or more were subject to RACT requirements; and all sources of 50 tons or more were subject to permit requirements under Title IV.

• **NOx control.** Required the administrator to promulgate within one year guidance concerning conditions under which control of NOx could be substituted for, or combined with, control of VOCs in order to reach attainment of ozone air pollution.

• **Vehicle inspection and maintenance.** Required a state to implement within two years an enhanced program of motor vehicle inspection and maintenance, with extensive requirements. The program was to apply in each urbanized serious area with a population of 200,000 or more. The program had to include annual emissions testing unless the administrator was satisfied that a biennial inspection was at least as effective.

• **Economic incentives for clean-fuel vehicles.** Required states to submit state implementation plan revisions for areas covered by the clean-fuel vehicle program (Title II), to make use of clean alternative fuels in clean-fuel vehicles economical for vehicle owners.

• **Transportation controls.** Required states, beginning six years after enactment and each three years thereafter, to determine whether vehicle miles traveled, vehicle emissions, congestion levels and other relevant factors matched the assumptions used in the area's demonstration of attainment. If not, the state would have 18 months to revise its implementation plan to include transportation control measures to reduce emissions.

• **25-ton 'de minimis' rule.** Required that, in applying new source review provisions to serious areas, any physical or operational change in a stationary source could not be considered "de minimis" (so small as to be unimportant) unless the increase in net emissions from the source, taken together with all other increases in net emissions over any five-year period, did not exceed 25 tons.

• **Modifications of sources.** Established special rules for modification of major sources. These provisions were to be triggered by a physical or operational change in the source and an exceedance of the de minimis threshold. Once triggered, the provisions required the unit (if the source was less than 100 tons per year) to meet the best available control technology (BACT) level. If the source obtained internal offsets of at least 1.3 to 1, there would not have been a modification under the bill.

For units at sources greater than 100 tons per year, lowest achievable emissions rate (LAER) technology and offsets were to be required, unless internal offsets of at least 1.3 to 1 were obtained.

• **Serious area offsets.** Required serious areas to have an offset ratio of total required emissions offsets to total increased emissions from a new or modified facility of at least 1.2 to 1.

Severe Areas

• **General.** Required that severe ozone non-attainment areas meet all requirements applicable to serious areas, plus these additional requirements:

• **Sources as small as 25 tons.** Required that the terms "major source" and "major stationary source" apply to any stationary source or group of sources within a contiguous area and under common control that emitted or had the potential to emit 25 tons or more of VOCs.

• **Vehicle miles traveled.** Required a state to submit, within two years of enactment, a state implementation plan revision including all reasonably available techniques for reducing aggregate vehicle emissions. At a minimum, the revision had to include specific enforceable strategies and transportation control measures adequate to offset any growth in emissions from increases in vehicle miles traveled (VMT).

• **Severe area offsets.** Required severe areas to have an offset ratio of total required emissions offsets to total increased emissions from a new or modified facility of at least 1.3 to 1. However, the required offset ratio was to be 1.2 to 1 if the state air quality plan required all existing major sources in the non-attainment area to use BACT instead of RACT for the control of VOCs.

Extreme Areas

• **General.** Required that extreme areas meet all requirements applicable for severe areas, plus these additional requirements:

• **Sourçes as small as 10 tons.** Required that the terms "major source" and "major stationary source" apply to any stationary source or group of sources within a contiguous area and under common control that emitted or had the potential to emit 10 tons or more of VOCs.

• **No exemptions.** Prohibited extreme areas from taking advantage of exemptions available to other qualifying non-attainment areas to allow them to achieve less than the required 15 percent emissions reduction in the first six years after enactment, or to achieve less than the required annual 3 percent reduction requirement.

• **Extreme area offsets.** Required extreme areas to have an offset ratio of total required emissions offsets to total increased emissions from a new or modified facility of at least 1.5 to 1. However, the required offset ratio was to be 1.2 to 1 if the state air quality plan required all existing major sources to use BACT instead of RACT for control of VOCs.

• **Modifications.** Required that any change at a major stationary source that resulted in any increase in emissions from any pollutant-emitting activity be considered a modification that was to require installation of technology to achieve the lowest achievable emissions rate. In effect, this provided that there would be no de minimis level of emissions increase in evaluating whether a change at a unit had produced an emissions increase.

In addition, any change at a major stationary source that resulted in any increase in emissions from any pollutant-emitting activity would require a 1.5-to-1 offset, unless the source offset the increase by a greater reduction in emissions from other discrete operations, units or activities within the source to achieve an internal offset ratio of 1.3 to 1.

• **Clean fuels or advanced control technology.** Required that, effective eight years after enactment, each new, modified or existing electric utility, industrial or commercial boiler emitting more than 25 tons per year of NOx must either: burn natural gas, ethanol, methanol or a comparably low-emitting fuel as its primary fuel; or use advanced control technology, such as catalytic control technology, or comparably available methods for the reduction of emissions of NOx.

• **Control of NOx.** Provided that state implementation plan provisions required for major stationary sources of VOCs also applied to major stationary sources of NOx. This requirement was not to apply to NOx sources for which net air quality benefits would be greater in the absence of NOx reductions. The requirement would not apply to non-attainment areas if additional reductions of NOx would not contribute to attainment in the area or produce net ozone air quality benefits in a relevant ozone transport region. The administrator could limit the application of VOC control requirements to NOx sources if the result would be excess reductions in emissions of NOx.

Commercial and Consumer Products

• **Study.** Required the EPA administrator to conduct a study and report to Congress within three years on VOC emissions from consumer and commercial products, their contribution to ozone non-attainment and criteria for regulating them. In setting those criteria, the administrator had to consider, in addition to the availability of alternatives, a product's uses, benefits and commercial demand; health or safety functions; emissions of highly reactive VOCs; and susceptibility to cost-effective controls.

• **Regulations.** Required the administrator, upon submission of the report, to list those categories of products that accounted for at least 80 percent of VOC emissions from such products in ozone non-attainment areas. The administrator could control or prohibit any activity, including the manufacture or sale of any consumer or commercial product that emitted VOCs into the ambient air.

States were not be pre-empted from proposing or adopting regulations affecting such products.

CO Non-Attainment Areas

• **Classification and attainment dates.** Classified CO non-attainment areas as follows (the administrator had discretion to adjust the classification for an area that was within 5 percent of the cutoff point):

Area classification	Design value	Attainment date
Moderate	9.1-16.4 ppm	Dec. 31, 1995
Serious	16.5 ppm and above	Dec. 31, 2000

• **Extensions.** Allowed the administrator to permit up to two one-year extensions of the attainment date if the state had met all state implementation plan commitments and had not recorded more than one exceedance of the standard in the year preceding the extension year.

• **Failure to attain; reclassification.** Provided that no later than six months after the attainment date, the administrator had to publish a notice identifying areas failing to attain. Any moderate area that failed to attain would be reclassified as a serious area.

• **Requirements for moderate areas.** Required moderate areas to submit state implementation plan revisions within two years of attainment for areas with a design value greater than 12.7 ppm, providing: 1) a comprehensive inventory of actual emissions from all sources; 2) a forecast of VMT for each year before projected attainment, to be updated annually; 3) specific measures to be taken if any estimate of VMT exceeded the most recent forecast or if the area failed to attain by the attainment date; 4) an enhanced motor vehicle inspection and maintenance program as required for serious ozone non-attainment areas (but geared to reducing CO emissions); 5) a demonstration that the plan would provide for attainment by the attainment deadline, and 6) provisions for annual emissions reductions necessary to attain by the deadline.

Vehicle inspection and maintenance. Immediately after enactment, the state had to submit corrections to any vehicle inspection and maintenance program to ensure that the program complied with existing EPA regulations.

• **Requirements for serious areas.** Required that all serious areas meet the requirements for moderate areas with a design value of greater than 12.7 ppm and also submit provisions within two years to comply with the requirements for transportation control measures required for severe ozone non-attainment areas.

• **Stationary source emissions control.** Provided that serious CO non-attainment areas in which stationary sources contributed significantly to CO levels had to submit a plan revision within two years of enactment providing that any stationary source emitting 50 tons per year or more of CO would be considered a major stationary source.

• **Waivers of motor vehicle requirements.** Allowed the EPA administrator to waive, on a case-by-case basis, any requirements that pertained to transportation controls, auto inspection and maintenance, or oxygenated fuels under Title II, if the administrator determined that mobile sources did not contribute significantly to CO levels in the area.

• **Carbon monoxide milestones.** Required that by March 31, 1996, serious CO non-attainment areas submit to the EPA administrator a demonstration that the area had achieved an aggregate reduction in CO emissions at least equivalent to the total of the specific annual emissions reductions required to be achieved by Dec. 31, 1995.

If the state failed to submit the required demonstration or achieve the emissions reductions required to meet the milestone, the state had to submit, within nine months of such failure or of EPA notice of such failure, a plan revision to implement an economic incentive and transportation planning program sufficient to achieve the emissions reduction set forth in the plan by the attainment date.

• **Serious areas that failed to attain.** Provided that any serious area that failed to attain had to submit, within nine months of such failure, a state implementation plan revision to implement a program of economic incentives and requirements.

The program had to be sufficient, in combination with other elements of the revised plan, to reduce the total tonnage of emissions of CO in the area by at least 5 percent a year until attainment.

PM-10 Non-Attainment Areas

• **Initial classification as moderate.** Provided that all particulate matter (PM-10) non-attainment areas initially be classified as moderate.

• **Reclassification as serious.** Provided that the administrator could redesignate as serious those areas that could not practically reach attainment by the moderate attainment date. Within six months after the attainment date, the administrator had to reclassify as serious all moderate areas that had failed to attain.

• **Attainment dates.** Provided that all areas had to attain as expeditiously as practicable, within the following outside dates:

Moderate areas had to generally attain no later than Dec. 31, 1994, or for certain other moderate areas, no later than six years after designation.

Serious areas had to generally attain no later than Dec. 31, 2001, or for certain other serious areas, no later than 10 years after the date of designation to non-attainment.

• **Extension for moderate areas.** Allowed the administrator to grant up to two one-year extensions of the attainment date if the state had met all state implementation plan commitments and had not recorded more than one exceedance of the standard in the year preceding the extension year.

• **Extension for serious areas.** Provided that serious areas could receive an extension of no more than five years if the otherwise applicable attainment date was impracticable; the state implementation plan had been fully implemented; the state implementation plan included the most stringent measures of any other state's implementation plan that was feasible for the areas; and the state submitted a demonstration of attainment by the most expeditious alternative date practicable.

• **Waivers for certain areas.** Allowed the EPA administrator to waive any requirement applicable to a serious area if the administrator determined that man-made sources did not contribute significantly to the PM-10 problem in that area.

• **Requirements for moderate areas.** Required moderate areas to submit revisions to their state implementation plans to require a new source review permit program and submit either a demonstration that the plan would provide for attainment by the attainment date or a demonstration that attainment by that date would be impracticable.

In addition, moderate areas had to include provisions in their submissions to require that reasonably available control measures (RACM) for the control of PM-10 emissions be implemented no later than Dec. 10, 1993, or four years after designation.

• **Serious areas.** Required serious areas to meet the requirements applicable to moderate areas and provide either a demonstration that the plan would provide for attainment by the attainment date or (for those areas for which the state was seeking an extension) a demonstration of attainment by the most expeditious alternative date practicable.

In addition, serious areas had to include in their submissions provisions to require that best available control measures for the control of PM-10 emissions be implemented no later than four years after the area was classified or reclassified as serious.

• **Major source size.** Defined "major source" and "major stationary source" as any stationary source or group of sources within a contiguous area and under common control that emitted or had the potential to emit 70 tons or more per year of PM-10.

• **PM-10 milestones.** Established a milestone program for PM-10 areas. Plan revisions had to include quantitative emissions reduction milestones to be achieved every three years until the area reached attainment.

• **Failure to attain.** Provided that where a serious PM-10 non-attainment area had not attained by the attainment date, the state had to submit within 12 months plan revisions that provided for attainment as expeditiously as practicable and that included a program of specific emissions reduction measures sufficient, in combination with other elements of the revised plan, to reduce the total tonnage of emissions of PM-10 in the area by at least 5 percent per year until attainment.

• **Control of PM-10 precursors.** Provided that the control requirements in effect under this part for major stationary sources of PM-10 also applied to major stationary sources of PM-10 precursors, except where the administrator determined that such sources did not contribute significantly to PM-10 levels that exceeded the standard in the area.

SO_2, NO_2 and Lead Non-Attainment

• **General.** Establisheed state implementation plan submittal and attainment dates for areas that needed to do additional planning to attain standards for sulfur oxides (SOx), nitrogen dioxide (NO_2) and lead.

• **Plan submission deadlines.** Required areas newly designated non-attainment for one of these pollutants to submit a new plan within 18 months of the designation. Such plans had to demonstrate attainment within five years of the designation.

Title II — Motor Vehicles

Heavy-Duty Trucks

• **Standards.** Allowed the administrator of the EPA to promulgate emissions regulations for pollutants from heavy-duty vehicles or engines and from other mobile sources on the basis of information available concerning the effects of such air pollutants on the public health and welfare, taking costs into account.

Effective for model year (MY) 1998 and thereafter, the regulations had to limit emissions of nitrogen oxides (NOx) from gasoline and diesel-fueled heavy-duty trucks to 4.0 grams per brake horsepower hour (gbh).

In-Use Certification Emissions Standards

• **Passenger cars and light-duty trucks.** Required emissions standards for non-methane hydrocarbons (NMHC), carbon monoxide (CO) and NOx for passenger cars and light-duty trucks of 6,000 pounds gross vehicle weight rating or less. For MY 1994, 40 percent of each automaker's passenger cars and light-duty trucks had to comply, increasing to 80 percent for MY 1995 and to 100 percent thereafter.

Emissions standards for the first five years or 50,000 miles, whichever came first, were 0.25 grams per mile (gpm) for NMHC, 3.4 gpm for CO and 0.4 gpm for NOx for passenger cars and light-duty trucks weighing 3,750 pounds loaded vehicle weight or less. For 10 years or 100,000 miles, whichever came first, emissions standards were to drop to 0.31 gpm for NMHC, 4.2 gpm for CO and 0.6 gpm for NOx.

• **Particulate matter (PM).** Established emissions standards for PM for passenger cars in MY 1994 and thereafter and for light-duty trucks of 6,000 pounds gross vehicle weight rating (gvwr) or less produced in MY 1995 and thereafter.

In the case of light-duty trucks, 40 percent had to comply in MY 1995, 80 percent in MY 1996 and 100 percent thereafter. For passenger cars and trucks weighing 3,750 pounds loaded vehicle weight or less, 40 percent were to comply in 1994, 80 percent in 1995 and 100 percent thereafter.

Emissions standards for the first five years or 50,000 miles were 0.08 gpm, then 0.10 gpm for the first 10 years or 10,000 miles.

• **Truck emissions.** Established emissions standards for gasoline-fueled and diesel-fueled trucks of more than 6,000 gvwr beginning with MY 1996. In 1996, 50 percent of such vehicles were to comply, rising to 100 percent thereafter.

Trucks from 3,751 pounds to less than 5,750 pounds, loaded vehicle weight, for the first five years or 50,000 miles: NMHC — 0.32; CO — 4.4 gpm; NOx — 0.7 gpm. For a useful life of 11 years or 120,000 miles: NMHC — 0.46; CO — 6.4 gpm; NOx — 0.98 gpm; PM — 0.10 gpm.

For trucks of more than 5,750 pounds gvwr, for five years or 50,000 miles: NMHC — 0.39 gpm; CO — 5.0 gmp; NOx — 1.1 gpm.

For 11 years or 120,000 miles: NMHC — 0.56; CO — 7.3 gpm; NOx — 1.53 gpm; PM — 0.12 gpm.

• **Tier II standards.** Directed the EPA administrator, with the participation of the Office of Technology Assessment, to study whether to establish in MY 2003 and later the following emissions standards on a nationwide basis for passenger cars and trucks weighing less than 3,750 pounds loaded vehicle weight: 0.125 gpm for NMHC; 0.2 gpm NOx; 1.7 gpm CO. The useful-life period accompanying these standards was to be 10 years or 100,000 miles, whichever came first.

The administrator had to submit the report to Congress no later than June 1, 1997. No later than Dec. 31, 1999, the administrator had to decide whether to further reduce emissions to attain or maintain the national ambient air quality standard (NAAQS), whether the technology for meeting more stringent emissions standards was available and whether further emissions reductions from such vehicles were needed and cost-effective.

The standards and useful-life periods specified were to go into effect unless the administrator determined by rule that such standards should be more stringent or should be postponed.

In-Use Compliance

• **Intermediate in-use standards.** Established intermediate standards in MY 1994-95, upon which recall decisions would be made, for motor vehicles of less than 6,000 pounds gvwr subject to the NMHC, CO and NOx emissions standards. The intermediate standards were to apply to 40 percent of each manufacturer's sales volume in MY 1994 and 80 percent in MY 1995.

Emissions standards for passenger cars were 0.32 gpm for NMHC, 3.4 gpm for CO and 0.4 gpm for NOx.

Standards for light-duty trucks weighing 3,750 pounds loaded vehicle weight or less were 0.32 gpm for NMHC, 5.2 gpm for CO and 0.4 for NOx.

Light-duty trucks weighing up to 5,750 loaded vehicle weight had to cut emissions of NMHC to 0.41 gpm, CO to 6.7 gpm and NOx to 0.7 gpm.

Emissions standards for trucks weighing more than 6,000 gvwr were 0.49 gpm for NMHC, 6.2 gpm for CO and 1.38 gpm for NOx.

• **Useful life.** Set useful life standards for the purposes of determining compliance with emissions reductions for NMHC, CO, and NOx at five years or 50,000 miles, whichever came first. For the purposes of certification, the useful life was to be 10 years or 100,000 miles, except that no testing was to be done beyond seven years or 75,000 miles.

Other Emissions Standards

• **CO emissions at cold temperatures.** Required the EPA administrator to promulgate regulations for emissions of CO from light-duty vehicles and trucks in MY 1994 and later when tested at 20 degrees Fahrenheit. Beginning with MY 1994, emissions from 40 percent of a manufacturer's vehicles could not exceed 10.0 gpm. In 1995, 80 percent of vehicles were to have to comply, rising to 100 percent thereafter. The administrator could also issue regulations applicable to emissions of carbon monoxide from heavy-duty vehicles and engines. If, by June 1, 1997, six or more non-attainment areas (excluding Steubenville, Ohio, and Oshkosh, Wis.) had a CO design value of 9.5 ppm or greater, an emission standard of 3.4 gpm was to take effect for light-duty vehicles (4.4 gpm for light-duty trucks) beginning with MY 2002.

• **Evaporative emissions.** Required the administrator to issue regulations within 33 months to require reductions in evaporative emissions of hydrocarbons from all gasoline-fueled vehicles during operation and during sustained periods of non-use under summertime conditions conducive to the formation of ozone. Reductions had to be the greatest possible from means expected to be available when the regulations go into effect.

• **Onboard vapor recovery.** Required the administrator within one year to issue standards requiring onboard systems for the control of vehicle refueling emissions for light-duty vehicles manufactured, beginning with the fourth model year after the model year in which the standards were issued. The standards had to apply to a percentage of each manufacturer's fleet of new light-duty vehicles and to require that such systems provide a minimum evaporative emission capture efficiency of 95 percent.

Requirements relating to Stage II gasoline vapor recovery for areas classified as moderate for ozone were not to apply after promulgation of such standards. The administrator could also waive those Stage II requirements for serious, severe or extreme ozone areas if onboard emissions control systems were in widespread use.

• **Air toxics.** Required the administrator to complete within 18 months a study of the need for and feasibility of controlling toxic emissions associated with motor vehicles and motor vehicle fuels not regulated under Title II, particularly benzene, formaldehyde and 1,3-butadiene. Within 54 months of enactment, the administrator had to issue regulations containing reasonable requirements for control of such hazardous emissions from motor vehicles and motor vehicle fuels.

• **Emission control diagnostics systems.** Required the administrator to promulgate regulations within 18 months of enactment to require installation by MY 1994 of onboard diagnostic systems on all light-duty passenger vehicles and trucks. The administrator could extend the requirement to heavy-duty vehicles and engines. The administrator could waive compliance with the regulations in 1994 or 1995, or both.

The diagnostic systems had to identify emissions-system malfunctions that could cause vehicles to fail to comply with emissions requirements, including, at least, any failures in the catalytic converter or the oxygen sensor. States had to update their state implementation plans to require vehicle inspection and maintenance programs to include onboard diagnostic systems in their inspections.

• **Testing and certification.** Directed the administrator to develop certification test procedures to determine whether light-duty vehicles and trucks from MY 1993 and thereafter complied with required inspection methods and procedures. EPA had to review and revise requirements for testing to ensure that test conditions reflected driving conditions.

• **Auto warranties.** Established a warranty period beginning with MY 1995 under which new light-duty trucks and light-duty vehicles and engines had to be free from pollution control defects for two years or 24,000 miles. This warranty period was to apply to all automotive parts and systems except the catalytic converter, the electronic control unit and an onboard emissions diagnostic device, which was listed as "major emission control components" subject to a warranty period of eight years or 80,000 miles. The administrator could include other equipment in the extended warranty category if the device was not in general use before MY 1990 and the retail cost exceeded $200.

Fuel Volatility

• **Reid pressure.** Required the EPA administrator to promulgate within six months regulations requiring additional reductions in the volatility of gasoline during the high ozone season (mainly the summer months). The regulations had to include a maximum Reid vapor pressure standard of 9.0 pounds per square inch (psi), and the administrator had to establish more stringent Reid vapor pressure standards as needed to achieve comparable evaporative emissions (on a per-vehicle basis) in non-attainment areas. The regulations had to take effect no later than the high ozone season of 1992.

• **Ethanol exemption.** Permitted gasoline containing at least 9 percent but not more than 10 percent ethanol (by volume) to exceed the volatility requirements by up to 1.0 psi.

Diesel Fuel

• **Sulfur content.** Barred as of Oct. 1, 1993, the manufacture, sale or transport of motor vehicle diesel fuel having a sulfur content of greater than 0.05 percent by weight or a cetane index below 40.

• **Certification fuel.** Required the sulfur content of fuel used to certify heavy-duty diesel engines for MY 1991-93 to be 0.10 percent by weight. Certification fuel for diesel engines for MY 1994 and later had to comply with the stricter requirements in the above paragraph.

Reformulated Gasoline

• **Formula and emissions limits.** Directed the EPA administrator within one year to issue regulations requiring use of cleaner, reformulated gasoline in nine ozone non-attainment areas with the highest design values for the period of 1987-89, beginning in 1995. The reformulated gasoline had to meet the more stringent of the following emissions standards: either 1.0 percent benzene content by volume, 25 percent aromatic hydrocarbon content by volume, no lead or other heavy metal content and 2.0 percent oxygen content by weight; or 15 percent below the total emissions of ozone-forming volatile organic compounds (VOCs) and hazardous air pollutants from representative MY 1990 vehicles when using 1990 certification fuel during the high ozone season. The last standard was to increase to 25 percent in 2000 if feasible, taking costs into account, but could be no less than 20 percent.

• **Nitrogen oxides.** Required that total emissions of NOx be no greater than the level of such emissions when using conventional gasoline of the same grade that met the reformulated gasoline requirements. If compliance with the limitation on NOx emissions was technically infeasible, the administrator could adjust or waive the reformulated gasoline content requirements.

• **Fuel certification.** Required the administrator to certify alternative fuel formulations if they would achieve equivalent or greater reductions in emissions of VOCs and hazardous air pollutants than were achieved by a fuel meeting the requirements in the above paragraphs. The administrator was to approve or deny petitions to certify such fuel within 180 days.

• **Fuel sales.** Prohibited fuel refiners or marketers from selling uncertified fuel after Jan. 1, 1995, in any covered ozone non-attainment area.

• **Opt in.** Required the administrator to apply the above prohibition on conventional fuels sales to marginal, moderate, serious or severe non-attainment areas by 1995, or one year after receiving an application to do so from the governor of a state, whichever was later. If the administrator determined in consultation with the secretary of Energy that there was insufficient domestic capacity to produce the certified fuel, the administrator had to extend the effective date of the conventional fuels sales prohibition in marginal, moderate, serious or severe areas for one year. That prohibition could be extended for two additional one-year periods.

• **Credits.** Required that credits be granted for fuel that exceeded the minimum oxygen content requirements, included lower aromatic hydrocarbon content or had a benzene content less than the maximum specified. Credits could be transferred to another fuel producer for the purpose of compliance, but they could not be used in a non-attainment area if they raised average fuel aromatic hydrocarbon and benzene content or lowered average fuel oxygen content.

• **Antidumping rules.** Barred the sale of gasoline in areas not covered by the reformulated gasoline requirements that resulted in average per gallon emissions of VOCs, NOx, CO or toxic air pollutants greater than that refiner, blender or importer sold in 1990. That prohibition would be effective beginning in 1995.

CO Non-Attainment Areas

• **Oxygenated Fuels.** Required each state in which there was all or part of a moderate or serious CO area to submit a state implementation plan within one year after classification of the area to ensure that gasoline sold in the non-attainment area be blended to contain not less than 2.7 percent oxygen as of Nov. 1, 1992. The EPA administrator had to waive this requirement if the state demonstrated that use of oxygenated fuels would interfere with attainment of a national or local ambient air quality standard for any air pollutant other than CO or if the state demonstrated that mobile sources did not contribute significantly to CO levels in the area.

• **Oxygen credits.** Required the administrator within nine months after enactment to allow use of marketable oxygen credits from fuels with higher oxygen content than required to offset the sale of fuels with lower oxygen content.

• **Serious non-attainment areas.** Required states to submit a plan revision within nine months after the administrator determined that the NAAQS for carbon monoxide was not met in a serious area by the applicable date to require that gasoline be blended to contain not less than 3.1 percent oxygen.

Non-Road Vehicles and Engines

• **CO, VOCs and NOx.** Directed the EPA administrator to complete within one year a study on emissions from non-road engines and vehicles. If the administrator determined that emissions of CO, VOCs and NOx from new non-road engines were significant contributors to ozone or CO concentrations in more than one area that failed to attain the NAAQS for ozone or CO, the administrator was required within one additional year to issue standards for emissions from non-road vehicles that contributed to such air pollution. The regulations had to apply to the useful life of the vehicle.

• **Pre-emption.** Barred any state or political subdivision from adopting or enforcing standards relating to the control of emissions from new locomotives or non-road vehicles or engines smaller than 175 horsepower used in construction or farm equipment. Within five years, the administrator had to issue regulations to control emissions from new locomotives.

The administrator could authorize California to adopt and enforce standards and other requirements relating to the control of emissions from other non-road vehicles or engines if they were at least as protective of public health and welfare. Other states could adopt the California standards.

• **Prohibition on engines requiring lead.** Directed the administrator to issue regulations for motor vehicle and non-road engines manufactured after MY 1992 to prohibit the manufacture or sale of engines that required leaded gasoline.

Enforcement

• **Testing.** Prohibited refusal by a manufacturer to pay for procurement or testing of vehicles to determine whether a vehicle met in-use standards throughout its life.

• **Tampering.** Made it illegal for anyone to remove or disable any component of a vehicle emission-control system or to manufacture, sell or offer to sell any device designed to bypass or disable an emission-control system.

• **Civil penalties.** Raised the maximum civil penalty for a violation of certain vehicle requirements from $10,000 (set in 1970) to $25,000.

Administrative penalties could total no more than $200,000, unless the EPA administrator and the attorney general determined that a larger penalty was appropriate. An existing penalty provision providing for a forfeiture of $10,000 per day for fuel-regulation violations was replaced with a civil penalty of up to $25,000 per day for each violation plus the economic benefit of non-compliance.

In the case of violations of fuels standards based on a multiday averaging period, each day was a separate day of violation.

Clean-Fuel Vehicles and Fuels

• **General.** Required the EPA administrator within two years to issue regulations including clean-fuel standards for fleets of 10 or more motor vehicles capable of being centrally fueled, excluding those garaged at a personal residence at night, held for lease or sale to the public, or used for product evaluation, law enforcement or emergency. The standards were to be adopted beginning in MY 1996 in all serious, severe and extreme ozone non-attainment areas with a 1980 population of 250,000 or more and in all CO non-attainment areas with a design value of 16.0 ppm or more and a population of 250,000, excluding those areas where mobile sources did not significantly contribute to the CO problem.

State implementation plans had to phase in these requirements so that 30 percent of fleet cars and light-duty trucks up to 6,000 pounds gvwr met the requirements by MY 1998, 50 percent by MY 1999 and 70 percent by MY 2001. For heavy-duty trucks above 8,500 pounds gvwr, 50 percent had to comply by MY 1998 and thereafter.

Specific standards were as follows:

• **Phase I, cars and light-duty trucks.** Required emissions standards for a useful life of 50,000 miles for all light-duty vehicles and light-duty trucks weighing up to 3,750 pounds loaded vehicle weight and up to 6,000 gvwr. The standards were as follows: non-methane organic gas (NMOG) — 0.125 gpm; CO — 3.4 gpm; NOx — 0.4 gpm; and formaldehyde (HCHO) — 0.015 gpm.

For a useful life of 100,000 miles, the standards were as follows: NMOG — 0.156 gpm; CO — 4.2 gpm; NOx — 0.6 gpm; HCHO — 0.018 gpm; and PM — 0.08 gpm (diesel-fueled vehicles only).

• **Light-duty trucks.** Required emissions standards for a useful life of 50,000 miles for light-duty trucks weighing more than 3,750 pounds and up to 5,750 pounds loaded vehicle weight and up to 6,000 pounds gvwr: NMOG — 0.160 gpm; CO — 4.4 gpm; NOx — 0.7 gpm; HCHO — 0.018 gpm. For a useful life of 100,000 miles, the standards were as follows: NMOG — 0.2 gpm; CO — 5.5 gpm; NOx — 0.9 gpm; HCHO — 0.023 gpm; PM — 0.08 gpm (diesel-fueled vehicles only).

• **Heavy-duty vehicles.** Required heavy-duty vehicles or engines beginning in MY 1998 and having a gvwr greater than 8,500 pounds and up to 26,000 pounds gvwr to have combined emissions of NOx and NMHC that did not exceed 3.15 grams per brake horsepower hour (50 percent less than the emissions that would result from heavy-duty diesel vehicles of MY 1994 using baseline fuel), unless the administrator determined that the standard was not feasible based on durability, cost, lead-time, safety and other factors.

• **Phase II, cars and light-duty trucks.** Required emissions standards for a useful life of 50,000 miles for light-duty vehicles and light-duty trucks weighing up to 6,000 pounds, beginning with MY 2001: NMOG — 0.075 gpm; CO — 3.4 gpm; NOx — 0.2 gpm; and HCHO — 0.015 gpm.

For a useful life of 100,000 miles: NMOG — 0.090 gpm; CO — 4.2 gpm; NOx — 0.3 gpm; HCHO — 0.018 gpm; and PM — 0.08 (diesel-fueled vehicles only).

• **Light-duty trucks up to 6,000 pounds gvwr.** Required emissions standards for a useful life of 50,000 miles for light-duty trucks weighing more than 3,750 pounds and up to 5,750 pounds loaded vehicle weight and up to 6,000 pounds gvwr: NMOG — 0.1 gpm; CO — 4.4 gpm; NOx — 0.4 gpm; and HCHO — 0.018 gpm.

For a useful life of 100,000 miles: NMOG — 0.13 gpm; CO — 5.5 gpm; NOx — 0.5 gpm; HCHO — 0.023 gpm; and PM — 0.08 gpm (diesel-fueled vehicles only).

• **Light-duty trucks greater than 6,000 pounds gvwr.** Required emissions standards for trucks of more than 6,000 pounds gvwr and less than or equal to 8,500 pounds gvwr, beginning with MY 1998. For a useful life of 50,000 miles, those standards varied by weight category.

California Clean-Fuel Vehicle Standards

• **CARB standards.** Allowed the California Air Resources Board to adopt more stringent standards for clean-fuel vehicles that could be adopted for fleets nationwide. California could also adopt less stringent standards, which would delay application of the above standards for two years.

California Pilot Program

• **Clean-fuel vehicles.** Required the EPA administrator to issue regulations within two years mandating the sale of 150,000 clean-fueled vehicles in California in MY 1996, 1997 and 1998, increasing to 300,000 vehicles in 1999 and thereafter. California was required to revise its state implementation plan (SIP) to ensure that sufficient amounts of clean fuels were produced and distributed. Other states could opt into the program, although there were no provisions to mandate the sale or production of clean vehicles or fuels in other states. States were not authorized to prohibit or limit the manufacture or sale of vehicles or engines certified by California as being in compliance with California's standards, or to take action that would result in the creation of a vehicle or engine different from one certified by California (a "third vehicle").

Urban Buses

• **Emissions standards for clean-fuel buses.** Required the EPA administrator to promulgate by Jan. 1, 1992, emissions standards for clean-fuel buses for MY 1994 and thereafter. The standards had to be based on the best technology that could reasonably be anticipated to be available at the time the standards were implemented, taking into account cost, safety, energy, lead time and other relevant factors. Except for the specific requirements referred to in the next paragraph, the standards had to require compliance with emissions standards for conventional heavy-duty vehicles of the same type and model year.

• **Specific requirements for buses.** Required that clean-fuel bus emissions of PM not exceed 50 percent of the emissions allowed for conventional heavy-duty vehicles or engines in MY 1994 and thereafter. The administrator could exceed the 50 percent level if it was technologically achievable but could not increase allowable emissions above 70 percent.

• **Additional fuel requirement.** Required the administrator annually to test urban buses subject to the PM standard to determine if they complied over their full useful life. If not, the administrator had to require that all buses purchased or put into service in metropolitan statistical areas (MSAs) or consolidated metropolitan statistical areas (CMSAs) with a 1980 population of 750,000 be operated on clean fuels (methanol, ethanol, propane, natural gas or any comparable low-polluting fuel).

The administrator had to phase in the requirement over five years, beginning three years after the administrator's determination above.

• **Existing urban buses.** Required that the foregoing clean-fuel regulations also applied to existing buses that had their engines rebuilt or replaced after Jan. 1, 1995, and that operated in the areas described.

• **PM.** Required that emissions of PM from buses before 1994 not exceed 0.25 gram per brake horsepower hour in MY 1991 and MY 1992 and 0.10 gram per brake horsepower hour in MY 1993 and thereafter.

Title III — Air Toxics

Hazardous Air Pollutants

• **Major sources.** Defined "major source" to mean any stationary source of air pollutants that emitted an aggregate of at least 10 tons per year of any hazardous air pollutant or at least 25 tons per year of a combination of hazardous air pollutants.

The EPA administrator could establish a lesser quantity or different criteria in the case of radionuclides, on the basis of a pollutant's potency, persistence, potential for bioaccumulation or other factors.

• **Area sources.** Defined "area source" as any stationary source of hazardous air pollutants that was not a major source. The definition did not include motor vehicles or non-road vehicles subject to regulation under Title II.

• **Stationary sources.** Defined "stationary source" to mean a facility or installation (or unit thereof) that emitted or might emit hazardous air pollutants.

• **New sources.** Defined "new source" to mean a source whose construction or reconstruction was begun after the administrator first proposed regulations applicable to that source.

• **Hazardous air pollutants.** Defined hazardous air pollutants to mean any air pollutant listed by the bill.

• **Adverse environmental effects.** Defined "adverse environmental effects" to mean any threat of significant adverse effects that could reasonably be anticipated to wildlife, aquatic life or other natural resources, including disruption of local ecosystems, impacts on populations of endangered or threatened species, significant degradation of environmental quality over broad areas or other comparable effects.

List of Pollutants

• **List.** Established a list of 189 substances and compounds that had to be considered hazardous air pollutants. *(Air toxics box, p. 255)*

• **Review.** Required the EPA administrator periodically to review and revise the list by adding pollutants that presented a threat of adverse human health or environmental effects.

• **Add or delete.** Allowed any person to petition the administrator to add or delete substances. A petition had to contain adequate data on the health effects of the substance or other evidence sufficient to support the petition.

The administrator had to accept the petition or deny it and explain why within 18 months. Such a petition could not be denied on the grounds that the administrator did not have the time or the resources to review it.

The administrator had to add a pollutant to the list if it was known or reasonably anticipated to cause adverse human health or environmental effects.

Conversely, the administrator had to remove a pollutant from the list if it was not known or reasonably anticipated to cause adverse health or environmental effects.

• **Lead.** Prohibited the administrator from listing elemental lead as a hazardous air pollutant.

Source Categories

• **Major sources.** Required the EPA administrator to publish a list within 12 months of all categories and subcategories of major sources of hazardous air pollutants. The list had to be revised at least every eight years.

• **Area sources.** Required the administrator to list and desig-

Hazardous Air Pollutants

CAS #	Chemical Name
75070	Acetaldehyde
60355	Acetamide
75058	Acetonitrile
98862	Acetophenone
53963	2-Acetylaminofluorene
107028	Acrolein
79061	Acrylamide
79107	Acrylic acid
107131	Acrylonitrile
107051	Allyl chloride
92671	4-Aminobiphenyl
62533	Aniline
90040	o-Anisidine
1332214	Asbestos
71432	Benzene (including from gasoline)
92875	Benzidine
98077	Benzotrichloride
100447	Benzyl chloride
92524	Biphenyl
117817	Bis((2-ethylhexyl)) phthalate (DEHP)
542881	Bis(chloromethyl)ether
75252	Bromoform
106990	1,3-Butadiene
156627	Calcium cyanamide
105602	Caprolactam
133062	Captan
63252	Carbaryl
75150	Carbon disulfide
56235	Carbon tetrachloride
463581	Carbonyl sulfide
120809	Catechol
133904	Chloramben
57749	Chlordane
7782505	Chlorine
79118	Chloroacetic acid
532274	2-Chloroacetophenone
108907	Chlorobenzene
510156	Chlorobenzilate
67663	Chloroform
107302	Chloromethyl methyl ether
126998	Chloroprene
1319773	Cresols/Cresylic acid (isomers and mixture)
95487	o-Cresol
108394	m-Cresol
106445	p-Cresol
98828	Cumene
94757	2,4-D, salts and esters
3547044	DDE
334883	Diazomethane
132649	Dibenzofurans
96128	1,2-Dibromo-3-chloropropane
84742	Dibutylphthalate
106467	1,4-Dichlorobenzene(p)
91941	3,3-Dichlorobenzidene
111444	Dichloroethyl ether (Bis(2-chloroethyl)ether)
542756	1,3-Dichloropropene
62737	Dichlorvos
111422	Diethanolamine
121697	N,N-Diethyl aniline (N,N-Dimethylaniline)
64675	Diethyl sulfate
119904	3,3-Dimethoxybenzidine
60117	Dimethyl aminoazobenzene
119937	3,3'-Dimethyl benzidine
79447	Dimethyl carbamoyl chloride
68122	Dimethyl formamide
57147	1,1-Dimethyl hydrazine
131113	Dimethyl phthalate
77781	Dimethyl sulfate
534521	4,6-Dinitro-o-cresol, and salts
51285	2,4-Dinitrophenol
121142	2,4-Dinitrotoluene
123911	1,4-Dioxane (1,4-Diethyleneoxide)
122667	1,2-Diphenylhydrazine
106898	Epichlorohydrin (1-Chloro-2,3-epoxypropane)
106887	1,2-Epoxybutane
140885	Ethyl acrylate
100414	Ethyl benzene
51796	Ethyl carbamate (Urethane)
75003	Ethyl chloride (Chloroethane)
106934	Ethylene dibromide (Dibromoethane)
107062	Ethylene dichloride (1,2-Dichloroethane)
107211	Ethylene glycol
151564	Ethylene imine (Aziridine)
75218	Ethylene oxide
96457	Ethylene thiourea
75343	Ethylidene dichloride (1,1-Dichloroethane)
50000	Formaldehyde
76448	Heptachlor
118741	Hexachlorobenzene
87683	Hexachlorobutadiene
77474	Hexachlorocyclopentadiene
67721	Hexachloroethane
822060	Hexamethylene-1,6-diisocyanate
680319	Hexamethylphosphoramide
110543	Hexane
302012	Hydrazine
7647010	Hydrochloric acid
7664393	Hydrogen fluoride (hydrofluoric acid)
123319	Hydroquinone
78591	Isophorone
58899	Lindane (all isomers)
108316	Maleic anhydride
67561	Methanol
72435	Methoxychlor
74839	Methyl bromide (Bromomethane)
74873	Methyl chloride (Chloromethane)
71556	Methyl chloroform (1,1,1-Trichloroethane)
78933	Methyl ethyl ketone (2-Butanone)
60344	Methyl hydrazine
74884	Methyl iodide (Iodomethane)
108101	Methyl isobutyl ketone (Hexone)
624839	Methyl isocyanate
80626	Methyl methacrylate
1634044	Methyl tert butyl ether
101144	4,4-Methylene bis(2-chloroaniline)
75092	Methylene chloride (Dichloromethane)
101688	Methylene diphenyl diisocyanate (MDI)
101779	4,4'-Methylenedianiline
91203	Naphthalene
98953	Nitrobenzene
92933	4-Nitrobiphenyl
100027	4-Nitrophenol
79469	2-Nitropropane
684935	N-Nitroso-N-methylurea
62759	N-Nitrosodimethylamine
59892	N-Nitrosomorpholine
56382	Parathion
82688	Pentachloronitrobenzene (Quintobenzene)
87865	Pentachlorophenol
108952	Phenol
106503	p-Phenylenediamine
75445	Phosgene
7803512	Phosphine
7723140	Phosphorus
85449	Phthalic anhydride
1336363	Polychlorinated biphenyls (Aroclors)
1120714	1,3-Propane sultone
57578	beta-Propiolactone
123386	Propionaldehyde
114261	Propoxur (Baygon)
78875	Propylene dichloride (1,2-Dichloropropane)
75569	Propylene oxide
75558	1,2-Propylenimine (2-Methyl aziridine)
91225	Quinoline
106514	Quinone
100425	Styrene
96093	Styrene oxide
1746016	2,3,7,8-Tetrachlorodibenzo-p-dioxin
79345	1,1,2,2-Tetrachloroethane
127184	Tetrachloroethylene (Perchloroethylene)
7550450	Titanium tetrachloride
108883	Toluene
95807	2,4-Toluene diamine
584849	2,4-Toluene diisocyanate
95534	o-Toluidine
8001352	Toxaphene (chlorinated camphene)
120821	1,2,4-Trichlorobenzene
79005	1,1,2-Trichloroethane
79016	Trichloroethylene
95954	2,4,5-Trichlorophenol
88062	2,4,6-Trichlorophenol
121448	Triethylamine
1582098	Trifluralin
540841	2,2,4-Trimethylpentane
108054	Vinyl acetate
593602	Vinyl bromide
75014	Vinyl chloride
75354	Vinylidene chloride (1,1-Dichloroethylene)
1330207	Xylenes (isomers and mixture)
95476	o-Xylenes
108383	m-Xylenes
106423	p-Xylenes
0	Antimony compounds
0	Arsenic compounds (inorganic including arsine)
0	Beryllium compounds
0	Cadmium compounds
0	Chromium compounds
0	Cobalt compounds
0	Coke oven emissions
0	Cyanide compounds [1]
0	Glycol ethers [2]
0	Lead compounds
0	Manganese compounds
0	Mercury compounds
0	Mineral fibers [3]
0	Nickel compounds
0	Polycylic organic matter [4]
0	Radionuclides (including radon) [5]
0	Selenium compounds

NOTE: For all listings above that contain the word "compounds" and for glycol ethers, the following applies: Unless otherwise specified, these listings are defined as including any unique chemical substance that contains the named chemical (i.e., antimony, arsenic, etc.) as part of that chemical's infrastructure.

[1] *X'CN where X = H' or any other group where a formal dissociation may occur. For example, KCN or* $Ca(CN)_2$.

[2] *Includes mono- and diethers of ethylene glycol, diethylene glycol, and triethylene glycol* $R\text{-}(OCH_2CH_2)_n\text{-}OR'$ *where n = 1, 2, or 3; R = alkyl or aryl groups; R' = R, H, or groups which, when removed, yield glycol ethers with the structure* $R\text{-}(OCH_2CH_2)_n\text{-}OH$. *Polymers are excluded from the glycol category.*

[3] *Includes glass microfibers, glass wool fibers, rock wool fibers, and slag wool fibers, each characterized as "respirable" (fiber diameter less than 3.5 micrometers) and possessing an aspect ratio (fiber length divided by fiber diameter) greater than or equal to 3, as emitted from production of fiber and fiber products.*

[4] *Includes organic compounds with more than one benzene ring, and which have a boiling point greater than or equal to 100 degrees Celsius.*

[5] *A type of atom which spontaneously undergoes radioactive decay.*

nate for regulation each category or subcategory of area sources that the administrator found presented a threat of adverse effects to human health or the environment. The administrator within five years had to list sufficient categories or subcategories of area sources to ensure that area sources representing 90 percent of the 30 most hazardous air pollutants in the largest number of urban areas were regulated. Regulations had to take effect within 10 years.

• **Specific pollutants.** Required the administrator within five years to list categories and subcategories of sources to assure that 90 percent of the aggregate emissions of alkylated lead compounds, polycyclic organic matter, hexachlorobenzene, polychlorinated biphenyls, 2,3,7,8-tetrachlorodibenzo-furans and 2,3,7,8-tetrachlorodibenzo-p-dioxin were subject to emissions-reduction standards.

• **Research facilities.** Directed the administrator to establish a separate category covering research or laboratory facilities, as necessary to assure the equitable treatment of such facilities.

• **Low-risk categories.** Allowed the administrator to delete from the list of source categories any category of sources that emitted carcinogens in quantities that caused a lifetime risk of carcinogenic effects (to the most-exposed individual) of 1 in 1 million or less, or, in the case of hazardous air pollutants that could result in adverse environmental effects or health effects other than cancer, emitted pollutants at a level adequate to protect public health with an "ample margin of safety" and with no adverse environmental effect.

First-Round Standards

• **Affected categories.** Required the EPA administrator to set a first round of technology-based emissions standards for every category and subcategory on the list of sources. The administrator could differentiate among classes, types and sizes of sources, but such differentiation could not result in a delay in compliance.

• **General standard.** Mandated that the first-round standards required the maximum emissions reduction achievable for new or existing sources, taking into consideration cost and any non-air-quality health and environmental impacts and energy requirements. Such reductions could be achieved by any means, including technological pollution controls, process changes, substitution of materials or special operator training and certification (otherwise known as maximum achievable control technology, or MACT).

• **New source.** Mandated that the emissions-reduction standard for new sources be at least as stringent as the most stringent emissions level achieved by a source in the same category or subcategory. It could be more stringent.

• **Existing sources.** Allowed that the emissions-reduction standard for existing sources be less stringent than the standard for new sources in the same category or subcategory, as long as the standard was at least as stringent as: 1) the average emissions limitation of the best-performing 12 percent of sources in a similar category or subcategory, excluding those sources that had, within 18 months before the emissions standard was proposed or within 30 months before it was issued, whichever was later, already achieved the lowest achievable emission rate applicable to a source category with 30 or more sources; or 2) the average emissions limitation of the five best-performing sources in a category or subcategory with fewer than 30 sources.

• **Health threshold.** Authorized the administrator, for pollutants for which a health threshold could be established, to consider that threshold, with an ample margin of safety, when setting emissions standards.

• **Area sources.** Authorized the administrator to promulgate emissions-reduction standards or requirements for area sources that provided for the use of cost-effective and generally achievable control technologies (GACT) or management practices.

• **Review.** Required the administrator to review and, if necessary, revise emissions standards at least every eight years.

• **Pre-emption.** Allowed no emissions standard set under this section of the bill to take precedence over stricter standards set in other relevant sections of the Clean Air Act or by a state.

• **Coke ovens.** Required the administrator to set emissions standards by Dec. 31, 1992, for coke ovens to provide no more than: 1) 8 percent leaking doors; 2) 1 percent leaking lids; 3) 5 percent leaking offtakes; and 4) 16 seconds visible emissions per charge, with no exclusion for emissions during the period after the closing of self-sealing oven doors. The compliance date for such emission standards for existing coke oven batteries was December 31, 1995.

For coke oven batteries electing to qualify for an extension of the compliance date for residual risk, the standards must be met within three years.

• **'Hammer' clause.** Required the owner or operator of any major source to submit a permit application within 18 months to operate a major source, under MACT standards, if the administrator failed to promulgate a standard for a category or subcategory of major sources by the applicable date.

• **Radionuclides.** Allowed the administrator not to set emissions standards for radionuclides emissions from a facility licensed by the Nuclear Regulatory Commission (NRC) if the administrator, after consulting with the NRC, determined that the NRC regulatory program protected public health with an ample margin of safety. This provision did not preclude a state or political subdivision of a state from setting its own radionuclides-emissions standards.

• **Effective date.** Required emissions standards to be put into effect upon promulgation.

Standards and Review Schedules

• **Emissions standards.** Required the EPA administrator to promulgate first-round, technology-based emissions standards for at least 40 categories and subcategories (not counting coke oven batteries) as expeditiously as possible, assuring that: 1) regulations for coke ovens be issued by Dec. 31, 1992; 2) emissions standards for 25 percent of the listed categories and subcategories be issued within four years; 3) an additional 25 percent of listed categories and subcategories be promulgated within seven years; and 4) emissions standards for all categories and subcategories be issued within 10 years.

• **Priorities.** Required the administrator, in determining the order in which to set emissions standards for various source categories and subcategories, to consider: 1) known and anticipated adverse effects on health and the environment; 2) quantities of hazardous air pollutants emitted; and 4) the efficiency of grouping various categories or subcategories.

• **Publicly owned treatment works (POTWs).** Required the administrator five years after enactment to promulgate emissions standards for publicly owned (sewage) treatment works.

Residual Risk

• **Report to Congress.** Required the EPA administrator, in consultation with the surgeon general, to report within six years on residual risk matters, including: 1) the risk to public health remaining, or likely to remain, from sources subject to regulation under this section after the application of MACT standards; 2) the public health significance of such estimated remaining risk and the available methods and costs of reducing such risks; 3) the actual health effects on people living in the vicinity of sources; and 4) recommendations on legislation regarding such risks.

• **Reversion to original standards.** Provided that, if Congress did not act on any EPA recommendation, the administrator had to, within eight years after promulgating MACT standards for a particular category or subcategory of sources, issue additional standards in accordance with laws preceding enactment of the Clean Air Act of 1990, which required that the EPA set standards for hazardous air pollutants to provide an "ample margin of safety" (consistent with interpretation of the recent benzene court decision) to protect the public health. The administrator could determine that a more stringent standard was necessary to prevent an adverse environmental effect. Such standards were required for pollutants classified as known, probable or possible human carcinogens if cancer risks to the most exposed individual were not reduced to less than 1 in 1 million.

• **Certain categories.** Provided that, in the case of categories or subcategories for which MACT standards had to be promulgated two years after enactment, the administrator had nine years to determine whether additional standards were required and, if so, to issue them.

• **Effective date, extensions.** Mandated that residual risk standards be effective on promulgation. In the case of an existing source, the standard could not apply until 90 days after its effective date. The administrator could grant a waiver allowing up to two additional years for the source to comply, if the delay was necessary for the installation of controls and if steps would be taken during the period of the waiver to ensure that public health would be protected from imminent endangerment.

Modifications

• **Offsets.** Provided that any physical change in, or change in the method of operation of, a major source that resulted in a greater than de minimis increase in actual emissions of a hazardous air pollutant not be considered a modification, if the increase would be offset by an equal or greater decrease in the quantity of emissions of a more hazardous air pollutant (or pollutants) from the source.

The EPA administrator within 18 months had to publish guidance on meeting such offset requirements, including identification, to the extent practicable, of the relative hazard to human health resulting from emissions of hazardous pollutants.

• **MACT standards.** Provided that, after the effective date of a permit program under Title V, major sources of hazardous air pollutants could not be modified, constructed or reconstructed unless the administrator (or the state) determined that MACT standards for existing sources would be met.

• **Work practice standards.** Authorized the administrator, in addition to any numerical emissions limit, to set design, equipment, work practice or operational standards for various sources.

The administrator had to set such standards whenever it was not feasible to prescribe or enforce an emissions standard — for instance, if the relevant pollutant could not be emitted through equipment designed or constructed to emit or capture that pollutant. The administrator could set an alternative means of emissions limitation if it would achieve reductions equal to those achieved by the primary design, equipment, work practice or operational standards.

Compliance Schedule

• **Special rule.** Provided that a new source that began construction or reconstruction after a standard was proposed and before it was promulgated was not required to comply with the promulgated standard until three years after the date of promulgation, if the promulgated standard was more stringent than the proposed standard and if the source complies with the proposed standard during the three years immediately after promulgation.

• **Existing sources.** Allowed the compliance date for any category or subcategory of existing sources to be as much as three years after the effective date of the standard or limitation.

• **Extension.** Allowed the administrator or state to issue a permit that granted an extension giving an existing source up to one additional year to comply, if the extra year was necessary for the installation of emissions controls.

• **Mining.** Allowed an additional extension of up to three years for mining waste operations, if a four-year compliance deadline was insufficient to dry and cover mining waste to reduce emissions of hazardous pollutants.

• **Presidential exemption.** Allowed the president to exempt any stationary source from compliance for two years if the president determined that the technology to implement the standard was not available and that the extension was in the national security interests of the United States. The exemption could be extended for an additional four years.

Alternative Emissions Limitations

• **General.** Allowed a state with a program approved under Title V (permits) to issue a permit that authorized a source to comply with alternative emissions limitations in lieu of standards under this section if the source met specified requirements:

• **Early reduction — pre-MACT.** Authorized alternative emissions limitations when an existing source showed that it had achieved a 90 percent reduction or more in emissions of hazardous air pollutants (95 percent in the case of particulates) prior to proposal of MACT standards.

The emissions reduction had to be determined with respect to verifiable and actual emissions on an annual average basis in a representative year not earlier than calendar year 1987 (unless the EPA administrator permitted 1985 or 1986 to be used as the base year).

Such alternative emissions limitations could be permitted in lieu of the MACT standard for a period of six years from the otherwise applicable compliance date, after which the source had to comply with the MACT standard.

• **Early reductions — post-MACT.** Provided that the alternative emissions limitation for early reductions also be available under narrow circumstances for emissions reductions achieved after MACT standards were proposed. If the early reductions were achieved by Jan. 1, 1994, the source could be granted an alternative emissions limitation, provided the source made an enforceable commitment to achieve the required early reductions before the proposal of the MACT regulations.

• **MACT extension.** Allowed an existing source five years to comply with MACT standards, once they were proposed, if it achieved a level of emissions reduction that complied with the best available control technology (BACT) or lowest achievable emissions rate (LAER) within five years prior to proposal of the MACT standard.

• **High-risk pollutants.** Provided that, with respect to high-risk pollutants such as chlorinated dioxins and furans (where adverse health effects were associated with small exposures), the administrator had to limit the use of offsetting reductions in emissions of other hazardous air pollutants as counting toward the 90 percent reduction qualifying sources for an alternative emissions limitation.

• **Extension for new sources.** Provided that a new source that began construction or reconstruction after a MACT standard was proposed, but before a residual risk standard was proposed, would not be required to comply with the residual risk standard until 10 years after the date construction or reconstruction commenced.

• **Coke ovens.** Allowed an extension from residual risk standards for coke ovens until 2020 if they met certain interim standards: a preliminary standard of 8 percent leaking doors, 1 percent leaking lids, 5 percent leaking offtakes and 16 seconds visible emissions per charge by 1993; MACT standards by 1995; LAER standards by 1998. LAER standards at a minimum had to require 3 percent leaking doors (5 percent for six-meter batteries); 1 percent leaking lids; 4 percent leaking offtakes; and 16 seconds visible emissions per charge, with an exclusion for emissions during the period after the closing of self-sealing oven doors (or the total mass emissions equivalent).

The EPA had to review but not necessarily revise the LAER standard in 2007. If it tightened LAER, coke ovens had to comply by 2010.

Area Source Program

• **75 percent reduction in attributable cancers.** Stated the sense of Congress that area sources of hazardous air pollutants presented a significant public health risk in urban areas and that area-source emissions should be reduced to the extent necessary to bring about a 75 percent reduction in cancers attributable to such sources.

• **Urban strategy.** Required the EPA administrator, within five years of enactment, to send to Congress a comprehensive strategy for dealing with hazardous air pollutants emitted by sources in urban areas with populations more than 250,000.

The strategy had to identify at least 30 pollutants that presented the greatest health threat in the largest number of cities and identify their source categories.

The administrator had to assure that sources emitting at least 90 percent of the 30 pollutants named would be regulated under the provision requiring establishment of first-round emissions standards.

• **Other strategies.** Required the administrator to encourage and support area-source strategies developed by state or local air pollution control agencies.

The administrator had to set aside 10 percent of the funds available for grants under this section to support those strategies.

State Programs

• **State submittals.** Allowed states to submit for approval by the EPA administrator programs for state implementation and enforcement of emissions standards for hazardous air pollutants or for prevention of accidental releases.

State programs could permit partial or complete delegation of the administrator's authorities and responsibilities but could not include authority to set standards less stringent than those promulgated by the administrator.

• **EPA guidance.** Required the administrator to publish guidance within 12 months of enactment to assist states in developing state programs. The administrator had to set up an air toxics clearinghouse, control technology center and risk information center to provide technical assistance and information to states, local agencies and (on a cost-reimbursable basis) to others. The administrator could make grants to a state to help it develop a submittal.

If the administrator determined that a state was not properly administering an approved program, the administrator had to notify the state; if the state failed to resolve the problem within 90 days, the administrator had to withdraw approval of the program.

The administrator could approve a program submitted by a local pollution control agency; if approved, that agency could take any action a state could take.

Atmospheric Deposition

- **Research program.** Required the EPA administrator to conduct a program to identify and assess the extent of atmospheric deposition of hazardous air pollutants and other air pollutants to the Great Lakes, Lake Champlain and coastal waters. The program had to include: 1) monitoring of the Great Lakes and coastal waters; 2) investigation of the sources of air pollutant deposition to those waters; 3) research to improve monitoring and determine the relative contribution of atmospheric deposition to total pollution loadings in those waters; 4) an evaluation of adverse human health effects; and 5) a sampling for pollutants in flora and fauna in those waters.
- **Great Lakes.** Required the administrator to oversee the establishment and operation of a Great Lakes atmospheric deposition network, including at least one facility in each of the five lakes, and to conduct certain research.
- **Coastal networks.** Required the administrator to design and deploy atmospheric deposition networks for coastal waters and their watersheds and to conduct certain research.

Miscellaneous

- **Electric utility steam generating units.** Required the EPA administrator to study and report within three years on hazardous pollutants from emissions of electric utility steam generating units. The administrator had to regulate electric utility steam generating units if appropriate, based on the results of the study.

The administrator also had to report to Congress within four years on mercury emissions from electric utility steam generating units, municipal waste combustion units and other sources, including area sources. The study had to consider the rate and mass of such emissions, the health and environmental effects, available control technologies and the costs of such technologies.

- **Coke-oven production technology.** Required the administrator and the Energy secretary to jointly undertake a six-year, $30 million study of coke-oven production emission control technologies and to assist in the development and commercialization of technically practical and economically viable control technologies that could significantly reduce the emissions of hazardous air pollutants from coke ovens.
- **Publicly owned treatment works.** Allowed the administrator to conduct studies jointly with the owners of publicly owned treatment works to characterize the hazardous air pollutants emitted by POTWs, identify the sources of those pollutants and demonstrate control measures for such emissions.
- **Hydrogen sulfide.** Directed the administrator to assess the human health risk of hydrogen sulfide emissions generated by oil and gas production. The administrator had to report to Congress within 24 months of enactment.
- **Savings clause.** Required that nothing in the bill affected the emissions standards already promulgated for hazardous air pollutants prior to enactment (standards for some sources of seven pollutants were set under existing language). No standard could be established for radionuclide emissions from certain plants and stacks except at the discretion of the administrator.

No standard promulgated prior to enactment with respect to medical research or treatment facilities could take effect until two years after enactment, unless the administrator determined that the regulatory program established by the Nuclear Regulatory Commission for such facilities did not provide an ample margin of safety to protect public health.

Accident Prevention

- **Purpose and general duty.** Set a general objective to prevent the sudden, accidental release of extremely hazardous substances and to minimize the consequences of any such release. The owners and operators of facilities that dealt with such substances had to use hazard-assessment techniques to identify hazards from such releases, design and maintain a safe facility, and minimize the consequences of accidental releases.
- **Definitions.** Defined "accidental release" to mean the unanticipated emissions of a regulated substance or other extremely hazardous substance into the air from a stationary source.
- **List of substances.** Required the EPA administrator to propose (within 12 months of enactment) and promulgate (within 24 months of enactment) a list of at least 100 substances that might suddenly be released in concentrations that could reasonably be anticipated to cause death, injury or serious adverse effects to human health or the environment.

The initial list had to include: chlorine, anhydrous ammonia, hydrochloric acid, methyl chloride, ethylene oxide, vinyl chloride, methyl isocyanate, hydrogen cyanide, ammonia, hydrogen sulfide, toluene diisocyanate, phosgene, bromine, anhydrous hydrogen chloride, hydrogen fluoride, anhydrous sulfur dioxide and sulfur trioxide.

The administrator had to review and revise the list at least once every five years. Upon adding a substance to the list, the administrator had to set a threshold for it.

- **Chemical safety board.** Established within the EPA an independent Chemical Safety and Hazard Investigation Board, consisting of five persons appointed to five-year terms by the president with the advice and consent of the Senate.

The board was to: 1) investigate and report to the public the cause or probable cause of sudden, accidental releases of chemical substances that caused a fatality, serious injury or substantial property damage; 2) issue periodic reports to Congress and federal, state and local agencies recommending measures to reduce the likelihood or consequences of accidental releases; and 3) establish by regulation requirements binding on persons for reporting accidental releases.

Within 18 months of enactment, the board had to publish a report with recommendations to the administrator on the use of hazard assessments in preventing or minimizing the consequences of accidental releases. The recommendations had to include a list of extremely hazardous substances and categories of facilities for which assessments were appropriate for preventing or minimizing accidents.

Whenever the board submitted a recommendation to the administrator or the secretary of Labor, the administrator or the Labor secretary had to respond formally in writing within 180 days, indicating whether a rulemaking would be initiated or orders issued to implement the recommendation.

- **Accident prevention.** Required the administrator to promulgate regulations and guidance within three years for the prevention, detection and correction of accidental releases. Requirements were to include monitoring, recordkeeping, reporting, training, vapor recovery, secondary containment, and other design, equipment, work practice and operational requirements.

The regulations were to require a facility handling an extremely hazardous substance to prepare and implement an approved risk-management plan. Neither the administrator nor the Chemical Safety and Hazard Investigation Board was allowed to regulate the accidental release of radionuclides arising from the construction and operation of facilities licensed by the Nuclear Regulatory Commission.

- **Presidential review.** Required the president to review accidental-release prevention, mitigation and response authorities of the various federal agencies and clarify and coordinate agency responsibilities to assure that they were implemented effectively and any deficiencies in authority or resources were identified.

Within 24 months of enactment, the president had to recommend to Congress any appropriate changes in the law.

- **State authority.** Stipulated that nothing in this section limited the right of state or local governments to adopt any regulations, requirements or standards stricter than those in this section.
- **Risk assessment and management.** Established a Risk Assessment and Management Commission that was to begin work no later than 18 months after enactment and investigate the policy

implications and appropriate uses of risk assessment in regulating hazardous air pollutants that posed a risk of cancer.

The commission had to report to Congress and the president within 48 months, making recommendations on the appropriate regulation of any cancer risks that remained after first-round emissions standards were put into effect.

The commission would cease to exist no later than nine months after submitting its report.

• **Chemical process safety management.** Required the Labor secretary to act under the Occupational Safety and Health Act of 1970 to prevent accidental releases of chemicals that could pose a threat to employees.

Within 12 months of enactment, the secretary and the EPA administrator had to promulgate a chemical process safety standard to protect employees from accidental releases of highly hazardous chemicals in the workplace. The secretary had to include in that standard a list of highly hazardous chemicals.

Municipal Waste Combustion

• **Performance standards.** Required the EPA administrator to establish performance standards and other requirements for each category of solid-waste incineration units. Standards were to include emissions limitations and other guidelines for both new and existing units.

Standards had to be promulgated as follows:

Within 12 months of enactment for solid-waste incineration units with a capacity of more than 250 tons per day that burned municipal waste.

Within 24 months of enactment for solid-waste incineration units with a capacity of 250 tons or less per day that burned municipal waste or hospital, medical and infectious waste.

Within 48 months of enactment (after being proposed within 36 months) for solid-waste incineration units burning commercial or industrial waste.

Within 18 months of enactment, the administrator had to publish a schedule for promulgating standards for other categories of units.

• **Standards.** Mandated that standards for solid-waste incineration units reflect the greatest degree of emission reduction achievable through application of best available control technologies and practices.

The degree of reduction in emissions that was deemed achievable for new units in a category could not be less stringent than the emissions control that was achieved in practice by the best controlled similar unit.

Emissions standards for existing units could be less stringent than standards for new units in the same category but could not be less stringent than the average emissions limitation achieved by the best performing 12 percent of units in the category (excluding units that met LAER standards 18 months before such standards were proposed or 30 months before they were promulgated, whichever was later).

Standards had to specify numerical emission limitations for particulate matter (total and fine), opacity (as appropriate), sulfur dioxide, hydrogen chloride, oxides of nitrogen, carbon monoxide, lead, cadmium, mercury, and dioxins and dibenzofurans. The administrator had to review the standards every five years.

• **State plans.** Required states, within one year after the administrator had promulgated guidelines for a category of solid-waste incineration units, to submit to the administrator a plan to implement and enforce the guidelines.

The state plan had to be at least as stringent as the guidelines and had to provide that all affected units be in compliance no later than three years after the state plan was approved (but no later than five years after the guidelines were promulgated).

The administrator had to approve or disapprove any state plan within 180 days of submission.

• **Administrator's plan.** Required the administrator to develop, implement and enforce a plan for solid-waste incineration units in any state that had not submitted an approvable plan of its own within two years of the administrator's promulgation of the relevant guidelines.

The plan had to provide for compliance by all units within five years of the promulgation of the guidelines.

• **Monitoring.** Required the administrator to promulgate regulations requiring each solid-waste incineration unit to monitor emissions at the appropriate points necessary to protect human health, to monitor other appropriate incinerator functions and to report the results of such monitoring.

• **Operator training.** Required the administrator to develop and promote, within 24 months of enactment, a model state program for the training of solid-waste incineration unit operators. The administrator could authorize any state or private entity to implement the training program if the program was at least as effective as the model program.

Beginning 36 months after the promulgation of the relevant performance standards and guidelines, it would be unlawful to operate an incinerator unless each person with control over the processes affecting emissions from the unit had passed a training program approved by the administrator.

• **Permits.** Required each solid-waste incineration unit to have a permit, beginning 36 months after promulgation of a performance standard, or by the effective date of a permit program under Title V, whichever was later.

Permits for municipal incinerators were to be issued for up to 12 years, subject to review every five years.

• **Effective date.** Made performance standards and other requirements for new solid-waste incineration units effective six months after promulgation. Standards for existing units were to take effect as expeditiously as practicable after approval of a state enforcement plan, but no more than five years after promulgation of the relevant standards or requirements.

• **State authority.** Stipulated that nothing would preclude a state or local government from enforcing any requirement for a solid-waste incineration unit that was stricter than one in effect under this section or any other provision of the bill.

• **Residual risk.** Provided that the administrator issue residual risk standards for incinerators if required under that section.

• **Acid rain.** Stipulated that an incinerator was not a utility unit as defined in Title IV provided that more than 80 percent of its annual average fuel consumption measured on a British thermal unit basis was from a fuel other than a fossil fuel.

• **Acid gas scrubbers.** Required the administrator, before promulgating any performance standards for municipal incinerators, to review the availability of acid gas scrubbers as a control technology for small new units and existing units.

• **Ash management.** Barred the administrator from regulating ash from solid-waste incineration units burning municipal waste for two years after enactment.

Title IV — Acid Rain

Findings and Purposes

• **Findings.** Found that acidic compounds and their precursors in the atmosphere and in deposition from the atmosphere ("acid rain") threatened natural resources, ecosystems, materials, visibility and public health; that the principal sources of acid rain were the emissions of sulfur dioxide (SO_2) and nitrogen oxides (NOx) from the combustion of fossil fuels; that the problem was of national and international significance; that economically feasible control strategies were available; that current and future generations would be adversely affected by delaying remedies; and that control measures to reduce precursor emissions from steam-electric generating units should begin without delay.

• **Purposes.** Stipulated that among the purposes of the title were reductions of annual SO_2 emissions by 10 million tons from 1980 levels and of annual NOx emissions by approximately 2 million tons from 1980 levels in the 48 contiguous states and the District of Columbia.

• **Compliance.** Established two deadlines for achieving reductions of SO_2 emissions and for generating extra "allowances" for emitting SO_2. Phase I was was to be 1995; Phase II, 2000.

Definitions

• **Affected sources and units.** Defined as a source that included one or more affected units, which were defined as a unit subject to emissions reduction requirements or limitations under several specific sections of this title. A unit was defined as a fossil-fuel-fired combustion device.

• **Utility unit.** Defined as a unit that served a generator in any state that produced electricity for sale.

A unit that cogenerated steam and electricity was considered a utility unit if the unit supplied more than one-third of its potential electric output capacity and more than 25 megawatts electrical output (MWe) to any utility power distribution system for sale.

• **Industrial source.** Defined as a unit that did not serve a generator that produced electricity, a "non-utility unit" as defined in this section or a process source.

• **Non-utility unit.** Defined as a unit that served a generator that produced electricity that sold no more than one-third of its potential electrical output capacity and no more than 25 MWe to any utility power distribution system.

• **Allowance.** Defined as an authorization, issued to an affected source by the EPA administrator, to emit, during or after a specified calendar year, one ton of SO_2.

• **Baseline.** Defined as the annual quantity of fossil fuel consumed by an affected unit, measured in millions of British thermal units (mmBtu), calculated as follows:

For each utility unit in commercial operation before Jan. 1, 1985, the baseline would be the annual average quantity of mmBtu consumed in fuel during the years 1985-87, according to certain Energy Department data.

For a utility unit for which those data were not recorded by the Energy Department and for non-utility units, the baseline would be the level specified in certain 1985 National Acid Precipitation Assessment Program (NAPAP) data, or in a corrected data base established by the administrator.

The administrator could exclude periods during which a unit was shut down for a continuous period of four calendar months or longer.

For any other non-utility unit not included in the NAPAP data, the baseline was to be the average annual quantity of mmBtu as calculated by a method the administrator has to promulgate within 18 months of enactment.

• **Capacity factor.** Defined as the ratio between a unit's actual electrical output and its potential electrical output.

• **Existing unit.** Defined as a unit that began commercial operation before enactment or any such unit that was subsequently modified, reconstructed or repowered after enactment. Existing units did not include simple combustion turbines or units that served a generator with a nameplate capacity of 25MWe or less.

• **Repowering.** Defined as replacement of an existing coal-fired boiler with one of several specified clean coal technologies or any other technology capable of controlling multiple combustion emissions simultaneously with improved boiler generation efficiency and with significantly greater solid waste reduction relative to the performance of technology in widespread commercial use as of enactment.

The term also meant any oil- and/or gas-fired unit awarded clean coal technology demonstration funding by the Energy Department by Jan. 1, 1991.

• **Reserve.** Defined as the bank of allowances established by the administrator under subsequent provisions.

• **State.** Defined as one of the 48 contiguous states and the District of Columbia (excluding Alaska and Hawaii).

• **Actual 1985 emission rate.** Defined as, for electric utility units or non-utility units, the annual SO_2 or NOx emissions rate as reported by NAPAP.

• **Allowable 1985 emission rate.** Defined as a federally enforceable emissions limitation for SO_2 or NOx, applicable to the unit in 1985.

• **Qualifying Phase I technology.** Defined as a technological system of continuous emissions reduction that achieved a 90 percent reduction in emissions of a pollutant. This was also called a scrubber.

• **Life-of-the-unit, firm power contractual arrangement.** Defined as a contractual arrangement under which a utility received a specified amount or percentage of capacity and associated energy generated by a specified generating unit (or units) and paid its proportional amount of such unit's total costs, for the life of the unit.

SO_2 Allowance Program

• **Allocations for existing and new units.** Required that the EPA administrator allocate annual allowances for a unit in an amount equal to its annual tonnage emissions limitation (as calculated under succeeding provisions).

• **Phase II emissions cap.** Prohibited, except as otherwise provided, beginning Jan. 1, 2000, the administrator from allocating or issuing SO_2 allowances for Phase II that would result in total annual SO_2 emissions from utility units in excess of 8.9 million tons.

The administrator could not take into account unused allowances carried forward by affected units or such allowances held by others following the year for which they were issued.

If necessary to meet this restriction, the administrator had to reduce, pro rata, the annual allowances allocated for each unit subject to Phase II requirements.

Subject to provisions requiring sale or auction of allowances by the administrator, the administrator had to issue allowances annually for each affected unit at an affected source.

If a unit eligible for Phase I, Phase II or clean-state allowances were removed from operation after enactment, the administrator had to continue to issue allowances annually for that unit.

• **Allowance transfer system.** Permitted allowances to be transferred among any lawful allowance holders or their designated representatives, as provided by allowance-system regulations promulgated 18 months after enactment. The regulations had to provide for the carrying forward of unused allowances, to be added to those allocated in subsequent years; this process included allowances issued to units subject to Phase I requirements but applied to emissions-limitation requirements in Phase II. Allowances could be transferred before they were actually issued; that would not affect the prohibition against using any allowance before the year for which it was issued.

• **Interpollutant trading study.** Required the administrator to deliver a study to Congress by Jan. 1, 1994, on the environmental and economic consequences of permitting the trading of SO_2 allowances for NOx allowances.

• **Allowance tracking system.** Required the administrator to promulgate a system within 18 months to provide for the issuing, recording and tracking of allowances.

• **New utility units — emissions cap.** Prohibited a new utility unit from emitting, after Jan. 1, 2000, an annual tonnage of SO_2 in excess of the number of allowances held. Such units were not eligible for SO_2 allowances (unless they qualified for allowances under special allowance provisions). If they did not otherwise qualify for allowances, they had to obtain them from other units with allowances. New utility units could obtain allowances from any person.

• **Nature of allowances.** Provided that an allowance was a limited authorization to emit SO_2. An allowance could be limited, revoked or otherwise modified. An allowance did not constitute a property right.

• **Public Utility Holding Company Act.** Provided that the acquisition or disposition of allowances not be subject to the provisions of the Public Utility Holding Company Act of 1935.

• **Prohibition.** Barred anyone from holding, using or transferring any allowance except in accordance with this subsection. No unit could emit sulfur dioxide in excess of the number of allowances held for that unit for that year.

• **Competitive bidding for power supply.** Stipulated that nothing in the title interfered or impaired programs for competitive bidding for power supply in any state.

• **Applicability of antitrust laws.** Provided that nothing in this section affected the applicability of antitrust laws to the transfer, use or sale of allowances or the authority of the Federal Energy Regulatory Commission regarding unfair methods of competition or anticompetitive acts or practices.

Phase I SO_2 Requirements

• **Emissions limitations.** Required that, after Jan. 1, 1995, 111 utility power plants emitting at a rate above 2.5 pounds of sulfur dioxide per million Btu (pounds/mmBtu) reduce SO_2 emissions to a level equal to 2.5 pounds/mmBtu multiplied by their average 1985-87 fuel consumption. *(Utility power plants chart, p. 261)*

• **Reserve.** Required the EPA administrator to determine, by Dec. 31, 1991, the total tonnage of reductions in SO_2 emissions from all utility units in 1995 that would occur as a result of compliance with this section and to establish a reserve of bonus allowances in that amount, not to exceed 3.5 million tons.

Acid Rain — Targeted Utilities

(Sulfur dioxide allowances in tons)

Utility	Allowance
Alabama	
Colbert-1	13,570
Colbert-2	15,310
Colbert-3	15,400
Colbert-4	15,410
Colbert-5	37,180
E. C. Gaston-1	18,100
E. C. Gaston-2	18,540
E. C. Gaston-3	18,310
E. C. Gaston-4	19,280
E. C. Gaston-5	59,840
Florida	
Big Bend-1	28,410
Big Bend-2	27,100
Big Bend-3	26,740
Crist-6	19,200
Crist-7	31,680
Georgia	
Bowen-1	56,320
Bowen-2	54,770
Bowen-3	71,750
Bowen-4	71,740
Hammond-1	8,780
Hammond-2	9,220
Hammond-3	8,910
Hammond-4	37,640
J. McDonough-1	19,910
J. McDonough-2	20,600
Wansley-1	70,770
Wansley-2	65,430
Yates-1	7,210
Yates-2	7,040
Yates-3	6,950
Yates-4	8,910
Yates-5	9,410
Yates-6	24,760
Yates-7	21,480
Illinois	
Baldwin-1	42,010
Baldwin-2	44,420
Baldwin-3	42,550
Coffeen-1	11,790
Coffeen-2	35,670
Grand Tower-4	5,910
Hennepin-2	18,410
Joppa Steam-1	12,590
Joppa Steam-2	10,770
Joppa Steam-3	12,270
Joppa Steam-4	11,360
Joppa Steam-5	11,420
Joppa Steam-6	10,620
Kincaid-1	31,530
Kincaid-2	33,810
Meredosia-3	13,890
Vermilion-2	8,880
Indiana	
Bailly-7	11,180
Bailly-8	15,630
Breed-1	18,500
Cayuga-1	33,370
Cayuga-2	34,130
Clifty Creek-1	20,150
Clifty Creek-2	19,810
Clifty Creek-3	20,410
Clifty Creek-4	20,080
Clifty Creek-5	19,360
Clifty Creek-6	20,380
E. W. Stout-5	3,880
E. W. Stout-6	4,770
E. W. Stout-7	23,610
Indiana	
F. B. Culley-2	4,290
F. B. Culley-3	16,970
F. E. Ratts-1	8,330
F. E. Ratts-2	8,480
Gibson-1	40,400
Gibson-2	41,010
Gibson-3	41,080
Gibson-4	40,320
H. T. Pritchard-6	5,770
Michigan City-12	23,310
Petersburg-1	16,430
Petersburg-2	32,380
R. Gallagher-1	6,490
R. Gallagher-2	7,280
R. Gallagher-3	6,530
R. Gallagher-4	7,650
Tanners Creek-4	24,820
Wabash River-1	4,000
Wabash River-2	2,860
Wabash River-3	3,750
Wabash River-5	3,670
Wabash River-6	12,280
Warrick-4	26,980
Iowa	
Burlington-1	10,710
Des Moines-7	2,320
George Neal-1	1,290
M. L. Kapp-2	13,800
Prairie Creek-4	8,180
Riverside-5	3,990
Kansas	
Quindaro-2	4,220
Kentucky	
Coleman-1	1,125
Coleman-2	12,840
Coleman-3	12,340
Cooper-1	7,450
Cooper-2	15,320
E. W. Brown-1	7,110
E. W. Brown-2	10,910
E. W. Brown-3	26,100
Elmer Smith-1	6,520
Elmer Smith-2	14,410
Ghent-1	28,410
Green River-4	7,820
H. L. Spurlock-1	22,780
Henderson II-1	13,340
Henderson II-2	12,310
Paradise-3	59,170
Shawnee-10	10,170
Maryland	
Chalk Point-1	21,890
Chalk Point-2	24,330
C. P. Crane-1	10,330
C. P. Crane-2	9,230
Morgantown-1	35,260
Morgantown-2	38,480
Michigan	
J. H. Campbell-1	19,280
J. H. Campbell-2	23,060
Minnesota	
High Bridge-6	4,270
Mississippi	
Jack Watson-4	17,910
Jack Watson-5	36,700
Missouri	
Asbury-1	16,190
James River-55	4,850
Labadie-1	40,110
Labadie-2	37,710
Labadie-3	40,310
Labadie-4	35,940
Montrose-1	7,390
Montrose-2	8,200
Montrose-3	10,090
New Madrid-1	28,240
New Madrid-2	32,490
Sibley-3	15,580
Sioux-1	22,570
Sioux-2	23,690
Thomas Hill-11	10,250
Thomas Hill-2	19,390
New Hampshire	
Merrimack-1	10,190
Merrimack-2	22,000
New Jersey	
B. L. England-1	9,060
B. L. England-2	11,720
New York	
Dunkirk-3	12,600
Dunkirk-4	14,060
Greenidge-4	7,540
Milliken-1	11,170
Milliken-2	12,410
Northport-1	19,810
Northport-2	24,110
Northport-3	26,480
Port Jefferson-3	10,470
Port Jefferson-4	12,330
Ohio	
Ashtabula-5	16,740
Avon Lake-8	11,650
Avon Lake-9	30,480
Cardinal-1	34,270
Cardinal-2	38,320
Conesville-1	4,210
Conesville-2	4,890
Conesville-3	5,500
Conesville-4	48,770
Eastlake-1	7,800
Eastlake-2	8,640
Eastlake-3	10,020
Eastlake-4	14,510
Eastlake-5	34,070
Edgewater-4	5,050
Gen. J. M. Gavin-1	79,080
Gen. J. M. Gavin-2	80,560
Kyger Creek-1	19,280
Kyger Creek-2	18,560
Kyger Creek-3	17,910
Kyger Creek-4	18,710
Kyger Creek-5	18,740
Miami Fort-5	760
Miami Fort-6	11,380
Miami Fort-7	38,510
Muskingum River-1	14,880
Muskingum River-2	14,170
Muskingum River-3	13,950
Muskingum River-4	11,780
Muskingum River-5	40,470
Niles-1	6,940
Niles-2	9,100
Picway-5	4,930
R. E. Burger-3	6,150
R. E. Burger-4	10,780
R. E. Burger-5	12,430
W. H. Sammis-5	24,170
W. H. Sammis-6	39,930
W. H. Sammis-7	43,220
W. C. Beckjord-5	8,950
W. C. Beckjord-6	23,020
Pennsylvania	
Armstrong-1	14,410
Armstrong-2	15,430
Brunner Island-1	27,760
Brunner Island-2	31,100
Brunner Island-3	53,820
Cheswick-1	39,170
Conemaugh-1	59,790
Conemaugh-2	66,450
Hatfield's Ferry-1	37,830
Hatfield's Ferry-2	37,320
Hatfield's Ferry-3	40,270
Martins Creek-1	12,660
Martins Creek-2	12,820
Portland-1	5,940
Portland-2	10,230
Shawville-1	10,320
Shawville-2	10,320
Shawville-3	14,220
Shawville-4	14,070
Sunbury-3	8,760
Sunbury-4	11,450
Tennessee	
Allen-1	15,320
Allen-2	16,770
Allen-3	15,670
Cumberland-1	86,700
Cumberland-2	94,840
Gallatin-1	17,870
Gallatin-2	17,310
Gallatin-3	20,020
Gallatin-4	21,260
Johnsonville-1	7,790
Johnsonville-2	8,040
Johnsonville-3	8,410
Johnsonville-4	7,990
Johnsonville-5	8,240
Johnsonville-6	7,890
Johnsonville-7	8,980
Johnsonville-8	8,700
Johnsonville-9	7,080
Johnsonville-10	7,550
West Virginia	
Albright-3	12,000
Fort Martin-1	41,590
Fort Martin-2	41,200
Harrison-1	48,620
Harrison-2	46,150
Harrison-3	41,500
Kammer-1	18,740
Kammer-2	19,460
Kammer-3	17,390
Mitchell-1	43,980
Mitchell-2	45,510
Mount Storm-1	43,720
Mount Storm-2	35,580
Mount Storm-3	42,430
Wisconsin	
Edgewater-4	24,750
La Crosse Genoa-3	22,700
Nelson Dewey-1	6,010
Nelson Dewey-2	6,680
N. Oak Creek-1	5,220
N. Oak Creek-2	5,140
N. Oak Creek-3	5,370
N. Oak Creek-4	6,320
Pulliam-8	7,510
S. Oak Creek-5	9,670
S. Oak Creek-6	12,040
S. Oak Creek-7	16,180
S. Oak Creek-8	15,790

The bill specified how to calculate a unit's reductions and how to adjust the calculation for reductions that would have occurred without the bill.

The administrator could issue allowances from the reserve until the reserve was exhausted, or until Dec. 31, 1999, whichever was earlier.

• **Extra Midwest allowances.** Granted, beginning in 1995 and ending in 1999, an additional 200,000 allowances to affected units in Illinois, Indiana or Ohio (other than units at Kyger Creek, Clifty Creek and Joppa Steam). The allowances had to be excluded from the calculation of the reserve.

• **Substitutions.** Allowed the owner or operator of an affected Phase I unit to include in its permit application and proposed compliance plan a proposal to reassign all or part of the unit's SO_2 reduction requirements to any other unit(s) under the control of the owner or operator. The proposal had to specify certain information and had to satisfy the administrator that the reassignment would achieve the same or greater emissions reduction than would have been achieved without the reassignment.

• **Eligible Phase I extension units.** Allowed the owner or operator of an affected unit to petition the administrator for a two-year extension of the deadline for meeting the Phase I emissions-limitation requirement.

To qualify for the extension, a unit had to either use qualifying Phase I technology (a scrubber) or transfer its Phase I obligation to a unit using such technology. The bill specified several technical conditions for an extension proposal, including a requirement that the unit provide an executed contract for the construction of qualifying Phase I technology.

A unit approved for such an extension received its normal complement of allowances (representing the amount of SO_2 emissions it was be allowed under Phase I emissions limitations).

Such a unit also had to be awarded by the administrator, from the bonus allowances available under the reserve, sufficient allowances to cover the difference between actual emissions and the limit the unit would otherwise have to meet.

In addition, any extension unit that reduced its SO_2 emissions below 1.2 lbs/mmBtu with qualifying Phase I technology during the period 1997-99 would get allowances from the reserve equal to those reductions.

After Jan. 1, 1997, an extension unit would have had to meet normal provisions of the bill, including penalties and offsets for excess SO_2 emissions. If any such unit exceeded its emissions limit, the administrator would have had to deduct allowances equal to that excess from the unit's allocation in the following year.

• **Renewable Energy Technology Reserve.** Provided that for each ton of sulfur dioxide emissions avoided by an electric utility, during the applicable period, through the use of qualified energy conservation measures or qualified renewable energy, the administrator would have to allocate a single allowance to the electric utility, on a first come, first served basis. Allowances totaling 300,000 could be granted, beginning Jan. 1, 1995, from the Conservation and Renewable Energy Reserve (CRER).

From 2000 to 2009, the administrator would have to deduct, on a pro rata basis, 30,000 tons a year for 10 years from the annual allocation of Phase II allowances to deposit in the CRER.

• **Midwest allowances.** Granted a special allocation of 200,000 annual allowances in each of the five years of Phase I to power plants in Illinois, Indiana and Ohio that were required to make reductions in Phase I.

Phase II Requirements

• **Applicability.** Required that after Jan. 1, 2000, each steam-electric existing utility be subject to the emissions limitations and other requirements of this section. Existing units that were not in operation during 1985 could use a baseline emissions rate for a subsequent year, as determined by the EPA administrator. The owner or operator of any unit operated in violation of this section would be fully liable for fulfilling requirements calling for excess emissions penalties and offsets.

• **Bonus allowances**. Required the administrator to distribute bonus allowances to accommodate growth in states with statewide average emissions below 0.8 pounds/mmBtu.

Plants that had increased utilization in the five years before enactment also could receive bonus allowances.

• **Extra allowances for the Midwest.** Allocated 50,000 extra allowances a year beginning Jan. 1, 2000, to plants in 10 states (Illinois, Indiana, Ohio, Georgia, Alabama, Missouri, Pennsylvania, West Virginia, Kentucky and Tennessee, other than units at Kyger Creek, Clifty Creek and Joppa Steam). These allowances were not subject to the 8.9 million ton cap on emissions.

• **Units at or above 75 MWe and 1.2 lbs./mmBtu.** Prohibited after Jan. 1, 2000, with certain exceptions, any existing utility unit that served a generator with a capacity of at least 75 megawatts of electricity (MWe) and an actual 1985 emissions rate of at least 1.2 lbs./mmBtu of SO_2 from exceeding an annual SO_2 tonnage limitation. That tonnage limitation would be equal to the product of the unit's baseline, multiplied by an emissions rate equal to 1.2 lbs./mmBtu, divided by 2,000.

This would be the general Phase II emissions limitation. Plants above 1.2 lbs./mmBtu had to reduce to that level or below.

• **Allowances for units below 60 percent capacity factor.** Required the administrator, from Jan. 1, 2000, through 2009, to issue annual allowances from the reserve to units with an actual 1985 emissions rate greater than 1.2 lbs./mmBtu and less than 2.5 lbs./mmBtu and a baseline capacity factor of less than 60 percent.

Such units were to get allowances equal to 1.2 lbs./mmBtu multiplied by 50 percent of the difference between the unit's baseline capacity factor and a 60 percent capacity factor.

• **Emissions limits for lignite-fired units.** Required that, after Jan. 1, 2000, any existing utility unit that: 1) had an actual 1985 emissions rate of at least 1.2 lbs./mmBtu; and 2) whose annual average fuel consumption during 1985-87 was more than 90 percent lignite coal; and 3) was in a state that had no non-attainment counties as of July 1, 1989, could not exceed an annual SO_2 tonnage limit equal to the product of its baseline multiplied by the lesser of the unit's actual 1985 emissions rate or its allowable 1985 emissions rate, divided by 2,000, unless the unit had allowances for the excess.

• **Allowances for oil-to-coal conversion units.** Required the administrator, after Jan. 1, 2000, to issue allowances to any unit in a state with an installed electrical generating capacity of more than 30 million kilowatts in 1988 that was issued a prohibition order or proposed order (to stop burning oil) and converted to coal between Jan. 1, 1980, and Dec. 31, 1985.

A unit was to get allowances equal to the difference between: 1) the unit's annual fuel consumption at a 65 percent capacity factor multiplied by the lesser of its actual or allowable emissions rate during the first full year after conversion, divided by 2,000; and 2) the number of allowances normally allocated for the unit under this section. The administrator could allocate no more than 5,000 allowances a year to such units; the administrator could meet that requirement by reducing, pro rata, the allowances issued to each unit.

• **Coal- or oil-fired units below 75 MWe and above 1.2 lbs./mmBtu.** Prohibited after Jan. 1, 2000, any coal- or oil-fired existing utility unit (with certain exceptions) that served a generator with a capacity of less than 75 MWe and an actual 1985 emissions rate of at least 1.2 lbs./mmBtu and which was owned by a utility whose fossil-fuel, steam-electric capacity was (as of Dec. 31, 1989) at least 250 MWe, to exceed an annual SO_2 emissions limitation. That limit would be equal to the unit's baseline multiplied by an emissions rate of 1.2 lbs./mmBtu, divided by 2,000, unless it had allowances for the excess.

• **Units owned by utilities with less than 250 MWe.** Required that any unit identical to those in the preceding paragraph (except that it was owned by a utility whose fossil-fuel, steam-electric capacity was less than 250 MWe as of Dec. 31, 1989) — not exceed, after Jan. 1, 2000, an annual SO_2 tonnage emissions limitation equal to the unit's baseline, multiplied by the lesser of its actual or allowable 1985 emissions rate, divided by 2,000, unless it had allowances for the excess.

• **Units in operation before 1966.** Prohibited, after Jan. 1, 2000, any existing utility unit:

1) with a capacity less than 75 MWe and an actual 1985 emissions rate of at least 1.2 lbs./mmBtu; and 2) that began operation on or before Dec. 31, 1965; and 3) that was owned by a utility whose fossil-fuel, steam-electric capacity was more than 250

MWe but less than 450 MWe (as of Dec. 31, 1989) and that served fewer than 78,000 electrical customers as of the date of enactment, from exceeding an annual SO_2 emissions tonnage limitation. That limitation was to be equal to its baseline multiplied by the lesser of its actual or allowable 1985 emissions rate, divided by 2,000, unless the unit had allowances for the excess.

After Jan. 1, 2010, such a unit could not exceed an annual emissions tonnage limitation equal to its baseline multiplied by 1.2 lbs./mmBtu, divided by 2,000, unless the unit had allowances for the excess.

- Barred any existing utility unit with a capacity below 75Mwe and an actual 1985 emissions rate equal to, or greater than, 1.2 pounds/mmBtu that was part of an electric utility system that at the time of enactment had at least 20 percent of its fossil-fuel capacity controlled by flue gas desulfurization devices, and that had more than 10 percent of its fossil-fuel capacity consisting of coal-fired units of less than 75Mwe, and had large units (greater than 400 Mwe), all of which had difficult or very difficult retrofit cost factors, from exceeding annual SO_2 emissions limitations. Those limitations would be equal to the product of its baseline multiplied by an emissions rate of 1.2 pounds/mmBtu, divided by 2,000, unless the owner or operator had allowances for the excess.

After Jan. 1, 2010, those units could not exceed an annual emissions tonnage limitation equal to the product of its baseline multiplied by an emissions rate of 1.2 pounds/mmBtu, divided by 2,000, unless the owner or operator had allowances for the excess.

- **Coal-fired units below 1.2 lbs./mmBtu.** Required that, after Jan. 1, 2000, any coal-fired unit the lesser of whose actual or allowable 1985 SO_2 emissions rate was less than 0.6 lbs./mmBtu, could not exceed an annual SO_2 tonnage emissions limitation. That limitation was to be equal to the unit's baseline multiplied by 1) the lesser of 0.6 lbs./mmBtu or the unit's 1985 emissions rate and 2) a numerical factor of 120 percent, divided by 2,000, unless the unit had allowances for the excess.

After Jan. 1, 2000, any coal-fired utility unit, the lesser of whose actual or allowable 1985 SO_2 emissions rate was at least 0.6 lbs./mmBtu but less than 1.2 lbs./mmBtu, could not exceed an annual SO_2 tonnage emissions limitation. That limit was to be equal to the unit's baseline multiplied by the lesser of its actual or allowable 1985 emissions rate divided by 2,000, unless the unit had allowances for the excess.

At the option of an operating company, the administrator could allocate to such a unit, from Jan. 1, 2000, through 2009, annual allowances equal to the amount by which 1) the lesser of 0.6 lbs/mmBtu or the unit's 1985 emissions rate multiplied by the unit's baseline adjusted to reflect operation at a 60 percent capacity factor, divided by 2,000, exceeded 2) the number of allowances allocated to the unit as basic Phase II allowance allocations.

In addition, also at the option of an operating company, the administrator could allocate to such a unit, from Jan. 1, 2000, through 2009, annual allowances (in addition to the unit's ordinary allocation) equal to the amount by which: 1) the lesser of the unit's actual or allowable 1985 emissions rate multiplied by the difference between its baseline capacity factor and a 60 percent capacity factor, divided by 2,000, exceeded 2) basic Phase II allowance allocations.

An operating company with units subject to this subsection could elect only one of the two alternative formulas for receiving additional allowances; that formula was to apply to the annual allowance allocation for every unit in the company subject to this subsection.

Notwithstanding other provisions, an owner or operator could choose to have allowances allocated to a unit that was subject to the emissions limitations of this subsection and had begun commercial operation on or after Jan. 1, 1981, but before Dec. 31, 1985, in this manner: The unit could receive allowances equal to its annual fuel consumption at a 65 percent capacity factor multiplied by the unit's allowable 1985 emissions rate, divided by 2,000.

In the case of an oil- or gas-fired unit that had been awarded a clean coal technology demonstration grant as of Jan. 1, 1991, the administrator was to allocate, beginning Jan. 1, 2000, allowances in an amount equal to the unit's baseline multiplied by 1.2 lbs/mmBtu, divided by 2,000.

- **Oil- or gas-fired units equal to or greater than 0.6 lbs./mmBtu but less than 1.2 lbs./mmBtu.** Prohibited, after Jan. 1, 2000, any oil- or gas-fired utility unit, the lesser of whose actual or allowable 1985 SO_2 emissions rate was equal to or greater than 0.6 lbs./mmBtu but less than 1.2 lbs./mmBtu, to exceed an annual SO_2 tonnage limitation. That limit was to be equal to the unit's baseline multiplied by the lesser of the unit's allowable or actual 1985 emissions rate and a numerical factor of 120 percent, divided by 2,000, unless the unit had allowances for the excess.
- **Oil- or gas-fired units less than 0.6 lbs./mmBtu.** Prohibited, after Jan. 1, 2000, any oil- or gas-fired utility unit, the lesser of whose actual or allowable 1985 emissions rate was less than 0.6 lbs./mmBtu and whose average fuel consumption during 1980-89 was 90 percent or less in the form of natural gas, to exceed an annual SO_2 tonnage emissions limitation equal to the unit's baseline multiplied by the lesser of 0.6 lbs./mmBtu or the unit's allowable 1985 emissions rate and a numerical factor of 120 percent, divided by 2,000, unless the unit had allowances for the excess.

In addition, beginning Jan. 1, 2000, the administrator was to allocate additional allowances to units operated by a utility that furnished electricity, electric energy, steam and natural gas within an area consisting of a city and one contiguous county, and in the case of any unit owned by a state authority, the output of which unit was furnished within that same area consisting of one city and one county.

The administrator was to allocate for each unit in the utility its pro rata share of 7,000 allowances and for each unit in the state authority its pro rata share of 2,000 allowances.

- **Units beginning operation between 1986 and Dec. 31, 1995.** Required that, after Jan. 1, 2000, no utility unit that had begun operation on or after Jan. 1, 1986, but no later than Sept. 30, 1990, not exceed an annual SO_2 tonnage emissions limitation. The limit was to be equal to the unit's annual fuel consumption at a 65 percent capacity factor multiplied by the unit's allowable 1985 SO_2 emissions rate, divided by 2,000, unless the unit had allowances for the excess.

After Jan. 1, 2000, the administrator was to allocate allowances to each unit listed below in the amount specified:

Unit	Allowances
Brandon Shores	8,907
Miller 4	9,197
TNP One 2	4,000
Zimmer 1	18,458
Spruce 1	7,647
Clover 1	2,796
Clover 2	2,796
Twin Oak 2	1,760
Twin Oak 1	9,158
Cross 1	6,401
Malakoff 1	1,759

After Jan. 1, 2000, the administrator was to allocate to any utility unit that began commercial operation, or had begun commercial operation, on or after Oct. 1, 1990, but not later than Dec. 31, 1992, allowances equal to the unit's annual fuel consumption at a 65 percent capacity factor multiplied by the lesser of 0.3 lbs./mmBtu or the unit's allowable SO_2 emissions rate, divided by 2,000.

For units that commenced construction before Dec. 31, 1990, and commercial operation between Jan. 1, 1993, and Dec. 31, 1995, allowances had to be granted in an amount equal to the product of the unit's annual fuel consumption, on a Btu basis, at a 65 percent capacity factor multiplied by the lesser of 0.30 lbs/mmBtu or the unit's allowable sulfur dioxide emission rate, divided by 2,000.

Utilities that had completed conversion from predominantly gas-fired existing operation to coal-fired operation between Jan. 1, 1985, and Dec. 31, 1987, for which there had been allocated a proposed or final prohibition order under the Powerplant and Industrial Fuel Use Act of 1978, were barred from exceeding an annual sulfur dioxide tonnage emissions limitation equal to the product of the unit's annual fuel consumption, on a Btu basis, at a 65 percent capacity factor multiplied by the lesser of 1.20 lbs/

mmBtu or the unit's allowable 1987 sulfur dioxide emissions rate, divided by 2,000, unless the owner or operator of such unit had obtained allowances equal to its actual emissions.

• **Exemption for small facilities and cogeneration facilities.** Exempted any unit that was a qualifying small power production facility or qualifying cogeneration facility under the Federal Power Act (PL 99-495), or a new independent power production facility, from the emissions limitations of this section if, by the date of enactment, an applicable power sales agreement had been executed, the facility was subject to a state regulatory authority order requiring an electric utility to enter into a power sales agreement, or an electric utility had issued a letter of intent or similar instrument committing to purchase power from the facility at a previously offered or lower price, or the facility had been selected as a winning bidder in a utility competitive bid solicitation.

• **Oil- and gas-fired units with less than 10 percent oil consumed.** Prohibited, after Jan. 1, 2000, any oil- or gas-fired utility unit whose average annual fuel consumption during 1980-89 exceeded 90 percent in the form of natural gas from exceeding an annual SO_2 tonnage emissions limitation. That limit was to be equal to the unit's baseline multiplied by the unit's actual 1985 emissions rate, divided by 2,000, unless the unit had allowances for the excess.

Beginning on Jan. 1, 2000, until the end of 2009, the administrator was to allocate from the reserve annual allowances for each such unit. The allowances were to be equal to the unit's baseline multiplied by 0.05 lbs./mmBtu, divided by 2,000. Beginning Jan. 1, 2010, the administrator was to allocate allowances equal to the unit's baseline multiplied by 0.05 lbs./mmBtu, divided by 2,000.

• **Florida allowances.** Required the administrator to issue further allowances, in addition to other Phase II allowances, to units subject to Phase II emissions limitations in a state that had experienced population growth greater than 25 percent between 1980 and 1988 and that had installed capacity of more than 30 million kilowatts in 1988.

The only state that met these requirements was Florida.

The allowances would be allocated in an amount equal to the difference between: 1) the number of allowances that would be allocated for the unit pursuant to the emissions limitation requirements of this section applicable to the unit, adjusted to reflect the unit's annual average fuel consumption of any three consecutive years during 1980-89 as elected by the owner or operator; and 2) the number of allowances allocated for the unit pursuant to the emissions limitation requirements of this section. However, no more than 40,000 allowances could be annually allocated under this provision.

If necessary to meet that restriction, the administrator could reduce, pro rata, the additional allowances allocated to each unit.

• **Allowances for certain units.** Required that, after Jan. 1, 2000, the administrator annually allocate certain allowances for each unit subject to the Phase II emissions limitations for units of 75 MWe or larger that met these conditions: 1) the lesser of whose actual or allowable 1980 emissions rate had declined by 50 percent or more by enactment; 2) whose actual emissions rate was less than 1.2 lbs./mmBtu as of Jan. 1, 2000; 3) which began operation after Jan. 1, 1970; and 4) which was owned by a utility company whose combined kilowatt-hour sales had increased by more than 20 percent between 1980 and the date of enactment.

This provision was drawn to specify a utility in Michigan.

The allowances were to be allocated in an amount equal to the difference between: 1) the number of allowances that would be allocated for the unit under the general emissions limitation provision, adjusted to reflect the unit's annual average fuel consumption for any three consecutive years during 1980-89 as chosen by the owner or operator; and 2) the number of allowances allocated for the unit under the general emissions limitation provision without adjustment. However, no more than 5,000 allowances could be allocated under this provision.

If necessary to meet that restriction, the administrator could reduce, pro rata, the allowances allocated to each unit affected by this provision.

• **Certain municipally owned power plants.** Required that the administrator annually allocate, after Jan. 1, 2000, for each existing municipally owned oil- or gas-fired utility unit with a capacity of 40 MWe or less, the lesser of whose actual or allowable 1985 SO_2 emissions rate was less than 1.2 lbs./mmBtu, allowances in an amount equal to the unit's annual fuel consumption at a 60 percent capacity factor, multiplied by the lesser of its allowable or actual 1985 emissions rate, divided by 2,000.

Allowances for "Clean States"

• **Governor's choice.** Required that, in addition to ordinary Phase II allowances, the governor of any state with a 1985 statewide annual SO_2 emissions rate no greater than 0.8 lbs./mmBtu (averaged over all fossil-fuel-fired utility steam generating units) could choose to receive additional allowances for Phase II units in the following manner (in lieu of additional allowances those units could have qualified for under other formulas):

The EPA administrator had to allocate allowances from the Phase II reserve to all such units in an amount equal to 125,000, multiplied by a unit's pro rata share of electricity generated in 1985 at fossil-fuel-fired steam units in all states eligible for the program.

Each governor of an eligible state had to notify the administrator whether that state chose to participate. If the governor failed to notify the administrator, units in the state would receive allowances under the normal Phase II procedures.

After Jan. 1, 2010, clean-state units were to receive allowances according to the normal Phase II procedures.

NOx Emissions

• **Applicability.** Required that, on the date a coal-fired utility unit became an affected unit under Phase I, Phase II or repowered-source requirements, or on the date a unit would have to meet SO_2 reduction requirements provisions covering Phase I extension units or units that qualified for an extension for clean coal technology, each such unit would become an affected unit under this section and would have to meet NOx emissions limitations.

• **First-round limitations.** Required that, no more than 18 months after enactment, the EPA administrator set the following annual NOx emissions limitations: a maximum rate of 0.45 lbs./mmBtu for tangentially fired boilers; a rate of 0.5 lbs./mmBtu for dry-bottom, wall-fired boilers and for cell burners.

The administrator could set a rate higher than these for any type of utility boiler if the administrator found that the maximum listed rate for that boiler type could not be achieved using low-NOx burner technology.

After Jan. 1, 1995, no affected unit could exceed rates set by the administrator.

• **Second-round limitations.** Required that, by Jan. 1, 1997, the administrator promulgate annual, average, allowable emissions limitations for NOx for wet-bottom, wall-fired boilers; cyclones; and all other types of utility boilers.

The administrator was to base such limitations on the degree of reduction: 1) that was achievable through the retrofit application of the best system of continuous emissions reduction, taking into account available technology, costs and energy and environmental impacts; and 2) whose costs were comparable to the first-round controls.

The administrator could, by Jan. 1, 1997, revise those first-round limitations for tangentially fired and dry-bottom, wall-fired boilers (including cell burners) to be more stringent if the administrator determined that more effective low-NOx burner technology was available. However, no affected Phase I SO_2 unit that was also subject to the first-round NOx limitations was subject to any revised limitations.

• **Revised performance standards.** Required that, by Jan. 1, 1993, the administrator propose revised performance standards for NOx from fossil-fuel-fired steam generating units, including both utility and non-utility units. The administrator had to promulgate those revised standards by Jan. 1, 1994. The revisions had to reflect improvements in methods for NOx reduction.

• **Alternative emissions limitations.** Required the permitting authority, at the request of an owner or operator, to authorize a less stringent emissions standard if it was determined that: 1) a unit subject to the first-round limits could not meet those limits using low-NOx burner technology; or 2) a unit subject to the second-round limits could not meet the applicable rate using the technology on which the administrator based the limit.

The permitting authority had to issue an operating permit to such a unit that would permit the unit to emit at a rate in excess of the applicable emissions rate during the demonstration period. At the end of the demonstration period, the permitting authority had to modify the permit to reflect the alternative emissions rate.

Units subject to the first-round emissions limitations and for which an alternative limitation had been established would not be required to install any additional control technology beyond low-NOx burners.

Nothing would preclude an owner or operator from using an alternative NOx control technology that could meet the applicable emissions limits.

If the owner or operator demonstrated that the technology necessary to meet such requirements was not in adequate supply to enable its installation and operation at the unit by Jan. 1, 1995, the administrator should extend the deadline for compliance for the unit by a period of 15 months.

• **Emissions averaging.** Allowed the owner or operator of two or more units subject to NOx emissions limitations to petition the permitting authority for emissions averaging, instead of complying with the unit-specific first- and second-round or alternative emissions limitations. The averaging program had to ensure that the actual annual emissions rate averaged over the relevant units was less than or equal to the Btu-weighted, average annual emissions rate for the same units if they had been operated, during the same period of time, in compliance with the first- and second-round NOx limits.

Permits and Compliance Plans

• **Permit program.** Required that the provisions of this title be implemented by five-year operating permits issued in accordance with certain specifications. Any permit issued by the administrator (or a state with an approved permit program) had to prohibit annual emissions of SO_2 in excess of the number of allowances to emit SO_2, and had to bar use of any allowance prior to the year for which it was allocated.

• **Phase I permits.** Required the administrator to issue permits to affected Phase I sources.

Within 27 months of enactment, an affected source under Phase I SO_2 requirements and the NOx reduction provisions had to submit a permit application and proposed compliance plan, which was binding and enforceable until the administrator issued a permit for the source.

In the case of a compliance plan for an affected source that proposed to meet emissions limitations by reducing utilization of the unit compared with its baseline, or by shutting down the unit, the source had to include in its proposed compliance plan a specification of the unit or units that would provide electrical generation to compensate for the affected source, or a demonstration that such reduced utilization would be accomplished by energy conservation or improved unit efficiency.

The unit to be used for such compensating generation, which was not otherwise an affected unit under Phase 1 SO_2 or NOx program requirements, would be deemed an affected unit under the Phase I SO_2 requirements and subject to the same requirements for all such units.

However, allowances would be allocated to the compensating unit in the amount of an annual limitation equal to the unit's baseline multiplied by the lesser of the unit's actual or allowable 1985 emissions rate, divided by 2,000.

The administrator had to review each proposed compliance plan and approve or disapprove it within six months after submission. Within 18 months of enactment, the administrator had to issue regulations in accordance with Title V (permits) to supersede any permit application and compliance plan.

• **Phase II permits.** Required that, in order to implement portions of this title other than Phase I SO_2 requirements, each state with an affected unit submit a comprehensive and enforceable permit program for approval by the administrator. The administrator had to approve any such program that met the requirements of this title and the existing Clean Air Act.

By Jan. 1, 1996, each affected Phase II source, including affected units under the repowered sources provisions, was to submit a permit application and a proposed compliance plan (including a description of any alternative method of compliance).

By Dec. 31, 1997, each state with an approved permits program was to issue permits for affected Phase II sources that satisfied the relevant requirements. In the case of a state without an approved permits program or a state that failed to issue permits to all its affected sources by July 1, 1996, the administrator was to issue permits for each affected source by Jan. 1, 1998.

• **New units.** Required each state to submit to the administrator a comprehensive and enforceable operating permit program for new units no later than 24 months before: 1) Jan. 1, 2000, or 2) the date on which the unit commenced operation.

• **Units subject to NOx limits.** Required sources subject to NOx emissions limits to submit a permit application and compliance plan before Jan. 1, 1998.

• **Amendment of application and compliance plan.** Allowed a permit applicant to submit a revised permit application and compliance plan at any time after submission of the originals.

• **Multiple owners.** Prohibited issuance of any permit under this section to an affected unit until the designated representative of the owner or operator had filed a certification concerning the holding and distribution of allowances. The bill set specifications for such certifications.

Repowered Sources

• **Availability.** Permitted the owner or operator of a Phase II existing unit to demonstrate to the permitting authority by Dec. 31, 1997, that one or more units would be repowered with a qualifying clean coal technology to comply with Phase II requirements. As part of that demonstration, the owner or operator had to provide, by Jan. 1, 2000, satisfactory documentation of a preliminary design and engineering effort for such repowering and a binding contract for the majority of the equipment.

• **Extension.** Required that an owner or operator that satisfied the preceding requirements be granted a three-year extension of the emissions limitation compliance date for that unit (from Jan. 1, 2000, to Dec. 31, 2003). Any unit granted an extension under this provision would not be subject to the new-source waiver in the Clean Air Act and would continue to be subject to requirements of this title as if it were a unit subject to Phase II requirements.

If an existing unit had been granted an extension for repowering with a clean coal unit, but satisfied the administrator that the clean coal technology to be utilized had been properly tested and constructed, but nevertheless was unable to achieve the emissions reduction limitations in an economically or technologically feasible manner, the existing unit could be retrofitted or repowered with equipment or facilities utilizing another clean coal technology or other available control technology.

• **Allowances.** Required the administrator to issue to the owner or operator of the affected unit, for the period of the extension, annual allowances for SO_2 emissions equal to the affected unit's baseline, multiplied by the lesser of the unit's federally approved state implementation plan (SIP) emissions limitation or its actual emissions rate in 1995. Such allowances could not be transferred or used by any other source to meet emissions requirements.

The owner or operator had to notify the administrator 60 days before the extension unit was removed from operation to install the repowering technology. Effective on that date, the unit would be subject to Phase II requirements. Allowances for the year during which the unit was removed from operation would be calculated as the product of the unit's baseline multiplied by 1.2 lbs./mmBtu, divided by 2,000, and prorated accordingly.

Allowances for such existing utility units for the years following completion of repowering would be equal to the unit's baseline multiplied by 1.2 lbs./mmBtu, divided by 2,000.

• **Control requirements.** Required that any extension unit that did not increase actual hourly emissions of any regulated pollutant not be subject to any performance standard under the Clean Air Act.

Election for Additional Sources

• **Applicability.** Allowed the owner or operator of any unit that emitted SO_2 but was not, and would not become, an affected unit under provisions covering new utility units or Phase I and Phase II units, or that was a process source, to elect to designate that unit or source to become an affected unit and receive allowances. The administrator had to approve a designation that met the requirements of this section.

• **Baseline.** Required the administrator to set a baseline for an election unit based on fuel consumption and operating data for 1985-87 (or other data if those were not available).

• **Emissions limitations.** Required that annual SO_2 emissions limitations be equal to the unit's baseline multiplied by the lesser of the unit's actual or allowable 1985 emissions rate, or, if the unit did not operate in 1985, by the lesser of the unit's actual or allowable emissions rate for a subsequent year, divided by 2,000.

• **Process sources.** Required the administrator, within 18 months, to establish a program under which the owner or operator of a process source that emitted SO_2 could elect to designate that source as an affected source for the purpose of receiving allowances.

• **Limitation.** Prohibited any unit designated under this section from transferring or banking allowances produced as a result of reduced utilization or shutdown. Such allowances could be transferred or carried forward for use in subsequent years, however, to the extent that the reduced utilization or shutdown resulted from the replacement of thermal energy from the designated unit, with thermal energy from any other unit subject to the requirements of this title, and the designated unit's allowances were transferred or carried forward for use at those other replacement units (or unit).

In no case could the administrator allocate to a source designated under this section allowances in an amount greater than the emissions resulting from operation of the source in full compliance with the requirements of the bill. Such allowances did not allow a unit to operate in violation of any other requirements of the bill.

The administrator had to issue regulations to put this limitation into effect within 18 months.

• **Small diesel refineries.** Required the administrator to issue allowances to owners or operators of small diesel refineries who produced diesel fuel after Oct. 1, 1993, meeting certain requirements of the act. Allowances could be issued under this provision only for the period from Oct. 1, 1993, to Dec. 31, 1999.

The allowances were to be equal to the pounds of SO_2 reduction attributable to desulfurization by the small refinery, divided by 2,000. For this calculation, the concentration of sulfur removed from diesel fuel was to be the difference between 0.274 percent and 0.05 percent (by weight). No more than 1,500 allowances could be issued to a small refinery in a single year. In any given year, no more than 35,000 allowances could be issued under this program.

Excess Emissions Penalty

• **SO_2 and NOx.** Required that a penalty be paid by the owner or operator of any unit or process source subject to the emissions limitations of this title that emitted SO_2 or NOx in excess of the unit's emissions limitation, or, in the case of SO_2, in excess of its allowances. That penalty was to be calculated on the basis of the number of tons emitted in excess of the unit's emissions limitation requirement or, in the case of sulfur dioxide, of the allowances the operator held for use for the unit for that year, multiplied by $2,000 and adjusted for inflation.

That penalty would not diminish the liability of the unit's owner or operator for any fine, penalty or assessment against the unit for the same violation under any other section of the bill.

• **Offset for SO_2.** Required the owner or operator of any affected source that emitted SO_2 in excess of the unit's emissions limitation or its allowances to offset the excess emissions by an equal tonnage amount in the following year, or a longer period at the discretion of the administrator.

Within 60 days of the end of the year in which the excess occurred, the owner or operator had to submit a plan to the administrator and to the state to achieve the required offsets. The administrator also had to deduct allowances equal to the excess tonnage from those issued to the source during the years following the year in which the excess emissions occurred.

Monitoring, Reporting and Recordkeeping

• **Applicability.** Required the owner or operator of any source subject to this title to install and operate a continuous emission monitoring system (CEMS) on each affected unit at the source and to quality-assure the data for SO_2, NOx, opacity and volumetric flow. The EPA administrator had to promulgate regulations within 18 months of enactment to specify the requirements for CEMS, for any alternative monitoring systems and for recordkeeping and reporting of information from such systems.

• **Phase I requirements.** Required that any unit subject to Phase I SO_2 emissions limitation requirements install, operate and keep records from CEMS no later than 36 months after enactment.

• **Phase II requirements.** Required that, no later than Jan. 1, 1995, the owner or operator of each affected unit that had not yet installed CEMS do so and operate the system and keep relevant records.

• **Unavailability of data.** Required that, if CEMS data or alternative data was unavailable for a unit during any period when that data was required, and the owner or operator could not provide emissions data satisfactory to the administrator, the administrator had to deem that unit to have been operating in an uncontrolled manner during the period for which data was unavailable.

The administrator had to promulgate regulations within 18 months of enactment to prescribe a means for calculating emissions for that period. The owner or operator would be liable for excess emissions fees and offsets.

Clean Coal Technology Incentives

• **Definition.** Defined "clean coal technology" to mean any technology, including technologies applied at the pre-combustion, combustion or post-combustion stage at a new or existing facility, that would achieve significant reductions in air emissions of SO_2 or NOx associated with the use of coal in the generation of electricity, process steam or industrial products, and which was not in widespread use as of the date of enactment.

A clean coal technology demonstration project meant a project using funds appropriated under the heading "Department of Energy-Clean Coal Technology" up to a total amount of $2.5 billion for the commercial demonstration of clean coal technology, or similar projects funded through appropriations for the EPA. The federal contribution for a qualifying project had to be at least 20 percent of the total cost of the project.

• **Temporary projects.** Stipulated that installation, operation, cessation or removal of a temporary clean coal technology demonstration project that was operated for a period of five years or less, and which complied with the state implementation plan and other requirements necessary to attain and maintain NAAQS, was not required to comply with new source performance standards, PSD requirements or non-attainment requirements under Title I.

• **Permanent projects.** Provided that permanent clean coal technology demonstration projects that constituted repowering were not subject to new source performance standards or review and permitting PSD requirements for any pollutant whose emissions would not increase as a result of the demonstration project.

• **EPA regulations.** Required the administrator within 12 months to issue regulations or interpretive rulings to revise requirements under new source performance standards, PSD requirements or non-attainment requirements under Title I to facilitate projects consistent in this subsection.

• **Exemption.** Provided that physical changes or changes in the method of operation associated with the commencement of commercial operations by a coal-fired utility unit after a period of discontinued operation not subject the unit to new source performance standards or PSD requirements under Title I if the unit: 1) was not in operation for the two-year period prior to enactment; 2) the emissions were carried in the permitting authority's emissions inventory at the time of enactment; 3) was equipped before shutdown with a continuous system of emissions control that achieved a removal efficiency for SO_2 of no less than 85 percent and a removal efficiency for particulates of no less than 98 percent; 4) was equipped with low-NOx burners prior to the time of commencement; and 5) was otherwise in compliance with the requirements of the act.

Contingency Guarantee, Auctions

• **Special reserve of allowances.** Required the EPA administrator within 36 months to set up a Special Allowance Reserve containing allowances to be sold under this section. To set up the reserve, the administrator had to withhold 2.8 percent of the allocation of allowances for each of the years 1995-99 and 2.8 percent of the basic Phase II allowance allocation beginning in 2000.

• **Fixed-price sale.** Required the administrator to offer to sell allowances at $1,500 per ton (adjusted for inflation).

The administrator could sell no more than 50,000 allowances usable in any calendar year. No allowance sold under this program could become usable before the year 2000.

- **Allowance auction.** Required the administrator to conduct auctions of 150,000 allowances each year from 1995 through 1999 and 250,000 tons in each year beginning in 2000.

Fossil Fuel Use

- Required that any person who entered a contract to receive hydroelectric energy in return for the provision of electric energy would have to use his own allowances to satisfy his obligations under the contract. A Federal Power Marketing Administration (FPMA) was not subject to these requirements for electric energy generated by hydroelectric facilities and sold by that FPMA, but anyone who sold or provided electric energy to any FPMA had to comply.

Repeal of Percentage Reduction

- Repealed the 1977 amendments regarding percentage reduction by modifying the way in which the definition of a standard of performance for new fossil-fuel-fired stationary sources was expressed. "Standard of performance" meant an emissions standard that reflected the degree of emissions limitation achievable through the best system of reduction, which (taking into account cost and any non-air-quality health and environmental impact and energy requirements) the EPA administrator determined had been adequately demonstrated.
- **Revised regulations.** Required the administrator, within three years, to promulgate revised regulations for standards of performance for new fossil-fuel-fired electric utility units beginning construction after the date on which the regulations were proposed. The regulations were to require any source subject to the revised standards to emit SO_2 at a rate not greater than would have resulted from compliance with the standards before revision.
- **Conditionality.** Required that the repeal of percentage reductions and the requirement for revised regulations apply only as long as the SO_2 emissions cap remained in force.

Miscellaneous

- **Acid deposition standards.** Required the EPA administrator to report to Congress within 36 months on the feasibility and effectiveness of an acid deposition standard or standards to protect sensitive and critically sensitive aquatic and terrestrial resources.
- **National Acid Lakes Registry.** Required the administrator to create and publish, within one year, a National Acid Lakes Registry listing all lakes known to be acidified due to acid deposition.
- **Industrial SO_2 emissions.** Required the administrator to send to Congress by Jan. 1, 1995, and every five years thereafter, an inventory of national annual SO_2 emissions from industrial sources, including qualifying small power production facilities and qualifying cogeneration facilities ordinarily not subject to the provisions of this title.

The administrator had to report on the likely SO_2 emissions trends over the next 20 years and give estimates of actual emissions reductions achieved by promulgation of the diesel-fuel desulfurization regulations. *(Title II: Motor vehicles, p. 251)*

Whenever the inventory indicated that industrial SO_2 emissions could reasonably be expected to exceed 5.6 million tons, the administrator would have to take actions under the Clean Air Act to prevent that, including promulgating new and revised standards of performance for new or existing sources (including small power production facilities and cogeneration facilities).

- **Cost sharing.** Expressed the sense of the Congress that the bill's allowance program allocated the costs of achieving the required reductions of SO_2 and NOx emissions among U.S. sources. Broad-based taxes and emissions fees (cost sharing) that would have anyone other than those required to make the reductions pay the costs were deemed "undesirable."
- **Canadian acid rain program.** Required the administrator to report to Congress on Canada's acid rain program.
- **Clean coal technologies export programs.** Required the Energy secretary in consultation with the Commerce secretary to report to Congress within one year on a study of clean coal technologies export programs within federal agencies. The study had to look at the effectiveness of interagency coordination of export promotion and determine the feasibility of setting up an interagency commission for that purpose.
- **Studies by the U.S. Fish and Wildlife Service and the University of Wyoming.** Authorized $500,000 for the U.S. Fish and Wildlife Service (FWS) to fund research on acid deposition and the monitoring of high-altitude mountain lakes in the Wind River Reservation in Wyoming, to be conducted through the Management Assistance Office of the FWS located in Lander, Wyo., and by the University of Wyoming.

In addition, $250,000 was authorized for the U.S. Fish and Wildlife Service to fund a study to be conducted in conjunction with the University of Wyoming on the effectiveness of various buffering and neutralizing agents used to restore lakes and streams damaged by acid deposition.

Title V — Permits

Permit Programs

- **General.** Required that, after the effective date of any permit program approved or promulgated under this title, it would be unlawful to violate any requirement of a permit issued under this title or operate, except in compliance with a permit, a major source, or any source (including an area source) subject to regulation under certain provisions of the Clean Air Act, or any source designated by regulations promulgated by the EPA administrator.
- **Definitions.** Defined "major source" as any stationary source, or any group of stationary sources within a contiguous area and under common control, that emitted or had the potential to emit 10 tons per year (tpy) or more of any hazardous air pollutant or 25 tpy or more of any combination of hazardous air pollutants, unless the administrator established a lesser quantity for a major source on the basis of potency, characteristics of the air pollutant or other relevant factors; or that emitted or had the potential to emit 100 tpy or more of any air pollutant.

"Area source" was defined as any source that was not a major source but that was a member of a source category based on aggregate emissions, or potential aggregate emissions, of a listed pollutant.

- **Exemptions.** Allowed the EPA by rule to expand the list of sources that would be required to obtain a permit after public notice and comment, and also authorized the EPA to exempt one or more source categories from such permit requirements if the administrator found that compliance would be impracticable, infeasible or unnecessarily burdensome, but only if such exemption remained consistent with the bill's mandate to protect the public health, welfare and the environment.

No major source could be exempt from the requirements.

- **Minimum elements.** Required the administrator, within 12 months of enactment, to promulgate regulations establishing several minimum elements of a permit program to be administered by a state or local air pollution control agency. Among those would be a requirement that permittees pay an annual fee of at least $25 a ton, or whatever figure the administrator determined was necessary to cover the direct and indirect costs of the permit program, for any registered pollutant.

In calculating the tonnage fee to be collected, the permitting authority had to exclude emissions in excess of 4,000 tons a year. The fee was to be increased for inflation.

- **Required authority.** Mandated that adequate personnel and funding be available to administer the program; that the permitting authority be able to issue permits for a fixed term of no more than five years, ensure compliance, and enforce permits and recover civil penalties up to $10,000 a day for violations.

In addition, the permitting authority in each state had to be empowered to ensure that no permit would be issued to any source in the event the administrator objected to the issuance of that permit.

- **Processing procedures.** Required permitting authorities to establish expeditious processing procedures for permit applications and also required permitting authorities to allow an opportunity for judicial review in state courts of the final permit action by the applicant or by any person who participated in the public comment process on the application.
- **Permit revisions.** Required permits for major sources with a term of three years or more to be revised before the expiration of

the permit term, in order to incorporate applicable standards and regulations that were promulgated after issuance of the permit. The revisions would have to occur within 18 months of the promulgation of the standards or regulations.

- **Single permit.** Allowed a single permit to be issued for a facility with multiple sources.
- **State programs.** Required that, within three years of enactment, the governor of each state would have to submit to the administrator a permit program meeting the requirements of this title. The governor would also have to submit a legal opinion that state, local or interstate compact laws had sufficient authority to carry out the permit program. The administrator would have to approve or disapprove such a program in whole or in part within one year of receiving it.

If the program was disapproved in whole or in part, the administrator would have to notify the governor of any necessary changes; the governor would have to revise and resubmit the program within 180 days. If the governor failed to resubmit an approvable program, the administrator could apply a sanction (see Title I) and could promulgate, administer and enforce a program.

The administrator would have to suspend issuance of federal permits as soon as a state program was approved and implemented. However, the administrator would have to continue to administer and enforce federally issued permits until they were replaced by state-issued permits.

- **Sanctions.** Allowed the administrator to deny highway funds or increase emissions reduction requirements if a state did not submit a program as required or if the administrator disapproved the program in whole or in part within 18 months after the date required for such submittal or the date of such disapproval. If more than 18 months elapsed without state submission, the EPA was required to apply a sanction.
- **Pre-emption.** Required the administrator to issue a federal permit program for a state if a state permit program had not been approved in whole or part within two years after the submission deadline.
- **Interim approval.** Required that interim approval, for a period not to exceed two years, be made available by rule for state permit programs, including partial programs, that substantially met the permit requirements but were not fully approvable.
- **Effective date.** Required that the permit program become effective on approval by the EPA.
- **Administration and enforcement.** Required the administrator to withdraw approval of a permit program or apply sanctions or promulgate a program if a state failed to implement its program within 18 months.

Permit Applications

- **Applicable date.** Provided that any stationary source required to have an operating permit become subject to a permit program on the latter of the following dates: the effective date of a permit program (or partial or interim program) applicable to the source, or the date a source became subject to permit requirements.
- **Compliance plan.** Required that permit applications be accompanied by a compliance plan describing how the source would comply with the state implementation plan and emissions standard, limitation or prohibition, as well as a schedule for submitting progress reports at least every six months.
- **Reporting.** Required the permittee to certify at least annually that it was in compliance with applicable terms of the permit and to report promptly any deviations from permit requirements.
- **Deadline.** Required that within one year, an entity that owned a stationary source that became subject to the permit program would have to file with the permitting authority the application and compliance plan. The permitting authority would have to approve or disapprove the application within 18 months after receipt. Action on permit applications submitted within the first year after the effective date of a permit program would be phased in so that at least one-quarter of the permits would be acted on annually over a period not to exceed four years after the effective date.
- **Timely and complete applications.** Provided for continued operation of stationary sources subject to the permit program, with the exception of sources required to have a permit before construction, so long as the applicant filed an application for a permit on a timely basis and the application complied with the criteria of the regulations.
- **Copies and availability.** Provided that a permit application, compliance plan, emissions or compliance monitoring report, certification and issue permit be made available to the public, with certain exceptions for trade secrets.

Permit Requirements and Conditions

- **Conditions.** Provided that each permit include a schedule of compliance, including emissions standards and limitations and other appropriate conditions to ensure compliance.
- **Monitoring and analysis.** Gave the EPA authority to prescribe by rule procedures and methods for determining compliance and for monitoring regulated pollutants.

Continuous emissions monitoring would not be required if alternative methods were available that provided sufficiently reliable and timely information for determining compliance or if the technology for such continuous monitoring were not available.

- **Inspection.** Provided that permits include provisions on inspections, entry, monitoring, compliance, certification and reporting to ensure compliance.
- **General permits.** Allowed the permitting authority to issue general permits for numerous similar sources within a geographical area.
- **Temporary sources.** Allowed permittees to receive permits authorizing operations at numerous fixed locations without requiring a new permit at each site.
- **'Permit shield.'** Provided that compliance with a permit be deemed compliance with all requirements of this bill that were explicitly addressed by the permit; however, compliance with a permit would not alter, modify or otherwise affect the authority of the EPA administrator to act under his emergency powers. Any determination that a source would be shielded from any requirement of the Clean Air Act would have to be open to public review.

Notification

- **Transmission and notice.** Required each permitting authority to transmit to the EPA copies of permit applications and to give notice in accordance with EPA regulations of every action related to the consideration of the application.

Permitting authorities would be required to notify of the application contiguous states in which the emission originated or any state within 50 miles of the source and to notify them of each proposal forwarded to the EPA and to provide an opportunity to the states to submit written recommendations concerning the permit and its terms and conditions.

If the recommendations were not adopted by the permitting authority, it would be required to notify the applicable state and the EPA in writing of its failure to accept the recommendations and provide a statement of reasons.

The EPA was authorized to expand the 50-mile limit for notice and to require notice to non-contiguous states in appropriate circumstances.

- **Objection by the EPA.** Required the administrator to object to the issuance of a permit if the administrator determined that the permit contained provisions that were not in compliance with the act, including the requirements of an applicable implementation plan. If the proposed permit did change a state implementation plan requirement or was otherwise not in compliance with the Clean Air Act, and the administrator failed to notify the permitting authority, any person could commence a citizen suit to compel the administrator to object to the permit, although such a petition would have to be based only on objections that were raised during the public comment period on the permit unless the petitioner demonstrated that it was not possible to raise such objections at that time.
- **Issuance or denial.** Required the EPA to issue or deny the permit if the permitting authority failed within 90 days after the date of the above objection to revise the permit to meet the objection.
- **Waiver of notification.** Authorized the EPA to waive, at the time of permit approval, the provisions requiring notice to the EPA and contiguous states for any category of sources other than major sources.
- **Refusal to terminate.** Required the EPA to notify the per-

mitting authority if it found cause to terminate, modify or revoke and reissue a state permit.

Other Authorities

• **State or interstate.** Allowed state or interstate permitting authorities to establish additional permitting requirements consistent with the act and the EPA's regulations.

• **Small sources.** Required each state to submit to the EPA within two years, as part of a state implementation plan or as a revision to a state implementation plan, a plan for establishing a technical and environmental compliance assistance program for small business stationary sources. Those sources were defined as those that emitted 50 tons per year or less of any regulated pollutant and 75 tons per year or less of all regulated pollutants, that had 100 or fewer employees, and that qualified for assistance from the Small Business Administration. Other sources that emitted less than 100 tons per year of all regulated pollutants could petition for inclusion.

Among the elements of an acceptable state plan were adequate mechanisms for: coordinating information about compliance methods and technologies for small sources, advising small sources on pollution prevention and pollution-reducing methods of operation, and setting up a state office to serve as an ombudsman for small sources in dealing with the state air pollution agency.

• **EPA program.** Required the EPA to set up a small-source technical assistance program within nine months after enactment to provide technical guidance to states to implement this program and to provide for implementation of the program in any state that failed to comply.

• **Continuous emission monitors.** Required the EPA to consider the necessity and appropriateness of continuous emission monitoring requirements for small business stationary sources before applying such requirements to those sources.

The EPA also had to consider the size, type and technical capabilities of small business stationary sources in developing control technique guidelines. States could consider modifying the methods by which small business stationary sources could comply with permit requirements as long as such modifications did not relax any deadlines or requirements of the Clean Air Act.

Title VI — Stratospheric Ozone

Definitions

• **Ozone-depleting substance.** Defined as any substance that was known or could reasonably be anticipated to cause or contribute to stratospheric ozone depletion. Such term included, at a minimum, all Class I and Class II substances listed below.

• **Ozone-depletion factor.** Defined as a factor established by the EPA administrator to reflect the ozone-depletion potential of a substance, on a mass per kilogram basis, as compared with trichlorofluoromethane (CFC-11).

Control of CFCs

• **Lists.** Required the EPA administrator to publish two phase-out lists, within 60 days, of manufactured substances known or anticipated to cause or contribute significantly to changes in the atmosphere or the Earth's climate, including ozone depletion.

Class I covered all fully halogenated chlorofluorocarbons (CFCs), halons, carbon tetrachloride, and methyl chloroform.

Class II covered all transitional substances, or partially halogenated chlorine-containing halocarbons (HCFCs), including hydrochlorofluorocarbon-22, HCFC-123, HCFC-124, HCFC-141(b), and HCFC-142(b).

• **Additions.** Allowed the administrator to add, in accordance with the criteria above, any substance to the list of Class I or Class II substances.

No less frequently than every three years after enactment, the administrator had to list any additional Class I or Class II substances, allowing citizens to petition for additions and providing for extension of the applicable deadlines if the statutory deadlines were not attainable considering when the substance was added.

• **Removals.** Barred any substance from being removed from the list of Class II substances unless it were added to the list of Class I substances.

No Class I substance, above, could be removed from the list of Class I substances.

• **Ozone-depletion factors.** Required the administrator to assign to each listed substance a numerical value representing the substance's ozone-depletion potential.

In addition, the administrator had to publish the chlorine-loading potential and the atmospheric lifetime of each listed substance. Minimum values would had to be assigned to the following substances.

Table

Substance	Ozone-depletion factor
CFC-11, CFC-12, CFC-13, CFC-111, CFC-112	1.00
CFC-113	0.80
CFC-114	1.00
CFC-115	0.60
CFC-211, CFC-212, CFC-213, CFC-214, CFC-215, CFC-216, CFC-217	1.00
Halon-1211	3.00
Halon-1301	10.00
Carbon tetrachloride	1.10
Methyl chloroform	0.10
HCFC-22	0.05
HCFC-123, HCFC-124	0.02
HCFC-141(b)	0.10
HCFC-142(b)	0.06

• **Montreal Protocol.** Required the numerical value of the ozone-depletion potential of a substance to be consistent with any specification in the Montreal Protocol.

Monitoring and Reporting Requirements

• **Regulations.** Required the EPA administrator to amend existing regulations regarding monitoring and reporting of Class I and Class II substances within 180 days of enactment to conform to the new requirements.

• **Annual production level reports.** Required each person producing a Class I or Class II substance to file a report with the administrator setting forth the amount of the substance that person produced in the preceding calendar year.

• **Baseline reports.** Required that on the date the first annual report was filed, each person producing a Class I substance, other than a substance added to the list after enactment, file a report setting forth the amount of such substance that was produced during the baseline year.

• **Monitoring and reports.** Required the administrator to monitor and, not less often than every two years following enactment, submit a report to Congress on the production and use of Class I and Class II substances, including data on domestic production and use and an estimate of worldwide production.

Production Phaseout, Class I

• **Phase-out schedule.** Made it unlawful for a person to produce in excess of the percentage of annual quantities specified in the table below. Consumption also had to be phased out in accordance with the schedule.

Date	Carbon Tetrachloride	Methyl Chloroform	Other Class I Substances
1991	100	100	85
1992	90	100	80
1993	80	100	75
1994	70	85	65
1995	15	70	50
1996	15	50	40
1997	15	50	15
1998	15	50	15
1999	15	50	15
2000	—	20	—
2001	—	20	—

• **Termination of Class I substances.** Made it unlawful for any person to produce any amount of a Class I substance after Jan. 1, 2000 (Jan. 1, 2002, in the case of methyl chloroform).

• **Exceptions.** Provided exceptions to the ban for necessary medical and aviation safety purposes and for export to developing countries that were party to the Montreal Protocol and required the substances for basic domestic needs. Total exceptions by any one producer could not result in production of annual quantities greater than 10 percent of that producer's 1986 levels.

The bill provided additional, more expansive exceptions, not subject to the cap, for national security purposes, for certain uses and production of CFC-114, halon-1211, halon-1301 and halon-2402. The president would have to explain the reason for the exception to Congress within 30 days. National security interests included the domestic production of crude oil and natural gas on the North Slope of Alaska.

• **Fire suppression.** Allowed the EPA administrator to authorize production of limited quantities of halon-1211, halon-1301 and halon-2402 solely for purposes of fire suppression if the administrator, in consultation with the administrator of the U.S. Fire Administration, determined that no safe and effective substitute had been developed. No exception could be granted to permit production after Dec. 31, 1999.

Production Phaseout, Class II

• **Production and use freeze.** Made it unlawful, effective Jan. 1, 2015, for any person to produce or use any Class II substance unless it had been used, recovered and recycled; was used and entirely consumed in the production of other chemicals; or was used to maintain and service household and commercial appliances manufactured before Jan. 1, 2020.

By Dec. 31, 1999, the EPA administrator had to promulgate regulations phasing out production and restricting the use of Class II substances according to this schedule.

• **Production ban.** Made it unlawful, effective Jan. 2, 2030, for any person to produce any Class II substance.

Accelerated Schedule

• **Regulations.** Required the EPA administrator to establish more stringent schedules for phasing out production of Class I or Class II substances, or both, if: 1) the administrator determined that it was necessary to protect human health and the environment, 2) the faster schedule(s) were attainable based on the availability of substitutes for a listed substance, or 3) if the Montreal Protocol was modified to include a schedule faster.

Exchanges

• **Transfers and trades.** Provided for the issuance of Class I and Class II substance allowances if exchanges among producers would result in greater total reductions in production of the substances than would occur in the absence of the trade, including interpollutant trades.

Recycling and Disposal

• **Schedule.** Required the EPA administrator to establish regulations by Jan. 1, 1992, on the use and disposal of Class I and Class II substances during the service, repair or disposal of appliances and industrial process refrigeration. Such regulations had to become effective by July 1, 1992.

Within four years of enactment, the EPA would have to issue regulations regarding recycling and disposal of both Class I and Class II substances not covered by the earlier regulations.

The regulations had to reduce the emissions to the lowest achievable level and maximize the recapture and recycling of such substances and could require the use of alternatives. Regulations on the production of other substances that directly or indirectly exacerbate global warming also were required.

• **Disposal.** Required substances contained in bulk in appliances and other machines to be removed before such machines were thrown out. New appliances had to include design features that allowed the substances to be recaptured during servicing and disposal. Such items had to be disposed of in such a way that reduced emissions to the maximum extent practicable.

• **Servicing.** Made illegal, as of Jan. 1, 1992, the release of refrigerant substances, except for the smallest amounts, while servicing or repairing household appliances or commercial refrigerators and air conditioners.

Motor Vehicle Air Conditioners

• **Regulations.** Required the EPA administrator within one year to establish standards and requirements for servicing motor vehicle air conditioners.

• **Definitions.** Defined "refrigerant" as any Class I or Class II substance used in a motor vehicle air conditioner. The term "approved refrigerant recycling equipment" meant equipment certified by the administrator (or an independent standards testing organization approved by the administrator) for the extraction and reclamation of refrigerants from motor vehicle air conditioners.

• **Servicing air conditioners.** Barred any person from undertaking repair or servicing of a motor vehicle air conditioner that involved the refrigerant without proper use of approved refrigerant recycling equipment.

No person could perform such service unless properly trained and certified. The prohibition was to take effect two years after enactment.

• **Extension.** Extended the effective date of the prohibition to three years after enactment in the case of a person repairing or servicing motor vehicles at an entity that performed service on fewer than 100 motor vehicle air conditioners during calendar year 1990.

• **Small containers.** Made it unlawful, effective two years after enactment, for anyone to sell or distribute in interstate commerce to any non-certified person any motor vehicle refrigerant under regulation that was in a container carrying less than 20 pounds of the substance.

Non-Essential Chlorofluorocarbon Products

• **Plastic party streamers.** Required the EPA administrator to identify and, within two years of enactment, bar the sale or distribution in interstate commerce of non-essential products that released Class I substances into the environment (including any release occurring during manufacture, use, storage or disposal). At a minimum, the regulations were to apply to chlorofluorocarbon-propelled plastic party streamers and noise horns and chlorofluorocarbon-containing cleaning fluids for non-commercial electronic and photographic equipment.

• **Other products.** Barred any person, effective Jan. 1, 1994, from selling or distributing or offering for sale or distribution in interstate commerce any aerosol product or other pressurized dispenser that contained a Class II substance or any plastic foam product (other than a foam insulation product) that contained, or was manufactured with, a Class II substance, except where the use of the aerosol produce or pressurized dispenser was determined to be essential as a result of flammability or worker safety concerns, and the only available alternative was a Class I substance that legally could be substituted for such Class II substances.

• **Exemption.** Exempted from these limitations any medical device, as defined by the bill.

Labeling

• **Regulations.** Required the EPA administrator to issue regulations to implement labeling requirements within 18 months after enactment.

• **Class I substances.** Required, effective 30 months after enactment, that containers in which a Class I substance was stored or transported, and products containing such substance or manufactured with a process that used such substance, not be introduced into interstate commerce unless they bore a clearly legible and conspicuous label stating either "Warning: Contains (name of substance), a substance which harms public health and environment by destroying ozone in the upper atmosphere," or "Warning: Manufactured with (name of substance), a substance which harms public health and environment by destroying ozone in the upper atmosphere."

• **Class II substances.** Applied the labeling requirements to any container in which a Class II substance was stored or transported and to any product containing a Class II substance or manufactured with a process that used a Class II substance if the administrator found that there was an alternative for such substance or for the use of such substance and that the alternative reduced the overall risk to human health and the environment and was available at the time or potentially available.

Effective Jan. 1, 2015, the requirements for labeling of Class I substances were to apply equally to Class II substances.

Safe Alternatives Policy

• **Replacement.** Required the EPA administrator to issue rules within two years requiring that replacement chemicals, product substitutes and alternative production processes, products and raw materials that reduced overall risks to human health and the environment be used, to the maximum extent practicable, for the replacement of Class I and Class II substances.

• **Research.** Required the administrator, in consultation with other agencies, to recommend federal research programs and other activities to promote the development and use of substitutes for refrigerants, solvents, fire retardants, foam blowing agents and other commercial applications that used covered substances.

The administrator also had to examine federal practices and recommend ways that they could be converted to the use of safe substitutes and maintain a public clearinghouse for information on safe substitutes.

• **Disclosure.** Required the administrator to require producers of chemical substitutes to provide all published and unpublished health studies related to the chemical. Such producers had to give 90 days' notice to the EPA before introducing such products to the market.

• **Alternatives.** Required that those rules bar, not more than two years after enactment, replacement of any Class I substance with any substitute substance that the administrator determined might present adverse effects to human health or the environment. These rules would apply only if the administrator had identified an alternative to such replacement that would reduce the overall risk to human health and the environment and was available at the time or potentially available. The administrator was required to publish a list of the substitutes prohibited for specific uses and the safe alternatives identified.

Federal Procurement

• **Conformation.** Required the EPA administrator or the General Services Administration (GSA), in consultation with the administrator, to promulgate regulations requiring each federal department, agency and instrumentality to conform its procurement regulations to the policies and requirements of this title and to maximize the substitution of safe alternatives for those listed ozone-depleting, global-warming substances.

• **Application.** Required every federal agency or department, within 30 months of enactment, to conform its procurement regulations and specifications to the GSA plan.

State and International Laws

• **State pre-emption.** Prohibited states, for the first two years after enactment, from enforcing any requirement concerning the design of any new or recalled appliance for the purpose of protecting the ozone layer.

• **Montreal Protocol.** Stated that the title was to be considered a supplement to the Montreal Protocol, did not supplant the protocol and did not abrogate the responsibilities or obligations of the United States to implement fully the provisions of the protocol.

• **Technology transfers.** Required the president to prohibit the export of technologies used to produce Class I substances; to prohibit direct or indirect investments in facilities designed to produce a Class I or Class II substance in nations that were not parties to the Montreal Protocol; and to direct that no government agency provide subsidies or assistance for the purpose of producing a Class I substance.

• **International trading.** Allowed for international trading among parties to the Montreal Protocol if any transfer resulted in a net reduction in production in that year.

International Cooperation

• **Treaties.** Required the president to enter into international agreements to foster cooperative research that complemented studies and research authorized by this title, and to develop standards and regulations that protected the stratosphere consistent with regulations applicable within the United States.

For these purposes, the president was required to negotiate multilateral treaties, conventions, resolutions or other agreements and to formulate or support proposals at the United Nations or other international forums.

The president also had to report to Congress periodically on efforts to arrive at such agreements.

• **Montreal Protocol.** Required the EPA administrator, in consultation with the secretary of State, to support global participation in the Montreal Protocol on Substances that Deplete the Ozone Layer. The bill authorized up to $30 million for this purpose over fiscal 1991-93, and an additional $30 million if China and India joined the Montreal Protocol as parties.

Methane Assessment

• **National goals.** Established a goal of identifying and analyzing options to reduce the risks of tropospheric ozone formation and global climate change by reducing global methane emissions enough to ensure that the atmospheric concentration of methane did not rise above existing levels.

• **Information collection.** Authorized the EPA administrator to collect information from people responsible for the release of methane to the atmosphere during manufacturing, processing, resource recovery or distribution, waste management or other economic activities.

Failure to comply with such requests would constitute a civil violation.

• **Economically justified actions.** Required the administrator within two years of enactment to report to Congress identifying activities, substances or processes that could reduce methane emissions and were economically justified with or without consideration of environmental benefit.

• **Source inventory.** Required the administrator within two years, in conjunction with the secretaries of Energy and Agriculture, to submit a report to Congress with an inventory of methane emissions associated with 1) natural gas extraction, transportation, distribution, storage and use; 2) coal extraction; 3) management of solid waste; 4) agriculture; and 5) human activities.

The administrator also had to develop a plan outlining measures that could be used to stop the growth in atmospheric concentrations of methane from sources within the United States.

• **International studies.** Required the administrator within two years to submit a report on methane emissions from other countries, with inventories of methane emissions and analysis of the potential for preventing an increase in atmospheric concentrations from activities in other countries. The report had to identify technology transfer programs that could promote methane emissions reductions in lesser developed countries.

• **Natural sources.** Required the administrator within two years to report on methane emissions from biogenic sources such as tropical, temperate and subarctic forests; tundra; and freshwater and saltwater wetlands.

Title VII — Enforcement

Federal and State Enforcement

• **Implementation plan.** Required the EPA administrator to notify a person and state of any violation of an implementation plan or permit. One month after the notification, the administrator could, without regard to the period of violation, issue an order requiring compliance with the plan or permit, issue an administrative penalty order or bring a civil action.

• **State enforcement.** Required the administrator to notify the state if violations of an implementation plan or an approved permit program were so widespread that they appeared to result from the state's failure to enforce the plan or permit program effectively. If the failure extended more than 30 days after such notice (90 days in the case of a permit program), the administrator had to give public notice of that finding. The administrator could then enforce any requirements of the plan or permit program by issuing an order requiring the person to comply, issuing an administrative penalty order or bringing a civil action.

• **Other requirements.** Required the administrator to take action if any person violated provisions relating to new source performance standards, hazardous emissions standards, inspection or permit requirements, or acid-deposition control. Action could include issuing an administrative penalty order or an order requiring such person to comply, taking civil action or requesting the attorney general to commence a criminal action.

• **Order requirements.** Required that an order (other than for a violation of hazardous emissions standards) not take effect until the person to whom it was issued had an opportunity to confer with the administrator. The order had to require the person to whom it was issued to comply as expeditiously as practicable but in no event later than one year after the order was issued.

Issuance of an order did not limit the authority of the state or the administrator to assess penalties or take other enforcement action, nor affect any person's obligations to comply with any terms or conditions of any permit or implementation plan.

• **Failure to comply.** Allowed the administrator to take the following actions if a state was not acting in compliance with provisions to prevent significant deterioration of air quality or with plan requirements for non-attainment areas: issue an order prohibiting the construction or modification of any major stationary source in any area to which such requirement applied, issue an administrative penalty order or bring a civil action.

Judicial Enforcement

• **Injunctive relief.** Required the EPA administrator, as appropriate, to commence a civil action for permanent or temporary injunction, or assess and recover a civil penalty of up to $25,000 per day for each violation, or both, in the following instances: if an owner or operator of an affected source, a major emitting facility, or a major stationary source: 1) violated any requirement of an applicable implementation plan or permit, 2) violated any other requirement for attainment or maintenance of national air quality standards, control of hazardous air pollution, permits or acid deposition control, including, but not limited to, a requirement of any rule, order, waiver or permit or for the payment of any fee, or 3) tried to build or modify a major stationary source in any area where the administrator had found that the state was not acting in compliance with provisions for non-attainment areas or for prevention of significant deterioration of air quality.

Issuance of an order did not limit the authority of the state or the administrator to assess penalties or take other enforcement action, nor affect any person's obligations to comply with any terms or conditions of any permit or implementation plan.

• **Failure to comply.** Allowed the administrator to take the following actions if a state was not acting in compliance with provisions to prevent significant deterioration of air quality or with plan requirements for non-attainment areas: issue an order prohibiting the construction or modification of any major stationary source in any area to which such requirement applied, issue an administrative penalty order or bring a civil action.

Judicial Enforcement

• **Injunctive relief.** Required the EPA administrator, as appropriate, to commence a civil action for permanent or temporary injunction, or assess and recover a civil penalty of up to $25,000 per day for each violation, or both, in the following instances: if an owner or operator of an affected source, a major emitting facility, or a major stationary source: 1) violated any requirement of an applicable implementation plan or permit, 2) violated any other requirement for attainment or maintenance of national air quality standards, control of hazardous air pollution, permits or acid deposition control, including, but not limited to, a requirement of any rule, order, waiver or permit or for the payment of any fee, or 3) tried to build or modify a major stationary source in any area where the administrator had found that the state was not acting in compliance with provisions for non-attainment areas or for prevention of significant deterioration of air quality.

Criminal Penalties

• **Violations.** Required that any person who knowingly violated the following provisions be punished, upon conviction, by a maximum fine of $250,000 for individuals and $500,000 for organizations or by imprisonment for a period not to exceed five years, or both. In the case of a second conviction for one of the following violations, the maximum fine and punishment would be doubled. Subject to these criminal penalties were violations of the following: any rule, order, waiver or permit promulgated or approved, including any requirement for the payment of any fee owed the United States under requirements regarding state implementation plans; an order to comply with a state implementation plan or standards or requirements for ozone protection, new source performance, hazardous emissions, inspections or preconstruction requirements; an emergency order; and provisions regarding permits and acid-deposition control.

• **False statements.** Required a maximum fine of $250,000 for individuals and $500,000 for corporations, or imprisonment for not more than two years, or both, upon conviction of any person who: 1) knowingly made any false statement, representation or certification, or omitted material information from, or knowingly altered, concealed or failed to file or maintain any notice, application, record, report, plan or other document required to be filed or maintained, 2) failed to notify or report as required, or 3) falsified, tampered with or rendered inaccurate, or failed to install, any monitoring device or method required.

• **Failure to pay.** Required a fine of up to $250,000 for individuals or $500,000 for corporations, or imprisonment for up to one year, or both, upon conviction of any person who knowingly failed to pay any fee owed the United States under provisions regarding attainment and maintenance of national air quality standards, control of hazardous air pollutants, permits or control of acid depositions. A second conviction would subject a violator to a doubling of the maximum fine and punishment.

• **Negligent releases.** Required a fine of up to $250,000 for individuals and $500,000 for corporations, or imprisonment for not more than one year, or both, upon conviction of any person who negligently released into the ambient air any hazardous air pollutant listed under national emissions standards for hazardous air pollutants, or under the Superfund Amendments and Reauthorization Act of 1986 list of extremely hazardous substances that was not listed under the national emissions standards, and who at the time negligently placed another person in imminent danger of death or serious bodily injury. A second conviction would subject a violator to a doubling of the maximum punishment.

• **Knowing releases.** Required a fine of up to $250,000 for individuals and $500,000 for corporations, or imprisonment of not more than 15 years, or both, for any person convicted of knowingly releasing into the ambient air any hazardous air pollutant listed under Clean Air Act national emissions standards for hazardous air pollutants, or under the superfund list of extremely hazardous substances that was not listed under the national emissions standards, and who knew at the time that he thereby placed another person in imminent danger of death or serious bodily injury.

For any air pollutant for which the EPA administrator had set an emissions standard or for any source for which a permit had been issued, a release of such pollutant in accordance with that standard or permit would not constitute a violation for negligent or knowing releases. Any "person" committing such violation that was an organization would, upon conviction, be subject to a fine of not more than $1 million for each violation.

A second conviction would subject a violator to a doubling of the maximum punishment.

• **Definitions.** Defined "person" as an individual, corporation, responsible corporate officer, partnership, association, state, municipality, political subdivision of a state, and any agency, department or instrumentality of the United States and any officer, agent or employee thereof.

With the exception of a separate definition in the paragraph on Negligent Releases, "a person" would not include an employee who was carrying out his normal activities and who was acting under orders from the employers.

Civil Penalties

• **Violations.** Allowed the EPA administrator to assess against any person a civil administrative penalty of up to $25,000 per day of violation, whenever the administrator found that such person: 1) violated any requirement of an implementation plan, 2) violated any other requirement of provisions regarding attainment and maintenance of national air quality standards, control of hazardous air pollution, permits or acid deposition control, including a requirement of any rule, order, waiver or permit promulgated or approved or for the payment of any fee owed the United States, or 3) attempted to construct or modify a major stationary source in any area where the administrator had found that the state was not acting in compliance with provisions for non-attainment areas or for prevention of significant deterioration of air quality.

• **Penalty cap.** Limited the administrator's authority to matters where the total penalty sought did not exceed $200,000 and the first alleged date of violation occurred no more than one year before the initiation of the administrative action, except where the administrator and the attorney general jointly determined that a matter involving a larger penalty amount or longer period of violation was appropriate.

• **Field citations.** Allowed the administrator, after consultation with the attorney general and the states, to implement a field citation program through regulations assessing civil penalties not to exceed $5,000 per day of violation. The administrator had to provide a reasonable opportunity for a person receiving the citation to be heard and to present evidence.

• **Court review.** Allowed any person against whom a civil penalty was assessed to seek review in U.S. District Court.

• **Penalty assessment criteria.** Required the administrator or the court, in determining the amount of any penalty, to consider the size of the business, the economic impact of the penalty on the business, the violator's full compliance history and good-faith efforts to comply, the duration of the violation, payment by the violator of penalties previously assessed for the same violation, the economic benefit of non-compliance, and the seriousness of the violation.

Miscellaneous

• **Rewards.** Allowed the EPA administrator to pay a reward, not to exceed $10,000, to any person who furnished information or services that led to a criminal conviction or a judicial or administrative civil penalty for any violation of provisions regarding attainment and maintenance of national air quality standards, control of hazardous air pollution, permits, or acid deposition control. Any officer or employee of the United States or any state or local government who furnished information or rendered service in the performance of an official duty was ineligible.

• **Settlements; public participation.** Required the administrator, at least 30 days before a consent order or settlement agreement of any kind was final or filed with a court, to provide a reasonable opportunity by notice in the Federal Register to persons not named as parties or intervenors to the action or matter to comment in writing. This notice provision did not apply to civil or criminal penalties.

• **Operator.** Defined "operator" as any person who was a part of senior management personnel or a corporate officer. Except in the case of knowing and willful violations, the term did not include any person who was a stationary engineer or technician who was not a part of senior management personnel or a corporate officer.

• **Compliance certification.** Allowed the administrator to require any person who owned or operated any emission source, who manufactured emission control equipment, or who was subject to any requirement of the Clean Air Act, to maintain records, make reports and install monitoring equipment and provide relevant information for the purposes of enforcing the law.

The administrator could also require enhanced monitoring and submission of compliance certification of any owner and operator of a major stationary source.

• **Subpoenas.** Gave the administrator authority under some circumstances to issue administrative subpoenas in support of enforcement activities.

• **Emergency orders.** Authorized the EPA to take emergency action to protect the "public health or welfare, or the environment" (existing law stated simply "health of persons") and deleted the requirement that inaction by local or state authorities would have to be a precondition to EPA action.

• **Contractor listings.** Allowed the administrator to exclude from federal government contracts, grants or loans any facility owned or operated by a person criminally convicted under specified sections.

• **Citizen suits.** Authorized citizens to file suits against sources that had violated the Clean Air Act two or more times in the past.

Citizens were authorized to sue to enforce the terms and conditions of any permits, as well as the requirement to obtain a permit. They also were authorized to seek civil penalties in citizen suits for past violations, provided the violation occurred two or more times.

Courts were permitted to award up to $100,000 to projects that would enhance protection of the public health or the environment. Citizens could sue the EPA if the administrator unreasonably delayed performing any non-discretionary action.

• **New source review.** Clarified and confirmed that the administrator could prohibit the operation or modification, as well as construction, of a new source that had violated new source requirements.

• **Movable stationary sources.** Expanded non-compliance penalty provisions in existing law to cover violations of the permit program and acid deposition controls.

Exempted from the definition of stationary source were emissions resulting directly from an internal combustion engine for transportation purposes or from a non-road engine or non-road vehicle.

Titles VIII-X — Miscellaneous

Air Pollution from OCS Activities

• **Regulations.** Required the EPA administrator, in consultation with the secretary of the Interior and the commandant of the U.S. Coast Guard, to issue rules within one year to control air pollution from outer continental shelf (OCS) oil and gas sources located offshore of states along the Pacific, Arctic and Atlantic coasts, and along the U.S. Gulf Coast off Florida eastward of longitude 87 degrees and 30 minutes; to attain and maintain federal and state ambient air quality standards; and to comply with the provisions in existing law for the prevention of significant deterioration of air quality.

• **25 miles.** Required that sources within 25 miles of the seaward boundary of such states comply with the same standards applicable to the corresponding onshore area.

The requirements included, but were not limited to, state and local standards for emission controls, emission limitations, offsets, permitting, monitoring, testing and reporting. New OCS sources had to comply on the date the regulations were issued; existing OCS sources had two additional years to comply.

• **Exemptions.** Allowed the administrator to exempt an OCS source from a specific requirement if the administrator found that compliance with a pollution control technology requirement was technically infeasible or would cause an unreasonable threat to health and safety.

Any increase in emissions due to such an exemption would have to be offset.

Air Pollution Planning and Control

• **Grants.** Authorized the EPA administrator to make grants to air pollution control agencies in amounts up to three-fifths of the costs of planning, developing and carrying out an air pollution control program.

• **Annual report repeal.** Repealed the existing requirement that the administrator submit an annual report on measures taken to implement the Clean Air Act.

Emissions Factors

• Required the EPA administrator within six months and every three years thereafter to review and, if necessary, revise the methods used to estimate the quantity of emissions of carbon monoxide, volatile organic compounds and nitrogen oxides from sources of such air pollution (including area sources and mobile sources).

The administrator had to establish emission factors for sources for which no such methods had been previously established.

In addition, the administrator would have to permit any person to demonstrate improved emissions estimating techniques, and following approval of such techniques after appropriate public participation, the administrator would have to authorize their use.

Hydrogen Fuel Cells

• **Research.** Required the EPA administrator, in conjunction with NASA and the Energy Department, to conduct a test program of a hydrogen fuel cell electric vehicle, and to determine how best to transfer existing NASA technology into the form of a mass-producible, cost-effective vehicle.

The test program had to include construction of a prototype, and be completed within three years. The test program had to be performed at a university with the best facilities and expertise.

Other

• **Solar and renewable energy.** Required the Federal Regulatory Energy Commission, within 24 months of enactment, to complete rulemaking to establish a demonstration program for regulatory incentives to promote and encourage solar and renewable energy.

The commission had to complete a study that calculated the net environmental benefits of renewable energy, compared with non-renewable energy, and assign numerical values to them.

• **Southwestern New Mexico.** Required the EPA administrator to study the causes of degraded visibility in southwestern New Mexico and authorized the administrator, in consultation with the secretary of State, to work with the government of Mexico in conducting the study.

• **Small communities.** Required the administrator, before putting provisions of the bill into effect, to consult with the EPA Small Communities Coordinator to determine the impact of a provision on small communities, including the estimated cost of compliance with a provision.

• **Trading nations.** Required the president, within 18 months of enactment, to report to Congress on the economic effects of the differences between U.S. air pollution law and standards of the nation's major trading partners. The president had to provide a strategy for addressing such economic effects through trade consultations and negotiations, with recommendations for reducing or eliminating competitive disadvantages for U.S. manufacturers. The president had to make an interim report within nine months.

• **Economic impact analyses.** Required the administrator, in consultation with the Commerce and Labor secretaries and a new Council on Clean Air Compliance Analysis, to conduct a study of the impact of the new Clean Air laws on the public health, economy and environment of the United States, considering the costs, benefits and other effects associated with compliance of new clean air standards.

The report was to be submitted to Congress within 12 months and updated one year after that and every two years thereafter.

Within six months the administrator, in consultation with the Commerce and Labor secretaries, would appoint an Advisory Council on Clean Air Compliance consisting of nine members who were recognized experts in the fields of health and environmental effects of air pollution and other relevant fields.

• **U.S.-Mexico border.** Authorized the administrator, in cooperation with the secretary of State, to negotiate with representatives of Mexico to establish a program to monitor and improve air quality along the U.S.-Mexico border. (EPA had been engaged in such an effort since July 1984.) The monitoring component would have to identify the sources of air pollution along the border region and the level of emission reductions needed to achieve national ambient air quality standards and other air quality goals. The program could also include measures to reduce air pollution along the border region.

• **International border impact.** Directed the administrator to take into account the impacts of air pollution originating from outside the United States when acting on state implementation plans for non-attainment areas of ozone, carbon monoxide and particulate matter.

The administrator had to approve the state implementation plan of any state that demonstrated that it would have achieved attainment by the required date but for emissions emanating from outside the United States.

• **National parks visibility.** Required the administrator, in conjunction with the National Park Service and other agencies, to conduct research to identify and evaluate sources and source regions of visibility impairment in national parks, and to report interim findings to Congress within three years. The bill authorized $8 million a year for five years to conduct the research.

The administrator also could establish visibility transport regions and commissions whenever the administrator had reason to believe that interstate transport of air pollutants from one or more states contributed to visibility impairment in national parks, with state governors or their designees as members of the commission. The commission had to issue a report within four years of establishment recommending what measure should be taken to remedy such adverse impacts.

A commission for the Grand Canyon had to be established within 12 months of enactment.

• **Stripper wells.** Exempted from provisions of Title I (ambient air quality), other than areas designated as severe or extreme, the production of and equipment used in the exploration, production, development, storage and processing of oil from a stripper well property and stripper well natural gas.

• **Greenhouse gases.** Required the administrator within 18 months to issue regulations requiring that all affected sources subject to provisions on acid rain control also monitor carbon dioxide emissions according to the same timetable as sulfur dioxide emissions. The data was to be available to the public.

Authorization

• Authorized such sums as necessary for fiscal 1991-98 for research and development programs and for the EPA to carry out requirements of the bill. The bill authorized up to $50 million a year for grants to states to develop state implementation plan revisions for areas that were non-attainment for ozone, carbon monoxide or PM-10, and up to $15 million a year for grants to states to prepare implementation plans for air pollution abatement and control programs (Title I).

Clean Air Research

• **Research and development program.** Amended existing Clean Air Act provisions that authorized the EPA administrator to establish a national research and development program for the prevention and control of air pollution by adding a provision authorizing the administrator to "construct such facilities and employ staff as are necessary to carry out this act."

• **Monitoring and inventories.** Required the administrator to conduct a program of research, testing and development of methods for sampling, measuring, monitoring, analyzing and modeling air pollutants, including precursors of acid rain.

Among other things, the program had to establish a national network to monitor, collect and compile data on the status and trends of air emissions, deposition, air quality, surface water quality, forest condition and visibility impairment.

• **Improved monitoring and modeling techniques.** Required the development of improved monitoring and modeling techniques to increase understanding of the sources of ozone precursors, ozone formation, ozone transport, regional influences on urban ozone, regional ozone trends and interactions of ozone with other pollutants.

• **Health effects.** Required the administrator to conduct a research program on the short- and long-term effects of air pollutants, including wood smoke, on human health. The program was to be coordinated by an interagency task force of representatives of seven federal agencies. The program was to require an evaluation within 12 months of enactment of each of the hazardous air pollutants listed under the provisions of Title III (air toxics), to determine their relative priority for preparation of environmental health assessments. At least 24 assessments had to be published annually.

• **Ecosystem studies.** Required the administrator to conduct a research program to improve understanding of the causes, effects and trends of ecosystem damage from air pollutants, including acid rain. The program had to identify regionally representative and critical ecosystems for research.

• **Liquefied gas.** Required the administrator, in consultation with the Energy secretary, to oversee an experimental and analytical research effort at the Liquefied Gaseous Fuels Spill Test Facility.

The administrator, in consultation with the Energy secretary, had to select at least 10 chemicals each year for such research activities, with at least two chemicals chosen for field testing, giving highest priority to those posing the greatest threat to human health and the environment.

The secretary was authorized to enter into contracts or make grants to nonprofit entities affiliated with the University of Nevada and the University of Wyoming, with a requirement for permanent research facilities.

The bill authorized $3 million in fiscal 1991 and such sums as necessary for future years.

• **Pollution prevention and emissions control.** Required the administrator to conduct a basic engineering research and technology program to develop, evaluate and demonstrate strategies and technologies for air pollution prevention, including the prevention of acid rain, with special attention to pollutants that posed a significant risk to human health and the environment.

• **Coordination of research.** Required the administrator to develop and implement a plan for identifying areas in which the research programs described above could be carried out in conjunction with other federal ecological and air pollution research efforts.

• **Acid rain response action.** Required the president to submit to Congress within six months a plan describing activities and assigning responsibilities for federal research on acid rain, and including coordination of the activities of the administrator under this subsection. The president had to develop and submit to Congress, within one year of enactment, an assessment framework for reporting complicated technical information about acid rain to policy-makers and the public. The president had to report to Congress every two years on the reduction in acid deposition rates that would have to be achieved in order to prevent adverse ecological effects.

- **Clean alternative fuels.** Required the administrator to conduct a research program to identify, characterize and predict air emissions and other potential environmental effects related to the production, distribution, storage and use of clean alternative fuels to determine the risks and benefits to human health and the environment, in comparison with gasoline and diesel fuels.
- **Adirondack destruction assessment.** Required the administrator to establish a program to research the effects of acid rain on waters where acid deposition had been most acute. The research had to be conducted under a multi-year contract at Rensselaer Polytechnic Institute, Troy, N.Y. The bill authorized a minimum of $6 million to carry out this program.

Disadvantaged Business Concerns

- **Research.** Required that at least 10 percent of the research of EPA-funded research contracts be conducted by disadvantaged business concerns.
- **Definition.** Defined a disadvantaged business concern as one in which 51 percent of the company, or 51 percent of the stock, was owned by one or more socially and economically disadvantaged individuals, or in which the management and daily business operations were controlled by such individuals.

The following institutions were presumed to be disadvantaged: historically black colleges and universities, colleges and universities with at least 40 percent Hispanic students, minority institutions, and private and voluntary organizations controlled by individuals who were socially and economically disadvantaged.

- **Quota prohibition.** Barred the use of quotas or a requirement that had the effect of a quota in determining eligibility.

Title XI — Job-Loss Benefits

- **Job displacement.** Required the Labor secretary to make grants to states or sub-state grant-making entities (such as employers, labor unions or employer associations) to provide needs-based payments, training and employment services to eligible workers laid off or fired due to the employers' compliance with the Clean Air Act. Priority for grants was to be given to areas that had the greatest number of eligible individuals.

Grant applicants had to assure that funds would provide needs-based payments.

- **Needs-related payments.** Required the secretary to prescribe regulations detailing the use of funds for needs-related payments, which were designed to enable eligible individuals to complete retraining programs. Payments could be made only to an individual who did not qualify or had ceased to qualify for unemployment compensation, and who had been an enrolled participant in training by the end of the 13th week of the individual's unemployment compensation benefit period, or, if later, the end of the eighth week after an individual was informed that a short-term layoff would exceed six months.

To qualify for such payments, the individual's total family income — not counting unemployment compensation, child support or welfare payments — could not be in excess of the lower-living standard income level, in relation to family size. Payments had to be equal to the former level of unemployment compensation or the family's poverty level, whichever was higher.

- **Job-search allowance.** Allowed reimbursement for not more than 90 percent of the worker's job search expenses but not to exceed $800 unless approved by the secretary.
- **Relocation allowance.** Allowed reimbursement for relocation expenses if the secretary determined that an eligible worker could not reasonably be expected to find suitable employment in the commuting area in which the employee resided and if that worker had received an offer for suitable employment with a reasonable expectation of long-term duration in the area in which the employer wished to relocate.

The amount of relocation allowance for any one worker could not exceed 90 percent of the reasonable expenses incurred by a worker and the worker's family and any household effects. The worker also could receive a lump-sum payment equal to three times the employee's average weekly wage, up to $800, unless a higher amount was approved by the secretary.

- **Authorization of appropriations.** Authorized $50 million for fiscal 1991, and such sums as may be necessary for each of fiscal 1992-95. The total amount for the five fiscal years could not exceed $250 million. ■

Continued from p. 247

what was widely recognized as a failed federal program to control the most hazardous airborne pollutants, such as benzene and asbestos, emitted by industrial facilities. The EPA was required under the 1970 Clean Air Act to identify hazardous pollutants that contributed to death or serious illness and to set emissions standards for those pollutants. The standards were to be set at a level that provided "an ample margin of safety" to protect the public health.

But because of funding shortages, industry pressure and what many viewed as unrealistic standards for reducing health risks, the EPA had listed only eight of the 275 toxic substances known to be emitted by industrial facilities. Standards had been issued for only seven.

Under the new air toxics pact, about 250 major industrial polluters, such as chemical plants and oil refineries, had to install "maximum achievable control technology" — the average emissions limitations of the cleanest 12 percent of similar facilities — to reduce toxic emissions by 2003. The controls were required earlier, in 1995, for 41 of those sources. New plants had to meet higher emissions limits.

If significant risks to public health still remained after those controls were installed, the EPA had to further tighten emissions standards to ensure that nearby residents were not exposed to more than a 1-in-10,000 "residual risk" of cancer. Otherwise, the plants had to shut down.

In addition to regulating major sources of emissions, the agency had to ensure that emissions of the 30 most serious air pollutants from smaller "area sources," such as dry cleaners and gas stations, be reduced by 90 percent.

The new controls on major sources proved to be the most controversial. Much of the wrangling during the negotiations centered on whether more lenient standards should be issued for steel plant coke ovens. Industry lobbyists argued that the nation's 30 remaining steel plants might have to shut down if they had to meet the same standard for residual cancer risks imposed on other polluters.

Steel plants were among the dirtiest industrial facilities in the nation, posing, in some cases, cancer risks of as high as 1-in-55 to nearby residents.

Complicating negotiations was the fact that many conferees liked the other chamber's version of the bill better than their own. While the House bill had no special break for the steel industry, conference leaders Dingell and Lent, as well as Democrats Eckart and Boucher, who both had steel plants in their states, wanted to move closer to the Senate bill, which would have given steelmakers until 2020 to cut cancer risks to the same level required of other major sources by 2003. The more pro-environment Senate conferees, on the other hand, were eager to weaken the Senate-passed extension for the steel industry in favor of the House's tougher controls.

The resulting deadlock was finally broken with an agreement to give steelmakers until 2020 to reduce cancer risks to nearby residents to 1-in-10,000, but only if they cleaned up significantly in the meantime. In fact, by 1998, they had to meet a tighter emissions standard than any other industry had to meet in that year. Steel industry lobbyists said they could live with the proposal. John M. Stinson of National Steel Corp. said steelmakers would spend about $6 billion between 1993 and 1998 to bring facilities up to the new standard, but he added that a number of steel plants would have had to modernize anyway. "It gives us the certainty to go about running our business," he said.

Environmentalists, however, were disappointed. "It's very distressing," said Doniger, the Natural Resources Defense Council lawyer. "A generation or more of people will be exposed to very serious cancer risks."

Equally distressing, Doniger said, was the conferees' decision not to regulate emissions of two highly toxic metals — mercury and cadmium — by utilities. The Sierra Club's Weiss called that omission a "special-interest provision of the worst sort."

Environmental groups fared better with the agreement on municipal waste incinerators. The Senate required that toxic ash left behind after city garbage was burned be disposed of under standards less rigorous than required for hazardous waste, but more stringent than regular garbage. The House bill had no such provision.

Environmentalists supported the House bill, hoping to win stronger hazardous-waste disposal standards during reauthorization, probably in 1991, of the Resource Conservation and Recovery Act (RCRA).

At the insistence of Lent, however, whose state of New York relied increasingly on garbage incineration, a compromise was reached to bar the EPA from issuing standards within the following two years requiring that ash be regulated as hazardous. Lent said localities investing in incinerators "want to know what they can do with the garbage."

Job Benefits

After yet another marathon, all-night negotiating session, a decade of legislative gridlock and bitter rivalry dissolved into a festival of back-patting as conferees on Oct. 22 cheerily ratified the basic ingredients of a final agreement on the bill.

The final roadblock was cleared in the wee hours of the morning Oct. 22, when White House domestic policy adviser Porter and Bob Grady, an aide to budget director Richard G. Darman, gave conferees the thumbs up on a compromise to provide up to $250 million in assistance to workers, particularly coal miners, thrown out of work by clean air controls. *(Aid to displaced workers, p. 277)*

Chances of a last-minute filibuster by Western senators subsided as well, as conferees unceremoniously dropped a proposal by Oregon Democrat Wyden to improve air visibility in national parks, such as the Grand Canyon, in the Western United States. Montana Democrat Baucus, who headed the Senate conferees, and Wyoming Republican Simpson refused to budge from language in the Senate proposal calling merely for a study of the problem.

Wyden planned to push the EPA to tighten regulations without congressional action. "You're talking about tremendous national treasures that all Americans are enjoying," he said.

Acid Rain Agreement

A final marathon negotiating session began late the week of Oct. 15, when conferees worked to resolve their differences on acid rain.

Compromise had been elusive because a control strategy had to balance the needs of two broad camps. On one side were the clean states — those with utilities that burned less polluting, low-sulfur coal or that had installed scrubbers or other pollution control devices. On the other were the dirty states, which were located mostly in the Midwest and mined and burned high-sulfur coal.

The "cleans" wanted to ensure that they got credit for earlier emissions reductions and could expand their electric utility capacity, if needed, without busting tight emissions caps. They also did not want to pay for the Midwest's costly cleanup. "Why should you have to pay the Midwest because they're dirtier?" asked Ned Helme, director of the Alliance for Acid Rain Control, a coalition of clean states, many of which were the recipients of acid rain.

The "dirties," on the other hand, wanted to preserve jobs for high-sulfur coal miners in the Midwest and the Appalachian states. They also wanted cost sharing among states to keep the cleanup from further depressing the economies of Midwestern states.

Acid rain legislation in previous years had involved such a cost-sharing component, but Bush opposed that approach. Instead, his bill put forth a market-based system of pollution "allowances" that could be granted to utilities that limited sulfur dioxide emissions. That proposal became the key ingredient in political trade-offs that eventually cemented an acid rain agreement.

The idea behind the Bush proposal was to give plants the flexibility to clean up in the most cost-effective manner. Because dirty utilities could sell or trade their allowances, they were encouraged to clean up more than required and recover their costs by selling valuable credits. The buyers: clean utilities that wanted to expand but had little or no room to do so under tough new emissions caps. With variations, both bills adopted this approach.

As had been the case with most clean air issues, the debate in conference began with House members wrangling among themselves over how, or whether, to move toward the Senate position. Both bills hinged on a complex and intertwined set of agreements among members who had fought to get the best deal for electric utilities and workers in their states.

Environmentalists, the administration and many House conferees preferred the simpler system in the Senate bill. But central to that agreement was a requirement that two-phase emissions limits be imposed one year earlier, in 1995 and 2000 — deadlines that House Midwesterners, particularly Indiana Democrat Sharp, said would be too costly.

Members from other regions countered — to little avail — with data to show that the Senate agreement would actually be cheaper for the Midwest than the House bill.

Resistance to the Senate proposal began to soften on Oct. 19, when House conferees agreed to placate angry Midwesterners with an offer of 275,000 extra pollution allowances to ease the burden on utilities in their states.

In that initial House proposal, the extra allowances were to come from installing scrubbers at taxpayers' expense in Midwestern utility plants that served Energy Department facilities. Scrubbers captured up to 95 percent of sulfur dioxide emissions, but cost $300 to $600 for every ton of the pollutant removed. That plan was panned in the Senate, particularly by Wendell H. Ford, D-Ky., who said it could push up electricity rates and force a federal uranium enrichment plant in his state to shut down.

Proposals were then shuttled back and forth until about 5 a.m. on Oct. 22, with conferees eventually agreeing to

Continued on p. 278

Assistance for Displaced Workers

Any time Congress imposes new regulations on industry, as the clean air package did, another time-tested issue surfaces — what to do about the workers who lost their jobs in the process.

In past years, Congress invariably came through with some kind of relief. But it rarely happened without a fight — and 1990 was no different.

After a bruising defeat in the Senate and veto threats aimed at the House, clean air conferees agreed that the government should give income assistance and retraining to coal miners and others who might lose their jobs as a result of the legislation (S 1630 — PL 101-549).

The compromise, while narrower in scope than the original provision by Rep. Bob Wise, D-W.Va., marked the first time since the 1970s that Congress had agreed to give cash payments to workers dislocated by new legislation.

The Bush administration was adamantly opposed to the original Wise amendment, passed by the House in May, which it considered an open-ended entitlement for workers.

It would have authorized $250 million over five years to allow workers an additional 26 weeks of unemployment benefits and retraining if they showed the new clean air law was "an important contributing factor" to their job loss.

The clean air package's acid rain controls were expected to shift jobs from the high-sulfur coal industry in the East to low-sulfur coal workers in Western states. Other provisions could cost jobs in the oil, chemical and auto industries.

That prospect prompted a related Senate proposal by Robert C. Byrd, D-W.Va., which failed by one vote in March.

It would have cost $500 million and was aimed at helping only displaced coal miners.

White House Compromise

During the House-Senate conference on the clean air bill, the administration sent signals that the Wise provision was a bill-killer.

Surprisingly, however, President Bush was willing to deal. Domestic policy adviser Roger B. Porter and other White House aides worked with congressional staff into the early morning hours of Oct. 22 to reach a compromise on the issue.

"They realized the bill was not going to get to the White House without some worker-adjustment amendment in it," said William Samuel, legislative director for the United Mine Workers of America. "So they cut their losses."

The result altered the original provision but left its intent largely intact. Displaced workers could receive cash after their unemployment assistance ran out as long as they remained in a retraining program. The authorization remained at $250 million over five years, but the biggest change involved the source of the funds.

Instead of making the plan part of the mandatory unemployment benefits program, which Bush opposed, conferees put all funding under the Economically Dislocated Workers Assistance Act, a part of the larger Job Training Partnership Act (JTPA), which was dependent on yearly appropriations.

Wise, aware that employment agencies and unions that received JTPA funds rarely used their discretion to give cash to workers as well as retraining, insisted on language ensuring that workers would get both. The payments were to be equal to the unemployment insurance level or enough to keep family income above the poverty level, whichever was higher.

"We lost the strict, mandatory nature of the unemployment insurance," Wise said. "But my feeling is, what we got achieves exactly the same result."

A Recurrent Problem

Typically, unemployment in a market economy was caused by forces such as shifts in production techniques, drops in demand or corporate belt-tightening. But the federal government, through its economic regulations, also has handed its share of pink slips to private-sector workers.

Congress over the years had offered a patchwork of assistance. In fact, instances of Congress leaving workers it displaced without some kind of help were hard to find.

In 1962, workers who lost jobs because of that year's trade law were given "trade adjustment assistance." The criteria for eligibility were eased in 1974, in a decade that was a watershed for such laws. Congress in 1973 granted workers fired as a result of that year's bailout of bankrupt railroads $250 million in lost wages.

In 1978, Congress agreed to pay full salaries for up to six years to 2,900 workers displaced by that year's expansion of the Redwood National Park. Sen. Ted Stevens, R-Alaska, at the time called the provision to aid timber workers a precedent of "substantial magnitude."

Months later, Congress extended similar protections to air carrier workers who lost jobs as a result of airline deregulation legislation.

The deregulation era of the 1980s meant Congress enacted few regulatory bills that directly cut jobs. In 1988, however, Congress revamped the JPTA law to include dislocated workers assistance programs. *(1988 Almanac, p. 215)*

Labor groups were hoping that Wise's victory would revive the trend of the 1970s. Coming in 1991 were bills to raise automobile fuel-economy standards, convert some defense industries into civilian uses and protect spotted owls, dolphins and red-cockaded woodpeckers from industry.

Some House members favored setting up an agency to help all workers cut out of jobs by new laws. Hearings on sweeping efforts to help defense industry as well as timber workers went nowhere after Iraq invaded Kuwait.

Others criticized broad-scale relief as unrealistic.

"Workers should not be left out there naked in the cold weather with no assistance at all as a direct result of a congressional action," said Jay Power, a lobbyist for the AFL-CIO. "But it has to be done on an individual basis. Creating a pot of money is not the way to go."

Continued from p. 276
grant plants in Ohio, Illinois and Indiana 200,000 extra allowances a year for the following five years. After the year 2000, 10 Midwestern states would get 50,000 extra allowances every year.

In exchange for that concession, Midwesterners caved in on some other demands, including a provision in the House bill that would have allowed governors to veto the use of anything other than local coal in electric utilities. That could have protected Midwestern coal-mining jobs, as well as created new jobs, by requiring utilities to install scrubbers or other emissions-reduction technology instead of switching to out-of-state low-sulfur coal.

The result of the weekend talks was an acid rain agreement that, with the exception of additional allowances for the Midwest, followed the Senate bill closely. It required annual sulfur dioxide emissions to be reduced by about 10 million tons by the year 2000. Annual nitrogen oxide emissions had to be cut by 2.7 million tons by that year.

Midwestern plants had to clean up first; beginning in 1995, 111 of the dirtiest coal-fired plants in 21 states had to reduce sulfur dioxide emissions. About 200 more would have to comply by 2000. Plants that committed to using scrubbers to clean up emissions in the first phase could delay compliance until 1997. After 2000, the amount of sulfur dioxide emissions could not exceed 8.9 million tons a year, meaning plants had to offset the extra pollution generated by new units or expansions.

Environmental groups opposed the additional allowances for Midwest utilities. "Our basic position was that the Midwest did not need the extra tons," said Marchant Wentworth, a lobbyist for the Izaak Walton League. "The data supports that. But it was a political problem, not a data problem. Sharp needed something big to take back."

Yet despite the Midwest's final gains, the bill was far more costly for their states than acid rain proposals debated in previous years. In 1984, Midwesterners, backed by Republican conservatives, scuttled a bill by Reps. Waxman and Sikorski that would have imposed a nationwide utility tax — amounting to a $2.2 billion a year subsidy — to pay for scrubbers on the dirtiest 50 utility plants.

"The burden of that decision falls directly on the shoulders of the electric utility industry," said Rep. Madigan. "They felt they would never have to deal with this problem. They were wrong."

FINAL ACTION

As the clean air bill headed toward overwhelming final approval in both chambers, its passage had become almost inevitable. Over the 16 months since Bush had introduced legislation to rewrite the nation's main antipollution law, it had evolved into an election-year trophy that was too precious for anyone to steal away. With Congress' image battered by months of budget impasse and anti-incumbency sentiment, Democrats in particular wanted a big environmental victory to take home.

House, Senate Votes

Montana's Baucus, who chaired the conference, called the bill "the most comprehensive and sweeping environmental legislation that Congress has passed in this century." But as he presented the conference report to the Senate on Oct. 27, Baucus freely acknowledged the Democrats' debt to Bush for his support.

"George Bush turned around the previous administration's point of view," Baucus said on the Senate floor. "The Reagan administration was very much opposed to clean air. The Bush administration is very much in favor of clean air legislation. George Bush deserves major credit."

The conference agreement did depart significantly from the bill Bush proposed in June 1989, and administration officials were often shut out of substantive negotiations. Still, there would have been no bill without Bush, and the final product reflected many accommodations to the administration's positions.

Supporters of the legislation also owed a debt to House Energy Chairman Dingell, who supported the rewrite after having helped bottle up bills through the 1980s. Dingell did not recite that history as he presented the measure to the House for approval on Oct. 26. Instead, he stressed his role in helping write "every clean air bill ever passed" and praised the 1990 bill despite the "sacrifices" it would require in the interests of a cleaner environment.

The House voted 401-25 to approve the conference report. Voting against the measure were 20 Republicans — six from Midwestern states that would be hurt by the bill's acid rain provisions — and five Democrats, including four Midwesterners. *(Vote 525, p. 166-H)*

The Senate's 89-10 vote on Oct. 27 clearing the measure for Bush was a virtual replay of its 89-11 vote in April. The same five Democrats who opposed the measure in April voted against it again: Dixon and Simon, Ill; Glenn, Ohio; and Byrd and Rockefeller, W. Va. Among Republicans, Nickles of Oklahoma and Wallop of Wyoming shifted to supporting the bill, Utah's Hatch changed to opposition, and Oregon's Mark O. Hatfield missed the vote while campaigning for re-election. *(Vote 324, p. 63-S)*

Interest Group Assessments

The competing lobbying groups on the bill did not completely share the lawmakers' enthusiasm for the final product. Environmentalists and industry alike found cause for discontent.

From industry's perspective, Congress had approved controls that would be tougher and far more costly than those backed by the administration. "In almost every title we have provisions that are stronger than those we were advocating through the years," said California's Waxman, the main House champion of clean air legislation.

Under pressure from industry, Bush also began backpedaling almost immediately on some of his own proposals — particularly an aggressive alternative-fuels program that would have mandated production of about 1 million methanol-fueled cars. Congress dropped that in favor of a California pilot program requiring Detroit to manufacture whole new lines of clean-fueled cars, along with provisions requiring oil companies to sell cleaner, reformulated gasoline in the nation's most polluted cities.

But by the time the administration sent the conferees a counterproposal on the bill Sept. 26, it was too late to make much of a difference. The Senate, for example, had already given in, without a fight, to House provisions requiring much more stringent urban smog controls on businesses ranging from dry cleaners to oil refineries. Industry lobbyists counted that as their most serious clean air loss.

Congress felt free, in part, to opt for the stronger controls because of skepticism that Bush would veto the bill over its price tag in the waning days of an election-year session. "I don't think there was ever a serious consideration given to a veto of this legislation," said House conferee Sherwood Boehlert, R-N.Y.

At the start of the year, on Jan. 19, Bush had written to Senate Minority Leader Dole that he would send back any proposal that would cost the economy more than 10 percent more than the administration bill, whose cost was estimated at about $20 billion. Yet the latest estimates were that the legislation would cost $25 billion to $35 billion. "If the president holds true to his 10 percent cost veto threat, this bill won't become law," Fay of the Clean Air Working Group said as the bill headed for the White House.

Still, environmentalists bemoaned a number of compromises to Bush that extended into the late 1990s the imposition of controls to reduce pollution from automobiles and fuels, and a 17-year delay, until 2020, won by the steel industry on a requirement that plants shut down if they could not significantly reduce cancer risks from toxic emissions. "This bill will not be technology-forcing until the 21st century," predicted the Sierra Club's Weiss.

Industry lobbyists, meanwhile, prepared for life after the clean air bill.

They said auto controls would add hundreds of dollars to the cost of cars, gas and electricity prices would go up, plants would spend millions on new pollution controls, and small businesses would have to scramble to comply with tough and expensive new permit requirements.

"The American consumer and ratepayer better brace themselves for the cost of this bill," Fay said.

Bush Signing

Business complaints about the costs, however, were no threat to Bush's signing a bill that he had helped nurture for more than 16 months. In the Nov. 15 bill-signing ceremony, Bush took credit for his role in breaking what he called "the logjam that hindered progress on clean air for 13 years." He termed the bill "the most significant air pollution legislation in our nation's history" and ticked off the environmental progress that it promised to accomplish:

- A 56 billion pound reduction in air pollution — "224 pounds for every man, woman, and child in America."
- A 40 percent reduction in smog by the year 2000.
- A 75 percent reduction in dangerous air toxics emissions.
- Reduced dependence on foreign oil "by the next decade" because of the alternative fuel provisions.

In a nod to business concerns, however, Bush stressed that the bill was "balanced" and imposed "reasonable deadlines for those who must comply." And in a written statement, he said he was directing EPA Administrator Reilly to implement the act "in the most cost-effective manner possible." ■

Fuel-Efficiency Effort Defeated in Senate

Heavy lobbying by the auto industry and the Bush administration stalled a Senate attempt to raise federal automobile fuel-efficiency standards Sept. 25, killing the issue for the 101st Congress.

The Senate voted 57-42, three votes short of the 60 votes needed to limit debate on a bill (S 1224) that would have forced automakers to increase 1988 Corporate Average Fuel Economy (CAFE) levels by 20 percent by 1995 and 40 percent by 2001. The existing standard was 27.5 miles per gallon (mpg). *(Vote 248, p. 50-S)*

After the vote, sponsors Richard H. Bryan, D-Nev., and Slade Gorton, R-Wash., agreed to pull the bill from consideration. "The minority won a small and shortsighted victory," Bryan said. "We will be back next year."

BOXSCORE

Legislation: Motor Vehicle Fuel Efficiency Act (S 1224).

Major action: Senate rejected cloture motion, 57-42, Sept. 25; cloture invoked on motion to proceed to the bill, 68-28, Sept. 14; approved by Senate Commerce, Science and Transportation Committee, April 3.

Reports: Commerce, Science and Transportation (S Rept 101-329).

The legislation, dropped from the clean air package in March in exchange for separate floor consideration, got a big boost after the Aug. 2 Iraqi invasion of Kuwait set off renewed debate over U.S. energy policy. Bryan said the bill would have saved 2.8 million barrels of oil per day and led to 40 mpg fleet averages.

But opposition from the Bush administration offset any momentum Bryan gained from the Persian Gulf crisis. The administration argued that the bill was not economically sound or technically feasible. Energy Secretary James D. Watkins told senators at a Sept. 13 hearing that he and Transportation Secretary Samuel K. Skinner would recommend a veto on those grounds.

The auto industry lobbied heavily against the bill, arguing that it would require further downsizing, which would lead to small, unsafe cars.

Proponents of the bill disagreed, saying the technology existed or could be developed to allow cars to meet the tougher requirements without downsizing. They played heavily to the Middle East oil crisis.

"Today the gas guzzler won, and they're popping the champagne corks in [Iraqi President] Saddam Hussein's palace," said Dan Becker of the Sierra Club.

Cabinet members took the offensive shortly before the Senate voted Sept. 14 to cut off debate on the motion to proceed to the bill.

That first cloture vote, 68-28, was a strong showing for Bryan's camp, but then 11 senators — eight of them Republicans — switched their votes on the Sept. 25 motion to cut off debate on the bill. *(Vote 235, p. 48-S)*

BACKGROUND

Fuel-efficiency standards were first mandated in the 1975 Energy Policy and Conservation Act (PL 94-163). Under the 1975 law, automakers had to meet across-the-board, incremental increases in fuel economy — beginning with 14 mpg in 1974 and increasing by 1985 to 27.5 mpg, the existing standard. *(1975 Almanac, p. 220)*

Bryan said his bill to further increase the standards would help reduce air pollution. If put into full effect, he said, his legislation would have cut carbon dioxide emissions by 500 million tons a year.

But it was the new uncertainty about the nation's dependence on oil from abroad — spurred by Iraq's invasion of Kuwait — that gave the CAFE bill its new thrust. Bryan said his bill would have resulted in vastly improved new fleet mileage averages and would have saved nearly 3 million barrels of oil a day.

Bryan's bill was controversial largely because it would have changed the basic approach of the government's CAFE standards. Unlike the 1975 law, Bryan would have required percentage increases in CAFE based on the 1988 fuel-economy averages of each manufacturer's fleet.

Thus, Japanese companies that made smaller, more fuel-efficient cars would have been forced to meet higher standards than U.S. companies, which catered to larger-car markets.

The bill would have pushed all auto companies to improve gas-mileage standards by a certain percentage over their 1988 fleetwide average. "It requires everyone to put their shoulder to the wheel to do better," Bryan said.

Industry Concerns

Both domestic and foreign automakers opposed CAFE bills though foreign manufacturers more strenuously opposed Bryan's percentage approach, which would have affected them more. The Chrysler Corp. and the Ford Motor Co. (along with the United Auto Workers union) would have parted company with the Japanese and backed Bryan's approach if CAFE legislation had become inevitable. (the General Motors Corp. opposed any change in the standards.)

Chrysler and Ford officials argued that the percentage formula in Bryan's bill was better than existing law, which they said gave Asian manufacturers the competitive edge because the standards were easy to satisfy with their small-car fleets.

As an alternative, early in the debate, import manufacturers pushed to raise CAFE standards based on vehicle size or class. This would have meant different overall fuel-economy standards for companies based on their mix of vehicle sizes: companies that made more small cars would have to have met higher standards, which would have fallen if the company began producing larger vehicles.

Such a system would also have favored domestic producers over the Japanese. Similarly, it would not have required nor necessarily encouraged domestic manufacturers to produce smaller, more fuel-efficient vehicles.

Environmentalists worked hard to keep this size-class option on the shelf. They argued that it would have encouraged U.S. automakers to stick with what they made best: larger, more profitable, less efficient vehicles.

For environmentalists, any incentives for larger cars would have defeated the original purpose of the legislation — reducing carbon dioxide emissions, which some scientists said were adding to dangerous changes in the temperature of the atmosphere. It was largely concern about such global warming — as well as about rising U.S. dependence on foreign oil — that gave political impetus to the long-dormant issue.

Environmentalists pushed hard for the highest standards they thought possible: perhaps 45 mpg by the year 2000.

"The technology that will be required to achieve a 45-miles-per-gallon fuel economy standard is already on the shelf and is just not being put on the cars by most of the manufacturers," says the Sierra Club's Becker. "These are not exotic technologies."

Supporters of new CAFE standards said domestic automakers might have to be forced to stake a claim to a U.S. technological edge in fuel-efficient cars.

From the industry's perspective, any standard above about 30 mpg was not possible without dramatic changes in U.S. consumers' car-buying behavior. "Sales of Festivas and Escorts would have to go up dramatically," said David Kulp, manager of fuel economy, planning and compliance at Ford's automotive emissions office, speaking of two small cars on the 1990 market.

Sens. Donald W. Riegle Jr., D-Mich., Don Nickles, R-Okla., and other opponents of the bill said the standards under the Bryan bill were so tough they would force automakers to offer only smaller, less safe cars, which in turn would mean a loss of autoworkers' jobs.

Commerce Committee Chairman Ernest F. Hollings, D-S.C., said arguments by domestic automakers that they could not meet the standards and still remain competitive would be "very disturbing, if not for the fact that they said the same things in the 1970s," when earlier CAFE legislation was debated.

Domestic automakers argued in 1974 and again in hearings in 1989 that new standards would force them to make subcompact cars that U.S. consumers did not want. But Bryan said the industry could meet the standards with existing technology and with cars the size of the 1987 fleet.

Japanese Involvement

Meanwhile, the Japanese were worried that tougher fuel-economy proposals would shut them out of the U.S. luxury-car market. They most strongly opposed the percentage formula in Bryan's bill.

Asian automakers said Bryan's legislation was unfair to companies that had made the most progress in increasing fuel economy. "Punishing people for good works just seems to be bad public policy," says Charles E. Ing, a lobbyist for Toyota Motor Sales U.S.A. Inc. "It certainly doesn't provide any incentive to better government mandates."

Foreign automakers and their U.S. dealers were ready early to test their substantial lobbying muscle to make sure Bryan's plan did not become law. Kathleen Mordini, vice president of public affairs for the American International Auto Dealers Association, which represented about 9,200 import car franchises, said U.S. dealers began visiting members of Congress in May 1989 to fight the bill.

Japanese corporate officials also got involved, making an unusual appearance at congressional hearings in September 1989 to testify against the CAFE legislation. Toni Harrington, manager of industry and government relations for Honda North America, said Honda "strongly, strongly, strongly" opposed Bryan's bill.

Suzuki Motor Co. Ltd. took a more aggressive and politically charged stance — circulating a legal analysis prepared by Petit & Martin, a Los Angeles-based law firm, arguing that Bryan's bill would discriminate against imports and violate U.S. obligations under the General Agreement on Tariffs and Trade, the international treaty governing nearly all world trade.

Both domestic and foreign auto dealers also showed their political might during the electoral season. According to the Federal Election Commission, the imported-car industry's political action committee, Auto Dealers and Drivers for Free Trade (AUTOPAC), contributed $3.8 million in the 1988 elections while Detroit's "Big Three" — Ford,

General Motors and Chrysler — spent $1.2 million.

In an attempt that could have pre-empted some of the issue, AUTOPAC poured approximately $365,000 into the close 1988 Senate race in Nevada between Bryan and Republican Sen. Chic Hecht (1983-89). Most of the money went into television ads praising Hecht for his stands on trade issues though some went into ads criticizing a stand taken by Bryan.

The car dealers actually picked an issue they considered effective with Nevada voters, but which had little to do with automobiles — the dealers' ads attacked Bryan for a position he had once taken on Social Security.

COMMITTEE ACTION

CAFE legislation received Senate committee approval in 1990, but never got beyond a subcommittee hearing in the House.

Senate proponents had little difficulty garnering the necessary votes to report the measure to the full chamber.

In the House, though, all fuel-economy initiatives had to face the bulwark of Energy and Commerce Committee Chairman John D. Dingell, D-Mich., the Big Three's strongest political ally. And Dingell staunchly championed industry efforts to fight higher gas-mileage standards.

Senate Commerce

On a 14-4 vote, the Senate Commerce, Science and Transportation Committee on April 3 approved S 1224.

The vote was a victory for environmentalists and a setback for automakers, who had argued that the levels of fuel efficiency called for in the bill would be impossible to achieve without radically reducing the size of cars.

Nevertheless, the bill was ordered reported to the floor after little debate.

"It's time that we do some of the tough things that are necessary to encourage conservation in this country," said committee member Lloyd Bentsen, D-Texas.

A few members of the committee came to the automakers' defense. "Just so this won't turn into a complete love-in, I don't support this legislation," said Trent Lott, R-Miss.

He and the other Republicans who opposed the bill said the standards imposed were too stringent and would have reduced consumer choice as a result of the massive downsizing that manufacturers would have to pursue to meet the standards.

Transportation Secretary Skinner wrote in a letter March 7 that the bill would have a "devastating impact on American consumers, auto workers, highway safety and our vehicle industry."

To address the concern that smaller cars would be less safe, the Senate included a proposal by John C. Danforth, R-Mo., to give automakers credit for a 10 percent boost in fuel-economy ratings if they installed air bags on the driver and front-passenger sides of the car. Companies would get credit for a 5 percent increase if an air bag were installed just on the driver's side.

House Subcommittee Hearing

The presence of Energy and Commerce Chairman Dingell had hampered CAFE proponents in the House. Dingell consistently backed industry efforts to keep rising concern about air pollutants from being translated into gas-mileage standards the industry called impossible to achieve.

In 1990, though, Dingell and the House showed some signs of movement on the issue. The Energy Subcommittee on Energy and Power held a hearing on Sept. 19 — the first time in five years that Dingell allowed the issue such a forum.

The announcement came after environmental groups made pleas to the House leadership on Sept. 4 to allow a CAFE bill (HR 5560) by Barbara Boxer, D-Calif., to bypass Dingell.

The pros and cons of CAFE standards were vigorously debated at the rancorous hearing. Backers of the measure who testified at the hearing included Bryan and Boxer.

Opponents, led by representatives of the auto industry and Dingell, argued that the smaller, lighter cars that would have to be built to satisfy the new requirements would be more dangerous and less convenient for motorists.

But a representative of the Center for Auto Safety, which supported the legislation, told the subcommittee that safe, fuel-efficient cars could be built.

With the Senate's action a few weeks later killing the measure for the Congress, the House acted no further on the matter. The subcommittee never even acted on the measure other than holding the hearings; the full committee did not touch the issue.

SENATE FLOOR ACTION

The Senate's 57-42 vote on Sept. 25 to invoke cloture on S 1224 — three votes short of the 60 votes needed to limit debate — effectively killed the bill for 1990. Eleven days earlier, on a 68-28 vote, senators had voted to cut off debate on a motion to proceed to the bill.

After the first cloture vote, Riegle said that he and Nickles had a good chance of swinging more votes their way before the second vote.

In the meantime, they planned to offer several amendments to the bill in an effort to kill the measure.

"The auto industry is an immense lobby," said Bryan aide James Mulhall. "They're going to try to load this thing with the kitchen sink and try to sink us."

Auto industry and labor union officials also arranged meetings with key undecided senators before the final vote. Car dealers and autoworkers bombarded Capitol Hill with phone calls and letters.

Before rejecting the cloture motion, the Senate did approve six amendments to the bill. One, by Nickles, would have required government vehicles to meet the proposed new standards.

But the chamber rejected, 49-46, an amendment by Paul Simon, D-Ill., to provide financial assistance to autoworkers who would lose their jobs because of the proposed fuel standards. *(Vote 246, p. 46-S)*

While the auto companies ultimately prevailed, their warnings were viewed with increasing skepticism. Bryan and others, including Sen. Howard M. Metzenbaum, D-Ohio, the sponsor of another CAFE bill (S 984), reminded automakers of the industry's 1974 prediction that new gas-mileage standards would force them to produce only Pinto-sized subcompacts by 1985. "The automakers, obviously, were dead wrong," Metzenbaum said.

Bryan added: "Their testimony now is almost a carbon copy of their testimony in 1974, the thrust of which is: It can't be done."

This drew sighs from auto industry officials. Kulp said, "Some things we said in the mid-1970s we would have preferred that we didn't say." ■

House-Passed Octane-Labeling Bill Dies

The House passed Oct. 23, by voice vote and after perfunctory debate, legislation to encourage states to crack down on gasoline dealers who sold low-octane fuel at high-octane prices, cheating customers out of millions of dollars a year.

The legislation (HR 5520 — H Rept 101-823), which the Senate never acted on, would have made it easier to prosecute service station owners, allowed states to order businesses to stop selling mislabeled gas immediately and broadened the octane-labeling law to include new fuels such as gasohol.

"Octane mislabeling is consumer fraud," said Carlos J. Moorhead of California, ranking Republican on the Energy and Power Subcommittee.

Subcommittee Chairman Philip R. Sharp, D-Ind., was kinder to the industry: "The majority of gasoline distributors and dealers are honest businessmen and women," he said.

"Much of the mislabeling is accidental. However, there are known instances of octane cheating or fraud."

Moorhead called efforts to pass the bill "a textbook way to craft a bipartisan legislative package." He had worked with Sharp to pass the measure and, aside from a question posed by Austin J. Murphy, D-Pa., they were the only two members to address the bill when it reached the floor.

The Energy and Commerce Committee approved the bill Sept. 25. The measure was approved in virtually the same form as it had been crafted Aug. 1 by the Energy and Power Subcommittee.

Background

Octane ratings measured gasoline's resistance to engine knock, the metallic pinging sound caused by improper combustion. Different engines required different octane levels; most were designed to use regular 87 octane, but about a third of all gasoline sold was mid- or high-test quality, generally 89 to 94 octane.

The General Accounting Office (GAO) had cited cases in which gasoline from pumps posted with different octane ratings came from the same storage tanks.

The GAO issued a report on the problem in April at the request of Sharp and Charles E. Schumer, a Democrat from New York City, where the problem was said to be severe.

According to the report, there was relatively little mislabeling in 20 states with active octane-testing programs.

In some states that did not regularly test, big problems were found. In some areas tested for the GAO, more than half of the gasoline was below octane by as much as six points.

That meant some cars were getting fewer miles to the gallon and consumers were unknowingly damaging their engines — and being cheated out of lots of money in the process.

Though no concrete nationwide figures existed, the report said that 1979-87 statistics from the Motor Vehicle Manufacturers Association showed that more than 9 percent of all gasoline sampled by the group was mislabeled by more than half a point.

"Assuming that 9 percent of the gasoline sold in 1988 was mislabeled by only one-half an octane number, GAO estimates that consumers could have paid about $150 million for octane they did not receive," the report said.

That was probably the minimum. "This is a serious problem costing the consumer hundreds of millions of dollars a year," Sharp said.

Congress, following the lead of several states that had detected abuse, first tried to address the problem in 1978 with the Petroleum Marketing Practices Act (PL 95-297). It mandated the uniform posting of octane levels, prompting rules that required small yellow stickers on all gas pumps. It required refiners, importers and distributors to test and certify octane ratings. *(1978 Almanac, p. 748)*

The Environmental Protection Agency (EPA) was given responsibility for the testing of octane ratings nationwide and the Federal Trade Commission (FTC) was supposed to prosecute violations. But the EPA tested for only two years, and the FTC never prosecuted a single case. Both blamed Congress for not appropriating enough money to do the job.

That left the problem to the states. But, as the GAO study showed, enforcement was spotty.

The problem became more acute, state officials testified, when California prosecutors in 1988 decided that they had to drop mislabeling charges against a large distributor because they discovered that the federal law pre-empted stricter state laws.

The federal law only provided for civil fines, although several states had criminal statutes and allowed officials to issue immediate "administrative stop-sale orders" to offending dealers.

Referring to such stop orders, the GAO said that the 1978 law "would seem to pre-empt this option."

Legislative Action

HR 5520 would have given states a freer hand, though not much else. It would not have forced states to establish testing programs, and energy policy-makers on Capitol Hill had little inclination to press the EPA and FTC to follow the 1978 law's original mandate — if only because it would have cost too much. The bill, in fact, would have changed the law to make the EPA's mandatory testing authority discretionary.

As much as anything, the purpose of moving the bill appeared to be to raise the consciousness level of the issue. That tack appeared to be working. After Congress began looking into the matter, several states began testing programs or considered doing so.

The bill would also have:

- Made it easier to prosecute retailers by lowering the threshold of proof needed to show that they knew that they had sold mislabeled gasoline.
- Broadened the 1978 law to include new types of fuel because the FTC had ruled that gasohol was not a gasoline. The increasing use of alcohol blends and other alternative fuels was expected to accelerate under the Clean Air Act revision enacted in 1990. *(Clean Air Act, p. 229)*
- Required the administration and the FTC to study several issues, including whether colored dyes should be added to gas supplies to help customers distinguish between octane ratings.

Though the House panels and full chamber approved the measure, the Senate never took up the legislation. The bill was referred to the Senate Commerce, Science and Transportation Committee, which did not act. ■

Oil Spill Liability, Prevention Bill Enacted

Congress ended 16 years of deadlock over oil pollution Aug. 4 when it sent President Bush a long-awaited get-tough bill meant to prevent oil spills and punish spillers. The president signed the bill on Aug. 18.

Congress, the Bush administration, environmentalists, and industry representatives overcame disputes on a number of sticking points — state preemption, double hulls, liability limits and international protocols — before producing the compromise measure.

The House early on Aug. 4 cleared the bill (HR 1465) for the president's signature, when it adopted the House-Senate conference report on a 360-0 vote. The Senate had adopted the final version on Aug. 2 by a vote of 99-0. The final product was a compromise bill that had been stitched together from versions passed by both chambers in 1989. *(House vote 320, p. 104-H; Senate vote 206, p. 43-S)*

A final floor fight in the House — over a conference agreement to ban oil and gas drilling off North Carolina — fizzled quickly. Ralph Regula, R-Ohio, failed to force a vote on the drilling ban when the House approved a restrictive rule governing floor debate, 281-82. *(Vote 319, p. 104-H)*

In the end, environmentalists won much more than they lost in their campaign to toughen federal laws and increase spillers' liability. They effectively rode a wave of public outrage over 1989's catastrophic *Exxon Valdez* spill in Alaska and a series of other accidents.

Yet in the 16 months between the Alaska spill and final passage of the measure, the oil and shipping industries managed to pull off several significant feats of damage control.

Expensive safety requirements were imposed on shipowners, but not as quickly as environmentalists would have liked. Damage liability limits for shippers were increased greatly, but not enough for the environmentalists. And, to environmentalists' chagrin, oil owners and cleanup teams were partly shielded from direct financial risks.

"They got a number of their concerns addressed," said Clifton E. Curtis, a lobbyist for Friends of the Earth. George Miller, D-Calif., one of the House's leading environmentalists, agreed: "Their fingerprints are on the bill."

Ernest J. Corrado, who represented tanker owners and operators as president of the American Institute of Merchant Shipping, had a similar view from a different perspective: "Relative to where we are now, it's horrendous; relative to what it might have been, it's a little better. It could have been a lot worse."

Despite his reservations, Curtis tried not to appear ungrateful. "Overall, we're extremely pleased with the legislation," he said.

BOXSCORE

Legislation: Oil Pollution Prevention, Response, Liability and Compensation Act, PL 101-380 (HR 1465).

Major action: Signed, Aug. 18. Conference report adopted by House, 360-0, Aug. 4 (session of Aug. 3); by Senate, 99-0, Aug. 2. Passed Senate, Nov. 19, 1989; House, 375-5, Nov. 9, 1989.

Reports: Conference report (H Rept 101-653). Public Works and Transportation (H Rept 101-242, Part I); Merchant Marine and Fisheries (Part II); Science, Space and Technology (Part III); Public Works (Supplemental, Part IV); Merchant Marine (Supplemental, Part V).

BACKGROUND

Congress, unable to enact a law revamping the nation's oil-spill liability and prevention laws since it began trying in 1974, was finally spurred to action by the *Exxon Valdez* spill.

Previously existing law was a hodgepodge. Various types of spills were covered in several laws enacted in the 1970s, including the Clean Water Act and the Trans-Alaska Pipeline Authorization Act. Many states enacted their own laws, with some setting up compensatory cleanup funds and imposing unlimited liability on spillers.

Environmentalists had been pressing Congress to enact a comprehensive oil-spill bill since the mid-1970s, but disputes among interest groups stymied action. That was fine with many in industry, who benefited from low federal liability limits.

Several attempts to enact a comprehensive federal law fell short of passage at various stages in the process over the years. Chief among the reasons was the House's insistence on a provision to pre-empt strict state laws and the Senate's equally hard-line position against the idea. (In 1990, 19 states had laws imposing unlimited liability on oil spillers.)

The *Exxon Valdez* spill removed that obstacle, prompting the House to do a complete about-face and abandon its position by an overwhelming margin after lobbyists representing environmental groups threatened lawmakers with negative publicity for voting against them on the issue.

After agreeing to prohibit pre-emption, the House voted 375-5 on Nov. 9 for its oil-spill liability, compensation, prevention and cleanup bill. The Senate had passed a similar bill (S 686) on Aug. 4 by a vote of 99-0. *(1989 Almanac, p. 682)*

Later spills off Texas and California helped create pressure to resolve other disputes.

The rest of the bill fell into place very slowly, however. The industry managed to limit its cost in significant ways, but said the measure could still end up costing energy producers and transporters billions.

Provisions

Following are the major provisions of HR 1465 as cleared for the president:

- Increased spillers' liability many times over existing federal limits and imposed stiffer civil and criminal penalties. Liability could top $200 million for big tankers.
- Required spillers to pay for cleaning up oil spills and compensated parties economically injured by them.
- Continued to allow states to impose unlimited liability on shippers.
- Authorized using money from a federal fund, subject to annual appropriations, to pay for cleanup and compensation costs not covered by spillers. The fund, designed eventually to contain $1 billion, was to be financed by a recent 5-cents-a-barrel oil tax.

- Required shippers to draft "worst-case" oil-spill response plans for quick cleanup.
- Enhanced the federal government's oil-spill response capability. District response groups were to be positioned across the country to aid strike teams, and a new national command center was to be established in Elizabeth City, N.C.
- Expanded the president's power to take control of a spiller's cleanup operations.
- Required the government to do an audit of the structural soundness of the Trans-Alaska Pipeline, taking into account safety, health and environmental protection.
- Established a multi-agency oil-pollution panel to coordinate federal research.
- Stiffened anti-drug and anti-alcohol laws for ship operators by requiring testing for certain workers and threatening substance abusers with license revocation.
- Blocked oil or gas drilling off the coast of North Carolina until Oct. 1, 1991.

CONFERENCE ACTION

Senate and House conferees finally met on April 25 to finish crafting oil-spill legislation, which had passed both houses in 1989. They did not meet again until late in June and then completed the legislation on July 26.

Though both chambers had resolved most of the major issues that had stymied final action on oil-spill bills in past years, they started feuding again over a couple of sticking points — including a relatively minor but key issue that threatened to block chances for a quick compromise.

International Protocols

One of the first issues in contention was a House-approved section of the bill that would have implemented, subject to Senate ratification, a 43-nation oil-spill agreement. That pact set liability limits for oil spills by ocean tankers and established an international fund to pay for damage — up to a specified cap — over the liability limits.

The agreement, prompted by a big spill off the coast of England, encompassed two international conventions from 1969 and 1971 and amendments in the form of "protocols" drafted in 1984.

The Senate had refused to ratify the original conventions because a substantial bloc of senators believed the liability limits were too low and would have effectively pre-empted stiffer state and federal laws.

Several House conferees, seeking to pressure the Senate to act on the treaty, insisted that the implementing language remain in the oil-spill liability bill.

Senate conferees, whose position was outlined by Majority Leader George J. Mitchell, D-Maine, remained adamantly opposed not only because of the pre-emption issue, but also because senators considered the House's protocol-implementing provision an invasion of their constitutional prerogative to dispose of treaties as they saw fit.

At the conference meeting, Rep. Robert W. Davis, R-Mich., complained about the industry vs. environmentalist nature of the split. "We must not allow this issue to become a litmus test for those who want to play the greener-than-thou game," he said.

The Bush administration argued that the protocols would not pre-empt state liability laws under the House bill because all cleanup costs could be recovered — first from the spiller and other responsible parties, second from the international fund and last from the federal fund.

States still would be free, the administration argued, to bring criminal and civil actions to further punish spillers.

Senate opponents argued that only a very few additional ships would be covered by the international fund that were not covered by federal or state law — those owned by parties with no financial interests in the United States, which were passing by the country, but not stopping in, any U.S. port.

"Only a small percentage of vessels fall into this category," said Mitchell, who devoted almost his entire opening statement at the conference to the issue. "I am inalterably convinced that the 1984 protocols are not worth the price."

Mitchell used the *Exxon Valdez* spill to illustrate his point. He said that under the Senate version and the House bill without the protocols, the Exxon Corp. "would have been strictly liable for all cleanup costs and damages incurred as a result of its spill in Alaska's Prince William Sound. Cleanup costs alone are estimated at approximately $2 billion."

Under the protocols, he added, Exxon's liability would have been limited to less than $60 million — and taxpayers would have had to pay nearly all the rest.

The second conference meeting did not take place for another two months — during which there was a major spill off the coast of Texas and smaller spills elsewhere. On June 28, when conferees finally met, industry-backed House negotiators finally bowed to pressure from Senate environmentalists on the international oil-spill agreement.

In what seemed like a halfhearted effort to break the stalemate, Rep. Gerry E. Studds, D-Mass., offered a compromise. His proposal would have had the United States participate in the agreement for five years "on a trial basis."

If the other signatories did not make the accord tougher, Studds said, the United States would cease to participate: "International protection should not come at the expense of strong federal or state laws. The international protocols must be renegotiated."

Davis, leading the House forces in favor of the industry position, urged the Senate to accept Studds' proposal. He argued that federal and state laws had little or no effect on many foreign shippers. That fact, he said, constituted "a loophole the size of the *Mega Borg*," the listing tanker that burned for more than a week off the coast of Texas after exploding June 8.

The Bush administration also weighed in on the final day with a package of letters from foreign governments urging the United States to join the accords.

Despite the urgings, Senate conferees rejected Studds' amendment by voice vote. Studds then proposed a nonbinding statement supporting an "effective" international agreement.

Rep. Don Young, R-Alaska, a supporter of the protocols and then of Studds' compromise, was bitter in defeat: "This is an amendment that means very little or nothing. It's a small crumb."

Mitchell, acknowledging Young's interpretation of the proposal's legislative intent, persuaded his colleagues to support the statement by voice vote.

Compromise on Double Hulls

One of the other major issues of contention in the legislation was a debate over whether, or how, to require oil tankers to have double hulls, a design long recommended by environmentalists to prevent spills.

Indeed, the first action taken in 1990 on the oil-spill

legislation was a Feb. 7 House vote in favor of requiring new and existing oil tankers and barges to be outfitted with double hulls or double bottoms. The non-binding 376-37 vote came on a motion to instruct conferees to insist on such a provision when negotiating with senators on the measure. *(Vote 12, p. 6-H)*

Offered by Dean A. Gallo, R-N.J., the motion received only token opposition partly because of its vagueness. It did not instruct the conferees to accept the House's double-hull-and-bottom provision specifically. But it appeared to call for one that was stricter than the Senate's.

The House bill required all tankers and barges traveling in U.S. waters to have double hulls within 15 years. As an interim step, the biggest tankers would have to have double bottoms (a component of double hulls) within seven years. Altogether, the provision forced the owners of about 1,800 barges and several hundred tankers to spend hundreds of millions — perhaps billions — of dollars to stitch another layer of metal on their vessels.

The shipping and oil industries and the Bush administration much preferred the Senate version, which imposed the double-hull requirement only on new tankers (not barges). The requirement would have gone into effect a year after enactment and would have allowed the secretary of Transportation to decline to impose the provision.

Corrado of the shippers' group said if the tanker owners had to accept mandatory double-hulls, they would fight for more time. Curtis from Friends of the Earth expressed a willingness to compromise on the seven- and 15-year deadlines in the House bill.

"It's terribly expensive," said House Public Works and Transportation Committee Chairman Glenn M. Anderson, D-Calif. "I don't want to see us put prohibitive costs on the people that own these ships. If the cost is as high as they claim, it's going to raise the price of oil."

On top of the expense, it would also take a long time to retrofit ships — about two years for each, according to the shippers' estimates. They said U.S. shipyards did not have the capacity to handle all the work, but the shipbuilders insisted they did.

At the April 25 conference, members officially acknowledged that the double-hull issue should be among the first to be settled. Conferees approved a compromise July 12. Under the compromise, almost all U.S. oil tankers were required to have double hulls by the year 2010.

According to figures provided by members and their aides, the agreement phased out 45 percent of the nation's single-hulled fleet's oil capacity by the year 2000, 85 percent by 2005 and all by 2010. The compromise was based on a sliding-scale phaseout schedule that forced the biggest and oldest ships to be retired or retrofitted sooner than smaller vessels.

Approved without public discussion, the agreement was less stringent than the original House language but stricter than the Senate bill — though still not enough to satisfy environmental groups. The environmentalists were pushing conferees to phase out single-hulled ships by 2005, while the oil industry was pushing for 2015.

Friends of the Earth's Curtis criticized the compromise, accusing conferees of giving "Mother Nature a kiss on the cheek — followed by a slap in the face."

Industry lobbyists were satisfied. "Double hulls came out pretty well," Corrado said. "At least it's reasonable."

Members said it was a fair compromise because they split the requests down the middle. However, they also made several significant concessions to oil and shipping interests that upset the environmentalists.

Exempted until 2015 were inland barges, some coastal barges and big tankers that brought oil from overseas to be unloaded (lightered) well offshore. Less expensive spill-resistant designs known as "double containment systems" were allowed on some smaller vessels as long as the Transportation secretary deemed them to be as safe as double hulls. Ships with double bottoms or sides received an extra five years.

In behind-the-scenes negotiations leading up to the conference action, each delegation moved away from its chamber's original position.

That was because many House conferees — such as Anderson and W. J. "Billy" Tauzin, D-La. — were more inclined toward oil interests than those members who crafted and pushed the double-hull amendment on the floor in 1989. Conversely, the Senate conference group was dominated by pro-environmentalists, such as Mitchell and John H. Chafee, R-R.I..

However, a Feb. 7 oil spill off the coast of California and

Environmental Crimes

Legislation to stiffen criminal penalties for individuals and groups responsible for environmental disasters that cause death, injury or severe damage won approval March 29 from the House Judiciary Subcommittee on Criminal Justice, but went no further.

The bill (HR 3641), sponsored by subcommittee Chairman Charles E. Schumer, D-N.Y., was in part a response to the massive 1989 *Exxon Valdez* oil spill in Alaska.

"We need a law that makes a connection between the size of the environmental crime and the size of the punishment," Schumer said.

As approved by the Criminal Justice Subcommittee, the bill would have made it a felony to knowingly create a risk of death by polluting. Negligent endangerment, or "gross deviation from the standard of care that a reasonable person would exercise," would have been a misdemeanor.

Penalties under the bill could have reached $2 million in fines for corporations or $500,000 for individuals. Repeat offenders could have faced jail terms of up to 30 years.

In addition, courts would have been required to put guilty companies on probation and subject them to an environmental audit to identify pollutants and recommend measures to reduce emissions levels. The court then could require the company to put those measures into effect.

Schumer was cosponsoring the legislation with the subcommittee's ranking Republican, George W. Gekas, Pa. But they were negotiating details up to the time of the markup, and Gekas warned that Republicans might have additional objections at the full committee level.

The administration opposed the bill. Deputy Assistant Attorney General George W. Van Cleve told the subcommittee Dec. 12, 1989, that the administration believed the tougher penalties could backfire by making juries less likely to convict defendants in environmental cases.

Pipeline Inspection Measure Enacted

Legislation prompted by pipeline accidents off the Gulf of Mexico, requiring gas and pipeline owners in the gulf to inspect and rebury exposed lines, was signed into law by President Bush on Nov. 16.

The measure (HR 4888 — PL 101-599), sponsored by Rep. W. J. "Billy" Tauzin, D-La., cleared the Senate Oct. 27 after having passed the House Oct. 15.

Tauzin introduced the bill in response to two accidents in the gulf in which boats slammed into pipelines and set off explosions that claimed 13 lives. It was supported by a cross section of interest groups in the area, including pipeline owners, the fishing industry and vessel operators who serviced the gulf's oil platforms.

The bill was limited to pipelines in the gulf in order to ease its passage through three House committees: Merchant Marine and Fisheries, Public Works and Transportation, and Energy and Commerce. Tauzin's Louisiana colleague, Democratic Sen. John B. Breaux, persuaded his chamber to accept the committees' work.

BACKGROUND

In shallow waters of the Gulf of Mexico near the Texas-Louisiana border Oct. 3, 1989, 14 fishermen aboard the *Northumberland* were netting menhaden, small fish used in livestock feed. As dusk approached, Capt. Wayne Gough backed up the 168-foot vessel to prepare for another catch and slammed the stern into an underwater natural gas line. Unbeknown to Gough and anyone else who traveled those waters, shifting currents had uncovered the pipeline from beneath the gulf floor.

The resulting explosion triggered a 100-foot jet of flame that burned for about 18 hours. Eleven men died, and two were seriously injured. Only Gough came out largely unscathed; he managed to dive off the side of the boat just before the fire engulfed the ship's bow.

The tragedy could have been prevented, the fishing industry said. So it pushed Congress to require gas and oil companies to inspect all shallow-water pipelines annually and to rebury uncovered tubes.

"That was an exposed pipeline that obviously was exposed for several years and should have been checked and should have been reburied," said Richard E. Gutting Jr., a lobbyist for the National Fisheries Institute.

Shifting Sands

Under existing law, pipelines were required to be buried at least three feet below the ocean bottom. But, said proponents of the bill, gulf-water streams constantly shifted and eroded floor sands and soils, uncovering pipelines that had not been inspected in years.

Federal officials disclosed after the *Northumberland* accident that there had been other fatal accidents caused by vessels striking uncovered gas lines. On July 24, 1987, a fishing vessel struck a natural gas pipeline in the gulf, and two crewmen were killed in the fire.

"That's what made us aware that this was an emerging issue," said Barney White, a vice president of Zapata Corp., a Houston-based energy-production company that owned the *Northumberland* as part of a fishing subsidiary. "We're afraid that there might be more of these time bombs out there."

Tauzin, chairman of the Merchant Marine Subcommittee on Coast Guard and Navigation and a member of the Energy Committee, introduced HR 4888 on May 23: "It is my hope that passage of this bill will help ensure that there will never be another disaster."

COMMITTEE ACTION

Tauzin's bill moved fairly quickly through three committees — Merchant Marine, Energy and Public Works — after pipeline owners and the fishing industry agreed to a compromise version.

Tauzin's original version would have applied to all gas and oil pipelines in up to 22 feet of offshore water and in inland waterways, not just pipelines in the Gulf of Mexico. The bill also would have required owners to undertake several expensive tasks. They would have had to pay new fees, face surprise Coast Guard inspections, inspect their pipes yearly and comply with numerous reporting requirements.

Pipeline owners said they were willing to accept new requirements but lobbied to limit the cost of the bill.

Fishing groups, who favored the broad bill introduced by Tauzin, agreed, at Tauzin's request, to compromise with pipeline owners on a narrower measure as a temporary solution. Tauzin, historically among the gas and oil industries' most faithful allies, was also a big protector of Louisiana's fishing industry.

Narrow Bill

The version approved Sept. 13 (H Rept 101-814, Part III) by the House Merchant Marine panel — the first of the three House panels to approve the bill — applied only to natural gas pipelines in the Gulf of Mexico in up to 15 feet of water.

Gone were the fees, most of the reporting requirements and any mention of surprise inspections.

The Energy and Commerce Committee, with the agreement of Merchant Marine, added oil pipelines to the bill's coverage and approved the measure Sept. 25 (H Rept 101-814, Part II). The Public Works Committee then approved this version of the bill on Oct 5 (H Rept 101-814, Part I)

FLOOR ACTION

The House gave voice-vote approval to the pipeline bill Oct. 15 as it had been agreed on by the three committees. The Senate cleared the legislation by voice vote Oct. 27, after Breaux persuaded his colleagues to take up and accept the House measure without Senate committee action.

As enacted, the law applied to pipelines in the Gulf of Mexico in up to 15 feet of water. The law required pipeline owners to inspect each pipeline periodically, to mark exposed pipelines with buoys until buried as required and to tell the government about them so vessel owners and operators could be warned of the danger.

near Anderson's district helped environmentalists during the double-hull debate.

Long an ally of the oil and shipping interests that frequented the harbor in his Long Beach district, Anderson took a helicopter tour that hovered just feet above the beaches soiled by oil spilled from the *American Trader* off Huntington Beach, just south of Long Beach. The spill helped shift his position on the double-hull issue, he said.

"They told us out there that if it had a double hull, it wouldn't have ruptured," Anderson remarked.

Liability Limits and Impact

The other main conference issue in dispute centered around liability limits — the amount of money spillers pay for damage before money from a government pot was used.

The bill authorized a $1 billion federal cleanup fund — financed by a recently imposed tax on the oil industry of 5 cents a barrel — to be used only after the shipper's liability money was used up.

The two chambers differed over liability limits. The House approved $1,200-per-ton limits split between cargo and shipowners, while the Senate's $1,000 figure applied only to shipowners. The environmentalist coalition pressed for up to $2,000 a ton, split between cargo and shipowners.

Conferees agreed to $1,200 per ton, a potentially hefty sum for huge tankers that held 200,000 tons and well over the existing top cap of $150 per ton. But at the urging of independent oil companies, which said they often had little control over who transported their product, conferees declined to hold oil owners directly liable.

"Cargo owners should not be held liable for the conduct of another party," the American Petroleum Institute argued in a position paper.

Conferees also acceded to industry requests on whether cleanup crews should be shielded from federal liability. The oil industry portrayed them as "good Samaritans."

The environmental groups favored the Senate bill on this score because it contained no such exemption, but industry's argument won out. "Absent this immunity," the oil institute argued, "the radically changed liability exposure facing clean-up organizations would likely render their operations uninsurable — and unavailable."

Oil interests also managed to kill a move by environmentalists to punish spillers for "simple negligence." Under the bill, spillers faced unlimited federal liability only if found guilty of "willful misconduct or gross negligence."

During the conference, members also rejected environmentalists' pleas to give states a strong hand in deciding how extensive cleanup efforts must be.

Under the agreement, the president would have the sole authority to declare a federal cleanup effort complete, although states would be able to do extra work and try to recover costs from spillers. That was a compromise with environmentalists, who had backed a Senate provision to give affected state governors and the president equal say over when federal cleanup efforts could be declared finished and halted.

Pro-industry conferees also rejected a Senate attempt, backed by environmentalists, to impose fees on shippers to pay for administering some of the bill's Coast Guard inspection and oversight requirements.

Even though the oil industry received certain concessions on some of the liability issues, the bill was expected to cost the industry hundreds of millions and perhaps billions of dollars, with much of that to be paid by consumers.

Stiff increases in federal liability limits, expanded civil and criminal sanctions and the tacit acceptance of tougher state liability laws were also expected to drive shipping insurance premiums up considerably. Shippers also could spend untold amounts buying new, safer vessels or improving old ones, preparing elaborate "worst-case" spill contingency plans, and making sure they have proper cleanup equipment and trained personnel on call.

In a big spill, shippers could find themselves taking orders from the federal government, which was empowered to direct cleanup efforts with an enhanced system of expert Coast Guard strike teams whose chief concern would not be controlling costs.

Miller, who had pressed unsuccessfully on the House floor for even tougher liability standards for oil-spillers, declared final victory. "This oil-spill bill says the safe transportation of oil is going to be part of the cost of doing business." The industry, he added, "was trying to avoid that, but the environmental camp won that debate."

Tauzin, who frequently opposed Miller's positions on the bill, agreed with that assessment. "It's clearly a big environmental win," he said.

But Tauzin complained that the bill was still too stringent, particularly in allowing states to impose unlimited liability on shippers. "We've gone too far in some cases," he said. "That's a mistake, and we're going to live to regret it."

Industry representatives warned that some smaller shippers could be forced out of business. A few of the bigger international shippers were already boycotting U.S. ports, prompting fears among industry-leaning members that underinsured companies would soon take over part of the U.S. oil transportation market.

FINAL ACTION

The Senate passed the final version of the bill Aug. 2 by a vote of 99-0. *(Vote 206, p. 43-S)*

Once the measure made its way back to the House floor Aug. 3, few contentious issues remained. The only remaining skirmish was over the bill's one-year moratorium on gas and oil drilling off North Carolina — manifested in the House vote on the rule for floor consideration of the bill.

One of the bill's chief sponsors, Rep. Walter B. Jones, a Democrat from a North Carolina coastal district, had added the provision late in the House-Senate conference. Jones persuaded the Interior Appropriations Subcommittee in July to propose barring new drilling leases off North Carolina in fiscal 1991. His addition to the oil-spill bill went a step further to block the Mobil Corp. from drilling an exploratory well under an existing lease to make time for more studies.

Early in the week, Jones had been expected to prevail easily, despite administration opposition. But opponents were emboldened by Iraq's invasion of Kuwait on Aug. 2, which prompted an oil-price surge and renewed jitters over U.S. reliance on oil imports. *(Persian Gulf crisis, p. 717)*

Still, some administration officials knew the effort to remove the provision was a long shot because the White House never objected very strenously. Bush had struggled to establish pro-environment credentials and issued no veto threats.

The Rules Committee, by voice vote on Aug. 2, approved a resolution that protected the amendment from a separate vote. To kill the provision and force a vote on the drilling ban, opponents had to defeat the rule. They failed by a vote of 281-82, and the House proceeded to pass the bill unanimously, 360-0. *(Votes 319, 320, p. 104-H)* ■

States Get More Say in Offshore Activity

Congress cleared a measure revamping and expanding the 1972 Coastal Zone Management Act (CZMA) after key members agreed to include the legislation in the fiscal 1991 budget-reconciliation bill (HR 5835 — PL 101-508).

Differing versions of the rewrite already had been approved by the House (HR 4450) and the Senate Commerce Committee (S 2782). The House approved the revamping of the law again as part of the Merchant Marine Committee's contribution to the deficit-reduction bill, leaving it to conferees from Senate Commerce and House Merchant Marine to agree on its final form.

The bill, which extended the CZMA through fiscal 1995, gave states more say over federal activities off their shores *(Provisions: Budget Reconciliation, Title VI, p. 154)*.

Separately, Congress renewed and expanded a moratorium on federal offshore oil and gas leases as part of the Interior appropriations bill (HR 5769 — PL 101-512). *(Interior appropriations, p. 870)*

BACKGROUND

The 1972 Coastal Zone Management Act (PL 92-583) used federal grants to entice states into drafting plans for protecting their shore areas from the adverse impacts of development. It also promised states that federal coastline activities would be "consistent" with federally approved state plans. *(1972 Almanac, p. 970)*

The rewrite's crafters wanted to bolster that consistency provision in a way that the Bush administration and some Republicans opposed.

The bill attempted to overturn a 1984 Supreme Court decision (*Secretary of the Interior v. California*) that watered down the consistency provision by declaring that the law did not cover federal outer continental shelf oil- and gas-drilling lease sales. *(1984 Almanac, p. 335)*

The new consistency provision in the legislation was popular with many shore-state members from both parties because it gave states more power to try to block or alter federal decisions that affected their coastal zones — even those that involved activities outside the zones, such as oil and gas drilling. In many states, most notably California and Florida, offshore oil and gas drilling was widely unpopular with voters, so many members wanted to help enhance the states' say in such matters.

Administration officials threatened to veto the House bill over this issue and lobbied GOP senators hard against the provision. Especially concerned about it were the Interior Department, which oversaw drilling leases, and the Defense Department, which was worried that states might attempt to block shore-area training exercises, aides said.

HOUSE ACTION

The House passed its bill (HR 4550) to extend and strengthen the CZMA on Sept. 26, giving it overwhelming approval despite a veto threat from the administration.

Committee Action

Legislation approved by the Merchant Marine and Fisheries Committee on April 18 to renew and expand the CZMA was aimed at giving states more power to block oil and gas drilling off their shores.

The bill (HR 4030) was approved by voice vote but never reported because its broad scope would have enabled several other committees to claim sequential referral.

Instead, the panel approved a narrower bill (HR 4550 — H Rept 101-535) on May 23 that made largely technical changes in existing law without touching on the broader issues in HR 4030, such as state authority to block federal oil and gas leasing and coastal water quality improvement.

Provisions dealing with these issues were then added as part of a substitute amendment when the House considered the bill.

Floor Action

The House voted 391-32 on Sept. 26 to approve the revised HR 4450, reauthorizing the CZMA for five years and enhancing the power of states to block oil drilling off their shores. *(Vote 386, p. 124-H)*

Expected fights over offshore drilling fizzled after it became clear that antidrilling forces would win.

The existing law provided funds, policy guidance and technical assistance to help coastal and Great Lakes states establish and maintain coastal zone management plans.

States opposed to federal attempts to lease oil- and gas-drilling rights in the outer continental shelf off their shores had long argued that the 1972 law gave them some say over such matters. But the 1984 ruling by the Supreme Court declared that lease sales did not "directly affect" coastal zones, which did not extend into the continental shelf.

The House bill was aimed at overturning the ruling by stating that the consistency provision covered any federal activity "in or outside the coastal zone" and by deleting the word "directly" so the provision would cover any activity merely "affecting" coastal zones. The Bush administration threatened to veto the House bill over the issue.

Attempting to appease the White House, Norman D. Shumway, R-Calif., had planned to offer an amendment to weaken the new provision, which he said would have given the "upper hand" back to the federal government. But he decided against offering the amendment after it became clear that he would have lost.

In a deal with Leon E. Panetta, D-Calif., leader of the antidrilling forces, Shumway agreed not to offer his amendment and Panetta dropped plans for another amendment that would have further enhanced state powers by stating explicitly that the drilling leases were covered by the consistency provision.

SENATE ACTION

The Senate Commerce Committee approved its overhaul of the CZMA (S 2782 — S Rept 101-445) on June 27.

Like the House bill, the Senate measure would have strengthened state powers by clarifying that all federal agency activities were subject to the consistency requirements of the CZMA if they affected natural resources, land uses or water uses in the coastal zone.

The bill, which would have renewed the CZMA for five years, also would have required states to establish coastal water quality protection programs. And similar to the House bill, the Senate measure would have established a new grant program to encourage states to incorporate into their coastal management programs a number of high-priority national objectives, such as wetlands protection.

Trent Lott, R-Miss., complained that the provisions to preserve wetlands were too broad, potentially prohibiting Mississippi's coastal counties from any development.

"There is no effort here to restrict development," said bill sponsor John Kerry, D-Mass., noting that the coastal zone management process was voluntary and states could choose not to participate. The bill simply tried to encourage and entice states to protect their wetlands, he said.

But the Senate never took up the measure because of Republican objections.

RECONCILIATION ACTION

After the Senate failed to act on a bill, the House Merchant Marine panel added the coastal zone management legislation to its piece of the deficit-reduction package. The House included the CZMA language when it passed its deficit-reduction bill on Oct. 16.

Though some Senate Commerce Republicans opposed including the coastal-zone rewrite in the deficit bill, it became clear at an informal meeting Oct. 25 that Commerce panel Democrats had enough votes. Paving the way for final action, reconciliation conferees from the Commerce and Merchant Marine panels ultimately agreed on a five-year measure that authorized appropriations at continually increased levels, starting at $58.75 million in fiscal 1991 and rising to $119.24 million in fiscal 1995.

Conferees killed a controversial provision that would have encouraged states to adopt "no net loss" wetlands policies with some of the bill's new grants. Members from states with sizable amounts of wetlands feared it would stifle development.

As cleared and signed into law by President Bush, other CMZA provisions of the reconciliation bill bolstered states' authority to block oil and gas leasing off their coasts as well as other federal activities that were inconsistent with state coastal protection plans.

The measure also did the following:

- Established Coastal Zone Enhancement Grants to encourage states to improve their coastal protection plans in one or more of eight areas: coastal wetlands protection; natural hazards management (including potential rises in sea and Great Lakes levels); public access improvements; reduction of marine debris; coastal growth and development impact assessments; special area management planning for important coastal areas; ocean resource planning; and siting of coastal energy and government facilities.
- Established a coastal non-point-source pollution control program, requiring shoreline states to develop plans for protecting their waters from non-point-source pollution (runoff from city streets and farms). States were to get new grants to help them develop their programs, but the government would withhold parts of their CZMA and Water Pollution Control Act grants starting in 1996 if they failed to submit acceptable non-point-pollution plans.
- Required the Environmental Protection Agency to establish uniform national guidelines for controlling non-point-source pollution to coastal waters. States had to follow these guidelines in developing their plans. ■

Coastal, Great Lakes Cleanup Efforts Stall

Ambitious bills aimed at cleaning the muck out of coastal and Great Lakes waters gained House and Senate committee approval during the 101st Congress but stalled before reaching the floor.

The bills faced opposition from some Republicans who said that the bills would have made piecemeal changes in the Clean Water Act (PL 92-500) that were better addressed during the scheduled reauthorization of that law the following year. The Clean Water Act governed both inland and coastal waters.

The House bill (HR 2647) was reported by the Merchant Marine and Fisheries and Public Works committees, but the versions were never reconciled and the bill did not reach the floor. It would have required the Environmental Protection Agency (EPA) to revise its coastal water-quality standards within five years. For the 16 worst pollutants, new criteria would have to be issued within two years.

The House measure also would have required coastal states to develop water-quality protection plans. If a plan was not approved by the EPA and the National Oceanic and Atmospheric Administration (NOAA) within three years, states would have lost some forms of federal aid.

The Senate Environment and Public Works Committee also reported a coastal bill (S 1178 — S Rept 101-339), which included provisions related to improvement of the Great Lakes that became law via another bill.

House Action

Action on HR 2647 kicked off at a joint markup by the Fisheries and Wildlife and Oceanography subcommittees of Merchant Marine on April 4, as members approved a substitute amendment to the bill as introduced. The full Merchant Marine Committee approved the bill April 18 (H Rept 101-605, Part I).

As reported by Merchant Marine, HR 2647 would have strengthened coastal water-quality standards and toughened federal enforcement of those standards, required states to adopt water-quality protection plans, authorized long-term monitoring programs and barred states and federal contractors who abused clean-water standards from receiving new grants and contracts.

State coastal zone management agencies could also have lost federal grants if programs were not developed to reduce "non-point" runoff from cities' streets and farms. The measure would also have required the development of a national strategy to monitor coastal water quality.

The Public Works Water Resources Subcommittee approved the bill July 31, even as some environmentalists criticized the measure for not being tough enough on "combined sewer overflows" from outdated sewage systems that dumped untreated waste into oceans during heavy rainfalls.

They also wanted new controls on sediments contaminated from industrial discharges.

The subcommittee removed provisions in the Merchant Marine bill to require that "effluent fees" be paid by municipal sewage treatment plants and industrial facilities based on the toxicity and amount of pollutants discharged.

Also stripped from the bill was language to allow industries to trade credits for pollution compliance.

The full Public Works Committee approved the bill Oct. 5 (H Rept 101-605, Part II) after toughening the measure's language on combined sewer overflows. The new version would have required the EPA to implement interim measures to treat the worst overflows.

The bill would have authorized $150 million for grants to states, some of which would come from fines and outer continental shelf mineral receipts.

Senate Action

The Senate Environment and Public Works Committee voted 16-0 to approve S 1178 on June 12 (S Rept 101-339). The bill, sponsored by Majority Leader George J. Mitchell, D-Maine, included tougher language on combined sewer overflows and industrial sediments than the House bill.

The Senate measure also included language to require Great Lakes states and the EPA to draw up water-quality standards for the lakes. The language was aimed at implementing the 1987 U.S.-Canada Great Lakes Water Quality Agreement.

As reported by the committee, the bill would have authorized additional research and monitoring of coastal waters and provided greater authority to the EPA to take steps — such as tougher discharge permits — to improve coastal water quality.

The measure also would have required the EPA and the states to develop long-term plans to combat combined sewer overflows. In addition, the bill would have set up a program to monitor the dumping of contaminated sediment and require EPA permits for especially contaminated sediments.

But S 1178 did not make it to the floor. The Great Lakes provisions of the measure were instead added to a separate Great Lakes bill (HR 4323 — PL 101-596) that cleared the House on the last day of the 101st Congress. *(Great Lakes, p. 301)* ■

Beach Pollution Bill Dies

A compromise bill aimed at providing the public better information about beach water pollution passed the House late in the session, but the Senate did not act on it.

The bill (HR 4333) was also attached to the must-pass budget-reconciliation bill by the House Merchant Marine and Fisheries Committee, but was stripped out in conference with the Senate.

The Senate Environment and Public Works Committee also approved a version of the measure (S 2706).

The measure would have required the Environmental Protection Agency (EPA) to develop criteria for beach water quality and require states to test beach water and post signs should the water violate acceptable standards.

As introduced, the measure would have required states to close such beaches. The bill was also amended to authorize $3 million a year to provide grants to states to assist them in carrying out the new standards.

The bill was pushed by members of the New Jersey delegation. They believed their state, which had a strict testing and beach closure program, was at risk of losing tourist dollars to states with less stringent requirements.

House Action

The Merchant Marine Subcommittee on Oceanography and Great Lakes approved HR 4333, by voice vote, on July 19. As approved by the subcommittee, the bill would have required the EPA to develop water-quality criteria for coastal recreation waters within one year.

The subcommittee-approved measure would have also required the EPA to develop standards for closing and reopening beaches because of floatable materials, such as medical wastes. If states did not adopt standards within two years, the federal regulations would have applied.

Under existing law, water-testing standards could not be enforced unless adopted by states as part of their own standards.

The legislation also called for a study to identify indicators for "human-specific pathogens" — bacteria and viruses from sewage in coastal waters that threatened public health. The results would have been incorporated into the federal standards.

State coastal-zone management agencies would have been required to identify all the coastal recreation waters in the state and provide technical assistance to local governments to ensure that beaches and beach waters were as free as possible from floating waste. Water quality would have to be tested at least once a week during periods of heavy recreational use, as New Jersey law already required.

The bill would have authorized $1 million for each of fiscal years 1992 and 1993 to carry out the program.

Members from some other coastal areas indicated that they had strong concerns about the bill. Gerry E. Studds, D-Mass., who chaired the Merchant Marine Environment Subcommittee, said the measure would have trampled the rights of states to come up with their own beach-water protection plans.

The bill's author, William J. Hughes, D-N.J., , and Studds worked out a compromise that was ordered reported by the full Merchant Marine Committee on Sept. 13 (H Rept 101-844, Part I).

The revised bill would have required that states post signs to inform the public when beach water exceeded the new standards. But states would not have had to close the beaches as required under the original bill.

The compromise also included a $3 million authorization to the EPA to provide grants to states to assist them do the testing.

The House Public Works and Transportation Committee approved the bill Oct. 5 (H Rept 101-844, Part II).

The measure received a big push when the Merchant Marine Committee attached it to the omnibus budget-reconciliation bill (HR 5835). But the Senate did not go along, and the language was dropped in conference.

The bill also passed the House on Oct. 23, under suspension of the rules, by a 326-89 vote. *(Vote 510, p. 160-H)*

Senate Action

The Senate version of the beach water bill (S 2706) was ordered reported by the Environment and Public Works Committee on Oct. 4 (S Rept 101-550) but was not taken up on the floor.

The Senate bill contained similar provisions to the final House version. The Environment Committee, in amending the bill, shifted the emphasis of the bill from beach closings to public notification of a potential health threat. ■

Hill-Bush Impasse Kills EPA Measure

Legislation to elevate the Environmental Protection Agency (EPA) to Cabinet-level status died in 1990 after a standoff between Congress and the White House over provisions that would have strengthened environmental laws.

President Bush supported the idea in principle. But when lawmakers tried to tighten environmental laws and give the proposed Department of the Environment added clout, Bush announced his opposition.

One of his main objections was a provision in the House bill (HR 3847) that would have given states the power to prosecute federal agencies for failing to comply with environmental laws at nuclear weapons plants and other federal facilities. While states were able to prosecute private firms for environmental violations, the federal government claimed "sovereign immunity" for its own facilities. *(Federal facilities, p. 308)*

Bush also objected to provisions to create an independent Bureau of Environmental Statistics. The bureau would have been able to release data on environmental quality and its effect on public health without review by the executive branch, notably the Office of Management and Budget (OMB) or the new Environment secretary.

Finally, the administration opposed a provision that would have limited the number of political appointees in the new department.

The Senate bill (S 2006) was blocked from floor consideration because of concerns that there would be an attempt to attach an amendment on federal facilities and because of turf battles between the Governmental Affairs Committee and the Commerce, Energy and Environment panels.

BOXSCORE

Legislation: EPA Cabinet-level status (HR 3847, S 2006).

Major action: HR 3847 passed by House, 371-55, March 28; S 2006 approved by Governmental Affairs Committee, Feb. 28.

Reports: Governmental Affairs (S Rept 101-262); Government Operations (H Rept 101-428).

BACKGROUND

President Richard M. Nixon created the EPA under his executive reorganization powers in 1970. The new agency consolidated existing environmental programs from the Departments of Interior, Agriculture and Health, Education, and Welfare; Atomic Energy Commission; Federal Radiation Council; and Council on Environmental Quality.

No vote was needed on the plan unless Congress wanted to veto it. The House Government Operations Committee, however, endorsed creation of the EPA as "a favored step in the Federal Government's effort to improve our environment," and the House rejected by voice vote a resolution to disapprove the action. *(1970 Almanac, p. 465)*

Twenty years later, the EPA had established itself as the lead federal agency on environmental issues, and its administrators had been key figures in environmental policy-making in successive administrations. Environmentalists hoping to increase the agency's clout began pushing to raise it to Cabinet-level status.

Legislation had been introduced by members of both houses on Jan. 23. Both bills called for elevation of the EPA to a Department of the Environment, establishment of an office to coordinate and compile environmental statistics, and other restructuring of the agency.

Bush endorsed the idea the next day. "I'm pleased to endorse the elevation of the EPA," Bush announced at a news conference. "Many countries have environmental ministers with Cabinet status, and I'm convinced that Cabinet status will help influence the world's environmental policy."

Spokesmen from the administration, Congress and environmental groups predicted a bill would be on the president's desk by Earth Day, April 22.

More Clout

Proponents of the legislation pointed to benefits such as better interagency communication, more clout with foreign governments, more prestige within domestic government and better efficiency through restructuring.

"By almost any measure, EPA deserves Cabinet status," said William Howard, the National Wildlife Federation's executive vice president. "The agency has a larger budget than either the State Department or the Commerce Department and employs more people than the Education Department or HUD [the Department of Housing and Urban Development]."

Some groups, however, saw the action as a mostly symbolic way of delivering on Bush's promise during the 1988 campaign to be the "environmental president."

"It's kind of a trump card for the Bush administration," said Nancy Light of the Sierra Club. "It's something they can point to and say, 'We know the environment is very important.' ... As far as the media and the public are concerned, it makes a statement."

Sen. Al Gore, D-Tenn., was cautious. "It's not enough to just pull an extra chair to the Cabinet table. This administration has to prove this represents a substantive commitment to policy action — not just a new decorator at the White House."

SENATE ACTION

The Senate Governmental Affairs Committee approved the bill (S 2006) to elevate the EPA to a Cabinet-level position Feb. 28. The measure, sponsored by John Glenn, D-Ohio, and William V. Roth Jr., R-Del., called for a Bureau of Environmental Statistics, an Interagency Committee on Global Environmental Change, new measures to promote energy conservation, an international meeting on energy efficiency and renewable resources, and an international meeting on global climate protection.

An amendment by Jeff Bingaman, D-N.M., to preserve the independence of the proposed Bureau of Environmental Statistics failed on a 6-6 vote. Bingaman appealed to the committee "to assure the bureau's right to collect and publish statistical data without interference."

But Ted Stevens, R-Alaska, said the amendment would prevent the new Environment secretary from setting policy for statistical output.

In another close vote, the panel approved, 7-6, an amendment by Joseph I. Lieberman, D-Conn., to require the secretary of Environment to serve as chairman of a proposed interagency commission on global environmental policy.

Several senators saw the move as circumscribing the president's power to appoint officials within the executive branch. But the bill was never taken up by the full Senate. One reason was that some senators feared that the Senate would attach language requiring federal facilities to comply with hazardous- and solid-waste laws, as in the House. The bill also languished because of jurisdictional disputes between the Governmental Affairs Committee and the Commerce, Energy and Environment panels, which did not have sequential referral of the bill.

HOUSE ACTION

The House Government Operations Committee gave voice vote approval March 13 to its bill (HR 3847) creating a new Department of Environmental Protection and chartering new bureaus within it.

HR 3847 called for a new Bureau of Environmental Statistics, which would have collected environmental and related public-health data and made it accessible to the public.

The bill would have created an Office of Pollution Prevention with a goal of reducing pollution emissions and waste generation and promoting recycling.

The bill also would have established an Office of International Environmental Affairs, through which the secretary of Environment would assist the secretary of State in negotiating international agreements to protect the environment.

The committee approved by voice vote an amendment by Mike Synar, D-Okla., stipulating that political affiliation could not be the "primary factor" considered in appointing regional administrators for the department.

Members also approved, on a 25-11 vote, an amendment by committee Chairman John Conyers Jr., D-Mich., to require individuals being considered for departmental advisory panels to make financial disclosures to determine whether they might have conflicts of interest.

Floor Action

Despite repeated veto threats from the Bush administration, the House voted overwhelmingly March 28 to elevate the EPA to full department status and to make its administrator a member of the president's Cabinet.

The 371-55 vote on the bill included 132 Republicans and 239 Democrats in favor of creating a Department of Environmental Protection. In an unexpected move, the House also agreed to attach the contents of another bill (HR 1056), which would have required federal agencies to comply with solid- and hazardous-waste regulations. *(Vote 50, p. 22-H)*

The White House, which had voiced support for the general goal, issued a statement March 22 listing its objections to the House bill.

The main point of contention was the bill's provision for a new Bureau of Environmental Statistics, which would have functioned as an independent arm of the department in gathering data to determine environmental quality and its effect on public health.

All information analysis, collection and dissemination would have been delegated to the bureau by the new secretary, who would have been unable to review the bureau's reports.

EPA Investigators

Congress cleared legislation on Oct. 27 that included provisions to boost the number of civil and criminal investigators at the Environmental Protection Agency (EPA).

Both the House and Senate had approved the increased manpower for the EPA earlier in the year. The provisions were added to an unrelated bill (HR 3338), which cleared Congress in its final days before adjournment. President Bush signed the bill Nov. 16 (PL 101-593).

The provisions required an increase in the number of EPA investigators from 54 to 200 over a five-year period. The act provided for an increase of 50 civil investigators by the end of fiscal 1991 to assist in the development and prosecution of civil cases and administrative enforcement actions.

As enacted, the bill called for the creation of a national institute to train environmental lawyers, inspectors, investigators and technical experts.

Joseph I. Lieberman, D-Conn., the sponsor of a stand-alone Senate bill for more EPA investigators (S 2176), said the agency had only a fourth as many investigators as the U.S. Fish and Wildlife Service — too few to take tough action against polluters.

Lieberman's bill was reported by the the Environment and Public Works Committee on July 13 (S Rept 101-366) and passed by the Senate, by voice vote, in the early hours of Aug. 4 (session of Aug. 3).

The House had included a similar section in its bill (HR 3847) to raise the EPA to Cabinet status, but that bill stalled after House passage March 28.

HR 3338 was originally a bill to transfer all federal interest in a fish hatchery to the state of South Carolina. The bill was amended to include provisions to establish regional marine research programs and to increase the number of EPA investigators, among other things.

By voice vote, the House on Oct. 27 cleared the Senate version of the bill, which included the title on EPA investigators. The Senate had passed the measure by voice vote on Oct. 26. House members originally had passed the bill — without the EPA enforcement provisions — by voice vote on July 16.

The House Merchant Marine Committee approved HR 3338 on May 23 (H Rept 101-586). The Senate Environment Committee approved the bill, with the EPA enforcement provisions, on Sept. 25 (S Rept 101-522).

White House officials said they could not support the bill because it would bypass the president's authority over executive branch agencies and would "restrict executive branch oversight of the new bureau," according to a statement issued by the OMB. The White House wanted the House bill amended to make the bureau director a presidential appointee.

At a news conference called March 28 to answer the veto threat, the bill's lead sponsor, Conyers, said the OMB and its director, Richard G. Darman, had a history of manipulating data to conform with administration policy.

"We don't want any more cooking of books or skewing

of testimony," he said. "It will not take that familiar route through Darman's office at OMB."

White House Threatens Veto

The Bush administration and supporters of EPA Cabinet legislation in Congress said raising the agency to department status would give the new secretary more leverage to negotiate solutions to environmental matters in the United States and abroad.

The administration supported a substitute offered by Dennis Hastert, R-Ill., that would have simply elevated the agency and its administrator to the Cabinet. But virtually all other provisions, as well as nine amendments proposed by members of both parties, were left out.

Although Hastert's amendment was rejected, 161-266, the vote was an indication that the House might have had difficulty mustering the two-thirds majority needed to override a Bush veto. *(Vote 49, p. 22-H)*

After the House action, White House spokesman Marlin Fitzwater said March 29 that Bush "will not be reluctant to use his veto powers" on the EPA measure, but he might "end up vetoing and then fighting to sustain that veto as a way of forcing legitimate compromise on reconsideration."

Bush's other objections to the House bill included:

- A provision that appointment of 11 regional administrators by the secretary would not be based primarily on political affiliation. Synar, who had proposed the provision during committee markup, argued that these positions would be substantive jobs requiring environmental knowledge and expertise. The language would not preclude the new secretary from appointing Republicans, he said, as long as they were qualified.
- A provision to restrict private contractors from performing "inherently government functions." Members complained that the EPA used too many private contractors, often with conflicts of interest, to do jobs that should have been performed only by government employees.

Expanding the RCRA

In a further challenge to the administration, the House approved on a voice vote an amendment by Dennis E. Eckart, D-Ohio, to reaffirm the power of the new Environmental Protection Department and of state governments to enforce compliance with the Resource Conservation and Recovery Act (RCRA) at federal facilities.

Eckart's amendment would have waived all federal departments' and agencies' sovereign immunity to the RCRA regulations, making them subject to the same penalties imposed on private individuals, businesses, and state and local governments. The House passed identical language in HR 1056 on July 19, 1989, on a 380-39 vote. The Defense and Energy departments had gone to court to challenge RCRA regulation of federal facilities, particularly nuclear-weapons production plants. *(1989 Almanac, p. 679)*

Other amendments adopted on voice votes included one by Lynn Martin, R-Ill., to increase the number of professional criminal investigators assigned to the new department's Office of Criminal Investigations by at least 30 percent each fiscal year for five years. The measure would also have required the department to hire 50 more civil investigators. Providing the EPA more enforcement manpower had broad, bipartisan support, and a provision to nearly quadruple the number of investigators over a five-year period was folded into an unrelated measure at the end of the session and signed into law (HR 3338 — PL 101-593). *(EPA investigators, p. 292)* ■

Environmental Education Office Authorized

Legislation (S 3176 — PL 101-619) setting up an Office of Environmental Education in the Environmental Protection Agency (EPA) and authorizing grants for environmental education and training programs cleared Congress by voice vote Oct. 26 and was signed into law by President Bush Nov. 16.

The legislation established the Office of Environmental Education at the EPA to administer and coordinate the federal government's environmental education programs.

The bill also included provisions to set up an Environmental Education Foundation that would support EPA environmental education efforts through private donations.

The foundation could not accept gifts that would require an education program to represent the economic interests of the giver.

The legislation authorized up to $12 million annually in fiscal 1992-93, rising to $14 million annually by fiscal 1996. Of that, about $5 million a year would go to grants to school systems, colleges, environmental agencies or nonprofit organizations.

Legislative Action

The Senate passed S 3176 by voice vote on Oct. 26, and the House cleared the measure for the president the same day, also by voice vote.

The legislation was based on similar bills that had passed the Senate on July 18 (S 1076 — S Rept 101-284) and the House on Sept. 28 (HR 3684 — H Rept 101-671). To avoid a conference and quickly reconcile differences between the House and the Senate, proponents introduced S 3176 on Oct. 10.

Among the changes was the inclusion of the nonprofit Environmental Education Foundation, which had been in the House measure but not the Senate bill.

The compromise bill also reduced funding for fiscal 1992-93 from the $15 million annually in the original Senate bill to $12 million annually. The House measure had authorized $10 million annually.

In signing the bill Nov. 16, President Bush expressed reservations about the constitutionality of two provisions.

First, he questioned the wisdom of creating a nonprofit foundation that would neither be private nor governmental. Bush said the setup undermined the separation of powers principles in the Constitution and diminished the way in which government would be held accountable.

Second, he called unconstitutional a provision requiring the EPA administrator to receive advice from the newly created National Environmental Education Advisory Council concerning the execution of his functions under the act. Bush said the requirement unconstitutionally limited the range of advice that the administrator could receive. ■

Compromise To Protect Tongass Forest

Compromise legislation that withheld more than 1 million additional acres of the Alaskan Tongass National Forest from timber-cutting cleared late in the 101st Congress.

The measure (HR 987 — PL 101-626) designated 296,000 acres of the forest as wilderness (meaning no logging, mining or road-building) and another 722,000 acres on which some mining and road-building could occur. In addition, the bill repealed a requirement that 4.5 billion board feet of timber be harvested each decade and an automatic appropriation of $40 million that paid for roads and other measures needed to cut and remove the timber.

The legislation also required that long-term contracts under which pulp mills in the region were guaranteed cheap timber be renegotiated so that the timber sales would be profitable to the government.

Environmentalists had pushed for Tongass legislation for years.

But the Alaska delegation had thwarted their efforts, contending that limits on Tongass logging would hurt the Alaskan economy.

By 1990, however, the state's lawmakers realized that pressure for a bill was strong and decided to participate in crafting the compromise.

The final bill included most of the Senate bill's policy language and essentially split the difference between the House and Senate on the amount of Tongass timber acreage that was set aside.

The House cleared the conference report Oct. 26, after Senate adoption on Oct. 24. President Bush signed the bill into law Nov. 28.

BOXSCORE

Legislation: Tongass Timber Reform Act, PL 101-626 (HR 987).

Major action: Signed, Nov. 28. Conference report adopted by House, Oct. 26; by Senate, Oct. 24. Passed by Senate, 99-0, June 13; by House, 356-60, July 13, 1989.

Reports: Conference report (H Rept 101-931); Energy and Natural Resources Committee (S Rept 101-261); Interior Committee (H Rept 101-84, Part I); Agriculture Committee (Part II).

BACKGROUND

The Tongass National Forest, a 16.7 million-acre preserve located in southeastern Alaska, was one of the world's last remaining temperate rain forests.

The below-cost timber sales dated to a 1947 decision by Congress that allowed the Forest Service to enter into 50-year contracts with companies that agreed to build pulp mills in the Tongass region in exchange for long-term sales of timber.

Under the contracts, the U.S. Forest Service made available 4.5 billion board feet (bbf) per decade to pulp mills in the Tongass region, regardless of market conditions.

As a result, the timber had sold for as little as $3 per 1,000 board feet, as opposed to $200 on the open market.

As of 1990, two of those contracts remained in effect.

Much of the timber and pulp was exported to the Far East, and one of the affected mills was Japanese-owned — a fact that allowed environmentalist critics to use trade arguments to buttress their case against the practice.

Alaska lawmakers insisted that the timber sales were vital to the southeastern Alaska economy and that cancellation of the arrangement would devastate the region.

After a decade of controversy over the issue, Congress crafted a compromise as part of the 1980 Alaska Lands Conservation Act (PL 96-487).

The act, which restricted development on more than 100 million acres of federal lands in Alaska, set aside 5.5 million acres of wilderness in the Tongass.

Alaska lawmakers won inclusion of provisions mandating the 4.5 bbf requirement and creating a permanent $40 million annual appropriation for the Forest Service to facilitate timber harvesting. *(1980 Almanac, p. 575)*

The compromise did not satisfy critics, who stepped up pressure through the 1980s to further curtail the timber harvests.

"Since 1980, it has become increasingly clear that the Alaska Lands Act failed to establish a reasonable balance between timber harvest and other uses of the resources of the Tongass National Forest," said Rep. George Miller, D-Calif. Miller had guided HR 987 through the House in 1989.

HOUSE ACTION

The House Agriculture and Interior committees developed competing versions of HR 987 in the spring of 1989. The Interior panel's version called for canceling the contracts altogether, while the Agriculture bill would have ordered the Agriculture secretary to renegotiate them. *(1989 Almanac, p. 678)*

The Agriculture Forest, Family Farms and Energy Subcommittee approved the measure on April 13, 1989, by voice vote.

The bill would have cut off the $40 million annual appropriation, eliminated the requirement to sell 4.5 bbf per decade and required renegotiation of the long-term timber contracts.

The full committee approved the measure June 21, 1989, also by voice vote (H Rept 101-84, Part II).

The Interior Committee, on a 23-15 vote May 31, 1989, approved a tougher version of HR 987 (H Rept 101-84, Part I) to cancel the 50-year pulp mill contracts.

Bob Smith, R-Ore., offered the Agriculture Committee bill as a substitute at the Interior markup, but it was rejected 15-24.

Both bills would have preserved 1.8 million additional acres of the Tongass in 23 new wilderness areas, expanding the 5.5 million acres designated in 1980.

The legislation came to the House floor July 13, 1989. Members chose the tougher Interior version of HR 987, rejecting the substitute offered by the Agriculture Committee by a 144-269 vote.

The Interior Committee measure subsequently passed 356-60, offering members an unusual three-for-one opportunity to vote for the environment, fiscal responsibility and a small dose of Japan-bashing.

SENATE ACTION

In the Senate, Energy and Natural Resources Committee Chairman J. Bennett Johnston, D-La., worked hard to craft a compromise Tongass bill that could bring together the two wings of his committee: the pro-environmentalists, who were led on the issue by Tim Wirth, D-Colo., and those such as Alaska Republican Frank H. Murkowski, who wanted to protect the sectors of the economy in the southeastern Alaskan Panhandle dependent on the Tongass.

Committee Markup

The Energy Committee on March 7 approved its version of HR 987 by a vote of 19-0 (S Rept 101-261).

But the unanimity of the vote was deceiving: The pro-timber and pro-environmental forces on the committee began the day tenuously united on a compromise bill.

They ended in sharp disagreement over several amendments to the bill, united only in their intention to go to the Senate floor to fight out their differences. "The consensus, to some extent, was broken," Johnston said after the vote.

As in the House version, the Senate bill would have canceled the annual $40 million appropriation the Forest Service received for road building in the Tongass. The bill also eliminated the requirement that 4.5 bbf of timber be harvested each decade; instead, the bill directed the Agriculture secretary to "seek to meet market demand for timber."

The most divisive fight came over a provision to require that the Forest Service not allow timber cutting within a buffer zone 100 feet wide along rivers and tributaries that supported fish (Class I and Class II streams, respectively). The idea was to prevent harm to fish from sedimentation that occurred after logging.

Murkowski offered an amendment that would have eliminated buffer strips along Class II tributaries, except for a 300-foot swath above where they joined Class I streams. Environmental groups, as well as United Fisheries of Alaska, a group that represented the state's fish industry, supported more extensive buffer zones.

Murkowski's amendment was adopted, 10-9, with Alabama Democrat Howell Heflin joining with the committee's nine Republicans in voting for it.

Wirth later implied that the amendment had changed his mind about supporting the committee bill.

"It directly contradicts what we agreed to do," Wirth said, adding that it was "perfectly possible" that he would offer a tougher substitute very similar to the House measure when the Senate took up its bill on the floor.

While the House bill would have canceled the contracts, the Senate measure would have broadly changed the contracts to cut back harvesting of old-growth timber to raise timber prices. And the Forest Service, not the companies, would have had responsibility to choose the site and size of the cutting areas.

In addition, the Senate committee bill would have placed 673,000 acres of land in the Tongass off-limits to timber harvesting, about 1.1 million acres fewer than the House measure.

Floor Action

The Senate passed the Tongass bill June 13 by a 99-0 vote after adopting by voice vote a substitute amendment by Johnston providing tougher protections for streams than the Murkowski language adopted in committee. Johnston's amendment would bar timber cutting within a 100-foot buffer zone along rivers that supported fish and along their tributaries. *(Vote 116, p. 27-S)*

Murkowski and fellow Alaska Republican Ted Stevens had delayed the bill, but conceded that the pressure for action was too great for them to resist. In voting for the measure, they said it would not impose as much hardship on the Alaska economy as the tougher House-passed version of the bill.

But Stevens warned his colleagues to hold to the Senate position in conference.

"If this conference committee drastically changes this bill and spells out a more immediate death to the timber industry in southeastern Alaska, I shall be back on this floor and shall oppose the bill with every bit of my strength," he said.

FINAL ACTION

Conferees reached an agreement late in the session after breaking a standoff that threatened to kill the bill. The House and Senate had remained far apart after they exchanged their initial offers on Oct. 11.

But the House eased off its demand to cancel the timber contracts that had guaranteed timber at cheap prices to two pulp mills in the region. Instead, the contracts were to be modified to prevent below-cost sales.

The language removed the mandate to harvest 4.5 billion bbf of timber each decade. Instead, the Forest Service was directed, in setting the timber harvest level each year, to meet "market demand" for logs, and sell them at a profitable price.

As cleared, the bill ended the automatic appropriation of $40 million a year to pay for roads and other measures necessary to cut and remove the timber. Both versions had included that language.

House members wanted more of the Tongass designated as wilderness (meaning no logging, mining or road-building would be allowed) than the Senate.

The House's initial offer was to protect 863,500 additional acres as wilderness areas and another 648,299 acres on which some road building and mining — but no logging — could take place.

The Senate proposed 201,443 acres of new wilderness, with another 734,597 acres to be protected.

As cleared, the bill protected over 1 million more acres of the forest from timber cutting. Of that, 296,000 acres would be designated as wilderness (meaning no logging, mining or road building) and another 722,000 on which some road building and mining — but no logging — could occur.

In the end, Alaska lawmakers could not kill the bill, but they claimed credit for lessening its restrictions.

Supporters of the legislation were pleased with the outcome.

"[A] decade of disgrace in the Tongass ... will end when this conference is enacted into law," said Bruce F. Vento, D-Minn.

For their part, Alaska lawmakers claimed credit for lessening the restrictions and hoped that the issue had been resolved. "While this legislation errs too far on the side of preservation," Murkowski said, "... we have received assurances that it should bring some finality to the Tongass issue." ■

Timber, Spotted Owl Forces in Standoff

An impasse over the fate of the northern spotted owl and timber jobs in the Pacific Northwest remained unbroken when the 101st Congress adjourned, as authorizing committees were unable to referee a longstanding fight between timber interests and environmentalists.

The impasse left the issue for the time being to the courts, which had struck down the most recent appropriations bill rider limiting courts' power to block timber sales.

Under existing law, the federal government was not supposed to allow logging on Forest Service lands that would have jeopardized threatened or endangered species or their habitats. When faced with the potential loss of thousands of timber jobs, however, lawmakers repeatedly acted to allow continued limited logging in the owl's habitat by passing appropriations riders limiting judicial review of the federal government's logging practices.

On Sept. 19, however, a federal appeals court struck down the 1989 rider. The 9th U.S. Circuit Court of Appeals in San Francisco said Congress could waive or modify environmental laws but could not prevent the courts from reviewing whether agencies were complying with them.

With its options limited and the issue increasingly polarized between environmentalists and logging interests, Congress could agree only on a limited step before adjourning. Authorizing committees failed to complete legislation, but Appropriations committees did include timber language in their must-pass spending bills.

The Interior appropriations bill (HR 5769 — PL 101-512) set a target of 3.2 billion board feet (bbf) to be sold in fiscal 1991 from Washington and Oregon — a 20 percent reduction from the 3.85 bbf in fiscal 1990. *(Interior appropriations, p. 870)*

But House Agriculture Committee and Interior Committee subcommittees staged last-minute and futile attempts to move legislation to regulate federal timber sales in the Northwest.

For its part, the Bush administration waited until mid-September to weigh in with a proposal that asked Congress to exempt timber sales in the region from environmental laws. The plan was widely seen as unrealistic.

Bruce F. Vento, D-Minn., chairman of the House Interior Subcommittee on National Parks and Public Lands, said, "The likely scenario based on the administration's proposal and the attitude here is: Let the crisis occur."

BACKGROUND

The federal timber sales controversy highlighted longstanding tension over the dual roles of the Agriculture Department's Forest Service. The agency was expected to keep timber harvest levels high, but was also supposed to emphasize values such as wilderness, wildlife and recreational use of public lands.

Since 1960, Congress had repeatedly passed laws that required the Forest Service to consider values other than timber in managing the national forests. Those laws were aimed at correcting what many viewed as the agency's timber bias. But the timber industry and its supporters used their influence to win approval of annual Forest Service budgets that allowed logging levels above what environmentalists said the national forests could sustain.

Though Congress had kept timber sales fairly high, it had also passed laws aimed at preserving the forests and their wildlife habitats. One of the key environmental laws, the Endangered Species Act of 1973 (PL 93-205), required the Interior Department's U.S. Fish and Wildlife Service to determine which land species should be listed as threatened or endangered. Federal agencies were then required to ensure that their actions did not jeopardize listed species or harm their habitats.

But environmental laws — and the extent to which Congress and the administration would go to enforce them — were severely tested by the northern spotted owl, a threatened species that inhabited the western portions of Northern California, Oregon and Washington. Full protection of the spotted owl and other species had the potential to disrupt jobs and communities throughout the Pacific Northwest and beyond.

In preceding years, Congress had sidestepped the wildlife vs. jobs issue, passing legislation that directed courts to assume the federal government's logging practices complied with environmental laws. Such limits on judicial review were designed to keep timber sales from being bogged down in the courts. Since 1984, court injunctions had been issued six times in Washington and Oregon against the Forest Service or the Bureau of Land Management (BLM).

In 1989, Congress reached a compromise that had temporarily freed timber sales in Washington and Oregon from court-ordered bans, in return for lower limits on timber harvests and additional protection for wildlife habitats. *(1989 Almanac, p. 736)*

LEGISLATIVE ACTION

Congress was under its own deadline to act on the logging issue because the 1989 interim agreement to lift court-ordered bans on timber sales in exchange for some owl habitat preservation was to expire Sept. 30. But the big differences among the authorizing committees made it apparent that Congress was likely to do nothing more than attach another one-year Band-Aid to the fiscal 1991 Interior spending bill.

Interior Appropriations

The House Appropriations Subcommittee on the Interior marked up HR 5769 on July 24 and proposed cutting timber sales in the owl's old-growth habitat by 20 percent, to the lowest level in 30 years (H Rept 101-789).

The bill would have provided enough funding for about 3 bbf on Forest Service lands in Washington and Oregon, but would also have allowed 200 million board feet be carried over from fiscal 1990. The timber sales language was not significantly amended later in the legislative process. The Senate version of the bill also approved timber sales of 3.2 bbf from the region.

Timber lobbyists said the funding levels were too low, while environmentalists said the harvest levels in the bill were too high to allow the spotted owl to be saved.

Authorizing Committees

Two House subcommittees worked on legislation to reach a long-term solution to the timber sales question, but it became apparent that a compromise was not in sight.

The House Interior Subcommittee on National Parks

and Public Lands weighed in with its proposal on Sept. 13, approving 19-13 a bill (HR 5295) by Vento that would have protected 6.3 million acres of old-growth forests from commercial logging. That acreage would have been drawn from 17 national forests and six BLM districts in Oregon, Washington and Northern California.

Vento's bill also would have set minimum timber sales in the region at 2.6 bbf annually on Forest Service lands and 450 million board feet on BLM lands annually for three years, a much lower level than was then being harvested.

Members of the House Agriculture Subcommittee on Forests, Family Farms and Energy also debated draft legislation Sept. 13. The panel was deeply split, however, and no bill was approved.

Subcommittee Chairman Harold L. Volkmer, D-Mo., advanced an outline of a far broader proposal that would have set up an old-growth forest reserve similar to that in Vento's bill and provided aid to timber communities. But his plan also envisioned major changes in the management of federal forests throughout the country.

"We're trying to give a little more certainty to the timber industry so they have some idea of what's going to be available in the future," Volkmer said.

Environmentalists objected to the pro-timber bent of the Volkmer proposal. "You're putting resource outputs above all other objectives," said Jim Jontz, D-Ind.

One proposed change, to limit the ability of environmental groups and others to take the Forest Service to court over logging plans, drew heavy fire from environmental and civil rights groups as well as from senior members of Congress.

Administration Proposal

After a U.S. Fish and Wildlife Service decision June 22 to officially designate the spotted owl as a threatened species, the administration was required by Sept. 1 to come up with a plan to preserve the owl and its habitat.

The Bush administration finally unveiled its plan on Sept. 21. But members who expected an initiative that could have broken the congressional logjam were disappointed.

The administration's plan asked Congress to exempt timber sales in the Pacific Northwest from environmental laws. The administration also asked Congress to amend the Endangered Species Act to allow economic factors to play a greater role in decisions about how, or whether, to protect the spotted owl.

Environmentally oriented members criticized the plan as an attempt to sidestep environmental laws without charting a long-term solution. And pro-timber members, such as Sid Morrison, R-Wash., acknowledged that the administration package asked for "congressional action that is not within the realm of the possible." ■

Water Projects Trimmed To Satisfy Bush

After trimming the measure in response to administration objections, Congress cleared a two-year authorization bill for Army Corps of Engineers water projects on Oct. 7. President Bush signed the bill Nov. 8.

The measure (S 740), passed by voice votes in the House and Senate, authorized 27 new projects with a projected initial federal cost of $2 billion. Conferees removed from the bill two large lock and dam projects that were slated to cost $750 million. The two lock and dam projects had not received final corps approval.

By far, the largest new project authorization in the legislation was a $1.2 billion flood control project along the Passaic River in New York and New Jersey, with a federal share of $890 million. *(New projects, p. 299)*

The measure also authorized 30 modifications to previously authorized projects. The original Senate bill contained 11 proposed project modifications, while the House version would have authorized 46.

But the conferees dropped the largest project modification, a $270 million proposal to restore wetlands along the Kissimmee River in Florida that were damaged by a corps navigation project in the 1960s. The Bush administration had threatened to veto the bill over the project, because the required environmental impact study had not been completed. However, the conferees approved a feasibility study aimed at accelerating authorization of the project in the 102nd Congress.

The Senate subsequently passed, by voice vote, a stand-alone bill (S 262) to authorize the Kissimmee River project modification, but the House did not take up the measure.

The conference agreement was hammered out after staff negotiations and was adopted by both chambers on Oct. 7, the last day of the session. Major sticking points in the negotiations were the Kissimmee project and a disagreement between members from North Carolina and Virginia over a plan of the city of Virginia Beach to take drinking water from Lake Gaston, which straddles the states' borders.

Also dropped in conference were two smaller projects that had not received corps approval. But a $327 million flood control project for Los Angeles County that was sought by House Public Works Chairman Glenn M. Anderson, D-Calif., survived despite not having corps approval.

But these disagreements were minor compared with the logjams that had held up water projects bills between 1976 and 1986. Objections from Presidents Jimmy Carter and Ronald Reagan blocked corps authorizations bills during those years. *(1986 Almanac, p. 127)*

Perhaps most noteworthy about the legislation was how smoothly it passed. "This bill is a harbinger for regularizing

BOXSCORE

Legislation: Water Resources Development Act, PL 101-640 (S 2740).

Major action: Signed, Nov. 28; conference report adopted by Senate, Oct. 27; by House, Oct. 27; passed by House, 350-55, Sept. 26; by Senate, Aug. 1.

Reports: Conference report (H Rept 101-966). Public Works and Transportation (H Rept 101-705). Environment and Public Works (S Rept 101-333).

this process," said a Senate aide. "It's a pretty major accomplishment."

The law was the third biennial authorization since 1986, when Congress began requiring states, localities and project users to contribute a higher share of construction costs. User costs averaged about 25 percent. In addition, authorizations for the projects expired automatically if they did not receive appropriations to begin construction within five years. Before 1986, there had accumulated a huge backlog of projects that had never received funding. *(1988 Almanac, p. 152)*

SENATE ACTION

The Senate Environment and Public Works Committee on May 22 approved a committee draft of S 2740 by voice vote. As reported, the bill included 22 new flood control, navigation and recreation projects. At the markup, committee members added the $270 million Kissimmee project modification and also raised the authorization for the huge Passaic River project from $913.5 million to $1.2 billion.

The committee also added language offered by Daniel Patrick Moynihan, D-N.Y., to authorize $37.5 million over five years for grants to research and control the zebra mussel, the fast-spreading mollusk that had infested the Great Lakes and caused big problems at drinking water and power plants as it clogged up intake and outflow pipes.

The Senate bill also included language that would have required management changes within the corps. Some local officials had criticized the corps for making detrimental changes in projects without consulting them. The officials, whose localities had contributed to the costs of the projects, pushed for language that would have required the corps to justify such project changes and the secretary of the Army to determine that the changes were in accord with the original congressional authorizing intent.

The bill also would have required that the public be allowed to comment on water project plans before they became effective.

Five additional projects that had since obtained corps approval were added to the bill when it passed the Senate by voice vote Aug. 1. The projects were added to the bill via an amendment, adopted by voice vote, offered by Environment and Public Works Chairman Quentin N. Burdick, D-N.D.

HOUSE ACTION

The House Public Works Water Resources Subcommittee unveiled its version of the bill (HR 5314) July 26. The original House bill would have authorized 28 new projects with a federal cost of $1.8 billion.

The subcommittee approved the bill, sponsored by committee Chairman Anderson without amendment. Subcommittee Chairman Henry J. Nowak, D-N.Y., requested that members withhold their amendments until the full committee markup.

The full committee ordered the bill reported Aug. 1 after adding two large lock and dam projects, slated to cost $750 million, to the measure. The committee added $450 million for a Monongahela River navigation project in Pennsylvania and $300 million for a project on the Kanawha River in West Virginia.

The committee attached 61 amendments to the bill, including an en bloc package of 57 amendments that were developed under Nowak's coordination. In addition to the two new projects, Nowak's package proposed to modify 14 existing corps projects, bringing the total to 36 proposed project modifications.

The committee also adopted an amendment, offered by Arlan Stangeland, R-Minn., aimed at improving the corps' environmental performance. The amendment was the text of a Stangeland bill (HR 5370) to establish environmental protection as one of the corps' primary missions as it designed, constructed and operated water projects.

The language — worked out with the input of both the corps and the National Wildlife Federation — required the corps to construct projects that would lead to no net loss of wetlands. The amendment would have barred the corps from undertaking beach stabilization or sand replacement projects unless the projects were located in states that had beachfront management programs restricting development in unstable beach areas.

Also authorized was an annual $50 million authorization over five years for federal contributions to help fund environmental dredging projects. Local governments were required to pay 50 percent for such projects.

Floor Action

In the face of a veto threat from the administration, the House passed its version of the legislation Sept. 26.

The bill passed overwhelmingly 350-55, which would have been enough to override a veto. But leading Republicans said their support was conditional on removing from the bill in conference several projects the administration opposed. *(Vote 387, p. 124-H)*

The administration wanted to remove 18 projects whose environmental and economic feasibility studies were not approved by the Office of Management and Budget (OMB) and five projects that were conditionally authorized pending Corps of Engineers approval.

Water Resources Subcommittee Chairman Nowak said he was hopeful of a compromise "if the administration is reasonable."

In 1988, after a veto threat, conferees dropped several projects that were conditionally authorized.

"Everybody anticipates the House bill will be pared down significantly in conference," said an administration aide.

The bill's price tag also continued to grow on the floor, as members adopted an amendment by Stangeland that adjusted the cost estimates of 12 proposed projects and boosted the total cost of the new projects by $220 million, to $3.8 billion.

Members adopted, by voice vote, an amendment by John Paul Hammerschmidt, Ark., ranking Republican on the Public Works Committee, that would have extended to fiscal 1993 the existing $1.8 billion ceiling on annual obligations for all projects. Hammerschmidt said the amendment made the bill more palatable to the White House.

Ten additional project modifications found their way into the bill on the floor, via amendment.

The bill attracted several amendments on the House floor, all adopted by voice vote, including proposals by:

- Anderson to establish as corps policy an interim goal of no overall net loss of wetlands, with a long-term goal of increasing wetlands acreage.
- James A. Traficant Jr., D-Ohio, to require that all materials and products purchased to carry out corps projects be produced in the United States, with certain exceptions.

But members rejected an amendment by Owen B. Pickett, D-Va., that would have removed restrictions on con-

Water Resources Act: New Projects

Following are new water resources projects authorized by the Water Resources Development Act (S 2740 — PL 101-640) and described in the conference report (H Rept 101-966):

- **Bayou La Batre, Ala.** Navigation project for Bayou La Batre, Ala.; total cost, $16.2 million; federal share, $4.5 million.
- **Homer Spit, Alaska.** Storm damage prevention project for Homer Spit, Alaska; total cost, $4.7 million; federal share, $3.1 million.
- **San Francisco River, Ariz.** Flood control project on the San Francisco River at Clifton, Ariz.; total cost, $12.5 million; federal share, $9.2 million.
- **Nogales Wash and tributaries, Ariz.** Flood control project for the Nogales Wash and tributaries, Ariz.; total cost, $11.1 million; federal share, $8.3 million.
- **Coyote and Berryessa Creeks, Calif.** Flood control project for the Coyote and Berryessa Creeks, Calif.; total cost, $53.3 million; federal share, $39 million.
- **Oceanside Harbor, Calif.** Navigation and storm damage reduction project, Oceanside Harbor, Calif.; total cost, $5.1 million; federal share, $3.4 million.
- **Ventura Harbor, Calif.** Navigation project, Ventura Harbor, Calif.; total cost, $6.5 million; federal share, $5.2 million.
- **Martin County, Fla.** Storm damage reduction project, Martin County, Fla.; total cost, $9.4 million; federal share, $3.9 million.
- **Miami Harbor Channel, Fla.** Navigation project, Miami Harbor Channel, Fla.; total cost, $67.1 million; federal share, $42.8 million.
- **McAlpine Lock and Dam, Ind. and Ky.** Navigation Project, McAlpine Lock and Dam, Ind. and Ky.; total cost, $219.6 million, half from appropriations, half from Inland Waterways Trust Fund.
- **Fort Wayne, St. Mary's and Maumee Rivers, Ind.** Flood control project, Fort Wayne, St. Mary's and Maumee Rivers, Ind.; total cost, $35.6 million; federal share, $26.5 million.
- **Aloha-Rigolette, La.** Flood control project, Aloha-Rigolette Area, La.; total cost, $8.3 million; federal share, $6.2 million.
- **Boston Harbor, Mass.** Navigation project, Boston Harbor, Mass.; total cost, $26.2 million; federal share, $16.2 million.
- **Ecorse Creek, Mich.** Flood control project, Ecorse Creek, Wayne County, Mich.; total cost, $9.3 million; federal share, $6.8 million.
- **Great Lakes Connecting Channels and Harbors, Mich. and Minn.** Navigation project, Great Lakes Connecting Channels and Harbors, Mich. and Minn.; total cost, $13.1 million; federal share, $8.8 million.
- **Coldwater Creek, Mo.** Flood control project, Coldwater Creek, Mo.; total cost, $21.3 million; federal share, $15.5 million.
- **River Des Peres, Mo.** Flood control project, River Des Peres, Mo.; total cost, $21.3 million; federal share, $15.8 million.
- **Passaic River, N.Y. and N.J.** Flood control project, Passaic River Main Stem, N.Y. and N.J.; total cost, $1.2 billion; federal share, $890 million.
- **Rio De La Plata, Puerto Rico.** Flood control project, Rio De La Plata, Puerto Rico; total cost, $59 million; federal share, $35.9 million.
- **Myrtle Beach, S.C.** Storm damage reduction project, Myrtle Beach, S.C.; total cost, $59.7 million; federal share, $38.8 million.
- **Buffalo Bayou, Texas.** Flood control project for the Buffalo Bayou and tributaries, Texas; total cost, $727.4 million; federal share, $403.4 million.
- **Ray Roberts Lake, Texas.** Multiple purpose project, Ray Roberts Lake, Greenbelt, Texas; total cost, $8.5 million; federal share, $3.2 million.
- **Upper Jordan River, Utah.** Flood control project, Upper Jordan River, Utah; total cost, $7.9 million; federal share, $5.2 million.
- **Buena Vista Lake, Va.** Flood control project, Buena Vista, Va.; total cost, $55.1 million; federal share, $41.3 million.
- **Moorefield, W.Va.** Flood control project, Moorefield, W.Va.; total cost, $16.3 million; federal share, $11.7 million.
- **Petersburg, W.Va.** Flood control project, Petersburg, W.Va.; total cost, $17.9 million; federal share, $10 million.
- **Los Angeles County, Calif.** Flood control project, Los Angeles County Drainage Area, Calif., subject to favorable review of chief of Army Corps of Engineers; total cost, $327 million; federal share, $163.5 million. ■

struction of a pipeline from Virginia Beach, Va., to Lake Gaston on the Virginia-North Carolina border.

Members from North Carolina said that the project would have threatened the striped bass population downstream from the lake in the Roanoke River and Albemarle Sound. In rejecting the amendment, members kept intact a provision that would have barred construction on the project until an environmental impact report ordered by Congress in 1988 had been received and evaluated by the corps.

Some sparks flew during debate over an amendment — subsequently withdrawn — by Byron L. Dorgan, D-N.D., to require local input on operations of dams and water projects in the Missouri River basin.

The amendment was spurred by dissatisfaction over corps operation of dams in the Upper Missouri River Basin. Dorgan said corps actions had resulted in lower water levels in recreational lakes. Dorgan withdrew the amendment after Nowak promised to hold hearings on the matter during the 102nd Congress.

Both the House and Senate bills were broader than the administration's proposal (HR 4867), which would have authorized four new flood control projects and modification of an existing project.

The administration's bill also would have allowed the federal government to charge user fees for recreational facilities such as beaches and boat launching ramps contained in corps projects.

FINAL ACTION

As the bills headed toward conference, it was apparent that they would have to be cut to avoid a presidential veto. OMB officials threatened to recommend a veto if the bills were not trimmed. "I think we'll have to [make cuts], or we won't get a bill," said Hammerschmidt .

Conferees dropped four of the five projects that were to be conditionally authorized, subject to favorable review by the chief of the corps, including the two large lock and dam projects.

Conferees also dropped a $37.5 million Senate provision to combat the zebra mussel, but separate legislation to fight the pest (HR 5390 — PL 101-646) also became law. *(Zebra mussels, p. 303)*

The Lake Gaston issue proved to be a particularly sticky conference issue. "That took a lot of personal member involvement," said an aide involved in the conference negotiations. Most of the rest of the conference agreement was worked out by staff.

As passed by the House, no construction of the project was to be permitted until the secretary of the Army had reviewed an environmental impact study required under the 1988 Atlantic Striped Bass Conservation Act (PL 100-589). The conferees reached a compromise that permitted the City of Virginia Beach (which bore the full cost of the project) to begin construction, but also allowed the secretary to modify the project in light of the environmental impact report. The compromise also required the report be submitted by Jan. 1, 1992.

Despite administration objections, conferees kept in the bill a $115 million authorization to replace a bridge in Delaware over the Chesapeake and Delaware Canal.

The Senate language on revision of corps management practices and on public comment on proposed projects was dropped, as was the House language to extend the $1.8 billion ceiling on annual obligations for all projects.

Conferees kept language in both House and Senate bills that modified existing cost-sharing requirements included in the 1986 and 1988 laws. Under this requirement, the local contribution to a project was partially determined by its ability to pay. The new language eliminated the minimum local contribution of 25 percent and broadened the criteria used to judge local jurisdictions' ability to pay. The new language required that the economic conditions of localities be taken into account when determining eligibility for reduction of the local contribution to projects. ■

Bill To Control Grand Canyon Erosion Dies

The House and Senate both acted to protect the Grand Canyon from man-made erosion caused by large volumes of water rushing out of the Colorado River's Glen Canyon Dam. But the effort fell victim in Congress' final week to unrelated disputes over a water project bill that was carrying the environmentalist-backed measure.

Arizona's congressional delegation and key environmentalist-minded lawmakers had been pushing bills (HR 4498, S 2807) to control the fluctuating flows from Glen Canyon Dam, located 30 miles upstream from the Grand Canyon.

The bills were strongly backed by environmentalists and outdoor enthusiasts, but opposed by the Bush administration and by Western power users that feared the dam's power production would be reduced.

The House passed HR 4498 by voice vote on July 30 after revising it to conform with S 2807. In the Senate, S 2807 was then folded into another House-passed measure (HR 2567) authorizing a number of water reclamation projects.

That bill, however, died in Congress' final week in a dispute over a House-backed amendment to limit irrigation subsidies for large agricultural operations. *(Water subsidy fight, p. 356)*

BACKGROUND

The Glen Canyon Dam, authorized by the Colorado River Storage Project Act of 1956 and completed in 1963, was a key flood-control and power-generating structure for the lower Colorado River Basin states. *(1956 Almanac, p. 408)*

Monthly and annual dam operations were governed by many agreements, including the Mexican Water Treaty, the Colorado River Compact, the Upper Colorado River Basin Compact, the Colorado River Basin Project Act of 1968 and others. As a result of its many obligations to supply different areas with annual amounts of water, the volume of water let through the dam fluctuated often.

Environmentalists and outdoor enthusiasts had been complaining that widely fluctuating releases from the dam were damaging the Grand Canyon.

They found support in a 1988 Interior Department study that found that the fluctuations — which varied the river level by as much as 13 feet a day — were having adverse effects on downstream environmental and recreational resources.

The Interior Department study had not been intended to lead directly to changes in dam operations, but several lawmakers stepped up pressure for concrete action.

"Park Service employees and Colorado River rafting guides have known for years that the daily operation of the dam was wreaking havoc on the beaches and wildlife habitat at the bottom of the Grand Canyon," Rep. George Miller, D-Calif., chairman of the House Interior Energy and Water Subcommittee, said in introducing HR 4498 on April 4. "Now the word is getting out. We have a problem of crisis proportions at Glen Canyon Dam, and emergency action is needed before it is too late for the Grand Canyon."

Utilities, with the support of the Bush administration, countered that a minimum of erosion was occurring and that strict controls on outflow would result in higher electricity prices.

LEGISLATIVE ACTION

The House Interior Committee's subcommittee on Water, Power and Offshore Energy approved HR 4498 on June 26.

The legislation (HR 4498 — H Rept 101-641) sought to order the Interior Department to protect the Grand Canyon by moderating the amount of water released from the dam. Moderate release levels also would have been ordered until completion of an environmental impact statement on the dam's effect on the Grand Canyon. The bill also called for a long-term monitoring of the dam and its water flow operations.

Bill supporters argued that the Interior Department was running the dam at peak output to increase power supply while disregarding resource protection responsibilities listed under various compacts.

Things heated up a bit in the subcommittee hearing June 26 when Miller refused to accept testimony from two administration witnesses during a hearing because Interior Secretary Manuel Lujan Jr. had reportedly prevented two other key department officials from appearing at the session.

Steve Goldstein, chief spokesman for the Interior Department, said the agency had interpreted Miller's letter of invitation as a request for an administration representative to speak on dam operations. But Miller saw Lujan's decision as a maneuver against the committee and the bill, which Lujan and the administration opposed.

The full Interior Committee on July 18 gave voice vote approval to HR 4498 after approving a substitute draft of the measure that made minor changes to the bill as reported by subcommittee. The substitute adopted much of the language of the Senate version of the bill (S 2807).

The House passed the bill by voice vote July 30, calling on the Interior secretary to protect the Grand Canyon by establishing moderate flows from Glen Canyon Dam until an ongoing environmental impact statement on its operation was completed.

Senate Acts, Bill Dies

The Senate Energy Subcommittee on Water and Power held a hearing July 24 on the Senate version of the Grand Canyon legislation (S 2807) introduced by Arizona's two senators, Democrat Dennis DeConcini and Republican John McCain.

Stewart Udall, who served as Interior secretary when the dam was being built and first put into service, testified at the hearing that dam operations were violating the National Park Act of 1960.

"That act says protect, use, but do not impair," said Udall, brother of House Interior Committee Chairman Morris K. Udall, D-Ariz.

"We have seen through the operation of the Glen Canyon Dam the massive impairment of a national park."

The Bush administration, however, opposed the measures as did representatives of Western power authorities, who maintained that the legislation would increase consumers' electric bills by compromising the dam's ability to meet peak power needs.

Opponents of the bill also maintained that only marginal erosion was occurring at the Grand Canyon, which itself was the result of millions of years of water erosion.

The administration also argued that moderating release levels before a study was done could interfere with the scientific research that was being conducted for the environmental impact statement.

Most of the text of S 2807 was inserted into HR 2567, a water projects bill that Miller had used as a vehicle for trying to limit water subsidies for large Western farm operations. Sen. Pete Wilson, R-Calif., however, put a hold on the bill to block the subsidy limits, relenting only when the provisions were stripped out.

The Senate then passed HR 2567, with the Grand Canyon provisions included, on Oct. 26. But Miller refused to accept the bill without the water subsidy limits, and the measure died in the impasse. ■

Great Lakes Cleanup Efforts Boosted

Legislation to strengthen Great Lakes pollution-control efforts became law during the 101st Congress, after the Senate made substantial changes to the House-passed version of the measure (HR 4323).

The new law (PL 101-596) put more pressure on the Environmental Protection Agency (EPA) and Great Lakes states to improve the lakes' water quality. It also directed the EPA to redouble U.S. efforts to implement the 1978 U.S.-Canada Great Lakes Water Quality Agreement.

The bill passed the House under suspension of the rules Sept. 24. It was amended and passed the Senate on Oct. 18, by voice vote. The House agreed to the Senate changes and cleared the bill Oct. 27, the final full day of the session.

Supporters of the measure said that the EPA and the states had done little to implement the U.S.-Canada agreement, under which the two nations had pledged to develop cleanup plans for 42 badly polluted areas of the lakes. They said that the measure required the states to develop such plans, which were previously developed under voluntary deadlines.

House Action

The Public Works Water Resources Subcommittee approved HR 4323 by voice vote on July 26. As approved by the subcommittee, the bill set up a framework to implement the U.S.-Canadian accord. The bill directed Great Lakes states to develop lakewide management plans and submit "remedial action plans" to clean up badly polluted areas.

The states were also directed to develop, with EPA guidance, Great Lakes water quality standards for certain pollutants, including biological agents. The measure placed added emphasis on demonstration projects to combat contaminated sediments.

The subcommittee-approved bill would have authorized $30 million per year for fiscal 1992-97.

The full committee approved HR 4323 on Aug. 1, by voice vote (H Rept 101-704).

The House passed the bill on Sept. 24, by a 376-37 vote. *(Vote 365, p. 118-H)*

Senate Action

Great Lakes language was originally included in the Marine Protection Act of 1989 (S 1178), which was reported by the Environment and Public Works Committee (S Rept 101-339) but went no further.

The Great Lakes language in S 1178 subsequently came directly to the Senate floor as a substitute amendment to HR 4323. The bill then passed by voice vote. The Senate language made several changes and additions to the House bill.

The Senate amendment added provisions designed to improve federal, state and local coordination of cleanup efforts for three other polluted bodies of water: the Long Island Sound, Lake Champlain on the New York-Vermont border and Lake Onondaga, near Syracuse, N.Y.

The new bill also authorized $9 million over fiscal 1992-94 for research on the effects of human consumption of contaminated Great Lakes fish. The Senate also added a requirement that the EPA develop and implement management plans of confined disposal facilities used to contain contaminated sediments dredged from the lakes.

But the Senate bill did not include grants to states to develop the remedial-action plans to clean up badly polluted lakes areas, while at the same time it required such plans be readied by Jan. 1, 1993, 18 months earlier than the House bill.

In addition, because the Clean Water Act was due to be reauthorized the following year, in 1991, the Senate language only authorized funding for the Great Lakes programs for fiscal 1991. The amount of the authorization was $25 million, $5 million less than the House measure. ■

Barrier Islands Protection Bill Enacted

Legislation more than doubling the acreage of coastal barrier islands that would be barred from federal development aid cleared Congress on Oct. 27 and was signed by President Bush on Nov. 16 (HR 2840 — PL 101-591).

Passed on a voice vote in both chambers, the measure added 700,000 acres to the barrier island system, established in 1982 to save the fragile environments by limiting federal aid that encouraged development.

BACKGROUND

Barrier islands are long, narrow, mostly sand-based land formations or atolls that sit off mainland coasts. They exist as a protective buffer for lagoons, wetlands, and salt marshes and the marine species that thrive in them.

Though unstable and far from permanent, many barrier islands had been developed over the years, and some, such as Atlantic City, N.J., and Miami Beach, Fla., became among the biggest resorts and most densely populated areas of the country.

For decades, the government had financially aided development of barrier islands, directly and indirectly, through flood insurance, flood control and other public works projects; disaster relief; housing subsidies and mortgage insurance; beach restoration and erosion protection efforts; community development grants; wastewater-treatment grants and other forms of assistance.

1982 Law

Environmentalist concerns, buttressed by budgetary considerations, led Congress in 1982 to enact the Coastal Barrier Resources Act (CBRA) (PL 97-348) to slow federal spending and discourage development on the fragile coastal barriers. *(1982 Almanac, p. 436)*

The law, supported by environmental groups and the Reagan administration, prohibited most federal assistance to a specified list of still-undeveloped coastal barrier lands comprising about 453,000 acres of shoreline from Maine to Texas. Exceptions were made for extracting or transporting energy resources, maintaining existing navigation channels, Coast Guard facilities and expenditures related to national security.

The law did not bar people from building on their land, but made it quite difficult because developers almost always needed federal flood insurance to secure mortgages. Environmental Protection Agency Administrator James B. Watt stressed the budget-cutting effect of the law in the active support he gave to the bill.

In 1988, the Interior Department recommended expanding the acreage covered by the law by about 791,000 acres and 423 miles of coastline.

Once in office, the Bush administration also supported expanding the law's coverage.

COMMITTEE ACTION

Legislation to expand the acreage covered by CBRA was introduced in the House by Gerry E. Studds, D-Mass., chairman of one of two Merchant Marine and Fisheries subcommittees with jurisdiction over the issue.

HR 2840 included numerous recommendations offered by the Interior Department, though some proposals were dropped after aides visited the sites and determined that they were ineligible, often because the land had already been developed.

Companion legislation was introduced in the Senate by John H. Chafee, R-R.I. S 2729 was slightly different from the House version in the acreage covered under coastal barrier maps and in the manner of classifying federal property in the coastal barrier system.

In a break with the past, some members of Congress fought to have land in their districts included in the system. But lawmakers were also lobbied by landowners and developers in some cases to keep their land out of the system.

Some of the biggest cuts to the Interior Department's recommendations were in the Florida Keys. More than half of the area's 100,000-plus acres proposed for inclusion were removed in a deal meant to appease Democratic Rep. Dante B. Fascell, who represented that part of the state and objected to any of it being included.

In another move to help appease Fascell, the bill was being moved in tandem with a measure (HR 3719) he sponsored to make the Florida Keys a national marine sanctuary. That bill also cleared Congress late in the session. *(Florida Keys sanctuary, p. 303)*

House Markups

HR 2840 was approved by the House Merchant Marine and Fisheries Committee on June 27 (H Rept 101-657, Part I) after two of its subcommittees, Fisheries and Oceanography, had approved the measure the week before.

Two system-expanding amendments, by Claudine Schneider, R-R.I., and Frank Pallone Jr., D-N.J., were adopted in the Fisheries Subcommittee markup June 20. Another New Jersey addition was successfully offered in full committee by Republican H. James Saxton. The legislation next went to the House Banking Subcommittee on Policy Research and Insurance.

The subcommittee approved amendments to HR 2840 on Sept. 11 to prohibit federal flood insurance to offshore islands covered by legislation protecting coastal barrier islands.

Many of the lands exempted from the bill, such as along the Texas coast, off the Great Lakes and in the Florida Keys, were deleted at the behest of individual members of the Banking Committee.

On the other hand, Ben Erdreich, D-Ala., chairman of the Banking Subcommittee on Insurance, offered an amendment to bar housing aid or federal insurance for development of Mobile Point in his district.

And Banking Committee Chairman Henry B. Gonzalez, D-Texas, offered a similar amendment affecting a swamp in Texas.

The full Banking Committee approved the bill on Sept. 18 (H Rept 101-657, Part II).

Senate Markups

The Senate Environment and Public Works Subcommittee on Environmental Protection approved S 2729 on Sept. 25 and the full committee followed on Oct. 12 (S Rept 101-529).

While the legislation was well received, committee members did caution in their report that local tax revenues in areas with coastal barrier lands might suffer from "constraining new development of private property."

The committee report also noted that while the federal government would save money by not having to pay for things like disaster insurance, it stood to lose money from expected lower values on federal lands following expansion of the coastal barrier system.

The Congressional Budget Office, according to the report, also determined that inclusion of some Texas lands that had federal agency guarantees in the barrier system would cost the government between $5 million and $15 million in direct spending costs by 1998.

FLOOR ACTION

The House passed HR 2840 on Sept. 28 by voice vote after brief debate. No one spoke in opposition.

The Senate passed HR 2840 by voice vote on Oct. 26, with minor amendments.

House action Oct. 27 concurring in the amendments cleared the measure for the president.

Provisions

Most of the acreage added to the system under the bill was along the Atlantic and Gulf coasts. However, it also included for the first time about 30,000 acres along the shores of the Great Lakes, 48,000 acres in the Florida Keys, 20,000 acres in Puerto Rico and 3,700 acres in U.S. Virgin Islands.

In addition, the bill established a mechanism for states or localities to bring areas into the system.

And it directed the Interior Department to begin mapping undeveloped barriers along the Pacific coast for possible inclusion in the system. ■

Florida Keys Declared Marine Sanctuary

The Florida Keys were declared a national marine sanctuary and protected from oil drilling and ships under legislation cleared by the Senate on Oct. 27 and signed by President Bush on Nov. 16.

The measure (HR 5909 — PL 101-605), sponsored by Rep. Dante B. Fascell, D-Fla., protected the Keys from oil drilling and from certain ships that could disrupt marine life and fragile coral reefs that meander through the Keys.

HR 5909 also required development by the Commerce Department of a comprehensive management plan and a water quality program intended for the Keys. The bill bypassed the usual route — an extensive Commerce Department evaluation — to qualify areas as sanctuaries.

Fascell and Florida's Democratic senator, Bob Graham, introduced parallel bills (HR 3719, S 2247) in late 1989 after three freighter groundings earlier in the year had destroyed over 5,000 square meters of reefs in the Keys. Fascell and Graham said day-to-day use by tourists and divers also posed a risk for the reefs.

Fascell's bill was approved by the House Merchant Marine and Fisheries Committee (H Rept 101-593) and passed by the House by voice vote on July 23. Graham's bill was being considered in the Senate as part of a broader measure to reauthorize the National Oceanic and Atmospheric Administration that was not enacted.

After House passage of HR 3719, Fascell worked to attach his proposal to a bill (HR 2840) to stop federal aid and insurance for private and commercial development of coastal barrier islands. But late in the session Fascell reached an accord on the Keys legislation with the main players in the Senate to avert any last-minute glitch that could have killed the bill. *(Coastal barrier act, p. 302)*

After the accord, HR 5909 was passed by voice votes in the House on Oct. 26 and the Senate on Oct. 27. ■

Zebra Mussels Control Program Established

Congress enacted legislation in 1990 to combat small, tenacious mullusks known as zebra mussels, which were threatening to take over the Great Lakes and other water systems.

The House cleared the measure (HR 5390 — PL 101-646) Oct. 27, and President Bush signed it Nov. 29.

The measure — the Nonindigenous Aquatic Nuisance Act of 1990 — set up programs to monitor and eradicate zebra mussels and other foreign organisms that might cause harm to waterways.

The legislation was prompted by a population explosion of zebra mussels throughout the Great Lakes that posed serious threats to commerce and regional communities.

The mussels inhabited large swaths of the coastal areas of the Great Lakes, attaching themselves to water intake pipes and grills, power plant water lines, and boat motors. By 1986 almost 10,000 square miles of the Great Lakes had been infested.

If left unchecked, water ecology experts predicted, the mussels would eventually inhabit two-thirds of the nation's drinking water systems over time, according to a Senate committee report.

The original mussels were thought to have arrived in the ballast discharge of a merchant ship perhaps in the early 1980s.

Only a few mussels were needed for the infestation to begin. A zebra mussel produced as many as 40,000 offspring per year, most of which could thrive in the waters of the Great Lakes, which contained few of the mussel's natural predators.

As enacted, the legislation required the U.S. Coast Guard to issue binding regulations to prevent ships from introducing "aquatic nuisance species" into the United States.

The legislation also called for the establishment of an Aquatic Nuisance Species Task Force to coordinate efforts among six federal agencies to halt the introduction of foreign species in U.S. water systems.

The task force was also ordered to research the introduction, direction and dispersal rate of non-indigenous species in U.S. waters.

The secretary of the Interior, under the measure, was ordered to list the zebra mussel as an injurious species and to prohibit the interstate transport of the mussels for commercial purposes.

Additionally, the legislation encouraged the secretary of State to negotiate international efforts to stop the spread of non-indigenous species in waters shared for commercial and other forms of passage.

At one point, zebra mussel prevention language was attached to a large water projects bill (HR 5314), but it was dropped before enactment. *(Water projects, p. 297)*

The House first passed the zebra-mussels bill on Oct. 1.

The Senate passed a somewhat different version (S 2254 — S Rept 101-523) on Oct. 26, and the next day the House accepted the Senate changes, thus clearing the bill for the president.

All action came on voice votes. ■

Arizona Wilderness Gains Protection

Legislation reclassifying 1.1 million acres of land in Arizona as wilderness protected from development, mining or motor vehicles cleared Congress in its final hours.

The legislation (HR 2570), which set aside 39 areas of differing sizes in Arizona as wilderness, had passed the House early in the year, but was delayed by disagreements within the Arizona delegation over the exact boundaries of the new wilderness areas and opposition from interests that traditionally resisted wilderness expansion.

Senate approval came only on Congress' last full day, Oct. 27. The measure cleared after midnight only after the House insisted on — and the Senate acceded to — deletion of some extraneous amendments senators had added.

The law reclassified multiple-use parcels of land throughout the state that were controlled by the Bureau of Land Management, prohibiting development and motor vehicle use and limiting use to restricted forms of recreation such as hiking.

President Bush signed the bill into law on Nov. 28 (PL 101-405).

House Action

The House easily passed the legislation on Feb. 28 by a vote of 356-45. *(Vote 18, p. 10-H)*

The Interior and Insular Affairs Committee had approved the bill Feb. 7 by voice vote (H Rept 101-405).

The bill was sponsored by Arizona's Morris K. Udall, the Democratic chairman of the Interior Committee and also a champion of federal efforts to save national parks and other lands.

Despite the overwhelming approval, the bill advanced only after members of the Arizona delegation and the Interior Committee negotiated a last-minute compromise on the bill's water-rights language.

Disagreement over who would decide water rights in the new wilderness was the main stumbling block to unity among Arizona's five-member House delegation.

Although all five agreed that federal water rights must be decided in state court, Arizona Republicans John J. Rhodes III and Jon Kyl wanted such procedures stated explicitly in the bill.

Under federal law, the federal government had the option to file in either state or federal court.

A compromise provision directed the Interior secretary to file for those water rights in Arizona state courts first, but it kept the federal court option open.

Despite the compromise, Arizona members did not totally agree. Republican Bob Stump of the state's large 3rd District voted against the bill, saying it did not "represent a reasonable balance between multiple-use and environmental concerns."

Stump, a strong multiple-use advocate, said nearly 75 percent of the land to be designated as wilderness was in his district, which covered most of western Arizona, from Utah almost to the Mexican border.

Senate Action

Opposition to the bill increased as it moved through the Senate. The Senate Energy and Natural Resources Committee approved the bill 13-6 on June 20 (S Rept 101-359).

Opposing the bill were senators from large Western states, who argued that millions of acres of land in their states were already owned or managed by the federal government and that a further expansion of the wilderness system was not needed.

Also working to kill the bill in both the Senate and the House were industrial mining companies such as Asarco, which had operations that had expanded near mineral-rich lands slated to become untouchable wilderness by the bill.

Outdoor enthusiasts were against the bill as well since off-road motorcycling and other sports were prohibited by the wilderness language in the bill.

The opposition slowed the bill, but so, too, did the Senate's penchant for adding extraneous measures. As approved by voice vote Oct. 27, the bill contained what Udall later called "a grab bag" of "unconstructive" amendments.

Some provisions — such as a new Take Pride in America program and a study of Civil War sites — represented bills previously approved in one or both chambers, but senators added others — mostly dealing with water issues — without floor consideration.

The House got the bill as Congress was struggling toward adjournment in the early hours of Oct. 28. Despite the hour, the House insisted on some deletions and amendments before passing the bill again. The Senate accepted the changes, clearing the bill for the president.

Other Wilderness Bills

Among the other wilderness bills passed by Congress during the year were:

- HR 5428, signed by Bush on Nov. 28 (PL 101-633), to designate as wilderness about 26,000 acres of the Shawnee National Forest in southern Illinois.
- S 2205, signed into law Sept. 28 (PL 101-401), to designate as wilderness about 12,000 acres in the White Mountain National Forest in Maine. ■

Congress Bans U.S Mining in Antarctica

Congress, seeking to avert environmental despoliation of Antarctica, enacted legislation to bar U.S. exploration or development of minerals on the ice-covered continent. Lawmakers also passed a joint resolution calling on President Bush to begin negotiations aimed at tighter international guardianship of the continent.

The legislation (HR 3977) was pushed by lawmakers concerned with preserving Antarctica's near-pristine environment, but resisted by those who believed that it would tie the administrations's hands in international negotiations.

The legislative moves reflected a broad agreement in Congress on the importance of protecting Antarctica's environment. The administration professed it shared those goals, but originally opposed the measure, fearing that Congress would have hampered the administration's ability to conduct foreign policy.

> **BOXSCORE**
>
> **Legislation:** Antarctic Protection Act, PL 101-594 (HR 3977); global commons resolution, S J Res 206 (PL 101-620).
>
> **Major action:** HR 3977: Signed, Nov. 16. Cleared by House, Oct. 26; passed by Senate, with amendment, Oct. 25 (session of Oct. 24); by House, Oct. 15. S J Res 206: Signed, Nov. 16. Cleared by Senate, Oct. 25 (session of Oct. 24); passed by House, with amendment, Oct. 23; by Senate, Oct. 4.
>
> **Reports:** HR 3977: Merchant Marine and Fisheries (H Rept 101-692, Part I).

Enactment of the ban on U.S. development and exploration came only after supporters of the bill agreed to the administration's insistence that U.S. environmental laws not be applied to government activities in Antarctica. The bill cleared Congress on Oct. 26 and was signed by Bush on Nov. 16 (PL 101-594).

As cleared, HR 3977 made it illegal for any U.S. citizen to engage in, finance or otherwise assist in any mineral development in Antarctica. The regulation was to stay in effect until the conclusion of an international treaty that indefinitely prohibited any Antarctic mineral activity. Violations would be punished under the regulations of the 1984 Antarctic Marine Living Resources Convention Act.

The measure also stated that it was the sense of Congress that the president should urge the secretary of State to negotiate the international treaty to indefinitely ban mineral activity in Antarctica. The legislation authorized $1 million in fiscal 1991-92 for the under secretary of Commerce to carry out the provisions of the bill and $500,000 for the secretary of State in fiscal 1991-92 to carry out the treaty negotiations.

Congress also passed a joint resolution (S J Res 206 — PL 101-620) that called on the Bush administration to begin international negotiations concerning the administration of Antarctica. The resolution urged the Bush administration to regard Antarctica as a part of the global ecological commons and to push for this classification during the multination discussions.

The administration preferred this language to HR 3977 that would have banned U.S. mining and pressed for negotiation of a permanent international ban.

BACKGROUND

Antarctica had been administered under international agreements since the first Antarctica treaty of 1959. Thirty-nine countries were party to the treaty, including the United States. The treaty was supplemented later by other international agreements drawn to protect the animal and plant life on the icy continent.

In 1978, Congress passed the Antarctic Conservation Act (PL 95-541), formally adopting the provisions of the Agreed Measures for the Conservation of Antarctic Flora and Fauna, a 1964 document drawn up by the parties to the Antarctic Treaty.

The act provided for the protection of the native wildlife on Antarctica and established regulations for the export or import of non-indigenous plant or animal life into Antarctica. Under the law, the National Science Foundation (NSF) was made responsible for creating a system for the regulation of most U.S. activities on the continent.

In addition, Congress passed the Antarctic Marine Living Resource Convention in 1984 as a part of a group of international agreements that also included a fishing agreement with Iceland and the European Economic Community (PL 98-623). This agreement established international mechanisms for the conservation and protection of marine life in Antarctica.

Though no mineral deposits were known to exist in the Antarctic, some parties to the Antarctica treaty wanted to set out a framework to control mining, should any minerals be discovered there. The final 1988 treaty, the Convention on the Regulation of Antarctic Mineral Resource Activities, known as the Wellington Convention, would have limited mining and provided some environmental protections of the Antarctic.

But opponents of the treaty argued that the Wellington Convention, by allowing mineral exploration, could have led to the exploitation of the continent, despite the environmental protections built into the treaty.

These concerns led at least two countries — France and Australia — to refuse to ratify the minerals convention.

Congressional opponents of mining in Antarctica, led by Rep. Silvio O. Conte, R-Mass., introduced legislation on Feb. 7 to enact a unilateral permanent ban on U.S. mining in Antarctica and to encourage talks to make that ban international.

While Conte found wide support in Congress for his measure, he encountered strong resistance from the Bush administration, which argued that there was no international consensus to support such a permanent prohibition on mining.

The administration objected to passing a law that took unilateral U.S. action while the international discussions were still going on.

COMMITTEE ACTION

By September, both the Merchant Marine and the Foreign Affairs committees had approved HR 3977 in identical form. But administration objections to some provisions of the measure threatened the future of the bill.

The Foreign Affairs panel in September also passed H J Res 418 to call on the administration to negotiate with other countries concerned with the administration of Antarctica for an international ban on mineral development in the region.

Merchant Marine Committee

Two House Merchant Marine subcommittees — Fisheries and Wildlife Conservation and Oceanography — approved HR 3977 in a joint markup session July 19.

Oceanography Subcommittee Chairman Dennis M. Hertel, D-Mich., said he wanted to protect the continent from all environmental degradation but recognized that no single nation had jurisdiction over the region. The 39 nations that had claimed a stake in the region had been unable to agree on how to protect it, particularly if valuable mineral deposits were to be discovered.

The legislation would have required the secretary of State to enter into international negotiations for more comprehensive environmental protections that would bar all mining.

As a first step, the measure would have prohibited exploration and development of mineral resources by U.S. citizens.

The bill also would have required the Commerce Department to issue regulations governing the growing number of tourist expeditions to the area. And the measure would have added new regulations on commercial fishing expeditions to the Antarctic region.

Finally, under the bill, all federal activities in Antarctica would have been covered by the National Environmental Policy Act (NEPA) of 1969 to ensure that environmental impact assessments would have been done on all proposed federal activity in Antarctica.

During the markup, Gerry E. Studds, D-Mass., and Hertel offered a substitute that made several technical changes to the bill and deleted the section on fishing regulations.

The subcommittees approved the substitute and sent HR 3977 on to the full committee by voice vote.

On Aug. 1, the full Merchant Marine Committee followed suit, approving the measure by voice vote.

During its consideration, the full committee approved an amendment by Studds that struck the tourism regulation provisions and added an authorization for $500,000 for the State Department to negotiate the international agreement called for in the bill.

Foreign Affairs Committee

Before taking up HR 3977, the Foreign Affairs Committee turned to H J Res 418.

The Subcommittee on Human Rights and International Organizations on July 25 approved the resolution by voice vote.

Sponsored by Wayne Owens, D-Utah, the measure called for Antarctica to be managed as a "global ecological commons" under a new international agreement.

The Antarctic Minerals Convention, which the United States had signed but had not ratified, was not adequate to protect the Antarctic environment, according to the resolution.

The full committee approved H J Res 418 on Sept. 13. Foreign Affairs Chairman Dante B. Fascell, D-Fla., called HR 3977 "the next logical step."

On Sept. 26, the Human Rights Subcommittee approved by voice vote an amendment that made the bill the same as the one approved earlier by the Merchant Marine panel and then sent the bill to full committee.

The committee considered HR 3977 the following day and approved it by voice vote in the same form it had been reported by the Merchant Marine Committee.

The Bush administration had indicated unhappiness with some parts of the measure, and bill sponsors said they had worked with the administration to avoid a veto.

"This legislation [HR 3977] is very important in pushing, nudging the administration to take a strong leadership position," said Owens.

Studds said that the administration could live with the bill, but "I know personally the names of penguins who can't live without it."

The only controversy during the Foreign Affairs markup of HR 3977 came over a matter of committee jurisdiction. Robert G. Torricelli, D-N.J., offered an amendment to strike the provision applying the 1969 environmental law. Instead, it would have put the NSF in charge of issuing regulations for environmental assessment of all U.S.-sponsored activities in Antarctica.

Torricelli complained that the bill had not passed through the Science Committee, which generally dealt with Antarctica issues. He said his provision would have merely ensured the Science Committee's participation.

Torricelli, a member of the committee, was also protecting the turf of another New Jersey Democrat, Science Committee Chairman Robert A. Roe.

Opposing the amendment, Studds said that giving the NSF control of U.S. activity in Antarctica would be like "putting the fox in charge of the chicken coop. They [NSF officials] are the last people to put in charge of cleaning up their mess."

The NSF had been sponsoring research in the Antarctic region for more than 30 years. It was sued by the nonprofit interest group Environmental Defense Fund, which sought to force the NSF to stop burning garbage and dumping junk in landfills close to the water in Antarctica.

Torricelli's amendment failed on a voice vote. But Torricelli warned that members were headed toward a "needless jurisdictional conflict" when the bill went to the floor.

FLOOR ACTION

The House passed H J Res 418 on Oct. 1 by a vote of 398-11. The Senate first approved S J Res 206 on Oct. 4 by voice vote. *(Vote 395, p. 128-H)*

The full House then considered HR 3977 on Oct. 15, passing the committee-approved version by voice vote after little discussion.

The Senate passed a separate version (S 2575) on Oct. 16 after several holds were lifted and then took up the House-passed measure.

The House bill would have required environmental impact reports to be prepared before U.S. scientific activities in the region could go forward, a provision that was dropped from the Senate bill because of administration objections. The stronger House language was not expected to survive in conference.

The bill, however, still faced considerable opposition from the administration. The White House did not approve of the provision to apply NEPA to Antarctica.

Administration officials argued that it might have impinged on the execution of U.S. foreign policy or resulted in a conflict of laws with other nations.

When the Senate took up HR 3977 in the early hours of Oct. 25 (session of Oct. 24), after lengthy negotiations between the bill-supporters in the House and Senate and the administration, the Senate approved an amendment to drop the NEPA provision from the bill. The full chamber then passed the bill by voice vote.

Despite vows from some members of the House to revisit the NEPA idea in 1991, the House agreed to the Senate amendment on Oct. 26, clearing the measure for the president.

The Senate, meanwhile, had cleared S J Res 206 on Oct. 25 (session of Oct. 24) just before it acted on HR 3977. The House had passed an amended version of the resolution Oct. 23.

Bush signed the resolution (PL 101-620) on Nov. 16. ■

Global Warming Research Measure Enacted

Congress cleared for the president a measure (S 169) to provide for a national plan to improve scientific understanding of global warming changes. Some scientists said the buildup of carbon dioxide in the atmosphere from burning fossil fuels would lead to a dangerous increase in the Earth's temperature.

The House by voice vote passed an amended version of the legislation on Oct. 26 based largely on HR 2984, approved in committee earlier in the year. The Senate cleared the House-passed version in the early hours of Oct. 28, shortly before its adjournment. President Bush signed the measure (PL 101-606) on Nov. 16.

The Senate first passed S 169, sponsored by Ernest F. Hollings, D-S.C., on Feb. 6 by a 100-0 vote. *(Vote 5, p. 416)*

Lawmakers, however, failed to clear a more extensive bill (S 324) designed to establish a national energy policy to reduce the threat of global warming. The Senate passed S 324 on Aug. 4 to stem emissions of carbon dioxide, methane and other greenhouse gases, but the House took no action on the measure.

In the House, HR 2984 — to promote international cooperation in research on global climate change — won approval from a Foreign Affairs subcommittee, on May 2, and from the full Science Committee. The bill would have established an Office of Global Change within the White House and encouraged the involvement of scientists from developing nations. It called for discussions leading to international agreements to coordinate research on global climate change.

The Science Committee on April 18 approved HR 2984 by voice vote to create a global change research program to study the effects of global warming and develop policies to deal with it. The bill would have established a permanent program and provided the Committee on Earth Sciences with resources to coordinate the effort.

Senate Action on S 324

The Senate Energy Committee on May 16 approved a bill to establish a national energy conservation policy to reduce the threat of global warming. The 19-0 vote came after Chairman J. Bennett Johnston, D-La., persuaded members not to "load down" the measure with amendments that might jeopardize passage on the Senate floor.

The bill (S 324 — S Rept 101-361), sponsored by Tim Wirth, D-Colo., would have required the Energy Department to develop a "least-cost national energy plan" designed to stabilize the volume of carbon dioxide and other greenhouse gas emissions.

Wirth's bill would have required the Energy Department to establish research and development programs for renewable and other energy resource alternatives. It would also have required the department to put into effect initiatives to use natural gas as a motor vehicle fuel.

The measure also would have encouraged partnerships between federal and state agencies to help achieve a 20 percent reduction in carbon dioxide emissions by the year 2005. It would have authorized $163 million for the programs in fiscal 1992, $168 million in 1993 and $183 million in 1994.

The committee May 9 began consideration of S 324, which originally proposed a wide range of solutions to the global-warming threat, such as curbing the world's birthrate, discouraging deforestation, encouraging development of alternative fuels and imposing fuel taxes to cut carbon dioxide emissions 20 percent by 2000.

Democratic and Republican staff members worked out the less ambitious compromise.

Wirth said he agreed to the compromise to move the bill through committee and the full Senate without controversial baggage that could damage its chances of passage. He had planned from the beginning to tear off part of his omnibus bill and deal separately with such issues as energy efficiency, conservation and clean coal technologies, thus keeping jurisdiction within the Energy panel.

The committee had considered variations of the global-warming legislation for the past three years. But interest heightened in 1990 with action on the Clean Air Act and increased anxieties among the voting public about air, water and soil pollution. *(Clean Air Act, p. 229)*

At Johnston's urging, ranking Republican James A. McClure of Idaho withheld an amendment to institute a research and development program for the use of nuclear energy in fighting greenhouse effects. Instead, McClure settled for language giving the Energy Department six months to conduct a study to determine whether nuclear energy could help clean up the environment.

Johnston, however, pushed through an amendment that would authorize $27 million over three years for a research and development program for more efficient uses of coal-firing technologies. The panel also adopted an amendment by John D. Rockefeller IV, D-W.Va., to authorize $20 million for a three-year research and development program for the non-fuel use of coal. Rockefeller originally sought $95 million over three years but at Johnston's urging Rockefeller submitted the less costly version.

The full Senate passed S 324 on Aug. 4 by voice vote. Wirth called the compromise on S 324 "a guide, not a mandate" to reducing greenhouse gas emissions. Amendments included provisions for encouraging energy efficiency and renewable energy technologies, commercial applications of fuel cell systems and construction of geothermal small-power production facilities. ■

Moves on Waste Laws for U.S. Sites Stall

Measures that would have allowed states to levy fines against federal facilities that failed to comply with hazardous and solid waste laws moved ahead in the House and Senate but fell short of final passage.

The bills (S 1140, HR 1056) sought to establish the power of the Environmental Protection Agency (EPA) and state governments to enforce compliance with the Resource Conservation and Recovery Act (RCRA) at federal facilities. RCRA was the 1976 law that regulated hazardous and solid waste.

The measure won approval in the Senate Environment Committee but never made it to the floor. In the House, members attached their proposal to a separate bill elevating the status of the EPA, but that bill went no further. President Bush had threatened to veto the measure over the federal-facilities provision.

The application of RCRA regulations to federal facilities — particularly nuclear weapons production plants — had been challenged in court by the Defense and Energy departments.

When Rep. Dennis E. Eckart, D-Ohio, introduced HR 1056 in February 1989, he called the environmental record of federal agencies a "national disgrace." Discoveries of seepage of radioactive and hazardous waste at the Energy Department's Feed Material Production Center in Fernald, Ohio, and the Rocky Flats nuclear arsenal plant in Golden, Colo., had made headline news and helped fuel support for the bill.

State officials, labor unions and environmentalists, including the National Audubon Society, Sierra Club, National Association of Attorneys General and the AFL-CIO, had been pushing hard for the legislation in the hope that it would give states leverage to speed action on thousands of hazardous waste sites at Energy and Defense Department facilities.

BACKGROUND

After defeating last-ditch efforts to limit the scope of the bill, the House on July 19, 1989, passed HR 1056 by a vote of 380-39. The Senate companion measure on federal-facilities compliance never moved in 1989. *(1989 Almanac, p. 679)*

A similar federal-facilities compliance bill was introduced in 1988, but it died in committee along with other bills that would have amended RCRA.

Appropriations had kept RCRA alive since the law expired in November 1989.

State governments, which the Reagan administration made mostly responsible for setting environmental standards, had begun to take a hard line on environmental, health and safety standards at nuclear weapons plants. Governors were challenging the longstanding "sovereign immunity" of the federal government against states' efforts to enforce their environmental regulations.

In an estimate released early in 1989, the Department of Energy (DOE) said modernization and cleanup of the nuclear weapons complex would cost at least $81 billion through the year 2010. A July 1990 report by the DOE said that the cost over the next five years would be 50 percent higher than the department had estimated in 1989.

In an earlier report, the General Accounting Office (GAO) estimated the cost at between $100 billion and $155 billion. Other estimates put the cost of cleaning up the weapons industry at $200 billion or more over the next 30 years.

Nuclear weapons plants were not the only costly, environmental hot spots for the U.S. military complex. Routine industrial and maintenance activities at more than 1,000 installations across the country were generating about 400,000 tons of hazardous waste annually, according to the GAO.

The Pentagon estimated that proper disposal of effluents such as crankcase oil, cleaning solvents and lead-based paints would cost as much as $15 billion over 25 years, which did not include the cost of cleaning up installations the Pentagon had sold or abandoned.

Of all the federal facilities regulated by existing environmental laws, 70 percent to 90 percent belonged to the Pentagon, according to a House Armed Services panel reviewing that cleanup.

LEGISLATIVE ACTION

In an attempt to give the measure new life in 1990, Eckart offered HR 1056 as an amendment to legislation (HR 3847) that would have elevated the EPA to Cabinet-level status.

The House approved the amendment on March 28 by voice vote and with little debate. The amendment was identical to the bill the House had passed overwhelmingly in 1989.

Though the House passed the EPA measure in March, the bill stalled after Bush threatened a veto. *(EPA Cabinet status, p. 291)*

Despite GOP objections that the bill would delay costly cleanup of hazardous waste at federal facilities, the Senate Environment Committee on Oct. 4 approved S 1140 (S Rept 101-553) to force the federal government to comply with its own environmental laws.

The committee approved the bill 15-0, but the measure never saw floor action because of objections from several senators.

Majority Leader George J. Mitchell, D-Maine, said the legislation would clarify an issue that had divided the judiciary: Three federal appeals courts had ruled that a particular section of RCRA did not waive the federal government's sovereign immunity — that is, did not allow states to sue federal facilities — but a district court in Maine had ruled otherwise.

Mitchell's proposal also would have given the EPA authority to force other federal agencies and departments to comply with environmental regulations.

"The bill involves a simple principle: The federal government should be subject to the laws which it imposes on others," Mitchell said.

"Our entire legal system is based on the premise that there cannot be compliance with any law without enforcement," he added.

But ranking Republican John H. Chafee, R.I., said the bill would simply funnel money needed to clean up federal facilities into penalties and fines to states.

Chafee said, "The majority leader certainly shows his loyalty to his home state by balancing three federal appeals court decisions against one district court decision in Maine."

Members first defeated, on a party-line vote of 6-9, an amendment by Chafee to narrow the number of facilities that would be subject to the waiver of federal sovereign immunity.

Chafee's amendment, among other things, would have barred states from collecting fines and penalties from older facilities that had not received hazardous and solid waste since July 1982. States also could not have sued agencies for failing to meet facility-closure requirements if complying with them would have cost more than $25 million.

The committee did agree, by voice vote, to an amendment by James M. Jeffords, R-Vt., requiring that the cost of EPA inspections of federal facilities be borne by the agencies involved, not by the EPA. ■

Stello Withdraws Bid for DOE Nuclear Post

The White House announced April 24 that President Bush had accepted Victor Stello Jr.'s request to withdraw his nomination to be assistant secretary of Energy in charge of defense programs. Bush had nominated Stello in July 1989 to head the nation's nuclear bomb production program.

The action, forestalling a likely Senate floor confirmation fight, was a victory for a coalition of environmentalists, anti-nuclear activists and their allies in Congress. They had charged that Stello was too cozy with the industry during his 24-year career as a nuclear regulator and repeatedly impeded criminal investigations of wrongdoing by industry players. Members of Congress accused Stello of helping to orchestrate an effort to have another top Nuclear Regulatory Commission (NRC) official fired for being too aggressive in investigating industry wrongdoing. They also said Stello might have lied to Congress to justify his actions.

Stello's withdrawal came just days before NRC Inspector General David C. Williams was to have briefed Senate Armed Services Committee leaders on his investigation of Stello, formerly the NRC's chief staffer.

Williams' report, first reported publicly by The New York Times on June 20, strongly criticized and questioned the truthfulness of Stello's statements to Congress. The results of the investigation reflected the findings of a harsh report issued by a House Interior subcommittee April 5. Williams concluded, among other things, that Stello had improperly delayed an investigation of unsafe conditions at a New York nuclear reactor and had given explanations in congressional testimony that were "not credible."

Armed Services Committee aides and Energy Secretary James D. Watkins, whose department ran the bomb programs, heard Williams' briefing 11 days before Stello asked Bush to withdraw his name.

Stello told Bush in an April 20 letter that he was certain that "final Senate action on my nomination will not take place in the foreseeable future." He said the nation needed an assistant secretary of Energy for defense programs to be confirmed and in place "at the earliest opportunity."

"It has become clear to me that I cannot be that person," wrote Stello, who added that injuries suffered during a January skiing accident "also weigh on my decision."

Bush nominated Richard A. Claytor, the principal deputy assistant secretary for nuclear energy, for the post on Sept. 10. Claytor was approved by the Senate on Oct. 10 with no debate.

Throughout the investigations into his actions, Stello denied all wrongdoing and, along with his supporters in Congress and the Bush administration, dismissed his critics as antinuclear ideologues who wanted to dismantle the government's bomb-building system. Watkins kept Stello as a deputy assistant secretary for facilities — a lower-level job in the department's crippled weapons program.

The Fortuna Affair

Stello's undoing focused on his dealings with another top NRC official who was fired for apparently being too aggressive in investigating industry wrongdoing. The event became known as the Fortuna affair.

Roger Fortuna was the NRC's aggressive second-ranking investigator of criminal wrongdoing within the nuclear industry. Long unpopular with Stello and his allies, Fortuna became the target of a lengthy investigation when an informant sold to the NRC tapes of Fortuna talking to an antinuclear activist.

With Stello's approval, NRC officials paid the informant more than $6,000 in 1988 for the tapes. From the tapes, officials decided that Fortuna might have been engaged in a conspiracy "to topple" the agency. He was suspended and demoted for 11 months but was finally reinstated in February after subsequent investigations determined that he had not violated any laws or rules.

Fortuna's Office of Investigations was responsible for developing criminal allegations that it then sent to the Justice Department. Fortuna said that Stello wanted to reduce the flow of such allegations.

Stello repeatedly clashed with Fortuna's office over such matters, but Stello said his motivation in those debates was to make sure criminal investigations did not interfere with his job: making sure nuclear plants were safe.

Many who looked into the affair, including several congressional committees and several outsiders hired by the NRC, concluded that the evidence proved no wrongdoing by Fortuna, who said that he was cultivating the activist as a source. Though some questioned Fortuna's judgment, most decided that a desire to get Fortuna fired played a role in the investigation.

In his zest to pursue the Fortuna inquiry, Stello admitted that he sat on significant safety-related allegations, some involving drugs, made by the informant about a nuclear plant in upstate New York. Stello said he did not want to compromise the Fortuna investigation by letting him know that the informant was in contact with the NRC.

Stello repeatedly testified to Congress that his motives in pursuing Fortuna were based on public health and safety concerns, but members said his claim had been undermined by voluminous evidence to the contrary.

Action Delayed

The Senate Armed Services Committee in January had been on the verge of recommending Stello's nomination to the full Senate, but members balked on learning that

Stello's actions and his allegedly misleading statements to Congress were the focus of an ongoing investigation by the NRC's inspector general.

Williams began his review shortly after Dec. 3, 1989, when he became the NRC's first Senate-confirmed inspector general. Congress created the quasi-independent job in 1988 to combat management interference with NRC investigations. On Jan. 26, Williams briefed committee Chairman Sam Nunn, D-Ga., and ranking Republican John W. Warner, Va., on the scope of his probe.

Its three tiers, he told them, included the actual allegations against Fortuna, the conduct of the inquiry against him and the truthfulness of Stello's statements to Congress about it.

Nunn announced Jan. 31 after a closed-door committee meeting that action on the Stello nomination had been delayed indefinitely.

Opponents Tim Wirth, D-Colo., and John Glenn, D-Ohio, already had given up the fight and drafted a dissenting opinion to explain their votes against Stello.

"We did not know that the Fortuna investigation was focused to the degree it is on Mr. Stello," Nunn said, after receiving Williams' Jan. 26 briefing. "We did not know how serious the allegations were regarding Stello."

When committee members agreed to the delay, Wirth was delighted. "I think they're finally catching on," he said. "I think the momentum is going in the direction where I think Secretary Watkins would be very wise to withdraw the nomination."

Subcommittee Report

The House Interior Investigations Subcommittee, ending its yearlong probe, approved by voice vote a report April 5 that stopped just short of accusing Stello of lying to Congress. Republicans on the subcommittee assented to the publication of the report, but added in a supplement, "We have not concluded that sufficient evidence exists to date to disqualify Mr. Stello" from serving as the Energy Department's assistant secretary for defense programs.

In the supplement, the Republicans also "questioned the veracity" of Stello, agreeing with the report's conclusion that he was at times "not credible" and "disingenuous" and "exercised poor judgment" during the Fortuna affair.

The subcommittee report concluded that there was "no compelling evidence of wrongdoing by Mr. Fortuna." It added: "The fact that the investigation has been pursued over such an extended period . . . suggests that senior NRC officials abused their authority in order to indulge personal and professional antagonisms toward Mr. Fortuna."

The report also called the cash payment "highly inadvisable" and concluded that the investigation of Fortuna was "sloppy and unprofessional" and that Stello "improperly participated" in it.

It added, "The Subcommittee believes that Mr. Victor Stello, in formulating a justification for his actions in this matter, has misstated the facts to this subcommittee and other committees of the Congress."

Less than three weeks after the subcommittee issued its report, Stello asked that his nomination be withdrawn. The withdrawal came as Williams was preparing to release his findings to Senate committee members.

When Stello withdrew, Warner, an ally of Watkins from the senator's days as Navy secretary, insisted the nomination had not been a lost cause on the Senate floor. "I was prepared to wage a tough battle," he said.

But Stello's opponents said they were relieved. "Victor Stello should not have been nominated for this job in the first place," said Wirth, Stello's most vocal critic. "It's time to move on." ■

Uranium Enrichment Spinoff Blocked

Legislation to revise and strengthen the Energy Department's troubled uranium enrichment enterprise failed to win enactment in the 101st Congress.The Senate in 1989 had passed a bill (S 83) sponsored by Wendell H. Ford, D-Ky., to spin off the uranium enrichment enterprise into a government corporation designed to operate at a profit. But the House balked. *(1989 Almanac, p. 690)*

Biding his time, Ford waited until the fiscal 1991 budget-reconciliation bill (HR 5835) was being assembled. From his position as chairman of the Energy Subcommittee on Research and Development, he attached S 83 to the reconciliation bill when the Energy and Natural Resources Committee added its recommendations to that package. But the measure was stripped from the final version in conference with the House. *(Reconciliation, p. 138)*

An unrelated proposal to ease licensing requirements for private uranium enrichment facilities, including one planned for northern Louisiana, was attached to a separate bill on alternative energy (HR 4808 — PL 101-575) by Senate Energy Committee Chairman J. Bennett Johnston, D-La. That bill did clear Congress on Oct. 28. *(Alternative energy, p. 317)*

The Senate committee, at Ford's behest, had attached S 83 to its own version (S 2415 — S Rept 101-470) of the alternative energy bill, which was reported Sept. 21 and passed by the Senate on Sept. 26. But the House refused to act on that measure, and Ford ultimately agreed to let HR 4808 clear without such a provision.

Though the Senate over the years had repeatedly approved bills on the government's uranium enrichment program, antinuclear forces and environmentalists in the House always fiercely opposed such legislation. *(1988 Almanac, p. 171; 1987 Almanac, p. 318)*

The Energy Department enterprise sold nuclear fuel to utilities and provided core material for some of the government's deadliest warheads.

One of the nation's two enrichment facilities employed 1,572 workers in Paducah, Ky., and Ford feared that those jobs could vanish unless the program was restructured.

The U.S. government, which was once in control of a worldwide enriched uranium monopoly, had seen its share of the market slip to less than 50 percent.

"We're not being competitive," Ford said, because prices were artificially high compared with those offered by the Soviets and Europeans. Ford wanted to create a new government corporation to run the program. In doing so, his plan would have allowed the enterprise to write off billions of dollars of past costs that critics of the program

NRC To Collect Costs From Industry Fees

The Nuclear Regulatory Commission (NRC) was ordered to collect all its operating costs for a five-year period from fees imposed on the nuclear power industry under a provision rolled into the fiscal 1991 budget-reconciliation bill.

Conferees on the Omnibus Budget Reconciliation Act (HR 5835 — PL 101-508) agreed to impose a projected $287 million a year in new fees on nuclear power producers to reduce the deficit by $1.6 billion over a five-year period. *(Budget-reconciliation act, provisions: Title VI, Energy, Environment, p. 154)*

The NRC had been under a congressional mandate to recover 45 percent of its costs from such fees. The compromise provision raised that figure to 100 percent through fiscal 1995.

The agreement — by leaders of the Senate Environment Committee and the House Interior and Energy committees — represented a major concession by the Senate, which in the past had resisted House and administration attempts to raise NRC fees substantially.

In return, House members accepted a Senate proposal to limit the fee increase to five years.

Background

The NRC, like other federal regulatory agencies, had collected fees for services provided to its licensees under the 1952 Independent Offices Appropriation Act (IOAA). The fees, based on special services to users, recovered only a small portion of the NRC's budget (roughly 10 percent).

In December 1985, the House Energy and Commerce Committee recommended a budget-reconciliation provision to direct the NRC to impose "annual charges" on its licensees that, when added to amounts collected under the IOAA, would equal 50 percent of the agency's annual budget. In conference, the figure was reduced to 33 percent, and the provision was enacted as part of the 1985 budget-reconciliation package (PL 99-272).

The NRC rule implementing this law imposed a standard annual charge of $950,000 on each operating power reactor, regardless of size or costs to operate.

In 1986, before the rule took effect, the Reagan administration, the NRC and members of Congress began debating changes.

The administration recommended that Congress specify a standard charge per amount of electricity each power reactor was capable of producing.

The House Interior Committee proposed legislation taking this approach, specifying a fee of $750 per megawatt of capacity, which would have recovered about 60 percent of the NRC's fiscal 1987 budget. The House Energy and Commerce Committee reported legislation that retained the NRC's existing standard approach but would have increased the percentage of budget recovered from 33 percent to 100 percent.

The Senate Environment and Public Works Committee reported a bill increasing the percentage to 38 percent. The legislation stalled when House and Senate conferees failed to resolve these differences. *(1986 Almanac, p. 147)*

The House Energy Committee, during discussion of the NRC reauthorization bill in 1987, again discussed raising the amount to be recovered through user fees. The 1987 budget reconciliation act retained the NRC's authority to collect annual charges, but increased the percentage of the budget to be recovered from 33 percent to 45 percent for fiscal 1988 and 1989 only. *(1987 Almanac, p. 321)*

The 1989 budget-reconciliation act amended the law to allow the percentage to remain at 45 percent for a third year, fiscal 1990. Without new legislation, the amount was to revert to 33 percent in fiscal 1991.

Legislative Action

Early in the 101st Congress, on May 17, 1989, the House Interior Committee amended the NRC authorization bill (HR 1549) to direct the NRC to collect user fees in an amount necessary to recover 100 percent of the agency's annual budget. But that legislation stalled.

In the budget-reconciliation process in 1990, the Senate proposed amending the 1985 law to recover 100 percent of NRC operating costs. But its proposal differed from the House provision in that it would have required the NRC to impose annual charges for only five years.

Conferees followed the Senate bill, with an amendment to provide a "floor" on the fees and annual charges equal to 33 percent of the NRC's budget.

The provision was projected to bring in an extra $287 million in fiscal 1991 and $1.55 billion through fiscal 1995. Without further action, the 100 percent figure was to revert to 33 percent for fiscal 1996.

said should be recouped from customers — something Ford and his allies said would only make matters worse.

House critics such as George Miller, D-Calif., and the National Taxpayers Union called the bill a "bailout" for the nuclear industry. It "saddles the taxpayers with a multibillion-dollar bill," said Miller and several allies in a letter protesting Ford's move. "It would be a serious mistake to attach such a bill to deficit-reduction legislation."

Ford took a step toward appeasing his critics by attaching to the budget bill about $100 million-a-year worth of nuclear industry fees to pay for cleaning up environmental damage at existing uranium enrichment facilities. Ford's proposal also would have required the enrichment enterprise to pay dividends to the U.S. Treasury for the next five years.

Ford's changes produced enough in projected deficit cuts to protect the entire uranium measure from being stripped outright from the reconciliation bill — an easy move in the Senate, where the rules allowed a member to block any item deemed extraneous to its real purpose, deficit reduction. Sixty votes were needed to overturn such a move.

Nevertheless, even those in the House willing to compromise said there was not enough time to settle the issue. "It's just too controversial to do on reconciliation," said an Interior Committee aide. ■

Little Action on Energy Policy in 1990

Congress enacted a handful of energy-related proposals in 1990 but left debate over a national energy policy for 1991.

Iraq's invasion of oil-rich Kuwait, the most immediate threat to the nation's energy security since the crisis-ridden 1970s, heated up the moribund debate over U.S. energy security, but did little more in the debate over energy policy than sharpen the rhetoric.

On the core question facing energy policy-makers — whether to increase domestic fossil fuel production on public lands — the invasion merely bolstered both sides' arguments.

Pro-industry lawmakers argued for increased exploration to reduce imports from the unstable Middle East; environmentalists parried that the oil war should persuade the United States to wean itself from fossil fuels with alternative energy sources and diligent conservation.

The Bush administration, meanwhile, continued to prepare a big new national energy policy to be submitted to lawmakers in early 1991.

Officials promised that it would include significant alternative energy and conservation proposals to balance pro-development initiatives.

While expressing concern for what Energy Secretary James D. Watkins called an addiction to foreign oil, officials throughout the year were crafting the National Energy Strategy largely around environmental concerns.

"It's become clear that unless conservation and efficiency are at the focal point of our attention, then we're not going to get anywhere," Watkins said, dropping key buzzwords of the environmental movement.

The biggest change in energy policy in 1990 came with enactment of a bill expanding the Strategic Petroleum Reserve (SPR), the nation's rainy day supply of crude oil, and creating a second reserve for refined products.

The Iraqi invasion forced Bush to accept the measure, even though he opposed its expansion provisions as too expensive and unnecessary.

On the other hand, Bush successfully resisted congressional pressure to begin selling off large amounts of the reserve to curb rising oil prices.

Bush's bid to end the decadelong stalemate over offshore oil drilling failed. He imposed his own drilling ban off much of the East and West coasts in June in the hope that Congress would allow drilling elsewhere. But lawmakers insisted on using the annual Interior spending bill to continue — and expand — existing moratoriums.

"The environmental movement is still too strong," said Rep. W. J. "Billy" Tauzin, D-La., a pro-development oilstater.

"It's going to take long lines again; it's going to take shortages; it's going to take people getting cold."

Just 55 hours after Iraqi troops charged into Kuwait, the question was posed squarely to the House early on Aug. 4. Members had a chance to speed the development of what was described as one of the nation's largest untapped sources of energy — a natural gas field off North Carolina.

Lawmakers overwhelmingly declined the opportunity, in effect approving a one-year drilling ban off the Outer Banks; the Senate had earlier accepted the ban without debate.

A measure opposed by Bush that would enhance states' powers to block federal decisions to permit oil drilling off their shores was approved as part of a reauthorization of the Coastal Zone Management Act, which was attached to the fiscal 1991 deficit-cutting reconciliation bill. *(Coastal Zone Management Act, p. 288)*

Bush's only significant victory on energy policy was to gain approval of a new set of tax breaks to encourage domestic energy production, which also was part of the deficit bill.

The bill also included a 5-cents-a-gallon gas tax increase; a broad-based energy tax proposed during negotiations between Congress and the White House never made it out of the summit.

Background

Few experts or politicians doubted that the nation needed some sort of energy policy and that the federal government needed to assert a role — perhaps the leading role — in steering the country's energy marketplace from production to end use.

Although some free-marketeers, including Reagan administration hard-liners, argued that the United States' energy "vulnerability" was not as great as its "dependence" suggested, most energy experts and officials or lawmakers who addressed the issue considered the situation increasingly grave. Shortly after taking office, Bush declared increasing oil imports an unacceptable threat to national security.

That scare line, however, was wearing thin.

With widely varying approaches and degrees of urgency, every president since 1973 emphasized that danger and tried unsuccessfully to spur the nation into accepting their prescriptions for a cure. Nixon said that "we are running out of energy." Gerald R. Ford spoke of "a future of shortages," and Jimmy Carter declared "the moral equivalent of war" on a potential "national catastrophe." Even Ronald Reagan announced that "petroleum imports threaten to impair our national security."

U.S. oil production continued to plummet in 1989 to its lowest point in 26 years. Imports took up the slack, accounting for 46 percent of consumption. The nation was more dependent on imports only once, in 1977, when imports accounted for 48 percent of consumption, precipitating the energy crisis of 1979.

Iraq's annexation of Kuwait, meanwhile, doubled Iraqi President Saddam Hussein's control over crude oil reserves from 10 percent of the world total to nearly 20 percent. Bush's decision to prohibit trade with Iraq and Kuwait effectively cut off more than one-tenth of the oil imported into the United States.

The impact was immediate, exacerbating recession jitters. Per-barrel prices of oil skyrocketed, approaching $30 before receding some, up from the mid-teens in June and about $20 right before the invasion. Gasoline prices, reflecting fear about the future rather than actual costs, immediately rose by as much as 20 cents a gallon.

Legislative Action

Following is a brief summary of some of the energy-related issues that the 101st Congress confronted in 1990:

- **SPR expansion.** Bush on Sept. 15 signed a bill to

Energy Tax Breaks, Higher Gas Levy Passed

One of President Bush's only victories on energy policy in 1990 was the passage of a new set of tax breaks to encourage domestic energy production as part of the deficit-reduction bill (HR 5835 — PL 101-508).

The bill also included a 5-cents-a-gallon gas tax increase; a broad-based energy tax proposed during negotiations between Congress and the White House never made it out of the budget summit.

The deficit-reduction bill provided $2.5 billion in energy-related tax breaks, primarily to benefit oil and gas operations, over the following five years. The bill extended tax credits for the production of non-conventional and alcohol fuels; provided new credits for ethanol production and costs associated with certain difficult oil-recovery projects; expanded percentage-depletion deductions allowed independent oil and gas producers; and provided alternative minimum tax relief for oil and gas producers.

The bill also extended through the end of 1991 tax credits for businesses that invested in solar or geothermal energy. A credit for ocean thermal energy was allowed to expire.

Under the legislation, the excise tax on gasoline, diesel and other motor fuels increased by 5 cents a gallon. That brought the federal tax on gasoline to 14 cents a gallon. The House wanted no increase; the Senate wanted a boost of 9.5 cents a gallon.

A fight over home heating oil taxes that pitted the Northeast against the Southwest helped doom the budget-summit agreement when it reached the House floor Oct. 5.

It was over the petroleum tax that two summit members — Massachusetts Rep. Silvio O. Conte and Texas Sen. Lloyd Bentsen — did battle in the negotiation's final 30 minutes.

When these forces emerged from the summit, they had rejected a broad-based energy tax that many had considered a sure bet.

Conte, the Appropriations Committee's top Republican, wanted to give his constituents a break. Top White House and congressional negotiators agreed that home heating oil, the source of warmth for most of Massachusetts, would be exempt from the proposed tax.

Conte savored his brief victory, but Democrat Bentsen, sore that the package's oil and gas taxes would hit producers in his state hard, insisted that the Northeast share the pain. The exemption was unceremoniously removed from the agreement.

The summit negotiators instead settled on $57.4 billion in levies over five years — almost all of it from a proposed new 2-cents-a-gallon petroleum tax and an additional 10-cents-a-gallon increase on motor fuels taxes. The budget-summit agreement, however, suffered a major defeat on the House floor on Oct. 5, and lawmakers were forced to begin their negotiations anew.

expand the nation's rainy-day supply of crude oil and create a second reserve for refined products such as heating oil. Bush retreated from veto threats after events in the Middle East heightened concern over U.S. dependency on foreign oil. Congress failed to clear legislation aimed at pressuring Bush to sell off 15 million barrels of oil from the reserve. *(Strategic petroleum reserve, p. 314)*

- **Energy taxes.** One of Bush's few victories on energy policy was the passage of a new set of tax breaks to encourage domestic energy production. The bill also included a 5-cents-a-gallon gas tax increase, though a broad-based energy tax never made it out of the budget summit. *(Energy taxes, this page)*
- **Fuel-efficiency standards.** Heavy lobbying by the auto industry and the Bush administration stalled a Senate attempt to raise automobile fuel-efficiency standards. The Senate fell three votes short of the 60 votes needed to limit debate on a bill that would have forced automakers to increase 1988 Corporate Average Fuel Economy (CAFE) levels. *(Fuel economy standards, p. 279)*
- **Alternative-power regulatory breaks.** A last-minute controversy delayed but did not derail legislation providing regulatory breaks to alternative-power producers. The measure was finally approved by the Senate on Oct. 27 and by the House in the early morning hours of Oct. 28. *(Alternative-energy breaks, p. 317)*
- **Alaska oil drilling.** The Senate Energy Committee on Oct. 11 decided against an end-of-the-session bid to persuade Congress to open Alaska's Arctic National Wildlife Refuge (ANWR) to oil drilling. The issue received a boost after Iraq's invasion of Kuwait reopened the issue of enery dependency. *(Arctic refuge, p. 315)*
- **Offshore drilling bans.** One-year moratoriums on oil drilling off most U.S. shores survived late-night conference negotiations on the fiscal 1991 spending bill for the Interior Department. The moratorium on offshore drilling encompassed all the areas included in the Bush administration's decadelong drilling ban, as well as Alaska's Bristol Bay, the Florida Panhandle and a portion of the mid-Atlantic, stretching from New Jersey to Maryland. *(Interior appropriations, p. 870)*
- **State conservation goals.** Legislation to redefine national energy conservation goals and to promote state energy-efficiency programs was signed into law on Oct. 18. The measure encouraged the efficient use of available energy sources by updating and widening the scope of Department of Energy (DOE) programs that funded state conservation initiatives. *(State conservation, p. 319)*
- **Hydrogen fuel research.** Congress created an Energy Department hydrogen fuel research program and named it for the late Sen. Spark M. Matsunaga, D-Hawaii, who had been pressing the government to investigate hydrogen as an alternative energy source for years before his death April 15. *(Hydrogen research, p. 318)*
- **Oil-shale claims.** Congressional attempts to block the "giveaway" of federal oil-shale lands inched forward in 1990, but were dropped from the budget-reconciliation bill after Senate objections. *(Oil-shale claims, p. 316)* ■

Bush Signs Bill To Expand Oil Reserve

Backing off repeated veto threats, President Bush on Sept. 15 signed a bill to expand the nation's rainy-day supply of crude oil and create a second reserve for refined products such as heating oil. Bush retreated from his veto threats after events in the Middle East heightened concern in the United States over dependency on foreign oil.

Congress failed, however, to clear legislation aimed at pressuring Bush to sell off 10 million more barrels of oil from the Strategic Petroleum Reserve (SPR). Both chambers unanimously approved the SPR expansion bill (S 2088 — PL 101-383) on Sept. 13. The House acted first on a 391-0 vote; the Senate followed suit by voice vote, clearing the measure for the president. *(Vote 331, p. 108-H)*

House and Senate negotiators had reconciled conflicting versions of the bill the night before. Members were in such a rush to approve the measure before legislative authority for the reserve expired Sept. 15 that they acted before official copies of the House-Senate conference committee's report (H Rept 101-698) were available.

On Aug. 10, Bush had signed a one-month extension of the SPR (S 2952 — PL 101-360), pending approval of the broader S 2088. The crude-oil stockpile's existing authority expired Aug. 15. The Senate passed the bill Aug. 2; the House cleared the extension on Aug. 4.

Energy Department officials told Congress earlier in the year that they would urge Bush to veto the bills that had been approved by the House and Senate. They opposed the Senate's expansion of the crude-oil supply and the House's refined products reserve.

But proponents of the two controversial provisions were emboldened by Iraq's Aug. 2 invasion of Kuwait. The resulting worldwide embargo against Iraq crimped oil supplies, raised gasoline prices and renewed concerns over the country's dependence on foreign fuel. The provisions had wide support in Congress before the invasion and overwhelming support after, making it unlikely that either house would have sustained a Bush veto.

The administration's position was weakened by the rhetorical beating that lawmakers from both parties laid on Bush for refusing to draw oil from the 590 million-barrel reserve, which they said would not only have offset the loss of Iraqi and Kuwaiti oil but also would have helped hold down the sharply rising price of gasoline.

For those reasons, Energy Department officials dropped their opposition to both provisions. Deputy Energy Secretary W. Henson Moore told the Senate Energy Committee on Sept. 13 that the administration would not oppose the conference report. The decision, Moore said, reflected "political reality," not a change in the administration's philosophical objection: that the multibillion-dollar cost of the provisions was too high.

Background

The Energy Department's strategic petroleum reserve was a huge supply of unrefined crude set up in 1975 in response to the 1973-74 oil embargo. The reserve, stored in salt domes in Louisiana and Texas, had grown fairly constantly since 1977 and by mid-1990 contained nearly 580 million barrels. But the number of days of protection the reserve provided dropped as energy use and imports increased. The system could have replaced up to 110 days of imports in the mid-1980s, but that figure had dipped to less than 80 days, according to the Senate Energy Committee.

Even if the system reached its 750 million-barrel goal within the next several years — it was being filled at a rate of 40,000 barrels a day — that cushion could have dropped to as low as 50 days by 2010, the committee said.

The administration said increasing the reserve to 1 billion barrels would be too expensive. The country already spent about $20 billion on the stockpile, and it was expected to cost several billion dollars more to reach 750 million barrels. It would cost many billions of dollars more than that to hit 1 billion barrels.

As signed by Bush, the bill:

- Forced the administration to expand its plan to fill the reserve to 1 billion barrels from the existing goal of 750 million.
- Created a reserve for refined petroleum products. In a compromise, the House agreed that the reserve would be undertaken only as a three-year test and would contain much less than the 20 million barrels originally envisioned. The president would also be allowed to trade crude oil for imported refined products.
- Expanded the president's authority to sell off oil from the reserve. At the time, he could dip into the reserve only to respond to an emergency caused by an import disruption, an act of God or sabotage. The bill allowed him to act any time "a domestic energy supply shortage of significant scope or duration" existed or was imminent.

Senate Action

The Senate on May 22 passed S 2088 to expand the reserve from 750 million to 1 billion barrels, at an estimated cost of $12 billion. The Bush administration opposed the expansion, which the Senate approved on a voice vote.

The bill's billion-barrel provision was drafted under the leadership of Energy Committee Chairman J. Bennett Johnston, D-La. Arguing that the nation needed a bigger fuel cushion in case of another embargo, Johnston had pushed for a billion-barrel reserve for some time. The committee approved the bill April 23 (S Rept 101-289).

The Louisiana Land and Exploration Co., a big oil and gas producer, wanted Congress to increase the 750 million-barrel cap so it could lease the government some of its extra salt domes for storage, a deal that could be worth millions of dollars a year. (Both chambers' bills included provisions that would allow storage facilities to be leased.)

House Action

The House on July 16 approved its version of the SPR bill (HR 3193) requiring the Energy Department to stockpile refined oil products as part of the reserve. The House passed its bill on a voice vote and cleared the way for a conference by inserting its version into the Senate's.

Bucking a last-minute veto threat, the House Energy Committee had approved the bill June 27 (H Rept 101-604). The administration's threat annoyed the panel's top Republicans, who felt that they had been taken advantage of and allowed the measure to be approved by voice vote.

Responding to an earlier veto threat, the Republicans had followed the administration's bidding and fought hard to kill a provision that would have increased the reserve's

Arctic Refuge Bill Stalls Once Again

The Senate Energy Committee on Oct. 11 decided against an end-of-the-session bid to persuade Congress to open Alaska's Arctic National Wildlife Refuge (ANWR) to oil drilling. The issue received a boost after Iraq's invasion of Kuwait reopened the issue of energy dependency.

Frank H. Murkowski, R-Alaska, wanted the committee to include the panel's ANWR-drilling bill (S 684) in the budget-reconciliation bill. But he backed off after hearing that the move was opposed by Senate and House Democratic leaders. "It seems to me you would be doing damage to your cause by bringing it up and losing," committee Chairman J. Bennett Johnston, D-La., warned Murkowski.

Debate over drilling within the refuge's 1.5 million-acre coastal plain (about half the size of Connecticut) had raged since before 1980, when Congress abandoned efforts to settle the issue by ordering the administration to study the question for a while. *(1980 Almanac, p. 575)*

In response to a 1987 report by the Reagan administration, committees dominated by pro-industry members — House Merchant Marine and Senate Energy — reported out bills during the 100th Congress to open the ANWR to oil exploration. Both bills sought to safeguard against environmental damage.

Nevertheless, attempts to appease drilling opponents failed, and the legislation went nowhere. The high hopes oil-drilling proponents held going into the 101st Congress were dashed when the *Exxon Valdez* spilled 11 million barrels of crude oil in Alaska's Prince William Sound on March 24, 1989 — just eight days after Senate Energy approved S 684. *(1989 Almanac, p. 678)*

The issue was sidelined indefinitely. But Iraq's invasion of Kuwait in August 1990 shifted the political landscape. *(Persian Gulf crisis, p. 717)*

The Bush administration estimated that there could be enough recoverable crude beneath the plain to produce 600,000 barrels a day over 15 years — roughly what the United States was importing from Iraq and Kuwait before the invasion.

Environmentalists who wanted to preserve the virtually untouched landscape were suddenly on the defensive as both sides girded for a renewed confrontation in the decadelong struggle.

"The Middle East crisis wiped the *Exxon Valdez* off the ANWR map as quickly as the *Exxon Valdez* wiped ANWR off the legislative map," said one House aide.

But even some who favored drilling said the long stalemate very well would continue into the 102nd Congress, leaving the wilderness off-limits at least through the next two years. That was because drilling advocates faced tough foes with a formidable advantage — stubborn environmentalists who could prevent drilling merely by obstructing any effort to change the status quo.

Environmentalists had "the home-field advantage because all they have to do is block us," said Jim Hughes, a deputy assistant secretary of the Interior. "Blocking something is always easier than doing something affirmative, so in a 50-50 battle, that certainly could tip the scales in their favor."

goal. In doing so, they acted against the wishes of some in their party, in addition to powerful Democrats who had appeared locked into the idea.

Some of Johnston's allies on the House Energy Committee, including W. J. "Billy" Tauzin, D-La., were not yet willing to give up the fight for the billion-barrel reserve. "To do less is to compromise the security of this nation," Tauzin said in arguing that the nation needed a bigger fuel cushion in case of another embargo.

During that behind-the-scenes fight over the size of the crude-oil reserve, the administration failed to mention that the bill's refined-products stockpile was equally objectionable, members said. Once the billion-barrel provision had been knocked out, however, the Energy Department sent members a letter congratulating them for that move — and informing them for the first time that the refined-products reserve might also provoke a veto.

The provision in question would have required the Energy Department to set up a 20 million-barrel system of reserves for refined products such as heating oil and gasoline. Under an amendment by Edward J. Markey, D-Mass., new stockpiles would have to be located in at least one area that was especially dependent on imports.

Carlos J. Moorhead, R-Calif., said the refined product reserve, at less than $500 million, was a better deal for the administration than the crude-oil reserve expansion. "That's a pretty good bargain — particularly when there are sound policy reasons for storing some refined products, given refinery constraints and transportation bottlenecks," he said.

Though not explicitly stated in the bill, members from colder climes wanted heating oil stored in their region, a concept that gained favor after 1989's winter deep freeze constricted supplies and sent prices soaring.

As crafted by Energy Subcommittee Chairman Philip R. Sharp, D-Ind., the provision was aimed at facilitating a more rapid crisis response than was then possible. As the reserve was set up then, it could have taken weeks of transport and refining to get crude oil from hollowed-out salt domes in Louisiana and Texas to consumers.

"As our refining capacity dwindles," Lent said, "it is important that we begin to store some refined products in the event of a significant energy emergency."

In a June 22 letter to committee leaders, Deputy Energy Secretary Moore said the provision "would increase costs, be ineffective, distort the marketplace, produce economic inefficiencies and lower industry stocks while producing no net benefits to the public."

However, the events in Iraq and the Middle East completely changed the climate for the legislation. Both provisions opposed by the administration made their way into the final bill and Bush reluctantly signed it.

Postscript

Less than two weeks after he signed the SPR-expansion bill, Bush issued a surprise announcement that he would release 5 million barrels for sale from the reserve. Democrats, eager for Bush to undertake a much bigger sale from the supply to calm soaring oil prices, pushed legislation (HR 5731) to pressure Bush to sell off 10 million more barrels of oil. The House on Sept. 28 approved HR 5731 and the Senate Energy Committee on Oct. 11 approved the House-passed bill (S Rept 101-548).

The measure would have increased from 5 million barrels to 15 million the amount of oil Bush was authorized to sell to test the reserve's distribution system.

Bush had been under heavy bipartisan fire to sell off some of the reserve to calm oil markets as prices spiraled upward to $40 a barrel in response to the crisis in the Middle East. Oil prices, though, declined significantly after peaking in early October. By the end of the year, the weekly world average had dropped back to $25 a barrel.

The White House at first had resisted, insisting that there was not a sufficient shortage of oil to justify such a move and that it was improper to use the reserve merely to manipulate market prices.

When the pressure did not let up and prices continued to climb, the administration decided to release 5 million barrels, roughly one-third of what the nation imported on any given day. The president was relying in part on a provision in the SPR-expansion bill that allowed him to draw out 5 million barrels as a test of the system.

House Energy Subcommittee Chairman Sharp had his staff draw up the bill authorizing the president to draw out 15 million barrels. Senior members of the Energy Committee from both parties quickly signed on as cosponsors.

The bill was brought to the floor and passed by voice vote under an expedited procedure the next day, Sept. 28. The full Senate, though, did not take the measure up before adjournment. ■

Oil-Shale Lands Bill Balked

Congressional attempts to block the "giveaway" of federal oil-shale lands inched forward in 1990, but were dropped from the must-pass budget-reconciliation bill after Senate objections.

In 1989, the House had passed a bill (HR 2392) designed to stop the sale of federal lands claimed for oil-shale exploration. Under existing law, the claims could be legally "patented," or converted into private property for $2.50 per acre. But the process by which oil could be extracted from oil shale was not commercially viable.

The Senate Energy and Natural Resources Committee approved a similar measure in March 1900 — after several years of work on the issue by Tim Wirth, D-Colo. But Wirth's Republican colleague from Colorado, William L. Armstrong, held up floor consideration.

The House Interior Committee succeeded in attaching the measure to the budget-reconciliation bill (HR 5835) that passed the House, but conferees were unable to reach a compromise and the language was dropped.

The issue began in 1986 when the Interior Department transferred 82,000 acres of oil-shale land in Colorado to claimants for $2.50 an acre. Some was later resold to major oil companies for $2,000 an acre.

A bill to prevent the recurrence of such a windfall was introduced in 1986 but died in a House committee. In 1987, the House passed a similar measure, 295-93, but the bill languished in the Senate. *(1987 Almanac, p. 322)*

House Action

In the 101st Congress, the House Interior Committee approved HR 2392 on May 10, 1989, over the objections of committee Republicans who said the measure would have infringed upon claim-holders' property rights. The bill gained House approval on June 1, 1989. *(1989 Almanac, p. 687)*

The House measure would have required the Interior secretary to determine which claims were valid and sort them into three categories, depending on the degree to what extent the claimants had met patent requirements.

Under the House bill, only about 7,000 acres would have been eligible to be sold for $2.50 per acre. The House bill would have cut off eligibility for claiming title to the land as of Jan. 24, 1989, as in the original Senate version. Under the other two categories of claims in the House bill, claim holders would not have been able to receive ownership of their claims. Instead, they could hold mining rights to the land in exchange for higher fees to the government.

The House bill would have allowed claim holders who had initiated a patent application by Jan. 24, 1989, to patent limited mineral rights for $2,000 per acre, vs. $2.50 per acre in the Senate bill.

The remaining claimants who had not applied for patents by Jan. 24, 1989, would have been required to spend $5,000 a year to "diligently develop" their claim and pay the government fees of 50 cents a year per acre during a 20-year lease. Under the Senate bill, they could have maintained the claim for a $550 annual fee or obtained a limited patent for fair market value.

Senate Action

The Senate Energy and Natural Resources Committee on March 8 approved a bill (S 30 — S Rept 101-259) that would have set different guidelines to claims to more than 250,000 acres of federal oil-shale land in three Western states. The committee had failed repeatedly to reach a consensus on the measure because of a dispute between Wirth and the committee's ranking Republican, Idaho's James A. McClure. Wirth wanted to cut off eligibility for claiming title to the land as of Jan. 25, 1989, the date the measure was introduced. But McClure initially wanted to give claimants up to 30 months to apply for a full patent to the federal land in Colorado, Wyoming and Utah.

In 1990, Wirth and McClure agreed on a compromise — though with reservations on both their parts. Under their agreement, the cutoff for applying for a patent would have been the date the committee approved the bill.

Under S 30, holders of valid oil-shale claims who had not filed a patent application could have obtained a limited patent to oil shale only for fair market value or they could have maintained the claim for a $550 annual fee.

McClure said he was not happy with the annual fee or the limited patent provision, but wanted to end the controversy. Wirth also had misgivings but said he was satisfied that at least "the cup is half full."

Despite the Wirth-McClure accord, Armstrong continued to oppose the measure. He placed an informal "hold" on floor consideration of the bill because he could not obtain assurances that the Senate bill would not have been changed in conference with the House. ■

Regulatory Breaks for Alternative Power

A last-minute controversy over a power line in California delayed but did not derail legislation providing regulatory breaks to alternative-power producers. The power line imbroglio was the last of several that had threatened to kill the bill, but the problem was worked out before Congress adjourned on Oct. 28.

The measure was finally approved by the Senate on Oct. 27 and the House a few hours later in the early morning hours of Oct. 28. President Bush signed the bill (HR 4808 — PL 101-575) on Nov. 15.

The legislation removed limits on the size of wind, solar, geothermal and waste-based power plants that could take advantage of breaks first provided only to small plants under the Public Utilities Regulatory Policies Act of 1978 (PL 95-617).

Another provision, inserted by Senate Energy Committee Chairman J. Bennett Johnston, D-La., eased license requirements for private uranium enrichment facilities, including one planned for northern Louisiana.

Proponents in the House earlier in the session had attached the provisions of the alternative-energy bill to the budget-reconciliation measure. Conferees, though, killed the extraneous provision at the insistence of Sen. Wendell H. Ford, D-Ky., who was upset that a provision of his was killed.

Senate supporters of the legislation, meanwhile, had attached the provisions from their version (S 2415) to a global-warming bill in August.

BACKGROUND

Congress in 1978 enacted the Public Utility Regulatory Policies Act (PURPA) to attempt to foster the fledgling alternative-energy industry by exempting small producers from state and federal utility regulations and requiring existing local utilities to buy electricity from them. That law was enacted when the nation was looking for ways to maximize domestic power sources as it rebounded from its first major energy crisis and headed right into its second. *(1978 Almanac, p. 639)*

To appease utilities worried about unfair competition, Congress limited eligibility to alternative producers with only a small fraction of the capacity of the biggest conventional plants: 30 megawatts to 80 megawatts, depending on the technology involved, compared with 1,100 megawatts for big traditional plants.

The existing law and market forces fostered a growing alternative-energy industry, although it still provided just a small percentage of the nation's electricity needs.

A House Energy Committee staff memo in 1990 said that wind and solar energy producers nationwide had grown from "virtually nothing" in 1978 to 1,500 megawatts and 2,500 megawatts, respectively — "enough power each year for the residential needs of a city the size of San Francisco." Likewise, geothermal production (tapping heat from beneath the Earth's surface) increased from 900 megawatts in 1980 to 2,600 in 1989.

Nevertheless, only about 2 percent of the generating capacity installed from fiscal 1980 to 1988 came from all renewable sources, according to the Congressional Research Service.

Renewable-energy companies said they needed more room to grow. The law's limits did not bother them in years past because all alternative-energy plants were small; by 1990 bigger plants were technologically feasible.

HOUSE COMMITTEE ACTION

The House Energy Committee approved HR 4808 by voice vote on July 17 (H Rept 101-885) to boost the alternative-energy industry by removing size restrictions on solar, wind and geothermal power plants that qualified for regulatory benefits. Caps for other, more environmentally hazardous renewable energy sources, such as municipal waste-based systems would be retained. The Subcommittee on Energy and Power had approved the bill on June 14.

The Bush administration contended the House position did not go far enough. The Energy Department asked Congress to lift the limit for all alternative-energy sources — including waste coal and oil, solid waste and "biomass," such as lawn clippings. The administration wanted Congress to give equal opportunity to all alternative-energy producers.

But Energy Subcommittee Chairman Philip R. Sharp, D-Ind., the bill's sponsor, decided that eliminating the limit for all alternative producers could raise more pollution problems than he wanted to deal with in what was a simple, one-page bill, an aide said. Sharp's position was supported by environmental lobbyists.

SENATE ACTION

The Senate was dealing with a companion bill (S 2415) that differed significantly from the House measure. Unlike the House bill, the Senate measure included companies that used waste products to produce energy. Environmentalists opposed the addition, fearing increased pollution from burning waste. The Senate bill also contained a sunset provision forcing producers to act by Dec. 31, 1992, to take advantage of the expanded breaks.

Pete V. Domenici, R-N.M., wanted to attach S 2415 to a global-warming bill (S 324) that the Energy Committee had approved in May. But Louisiana's Johnston, chairman of the Senate Energy Committee, objected.

Johnston, a powerful proponent of Louisiana's oil interests, was skeptical of solar and wind energy. He believed that renewable-energy sources remained worthy of some regulatory breaks, but he questioned whether public utilities should be forced to purchase their product. "Why, if you're competitive, do you need to force people to buy you?" asked an aide in summing up Johnston's concern.

On Aug. 4, though, the Senate passed S 324 by voice vote and attached the alternative-energy provisions. *(Global warming, p. 307)*

The Senate Energy Committee, meanwhile, was trying to use the alternative-energy bill as a bargaining chip to force House action on another of its top legislative priorities — a bill (S 83) sponsored by Ford to revamp the Energy Department's uranium enrichment enterprise, which sold fuel to nuclear power producers.

The committee voted 18-0 to approve S 2415, and the full Senate passed the bill on Sept. 26 by voice vote. When the Senate approved S 2415, Ford attached the text of S 83 to it. The uranium enrichment measure had passed the Senate on July 20, 1989. *(1989 Almanac, p. 690)*

Senators linked the two measures to spur the House to act on S 83. The uranium enrichment measure, however, faced stiff opposition in the House, so members there refused to act on S 2415, as long as it had the provisions attached. *(Uranium enrichment, p. 310)*

HOUSE FLOOR ACTION

Continuing the multipronged attack to get alternative-energy legislation enacted, House members tried attaching their alternative-energy bill to the fiscal 1991 deficit-cutting reconciliation bill (HR 5835). But as they were trying that, Ford did the same thing with his uranium bill.

House conferees on the budget bill refused to negotiate on Ford's uranium provisions, forcing them off the budget measure, so Ford rejected their alternative-energy measure, and it, too, was dropped from the final budget package.

And so, while alternative-energy legislation had proven that it enjoyed wide support in both chambers — the House and Senate approved versions of it twice each, but as part of different bills — the issue became mired in an unrelated brink-of-adjournment dispute among Congress' top energy lawmakers.

The next action came when the House passed its version (HR 4808) by voice vote Oct. 23. House Energy Committee members badly wanted to see the bill enacted. They had altered their measure substantially to make it more to the liking of the Senate Energy Committee, where Johnston was no fan of the proposal.

House members agreed to sunset the expanded breaks in four years, instead of making them permanent, as they had originally planned. The Senate version contained a two-year sunset. Moreover, House members agreed to include waste-based energy producers, something they were hesitant to do at first but later accepted. Johnston had earlier made the same change to his chamber's proposal when it was added to the global-warming bill.

Final Bids

The House made a final bid to get its bill enacted on Oct. 23, when members approved HR 4808 by voice vote. Seeking to pressure Ford into allowing it to become law, House members attached a provision dear to Johnston.

The new provision would make it much easier for several U.S. utilities and a European firm to get an operating license for a $750 million uranium enrichment plant they planned to build in northern Louisiana.

Johnston had been pushing a slightly less strict version of the licensing provision as part of other Senate bills, including Ford's uranium bill, but hopes for enactment had dimmed.

Ford, upset that his bill had died, threatened to hold up the new House alternative-energy bill, but backed off. That cleared the way for final action by the Senate.

But then another controversy emerged over a tiny provision added by George Miller, D-Calif., chairman of the House Interior Subcommittee on Water, Power and Offshore Energy Resources.

Miller wanted to block a new power line through the properties of some of his Contra Costa County constituents.

Miller used the bill to force the consortium of West Coast utilities behind the project to relocate the proposed power line at the behest of a group of landowners and local government officials.

Miller had first inserted a provision to require the utilities to use an existing power line right of way for the new line. Utilities involved in the project argued that they would have to spend more than $100 million to change their plans.

But they were afraid of derailing the alternative-energy bill, which they favored, or angering Johnston by killing the Louisiana provisions.

The controversy held up final approval of the bill late Oct. 26.

Miller finally agreed to a provision that merely rejected the proposed alignment and ordered the Energy Department, which was helping to oversee the project through the Western Area Power Administration, to submit a new one by Jan. 30, 1991. Congress would have to act by March 1 if it wanted to reject the new plan.

The bill was finally approved by the Senate on Oct. 27 and the House in the early morning hours of Oct. 28. ■

Hydrogen Fuel Research Program OK'd

Congress created an Energy Department hydrogen fuel research program and named it for the late Sen. Spark M. Matsunaga, D-Hawaii, who had been pressing the government to investigate hydrogen as an alternative energy source for years before his death April 15.

The House on Oct. 23 gave final approval to the bill (S 639), clearing the measure for President Bush. The Senate had approved the bill on Oct. 16. Both chambers acted by voice vote.

Bush signed the bill on Nov. 15 (PL 101-566).

The House action clearing the bill came just days after Congress approved a final energy and water projects spending bill for fiscal 1991 (HR 5019) that had been stripped of a $4 million earmark for hydrogen research.

The authorization bill called for spending $20 million for the new hydrogen research program in fiscal 1992-95. Removed from the final measure was a separate NASA program to investigate the use of hydrogen as a fuel for domestic aircraft. That provision had been in earlier versions of the bill, including one approved by the House on May 9 (HR 4521).

The Benefits of Hydrogen

Hydrogen was considered to have a very important potential role as an energy storage medium, especially for solar energy, which could be produced efficiently only during certain daylight hours — and at that, only when the sky was clear.

By 1990, however, the only widespread use of hydrogen as a fuel occurred in the space program, where there were no practical alternatives available. For other than space applications, the lower cost and convenience of more easily available fuels overwhelmed any advantages of hydrogen.

There was a growing feeling among some members of

Congress that any new applications for hydrogen would remain infeasible until the cost of producing hydrogen was reduced significantly.

The Energy Department carried out research and development on hydrogen as an energy medium under numerous programs, but the department did not have a consolidated effort to reduce the cost of producing hydrogen.

Matsunaga introduced S 639 on March 16, 1989, to support a strong federal research, development and demonstration program to develop low-cost hydrogen production technologies. He had been pushing similar legislation for the past decade, arguing that until the production cost of hydrogen was reduced, consumers would be denied the benefits of the alternative fuel, especially its environmental advantages.

Legislative Action

Two House Science subcommittees on April 4, 1990, separately approved legislation (HR 2793) to create a research program within the Energy Department to develop ways of using hydrogen as an energy source.

The Energy Research and Development Subcommittee gave the bill approval by voice vote during a morning session, followed by the Transportation, Aviation and Materials Subcommittee, also by voice vote, later that day.

Under the legislation, the Energy Department's hydrogen research program would receive $4 million in fiscal 1991, $5 million in 1992 and $6 million in 1993.

The authorization would be increased to $15 million in 1994 and $20 million in 1995.

Supporters of the legislation argued that liquefied hydrogen was a clean-burning and efficient fuel, but that research was needed to learn how to produce it cheaply.

Matsunaga died April 15. On April 18, the House Science Committee approved by voice vote different legislation (HR 4521) also to establish an Energy Department research program to increase the nation's ability to use hydrogen as a fuel (H Rept 101-474).

The House committee approved an amendment to rename the bill the Matsunaga Hydrogen Research and Development Act, after committee Chairman Robert A. Roe, D-N.J., noted Matsunaga's long interest in the issue.

In the Senate, the Energy and Natural Resources Committee on June 20 approved, 19-0, Matsunaga's bill (S 639) to establish programs to research and develop hydrogen as an alternative fuel (S Rept 101-385).

Under the bill, NASA would seek to develop hydrogen as a fuel for commercial aircraft. The Energy Department also would be required to develop technologies for producing and using the fuel.

The Energy Committee ordered S 639 reported as a substitute for HR 4521; the NASA provisions were removed and contained in a separate bill (S 2613) that was not enacted. ■

Energy Conservation, Efficiency Programs

Legislation to redefine national energy conservation goals and to promote state energy efficiency programs was signed into law by President Bush on Oct. 18. The measure (S 247 — PL 101-440) encouraged the efficient use of available energy sources by updating and widening the scope of Department of Energy (DOE) programs that funded state energy conservation initiatives.

Bill backers saw the legislation as useful in helping the nation become less dependent on foreign oil, a situation made more precarious by the Persian Gulf crisis.

The legislation, the State Energy Efficiency Programs Improvement Act, updated parts of the wide-ranging Energy Policy and Conservation Act (EPCA) enacted in 1975 (PL 94-163) following an energy scare in the nation brought on by escalating oil prices during the oil embargo of 1973. *(1975 Almanac, p. 223)*

S 247 updated provisions in the 1975 law authorizing the State and Local Assistance Programs (SLAP) by:

- Calling for statewide energy goals for the year 2000.
- Ordering a review of a funding formula used to allocate low-income weatherization financing.
- Ordering development and coordination of state emergency energy policies for times of low supply.

S 247 amended EPCA by requiring states seeking federal funds for conservation projects to set a goal of increasing statewide energy efficiency by 10 percent by the year 2000.

SLAP programs, administered through the DOE, provided states with federal funds for conservation programs such as low-income home weatherization, school and hospital energy saving projects, and statewide conservation training. The bill also required states to have comprehensive energy emergency policies in place for supply disruptions and to improve integration of state and local energy conservation programs.

S 247 also provided for a State Energy Advisory Board to advise the DOE on the efficiency of the state programs. The advisory board also provided the DOE with direct access to state energy program data.

The legislation also ordered the DOE to review and revise, if warranted, a formula it was using for determining the allocation of DOE Weatherization Program funds to states. The DOE was told to determine whether the funding formula should be revamped to give more weight to energy assistance for cooling.

The old formula had emphasized heating assistance, which meant warmer states stood to receive fewer funds. The DOE was also ordered to annually update the data banks that it used for allocating the funds.

The Senate Energy Committee approved S 247, 19-0, on Nov. 15, 1989 (S Rept 101-235). The full Senate passed the bill on Jan. 25, 1990, by voice vote.

The House moved more slowly on similar legislation (HR 711), which the Energy and Commerce Subcommittee on Energy and Power approved by a 14-1 vote June 14. The full committee approved the bill (H Rept 101-646) by voice vote June 19.

Committee members agreed to an amendment by Tom Tauke, R-Iowa, and Ron Wyden, D-Ore., allowing states greater flexibility to spend money granted for technical audits in hospitals and schools.

The full House, after inserting the language of HR 711, passed S 247 by voice vote Oct. 1. The Senate by voice vote cleared the House version Oct. 4. ■

Chapter 5

COMMERCE

1990 Farm Bill . . . 323
Great Lakes Ports . . . 338
Farm Bill Provisions . . . 342
Rural Development Aid . . . 352
Food Stamp Program . . . 354
Nutrition-Monitoring Bill . . . 355
Screwworm Bill . . . 355
Irrigation Subsidies . . . 356
Low-Cost Timber Sales . . . 358
Pesticide-Residue Regulation . . . 358
Mandated Family Leave Bill . . . 359
Veto Message . . . 361
Age Protection Bill . . . 362
Whistleblower Bill . . . 364
Job-Training Bill . . . 365
Displaced Homemakers Bill . . . 366
Pension Reversions . . . 367
Pension Benefit Guaranty Corporation . . . 368
Jobless Pay Increase Bill . . . 368
Unemployment Benefits . . . 368
Eastern Airlines Strike Veto . . . 369
Martin Named to Labor Department . . . 369
Cable Reregulation . . . 370
FCC Authorization . . . 372
Ads During Children's TV . . . 373
TV Violence . . . 374
Closed-Captioning Bill . . . 375
Radio Frequencies Shift . . . 376
Business Curbs on 'Baby Bells' . . . 377
Operator Services Rates . . . 378
'Junk Fax' Curbs . . . 379
FCC Minority Preference Policies . . . 379
Transporting Hazardous Materials . . . 380
'Backhauling' Limits . . . 382
Aviation Package . . . 384
Coast Guard Fees . . . 386
Airline Leveraged Buyouts . . . 388
Aviation Security Bills . . . 389
Airline Rights Bill . . . 389
Amtrak Reauthorization . . . 390
Veto Message . . . 391
Amtrak Waste Disposal . . . 392
Consumer Product Safety Commission . . . 393
SBA Bill . . . 395
Fastener Standards . . . 395
Fish Inspection Bill . . . 396
'Dolphin-Safe' Tuna Labeling . . . 399
Product Liability . . . 400
Insurance Antitrust Bill . . . 401
Hotel Fire Safety . . . 402
'Fire-Safe' Cigarettes . . . 402
Telemarketing Fraud . . . 402

Congress Enacts Lean Farm Package

Price supports frozen; subsidized acreage reduced

In a year when the farm economy was improving and the federal budget tightening, Congress worked out a deal on the omnibus, five-year farm bill to reauthorize crop subsidies, conservation and nutrition programs and to reduce projected federal subsidies by nearly $14 billion.

The farm bill (S 2830), cleared by the Senate on Oct. 25, was less generous than farm-state lawmakers had hoped it would be when deliberations began in the spring. But it passed both chambers by solid majorities shortly before the August recess and, after being held up to make spending cuts mandated by the congressional budget resolution, won final approval by similar majorities as the session neared an end.

In signing the measure (PL 101-624) on Nov. 28, President Bush said he was pleased that it would "continue the market-oriented shift" begun in the last farm bill, enacted in 1985 and due to expire at the end of 1990.

BOXSCORE

Legislation: Food, Agriculture, Conservation and Trade Act, PL 101-624 (S 2830).

Major action: Signed, Nov. 28. Conference report adopted by Senate, 60-36, Oct. 25; by House, 318-102, Oct. 23. HR 3950 passed by House, 327-91, Aug. 1; S 2830 passed by Senate, 70-21, July 27.

Reports: Conference report (H Rept 101-916). Agriculture (H Rept 101-569, Part I; Supplemental, Part III); Foreign Affairs (Part II); Education and Labor (Part IV); Ways and Means (Part V). Agriculture, Nutrition and Forestry (S Rept 101-357).

The 1990 bill itself did not reduce subsidy levels or make other cuts, but froze farm price- and income-support rates at their existing levels. As part of the omnibus budget-reconciliation act, however, Congress approved provisions to reduce the overall cost of the farm bill from $54 billion to just over $40 billion. *(Budget reconciliation, p. 138; provisions: Title I, p. 141)*

"Almost all of those things that are good for agriculture come in the farm bill. All of the pain comes in reconciliation," said Richard G. Lugar of Indiana, the ranking Republican on the Senate Agriculture Committee.

As in the past, the farm bill amended and added to — but did not repeal — permanent enabling legislation of 1938 and 1949, authorizing programs through 1995 for commodity price supports, agricultural exports, soil conservation, farm credit, and agricultural research. *(Farm bill provisions, p. 342)*

The bill also reauthorized the federal food stamp program for five years and somewhat strengthened penalties for fraud and misuse of food coupons. *(Food stamps, p. 354)*

Most of the savings from the bill — an estimated $7 billion over five years — was to come from putting into law the so-called triple base acreage-reduction plan. Under the plan, 15 percent of farmland was to be ineligible for crop subsidy payments, though farmers could grow other crops on the land and take those crops to market.

Farm-state lawmakers gained one big concession in the final conference: a provision that the secretary of Agriculture was to increase export subsidies and loans and ease production restrictions if the U.S. did not achieve a reduction in world agriculture subsidies in the so-called Uruguay Round of negotiations on the international General Agreement on Tariffs and Trade (GATT). *(GATT, p. 209)*

The measure also contained important environmental provisions, including a 1 million-acre wetlands reserve, mandated recordkeeping for farmers' use of dangerous chemicals and national standards for foods labeled as "organically grown." But environmentalists lost on one of their key fights — a "circle of poison" provision to restrict the export of banned pesticides that were used on crops abroad and then carried back into the United States as residue on foods.

In other major provisions, the farm bill consolidated rural development programs in the Department of Agriculture and overhauled the Food for Peace (PL 480) program. *(Rural development, p. 352; Food for Peace, p. 803)*

BACKGROUND

Farm bills set federal policy, usually over a four- or five-year period, for a host of programs, including commodity price and income supports, rural housing and farm lending, food stamps and school lunches, agricultural research, export subsidies, and soil and water conservation.

History of Federal Role

The programs dated to President Franklin D. Roosevelt's New Deal, when protective federal intervention was deemed essential to shore up farm income. The most important congressional enactment, the Agricultural Adjustment Act of 1938, established the basic price-support and production control system for non-perishable agricultural commodities that remained in existence more than 50 years later.

The Agricultural Act of 1949 revised the system by giving the secretary of Agriculture more flexibility in setting price-support levels. Passage of the legislation in effect reflected a middle position in the debate that Congress would revisit time and time again between those who favored government management of farm prices and those who advocated a free market for agricultural products.

Democratic presidents — Harry S Truman, John F. Kennedy and Lyndon B. Johnson — all favored continuation of the New Deal policies of price supports and production controls, while Republican Dwight D. Eisenhower steered a middle course of maintaining price supports at lower levels. *(Congress and the Nation Vol. I, p. 665)*

By the late 1960s, however, political and economic conditions were threatening the survival of the New Deal-era mechanisms. The increased mechanization of U.S. agriculture was contributing to the exodus of many small farmers, which in turn led to diminishing political clout for the

Farm Belt in Congress. The era of Republican presidents beginning with Richard M. Nixon's six years in the White House initiated a series of steps away from government management of farm prices that continued under Democrat Jimmy Carter and that Republican Ronald Reagan vowed to accelerate in the 1980s.

Under Nixon, the Agricultural Act of 1970 (PL 91-524) maintained the system of crop and price controls, but added a "set-aside" program that allowed farmers to be compensated for taking a portion of their land out of production and then to raise whatever they wanted on the remaining land. The Agriculture and Consumer Protection Act of 1973 (PL 93-86) replaced the old support prices for the major commodities of cotton, wheat, corn and other feed grains with lower "target prices" that would reimburse farmers only in the event of sharp market-price drops.

Carter, a peanut farmer before turning to politics, continued his Republican predecessors' movement toward lower price supports and reduced interference in farmers' planting decisions. He repeatedly threatened to veto the 1977 farm bill if it cost too much. And he ended his administration on a sour note by imposing a grain embargo against the Soviet Union — a foreign policy move that generated a domestic backlash among the farmers who had made the United States the world's largest grain supplier.

Reagan capitalized on the backlash by forswearing use of grain embargoes as a foreign policy weapon, but increased the rhetorical push for reducing federal support for agriculture and moving farmers toward the free market. Despite that rhetoric, the 1981 farm bill (PL 97-98) crafted by Congress and signed by Reagan maintained price supports and even added a new support program for sugar. *(1981 Almanac, p. 535)*

Outlays under the 1981 bill were projected at the time to be about $11 billion over its four-year duration. But a devastating farm depression forced the government to buy up huge amounts of surplus commodities and support farmers' incomes with artificially high prices — at a final, four-year cost of $54.7 billion.

In the midst of that depression, Congress in 1985 produced a farm bill (PL 99-198) that lowered artificially high prices, but kept a lifeline to struggling farmers through massive income-support payments. The bill probably did more to nurse American agriculture back to health than any collection of government programs since the Great Depression — but again, at a high cost: $88.6 billion over five years. *(1985 Almanac, p. 517)*

'A Real Addiction'

Yet even though many farmers regained their vigor after some devastating years in the 1980s, Congress did not face an easy time as it began to work on the 1990 farm bill.

The farm program did not work so logically:

- It could seem stunningly generous and, simultaneously, soberly frugal. More taxpayer dollars had been spent on agriculture during the previous five years than at any time in U.S. history. Yet agriculture spending had recently become the fastest shrinking portion of the federal budget.
- Even bad weather could be a boon. In 1988, the worst drought in half a century scorched millions of acres of cropland across the country. In 1989, there was more terrible weather and crop losses in many regions. Yet total farm income climbed to record levels. *(1989 Almanac, p. 387)*
- Myth did not match reality. The farm program was often depicted as a safety net to see farmers through the hard times. Yet in 1989, 82 percent of all growers of major crops such as wheat, corn and rice collected federal subsidies. And government payments as a percentage of their annual family budgets jumped from 8.1 percent in 1980 to 31.7 percent in 1988.

By the beginning of 1990, massive government assistance had put color back in agriculture's cheeks. The agriculture economy was rebounding. The value of U.S. exports was again above $40 billion after dropping below $30 billion four years before. Farmland values had revived and farm foreclosures had slowed substantially.

By then, even the $10 billion to $11 billion agriculture budget looked positively spartan — and certainly more defensible — compared with several years before, when farm program spending soared as high as $25.8 billion.

But the bargain had been doubly Faustian: The web of cash that fueled the recovery bound farmers to government programs as never before. So important had farm subsidies become to their economic well-being that many farmers who once looked askance at government assistance could no longer afford to refuse it.

And farm-state lawmakers, having seen farmers through the lean years with unparalleled generosity, were using their success to justify preserving the same level of benefits, despite continuing pressure to cut the federal deficit. "There is a real addiction," said Robert L. Thompson, dean of agriculture at Purdue University. "Farm programs are not unlike cocaine."

That addiction was the most troublesome legacy of the 1985 farm bill. Yet the bill had been so successful in other ways that discussions about dismantling or redirecting federal agriculture programs, the subject of plenty of yeasty ideological debate throughout the laissez-faire Reagan era, had become moribund in the Bush administration.

Political Considerations

Many in Congress, particularly Republicans, preferred it that way. The 1985 farm bill debate was a brutally partisan affair and a rallying point for populist Democrats. They attacked Senate Republicans, several of whom were up for re-election in 1986, as co-conspirators with the Reagan White House in a plot to extricate the federal government from agriculture in the midst of the worst farm depression in years.

Republicans spent the year trying to prove, as Sen. Bob Dole of Kansas put it, that the Democrats were not the only "self-appointed protectors of American farmers."

They did not fully succeed. Three Republicans from farm states were defeated for re-election — Mack Mattingly of Georgia, James Abdnor of South Dakota, and Mark Andrews of North Dakota — and the GOP lost control of the Senate. Each of the victorious Democrats — Wyche Fowler Jr. of Georgia, Tom Daschle of South Dakota and Kent Conrad of North Dakota — became members of the Senate Agriculture Committee.

After such a bloodletting, there was an understandable wariness in both parties about renewing the farm fight in 1990. "I doubt that the debate on the 1990 farm bill will be as divisive as it was in 1985," said Patrick J. Leahy, D-Vt., chairman of the Senate Agriculture Committee.

Little Interest in Major Changes

Given the apparent tranquillity in farm country, there was little interest in Congress in making drastic changes in the basic structure of farm price supports as they were established in the 1985 farm bill.

Until then, a farmer could rely on the federal government dutifully buying most of his surplus crops of wheat, corn, cotton, rice and other subsidized commodities. The 1981 farm bill, crafted in a time of rapid inflation, had created an arbitrary system of constantly rising price supports. Although it forced the government to buy huge amounts of surplus commodities, the system helped limit supply on the U.S. market and kept prices up. In this way, the government indirectly supported farmers' incomes with artificially high prices.

The 1985 farm bill switched course, allowing price supports to fall more in line with lower world-market prices. Essentially, it told the farmer to get what he could for his crop on the open market. The federal government would not buy up so much of his surplus anymore. But, if it happened that his profit was lower than what Congress thought it ought to be, a check would arrive in the mail to make up the difference.

Not surprisingly, Congress' notion of what farmers ought to get for their crops — the "target price" — had been a good deal more generous than the market's. The 1985 farm bill kept target prices relatively high and had brought them down gradually only in recent years. As a result, direct income support to farmers — known as deficiency payments — increased dramatically.

The fundamental shift in the 1985 farm bill — removing the artificially high government support on commodity prices — stanched the hemorrhaging of the Farm Belt. Foreign producers could no longer easily undersell U.S. commodity exports. "We had taken a lot of the risk out of international agriculture" in 1981, said consultant William G. Lesher, who was the Agriculture Department's chief economist during the Reagan administration. "But the 1985 farm bill signaled that times had changed. We spent billions, but we got something for it."

As a result, the Bush White House was not about to fall on its sword over economic principles the way the Reagan administration did in proposing to severely restrict farm payments. Bush and Agriculture Secretary Clayton Yeutter wanted to give Democrats no grist for partisan attacks.

Still, they did have the ongoing international trade negotiations to consider. The U.S. position at the GATT talks was that "trade distorting" agriculture subsidies should be eliminated worldwide.

Although an agreement on that principle seemed increasingly unlikely at the beginning of the year, Yeutter, the U.S. trade representative under Reagan, had staked his reputation on making some sort of groundbreaking deal with the United States' main agricultural nemeses, the European Community and Japan.

But U.S. producers were loath to relinquish even a portion of their subsidies without a comparable sacrifice from producers abroad. Suggestions to do so drew cries from farmers that the U.S. was engaged in "unilateral disarmament." So, in its proposals for the 1990 farm bill, the administration did not even bother to suggest it, even though that was the official U.S. policy at the GATT talks.

ADMINISTRATION PROPOSAL

At the beginning of the year, the Bush administration offered Congress a pragmatic package of farm policy recommendations for the 1990s, but the package left out specific instructions on how to cut agriculture subsidies, perhaps the most contentious issue in the 1990 debate.

Instead of the usual practice of sending Congress formal legislation to retool farm programs, Agriculture Secretary Yeutter on Feb. 6 offered a multitude of recommendations — some detailed and some not.

'All Our Necks on the Line'

Yeutter called for more flexibility for farmers receiving subsidies to respond to market signals and proposed modest changes in federal farm policy. But he declined to give much insight into the matter of most concern to farm-state lawmakers: how farm subsidies should be cut in order to reduce the deficit. Nor did he offer an overall price tag the administration would accept for farm programs over the following five years.

In so doing, the administration embarked on a strategy intended to sustain its leverage in the upcoming farm bill debate. The idea was to avoid taking hard positions early in the debate and to keep the administration from looking like an enemy of the politically popular farm program.

The strategy seemed to work. No political uproar confronted the unveiling of the Bush plan, as it did in 1985 when the Reagan administration proposed dismantling federal farm programs. To lawmakers, many of whom predicted that farm subsidies would continue to decline, the administration's vagueness on farm spending was unnerving. They wanted specifics.

"All our necks will be on the line, but yours first," Senate Agriculture Chairman Leahy suggested to Yeutter at a Feb. 7 hearing on the farm bill proposals. Yeutter promised to negotiate the budget details with the 19-member Agriculture Committee quickly. "I want to make sure there are 20 necks out there, instead of just one," he said.

Stressing Flexibility

When the administration did stick out its neck, it often found members of Congress willing to take a whack, as they did with Yeutter's detailed proposals to loosen restrictions governing participation in federal farm programs that deterred farmers from planting certain crops such as soybeans — even when the market price was attractive.

Giving farmers the flexibility to respond better to market conditions promised to be the major thrust of the farm bill. The administration made its flexibility proposal the centerpiece of its recommendations.

"Farmers throughout the country feel that the ability to handle their operations in the most efficient manner is hampered," Yeutter said. "They have to plant for the program and not for the market."

To correct the problem, the administration proposed overhauling the existing base acreage system. That system determined what share of farmers' land was eligible for federal farm payments. Producers of so-called program crops (wheat, feed grains, cotton and rice) were assigned a base acreage for specific crops, which was calculated as a five-year average of plantings on their farms.

If a farmer planted a crop other than that which he had a base for, he lost part of his subsidy payments. His base also shrank in the future. Crops such as corn paid such attractive government benefits that potential alternatives such as soybeans were not comparably profitable to plant, even when the market price was high.

The administration proposed to substitute a system much like the one in place during the 1970s. Instead of a base acreage for each crop, a farmer would have one overall base. It would include all the acreage a farmer planted to any program crop as well as his acreage planted to oilseeds (soybeans, sunflowers and rapeseed).

On that base, called a Normal Crop Acreage, the farmer

could plant any of the program crops or oilseeds in any proportion. Thus a farmer with a 300-acre farm who had a 100-acre wheat base and a 100-acre corn base could potentially devote all his acres to corn. Or he could plant half to wheat and half to soybeans. If he wanted, he could even grow 300 acres of canola, an oilseed.

Under the administration plan, the farmer's support check from the government would remain the same — regardless of what proportion he planted. The farmer would still receive the subsidy payment for 100 acres of wheat and 100 acres of corn, even if he grew neither crop.

Proposal Criticized

While most farm-state lawmakers were also calling for flexibility, the administration plan proved controversial. Some lawmakers worried about the symbolism of removing the link between support payments and actual production. Doing so made government support for farmers look much more like welfare, much less like a program to ensure a stable food supply.

Farmers "don't want a welfare check," said Daschle.

Yeutter responded that the administration did not propose to give them one. "I don't see the program as being at all comparable to a welfare program," Yeutter said.

Other lawmakers objected to the administration plan on more parochial grounds. In particular, some soybean growers worried that flexibility provisions would lead other farmers to plant more soybeans, thus lowering the price they received. Some soybean growers were asking Congress to enact a complicated income-support program to cushion them from the ill effects of flexibility. "We're going to have to do something for soybeans beyond just flexible planting," Christopher S. Bond, R-Mo., told Yeutter.

Environmental Issues

Flexibility was also a key element of the administration's proposals for dealing with environmental problems resulting from agriculture. Allow farmers to respond better to market signals, Yeutter argued, and they would become more efficient and frugal in their use of synthetic pesticides and fertilizers. They would rotate their crops more, too. Ultimately, the environment would benefit, he said.

The administration also called for offering farmers incentives to become better environmental stewards. New environmental controls, as called for by some environmental groups, were not the administration's answer. "I don't happen to think that regulatory demands are the best way to go about dealing with these issues," Yeutter said.

The administration proposed extending the Conservation Reserve Program (CRP), under which farmers were paid to take environmentally fragile land out of production. New land enrolled in the CRP would have to meet tougher erosion-control standards if returned to production.

Also, the CRP would be reoriented to deal with groundwater contamination problems and wetlands loss. Farmers would be paid to withdraw land susceptible to groundwater contamination from production. Existing cropped wetlands would be eligible for CRP payments beyond 1990, the deadline for enrolling fragile land in the program. Farmers who agreed to take the land permanently out of production would be offered payments.

Other Areas

Among other areas in which the administration made recommendations were:

- **Loan rates.** The administration wanted to set all loan rates — the price at which the government provided loans to farmers to enable them to hold their crops for later sale — using the same formula. Specifically, the administration called for loan rates for each program crop and soybeans to be set at 75 percent to 85 percent of the average price for the commodity over the last five years. The 1985 farm bill established different methods for determining loan rates.
- **Acreage Reduction Programs (ARPs).** A change was proposed in the way the federal government determined how much land to idle to control production and limit budget outlays. Instead of ARPs being required when year-end commodity stocks reached a certain level, the administration proposed a broader criterion to determine set-aside levels: how much of a commodity the Agriculture Department projected would be used domestically and in export markets, in addition to year-end stock levels.

For wheat and feed grains, if the ratio of ending stocks to use for the preceding year was estimated to be over 40 percent for wheat and 25 percent for corn, the ARP level would be 12.5 percent to 20 percent of each farmer's base acreages.

If the stocks-to-use ratio was 40 percent or less for wheat and 25 percent or less for corn, the ARP level would be 0 percent to 12.5 percent. The Agriculture secretary would have discretion to set the actual ARP within the established ranges.

ARPs would be used to achieve a stocks-to-use ratio of 30 percent for cotton and 20 percent for rice.

- **Disaster assistance.** The administration proposed to scrap the federally subsidized crop insurance program and rely exclusively on direct disaster payments for farmers whose crops were damaged by the weather. Most crops would be eligible.

Farmers would be eligible for the payments in counties where harvests fell 65 percent below normal. Individual farmers would be paid disaster benefits for any shortfall in their output below 60 percent of the county average yield. Producers would receive 65 percent of the average market price for the last three years for each eligible commodity.

- **Farm credit.** The administration also proposed broadly restructuring the Farmers Home Administration (FmHA) lending priorities, targeting "socially disadvantaged" and beginning farmers, drastically cutting back direct FmHA lending and restricting opportunities for restructuring debt. As did the Reagan administration, Bush proposed shifting FmHA lending from direct to guaranteed loans.
- **Food stamps.** The administration proposed reauthorizing the food stamp program at a level sufficient to provide current services. Several provisions cracking down on fraud and abuse in nutrition programs were also proposed, and special grants would be offered to nonprofit groups to test ways of extending food stamp benefits to the homeless.

HOUSE COMMITTEE ACTION

It took 85 days, but the House Agriculture Committee on June 14 finally completed work on a 1990 farm bill that acknowledged there was no money for a major policy change — and little sentiment for it among farmers.

Working all day June 13 and early into the next morning, the House committee finished deliberations on its massive bill (HR 3950), an omnibus measure to reauthorize most farm and nutrition programs for five more years.

The committee tried to make sure the bill cast a reassuring environmental aura and was within budget, if only to ward off the attacks of farm program skeptics when it went to the House floor. In general, the bill froze support levels for major commodities, such as wheat, corn, cotton and rice, for the following five years.

Higher Support Prices Rejected

The biggest fight in the committee — over the fundamental direction of U.S. farm policy — had ended May 24 with the defeat of a group of junior Democrats who had hoped to go home for the Memorial Day recess promising farmers large increases in crop prices.

Senior members warned that the plan could return agriculture to its mid-1980s' woes, when constantly increasing price supports caused U.S. commodity exports to plunge and forced the government to buy the huge crop surpluses.

Upper-tier Democrats joined a nearly united bloc of Republicans to vote down the plan, which was put forward by Iowa Democrat Dave Nagle. It would have reversed the course established in the 1985 farm bill, which brought U.S. prices more in line with lower world market prices and kept a lifeline to struggling farmers by providing billions of dollars in direct income-support payments.

"The choice was whether you go back to the 1981-1985 system in which the government raised prices and then tried to deal with the consequences. Our view is that the consequences would have been very adverse," said Deputy Under Secretary of Agriculture John B. Campbell.

Nagle said some estimates showed that as many as 500,000 farmers would leave agriculture over the following five years if Congress merely froze support levels. "I don't want the blood of those farmers who leave their farms on my hands," he said.

But senior committee members recalled the effects of raising price-support levels above international prices. "If you raise the loan rate over the market price, you will not raise farm income — you will lower farm income," said Kansas Republican Pat Roberts.

The amendment was rejected by a vote of 17-28. Most of the Democrats voting for the amendment were not in Congress when the 1985 bill was written. The only Republican to vote with Nagle was Montana's Ron Marlenee.

The committee was able to resolve the most controversial part of the bill, the commodity programs, after disposing of the Nagle amendment. Lawmakers voted to retain the thrust of the 1985 farm bill by freezing support rates for crops such as wheat, corn, cotton and rice, while giving farmers modest new freedom to rotate their crops without losing eligibility for the same level of government subsidies. The bill also established an inexpensive subsidy program for growers of soybeans and other oilseeds.

Wheat, Feed Grains and Soybeans

The Agriculture Committee had to rip up its wish list in order to comply with the budget and insulate the 1990 farm bill from attack.

Committee leaders asked members May 17 to revoke nearly $14 billion in subsidy increases that had been proposed during subcommittee markups in April. After some anguished protests, lawmakers appeared willing to relent, even though it dampened their election-year hopes to increase payments to farmers. The leadership plan froze support rates for major crops, such as wheat, corn, cotton and rice.

"We think that is the best protection" against opponents of the farm program, said Dan Glickman, D-Kan., chairman of the Subcommittee on Wheat, Soybeans and Feed Grains.

In his budget for fiscal 1991, President Bush called for cuts of $1.5 billion in farm subsidies. Administration officials never said explicitly what price tag they would accept for the five-year farm bill, but they implied that Bush would sign a five-year bill costing about $53 billion.

Over the previous two months, House Agriculture subcommittees had adopted a number of proposals to increase payments to farmers:

- Target prices — the support levels Congress set to guarantee farmers a minimum income — would increase roughly 10 percent over the following five years for wheat and feed grains under a plan adopted March 29. Target prices had declined by the same amount since 1987. The Bush administration said sending them back upward would cost $6.5 billion in 1991-95.
- Loan rates — the per-bushel subsidy rate at which the government provided short-term loans — would increase between 7 cents and 30 cents for wheat and feed grains under the subcommittee plan. Loan rates had come down dramatically since 1985. Increasing them over the following five years would cost $1.1 billion and could make U.S. commodity prices less competitive internationally, according to administration officials.

But House members finally heeded warnings that their colleagues on the floor were not in the mood to accept a more generous farm program.

New York Democrat Charles E. Schumer and Texas Republican Dick Armey were putting together a coalition to cut spending when the farm bill came to the floor. But, Glickman said, "it's not Armey and it's not Schumer" who concern the committee. "It's kind of an attitude among members that we are going to be a little more under siege than we have in the past."

A task force created by committee Chairman E. "Kika" de la Garza, D-Texas, recommended that the committee freeze target prices for major commodities at 1990 levels for the next five years and limit dairy program spending to existing levels. A soybean marketing loan would be established but at a rate of about $5.25 a bushel, low enough to minimize the cost to the government.

Aides and lawmakers who attended a May 17 committee caucus said members agreed to accept the package even though it was a far cry from the increases that many of them had sought. "I feel we are not meeting the needs of the producer," said Indiana Democrat Jim Jontz, whose idea to tie government support rates to increases in the cost of production was eventually dropped.

Lawmakers also agreed to slightly loosen government rules that required farmers to plant the same crop year after year to remain eligible for government payments.

Under the task force's recommendations, farmers would be allowed to plant any mix of program crops — wheat, feed grains, cotton, rice, and oilseeds, such as soybeans or sunflowers — on 20 percent of their land reserved for subsidized crops. The idea, known as "flexibility," was to encourage farmers to rotate crops and respond to market signals. But farmers would not receive subsidy payments on that 20 percent of their land.

Administration officials applauded the committee for reducing its subsidy proposals, which would trim about $10 billion of previously approved subsidy expansions. "All in all, this has been a major improvement," said the Agriculture Department's Campbell.

The administration still wanted much more flexibility.

But the subject caused all sorts of regional and philosophical divisions on the committee, because allowing farmers to plant more of a commodity in response to high market prices created competition that hurt producers already planting that crop.

Soybeans caused similar problems. In the South, where it was more expensive and less profitable to grow soybeans, farmers wanted a loan rate of about $6.25. But according to lawmakers and aides, no one on the committee was willing to use part of the subsidies that went to other crops to pay for a higher loan rate for soybeans.

"There's no money for soybeans unless you take it out of other commodities," said Jerry Huckaby, D-La..

Sugar Program

The House committee's action did not solve all the problems with the commodity section. The Bush administration remained bitterly opposed to several changes in the government sugar program.

The committee already had done a lot to overcome opposition to the sugar program, but it was not enough to satisfy the administration. During deliberations May 23, the committee removed a provision that would have tied price supports for domestic sugar — at the time, 18 cents a pound — to increases in the Consumer Price Index.

To secure the support of the corn sweetener industry, Huckaby agreed to scale back a proposal that had been approved April 19 by the Rice, Cotton and Sugar Subcommittee, which he chaired. The proposal would have imposed marketing controls on both the sugar and corn sweetener industries during times of overproduction.

An unusual coalition had united behind Huckaby's byzantine plan, including the usually protectionist domestic cane and beet-sugar industries, as well as their longtime rivals, the Caribbean and Central American nations that had long complained about the stiff U.S. import barriers.

The battle lines, though not altogether clear, radiated outward from Capitol Hill, crossed most of the Farm Belt and extended far overseas.

The corn sweetener industry was pitted against sugar cane and sugar-beet growers and processors. All of them were arrayed against soft drink and candy companies, which wanted lower sugar prices.

Meanwhile, Caribbean nations were competing with the rest of the sugar-exporting world for special access to the restricted U.S. market, while the Bush administration and sugar program critics in Congress were battling the program's dedicated defenders on the Agriculture Committee.

Weeks of negotiations among these various forces produced Huckaby's plan to overhaul the sugar program. He proposed to loosen the sharp restrictions on sugar imports that Congress had forced on the administration in the 1985 farm bill. He also wanted to raise the federal price-support levels for domestic sugar even though U.S. prices were already well above world prices.

But there remained bitter opposition from several quarters, including the Bush administration. Administration officials did not want Congress to adopt more measures to protect U.S. sugar producers because they feared that it would undermine the GATT negotiations in Geneva.

Huckaby's bill, however, contained three such measures: The first would have barred any nation that imported Cuban sugar from exporting sugar to the United States. Countries affected would have included Mexico and Canada, according to administration officials.

A second provision would have provided Caribbean Basin countries — along with other sugar-exporting nations with per-capita incomes of less than $1,500 — a 5-cent premium on sugar they sent to the United States for refining and re-export.

Administration officials said the 5-cent premium was merely an attempt to buy the support of Caribbean exporters for a proposal that GATT would bar. And they argued that the plan could prompt retaliation by other sugar-exporting nations that relied on U.S. sales.

In a third attempt to protect U.S. sugar producers, Huckaby proposed making the price-support program even more generous. Since 1985, U.S. sugar prices had been supported at roughly 21 cents a pound — a support price of 18 cents plus a 3-cent "differential" for transportation costs. The world price, meanwhile, had fluctuated from a low of $4.04 in 1985 to $14.03 in 1989.

Huckaby's bill, beginning in 1992, would have increased the U.S. support price on a scale pegged to the Consumer Price Index, the government's annual inflation gauge. According to the Congressional Budget Office (CBO), that inflation rate would run slightly more than 4 percent a year over the following five years.

As the bill headed to the full committee and the House floor, there was the ever-present threat that Huckaby's coalition could collapse. "I believe we have what can best be termed a tenuous agreement among the sweetener industry," said Minnesota's Arlan Stangeland, the subcommittee's ranking Republican.

Corn industry officials saw the marketing controls as an effort to curtail their growth, which had been substantial during the 1980s — largely at the expense of sugar cane and beet growers. Of most concern to the industry were the limits on high-fructose corn syrup, which had a 45 percent share of the sweetener market.

When his plan went to the full Agriculture Committee, Huckaby agreed to remove the controls on all corn sweeteners except crystalline fructose, which was a relatively minor part of the corn sweetener market. Sales would be capped at 200,000 tons during years when marketing controls were in effect for the sugar industry.

Among other changes, the committee removed the provision that would have barred any nation that imported Cuban sugar from exporting sugar to the United States, agreed to scale back a program to boost imports of Caribbean sugar for refining and re-export that would be financed by an assessment on domestic sugar and fructose, and removed a provision requiring import quotas on sugar-containing products.

But the administration still opposed the sugar section because, officials said, it could no longer be operated without cost to the federal government, it would violate international trading rules and it would provide disaster payments to sugar cane farmers in Louisiana whose crops had been damaged by freezing.

Administration officials said the farm bill had too far to go along the legislative pathway to be in danger of a veto yet. But unless Congress addressed administration concerns, said Campbell, "sugar could be the issue that tips the balance for an otherwise signable bill."

Dairy Production Problems

The dairy program was also a sore spot for the committee. During deliberations May 22, the committee voted to set a five-year floor on the government price support level at $10.10 per hundredweight, the existing level.

But lawmakers were split on how to handle the dairy

industry's recurring overproduction problem.

Under the bill, the price-support level would increase by at least 25 cents if government purchases of dairy products, which were used to support the price, fell below 3.5 billion pounds in a year.

If purchases exceeded 7 billion pounds a year beginning in 1992, the Agriculture secretary would have authority to impose marketing controls on the dairy industry. The idea was to eliminate the incentive for dairy farmers to produce pound after pound of surplus.

A compromise worked out by Dairy Subcommittee Chairman Charles W. Stenholm, D-Texas, and the subcommittee's ranking Republican, Steve Gunderson of Wisconsin, was adopted by the committee. That came after the defeat of competing plans offered by Harold L. Volkmer, D-Mo., and Tim Johnson, D-S.D.

The Stenholm-Gunderson plan had the virtue of vagueness. The dairy industry was uncomfortable with rigid quota schemes to control overproduction and with assessments on producers. So the Stenholm-Gunderson plan did not specify how the secretary was supposed to control production; it required him to study the matter and report back to Congress. Most lawmakers expected that the final mechanism would involve some sort of so-called two-tier pricing.

That meant a dairy farmer would get the support price of at least $10.10 per hundredweight for his milk until there was overproduction, after which some sort of brake would be applied — such as lowering the support price on additional milk produced.

At bottom, however, the dairy fight arose from the 1985 farm bill, which set dairy price supports on a downward path. Many dairy-state lawmakers wanted to end that decline — and even send price supports back up.

"If we can work within the budget to provide more money for farmers, I think we should be doing it, even if it means the consumer has to pay 10 cents more a gallon for milk," said Volkmer.

Volkmer's plan to overhaul the dairy price-support program and ensure farmers a higher price for milk had previously been approved on April 3 by the House Agriculture Subcommittee on Livestock, Dairy and Poultry despite warnings from the panel's leadership that it would not work and from the Bush administration that it was not needed.

In the process, the panel exacerbated regional splits in the dairy industry. "We still do not have the kind of consensus that will be necessary to pass the dairy title," said Stenholm after the subcommittee action.

"What is the crisis? Why are we . . . revamping the dairy program?" asked Virginia Democrat Jim Olin, who pointed out that milk surpluses and the cost of the program had come down since the last overhaul in 1985.

The "crisis" the dairy industry saw was caused by the falling dairy support price. To keep the price of dairy products above the world price, the government bought surplus butter, cheese and other milk products at a generally higher price established by Congress.

Under existing law, though, the price fell by 50 cents per 100 pounds every year that the government purchased more than 5 billion pounds of milk products. Since 1985, the support level had fallen $2 to $10.10.

However, the subcommittee took care of industry objections to the price cuts. Volkmer offered an amendment adopted by voice vote that would have increased the support price 50 cents to $10.60 and barred any decreases below that level for the five-year life of the farm bill.

Raising the support price, however, threatened to worsen the milk surplus problem that had plagued the dairy industry for decades. So did new technology and products such as bovine somatatropin, a synthetic hormone (likely to become available in the near future) that significantly increased cows' milk output.

To address the continuing problem of overproduction, the subcommittee bill created a quota system intended to deter farmers from squeezing out pound after pound of surplus. The basic idea put forward by Stenholm and Gunderson was to create a two-tier pricing system, under which the farmer would be offered the artificially high support price for some portion of his production and a lower price for excess milk.

But the subcommittee ended up adopting, by voice vote, a less severe Volkmer amendment after a test vote showed the panel favored it by 7-5.

Instead of a sharply lower price for overproduction, the Volkmer plan would have assigned dairy farmers a production level based on the amount of milk they had sold for commercial use during recent years. During periods of overproduction, a farmer would be charged an assessment on any milk sold to the government that exceeded his base. The assessment would be equal to the difference between the support price and the market price.

The pricing system would go into effect only if government purchases of dairy products were expected to exceed 7 billion pounds (of which 260 million pounds was milkfat and 600 million pounds was nonfat solid dairy products).

However, there was deep division about the wisdom of the Volkmer plan and two-tier pricing in general. The disagreement revolved around three issues: How would excess milk be disposed of? Which dairy-producing regions of the country would benefit (and which would be hurt) by two-tier pricing? And would milk production reach such high levels that the two-tier pricing structure would be in effect permanently?

Stenholm and Gunderson criticized the Volkmer pricing structure because, they said, it would not create an incentive to get rid of surplus dairy products; it would continue the incentive to sell them to the government. An effective two-tier system, they argued, would require that the artificially high support price be removed on any overproduction. That way, there would be an incentive to get rid of the surplus.

But because Volkmer's amendment imposed an assessment on overproduction, rather than lowering the support price, Stenholm and Gunderson argued, farmers would continue to overproduce as long as the government continued to buy surplus milk at above-market prices.

When the bill came before the full committee, Volkmer's amendment to raise the dairy price support to $10.60 was defeated by a vote of 14-24. Johnson's amendment to raise the support level $3 to $13.10 was rejected 13-28.

Peanuts

The Agriculture Subcommittee on Tobacco and Peanuts on March 29 approved provisions to renew and modify the federal peanut quota and price-support program, but disagreements remained between major manufacturers and Georgia peanut growers, on one side, and farmers from other states on the other.

A marathon closed-door meeting two days earlier between growers and manufacturers failed to produce accord on several provisions.

The peanut title of the farm bill, approved by the panel on a voice vote, would continue the government's two-tier price-support program for peanuts — one level for those grown under a nationally imposed quota system and a lower support level for "additional" peanuts sold overseas.

The market-linked quota was the amount of peanuts estimated by the Agriculture secretary to be needed for domestic edible and seed uses. The bill raised the national peanut production quota floor to 1.35 million tons from 1.1 million tons.

As put forward by subcommittee Chairman Charlie Rose, D-N.C., the bill also made other changes to the 1985 law but essentially retained most of the key provisions.

That flew in the face of the Bush administration, which wanted to eliminate key elements of the peanut program, such as restrictions on the sale of quota peanuts, a cost-of-production escalator and the $631 per ton quota price-support rate. Administration officials argued that the existing formula resulted in a price-support level well above worldwide prices, making peanuts consumed in the United States much more expensive than those sold overseas.

The subcommittee's opening markup March 27 was hastily adjourned when panel member Charles Hatcher, D-Ga., said he would soon have amendments stemming from an agreement between growers in his state and manufacturers. The manufacturers — major candy and peanut butter companies such as Mars Inc. and Procter & Gamble Co. — had long opposed the peanut price-support program, while peanut growers and their supporters in Congress considered it vital.

Rose and Hatcher arranged a private meeting between national grower groups and the manufacturers, excluding administration officials, but no agreement was reached.

"I would love to have the manufacturers on board for the 1990 peanut program," Rose said. But, he added, "I'd like to see [the parties involved] get a little closer together.... I don't want the growers to make unreasonable compromises that will be harmful to them."

Hatcher said that manufacturers' willingness to endorse the program with conditions was a major concession in itself. He noted that manufacturers backed the existing $631 per ton price support and a connected cost-of-production escalator, rather than the administration's $503 per ton proposal.

But a panel aide said manufacturers had insisted their provisions be accepted as a package. "That's like cramming something down someone's throat," the aide said.

The staff member noted that Georgia peanut farmers "really don't have any power to negotiate or discuss for other areas of the country." A Hatcher aide, however, predicted that growers in other regions "will come around."

Also, the aide said, the cost-of-production escalator proposed by manufacturers would amount to a maximum 24 percent increase over five years rather than the 30 percent maximum in effect at the time.

Environmental Debate

The House bill also included the terms of a deal between environmentalists and farm groups.

Officials of key environmental and farm organizations vowed to support three areas of the controversial conservation section: the so-called swampbuster program, which denied government subsidies to farmers who drained and planted wetlands; an initiative calling for incentive payments to farmers to reduce water pollution on as much as 20 million acres of farmland; and a new five-year program to pay farmers to retire 2.5 million acres of wetlands from production.

"Many felt that the gap could not be bridged," Glenn English, D-Okla., said of the accord between environmentalists and farm groups. "It took a lot of meetings,... table-pounding and hand-wringing."

English said the compromise would impose no additional mandatory controls on farming practices. Many farmers were hoping to reverse several of the more stringent provisions of the 1985 farm bill, particularly swampbuster, which linked farm program payments to environmental controls for the first time.

The bill tried to clear up confusion about which areas were subject to swampbuster and allowed some draining of small wetlands if a swamp area nearby was restored to its natural condition. Farmers violating the law would not have their program benefits ended for first violations; they would be fined $750.

"It does provide relief for farmers," English said.

Environmentalists managed to prevent a broad loosening of existing law by threatening a showdown on the floor.

But many of their more ambitious proposals to build on the mandatory controls in the 1985 law, such as requiring farmers to keep records of their pesticide use and reduce their use of agricultural chemicals in polluted areas, were left out. They had to settle for voluntary programs.

Maureen Hinkle, a lobbyist for the National Audubon Society, praised the committee for "deciding their own environmental future, instead of having it happen to them."

Trade

The House Agriculture Subcommittee on Department Operations, Research and Foreign Agriculture agreed April 25 to extend for another five years several programs that subsidized exports of U.S. commodities and provided food aid to needy foreign nations.

In the process, the panel approved measures intended to tighten controls on how the Agriculture Department was required to operate such export-related programs. Audits by the General Accounting Office and others had found numerous problems, such as commodities being subsidized for export under U.S. programs that were not grown in the United States.

In the Food for Peace program (PL 480), the subcommittee measure expanded authority to donate government-owned commodities to countries meeting poverty criteria established by the World Bank. The government had authority for donations and sales, but the donations were limited because they had to be funneled through private organizations. Existing law provided for a minimum of 1.9 metric tons of grain to be provided annually, of which 1.425 million tons had to be distributed by private voluntary organizations.

In addition, the bill called on the Agriculture secretary to try "to maintain a stable level of commodities" for use in PL 480. Because the program relied on surplus commodities purchased by the government, food aid often languished when surpluses were low.

For the Export Enhancement Program (EEP), a popular subsidy for grain exporters, the subcommittee authorized appropriations of not less than $500 million for each of the following five years. In addition, the bill required the secretary to establish a uniform procedure for calculating how much of a premium exporters received for subsidized sales. The Agriculture Department had been criticized for lacking consistent procedures.

The bill also broadened the scope of the Targeted Export Assistance Program (TEAP) by permitting it to be used to stimulate exports in countries with market potential — not just where there were unfair trade practices, as existing law required.

Research

Government research into more environmentally sensitive farming methods was voted a hefty increase under legislation approved April 25 by the House Agriculture Subcommittee on Department Operations and Research.

The measure reauthorized the $1.3 billion Agriculture Department research and extension budget. Overall, the panel approved roughly $600 million in new spending over five years. More than half of the increase — $350 million — went to competitive research grants, $100 million more than requested by the Bush administration.

The subcommittee agreed to dramatically expand the government's emphasis on what was known as sustainable agriculture — a loosely defined concept involving crop diversification, rotation, cultivation to control pests, and other practices aimed at reducing the need for pesticides and other common agricultural production inputs.

The panel proposed a substantial increase, to $40 million a year, for such research. Members also approved an amendment authorizing another $40 million to train government extension agents in sustainable agriculture techniques. The government's low-input sustainable agriculture (LISA) program was receiving $4.4 million.

HOUSE FLOOR ACTION

The House on Aug. 1 easily passed its version of the 1990 farm bill (HR 3950), on a 327-91 vote, despite a much-ballyhooed coalition of urban Democrats and suburban Republicans, which proved more adept at drawing attention to its attacks on farm programs than at attracting votes. *(Vote 299, p. 96-H)*

The centerpiece of the coalition's assault — an amendment to deny crop subsidies to prosperous farmers — was easily defeated, 159-263, on July 26. *(Vote 266, p. 88-H)*

In general, the House measures froze the existing income-subsidy levels for crops such as wheat, corn, cotton and rice. While significant — and potentially expensive — changes were proposed in the system of price-support "loan" rates offered to farmers, the bill did not greatly increase overall payments to farmers.

Nevertheless, veto threats from the administration proliferated. Rep. Edward Madigan of Illinois, ranking Republican on the House Agriculture Committee, said Bush budget director Richard G. Darman told him that "if anything like what we passed today was put before the president, he would veto it."

The House bill would cost about $55 billion, according to a House Agriculture Committee estimate — $2 billion more than the five-year House budget allocation for farm programs. It was anticipated that another $8 billion to $20 billion might have to be cut from the bill pending a White House-congressional budget agreement to trim the deficit.

But the almost certain prospect of having to make deep cuts in farm spending before the end of the year — either from a budget-summit agreement or from automatic cuts required under the Gramm-Rudman antideficit law — helped to stave off cost-cutting efforts while the bill was on the House floor.

"People figure: 'Why should we vote against farmers? Why should we do the right thing and take political hits for it, if the summit is going to take care of it?' " said Deputy Under Secretary of Agriculture Campbell.

As a result, the bill reported from the House Agriculture Committee proved sturdy on the House floor. Chairman De la Garza and his lieutenants had beaten back virtually every amendment to alter the bill the week of July 23. And when floor deliberations resumed Aug. 1, the victories continued.

Sweet Day for Sugar Farmers

Despite doomsday scenarios for farm-subsidy programs, even a target as large as the government sugar program emerged unscathed.

Although the sugar program by law cost the government nothing (and thus was not likely to be affected by the coming budget cuts), many farm-state lawmakers feared that it might be the one subsidy program not to survive on the floor.

But during deliberations July 24, the House rejected a 2-cent cut in the 18-cent-per-pound sugar price support. The amendment fell 150-271. "We got waxed," said Thomas J. Downey, D-N.Y., who sponsored the House amendment with Bill Gradison, R-Ohio. *(Vote 258, p. 86-H)*

Supporters of the 2-cent cut argued that no other crop program was more blatantly protectionist than sugar and that, although it cost the taxpayer nothing, no other imposed such a burden, both on consumers in higher sugar prices and on U.S. sugar-exporting allies, whose exports to the U.S. market were severely limited.

Many signs seemed to point toward a victory in the House for Downey and Gradison. The Bush administration had publicly endorsed their amendment. Cargill Inc., the giant Midwestern agribusiness company, had expressed support for the cut as well, thus raising the possibility that the farm coalition, which usually banded together to protect attacks on individual programs, might split its votes.

In addition, Ways and Means Committee Chairman Dan Rostenkowski, D-Ill., had succeeded in removing a key feature of a deal that Huckaby, chairman of the Agriculture Subcommittee on Sugar, had struck to win support for the House sugar section: a 5-cent premium on sugar exported to the United States for refining and re-export.

Huckaby had included the provision to mute the principal foreign policy objection to the sugar program — namely, that the import restrictions it contained hurt some of the best and poorest U.S. allies, such as Caribbean nations and the Philippines. But Ways and Means, which had primary jurisdiction over tariff and trade issues, voted to strip the provision from the bill, and when the measure went to the Rules Committee for a resolution governing floor debate, Rules members voted not to allow Huckaby a chance to restore his 5-cent premium.

None of these gains for farm-program critics seemed to make much difference on the floor, however.

Republicans defected in droves from the administration, whose lobbying in behalf of the cut was only "lukewarm," Campbell acknowledged.

Two House Republicans, Patricia Saiki of Hawaii and Bill Schuette of Michigan, were running for the Senate from sugar cane- and sugar beet-producing states. Another, Arlan Stangeland of Minnesota, was in a tough race for reelection. All three lobbied hard against the cut, said lawmakers and aides.

In addition, Minority Leader Robert H. Michel of Illinois and GOP Whip Newt Gingrich of Georgia voted against the cut.

Huckaby and Agriculture Committee Chairman de la Garza worked hard to round up votes among Democrats. "The sugar guys did a much better job in trading votes," Downey said. "They used fundraising and other relationships and worked it very hard."

Sugar-industry advocates insisted that the cut would devastate parts of the U.S. sweetener industry. The principal beneficiaries, they claimed, would be the European Community, which subsidized its sugar growers by as much as 30 cents a pound. De la Garza, who represented south Texas sugar cane growers, ended the debate with a rousing chorus: "Vote 'no' on the Downey amendment. It is jobs U.S.A., jobs U.S.A., jobs U.S.A.! You cannot cut it anymore. You cannot hide it anymore."

Payment Limits

In the last of a series of unsuccessful amendments designed to reduce the proportion of government benefits going to affluent farmers, Silvio O. Conte, R-Mass., proposed to tighten loopholes that permitted widespread evasion of a $50,000 limit on income subsidies and a $250,000 cap on government benefits paid to individual farmers.

Heaping scorn on farm programs, Conte reminded the House that it had ostensibly closed such loopholes in 1987 but that big producers had skirted the limits by subdividing their farms into smaller units, each of which qualified for payments. "You've been had," Conte bellowed to his colleagues. "A gigantic loophole allows a small number of farmers to double their take."

At the time, a producer could collect payments from three different entities: his own farm (which was eligible for the maximum $50,000 and $250,000) and two other farming operations in which he was allowed no more than half-ownership (each of which was eligible for half the limit).

From these three entities, a farmer could legally double his take, for a total of $100,000 in income subsidies and $500,000 in total benefits.

But instead of closing that loophole, the House adopted an alternative amendment offered by Agriculture Committee member Huckaby. It lowered the total benefits allowed to $200,000 but retained provisions that permitted large farmers to double their income subsidies.

Huckaby said this so-called "three-entity" rule encouraged father-son farming and equipment sharing. "We want our government programs to encourage efficient-sized operations, not to encourage our farmers to break up their operations into smaller and smaller entities," he said.

Seeing little support for his original amendment, Conte tried to attach his language eliminating the three-entity exemptions to Huckaby's substitute.

But the House rejected that concession, 171-250, before adopting Huckaby's initial proposal on a 375-45 vote. *(Votes 295-296, p. 96-H)*

'A Meat-Ax Approach'

An amendment to deny crop subsidies to farmers with gross adjusted incomes of more than $100,000 a year fared only nine votes better.

Sponsors Armey and Schumer appealed for farm-state support by portraying their amendment as an attack on rich farmers that would lead to a greater proportion of federal payments going to small, family-run operations. The ban would affect only 21,000 of the nation's 750,000 commercial farmers, they said, but it would save up to $700 million a year.

The four-hour debate cut to the heart of the philosophical underpinnings of federal farm programs.

"The Schumer-Armey amendment will fix the farm program," Schumer said. "It will say, 'Money goes to the family working the soil, but it does not go to the well-to-do hobby farmers, the large agribusinesses and the investors who are now milking the federal government for $700 million a year.' "

Farm-state lawmakers responded that "means-testing" farm programs would undermine the farm program and cause overproduction, food price swings and greater payments to those farmers who stayed in the program.

"This amendment is a meat-ax approach," de la Garza said. "Can you imagine the former shoeshine boy from Mission, Texas, being accused of protecting the rich and the greedy? Ridiculous!"

According to aides and lawmakers, one of the factors that hurt the amendment was the perception that Armey and Schumer were "anti-farmer" and that the amendment, which was supported by the Bush administration, was offered merely to cut the agriculture budget, not to help family farmers.

The farm bloc also drew support from organized labor in fending off Armey-Schumer. The AFL-CIO said in a letter to members that "the exclusion of big producers seems enticing on the surface" but "the amendment would make farm programs inoperable."

Several members and aides suggested that pro-labor Democrats, who voted overwhelmingly against the amendment, were fulfilling their end of a trade: A vote against Armey-Schumer in exchange for farm-state support for a textile protection bill that was coming to the floor soon. *(Textile bill, p. 221)*

Moreover, opponents of the Armey-Schumer amendment were aided by several environmental groups, including the National Audubon Society and the National Wildlife Federation. They argued that kicking big farmers out of federal farm programs would hurt environmental quality because, to qualify for federal payments, farmers had to comply with numerous environmental controls, including a ban on draining wetlands and plowing highly erodible land.

Another environmental group, the Natural Resources Defense Council, came out in favor of the Armey-Schumer proposal. "If anything drives the overproduction of commodity crops, it is the status quo, not restrictions on subsidies to the wealthy," the group said in a letter to members of Congress.

The status quo prevailed, however. The amendment was defeated, 159-263. *(Vote 266, p. 88-H)*

The Organic Label

Only a few amendments significantly altered the philosophical bent of the Agriculture Committee bill.

In one of the closest votes of the debate, the House adopted, 234-187, an organic foods amendment by Peter A. DeFazio, D-Ore., to replace a hodgepodge of state laws with a national standard governing what foods could be labeled organic. *(Vote 297, p. 96-H)*

While the amendment prescribed certain broad criteria, authority for devising most of the specific standards for production, handling and testing of organic food was given to a board to be composed of organic farmers, consumers, retailers and others.

Agriculture Committee member Stenholm offered an

alternative amendment that gave authority for setting organic standards to the Agriculture Department. But DeFazio maintained that that approach was a ploy to kill the organic standard by lawmakers who felt it was a threat to traditional, chemical-intensive agriculture.

"There's a philosophical gap," DeFazio said. "There are those like Mr. Stenholm and others who don't believe in organic production. They wanted to push this to the wall."

'Circle of Poison'

Later, de la Garza accepted an amendment to greatly restrict the export of pesticides considered too dangerous for use in the United States (and which could return to this country on imported food). But de la Garza managed to secure a provision to partly mollify farm-state lawmakers and agricultural chemical companies that opposed the "circle of poison" amendment.

The compromise revolved around the treatment of so-called "unregistered" pesticides — those that could not be used domestically. Instead of an absolute ban on exports of these pesticides, they could be legally shipped out if registered in a country that was a member of the Organization for Economic Cooperation and Development (OECD), a group of 24 industrialized nations, and if the Environmental Protection Agency (EPA) concurred.

SENATE COMMITTEE ACTION

Stepping back from a partisan abyss, senior Democrats on the Senate Agriculture Committee joined Republicans on June 21 in approving, 15-4, an omnibus five-year farm bill (S 2830) containing a package of modest changes to federal crop-subsidy programs.

But a vocal bloc of prairie-populist Democrats, insisting that the package was not generous enough, remained poised to leap off the edge and take the whole package down with them.

Deceptive Unity

Beneath the deceivingly unified vote approving the bill, there were deep divisions about the policy course being taken — and about political strategy.

Thus the bill was sent to the floor threatened from without by farm program skeptics and from within by farm-state lawmakers unhappy with the deal. The deal threatened to unravel on the floor if Democrats made good on their vow to offer generous subsidy increases or schemes to direct a greater proportion of benefits to needy farmers.

According to committee estimates, the bill as reported to the floor would cost roughly $55 billion over five years, about $500 million more than was assumed in the Senate "baseline" — the amount that would be spent if existing law were extended. Administration officials said the price tag would be higher.

"It could be worse, but I think there are a lot of problems with it," said Bruce Gardner, assistant secretary of Agriculture for economics.

Among other objections, the administration disliked provisions that would limit its discretion to adjust price support levels based on market conditions and that would change existing crop programs for wheat, feed grains and soybeans, as well as the dairy price-support system.

The package had to be reworked many times in the weeks before final committee action. In the end, it gave enough lawmakers enough of what they sought to allow them to declare partial victory.

"If everybody got everything they wanted, we would have 19 different bills," said committee Chairman Leahy.

Prairie Populist Bloc

The bill froze income-subsidy levels for crops such as wheat, corn, cotton and rice, as well as dairy products. And though it made significant changes in the system of price supports offered to farmers, the bill provided no increase in overall payments provided under these so-called loan rates.

Those were the key conditions demanded by Lugar, the committee's ranking Republican. Senior Democrats were willing to comply in exchange for his and other Republicans' support. They said they wanted a bipartisan deal, not a lot of divisive votes. But the deal did not please the prairie Democrats, who had hoped to achieve either higher subsidy levels or a clear-cut split between Republicans and Democrats over farm policy — preferably both.

Several of them, such as Nebraska's Bob Kerrey and Iowa's Tom Harkin, voted for the final package even though they said they did not like it.

"We tinkered around the edges. Part of it was face-saving, and part of it was a determination by some not to budge," said South Dakota Democrat Daschle, who opposed the final package.

By not budging, Lugar maneuvered the Democrats into preserving, with some notable exceptions, the course established in the 1985 farm bill. "Essentially, we have a continuation of the farm policy we've had for the past five years," Lugar said.

There were some significant concessions: Growers of wheat, feed grains and soybeans would be offered so-called marketing loans, under which farmers, using their crops as collateral, received harvest-time advances from the government. Only cotton and rice producers at the time were given marketing loans.

Marketing loans required a producer to repay only as much of the loan as he got for his crop at market any time during the ensuing nine months. The remainder of the loan could be kept as a subsidy.

In addition, at Democrats' insistence, the bill put new constraints on the power the Agriculture secretary had to lower the loan rate — the amount the government would lend a farmer on a crop — by up to 20 percent each year for wheat and feed grains.

Under the bill, every 1-cent reduction in the loan rate would have to be accompanied by an offsetting 0.75-cent payment to farmers before planting. The payment would have to repaid within nine months.

Democrats such as Kerrey insisted that the Bush and Reagan administrations had lowered loan rates too far, making the government floor under market prices irrelevant and reducing the advance payments farmers got from the government. The loan rate was at the center of a three-week impasse over commodity programs.

In the end, Kerrey, Daschle and other Democrats could not muster enough support. On June 20, the committee rejected their amendment, 7-11, to strip the secretary's authority to lower loan rates. Every Republican voted against it, as did senior Democrats David Pryor of Arkansas and David L. Boren of Oklahoma. Leahy did not vote.

That defeat for the prairie populists came immediately after another one on an amendment by Max Baucus, D-Mont., that would have increased so-called target prices — the guaranteed minimum prices farmers received for their crops. The amendment would have increased target prices in years when the inflation rate exceeded 4.3 percent.

The same coalition of Republicans and senior Democrats united to defeat the target-price hike. It was rejected 7-12, with Leahy voting in opposition this time.

Political Considerations

Those two votes were perhaps the most significant of the farm bill. They showed two things: first, that Lugar could command the allegiance of the eight other Republicans in his quest to prevent subsidy increases; and second, that senior Democrats would take the politically dangerous step of voting against subsidy increases to preserve the possibility of a final compromise with Republicans.

"It was my concern that we either had to reach an agreement or it would be a long, long time before we would get the farm bill out of this committee," said Leahy.

In addition, several Southern lawmakers, including Pryor and Howell Heflin, D-Ala., apparently were concerned about threats from both Lugar and Daschle to expose apparent payment inequities in farm programs and to require that benefits be targeted to needy farmers.

Payments in the cotton and rice program historically had gone to relatively few — and frequently wealthy — producers in the South. According to their aides, Southern lawmakers thought the best way to avoid a messy fight over targeting was to reach a compromise with Republicans that ensured as many votes for the farm bill package as possible.

But accommodating Republicans meant disappointing the prairie-state Democrats, who clearly resented members of their own party giving Republicans the cover of a compromise rather than a battle. "Dick Lugar would like a package because he does not want to strip away the façade that there are deep philosophical differences between us," said Daschle. "But for a lot of us, there's just too much at stake to just go along and be a good guy."

Several of the junior Democrats on the committee had been elected since 1985, when they ran against the policy of lower subsidy rates enshrined in the 1985 bill. These Democrats preferred to be identified with higher government spending on farmers, a difference with Republicans that, they believed, could prove crucial in several Farm Belt Senate races in the fall.

Pressure on Republicans

Ironically, after losing in a series of key votes June 20, the prairie populists seemed to be on the verge of getting the partisan split many of them wanted. The committee had rejected a series of amendments, but it had not adopted anything yet. "We're back to where we started on loan rates," said Lugar.

Then suddenly the votes seemed in danger of breaking along party lines.

Boren dramatically announced that, in opposing higher target prices and an end to the loan rate reductions, he had "cast three votes against my policy positions . . . because of my view that it is so important that we get a compromise."

Unless Republicans agreed to a compromise by the next day, Boren declared, he would switch his votes — and call for a revote on several of the amendments. Leahy and Pryor made the same threat, thus raising the possibility that Democrats would unite behind a plan to raise target prices and loan rates, overriding the Republicans entirely.

The pressure on Republicans to reach an agreement increased.

Boren and Leahy never carried out their threat. By the morning of June 21, a revised compromise fashioned by Republican and Democratic staff was on the table. It showed enough give on the part of Republicans to satisfy Boren, Leahy and Pryor. Then the problem became selling it to prairie Democrats.

At 8 o'clock that night, the Democrats were still holding out. Leahy seemed intent on finishing the farm bill that evening, yet the prairie Democrats had revived a proposal that had already been rejected: to increase target prices by partly offsetting inflation of more than 4.3 percent a year.

At that point, according to aides present, a senior Democrat announced that the stalling had gone on long enough and that the prairie Democrats would have to abandon their demand for a target-price increase or he was leaving.

It was clear then, said an aide, that the junior Democrats were being offered the compromise — and being told to take it or leave it. "With that, they gave up," said the aide.

Daschle acknowledged afterwards: "We just didn't have the votes."

It would be possible for a farmer to get an increase in his target price under the bill, but only if he agreed to idle more of his land in order to limit output. The idea was for the target-price increase to cost the government nothing, since there would be a corresponding decrease in the production of a commodity eligible for government subsidies.

Dairy, Soybeans and Sugar

In other action, the committee voted to keep the dairy price support at the existing $10.10 per hundredweight for five years. If government purchases of surplus dairy products exceeded 7 billion pounds in a year, the Agriculture secretary would be authorized to take steps to control production.

By a 16-2 tally, the committee voted to bar the secretary from taking one step: buying up and slaughtering dairy herds. Congress ordered a so-called whole-herd buyout in the 1985 farm bill, but that aroused opposition from cattlemen because it created a temporary glut of beef, thus lowering prices. The amendment, offered by Baucus, was opposed by Leahy and Rudy Boschwitz, R-Minn.

On June 14, the Senate committee voted to renew the government sugar program with few changes. U.S. sugar prices would continue to be supported at roughly 21 cents a pound, a support price of 18 cents plus a 3-cent "differential" for transportation and other costs. Lugar's amendment to do away with the sugar program was rejected 2-16. His subsequent amendment to cut sugar price supports by roughly 10 percent was rejected 5-12.

Environment

An hour after the Senate Agriculture Committee had intended to begin its May 3 deliberations on a compromise measure to revamp federal wetlands protections, supporters were still closeted in a back room, virtually daring North Dakota Democrat Kent Conrad to break the deal.

"It got fairly contentious in there," Conrad conceded later.

But the threat of a fight with the environmental lobby proved an effective deterrent. Even though Conrad and some other farm-state members favored extensive loosening of a federal law — known as "swampbuster" — that barred the draining of swamps and marshes for farming, they were not certain they could succeed.

Rather than fight it out, the committee agreed by voice vote to accept an agreement brokered by Leahy that would toughen some elements of swampbuster and relax others, but keep the essence of the 1985 law intact. Conrad voiced the only "no" vote but did not try to challenge the agreement with deal-busting amendments.

The committee May 2 also reauthorized and, in some cases, expanded other Agriculture Department soil- and water-conservation programs.

The wetlands fight illustrated the extent to which the environmental lobby had managed to sustain a sphere of influence in agricultural policy-making that it carved out in 1985, the year of the last omnibus farm bill.

Farm organizations and their allies on the Agriculture Committee began the 1990 debate with the intention of reversing some of the more stringent environmental controls that the 1985 law imposed on farming practices. The law was simple and tough: Farmers who drained and cultivated wetlands were denied federal farm benefits — which, for many, totaled hundreds of thousands of dollars.

But the politics of agriculture were changing. The power of the farm coalition — at least in environmental matters — was being challenged, even in the friendly confines of the Agriculture Committee, as lawmakers contended with the growing public insistence on environmental protection.

The stakes increased when President Bush took office with a policy of "no net loss" of wetlands. Various agencies had been debating about how to carry out the mandate, but no changes were recommended in swampbuster "because of the diverse opinion within the administration," said Campbell, deputy under secretary of Agriculture.

Neither environmental groups nor farm organizations professed complete satisfaction with the changes approved by the committee, but both sides vowed to support the compromise on the Senate floor.

"The compromise moved in the right direction. A month ago, we were down at the bottom of the hill. Now we're closer to the top," said Kenneth A. Cook of the Center for Resource Economics, an environmental group.

"Whether or not exactly what we put on the table was adopted, it will provide farmers with a small amount of relief," said Mark Nestlen, director of congressional relations for the American Soybean Association.

Environmental organizations such as the Natural Resources Defense Council and the National Wildlife Federation did not have broad support on the committee. But they did have a strong advocate for their agenda in Leahy. And, as public concern about farming's adverse effects on the environment increased, they gained the support of more lawmakers who were not on the committee but who might try to amend an environmentally suspect farm bill on the Senate floor.

Many environmental lobbyists at first predicted a floor fight would be necessary to preserve swampbuster. A bill introduced by Georgia Democrat Fowler and supported by 11 others on the 19-member committee would have loosened swampbuster by, among other things, exempting wetlands that had been previously cropped.

Farm organizations such as the National Corn Growers Association and the National Association of Wheat Growers complained that existing law was overly restrictive and that the penalty was draconian. Often, organization officials argued, it prevented farmers from draining small, inconsequential "prairie potholes" that had none of the ecological benefits that the environmentalists were trying to protect.

Environmental groups argued that the changes to swampbuster proposed by the commodity groups would have exempted millions of acres of wetlands, mostly in the Great Plains and Midwest. Moreover, they pointed out that fewer than 200 producers were denied benefits since the program began, even though an estimated 500,000 acres of wetlands were lost each year, much because of agriculture.

With help from ranking Republican Lugar, Leahy and his staff managed to quell a revolt against swampbuster that had been building for months among committee members. According to lawmakers, staff and lobbyists, Leahy warned repeatedly that the Fowler bill could not survive on the floor, nor would he defend it from possible amendments intended to toughen the wetlands controls.

But Leahy offered a promise as well: If the committee could craft a compromise that was acceptable to both environmental and farm organizations, he would give it his imprimatur. And he brought a guarantee from a coalition of environmental organizations that they would stick with the compromise on the floor.

Then the negotiations began in earnest. "The breakthrough came when Leahy promised no floor votes from the environmentalists," said a top-level Senate aide involved in the negotiations.

As approved by the committee, the new swampbuster provision:

- Required the Agriculture Department to withhold farm program payments from producers who merely drained wetlands for the purpose of planting on them. The existing statute required farm benefits to be denied when a farmer both drained and planted a crop on the land. Environmental groups demanded this key change.
- Allowed planting on wetlands that, because of natural and seasonal characteristics, had been planted with a crop but not drained before the blanket ban prohibiting such planting was imposed in 1985.
- Allowed the draining of land that had been extensively farmed but still had wetlands characteristics, as long as the drainage would have a "minimal effect" on ecology and wildlife habitat. Commodity organizations sought this allowance, although they wanted a more explicit exemption.
- Established a case-by-case procedure for determining what qualified for the minimal-effect exemption. In some cases, a farmer who drained swamp or marshland would be required to restore a wetland of equal size or ecological benefit nearby.
- Required that officials of both the Fish and Wildlife Service and the Agriculture Department's Soil Conservation Service approve farmers' plans to restore wetlands. Environmental groups wanted to bring Fish and Wildlife into the process in hope that it would be more protective of wetlands than the Agriculture Department.
- Lessened the penalty against first-time violators for draining wetlands. Instead of resulting in the loss of all farm program benefits, such violations would result in fines of $1,000 to $10,000. The producer also would have to restore the wetland. If the producer violated the provision again within the next 10 years, he would lose his benefits.

In separate action May 2, the Senate committee voted to create conservation programs that would give farmers financial incentives to enroll wetlands in government easements and to prevent contamination of ground and surface water as a result of agricultural practices.

And for the first time, the committee voted to require farmers to keep records of their use of certain pesticides thought to harm the health of humans when applied in high concentrations. The Agriculture Department would have to assist farmers in devising plans to reduce the harmful effect of agricultural chemicals on water. Farmers would be eligible for incentive payments for three to five years, not to exceed $3,500 annually, to carry out the plans.

The measure also encouraged the secretary to enroll 1 million acres of wetlands over five years in the Conservation Reserve Program (CRP), which paid farmers to remove land from production for 10-year stretches. The CRP, which was established in 1985 to protect highly erodible land, was renamed the Conservation Stewardship Program (CSP).

While the CRP was primarily intended to reduce soil erosion, its descendant, the CSP, would be much broader. There was broad authority to enroll land that "will prevent or ameliorate an on-farm or off-farm threat to water quality," according to the bill. That meant that wellheads, cropland underlaid with karst, and cropland in important watershed areas would be eligible.

The bill included generous provisions to promote the planting of trees on retired land through government cost-sharing and other arrangements. For example, pastureland on which only trees were to be planted could be enrolled. The bill would require the Agriculture Department to pay from 50 percent to 75 percent of the costs of maintaining tree-planting for two to four years. Also, landowners planting trees would be eligible for land-retirement contracts of from 10 to 15 years. Previous contracts were limited to 10 years.

Circle of Poison

Shedding its traditional agribusiness loyalties, the Agriculture Committee on June 6 repudiated the chemical industry and voted to severely restrict exports of pesticides considered too dangerous to use in the United States.

The Senate panel took the first step toward curtailing what some environmental groups called the circle of poison, in which domestically banned pesticides were exported for use abroad. Illegal residues of these pesticides, including some suspected carcinogens, were regularly detected in food — mostly fruits and vegetables — that came into the United States.

The provision, which would have amended the Federal Insecticide, Fungicide and Rodenticide Act (FIFRA), became part of the committee's farm bill.

Environmentalists and consumer advocates had long contended that it was an immoral policy to export pesticides that were banned in the United States. But the issue gained momentum in Congress only as critics chose to emphasize that pesticide exports could ultimately pose health risks to U.S. consumers.

The amendment, pushed by Leahy would have barred exports of those pesticides that could not be used domestically or be present as residue on food sold in the U.S.

"It eliminates the double standard between our export policy and our domestic pesticide policy," said William J. McNichol of the National Coalition Against the Misuse of Pesticides.

The amendment was adopted by voice vote, in spite of vehement objections by committee Republicans.

As drafted, the bill would have imposed a blanket restriction on exports of pesticides that the EPA had not registered for use in the United States. But chemical company lobbyists argued the provision was unduly restrictive.

A pesticide intended for use on bananas, for example, might never be registered in the United States, because bananas were hardly grown domestically.

To win the support of several Democrats, Leahy agreed to loosen the ban. As approved, the amendment would allow the export of some unregistered pesticides as long as the EPA had ruled that they could be present on food below a certain level. If the EPA established no such "tolerance level" for an unregistered pesticide, it could not be exported.

It was legal to import food products containing the residue of pesticides for which the EPA had established tolerance levels, even if the pesticides present were unregistered. The bill sought to end that loophole by revoking those "tolerances" for banned pesticides.

But because so little imported food was inspected by the Food and Drug Administration (FDA), critics said, the Senate bill would not make food any safer. Foreign producers would simply buy the banned pesticides from manufacturers in other countries, said Jay J. Vroom, president of the National Agricultural Chemicals Association.

Leahy argued that Congress still had a responsibility to act. About 5 percent of the imported food sampled by the FDA was contaminated with illegal pesticides, twice the rate for domestic food. "Because FDA waves through virtually all imported food without inspection, these chemicals often end up on America's dinner table," Leahy said.

Republicans argued that the bill would force some pesticide production out of the United States, costing jobs and reducing the government's controls over pesticides. "If these pesticides can be manufactured offshore, we will then be in a position to have no control over them," said Missouri's Bond.

Lugar said he would prefer to consider the issue as part of a broader effort to revise FIFRA, which was due to be renewed in 1991. The Bush administration, Lugar and several other lawmakers had introduced food safety legislation to overhaul FIFRA; Lugar warned that he might try to reopen the issue on the floor.

Leahy's bill would also control exports of certain pesticides that were considered hazardous but that could be legally used in the United States. Such pesticides would be barred from going to countries that asked the U.S. government not to export them, as long as the country was not producing the chemical itself or importing it from a third country.

Research

The Agriculture Committee agreed April 19 to give a boost to alternative farming techniques that reduced the use of toxic chemicals, approving provisions to authorize $40 million in new spending to research such methods.

Those funds, a marked increase over the existing $4.5 million authorization, would create a program to explore alternative or organic farming methods — also known as low-input sustainable agriculture (LISA) — that reduced reliance on pesticides, herbicides and fertilizer.

The funds could be used for laboratory and field research, education and training, and to establish a matching-grant program to help states carry out their own LISA programs. An additional $10 million would be earmarked to train agricultural extension agents in alternative farming production.

The research provisions, approved by voice vote, would set up public-private partnerships to develop products made from crops and provide federal seed money to help market them. These included backpacking equipment made from milkweed, and disposable diapers made from corn and wheat.

By voice vote, members rejected a substitute amendment drafted by Jesse Helms, R-N.C., representing the

Bush administration's proposals. Panel Chairman Leahy and fellow Democrat Daschle urged rejection of the substitute. Aides said it did not put as much emphasis on reducing chemical inputs through alternative farming methods.

Grain Quality

Also on April 19, the committee handily adopted new farm bill provisions to improve U.S. grain, although sponsors conceded that the measure was only a first step in establishing an effective grain-quality program.

Daschle, sponsor of a bill (S 1977) to create a system to assure clean grain exports, said he would have preferred stronger legislation but could not attract widespread support for such a program. He said his amended version would provide a "carrot rather than a stick" to achieve its goals.

Cosponsor Bond also acknowledged the lack of enforcement powers but said the bill would send an important signal to buyers of U.S. grain. "This is extremely important to our farmers and for our producers," the Missouri Republican said, adding that failing to provide high-quality grain in the United States and abroad would mean that "we're going to lose out on sales."

Despite many charges over the past decade that U.S. grain did not match the quality of other foreign producers', existing farm law did not address grain cleanliness and gave federal agencies no specific direction on improving the quality of wheat, corn and other grains.

As approved on a voice vote by the Agriculture Committee, S 1977 established a grain-quality coordinator in the Agriculture Department and created a system by which the head of the Federal Grain Inspection Service could determine future grain standards.

The focus for the new coordinator, who would head a new grain-quality committee within the department, would be oversight of all government grain-quality improvement efforts.

The measure would standardize commercial grain inspection and allow the inspection service to prohibit combining defective and higher-quality grains.

Peanuts

Brushing aside a Bush administration proposal to scale back price-support rates for peanuts, the committee on April 26 gave voice vote approval to provisions extending the existing program.

The legislation renewed a two-tier price-support system created in 1985 that provided subsidies for peanuts grown under a national domestic sales quota, with a lower support level for "additional" peanuts sold overseas.

The committee agreed to raise the national quota from 1.1 million tons to 1.35 million tons and keep in place a cost-of-production escalator as part of the price-support rate.

As in existing law, the support rate was the same as for the previous year's crop, adjusted upward for increases in production costs, although it could not increase by more than 6 percent a year. The existing domestic support rate was $631 a ton.

On a voice vote, the committee rejected an amendment by ranking Republican Lugar to eliminate the cost-of-production escalator and cut the support rate. Lugar was sponsor of a bill (S 2292) that embraced Bush administration proposals to scale back the peanut program.

Lugar complained that the price support for quota peanuts had increased 13 percent since 1985, and he said peanut farmers received better treatment from the government than growers of other crops.

Wool, Mohair, Honey

Warning that the government subsidy programs for wool, mohair and honey were "vulnerable" on the Senate and House floors, Lugar went after them himself April 24. But he was turned back by the committee Democrats, led by lawmakers whose states were home to the few beekeepers and ranchers who collected the subsidies.

Instead, the committee voted to reauthorize the controversial programs for another five years at the same or slightly higher subsidy levels than were then being offered.

Lugar warned that it would be difficult to defend the existence of these programs when the farm bill reached the floor, particularly since some critics were saying they were specialized commodities that the government should not be subsidizing. "The wool program, at some point, is going to be a casualty of the debate this year," Lugar predicted, adding that "the honey program is even more vulnerable."

Instead of eliminating the programs, however, Lugar proposed that subsidy levels for the three commodities be adjusted by the same percentage as wheat, corn, cotton and other major crops. The committee had not acted on those crops yet, but Lugar said he assumed that support levels would come down — thus necessitating reductions for wool, mohair and honey.

The committee rejected Lugar's amendment to adjust subsidy levels downward for wool and mohair, 8-10, and a similar proposal for honey, 9-10, both on party-line votes.

Trade

The Agriculture Committee's trade title, approved by voice vote on April 5, "makes the most dramatic change in American foreign food policy in a decade," Chairman Leahy said, adding that it would strengthen the government's ability to provide food aid to emerging democracies in Eastern Europe and elsewhere.

The measure would change agricultural trade laws by consolidating most commercial trade authorities under one statute, eliminating redundant and contradictory programs and calling for a long-term trade strategy.

For example, it consolidated various barter authorities of the Agriculture Department. "These authorities are confusing in current law as they are stated several times in several places," said a committee document.

The bill sought to reform the 1954 Food for Peace Program, Leahy said, by providing food grants to the poorest countries and by cleaning up the "bureaucratic morass" that slowed such aid. It also created a new "Food for Freedom" program, described by one committee aide as a "mini-Marshall Plan" to help new democracies.

It created a new marketing-assistance program to improve the nation's competitive posture in foreign sales and sought to curb unfair competition by putting more punch behind the Export Enhancement Program (EEP).

The EEP awarded subsidies in the form of surplus commodities to exporters who sold agricultural goods abroad at lower world prices.

An amendment by Harkin adopted by the panel called on the department to use definite and publicized criteria for determining unfair trade practices and to maintain a set of procedures for reviewing bonuses awarded under EEP.

During the panel's opening markup session April 4, senators accepted two amendments by Leahy and Lugar to authorize the president to spend $3 billion to forgive the

Great Lakes Ports Win Protections . . .

When Senate farm bill managers abruptly halted an all-out regional battle over agricultural shipping subsidies late on July 26, they were determined not to let history repeat itself.

The same debate, over whether to give Great Lakes ports preference in shipping food-aid cargo to needy nations, had tied up the 1985 farm bill for days before managers gave in to Great Lakes senators and included provisions to give special breaks to their dying ports.

In 1990, Agriculture Committee floor managers had less patience. Senators from Illinois, Wisconsin and Ohio were seeking renewal of the favors when their main rivals from the states bordering the Gulf of Mexico took the floor and lectured on the topic late into the night. It took diplomacy and some hardball threats to persuade both sides to call it quits.

On July 27, the battle resumed behind closed doors, where Great Lakes senators managed to claim a limited win to take into a conference with the House.

Despite its proven ability to bottle up farm bills, the age-old "cargo preference" issue was less about farming than it was about waterfront rivalry and the power of the merchant marine lobby to defend its dying industry. Modern commercial cargo preferences dated to 1954, when Congress saw the need to ensure a robust postwar shipping industry in the interest of national security.

But by 1990 the shipping trade had been anything but robust. Inefficiency, competition from abroad and newer ships with more capacity had eaten away the industry. The active U.S. commercial fleet had shrunk by 31 percent over the past decade to 383 vessels, according to the General Accounting Office.

Great Lakes members said their region was hit the hardest. Ships, foreign or domestic, had little incentive to use lake ports. And newer ships could not fit through the Welland Canal, connecting Lakes Erie and Ontario.

But the region's members also blamed the 1985 farm bill for the loss of trade. Before 1985, half of all federally subsidized farm exports had to be shipped aboard U.S.-flag ships. Congress increased the requirement for food-donation shipments to 75 percent but dropped the requirement for other types of commercial exports.

The arrangement was part of a deal between farm-staters, who wanted to use cheaper foreign vessels, and the merchant marine industry, whose political clout kept farm-state members from repealing cargo preference rules entirely. The subsidy amounted to $150 million a year and accounted for 3.2 percent of all food exports.

But the increase to 75 percent hurt the Great Lakes, the region's lawmakers said, because no U.S. carrier made regularly scheduled trips through the St. Lawrence Seaway.

debts of the poorest nations borrowing under the Food for Peace Program.

The committee also established tough criteria for eligibility, including a provision that only countries with multilaterally sanctioned debt restructuring programs could qualify.

Nebraska's Kerrey and other members voiced concern that such a provision might limit the president's ability to forgive the debts of needy countries the U.S. government wanted to help, including its Latin American neighbors.

"I have some moral difficulty saying to someone who's hungry, 'You will have to remain hungry until your government has structural reform,' " Kerrey said.

But Leahy said there was a limited amount of money for debt forgiveness. "That's one of the reasons for the tough criteria," he said.

Another Leahy-Lugar amendment was aimed at preventing program abuse by agents for foreign countries receiving U.S. food aid under Food for Peace.

Leahy noted reports that some of the agents had been serving simultaneously as ship brokers for foreign and U.S.-flag vessels, creating a potential conflict of interest.

The measure, which let the Agriculture Department arrange for the shipping itself, "not only makes it much tighter but turns off what I think is a ticking time bomb of a scandal" in the Food for Peace program, said Leahy.

The amendment forbade freight agents hired by the Agriculture Department or the Agency for International Development from representing any supplier of commodities or cargo or any foreign government.

The committee accepted other amendments to provide more funds for export promotion and overseas marketing development programs.

The EEP was authorized at a minimum $900 million in fiscal 1991 and between $500 million and $900 million a year from fiscal 1992 through fiscal 1995, under an amendment by Kerrey. He noted that the administration had requested $900 million for the program in its fiscal 1991 budget. The EEP at the time was authorized for $500 million but got only $300 million, committee aides said.

The panel on April 5 rejected, 1-17, an amendment by Pete Wilson, R-Calif., to authorize at least $325 million annually for the Targeted Export Assistance program, which helped private agricultural organizations promote U.S. products in foreign markets.

Wilson wanted to alter an amendment by Montana's Baucus that had been accepted the day before calling for a minimum of $225 million and a maximum of $325 million for targeted export assistance. Although the program was already authorized at $325 million, the administration was spending only about $200 million a year.

Thad Cochran, R-Miss., expressed concern that the committee was trying to direct spending by imposing minimum spending levels, thus "encroaching on the jurisdiction of the Appropriations Committee." Cochran, who also served on the spending panel, warned that "we're going to run into trouble on the floor."

SENATE FLOOR ACTION

The Senate's 70-21 vote on July 27 approving its five-year farm bill (S 2830) largely reaffirmed the basic course of U.S. agriculture policy as set in 1985. *(Vote 187, p. 41-S)*

Senators rejected appeals by farm-state lawmakers to raise the subsidy levels in the bill and direct more government payments to small, family-run farming operations.

... In Farm Bill Battle of the Waterfronts

The 1985 bill did establish a "set-aside" provision to guarantee that 240,000 tons of "Food for Peace," or PL 480, U.S.-flag shipments originated from Great Lakes ports. U.S. ships were thus forced to travel the lakes, providing a base for shipping other goods.

But the set-aside expired at the end of 1989, and Great Lakes ports had no business from U.S.-flag ocean-going ships since.

So when the 1990 farm bill came to the Senate floor, Democrats John Glenn of Ohio, Alan J. Dixon of Illinois and Herb Kohl of Wisconsin sought to restore the Great Lakes set-aside.

Under their proposal, the set-aside would end in 1993. And, to help ailing Great Lakes ports get more business, the measure would waive the three-year waiting period for buyers of foreign ships who put U.S. flags on them.

Gulf-state senators, led by Mississippi Republicans Thad Cochran and Trent Lott, fought the plan vigorously. Southern lawmakers had argued since 1985 that the set-aside unfairly favored the Great Lakes at the expense of gulf-state ports. J. Bennett Johnston, D-La., called the set-aside a "jobs grab from the cheaper ports on the gulf to those along the Great Lakes." But Cochran's attempt to kill the Great Lakes amendment failed narrowly, 46-50, with Great Lakes members drawing surprising support from Maryland, California, Washington and New Jersey. *(Vote 177, p. 39-S)*

Cochran and Lott then went long into the night, explaining the history of the issue on the floor. By midnight, Agriculture Committee Chairman Patrick J. Leahy, D-Vt., and Majority Leader George J. Mitchell, D-Maine — who had both voted with the Great Lakes bloc to fend off Cochran — called for a truce.

Dixon, Glenn and Kohl backed off after Leahy and Mitchell threatened to switch their votes on the amendment. The next day gulf-state members struck a deal that gave Great Lakes members some semblance of victory. Merchant-marine lobbyists came up with a plan to allow Great Lakes ports the new reflagging rules but replace the set-aside with complicated new bidding rules on PL 480 cargo. When asked what impact the deal would have on gulf-state ports, Cochran just smiled and said, "Nothing."

But it gave the Great Lakes senators some clout in conference, where they joined forces with a stronger House position. Conferees approved a provision stipulating that Great Lakes ports would have to be assured of the same percentage of PL 480 cargo as they had in 1984. Foreign vessels were exempted from the normal three-year wait for reflagging so they could qualify to ship PL 480 commodities from Great Lakes ports.

But, except for one successful amendment to do away with the federal honey program, proposals to lower payments or eliminate certain crop programs were also defeated.

The Senate completed floor debate after only six days — a far cry from 1985, when a sharply partisan Senate debated the measure from Oct. 25 until Nov. 23. One of the last items to be resolved in the Senate was a battle between Great Lakes states and other harbor areas over the age-old "cargo preference" requirement that a percentage of federally subsidized agriculture exports be carried on U.S.-flag ships. *(Cargo preference, p. 338)*

Arguments Over Costs

With floor debate on the 1990 farm bill beginning under the threat of a veto, the Senate on July 19 showed that it was willing to slash federal farm programs if the budget required it — but not by depriving affluent farmers of their sizable share of the payments.

Arguing that large farmers were crucial to the smooth operation of federal crop-subsidy programs, farm-state lawmakers easily parried an amendment by Harry Reid, D-Nev., that would have barred farmers who made gross sales of more than $500,000 a year from receiving most federal subsidies. The amendment was killed on a tabling motion, 66-30. *(Vote 162, p. 36-S)*

Earlier, the Senate had accepted an amendment by Agriculture Committee Chairman Leahy and ranking Republican Lugar that cut $3.5 billion out of the cost of the bill. The amendment brought the estimated $54 billion bill just slightly under the allocation for agriculture in the Senate budget resolution.

But it did not satisfy the Bush administration, which broke its high-level silence the week of July 16 with a barrage of criticism of the Senate bill and its House companion. Agriculture Secretary Yeutter said the Senate bill, which sought to freeze most subsidy levels, was sending farmers the wrong signal because White House and congressional negotiators were trying to craft a deficit-reduction package that might require still deeper cuts in agriculture spending.

If Congress sent the final bill to the president before the budget-summit talks concluded and without changes to make it more market-oriented, Yeutter said, he would recommend a veto. "The administration expects the budget summit to achieve substantial, multi-year savings," said a companion statement from the White House's Office of Management and Budget (OMB). "It would be a mistake for Congress to complete action on a bill that gives producers the wrong impression by sending them inaccurate signals about likely program parameters."

The Yeutter complaint brought a quick retort from Chairman Leahy. "At the eleventh hour USDA has cooked up new numbers," he said. "The reality is the Senate farm bill is over $6 billion less than what the president proposed in January."

GOP Divisions Over Savings

A rather typical farm bill dynamic had begun to emerge.

The administration was accusing Congress of being overly generous with farmers. Democrats in the House and Senate were blaming the president and his lieutenants for threatening the economic health of the farm sector. Opponents of the farm program were attacking it as wasteful and inequitable. And farm-state Republicans were wrestling with whether to support the administration's calls for lower farm spending — or side with the Democrats.

Division was already apparent within GOP ranks as Lugar, for one, complained of the administration's tactics.

Lugar had won a hard-fought victory in the Agriculture Committee against increases in price- and income-support rates — known as target prices and loan rates — for wheat, corn, cotton and rice. He said he felt somewhat aggrieved because he achieved basically what the administration demanded: a continuation of current farm policy.

"Without a great deal of assistance, I've managed to achieve a freeze of target prices and loan rates," Lugar said in an interview. "And the failure of the administration to acknowledge this strikes me as curious."

But Minority Leader Dole, according to several Republican aides, believed that Lugar had bargained away too much in committee.

Notably, there remained in the bill a potentially expensive new loan program, the marketing loan, for soybean, wheat and corn growers; a requirement that the Agriculture secretary increase pre-harvest loans if he exercised his authority to lower loan rates; and an end to automatic cuts in the dairy price support during overproduction.

In a letter sent to senators July 16, Yeutter said these and other provisions "depart from the market-oriented focus of the 1985 farm bill."

In addition, although most of the provisions were estimated by the CBO to have little or no cost, the administration said the assumptions built into those estimates were likely to be wrong. The commodity provisions could cost more than $5 billion in 1991-95, the Yeutter letter said.

Leahy and Lugar's floor amendment to trim $3.5 billion from the bill was not sufficient, administration officials said, because it tinkered with farm programs and did not reduce significantly the potential subsidy payments the government would be obligated to make if crop prices fell.

Unless "some real savings" were found on the floor, Dole said, he would offer an amendment to reduce the cost of the farm bill and restore many of the deviations it took from existing law. But neither Dole nor his staff could provide details.

"If we cannot strike an agreement to get this bill under budget, I will not be able to cast a favorable vote," Dole said. "And if we arrive at a point where progress on the committee bill stalls, I believe my substitute ... can be supported by a bipartisan cast of senators."

The Dole-Lugar split was unusual because the two lawmakers appeared to have reversed roles: Usually, on farm matters, it was Lugar who upheld the administration's budget principles and Dole who relished cutting deals with the Democrats to move legislation.

In this case, Lugar helped craft the deal that bound him to the committee bill along with several other Republicans and a bloc of moderate farm-state Democrats, such as Pryor of Arkansas. Dole and the administration hardly participated in the drafting and only after it was reported to the floor did they attempt to regain influence over the final product.

Targeting Subsidies Rejected

Still, the coalition backing the bill seemed in no danger of unraveling.

Reid's amendment to withhold payments from farmers with annual gross sales of more than $500,000 was expected to be a serious challenge, because the idea of "means-testing" farm programs, instead of allowing all producers to participate, was an idea that had acquired growing cachet.

But 2½ hours into the debate, Reid still had not found another senator willing to speak in favor of his amendment.

Reid portrayed the amendment as an opportunity to eliminate the $1.2 billion in federal crop subsidies that was being paid to 14,000 "farmer fat cats" and put the savings to better use, such as improving health care.

But farm-state lawmakers countered that subsidies were paid according to production levels, not need, for an important reason: The biggest farmers were responsible for as much as 40 percent of the nation's agricultural output.

Farm-state lawmakers portrayed the farm program as at least as much a constraint for those farmers as a windfall. Make them ineligible for the farm payments, said Pryor, and "they will be free to grow anything they want. They will double and triple their production. We're going to see massive overproduction, massive decreases in farm prices, massive declines in farm income and, ultimately, rural chaos."

Whether or not fear of such an upheaval influenced the vote, only 14 Republicans and 16 Democrats voted against the motion to table the amendment, although Leahy and Majority Leader George J. Mitchell, D-Maine, were among them.

There remained a potentially bigger threat to the farm bill from those who acknowledged Reid's point — that farm program payments disproportionately went to wealthy corporate farming operations — but did not support his methods. Instead of cutting overall spending on crop subsidies, some farm-state populists, such as South Dakota's Daschle, had amendments in mind to redirect the money to smaller family farmers.

If some of the more expensive proposals passed, Republicans such as Lugar who were supporting the farm bill vowed to withdraw their support. Alternatively, if Republicans such as Dole or Minnesota's Boschwitz succeeded in attaching amendments that trimmed farm spending or upset the committee deal, Democrats threatened to desert the compromise as well.

"It's not the bill I wanted, but I can defend it because we had to have a bipartisan bill to get it passed," said Nebraska Democrat Kerrey, who threatened to offer a targeting amendment if Republicans launched an assault on farm-program spending.

Daschle considered offering an amendment to establish a two-tier income-support structure. Farmers would be offered two target prices: a higher price for a certain amount of their production and a sharply lower price for the rest. Thus, said Daschle, many smaller farmers would effectively get a target price increase, because their total production might not exceed the total output eligible for the higher price.

"The 1980s were the worst period for farm income since records have been kept," Daschle said. "The committee bill as it stands offers no improvement. Even given the budget limits, we can write a farm bill that does more to improve farm income and that does it more fairly than this proposal."

Fellow prairie Democrat Baucus promised to resurrect an amendment he offered unsuccessfully in the Agriculture Committee that would increase target prices with inflation. Under his proposal, target prices would go up by whatever percentage inflation exceeded 4.3 percent.

Sugar and Honey

While members of the Agriculture Committee were still arguing among themselves over the broad outlines of farm policy, other senators were gearing up for selected attacks on key farm programs. The carefully fashioned coalition of farm-state Republicans and Democrats managed, however, to withstand most assaults from both sides: those who wanted to make the bill more generous to farmers and those who wanted to cut subsidies.

Floor managers Leahy and Lugar argued that amendments that greatly altered the basic deal they had worked out in committee would lead to a free-for-all, whose outcome no one could predict.

An important test of their coalition came in an amendment to gut the sugar program. Although the sugar program by law cost the government nothing (and thus was not likely to be affected by the coming budget cuts), many farm-state lawmakers feared that it might be the one subsidy program not to survive on the floor.

But during deliberations July 24, the Senate rejected a 2-cent cut in the 18-cent-per-pound sugar price support. The amendment, offered by Bill Bradley, D-N.J., was tabled, or killed, by a vote of 54-44. *(Vote 166, p. 37-S)*

Later that day, the House defeated the same amendment.

Lugar, however, did not even try to save the government honey program. Lawmakers voted for a four-year phaseout of the controversial price-support mechanism, which provided an average of $77 million a year in subsidies to 6,000 beekeepers. A tabling motion to kill the amendment, which was offered by John H. Chafee, R-R.I., was defeated 46-52, and the amendment was adopted on a voice vote. *(Vote 168, p. 37-S)*

The honey program was not pronouced dead yet, however. In 1985, the program had also been eliminated in the Senate, but restored in conference with the House. Supporters expressed hope that the same would happen again in 1990, arguing that the honey program was important because it helped keep beekeepers in business to pollinate other crops. "You can't import pollination," said Daschle.

Other Subsidies

The Senate was not inclined to make a broad attack on other controversial subsidy programs that benefited a relatively few growers. The Senate rejected an amendment by William V. Roth Jr., R-Del., to repeal the peanut quota system, which artificially raised the cost of domestic peanuts and kept peanut production concentrated in Southeastern states. A tabling motion carried 57-41. *(Vote 173, p. 38-S)*

A group of Democrats from the upper Midwest proved equally incapable of beating Leahy and Lugar on several amendments to raise subsidy levels and direct more of the benefits to smaller farmers.

Daschle offered his amendment to restructure income-support programs for wheat and feed grain producers by offering them two target prices. Wheat farmers, for example, would have received a guaranteed price of $4.10 for the first 12,500 bushels they produced. Additional wheat produced would be supported at only $3.40 a bushel.

The Leahy-Lugar deal, on the other hand, froze the wheat target price at its existing level, $4.

Daschle argued that, under his amendment, small farmers would effectively get a target price increase, because their entire output might be eligible for the higher price. "We have been told time and again that only if the budget would allow, we could get a program that could ensure small farmers long-term viability," he said.

But Lugar and Leahy opposed the amendment because, they said, it would destroy their fragile coalition. "I find the logic of the situation that brought forth this amendment incomprehensible, except with the thought that there are still persons in our society who believe that raising the target price, raising the government price, somehow brings more income," Lugar said.

Leahy said the farm bill was like a Rubik's cube, a puzzle with many interlocking parts. "I believe the deal would begin to fall apart if we changed a face."

Daschle's amendment was defeated 24-72. So was Baucus' amendment to provide target-price increases to partly offset inflation in years when it exceeded 4.3 percent. It was rejected 26-72. *(Votes 170, 172, p. 38-S)*

CONFERENCE ACTION

As the 1990 farm bill moved to conference at the end of the year, it became the chaser in a laborious game of shadow tag — it moved and stopped when the budget did.

When the House soundly rejected the budget-summit agreement Oct. 5, it put a freeze on the House-Senate conference negotiating a final version of the $55 billion farm bill.

Without a budget, the most important question of the conference — how much to cut crop subsidies — no longer had an answer. "It puts the conference on hold," said House Agriculture Committee member Glickman.

The House action threw the farm bill into chaos and forced conferees to rethink their strategies. The administration had hoped to use the budget to force fundamental changes in the bill's thrust. Some lawmakers, dissatisfied with some stringent environmental controls in the bill, had hoped they could be stripped out in the time crunch to meet the budget. Now both strategies were in doubt.

Farm-state lawmakers sensed that they might be vulnerable again to even deeper cuts than the $13 billion from farm programs the summit demanded. But, with the congressional elections approaching, both Democrats and Republicans were vowing to defend the farmer at all costs. "I think the number was as high as it's ever going to get," said Glickman of the summit agreement.

Agriculture Secretary Yeutter called the House action a "betrayal of political responsibility [that] makes many meritorious agricultural programs more vulnerable to cuts than before." He added, "I will strongly resist any effort to cut agricultural expenditures further."

Even before the budget vote, the farm-bill conference was proceeding at a glacial pace. Two weeks after deliberations had begun, the members only completed work on four of the Senate bill's 24 sections. And those two — forestry and credit — were relatively minor and uncontroversial.

"It certainly has been slow-moving, but that is almost inevitable with many members preoccupied with the budget question," said Lugar, ranking Republican on the Senate Agriculture Committee.

House conferees were not even finally selected until the week of Oct. 1. With eight committees claiming jurisdiction over the 1,000-page bill, Speaker Thomas S. Foley, D-Wash., finally named 121 members to negotiate for the House, including 42 from Agriculture.

Very few members not on the Agriculture Committee showed up for the meetings. Yet their staffs met regularly to resolve differences between the two bills. That delayed matters somewhat.

A standoff between members of the House and Senate Agriculture committees also slowed the conference. Some

Continued on p. 347

1990 Farm Bill Provisions

Following are provisions of the Food, Agriculture, Conservation, and Trade Act (S 2830 — PL 101-624) as cleared by Congress on Oct. 25 and signed by President Bush on Nov. 28, along with agriculture provisions of the Omnibus Budget Reconciliation Act (HR 5835 — PL 101-508) as signed by Bush on Nov. 5:

Commodities

Wheat and Feed Grains

• **Price and income supports.** Maintained the existing system of offering crop loans to farmers at harvest, with farmers using their crops as collateral and having the option of repaying the loans plus interest, or defaulting on the loans, keeping the principal and leaving the government with no recourse except to take possession of the crops.

• **Target price.** Maintained a system of offering "deficiency" payments to farmers to make up any shortfall between the national weighted average market sale prices received by farmers during the year and certain "target" prices.

The bill set a floor under target prices for wheat and feed grains, effectively freezing them at 1990 levels — $4 per bushel of wheat and $2.75 per bushel of corn.

Sorghum was set at a level the Agriculture secretary determined to be fair and reasonable in relation to corn. The same was true for oats, though the price could not be less than $1.45 per bushel. The price for barley could not be less than 85.8 percent of the target price for corn.

• **Loan rates.** Changed the formula for setting loan rates. Instead of giving the secretary discretion to set the basic loan rate at 75 percent to 85 percent of the previous five-year moving average of market prices, excluding the high and low years, the bill mandated that the loan rates be set at 85 percent of the previous five-year average, excluding the high and low years. The decline in the basic loan rate was limited to no more than 5 percent a year.

The secretary was given authority to reduce the loan rate, based on estimates of surplus levels.

For wheat, if the estimated year-end surplus was at least 30 percent, the secretary could reduce the loan level by up to 10 percent. If the ratio was less than 30 percent but not less than 15 percent, the loan rate could be lowered by up to 5 percent.

For feed grains, if the estimated year-end surplus was at least 25 percent, the loan rate could be reduced up to 10 percent. If the ratio was less than 25 percent but not less than 12.5 percent, the loan rate could be reduced by up to 5 percent.

The secretary was given the authority to reduce the loan rate an additional 10 percent if he determined that it was necessary to keep U.S. wheat and feed grains competitive in the world market. The loan rate could not be lower than $2.44 a bushel for wheat and $1.76 a bushel for corn, except under the basic 85 percent formula.

• **Acreage Reduction Program (ARP).** Set acreage-reduction requirements for producers as a condition for receiving price- and crop-support loans. For wheat in 1992-1995, if surpluses exceeded 40 percent, the percentage of land that producers had to retire had to be from 10 percent to 20 percent.

If surpluses were 40 percent or less, the secretary could provide for an ARP of no greater than 15 percent.

For feed grains in 1991-1995, if surpluses were greater than 25 percent, the ARP would have to be at least 10 percent but no more than 20 percent. If surpluses were 25 percent or less, the secretary could set the ARP at 12.5 percent or less.

The secretary was not required to establish an ARP. For the 1991 crop of wheat, the ARP would be set at 15 percent.

• **0/92 program.** Reauthorized the 0/92 program, in which producers who did not plant wheat and feed grains were eligible for 92 percent of the deficiency payment they collected for these crops. Producers would be allowed to plant oilseeds other than soybeans (including canola, sunflowers, safflower and flaxseed) on 0/92 acres devoted to conservation uses.

The secretary had the option to offer producers an increase or decrease in their acreage-reduction program percentages in return for a corresponding increase or decrease in their target price.

For wheat, the allowable increase in the ARP would be 10 percent for 1991 and 15 percent for the following crop years, with a maximum overall ARP of 25 percent.

For feed grains, the allowable ARP adjustment in 1991 would be 5 percent and 10 percent the following years, not to exceed a total ARP of 20 percent.

For every 1 percentage-point increase in the ARP, the Agriculture Department would have to increase the producer's target price by 0.5 percent to 1 percent. This option was not supposed to cause additional outlays.

When the secretary determined that domestic oat production would not meet domestic demand, he was authorized to let producers plant oats on their set-aside acreage. If domestic oat production was estimated to exceed domestic demand, the secretary was authorized to limit the amount of oat acreage so that output met demand.

Cotton

• **Target price.** Set a floor under the upland cotton target price at 73 cents a pound, effectively freezing it at the existing 1990 level for 1991 through 1995. For extra long staple cotton, the target price would be set at 120 percent of the loan rate.

• **Loan rate.** Kept the existing formula for setting the loan rate. For upland cotton, the loan level would have to be either 85 percent of the five-year moving average, dropping the high and low years, or 90 percent of a 15-week average of the five lowest cotton-price quotes for Northern Europe, whichever was lower.

The loan rate could not be reduced more than 5 percent a year or fall below 50 cents a pound.

For extra long staple cotton, the loan rate would have to be set at 85 percent of the five-year moving average of market prices, dropping the high and low years.

• **Marketing loan.** Continued the "marketing loan" for cotton, which permitted producers to repay their government loans at the world market price when it was lower than the loan rate.

The bill established a new procedure for ensuring that the price of U.S. cotton was competitive abroad. Marketing certificates must be issued to domestic users and exporters when the lowest U.S. price as quoted in Northern Europe exceeded the average of the five cheapest Northern European prices by more than 1.25 cents per pound for four consecutive weeks.

• **Import quota.** Required a quota on imported cotton if U.S. cotton was uncompetitive in world markets for 10 consecutive weeks. The quota was equal to one week's consumption of upland cotton by domestic mills at the average price during the most recent three months.

• **Acreage Reduction Program (ARP).** Required the Agriculture secretary to announce no later than Jan. 1 the percentage of land farmers would have to idle in the coming year to qualify for price and income supports.

The secretary was directed to achieve a 30 percent surplus of stocks, but he was barred from imposing an acreage reduction of more than 25 percent. The secretary was required also to use a paid land diversion to achieve the surplus target.

The bill maintained the 50/92 option, which gave producers 92 percent of their annual deficiency payments if they idled at least 50 percent of their acreage.

The secretary had the option of offering producers not participating in 50/92 an increase or decrease in their ARP percentages in return for a corresponding increase or decrease in their target price.

ARPs could be increased a maximum of 10 percent, with a maximum overall ARP of 25 percent. For every percentage point increase or decrease in the ARP, the secretary was required to increase or decrease the producer's target price by 0.5 percent to 1 percent.

Rice

• **Target price.** Set a floor under the target price for the 1991 through 1995 crops of rice, effectively freezing it at the existing 1990 level of $10.71 per hundredweight.

• **Loan rate.** Established the loan level at 85 percent of the moving average of market prices, dropping the high and low years. The loan rate could not be reduced more than 5 percent a year and could not be below $6.50 per hundredweight.

• **Marketing loan.** Continued the marketing loan for rice, which permited producers to repay their government loans at the world market price when it was lower than the loan rate.

The bill required that payments to rice producers be made in the form of negotiable marketing certificates, redeemable for cash or government-owned commodities, whenever the world price was below the loan rate.

• **Acreage Reduction Program (ARP).** Directed the Agriculture secretary to employ an acreage reduction program to achieve an annual surplus that was equal to 16.5 percent to 20 percent of the average production over the three preceding years. The acreage reduction could not exceed 35 percent.

The bill continued to give producers the 50/92 option to idle at least 50 percent of their land and still receive 92 percent of their annual deficiency payments. The secretary had the option to provide 92 percent payment to producers who planted none of their acreage, but was required to do so for producers prevented from planting rice by natural disasters.

The secretary had the option of offering producers not participating an increase or decrease in their ARP percentages in return for a corresponding increase or decrease in their target price. The secretary could offer this option only if the ARP was 20 percent or less.

ARPs could be increased a maximum of 10 percent, with a maximum overall ARP of 25 percent. For every percentage point increase or decrease in the ARP, the secretary was required to increase or decrease the producer's target price by 0.5 percent to 1 percent.

Soybeans

• **Marketing loan.** Restructured the soybean price-support program by mandating the use of a marketing loan, in which producers repaid their government loans at the world price when it was lower than the loan rate. A marketing loan also would be required for other oilseeds, including sunflower, canola, safflower, mustard seed, flaxseed and other crops designated by the Agriculture Department.

• **Loan rate.** Set the soybean loan rate at $5.02 per bushel for the 1991-95 crop years.

The loan level for sunflower seed, canola seed, rapeseed, safflower seed, flaxseed, and mustard seed was 89 cents per pound. For other oilseeds, the Agriculture secretary was directed to set a loan level that was "fair and reasonable" in relation to soybeans.

• **Acreage limitation.** Barred the secretary from requiring producers to participate in production adjustment programs as a condition of eligibility.

Sugar

• **Price support.** Continued the existing system of giving non-recourse loans to sugar processors who agreed to pay the support price to sugar cane and beet producers. The bill maintained the existing loan rate at 18 cents a pound for raw cane sugar (plus a 3-cent transportation differential) and gave the Agriculture secretary authority to increase the loan rate based on the cost of production and other factors. The bill set the beet loan level based on the weighted averages of the most recent five years of producer returns for sugar beets relative to cane.

The secretary would have to continue to operate the program at no cost to the federal government, effectively requiring the government to limit sugar imports to maintain domestic prices above the loan rate.

• **Imports.** Set a minimum import level of 1.25 million short tons a year. The bill authorized a tariff rate quota system to replace import quotas.

• **Marketing controls.** Required the secretary to establish marketing allotments for sugar processors if the secretary estimated that imports would fall below 1.25 million short tons. Processors would be prohibited from marketing, including pledging as loan collateral, any sugar in excess of their marketing allotment. The bill required a proportionate allocation of allotments among producers of sugar cane in states with more than 250 producers. It imposed a marketing control on crystalline fructose equivalent to 200,000 tons of sugar, but none on high fructose corn syrup.

• **Disaster payments.** Required disaster payments to producers who lost more than 40 percent of their crop in 1990. The payment would have to be at a rate of 50 percent of the loan rate and made on the amount of sugar that was harvested. The payments would be subject to advance appropriation.

Dairy

• **Price support.** Continued the system of government purchases of milk products (butter, cheese and dry milk) from processors in order to enure a minimum price to producers during periods of oversupply. The bill set a floor for the support price at $10.10 per hundredweight through 1995.

The bill mandated at least a 25-cent increase in the support price if purchases by the Commodity Credit Corporation (CCC) were projected to be less than 3.5 billion pounds in a year. The support price would have to be lowered between 25 cents and 50 cents if purchases were projected to exceed 5 billion pounds. The support price would remain unchanged if purchases were from 3.5 billion pounds to 5 billion pounds.

The bill excluded any increase in imports of dairy products from projections of annual surpluses, allowing greater accumulation of surplus before triggering price-support cuts.

• **Supply management.** Required the Agriculture secretary to recommend measures for limiting government purchases of surplus dairy products. The study could not consider such measures as mandatory cattle slaughter or price-support cuts.

The bill directed the secretary to impose assessments on dairy farmers beginning in 1992 if CCC purchases were projected to exceed 7 billion pounds. The assessments could be imposed only if Congress failed to enact legislation to limit production of surplus milk.

The amount of the assessments was intended to cover the cost of the CCC purchasing dairy products above the 7 billion pound level.

• **Make allowances.** Prohibited the states, effective 12 months after enactment, from using a greater allowance than provided for in the federal program to establish a Grade A price for milk for manufacturing butter, nonfat milk or cheese.

• **Export sales.** Continued the existing mandate to make export sales by the CCC of not less than 150,000 metric tons of dairy products (not less than 100,000 metric tons of butter and not less than 20,000 metric tons of cheese) if it did not interfere with regular commercial trade.

Wool and Mohair

• **Price support.** Extended the existing price-support program, freezing the wool price support at 77.5 percent of an amount formulated from production costs and continuing the support level for pulled wool and mohair in relation to the level for shorn wool.

The bill set an annual per farmer payment limitation of $200,000 in 1991, $175,000 in 1992, $150,000 in 1993, and $125,000 in 1994 and 1995.

Honey

• **Price support.** Extended the non-recourse loan program for honey, including the marketing loan, in which producers repaid their government loans at a level determined by the Agriculture secretary when the world price was lower than the support rate. A floor was set at the existing support rate of 53.8 cents per pound.

• **Payment limits.** Set a total per-farmer payment limitation of $200,000 in 1991, $175,000 in 1992, $150,000 in 1993, and $125,000 in 1994.

Peanuts

• **Quota system.** Continued the existing peanut program, in which the government supported the price of peanuts through a quota system. Growers who held marketing quotas for domestic sales would have to comply with those quotas in order to qualify for price supports. The bill set a national marketing quota floor of 1.35 million tons. When the Agriculture Department made adjustments in the national quota, state quota allocations would have to be based on a state's 1990 share of the national quota.

The bill permitted the distribution of up to 25 percent of all poundage quotas released in the state to farms not having a poundage quota in the previous year. In Texas only, one-third of poundage quota increases would have to be distributed to quota farms producing contract non-quota "additional" peanuts, and two-thirds of additional poundage quota increases would be distributed to other farms in the state.

The bill required a tenant to share equally in any increase in the quota resulting from the tenant's production.

• **Support level.** Continued non-recourse loans, which were available for all peanuts produced at two support levels. The higher loan rate, available only for quota peanuts, was set at the previous year's support level. The department was authorized to increase the quota price up to 5 percent annually to mitigate the cost of production. "Additional" peanuts produced in excess of the quotas or by producers without a quota would be supported at a lower rate.

General Commodity Provisions

• **Flexibility.** Permitted producers limited flexibility to alter their crop mix without losing base acreage for program crops such as wheat, feed grains, cotton and rice. The goal was to allow producers to respond better to market signals, instead of producing crops merely to bring in subsidies.

Base acreage was the average of acres planted to particular crops and considered planted for harvest during the five preceding years. Losing base acreage for specific crops reduced the amount of price-support loans and other benefits available to a producer in the future.

The bill allowed producers to plant up to 25 percent of their wheat, feed grains, cotton and rice base acreage with other crops, including any program crop, oilseed crop, industrial and experimental crop, except any fruit and vegetable crop, including potatoes and dry edible beans not designated by the Agriculture secretary as experimental or industrial. No deficiency payments could be made on flexible acres.

If the secretary estimated that the national average soybean price would be less than 105 percent of the loan rate, the quantity of crop acreage that could be planted with soybeans could not exceed 15 percent.

In addition, to make required deficit-reduction savings in agriculture programs, the reconciliation made a mandatory reduction of 15 percent in the amount of acreage that was eligible for government subsidy payments from 1991 to 1995. In effect, producers could not plant whatever they wanted on up to 25 percent of their acreage usually devoted to program crops. On 15 percent of that, the producer was ineligible for program payments, no matter what he planted. On the remaining 10 percent, the producer had the option of planting something other than program crops, but he would have to forgo payments.

• **Payment limitations.** Maintained the existing $50,000 limit on direct payments and deficiency payments, adding a new limit of $75,000 on total marketing loan payments and so-called Findley payments that resulted from lowered loan rates. The effective cap on total payments was lowered from $500,000 to $250,000.

Most farm program payments would be allocated directly to individuals for the purpose of payment limitations, while deficiency and land diversion payments would continue to be attributed to farming entities.

• **Commodity reserves.** Extended the operation of the long-term Farmer-Owned Reserve, which kept wheat and feed-grain stocks off the market as long as prices were below designated release levels.

The bill requireed the Agriculture Department to replenish, within 18 months, the Food Security Wheat Reserve, which was used during periods of tight U.S. wheat supplies to provide international food aid, either by using appropriated funds or drawing on stocks of the Commodity Credit Corporation.

The levels in the reserve could not be less than 300 million bushels or more than 450 million bushels of wheat, and not less than 600 million bushels nor more than 900 million bushels of feed grains.

Crops could be stored in the reserve when the average price for wheat or corn during the previous 90 days exceeded 120 percent of the loan rate, and when the projected surplus-to-use ratio was at least 37.5 percent for wheat and 22.5 percent for corn.

Deficit-Reduction Provisions

• **Triple base.** In order to comply with the deficit-reduction "reconciliation" target for agriculture, the bill (HR 5835) reduced by 15 percent the amount of program crop acreage on which the government made subsidy payments from 1991 through 1995.

Under the so-called triple base plan, farms receiving subsidies had three categories of land: the annually announced acreage reduction percentage, which took land out of production; the permitted acreage on which the program crop was planted and which was eligible for deficiency payments; and the 15 percent of their land which was not eligible for payments.

On the third category, producers could plant any program crop (wheat, corn, cotton and rice), oilseeds (such as soybeans, canola and sunflower) or non-program crops except fruits and vegetables. Crops planted on this land were eligible for loans and marketing loans.

For the 1991 crop of winter wheat only, producers had the option to participate in the 15 percent triple base plan or to have their deficiency payments calculated on a 12-month average.

For other crops of wheat, feed grains and rice, the deficiency payment would have to be calculated on a 12-month basis, rather than the existing five-month basis, in 1994 and 1995. The change would reduce government outlays.

• **Acreage Reduction Program (ARP).** Established maximum acreage levels of 20 percent for wheat and feed grains, 25 percent for cotton, and 35 percent for rice, based on certain surplus levels. The reconciliation bill set a minimum ARP level for wheat of 6 percent in 1992, 5 percent in 1993, 7 percent in 1994, and 5 percent in 1995, and a minimum ARP level of 7.5 percent for feed grains.

• **Other commodities.** Authorized loan origination fees and other assessments on other commodities. Dairy producers would have to pay a 5-cent fee in fiscal 1991 and an 11-cent fee for 1992 through 1995. The Agriculture secretary had authority to refund this fee if a producer could prove his milk production had not increased from the previous year's level. Producers of oilseeds would have to pay a 2 percent loan-origination fee. Peanuts, honey and tobacco were subject to a 1 percent loan fee. Wool and mohair producers would have 1 percent deducted from their incentive payments.

• **Loan authorizations.** Established loan levels for the Rural Electrification and Telephone Revolving Fund, then reduced the levels to be able to claim the savings, as follows: an $896 million authorization in fiscal 1991 reduced by $224 million; a $932 million authorization in fiscal 1992 reduced by $234 million; a $969 million authorization in fiscal 1993 reduced by $244 million; a $1.01 billion authorization in fiscal 1994 reduced by $256 million; and a $1.05 billion authorization for fiscal 1995 reduced by $267 million.

The bill established loan levels for the Farmers Home Administration (FmHA) Agricultural Credit Insurance Fund, then reduced the levels in order to be able to claim the savings, as follows: a $4.2 billion authorization in fiscal 1991 and a reduction in direct loans of $482 million; a $4.3 billion authorization for fiscal 1992 and a reduction in direct loans of $614 million; a $4.5 billion authorization for fiscal 1993 and a reduction in direct loans of $760 million; a $4.7 billion authorization in fiscal 1994 and a reduction in direct loans of $859 million; and a $4.9 billion authorization for fiscal 1995 and a reduction in direct loans of $907 million.

• **GATT.** Required the secretary, if the United States did not enter into an agreement under the General Agreement on Tariffs and Trade (GATT) by June 30, 1992, to increase by $1 billion the level of spending in fiscal 1994 and 1995 on export promotion programs for agricultural goods. The secretary was also authorized to waive minimum levels of acreage that would have to be retired by producers of program crops in 1993, 1994 and 1995. And the secretary could allow producers to repay their crop loans for wheat and feed grains at levels established in the Agricultural Act of 1949.

If there was no GATT agreement by June 30, 1993, the secretary could waive all cuts required in agriculture spending to meet the deficit-reduction targets, in addition to the other measures.

Trade

Food for Peace (PL 480)

• **Authorization.** Overhauled the Food for Peace program, also known as PL 480, in which U.S. commodities were donated and sold overseas to combat hunger and stimulate export markets. The bill extended the credit sales program (Title I) as well as the grant program (Title II), in which commodities were donated through private voluntary organizations, but it established another government-to-government grant program (Title III).

The bill repealed the authorization ceiling on total costs of the concessional sales and government-to-government grant programs. Annual Title II appropriations were limited to no more than $1 billion, unless the president determined that more was necessary to meet urgent humanitarian needs. Not less than 40 percent of the amounts available for Title I could be used to carry out sales programs and not less than 40 percent could be used for the grant program.

• **Delegation of authority.** Specified that the president should designate the Agriculture Department to carry out the credit sales program and the Agency for International Development (AID) to carry out the grant programs. The bill maintained the Agriculture secretary's authority to determine commodities available for export; however, such determination would have to be made before the beginning of the fiscal year, and the secretary's authority to change the "docket" during the year was limited.

The bill continued to allow the program to be used to advance U.S. foreign policy goals, but it narrowed the definition of foreign policy to include only improving the food security of recipient nations. It removed a requirement that countries be termed "friendly" before thay could receive PL 480 funds.

• **Eligible countries.** Maintained a requirement that 75 percent of PL 480 funds be programmed to poorer developing countries, as defined by the World Bank. The bill authorized the department to determine which countries were eligible for Title I, but they would have to be countries with a demonstrated potential to become U.S. markets. AID had the authority to determine eligibility for Title III, giving priority to countries with high levels of malnutrition, a daily per capita consumption of less than 2,300 calories, an under-5 child mortality rate of more than 100 per 1,000 births, and an inability to meet its food requirements through domestic production or imports.

• **Shipping agents.** Gave the secretary or the Commodity Credit Corporation authority to serve as shipping agent for Title I transactions and required full and open competition for the purchase of commodities and ocean transportation.

• **Cargo preference.** Renewed a requirement that 50 percent of PL 480 shipments be transported on U.S.-flag vessels. Great Lakes ports would have to be assured of the same percentage of such cargo as they had in 1984. Foreign vessels would be exempt from the normal three-year wait for reflagging so that they could qualify to ship PL 480 commodities from Great Lakes ports.

Exports

• **Export Enhancement Program (EEP).** Extended through 1995 the Export Enhancement Program, in which the government subsidized exports of U.S. farm products by paying cash bonuses or surplus commodities to exporters. The bill established a minimum funding level of $500 million a year.

The bill required exporters, users or processors who received EEP bonuses to maintain records of the transaction for five years, and permitted the Agriculture secretary to have complete access. The secretary could require participants to maintain and make available all of their transaction records for the five previous years, even transactions not conducted through EEP.

• **Market Promotion Program.** Reauthorized and broadened the scope of the old Targeted Export Assistance program (TEA), which provided funds and commodities to trade organizations for the purpose of promoting U.S. exports, and renamed it the Market Promotion Program (MPP). While priority would still have to be given to markets that were subject to unfair trade practices, the program could be used to help encourage the development and expansion of foreign markets generally.

The bill allowed program funds to be used to advertise specific brands of products in a foreign country under terms and conditions established by the secretary. The bill authorizeed funding of $200 million a year through fiscal 1995.

• **Export credit guarantees.** Reauthorized the program providing short-term (up to three years) and intermediate-term (three to 10 years) export credit guarantees. The bill provided at least $5 billion annually for five years in short-term credits and $500 million annually for intermediate credit guarantees. It requireed that only the export of commodities with U.S. components as defined by the revised 1978 Trade Act could be financed or guaranteed.

The bill prohibited the granting of credit to countries that had a pattern of human rights violations. It authorized the secretary to waive restrictions on loans that would be detrimental to U.S. farmers.

• **High-value products.** Required that at least 25 percent of the funds for export subsidy programs be used to promote the export of high-value commodities and value-added products.

• **Emerging democracies.** Authorized additional short-term export credit guarantees of $1 billion for fiscal 1991-95 for short- and intermediate-term credit guarantees to emerging democracies.

Other Farm Programs

Research

• **General research.** Authorized spending ceilings for federal agriculture research of $850 million annually, including funds for several new programs; $310 million for state agricultural experiment stations; $420 million for extension programs; and $50 million for research facilities. The bill also authorized $63 million in fiscal 1991 for food and nutrition education with annual increases to $83 million by fiscal 1995; $60 million for animal health and disease programs; and $50 million for higher education grants and fellowships.

• **Competitive grants.** Expanded the competitive grant program for high-priority agricultural research, including plant systems; animal systems; nutrition, food quality, and health; natural resources and the environment; engineering products and processes; and markets, trade and policy.

The bill authorized $150 million in fiscal 1991, $275 million in fiscal 1992, $350 million in fiscal 1993, $400 million for fiscal 1994, and $500 million for fiscal 1995.

• **Sustainable agriculture.** Authorized $40 million for research into sustainable agriculture. The bill defined sustainable agriculture as an integrated system of plant and animal production practices having a site-specific application that would, over the long-term, satisfy human food and fiber needs; enhance environmental quality and the natural resource base upon which the agriculture economy depended; make the most efficient use of non-renewable resources and on-farm resources and integrate, where appropriate, natural biological cycles and controls; sustain the economic viability of farm operations; and enhance the quality of life for farmers and society.

Authorized programs included matching grants for state programs, cooperative research with colleges and universities, and training for agricultural extension agents.

• **Alternative agriculture.** Established an Applied Agricultural Research Commercialization Center within the Agriculture Department to promote the development of marketable farm products other than food and other traditional forest or fiber products and foster economic development in rural areas. The board was authorized to make low-interest loans and loan guarantees to researchers and consortia, including up to six regional centers created by the bill.

The bill authorized funding of $10 million in fiscal 1991, increasing to $75 million by 1994.

Conservation

• **'Sodbuster.'** Reauthorized the "sodbuster" program to discourage cultivation of fragile soils. Monetary penalties ranging from $500 to $5,000 could be imposed on producers for inadvertent violations, but they would lose all of their federal benefits if they violated the statute more than once in a five-year period.

The bill expanded the list of federal benefits denied farmers who cultivated such land without an approved conservation plan to include disaster-assistance payments for tree-planting, conservation program payments, Conservation Reserve Program (CRP) payments, Wetland and Environmental Easement program payments, Natural Resource payments and funds under the Small Watersheds Program.

• **'Swampbuster.'** Reauthorized the "swampbuster" program to deny federal benefits to producers who drained and cultivated wetlands. The bill specified that all three characteristics of a wetland — hydric soils, hydrology and hydropytic vegetation — would have to be present for a wetland to be subject to the restrictions. The Agriculture Department would have to exempt farmers from swampbuster when draining would have a minimal effect.

Swampbuster was triggered at the time a wetland was drained, not when it was cropped, as existing law provided. The bill allowed the use of graduated penalties (ranging from $750 to $10,000) for inadvertent drainings, as long as the producer agreed to restore the wetlands. However, the producer would lose all of his benefits if he violated the statute more than once during a 10-year period. The bill expanded the list of federal benefits denied farmers who cultivated such land without an approved conservation plan to include disaster-assistance payments for tree-planting, conservation program payments, CRP payments, Wetland and Environmental Easement program payments, Natural Resource payments and funds under the Small Watersheds Program.

The bill exempted producers from loss of benefits if the wetland had been farmed in the past and its conversion was mitigated by the restoration of another drained wetland.

• **Conservation reserves.** Created an Agricultural Resources Conservation Program (ARC) to protect highly erodible land, wetlands and land susceptible to water pollution caused by farming. Included in the ARC umbrella were three programs: the existing Conservation Reserve Program, in which producers were paid to remove highly erodible land from production for 10 years; a new Wetlands Reserve Program, which paid farmers to place wetlands in easements for 30 years or longer; and a new Water Quality Incentives Program, which gave producers financial assistance for the purpose of reducing water pollution caused by farming.

Enrollment in the CRP was targeted to reach not less than 40 million acres nor more than 45 million acres by 1995. That could include environmentally sensitive land, shelterbelts, windbreaks and marginal pastureland on which trees had been planted. Up to 1 million acres of wetlands could be enrolled in the wetlands reserve, while there was a 10-million acre target for the water quality program.

• **Crop rotation.** Established a new program to encourage farmers to rotate their crops and plant beneficial resource-conserving crops, without losing eligibility for the same level of crop subsidy payments.

• **Pesticide recordkeeping.** Required farmers to keep a record of their application of certain hazardous chemicals, known as "restricted use" pesticides. The records would have to be provided to the Agriculture Department and made available to health-care professionals who requested information about specific cases. The public could gain access to the pesticide-use information through a Freedom of Information Act request, but the names of producers and the specific location of their farms could not be released.

Forestry

• **Forest stewardship.** Reauthorized and created several programs to encourage better stewardship of private forests and offered financial assistance for timber and conservation activities.

• **America the Beautiful.** Establishsd a private, nonprofit foundation to promote tree-planting and related conservation activities. The foundation provided grants to help support planting, protection and cultivation of trees. The goal was to plant 1 billion trees. The bill authorized a $25 million grant in fiscal 1991 with future support to come from private sources.

• **Disaster assistance.** Authorized the Agriculture Department to provide disaster assistance to forestland owners who suffered losses due to damaging weather or wildfire. Disasters after October 1989 were covered. Landowners could be reimbursed for up to 65 percent of the cost of re-establishing tree stands or given sufficient tree seedlings to reforest the areas. Individuals could not receive more than $25,000 a year in assistance, and the bill barred landowners with gross revenues of more than $2 million a year from receiving assistance.

Nutrition Programs

Food Stamps

• **Benefits and eligibility.** Reauthorized the food stamp program for five years. Basic benefits would have to be be kept at the existing 103 percent of the Thrifty Food Plan (a government estimate of the market-basket value of common foodstuffs). The excess shelter expense ceiling would have to be kept at the existing $177 a month.

States were authorized to allow approved restaurants to accept food stamps for the purpose of feeding the homeless. Residents of Guam and the Virgin Islands were allowed to use food stamps for meals in senior citizens' centers and private establishments offering meals at reduced prices.

The bill excluded from the calculation of income in determining food stamp eligibility the following: education loans, grants and scholarships, clothing allowances provided by state assistance programs, assistance payments made to a third party on behalf of a household residing in transitional housing, and general state welfare payments.

• **Electronic benefit transfer.** Authorized online electronic benefit transfer systems replacing coupons with plastic cards as an operational alternative. The bill required that all checkout lanes in grocery stores in which food stamps were used in at least 15 percent of its sales be equipped with special devices, at the Agriculture Department's expense.

• **Minimum benefit.** Required the existing $410 minimum benefit for one- and two-person households to be adjusted for inflation each October and rounded to the nearest $5.

• **Fraud and misuse.** Strengthened various reporting requirements and imposed fines on retail and wholesale food operations that accepted loose coupons or food stamps from unauthorized third parties or used food stamps in money laundering schemes or computer fraud. Retail food stores would be permanently disqualified from handling food stamps if firearms or illegal drugs were sold for food stamp coupons. The bill authorized a fine of up to $250,000 and a prison term of up to 20 years for laundering coupons or authorization cards worth more than $5,000.

Other Nutrition Programs

• **Emergency food assistance.** Reauthorized the Temporary Emergency Food Assistance Program (TEFAP) for five years, eliminating the word "temporary" and requiring the Agriculture secretary to make surplus commodities from the Commodity Credit Corporation (CCC) available to feeding organizations. The secretary was required to spend $175 million in fiscal 1991, $190 million in fiscal 1992 and $220 million a year from fiscal 1993-95.

• **Puerto Rico.** Set authorization levels for nutrition block grants to Puerto Rico at $985 million in fiscal 1991, gradually increasing through 1995.

• **Other nutrition programs.** Reauthorized distribution of commodities to soup kitchens and food banks, with a requirement that $32 million of commodities be purchased annually.

The bill also reauthorized the Commodity Supplemental Food program, requiring the CCC, to the extent inventories existed, to provide 7 million pounds of cheese a year from fiscal 1991-95.

Miscellaneous

• **Disaster protection.** Required that crops covered by crop insurance in one county of a state be covered throughout the state and that rates be adjusted to achieve actuarial sufficiency. However, it would cap rate increases at no more than 20 percent of the previous year's rate. The bill directed the Agriculture secretary to use the Agricultural Stabilization and Conservation Service in providing crop insurance information and agent lists to farmers. It included a sense of Congress resolution supporting the continuation of crop insurance and the use of funds borrowed from the Commodity Credit Corporation to continue the program.

Direct disaster payments were authorized for 1990 crops.

• **Rural development.** Established a new Rural Development Administration within the Agriculture Department and transfered most duties relating to rural development to the agency. New programs were authorized to promote economic development and improve schools, health care and water supply in rural areas.

The bill permitted up to five states to set up state rural economic development review panels, whose job would be to rank applications for funds within the state's allocation of federal funds. The secretary retained authority for distributing funds. The bill authorized appropriations to establish revolving loan funds in up to five states, which would provide lines of credit to nonprofit corporations and public agencies in rural development.

The bill removed the cap on authorization of appropriations for rural water and waste facilities and authorized the secretary to make loans to Rural Electrification Administration (REA) borrowers for water and sewer projects. Up to 50 percent of the cost of the projects could be loaned. The bill expanded the authority of the banks for cooperatives of the Farm Credit System to make water and sewer loans to communities with populations of less than 20,000.

The FmHA was authorized to make up to $25 million in loans to small communities for emergency water and waste-facility projects. Another $30 million was authorized for loans to communities facing significant health risks due to lack of sewer and water treatment facilities.

The bill established grants to encourage and improve the use of telecommunications and computer networks. It authorized low- and market-rate loans to businesses, local governments or public agencies to fund facilities in which participants shared telecommunications equipment, computers and software. It authorized $15 million annually for fiscal 1991-94.

The bill allowed REA borrowers to defer making any loan payments if funds in an amount equal to the deferment of five or 10 years were used for rural development projects, as long as the deferral was not more than half the cost of the project and the borrower made a payment to REA equal to the amount deferred. The bill created a Rural Business Incubator fund and permited the REA to make grants or low-interest loans (5 percent or less) to its borrowers and other nonprofit entities to support the operation of incubators, designed to promote business creation and relocation at certain sites.

- **Organic certification.** Required the department to set national minimum standards (and permited states to adopt more restrictive standards) for the production and labeling of organic foods.
- **Credit.** Reduced from three years to one year the time during which the FmHA would have to dispose of land in its inventory. People who had leased property acquired by FmHA before Jan. 6, 1988, had the right of first refusal on the sale of the property during a limited period. Beginning farmers and ranchers also had preference to purchase inventory property.

The bill required that the continued viability of farms be maintained when conservation easements were placed on inventory property. Easements placed on drained wetlands could not exceed 10 percent of the existing cropland. Easements placed on frequently cropped wetlands could not exceed 20 percent of the farm. The bill increased the interest rate subsidy on certain guaranteed loans to 4 percent. It also provided for a gradual shift from direct government lending to farmers in favor of government guarantees of private loans.

It limited FmHA borrowers to a single write-down for loans made after Jan. 6, 1988. There was a lifetime cap of $300,000 in principal and interest on FmHA borrowers. The Farm Credit Administration was authorized to oversee the financial condition of the Federal Agricultural Mortgage Corporation (Farmer Mac). The bill also created a secondary market for FmHA loans through Farmer Mac. ■

Continued from p. 341

House members wanted to move quickly to negotiations on the commodity sections, which set subsidy levels for the big program crops of wheat, corn, cotton and rice. But Senate participants resisted that suggestion, believing it would reduce the incentive to get agreement on the more controversial environmental sections.

"When Chairman Leahy suggested that time was running out, the suggestion from the House side was that we move onto the commodity titles," said Lugar. "That's not in the cards."

Organic Farming

Meeting Oct. 5, after the early-morning budget vote, House and Senate members completed action on a section establishing national standards for organic agricultural production.

The day before, House conferee Stenholm had objected to applying the organic definition to livestock producers. When Leahy proposed to remove livestock from the scope of the bill, the Texas Democrat and others raised broader concerns.

"Somehow it has gotten out of hand, [the idea] that organic is good for you," said House Agriculture Chairman de la Garza, a fellow Texan. "All this organics is going to be very, very expensive."

Both House and Senate bills set up a voluntary program in which crops raised according to certain production practices would be certified as organic. But some House Agriculture members did not like the program, which was attached as a floor amendment in the House. Finally, House members agreed to accept the provision, provided that the Agriculture Department held hearings on organic livestock production.

Conferees also finished the research section and part of the conservation section.

They resolved a dispute over low-input agriculture, which relied on lower pesticide use, by authorizing $40 million in research funds and reducing the emphasis on helping small family farmers.

'Triple Base'

As the conference slogged through such disputes, members were privately trying to fathom how they could meet the budget with the least pain for farmers. The summit document listed several options to achieve most of the $13 billion in farm-program cuts.

An annual 2 percent cut in target prices (the per-bushel amount guaranteed to program-crop farmers) and a 3 percent annual reduction in the acreage that qualified for crop subsidies would yield $12.4 billion, according to the OMB.

Or, the summit agreement suggested, the Agriculture committees could adopt a "triple-base" policy. At the time, farmers had two categories of land — land that was eligible for subsidy payments and land that they had to idle as part of the government effort to control production. Under the triple-base concept, farmers would get a third category: land on which they were allowed to plant other crops, but which was not eligible for crop payments. The government did not have to pay as much in subsidies, while the farmer maintained income by selling marketable commodities.

Requiring the Agriculture Department to offer a one-time, 15 percent triple base along with a 2 percent target-price cut would save $12.2 billion over five years, according to the OMB. A one-year, 25 percent triple base alone would save $13.8 billion.

Bush administration officials had called for target-price cuts and indicated support for the triple-base concept throughout the farm-bill deliberations. They argued that these approaches would continue the market-oriented approach to farm policy of the 1985 farm bill.

But the administration's suggestions were largely ignored in Congress, even by Republicans. Both House and Senate farm bills froze subsidy rates at existing levels.

When the summit agreement resurrected the savings proposals, some farm-state lawmakers interpreted it as a

White House attempt to dictate how the farm-bill conference should proceed.

The suggestions were not binding. Nor had the budget yet been approved. But administration officials, including Deputy Under Secretary of Agriculture Campbell, said a side summit agreement existed that purportedly would prevent the Agriculture committees from straying too far from the proposals. The administration had a list of 19 other options — mostly budget gimmicks and other ways of getting around direct cuts in farm-income subsidies — that were considered unacceptable.

Among the options were raising loan rates, increasing the amount of idled land, switching payments into different fiscal years and relying on unjustified economic assumptions. Lawmakers said they did not feel bound by it.

"We have not quite reached the point of constitutional irrelevancy where OMB and the White House write the farm bill," said Leahy.

In fact, Democrats in both the House and Senate said the House Democratic leadership had assured them that they could exempt agriculture from cuts entirely after 1992 if there was no international agreement restructuring agricultural trade as part of the ongoing GATT negotiations.

"That's a fairy tale," said Madigan, House Agriculture's ranking Republican. Then he crooned: "Fairy tales may come true."

Moving Toward Completion

The farm bill moved toward completion Oct. 12 as Senate negotiators began considering a package of more than $13 billion in farm program cuts recommended by an anguished House Agriculture Committee.

Farm-state lawmakers took pains to avoid making any direct hits on farmers' income subsidies, but many of the proposed cuts in the $54 billion measure appeared certain to have an impact on farmers' pocketbooks.

Nevertheless, the House deal cleared the way for conferees to wrap up a plethora of other issues on the bill. House and Senate negotiators met throughout the day and through the weekend in order to complete action on the budget portion of the bill.

Progress on resolving the differences between the House- and Senate-passed bills had been slow. Members had known since the beginning of the year that the budget would require deep cuts in farm program spending. But they did not really begin to negotiate — either with the Bush administration or their legislative counterparts — until they were told by congressional budget writers to come up with $13.6 billion in five-year deficit-savings.

"We have run out of time," said Leahy.

Since the beginning of the farm bill debate, farm-state lawmakers had complained that the administration had opted out of the negotiations over the bill. That changed Oct. 10, when Yeutter came to a House Agriculture session that was considering options to achieve the budget target.

Out of that session came a package of farm policy changes that, according to committee aides, Yeutter said would provide all but $1.5 billion of the savings required of agriculture. More importantly, the package did not seem to contain any policy changes that the administration found objectionable enough to threaten to veto the bill.

After more massaging Oct. 11, senior House committee members made up the $1.5 billion shortfall. They approved the package by a voice vote late in the evening.

"Pain, pain, pain," said House Agriculture Committee Chairman de la Garza, reflecting the difficulty lawmakers had cutting payments to farmers just weeks before Election Day. The House package avoided direct cuts in price- and income-support levels, although several of the changes had the effect of lowering the size of the check farmers received from the government.

Most of the savings — $5.8 billion over four years — came from putting into law the triple-base acreage-reduction plan.

The House triple-base plan was to go into effect in 1992, when farmers were not to receive subsidies on 15 percent of the land portion devoted to program crops. The percentage was to remain at 15 percent in 1993 and then increase to 20 percent in 1994 and 25 percent in 1995.

The House package also included a change in the arcane method of calculating deficiency payments that went to farmers as income subsidies. The effect, though masked as a technical change in the formula, was to shrink the size of benefit checks to farmers.

Instead of using a six-month average of market prices to determine the support payment, the committee shifted to a 12-month average. The change effectively increased the market-price average. Thus the government, which made up the shortfall between the market price and a congressionally set target price, ended up paying smaller amounts.

While that change saved $2.9 billion over five years, some Senate Democrats balked at its potential effect on farm incomes. The committee worked into the evening Oct. 12 in search of a alternatives that would be acceptable to Yeutter.

To distribute the cuts evenly, House lawmakers wanted to assess producers of other subsidized crops that did not receive direct support payments — such as dairy, sugar and peanuts — with a 1 percent fee on loans and support rates. The assessments brought in more than $1 billion.

Other government loan programs also were slashed to get savings. Direct lending by the FmHA and the Rural Electrification Administration was replaced with government guarantees on private loans, for savings of $2.2 billion over five years.

In addition to the cuts in existing programs, the committee voted to drop several expensive provisions from the House-passed farm bill, including a proposed $5.3 billion increase in food stamp and nutrition programs.

House members also agreed to drop a $2.3 billion program under which farmers would be paid subsidies on their actual yields rather than a historical calculation of their output.

The Senate had not formulated a savings package of its own. Some Senate Agriculture aides had said their committee might produce something very similar. However, late on Oct. 12, Nebraska's Kerrey threw up a red flag against the House plan, particularly the 12-month deficiency payment calculation and what he believed was an unfair burden on wheat and corn farmers.

Conservation Program

During the week of Oct. 8, conferees completed action on several other sections of the bill, including the controversial conservation title. Environmental organizations had expressed fear that farm-state lawmakers would jettison several provisions from the conservation section, which had been adopted in order to win support for the bill on the House and Senate floors.

But environmentalists said that the conservation title emerged relatively unscathed.

"Not only was there no backsliding," said Ken Cook of

the Center for Resource Economics, "the conference made some major improvements."

Conferees agreed to reauthorize the CRP, in which farmers were paid to take highly erodible land out of production, though they renamed it the Agricultural Resource Conservation program. The bill directed the Agriculture secretary to add 6 million acres of land to the 34 million-acre reserve, including 1 million acres of wetlands. The bill also provided for a voluntary program offering farmers incentives to reduce and prevent water pollution from agriculture.

For environmental organizations, a major goal was to get the wetlands and water-quality incentive program funded through the CRP. Congress was much more likely to fund the CRP than a new program, lobbyists argued, because farmers depended on the CRP payments. Conferees agreed.

House members, many of whom were skeptical of the conservation provisions, claimed credit for streamlining what they described as a hodgepodge of proposals in both bills.

Circle of Poison

One provision of both House and Senate farm bills that was inspired by environmental concerns caused no end of acrimony among farm-state lawmakers.

The provision was known as the circle of poison, the name that environmental organizations used to describe how pesticides banned for use in this country could be exported, used on crops abroad, then carried back into the United States as residue on food.

The farm bills contained provisions designed to break the circle of poison by greatly restricting the export of banned pesticides.

But the provisions had produced a potent counterattack from pesticide companies and farm organizations, which argued that American jobs, not the safety of the food supply, was at stake.

As the House and Senate neared completion of negotiations on the farm bill, Lugar stepped forward with an amendment that he said would make the pesticide restrictions less draconian, allowing U.S. chemical companies to continue producing pesticides for crops that were not grown in this country but were crucial to agricultural production abroad.

"I think it's important for the U.S. to be able to export chemicals that are perfectly safe," Lugar said.

Opponents said Lugar's proposal was a last-ditch effort by large chemical companies to escape some of the most important restrictions in the bill. "We should not force a country to receive a pesticide that it does not want," said Mike Synar, D-Okla., author of the provision in the House.

At the very least, the Lugar effort strained relations between him and his committee chairman, Leahy, who considered the pesticide provisions a key trophy of his chairmanship. "Adoption of this amendment would be a triumph of special interests over the public interest," Leahy said.

Both the House and Senate farm bills allowed the export of pesticides that the EPA had approved for domestic use and that might appear in low levels on food.

The House bill went further by allowing the export of pesticides without EPA registration or tolerable residue level, as long as the pesticides were registered for use in a country that was a member of the OECD group of 24 industrialized countries. The EPA had to certify that the pesticides met health and safety standards.

The Lugar amendment removed the requirement that the EPA approve unregistered pesticides before they could be exported. As long as the chemical had an OECD registration, it could be shipped abroad, although an exporter had to provide basic information to EPA about the chemical components. The amendment also removed a requirement that recipient countries affirm that they wanted the pesticide before it could be shipped.

Some House Agriculture Committee members disliked the circle of poison provision in their bill. They adopted it to win environmentalists' support for the farm bill. Synar, Leahy and others subsequently worried that it would be dropped in favor of the Lugar proposal.

Synar offered a motion on the House floor Oct. 11 instructing conferees to insist "at a minimum" on the pesticide provision passed by the House. Kansas Republican Roberts denounced the move, saying it was a "seriously flawed provision that will eliminate highly skilled, well-paying jobs without any contribution to improved food safety."

The House rejected Synar's motion, 162-248. After that vote, farm-bill conferees, who had never been fond of the antipesticide provision, dropped it from the bill altogether. *(Vote 450, p. 144-H)*

Final Agreement

The 1990 farm bill promised to be a historic document that freed the American farmer from the straitjacket of government subsidies. Or it threatened to be a hack job that would inflict pain on the farmer and cost the taxpayer dearly. After completing their final, marathon negotiating session on the five-year, $40.8 billion bill at 3:45 a.m. on Oct. 16, farm-state lawmakers were not sure which.

House and Senate conferees on the bill managed to cut $13.6 billion out of farm subsidies in accordance with their budget instructions. And they secured the blessing of the Bush administration, which had held out repeated veto threats against a bill that set the course for nearly all federal agriculture and nutrition programs through 1995.

Even the authors did not know where the new agriculture policy they crafted was headed. "Freedom is a wonderful thing. That's what scares everybody," said Lugar.

"We are moving into uncharted seas," de la Garza agreed. It was the budget crisis that led them there. After decades of building the web of government subsidies and loans for farmers, farm-state lawmakers were issued blunt instructions to cut the cost of their programs by 25 percent — and to do it less than a month before Election Day.

They complied not by paring the target prices, marketing loans, quota systems and other trappings of the farm program. Instead, they added new layers of complexity.

At the same time, the bill freed farmers from some government controls that made their planting decisions predictable and gave the Agriculture Department great power over the price and supply of farm commodities.

The result was a hodgepodge of changes — and much contradictory policy. For example:

- The bill paid farmers with one hand and took money away with the other. The support levels for dairy and sugar were frozen at their existing levels. But dairy producers and sugar growers also faced being hit with an assessment to pay for the cost of their program.

"It's levying taxes on yourself to pay for a program because you didn't want to reduce the support levels on these crops," said William Lesher, a former Agriculture

Department official in the Reagan administration.

• Farm-state lawmakers, including Leahy, hailed the bill as the most environmentally conscious farm bill ever, but environmental groups said the bill lost some of its luster when conferees made several last-minute changes.

Specifically, the conference dropped the circle of poison provision that would have banned the export of most pesticides prohibited for use in the U.S. And a provision requiring farmers to keep a record of their pesticide use was changed so that only the most hazardous chemicals were covered and access to the records severely restricted.

• The Bush administration was pleased with changes in the bill that were expected to allow the agricultural sector to respond more to market signals and less to government payment levels. But, as part of the final deal, administration officials agreed to accept high price-support levels that experts believed could price U.S. wheat out of the international market.

Even the claim that the bill achieved $13.6 billion in savings was suspect since the economic assumptions and estimates contained in the bill were already out of date. "This bill will not cost $40 billion," said Campbell, deputy under secretary of Agriculture. "It will cost more."

A Third Category

The centerpiece of the bill was a plan to reduce by 15 percent the amount of cropland eligible for government income-support payments. Every farmer who participated in government crop programs was free to plant whatever he wanted (except for fruits and vegetables) on 15 percent of the land on which he usually raised subsidized crops (wheat, corn and other feed grains, and cotton and rice).

Among farm policy-makers, this triple-base change gave farmers receiving subsidies a third category of land in addition to the acreage on which they received subsidies and the land the government, as a condition of federal benefits, required them to idle.

Simple as it sounded, triple base was a major development in farm policy. Under existing law, farmers tended to continue planting crops that were subsidized. Even if market conditions suggested that they should rotate crops to meet changing demand, they usually stuck with the subsidized crop because of the guaranteed return from the government. Under the new program, on at least 15 percent of their land, farmers had an incentive to grow the crop that was best suited to their region — and that was bringing the highest market price.

For example, farmers in the Midwest who historically had planted mostly corn because of the relatively high subsidies were expected to shift heavily into soybean production. "The beauty of it," said Campbell, "is that we do not know exactly what farmers will do."

Yet this "flexible" farm policy had its potential pitfalls.

In some regions, farmers did not have a lot of alternatives. Wheat farmers in Kansas, Oklahoma and Colorado planted wheat year after year because it was one of the few crops their arid land supported. Then there were producers in the South who raised mainly soybeans. They feared that if Midwesterners started growing a lot more soybeans it would drive down the price of their staple crop.

"For many small and moderate-sized farms, the much-ballyhooed flexibility of the new farm program only will mean the flexibility to go broke," said Ron Kroese, director of the Land Stewardship Project, a farm organization based in Minnesota.

The Bush administration supported triple base because it allowed farmers to get more of their income from the marketplace, rather than from the government.

For the House and Senate conferees, however, the decision to adopt triple base reflected political concerns.

Lawmakers had to come up with deep savings in crop programs, but they did not want to do it directly — by lowering price- and income-support levels — particularly after promising farmers that this farm bill would arrest the decrease in subsidies that had occurred over the previous three years. A further cut in target prices would have translated into a direct cut in payments to farmers.

"They're politicians, and that's just not in their repertoire," Lesher said.

So the conferees decided to cut government payments to farmers indirectly, using triple base. The 15 percent reduction in acreage eligible for subsidies was expected to reduce spending on government crop programs by roughly $7 billion from 1991 through 1995, according to a Senate Agriculture Committee aide.

House members, notably Democrat Stenholm and Republican Roberts, had long favored using triple base to achieve the budget savings required of agriculture. But the concept was kept under wraps until fall.

Their committee colleagues were still harboring hopes that they would win a freeze in subsidy levels without a cut in payments to farmers. Earlier in October, however, when the House and Senate finally passed budget resolutions calling for cuts of over $13 billion from agriculture programs, those hopes faded.

"It became clear that this was the first time they were developing a farm bill under real budget pressure and that the cuts would have to be more real than smoke and mirrors," Lesher said.

At that point, passing the farm bill became an exercise in spreading the pain as equally as possible among the various commodities and farm interests under the government subsidy umbrella. Also, the package had to be made acceptable to the Bush administration, which had a long list of objections to both the Senate and House farm bills.

The crucial moment may have arrived the evening of Oct. 12, when Yeutter came to a meeting of senior House and Senate conferees, including Leahy, Lugar, de la Garza and Madigan.

According to aides and lawmakers in the room, Yeutter offered this deal: Give him changes in the sugar and dairy sections of the bill, which strayed too far from the free-market approach favored by the administration, along with a few other demands. In return, Yeutter said he would not object to provisions in the House bill raising the price support loan rates for wheat and feed grains. In addition, he agreed to let the conferees claim $650 million in additional savings with a provision requiring corn farmers to idle more land.

The savings came in handy as the conferees worked toward achieving their $13 billion target. But the real concession by Yeutter and the administration was on loan rates. For months, the administration had been criticizing congressional efforts to raise loan rates, which acted as a floor on U.S. prices.

The government made crop loans to farmers at harvest to control the flow of commodities going to market. The crop became the collateral.

Farmers used the money, lent to them at a per-bushel rate established under the farm bill, to tide them over until market prices seemed favorable for sale. If prices failed to rise above the loan rate, farmers could keep the money and turn their crop over to the government.

This system generally thrived for both farmers and the government in the 1970s, when prices remained high. During the mid-1980s, however, grain exports plunged, in part because Congress had set such high loan rates that U.S. commodities were uncompetitive in international markets. The 1985 farm bill tried to address this anomaly by giving the Agriculture secretary wide discretion to lower loan rates to below world market prices.

The tradeoff Congress got in 1985, in agreeing to lower loan rates, was a promise that farm-income subsidies, which were tied to much higher target prices, would remain lucrative enough to keep farmers from feeling the pinch.

Since then, the Reagan and Bush administrations had used their loan-rate discretion to full effect, keeping commodity prices low so that U.S. exports could reclaim a larger share of the foreign market. Of course, the federal government had to pay the price in the form of income subsidies, which kept farm-program costs from $10 billion to $20 billion a year.

In 1990, House and Senate Agriculture Committee members sought to reclaim some control over price supports with provisions in the new farm bill to raise loan rates.

When Yeutter agreed to the House loan-rate provisions, it stunned many in the room, particularly Democrats, who were convinced that low loan rates were "a religious issue" for the administration, as one Senate aide put it.

Indeed, all the while he was negotiating a farm bill with Congress, Yeutter had been trying to secure a landmark international agreement to eliminate "trade-distorting" agriculture subsidies throughout the world. As U.S. trade representative in the Reagan administration, Yeutter had put forth such a proposal for the GATT negotiations. But, as the talks were being extended into 1991, the United States had gotten nowhere in its attempts to win concessions on agriculture. To Europeans, in particular, farm subsidies were just as politically potent, if not more so, than in the United States.

While Yeutter needed to wrap up the farm bill to get negotiating room for GATT, lawmakers clearly felt they had the upper hand. Yeutter did manage to persuade conferees to insert broad authority in the farm bill for the department to continue paying farmers with payment-in-kind certificates for government-controlled commodities. These "PIK" certificates had been a powerful tool for the government in moving grain and manipulating prices.

As for loan-rate provisions, "We just decided it wasn't worth the trouble," said Campbell, who was advising Yeutter. Lugar offered another explanation: "Yeutter didn't have the votes" to defeat higher loan rates.

Many lawmakers took Yeutter's offer as a sign that the administration would not carry out its threats to veto the bill as long they agreed to some modest concessions.

In the case of the dairy program, for example, the conferees agreed to remove a provision requiring supply controls on dairy producers during times of surplus. The dairy industry had never liked the idea of supply controls.

But the conferees rejected an administration demand that they not tamper with a market-oriented feature of the current dairy program — a controversial trigger system that automatically cut the dairy subsidy level during times of surplus production. The conferees did away with the subsidy cuts altogether, establishing a floor under the dairy price support at its existing level of $10.10 per hundred pounds of milk products.

Finally, during a 14-hour session on Oct. 15 and into the morning of the next day, the conference evolved into a free-for-all bargaining session. Lawmakers got down to negotiating the best deal they could for the crops raised in their home states, while keeping one eye out to make sure other crops were sharing in the pain of budget cuts.

Soybean loan levels arguably fell the furthest. At the beginning of the year, lawmakers talked about increasing the level by $1.75 a bushel, to $6.25. But it cost too much. During committee deliberations in the spring and early summer, members in both the House and Senate yielded to calls for fiscal restraint by trimming the proposed level to between $5.25 and $5.50 a bushel.

But by the time farm-bill conferees finished their work, the soybean loan rate had sunk all the way to $5.02. On top of that, soybean producers were slapped with an assessment that made the effective loan rate $4.92 — still an increase, though only 42 cents above where it started.

It was a bitter defeat for lawmakers from Southern soybean-producing states, particularly since the existing soybean program cost the government relatively little. "It's hard for soybeans to contribute to deficit reduction when they don't contribute to the deficit," said Arkansas Democrat Pryor.

Final Assessments

After the House and Senate negotiators reached agreement on the final version of the bill on Oct. 16, it still took more than a week to finish the drafting and paperwork to allow the House and Senate to complete action. And the key lawmakers, in urging approval of the mammoth bill, were restrained in their enthusiasm.

"It is a good piece of legislation, within the constraints that we have," Agriculture Chairman de la Garza told his colleagues Oct. 23.

"There is pain here," Senate Agriculture Chairman Leahy said Oct. 25. "It is not an easy thing to vote for, when you're dealing with programs that will be cut. For once, it's not smoke and mirrors."

South Dakota Democrat Daschle told Senate colleagues the bill would lead to a 25-percent cut in farm income that would fall disproportionately on smaller, midsized family farmers.

Despite the reservations and warnings, the conference report won overwhelming approval in both chambers. The House voted 318-102 to adopt the report Oct. 23; the Senate followed Oct. 25 by a vote of 60-36. *(House vote 508, p. 160-H; Senate vote 317, p. 62-S)*

In both chambers, farm-state lawmakers voting against the bill were joined by a disparate bloc of conservative Republicans and moderate to liberal urban members from both parties. The 36 senators who voted against the measure included 12 Democrats and six Republicans from farm or prairie states along with 11 moderate to liberal Democrats and seven Republicans ranging the political spectrum from North Carolina conservative Helms to Maine's moderate William S. Cohen.

When he signed the bill Nov. 28, Bush voiced no reservations, viewing the measure as a continuation of a shift toward market-oriented policies and a good base for maintaining pressure to reduce worldwide agriculture subsidies.

"Increased flexibility in planting choices contained in the 1990 farm bill will allow farmers to break out of the traditional farm program straitjacket, which bound them to produce the same crop year after year, regardless of market opportunities," Bush said. ■

Rural Development Aid Consolidated

As part of its massive farm bill, Congress included provisions to stimulate rural economic development. The provisions were taken from measures (S 1036, HR 3581) that passed both chambers earlier in the 101st Congress and were attached to the omnibus, five-year bill.

The farm bill (S 2830 — PL 101-624) established a new Rural Development Administration within the Agriculture Department and transferred most duties relating to rural development to the agency.

New programs were authorized to promote economic development and improve schools, health care and water supply in rural areas.

Also under the bill, up to five states could set up state rural economic development review panels, whose job would be to rank applications for funds within the state's allocation of federal funds. The Agriculture secretary retained authority for distributing funds. The bill authorized appropriations to establish revolving loan funds in up to five states, which would provide lines of credit to nonprofit corporations and public agencies in rural development.

The bill removed the cap on authorization of appropriations for rural water and waste facilities and authorized the secretary to make loans to Rural Electrification Administration (REA) borrowers for water and sewer projects. Up to 50 percent of the cost of the projects could be lent. The bill expanded the authority of the banks for cooperatives of the Farm Credit System to make water and sewer loans to communities with populations of less than 20,000.

The measure authorized the Farmers Home Administration (FmHA) to make up to $25 million in loans to small communities for emergency water and waste-facility projects.

Another $30 million was authorized for loans to communities facing significant health risks due to lack of sewer and water treatment facilities.

The bill established grants to encourage and improve the use of telecommunications and computer networks. It authorized low- and market-rate loans to businesses, local governments or public agencies to fund facilities in which participants shared telecommunications equipment, computers and software. It authorized $15 million annually for fiscal 1991-94.

The bill allowed REA borrowers to defer making any loan payments if funds in an amount equal to the deferment of five or 10 years were used for rural development projects, as long as the deferral was not more than half the cost of the project and the borrower made a payment to the REA equal to the amount deferred. The bill created a Rural Business Incubator fund and permitted the REA to make grants or low-interest loans (5 percent or less) to its borrowers and other nonprofit entities to support the operation of incubators, designed to promote business creation and relocation at certain sites.

Before being rolled into the farm bill, HR 3581 had passed the House on March 22. The Senate on Aug. 2, 1989, had passed S 1036.

BACKGROUND

When the Senate Agriculture Committee began crafting legislation in June 1988 to foster rural economic development, the effort quickly collapsed in vitriolic disagreement over philosophical differences as well as a shortage of funds. In 1989, supporters came back with less expensive legislation. *(1989 Almanac, p. 390)*

The new measure (S 1036) made it easier for rural businesses to get credit, expanded federal programs for financing water and sewer projects, and authorized loans and grants to help modernize telecommunications technology in rural schools, hospitals and businesses, as well as other infrastructure and economic-development projects. The bill authorized $300 million in new spending in fiscal 1990 and slightly more in each of the following two years.

Several factors were working in the bill's favor. There was already a modest sum of money for rural development in the Senate's fiscal 1990 budget resolution: $150 million in budget authority over 1989's inflation-adjusted agriculture baseline. And Majority Leader George J. Mitchell, D-Maine, appeared strongly supportive.

But there was no shortage of threats to the bill. Several committee Republicans took a dim view of expanding the federal bureaucracy to attack rural problems. And, unlike the Senate, the House had shown little interest in moving a free-standing rural-development bill in 1989.

Lacking a cohesive constituency to lobby for funds, rural development was more popular as a campaign theme than as legislation.

"Everyone who runs for office is happy to say they support rural development," said Agriculture Chairman Patrick J. Leahy, D-Vt. "It's time to put up or shut up."

Senate Action in 1989

The Senate on Aug. 2, 1989, passed S 1036. While it was a high priority of Leahy, fundamental disagreements among his counterparts on the House Agriculture Committee delayed action on comparable legislation until 1990.

Moreover, the Senate bill differed markedly from the approach taken in the House. The House bill pooled roughly $1 billion in existing rural development funds and decentralized the funding process by allowing states to allocate their share of the funds among projects that they decided were worthy.

The Senate bill left existing rural-development programs largely intact, while establishing new loan programs to entice businesses to rural areas and improve schools, health care and infrastructure.

The Senate bill had been Leahy's pet project since he took over the committee in 1987. But rural development proved particularly controversial because there was little money to back up such initiatives and little agreement about what was needed.

Before the bill passed the Senate, Leahy agreed to accept more than 30 floor amendments in order to get the support of various farm-state senators. Leahy did succeed in forestalling amendments that would have funneled more money to individual farmers, but that success came at a price. Member after member stepped forward with parochial amendments, and, in the end, member after member was accommodated.

HOUSE COMMITTEE ACTION

The House Agriculture Committee spent eight hours Feb. 27 disposing of nearly 40 amendments, but finally succeeded in approving controversial legislation that would consolidate and streamline the hodgepodge of federal programs providing economic assistance to rural areas. After all the amendments, the bill (HR 3581) was reported on a voice vote.

Sponsored by Glenn English, D-Okla., and E. Thomas Coleman, R-Mo., the bill was particularly controversial because it acknowledged the central problem with rural development: There was no new money in the budget for it.

Unlike the Senate bill, the English-Coleman bill did not propose a raft of new spending. It sought to provide modest new authority for certain rural lending institutions to expand their offerings. And it would have overhauled the way the federal government delivered roughly $1 billion in assistance to rural areas.

On one hand, the bill would have centralized federal efforts by pooling the existing funds and giving authority for distributing them to a new agency within the Agriculture Department, the Rural Development Administration.

On the other hand, the legislation would have decentralized the funding process by giving state-appointed boards authority for allocating their share of the funds among projects they decided were worthy.

Yet that flexibility was controversial — to Agriculture Department agencies like the FmHA and the Extension Service that delivered federal assistance to the banks that dominated private lending in rural areas, and, most of all, to those states that received the most money.

Controversial Amendments

Despite the final compromise, the markup did not go smoothly. Charlie Rose, D-N.C., offered an amendment that would have kept $400 million the FmHA used for rural water and sewer loans and grants out of the $1 billion funding pool the bill would have established.

Rose argued that money for basic infrastructure such as water projects, which was already tight, would dry up completely if it was grouped in a large pot of money intended to stimulate jobs in rural areas. "You're basically being asked to fund rural economic development at the expense of rural water and sewer loans," Rose said. "That's a terrible choice."

There were powerful forces behind Rose's position: The National Association of Home Builders sent a letter to members of the committee Feb. 26 urging support for Rose's amendment.

And no less a figure than Jamie L. Whitten, D-Miss., the chairman of the House Appropriations Committee, called pooling of the funds "a serious step backward" that his committee would "write provisions to avoid," if necessary.

But other lawmakers argued that Rose's amendment would gut the bill by removing the largest chunk of existing rural development funds from the pool.

In order to ward off Rose, English offered a compromise. He proposed to increase authority for water and sewer grants to $500 million from $155 million. And he proposed to reserve up to $34 million annually for water and sewer grants, which could not be transferred into the rural development pool, according to a committee aide.

English's amendment was adopted by a vote of 25-18.

Also controversial was a section of the bill that encouraged certain government-subsidized entities such as rural electric cooperatives and rural telephone banks to expand their loan-making, despite the Bush administration's opposition to these programs.

The bill would have encouraged cooperatives to make rural development loans by allowing them to defer repaying their loan obligations to the federal government, sponsors said.

Also, the bill would have diminished the latitude that rural telephone bank officials had to not use some of their loan funds during the fiscal year.

The Bush administration strongly opposed the provisions because it said there would be significant cost involved. Agriculture Under Secretary Roland R. Vatour said that the telephone provisions could cost up to $544 million and could prompt a veto. The Congressional Budget Office said that the provisions were cost-free, according to committee aides.

HOUSE FLOOR ACTION

HR 3581 was abruptly pulled from the floor March 15 after an amendment that undermined the heart of the bill won approval on a 204-193 vote. The amendment, offered by Rose, removed provisions that would have permitted the Agriculture secretary to transfer funds among various federal loan and grant programs that were used by rural communities to improve infrastructure and economic opportunity. *(Vote 27, p. 14-H)*

The transfer authority was considered vital to the bill. The House measure expanded spending authority for agriculture loan and grant programs — as would the companion S 1036 — but it also pooled roughly $ 1 billion in such funds and let state-appointed boards decide how to spend their share of the money.

But Rose's amendment would have barred transferring funds among various rural development accounts. Water and sewer loan money would have to be used for water and sewer projects. "It takes us back to the status quo," said English.

The status quo was what Rose wanted. Ever since the Agriculture Committee rejected a similar amendment he offered to strike the transfer provision, Rose had insisted that the bill would promote flashy economic development projects at the expense of infrastructure.

"I got just one problem here," said Rose in a folksy floor speech. "It ain't been explained real well, brothers and sisters, that the money for this bill comes out of something else that's real important."

The proposal for giving significant authority for doling out money to state-appointed boards concerned many federal lawmakers.

"I have more influence under the present system than I would under the system created by the bill," said Bill Alexander, D-Ark.

After the vote, English blamed the defeat on general "confusion" about the bill's effect and "misinformation" put out by opponents. He said committee leaders would try to bring it up again the following week.

Chamber Passage

On March 22 the House revived and passed the rural development bill, undoing the action it had taken a week earlier.

Bill sponsors English and Coleman worked out a compromise with Rose that restored some of the transfer authority that Rose's amendment had eliminated. Members adopted the compromise by voice vote before passing the bill by 360-45. *(Vote 40, p. 18-H)*

English and Coleman managed to get Rose to support

limited authority for the secretary to shift about $1 billion in loan and grant funds distributed by the FmHA.

Rose said he was particularly concerned about allowing about $500 million in loan and grant funds for rural water and sewer projects to be transferred into other areas. But he agreed to accept a complicated compromise that protected most water and sewer funds while retaining some transfer authority.

On March 27, the House inserted the text of HR 3581 into S 1036 in preparation for a conference on the measure.

While the Senate's measure differed substantially from the House version, most of the provisions of the two bills did not directly conflict. So, English said, it could be possible to simply "marry the two together" in a House-Senate conference.

Before the chambers met in conference on the rural development legislation, though, both the House and Senate rolled their bills into the farm package, which cleared the Senate on Oct. 25 and was signed by President Bush on Nov. 28. ■

Food Stamp Program Extended Five Years

Food-assistance provisions such as the food stamp program were always a part of farm bills since the 1960s; the 1990 omnibus farm bill was no exception.

The farm bill (S 2830 — PL 101-624) extended the federal food stamp program for five years and imposed additional penalties for fraud and misuse of food coupons. Domestic commodity donation programs were reauthorized, including the Emergency Food Assistance Program and the Commodity Supplemental Food Program.

Under the bill, basic food stamp benefits would have to be kept at the existing 103 percent of the Thrifty Food Plan (a government estimate of the market-basket value of common foodstuffs).

The excess shelter expense ceiling would have to be kept at the existing $ 177 a month.

Many of the details of the food stamp provisions were taken from a separate piece of legislation (HR 4100) and from the earlier House version of the farm bill.

The Senate version of the farm bill did not address reauthorization of the food stamp program because Agriculture Committee leaders wanted to avoid procedural and political complications related to the Gramm-Rudman antideficit law and deficit-reduction negotiations.

However, committee leaders did plan to negotiate for a full reauthorization with the House in conference.

The fiscal 1991 agriculture spending bill (HR 5268 — PL 101-506), meanwhile, appropriated $19.1 billion for food stamps, an increase of $2.2 billion over fiscal 1990 and nearly $1 billion more than the total requested by Bush. *(Agriculture appropriations, p. 867)*

BACKGROUND

Food-assistance provisions — including the food stamp program, the $2 billion Women, Infants and Children program, and the $170 million food-giveaway program called the Temporary Emergency Food Assistance Program (TEFAP) — were part and parcel of farm bills ever since their inception with other Great Society welfare programs of the 1960s.

While these Agriculture Department programs had always been viewed favorably by farmers and farm-state lawmakers — mainly because they provided a ready-made, government-subsidized market for farm commodities — the food-assistance provisions of the farm bill also served an important political function.

They were used to win urban support for farm subsidies, which annually funneled billions of federal dollars to an ever-dwindling number of rural constituents. Indeed, this marriage of convenience between rural and urban lawmakers helped fend off broadside attacks of both farm subsidies and food-assistance subsidies.

President Ronald Reagan's personal antipathy to so-called welfare queens and the increasing clout of Jesse Helms, R-N.C., who was chairman of the Senate Agriculture Committee from 1981 to 1987, had enabled conservatives to push through legislation (PL 97-35) in 1981 that cut the food stamp program by $6 billion over three years. *(1981 Almanac, p. 466)*

But during the last farm bill debate in 1985, reports of increased poverty prompted Congress to expand food stamp benefits and broaden eligibility for a program that assisted 19 million low-income people. *(1985 Almanac, p. 305)*

In 1990, with Reagan gone and Helms no longer Agriculture Committee chairman, nutrition programs not only appeared safe for the new farm bill, but some lawmakers were looking for ways to make up for the lean years.

Other than discretion over TEFAP spending and a proposal to limit school lunch subsidies, the Bush administration showed little taste for doing battle over food stamps and other big-ticket nutrition programs.

Indeed, the political momentum appeared to be moving toward conciliation rather than conflict over food assistance programs.

Other Provisions

Under the 1990 bill, states were authorized to allow approved restaurants to accept food stamps for the purpose of feeding the homeless. Residents of Guam and the Virgin Islands were allowed to use food stamps for meals in senior citizens' centers and private establishments offering meals at reduced prices.

The bill excluded from the calculation of income in determining food stamp eligibility: education loans, grants and scholarships, clothing allowances provided by state assistance programs, assistance payments made to a third party on behalf of a household residing in transitional housing, and general state welfare payments.

The bill also strengthened various reporting requirements and imposed fines on retail and wholesale food operations that accepted loose coupons or food stamps from unauthorized third parties or used food stamps in money-laundering schemes or computer fraud.

Retail food stores would be permanently disqualified from handling food stamps if firearms or illegal drugs were sold for food stamp coupons. The bill authorized a fine of up to $250,000 and a prison term of up to 20 years for laundering coupons or authorization cards worth more than $5,000.

EARLY HOUSE ACTION

A House Agriculture subcommittee March 22 approved HR 4100 to expand federal nutrition programs, such as food stamps. The bill, which the Domestic Marketing, Consumer Relations and Nutrition Subcommittee approved by voice vote, comprised domestic hunger-relief and nutrition sections that were later folded into the farm bill.

The measure authorized higher spending levels for several low-income food aid and nutrition programs administered by the Agriculture Department, such as food stamps and TEFAP. It also included provisions to promote self-sufficiency among poor Americans, simplify assistance programs and combat food stamp fraud.

The bill was named after the late Rep. Mickey Leland, a Texas Democrat who died in August 1989 while on a hunger-relief mission to Ethiopia. Its sponsor was Leon E. Panetta, D-Calif.

The measure authorized about $600 million in new spending on food stamps, TEFAP and smaller nutrition programs in fiscal 1991, $800 million in fiscal 1992 and $900 million in fiscal 1993. Overall, food stamps were earmarked for about $15 billion and TEFAP at $120 million in fiscal 1990. Those levels would be increased by roughly $400 million and $70 million, respectively, in fiscal 1991.

The bill would expand eligibility for food stamps by phasing out the limit on shelter costs that food stamp recipients could deduct from their income, raising it to $300 a month from $177 a month by September 1992 and lifting it higher in fiscal 1994.

The Bush administration expressed concern about the bill's costs, estimating that it would increase food stamp spending by $5.2 billion over five years and overall nutrition funding by $7.1 billion during that time. Officials also opposed a provision that would forgive the debts states owed the food stamp program for overpayments since 1983.

Several amendments were accepted by voice vote. One, by Dan Glickman, D-Kan., would increase penalties for grocers who illegally trafficked in food stamps to the same levels as those imposed on money launderers, including a $500,000 fine and prison time.

Also adopted by voice vote were amendments by Harley O. Staggers Jr., D-W.Va., to help low-income single parents enrolled as full-time college students remain eligible for food stamps, and by Bill Sarpalius, D-Texas, dealing with reimbursement for child-care expenses. ■

Nutrition-Monitoring Measure Enacted

The Senate on Oct. 5 cleared legislation aimed at better coordinating the federal government's nutrition-monitoring efforts, sending the measure to President Bush. The House had passed the bill on Oct. 2.

Bush signed the measure (HR 1608 — PL 101-445) on Oct. 22.

The bill required the Departments of Agriculture and Health and Human Services to develop a 10-year plan to determine what kinds of food Americans ate (traditionally an Agriculture Department function) and how nutritious they were (a Health and Human Services function).

The administration also would have to establish a National Nutrition Monitoring Advisory Council and publish a comprehensive report every five years called "Dietary Guidelines for Americans."

The key compromise gave opposing sides a voice in challenging the findings in the report.

Under the legislation, the secretaries of Agriculture and Health and Human Services were charged with making sure that any other nutritional advice issued by any federal agency was consistent with the dietary guidelines report or with new information.

The Senate had passed a similar bill (S 253 — S Rept 101-137) by voice vote on Nov. 3, 1989. Rep. George E. Brown Jr., D-Calif., one of the bill's main proponents, said the two measures were "virtually identical."

Rep. Robert A. Roe, D-N.J., another key supporter, said that the 1990 version was only "slightly modified" from one cleared by Congress in 1988.

Bills to set up a system to make sure that the government spoke with one voice when agencies said anything about the nutritional value of different types of food had been kicking around for a decade. However, President Ronald Reagan vetoed the 1988 measure on the grounds that it was unnecessary and cumbersome. Farm commodity groups, in particular, had feared the bill would result in the government declaring certain foods, such as beef and eggs, unhealthful. *(1988 Almanac, p. 645)*

The Bush administration took no position on either bill in the 101st Congress, although administration officials did persuade the House to make small modifications to the legislation. The final bill was a compromise crafted by three House committees with jurisdiction over such issues: Science, Energy and Agriculture. ■

Screwworm Bill Cleared

The Senate on March 5 cleared by voice vote a bill that authorized the Agriculture Department (USDA) to produce sterile screwworms and sell them to foreign countries to eradicate fertile screwworms.

The measure was passed by the House on Feb. 27 also on a voice vote.

President Bush signed the bill (HR 4010 — PL 101-255) on March 15.

Sponsors said the bill was needed because screwworms — flesh-eating parasites — were a growing problem in Central and South America and had recently spread to North Africa. The screwworm was eradicated in the United States in 1982.

The United States and the government of Mexico jointly operated a facility in Mexico that produced the sterile screwworms. The legislation allowed the USDA to sell the sterile screwworms to foreign countries, with the funds to be directed back into the program. ■

Large Farms Keep Irrigation Subsidies

Provisions to eliminate federal irrigation subsidies for large farm operations and for Western farmers who grew surplus crops were approved by the House, but killed by an adamant Sen. Pete Wilson, R-Calif., in the final week of the session.

The dispute concerned millions of dollars in federal irrigation subsidies received by large Western farm operations. Urban and environmentalist-minded lawmakers wanted to tighten enforcement of acreage limitations designed to target the subsidies to small and midsize farms.

The House adopted the water-subsidy limits by solid margins on June 14 as amendments to a non-controversial Bureau of Reclamation water and power projects authorization bill (HR 2567). When the bill reached the Senate, however, Wilson, a strong supporter of his state's giant agricultural sector, blocked consideration of the measure unless the restrictions were removed.

Wilson prevailed, and the Senate passed the bill without the subsidy limits Oct. 26. But the House sponsor of the amendment, George Miller, D-Calif., responded by trying to reattach the subsidy limits. When neither side gave way in last-minute negotiations, the bill died.

When the bill died, it took down with it a dozen water project authorizations intended mostly for Western states. In addition, the bill contained environmentalist-backed provisions to protect the Grand Canyon from excess man-made erosion caused by high volumes of water being sent through the Glen Canyon Dam, situated 30 miles upstream of the Grand Canyon. *(Grand Canyon, p. 300)*

BACKGROUND

Western farms had been receiving low-cost federal water since 1902, under a reclamation statute that limited the subsidies to farms of 160 acres for an individual or 320 acres for a farmer and spouse.

As mechanized agribusiness operations supplanted family farms, however, the acreage limit became outdated and was often evaded through leasing or other arrangements; enforcement, critics maintained, was lax. In California, federally irrigated farms often covered thousands of acres.

A federal court ruling in 1976 upholding the 160-acre limit set the stage for an effort in the Carter administration to tighten enforcement, which in turn prompted agricultural interests to press Congress to loosen the restrictions. Their efforts finally bore fruit in 1982, with a law depicted as a compromise between growers and their congressional supporters on one side and urban and environmentalist-minded lawmakers on the other.

The 1982 Reclamation Reform Act (PL 97-293) raised the acreage limit for low-cost water to 960 acres for an individual or small corporation. It permitted water service to leased acreage beyond that limit but at a higher price — bringing the government closer to recovering the costs of constructing and operating Western water projects. *(1982 Almanac, p. 353)*

The tenuous compromise of the 1982 act yielded to renewed dispute when the Bureau of Reclamation issued regulations in 1985 and 1986. Critics charged that the rules sanctioned abusive arrangements by growers to get around the limitations — through family or employee trusts or multiple corporations or partnerships.

Miller, an urban California lawmaker who chaired the Interior Water and Power Subcommittee, sought legislation in 1987 to plug the loopholes. He failed to get a broad revision, but did attach provisions to that year's budget-reconciliation bill curbing the use of revocable trusts to skirt the acreage limit and requiring the Bureau of Reclamation to audit large farm operations to make sure they qualified for the subsidies.

At the same time, Miller requested the General Accounting Office (GAO) to examine implementation of the law. Its October 1989 report concluded that the 1982 law "has not stopped federally subsidized water from being delivered to owned and/or leased land over 960 acres being operated as one farm." One consequence, the GAO noted, was a reduction in revenues to the federal government.

In California's lush Central Valley — where critics said most of the abuses were located — water subsidies cost $135 million per year, the Interior Department said.

The GAO report helped lay the groundwork for Miller and Bill Bradley, D-N.J., who chaired the Senate Energy Water and Power Subcommittee, to renew the water-subsidy fight in 1990.

HOUSE ACTION

The showdown between Western agricultural interests and water-subsidy reform advocates came on the House floor June 14 on a largely non-controversial water projects bill (HR 2567 — H Rept 101-336) that had been approved by the Interior Committee on Nov. 8, 1989. The measure contained a grab bag of projects with a total price tag in the range of $100 million to $150 million.

On the eve of the scheduled floor action on the bill, Miller introduced his amendment to tighten the 960-acre limit to apply to any "farm or farm operation," including trust arrangements.

Several Western lawmakers, led by Richard H. Lehman, D-Calif., tried to block consideration of the amendment, arguing it was too complex to be debated for the first time on the floor. But the rule permitting Miller's amendment and a second amendment, by Sam Gejdenson, D-Conn., to limit water subsidies for growing surplus crops, was approved June 13, 250-167. *(Vote 165, p. 58-H)*

Water Subsidies

The House adopted Miller's amendment, 316-97, after an emotional debate pitting populist and cost-cutting appeals against warnings of federally mandating business practices on efficient farm operations. *(Vote 170, p. 60-H)*

Miller said his amendment would end "abuses" that allowed some farmers "to enjoy the multimillion-dollar water subsidies intended only for family farmers."

But Lehman and his Republican colleague from the Central Valley, Charles "Chip" Pashayan Jr., argued that the subsidy restrictions would end up hurting family farms operated through trust arrangements or large farm operations owned through employee trusts.

Lehman, saying that Miller's amendment would lead to "a centrally planned government farming program," sought to narrow it with an amendment exempting family trusts that owned large farms.

But Lehman's amendment failed, 118-297, setting the

stage for the overwhelming vote adopting Miller's amendment. *(Vote 169, p. 60-H)*

Surplus Crops

Gejdenson's amendment, adopted 338-55, was aimed at what critics called a double subsidy for farmers receiving both federal irrigation water and government payments for surplus crops. *(Vote 171, p. 60-H)*

Surplus crops were commodities, such as cotton, rice, wheat and corn, for which the federal government had an acreage reduction program.

Gejdenson said the measure would save taxpayers almost $1 billion a year by ending "an unjust, unsound and outrageous practice by a select group of Western farmers who continually use federally subsidized water to grow surplus crops which are bought back by the government."

His amendment sought to phase out irrigation subsidies for those crops starting two years after enactment of the legislation, when the farmers would have had to pay half the cost of the water. They would have been required to pay the entire water bill four years after enactment.

The elimination of water subsidies for surplus crops would not have applied to irrigation on Indian lands or to water districts that shared in at least 20 percent of the project's costs, nor would it have affected farmers who grew those crops but did not receive federal payments for them.

Pashayan, arguing against Gejdenson's amendment, said it would hurt small farms and discourage agricultural production. "It is not only the policy, but the details behind it," he said.

Before the final vote, the House amended Gejdenson's proposal to specify that the water-subsidy phase-out would occur only if the Agriculture secretary determined that there was a sufficient amount of surplus commodities in government storage to meet any emergency, such as a drought. As amended, HR 2567 was approved by voice vote and sent to the Senate.

SENATE ACTION

The water-subsidy limits in HR 2567 were unwelcome in the Senate, where the 17 Western states served by the Bureau of Reclamation had more clout to press the interests of growers benefiting from the subsidies.

Energy Committee Chairman J. Bennett Johnston, D-La., and the committee's ranking Republican, James A. McClure, Idaho, had opposed reform efforts in the past. But urban Democrat Bradley was using his Water and Power Subcommittee chairmanship to push the issue.

An amended version of HR 2567 without the water-subsidy limits passed the Energy Committee, 18-0, on Sept. 19 (S Rept 101-499). The bill was expanded, however, to include the $250 million Lake Andes irrigation project in South Dakota and the Grand Canyon protection provisions, passed by the House on July 30.

The committee's report was filed Oct. 5, setting the stage for high-stakes maneuvering in Congress' final weeks.

Central Utah Project

Miller made the first move by tying the water-subsidy limits to a new bill (HR 3960 — H Rept 101-764) authorizing a $750-million expansion of the Central Utah Project.

Utah's congressional delegation — including Republican Sen. Jake Garn — had pushed hard for the project, but environmentalists and the Bush administration had been opposed or skeptical. Miller, however, helped broker a compromise that included cost-sharing and environmental mitigation provisions making the bill acceptable to environmental groups and the administration.

When the bill was brought to the House floor Oct. 15, Miller included the House-passed version of HR 2567 as an amendment. Opponents of the water-subsidy limits renewed their arguments against the provisions, but made no move to block the maneuver. The 211-143 vote approving the bill, shortly after midnight, had the effect of enlisting the Utah delegation as strong allies for reclamation reform. *(Vote 467, p. 148-H)*

Floor Action

In the Senate, Wilson, campaigning for his state's governorship, had said during the summer that he would stay neutral in the politically sensitive water-subsidy fight. But as floor action loomed, he shifted his stance to strong opposition, with his aides putting out the word that his hand had been forced by the neutrality of the state's other senator, Democrat Alan Cranston.

Wilson opposed not only the Miller-backed provisions in HR 2567 but also a compromise developed by Bradley. Bradley's amendment would have provided for a tighter definition of farming operation to be applied in just four states, including California, and for a phased-in restriction on subsidies for farms operated through trust arrangements to be applied throughout the West. McClure said he would not object to the amendment, but, according to a memo circulated Oct. 19, also said it "must, of course, be acceptable to all Senators from Reclamation states."

Wilson refused to budge. He put a hold on HR 2567 — the procedure allowing any senator to block consideration of a bill — unless the water-subsidy limits were removed. He told the Los Angeles Times that Miller was "trying to pass this provision by extortion. He is coupling a number of legitimately needed projects throughout the Western states with these unfair proposals he calls reform."

Garn was described as furious. The San Francisco Chronicle quoted a source as saying that Garn told Wilson on the Senate floor, "You damn well better hope you get elected [governor], because if you come back here, you're never passing another piece of legislation." (Garn apparently apologized later; Wilson was elected governor Nov. 6.)

To satisfy Wilson, the water-subsidy limits were removed, and HR 2567 was brought to the Senate floor on Oct. 26 — with the Central Utah Project rolled into the bill as debate opened. Wilson did not speak during the brief floor debate.

After voice vote approval of the bill, Bradley told his colleagues that Wilson's decision to block the reclamation reform provisions "endangers the prospect of the package in conference. But we had to abide by the senator's wish because one senator at this stage of the year can block any piece of legislation."

FINAL ACTION

As the House and Senate began their last full day of business, Oct. 27, Miller was insisting that the water-subsidy provisions be restored to the water projects bill in some form. But hectic negotiations with California grower groups and environmental organizations failed to produce a compromise that Miller and Wilson would both accept.

After Congress adjourned, an aide to Miller indicated that any water projects bill in the 102nd Congress would again be tied to the water-subsidy limits issue. ■

Plan To Bar Low-Cost Timber Sales OK'd

A House Agriculture subcommittee tried but failed to block a Bush administration budget initiative to phase out money-losing timber sales on some federal lands.

The House Agriculture Forests, Family Farms and Energy Subcommittee on July 18 approved a bill (HR 5292) to prohibit the Agriculture Department from implementing a below-cost timber sale pilot test included in President Bush's fiscal 1991 budget.

But the more powerful Interior Appropriations Subcommittee on July 24 approved funding for the administration's proposal as it crafted the Interior appropriations bill. The spending bill (HR 5769 — PL 101-512) included funds for the Forest Service.

The administration was proposing a test in nine national-forest administrative units to determine whether a loss of jobs in the timber industry could be offset by increased recreational activities in the forests.

Under the administration's plan, the amount of timber sold from the national forests would have been reduced from 198 million board feet to 120 million board feet a year.

The bill to bar the pilot test was sponsored by Forests Subcommittee Chairman Harold L. Volkmer, D-Mo., and backed by the timber industry and members from affected states. They argued that the plan was poorly conceived and would have thrown too many loggers out of work.

Enough sparks flew during subcommittee debate, however, to persuade Volkmer to pull the legislation from full committee consideration later that afternoon. Volkmer had said at the start of the subcommittee markup that he intended to send a signal to the administration and to the Appropriations Committee, not necessarily to bring a bill to the floor.

The administration indicated it was more interested in what appropriators had to say. "It all depends on what the Congress does through the Appropriations Committee and to what extent they respond to Chairman Volkmer's position on the matter," said Steven Sautterfield, assistant director of program development and budget in the Forest Service. "That will be our first indication of where the House of Representatives is on this."

The Forest Service estimated that 59 of the 115 national-forest administrative units operated "below cost" — that is, they brought in less revenue from timber sales than the federal government spent to prepare the parcels for sale, based on a three-year average. Most of the preparation costs went into building logging roads. ■

Pesticide-Residue Regulation Shelved

Legislation to stiffen regulation of pesticide residues in food advanced in the Senate in the 101st Congress, but was shelved by session's end.

The Senate Labor and Human Resources Committee approved the measure (S 722). But the main sponsor of the bill, Labor Committee Chairman Edward M. Kennedy, D-Mass., was unable to reach agreement with the Bush administration, which had unveiled its own proposal to overhaul pesticides laws in 1989. *(1989 Almanac, p. 396)*

At the heart of the impasse was the issue of state preemption. The Kennedy bill would have allowed states to set tougher food safety standards than the federal government. The administration proposed to set a uniform federal standard, which would have done away with tougher state laws.

The Labor Committee approved the legislation June 27 by voice vote, despite protests by Orrin G. Hatch, R-Utah, and other Republicans that it would not provide for preemption of state laws. Kennedy said he did not want to bring the bill to the floor without GOP support.

The House took no legislative action on an identical bill (HR 1725).

Both environmentalists and farmers desired changes in pesticide regulations. Consumers were concerned about food purity and agricultural interests wanted to avoid a polyglot of potentially stricter state regulations.

Overshadowing the debate was "Big Green," an environmental initiative on the Nov. 6 ballot in California, that would have required California farmers to phase out pesticides shown to cause cancer in animals. It also would have barred food containing these chemicals from being sold in the state. Big Green — which California voters rejected by more than a 3-2 margin — was an archetypical example of the type of strict state regulation that farmers feared and that the administration wanted federal law to pre-empt.

In addition to pre-emption, there was controversy over a provision to establish a "negligible risk" standard for evaluating the health dangers of pesticides. The Environmental Protection Agency (EPA) would have been required to limit pesticide residues in raw and processed foods to ensure that the risk of cancer from consuming the food was not greater than one in a million.

The bill would have clarified existing law to permit the EPA to consider only health risks when determining what level of pesticide residue could be present in foods. The administration had proposed to allow the EPA also to consider the economic benefits of the pesticide to the food industry.

The Kennedy bill would have effectively loosened existing law for processed foods, which were barred from containing any trace of pesticides considered to be carcinogenic. The bill, however, would have subjected pesticides found on raw foods to a stricter standard. Under existing law, the EPA considered both health risks and economic benefits, but Kennedy wanted to make both raw and processed foods subject to the one-in-a-million health-risk standard.

But the bills both would have barred a controversial feature of existing pesticides regulations, which allowed the use of older, potentially more dangerous pesticides that had gained approval while employing more rigorous standards to bar the use of newer, safer ones. Both proposals also would have strengthened the EPA's power to ban potentially dangerous pesticides. ■

House Sustains Family Leave Veto

> **BOXSCORE**
>
> **Legislation:** Family and Medical Leave Act (HR 770, S 345).
>
> **Major action:** House sustained veto, 232-195, July 25; vetoed, June 29. Passed by Senate, June 14; by House, 237-187, May 10.
>
> **Reports:** Labor and Human Resources (S Rept 101-77). Education and Labor (H Rept 101-28, Part I); Post Office and Civil Service (Part II); House Administration (Part III).

Despite intense lobbying by Democrats hoping to score an election-year upset, Congress on July 25 failed to override President Bush's veto of a bill that would have required employees to grant unpaid leave to workers caring for newborn children or sick relatives.

The vote, 232-195, fell 54 short of the two-thirds majority necessary to override the June 29 veto of the measure (HR 770). *(Vote 262, p. 88-H)*

The vote put family and medical leave to rest for the year, although Democrats vowed to keep fighting. "We shall override someday," said Rep. Patricia Schroeder, D-Colo., a longtime advocate of a federal mandated-leave policy.

The legislation would have protected jobs for workers in businesses with at least 50 employees who took up to 12 weeks of unpaid leave to care for a newborn, adopted or ill child. It also would have covered time off for personal medical emergencies, including caring for family members.

Bush said he supported the concept of parental and medical leave but believed that such arrangements were the domain of labor-management negotiations. In his veto message, Bush criticized the bill's "rigid, federally imposed requirements." *(Veto message, p. 361)*

In floor debate before the vote, Steve Bartlett, R-Texas, called the legislation a "cruel hoax" on American workers, because it prescribed a "one size fits all" leave policy for all workers.

But Marge Roukema, R-N.J., a leading proponent of the legislation, disagreed. "This bill represents not only decency, but what is required in the workplace today," Roukema said.

BACKGROUND

Supporters of family leave had been pushing their legislation for years; Schroeder introduced the first parental leave bill in 1985. A bill similar to the 1990 version made it to the Senate floor in 1988 but was killed there after getting mired in election-year politics. *(1988 Almanac, p. 261)*

In 1989, family leave legislation was approved by three House committees and a Senate committee early in the year but failed to reach the floor in either chamber. *(1989 Almanac, p. 348)*

Supporters of a national, mandatory parental leave policy, primarily labor and women's groups, said the country was overdue for federal minimum requirements to bring business in line with the changing demographics of the workplace. About 60 percent of mothers worked outside the home, they said, and the United States was the only major industrialized nation other than South Africa that had no family leave policy.

In contrast, at least 75 other countries, including all other Western industrialized nations and Japan, required various standard family-related benefits.

A 50-state review by the Women's Legal Defense Fund showed that even within the United States protection for family or medical needs was limited. Twenty-five states had no laws guaranteeing family or medical leave, and no state guaranteed employees the breadth or length of protection HR 770 would have provided.

What the Bill Would Have Done

As approved by the House and the Senate, the legislation would have required businesses with 50 or more employees to offer 12 weeks a year of unpaid medical or parental leave. Only one parent could have taken parental leave at a time. Medical leave, when certified by a doctor, could have been used to care for a sick spouse, parent or child. Employees who had worked in a job for at least 1,000 hours over the course of a year would have been eligible.

The legislation would have given federal workers more comprehensive benefits: 18 weeks over two years for parental leave and 26 weeks a year for medical leave. House workers would have received the same protections as private employees; the bill was not amended to include Senate workers.

Among the bill's other provisions were:

- Exemption of highly paid employees if eligibility for the unpaid leave would cause "substantial and grievous" economic injury to an employer. Such employees were defined as among the highest-paid 10 percent within a 75-mile radius of where they worked.
- Extension of unpaid leave coverage to federal and House employees. Federal workers would have gotten 18 weeks over two years for parental leave and 26 weeks each year for medical leave. Home workers would have received the same protections as private employees.
- Making violators liable to pay an employee's lost wages, benefits and other compensation and up to three times that amount in damages.

Business Concerns

The bill was opposed by the U.S. Chamber of Commerce, the Bush administration and a number of conservative Republicans. They argued that mandated leave would remove employers' flexibility and lead them to cut other benefits workers might prefer. "This bill is not going to be the doom of our economy," said Rep. Tom DeLay, R-Texas. "But it is another nail in the coffin of competitiveness and productivity."

Businesses were also concerned that this measure was merely the next step toward more intrusive legislation that might eventually encompass mandated employee health benefits as well.

"What we're fearful of is a deluge of these proposals similar to what was enacted in the 1930s," when Social Security, workers' compensation and other benefits became law, said John J. Motley, vice president for federal government relations at the National Federation of Independent Business.

Supporters and opponents also disagreed over the cost of the bill. Because employers would have had to maintain only health insurance for workers who chose to take unpaid leave, bill sponsors said the cost would be less than $5.30 a year per covered employee.

In addition, according to a 1989 study by the Family Medical Leave Coalition, working women who had no parental leave benefits lost an aggregate of about $607 million a year in earnings. The study also said that it cost $108 million a year in lost taxes and payments for assistance to women who were unemployed or on welfare because they did not get parental leave.

Opponents said the $5.30-a-year estimate of the burden to business was far too low and did not take into account hidden costs, such as litigation and training temporary employees. "To tell people that this bill doesn't cost anything is an outrageous lie," said Rep. Fred Grandy, R-Iowa.

Estimates by the Chamber on the cost to business, made on the basis of earlier parental leave bills, ranged as high as $23.8 billion a year. But the General Accounting Office, an investigative arm of Congress, said that estimate was based on unrealistic assumptions, including how many employees would take leave and how many would be replaced by temporary workers.

HOUSE ACTION

The House on May 10 became the first chamber to pass the family leave bill. The measure approved by the House, though, had been scaled back to gain support from wavering Republicans and conservative Democrats — among them Illinois Republicans Henry J. Hyde and Lynn Martin; Gerald B. H. Solomon, R-N.Y.; and Ed Jenkins, D-Ga.

Noting that the bill passed just three days before Mother's Day, sponsor Schroeder said, "We finally did something real besides chocolate and cards."

A total of 39 Republicans voted for the bill; of the 28 female members in the House, 22 voted in favor.

Although parental leave backers said they won by more votes than expected, the 237-187 vote on final passage fell 46 short of the two-thirds needed for an override. *(Vote 107, p. 38-H)*

Earlier, the House watered down the committee version, approving a substitute by Bart Gordon, D-Tenn., and Curt Weldon, R-Pa., by a wider margin of 259-157. *(Vote 105, p. 38-H)*

The committee-approved version would have tightened the small-business exemption after three years to apply to companies with 35 or more employees. Workers would also have qualified for more unpaid leave: up to 15 weeks a year of medical leave and 10 weeks a year of parental leave. The medical leave would have applied to parents, parents-in-law, stepparents or legal guardians, but not to spouses.

But with the House certain to approve the bill as amended, nine Republicans and a large bloc of Southern Democrats, who typically were supported by business, switched their "aye" votes and opposed it on final passage.

"They were identical [votes], but you could explain it different at home," said Charles W. Stenholm, D-Texas, who voted against the legislation in both instances.

Sponsors said they were confident that Bush would retract his veto threat by the time the bill reached his desk. Roukema, ranking Republican on the Education and Labor Subcommittee on Labor-Management Relations, said she and other GOP supporters of parental leave would push for a meeting with the president to convince him that it was a "bedrock family issue worthy of his support."

But business lobbyists, who met with White House Chief of Staff John H. Sununu on May 7, said Bush would not change his mind. "I had John Sununu look me straight in the eye and say that the president would veto it," said Mary T. Tavenner, a lobbyist for the National Association of Wholesaler-Distributors.

The substitute language — sponsored by Weldon and Gordon, neither of whom had backed the earlier parental leave bill — was worked out in about a month of negotiations with undecided members. While proponents promoted it as a bipartisan compromise, opponents called it no compromise at all.

"It was a Clay compromise with Schroeder," complained Bartlett. Schroeder and William L. Clay, D-Mo., chairman of the Labor-Management Relations Subcommittee, were longtime supporters of parental leave legislation.

Business lobbyists said they played no role in the negotiations. "The area that has always been critical from the business community standpoint is the mandate, and there was no attempt to change that," Motley said.

But Schroeder said the bill — which had gone through several changes — barely resembled the leave policy she pushed in 1985: "I have trouble supporting this compromise because it has been watered down so much."

Amendments Withdrawn

Six weakening amendments had been scheduled for floor debate, but none were offered. Bartlett said three GOP amendments were withdrawn after discussions with the White House because they might have increased support for the legislation.

"The bill is dead," he said. "Any modest improvement in the bill had some potential risk for reviving it."

Bartlett's amendments would have made only full-time employees eligible for leave and would have required workers to give a month's notice before taking the leave and a month's notice before returning to work.

Amendments by Democrats Timothy J. Penny, Minn., and Stenholm also fell by the wayside, aides said, in part because they did not have the votes. A Clay amendment also was not offered. Stenholm and Clay had targeted their amendments at conditions under which employees would have resumed work.

Penny had planned to offer his own leave bill (HR 3445) as a substitute amendment. It would have mandated 10 weeks of unpaid leave a year, but only to care for newborns or adopted children.

Penny said he withdrew his amendment in part because House members had turned the issue into a "political screaming match."

"The debate we will have today and tomorrow is about key votes by special interest groups and political gamesmanship by the political parties," Penny said May 9. "It is not a serious attempt to address the issue."

SENATE ACTION

Amid little of the partisan struggle that marked earlier efforts on the legislation, the Senate on June 14 passed HR 770 by voice vote.

Republican opponents conceded that they were uncertain they had the votes to prevent Senate passage of the scaled-back proposal, and, with a presidential veto looming, saw little point in putting up a fight.

By approving the bill as part of a broader unanimous-

Veto of Mandated Leave Bill

Following is the text of President Bush's June 29 veto message of the Family and Medical Leave Act (HR 770).

I am returning herewith without my approval HR 770, the "Family and Medical Leave Act of 1990." This bill would mandate that public and private employers with 50 or more employees, and the Federal Government, provide their employees with leave under specified circumstances.

In vetoing this legislation with its rigid, federally imposed requirements, I want to emphasize my belief that time off for a child's birth or adoption or for family illness is an important benefit for employers to offer employees. I strongly object, however, to the Federal Government mandating leave policies for America's employers and work force. HR 770 would do just that.

America faces its stiffest economic competition in history. If our Nation's employers are to succeed in an increasingly complex and competitive global marketplace, they must have the flexibility to meet both this challenge and the needs of their employees. We must ensure that Federal policies do not stifle the creation of new jobs, nor result in the elimination of existing jobs. The Administration is committed to policies that create jobs throughout the economy — serving the most fundamental need of working families.

The strong American labor market of the past decade is a sign of how effectively our current labor policies work. Between 1980 and 1989, the United States created more than 18 million new jobs. In contrast, within European countries, where mandated benefits are more extensive and labor markets less flexible, job growth has been weak. Between 1980 and 1989, all of Europe generated only 5 million new jobs.

As a Nation, we must continue the policies that have been so effective in fostering the creation of jobs throughout our economy. HR 770 is fundamentally at odds with this crucial objective.

HR 770 ignored the realities of today's work place and the diverse needs of workers. Some employees may believe that shorter paid leave is more important than the lengthy, unpaid leave mandated by this legislation. Caring for a sick friend, aunt or brother might be just as critical to one employee as caring for a child is to another. In other cases, some employees may prefer increased health insurance or pension coverage rather than unpaid family and medical leave.

Choosing among these options traditionally has been within the purview of employer-employee negotiation or the collective bargaining process. By substituting a "one size fits all" Government mandate for innovative individual agreements, this bill ignores the differing family needs and preferences of employees and unduly limits the role of labor-management negotiations.

We must also recognize that mandated benefits may limit the ability of some employers to provide other benefits of importance to their employees. Over the past few years, we have seen a dramatic increase in the number of employers who are offering child-care assistance, pregnancy leave, parental leave, flexible scheduling and cafeteria benefits. The number of innovative benefit plans will continue to grow as employers endeavor to attract and keep skilled workers. Mandated benefits raise the risk of stifling the development of such innovative benefit plans.

My Administration is strongly committed to policies that recognize that the relationship between work and family must be complementary, and not one that involves conflict. If these policies are to meet the diverse needs of our Nation, they must be carefully, flexibly and sensitively crafted at the work place by employers and employees, and not through Government mandates imposed by legislation such as HR 770. ■

---

consent agreement involving several contentious bills, GOP opponents were also able to avoid a recorded vote on an issue that had been widely portrayed as pro-family.

The Office of Management and Budget issued a statement June 14, the day of the Senate vote, reiterating that the administration "strongly opposes" the measure. The statement said the White House supported the objective of parental and medical leave, but preferred voluntary benefits that had been worked out through employer-employee negotiations.

After the House vote, business lobbyists had been working to ensure their veto-proof margin in that chamber, even before debate was completed in the Senate.

The chief Senate sponsor, Christopher J. Dodd, D-Conn., abandoned a stronger bill (S 345) that he had introduced in February 1989. It would have required businesses with 20 or more employees to offer 10 weeks of unpaid leave over two years to workers who had a baby, adopted a child or had a seriously ill child or parent. Workers would have received up to 13 weeks of unpaid leave a year if they became seriously ill themselves. Employees who had worked at least 900 hours over the course of a year would have been eligible for the leave.

FINAL ACTION

The House on July 25 easily sustained President Bush's veto of the family leave bill. Backers actually won eight fewer votes than when the House passed the measure.

Though Senate passage had come without a recorded vote, Dodd said he was "within two or three votes" of a two-thirds majority. The failed House vote, though, made a Senate vote unnecessary.

Democrats immediately moved to capture the political high ground after the failed override attempt. Dodd recalled a presidential campaign statement Bush made in support of unpaid leave for workers. In "one of the first opportunities [Bush] had to live up to a campaign pledge, he walked away from it," Dodd said.

"I want to emphasize my belief that time off for a child's birth or adoption or for family illness is an important benefit for employers to offer employees," Bush said in his veto message. "I strongly object, however, to the federal government mandating leave policies."

During the 1988 presidential campaign Bush had opposed the mandatory-leave legislation, stating his support even then for encouraging employers to provide parental leave voluntarily.

A partisan clash seemed inevitable, with Democrats trying to pin an anti-family label on Bush, while peeling off enough Republicans and conservatives in their own party to override. "The president should be ashamed for vetoing this bill and making a mockery of the term 'family values,'" House Majority Leader Richard A. Gephardt, D-Mo., said in a statement.

Bush said the bill would have placed undue burdens on business. "We must ensure that federal policies do not stifle the creation of new jobs, nor result in the elimination of existing jobs," Bush said in his statement.

Republicans had criticized the bill as an election-year tribute to labor unions, which had strongly backed it.

Dodd, though, vowed to revisit the issue. "George Bush is going to have a family leave bill on his desk every year that he's in office," Dodd said. ■

Compromise Age Protection Bill Passed

Compromise legislation reversing a 1989 Supreme Court ruling that allowed age-based discrimination in employee benefits cleared Congress late in the session and, despite previous reservations from the administration, was signed into law by President Bush on Oct. 16.

The court, in a 7-2 ruling June 23, 1989, had held that the strict antibias provisions of the 1967 Age Discrimination in Employment Act did not extend to retirement benefits. Lawmakers promptly introduced bills to overturn the decision, but the proposals encountered resistance from business organizations and some labor unions.

Democratic-backed bills moved out of committee in both chambers in early 1990, but continued to draw opposition from GOP lawmakers and business groups that feared the legislation would restrict early-retirement incentive plans — an important method of trimming personnel costs. The Bush administration threatened to veto the legislation.

Late in the session, however, Sens. Howard M. Metzenbaum, D-Ohio, and Orrin G. Hatch, R-Utah, put together a complex compromise aimed at neutralizing opposition from employers by exempting most early-retirement incentive plans. The Senate approved the measure 94-1 on Sept. 24, and the House followed suit, on a 406-17 vote, Oct. 3. *(Senate vote 245, p. 50-S; House vote 407, p. 132-H)*

BOXSCORE

Legislation: Older Workers Benefit Protection Act, PL 101-433 (S 1511, HR 3200).

Major action: Signed, Oct. 16. Passed by House, 460-17, Oct. 3; by Senate, 94-1, Sept. 24.

Reports: Labor and Human Resources (S Rept 101-263); Education and Labor (H Rept 101-664).

BACKGROUND

The Age Discrimination in Employment Act (ADEA), originally enacted in 1967, prohibited private and public employers from discriminating on the basis of age against employees age 40 or older in hiring, promotion or compensation. But it contained an exemption for "any bona fide employee benefit plan such as a retirement, pension, or insurance plan, which is not a subterfuge to evade the purposes" of the act. *(1967 Almanac, p. 658)*

Regulations dating from 1969 interpreted that provision to prohibit age-based differentials in benefits unless they were justified by "significant cost considerations." But the so-called equal cost or equal benefit regulations were invalidated by the Supreme Court in a 7-2 decision in 1989.

The ruling came in a case, *Public Employees Retirement System of Ohio v. Betts*, brought by a former state of Ohio employee forced to retire at age 61 because of an Alzheimer's-related disease. Under Ohio's pension system, her retirement benefits were less than half what she would have received had she been under age 60 when she retired.

Justice Anthony M. Kennedy, writing for the court, said that the language of the ADEA did not expressly bar discrimination in employee benefits. The only way to successfully challenge a benefits plan, he said, was to show it was aimed at discriminating in some non-fringe-benefit area, such as hiring or firing. *(1989 Almanac, p. 315)*

Bills Introduced

Several members of Congress, saying the court had misconstrued the law, began drafting legislation to overturn the decision within weeks of the ruling. "Congress did not intend for older workers to go unprotected from age discrimination in an employment area as critical as employee benefits," said Rep. Edward R. Roybal, D-Calif., chairman of the House Select Committee on Aging.

Roybal and David Pryor, D-Ark., chairman of the Senate Special Committee on Aging, introduced companion measures (HR 3200, S 1511) in early August 1989. Roybal's bill had 115 cosponsors; 45 senators signed on to Pryor's measure.

Hearings in September brought strong support for the bill from senior citizens' and civil rights groups. The Equal Employment Opportunity Commission (EEOC), whose regulations had been invalidated by the court's ruling, said it would endorse the bill if some changes were made.

But business groups warned that the proposed legislation would jeopardize many retirement plans and invalidate some widely used benefit practices, especially early-retirement incentives for younger workers. In a letter, the United Auto Workers (UAW) echoed that concern, saying it favored retaining severance pay options and early-retirement incentives that treated workers differently based on age.

COMMITTEE ACTION

Voting largely along party lines, the Senate Labor and Human Resources Committee and the House Education and Labor Committee approved bills to overturn the *Betts* decision early in 1990.

Senate Committee Markup

The Senate Labor Committee voted 11-5 on Feb. 28 in favor of a substitute version of S 1511 developed by Metzenbaum and James M. Jeffords, R-Vt. Voting against the measure were five of the panel's seven Republican members.

The revised bill picked up support from organized labor, including the UAW and the AFL-CIO, by sanctioning early-retirement incentives. But it was still opposed by such business groups as the U.S. Chamber of Commerce.

Metzenbaum said the main purpose of the bill was to make clear that the 1967 act covered discrimination against older workers in benefits unless the disparate treatment was justified by "significant cost considerations."

"The Supreme Court was wrong, and the bill before us is designed to correct the court's mistake," he said.

The substitute included three major changes urged by the EEOC and labor unions. It clarified that early-retirement incentive programs that were "truly voluntary" would still be legal. It also provided that workers who retired before they were entitled to a full pension could receive a subsidized pension, even though workers who had reached 65 years of age would not receive such subsidies.

Finally, the revised bill also permitted "bridge payments" that were given to some early retirees to subsidize their income until they began collecting Social Security, even though workers who retired at age 65 were not entitled to such payments.

The revised bill also contained a partial concession to employers and unions concerned about the original measure's effect on the practice of "integrating" or coordinating severance pay with pension benefits. In layoffs or plant shutdowns, employers often gave younger workers more in severance pay than they gave older, pension-eligible workers — in recognition that the pensions afforded older workers an income stream that younger workers would not have.

Metzenbaum and Jeffords refused to give blanket approval for the practice, but did modify the bill to allow severance pay for retirement-eligible employees to be offset by the value of any retirement health benefits. In addition, employers offering retirement health benefits could get an additional offset for so-called pension sweeteners — increases beyond the pension an employee would receive based on length of service.

Hatch, however, who led GOP efforts to amend the bill, complained the provision did not go far enough and argued for a broader exemption for integrated benefits.

In markup, the committee also approved an amendment by Jeffords to deal with a separate but related issue: the increasing practice among employers of shielding themselves from age-discrimination suits by seeking waivers from affected employees.

The amendment set a series of standards to ensure that workers who waived their rights to file age-discrimination claims in exchange for generous early-retirement plans knew what they were doing. Specifically, it provided that waivers be in writing and include a recommendation to consult with an attorney, that employees have a period of time after the agreement to change their minds, and that in cases affecting groups of employees the employer reimburse any employee for 80 percent of the cost of consulting a lawyer for up to 10 hours of the attorney's time.

One other provision — making the bill retroactively effective to the date of the *Betts* ruling, June 23, 1989 — was particularly troublesome to business groups. "Companies who have been operating and think they are fine might discover they are not," said Lisa Sprague, manager of employee benefits policy for the U.S. Chamber of Commerce.

House Committee Markup

The House Labor Committee approved a substantially similar bill by a near party-line vote of 20-13 on April 4 after a quarrelsome markup that ended with outvoted Republicans walking out in an effort to deny Democrats the quorum needed to order the bill reported.

Prior to the committee markup, the White House raised the possibility of a veto. In a letter March 27 to the committee's ranking Republican, Bill Goodling, Pa., White House domestic policy adviser Roger Porter listed five areas of concern in the Senate committee's version of the bill: retroactivity; integration or coordination of benefits; waiver of rights; effects on pension plans; and effects on state and local governments. He also criticized as overly restrictive a provision that would permit early-retirement plans as long as they were voluntary and they would "further the purposes" of the age-discrimination law.

Porter said that without "substantial changes" in the bill, "several of the President's advisors would recommend that he veto the legislation."

In the House committee markup, bickering over the bill began as the panel came to order. Marge Roukema, R-N.J., accused acting Chairman William L. Clay, D-Mo., of breaking a gentlemen's agreement to allow 2½ hours for debate. Clay still limited debate to two hours. That set off a cacophony of GOP protests until Goodling intervened. "Can we all stipulate that we're very resentful and get on with business?" he snapped.

When the panel turned to amendments, GOP members began by attacking the provision on early-retirement plans. "It's vague, it's mysterious, and it's problematic," said Cass Ballenger, R-N.C., echoing the White House stance. But the committee defeated, 12-21, his amendment to substitute language allowing employers to use age distinctions when offering benefit packages.

The committee also rejected these amendments:

- By Thomas E. Petri, R-Wis., to shift the burden of proof in lawsuits from the employer to the employee, 11-23.
- By Goodling, to allow employers to "integrate" severance with a retiree's pension, 11-22.
- By Roukema, to make the legislation effective on the date of enactment, rather than the day of the *Betts* decision, 13-20.

The House panel followed the Senate committee's example in expanding the original legislation to deal with the question of legal waivers in exchange for early-retirement payments. But it adopted a stricter limitation — sponsored by Clay and Matthew G. Martinez, D-Calif. — barring any waiver unless it was part of a settlement of an allegation of age discrimination made by a worker against an employer.

FLOOR ACTION

The Senate took up the legislation Sept. 17, with business opposition still strong. Republican Sens. Hatch and Nancy Landon Kassebaum, Kan., had a substitute that also called for overruling *Betts* but provided more flexibility to employers.

But Hatch first offered an amendment that would have gutted the bill by providing that it would not apply to state or local governments or to private employers unless federal employers also were included.

Sponsors of the legislation moved to deflect the attack with an amendment stipulating that the federal government would be covered two years after enactment of the legislation and that the Office of Personnel Management would conduct a study within one year on any changes needed in federal benefit plans to comply.

"A vote for the Hatch amendment is a vote to kill this bill," Metzenbaum said, closing debate on the amendments Sept. 18. The Senate agreed, voting 80-19 to extend the bill to federal employers and then adopting Hatch's language as amended by voice vote. *(Vote 243, p. 49-S)*

Metzenbaum-Hatch Compromise

Despite the victory over Hatch's amendment, the Democratic managers of the bill recognized they did not have the votes or the time to pass the bill as written and overcome a possible presidential veto. So over the weekend, with the blessing of Majority Leader George J. Mitchell, D-Maine, staff for Metzenbaum and Hatch conducted intricate negotiations aimed at drafting a measure that both senators could endorse.

The compromise unveiled Sept. 24 left no one completely happy, but Metzenbaum and Hatch both appealed to colleagues to vote for it.

"The best way to get a law at this late stage of the session is by consensus," Metzenbaum said. "Now that Senator Hatch is on our side, we will work together to ensure quick passage by the House and final approval by the president."

"It is certainly not perfect," Hatch said. He predicted that if the legislation was enacted, it might come back to Congress for fine-tuning within a short time.

The compromise preserved the essential features of the original bills, extending the age-discrimination law to employee benefits and codifying the EEOC's "equal cost or equal benefit" rules that the Supreme Court had invalidated. But it also gave employers "safe harbors" for the two most widely used types of early-retirement incentives — pension subsidies and Social Security "bridge" payments. Employees participating in those types of incentive programs could sue for age discrimination only if they claimed their participation was coerced.

With other types of early-retirement programs, workers could sue on grounds that their employer's plan was not consistent with the "relevant purposes" of the 1967 age-discrimination law. That language was another compromise between Metzenbaum, who wanted strict adherence to all three specifically stated purposes of the ADEA, and Hatch, who wanted plans to be upheld if an employer could show "legitimate business purposes."

The compromise also gave employers an additional, partial concession on the issue of integrating severance pay and pension benefits. It allowed employers an offset for plant-shutdown sweeteners even if they did not offer retirement health benefits, omitting a requirement from the committee-passed bill.

On a related issue that had divided the two senators, the compromise allowed employers to offset long-term disability payments with pension benefits when an employee chose to begin receiving a pension or reached normal retirement age. Metzenbaum had wanted to allow the offset only in case of voluntary retirement; Hatch had wanted a broader offset in every case, based on a worker's accrued pension eligibility.

Employers got further concessions. The burden of proof in employee-benefit claims was placed on workers. Retroactivity was eliminated; instead, the law was to take effect for non-union employees 180 days after enactment and for union employers at the end of existing collective-bargaining agreements or by June 1, 1992. And the waiver provision was amended to drop any requirement for employers to pay employees' legal fees.

The provision for covering federal employees was also dropped. State and local governments were given two years to comply with the new law.

Despite the reservations from the authors of the compromise, no senator spoke in opposition to the revised measure. It passed 94-1, with James A. McClure, R-Idaho, casting the lone dissenting vote. *(Vote 245, p. 50-S)*

Final Action

The House moved quickly after the Senate action. The bill was brought to the floor Oct. 2 under suspension of the rules — limited debate and no amendments. Clay, after explaining the compromise, told members, "If we pass the Senate bill today, we have been informed that the president will sign it."

The roll call was delayed to the next day when the bill passed, 406-17, with Republicans casting all the "no" votes. ■

Whistleblower Bill Fails

Legislation aimed at better protecting private-sector employees who "blow the whistle" on health and safety violations by their companies was approved by the Senate Labor Committee but never taken up by the full Senate. Companion legislation in the House received one subcommittee hearing in 1989, but saw no action in 1990.

The bills (S 436, HR 3368) would have closed some loopholes in federal laws designed to protect so-called whistleblowers from management reprisals.

The chief sponsors — Sen. Howard M. Metzenbaum, D-Ohio, and Rep. William D. Ford, D-Mich. — sought to protect private-sector workers from retaliation if they disclosed federal health and safety violations or refused to participate in an illegal or extremely hazardous activity as long as the employee first tried to correct the violation.

The protections in their bills would have applied to any industry subject to federal health and safety standards.

The Bush administration and GOP lawmakers opposed the bill, arguing that it was too broad and could encourage malicious disclosures by disgruntled employees.

Whistleblowers employed in government agencies and by government contractors were already protected from reprisals by a measure (S 20 — PL 101-12) signed by President Bush on April 10, 1989. *(1989 Almanac, p. 353)*

Legislative Action

The Senate Labor and Human Resources Committee approved S 436 on a party-line, 8-7 vote on April 25.

In its report (S Rept 101-349), the committee said that without federal protection statutes for whistleblowing "private citizens will continue to be reluctant to assist health and safety enforcement efforts if they know that they may be punished for providing such assistance."

Bill proponents also argued that related whistleblower measures that were already enacted into law contained numerous inconsistencies that S 436 could have cleared up.

Under laws already enacted, some private-sector employees, such as miners, longshoremen, migrant workers and truckers, were covered in the same respect as federal workers, for reports of health and safety violations, but not for waste, fraud or abuse, as federal workers were.

S 436 and HR 3368 would have extended protections to workers in industries that were not already covered, such as aviation, food processing and nuclear-weapons production.

Under Metzenbaum's bill, a private-sector employee who alleged discrimination on the basis of whistleblowing would have had to file a complaint within 180 days of the alleged discriminatory action or incident.

If after 60 days an investigative office within the Labor Department found "reasonable cause to believe" the complaint had merit, the employee would have to be temporarily reinstated. An employee prevailing on a reprisal claim could be awarded back pay and costs, including legal fees.

In dissenting views, GOP committee members argued the bill "would provide millions of workers, including those covered by existing whistleblower laws, with a new, expansive, and virtually unprecedented right to refuse work." ■

Funding Dispute Kills Job-Training Bill

The House and the Senate crafted legislation to refocus and overhaul the federal government's major job-training program for disadvantaged youths, but the effort fell short because of disagreements over funding allocations.

Both chambers' bills sought to alter the funding formula that determined the amount of money states received for job training.

While competing measures were approved by the House on Sept. 27 — and the Senate Labor Committee on July 26, 1989 — the Senate legislation stalled in 1990 because of opposition from states that would have received less funding under its allocation formula. A last-ditch effort also failed to attach the measure to the Labor, Health and Human Services, and Education appropriations conference report in the days before adjournment.

> **BOXSCORE**
>
> **Legislation:** Job Training Partnership Act amendments (HR 2039, S 543).
>
> **Major action:** HR 2039 passed by House, 416-1, Sept. 27. S 543 approved by Senate Labor Committee, July 26, 1989.
>
> **Reports:** Education and Labor (H Rept 101-747). Labor and Human Resources (S Rept 101-129).

Under the existing Job Training Partnership Act (JTPA), job-training allocations were based largely on the number of unemployed people in states and local communities. The House bill (HR 2039) would have changed the government's formula for figuring the federal funding that each state received for summer youth programs, while leaving intact the formula for determining funding for adult programs. It passed the House by a vote of 416-1. *(Vote 389, p. 126-H)*

Under the measure, the new funding formula for youth programs would have allotted 60 percent of funding on the basis of the number of unemployed in the state, 20 percent on the number of residents receiving Aid to Families with Dependent Children (AFDC) and 20 percent on the number of economically disadvantaged people in the state.

Some senators, meanwhile, raised concerns that the measure introduced in the Senate (S 543) would have altered the funding formula for all job programs under JTPA. Lawmakers said some states — including Texas, Louisiana, Michigan and Indiana — would lose money.

The House bill would have authorized about $3 billion in fiscal 1991 for a variety of programs in JTPA. The Senate bill would have authorized up to $1.2 billion to train needy adults and youths and $1.6 billion for a summer youth job-training program. Under the Labor-HHS spending bill, $4.07 billion was appropriated for all JTPA programs and grants in fiscal 1991. JTPA received $3.92 billion in fiscal 1989 appropriations.

The Bush administration objected to the funding increases in both bills and a number of other provisions, including the establishment of a program of federally subsidized jobs to provide assistance in disaster areas.

Congress was successful in amending the JTPA in a separate piece of legislation to provide job training to displaced homemakers (HR 3069 — PL 101-554). *(Displaced homemakers, p. 366)*

BACKGROUND

The House and Senate bills were the first major attempts to amend the 1982 job-training law, which was coauthored by Sen. Edward M. Kennedy, D-Mass., and Vice President Dan Quayle, then a GOP senator from Indiana.

Quayle repeatedly cited the JPTA during the 1988 presidential campaign as one of his main legislative accomplishments. *(1988 Almanac p. 44-A; 1982 Almanac, p. 39)*

JTPA replaced a problem- and abuse-plagued public-service employment program known as CETA (the Comprehensive Employment and Training Act). The job-training act was administered by service delivery areas (SDAs) established by the governors of each state. For each SDA, local officials designated a private industry council to help plan and administer the job-training programs.

During hearings on the bills, job-training officials criticized the program for not serving such people as the homeless, who were the most needy and often the most difficult to train and place. They complained that an incentive system in the program awarded programs with higher placement rates, prompting administrators to target people who were easier to train.

Senate and House sponsors of the new legislation tried to address these underlying concerns.

The newly devised formulas sought to emphasize poverty rates, rather than unemployment rates as the chief determinant of federal funding. That proposed shift under the Senate bill generally favored the nation's poorest, inner-city areas at the expense of suburban sections of the country.

In July 1989, the Senate Labor Committee approved S 543 by a vote of 15-1. The lone dissenter was Democrat Brock Adams of Washington, who worried that his state also would lose funding under the bill.

Sponsored by Paul Simon, D-Ill., the measure never reached the Senate floor because members were concerned that a number of states would lose money.

In a vain attempt to minimize disruption in the existing program — and dampen political opposition from regions threatened by the new formula — the Senate bill provided that each state through fiscal 1992 would receive at least as much money as it was already getting.

HOUSE COMMITTEE ACTION

The House Education and Labor Committee approved HR 2309 by voice vote July 31. Approval of the measure followed a number of heated and contentious markups by the committee and its Subcommittee on Employment Opportunities.

Committee members dealt with a barrage of amendments at its first markup July 19. They settled the most controversial issues — the funding formula, emergency disaster-relief employment and "flexible" job placement — on July 26 before finally sending the legislation to the full House on July 31.

The action followed a turf battle between subcommittee

and committee members over which draft bill to work from.

Subcommittee Markup

Education and Labor Committee Chairman Augustus F. Hawkins, D-Calif., and ranking Republican Bill Goodling, Pa., said they had spent a year working out a bipartisan compromise. The bill was sent to subcommittee for consideration, where Chairman Matthew G. Martinez, D-Calif., added a number of amendments, some of which were opposed by Hawkins, committee Republicans and Labor Secretary Elizabeth H. Dole.

Dole called the funding increases in the bills "excessive" and sent a letter on July 19 to Hawkins outlining her objections to much of the legislation.

After the changes, instead of considering the Hawkins bill, the committee began considering a substitute by Martinez that incorporated Hawkins' bill and some of the changes Martinez favored. Committee leaders, particularly Republicans, said they were blindsided. "We've spent a year, day and night, working on a piece of legislation, and we seemed to have a consensus, and all of a sudden we go to a piece of legislation that I don't think anyone understands the implications of," Goodling said.

At the July 17 subcommittee markup, Martinez offered several amendments that drew fire from Republicans, including Goodling.

One amendment would have provided for emergency disaster-relief employment through the JTPA. Another would have applied the Fair Labor Standards Act, which exempted Puerto Rico from minimum-wage requirements, to the JTPA in Puerto Rico. A third amendment would have allowed county and city "service delivery areas" set up by the JTPA to serve one another's residents.

Goodling argued that the JTPA was a training bill, not an employment service. "We're mixing apples and oranges," he said.

Although only three members were present at the subcommittee session, Martinez called for a vote on the amendments as a package. The amendments were approved by a roll-call vote of 6-4, with Martinez casting a number of proxy votes.

Republicans later complained that there was no quorum. Martinez said that he had acted in good faith and that it was agreeable to everyone that the vote be taken; Republicans, he said, were objecting because they disagreed with the changes.

Goodling said Republicans did not actively protest the unusual procedure, but he objected to using the Martinez substitute as the working document when the Hawkins bill had been agreed to by all sides.

Hawkins settled the issue by deciding that the committee would work from the Martinez version rather than the compromise bill.

Hawkins tried to soothe all sides. "In the final process, it really doesn't make much difference what we work off of, as long as we work to get a bipartisan bill."

Committee Markups

Adopted by voice vote July 31, the committee-approved measure included a compromise amendment by Pat Williams, D-Mont., to change the funding formula that determined how much each state received for youth employment training, while keeping the old formula for adult programs.

Committee members agreed to the Williams amendment July 26, removing a major obstacle to approval of JTPA legislation. The amendment sought to change the funding formula for youth programs in states to allot 60 percent of funding on the basis of unemployment, 20 percent on the number of AFDC recipients and 20 percent on the number of economically disadvantaged people.

Williams described his amendment as a compromise to satisfy those members whose states had previously received the largest funding shares and who may have been afraid of losing funds and those who believed their states were not getting a fair share.

Another amendment that sparked heated debate would have authorized $15 million to provide emergency employment to disaster victims.

The committee agreed to a compromise by Goodling to limit eligibility to those who both qualified for the JTPA dislocated-worker program and were unemployed because of a disaster.

The amendment, first offered by Cass Ballenger, R-N.C., originally sought to delete the earlier provision added by Martinez to authorize $15 million to provide emergency disaster-relief employment.

Displaced Homemakers

The House on Oct. 24 cleared and sent to the president a bill to provide job training to displaced homemakers.

The Senate passed the measure by voice vote in the early morning hours of Oct. 20 (during the session of Oct. 19) with an amendment to reduce the fiscal 1991 authorization to $35 million. Sen. Strom Thurmond, R-S.C., had objected to the $50 million figure approved by the House on Oct. 15. The House agreed to the Senate change.

President Bush signed the bill into law (HR 3069 — PL 101-554) on Nov. 15.

The legislation amended the 1982 Job Training Partnership Act (JTPA) by authorizing funding to train the nation's estimated 15.6 million displaced homemakers — women whose long-term roles as homemakers ended because of divorce or the death or disability of their husbands. The provision was contained in House and Senate versions of a broader overhaul of the act and then stripped out as a separate measure when those bills stalled.

The funding for the homemakers bill would be used to expand and coordinate existing training and support services at the state and local levels.

The House Education Committee's ranking Republican, Bill Goodling of Pennsylvania, said the number of displaced homemakers had grown an estimated 12 percent in the past decade. Approximately 60 percent of the women were unemployed.

Under the bill, states would have to give special consideration to women 40 and older as well as minority displaced homemakers.

The measure was introduced in August 1989 by Matthew G. Martinez, D-Calif., chairman of the House Education and Labor Committee Employment Opportunities Subcommittee. It was referred to the subcommittee where it remained until October 1990; the subcommittee held one hearing, on Sept. 28, 1989.

Ballenger and other Republicans argued the amendment would create a public service program, contrary to the JTPA's original intent. "It almost goes back to being CETA again," he said, referring to the program JTPA replaced.

But Williams argued that Labor Secretary Dole had already been forced to use funding to employ disaster victims. "This section simply faces up to the reality that [Dole] has been facing up to for the past year," he said.

Voting along party lines, the committee rejected, 14-21, an amendment by Texas Republican Steve Bartlett that would have let participants trained for specific jobs to be placed in related fields.

Bartlett argued that many JTPA participants were trained to do particular work but could not find employment in those specific areas because, under existing law, JTPA funds could only be used to place people in jobs for which they had been trained. Bartlett said the restriction could keep some employers from participating in the program, thus defeating the bill's purpose of targeting the nation's most disadvantaged.

"They are not going to train people that are hard to train and hard to place," Bartlett said. "They won't take risks."

"We must have some kind of relationship between the training and the job in this business," Martinez said in opposing the amendment. "If we don't, we could have a worse situation develop."

HOUSE FLOOR ACTION

The House passed HR 2039 on Sept. 27 by an overwhelming vote of 416-1. The lopsided margin of victory masked the sometimes-heated debate the bill had sparked in committee. Because of the continuing controversy over the funding formula, though, no bill ever reached the Senate floor in 1990.

In addition to the Williams compromise on the funding formula to implement the 60-20-20 percent allotment formula for unemployed people, AFDC recipients and the economically disadvantaged, three amendments received voice-vote approval on the floor:

- An amendment offered by Gary Condit, D-Calif., to revise JTPA eligibility requirements to increase participation of migrant and seasonal farmworkers.
- An amendment offered by Goodling, to require local grant recipients to keep records to enable the Labor Department to better collect information about the program's effectiveness.
- An amendment offered by Bartlett, to increase the chances for participation for some youths who cannot show that they are economically disadvantaged.

One Last Chance

Just when it appeared that JTPA legislation was dead for the year, dramatic events surrounding passage of the Labor, Health and Human Services, and Education appropriations bill (HR 5257 — PL 101-517) gave the issue a final chance. *(Labor-HHS appropriations, p. 847)*

Before being cleared by the Senate on Oct. 26, the conference report spent four days bouncing back and forth between the two chambers.

New Mexico Democrat Jeff Bingaman on Oct. 25 successfully attached to the bill a $2 million allocation for the National Council on Educational Goals.

Republicans who opposed the education commission fought back by successfully appending to the bill a big separate bill to revise the JTPA.

"If the majority wants to use appropriations bills to carry authorizing legislation, then we ought to give it some legislation to carry," said Orrin G. Hatch, R-Utah.

The job-training legislation was adopted by a roll-call vote of 95-1. The lone holdout was Senate Appropriations Committee Chairman Robert C. Byrd, D-W.Va. "I don't want to see the legislative process perverted here, and that's exactly what we're doing when we put authorizing legislation into appropriations bills," Byrd complained. "We're going to kill this bill right here. It's going to die if we don't stop playing games with it." *(Vote 318, p. 104-H)*

The House stripped off the jobs bill early Oct. 26, before sending the measure back to the Senate for clearance.

Supporters of revamping the 1982 act said they would renew their efforts in 1991. Most observers expected the Senate to take up a new bill resembling the one the House passed with the less controversial funding allocation.

Said Williams, author of the compromise funding formula, "The Senate bill has been stalled since last year because of the formula." ■

Tax on Pension Moves

A labor-backed measure designed to discourage employers from terminating overfunded pension plans stalled in 1990, though Congress did pass tax penalty provisions expected to slow the practice.

S 685, a modified version of a bill nearly enacted in 1989, was approved by the Senate Labor and Human Resources Committee on Feb. 28, but saw no further action.

However, provisions sharply increasing taxation of any excess pension plan funds retained by an employer were included in the omnibus deficit-reduction bill (HR 5835 — PL 101-508). *(Reconciliation provisions, Title XII, p. 161)*

BACKGROUND

Pension plan reversions — the process by which an employer terminated a plan and used the excess funds for other activities — increased following a Labor Department ruling in 1983 that the practice was not regulated under the 1974 Employee Retirement Income Security Act (ERISA). Many companies then took the opportunity to cash out their pension plans and use the excess cash to finance corporate takeovers or other activities.

Organized labor and retired workers' groups sought legislation to curb the practice.

But business organizations argued that any legislation restricting what an employer could do with excess pension money would discourage employers from creating pension plans.

Congress tried to dampen employers' enthusiasm for terminating plans in 1986 by levying a 10 percent excise tax on the surplus funds, increasing the rate to 15 percent in 1988. *(1986 Almanac, p. 491)*

In 1989, bills severely restricting an employer's ability to cash out plans were approved by the Senate and House Labor committees (S 685, HR 1661) and then attached to that year's budget-reconciliation bill. But the pension-reversion provisions were stripped at the last minute along with other extraneous measures. *(1989 Almanac, p. 350)*

LEGISLATIVE ACTION

The Senate Labor Committee returned to the issue Feb. 28, approving a modified form of S 685 (S Rept 101-294). Voting for the bill were the panel's eight Democrats and two Republicans who had voted in 1989 against including the measure in budget reconciliation: James M. Jeffords, Vt., and Nancy Landon Kassebaum, Kan.

As modified, S 685 would have applied ERISA standards to pension plan terminations by requiring the manager of the plan to allow a termination only if it was determined to be in the best interest of the plan participants.

The measure also included a provision to create a system of "portable pensions" to enable employees to carry their pension funds with them as they changed jobs.

Budget Reconciliation

While S 685 saw no further action, supporters of the legislation again tried to use the budget-reconciliation bill as a vehicle, and this time succeeded.

As enacted, Title XII increased to 20 percent from 5 percent the excise tax employers would have to pay to cash out their pension plans.

The rate would be 50 percent if an employer decided not to set up a new pension plan.

When an employer terminated a pension plan, it would then either have to keep a "cushion" of 25 percent of the surplus in a new pension plan or pay out 20 percent of the surplus in cash to retirees and workers.

Employers would not be penalized, however, if they used the excess pension funds to pay premiums on retiree health plans.

The Congressional Budget Office estimated that the pension-reversion provision would lose about $388 million in federal revenues over the five years of the budget agreement by discouraging the practice. ■

Pension Board Backed

The Supreme Court, in an 8-1 ruling on June 18, upheld the authority of the Pension Benefit Guaranty Corporation (PBGC) to make financially ailing companies take back the responsibility for pension plans.

The decision in *Pension Benefit Guaranty Corp. v. LTV* was an important victory for the government-owned entity created by the 1974 Employee Retirement Income Security Act (ERISA) to insure private pension plans. It came at a time when the agency faced a possible $1.5 billion deficit of liabilities over assets.

The ruling upheld a PBGC order that LTV Corp., a diversified corporation that included one of the nation's largest steel companies, resume responsibility for three pension plans with liabilities totaling $2.3 billion. LTV filed for reorganization under Chapter 11 of the federal bankruptcy code in 1986 and informed the PBGC that it could no longer fund the pension plans.

Senate Minority Leader Bob Dole, R-Kan., said the decision "sends a strong and clear message to employers that they cannot escape their own plan funding obligations by declaring bankruptcy, shifting billions of dollars of liability to the government, and then going back into business and setting up new plans." ■

No Hike in Jobless Pay

A bill that would have increased unemployment benefits — and also raised unemployment taxes — was pulled from House committee consideration July 25 by its sponsor, Thomas J. Downey, D-N.Y., when it became clear that it lacked the requisite support.

Downey quickly removed the measure from consideration when it became clear that even some liberal Democrats on the Ways and Means Committee were wavering in their support of the bill (HR 3896). Downey had expected his bill to face major opposition from Republicans on the committee.

"We looked like we were about one vote short," Downey said later. "People got cold feet."

As approved by voice vote March 13 by the Human Resources Subcommittee, HR 3896 sought to extend unemployment benefits by creating a "substate" trigger. This would have allowed a state's governor to activate extended unemployment benefits in one area of the state, even if the unemployment rate in the state as a whole was not high enough to trigger the extended benefits program.

Jobless people were eligible for 13 weeks of extended benefits after they had exhausted the 26-week state plans, but only if the state as a whole had high enough unemployment rates to trigger the program.

Preliminary estimates by the Ways and Means staff showed the bill would have cost $3.3 billion over the next three fiscal years and a total of $6.5 billion by fiscal 1995.

To pay for these extra benefits, the bill provided for an increase in the federal wage base on which employers paid unemployment taxes. The minimum taxable wage base used to calculate employers' unemployment insurance tax would have risen annually from its existing level of $7,000 to $10,000 by fiscal 1993.

The proposed tax increase drew scornful comments from the committee minority — and even some Democrats.

Ranking Republican Bill Archer of Texas said the committee would be "sending a strange signal" to the White House and congressional budget negotiators if they "continued to tax and spend as if we have no budget deficit."

Downey defended his proposal, saying that unemployment reserves were inadequate to cover a possible recession and that "this is a preparation for bad times to come."

But he had a hard time persuading his Democratic colleagues. "I don't take lightly the idea of adding to the payroll taxes," said Byron L. Dorgan, D-N.D.

Downey tried to increase support for the bill with an amendment to authorize a five-year program for dislocated workers who lost their jobs because of action by the federal government, but this proposal also drew opposition.

Rod Chandler, R-Wash., told members that it would not help "salve your conscience by shutting down an industry, then turning around and saying, 'We gave you compensation.' " ■

House Sustains Veto On Eastern Strike

The House on March 7 sounded the death knell for Democratic efforts to force the Bush administration to intervene in the dispute between Eastern Airlines and its unions.

Members voted to sustain the president's veto of a bill (HR 1231) that would have set up a blue-ribbon commission to recommend solutions to the yearlong strike. The 261-160 vote was 21 votes short of the two-thirds majority needed to override Bush's veto. *(Vote 22, p. 12-H)*

The largely party-line vote was a setback for organized labor and for the Eastern Airlines pilots who had lined the House gallery in dwindling numbers during much of 1989 and early 1990. Stronger legislation to suspend the strike for 26 days while a presidentially appointed emergency board worked to resolve the dispute fell victim to a Senate filibuster threat in 1989.

The compromise measure, offered by Senate Majority Leader George J. Mitchell, D-Maine, was intended to placate GOP opponents while forcing the president to take some action — or, at the least, to pay a political price for refusing to act.

Democrats said the Bush and Reagan administrations had parted with precedent by ignoring federal strike mediators' recommendations to set up an emergency board.

BACKGROUND

The strike at Eastern, the nation's seventh-largest air carrier, began March 4, 1989. Five days later, the airline filed for Chapter 11 bankruptcy to gain protection from its creditors.

Many leading Democrats urged Bush to follow the advice of federal mediators and establish an emergency panel to recommend a settlement to the dispute.

This procedure, often used in transportation disputes, also would have sent strikers back to work for a 60-day "cooling-off" period.

Strikers said they would have welcomed intervention; Eastern's management opposed it.

On Oct. 26, 1989, the Senate passed the bill to establish a four-member commission to make recommendations on ending the strike; the House followed suit on Nov. 7. But Bush, citing objections to government intervention, vetoed the bill on Nov. 21. *(Veto message, 1989 Almanac, p. 43-C)*

Eastern's Last Hope?

As in the past, the legislation became embroiled in debate over what effect it would have had on the bankruptcy proceedings involving the airline and on remaining Eastern employees.

It also gave Democrats a chance to rail against Frank A. Lorenzo, chief of Texas Air Corp., Eastern's parent company, for what Peter A. DeFazio, D-Ore., called "corporate recklessness." DeFazio said the bill represented Congress' "last hope of restoring Eastern as a competitive airline."

But Texas Republican Jack Fields criticized his Democratic colleagues for carrying out "personal vendettas through legislation." He and other Republicans — with the vocal exception of Minority Whip Newt Gingrich of Georgia, whose district had a lot of Eastern employees — said Congress risked forcing the airline out of business altogether by increasing bitterness between management and the unions and making a resolution of the strike less likely.

"I acknowledge the temptation to side with the frustrations of labor," said Hamilton Fish Jr., R-N.Y. "But the courts should be permitted to act unfettered by legislative interference."

Bankruptcy examiner David I. Shapiro had written House GOP Leader Robert H. Michel, Ill., on March 5 to urge Congress to stay out of the dispute, saying the legislation would be "disastrous" for Eastern. Shapiro said the further delay could force Eastern out of business, jeopardizing the pensions of its 12,000 retirees and putting 17,000 employees out of work.

Shapiro issued a report the week of Feb. 26 that found "reasonable grounds" for challenging 12 of 15 transactions between Texas Air Corp. and Eastern.

While unions used the findings to lobby in favor of legislation, Republicans opposing the veto override cited the report as evidence the issue was being investigated fully without congressional intervention. ■

Lynn Martin Picked For Labor Post

President Bush on Dec. 14 announced his selection of Lynn Martin, a moderate Republican congresswoman who lost her bid to be elected senator from Illinois, to succeed Elizabeth H. Dole as secretary of Labor. Dole became the first member of Bush's original Cabinet to leave when she resigned effective Nov. 23 to head the American Red Cross.

Martin, who served 10 years in the House, was defeated by nearly a 2-1 margin in her bid for the Senate by incumbent Democrat Paul Simon.

Martin's AFL-CIO rating from 1981 through 1989 averaged 24 percent in non-election years and 37 percent in election years.

She voted the position of the U.S. Chamber of Commerce an average of about 75 percent of the time during her 10 years in Congress.

Martin had longstanding ties to Bush, having backed him in his first presidential bid in 1980 and served as a national co-chairman of his 1988 campaign. But she had only a 56 percent score on presidential support during 1990. She voted for the civil rights and parental leave bills, both vetoed by Bush, and in 1989 she voted to override his veto of a minimum-wage bill.

In her nearly two years in the Labor post, Dole was credited with negotiating an agreement on an increase in the minimum wage, increasing enforcement of job safety and child-labor laws, using government contracts to encourage companies to move women and minorities into management positions, and moving more women and minorities into policy positions at the Labor Department itself. *(Dole confirmation, 1989 Almanac, p. 398)*

But some Democrats questioned her effectiveness. "It cannot have been easy," said Sen. Edward M. Kennedy, D-Mass., "serving as a pro-labor secretary in an anti-labor administration."

Cable Reregulation Blocked in Senate

Legislation to reregulate the cable television industry died on the Senate floor Sept. 28 despite strong backing fueled by consumer complaints about price increases during nearly four years of deregulation.

Three senators who viewed the bill as too tough on cable operators — Democrat Tim Wirth, Colo., and Republicans Bob Packwood, Ore., and Malcolm Wallop, Wyo. — blocked a move to bring the bill (S 1880) up for floor debate.

A similar bill (HR 5267), somewhat more to the liking of the cable industry, had cleared the House by voice vote Sept. 10.

Both bills would have allowed the Federal Communications Commission (FCC) to regulate rates for basic cable service. State and local governments had regulated cable rates through their franchising authority before Congress' decision to deregulate cable took effect at the end of 1986.

Both bills also sought to increase competition in the video marketplace by prohibiting cable programmers with ties to cable operators from discriminating against competing multichannel video services such as wireless cable, direct broadcast satellite and home satellite dish users.

The cable industry had been neutral on the House measure and actively opposed the Senate bill. Wirth and Packwood were authors of the 1984 deregulation measure.

Supporters of the reregulation bills said they planned to push their proposals again in the 102nd Congress. Hearings had already been promised in 1991 on a related issue: allowing telephone companies to operate cable systems. That issue had been put aside in hope of avoiding cable industry opposition to the 1990 measures.

BOXSCORE

Legislation: Cable Television Consumer Protection and Competition Act (HR 5267); Cable Television Consumer Protection Act (S 1880).

Major action: HR 5267, passed by House, Sept. 10; S 1880, unanimous-consent request to proceed to immediate consideration objected to, Sept. 28.

Reports: Commerce (S Rept 101-381); Energy and Commerce (H Rept 101-682).

BACKGROUND

Congress in 1984 passed legislation, the Cable Communications Policy Act, that largely deregulated the cable television industry. The law, climaxing two decades of resistance to restrictive regulation by the FCC and by state and local governments, marked a watershed in cable's growth from an auxiliary video service for outlying areas to a full-fledged competitor in the burgeoning video marketplace. *(1984 Almanac, p. 286)*

The law eliminated the authority of state and local governments to regulate rates cable operators charged to subscribers as of Dec. 29, 1986, unless the cable system was not subject to "effective competition" — later defined by the FCC as at least three broadcast stations. The act also capped the franchise fee a local government could charge a cable operator at 5 percent of the system's gross revenue.

Cable operators and their trade association, the National Cable Television Association (NCTA), argued that rate regulation, high franchise fees and other restrictions imposed in the franchising process limited cable's ability to finance investments needed to reach more subscribers and to increase program offerings.

An FCC report issued in July 1990 contended that deregulation had contributed to a growth in cable service. Investment in new and expanded capacity increased from $1.1 billion in 1984 to $1.7 billion in 1989. Spending on cable programming tripled, from $302 million to $965 million. And the percentage of households with cable service available to them increased from 70 percent to 90 percent.

At the same time, though, rates for cable service increased faster than the rate of inflation. A survey by the General Accounting Office, issued in June 1990, showed that in the three years since deregulation the average cable subscriber's monthly rate for the lowest-priced basic services had increased 43 percent. Members of Congress, citing individual instances of rates doubling or tripling in the same period, charged that cable operators had engaged in monopolistic price-gouging.

As a result, pressure mounted during the 101st Congress for legislation to restore some government regulation of cable rates. In addition, some lawmakers wanted to deal with concerns of broadcasters, wireless cable providers and satellite dish makers that the increasingly integrated cable industry was choking off competitors by keeping cable programming from other multichannel services, shutting out other program suppliers and disadvantaging broadcasters in their placement on cable systems.

Two Major Bills Introduced

Two major cable bills were introduced in 1989.

The first measure — S 1068/HR 2437, introduced May 18, 1989, by Sen. Al Gore, D-Tenn., and Rep. Rick Boucher, D-Va. — would have allowed local government regulation of cable rates in areas with only one cable system. It also would have barred cable operators and their affiliated program suppliers from discriminatory practices against other cable systems.

Most troublingly to the cable industry, the Gore-Boucher bill also would have allowed telephone companies — telcos, in the industry's jargon — to offer cable services as long as the funds were not provided by telephone ratepayers. The 1984 cable deregulation act and a federal court order that governed the breakup of the American Telephone & Telegraph Co. prohibited phone companies from offering cable in all but some small rural communities.

The second bill — S 1880/HR 3826, introduced Nov. 15, 1989, by Sen. John C. Danforth, R-Mo., and Rep. Jim Cooper, D-Tenn. — also would have allowed local rate regulation in areas with only one cable system and barred programmers with connections to cable operators from discriminating against other cable systems. It did not contain a provision to allow telephone companies to operate cable systems, but did include two other provisions aimed at curbing the cable industry's marketplace clout.

One provision, sought by broadcasters, would have restored so-called must-carry rules that required cable operators to air most local television broadcasts. Federal courts had struck down the must-carry rules in 1985 and then again in 1987 after the FCC moved, under pressure from Congress, to restore them.

A second provision in Danforth's bill responded to the increased concentration of the cable industry by proposing to limit any multiple cable system operator's overall number of subscribers to 15 percent of the national total. The largest cable conglomerate, Tele-Communications Inc., headquartered in Denver, owned nearly 400 systems with 4.5 million subscribers — 9.3 percent of the national share. It also had equity interests in more than a dozen program services, including Movietime, the Discovery Channel and Cable News Network (CNN), the 24-hour news service.

Variety of Interests

The host of interest groups staked out their positions on cable issues during hearings by the House and Senate communications subcommittees that began in June 1989 and continued into spring 1990.

The cable industry made clear its distaste for any new legislation. NCTA President James P. Mooney told senators Nov. 16, 1989, that choosing between the two major legislative options — reregulation or telco competition — was like choosing between being "boiled in oil or vinegar."

The U.S. Telephone Association actively backed the Gore-Boucher bill, echoing the lawmakers' argument that allowing telcos to operate cable systems would hasten new services through fiber-optic technology. So did the National League of Cities and the U.S. Conference of Mayors.

But the cable industry was joined in its opposition to the provision by the newspaper industry, which wanted to keep telephone companies out of information services, and by the Consumer Federation of America, which doubted the adequacy of safeguards to keep telephone ratepayers from subsidizing the telcos' new cable ventures.

Broadcasters and their trade association, the National Association of Broadcasters, lined up behind Danforth's bill with its must-carry provision and limits on cable conglomerates. The limits on cable's marketplace clout also were supported by the fledgling Wireless Cable Association, whose members used microwave transmissions rather than hard wire to offer cable services, and from the satellite dish industry's trade association, the Satellite Broadcasting and Communications Association.

COMMITTEE ACTION

A consensus began to emerge among members of both the House and the Senate Commerce committees on the need to re-establish some controls over the cable industry. Compromise measures, crafted to neutralize potential cable industry opposition, moved through these committees in June and July 1990.

Senate Committee Markup

The Senate Commerce Committee moved first, approving a substitute version of S 1880 on June 7 drafted by the committee's chairman, Ernest F. Hollings, D-S.C.; Communications Subcommittee Chairman Daniel K. Inouye, D-Hawaii; and Danforth. The vote was 18-1, with Packwood casting the lone dissenting vote.

The substitute was more to cable's liking than Danforth's original bill; for example, it shifted rate regulation from local governments to the FCC. And the committee's markup session was delayed an hour in an effort to nail down an agreement by NCTA not to oppose the measure.

The tenuous accord dissolved, however, over NCTA's objection to language barring cable operators from "unreasonably" refusing to deal with other multichannel video programming distributors. Senators pointed to language in introductory "findings" that sanctioned exclusive agreements between programmers and cable operators as a "legitimate competitive strategy," but NCTA President Mooney said he wanted more explicit protections.

Angered by what he called the cable industry's decision to pull out of the deal "at the very last minute," Gore offered an amendment to delete the finding on exclusive business arrangements. The amendment, which carried by voice vote, also required sale of cable programming carried on satellites to home satellite dish users.

The cable industry did secure one victory, however: postponement of consideration of an amendment by Conrad Burns, R-Mont., to allow telco entry into cable. Hollings and Inouye both said the issue would derail the bill, and Burns agreed to withdraw his proposal on a promise of a separate markup session in July.

Senate Bill Provisions

As approved by the committee, the bill would have:

- Allowed the FCC to set rates for "basic tier" cable service — which could be limited to carrying local television stations — in areas where the agency determined that cable systems were not subject to "effective competition." The provision exempted systems used by fewer than 30 percent of households in a cable area and cable operators in communities that had access to a "sufficient number" of local broadcast stations and at least one other multichannel video programming distributor.
- Allowed the FCC to regulate rates for ad-supported cable channels such as CNN and the sports channel ESPN based on consumer complaints that rates were "significantly excessive." Pay-for-view and premium services such as HBO and Showtime would not have been regulated.
- Barred cable programmers with ties to cable operators from discriminating in price and other conditions against the cable company's competitors.
- Forced cable companies to carry local television stations on the same channel number they used over the air, or, at the broadcaster's discretion, on the channel used before the 1985 court ruling.
- Directed the FCC, within a year, to limit the number of subscribers a single cable operator could reach and to restrict the number of channels a cable operator could devote to affiliated programming.

House Markups

The House Commerce Telecommunications Subcommittee followed with approval of a bill with further concessions to the cable industry. The late-drafted bill, developed by the subcommittee's chairman, Edward J. Markey, D-Mass., and ranking Republican, Matthew J. Rinaldo, N.J., was approved by the subcommittee on voice vote June 25.

The bill (HR 5267) contained the explicit protection the cable industry sought for exclusive programming agreements as long as the cable market was deemed competitive. It also took a less aggressive approach than the Senate bill to limiting monopolistic practices by calling for a study, rather than issuance of rules, on limiting horizontal and vertical integration in the cable industry.

On rates, the House bill would have required the FCC to cap prices for the "basic tier" of cable programming —

local broadcasts and public-access channels — and to reduce rates for other programming deemed "unreasonable or abusive." The bill would have made it slightly easier to roll back rate increases than the Senate committee's bill.

The House bill also included a new compromise reached among the cable industry, broadcasters and public television over the must-carry issue. The accord called for cable operators to devote about 25 percent of their channels to local broadcasts and to carry those broadcasts on the same channel number that TV stations used.

As in the Senate, the issue of letting telcos into cable was deferred. Boucher, acknowledging he did not have the votes to win on the issue in subcommittee, said he would wait until full committee to raise the issue.

Boucher and Cooper both said the subcommittee bill was too weak. But other subcommittee members said the compromise was adequate to deal with the few "renegade" cable operators that had engaged in excessive rate hikes.

The subcommittee's bill was approved with little change by the full Commerce Committee July 27. And Boucher, saying he was two votes short, decided again to withhold his amendment on the telco-cable issue. Markey promised hearings would be held on the subject in 1991.

Administration, FCC Positions

Both the Bush administration and the FCC opposed the moves to re-establish regulation of cable rates.

The administration, in letters written prior to the Senate and House committee markups, said deregulation had brought "substantial benefits" and that reregulatory proposals would "put these gains at risk."

The letters, signed by Commerce Secretary Robert A. Mosbacher and James Rill, head of the Justice Department's antitrust division, called instead for emphasizing "competitive principles, such as promoting new entry. . . ."

The FCC adopted a similar stance in a study of the effects of the 1984 act issued July 26, the day before the Commerce Committee was scheduled to mark up HR 5267.

The commission, concluding that deregulation had fostered a growth in cable service, rejected the need for "far-reaching rate regulation." But it did call for removing barriers to other multichannel providers, backed some form of must-carry provision for local broadcasters and supported legislative limits on anticompetitive practices by cable conglomerates.

FLOOR ACTION

With most of the controversies removed from HR 5267, House leaders brought it to the floor Sept. 10 under suspension of the rules — with limited debate and no amendments permitted. The administration issued a statement the same day saying it "strongly" opposed the bill. Besides objecting to regulating rates and restricting cable programmers' distribution systems, the administration also warned against the constitutionality of the must-carry provision and criticized a provision unique to the House bill to restrict foreign ownership of cable systems. In its existing form, the statement concluded, the president's senior advisers would recommend the bill be vetoed.

Despite the administration's stand, no one opposed the bill on the House floor, and it passed by voice vote.

Objections Block Senate Bill

Efforts to defuse controversies over the Senate bill, however, failed.

When Majority Leader George J. Mitchell, D-Maine, sought to bring S 1880 to the floor under a procedure requiring unanimous consent Sept. 28, Wirth and Packwood said they would object.

Wirth, acknowledging the industry's importance to his state, said he supported a bill to deal with complaints about soaring rates and declining service.

But Wirth criticized the provisions that questioned exclusivity agreements or volume discounts.

Packwood said cable deregulation had achieved "the goals we set out to achieve" — wider availability of cable service and expanded cable programming — and called the reregulation bill "an overreaction." Wallop, speaking later, voiced similar criticisms.

With the bill blocked, Danforth rose to express his disappointment and vowed to revisit the issue in 1991.

Wirth and Gore, however, made a last-ditch attempt to revive the bill in 1990 by agreeing Oct. 11 on an amendment to preserve some forms of exclusive agreements between cable operators and programmers.

Wirth's change of heart proved inadequate, though. The White House repeated its opposition to the bill and the cable industry voiced concerns about a host of potential amendments from Democratic senators to strengthen the bill's regulatory provisions.

After Congress adjourned, however, the FCC moved to restore some regulation of cable systems by proposing on Dec. 13 to tighten the definition of "effective competition" for purposes of determining whether a cable operator was exempt from rate regulation by state or local governments. The commission was expected to act on the proposed rule in spring 1991.

While the FCC rule was viewed as possibly mooting the rate regulation issue, congressional supporters of reregulation said they still wanted to pursue other goals of the legislative measures. ■

FCC Reauthorized

The House on Sept. 13 cleared a bill to reauthorize the Federal Communications Commission (FCC). President Bush signed the measure (HR 3265 — PL 101-396) on Sept. 28.

By voice vote and after virtually no debate, the House accepted the measure as amended by the Senate on July 19. The final compromise authorized $119.8 million for fiscal 1991 and $109.8 million for fiscal 1990.

The fiscal 1991 Commerce, Justice, State and spending measure (HR 5021, PL 101-515) appropriated $115.8 million for fiscal 1991 while the fiscal 1990 measure (HR 2991) provided $109 million. *(Commerce, Justice, State appropriations, p. 881; 1989 Almanac, p. 724)*

The authorization measure also:

- Provided for FCC fee retention by allowing the agency to keep 4 percent of the cost of regulation fees that it collected in fiscal year 1990 in order to defray the costs of collecting such fees.
- Granted the FCC additional power to prevent willful or malicious interference to radio communications.

An earlier version of the measure had passed the House on Oct. 30, 1989. The bill had been reported from the Energy and Commerce Committee (H Rept 101-316) on Sept. 13 of that year. ■

Congress Restricts Ads During Kids' TV

A bill limiting advertising during children's television shows became law at midnight Oct. 17 without President Bush's signature.

The final version of the legislation (HR 1677), by Rep. John Bryant, D-Texas, was cleared by the House on Oct. 1 amid uncertainty over whether it would draw a veto. The Senate had passed it on Sept. 24.

Bush said in an Oct. 17 statement that he "wholeheartedly" supported the bill's goals but objected to its methods.

"In an effort to improve children's television, this legislation imposes content-based restrictions on programming," said Bush. "The First Amendment, however, does not contemplate that government will dictate the quality or quantity of what Americans should hear. Rather, it leaves this to be decided by free choices of individual consumers."

Bush's statement cited numerous criticisms he had of the bill and, other than his praise of its objectives, gave no reason for his letting the measure become law.

Starting in April 1991, commercials on children's programs would be limited to 12 minutes per hour on weekdays and 10½ minutes per hour on weekends. Previous commercial limits were repealed by the Federal Communications Commission (FCC) in 1984.

As a condition of license renewal, the bill required TV stations to show that their overall programming, as well as shows for youths, met children's educational needs. The bill represented the first major move back to broadcast regulation since the Reagan administration.

The bill also authorized $6 million over two years to develop better programs for children. In addition, it mandated that the FCC complete within 180 days a study of "program-length commercials" — half-hour television programs such as "G. I. Joe: A Real American Hero," and "The Transformers," which critics said were designed exclusively to sell the toys based on their main characters.

BOXSCORE

Legislation: Children's Television Act, PL 101-437 (HR 1677, S 1992)

Major action: Became law Oct. 17 without president's signature. Passed by House, Oct. 1; by Senate, Sept. 24. Earlier versions passed by House, July 23; by Senate, July 19.

Reports: Energy and Commerce (H Rept 101-385). Commerce, Science and Transportation (S Rept 101-227).

BACKGROUND

The measures before both chambers of Congress were based on the argument, vigorously disputed by the broadcast industry, that deregulation of broadcasting under President Ronald Reagan had led to a sharp decline in the amount and quality of educational programs available to children.

Advocates of more controls saw the measures as the first step in turning back the deregulation policies of the FCC under Reagan and its former chairmen, Dennis R. Patrick and Mark Fowler. As part of its goal to deregulate the broadcast industry, the FCC in 1984 abolished guidelines that set children's programming quotas and commercial restrictions. The FCC maintained that the marketplace best decided what was in the public interest.

Critics said, though, that after 1984 the amount of educational children's programming had declined while the number of shows that hawked children's products had increased: in particular, program-length commercials.

Proponents of advertising time restrictions argued that young children were far more susceptible to commercials than adults because they often could not distinguish television programs from commercials.

Advertisers and a number of Republicans opposed limits on truthful advertising as a violation of First Amendment protections of commercial speech and a dangerous first step to more government intrusion.

Action in 1989

The push to enact legislation began early in the 101st Congress. Committees in 1989 adopted bills to place strict time limits on the amount of advertising that could be shown during children's TV shows and to direct the FCC to consider, as a condition of license renewal, whether broadcasters had served the educational and informational needs of children in their "overall programming."

By voice votes and without any changes, the Energy and Commerce Committee on April 11 approved HR 1677 by Edward J. Markey, D-Mass. Markey's bill was identical to a bill passed by Congress in 1988 but pocket-vetoed by Reagan after the 101st Congress adjourned. The Telecommunications and Finance Subcommittee, which Markey chaired, had approved HR 1677 on April 6.

Reagan had called the legislation an unneeded intrusion into broadcasters' programming and license renewals.

The Senate Commerce, Science and Transportation Committee Oct. 5 approved an unnumbered Senate bill to cut back on the commercial content of children's television programs. The legislation straddled two proposals introduced earlier in the year: S 707 by Howard M. Metzenbaum, D-Ohio, which was identical to Markey's, and S 1215 by Tim Wirth, D-Colo., which was favored by Democrats but viewed as politically unrealistic.

The new Senate bill, approved by voice vote, adopted the less stringent time limits in the Metzenbaum-Markey bill on commercials aired during children's programs — 10½ minutes per hour on weekends and 12 minutes on weekdays. But it opted for language in the Wirth bill requiring that broadcasters air shows specifically designed for the educational needs of children.

The House legislation was the result of extensive negotiations between Markey and the National Association of Broadcasters (NAB), which decided not to oppose the requirements in hope of gaining congressional support for other industry priorities. In particular, the industry wanted so-called must-carry legislation to force cable companies to air local television stations. *(1989 Almanac, p. 380; 1988 Almanac, p. 578)*

Democrats had also made it clear they viewed Bush's support for the measure as a test of his campaign promise to be the "education president."

Resistance to reregulation from the industry and from

Republicans, as well as the ever-present threat of a presidential veto, stymied action on stronger legislation, however.

FLOOR ACTION

After months of negotiations to quell the opposition of Republicans and the broadcast industry, Senate Democrats on July 19 won voice-vote approval of their version of the bill (S 1992), offered by Wirth and Alan Cranston, D-Calif.

The House on July 23 passed its version of HR 1677 after Democratic sponsors made a number of concessions to Republicans and the Bush administration, which had threatened a veto over earlier drafts of the legislation. The House bill, approved by voice vote, was nearly identical to S 1992.

Both measures limited advertising on children's television shows to 10½ minutes per hour on weekends and 12 minutes per hour on weekdays.

Both bills also required the FCC to consider how well a station's overall programming had served children's educational needs. The FCC also would have to consider programming specifically designed to educate children.

"For far too long, we have allowed children's television to be driven solely by commercial considerations," said Markey, chief author of the bill. "Children's television should and can be the video equivalent of textbooks and the classics, rather than the video equivalent of a 'Toys-R-Us' catalog."

The Senate bill approved by committee in 1989 would have required more explicitly that broadcasters air shows designed for the educational needs of children. The broadcast industry adamantly opposed that language, calling it an unconstitutional intrusion into programming.

Under the amended Senate bill, broadcasters could point to family programs such as "The Cosby Show" to demonstrate that children were being addressed in "overall programming." The new Senate bill also deleted a provision that would have required the FCC to act within 90 days on complaints about advertising on children's TV.

The only item requiring a House-Senate conference was a Senate provision to authorize a $10 million National Endowment for Children's Educational Television. Sponsors' aides on both sides of the aisle said they did not expect much trouble in fashioning a compromise on the endowment.

Talks on TV Violence Encouraged

In the waning hours of the 101st Congress, Senate sponsors of a bill designed to encourage television industry officials to develop guidelines on violence in TV programming successfully attached their measure to the federal judgeships bill (HR 5316 — PL 101-650).

Congress cleared the legislation in the early morning hours of Oct. 28.

Paul Simon, D-Ill., got his colleagues to add a proposal to exempt television industry officials from antitrust law so they could meet to discuss stemming the "negative impact" of TV violence. The legislation arose from Hill concerns about mayhem on TV and some networks' belief that antitrust laws barred them from jointly weighing programming guidelines.

An earlier Senate version of the measure (S 593) urged TV officials also to talk about guidelines for the depiction of illegal drug use and explicit sex. The drugs element was added before Judiciary Committee approval in early 1989; the explicit-sex provision was an amendment by Jesse Helms, R-N.C., adopted by the Senate 91-0 on May 31, 1989. *(1989 Almanac, p. 286)*

But House Judiciary Committee members refused to accept any topics beyond TV violence, arguing that the bill should be as narrow as possible to avoid steps toward censorship.

They blocked the appointment of conferees to resolve differences between House and Senate bills until they could get Helms' guarantee that the legislation could proceed without the topic of sexually explicit material. Senate sponsors of adding the drugs topic agreed to drop it after House protests.

Helms insisted on his amendment until the last days of the session, when it appeared that either the television antitrust exemption would not become law or that inclusion of the sex-on-TV language would kill the judges bill in the House. Lobbied by GOP colleagues interested in passage of the judgeship bill, and running in a close election campaign, Helms backed down.

Action in 1989

Both chambers had approved similar bills in 1989, but no legislation cleared. The Senate gave voice-vote approval May 31, 1989, to its earlier version of the legislation; the House acted Aug. 1, 1989, on a 399-18 vote.

Spokesmen from the three major networks said the legislation was not necessary and suggested it would not change their programming approach.

Lawmakers, though, said there was far too much violence on television and that it likely contributed to aggressive behavior, especially among children.

Simon said, "I think the reality is that television shapes our society in powerful ways, and there is no question that violence on television influences how young children view the world and themselves."

Rep. Don Edwards, D-Calif., led the congressional protest against the bill in 1989.

"HR 1391 is saying the kind of programming that the government favors and the TV industry should produce. That is indirect censorship, clear and simple," said Edwards, who chaired the Judiciary Subcommittee on Civil and Constitutional Rights.

The American Civil Liberties Union also opposed the bill, calling it "a wholly inappropriate and unconstitutional effort to shape the content of American television."

House Judiciary Committee Chairman Jack Brooks, D-Texas, disagreed. "It should be noted that this bill does not, and is not intended to, coerce any conduct," he said. "No sanctions for failing to meet, failing to adopt guidelines, or failing to adhere to any guidelines that might be developed, are included in this bill."

The bills also stopped short of banning program-length commercials and instead ordered the FCC to review such shows within six months of the legislation's enactment.

The children's television lobby lost efforts to include provisions aimed at beating back the trend toward such commercials. Wirth had hoped his bill would effectively abolish the program-length commercials by defining them as commercial matter subject to the minutes-per-hour advertising limits.

The licensing of animated characters for both television shows and toys became a billion-dollar industry during the 1980s, with such characters as the Smurfs and Strawberry Shortcake leading the march on Saturday morning audiences. Program-length commercials proliferated after 1984, when the FCC dropped a ban against such programs.

CONFERENCE/FINAL ACTION

During the week of Sept. 17, the House and Senate ironed out the minor differences between the chambers' bills — the Senate provision to create a $10 million national endowment for the development of children's television programming. The House had no such provision.

Both chambers agreed after informal negotiations to lower the amount of the endowment to $2 million in fiscal 1991 and $4 million in fiscal 1992.

"American children spend more time watching television than any other activity other than sleep," said Daniel K. Inouye, D-Hawaii, chairman of the Senate Commerce Subcommittee on Communications.

"The commercial broadcaster is a public trustee, given free use of a valuable portion of the spectrum in exchange for volunteering to serve the public interest."

In a Sept. 17 statement, the administration — again without making an official veto threat — said it strongly opposed enactment of the bill because it raised "extremely serious" First Amendment questions. One was the denial of broadcast licenses to stations that did not carry what the government considered to be adequate children's programming. Another was the bill's imposition of limits on advertising.

Despite the administration's protestations, few supporters of the measure expected Bush to veto it.

"How on earth can he veto a bill directed to the needs of children that costs nothing? With bipartisan support and no industry opposition," asked Andrew Jay Schwartzman, executive director of the public interest group Media Access Project. "What's in it for him?"

Despite its First Amendment concerns, the NAB did not oppose the bill. NAB officials even met with White House aides the week of Sept. 17 to urge the president to sign it.

"It's such an opportunity for the president, who after all can't do a hell of a lot about education without spending some money," said Peggy Charren, president of Action for Children's Television.

With wide expectation that Bush would allow it to become law, the House on Oct. 1 cleared HR 1677 by voice vote. The Senate passed it on Sept. 24.

Ultimately, Bush's interest in becoming the "education president" was thought to be stronger than the Justice Department's First Amendment arguments against the bill's provisions requiring broadcasters to show that they were meeting children's educational needs. ■

Closed-Captioning Bill

Congress enacted legislation to increase the accessibility of closed-captioned television broadcasts — a service for hearing-impaired viewers — by requiring television sets to be equipped with built-in decoder circuitry capable of displaying closed-captioned transmissions.

Under the measure, cleared by the House on Oct. 1, all television sets with screens 13 inches or larger manufactured in or imported to the United States had to be equipped with the circuitry. The requirement was to take effect after July 1, 1993.

The legislation sought to ensure that closed-captioned television signals that reached only a fraction of the nation's viewers in 1990 would begin appearing in millions of households by 1993.

An agreement between television manufacturers and sponsors paved the way for Senate passage of the bill (S 1974 — S Rept 101-393) on Aug. 2, also by voice vote. President Bush signed the measure (PL 101-431) Oct. 15.

Only 300,000 TV sets in the United States in 1990 had closed-captioning decoders attached to them. The decoders were expensive ($160 to $200 each) and difficult to install.

Captioning involved converting the spoken parts of TV programs into printed words for display on the television screen, similar to subtitles in foreign movies. The captions were transmitted as encoded data in video-broadcast signals and seen only by viewers having decoding equipment.

By guaranteeing wider access to closed-captioning, the legislation sought to help not only the hearing impaired but also children learning to read, immigrants trying to learn English and adults seeking to improve their literacy.

In its report on the House version (HR 4267 — H Rept 101-767), the Energy and Commerce Committee estimated the potential audience for closed-captioned programming at 24 million hearing-impaired people, including millions of elderly Americans; 23 million to 27 million functionally illiterate adults; 3 million to 4 million immigrants; and 18 million children in kindergarten through third grade.

The Commerce Committee reported the bill on Sept. 25. Its Subcommittee on Telecommunications and Finance had approved the bill July 12.

"All Americans have not been able to participate in the video revolution on an equal basis," sponsor and Telecommunications Subcommittee Chairman Edward J. Markey, D-Mass., said at the committee markup.

One amendment, to change the compliance date for manufacturers to July 1993 from October 1992, was adopted by the committee by voice vote. That brought the bill in line with the Senate's companion measure passed by its Commerce Committee.

Cost estimates for the decoding computer chips ranged from about $3 to $15 per set, to be passed along to consumers in the price of TV sets.

All prime-time network television programming was closed-captioned, as were many sporting events and independent TV and cable programs. But producers of closed-captioned programs voiced concern that without legislation, the low numbers of decoders being purchased would discourage the expansion of closed-captioning, an expensive procedure. ■

House Backs Shift of Radio Frequencies

After some last-minute changes, the House on July 30 passed by voice vote a measure ordering the Federal Communications Commission (FCC) to transfer 175 megahertz of government radio spectrum to civilian commercial use to help ease an existing spectrum shortage.

The measure (HR 2965 — H Rept 101-634) sought to shift spectrum space from defense and other federal uses to the private sector.

Daniel K. Inouye, D-Hawaii, introduced a similar bill (S 2904) in the Senate, but it stalled in committee. Pentagon officials and some senators had reservations about the bill, and with Congress' late-session schedule unpredictable amid the Middle East crisis, the measure died.

Supporters said the legislation was needed to push the administration and the FCC to improve their spectrum coordination and assignment policies.

Energy and Commerce Committee Chairman John D. Dingell, D-Mich., chief sponsor of HR 2965, called the bill "one of the most important initiatives for our long-term economic prosperity to come before the House."

The House bill was modified before reaching the floor to accommodate some concerns of the Bush administration. The minimum amount of space to be turned over was reduced from 200 megahertz — the equivalent of 30 new TV channels — to 175 megahertz, and the range from which the FCC could conduct spectrum space transfers was broadened. Agencies also would have had three years, not six months, to vacate the frequencies.

The 175 megahertz was about one-third of the total spectrum reserved exclusively for the government, which controlled 13 percent of the usable spectrum. (The private sector had 28 percent to itself; the other 59 percent was shared.)

The measure had gained voice-vote approval June 19 from the Energy and Commerce Committee. The Subcommittee on Telecommunications and Finance had approved it June 7, also by voice vote.

In response to Bush administration objections, the committee omitted bill language that would have barred auctioning of the newly available spectrum.

BACKGROUND

Calls for the government to give up some excess frequencies stemmed from the growth in radio spectrum use by cellular telephones, pagers and remote control devices and the prospect of new services such as high-definition television and personal-communications networks.

The radio band, part of the broader electromagnetic spectrum, was measured in meters of wavelength and cycles per second, or "hertz." Radio waves ranged from 3 kilohertz (thousands) up to 300 gigahertz (billions), with AM radio at the lower end, television in the middle and satellites and microwave at the top.

Nearly 200 new radio stations went on the air in the United States in 1926, operating at random and creating interference range wars. Congress subsequently passed the Radio Act of 1927 and the 1934 Communications Act to set up new rules for allocation and licensing.

By 1990, "all the desirable areas of the spectrum [were] pretty much committed," said Thomas P. Stanley, the FCC's chief engineer.

The most valuable commercial space around the center of the spectrum was held by TV and radio broadcasters, who made $34 billion in annual revenues off the airwaves in 1989, according to industry analyst Paul Kagan Associates of Carmel, Calif.

Cellular telephone, at a higher end of the band, was the prosperous newcomer, with 1989 revenues of $3.6 billion. The industry's 50 megahertz (millions) of bandwidth had an estimated market value of $66 billion to $88 billion, according to an internal Commerce Department memo.

Foreign Competition, Domestic Opposition

Meanwhile, entrepreneurs said, the congestion allowed competitors from Europe and Japan to gain an upper hand in the field. Broadcasting in most other countries, especially in Europe, was primarily government-run, meaning fewer spectrum-crowding problems. "Somehow the availability of spectrum in those countries, where blocks of spectrum have been set aside, seems to have encouraged new ideas, new communications systems," said the FCC's Stanley. "If falling behind means the ideas are coming from elsewhere, it looks like we're falling behind."

U.S. companies hoped to have a domestic spectrum-allocation plan by 1992, when Spain was scheduled to host a World Administrative Radio Conference on spectrum that would help define new global allocation standards.

Edward J. Markey, D-Mass., chairman of the Telecommunications Subcommittee, concurred. "If we do not make these kinds of decisions, we are going to wind up in a situation where the Germans, the French and the Japanese have made the allocations, have given the incentives for entrepreneurs to invest in new technologies, because spectrum is available in their countries," he said.

A developing European spectrum standard for new telephone technologies was between 1,700 and 2,300 megahertz. In the United States, however, the Pentagon used that space for, among other things, new satellites that monitored global troop movements.

"If they took all of that, we'd have some heartburn," said Lt. Gen. James S. Cassity Jr., director of command, control and communications systems for the Defense Department's Joint Staff. "It would cost literally tens of millions of dollars if we had to give up those frequencies."

Concern over the large U.S. military force in the Middle East also heightened hesitancy to alter the military's use of spectrum space until that situation became more settled.

In addition to the military, broadcasters saw their spectrum space threatened by telephone technologies. An administration draft legislative proposal leaked from the Hill during the summer of 1990 recommended phasing out ultrahigh frequency (UHF) broadcasting in favor of mobile communications and wireless telephone technologies. Broadcasters opposed the idea, valuing their UHF and very high frequency (VHF) spectrum space.

The plan came from the National Telecommunications and Information Administration, which advised the FCC and governed federal spectrum space.

DEBATE OVER REVENUES

The spectrum allocation measures stoked a 63-year-old debate over U.S. communications policy: whether the government should charge for spectrum space.

The Bush administration, eager for sources of new revenue, at the very least wanted the Dingell-Inouye legislation to make private-sector users of any transferred spectrum pay for relocation costs incurred by federal agencies that gave up spectrum slots.

Much more controversial were spectrum license auctions and user fees. For decades, economists recommended that the federal government glean revenue from the airwaves. But Congress had balked, fearing that only the wealthy would control the frequencies, excluding cash-poor minority and female owners.

Advocates of charging for spectrum argued that the private sector already was controlling the airwaves with cash. On Aug. 22, for the first time since Congress in 1981 abolished a law against profiteering from license competitions, a formal private auction for the right to bid on a license for a new FM radio station was held in Kentucky.

The administration wanted to make public auctions part of the FCC license process. Bush's past two budget proposals had called for auctioning 6 megahertz of underused spectrum to raise about $3.4 billion over two years.

A Dingell provision banning such auctions was removed from the House spectrum transfer bill to appease the administration.

Auction advocates pointed to the millions in profits made by cellular phone companies that sold licenses after receiving them free, by lottery, from the FCC. "That was giving away the store, as far as I'm concerned," said communications entrepreneur Peter Dolan. "The government certainly lost needed revenues."

TV and radio stations also had been bought and sold by profiteers, after the FCC abolished a three-year-minimum ownership rule in 1982.

A federal appeals court Aug. 28 upheld the rule's demise, agreeing with the FCC's assertion that market forces best determined the public interest.

The Public Interest

While the National Association of Broadcasters (NAB) saw merit in auctioning licenses of spectrum newcomers such as mobile communications, it argued for years that broadcasters were different and should not be made to pay fees for spectrum.

Their longtime fears were realized in late July when the White House's Office of Management and Budget (OMB) began floating a budget-summit idea of a user fee on all radio spectrum space, amounting to 4 percent of a licensee's gross receipts. OMB hoped to raise an estimated $6 billion to $9 billion over five years with the fee.

The NAB moved quickly into action, sending radio and television stations packages with instructions on how to lobby key lawmakers against the idea. Ranking minority members Norman F. Lent, R-N.Y., of the House Energy and Commerce Committee, and Matthew J. Rinaldo, R-N.J., of the Telecommunications Subcommittee, wrote budget-summit members to argue against the tax.

Broadcasters had a litany of arguments against spectrum user fees. They would be hit hardest by such a fee, the NAB argued, because theirs was a free service to the public, with revenue coming primarily from advertising rates. If those rates went up, the number of ads would go down, making it hard for broadcasters to recoup their losses.

The user fee would deal a fatal blow to many smaller stations that already were on the edge financially, the NAB asserted, and would deteriorate local programming.

Their biggest weapon against the fee, though, was a thinly veiled threat: Broadcasters would no longer necessarily feel beholden to the concept of operating in the public interest, a keystone of U.S. broadcasting theory.

Broadcasters were the only spectrum users who had to provide public service functions, ranging from public service announcements, equal-access rules, commitments to providing local news and an emergency broadcast system.

User fees "could modify or destroy the public service obligations of broadcasters and others under the law," the Lent-Rinaldo letter warned. Such a fee, said James C. May, the NAB's executive vice president for government relations, "would be the first and most serious breach of the contract that exists between broadcasters and government."

Critics called broadcasters' arguments ironic, coming from an industry that had worked with the Reagan-era FCC to dismantle public service regulations, such as children's television advertising and content rules, the so-called fairness doctrine governing political advertisements and rules to prevent license trafficking. "We're glad to see broadcasters are acknowledging their public responsibilities," said Andrew J. Schwartzman of the public interest group Media Access Project. ■

'Baby Bells' Ask To Ease Curbs on Business

For the first time since the breakup of American Telephone and Telegraph Co. (AT&T) in 1984, lawmakers acted to loosen court restrictions on the seven regional telephone companies.

The Senate Commerce, Science and Transportation Committee approved a bill (S 1981 — S Rept 101-355) on May 23 to let the so-called Baby Bells make telephone equipment. But the bill never reached the Senate floor.

A more controversial draft bill left pending before the House Energy and Commerce Subcommittee on Telecommunications would also have let the regional phone companies offer electronic information services— a move strongly opposed by newspapers and other information industries.

The courts had closed both business areas, as well as long distance phone service, to the Baby Bells in 1984.

A three-judge panel of the U.S. Court of Appeals for the District of Columbia Circuit on April 3, though, issued a ruling that gave the Baby Bells a second chance on electronic information services. While upholding the earlier decision as it dealt with restrictions on long distance and equipment manufacturing, the court sent the matter of electronic information services back to the lower court with new instructions.

By dealing with the most highly charged political issue, the appeals court ruling blunted the companies' push for legislative relief.

The Senate bill, by Commerce Committee Chairman Ernest F. Hollings, D-S.C., would have let the regional phone companies enter joint manufacturing ventures, as long as they were not with other Baby Bells.

Under the House bill, the phone companies could research and design, but not actually fabricate, phone equipment, unless it was determined to be in the public interest.

BACKGROUND

The 1982 consent decree that led to the breakup of AT&T, overseen and subsequently enforced by U.S. District Judge Harold H. Greene, restricted the Bell companies' activities in the areas of long distance, telecommunications equipment manufacturing and information services. The restrictions were put in place to keep the fledgling Baby Bells from committing monopolistic practices and choking off potential competitors.

Greene oversaw the agreement that settled the antitrust case and determined what business activities the phone companies could be involved in. A growing number in Congress, though, complained that the unintended result of the entire breakup was to give a federal judge single-handed control over U.S. telecommunications policy.

The Bell companies and other backers of wresting telecommunications policy from Greene argued that the business restrictions hurt U.S. competitiveness by slowing the introduction of new technologies that were available abroad. They said other countries such as Japan, France and West Germany, whose industries were not subject to such limits, were gearing up to usurp the United States' leading role in technology.

But companies that saw their interests threatened by efforts to unleash the phone companies into new business areas — such as the politically powerful newspaper industry — countered that it would be impossible to keep the Baby Bells from using their monopoly over phone lines to run competitors out of business.

Consumer groups were concerned that the phone companies would dip into funds from phone ratepayers to pay for expensive new technologies.

House Draft Proposal

Key members of the House Energy and Commerce Committee developed a draft proposal aimed at breaking the congressional deadlock over allowing the regional Baby Bell telephone companies into new businesses.

The proposal, hammered out during 1989 and early 1990 between Democratic and Republican staff members on the committee and its Telecommunications Subcommittee, sought to lift the business restrictions and give authority to regulate the Baby Bells back to the FCC.

Under the proposal, the Bell companies would be allowed to research, design and develop telecommunications equipment and, under certain conditions, to gain FCC approval to fabricate equipment. The companies could also produce telecommunications software.

The Baby Bells would also be allowed to offer information services, including electronic publishing, in areas outside their own regions where they did not have a monopoly over telephone lines. The regional Bells already were allowed to offer "gateways" — the conduit through which consumers could gain access to information services offered by competitors — but not the actual information content.

In response to concerns from the newspaper industry about advertising competition, the draft provided that the Bell companies could offer electronic Yellow Pages, but they could be updated only once a month for two years.

These information and manufacturing services would have to be set up in separate subsidiaries to aid regulators in ensuring that the phone companies did not "cross-subsidize" — that is, finance new ventures with funds from phone ratepayers.

LEGISLATIVE ACTION

The Senate Commerce, Science and Transportation Committee approved S 1981 by voice vote May 23 to let the Baby Bells make telephone equipment.

Hollings had introduced the measure Nov. 21, 1989. Two hearings were held on the measure on April 25 and May 9 by the Communications Subcommittee.

Two members included minority views in the committee report filed June 29. Daniel K. Inouye, D-Hawaii, and Bob Kerrey, D-Neb., argued that given the opportunity to expand their dealings, the Bell companies would "use their essential facilities to undermine the competition" as they had done before divestiture.

The House Telecommunications Subcommittee, meanwhile, had held hearings on its draft legislation in May and June 1989 and returned to the subject with further hear-

Operator Services Rates

Legislation to beef up regulatory oversight of a burgeoning telephone-operator services industry was cleared for President Bush's signature by the House on Oct. 3.

The bill (HR 971 — PL 101-435), sent to the White House on a voice vote, required the Federal Communications Commission (FCC) to review rates of "alternative operator services" that sprung up after the breakup of the American Telephone & Telegraph Co. in 1984. These unregulated companies leased phone lines and served hotels, airports, hospitals and universities; consumers complained they charged excessive rates and sometimes blocked individuals from using their own long-distance service.

The bill required the FCC to review rates filed by each operator-service provider and, if they appeared unreasonable, to force the provider either to justify the rates or to announce them to consumers at the beginning of calls. The FCC would regulate the rates if they ultimately were found to be unreasonable.

The FCC, acting on a complaint by the consumer group Telecommunications Research and Action Center in 1988, had refused to investigate rates or propose rules for the industry, although it did order carriers not to block access to other carriers.

The House bill, sponsored by Jim Cooper, D-Tenn., was passed by voice vote Sept. 25, 1989, after having been approved by the Energy and Commerce Committee on June 27 of that year (H Rept 101-213). The Senate Commerce, Science and Transportation Committee approved a substantially similar bill (S 1660 — S Rept 101-439) on June 27. After negotiations between lawmakers, the industry and the FCC, the Senate passed a compromise substitute by voice vote on Oct. 1. House action agreeing to the amended version cleared the measure for the president, who signed it Oct. 17.

ings in 1990, the first on March 7. The issue, though, took on a new perspective with the appeals court ruling April 3 giving the Baby Bells a second chance to persuade Judge Greene to let them offer electronic information services.

Subsequently, on April 18 the subcommittee held a hearing dealing specifically with information services and the impact of the court ruling. Other hearings were held in late April and May to re-evaluate the issue in light of the decision.

During the March 7 hearing, subcommittee members indicated that vast differences remained on how to navigate the mine field between the seven regional phone companies, their major competitors and consumer groups. All still had reservations about the proposal. ■

'Junk Fax' Curbs Eyed

Seeking to provide relief to many office workers, the House on July 30 passed a bill (HR 2921 — H Rept 101-633) to restrict unsolicited advertising over telephones and fax machines.

The bill, passed by voice vote, would have allowed people and businesses who did not want their phone numbers used for unsolicited advertisements to put their numbers on a nationwide list. Telemarketers would have faced fines if calls or transmissions were made to any number on the list. The Federal Communications Commission (FCC) was to compile the list and punish offenders.

The measure also would have made it unlawful for autodialers — computers that dialed large blocks of numbers in sequence or at random and delivered prerecorded messages — to place unsolicited sales pitches to any emergency phone line of a hospital, law enforcement agency, fire station or physician's office.

Similarly, the FCC was directed to require — as soon as it was "technically practicable" — autodialers to disconnect when the called party hung up. The original legislation would have required autodialers to disconnect within five seconds, but businesses said that was not technically feasible with some autodialer systems.

Many marketing firms had computers that could automatically dial up to 1,000 phones a day to deliver prerecorded messages. In some instances, the devices were not capable of disconnecting the call until many seconds after the party hung up. "Such random programming not only makes the machine an equal opportunity nuisance, but an equal opportunity hazard," said the bill's sponsor, Edward J. Markey, D-Mass., chairman of the Energy and Commerce Subcommittee on Telecommunications. HR 2921 was approved by the subcommittee July 20, 1989.

President Bush had promised to veto the measure. "The number of complaints are small, and there are already systems and infrastructures in place to deal with them," a spokeswoman said.

The legislation won quick voice-vote approval from the House Energy and Commerce Committee on May 15.

A somewhat related and weaker measure (S 2494) passed the Senate by voice vote Oct. 23. It sought to strengthen the authority of the Federal Trade Commission regarding fraud committed in connection with telephone sales. That bill also provided for restrictions on autodialers. *(Telemarketing fraud, p. 402)* ■

Supreme Court Backs Affirmative Action

In a surprising endorsement of affirmative action, the Supreme Court on June 27 ruled that Congress could mandate preferential treatment of minorities to increase their ownership of broadcast licenses.

The court said "benign race-conscious measures," including those that did not compensate victims of past discrimination, were constitutional as long as they served important government objectives.

The 5-4 decision in *Metro Broadcasting Inc. v. Federal Communications Commission* upheld policies that Congress had forced on a reluctant Federal Communications Commission (FCC). It marked the first time the court had upheld an affirmative-action program not devised to remedy past discrimination.

At issue in the companion cases of *Metro Broadcasting* and *Astroline Communications Co. v. Shurberg Broadcasting of Hartford* were two types of minority set-aside programs: one giving special credit to minorities in proceedings for new licenses and the other, in a "distress sale" program, allowing some radio and television stations to be sold only to minority-controlled companies.

In the Reagan years, the FCC had tried to dismantle its race-preference system, but Congress beginning in 1987 blocked the commission from spending any of its appropriated money to examine or change the two programs.

White-owned broadcasting companies challenged the policies as violating constitutional equal-protection guarantees. Other opponents of the policies, including the Bush administration, contended that the policies were not linked to proof of past discrimination.

In his opinion for the court, Justice William J. Brennan Jr. stressed Congress' determination that race-based preferences were necessary for broadcast diversity and that lawmakers had long dictated protection for minorities. The court said the federal government had more authority than state and local governments to set aside contracts for minorities.

"It is of overriding significance in these cases that the FCC's minority ownership programs have been specifically approved — indeed, mandated — by Congress," Brennan wrote.

Brennan said minority-ownership policies served an important government objective of broadcast diversity and endorsed the implication from Congress that "the American public will benefit by having access to a wider diversity of information sources."

Sandra Day O'Connor, writing for the dissenting justices, said the court had taken a great step backward with its opinion: "This departure marks a renewed toleration of racial classifications and a repudiation of our recent affirmation that the Constitution's equal protection guarantees extend equally to all citizens." She added that in providing benefits to blacks and other minorities, the FCC was denying benefits to whites based on their race.

Hazardous Materials Law Strengthened

Legislation that beefed up laws governing the transportation of hazardous materials became law during the 101st Congress.

The measure (S 2936), the first major revision of the nation's hazardous materials transportation laws, was cleared by Congress on Oct. 26 and signed into law by President Bush on Nov. 16.

The House and Senate had to work out substantial differences on proposals to overhaul the Hazardous Materials Transportation Act, a 15-year-old law that was designed to prevent releases of chemicals and other hazardous materials being shipped across the country.

The bills focused on stricter enforcement of laws governing transport of such hazardous materials as poisonous gases or toxic chemicals and were aimed at helping states to respond better to accidents involving the materials. More than 4 billion tons of such materials were shipped each year.

Two House committees — Energy and Commerce and Public Works and Transportation — approved versions to impose fees on industry to pay for the tougher program, an approach the Bush administration opposed. The Energy and Commerce bill would have used those funds to hire more federal inspectors; the Public Works bill emphasized grants to states for training of emergency response personnel.

The Senate bill, on the other hand, would have imposed no fees on industry but would have authorized appropriations for the program.

In the last week of the 101st Congress, the Senate decided to go along with the fees and accept a compromise worked out among the House and Senate committees.

As enacted, the bill also:

- Increased civil and criminal penalties for hazardous materials transport violations. The maximum penalty was raised to $25,000 per violation per day. A minimum penalty of $250 was established.
- Provided additional federal inspectors for all transportation modes to enforce the regulations.
- Required the Transportation Department to look for ways to improve the existing system of placard notices on vehicles and study the idea of a computerized central reporting system.
- Required safety permits for shippers who transported ultrahazardous materials such as explosives, poison gases and radioactive materials.

BOXSCORE

Legislation: Hazardous Materials Transportation Uniform Safety Act (S 2936 — PL 101-615).

Major action: Signed Nov. 16. Cleared by Senate, as amended, Oct. 26; passed by House, Oct. 25; by Senate, Oct. 23.

Reports: Energy and Commerce (H Rept 101-444, Part I); Public Works and Transportation (Part II); Commerce, Science and Transportation (S Rept 101-449).

BACKGROUND

The Hazardous Materials Transportation Act (PL 93-633) — passed by Congress in late December 1974 and signed into law Jan. 3, 1975 — governed oversight by various federal agencies of the estimated 4 billion tons of hazardous materials that were transported across the country each year, about 500,000 shipments a day. The law was spurred by reports of numerous accidents involving releases of hazardous materials, especially due to defective railroad tracks. *(1974 Almanac, p. 698)*

In pushing the measure, members of Congress criticized the Transportation Department's enforcement of existing regulations. At the time, the department itself estimated that 75 percent of all hazardous materials shipments violated regulations. Much of the blame was placed on the fragmented nature of the federal regulatory effort, as several federal agencies had jurisdiction in different transportation areas but did not coordinate their efforts.

To address the problem, the law:

- Authorized the secretary of Transportation to issue tougher regulations for shipment of hazardous materials.
- Permitted the secretary to require registration of those who transported hazardous materials or manufactured containers for shipping such materials.
- Set civil penalties of up to $10,000 for each violation of the regulations by shippers or container manufacturers.
- Set criminal penalties for willful violations of the regulations of a fine of up to $25,000 or five years in prison.

As the number of hazardous materials shipments increased, a consensus emerged that the 1974 legislation needed to be revamped. The penalties established in the 1974 bill were seen as inadequate deterrents 15 years later.

In addition, even though the volume of hazardous materials shipments had increased, Transportation Department inspection and enforcement efforts had been cut. A 1986 Office of Technology Assessment report showed that from 1979 to 1984, department manpower devoted to hazardous materials inspections had been cut in half.

A report by the General Accounting Office in November 1989 similarly found that the Federal Railroad Administration lacked the budget and systematic approach necessary to ensure safe rail shipments of hazardous materials.

The last previous authorization for the Hazardous Materials Transportation Act (PL 98-559) expired in 1986.

'Woefully Inadequate' Enforcement

A major proponent of revising the law was Thomas A. Luken, D-Ohio, who chaired the Energy and Commerce Committee's Transportation and Hazardous Materials Subcommittee.

Luken maintained that outdated regulations and the limited number of inspectors had led to "woefully inadequate" enforcement of safety laws by the administration. "The potential for a Bhopal-on-wheels accident is ever-present," he said, referring to the 1984 catastrophic gas leak in India.

In opening hearings on the bill, Luken also criticized the Transportation Department for not exercising the power it had been given to establish a comprehensive registration program for those involved in transporting hazardous materials. Luken said the lack of such a program meant that the department had an inadequate information base.

At the hearings, firefighters and police officers also said they needed additional training to better respond to hazardous materials accidents.

By the opening of the second session of the 101st Congress, it was apparent that lawmakers were ready for a major revamping of the act.

HOUSE COMMITTEE ACTION

Luken's Transportation and Hazardous Materials Subcommittee approved his bill by an 11-0 vote on Jan. 31.

HR 3520 would have required all persons involved in hazardous waste transportation to register with the Transportation Department. It would also have required the department to set up a safety permit program for carriers that hauled extremely hazardous cargo, such as explosives, poisonous gases and radioactive materials.

The legislation would have expanded federal authority to prosecute violators and increase civil and criminal penalties. Tampering with containers or vehicles used for hazardous materials transportation or with labels identifying their content would have been made a crime.

The subcommittee's version would have authorized 200 new inspectors to enforce the new regulations.

The measure easily gained subcommittee approval, but several controversial amendments were readied for the full committee markup.

Matthew J. Rinaldo, R-N.J., urged Luken to incorporate a bill (HR 2584) by Public Works Committee member Doug Applegate, D-Ohio, to require the Transportation Department to contract with a private agency to set up a centralized data bank on hazardous shipments. Firms would have had to submit information on their cargo in advance so emergency personnel could know of the cargo's makeup in case of an accident.

Firefighter groups pushed hard for the Applegate language, but critics said it would have been too costly to transporters.

Subcommittee members approved, by voice vote, an amendment by W. J. "Billy" Tauzin, D-La., to allow states to take over enforcement of hazardous materials transport laws if they passed laws identical to the federal regulations.

Luken's bill also would have barred the shipment of food, drugs or other items for human consumption in vehicles used to ship hazardous materials or garbage unless the containers had been decontaminated in accordance with federal regulations.

Identical "backhauling" provisions were approved by the subcommittee as a separate bill (HR 3634) on Nov. 14, 1989.

Commerce Committee Approval

Despite the rumblings at the subcommittee markup, the full Energy and Commerce Committee approved the bill March 13 after barely a word of dissent.

The only major amendment to HR 3520 was a compromise worked out between the Energy and Public Works committees on the backhauling legislation.

The legislation was spurred by reports that trucks were carrying food, drugs and other perishables to the East Coast and returning with garbage or chemical wastes destined for Western landfills.

The committee also approved the backhauling provision as a separate bill (HR 3386) as well, to try to get early floor action on it. *(Backhauling, p. 382)*

The Applegate bill was not added as an amendment. Luken opposed the language because he thought it premature to mandate the adoption of the centralized data center. There were other feasible technologies under development, he said, and the proposed data center might quickly have become obsolete. Shippers also objected to the proposed reporting requirement because of the extra burden it would have placed on them.

Gerry Sikorski, D-Minn., decided not to offer an amendment to allow states to enforce stricter hazardous materials transportation laws. The bill largely pre-empted state regulations for uniform federal standards. Sikorsky was apparently satisfied with the language to allow state enforcement of federal standards.

Public Works Approval

The Public Works Surface Transportation Subcommittee unveiled its version of HR 3520 on Aug. 2 and doused firefighters' hopes for a computerized program to track hazardous waste shipments across the country.

Applegate decided not to offer his data base bill as an amendment to the broader legislation. In exchange, he secured an agreement to have the National Academy of Sciences study the issue and submit legislative recommendations. He said he lacked the votes for approval but was satisfied with the compromise language included in the bill to require the Transportation secretary to review alternatives to the existing placarding system for identifying cargo content. Applegate said the placarding system, which was run by chemical manufacturers, was "inadequate, completely" and amounted to "the fox running the chicken coop."

The Public Works bill had a different focus than the Energy Committee version. The Public Works focus would have authorized $25 million in state and local grants in fiscal 1993 for emergency-response planning and training. Energy's version would have authorized $13 million to hire 200 new inspectors.

Both approaches were to be funded through registration and permit fees paid by transport companies.

An Energy and Commerce staff member said Public Works' grants-oriented approach reflected that committee's reputation for having a "pork barrel" orientation.

Energy Committee members said the Public Works approach would have discouraged privately funded efforts to train emergency personnel. In their view, government funds would have been better used for enforcement of transportation laws governing hazardous materials.

The bill was approved for full Public Works Committee action by voice vote. With little fanfare, the full committee ordered HR 3520 reported on Sept. 26.

SENATE COMMITTEE ACTION

Meanwhile, the Senate Commerce, Science and Transportation Committee had approved its version of the legislation (S 2936) on July 31, also by voice vote.

The Senate legislation did not contain language included in both House bills to require the Transportation Department to register companies that transport hazardous waste. Instead, the department would have been directed to determine within 30 months whether annual registration requirements were necessary.

The Senate bill also included no registration fee requirement; instead, it proposed authorizing $10 million in fiscal 1991 and $25 million in fiscal 1992 for grants to states. It would have required that the Transportation

Department add 10 inspectors above those authorized for fiscal 1990.

All three bills contained the same broad guidelines, however. Each would have set up a safety permit program for carriers that hauled extremely hazardous cargo, expanded federal authority to prosecute violators and increased civil and criminal penalties.

But differences remained over whether federal law should have pre-empted tougher state laws — a provision industry avidly sought. The Senate did not address the issue at all. The House Energy and Commerce Committee bill called for federal pre-emption whenever state regulations differed from federal law, while the Public Works bill outlined more limited pre-emption standards.

FLOOR ACTION

The Senate passed its version of the bill by voice vote on Oct. 23, even as members and staff were working out a compromise bill with the House. The House then passed S 2936 on Oct. 25, also by voice vote, after inserting a substitute amendment that incorporated the compromise. The Senate cleared the bill the next day.

The measure cleared with the help of an 11th-hour compromise crafted with considerable input from Luken, who was retiring from the House. Luken found middle ground on several key issues with lawmakers from the House Public Works and Senate Commerce committees.

Among the most contentious were the fee on haulers to pay for emergency-response training and the extent to which states would be pre-empted by federal law.

The Senate accepted House language to require hazardous cargo haulers to register and pay fees ranging from $250 to $5,000. The fees were to fund the grants to states to train state emergency response crews.

Under the original Senate bill, the financing would have come through a separate appropriation rather than a dedicated funding source.

The Senate also accepted House language aimed at better delineating the federal and state regulatory roles. Haulers, who had feared stricter state regulation, had pushed hard for the language to pre-empt states from surpassing federal guidelines.

The compromise authorized $30 million over six years for states to develop emergency response plans and $54.8 million for response training and curriculum.

States were given some latitude over regulating the hazardous materials, but in most cases they were to follow federal guidelines. For instance, states were allowed to use federal guidelines when designating highway routes for hazardous materials.

But they were pre-empted from regulating the classification, packaging, handling and marking of hazardous materials unless state or local law was substantially the same as federal regulations.

The backhauling bill, which had cleared the Senate on Oct. 19, was not included in the final version.

The Bush administration initially opposed the hazardous materials transportation bills, particularly the requirements that companies involved in the transport of hazardous materials register each year and pay fees. But those reservations were not enough to prompt a veto of the bill. ■

Strict Limits on 'Backhauling' Enacted

The practice of alternating shipments of food in trucks or rail cars that had earlier been used to transport potentially hazardous materials came under strict new regulations under a law enacted by the 101st Congress.

The bill (HR 3386 — PL 101-500) cleared Congress on Oct. 19 and was signed by President Bush on Nov. 3.

Such "backhauling" was especially common east of the Mississippi, as trucks were used to haul trash from the Northeast and returned with food from the Midwest. Backhauling had increased in the years immediately before the new law because the shortage of landfill space in Eastern states had made interstate garbage transport more common and lucrative.

Under the new law, the Transportation Department was required to set standards for what materials could be shipped in trucks and rail cars used to haul food and what decontamination procedures would be required between loads. It barred outright food transport by cargo tanks that hauled ultrahazardous materials, such as asbestos.

The measure had been passed overwhelmingly by the House on March 27, but then stalled for months in the Senate because Daniel R. Coats, R-Ind., wanted to attach an unrelated amendment allowing states to bar imports of garbage from other regions.

But after Coats found another vehicle for his amendment, the Senate approved the backhauling bill easily, clearing it for the president by voice vote on Oct. 19.

BOXSCORE

Legislation: Safe Transportation of Food Act, PL 101-500 (HR 3386).

Major action: Signed, Nov. 3. Cleared by Senate, Oct. 19; House agreed to Senate amendments, with amendments, Oct. 16 (session of Oct. 15). Passed by Senate, Sept. 20; by House, 410-15, March 27.

Reports: Public Works and Transportation (H Rept 101-390, Part I); Energy and Commerce (Part II).

BACKGROUND

Congressional support for banning backhauling of foodstuffs in garbage trucks had mushroomed since a small Pennsylvania newspaper first wrote about the practice in early 1989.

The momentum toward strictly regulated backhauling began in the House Public Works Oversight and Investigations Subcommittee, which first held hearings in August 1989 that exposed the prevalence of the practice.

The Subcommittee heard testimony from truck drivers and food inspectors, who testified that backhauling was widespread.

The Public Works Committee also commissioned a General Accounting Office (GAO) report on backhauling.

The report — titled "Little Is Known About Hauling Garbage and Food in the Same Vehicles" — was unable to document hard evidence of the practice but did document the increasing number of long-distance shipments of garbage. The report revealed that New York and New Jersey shipped about 200,000 truckloads of garbage each to out-of-state landfills.

Trucking officials testified before congressional committees that up to 60 percent of refrigerated carriers alternated shipments of meat with garbage. Citizen activists displayed pictures of maggots that swam in the disinfectant used to clean trucks between loads.

There was no dispute that backhauling should have been stopped; even the nonpartisan GAO called the practice "disgusting." But the Bush administration maintained that laws already on the books prevented truckers or rail car operators from delivering soiled food.

HOUSE COMMITTEE ACTION

The full Public Works Committee ordered HR 3386 reported Nov. 17, 1989, by voice vote. The Public Works bill would have banned refrigerated trucks from backhauling. That provision was spurred by testimony that it was virtually impossible to clear the refrigeration systems of bacteria once the trucks were used to haul garbage.

The bill would also have prohibited cargo tank trucks from alternating between food and non-food products. The committee had heard testimony that juice concentrates had been hauled in the same trucks used to haul formaldehyde.

The Energy and Commerce Committee's Transportation and Hazardous Materials Subcommittee had approved another backhauling bill Nov. 14. The more expansive Energy Committee measure (HR 3634) would have required that the Transportation secretary develop two categories of hazardous materials: more dangerous substances that could never have been shipped in vehicles used to transport food, and less hazardous materials that could have been shipped in the same vehicles if disposal and decontamination procedures were followed.

The Energy Committee bill would also have covered rail transportation; the Public Works Committee did not have jurisdiction over railroads.

The Energy Committee measure was originally included in broader hazardous materials legislation (S 2936) but was introduced as a separate bill because members wanted to move it quickly. *(Hazardous materials, p. 380)*

Energy and Commerce Committee Chairman John D. Dingell, D-Mich., indicated he wanted to move quickly on backhauling legislation. But he also exerted his wish for jurisdiction over the Public Works version and snared the legislation in a turf dispute.

The full Energy Committee approved a compromise version of HR 3386 on March 13. The compromise bill would have required the Department of Transportation, in consultation with the Environmental Protection Agency and the Department of Health and Human Services, to set standards for what materials could be shipped in trucks and rail cars used to haul food.

SENATE COMMITTEE ACTION

One week after the House overwhelmingly had passed its bill to prohibit backhauling, the Senate Commerce Committee on April 3 approved its measure (S 2393) by voice vote after no debate.

The legislation combined two earlier backhauling proposals: S 1751, by Slade Gorton, R-Wash., and S 1904 by Al Gore, D-Tenn. The Senate bills also would have required the Department of Transportation to set standards for what materials could be shipped in trucks and rail cars used to haul food, as well as what decontamination procedures would be required between loads.

The Senate bill also included the language to bar cargo tanks that hauled ultrahazardous materials from shipping food. In addition, it contained a broader provision to require the Transportation Department to issue regulations governing non-refrigerated, or "dry," trucks and rail cars.

Also included in the Senate legislation was separate truck-safety language from a bill (S 819) the Senate had passed Aug. 3, 1989. *(1989 Almanac, p. 384)*

Those provisions would have stiffened federal penalties for selling drugs at truck stops and roadside rest areas. They would also have required the department to make available to the public a listing of those carriers with an unsatisfactory safety rating. Bus companies would have been barred from carrying passengers and trucking companies from transporting hazardous materials until they improved their safety status.

FLOOR ACTION

The House passed HR 3386 on March 27 by a vote of 410-15. No member spoke in opposition to the bill. *(Vote 45, p. 20-H)*

"We don't eat food out of garbage cans, and we shouldn't be expected to eat food out of garbage trucks," said William F. Clinger Jr., R-Pa., sponsor of the original bill.

In the Senate, however, the backhauling bill was held up for months by Coats' effort to attach unrelated language to bar states with overflowing landfills, such as New York and New Jersey, from shipping garbage to states that did not want it. The Indiana Republican's amendment was strongly opposed by New Jersey's two Democratic senators, Frank R. Lautenberg and Bill Bradley.

On Sept. 18, Coats found another vehicle for his amendment: the District of Columbia spending bill (HR 5311). Despite an argument from D.C. Appropriations Subcommittee Chairman Brock Adams, D-Wash., that the provision was not germane to the bill, the Senate approved Coats' amendment, 68-31. *(Vote 244, p. 49-S)*

With that action, the backhauling legislation was free to move forward. The Senate approved it by voice vote Sept. 20. A month later, House-Senate conferees stripped Coats' amendment from the D.C. spending bill.

Differences remained between the House and Senate versions, however. Farm-state senators had amended the Senate bill to allow state to exempt from commercial license requirements drivers of vehicles who delivered agriculture equipment or provided harvesting assistance to farmers. A compromise version passed the House in the early morning hours of Oct. 16, by voice vote. It cleared the Senate on Oct. 19, also by voice.

The final version of the bill retained some of the truck safety provisions included in the Senate bill. But the compromise dropped the Senate provision to double penalties on drug dealing at truck and rest stops in the face of opposition from the House Judiciary Committee. The Senate language concerning farm-related license exemptions was also dropped, after opposition by House Public Works members. ■

Bush Gets Parts of Aviation Package

President Bush achieved some of his administration's major transportation policy objectives when both chambers passed an aviation package as part of the final budget package Oct. 27.

New airline ticket fees of up to $3 per flight and new guidelines on aviation noise were approved by Congress as part of the budget-reconciliation legislation (HR 5835 — PL 101-508). Bush had sought to levy a passenger ticket tax to pay for airport facility improvements.

"We achieved a resounding victory this year in reauthorizing the Federal Aviation Act," said Transportation Secretary Samuel K. Skinner after passage. "In fact, it proved to be the most significant aviation legislation since deregulation," he added in a Dec. 10 address to the American Association of State Highway Transportation Officials.

In March, Bush had sent Congress a $22 billion, five-year plan for commercial aviation programs that continued the administration's approach to funding the nation's infrastructure needs: user fees.

Bush's bid to levy the ticket fees had been passed by the House in August as part of a reauthorization of the Airport and Airway Trust Fund (HR 5170).

During the Senate Commerce Committee's markup of its budget-reconciliation measure, Wendell H. Ford, D-Ky., chairman of the Aviation Subcommittee, attached his own proposal for the passenger facility charge (PFC). But he linked it to adoption of a federal noise policy and revision of the slot system governing takeoffs and landings at four of the nation's busiest airports.

After weeks of negotiation between Ford and Rep. James L. Oberstar, D-Minn., chairman of the House Public Works Subcommittee on Aviation, a deal was struck just before Congress voted on the final budget package of the year. The deal phased out the noisiest jets, so-called Stage 2 aircraft, by 2003. The Department of Transportation (DOT) was required to adopt a noise policy by July 1991 and to approve any local restrictions on newer Stage 3 planes. All existing local noise restrictions were not affected.

The compromise removed all changes Ford proposed on airport slots, including an attempt to open more landing slots at LaGuardia and Washington National airports.

The fiscal 1991 Transportation spending bill called for a 14 percent increase in Federal Aviation Administration (FAA) spending, providing $6.1 billion for the FAA in fiscal 1991. Spending was also increased 11 percent for the Federal Highway Administration and 24 percent for the Coast Guard. *(Transportation appropriations, p. 876)*

BUSH'S TRANSPORTATION PLAN

The Bush administration on March 8 unveiled a major policy initiative for financing the nation's transportation needs that called for new user fees, more state and local spending, and a decreased federal commitment to mass transit programs.

The new National Transportation Policy, titled "Moving America into the 21st Century," built on a number of proposals revealed in Bush's fiscal 1991 budget request.

On March 19, Bush sent Congress his $22 billion, five-year plan for commercial aviation programs.

The proposal sought to increase fuel and departure taxes for airline passengers and add a new airport tax of up to $12 for each round-trip ticket. The money would be used to increase spending on airports and air-traffic control.

The Transportation Department report underscored the seriousness of the problem: 21 primary airports had more than 20,000 hours of flight delay a year; 42 percent of the nation's highway bridges were structurally deficient or obsolete; 65 percent of peak-hour travel on urban Interstate highways was congested in 1987.

Skinner said generating more money at the state level — for example, through tolls on federal-aid highways (prohibited under existing law), airport passenger user fees or state gasoline tax increases — would ensure more local flexibility and better management of resources.

Skinner's report also envisioned more private-sector involvement in mass transit facilities and airports, and it would have provided no federal subsidies for the Amtrak national passenger railroad. Such proposals had been summarily rejected in congressional budget fights in the past.

Congressional Resistance

In a hearing March 8 before the House Public Works Subcommittee on Surface Transportation, Skinner came under sharp attack from members — most of them Democrats — who criticized the administration for being tall on ideas and short on funds.

"Of course, we want to get more bang for our buck," said Nick J. Rahall II, D-W.Va., "but we need to put money toward infrastructure needs. Our threat is not communism; it's competition."

Critics in Congress objected to much of the administration's plan. They said the money for the aviation programs should come exclusively from a projected $7.6 billion surplus in the Airport and Airway Trust Fund, not from new taxes. The trust fund was collected through fees on tickets and fuel, although the revenues were not directly earmarked for air transportation programs, and program expenditures were still subject to general appropriations.

"Before we talk about saddling air travelers with another tax, we should spend the $7 billion that [the Office of Management and Budget (OMB)] has stashed away in the aviation trust fund," said Oberstar. "Any new tax — call it a user fee, call it a facility charge, it's still a tax — will just add to that stash." (Oberstar would later become one of the major supporters of the fee, however.)

Ford said March 21 that the increases called for in FAA spending were also unrealistic in light of other transportation cuts, such as the proposed elimination of funds for Amtrak and large cuts in mass transit subsidies.

Ford said some of the funds for FAA facilities and equipment and airport improvement grants would have to be diverted to these programs. "You cannot have an increased budget for FAA and adequately fund the other transportation programs," he said. "Everyone in town seems to know this fact except for DOT and OMB."

State and local officials had already begun airing concerns that Skinner's proposals would shift too much of the burden of tackling traffic congestion and crumbling highways and bridges to the states.

Passenger Facility Charges

Under the administration's proposal, federal airline ticket taxes would be increased to 10 percent from 8 percent, and airports would be permitted to raise their own revenues for capital improvement projects through a PFC of up to $12 per round-trip ticket.

The administration estimated that these fees would bring an additional $1 billion a year into airport development, assuming the largest 45 airports imposed the tax. For every $1 an airport raised through PFCs, federal funds for airport projects would be cut by 50 cents.

Capitol Hill was no stranger to the idea of a PFC. Congress banned such fees in 1973 after members learned that some local airport authorities were using the money for things other than runways and terminals. *(1973 Almanac, p. 453)*

Congress also assumed that the airport trust fund, created in 1970 and financed in part through an 8 percent surcharge on passenger tickets, would take over for what was pejoratively called a "head tax" on airline passengers.

Under the administration's plan, freight fees would also have increased to 6 percent from 5 percent. Aviation gasoline taxes would have risen to 15 cents a gallon from 12 cents and jet fuel taxes to 18 cents a gallon from 14 cents.

Trust Fund Debate

Also under Bush's budget, the Airport and Airway Trust Fund surplus would be reduced from about $7.6 billion to $3 billion by 1995 through spending on capital improvement projects and FAA operations.

DOT proposed "spending down" the trust fund — that is, spending more on aviation programs than was received each year in new revenues.

The president's budget called for reducing the fund to $3 billion by fiscal 1995 and spending a greater percentage of trust funds (and a smaller percentage of general revenues) on FAA operations.

But critics said the proposal did not envision spending the fund fast enough. Lawmakers also opposed spending the trust fund on FAA operations, arguing that such money should go toward capital improvements.

Much of the transportation debate in Congress also centered on how far to go in spending the $10 billion surplus in the Highway Trust Fund, which was made up of taxes on motor fuel. Critics said the administration and its allies in Congress were hoarding the trust fund money — using revenues supposedly earmarked for transportation needs to help pay for other domestic programs — to mask the true size of the government's general fund deficit. They wanted the highway money spent on capital improvements.

"This money has been paid by the American highway users in the expectation that it will be used for transportation purposes," said Public Works Chairman Glenn M. Anderson, D-Calif.

Bush's budget estimated spending slightly more than the revenues taken in by the Highway Trust Fund in fiscal 1991 — not including interest.

Although the highway fund had a surplus of $10 billion, Skinner said there were more than $30 billion in transportation-related commitments against that balance.

Bill Highlights

As part of its fiscal 1991 budget-reconciliation package, Congress, among other things, enacted the passenger facility fee and sought to establish a national noise-abatement plan. *(Reconciliation provisions, Title IX, p. 156)*

The measure allowed airports to impose ticket fees of $1, $2 or $3 on passengers to pay for facility improvements. The charges were limited to two boardings per one-way trip and could not be levied on passengers traveling to or from cities receiving subsidized essential air service.

The bill required the Transportation secretary, by July 1, 1991, to issue regulations establishing a national aviation noise policy that included the phaseout of older, Stage 2 aircraft by Dec. 31, 1999.

Aircraft flying solely outside the continental United States were not subject to the noise guidelines.

The bill also required the Transportation secretary by July 1, 1991, to initiate a rulemaking proceeding to consider more efficient methods of allocating existing capacity at high-traffic airports, in order to provide improved opportunities for operations by new entrant air carriers (defined as a carrier having less than 12 operating rights at such airports).

COMMITTEE ACTION

A variety of committees dealt with appropriations, proposed user fees and other aviation and transportation-related matters. While the fiscal 1991 transportation spending bill and the budget-reconciliation measure were the ultimate vehicles for transportation policy, other bills were also being moved through the legislative process.

Committees dealt with, among other things, user fees, trust fund spending and airport slots. Congress also passed two measures to improve aviation security in the United States. *(Aviation security, p. 389)*

Aviation Fees, Spending

Bush's proposal for a PFC — imposed directly by airports on each airline ticket — won unexpected approval from the House Public Works Committee on June 28. The funds raised would have to be used to pay for needed improvements at those airports to increase capacity.

Authority for the fee was a key part of broader legislation (HR 5170 — H Rept 101-581) to also authorize a big increase in Airport Trust Fund spending. Those provisions had been approved separately, as HR 4986, by the Public Works Subcommittee on Aviation on June 14. The full committee approved HR 5170 on a 37-10 vote.

Oberstar, one of the early critics of the Bush plan, called the new fee "a major step forward in improving airport capacity and improving the nation's air-traffic control system."

Oberstar told his colleagues that $10 billion a year should be spent for airport improvement projects. He estimated that the new fee would raise more than $1 billion a year to supplement spending from the trust fund.

But to ensure that federal trust fund spending was not reduced as a result of increased passenger fees, the committee included a provision to repeal the fee if federal airport-improvement spending dropped below $3.7 billion over fiscal 1991-92.

Backers of the bill assumed that only medium- and large-sized airports would elect to collect the fee. Those airports' share of airport-improvement project money from the trust fund would be reduced by 50 cents for every $1 they collected in passenger fees.

As approved, the bill would have:

- Required airports wishing to collect the fee to seek approval from the secretary of Transportation. The fee would have to be spent on an airport-improvement project specifically approved by the secretary.
- Required airlines to collect fees of $1, $2 or $3 for each passenger and turn the proceeds over to that airport. Pas-

sengers would have to pay only at the first two airports used on a one-way trip.

- Reallocated trust fund money not distributed, mostly for the benefit of small airports.
- Prohibited small airports that received federal essential air service subsidies from imposing the fee.

Opponents of the new fee failed, on a 25-11 vote, to stop the new charge June 27 when the Aviation Subcommittee marked up the measure. They declined to press the matter in full committee the next day.

During subcommittee debate, Norman Y. Mineta, D-Calif., complained that "this will drive travel agents up the wall" because not every airport would impose the fee and because the fee could differ from airport to airport.

Several members complained that airline passengers would be taxed doubly — once by the existing 8 percent airline ticket tax that went into the trust fund and again by the new fee — both for the same purpose. "The consumer will be hit by a one-two punch," Mineta said.

Douglas H. Bosco, D-Calif., warned that "airports will become 'taxports,' " and said that airline passengers should not have to pay the added charge "while there is $8 billion sitting in the trust fund."

The latter argument was greeted with some sympathy by many panel members, who had long complained that the trust fund had been building up a huge, nominal surplus for years. The Public Works Committee had made annual attempts, without success, to remove the trust fund from the unified federal budget, which benefited from the trust fund surplus by showing a smaller overall deficit.

But Oberstar convinced the majority of the panel that the administration had agreed to support increased trust fund spending, enough to reduce the trust fund surplus by about $1 billion over the next five years.

Oberstar agreed that passengers were being asked to pay more, "but we all know that there is no free lunch."

Airport Slots

A handful of small regional air carriers, meanwhile, were working to repeal an airport scheduling system in which the largest airlines traded millions of dollars to control takeoff and landing slots at the nation's four busiest airports.

Saying they had been put at a competitive disadvantage because of the "buy-sell" rule, two of the smaller carriers — Midwest Express Airlines Inc. of Milwaukee and America West Airlines Inc. of Phoenix — pushed a bill in the Senate to repeal it.

The bill (S 2851 — S Rept 101-447), sponsored by Republicans Bob Kasten of Wisconsin and John McCain of Arizona, was approved on a voice vote July 31 by the Senate Commerce Committee. It still faced opposition, however, from New York and Virginia senators, who feared that the airports in their states would quickly be gridlocked by more flights.

Trouble with runway congestion at the nation's busiest airports — including John F. Kennedy and LaGuardia in New York, O'Hare in Chicago and National Airport in Washington — led to a 1969 High Density Traffic Airport Rule that limited the number of hourly takeoffs and landings.

Slots at those airports at first were distributed by a committee of air carriers. But that system broke down in 1981 amid the air-traffic controllers' strike and heated competition in the airline industry.

In its place came the buy-sell rule, a 1986 invention of

Boat Owners To Pay Coast Guard Fees

Conferees from the House Merchant Marine and Fisheries Committee and the Senate Commerce Committee agreed to require recreational boat owners to buy yearly Coast Guard decals. The provisions were included in the budget-reconciliation package (HR 5835 — PL 101-508) approved by Congress on Oct. 27.

Two weeks earlier, Merchant Marine Committee members thought they had found a way around the fees, which had been in administration budget requests for a decade. But their alternative, imposing new tonnage taxes on shippers from foreign ports, drew strong opposition from shipowners, importers and lawmakers who represented ports that did a lot of foreign business.

The panel had proposed raising the duty on tonnage shipped to the United States from Western Hemisphere ports from 2 cents a ton to 27 cents, and levies on ships from other foreign ports from 6 cents to 81 cents. The new rates, which would have affected U.S.-flag and foreign vessels, were expected to raise $182 million in fiscal 1991.

Merchant Marine finally acquiesced on the user fees, but only after modifying the Senate's language by adopting a sliding scale ranging from $25 for boats 16 feet or longer to $100 for boats 40 feet or longer.

The proposed tonnage rates were also increased to 9 cents per ton for all ships originating from Western Hemisphere ports and 27 cents per ton for ships from all other foreign ports — much smaller increases than the committee originally approved.

The Merchant Marine Committee had agreed Oct. 12 that shippers from foreign ports, not U.S. recreational boat owners, should be recruited to help the panel meet budget-reconciliation targets.

Congressional budget writers and the Bush administration had sought $200 million from fees for Coast Guard services.

The Senate Commerce Committee complied in an Oct. 10 markup, agreeing to impose direct and indirect Coast Guard fees to raise $200 million in fiscal 1991. Other savings included railroad inspection fees, which would raise $20 million in fiscal 1991; per-passenger fees on airlines and cruise ships to fund the U.S. Travel and Tourism Administration, which would raise $7 million; and weather service fees for the National Oceanic and Atmospheric Administration, which would raise $5 million.

The final provisions directed the Coast Guard to set up the system for the collection of $200 million from payments by users of Coast Guard services. The fee system went into effect immediately and was to continue through fiscal 1995.

The Coast Guard's authority to collect fees was extended to include direct user fees for inspection and examination of certain vessels and licensing, certification and documentation of personnel. *(Budget-reconciliation provisions, Title X, p. 157)*

the Reagan administration's deregulation-minded FAA. It let carriers purchase or lease slots from competitors for any length of time.

Much of the trading had gone on privately between carriers for upward of $1.5 million for one 15-minute slot. The FAA asked only that it be told which airline controlled each slot.

The Kasten-McCain bill sought to repeal the buy-sell rule, increase the number of slots available to new airlines in an airport by 5 percent and phase out the underlying high-density rule.

The Bush administration, however, saw no problem with the buy-sell approach. It allowed slots to be allocated by "market demand and, therefore, be put to their most productive use with minimal interference by the government," said Jeffrey N. Shane, the assistant Transportation secretary for policy and international affairs.

The half-dozen smaller commercial carriers that remained active, though, said the buy-sell approach had become prohibitively expensive and anticompetitive, as the larger carriers dominated the busiest hubs.

Though the larger airlines were said to benefit by the slot system, most wanted it repealed. Little, if any, money was made by selling the slots unless a business was leaving the industry, officials said. And carriers had long complained that the high-density rule tied their flight schedules to government-imposed slots rather than market demand.

While airline officials liked the Kasten-McCain bill's 18-month sunset of the high-density rule, they did not want to give up the buy-sell system immediately, as the bill would have done, until the FAA found an alternative.

The Pan Am and Trump shuttles were virtually alone among airlines in their defense of the slot system and the buy-sell rule. The shuttles, which offered hourly flights between Washington, New York and Boston, were dependent on reliable slots.

Removing the high-density rule, meanwhile, could have meant "a large increase in traffic ... major traffic delays and diversions to unplanned airports," said Morris Sloane, director of aviation operations for the Port Authority of New York and New Jersey.

Several senators also expressed concern at a July 31 markup of the bill about airport congestion. "Anything that allows more planes to take off and land at National Airport ... would be absolutely the wrong approach," said John B. Breaux, D-La.

FLOOR ACTION

The House on Aug. 2 easily passed HR 5170 outlining a $22 billion, five-year plan to increase spending from the Airport and Airway Trust Fund. The vote was 405-15. The legislation included the plan to impose new PFCs and boost the cost of round-trip airfares by up to $12 a ticket. *(Vote 302, p. 98-H)*

Those who once adamantly opposed the idea of the PFC, including major airlines and leading Democratic policy-makers, pulled surprising turnarounds and ended up backing the new fees. Oberstar, an early critic of the fee plan, eventually became its sponsor.

Bosco, a Public Works member and sponsor of the amendment to kill the fee, labeled such reversals "religious conversion."

Observers credited Secretary Skinner, airport operators from across the country and politically powerful Chicago lawmakers who hoped the fee could help them win a new city airport.

The House rejected an attempt to kill the fee by a vote of 171-252. The vote split across partisan and ideological lines. Regional interests were somewhat more evident; for example, only three of Illinois' 22 members voted against the fee. *(Vote 301, p. 98-H)*

The revenue raised from the fees could be used only to pay for facility improvements; small airports also would get a portion of the revenue received from large and medium-sized hub airports.

A PFC was especially attractive to most Chicago-area lawmakers, who hoped a new passenger fee at bottled-up O'Hare International Airport would give them the edge in a competition over a new area airport.

Some critics of the fee said airlines may have been swayed because they depended on good relations with the Transportation Department, which held sway over lucrative route assignments and played a role in decisions about acquisitions and mergers.

On Aug. 2, United Airlines got a favorable recommendation over its competitors by a Transportation Department administrative law judge to receive a Chicago-to-Tokyo route worth up to $300 million yearly. United backed the passenger fee by the time of the House vote after opposing it earlier in 1990.

Airline executives were not the only ones making midair turnabouts on the matter of passenger service fees.

Oberstar went from speaking loudly against the fee in March and June to sponsoring the idea and pushing for its approval in July. He said he switched his position because he was able to reach an agreement with the Appropriations Committee to spend more from the trust fund. With that deal in hand, Oberstar said, he realized that even more money would be needed for airport improvements than the trust fund would have allowed.

Chicago Clout

Political muscle from Chicago, the nation's busiest air-traffic center, also played a key role in promoting the passenger charge.

The city of Chicago owned O'Hare and Midway airports and would have liked to own the new airport.

The passenger charge language, as it was written, could have given Chicago a big edge over the competition. O'Hare would get up to $90 million a year through the new charge. The money would give the city's airport authority instant leverage for future bond issues, making Chicago's financing more attractive to the site-selection committee.

Mayor Richard M. Daley visited Capitol Hill to lobby for the fee and had the help of Illinois Democrats Dan Rostenkowski, chairman of the House Ways and Means Committee, and William O. Lipinski, a five-term member representing south and central Chicago.

One part of the measure specified that airport authorities collecting the fees would be able to use them for other airports under their control. That would give O'Hare license to subsidize construction of the new airport. Because the fee would draw more from the pockets of out-of-towners than local voters, members saw little political risk in supporting a measure that would bring money home.

RECONCILIATION

"It's always easier to levy taxes on the transient," said fee opponent Bob Carr, D-Mich.

Both chambers passed the aviation package as part of the budget-reconciliation bill Oct. 27.

As the 101st Congress was drawing to a close, Ford was forcing action on a number of his top legislative priorities — including the aviation package — by attaching them to the must-pass deficit-reduction package. Frustrated that many had stalled, Ford was eager to get some enacted before Congress adjourned.

"You have to look at what's available to you," Ford said. "I've been thinking about this for some time."

Committee Action

The Senate Commerce Committee on Oct. 10 voted for the passenger fees as part of its budget-reconciliation plan.

Committee members stipulated, however, that the fees could go into effect only if and when a federal airport noise policy was adopted and the $7.6 billion Airport and Airway Trust Fund was spent to below $4 billion.

Ford succeeded not only in linking the fees to issues of concern to him but also in attaching practically his entire aviation agenda for the year to the committee's fiscal 1991 budget-reconciliation legislation.

The package, originally introduced as part of the airport-capacity expansion bill (S 3094), was agreed to by voice vote, despite protests by some panelists that it was not germane to the budget bill.

The Public Works Committee on Oct. 12 also included the package in its reconciliation package.

Ford and Oberstar originally had opposed the charge on grounds that appropriators should instead accelerate spending from the trust fund.

But Oberstar reversed his view in July, saying funds were needed to help build and repair the nation's airport network beyond any increase in trust fund spending. Ford finally acknowledged a need for the PFC, but said it should go hand in hand with a federal noise-abatement policy.

"The greatest obstacle to expanding airports and increasing air carrier service is the opposition to aircraft noise," Ford said in announcing his package Sept. 24. No new major U.S. airport had been built in the United States since 1973.

Local communities continued to enact a patchwork of noise-abatement laws, forcing airports to restrict flight times and types of aircraft allowed on runways. Aircraft manufacturers said the resulting confusion reinforced the need for a uniform national noise policy.

Oberstar had held several days of hearings on the noise issue and had planned to act on the matter in 1991. Oberstar also had previously worked out an agreement with House appropriators to spend more money from the trust fund in fiscal 1991, but the Senate Commerce panel made no such deal with Senate appropriators.

Ford's amendment also would have:

- Repealed the buy-sell rule that allowed airlines at four of the nation's busiest airports to purchase or lease takeoff and landing time slots from each other.
- Exempted Washington National Airport from the repeal of the buy-sell and high-density rules. Commerce panelist Charles S. Robb, D-Va., argued that repeal of the rules would only worsen congestion and noise problems at the airport.
- Allowed funds for the rural essential air service program to come from the airport trust fund, making them less vulnerable to yearly cuts in appropriations. Essential air service was a program dear to Appropriations Chairman Robert C. Byrd, D-W.Va., whose support would be helpful should senators challenge Ford's aviation package as not germane.

Final Action

After weeks of negotiation between Ford and Oberstar, a deal was struck just before Congress voted on the final budget package.

The deal phased out the noisy Stage 2 jets by 2003. The agreement required the Transportation Department to adopt a noise policy by July 1991 and approve of any local restrictions on newer Stage 3 planes. All existing local noise restrictions were not affected.

The compromise removed the changes Ford had proposed regarding airport slots. The changes, contained in S 2851, would have given small airlines a chance to compete for business at the nation's busiest air-traffic hubs.

In the Senate bill, Ford had made sure the PFCs were included only as part of a quid pro quo for several proposals more to the liking of various forces within the airline industry. Ford's committee proposal would have shielded airlines from a patchwork of local noise controls with a single federal policy; protected air-traffic subsidies for rural areas in Kentucky and elsewhere; and pressured appropriators into spending billions of dollars to expand airports across the country.

On the floor Oct. 18, Ford had to compromise to get the votes needed to pass the package. He agreed to change the noise policy to grandfather existing local rules and limit federal control over new ones.

He also altered the McCain proposal so that it opened up only two airports — LaGuardia and Washington National — to more competition.

The Senate approved the compromise, 69-31. The measure received strong support from both parties, with Republicans favoring the compromise 30-15 and Democrats backing the plan 39-16. *(Vote 290, p. 94-H)*

Nine days later, during their final sessions, the House and Senate passed the budget-reconciliation measure, including the aviation and transportation initiatives. ■

No Curbs on Airline LBOs

House-passed legislation to restrict airline takeovers died in 1990 after the collapse of two attempted buyouts diminished the urgency of the issue on Capitol Hill.

The bill (HR 3443 — H Rept 101-303), which the House passed 301-113 on Nov. 1, 1989, would have given the secretary of Transportation new powers to disapprove airline takeovers under certain conditions. In the Senate, Wendell H. Ford, D-Ky., was sponsoring a similar bill (S 1277 — S Rept 101-169), which he had vowed to try to bring to the floor early in 1990. *(1989 Almanac, p. 373)*

The bills responded to a rash of debt-financed takeovers or takeover attempts of U.S.-based airlines during the 1980s. But by late 1989, the financial climate for such leveraged buyouts (LBOs) had chilled.

Two pending deals — financier Donald J. Trump's bid for American Airlines and a union-backed bid for United Airlines — collapsed. As a result, "the sense of urgency has lessened," a Senate aide said.

The Bush administration initially had been receptive to the legislation but by fall 1989 had shifted to opposition and had threatened a veto. ■

Aviation Security Bills Cleared by Congress

Congress sent bills to the president in August and October aimed at improving aviation security.

One measure extended a program to allow the Federal Aviation Administration (FAA) to levy civil penalties against violators of safety guidelines.

Another strengthened federal aviation security procedures by creating new safety-related positions within the Department of Transportation.

A measure aimed at improving inspection requirements for aging aircraft passed the House but did not reach the Senate floor.

Safety Guidelines Extended

The Senate by voice vote Aug. 4 cleared a bill extending a program to allow the FAA to levy civil penalties against airlines and pilots who violated airline safety guidelines.

The House had passed the measure July 16, also by voice vote. President Bush signed the legislation (HR 5131 — PL 101-370) on Aug. 15.

Under the bill, the FAA would be able to continue issuing fines of up to $50,000 for infractions ranging from inadequate X-ray screening to air-traffic violations. Such enforcement had been handled by the Justice Department prior to 1987. FAA officials received the power to assess fines in 1987 because the Justice Department had limited resources to prosecute such minor cases.

The legislation's two-year extension of the program was retroactive to July 31, the date the program expired.

The program was started in 1987 to give FAA officials the power to assess fines less than $50,000 for various infractions. *(1986 Almanac, p. 293)*

After the FAA took over enforcing penalties, X-ray detectors picked up 95 percent of test weapons, as opposed to 85 percent before 1987, said the bill's sponsor, House Public Works Aviation Subcommittee Chairman James L. Oberstar, D-Minn.

The airline industry, however, criticized the FAA's enforcement methods as heavy-handed.

A federal appeals court also found the agency issued its new regulations without proper opportunity for public comment.

For those reasons, industry lobbyists in 1990 persuaded the bill's sponsors, who had wanted to make the program permanent, to seek only two years.

The Senate Commerce, Science and Transportation Committee reported the bill (S Rept 101-425) on Aug. 3; the House Public Works and Transportation Committee reported its version (H Rept 101-602) on July 13.

Security Procedures Strengthened

The Senate on Oct. 23 sent to the president legislation to beef up federal aviation security procedures. Bush signed the measure into law (HR 5732 — PL 101-604) on Nov. 16.

The legislation, passed by voice vote, would establish new Department of Transportation positions, including a director of intelligence and security, an assistant administrator for civil aviation security and federal security managers, who would be responsible for monitoring security activities at select airports.

The bill also would develop new personnel standards for

Airline Rights Bill Dies

The Senate in June considered legislation to end a practice by commercial airlines that prohibited blind passengers from sitting in exit-row seats. After three days of consideration, though, the Senate failed to cut off debate on the bill (S 341) because some senators saw it as an excellent vehicle on which to attach favored bills as amendments.

The Senate on June 12 failed, 56-44, to limit debate on the measure. Sixty votes were needed to invoke cloture. Majority Leader George J. Mitchell, D-Maine, pulled the bill from consideration after the cloture vote failed. The Senate had considered the measure June 6, 8 and 12. *(Vote 114, p. 42-H)*

As soon as the bill came to the Senate floor, the White House issued a statement opposing it. The administration maintained that legislation was no longer necessary because the Federal Aviation Administration (FAA) had issued a rule allowing only passengers able to perform basic escape functions during emergency evacuations to sit on the exit rows of a commercial aircraft. Thus, the FAA maintained, blind people were no longer being discriminated against by airlines solely on their inability to see.

In March 1989, the FAA proposed a regulation aimed at limiting exit-row seats to people able to operate emergency exits without assistance. The list of those to be barred included the physically and mentally disabled, obese and frail people, and children traveling alone.

Groups representing the blind strongly opposed the FAA proposal. State chapters of the National Federation of the Blind lobbied lawmakers, saying such restrictions were an affront to blind people's dignity and presumed, on the basis of no evidence, that they were unable to operate the exits.

The Senate Commerce Committee had approved the bill (S Rept 101-45) on May 16, 1989, by voice vote. *(1989 Almanac, p. 377)*

Alan Cranston, D-Calif., said he was disappointed to learn that blind people were still being discriminated against despite the provision of the Air Carrier Access Act of 1986 (PL 95-435) that prohibited airlines from discriminating against the disabled. Cranston, a sponsor of the 1986 act, also supported the 1990 bill. *(1986 Almanac, p. 291)*

During consideration of the measure June 6, bill sponsor Ernest F. Hollings, D-S.C., accepted an amendment by Christopher S. Bond, R-Mo., to require commercial airlines to have child-safety systems. Bond argued that children should have the same protection in airplanes as in cars.

The Senate also grappled with an amendment by Nancy Landon Kassebaum, R-Kan., to absolve general-aviation manufacturers from liability in lawsuits arising from crashes of airplanes more than 20 years old. No final action was taken on the amendment before the bill died.

The amendment was the same as S 640, a bill Kassebaum had been trying to pass for several years in behalf of three large aviation manufacturers in her home state.

airport security employees, accelerate the FAA's security research program and prohibit the selective notification of passengers about terrorist threats.

An identical bill passed the House by voice vote Oct. 1, after some last-minute changes aimed at answering administration objections. HR 5732 was based on HR 5200, which was approved in committee.

The legislation was largely the result of a report by a presidential commission that explored the terrorist bombing of Pan Am Flight 103 over Lockerbie, Scotland, in 1988. Most of those recommendations already had been put into effect by the administration.

The Aviation Subcommittee had approved HR 5200 on Sept. 13.

Subcommittee Chairman Oberstar blocked two amendments, by James M. Inhofe, R-Okla., and Mel Hancock, R-Mo., to require mandatory death penalties for airline terrorists. The sponsors withdrew their amendments after Oberstar expressed doubts about their germaneness.

The Transportation Committee on Sept. 26 reported titles of HR 5200 (H Rept 101-845, Part I) that affected the FAA and the Transportation Department.

The Foreign Affairs Committee on Sept. 27 approved parts of the bill that would change State Department aviation security programs.

The committees' versions would have created a new assistant secretary of Transportation for security and intelligence, set up new security procedures and expanded research programs on bomb-detection devices.

To accommodate administration objections, a committee amendment changed the provision to create the new assistant secretary. Instead, the lower-level position of director of intelligence and security would be created. The director would report to the Transportation secretary.

"Aviation cannot continue to be put on the back burner, as it clearly was before Pan Am 103," said Frank R. Lautenberg, D-N.J., chairman of the Senate Transportation Appropriations Subcommittee and sponsor of the bill.

The administration had opposed the bill, saying it would micromanage the Transportation Department's efforts to adopt the panel's recommendations.

President Bush, however, never issued a formal veto threat.

Aging Aircraft

When the House passed HR 5131 on July 16, it also passed another aviation bill (HR 3774) — to improve inspection requirements for aging commercial aircraft. That measure, though, drew little interest in the Senate and died.

The bill had been reported by the Public Works and Transportation Committee (H Rept 101-606) on July 16.

Passed on a voice vote, the aging-aircraft measure would have ordered the FAA to require that planes 15 years old or more be inspected for metal fatigue and other effects of aging during their regular heavy-maintenance checks.

It was drafted in response to an incident in 1988, when an Aloha Airlines plane lost the top of its fuselage, killing a flight attendant. An estimated 2,400 of the nation's jetliners, or 28 percent, were more than 20 years old, and the number was expected to increase to 5,700 by the end of the 1990s.

The Senate did not take up companion legislation or mark up the House bill. Many senators said they felt the legislation was not needed, as the FAA had already ordered new structural modifications and inspection procedures for older planes. ■

After Veto, Amtrak Renewed for Two Years

The Senate on June 25 cleared by voice vote legislation that reauthorized funding for the Amtrak national passenger railway after stripping out an antitakeover provision that had prompted President Bush to veto a previous reauthorizing measure earlier in June.

The Senate passed the bill (HR 5075 — PL 101-322) shortly after the House had done so, also by voice vote. It authorized $684 million for Amtrak in fiscal 1991 and $712 million in fiscal 1992.

The president signed the legislation July 6.

Bush had vetoed the earlier version (HR 2364), objecting to a requirement that the Interstate Commerce Commission (ICC) review the acquisition of major railroads by non-railroad companies. *(Veto message, p. 391)*

The administration had first threatened in 1989 to veto Amtrak legislation and Bush had requested no railroad funds in his 1989 budget.

The Senate on June 12 sustained Bush's veto as supporters fell two votes short of the two-thirds needed to override. Five days earlier, the House had voted 294-123 to override, 16 votes more than necessary.

The new bill retained a provision sought by the Virginia delegation to allow construction of the Northern Virginia commuter rail line. Progress required a federal liability waiver involving the use of Conrail freight railroad lines. "All of Northern Virginia's battle-weary commuters are grateful," said Rep. Stan Parris, R-Va.

BACKGROUND

Bush, following the lead of his predecessor Ronald Reagan, proposed in his fiscal 1989 and fiscal 1990 budgets the elimination of federal assistance to Amtrak. But federal funding of Amtrak had remained popular in Congress, particularly among members from the Northeast, where the railroad's operations were concentrated, and Congress routinely rejected such requests.

In September 1989, the House passed its version of HR 2364 (H Rept 101-207). The Senate passed its version of Amtrak reauthorization legislation in November 1989. Both bills authorized up to $656 million in new budget obligations for the railroad in fiscal 1990, $684 million in fiscal 1991 and $712 million in fiscal 1992.

The Senate in 1989 approved four amendments, included a proposal requiring the Transportation secretary to conduct a study to determine the demand among certain railroads for federal guarantees of obligations.

Proponents of the measure said continued government help was necessary even though Amtrak had made progress toward financial independence. Ticket revenues covered approximately 75 percent of costs in 1990, up from 48 percent in 1981. *(1989 Almanac, p. 378)*

Conference Action

Acting on a voice vote without debate, the Senate on May 10 cleared HR 2364 to reauthorize federal funding for the Amtrak national passenger railroad.

The House had approved the conference report (H Rept 101-471) May 9 on a 322-93 vote. *(Vote 103, p. 36-H)*

Both chambers acted despite advance warnings of a probable presidential veto. Chief among the Bush administration's objections was a House provision to require the ICC to review proposed acquisitions of major railroads by non-railroad companies.

The provision — to expand the ICC's authority to prevent takeovers of railroads that threatened to hurt employees or rail service — was in the House-Senate conference agreement on HR 2364. The agreement also authorized $684 million for the railroad in fiscal 1991 and $712 million in fiscal 1992.

Conferees accepted language in the House bill (H Rept 101-207) that would have required the ICC to approve acquisitions of railroads by companies not involved in the rail business. The ICC already had the authority to oversee mergers between railroads.

Backers argued that the ICC provision would have simply closed a loophole in existing law, while opponents, including the Bush administration, said the 100-day review period in the provision would have had a chilling effect on investment in the rail industry.

Transportation Secretary Samuel K. Skinner wrote to House Energy and Commerce Committee Chairman John D. Dingell, D-Mich., on May 1 that he would recommend that President Bush veto the bill because of the ICC provision and "unjustified new authorization levels." Bush requested no money for Amtrak in fiscal 1991.

At a conference meeting May 2, Sen. Charles S. Robb, D-Va., sought assurances from Dingell that the ICC provision would be stripped from the bill if Bush vetoed it, but Dingell would not give them. "It is not my belief that we should in any way indicate that we will accept a veto," Dingell said.

Robb said he wanted to ensure passage of language that would limit liability for compensatory and punitive damages for accidents on part of the Virginia commuter rail.

FINAL ACTION

Bush then issued the first veto of 1990 and the 11th of his presidency when he vetoed HR 2364 on May 24, citing the provision in the legislation to bring railroad acquisitions under new government scrutiny. "HR 2364 contains an unprecedented new regulatory review requirement and represents a step backward for the entire rail industry," Bush said in his veto message to Congress.

Though the House had no trouble overriding the veto — the June 7 vote was 294-123, well more than the two-thirds majority required — the Senate fell two votes short of the two-thirds needed to override.

In the House, 58 Republicans joined 236 Democrats in voting to override. *(Vote 162, p. 56-H)*

Senate Majority Leader George J. Mitchell, D-Maine, had wanted a Senate vote soon after the House action, but Republican leader Bob Dole of Kansas insisted on a delay because several GOP senators were not present.

The Senate's June 12 override vote on Amtrak was 65-35 at first, but then Mitchell switched his vote from "yea" to "nay" to preserve the right to move to reconsider. Only senators voting with the prevailing side could make such a request. With Mitchell's switch, the official vote became 64-36. *(Vote 115, p. 27-S)*

By June 14, however, Democrats had abandoned hope of a second override attempt after they failed to pick up the two votes they needed. Doing so seemed unlikely from the start because all the senators who supported Bush were Republicans.

Amtrak Veto Cites Regulatory Provision

Following is the May 24 White House memorandum of disapproval from President Bush saying that he would not sign HR 2364, a bill to reauthorize the Amtrak national railway passenger system:

I am returning herewith without my approval HR 2364, the Amtrak Reauthorization and Improvement Act of 1990.

HR 2364 contains an unprecedented new regulatory review requirement and represents a step backward for the entire rail industry.

This new regulatory burden would interfere with the ability of the nation's largest freight railroads to obtain needed capital or to change existing capital structure. The provision would institute for the first time, and for the railroad industry alone, government review and approval of acquisitions by entities that are not actual or potential competitors, including a carrier's own management or employees. This requirement is an unwarranted regulatory roadblock to financial restructuring of the railroad industry.

There is already adequate authority to protect the public interest in acquisition situations. Acquisitions of railroads by other railroads are now closely scrutinized under existing law to prevent reductions in competition. Dispositions of rail line segments are also subject to scrutiny when appropriated. Any financing of an acquisition, whether or not by another carrier, that involved the issuance of securities or new obligation by the target carrier is subject to review as well.

This review focuses on the acquisition's effect on the public interest and on the carrier's ability to provide service. Current law is therefore more than sufficient to protect shippers and the general public.

The rejuvenation of the rail industry since 1980 is due in large part to the Congress' decision to lift outdated and counterproductive government oversight from the railroads. The result was the creation of a favorable environment for capital investment for the first time in decades. The new regulatory hurdle in HR 2364 would counter this progress by adding uncertainty to refinancing and by delaying the infusion of cash when it may be most needed. Further, this delay and uncertainty would likely drive up the railroad industry's cost of capital, which could ultimately jeopardize the industry's financial stability and endanger needed rail service. For no justifiable reason, the bill could inhibit the future flexibility of Class I freight railroads to use capital restructuring to adapt to ever-changing markets and economic circumstances.

Existing law is adequate to ensure protection of the public interest when railroad acquisitions are being proposed. Because HR 2364 would impose a new, unprecedented and unjustified regulatory review requirement for railroad acquisitions, I am compelled to veto the bill. ■

"We're pleased that we were able to sustain the veto," White House spokesman Stephen Hart said immediately after the vote. Hart said Bush had been on the telephone with Republican senators throughout the day to make sure they knew he gave the issue high priority.

In vetoing the bill, Bush cited only the ICC provision, which he said would have had unfortunate economic consequences. "This requirement is an unwarranted regulatory roadblock to financial restructuring of the railroad industry," he said in his veto message.

Some Democrats said the veto was a backdoor effort to scuttle support for Amtrak — a course followed unsuccessfully by the Reagan administration. "They're trying to railroad us," said Frank R. Lautenberg, N.J.

But Republicans denied that that was the case. House GOP leader Robert H. Michel of Illinois even produced a letter from Bush pledging to sign the measure if it were passed again without the ICC provision.

Bob Kasten, R-Wis., said a bill without the objectionable part had been introduced in the House (HR 4984) and was ready for Senate introduction if necessary. "The fight is not over the funding of Amtrak," he said.

An Amtrak spokesman said the veto would not have affected daily operations because the railroad was working from money Congress already had appropriated for fiscal 1989-1992. But he said the veto would have indefinitely postponed plans for the commuter line being developed between Washington and Northern Virginia suburbs. ■

Amtrak Told To Curb Waste Disposal

Congress gave Amtrak, the nationwide system of passenger railroad service, six years to stop flushing human waste onto the tracks, thus giving it time and protection from several states that had filed suit against the rail service. The provision was attached to an unrelated bill (S 1430) that set up a national service program.

The provision that gave the private rail corporation the relief was written by Sen. Orrin G. Hatch, R-Utah, in the closing days of the 101st Congress. S 1430 was passed by the Senate on Oct. 16, cleared by the House on Oct. 24 and signed by President Bush on Nov. 16. *(Community service, p. 559)*

Amtrak officials were quick to point out that 20,000 trains a day were flushing waste onto railroad beds in the 1920s, and that trains worldwide continued to do so in the '90s. Amtrak ran 220 routes a day in 1990, 100 of those in short distances where waste disposal was not a problem.

Even by 1990, though, Amtrak had yet to find a way to fit trains with human-waste retention tanks capable of making long trips without being emptied periodically.

While Amtrak officials pointed to studies saying the time-honored method of dumping did not spread disease, they conceded that it was a public relations albatross.

"When people hear about it, they laugh about it for a few minutes," said David J. Carol, Amtrak's government affairs director. "Then they just find it disgusting."

Background

Up to 500 of Amtrak's long-distance passenger cars built before 1971 had toilets that flushed directly onto the tracks. Cars built since then had 30-gallon retention tanks with a six- or seven-hour capacity. When full, they automatically sprayed liquefied waste from their storage tanks onto the tracks, but only at speeds over 35 miles per hour.

Federal law prohibited the unregulated public dumping of human waste, but in 1976 Amtrak was exempted. A government study commissioned that year found no epidemiological link between such waste disposal and the spread of disease.

In the 1980s, the AIDS epidemic spurred railroad-bed workers in Utah to push Amtrak to change the method of disposing of waste. "That was the spark that got this issue going," said Amtrak's Carol, "even though the surgeon general insisted you cannot get AIDS from human waste."

Carol added, however, that he empathized with the plight of those who worked the railroad beds.

Amtrak remained unchallenged by the patchwork of state and local laws until a Florida case went to trial in 1989. In one frequently cited witness account, an Amtrak train emptied its retention tanks over a bridge in Putnam County, Fla. The liquefied waste sprayed down on William and Mary Trammell, two residents who were bass fishing on the St. Johns River with a couple from Alaska.

A Florida jury convicted Amtrak in November 1989 of four counts of commercial littering. Amtrak, facing up to $20,000 in fines, won the right to an appeal that was still pending by the end of 1990. Nevada, California, Idaho and Oregon also had cases pending, and a dozen other states were considering similar action.

Amtrak suddenly found itself facing a possible shutdown of service in several states. "You can't get to California if you can't operate through Nevada," Carol said.

The Florida case inspired Amtrak to push harder for legislative changes that would give the company more time to upgrade its trains with new waste-disposal technology.

Amtrak was testing different systems being developed by private companies.

Part of the problem was the volume of waste to be retained. Researchers were exploring vacuum methods used in airplanes as a way to use less water in the septic systems. But those systems had to be modified to work for up to three days at a stretch at widely fluctuating and extreme temperatures.

Legislative Details

The Hatch provision exempted Amtrak from all federal, state and local laws governing waste disposal, while giving the rail service six years to retrofit its fleet.

Prosecutors in Florida and other states were unhappy with a provision making the law retroactive to Feb. 5, 1976. That wording, insisted on by House Energy and Commerce Chairman John D. Dingell, D-Mich., meant pending cases likely would be dismissed.

Amtrak estimated the upgrades would cost $50 million to $80 million. But the provision did not explicitly authorize any funds. It simply said the upgrades were "subject to the appropriation of funds." That bothered critics such as Sen. Bob Graham, D-Fla.

"My concern is that we're going to get the worst of both deals," Graham said. "We're going to have no protection at the federal, state or local level from this odious activity, and we're going to have difficulty in these very tight fiscal times securing the necessary appropriations." ■

Troubled Consumer Agency Is Renewed

In a long-sought victory for consumer activists, Congress passed legislation to reauthorize the troubled Consumer Product Safety Commission (CPSC). It was the first stand-alone reauthorization of the watchdog agency since 1981.

The House cleared the bill Oct. 25 by adopting a House-Senate conference report, 375-41. The Senate had approved the measure on Oct. 22 by voice vote. President Bush signed the bill Nov. 16. *(Vote 520, p. 164-H)*

The two-year bill eased the commission's quorum requirements, raised civil penalties for rules violations and speeded up CPSC rulemaking. It also tightened procedures under which the agency could defer rulemaking in favor of voluntary industry standards. In addition, the measure contained compromise language that required manufacturers to notify the agency when they settled or lost three lawsuits concerning a hazardous product within a two-year period.

The bill was aimed at jump-starting the commission, which had languished through the preceding 10 years as its budget and staff were cut and as Reagan administration appointees, especially former Chairman Terrence M. Scanlon, were less responsive to consumer activism.

Final approval came after the House moved toward the Senate's less stringent position on the lawsuit-disclosure issue and agreed to drop language directing the agency to regulate several specific products listed in the bill.

Funding for the agency was authorized at $42 million in fiscal 1991 and $45 million in 1992. The VA, HUD and independent agencies spending bill (HR 5158 — PL 101-507) provided $37.1 million in 1991. *(VA, HUD, independent agencies appropriations, p. 854)*

BOXSCORE

Legislation: Consumer Product Safety Commission Reauthorization, PL 101-608 (S 605).

Major action: Signed, Nov. 16; conference report adopted by House, 375-41, Oct. 25; by Senate, Oct. 22. House version (HR 4952) passed, July 16; S 605 passed by Senate, Aug. 3, 1989.

Reports: Conference report (H Rept 101-914); Energy and Commerce Committee (H Rept 101-567); Commerce, Science and Transportation Committee (S Rept 101-37).

BACKGROUND

Congress created the CPSC in 1972 as an independent safety watchdog agency over potentially dangerous consumer products. *(1972 Almanac, p. 141)*

In its early years, the commission was buffeted by criticism from consumers, businesses and Congress for inefficiency and poor management, but there was never enough discontent on Capitol Hill to spur a major revamp of its structure or mandate.

With the election of President Ronald Reagan in 1980, controversies intensified as the agency became a battleground between consumer advocates and a free-market, deregulation-minded Republican administration.

Reagan failed in efforts to abolish the agency outright, but he was able to rein it in by cutting its budget and staff and appointing commissioners who critics said were less than effective.

Impasse in Congress

As a result of the continuing political controversies, Congress had failed to reauthorize the CPSC since 1981. Lawmakers tried, however, to assert control over the agency through the appropriations process.

In 1985, for example, Congress cut funds for two commissioners, reducing the agency's membership to three. Ostensibly a budget-driven move, the provision also reduced the number of Reagan appointees.

Because an accompanying provision to cut the quorum needed to conduct commission business from three to two was stuck in reauthorization bills, however, the reduction effectively allowed one commissioner to halt the agency's work simply by not showing up for meetings. Scanlon, who served on the agency from 1983-89 and headed it from 1986-89, was accused of using this tactic, but he denied it.

In the 100th Congress, CPSC reauthorization bills won approval from both the House and Senate Commerce committees. But the Senate measure, approved in 1987, was blocked by objections from Idaho's Republican senators, James A. McClure and Steve Symms. They indicated they would block the measure as long as the CPSC persisted in efforts to shut down a mom-and-pop operation in their state that manufactured a product called the "Worm Gett'r." Such "product-specific" language had blocked reauthorizations in previous years as well. *(1988 Almanac, p. 580)*

After Scanlon resigned in January 1989, the agency languished for almost a year with no quorum at all. President Bush in October nominated Jacqueline Jones-Smith, a Federal Election Commission lawyer, to replace Scanlon. The Senate confirmed her on Nov. 18, 1989.

By 1989, the commission's budget had dropped to $35 million, down from a high of $43 million in fiscal 1979, and staff had been cut almost in half. Even so, the agency still oversaw the safety of an estimated 15,000 consumer products.

Reagan and Bush administration officials maintained that the agency, as a result of the cutbacks, had been more effective and less adversarial. But consumer groups said that the real goal was to gut the agency's effectiveness.

SENATE ACTION

CPSC reauthorization legislation began moving again early in the 101st Congress when the Senate Commerce Committee approved S 605 by voice vote on April 18, 1989. The two-year reauthorization called for up to $36.5 million in fiscal 1990 and $38.2 million in fiscal 1991.

McClure again held up floor consideration over the Worm-Gett'r issue. When the company went bankrupt, however, McClure dropped his hold on the bill, and the Senate passed the measure by voice vote on Aug. 3, 1989.

On the floor, the Senate adopted by voice vote an amendment by Frank R. Lautenberg, D-N.J., to index to inflation the maximum level of civil penalties levied for violations of federal law.

The amendment raised the $2,000 civil penalty to $5,000 and the $500,000 penalty for a related series of violations to $1,250,000. These penalties would have to be adjusted every five years based on increases in the Consumer Price Index.

Richard H. Bryan, D-Nev., chairman of the Senate Commerce Subcommittee on the Consumer, eventually succeeded in keeping the bill free of the product-specific provisions that had stopped earlier bills.

The bill also eased the CPSC's quorum requirements by lowering the number of commissioners from three to two. The number of members on the commission was reduced from five to three. *(1989 Almanac, p. 385)*

HOUSE ACTION

The legislation cleared its first hurdle in the House on June 6, 1990, as the Energy and Commerce Subcommittee on Commerce and Consumer Protection approved HR 4952 by a 3-2 vote.

The House bill would have authorized $42 million in fiscal 1991 for the CPSC. The legislation would have required the CPSC to more carefully monitor industry compliance with voluntary safety standards, increased civil penalties and required manufacturers to report to the agency lawsuits alleging "death or grievous bodily injury" from dangerous products. It also included the language to lower the quorum requirement.

But controversies that had killed the reauthorizations in the preceding nine years remained in the bill.

Subcommittee Amendments

Republican lawmakers continued to object to portions of the bill to require the CPSC to take action on specific products, such as reclining chairs, children's toys and amusement park rides.

"We have a commission whose duty it is to decide which products should be subject to regulation," said Howard C. Nielson, R-Utah. "We shouldn't take that responsibility away from them."

An amendment by William E. Dannemeyer, R-Calif., to strip all the product-specific language from the bill was defeated on a vote of 2-3. Instead, the subcommittee adopted proposals to add two new products to the list.

An amendment by Joe L. Barton, R-Texas, approved 4-2, would have essentially codified a 1988 consent decree that barred the sale of three-wheel all-terrain vehicles (ATVs) and required manufacturers to develop a lateral stability standard for four-wheel ATVs. Manufacturers had not yet developed the standard, even though the CPSC deadline expired in May.

Another amendment, by Gerry Sikorski, D-Minn., would have mandated a voluntary standard to require safety devices on garage doors that operate automatically. Sikorski said at least 68 children had been killed and 26,959 injured since the voluntary standard went into effect in 1973.

The amendment, supported by consumer groups and garage-door manufacturers, was approved by voice vote.

Disclosure Issue

The subcommittee had approved a stronger CPSC bill (unnumbered) in 1989. But the panel's new chairman, Doug Walgren, D-Pa., subsequently agreed to weaken or remove several provisions strongly opposed by business groups to gain the backing of moderate Republicans.

In particular, Walgren stripped language strongly supported by consumer groups that would have allowed the CPSC to disclose reports of product hazards to the public. Most other health and safety agencies had that authority.

The reports would have included a disclaimer if the CPSC had not verified the hazards. But business groups were concerned that the allegations would scare off consumers before manufacturers could prove them false.

Even with this provision removed, sponsors had to stave off several GOP attempts to gut the legislation. Eventually, though, Walgren obtained the cosponsorship of all but two of the 11 members of his subcommittee.

Committee Approval

The full Energy and Commerce Committee approved HR 4952 by voice vote on June 19. Walgren said he was optimistic about the bill's chances.

"We have every reason to believe that this bill will have a chance to be approved by the full House," a Walgren aide said.

At the markup, opponents of the product-specific language made clear their determination to cut the language out of the bill at a later stage in the legislative process.

Said Norman F. Lent, R-N.Y., ranking minority member of Energy and Commerce: "It's only a small agency. And when faced with a product-specific agenda dictated by this committee, something's going to have to give, and I suspect that the commission's priorities . . . will be less than well-addressed."

Walgren maintained that the activities mandated by the product-specific language would take up about 2 percent of the CPSC's budget.

Two amendments to strip the language were defeated by voice vote. The committee then ordered the bill reported to the floor by voice vote, with William E. Dannemeyer, R-Calif., expressing the only opposition.

Floor Action

The House on July 16 passed HR 4952 by voice vote under suspension of the rules.

There was little debate, although Nielson — describing himself as "a repentant cosponsor" of the legislation — criticized the product-specific provisions as "micromanagement" of the agency.

CONFERENCE

The product-specific language remained the biggest difference between the House and Senate bills, and it was clear that the House had to give in to obtain agreement.

Another stumbling block to final passage was House language to require manufacturers to report to the CPSC when they were sued on allegations that their products caused "death or grievous bodily injury."

The chambers also differed over the commission's scope and structure. The House bill called for eased quorum requirements for a five-member CPSC, while the Senate bill would have reduced the number of seats on the panel to three.

Final Provisions

The House acceded to Senate demands to remove language that would have directed the agency to regulate specific products, such as ATVs, amusement park rides, and children's toys and sleepwear.

As in 1988, Symms and McClure indicated to the conferees that they would block the bill if the product-specific language were not removed.

Conferees retained four other product-specific provisions, however, that were acceptable to the industries involved. Retained were provisions to direct the CPSC to develop safety standards for cigarette lighters and automatic garage-door openers. In addition, the agency was required to study the effectiveness of the use of bittering agents to prevent poisonings and also report to Congress on its efforts to reduce indoor air pollution.

The ATV industry lobbied particularly hard to remove a provision that would have banned sales of three-wheeled ATVs by companies that had not signed on to an existing voluntary agreement that banned sales through 1998. The deleted language would also have made the ban permanent and would have required the development of stability standards for four-wheeled ATVs.

Conferees also agreed on compromise language that required manufacturers to report to the CPSC when they settled or lost three lawsuits concerning a hazardous product within a two-year period.

Senators argued that complaints in a lawsuit were only allegations and that, under the original House language, the agency would have been swamped with inaccurate information. House members said the stricter reporting requirements would have created an "early warning" system to discover dangerous products.

The final bill lowered the quorum to two members as long as the commission consisted of three members.

The final bill also responded to criticisms of the agency for the practice of suspending rulemaking procedures after manufacturers promised to develop voluntary standards. Under the House language kept in the final bill, promises were not enough; voluntary standards had to actually exist before the rulemaking threat could be removed. ■

Fastener Standards Set

Legislation cleared by Congress on Oct. 26 required that high-strength metal fasteners sold in commerce conform to the specifications to which they were represented to be manufactured. President Bush signed the bill (HR 3000 — PL 101-592) on Nov. 16.

The legislation, championed by House Energy and Commerce Committee Chairman John D. Dingell, D-Mich., was aimed at stopping distribution by foreign and domestic counterfeiters who were selling substandard nuts, bolts, screws and washers. *(1989 Almanac, p. 379)*

The legislation also required that samples from each lot of high-strength fasteners used in critical areas of nuclear power plants, commercial airliners and military vehicles be tested by a laboratory accredited by the National Institutes of Standards and Technology.

The House had passed the bill by voice vote on Sept. 19, 1989. The Senate passed an amended version on Oct. 26, 1990, and the House concurred with the Senate version the same day. ■

SBA Bill Trimmed, Passed

The House sent to the president a four-year reauthorization of the Small Business Administration (SBA) in the closing hours of the 101st Congress.

The bill cleared the House by a 250-0 vote in the early morning hours of Oct. 28 (the session of Oct. 27) after the House agreed to Senate amendments aimed at trimming the price tag of the bill.

The House vote was its second to last before adjourning; the Senate had passed the measure by voice vote Oct. 27. *(Vote 535, p. 168-H)*

Despite lingering concerns about its cost, President Bush signed the bill (HR 4793 — PL 101-574) on Nov. 15.

Hoping to address administration and Budget Committee objections to the bill's costs, the Senate had removed a House effort to provide $42 million over three years for pilot grant programs to spur marketing, tourism and "incubator" or shared office facilities for fledgling small businesses in rural areas.

Instead, the Senate directed the SBA to hold five regional conferences on rural development. The final bill also encouraged lenders in a pilot program to make guaranteed loans of up to $75,000 to rural businesses.

Senators also removed a House provision that would have allowed borrowers to refinance SBA-guaranteed loans with lower penalties than under existing law. The bill raised spending for most SBA programs by 5 percent in each fiscal year. It provided $3.55 billion for small business guaranteed loans, $440 million more than Bush requested.

The SBA, set up in 1953, guaranteed commercial loans to owners of small businesses who were unable to get credit on their own. It also offered direct loans to veterans, the disabled, minority businesses and some disaster victims.

The fiscal 1991 Commerce, Justice, State spending bill (HR 5021) appropriated $469.6 million for the SBA; the 1990 spending bill had appropriated $432.9 million.

Earlier Action

The House had passed HR 4793 by a vote of 398-26 on Sept. 25, after defeating efforts to kill off tree-planting and loan-refinancing incentives. *(Vote 380, p. 122-H)*

The House bill called for $10 million in minority development contract assistance loans for fiscal 1991. Bush had asked for $5 million.

For other forms of direct loans, the House bill would spend $19 million for the disabled, $24 million for economic opportunity and $19 million for veterans in fiscal 1991. The White House asked for no money to be authorized for those types of loans.

Despite the discrepancies, the amounts made it into the final bill and the president signed it.

An amendment by Andy Ireland, R-Fla., rejected 150-269, would have struck language that would provide $180 million in grants over four years to encourage tree-planting. The Bush administration, which had its own tree-planting program in the omnibus farm bill, opposed the language. *(Vote 378, p. 122-H)*

By voice vote, the House accepted an amendment by Ron Wyden, D-Ore., that would create a $22 million pilot program over five years to shepherd new technologies from federal laboratories to small businesses.

The House Small Business Committee had reported the measure (H Rept 101-667) on Aug. 3; no Senate committee marked up the legislation. ■

Fish Inspection Bill Dies in Hill Turf Fight

A bill that would have established mandatory federal inspection of fish and shellfish for the first time died after having passed both chambers in 1990. The legislation fell victim to a turf fight in Congress and the Bush administration over which agencies would have the responsibility for overseeing the program.

The House passed the bill (S 2924) by a vote of 324-106 on Oct. 24 after the Senate passed its version by voice vote Sept. 12.

With the strong backing of Senate Majority Leader George J. Mitchell, D-Maine, the Senate-passed bill gave the U.S. Department of Agriculture (USDA) the job of inspecting and licensing processing plants, the Commerce Department authority to bar fishing in contaminated waters, and the Food and Drug Administration (FDA) the role of setting contaminant standards.

Late in the session, after turning aside a measure similar to the Senate's, the House passed its bill giving the inspection duties to the FDA and the National Oceanic and Atmospheric Administration (NOAA). By that point, there was neither the time nor the inclination among House and Senate lawmakers to hold a conference and reach a compromise on the bill.

Three House committees tussled over which agency should be given the duty to inspect the fish. Each committee predictably wanted to give the responsibility to the agency it oversaw.

An Agriculture Committee bill (HR 3508) would have given primary responsibility to the USDA. An Energy and Commerce Committee version (HR 3155) would have assigned the duty entirely to the FDA. A third bill (HR 2511), backed by Gerry E. Studds, D-Mass., of the Merchant Marine and Fisheries Committee, would have split the inspection program between the Commerce Department and the FDA, phasing it in over time.

In the Senate, the Agriculture Committee bill (S 1245) sought to require the USDA to administer a program using FDA standards. The Commerce Committee bill (S 2228) directed the Commerce Department to carry out inspections of plants and vessels that processed fish with the FDA having responsibility for setting processing standards.

BOXSCORE

Legislation: Mandatory fish inspection (S 2924, S 2228, S 1245, HR 3508, HR 3155, HR 2511).

Major action: S 2924 passed by House, 324-106, Oct. 24; by Senate, Sept. 12.

Reports: Merchant Marine and Fisheries (HR 2511 — H Rept 101-874, Part I); Energy and Commerce (HR 3155 — H Rept 101-875, Part I). Commerce (S 2228 — S Rept 101-369); Agriculture (S 1245 — S Rept 101-335).

BACKGROUND

Throughout the 1980s the amount of seafood eaten in the United States grew significantly. Annual consumption increased by 23 percent to a record high in 1989 of 15.9 pounds per person. According to a Department of Commerce report published in May, U.S. consumers spent $28.3 billion on fish and shellfish in 1989.

After a decade on the upswing, however, fish sales by 1990 began to experience a slide that many officials attributed to a crisis of consumer confidence.

Efforts to create a mandatory inspection program, like those for meat and poultry, had been held up because lawmakers had been unable to agree on who would handle inspections. While the USDA oversaw mandatory meat and poultry inspection, fish was governed only by a voluntary, industry-regulated program. Fish was the only major flesh food not subject to mandatory federal inspection.

Senate Agriculture Committee Chairman Patrick J. Leahy, D-Vt., said self-regulation by the fish industry had not been beneficial to consumers. Only 12 percent of U.S. seafood underwent inspection, he said, and only 7 percent of the country's 2,000 fish processors participated in voluntary programs.

"While mandatory federal inspection cannot completely eliminate all contaminants from the marketplace, it will make our seafood safer and reduce the risk of illness to consumers," Leahy said.

Public Voice for Food and Health Policy, a consumer advocacy organization, had campaigned since 1986 for adoption of fish inspection legislation.

HOUSE COMMITTEE ACTION

As evidence of a contentious turf battle, three House committees in 1990 held hearings and markups on fish inspection legislation. All three committees — Energy and Commerce, Agriculture, and Merchant Marine and Fisheries — approved different bills, establishing some of the major jurisdictional and policy obstacles for seafood inspection legislation to overcome.

Energy and Commerce

The Energy and Commerce Committee approved a bill (HR 3155) on March 13 to require the FDA to inspect food processing plants "frequently and randomly." The bill sought to convert the government's voluntary seafood inspection into a mandatory program run by the FDA.

Only a trace of the controversy surrounding the issue of fish inspection was evident at the markup. Edward Madigan, R-Ill., reiterated his view that the USDA, which inspected meat and poultry, was better equipped than the FDA to inspect fish.

But Henry A. Waxman, D-Calif., chairman of the Health and the Environment Subcommittee, defended the bill. Only the FDA had the scientific expertise necessary to enforce standards that would be imposed for microbiological contaminants and chemical residues, he said. And unlike the USDA, which promoted and helped market U.S.-produced food and commodities, the FDA "has no mandate to promote the products it regulates," he said.

The consumer group Public Voice had objected to the lack of additional funds to carry out fish inspection. Consequently, Madigan offered an amendment to authorize $75 million in fiscal 1991 for the FDA to carry out the program. It was adopted by voice vote.

Agriculture

The Agriculture Committee approved its fish inspection bill (HR 3508) by voice vote July 18.

"Seafood is safe," said Roy Dyson, D-Md. "I think what we're trying to do with this legislation is restore some confidence."

The bill would have divided the fish inspection duties among three agencies: The USDA would have licensed and inspected fish processing plants, including processing ships. The Commerce Department would have had authority to bar fishing in waters found to be contaminated, and the FDA would have been responsible for setting standards governing acceptable levels of contaminants in fish.

The Energy and Commerce bill (HR 3155) and a similar Senate Commerce version (S 2228) would have given the duty entirely to the FDA.

House Agriculture's bill would have exempted fishing vessels from inspection. However, the bill would have provided for a study by the Agriculture and Commerce departments to determine the need and feasibility of licensing fishing vessels.

The fishing industry and consumer groups also clashed over whether states should be allowed to set more stringent fish-cleanliness standards than the federal government. Consumer groups thought they should. Industry representatives argued that a patchwork of state laws could disrupt the industry.

The Agriculture Committee adopted a compromise provision that would have enabled states to petition the federal government for the right to set tougher fish-safety laws. The amendment, sponsored by Dan Glickman, D-Kan., was adopted on a 15-10 vote.

Merchant Marine and Fisheries

The Merchant Marine and Fisheries Committee on Aug. 1 became the third House panel to approve a federal fish-inspection program. The panel approved HR 2511 (H Rept 101-874, Part I) by voice vote to give the Commerce Department authority over the program.

Before approving the measure the committee adopted a series of amendments offered by Studds that made a number of technical and conforming changes to the bill.

A week earlier, on July 25, the Subcommittee on Fisheries and Wildlife Conservation had held a markup on the legislation. At the markup, Studds and Don Young, R-Alaska, offered a substitute amendment that differed significantly from the bill as introduced and from a staff draft that had been discussed at the subcommittee's April 25 hearing on the legislation.

The substitute, adopted by voice vote, called for the two-stage seafood safety program to be developed by the Commerce secretary.

SENATE COMMITTEE ACTION

In the Senate, the Agriculture and Commerce committees approved competing seafood safety measures during 1990. The measures, though, left unresolved the issue of who would carry out any mandatory inspection program.

Agriculture

The Agriculture Committee approved by voice vote May 22 a bill (S 1245 — S Rept 101-335) to require the USDA to administer a mandatory fish inspection program — using standards set by the FDA.

As approved, S 1245 would have put fish processing plants under one of three inspection programs. Two of the programs — intrastate and interstate — would have been established by the states, but the federal government would have shared half the cost of their operation.

Where no inspection program was imposed by a state, the federal government would have been responsible.

The FDA would have set inspection standards for contaminants such as microbiological organisms and chemical residues. If fish were found to exceed those standards, the government could have prohibited fishing and harvesting in the waters where they were caught.

Although Democrats and Republicans on the committee had privately worked out most of the key elements of S 1245, they debated over a provision that would have protected employees at fish processing plants who reported public health or sanitary violations.

An amendment by Thad Cochran, R-Miss., to delete the whistleblower provision was approved 10-9. Cochran said the provision would have duplicated a pending whistleblower protection bill (S 436) for private-sector employees who exposed health and safety violations in their companies. S 436 ultimately died.

Democrats argued that the legislation was already a compromise because it would not impose continuous government inspection for fish, as was the practice with meat and poultry. Because of that, they said, it was imperative for employees to be part of the self-regulation procedure at fish processing plants.

Under the measure, inspectors of processing plants would have had the authority to scrutinize fish and fish products, packages, containers, labels and all processing equipment. "Adulterated or misbranded" fish would have been seized and condemned.

All fish processing plants would have to be certified by the USDA annually and would be subject to restrictions or cancellations for non-compliance.

The legislation also would have prohibited importation of seafood that did not meet the inspection standards set for domestic fish.

However, fish not meeting minimum U.S. health and safety standards could be exported to a country that set less stringent conditions.

The bill also would have given the Commerce Department authority to prohibit fishing in contaminated waters.

Commerce

The Commerce Committee on June 27 approved legislation (S 2228) to improve seafood safety, but left unresolved the dispute with the Agriculture Committee over which agencies would carry out the inspection program.

The bill, approved by voice vote, directed the Commerce Department to carry out periodic inspections of plants and vessels that processed fish. The FDA would have had responsibility for setting standards governing the permissible level of contaminants in seafood and sanitation in processing facilities.

The Commerce Committee bill would not have allowed user fees, although the government would have had the authority to recover certain costs from the industry. The USDA's beef and poultry inspection programs were paid for by the government; the seafood industry was concerned about user fees.

Under the bill, federal agencies could have delegated inspection authority to states that were at least as stringent about inspection as the federal government. In addition, all imported fish and fish products would had to have been inspected if they came from countries without a comparable inspection program.

SENATE FLOOR ACTION

The Senate on Sept. 12 passed S 2924 to require federal fish inspection, resolving, at least within the Senate, the jurisdictional dispute over which agencies should oversee the fishing industry. The bill was a clean version of S 1245 approved by the Agriculture Committee in May.

Under the measure, passed by voice vote, fish and seafood sold in the United States would for the first time have to receive a stamp of approval from the USDA, just as beef and poultry did.

"No longer will consumers have to guess whether or not the fish they eat is safe," said Leahy, who sponsored the bill with Mitchell.

The Senate rejected, 39-59, a competing bill, sponsored by Ernest F. Hollings, D-S.C., Edward M. Kennedy, D-Mass., and Ted Stevens, R-Alaska, that would have given responsibility for fish inspection exclusively to the Commerce Department and the FDA. *(Vote 232, p. 47-S)*

Under the Mitchell-Leahy bill, the USDA would license and inspect fish processing plants, including processing vessels. The Commerce Department would continue to oversee fishing waters and have authority to bar fishing and shellfish harvesting in contaminated waters. The FDA would set standards for acceptable levels of contaminants in fish.

To Hollings, the chairman of the Commerce Committee, the Mitchell-Leahy bill was a blatant turf grab by the Agriculture Committee, which Leahy chaired.

"There is no seafood inspection crisis," Hollings said. "Yet we have this proposal to take a good program and try to give it to a department that is itself under investigation by the Congress because of deficiencies with respect to food, meat and poultry inspection."

However, Mitchell argued that the Hollings-Stevens plan did not provide for a lead agency or take advantage of the food safety expertise at the USDA.

Administration, Interest Groups Respond

The Bush administration opposed the Mitchell-Leahy bill. Officials had called for expanding the existing seafood inspection program at the FDA and Commerce, in the manner of the Hollings-Stevens substitute. According to an administration policy statement, senior advisers would have recommended a veto if Congress tried to transfer the duty to the USDA.

The Senate-passed bill would have required the USDA to certify foreign processing plants that exported to the United States. Fish from uncertified plants would have to be inspected. The bill would have provided for periodic and unannounced inspections of domestic processing plants.

However, consumer groups backing the legislation were split over whether the bill contained sufficient protection for whistleblowers.

Even though whistleblower protections were stripped out of the bill during committee deliberations, Public Voice for Food and Health Policy continued to support the Mitchell-Leahy measure. Most other consumer groups, including the Consumer Federation of America and Public Citizen's Congress Watch, supported the Hollings-Stevens measure because it would have protected whistleblowers from reprisals.

Labor unions supported the Hollings-Stevens measure as well. "It is essential that employees involved in the processing operation feel free to report violations without fear of losing their jobs," said Kennedy, chairman of the Labor Committee.

But Ellen Haas, executive director of Public Voice, said that only Mitchell and Leahy kept up the pressure to move fish inspection legislation.

"Without their leadership, we clearly would not have seen a fish inspection bill pass the Senate during this session of Congress," Haas said.

Haas said they had agreed to seek to restore the whistleblower language in conference with the House.

HOUSE FLOOR ACTION

Though the House was the first chamber to see a committee complete action on seafood inspection — Energy and Commerce in March — it did not take up the legislation on the floor until the end of October. By that time, the 101st Congress was drawing to a close and chances of passage of the legislation had grown slim.

On Oct. 24, though, the House settled its yearlong turf battle over which federal agency should inspect fish. With the end of the session near, lawmakers decided to fight it out on the floor. The debate quickly turned into an acrimonious bloodletting, with Agriculture on one side and Energy and Commerce and Merchant Marine on the other.

In voting 277-153 for an amendment by Studds and John D. Dingell, D-Mich., lawmakers endorsed mandatory federal inspection, but only for shellfish. The program would have been carried out by the FDA and the NOAA, the two agencies that ran the modest, voluntary seafood inspection program.

The bill itself (S 2924) passed by a vote of 324-106. But there was almost no time — or interest — to forge a compromise with the Senate. *(Votes 514-515, p. 162-H)*

Jurisdictional Dispute

Agriculture Committee members, led by Chairman E. "Kika" de la Garza, D-Texas, argued that a fish inspection bill would clear Congress only if the House adopted the Senate bill with few changes. But Dingell, a master of jurisdictional maneuvering, accused the Agriculture Committee of employing brinkmanship in an effort to steal jurisdiction over fish from Energy and Commerce.

De la Garza countered that it was Dingell who was renowned for aggrandizing the power of his committee.

However, opponents of putting the fish inspection program in the USDA reminded lawmakers that the meat and poultry inspection system the department already ran was frequently accused of laxity. "It is no secret that the USDA has not done the greatest job in the world of inspecting meat," said John Conyers Jr., D-Mich., chairman of the House Government Operations Committee.

The Dingell-Studds amendment would have covered only shellfish because they presented a much higher risk of contamination than other types of seafood. According to Studds, the chance of contracting illness from a serving of shellfish was 1-in-250, while it was 1-in-5 million from a serving of finfish.

The bill also included a provision designed to deflect criticism that the bill did not go far enough. Within 18 months after enactment, the administration would have to submit to Congress a proposal for inspecting all fish and fish products.

The administration supported an expansion of the existing program in the FDA and the NOAA.

Whistleblower Protection

The Agriculture panel attempted to win labor support for its plan by including protection for whistleblowers. But the Dingell-Studds plan included even stronger whistleblower protections, which won broad support for the plan from labor unions and consumer groups.

Public Voice continued to support the Agriculture Committee plan because it might not have required a conference with the Senate and could have been cleared quickly for the president. That bill, which was strongly pushed by Mitchell, would have involved three agencies in the inspection process. The USDA would have licensed and inspected fish processing plants, including processing vessels. The Commerce Department would have overseen fishing waters and had the authority to bar fishing and shellfish harvesting in contaminated waters. And the FDA would have set standards governing contaminant levels in fish.

Though Dingell kept reminding other lawmakers that the administration had threatened to veto the Senate bill, Agriculture Committee members warned that not adopting the Senate bill would have meant a year's worth of work on the issue would be lost. "If the Dingell-Studds substitute passes," said Charles W. Stenholm, D-Texas, "the bill is dead for the year." ■

Labeling of 'Dolphin-Safe' Tuna Regulated

Supporters of bills to protect marine life won a partial victory in the 101st Congress as legislation to regulate the labeling of "dolphin safe" tuna became law. The language was attached to the reauthorization (HR 2061) of the 1976 Magnuson Fishery Conservation and Management Act, which regulated fishery management.

The measure required that companies that sell dolphin safe tuna be able to prove that the fish was not caught with methods that killed dolphins.

Also attached to the bill was an amendment that banned the use of large drift nets in U.S. waters and called on the administration to pursue an international agreement to end use of large-scale drift nets on the high seas.

The bill also quadrupled the maximum penalty for violating U.S. fishing laws. Under the Magnuson fishery conservation law, the United States had exclusive authority over living resources in a 200-mile zone off U.S. shores.

The Senate passed the fisheries legislation Oct. 27, and the House cleared it for the president the same day. President Bush signed it into law Nov. 28 (PL 101-627).

Background

The tuna-labeling language reflected consumer and congressional concern over the killing of dolphins in the eastern Pacific Ocean. For reasons unknown, dolphins swam along with tuna and were being drowned in purse seine nets used to harvest tuna. Earlier in the year, the three largest U.S. tuna processors had voluntarily pledged to purchase only tuna caught with dolphin-safe methods.

But dolphin advocates said that other processors were mislabeling "dolphin unsafe" tuna as being dolphin safe.

Drift nets — miles-long nets that trapped fish indiscriminately — were also blamed for killing other marine life, such as dolphins and birds. The major users of drift nets were Taiwan, South Korea and Japan.

The Magnuson Act created eight regional councils to oversee regulation of the nation's fisheries resources within the 200-mile limit. The fisheries councils set up and enforced management plans aimed at preventing overfishing.

Legislative Action

The dolphin-safe language was a weaker version than contained in a bill (HR 2926) that was ordered reported out of the House Merchant Marine Committee on May 23. That bill would have required the labeling of tuna in accordance with the method used to catch it. Tuna caught with methods that did not harm dolphins could have been labeled "dolphin safe," while other tuna would have been required to be labeled that it was caught "with technologies that are known to kill dolphins."

As introduced, HR 2926 framed the issue as one of consumer choice. But at the full committee markup, the bill's most vociferous opponent, Don Young, R-Alaska, won adoption of an amendment that stiffened the bill to include a ban on the import and sale of any dolphin-unsafe tuna. Young's amendment was aimed at broadsiding the bill. The amendment would have set a precedent that food processors would have found odious and could have forced referral of the bill to the Ways and Means Committee, which had jurisdiction over trade issues.

In the Senate, Joseph R. Biden Jr., D-Del., won adoption, by voice vote, of the modified dolphin protection language as an amendment to the fisheries bill.

"I would like to pass stronger legislation," said Biden. "But I think it is more important that as dolphin-safe tuna enters the market we provide consumers with the strongest assurance possible that their good intentions in selecting dolphin-safe tuna are not being taken advantage of."

Biden worked out the compromise with John B. Breaux, D-La., who had threatened to block the tougher language that Biden had introduced as S 2044.

The Magnuson reauthorization originally passed the House on Feb. 6 by voice vote, under suspension of the rules. It passed the Senate, amended, on Oct. 11 by a vote of 98-0. Both bodies subsequently re-passed the bill, and the House ultimately cleared the bill by agreeing to the Senate amendment to the House amendment to the Senate amendment of the bill. *(Vote 264, p. 53-S)*

The final version of the bill dropped a Senate provision that would have authorized the Commerce secretary to bar new fishermen from harvesting in overfished fisheries.

The Magnuson Act was reauthorized through fiscal 1993. The new law authorized $94 million for fisheries programs in 1991, an almost $13 million boost over 1990 spending levels. Most of the additional money was to be aimed at increased enforcement and research.

The new law also extended the jurisdiction of the U.S. fisheries councils to include tuna, a highly migratory species that had been regulated through international agreements. It also called on the secretary of State to pursue an international agreement to prevent overfishing of other highly migratory species such as swordfish. ■

Bill To Curb Product Suits Stalled Again

A scaled-back bill to establish federal standards for product liability suits was approved by the Senate Commerce Committee on May 22, but never reached the floor for debate. It was the fifth time since 1980 that the industry coalition pushing measures aimed at reducing payments to consumers injured by dangerous or defective products had won committee approval of its legislation but failed to get a floor vote.

The legislation got a small boost early in the year when President Bush included product liability reform in a laundry list of legislative items in his State of the Union address. Vice President Dan Quayle, who had supported previous bills on the subject while in the Senate, was given the job as head of the President's Council on Competitiveness to lobby Congress on the issue.

Sen. Bob Kasten, R-Wis., sponsor of the 1990 proposal (S 1400), dropped some of the most controversial provisions from measures he had sponsored in previous Congresses in order to gain Democratic support. Five Democrats joined eight Republicans to produce the Commerce Committee's 13-7 vote in favor of the bill; Bob Packwood, Ore., was the only Republican to vote against it.

The bill languished in the Senate Judiciary Committee for two months until the panel discharged it without recommendation after a one-day hearing July 31 — too late for sponsors to try to push it for floor action.

Kasten tried but failed late in the session to add product liability provisions to a technology programs bill designed to spur U.S. competitiveness. *(Technology bill, p. 440)*

A parallel product liability bill (HR 2700) was introduced in the House, but the Energy and Commerce Committee never held hearings on the measure.

BACKGROUND

Manufacturers had been lobbying since 1980 for a federal product liability law that they said would protect industry from burdensome litigation and skyrocketing insurance premiums by establishing uniform standards governing suits by victims of unsafe products. While the bills changed over time, they all proposed standards more restrictive than those on the books in many states — for example, establishing a higher standard of proof for plaintiffs or limiting punitive damage awards against manufacturers.

Consumer groups, backed by the powerful trial lawyers lobby, opposed the bills as an attack on victims' rights and states' prerogatives over personal injury suits. They also challenged the insurance industry's contention that product liability laws were causing the insurance crisis, blaming instead what they called the industry's own anticompetitive practices.

The Senate Commerce Committee approved product liability legislation three times. In 1982 and 1984, the bill was not brought to the floor. In 1986, proponents won an 84-13 floor vote to proceed to consideration of the bill, but it was then pulled in the face of a promised filibuster by the leading opponent of the measure, Ernest F. Hollings, D-S.C. *(1986 Almanac, p. 287; 1984 Almanac, p. 296; 1982 Almanac, p. 330)*

In 1988, proponents concentrated on the House and, for the first time, got a bill through the Energy and Commerce Committee. But the bill went next to the Judiciary Committee, which took no action. The chairman of the committee, Peter W. Rodino Jr., D-N.J., opposed the measure, as did many of the other Democrats on the panel. *(1988 Almanac, p. 573)*

Bills Introduced

Product liability bills containing slightly different variations on industry-backed proposals were introduced in 1989 in the Senate by Kasten and in the House by Thomas A. Luken, D-Ohio, a senior member of the Commerce Committee.

Kasten's bill included provisions to establish a higher burden of proof ("clear and convincing evidence" rather than "preponderance of the evidence") for consumers bringing product liability suits, to prevent awards to people who were intoxicated or using drugs if that was the primary cause of their injury, and to limit pain and suffering damages to the proportion of a manufacturer's fault.

The bill would also have established a "collateral source rule" allowing a reduction in damage awards against a defendant for any payment a plaintiff received from another source, such as a workers' compensation award. It would have limited the liability of product sellers to cases in which the seller was at fault or the manufacturer could not be sued. And it would have imposed a uniform statute of limitations allowing plaintiffs two years to file a suit after discovering an injury and its cause.

Kasten dropped from his proposal, however, business' long-sought-after cap on punitive damages — the damages ostensibly imposed to punish companies for extreme negligence or wrongdoing rather than to compensate the individual plaintiff for injuries.

Luken's bill contained some of the same features as Kasten's — for example, the higher burden of proof, limit on seller liability, collateral source rule and statute of limitations. In addition, it contained one feature not included in Kasten's: a "state-of-the-art defense" allowing manufacturers to avoid liability if, at the time the product was made, it could not have been more safely designed or the manufacturer could not have known and warned the consumer of the product's dangerous effect.

Lobbying Positions

Consumer groups and trial lawyers again rallied to oppose the bills and cited new evidence for their position.

In September 1989, a study by the General Accounting Office found that the size of awards in product liability suits was closely linked with the severity of injury and the amount of economic loss — undercutting manufacturers' claims of unpredictable damage awards by runaway juries.

In another study of tens of thousands of product liability decisions, two Cornell University Law School professors documented a "quiet revolution," beginning in the early to mid-1980s, in which the law shifted to favor manufacturers. "What surprised me was that the data bore it out so starkly," said one of the authors, James A. Henderson Jr., who had testified in favor of product liability legislation. "Sweeping reform of the type that I was trying to push a decade ago seems questionable now."

For their part, supporters of the bill tied their previous

arguments to a new theme being stressed by the administration: competitiveness. "A manufacturer is more likely to be willing to introduce a product in the marketplace if he knows what the rules are," said Victor Schwartz, a Washington lawyer who represented the Product Liability Alliance, a coalition of businesses pushing the legislation.

SENATE COMMITTEE ACTION

The Senate Commerce Committee's approval of Kasten's bill followed a one-day hearing on the bill by its Consumer Subcommittee on May 11.

Henderson, the Cornell professor, told the panel the bill was not anticonsumer because consumers ordinarily bore the brunt of liability suits by paying higher costs for products. "If S 1400 is anti-anything, it is anti-trial lawyer," said Henderson, who added that successful plaintiffs in lawsuits get to keep less than half of what they are awarded.

But representatives of consumer groups disagreed with Henderson. Linda Lipsen, legislative counsel for Consumers Union, said claims of a "litigation explosion" in liability cases were overstated and the measure was not needed.

Consumer groups also attacked a provision to exempt companies that produced or sold medical devices or drugs approved by the government from paying punitive damages in cases involving agency-approved products.

The U.S. Public Interest Research Group released a report May 10 that found at least 10 Food and Drug Administration-approved drugs and medical devices that manufacturers discovered were hazardous but continued to sell anyway.

Committee Markup

The debate over the costs of the existing rules for handling product liability suits carried over into the committee markup on May 22. Kasten told his colleagues the existing system was "wasteful," failed to compensate victims adequately and placed "an undue burden on American business."

Another supporter, John C. Danforth, R-Mo., said that existing practice, "where 75 cents or so on the dollar goes into the pockets of lawyers, is just haywire."

But opponent John B. Breaux, D-La., said the measure would amount to "rolling over the states" by pre-empting their laws. And committee Chairman Hollings said, "I hate to see a committee report out a bad bill all in the name of uniformity."

The 13-7 vote to report the bill reflected bipartisan support. Five Democrats voted for the bill — Daniel K. Inouye of Hawaii, Jim Exon of Nebraska, John D. Rockefeller IV of West Virginia, Lloyd Bentsen of Texas and Charles S. Robb of Virginia — along with eight Republican senators. Packwood was the only Republican to vote against it.

Judiciary Committee

Kasten's bill went next to the Senate Judiciary Committee. Product liability legislation had traditionally encountered more resistance from the lawyer-dominated Judiciary committees than from the more business-oriented Commerce panels.

After a one-day hearing on July 31, the Senate Judiciary Committee decided to release the bill without recommendation or report. By the time the bill was calendared Aug. 31, it was competing for floor time with budget and appropriations measures and a host of other urgent legislative items.

Sponsors vowed to try again in the 102nd Congress, although Luken's retirement deprived them of their point man in the House and both Judiciary panels were deemed likely to remain reluctant to consider the legislation. ■

Effort To Bar Insurers' Price-Sharing Stalls

A bill to restrict insurance companies from sharing price information and engaging in monopolistic practices narrowly won approval from the House Judiciary Committee on June 20, but then stalled.

The Judiciary Committee approved HR 1663 on a 19-17 vote, with three Democrats joining the panel's 14 Republicans in voting against it (H Rept 101-976). If enacted, the bill would have been the first congressional revision of the McCarran-Ferguson Act of 1945, which exempted the insurance industry from antitrust laws.

Similar measures had been pushed unsuccessfully in the 99th and 100th Congresses. A House Judiciary subcommittee in 1988 approved a bill partially lifting insurers' antitrust immunity, but it died before the full committee in the face of concerted opposition from the insurance industry. *(1988 Almanac, p. 574)*

HR 1663 would have prohibited monopolization, price-fixing, allocation of territories among competing insurance companies, and unlawful "tying," the practice of forcing a consumer to purchase one type of insurance in order to be eligible to buy another. It provided for a five-year transition period for insurers to comply.

Committee Chairman Jack Brooks, D-Texas, said the bill would "allow the brisk winds of competition to blow once again in the insurance industry." But committee Republicans argued that the bill would call into question the legality of many industry practices and do nothing to provide increased availability or affordability of insurance.

In markup, Dan Glickman, D-Kan., unsuccessfully pushed an amendment to ensure that insurance companies could continue to engage in "trending" — the practice of sharing historical data on the volume of claims.

Under the bill, companies could not use information they shared with each other to fix premium prices or try to monopolize the insurance industry. Brooks, who crafted the provision to deflect Glickman's amendment in subcommittee, argued the language would not prohibit trending. In full committee, Glickman's amendment was defeated, 6-30.

On final approval, Glickman and two other Democrats — Edward F. Feighan, Ohio, and Bruce A. Morrison, Conn. — joined 14 Republicans in voting against the bill. But the bill saw no further action, and the committee report was not filed until the last full day of the session.

Hotel Fire Safety Pushed

The House on Sept. 10 cleared for the president a bill that put added pressure on hotels and motels to install sprinklers and smoke detectors by steering federal business from those that lacked the fire safety equipment.

The bill (HR 94 — PL 101-391), passed on a voice vote, would prohibit most government employees from staying in hotels that failed to meet the new sprinkler-smoke detector guidelines and would forbid federally funded conferences from being held in such places.

The Senate had passed the bill by voice vote on Aug. 3. President Bush signed the measure Sept. 25.

While the bill arrived on the House floor with broad support from the hotel-motel industry, fire safety officials and others, it endured a long and obstacle-ridden path of negotiation and compromise to get there.

"I'm delighted to see this bill about to become law after three years of extensive negotiations," said Rep. Sherwood Boehlert, R-N.Y., sponsor of the legislation that was spurred by the Dec. 31, 1986, Dupont Plaza Hotel fire in Puerto Rico, in which 97 people were killed.

Of the 3 million hotel rooms in the country, just under half had sprinklers, said Jim Gaffigan of the American Hotel and Motel Association. Large, high-rise hotels almost all had sprinklers, he said, adding that the bill would have the biggest effect on medium-sized hotels and motels.

Industry Concerns, Compromises

David J. Goldston, a GOP staff member for the House Science Subcommittee on Research and Technology, said the larger hotel chains such as Marriott, Hilton and Sheraton, which were already equipped with sprinklers, never had big problems with the bill. It was the mid-sized groups that pushed for changes. Holiday Inn Inc., arguing that its hotels were constructed with fire safety in mind, was one of the last holdouts, Goldston said. The chain unsuccessfully sought an exemption for hotels built like Holiday Inns but came on board when the Senate Commerce Committee adopted the measure, he said.

As passed by the House, the bill would have exempted from the guidelines only hotels and motels shorter than three stories, with no interior corridors and with immediate means of exit to the ground level from all rooms.

These "almost nonsensical" requirements "flew in the face of modern construction techniques" and security considerations, said Dan Tate, the lobbyist for such mid-sized motels as Super 8, Econolodge and Days Inn.

The Senate amended the bill to exempt all hotels shorter than four stories from the sprinkler provisions. Those smaller hotels would only have to install smoke detectors to be in compliance with the guidelines.

Under the final version of the bill, states were given two years to compile lists of hotels within their borders that had complied with the new sprinkler and smoke detector guidelines. Within four years, 65 percent of any federal agency's travel nights would have to be spent at hotels with sprinklers. By the seventh year, 90 percent of federal travel would have to go to such hotels. ■

'Fire-Safe' Cigarettes

Acting by voice vote, the Senate on July 30 cleared for the president's signature a bill aimed at developing a cigarette that would extinguish before starting a fire. The House passed the bill earlier that day, also on a voice vote.

President Bush signed the measure (HR 293 — PL 101-352) on Aug. 10.

The legislation, sponsored by Rep. Joe Moakley, D-Mass., directed the Consumer Product Safety Commission (CPSC) to supervise a study of cigarette safety and the technical feasibility of devising fire-safe cigarettes.

The House Energy Committee on July 26 approved the measure by voice vote. Its Consumer Protection Subcommittee had approved the bill July 19 after reaching a compromise that satisfied the tobacco industry.

The subcommittee adopted a substitute offered by Rick Boucher, D-Va. The amendment dropped a provision in the original bill that would have required the CPSC to establish a mandatory fire safety standard for cigarettes.

Instead, the bill directed the CPSC to supervise a study of cigarette safety, with an eye toward developing safer cigarettes that would also be acceptable to smokers. Previous studies of such cigarettes had shown that safer cigarettes were technically feasible but did not address whether they were commercially feasible. ■

Telemarketing Fraud

The Senate on Oct. 23 passed a bill (S 2494 — S Rept 101-396) to strengthen the authority of the Federal Trade Commission (FTC) regarding fraud committed in connection with telephone sales.

Richard H. Bryan, D-Nev., one of the bill's sponsors, said the legislation was needed to combat the "bad actors who are out to defraud and harass the consumer."

The measure, adopted by voice vote, would have required the FTC to prescribe new rules regarding telemarketing activities. It urged the commission to consider: mandating timely delivery of telemarketed goods and services; requiring a "cooling off" period in which buyers could cancel orders; restricting and limiting the hours when unsolicited calls could be made; and prohibiting the use of autodialers — computers that dialed large blocks of numbers in sequence or at random and delivered prerecorded messages — that did not disconnect as soon as the called party hung up.

Supporters of the measure pointed out that the measure in no way pre-empted state laws or altered the FTC's existing authority. "The bill provides the FTC with enhanced enforcement tools, such as increased subpoena power, to carry out its consumer protection functions," said Bryan.

Bryan added that he supported legislation "carefully crafted to avoid unduly burdening the many legitimate telemarketers."

S 2494 had been approved by the Commerce Committee on July 26.

The House on July 30 had passed a somewhat related and stronger bill (HR 2921) that sought to prohibit unsolicited advertising over telephones and fax machines. *('Junk fax' curbs, p. 379)* ■

Chapter 6

GENERAL GOVERNMENT

Federal Workers' Pay Overhaul . . . 405
Lump-Sum Retirement Benefits . . . 406
Hatch Act Revisions . . . 408
Veto Message . . . 410
Paperwork Reduction Act . . . 411
OMB's Review Powers Curbed . . . 412
Regulatory Negotiation Guidelines . . . 413
Pacts on Fund Transfers . . . 414
Census Undercount Claimed . . . 415
Federal Financial Centralization . . . 416
Deceptive Mailings . . . 417
Anti-Pornographic Mail Bill . . . 417
Child-Proof Packaging . . . 417
Veterans Affairs . . . 418
Federal Indian Policy . . . 421
Bush Indian Preference Act Veto . . . 423
Puerto Rico's Status . . . 424
D.C. Mayor, 'Shadow' Delegation . . . 428
Aid to D.C. Metro Rail . . . 429
Acid-Free Paper . . . 429
National Endowment for the Arts . . . 430
NASA . . . 434
Space Station Design Overhaul . . . 436
Space Patent Law . . . 437
Superconducting Super Collider . . . 438
Technology Programs . . . 440
Animal Rights Protests . . . 441
Earthquake Research and Preparedness Act . . . 442
Mining Research . . . 442

Federal Workers' Pay Overhaul Enacted

A sweeping overhaul of the federal pay system was the centerpiece of the $20.9 billion fiscal 1991 spending package for the Treasury Department and U.S. Postal Service. The House cleared the bill on Oct. 24, and President Bush signed it Nov. 5.

Under pay revision provisions agreed to the week of Oct. 15 by the administration and House and Senate conferees, federal workers would receive raises equal to the average annual salary increases in the private sector beginning in 1992. Employees were guaranteed salary increases of up to 5 percent annually, based on the Employment Cost Index (ECI), which kept track of changes in the private local labor markets.

The aim of the bill was to close the gap between federal and private-sector salaries. According to the president's pay advisers, federal pay had fallen an average of 30 percent behind private-sector wages.

The final provisions came from two separate bills (HR 3979, S 2274) that were approved by committees in both chambers earlier in the year.

Under existing law, federal workers of the same rank received the same pay, regardless of where they lived. Beginning in fiscal 1994, federal workers in high-cost cities would qualify for extra locality-based pay increases. For nine years, starting in 1995, the remaining gap would be closed by 10 percent.

Under the bill, the president could opt not to increase salaries only in the event of war or negative growth of the gross national product for two consecutive quarters. After 1995, the president would have broader discretion to alter the agreement.

The bill also gave all federal workers a 4.1 percent pay increase effective Jan. 1, 1991. Bush had asked for a 3.5 percent increase.

The House originally had approved the conference report on the bill on Oct. 22, on a 343-67 vote. The Senate approved the package Oct. 23 on a voice vote but added two minor amendments unrelated to the pay increase. The House accepted the amendments Oct. 24, clearing the bill for the president's signature. *(Vote 505, p. 160-H; Treasury, Postal Service appropriation, p. 886)*

In other action on federal pay, Congress suspended for five years the option that federal workers had to receive a portion of their pension in a lump-sum payment when they retired. Officials estimated that the provision, included in the budget-reconciliation bill, would save $8.1 billion over five years. *(Lump-sum suspension, p. 407)*

BOXSCORE

Legislation: Federal pay system overhaul (HR 3979, S 2274), enacted as part of fiscal 1991 Treasury Department and Postal Service appropriations, PL 101-601 (HR 5241).

Major action: Signed, Nov. 5. Conference report cleared by House, Oct. 24; adopted by Senate, Oct. 23; adopted by House, 343-67, Oct. 22. Senate passed HR 5241, 93-6, Sept. 11. Senate Governmental Affairs Committee approved S 2274, July 25. House Post Office and Civil Service Committee approved HR 3979, July 18.

Reports: Conference report on HR 5241 (H Rept 101-906). HR 3979: Post Office and Civil Service (H Rept 101-730). S 2274: Governmental Affairs (S Rept 101-457).

BACKGROUND

The General Schedule (GS) — a nationwide ranking system for federal workers — was the result of efforts dating back to the mid-19th century striving for uniformity and pay equity for all government employees. A major breakthrough toward that end, the 1923 Classification Act, created a classification system for federal workers in Washington. Legislation mandating a comprehensive nationwide system was enacted in 1949.

Although these systems achieved internal consistency, they did not address the question of parity with private industry.

In the 1980s, a number of studies suggested that the federal government could no longer compete with the private sector and had to hire inferior employees or leave positions vacant and often cut back its services.

"We have a pay system that is not market-sensitive," said Constance Newman, director of the Office of Personnel Management (OPM).

"We have lost many of our best, brightest and most dedicated to the private sector because of our non-competitive pay rates," said Rep. Gary L. Ackerman, D-N.Y.

The principle of pay comparability with the private sector was not enacted until 1970. Beginning in 1978, citing economic conditions, successive presidents disregarded the recommendations of their pay agents — a group of federal officials who reported annually to the president and made a pay-adjustment recommendation based on national survey data — and granted smaller annual salary increases than recommended. *(1970 Almanac, p. 861)*

Although it had the power to do so, no Congress had chosen to override the president's final pay determination and grant a full pay raise as recommended by the pay agent. Members of Congress did blame the White House for the resulting problems in recruiting and keeping federal workers, but successive administrations argued that economic conditions made it impossible to provide the recommended increases.

As the federal/private-sector pay gap grew, the government found it increasingly difficult to attract and retain highly skilled workers. A number of studies analyzing the problem pointed to the pay disparity as the major cause of the difficulties.

The National Commission on the Public Service, headed by former Federal Reserve Board Chairman Paul A. Volcker, in March 1989 released a report recommending, among other things, immediate 25 percent pay raises for top-level government employees — including members of Congress. Like several studies before it, the Volcker commission also proposed a major overhaul of the GS, recommending a locality-based pay system that would raise existing salaries to reflect real differences in costs in different parts of the country. *(1989 Almanac, p. 366)*

In an attempt to address the pay problems of government workers, Congress acted on a number of bills.

The House Post Office and Civil Service Committee on

Oct. 25, 1989, approved a measure (HR 2544), based on recommendations of the Volcker report, to make the federal government more attractive to university graduates. The bill would have allowed agencies to repay outstanding federal student loans of new recruits.

Congress also cleared a measure in 1989 to make mid- and upper-level federal employees eligible for overtime pay. *(1989 Almanac, p. 366)*

Earlier Versions

In early 1989, members introduced measures in each chamber to attempt once again to make federal salaries competitive with private-sector wages. The House bill would have authorized sufficient raises to close the gap between federal and private sectors over a 10-year period.

Under the locality-based increase, workers in New York and Washington, for example, would earn more than their same-grade counterparts in less expensive areas of the country. This locality-based feature marked a major innovation in the government's GS salary structure.

The general across-the-board pay adjustments would be based on two of the many types of ECI available from the Bureau of Labor Statistics (BLS).

The ECI figure called for in the House bill would have measured the average annual wage and salary increases of private-sector workers, excluding salespeople. The ECI selected by the Senate would have combined the average annual wage and salary increases of private-sector workers with the average yearly wage and salary increases of state and local government employees — whose salaries were increasing at a slightly faster rate than those of private-sector workers. Both ECIs would be based on wage and salary increases only and would not include benefits.

The House bill would have made the annual salary increases automatic, but the Senate bill would have allowed the president to grant somewhat smaller increases than recommended. The Senate bill would have permitted the president to reduce pay increases by 0.5 percent when the ECI was 5 percent or less and by 1 percent when the ECI was between 5 percent and 8 percent.

The administration rejected both bills, insisting instead on full presidential discretion. Claudia Cooley, Personnel Systems and Oversight Group associate director at OPM, said, "No employer gives raises whether they can afford to or not, no matter what some survey says. That's not normally how employers function."

The House's move to close the pay gap and the issue of presidential discretion accounted for the considerable difference in the bills' total costs.

If exercised in full, the executive prerogative to limit pay increases would have reduced the Senate bill's $7 billion price tag to $3.8 billion over a five-year period, according to a committee aide. The House bill would have cost more than $15 billion over five years, according to the Congressional Budget Office.

Another difference between the House and Senate bills was how the locality-based pay adjustments would be calculated. The Senate version determined locality-based adjustments on BLS "pay relatives" — the difference between private-sector salaries in a given city and the private-sector national average.

Locality-based adjustments in the House bill came from the ECI differentials between federal and non-federal pay — a gap the House bill sought to close in 10 years. The Senate bill imposed no time limits on closing the gap, but instead called for a study within three years.

At the July 25 Senate committee markup of S 2274, Carl Levin, D-Mich., opposed the bill and the locality-based provisions. An aide to Levin said that paying urban workers more than rural workers for the same job was at bottom "divisive" and "tough ... to justify."

The administration, meanwhile, proposed its own solution, which entailed restructuring the pay system to redirect funds to critical pay categories rather than pumping scarce dollars into a broad program of increases.

But neither the House nor Senate marked up the administration alternative (HR 4716, S 2547), preferring instead to incorporate its workable elements into the two measures already under consideration.

COMMITTEE ACTION

House and Senate committees approved federal pay revision bills in 1990 but neither bill moved to the floor of the chamber. Members finally found the right vehicle for the measure when they attached it to the Treasury spending bill.

The House Post Office and Civil Service Committee approved HR 3979 on July 18 and the Senate Governmental Affairs Committee approved S 2274 on July 25.

House Committee

The House Post Office and Civil Service Committee on July 18 voted 19-4 to approve HR 3979 calling for comprehensive revisions in the federal pay structure to make government workers' salaries competitive with those in the private sector.

Committee Chairman William D. Ford, D-Mich., called the measure's approval historic, saying, "There has not been an attempt to modernize and revise the federal pay structure in this century."

The bill would have authorized the president to make adjustments in federal pay scales in areas with especially large gaps between federal and non-federal pay starting Oct. 1, 1992, and to increase pay by as much as 8 percent in New York, San Francisco and Los Angeles in the interim.

Special pay systems could be established for certain occupations, such as federal firefighters, law enforcement officers and health officials.

The Post Office Subcommittee on Compensation and Employee Benefits approved the bill, 4-1, on July 17.

Senate Committee

The Senate Governmental Affairs Committee on July 25 approved S 2274 to overhaul the federal pay system.

Approved on a voice vote, the act would have granted all white-collar government workers an annual pay increase based on the ECI. The ECI average would be based on annual wage increases of private-sector workers, excluding salespeople, as well as on yearly salary increases for state and local government employees.

In addition to the general increase, the bill would have authorized locality-based pay increases for federal workers in particularly expensive cities.

This feature would increase the government's "ability to recruit and retain valued employees," said William V. Roth Jr. of Delaware, the committee's ranking Republican.

Unlike the Senate bill, which would impose no time limits on narrowing the federal/private-sector pay gap, the House bill sought to redress the problem in 10 years.

Among several amendments approved in committee was a proposal by Roth to provide for travel and interview expenses for government job applicants. The amendment would also provide for a special retention bonus to prevent highly qualified government workers from defecting to high-bidding private companies.

A provision in the bill would have given the president discretion to reduce the ECI-based pay adjustments by half a percentage point in a "national emergency" or "serious economic conditions." When Roth offered the amendment in the markup, however, committee Chairman John Glenn, D-Ohio, said "Every president has thought he's been in 'serious economic conditions,'" and warned that the wording could effectively nullify the bill. Roth then withdrew the amendment.

FINAL ACTION: APPROPRIATIONS

Supporters of the overhaul of the federal pay system advanced their cause on Sept. 11. On a 93-6 vote, the Senate passed its version of the fiscal 1991 Treasury spending bill, after adopting by voice vote the amendment on the pay system. *(Vote 231, p. 47-S)*

The overhaul plan was offered by Glenn and Roth, chairman and ranking Republican, respectively, of the Governmental Affairs Committee, and incorporated the language of S 2274, approved by their committee July 25.

The amendment incorporated several changes to the language in S 2274. Most important, it retained the unlimited discretion the president had to limit or deny pay raises in the event of "serious economic conditions affecting the general welfare."

As approved by the Governmental Affairs Committee, the pay overhaul measure would have imposed some limits on the president's authority to override the annual report of his pay agent and grant smaller pay increases than would be required to keep up with salary increases in the private sector.

The provision had been a major sticking point in negotiations between the administration and Congress.

The revised language also would create a separate pay system for law enforcement agencies, some of which were particularly hard hit by the public/private-sector pay disparity.

The Senate gave voice-vote approval to an amendment by Dennis DeConcini, D-Ariz., to raise the starting salaries of federal officers by $3,000 a year; grant cost of living bonuses to officers assigned to the nation's 13 highest costing cities; and provide relocation, retention and language-skill bonuses.

Conferees Negotiate

House and Senate conferees approved the fiscal 1991 Treasury spending bill on Oct. 19, after days of negotiations with the Bush administration over concerns that the pay-overhaul proposal might erode the president's authority to limit or deny pay raises.

An agreement was negotiated by Rep. Steny H. Hoyer, D-Md., representing the conferees, and officials from the White House Office of Management and Budget (OMB) and the OPM.

The resulting language was a combination of the administration's own proposals and the earlier bills introduced by Ackerman and Hoyer, and Glenn and Roth.

Barring unusual economic circumstances, the president would have to increase salaries for federal employees in areas with a gap of 5 percent or greater.

The gap would have to be closed by at least 20 percent in the first year and an additional 10 percent each year until federal workers were brought to within 95 percent of full comparability.

After 1995, the president would have broad discretion to alter the agreement.

After some debate, conferees also agreed to provide a 4.1 percent cost of living adjustment for federal workers for fiscal 1991; Bush had asked for a 3.5 percent increase.

DeConcini, chairman of the Senate Appropriations Subcommittee on the Treasury, Postal Service and General Government, said the full committee's chairman, Robert C. Byrd, D-W.Va., and ranking Republican, Mark O. Hatfield of Oregon, were "really upset," about the increase because it would raise the overall cost of the $20.6 billion bill.

Despite the concerns, the House approved the conference report on Oct. 22. The Senate approved a slightly amended package Oct. 23 and the House accepted the amendments Oct. 24, clearing the bill for Bush. ■

Retirement Benefits

In a budget-cutting move, Congress acted in 1990 to take away federal workers' right to take their retirement benefits in a lump sum upon retirement.

As part of the fiscal 1991 budget-reconciliation bill, Congress suspended for five years lump-sum benefits for federal employee retirees. Workers retiring on or before Nov. 30, 1990, or after Sept. 30, 1995, would not be affected. *(Reconciliation provisions, Title VII, p. 155)*

The Office of Management and Budget and the Congressional Budget Office calculated that eliminating the lump-sum option would save $1 billion in fiscal 1991 and $8.1 billion over the five years. Many observers — federal employees, union representatives and government officials — doubted that the option would be reinstated in 1995.

Under the lump-sum option, employees would receive two taxable payments equal to the amount they had contributed to their pension plan. Workers entitled to the 50/50 lump-sum payments would receive payments in two calendar years — one received shortly after retirement and one a year later. Acceptance of the payment would reduce a retiree's annual annuity check by 5 percent to 20 percent.

Employees "involuntarily separated" from their jobs would continue to receive a 50/50 lump-sum benefit, as would critically ill employees. U.S. armed forces or Defense Department workers employed because of Operation Desert Shield were given an extra year — until Nov. 30, 1991 — to retire and claim the payment.

Personnel managers in various departments throughout the government — such as the Department of Health and Human Services and the Office of Personnel Management (OPM) — reported increases in the number of employees who retired during the later months of 1990. OPM officials attributed some of the increase to the new congressional regulations.

The option had become so popular that by November up to 80 percent of those employees eligible to collect the payments had chosen to do so.

Bush Veto Leaves Hatch Act Intact

After intensive lobbying by the White House, the Senate on June 21 fell two votes short of overriding President Bush's veto of a bipartisan bill (HR 20) to amend the so-called Hatch Act, which prohibited the nation's 3 million federal employees from taking part in partisan politics. *(Veto message, p. 410)*

As a result, the effort to rewrite the 51-year-old law ended where it began two years earlier, as a wishful goal of federal union leaders and their growing number of allies in Congress. Among those strongly supporting the legislation were the American Federation of Government Employees (AFGE) and the American Postal Workers Union.

Groups that lined up against the bill included the U.S. Chamber of Commerce, the American Civil Liberties Union and the independent citizens' lobbying group Common Cause.

BOXSCORE

Legislation: Hatch Act revisions (HR 20).

Major action: Senate sustained veto, 65-35, June 21; House voted to override veto, 327-93, June 20; vetoed, June 15. House agreed to bill as passed by Senate, 334-87, June 12; passed by Senate, 67-30, May 10; originally passed by House, 297-90, April 17, 1989.

Reports: Post Office and Civil Service Committee (H Rept 101-27).

The 65-35 Senate vote — 67 "ayes" were needed to achieve the two-thirds majority to override — came on the heels of a 327-93 vote in the House on June 20. All but three House Democrats and nearly half their GOP counterparts voted to make the bill law over Bush's objections. *(Senate vote 121, p. 29-S; House vote 184, p. 64-H)*

Still, the overwhelming House vote was not enough to prevent Bush from racking up the 12th straight veto win of his presidency. In the Senate, bill supporters could not staunch the tide of presidential persuasion.

On May 10, the Senate had passed the measure on a 67-30 vote, just enough to override a veto. All 54 Democrats and 13 Republicans voted for the bill in what union leaders saw as a pivotal moment in their efforts to recast a previously partisan issue into a bipartisan one. Between that vote and the override attempt, Hawaii Democrat Daniel K. Akaka joined the Senate to give bill proponents another supporter.

Senate aides said the Bush administration, needing at least two votes to sustain the veto, had targeted Republicans Arlen Specter of Pennsylvania and Pete V. Domenici of New Mexico for strong arm-twisting. White House Chief of Staff John H. Sununu and Attorney General Dick Thornburgh, a former governor of Pennsylvania, personally lobbied Specter, according to congressional aides and union officials.

In the end, Specter maintained his support for the bill, but Domenici and two other Republicans, Trent Lott of Mississippi and Alfonse M. D'Amato of New York, changed their earlier votes and supported Bush, allowing the president's veto to stand.

BACKGROUND

In 1939, when the Hatch Act was passed, few doubted that it was needed to address a growing problem.

By the end of 1934, more than 60 new federal agencies had been created and 300,000 new federal jobs had come into being. Lawmakers feared that most were being staffed on the basis of political patronage.

In 1938, a Senate panel found that some federal workers had been coerced into contributing to the re-election fund of Sen. Alben W. Barkley, D-Ky. (1927-49, 1955-56). A Senate investigation the next year disclosed that political appointees in the Works Progress Administration had coerced workers into making political contributions to protect their jobs.

It was his concern about such an expanding federal government and subsequent corrupt political practices that led Sen. Carl A. Hatch, D-N.M. (1933-49), to become an advocate of strict limits on political activity by federal employees as a means of ensuring clean elections.

Hatch's bill passed the Senate with no hearings and little debate. In fact, congressional action was so fast that an amendment had to be offered later to exempt the president, the vice president and members of Congress from the restrictions, which would have prevented them from even seeking re-election.

Efforts to revise the law, which remained controversial since its passage, were repeatedly blocked.

In 1966, Congress established an independent bipartisan commission, which urged that federal workers be allowed to participate in politics. Similar legislation cleared Congress in 1976, but President Gerald R. Ford vetoed it. *(1976 Almanac, p. 490)*

Revision efforts again fell short in the 100th Congress but were revived in the 101st Congress. On April 17, 1989, the House passed a similar measure (HR 20 — H Rept 101-27) by 297-90. Meanwhile, the Senate Governmental Affairs Committee in July 1989 approved S 135 (S Rept 101-165), sponsored by committee Chairman John Glenn, D-Ohio. *(1989 Almanac, p. 365)*

Provisions

The House bill was more sweeping than the Senate's. It would have allowed federal workers to run for public office and would have given employees a limited opportunity to raise money for political purposes.

The Senate bill, which supporters in both chambers knew stood a better chance of passage, would not have allowed employees to run for partisan political office, but it would have allowed them to organize voter registration drives and act as delegates to the presidential nominating conventions. The bill would have barred a federal worker from raising money for a candidate's campaign or for most political action committees (PACs) other than the one representing the worker.

While off duty, a federal worker also could have held an office in a party, distributed campaign literature, solicited votes or publicly endorsed candidates.

The Senate bill also would have:

- Prohibited employees from using their official authority to affect or influence an election's outcome.

• Prohibited workers from knowingly receiving, accepting or soliciting a political contribution from any person who was not a member of their federal employee organization.

Workers also would have been prohibited from accepting political contributions not intended for use by the PAC of that federal employee organization.

This anti-coercion provision included prohibitions against pressure to contribute to political campaigns and attend political functions.

However, employee groups could have solicited contributions from their members for PACs.

• Prohibited employees from running for election to a partisan political office. However, they would have been permitted to hold offices in party organizations and affiliated groups, including convention delegate positions.

While on duty, a federal worker would have been barred from participation in political activities — such as wearing campaign buttons — while in government uniform or wearing official insignia identifying the office or position of the employee; operating a government vehicle; or occupying any room or building used for official duties by employees or officeholders of the government, federal agencies or other government offices.

Excluded from the bill's restrictions were "certain high-level political appointees" whose duties extended outside normal work hours and took them away from their place of work.

They would have been excluded as long as the employees were appointed by the president with approval from the Senate, participated in activities not paid for by the government and determined foreign policy or the "nationwide administration of federal laws."

SENATE ACTION

In May 1990 the Senate finally picked up where it left off in July 1989.

After eight days of debate and a barrage of Republican amendments, the Senate on May 10 passed its version of the Hatch Act revision bill, HR 20. The tally was 67-30, just enough votes to override a veto. Before approving HR 20, the Senate substituted the amended text of its bill (S 135), approved in Glenn's committee in July 1989. *(Vote 90, p. 21-S)*

After the vote, White House spokesman Marlin Fitzwater reiterated that the president would veto the bill. "We believe it politicizes the civil service in an inappropriate fashion, makes them vulnerable to political manipulation as well as political solicitation," he said.

Senate Majority Leader George J. Mitchell, D-Maine, had forced the bill to the floor May 1, when he won a 70-28 vote to shut off debate on a motion to proceed to consideration of the measure.

Seventeen Republicans, most of them from the Northeast and the Southwest, joined the Democrats in voting for cloture. *(Vote 76, p. 19-S)*

In a series of test votes May 1-3, Democratic supporters of the bill showed that they had enough Republican votes to shut off debate and pass the bill, despite the threat of a presidential veto.

Republicans, unwilling to admit defeat, offered amendment after amendment in what Democrats described as a stalling effort. Glenn, the bill's floor manager, accused Republicans of attempting to "filibuster" through use of the amendment process.

Two substitute amendments offered by Governmental Affairs' ranking Republican, William V. Roth Jr. of Delaware, were turned back May 3 on votes of 67-30 and 66-29 after Glenn complained that they failed to solve the main problem: the federal workers' inability to participate in the political system. *(Votes 77, 78, p. 19-S)*

Roth, like the Bush administration, argued that the bill's safeguards against coercion were inadequate.

Charles S. Robb, D-Va., and John W. Warner, R-Va., who supported the bill, then offered an amendment to strengthen its anti-coercion provisions.

Their amendment, which was agreed to on a voice vote, would have included a maximum fine of $5,000 or a prison sentence of up to three years for attempts to coerce an employee into participating in the political process or into making a contribution.

"It is our view," Warner said, "that this amendment will help put teeth into the legislation by thus strengthening the U.S. Criminal Code."

Glenn then mustered his forces to kill, 59-35, an amendment by Pete Wilson, R-Calif., that would have required the General Accounting Office to review implementation of the law and to report whether there was a pattern of illegal political activity. *(Vote 79, p. 19-S)*

Democrats also argued that the Hatch Act was outdated and that, because of hundreds of unclear rules, it intimidated federal workers from any political participation.

"If 'Hatched,' you cannot wave a political poster at a rally, but you can put it on your car or post it on your front lawn," Glenn said.

Likewise, he said, existing rulings allowed a worker to wear a campaign button on the job and write a $1,000 check to a candidate, but not to give time for such activities as stuffing envelopes or circulating petitions.

"We must balance the need to protect the integrity of the civil servants with our duty to protect the constitutional right of all citizens who participate in the nation's political processes," Glenn said.

Campaign Finance Issues

Several GOP amendments were aimed at trying to tie the Hatch Act revisions to the broader issue of campaign finance reform. Republicans failed in a number of efforts to amend sections of the bill that would have allowed federal employees to solicit funds from colleagues for union PACs. Republicans argued that, because the unions were largely Democratic, the provisions would have meant more dollars for Democrats.

On May 9, members defeated an amendment by Mitch McConnell, R-Ky., that would have allowed federal employees to refuse to pay any part of union dues that was funneled to political campaigns without losing their right to vote on collective-bargaining issues. The amendment was killed on a tabling motion, 63-35. *(Vote 84, p. 20-S)*

Also on May 9, Minority Leader Bob Dole, R-Kan., offered an amendment that would have called for federal employees to decide through agency-by-agency referendums every five years whether to exercise their right to participate in political activities. Dole's amendment was tabled, 62-36. *(Vote 85, p. 20-S)*

The Senate also voted, 63-35, to table a Roth amendment that would have prohibited federal employees from soliciting political contributions from co-workers. *(Vote 86, p. 20-S)*

An attempt by Domenici to maintain Hatch Act restrictions on employees of federal agencies such as the Central Intelligence Agency, the Internal Revenue Service and the

Bush Veto Message on Hatch Act Revisions

Following is the June 15 memorandum of disapproval from President Bush saying that he would not sign the Hatch Act revisions bill (HR 20):

I am returning herewith without my approval HR 20, the "Hatch Reform Act Amendments of 1990." This bill would alter unacceptably the provisions of Federal law, commonly known as the Hatch Act, that bar Federal employees from active participation in partisan politics.

As one who has devoted much of his life to public service, I take great pride in the integrity of our Federal work force. Thus, to protect Federal employees from political pressure and preserve the impartial, evenhanded conduct of Government business, I am obligated to disapprove HR 20.

Originally enacted in 1939 as a bulwark against political coercion, the Hatch Act has successfully insulated the Federal service from the undue political influence that would destroy its essential political neutrality. It has been manifestly successful over the years in shielding civil servants, and the programs they administer, from political exploitation and abuse. The Hatch Act has upheld the integrity of the civil service by assuring that Federal employees are hired and promoted based upon their qualifications and not their political loyalties. It also has assured that Federal programs are administered in a nonpartisan manner, which is critical to maintaining the public's confidence and trust in the operations of Government.

HR 20 would effectively repeal the Hatch Act's essential prohibitions on partisan political activity by Federal civil servants. It also would convert the present rule that partisan politicking by Federal civil servants is prohibited, into a presumption that such partisan campaigning should be encouraged. Under this legislation, Federal employees would be able to participate actively in partisan political campaigns and hold official positions in political parties; actively endorse partisan political candidates in the public media; and solicit political contributions in most situations from other employees who are members of the same "employee labor organization" for that organization's political action committee. The obvious result of the enactment of HR 20 would be unstated but enormous pressure to participate in partisan political activity.

History shows that such a reversal in the role of partisan politics in the ethic of public service would inevitably lead to re-politicizing the Federal work force. The sanctions provided in the bill would add little if anything to the effectiveness of existing criminal prohibitions.

Moreover, experience with enforcement of criminal anti-patronage laws shows that the Federal criminal justice process is ill-suited to the task of protecting Federal employees from subtle political coercion. Public servants who are subjected to direct or indirect partisan political pressures understandably would often be reluctant to file criminal complaints against their superiors or peers, possibly putting their livelihoods in jeopardy. They deserve better protection than that.

Overt coercion is difficult enough by itself to guard against and detect. The more subtle forms of coercion are almost impossible to regulate, especially when they arise in a climate in which the unspoken assumption is that political conformity is the route to achievement and security. Such a climate leads inexorably to subtle, self-imposed pressures on employees to conform, or appear to conform, to whatever political tendency will assure greater job security.

After all the debate, no real need to repeal the existing Hatch Act has been demonstrated. Under present law, the Hatch Act allows Federal employees to engage in a variety of forms of political expression. Only forms of active participation on behalf of partisan political causes and candidates are barred. The Supreme Court has twice determined that these limits on active partisan political activity are constitutional. These rules provide reasonable balance between participation in the political process by Federal civil servants and the need to protect them from harassment and coercion that would jeopardize the fair and impartial operation of the Government. HR 20 poses a grave threat to that delicate balance.

Indeed, the lack of any grass-roots clamor for repeal of the Hatch Act either now, or at any time during its 50-year existence, testifies to the support this statute has received within the ranks of the Federal civil service and among the general public.

I am firmly convinced that any appreciable lessening of the current protections afforded to Federal civil servants by the Hatch Act will lead to the repoliticization of the civil service and of the programs it administers. We cannot afford, in the final decade of this century, to embark on a retreat into the very worst aspects of public administration from the last century. ■

National Security Council was also killed, 58-39. *(Vote 87, p. 20-S)*

HOUSE ACTION

A month after the Senate acted on the legislation, the House followed suit — despite the clear threat of a presidential veto.

Robert S. Walker, R-Pa., read on the House floor a letter stating Attorney General Thornburgh's "grave and unequivocal objections to HR 20." The bill, the letter said, "would permit virtually unbridled partisan activities by federal employees, which, history shows, would in turn inevitably lead to the politicization of public administration." Nevertheless, on a 334-87 vote, the House June 12 passed without amendment or conference the Senate version of HR 20, with 90 Republicans voting for it. *(Vote 163, p. 58-H)*

FINAL ACTION

True to his often-repeated word, President Bush vetoed the Hatch Act revisions on June 15, just three days after the House had cleared the measure. Bush said that "after all the debate, no real need to repeal the existing Hatch Act has been demonstrated."

Five days later, despite the partisan rhetoric from the White House and Senate Republicans, the House voted 327-93 to override Bush's veto. More House Republicans supported the measure than at any other time since legislation to revise the Hatch Act was introduced in 1975.

Among the Republicans voting to override was Minority Leader Robert H. Michel of Illinois. Michel's vote came as something of a surprise to Jeff Johnson, president of the Association of Letter Carriers' local chapter in Peoria, Ill., Michel's hometown. "Michel traditionally has a very poor voting record with us, 14 or 15 percent," Johnson said. "Most [Republicans] are not strong union supporters."

In Virginia and Maryland, home to thousands of federal workers who commute to jobs in metropolitan Washington, the measure found the eager support of most Republicans. Helen Delich Bentley and Constance A. Morella of Maryland supported the bill, as did Thomas J. Bliley Jr. and Stan Parris of Virginia.

But Republican opponents argued that there was little or no grass-roots support for the bill, merely union members who wanted to buy influence with PAC dollars.

Bush said in his veto message, "The lack of any grass-roots clamor for repeal for the Hatch Act... testifies to the support this statute has received within the ranks of the federal civil service and among the general public."

Even Maryland's Morella doubted that Republicans were convinced by rank-and-file federal workers or unions. Although her district had among the largest numbers of federal employees, she said, she got little direct pressure from constituents.

"I didn't get a lot of mail on the issue," she said. "With the rank and file, it was not one of the real biggies."

Federal workers were more concerned about such issues as health insurance reform, Morella said. "I don't think the revision of the Hatch Act would make any big difference in politics."

Back to the Senate

The House vote sent the measure back to the Senate where a close, bitter and contentious fight followed.

"A veto override is going to be a priority for this union," said Janice Lachance, a spokeswoman for the AFGE. "We're going to see if we can hold on to those 67 votes," she said before the override attempt.

Once again, the Senate debate became a partisan contest between Democrats, who argued that the bill was a civil rights issue, and Republican opponents, who countered that Democrats' support was based largely on their desire for PAC dollars.

Led by Dole, Republicans said federal workers' unions contributed most of their PAC dollars to Democrats. Republicans could only lose with passage of the bill, he said.

Dole said the postal carriers' union "helped hand out $769,000" in PAC money in 1989, with most of it going to Democrats. "They want to get [this passed] before this election," he said. "This is what they want, more power.... That's how it works around here. Money is power."

David Pryor, D-Ark., accused Republicans of strapping the federal worker with regulations they refused to live under themselves. Presidential appointees, including Sununu and Drug Policy Director William J. Bennett, regularly took part in partisan politics, campaigning for candidates, he said.

"The GS-5 government secretary who types letters should have at least the same rights as the secretary of Labor for whom she works," Pryor said in a pointed reference to Dole's wife, Labor Secretary Elizabeth H. Dole.

Federal employees once again demonstrated their strong presence in numerous states, a fact reflected in the bipartisan votes of some delegations.

George B. Gould, chief lobbyist for the American Association of Letter Carriers, denied that the bill would ultimately favor Democrats over Republicans. "We contribute to our friends. There's nothing mysterious about that," he said.

A good example, he said, was Sen. Ted Stevens, R-Alaska. "[He] has always supported us," Gould said.

Gould said he believed that most members from both houses voted for the measure simply on its merits. "I think we've gotten so cynical" in analyzing voting choices, he said. Gould pointed to states such as Mississippi, Alaska and New Mexico, which had few federal workers and whose senators voted for the measure before Bush's veto.

However, Pete Domenici of New Mexico was one of the three Republicans to change his earlier vote and support Bush in the June 21 vote. ■

Paperwork Reduction Renewal Stymied

Legislation (S 1742, HR 3695) to reauthorize the 1980 Paperwork Reduction Act (PL 96-511) failed to clear, falling victim to battles between Congress and the Bush administration over proposed restrictions on the Office of Management and Budget's (OMB) authority to review government regulations.

For much of the year, the administration strongly opposed provisions in both bills that would have limited control of OMB's Office of Information and Regulatory Affairs (OIRA) over the regulatory review process.

When a compromise finally was reached between the administration and Congress, there was only a week left in the session — too little time to overcome delays in the Senate.

OIRA funding was continued, however, within OMB's general appropriations fund.

The House passed HR 3695 by voice vote on Oct. 23. House backers of the legislation believed the Senate would quickly pass its version of the bill, which would then be accepted by the House.

But Senate action on the measure before adjournment was thwarted by several members, including Republican Phil Gramm of Texas, who placed holds on the bill, warning the leadership they would object to its consideration.

Meanwhile, the Supreme Court handed down early in the year an important ruling limiting OMB's power under the law.

Congressional critics of OMB hailed the ruling as a vindication of their criticisms. *(Court ruling, p. 412)*

BACKGROUND

The main goal of the 1980 Paperwork Reduction Act was to reduce, by 25 percent, the public's paperwork burden on such tasks as federal employment guidelines for small businesses, defense procurement contracts and even individual income tax forms. OIRA was created to review requests by federal agencies for information and to make sure that the information requested was necessary, that it could not be found elsewhere and that it was being collected efficiently. *(1980 Almanac, p. 528)*

The effect of the 1980 law was to give the executive branch — specifically the OIRA — growing control over the form and content of regulations issued by federal departments and agencies.

President Ronald Reagan issued a number of executive orders moving OMB toward increased regulatory oversight power. *(1981 Almanac, p. 404)*

The legislative and executive branches had fought for years for control of the regulatory process. Because the regulatory review power had accrued to OMB under Republican administrations, it particularly drew the ire of congressional Democrats.

Many Democrats resented OMB's OIRA, accusing it of

misusing its authority to review agency regulations by delaying proposed rules that the administration disagreed with and changing others to suit administration policy.

From 1983 to 1986, Congress withheld authorization of the OIRA. In 1986 leading House Democrats threatened to withhold OIRA's fiscal 1987 funding.

In the face of that threat, OIRA Director Wendy Lee Gramm agreed to make available to Congress and the public some of its review information, including correspondence between agency heads and the OIRA.

Congress renewed the OIRA's authorization through fiscal 1989. *(1986 Almanac, p. 325)*

But members of Congress continued to voice complaints about the OIRA. Some highly publicized cases included a delay and subsequent weakening of a regulation that would have required manufacturers to inform employees about toxic chemicals used in the workplace and an OIRA request that the Census Bureau drop one-third of the questions in the 1990 census.

LEGISLATIVE ACTION

In early 1990, some key lawmakers thought they had an agreement with the administration to pass a simple reauthorization for the OIRA in return for OMB's limiting its regulatory power. But the accord dissolved, and at year's end no bill had passed.

House Committee

In March 1990, House Government Operations Committee Chairman John Conyers Jr., D-Mich., and the ranking Republican on the panel, Frank Horton of New York, were sure they had reached agreement with OMB Director Richard G. Darman: If Congress approved a simple re-

OMB's Regulatory Review Powers Curbed

In a decision rendered on Feb. 21, the Supreme Court curbed the power of the Office of Management and Budget (OMB) to override health and safety disclosure regulations.

The decision was hailed by members of Congress who thought OMB exercised too much control over other agencies. The justices ruled, 7-2, that OMB had no authority under the Paperwork Reduction Act to block another agency's directive that businesses disclose health and safety data to their workers or the public.

The court said the law empowered OMB to review requests for data intended for government use but did not extend to regulations intended to generate information for the benefit of a third party.

The paperwork law (PL 96-511) had been a powerful tool in both Reagan and Bush administration efforts to rein in the federal regulatory process. OMB used the 1980 law to derail agency rules affecting workplace hazards, wood stoves and food labeling.

The case of *Dole v. United Steelworkers of America* involved a regulation from the Labor Department's Occupational Safety and Health Administration (OSHA) that required employers to make sure that their employees were told of potential hazards posed by chemicals at their workplace. The OSHA regulation at issue required employers to put warning labels on chemical containers, make available work sheets on hazardous chemicals, and train workers to understand and handle hazardous materials.

When OSHA first created the Health Communication Standard in 1983, it was confined to manufacturers; OMB approved the standard. But unions and consumers sued, and after a federal appellate court in 1987 ordered OSHA to extend the standard's coverage to other employers, OMB rejected OSHA's revised disclosure requirements. It said the requirements were not necessary to protect employees.

The Supreme Court affirmed the ruling of the 3rd U.S. Circuit Court of Appeals.

In the opinion written by Justice William J. Brennan Jr., the court said, "Because Congress expressed concern [in writing the paperwork law] only for the burden imposed by requirements to provide information to a federal agency, and not for any burden imposed by requirements to provide information to a third party, OMB review of disclosure rules would not further this congressional aim."

Joining Brennan were Justices Thurgood Marshall, Harry A. Blackmun, John Paul Stevens, Sandra Day O'Connor, Antonin Scalia and Anthony M. Kennedy.

In a dissenting opinion, Justice Byron R. White, joined by Chief Justice William H. Rehnquist, said that OMB for years had been reviewing proposals similar to the standard at issue in the case.

Rehnquist said the court should have given more deference to OMB's interpretation of its power under the paperwork law.

House Government Operations Committee Chairman John Conyers Jr., D-Mich., called the court's decision an "overwhelming reaffirmation of Congress' original intention" in passing the paperwork law.

"This is a victory for all Americans who have suffered — or perhaps lost their lives — over the last 10 years as a result of the Reagan and Bush administrations' denial or gutting of information needed to protect the public's health," said Conyers.

OMB officials testifying before the Senate Governmental Affairs Committee when the court ruling was announced declined to speculate on its effect, and an OMB spokesman said later that the agency would have no comment on the decision.

Gary Bass, executive director of OMB Watch, a private watchdog group, commented that the ruling "greatly limits OMB's authority," but that the agency still "has an arsenal of weapons."

He cited Reagan-era executive orders that required all agencies to submit proposed regulations to OMB for cost-benefit analysis and for a determination of whether they were consistent with the president's policies.

The two government operations committees were working on a reauthorization of the Paperwork Reduction Act when the court's decision was handed down, but the bills stalled at the end of the session in an impasse between Congress and the administration.

authorization for the OIRA, OMB would agree to limit its regulatory power.

Conyers' panel approved HR 3695, a three-year reauthorization of the OIRA, on March 13 without the limitations on OMB (H Rept 101-927). Instead, the restrictions negotiated by Conyers, Horton and Darman were spelled out in an administrative agreement separate from the legislation, to become effective when the reauthorization became law.

The agreement called for the OIRA to provide, in writing, a detailed explanation of the reasons for all substantive changes in proposed regulations and would have set deadlines for the OIRA's review of regulations.

The House bill contained provisions requiring the OIRA to make available to the public an explanation of any decision to change a regulatory paperwork proposal. It also would have limited the OIRA's ability to overrule agency decisions on rulemaking.

Both of these provisions were opposed by the White House, but House backers of the measure believed they had a deal with the administration.

But, on April 5, as leaders of the House committee were preparing to take HR 3695 to the floor, White House Chief of Staff John H. Sununu met with Conyers to raise several questions about the agreement. In a subsequent letter to Conyers, White House legal counsel C. Boyden Gray said the administration would not back the deal.

Senate Committee

At the same time, the Senate Governmental Affairs Committee was encountering difficulty in marking up S 1742, which, unlike HR 3695, contained many restrictions on the OIRA. Republicans on the Senate panel objected to the restrictions and boycotted a scheduled April 5 markup.

The sponsor of S 1742, Jeff Bingaman, D-N.M., argued that the agreement between the House panel and Darman would be unenforceable.

S 1742 would have given OMB 60 days to review proposed regulations and would have given the OIRA the right to review regulations only if it found the agency's request for information and consequent paperwork demands unreasonable or incomplete.

Finally, on June 7 the Senate Governmental Affairs Committee approved S 1742 by a 14-0 vote, after narrowly defeating an amendment that backers said would have gutted the bill (S Rept 101-487).

The amendment, defeated on a 7-7 tie, would have eliminated provisions requiring OMB to make information dealing with regulatory reviews available to the public. Republicans, joined by Democrat Sam Nunn, Ga., backed the amendment, claiming that the disclosure requirement would interfere with the president's ability to run the executive branch.

The Senate bill included provisions, insisted upon by Nunn, that were designed to protect small businesses from any increase in paperwork that the legislation might create.

Floor Action

After the legislation had languished for several months, the administration and key members of Congress finally agreed to another compromise during the last week of the session: Administration officials and Senate Governmental Affairs Committee leaders reached a handshake deal over control of OMB's regulatory rulemaking oversight. The administration promised to rein in its own regulatory power if Congress agreed not to write restrictions into law. Senate panel leaders agreed to bring a stripped-down version of S 1742 to the floor.

Believing that final action was at hand, the House passed HR 3695 by voice vote Oct. 23 after about 15 minutes of debate.

The administration agreement would have required some notification when the OIRA was considering a new regulation, would have required the OIRA to explain why it changed a proposed rule and would have set limits on the amount of time the agency had to review regulations.

On Oct. 24, OMB released a statement saying that the administration "strongly supports" the Senate bill containing a straightforward, four-year reauthorization of the OIRA. But several Republican senators placed anonymous holds on the measure during the final days of the session and the bill died.

Another casualty of the last-minute holds was the nomination of Vanderbilt University law Professor James F. Blumstein to head the OIRA. The job was vacant after the Oct. 1, 1989, departure of S. Jay Plager and James B. MacRae served as acting director.

The Governmental Affairs Committee endorsed Blumstein's nomination on a 5-3 vote on Oct. 26, but without any great enthusiasm. The nomination was not formally reported to the full Senate before adjournment.

Leaders of the panel had made it clear there would be no action on the nomination unless the legislation cleared. S 1742 contained provisions spelling out in more detail the qualifications of background and knowledge required of the director of the OIRA and congressional leaders wanted to consider the appointment in the context of the new qualifications. ■

Guidelines on Regulatory Negotiation

Acting by voice vote, the House on Oct. 22 agreed to Senate amendments and cleared for the president a bill that sought to promote a procedure whereby parties with an interest in a federal regulation could come together in a negotiation session.

President Bush signed the measure (S 303 — PL 101-648) Nov. 29.

The bill gave explicit authority to a procedure known as regulatory negotiation and established so-called reg-neg guidelines for agencies and affected outside parties when both agreed to work together in drawing up regulations. By providing a framework by which interested parties and regulatory agencies could negotiate rules together, the measure sought to limit costly litigation and other delays caused by legal challenges and resistance to regulations.

Rep. Don J. Pease, D-Ohio, sponsor of the bill, said the measure was "aimed at providing an alternative to the present adversarial rulemaking process by establishing an optional procedure through which interested parties could negotiate a compromise rule."

The bill did not supersede the practiced method of rulemaking, whereby agencies solicited commentary and information on a proposed rule for study and consideration before issuing a final rule.

It did define, however, conditions under which negotiated rulemaking might be appropriate.

The measure authorized the Administrative Conference of the United States (ACUS) — an agency charged with studying and recommending improvements in federal administration and legal procedures — to serve as an information clearinghouse and adviser to agencies and parties participating in negotiated rulemaking procedures. The bill also authorized $500,000 for the ACUS annually for three years.

In a related matter, the House on Oct. 26 cleared HR 2497 to authorize federal agencies to use alternative dispute resolution techniques, including settlement negotiations, mediation, "mini-trials" and arbitration, to resolve administrative disputes.

Proponents said alternative dispute resolutions could be faster, cheaper and less contentious than court battles. The use of such alternatives to litigation would be voluntary for both parties under the legislation (PL 101-552) signed by Bush on Nov. 15.

The Senate had passed an amended version of the bill Oct. 25. The House originally passed the measure June 5, four days after the Judiciary Committee reported the bill (H Rept 101-513).

BACKGROUND

The most widely used method of rulemaking by federal regulatory agencies had been the 1946 Administrative Procedure Act (APA). Under this statute, an agency published in the Federal Register a draft of a proposed regulation and provided an opportunity for public comment. After reviewing responses, the agency made revisions and promulgated a final rule.

Over time, additional requirements were imposed upon agencies to ensure that federal rules were not capricious or arbitrary.

Agencies were held accountable for their actions by a formal record of materials used for rulemaking decisions. Agencies challenged on a rule and unable to justify their decisions in light of their record could face judicial intervention and have their rules altered or stricken.

The rulemaking process led to adversarial relationships among agencies and affected parties. Some interested parties tried to skew the record in their favor by taking extreme positions and withholding relevant information. Also the process offered little opportunity for direct communication, exchange of information and expertise, and compromise among affected parties and agencies.

In 1982, the Administrative Conference published a report endorsing the process of negotiated rulemaking between interested parties and federal regulatory agencies. Several agencies subsequently adopted the ACUS's conclusions and tried negotiations in the rulemaking process.

The 100th Congress began passing legislation containing reg-neg provisions on an ad hoc basis, but deferred enactment of governmentwide negotiated rulemaking legislation to permit individual agencies to experiment with the procedure.

In 1988, the Senate passed S 1504, a version of reg-neg legislation, but the measure died in the House. Sen. Carl Levin, D-Mich., introduced S 303 on Jan. 31, 1989, a revised version of S 1504. On July 13, the Governmental Affairs Committee passed the measure (S Rept 101-97) and the full Senate passed it by voice vote Aug. 3.

House Action

The House took action on its version of the reg-neg bill (HR 743) in early 1990. The Judiciary Subcommittee on Administrative Law and Governmental Relations on Feb. 7 approved the bill after adopting an amendment to provide that a notice of the formation of a negotiated rulemaking committee — composed of representatives of each interested party — be placed in trade and specialty journals in addition to the Federal Register.

On March 28, the Judiciary Committee ordered the bill reported favorably as passed in subcommittee (H Rept 101-461).

The House then passed HR 743 on May 1 by a vote of 411-0. After passing the legislation, the House inserted the text of the bill into S 303 and passed it by voice vote. *(Vote 86, p. 32-H)*

Senate Action

The Senate on Oct. 4 took up the bill as passed by the House, adopting several amendments by Ted Stevens, R-Alaska, aimed at better notifying residents in rural states.

The amendments stipulated, among other things, language requiring the publication in trade and specialty journals of decisions not to proceed with negotiated rulemaking committees and a requirement that agencies notify applicants or nominees to such a committee of their decision not to proceed with the committee.

The Senate passed the amended bill by voice vote and returned it to the House, which concurred with the Senate amendments Oct. 22, clearing the bill for the president. ■

Pacts on Fund Transfers

Acting on voice vote, the Senate on Oct. 10 cleared legislation (HR 4279) designed to eliminate friction between the states and the federal government over the transfers of money to states for funding grant programs.

The bill, signed by President Bush on Oct. 24 (PL 101-453), gave the Treasury secretary authority to negotiate state-by-state agreements on how cash would be transferred.

States choosing to receive funds in advance would have to make annual interest payments to the federal government.

A state would be owed interest by the federal government if it had to advance funds for a federal grant program.

Federal officials had complained that states often withdrew funds before they needed them and put them in interest-bearing accounts. Existing law did not require states to account for the interest earned.

Many states, in turn, contended that the federal government was often late in reimbursing states for money advanced for use in federal programs.

The bill had been cosponsored by House Government Operations Committee Chairman John Conyers Jr., D-Mich., and ranking Republican Frank Horton, N.Y., and approved by the committee Aug. 2 (H Rept 101-696).

The House passed the bill, 410-4, on Sept. 24. *(Vote 362, p. 118-H)* ■

Cities Fault Census for Undercount

The official 1990 census results pegged the national population at 249,632,692 — an increase of more than 23 million people (10.2 percent) over the 1980 total.

The final tally, released Dec. 26, added about 4 million people to the preliminary fall numbers issued by the Census Bureau. Bureau Director Barbara Everitt Bryant said the final number depicted an increase in many cities that had complained about undercounts. The Commerce Department said it would decide by July 15, 1991, whether to use its authority to adjust the census tally to correct for undercounting.

Rural areas, a comeback story in the 1970s, experienced renewed deterioration in the '80s. Big cities, braced for bad news, were nonetheless disturbed at the magnitude of their decline. Mayor David N. Dinkins of New York called the head count for his city "unadulterated nonsense."

State and local governments had perhaps the greatest stake in an accurate count of each person within their borders. Apart from determining political representation, that head count fit into sometimes complex formulas for the distribution of federal funds.

The fiscal 1991 spending bill for the State, Commerce and Justice departments appropriated $383 million for the Census Bureau, $48.4 million less than requested by the administration. The fiscal 1990 supplemental spending bill appropriated $110 million to cover expenses related to the lower-than-expected response rates for the 1990 count; the bureau had already received $1.42 billion in fiscal 1990.

Background

The decennial census, a mandate of the Constitution, by 1990 had become far more than a method to count people and reapportion congressional districts. To many observers, it was the crank that ran the nation's information machine. *(Reapportionment and redistricting, p. 930)*

State and local governments tapped the information to plan for child-care and transportation needs; the Pentagon used it to search out areas ripe for U.S. armed forces recruitment. Congress, for its part, required agencies to use census information to distribute federal aid to state and local governments — about $31 billion in fiscal 1989.

"It's hard to think about anyone not being concerned about the census," said Katherine Wallman, executive director of the Association of Data Users.

The U.S. Census Bureau, a division of the Commerce Department, spent much of 1990 in the throes of counting the U.S. population for the 21st time since the founding of the Union. Director Bryant said earlier in the year that when the monumental effort was completed it would be a good census — though it would also carry a big price tag.

Bryant's assurances did not quiet critics in Congress and across the nation who called the initiative bungled and inept. "The Census Bureau has not been able to adapt to America 1990," said Rep. Charles E. Schumer, D-N.Y.

The preliminary population figures — released by the Census Bureau on Aug. 29 — featured unpleasant surprises for some. Many government officials were upset with the low counts in their states or cities and argued that the bureau had failed to perform its job adequately.

After their release, the preliminary population figures were subjected to four months of tabulation, review and legal challenges. They were mailed by the Census Bureau to 39,000 state and local governments, which had three weeks to provide evidence of error or omission by census enumerators.

"The local governments have a real opportunity to have an impact," said Kimball W. Brace of Election Data Services. "Because a little work on their part now in local review and finding people the Census Bureau has missed can go a long way in swinging some of these [congressional] seats."

An undercount was nothing new. In 1980, the Census Bureau estimated that it counted about 99 percent of the white population but only about 94 percent of blacks.

Calls for an adjusted count were not new either. Several cities with large minority populations sought but failed to win adjustment of the 1980 census count.

The latest debate began in 1987, when the Commerce Department announced that it would not adjust the 1990 count. That fueled charges that the Republican administration was undercounting a Democratic constituency. It was not long before a lawsuit was brought by New York City (along with other cities, states and civil rights groups) calling on the Census Bureau to make a statistical adjustment of the tally to account for people who were missed.

In response to the lawsuit, the Commerce Department in 1989 agreed to defer a final judgment on the adjustment question until as late as mid-July 1991.

Early in 1990, the plaintiffs in the New York City case reopened their lawsuit in an effort to get the Commerce Department to draft new guidelines that would require the department to adjust the count in 1991, unless it could demonstrate that a statistical change would not be more accurate than the actual tally.

In something of a split decision, a federal district court in New York ruled June 7 that an adjustment would be constitutional and that the Commerce Department would "clearly incur a heavier burden" to explain an anti-adjustment decision in 1991. But Judge Joseph M. McLaughlin also ruled that the Commerce Department's guidelines on the matter were not inadequate or biased.

State and Local Interests

After a decade of cuts in federal aid for housing, employment and other programs, no state wanted to be short shrifted in a national reckoning that would provide the basis for federal allocations over the next 10 years.

As a result, local officials were the most critical of the 1990 census effort. Big-city mayors such as New York's Dinkins and Houston's Kathy Whitmire worried that undercounting, particularly of hard-to-reach minority groups, would mean big losses in federal funds.

The General Accounting Office, an investigative agency of Congress, estimated that 100 federal programs were doled out in part on the basis of census population data, including job training funds, Community Development Block Grants and Head Start. The Medicaid Assistance Program relied on per capita income data from the census to distribute 50 percent of its funds.

Members of Congress expected federal funds to follow population shifts from the Northeast and Midwest to the Sun Belt states. With undercounts in inner-city areas, that drop in funds could be exacerbated; Schumer said New

York City could lose more than $1 billion in federal aid because the census enumerators were passing by many people, particularly illegal aliens.

Other followers of the census, though, said the problem was overstated.

"There tends to be an exaggerated view of the importance of census data for federal aid," said Richard P. Nathan, provost of Rockefeller College of Public Affairs at the State University of New York and a researcher on state and local census issues. "Most of the big federal programs are open-ended matching grants."

States that lost population actually would gain money under other programs, such as Community Development Block Grants, he said.

In addition, some federal programs offset population data with other factors, such as per capita income, or, in the case of transportation funding, a state's share of public road mileage. These factors could mitigate the impact of population losses on federal funds.

Response Problems

The problem, as Bryant told Congress on April 19, was that of the 106 million census questionnaires sent out by the bureau, only 63 percent were filled out and returned.

Starting April 26, census enumerators visited households that did not respond; because of the low response rate, they had to visit many more than had been expected. The mail-in response rate for the 1980 count was 75 percent, and the bureau budgeted for a 70 percent response rate in 1990. Bryant said the dropoff generally seemed to be across the board, rather than confined to certain areas.

To improve the accuracy of the 1990 count, the Census Bureau said it had put 90 percent of its promotional effort into reaching the 10 percent of the population that was most difficult to count. The bureau said it was involving more organizations, cities and people than ever before in the tally.

Bryant estimated that each 1 percentage point shortfall in the targeted mail response rate increased follow-up costs by $10 million.

If the response rate stayed at 63 percent, or 7 percentage points below the target, about $70 million more would be needed. For each percentage point of the population that failed to send back the questionnaire, enumerators had to visit an additional 950,000 households, meaning census workers would have had to knock on 35.2 million doors to complete their constitutional mandate.

Critics of the 1990 effort pointed to numerous incidents and tactics to explain some of the bureau's problems.

Schumer said the bureau refused to use city data to help find residents who were doubled-up in public housing against regulations and might have been eager to avoid census-takers.

Schumer also complained that many residents who did not speak English probably did not respond because they had received questionnaires written in English and had to call a toll-free number to get one in another language.

Bureau spokesman Peter A. Bounpane said Schumer neglected to mention many changes the bureau had made at the city's request, including giving localities more review of census maps. Bounpane also said census improvements in 1990 included a new foreign-language pre-mailing. ■

Financial Centralization

Legislation cleared in the final hours of the session created a centralized financial management system within the federal government. The aim of the measure was to improve the government's financial management practices and to prevent waste, fraud and abuse.

The House, which originally passed the bill (HR 5687) by voice vote on Oct. 15, cleared it in the early hours of Oct. 28 (session of Oct. 27) by accepting amendments the Senate made in passing the bill Oct. 26. President Bush signed the bill on Nov. 15 (PL 101-576).

The bill's principal sponsor, House Government Operations Committee Chairman John Conyers Jr., D-Mich., said the measure would guard against future cases of mismanagement by creating "a means by which Congress can hold agencies more accountable for how their money gets spent — and how it gets wasted."

Conyers said that government studies had "identified 78 different problems which potentially pose hundreds of billions of more dollars in liabilities." The Government Operations Committee approved the bill on Oct. 6 by voice vote (H Rept 101-818, Part I). The Government Operations Subcommittee on Legislation and National Security had approved the measure Sept. 25. The bill was jointly referred to the Committee on Post Office and Civil Service, which discharged it Oct. 10.

Sen. John Glenn, D-Ohio, had introduced companion legislation (S 2840), but the Senate Governmental Affairs Committee never acted upon it.

As enacted, the bill established a deputy director of mangagement at the Office of Management and Budget (OMB). It split the position of the assistant to the director at OMB into a deputy director for budget and a deputy director for management — who, Glenn said, "will be responsible for the 'M' in OMB."

In addition, the bill created statutory chief financial officers at 14 executive departments and nine federal agencies as well as an Office of Federal Financial Management at OMB, to be headed by a controller.

According to a House committee aide, the new financial management scheme would merge the government's budgeting and accounting functions and enable cost-comparisons across agencies.

The law required that OMB report to Congress annually on the status of financial management along with a five-year plan for improving management operations. By the end of 1991, agencies were to be required to start issuing annual audited financial statements.

Among the changes lawmakers made to the bill during negotiations was a compromise to expand the scope of its provisions to include more agencies.

The Bush administration had preferred comprehensive legislation that would have required all agencies to produce financial statements accounting for all their activities. As enacted, the bill authorized agencywide, two-year pilot projects for some agencies and for others a "go-slow approach" requiring financial statements only "where the problems are — in real estate transactions, loans and loan guarantees, trust funds and revolving funds," said Conyers.

Congress was to vote on expanding the program to all agencies after reviewing an OMB cost-analysis report on the program scheduled for 1993. ■

Hill Cracks Down on Deceptive Mailings

The House on Oct. 19 cleared legislation to curb the use of potentially deceptive mailings by advertisers and fund-raisers.

Acting on a voice vote, the House accepted Senate amendments to a bill sponsored by Frank McCloskey, D-Ind., chairman of the House Post Office Subcommittee on Postal Operations and Services.

President Bush signed the measure Nov. 6 (HR 2331 — PL 101-524).

The Senate had passed its version of the legislation (S 273) on Oct. 4 by voice vote.

The measure was designed to stop solicitations, especially for the elderly, made to look like federal checks or other correspondence. The U.S. Postal Service could not deliver such "deceptive" mail unless it carried an insignia advising the recipient that the product or service was not endorsed by the federal government.

The bill required commercial mailings that contained any symbols, insignias or seals that could imply a federal government connection to be disposed of by the Postal Service unless it bore a disclaimer such as: "THIS PRODUCT OR SERVICE HAS NOT BEEN APPROVED OR ENDORSED BY THE FEDERAL GOVERNMENT, AND THIS OFFER IS NOT BEING MADE BY AN AGENCY OF THE FEDERAL GOVERNMENT."

Envelopes containing such solicitations would be required to carry — also in capital letters — the legend: "THIS IS NOT A GOVERNMENT DOCUMENT."

Lawmakers expected that the bill would apply to such mailings as a "national medical census" sent out in 1988 to raise funds for the National Kidney Foundation and a come-on for vacation homes that came in an envelope bearing "Internal Review Service, Accounting Department" as its return address.

One group, the National Committee to Preserve Social Security and Medicare, employed such attention-grabbing phrases as "time-dated legal documents" on envelopes addressed to senior citizens.

The original House bill, passed on July 31, 1989, would have given the Postal Service eight months to review its procedure for declaring items "non-mailable." *(1989 Almanac, p. 368)*

The final bill incorporated language in the Senate bill written by David Pryor, D-Ark., chairman of the Governmental Affairs subcommittee that oversaw the U.S. Postal Service, to make the bill effective within 180 days. ■

Anti-Porn Mail Bill Shelved

Unable to untangle the constitutional questions on proposed legislation to impose civil fines on mailers of sexually explicit advertisements, the House Post Office and Civil Service Committee on June 21 sent the bill back to subcommittee where the measure languished and died.

The Subcommittee on Postal Personnel and Modernization had approved the bill (HR 3805) on March 27 and deadlocked over language to subject pornographic mailers to civil penalties of $500 to $1,500 for each violation.

Under existing law, companies were prohibited from mailing pornographic materials to households that had requested that the U.S. Postal Service place them on a list designed to shield them from unwanted mail. But that law did not specifically call for civil penalties.

Testimony before the subcommittee in 1989 indicated that lax enforcement by the Justice Department and the Postal Service had allowed companies to continue sending mailings touting X-rated videos and other pornographic materials to people who did not want them and who had specifically asked that those materials not be delivered to their homes.

"HR 3805 would put teeth into the current statutes regarding the mailing of pornographic materials," said subcommittee Chairman Charles A. Hayes, D-Ill. "Mailers would certainly think twice before arbitrarily mailing their materials to those households."

The constitutional question arose when Tom Ridge, R-Pa., submitted an amendment that would also have imposed civil penalties on companies or individuals who mailed unsolicited sexually oriented advertisements, regardless of whether the ads were obscene. The Justice Department told the committee that the amendment was too broad and would be found unconstitutional.

In a letter to the committee, the Justice Department said there were sexually oriented advertisements that solicited for "entirely lawful materials" on sex education, reproduction science or sexual disease.

The bill, sponsored by committee member Frank McCloskey, D-Ind., also would have removed the $10,000 price tag the Postal Service charged advertisers who wanted a copy of the restricted mailing list. McCloskey said most companies had refused to pay to get the list. ■

Kid-Proof Packaging OK'd

Congress on Oct. 16 cleared legislation to prevent the mailing of any unsolicited sample of a drug or other hazardous household substances that did not meet child-resistant packaging requirements.

The bill (HR 5209 — PL 101-493) passed the Senate by voice vote Oct. 16 after being amended and passed by the House by voice vote Oct. 1.

President Bush signed the measure Oct. 31.

The legislation, effective 180 days after its enactment, authorized the U.S. Postal Service to dispose of improperly packaged samples. Lawmakers said the Postal Service supported the legislation.

Rep. Frank McCloskey, D-Ind., sponsored the bill and said it was designed to prevent children from ingesting medicine and household product samples received through the mail.

McCloskey served on the Post Office and Civil Service Committee, which reported the legislation (H Rept 101-758) on Sept. 26. The bill had been approved for full committee action on Sept. 25 by the Subcommittee on Postal Operations and Services. ■

Agent Orange Again Stalls Vets' Bill

A floor challenge to Agent Orange provisions in the Senate's omnibus veterans' health package proved to be the death of House and Senate bills in 1990 that would have provided a significant cost of living increase for veterans. As a result, only one significant piece of veterans legislation — a nurses' pay bill — cleared Congress in 1990.

House Veterans' Affairs Committee Chairman G. V. "Sonny" Montgomery, D-Miss., blamed the Senate for Congress' inaction, saying the House had sent 11 bills to the Senate. Senate Veterans' Affairs Committee Chairman Alan Cranston, D-Calif., accused Republicans of preventing action on legislation by constantly raising objections.

With national attention riveted on U.S. military forces in the Persian Gulf, Congress in January 1991 hastened to approve the 5.4 percent cost of living adjustment (COLA) for disabled veterans. The bill (HR 3) moved quickly after members agreed to push through separate legislation (HR 556) ensuring that veterans suffering from exposure to Agent Orange would get disability compensation.

Both chambers passed the bills unanimously, and President Bush signed them Feb. 6, 1991 (COLA, PL 102-3; Agent Orange, PL 102-4). The bipartisan compromise marked the first time in more than a decade that House and Senate committee leaders agreed that the government should compensate veterans exposed to Agent Orange for specific illnesses. The chemical defoliant, used in Vietnam, had been linked to some forms of cancer.

The bills provided the COLA for veterans suffering from service-connected disabilities and for survivors of veterans who died of service-related injuries. The bills also codified decisions by the Department of Veterans Affairs (VA) to provide permanent benefits to Vietnam veterans suffering from two forms of cancer and "chloracne," a skin ailment associated with the spraying of Agent Orange.

The House had passed its COLA bill (HR 5326) by voice vote Oct. 15. S 2100, the Senate omnibus bill, died at the close of the session when Republicans Alan K. Simpson of Wyoming and Frank H. Murkowski of Alaska objected to its Agent Orange provisions.

BACKGROUND

Congress in 1989 cleared a wide-ranging bill (HR 901 — PL 101-237) providing health, education and home-loan benefits to veterans. The measure bundled a number of veterans' bills passed during the year by one chamber or the other.

Dropped from the final version, however, and left for continuing discussions in 1990 were the Senate-passed provisions to provide disability benefits to certain victims of Agent Orange and House-passed provisions to allow VA medical centers to set competitive salary levels for nurses. *(1989 Almanac, p. 361)*

The issues that held up the legislation demonstrated that the Vietnam War, which 20 years before had fomented a war at home between generations, continued to divide members of Congress who had to deal with the battlefield's wrenching aftermath.

The focal point was Agent Orange, the chemical defoliant sprayed so extensively in Southeast Asian jungles that many American soldiers were exposed to its potentially toxic properties — to as yet uncertain effects.

Thousands of Vietnam veterans had sought federal veterans' compensation benefits based on claims that their exposure to Agent Orange resulted in various forms of cancer. Their claims went nowhere under the Reagan administration, which maintained that a causal link between Agent Orange and cancer could not be established.

The Senate in 1989 passed legislation (S 1153) to expand compensation for veterans, and Rep. Lane Evans, D-Ill., in 1990 pushed a companion bill, HR 3004. The Evans bill, though, remained bottled up in the Veterans' Affairs Committee throughout much of 1990.

Evans' bill would have provided for a presumption of service connection for five diseases suffered by Vietnam veterans: non-Hodgkins lymphoma (NHL), soft-tissue sarcoma, melanoma, basal cell carcinoma and chloracne. Under the bill, the VA secretary could include additional diseases based on the findings of independent reviews of pertinent studies.

The key opponent of the bill was committee Chairman Montgomery. Aides said Montgomery wanted decisions on compensation to be "made by the experts," not legislators.

Unlike its predecessor, the Bush administration early in its term signaled a willingness to consider Agent Orange cancer claims, but VA Secretary Edward J. Derwinski later hedged that possibility with an announcement Nov. 24, 1989, that his decision would await the results of a study by the federal Centers for Disease Control (CDC) due in early 1990.

Derwinski's Decisions

Ironically, despite a report released early in 1990 that the CDC could find no causal link between cancer and exposure to Agent Orange, Derwinski announced March 29 that the VA would compensate Vietnam veterans who were sufferers of NHL and soft-tissue sarcoma; the VA had issued a 1985 decision to compensate for chloracne.

A panel of scientists assembled by the American Legion, the Vietnam Veterans of America and the National Veterans Legal Services Project released a study May 1 that sharply disagreed with the CDC findings. Their report linked Agent Orange to at least eight disease categories in Vietnam veterans.

Derwinski decided on May 18 to compensate Vietnam veterans who suffered from soft-tissue sarcomas, a group of cancers. As a result, about 1,100 veterans or their survivors were expected to receive compensation, at a projected cost of $8 million a year.

Meanwhile, the VA on May 2 asked members of the House Veterans' Affairs Subcommittee on Compensation to postpone until October consideration of Agent Orange legislation so the department could complete its regulations for compensating Vietnam veterans who suffered from NHL.

Bill sponsor Evans said that Vietnam veterans had already waited long enough and that the committee should not hold off until October.

HR 3004 sought to provide for "statutory presumptions of service connection" and require compensation to Vietnam veterans exposed to the herbicide who suffered from chloracne, NHL, soft-tissue sarcoma, melanoma and basal cell carcinoma.

The bill would also have required the VA to contract

with a non-governmental scientific organization to conduct independent reviews of pertinent studies on Agent Orange and submit their findings to the secretary. Under the bill, the secretary could compensate veterans for additional diseases, based on findings from the organizations.

AGENT ORANGE DEBATE

As it had in the past, debate over Agent Orange provisions dominated, and eventually stalled, efforts to pass veterans' legislation in 1990. While the House passed its bill Oct. 15, it could not reach agreement with the Senate, leaving the matter to be handled in early 1991.

Committee Action

The Senate Veterans' Affairs Committee on July 12 approved S 2100 (S Rept 101-379) by voice vote. The omnibus bill would have provided physicians at VA hospitals with pay increases and exempted veterans' medical care dollars from across-the-board cuts under the Gramm-Rudman antideficit law.

The House Veterans' Affairs Compensation Subcommittee approved HR 5326 on July 26 by voice vote but voted 6-4 to delete the Agent Orange provision. Evans, sponsor of HR 3004 from which the provision was drawn, argued that the government was "morally obligated" to compensate the Vietnam veterans.

In deleting the Agent Orange provision, the subcommittee substituted a provision by Timothy J. Penny, D-Minn., that would have required the VA to set up a system to keep tissue archives for all veterans exposed to Agent Orange.

The Penny provision would have allowed the National Academy of Sciences (NAS) to be the "one last authority" on the link between Agent Orange and cancer. The NAS also would have to organize within a year a medical conference "to resolve this issue," Penny said.

The full Veterans' Affairs Committee gave voice vote approval to HR 5326 on Oct. 12 and reattached the controversial Agent Orange provision. The amendment was adopted on a tight 16-14 vote, with Montgomery and ranking Republican Bob Stump of Arizona voting against it.

"Congress should not legislatively establish presumptions of service connection ... until convincing scientific evidence is confirmed," Stump said. Other members objected to the bill language that Congress found "sufficient scientific evidence" to presume a connection between the diseases and Agent Orange.

Floor Action

On Oct. 27, the final full day of the 101st Congress, the battle over Agent Orange provisions killed HR 5326 — and with it, a 5.4 percent COLA for certain veterans. According to the VA, the defeat marked the first time Congress had failed to pass such an increase in the same year in which it granted increases to Social Security recipients.

Montgomery made an eleventh-hour attempt to push through a substitute bill (HR 5962) without the Agent Orange provisions he opposed. But his request for "unanimous consent" to bring up the bill was thwarted on the House floor when Ted Weiss, D-N.Y., a longtime advocate of compensation for victims of Agent Orange, objected.

The House had passed an earlier version of HR 5326 on Oct. 15 by voice vote with the Agent Orange provision.

Meanwhile, in the Senate, Simpson and Murkowski for weeks stymied action on an omnibus health package (S 2100) over similar Agent Orange provisions, which senators had overwhelmingly approved in 1989.

Montgomery long opposed any compensation for veterans suffering from ailments linked to exposure to the chemical, arguing that there was no scientific evidence proving a definite link. For the past four years, Montgomery had successfully blocked efforts by Evans to push Agent Orange legislation through the Veterans' Affairs Committee.

Montgomery continued to oppose the inclusion of the Agent Orange amendment in the House, while Simpson, who had worked closely with Montgomery during his years as Senate Veterans' Affairs chairman, opposed similar provisions in the Senate bill.

When Congress adjourned without passing a COLA increase for disabled veterans, Montgomery immediately blamed Weiss. A news release from the House committee referred to Weiss as "the New York Congressman" who had killed the COLA.

Veterans' organizations, however, hailed Weiss' last-minute move. "What Ted Weiss did was heroic and positive as we look forward to next year," said Paul S. Egan, legislative director for the Vietnam Veterans of America. "Our hat's off to him."

American Legion officials agreed. "We support what he was doing in regard to Agent Orange legislation," said legislative director Philip Riggin. "Ted Weiss is not a bystander in this thing."

OTHER VETERANS' ISSUES

Congress acted on a number of veterans' bills in 1990, though only one cleared — an increase in the salaries for nurses employed by VA hospitals. Other issues that the 101st Congress dealt with, but failed to resolve, included veterans' housing needs, VA recruitment and retention of medical personnel, establishment of medical research grants and improved disability pay.

Competitive Salaries

Acting on a voice vote, the House on Aug. 3 cleared for the president a bill (HR 1199) to make salaries for nurses employed by VA hospitals competitive with local labor markets. HR 1199 was the only significant piece of veterans' legislation that became law in 1990.

The Senate passed the measure on Aug. 2, also by voice vote. President Bush signed the bill into law (PL 101-366) on Aug. 15.

Sponsored by Rep. Joseph P. Kennedy II, D-Mass., the bill would affect the salaries of about 35,000 registered nurses and nurse anesthetists. It required the VA to use data from the Bureau of Labor Statistics to determine local salaries. In small communities where data was not available, the bill required local VA medical centers to conduct a survey of area nursing salaries and set wages competitive with the market.

The House had originally passed HR 1199 on June 27, 1989. The Senate in 1989 included similar nursing pay provisions in an omnibus veterans bill (S 13), but the provisions were dropped in conference.

In 1990, the House on May 1 passed by voice vote a related bill (HR 4557) to raise the salaries of VA physicians, dentists and nurses. The bill would have allowed VA hospital administrators to give "special pay" to health professionals in areas in which federal salary levels were not competitive. The bill also included the nursing pay provisions from HR 1199.

Montgomery said the bill was designed to address the "crisis in recruiting and retaining physicians and dentists" because of low salary scales in VA hospitals.

The House Veterans' Affairs Committee had approved HR 4557 on April 26.

Veterans' Housing Needs

In an attempt to deal with veterans' housing needs, the House on July 16 passed HR 5002. The House Veterans' Affairs Committee approved the measure on June 27, one week after its Subcommittee on Housing and Memorial Affairs had approved it.

The bill contained a number of provisions, including one to require the VA secretary to establish a three-year program of transitional housing for participants in the Compensated Work Therapy program, a rehabilitative program for veterans with psychological or physical problems.

Funds to establish the temporary housing units would have come from the discretionary General Post Fund. The VA also could have provided loans of up to $4,500 to assist nonprofit organizations in leasing housing units for group residences for veterans with substance abuse problems.

The measure would have authorized mortgage payment assistance up to $10,000 to help veterans avoid foreclosure of their home loans guaranteed by the VA. The provision — which had been a free-standing bill (HR 5069) and was added to HR 5002 in subcommittee — would also have authorized the VA secretary to provide a demonstration program of transition housing for people enrolled in the VA's work-therapy programs.

Another provision of HR 5002 would have entitled individuals who had served in the National Guard or the reserves for at least six years to be eligible for the VA's Home Loan Guaranty program.

The government, however, would not make a contribution to the purchase of the home as it did for active-duty veterans. Reservists who placed no down payment would be required to pay 2 percent of the loan amount in closing costs. Those who put down 5 percent would pay 1.5 percent, and those who put down 10 percent or more would pay 1.25 percent.

House members dealt with the most controversial issue related to HR 5002 — an ambitious effort to provide more assistance to homeless veterans — during the June 27 committee markup.

Kennedy and Tom Ridge, R-Pa., offered an amendment in committee to help homeless veterans, who Kennedy said constituted at least one-third of America's homeless population. Their amendment would have authorized $10 million to forge a "voluntary relationship" between the VA and the Department of Housing and Urban Development (HUD) to help homeless veterans find affordable housing.

The amendment would have given preferential treatment to homeless veterans trying to enroll in HUD's Section 8 subsidized housing program.

Ridge argued that preferential treatment for homeless veterans was consistent with many government programs because some groups — such as the elderly and AIDS victims — were allowed privileges in receiving subsidized housing.

The proposal immediately gained sympathy — but little support — from fellow committee members. Montgomery said money was not available and the VA was already providing sufficient help to troubled veterans.

Republicans quickly took up Montgomery's theme: To give Kennedy and Ridge the money they wanted would probably take away from already dwindling medical care and hospital funds for veterans.

The Kennedy-Ridge amendment was defeated by the committee, 8-17.

VA Personnel Retention

The House on Oct. 15 passed by voice vote a number of veterans' bills, including HR 5740, legislation crafted to help the VA recruit and retain medical personnel. The bill would have allowed part-time medical personnel to accept honoraria for speeches and articles, as long as the payment did not represent a conflict of interest.

The bill also would have prohibited appropriations for major medical projects or leases unless the funds had been specifically authorized by the Veterans' Affairs Committee.

The House Veterans' Affairs Subcommittee on Hospitals and Health Care passed HR 5740 by voice vote Oct. 2 — after it had been stripped of all provisions that would cost money.

Because of the new budget agreement between the White House and bipartisan congressional leaders, which required $620 million in savings and fees in fiscal 1991 from VA programs and $3.35 billion over five years, the panel took out a number of provisions to expand dental care to veterans. It was an immediate example of how the summit agreement caused Veterans' Affairs Committee leaders to re-examine some of the concepts behind their legislative agenda for 1990.

Montgomery said the chambers' committees would be hard pressed to find $620 million. "This is a great amount of money," he said, "especially as the VA cannot even operate all of its programs today."

Senate committee Chairman Cranston agreed, saying the reduction "is higher than expected and will not be painless."

The only thing that seemed to be safe was a proposal for pay increases for VA medical personnel, perhaps the highest priority of the veterans' lobby in 1990. The pay increase was under the purview of the Appropriations committees and thus not within the immediate jurisdiction of the Veterans' Affairs committees.

Yet as unappealing as the budget-summit cuts were, said the Vietnam Veterans of America's Egan, veterans' groups confronted an even more forbidding specter in the massive, across-the-board cuts that would have been exacted under the Gramm-Rudman law if no budget agreement was approved. Gramm-Rudman cuts would have doubled the $620 million in savings the summit wanted from veterans' programs.

The summit negotiators listed a number of cost-saving options in veterans' programs. The VA could collect more from third-party insurers of medical care. It could limit eligibility for VA home loans to veterans who had been out of military service no longer than 10 years. And it could limit inheritance of compensation and pension by remote heirs. The Office of Management and Budget (OMB) estimated that verification of pension eligibility and revision of eligibility requirements for veterans over the age of 65 would also save money.

OMB also suggested charging user fees for services and increasing copayments for high-income veterans.

Miscellaneous Matters

- **Medical research grants.** By voice vote, the House on June 12 passed HR 4390 after little debate and without opposition. The Veterans' Affairs Committee had approved the bill on April 26. The measure would have created a VA medical research grant program that would have built on existing cooperative research efforts between the VA and the Defense Department. It would have allowed the VA to accept private as well as federal funds for research.

• **Disability pay.** Besides the prospect of coming up with cuts in existing programs, a number of veterans' initiatives moving forward in the House and Senate were affected by summit cuts.

Among them were bills (S 190 and HR 303), referred jointly to the Veterans' Affairs and Armed Services committees, that would have allowed disabled veterans to receive both disability and retirement pay. Under existing law, a retiree had to choose between the two. Sen. Bob Graham, D-Fla., said the law was unfair because civil service retirees were eligible to receive military disability payments in addition to their pensions.

The Senate Veterans' Affairs Committee on June 28 approved S 190 by a 5-4 vote. HR 303 was left pending in the House Veterans' Affairs Committee and went nowhere during the session. Both bills were bogged down because of the potential $1.2 billion cost.

• **Recruitment and hiring.** The House passed HR 4088 on June 12 by voice vote. The legislation would have established a permanent Veterans Recruitment Authority to give preference in federal hiring to veterans, especially disabled ones.

• **Employment and training.** By voice vote, the House passed HR 4087 on July 10. The bill would have offered VA employment, training and other services to members of the military who had no more than 180 days of service remaining.

• **Educational services.** The House passed HR 4089 on July 10 by voice vote. The measure sought to extend educational and vocational services to a variety of people, including veterans who had been out of the service for less than a year, those still active with 180 days or less of duty remaining and some disabled military personnel with service-related injuries who were in VA hospitals.

• **Veterans' rehabilitation.** The House Veterans' Affairs Committee on May 17 approved by voice vote HR 3053, calling for the issuance of rehabilitation certificates to veterans who received dishonorable or general discharges if they proved that their conduct had been exemplary for at least three years. The legislation would have required the Labor Department to issue the certificate showing prospective employers that the veteran would be a good risk.

The panel rejected, 9-15, an effort by Robert C. Smith, R-N.H., to kill the bill on a tabling motion. Smith said it was improper for the federal government to certify whether a veteran had been rehabilitated.

The House Veterans' Affairs Subcommittee on Education, Training and Employment approved those four bills — HR 4087, HR 4088, HR 4089 and HR 3053 — by voice vote on May 3. ■

Little Change on American Indian Policies

Despite extensive evidence of major problems in Indian programs, and recommendations to take drastic preventive and corrective action, Congress in 1990 tampered little with federal Indian policy.

After two years of investigating fraud and mismanagement in federal agencies that were responsible for overseeing Indian programs, a special Senate investigative committee had recommended late in 1989 that those agencies be largely abandoned and that federal funds be given directly to tribal governments.

The report cited many examples of neglect and corruption in a number of federal agencies.

However, nearly all 1990 congressional legislative activity on Indian issues was limited to fine-tuning existing programs or establishing relatively inexpensive new ones — rather than the major overhaul urged in 1989.

During the year, President Bush did pocket-veto a bill to revise provisions of a law that provided a preference to Indian businesses.

The action marked the most noteworthy and controversial action on Indian legislation.

Also in 1990, Congress cleared bills to protect American Indian grave sites and return remains to the tribes; strengthen the authority of Interior Department law enforcement services and officers on Indian land; establish a grant program to help Indian tribes clean up environmental problems; and prevent child abuse and improve health care.

Meanwhile, Congress appropriated $1.57 billion in fiscal 1991 for the Bureau of Indian Affairs (BIA). The total was $381.6 million more than the president had requested and nearly $200 million more than the bureau received in fiscal 1990. *(Interior appropriations, p. 870)*

BACKGROUND

A highly publicized Senate report, released in November 1989, called for the abolishment of the BIA. The 238-page report by a special Senate committee, detailed fraud and abuse in Indian programs and advocated dismantling the BIA. It also recommended giving Indian tribes control over the $3.3 billion federal budget for Indian programs in what the panel hailed as a "new federalism" for American Indians. *(1989 Almanac, p. 369)*

Many Indians had reason to be skeptical, though. Congress had cited federal agencies for mismanagement in their handling of Indian programs on 42 occasions in the past 83 years. Each time, congressional investigators urged reforms that either were not adopted or proved ineffective.

"Indians have never had any political clout and very little voice in congressional matters," said Rep. Ben Nighthorse Campbell, D-Colo., the only Indian in Congress.

Indians have not exhibited much clout in Congress. Numbers helped explain the lack of influence. Fewer than 1 million Indians lived on U.S. reservations, and most of them never voted in congressional elections.

Federal Indian Policy

In 1824, BIA was created as an agency within the War Department, and the United States treated Indian tribes like foreign countries, signing treaties and operating on a government-to-government basis. Even in modern times, tribes retained a special brand of sovereignty, subject to federal laws but insulated from most state and local laws.

Soon after BIA was transferred to the Interior Department in 1849, however, the government started isolating Indians on reservations. Throughout the 20th century, the federal government see-sawed from one extreme to another, first encouraging tribal life and later calling for an end to all special federal treatment for Indians. *(Congress and the Nation Vol. I, p. 1096)*

In 1974, the pendulum swung back again when Congress passed the Indian Self-Determination Act (PL 93-638). The law acknowledged the federal government's role as trustee but also shifted much of the control of federal programs to the tribes. *(1974 Almanac, p. 672)*

But passing Indian legislation had not been simple. It took six years just to enact a law regulating tribal gambling. During the 1980s, a number of other relatively minor Indian measures cleared Congress, only to be vetoed by President Ronald Reagan.

LEGISLATIVE ACTION

Congress cleared a number of Indian measures during 1990, encountering resistance from the administration on some. Bush pocket-vetoed one bill.

'Indian Preference' Measure Vetoed

Bush on Nov. 16 announced that he would not sign the bill (S 321) to revise provisions of a law that provided a preference to Indian businesses. He called the bill "seriously flawed" and said it "would create more problems than it would solve." *(Text, p. 423)*

The Senate had cleared the bill Oct. 23, three days after the House had acted. The Senate had passed an earlier version of the legislation Feb. 7.

S 321, as outlined in the special committee's 1989 report, would have made the BIA set-aside program for Indian firms more resistant to abuse. The Indian Affairs Committee first reported the bill Nov. 20, 1989.

In the House, HR 1714 was an early Interior Committee companion to S 321 that sought to strengthen the Indian preference in contracting on the reservations.

The House in 1990, though, chose to work off of the Senate bill. The chamber referred S 321 to the Interior and Insular Affairs Committee, which reported the amended bill (H Rept 101-904) on Oct. 19. The full House then passed the measure the next day.

In announcing his pocket veto, Bush's statement said that the bill "would impose new, expensive and often duplicative program responsibilities on the secretary of the Interior that would be difficult to implement." He added that he supported "the goals of S 321" and was "committed to helping alleviate the widespread unemployment and underemployment on Indian reservations."

Bush expressed concern that the measure was cleared in the final days of the 101st Congress without sufficient consideration having been given to complex issues.

Tribal Remains

Legislation to protect American Indian grave sites and return remains to the tribes was cleared by the House on Oct. 27. Bush signed the bill (HR 5237 — PL 101-601) on Nov. 16, despite having opposed an earlier version of the measure.

The bill was an attempt to balance the emotional requests of Indian tribes for the return of the remains of their ancestors with the scholarly interests of scientists and museum officials. Under existing law, human remains unearthed on federal lands were considered federal property to be preserved in museums or educational institutions.

Before approving the measure, the House agreed to some Senate changes, including an amendment that excluded the Smithsonian Institution from the mandates of the bill. The Smithsonian was often criticized by American Indians for holding thousands of Indian skeletons.

Rep. Bill Richardson, D-N.M., said the House agreed to the Senate amendment "in favor of similar legislation dealing specifically with the Smithsonian in the next Congress."

Indian grave sites on federal and tribal land were protected from looting. The bill also established guidelines for museums to return human remains and cultural items.

However, the bill covered only skeletal remains and funeral objects buried with the bodies. In addition, the claimants would have to prove that the remains and objects belonged to their particular tribe.

The Senate passed the bill as amended by Wendell H. Ford, D-Ky., on Oct. 26. The House first passed the bill Oct. 22. The House Interior Committee approved the measure Oct. 10.

Health-Related Issues

Congress dealt with a number of Indian health and human service issues in 1990. Measures to prevent child abuse and improve health care were enacted while bills to curb alcohol and substance abuse and to provide greater federal benefits stalled at the committee level.

The need for child-abuse legislation was made clear in 1989. According to the special Senate report, the BIA had employed teachers who had admitted to child molestation, including one who sexually abused at least 25 Indian students over 14 years.

The bureau did not issue child-abuse reporting guidelines until 1988, after the investigative committee had held hearings on the subject.

The House cleared legislation (HR 3703) on Oct. 27 designed to prevent child abuse on Indian reservations. Originally introduced in the Senate as S 1783 by John McCain, R-Ariz., the child-abuse language was attached to a House bill authorizing the Rumsey Indian Rancheria, a small tribe in California, to sell a tract of its land.

Bush signed the bill into law (PL 101-630) on Nov. 28.

The measure stemmed from hearings that revealed numerous cases of sexual abuse of Indian children by BIA employees. The House Interior Committee approved the bill Oct. 10; the Senate had passed it Nov. 19, 1989.

The bill ensured that workers dealing with Indian children had no criminal record and established financial penalties and prison terms for officials who were aware of abuse and did not report it.

Also included under HR 3703 were a number of other Indian bills, including legislation (S 2645) aimed at improving the quality and scope of health care available to urban American Indians. The measure included funding for immunization services, mental health care, child-abuse treatment and a health-promotion and disease-prevention program.

The program was expected to benefit half the off-reservation Native American population, which was estimated at from 750,000 to 1 million people.

The Senate Select Indian Affairs Committee originally approved S 2645 on Sept. 18. Urban Indian health pro-

Bush Vetoes Indian Preference Act

Following is the memorandum of disapproval issued by President Bush on Nov. 16 announcing that he would not sign the bill (S 321) that would have revised provisions of a law that provided a preference to Indian businesses:

I am withholding my approval of S 321, the Indian Preference Act of 1990. S 321 would establish, among other things, a program to provide preferences to qualifying Indian enterprises in the award of federal grants or contracts using funds appropriated for the benefit of Indians.

The bill would impose new, expensive and often duplicative program responsibilities on the secretary of the Interior that would be difficult to implement. It would also likely result in federal agencies assuming new, unfunded liabilities related to Indian preference enterprises.

My administration strongly supports the goals of S 321 and is committed to helping alleviate the widespread unemployment and underemployment on Indian reservations. Moreover, the administration supports efforts to prevent companies from misusing federal Indian preference programs. Accordingly, amendments are needed to the "Buy Indian Act" to increase Indian economic self-sufficiency and employment opportunities and to prevent utilization of preference provisions by non-qualifying companies. However, S 321 is seriously flawed and would create more problems than it would solve.

I am withholding my approval of S 321 to allow further review of the issues in the 102nd Congress. Many of the issues raised by S 321 are complex and deserve a full airing in both houses of Congress. The House passed S 321 in the final days of the 101st Congress without sufficient consideration of these complex issues.

In the interim, I am directing the secretary of the Interior to take the necessary steps to address the contracting problems identified in the November 1989 report of the Special Committee on Investigations of the Senate Select Committee on Indian Affairs.

In particular, I am directing the secretary to issue guidelines that set forth specific procedures to govern Bureau of Indian Affairs field contracting officers in conducting pre-award reviews of grants and contracts. I am also directing the secretary to develop and submit proposed regulations to implement the "Buy Indian Act" for executive review within 90 days. ■

grams had been authorized to receive $13.1 million. The bill sought to increase that level by $9 million in fiscal 1991 and, in deference to White House wishes, would first have made some funds available for studies by the Indian Health Service — a branch of the Department of Health and Human Services — to determine where government money was most needed. The programs would then have received $18 million in fiscal 1992, $23 million in fiscal 1993 and $28 million in fiscal 1994.

The Indian Health Service received $1.59 billion in fiscal 1991 as provided by the Interior appropriations bill.

Meanwhile, a separate measure that would have authorized up to $30 million annually over five years to develop programs designed to prevent child and family violence passed the Senate by voice vote on Aug. 3. Under that bill (S 2340 — S Rept 101-403), counseling and training would have been provided, and a caseworker would have been assigned to each tribe. The bill stalled in the House Interior and Insular Affairs Committee.

Two other measures made it through the Senate Indian Affairs Committee but went no further.

On June 21, the panel approved legislation (S 2297) to provide funding for alcohol and substance abuse treatment for American Indian tribes. The bill, introduced by McCain and approved by voice vote, included a program to treat fetal alcohol syndrome.

The committee Sept. 12 approved a bill (S 2995) to allow American Indians to earn up to $4,000 from reservation lands without the income counting against them in determining eligibility for federal programs.

The bill, approved by voice vote, was sponsored by Tom Daschle, D-S.D., who argued that federal benefits, including Supplemental Security Income and food stamps, were often delayed or denied to American Indians because of inaccurate federal estimates of their income from land leases.

Miscellaneous Matters

Congress grappled with a wide range of Indian issues throughout 1990. A number of bills cleared and were signed into law by Bush, despite his occasional objections to portions of the bills.

Following are some of the Indian matters from the second session of the 101st Congress:

- **Environmental concerns.** Congress on Sept. 24 cleared a bill (S 2075) to establish a grant program to help Indian tribes clean up environmental problems. The House voted 316-99 to send the measure to the president; the Senate had passed it May 23. *(Vote 364, p. 118-H)*

The bill authorized $8 million for each of fiscal 1991-96 for grants to improve the capability of tribal governments to regulate environmental quality on Indian reservations

Bush opposed passage of the bill but never issued a formal veto threat and signed the measure Oct. 4 (PL 101-408).

The House Interior and Insular Affairs Committee reported the bill (H Rept 101-743) on Sept. 24, the day the measure cleared. The Senate Indian Affairs Committee on May 1 approved the bill (S Rept 101-295), though that version did not authorize a specific funding amount.

The Senate Indian Affairs Committee also on May 1 approved a measure (S 2354 — S Rept 101-293) that would have authorized funds for Community Development Block Grants to Indian tribes. The legislation would have freed $27 million already appropriated for fiscal 1990. The full Senate passed the bill May 22, but it stalled in the House Banking, Finance and Urban Affairs Committee.

- **Education.** The House on Oct. 12 cleared legislation to reauthorize funding for tribally controlled community colleges; the Senate had approved the bill Oct. 11. Bush signed the measure (S 2167 — PL 101-477) on Oct. 30.

The bill increased from $350,000 to $750,000 the federal contribution to the tribally controlled Community College Endowment Program. Indian education programs received $75.8 million in fiscal 1991 through the Interior appropriations bill.

The Senate Select Committee on Indian Affairs approved S 2167 (S Rept 101-371) on June 21.

- **Law Enforcement.** The Senate cleared legislation (HR 498) on Aug. 4 to strengthen the authority of Interior Department law enforcement services and officers on Indian land. The House had passed the measure Aug. 1.

Bush signed the legislation (HR 498 — PL 101-379) on Aug. 18.

Both chambers had passed slightly differing versions of the bill in 1989 — the Senate on Nov. 18 and the House on May 23. *(1989 Almanac, p. 372)*

The measure gave BIA law enforcement officials the right to carry guns and arrest people who committed crimes on Indian lands. The U.S. government was responsible for enforcing federal laws on Indian reservations, but that authority had never been put into statutory language that carried the weight of law.

BIA officials generally acted as a police force on reservations and aided FBI investigations of major crimes, such as murder and rape, on Indian lands. HR 498 created a criminal inquiry arm within the BIA's law enforcement branch to boost BIA officials' role in such probes.

• **Seminole Indians.** The Senate on April 5 cleared on a voice vote a bill to distribute about $47 million to Seminole Indians for claims arising over inadequate compensation for lands in the early 1980s. The House passed the bill on a voice vote April 3.

Bush signed the measure (S 1096 — PL 101-277) on April 30.

Both chambers adopted an agreement (H Rept 101-439) to allocate 75.4 percent of the money to the Seminole Nation of Oklahoma and 24.6 percent to the Seminole Tribe, the Miccousukee Tribe of Indians and the independent Seminole Indians, all of Florida.

The Indian Claims Commission had awarded the Seminole Indians $16 million in 1976.

The funds were never distributed, however, because of litigation over the distribution method recommended by the Interior Department, which submitted a plan based on population during the period spanning 1906-1914.

The conference agreement essentially adopted the Interior plan. The House originally passed a bill Feb. 6 allocating 73 percent of the funds to Oklahoma Seminoles. The Senate had passed its first version of the bill in November 1989.

• **Micmac Settlement Act.** The House on Oct. 10 failed to garner the two-thirds majority necessary to suspend the rules and pass the Aroostook Band of Micmacs Settlement Act. The bill (S 1413) sought to provide federal recognition of the Aroostook Band of Micmacs as an Indian tribe, making all members of the band eligible to receive all of the federal benefits and services available to recognized Indian tribes. The Congressional Budget Office estimated that if the full amount had been authorized and appropriated, outlays would have been $900,000 in fiscal 1991, and the cost of providing federal benefits and services to the band would have been $1 million annually. The bill was rejected 248-172, failing to get the 280 votes required for passage. *(Vote 442, p. 142-H)*

• **Forest management.** The House on Oct. 10 passed S 1289 to improve the management of forests and woodlands and the production of forest resources on Indian lands. The measure would have required tribes to institute "forest management plans" approved by the tribes and the Interior secretary. Special committee investigators in 1989 found that forestry planning and timber marketing in Indian country were grossly inefficient and outdated. The Senate had passed an earlier version in the early morning hours of Aug. 4, but the differences between the two versions were not reconciled before Congress adjourned. ■

Puerto Rico's Status Remains Unresolved

After emerging in 1989, legislation to give Puerto Ricans the right to determine their future relationship with the United States stalled at the end of the 1990 session. The legislation died at the end of the 101st Congress after J. Bennett Johnston, D-La., chairman of the Energy and Natural Resources Committee, which had primary jurisdiction over Puerto Rico, announced that fundamental differences between his bill (S 712) and the House version (HR 4765) could not be resolved in time.

Johnston pledged that a bill calling for a plebiscite on Puerto Rican status would be signed into law by 1991's July Fourth recess — allowing enough time to set up an islandwide referendum by the spring of 1992. House Speaker Thomas S. Foley, D-Wash., also pledged his cooperation as did Virgin Islands Democratic Del. Ron de Lugo, chairman of the Interior Subcommittee on Insular and International Affairs.

The Senate bill would have provided for a self-executing referendum (one whose result would automatically take effect) in Puerto Rico to decide among statehood, independence or "enhanced" commonwealth status. The House bill also called for a referendum but one that would not be self-executing.

On Oct. 10, the day the House passed its bill by voice vote, Johnston announced that he would not pursue passage of the Senate bill because not enough time remained in the session for a conference with the House. Johnston said then that a self-executing bill was the way to go and that he would not accept the House bill; he later changed his view on a self-executing bill.

The Senate Energy and Natural Resources Committee approved S 712 on Aug. 2, 1989. The Senate Finance Committee, with jurisdiction over the Social Security, tax and trade provisions, sent the bill to the floor without a recommendation Aug. 1, 1990. The Agriculture Committee, which oversaw food stamp provisions, failed to act. *(1989 Almanac, p. 356)*

BACKGROUND

Throughout Puerto Rico's nearly 40-year history as a U.S. commonwealth, island voters have had a demonstrated knack for the political dogfight.

Puerto Ricans referred to celebrating an election rather than just holding one. Election Day featured motorcades and street parades, and about 80 percent of those eligible usually voted.

Yet Puerto Ricans also saw the necessity to compensate for the commonwealth's lack of a vote in Congress and assiduously courted U.S. officials and hired lobbyists to help protect its interests. In the process, they made their voices heard above thousands of special interests that competed for attention in Washington. Indeed, lobbying Congress and the president was a central function of Puerto Rican government.

Puerto Rico had been struggling to take charge of its

own affairs even before the Spanish-American War in 1898, when Spain ceded control of the island to the United States after four centuries of control.

The island began its relationship with the United States as a powerless possession but pushed continually for increasing authority to govern itself. Congress, for the most part, went along.

Over the first half-century of federal control, Congress extended U.S. citizenship to Puerto Ricans and gave them the power to elect a legislature and a governor. In addition, in 1921, the federal government sought to boost the local economy by exempting from federal taxes U.S. corporations doing business in Puerto Rico.

The tax credit, later known as Section 936 of the Internal Revenue Code, provided a major incentive for U.S. businesses to operate on the island. With an influx of manufacturing interests, the island moved from an agrarian to an industrialized economy. The corporations were credited with elevating the standard of living, making Puerto Rico's per capita income one of the highest in the Caribbean.

Even so, more than 60 percent of the population remained below the United States' official poverty line, putting it below even the poorest of states. As a result, island residents had always been dissatisfied with their relationship to the federal government. *(Chart, Profile of Puerto Rico, 1989 Almanac, p. 359)*

In 1951, the island adopted a commonwealth constitution, and Congress approved it a year later, granting full local authority to Puerto Rico's elected officials. The tax credits remained under the commonwealth status. Puerto Ricans also were exempted from the requirement to pay federal income taxes, though they retained basic citizenship rights.

The ink was barely dry on the commonwealth constitution, however, before Puerto Rico again expressed concern about its status.

The island government pushed members of Congress to introduce a number of bills to expand its power. None were successful.

Although Puerto Ricans voted to continue commonwealth status in a 1967 referendum, the next year, Luis A. Ferré, a statehood party member, was elected governor. The governorship had changed hands between the two parties several times since then.

Legislative Maneuvering

Status had been the dominant political issue in Puerto Rico for decades, but it took the coalescence of a number of political factors on the mainland and on the island to jump-start legislation allowing a plebiscite to choose among statehood, independence and "enhanced" commonwealth status.

Few even on Capitol Hill were familiar with the complex legislation enabling this process. But driven by Sens. Johnston and James A. McClure, R-Idaho, it was put on the legislative fast track in the 100th Congress.

In November 1988, Puerto Rican Gov. Rafael Hernández Colón, who supported commonwealth status, won re-election with a scant plurality over a statehood candidate. It was the fourth consecutive election in which no candidate received a majority, and Hernández, a member of the Popular Democratic Party (PDP), pledged to resolve the issue once and for all.

The Puerto Rican Independence Party (PIP), which supported a complete break with the United States, had never been a strong force on the island but took the chance to enhance its legitimacy by joining the compact. The New Progressive Party (NPP), which supported statehood, had suffered electoral setbacks in 1988, and leaders apparently decided that promoting the one issue that united the NPP could re-energize its troops.

Weeks later, President Bush surprised the nation by making special mention of Puerto Rico in his first appearance before Congress on Feb. 9, 1989. A longtime supporter of statehood, Bush asked Congress to take the necessary steps to allow for the island's self-determination.

With this support in hand, Johnston and McClure shifted into high gear. Their goal from the outset was to draft a self-executing bill — one that would fully and finally commit the U.S. government to specific plans for implementation of each option. The two senators invited Puerto Rican officials from each party to submit a wish list of implementing language, all of which was incorporated into their bill (S 712).

The effort to give Puerto Ricans the right to determine their future relationship with the United States survived its first major test on Aug. 2, 1989, when the Senate Energy and Natural Resources Committee approved S 712. The committee ordered the bill reported to the full Senate on an 11-8 vote, with the backing of a majority of both Democrats and Republicans.

In contrast with the Senate, no comparable legislation was introduced in the House in 1989, the proposal lacking a legislative point man.

Economic, Political Interests

Among those with a big interest in commonwealth status were the U.S. companies that operated on the island. To help further their cause in Congress, they established the Puerto Rico U.S.A. Foundation, which had 70 members in 1990.

Peter Holmes, a spokesman for the foundation, said that if statehood were adopted, 50 percent of U.S. companies would leave the island.

"It would be a very different economy for Puerto Rico," he said, noting that U.S. businesses were major employers on the island.

The corporations, including some of the nation's largest pharmaceutical companies, said they could use the money they saved in taxes for research and development, keeping the United States ahead of the rest of the world in drug research.

BOXSCORE

Legislation: Puerto Rico self-determination (HR 4765, S 712).

Major action: S 712 died on Senate floor, Oct. 10; House passed HR 4765, Oct. 10. Senate Finance Committee sent S 712 to the floor without recommendation, Aug. 1; Senate Energy and Natural Resources Committee approved S 712, Aug. 2, 1989.

Reports: Finance (S Rept 101-481); Energy and Natural Resources (S Rept 101-120). Interior and Insular Affairs (H Rept 101-790, Part I); Rules (H Rept 101-790, Part II).

Supporters of statehood said its benefits outweighed the potential economic sacrifices.

Statehood would give Puerto Rico two senators and six or seven voting House members.

Puerto Rico would be eligible for more federal dollars, including full food stamp benefits and other welfare payments.

In addition, statehood would allow Puerto Ricans, who had fought in every U.S. conflict in this century along with mainland soldiers but were not allowed to vote in presidential elections, full voting rights of citizenship.

Although statehood appeared to be an attractive option, Harold Seidman, a former White House budget official who dealt with U.S. territorial affairs since the Eisenhower administration, noted that it also had drawbacks. Besides the loss of the tax credits, many people in Puerto Rico feared that the future of their culture and language would be in jeopardy under statehood.

"They don't want to be completely assimilated," Seidman said.

The question was also not an easy one for members of Congress and mainland parties.

Admittance to the Union would bring in two new senators, threatening to upend the Senate's tenuous balance of power.

The inclusion of a state of Puerto Rico could also upset the House. Because the size of the House was set at 435, other states would lose congressional numerical clout.

Poorer states also feared that Puerto Rican statehood might take federal dollars away from them.

Still, Puerto Rico's status rested largely with the island's political parties. And because their alliance in favor of the referendum was shaky, so were chances for the legislation.

A major roadblock to legislation was the absence of a clear majority on either side of the status question, unlike the clear consensus that accompanied Alaska's and Hawaii's admittance to the Union in 1959.

In January 1989, public opinion polls showed that residents favored commonwealth 52 percent to 41 percent. A later poll showed that islanders favored statehood 48 percent to 42 percent.

What the Bills Would Have Done

Both bills before Congress would have directed the Puerto Rican government to hold a referendum to allow the island's 3.6 million residents to choose among statehood, independence or "enhanced" commonwealth status. However, the Senate bill would have been self-executing, putting immediately into effect whatever option Puerto Rican voters chose.

The House bill called for a non-binding referendum and would merely have set up an expedited procedure for Congress to follow up on the results.

Besides the question of whether to make the referendum self-executing, a key difference between House and Senate bills was how the choices would be framed to Puerto Rican voters.

The Senate bill attempted to strictly define the three options before the plebiscite, including financial benefits or liabilities for the island and the United States.

The House bill would simply have authorized the plebiscite, allowing Congress to outline the details of the chosen option later.

The bill would have directed the House Interior and the Senate Energy committees to draft new bills after the referendum to put into effect the status chosen by a majority of the voters.

That bill, if enacted, would have become effective only if approved by another vote of Puerto Rican residents.

S 712 had been criticized for favoring the statehood option. The Senate Finance Committee scaled back the benefits section and amended the bill so that the same benefits would be provided under statehood or commonwealth status.

HOUSE ACTION

The House Interior Subcommittee on Insular Affairs on Aug. 3 approved HR 4765 to grant islanders a referendum on their status.

The House bill would have directed House Interior and the Senate Energy Committee to draft bills after the referendum to implement the status chosen by a majority of the island's voters.

That bill, if enacted, would have become effective in 1992 if approved by another vote of Puerto Rican residents.

The full committee on Sept. 19 approved HR 4765 on a 37-1 vote. However, unlike S 712, to make the results of the referendum self-executing, the House bill would have given Congress another vote on whether to change the island's existing status as a commonwealth.

If that bill were enacted, it would go to another vote among Puerto Rican citizens.

The House measure represented a hard-won compromise between committee members who favored widely different options.

Among them, Robert J. Lagomarsino, R-Calif., following Bush's stated position, favored statehood.

Lagomarsino introduced legislation in 1987 at the request of then-Vice President Bush calling for Puerto Rican statehood.

Statehood was strongly opposed by Puerto Rico's resident commissioner, Jaime B. Fuster, Pop. Dem., a nonvoting member in the U.S. House. Fuster said the new bill was "imperfect" because of the many compromises made "between many different parties that do not all share the sense of purpose and the high-mindedness that should have prevailed."

The negotiations were complicated by a push by Jose E. Serrano, D-N.Y., to include a provision that would have allowed 2.5 million Puerto Ricans who lived on the mainland to vote in the island's plebiscite. Serrano's provision was excluded because of opposition from Puerto Rico's political parties.

However, the bill would have established a "dialogue committee" made up of members of the three powerful political parties on the island, which were aligned with each of the three options.

If two of the three parties agreed, the Puerto Rican government could allow Puerto Ricans on the mainland to vote in the plebiscite.

The final product was agreeable to all committee members except Ron Marlenee, R-Mont., who voted against the measure to protest the system of reapportionment, under which Montana would lose one of its two House seats.

The House Rules Subcommittee on Rules of the House held a hearing and markup on Sept. 27 and approved HR 4765. The panel approved the Interior Committee's version of the legislation and reported it favorably to committee. The full Rules Committee on Oct. 2 approved HR 4765 by voice vote.

Floor Passage

HR 4765 then won quick, voice vote passage in the House on Oct. 10, before stalling in the Senate. Just moments before Johnston declared the legislation dead, de Lugo, the Virgin Islands delegate and head of the Interior's Insular Affairs Subcommittee, was relishing the House victory after months of tortuous negotiations.

De Lugo expressed hope that the Senate would move on the bill, despite statements from Johnston earlier in the day that the measure would not get floor time. "There's plenty of time," de Lugo said.

Temporarily buoyed by the House's unexpectedly easy passage of the legislation, referendum supporters grasped to save the measure in the 101st Congress. The presidents of the island's three political parties wrote Johnston on Oct. 11 urging him to accept the House bill "with amendments."

"As you know, there is simply no inclination on the part of Congress to pass a bill like S 712," the letter said.

SENATE ACTION

The Senate Finance Committee on Aug. 1 ordered S 712 reported to the floor, although without a favorable recommendation, highlighting a lack of key support for the measure in the chamber.

The committee cut out provisions previously approved by the Energy and Natural Resources Committee that would have given the island millions of dollars in special social-program benefits if its citizens chose statehood.

Finance Chairman Lloyd Bentsen, D-Texas, said the amended bill would have provided the same funding for social programs under the statehood and commonwealth options.

"What we're trying to do is make this a level playing field for the people of Puerto Rico," Bentsen said.

The move thrilled commonwealth supporters, including Puerto Rican Gov. Hernández. "Yesterday was a major victory for commonwealth," said Jose Berrocal, counselor to the governor.

The Senate action came nearly a year to the day after a version of the bill was approved by the Energy and Natural Resources Committee and sent to the Finance panel to consider the Social Security, tax and trade provisions.

While the bill committed the U.S. government to carrying out the will of a majority of Puerto Rican voters, it had come under increasing fire for favoring the statehood option. Proponents of both statehood and commonwealth had remained angrily divided over the bill's "slant."

For example, as happy as commonwealth supporters were with the changes made by the Finance Committee, statehood supporters also saw reason for hope. Former Puerto Rican Gov. Carlos Romero Barcelo, president of the pro-statehood New Progressive Party, said the committee's action was instead "a real blow to commonwealth."

Under the commonwealth option, he said, island residents would not have fiscal autonomy, which commonwealth supporters advocated. Instead, they would lose some tax credits and customs duties and would have to provide matching funds for social programs.

Besides scaling back the benefits section, the Finance Committee also departed from the Energy panel by inserting a provision to establish a "transition period" to effectively delay statehood until 1996.

The provision would have allowed for a gradual phase-out — 25 percent a year — of federal tax credits for U.S. corporations that located in Puerto Rico. A major concern for those who opposed statehood was the potential loss of millions of dollars in corporate tax credits. During the transition period, federal income and excise taxes would also be phased in, at 25 percent per year.

Under existing law, Puerto Ricans did not pay federal income taxes, and proceeds of federal excise taxes on rum exported to the mainland and from customs duties were turned over to the Puerto Rican government.

"The Finance Committee amendments would eliminate this special treatment upon statehood admission," according to a committee statement. If the island chose independence, tax credits to U.S. corporations would also be phased out over a five-year transition period.

Social programs would be discontinued during the transition period, although U.S. Social Security payments would continue for up to five years while the two countries worked out an agreement on future payments.

Island residents would retain U.S. citizenship under independence.

Meanwhile, both Republicans and Democrats were wary of supporting the bill because of its possible costs as their own states faced tighter budget constraints.

John D. Rockefeller IV, D-W.Va., said he was concerned about the effect that a change in Puerto Rico's status might have on other areas of the U.S. economy. "I am unable to separate the representation of my state from the consideration of this amendment," he said.

Rockefeller, a member of both the Finance and Energy committees, criticized the Energy panel's version. "I voted against the Energy bill very, very strongly and very, very easily," he said.

Floor, Final Action

Moments after the House on Oct. 10 gave voice vote approval to HR 4765, Johnston effectively killed its chances with a few words on the Senate floor.

"With probably only 10 days remaining in this Congress, it has become clear that enactment of a Puerto Rico referendum bill is not possible," said Johnston.

A committee aide to Johnston said that too many differences remained between the House and Senate as the two chambers attempted to wrap up a long list of congressional business. Johnston, the aide said, was not willing to accept the House version.

The major difference was that the Senate bill would have been self-executing, putting immediately into effect whatever option Puerto Rican voters chose while the House bill called for a non-binding referendum.

Johnston restated his support for the measure and said he hoped that the Senate would pass a bill early in 1991 and work out its differences with the House so that a referendum could be held in the fall of 1991 or spring of 1992, before island elections for governor and municipal offices.

Officials from the island's three main political parties were upset by the turn of events, if only because they would have liked to resolve an issue that had become a political obsession to thousands of island residents.

"We have pleaded with him [Johnston]," said David Gerkin, a lobbyist for the statehood movement. "We don't prefer the approach taken by the House, but we see it as the only realistic vehicle."

Johnston sought to assure Puerto Ricans that quick action was possible in 1991. But on Feb. 27, 1991, the Senate Energy Committee killed, on a 10-10 vote, the plebiscite bill Johnston introduced at the start of the 102nd Congress. ■

D.C. Elects Mayor, 'Shadow' Delegation

District of Columbia voters in November elected a new mayor, a new non-voting House delegate and its first "shadow" congressional delegation in the hope of bolstering the District's bruised image. The shadow delegation — two senators and one House representative — was also given the mandate of lobbying Congress for statehood and included as a senator one of statehood's most prominent supporters, Jesse Jackson.

The D.C. City Council in February had authorized the election of the shadow delegation but stopped short of appropriating $1.3 million it had estimated would be needed to pay the delegation and its staff. The delegation — Jackson, fellow shadow senator Florence Pendleton and shadow congressman Charles Moreland — carried no congressional recognition, public budget or salaries.

The winner of the mayoral election was Sharon Pratt Dixon, a former utility company executive, who won a crowded September primary and then crushed former D.C. Police Chief Maurice T. Turner Jr. in November. Dixon tried to capitalize on her status as a political outsider and as a harsh critic of outgoing Mayor Marion S. Barry Jr. Barry's woes had contributed to the District's image problems on Capitol Hill throughout the year.

Eleanor Holmes Norton, a civil rights lawyer, was elected to replace Walter E. Fauntroy as the District's non-voting delegate to Congress. Some observers, however, questioned how effective and positive a force she would be after disclosures during the campaign that she and her husband had not filed local income taxes for many years.

Fauntroy, the District's delegate for 19 years, announced March 3 that he would run for mayor. He finished fifth in the Sept. 8 Democratic primary. Fauntroy had risen to the third-ranking position on the Banking, Finance and Urban Affairs Committee.

Mayor Barry's Troubles

The elections were the culmination of a troubled year for the District, as its standing deteriorated even further on Capitol Hill — especially in light of Barry's troubles.

Barry was convicted on Aug. 10 of one misdemeanor count of drug possession and acquitted of another misdemeanor drug charge. A mistrial was declared on the 12 remaining charges when the jury reported that it was deadlocked.

Barry's arrest Jan. 18 on cocaine charges — and the possibility of further revelations of D.C. government corruption — had introduced an element of uncertainty into relations between Capitol Hill and the District.

"Congress cannot — and will not — hold the city responsible for the actions of its mayor," said Iowa Democrat Tom Harkin, the former chairman of the Senate Appropriations Subcommittee on the District of Columbia.

But critics of the D.C. government saw the Barry problems as one more reason to oppose statehood or any enhancement of the District's status.

Congress reiterated its low opinion of statehood July 24 when a Senate Appropriations subcommittee gave bipartisan, voice vote approval to an amendment to the District's fiscal 1991 spending bill (HR 5311) prohibiting the city from using federal or locally raised revenues to fund its shadow delegation.

The District also could not use its funding to pay for any other attempts to push for statehood.

The Senate on Oct. 26 cleared the appropriations measure, complete with the amendment. *(D.C. appropriations, p. 891)*

Jackson, who declared his candidacy for shadow senator July 5, had said he would ask Senate Democratic leaders to give him office space and access to the Senate floor if elected.

Tennessee was the first territory to send a shadow delegation to Congress when it acted in 1796. Since then, six prospective states had done the same, though Tennessee's representatives were the only ones allowed on the floor of the Senate during sessions.

Because the District never asked Congress to approve funding for the shadow delegation, the amendment offered by the subcommittee's ranking Republican, Phil Gramm of Texas, was understood by D.C. officials as a political gesture.

Congress had been unwavering in its recent opposition to D.C. statehood. While Congress had approved a constitutional amendment in 1978 to give the District voting representation in Congress, the effort died in 1985 when the statutory deadline for ratification expired. *(1985 Almanac, p. 404; 1978 Almanac, p. 793)*

More recently, in 1989, Congress would not allow the city to spend $150,000 for a statehood lobbying office.

Legislative Proposals in 1990

Congress had a constitutional right to legislate for the District. It pointedly reserved that prerogative for itself when it passed limited home rule in 1973 (PL 93-198). Residents had since been allowed to elect their own mayor and council members. But District laws were still subject to congressional oversight.

Meanwhile, there was no shortage of suggestions in 1990 on what to do about the District's disputed political status.

On Feb. 25, Maryland Gov. William Donald Schaefer, D, offered to annex the District back into the state. His retrocession offer, he said, would provide residents the opportunity to vote for Maryland's two U.S. senators and an additional voting House member.

Jackson immediately blasted Schaefer's proposal, saying it was akin to the South African "Bantustan" concept of segregated black homelands.

On March 6, Ralph Regula, R-Ohio, introduced a retrocession bill (HR 4195), to carry out Schaefer's proposal. Also on March 6, Stan Parris, R-Va., a longtime opponent of statehood who represented Virginia suburbs of the District, announced his "alternative" to statehood. He introduced a bill (HR 4193) to give D.C. residents the right to vote — but only in Maryland.

Under Parris' bill, the District would remain autonomous, maintain limited home rule and its mayor and council, and Congress would still approve the city's budget. But D.C. residents would be allowed to vote for a representative and two senators in Maryland.

Parris chose Maryland, he said, because in 1790, when Maryland ceded land to form the nation's capital, District residents continued to vote in that state. Congress withdrew those voting rights in 1801. "I think it's in their best interest to want this," Parris said.

Sens. Edward M. Kennedy, D-Mass., and Paul Simon,

D-Ill., on May 17 introduced legislation (S 2647) to make the District the nation's 51st state. The bill would have named the state New Columbia and allowed District residents to elect two U.S. senators and a House member with full voting rights.

Kennedy, who backed previously unsuccessful statehood bills, predicted a rocky future for the new bill. But he also chided federal lawmakers for clinging to control over the District.

"As we begin this new national campaign for statehood," Kennedy said, "we hope public opinion around the country will hasten the end of this harsh plantation mentality in Congress."

Fauntroy sponsored a similar bill (HR 51) in the House, but the District of Columbia Committee did not act on it.

Some statehood opponents feared that involvement by Jackson could unstick the statehood debate. "I have never believed there are enough votes for [a statehood bill] to pass," said Parris. "But Jesse Jackson's presence might have an impact on the scheduling of a vote on statehood."

If Democrats in Congress insisted on pressing for statehood, Parris said, his response would be "to increase the stakes by suggesting the alternative to statehood is repeal of home rule."

But that argument ignored the reasons Congress had granted home rule in the first place. The civil rights movement in the 1960s had generated too much political pressure to sustain a system in which the District, a majority-black city, was in effect governed by members of Congress, particularly the white Southerners who dominated the House District of Columbia Committee.

Moreover, as the problems of running a city accumulated in the 1960s, Congress simply tired of acting as the District's municipal authority. Neither of those realities had changed.

Home rule itself, however, was not in jeopardy. "When you have a mayor in trouble it gives people who do not like home rule [a chance] to grandstand," said Democratic Rep. Steny H. Hoyer, who represented a Maryland district in the D.C. suburbs. "But the basic principle that the residents of the District of Columbia should be entitled to govern themselves is not in question." ■

Congress OKs Metro Aid

The House on Oct. 26 cleared legislation to authorize $2.1 billion to fund the Washington, D.C.-area Metro rail system to near-completion. The bill passed the Senate Oct. 25.

Under pressure from the Bush administration, members crafted a compromise to raise the requirement for local contributions to construction from 20 percent — as approved by the House in March — to 37.5 percent. Under the final bill, the federal contribution would be $1.3 billion over the next eight years.

Both chambers approved the compromise by voice vote in the final week of the session. President Bush signed the measure (HR 1463 — PL 101-551) on Nov. 15.

The transportation funding measure (HR 5229) appropriated $51.7 million for the Washington rail system in fiscal 1991. *(Transportation appropriations, p. 876)*

The House had voted March 28 to authorize funds to complete the final 13.5 miles of the rail system, ignoring administration arguments that the District should fall into line with the other regions competing for federal transportation dollars.

The legislation, passed on a 260-150 vote, would have authorized $2 billion over the next 11 years — in annual installments of almost $200 million — to complete the projected 103-mile system. The remaining $675 million, which represented 25 percent of the estimated $2.7 billion needed for the project, would have come from Washington-area taxpayers. *(Vote 52, p. 22-H)*

Stan Parris, R-Va., called the vote a "victory for the Washington metropolitan area." But Dana Rohrabacher, R-Calif., said it was a "budget-buster which takes tax dollars from all parts of the country to help one of the richest areas" solve its transportation problems.

The District of Columbia Committee had reported the measure (H Rept 101-430) on March 23. ■

Acid-Free Papers Urged

In a move to preserve government papers considered part of the national heritage, Congress on Sept. 26 cleared a measure providing for the use of acid-free "permanent" paper to preserve federal records, documents and other publications of enduring national value. President Bush signed the joint resolution (S J Res 57 — PL 101-423) on Oct. 12.

The resolution also urged federal agencies and state and local governments to use acid-free paper for "permanently valuable" records.

House members on Sept. 17 adopted an amended version of the resolution and the Senate agreed to the amendment Sept. 26. The amendment called for three Library of Congress reports over five years on government use of acid-free paper; the Senate had originally wanted annual reports. The library had already begun a program to de-acidify volumes of books that had been printed on acid paper.

Typical acid-based paper had a life expectancy of decades while acid-free paper, if well protected, could last for many centuries. A House committee report noted: "Eventually, acid-free permanent papers will reduce the need for microfilming or de-acidification of books. While the benefits will not be realized for several decades, the savings at that time will be millions of dollars nationwide."

The resolution first passed the Senate on July 31, 1989.

In 1990, the House Government Operations Subcommittee on Government Information on May 16 unanimously approved its own resolution (H J Res 226 — H Rept 101-680) calling for the establishment of a national policy on the use of acid-free paper. The full committee passed the measure by voice vote Aug. 2.

The House passed its measure on Sept. 17 and then passed S J Res 357 in lieu, amending it to contain the text of the just-passed H J Res 226. The Senate cleared the measure for the president Sept. 26. ■

Restrictions Removed on Arts Funding

A year after lawmakers first prohibited the National Endowment for the Arts (NEA) from underwriting projects that could be considered obscene, sadomasochistic or homoerotic, the ban was dropped. Instead, Congress empowered the NEA chairman in 1990 to ensure that grants were made on "general standards of decency and respect for the diverse beliefs and values of the American public." The controversial issue of obscenity was passed to the courts.

Throughout the summer, the Senate Labor and Human Resources Committee had worked on an NEA reauthorization (S 2724) compromise that broached the topic of letting the courts rule on obscenity. The compromise, offered by Orrin G. Hatch, R-Utah, was one of the least intrusive methods for awarding arts grants — while still addressing obscenity and pornography — that had been proposed in Congress so far.

Meanwhile, Pat Williams, D-Mont., who chaired the House Education and Labor Subcommittee on Postsecondary Education, worked on an agreement with E. Thomas Coleman, Mo., the subcommittee's ranking Republican, to reauthorize the NEA and leave the obscenity issue to the courts.

The Williams-Coleman compromise (HR 4825) became the chief vehicle that first passed the House on Oct. 11 as a straight reauthorization for the endowment. When the Senate failed to act quickly on a reauthorization, NEA supporters in the House turned their attention instead to the NEA's spending bill.

The fiscal 1991 Interior appropriations bill (HR 5769 — PL 101-512) was amended to include a three-year reauthorization of the NEA with no restrictions on the kind of art it might fund. Congress required grant recipients to return money used to produce any work of art that the courts declared obscene. Artists could be barred from receiving additional grants for three years unless they paid the money back.

In a House-Senate conference, the Senate agreed to drop an amendment by Jesse Helms, R-N.C., to ban funding of works that denigrated religion. The Senate then accepted the House language, which instructed the NEA, in judging applications, to take into account "general standards of decency and respect for the diverse beliefs and values of the American public."

The legislation shifted 35 percent of the NEA's money to state arts councils, up from 20 percent. *(Interior appropriations, p. 870)*

BOXSCORE

Legislation: National Endowment for the Arts reauthorization (S 2724, HR 4825), enacted as part of fiscal 1990 Interior appropriations, PL 101-512 (HR 5769).

Major action: Signed, Nov. 5. Conference report cleared by Senate, Oct. 27; adopted by House, 298-43, Oct. 27. HR 5769 passed by Senate, Oct. 24; by House, Oct. 15. House passed HR 4825, 349-76, Oct. 11. Senate Labor and Human Resources Committee approved S 2724, Sept. 12. House Education and Labor Committee approved HR 4825, June 19.

Reports: Conference report on HR 5769 (H Rept 101-971). S 2724: Labor and Human Resources (S Rept 101-472). HR 4825: Education and Labor (H Rept 101-566).

BACKGROUND

After several years of growing congressional and private support for the study, development and presentation of the arts and humanities, Congress in 1965 established the National Foundation on the Arts and Humanities. The foundation consisted of two autonomous subdivisions, the National Endowment for the Arts and the National Endowment for the Humanities.

Each endowment was authorized to make grants, most of them matched, for a wide range of activities. The operations of the National Foundation were coordinated with other federal activities.

In his Jan. 6, 1965, State of the Union address, President Lyndon B. Johnson said, "To help promote and honor creative achievements, I will propose a National Foundation on the Arts." Johnson added in March that "pursuit of artistic achievement ... is also among the hallmarks of a Great Society."

Before the establishment of the foundation, the federal government's support for the arts and humanities in general had been expressed through occasional patronage rather than direct subsidies. Much of the government's involvement had been through federally connected activities in the District of Columbia, such as the commissioning of parks, buildings and monuments and support of the Library of Congress, the Smithsonian Institution and the National Gallery of Art. *(1965 Almanac, p. 621)*

Since its inception, the endowment had served as a catalyst to encourage record levels of new private and public support for artists and arts organizations. Historically, each federal dollar awarded had attracted more than $6 in matching funds.

Recent Controversies

NEA funding for exhibitions of works that members of Congress found pornographic or sacrilegious had boiled into a major controversy on Capitol Hill in 1989. Triggering the outcry were two artists: Andres Serrano, creator of "Piss Christ," a photograph of a crucifix in a jar of urine; and the late Robert Mapplethorpe, known for his homoerotic photographs.

NEA advocates in Congress faced the uphill task of pushing two sets of legislation — the reauthorization and the appropriation — through a barrage of restrictive amendments.

Corralling the move to squelch NEA funding of the controversial works was the outspoken Republican from North Carolina. Helms had warned his colleagues that he would resurrect the NEA brouhaha each year until strict guidelines on federal arts funding were imposed. He told them: "Old Helms has been beat before. But old Helms does not quit."

The endowment's watchdog in the House was Dana

Rohrabacher, R-Calif. Neither Rohrabacher nor Helms were members of panels with jurisdiction over the agency.

As the public got increasingly involved in the controversy, representatives of the evangelist right — the Rev. Donald E. Wildmon and former Republican presidential contender Pat Robertson — cranked up letter-writing campaigns to members calling for the abolition of the agency.

Over 85,000 NEA grants had been awarded by 1990 and supporters argued that detractors were using a handful of controversial projects to destroy a quarter-century of work.

Helms offered an amendment in 1989 that would have prohibited federal funding for materials that were "obscene" or depicted various activities or human organs. Although he gained some support, his colleagues in the Senate eventually rejected that proposal 62-35.

Helms revised his instructions and asked for a ban on funding for "obscene or indecent" works. The amendment was approved by voice vote at the same time the Senate approved a proposal by Wyche Fowler Jr., D-Ga., to delete the word "indecent," sending a mixed signal to the House.

Conferees finally agreed on relatively modest compromise language in the fiscal 1990 Interior appropriations bill (HR 2788 — PL 101-121). The bill banned the use of federal funds for artworks that could be determined obscene. *(1989 Almanac, p. 731)*

Under the new law, the NEA required grant recipients to sign a pledge of compliance with the new set of restrictions. Some of the arts groups protested by rejecting the NEA money; several lawsuits challenged the constitutionality of the certification requirement.

True to his word, Helms' campaign for another Senate term in North Carolina used the NEA as a platform centerpiece. Although he won the 1990 election, Helms again lost the NEA battle.

COMMITTEE ACTION

As the arts community grappled with the new ban on funding artworks that might be considered obscene, House and Senate committee members in mid-1990 faced a new round of NEA authorization and appropriation bills. The immediate challenge was to craft language that could address the obscenity issue without sparking the ire of either detractors or supporters of the endowment.

Senate Action

After a summer of closed-door talks among its leaders, the Senate Labor and Human Resources Committee on Sept. 12 approved an NEA reauthorization (S 2724) by 15-1. The bill included a compromise that would pass to the courts the controversial issue of obscenity.

The compromise, offered by Hatch, would not forbid the NEA from funding any art on obscene, homoerotic, sacrilegious or other grounds. But artists or arts organizations would be required to return any federal dollars if a court found that works they created were obscene or violated child pornography laws. In addition, they would be ineligible for NEA grants for at least three years from the date of conviction.

If an artist could not repay the grant money, the endowment could require that the state or local arts agency that passed the money along to the artist make the repayment.

"I think they have put together a pretty good blueprint for the resolution of this," said Anne G. Murphy, executive director of the American Arts Alliance, a consortium of performing and exhibiting arts groups. And Marsha Adler, deputy director of public policy for People for the American Way, called it an "artful compromise."

But in Tupelo, Miss., Wildmon was unimpressed. As director of the American Family Association, he and his members lobbied heavily against the endowment. "What Sen. Hatch has done is given the NEA the best green light they can get," Wildmon said. "His proposal would not prohibit 'Piss Christ.' His proposal would not prohibit Mapplethorpe. His proposal would prohibit absolutely nothing."

Hatch, however, said the solution was a constitutional method for sanctions against obscenity. "I completely agree that we cannot tolerate spending hard-earned tax dollars on art that is obscene or involves child pornography. Taxpayers should certainly not be expected to subsidize such filth under the principle of free expression."

Daniel R. Coats, R-Ind., opposed the measure. He complained that the compromise would do nothing to prevent obscene works from getting federal dollars. "If we don't address it here, we're going to hear about it on the floor. If we don't address it on the floor, we're going to hear about it from the American people, and I think the future of the National Endowment for the Arts will be in jeopardy."

Coats offered an amendment that would bar grants for obscene projects, for the sexual exploitation of minors and for attacking historically religious tenets, traditions, symbols or figures.

Hatch dismissed Coats' proposal as unconstitutional and a prior restraint of freedom of expression. The amendment was defeated, 2-14, with only Strom Thurmond, R-S.C., supporting Coats.

With the bipartisan committee backing, the NEA reauthorization was considered in a good position to fend off expected attacks from Helms.

Arts advocates were optimistic that the combination of the Hatch plan and an independent commission's report Sept. 11 opposing legislative restrictions on the content of NEA-funded art would protect the endowment from efforts on the House floor to tighten restrictions.

In addition to letting the courts decide whether a project was obscene or violated child pornography laws, the Senate legislation would eliminate the controversial requirement that artists sign a pledge not to create obscene works. Instead, grant recipients would be requested "to note" the sanctions that would be incurred if they created an obscene work.

To make the agency more responsive to the public, the bill called for:

- A "wide geographic, aesthetic, ethnic and minority representation" on the panels selecting grant recipients.
- Standardized panel procedures.
- Increased visits to see applicants' works.
- A verbatim record of all deliberations and recommendations of each panel.
- Open meetings of the National Council on the Arts.

The legislation would authorize $195 million in fiscal 1991 and such sums as may be necessary through 1995 for the NEA.

House Action

As the debate unfolded in the House, Sidney R. Yates, D-Ill., squelched a proposal July 24 by House Appropriations Committee Chairman Jamie L. Whitten, D-Miss., to ban funding of "obscenity."

Whitten had inserted language in a report on the continuing resolution (H J Res 655) that would bar federal funds from being used to support or finance "any indecent, antireligious or obscene picture, play or writing." The report would have required that anyone violating the guidelines return the money.

Whitten visited the Interior Appropriations Subcommittee, which Yates chaired, and requested a ban on funding "filthy pictures." The subcommittee, however, decided to hold off and debate the issue in full committee.

At the appropriations hearing Sept. 25, Yates complained that Whitten's resolution was only for 20 days. And he noted that the law allowed the federal government to recapture NEA funds used to create obscene works.

Siding with Yates, Silvio O. Conte, R-Mass., said Whitten's language was vague and most likely unconstitutional. And he said Whitten did not consult other members on the amendment, which Conte said represented the views of "only one person, one man, sort of a politburo of sorts."

Yates' motion to delete the language was approved by voice vote.

Williams-Coleman Compromise

On Oct. 4, Williams and Coleman of the Education and Labor Subcommittee on Postsecondary Education, unveiled a compromise version of an NEA reauthorization bill (HR 4825). The compromise stated that the NEA could not fund obscene art but would leave it to the courts to judge whether a project had crossed that line.

After a hearing, the NEA could order grant recipients to return the federal money if they were found guilty of violating obscenity standards. In addition, offending artists would be barred from receiving grants for three years.

"The heart of the issue here is whether members of the House of Representatives were going to hold ourselves up as determiners of art in America," Williams said. "With this, we say 'no.' "

Other Republicans who backed the compromise were Steve Gunderson, Wis., and Paul B. Henry, Mich.

Coleman and Gunderson had initially wanted to require the NEA chairman to determine whether an artist had created an obscene work, and if so, to stop the grant and recoup the money. The artist could have appealed the decision in U.S. District Court. Critics said the plan would have turned due process on its head.

Coleman and Gunderson also proposed increasing the distribution of all NEA funds to state arts agencies from 20 percent to 60 percent.

Henry had proposed language that would have directed the NEA to avoid funding projects that "deliberately denigrate" the cultural heritage of the United States, its religious traditions, or racial or ethnic groups. He would also have barred funding any project that was obscene according to Supreme Court standards or indecent under the Federal Communications Commission's definition.

In a nod to Henry, the compromise would instruct the NEA chairman to ensure that "artistic excellence and artistic merit" were the criteria used to judge applications, while taking into account "general standards of decency and respect for the diverse beliefs and values of the American public."

Provisions in the compromise would have also tightened the application process, making the chairman more accountable for the art the NEA funded.

When no consensus emerged on the obscenity issue during a markup on the legislation reauthorizing the agency for three years, HR 4825 was sent to the floor without it.

There were 26 amendments pending, including one to abolish the agency.

FLOOR ACTION

Endowment supporters in the House guided the compromise reauthorization bill toward successful passage, easily defeating Rohrabacher's attempts to add restrictions.

Bogged down by other legislation, the Senate did not move as quickly. No supporter appeared willing to introduce S 2724 and face another floor fight with Helms.

With the reauthorization stalled, congressional attention shifted to appropriations. The House passed a funding bill (HR 5769) on Oct. 15 and attached the entire three-year reauthorization, again throwing the ball to the Senate.

Senate Action

The NEA reauthorization bid was adopted as an amendment to the Interior appropriations spending bill (HR 5769) on Oct. 24. The Senate voted 73-24 on the amendment, offered by Hatch, that reflected a compromise hammered out earlier in the Labor and Human Resources Committee. *(Vote 308, p. 60-S)*

The Hatch amendment supplanted language in the Appropriations Committee version of the bill that would have continued to ban funding of projects that "may be considered obscene, including but not limited to, depictions of sadomasochism, homoeroticism, the sexual exploitation of children, or individuals engaged in sex acts and which, when taken as a whole, do not have serious literary, artistic, political or scientific value."

But in the excitement of winning that fight and beating back even stiffer obscenity restrictions offered by Helms, arts supporters left the floor before work on the bill had been completed.

That allowed Helms to win voice vote approval, in a nearly empty chamber, of an amendment to ban funding of works that denigrated religion. Helms complained that the funding ban in existing law left "a loophole wide enough to drive six Mack trucks abreast through."

He said the language "doesn't prevent these sleazeballs from getting themselves naked on a stage, rubbing themselves with chocolate and saying, 'Look at me, I'm an artist.' "

Hatch, however, framed the debate this way: "Do we want to do away with the endowment, or do we want artists to have freedom of expression?"

Helms' first amendment, which would have forbidden NEA funding for projects that "depict or describe, in a patently offensive way, sexual or excretory activities or organs," was defeated, 29-70. *(Vote 307, p. 60-S)*

The Senate then adopted the Hatch plan to require artists to pay back the government if they were convicted of violating obscenity or child pornography laws and to ban artists from receiving federal grants for three years after a conviction.

The huge margins in both votes convinced members the debate was essentially over. Claiborne Pell, D-R.I., who had worked with Hatch on the compromise, issued a news release proclaiming victory for restriction-free legislation.

But Helms was not through. First he offered an amendment to prevent grants from being awarded to people whose family income was 1,500 percent of the poverty line. It was rejected by voice vote.

Then he offered his religion amendment. Hatch, however, had left the floor. Only Pell and Robert C. Byrd,

D-W.Va., remained. Byrd, who said he would accept the amendment for discussion in conference, had voted with Helms on the two prior roll call votes. Pell, who could have asked for a roll call vote, simply said "no."

Hatch said it would be up to the House to take the language out of the bill. Even with a roll call vote in the Senate, he said, "I'm not sure it could have been stopped anyway."

Williams, the chief sponsor of restriction-free legislation in the House, called the Helms amendment "a wart on an unblemished face."

The ban on funding sacrilegious art inserted by Helms dealt a wild card to conferees ironing out the differences between the two chambers' Interior appropriations bills. Most members expected conferees to drop the language before returning the Interior bill to both chambers for final approval.

House Action

After a debate punctuated with strident warnings about obscenity and pornography, the House on Oct. 11 rejected attempts to restrict and kill the NEA and voted overwhelmingly to reauthorize the agency. The 349-76 vote on HR 4825 followed months of stalemate between arts advocates who wanted to preserve the endowment as it was, moderate Republicans who wanted to include language opposing obscenity, and conservatives who wanted to abolish the agency altogether. *(Vote 449, p. 144-H)*

The compromise crafted by Williams and Coleman finally paved the way for passage. The compromise stated that the NEA should not fund obscene projects, but it left the determination of what was obscene to the courts.

Rohrabacher framed the debate by telling his colleagues that they could either vote to provide guidelines for the NEA or they could "gut the standards" by voting for the Williams-Coleman substitute.

The House first rejected, 64-361, an amendment by Philip M. Crane, R-Ill., that would have abolished the NEA. *(Vote 446, p. 144-H)*

Rohrabacher then offered his amendment, which would have restricted the endowment from funding projects that were obscene; that depicted human sexual or excretory activities or organs; that denigrated the beliefs, tenets or objects of a particular religion; or that denigrated a person or group on the basis of race, sex, handicap or national origin.

Defending his language, Rohrabacher asked, "Is it censorship not to fund projects indistinguishable from hardcore pornography?"

He complained about an NEA grant to the San Francisco Lesbian and Gay Film Festival, which had used the money to show films with pornographic titles.

But Amo Houghton, R-N.Y., objected strongly, saying "The pornography issue is a ruse," designed to gut federal arts spending.

The amendment was defeated 175-249. *(Vote 447, p. 144-H)*

Lawmakers approved the Williams-Coleman substitute with little dissent, 382-42. *(Vote 448, p. 144-H)*

An amendment by Fred Grandy, R-Iowa, softened one provision in the compromise, which would have barred artists from receiving grants for three years after being found guilty of violating obscenity standards.

Grandy's amendment, approved by voice vote, would allow artists to receive grants once they repaid their original grant.

Rather than revise the controversy when the reauthorization bill floundered in the Senate, the House passed HR 5769 on Oct. 15 and attached the entire reauthorization measure — complete with the three-year extension of the endowment, the obscenity penalty provisions and the shift in funding to the states.

The Senate insisted on amendments to HR 5769 on Oct. 24; the House disagreed with the new provisions and asked for a conference on Oct. 25.

FINAL ACTION

Both the House and Senate agreed to a conference after each chamber passed HR 5769, the Interior appropriations bill, with conflicting amendments on reauthorizing the NEA.

Avoiding another series of heated arguments, the Senate conferees accepted the House version, including the Williams-Coleman compromise, without much discussion.

The conference report filed in the House on Oct. 27 (H Rept 101-971) appropriated $147 million for the endowment. The House agreed to the Interior conference report Oct. 27 by a vote of 298-43. The Senate cleared the bill by voice vote Oct. 27 and President Bush signed the measure Nov. 5. *(Vote 532, p. 168-H)*

As expected, the conferees deleted the Helms provision that would have banned funding works that denigrated religion. Slightly more controversial was the complete deletion of the Hatch amendment.

Rep. Conte of Massachusetts spoke in support of Sen. Hatch's reform provision, calling it a "a workable mechanism for excluding art not worthy of federal funding."

By contrast, he pointed out that the Williams-Coleman provision would require the NEA chairman to ensure that grants were made on "general standards of decency and respect for the diverse beliefs and values of the American public."

"Now that sounds like apple pie and motherhood, but in reality the NEA will have a difficult, if not impossible, time implementing this provision in a constitutional manner," Conte said.

Critics Promise More Pressure

Critics of the NEA vowed to maintain the pressure despite their final setback. "I say to the arts community and all homosexuals upset about this amendment: What is past is prologue," Helms said. "You ain't seen nothing yet."

Even Hatch, who helped broker the conference agreement, warned that the endowment could face trouble in the future. "If there are any of these [offensive projects] funded in the future, they're going to be in trouble, and I'm going to be upset, too," he said.

For its part, the NEA was torn as to how to proceed.

The National Council on the Arts, which advised the NEA chairman, voted on Dec. 14 not to impose standards of decency on panelists who recommended arts grants. Instead, the council instructed panel members that "by virtue of your backgrounds and diversity you represent general standards of decency — you bring that with you."

In January 1991, U.S. District Court Judge John Davies in Los Angeles ruled that the antiobscenity pledge that grant recipients had been required to sign under the fiscal 1990 provision was unconstitutional. On Feb. 20, the endowment announced that it was dropping the requirement to settle a similar suit brought by the New School of Social Research in New York. ■

NASA Cuts Slow Ambitious Plans

In a year of space mishaps, Congress approved $13.9 billion for the National Aeronautics and Space Administration (NASA), a higher amount than in fiscal 1990 but less than President Bush had requested for an ambitious moon-Mars exploration mission.

A compromise one-year authorization bill (S 2287) effectively calling for $15 billion in new spending cleared the Senate on Oct. 25 following action the same day by the House, which had passed a three-year authorization (HR 5649) on Sept. 28. President Bush signed the bill Nov. 16.

The authorization bills were only blueprints, though. Congress provided just $13.9 billion in the NASA appropriations bill (HR 5158 — PL 101-507) that was cleared on Oct. 26 and signed into law Nov. 5. *(VA, HUD, independent agencies appropriations, p. 854)*

Bush had requested $15.1 billion for NASA in fiscal 1991, a 24 percent increase over the $12.2 billion provided in fiscal 1990. The final spending figure was a healthy 14 percent increase but not enough to launch some administration priorities — most notably the multibillion-dollar effort to send explorers to the moon and on to Mars.

NASA's contribution to global environmental monitoring — Mission to Planet Earth — escaped the legislators' heavy cuts. Even so, all new space endeavors were closely scrutinized as NASA's image suffered after the $2 billion-plus Hubble Space Telescope was discovered to have a focusing flaw, the shuttle fleet was grounded for months by fuel leaks, and the $20 billion-plus space station was troubled by serious design flaws. *(Space station, p. 436)*

"The damn agency is dying of a thousand nicks," said Dave Nagle, D-Iowa, a sharp critic of the agency who nonetheless supported many of its goals from his seat on the House Science Committee.

Growing public concern over further space expenditures triggered the White House to convene a blue-ribbon task force in July that closely scrutinized the agency. A report issued Dec. 10 recommended that NASA concentrate on science and on building a new launch system for the commercial space program.

Before the problems started to unfold, the House Science, Space and Technology Committee led by Chairman Robert A. Roe, D-N.J., again pushed a multi-year authorization bill. Meanwhile, the Senate Commerce, Science and Transportation Committee's chairman, Ernest F. Hollings, D-S.C., exerted additional influence as a top member of the Senate Appropriations Committee and successfully resisted the three-year measure.

BOXSCORE

Legislation: NASA authorization, PL 101-611 (S 2287, HR 5649).

Major action: Signed, Nov. 16. Passed by House, Oct. 25; by Senate, Oct. 25 (session of Oct. 24); HR 5649 passed by House, Sept. 28.

Reports: Commerce, Science and Transportation (S Rept 101-455); Science, Space and Technology (H Rept 101-763).

BACKGROUND

The House and Senate had deadlocked on NASA authorization measures at the end of 1989 after the House approved a three-year authorization (HR 1759) and the Senate a one-year bill (S 916). *(1989 Almanac, p. 695)*

The new year opened with expectations of an exciting new start for space science and exploration. Not since the Kennedy administration had there been so much enthusiasm for exploring the universe.

NASA was preparing to launch the first of the grand observatories — the Hubble Space Telescope, and the National Space Council was charting a lunar and Mars mission.

In his budget request, Bush asked Congress for a 24 percent increase in the agency's funding, including $1.3 billion for space exploration and a 36 percent increase — to $2.6 billion — for the space station.

By June, however, space agency officials were facing an angry and scrutinizing Congress. NASA was in the midst of its worst crisis since the *Challenger* exploded shortly after launch in January 1986, killing its crew and burying immediate hopes for a civilian space shuttle program. Investigations by congressional committees and a special presidential commission resulted in sharp criticism of NASA management, budgeting and quality control. *(1986 Almanac, p. 326)*

NASA's hope to restore its tarnished image was set back when officials were forced to reveal that the main viewing device in the $2 billion-plus Hubble telescope, launched April 24, did not work.

Compounding the problem, NASA announced June 29 that it would ground its space shuttle fleet until it could find the cause of hydrogen leaks in the *Atlantis* and *Columbia* spacecraft. Soon after, an outside task force was put together to consider the future long-term direction of the agency.

The unraveling of these difficulties threatened to cloud future funding prospects, especially as NASA was entering the costly hardware development stage for several big projects, including space station Freedom and the Earth Observing System.

Pressures to increase funding for these multi-year, multibillion-dollar space endeavors were pitted against major domestic programs such as housing and veterans' health care, which fell under the same appropriations subcommittees that oversaw NASA.

Meanwhile, the debate over the authorization bill became more over turf than policy. The House Science Committee technically had jurisdiction over the space program but over the years had lost power to the Appropriations Committee, which funded space programs and often dictated the scope and size of important programs.

The House Science Committee had tried for three years to authorize multi-year appropriations for NASA, only to be continuously rebuffed by Appropriations panels. Science Committee members said NASA's relationship with international partners would improve if longer-term funding was guaranteed; appropriators countered that the multi-year funding would not make the agency more efficient.

The House Committee's vision for longer-term funding was again articulated in a bill (HR 5649) in 1990 that would have authorized the agency's endeavors for a three-year period even though NASA struggled through one of the most troubled times in its history.

The one-year authorization that finally passed in 1990 reflected growing budget constraints and Congress' skepticism of the space agency's ability to effectively administer multi-year, multibillion-dollar projects.

Congress' slashing of funds to an expanded human exploration program to the moon and Mars was a direct blow to Bush, who called the program a national priority. The plan called for returning to the moon by 2000, establishing a lunar base and reaching Mars by 2010.

COMMITTEE ACTION

The House and Senate committees overseeing NASA's policies and programs were forced to rethink the direction of big space projects in 1990 as funding constraints dictated cutting the president's ambitious request. Compounding the money problems were a series of major blows to the agency, as technical and managerial problems emerged throughout the year.

Senate Committee

The Senate Commerce Committee on June 27 approved by voice vote a 20 percent increase in NASA authorization levels for fiscal 1991 but cut Bush's proposal for a moon-Mars mission.

As reported, S 2287 authorized $14.8 billion for the agency, deleting virtually all of the $188 million the president had asked for the moon-Mars project.

Al Gore, D-Tenn., chairman of the Science, Technology and Space Subcommittee, urged colleagues to cut funds for the mission, saying the venture "can benefit from a little more thought ahead of time." Projected costs of the president's plan would rise from $188 million in fiscal 1991 to $1.1 billion by fiscal 1995, Gore said.

The panel's lone advocate for authorizing the program in fiscal 1991, ranking Republican John C. Danforth, Mo., said the mission was "the one program where we are offering a futuristic view of what this nation can do."

The committee's markup came the same week that problems with the Hubble telescope and the space shuttle program had developed. The emerging technical and oversight problems contributed to an increasing reluctance on the part of senators to rubber-stamp the administration's priorities as the authorization and appropriations bills progressed.

House Committee

The House Science Committee was more supportive of the space program, giving NASA a full vote of confidence on Sept. 19 as it approved a multi-year reauthorization by voice vote.

HR 5649 would have authorized nearly $17 billion for NASA in fiscal 1991, including the president's full requests for the space station and the moon-Mars mission, and even more in fiscal 1992-93.

One rationale for a three-year bill was that longer funding would mean more efficient program development unencumbered by what Space Subcommittee Chairman Bill Nelson, D-Fla., called "fits and starts" in annual funding.

The Science Committee was the only Capitol Hill supporter of President Bush's moon-Mars mission, however. And it had to reckon with members' frustration at their declining influence in the budgetary process.

F. James Sensenbrenner Jr. of Wisconsin, the Space Subcommittee's ranking Republican, said committee members had themselves to blame for their diminished clout. "This committee has simply rubber-stamped NASA's wish list without prioritizing," he said.

As approved by the committee, HR 5649 would authorize $14 billion in new budget authority for fiscal 1991. Together with $2.9 billion already authorized for the space station, total NASA budget authority would be $16.9 billion — $1.8 billion more than the Bush request.

The authorization bill's funding levels were little more than a statement of best-case priorities, though. The bill won approval from the House by voice vote Sept. 28 — too late to have much influence on the appropriations process.

One reason for the bill's delay was Nelson's absence during much of 1990 for an unsuccessful bid for the Democratic gubernatorial nomination in Flordia. The Space Subcommittee approved a version of the NASA bill in March, but Nelson was not around to push it toward the floor.

FLOOR ACTION

The two chambers succeeded in crafting a compromise in 1990, a process that had failed in 1989 because of major differences over the number of years to be authorized. The Senate's bill for a one-year authorization prevailed during the conference sessions, although the final measure sent to the president reflected many House priorities.

House Action

The House had passed a bill (HR 1759) on Sept. 21, 1989, authorizing $12.8 billion for NASA programs in fiscal 1990. It also authorized funds for most NASA programs for the next three fiscal years.

After a volley between the chambers failed to pass a compromise measure, the House on Nov. 20, 1989, passed HR 3729, which would have authorized two years' worth of spending for most programs and three years for the space station. The House bill also called for a total of $1.6 billion for two new deep-space probes — one to Saturn, the other a comet flyby.

On the last day of the 1989 session, the Senate stripped the bill of all its two-year authorizations but left the space station and deep-space probes.

The bill (HR 5649), approved by the House on Sept. 28, 1990, again authorized funding for three years. Although the one-year Senate bill prevailed, the final measure contained some key House provisions.

The House passed the three-year NASA authorization bill (HR 5649) by voice vote with no debate Sept. 28.

Appropriations Bill

Appropriators had voted to give NASA some of what it wanted but less than the president had asked or the authorizing committees had recommended. As approved by the House on June 29, the NASA spending bill provided $14 billion for the space agency.

The Senate cut the figure to $13.5 billion as it approved HR 5158 on Oct. 3. Utah's Jake Garn, ranking Republican on the Appropriations subcommittee for NASA, withheld an amendment to increase space funding because of the spending levels agreed to the previous weekend in the congressional-White House budget summit.

Senate Action

As appropriators completed their work, the two authorizing committees worked to resolve their differences, too. A compromise version of S 2287 went first to the Senate, where it was approved by voice vote shortly after midnight on Oct. 25, and then to the House, where voice vote approval followed later the same day.

Officially, the final bill authorized new spending of $13.9 billion, but it effectively called for spending about $15 billion in fiscal 1991 — roughly $100 million less than Bush had requested. Included in the bill was a $1.6 billion multi-year authorization to develop a pair of deep-space probes known as CRAFT-Cassini. The bill also limited previously authorized spending on the space station in fiscal 1991 to $2.5 billion.

Although the bill was a one-year measure, not the three-year authorization the House had hoped for, Roe did manage to retain some of the key provisions from the original House-passed bill.

The bill pushed NASA to use more unmanned rockets; helped the commercial space industry by requiring NASA to use outside vendors for some services; attempted to limit the proliferation of man-made debris in outer space; and required NASA to spread research money nationwide.

The authorization bill also reflected lawmakers' interest in another major undertaking, the global monitoring program known as Mission to Planet Earth. It funded a new start on the Earth Observing System (EOS) designed to study the environmental problems that affected our planet.

FINAL ACTION

The day afer the authorization measure was cleared, Congress completed work on the NASA appropriations bill, providing to the agency $13.9 billion for fiscal 1991.

The appropriations bill reached Bush's desk first, and he voiced regret as he signed it Nov. 5. While noting the 13.5 percent increase over the fiscal 1990 budget, Bush said he was "disappointed that the Congress would not provide the small amount of funding requested for technology development to enable future manned missions to the moon and Mars. . . ."

Bush signed the authorization measure Nov. 16. ■

Overhaul Ordered for Space Station Design

Congress struck a major blow to NASA's "Freedom" when it called for a design overhaul of the multibillion-dollar permanently manned space station.

Strongly worded instructions in the conference report on NASA's spending bill (HR 5158 — H Rept 101-900) cut $551 million from the $2.5 billion space station Freedom request for fiscal 1991 and ordered NASA to report back to Congress in 90 days with a "new approach" for its massive undertaking. *(VA, HUD, independent agencies appropriations, p. 854)*

Although NASA's authorization bill (S 2287 — PL 101-611) approved President Bush's request for the multi-billion-dollar space endeavor, the spending bill cleared by Congress instructed the space agency to scale back the plan.

William Lenoir, NASA's associate administrator for space flight, and Richard Kohrs, director of the space station program, said at a news conference in November that budget cuts would require that the station be built in phases and put into limited use until the next section was completed.

Congress had ordered NASA to base its new approach on an "incremental concept" that would permit each phase to be discrete and independent of the next. The space station program was capped at $640 million until the 90-day study was completed and Congress was satisfied with the direction of the project.

The original plan called for the space station to be constructed in orbit from 1995 to 1999 and then be permanently occupied by a crew of up to eight scientists and astronauts. The project, which space experts estimated in 1990 would cost about $40 billion, had become too large and ambitious during a period of shrinking budgets, NASA officials said.

Bits and Pieces

Orbiting a habitat and laboratory into space was an idea launched in 1984 by President Ronald Reagan, who dubbed it "Freedom" and pushed Congress to include enough money to guarantee the project's survival. But the multi-billion-dollar endeavor was too expensive to fund fully and instead got its start in bits and pieces. *(1989 Almanac, p. 697)*

President Bush threw his weight behind the project, too, but in 1990 the space station hit major obstacles when a long-awaited study concluded that the station would require so much maintenance by spacewalking astronauts that it might not be feasible to build as designed. A report published in The New York Times in July said 3,800 man-hours of maintenance would be required each year, a sizable increase from the 2,200-hour prediction made in March that had caused an uproar in Congress.

A NASA investigation team headed by Dr. William F. Fisher and Charles R. Price of the Johnson Space Center in Houston found that the space station could not be built as designed because its vast array of parts would start to break down before the station was complete.

The report came amid growing concern about other design aspects of the station. As the scope of the plan developed, the weight kept increasing, which would have meant more expensive shuttle flights.

Congress also questioned whether the existing spacesuit would be sufficient for astronauts involved in outside construction and maintenance of the orbiting station.

"There'll be a point at which we will be wondering whether it's worth going forward," said Robert A. Roe, D-N.J., chairman of the House Science Committee.

Rep. Bob Traxler, D-Mich., chairman of NASA's Appropriations subcommittee, added: "It's too early to pass judgment on whether the station is . . . a dead duck. It might be an endangered species right now."

Traxler's Republican counterpart, New York's Bill Green, agreed. "There's a lot of frustration with NASA and more and more willingness to look at these big-ticket programs and wonder, 'Do we need this?' "

Roe, Traxler and Green had played crucial roles in allowing the government to spend nearly $4 billion on the space station during its initial six-year design phase.

Despite that money, Traxler and Green sent NASA a strong signal in 1990 that they might soon be ready to cut their losses.

In its report on NASA's spending bill (H Rept 101-556), the House Appropriations Committee told NASA not to spend any more than $750 million on the station in fiscal 1991 (of a total $2.3 billion) without permission from the House and Senate committees. The cap, the report said, was intended to make sure that the design problems were worked out before NASA got too far into the actual bending of metal.

Shrinking the Design

The design in 1990 envisioned a station made up of four main pressurized modules built by the United States, Japan and the European Space Agency, each to be affixed to a 500-foot-long beam. There would be solar panels to power the station and a robot arm to function in the space environment.

NASA's Kohrs said in November that the redesign effort would look at reducing by 90 feet the length of the beam and eliminating attachment points for scientific experiments outside the station modules.

There was also growing concern at the space agency on how the shrinking budget would ever accommodate an anticipated construction budget for 1993, estimated at $3 billion.

The conference committee, in its report, had said that the maximum annual growth in NASA's budget could not exceed 8 percent to 10 percent. The fiscal 1991 appropriation of $1.9 billion could not meet the projected costs, even if a design would be ready for construction in two years.

The appropriators' specific cuts to the space station in 1990 included $12 million from the $15 million requested for space station integrated and attached payload activities; $2.3 million from the planning office in Reston, Va.; and $15 million for the neutral buoyancy laboratory.

However, the budget request of $106.3 million for the flight telerobotic servicer — a program within NASA's Goddard Space Flight Center in Greenbelt, Md. — escaped the budget ax. Barbara A. Mikulski, D-Md., chairman of the Senate Appropriations subcommittee that handled NASA spending, had kept a close eye over that space station component. ■

Space Patent Law Enacted

A measure pushed by space industry interests to explicitly extend U.S. patent law protections to inventions developed in space cleared Congress on Oct. 26 and was signed by President Bush on Nov. 15 (S 459 — PL 101-580).

The measure, aimed at encouraging private investment in space-based research and manufacturing, provided that inventions "made, used or sold in outer space" on U.S. spacecraft would be covered by U.S. patent laws.

Sen. Al Gore, D-Tenn., who sponsored the Senate version of the legislation, said the law would allow U.S. space interests to "get on with the challenges of space-based activities so that working in space will be as commonplace as working on Earth."

The Senate passed the bill by voice vote May 1; the House followed suit Oct. 26, two days before the session ended.

The House had passed similar bills in 1986 and 1988, but they were not acted on by the Senate. Gore, chairman of the Senate Commerce Science Subcommittee, helped shepherd the legislation through the Senate in 1990, along with the chairman of the Judiciary Patents Subcommittee, Dennis DeConcini, D-Ariz.

Background

U.S. entrepreneurs were increasingly eyeing the commercial potential of space, but were uncertain how existing patent law would apply beyond the Earth's surface. International partners in major space endeavors were also concerned about patent rights.

House-passed bills in 1986 and 1988 aimed at resolving the issue went unacted on by the Senate. In 1988, after the bill reached DeConcini's subcommittee late in the session, he declined to take it up but promised to make the issue a priority in the 101st Congress. *(1988 Almanac, p. 644; 1986 Almanac, p. 89)*

The issue gained relevance in 1990 because the proposed space station Freedom, an international effort that planned to contain experiments sponsored by different nations, was gaining attention in Congress and moving closer to reality. *(Space station, p. 436)*

Without a new law, patent issues raised by space station inventions would have been left up to the courts to settle — an uncertainty that concerned some international participants in the project.

S 459 addressed these uncertainties by exempting from U.S. patent law spacecraft or modules of spacecraft that were covered by international agreements dealing with patent rights or that were registered to foreign nations.

That left enough room for space station nations, including Japan, to bargain over such rights without having to worry about how the courts would deal with patent issues.

Legislative Action

With Gore pushing the legislation, the Senate Judiciary Committee approved S 459 by voice vote on March 22 (S Rept 101-266).

The full Senate passed the bill by unanimous consent May 1.

In the House, a similar measure (HR 2946) had won approval by the Science Subcommittee on Space Science and Applications on Sept. 21, 1989.

Although the full Science Committee never formally acted on the measure, the House Judiciary Committee included HR 2946 as one of five titles in another bill (HR 5598).

Another title dealt with a more controversial issue by proposing to authorize the patenting of genetically engineered animals but not humans.

The Judiciary Committee approved HR 5598 by voice vote on Sept. 18 (H Rept 101-960, Part I).

On Oct. 26, Rep. Robert W. Kastenmeier, D-Wis., chairman of the Judiciary Patents Subcommittee, brought the narrower HR 2946 to the House floor, saying the other titles in HR 5598 would be held until the next Congress.

After brief statements all in support of the bill, the House passed HR 2946 by voice vote and then laid it on the table in lieu of S 459.

Voice vote passage then cleared the measure for the president. ■

Super Collider Funds Request Trimmed

Congress provided $243 million in funding to build the world's largest atom smasher in Texas — less than President Bush requested — as spiraling cost estimates for the Energy Department project brought forth renewed efforts in the House to cap spending.

As part of an authorization measure (HR 4380) passed May 2, the House included a provision to cap federal spending on the superconducting super collider (SSC) at $5 billion. But the authorization bill died in the Senate, just as a similar House bill had done in 1988.

The super collider was conceived as a 53-mile, underground, racetrack-shaped tunnel in which 10,000 giant magnets would hurl subatomic particles into each other at nearly the speed of light. Scientists planned to use the powerful computers to study the resulting subatomic debris to learn about the basic nature of matter and energy.

Once projected to cost $5.3 billion, the super collider was officially estimated in 1990 to cost $8.6 billion. Congress had been pressing the Energy Department to send it a hard estimate, but the Bush administration had delayed putting its imprimatur on a figure.

President Bush's $318 million fiscal 1991 request for the project was cut by $75 million in the Energy Department's spending bill (HR 5019 — PL 101-514) after its estimated cost continued to rise. *(Energy, water appropriations, p. 861)*

Both houses initially had approved Bush's full request. But when the fiscal 1991 budget agreement forced appropriators to cut hundreds of millions of dollars from domestic programs in the energy and water bill's final version, the super collider proved an easy target. It ended up with only $243 million, though key members insisted that Congress was committed to seeing the project completed.

The $5 billion cap approved by the House called for foreign countries and Texas to pay for the rest. In the Senate, though, Energy Committee Chairman J. Bennett Johnston, D-La., a big supporter of the project, had no intention of moving an authorization bill because he could control funding through his other chairmanship — the Appropriations Subcommittee on Energy and Water Development.

BACKGROUND

A vigorous debate marked the super collider since the government began studying the idea in 1984.

High-energy physicists and other proponents said the atom smasher would unlock great secrets about the nature of matter, energy and the universe. Detractors labeled it as pork that would drain scarce dollars from more important science projects.

The project had attracted broad congressional support, as 38 states competed to be the host site. Some of that support faded, however, after the Energy Department decided in November 1988 to build it in President Bush's home state of Texas — in Waxahachie, 25 miles south of Dallas.

Personal appeals by Bush — along with the promise of substantial foreign participation — resulted in a $225 million appropriation for fiscal 1990. The funds were to be used for research and development and initial construction of the super collider. *(1989 Almanac, p. 737)*

Congress had appropriated $430 million so far for the project, including the $225 million in fiscal 1990 funds, but had never passed a bill to authorize the project.

The House approved a bill in 1988 to authorize funding for the super collider, but the measure was not acted on in the Senate. The House killed an amendment in 1989 that would have delayed construction of the project. *(1988 Almanac, p. 640)*

Costs for the super collider continued to escalate. Once estimated to cost about $5.3 billion, then $5.9 billion, by 1990 the project was being given a price tag of $8 billion.

The figure rose again in midsummer — to $8.6 billion — just after congressional proponents of the project had won backing for full funding from the House and Senate Appropriations committees.

The $8.6 billion figure came July 25 from the Energy Department's High Energy Physics Advisory Panel, a group of outside experts. Deputy Energy Secretary W. Henson Moore's disclosure marked the second consecutive year that the department revealed higher costs after the annual appropriation for the project had been pretty much nailed down.

HOUSE ACTION

The House Committee on Science, Space and Technology tried again in 1990 to push through an authorization measure for the super collider, but the bill also provided critics a legislative vehicle for trying to cap federal spending on the project.

Committee Action

The House Science Committee approved HR 4380 by a vote of 32-9 on March 28 after a 4½-hour markup (H Rept 101-448). Committee Chairman Robert A. Roe, D-N.J., a super collider enthusiast, argued strongly for passage of the authorization bill. "It's our responsibility to make a decision," he said. "The problem we're faced with — if we don't authorize, we don't have an SSC."

As originally proposed, the bill would have set an overall spending limit for the SSC of $7.5 billion — a federal cap of $5 billion, a $1 billion contribution from Texas and the rest to come from foreign investment.

Before approving the bill, however, the panel agreed by voice vote to an amendment by Ralph M. Hall, D-Texas, that removed the $7.5 billion overall cap. Committee members said the limit would hamper negotiations to secure foreign funding, which would be set at between 20 percent and 33 percent of the total cost.

Roe also deflected an effort by critic Sherwood Boehlert, R-N.Y., to stretch out work on the project.

Boehlert offered an amendment that would have delayed all construction and most design work until the Energy Department certified the prototype magnets needed for the project. He argued that caution was called for because the industry did not know whether it could produce the 10,000 magnets the project needed. "How can we give a green light to turning earth on this project when so much is uncertain?" he asked.

Roe told Boehlert that his amendment would delay the project by up to 18 months and would cost $1.5 billion to $2 billion more. He offered a substitute to Boehlert's amendment that effectively removed most of its provisions. The Roe amendment was approved, 33-13.

Floor Action

The House passed the authorization bill on a 309-109 vote on May 2 with a cap limiting total federal spending to $5 billion and calling for $2.4 billion in outside contributions. *(Vote 94, p. 34-H)*

With Roe's endorsement, the cap appeared to be a key compromise that quieted opposition while limiting the government's obligation to the project.

Pennsylvania's Robert S. Walker, the ranking Republican on House Science, said that with the spending cap and a call for at least 20 percent funding from foreign sources, the bill "is a step in the right direction."

Roe was again passionate in urging support for the project. "What is at stake in HR 4380 is nothing less than American leadership in science, technology and education," he told his colleagues. "And if we are not willing to fight for leadership in these areas, we are not going to create the new wealth of tomorrow."

But Boehlert implored the project's staunchest backers to practice moderation.

The legislation specified that $1 billion of the project's costs would be paid by Texas — as the state had promised — and 20 percent to 33 percent by foreign sources.

More important, it would allow spending on the project to proceed in phases only as certain milestones were achieved. For example, the first $1.17 billion could be released only after the Energy Department submitted to Congress plans for the site, magnet development, management, organization and cost estimates. Another $5.98 billion could be released after other goals were met, such as magnet assembly tests.

With Roe's blessing, members adopted by voice vote a Boehlert amendment that aimed to seal the federal obligation at 1990 estimates. It specified that before the Energy Department could obligate $5.9 billion of the project's funding, it would have to certify that the super collider could be built without exceeding the $5 billion limit.

In a blow to the host state, Roe and other super collider boosters failed to stop an amendment, adopted 256-163, deleting a provision of the bill that would have guaranteed Texas a refund of its $1 billion investment if the project was scrapped before Oct. 1, 1995. *(Vote 93, p. 34-H)*

Joe L. Barton, R-Texas, who represented Waxahachie, argued that his state was being asked to "front-load its contribution" to the super collider. Texas taxpayers would shoulder an undue share of the losses should the project be canceled in the next few years, he said.

Texas lawmakers and Roe warned that other states would hesitate to enter into partnerships with the federal government in the future if Texas lost its contribution.

But the amendment's author, F. James Sensenbrenner Jr., R-Wis., characterized the refund guarantee as a bailout provision that would have changed the nature of the state-federal partnership. Deleting it would assure that the partnership was one of "risk sharing," he said.

Sensenbrenner also noted that the nation's highest-ranking Texan, Bush, supported the move to strike the Texas refund provision.

Boehlert and other critics hailed the spending cap and deletion of the refund provision as significant victories in holding down super collider spending.

Among other amendments, the House:

- Adopted, 420-0, a proposal by Howard Wolpe, D-Mich., to require the General Accounting Office, an investigative agency of Congress, to review the various Energy Department reports on the super collider required under the bill. Those reports included the department's certification of successful completion of magnet assembly tests and its confirmation of commitments for contributions from Texas and foreign sources. *(Vote 92, p. 34-H)*
- Adopted by voice vote a proposal by James A. Traficant Jr., D-Ohio, to prohibit companies based in countries engaged in unfair trading practices against the United States from bidding for super collider contracts.
- Adopted by voice vote a proposal by Louis Stokes, D-Ohio, calling on the Energy Department to set aside 10 percent of the super collider funds for contracts to businesses or other groups operated by blacks, Hispanics, women and American Indians, and to take steps to ensure participation of such groups in the development, construction and operation of the super collider.

FINAL ACTION

In the Senate, Johnston used his dual committee positions to ensure that the House's cost-containment effort went no further. But budget necessities did force lawmakers to reduce funding for the super collider in 1991 even after both chambers had initially supported full funding in the energy-water appropriations bill.

Johnston had been widely regarded as skeptical about the super collider project, but by 1990 he had become a solid supporter. A good-sized chunk of money from the project was expected to end up in Louisiana. Two companies bidding on the project's $1 billion-plus contract to build the massive magnets for the experimental device promised to set up factories in the oil-depressed state.

As head of the Energy and Water Appropriations Subcommittee, Johnston on July 19 pushed through approval of Bush's full 1991 request of $318 million and a highly favorable committee report (S Rept 101-378) that contained no mention of the $2 billion cost increase for the project. The report also rejected the House's premise of requiring foreign investment to cover any cost overruns.

"It is the continued consensus of the committee that the SSC should proceed whether foreign participation is forthcoming or not," the report said. "The benefits to be gained ... outweigh the budgetary requirements that appear to require foreign participation."

Meanwhile, as Energy Committee chairman, Johnston said that he had no plans to do a separate authorization because many of the players who would draft such a bill already oversaw the project's annual budget on the Appropriations Committee. "We think it might be redundant," he said.

Budget Necessities

House appropriators were also supportive of the project, approving the full $318 million requested in the energy-water spending bill that the House passed June 19. The Senate approved HR 5019 on Aug. 1, again with full funding for the SSC.

When House and Senate negotiators met in October to bring their spending in line with the final congressional budget resolution (H Con Res 310), they had to cut $750 million. The super collider was the first project to feel the pinch as conferees cut its funding by $75 million; the conference report cleared Congress on Oct. 20 and was signed by Bush on Nov. 5. ■

Technology Programs Stalled by Side Issue

An eleventh-hour fight over a side issue dashed efforts to reauthorize and expand several Commerce Department programs to bolster manufacturing and technology in the 101st Congress.

Although both chambers had passed bills (S 1191, HR 4329), final legislation failed after Sen. Bob Kasten, R-Wis., insisted that the bill include product-liability reforms. Commerce Committee Chairman Ernest F. Hollings, D-S.C., a strong opponent of the product-liability measure, blocked Kasten's move. *(Product liability, p. 400)*

The technology bills were largely a response to countries such as Japan that aggressively aided their own industries' high-tech efforts, giving them an edge over U.S. companies.

Science-minded lawmakers pushed the legislation, but the Bush administration had strongly signaled it did not want the federal government choosing industrial "winners and losers."

The House would have provided $290 million in fiscal 1991 and $468 million in fiscal 1992 for the Commerce Department's Technology Administration program, which was created in 1988 and included the National Institute of Standards and Technology (NIST).

The Senate had approved a bill in 1989 that would have authorized $320 million in fiscal 1990 for the technology programs.

Included in both chambers' bills were expansions of the department's Advanced Technology Program, which provided seed money for consortia aimed at commercializing new technologies, such as high-definition television (HDTV), advanced manufacturing and superconductivity.

BACKGROUND

Fearful of Japan and other competitors capitalizing on U.S. technology, many members of Congress urged passage of legislation considered crucial to bolstering new technologies. But the Bush administration wanted private industry, not the federal government, to take the lead.

A Senate-passed bill (S 1191) to reauthorize the Commerce Department's one-year-old Technology Administration program failed in 1989 when the House did not act on the reauthorization before adjourning. The Senate had passed the bill by voice vote on Oct. 26, 1989. *(1989 Almanac, p. 699)*

The urgency for promoting technology was heightened in 1990 when a Commerce Department study showed that the Japanese and Europeans had made great strides toward carving out market shares in 12 emerging technologies, while the United States had become even less competitive.

Senate Commerce Chairman Hollings was particularly interested in getting funds for NIST's Advanced Technology Program (ATP), which Congress had created in the 1988 trade law (PL 100-418).

ATP — a civilian counterpart to the Defense Advanced Research Projects Agency (DARPA), which provided funds to innovative high-tech defense endeavors — was designed to provide seed money for research consortia and small businesses to speed commercialization of new technology.

Commerce's new Technology Administration also included another favorite Hollings project: manufacturing-technology centers. The centers, called Hollings Centers, were located around the country for research into transferring technology to small and medium-sized businesses.

LEGISLATIVE ACTION

Strong support for the technology programs from science- and trade-minded lawmakers propelled bills through the Senate in 1989 and the House in July 1990.

Senate Passage

The Senate passed S 1191 by voice vote on Oct. 26, 1989. As approved by the Senate Commerce Committee on Aug. 1, 1989, the bill authorized $320 million in fiscal 1990 funds, including up to $100 million for the ATP (S Rept 101-159).

The committee had removed $30 million for HDTV and several other earmarks in the hope of attracting administration support for the bill. However, the bill did set aside $75 million for the secretary of Commerce to fund research in HDTV, advanced manufacturing, high-temperature superconductivity, ceramics and composite materials, and X-ray lithography.

The bill included $12 million for the regional manufacturing facilities — the Hollings Centers.

House Action

The House Science Committee's Research and Technology Subcommittee approved a three-year authorization (HR 3042) for NIST in July 1989 that included $331 million for technology programs in fiscal 1990.

The House bill called for $150 million for ATP, $50 million more than in the Senate bill. However, the House failed to act on the reauthorization that year.

When the topic was revisited in the second session, the House Science Committee on March 21 sent a strong signal to the Bush administration in favor of throwing government support behind emerging technologies and lifting some antitrust barriers to boost U.S. competitiveness.

The committee approved, 49-0, a bill (HR 4329 — H Rept 101-481) to reauthorize NIST and to provide seed money to research consortia to speed commercialization of new technologies. Before final passage, the House approved minor, mostly technical changes that had been introduced as a substitute bill (HR 5072).

The most significant change removed a section that would have relaxed antitrust laws for certain joint ventures. The Judiciary Committee, which also had jurisdiction over the bill, voted June 12 to strip that section because the House had already passed a similar antitrust measure (HR 4611) June 5. *(Antitrust bills, p. 540)*

The House passed HR 4329 on a 327-93 vote July 11. It would have provided $290 million in fiscal 1991 for the technology programs and $468 million in fiscal 1992, compared with $159 million for the same programs in fiscal 1990. *(Vote 221, p. 45-S)*

Administration Position

The Bush administration, which had requested less than $200 million for the programs in its fiscal 1991 budget, opposed the measure, objecting to hefty increases for the bill's centerpiece Advanced Technology Program. The House would have authorized $50 million in funding for

ATP in fiscal 1990, rising to $100 million in fiscal 1991, and $210 million in 1992.

The overwhelming vote for passage in the House and the substantial Republican support represented a significant shift away from the hands-off approach to commercial technology issues advocated by the Reagan administration.

Even some of the House's staunchest conservatives openly disagreed with the Bush White House's continued opposition to activist technology policies. Among them were Robert S. Walker of Pennsylvania, the Science Committee's ranking Republican; Newt Gingrich of Georgia, the GOP whip; and Don Ritter, R-Pa., considered the resident scientist.

FINAL ACTION

The House set the stage for a conference by inserting its version of the reauthorization package into the Senate bill.

Negotiators then informally crafted a compromise bill. But Kasten, who had won Commerce Committee approval of his product-liability bill (S 1400) in May, insisted any technology measure address that issue, too.

Hollings, who had fought product-liability legislation for a decade, objected, creating an impasse that killed the technology bill.

A last-ditch effort to enact a supercomputer bill separately failed. The Senate approved a three-year, $700 million-plus Commerce-Energy compromise (S 1067) by voice vote Oct. 24, but the House Science Committee declined to bring the measure to the floor.

Although the authorization bills stalled, Congress appropriated $166.2 million in fiscal 1991 for the technology programs, which included $35.9 million for ATP and $11.9 million for the Hollings Centers. Congress had appropriated $9.9 million for ATP in fiscal 1990. *(Commerce, Justice, State appropriations, p. 881)* ■

Animal Rights Activists Survive Session

Legislation to clamp down on animal rights activists who resorted to illegal means to further their agenda fell off Congress' agenda before it adjourned Oct. 28.

The effort to federalize such crimes was being pushed by farmers and researchers but was opposed by animal welfare groups, who denounced it as a mere public relations effort to brand them as terrorists and stifle whistleblowers who exposed cruelty to animals.

The Senate had passed a bill (S 727) by Howell Heflin, D-Ala., late in 1989 to make a federal offense out of burglary and other crimes perpetrated against animal research labs.

But the House Agriculture Committee did not get around to marking up a similar measure, sponsored by Charles W. Stenholm, D-Texas, until the final days of the 1990 session.

The Judiciary Committee claimed jurisdiction over the matter, but members there never got a chance to review it because the Agriculture panel did not officially report its bill (HR 3270 — H Rept 101-953, Part I) out of committee until Oct. 26.

Meanwhile, a similar bill (HR 3349) pushed by animal researchers — introduced by Rep. Henry A. Waxman, D-Calif. — also died when members crafting a last-minute National Institutes of Health (NIH) reauthorization (S 2857 — PL 101-613) decided to keep their bill free of controversial provisions.

BACKGROUND

Chances looked good early in 1990 that lawmakers would enact legislation to protect farms and research labs from animal rights activists.

Several bills that faced Congress would have brought the investigative and prosecutorial powers of the U.S. government to bear on radicals who had gone to extremes in promoting their causes.

The animal activists were also losing crucial behind-the-scenes fights over federal animal-care rules.

Biomedical researchers and farmers who had long been virtually silent were fighting back against a decades-long public relations barrage, undertaken by groups such as People for the Ethical Treatment of Animals (PETA).

"We're in a battle for the hearts and minds of the American public," said Frankie Trull, president of the National Association for Biomedical Research.

The battle was initially waged over legislation crafted by the House Agriculture Committee (HR 3270) that would make it a federal crime to trespass or commit other illegal acts against farms and animal-research labs, an occasional tactic of the radical fringe of the animal rights movement.

Animal-protection groups fought harder against the measures in 1990, arguing that they were designed to intimidate whistleblowers, inhibit the flow of negative information and unfairly brand their entire movement as terrorist.

Behind the legislation were hundreds of farm and research groups, headed by Trull's National Association for Biomedical Research, who feared that the violence would escalate as it had in England, where the groups said animal rights activists had bombed two cars earlier in 1990, seriously injuring a baby in one.

LEGISLATIVE ACTION

The Senate acted in 1989 on legislation (S 727) to clamp down on animal rights activists.

The bill, approved by voice vote Nov. 20, was aimed at more serious acts such as burglary but was limited to illegal acts against research labs.

In the House, Stenholm introduced his bill (HR 3270) in September 1989 to make it a federal crime to trespass or commit other illegal acts against farms and animal-research labs.

By the time of the Agriculture Research Subcommittee's hearing on the bill July 17, Stenholm had gathered more than 200 cosponsors, including virtually all of the subcommittee and full committee members.

Supporters of the bill viewed it as a way to curtail the wave of violence. But some lawmakers had doubts, including subcommittee Chairman George E. Brown, D-Calif., who said he thought the measure went too far.

The Bush administration's science adviser, D. Allan Bromley, endorsed the bill, as did Health and Human Services Secretary Louis W. Sullivan and former Surgeon General C. Everett Koop. But the Justice Department said it opposed the measure, arguing that it and other similar measures duplicated existing statutes and could raise false hopes that the FBI would jump into every future case.

"We do not need any additional jurisdictional hooks," Paul Maloney, a deputy assistant attorney general, told Brown's panel.

The Justice Department found a sympathetic ear with one of Stenholm's cosponsors, Dan Glickman, D-Kan., who said the bill was so vague that it could be interpreted to protect the home of every pet owner from trespass.

"We ought not make simple trespass a federal crime. Our judiciary is overloaded as it is," he said.

Glickman said he favored "going after the zealots" by narrowly focusing the bill to include only the most severe acts, and he offered to broker a compromise with Stenholm. But the subcommittee proceeded to report the bill unamended.

At that point, however, the bill ran into scheduling problems. With the Agriculture Committee preoccupied with the 1990 farm bill, full committee markup was not held until Oct. 22. The bill was approved, a formal report issued Oct. 26, and the measure referred to the Judiciary Committee. But by then, it was too late for the measure to be brought to the House floor.

Meanwhile, the Energy and Commerce Subcommittee on Health and the Environment had approved an NIH reauthorization bill (HR 5661) Sept. 18 with provisions aimed at violence against animal-research labs.

Among other things, the bill, written by subcommittee Chairman Waxman, sought to create federal civil and criminal penalties for animal rights activists who broke into federally funded animal-research facilities.

The subcommittee bill included a modified version of a bill (HR 3349) introduced by Waxman earlier in 1990 aimed at deterring break-ins at research facilities by opponents of animal experimentation.

The House Energy and Commerce Committee approved HR 5661 (H Rept 101-869) on Sept. 26.

The measure made it a federal offense to knowingly release or injure any research animal in a federally funded facility, to knowingly destroy or alter research records, or to knowingly deter, through intimidation or any degree of physical restraint, people from entering or exiting such facilities.

Violators could be subject to jail terms of up to five years and ordered to pay restitution to the facility. The bill also permitted the facility in question to file civil lawsuits.

After a brief debate and adoption of three minor amendments offered by Democrats, the committee approved the bill by voice vote.

With time running out in the 101st Congress, however, and the administration opposed to most provisions of the legislation, sponsors decided to strip the NIH bill of all but a couple of non-controversial sections. ■

Earthquake Act Expanded

The House on Oct. 20 cleared for the president a $363 million three-year authorization bill for earthquake research and preparedness programs.

President Bush signed the measure (S 2789 — PL 101-614) on Nov. 16.

The measure authorized $102 million in fiscal 1991, $120 million in fiscal 1992 and $141 million in fiscal 1993. Funding for fiscal 1990 was about $73 million.

Passed by voice vote, the bill reauthorized and expanded the 1977 Earthquake Hazards Reduction Act. The Senate had passed identical legislation Oct. 19.

Studies continued to forecast major earthquakes in both Northern and Southern California in the next decade. Seismologists also said there was a 40 percent to 60 percent chance of a major earthquake along the fault line region around New Madrid, Mo., within the next 30 years.

Under the bill, the National Science Foundation would work with the U.S. Geological Survey to identify geographic regions that should be the targets for earthquake research proposals. States also would be eligible to receive earthquake preparedness matching grants from the Federal Emergency Management Agency.

The Senate Commerce, Science and Transportation Committee reported S 2789 (S Rept 101-446) on Aug. 30. The committee measure authorized the same amounts approved in the final version. An earlier version of the legislation (HR 3533) passed the House on Sept. 24 by a vote of 283-132. *(Vote 369, p. 120-H)*

The House Science Committee on June 13 had approved HR 3533 (H Rept 101-464, Part II) by voice vote. It would have authorized $110 million in fiscal 1991, $136 million in 1992, $170.5 million in 1993 and $210.5 million in 1994.

The House Interior committee on April 4 gave voice-vote approval to HR 3533 (H Rept 101-464, Part I), authorizing those same amounts for fiscal 1991-93 and $210.8 million in fiscal 1994. ■

Mining Research Aided

Congress authorized the creation of a new research institute in 1990 that was expected to develop new and innovative ways of mining and processing rare minerals critical to U.S. defense and industry.

Minerals such as platinum, vanadium, chromium, cobalt and manganese, which were used in a wide variety of consumer products and weapons, were supplied almost entirely from foreign sources.

The Strategic and Critical Minerals Act (HR 4111 — PL 101-498), introduced Feb. 27 by Rep. Larry E. Craig, R-Idaho, called for the secretary of the Interior to select the site. The bill authorized a minimum of $1.5 million annually for the center.

Among the criteria for choosing the site, envisioned as a consortium with a leading university and several cooperative affiliates, was that the university not already host a generic mineral technology center. There were six such centers at various universities throughout the country.

The host site was also to be located west of the 100th

meridian and offer advanced degree programs in geology and geological engineering. The University of Idaho at Moscow, which met all the criteria, was discussed as a strong possibility, though the bill did not exclude other candidates.

Once established, the center's research was to be aimed at domestic ore that could not be mined or processed efficiently or economically using existing technologies.

Another major responsibility of the center was to identify new deposits of strategic and critical mineral resources.

"As we move into the next century, this nation must have the natural resources to compete and move forward with new and emerging technology," Craig said.

U.S. Bureau of Mines studies showed that 95 percent of world production of the platinum group metals came from the Soviet Union and southern Africa. These minerals and other critical materials were considered crucial to U.S. defense and economic well-being.

For example, the minerals were considered essential for producing high-temperature tolerant metals for use in jet and rocket engines and turbines.

The science of superconductivity was also considered dependent on forging a stable supply of these materials.

Legislation (HR 4111) to authorize a new research center to focus on domestic production of rare and much-needed materials won voice-vote approval March 27 from the House Interior Subcommittee on Mining.

Craig, as a member of the subcommittee, said he introduced the bill because the future availability of the materials from foreign sources was unknown.

The House Interior Committee on April 4 gave voice-vote approval to the legislation (H Rept 101-465).

The bill, approved by the House under a suspension of the rules on July 10, also called for studies and research to improve and develop mineral extraction.

The center was directed to develop substitutes for critical and strategic minerals, improve recycling and develop new processing and fabrication methods. It would also serve as a focal point to identify new deposits of these minerals.

The Senate Energy Committee gave voice-vote approval Sept. 26 to HR 4111 (S Rept 101-496).

The Senate passed the bill by voice vote Oct. 16, clearing it for President Bush, who signed it Nov. 2. ■

Chapter 7

LAW & JUDICIARY

Americans With Disabilities Act 447
ADA Provisions 452
Civil Rights Bill 462
Civil Rights Division Head 465
Veto Message 472
Immigration Act of 1990 474
AIDS Exclusion Policy 480
Immigration Act Provisions 482
Crime Control Act of 1990 486
Death Row Appeals 488
Crime Act: Major Provisions 499
Gun Control 500
Antidrug Measures 502
Martinez Named to 'Drug Czar' Post 503
Juvenile Justice Agency Head 506
'Hate Crime' Statistics 506
Biological Weapons Ban 507
Violence Against Women 507
Souter Supreme Court Confirmation 508
Bush Nomination Announcement 509
Brennan's Judicial Legacy 510
Souter's Statement at Hearings 512
Bush's Nominations to U.S. Courts 515
Imprints on the Bench 517
Thomas Confirmed to D.C. Circuit 518
New Judgeships 520
Judicial Improvements Act of 1990 522
Administrative Law Judges Corps 523
Flag Protection Amendment 524
Abortion Issue in 1990 528
Legal Services Corporation 531
North's Iran-Contra Convictions Set Aside 534
RICO Limitations 536
Vertical Price-Fixing 539
Antitrust Penalties Raised 540
Copyright Bills 541
Disaster Litigation 543

Sweeping Law for Rights of Disabled

Private discrimination barred; access mandated

After years of effort and months of final negotiations, Congress on July 13 cleared landmark legislation to extend broad civil rights protections to an estimated 43 million Americans with mental and physical disabilities.

"It may be raining outside, but this is truly a day of sunshine for all Americans with disabilities," said Sen. Tom Harkin, D-Iowa, chief sponsor of the Americans with Disabilities Act — known as ADA.

President Bush had supported the measure almost since its inception in 1988 and signed it into law at a White House ceremony July 26.

Passage of the bill (S 933) was a major triumph for the coalition of civil rights, disability rights, public health and AIDS support groups that had laid meticulous groundwork since 1988 for passage of the legislation.

The bill in 1989 passed the Senate and advanced through one of the four House committees with jurisdiction over it. *(1989 Almanac, p. 249)*

BOXSCORE

Legislation: Americans with Disabilities Act, PL 101-336 (S 933, HR 2273).

Major action: Signed, July 26. Conference report adopted by Senate, 91-6, July 13; by House, 377-28, July 12. Passed by House, 403-20, May 22; by Senate, 76-8, Sept. 7, 1989.

Reports: Conference reports (H Rept 101-596, H Rept 101-558). Public Works and Transportation (H Rept 101-485, Part I); Education and Labor (Part II); Judiciary (Part III); Energy and Commerce (Part IV). Labor and Human Resources (S Rept 101-116).

Bipartisan Support

The strong, bipartisan support in Congress for the ADA also reflected the public's growing endorsement of the goal of helping the disabled have greater access to the activities of daily life.

A Gallup News Poll released Dec. 20, 1989, found that 81 percent of those queried believed that insufficient attention had been paid to the civil rights of the disabled.

While support for the measure was strong, it was not unanimous.

Some business interests worried that compliance with the law would saddle the private sector with expensive outlays.

As cleared for the president, the ADA extended to people with disabilities protections from discrimination in employment and public accommodations similar to those the 1964 Civil Rights Act afforded women and racial and ethnic minorities.

The measure also required that public transportation systems, other public services and telecommunications systems be accessible to those with disabilities.

The House approved the conference report by a vote of 377-28 on July 12. *(Vote 228, p. 78-H)*

The Senate cleared the bill July 13, approving the conference report by a vote of 91-6. *(Vote 152, p. 34-S)*

Although the final votes on the measure reflected the widespread bipartisan support it enjoyed in both chambers, enactment came only after floor battles at each end of the Capitol the week of July 9 and a second conference to settle two remaining differences concerning how Senate employees were to be covered and whether employers should be allowed to transfer workers with AIDS away from food-handling jobs.

BACKGROUND

Discrimination against the disabled was already prohibited in federally funded activities by the 1973 Rehabilitation Act and in housing by the 1988 Fair Housing Act amendments. But the disabled were not among the classes covered by the landmark 1964 Civil Rights Act, which barred discrimination in employment and public accommodations on the basis of race, sex, religion or national origin.

"You can't legislate attitudes," said Pat Wright, executive director of the Disability Rights Education and Defense Fund. "But you can level the playing field, and that's what the ADA is all about."

Before the 1964 act, said Harkin, "if you were black, you couldn't sit at the lunch table, or you had to sit at the back of the bus. All [business] had to do to accommodate was to let them sit wherever they wanted." But disabled people "can't even get on the bus or into the restaurant, so over time, the impact will be greater."

Wright agreed. "Sometimes there are barriers that prevent people from getting in to be discriminated against. The problem has been getting them in the door."

Because physical as well as psychological barriers were involved, the ADA was considerably broader in scope than the 1964 act.

What the Bill Does

S 933 prohibited discrimination against the disabled in employment, public services and public accommodations, and required that telecommunications be made accessible to those with speech and hearing impairments through the use of special relay systems.

The bill required employers to make "reasonable accommodations" for disabled workers, but not changes that would involve "undue hardship."

The employment provisions were to take effect in two years for employers of 25 or more people and in four years for employers of 15 or more.

"This bill does not guarantee a job — or anything else," said Steny H. Hoyer, D-Md., who served as midwife for the measure as it moved through four House committees. "It guarantees a level playing field: that qualified individuals won't be discriminated against because of their disability."

Steve Bartlett of Texas, who led Republican supporters of the bill, said, "The ADA should reach every community and reshape attitudes toward disability, so that differences among us become more a question of interest than bias."

Although it was patterned after the 1964 act, the ADA went well beyond that law. Its public accommodations section applied not only to the restaurants, lodgings, places of entertainment and gasoline stations covered by the earlier law, but also to museums and sports stadiums, doctors' offices and hospitals, dry cleaners, pharmacies, grocery stores and all other retail and service establishments.

Establishments were required to make new and renovated facilities accessible to the disabled and to make whatever "readily achievable" modifications in existing facilities were needed to accommodate the disabled.

The bill also required all new purchased or leased buses and rail cars to be accessible to the disabled but did not require retrofitting of existing vehicles.

Business Complaints

The business community, which had long expressed concern about the potential costs of compliance with the bill's employment and public accommodations provisions, kept up its efforts. To many businesses, the bill was a nightmare of details and definitions that would dictate what this latest public-policy pledge of equal opportunity meant in practice. "This bill is very scary in the potential burdens it puts on small businesses," said John Sloan Jr., president of the National Federation of Independent Business (NFIB), one of a handful of groups that lobbied against the bill. "We consider it a good idea gone bad."

Backers of the measure said that they had already compromised repeatedly to address business concerns. "We are dealing with an obstructionist element bound and determined to block this legislation regardless of what compromises we might make," testified Lex Frieden, former executive director of the National Council on Disability, which wrote the original draft of the ADA.

Other ADA backers said business was grossly overestimating the cost of complying with the bill. At one meeting, recalled Wright, a business owner was complaining that it was going to cost him $15,000 to lower his drinking fountains in order to make them accessible to those in wheelchairs. "I told him, 'You know, you could just go down to Safeway and buy a $1.98 Dixie cup dispenser and that would bring you into compliance, too.' "

James P. Turner, the acting assistant attorney general for the Justice Department's civil rights division, pointed out that many of the provisions in the ADA bill that business lobbyists said were too vague "are drawn directly, and in many instances even taken verbatim, from the federal regulations" that were in force for many years.

Action and Delay in 1989

The Senate approved its version of the ADA in September 1989. Only one committee — Labor and Human Resources — had jurisdiction over the bill in the Senate, smoothing its road to passage in the chamber.

The bill also had the strong backing of Bush, who talked glowingly of the ADA bill on the campaign trail in 1988. In his acceptance speech before the Republican convention, Bush said, "I am going to do whatever it takes to make sure the disabled are included in the mainstream. For too long they've been left out. But they're not going to be left out anymore."

Bush again endorsed the bill Jan. 18, 1989, just two days before his inauguration.

In a speech at the Department of Health and Human Services (HHS), he said, "One step that I've discussed will be action on the Americans with Disabilities Act, in simple fairness, to provide the disabled with the same rights afforded other minorities."

As the bill weaved its way through each chamber and every committee, Bush did not retreat from his support for the measure even when the administration had disagreements or qualms over certain provisions.

A few problems arose that complicated matters in the House, though. Four committees had jurisdiction over various components of its bill (HR 2273), for example, and only the Education and Labor Committee got around to approving the measure in 1989.

The Energy and Commerce Subcommittee on Telecommunications and Finance did approve its section of the measure in 1989, requiring telephone companies to establish better methods for helping hearing-impaired people communicate over the telephone.

Another difficulty in 1989 was the resignation of the bill's chief sponsor and leading advocate in the House: Majority Whip Tony Coelho, D-Calif. (1979-89), who left Congress in June 1989 following allegations of questionable financial dealings. *(1989 Almanac, p. 43)*

Coelho resigned before the ADA began moving, and he asked Hoyer to head House efforts to pass the bill.

"I was an original cosponsor in the 100th Congress," said Hoyer. "I had worked with him and was one of his closest friends, and I guess I was the logical choice. Tony asked me to do it, and I did it."

HOUSE COMMITTEE ACTION

Just as the House committees were beginning to move on ADA legislation, Bush and administration officials voiced disagreement with Democratic sponsors over a crucial element of a deal struck in 1989.

At issue were the proposed remedies for employment discrimination against the disabled. The compromise language negotiated in 1989 specified that remedies under ADA were to be the same as those provided to women and minorities under Title VII of the 1964 Civil Rights Act. Under existing law, those remedies were primarily injunctive relief and back pay.

But in response to a series of 1989 Supreme Court rulings, separate legislation (HR 4000, S 2104) was introduced to amend Title VII to permit aggrieved parties to sue for monetary damages. *(Civil rights bill, p. 462)*

The administration opposed expansion of Title VII remedies and wanted to make sure that no monetary damages were possible under the ADA, either.

"A very critical element of this bill was that, as under Title VII of the Civil Rights Act of 1964, the remedies it made available for violations of the employment title were limited to non-damage remedies that can be obtained in a trial before a judge," Attorney General Dick Thornburgh said in a March 12 letter to Hoyer.

"In return," he said, "the administration agreed to broad coverage under the public accommodations title," coverage that "is much broader" than that provided under the 1964 law to women and minorities.

But backers of the ADA resisted changing the bill. They maintained that their agreement with the administration was not merely to give the disabled existing Title VII remedies, but to ensure that the disabled had access to the same remedies for employment discrimination that women and minorities had.

Energy and Commerce

On March 13 — the day after the administration released its letter on the remedies issue — the Energy and

Commerce Committee approved the bill by a vote of 40-3, becoming the first House committee in 1990 (and second overall) to approve the ADA.

The committee had primary jurisdiction only over portions of the bill relating to railroads and telecommunications (and therefore could not address the administration's concerns). Members adopted substitute provisions on those sections offered by committee Chairman John D. Dingell, D-Mich., and ranking Republican Norman F. Lent, N.Y.

Among other things, the substitute required Amtrak and other commuter rail systems to make at least one car per train accessible to the disabled within five years; all new cars purchased or leased by Amtrak or commuter authorities would have to be accessible from the outset.

The measure required common carriers to provide telecommunications relay services within three years. Such services permitted hearing-impaired people to use telephones. And it required public service announcements on television that were produced with federal funds to be closed-captioned for the hearing-impaired.

Committee members spent the better part of two hours fending off amendments aimed at narrowing the bill's broad protections. All were rejected by a show of hands.

A handful of members led by William E. Dannemeyer, R-Calif., tried unsuccessfully to limit those covered by the measure and the types of discrimination to be outlawed.

Dannemeyer first tried to eliminate from coverage people who were "regarded as having a disability."

He said, "When we get into the never-never land of 'regarded' as having an impairment, it's subjective."

Backers of the provisions, led by Henry A. Waxman, D-Calif., said the category was needed to protect people such as recovered burn victims who were not actually disabled but might be subjected to discrimination because of their appearance or other factors.

He noted that identical language was included in Section 504 of the 1973 Rehabilitation Act, which prohibited discrimination on the basis of disability in federally funded activities.

Dannemeyer also said he did not want the bill to apply to carriers of HIV, the AIDS virus, who were homosexuals or users of illegal drugs. Those with AIDS or HIV were considered disabled under both the Rehabilitation Act and the ADA.

Waxman said Dannemeyer "wants to make a judgment that some people who are disabled shouldn't be protected because they deserve to be discriminated against."

The amendment was defeated on a 2-15 show of hands.

Dannemeyer received only slightly more support for an amendment to strike a provision allowing remedies to a person "who believes that he or she is about to be subject to discrimination on the basis of disability."

Dannemeyer said, "This is weird, to say the least. There would be no end to claims of anticipatory discrimination."

Advocates said such language was needed to give the disabled a chance, among other things, to obtain injunctions to bar construction of a building if blueprints indicated it would not be accessible.

The amendment failed, 4-14.

A third Dannemeyer amendment would have excluded from coverage anyone with a "currently contagious or sexually transmissible disease or infection" and those with behavioral disorders.

Backers pointed out that the bill excluded from coverage those who posed a direct threat to the health or safety of others. It also excluded those with any of a long list of behavioral disorders, including transvestism, transsexualism, pedophilia, exhibitionism and voyeurism. The amendment failed by 5-17.

Public Works and Transportation

On April 3 the third of four House committees considering the ADA measure gave its approval. The House Public Works and Transportation Committee endorsed the measure by a vote of 45-5. That left only the Judiciary Committee as the final hurdle before a vote on the House floor.

Public Works had jurisdiction over transportation provisions, which were considered vital by the groups pressing for enactment of the ADA.

"Transportation is the linchpin of the bill," said Wright of the Disability Rights Education and Defense Fund. "Making buildings accessible is a waste of money if people can't get to them."

While virtually all who spoke at the markup endorsed the goal of full access to transportation systems, some members expressed skepticism over whether the measure before the committee would foster that goal.

"Good intentions can produce unintended consequences," said Bud Shuster, Pa., ranking Republican on the Surface Transportation Subcommittee, which approved the measure March 6. Shuster called the bill "feel-good legislation," warning that without providing new funds for transit systems to pay for needed changes, "we could end up creating problems rather than solutions."

Although the votes broke largely along partisan lines as the committee rejected a half-dozen amendments to the bill, the disputes were actually more regional in nature.

Republicans complained that many of the "refinements" to the Senate version of the bill tended to benefit large urban areas represented by Democrats. Most of the changes "came from your side of the aisle, while our efforts have fallen on deaf ears," ranking Republican John Paul Hammerschmidt, Ark., told committee Democrats.

But Hammerschmidt was rebuffed when he tried to return to the language of the Senate-passed bill. His amendment failed on a party-line vote of 19-30. The same amendment had failed in subcommittee, 14-24.

An earlier attempt to eliminate all exceptions and time extensions for transit systems to be made accessible was also defeated, by a vote of 17-31.

"These concessions are inconsistent with the concept of a civil rights bill," Hammerschmidt said. In any case, he added, the measure "should not provide exceptions for some areas and not for others."

Norman Y. Mineta, D-Calif., denied that the exceptions in the bill benefited only large urban areas. He said a change to allow more flexibility in paratransit systems that serve those unable to use regular fixed-route buses was more likely to help small cities than large ones.

Democrats also managed to fend off another Hammerschmidt amendment that would have set aside $200 million from the Urban Mass Transportation Administration's (UMTA) discretionary fund to help public transit systems pay for bus lifts for wheelchairs and other needed changes.

"The ADA mandates significant expenditures without any way to help pay the additional costs," Hammerschmidt said.

But Public Works Chairman Glenn M. Anderson, D-Calif., called the proposal a "killer amendment." It was unnecessary, said Anderson, because the costs of making needed changes were already reimbursable under the UMTA law, adding that a funding title would threaten the movement of the measure, because no other committee had added funding. "We would be destroying the considerable progress of this bill," he warned.

The amendment was defeated, 18-31.

One of the most contested amendments, by Thomas E. Petri, R-Wis., sought to give local public transit agencies the option of putting lifts on fixed-route buses or providing paratransit services, or some combination of both. Under the measure, all new buses were required to have wheelchair lifts, and paratransit would also have to be provided for those otherwise unable to use the regular buses.

"Being against mandatory bus lifts does not mean one is against transportation services for the disabled," said Petri.

But even some Republicans disagreed. "Civil rights is never something we've left up to local option," said Sherwood Boehlert, N.Y.

Petri's amendment was defeated by voice vote.

During the subcommittee markup the month before, committee Republicans praised several of the compromises worked out over several weeks of negotiations. They included a special three-year study by the Office of Technology Assessment to determine how intercity buses could best be made accessible to the disabled and a 10-year delay in the requirement that key commuter rail and subway stations be made accessible within 20 years.

Backers of the measure suffered only one setback at the markup when the panel adopted, 20-18, an amendment by Dennis Hastert, R-Ill., requiring that only one car per train in commuter rail systems be made accessible, instead of every car.

The subcommittee did, however, defeat two other attempts to provide exceptions to the requirements.

By a vote of 14-24, members rejected a Shuster amendment that would have allowed waivers of the rule that all new buses be accessible to the disabled in communities with populations of less than 200,000 if sufficient alternative services were available.

Members also rejected, also by a vote of 14-24, a Shuster amendment that would have waived the requirement for private companies not primarily in the business of providing transportation services (such as hotels that operated shuttle systems) to make vehicles holding more than 16 passengers fully accessible.

Judiciary

The Judiciary Committee on May 2 became the fourth and final House panel to approve HR 2273.

The 32-3 Judiciary vote followed two days of markup during which members considered nearly two dozen amendments. Eleven of the 14 rejected amendments were offered by the three Republicans who voted against the bill: Dannemeyer; Bill McCollum, Fla.; and Chuck Douglas, N.H.

An anticipated fight over the remedies available to those who suffered illegal job discrimination fizzled, with Republicans not even calling for a recorded vote on an administration-backed amendment that failed. That issue dominated the April 25 markup by the Civil and Constitutional Rights Subcommittee, which approved the bill 7-1.

The bill provided the disabled the same remedies available to women and minorities under Title VII of the 1964 Civil Rights Act. While that law allowed only injunctive relief, back pay and attorneys' fees, separate civil rights legislation moving through both chambers — and ultimately vetoed by Bush — called for adding monetary damages under Title VII. The administration opposed such damages except for blacks, who already could obtain them under a separate civil rights statute.

F. James Sensenbrenner Jr., R-Wis., offered a Bush-backed amendment — which lost in subcommittee on a 3-5 party-line vote — to limit ADA remedies to the existing ones available under Title VII. He said bill sponsors were reneging on the deal they made with the administration in 1989 to eschew monetary damages in exchange for broad public accommodations coverage.

But supporters of the bill insisted that the disabled deserved the same job-bias remedies as women and minorities, whatever those were at any given time.

Backers of the measure also had little trouble fending off amendments to limit the bill's coverage. Most of those came from Dannemeyer, who charged that the measure "surreptitiously extends civil rights protections to homosexuals" because it included as a protected disability both AIDS and HIV infection.

What the committee fought about most heatedly was an issue that had simmered since the bill's introduction — whether its sweeping requirement that public accommodations be made accessible to the disabled would unduly burden small businesses.

But members ultimately defeated by 15-20 — the narrowest margin of any amendment voted on — a proposal by Tom Campbell, R-Calif., that would have delayed the effective dates of the public accommodations provisions for small businesses.

The committee did make some substantive changes to the bill, although most of them clarified provisions already included or otherwise built on themes in the bill.

A key compromise was a package of amendments offered by ranking Republican Hamilton Fish Jr., N.Y. The Fish package was worked out with the White House; Don Edwards, D-Calif., and Sensenbrenner, chairman and ranking Republican, respectively, of the subcommittee that considered the bill; and McCollum. It included three amendments sought by small-business interests and three sought by lobbyists for the disabled.

The business-backed changes included one to define more specifically the "direct threat" a person with a disabling communicable disease must pose before he or she may be discriminated against. The amendment said direct threat would mean "a significant risk to the health or safety of others that cannot be eliminated by reasonable accommodation."

A second change required that consideration be given to an employer's judgment in determining the "essential functions" of a job. The bill barred discrimination against a disabled person if he or she was capable of performing those essential functions.

Finally, the changes clarified that a cause of action for "anticipatory" discrimination extended only to situations in which a structure was about to be built or altered in such a way as to render it inaccessible to the disabled.

The changes sought by the disability community included ensuring that alterations made to accessible structures not render them inaccessible, that review courses and examinations necessary for professional licensing and certification be given in accessible locations or that special accommodations be made so that the disabled were not excluded, and that the general prohibition against discrimination in public accommodations cover those who owned, leased or operated such places.

Other amendments adopted, all by voice vote, included:

- By Dan Glickman, D-Kan., to encourage "where appropriate and to the extent authorized by law" the use of dispute-resolution methods other than going to court.

• By William J. Hughes, D-N.J., to clarify the definitions of "undue hardship" and "readily achievable," in determining whether business owners must make changes necessary to accommodate those with disabilities.

Small-business groups, led by the National Federation of Independent Business, lobbied heavily for changes to ease burdens that would be imposed on them by the bill.

But bill sponsors, as well as Bush administration officials, said the measure contained dozens of provisions to minimize any adverse impact on businesses, particularly small businesses.

Backers managed to fend off most of the business-backed amendments.

For example, the committee rejected one amendment by George W. Gekas, R-Pa., that would have created a rebuttable presumption that a business with fewer than 100 employees met the bill's requirements if it had spent a total of $1,500 over the preceding three years to accommodate the disabled. Sensenbrenner said the proposal "allows someone to cop out by spending one penny more, even if it does not do the job."

With such a cap, said Edwards, "businesses would focus on meeting the cap and not making the necessary changes."

Backers had more difficulty with Campbell's amendment, which would have delayed the effective date of the public accommodations provisions until 18 months after the issuance of final implementing regulations, instead of 18 months after the bill's enactment.

Campbell said his goal was "to avoid the situation we had with Section 89, where small businesses did not understand the requirement." Congress in 1989 repealed Section 89, a tax code provision concerning discrimination in the provision of employee benefits, after a storm of business protests. *(1989 Almanac, p. 341)*

But backers insisted that the 18-month delay already in the bill was sufficient.

Also rejected were the following amendments offered by Dannemeyer:

• To exclude homosexuals from coverage if they were regarded as having AIDS or HIV, defeated by voice vote.

• To exclude communicable diseases from the definition of protected disabilities, rejected 11-25.

• To provide a legal cause of action against the U.S. government for co-workers infected because an employer hired someone with a communicable disease, defeated 2-31.

• To stipulate that nothing in the act created, "directly or indirectly," any right for any person on the basis of his or her sexual preference, rejected 4-31.

Dannemeyer said the last amendment was needed to prevent the ADA "from being turned into a homosexual bill of rights."

Noting that the bill already explicitly excluded homosexuality from conditions regarded as disabling, Barney Frank, D-Mass., an acknowledged homosexual, replied, "This is not a case on which the statute is silent. I would like to give the gentleman my personal assurance that this will not be viewed as a homosexual bill of rights."

HOUSE FLOOR ACTION

On May 22 the House overwhelmingly passed the ADA by a vote of 403-20. *(Vote 123, p. 44-H)*

Support for the bill was so strong in both chambers that a House-Senate conference probably would not have been necessary had the House not adopted a controversial amendment May 17.

By 199-187, members approved an amendment that would have permitted employers to transfer workers with contagious diseases out of food-handling jobs, even if the disease could not be transmitted through food. Lawmakers on both sides of the issue said the amendment was aimed at people with AIDS. *(Vote 118, p. 42-H)*

Although the bill already specified that its antidiscrimination protections did not apply to workers with contagious diseases that posed a "direct threat" to the health or safety of others, an amendment by Jim Chapman, D-Texas, would have allowed the transfer of workers with diseases that were not transmissible through food but were wrongly perceived to be so by much of the general public.

Supporters of the amendment argued that restaurant owners needed the flexibility to transfer workers with AIDS or HIV out of food-handling positions — not because the virus could be spread via food (AIDS experts said it could not) but because of public perceptions that such workers would present a danger.

Opponents, including most of the bill's key sponsors, said permitting discrimination on the basis of an incorrect perception was exactly what the bill was intended to outlaw. Even representatives of the restaurant industry conceded that the problem they sought to address was not actual risk but the fear of risk.

"With AIDS, for instance, we know it's not transmissible through food," said Elaine Graham, director of federal relations for the National Restaurant Association. "But there is a public perception out there that there is [a risk]. We consider ourselves between a rock and a hard place."

Those opposing the amendment said such perceptions had no place in a civil rights bill. "Twenty-five years after the passage of the major civil rights legislation of the 1960s, we are still hearing the same tired arguments that were used to justify segregated restaurants," said John Lewis, D-Ga., a leader of the 1960s civil rights movement. "They have been dusted off and used again to defend discrimination."

The White House officially opposed the Chapman amendment in a letter from HHS Secretary Louis W. Sullivan to House Speaker Thomas S. Foley, D-Wash. But the letter did not arrive on Capitol Hill until after debate on the amendment was under way.

"Since the act limits coverage for persons who pose a direct threat to others, relaxing the anti-discrimination protection for food service workers is not needed or justified in terms of the protection of the public health," wrote Sullivan.

ADA backers called the letter too little, too late. If the White House had made its opposition known earlier, "I think [the outcome] could possibly have been different," said Hoyer. But he added, "I'm sure the Senate will now ask for a conference because this amendment will not be acceptable."

Bartlett predicted trouble if the conference did not leave the Chapman amendment intact. "My view is the Chapman amendment needs to survive conference. If not, it will require another vote of the House," he said.

The other significant issue left to the conference was the question of congressional coverage. The House bill included Congress under its purview, with enforcement to be handled through the internal grievance procedures set up in 1988 and extended in 1989 to deal with other employee discrimination complaints. *(1988 Almanac, p. 53)*

Continued on p. 459

Americans With Disabilities Act

Following are provisions of the Americans with Disabilities Act (ADA), PL 101-336 (S 933):

Purpose

• Stated that the purposes of the act were to "provide a clear and comprehensive national mandate for the elimination of discrimination against individuals with disabilities; to provide clear, strong, consistent enforceable standards addressing discrimination against individuals with disabilities"; to ensure that the federal government played a central role in enforcing the standards established under the act; and "to invoke the sweep of congressional authority, including the power to enforce the 14th Amendment and to regulate commerce, in order to address the major areas of discrimination faced day-to-day by people with disabilities."

General Definitions

• Defined "individual with a disability" as a person who had a physical or mental impairment that substantially limited one or more major life activities, had a record of such an impairment or was regarded as having such an impairment.

• Defined "auxiliary aids and services" to include qualified interpreters or other effective methods of making aurally delivered materials available to those with hearing impairments; qualified readers, taped text or other effective methods of making visual materials available to those with visual impairments; acquisition or modification of equipment or devices, and other similar services and actions.

Title I: Employment Discrimination

• **Discrimination prohibitions.** Beginning two years after enactment, prohibited a covered entity (defined as an employer, employment agency, labor organization or joint labor-management committee) from discriminating against a qualified individual with a disability in job application procedures, in hiring, advancing, training, compensating and discharging employees, and in other terms, conditions and privileges of employment.

• **Coverage.** Defined "qualified individual with a disability" as a person with a disability who, with or without reasonable accommodation, could perform the essential functions of the job that such individual held or desired. Required that consideration be given to the employer's judgment in determining which functions of a job were essential and that, if an employer had written a job description before advertising or interviewing applicants, that such description be considered evidence of the essential functions of the job.

• **Exclusions.** Specifically excluded from that definition any employee or applicant who at that time used illegal drugs, when the employer acted on the basis of such use. Not excluded were people who had been rehabilitated and were no longer using drugs, were participating in a supervised rehabilitation program and were no longer using drugs or who were erroneously regarded as using drugs. Permitted entities to adopt procedures and policies, including drug tests, to ensure that former drug users were no longer engaged in such use.

• Provided that homosexuality and bisexuality were not impairments and as such were not disabilities under the act. Specified that for purposes of the act the term "disabled" or "disability" did not apply to an individual solely because that individual was a transvestite. Further excluded from the definition of disability "transvestism, transsexualism, pedophilia, exhibitionism, voyeurism, gender identity disorders not resulting from physical impairments, or other sexual behavior disorders; compulsive gambling, kleptomania, or pyromania; or psychoactive substance use disorders resulting from current illegal use of drugs."

• Permitted as a "qualification standard" a requirement that an individual not pose a direct threat to the health or safety of other individuals in the workplace. Defined "direct threat" to mean a significant risk to the health or safety of others that cannot be eliminated by reasonable accommodation.

• **Prohibited activities.** Defined "discrimination" to include:

1) Limiting, segregating or classifying a job applicant or employee in a way that adversely affected the opportunities or status of such person because of his or her disability.

2) Participating in a contractual or other arrangement or relationship that subjected a covered entity's qualified applicant or employee to prohibited discrimination (including arrangements with employment agencies, labor unions, providers of fringe benefits, and training and apprenticeship programs).

For example, a company could be found to be discriminatory if its employment agency refused to accept applicants with disabilities.

3) Using standards, criteria or methods of administration that discriminated on the basis of disability or that perpetuated the discrimination of others who were subject to common administrative control.

4) Excluding or otherwise denying equal jobs or benefits to a qualified individual because of the disability of a person with whom the qualified individual was known to have had a relationship or association (such as a disabled spouse).

5) Failing to make "reasonable accommodations" to the known physical or mental limitations of a qualified applicant or employee, unless the employer could demonstrate that the accommodations would impose an "undue hardship" on its operations.

6) Denying job opportunities to a qualified applicant or employee based on the need to make reasonable accommodation to the person's physical or mental impairment.

7) Using qualification standards, employment tests or other selection criteria that tended to screen out an individual with a disability or a class of individuals with disabilities unless the tests or other selection criteria were shown to be job-related for the position in question and were "consistent with business necessity."

8) Failing to select and administer employment tests so that the test results accurately reflected the skills, aptitude or other factors the tests purported to measure of individuals with a disability that impaired sensory, manual or speaking skills (unless those were the skills to be measured).

• Defined "reasonable accommodation" to include making existing facilities used by employees readily accessible to and usable by individuals with disabilities, job-restructuring, part-time or modified work schedules, reassignment to a vacant position, acquisition or modification of equipment or devices, appropriate adjustment or modification of examinations, training materials or policies, the provision of qualified readers or interpreters, and similar accommodations.

• Defined "undue hardship" as an action requiring significant difficulty or expense. Stipulated that factors to be considered in determining whether a specific accommodation would impose an undue hardship included:

1) the nature and cost of the accommodation needed,

2) the overall financial resources of the facility or facilities involved in the accommodation, the number of people employed at the facility, and the effect of expenses and resources or other impact of the accommodation on the facility's operation,

3) the overall financial resources of the covered entity and its size, including number of employees and number, type and location of its facilities, and

4) the type of operation or operations of the covered entity, including the composition, structure and functions of its work force, geographic separateness, and administrative or fiscal relationship of the facility or facilities to the covered entity.

• **Medical examinations.** Prohibited employers from requiring medical examinations or asking job applicants whether they had a disability, although employers could make pre-employment inquiries into the ability of an applicant to perform job-related functions and could conduct voluntary medical examinations that were part of an employee health program.

• Permitted employers to require medical examinations after making a job offer but before the applicant began work and allowed them to condition the offer on the examination results, but only if all entering employees were subjected to such examinations and they were job-related and consistent with business necessity.

• Required information collected as a result of such examinations to be kept confidential and separate from other personnel information, except that supervisors and managers could be informed regarding necessary restrictions on the work or duties or necessary accommodations for the employee. First-aid and safety personnel could also be informed, when appropriate, if the disability could require emergency treatment, and government officials investigating compliance could be provided relevant information on request.

• Stipulated that tests to determine illegal drug use were not considered medical examinations, although it stated that "nothing in this title shall be construed to encourage, prohibit or authorize the conducting of drug testing for the illegal use of drugs by job applicants or employees or making employment decisions based on such test results."

The act also specifically reserved the right of the Department of Transportation to test employees in safety-sensitive positions both for illegal drug use and impairment by alcohol and to remove those who tested positive from such jobs.

• **Coverage phase-in.** For the first two years following the effective date of the employment section, defined "employer" as a person in an industry affecting commerce who had 25 or more employees for each working day in each of 20 or more calendar weeks in the current or preceding calendar year. After two years, employers with 15 or more employees would be covered.

• **Exempted employers.** Exempted as "employers" the U.S. government, corporations wholly owned by the U.S. government or by an Indian tribe, and bona fide private membership clubs (other than labor organizations) exempted from federal taxation under Section 501(c) of the Internal Revenue Code of 1986. [Federal agencies and those receiving federal financial assistance were already prohibited from discriminating against those with disabilities by Sections 501 and 504 of the 1973 Rehabilitation Act (PL 93-112). Congressional coverage was addressed in Title V of the act.]

• **Defenses.** Permitted an employer accused of discriminatory qualification standards, tests or other selection criteria to use as a defense that such standards — including the requirement that an individual not pose a direct threat to the health or safety of others in the workplace — were job-related and consistent with business necessity and that no reasonable accommodation was possible.

• Specifically permitted a religious corporation, association, educational institution or society to give employment preference to individuals of a particular religion to perform work connected with its activities. Also permitted a religious organization to require that all job applicants and employees conform to its religious tenets.

• **Communicable diseases.** Required the secretary of Health and Human Services, within six months of enactment, to review all infections and communicable diseases that could be transmitted through food handling, publish a list of diseases the secretary determined were transmissible through the food supply, and "widely disseminate" the list of diseases and their modes of transmission to the public. The secretary would be required to update the list annually.

• Permitted employers to refuse to assign or continue to assign to a job involving food handling an individual with a disease on the list for which risk of transmission could not be eliminated by reasonable accommodation.

• Stipulated that language relating to food handling not be construed to "pre-empt, modify or amend" any state or local law, ordinance or regulation regarding food handling designed to protect the public health from individuals who posed a significant health or safety risk that could not be eliminated by reasonable accommodation.

• **Drug, alcohol use.** Permitted employers to prohibit the use of alcohol or illegal drugs at the workplace by all employees, to require that employees not be under the influence of alcohol or illegal drugs at the workplace, and to require that employees conform to the Drug-Free Work Place Act of 1988 (PL 100-690).

Also permitted employers to hold an employee who was a drug user or alcoholic to the same qualification standards for employment or job performance and behavior as other employees, even if any unsatisfactory performance or behavior was related to the drug use or alcoholism of such employee.

Also permitted employers to require that employees meet alcohol and illegal drug-use standards, if applicable, established by the Department of Defense, the Nuclear Regulatory Commission or the Department of Transportation.

• **Posting of notices.** Required every employer, employment agency, labor organization or joint labor-management committee covered under Title I to post notices accessible to job applicants, employees and members describing the applicable provisions of the act, in the manner prescribed by the Civil Rights Act of 1964 (PL 88-352).

• **Regulations.** Required the Equal Employment Opportunity Commission (EEOC) to issue regulations within one year of enactment to carry out the requirements of the title.

• **Enforcement.** Stipulated that the same powers, remedies and procedures set forth in the 1964 Civil Rights Act should be available to the EEOC, the attorney general or any person who believed that he was being discriminated against on the basis of disability in violation of any provisions of Title I or regulations to enforce the employment provisions.

• **Rehabilitation Act amendments.** Directed federal agencies with enforcement authority over employment discrimination in the Americans with Disabilities Act (ADA) and the 1973 Rehabilitation Act to develop coordination procedures to avoid duplicating effort and imposing inconsistent or conflicting standards.

Title II — Public Services

Subtitle A: General Prohibitions Against Discrimination

• **Definitions.** Defined as a "public entity" any state or local government, any department, agency, or other instrumentality of a state or states or local government, Amtrak, and any commuter rail authority (as defined in the Rail Passenger Service Act).

For the purposes of Title II, defined "qualified individual with a disability" as one who, with or without reasonable modifications to rules, policies and practices, the removal of architectural, communication and transportation barriers, or the provision of auxiliary aids and services, met the essential eligibility requirements for the receipt of services or participation in programs or activities provided by a public entity.

• **Prohibited activities.** Prohibited a qualified person with a disability from being excluded from or denied the benefits of the services, programs or activities of a public entity or from being subjected to discrimination by any such entity.

Conferees specified in their report their intent that the above provision required that 911 telephone emergency services be made available to individuals with speech or hearing impairments.

• **Enforcement.** Provided that the remedies, procedures and rights set forth in Section 505 of the Rehabilitation Act of 1973 (primarily the right to obtain a court or administrative order against the discriminatory behavior and to have attorneys' fees paid) should be the remedies, procedures and rights Title II provided to any person alleging discrimination on the basis of disability in the provision of public services.

• **Regulations.** Required the attorney general to promulgate regulations within one year to implement the requirements of Subtitle A of Title II, with the exceptions of matters in the secretary of Transportation's scope. Required the regulations to include standards applicable to facilities and vehicles covered by Subtitle A, other than facilities, stations, rail passenger cars and vehicles covered by Subtitle B.

• **Effective date.** Except for the requirement regarding regulations, above, provided that provisions of Subtitle A of Title II were effective beginning 18 months after the date of enactment.

Subtitle B: Public Transportation Provided by Public Entities

Part I: Public transportation other than by aircraft, commuter rail, or Amtrak.

• **Definitions.** Defined "demand responsive system" as any system of providing designated public transportation that was not a fixed route. Defined "designated public transportation" as transportation (other than public school transportation) by bus, rail or other conveyance (other than by aircraft or commuter or intercity rail) that provided the public with general or special service (including charter service) on a regular and continuing basis. [Aircraft were covered by the Air-Carrier Access Act. Intercity rail transportation was covered in Part II, below.] Defined "fixed route system" as a system in which a vehicle was operated along a prescribed route according to a fixed schedule. Stipulated that the word "operates" included operation of a system by a person under contract or other arrangement or relationship with a public entity.

• **New vehicles.** Provided that beginning 30 days after enactment, all new fixed-route buses, rapid- or light-rail vehicles or other vehicles purchased or leased or solicited for public transportation must be "readily accessible to and usable by" individuals with disabilities, including those who used wheelchairs.

• **Used vehicles.** Provided that beginning 30 days after enactment, public entities purchasing or leasing used vehicles for public transportation must make "demonstrated good-faith efforts" to purchase vehicles that were readily accessible to and usable by disabled individuals, including those who used wheelchairs.

• **Remanufactured vehicles.** Provided that beginning 30 days after enactment if a public entity remanufactured a vehicle or purchased or leased a remanufactured vehicle for public transportation so as to extend its usable life for five years or more, that vehicle, to the maximum extent feasible, must be readily accessible to and usable by disabled individuals, including those who used wheelchairs.

• **Historic vehicles.** Provided an exception for historic vehicles used solely on segments of a fixed-route system included on the National Register of Historic Places if making such a vehicle accessible would "significantly alter the historic character of such vehicle." In that case, only modifications that did not significantly alter the historic character of the vehicle would be required.

• **Paratransit.** Provided that if a public entity operated a fixed-route public transportation system (other than a system providing commuter bus service only), it had to also provide paratransit or other special transportation services to individuals with disabilities, including those using wheelchairs, who otherwise could not use fixed-route systems. [Paratransit was transportation for those unable to board, ride, or exit from regular buses. Such service would have to provide a level of services comparable to that of the fixed-route system.] Response time would have to be comparable only to the extent practicable.

Required the secretary of Transportation to promulgate within one year of enactment final paratransit regulations. Such regulations had to require the following:

• That paratransit be available to anyone with a physical or mental impairment (including a vision impairment) who was unable to board, ride or exit any vehicle on the system that was readily accessible to and usable by individuals with disabilities; to anyone who, with the assistance of a wheelchair lift, was able to ride on the regular fixed-route system, but who wished to travel on a route at a time when no vehicle with a lift was available; and to anyone with a disability whose condition prevented him or her from traveling to a boarding location or from a disembarking location on the fixed-route system.

In all cases, paratransit would also have to be available to one person accompanying the person with the disability and to more than one person if space were available and would not result in the denial of service to individuals with disabilities.

• That if the public entity could demonstrate that the provision of such paratransit services would impose an undue financial burden on the public transit entity, it would be required to provide such services only to the extent that doing so would not impose such a burden. However, the secretary could establish circumstances in which he could require a public entity to provide services beyond what would otherwise be required.

Stipulated that the language not be construed to prevent a public entity from providing paratransit or other special transportation services at a greater level than the ADA required, or to persons other than those with disabilities.

• **Demand-responsive systems.** Provided that new vehicles purchased or leased more than 30 days after enactment by public entities that operated demand-responsive systems (in which a person had to request transportation before any service was rendered) had to be readily accessible to and usable by disabled individuals, including those who used wheelchairs, unless the entity could demonstrate that its system provided service to individuals with disabilities equivalent to that provided to the public.

• **Temporary relief/lifts.** Permitted the secretary of Transportation temporarily to relieve public entities of the obligation to purchase new buses accessible to the disabled if the entity demonstrated that buses with lifts were unavailable and that further delay in purchasing new buses would significantly impair transportation services.

• **New facilities.** Required that new facilities to provide designated public transportation services be readily accessible to and usable by those with disabilities, including those who used wheelchairs.

• **Alterations of existing facilities.** Provided that facilities or any part thereof used for public transportation that were altered by, on behalf of, or for the use of a public entity in a manner that affected or could affect their usability must, to the maximum extent feasible, be made readily accessible to and usable by those with disabilities, including those who used wheelchairs.

• **Key stations.** Required that all stations in intercity rail systems and "key stations" in rapid-rail and light-rail systems be readily accessible to and usable by those with disabilities, including those who used wheelchairs, "as soon as practicable." What constituted "key stations" was to be determined by the secretary of Transportation by regulation. Key stations were generally required to be accessible within three years after enactment, but the secretary was permitted to extend that up to 30 years for stations that required "extraordinarily expensive structural changes" or replacement as long as two-thirds of such stations were accessible in 20 years. Public entities were to develop and submit to the secretary plans to achieve necessary changes.

• **Non-key stations.** Generally required that, when viewed in their entirety, public transportation systems be readily accessible to and usable by individuals with disabilities. Except for key stations, however, public entities were neither required to alter existing facilities to make them accessible — unless alterations were otherwise planned — nor required to provide access to individuals in wheelchairs to facilities from which those in wheelchairs would be unable to benefit.

• **One car per train rule.** Required, as soon as was practicable but no later than five years after enactment, that at least one car on every train with two or more cars in light- and rapid-rail systems be accessible to those with disabilities, including those who use wheelchairs. A special rule applied to historic trains similar to that for historic vehicles, above.

• **Regulations.** Required the secretary of Transportation, within one year of enactment, to issue regulations to carry out the provisions of this subtitle other than for paratransit (which had its own requirement for regulations, above). The regulations were to include standards for facilities and vehicles consistent with the minimum guidelines and requirements issued by the Architectural and Transportation Barriers Compliance Board.

Provided for special consideration for building and alterations if the required regulations were not issued within one year.

• **Effective date.** Except where indicated above, provided that the effective date for Part I of Subtitle B was 18 months after enactment.

Part II: Public transportation by intercity and commuter rail

• **One car per train rule for intercity rail transportation (Amtrak).** Required, as soon as practicable but no later than five years after enactment, that at least one car on every Amtrak train be accessible to those with disabilities, including those who used wheelchairs.

• **New intercity cars.** Generally required, as for other categories of train cars, that new Amtrak cars purchased or leased beginning 30 days after enactment be fully accessible. However, special rules applied for different categories of cars.

Single-level passenger coaches were required to have space in which to park and secure a wheelchair, a seat to which a passenger in a wheelchair could transfer, space to store a folded wheelchair and a wheelchair-accessible restroom. Different rules applied to bilevel passenger cars and single- and bilevel dining cars.

• **One car per train rule for commuter rail cars.** Required, as soon as practicable but no later than five years after enactment, that at least one car on every commuter train be accessible to those with disabilities, including those who used wheelchairs. Specified that "readily accessible to and usable by" not be construed to require a restroom usable by those in wheelchairs if no restroom was provided for other passengers, or a seat to which a person in a wheelchair could transfer or space in which to store a folded wheelchair.

• **Used and remanufactured rail cars.** Required that those purchasing or leasing used rail cars for intercity or commuter rail systems make "demonstrated good-faith efforts" to purchase vehicles that were readily accessible to and usable by disabled individuals, including those who used wheelchairs. Also required that remanufactured cars that were purchased or leased, or existing cars that were remanufactured to extend their usable life by 10 years or more, be readily accessible to and usable by disabled individuals, including those who used wheelchairs, to the maximum extent feasible.

• **New and existing stations.** Required new stations to be readily accessible to and usable by disabled individuals, including those who used wheelchairs. All existing Amtrak stations would have to be made accessible as soon as practicable but in no event later than 20 years after the date of enactment. Existing key stations in commuter rail systems would have to be made accessible as soon as practicable but in no event later than three years after the date of enactment. The secretary of Transportation could extend that up to 20 years if the stations could be made accessible only by raising the entire passenger platform or through other extraordinarily expensive structural changes.

Required the commuter authority to designate which stations were key, to consult with individuals with disabilities and groups representing the disabled and to hold public hearings in making such designation, and to take into account such factors as high ridership or whether such station was a transfer or feeder station.

• **Alterations of existing facilities.** Provided that facilities or any part of them used for public transportation that were altered in a manner that affected or could affect their usability must, to the maximum extent feasible, be made readily accessible to and usable by those with disabilities, including those who used wheelchairs.

• **Regulations.** Required the secretary of Transportation to issue regulations to carry out provisions of this subtitle within one year of enactment. Special standards would apply if the regulations were not complete after one year.

Title III — Public Accommodations

• **Definitions.** Defined as "public accommodations" the following:

1) privately operated entities whose operations affected commerce, including inns, hotels, motels or other places of lodging (exempting establishments located within an owner-occupied residence and containing no more than five rooms for rent or hire),

2) restaurants, bars or other establishments serving food or drink,

3) movie theaters, other theaters, concert halls, stadiums or other places of exhibition or entertainment,

4) auditoriums, convention centers, lecture halls or other places of public gathering,

5) retail sales establishments, including bakeries, grocery stores, clothing stores, hardware stores and shopping centers,

6) service establishments, including laundromats, dry cleaners, banks, barber shops, beauty shops, travel services, shoe repair services, funeral parlors, gas stations, accountants' or lawyers' offices, pharmacies, insurance offices, doctors' and other health providers' offices and hospitals,

7) terminals, depots or other stations used for specified public transportation,

8) museums, libraries, galleries and other places of public display or collection,

9) parks, zoos, amusement parks or other places of recreation,

10) schools of all levels,

11) social service centers, including day-care and senior citizen centers, homeless shelters, food banks and adoption agencies, and

12) places of exercise or recreation, including gyms, health spas, bowling alleys and golf courses.

• Defined "specified public transportation" as transportation by bus, rail or any other conveyance (other than airplanes) that provided the public with general or special service (including charter service) on a regular and continuing basis. Stipulated that "vehicle" not include rail passenger cars, locomotives, freight cars, cabooses, or cars otherwise referred to in Title II, above.

• Defined "readily achievable" to mean easy to accomplish and able to be carried out without much difficulty or expense. Stipulated that factors to be considered in determining whether a specific accommodation would be readily achievable included the following:

1) the nature and cost of the action needed,

2) the overall financial resources of the facility or facilities involved in the action,

3) the number of employees at the facility,

4) the effect on expenses and resources or other impact of the action on the facility's operation,

5) the overall financial resources of the covered entity,

6) the overall size of the business of a covered entity with respect to the number of its employees,

7) the number, type and location of a covered entity's facilities,

8) the type of operation or operations of the covered entity, including the composition, structure and functions of the entity's work force,

9) the geographic separateness and administrative or fiscal relationship of the facility or facilities in question to the covered entity.

• **General prohibitions.** Generally forbade discrimination on the basis of disability in the full and equal enjoyment of goods, services, facilities, privileges, advantages and accommodations of any place of public accommodation by any person who owned, leased (or leased to) or operated a place of public accommodation.

• Deemed discriminatory:

1) Direct discrimination against an individual or class of individuals on the basis of disability or through contractual, licensing or other arrangements (although covered entities were only liable in contractual arrangements for discrimination against the entity's own customers and clients and not the contractor's customers and clients),

2) Providing opportunities not equal to those afforded other individuals,

3) Providing a good, service, facility, privilege, advantage or accommodation that was different or separate from that provided to other individuals, unless such action was necessary to provide an opportunity as effective as that provided to others.

• Required that goods, facilities, privileges, advantages, accommodations and services be provided in the most integrated setting appropriate to the needs of the individual.

• Notwithstanding the existence of separate or different programs or activities, required that individuals with disabilities not be denied the opportunity to participate in programs or activities not separate or different.

• Forbade the use, directly or through contracts or other arrangements, of standards or criteria or methods of administration that discriminated on the basis of disability or that perpetuated the discrimination of others who were subject to common administrative control.

• Also defined as discriminatory the exclusion or other denial of equal goods, services, facilities, privileges, advantages and accommodations or other opportunities to an individual or entity because of the known disability of an individual with whom the individual or entity was known to have had a relationship or association.

• **Specific prohibitions.** Specifically defined as discriminatory:

1) Imposing or applying eligibility criteria that screened out or tended to screen out an individual with a disability or any class of individuals with disabilities from full and equal enjoyment of goods, services, facilities, privileges, advantages and accommodations, unless such criteria could be shown to be necessary for the provision of the goods, services, facilities, privileges, advantages and accommodations,

2) Failing to make reasonable modifications in policies, practices or procedures when such modifications were necessary to afford such goods, services, facilities, privileges, advantages and accommodations to individuals with disabilities, unless the entity

could demonstrate that making such modifications would fundamentally alter the nature of the goods, services, facilities, privileges, advantages and accommodations,

3) Failing to take "such steps as may be necessary" to ensure that no individual with a disability was excluded, denied services, segregated or otherwise treated differently because of the absence of auxiliary aids and services, unless the entity could demonstrate that taking such steps would fundamentally alter the nature of the good, service, facility, privilege, advantage or accommodation being offered or would result in an undue burden,

4) Failing to remove architectural and communication barriers that were structural in nature in existing facilities and transportation barriers in existing vehicles and rail passenger cars used by an establishment for transporting individuals (not including barriers that could be removed only through the retrofitting of vehicles or rail passenger cars by the installation of a hydraulic or other lift), where such removal was readily achievable,

5) In cases in which an entity could demonstrate that such barrier removal was not readily achievable, failing to provide alternative methods if such methods were readily achievable.

• **Transportation.** Beginning 30 days after enactment, defined as discriminatory the failure of a private entity that provided public transportation, but not as a primary business activity (such as a hotel that operated an airport shuttle), to purchase or lease new vehicles with a seating capacity of more than 16 passengers that were not fully accessible to those with disabilities, including those who used wheelchairs. Such an entity could purchase or lease inaccessible vehicles, however, if its overall transportation system provided a level of service to individuals with disabilities equivalent to that provided to persons without disabilities.

• **Health or safety.** Stipulated that nothing in the act required an entity to permit an individual to participate in or benefit from the goods, services, facilities, privileges, advantages and accommodations of that entity if the individual would pose a direct threat to the health or safety of others. Direct threat was defined as posing "a significant risk to the health or safety of others that cannot be eliminated by a modification of policies, practices, or procedures or by the provisions of auxiliary aids or services."

• **New construction.** Deemed discriminatory the failure to design or construct facilities for first occupancy later than 30 months following the date of enactment that were not readily accessible to and usable by individuals with disabilities, except where an entity could demonstrate that it was structurally impracticable to meet the requirements of standards set forth in regulations to put the act into effect.

• **Alterations of existing facilities.** Required that alterations to a facility or any part of it "to the maximum extent feasible" render the facility readily accessible to and usable by individuals with disabilities, including those who used wheelchairs. Where an entity was altering an area of the facility containing a primary function, such as the ticket counter of a bus terminal, it required the entity to make the alterations so that, to the maximum extent feasible, the path of travel to the altered area and the bathrooms, telephones and drinking fountains serving the remodeled area were readily accessible to and usable by individuals with disabilities. The latter requirement would not apply in cases in which alterations to the paths of travel were disproportionate to the overall alterations in terms of cost and scope (as determined under criteria established by the attorney general).

• **Elevators.** Specified that the bill did not generally require that elevators be installed in facilities of fewer than three stories or less than 3,000 square feet per story. Elevators, however, would be required in buildings to be used as shopping centers, shopping malls or as professional offices of health-care providers. The attorney general also could determine that elevators were needed in otherwise excluded buildings based on the type and amount of usage the facility received.

• **Privately owned public transportation systems.** Generally barred discrimination on the basis of disability in the full and equal enjoyment of public transportation services provided by private entities primarily engaged in the business of transporting people (except by air) and whose operations affected commerce.

• Deemed discriminatory imposing or applying eligibility criteria that screened or tended to screen out individuals with disabilities or classes of individuals with disabilities from "fully enjoying" the public transportation services, or failing to make reasonable modifications, provided auxiliary aids and services or removed barriers as required above in Title III (unless such criteria could be shown to be necessary for the provision of the services being offered).

Beginning 30 days following enactment, also deemed discriminatory the purchase or lease of a new vehicle (other than an automobile, a van with a seating capacity of less than eight passengers or an over-the-road bus) that was not readily accessible to and usable by individuals with disabilities (including those who used wheelchairs).

For vehicles used in demand-responsive systems, new vehicles did not have to be readily accessible to and usable by individuals with disabilities if the entity could demonstrate that the overall system provided a level of service to people with disabilities equivalent to that given to the public.

Similarly, beginning 30 days following enactment, vans that seated fewer than eight passengers had to be fully accessible unless the entity could demonstrate that the system for which the van was being purchased or leased, when viewed in its entirety, provided a level of service to people with disabilities equivalent to that provided to those without disabilities.

• **Rail cars.** Beginning 30 days following enactment, deemed discriminatory the purchase or lease of a new rail passenger car that was not readily accessible to and usable by individuals with disabilities, including those who used wheelchairs. Also required the remanufacture of such a car that would extend its usable life by 10 years or more — or the purchase or lease of such a remanufactured car — to be accessible "to the maximum extent feasible."

• **Historical or antiquated rail cars.** Provided an exception to the extent that compliance with the above requirements would "significantly alter the historic or antiquated character" of a rail passenger car or rail station used exclusively by such cars or would violate safety rules issued by the secretary of Transportation. Defined historical or antiquated rail passenger cars as those at least 30 years old whose manufacturer had left the business and which either had "a consequential association with events or persons significant to the past," embodied the distinctive characteristics of a type of rail passenger car used in the past or represented a past time period.

• **Over-the-road buses.** Required the Office of Technology Assessment (OTA) to undertake a study to determine the access needs of individuals with disabilities to over-the-road buses (defined as a bus with an elevated passenger deck located over a baggage compartment) and the most cost-effective methods for providing access to such buses and bus service by those who used wheelchairs, through all forms of boarding options.

Required the study to be submitted to the president and Congress within 36 months of enactment.

Required that final regulations regarding over-the-road buses be issued by the secretary of Transportation within one year after the study was submitted. The regulations, which were to be based on the results of the OTA study, would require that every private provider of transportation by over-the-road bus must provide accessibility to individuals with disabilities, including individuals who used wheelchairs.

The regulations would have to require compliance seven years from the date of enactment for small providers (to be defined by the Transportation secretary) and six years for other providers. Permitted the president, if he determined as a result of the study that compliance with the over-the-road bus requirements on or before the deadlines would significantly reduce intercity bus services, to extend each of the deadlines by one year. Stipulated that the final regulations could not require installation of accessible restrooms in over-the-road buses if such installation would result in a loss of seating capacity.

Within one year of enactment, required the Transportation secretary to issue interim accessibility regulations. But those interim rules could not require that structural changes be made to over-the-road buses or that boarding assistance devices be purchased to provide access.

• **Regulations.** Within one year of enactment, required the attorney general to issue regulations regarding transportation and other services covered under the public accommodations title (except for those concerning over-the-road buses, above). Required that any standards included in the final regulations be consistent with the minimum guidelines and requirements issued by the Architectural and Transportation Barriers Compliance Board.

• **Interim accessibility standards.** If final regulations were not issued within the required year, provided that in cases of new construction or alterations for which a valid building permit was obtained before final regulations were issued and on which construction began within one year after the permit was received that compliance with the Uniform Federal Accessibility Standards in effect at the time the permit was issued should suffice to meet the accessibility requirement.

Similarly, vehicles and rail passenger cars whose design complied with the laws and regulations governing accessibility of such vehicles or cars at the time the design was "substantially completed" would be deemed to meet the accessibility requirement.

• **Exemptions, private clubs and religious organizations.** Exempted from the requirements of the public accommodations section private clubs or establishments exempt under Title II of the 1964 Civil Rights Act as well as religious organizations or entities controlled by religious organizations.

• **Enforcement.** Provided that the same remedies and procedures set forth in the 1964 Civil Rights Act [preventive relief, including an application for a permanent or temporary injunction, restraining order or other order, and attorneys' fees] were the same remedies and procedures available to any person who was being discriminated against on the basis of disability in violation of Title III provisions or "who has reasonable grounds for believing that such person is about to be subjected" to discrimination in violation of provisions regarding new construction or structural alteration of a facility. Specified that nothing in the section "shall require a person with a disability to engage in a futile gesture if such person has actual notice that a person or organization covered by this title does not intend to comply with its provisions."

• With respect to violations pertaining to removing barriers in existing facilities, altering existing facilities and undertaking new construction, provided that remedies should include an order to alter facilities to make them readily accessible to and usable by individuals with disabilities. Where appropriate, required that courts could also require providing an auxiliary aid or service, modifying a policy or providing alternative methods, to the extent required under Title III.

• **Attorney general's powers.** Required the attorney general to investigate alleged violations of the public accommodations provisions, including periodically reviewing compliance by covered entities.

• Permitted state and local governments to apply to the attorney general to certify that building codes met or exceeded minimum requirements for accessibility to and usability of covered facilities by persons with disabilities. Specified that such certification could be used as a "rebuttable presumption" that the codes met the requirements of the act at any enforcement proceeding. Under a rebuttable presumption, unless the party claiming discrimination could show compelling evidence to the contrary, any certified code was presumed to meet the accessibility requirements of the act.

• Authorized the attorney general to file a civil suit in U.S. District Court if he "has reasonable cause to believe that any person or group of persons is engaged in a pattern or practice of discrimination under this title" or that any person or group of persons had been discriminated against and that such discrimination raised an issue of general public importance.

• Authorized the court in such civil suits to grant temporary, preliminary or permanent relief, require the provision of an auxiliary aid or service, modification of policy, practice, procedure, or alternative method, or to make facilities readily accessible to and usable by individuals with disabilities.

• Authorized the award of other relief as the court considered appropriate, including monetary damages to aggrieved persons when such damages were requested by the attorney general, as well as civil fines "to vindicate the public interest." Such fines could not exceed $50,000 for a first violation and $100,000 for any subsequent violation.

Stipulated that in "pattern or practice" cases, all violations included in an attorney general suit counted as a single first violation in assessing the maximum civil penalty, and that the $100,000 fine could only be applied in a subsequent case. Also specified that the terms "monetary damages" and "such other relief" did not include punitive damages.

• In determining civil penalties, required the court to give consideration to any good-faith effort or attempt to comply with the requirements of Title III by the entity in question. In evaluating "good faith," required the court to consider, among other factors it deemed relevant, whether the entity could have reasonably anticipated that an appropriate type of auxiliary aid would have been needed to accommodate the unique needs of a particular individual with a disability.

• **Examinations and courses.** Required that examinations or courses related to applications, licensing, certification or issuing credentials for secondary or postsecondary education, professional, or trade purposes be offered in a place and manner accessible to those with disabilities or that alternative accessible arrangements for such individuals be made.

• **Effective date.** Specified that, except for the provisions noted above regarding regulations and accessibility of transportation services, the requirements of the title should become effective 18 months after the date of enactment.

• **Delay in civil actions for small business.** Except for actions related to the section concerning new construction and structural alterations of facilities, precluded civil actions against certain small businesses for a certain period of time.

For businesses that employed 25 or fewer employees and had gross receipts of $1 million or less, civil suits would not be permitted for acts or omissions occurring for six months following the effective date.

For businesses that employed 10 or fewer employees and had gross receipts of $500,000 or less, civil suits would be barred for acts or omissions occurring up to one year following the effective date.

[In their report, conferees noted that the extended time period "gives small businesses additional time to learn the requirements of the ADA and to come into compliance with the Act before they will be subject to a civil action. The conferees fully expect that businesses will, however, make good-faith efforts to comply with the Act during this additional phase-in period."]

Title IV: Telecommunications Relays

• **Definitions.** Defined TDD as a Telecommunications Device for the Deaf, a machine that employed graphic communication in the transmission of coded signals through a wire or radio communication system.

• Defined "Telecommunications Relay Services" as telephone transmission services that permitted an individual who had a hearing or speech impairment to communicate by wire or radio with a hearing individual in a manner functionally equivalent to that of someone without an impairment.

• **Services required.** Amended the Communications Act of 1934 to require the Federal Communications Commission (FCC) to ensure that interstate and intrastate telecommunications relay services were available, "to the extent possible and in the most efficient manner" to hearing- and speech-impaired individuals.

• For purposes of administering and enforcing provisions of Title IV, granted the FCC the same authority, power and functions with respect to common carriers engaged in intrastate communications as it had for common carriers engaged in interstate communications.

• Required each common carrier providing telephone voice transmission services to provide telecommunications relay services within the area in which it offered service. Such services would have to be provided either individually, through designees, through a competitively selected vendor or with other carriers within three years after enactment.

• **Regulations.** Required the FCC, within one year of enactment, to prescribe regulations to implement the requirement, including establishing functional requirements, guidelines and operations procedures and minimum standards, and requiring that such relay services operate continuously.

The regulations had to also require that users of telecommunications relay services pay rates no greater than those paid for functionally equivalent voice communication services with respect to such factors as duration of the call, time of day, and distance from the point of origin to the point of termination.

Regulations had to also prohibit relay operators from refusing calls or limiting length of calls that used telecommunications relay services, prohibit relay operators from disclosing the content of any relayed conversation and from keeping records of any such conversation beyond the duration of the call, and prohibit relay operators from intentionally altering a relayed conversation.

The regulations were also to encourage the use of existing technology and not discourage or impair the development of improved technology.

• **Separation of costs.** Required the FCC to issue regulations governing the jurisdictional separation of costs of such services, generally providing that the costs of interstate telecommunications relay services be collected from interstate jurisdiction and intrastate telecommunications relay services be collected from intrastate jurisdiction.

• **Enforcement.** Required the FCC to resolve a complaint alleging a violation by a final order within 180 days after the complaint was filed.

• **Closed-captioning of public service announcements.** Required that television public service announcements funded in whole or part by the federal government be closed-captioned for the hearing-impaired.

Title V: Miscellaneous

• **Congressional coverage — Senate.** Reaffirmed the Senate's commitment to Rule XLII, which barred discrimination in employment on the basis of "race, color, religion, sex, national origin, age, or state of physical handicap."

Generally provided that the rights and protections provided pursuant to the ADA, the Civil Rights Act of 1990 (S 2104), the Civil Rights Act of 1964, the Age Discrimination in Employment Act of 1967 and the Rehabilitation Act of 1973 should apply to employees of the Senate. Provided, however, that claims of discrimination be investigated and adjudicated exclusively by the Select Committee on Ethics or other entity the Senate designated. Specified that remedies, if warranted, "to the extent practicable" should be the same as those available to others under the acts named above. Provided that the Architect of the Capitol establish remedies and procedures for matters not related to employment (primarily public accommodations). Such remedies and procedures were to be effective on their approval by the Senate Committee on Rules and Administration.

• **Congressional coverage — House.** Provided that employment protections provided under the act be available to employees of the House of Representatives or any employing authority of the House and that complaints be handled by the Fair Employment Practices Board as approved in H Res 15 of the 101st Congress. Provided that the Architect of the Capitol establish remedies and procedures for matters not related to employment (primarily public accommodations).

Such remedies and procedures were to be effective on their approval by the Speaker of the House, after consultation with the House Office Building Commission.

• **Congressional coverage — Instrumentalities of Congress.** Provided that the ADA applied to each instrumentality of Congress. Instrumentalities included the Architect of the Capitol, Congressional Budget Office, General Accounting Office, Government Printing Office, Library of Congress, Office of Technology Assessment and U.S. Botanic Garden. Required the chief official of each instrumentality to establish remedies and procedures (to be applied exclusively) to carry out the purposes of the ADA and to report to Congress describing the remedies and procedures. Stipulated that nothing in the act alter enforcement procedures for individuals with disabilities provided in the General Accounting Office Personnel Act of 1980 and regulations stemming from that act.

• **Rehabilitation Act of 1973.** Stipulated that "except as otherwise provided" nothing in the act should be construed to reduce the scope of coverage or apply a lesser standard than provided under Title V of the Rehabilitation Act of 1973 or federal regulations issued pursuant to that title.

• **Other laws.** Stipulated that nothing in the act should be construed to invalidate or limit the remedies, rights and procedures of any other federal, state or local law that provided greater or equal protection for the rights of individuals with disabilities than those afforded under the act.

Did not, however, prevent the prohibition or imposition of restrictions on smoking in places of employment covered by Title I, in transportation covered by Title II or in places of public accommodation covered by Title III.

• **Insurance and employee benefits.** Stipulated that Titles I through IV did not prohibit or restrict insurers or other organizations from normal underwriting practices consistent with state law. Also stipulated that the titles did not prevent persons or organizations from establishing, sponsoring, observing or administering bona fide benefit plans, as long as such plans or insurance were not used to evade the purposes of Titles I, II or III.

• **Opportunity to decline.** Stipulated that nothing in the act required an individual with a disability to accept an accommodation, aid, service, opportunity or benefit.

• **State immunity.** Provided that a state was not immune under the 11th Amendment to the Constitution from an action in federal court or a state court of competent jurisdiction for a violation of the act. [The 11th Amendment generally prevented states from being sued in federal courts.] Provided that the same remedies were available for a violation committed by a state as would be available in an action against any other public or private entity.

• **Whistleblower protection.** Prohibited discrimination against any individual because that person had opposed any act or practice outlawed by the act or because that person had made a charge, testified, assisted or participated in any manner in an investigation, proceeding or hearing under the act.

• **Interference or coercion.** Made it unlawful to coerce, intimidate, threaten or interfere with any person "in the exercise and enjoyment of, or on account of his or her having exercised or enjoyed, or on account of his or her having aided or encouraged any other individual in the exercise or enjoyment of, any right granted or protected" by the act.

• **Architectural and Transportation Barriers Compliance Board.** Within nine months of enactment, required that the Architectural and Transportation Barriers Compliance Board issue minimum guidelines to supplement the existing Minimum Guidelines and Requirement for Accessible Design. Required the guidelines to establish additional requirements to ensure that buildings, facilities, vehicles and rail passenger cars were accessible in architecture and design, transportation and communication to individuals with disabilities.

• **Historic buildings.** Required that for alterations of buildings or facilities eligible for listing in the National Register of Historic Places or designated as historic under state or local law, the minimum guidelines established procedures at least equivalent to those established by applicable sections of the Uniform Federal Accessibility Standards.

• **Attorneys' fees.** Authorized the awarding of "a reasonable attorney's fee," including litigation expenses and costs, to the prevailing party (other than the United States) in any action or administrative proceeding under the act.

• **Technical assistance.** Within 180 days, required the attorney general, in consultation with the chairman of the EEOC, the secretary of Transportation, the chairman of the Architectural and Transportation Barriers Compliance Board and the chairman of the FCC to develop a plan to assist covered entities, along with other executive agencies and commissions, in understanding their responsibilities under the act. Permitted the attorney general, in developing the plan, to get assistance from other federal agencies, including the National Council on Disability, the President's Committee on Employment of People with Disabilities, the Small Business Administration and the Department of Commerce.

• Authorized each federal department or agency with responsibility for putting sections of the act into effect to render technical assistance to individuals and institutions that had rights or responsibilities under the act. Required the agencies to ensure the availability and provision of appropriate technical assistance manuals no later than six months after applicable final regulations were published under Titles I, II, III and IV. Also permitted each federal department or agency to make grants or award contracts to effectuate the purposes of the act. Such grants and contracts had to be designed to ensure wide dissemination of information about the rights and duties established by the act and to provide information and technical assistance about techniques for effective compliance.

• Stipulated that failure to receive technical assistance, including failure by other entities to develop or disseminate any technical-assistance manual, did not excuse an employer, public accommodation or other entity from complying with applicable provisions and requirements of the act.

• **Wilderness areas.** Required the National Council on Disability to study and report within one year the effect that wilderness designations and wilderness land management practices had on the ability of people with disabilities to use and enjoy the National Wilderness Preservation System.

• Reaffirmed that Congress did not intend that the Wilderness Act be construed as prohibiting the use of a wheelchair in a wilderness area by someone whose disability required its use and that, consistent with the Wilderness Act, no agency was required to provide special treatment or accommodation or to construct facilities or modify conditions of lands within a wilderness area to facilitate such use.

• **Illegal use of drugs.** Specified that for both the ADA and the Rehabilitation Act of 1973, the term "individual with a disability" did not include an individual who was currently using illegal drugs if the covered entity acted on the basis of such use.

However, the act stipulated that the above not exclude an individual with a disability who had completed a supervised drug rehabilitation program and was no longer illegally using drugs or who had otherwise been rehabilitated or was erroneously regarded as engaging in such use.

• Permitted covered entities to adopt or administer "reasonable policies or procedures," including but not limited to drug testing, designed to ensure that a former user of illegal drugs was no longer engaged in such use.

• Required that individuals not be denied health services or services provided in connection with drug rehabilitation on the basis of current illegal use of drugs if the individual was otherwise entitled to such services.

• For purposes of the Rehabilitation Act, provided that programs and activities providing health or rehabilitation services not exclude any individual from the benefits of such programs or activities on the basis of current illegal drug use if he was otherwise entitled to such services. Provided that for programs and activities providing educational services, local educational agencies could take disciplinary action for the use or possession of illegal drugs or alcohol against any handicapped student who was using alcohol or drugs illegally to the same extent that such action was taken against non-handicapped students.

• For purposes of Sections 503 and 504 of the Rehabilitation Act as they related to employment, stipulated that the term "individual with handicaps" did not include alcoholics whose alcohol use prevented them from performing the duties of the job or whose employment, because of alcohol abuse, directly threatened the property or the safety of others.

• Defined "illegal use of drugs" as drugs whose use, possession or distribution was unlawful under the Controlled Substances Act but did not include use of a drug taken under supervision of a licensed health-care professional or other uses authorized by the Controlled Substances Act or other provisions of federal law.

• **Miscellaneous exclusions.** Provided that homosexuality and bisexuality were not impairments and as such were not disabilities under the act. Specified that for purposes of the act the term "disabled" or "disability" did not apply to an individual solely because that individual was a transvestite.

Also excluded from the definition of disability "transvestism, transsexualism, pedophilia, exhibitionism, voyeurism, gender identity disorders not resulting from physical impairments, or other sexual behavior disorders; compulsive gambling, kleptomania, or pyromania; or psychoactive substance use disorders resulting from current illegal use of drugs."

• **Alternative means of dispute resolution.** Where appropriate and to the extent authorized by law, encouraged the use of alternative means of dispute resolution, including settlement negotiations, conciliation, facilitation, mediation, fact finding, minitrials and arbitration to resolve disputes arising under the act.

• **Severability provision.** Stipulated that if any provision of the act was held unconstitutional, it should be severed from the rest of the act and not affect the enforceability of the remaining provisions. ■

Continued from p. 451

Those procedures allowed House employees to seek a formal hearing on their complaints if mediation failed, to obtain a ruling from a hearing examiner and to appeal to a board composed of House members and non-members. Remedies included injunctive relief and back pay.

The Senate version of S 933 also covered Congress, but was silent on enforcement, leaving Congress — like private employers — subject to enforcement by the executive branch. Some members said that raised separation-of-powers problems — an argument that had prevailed in the past when Congress exempted itself from other labor and anti-discrimination laws.

Bill supporters were upset with the administration for not working hard enough to fend off weakening amendments and for refusing to take a position on an amendment offered by Jim Olin, D-Va., that would have defined as an "undue hardship" any accommodation for a disabled person that cost an employer more than 10 percent of the disabled employee's annual salary. Olin's amendment was ultimately rejected, 187-213. *(Vote 117, p. 42-H)*

After negotiations, three other amendments were accepted by ADA supporters and adopted:

• By John J. LaFalce, D-N.Y., by 401-0, to delay enforcement of the public accommodations provisions of the bill for small businesses. *(Vote 116, p. 42-H)*

Provisions barring discrimination would take effect as scheduled 18 months following enactment, but enforcement actions against businesses with 25 or fewer employees and gross receipts of $1 million or less would be barred for an additional six months. Such civil actions would be barred for an additional year for businesses with 10 or fewer employees and gross receipts of $500,000 or less.

• By McCollum, by voice vote, to stipulate that if an employer accused of job discrimination had a written job description, that description must be considered as evidence in determining the "essential functions" of the job.

• By James V. Hansen, R-Utah, by voice vote, to permit wheelchair access to designated wilderness areas. Before approving the amendment, members accepted modified language proposed by Bruce F. Vento, D-Minn., chairman of the Interior Subcommittee on National Parks and Public Lands, stipulating that "no agency is required to provide any form of special treatment or accommodation, or to construct any facilities or modify any conditions of lands within a wilderness area, in order to facilitate such use."

Before passing the bill, the House rejected three other amendments. The most contentious was the Bush-backed Sensenbrenner amendment that would have written into the ADA bill the existing remedies available under Title VII of the 1964 Civil Rights Act — injunctive relief, back pay and attorneys' fees.

The amendment, previously rejected by a House Judiciary subcommittee and by the full committee, failed, 192-227. *(Vote 121, p. 44-H)*

The other two amendments rejected, both of which

concerned public transportation, also had been considered at the committee level.

One, offered by William O. Lipinski, D-Ill., would have restored bill language approved by the Public Works Committee — over the objections of the disability community and bill sponsors — requiring that only one car per train in commuter rail systems be accessible to those in wheelchairs. The Energy and Commerce Committee approved commuter-rail provisions without that language, and its version was the one that went to the floor.

The amendment failed by a vote of 110-290. *(Vote 119, p. 44-H)*

Members also rejected, 148-266, an amendment offered by Shuster that would have permitted a waiver in cities with fewer than 200,000 residents of the bill's requirement that all new buses be equipped with wheelchair lifts. *(Vote 120, p. 44-H)*

Critics of the amendment said civil rights should not vary with population density. "A civil right to equal transportation services does not diminish according to a city's population in the latest census," said California's Mineta. "How can we let the census control someone's civil rights?"

CONFERENCE ACTION

With only two major items in dispute between the versions of the bill passed by the House on May 22 and by the Senate in September 1989, conferees were able to reach agreement after only a single two-hour meeting June 25.

But those two issues — how Congress should be covered by the new antidiscrimination requirements and whether people with AIDS or other diseases could be transferred out of food-handling jobs — continued to bog down the bill even after they were ostensibly settled by conferees.

While members in both chambers agreed that Congress should be subject to the bill's ban on discrimination in employment and public accommodations, they still disagreed on how the ban should be enforced.

The House bill provided for a wholly internal mechanism both for House employees and those of Congress' "instrumentalities," including the Architect of the Capitol and the General Accounting Office. Under that measure, complaints would be handled pursuant to the House ruling authorizing that chamber's Office of Fair Employment Practices.

The Senate bill, however, as part of an amendment added by Charles E. Grassley, R-Iowa, simply made the provisions of the law applicable to the Senate and the instrumentalities.

Conferees agreed that the internal mechanism would apply in the House and to the instrumentalities and that while the Senate would set up its own internal procedure to handle complaints, those not satisfied with the outcome could still sue in federal court.

"We shouldn't saddle the private sector with something we're not willing to saddle ourselves with," said Orrin G. Hatch, R-Utah, a backer of Grassley's language.

But others in the Senate argued just as vehemently that allowing individuals to sue in federal court violated the constitutional separation of powers as much as allowing members of the executive branch to administer the law.

Chapman Amendment

But while some senators were not satisfied with the proposed resolution of the congressional coverage issue, others were equally unhappy that conferees dropped the controversial Chapman AIDS amendment.

This issue took on a new twist when the Senate on June 6 instructed its conferees to accept the House's amendment. The motion to instruct, offered by Jesse Helms, R-N.C., was approved by voice vote after senators by 40-53 refused to table (kill) it. *(Vote 110, p. 26-S)*

In contrast to the House, which often went on record urging conferees to take a particular position, the Senate rarely voted on such motions. And while no one said the vote was unprecedented, not even longtime Senate observers could remember a case in which the chamber's conferees were instructed to accept a House-passed provision.

Helms' motion was technically not binding on the Senate conferees, but it put them in an awkward position. While a majority of both House and Senate conferees voted against the language, both chambers went on record in support of the provision.

Opponents of Helms' motion brandished letters from a raft of experts, including HHS Secretary Sullivan and Centers for Disease Control Director William L. Roper, saying that the language was unnecessary and unwise. The health authorities warned it could harm efforts to educate the public about how AIDS was spread.

Helms had letters from key backers of the language, including the National Restaurant Association and the NFIB.

After the vote, an angry Harkin accused the NFIB, which had targeted him for defeat in November, of "playing politics" with the issue. "If you want to pander to perception," he said, "why don't we take everyone with AIDS and put them in a colony like you used to do with lepers?"

Representatives of AIDS and disability groups said a more important factor in their defeat was Minority Leader Bob Dole's support of the Helms motion. Dole, R-Kan., was a key supporter not only of the ADA bill but also of various bills and amendments to boost federal support of AIDS research, prevention and treatment. Dole was one of several senators with a disability, having lost use of one arm in World War II, and he usually voted with the disability groups.

This time, after Dole voted with Helms, at least two Republicans who initially voted the other way switched, and several Southern Democrats who had not voted cast their votes with Helms.

"They don't own me," said Dole when asked later why he didn't support the position favored by disability-rights groups. "Just because you have a handicap doesn't mean you have to be for every screwball thing."

Backers of the Chapman amendment in both chambers argued that even a mistaken perception that someone with AIDS could represent a health threat could threaten the viability of a restaurant.

Said Rep. Bartlett, one of the ADA's primary backers in the House, "If you have [a worker with] AIDS, you can be put out of business, and I suggest that violates the spirit of the law."

But Sen. Edward M. Kennedy, D-Mass., chairman of the Labor and Human Resources Committee, who chaired the conference, said that tradition and precedents had given Senate instructions to conferees far less weight than similar motions receive in the House (the measures were non-binding in both cases). The instructions to accept the amendment "are basically meaningless," he said, in announcing that Senate conferees proposed to drop the provision.

House conferees were considerably more divided, voting 12-10 to strike the amendment.

FINAL ACTION

With the conference completed on June 25, supporters hoped for prompt action on the conference report. But last-minute maneuvering had Democrats in both chambers accusing Republicans of efforts to delay the bill and Republicans hotly denying ill intentions.

When it was apparent that the Senate had not yet ironed out the congressional coverage problem, sponsors decided to have the House proceed. However, Hatch and Dole blocked Democratic efforts to get the House to act on the conference report.

Democrats in both chambers said (and Republicans privately confirmed) that a key reason was the expectation that the House would defeat a motion to recommit the report to conference with instructions to restore the Chapman amendment.

If the House had then approved the conference report, the Senate would have been unable to consider a similar recommittal motion because the conference would have ceased to officially exist after the first chamber approved the report. That would have left the Senate with the choice of accepting the report in its existing form or killing the bill.

Instead, neither chamber took up the conference report until the second week in July.

The task still ahead was resolving differences over coverage of congressional employees and the Chapman amendment.

In effect, the Senate fought its final battle over congressional coverage for the ADA during July 10 consideration of the Civil Rights Act of 1990 (S 2104).

After a day of debate, the Senate approved an amendment to that bill offered by Rules Committee Chairman Wendell H. Ford, D-Ky., to codify an existing Senate rule providing civil rights protections for Senate employees.

That was a significant change from provisions House and Senate conferees agreed to June 25 on the ADA bill. Those would have permitted — because of an amendment by Grassley — Senate employees alleging discrimination to sue in federal court if they were dissatisfied with the outcome of the Senate's internal grievance procedure.

But Ford, along with ranking Republican Ted Stevens of Alaska and the leaders of the Ethics Committee, Howell Heflin, D-Ala., and Warren B. Rudman, R-N.H., argued successfully that allowing courts to second-guess congressional actions would be a dangerous violation of the Constitution's separation of powers between branches.

Such power, suggested J. Bennett Johnston, D-La., could result in a judge's ordering a senator to hire someone as a "confidential political adviser who was neither sympathetic with his politics or perhaps not even of the same party."

After the Senate made clear it preferred Ford's approach to Grassley's on the civil rights bill, ADA sponsors agreed July 11 to permit the Senate to send that measure back to conference to replace the language permitting Senate employees to go to court with the text of Ford's amendment. The recommittal motion July 11 was by voice vote.

When the ADA went back to conference, it gave proponents of the Chapman amendment one more chance to get it included in the final version.

"You can call it hysteria all you want to, but you better believe that the vast majority of people who eat in restaurants do not want to have their food prepared or handled by people who have AIDS or who are HIV-positive," said Helms, who in June had sponsored the successful motion to instruct Senate conferees to accept the Chapman language.

When the motion to send the bill back to conference to deal with the court issue was on the floor, Helms tried to amend it to instruct conferees on the Chapman language. Helms' amendment failed, 39-61. *(Vote 148, p. 33-S)*

After that, members approved, 99-1, a compromise by Hatch that called for the secretary of HHS to develop and disseminate a list of infections and communicable diseases that can be transmitted through food. Those with such diseases could then be transferred out of food-handling positions. *(Vote 149, p. 33-S)*

Dole, who earlier had supported Helms' efforts, changed his position.

"The Chapman amendment would send a false and dangerous message that would undermine the efforts of our public health officials to calm necessary public fears about AIDS transmission," he explained. "Public ignorance has never before been considered a valid excuse for discrimination."

The reconvened conference quickly ratified the two changes on July 12.

"This amendment does speak to the health concerns of the American public," said Hoyer. Unlike the original Chapman language, Hoyer said, the Hatch "language is consistent with the bill."

But House backers of the Chapman language were still unhappy.

Hatch's amendment, complained Bartlett, who otherwise strongly backed the bill, "flipped Chapman on its head. The fact is AIDS cannot be transmitted by food handling, but the reality is in small and medium-sized towns, if you don't give people flexibility to move cooks with AIDS out of the kitchen, it's just a lottery" as to whether restaurants can stay in business. "The reality is other people have rights, too," he added.

Though some House members were disappointed with Hatch's compromise, enough went along with it to permit approval of the conference report. By 180-224, members rejected a motion by Dannemeyer to recommit the bill to conference for a third time in order to put the language back. *(Vote 227, p. 78-H)*

With the major issues decided and obstacles cleared, both chambers gave their overwhelming approval to the ADA.

During final consideration of the measure in the Senate, emotions were high as the landmark legislation neared clearance.

Harkin delivered a portion of his floor speech in sign language; that was, he said, a message to his brother Frank, who was deaf.

"I told him that today Congress opens the doors to all Americans with disabilities — that today we say no to ignorance, no to fear, no to prejudice," Harkin said.

Hatch broke down briefly as he spoke of the courage of his late brother-in-law who battled polio. And Kennedy, Harkin's key ally on the measure, spoke of his mentally retarded sister, Rosemary, and his son, Teddy Jr., who lost a leg to cancer.

"Americans with disabilities deserve more than good intentions," Kennedy said. "They deserve emancipation from generations of prejudice and discrimination, some of it well-meaning but all of it wrong-minded." ■

Bush Vetoes Job Bias Bill; Override Fails

In the first defeat of a major civil rights bill in the last quarter-century, the Senate on Oct. 24 failed by one vote to override President Bush's veto of a bill (S 2104) intended to protect workers against job bias.

The measure targeted six 1989 Supreme Court decisions that narrowed the reach and remedies of laws prohibiting employment discrimination and made it harder to prove job discrimination and easier to challenge affirmative-action programs.

Absent from the eight months of negotiations over the Civil Rights Act of 1990 was the successful give and take that saw two other civil rights-related bills become law during the same session: one to prohibit discrimination against disabled people (S 933 — PL 101-336), the other to prevent age discrimination in employee benefits (S 1530 — PL 101-433). *(Disabled antidiscrimination, p. 447; age discrimination, p. 362)*

Unlike those measures, the civil rights bill received a veto threat within weeks of being offered in February. In May, Bush effectively disowned the threat and said he wanted to sign a civil rights bill. But he said he would not agree to a bill that led to hiring quotas.

Business groups said that if standards established by the Supreme Court for a defense of employment practices were reversed, companies would adopt hiring quotas for women and minorities so that the companies would not be subject to frivolous discrimination lawsuits based on a higher percentage of male or white workers.

The argument was critical in the debate as Bush and other Republicans helped make the tag "quota bill" stick.

Meanwhile, there was discord among civil rights ranks over how strong a hand they had and what they needed to give up. Most were unwilling to yield significant ground because they were confident that Bush would not risk the political cost of a veto.

The Senate had adopted the conference report on S 2104 by 62-34 on Oct. 16 and the House by 273-154 on Oct. 17. The votes left civil rights activists three Senate votes and 12 House votes shy of the two-thirds needed to override Bush's anticipated veto. *(Senate vote 276, p. 55-S; House vote 478, p. 152-H; veto message, p. 472)*

On the day of the override attempt, black House members ringed the Senate floor watching as the votes were cast. Above in the gallery sat David Duke, the unsuccessful Louisiana senatorial candidate and former Ku Klux Klan leader who had run against affirmative action and programs favoring blacks. Jesse Jackson, a black leader and former Democratic presidential contender, earlier had sat in the gallery watching debate.

The only senator to switch sides after the Oct. 16 vote on the conference report was Rudy Boschwitz, R-Minn., who had earlier opposed the bill. Boschwitz, who was up for re-election, waited, however, to cast his vote until it was clear that he would be the 66th vote, not the decisive 67th.

BOXSCORE

Legislation: Civil Rights Act of 1990, S 2104 (HR 4000).

Major action: Senate sustained veto, 66-34, Oct. 24; vetoed, Oct. 22. Conference report adopted by House, 273-154, Oct. 17; by Senate, 62-34, Oct. 16. Passed by Senate, 65-34, July 18; by House, 272-154, Aug. 3.

Reports: Conference reports (H Rept 101-755, H Rept 101-856). Labor and Human Resources (S Rept 101-315). Education and Labor (H Rept 101-644, Part I); Judiciary (Part II).

In all, 11 Republicans joined all 55 Democrats in voting for the veto override, which failed 66-34. *(Vote 304, p. 60-S)*

Edward M. Kennedy, D-Mass., the bill's Senate sponsor, said he would reintroduce the bill in 1991. Civil rights activists were predicting passage by early spring, but the administration was signaling it would continue to resist any legislation it viewed as a quota bill.

BACKGROUND

In a series of decisions during its 1988-89 term, the Supreme Court significantly restricted both the reach and the remedies of federal civil rights laws. The rulings stunned groups representing minorities and women, and prompted calls for legislation to modify the decisions. But by the end of 1989, the civil rights coalition had not yet finished drafting omnibus legislation to counter the rulings. *(1989 Almanac, p. 314)*

Lawyers who handled job-bias cases said that because of the tight new standards set by the court, many legitimate claims simply were not being filed, some complaints were being dismissed and remedies were being limited.

Proponents in Action

After months of negotiations, a bipartisan coalition of civil rights advocates Feb. 7 launched a legislative campaign to counter six of the 1989 decisions. All had narrowed the laws against employment discrimination.

Members unveiled the legislation at a large news conference that included Coretta Scott King, widow of the Rev. Dr. Martin Luther King Jr. Also there to support the initiative were leaders from various women's, minority and religious organizations.

Companion measures (S 2104, HR 4000) were introduced in Congress by Kennedy and Rep. Augustus F. Hawkins, D-Calif., with scores of cosponsors.

Kennedy said rights activists had more Senate cosponsors — 37 as of Feb. 8 — than they had at the start of successful efforts to reverse 1980 and 1984 Supreme Court rulings on voting rights and discrimination in federally funded programs.

"There are those who say we need no action," Hawkins said. "They say these decisions were merely technical adjustments. That we should wait and see what the impact will be. But racial and sexual harassment are not technicalities. They are abominations."

Part of the delay in drafting legislation in 1989 to overturn the decisions, according to key staff members, was that the same Judiciary and Labor Committee aides who had to draft the civil rights bill had been involved until then with legislation to protect the U.S. flag, broaden the death penalty, increase the minimum wage and outlaw discrimination against the disabled.

With Congress busy on these and other bills, staff members said, even if a bill had been introduced, it could not have been acted on promptly.

What the Bill Would Have Done

The Kennedy and Hawkins measures were broad in scope, seeking to overturn the six Supreme Court cases as well as amend other existing rules. The ambitious nature of the legislation set it apart from less controversial civil rights measures of the 1980s that overturned single high court decisions.

The proposed bills sought to amend Title VII of the 1964 Civil Rights Act, which barred employment discrimination based on race, color, religion, sex or national origin. Title VII remedies were limited to back pay and benefits, attorneys' fees and injunctive relief.

The bill would have changed that to allow financial compensation for pain and suffering and punitive damages in intentional-discrimination cases. Unlike existing rules, the bill also would have allowed jury trials. And the bill would have extended the statute of limitations in Title VII job discrimination cases from six months to two years.

In addition to the Title VII changes, the civil rights measure sought to overturn or modify the following 1989 Supreme Court decisions:

- *Patterson v. McLean Credit Union*, which held that Section 1981 of Title 42 of the U.S. Code prohibited racial discrimination only in hiring, not subsequent on-the-job activity. The bill would have made clear that Section 1981 covered all aspects of a job relationship.

The Kennedy-Hawkins legislation stated that Section 1981 outlawed racial discrimination in the "making, performance, modification and termination of contracts and the enjoyment of all benefits, privileges, terms and conditions of the contractual relationship."

It would have ensured that the statute covered complaints of racial harassment, and it would have applied the new standards to all legal actions begun after June 15, 1989, the date of the *Patterson* decision, or pending at the time of that ruling.

- *Wards Cove v. Atonio*, which required workers to identify the specific employment practices alleged to have resulted in racial disparities in a workplace and shifted to complaining workers the burden of proving that an employer had no business necessity for the challenged practices. The bill would have returned to the employer the burden of proving that a practice with a "disparate impact" on minorities or women was necessary to the business. It would have allowed employee-plaintiffs to establish that a practice had a disparate impact without pinpointing the specific cause of the discrimination.

Some practices that had been cited as having a disparate impact were aptitude tests that resulted in ethnic minorities being kept out of jobs or physical strength requirements that caused women to lose promotions.

The court held, 5-4, that an employee who claimed that a company's practices had a disparate impact on women, blacks or other minorities had to identify the specific employment practices that resulted in the discrimination. The court said the burden rested on the employee to disprove an employer's assertion that the practices served a legitimate business purpose.

The decision involving Alaskan cannery workers effectively overturned the 18-year-old standard of *Griggs v. Duke Power Co.*, which had required employers to prove a business necessity for practices that adversely affected minorities and women.

The bill would have returned the law to the *Griggs* standard and made clear that workers did not have to pinpoint the specific practices that resulted in an adverse impact on women and minorities.

- *Martin v. Wilks*, which allowed court-approved affirmative-action plans to be challenged later by individuals affected by a consent decree, even if they did not protest at the time the matter was being negotiated. The bill would have made consent decrees final, provided that all potentially affected parties were given adequate notice that a court order was being negotiated.
- *Lorance v. AT&T Technologies*, which required workers who thought a seniority system was discriminatory to file suit soon after the system was adopted. The bill would have allowed challenges to seniority systems under deadlines that would not begin running until an individual was adversely affected by the plan.
- *Independent Federation of Flight Attendants v. Zipes*, which barred successful plaintiffs from obtaining attorneys' fees for their efforts to defend against intervenors. The bill would have allowed successful plaintiffs to obtain attorneys' fees from intervenors.

The bill also would have responded to a series of court decisions since 1985 cutting back on attorneys' fees for prevailing plaintiffs in civil rights cases.

- *Price Waterhouse v. Hopkins*, which allowed an employer to defend a discriminatory employment decision if it could prove the same decision would have been made in the absence of bias. The bill would have made employers liable for intentional discrimination even if the same decision would have been made for non-discriminatory reasons.

Business Complaints

The Supreme Court rulings cheered conservative legal organizations and, to a lesser extent, business groups. Administration reaction to the decisions was ambivalent. A Justice Department spokesman initially said the administration would have to study what stance it would take on congressional efforts to overturn the rulings.

As legislation was introduced, the *Wards Cove* decision became the focal point. Civil rights activists found the *Wards Cove* provision especially important because of its broad effect on the ability of workers to win job discrimination claims.

Employer groups, conservative organizations and the administration, on the other hand, came to embrace the decision. They depicted any effort to modify it as all but forcing employers to adopt hiring and promotion quotas in order to avoid lawsuits.

Deputy Attorney General Donald B. Ayer said the proposed legislation would snare employers whose legitimate business practices inadvertently led to disproportionately low numbers of minority workers.

"Employers will fall back on quotas," Ayer predicted. "They will make sure they have so many blacks, so many Hispanics and be done with it. ... The whole issue of *Wards Cove* is whether we're going to put employers in the position that the only safe course is to have quotas."

Proponents of the bill insisted that the measure had nothing to do with quotas and would not encourage them.

"This legislation specifically does not deal with affirmative action or quotas, even though there are those — primarily those who will not support this legislation — who say it does," Kennedy said.

Ralph G. Neas, executive director of the Leadership Conference on Civil Rights and a key lobbyist working on the legislation, rejected suggestions that potential stumbling blocks — such as the quota issue — might make it more difficult to draw support for a broad antidiscrimination measure.

"Over the past decade, 70 percent majorities in both houses of Congress have supported major civil rights bills," said Neas. "We are quite confident that that same bipartisan majority will pass this bill."

Administration Proposal

After the Kennedy-Hawkins bill was introduced with its considerable fanfare, the administration countered with its own one-page bill to reverse the *Patterson* and *Lorance* decisions.

But while Bush supported bills (S 2166, HR 4081) to overturn *Patterson* — by authorizing monetary damages for the victims of racial discrimination in all phases of a job relationship — the administration opposed provisions of S 2104 and HR 4000 that would also grant such damages to women, religious minorities, ethnic minorities and, indirectly, the disabled.

Not only did civil rights lobbyists and their primarily Democratic supporters in Congress insist that Bush's position was unfair and illogical, but some prominent administration allies also agreed.

"The administration has put itself in a position that makes it look like it's arguing against itself," said William Bradford Reynolds, the conservative head of the Justice Department's Civil Rights Division during the Reagan administration.

Administration officials disagreed with that assessment.

"Given the history of slavery in this country and deep-seated bitterness of the Civil War — and a history of demonstrations and violence over race — there is no question that race is different," Ayer said. "So it is not inherently irrational to say that we will have a separate statute and separate remedies for race."

Bush had gone to some lengths to portray himself as more concerned about civil rights than Ronald Reagan, who vetoed an important civil rights bill and nominated Robert H. Bork to the Supreme Court despite vehement opposition of many blacks and women's groups. In both cases, the civil rights lobby prevailed. *(Grove City law, 1988 Almanac, p. 63; Bork fight, 1987 Almanac, p. 271)*

Bush had appeared before leading black groups, appointed women and minorities to his Cabinet and other important government positions, and compromised with civil rights groups and congressional Democrats on legislation to prohibit discrimination against the disabled.

Although some critics said his efforts had been largely cosmetic, Bush had the highest sustained poll ratings among blacks of any Republican president in 30 years. A New York Times/CBS News poll published April 13 showed that 56 percent of blacks approved of Bush's job performance.

But the administration's opposition to the civil rights bill had begun to jeopardize his standing among black leaders. The Leadership Conference, which included all major civil rights organizations, made the legislation its 1990 priority.

Attorney General Dick Thornburgh had already antagonized the groups by saying Bush should veto the Kennedy-Hawkins bill.

Julius Chambers, director-counsel for the NAACP Legal Defense and Educational Fund, said at a commencement speech at the University of North Carolina on May 13, "In civil rights, actions speak louder than words. The course of action being urged by the Justice Department will drown out all the lofty rhetoric and fine-sounding speeches that we have heard from the Oval Office."

One day later, Bush met with minority leaders at the White House, and White House spokesman Marlin Fitzwater described differences between the administration's position and the Kennedy-Hawkins bill as "minimal."

On May 17, Bush said at a White House Rose Garden ceremony, "I want to sign a civil rights bill, but I will not sign a quota bill." Thus, Bush found himself in the difficult position of wanting to support a civil rights bill but opposing the major vehicle for civil rights in Congress.

Fight Over Title VII

Much of the debate over the bill centered on the proposed expansion of Title VII remedies. The Kennedy-Hawkins bill sought to grant similar remedies to all victims of job bias and would have allowed a worker to sue for both compensatory and punitive damages, and demand a jury trial.

The administration objected, maintaining that by introducing the possibility of monetary damages and a jury trial, the bill would transform a conciliatory process before the Equal Employment Opportunity Commission (EEOC) into an adversarial one before the courts.

Existing law required a worker alleging discrimination to file a complaint with the EEOC, which tried to mediate the complaint. To sue, a worker had to obtain EEOC permission.

Ayer said the main purposes of Title VII were to make peace between the employer and the employee and to get the worker back on the job.

"In 1964, Congress went through a very lengthy, thought-provoking and painful process [to develop Title VII]. And the statute works well," he said. "By providing a process for mediation and not incorporating more extensive and threatening remedies, Title VII creates an environment that gives employers and employees a better chance of getting an individual back on the job.

"What the [Kennedy-Hawkins] bill does is essentially abandon that view in favor of what I think is an overly simple view that more remedies are better for the plaintiffs."

But bill supporters said the bonanza predicted for plaintiffs and their lawyers would not materialize. They pointed to a study by the Washington law firm of Shea & Gardner for the National Women's Law Center that found that racial minorities who sued under Section 1981 during the past decade did not win huge jury awards.

In fact, according to the firm's data, in many of the cases that went to trial, compensatory or punitive damages were not awarded because the court specifically concluded that the remedies afforded under Title VII were enough to make the plaintiff whole for the damage suffered.

The firm found that of 576 cases decided from 1980 to 1990 under Section 1981, 144 were settled, reversed or remanded, and 314 were dismissed.

In the 118 other cases, the plaintiff proved that the employer intentionally engaged in unlawful racial discrimination, the study said. In 50 of those cases, however, workers did not get compensatory relief or punitive damages. Instead, the plaintiff got only back pay or a remedy similar to those available under Title VII.

The research found that plaintiffs won compensatory or punitive damages in 68 cases and that damages were less

Civil Rights Division Head Confirmed

The Senate on March 9 confirmed by voice vote former New York state GOP Sen. John R. Dunne to be assistant attorney general for the Justice Department's Civil Rights Division. The nomination proceeded rather smoothly, especially when compared with the controversial, and unsuccessful, nomination in 1989 of William Lucas to the post.

Dunne was a graduate of Yale Law School, a 24-year veteran of the state Senate and a partner in a Long Island law firm. He was approved by the Senate Judiciary Committee on March 8 after a two-hour confirmation hearing two days earlier. Bush had nominated Dunne on Jan. 25.

Known as a moderate, Dunne was backed by many influential politicians in and out of Congress. He was introduced by New York Sens. Daniel Patrick Moynihan, a Democrat, and Alfonse M. D'Amato, a Republican, and New York Gov. Mario M. Cuomo, a Democrat, praised him.

Among Dunne's most mentioned accomplishments was his mediation during the 1971 Attica prison riots.

The post had not been permanently filled since William Bradford Reynolds resigned in 1988. Reynolds alienated civil rights groups during his tenure, opposing affirmative action and school busing as remedies against discrimination.

Civil rights groups led the opposition to Lucas, Bush's first nominee for the post. Lucas' nomination was killed by the Judiciary Committee on Aug. 1, 1989, on a 7-7 vote. Critics said he lacked knowledge of civil rights law and raised questions about his management ability and character. *(1989 Almanac, p. 236)*

Much of the congressional questioning of Dunne focused on a number of Supreme Court decisions from the 1988-89 term that made it harder to prove job discrimination and that narrowed the remedies once a worker showed bias.

Dunne said that while the court appeared to have made it harder to assert discrimination, it might have produced a fairer balance of legal rights for employers and employees. He said the rulings might mean only that groundless cases would not go forward.

But he said of the rulings: "They were legally sound. Now we have to see if they are socially sound." In response to questions, he added: "They triggered my concern. I'm not offended by them. I'm concerned."

Dunne also faced questioning about his membership in two all-male clubs in New York. One had since begun admitting women, and Dunne resigned from the other after Bush began considering him for the nomination. Dunne acknowledged that he had never tried to change either club's policies and was not offended by them.

Dunne said his belonging to two restrictive clubs "might give people pause," but he said that on balance his record demonstrated his commitment to minorities and the disadvantaged. He mentioned his work for prisoners' rights and sponsorship of a bill for AIDS-testing confidentiality.

Civil rights groups — such as the NAACP and the Leadership Conference on Civil Rights — reacted cautiously to the nomination and ended up neither endorsing nor opposing Dunne.

than $50,000 in 42 of those cases. Only three cases brought damages of more than $200,000.

SENATE COMMITTEE ACTION

After two hours of debate April 4, the Senate Labor and Human Resources Committee approved S 2104 by a vote of 11-5.

Republicans James M. Jeffords, Vt., and Dave Durenberger, Minn., joined all the committee Democrats in supporting the measure.

Thornburgh said in an April 3 letter to the committee that he and "other senior advisers" would recommend that President Bush veto the bill.

In committee, Orrin G. Hatch, R-Utah, was most outspoken in opposition to the bill and proposed three amendments.

The only one that was accepted amended the section relating to practices that had disparate impact on women and minorities, stemming from the *Wards Cove* decision.

The amendment provided that employers could bar employees from using or possessing illegal drugs, as long as the no-drug rule was not adopted to discriminate intentionally against minorities.

The committee adopted the Hatch provision after accepting a Kennedy amendment to clarify that it applied only to current drug users and exempted individuals who were taking drugs under a doctor's supervision.

The committee rejected 4-12 a Hatch amendment that would have left with complaining workers the burden of proving that an employer had no business necessity for practices that were significantly related to the health or safety of employees, consumers, patients or other persons affected by the business operation.

Kennedy said such an amendment would give employers authority to discriminate under the guise of protecting health and safety.

The Supreme Court already had agreed to hear a case in its next term challenging a battery manufacturer's work rules that excluded women of child-bearing age from jobs in which they could be exposed to lead, which could cause birth defects. Women's groups called the case one of the most important sex discrimination issues of recent years.

The committee also rejected, 5-11, a Hatch amendment to the *Martin* section that would have allowed adversely affected parties to challenge consent decrees in a discrimination case at a later time.

Hatch, who maintained that the entire bill was a "radical reworking" of Title VII, had brought several other amendments to dilute the legislation but did not press them in committee. He said he would offer them when the bill came up on the floor.

Administration Threats

Bush's veto threat and the hard-nosed tone of Thornburgh's April 3 letter to the Senate Labor Committee did little to improve relations between the administration and civil rights groups.

The Leadership Conference on Civil Rights, which fought with the Reagan administration for eight years, accused the Bush administration of "bowing to the right wing of the Republican Party."

Kennedy said he hoped the administration would eventually support enactment of the bill.

But Senate Minority Leader Bob Dole, R-Kan., whose support was critical in winning enactment of civil rights in the 1980s, was a cosponsor of the administration bill and had not, according to an aide, been working on any compromise with sponsors of S 2104.

The administration opposed the attempts to counter any of the court rulings except *Patterson* (racial harassment) and *Lorance* (seniority system).

In his letter to Kennedy, Thornburgh spelled out the administration's criticism of the proposals affecting the other four cases and the expansion of Title VII remedies.

Regarding *Wards Cove*, the attorney general said, "Asking the plaintiff to identify the specific practices that produce a disparate impact before employers are asked to justify them is consistent with traditional rules allocating burdens of proof.

"This allocation of responsibilities strikes us as more efficient and equitable than allowing plaintiffs simply to allege that a hiring system produces a disparate impact and forcing employers to demonstrate that each individual employment practice within that system does not have a disparate impact, as S 2104 would."

In the provision to counter the *Price Waterhouse* decision, Thornburgh said that a recovery based on an employer's motivation, or state of mind, would be "contrary not only to the spirit of Title VII, but to the spirit of our legal system as well."

Thornburgh said that the finality sought in the bill regarding the *Martin* decision raised constitutional concerns about due process.

The administration supported the result in *Independent Federation of Flight Attendants v. Zipes*, agreeing with the court that attorneys' fees should be recovered only if an intervenor's attack on a prevailing plaintiff was frivolous.

The administration objected to the new remedies proposed for Title VII.

"Under the bill's regime," Thornburgh wrote, "plaintiffs' lawyers will inevitably include claims for pain and suffering, emotional harm and the like as a matter of course. Placing these issues before a jury, as well as the complex and emotional issues of liability that are often involved in Title VII cases, will turn Title VII litigation into a time-consuming, high risk venture for both plaintiffs and defendants."

Durenberger, one of the two Republicans who voted for the bill, questioned the administration's commitment to any legislation. "If this committee didn't act, the administration wouldn't either," he said.

SENATE FLOOR ACTION

The fragile bipartisanship that had marked passage of civil rights legislation in the 1980s shattered July 18 as the Senate passed its major antidiscrimination bill over the furious objections of the GOP leadership and in the face of a veto threat.

The Senate's 65-34 vote for S 2104 came after eight weeks of talks between Kennedy and White House Chief of Staff John H. Sununu collapsed in mutual recriminations. *(Vote 161, p. 36-S)*

In the vote on the bill, 10 Republicans joined 55 Democrats to pass the measure. No Democrats opposed it, although some threatened that if pro-business changes were not made in conference, they might drop their support. In the other key vote, the chamber voted the day before to invoke cloture on the bill. That vote was 62-38, two more than needed to limit debate. *(Vote 158, p. 35-S)*

In the wake of the Senate's vote, the White House's Fitzwater held out hope for an eventual compromise, saying the administration expected to work to change the bill in the House. "We still want a bill we can sign," he said July 18. But Fitzwater issued a statement later saying the "president wants a bill that ends discrimination, not one that starts a quota system."

Minority Leader Dole angrily accused Democrats of forcing action on the bill as "an opportunity to put the Republicans on record as being against civil rights."

Dole said, "This senator's never voted against a civil rights bill. But he has never had one shoved down his throat before."

Majority Leader George J. Mitchell, D-Maine, insisted, however, that he would not have called the vote if he had believed an agreement was near or if Republicans had offered to work to complete debate by a certain deadline.

"If there is one thing I have tried to do since I became majority leader, it is to establish a sense of fairness and comity in the Senate," Mitchell said.

Bush, his Hill allies, and the business community contended that the bill threatened legitimate employer practices because it broadened existing bases for lawsuits and increased awards available. To avoid frivolous suits, businesses would resort to hiring quotas, they argued.

"Quotas, schmotas," Kennedy bellowed to his colleagues on the floor. "Quotas are not the issue; job discrimination is the issue." He and others insisted that the legislation was necessary to help people seek redress when they were denied jobs or promotions on the basis of race or sex. They said existing law unfairly burdened discrimination victims and did not deter employers from violating workers' rights.

Fight Over Cloture, Remedies

Mitchell twice before had filed petitions for cloture to put pressure on the factions to resolve their differences and get S 2104 to the floor. But he had revoked the requests when a compromise seemed near.

When he persisted on July 17 to require a vote to cut off amendments and limit debate on the bill, Republicans were furious. More than 80 amendments were pending.

After the 62-38 cloture vote, when a cheer was heard from civil rights lobbyists near the chamber, Dole said, "This is a political game. You can hear the thunder or the roar out in the hall, after the score, after the touchdown, after the victory."

Kennedy later rejoined, "I wish we could see that kind of indignation about the unfairness that is taking place in job discrimination all over this country against women and against minorities."

The issue that had derailed negotiations and triggered the cloture vote involved legal remedies for employment practices that disproportionately hurt women and minorities — the *Wards Cove* ruling.

As introduced, S 2104 would have required employers

to prove that an employment practice that had an adverse impact on women or minorities was "essential to effective job performance." But Sens. Kennedy and John C. Danforth, R-Mo., announced on May 17 that they would amend the bill to ensure that it did not lead to quotas. Built upon concessions supporters already had made in the House, their amendment would have required proof that the practice bore "a substantial and demonstrable relationship to effective job performance."

The latest compromise brought support for S 2104 from Danforth, John Heinz, R-Pa., and five Southern and Western Democrats. But Hatch said Bush and his advisers were "too smart to be taken in by this new language. The right of employers to hire the most qualified employees ought to be maintained."

Kennedy's amended bill also stated that nothing in the act should be construed to require an employer to adopt hiring or promotion quotas. Hatch called that provision "totally useless."

"First of all, we admit that the act does not require quotas," Hatch said. "We have never argued that the bill expressly requires or demands quotas. But as a result of the way this bill rewrites the disparate impact theory, the only way that employers can avoid costly lawsuits they are almost certain to lose is to adopt quotas."

Kennedy's revision on the quota issue was included in an amendment adopted 65-34. *(Vote 160, p. 36-S)*

The Senate then adopted by voice vote a Kennedy substitute for S 2104 that had been reported by the Labor and Human Resources Committee.

Other Amendments

Some politically meaningful amendments did not come to a vote. A number of Southern Democrats tried to get the chamber to consider two proposals that would have made the bill more acceptable to business.

David Pryor, D-Ark., attempted to make sure that employer practices would not be found discriminatory simply because statistics showed that a plant had a higher percentage of whites than minorities.

Another proposal, offered by David L. Boren, D-Okla., would have limited punitive damage awards to $150,000 or to the amount of compensatory damages.

Boren said assurances were needed that any new law would not produce frivolous litigation when the goal was to protect the rights of people who suffered discrimination.

But Dole objected to Kennedy's effort to get procedure waived and the amendments added. Dole's move effectively ensured that the bill would remain unpalatable to Bush.

Dole said he thought it was fair that because GOP members' amendments had been choked off, Democratic proposals should be blocked.

The Southern Democrats, unhappy with the outcome, nevertheless voted for the bill on final passage and said they hoped the two provisions would be adopted in conference. Kennedy promised that he would work for them.

Among the senators who were reluctant to vote for the bill without the amendments was Dale Bumpers, D-Ark. He said, "You do not have to be a rocket scientist to figure out that the whole goal is to make the bill as bad as possible or to try to make it as bad as possible to give the president more cover in vetoing the bill."

Earlier Floor Action

A week before the measure passed the Senate, civil rights activists, Bush administration officials and their Senate allies dickered over the complicated questions of legal remedies — the disparate impact issue.

Though Mitchell said "considerable progress" had been made in negotiations, he still filed a cloture petition for July 17 to keep up pressure on the administration and party factions to resolve their differences.

Hatch had been trying to persuade the administration to take a hard line. "They keep trying to pacify Kennedy," said Hatch, who had become as much a critic of White House alternatives as some Democrats, albeit for different reasons.

But the White House's Sununu indicated in a letter to Kennedy that once that dispute was solved, the administration might drop its opposition to the bill and an agreement could be at hand.

"If we can deal quickly with these issues so directly related to our concerns on the quota implications and the potential for quota practices that could result from your proposed bill," Sununu wrote July 10, "then I am sure we can develop a way to handle the remaining issues.

"The administration's basic concern is that the bill as crafted now, will, even if unintentionally, compel businesses to adopt quota policies in hiring and promotion as the only or best defense against the likelihood of legal action."

At the same time, a moderate Republican, Nancy Landon Kassebaum, Kan., tried to draft an entirely new bill that could draw support from Republicans and conservative Democrats who, while shunning the Kennedy bill, believed antidiscrimination laws needed some revision. Her proposal eventually died without a vote.

In earlier floor action on S 2104, the Senate on July 10 adopted an amendment to extend the provisions of the bill, as well as the pending Americans with Disabilities Act (S 933) and some other civil rights laws, to Senate workers. Senate aides would not have the right to sue in court but would have been able to present their grievances to a Senate panel.

The amendment, offered by Wendell H. Ford, D-Ky., was an attempt to find a middle ground in a long-running dispute over how Congress could be held to the same labor practices as other institutions without violating the traditional separation of powers.

Ford, chairman of the Senate Committee on Rules and Administration, had objected to a provision in S 933 that would have allowed Hill workers to sue their bosses. His amendment would write into the U.S. Code a Senate rule against bias.

Charles E. Grassley, R-Iowa, moved to table the Ford amendment; that effort failed, 18-74. The Senate then adopted the Ford amendment by voice vote. *(Vote 144, p. 33-S)*

Grassley then tried to give congressional employees the right to bring their discrimination complaints to federal court. The Senate rebuffed his amendment on a 63-26 tabling vote. *(Vote 145, p. 33-S)*

Both proposals by Ford and Grassley involved a dispute on the disabilities bill and paved the way for final action on that measure.

HOUSE COMMITTEE ACTION: EDUCATION AND LABOR

The House Education and Labor Committee on May 8 approved HR 4000 after four days of consideration. The 23-10 vote saw a single Republican, Peter Smith of Vermont, join a phalanx of Democrats in support of the bill.

When the bill was amended May 2 to soften one of its more controversial provisions, Republican members apparently were caught unaware and said they needed time to reconsider their position and what amendments they would subsequently offer.

The committee had voted 33-0 to redefine the test an employer had to meet in defending a job practice shown to have a negative impact on women or minorities.

Vermont's Smith, who sponsored the amendment with Hawkins, said the change in the business-necessity test would improve the bill substantively and politically. "It breaks one of the fundamental impasses," he said.

While 33 committee members voted for the amendment, Rep. Harris W. Fawell, R-Ill., who protested the bill at every turn, voted "present." Fawell said he believed the legislation would hurt businesses and end up helping mostly lawyers.

Though nearly all GOP committee members voted for the change, some later agreed with statements from business groups that the change was "at best cosmetic."

On May 3, Steve Gunderson, R-Wis., returned to the issue, offering an amendment that would have required an employee charging discrimination to demonstrate which specific practice or practices within a group resulted in the alleged disparate impact.

Gunderson said that an employer needed to know what to defend himself against when confronted with a discrimination suit.

Hawkins said Gunderson's amendment would simply conform the bill to the language of *Wards Cove* and, as a result, do the opposite of what the bill's sponsors intended. The amendment was defeated, 10-22.

Other Amendments Adopted

Another Hawkins amendment was vigorously opposed by committee Republicans before being adopted by 22-11 along party lines May 3.

The bill would prohibit an employer-defendant from requiring a plaintiff to waive any claim to payment of attorneys' fees as a condition of a negotiated settlement or consent decree.

The amendment extended this ban to negotiated lawsuit dismissals.

Hawkins said lawyers would be discouraged from taking job-discrimination cases unless they knew they could collect their fees from the business-defendant if they prevailed. Few worker-plaintiffs could afford significant legal fees.

Eight other amendments offered by Hawkins were adopted by voice vote with little discussion. They sought to:

- Clarify that a plaintiff-employee could not challenge all of an employer's practices but had to identify the particular group of practices alleged to have a discriminatory impact.
- Specify the types of labor-management committees that were included in the definition of "respondent" in the bill, to conform to other provisions of Title VII.
- Clarify that monetary damages authorized in the bill were only for cases of intentional discrimination and not for disparate-impact claims.
- Ensure that requirements that all potentially affected parties be notified when affirmative-action consent decrees were being negotiated conform to constitutional dictates.

As introduced, the bill would bar subsequent challenges to court-approved agreements, reversing the *Martin* decision. The amendment made clear the new language was not intended to threaten anyone's right to due process.

- Clarify that the provisions relating to challenges to consent decrees did not change the federal statute governing venue.
- State that the intent of the measure was to achieve equality of opportunity, rather than of results, and codify the principle that courts should construe civil rights laws broadly to remedy discrimination.
- Clarify that only provisions allowing challenges to seniority systems at the time an employee was affected would be retroactive to the June 12, 1989, date of the court's decision in *Lorance*. Other provisions, which extended the statute of limitations for challenges from 180 days to two years, would be effective upon enactment of the bill.
- Clarify that an employer could adopt a rule barring the employment of current users of illegal drugs without incurring liability under Title VII.

The committee also adopted May 3, by voice vote, an amendment by Steve Bartlett, R-Texas, to require a study by the Administrative Office of the U.S. Courts assessing the disposition, timeliness, quantity and costs of employment discrimination cases processed by the federal courts since the 1964 Civil Rights Act was enacted.

Amendments Rejected

Twice during the May 3 markup, angry Republicans walked out of the committee room. At first, Hawkins tried to limit debate on the remaining amendments, all of which were GOP-sponsored, saying he wanted a final vote on the bill that day.

Gunderson objected, saying the bill was too complex to be disposed of quickly. "These are all serious amendments, and you can't just cut off debate," he said.

But Hawkins complained that the Republicans had introduced new amendments that had not been shown to the Democrats.

"You don't want to discuss these amendments, so why don't you all just go ahead and pass the bill?" Gunderson responded. "This is a civil rights bill, but you don't want to protect the rights of the minority on this committee."

With that, Gunderson walked out. He returned later after Hawkins agreed to extend the debate time.

Later in the markup, Bartlett offered an amendment that would have extended Title VII coverage to House employees. He argued that the House should not have a separate set of employment rules from those it expected private employers to follow.

Democrat William L. Clay of Missouri wondered why only House employees were mentioned, not Senate workers. He accused Bartlett of offering "mischievous" amendments, which the Texas lawmaker would not even vote for himself. Clay said he was tired of "frivolous debate over frivolous amendments."

Ranking Republican Bill Goodling, Pa., said Clay was violating House rules by questioning another member's motives. He demanded that Clay strike his remarks from the record. Clay refused, and Goodling walked out.

Bartlett remained to defend his amendment, and eventually Clay conceded that he was wrong in questioning Bartlett's motives. He asked that his previous remarks be removed. Goodling returned, the markup went on, and Bartlett's amendment was rejected on a 9-21 vote.

The committee's final day of markups on May 8 had a conciliatory tone. But despite the less fiery tone of debate, the committee by voice vote rejected all amendments offered by Republicans, including the following:

- By Fawell, to delete a section reversing the court's decision in *Martin.* The section would give finality to a court's consent decree resolving challenges to employment discrimination.
- By Bartlett, to delete from the bill the Title VII provisions that would permit the award of compensatory damages and, in egregious cases, punitive damages.
- By Bartlett, to overhaul several laws in an effort to move toward creation of a uniform, national antidiscrimination statute.

Other amendments that had been rejected during the markup May 3 included:

- By Fawell, 7-24, to limit the use of disparate-impact analysis to the hiring process; working conditions, wage levels and employee benefits would not be covered.
- By Thomas E. Petri, R-Wis., to delete from the bill language that would extend the statute of limitations under Title VII for challenges to discriminatory seniority systems; by voice vote.
- By Fawell, 10-24, to remove a section of the bill specifying that discrimination based on race, sex, national origin or religion may play no role in employment decisions.

The provision was aimed at reversing the *Price Waterhouse* ruling.

Fawell said the bill provided no defense for an employer because an employee need only show that a discriminatory motive was involved.

But Ford countered that the language was important because it made clear that a "little bit of discrimination" was enough to get an employer into court. What the bill said, Ford added, was, "You may not get your job back, but you do get some sort of recompense."

- By Paul B. Henry, R-Mich., 13-21, to preclude prevailing plaintiffs from collecting attorneys' fees from the original defendants when other parties subsequently intervened to contest the judgment. Henry said the intervenors should then become responsible for paying the attorneys' fees.
- By Cass Ballenger, R-N.C., to delete language allowing prevailing plaintiffs to recover expert witness fees in Title VII cases; by voice vote.

HOUSE COMMITTEE ACTION: JUDICIARY

The House Judiciary Committee, taking up the bill the week after the Senate had approved its version of the legislation, approved HR 4000 on July 25; after rejecting several Republican-backed amendments aimed at limiting its scope, the committee accepted the measure 24-12.

The Judiciary Subcommittee on Civil and Constitutional Rights on July 12 had voted 5-3 to approve the bill.

The version adopted by the committee closely resembled S 2104 passed by the Senate on July 18 over the objections of the White House.

Barney Frank, D-Mass., responding to GOP predictions of dire consequences for U.S. courts and businesses, said antidiscrimination laws had been "historically underenforced."

"It's still much easier for a smart bigot to get away with it" than it was for a victim to get compensated, he said, "and it still will be after we pass this bill."

Two panel Republicans, ranking GOP member Hamilton Fish Jr. of New York and Tom Campbell of California, joined the 22 Democrats in supporting the measure.

But bill opponent F. James Sensenbrenner Jr., Wis., ranking Republican on the Civil and Constitutional Rights Subcommittee, called the measure "the plaintiffs' lawyers' full employment law of 1990," saying it would not help the victims and would only clog the courts.

Sensenbrenner's amendment to strike the portion of the bill calling for punitive and compensatory damages for intentional discrimination was defeated, 12-23. It would have replaced that provision with immediate injunctive remedy for victims of on-the-job harassment, capping potential compensation at $30,000.

Panel Democrats, including Civil and Constitutional Rights Subcommittee Chairman Don Edwards, Calif., argued that Sensenbrenner's amendment would unfairly limit juries' ability to award damages in harassment cases.

Craig Washington, D-Texas, recalled the case of a woman whose co-workers had exposed their buttocks to her, and said that under the amendment "the jury that elected Mr. Sensenbrenner" would not be trusted to set damages for her.

But Henry J. Hyde, R-Ill., called Sensenbrenner's proposal an "effective and speedy remedy," adding that "someone can show me their buttocks all day if I can get $30,000 per view."

Other Amendments Defeated

The committee defeated several other amendments, including:

- A proposal by Sensenbrenner, on a 16-20 vote, to make Congress subject to the same antidiscrimination laws as other employers. Opponents, citing constitutional problems, said the bill was the wrong vehicle for such a law.

The subcommittee also beat back, 3-5, a Sensenbrenner amendment to let congressional workers sue their employers in federal court based on the bill.

"We ought to subject ourselves to the same liability that we are subjecting employers in the private sector to," said Sensenbrenner.

In subcommittee, Sensenbrenner also tried to strike from the bill the section allowing expanded damages for intentional discrimination under Title VII. That amendment failed on a voice vote.

- A proposal by Hyde, 13-23, which, like the underlying bill, would have returned the burden of proof in job discrimination cases from employees to employers.

But it would have imposed a special requirement for workers in job discrimination suits involving disparate impact. Those plaintiffs would have had to show a link between the statistical disparity and discriminatory work practices.

- A proposal by Carlos J. Moorhead, R-Calif., 18-18, that would have removed provisions making the legislation retroactive. "It is very unfair to the American people to pass bills that apply to previous actions," Moorhead said.

The amendment appeared to have been approved, 18-17, but Lawrence J. Smith, D-Fla., who had passed on the initial tally, cast a "no" vote after hearing that count.

- Two amendments by Chuck Douglas, R-N.H., to put tight statutes of limitations on the filing of discrimination suits and another Douglas amendment to allow some settled class-action cases to be reopened later by new plaintiffs.

A similar amendment by Campbell also was rejected.

- A Campbell amendment to prevent attorneys from vetoing out-of-court settlements in discrimination cases because attorneys' fees were waived. The amendment would have stricken a portion of the bill that would prohibit any settlement unless the parties or the counsel attested that a waiver of attorneys' fees was not compelled as a condition of settlement.

The committee adopted, by voice vote, an amendment by Patricia Schroeder, D-Colo., and Dan Glickman, D-Kan., encouraging alternative avenues of dispute resolution, such as arbitration, mini-trials and settlement.

HOUSE FLOOR ACTION

In voting 272-154 for HR 4000, the House on Aug. 3 joined the Senate in a standoff with the Bush administration. Thirty-two Republicans voted with 240 Democrats for the bill; voting against it were 142 GOP members and 12 Democrats. *(Vote 310, p. 100-H)*

The House followed the Senate's lead in passing the civil rights bill over President Bush's objections but only after adopting two politically inspired amendments aimed at shoring up the crucial support of conservative Democrats and getting within striking distance of overriding a veto.

The House's vote was 12 short of the two-thirds voting necessary to override a veto. The Senate came within two votes of the 67 it would need.

During the House debate, members relayed bitter tales of firsthand discrimination: being thrown out of restaurants and barber shops and losing jobs.

Dave McCurdy, D-Okla., spoke of his childhood, a white boy growing up in southwest Oklahoma.

"I was aware of racism, both open and subtle," McCurdy said. "I was bothered by it but accustomed to hearing the word 'nigger' or 'wetback.' I heard Jews and Catholics referred to in derogatory terms. I regret that for a while, such terms were used even in my own family until I fought against it."

Albert G. Bustamante, D-Texas, a Hispanic, offered some personal observations. "It is no fun to be run out of restaurants, out of barber shops, to be denied employment simply because you are a Mexican or a wetback or a Mescin or whatever other title they used to use for us," he said.

Before passing the bill, the House defeated a substitute measure that was partially written by White House officials and initially sponsored by House Small Business Committee Chairman John J. LaFalce, D-N.Y.

House leaders denounced the proposal as raising the obstacles and lowering awards for workers who alleged discrimination. It lost 188-238. *(Vote 309, p. 100-H)*

The two amendments accepted in the House made the bill more palatable to moderates by ostensibly softening the bill's impact on business. One of them gave members a chance to vote against quotas, and the second let them vote against big damage awards.

Even with the changes, though, Bush's opposition was firm.

In addition to his allegation that the bill would lead to quotas, Bush wrote Aug. 2 that it "will also foster divisiveness and litigation rather than conciliation and do more to promote legal fees than civil rights."

Quotas

The sensitivity of the quota issue was underscored by members' determination to vote for an antiquota amendment — even though the wording was already in the bill.

House members wanted specifically to vote for an amendment that said, "Nothing in ... this act shall be construed to require an employer to adopt hiring or promotion quotas on the basis of race, color, religion, sex or national origin."

The amendment by Michael A. Andrews, D-Texas, and Stephen L. Neal, D-N.C., also said that a mere statistical imbalance in an employer's shop on account of race, color, religion, sex or national origin could not establish that a boss discriminated.

Similar language had been added to the bill during Judiciary Committee action July 25, and committee members chafed at the idea of the superfluous provision. But they acquiesced after the House leadership said a vote against quotas would help Southern Democrats answer worried business constituents.

"The amendment was necessary to remove any smidgen of doubt that this is a quota bill," said Mike Synar, D-Okla., a member of the Judiciary Committee.

But Sensenbrenner, a chief foe of the bill, called the amendment a "fig leaf" for political cover that would do no more than assuage fears that the bill would lead — as Sensenbrenner insisted — to quotas.

The amendment was adopted 397-24 on Aug. 2. *(Vote 306, p. 100-H)*

The Office of Management and Budget (OMB) summed up the administration's principal objection to the bill: "HR 4000 will result in quotas, not by requiring them directly, but by inducing employers to adopt surreptitious quotas in order to avoid the cost and trouble of disparate impact lawsuits, which HR 4000 makes extremely difficult for employers to win."

OMB continued, repeating the language of the Andrews-Neal amendment, "It is never the 'mere existence of a statistical imbalance' that is alleged in a disparate-impact case, but rather an imbalance *caused*, albeit unintentionally, by a challenged practice."

Cap on Punitive Damages

A second amendment that solidified moderates' support of the bill, to cap punitive damages that could be awarded a victim of intentional discrimination, also was adopted Aug. 2. The vote was 289-134. *(Vote 307, p. 100-H)*

Responding to fears that employers would be saddled with million-dollar damage awards for discrimination, Hawkins and Judiciary Chairman Jack Brooks, D-Texas, imposed a cap on punitive damages for employers with fewer than 100 workers of $150,000 or the amount of compensatory damages.

The cap amendment in part destroyed the equality that bill sponsors were trying to reach for racial, sexual and religious victims of bias.

Workers who had been subject to racial discrimination on the job could win unlimited damages under Section 1981 of Title 42 of the U.S. Code.

Other victims, covered by a separate law, would fall under the $150,000 limit.

The administration attacked the caps as "a minor change at best." OMB said the administration still objected to transforming the administrative nature of Title VII, what it called a "carefully balanced remedial framework," to provide money damages and jury trials, "a radically different tort-style approach."

Brooks said the cap would apply to more than 97 percent of U.S. businesses. He said it was necessary to convince employers that they would not be subject to multimillion-dollar lawsuits because of the bill.

Hawkins said he did not believe in limits for people who

were wronged but acknowledged that a majority of the House wanted a limit on potential court awards.

The LaFalce Amendment

The final amendment considered during the two days of House action was crafted by LaFalce, but offered by House Minority Leader Robert H. Michel, R-Ill., after the Democratic leadership blocked LaFalce from offering it as a Democratic alternative.

Earlier in the week, it appeared that the LaFalce alternative might draw a significant majority of conservative Democrats, but extensive lobbying by civil rights activists and the offering of the antiquota language and damages cap shut down most Democratic support. In the Aug. 3 vote, 224 Democrats and 14 Republicans voted against the substitute; 28 Democrats and 160 Republicans voted for it.

LaFalce had entered the fray unexpectedly in late July and became a conduit for an administration offering. The New York Democrat acknowledged he had not been following the yearlong Hill deliberations over the court decisions and other elements of the bill.

But he said he wanted to wring a compromise between the White House and congressional leaders and adopted an alternative that had been offered by Kassebaum during Senate debate.

Although the LaFalce substitute responded to some of the court decisions addressed in HR 4000, it would have established an easier test for employers who had to defend themselves in discrimination suits and would have gone only part way in modifying Title VII. LaFalce's amendment would have allowed up to $100,000 in relief for victims of intentional discrimination.

Hawkins, Brooks and House Democratic leaders blasted LaFalce's last-minute attempt to push through a White House plan that had already been turned down by the Senate.

Judiciary Committee Chairman Brooks described the substitute as a "civil wrongs" bill. But a fellow Texas Democrat, Charles W. Stenholm, said he was voting for the LaFalce plan because it would not lead to endless litigation, as he predicted the Hawkins bill would.

CONFERENCE ACTION

House and Senate conferees Oct. 11 scaled back the omnibus bill in an effort to send Bush a measure he would accept. But the legislation still faced a veto and some civil rights activists said conferees made concessions with no payoff.

While Kennedy predicted that S 2104 would draw a veto-proof majority in the Senate, other sponsors remained skeptical, and talks with the White House continued.

As the legislation moved in conference in late September, the momentum that civil rights activists had earlier in the year was being eclipsed by the campaign by the White House and the business community to label the measure a quota bill.

So when the measure was first approved by a House-Senate conference committee Sept. 25, its chances of enactment were still far from likely. Bush's veto threat loomed as the legislation prepared to make its way back to the House and Senate floors in early October.

In the meantime, Kennedy continued to try to broker an agreement with the White House to rescue the comprehensive anti-job-discrimination measure.

Meeting Sept. 24-25, conferees went only a small way toward responding to the administration's objections: They agreed to limit potential punitive damages for employers who intentionally discriminated in violation of Title VII. The conferees voted 9-7 to cap punitive damages at $150,000, or compensatory damages plus lost pay, whichever was greater.

The Oct. 11 changes attempted to dispel some of the administration's objections by further easing employers' burden of proof of non-discriminatory practices. By a 375-45 vote earlier Oct. 11, the House sent the bill back to the conference. *(Vote 445, p. 142-H)*

Final Compromises

All along, Democrats had questioned the White House commitment to a bill. Since the spring, lawmakers and Bush officials had dickered over language that would help bias victims but not burden employers unfairly.

Supporters of S 2104 tried to persuade "no" voters to back the conference report approved Sept. 25. Meanwhile, key members continued negotiating with the White House. One broker, William T. Coleman Jr., former Transportation secretary under President Gerald R. Ford, said Oct. 11 that the new conference report "takes care of every legitimate concern" of the administration, adding that he predicted that Bush would sign the bill.

Under the new language:

- When an employer tried to defend as a "business necessity" a practice that ended up discriminating disproportionately against women or minorities, its burden of proof would be lower than what the bill originally proposed in most situations, including when employees' use of methadone, alcohol or tobacco was involved. In cases of hiring and promotion, the burden of proof required by the bill would remain higher.
- Workers in disparate impact cases would have to pinpoint specific practices that excluded women, blacks or other minorities. The original bill did not require such precision. The new bill stated, however, that specific practices would not have to be proved when the employer did not produce relevant records.
- The bill said that it should not be interpreted "to encourage" quotas.
- People hurt by court-approved affirmative-action orders would have a greater opportunity to challenge those orders than allowed under the original bill.
- In cases of intentional discrimination, a worker could not win compensatory or punitive damages if an employer could prove that it would have taken the same action even without discrimination.

The new language arose from intervention by Hatch, who had been one of the strongest foes of S 2104 but who contended that he wanted a bill.

Hatch, however, did not endorse the revised language. Sen. Arlen Specter, R-Pa., who was not a conferee on the bill but who negotiated with the White House, said that Hatch switched because the White House was not mollified by the new provisions.

Specter said that Hatch had said the new language "was acceptable."

Hatch explained Oct. 12 that he had some objections to the compromise although he would have been willing to dismiss them had the White House accepted the changes. "For it to work, all sides had to agree," he said. "I told Bill Coleman that if the president still maintains his veto posture, I will lead the fight against it." Hatch added that the changes were definite "improvements." The administra-

Bush Cites 'Quotas' in Rights Bill Veto

Following is the text accompanying President Bush's Oct. 22 veto of the Civil Rights Act of 1990 (S 2104):

I am today returning without my approval S 2104, the Civil Rights Act of 1990. I deeply regret having to take this action with respect to a bill bearing such a title, especially since it contains certain provisions that I strongly endorse. Discrimination, whether on the basis of race, national origin, sex, religion, or disability, is worse than wrong.

It is a fundamental evil that tears at the fabric of our society, and one that all Americans should and must oppose. That requires rigorous enforcement of existing antidiscrimination laws. It also requires vigorously promoting new measures such as this year's Americans with Disabilities Act, which for the first time adequately protects persons with disabilities against invidious discrimination.

One step that the Congress can take to fight discrimination right now is to act promptly on the civil rights bill that I transmitted on Oct. 20, 1990. This accomplishes the stated purpose of S 2104 in strengthening our nation's laws against employment discrimination. Indeed, this bill contains several important provisions that are similar to provisions in S 2104:

- Both shift the burden of proof to the employer on the issue of "business necessity" in disparate impact cases.
- Both create expanded protections against on-the-job racial discrimination by extending 42 U.S.C. 1981 to the performance as well as the making of contracts.
- Both expand the right to challenge discriminatory seniority systems by providing that suit may be brought when they cause harm to plaintiffs.
- Both have provisions creating new monetary remedies for the victims of practices such as sexual harassment. (The administration bill allows equitable awards up to $150,000 under this new monetary provision, in addition to existing remedies under Title VII.)
- Both have provisions ensuring that employers can be held liable if invidious discrimination was a motivating factor in an employment decision.
- Both provide for plaintiffs in civil rights cases to receive expert witness fees under the same standards that apply to attorneys' fees.
- Both provide that the federal government, when it is a defendant under Title VII, will have the same obligation to pay interest to compensate for delay in payment as a non-public party. The filing period in such actions is also lengthened.
- Both contain a provision encouraging the use of alternative dispute resolution mechanisms.

The congressional majority and I are on common ground regarding these important provisions. Disputes about other controversial provisions in S 2104 should not be allowed to impede the enactment of these proposals. Along with the significant similarities between my administration's bill and S 2l04, however, are crucial differences. Despite the use of the term "civil rights" in the title of S 2104, the bill actually employs a maze of highly legalistic language to introduce the destructive force of quotas into our nation's employment system. Primarily through provisions governing cases in which employment practices are alleged to have unintentionally caused the disproportionate exclusion of members of certain groups, S 2104 creates powerful incentives for employers to adopt hiring and promotion quotas. These incentives are created by the bill's new and very technical rules of litigation, which will make it difficult for employers to defend legitimate employment practices. In many cases, a defense against unfounded allegations will be impossible. Among other problems, the plaintiff often need not even show that any of the employer's practices caused a significant statistical disparity. In other cases, the employer's defense is confined to an unduly narrow definition of "business necessity" that is significantly more restrictive than that established by the Supreme Court in [*Griggs v. Duke Power Co.*] and in two decades of subsequent decisions. Thus, unable to defend legitimate practices in court, employers will be driven to adopt quotas . . . to avoid liability.

Proponents of S 2104 assert that it is needed to overturn the Supreme Court's [*Ward's Cove Packing v. Atonio*] decision and restore the law that had existed since the *Griggs* case in 1971. S 2104, however, does not in fact codify *Griggs* or the court's subsequent decisions prior to *Ward's Cove*. Instead, S 2104 engages in a sweeping rewrite of two decades of Supreme Court jurisprudence, using language that appears in no decision of the court and that is contrary to principles acknowledged even by Justice Stevens' dissent in *Ward's Cove*: "The opinion in *Griggs* made it clear that a neutral practice that operates to exclude minorities is nevertheless lawful if it serves a valid business purpose." I am aware of the dispute among lawyers about the proper interpretation of certain critical language used in this portion of S 2104. The very fact of this dispute suggests that the bill is not codifying the law developed by the Supreme Court in *Griggs* and subsequent cases.

This debate, moreover, is a sure sign that S 2104 will lead to years — perhaps decades — of uncertainty and expensive litigation. It is neither fair nor sensible to give the employers of our country a difficult choice between using quotas and seeking a clarification of the law through costly and very risky litigation. S 2104 contains several other unacceptable provisions as well. One section unfairly closes the courts, in many instances, to individuals victimized by agreements, to which they were not a party, involving the use of quotas. Another section radically alters the remedial provisions in Title VII of the Civil Rights Act of 1964, replacing measures designed to foster conciliation and settlement with a new scheme modeled on a tort system widely acknowledged to be in a state of crisis. The bill also contains a number of provisions that will create unnecessary and inappropriate incentives for litigation. These include unfair retroactivity rules; attorneys' fee provisions that will discourage settlements; unreasonable new statutes of limitation; and a "rule of construction" that will make it extremely difficult to know how courts can be expected to apply the law. In order to assist the Congress regarding legislation in this area, I enclose herewith a memorandum from the attorney general explaining in detail the defects that make S 2104 unacceptable.

Our goal and our promise has been equal opportunity and equal protection under the law. That is a bedrock principle from which we cannot retreat. The temptation to support a bill — any bill — simply because its title includes the words "civil rights" is very strong. This impulse is not entirely bad. Presumptions have too often run the other way, and our nation's history on racial questions cautions against complacency. But when our efforts, however well intentioned, result in quotas, equal opportunity is not advanced but thwarted. The very commitment to justice and equality that is offered as the reason why this bill should be signed requires me to veto it. Again, I urge the Congress to act on my legislation before adjournment. In order truly to enhance equal opportunity, however, the Congress must also take action in several related areas. The elimination of employment discrimination is a vital element in achieving the American dream, but it is not enough. The absence of discrimination will have little concrete meaning unless jobs are available and the members of all groups have the skills and education needed to qualify for those jobs. Nor can we expect that our young people will work hard to prepare for the future if they grow up in a climate of violence, drugs and hopelessness.

In order to address these problems, attention must be given to measures that promote accountability and parental choice in the schools; that strengthen the fight against violent criminals and drug dealers in our inner cities; and that help to combat poverty and inadequate housing. We need initiatives that will empower individual Americans and enable then to reclaim control of their lives, thus helping to make our country's promise of opportunity a reality for all. Enactment of such initiatives, along with my administration's civil rights bill, will achieve real advances for the cause of equal opportunity. ■

tion, however, renewed the veto threat Oct. 12.

The conferees accepted the senators' changes, 11-8. All of the opponents were Republicans, except for Texas' Washington, who had urged bill sponsors not to water down the bill without some guarantee of White House approval. He said the legislation had become a "hollow shell of a civil rights bill." GOP conferees said the bill still placed too heavy a burden on employers.

Initial Agreement

The Sept. 25 compromise centered on punitive damages for intentional discrimination in violation of Title VII. While the conferees agreed to a cap, not everyone was pleased with the arrangement.

Four House Democrats who strongly backed the legislation abstained from voting in protest of the cap. They were Washington, Schroeder, Edwards and Kweisi Mfume, Md.

But Kennedy and other Senate Democratic conferees said the cap was key to that chamber's approval of the bill. During the Senate's consideration of the measure July 18, proponents won votes to limit debate and pass the bill after Kennedy promised wavering Southern Democrats that he would try to get the cap in the conference.

The cap would apply only to damages under Title VII, which forbade racial, sex, religious and ethnic discrimination on the job. Victims of racial bias, however, could sue under Section 1981, which allowed unlimited damages.

At the time that negotiations were plodding along, business groups began making further inroads. Small-business owners wrote to their senators and representatives to protest their increased liability to charges of discrimination. These concerns were picked up in editorials in several major newspapers and magazines.

Civil rights supporters also argued among themselves over how to sell the bill and how to counter the perception that the legislation would put employees on more than equal footing with employers. They generally played up the provisions to reverse the court and make it easier for victims of bias to sue their employers, rather than the change in damages under Title VII, aimed specifically at increasing remedies for women who met discrimination.

After the House-Senate conference committee had finished its work on S 2104, a White House spokesman called the cap on punitive damages a "positive change," but said the bill still faced a veto.

The Senate version had had no cap on damages. The House bill had included a cap, but it would have applied only to businesses with fewer than 100 workers.

Hawkins, lead House sponsor of the legislation, said he, too, opposed a limit on punitive damages but acknowledged the reality that concessions had to be made to move the bill. Said Hawkins, "I think it's a small price to pay for the other benefits in the bill."

FINAL ACTION

With proponents of the bill still short of the two-thirds vote needed to override the expected veto, Congress nevertheless took up the civil rights conference report.

The Senate adopted the conference report, 62-34, on Oct. 16, and the House, 273-154, on Oct. 17. The votes left supporters three Senate votes and 12 House votes shy of the two-thirds needed to override the threatened veto.

Five days later, on Oct. 22, Bush followed through with his threat and vetoed the bill, citing once again his concerns that it would lead employers to adopt hiring quotas.

The Senate on Oct. 24 failed, 66-34, to override the veto of S 2104, and the measure was dead in the 101st Congress. *(Vote 304, p. 60-S)*

The only senator to switch sides after the Oct. 16 vote on the conference report was Minnesota's Boschwitz, who had opposed the bill earlier.

Other GOP senators close to switching to vote for the bill said they did not want to abandon Bush during the difficult budget negotiations and ongoing trouble in the Persian Gulf.

Warren B. Rudman, R-N.H., came as close as any senator to switching from a "nay" to a "yea" on the conference report. But after up-to-the-end pressure by the White House, including a call from Bush, Rudman opposed the legislation.

Rudman said Oct. 18, "It was a very, very close call. I was convinced that it would take some minor changes to make it satisfactory to me, but the changes could not be done at that late date. When it came down to it, I thought the administration was a mite unreasonable, ... but I didn't want to get into a position of overriding the president's veto."

Lasting Effects?

Bush wrote to senators Oct. 16 before their vote on the conference report that he believed the bill would still cause businesses to adopt quotas in hiring and promotion. "It will also foster divisiveness and litigation rather than conciliation and do more to promote legal fees than civil rights. If this bill is presented to me, I will be compelled to veto it."

Neas, of the Leadership Conference on Civil Rights, said in a statement after the votes that "George Bush is a Ronald Reagan in sheep's clothing."

"While his style and rhetoric may differ, his substantive civil rights policies are just as deadly to those who are the victims of job discrimination."

Missouri's Danforth said on the Senate floor that the discussions over basic job rights lost sight of the individual worker and became consumed in legal minutiae.

"I believe that it is very important in this country to have business that can compete and that can be successful," Danforth said. "But in the end, as a matter of national identity, national value, clearly if we are forced to make the choice, the choice must be in favor of equal opportunity for employment."

But it was the quota issue that eclipsed debate on all other provisions and contributed heavily to the legislation's downfall. During debate to override Bush's veto, Alan K. Simpson, R-Wyo., summed up the opponents' position: "If you get sued by the numbers, you'll hire by the numbers."

But Democrats continued to insist that quotas were not the real problem. "The issue for the president isn't quotas — it's politics," said party Chairman Ronald H. Brown in a statement. "George Bush got to the White House by pandering to fear. Having abandoned his no-tax pledge, he feels compelled to keep his real base intact."

Specter, a Republican supporter of the bill, feared for the electoral well-being of his party. He said before the override vote, "I am very concerned about my party, which has been tagged as the party of the rich, and unfairly so, in the arguments now going on about the tax bill.... I am concerned about my colleagues who want to vote for this bill, who have urged the president to sign a civil rights bill. But out of loyalty to the president, they may stay with him here, and they will suffer defeat at the polls, because this is a bill which ought to be signed for America." ■

Sizable Boost in Immigration OK'd

Congress in 1990 cleared the most sweeping revision of legal-immigration laws in a quarter century, moving to admit more immigrants — especially those with education and skills needed in the United States.

The legislation, several years in the making, comprehensively revised the country's 25-year-old visa system, with a primary goal of increasing the immigration of Europeans and specially trained workers.

The House cleared the bill (S 358) on Oct. 27, the last full day of the session, but only after a last-minute showdown with one of the prime Senate sponsors of the bill, Alan K. Simpson, R-Wyo., over a provision he had added in conference. When Simpson backed down, the House approved the final version and sent the bill to President Bush, who signed it Nov. 29.

BOXSCORE

Legislation: Legal immigration, PL 101-649 (S 358).

Major action: Signed, Nov. 29. Conference report adopted by House, 264-118, Oct. 27; by Senate, 89-8, Oct. 26. HR 4300 passed by House, 231-192, Oct. 3; S 358 passed by Senate, 81-17, July 13, 1989.

Reports: Conference report (H Rept 101-955); Judiciary (H Rept 101-723, Part I); Ways and Means (Part II); Judiciary (S Rept 101-55).

Under the existing law, which favored foreigners with immediate relatives in the United States, all but about 10 percent of the people who qualified for visas came from Asia and Latin America.

The new law, which was to take effect Oct. 1, 1991, would allow legal immigration to climb from about 500,000 people to about 700,000 during each of the first three years of the act. After that, a permanent level of 675,000 people would be in place. A category of "diversity" visas would be created to benefit nationals of countries, primarily in Europe, adversely affected by the 1965 law. *(Provisions, p. 482)*

The totals did not include refugees or people granted asylum because they were fleeing persecution in their own countries. In fiscal 1991, the administration planned to admit 131,000 refugees, most from East Asia and the Soviet Union.

The measure also:

- Increased the number of visas for people with family members already in the United States.
- Included an 18-month stay of deportation for people from El Salvador living illegally in the United States. This provision was sought by members of Congress who wanted to protect Salvadorans who fled their war-torn homeland.
- Made it harder to exclude foreigners because of their political beliefs or sexual orientation. Chief House sponsor Bruce A. Morrison, D-Conn., said specifically of the revision of the 1952 McCarran-Walter Act, "It finally does away with the Cold War-era ideological excess that has kept many important artists and scholars from visiting the United States, while at the same time strengthening provisions to exclude criminals and terrorists."
- Opened the door to easing restrictions on people with the AIDS virus, specifying that an alien could be excluded only if he or she had "communicable diseases of public health significance." *(AIDS, p. 480)*

The House version of the legislation (HR 4300) was more generous than the Senate version in allocating new visas and aiding specific countries. Simpson, who long had wanted a ceiling on immigration and greater efforts to keep out illegal aliens, held up the bill until House conferees approved an overall limit and increased border protection.

Edward M. Kennedy, D-Mass., the lead Senate sponsor, said, "By rejecting the imbalances which have inadvertently developed in recent years, we will again open our doors to those who no longer have immediate family ties to the United States."

Ethnic, religious, labor and business groups all praised the legislation, which until the final hours of the conference appeared in jeopardy because of competing interests. Conferees approved the bill on Oct. 24.

Although some ethnic groups had sought higher visa increases and opposed provisions targeting illegal aliens, the compromise bill was widely embraced.

Raul Yzaguirre, president of the National Council of LaRaza, said, "This legislation represents a new era in the immigration policy debate. The votes [during original action on the bills] in both the House and Senate have shattered the myth that Congress is unwilling to adopt fair, humane immigration policy."

White House aides were involved in the compromise negotiations, though the administration had not been closely involved with the bill as it moved from Senate passage in July 1989 to House passage 15 months later.

In signing the bill Nov. 29, however, Bush said it met "several objectives of this administration's domestic policy agenda — cultivation of a more competitive economy, support for the family as the essential unit of society, and swift and effective punishment for drug-related and other violent crime."

BACKGROUND, SENATE PASSAGE

Congress undertook revision of the 1965 legal-immigration statutes after spending half a decade in the 1980s transforming the illegal-immigration laws. The 1986 Immigration Reform and Control Act (PL 99-603) gave millions of illegal aliens amnesty and instituted sanctions for employers who hired undocumented workers. *(1986 Almanac, p. 61)*

Although members of Congress disagreed over the approach, there was consensus that the system of legal immigration was too rigid and needed to be more open to immigrants from nations shortchanged by existing law.

Until 1965, immigration policy was based on nationality and reflected narrow attitudes toward race and national origin. Then Congress repealed the country-based quotas and replaced them with a system based primarily on reuniting families and allowing in immigrants with needed skills. *(1965 Almanac, p. 459)*

The result, however, was a new lopsidedness. In 1965, more than one-third of those admitted were from Europe and only 7 percent were from Asia. In 1990, 85 percent of all immigration came from two areas of the globe, Latin America and Asia.

Under existing law, only immediate relatives (spouses, minor children and parents) of U.S. citizens were not subject to annual limits on the number of visas.

The existing visa-allotment system heavily emphasized family unification, reserving most visas for immediate relatives of U.S. citizens and permanent residents.

Many in Congress were frustrated by the system's unintended exclusion of immigrants from "old seed" European countries and by its failure to respond to U.S. labor shortages.

Even people who readily qualified for visas spent years on waiting lists, and members of Congress wanted to help clear out backlogs — particularly for spouses and unmarried children of permanent residents, and adult brothers and sisters of U.S. citizens and permanent residents.

And members agreed generally that a new "independent" category of visas was needed for immigrants who had special skills in a particular field, education or knowledge of English.

Kennedy and Simpson pushed an ambitious legal-immigration bill through the Senate in 1988, but it was stymied in the House.

Instead, Congress cleared a stopgap measure (PL 100-658) that gave a one-year visa extension to foreign nurses working in the United States and created a means for more Irish citizens to immigrate — a special concern of Kennedy, who had a large Irish-American constituency. *(1988 Almanac, p. 266)*

The following year, the Senate tried again, approving a bill (S 358) on July 13 that placed a new emphasis on immigrants' skills and talents and authorized entry of thousands more foreigners each year.

The measure capped overall immigration at 630,000 people annually, although floor amendments made that limit relatively flexible.

The Bush administration had given qualified support to S 358. The Senate's vote to pass it was 81-17. *(1989 Almanac, p. 265; Senate provisions, 1989 Almanac, p. 270; Senate vote 117, 1989 Almanac, p. 24-S)*

HOUSE COMMITTEE ACTION

The House did not act on the legislation in 1989, but its Judiciary Subcommittee on Immigration, Refugees and International Law did begin hearings on Sept. 27, 1989, with the intention of taking up the measure in 1990.

Action was slowed, however, by differences among subcommittee members and by the competing demands on the time of the subcommittee chairman, Morrison, who was in a campaign (ultimately unsuccessful) to be elected governor of Connecticut.

Warming Up in the House

Morrison's draft of the legislation was substantially more generous than the Senate's bill. His proposal sought to increase the number of foreigners who would have unlimited immigration opportunities and create a plan for admitting people based on job shortages.

In two subcommittee hearings Feb. 21, Bush administration officials declined to comment on the Morrison plan, saying they had not had sufficient time to study it. But officials of the Immigration and Naturalization Service (INS), State Department and Department of Labor expressed reservations about the open-ended nature.

Morrison's plan would have allowed unlimited visas for spouses and minor children of permanent U.S. residents — a group already on a waiting list in the "Second Preference" category. The change could bring in 235,000 more immigrants the first year and then 75,000 more immigrants annually, a State Department official said.

Like the Senate measure, Morrison's bill emphasized immigrants' education and professional skills, permitting foreigners who did not have close relatives or a job waiting in the United States to qualify for visas. It created a category for these "independent" immigrants and allocated 54,000 visas to them annually.

But Morrison's bill differed in its approach. Besides adding possibly 100,000 more visas than S 358 would permit, Morrison sought to link the non-family visa allotments more closely to U.S. labor needs.

He proposed a system for state and federal certification of labor shortages that would lead to new slots for foreign workers.

He suggested requiring employers who hired immigrants for those shortages to pay the immigrants and all their other workers at least 105 percent of the prevailing wage. There would also be a 15 percent tax on the wages of a new immigrant that would go into a job-training fund for U.S. workers.

Other House members offered proposals: HR 4165, by Charles E. Schumer, D-N.Y., to increase visas for workers; HR 672, by Howard L. Berman, D-Calif., to grant more visas for family members and workers and set up a category for "independent" immigrants; HR 2646, by Lamar Smith, R-Texas, to set aside an additional 30,000 visas annually for a special category of aliens to be admitted by the administration for foreign policy reasons; and HR 2448, by Hamilton Fish Jr., R-N.Y., to allow unlimited immigration for spouses and unmarried minor children of permanent residents.

Subcommittee Markup

After delays because of differences among subcommittee members on a number of issues, most pertaining to employment-related visas, Morrison's panel began marking up HR 4300 in early April and finished April 18.

By 6-4, the subcommittee sent to the full Judiciary Committee a measure that would have increased the number of visas allowed for family members, workers and foreigners who met criteria of a new "diversity" classification.

That category was intended to ensure a broader mix of immigrants, increasing the number of Europeans who could get visas. Under existing law, favoring immediate relatives in the United States, 43 percent of all immigrants came from Asia and 41 percent came from Latin America. Ten percent came from Europe.

Overall, the bill raised the prospect of doubling U.S. visa quotas, because it removed or increased numerical limits on a host of categories.

For example, an unlimited number of spouses and minor children of permanent U.S. residents would be admitted, compared with the 70,200 visas being granted annually to those groups.

The bill would have increased from 54,000 to 95,000 the visas available to workers who either had jobs waiting for them in the United States or who had education and job skills needed in the United States. The total number of visas that would go to workers, their spouses and minor children was estimated at 235,000.

The measure also would have allowed stays of deportation for the spouses and minor children of aliens legalized under the 1986 Immigration Reform and Control Act and established a conditional residency program for aliens who were in the United States as of Jan. 1 and had job offers.

Major Provisions

The House subcommittee had delayed action for several weeks on the bill's employer-related sections and on the proposal for diversity visas while Morrison and Schumer worked on a compromise.

Morrison agreed to ease some of his proposed conditions for employers who wanted to hire foreign workers. And he accepted Schumer's plan to grant ethnic-diversity visas inversely proportionate to current admissions.

Under HR 4300, employers seeking to hire immigrant workers would have to attest to the Labor Department that they had tried without success to recruit U.S. workers and then wait 30 days to see whether protests were lodged.

Morrison had proposed that immigrant workers be paid 105 percent of the prevailing wage, as an incentive for companies to hire U.S. workers, but that provision was amended in subcommittee to require payment only of the prevailing wage.

A fund for the education and training of U.S. workers would have been established from a head tax of sorts paid by large employers who brought in immigrant workers.

Within the employment-based categories, 30,000 visas would have been set aside for workers and their families from low-admissions countries.

Under a separate section, 25,000 visas would have been granted annually during the following three years for individuals from those countries.

Another provision of the bill was tied specifically to regions of the globe, allocating visas inversely proportionate to the number of immigrants coming from a region. It would have granted 10,000 visas in each of the first three years and 75,000 annually thereafter.

Europeans would have received 44 percent of the diversity admissions. Asians would have received 11 percent.

Family Unification

As approved by the subcommittee, the bill would have provided 185,000 visas a year for immigrants seeking to join family members in the U.S. and 95,000 for workers.

Many foreigners would not have been subject to the limits: parents, spouses or minor children of U.S. citizens; spouses and minor children of permanent U.S. residents; refugees; and special immigrants, such as employees of the U.S. government abroad and retired employees of international organizations.

The unlimited visas for spouses and minor children of permanent U.S. residents — a policy to be phased in over five years — would have been a change from existing law. The State Department projected it could result in 235,000 more immigrants the first year, then 75,000 more immigrants annually. Spouses and minor children of permanent residents were on a waiting list in the Second Preference category.

The family-sponsored preference system would have been restructured and gained more visas under the bill: 55,000 visas for adult unmarried sons and daughters of U.S. citizens, 35,000 visas for adult unmarried sons and daughters of permanent U.S. residents, 30,000 for adult married sons and daughters of citizens, and 65,000 for brothers and sisters of citizens.

Other provisions of the bill would have increased visas for individuals from certain countries. The measure would have granted 25,000 visas a year through 1993 for foreigners from countries adversely affected by the existing immigration system — primarily the Irish and other Western Europeans — who entered the United States before Jan. 1, 1990, and who had a job commitment for at least one year.

Many of the individuals who would have been covered by this section came to the United States on temporary visas that had since expired and were living a sort of underground existence.

The bill also would have allowed family members of illegal aliens granted amnesty under the 1986 immigration law to remain in the United States if they had entered before Jan. 1, 1990, and had applied for visas. The bill would have allowed them to get work permits but would not have made them eligible for public assistance programs.

Amendments Adopted

The subcommittee considered 25 amendments during its meetings April 3-4, six of which were withdrawn. The following amendments were adopted by voice vote unless otherwise indicated:

- By Berman and Fish, adopted 5-3, to offer an additional 43,000 visas for each of the following five years to spouses and children of permanent U.S. residents who were on waiting lists (the existing Second Preference), and an additional 57,000 visas for each of the next five years to adult brothers and sisters of U.S. citizens and their spouses and children on waiting lists for the Fifth Preference.
- By Berman, to allow spouses and children of aliens in a seasonal-agriculture worker program to avoid deportation if they were in the United States illegally.
- By Berman, to waive an English-language requirement for naturalization for individuals who had met certain age and residency terms.
- By Berman, to ensure that State Legalization Impact Assistance Grants (SLIAG) covered aliens while they were applying for lawful temporary status.
- By Barney Frank, D-Mass., to allow displaced Tibetans in India or Nepal to qualify for special immigrant visas.
- By Frank, to allow an individual in Hong Kong to use a valid U.S. visa any time through the year 2002, as opposed to the usual expiration of four months.
- By Morrison, to clarify notification for deportation hearings and, if an alien was to be ordered deported in absentia, require clear and convincing evidence that written notice had been provided.
- By Lamar Smith, to include in SLIAG formulas calculations for spouses and children of legalized aliens who were here illegally but whose deportation was barred.

Amendments Rejected

The subcommittee defeated numerous amendments offered by ranking Republican Smith, who sought to limit additional visas and had constantly raised concerns about how states were accommodating legal and illegal aliens.

Among Smith's proposals were the following, which, unless otherwise noted, were defeated by voice vote:

- To include spouses and children of permanent U.S. residents within numerical limits, as in existing law, rather than in a category of unlimited visas.
- To require the attorney general to compute the difference between how many foreigners were eligible for immigration under the Morrison bill and under existing law, and to authorize an appropriation to the states to handle the increased number of aliens.
- To remove from the bill a Jan. 1, 1990, cutoff date for spouses and children of legalized aliens who would be pro-

tected from deportation; rejected 4-6.

- To remove from the bill all sections relating to employer sanctions for those who hired illegal aliens and all other provisions relating to the 1986 immigration law.
- To make clear that certain legalized aliens were disqualified from cash welfare programs.
- To make several changes in the labor certification procedure, prevailing wage and seasonal-worker requirement of a temporary-worker program primarily for agricultural workers.

Committee Action

The House Immigration Subcommittee's bill was such a departure from current law that it looked as though it would be impossible to get through the full Judiciary Committee or to reconcile with the Senate bill.

But Kennedy, the main sponsor of S 358, elicited a promise from House Judiciary Chairman Jack Brooks, D-Texas, that the committee would consider the bill in time for passage in 1990.

Brooks, who wanted a more modest proposal, persuaded Morrison to scale back HR 4300 as approved by the subcommittee. That paved the way for the full committee to approve the bill on Aug. 1.

Originally, the bill would have allowed the granting of 95,000 visas to workers who either had jobs waiting for them in the United States or who had education and job skills needed here. The new bill called instead for admitting 65,000 foreigners annually for employment.

Morrison's substitute bill also would have lowered the number of visas available on an intermediate basis to reduce backlogs in family-related categories, from 100,000 a year to 50,000.

The committee's 23-12 vote for the bill came after two days of debate that centered on just how generous U.S. immigration policy should be.

The Bush administration threatened to veto the House bill as approved by the Judiciary Committee, specifically citing increases in the number of visas for relatives of legal residents who were not naturalized as U.S. citizens.

Brooks tried in vain to discourage amendments, warning, "If you keep adding little arms and fingers and legs to this bill, you're going to jeopardize it."

Brooks ended up voting for the measure with reservations.

His committee's version, like the Senate's legislation, placed a new emphasis on immigrants' skills and talents. But the House bill called for admitting an estimated 800,000 foreigners a year, in contrast to the 630,000 visas envisioned under the Senate measure and the existing number of about 500,000.

The House bill also departed from the Senate bill by providing a stay of deportation for spouses and children of individuals who became legal residents under the 1986 immigration law. To qualify for the amnesty, the spouses and children had to have been in the United States as of Jan. 1, 1990.

Bush administration policy provided a stay of deportation to spouses and children of legalized aliens only if they were here by 1986.

The House bill also would have granted amnesty and visas for 25,000 foreigners annually who were here illegally but who came from countries hurt by the 1965 law and who already had a job. The "Irish" lobby had been pushing particularly for such language because Ireland was a low-admissions country and its faltering economy had spurred many young people to leave for better opportunities.

The House bill also called for Northern Ireland and the Republic of Ireland to be considered as separate countries for purposes of diversity visas, raising the number of visas that could go to that region.

Newly arrived Irish settled predominantly in Boston and New York, and the Irish Embassy in Washington estimated that 50,000 Irish citizens were here illegally.

Morrison said the country's immigration law needed to be updated to help clear years-long waiting lists of relatives trying to get into the country and to shore up U.S. competitiveness by admitting more immigrants with special talents. "But this bill also responds to the adverse impact of the 1965 law and is an attempt to move to a permanent 'diversity' visa," Morrison said.

John Bryant, D-Texas, said the country was "diverse enough" and questioned the policy of increasing immigration at a time when domestic resources were strained.

"At some point we have to use our marginal resources to build a strong American population to fill jobs," Bryant said.

Another opponent, the subcommittee's ranking Republican Lamar Smith, suggested higher immigration would increase joblessness, lower wages and increase crime. "If you favor increasing immigration," he said, "you have to take responsibility for the consequences."

Morrison and other supporters of the bill said immigrants contributed far more to the U.S. economy than they took. "This is not an obligation" to admit non-refugee foreigners, Morrison said. "This is what is in the best interest of the United States."

Massachusetts Democrat Frank agreed. "Lazy people don't immigrate," he said.

Texans Bryant and Smith were two of the most vocal opponents of the bill. But others from Texas and border states like California supported the measure. Similarly, while mostly Northeastern members were the driving force for immigration revision — to help the "old seed" countries — a handful opposed the bill.

Major Provisions

The House bill retained as the centerpiece of immigration policy the reuniting of families.

Under existing law, there was no limit on spouses, minor children or parents of U.S. citizens who could enter the country; and there would be no limit under the House bill. About 220,000 immediate-family members came to the United States each year.

All other relatives of U.S. citizens and permanent residents — for example, adult sons and daughters, brothers and sisters — were eligible for 216,000 visas a year.

Under the House bill, that limit would have increased to 300,000 to be divided as follows:

- Spouses and minor children of permanent residents, 115,000 visas.
- Adult unmarried sons and daughters of U.S. citizens, 55,000.
- Adult, unmarried sons and daughters of permanent residents, 35,000.
- Married sons and daughters of citizens, 30,000.
- Brothers and sisters of citizens, 65,000.

The Senate bill would have have increased the family preference visas to 260,000.

Existing law allowed 54,000 visas for permanent workers and an unlimited number of visas for temporary workers. The House bill would have raised permanent employment-based immigrants to 65,000 a year (75,000 after 1997) and provided a new ceiling — 66,000 annually — on temporary workers.

While the number of foreign workers allowed would have increased, some provisions would have served as a disincentive to foreign labor. Morrison said he wanted to ensure that jobs were not taken away from Americans.

The bill would have taxed employers for each foreign worker hired: $1,000 for companies with 200 employees or more, $500 for companies with 50-199 workers, and no fee for those with fewer than 50. The proceeds would have been used for education and training of U.S. workers.

The bill also would have required employers seeking to hire immigrant workers to attest to the Labor Department that they had tried to recruit U.S. workers and then to wait 30 days to see if protests were lodged.

Amnesty Provisions

Between subcommittee and committee action, Morrison dropped from the bill language to shield from deportation the spouses and children of persons legalized under the "amnesty" provisions of the 1986 act.

But Berman got the full committee to amend the bill to reinsert the proposal, which the California Democrat said was intended to stop the breakup of families formed since 1986. The committee approved the amendment, 28-8, over objections that it undermined the 1986 law by granting another amnesty.

At one point, Bryant proposed scrapping the entire bill but keeping the Berman provision, which would primarily have helped people in border states like Bryant's Texas. The move failed 14-22.

Favoring the Excluded

For three years, the House bill would have allowed 25,000 visas annually for foreigners from countries largely excluded under the 1965 law and already holding jobs in the United States illegally.

Also during the following three years, 15,000 visas were to be set aside for natives of Eastern Europe who since Oct. 1, 1989, had been living in another foreign country but were not resettled. Another 15,000 visas annually would have been available for natives of Africa.

In 1994, a permanent diversity-visa program would have kicked in, giving preference to people applying from countries that had low admissions under the family-related and employment criteria. A total of 50,000 visas would have been available annually.

Among the amendments accepted by the full committee was a proposal by Frank to revise existing grounds, in a 1952 law, for exclusion of foreigners. It refined the language for those with drug addictions or mental disorders, removed language excluding the mentally retarded and repealed an exclusion based on homosexuality and polygamy.

The panel adopted the amendment, 23-12, with 19 Democrats and four Republicans voting for it and three Democrats and eight Republicans opposing it.

The committee's final approval of the bill came on a largely party-line vote of 23-12. Four Republicans — including Fish, the panel's ranking minority member; Mike DeWine, Ohio; Chuck Douglas, N.H.; and Tom Campbell, Calif. — joined 19 Democrats in endorsing the bill. Three Democrats — Bryant, Hughes, and Harley O. Staggers Jr., W.Va. — joined nine Republicans in voting against it.

Eight of the nine GOP lawmakers signed dissenting views that cited polls showing that most Americans opposed increased immigration. But the committee report argued that the increased immigration under the bill was "well within this nation's absorptive capacity."

HOUSE FLOOR ACTION

After turning back efforts to water down or gut the legislation, the House on Oct. 3 voted 231-192 to pass HR 4300. The vote followed two days of debate and one major change from the bill approved by the House Judiciary Committee on Aug. 1. *(Vote 406, p. 130-H)*

While a number of amendments were accepted by voice vote on the floor, the most significant change in the committee's bill was the addition of a three-year stay of deportation for illegal immigrants from four war-torn countries: El Salvador, Lebanon, Liberia and Kuwait. The provision was added by the House Rules Committee, whose chairman, Joe Moakley, D-Mass., long had sought to suspend deportation for certain Central Americans.

The Rules Committee allowed a vote on an amendment to strike the provision. It was offered by Bill McCollum, R-Fla., Oct. 2 and was defeated, 131-285. *(Vote 402, p. 130-H)*

The House in October 1989 passed a bill (HR 45) that included a stay of deportation for Salvadorans and Nicaraguans. The idea was to give Central Americans a safe haven until turmoil in their homeland stopped and to acknowledge that thousands of Central Americans were living in the U.S. illegally and that the government was not prepared to deport them.

That bill never made it through the Senate, however. *(1989 Almanac, p. 273)*

Requirements for Employers

One of the most controversial sections of HR 4300 was deleted by the House Rules Committee, at the request of the Ways and Means Committee: the head tax on employers that brought in foreign workers. Money from the tax would have gone to a training fund for domestic workers.

The Ways and Means panel called the fee a revenue measure that was within its jurisdiction.

As an alternative, Morrison sought to require employers who hired foreign workers to certify that they had agreed to provide education and training for U.S. workers or students. His amendment, offered during floor debate, would have compelled an employer of more than 200 workers to certify that 100 hours of tutoring for students in math, science or computer skills, or 100 hours of skilled training had been provided. Companies with more than 49 workers but fewer than 200 would have had to provide 50 hours of such training.

The amendment was rejected 194-229. *(Vote 400, p. 130-H)*

While the bill was intended to increase the number of trained immigrants, House authors tried to make sure that U.S. workers were not displaced.

Employers who wanted to bring in foreigners would have had to certify that there was a shortage of domestic workers in the specific field.

As amended by voice vote on the floor, the bill would have offered two options: a firm could continue to go through the existing labor certification process, in which the Labor Department determined whether there was a shortage of U.S. workers in a certain field, or the firm could follow a new verification procedure in which it attested to the department that it had tried to recruit U.S. workers. Under the latter approach, a company would have had to wait 30 days to see if any protests were lodged by domestic workers.

Holding Firm on Visas

The House floor beat back several attempts to decrease the number of new visas. The clashes repeated divisions in the Judiciary Committee action, with committee Republicans McCollum and Lamar Smith and Democrat Bryant the strongest advocates of restrictions on immigration policy. "We have a shortage of jobs and training, not a shortage of people," Bryant said.

Smith sought to limit total immigration to 630,000 a year, the limit set in the Senate bill and favored by the White House. But his amendment was rejected 143-266. *(Vote 399, p. 128-H)*

Another Smith amendment that would have ordered increased federal funds to states to pay for the education and health costs for newly legalized aliens was rejected 53-368. *(Vote 401, p. 130-H)*

An amendment by Tom Lewis, R-Fla., would have provided $500 million annually for five years to reimburse states for cash and medical assistance for newly arrived foreigners. It was rejected 99-319. *(Vote 403, p. 130-H)*

An amendment that could have been most devastating for the legislation also was defeated, 165-257. Offered by Bryant, it would have stripped all the provisions of the bill except those barring the deportation of spouses and children of legalized aliens. *(Vote 404, p. 130-H)*

HOUSE-SENATE DIFFERENCES

The next hurdle facing the bill was Simpson, who had sponsored the less sweeping Senate version. Simpson wanted to press for a cap on immigration and opposed many of the key sections of the House measure, particularly those granting amnesty to illegal aliens.

Ranking minority member of the Judiciary Subcommittee on Immigration and assistant minority leader, Simpson raised the threat of a filibuster against the appointment of conferees for the legislation.

Simpson and administration officials acknowledged a need for more immigrants, particularly to bolster the labor force, but opposed policies that might reward illegal immigrants over foreigners who had waited in line for years.

On Sept. 24, Simpson had introduced a bill (S 3099) to amend the 1986 law to try to stem document fraud by illegal aliens, educate employers who might be discriminating against foreign workers in fear of sanctions, and beef up border security. Simpson said he would be reluctant to support a legal-immigration bill unless S 3099 was passed.

He said the number of foreigners trying to sneak through the U.S. southern border was increasing. "With apprehensions likely to exceed 1 million persons during this fiscal year," Simpson warned, "I am no longer comfortable with increasing our immigration levels by over 25 percent."

Simpson also had made clear his opposition to the Moakley provision for a stay of deportation. In 1989, he stalled Senate Judiciary Committee business for several weeks when a related bill (S 458) by Dennis DeConcini, D-Ariz., was before the panel. That bill, which would have suspended for two years deportation of Salvadorans and Nicaraguans, was approved by the committee but never came to the floor.

With the 1990 session nearing an end, Simpson presented House and Senate leaders on the issue with a list of demands that would have significantly altered the focus of S 358.

"I've let bills die before," he said Oct. 10. But he maintained that contrary to appearances, he wanted a bill. "I am not a blunderbuss who only wants my way," he said. "I am not going to go in there" to meetings with other members of Congress "and say, 'Take it or leave it.'"

Kennedy, who preferred the expansive House approach, held meetings with Simpson, trying to broker a compromise on S 358 before the 101st Congress ran out.

Simpson's Demands

Simpson contended that the nation needed to know the number of immigrants it would have to absorb each year. He wanted a cap on legal immigrants and stepped-up efforts to keep illegal aliens out.

Under Simpson's requirement, total immigration would be capped at 675,000 visas annually. While the Senate bill set a limit of 630,000 immigrants a year, that cap was porous because the bill would allow unlimited immediate relatives (spouses and children) of U.S. citizens to immigrate.

Under the Senate bill, about 10 percent of all visas granted would be "independent" — going to people not sponsored by family members or employers. They would be allocated based on a point system.

Simpson wanted immigrants who applied under this category to get credit for speaking English, saying he believed speaking English would greatly enhance an immigrant's chance to succeed here.

On another issue, Simpson didn't want amnesty for people who either sneaked into the United States or who came here on temporary visas that had since expired.

Much of what Simpson wanted, such as the firm cap on immigration and credit for English, was rejected during Senate floor debate in July 1989. And his ideas never went far in the House, where members sought to open the door wider than the Senate proposed.

Following are some other demands made by Simpson:

- In addition to beefing up the ability to catch illegal aliens, he wanted criminal aliens deported. He said U.S. detention centers were overflowing.
- Contrary to a provision in HR 4300, Simpson did not want spouses and children of permanent residents to be allowed unrestricted entry. The House bill reclassified those immigrants to give them virtually unrestricted status similar to immediate relatives of U.S. citizens, but it imposed a limit of 115,000 visas a year.
- Also differing from the House bill, Simpson wanted no limit on temporary visas for skilled workers. HR 4300 called for a ceiling on the number of visas allowed annually for people in specialized occupations, such as entertainers and athletes, while the Senate bill did not address temporary visas. Business groups objected to limits on temporary visas, but labor interests complained that foreign workers coming in for temporary assignments deprived domestic workers of jobs.

The Politics of Delay

The House had helped deal Simpson a strong hand.

After the Senate passed its bill, the House took 15 months to pass its own, in part because of members' differences over the sweeping approach of the bill's lead sponsor, Morrison. House negotiations also were slowed at times because Morrison's attention was divided between Congress and his gubernatorial campaign.

AIDS Exclusion Policy Lifted by HHS . . .

In 1987, Sen. Jesse Helms, R-N.C., persuaded Congress to take the unusual step of adding the AIDS virus — by law — to a list of "dangerous contagious diseases" that were grounds for exclusion from the United States.

"Other countries are trying to stop the import of the AIDS virus. They do not want it to come into their country, and neither should we," Helms said. With barely a murmur of dissent, the Senate adopted his amendment, 96-0, and the House accepted the provision as part of a 1987 supplemental appropriations bill (PL 100-71). *(1987 Almanac, p. 403)*

The AIDS-exclusion policy was denounced by the health community, AIDS advocates and their allies in Congress. Three years later, while working on a broad overhaul of U.S. law governing legal immigration, Congress reversed itself and restored to the secretary of Health and Human Services (HHS) discretion to redraw the list of diseases.

To the applause of lawmakers, HHS Secretary Louis W. Sullivan at the turn of the year used his newly restored power to remove AIDS-virus infection from the list of sicknesses that could keep someone from entering the United States. The new policy, disclosed Jan. 3, 1991, was to take effect June 1, 1991.

"The administration's decision is as welcome as it is long overdue," said Sen. Edward M. Kennedy, D-Mass., the prime Senate sponsor of the immigration bill (S 358) that served as the vehicle for repealing the mandatory AIDS exclusion. *(Immigration bill, p. 474)*

Background

The 1952 McCarran-Walter Act prohibited the entry into the United States of individuals who fell into 33 categories. In recent years, its exclusions based on political ideology had raised protests and brought some revisions of the law. Among those the act still barred were the mentally retarded, the "insane," and people afflicted with a "sexual deviation" or with any dangerous contagious disease.

The HHS secretary normally specified by regulation which diseases were grounds for exclusion. In 1990, those on the list were five sexually transmitted diseases (chancroid, gonorrhea, granuloma inguinale, lymphogranuloma venereum and infectious syphilis); infectious leprosy; active tuberculosis; and human immunodeficiency virus (HIV) infection. HIV infection — the AIDS virus — was the only one set by law.

The government estimated that about 1 million people infected with HIV were in the United States, which in 1990 had the largest number of AIDS victims worldwide. Many physicians and scientists, including the director of the U.S. Public Health Service, argued that it was safe to allow individuals with the AIDS virus to visit this country.

A person with the HIV virus could still apply for a waiver to enter the United States — the same as any individual ineligible under the exclusions of the McCarran-Walter Act. And the government sought to ease that procedure to avert a potential embarrassment for the United States as San Francisco prepared to host a major worldwide conference on AIDS in June.

Several countries and international groups recommended boycotting the meeting to protest the U.S. policy. Said Jean McGuire, executive director of the Washington-based AIDS Action Council, "We have become an embarrassment in the global community."

Each side had offered a number of proposals, but no agreements had been made.

Meanwhile, some of Simpson's Republican colleagues — Orrin G. Hatch, Utah; Arlen Specter, Pa.; and Rudy Boschwitz, Minn. — wrote to Senate and House Immigration Subcommittee members urging compromise.

"We are convinced that the differences between these two measures can be reconciled and that immigration reform legislation in the national interest can be enacted this year," they said in an Oct. 9 letter.

They said they were primarily interested in increasing the visas available for family members, preferred the House levels but urged the panels to "split the difference."

Rick Swartz, a longtime immigration lobbyist, said, "There is every opportunity now to enact a good compromise bill. If Simpson succeeds in obstructing the process, that opportunity will be lost for at least three years, until past the elections."

CONFERENCE AGREEMENT

House-Senate conferees and White House aides finally reached agreement on the complex bill on Oct. 24, as lawmakers were struggling toward adjournment.

On the key issue — immigration levels — conferees roughly split the difference between the House-approved level of about 800,000 per year and the Senate's 630,000 figure. Under S 358 as approved by the conferees, legal immigration would increase to 700,000 annually during the first three years of the act. After that, a permanent level of 675,000 would be set.

Family-Related Immigration

Of the total, 520,000 visas would be reserved in the first three years for people with relatives in the United States. In fiscal 1996, that total would be scaled back to a permanent 480,000 visas.

Under existing law, about 500,000 immigrants were coming to the United States every year. All immediate relatives of U.S. citizens (spouses, parents and minor children) were admitted without regard to visa-allocation limits. Immigration officials estimated that 220,000 immigrants a year gained entry as immediate relatives.

Those immediate relatives would fall under the eventual 675,000 limit on family-related visas.

The other large family category involved visas for siblings of U.S. citizens and for the spouses, parents and minor children of people who were legal permanent residents. Under existing law, 216,000 visas were being allocated in the so-called family-preference system. The bill called for a guaranteed 226,000 visas annually for these relatives.

. . . After Congress Repeals Mandatory Ban

In February, the Immigration and Naturalization Service (INS) and the State Department, whose consular officers screened people for entry, issued guidelines to deal with the "significant number of foreign HIV-infected individuals" expected to attend the International Conference on AIDS.

If an applicant objected to having the visa and waiver notation placed in his or her passport, consular officers would stamp the visa and note the waiver on a separate sheet that would be attached to the passport.

Despite the attempts to make the waiver process simpler, a congressional sponsor of legislation to overturn the ban, Rep. J. Roy Rowland, D-Ga., said it was still onerous. "It's burdensome and it is stigmatizing," Rowland said in April.

In response to the clamor, the INS on April 13 announced creation of a special, 10-day visa that could be used to attend the conference. Those applying for the visa would not have to say whether they were HIV carriers. The new visa would be in addition to the government's existing waiver policy, which would stay in effect.

Legislative Action

Rowland's bill (HR 4506), introduced April 4, called for the HHS secretary to review whether HIV should be on the list of excludable diseases.

Rowland, a physician, said he hoped that President Bush would support the bill. But on April 12, a spokesman said the president had no position and the administration was still studying the issue.

In May, Rowland and Henry A. Waxman, D-Calif., chairman of the House Energy and Commerce Health Subcommittee, produced an opinion from the General Accounting Office that said the president and HHS secretary already had the power to remove AIDS from the exclusion list. But the administration disagreed.

"The administration continues to believe that the issue of amending or reversing this recent congressional mandate imposed on the president by a vote of 96-0 rests with the Congress," an HHS statement said.

Waxman's subcommittee held a hearing June 27, but the bill went no further on its own. At the end of the session, however, Rowland succeeded in attaching it to the legal-immigration overhaul working its way through Congress.

Conferees on the bill included Rowland's amendment in their agreement reached Oct. 24. AIDS advocacy groups were pleased. "This bill finally exorcises the ghost of Joe McCarthy from the law," said Tom Stoddard, director of the Lambda Legal Defense Fund, an organization representing homosexuals.

The bill cleared Congress on Oct. 27, and Bush signed it into law (PL 101-649) on Nov. 29. In a statement, he noted that the revised grounds for exclusion "lift unnecessary restrictions on those who may enter the United States" but made no specific reference to the AIDS issue.

On Jan. 3, 1991, however, HHS officials disclosed that Secretary Sullivan had revised the list to include just one disease — infectious tuberculosis, the only common deadly disease that could be passed by casual contact.

Waxman said he was pleased, but he pointedly noted the administration's long delay in making the decision. "Since May, the president has known he had the power to make this change, but it has taken an act of Congress for him to consider his own health advisers' recommendations," Waxman said.

One badly backlogged category — spouses and minor children of permanent residents — would get 114,200 visas annually, double the existing number.

Worker and 'Diversity' Visas

Under the existing system, 54,000 visas went each year to workers needed to fill U.S. jobs and their families. The bill would provide 140,000 visas annually for people coming here for a guaranteed job.

Of that total, 40,000 visas would be for workers with "extraordinary abilities," managers and university professors. Another 40,000 would be for workers with high abilities and advanced degrees, and 30,000 for skilled workers.

The rest of the job visas would go to unskilled workers (10,000), foreign investors (10,000) and "special" immigrants, such as ministers (10,000).

The bill would dictate that after an employer applied for labor-shortage certification with the Department of Labor, expressing a need for a foreign worker, any U.S. worker could submit evidence to challenge the request.

A new "independent" or "diversity" visa would be created, mainly for people from countries disadvantaged under existing immigration law. To be eligible, an immigrant would have to have a high school diploma or its equivalent, or one year of experience in an occupation that required at least two years of experience or training.

A permanent diversity visa would be established in fiscal 1994, with 55,000 granted each year.

In the intervening years, there would be 40,000 visas a year set aside for people from countries disadvantaged under existing law.

Nearly half of those would be granted to people from Ireland and other Western European countries who came here under temporary visas and had a guaranteed job in the United States.

Hong Kong was one of the few homelands that got special treatment under the compromise bill. The provisions were adopted mostly because of fears associated with the Chinese government's planned 1997 takeover of that British colony.

Under existing law, Hong Kong nationals received 5,000 visas. The compromise bill would raise that to 10,000 in each of the next three years, then increase the quota to 20,000. In fiscal 1992 through 1994, an additional 12,000 visas would be granted to executives and managers of U.S. companies in Hong Kong who would be transferred to the United States.

Salvadoran Deportation, Amnesty

One key provision in the bill related to the 1986 illegal-immigration law. It would allow a stay of deportation and

Continued on p. 484

Provisions of 1990 Immigration Act

Following are major provisions of the Immigration Act of 1990 as signed into law Nov. 29 (S 358 — PL 101-649):

Total Visa Allotments

• **Total immigration level.** Established a national level of 700,000 visas annually in fiscal 1992-94 and 675,000 annually after that and described the categories of immigrants that were included within that national level.

Dictated that for 1992-94, 55,000 visas be granted to spouses and children of people who received amnesty under the Immigration Reform and Control Act of 1986 (IRCA). Required that those spouses and children had to have entered the country before May 5, 1988.

Defined "immediate relatives" as children, spouses and parents of U.S. citizens. Provided no numerical limit on the admission of immediate relatives of U.S. citizens. Required that if immigration of immediate relatives exceeded 239,000 during fiscal 1992-94, the amount of the excess be subtracted from the 55,000 additional visas for spouses and children of those granted amnesty.

• **Visa categories within the totals.** Set aside 520,000 visas per year for family preference immigrants in fiscal 1992-94, including 55,000 specifically earmarked for the spouses and children of aliens legalized under IRCA; after that, 480,000 visas per year would be set aside. Allocated an additional 140,000 visas for employment-based immigrants. Set aside an additional 55,000 diversity visas.

Provided that the number of family preference visas be reduced each fiscal year by the number of immediate relative visas issued in the previous fiscal year, subject to a floor of 226,000 beginning in fiscal 1992. In any fiscal year if the family preference number was 226,000 or above, any additional visas would be allocated to the so-called Second Preference category, made up of spouses and children of permanent residents. Dictated that in all years, a minimum of 226,000 visas would be reserved for family preference immigrants, thereby allowing the 675,000 level to be exceeded.

• **Per-country limits**. Established an annual limit on immigrants from any single foreign state of no more than 7 percent for family connection visas and employment-based immigrants.

• **Hong Kong.** Allowed Hong Kong to be treated as a separate foreign state, not as a colony, for purposes of visa allocations. But dictated that the number of visas available to natives of Hong Kong not exceed 10,000 per year in fiscal 1991-93.

Allowed Hong Kong natives who obtained visas to delay using them until Sept. 30, 2001. Provided 12,000 visas per year for fiscal 1991-93 for Hong Kong nationals who were high-level employees of large U.S. corporations in Hong Kong.

The corporation had to employ at least 100 workers in the United States and at least 50 workers abroad and have a gross annual income of at least $50 million.

• **Limits on asylum.** Increased the limit on people who had been granted asylum and were seeking permanent residency from 5,000 per year to 10,000 per year.

Exempted from the 10,000 limit people granted asylum who had applied for permanent residence on or before June 1, 1990.

Family Preference System

• **Totals.** Provided 520,000 visas annually for family sponsored immigrants (including immediate relatives) during fiscal 1992-94. Provided 480,000 visas annually in subsequent years.

• **Categories.** Dictated that the existing family preference system be retained, except that the Second Preference category (for spouses and minor children of permanent residents) be divided so that 75 percent of visas issued would be without regard to per-country limits, and 25 percent of the visas would be issued within the confines of per-country limits. The split was intended to allow high-demand countries to continue to claim most of the visas but also to ensure that low-demand countries were not squeezed out.

• **Minimum levels.** Dictated that family preference visas never fall below the following levels:

23,400 visas annually to unmarried sons and daughters of U.S. citizens;

114,200 visas annually to spouses, and unmarried sons and daughters, of permanent residents;

23,400 to married sons and married daughters of U.S. citizens;

65,000 to brothers and sisters of U.S. citizens, if such citizens were at least 21 years old.

Further divided the category for spouses, and unmarried sons and daughters, of permanent residents (Second Preference):

77 percent of the 114,200 visas would go to spouses and children under 21 years of age;

23 percent would go to unmarried children over 21 years of age.

Employment-Based Immigration

• **Categories.** Established five categories for job-based visas: priority workers; aliens with exceptional ability or members of the professions; skilled and unskilled workers; special immigrants; and employment-creating investors.

Provided 40,000 visas per year for priority workers, described as aliens of extraordinary ability in the sciences, arts, education, business or athletics; outstanding professors and researchers with at least three years' experience; and multinational executives and managers who would continue working for the same U.S. employer.

Provided 40,000 visas per year for aliens with exceptional ability or who were members of a profession requiring an advanced degree or its equivalent. Provided 40,000 visas per year for foreigners who were members of a profession requiring a bachelor's degree; who were coming to perform skilled labor or who were coming to perform unskilled labor for which qualified workers were not available in the United States. Limited to 10,000 visas the category for unskilled immigrants.

Provided 10,000 visas for aliens who were "special immigrants." Required that no more than 5,000 such visas be issued to aliens coming as professionals working for a religious organization or religious functionaries. Provided 10,000 visas for foreigners who invested substantial capital in a new commercial enterprise that would create at least 10 new jobs for U.S. workers. Investment would have to be at least $1 million or at least $500,000 in a rural area or an area of high unemployment.

Required that at least 3,000 of the visas available in this section be set aside for enterprises in targeted employment areas (rural or with an unemployment rate at least 150 percent of the national average).

• **Labor certification required.** Dictated that a job visa not be issued to an immigrant until the consular officer received a determination from the secretary of Labor that the worker was needed.

Created a three-year pilot program to examine use of "scheduling" certain occupations for faster determination of labor certification applications. Allowed for job-offer notices and the right of interested parties to submit evidence relating to the application for labor certification. Created a modified attestation process for H-1B "specialty occupation" non-immigrants.

'Diversity' Visas

• **Permanent diversity program.** Provided 55,000 visas beginning in fiscal 1995. Dictated that the visas be allocated to nationals from countries that had been sending few immigrants to the United States under existing law. Required the individual to possess minimum skills.

Provided that the attorney general determine high- and low-admissions countries based on data from the most recent five-year period. Stated that foreigners who benefited from this program had to have minimum education or occupational skills: at least a high school education or its equivalent, or at least two years of work experience in an occupation that requireed at least two years of training or experience.

Provided that Northern Ireland should be treated as a separate foreign state, rather than as part of the United Kingdom, thereby increasing the number of visas allowed for that area.

• **Transition diversity program.** Granted 40,000 visas per year for fiscal 1992 through 1994 to nationals from countries adversely affected under existing immigration law. Dictated that 40 percent of the visas be reserved for nationals of high-qualifying countries under the 1986 "NP-5" program, primarily Ireland.

Required that a person qualifying under the transitional diversity program have a commitment for a job for at least one year. Provided that aliens notified of visa availability under the 1986 "NP-5" program be allocated visas during fiscal 1991. Notification would have to have been made by May 1, 1990. This provision was intended to cover people from countries adversely affected by existing law but who could not be considered to be natives of the country because they were either not born in the country or that because of changes in national borders, the place of birth was now within the borders of a different country.

• **Tibet.** Required that 1,000 visas be allocated to displaced nationals from Tibet over the following three years.

Commission on Immigration Reform

• **Commission on immigration reform.** Set up a nine-member commission: one member who would serve as chairman (to be appointed by the president); two members to be appointed by the Speaker of the House (to be selected from a list of nominees provided by the chairman of the House Judiciary Subcommittee on Immigration, Refugees and International Law); two members to be appointed by the minority leader of the House (from a list of nominees provided by the ranking minority member of the Immigration Subcommittee); two members to be appointed by the majority leader of the Senate (from a list of nominees provided by the chairman of the Senate Judiciary Subcommittee on Immigration and Refugee Affairs; two members to be appointed by the minority leader of the Senate (from a list of nominees provided by the ranking minority member of the Immigration Subcommittee). Appointments would begin in fiscal 1992.

Provided that the commission review and evaluate the effect of the act and the amendments made by it and report to Congress by Sept. 30, 1994. Items among those to be considered: the effect of a national level of immigration on the availability and priority of family preference visas; the effect of the employment-based and diversity programs on labor needs, employment and other economic and domestic conditions in the United States; the social, demographic and natural resources effect of immigration; the effect of immigration on foreign policy and national security; and the effect of per-country levels on family sponsored immigration.

Ordered the commission also to examine the characteristics of the individuals admitted under the new diversity program and how those characteristics compared with characteristics of family sponsored and employment-based immigrants.

Non-Immigrant Status

• Expanded an existing "visa waiver" pilot program for foreign visitors beyond the existing eight countries and extended it for three additional years.

• **Labor problems.** Provided that no non-immigrant would be entitled to arrive in the United States to perform service on a U.S. vessel or aircraft during a labor dispute when there was a strike or lockout in the bargaining unit of the employer for whom the alien intended to work.

• **Longshore work.** Prohibited foreign crew workers from performing longshore work in U.S. ports. Defined longshore work as any activity relating to the loading or unloading of cargo, the operation of cargo-related equipment and the handling of mooring lines on the dock when the vessel was made fast or let go in the United States or the surrounding coastal waters.

Allowed for the following exceptions: when a collective-bargaining agreement would allow a foreign crew to perform the work; when prevailing port practice would allow the crew to do the work; when reciprocal rights were given to a U.S. crew to perform longshore work; or when safety certification was required for longshore work, and only the foreign crew possessed such certification.

• **"E" visas.** Expanded the availability of the "E" visa to include trade in services and technology. Extended reciprocal "treaty trader" status to Australia and Sweden.

Temporary Workers

• **Temporary workers.** Established a limit of 65,000 visas per year for highly skilled aliens coming to work temporarily for U.S. employers (H-1B) and a limit of 66,000 for H2-B non-agricultural temporary workers.

Defined "specialty occupation" as one that required theoretical and practical application of a body of highly specialized knowledge and attainment of a bachelor's or higher degree in the specific specialty (or its equivalent) as a minimum for entry into the occupation in the United States.

Provided that after an H-1B alien was granted a visa, an employer would have to attest that the worker had met certain employment standards. Required an employer to pay the prevailing wage level. Dictated that overall visa limits on temporary workers apply only to principals and not to spouses and children and that holders of H-1B visas could not stay longer than six years.

• **New non-immigrant class for artists and entertainers.** Set up new visa categories separate from the H-1 system for artists and entertainers of "extraordinary ability" (O visas) and for artists and entertainers with the proper level of international recognition (P visas). Allowed entry to foreigners accompanying aliens who were an integral part of the performance.

Established a cap of 25,000 "P" visas per year and set a limit of five years on the stay in the United States.

Set up a new classification of "Q" visas for foreigners who would come here temporarily (not more than 15 months) on a cultural exchange program. Stated that the attorney general would oversee the program for the purpose of providing practical training, employment and the sharing of the history, culture and traditions of the foreigner's homeland. Required the alien to be employed under the same wages and working conditions as domestic workers.

• **Religious workers.** Created a new visa category for professionals and functionaries working for a religious organization. Required the immigrant to have been a member of the religious organization for at least two years immediately preceding the time of application for admission. The limit on the visa would be five years. Dictated that the category would expire on Oct. 1, 1994.

Family Unity and Temporary Protected Status

• **Family unity.** Suspended deportation and granted work authorization to spouses and children of aliens granted amnesty in 1986, provided that the spouses and children entered the United States before May 5, 1988.

• **Temporary protected status.** Established a new statutory program to replace existing executive branch authority to grant extended voluntary-departure status to nationals from specially designated countries.

Retained with the administration the authority to designate countries or portions of countries as beneficiaries of temporary protected status. Dictated that the attorney general could designate any foreign state for such status if the attorney general found any of the following conditions: ongoing armed conflict within the state that would pose a serious threat to nationals required to return to that state; an earthquake, flood, drought, epidemic or other environmental disaster in the state resulting in a substantial but temporary disruption of living conditions in the area affected; extraordinary and temporary conditions in the foreign state that prevented aliens who were nationals of the state from returning to the state in safety. Provided for periodic review, terminations and extensions of protected status.

• **El Salvador.** Granted to nationals of El Salvador immediate temporary protected status until June 1, 1992. A conference report accompanying the legislation stated that Congress strongly urged the attorney general to grant temporary protected status to nationals of Kuwait, Lebanon and Liberia.

Stated in the conference report that Congress intended that the president's executive order barring the return of Chinese nationals remain in effect as the president had indicated until 1994.

Naturalization

• **Administrative naturalization.** Provided that permanent resident aliens seeking naturalization could appear before a U.S. district court, as was existing law, or follow an administrative procedure. The latter process had been created with the aim of reducing delays.

Provided that an applicant for naturalization who was denied naturalization after a hearing before an immigration officer could seek review of such denial before a U.S. district judge. The review would be de novo, and the court would make its own finding of fact and conclusions of law.

Reduced the requirement for naturalization from six months' residence in a state to three months' residence in a state or in an Immigration and Naturalization Service (INS) district.

• **Filipino war veterans.** Allowed a waiver of residency and the naturalization process and awarded citizenship to natives of the Philippines who fought on the side of the United States in World War II.

Criminal Aliens

• **Criminal aliens.** Revised procedures for removing criminal aliens from the United States. Limited defenses to deportation that a criminal alien could assert. Required state court systems to provide information to the INS on convicted aliens. Expanded INS arrest authority of aliens believed to have committed a felony. Provided additional resources to the Executive Office for Immigration Review.

• **Report on criminal aliens.** Required the attorney general to submit to Congress by Dec. 1, 1991, a report that described the efforts of the INS to identify, apprehend, detain and remove from the United States aliens who had been convicted of crimes here.

• **Employer sanctions and antidiscrimination.** Required that the Justice Department, with the chairman of the Equal Employment Opportunity Commission, the secretary of Labor and the head of the Small Business Administration, conduct a campaign to disseminate information respecting the rights and remedies for victims of discrimination in connection with unfair immigration-related employment practices. Such a campaign would be aimed at increasing the knowledge of employers, employees and the general public concerning employer and employee rights, responsibilities and remedies under this section and title.

Authorized $10 million for dissemination of information concerning antidiscrimination provisions. Eliminated a requirement that aliens submit a declaration of intention to become a citizen to qualify to file an antidiscrimination complaint.

Removed sanctions for recruiting agencies that did not verify clients' work eligibility. The burden of verifying worker eligibility would lie with the employer.

• **Enhanced enforcement.** Provided for repair and construction of barriers to deter illegal entry on U.S. borders.

Authorized an increase of 1,000 border patrol officers of the INS. Imposed new civil penalties against persons who knowingly used or accepted fraudulent documents for immigration purposes and raised criminal fine levels for those who concealed aliens.

• **Deportation procedures.** Required that aliens subject to deportation be given notice of such, the date of a hearing and possible defenses. Required aliens to keep the INS informed of their address.

Dictated that any alien who failed to appear for a scheduled deportation hearing or who failed to keep the INS apprised of his or her address could be ordered deported in absentia. Required the attorney general to issue regulations and report to Congress on consolidating and expediting existing deportation procedures.

Exclusions

• **Exclusions for people seeking immigration.** Revised the existing grounds for exclusion and deportation, repealing outmoded grounds and expanding possible waivers.

• **Health exclusions.** Dictated that people be excluded only for diseases that posed a public health risk. Barred entry of aliens who had a communicable disease of "public health significance," in accordance with regulations prescribed by the secretary of Health and Human Services (HHS); who had a physical or mental disorder accompanied by behavior that posed a threat to the property, safety or welfare of the individual or others; who were drug abusers or addicts, in accordance with regulations prescribed by the secretary of HHS. Allowed greater grounds for waivers, at the attorney general's discretion.

• **Foreign policy.** Dictated that aliens not be barred from entry because of their political beliefs. Further specified that foreign-government workers could not be prohibited solely because of political beliefs. Generally excluded any alien whose entry or proposed activities in the United States would have serious adverse foreign policy consequences for the United States.

Stated that any immigrant who was or had been a member of the Communist Party or any other totalitarian party could be excluded. Allowed exception for involuntary membership, youth membership and membership that ended at least two years before the date of the application. Also specified that aliens who were members of the Communist Party but had immediate relatives in the United States and were not security threats could obtain waivers.

Removed membership in or affiliation with the Communist Party as a ground for exclusion of non-immigrants.

• **Criminal activities.** Expanded the waiver possibility for exclusion based on long-past or non-violent criminal activities.

Miscellaneous

• **Marriage fraud law waivers.** Under existing law, an alien could not obtain permanent residence unless he or she was married for at least two years after entering the United States. The new law would waive the requirement if the alien was battered by a spouse. Provided that aliens who married while in deportation proceedings could seek a waiver of the "two-year return" requirement if they could establish by clear and convincing evidence that the marriage was bona fide.

• **Lebanese nationals.** Dictated that visas to Lebanese nationals qualifying for visas under the Second Preference (spouses or children of permanent residents) or Fifth Preference (adult brothers and sisters) be granted as early as possible in a fiscal year.

• **Permanent residence status.** Provided a one-year extension of a deadline for filing applications for adjustment from temporary to permanent residence for legalized aliens. ■

Continued from p. 481

work authorization for spouses and minor children of legalized aliens who had been in the U.S. since May 1988.

And another provision, the 18-month stay of deportation for people living in the United States illegally, was one of the last to be resolved by House and Senate conferees. It pitted Rules Chairman Moakley against lead Senate negotiators Kennedy and Simpson.

Kennedy and Simpson argued against singling out one country for special treatment. Opponents also contended that people who had come to the United States illegally should not be rewarded and that some of the Salvadorans had emigrated for economic rather than political reasons.

But Moakley, who had been trying since the 98th Congress to win a stay of deportation for the Salvadorans, noted that he had been willing in other years to back off in the interests of whatever immigration bill was on the table. This year, he said, he was not going to budge.

Eventually, Kennedy and Simpson did.

In addition to adopting the Moakley provision to help Salvadorans, the conferees also approved a new procedure for temporary stays of deportation for people fleeing armed conflict or natural disasters.

The attorney general would have discretion to grant such stays, and the conferees urged the Justice Department to give temporary protected status to immigrants from three other countries — Kuwait, Lebanon and Liberia.

Satisfying Simpson

Simpson withdrew a number of the demands he had made, such as a lower cap on immigration and no amnesty-related language. What the Wyoming Republican got in return was stiffer border patrol, stepped up deportation procedures, civil penalties for document fraud and a pilot program to create a forgery-proof driver's license that could be used by employers to screen out illegal workers. Three states would have the option of adopting such a license.

Ethnic groups and the American Civil Liberties Union opposed the license provision, saying they feared it might be the first step toward a national identification card.

Simpson strongly urged — and won — a provision to set aside 10,000 employment-related visas for individuals who invested at least $1 million in a new enterprise here and hired at least 10 U.S. workers.

Simpson said he thought the final bill was a good blend of priorities among immigration leaders.

Sen. Paul Simon, D-Ill., who helped bridge many of the rifts between House members and senators, said the final bill "revitalizes a system that has grown rusty and unresponsive."

FINAL ACTION

The bill had yet to clear its final hurdle, however. The 101st Congress ultimately was able to pass it only after an upset, a surprise and an ironic twist on the last day of the session.

The upset came as a small group of Hispanic members engineered a late-night defeat Oct. 26 of a rule for consideration of the conference report on the bill.

They opposed Simpson's pilot program to create a forgery-proof driver's license that could be used by employers to screen out illegal workers. They saw that as the first step toward a national identification card.

The surprise was that Simpson, who earlier had held up the bill until he got a deal that included the driver's license project, dropped it without a fight.

The ironic twist was that Moakley, long shut out on immigration matters, helped save the bill in the end.

Having won conferees' assent to his provision to stay deportation of Salvadorans, Moakley helped panicky bill sponsors in the early hours of Oct. 27 when they needed another rule that would allow the legislation to be put to a House vote.

"If that immigration bill had gone down, and I had not been a part of the bill, they'd still be looking for a rule," Moakley said Nov. 1.

The Senate had approved the conference report 89-8 about 10 p.m. Oct. 26. Sponsors thought the measure was headed toward swift approval in the House. *(Vote 323, p. 63-S)*

But California Democrats Edward R. Roybal and Esteban E. Torres and other Hispanics had worked the House floor for most of the day trying to persuade colleagues to vote against the rule.

Torres said later, "All we wanted to do was remove the [driver's license] section, not doom the legislation."

Torres and other opponents of the driver's license project made it a civil rights issue, warning that the plan was a threat to privacy and individual liberties. They won over black members, who had significant Hispanic populations in their districts and who were frustrated by Bush's veto of a civil rights bill (S 2104). *(Civil rights bill, p. 462)*

Liberal Democrats joined, too, because of the civil liberties issue, as did GOP members who were against the overall bill.

The vote on the rule was 186-235. *(Vote 526, p. 166-H)*

Bill proponents then came up with the idea of a concurrent resolution to strip out the license provision.

The idea was to get both chambers to pass a resolution dictating that when S 358 was enrolled, the driver's license section would be dropped. It was an alternative to sending the bill back to the Senate, where if the license provision were up for amendment, senators might rethink other sections.

House members, in a sweat, called Simpson. They worried that he might refuse to drop the license language. But to everyone's surprise, Simpson said his proposal had been diluted in conference and was hardly what he wanted anyway.

The License Proposal

The license proposal stemmed from a desire to slow the flood of illegal aliens into the country and to give employers, who faced penalties for hiring undocumented workers, an easier way to verify that an applicant was here legally. The General Accounting Office reported earlier in 1990 that employer sanctions were causing widespread bias against foreign-looking workers.

Simpson's plan drew opposition more for what it signified than for what it would have done. It would not have been mandatory anywhere, and only three states would have had the option of adopting such a license.

Simpson wanted the license to include a "biometric" component, such as a fingerprint, and a Social Security number, both of which could be verified when an individual applied for the license.

But in conference, the Social Security number proposal was dropped.

The provision had not been in either the original House or Senate immigration bills when they passed their respective chambers, but it was added to appease Simpson's desire to keep illegal aliens out of the country.

In floor debate, Roybal said, "It is ironic that South Africa has just abandoned its notorious pass-card identification program that has been an essential element of its hated apartheid system."

By voice vote Oct. 27, both chambers agreed to delete the license proposal. The House then adopted the conference report 264-118. The vote split party lines, with 64 Republicans and 54 Democrats opposing the final bill. *(Vote 530, p. 166-H)*

Signed by Bush

Bush signed the bill in a Nov. 29 ceremony that included Senate sponsors Kennedy and Simpson, House sponsor Morrison, and Lamar Smith, who had opposed the measure as ranking Republican on the House Immigration Subcommittee but ended up voting for the final bill.

Calling immigration "a bridge to America's future," Bush praised the bill's major provisions to increase the number of skilled workers allowed into the United States and strengthen family reunification. He also praised what sponsors regarded as the most important secondary feature: the revision of the politically related exclusion grounds.

On a bill that the administration had frequently been opposed to or uninterested in, however, Bush used minor sections to tie the measure to the administration's anti-crime rhetoric. He said provisions for deporting violent criminals would aid the war on drugs and also praised a provision that he said clarified the authority of INS agents to make arrests and carry firearms. ■

Bush Signs Stripped-Down Crime Bill

Time pressures and irreconcilable differences over some of the most emotional issues in criminal justice combined at the end of the 101st Congress to dilute a sweeping election-year anticrime package.

With the clock running out, House-Senate conferees on the legislation (HR 5269, S 1970) on Oct. 26 abandoned efforts to reach agreement on the most controversial provisions before them — a broadened federal death penalty, limits on legal challenges by condemned prisoners, and restrictions on semiautomatic assault-type weapons.

> **BOXSCORE**
>
> **Legislation:** Crime Control Act of 1990, PL 101-647 (S 3266).
>
> **Major action:** Signed, Nov. 29. Passed by Senate, Oct. 27; by House, 313-1, Oct. 27. HR 5269 passed by House, 368-55, Oct. 5; S 1970 passed by Senate, 94-6, July 11.
>
> **Reports:** Judiciary (H Rept 101-681, Part I); Ways and Means (Part II).

Also gone from the final version were provisions sought by the Bush administration that would have allowed courts to consider evidence gathered with flawed warrants, to shorten delays in carrying out executions and to impose tougher penalties for illegal firearm use.

Instead, both chambers approved a stripped-down bill (S 3266) on Oct. 27 that included only proposals acceptable to all. These involved increased penalties for child abuse; prison alternatives, such as house arrest; more funding for local law enforcement and increased authorizations for federal law enforcement agencies such as the FBI.

In a response to the thrift crisis, the measure also set up in the Justice Department an office of special counsel for financial institutions fraud, made it easier for federal banking agencies and the Justice Department to seize the assets of defendants in such cases, and limited defendants' ability to use bankruptcy to avoid civil or criminal penalties.

The Senate approved the bill by voice vote; the House passed it 313-1, clearing the measure for the president. *(House vote 534, p. 168-H; highlights of provisions, p. 499)*

President Bush signed the bill Nov. 29, while expressing "deep disappointment over many provisions noticeably absent from the legislation."

But, he said, "while this is not the crime bill I asked Congress to pass, I am pleased with the tools [it] provides for fighting financial institutions fraud."

When Bush unveiled his big anticrime package in May 1989, it centered on the first broad expansion of the federal death penalty since the Supreme Court reinstated capital punishment in 1976.

In the Senate, controversial provisions dealing with the death penalty, habeas corpus, gun controls and the exclusionary rule were rolled into a separate bill (S 1970) after they almost derailed antidrug legislation in 1989. *(1989 Almanac, pp. 259, 260)*

When senators took up the issues in May 1990, a surprise vote for restrictions on assault-style weapons almost sank the bill. But surviving a threatened filibuster, the bill was passed July 11.

On the House side, the Democratic leadership for months resisted pressure for a crime bill from Bush, GOP members and Democratic moderates. The Judiciary Committee approved a bill July 23, but its safeguards for defendants' rights drew a Bush veto threat. Most were stripped out during floor consideration, and the bill passed by the House on Oct. 5 was far tougher on criminals than the Judiciary Committee version.

The House bill contained a "racial justice" clause, which would have allowed defendants to get out of a death sentence if they could prove, initially with statistics of racial imbalances, that it was imposed because of racial bias. The House conferees would not give up on that provision, which the Senate had rejected. Senate conferees would not relinquish gun control.

Conferees resolved the impasse by dumping the controversial provisions altogether. With little time left, Republican critics of the outcome could do nothing but fume. The bill cleared both chambers on the last full day of its 1990 session, and Bush used the Nov. 29 bill signing ceremony to urge Congress to "implement the remainder of the comprehensive crime package" in 1991.

Gun control proponents also planned to try again in 1991 after a year in which their efforts to enact a ban on assault weapons and a waiting period for handgun purchases progressed but fell short of enactment. *(Gun control, p. 500)*

BACKGROUND

Since 1982, Congress cleared an anticrime or antidrug bill every two years, typically in the waning days of the session right before the final campaign swing. *(1988 Almanac, p. 85; 1986 Almanac, p. 92; 1984 Almanac, p. 215; 1982 Almanac, p. 419)*

Lawmakers broke the biennial rhythm in 1989 by acting on a big antidrug package in a non-election year. But to ensure speedy passage of that measure, Senate leaders in September agreed to peel off controversial anticrime provisions and bundle them for later consideration.

The unanimous-consent agreement, largely a concession to Republicans, called for the Senate to consider a broadened federal death penalty, firearms regulation, new limits on habeas corpus appeals, exceptions to the exclusionary rule barring use of illegally seized evidence, a Justice Department reorganization and proposals to combat international money laundering.

Debate on the package had been postponed three times since September 1989 because of the crush of other business. First it was to be brought up before the 1989 adjournment. Leaders in both parties agreed in November to postpone consideration until February 1990. Then, the package was rescheduled for April. Next, it was rescheduled for before the Memorial Day 1990 recess.

On the Senate calendar were S 1970, a bill introduced by Senate Judiciary Committee Chairman Joseph R. Biden Jr., D-Del., that covered items in the unanimous-consent agreement, and S 1971, an alternative offered by Strom Thurmond, S.C., ranking Republican on the Judiciary Committee.

Bush, who urged adoption of a number of the proposals already before the Senate, sent a new package of antidrug and anticrime proposals to Congress on May 16, 1990.

Included were provisions to stiffen criminal and civil asset-forfeiture laws and to permit the Immigration and Naturalization Service to summarily deport aliens who were in the United States legally if they were convicted of drug-related crimes or crimes involving the use or threat of physical force.

Political Currents

Republicans repeatedly used the crime issue as a club against Democrats since Richard M. Nixon made law and order a major theme of his 1968 presidential campaign.

The potency of that weapon was demonstrated again in 1988 when Democratic presidential nominee Michael S. Dukakis failed to counter the impact of Bush campaign commercials that in effect blamed the Massachusetts governor for the rampage of a murderer-rapist furloughed from the state's penitentiary, Willie Horton. Democrats' efforts to point out that the Massachusetts furlough program had originated under a Republican governor did little to counteract the powerful television image of prisoners' appearing to be let out of prison through a revolving door.

Democrats were still coping with the fallout from the 1988 campaign in 1990. In the next round of anticrime legislation, Democrats hoped to seize the initiative and "de-Dukakisize" the issue, as one key Democratic aide said.

Biden wanted to ensure that any Senate legislation was written largely by Democrats and that it would be seen as a tough, bold proposal. He rejected the notion that Democrats had to be defensive about their stance on crime issues, saying they were the ones who had pushed for more money for law enforcement.

But he acknowledged that, figuratively speaking, "one of my objectives, quite frankly, is to lock Willie Horton up in jail."

But while the debate represented an opportunity for Democrats, it was also a minefield.

Some of them opposed some of the Republican proposals, such as a broad federal death penalty and a limit on the appeals of prisoners on death row, leaving them potentially vulnerable to charges that they were soft on crime.

As a party, the GOP generally spoke with one voice for punishment over rehabilitation, harsher and harsher sentences and no gun control. In control of the White House for all but four years since Nixon was first inaugurated, Republicans had a valuable platform on crime and drugs.

Don Nickles, R-Okla., chairman of the National Republican Senatorial Committee, said that votes on the death penalty and other crime issues would help Republican candidates. "It's not necessarily that these issues are for political purpose," he explained, "but politically they fall to our advantage."

Nixon broke ground in 1968 with his use of television commercials that capitalized on the public's fear of crime. Despite years of imitation, the issue continued to resonate with voters and to be embraced by politicians.

The Associated Press, which in April reported the pervasiveness of the capital punishment issue in the year's gubernatorial races, quoted Democratic consultant Frank Greer as saying, "The death penalty has become a sort of simplistic litmus test or symbolic test of whether you're tough on crime."

Democratic campaign strategists insisted that most party incumbents were not defensive on crime because their positions were well-known and accepted by constituents. John B. Breaux, D-La., chairman of the Democratic Senatorial Campaign Committee, said the crime issue "is not a party concern at all."

And Biden argued that the stereotype of Democrats as permissive toward criminals did not hold up when placed next to Democratic action on anticrime and antidrug bills in recent years.

He pointed out that Democrats in 1989 more than doubled the funds sought by Bush for his antidrug program. Emergency antidrug funds added to the fiscal 1990 Transportation appropriations bill (HR 3015 — PL 101-164) brought total federal antidrug spending for the year to $8.8 billion, up from $5.7 billion the year before and about $900 million more than Bush had requested. *(1989 Almanac, p. 749)*

Death Penalty, Racial Bias

Complicating the capital punishment debate was a civil rights dispute.

The death-penalty provisions in S 1970 were drawn from a bill (S 32) ordered reported Oct. 17, 1989, by the Judiciary Committee. They would have authorized capital punishment for 30 federal crimes, primarily murder, espionage and treason. *(1989 Almanac, p. 260)*

But to the dismay of Thurmond, the sponsor of S 32, the committee adopted an amendment by Edward M. Kennedy, D-Mass., that would have prohibited the death sentence in state and federal cases if a defendant could prove with statistical or other evidence that his race, or that of the victim, played a role in sentencing.

Kennedy asserted that the death penalty was applied in a way that discriminated against blacks. Thurmond countered that studies were inconclusive and that juries judged each defendant individually.

Thurmond also said Kennedy was trying to undermine capital punishment with rules that would force prosecutors to spend their time developing race-based statistical evidence to prove that the race of the defendant or victim was incidental to the sentence sought.

GOP senators wanted to strip the Kennedy amendment from the bill.

In the previous two years, the Senate had approved two bills to authorize the death penalty for particular offenses. On Oct. 26, 1989, it passed a measure (S 1798) to provide the death penalty for terrorists who murdered U.S. citizens abroad. The vote was 79-20. *(Senate 1989 vote 275, 1989 Almanac, p. 51-S)*

In 1988, the Senate authorized the death penalty for so-called drug kingpins by a vote of 65-29, and the measure (S 2455) became part of the Anti-Drug Abuse Act of 1988 (HR 5210 — PL 100-690). *(Drug bill: death-penalty provisions, 1988 Almanac, p. 91)*

In floor action on the 1988 legislation, senators rejected a "racial justice" amendment similar to that which Kennedy added to the 1990 bill. But this time, the provision was in the legislation before the Senate, and the burden would be on its opponents to get it out.

Habeas Corpus Revisions

Another controversial section of the crime legislation was aimed at limiting both the number and timing of challenges that defendants sentenced to death could make in the federal courts after exhausting their state appeals.

A 1989 report by a judicial committee headed by retired Supreme Court Justice Lewis F. Powell Jr. found that the

Lawmakers Divided on Court Rulings . . .

Death row appeals, a perennially divisive issue that held up action on the 1990 crime bill, saw more action in the Supreme Court than in Congress.

That complicated the task as members tried to strike a balance between their traditional election-year toughness on defendants and the desire of some lawmakers, many in leadership positions, to rein in a court they believed was too harsh on defendants' rights.

A key question was whether a death row defendant should have the benefit of a favorable court opinion in another case after his own conviction had become final. The court in 1989 and 1990 generally barred inmates from using subsequent court decisions to challenge their convictions in habeas corpus petitions.

To some Democrats in Congress, the majority was trying to gut the habeas corpus process. They believed that for the ultimate punishment, speed and finality should take a back seat to thorough, if lengthy, review.

Leading this side in crime bill negotiations were Reps. William J. Hughes, D-N.J., chairman of the House Judiciary Subcommittee on Crime, and Robert W. Kastenmeier, D-Wis., chairman of the Judiciary Subcommittee on Courts, Intellectual Property and the Administration of Justice. Their provisions to counter the court were stripped from the bill (HR 5269) on the House floor Oct. 4. The Senate bill (S 1970) had no comparable provision.

At the same time, other members, primarily Republicans, wanted to greatly restrict the habeas corpus process. The average time from conviction to execution, according to a Hill-established study panel, was more than eight years.

These members said that although the court imposed new restrictions on inmates, they wanted to set in law time limits for appeals and confine the grounds on which an inmate could press his challenge.

A leader on this side was Henry J. Hyde, R-Ill., who got the House to amend its bill to allow inmates only one chance to make habeas corpus claims in federal court. The Bush administration also pressed to curtail the process.

Many others fell in the middle, saying the existing appeals process was too lengthy, but wanting to restore the more lenient standard for retroactive application of court opinions that helped an inmate.

Some questioned whether, with the Supreme Court's active interest in habeas corpus, lawmakers who wanted to hem in the appeals process even needed to enter the fray.

Leslie Harris, chief legislative counsel of the American Civil Liberties Union's Washington office, said, "As a political matter, Congress can still say it wants habeas corpus reform, but the court has already done what people have been pushing for and worse."

Even some members who wanted more limits on the appeals process said Congress should step aside and leave the matter to the courts.

In 1988, during consideration of the omnibus drug bill (PL 100-690), Congress failed to compromise on habeas corpus and set up a study panel instead. The panel, led by retired Supreme Court Justice Lewis F. Powell Jr., subsequently recommended that prisoners get a six-month period for filing a writ of habeas corpus, after exhausting state court appeals.

One round of federal habeas corpus petitions would be permitted. Hyde's amendment was drawn largely

average time between conviction and execution in capital cases was more than eight years. The delay stemmed from court backlogs and the numerous chances inmates had to challenge their death sentences at the state and federal level. *(Habeas corpus, this page)*

Under existing law, inmates on state death rows first had to challenge their convictions in state courts before beginning collateral attacks on their convictions by seeking a writ of habeas corpus from federal district courts.

Both S 1970 and S 1971 would have limited the number of habeas corpus petitions that could be filed in federal court by a person convicted under state law, and both would have required a prisoner to petition for habeas corpus relief within one year of exhausting his state appeals.

The Republicans' S 1971 went much further than the Democratic-sponsored S 1970 by barring a defendant's federal court appeal unless he could prove that he did not have a "full and fair" adjudication in state court.

While states that allowed capital punishment were frustrated by the length of time it could take for a murderer to be executed, some senators feared that streamlining the process could lead to judicial errors.

Biden's proposal would have allowed a prisoner to file a second habeas application in federal court in extraordinary cases in which there might be a "miscarriage of justice." His plan, embodied in S 1970, would have applied only to capital cases and would have required states to guarantee prisoners qualified counsel during their appeals.

S 1971 would have more extensively rewritten habeas corpus law for all federal and state offenses and would not have required the state to provide free counsel.

Slower Pace in the House

In the House, several proposals were the subject of Judiciary subcommittee hearings, but the Judiciary Committee did not hasten to report out an omnibus measure. The Crime Subcommittee on March 21 approved one bill (HR 4225) that would have banned assault-style firearms.

The bill sought to apply to domestic weapons the same restrictions that the Bush administration had imposed on foreign-made semiautomatics. It would have banned the possession and sale of any U.S.-made semiautomatic weapons that did not have a sporting purpose, as determined by the Bureau of Alcohol, Tobacco and Firearms.

The legislation would not have affected handguns and would not have barred any semiautomatics someone already owned.

"That is more like the left-wing concept of how you fight crime," said Rep. Robert S. Walker, R-Pa., one of the most vocal critics of House inaction on law enforcement proposals.

In April, Walker tried to engineer defeat of a rule for

... That Curb Death Penalty Challenges

from this proposal. *(1989 Almanac, p. 259)*

Critical court decisions in 1989-90 that limited death row defendants' appeals were decided 5-4. In the majority were Chief Justice William H. Rehnquist and Justices Byron R. White, Sandra Day O'Connor, Antonin Scalia and Anthony M. Kennedy. Dissenting were Justices William J. Brennan Jr., Thurgood Marshall, Harry A. Blackmun and John Paul Stevens.

- *Teague v. Lane*, a black man objected to his trial by an all-white jury; the prosecutor had used peremptory strikes to eliminate black jurors. The defendant based his petition in part on a high court ruling, after his conviction, allowing challenge of a jury and review of peremptory strikes. The court decided Feb. 22, 1989, that new constitutional rules of criminal procedure should not be applied retroactively unless the change went to the fundamental fairness of how a trial was conducted. In this case, White did not fully support the court's opinion but found the habeas limit acceptable.
- *Saffle v. Parks*, an inmate whose conviction and death sentence became final in 1983 claimed that an instruction in the penalty phase of his trial, telling the jury to avoid any influence of sympathy, violated the Eighth Amendment. He cited a 1987 court decision finding the antisympathy instruction unconstitutional. The court ruled March 5, 1990, that good-faith interpretations of legal principles at the time of a conviction could stand even when later rulings contradicted them.
- *Butler v. McKellar*, a defendant tried to get his conviction overturned based on a new court ruling that said if a suspect had asked for a lawyer in one inquiry, he could not be interrogated by police, without counsel, in another. The court, in another March 5 decision, held that a defendant could not challenge his conviction via a habeas corpus petition based on a new constitutional rule that a state appeals court could not reasonably have predicted at the time of the defendant's direct appeal.

Rehnquist wrote for the majority that federal courts should not second-guess "reasonable, good faith interpretations of existing precedents made by state courts even though they are shown to be contrary to later decisions." Dissenting justices criticized the opinion, saying that inmates would languish in jail or die "because state courts were reasonable, even though wrong."

- *Sawyer v. Smith*, a defendant challenged his death sentence based on the prosecutor's telling jurors that even if they recommended execution, they were not responsible for the sentence.

A 1985 ruling in a subsequent case prohibited the death sentence when jurors were misled about their role in capital punishment. The court ruled June 21, 1990, that a defendant was not entitled to federal habeas corpus relief based on a new court ruling in another case unless the principle of the new case was "fundamental to the integrity of the criminal proceeding."

In the end, the habeas corpus issue was too controversial for House and Senate conferees to resolve. The revisions approved by both chambers were dropped in conference, along with the expansion of the federal death penalty. Lawmakers on both sides of the aisle complained about the deletions, but the stripped-down bill cleared Congress on Oct. 27.

Bush signed the bill Nov. 29, but voiced regret that it lacked "comprehensive reform of habeas corpus proceedings that continue to nullify State death penalty laws through repetitive hearings and endless delays."

---

debate on an antitrust measure so that the Rules Committee could be instructed to make in order an amendment incorporating Bush's anticrime proposals. The move failed, but it did send a warning shot across the Democratic bow.

House Judiciary Chairman Jack Brooks, D-Texas, said he was not holding up anticrime legislation, but was trying to take a more deliberative approach to the issue. He assigned most of the Bush crime package to Judiciary subcommittees, and it was expected that the full committee would act on some legislation despite Brooks' avowed skepticism.

"All of us have voted for crime bills almost every year for the last few years," Brooks declared in April. "We have got almost as many crime bills passed as they have crimes committed."

SENATE FLOOR ACTION

The Senate passed its version of the crime bill (S 1970), 94-6, on July 11 after weeks of contentious debate and cloture votes. *(Vote 147, p. 33-S)*

Biden and GOP floor manager Thurmond praised the measure with superlatives.

"This is the toughest, most comprehensive crime bill in our history," said Biden.

"This bill will go down in history as one of the greatest pieces of legislation ever passed," Thurmond said.

Largely written on the floor — there was no committee report — S 1970 reflected more of Biden's original proposal (S 1972) than Bush's.

On the more contentious issues, the Senate:

- Voted to ban nine foreign and domestic semiautomatic assault guns.
- Approved a new death penalty, an option for more than 30 crimes. It was largely the handiwork of Republicans and had been a goal of Bush.
- Approved a compromise between Democrats and Republicans on revising the habeas corpus process under which death row inmates could challenge their sentences.
- Rejected a provision that would have prohibited a death sentence if a defendant could show that his or the victim's race played a role in sentencing. The "racial justice" proposal was stripped from the bill with the support of a majority of Republicans and just fewer than half the Democrats.
- Authorized 3,000 federal agents and prosecutors and included a Democratic proposal to authorize $900 million — nearly half the nearly $2 billion in the bill — for local law enforcement.

The White House opposed most of the big-money items attached to the bill in amendments June 28.

Before passage, the Senate voted 99-1 to add one final

amendment to the bill, a package of get-tough provisions aimed at savings and loan fraud. *(Vote 146, p. 33-S)*

Voting against the final bill were two liberal Democrats, Kennedy and Howard M. Metzenbaum of Ohio; two moderate Republicans, Dave Durenberger, Minn., and Mark O. Hatfield, Ore.; and two GOP conservatives, William L. Armstrong, Colo., and William V. Roth Jr., Del.

Seesawing Fortunes

The first four days of floor action May 21-24 were marked with partisan maneuvers and political upsets.

Democrats, eager to take the political offensive on the crime issue, won on a number of provisions. They hoped that if Republicans tried later to retaliate with "killer" amendments, the GOP would be viewed as trying to sandbag the crime bill.

But Orrin G. Hatch, R-Utah, accused the Democrats of "watering down" the death-penalty section and of working toward a bill that was "less than tough on crime."

The most serious threat to the bill's passage, however, came not from the debate over capital punishment and death-penalty appeals but from a narrow vote to preserve the committee-approved ban on assault weapons.

Habeas Corpus: Two Tries

The writ of habeas corpus — Latin for "you have the body" — was a centuries-old English legal procedure for prisoners to challenge the legality of their detention.

In the United States, death row inmates routinely sought writs of habeas corpus in state and federal courts in legal challenges after their regular appeals in an effort to reverse their sentences, overturn their convictions or at least delay executions.

Under existing law, inmates had to exhaust their petitions in state courts before making collateral attacks on their convictions in federal court. A committee appointed by Chief Justice William H. Rehnquist and headed by retired Justice Powell found in a 1989 report that the average time between conviction and execution in capital cases was more than eight years.

Biden and Bob Graham, D-Fla., had authored limited revisions of the habeas corpus process that were included in S 1970 as reported. On the floor, Thurmond and Arlen Specter, R-Pa., offered a substitute with tighter time limits and stricter requirements for second petitions in federal courts.

The Thurmond-Specter proposal was defeated, 47-50, on May 23. But the next day, a motion to reconsider was adopted 52-46, and the language was then accepted by voice vote. *(Vote 105, p. 24-S; vote 106, p. 25-S)*

Switching to allow reconsideration were Oklahoma Democrat David L. Boren and Minnesota Republican Durenberger, along with Specter, who had voted "no" the first time, when it was clear that the amendment was failing, to preserve his right to ask for a new vote.

Two senators who were absent May 23, Louisiana Democrats John B. Breaux and J. Bennett Johnston, voted for reconsideration May 24.

A Faster Review Process

Graham described the Thurmond-Specter plan as "90 to 95 percent identical" to his proposal.

The final language would have eliminated the exhaustion of state habeas corpus proceedings as a prerequisite for federal habeas corpus proceedings and would have required federal courts to complete review of such petitions within a year. States could adopt the faster procedure only if they provided competent counsel to the prisoner facing execution.

Specter maintained that the state reviews were "customarily pro forma" and unreasonably delayed the process.

"They go before the same court where the person is tried and sentenced to death," he said. "That case has already gone to the state supreme court, which has upheld the trial and the death penalty. The only additional ingredient customarily is the issue of competency of counsel. And as a matter of practice, it is pro forma. Several years are consumed in that process."

But Graham said a state court should first decide the state issues. He said that because there were no sanctions for federal judges who did not comply with the time periods, there was no point to setting deadlines.

Powell's committee did not recommend bypassing state habeas reviews. But it would have required prisoners to petition a federal court within six months of a final state order and would have barred added filings.

The Thurmond-Specter language would have required inmates to file a federal habeas petition within 60 days of the appointment of counsel and resolution of an appeal to the state's highest court.

The Graham-Biden version would have allowed a year for filings.

The Thurmond-Specter plan also would have set stricter limits on second petitions in federal district court, requiring that an inmate first get permission from a federal appeals court. A second petition would be allowed only if the facts of the claim would be enough, if proved, to undermine the court's confidence in the jury's determination of guilt or if newly discovered facts would compromise the court's confidence in the validity of the death sentence.

The bill would let a court consider a subsequent claim based on intervening decisions by the U.S. Supreme Court that "establish fundamental rights." Specter said it was unlikely that there would be many such intervening decisions because of the swift timetable ordered.

Broadening the Death Penalty

S 1970 would have authorized capital punishment for 30 federal crimes, primarily murder, espionage and treason. Most of these offenses carried a death penalty, but the sanction was invalidated in 1972 when the Supreme Court struck down all existing state and federal capital punishment laws.

The court later set out guidelines for how to impose the death penalty, outlining a two-stage procedure. Since then, states that allowed capital punishment had set up a process by which a trial was held to determine a defendant's guilt or innocence, and then a second proceeding was conducted to set the sentence. The first execution under the new guidelines was in 1977, and 123 people had been executed as of May 2, 1990, according to the NAACP Legal Defense and Educational Fund. The fund also reported that 2,327 people were on death rows as of that date.

In 1974 Congress approved capital punishment for airline hijackings that resulted in death, and in 1988, as part of an omnibus antidrug law, it approved capital punishment for certain drug-trafficking murders. *(1974 Almanac, p. 275; 1988 Almanac, p. 85)*

A sizable majority in the Senate supported a broader federal death penalty, and many members viewed Kennedy's "racial justice" proposal as an effort to deter capital punishment.

Under Kennedy's proposal, prosecutors would have to prove by "clear and convincing evidence" that racial disparities in sentencing were not the result of discrimination but simply reflected pertinent non-racial factors.

"In study after study, experts have found that those who kill white people are many times more likely to receive the death penalty than those who kill blacks," Kennedy said. "And there is disturbing evidence that black defendants are more likely to be given a death sentence than white defendants."

In 1987, the Supreme Court in *McCleskey v. Kemp* rejected challenges to capital punishment based on statistical evidence of racial disparities. The court said the defendant failed to demonstrate purposeful discrimination.

"I believe that the *McCleskey* decision was wrongly decided," Kennedy said, "and that the compelling evidence that McCleskey's sentence was affected by racial consideration should have been sufficient to set aside his sentence."

But Graham, a former governor of Florida who had long been a strong advocate of capital punishment, said Kennedy's provision would destroy a state's capital punishment procedures.

He said that the criminal justice process did not lend itself to statistical analysis and that a jury should be left to assess the specific acts of a defendant.

Graham moved on May 24 to strike Kennedy's language and prevailed 58-38, winning a majority of Republicans and just fewer than half the Democrats. *(Vote 108, p. 25-S)*

Executing the Mentally Retarded

Critics of capital punishment succeeded, however, in preserving two provisions of S 1970 to bar executing anyone under 17 at the time of a federal crime or who was mentally retarded. The amendments responded to two recent Supreme Court decisions that refused to impose such limitations as a matter of constitutional law.

"The Supreme Court says it is all right to put mentally retarded people to death," Biden said in explaining the proviso. "Just because the Supreme Court said we can, that does not mean we should."

By 38-59, the Senate rejected May 24 a Thurmond amendment to spare only the mentally retarded who were incapable of knowing right from wrong. *(Vote 107, p. 25-S)*

Ban on Assault Weapons

Democrats surprised themselves May 23 by mustering enough votes to defeat Hatch's motion to delete the ban on making, selling or possessing nine semiautomatic assault-style weapons. Among the weapons to be banned was the AK-47, which had been used in the January 1989 schoolyard massacre in Stockton, Calif., that sparked an outcry over criminal use of semiautomatics.

Hatch's motion to delete the weapons ban failed 48-52. Two hours later, gun control advocates prevailed again as a motion to reconsider fell short, 49-50. On the second roll call, seven Republicans joined 43 Democrats in protecting the gun ban. *(Votes 103, 104, p. 24-S)*

The day before the votes, the National Rifle Association (NRA) was predicting victory, and supporters of the gun ban were gloomy, despite intensive lobbying efforts by scores of law enforcement representatives who supported the provision.

But Dennis DeConcini, D-Ariz., whose sponsorship of the gun ban had touched off a recall effort, later abandoned, in Arizona, brought off the one-vote victory.

The vote marked the biggest Senate defeat for the NRA, which was known for its lobbying muscle and hefty campaign contributions.

In 1988, when the NRA was able to pressure Congress to keep a seven-day waiting period to buy handguns out of an omnibus crime bill, the action took place in the House. The only time the full Senate approved a gun control measure in 1988 was an 89-0 vote for an amendment to antidrug legislation that banned making, importing, selling or possessing firearms that could evade X-ray or metal-detecting devices. *(1988 Almanac: drug bill, p. 85; NRA, p. 100; plastic guns, p. 108)*

As recently as 1986, Congress had voted to significantly ease federal gun control laws, after many years of NRA lobbying to win relaxation of the landmark 1968 Gun Control Act. A major provision of the 1986 law (PL 99-308) lifted a 20-year ban on interstate sales of rifles and shotguns and lowered the number of people who were required to get licenses to sell firearms. *(1986 Almanac, p. 82)*

The DeConcini language would have banned five types of foreign and four types of domestic weapons for three years. Owners of listed weapons would have to get a proof-of-ownership form from a licensed dealer and keep a record of people to whom they sold the weapons.

Nine types of weapons were on the list to be banned. Five types were foreign-made and were already barred under an administration order: Norinco, Mitchell and Poly Technologies Avtomat Kalashnikovs (all models, the AK-47 included); Action Arms Israeli Military Industries Uzi and Galil; Beretta AR-70 (SC-70); Fabrique Nationale FN/FAL, FN/LAR and FNC; and Steyr AUG.

The four categories of domestic weapons listed were INTRATEC TEC-9; MAC 10 and MAC 11; Street Sweeper and Striker 12; and Colt AR-15 and CAR-15.

Stiffer Ban Rejected

A handful of Southern Democrats who generally opposed gun control supported DeConcini, including Lloyd Bentsen of Texas, David L. Boren of Oklahoma, Sam Nunn of Georgia and Al Gore of Tennessee. DeConcini also won the vote of Majority Leader George J. Mitchell, D-Maine, elected by a big sporting state and who had been quoted in the past as saying he did not believe in gun control.

DeConcini said, "If Mitchell hadn't done it, I don't think we would have won." Mitchell said DeConcini's proposal reflected a "reasonable, moderate and feasible recognition that our nation can accept some limits on firearms ownership when the firearms in question have no valid hunting or sporting purpose."

But while the vote was a success for Democrats, it cast uncertainty on the entire legislation.

The NRA vowed to work to make sure the provisions went no further. The Bush administration hinted the president would veto a bill with such restrictions.

A day earlier, the Senate had voted 82-17 to table an amendment by Metzenbaum that would have permanently banned 12 more types of semiautomatic rifles and pistols and limited ammunition magazines to 15 rounds. *(Vote 102, p. 24-S)*

Proponents of the gun control provisions said senators queasy about supporting DeConcini's ban liked the "cover" of being able to reject Metzenbaum's tougher curbs.

NRA Strikes Back

Caught off guard by the May 23 vote, the NRA wrote letters to its members in the districts of senators who had voted to retain the assault-weapons provision, saying that those senators had betrayed "honest gun owners."

"This vote sets America on the road to universal gun confiscation," the NRA told its members.

It asked them to write to senators saying, "Your gun ban vote is a double-cross, and if you think gun control is the same as crime control, you have no business being in the U.S. Senate."

An incensed Bob Kerrey, D-Neb., who had voted to keep the ban on semiautomatics, inserted into the Congressional Record on June 5 an NRA letter to one of his constituents, along with a response he sent to the organization accusing it of "irresponsible, inaccurate and misleading statements."

"Allow me to predict that your outrageous techniques will, in the end, prove to be counterproductive," Kerrey wrote to Wayne LaPierre, executive director of the NRA's lobbying group.

Cloture Efforts

The gun-control provision figured in two unsuccessful efforts to invoke cloture on the bill the week of June 4. Neither Democrats nor Republicans wanted the blame for killing the election-year bill, but inclusion of the assault-weapons ban changed the dynamics of the issue somewhat.

Attempts to invoke cloture and thereby limit debate failed 54-37 on June 5 and 57-37 on June 7. Sixty votes (three-fifths of the entire Senate) were required for cloture. *(Votes 109, 112, p. 26-S)*

On both roll calls, Republicans voted heavily against limiting debate, while most Democrats supported cloture. Senators' positions on gun control appeared to influence their votes.

Of the 37 senators voting against cloture, 35 had tried May 23 to strip from the bill the ban on the manufacture, sale and possession of nine semiautomatic assault-style weapons. When that effort failed, many Republicans who had previously supported the anticrime bill suddenly turned against it.

Most of the debate on June 7 centered on which party was responsible for jeopardizing the anticrime bill.

As he threatened to end further consideration of S 1970, Majority Leader Mitchell said, "Let's not have any misunderstanding where the responsibility lies for not getting a crime bill. It's not the majority leader who's taking the bill down but the Senate, specifically those who voted against cloture."

Both he and Biden pointed to the opponents of gun control, mostly Republicans, in particular.

When Republicans rejected that connection, Mitchell scoffed at the idea that it was mere coincidence that 32 of the 37 senators who voted against cloture on June 5 had fought the semiautomatics ban; on June 7, it was 35 of 37.

The two other senators who voted against cloture June 7 — Kennedy and Hatfield — opposed the death-penalty provisions.

Finger-Pointing

Republicans, who made up most of the anti-gun-control forces in the Senate, maintained that their votes against cloture had more to do with "gag" orders that Democrats had imposed on the bill to limit Republicans' ability to offer amendments.

Utah's Hatch said, "The real reason it [cloture] was not [invoked] was because there is a desire on the part of many senators on the floor to ... bring up additional amendments that happen to apply to the criminal aspects of the bill."

Minority Leader Bob Dole, R-Kan., who voted for cloture, chided Mitchell for giving up after two votes. He and other Republicans suggested that if Mitchell would not let the bill return to the floor, it was the Democrats who were in effect killing the bill.

"It's in the bag," Dole predicted of a third cloture vote.

Mitchell quickly rejoined, "We are told that cloture is in the bag. That is what I was told yesterday. That is what I was told this morning. And as we have just seen, cloture was not in the bag."

Biden said, "Everyone knew this was do-or-die time for the crime bill. And it just died."

The Bill Is Revived

Although Mitchell at first indicated that he did not want the Senate to spend more time on the anticrime bill, he soon agreed to allow Biden and Thurmond to search for a way to salvage the legislation.

What they came up with was a little something for everyone with a tough-on-crime agenda. After some false starts, an agreement on how amendments would be presented was reached June 28. And senators agreed not to reopen the contentious crime issues for the rest of the year.

The pact specified that when senators finished with S 1970, no motions would be allowed for the rest of the 101st Congress on the death penalty, assault weapons, the exclusionary rule, the availability of firearms for purchase or death row inmates' petitions for writs of habeas corpus.

The unanimous-consent agreement also dropped from the original version of S 1970 a proposal to reorganize the Justice Department's crime and dangerous-drug divisions and a plan to relax the so-called exclusionary rule to allow certain evidence seized without a valid search warrant to be introduced into court.

During the 10-hour crush June 28-29 to finish amending the bill before the Fourth of July recess, senators made headway only by agreeing to less debate and shorter votes. Several pet projects were dropped.

A host of amendments were adopted by voice votes, some of them subject to senators' concerns about constitutional problems.

Negotiations over the savings and loan fraud amendment lagged, however, so the bill was held over for final action July 11.

Another Shootout Over Guns

Phil Gramm, R-Texas, tried once more on June 28 to remove the assault-weapons ban from the bill.

Gramm proposed substituting provisions to mandate minimum sentences for firearms violations and for other drug-related and violent crimes. He said he offered members a choice between gun control and "criminal control."

"The sad, cold reality is that felons who are smuggling drugs into the country will smuggle in guns," Gramm said.

Countering Gramm, DeConcini moved to add his own antigun language to the Texan's amendment. That forced members to vote again to keep in the bill what would be the first federal ban on U.S.-made semiautomatics.

Despite the NRA's lobbying and the presence of Vice President Dan Quayle, presiding and ready to break a tie, the DeConcini gun ban prevailed in its June 28 test. The vote was 50-48. *(Vote 133, p. 31-S)*

Alfonse M. D'Amato, R-N.Y., the one member rumored ready to switch to oppose the weapons ban, was lobbied vigorously by both sides right up to the end of the vote. But he ended up voting for the prohibition.

With DeConcini's gun ban locked into the amendment, Gramm's proposal for stricter penalties passed 87-12. *(Vote 134, p. 31-S)*

It would have required that anyone using a firearm during a violent crime be sentenced to at least 10 years in prison without parole. The mandatory penalties would be higher if the weapon was fired or if the conviction was the defendant's second firearms offense.

Another Round on Death Penalty

On June 29, the Senate rejected 25-73 a motion by death-penalty opponent Hatfield that would have substituted mandatory life imprisonment for the 30 crimes. *(Vote 143, p. 33-S)*

In separate action earlier, the Senate also expanded the reach of capital punishment by authorizing the death penalty for so-called drug kingpins, defendants convicted as leaders of continuing criminal enterprises. The amendment by D'Amato was adopted 66-32. *(Vote 140, p. 33-S)*

But the Senate defeated, 43-55, an amendment by Pete Wilson, R-Calif., that would have authorized the death penalty in cases in which death resulted during an offense that violated a civil rights statute. *(Vote 141, p. 33-S)*

One of the more contentious changes to the death-penalty language was offered by Daniel K. Inouye, D-Hawaii. He proposed excluding Indian lands from the reach of the capital punishment provisions unless a tribe voted to have the law cover its land.

Inouye said without his amendment people on reservations in states that did not impose the death penalty would be liable for capital punishment because they were on federal lands. Most murder cases were covered by state law, and Indian land made up a significant portion of federal lands to which the new death-penalty law would apply.

The Senate rebuffed two challenges by James A. McClure, R-Idaho. One, to table Inouye's amendment, failed 37-62. The second, to narrow the Inouye amendment's scope, was tabled 51-47. *(Votes 136, 137, p. 31-S)*

The Senate then adopted Inouye's amendment by voice vote.

The role of race in a state's criminal justice system, including the imposition of the death penalty, would have been studied under an amendment that Graham offered on June 28. He proposed that Congress authorize $2 million annually for the next five years for state grants.

A skeptical Hatch suggested that the study might be used to overturn convictions of minorities. He tried to amend the proposal to limit the studies to whether the constitutional rights of criminal defendants were being violated. The Hatch amendment failed 44-55, and the Graham proposal then carried by voice vote. *(Vote 138, p. 31-S)*

A death-penalty provision already in S 1970, involving the petitions that prisoners made to federal courts to challenge the legality of their detention, was left unamended. The bill would have eliminated the exhaustion of state habeas corpus proceedings as a prerequisite for federal habeas corpus review and would have required federal courts to complete review of such petitions within a year.

Other Amendments

Following are other amendments considered by the Senate:

Law enforcement. A Biden proposal called for adding 1,000 FBI agents, 1,000 Drug Enforcement Administration agents, 500 border patrol officers and 480 prosecutors to the Justice Department.

The amendment, adopted 96-2 on June 28, had a projected price tag of $332 million. *(Vote 142, p. 32-S)*

A separate amendment by John Kerry, D-Mass., adopted by voice vote, would have authorized $900 million to the Bureau of Justice Assistance for state and local law enforcement assistance. Illegal drug activity would have been the target of the grants.

To improve the education and training of police officers, the Senate adopted an amendment to authorize $400 million in fiscal 1991 to states to provide college scholarships to individuals who promised to work four years after graduation for state or local police departments.

The police corps plan was offered by Specter and adopted 64-35 on June 28. The proposal was heartily praised and the only point of opposition was its cost. *(Vote 139, p. 32-S)*

Illegal drugs. The Senate adopted an amendment by Daniel K. Akaka, D-Hawaii, to impose tougher penalties for producing, manufacturing, selling or distributing "ice" — a pure and smokeable form of methamphetamine — after hearing warnings that it could become the fad illegal drug of the next decade.

The amendment was adopted June 28 after a proposal by Slade Gorton, R-Wash., was attached 79-20. Gorton's amendment sought to require that certain manufacturers of ice and other controlled substances be licensed. *(Vote 135, p. 31-S)*

Children, victims. By voice vote, the Senate adopted a Child Victims Bill of Rights, which would have increased the penalties for drug-related child abuse and set up a $20 million grant program to establish a child abuse investigation and prosecution program. The proposal by Harry Reid, D-Nev., was accepted after amendments by voice vote by Herb Kohl, D-Wis., and Thurmond.

Kohl's amendment would have authorized $15 million in fiscal 1991 for grants to programs that treated juvenile offenders who were abused. Thurmond's amendment would have increased the penalties for sex crimes against children and also made it a crime to possess or view certain pornography.

Members also adopted by voice vote separate amendments to increase victims' access to information during federal criminal proceedings and their ability to win restitution, offered by Charles E. Grassley, R-Iowa; to provide for a mandatory 30-year prison term for child kidnapping, by Rudy Boschwitz, R-Minn.; and to place a work requirement on federal prisoners, by Trent Lott, R-Miss.

Savings and Loan Fraud

The savings and loan fraud amendment stemmed from a compromise among members of the Judiciary and Banking committees and the Bush administration. It was approved 99-1, on July 11, with the only "no" vote coming from Colorado Republican Armstrong, who called the amendment a "knee-jerk response." *(Vote 146, p. 33-S)*

The amendment, sponsored primarily by Tim Wirth, D-Colo., and John Heinz, R-Pa., would have provided $162.5 million to beef up federal investigations of thrift fraud and increase the penalties for defendants, including mandatory life imprisonment for long-term, multimillion-dollar offenders. Violators who acted in concert with at least three other offenders and collected more than $5 million for their crimes over two years would be eligible for life in prison.

"Perhaps the amendment will provide senators a smoke screen to shift the culpability for the S&L mess from the Congress and on to a few unscrupulous businessmen," Armstrong said. "But the fact is the S&L mess, which the American taxpayer has been called upon to clean up, was not primarily the result of the wrongdoing of a few thrift executives, but of a collapse of a thrift system established by and overseen by the Congress."

With the addition of the savings and loan fraud amendment, the Senate called it quits on the bill. Attention then shifted to the House.

HOUSE COMMITTEE ACTION

On the House side, Republicans had tried for a year to force consideration of an array of bills containing Bush's anticrime proposals, only to have them languish in the Judiciary Committee. Meanwhile, Democrats, who had come to expect biennial, election-year crime bills, had been drafting their own proposals.

Judiciary Committee Chairman Brooks, skeptical about the need for crime bills, eventually changed his tune and scheduled a markup. "This is a tough, far-reaching package that fights back," Brooks said as his committee began its work July 17.

The committee completed work on its version of the crime bill (HR 5269) on July 23. The vote was 19-17.

Among the committee bill's key elements:

- It would have allowed capital punishment for 10 federal offenses, as opposed to 34 in the Senate bill.
- It contained a compromise aimed at clearing the federal courts of excessive appeals from death row inmates. It would have set deadlines for an inmate to petition for a writ of habeas corpus, a process by which an inmate challenged his detention.
- It would have allowed death row inmates to challenge their sentences if they could prove that their race or that of their victims was a factor in imposing the death penalty. The Senate eliminated that provision during floor debate.
- It would have more strongly emphasized improving the federal prison system and finding alternatives to traditional incarceration. It would have authorized $330 million for those efforts.

William J. Hughes, D-N.J., who chaired the Crime Subcommittee, called this provision the bill's "centerpiece."

- The bill also would have authorized $153 million each of the following three fiscal years for the Justice Department to investigate and prosecute fraud in the thrift industry.

The committee defeated amendments to outlaw semiautomatic pistols and cheap, easily concealed handguns, but voted to increase penalties for some firearms violations.

Death Penalty

Like the Senate version, the House committee bill backed an expansion of the federal death penalty.

HR 5269 would have allowed a sentence of death for anyone who killed the president or the vice president or injured them in the attempt.

The sentence could also have been applied to people convicted of murdering a foreign official or internationally protected person; a federal law officer in the Justice or Treasury departments, the Coast Guard or the Postal Service, or a federal prison guard; a federal witness in the Witness Protection Program; the victim of a kidnapping or hostage-taking; or the subject of a contract murder.

Capital punishment would also have been allowed for terrorism and skyjacking that resulted in the death of an innocent person and for espionage and treason.

The House measure would have prohibited death for people who were mentally retarded or who were under 18 at the time of their crimes. The restrictions were like those in the Senate bill, except that it used age 17 as the floor for a death sentence.

Harley O. Staggers Jr., D-W.Va., on July 17 tried to amend HR 5269 to provide a sentence of life in prison without parole for the crimes that the bill proposed to make capital offenses.

Staggers said he considered the death sentence morally wrong. Robert W. Kastenmeier, D-Wis., agreed, saying the punishment appealed "to a vengefulness that society seeks to satisfy."

While a handful of other Democrats agreed, Staggers' amendment was opposed by members who said they believed the penalty deterred violent crime.

Crime Subcommittee Chairman Hughes, a former state prosecutor, also argued that it was appropriate to reserve the ultimate penalty for the most egregious crimes.

The amendment was defeated by voice vote.

Don Edwards, D-Calif., pressed an amendment that would have taken off the House's death-penalty list three crimes that did not result in death: attempted assassination, espionage and treason. The committee rejected that amendment, too, 16-20.

When the committee returned to work July 18, George W. Gekas, R-Pa., tried to extend capital punishment to more than a dozen other death-penalty crimes that were in the statutes when the Supreme Court struck down the laws in 1972. Those crimes were formerly longstanding offenses such as bank robbery and wrecking a train — both only in which death resulted — and murder of a horse, meat, poultry or egg-products inspector.

Gekas said the death penalty should be allowed for all homicides involving federal officials. His amendment was rejected 14-22.

The committee also defeated, 14-22, a proposal by Bill McCollum, R-Fla., that would have allowed someone who ran a major drug-trafficking empire to be executed, even if his enterprise was not proved to have killed anyone.

Howard L. Berman, D-Calif., who fought the proposal, suggested that McCollum was applying "an eye for a tooth" justice.

McCollum rejoined that he was seeking "an eye for an eye," and ally Henry J. Hyde, R-Ill., added, "We are not being serious about the drug problem until we provide the ultimate penalty."

McCollum's "drug kingpin" provision was less sweeping than the Senate's, whih would have allowed the death penalty when the amounts of drugs and money involved were lower than the threshold McCollum proposed.

Habeas Corpus Petitions

On July 19, the Judiciary Committee approved a compromise amendment intended to reduce excessive habeas corpus appeals and to assure competent, court-appointed counsel for condemned inmates.

Offered by Kastenmeier and Hughes, the amendment would have required inmates to file petitions for writs of habeas corpus within one year of losing direct appeals of their sentences. The Senate bill would have required filing within six months.

The House measure would have kept the tradition of

appealing first to state courts, then to the federal bench. The Senate bill would have eliminated the exhaustion of state habeas corpus proceedings as a prerequisite for federal habeas corpus proceedings.

Assault Weapons

One of the more controversial provisions in the Senate package would have outlawed what police said were the nine most dangerous semiautomatic assault-style weapons.

The House bill did not have a similar provision to the Senate's highly controversial assault-gun ban, although the Judiciary Committee had already approved a ban on assault-style weapons.

Sponsored by Hughes and sent to the full House on June 12, HR 4225 would have required the Treasury secretary to outlaw domestic semiautomatics that did not meet the "sporting purposes" test under which foreign-made assault-style weapons were prohibited. The Customs Service estimated that 12 domestic rifles did not meet a sporting-purpose test.

The Judiciary Committee beat back two other gun-control moves. On July 18, it rejected 15-21 an amendment by Tom Campbell, R-Calif., to ban semiautomatic pistols. The next day, it defeated, 12-23, an amendment by Lawrence J. Smith, D-Fla., to outlaw making and importing cheap handguns known as Saturday night specials.

However, over Brooks' objections, the committee adopted, 19-15, an amendment by Dan Glickman, D-Kan., to increase from five to 10 years the mandatory prison sentence for using a sawed-off shotgun or rifle in drug crimes and to impose a 30-year sentence for using a bomb or a grenade during a drug-related crime.

Thrift-Industry Fraud

The savings and loan scandal contributed to the drive for an anticrime bill. With the thrift industry collapse expected to cost taxpayers billions of dollars, lawmakers wanted to show that they would punish wrongdoers.

House Speaker Thomas S. Foley, D-Wash., Brooks and other Democratic leaders used a news conference July 18 to announce an amendment to HR 5269 to give the Justice Department $153 million in additional money to go after savings and loan fraud and to stiffen criminal penalties and sentencing provisions.

The amendment also would have established new authority to freeze and seize assets of criminals and compel restitution for victims.

The bank fraud section was the result of a carefully crafted compromise between Charles E. Schumer, D-N.Y., and the panel's ranking Republican, Hamilton Fish Jr. of New York.

Many of the provisions in the thrift section were taken from a Republican-sponsored bill (HR 5050) that the House Banking Subcommittee on Financial Institutions had approved overwhelmingly June 28.

The thrift section would have made it illegal to conceal the assets of a failed thrift and would have established procedures for the government to seize U.S. any overseas assets of thrift officials convicted of fraud.

A 12-member bipartisan commission would also have been created to probe the causes of the thrift crisis and recommend strategies for law enforcement.

"The American people want solutions, and the Justice Department is responding," Schumer said. "And this gives the Justice Department all the resources they need to do the job."

Despite agreement on the need to spend more to investigate and penalize thrift fraud more harshly, the deliberations took on partisan overtones almost immediately after the bank fraud provisions were aired before the committee.

The bill would have authorized the Justice Department to set up a special counsel to investigate bank fraud. An acrimonious debate ensued over an amendment by Chuck Douglas, R-N.H., to authorize the special counsel to investigate past and current members of Congress.

Douglas linked the amendment to Democrats' call for an independent counsel to investigate Neil Bush, son of the president, for his role as a director of the failed Silverado Banking, Savings and Loan Association in Denver. Eleven Judiciary Committee Democrats had written Attorney General Dick Thornburgh on July 13 seeking appointment of a special prosecutor on the matter.

"We get 11 letters from Democrats [asking] to investigate Neil Bush, but they won't get a roll call vote to investigate their buddies," Douglas said.

Almost unanimously, the Democrats denounced Douglas for "painting with a broad brush" the relations of members of Congress with thrift officials tainted by the crisis. Some suggested that such a probe include inquiries into financial affairs of the president, the vice president, Cabinet members and their families.

Brooks objected to the whole idea, saying: "It's a bad attitude to be taking."

Douglas' amendment was narrowly defeated, 17-19. Joining Republicans in voting with Douglas were Democrats John Bryant, Texas; George E. Sangmeister, Ill.; and Craig Washington, Texas.

But Democrat Glickman then offered a different amendment, to give the special counsel authority to investigate executive branch officials and their families for involvement in bank and thrift irregularities. That amendment carried, 35-1.

The Judiciary panel adopted an amendment by Sangmeister to set mandatory sentences of 10 years to life in prison for certain high-ranking savings and loan "kingpins" convicted of fraud, part of an overall increase in penalties for bank fraud. All the new penalty provisions would have applied only to crimes that were uncovered in the future; allegations of fraud in the thrift industry that had already turned up would have been covered under existing law.

An amendment by Gekas that would have given the Federal Deposit Insurance Corporation top priority in trying to recoup property or money misappropriated from thrifts was defeated by voice vote.

The amendment, Schumer and other opponents argued, would have prevented shareholders from filing private lawsuits against officers of the savings institutions.

Other Issues

The committee approved miscellaneous amendments to the omnibus measure, many of them technical.

Among them were the following proposals:

- By McCollum, to disqualify those convicted of federal crimes from receiving government benefits other than pensions and retirement or welfare aid; by voice vote.
- By Bryant, to disallow sports lotteries for amateur and professional events and prohibit radio and television advertising for sports lotteries; by voice vote.

Bush Veto Threat

The House committee's version of the crime bill produced a veto threat from the administration. Bush and

Attorney General Thornburgh complained that it would be tougher on law enforcement than on crime.

"I simply will not accept anything that rolls back the clock on America's ability to fight crime and punish wrongdoers," Bush told a group of prosecutors at the White House on Sept. 12. "The bottom line is really this: I will not sign a crime bill that handcuffs the police."

While the administration raised a host of objections to HR 5269, it found most onerous the new standards on the death penalty and appeals.

On the racial disparity procedure, for example, the administration contended that prosecutors would have an "unrealistic burden" of disproving statistics offered by defendants. As a result, Thornburgh said in a Sept. 11 letter to House Speaker Foley, "this ill-conceived proposal would apply to every state defendant now on death row and would likely result in the invalidation of every capital sentence now in effect."

The House bill also would have required that before federal juries imposed the death penalty they find at least two aggravating circumstances, factors such as a prior murder conviction or exceptional brutality. Thornburgh said this constraint was "unprecedented." He also objected to the bill's death-penalty requirement for only 10 federal crimes (mostly involving murder) rather than the 30 offenses covered in the Senate bill.

Bush, in his speech, and Thornburgh, in his letter, also lashed out at the bill's standards for prisoners seeking habeas corpus review.

In three cases — the 1989 *Teague v. Lane* and the 1990 *Butler v. McKellar* and *Saffle v. Parks* — the high court had made it more difficult for defendants to challenge their convictions based on new, favorable court rulings in other cases. The House committee bill would have restored to defendants the chance to use new court rulings as a basis for appeal.

Democratic sponsors said these provisions were intended to balance the rights of defendants and the state's interest in carrying out a death sentence.

But Thornburgh said the effect would be to eliminate capital punishment: "These changes would vastly enlarge the opportunities for prisoners to attack and potentially overturn their convictions and sentences on the basis of alleged 'new law' that did not exist at the time the judgments in their cases became final."

Kastenmeier, who worked with Edwards and Crime Subcommittee Chairman Hughes on the death-penalty and habeas corpus provisions, said, "We don't regard this bill as favoring defendants. But we did try to balance things, no question about it."

HOUSE FLOOR ACTION

By the time HR 5269 came up for floor debate, the budget process was in turmoil and fears of anti-incumbent sentiment abounded. Approval of the bill on Oct. 5, by a vote of 368-55, came after an initial false start and then three days of debate and amendments that allowed members to show some pre-election muscle by making the bill tougher on defendants. *(Vote 427, p. 138-H)*

Derailing the Rule

Originally, the Rules Committee sought to preserve the tone of the Judiciary Committee's bill, barring floor amendments to strike the death-penalty provisions that Bush opposed.

But, in a surprise to both sides of the debate, that effort failed Sept. 25 when the House voted 166-258 against a rule that would have allowed consideration of the bill, without the disputed amendments. The GOP leadership was joined by 84 Democrats opposed to the rule. *(Vote 376, p. 120-H)*

Shortly before the House took up the bill Sept. 25, police groups accused the Democratic leadership, particularly Foley, of shutting out gun-control activists. The Rules Committee, which had allowed 46 amendments to the crime bill, had barred consideration of an amendment for a seven-day waiting period for handgun purchases.

Foley had voted in the past against gun control.

The Rules Committee had decided earlier that two proposals (HR 4225, HR 1154) for controls on semiautomatic assault-style weapons would be in order after a vote on the omnibus bill, HR 5269.

Hyde wanted to offer an amendment for an alternative habeas corpus proposal, but the Illinois Republican's proposal was barred by the Rules Committee. Hyde proposed requiring inmates to petition a federal court within six months; greatly restricting the grounds for subsequent appeal; and lessening requirements for competent counsel at trial and on appeal.

"If you want to do away with the death penalty, do it," Hyde said in floor debate opposing the limited rule. "Do not do it indirectly by reforming habeas corpus to produce a never-ending, never-final procedure. It is not fair to the prisoners. It is not fair to society. And it certainly is not fair to law enforcement."

National associations of district attorneys and attorneys general had written to members protesting the bill.

One of the 84 Democrats siding with the GOP leadership in voting down the rule was Claude Harris, of Tuscaloosa, Ala., who stood on the House floor and talked about his eight years as a trial judge and 10 years as a state prosecutor. He told his colleagues that if the House's omnibus crime bill became law, no state would be able to carry out the death penalty.

"A true crime-control act would not be without a single supporter among the entire prosecutorial population of this country, as this one is," Harris said.

The Rules Committee returned the following week with a rule that made in order proposed amendments the GOP sought — most importantly for them the Hyde proposal. The chamber resumed debate on the bill Oct. 3.

Raucous Debate

The Oct. 5 vote followed three days of raucous debate, in which opponents of capital punishment shouted derisively, "Kill! Kill! Kill!" as amendments were adopted to expand the death penalty to about 30 crimes and make it easier for states to impose and carry it out.

Stripped from the bill were provisions aimed at protecting defendants' rights, which in some cases might have resulted in blocking or delaying an execution. New limits on death row inmate appeals would be imposed.

Among the bill's other features:

- An increase in criminal penalties, mostly for drug crimes;
- Authorization of more money for local law enforcement;
- Requirement of new prison rehabilitation programs and sentencing alternatives.
- A loophole for the administration's ban on imported semiautomatic weapons: domestic parts could be used to make copies of banned foreign assault-style weapons.

While the majority had the momentum of public fears about crime, Charles B. Rangel, D-N.Y., complained that the House showed "a lust for blood."

Just before final passage, McCollum, ranking Republican on the Crime Subcommittee, who had been pushing the administration's law-and-order package, said, "I think we've done an excellent job in the war against crime in this bill."

But Crime Subcommittee Chairman Hughes, who supported the bill, nonetheless said, "I hope we never, ever bring up a crime bill again a month before an election."

Capital Punishment

As reported by committee, HR 5269 had 10 crimes that carried the potential of the death penalty. On Oct. 4, however, the House adopted, 271-159, a Gekas amendment to expand the list to an estimated 30 federal crimes. *(Vote 413, p. 134-H)*

Most on the list involved murder. Among them were the intentional killing of the president or vice president; of a member of Congress or Cabinet official; of a foreign official or other federally protected official; of a federal judge, prison guard or law enforcement officer; or of a kidnap victim or hostage.

Gekas' amendment also said that a judge or jury would be required to sentence a defendant to death if the judge or jury found the existence of one aggravating factor and either that it outweighed any mitigating factors or that it alone justified the death sentence.

The committee had given the jury or judge the discretion on a death-penalty decision and required two aggravating factors.

Gekas' amendment also would have allowed a prosecutor to ask the jury to consider aggravating factors that were not part of statute, without prior approval of a trial judge or notice to the defendant. It also would have barred challenges of a death sentence in a federal habeas corpus proceeding on grounds that the defense lawyer was incompetent. And it would have repealed a federal law that required counsel for indigent prisoners petitioning for habeas corpus relief.

Two other death-penalty amendments were accepted.

McCollum proposed allowing the death penalty for defendants who did not cause a murder but engaged in large-scale drug trafficking or who through "reckless disregard" caused a drug-related death. It was adopted 295-133. *(Vote 414, p. 134-H)*

Another amendment, offered by James A. Traficant Jr., D-Ohio, would have authorized the death penalty for anyone convicted of murdering a state or local law officer who had been working with a federal law officer. It was adopted by voice vote.

The House rejected, 108-319, a Hughes amendment similar to Gekas' that would have expanded the death penalty but would not have gone so far in removing procedural safeguards. *(Vote 412, p. 134-H)*

On Oct. 3, longtime death-penalty foe Staggers tried to get his colleagues to substitute mandatory life imprisonment without parole for the crimes in the bill. But his amendment failed, 103-322. *(Vote 410, p. 132-H)*

Inmates' Appeals

Under the bill as amended, death row inmates would have had six months to file habeas corpus petitions — unlike the unlimited time under existing law — and could generally petition the federal courts just once.

The modification, offered by Hyde, would have required states that wanted to impose the limit to provide lawyers for the inmates. But, unlike the committee bill, Hyde's language did not set standards for experience. The amendment was adopted, 285-146, on Oct. 4. *(Vote 418, p. 134-H)*

The Hyde amendment also contained language aimed at making it more difficult for defendants to challenge their convictions based on new, favorable court rulings in other cases.

A subsequent habeas corpus petition would be allowed only if the defendant was raising an issue that went to the validity of his conviction — a difficult test to meet. Ineffective counsel could not be used as a basis for a petition if the inmate had not made the complaint during a state appeal.

Hughes offered a compromise that would have allowed more exceptions for another attempt at an appeal. The House rejected it, 189-239. *(Vote 417, p. 134-H)*

Gun Control

As reported by committee, the bill would have barred use of either imported or domestic parts to make an AK-47, Uzi or any other foreign, assault-type semiautomatic weapon on the list of those banned by the administration.

But members, heavily lobbied by both sides of the gun control issue, weakened the bill on the floor, allowing domestic gun makers to assemble any semiautomatic rifle or shotgun identical to any rifle or shotgun banned from import. Under the amendment, by Jolene Unsoeld, D-Wash., only firearms assembled with foreign parts would be illegal. The Oct. 4 vote was 257-172. *(Vote 416, p. 134-H)*

The administration had blocked from import any semiautomatics that did not meet a sporting-purposes test. The drafters of HR 5269 had wanted to make sure that domestic manufacturers would not build copies of those outlawed weapons in U.S. plants. Unsoeld said her amendment would make sure that U.S.-made target and other sporting rifles would not be banned.

Racial Justice

The House adopted a compromise amendment offered by Hughes that would have allowed defendants to challenge their death sentences on grounds of racial discrimination. His amendment diluted the bill as reported but maintained the basic premise of establishing precautions against racism in sentencing.

The Judiciary Committee had sought to allow a defendant to establish a prima facie case through statistical evidence that either his race or that of the victim's led to the death penalty.

Accepted by a 218-186 vote on Oct. 5, the Hughes amendment would have required a court to examine the validity of the statistics and whether they provided a basis for finding a significant discriminatory pattern. The amendment would have reduced the weight of statistics and lessened the burden of proof necessary for the government to rebut the implication of racial discrimination. *(Vote 422, p. 138-H)*

Death-penalty hard-liners argued that statistics were misleading and that if the provision became law, prosecutors would be consumed with developing race-based statistics to prove that race was incidental to a jury's decision.

The House then defeated, 204-216, an amendment by F. James Sensenbrenner Jr., R-Wis., to eliminate all the racial-discrimination provisions. He and other GOP members argued unsuccessfully that the race-based standards would effectively end states' ability to impose capital punishment. *(Vote 423, p. 138-H)*

Other Issues

The House adopted, 265-157, on Oct. 5 an amendment, offered by Douglas, to extend the bill's "good faith" exception to the exclusionary rule to situations when there was no search warrant. *(Vote 424, p. 138-H)*

The committee's bill would have provided a "good faith" exception for evidence obtained with a faulty search warrant. Under the New Hampshire Republican's proposal, evidence obtained in a search or seizure that violated constitutional protections would not be excluded — even if officers had not obtained a warrant — if "the search or seizure was carried out in circumstances justifying an objectively reasonable belief that it was in conformity with the Fourth Amendment" of the U.S. Constitution.

In other action, the House:

- Adopted Oct. 3, 236-189, an amendment by Albert G. Bustamante, D-Texas, to delete language that would have taken away state discretion to distribute federal grant funds. The dropped provision would have set up a "direct pass through" from Washington to local governments, and states had protested that they should have the discretion to distribute the money. *(Vote 408, p. 132-H)*
- Adopted on Oct. 4, 309-120, an amendment by Carlos J. Moorhead, R-Calif., to remove a provision that would have blocked state and local law enforcement agencies from transferring forfeited assets to state and local law enforcement agencies if the transfer would circumvent state law. *(Vote 415, p. 134-H)*
- Adopted on Oct. 3, 415-3, an amendment by Lynn Martin, R-Ill., to cut 10 percent from antidrug and law enforcement block grants for states that did not have a law requiring a defendant convicted of rape to be tested for the AIDS virus at the request of the victim. *(Vote 409, p. 132-H)*
- Agreed on Oct. 5, 226-204, to an amendment by Barney Frank, D-Mass., to bar Federal Prison Industries from making any new item that was made by the footwear, apparel, textile or furniture industries, or expanding the production of any existing product made by these industries, until after a market study required by the bill had been submitted to Congress. The goal was to make sure that the virtually free prison labor did not compete with other U.S. workers. *(Vote 419, p. 136-H)*

CONFERENCE/FINAL ACTION

With the bill's future in doubt, members hedged their bets by tacking their favorite provisions onto other bills.

The House before the August recess broke out the savings and loan sanctions and passed them separately as HR 5401. The bill, approved July 31 by 424-4, contained provisions to create stiff penalties for bank fraud, make it easier to get stolen assets or prevent them from being protected by a bankruptcy filing, and provide more money for Justice Department enforcement activities. *(Vote 288, p. 94-H)*

The Senate Judiciary Committee Oct. 11 approved a related bill (S 3194), expanding on what was already in its omnibus crime legislation.

Meanwhile, both chambers appointed conferees — 94 from the House and 24 from the Senate — to try to resolve the disputes in time to permit enactment of a bill in some form.

Staff members from both chambers worked to settle the less difficult topics, such as new law enforcement programs, drug control, child-abuse penalties, prison expansion and victims' rights.

Saved for the members themselves were subjects related to the death penalty and guns.

On those issues, the chambers were far apart:

- The Senate wanted gun control. The House had voted against it.
- The House wanted "racial justice" safeguards for the death penalty. The Senate had voted them down.
- The House had a restrictive proposal for death row appeals, which its Democratic leadership fought in vain. The Senate had a convoluted appeals proposal that many senators were ready to scrap.

The strongest card held by opponents of the death penalty was the Racial Justice Act, which conservatives believed would make the imposition of capital punishment impossible. The House's provision would have let defendants escape execution if they could prove their sentence was imposed because of racial discrimination.

House Democrats used the section as leverage in negotiations to moderate the overall legislation. The White House threatened to veto a bill that included the race-based test. It also opposed the Senate's ban on semiautomatic assault-style weapons.

Some conferees suggested dropping the racial-justice section and the new restrictions on habeas corpus petitions. Another major sticking point was the Senate ban on sale or production of nine types of semiautomatic weapons.

House Judiciary Chairman Brooks suggested a bare-bones approach, stripping out the controversial provisions, but GOP conferees initially resisted.

"What would the bill amount to if we take out capital punishment?" asked Senate Judiciary ranking Republican Thurmond.

But Republicans gave in when a series of votes made it evident that agreement on a broad bill was unlikely.

Members fell to bickering over which party deserved the blame for failing to approve a broader bill. Republicans condemned Democrats for refusing to accept the death-penalty and habeas corpus provisions while Democrats lambasted GOP members for resisting controls on semi-automatic assault-style weapons.

Thurmond proposed that conferees remove from the bill all provisions relating to habeas corpus petitions and racial justice. That failed 3-5 among Senate conferees.

Florida's McCollum proposed a similar deal that failed among House conferees, 4-6. Because liberal Democrats dominated the House delegation, the conferees' votes did not reflect positions already adopted by the House as a whole during its consideration of the bill.

In another problem area, the House conferees refused to accept a Senate offer to accept the racial-justice provision if the House would accept the assault-guns provision. That idea failed, 4-6 — with Democrats Brooks and Crime Subcommittee Chairman Hughes joining the four Republicans in voting to nix it.

In the end, the controversial death-penalty and guns provisions were dropped, and a bill finally completed late on the evening of Oct. 26.

"It became clear that no possible agreement could be reached on these major issues," Senate Judiciary Chairman Biden said afterward.

Floor Action

The stripped-down bill went first to the Senate, where

1990 Crime Control Act: Major Provisions

Following are major provisions of the Crime Control Act of 1990 (S 3266 — PL 101-647) as cleared by Congress on Oct. 27 and signed into law by President Bush on Nov. 29.

• **Financial institutions.** The law raised the civil and criminal penalties for financial fraud and other wrongdoing. At the extreme, defendants who received $5 million or more in gross receipts from a continuing financial enterprise during any two-year period could get a fine of $10 million ($20 million for organizations) and a maximum sentence of life in prison.

The law also enhanced the ability of federal banking agencies and the Justice Department to seize assets fraudulently obtained from banks and savings and loans. A new office of special counsel for financial institutions fraud was to be established at the Justice Department. New prosecutors, FBI agents and Secret Service agents were authorized.

• **Prisons.** The law authorized $220 million for states to develop alternatives to incarcerating inmates in already-crowded prison buildings. It also gave the Bureau of Prisons the authority to set up a shock incarceration program (known as "boot camp"). The program would enforce a highly regimented schedule of discipline, physical training, labor, drill and ceremony characteristic of military basic training.

Separately, the act stated that all federal inmates should work, except for security, medical or disciplinary reasons.

• **Child abuse.** The law provided a statutory option and procedures for children who were witnesses at an abuse trial to testify outside the courtroom through a two-way closed-circuit television.

It authorized $10 million toward training for judges, prosecutors and child advocates on child-abuse issues. The aim was to prevent child abuse and better investigate and prosecute offenders.

The law also made possession of child pornography a federal offense and required producers to keep a record of the age of people appearing in hard-core pornography.

• **Steroids.** Anabolic steroids were to be covered under federal laws that applied to cocaine and other controlled substances, thereby increasing the penalties for steroid trafficking and allowing the Drug Enforcement Administration (DEA) to take charge of steroids investigations. The penalty for illegal steroids trade increased from three years in prison to a maximum of 20 years. New production and recordkeeping requirements were imposed on companies that made steroids.

• **Law enforcement, rural drug-abuse funding.** The law authorized up to $900 million in new federal aid for local law enforcement and called for an increase in federal agents, including 1,000 new DEA agents.

It also authorized $20 million for funding to help police and prosecutors in rural areas investigate illegal drug-trafficking.

• **Debt collection.** The law put in place a uniform federal system for collection of all debts owed the federal government, replacing a system that relied on differing state laws.

• **Money laundering.** The Treasury secretary was required to report to Congress every two years during the following four years on international money-laundering activities; investigations and prosecutions; and criminal indictments stemming from information provided by financial institutions.

The Treasury secretary was directed to appoint a task force to study the methods and costs of printing a serial number on U.S. currency that could be read by electronic scanning.

Also, the attorney general was given authority to transfer property civilly or criminally forfeited as part of a money-laundering offense to any foreign country that participated in the seizure of the property, provided the secretary of State agreed to the transfer and it was part of an agreement between the United States and the foreign country.

• **Drug-free school zones.** The law authorized an additional $15 million to train school personnel on drug-use intervention and counseling. It provided $1.5 million for a model drug-free school zone project. The goal was to prevent drug activities within schools and their surrounding environments. ■

Biden told colleagues Oct. 27 that he was "frustrated and disappointed that we could not get a bill" dealing with the major issues. But he insisted that the remaining provisions — including the S&L fraud package, child-abuse provisions, law enforcement assistance, debt-collection procedures, and stiffened penalties for use of steroids — added up to "a crime bill that merits [senators'] support nonetheless."

Republicans Thurmond and Alan K. Simpson, Wyo., joined in criticizing the omissions. Thurmond said the public should be "outraged," while Simpson said it was "a crime that after all the work we have done . . . , our efforts have been cast aside in the rush to complete some crime bill that will pass."

But the speeches and statements by most senators recited only the positive accomplishments in the bill, and the measure was passed without objection and forwarded to the House.

Later that evening, GOP House members took sharper aim at the removal of the death-penalty and habeas corpus provisions.

"This was a strong anticrime bill" when it left the House,·said Hyde, who had toughened the habeas corpus revision with his floor amendment. "It left here as Arnold Schwarzenegger and came back as Woody Allen."

Brandishing a copy of the 300-page bill, New Hampshire's Douglas said, "The only way a murderer has to fear this crime bill is if someone throws it at him. . . ." And Pennsylvania's Gekas, who had worked to toughen the death-penalty provisions in committee and on the floor, sarcastically congratulated death-penalty opponents for having "thwarted the will of the American people."

Democrats gamely defended the bill. Brooks and Hughes rattled off the provisions that had survived in conference, saying they added up to an important and strong anticrime measure. "To suggest that that is not an important anticrime meausre, I think, is unfair," Hughes concluded.

On a roll call vote, the bill passed 313-1, with only Gekas voting against it.

Signed by Bush

Bush reiterated the Republican lawmakers' complaints in signing the bill Nov. 29.

He noted that in 1989 he had offered an anticrime package that included death-penalty, habeas corpus, exclusionary rule, and gun-crime provisions.

"Despite the fact that each of these proposals passed one or both Houses of Congress," Bush said in a written statement, "*none* is included in the legislation I am signing today. At the eleventh hour, these reforms were stripped from the crime bill by the conference committee."

Bush said he was "pleased with the tools" the bill did provide against S&L fraud and also welcomed the debt-collection, child-abuse and child pornography provisions. But he closed by urging Congress to return to the issue in 1991. "The American people deserve tough, new laws to help us prevail in the fight against drugs and crime." ■

Assault Weapons Ban Is Dropped;

Gun control proponents gave a scare to the gun lobby in 1990, but ended up failing in three separate efforts to enact new federal restrictions on firearms.

A ban on assault-style weapons was included in the Senate's version of an omnibus anticrime bill (S 1970), but rejected by the House and stripped from the final measure (S 3266 — PL 101-647).

Two other gun control bills languished in the House.

The House Judiciary Committee on June 12 approved a bill (HR 4225) to outlaw certain semiautomatic weapons, but it was never brought to the floor.

A month later, the Judiciary Committee approved a bill (HR 467) to require a seven-day waiting period before a person could buy a handgun. But the so-called Brady bill was also never brought to the floor. The bill was named for former White House press secretary James S. Brady — wounded in a 1981 assassination attempt on President Ronald Reagan — and his wife Sarah Brady, who lobbied relentlessly for the measure.

Gun control opponents had traditionally held sway on the floors of both chambers, despite polls showing broad public support for tighter regulation of firearms. The major law on the books, the Gun Control Act of 1968 (PL 90-618), owed its enactment to the reaction in Congress and among the public to the assassinations that year of the Rev. Dr. Martin Luther King Jr. and Sen. Robert F. Kennedy, D-N.Y. *(Congress and the Nation Vol. II, p. 328)*

Efforts to relax the law, led by the National Rifle Association (NRA), began almost immediately afterward and finally bore fruit in 1986. Congress that year passed legislation (PL 99-360) that weakened the 1968 act by lifting the ban on interstate sales of rifles and shotguns and limiting the number of people who were required to get licenses to sell firearms. *(1986 Almanac, p. 82)*

In 1988, the NRA was able to pressure Congress to keep the Brady bill out of an omnibus crime measure. Instead, the bill (PL 100-690) contained a provision to require the attorney general to develop a felon identification system. *(1988 Almanac, p. 85; NRA, p. 100)*

Congress in 1990 showed signs of bucking the NRA's powerful lobbying network, but in the end gun control proponents lacked the clout needed to push any of their measures to enactment. The House Rules Committee agreed to let sponsors of the assault weapons ban bring HR 4225 up after the chamber acted on the omnibus crime bill. But backers of the bill did not try for a floor vote because they knew they lacked support — as indicated by the House's floor vote Oct. 4 to water down semiautomatic weapons restrictions already in the crime bill. *(Crime bill, p. 486)*

The Brady bill did not get a rule for floor action because of opposition from Speaker Thomas S. Foley, D-Wash., and other House leaders. Supporters' ability to muster the votes for passage was doubtful anyway.

ASSAULT WEAPONS BAN

The House Judiciary Committee on June 12 approved, 21-15, a bill (HR 4225) to ban U.S.-made assault-style semiautomatic weapons (H Rept 101-621).

The bill would have required the Treasury secretary to outlaw domestic semiautomatics that did not meet the "sporting purposes" test under which foreign-made assault weapons were barred. About 43 types of foreign weapons had been banned under the test set in 1989 by the Bureau of Alcohol, Tobacco and Firearms (BATF).

A spokesman said the bureau had no estimate of how many U.S.-made semiautomatics would be banned if HR 4225 became law. However, in January, the agency issued a memorandum to the U.S. Customs Service saying that 12 domestically produced rifles did not meet a sporting purposes test.

Gun control advocates counted the committee's action as their second victory in four weeks.

On May 23, the Senate had narrowly voted against stripping from its version of the anticrime bill (S 1970) provisions that would ban the manufacture, sale and possession of nine semiautomatic assault-style weapons, five of which already had been administratively banned under the sporting test for foreign firearms.

Senators initially voted 48-52 against an amendment by Orrin G. Hatch, R-Utah, to strike the provisions. Immediately afterward, a motion by Minority Leader Bob Dole, R-Kan., to reconsider the vote failed by just one vote, 49-50. *(Votes 103, 104, p. 24-S)*

Sarah Brady, serving as chairwoman of Handgun Control Inc., said the Senate vote and House committee action showed that lawmakers were "ready to help our law enforcement officers win the drug war by taking killing machines off America's streets."

But NRA lobbyist David Conover predicted HR 4225 would lose on the floor. "We think, as in the past, the vote in the Judiciary Committee will not be representative of votes taken on the floor," Conover said.

The Sporting Test

The sponsor of HR 4225, William J. Hughes, D-N.J., said the test he proposed was a natural outgrowth of the Bush administration's action against foreign firearms. "There is no difference between foreign and domestically made militarylike semiautomatic rifles in either their firepower or the devastation they can create," he said.

But the NRA's Conover said the bill would allow the Treasury Department to "pretty much ban any weapon by narrowly defining its sporting purpose test."

Under existing law, the Treasury secretary had authority to bar importation of weapons not "particularly suitable for or readily adaptable to sporting purposes."

The secretary would be able to evaluate U.S.-made weapons in the same fashion under HR 4225. Those that failed the test could not be bought, sold or owned in the future, but people who already owned weapons could keep them.

Factors already considered included whether the rifle could accept a grenade launcher or large-capacity magazine, or could accept a bayonet.

"These were among the specific factors used in compiling the list of banned foreign-made semiautomatic rifles, and they would be among the factors applied to

Waiting Period on Handguns Blocked

domestically made semiautomatic rifles," Hughes said.

The bill also would have made it illegal for anyone to own or sell an ammunition-feeding device with a capacity of more than seven rounds. Under the bill, the Treasury secretary would have 60 days to issue a list of the firearms to be banned.

In an effort to reduce violence associated with international drug trafficking, the bill also would have prohibited the exportation of domestically banned guns except by the U.S. government to a foreign government.

Breakdown of Vote

The 21-15 vote to send the bill to the floor was largely along party lines, with Democrats favoring the bill and Republicans opposing it.

Three Democrats crossed party lines to vote against the bill: committee Chairman Jack Brooks, Texas; Rick Boucher, Va.; and Harley O. Staggers Jr., W.Va.

Two Republicans voted for the bill: Tom Campbell, Calif., and Mike DeWine, Ohio.

Approval of the bill came after the committee had rejected, 16-20, an amendment by Bill McCollum, R-Fla., that would have allowed firearms to qualify for sporting purposes if they could "reasonably be construed as useful for recreational purposes, including hunting, competition, target shooting and collecting." Opponents said the definition was too broad.

Final Action

The Judiciary Committee's markup was the high-water mark for the assault-weapons ban in the House.

The Rules Committee agreed to make HR 4225 in order after the chamber completed action on the omnibus crime bill (HR 5269). But with time in the session running out, Hughes and other backers lacked the votes to push for floor action.

Instead, the House dealt with the semiautomatics issue during Oct. 4 debate on its version of the crime bill, softening restrictive firearms language in the measure.

The Judiciary Committee's version of the crime measure would have made it illegal to use either imported or domestic parts to make an AK-47, Uzi or any other foreign assault-style semiautomatic already banned by the administration.

But members weakened it on the floor, allowing domestic gun makers to assemble any semiautomatic rifle or shotgun that was identical to any rifle or shotgun already banned from import.

Under the amendment, by Jolene Unsoeld, D-Wash., only firearms assembled with foreign parts would be illegal. The vote was 257-172. *(Vote 416, p. 136-H)*

In the end, all of the firearms provisions were stripped from the bill that both chambers approved Oct. 27 and President Bush signed Nov. 29.

7-DAY WAITING PERIOD

The House Judiciary Committee on July 24 approved, 27-9, the measure (HR 467) that would have required a seven-day waiting period for people who wanted to buy handguns (H Rept 101-691).

Officially titled the Brady Handgun Violence Prevention Act, the bill would have given local law enforcement agencies a week to check a prospective gun-buyer's background.

If the buyer's profile revealed no grounds for blocking the sale — such as a felony conviction — the purchase could proceed.

The law would have applied only to private citizens making a purchase from a licensed handgun dealer.

James Brady, wheelchair-bound since the 1981 shooting, and Sarah Brady were both in the audience when the committee voted to send the bill to the House floor.

Breakdown of Voting

Eight of the committee's 14 Republicans joined all but three committee Democrats in voting for the bill.

Opposing the measure were Democrats Brooks, Staggers, and, by proxy, Boucher, and Republicans McCollum; William E. Dannemeyer, Calif.; Lamar Smith, Texas; Chuck Douglas, N.H.; Carlos J. Moorhead, Calif.; and, by proxy, George W. Gekas, Pa.

McCollum, the Crime Subcommittee's ranking Republican, led the opposition. He proposed an amendment that would have stricken the waiting period. Instead, it would have required states to spend 5 percent of their federal anticrime funds to keep criminal justice records.

The amendment failed, 12-24.

McCollum's amendment also would have required states to develop within a year a "point of purchase" telephone verification system that would allow gun dealers to check the buyer immediately.

"Why take seven days to do something that can be done in seven minutes?" McCollum argued.

But Hughes said that the amendment was simply a ploy to "gut the bill" and that bill opponents were concerned only with "the inconvenience" of making gun buyers wait seven days.

"How about Jim Brady and his inconvenience? The waiting period is the only thing we've got to buy some time to check the records," Hughes said.

Other members criticized the NRA's opposition to the bill. Conservative Republican F. James Sensenbrenner Jr. of Wisconsin lambasted the NRA for sending out "scurrilous mailings" to fight handgun legislation.

Final Action

Supporters hoped to offer HR 467 as an amendment to the omnibus anticrime bill. But the Rules Committee, which had allowed 46 amendments to that measure, barred consideration of a seven-day waiting period amendment. And the Rules panel never gave the bill a separate rule for floor consideration.

Police groups accused the Democratic leadership, particularly Speaker Foley, of shutting out gun control activists.

Foley said the bill was too controversial to bring to the floor at the end of a protracted session, but promised early consideration in the 102nd Congress.

Smaller Antidrug Measures Pass in 1990

Congress in 1990, unlike recent election years, passed no major antidrug package, but did enact a variety of smaller provisions and measures in areas such as treatment, education and law enforcement.

Meanwhile, the nation's highest ranking drug official, Director of National Drug Policy William J. Bennett, resigned in November after a somewhat stormy 20-month tenure as the first so-called drug czar. President Bush announced his intention to appoint Florida Gov. Bob Martinez to replace Bennett. Critics immediately attacked the appointment as a political prize for a man lacking adequate credentials for the job. *('Drug czar,' p. 503)*

Bush announced his second national drug-control strategy in January and called for a 12 percent increase in federal antidrug spending, to more than $10 billion in fiscal 1991. The proposal called for a substantial increase in federal law enforcement efforts, including hundreds of new Drug Enforcement Administration (DEA) and FBI agents and U.S. attorneys. Bush's initial plan also included a $155 million increase in federal treatment funding.

Since 1982, Congress cleared an antidrug or anticrime bill every two years, typically in the waning days of the session right before the final campaign swing. Lawmakers broke the biennial rhythm in 1989 by acting on a major antidrug package in a non-election year.

Numerous measures in 1990 stalled and died or were defeated. A bill to require mandatory drug testing of workers in the transportation industry died in conference when the House and Senate could not resolve differences over the scope of the testing. And a provision expanding the death penalty for drug-related crimes was dropped from 1990's anticrime bill. *(Crime bill, p. 486)*

BACKGROUND

In 1982, 1984, 1986 and 1988, Congress had cleared major antidrug legislation. The 1988 bill (PL 100-690) was the most comprehensive; it called for $2.8 billion to be spent on drug-abuse prevention, treatment and law enforcement. *(1988 Almanac, p. 85; 1986 Almanac, p. 92; 1984 Almanac, p. 215; 1982 Almanac, p. 419)*

That measure allowed the federal death penalty for major drug traffickers, created the Cabinet-level "drug czar" position to coordinate national drug policy, denied certain federal benefits to repeat drug-use offenders, included stiffer penalties for drug dealers, directed more funds at drug interdiction efforts, and provided a higher authorization level for drug-treatment programs.

In the final hours of the 1989 session, the Senate cleared conference reports on Bush's proposals to lend drug-fighting assistance to Colombia, Bolivia and Peru, and to require schools to implement programs aimed at preventing illegal substance abuse by students and employees. The fiscal 1990 Transportation appropriations bill, meanwhile, authorized $3.18 billion in new antidrug spending. *(1989 Almanac, p. 252)*

Lawmakers in 1989 acted on an antidrug package in a non-election year, but to ensure speedy passage Senate leaders removed controversial anticrime provisions and bundled them for later consideration.

Much of Bush's proposed antidrug legislation in 1989, though, fell victim to longstanding congressional disputes over narcotics-related matters. Two bills dealing with alcohol- and drug-abuse treatment programs (HR 3630) and the use of proceeds from assets seized during drug investigations (HR 3550) never emerged from conference.

The Senate on Aug. 3, 1989, had also passed a bill (S 819) to stiffen federal penalties for selling drugs at highway truck stops and roadside rest areas. The legislation was patterned after a plan to establish "drug-free school zones" contained in the 1988 antidrug package. The bill, though, sat in House committee after September 1989 and died. *(1989 Almanac, p. 384)*

The House and Senate in 1989 also headed toward a tough conference on legislation calling for random drug testing in the transportation industry. While both chambers passed legislation on the subject, the differences were so great that the measures never emerged from conference.

THE BUSH PLAN

Bush announced his second national drug-control strategy Jan. 25, 1990. He called for a 12 percent increase in federal antidrug spending, to $10.6 billion in fiscal 1991.

Critics, such as Joseph R. Biden Jr., D-Del., chairman of the Senate Judiciary Committee, said the administration's drug strategy focused too much on law enforcement and interdiction rather than on treatment and prevention of drug abuse. The new strategy largely reiterated proposals made in the administration's first antidrug plan, released in September 1989.

"We have to come up with a broader strategy," said Charles B. Rangel, D-N.Y., chairman of the House Select Committee on Narcotics Abuse and Control. "We've got to invest in one thing, human resources, and it's nowhere in this document."

Biden and others called for substantially higher funding of treatment and education programs, and greater efforts to provide economic assistance to Bolivia, Colombia and Peru, the three Andean nations that were the source of most of the cocaine used in the United States. *(Andean initiative, p. 805)*

Both the administration and Biden vehemently rejected the proposed legalization of drugs, an idea that had gained national attention but few, if any, backers on Capitol Hill.

Both also claimed that some progress had been made in the fight against substance abuse, especially in public attitudes and in international efforts to clamp down on the drug trade.

"It's becoming clear the war is winnable. . . . This is not mission impossible," said Bennett.

Death Penalty

While the strategy required very little legislative action other than by appropriators, one controversial proposal was an expansion of federal death penalty laws to include drug kingpins, even in cases not involving murder.

Bush wanted to expand the law to cover federal drug felons whose offenses resulted in death and drug kingpins who attempted to kill in order to obstruct justice. Under existing law, only drug kingpins who committed or ordered a murder were subject to the death penalty.

With time running out for the 101st Congress, though, House-Senate conferees on anticrime legislation (HR 5269,

Martinez To Follow Bennett as Drug Czar

William J. Bennett, who served 20 months as the nation's first "drug czar," announced his resignation on Nov. 8. President Bush on Nov. 30 announced his intention to nominate outgoing Florida Republican Gov. Bob Martinez to the post.

Martinez, decisively defeated in his bid for re-election Nov. 6, immediately came under criticism from congressional Democrats. His Senate confirmation hearings in 1991 seemed likely to examine critically his qualifications for the position.

Bennett had been a controversial figure as secretary of Education under President Ronald Reagan and continued to be outspoken and confrontational after Bush picked him to be hold the position formally called director of national drug policy created by the 1988 antidrug bill (PL 100-690). *(1988 Almanac, p. 85)*

The office was given Cabinet-level status, but Bush decided not to make the drug czar a member of the Cabinet. To some observers, that diminished from the start the clout and authority the office held.

Bennett showed no hesitancy, however, in using the office as a bully pulpit for pressuring Congress, state and local governments and the private sector for stronger action against use of illegal drugs. The office had a staff of about 130 and a budget of about $16.5 million.

In accepting his resignation, Bush praised Bennett for the job he had done and said there were "very promising signs that suggest the drug problem is diminishing, not only in the suburbs, but in the cities as well." Bush added that "we're on the road to victory."

A New York Times editorial on Bennett's tenure in office said that he had "brought a capacity for thorough study and rigorous analysis to the daunting complexities of drug abuse and trafficking." It also pointed out that during his nearly 20 months as drug czar, federal money for treatment nearly doubled to $1.5 billion.

Some Democrats, however, were critical. Senate Judiciary Committee Chairman Joseph R. Biden Jr., D-Del., frequently sparred with the administration over drug policy and often criticized it for over-emphasizing military and interdiction approaches at the expense of education and treatment.

Rep. Charles B. Rangel, D-N.Y., chairman of the House Select Committee on Narcotics Abuse and Control, was also a frequent critic of the administration's drug policies. In remarks to reporters Nov. 8, Bennett called Rangel "a gasbag" and said he "has nothing to do with drug policy." Rangel discounted the attacks and said Bennett was "frustrated."

Rumors of the Martinez appointment surfaced within a week after Bennett's resignation, and official announcement of his selection brought criticism from Capitol Hill.

"Unfortunately, Mr. Martinez lacks the background and record to suggest that he is well-suited for this task," Biden said in a statement.

During his four-year tenure as governor, Martinez stiffened penalties for drug dealers and was a strong proponent of increased use of U.S. military force in fighting international drug activities.

But the Miami Herald ran an editorial after rumors of the Martinez appointment surfaced. The paper said that Martinez was not "the ideal person" for the job. As governor, the editorial said, "he shortchanged drug education and treatment."

Despite the controversy, the Senate confirmed Martinez by a vote of 88-12 on March 21, 1991. Twelve Democrats — not including Biden — voted against him.

S 1970) abandoned efforts to reach agreement on the most controversial questions before them such as the death penalty, and the provisions were dumped. Instead, both chambers approved a stripped-down bill (S 3266) that included non-controversial proposals acceptable to all.

Law Enforcement

The administration proposal also called for a substantial increase in federal law enforcement efforts. Bush requested funds for 380 new DEA agents, 102 new FBI agents and 410 new U.S. attorneys. He called for a 53 percent funding increase — to $330 million — for the Organized Crime Drug Enforcement Task Force program, which coordinated federal, state and local efforts against sophisticated drug-related and money-laundering crimes.

Bush repeated his request from 1989 that states implement drug-testing programs throughout their criminal-justice systems as a condition for receipt of federal criminal-justice funds. That proposal made little headway in Congress, in large part because of state objections that such a testing program would be too costly.

To comply with the 1988 antidrug law, the administration also designated five "high-intensity drug-trafficking areas" eligible for additional law enforcement assistance. The five were metropolitan New York City, Los Angeles, Miami, Houston, and 35 counties along the Southwest border with Mexico. These areas would be eligible for $25 million in extra law enforcement assistance in fiscal 1990 and a proposed $50 million in fiscal 1991. Biden, though, called the administration proposal "grossly inadequate."

Treatment

Bush's plan included a $155 million increase in federal treatment funding, compared with a $2.2 billion increase proposed by Biden. Administration officials argued that there had been a tremendous increase in funding for state treatment programs over the past two years and that states needed to absorb those increases.

Most of the Bush increase — $100 million — was targeted for block grants to state drug-treatment agencies, bringing the total for that program to $577 million. The administration said it would push for legislation it proposed in 1989 to condition the receipt of such funds on the development of statewide treatment plans.

That legislation (HR 3630) stalled in conference, which deadlocked at the end of 1989 over a Senate-passed provision requiring random drug testing of transportation workers and a House provision to shift some of the treatment funds to categorical grants for rural antidrug efforts and the treatment of pregnant addicts. The administration opposed such a shift, although the latest plan did call for new research and demonstration programs to help pregnant addicts and their children. The plan also requested $6 million for demonstration grants to assist some of an estimated 100,000 "cocaine babies" born each year.

Interdiction

The administration called for a $344 million increase in interdiction efforts, for a total of $2.4 billion. This included a larger role for the Defense Department. The administration estimated that the Pentagon would spend $1.2 billion on antidrug efforts in fiscal 1991, compared with $200 million in fiscal 1988 and $800 million in fiscal 1990.

The administration also sought legislation giving federal law enforcement officials the authority to order U.S.-registered aircraft, or any aircraft flying over U.S. territory, to land if they were suspected of smuggling drugs.

The administration also proposed hiring 175 additional Customs Service inspectors and 174 new Border Patrol agents for the Immigration and Naturalization Service.

TREATMENT AND EDUCATION

Critics of the Bush administration's drug policy often focused on its emphasis on law enforcement rather than education and treatment. In 1990, though, Congress passed a variety of measures that increased both education programs aimed at reducing the demand for illegal drugs and at treating those addicted. Critics still maintained that not enough emphasis or money was given to those programs.

Treatment

Treatment programs in fiscal 1990 received more money than in fiscal 1989. In addition to established programs, Congress authorized an extra $40 million for a program to reduce the waiting period for addicts needing drug treatment and a Senate committee unanimously approved comprehensive legislation beefing up treatment and prevention programs.

Following are details on the measures:

- **Increased appropriations.** The fiscal 1991 spending bill for the Departments of Labor, Health and Human Services (HHS), and Education, and related agencies provided $2.1 billion for drug treatment.

The National Institute on Drug Abuse received $411 million, the Office for Treatment Improvement got $1.41 billion, and the Office for Substance Abuse Prevention was given $272 million. The total amount was $165 million more than in fiscal 1990 and $7.5 million less than the administration requested for fiscal 1991.

The House first passed its appropriations bill July 19. A day before the vote, Bennett criticized the bill because it provided $231.4 million less than the administration had asked for drug treatment and education programs.

"The conventional rap on us is that we're too much for law enforcement," Bennett told The Associated Press. "For a year now, we have been flogged for this. Now they cut our damned budget proposal on the demand side. Who are these clowns?"

Members on both sides of the aisle criticized Bennett for his comments but in the end agreed to restore the funding by drawing down a reserve set aside to pay for new programs expected to be enacted later in the year.

"We've been given a very bad rap by the czar," complained Silvio O. Conte, Mass., ranking Republican on the full Appropriations panel and the Labor-HHS Subcommittee. The panel did not provide the administration's full request, Conte said, because the antidrug programs "can't handle all the money we've been throwing at them."

- **Reduced waiting period.** The Senate on Aug. 4 cleared legislation to authorize an extra $40 million for a program to reduce the waiting period for addicts needing drug treatment, concurring with the technical amendments the House adopted when it passed the bill July 30. President Bush signed the measure (S 2461 — PL 101-374) Aug. 15.

Congress already had voted to appropriate the $40 million for fiscal 1990 but then had to approve the authorization before the funds could be spent. All the $100 million authorized in 1988 for the Waiting List Program — created by comprehensive antidrug legislation enacted that year — had been spent; drug treatment programs still had long waiting lists. The grants provided by the program aimed to help reduce the waiting lists at drug treatment centers.

S 2461 raised the authorization to $140 million and extended and modified the grants program. Drug abusers who were pregnant and addicted babies would be given priority for treatment under the revised program. Agencies that received the grants would be able to use half the money for follow-up programs to prevent patients from relapsing into drug abuse.

The inability of addicts to receive help in a timely manner had been a serious problem for communities and individuals battling drug abuse, especially in urban areas with high drug-abuse rates. New York City, for example, had a licensed treatment capacity for only 42,000 drug abusers but had an estimated 550,000 addicts, according to bill supporter Rep. Gary L. Ackerman, D-N.Y.

"Every day there are thousands of people in this country who come to terms with their drug addiction and decide to seek treatment, but cannot get it," said House sponsor Henry A. Waxman, D-Calif.

"They cannot get treatment for their addiction because when they finally get to the clinic doors, they are turned away; they are told there are no slots; they are told to come back in six weeks or six months, or maybe a year."

- **New prevention programs.** The Senate Labor and Human Resources Committee on Sept. 12 unanimously approved comprehensive legislation aimed at reducing the demand for illegal drugs by beefing up treatment and prevention programs.

The bill, a revised version of S 2649, was ordered reported on a 16-0 vote (S Rept 101-476). It would have authorized approximately $250 million in new funds for drug treatment and prevention programs in fiscal 1991. The measure died before any further action could be taken.

Many of the programs in the omnibus measure, noted bill sponsor and Labor Committee Chairman Edward M. Kennedy, D-Mass., were originally written by other senators as part of various antidrug bills in 1989.

Among the new programs included in the bill was one sponsored by Labor Committee member Christopher J. Dodd, D-Conn., that would have authorized $75 million to help coordinate services available to drug-addicted mothers and infants.

The House Energy and Commerce Subcommittee on Health and the Environment on Sept. 13 approved by voice vote its bill aimed at helping drug-addicted mothers and children.

Subcommittee Chairman Waxman said the unnumbered bill was drawn from provisions of HR 3630, a 1989 omnibus drug bill that had stalled in a House-Senate conference.

The Senate bill would also have altered the formula by which funds were distributed under the Alcohol, Drug Abuse and Mental Health Block Grant program. With a $1.2 billion appropriation in fiscal 1990, the block grant was the federal government's largest single antidrug and alcohol-abuse treatment and prevention program.

The new formula would have designated more funding for states with large rural populations, while taking into account that urban areas tended to have higher rates of drug- and alcohol-abuse problems.

"Drug use is a crime, but it is also a disease," said Kennedy. "We must respond to this disease with two tried-and-true weapons in the public health arsenal — treatment and prevention."

Education

Congress in 1990 dealt with a number of education measures that included drug-related provisions. Most of the pieces of legislation failed to clear during the 101st Congress, with supporters vowing to reintroduce the measures in the 102nd Congress.

Following are some of the education measures and their drug-related provisions that Congress dealt with in 1990:

- **HR 996.** Congress on Oct. 26 cleared a bill (HR 996 — PL 101-589) that established three scholarship programs to provide students grants in exchange for agreements to work or teach in science, math or engineering and for achieving outstanding work in the fields. The scholarship programs were authorized at $9.2 million in fiscal 1991.

The final bill contained a House provision to bar a convicted drug user or distributor from receiving any awards and would require that such a student repay any awards received plus punitive penalties.

- **S 695.** The Senate on Feb. 7 passed legislation (S 695) to authorize about $414 million in new education programs in fiscal 1991. The Senate passed the bill 92-8 after adopting numerous amendments by voice vote including one by Pete Wilson, R-Calif., to authorize $10 million for DARE (Drug Abuse Resistance Education), a drug-abuse prevention program that involved local law enforcement officials providing classroom instruction. *(Vote 10, p. 5-S)*

The bill also provided for $5 million annually in fiscal 1991-93 for a series of state grants to establish drug-testing programs for secondary school athletes.

The House on July 27 substituted the text of HR 5115 into the bill and passed the amended version; the measure went no further. HR 5115 had been passed by the House 350-25 on July 20. *(Vote 256, p. 86-H)*

A handful of amendments to HR 5115 were considered separately, including one to halt financial aid to students convicted of drug possession. Offered by Gerald B. H. Solomon, R-N.Y., it would have suspended financial aid for possession of a controlled substance for one year for the first offense, two years for the second conviction and indefinitely for the third. Students convicted of selling drugs would have lost their aid for two years the first time and indefinitely the second time. The measure was agreed to, 315-59. *(Vote 255, p. 86-H)*

- **HR 5064.** The House on July 10, by a vote of 388-13, passed HR 5064 (H Rept 101-572) to establish a $15 million grant program to develop a strategy for teaching elementary school pupils to resist pressures that could lead to drug abuse. The Education Department would be required to use funds appropriated for the Drug-Free Schools and Community Act. *(Vote 214, p. 74-H)*

The Bush administration opposed the bill, saying it would duplicate existing programs and was unnecessary.

The House Education and Labor Committee on June 27 had approved HR 5064. The Senate Labor and Human Resources Committee reported the legislation with an amendment on Sept. 27, but the bill went no further.

- **HR 5124.** The House on July 10 passed HR 5124 by voice vote to prevent student drug abuse. It included provisions that would establish criteria for drug-free school zones; require the Education Department to reserve $5 million of appropriated funds for grants to replicate successful drug-abuse education programs; and raise the authorization, from $35 million to $50 million, for the existing drug-abuse grant program for training of teachers and antidrug counselors.

The administration opposed the bill, arguing that its provisions were unnecessary, burdensome or redundant.

The Senate Labor and Human Resources Committee reported the bill with an amendment on Sept. 28, but the measure went no further.

DRUG TESTING AND ENFORCEMENT

Legislation calling for random drug testing in the transportation industry, passed by both chambers in 1989, went nowhere in conference in 1990. Similar legislation stalled in 1988 when the two chambers were unable to work out differences between House language addressing just railroad workers and a more far-reaching Senate measure. Both sides staked out similar positions in 1989 and 1990. *(1988 Almanac, p. 587)*

In other related action, the House on Oct. 19 adopted the conference report to the fiscal 1991 transportation appropriations bill, but only after conferees dropped Senate provisions that would have required drug testing for mass transit workers. The Senate gave in on an attempt by Alfonse M. D'Amato, R-N.Y., to require drug and alcohol testing for 179,000 mass transit workers. *(Transportation appropriations, p. 876)*

The Senate Commerce Committee on May 22 also approved a bill (S 2434 — S Rept 101-374) by voice vote, to require local mass transit programs that received federal funds to institute a Department of Transportation (DOT) drug-testing program for workers in safety-related positions. Roughly 195,000 transit workers would have been covered by the bill, which died.

The Supreme Court, meanwhile, on April 30 refused to consider a challenge to DOT's policy requiring random drug testing of employees in jobs with a direct impact on public health, safety or national security.

DOT officials approved a drug-testing program in 1987 for about 30,000 people in sensitive jobs, including air-traffic controllers. The U.S. Court of Appeals for the District of Columbia ruled in September 1989 that the program was "supported by sufficiently compelling circumstances to justify the invasions of privacy entailed."

Those who tested positive once for illegal drugs generally were transferred to non-sensitive jobs. If they tested positive again, they were fired.

The appeals court cited Supreme Court rulings from 1989 upholding drug and alcohol tests for railway workers involved in accidents and for U.S. Customs Service employees applying for certain jobs. But neither of those rulings determined the constitutionality of randomly administered drug tests.

Drug testing of federal workers stemmed from a 1986 order by President Ronald Reagan. The Bush administration endorsed the antidrug campaign. Neither the 1989 rulings nor the case acted on April 30 directly affected workers in the private sector.

Pressure on States

Congress attached a drug-related provision to its fiscal 1991 transportation appropriations measure (HR 5229). The House on Oct. 19 receded in its disagreement and concurred in the Senate amendment on the provision designed to crack down on drug offenders. The final bill would cut off 5 percent of a state's federal highway money in the first year and 10 percent in later years if that state did not suspend the driver's license for at least six months of anyone convicted of a drug offense.

Before passing the appropriations measure on July 12, the House had approved, 331-88, an amendment by Solomon to require 2 percent annual reductions in federal highway aid to states that did not suspend the driver's licenses of convicted drug offenders for at least six months. *(Vote 223, p. 78-H)*

The Senate, before passing its version of the spending bill Aug. 4, adopted the provision by D'Amato, the subcommittee's ranking Republican. D'Amato's provision was the one in the final bill. ■

Juvenile Agency Pick OK'd

The Senate on April 4 confirmed the nomination of Robert W. Sweet Jr. to head the Justice Department's Office of Juvenile Justice and Delinquency Prevention despite complaints by Democratic senators that Sweet had no experience specifically with troubled or delinquent youths.

Senate confirmation came on voice vote after just one senator, Judiciary Committee Chairman Joseph R. Biden Jr., D-Del., spoke out against Sweet on the floor. Biden said that he had "serious concerns" about Sweet's experience and that he was "not convinced" that Sweet was "firmly committed" to juvenile justice programs.

One other Democrat, John Kerry of Massachusetts, filed a statement opposing Sweet's nomination to head the Justice Department agency that administered federal programs for the prevention and treatment of juvenile delinquency and made grants to states and localities to help rehabilitate wayward youths.

In a detailed critique, Kerry noted that Sweet had been fired from an Education Department post during the Reagan administration by Secretary Terrel H. Bell for what Bell called a series of disruptive actions that amounted to an "end-run" around his superiors.

Republicans, however, defended Sweet's selection for the post. They contended that his work as a teacher, Education Department official and White House aide on education issues demonstrated his interest in juvenile justice issues.

When President Bush nominated him for the post, Sweet was serving as an education analyst for the Senate Republican Policy Committe.

Biden had also opposed Sweet when the Judiciary Committee voted 9-5 on March 22 to recommend that he be confirmed.

At the time, Biden said, "I don't have the stomach for leading any great crusade against Mr. Sweet."

A former high school teacher, Sweet had worked in the Department of Education as a special assistant in 1981-82. After that he worked as deputy director and acting director of the department's National Institute of Education in 1982-83 and then in the White House through 1988.

Democrats tied criticism of Sweet's lack of experience to a Bush administration proposal to delete funding for the juvenile justice agency, saying the two moves showed the president's low priority to juvenile justice issues. Congress in 1990 continued funding for the agency, which the Reagan administration had also proposed to eliminate. *(1988 Almanac, p. 119)*

Judiciary Committee Republicans defended Sweet's selection. Sen. Gordon J. Humphrey, R-N.H., who said he had been a friend of Sweet's for 15 years, said Sweet was "dedicated, above all things, to children and youth."

Voting to confirm the nomination in committee were Democrats Dennis DeConcini, Ariz.; Howell Heflin, Ala.; and Herb Kohl, Wis.; and Republicans Humphrey; Charles E. Grassley, Iowa; Orrin G. Hatch, Utah; Alan K. Simpson, Wyo.; Arlen Specter, Pa.; and Strom Thurmond, S.C.

Opposing Sweet were Biden; Edward M. Kennedy, D-Mass.; Patrick J. Leahy, D-Vt.; Howard M. Metzenbaum, D-Ohio; and Paul Simon, D-Ill. ■

'Hate Crime' Statistics To Be Published

In an effort to document the incidence of prejudice-inspired crimes in the United States, the House on April 4 cleared legislation requiring the Justice Department to gather and publish "hate crime" statistics for the next five years.

The bill was sent to the White House by a vote of 402-18. *(Vote 66, p. 26-H)*

President Bush signed the measure on April 23 (HR 1048 — PL 101-275).

The law required the attorney general to publish an annual summary showing how many crimes each year manifested evidence of prejudice based on race, religion, sexual orientation or ethnicity. Covered crimes included murder, manslaughter, forcible rape, assault, intimidation, arson and vandalism.

"This bill is a necessary first step toward combating hate crimes in a systematic and comprehensive way," said Charles E. Schumer, D-N.Y.

The only House member to speak against final approval of the bill was William E. Dannemeyer, R-Calif., who objected to including prejudice based on "sexual orientation." To do so, Dannemeyer said, would have treated homosexuals the same as constitutionally protected groups such as racial and religious minorities.

Similar legislation was passed by the House in both the 99th and 100th Congresses, only to die in the Senate. This time, the Senate passed HR 1048 by 92-4 on Feb. 8. *(Vote 13, p. 5-S)*

Before final passage, the Senate voted 96-0 to add language that "American family life is the foundation of American society" and that no funds provided under the bill could be spent to "promote or encourage homosexuality." *(Vote 11, p. 5-S)*

HR 1048 was introduced in February 1989 by Rep. John Conyers Jr., D-Mich., who also sponsored a similar measure in 1988. When he reintroduced the legislation, he referred to the much publicized killing of a black man in the Howard Beach area of Queens, N.Y., and said, "Few across the nation will ever know about the thousands of other lesser-known incidents unless information about them is compiled."

Paul Simon, D-Ill., the sponsor of the Senate bill (S 419) that was substituted into HR 1048, further commented on the reasons behind the measure. "When something happens at Howard Beach or somewhere else, we read about it and we may draw conclusions that incidents are going up or they are going down. But there is very little solid statistical evidence," he said.

The Senate rejected contentions by Jesse Helms, R-N.C., that Congress was being "hoodwinked" into passing the "flagship of the homosexual and lesbian legislative agenda."

It defeated 19-77 a Helms amendment that would have added language saying the "homosexual movement threatens the strength and survival of the American family as a basic unit of society" and that "state sodomy laws should be enforced because they are in the best interest of public health." *(Vote 12, p. 5-S)*

Joining Helms in opposing final passage of the legislation were William L. Armstrong, R-Colo.; Gordon J. Humphrey, R-N.H.; and Trent Lott, R-Miss.

Under the bill, the attorney general would set criteria for determining whether a crime was motivated by prejudice. Serious crimes such as murder, rape, assault and arson would be tracked for five years.

Barbara A. Mikulski, D-Md., captured the tone of much of the debate when she said, "I detest hate crimes" and cited "the letter bombs sent to judges and civil rights lawyers; the vandals who attack synagogues and leave swastikas as calling cards; the club-wielding gangs."

The Senate Judiciary Committee unanimously approved the bill on March 9, 1989. The House originally passed the bill by 368-47 on June 27, 1989. *(1989 Almanac, p. 40-H)* ■

Biological Weapons Ban

The House on May 8 cleared for the president legislation that made it a federal crime to develop, produce, sell or possess a biological weapon.

President Bush signed the measure May 22 (S 993 — PL 101-298).

The measure, which was passed by the Senate Nov. 21, 1989, was designed to implement a 1972 international convention on biological weapons that was unanimously ratified by the Senate in 1974 and had been signed by 111 nations.

The bill was sponsored by Herb Kohl, D-Wis., who said it "would strike a blow against terrorists" in addition to meeting the terms of the 1974 agreement. *(1989 Almanac, p. 292)*

Final action came when the House by 408-0 passed its version of the bill (HR 237), then substituted the text of the identical Senate-passed measure. *(Vote 99, p. 36-H)*

The Reagan administration did not pursue the legislation, saying existing laws were adequate. But the Bush administration supported S 993.

The bill authorized the attorney general to seize and destroy any biological agent, toxin or delivery system deemed to have no apparent peaceful purposes. The person whose property was seized would have an opportunity to protest, and the government would have to prove by a preponderance of the evidence that the biological substance in question was proscribed.

Anyone convicted of violating the act would be subject to a sentence of up to life imprisonment or a fine, or both.

The act did not restrict research or development for protection or other peaceful uses. ■

Bill To Deter Sex Violence

The Senate Judiciary Committee on Oct. 4 unanimously approved a bill designed to combat violence against women. But committee Chairman Joseph R. Biden Jr., D-Del., the sponsor, held off seeking floor action in the 101st Congress until the Justice Department completed a detailed review of it.

Violent crimes are often directed against women just "because they are women," Biden said at a June 20 hearing on the bill.

The measure (S 2754) would have done the following:

- Doubled minimum penalties for rape and aggravated assault, imposed new penalties for repeat offenders and provided more restitution for victims.
- Authorized $300 million for new police efforts to identify and combat sex crimes, with the majority of the funds going to the 40 metropolitan areas deemed most dangerous to women by the Bureau of Justice Statistics.
- Tripled funding for shelters for battered women.
- Authorized funds for increased lighting, camera surveillance and other security measures at public transit facilities.
- Created a National Commission on Violent Crime Against Women.
- Created federal penalties for spouse abuse.
- Required colleges to provide rape prevention programs.

Before approving the bill, the committee agreed to an amendment by Orrin G. Hatch, R-Utah, to require a state, on request, to supply rape victims with the results of attackers' AIDS tests.

An amendment by Edward M. Kennedy, D-Mass., to Hatch's amendment would deny 10 percent of the funds provided in the bill to any state that refused to act on such a request. ■

Senate Confirms Souter for High Court

After just four hours of debate, the Senate on Oct. 2 confirmed David H. Souter as an associate justice of the U.S. Supreme Court. The vote on President Bush's first nominee to the high court came nearly two weeks after the Senate Judiciary Committee completed five days of hearings on Souter.

Souter, 51, was sworn in Oct. 9, and started his working career at the court immediately, when the justices began the 1990-91 term's second week of hearing arguments in cases to be decided by July 1991.

The Senate vote to confirm Souter was 90-9 with nine Democrats opposing him mainly because of his refusal to state his position on privacy and abortion rights. *(Vote 259, p. 52-S)*

Bush nominated Souter to replace 84-year-old William J. Brennan Jr., who announced his retirement July 20, for health reasons. Brennan was the court's most senior member, having served for nearly 34 years, the seventh-longest tenure of any Supreme Court justice. *(Brennan career, p. 510)*

Though relatively unknown at the time of his appointment, Souter had been a short-list candidate in Ronald Reagan's 1987 search for a replacement for Justice Lewis F. Powell Jr.

Reagan eventually chose Robert H. Bork to replace Powell and a bitter confirmation battle ensued. Bork suffered the largest defeat of any Supreme Court nominee, failing in his confirmation bid by a 42-58 vote. Observers surmised that Souter was chosen by Bush in large part because he had no record to be dissected and used against him — as happened with Bork. *(Bork nomination, 1987 Almanac, p. 271)*

Souter's record, which included two years as New Hampshire attorney general, five years on a state trial court, seven years on the state Supreme Court and four months on a federal appeals court, offered little indication of how he would fit into the divided U.S. Supreme Court.

BACKGROUND

Bush nominated Souter to the Supreme Court on July 23, three days after Brennan's surprise retirement.

With the Souter nomination, Bush sought to set the ground rules for the relationship between the legislative and judicial branches by declaring that the court should not "legislate from the bench." *(Bush statement, p. 509)*

For Bush, Souter's ascension would ideally move the court more fully into an era in which the justices would reject a role as public policy-makers. That role was personified by Brennan, although it began eroding with the court's turnover during the Reagan years.

For his part, Souter immediately adopted the tight-lipped stance that senators would try hard to crack during confirmation hearings.

After thanking Bush for the nomination, Souter told the assembled reporters that he could not express "the realization that I have of the honor which the president has just done me. . . ."

"Beyond that," he added, "I hope you will understand that I think I must defer any further comments of mine until I am before the Senate in the confirmation process."

Despite Souter's guarded comments, it was clear that he would be a change from Brennan, who had helped shape the Supreme Court's broad constitutional rulings during the era of the Warren Court in the 1950s and '60s and then become a frequent and forceful dissenter as the court shifted to the right under Warren E. Burger (1969-87) and the current chief justice, William H. Rehnquist.

Souter, who became the youngest justice on the court, was expected to join a bloc of five conservative justices — Rehnquist and Associate Justices Byron R. White, Sandra Day O'Connor, Antonin Scalia, and Anthony M. Kennedy — who generally favored a narrower reading of the Constitution and federal statutes.

Souter Biography

Born in Melrose, Mass., on Sept. 17, 1939, Souter grew up in Weare, N.H., living in the same house since he was 11. He graduated from Harvard College in 1961, studied at Oxford University from 1961-63, and earned his law degree from Harvard Law School in 1966.

By all accounts, the former Rhodes scholar was a solitary, conscientious man with a diligent and straightforward approach to the law. He had only one published law article, a tribute to a state court justice in the New Hampshire Bar Journal.

Souter had practiced law in Concord, N.H., in the late 1960s before serving as assistant attorney general of New Hampshire from 1968-71. He then served as deputy attorney general from 1971-76 and was appointed attorney general of New Hampshire in 1976, succeeding his mentor Sen. Warren B. Rudman, R-N.H.

In 1978 Souter was named a judge on the Superior Court of New Hampshire, a trial court.

Five years later, then-Gov. John H. Sununu appointed him to the state Supreme Court, where he served until early 1990 when Bush — with Sununu as his chief of staff — plucked Souter to serve on the 1st U.S. Circuit Court of Appeals.

After Bush nominated Souter to the Court of Appeals, Souter skated through a Judiciary Committee nomination hearing April 5. The Senate confirmed him without objection April 27.

While his nomination to the appeals court generated little controversy or news, his nomination to the Supreme Court was a surprise to most — including Souter.

"The best news I have is that the blood is circulating to the brain well enough now so that I'm beginning to have some feelings," Souter said July 25.

The day before he had said he was "astonished" that he had been chosen.

When reporters shouted questions at the numerous photo sessions with senators, he declined to answer.

"I think it would be inappropriate for me to make any comments before the hearing," he said. Asked how it felt to be snatched from obscurity, he responded, "I must say, I never thought of myself as that obscure."

Preparing for the Hearings

With Souter's low profile a political plus for the Bush team, the administration tried to keep it that way.

Souter stayed out of the public eye during the summer, reviewing tapes from past nomination hearings, preparing his responses to predictable questions.

'A Remarkable Judge of Keen Intellect'

Following is the transcript of President Bush's announcement July 23 that he would nominate Judge David H. Souter of the 1st U.S. Circuit Court of Appeals to fill the Supreme Court vacancy created by the retirement of Associate Justice William J. Brennan Jr.:

Well, my oath to the Constitution charges me to faithfully execute the office of president, and to the best of my ability, preserve, protect and defend the Constitution of the United States. Few duties are more important in discharging that obligation than my responsibility under Article II, Section II, of our Constitution, to select from among all possible choices one nominee to fill a vacancy on the Supreme Court of the United States.

The task of narrowing the selection to one highly qualified jurist, committed to the rule of law and faithful to the Constitution, could never be easy. But I have found it enormously satisfying. My choice will serve the court and the Constitution well.

I am most pleased to announce that I will nominate as associate justice of the United States Supreme Court a remarkable judge of keen intellect and the highest ability, one whose scholarly commitment to the law and whose wealth of experience mark him of first rank: Judge David [H.] Souter of the United States Court of Appeals for the First Circuit.

Judge Souter, I believe with all my heart, will prove a most worthy member of the court. His tenure as an associate justice of the Supreme Court of the state of New Hampshire, as attorney general of that state, and more recently, as a federal appeals judge, unquestionably demonstrates his ability, his integrity and his dedication to public service.

And he has a keen appreciation of the proper judicial role rooted in fundamental belief in separation of powers and the democratic principles underlying our great system of government.

Let me pay tribute, too, to the justice whose retirement from the court created the vacancy, Justice William [J.] Brennan [Jr.]. His powerful intellect, his winning personality, and importantly, his commitment to civil discourse on emotional issues that at times tempt uncivil voices have made him one of the greatest figures of our age. No one can question his dedication to the nation and the energy that he has brought to his high office.

His retirement is marked by the dignity and honor that characterized his 34 years of service on the bench. And I told him the other day when I talked to him of the respect that Mrs. Bush and I have for him for his wonderful service.

In choosing to nominate Judge Souter, who, like Justice Brennan, is largely a product of the state court system, I have looked for the same dedication to public service and strength of intellect exemplified by Justice Brennan.

My selection process was not geared simply to any legal issue. It is not appropriate, in choosing a Supreme Court justice, to use any litmus test. And I want a justice who will ably and fairly interpret the law across the range of issues the court faces.

Our country serves as a model for the world at a time of special significance. And I stress within the White House, to the attorney general, that our process could not be dominated by politics or special interests. And I believe that we've set a good example of selecting a fair arbiter of the law.

Judge Souter will bring to the court a wealth of judicial experience on the Supreme Court of his state, and before that, as a state trial court judge. Prior to his appointment to the state bench, he was attorney general in the state of New Hampshire.

Judge Souter is a graduate of the Harvard Law School, Phi Beta Kappa graduate of Harvard College; he was also a Rhodes scholar. My respect for his outstanding record led me earlier this year to nominate him to his present position on the Court of Appeals.

The Senate unanimously confirmed him to that position because of his exceptional qualities and his experience. His opinions reflect a clean intellect — keen intellect, as well as wise balance between the theoretical and practical aspects of the law.

Judge Souter is committed to interpreting, not making, the law. He recognizes the proper role of judges in upholding the democratic choices of the people through their elected representatives with constitutional restraints.

Judge Brennan's retirement took effect last Friday. The court is now reduced to eight members. It is important to restore the bench to full strength by the first full Monday in October when the court begins its 1990 term.

I look forward to presenting Judge Souter's nomination to the Senate as quickly as possible and I look forward as well to a fair and expeditious confirmation process. . . . ■

He also went over what Bork did wrong.

Tom C. Korologos, a former top aide to Presidents Richard M. Nixon and Gerald R. Ford who handled hundreds of nominations for GOP administrations, said he hoped this one would stand out "for the ease with which it goes through."

But Democrats urged caution at the lack of immediate opposition to Souter.

Edward M. Kennedy, D-Mass., the Judiciary Committee's most prominent liberal, told the American Bar Association at its annual meeting in August, "In this day and age, the Senate will not confirm a blank slate to the Supreme Court of the United States."

As Souter spent the summer preparing for his September hearings, senators did the same. Judiciary Committee Chairman Joseph R. Biden Jr., D-Del., hired University of Chicago law Professor David A. Strauss to work with the committee's chief counsel and coordinate the efforts of outside constitutional scholars.

Senators scoured whatever materials they could find on Souter — from his tenure on the New Hampshire courts to his brief stint on the U.S. Court of Appeals — to flesh out his views on such issues as judicial activism, civil rights and abortion.

When Souter was nominated to the appeals court, a Senate Judiciary Committee questionnaire asked his views of judicial activism.

Souter's response, while not very revealing, indicated a willingness to go beyond the letter of a statute: "The obligation of any judge is to decide the case before the court, and the nature of the issue presented will largely determine the appropriate scope of the principle on which its decision should rest.

"Where that principle is not provided and controlled by black letter authority or existing precedent, the decision must honor the distinction between personal and judicially cognizable values. The foundation of judicial responsibility in statutory interpretation is respect for the enacted text and for the legislative purpose that may explain a text that is unclear. The expansively phrased provisions of the Constitution must be read in light of its divisions of power among the branches of government and the constituents of the federal system."

On abortion, White House congressional liaison Fred McClure said, "The judge alone will make the determination on how far he will go" in his testimony. Separately, Sununu had been assuring conservative activists that Souter was one of them and opposed abortion.

The president said that he never even asked Souter his position on abortion.

Brennan's Unique Judicial Stamp . . .

Justice William J. Brennan Jr., a bulwark for individual rights and liberties who kept alive the activism of the Earl Warren Court, left an imprint on Congress as he did on nearly every area of American life.

One of Brennan's more influential opinions, *Baker v. Carr*, ushered in an era of federal court involvement in reapportionment and congressional redistricting, which at the time of the 1962 ruling was the domain of governors and state legislators.

The court struck down apportionments that had resulted in state legislative districts with lopsided population variations. For the first time, the high court held that federal judges could resolve challenges to the distribution of voters. Brennan also wrote the majority opinion in two other major cases applying the "one person, one vote" doctrine to congressional line-drawing.

The rulings had the effect of shifting seats from rural areas to high-growth districts, especially suburbs, and they served as a basis for attacking racial gerrymandering. But the opinions and others upholding "one person, one vote" were a source of controversy because strict population equality often required splitting historically geographical entities like cities and counties.

It was hard to find an area that Brennan, the court's leading liberal and most senior justice, did not affect in nearly 34 years on the high court before his retirement on July 20 for reasons of health at the age of 84.

Brennan wrote decisions upholding affirmative action and broadening free speech and free press guarantees. One of his landmark opinions, the 1964 *New York Times Co. v. Sullivan*, gave for the first time First Amendment protection to defamatory statements against public officials and established a test that would leave news organizations liable only for publishing knowing or reckless falsehoods — the so-called actual malice standard.

Brennan was a defender of the rights of the accused. Although he failed to convince the court that the death penalty was cruel and unusual punishment — a constant crusade — he was a leader in other areas of defendants' rights: protection against self-incrimination, a right to counsel and the exclusion at trial of illegally obtained evidence, to name a few.

His 1970 *Goldberg v. Kelly* opinion extended the 14th Amendment guarantee of due process to entitle welfare recipients to a hearing before benefits were cut off.

Beyond his signed opinions, Brennan was a master at consensus. His magnetic personality, charm and sheer pragmatism allowed him to negotiate opinions to appeal to a majority on difficult issues. Court scholars said he helped shape the 1958 *Cooper v. Aaron* decision requiring the Little Rock, Ark., schools to desegregate and the 1973 *Roe v. Wade* decision recognizing a right to privacy in the 14th Amendment that protected a woman's decision to have an abortion.

Even his detractors, such as Robert H. Bork, former U.S. Appeals Court judge and rejected high court nominee, described Brennan as "the most powerful justice of this century."

View of Congress

For Congress, Brennan's mark was neither all positive nor all negative, just ringing and powerful. Without Brennan, there likely would not have been a congressional brouhaha over protection of the U.S. flag. He wrote the opinion for the 5-4 majority that struck down a Texas statute that outlawed flag burning, then a federal statute banning flag desecration, saying that both infringed on First Amendment protection of free speech and peaceful political protest. *(Flag burning debate, p. 524)*

In a decision also from the 1989-90 term — that ended up being Brennan's last hurrah — he wrote an opinion allowing Congress to order the Federal Communications Commission (FCC) to give preferential treatment to minorities applying for radio and TV licenses.

The 5-4 ruling in *Metro Broadcasting v. FCC* was a surprise, given the conservative majority's trend of rejecting favored treatment for blacks and women; and it

"There should be no litmus test in the process of confirmation," Bush said in a speech July 25, two days after he named Souter.

COMMITTEE ACTION

The Senate Judiciary Committee approved the Souter nomination Sept. 27 by a 13-1 vote, with Kennedy casting the only "no" vote.

While most members of the committee praised Souter's fairness and open-mindedness, some Democrats voiced reservations.

Republicans generally endorsed him as well qualified, though conservatives chafed a bit for not explicitly opposing abortion and for appearing to leave the door open to some hints of judicial activism.

Democrats' Ambivalence

During committee consideration, several Democratic senators said they hoped their positive impressions of Souter were accurate. Doubts arose from the fact that Souter's testimony in three days before the committee was exceptionally polished and more moderate than the conservative opinions he had written as a New Hampshire Supreme Court justice in 1983-90.

"Sometimes you have to vote with your instincts," said Howard M. Metzenbaum, D-Ohio, who separated himself from his allies in women's groups and civil rights organizations to support Souter.

"My instinct may be wrong," Metzenbaum said. "However, my sense is that David Souter is a fair and open-minded jurist who knows well the weight of the responsibilities which will be placed upon him. Maybe the wish is father to the thought. I hope not."

Kennedy said he was worried that Souter would erode abortion rights as well as civil rights. "We must vote our fears, not our hopes," Kennedy said.

The Leadership Conference on Civil Rights, which had led the fight against Bork in 1987 but was silent on the ultimate appointee, Anthony M. Kennedy, decided to op-

. . . Left His Mark on Congress, Too

was grounded in Brennan's idea of the authority of Congress. *(FCC ruling, p. 379)*

Rep. Don Edwards, D-Calif., said, "He had respect for the three branches of government, unlike other justices." Like other members of Congress, Edwards described Brennan as an institution within an institution.

While some justices had been inclined to reject legislative history in trying to interpret a federal statute, Brennan consistently found currency in the committee reports and floor statements of Congress.

And House legal counsel Steven R. Ross said, "Justice Brennan has always been one of the Congress' better friends on the court," noting that the justice had a broad reading of the Constitution's Speech or Debate Clause, which shielded lawmakers from criminal or civil action over their statements and acts.

In the 1975 *Eastland v. United States Servicemen's Fund*, Brennan concurred in an 8-1 opinion that said the clause barred an injunction seeking to block a Senate subcommittee's subpoena.

Four years later, Brennan was alone in an opinion that Sen. William Proxmire (D-Wis., 1957-88) should not have been liable for charges of defamation in his monthly "Golden Fleece" award. Brennan's dissent in *Hutchinson v. Proxmire* argued that lawmakers' public criticism of government wastefulness should be shielded by the Speech or Debate Clause, even when the statements were in a press release or newsletter.

But in writing the 5-4 majority opinion in the 1979 *Davis v. Passman*, Brennan avoided the question of whether the clause protected a congressman from an employee's discrimination suit and ruled that a worker denied due process and equal protection by federal action could sue for damages. It was the first time the court provided a constitutional basis for job discrimination charges by congressional employees.

That due process decision was typical of Brennan, who, when faced with a match between majority and individual rights, sided with the individual.

His retirement effectively closed an era of liberal activism, begun by the Warren Court, that Brennan kept alive for two decades after Warren's retirement.

The Warren Court (1953-69) took on social issues that previously had been the province of legislators. Its 1954 *Brown v. Board of Education* ruling, outlawing racial segregation in public schools, was a catalyst for the civil rights revolution of the late 1950s and '60s.

Brennan particularly eschewed the notion that the Constitution should be construed strictly in terms of the 18th-century framers. Instead, he read the Constitution with an overlay of modern times.

With his departure, Brennan left behind three justices generally viewed as liberals: Thurgood Marshall, Brennan's most consistent ally; Harry A. Blackmun; and John Paul Stevens.

A native of Newark, N.J., Brennan received a bachelor's degree from the University of Pennsylvania and a law degree from Harvard University. His experience on the bench began in his home state, first as a New Jersey Superior Court judge (1949-50), then as a judge in the appellate division (1950-52). He had been an associate judge on the New Jersey Supreme Court for four years when President Dwight D. Eisenhower in 1956 plucked the 50-year-old Brennan from obscurity and named him to the high court. Since then, Brennan had seen eight presidencies and written more than 1,200 opinions.

After suffering a small stroke earlier in July, Brennan decided to step down. "The strenuous demands of court work and its related duties required or expected of a justice appear at this time to be incompatible with my advancing age and medical condition," he wrote President Bush.

In a separate statement, he said, "It is my hope that the court during my years of service has built a legacy of interpreting the Constitution and federal laws to make them responsible to the needs of the people whom they were intended to benefit and protect. This legacy can and will withstand the test of time."

---

pose Souter. But the civil rights group and women's rights activists failed to sway Metzenbaum or Paul Simon, Ill., the two Democrats most likely to join Kennedy in voting against the nominee.

Biden, who joined with six Democrats and six Republicans to endorse Souter, was among those who said he had trouble making up his mind. It was, he said, a "close decision."

"As I see it, Judge Souter met his burden of proof with respect to some matters and failed to do so with respect to others. His philosophy was neither proven to be wholly inappropriate or wholly acceptable for confirmation," Biden said.

He voiced skepticism about what he called Souter's ambiguous position on many topics, among them abortion and remedies for racial and sex discrimination: "I found most troubling Judge Souter's initial refusal to discuss whether unmarried persons have any fundamental right of privacy — and worse still, his ultimate declaration that whether such rights exist is 'an open question.' "

Biden said the court, in 26 opinions written by 10 justices over the past 17 years, had recognized a fundamental right to privacy. He said in his mind the privacy right was not an open question.

But Biden said overall Souter was the best nominee committee Democrats could hope for from a GOP administration. Those sentiments were echoed by most of the other Democrats.

Simon called Souter's testimony better than his record. "On the basis of the testimony," Simon said, "my guess is that he will uphold *Roe v. Wade* [the 1973 Supreme Court case that legalized abortion nationwide], though his statements were tentative enough that I understand how reasonable people can reach opposite conclusions."

Committee Republicans described the nominee's judicial skill as exceptional and attacked those who would use abortion as a "litmus test."

"This nominee should be judged on his intellectual capacity, background and professional qualifications — not on his willingness to endorse the views or position of any

'Responsibility to Preserve Constitution'

Following is the opening statement by David H. Souter on Sept. 13 before the Senate Judiciary Committee hearings on his nomination to be associate justice of the Supreme Court:

... I would like to take a minute before we begin our dialogue together to say something to you about how I feel about the beginnings that I have come from and about the experiences that I have had that bear on the kind of judge that I am and the kind of judge that I can be expected to be.

I think you know that I spent most of my boyhood in a small town in New Hampshire — Weare, New Hampshire. It was a town large in geography, small in population.

The physical space, the open space between people, however, was not matched by the interspace between them because, as everybody knows who has lived in a small town, there is a closeness of people in a small town which is unattainable anywhere else.

There was in that town no section or place or neighborhood that was determined by anybody's occupation or by anybody's bank balance. Everybody knew everybody else's business, or at least thought they did.

And we were, in a very true sense, intimately aware of other lives. We were aware of lives that were easy, and we were aware of lives that were very hard.

Another thing that we were aware of in that place was the responsibility of people to govern themselves. It was a responsibility that they owed to themselves, and it was a responsibility that they owed and owe to their neighbors. I first learned about that or I first learned the practicalities of that when I used to go over to the town hall in Weare, New Hampshire, on Town Meeting Day. I would sit in the benches in the back of the town hall after school, and that is where I began my lessons in practical government.

As I think you know, I went to high school in Concord, New Hampshire, which is a bigger place, and I went on from there to college and to study law in Cambridge, Massachusetts, and Oxford, England, which are bigger places still. And after I had finished law school, I came back to New Hampshire, and I began the practice of law. And I think probably it is fair to say that I resumed the study of practical government.

I went to work for a law firm in Concord, New Hampshire, and I practiced there for several years. I then became, as I think you know, an assistant attorney general in the criminal division of that office. I was then lucky to be deputy attorney general to Warren [B.] Rudman, and I succeeded him as attorney general in 1976.

The experience of government, though, did not wait until the day came that I entered public as opposed to private law practice; because although in those years of private practice I served the private clients of the firm, I also did something in those days which was very common then.

Perhaps it is less common today — I know it is — but it was an accepted part of private practice in those days to take on a fair share of representation of clients who did not have the money to pay.

I remember very well the first day that I ever spent by myself in a courtroom. I spent [that day] representing a woman whose personal life had become such a shambles that she had lost the custody of her children, and she was trying to get them back. She was not the last of such clients. I represented clients with domestic relations problems who lived sometimes, it seemed to me, in appalling circumstances. I can remember representing a client who was trying to pull her life together after being evicted because she

---

one particular political constituency," said ranking Republican Strom Thurmond, S.C.

Souter Under Scrutiny

As the Souter hearings got under way, many senators remarked about the schism existing on the Supreme Court. Biden noted that the court was split on matters involving the First Amendment's guarantee of freedom of religion, on protections for civil liberties and defendants' rights, and on whether there was a basic right to abortion.

"Because of the close division on the court on the meaning of these constitutional guarantees," Biden told Souter, "if you are confirmed, you will have the power to determine which direction this nation will take, which path we will follow as we reach this critical constitutional crossroad."

The chairman added, "Judge, put bluntly, the burden of proof is on you. . . . A Supreme Court justice can assume his post only if the Senate is persuaded that the nominee is the right person for that position, at that particular junction in history."

Souter, though, took refuge in the history of legal principles and declined to comment, even indirectly, on most of the emotional social issues that might arise in cases at the court. He took pains to conceal his personal views.

He began his testimony by asserting that the greatest responsibility a judge faced was "to make the promises of the Constitution a reality for our time and to preserve that Constitution for the generations that will follow us after we are gone from here." *(Souter statement, this page)*

If Souter had a personal agenda for the bench, he did not reveal it. With few exceptions, Souter's testimony on Sept. 13, 14, and 17 gave little clue to how he would rule on particular disputes.

During his three days of questioning, Souter addressed the following topics:

- **Judicial activism.** Souter declined to cite any recent case in which the court had "improperly created new rights." He passed up chances to criticize judicial activism and refused to comment on an April court ruling that allowed a federal judge to order a school district to raise taxes to put school desegregation into effect.

In a rare use of loaded terminology, Souter said courts sometimes must fill a "vacuum" left by legislators.

Charles E. Grassley, R-Iowa, was among senators challenging the judge's comment. "If we are going to have a Supreme Court that thinks it can fill vacuums every time there is a perceived problem," he said, "then . . . you are going to be a very busy person, because democratic self-government does not always move with the speed or the consensus or the wisdom of philosopher kings who might best fill those vacuums."

Souter, whose forte was disarming the questioner, tried to dispel the notion that he would interpret the Constitution broadly. He said he was referring to a court's using existing rights in the Constitution to address social problems. He noted that in 1954, in *Brown v. Board of Education*, the court ordered school desegregation as Congress and states had declined to do.

In *Brown*, the court said separate public schools for black and white students violated the Equal Protection Clause of the 14th Amendment.

Grassley said, "If you are saying that when a state fails to live up to what the 14th Amendment says, in terms of equal protection and due process, that the court can step in, then that is fine. But if you mean that the court can otherwise fill vacuums, that is another thing."

couldn't pay the rent.

Although cases like that were not the cases upon which the firm paid the rent, those were not remarkable cases for lawyers in private practice in those days before governmentally funded legal services. And they were the cases that we took at that time because taking them was the only way to make good on the supposedly open door of our courts to the people who needed to get inside and to get what courts had to offer through the justice system.

I think it is fair to say — I am glad it is fair to say — that even today, with so much governmentally funded legal service, there are lawyers in private practice in our profession who are doing the same thing.

As you know, I did go on to public legal service, and in the course of doing that, I met not only legislators and the administrators that one finds in the government, but I began to become familiar with the criminal justice system in my state and in our nation. I met victims and sometimes I met the survivors of victims. I met defendants. I met that train of witnesses from the clergy to con artists who passed through our system and find themselves, either willingly or unwillingly, part of a search for truth and part of a search for those results that we try to sum up with the words of justice.

As you also know, after those years I became a trial judge, and my experience with the working of government and the judicial system broadened there because I was a trial judge of general jurisdiction, and I saw every sort and condition of the people of my state that a trial court of general jurisdiction is exposed to. I saw litigants in international commercial litigation for millions, and I saw children who were the unwitting victims of domestic disputes and custody fights which somehow seemed to defy any reasonable solution, however hard we worked at it.

I saw, once again, the denizens of the criminal justice system, and I saw domestic litigants. I saw appellants from the juvenile justice system who were appealing their findings of delinquency.

And, in fact, I had maybe one of the great experiences of my entire life in seeing week in and week out the members of the trial juries of our states who are rightly called the consciences of our communities. And I worked with them, and I learned from them, and I will never forget my days with them.

When those days on the trial court were over, there were two experiences that I took away with me or two lessons that I had learned, and the lessons remain with me today.

The first lesson, simple as it is, is that whatever court we are in, whatever we are doing, whether we are on a trial court or an appellate court, at the end of our task some human being is going to be affected. Some human life is going to be changed in some way by what we do, whether we do it as trial judges or whether we do it as appellate judges, as far removed from the trial arena as it is possible to be.

The second lesson that I learned in that time is that if, indeed, we are going to be trial judges, whose rulings will affect the lives of other people and who are going to change their lives by what we do, we had better use every power of our minds and our hearts and our beings to get those rulings right.

I am conscious of those two lessons, as I have been for all of the years that I was on an appellate course. I am conscious of them as I sit here today, suddenly finding myself the nominee of the president of the United States to undertake the greatest responsibility that any judge in our republic can undertake: The responsibility to join with eight other people, to make the promises of the Constitution a reality for our time, and to preserve that Constitution for the generations that will follow us after we are gone from here.

I am mindful of those two lessons when I tell you this: That if you believe and the Senate of the United States believes that it is right to confirm my nomination, then I will accept those responsibilities as obligations to all of the people in the United States whose lives will be affected by my stewardship of the Constitution. ■

Souter said he meant the former.

• **Abortion and privacy.** From the day Souter was selected, abortion dominated public interest in the nomination, and the Senate hearings reflected that interest.

Biden tried to draw out the judge's philosophy about rights that were not enumerated in the Constitution but had been inferred by the court. The Constitution contained no language about privacy, but the Supreme Court had extended the word "liberty" in the Due Process Clause of the 14th Amendment to protect privacy.

The Supreme Court's 1965 ruling in *Griswold v. Connecticut* relied on the term "privacy" to protect a married couple's use of contraception. The right to abortion flowed from this and other decisions.

Souter said, agreeing with the *Griswold* holding, "I believe that the Due Process Clause of the 14th Amendment does recognize and does protect an unenumerated right of privacy." He said marital privacy should be regarded as a fundamental right.

Biden asked, "Do you agree that procreation is a fundamental right?"

"I would assume that if we are going to have any core concept of marital privacy, that would certainly have to rank at its fundamental heart," Souter said.

Biden continued, "Now, let us say that a woman and/or her mate uses such a birth control device and it fails. Does she still have a constitutional right to choose not to become pregnant?" That was where Souter stopped. He said the question implicated *Roe v. Wade* and said because it was likely that the case would again be before the court, he could not answer.

He declined to be pinned down on the balance between a woman's "liberty interest" after conception and the state's interest in protecting the unborn.

Others tried to press Souter on legal principles or on his personal opinion on abortion. To questioning by Herb Kohl, D-Wis., Souter said, "I do not sit here under oath having any commitment about what I would do if that case were to come before me."

In response to questions from Metzenbaum, Souter said he understood the anguish of women facing an abortion decision and said he suddenly — in the middle of the questioning — had remembered an experience from 24 years earlier.

As a Harvard law student, Souter had been a proctor in an undergraduate dormitory. A student and his pregnant girlfriend came to Souter about the woman's desire to "self-abort." Souter said, "I spent two hours in a small dormitory bedroom that afternoon, in that room because that was the most private place we could get so that no one in the next suite of rooms could hear, listening to her and trying to counsel her to approach her problem in a way different from what she was doing, and your question has brought that back to me."

Metzenbaum said he believed Souter was more empathetic to the interests of people who oppose abortion.

One abortion opponent, Gordon J. Humphrey, R-N.H., in separate questioning rebuked Souter for saying he did not have a personal response to abortion while he was a trustee at a hospital that performed abortions. Similarly, Howard Phillips of The Conservative Caucus objected to Souter because Souter had approved that hospital policy.

The nominee again spurned abortion questioning during his final day testifying, and when asked what would happen if the Supreme Court overruled *Roe v. Wade*, he said legislators would pass a variety of laws. He did not immediately address problems that women who wanted abortions would have.

Abortion rights groups urged the committee to reject Souter because he would not say whether he believed there was a right to abortion.

Kate Michelman, director of the National Abortion Rights Action League, told the committee, "All the evidence points to the fact that he will vote to overrule *Roe v. Wade*." Souter insisted to senators that he had an open mind on the issue.

• **Criminal law.** Souter explicitly endorsed the death penalty, putting him in league with the existing court majority. Justices Brennan and Thurgood Marshall both had dissented from every capital punishment case.

Souter described the court's 1966 ruling in *Miranda v. Arizona*, requiring police to read suspects their rights, as a "pragmatic" effort by the court to make sure that defendants' confessions were not coerced. In earlier testimony he had said that some of the rulings of the Earl Warren era (1953-69) caused him, a former attorney general, to chafe at new restrictions on the state.

• **Voter reapportionment.** Souter said he sided with the majority in a 1962 court ruling, *Baker v. Carr*, that said federal courts had the power to resolve voter reapportionment disputes.

The one-person, one-vote decision had been used by some conservatives as an example of judicial activism. While Souter said he thought the dissent in the opinion was "very powerful," he said he subscribed to the majority view allowing the court to review the apportionment of state legislatures under the 14th Amendment's equal protection standard.

• **Civil rights.** Souter defended his civil rights record, said discrimination was a great national tragedy but was sketchy on the extent of government authority in remedying race bias.

In 1976, as New Hampshire attorney general, Souter submitted a brief to the U.S. Supreme Court defending New Hampshire's failure to comply with a federal equal-employment law that requested that employers file statistics on racial composition in the workplace. (The Supreme Court rejected Souter's appeal.)

And as an assistant attorney general, he had signed a brief supporting literacy tests for voters.

Kennedy, who raised both of these actions, had asserted early in the hearings, "There is little in his record that demonstrates real solicitude for the rights of those who are the weakest and most powerless in our society."

Souter's brief challenging requirements by the Equal Employment Opportunity Commission took the position that it was unconstitutional to require employers to compile reports of those statistics.

Kennedy said, "A reading of the brief would indicate that you did not believe that Congress had the power to implement and develop that legislation [aimed at job discrimination]."

Souter responded that at the time he had "no comprehensive personal view" of the constitutional authority of Congress in eradicating job discrimination. He said he was, first and foremost, representing the state as a client and that it was not clear in the mid-1970s how broad Congress' power on affirmative action was.

Kennedy admonished him that he was not only the lawyer for the governor but for all the people of the state.

Kennedy asked Souter about the state's contention that Congress did not have the authority to ban literacy tests for voting rights. "You said that if people who could not read were permitted to cast ballots, it would dilute the votes of literate citizens," the senator said.

Souter urged Kennedy to look at him today, not as he was 20 years ago, as an advocate for the New Hampshire governor's position.

"What troubles me," Kennedy said, "is that you said that the Congress did not have the power to collect data on race discrimination. Now, you say that Congress does not have the power to ban literacy tests for voting. Congress is attempting to deal with the profound historical, national problem that this country has ached at over its history and continues to do so today."

Souter rejoined, "I hope one thing will be clear . . . that with respect to the societal problems of the United States today there is none which, in my judgment, is more tragic or more demanding of the efforts of every American in the Congress and out of the Congress than the removal of societal discrimination in matters of race and in the matters of invidious discrimination, which we are unfortunately too familiar with."

In later questioning, he said the appropriate response to discrimination "is not to say, 'Stop doing it,' but to say 'Undo it.' "

He said one of "the most significant subjects" to be developed in the court in the near future was the extent of Congress' power in remedying discrimination.

• **Original intent.** Souter described himself as "an interpretist" and said that rather than looking for the original meaning of the words of the Constitution, the court should look at the original principle that the framers intended.

When Dennis DeConcini, D-Ariz., asked Souter to describe his approach to legislative history in the construction of statutes, Souter said he turned to legislative history that was a "reliable" guide to what Congress meant.

"What we are looking for is an intent which can be attributed to the institution itself . . . [evidence] we can genuinely point to and say, this represents not merely the statement of one committee member or committee staffer or one person on the floor, but . . . [the] institution or a sufficiently large enough number of the members of that institution."

• **Establishment Clause.** Arlen Specter, R-Pa., pressed Souter on his view of the Establishment Clause of the First Amendment. While Souter was cautious, he implied that he differed with an April 17 Supreme Court decision (*Employment Division, Department of Human Resources v. Smith*) that set a new standard for a state trying to justify a criminal law that conflicted with a religious practice. The standard made it easier for states to outlaw actions that incidentally were part of religious activity.

The case involved an Oregon statute barring use of the drug peyote, a traditional element of American Indian religious worship. The court, ruling 5-4 with conservative-leaning justices in the majority, upheld the Oregon law. Without commenting on the case itself, Souter said a prohibition that ended up affecting a religious practice must be balanced by a "compelling state interest." The five justices instead weighed whether a criminal statute was directed at religious practices.

• **Role of precedent.** Thurmond asked the judge about his philosophy for reversing past decisions.

When a judge thinks a case was wrongly decided, Souter said, he should look at whether it has come to be relied on by the public at large, legislatures and the courts. "We ask in some context whether private citizens in their lives have relied upon it in their own planning to such a degree that, in fact, it would be a great hardship in overruling it now," Souter said.

Souter stressed that his five years on a state trial court had left him with two lessons that he thought would help him as a high court justice.

One was that, "at the end of our task some human being is going to be affected, some human life is going to be changed in some way by what we do." The second was that people's behavior would be influenced by court rulings. "We had better use every power of our minds and our hearts and our beings to get those rulings right."

Committee Politics

After Souter's testimony, the committee heard from witnesses who were divided on whether he should be confirmed. He received bipartisan support from New Hampshire officials and national figures, including Griffin B. Bell, who was President Jimmy Carter's attorney general. Abortion rights and women's groups were most strongly opposed.

Souter's confirmation hearings ended Sept. 19. His knowledge of the law and his easy manner — a contrast to the combative approach of Reagan and some of his nominees — drew approval from a majority of the committee. Biden called Souter's presentation a "tour de force."

Immediately after the committee finished hearing testimony, four senators who had voted against Bork — Specter; John H. Chafee, R-R.I.; Jim Exon, D-Neb.; and John W. Warner, R-Va. — took to the floor to announce their support of Souter.

Meanwhile, five Democratic senators not on the committee had by Sept. 27 announced that they would oppose Souter: Brock Adams, Wash.; Bill Bradley, N.J.; Alan Cranston, Calif.; Frank R. Lautenberg, N.J.; and Barbara A. Mikulski, Md. They said they did not believe Souter would vote to uphold *Roe v. Wade*.

"Judge Souter's refusal to discuss the status of women under the Constitution stands in stark and disappointing contrast to his otherwise comprehensive discourse" on other constitutional issues, Mikulski said.

Many more senators spoke out in support of Souter. Alan J. Dixon, D-Ill., said, "Judge Souter has shown himself to be pragmatic, not doctrinaire, and with a respect for the rights and liberties of the individuals the Constitution protects."

FLOOR ACTION

The Senate's 90-9 vote to confirm Souter came Oct. 2 after less than four hours of debate.

Most senators praised Souter, who despite his brief tenure on the federal appeals court had gained the upper hand in his confirmation hearings by satisfying most members' queries and effectively deflecting questions on controversial issues.

Majority Leader George J. Mitchell, D-Maine, a former federal judge, said he believed Souter had a "a reasoned approach and sound understanding" of the Constitution. Of some senators' concerns that they did not know what kind of justice Souter would make, Mitchell said that Congress had a place, too, on constitutional matters and could respond if it believed the court was leaving a void.

Biden had said that less was known about Souter than any other high court nominee in the past quarter-century.

Before the vote, many of the nine senators opposing the nomination attacked Souter's refusal to state his position on privacy and abortion rights. Cranston said a vote for Souter placed "women's lives in jeopardy." He said, "I intend to do more than just hope for the best."

All the "no" votes were from Democrats. In addition to those who had previously announced their opposition, they were Daniel K. Akaka, Hawaii; Quentin N. Burdick, N.D.; and John Kerry, Mass. Pete Wilson, R-Calif., did not vote. He was in California campaigning for governor but earlier had said he supported Souter. ■

Bush Shifts U.S. Bench Further to the Right

Taking into account 85 new judgeships created under a 1990 law, 38 other vacancies and the 67 federal judges he appointed in 1989-90, President Bush had named or would be able to name at least 190 judges — about one-fourth of the federal judiciary.

Between Bush's and Ronald Reagan's judicial appointments — similar in their conservative profiles — the two GOP presidents by 1992 would have selected an overwhelming majority of the federal bench.

By then, said University of Massachusetts Professor Sheldon Goldman, the federal courts would have been as strikingly reshaped as they were after 12 years of Franklin D. Roosevelt's appointments. Goldman and other experts said that there was a potential for a major shift in how courts decided social policy issues.

Differences between Bush's and Reagan's nominees were few, according to observers across the political spectrum.

Edwin Meese III, a former Reagan attorney general working at the Heritage Foundation, said Bush administration officials "have done an excellent job." Meese, who while in office talked boldly of trying to remake the judiciary, added, "The results are the same as in the Reagan administration."

On the liberal side, George Kassouf, director of the Alliance for Justice's Judicial Selection Project, said Bush's nominees "don't bring out the same kind of controversies as the Reagan nominees, but they are the same good soldiers in the conservative movement." Kassouf's group criticized both administrations' dearth of female and minority appointments and contended that Bush appointed judges "insensitive to the needs of society's disadvantaged." Other outside monitoring groups and Democratic senators echoed the criticism.

The Bush administration, however, rejected that view and said it was trying to find more qualified female and minority candidates.

Goldman said that Bush appeared to be trying for more diversity than Reagan did. He pointed to Bush's record on the District of Columbia courts, in which the president was free from senators' recommendations. Of the four appointments made, one was a woman and one was a black man.

And the president was seeking help on Capitol Hill. He wrote to Senate Minority Leader Bob Dole, R-Kan., on Nov. 30, noting the role of GOP senators in choosing district court candidates and asking for more qualified female and minority recommendations.

At the same time, Bush emphasized to senators that he would not compromise on his goal of naming conservatives: "By 'qualified candidates,' I mean not only persons who have the training, intellect, character and temperament to be excellent judges, but also persons who understand the separation of powers and the judicial role within our constitutional system and who are committed to interpreting the law and not legislating from the bench."

Looking for Conservatives

In a judicial context, conservatism favored government's interest over an individual's. Conservative judges strictly construed the Constitution and federal statutes and generally left to legislators the establishment of new rights or remedies for societal ills. "Liberal" judges had the reverse priority.

The 1930s and '40s saw the evolution from an "economically conservative bench to a New Deal bench," said Goldman, who had written extensively on judicial selection. He said the influence of the Reagan-Bush appointments similarly would have "very profound consequences."

Citing the new judges' conservatism, Goldman predicted, "One of those consequences will be a revitalization of federalism. The ball for civil rights protection, for example, is now with state courts. Some state courts already have shown themselves to be more liberal [than federal courts] on civil rights and civil liberties issues. A majority still have not."

One notable distinction between the confirmation process under Bush and that under Reagan was the reaction from the public and Democratic senators to nominees.

The firestorms that met some of Reagan's choices were non-existent during the 101st Congress.

Bush's first appointment to the Supreme Court, David H. Souter, came through confirmation hearings largely unscathed and won an overwhelming 90-9 Senate confirmation vote Oct. 2. *(Vote 259, p. 52-S; Souter appointment, p. 508)*

That was the only recorded Senate vote on any of Bush's judicial nominees, although during a voice vote on Clarence Thomas' nomination to the U.S. Court of Appeals for the District of Columbia Circuit two senators registered their opposition. *(Thomas nomination, p. 518)*

And by the end of the 101st Congress, only three Bush nominees had not been approved, two of whom were submitted in the fall of 1990.

Liberals criticized the third, Floridian Kenneth L. Ryskamp for the 11th Circuit, covering Florida, Georgia and Alabama. After allegations arose regarding Ryskamp's record on civil rights and membership in a private club that reportedly had discriminated against blacks and Jews, the Senate Judiciary Committee shelved his nomination in the 101st Congress.

People for the American Way, a civil liberties group, also attacked Ryskamp, saying that he had ruled against civil rights plaintiffs more often than other judges in the Miami district or nationwide. But Justice Department officials disputed the group's figures and insisted that Ryskamp was committed to civil rights. And a majority of an American Bar Association (ABA) judicial screening panel gave Ryskamp its highest rating.

The private club in question, the Riviera Country Club in Coral Gables, had a reputation in the Miami area for discriminating against blacks and Jews. In 1990 it adopted a no-discrimination clause in its bylaws; the club's manager said that had been the unwritten policy for many years.

Judiciary Committee Chairman Joseph R. Biden Jr., D-Del., said at the end of the 101st Congress that there was not enough time to hold a hearing.

Ryskamp and the two other unconfirmed candidates were renominated Jan. 8, 1991. But on April 11, the Senate Judiciary Committee rejected Ryskamp's nomination on a party-line 8-6 vote.

Unlike some Reagan nominees, no Bush nominee was considered an engine for judicial conservatism. Reagan chose men who helped drive the conservative agenda, such as Antonin Scalia and Robert H. Bork. Both were named first to the D.C. Circuit Court of Appeals, then to the Supreme Court. Scalia was confirmed for the high court; Bork was denied confirmation in a highly publicized battle. *(1982 Almanac, p. 25-A; Scalia, 1986 Almanac, p. 67; Bork, 1987 Almanac, p. 271)*

Scalia, Bork and other well-known conservatives appointed by Reagan — mostly on the appeals courts — had "star quality," said Sen. Charles E. Grassley, R-Iowa, who speculated that Bush might have been trying to avoid controversy with lower-profile candidates.

Demographics

During the 101st Congress, Bush named, and the Senate confirmed, one Supreme Court justice, 18 appeals court judges and 48 district court judges. (Bush also appointed four judges to the U.S. Court of Appeals for the Federal Circuit, a court of limited jurisdiction, created in 1982, which was not included in these comparisons of appointments.)

Of the 18 appeals court appointees, two were women (11.1 percent); one appointee was a black (5.6 percent); and one was Hispanic (5.6 percent). Of the 48 district court judges, five were women (10.4 percent); one was black (2.1 percent); and one was Hispanic (2.1 percent).

The Bush percentages for women and minority appointments were slightly higher than Reagan's eight-year totals but did not come close to President Jimmy Carter's 1977-80 record.

Administration officials and GOP senators explained Bush's record by saying that women and minorities still were not at the top of the profession, from which nominees were drawn.

The ABA estimated that 20 percent of the legal profession was female. Most female lawyers worked in private firms, according to the ABA, yet only 6 percent of all partners were women; 25 percent of associates were women.

Racial minorities were an even smaller percentage of the profession. The National Law Journal reported as of September 1989 that in the country's largest law firms fewer than 2 percent of the partners were black or another minority.

"One doesn't need to be a partner to serve on the bench," said former Michigan Supreme Court Justice Dennis W. Archer (1986-90). Archer was chairman of the ABA's Commission on Opportunities for Minorities in the Profession and cited state supreme courts that had black justices.

"It is not accurate to say that the applicant pool doesn't exist," Archer said. "But it is more correct to say that they [Bush officials] do not seek minority or women applicants, and it is clear that Democrats need not apply."

The majority of blacks registered Democratic.

Archer argued that a person who had been on a court for a number of years usually shed his partisanship and dealt only with the law. "I can understand why Bush wouldn't want to appoint someone very active in [presidential opponent Michael S.] Dukakis' campaign." But he added that if he really wanted to appoint minorities, Bush would turn to Democrats who were not known for their partisanship and who had long court experience.

Before Reagan's years, it was not uncommon for between 5 percent and 10 percent of a president's nominations to come from the other party. With perhaps just four exceptions, Goldman said, all Bush appointees were Republican.

Senate Judiciary Committee Democrats criticized the race and gender profile.

Patrick J. Leahy of Vermont said of Bush aides, "They are just really comfortable with the good old boy network. They [the nominees] are the people who they would see back at their school clubs or who they hang around with, the wealthy people they grew up with."

Murray G. Dickman, assistant to Attorney General Dick Thornburgh, countered that the administration was trying to bolster the numbers of women and minorities. Dickman, who coordinated screening of candidates, said Bush was hamstrung in district court appointments by the tradition of accepting recommendations from GOP senators, who might not aggressively seek diverse candidates.

Imprints on the Bench

The following chart shows the impact on the federal bench of presidents from Franklin D. Roosevelt to George Bush. The 1990 law creating 85 new judgeships (HR 5316 — PL 101-650) took effect after Congress adjourned, so at year's end Bush had not filled any of the positions.

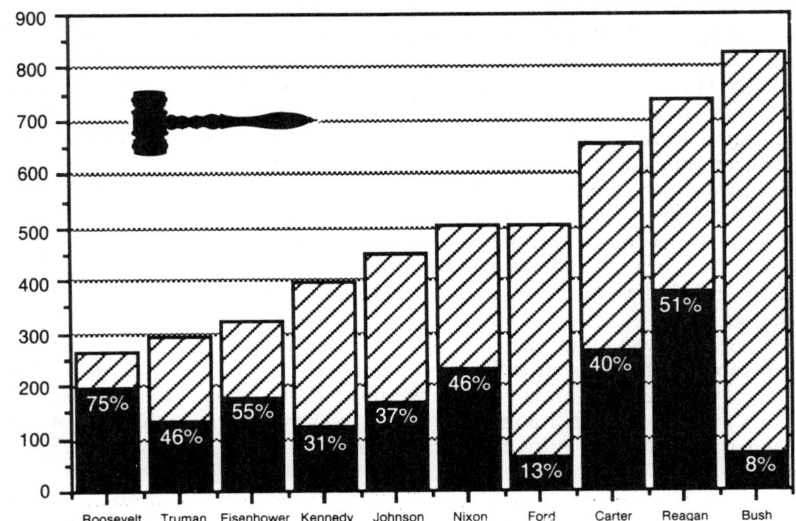

President	Supreme Court	Court of Appeals [1]	District Courts [2]	Total	Total Judgeships [3]
Roosevelt (1933-45)	9	52	136	197	262
Truman (1945-53)	4	27	102	133	292
Eisenhower (1953-61)	5	45	127	177	322
Kennedy (1961-63)	2	20	102	124	395
Johnson (1963-69)	2	41	125	168	449
Nixon (1969-74)	4	45	182	231	504
Ford (1974-77)	1	12	52	65	504
Carter (1977-81)	0	56	206	262	657
Reagan (1981-89)	3	83	292	378	740
Bush (1989-90)	1	18	48	67	825

[1] *Does not include the appeals court for the Federal Circuit.*
[2] *Includes district courts in the territories.* [3] *Total judgeships authorized in president's last year in office.*

SOURCE: Administrative Office of the U.S. Courts

Goldman said, "Until the Carter administration, the overwhelming portrait of the judiciary was white and male. With the Carter administration, they made very substantial inroads.... But even with Carter, the judges still were overwhelmingly white and male. There was backsliding with Reagan, but he did put the first woman on the Supreme Court."

Other statistics that emerged from questionnaires supplied to the Senate Judiciary Committee: The average age of the nominees was 50. A majority of them reported their net worth at more than $500,000. About one-third put their wealth at more than $1 million.

A majority attended schools that were privately funded rather than state-supported. Slightly more than half of the nominees had some judicial experience, either on a state or federal court or as a magistrate. The majority also received a unanimous "well-qualified" rating, the ABA's top and nearly one-third of all the appointees had worked for the Reagan administration.

People for the American Way, a liberal group that lobbied for scrutiny of candidates who belonged to private clubs, reported that 26 nominees said that they belonged to clubs that had discriminatory membership policies.

"Twelve nominees reported that they resigned from these clubs prior to their nomination, while others cited changes in the clubs' policies," its report said. "The remaining handful ultimately resigned their club memberships after tough questioning from the Senate Judiciary Committee."

In August 1990, the Judiciary Committee unanimously adopted a resolution saying that it was inappropriate for nominees or potential nominees to belong to discriminatory clubs "unless such persons are actively engaged in bona fide efforts to eliminate the discriminatory practices."

Judicial Philosophy

In his first year in office, Bush was slow to name judges and drew complaints from conservatives that he was allowing the Reagan judicial legacy to founder. He put 15 judges on the bench in 1989, the fewest of any president in a single year since 1963. There were 59 vacancies at the start of 1990, many of them since early 1989. *(1989 Almanac, p. 239)*

Clarence Thomas Easily Confirmed . . .

After an anticipated fight failed to materialize, the Senate on March 6 easily approved the nomination of Clarence Thomas for one of three vacancies on the U.S. Court of Appeals for the District of Columbia Circuit, a court often regarded as the second highest in the country and a steppingstone to the Supreme Court.

Sens. Howard M. Metzenbaum, D-Ohio, who cast the only vote against Thomas in the Judiciary Committee, and David Pryor, D-Ark., were the only members who registered opposition to Thomas on the floor. Both said Thomas did not understand age-discrimination law and blamed him for botched discrimination claims in the 1980s. The issue of lapsed complaints emerged in Thomas' confirmation hearing, but most senators appeared satisfied that the agency was ultimately able to track age-discrimination claims.

Pryor, who was chairman of the Senate Special Aging Committee, said, "Clarence Thomas has been responsible for allowing thousands of age-discrimination claims to lapse the statute of limitations." Pryor was referring to the time limit for pursuing private lawsuits for redress.

BACKGROUND

Thomas had been formally nominated Oct. 30, 1989, by President Bush, to replace Robert H. Bork, who resigned from the court in 1988. A black conservative, Thomas had been mentioned by some Republicans as a potential successor to the only black Supreme Court justice, 81-year-old Thurgood Marshall.

President Ronald Reagan chose three Supreme Court nominees from the D.C. Circuit: Antonin Scalia, whom the Senate confirmed in 1986; Bork, who was rejected in 1987; and Douglas H. Ginsburg, who withdrew from consideration for the position in 1987.

For the eight years before joining the court, Thomas was chairman of the Equal Employment Opportunity Commission (EEOC). He worked for Sen. John C. Danforth, R-Mo., as a legislative assistant in 1979-81 and served in the Department of Education as assistant secretary for civil rights in 1981-82, before being named to the EEOC. He was a staff attorney for Monsanto Co. in 1977-79.

Thomas was born in Savannah, Ga., and raised by his grandparents in rural Pinpoint, Ga. During his hearing, committee members and Thomas himself made much of his rise from poverty. Thomas graduated in 1971 from Holy Cross College and in 1974 from Yale Law School. He began his legal career as an assistant Missouri attorney general under Danforth, before Danforth's election to the Senate. The Missouri senator became one of Thomas' strongest backers in the confirmation process.

Republican Pre-emptive Strike

Stung by past defeats of conservative judicial nominees, Senate Judiciary Committee Republicans engaged in a pre-emptive strike to deter majority Democrats from attacking nominee Thomas. Conservatives in and out of Congress were embittered by the Senate's 1987 rejection of U.S. Supreme Court nominee Bork and by the Judiciary Committee's August 1989 vote blocking the nomination of William Lucas as assistant attorney general in charge of the Civil Rights Division.

"We can't be caught off guard this time," said Charles E. Grassley of Iowa, who joined other committee Republicans in loudly criticizing the questions that Chairman Joseph R. Biden Jr., Del., and other committee Democrats asked Thomas during the screening process before his appearance before the committee.

But Democratic members said the request presented legitimate demands of senators. They said the requests were specific and were necessitated by the numerous questions that had arisen about EEOC policies since Thomas had become chairman in May 1982.

The requests reflected concern over complaints about Thomas by members and outside groups and appeared partly intended to track possible bias against Hispanic EEOC employees and the commission's handling of age-discrimination cases.

Biden got a vote of confidence of sorts from ranking Republican Strom Thurmond, S.C., his predecessor as Judiciary chairman. Thurmond issued a statement saying, "The committee chairman has the right and responsibility to check the background of any appointee."

The committee requested, among other things, information on thousands of age-discrimination cases that had fallen through the cracks of the EEOC's enforcement proceedings in the 1980s.

The request also sought information on disparate-impact cases, which alleged discrimination based on neutral employment criteria that had been shown to have a disproportionate adverse impact on minorities.

Judiciary Democrats Metzenbaum and Paul Simon, Ill., were the only two members of the Labor and Human Resources Committee who voted against Thomas when he was reconfirmed in 1986 as head of the EEOC.

Before that 14-2 vote, Thomas was criticized for ordering EEOC attorneys to stop trying to meet minority hiring goals and timetables in job-discrimination cases.

But once Bush picked up the pace, conservatives were satisfied. Clint Bolick, director of the Landmark Legal Foundation Center for Civil Rights, said, "This is one area that conservatives have to be pleased with the Bush administration, from a quality and a philosophy standpoint."

Reagan sought judges who would not engage in judicial activism, defined by rulings prohibiting prayer in the public schools, establishing a constitutional right of privacy (including a woman's right to an abortion) and expanding the rights of defendants. His administration systematically screened the judicial philosophy of candidates, the president having adopted the GOP charge for judges who believed in "the decentralization of the federal government and efforts to return decision-making power to state and local elected officials."

The Supreme Court began swinging conservative during the late 1980s, and the lower courts began to follow as previous administrations' nominees retired and Reagan

. . .To Appeals Court for D.C. Circuit

He told the Labor Committee he would resume efforts to enforce goals and timetables. *(1986 Almanac, p. 581)*

COMMITTEE ACTION

Despite criticism from Republicans who thought he was using the information request as a means of delaying the start of Senate hearings, Biden did not delay and the Judiciary Committee on Feb. 22 voted 13-1 to approve Thomas for the vacancy on the court.

Metzenbaum, saying Thomas had displayed a lack of knowledge about age-discrimination law during his confirmation hearing, cast the only no vote. Other Democrats said Thomas was qualified to serve on the appeals court. But several made clear they were not addressing his qualifications for any future Supreme Court vacancy.

Despite warnings from conservatives that he would be skewered by the committee, Thomas fielded generally congenial questions during his Feb. 6 hearing and appeared to appease skeptical senators with a promise to keep his personal views in check.

"My obligation in all circumstances would be to follow Supreme Court precedent, not to establish law on my own," Thomas said. "I do not think that district court judges or court of appeals judges have the option of roaming unfettered on judicial terrain."

At the outset, Biden said that many of the concerns raised about Thomas' EEOC supervision, which were the basis for the lengthy document request, turned out to be "totally meritless."

Senior-citizens' groups and some civil rights organizations had criticized Thomas. After he was nominated, 23 organizations sent a letter to Biden saying that Thomas' actions at the EEOC "suggest that he lacks the commitment to equal justice, the qualifications and the judicial temperament for a lifetime appointment on one of the nation's most important courts."

But most of those groups neither testified at the hearing nor submitted statements.

Age-Discrimination Questions

Thomas' policies at the EEOC and his approach to job bias were the focus of much of the questioning.

Some of the most pointed remarks came from Metzenbaum, who criticized Thomas for allowing age-discrimination complaints to lapse at the EEOC. Because the commission did not process the complaints in a timely fashion, those employees were barred from pursuing private lawsuits for redress. As a result, in 1988, Congress extended by 18 months the statute of limitations for age claims that had slipped through the cracks.

While Thomas said that he accepted the blame for the delays, he said they stemmed in part from the EEOC policy of investigating each complaint. He also disputed the estimate of 13,000 delayed complaints, saying the actual number was 900. An EEOC spokesman later corrected the figure to 2,292 complaints. Thomas said the agency had since instituted a national data system to track age-discrimination filings.

Nonetheless, his nomination drew criticism from the National Council on Aging and from the Women Employed Institute. Both organizations sent representatives to testify at the hearing.

A statement from the council said that Thomas "fails the test of unbiased and unflagging enforcement" of federal age-discrimination laws.

Thomas said he had inherited an EEOC riddled with problems. "When I first arrived at EEOC, the agency quite simply did not function," he said. "I attempted over a period of almost eight years to bring leadership to the organization."

In contrast to Thomas' assertions, Nancy Kreiter, who was the research director of Women Employed, said, "The agency he inherited was in way better shape than the one he leaves behind."

Metzenbaum agreed. "I have some concerns about whether the agency has tried to remedy the effects of discrimination on women, minorities and the elderly," he said.

Thomas had resisted affirmative-action plans that called for numerical hiring goals and timetables to remedy discrimination. A number of senators questioned his sensitivity to other minorities.

Thomas' response: "The reason I became a lawyer was to make sure that minorities and individuals who have not had access gain access in society. Now, I may differ from others on how best to do that, but the objective has always been to include those who have been excluded."

Edward M. Kennedy, D-Mass., said, "That's a very fine statement and commentary. I don't think anyone can ask for any better assurances."

For those who still needed assurances, the support Thomas received from some senators answered many of their concerns. Democratic Sens. Sam Nunn, Ga., and Charles S. Robb, Va., testified in Thomas' behalf.

Several senators joked about Danforth's extensive effort to help Thomas win confirmation. "Sen. Danforth will be glad when this is over," Biden said. "He will quit calling us each three times a day."

---

and Bush judges took their place.

Said Goldman, "One thing does stand out: It is my sense that there was a deliberate effort to lower the thermostat. They have stayed away from the red-flag nominations."

Critics accused Bush of deliberately trying to avoid controversy, chastened by the Bork battle. Dickman, of the Justice Department, acknowledged that the bruising Bork fight in 1987 entered the thinking of administration officials, but he contended that they did not reject potential nominees because they were outspoken.

Meese attributed the comparative lack of controversy to Reagan's having begun the transformation on the judiciary. So now, he said, Bush's appointments were not startling. Reagan "was carrying out one of the major mandates on which he was elected," Meese said. "He needed to correct the judicial activism trend of the courts. He did that and changed it back to a course of constitutional fidelity." ■

Bill Creates 85 Judgeships for Bush To Fill

With relatively little controversy, the majority-Democratic Congress passed legislation (HR 5316) giving President Bush 85 new federal judgeships to fill — the first increase in the federal judiciary since 1984.

Attached to the legislation, which the House cleared in the early morning hours of Oct. 28, was a congressional mandate for judges to adopt special plans to speed up civil litigation. The directive, softened in response to opposition from federal judges, left the details of such plans up to federal judges in most districts, but required in 10 districts the adoption of specific guidelines, including an 18-month deadline for bringing cases to trial. *(Provisions, p. 522)*

> **BOXSCORE**
>
> **Legislation:** Federal judgeships, PL 101-650 (HR 5316, S 2648).
>
> **Major action:** Signed, Dec. 1. Cleared by House, Oct. 28 (session of Oct. 27). Passed by Senate, Oct. 27; by House, 387-18, Sept. 27.
>
> **Reports:** House Judiciary (H Rept 101-733); Senate Judiciary (S Rept 101-416).

The legislation, signed by Bush on Dec. 1, added 74 district court judgeships and 11 appellate posts. The Judicial Conference of the United States, the federal judiciary's policy-making body, had requested 96 new judgeships.

Pork-barrel politics shaped the allocation of new seats. Judgeships not recommended by the Judicial Conference were added for Republican senators on the Judiciary Committee and for members of both parties on the House subcommittee that handled the bill. Texas, home state of the Democratic chairman of the House Judiciary Committee, Jack Brooks, got the largest number of new seats — 11.

A separate bill (HR 1620) added to the legislation as it neared passage called for a national commission to consider alternatives to the unwieldy congressional process of impeaching tenured federal judges. Another measure folded into the final bill (HR 5381) put into effect a batch of largely non-controversial recommendations of the congressionally established Federal Courts Study Committee. *(Impeachment, 1989 Almanac, p. 229)*

The judgeships bill also attracted other late add-ons, including measures to encourage the networks to develop guidelines on TV violence and to give artists copyright protections against modifications of their works. But Sen. Howard M. Metzenbaum, D-Ohio, failed to attach a bill to tighten rules against manufacturers' fixing prices that dealers could charge for their products. *(TV violence, p. 374; artists' rights, p. 541; vertical price fixing, p. 539)*

BACKGROUND

Congress traditionally considered the federal judiciary's personnel needs against the backdrop of partisan politics.

When the Democratic-controlled Congress created a record 152 judgeships in 1978 for President Jimmy Carter to fill (PL 95-486), Republicans complained that the need for new judgeships had gone unacted upon under two GOP presidents. And in 1984, the majority Democratic Congress passed legislation (PL 98-353) creating 85 new judgeships, but stipulated that President Ronald Reagan could fill only 40 of the seats before the 1984 presidential election. *(1984 Almanac, p. 263; 1978 Almanac, p. 173)*

During Reagan's second term, the Judicial Conference asked for new judgeships, and GOP lawmakers tried to push the proposals. But Democrats never picked up the conference's request. As a result, the federal bench had remained at 168 appeals court judges and 575 district court judges.

Support for Judgeships

As the 101st Congress began, Chief Justice William H. Rehnquist stepped up the campaign to relieve pressures on the federal judicial system. In a rare formal news conference, Rehnquist complained that judges' workload was at an all-time high and morale at an all-time low; he urged Congress to create new judgeships and raise judicial salaries.

Bush endorsed the judges' pay increase in April 1989, and judges got a 7.9 percent increase as part of Congress' second effort to give itself and other federal officials a pay hike. *(1989 Almanac, p. 51)*

The request for new judgeships gained new urgency as lawmakers became aware of the caseload implications of the war against drugs. Drug cases increased 15 percent in 1988 and 1989, and judges in many areas said the rising drug caseloads were making it difficult for litigants in civil suits to get their cases to trial.

Overall, however, federal caseloads had actually declined from 299,164 in 1985 to 251,113 in 1990. Officials in the Administrative Office of the U.S. Courts attributed the decline to a higher minimum jurisdictional amount for so-called diversity of citizenship actions — suits heard in federal courts between citizens of different states — and a decline in filings by the United States in student loan default and veterans' benefits overpayment cases.

House Judiciary Chairman Brooks used the figures to question the need for more judges. Court officials, however, emphasized that even though the median time for disposition of civil cases had remained constant at nine months, the number of civil cases pending more than three years had shot up from 16,726 in 1985 to 25,207 in 1990.

For his part, Senate Judiciary Committee Chairman Joseph R. Biden Jr., D-Del., set up a task force in 1988 under the auspices of the Brookings Institution to examine the issues of delay and expense in civil litigation. The task force report in late 1989 concluded that judges needed to be better managers and listen to advice from the people who regularly used the civil justice system.

Biden used those principles to develop a bill (S 2027), introduced with bipartisan cosponsors on Jan. 25, 1990, to force federal judges to adopt specific plans to reduce delay and control expenses in civil litigation.

COMMITTEE ACTION

The Senate Judiciary Committee approved a revised version of Biden's caseload management proposal (S 2648), with a second title to create 77 new federal judgeships, by a 12-1 vote on July 12. Howell Heflin, D-Ala., a former state chief justice, cast the only "no" vote.

Brooks followed on July 19 with introduction of his own judgeships bill (HR 5316), originally containing 54 new judicial posts. Five more were added when Brooks' Economic and Commercial Law Subcommittee marked up the bill on Sept. 12; the measure then won voice-vote approval from the full Judiciary Committee on Sept. 18. At the same time, the committee approved a softened caseload management bill (HR 3898) paralleling Biden's proposal but with discretionary rather than mandatory guidelines.

Senate Committee Action

Approval of the combined caseload management-judgeships bill in the Senate Judiciary Committee came only after sharp exchanges between Biden and representatives of the federal judiciary. Many federal judges had objected to the detailed mandatory features of Biden's original bill. In response, Biden had agreed to work with a designated task force of the Judicial Conference to negotiate changes.

When the committee held a hearing June 26 on the revised bill, however, a representative of a different Judicial Conference committee gave the conference's formal position: It viewed the bill with "disfavor" as amounting to congressional micromanagement of the judiciary.

At the same hearing, Biden blasted the director of the Administrative Office of the U.S. Courts, Ralph Mecham, for a May 21 speech suggesting that politics was behind the location of new judgeships. Mecham told a judges' group that Biden's caseload management bill had picked up support from Republican committee members because their states had been given extra judgeships in the bill.

In fact, four judgeships not recommended by the Judicial Conference had been added for states represented by GOP senators on the Judiciary panel: Orrin G. Hatch, Utah; Gordon J. Humphrey, N.H.; Alan K. Simpson, Wyo.; and Arlen Specter, Pa. But Biden criticized Mecham and said he was tired of hearing complaints about his bill.

Despite the flap, Biden's bill won easy approval from the committee, with only Heflin voting no. As approved, the bill called for 77 new judgeships: 11 appellate positions and 66 trial-level posts, including nine the committee said it added in districts with high drug caseloads.

More pointedly, the bill mandated that all 94 federal judicial districts adopt detailed civil caseload delay- and expense-reduction plans that would include the following:

- Individualized case management.
- "Early and ongoing" judicial control of the pretrial process, including controlling discovery, setting deadlines for motions and setting firm trial dates within 18 months of filing unless that was certified to be impossible because of the complexity of the case or the number or complexity of pending criminal cases.
- "Careful and deliberate" monitoring of discovery and settlement talks in "complex or other appropriate" cases.
- Encouragement of cost-effective discovery through voluntary exchange of information between attorneys.
- Greater use of alternative dispute-resolution programs.

Each district court was to devise its plan in consultation with an advisory group, and the plans were to be reviewed by the court of appeals for that circuit and the Administrative Office. One other accountability provision called for the Administrative Office to release every six months a list of all cases pending for more than three years, all bench trials under advisement for more than six months and all motions pending for more than six months.

House Subcommittee Action

House Judiciary Committee work on the judgeships bill was less eventful, though Chairman Brooks used the mark-ups to question judges' claimed workload problems and criticize Bush for being slow to fill existing vacancies.

The Economic and Commercial Law Subcommittee, which Brooks chaired, had jurisdiction over the judgeships bill, while the Subcommittee on Courts, Intellectual Property and the Administration of Justice handled other judicial administration issues.

Brooks' subcommittee heard from just one witness from the Judicial Conference on July 30 before it proceeded to mark up HR 5316 on Sept. 12. In the markup, five judgeships were added to those Brooks originally included, all in areas represented by subcommittee members: Democrats Don Edwards, Calif.; Lawrence J. Smith, Fla.; and Harley O. Staggers Jr., W.Va.; and Republicans Hamilton Fish Jr., N.Y., and Carlos J. Moorhead, Calif.

Meanwhile, the Courts Subcommittee completed work on the caseload-management bill (HR 3898) after hearing from a Judicial Conference representative Sept. 6 opposing a mandatory approach. Chairman Robert W. Kastenmeier, D-Wis., long a major ally of the federal judiciary in Congress, agreed and offered a substitute bill making the details of the plans discretionary.

The Courts Subcommittee also sent to the full committee a bill to adopt some of the recommendations of the congressionally established Federal Courts Study Committee from its final report, issued April 2.

The group's major proposals — such as repealing mandatory minimum sentencing laws, routing virtually all drug cases to state courts and doing away with federal jurisdiction over diversity of citizenship suits — were too controversial to get serious consideration on Capitol Hill. But HR 5381 included dozens of minor recommendations such as increasing witness and juror fees, changing the name of U.S. magistrates to "U.S. magistrate judges" and providing for nearly equal representation of trial and appellate judges on judicial councils in each federal circuit.

Committee Markup

At its Sept. 18 markup, Brooks shepherded all three court bills through with no changes. As approved, the courts bill included 59 new judgeships: nine appeals court posts and 50 trial-level seats.

Two Republicans — George W. Gekas, Pa., and Bill McCollum, Fla. — tried to add judgeships for their states, but lost in party-line votes. After those votes, Dan Glickman, D-Kan., withheld an amendment to add a judgeship in his state "in deference to the chairman's strength."

Brooks underlined his view that the federal judiciary was facing no overall caseload crisis. He said new judgeships were needed in areas "overwhelmed" by high drug caseloads, but repeated the figures showing an overall decline in cases since 1985.

Brooks also noted that Bush had not submitted nominations for 30 of 42 existing vacancies on the federal bench. "It's clear that these new judgeships could do nothing to ease the courts' caseload unless the president acts decisively to fill these vacancies and makes nominations for these new positions," Brooks said.

All three court bills were approved by voice vote. With adjournment nearing, Brooks moved to bring them to the House floor the next week under suspension of the rules.

FLOOR ACTION

The House approved the three court bills separately on Sept. 27, the judgeships bill on a 387-18 vote and the

Judicial Improvements Act of 1990

Here are major court-related provisions of the Judicial Improvements Act of 1990 (HR 5316 — PL 101-650):

Title I: Civil Justice Expense and Delay Reduction Plans

Each U.S. district court shall implement a civil justice expense and delay reduction plan, developed either by the court itself or by the Judicial Conference of the United States.

• **Advisory Groups.** Each chief judge shall appoint a "balanced" advisory group for the district, composed of attorneys and "representatives of other major categories of litigants." The U.S. attorney or his or her designee was to be a permanent member; terms of other members were limited to four years.

• **Guidelines.** Each court "shall consider and may include" the following guidelines in adopting its plan:

(1) Systematic, differential treatment of cases, based on complexity, time needed to prepare for trial, and resources required and available for preparation and disposition of the case.

(2) Early and ongoing control of the pretrial process through involvement of a judicial officer in

(A) assessing and planning the progress of the case;

(B) setting early, firm trial dates, within 18 months of the filing of the complaint, unless a judicial officer certified that the demands of the case made such a trial date incompatible with serving the ends of justice or the trial could not reasonably be held within such time because of the complexity of the case or the number or complexity of pending criminal cases;

(C) controlling extent of and time for completion of discovery;

(D) setting deadlines for filing motions and a time framework for their disposition.

(3) Monitoring of complex cases through a discovery-case management conference or other conferences at which the judicial officer shall explore possibility of settlement, identify major issues, prepare a discovery schedule and set deadlines for filing motions.

(4) Encouragement of cost-effective discovery through voluntary exchange of information between attorneys.

(5) Prohibitions on consideration of discovery motions unless an attorney certified that a good-faith effort has been made to resolve the matter by agreement.

(6) Authorization to refer appropriate cases to alternative dispute resolution programs.

• **Techniques.** Each court "shall consider and may include" these management techniques:

(1) Requiring joint presentation of discovery-case management plan by opposing attorneys.

(2) Requiring that attorneys at pretrial conference be authorized to bind clients regarding all matters previously listed for discussion.

(3) Requiring that requests for extensions of deadlines or postponement of trial be signed by the attorney and party making the request.

(4) Presenting legal and factual basis of the case to a neutral court representative at a nonbinding conference early in litigation.

(5) Requiring that, upon notice by the court, representatives with authority to bind the parties be present or available by telephone during any settlement conference.

• **Review of plans.** Each plan shall be reviewed by a committee composed of the chief judge of the circuit and the chief judge of each district within the circuit.

• **Judicial information.** The director of the Administrative Office of the U.S. Courts shall prepare a semiannual report showing, for each judicial officer, the following:

(1) The number of motions pending for more than six months and the name of each such case;

(2) The pending number of bench trials under submission for more than six months and the name of each such case;

(3) The number and names of cases not terminated within three years of filing.

• **Pilot program.** The Judicial Conference shall designate 10 districts, including at least five in metropolitan areas, for a pilot program to adopt plans based on the six guidelines in the act. The programs were to be adopted by Dec. 31, 1991, and remain in effect for three years after.

Title II: Federal Judgeships

• **Circuit Courts of Appeals.** Eleven appellate positions as follows: 2 for the 3rd Circuit (based in Philadelphia); 4 for the 4th Circuit (Richmond, Va.); 2 for the 10th Circuit (Denver); and 1 each for the 5th (New Orleans), 6th (Cincinnati) and 8th (Kansas City, Mo.) circuits.

• **District Courts.** A total of 63 permanent judgeships and 11 temporary judgeships — which, traditionally, had been converted into permanent judgeships later — allocated among states as follows: Texas, 11; California, 9; 5 each for New York and Pennsylvania; Florida, 4; 3 each for Illinois, New Jersey and Tennessee; 2 each for Connecticut, Missouri, Ohio, Oklahoma, and West Virginia; and 1 each for Alabama, Arkansas, Georgia, Hawaii, Iowa, Kansas, Louisiana, Maine, Massachusetts, Michigan, Mississippi, Nebraska, New Hampshire, New Mexico, North Carolina, Oregon, South Carolina, Utah, Virginia, Washington and Wyoming.

• **GAO study.** An 18-month study by the General Accounting Office on policies, procedures and methodologies used by the Judicial Conference in recommending creation of new judgeships.

Title III: Implementation of Federal Courts' Study Committee Recommendations

The title enacted 25 sections of largely non-controversial matters, including provisions to:

• **Intercircuit conflicts.** Provide for a two-year study of frequency of conflicts between federal circuits and structural proposals to resolve them when the Supreme Court declined to do so. Five options, including a controversial national court of appeals, were included in the study committee's report.

• **Federal defenders.** Require a two-year study of the federal defender program — a substitute for the study committee's recommendation that appointment of federal defenders be by independent commissions rather than judges.

• **Claims Court.** Give quasi-independent status to judges of the U.S. Claims Court, appointed by the president for 15-year terms, by giving lifetime senior judge status and retirement benefits to any judge who sought but was denied reappointment.

• **Parole Commission.** Extend the life of the U.S. Parole Commission for five years to deal with cases of prisoners sentenced before abolition of parole by the 1987 federal sentencing law.

• **Administrative officers.** Require the chief justice to consult with the Judicial Conference in appointing the director and deputy director of the Administrative Office.

• **Judicial councils.** Require each circuit judicial council to be composed of an equal number of trial and appellate judges plus the chief judge of the circuit.

• **Magistrates.** Change the name of magistrates to "United States magistrate judges."

• **Juror and witness fees.** Increase to $40 from $30 the daily fees for jurors and witnesses in federal court.

• **Statute of limitations.** Establish a fallback four-year statute of limitations for new federal causes of action. The study committee had recommended that the uniform time period for filing suit be applied retroactively also.

Title IV: Judicial Discipline and Judicial Removal

• **Judicial discipline.** Several procedural changes aimed at expediting or simplifying disciplinary proceedings by judicial councils created by the Judicial Conduct and Disability Act of 1980.

• **National Commission on Judicial Impeachment.** A 13-member commission (three persons appointed by the president pro tem of the Senate, three by the Speaker of the House, three by the president, three by the chief justice of the United States and one by the Conference of Chief Justices of the States of the United States) to report within one year on advisability of new procedures for impeachment of federal judges. ■

caseload-management and study committee bills by voice votes. Senate action came a month later, delayed initially by action on the confirmation of Supreme Court nominee David H. Souter and then by negotiations over details of the caseload-management proposal. *(Vote 391, p. 126-H)*

House Action

House debate on the judgeships bill Sept. 27 was brief. Brooks reiterated his qualified endorsement of the need for the new positions, while Republican Moorhead noted that the bill did not go as far as the Bush administration or the Judicial Conference had recommended.

Without announcement, the bill had been amended before being brought to the floor to add trial-level judgeships for eastern Washington and central Illinois — areas represented in Congress by Democratic Speaker Thomas S. Foley and Minority Leader Robert H. Michel, respectively.

Immediately before the judgeships bill, the House had approved the caseload-management and study-committee bills, both by voice vote and with no speaker in opposition. Courts Subcommittee Chairman Kastenmeier said the revised HR 3898 — with discretionary management plans — had satisfied the concerns of the federal judiciary.

Final Action

When the House completed work on the court bills, Senate Judiciary Committee members and staff were busy with the Souter nomination. Once Souter was confirmed on Oct. 2, though, more delays resulted from negotiations over the content of the measures and over several senators' efforts to attach pet bills. *(Souter confirmation, p. 508)*

Final decisions were made in time for the Senate to take up the measures on Oct. 27, the last full day of the session.

On the judgeships, House and Senate negotiators "compromised" by including all the positions approved by either chamber: the 61 in the House bill plus 24 others contained in the Senate bill.

On caseload management, Biden agreed to a compromise calling for his detailed guidelines to be adopted only in 10 judicial districts chosen as pilot projects, with the other 84 districts free to tailor their own plans.

The court study committee recommendations were also rolled into S 2648, along with the bill to set up a study of judicial impeachment procedures, which the House had passed on June 5 (HR 1620 — H Rept 101-512).

Four other less germane titles were also added: an antitrust exemption for TV networks' talks on television violence, by Paul Simon, D-Ill.; artists' visual rights and copyright protection for architectural works, by Edward M. Kennedy, D-Mass.; and restrictions on computer software rental, by Orrin G. Hatch, R-Utah.

The consolidated bill was passed by voice vote, with no opposition, and then inserted as the text of HR 5316 to be passed again and sent to the House.

When the bill reached the House, Brooks complained mildly that it contained "a diverse collection of legislative initiatives," but noted that the House had passed all of the titles earlier in some form.

The House cleared the bill by voice vote shortly after midnight. ■

ALJ Corps Proposal Dies

Legislation to establish an independent government agency to handle disputes between federal agencies and private parties won approval from the Senate Judiciary Committee. But the measure was opposed by the Bush administration and saw no further action.

The bill (S 594) would have established an independent corps of administrative law judges (ALJs) to handle legal proceedings at the 29 federal agencies that had in-house ALJs. The Judiciary Committee approved the bill June 27 on a near party-line 9-5 vote (S Rept 101-467).

Under the Administrative Procedure Act of 1946, administrative law judges were assigned to a single agency, where they adjudicated disputes between private parties and the federal government on regulations, rulemaking and other matters.

The aim of the bill — sponsored by Howell Heflin, D-Ala., a former state chief justice — was to lessen the chances that an administrative law judge would be subject to coercion or improper reward by an agency involved in a dispute. By creating an independent ALJ corps as a separate federal agency and allowing judges to hear cases at different agencies, it was hoped the bill would assure the impartial resolution of administrative-law cases.

The Judiciary Committee took up the bill May 10, but postponed a vote in the absence of a quorum. When the committee voted on the bill June 27, Republican Arlen Specter, Pa., joined all eight committee Democrats in approving the measure while the committee's five other Republicans voted against it.

In the May 10 debate, Heflin said it would ensure the political independence of ALJs, who had come under fire for alleged abuse of power and "bad faith." Under existing conditions, Heflin said, ALJs were under pressure to make rulings that favored agency policies.

Fellow Democrat Paul Simon, Ill., compared the in-house ALJs to old-fashioned justices of the peace in his state, who were paid if they found drivers guilty of speeding and were not paid if the drivers were judged innocent.

"We're almost in that situation with the ALJs," Simon said. Those who don't support agency policy are "out of a job. That's no way to run a system of justice."

But Charles E. Grassley, R-Iowa, who opposed the bill, said it would weaken the credibility of ALJ rulings because independent judges would lack the specialized expertise of agency ALJs.

The Bush administration also opposed the measure, arguing that the system was intended to maintain specialist in-house ALJs to resolve arcane disputes. The administration also believed that the ALJ corps would add unnecessarily to government bureaucracy.

Under Heflin's bill, the ALJ corps was to be divided into eight divisions of ALJs with backgrounds in applicable areas, such as ratemaking.

Over two-thirds of the judges were employed by the Social Security Administration, which had come under attack during the Reagan administration for an allegedly budget-driven hostility to disability claimants. Other agencies that used ALJs were the Federal Trade Commission, Securities and Exchange Commission and Commodity Futures Trading Commission.

The Congressional Budget Office estimated that the creation of the ALJ corps would cost $10 million and that operating costs would come to about $5 million per year. ■

Amendment To Ban Flag Burning Fails

Supporters of a constitutional amendment aimed at outlawing flag burning failed for the second year in a row to get the measure through Congress, falling well short of the two-thirds majority needed in the House and Senate.

The furor over flag burning began anew in 1990 after a Supreme Court ruling June 11 *(United States v. Eichman)* that invalidated a 1989 federal statute designed to protect the flag. The court, reaffirming its 1989 decision in *Texas v. Johnson* that sparked the furor over the subject, once again held in a 5-4 ruling that flag burning was a form of political expression protected by the First Amendment and that Congress' statute — passed in response to the 1989 decision — was therefore unconstitutional.

Unlike 1989, though, opponents of the flag amendment were more prepared in the aftermath of the court's ruling. They quickly mounted an offensive that framed the battle as a fight over the sanctity of the Constitution in general and the First Amendment in particular.

Their efforts proved successful when the proposed constitutional amendments (H J Res 350, S J Res 332) made their way to the floors of both chambers.

In the House, resolutions offered by Minority Leader Robert H. Michel, R-Ill., and G. V. "Sonny" Montgomery, D-Miss., stated: "The Congress and the states shall have the power to prohibit the physical desecration of the flag of the United States."

The June 21 House vote — one year to the day after the *Johnson* decision — was 254-177, or 34 votes short of the two-thirds necessary for passage of an amendment. *(Vote 192, p. 66-H)*

Ninety-five Democrats joined 159 Republicans in voting for the amendment. Seventeen Republicans joined 160 Democrats in opposition.

In a vote that was moot, the Senate on June 26 also defeated a resolution for such an amendment. The measure failed 58-42, nine votes short of the required two-thirds of senators present and voting. *(Vote 128, p. 30-S)*

Thirty-eight Republicans and 20 Democrats supported the amendment, while seven Republicans joined 35 Democrats in opposition.

Polls had registered strong support for the amendment. A New York Times/CBS News poll in May found that 83 percent of the respondents believed flag burning should be against the law — and 59 percent of those favored a constitutional amendment if that were the only way to make flag desecration illegal. A USA Today poll conducted immediately after the court's June 11 ruling found that 69 percent of the respondents favored a constitutional amendment to make flag burning illegal.

By forcing an early vote on the amendment, however, opponents prevented its supporters from effectively mobilizing outside interest groups. And despite expectations the issue could figure in the November elections, it faded quickly after the amendment was defeated.

BACKGROUND

The flag uproar began in June 1989, when the Supreme Court by 5-4 ruled a Texas statute unconstitutional in *Texas v. Johnson.* After months of vocal outrage, public hearings and disagreements over whether to amend the Constitution, pass a statute or do nothing, Congress in October 1989 cleared the Flag Protection Act (PL 101-131).

The congressional drafters had said the statute was not intended to regulate the political expression of someone burning or otherwise defacing a flag.

The Senate in October 1989 rejected a proposed constitutional amendment (S J Res 180) to protect the flag. The result was 15 votes short of the required two-thirds of those present and voting. The House had never voted on an amendment. It cleared the flag statute by a 371-43 vote. The Senate approved the statute by a vote of 91-9. *(1989 Almanac, p. 307)*

New Law Challenged

The 1989 law, providing criminal penalties for anyone who "knowingly mutilates, defaces, physically defiles, burns, maintains on the floor or ground, or tramples upon any flag," received a quick challenge. Protesters in Seattle and in the District of Columbia burned flags shortly after the legislation took effect.

On Feb. 21, U.S. District Judge Barbara J. Rothstein in Seattle said that four people who burned a flag in front of a Seattle post office minutes after the flag law took effect were exercising their First Amendment rights.

U.S. District Judge June L. Green, of the District of Columbia, issued a similar ruling March 5 in the case of three protesters who burned a flag on the steps of the U.S. Capitol.

"The right to dissent is sometimes an albatross which burdens our society with its offensive sounds," Green said, in striking down the law. "Yet, political dissent lies at the heart of the First Amendment's protection."

The Justice Department had argued that the statute was drafted to protect the physical integrity of the flag and not to regulate speech. But Green disagreed, saying, "The government seeks to preserve the flag as a symbol only for those who would not damage or destroy it."

Senate Judiciary Committee Chairman Joseph R. Biden Jr., D-Del., and House Judiciary Committee Chairman Jack Brooks, D-Texas, insisted that the statute did not implicate the political motivations of a person who burned the flag, only the destructive act itself. Members had opted for a statute because, although they had questions about its effectiveness, they did not want to amend the Constitution.

Under a provision in the act, an appeal was to go directly to the U.S. Supreme Court for an expedited review.

Congress Reacts

As the court prepared to rule on the 1989 statute, supporters of a constitutional amendment to outlaw flag burning lay in waiting.

Senate Minority Leader Bob Dole, R-Kan., said, "I stand ready to reintroduce the amendment once the Supreme Court finally passes judgment on the flag statute."

Democrats in the House, though, hoped that the court would delay its ruling. The House counsel's advisory brief to the court, which GOP leaders had not seen, responded to a Justice Department request that parties' briefs be simultaneously exchanged and all responses filed by April 23. The brief contended that a hurried approach would harm the arguments in the two cases: *United States v. Eichman* and *United States v. Haggerty.*

Republicans responded that Democrats were trying to

delay another flag fight beyond the November elections. They said they expected the court to strike down the law and that they were ready to push for approval of the constitutional amendment when it did.

House Republicans who wanted a speedy ruling on March 22 forced the Democratic majority to withdraw the House request that the Supreme Court delay taking up the matter until the fall.

By 309-101, the House approved H Res 362, offered by Michel, to withdraw the brief. Later on March 22, a bipartisan advisory panel agreed to submit an amended brief that recommended no timetable for court action. *(Vote 39, p. 18-H)*

Supreme Court Redux

With an early decision expected, proponents of the statute hoped for a favorable ruling. They urged the Supreme Court to view the statute as "content-neutral," not an attempt to limit any type of political speech.

In arguing the case for the government, Solicitor General Kenneth W. Starr noted that the court often bowed to the judgment of Congress when the members specifically considered in drafting a law whether the act was constitutional. He contended that through passage of the new law, "the people's elected representatives have now made clear that the physical integrity of the flag of the United States, as the unique symbol of the nation, merits protection not accorded other national emblems."

But William M. Kunstler, a New York lawyer representing the demonstrators involved in the Washington, D.C., and Seattle cases, said the lower court rulings — that political dissent laid at the heart of the First Amendment's protection — should be upheld.

The House and Senate also filed amicus briefs, as did Biden, the law's Senate sponsor. They all argued the act was narrowly drawn to prohibit conduct, not expression.

But in a replay of its 1989 *Johnson* decision, the court June 11 struck down the statute as an infringement on the First Amendment.

Voting to strike down the law were Justices William J. Brennan Jr., Thurgood Marshall, Harry A. Blackmun, Antonin Scalia and Anthony M. Kennedy. Voting in the minority were Chief Justice William H. Rehnquist and Justices Byron R. White, John Paul Stevens and Sandra Day O'Connor.

Brennan, writing for the majority as he had in *Johnson*, rejected the idea that the language of the statute was "content-neutral," as its authors had intended.

"Each of the specified terms — with the possible exception of 'burns' — unmistakably connotes disrespectful treatment of the flag and suggests a focus on those acts likely to damage the flag's symbolic value," Brennan said.

"Although Congress cast the Flag Protection Act in somewhat broader terms than the Texas statute at issue in *Johnson*," he wrote, "the Act still suffers from the same fundamental flaw: it suppresses expression out of concern for its likely communicative impact."

HOUSE COMMITTEE ACTION

Within hours of the Supreme Court's decision, lawmakers were on the House and Senate floors demanding a constitutional amendment on the flag. Within two days, a House Judiciary subcommittee sent an amendment resolution to the full committee.

The proposed amendment was clearly on a fast track, with Republicans providing the engine. President Bush was in the forefront, saying June 12 that flag burning "endangers the fabric of our country, and I think it ought to be outlawed."

Opponents of the amendment were buoyed June 19 when the House Judiciary Committee voted 17-19 against recommending the amendment. The committee followed by voting 19-17 to send the resolution to the House without recommendation.

Subcommittee Politics

On June 13, the House Judiciary Subcommittee on Civil and Constitutional Rights had voted 5-3 to send H J Res 350 to the full committee with a recommendation to defeat it. Though its action was a boost for opponents of the amendment, the subcommittee, dominated by liberal Democrats, did not represent House sentiment. Voting for the adverse recommendation were all the Democrats on the subcommittee, many of whom were leading the fight against the amendment: subcommittee Chairman Don Edwards, Calif.; Robert W. Kastenmeier, Wis.; John Conyers Jr. and George W. Crockett Jr., Mich.; and Patricia Schroeder, Colo.

Voting against the recommendation were Republicans F. James Sensenbrenner Jr., Wis.; William E. Dannemeyer, Calif.; and Craig T. James, Fla.

The subcommittee also approved a draft resolution to condemn "desecration" of the U.S. flag while affirming congressional support and commitment to the values in the Bill of Rights.

Sensenbrenner and Dannemeyer voted against the resolution. Sensenbrenner said the resolution was offered only as "political cover" for Democrats who did not support the constitutional amendment.

Schroeder implicitly agreed, saying afterward, "It's so they don't get to say we're for flag burning."

Full Committee Action

Opponents of the amendment were further encouraged when the full committee voted against recommending it.

The opponents' victory was made possible when Harley O. Staggers Jr., D-W.Va., decided at the last minute to oppose the amendment because he thought the process was going too quickly. (Two days later, Staggers voted for the amendment on the House floor.)

The committee then voted to send the resolution to the House without recommendation.

Staggers was not the only member frustrated by the process. William J. Hughes, D-N.J., also a member of the Judiciary Committee, voted against the resolution while voicing discontent with the actions of both sides on the issue. "Form has taken over substance. Politics has taken over public interest," Hughes said.

In committee action, Hughes tried to amend the resolution so that a new constitutional amendment would allow only Congress, not the states or localities, to draft flag-desecration laws. He also tried to modify it to more narrowly define the term "desecration." Both attempts were voted down.

Later, Hughes suffered a similar defeat in the Rules Committee when he sought permission to offer these amendments on the floor.

Debate Over Rules

At a Rules Committee hearing on whether to waive the House rules and allow H J Res 350 to be taken up before the week of June 25, Gerald B. H. Solomon, R-N.Y., said, "I've been on the phone with 37 veterans' organizations, and they are appealing to you to wait until Tuesday [June 26]."

The Rules Committee voted 4-9 against Solomon's plan to delay action on the resolution, then approved by voice vote a request by Edwards and Brooks to allow a June 21 House vote.

On the floor, the rule was adopted 231-192, along party lines. *(Vote 191, p. 66-H)*

Backers of the constitutional amendment had tried to stop it from being brought to the floor June 21, saying they needed more time to persuade members to support their position.

But opponents counted enough votes to block the resolution and did not want to take any chances.

The Democratic leadership accurately noted that it had been GOP members who had originally pushed for speedy floor consideration of an amendment.

Opponents of the amendment got help in their effort to move H J Res 350 to the floor quickly from Judiciary Chairman Brooks. Brooks said he supported the amendment, but was angered by Republican hounding to move the resolution through his committee.

"If I delayed it, they would be jumping all over me," said Brooks, who had previously faced Republican accusations of holding up a number of bills, including anticrime legislation and a resolution for a balanced-budget amendment to the Constitution.

Pre-emptive Strategy

Some House members who opposed a constitutional amendment thought that the only way to win was to have a strategy in place well before the Supreme Court ruled.

So beginning in April, almost three months before the *Eichman* decision was expected, key members, including House Speaker Thomas S. Foley, D-Wash., and their staffs created a flag task force.

During those months the special task force carefully crafted the legal arguments against the amendment, devised political approaches, contacted newspaper editors and met with grass-roots groups.

Led by Edwards, and Chief Deputy Majority Whip David E. Bonior, D-Mich., task force members decided to use the Bill of Rights as both a legal argument and a symbol.

"We have to keep the debate focused on free speech," said Mike Synar, D-Okla. "I don't think we have to apologize for defending the First Amendment. No one wants the flag burned, but neither does anyone want their First Amendment rights trampled."

Democrats were not united, however, in their response to the ruling. "We are not taking a party position on it," said Foley, on behalf of the party leadership. "It is a matter for individual members' judgment and conscience how they vote on the issue."

Republicans were confident the issue would help them in the November campaign. "Democrats are definitely not going to get a free ride on this," said Edward J. Rollins, co-chairman of the GOP's House campaign committee.

But Foley disagreed. "I don't think people are going to react to the honest judgment of members of Congress about protecting the Constitution. Every country has a flag. We are one of the few countries that has a Bill of Rights."

While opponents were working feverishly, proponents of the amendment were just beginning to get organized.

The opponents had about 115 votes on June 11, but they quickly picked up strength. Supporters of the amendment, meanwhile, were being hurt in two major ways.

First, they relied heavily on veterans' groups to pressure members to support the amendment, but the veterans were too slow to mobilize and the pressure never came.

Second, the supporters were forced to defend themselves against charges that they were politicizing the flag.

The charges were prompted in part by a statement by Dole just after the court's ruling. Dole told reporters on June 11 that a vote against a constitutional amendment to protect the flag would make a good 30-second campaign commercial to use against Democrats.

Other GOP tacticians similarly framed the debate in terms of politics rather than the integrity of the flag.

By the week of June 18, when President Bush began calling undecided Democrats to urge them to back the amendment, it was too late. The undecideds had already been contacted a number of times by colleagues from the flag task force.

HOUSE FLOOR ACTION

Though nearly 60 percent of House members voted for the constitutional amendment, supporters still fell 34 votes short of the two-thirds vote needed.

The defeat of the amendment in committee provided valuable momentum to opponents. In the 48 hours after the Judiciary Committee vote a host of conservative Democrats turned against the amendment, influenced by their colleagues, their constituents or their own second thoughts.

Among the final names added to the "nay" vote count were Dave McCurdy, Okla., and Charles W. Stenholm, Texas.

Tim Valentine, D-N.C., changed his mind the night before the vote.

"For me, there was so much political risk involved that I guess I had just closed my eyes to the realities of the damage this could do to the Constitution," Valentine said.

David E. Skaggs, D-Colo., who was against the amendment, said he believed some members "literally risked their political futures" by opposing it.

Separately, Minority Whip Newt Gingrich, R-Ga., said, "How can it avoid being a big political issue? It's how you feel about the flag. This is going to be a legitimate, fair fight over values."

Gingrich said he expected another resolution for a flag amendment to be introduced in the new Congress in January 1991 and said that, in the meantime, candidates would be challenged to state whether they would vote for it.

But Majority Leader Richard A. Gephardt, D-Mo., predicted that Gingrich's political approach would fail.

"Everything can be turned into a 30-second [campaign] spot. I can run my own 30-second spot" to counterattack, Gephardt said.

Although polls still showed that a majority of the public favored an amendment to prohibit flag desecration, members of Congress noted a shift in their mail on the issue between the court's first ruling in *Johnson*, and the decision in *Eichman*.

"Last year, the theme was that this [court decision] is such a disgrace and that no one should be allowed to burn the flag," said an aide to a Republican member who actively sought the amendment. "This year, they [constituents] were saying, 'Don't tamper with the Constitution.'"

Proponents of the amendment tried to respond by saying they were not attempting to radically amend the Bill of Rights, but rather to correct an overly broad court interpretation of the First Amendment. But that legal explanation was never effectively communicated.

Tone of Debate

The seven hours of floor debate on June 21 appealed to party allegiances and emotions. "The Republicans believe they have found an issue they can use to win the election," said Texas Democrat John Bryant.

"They are so anxious to win they are willing to damage the Constitution to do it."

Craig Washington, D-Texas, a black lawyer, recalled defending a client who had been fired from his job because of the client's Ku Klux Klan activities, which included distributing material depicting blacks as savages. Washington said his pain and revulsion over the man's actions were secondary to his belief in the man's First Amendment right to free expression.

Minority Leader Michel, however, said the amendment posed no threat to freedom of speech.

"Anyone who truly believes that the First Amendment is so fragile that this amendment can in effect kill it, or that the American people are so weak in their love of free speech that they will begin to trample on their own First Amendment rights, doesn't in my view have faith in the people," Michel said.

Henry J. Hyde, R-Ill., who was designated to close the debate for GOP supporters of the amendment, called the flag a unique symbol.

"Can't we get a symbol and elevate it and say that it unites us as a country? . . . Too many people have paid for it with their blood. Too many people have marched behind it. Too many kids and parents and widows have accepted this triangle as the last remembrance of their most precious son. Too many to have this ever demeaned."

Hyde was applauded by members from both parties on both sides of the issue. He was followed by Foley, who likewise drew applause for an emotional appeal to patriotism and respect for the Constitution.

Foley said that "it would be a strange irony if we let those few people who burn or disrespect the flag push us, force us, into amending for the first time the First Amendment to the Constitution, the Bill of Rights."

To the mostly Republican proponents of the amendment, Foley added, "If it is not conservative to protect the Bill of Rights, I don't know what conservatism is today."

Foley, who had taken his usual low-key approach to the controversy but personally called wavering members, broke tradition and voted against the amendment. Historically, the Speaker seldom votes, except to break ties.

Despite the fact that the court rejected the earlier statutory approach to banning flag burning, some House members still wanted an approach other than a constitutional amendment.

Reps. Jim Cooper, D-Tenn., Rick Boucher, D-Va., and Ron Wyden, D-Ore., offered a bill to outlaw damage to the flag under certain circumstances, including actions promoting violence or damage to a federally owned flag.

Cooper said he was trying to draft a statute that would prohibit as many flag-damaging acts as possible without infringing on First Amendment rights.

But the bill (HR 5901) was defeated, 179-236, as a majority either wanted nothing less than a constitutional amendment or believed that such political protest should not be outlawed. *(Vote 193, p. 66-H)*

SENATE ACTION

Five days after the House effectively killed the chances of a constitutional amendment in the 101st Congress, the Senate did the same. Its 58-42 vote ended a chapter in the 101st Congress that began June 2, 1989, with the Supreme Court's first flag-burning ruling.

Strom Thurmond, R-S.C., was one of the few members who predicted the issue would return. "I do not think it is closed permanently, and I think you will see it come back again," he said. "I think you are going to see an aroused public because people believe in the flag."

Other members, though, said the debate and rancor over the issue had merely caused serious damage.

"I tell you that a wound has been opened in America over this debate, a real wound, not one that will be felt by us having ads run against us or for us, but a real wound," said Sen. Bob Kerrey, D-Neb.

"I have talked to older veterans who are angry with me, disappointed in me, disillusioned in me personally," he added.

Kerrey, a Vietnam War hero who earned the Medal of Honor, was among senators who fought hardest for rejection of the amendment.

Early Reactions, Actions

Despite the amendment's defeat, there was no keeping the flag issue off the immediate agenda — especially with an election just months away.

Republicans, well aware of Bush's 1988 success in using the flag issue against his Democratic opponent, Michael S. Dukakis, had dared the Democrats to vote against an amendment.

"I might make a 30-second spot," Dole said, suggesting that Democrats could be burned in campaign commercials for not supporting the flag amendment.

Dole was the first senator to speak on the floor about the flag June 11, suggesting that senators who supported the amendment were, in effect, on the side of the armed forces and that opponents were on the side of flag burners.

"I will place my money on the young men and women who serve in America's armed services, and the rest can place their money on [people] who were involved in this latest flag-desecration case," Dole said.

Senate Majority Leader George J. Mitchell, D-Maine, immediately responded that Dole's suggestion was "unfortunate and erroneous."

Noting that he had served in the Army, Mitchell said, "No useful purpose is served, other than to gain temporary tactical advantage, to suggest that disagreement on the issue of a constitutional amendment involves choice between those who burn the flag and those in the armed services."

Meanwhile, as the House debated the proposed constitutional amendment June 21, the Senate Judiciary Committee held a hearing on the subject.

Legal scholars, among them former U.S. appellate Judge Robert H. Bork, offered differing opinions on the wisdom of amending the Constitution. Bork supported it; most others opposed it.

Chairman Biden had scheduled the forum to help draft a narrower amendment than the one that went down to defeat in the House.

But midway through the hearing, Biden described it as a "futile exercise."

Biden said it was unlikely that an amendment would

pass the Senate. After the House vote, Dole said he agreed.

Nonetheless, the measure went to the full Senate.

Floor Considerations

The Senate first considered three alternatives to S J Res 332, which had been offered by Dole and Howell Heflin, D-Ala.

Dale Bumpers, D-Ark., proposed a statute that would have subjected anyone who knowingly and purposely desecrated the flag to a fine or one year in prison, or both. Bumpers said his was a "narrow legislative remedy," because "when you start talking about amending the Constitution for any purpose, I belong to the 'wait-just-a-minute club.' "

But some Republican senators termed the Bumpers amendment "a fig leaf" for political cover, and Pete Wilson, R-Calif., raised a point of order, contending that if the proposal were to become law the Supreme Court would declare it unconstitutional because it was as flawed as the 1989 statute. Wilson's point of order was upheld 51-48, in effect killing the Bumpers amendment. *(Vote 125, p. 30-S)*

Jesse Helms, R-N.C., then proposed an amendment to the resolution that would have led to a statute banning the public mutilation, defilement, incineration or other physical abuse of the flag and would have removed from the jurisdiction of the federal courts the power to hear any cases involving such acts.

Helms said he wanted the states to have exclusive jurisdiction over flag burning.

He charged that the Supreme Court had in a number of areas "clearly distorted the meaning of freedom and all of the good and decent things that America stands for."

Arlen Specter, R-Pa., said Helms was trying to undermine the Supreme Court's 1803 *Marbury v. Madison* deci sion, which had come to stand for the principle that the court was the final arbiter on constitutional issues.

Helms' amendment failed 10-90. *(Vote 126, p. 30-S)*

Biden proposed an amendment that would have given only Congress the power to pass laws against flag desecration. The amendment would have limited the prohibited acts to burning, mutilating or trampling on a flag.

Biden was attempting to adopt the language of the federal statute rejected by the Supreme Court into an amendment to the Constitution. He said he wanted to avoid a conflict with First Amendment rights but also to write as narrow an amendment as possible, keeping it "viewpoint neutral." His proposal was defeated 7-93. *(Vote 127, p. 30-S)*

Finally, senators cast their academic vote on S J Res 332. Voting for the amendment after having opposed it in 1989 because they preferred a statute were Democrats Max Baucus, Mont.; Kent Conrad, N.D.; and Bob Graham, Fla.; and Republicans William S. Cohen, Maine; Slade Gorton, Wash.; Mark O. Hatfield, Ore.; and Specter.

Charles S. Robb, D-Va., voted for the amendment in 1989 but opposed it this time, saying he no longer believed a constitutional amendment was needed to protect the flag.

Overall, there was a tone of fatigue to the Senate proceedings. Biden, who managed the floor debate, said he was sorry for "wasting the taxpayers' money in a sense in discussing something that is going nowhere." ■

Abortion Issue Non-Starter in 1990

The abortion issue, which loomed large in the country and on Capitol Hill as 1990 began, shrank to relative insignificance by year's end.

The Supreme Court, for the second year in a row, upheld state restrictions on abortion rights, but its rulings were narrow and did not arouse much public outcry.

That was a striking contrast to 1989, when the high court pushed abortion to the center of the political arena with a 5-4 ruling that undermined the landmark 1973 *Roe v. Wade* decision legalizing abortion nationwide.

The court's 1989 decision in *Webster v. Reproductive Health Services*, approving stiff Missouri restrictions on abortions, galvanized abortion rights advocates and produced a substantial shift of votes in Congress toward the pro-choice position. *(1989 Almanac, p. 296)*

Although the abortion issue figured prominently in a number of political campaigns in 1990, neither side could claim a clear victory. Anti-abortion contenders prevailed in some races, abortion rights supporters in others.

Faced with veto threats from President Bush if it did otherwise, Congress retained existing bans on federal funding of abortions except in cases where the woman's life would be endangered by carrying the pregnancy to term. For the District of Columbia, it extended an existing ban on use of either federal or local funds to pay for abortions.

Abortion rights supporters did not force a showdown on the funding issue on the appropriations bill for the Departments of Labor, Health and Human Services (HHS) and Education, traditionally the main battlefield for abortion fights. In part, they were discouraged by Bush's continued opposition to any easing of the existing ban. In 1989, the president repeatedly vetoed spending bills that contained abortion funding relaxations, forcing Congress to back down in the end.

But abortion rights advocates also were caught off guard by a new tactic adopted by anti-abortion forces. When the Senate voted, as it had in other years, to allow funding of abortions to end pregnancies resulting from rape or incest, abortion foes succeeded in attaching amendments requiring parental notification before abortions could be performed on minors. Abortion rights supporters considered such language unacceptable, and they gave up their efforts to win a rape and incest exception rather than see it linked to parental notification.

BACKGROUND

The *Webster* ruling dramatically changed the political dynamics of the abortion debate. From the early years following *Roe* until the 1989 ruling, anti-abortion forces had dominated the scene, staging protest rallies, pressing for new state restrictions and winning bans on public funding of abortions.

Abortion rights advocates resisted, but only sporadically. They were content for the most part to rely on the constitutional protection extended by the court, which guaranteed that women who could pay for their own abortions could legally obtain them.

President Ronald Reagan's relentless effort to reshape the Supreme Court changed all that. By 1989, Reagan — an ardent abortion foe — had named three justices to the high court, all of whom voted in *Webster* to uphold sweeping state restrictions on abortion.

Only Justice Sandra Day O'Connor, Reagan's first appointee, seemed to resist a complete reversal of *Roe v. Wade*. Although she voted with the majority to uphold Missouri's limits on abortion, she refused to overturn *Roe* as the Reagan administration had urged.

"When the constitutional validity of a state's abortion statute actually turns on the constitutional validity of *Roe v. Wade*, there will be time enough to re-examine *Roe,* and to do so carefully," she wrote.

The Votes Shift

Shocked into activism by the *Webster* decision, abortion rights advocates mobilized nationwide. They helped propel pro-choice Democrats L. Douglas Wilder of Virginia and James J. Florio of New Jersey to victory in their states' gubernatorial elections in 1989. And they swung 50 votes in Congress virtually overnight.

The key turnabout came in the House, which had consistently approved strict limits on abortion funding. For the first time since 1980, abortion rights supporters won a relaxation of the ban on funding of abortions except to save the life of the woman. The action played out first on the D.C. appropriations bill and then on the Labor-HHS funding bill. Lawmakers also approved language in the foreign aid appropriations bill that Bush found too lax on abortion.

Bush vetoed all three bills, and Congress eventually had to remove the offending language because abortion rights advocates could not muster the two-thirds majority needed to override Bush's vetoes.

But the stage was set for a renewed confrontation in 1990, and political candidates at all levels of government were put on notice that abortion would be a pivotal issue in the elections that year.

ABORTION AND THE COURT

Parental notification was at issue in two cases before the court in 1990. By a 5-4 vote, the court ruled June 25 in *Hodgson v. Minnesota* that states could require a woman under 18 to tell both parents before obtaining an abortion as long as she had the alternative of seeking permission from a judge. Separately, in *Ohio v. Akron Center for Reproductive Health*, the court by 6-3 also upheld an Ohio statute requiring one-parent notification.

It was indicative of the difficulty the abortion issue posed for the court that nine separate opinions were issued in the two abortion cases.

In the Minnesota case, the court ruled it was unconstitutional for a state to require both biological parents to be notified if there was no judicial-bypass alternative. Voting in the majority were Justices John Paul Stevens (who wrote for the court), William J. Brennan Jr., Thurgood Marshall, Harry A. Blackmun and Sandra Day O'Connor.

This was the first time O'Connor had found any abortion restriction unconstitutional.

O'Connor switched sides, however, to form a different 5-4 majority upholding an alternative form of the Minnesota law permitting a judicial bypass if a minor did not want to notify both parents. This time she was joined by Chief Justice William H. Rehnquist and Justices Byron R. White, Antonin Scalia and Anthony M. Kennedy.

In the Ohio case, the court ruled 6-3 that the state could require that a minor give notice to one parent or obtain a judge's permission before having an abortion.

While the court had previously ruled that minors must have access to a judicial-bypass procedure when parental consent was required for an abortion, it had never resolved the question on parental-notification laws.

The last time the court had reviewed parental notification, in the 1987 case of *Hartigan v. Zbaraz*, it had one vacancy and the justices split 4-4 on an Illinois statute requiring that parents be told before a physician performs an abortion on a minor.

Eight years earlier, in *Bellotti v. Baird*, the court struck down a Massachusetts parental-consent statute, saying that a minor must have access to a confidential, expeditious proceeding before a judge.

The judicial bypass was intended to allow a teenager to show either that she was mature enough and well-informed enough to make the abortion decision herself or that the abortion would be in her best interest.

Stevens, writing for a majority in part of the Minnesota case, said the court had considered the constitutionality of statutes providing for parental consent or parental notification in six abortion cases decided during the preceding 14 years, but none had ever involved two parents.

"The requirement of notice to both of the pregnant minor's parents is not reasonably related to legitimate state interests," Stevens said, noting that Minnesota made no exception for a divorced parent, a non-custodial parent, or a biological parent who never married or lived with the pregnant woman's mother.

Kennedy wrote for the dissenting justices, who had sought to uphold the constitutionality of the two-parent requirement without the judicial alternative.

He cited a "right of each parent to participate in the upbringing of her or his children. . . ."

Kennedy said no judicial alternative to a notice requirement should be demanded because, unlike with parental-consent laws, a notice requirement did not give a third party the right to make a decision on behalf of the minor.

In the Ohio case, Kennedy wrote for the majority, saying that one-parent notification, plus a 48-hour waiting period, did not impose an undue or otherwise unconstitutional burden on a minor seeking an abortion.

Stevens, who typically opposed abortion restrictions, voted with the conservative bloc — Rehnquist, White, O'Connor, Scalia and Kennedy — to uphold the Ohio law.

ABORTION AND POLITICS

The results of the Nov. 6 elections were mixed, but on balance abortion rights forces appeared to have made modest gains, picking up some votes in Congress and winning some gubernatorial contests in part, at least, on the strength of the abortion issue.

Gubernatorial Contests

Abortion rights activists counted Democratic victories in Florida and Texas as their clearest wins.

In Florida, GOP Gov. Bob Martinez outraged abortion rights advocates when he called a special session soon after the *Webster* decision to pass restrictive anti-abortion laws.

State legislators rebuffed Martinez, but activists did not forgive him in the campaign. One anti-Martinez bumper sticker urged, "Abort Martinez before a second term."

Former Democratic Sen. Lawton Chiles, who moved to an abortion rights stance after taking several anti-abortion positions during his years in the Senate, was initially reluctant to press the issue. But in the closing weeks of the fall campaign, Chiles did talk up his abortion rights views, seemingly to his benefit.

Texas also offered a clear choice between an abortion rights supporter — Democrat Ann W. Richards — and Republican Clayton Williams, an abortion opponent. Williams tried to frame the issue to his advantage, pressing Richards to join him in backing parental-notification laws for minors seeking abortion. But Richards' abortion rights views probably helped cement critical support among Republican women.

In Idaho, Democrat Cecil D. Andrus won re-election despite anger among anti-abortion groups over his veto of a post-*Webster* bill restricting abortion.

But anti-abortion governors were elected in Kansas, Ohio, Michigan and Alaska, seats previously held by abortion rights supporters.

After a much-publicized reversal on the issue, Ohio Attorney General Anthony J. Celebrezze Jr. hoped his new-found abortion rights stand would help him defeat Republican opponent George V. Voinovich, the former mayor of Cleveland. The issue did help keep the race close, but Voinovich won after a campaign that centered more on the ethics problems of the Democratic administration.

In Iowa, where many believed House Speaker Donald D. Avenson's abortion rights views would be a powerful weapon against Republican incumbent Terry E. Branstad, Branstad won handily. Several other anti-abortion governors considered potentially vulnerable on the issue — Democrat Robert P. Casey in Pennsylvania and Republicans Tommy G. Thompson in Wisconsin and Gregg in New Hampshire — were not noticeably damaged by the issue.

Abortion may have played a decisive role in the Oregon governor's race: as a spoiler. Both major-party nominees, Democrat Barbara Roberts and Republican Attorney General Dave Frohnmayer, supported abortion rights. But anti-abortion candidate Al Mobley drew 13 percent of the vote, votes Republicans believed came primarily at Frohnmayer's expense. Roberts won with 46 percent of the vote.

Congressional Races

The elections seemed to strengthen the ranks of abortion rights supporters in both chambers of Congress, but not enough to overcome a Bush veto.

The National Right to Life Committee (NRLC) estimated that it lost a net of eight anti-abortion votes in the House, which was closely divided on the issue in the 101st Congress. The National Abortion Rights Action League (NARAL) essentially agreed, projecting a pickup for its side of between seven and 10 votes.

Abortion opponents also lost two votes in the Senate. Those came in Minnesota, where abortion rights supporter Paul Wellstone ousted anti-abortion Republican incumbent Rudy Boschwitz, and in Colorado, where the open seat previously held by anti-abortion Sen. William L. Armstrong was filled by Rep. Hank Brown, also a Republican but generally a supporter of abortion rights.

The Senate change was likely to be the more significant of the two, because on several occasions in 1990, two votes could have choked off threatened filibusters on abortion-related issues on which abortion rights backers had majorities but not supermajorities.

Nonetheless, it appeared that abortion rights supporters still lacked the two-thirds majorities needed to override presidential vetoes of legislation to relax federal abortion restrictions. As a result, predicted NRLC Legislative Director Douglas Johnson, "It's unlikely there will be any drastic shift in abortion policy next year in either direction."

Mixed Message

As in gubernatorial races, the abortion issue cut both ways in congressional contests.

In Virginia's 8th District, Democrat and abortion rights supporter James P. Moran Jr. defeated incumbent Republican Stan Parris in a nasty fight in which abortion played a feature role.

But in North Carolina's Senate race, which also pitted a GOP abortion foe, Jesse Helms, against a Democrat who supported abortion rights, Harvey B. Gantt, abortion was just as prominently featured, and Helms won.

In several other races, abortion rights advocates were replaced with abortion opponents or vice versa, but it was unclear in many of those races how important the abortion aspect was. In Iowa, for example, abortion was a major issue in both the senatorial and gubernatorial races, but voters simultaneously returned incumbent pro-choice Democrat Tom Harkin to the Senate and incumbent anti-abortion Republican Branstad to the statehouse.

On balance, candidates who supported abortion rights were far more likely to advertise that position or use it as the spearhead of their campaigns. That represented a turnaround in the political use of the issue, one that had been apparent since the *Webster* decision in 1989 began energizing abortion rights voters.

Abortion rights forces also won the three major ballot initiatives. In Oregon, where GOP abortion opponent Mark O. Hatfield was returned to the Senate, voters rejected two anti-abortion initiatives. One, which would have seriously restricted legal abortions, was widely expected to fail. But even abortion rights advocates had expected the other to pass. It would have required that parents of minors be notified before the procedure could be performed.

Similarly, Nevada voters approved a proposal that codified the state's permissive abortion law and took potential changes out of the hands of the state Legislature.

FUNDING BANS

For all the fanfare and fireworks over abortion during the second session of the 101st Congress, in the end it was abortion opponents who prevailed, as abortion rights advocates failed on a half-dozen different measures to modify or overturn restrictive abortion-related policies.

As a result, in fiscal 1991 federal funds still could pay for abortions only for women whose lives would be endangered by continuing a pregnancy.

Also, no abortions were permitted in overseas military facilities; the District of Columbia remained barred from using local tax dollars to pay for the procedure; and organizations that provided family planning services overseas were not permitted to receive U.S. funds unless they agreed not to use their own funds to provide for or refer abortions.

Abortion controversies helped sink two bills that abortion rights advocates had hoped to pass. One would have reauthorized the federal family planning program, Title X of the Public Health Service Act. *(Family planning, p. 604)*

The other, which would have renewed expiring authorities within the National Institutes of Health (NIH), would have overturned an existing Bush administration ban on funding of research involving transplants of tissue from fetuses obtained through abortion. *(NIH, p. 600)*

The NIH bill also would have authorized the creation of new centers to study infertility and contraception. Abortion foes opposed the authorization, arguing that sponsors were seeking a backdoor way to authorize federal research funds for RU 486, an abortion-inducing drug on the market in France.

Abortion opponents were quick to trumpet their victories. "1990 Congressional Session Leaves Pro-abortion Groups Empty-Handed," proclaimed an end-of-session press release from the National Right to Life Committee.

But while opponents clearly won the war in 1990, abortion rights advocates won several battles they said would position them well for skirmishes in the 102nd Congress.

For example, the Senate on Sept. 25 voted 62-36 to overturn Reagan administration regulations that barred recipients of federal family planning funds from mentioning abortion as an option to women with unintended pregnancies. The Supreme Court was reviewing those rules, with a decision expected in 1991. *(Vote 252, p. 50-S)*

Abortion rights forces in the Senate also mustered majorities on amendments to permit abortions to be performed in military medical facilities (Aug. 3) and to provide foreign aid funds to overseas family planning programs that used their own money to offer information on abortion (Oct. 19). But both of those, along with the reauthorization bill for Title X, were scrapped when supporters could not produce the 60 votes needed to break filibusters threatened by anti-abortion senators. *(Military hospitals, vote 212, p. 44-S; foreign aid for family planning, vote 298, p. 59-S)*

"It's been a bumpy year after a very bright year last year," conceded Les AuCoin, D-Ore., a leader of the abortion rights forces in the House.

But AuCoin insisted that, in general, support for abortion rights in Congress had not fallen from the post-*Webster* peak in 1989. "It looks like a reversal, but what it was was tactical ingenuity," he said.

New Tactics by Abortion Foes

The key example of that ingenuity by anti-abortion lawmakers came during consideration of the $182 billion fiscal 1991 spending bill for the Departments of Labor, Health and Human Services (HHS) and Education. *(Labor-HHS bill, p. 847)*

During Senate committee consideration, members agreed to append to the bill a relaxation of the existing ban on federally funded abortions to permit funding in certain cases of rape or incest.

But the amendment had to be formally added to the bill on the floor, and before that could happen, abortion opponents — who lacked the votes to defeat the rape-incest language on the merits — instead successfully added to the amendment one of their own requiring that parents be notified before an abortion could be performed on a minor.

The amendment was added Oct. 12 only after a motion to kill it failed on a 48-48 tie. *(Vote 266, p. 54-S)*

That it was so close surprised both sides — parental notification was considered popular among lawmakers who otherwise supported abortion rights, just as rape and incest exceptions were considered popular among lawmakers who otherwise opposed the procedure.

Because the parental-notification language was appended to the bill in such a way that it could not be procedurally separated from the rape-incest language, however, abortion rights advocates decided it was better to drop both than to accept both.

Sometimes abortion got tied in with other issues, as with the appropriation for the District of Columbia. On that bill, the House twice rejected a conference report that would have permitted the use of federal funds to pay for abortions in cases or rape or incest, and would have restored to the city its right to use local tax funds to pay for any abortions. Both provisions were dropped. *(D.C. funding bill, p. 891)*

Such provisions were included in the fiscal 1990 spending measure but were dropped after President Bush vetoed the bill.

Abortion opponents hailed the twin rejections in 1990 as a sea change for the House, which had backed the changes repeatedly in 1989. But abortion rights advocates insisted that many of the negatives had less to do with abortion than with disgust with the District government, whose head, Mayor Marion S. Barry Jr., spent his summer as a defendant in a highly publicized criminal trial on drug and perjury charges. (Barry, who was convicted Aug. 10 on one misdemeanor drug possession count, did not seek reelection as mayor and was defeated in November for an at-large City Council seat.) ■

Legal Services Board Curbed on Rulemaking

The strife-torn Legal Services Corporation (LSC) remained blocked by Congress from putting into effect additional limits on state and local legal aid programs despite a new board of directors appointed by President Bush to try to quiet the controversies surrounding the agency.

A Senate-added rider on the 1991 spending bill for the LSC provided that until Oct. 1, 1991, the conservative-dominated board could not put into effect any new rules or regulations for the programs that received LSC funds. The bill also slightly raised the LSC's appropriation to $327 million and did not contain a package of restrictive amendments advocated by critics of legal aid programs. *(Commerce, Justice, State funding bill, p. 881)*

The appropriations bill was the only concrete action by Congress regarding the LSC during the year, though an effort was made to pass an authorization measure for the first time since 1981. The bill (HR 5271) was approved by the House Judiciary Subcommittee on Administrative Law on Aug. 3, but went no further.

Bush had begun the year by replacing a bitterly divided LSC board with his own appointees, installed under recess appointments that allowed them to serve without Senate confirmation.

The board lowered the rhetoric, but maintained the rightward tilt of Reagan-era boards on policy issues and on a key personnel matter: the selection of David H. Martin, a former Reagan administration official, as LSC president in August.

BACKGROUND

Congress created the LSC in 1974 as a quasi-independent corporation to dispense federal funds to legal aid programs free from political pressure by state and local officials. In debating the act, liberal and conservative lawmakers clashed sharply over the line between legal representation for the poor and political and social advocacy; that ideological battle persisted through both the Carter and Reagan administrations. *(1974 Almanac, p. 489)*

A three-year reauthorization was passed in 1977, but a new reauthorization had to be scuttled in 1980 in the face of opposition from conservative lawmakers. President Ronald Reagan tried to abolish the corporation. Congress refused, but Reagan succeeded in cutting its funds by 25 percent and naming sharp critics of legal aid to the 11-member LSC board of directors. *(1981 Almanac, p. 412; 1977 Almanac, p. 587)*

The Reagan-era LSC boards — kept in office under a series of recess appointments through Reagan's first term — adopted limits on class action suits and lobbying by legal aid lawyers and instituted more critical monitoring of local programs.

With Reagan's second term, a compromise of sorts resulted in Senate confirmation of a new board that had some liberal members but was still controlled by conservatives. *(1985 Almanac, p. 244)*

In the face of an anticipated Reagan veto, Congress did not try to pass reauthorizing legislation for the LSC after 1985. Appropriations bills instead were used to influence legal aid issues, and lawmakers added a number of riders limiting the board's power to impose new restrictions on LSC-funded programs.

Bush Appointments

Despite increased factionalization on the board, Bush left its members in place for his first 10 months in office. Then, in November 1989, when a resignation threatened to tip the balance of power to the liberal faction, Bush used recess appointments to name former Rep. John N. Erlenborn, R-Ill. (1965-85), to the vacancy and renamed another director whose previous recess appointment had expired, J. Blakeley Hall, son of Rep. Ralph M. Hall, D-Texas. *(1989 Almanac, p. 284)*

Bush followed by naming nine new board members on Jan. 22, the day before Congress was to return from a recess. As a result, Bush's board could serve until the end of the congressional session without Senate confirmation.

To chair the board, Bush designated George W. Wittgraf, an Iowa lawyer and Bush's 1988 campaign manager in the state. Others named were:

- John F. Collins, a former mayor of Boston and a Bush campaign supporter in 1988;
- Howard H. Dana Jr., a Maine lawyer who had been a liberal dissenter on an early Reagan-era board;
- Luis Guinot Jr., a lawyer from Washington, D.C., and Puerto Rico, and a Bush campaign supporter in 1988;
- Jo Betts Love, of Mississippi, the only black chosen, named to one of two seats for client-eligible groups; she said she had worked with senior citizens and the disabled;
- Guy V. Molinari, a former GOP congressman from New York (1981-89) and newly elected as Staten Island borough president;
- Penny L. Pullen, Republican leader of the Illinois House;
- Xavier L. Suarez, Miami mayor;
- Jeanine E. Wolbeck, of Minnesota, an anti-abortion activist chosen for the second client-eligible position.

Reaction to the Bush slate on Capitol Hill was mixed. Senate Labor and Human Resources Committee Chairman Edward M. Kennedy, D-Mass., whose committee would hold confirmation hearings on LSC nominees, was critical. "President Bush has had a year to choose these nominees," Kennedy said. "He should have waited another 18 hours and sent them to the Senate for confirmation, as the Constitution provides."

But New Hampshire Sen. Warren B. Rudman, a key supporter of legal aid programs as ranking Republican on the Appropriations subcommittee that handled LSC matters, significantly voiced no objection.

LEGISLATIVE ACTION

Once in office, the Bush board adopted a more conciliatory tone toward legal aid programs than its predecessors — pleasing both the legal aid community and its congressional supporters.

Funding Request

Two events in particular cheered legal aid groups.

First, the board announced in April it had asked for the resignation of LSC President Terrance J. Wear. During his two years in office, Wear, formerly an aide to Sen. Jesse Helms, R-N.C., an opponent of legal aid, had conducted what legal aid supporters viewed as a distorted campaign against wasteful spending by LSC-funded programs.

The board also decided to request an increase in LSC funding for fiscal 1991, from $321 million to $343 million. A year earlier, the last Reagan-era board had asked Congress to cut the LSC budget by 4 percent. *(1989 Almanac, p. 721)*

"We want to be as supportive as we can," Wittgraf told the Senate's Commerce, Justice, State Appropriations Subcommittee at an April 19 hearing on the 1991 budget request. Chairman Ernest F. Hollings, D-S.C., hailed the stance as signaling "a new day" at the LSC.

Rudman, who had been the main author of appropriations riders limiting the LSC board's powers, said he too was pleased. "I'm tired of micromanaging things," he said.

McCollum-Stenholm Amendment

Meanwhile, conservative lawmakers, backed by an umbrella group called the Legal Services Reform Coalition, were preparing for a second try at passing an omnibus package of restrictions and procedural requirements for legal aid programs. The amendment fell just seven votes short when its sponsors, Reps. Bill McCollum, R-Fla., and Charles W. Stenholm, D-Texas, tried to attach it to the LSC funding bill in October 1989. *(1989 Almanac, p. 721)*

Among other things, the amendment called for additional procedures for legal aid lawyers in representing farmworkers — a key goal of the American Farm Bureau Federation, the principal member of the Legal Services Reform Coalition. The National Legal Aid and Defender Association (NLADA) and other legal aid groups called the restrictions unnecessary, saying growers had failed to prove allegations of abusive conduct by legal aid lawyers.

McCollum and Stenholm held off announcing the 1990 version of their amendment, stirring hopes among legal aid groups that they would soften its provisions. Meanwhile,

Rep. Barney Frank, D-Mass., chairman of the Judiciary Administrative Law Subcommittee and a strong legal aid supporter, held two days of oversight hearings in May aimed at developing the first reauthorization measure for the legal aid agency since 1981.

The legislative work was momentarily overshadowed in June by the forced resignation of Erlenborn from the LSC board. Erlenborn was a partner in a Washington law firm with agricultural interests among its clients. Prodded by the American Farm Bureau Federation, they began complaining to the firm that Erlenborn's service on the board posed a conflict of interest. Erlenborn and independent legal experts said they saw no conflict, but Erlenborn decided to quit anyway to avoid embarrassing the firm.

In August, Bush picked Tom Rath, a former New Hampshire attorney general who was close to both Rudman and Supreme Court nominee David H. Souter, to succeed Erlenborn. With Congress in session, however, Rath could not be named to a recess appointment, and the board was reduced to 10 members for the remainder of the congressional session. By midsummer, it was clear that delays in the paperwork on the board nominations would make confirmation hearings impossible in the 101st Congress.

Authorization Bill

Frank's bill (HR 5271), introduced in July and approved 6-3 by the Administrative Law Subcommittee on Aug. 3, was a three-year reauthorization with no funding level set. It contained one conservative-backed provision: to attach federal civil and criminal penalties to the misuse of LSC funds. But it also included provisions sought by legal aid groups to strengthen the authority of local governing boards and limit LSC monitoring of legal aid programs.

By that time, McCollum and Stenholm had released their revised amendment and picked up a third cosponsor: Harley O. Staggers Jr., D-W.Va., a member of Frank's subcommittee, who said he would introduce the package at the markup of HR 5271. The new version slightly modified the farmworker restrictions, but it added one new provision to drastically curtail legal aid programs' ability to recover attorneys' fees in successful litigation.

Conservative interest in legislating restrictions on legal aid programs had increased because of a June 25 ruling by a federal judge in Washington that only Congress, not the LSC board, could set limits on the kinds of cases LSC grantees could undertake. The ruling, which the LSC appealed, blocked a rule adopted by the Reagan board to bar legal aid programs from handling cases involving congressional, state or local redistricting.

The subcommittee's markup, which began Aug. 2, proved a disappointment for the conservatives. Staggers' effort to add the entire package of restrictions failed, 3-6, and he made only modest gains in offering the provisions individually.

Frank deflected the two most contentious sections — banning work on redistricting cases or representation of drug defendants in public housing eviction cases — with softer provisions. Under his substitutes, only work on congressional redistricting cases, not state and local cases, was to be banned, while the drug-case restriction was to apply only to persons convicted of drug violations, not to those facing charges.

Conservatives suffered one other setback when Frank offered an amendment, adopted by voice vote, to lift the ban dating from 1974 on abortion-related litigation by LSC grantees. Staggers and two Republicans — Chuck Douglas, N.H., and Lamar Smith, Texas — appeared to vote against the amendment. But Frank, controlling three proxies, declared it adopted, and no roll call was requested.

Final Action

No work had been started in the Senate on an authorization measure, and Frank's bill was never put on the House Judiciary calendar. Attention instead focused on the LSC funding bill, and the conservative-backed drive to attach the McCollum-Stenholm-Staggers amendment to it.

Farm Bureau members staged a lobbying blitz on Capitol Hill on Sept. 11 to try to marshal support for the amendment. But two legal aid groups, NLADA and the Farmworker Justice Fund, countered by publicizing an Aug. 7 letter from Farm Bureau lobbyist Libby Whitley conceding that her group lacked documented evidence of abusive litigation by LSC-funded lawyers.

Despite the buildup, McCollum and Stenholm ended by not offering their amendment when the conference report on the LSC funding bill (HR 5021) reached the House floor Oct. 23. The bill did contain a provision, added in the Senate, that barred the LSC board from putting new rules into effect until Oct. 1, 1991.

PERSONNEL MATTERS

Meanwhile, the LSC board had voted 8-2 on Aug. 9 to pick David H. Martin, who was director of the Office of Government Ethics from 1983 to 1987, as its new president. Martin, who had no previous legal aid experience, was backed by the Legal Services Reform Coalition and picked over three finalists, all more to the liking of legal aid groups.

Martin took office in September after negotiating a three-year contract for the position, whose salary was to advance to $97,000 per year on Jan. 1, 1991. The position did not require Senate confirmation. In his ethics post during the Reagan administration, Martin had come under fire from some Democrats who viewed him as too timid in handling cases involving two White House aides: Edwin Meese III and Michael K. Deaver.

Once in the LSC post, Martin scored some points with legal aid groups with a softened rhetoric and a conciliatory trip to the NLADA's annual meeting in November. But in interviews, he lined up behind several of the items on the conservative coalition's agenda.

Any new initiatives, however, were put on hold when Bush failed to renew board members' recess appointments after Congress adjourned Oct. 28. For two months LSC went without a board before Bush made new recess appointments on Jan. 2, 1991 — again skirting immediate Senate confirmation.

Included on Bush's new slate were eight of the 10 members who had served on the board plus Rath, who had been nominated while Congress was in session. The two new appointees were Basile J. Uddo, a law professor at Loyola University in New Orleans and a member of the LSC board from 1985-90; and William Lee Kirk Jr., an Orlando, Fla., lawyer and former law partner of Florida Rep. McCollum.

The changes appeared to leave the board's ideological composition unchanged. Uddo, a swing vote on the board before conservatives blocked his reappointment, replaced Miami Mayor Suarez, who had voted against conservatives on some issues, including Martin's selection as president. Kirk, who was nominated for the post by McCollum, replaced former Boston Mayor Collins, who had been the most vocal of the board's conservatives. ■

North Convictions Set Aside on Appeal

A federal appeals court, citing the Iran-contra committees' decision to force former White House aide Oliver L. North to testify before the congressional panels under a grant of limited immunity, overturned North's convictions in the case.

In a split ruling July 20, a three-judge panel of the U.S. Court of Appeals for the District of Columbia Circuit set aside all three convictions against North and ordered a lower court to re-examine all the evidence used to convict him to determine whether any of it was influenced by North's immunized testimony in 1987 before Congress.

Members of Congress disagreed on whether the ruling proved the Iran-contra special investigating committees had erred in calling North to testify during the hearings.

"It was an inopportune and unnecessary way for the committee to operate," House Judiciary Chairman Jack Brooks, D-Texas, and a member of the House Iran-contra panel, commented after the ruling.

"But the committee didn't agree with my judgment. I think mine was right, and I think it was proven to be more than right."

But Warren B. Rudman, R-N.H., the Senate panel's vice chairman, said the congressional investigation could not have waited for completion of the criminal trial against North and other defendants.

"With Iran-contra, the hearings would have had to wait for more than three years," Rudman said. "The country couldn't afford that kind of paralysis."

Even though independent counsel Lawrence E. Walsh was preparing at year's end an appeal to the Supreme Court to reinstate the conviction, the appeals court ruling sent a clear signal to Congress that its interest in exposing wrongdoing could at times cripple prosecutors' efforts to put the wrongdoers behind bars.

BACKGROUND

North, a former Marine Corps lieutenant colonel and National Security Council (NSC) aide, was convicted on May 4, 1989, of three felony counts: altering and destroying NSC documents, aiding and abetting the obstruction of a November 1986 congressional inquiry into the Iran-contra affair and illegally accepting a home security system as a gift. *(1989 Almanac, p. 551)*

North had been fired from the NSC job with the initial disclosure on Nov. 25, 1986, that he helped mastermind the selling of arms to Iran in an effort to win release of U.S. hostages and the funneling of the proceeds of the arms sales to the U.S.-backed contras in Nicaragua.

His boss, national security adviser John M. Poindexter, resigned, and the scandal and investigations shadowed President Ronald Reagan for his remaining two years in office.

In December 1986, the House and Senate designated members of two special committees to conduct a joint investigation of the affair; the committees were officially constituted when the 100th Congress convened in January 1987.

Also in December, a three-judge panel picked Walsh, a deputy attorney general in the Eisenhower administration and one-time president of the American Bar Association, as independent counsel to investigate the affair and bring any prosecutions. *(Background, 1987 Almanac, p. 61; 1986 Almanac, p. 415)*

Clash Over Hearings

The committees wanted North and other key figures to testify before them, but Walsh strongly objected. In part because of Walsh's arguments, the committees delayed North's testimony for several months and initially questioned Poindexter, a retired rear admiral, in closed session.

While congressmen publicly voiced little opposition to immunity for North, members of the committees were engaged in a closed-door struggle over the issue. According to accounts that surfaced long after the committees completed their reports in 1987, many Democrats on the House panel had strong reservations about granting North immunity. Support for immunity was stronger on the Senate panel, especially among Republicans; in the end, immunity was supported by unanimous votes on the Senate committee and majority votes in the House.

More than 20 witnesses received immunity in the Iran-contra hearings, most of them lower-rung participants whom Walsh had also allowed immunity. At the time, committee members insisted that the witnesses would not necessarily escape prosecution.

Walsh's staff, meanwhile, was going to great lengths to shield themselves from the overwhelming media coverage of the congressional hearings. The precautions were designed to refute the anticipated arguments from any convicted defendants that prosecutors had improperly used information gained from the supposedly immunized testimony before the congressional committees.

A Relatively Rare Practice

The congressional practice of granting immunity from prosecution to obtain testimony from individuals who would otherwise claim their Fifth Amendment right to remain silent to avoid possible self-incrimination dated to 1857, but was relatively rare.

The most prominent example was the 1973 Senate hearings on the Watergate scandal. During those hearings, more than two dozen witnesses were granted immunity from prosecution based on their testimony. Special Prosecutor Archibald Cox had tried in vain to derail the immunity, arguing that it might prevent convictions, but eventually most of the major figures pleaded guilty or were convicted. *(Watergate scandal, 1973 Almanac, p. 1007)*

Since the 1987 Iran-contra hearings, House and Senate committees went to federal district court — a routine process — for authority to grant immunity seven times. Committees had also sought immunity for closed-door probes; those requests were filed in confidential court papers.

In the 1989 investigation into alleged influence-peddling and political favoritism at the Department of Housing and Urban Development (HUD), Congress sought immunity for only one relatively minor witness, even though six witnesses, including former HUD Secretary Samuel R. Pierce Jr., refused to testify. *(HUD scandal, p. 666; 1989 Almanac, p. 639)*

It took a two-thirds vote of a congressional committee to ask a federal district judge to grant the immunity. Once immunity was given, a witness was required to testify or face jail for contempt.

The 1970 law (PL 91-452) under which committees allowed immunity forbade the use of any compelled testimony against a defendant. But a witness could be prosecuted for crimes mentioned in his testimony if the evidence used in the prosecution was developed independently of the testimony. This type of "use" immunity was challenged in the 1972 Supreme Court case of *Kastigar v. United States*. The court upheld the practice as long as the government showed in any subsequent prosecution that it obtained its evidence from sources independent of testimony given under a grant of immunity.

COURT RULINGS

The appellate ruling in North's case was a decisive victory for his legal attack against the prosecution and also threatened the April 7 conviction of Poindexter.

Before North's trial began, U.S. District Judge Gerhard A. Gesell had heard three days of arguments on whether North's congressional testimony had influenced prosecutors and witnesses. After North's conviction, Gesell sentenced him on July 5, 1989, to 1,200 hours of community service and fined him $150,000.

Poindexter came to trial in 1990. He was convicted of five felony counts of conspiracy, obstruction of Congress and lying to Congress, and sentenced to six months in prison. Poindexter was the most senior official in the Reagan administration to be convicted of felony charges in the scandal and was the highest-ranking White House official to be convicted of criminal violations since Watergate.

North and Poindexter both pressed the immunity issue in challenging the convictions, and the appeals court panel in North's case agreed with him. The judges ordered Gesell to conduct a full hearing to determine whether North's congressional testimony affected his criminal case. And they also completely overturned North's conviction for altering, destroying and concerning documents because of an error in jury instructions.

'Soaked in Immunized Testimony'

In the court's per curiam opinion, the majority judges strongly criticized Gesell's original hearing on the issue.

"A central problem in this case is that many grand jury and trial witnesses were thoroughly soaked in North's immunized testimony, but no effort was made to determine what effect, if any, this extensive exposure had on their testimony," the court majority wrote.

"Papers filed under seal indicate that officials and attorneys from the Department of Justice, the Central Intelligence Agency, the White House and the Department of State gathered, studied and summarized North's immunized testimony in order to prepare themselves or their superiors and colleagues for their testimony before the investigating committees and the grand jury."

The appeals court said Gesell should not have focused on what the prosecutors might have learned from North's congressional testimony, but on what all witnesses might have picked up from the televised hearings or how their memories might have been refreshed by hearing North.

The judges gave several examples, including the trial testimony of Robert C. McFarlane, Poindexter's predecessor as national security adviser. They said McFarlane had altered his testimony before the congressional committees after listening to North testify and that Gessell made "no effort ... to determine what use, if any, this government witness made of North's testimony in his trial testimony."

The appeals judges said that Gesell had to review the testimony witness by witness and, if necessary, line by line. The prosecution had to show that no use whatsoever was made of any of the immunized testimony by the independent counsel's staff or by any witness. The rule also held true for grand jury proceedings.

The opinion was signed by Judges David B. Sentelle and Laurence H. Silberman — both Reagan appointees.

In dissent, Judge Patricia M. Wald, an appointee of President Jimmy Carter, argued that North had received a fair trial. "The majority effectively cuts off the trial judge's discretion in choosing the most practical means of ensuring defendant's *Kastigar* rights," she wrote, "and in so doing it makes a subsequent trial of any congressionally immunized witness virtually impossible."

Congressional Reaction

Despite the court's ruling, key figures in the congressional investigations defended the decisions to grant immunity to North and Poindexter.

Orrin G. Hatch, R-Utah, a member of the Senate committee who vigorously pushed for immunity for North, said he was willing to sacrifice potential convictions so that Congress could determine who directed and carried out the Iran-contra activities.

Some legal experts suggested that North's testimony should have been taken in private, but Hatch dismissed the idea. "In something like the highly explosive Iran-contra situation, the public wouldn't have stood for secret sessions," he said.

Rudman also defended the decision, but he acknowledged that immunity generally should be used sparingly because of the potential cost to the prosecution.

"There was a possible presidential abuse of power [in Iran-contra]. We were looking at a possible impeachment.... That's one thing," Rudman said. Then, using as an example the HUD probe, he added, "But when you have a question of thievery going on in agencies, it's another matter. In those [latter cases], prosecution and jail is far more important than finding out the truth early."

Further Appeals

On Nov. 27, the 12-member appeals court rejected Walsh's petition to rehear the case. At year's end, his office was preparing to appeal it to the Supreme Court. Poindexter's appeal was pending before the D.C. Circuit.

One other Iran-contra defendant was convicted in 1990. Former CIA agent Thomas G. Clines, who helped organize the secret arms supply network, was convicted Sept. 19 of four income tax charges of underreporting profits from the arms deals and failure to disclose control of foreign bank accounts. He was sentenced to 16 months in prison and fined $40,000.

Five other Iran-contra defendants had been convicted or pleaded guilty since 1987: McFarlane; retired Air Force Maj. Gen. Richard V. Secord; businessman and Secord partner Albert A. Hakim; conservative fundraiser Carl R. "Spitz" Channell; and Channell associate Richard R. Miller. *(Status of cases, 1989 Almanac, p. 555)*

Walsh had to drop conspiracy charges, however, against a former CIA station chief in Costa Rica, Joseph Fernandez, after the Justice Department refused to release information about CIA operations that Fernandez's lawyers said was essential to his defense. A federal appeals court in Richmond, Va., on Sept. 7 upheld a lower court's dismissal of the case. ■

Attempts To Limit RICO Fail Again

BOXSCORE

Legislation: Civil RICO revision (S 438, HR 5111).

Major action: HR 5111 approved by House Judiciary Committee, Sept. 18; S 438 approved by Senate Judiciary Committee, 12-2, Feb. 1.

Reports: Judiciary (H Rept 101-975); Judiciary (S Rept 101-269).

Differing bills aimed at cutting back private suits under the federal antiracketeering law known as RICO won approval from the Senate and House Judiciary committees in 1990, but the industry-dominated coalition behind the bills failed for the third consecutive Congress to push a measure to enactment.

Business groups and others maintained that the 1970 Racketeer Influenced and Corrupt Organizations Act (RICO) had been transformed from a weapon against organized crime into a bludgeon against established businesses, accountants, lawyers and other professionals. They wanted to limit the provisions for bringing triple-damage civil suits under the law and managed to get bills aimed at that goal far along in both the 99th and 100th Congresses.

The ad hoc Business Coalition for RICO Reform got bills introduced early in 1989 and voiced confidence that it would finally bring its drive to success in the 101st Congress. And as 1990 started, the coalition had reason for optimism.

The Senate Judiciary Committee, which had postponed a markup on the issue in the fall of 1989, moved on schedule Feb. 1 to approve the coalition-drafted bill (S 438) that would have virtually eliminated triple-damage private RICO suits.

In the House, William J. Hughes, D-N.J., chairman of the Judiciary Subcommittee on Crime, was negotiating with the coalition's House sponsor, Rick Boucher, D-Va., on a compromise bill that the coalition hoped could move quickly through that chamber.

The Hughes-Boucher compromise, however, was not unveiled until June 21. Its central feature — a so-called gatekeeper approach requiring federal judges to apply stricter standards in screening out RICO suits at an early stage — gave business groups less than the Senate bill, but the coalition embraced the new measure (HR 5111) in hope of speedy approval by the Judiciary Committee.

The committee's crowded agenda, however, delayed the RICO markup until Sept. 18. By that time, proponents were up against the legislative clock. When they were denied the chance to bring the bill to the House floor under expedited procedures, their effort was again doomed to fall short.

BACKGROUND

RICO, enacted as Title IX of the Organized Crime Control Act of 1970 (PL 91-452), was primarily intended to give federal prosecutors stronger weapons against organized crime. A laundry list of so-called predicate offenses could be used to fashion a criminal RICO charge, which carried with it a 20-year prison sentence, a fine of up to $25,000 and the threat of forfeiture of any proceeds from racketeering activities. *(1970 Almanac, p. 545)*

A less-noticed section also allowed private suits under RICO. A plaintiff could fashion a suit using the law's same broad definitions and, if successful, recover three times any monetary damages suffered from the racketeering activity, plus attorneys' fees.

The law was little used in its first decade, but during the 1980s prosecutors achieved dramatic successes with RICO cases against organized-crime groups in several major cities. In addition, prosecutors began to use the law's elastic coverage to go after corrupt politicians, drug dealers, white-collar criminals, labor racketeers, gamblers, terrorists, white supremacists and pornographers.

Civil RICO also went largely unused during the 1970s, but private lawyers began to develop its potential during the '80s. Plaintiffs ranging from forlorn investors and discontented utility customers to major corporations and fired executives cited RICO in suits against established businesses that included Fortune 500 corporations, major banks and securities dealers, and well-regarded law and accounting firms.

Business groups and others, including the American Civil Liberties Union (ACLU) and the American Bar Association (ABA), complained that civil RICO was being misused in routine commercial disputes that did not warrant enhanced penalties and more properly belonged in state courts.

The number of civil RICO cases rose dramatically after a 1985 Supreme Court ruling, *Sedima S.P.R.L. v. Imrex Co.*, that refused to limit suits to cases in which the defendant had already been convicted under RICO's criminal provisions.

From a trickle of cases before 1985, the number tallied by the Administrative Office of the U.S. Courts jumped to 614 in the next nine months and plateaued at about 1,000 a year through 1990. *(1985 Almanac, p. 8-A)*

Lobbying Drive

Three business groups with members often named as RICO defendants — the National Association of Manufacturers, the American Institute of Certified Public Accountants and the Securities Industry Association — had been pressing Congress to change the law since before the *Sedima* ruling. They stepped up their efforts after the Supreme Court decision.

In 1986, the coalition won House passage of a bill to impose the prior criminal conviction requirement on civil RICO suits, but the measure stalled in the Senate. In 1988, a recrafted bill won unanimous approval from the Senate Judiciary Committee, but was blocked from the floor by senators who objected to its retroactivity provision. *(1988 Almanac, p. 82)*

The bills introduced at the start of the 101st Congress — HR 1046 by Boucher and S 438 by Sen. Dennis DeConcini, D-Ariz. — retained the retroactivity provision and the limitation on triple-damage RICO suits except in cases brought by the federal government or those involving a prior criminal conviction.

But in a nod to consumer groups that had opposed sharp limits on civil RICO, the measures also contained a provision for plaintiffs to recover actual damages plus up to double punitive damages in three types of suits: insider trading, certain consumer-fraud cases, and suits brought by special local government bodies such as utility districts.

Hearings before the Senate Judiciary Committee in June 1989 and Hughes' Crime Subcommittee in May, June and July of that year allowed proponents and opponents of the bills to repeat their arguments over the extent of civil RICO abuse and the need for legislation to prevent it.

Representatives of two consumer groups associated with Ralph Nader — Public Citizen's Congress Watch and U.S. Public Interest Research Group (USPIRG) — and state law enforcement organizations insisted the business groups were exaggerating the alleged abuses under the law. They also pointed to the crisis in the savings and loan industry as proof of the need for strong legal weapons against sophisticated economic wrongdoing.

While the hearings were under way, the Supreme Court weighed in with a 5-4 decision, *H. J. Inc. v. Northwestern Bell Telephone Co.*, that again rejected pleas for judicial narrowing of the law. Proponents said the decision underlined the need for legislative change. *(1989 Almanac, p. 319)*

Setbacks for Proponents

After the Crime Subcommittee hearings had been concluded, however, Hughes made it known he wanted to take a different approach from the coalition-drafted measures. A former state prosecutor, he said he wanted to limit civil RICO while preserving it for serious white-collar fraud cases by writing stricter standards for racketeering suits to be enforced by federal judges at an early stage of litigation.

Hughes, Boucher and the subcommittee's ranking Republican, Bill McCollum of Florida, circulated a draft in late 1989. After getting sharply divergent views from the opposing interest groups, however, they decided to carry the quest for consensus over into 1990.

Meanwhile, DeConcini disappointed proponents by informing them he planned to delete the retroactivity provision from the bill. DeConcini had been buffeted by criticisms of his actions in behalf of Charles H. Keating Jr., a target of RICO counts in civil suits arising from the collapse of his California-based Lincoln Savings and Loan Association. *('Keating Five,' p. 78)*

Meeting with the business coalition's representatives in September, DeConcini told them the bill could only be jeopardized by allowing the consumer groups to depict it as a bailout for people implicated in the S&L scandals.

DeConcini readied his revised bill for introduction before the Senate Judiciary Committee on Nov. 16, 1989 — the panel's last scheduled meeting for the year — only to be blocked by a parliamentary maneuver by Howard M. Metzenbaum, D-Ohio.

Metzenbaum had sponsored the RICO overhaul in the 100th Congress, but — piqued by the business coalition's opposition to his amendment to preserve civil RICO in some investment-related suits — shifted positions in the 101st Congress. Citing a rule that barred committee markups while the Senate was in session, Metzenbaum forced postponement of the markup to 1990. "I'm willing to reform RICO, not gut it," Metzenbaum explained.

SENATE COMMITTEE MARKUP

Metzenbaum's objection proved to be only a temporary obstacle, however, as the Senate Judiciary Committee got back on schedule on Feb. 1, approving DeConcini's revised bill on a 12-2 vote. Only Metzenbaum and Edward M. Kennedy, D-Mass., voted against it.

There were no amendments after DeConcini offered his substitute for his original measure, and most of the debate focused not on the bill but on the savings and loan issue and the attacks on DeConcini.

"I, for one, am sick and tired of a colleague getting beat up," said Orrin G. Hatch, R-Utah, a bill cosponsor. "It's pathetic and it's criminal."

To underscore his decision to delete the bill's retroactivity provision, DeConcini waved a large tablet of paper toward reporters and cameras and recited the words on the page: "The RICO Reform Bill Does Not Apply to the Lawsuit Against Lincoln."

In a letter before the markup, Congress Watch and USPIRG made clear their plan to continue to link RICO to the savings and loan scandal.

"This nation is suffering through a white-collar crime wave, from insider trading on Wall Street to S&L fraud on Main Street; from commodities fraud in Chicago to telemarketing fraud in California," the letter stated. "It would be fitting cause for citizen outrage if Congress' response to this avalanche of sleaze is to weaken the laws against fraud."

Washington lawyer Richard Moe, a lobbyist for the accountants' group, praised the committee's action and criticized consumer groups that opposed the bill. "They are now trying to politicize this by linking it to the savings and loan crisis," he said.

Provisions

As approved by the committee, S 438 would have:

- Allowed triple-damage awards only in suits brought by the federal government or if the defendant already had been convicted of a RICO violation or related felony.
- Allowed awards of actual damages, costs and reasonable attorneys' fees, and punitive damages up to double the actual damages in suits by specialized units of local government, plaintiffs injured by insider trading and consumers defrauded in certain transactions, unless the securities or commodities laws already covered the behavior.

DeConcini's decision to allow the award of attorneys' fees was a partial concession to Metzenbaum. His original bill would not have allowed fee awards.

- Prohibited introduction of evidence on punitive damages until after a finding of liability, so that a jury would not be prejudiced by evidence of a defendant's wealth.
- Created an affirmative defense to RICO suits for defendant companies who were relying on some regulatory action or interpretation of law by an authorized federal or state agency.
- Barred RICO suits against someone who participated in "any non-violent demonstration, assembly, protest, rally or similar form of public speech undertaken for reasons other than economic or commercial gain or advantage."

The provision was a response to a small number of suits, including one successful action, arising from violent anti-abortion demonstrations outside clinics where abortions were performed.

HOUSE COMMITTEE ACTION

The House Judiciary Committee approved a modified RICO revision bill on Sept. 18 by voice vote, with four Democrats asking to be recorded as voting no (H Rept 101-

975). Intended as a consensus measure, the modified bill moved too slowly, however, to be pushed to enactment in the 101st Congress.

'Gatekeeper Plan'

Hughes, whose subcommittee got jurisdiction over RICO for the first time in the 101st Congress, described his "gatekeeper plan" as a better way of limiting civil RICO than the business coalition's proposal. Federal judges would be required to dismiss racketeering suits in early proceedings unless they met certain criteria for serious crimes.

The concept changed little from the initial draft in the fall of 1989 until its introduction by Hughes, McCollum and Boucher as HR 5111 in June. But the time spent in crafting the precise language proved fatal to the bill's chances.

Like the Senate bill, Hughes' measure retained the triple-damage remedy in cases where a defendant had already been convicted of a criminal offense related to the suit. Otherwise, however, the plaintiff would have to show all of the following:

- That the triple-damages remedy was "appropriate because of the magnitude of significance" of the injury.
- That the defendant was "a major participant" in criminal conduct responsible for the injury.
- That the remedy was "needed to deter future egregious criminal conduct" by the defendant or others.

In addition, Hughes included a provision to codify language from the Supreme Court's 1989 decision defining what constituted a "pattern of racketeering activity" under the law.

The RICO act only required proof of at least two offenses over a 10-year period; the bill would have added that the offenses be "related to one another" and "amount to or pose a threat of continuing racketeering."

The final bill was somewhat more favorable to RICO defendants than the original draft proposal.

It included provisions to raise the burden of proof for plaintiffs to "clear and convincing evidence" rather than the customary "preponderance of the evidence" standard, allow defendants an immediate appeal if a motion to dismiss was rejected and apply the new limits to some pending cases.

Subcommittee Markup

Hughes said at a June 21 news conference that the bill would be marked up by his subcommittee just five days later.

"It's going to move," he said. Nine of 11 subcommittee members signed on to the bill when introduced.

Boucher described the bill as better than his earlier measure "for the very practical reason that it enjoys a broad base of support."

Subcommittee approval of the bill on June 26 came by voice vote after a swift markup. John Conyers Jr., D-Mich., who had helped bottle up the 1988 legislation as chairman of the Criminal Justice Subcommittee, stopped short of opposing Hughes' bill but said he wanted to amend it to preserve civil RICO as a weapon in cases stemming from S&L suits:

Conyers lost on the only roll call vote of the session, however.

By a 4-6 vote, the panel refused to drop a retroactivity provision that Hughes, unlike DeConcini, had kept in his proposal. Conyers decided to withhold a second amendment — to preserve existing RICO procedures in any cases against banks, thrifts or other financial institutions — until full committee markup.

Committee Markup

The Judiciary Committee markup on Sept. 18, again played out against the backdrop of the thrift crisis, ended with voice-vote approval of the bill after sponsors made minor amendments aimed at neutralizing consumer groups' opposition.

In an unusual procedure, however, four Democrats asked to be recorded as voting no: Howard L. Berman, Don Edwards and Mel Levine of California and Craig Washington of Texas.

Hughes told the committee his bill was "a balanced approach" to revising the law. He said it would curb abuses but maintain civil RICO "as a useful tool to combat widespread criminal activities."

Several liberal Democrats, however, called for amending the bill to avoid weakening protections for victims of white-collar crimes.

"It is this law, of course, that is being used by elderly victims of Charles Keating's shenanigans," Conyers said as he introduced his amendment to preserve existing RICO procedures in suits against financial institutions.

To deflect the criticism, Hughes got the panel to amend the bill to provide that the new restrictions would apply only to future cases, not to pending suits such as the litigation against Keating.

Adoption of the amendment did not satisfy Dan Glickman, D-Kan., however, who urged that the effective date be changed to six months after enactment. Hughes grudgingly agreed.

Boucher introduced the second amendment aimed at defusing the thrifts issue. Under Boucher's amendment, a case involving a failed thrift would be presumed to involve "egregious criminal conduct," one of the new criteria for plaintiffs.

Boucher's effort to substitute his amendment for Conyers' broader change led to the one roll call vote of the markup, a 24-11 victory for the bill's supporters. Democrats divided 11-10 in favor of Boucher's version; Republicans voted solidly 13-1 for it.

FINAL ACTION

After the markup, attorney Moe also tried to neutralize the savings and loan issue, saying the approved bill would be "an effective tool for getting at fraud in S&Ls or anywhere else while at the same time weeding out the abuses that the present law has led to."

The key lobbyist against the bill, Congress Watch's Pamela Gilbert, however, said despite the modifications, the measure was still "a bailout for the savings and loan criminals, particularly the accountants and lawyers who facilitated the S&L crisis."

With the session scheduled to end in only a few weeks, the coalition's hopes for the bill's enactment depended on getting the bill onto the House floor under suspension of the rules — allowing for no amendments and only 40 minutes of debate.

But Conyers and a second committee chairman opposed to the bill, Banking Chairman Henry B. Gonzalez, D-Texas, raised objections, and the bill never reached the floor. With no House action, supporters of the Senate bill also did not push that measure to the floor. ■

Vertical Price-Fixing Bill Stalls Again

A bitterly fought antitrust bill to prevent manufacturers from fixing prices by their dealers died at the end of the 101st Congress. The House on April 18 approved a measure (HR 1236) designed to reduce conduct known as resale price maintenance, or vertical price fixing. But a related bill (S 865) stalled in the Senate as it had when the House passed similar legislation in 1987.

In an effort to get a floor vote on the bill, Sen. Howard M. Metzenbaum, D-Ohio, held up a bill creating 85 judgeships (HR 5316) until the last day of Congress. Metzenbaum finally relented after winning a promise from Senate Judiciary leaders, including bill opponent Strom Thurmond, R-S.C., for a floor vote early in 1991.

BOXSCORE

Legislation: Vertical price fixing (HR 1236, S 865).

Major action: Passed by House, 235-157, April 18; by Senate Judiciary Committee, 7-6, Feb. 22.

Reports: Judiciary Committee (S Rept 101-251); Judiciary Committee (H Rept 101-438).

Vertical price fixing occurred when a manufacturer conspired with a retailer to force a rival dealer to charge at least a certain price for the manufacturer's goods.

Typically, the type of case covered by the bill arose after a distributor decided to sell a particular product at a discount. Then another distributor — usually a bigger and more powerful one that was unwilling to lower its prices to meet the competition — persuaded the manufacturer to terminate the contract with the discounting distributor.

The chief sponsor of the House bill, Judiciary Chairman Jack Brooks, D-Texas, said price fixing was "experiencing a renaissance." At the beginning of 1990, he called HR 1236 his priority for the 101st Congress.

In the Senate, Metzenbaum, chairman of the Antitrust Subcommittee, termed S 865 "the most important, understated bill around, from the consumer standpoint."

Yet many members in both chambers insisted that the legislation was unnecessary and could have exposed businesses to legal actions when there was no agreement to fix prices. They said it could allow ambiguous evidence to be used to establish a conspiracy and in the end could hurt honest manufacturers.

The Justice Department also opposed the proposals, saying they would inhibit legitimate pacts between manufacturers and dealers and spawn endless litigation.

BACKGROUND

Since a 1911 Supreme Court decision, vertical price fixing had been automatically, or "per se," illegal. But administration policy and two court decisions in the past decade had created ambiguity about what was enough evidence to warrant a jury trial. They also cast doubt on whether vertical price fixing would be punished in the courts. The Justice Department had not brought a vertical price fixing case since 1980.

The 1990 legislation originated when it became apparent in the early 1980s that the Reagan administration did not intend to enforce the per se prohibition against resale price maintenance and was in fact supporting its reversal in court cases.

The Justice Department's position stemmed from a theory that such price maintenance could actually enhance rather than inhibit competition.

In 1983, to block the Justice Department from filing briefs in behalf of defendant-manufacturers charged with vertical price fixing, Congress approved a restriction saying no department money could be used to "overturn or alter the per se prohibition against resale price maintenance under the antitrust laws." *(1983 Almanac, p. 477)*

What the Bills Would Have Done

HR 1236 would in effect have reversed two Supreme Court decisions that made it much harder for plaintiffs to win vertical price fixing cases.

The first was a 1984 ruling in *Monsanto Co. v. Spray-Rite Service Corp.* that a complaining discounter must provide direct evidence that a manufacturer and another retailer had intended to maintain resale price levels. *(1984 Almanac, p. 12-A)*

The bill would have allowed a jury trial if the plaintiff could show that a supplier canceled its contract after receiving a communication from a rival dealer about the plaintiff's pricing policies. The plaintiff would have to demonstrate that the supplier's termination or refusal to supply was "substantially caused" by the competitor's communication.

A separate provision would have stated that minimum resale price maintenance was automatically illegal under antitrust law. The provision was intended to override the holding in the 1988 case *Business Electronics Corp. v. Sharp Electronics Corp.* that there was no per se violation of antitrust laws unless the manufacturer and the retailer agreed to set a specific price. *(1988 Almanac, p. 131)*

The bill would have codified the 1911 Supreme Court holding, in *Dr. Miles Medical Co. v. John D. Park and Sons Co.*, that minimum resale price fixing agreements were illegal per se.

Pros and Cons

Major groups fighting the legislation included the National Association of Manufacturers, the U.S. Chamber of Commerce and the American Bar Association (ABA).

Those supporting the bills included the International Mass Retail Association, the National Association of Catalog Showroom Merchandisers, the AFL-CIO and the National Association of Attorneys General.

Other bill supporters, including Sen. Herb Kohl, D-Wis., said that the legislation would still allow manufacturers to cut off dealers that were performing inadequately, as long as they did it on their own and not through an agreement with other dealers.

At the Judiciary Committee's hearing in June 1989, Kohl told his colleagues that dealer-retailer pacts had automatically been illegal since 1911 for a simple reason. "When a manufacturer conspires to require its distributors to charge a fixed price for a good or service, it eliminates price competition for consumers," he said.

While the 1988 *Sharp Electronics* decision helped focus congressional attention on manufacturers that cut off discount retailers, the provisions of the bills to reverse the decision provoked stiff opposition.

Sen. Dennis DeConcini, D-Ariz., who had supported related legislation in the 100th Congress, said the language of S 865 was so broad as to "put entirely innocent manufacturers at risk of triple-damages awards," which were allowed in antitrust cases.

Sims, of the ABA's Antitrust Law Section, maintained that the effect of the proposed legislation would be to limit a manufacturer's right — recognized since a 1919 Supreme Court decision in *U.S. v. Colgate & Co.* — to decide unilaterally with which customers it would do business.

It was an argument that many conservative members adopted. Thurmond contended that the bills amounted to unwarranted congressional intervention. "Nothing in this bill [S 865] mandates lower prices," he said. "In fact, because of increased litigation, costs to consumers will go up."

HOUSE ACTION

Despite a veto threat from Bush, the House on April 18 approved HR 1236, largely along party lines, by a vote of 235-157. *(Vote 74, p. 28-H)*

The House rejected three Republican-sponsored amendments to stiffen the standards of evidence a complaining retailer would have to meet. But members accepted, without objection, an amendment by Carlos J. Moorhead, R-Calif., to make the new evidentiary standards apply only to cases filed after enactment.

The Justice Department and the Federal Trade Commission said the bill would expose suppliers to unfounded antitrust liability when they canceled a dealer's contract for legitimate reasons, such as poor service.

The House Judiciary Committee had approved the bill June 20, 1989 (H Rept 101-438). *(1989 Almanac, p. 285)*

Hamilton Fish Jr., N.Y., ranking Judiciary Committee Republican, tried to amend the bill to require plaintiffs to produce evidence of a conspiracy to fix prices and to show that the price was "the major" cause for the manufacturer's decision to terminate the complaining retailer's contract.

Fish said he was concerned that the bill's language was too broad and that a manufacturer could be sued even if he had good reason to end a supply agreement.

"For example, a retail outlet may be terminated for not advertising a product as agreed upon, failure to provide adequate repair or warranty service, failure to hire trained sales or service personnel, failure to properly display the products of the manufacturer or simply because its sales are poor," Fish said. His amendment was rejected 192-204. *(Vote 72, p. 28-H)*

Chuck Douglas, R-N.H., tried to press a substitute amendment to codify the 1911 ruling but delete all evidentiary standards in the bill. It was defeated 155-242. *(Vote 71, p. 28-H)*

The final amendment rejected was offered by Tom Campbell, R-Calif., to allow a defense to price-fixing accusations that the defendant's share in the relevant market was so small that he lacked market power. It was defeated 190-199. *(Vote 73, p. 28-H)*

SENATE ACTION

The Senate Judiciary Committee on Feb. 22 approved S 685 (S Rept 101-251) to ensure that retailers could take legal action against vertical price fixing.

The bill was approved 7-6 after winning the vote of Dennis DeConcini, D-Ariz., who opposed the measure but had promised Metzenbaum that he would vote for the bill if it meant the difference between committee approval and rejection. Metzenbaum on Feb. 1 had dropped efforts to block committee consideration of a DeConcini bill overhauling RICO, the federal antiracketeering law. *(RICO revisions, p. 536)*

DeConcini sent a proxy to be used only in the event of a tie. There was some hesitation about whether it would be used because Arlen Specter, R-Pa., also had sent a proxy but had forbidden its use on the vote to approve the bill.

A Kohl amendment was adopted by voice vote. It said that to reach a jury, a retailer that alleged vertical price fixing would have to show that a competitor's price complaint was "the major cause" of a manufacturer's decision to terminate the plaintiff's right to distribute a product. The bill had used the phrase "major contributing cause."

In October, with the bill not having moved beyond committee, Metzenbaum sought to attach the measure to legislation bound to pass the chamber. Metzenbaum held up the federal judgeships bill (HR 5316) in an effort to get a vote on the unrelated antitrust bill. He relented when he was assured that S 865 would reach the floor early in the 102nd Congress. *(Federal judgeships, p. 520)* ■

Antitrust Fines Hiked; Director Curbs Eased

Legislation that eased the constraints on interlocking corporate directorships was cleared by the 101st Congress shortly before its adjournment, along with a late amendment to increase penalties in antitrust cases brought by the federal government.

Two other antitrust bills — to allow U.S. companies to pool their production efforts without fear of antitrust liability and to curtail vertical price fixing — stalled after winning House approval. *(Vertical price fixing, p. 539)*

Interlocking Directorates

Congress on Oct. 28 sent to the president a bill to ease the constraints on interlocking corporate directorships. The House cleared the measure Oct. 28 after the Senate had passed it the day before. President Bush signed the legislation (HR 29 — PL 101-588) on Nov. 16.

HR 29 updated the Clayton Antitrust Act of 1914 to prohibit individuals from serving on the boards of directors of competing companies if both had $10 million or more in assets. The threshold was indexed to keep pace with economic growth; previously, the prohibition applied if either company had $1 million or more in assets or profits. The legislation also extended the restrictions beyond directors to certain high-level officers.

In the waning hours of the 101st Congress, the Senate added an amendment to the bill that increased tenfold the maximum criminal fines for corporate violations of the Sherman Act — to $10 million from $1 million — and raised the maximum fine against an individual to $350,000 from $100,000. The amendment was essentially the same as the provisions of HR 3341 (H Rept 101-287), which had passed the House on Oct. 17, 1989. *(1989 Almanac, p. 287)*

The Senate also added an amendment providing for triple damages in civil suits brought by the United States against antitrust violators. Under existing law, private plaintiffs could obtain triple damages for antitrust injuries, while the U.S. government could win only actual damages. This provision was also originally part of a separate measure (S 996 — S Rept 101-288) that won the approval of the Judiciary Committee on March 22 but that never reached the floor.

The House originally approved HR 29, sponsored by Hamilton Fish, R-N.Y., the ranking Republican on the House Judiciary Committee's Economic and Commercial Law Subcommittee, by voice vote on May 15. The House Judiciary Committee had approved the bill (H Rept 101-483) on May 1.

Joint Ventures

The House on June 5 passed by voice vote legislation to encourage joint production ventures by U.S. companies. In the Senate, though, similar measures stalled in the Judiciary Committee's Antitrust, Monopolies and Business Rights Subcommittee.

The House bill (HR 4611) would have limited the antitrust liability of joint manufacturing ventures to single damages, rather than the usual triple damages, provided that companies notified the government in advance of their venture. The bill was intended to encourage U.S. companies to pool their resources and production efforts, without fear of antitrust liability, so they could be more competitive in the world market.

Jack Brooks, D-Texas, chairman of the Judiciary Committee, said, "There appears to be an overdrawn — yet real — perception in the business community that the antitrust laws generally discourage all collaborative activity, irrespective of the pro-competitive benefits achieved. Unfortunately, perceptions can affect behavior."

Congress in 1984 cleared the National Cooperative Research Act (PL 98-462), which provided similar limits on the antitrust liability of joint research and development ventures. HR 4611 would have amended the 1984 act. *(1984 Almanac, p. 258)*

Brooks said since then, more than 150 joint ventures had been formed in a wide range of industries — significantly more, he said, than before the law was enacted. "It is our hope that the collaborative activity at the production level will increase in a similar fashion," Brooks said.

The bill would have limited foreign involvement in any joint production venture to 30 percent and would have required that all the facilities of the venture be within the United States or its territories.

Bill Frenzel, R-Minn., criticized those provisions, saying they would discriminate against international investment. He said the bill could hurt relations with trading partners and could lead other countries to enact similar legislation that would restrict U.S. participation in ventures abroad.

Brooks defended his bill, saying it was designed to promote U.S. competitiveness, not "unduly favor" foreign firms.

The bill was approved May 1 by the Judiciary Committee (H Rept 101-516). The measure was not as extensive as proposals offered in 1989 that would also have provided antitrust exemptions for joint marketing and distribution ventures. The House Judiciary Subcommittee on Economic and Commercial Law had approved the measure April 26.

In the Senate, Howard M. Metzenbaum, D-Ohio, chairman of the Judiciary Committee's Antitrust, Monopolies and Business Rights Subcommittee, expressed deep misgivings about versions (S 1006, S 2692) similar to the one passed in the House, and the measures never advanced out of the subcommittee. ■

Assorted Copyright Bills Signed Into Law

Throughout the second session of the 101st Congress — especially during its waning days and hours — lawmakers passed an assortment of copyright measures that President Bush signed into law.

In the final hours of the session, the federal judgeships bill (HR 5316) became a vehicle for Senate sponsors of a couple of bills mired in complexity.

An artists' rights provision was adopted at the urging of Edward M. Kennedy, D-Mass. The judgeships bill also carried a Kennedy-backed provision extending copyright protection to architectural designs.

Another add-on, sponsored by Orrin G. Hatch, R-Utah, sought to protect the computer software industry against unfair profiteering by giving software copyright owners the option to refuse rental rights to software buyers.

Both chambers approved the bill by voice vote in the Oct. 27 session, with House action coming in the early hours of Oct. 28. President Bush signed the bill (HR 5316 — PL 101-650) on Dec. 1. *(Federal judgeships, p. 520)*

Legislation to allow publishers to collect damages from state governments and universities for infringement of copyrighted materials, meanwhile, cleared Congress shortly before its adjournment.

And minor bills to increase copyright fees and to reduce the number of commissioners on the Copyright Royalty Tribunal won congressional approval in June.

ARTISTS' RIGHTS

Under the Kennedy-backed legislation, visual artists — painters, sculptors and photographers — would have a legal right to prevent distortion or modification of their work even after it was sold.

The provision covered anyone who created a painting, drawing, print, sculpture or still photograph produced for exhibition purposes, but would not protect film directors. It would also cover works limited to 200 or fewer copies.

As approved, the measure would make it clear that anyone who created a painting, drawing, print, sculpture or still photographic image in a limited number of copies had a claim of authorship over the work.

The ownership of a right of integrity would be distinct

from actual ownership or possession of the work itself and from copyright.

The bill also would prevent the use of an artist's name on a work that he or she did not create.

Rep. Robert W. Kastenmeier, D-Wis., the bill's sponsor, said artists and museum directors had urged members to find a way for artists to protect their works and reputations.

By not applying the measure to filmmakers, lawmakers decided not to use this issue to tackle the controversy over whether black-and-white films should be "colorized" without the consent of the filmmaker.

Artists would be required to show that the distortion or mutilation prejudiced their honor or reputation. The protections would endure for the life of the artist plus 50 years.

Legislative Action

A Senate Judiciary subcommittee had approved a related proposal (S 1198) on June 28, and the House had passed a companion bill (HR 2690) on June 5.

HR 2690 won the approval of the House Judiciary Subcommittee on Courts, Intellectual Property and the Administration of Justice on Feb. 28.

The full committee approved the bill (H Rept 101-514) by voice vote March 28, and it passed the House on June 5 also by voice vote.

S 1198 was approved, 5-2, by the Senate Judiciary Subcommittee on Patents, Copyrights and Trademarks on June 28, but was never taken up in full committee during the last busy months of the session.

In the last hours of Congress, Kennedy, who sponsored S 1198, attached the measure to the judgeships bill in an attempt to assure passage.

COMPUTER SOFTWARE PROTECTION

In the waning hours of the 1990 session, Congress prohibited commercial leasing or rental of computer software without the permission of the copyright holders. The provisions of an earlier Senate-passed measure (S 198) were attached to the federal judgeships bill shortly before it cleared Congress on Oct. 28 (session of Oct. 27).

The bill was designed to forestall unauthorized copying of computer programs that often required millions of dollars to develop and that typically sold for several hundred dollars.

Computer software producers had long complained of businesses that rented expensive software to clients who then copied the program, essentially obtaining it at a greatly reduced cost.

"If these products can be rented and copied at a mere fraction of the retail cost, the potential for lost sales will almost certainly lead to the collapse of the U.S. software industry," bill sponsor Orrin Hatch, R-Utah, said.

The measure permitted nonprofit libraries and educational institutions to lend computer software to faculty, staff and students.

Legislative Action

S 198 was approved by the Senate Judiciary Committee (S Rept 101-265) by voice vote March 8. Its Subcommittee on Patents, Copyrights and Trademarks had approved the measure July 26, 1989.

The Senate passed the measure by voice vote May 1.

The House measure (HR 5498) contained only a few minor technical differences in its provisions concerning computer software protection. However, the legislation also dealt with the rights of artists, architects and video game manufacturers.

The Judiciary Committee approved HR 5498 on Sept. 18 (H Rept 101-735), and the full House passed the bill by voice vote Sept. 27. The House then passed S 198 after inserting the text of the just-passed HR 5498.

On Oct. 20, the Senate passed the amended S 198 by voice vote after stripping a provision designed to allow arcade owners to purchase video games from sources other than the manufacturers and authorized distributers.

Finally, both chambers decided to add the House version of S 198 to the judgeships bill in the Oct. 27 session.

STATE, UNIVERSITY COVERAGE

Legislation to allow publishers to collect damages from state governments and universities for infringement of copyrighted materials cleared Congress on Oct. 26 and was signed into law by President Bush on Nov. 15 (HR 3045 — PL 101-553).

The law responded to federal court rulings since the mid-1980s that held states and state-run universities immune from federal copyright infringement suits under the 11th Amendment to the Constitution, unless Congress specifically overrode that immunity.

The measure, which cleared both chambers by voice vote, allowed copyright owners to sue for actual and statutory damages, attorneys' fees and injunctive relief. The Senate had added a provision to limit attorneys' fees, but it was dropped in conference.

Publishers had sought the legislation, claiming that state universities and colleges were photocopying huge chunks of textbooks and other reference materials without fear of meaningful sanctions.

Legislative Action

Companion bills (HR 3045, S 497) to subject state universities to copyright infringement suits were introduced by the chairmen of the two subcommittees with jurisdiction over copyright and began moving in 1989. *(1989 Almanac, p. 291)*

Kastenmeier's HR 3045 was approved by his Subcommittee on Courts, Intellectual Property and the Administration of Justice on July 28, 1989, and by the full Judiciary Committee on Oct. 3, 1989 (H Rept 101-282).

The House approved the bill by voice vote less than two weeks later, on Oct. 16.

The Senate version, sponsored by Dennis DeConcini, D-Ariz., was approved by his Judiciary Copyrights Subcommittee on July 26, 1989, and then by the full committee on March 22, 1990 (S Rept 101-266).

During the full committee markup, Charles E. Grassley, R-Iowa, tried to amend the bill to protect states from paying attorneys' fees, one of the civil remedies available for prevailing plaintiffs under existing copyright law. But DeConcini argued that if state schools broke the law by copying protected material, they should be liable for damages that all copyright violators faced.

The committee rejected the amendment, but accepted a scaled-down version to cap fees at $75 per hour and limit their award to small businesses, tax-exempt organizations or individuals with a net worth of $1 million or less.

The full Senate took up the legislation on June 26, inserting the text of S 497 into HR 3045 and passing it by voice vote without debate.

Conferees dropped the Grassley amendment, calling it unnecessary because judges were unlikely to award attorneys' fees against the states (H Rept 101-887).

The Senate adopted the conference report on Oct. 19. House action approving the conference report on Oct. 26 cleared the bill for the president.

COPYRIGHT FEES, TRIBUNAL

Bills to increase copyright fees (HR 1622 — PL 101-318) and to reduce the number of commissioners on the Copyright Royalty Tribunal from five authorized positions to three (HR 3046 — PL 101-319) won congressional approval June 13 and were signed into law by President Bush on July 3.

The House had approved versions of both bills in 1989, but the Senate did not act on them. *(1989 Almanac, p. 291)*

Copyright Fees

HR 1622 changed the fee schedule of the Copyright Office, doubling copyright registration fees to $20 per work from $10 per work on Jan. 3, 1991, six months after the bill was signed into law. The legislation also provided for the adjustment of copyright fees every five years thereafter to account for inflation.

"The fees must be raised, or services diminished," said Kastenmeier, the bill's sponsor.

The existing fee schedule was set in 1976 and had not been changed since.

The House passed the measure by voice vote Oct. 16, 1989. The Judiciary Committee had reported it Oct. 13 (H Rept 101-279).

The Senate Judiciary Committee approved the bill on March 22 (S Rept 101-267).

A similar bill (S 1271), introduced by DeConcini, had been pending in Senate Judiciary in 1989 and was also approved by the committee on March 22. Subsequent to the committee vote, the panel inserted the text of HR 1622 into S 1271 and then sent the measure to the full chamber.

The Senate passed S 1271 on June 13, moments before clearing the identical HR 1622.

Copyright Tribunal

HR 3046 reduced the number of commissioners on the Copyright Royalty Tribunal from five to three and changed the salary classification rates for members of the tribunal and three other government offices.

The tribunal, responsible for distributing funds collected from transmission of cable and satellite television and from jukebox licenses, had been operating with only three of its authorized five commissioners and without any laws governing the contingency of lapsed terms. By reducing the number of commissioners and by allowing a commissioner whose term had expired to serve until a successor was confirmed, the legislation was designed to improve the tribunal's efficiency.

The legislation also shifted the commissioners from the General Schedule (GS) pay scale to the Senior Executive Service (SES) scale. The measure also moved top officials of three other agencies — the Copyright Office, the U.S. Patent and Trademark Office, and the U.S. Parole Commission — from the GS scale to the SES.

Introduced by Kastenmeier, HR 3046 was approved by voice vote by the House Judiciary Committee on Oct. 3, 1989 (H Rept 101-329). It first passed the House by voice vote Nov. 13, 1989.

The Senate Judiciary Committee approved both HR 3046 and the similar S 1272 on March 22 (S Rept 101-268). Subsequently, on March 30, the committee inserted the text of HR 3046 into S 1272 and sent the bill to the full chamber.

The Senate cleared HR 3046 on June 13, just after it passed the identical S 1272. ■

Disaster Litigation Stalls

Legislation to allow federal courts to consolidate multiple lawsuits stemming from disasters such as airplane crashes and bridge collapses was approved by the House on June 5, but was not taken up in the Senate.

The bill (HR 3406 — H Rept 101-515) would have amended the Federal Rules of Civil Procedure to permit consolidation in a single federal court of suits filed by disaster victims or their survivors if at least 25 people were killed or injured and damages sought exceeded $50,000 per person.

Under the bill, deciding compensatory damages would be returned in most cases to the state or federal court in which the individual suit had originally been filed.

The bill, sponsored by Robert W. Kastenmeier, D-Wis., passed the House by voice vote on June 5 after winning approval from the House Judiciary Committee March 28.

Kastenmeier, chairman of the Judiciary Subcommittee on Courts, Intellectual Property and the Administration of Justice, said that under existing law there was no way to consolidate state and federal lawsuits stemming from the same tragedy that presented identical issues of liability.

The House had approved a broader bill in 1988. In response to concerns from the Justice Department and the U.S. Judicial Conference, the measure was narrowed in the 101st Congress to apply only to suits arising from single accidents and not to multiple suits involving toxic torts or product-liability issues.

After House passage, the measure was referred to the Senate Judiciary Subcommittee on Courts and Administrative Practice, which did not act on the bill during 1990. ■

Chapter 8

HEALTH & HUMAN SERVICES/ EDUCATION

Child-Care Assistance 547
Head Start Expansion 552
WIC Program Emergency Funding 554
Children's Aid Bill 556
Social Security Earnings Test 557
Community Service Bill 559
Medicare Costs 563
Medicare Mammogram Coverage 564
'Living Will' Rights 566
Medicaid Help for Poor Children 569
Prescription Drug Discounts 570
Reimbursement Rates 571
Regulation of Medigap Plans 572
Nutrition Labeling 575
Orphan Drug Bill 577
Veto Message 578
Medical Devices Regulation 579
FDA Automation, Consolidation 581
AIDS Assistance 582
AIDS Resources Act Provisions 584
Disabilities Prevention 589
Nursing Home Regulations 589
Radiation Victims' Compensation 590
Childhood Vaccine Programs 591
Antismoking Bills 592
TB Prevention Program 594
National Health Service Corps 595
Health Programs for Minorities 596
Organ and Bone Marrow Programs 596
Emergency Services, Trauma Care 597
Injuries Research Grants 598
Elderly, Alzheimer's Programs 598
Mental Health Projects 599
National Institutes of Health 600
NIH Director 602
Family Planning Program 604
Cancer-Screening Grants 606
Pepper Commission Report 607
Health Planning Grants 609
Developmental Disabilities 609
Educational Excellence Act 610
Math, Science Education 612
Alexander Named to Education Department 614
Compensatory Education 615
Education for Disabled 616
Library Programs 617
Student Religious Groups Ruling 618
Dropout Prevention Program 618
Vocational Education Aid 619
Vocational Education Act Provisions 620
EEOC Probe of University Tenure 623
Student 'Right-to-Know' Act 624
Student Loan Defaults 626
Taft Institute Funding 628

Families Gain Help on Child Care

$22.5 billion package culminates three-year effort

In a belated response to one of the most sweeping social revolutions of the post-World War II era, Congress in 1990 cleared legislation to give American families billions of dollars in tax credits and other assistance for child care.

The five-year, $22.5 billion package, approved as part of the fiscal 1991 deficit-reduction bill, culminated a three-year legislative effort by a coalition of child-care advocacy groups, organized labor and educators.

Both chambers approved the conference report on the bill, HR 5835, on Oct. 27, clearing the measure for the president. The House vote was 228-200; the Senate vote, 54-45. *(Vote 528, p. 166-H; vote 326, p. 63-S)*

The legislation was the first major child-care measure to emerge from Congress since 1971, when President Richard M. Nixon vetoed a $2 billion child-care program on grounds that it could undermine the family by encouraging women to work outside the home. *(1971 Almanac, p. 504)*

BOXSCORE

Legislation: Child-care assistance (S 5, HR 3), enacted as part of budget-reconciliation bill, PL 101-508 (HR 5835).

Major action: Signed, Nov. 5. Conference report adopted by Senate, 54-45, Oct. 27; by House, 228-200, Oct. 27. House passed HR 3, 265-145, March 29; Senate passed S 5, June 23, 1989.

Reports: Conference report on HR 5835 (H Rept 101-964). HR 3: Education and Labor (H Rept 101-190, Part I); Ways and Means (Part II). S 5: Labor and Human Resources (S Rept 101-17).

That issue had become moot long before the 101st Congress. By 1990, 58 percent of all women with children under age 6 and 52 percent of those with babies under age 1 were in the work force.

The two-parent family with Dad at work and Mom at home with the children had become a vanishing model. Millions of women worked because they were the sole wage earners for their families. Millions of others worked because by 1990 it took two incomes to provide the standard of living once readily achievable on one.

Bill Highlights

The five-year package approved by Congress included $18.3 billion in tax credits to help low- and moderate-income families cope with the costs of child care and $4.25 billion for new grant programs to help states improve the quality and availability of such care. *(Reconciliation provisions: Title V — Child Care, p. 151)*

The tax credit package included a $12.4 billion expansion over five years in the earned-income tax credit (EITC) for working low-income families, with an extra credit for infants under age 1. It also created a new health insurance credit for families with children that was expected to cost $5.2 billion over five years.

The EITC was available to families with children in which at least one person worked, whether or not they owed any income tax. Those who owed no taxes received a refund from the government. Under the bill, by 1994 the maximum credit for a family of four was to be increased from a projected $1,127 to $2,013.

The final version of the bill made no change in the existing dependent-care tax credit, which at $3.9 billion in fiscal 1990 was the largest single source of government assistance for child care. Since that credit was not refundable, however, it was of no use to families who had so little income that they did not owe any taxes. That is why the child-care bill was targeted primarily at low-income families.

The grant funding in HR 5835 included $2.5 billion in appropriated funds over three years to help pay child-care expenses for families with incomes below 75 percent of the state's median income; $1.5 billion over five years for an entitlement program within Title IV of the Social Security Act to help provide care for low-income families not quite poor enough for welfare; and $200 million over five years in entitlement funds to help states improve the quality of child care.

To pay for the new child-care aid and the expanded EITC, Congress made permanent the 3 percent telephone excise tax, the financing mechanism included in both the free-standing bills passed by the House in 1990 (HR 3) and the Senate in 1989 (S 5).

The new spending not fully covered by the telephone tax was allowed as part of the delicate negotiations that produced the final budget-reconciliation bill, but no specific financing was designated.

BACKGROUND

Child-care legislation began moving in the 100th Congress and became an issue in the 1988 presidential campaign. Enactment of a child-care bill was one of the 101st Congress' top domestic priorities.

Both chambers passed child-care measures in 1989 (the House as part of that year's reconciliation bill), but sponsors had difficulty coming up with a final version that suited warring committees in the House and the Bush administration.

In 1988, attention had focused on the so-called ABC bill (Act for Better Child Care), which would have authorized $2.5 billion in its first year for a new program funding child-care services that met certain minimum health and safety standards.

Critics of the bill argued that by requiring day-care providers to meet federal standards, the measure could reduce rather than increase the amount of available care. Proponents, led by the Children's Defense Fund, organized labor and their allies on Capitol Hill, said uniform standards were needed to ensure the safety of all children, regardless of where they lived. State child-care standards, they noted, varied widely.

President Bush outlined his own child-care plan in August 1988, calling for expanded tax credits to help poor families pay for child care.

Although both the Senate Labor and Human Resources Committee and the House Education and Labor Committee reported the ABC bill in 1988, the measure went no further that year. *(1988 Almanac, p. 365)*

Senate Action, 1989

In 1989, both chambers passed child-care bills, although the measures were quite different.

The Senate moved first. On March 15, the Labor and Human Resources Committee by 11-5 approved a revised, $1.75 billion version of the ABC bill, S 5.

That same day, Bush formally outlined his tax-credit proposals for child care and urged an expansion of the popular Head Start program for low-income preschoolers.

On June 13, the Finance Committee got into the act, approving a tax credit plan of its own by 17-3. The package increased slightly and made refundable the existing dependent-care tax credit; it also created a credit of up to $500 for premiums paid for health insurance coverage by families with children.

By the time the full Senate passed S 5 by voice vote on June 23, the bill bore little resemblance to the version reported by Labor and Human Resources.

Majority Leader George J. Mitchell, D-Maine, put together a substitute incorporating a severely amended ABC bill, a Head Start expansion and the Finance Committee's tax credit package. On the floor, the measure was amended further to include a modest expansion of the EITC, a key element of the Bush plan.

House Committee Split, 1989

The House Education and Labor Committee approved its child-care bill, HR 3, by a near party-line vote of 23-11 on June 26, 1989.

The measure authorized $1.78 billion for an ABC grant program, a major Head Start expansion and a new program of school-based child care. Like the compromise Senate bill, the measure no longer mandated federal health and safety standards, instead calling on states to set their own and requiring creation of "model" standards they could adopt if they so desired.

On July 19, the Ways and Means Committee joined the fray, approving as part of its budget-reconciliation recommendations a package of tax credits and grants to the states totaling $16.04 billion over five years. A boost in the EITC accounted for $14.5 billion of the total; $1.55 billion was for an increase in the existing Social Services Block Grant (Title XX of the Social Security Act) earmarked for child care. On Sept. 7, Ways and Means substituted these provisions into the child-care bill, HR 3, knocking out the ABC grant program.

With Ways and Means at loggerheads with Education and Labor over how to fund grants for child care, all of the provisions were attached to the reconciliation bill by the House. But at year's end, House-Senate conferees stripped the child-care section from the budget bill, leaving the conflict unresolved. *(1989 Almanac, p. 203)*

HOUSE FLOOR ACTION, 1990

The intramural House dispute over how to fund a child-care program continued for more than eight months. It took House Democratic leaders until the week of March 12, 1990, to persuade the warring committees to compromise.

The dispute was not only long but also nasty at times.

In November 1989, the Children's Defense Fund (CDF), the leading backer of the Education and Labor bill, lashed out at the major authors of the Ways and Means proposal — Thomas J. Downey, D-N.Y., and George Miller, D-Calif. Downey was acting chairman of the Ways and Means Subcommittee on Human Resources; Miller was chairman of the Select Committee on Children, Youth and Families and a senior member of the Education and Labor Committee.

In a memo widely distributed to the media, CDF Executive Director Marian Wright Edelman accused Downey and Miller of trying to "sabotage ground-breaking child-care legislation for petty jurisdictional and power reasons."

The ill feelings did not die down during the congressional recess. On Jan. 8, members of the Illinois Alliance for Better Child Care marched outside the Chicago office of Ways and Means Chairman Dan Rostenkowski, D-Ill., demanding that he support the Education and Labor bill.

Downey and Miller fired back, sending out an "urgent child-care fact sheet" to their colleagues that criticized the "personalized and inaccurate accusations of some advocates who equate their personal preferences alone with 'good child-care legislation.'"

For months, the House leadership tried to negotiate peace between the committees, with little success.

The problem for the leadership was that while the Ways and Means plan appeared to have the support necessary to pass the House, the Education and Labor bill had the backing of the broad array of interest groups that put the issue on the national agenda in the first place.

Organized labor paved the way for a compromise by backing off from its insistence on keeping the ABC provisions in the House bill.

"Labor is looking at a package that is comprehensive, provides adequate resources and can pass the House," said Jerry D. Klepner of the American Federation of State, County and Municipal Employees.

The proposed compromise eliminated the ABC grant program, replacing it with an increase in Title XX funding, earmarked for child care, of $450 million in fiscal 1991 and $2.9 billion over five years. Unlike the ABC proposal, which would have been subject to annual appropriations, Title XX was an entitlement program funded automatically to its authorized ceiling.

Remaining in the measure were Education and Labor provisions to beef up the Head Start program, to create a school-based program of before- and after-school care, and to encourage businesses to offer child-care services. Also retained was a Ways and Means-approved increase in the EITC for working families with young children.

It was expected to cost $18.5 billion over five years, compared with $8.4 billion for the Senate's tax credit package.

More Complications

The compromise faced a challenge on the floor from a coalition of Republicans and conservative Democrats led by Reps. Charles W. Stenholm, D-Texas, and E. Clay Shaw Jr., R-Fla.

Downey and Miller united with Education and Labor Chairman Augustus F. Hawkins, D-Calif., and Dale E. Kildee, D-Mich., another leading ABC supporter, to fight off the Stenholm-Shaw alternative.

Stenholm-Shaw was in many ways very similar to the compromise Democratic bill. Both increased authorized funding for Head Start, increased funding for Title XX and expanded the EITC.

But the proposals differed in some key respects. Stenholm-Shaw did not include the school-based program for "latchkey" children. "The federal government should not mandate school-based care," Stenholm said.

Stenholm-Shaw also sought to finance about $1 billion of its net five-year cost of $20.45 billion by eliminating eligibility for the existing dependent-care tax credit for families with incomes higher than $90,000.

"It's really ridiculous that people with incomes of $100,000 can take a deduction for part of their child-care expenses," said Jim Slattery, D-Kan., a cosponsor of the plan.

Opponents of the Stenholm-Shaw plan fretted that it might be hard to beat. "It's enough like our bill to attract conservative and moderate Democrats," Downey said.

Church-State Controversy

Another issue snagging the child-care bill was how to funnel federal dollars to programs operated by religious institutions without running afoul of the Constitution. Churches and other religious organizations provided an estimated one-third of all center-based child care and in many areas offered the only care available.

The issue divided House members in both parties. But the distress was most obvious among Democrats.

"Obviously, it's a very controversial subject," said Speaker Thomas S. Foley, D-Wash. "There are deep disagreements in the party and in the House."

The church-state dispute turned on whether Congress should require or simply allow states to provide vouchers that parents could use to buy whatever sort of care they wanted for their children.

Both HR 3 and the Stenholm-Shaw plan sought to boost federal aid for child care through an increase in Title XX funds. Under existing law, states could use Title XX funds to pay for care either through vouchers or through contracts with child-care providers. Stenholm and Shaw wanted to require states to offer vouchers.

"Parents should be able to decide where they are going to send their children, and if they want to send them to the First Baptist Church or the local temple, they should be eligible for the same federal assistance as if they send them to the ABC child center," said Slattery.

Foley on March 22 told reporters that it was likely that the leadership would back vouchers.

"We made a commitment last year ... to provide an approach to this problem that moved toward the Senate language," Foley told reporters March 22. "We're meeting that commitment."

But the Senate voucher language, adopted largely in floor amendments, was confusing and contradictory.

On the one hand, S 5, in a new grant program authorized under the bill, gave states the option of funding care through vouchers, grants or contracts. It allowed vouchers to be offered only if resource and referral programs were available to help parents find care.

On the other hand, language added on the floor by Pete V. Domenici, R-N.M., required that parents be given the option of receiving vouchers.

Other Senate language by inference allowed the use of vouchers to pay for sectarian care but stipulated that funds "shall not be expended in a manner inconsistent with the Constitution."

It also said none of the requirements were intended to modify or supersede any provision of a state constitution or law prohibiting the use of public funds in or by sectarian institutions.

The Senate language permitted sectarian organizations to require that employees "adhere to the religious tenets and teachings of such organizations," language included in Stenholm-Shaw, and permitted religious providers to give preference to children whose families were members of the organization for slots not funded with public money.

Outside Lobbying

It was vouchers, however, that drew the most attention, and pressure to make them mandatory was intense.

In addition to the White House, the National Association of Evangelicals, which represented 50,000 churches from 77 denominations, weighed in strongly. Unless vouchers were mandatory, officials wrote in a March 7 letter to Bush, "a thoroughly secularized child-care system will shape the values of millions of America's children from their earliest years."

Lawmakers were flooded with phone calls supporting the Stenholm-Shaw bill and mandatory vouchers after former presidential candidate Pat Robertson and other religious broadcasters urged viewers of their television shows to call the Capitol.

A Stenholm staff member said she received a call from a Capitol switchboard operator asking her to explain the measure prompting so many calls.

But pressure against vouchers was strong, as well, and also came from a number of religious groups.

"In child care, as in education, the federal government must not finance religious or discriminatory practices. Government does not have the obligation to support, and indeed must not support, religious beliefs," said a letter signed by 47 organizations, including the National Education Association (NEA); the American Civil Liberties Union; and Jewish, Presbyterian, Episcopal and Baptist groups.

The NEA, which was leading the opponents, had long feared that vouchers for child care would lead directly to vouchers for school-age children, which it vehemently opposed.

Some governors also were unhappy with mandatory vouchers. A staffer for the National Governors' Association said that while many states were moving to voucher systems, such programs were expensive and time-consuming to set up.

House Floor Votes

The House Democratic leadership worked furiously to line up the votes needed to turn aside the administration-backed substitute offered by Stenholm and Shaw. And when the showdown came on March 29, it prevailed. Stenholm-Shaw failed, 195-225. *(Vote 57, p. 24-H)*

A similar proposal had drawn exactly the same number of "aye" votes in October 1989 during consideration of budget-reconciliation legislation.

Two efforts to change the provisions on sectarian care also were rejected during House debate.

By 182-243, members defeated an amendment by David E. Price, D-N.C., that would have allowed — instead of required — states to offer parents vouchers that could be used to pay for sectarian care. *(Vote 55, p. 24-H)*

Then, by 125-297, they rejected an amendment by Don Edwards, D-Calif., that would have barred the use of federal funds for sectarian worship or instruction and prohibited religious discrimination in the hiring of child-care workers by sectarian institutions that received federal funds. *(Vote 56, p. 24-H)*

The House passed the child-care bill, 265-145. *(Vote 60, p. 24-H)*

HOUSE-SENATE CONFERENCE

HR 3 finally made it to conference on May 9, after the House voted 411-0 to instruct conferees to reject the ABC child-care grant program included in S 5, the Senate version. *(Vote 102, p. 36-H)*

In the Senate, where motions to send measures to conference were normally routine, Republicans temporarily blocked proceedings while they considered trying either to reopen the measure or to attach a reduction in the tax rates on capital gains. In the end, they did neither after Senate Majority Leader George J. Mitchell, D-Maine, threatened in turn to hold up action on a supplemental funding bill that contained emergency aid Bush had requested for Panama and Nicaragua.

During debate on the motion to instruct conferees, House Ways and Means Chairman Rostenkowski urged rejection of the ABC plan, saying its inclusion would prompt a Bush veto that members could not override.

"No one will be helped if all we produce is a political issue for the next election," said Rostenkowski. "I have absolutely no interest in playing chicken with the president or jeopardizing the conference report on the House floor."

Education and Labor Chairman Hawkins, whose turf battle with Ways and Means had delayed House floor consideration for months, said he was not bothered by the non-binding vote.

"I urged a 'yes' vote," Hawkins said. "We intend to support the House position."

House Cedes Ground on ABC

Despite Hawkins' assurances, in mid-June he proposed that House conferees accept parts of the Senate bill that incorporated elements of the ABC grant program. He did so after conferees from the Senate Labor and Human Resources Committee rejected an initial House offer that did not include ABC.

"I find it astounding that we are preparing to abandon instructions from the House because the Senate rejected an offer," protested Downey, one of three Ways and Means conferees on the subconference and author of the Title XX provisions. "The Senate rejecting an offer is about as surprising as the sun rising in the east."

House Republicans were likewise miffed, arguing that any inclusion of ABC provisions would make the bill veto bait.

"Anything that smells of ABC is in the veto box," said Bill Goodling, Pa., ranking Republican on the Education and Labor Committee.

But Hawkins' 15 reliable votes among Education and Labor Democrats outnumbered both the nine Education and Labor Republicans and the three Ways and Means conferees eligible to vote on the offers. On June 19, conferees agreed to authorize $1.9 billion in child-care aid in fiscal 1991. That total included a yet-to-be-determined portion for a compromise ABC program, renamed the Child Care Block Grant.

The compromise would divide the funds three ways: the new block grant; a new program to enable part-day, part-year Head Start programs to offer full-day, year-round care; and a new program to help pay for school-based preschool and before- and after-school child care. Most Democrats on House Education and Labor supported it, outvoting all House GOP conferees and two Ways and Means Democrats.

"We have finished our job. That was our mandate," Christopher J. Dodd, D-Conn., chief sponsor of the Senate ABC bill, said after the subconference wrapped up.

But in the House the next day, Republicans and Democrats called for conferees to go back to the drawing board. The House voted 416-0 to instruct the conferees to reject what they had just accepted. *(Vote 186, p. 64-H)*

Several conferees said the major problem was structural: The conference was set up so that key issues were like ships passing in the night.

Because of committee jurisdictional lines, the Title XX portion of the bill was to be settled by the House Ways and Means and Senate Finance committees, while the ABC and other grant proposals remained the purview of the subconference between House Education and Labor and Senate Labor and Human Resources.

Therefore, the threshold question — whether to create a new grant program or use the Title XX approach — was not being directly addressed.

The bill was also burdened with unrelated Senate riders. On June 20, House members voted 384-36 to instruct conferees to accept provisions of the Senate bill to relax the Social Security earnings test for senior citizens ages 65 to 69. Under existing law, seniors who earned more than a specified amount each year faced reductions in Social Security benefits. *(Vote 185, p. 64-H)*

Senate conferees eventually dropped the earnings-test proposal. *(Earnings test, p. 557)*

The Closing Push

With lawmakers distracted by the budget negotiations, and with the amount of money available for child care dependent on the outcome of those talks, matters languished all summer long.

The Sept. 30 budget agreement between White House and congressional negotiators, even though it failed its first House test Oct. 5, effectively cut loose the child-care bill.

The budget accord carved out two ways to pay for a child-care initiative.

First, it assumed increased appropriations for the new grant program included in the Senate bill.

Second, it left out of the deficit-reduction package an extension of the 3 percent telephone tax, assuming those revenues would be used to pay for a new child-care tax credit for the poor and for a new child-care entitlement program under Social Security for families in danger of having to go on welfare.

Moving to Reconciliation

During the week of Oct. 15, the White House reached agreement on the outlines of a child-care plan with Senate negotiators, who proceeded to tuck the proposal into the fast-moving budget-reconciliation bill.

The compromise was struck between negotiators from the Senate Labor and Human Resources Committee and White House budget director Richard G. Darman.

For the first time, administration officials agreed to the creation of a new grant program for states aimed at making child care more available and affordable for working families. The White House had asserted that a new program would lead to creation of a federal child-care bureaucracy.

But Dodd, who championed the grant program, later said the timing of the negotiations had worked in his favor. "With everything else going sour, I don't think they wanted to be portrayed as against child care, too," Dodd said, in reference to the beating the administration was taking over the failed budget-summit agreement.

In the House, the Education and Labor Committee voted Oct. 15 to include its child-care package in the reconciliation bill (HR 5835) but the provisions were stripped during House floor consideration Oct. 16.

Such was not the case in the Senate, where the Finance Committee included in its reconciliation package its latest offer on the child-care bill. Finance also included in the reconciliation bill the grant provisions over which Labor and Human Resources had jurisdiction.

The Senate's action was the opposite of its stance in 1989, when the House sought to make child care part of the reconciliation bill and the Senate refused.

Grant Programs

The White House-Senate Labor Committee compromise authorized $2.5 billion over three years in new grants to states to finance child-care services for families with incomes lower than 75 percent of their state's median.

Twenty-five percent of the funds were to be reserved to pay for child-care quality improvements (such as increasing teacher salaries or writing new regulations) or for programs to provide early childhood education to preschool children or before- and after-school care for older children.

The compromise also called for a limited set of standards for child-care providers.

Administration officials had long complained that the ABC bill as passed by the Senate was overly prescriptive and burdensome and could serve to reduce instead of expand the supply of child care.

Under the compromise, all providers receiving federal funds had to be licensed, regulated or registered, and they had to meet specific state health and safety requirements. Dropped was a training requirement that had been included in both the Senate and House versions of the bill.

Funding for this grant program was to come through the regular appropriations process, which meant that child care would be pitted each year against other popular health, education and human services programs.

The proposal was considerably different from the House-passed version, which gave much more emphasis to school-based programs and included a major expansion of the Head Start program for preschoolers. It was also scaled back considerably from the proposal on which House and Senate conferees from the Labor panels had reached agreement in June.

The grant package was refined Oct. 20 to win the support of House Education and Labor Chairman Hawkins.

The $2.5 billion authorized for grants to states over three years included $750 million in fiscal 1991, $825 million in fiscal 1992 and $925 million in fiscal 1993.

States could use 75 percent of their grants either to provide child-care services directly to families with incomes below 75 percent of the state median income, or to increase the availability or quality of child care.

Of their remaining grant money, states were required to spend three-fourths on programs to provide preschool education or to serve school-age children before and/or after school.

Another 20 percent was to be spent on activities such as providing training for care-givers or increasing salaries for child-care workers. States could spend the remaining 5 percent of funds on either activity.

"The funding doesn't go as far as it should," Hawkins said, adding that available funding would serve only about 300,000 of the more than 10 million so-called latchkey children. "At that rate we certainly aren't doing much for children."

Indeed, even though the fiscal 1991 appropriations bill (HR 5257) for the Departments of Labor, Education, and Health and Human Services (HHS) technically provided the program with nearly the entire $750 million for fiscal 1991, it stipulated that none of the funds could be made available until Sept. 7, 1991 — less than a month before the end of the fiscal year. That was to result in estimated outlays of only about $40 million.

Still, Hawkins said, the bill was "a beachhead we may be able to use in the future."

Negotiators left in place most of the controversial church-state language. The final bill required that parents be given the opportunity to obtain a voucher that could be used to pay for religious child-care services, and permitted discrimination on the basis of religion in certain child-care settings.

Tax Credits

At 4 a.m. Oct. 26, House-Senate conferees agreed on tax credit and entitlement provisions of the big child-care package.

Before the package was folded into reconciliation, the committees had tentatively agreed to drop the House-backed Title XX expansion and instead create a small entitlement program within Title IV of Social Security. That program, within the section for child welfare services, was to help pay the child-care bills of low-income families not poor enough to qualify for welfare benefits.

As negotiations proceeded the week of Oct. 22, the Bush administration, having agreed to creation of a separate grant program, began to argue that the Title IV program was duplicative and unnecessary. And the Finance Committee, squeezed for funds, reduced the amount it was offering to put into Title IV.

But Ways and Means persisted, with members arguing that a new entitlement program, for which funding was assured and not subject to the whims of the appropriations process, was still necessary.

The compromise expanded the EITC and created the child-health credit championed by Senate Finance Committee Chairman Lloyd Bentsen, D-Texas. That credit was expected to cost $5.2 billion over five years.

The final compromise funded the new Title IV entitlement at $1.5 billion over five years. And it provided $200 million over five years for grants to states to help improve the quality of child care.

In a tradeoff, the Senate backed away from its insistence on making the existing dependent-care tax credit refundable. And the House dropped its proposal to put an income ceiling on eligibility for that credit.

The last item in the bill to be resolved involved a provision that would have increased by $500 the standard deduction (used by taxpayers who did not itemize) for families with children under age 1.

Although a "wee tot" allowance was a key demand of the administration, officials argued that the standard deduction increase would not help low-income families and would not encourage mothers to stay at home with their children, which was the intent.

Instead, the final package replaced the standard-deduction change with a special increase in the EITC for families with infants, adding up to $700 million over five years. ■

Major Expansion for Head Start Program

Brushing aside administration objections, Congress on Oct. 18 cleared for the president the biggest expansion of Head Start since the program's inception in 1965.

The Head Start provisions were part of an omnibus reauthorization of human services programs (HR 4151 — PL 101-501).

The Senate adopted the conference report on the bill by voice vote, clearing the measure for President Bush. The House had approved the agreement under suspension of the rules on Oct. 10.

Although Health and Human Services (HHS) Secretary Louis W. Sullivan had expressed "serious concerns" about the bill in a letter to conferees earlier in October, Bush signed the legislation on Nov. 3.

BOXSCORE

Legislation: Human Services Reauthorization Act, PL 101-501 (HR 4151).

Major action: Signed, Nov. 3. Conference report adopted by Senate, Oct. 18; by House, Oct. 10. Passed by Senate, Sept. 18; by House, 404-14, May 16.

Reports: Conference report (H Rept 101-816); Labor and Human Resources (S Rept 101-421); Education and Labor (H Rept 101-480).

In 1990, Head Start, a popular education, nutrition, health and social service program for poor preschoolers, served only about 20 percent of those eligible. HR 4151 authorized enough funding to serve all eligible preschoolers by 1994.

Budget constraints made it unlikely, however, that appropriations would match the authorizations, as conferees on the funding bill (HR 5257) for the Departments of Labor, HHS, Education and related agencies swiftly made clear.

HR 4151 authorized $2.4 billion for Head Start for fiscal 1991, but the Labor-HHS conferees on Oct. 19 approved just $1.95 billion. That was still a major increase over Head Start's fiscal 1990 funding of $1.55 billion. *(Labor-HHS appropriations bill, p. 847)*

The authorization bill called for $4.27 billion for Head Start in fiscal 1992, $5.92 billion for 1993 and $7.66 billion for 1994.

The bill required that 10 percent of the funds be reserved for "quality improvements," such as raising teacher salaries, buying equipment and refurbishing Head Start facilities. Such funds were to be available only to the extent they did not reduce the number of program participants.

LIHEAP, Other Programs

Also reauthorized under HR 4151 was the Low-Income Home Energy Assistance Program (LIHEAP), which provided funds to the states to help low-income households pay heating and cooling bills and weatherize their homes.

The measure authorized $2.1 billion for LIHEAP in fiscal 1991, $2.3 billion in 1992 and "such sums as may be necessary" for 1993 and 1994.

Again, actual appropriations were expected to fall well short of these targets. Conferees on the Labor-HHS spending bill voted $1.45 billion for LIHEAP in fiscal 1991, with a $200 million contingency reserve.

Among the other programs that HR 4151 reauthorized, and their funding ceilings, were the following:

- The Community Services Block Grant program (CSBG), which funded activities aimed at helping the poor become self-sufficient: $500 million by fiscal 1994.
- Follow Through, which provided Head Start-type services to children after they entered elementary school: $20 million in fiscal 1991 and "such sums" through fiscal 1994.
- The Community Food and Nutrition Program, which helped nonprofit agencies plan ways to meet the nutritional needs of the poor: $25 million by fiscal 1994.
- State Dependent Care Development Grants, which helped states run child-care information and referral services: $20 million in fiscal 1991 and "such sums" through fiscal 1994.
- The Comprehensive Child Development Centers program: $50 million, twice current levels, in each of fiscal 1991 through 1994. The program funded Head Start-type services to highly targeted populations of disadvantaged mothers, infants and toddlers.

BACKGROUND

Begun in 1965 as part of President Lyndon B. Johnson's War on Poverty, Head Start by 1990 had served more than 11 million children with a panoply of educational and social services intended to put economically disadvantaged preschool children on a comparable footing with their more affluent peers.

Although the law defined eligible children only as those below the age for compulsory school attendance (7 in most states), Head Start regulations said that children served should be at least 3 and that 90 percent of enrollees had to be from families with incomes below the federal poverty line ($10,060 for a family of three in 1989). Head Start programs also were required to serve children with disabilities. In 1990, according to HHS, which administered the program, 13 percent of enrollees were disabled.

Head Start in 1990 served 488,000 children in about 2,000 communities nationwide. Programs were operated by community action agencies, local governments, churches and other religious organizations, and public schools.

Head Start was designed to be comprehensive and intensive. In small groups with ample adult supervision, children participated in educational and social activities that prepared them to learn to read and write. They also received health, nutrition and social services.

Many Head Start parents participated in the program almost as intensively as did their children. Parents often were provided social services such as housing aid or legal assistance, and they in turn helped direct Head Start activities through parent councils.

Head Start also served as a job-training program for many parents. More than 30 percent of Head Start teachers were parents of current or former Head Start students.

Slots vs. Quality

Over the years, Head Start developed an enthusiastic following among elected officials. The business community, fearing a shortage of skilled labor and increasing worldwide competition, was also singing the praises of early childhood programs.

It was not surprising, therefore, that Bush chose to jump the gun on release of his fiscal 1991 budget to announce a week early that he was proposing a $500 million increase for Head Start. That was the largest increase ever proposed for the program.

Likewise, when Sen. Edward M. Kennedy, D-Mass., on April 9 delivered a speech at Georgetown University in Washington outlining "Democratic Values and the Challenge of the 1990s," the first priority he listed for spending the so-called peace dividend from the end of the Cold War was Head Start.

While everyone agreed that Head Start should be given more money, a major dispute erupted over how to spend the added dollars.

The administration wanted to enroll more children. "We think this year our priority is to make a big splash in expanding the program," said Wade F. Horn, commissioner of the Administration for Children, Youth and Families within HHS.

But Head Start operators and their allies in Congress said that before slots were added, the quality of existing programs needed to be improved. Those programs had seen per-child funding (in constant dollars) slide by 13 percent since 1981 — to $2,672 in 1989 from $3,084.

Edward F. Zigler, a Yale University psychologist who helped found Head Start, said, "I see a tremendous decline in the quality of Head Start from 25 years ago. . . . I'd rather serve fewer children well than more children badly."

"Whereas expansion is a noble objective, it should not be at the expense of quality," said Sister Barbara McMichael, director of the Providence, R.I., Head Start program, at hearing of the Senate Labor Subcommittee on Children on March 1. "If we have to water down services to enroll more children, we will have accomplished nothing."

Indeed, many experts said that what made Head Start work was the intensive nature of the program and that if programs were operated in a less comprehensive manner, they could not produce the desired results.

"There's a serious underfunding problem in current Head Start operations," said Don Bolce of the National Head Start Association, which represented those who ran the programs.

Bolce said Head Start programs were being squeezed by increasing rents and insurance premiums and the need to repair and renovate centers and replace toys and other equipment. To cover such costs, Bolce said, programs were being forced to cut back on transportation and social services and to increase the ratio of children to staff — sacrificing "all of those things that make Head Start work."

By far the most serious problem, advocates said, was low salaries. "Many of our dedicated, trained teachers and other staff cannot continue to work at approximately 50 percent of the wages [available] in the public schools," testified Providence's Sister McMichael. "They are committed, but you can't eat commitment."

Low salaries harmed children as well as teachers, because they caused rapid turnover. Eugenia Boggus, president of the National Head Start Association, testified March 1, "Frequent staff changes make children wonder if they did something wrong, when really the teacher just needed a job that paid enough to help get her own family above the poverty level."

Horn replied, "We know that salaries are low. It's not that we think Head Start teachers are all driving Mercedes." Still, he insisted, salaries had been increased over the past few years and, compared with other child-care programs, "we think we are retaining staff at an adequate level."

What Is Full Funding?

There was another question simmering in the Head Start debate: What was "full funding"?

The administration said the $500 million in added funds Bush was seeking for 1991 "could allow us to serve up to 70 percent of eligible children for at least one year and bring within reach our goal of a universal Head Start program."

Horn said full funding meant one year of Head Start for 90 percent of students, with an emphasis on 4-year-olds. The administration did not specify when it would reach that goal or at what cost, but Bush budget analysts said about $1 billion more than the fiscal 1990 appropriation would be needed to serve all 4-year-olds, and $1.6 billion on top of that would be needed to reach remaining eligible 3-year-olds. All those figures were based on the fiscal 1990 expenditure per child of $2,767.

James J. Renier, chairman and chief executive officer of Honeywell Inc., and a trustee of the Committee for Economic Development, testified: "All by itself, one year of preschool is not going to instill children, buffeted and battered by the culture of poverty, with the middle-class values and drive needed to help them compete successfully in school."

A definition of full funding also depended on the amount spent per child. "If you say $2,600 per child is sufficient, you come out with a very different figure for full funding," Bolce said. "We believe to deliver a high-quality program costs $4,000."

Another question was whether programs operated part-day or full-day, year-round or only when school was in session. Unless they operated all day, year-round, Head Start programs were unlikely to reach children whose parents were working or training for a job. Yet full-day programs had declined from about one-third to 15 percent of the total since 1972, according to the Society for Research in Child Development.

The big child-care bill (HR 3) passed by the House on March 29 authorized additional funds to make Head Start programs full-day, year-round to meet the needs of working parents. But those provisions were dropped from the final version of the measure, which was rolled into HR 5835, the budget-reconciliation bill. *(Child care, p. 547)*

ACTION IN THE HOUSE

The House Education and Labor Subcommittee on Human Resources kicked off the year's legislative action on Head Start on April 3 when it approved a four-year reauthorization that sought to improve quality and reach all eligible children by 1994.

The panel's version of HR 4151 authorized almost $2.4 billion for Head Start in fiscal 1991, increasing to nearly $7.7 billion in 1994, and set aside 10 percent of the total funding each year for quality improvements.

The fiscal 1991 authorization was $1 billion more than current funding and $500 million more than Bush requested. It assumed an expenditure of $3,500 per student and was enough money to serve all eligible 3- and 4-year-olds and the 30 percent of 5-year-olds not enrolled in kindergarten.

Dale E. Kildee, D-Mich., chairman of the subcommittee, pushed through a substitute that authorized $4.3 billion for Head Start in fiscal 1992, $5.9 billion in 1993 and almost $7.7 billion in 1994.

Originally, HR 4151 had set the authorizations for fiscal 1992-94 at "such sums as may be necessary," giving broad discretion to the Appropriations committees in both chambers to determine the funding levels. But Kildee said the bill's higher authorizations were needed to allow Head Start to enroll thousands more children.

Ranking Republican Tom Tauke of Iowa said that Head Start was already targeted for a large increase in fiscal 1991 and that the rest of the authorization should not be fixed in concrete so soon. "Given the variety of options that we have, it isn't prudent or wise for us to pick a number out of the air," Tauke said.

The panel also approved another Kildee amendment that set aside 10 percent of Head Start funds for quality-improvement programs. At least half of the funds were to be earmarked for salary increases for Head Start workers. One-fifth of the set-aside funds were for training and technical assistance programs. The HHS secretary could determine how the remainder should be spent.

Tauke did not oppose the amendment but voiced concern that the size of the set-aside would grow dramatically by 1994 under Kildee's proposal. "This is a ton of money to leave to the discretion of the secretary," he said.

Another Kildee amendment approved by the panel authorized $20 million in fiscal 1991 for the Follow Through program to help former Head Start students in kindergarten through third grade. The authorization was to increase by $10 million a year, reaching $50 million in fiscal 1994.

Tauke said he agreed that a follow-up program was essential because "there is evidence that the benefits of Head Start can get lost somewhere along the way." But he said the program should be tied to the Chapter 1 compensatory education program for disadvantaged children.

As approved by the subcommittee, HR 4151 included large authorization increases for LIHEAP and for the Community Services Block Grant program. Bush had sought to cut funding for both.

The bill authorized $2.15 billion in fiscal 1991 and

Emergency Funding for WIC Program

Moving with unusual speed, the Senate early June 29 cleared for President Bush an emergency funding authorization for the popular supplemental food program for women, infants and children (WIC).

The bill (HR 5149 — PL 101-330), introduced on June 25, was passed by the House on June 28. Action in both chambers was by voice vote.

Bush signed the bill into law July 12.

Numerous studies had shown that WIC, which provided food and other supplements to nutritionally at-risk pregnant women and young children, had been highly successful in preventing expensive health problems associated with inadequate nutrition. Congress had expanded WIC and reauthorized it for five years in 1989. *(1989 Almanac, p. 219)*

But the program, which reached only about half its eligible population, soon faced a severe funding crunch. Primarily because of a severe freeze over the winter of 1989-90, which resulted in large increases in the price of orange juice, and the drought of the year before, which caused the price of cereal to rise, funding shortfalls were expected to require 27 states to drop an estimated 280,000 women and children from the program, state WIC officials and the Agriculture Department reported the week of June 18.

According to the Center on Budget and Policy Priorities, which did its own survey, tens of thousands more participants were facing cutbacks in their WIC food packages.

Provisions of Bill

As introduced June 25 by Rep. Tony P. Hall, D-Ohio, HR 5149 would have allowed states not expecting funding shortfalls to return excess funds to the Treasury without having their next year's allocation reduced. It also would have allowed states to borrow against their fiscal 1991 allocations to maintain services at the level provided as of March 1, 1990. Under existing law, states could overspend against the next fiscal year by only 1 percent.

"We must not force innocent children to pay the price for inflation," Hall said. "If we fail to act now, we will consign these children to months of inadequate nutrition."

The House Education and Labor Committee approved the bill June 27 after dropping the first provision and altering the second to allow states with shortfalls to spend up to 5 percent of their next year's allocation.

But that was unacceptable to Appropriations Committee Chairman Jamie L. Whitten, D-Miss. Aides said Whitten was concerned that allowing states to spend so much of their next year's budget would only make the problem worse.

In the end, Whitten agreed to raise the overspending limit to 3 percent, which was expected to free an estimated $66 million. Congress approved that limit.

According to the Senate Agriculture Committee, at least $72 million in extra money was needed to allow all states to maintain their caseloads at the levels in effect before the cutbacks began.

"It's not enough," acknowledged Rep. George Miller, D-Calif., chairman of the Select Committee on Children, Youth and Families and one of the members who negotiated the final language. "We'll have to see if we can work out the rest later" in the regular fiscal 1991 Agriculture Department appropriations bill.

In fact, WIC fared relatively well in the $52.2 billion agriculture appropriations bill (HR 5268 — PL 101-506) that cleared Oct. 22.

The funding bill included a $3 billion increase — to $26.7 billion — for domestic nutrition programs. Most of that money, $19 billion, was for food stamps, which received an increase of $2.2 billion over fiscal 1990.

But WIC got $2.35 billion, an increase of $224 million over the previous year. *(Agriculture appropriations, p. 867)*

billion in fiscal 1992 for LIHEAP. The panel set no fixed ceiling for 1993 and 1994. Bush had requested $1.05 billion in fiscal 1991, below current funding of $1.4 billion.

HR 4151 authorized $451.5 million for the community services program in fiscal 1991, $460 million in 1992, $480 million in 1993 and $500 million in 1994.

States used funds from the program for projects dealing with problems such as homelessness and drug and alcohol abuse. The administration proposed killing the grants for fiscal 1991, except for $42 million to combat homelessness.

Full Committee Approval

The full House Education and Labor Committee approved HR 4151 on May 1 and the measure was formally reported on May 9.

The committee version set a $2.39 billion funding ceiling for Head Start in fiscal 1991, up from the $1.55 billion authorized and $1.4 billion appropriated for fiscal 1990. The authorization was set at $4.27 billion in fiscal 1992, $5.92 billion in 1993 and $7.66 billion in 1994.

Committee Chairman Augustus F. Hawkins, D-Calif., said it was "criminal" that such a small percentage of eligible children were being served by such "a successful, cost-effective program."

Republicans, led by Bill Goodling, Pa., and Tauke, lauded most elements of the measure, including the once-controversial set-aside of funds to improve the quality of existing Head Start programs. Bipartisan negotiations produced an agreement that whenever appropriations exceeded an inflation adjustment plus 10 percent, 10 percent of program funding should be set aside to improve teacher salaries and benefits, hire and train staff members, pay insurance premiums, pay for transportation and improve facilities.

The series of bipartisan amendments worked out before the meeting also included an authorization of "such sums as may be necessary" for a 20-year longitudinal study of the effects of Head Start, as well as for a shorter-term study to be completed before the program's next reauthorization in four years.

The amendments also required Head Start programs to make education services available to the preschoolers' parents "in order to better enable them to help their children reach their full potential."

In addition to Head Start, HR 4151 reauthorized the following:

- Follow Through, which provided Head Start-type educational and nutritional services to children after they entered elementary school, authorized at $20 million in fiscal 1991, rising to $50 million in fiscal 1994.
- State Dependent Care Development Grants, which helped states set up systems to provide information on, and improve the availability of, child-care services, authorized at "such sums as may be necessary."
- The Community Services Block Grant Program, authorized at $451.5 million in fiscal 1991, rising to $500 million in 1994.
- The Community Food and Nutrition Program, which provided grants to public and private nonprofit agencies to plan ways to meet the nutritional needs of low-income families, authorized at $10 million in fiscal 1991, rising to $20 million in 1994.
- The Child Development Associate Scholarship Assistance Program, which helped underwrite training of low-income individuals seeking to become licensed child-care providers, authorized at $3 million in fiscal 1991, and "such sums" through fiscal 1994.

Members agreed to drop the LIHEAP reauthorization from the bill. For LIHEAP, unlike the other programs, Education and Labor shared jurisdiction with the Energy and Commerce Committee. Kildee said he did not want to hold up the rest of the bill waiting for that panel to act. Kildee said he expected the LIHEAP provisions to be reunited with the rest of the bill either on the House floor or in a House-Senate conference.

There were only a few points of contention during the markup.

Tauke tried to link funding for Follow Through to the Chapter 1 program, but Kildee and Hawkins resisted that approach. Hawkins said the proposal would amount to "eliminating the program through the back door by commingling the funds for a $7 million program [Follow Through] with those for a $3 billion program [Chapter 1]." Tauke withdrew his amendment after Kildee promised to work with him on the proposal.

Members also sparred over a Hawkins amendment to require that $30 million of the Head Start funds be set aside in fiscal 1991, rising to $33.7 million in fiscal 1994, for Parent-Child Centers run by Head Start agencies. The centers provided services to parents and to children younger than 3 to prepare them for Head Start. Hawkins said his plan would double the program's current funding.

"Starting to deal with at-risk children at age 3 is late," Hawkins quoted pediatrician and child development expert T. Berry Brazelton.

Tauke, however, said he didn't want funds taken away from core Head Start activities. "I'd like to see [the Parent-Child Centers program] expanded but not at the expense of current Head Start programs," he said.

Hawkins' amendment was accepted after Tauke modified it to require that grants for the parent-child centers not be made unless Head Start agencies certified that they would not result in a reduction in Head Start services.

House Floor Action

Ignoring administration objections, the House approved HR 4151 on May 16 by 404-14. *(Vote 111, p. 40-H)*

The Office of Management and Budget (OMB) issued a statement saying the administration "strongly opposes" the bill. The OMB called the measure's funding "excessive" and opposed the quality set-aside. "Any expansion of Head Start should focus on increasing the number of children enrolled in the existing program," the statement said.

Before approving the bill, members by voice vote adopted two amendments offered by Tauke.

The first required that priority for Follow Through grants be given to schools that had a high concentration of former Head Start students and operated schoolwide programs under Chapter 1.

The other amendment renewed a special waiver permitting Colorado, Utah and Wyoming to distribute Community Services Block Grant funds through county agencies in areas that lacked their own community action agencies.

ACTION IN SENATE

The Senate Labor and Human Resources Committee on June 27 added its voice to the congressional chorus seeking full funding for the Head Start program as it approved HR 4151 by 16-0.

Like the House bill, the committee's version boosted Head Start's authorization to $2.39 billion in fiscal 1991 and to $7.7 billion in fiscal 1994.

The Senate committee bill, again like the House measure, set aside some of the funding to improve existing Head Start programs. Under the Senate plan, at least half the set-aside was to be used to improve teacher salaries and benefits.

The Senate bill also reauthorized all of the other programs in the House bill, at similar funding levels.

"These initiatives are at the heart of our federal antipoverty efforts," said Sen. Christopher J. Dodd, D-Conn., chairman of the Subcommittee on Children, Family, Drugs and Alcoholism. "They provide the assistance necessary for low-income families to have a surer footing in American society."

And the Senate bill included a four-year reauthorization of LIHEAP. The program, which had seen its appropriations decline since the early 1980s, was authorized at $2.15 billion in fiscal 1991, down from the $2.31 billion authorization for fiscal 1990. The program received $1.33 billion in fiscal 1990 appropriations.

Senate Floor Action

The Senate approved HR 4151 by voice vote on Sept. 18.

Funding levels for Head Start and the other programs were the same as those in the House bill, except as noted below:

- LIHEAP: $2.15 billion in fiscal 1991, $2.23 billion in fiscal 1992 and "such sums as may be necessary" for fiscal 1993 and 1994. The authorization was not included in the House version for jurisdictional reasons.
- Follow Through, authorized at $20 million in fiscal 1991 and at "such sums" through fiscal 1994.
- State Dependent Care Development Grants, authorized at $20 million in fiscal 1991 and "such sums" through fiscal 1994. The House bill authorized "such sums" for each of fiscal 1991 through 1994.
- The Community Services Block Grant Program, authorized at $451.5 million in fiscal 1991, rising to $500 million in fiscal 1994.
- The Community Food and Nutrition Program, authorized at $10 million in fiscal 1991, rising to $25 million in fiscal 1994. The House bill authorized $10 million in fiscal 1991, rising to $20 million in fiscal 1994.
- The Child Development Associate Scholarship Assistance Program, authorized at $3 million in fiscal 1991 and "such sums" through fiscal 1994.
- Demonstration Partnership Agreements Addressing the Needs of the Poor, authorized at $10 million for fiscal 1991 and at "such sums" through fiscal 1994.
- The Comprehensive Child Development Centers Program, authorized at $50 million in each of fiscal 1991 through 1994. The House bill did not include an authorization for the program, which had not been included in the omnibus bill before.

Also included in the Senate bill but not its House counterpart was a new authorization for a variety of programs aimed at better integrating and coordinating federal, state and local programs aimed at children and teenagers. The new programs, primarily the work of Sen. Dodd, were authorized at $60 million in fiscal 1991 and at "such sums" through fiscal 1994 for grants to establish family resource and support programs. Such programs were aimed at keeping troubled families together.

FINAL ACTION

In one of the briefest conferences ever held on Capitol Hill, House and Senate negotiators agreed Oct. 3 on the final version of HR 4151.

The 10 minutes it took conferees to finish the formalities and heap praise on one another and the bill was probably less time than it took for most of them to read the administration's seven-page, single-spaced letter of objections to the measure.

Although the Oct. 1 letter from HHS Secretary Sullivan expressed "serious concerns" about the bill, it stopped short of recommending a veto. And members considered it exceedingly unlikely that Bush would veto a measure calling for full funding by 1994 of Head Start, one of the goals he announced in his 1988 presidential campaign. ■

Children's Aid Bill Stalls

An ambitious five-year, $4.5 billion plan to help the nation's children won approval from a House Ways and Means subcommittee on June 27, but went no further in the 101st Congress.

While members of the Subcommittee on Human Resources voiced concerns about the cost of the measure, Democrats and Republicans insisted that the rising numbers of children whose families were homeless or addicted to drugs or alcohol or who required special services posed a serious enough risk to warrant the additional spending.

The panel approved the bill (HR 5020), sponsored by Thomas J. Downey, D-N.Y., by voice vote.

Dysfunctional families and the effect of neglect and abuse on young children "are the ticking time bomb in our society," said E. Clay Shaw Jr., Fla., the subcommittee's ranking Republican.

The bill drew opposition from only one subcommittee member — Don Sundquist, R-Tenn., who described himself as "the skunk at a garden party." The Bush administration also vehemently opposed the legislation.

"Such large program expansions under current budget conditions would be imprudent, and the proposals in HR 5020 do not address the problems of getting children out of the foster care program and into stable, permanent homes," Health and Human Services Secretary Louis W. Sullivan wrote in a June 27 letter to Downey.

The measure was intended to address a number of problems, such as the overall increase in the number of children requiring protective services or foster care and the sharp growth in the number of caseloads. Children entering the system also needed more comprehensive services than they had in the past.

HR 5020 would have built on the 1980 Adoption Assistance and Child Welfare Amendments (PL 96-272), the last major overhaul of child welfare and foster care programs. *(1980 Almanac, p. 417)*

In addition to providing more money for child welfare services, the bill also would have placed new obligations on the states, including requirements that services be available statewide, be aimed at preventing family breakups and at reunifying families with children in foster care, and include follow-up care to keep recently reunified families together and functioning. ■

Social Security Earnings Test Unchanged

Caught in a budget squeeze, Congress for the second year in a row reluctantly abandoned efforts to relax the Social Security retirement test, which reduced the benefits of working senior citizens who earned more than a certain amount each year.

Senior citizens' groups had been urging the change for years, and lawmakers on both sides of the aisle — keenly aware of the groups' lobbying clout — professed support for the change despite the anticipated revenue loss.

By a strange twist, the 1990 effort to ease the retirement test (also known as the earnings test) played out in negotiations over child-care legislation (HR 3), which was enacted as part of the budget-reconciliation package (HR 5835 — PL 101-508).

The proposed change would have increased from $9,360 in 1990 to $19,960 in 1991 the amount persons age 65-69 could earn before seeing a reduction in their Social Security checks.

The Senate Finance Committee had tacked a more modest liberalization onto its version (S 5) of the child-care bill in June 1989, then upped the ante in 1990. The language stayed in the bill until Oct. 4, when Senate conferees finally agreed to drop it. *(Child care, p. 547)*

Some Provisions Enacted

The final reconciliation bill did make a number of modifications in Social Security law, although nothing of the magnitude of the earnings test relaxation. *(Reconciliation provisions: Title V — Social Security, p. 150)*

Of the provisions enacted, perhaps the most popular was a requirement that the Social Security Administration (SSA) within six months restore telephone service to its local offices. Such service had been cut off in October 1989, a year after the SSA set up a toll-free network of 37 teleservice centers around the nation to respond to inquiries from the public.

The teleservice centers were supposed to relieve some of the burden on the agency's 1,300 district and branch offices, which were suffering from staff cutbacks. But matters did not work out that way.

In a survey conducted in early 1989, nine out of 10 workers at New Jersey's Social Security offices said that the teleservice had failed to reduce their workload, had done a poor job screening out people who could be taken care of without an office visit and had failed to properly inform those referred to the local offices about their situation.

Seniors themselves were even more unhappy. Busy signal rates, which were supposed to be no more than 5 percent, averaged 25 percent. They ranged from 8.2 percent in June 1989 to 51.4 percent in November 1989, according to the House Select Committee on Aging.

Even when callers got through, they often received the runaround or erroneous information.

Other significant provisions enacted did the following:

- Tightened controls over "representative payees," individuals appointed to receive Social Security or Supplemental Security Income (SSI) payments on behalf of beneficiaries unable to manage their own money.
- Made permanent the right of a Disability Insurance beneficiary to continue receiving benefits while appealing a ruling that he or she was no longer disabled. The right applied through two of the three appeals steps, and the beneficiary could be required to return the payments if the cutoff were upheld.
- Required the SSA to provide annual statements of earnings and benefits to all wage earners beginning Oct. 1, 1999.
- Gave immunity from prosecution for use of a false Social Security number to illegal aliens who were granted amnesty pursuant to provisions of the 1986 Immigration Reform and Control Act. *(IRCA, 1986 Almanac, p. 61)*

BACKGROUND

For the second year in a row, Congress dropped an earnings test provision from its final reconciliation bill. As in 1989, lawmakers could not figure out a way to offset the cost of the change. *(Previous action, 1989 Almanac, p. 221)*

Congress had relaxed the earnings test more than a dozen times since it was first imposed in 1939, but seniors continued to complain. During the 101st Congress, their cause was championed primarily by Republicans.

A May rally on the West Front of the Capitol, called to support repeal of the earnings test, featured dozens of Republicans, including House Minority Leader Robert H. Michel, Ill., and Minority Whip Newt Gingrich, Ga.

"Because of the earnings test, seniors are being forced out of the work force and into the rocking chair," Rep. Dennis Hastert, R-Ill., said at the rally.

The push for repeal was coming from some senior citizens groups as well, notably the National Committee to Preserve Social Security and Medicare, which also led the charge in 1989 to repeal the Medicare Catastrophic Coverage Act. *(1989 Almanac, p. 149)*

The Arguments

Proponents of repealing the test said it made no sense to discourage seniors from working at a time when the labor market faced future shortages. They also cited a 1989 study by economists Aldona and Gary Robbins that concluded that repeal of the test would produce a net gain in federal revenue because the increased costs of benefits not paid under existing law would be more than offset by taxes paid on new wages seniors would earn.

But many economists disputed the assertion that the earnings test was a deterrent to continued participation in the work force.

In the May 1990 Social Security Bulletin, Michael V. Leonesio wrote, "The evidence strongly suggests that the impact of the retirement test on the aggregate labor supply of older workers is fairly small."

A 1988 analysis by the Congressional Budget Office (CBO) found that most senior citizens were unaffected by the test. In 1986, fewer than one in 10 people age 65-69 who were eligible for Social Security benefits earned enough to lose benefits.

"I think it is fair to say that people retire for myriad reasons," Rep. Thomas J. Downey, D-N.Y., said during the June House debate on the issue. "They are not sitting at home waiting for Congress to change the earnings test so they can go to work."

Studies also showed that the primary beneficiaries of a substantial liberalization of the test would be the wealthiest of the elderly. While only one-eighth of Social Security beneficiaries age 65-69 had family incomes above $42,000 in 1986, more than 40 percent of those who lost benefits because of the retirement test were in that group, the CBO found.

Critics said that the retirement test was far less of a factor than age or health status when seniors decided whether to continue working.

House Ways and Means Committee Chairman Dan Rostenkowski, D-Ill., said, "If the House is genuinely interested in improving Social Security benefits, there are more equitable ways to do so. Two come readily to mind: improving benefits for the poorest Social Security beneficiaries — widows over the age of 85 — and eliminating some glaring inequities in the law affecting disabled widows."

Under existing law, future retirees could expect to recoup their lost benefits eventually. A "delayed retirement credit," which increased benefit levels for those who delayed the start of benefits or who lost benefits because of the retirement test, was too low in 1990 to make up fully for the lost benefits. But 1983 Social Security legislation (PL 98-21) was gradually increasing the credit to provide a total offset.

Why Child Care?

It was the Senate that originally added the retirement-test provisions to the child-care bill (then S 5) during floor consideration in June 1989. *(1989 Almanac, p. 213)*

By 100-0, senators approved an amendment to increase by about $1,200 the amount senior citizens age 65-69 could earn without having Social Security checks reduced.

In 1990 that amount was $9,360. (The retirement test did not apply to seniors over 70, and the provision would not have altered the rules for those age 62-64.)

The proposal was offered by Senate Finance Committee Chairman Lloyd Bentsen, D-Texas, but the issue was being pushed even harder by Senate Republicans, led by Finance member William L. Armstrong, Colo.

At the time, the fast-track child-care bill "seemed like a good vehicle," said Ron Pollack, executive director of Families USA, an advocacy group focusing on the problems of the low-income elderly. "They felt like this would be a very popular bill, and it was a good chance to get [the earnings test relaxation] into law."

The moves also came at a time when Congress was being deluged with complaints from affluent senior citizens about a new tax to pay for Medicare catastrophic-illness benefits. (Congress ultimately repealed the tax and the catastrophic-coverage program in November 1989.)

Bentsen acknowledged that relaxing the earnings test, which would have benefited many of the same seniors complaining the loudest about the catastrophic tax, would be politically advantageous for lawmakers.

LEGISLATIVE ACTION

The House Ways and Means Social Security Subcommittee on May 2 voted to ease the earnings test and to make the Social Security Administration an independent agency.

Those proposals were the most significant of 22 provisions approved by the panel. All had been included in the House version of the fiscal 1990 budget-reconciliation package, but were dropped in the frantic House-Senate negotiations that preceded adjournment Nov. 22, 1989.

The most contentious of the proposals sought to remove the SSA from the Department of Health and Human Services (HHS) and establish it as an independent agency. The agency was to be run by a three-member, bipartisan board appointed by the president. The board was to formulate policy and appoint an executive director to run Social Security's day-to-day operations.

SSA officials opposed creation of an independent agency, saying they would lose Cabinet-level representation to deal with budgetary and administrative concerns. But Hank Brown, Colo., the subcommittee's ranking Republican, said the agency would have more control of its affairs if it were an independent agency.

The subcommittee voted to raise the earnings exemption from $9,960 to $10,200 in 1991 and to $10,920 in 1992.

Another proposal called for the SSA to re-establish telephone access to its local offices.

Also approved were provisions that would have:

- Required HHS to set stiffer standards for, and conduct a more extensive investigation of, "representative payees," who received and managed Social Security checks for incompetent beneficiaries.
- Streamlined the procedure for SSA approval of attorneys' fees for those representing a successful claimant, allowing fees of up to 25 percent of past-due benefits, to a maximum of $4,000.
- Exempted from criminal penalties for fraudulent use of a Social Security card aliens who won amnesty under the 1986 immigration reform law (PL 99-603), provided they did not sell their cards or counterfeit them with the intent to sell them.
- Reduced, from $10,125 to $6,075 in 1991, the amount of annual earnings needed to gain a year of Social Security coverage. This was intended to help long-term, low-wage workers.

Conference/Final

Although the earnings test provision was not included in the version of the child-care bill the House passed in March 1990, the proposal was popular in that chamber as well as in the Senate.

More than 250 members cosponsored legislation (HR 2460) to eliminate the test.

Thus, it was not a surprise when the House voted 384-36 in June to instruct its child-care conferees to include in the bill a modified version of the Senate provision relaxing the retirement test. *(Vote 185, p. 64-H)*

Senate conferees, however, proceeded to up the ante. While the original Senate-passed proposal would have increased by $1,200 the amount a senior could earn without having benefits reduced, conferees on Aug. 3 proposed to increase it by more than $10,000, to $19,960 in 1991.

The Senate offer proposed to pay for the increase, which would have cost an estimated $1.2 billion the first year, by requiring state and local employees not already participating in a retirement program to participate in Social Security. Under existing law, states had the option of having such employees, mostly part-time and temporary workers, pay Social Security taxes.

The expanded Senate proposal carried a five-year cost of $9.47 billion, which exceeded the cost of the underlying child-care provisions.

One observer of the negotiations jokingly called the proposal "The Retirement Test and Minor Child Care Improvements Act of 1990." And when child-care negotiations got serious in early October, the Senate conferees dumped the costly earnings test relaxation. ■

Community Service Measure Enacted

Legislation to spur community service by the young and old was sent to President Bush despite the administration's objections that true volunteerism should not include financial incentives. The bill (S 1430) authorized grants to establish national, community- and school-based volunteer service programs.

The Senate approved the conference report, 75-21, on Oct. 16; the House cleared the legislation Oct. 24 by a vote of 235-186. *(Senate vote 274, p. 55-S; House vote 512, p. 162-H)*

Bush signed the measure Nov. 16, but noted his "reservations about the wisdom of employing 'paid volunteers' to the extent contemplated" by the bill.

Under the bill, grants were to be provided for programs with volunteers of all ages. Colleges and universities could apply for funds to run student community service programs, and community-based groups could seek grants to run programs involving adult volunteers.

Although community service was a major theme for Bush during his 1988 campaign, the administration previously had threatened to veto the bill because it disliked the financial incentives in the measure.

"The reward for voluntary service should never be seen as financial," said one administration statement.

In response, Senate Majority Leader George J. Mitchell, D-Maine, said, "In order for a broad array of young people to participate in service in their communities, we need to do more than simply encourage them."

The legislation, he said, would enable more than just those from wealthy families to serve their communities. For example, the bill included a three-year national service demonstration program, sponsored by Sen. Claiborne Pell, D-R.I. People who volunteered for one or two years in a community service program would be eligible to receive up to $5,000 in educational vouchers for each year of service.

In an effort to deter the veto threat, the legislation authorized the Points of Light Initiative Foundation proposed by Bush. That foundation would seek to foster volunteerism and administer service programs.

Conferees also agreed to drop the most contentious provision, a student-loan forgiveness proposal.

"The legislation is a call to action for the nation. It is a reaffirmation of our national commitment to lend a helping hand to our fellow citizens and our communities," said Edward M. Kennedy, D-Mass., who pushed the measure through the Senate.

The bill authorized $62 million in fiscal 1991, $105 million in fiscal 1992 and $120 million in fiscal 1993.

Lawmakers in both chambers in 1989 discarded proposals by Sen. Sam Nunn, D-Ga., and Rep. Dave McCurdy, D-Okla., to require students to perform community or national service in return for college aid.

BOXSCORE

Legislation: National and Community Service Act of 1990, PL 101-610 (S 1430, HR 4330).

Major action: Signed, Nov. 16. Conference report adopted by House, 235-186, Oct. 24; by Senate, 75-21, Oct. 16. Passed by House, Sept. 13; by Senate, 78-19, March 1.

Reports: Conference report (H Rept 101-893). Education and Labor (H Rept 101-844, Part I). Labor and Human Resources (S Rept 101-176).

BACKGROUND

What Bush envisioned in terms of legislation to encourage community service was still not clear more than a year after he first proposed a "Youth Engaged in Service to America" (YES) program in a campaign speech during his 1988 presidential race.

Since April 1989, administration officials had repeatedly promised that legislation to promote volunteerism was imminent. But none appeared for quite a while.

On Aug. 2, 1989, the Senate Labor and Human Resources Committee approved S 1430 — which it reported Oct. 27, 1989 — authorizing $300 million in activities to promote community service. *(1989 Almanac, p. 195)*

Most Republicans withheld support from the bill, saying the Senate should have waited to hear from the president but Democrats had run out of patience.

Kennedy's staff met with a variety of administration representatives, including people from the Office of National Service, from the staff of domestic affairs adviser Roger B. Porter and from the Office of Management and Budget. Kennedy also conferred with John H. Sununu, Bush's chief of staff. "We don't know who is drafting the legislation anymore," a Kennedy aide said.

On Jan. 4, Bush received the report of a special committee he set up to advise him. The committee, led by New Jersey Republican Gov. Thomas H. Kean, recommended legislation to create the Points of Light Foundation.

The Office of National Service recommended that the foundation set up "Points of Light Action Groups" in all 50 states to identify critical problems and encourage communities to tackle them. The foundation would point out model community service projects in schools, churches and synagogues and encourage other organizations to try similar projects.

Another idea for the foundation was to start a telephone hotline, a computer data base and an electronic bulletin board to disseminate information about volunteer opportunities. The foundation would also spread the word about volunteering by advertising and by providing stories about successful community service leaders and programs to the media.

Administration, Volunteer Groups' Concerns

The administration's stops and starts regarding national service legislation reflected an aversion to becoming enmeshed with the Senate's bill, which not only cost more than Bush's plan but also relied on post-service financial incentives to lure volunteers.

Bush said June 21, 1989: "YES is voluntary, truly voluntary. You don't need to be bribed with incentives and threatened with penalties to get engaged in community service."

An administration official said, "We were hesitant to

send up our package and have it attached to their $300 million package. The president's idea is for volunteers, not to create another VISTA. He wants true volunteerism."

VISTA (Volunteers in Service to America), a remnant of the "war on poverty" of the 1960s, paid its volunteers small stipends. The program was reauthorized in 1989, along with others overseen by the ACTION agency. *(1989 Almanac, p. 217)*

The Senate bill created programs for narrow segments of the population, he said. "The president's view is that service should be central to every American's life. The president is interested in a call to action to every single American and every single American institution."

Representatives of national volunteer organizations voiced frustration with the administration's pace and disappointment with the Kean commission's proposal.

"It's not real substantive," said Leonard W. Stern, executive director of the National Assembly of National Voluntary Health and Social Welfare Organizations. The group represented about 40 organizations, including the Red Cross, Boy Scouts, Girl Scouts and 4-H Clubs. "A lot of us were hoping that there would be more coming out of it than that," he said.

Frank J. Slobig, co-director of Youth Service America, a national umbrella organization for volunteer groups, said the president's interest was important.

But he worried that the Points of Light Foundation would simply encourage incidental volunteerism — such as a Boy Scout walking an old lady across the street. What he would rather see, he said, was young people making sustained commitments in rigorous, structured programs.

SENATE FLOOR ACTION

After four days of debate, a variety of extraneous amendments and pressure from the White House to cut costs, the Senate on March 1 passed S 1430. The bill, approved 78-19, authorized $125 million for various programs to encourage volunteerism. *(Vote 27, p. 8-S)*

Evoking the memory of his brother, President John F. Kennedy, Sen. Kennedy told the Senate, "It is time to rekindle the sense of community service and commitment to others."

After citing the example of Soviet, Eastern European and Chinese citizens risking their lives for democracy, Kennedy complained, "more and more young Americans do not vote and feel disconnected from their communities. They have forgotten that democracy means not only the right to pursue one's own interest, but the responsibility to participate in the life of the nation in return."

S 1430 called for grants to states and localities to create or expand school- and community-based service programs for students and adults. Senior citizens would be encouraged to volunteer in the schools; students would be enlisted to help in nursing homes, day-care centers, hospitals and other parts of the community. The bill sought to authorize a youth service corps for volunteers age 16 to 25 who enlisted for up to one year. They would receive a poverty-level living allowance and post-service benefits of up to $5,000.

The measure also would have authorized demonstration projects in 10 states for full-time and part-time national service programs. Full-time participants, who were to serve one or two years, would qualify for up to $5,000 per year in post-service vouchers to be used for tuition, student-loan payments or the down payment on a first home. Part-time volunteers, who would have to serve two weekends a month and two weeks per year for at least two years, could qualify for up to $2,000 per year in post-service benefits.

Full-time volunteers, but not part-timers, would also receive a poverty-level living allowance.

Administration Still Displeased

The bill brought to the floor on Feb. 26 was a compromise worked out between Kennedy and Orrin G. Hatch of Utah, the Labor and Human Resources Committee's ranking Republican. It slashed the total funding authorization from more than $300 million in the version approved by the committee in 1989 to $125 million in an effort to make the package more palatable to Bush.

Kennedy and Hatch also included a $25 million authorization over two years for the Points of Light Initiative Foundation the president wanted to create to coordinate and foster programs using volunteers.

One administration official complained that "Hatch was out there on his own," cutting deals with the Democrats that the administration did not want and then later telling the executive branch what he had done.

As he praised the bill, Hatch acknowledged the administration's concern. "While it is not precisely what President Bush has recommended, and I am aware that he still has concerns about the total authorization and other components of the bill, it is fair to say that this legislation reflects many changes that are compatible with the administration's vision for a national service program," he said.

The most controversial element of the bill, and the part Bush objected to most, was the national service demonstration with its post-service vouchers.

In a pointed barb at Bush and others who complained that the bill was not "true volunteerism" because it offered financial incentives, Nunn drew on his experience as chairman of the Senate Armed Services Committee.

"We could have used that argument in the [all-volunteer] military, but we did not because we knew it would not work," he said. "Some of the same people who are advocating that now were most vocal in the 1970s and 1980s in providing very large bonuses for people who served in the military."

Nunn said community service "should not be limited to those who have the luxury to serve without compensation."

It was Nunn who initially ignited an intense debate over the nature of community service when he, McCurdy and Charles S. Robb, D-Va., introduced legislation (S 3, HR 66) in 1989 that would have made military or civilian national service a prerequisite for receiving federal student aid.

The bill was denounced as discriminatory by those who said only the poor would have to serve and the affluent would pay their own college bills.

Nunn said he remained "fully committed" to the idea, but he settled for the demonstration program in the bill. Participants would serve in education, human services, environment or public safety, with a special emphasis on work related to poverty.

"This bill tests the concept of a civilian GI Bill, calling for a new basis of citizenship in which citizens are once again asked to give something back to their nation," Nunn said.

Even in its existing diluted form, Nunn's program touched off one of the more heated debates of the week.

Sen. John McCain, R-Ariz., a retired Navy officer who spent six years in a North Vietnamese prison camp, said the Senate would be making "a grave mistake" if it permitted post-service benefits for civilian national service to exceed the post-service education benefits available to military veterans.

S 1430, he noted, would allow full-time community service volunteers to receive educational and housing vouchers of up to $10,000 for two years of work, while military veterans received $9,000 in post-service educational benefits for two years' service. And that $9,000 required a $1,200 contribution from the enlistee.

"This is clearly not a fair situation," McCain said.

Nunn said he agreed that members of the military should be paid more than civilian volunteers. He insisted that the bill did not violate that principle because the combined in-service pay and post-service benefits of military enlistees far exceeded the combined total authorized for civilian volunteers.

"I do not think anyone ought to be deceived," Nunn said. "The military has a total package. It includes all sorts of benefits, including housing benefits, including food benefits, including a lot of things that are not part of this rather austere pilot program."

The Senate voted to table McCain's amendment, 54-41. *(Vote 19, p. 7-S)*

Amendments Adopted, Rejected

During debate on the bill, the Senate detoured from national service into the "peace dividend" when Phil Gramm, R-Texas, proposed an amendment stating the "sense of the Senate" that any savings from lower defense expenditures should be used to balance the budget and return money to the taxpayers, including through a capital gains tax cut.

Democrats offered their own opinion about what to do with the peace dividend with an amendment by Jim Sasser, D-Tenn., that urged deficit reduction and spending on "urgent national priorities," such as education, health care, the environment and antidrug and anticrime efforts.

The Senate rejected Gramm's amendment, 48-50, and adopted Sasser's, 79-19. *(Votes 22, 21, p. 7-S)*

Other amendments adopted, by voice vote unless otherwise indicated, included:

- By Pete V. Domenici, R-N.M., to include drug and alcohol abuse, education and treatment programs in the scope of service activities allowed under the bill.
- By Kennedy (for Kent Conrad, D-N.D.), to ensure that Indian tribes were eligible to receive program grants.
- By William L. Armstrong, R-Colo., to allow religious organizations to receive federal funds under the bill provided the money was not used for religious instruction, worship or other sectarian purposes, 91-3. *(Vote 18, p. 7-S)*
- By Bob Dole, R-Kan., to allow people with disabilities to participate in volunteer programs under the act.
- By Slade Gorton, R-Wash., to clarify the application of tort liabilities to remove risk from state employees.
- By Hatch (for Alfonse M. D'Amato, R-N.Y.), to make all groups receiving grants under the act subject to the drug-free workplace requirements in the Anti-Drug Abuse Act of 1988.
- By Armstrong, modified by Kennedy, to amend the District of Columbia Code to allow organizations to exclude adult homosexuals or bisexuals from coaching, teaching or serving as mentors to a minor if the minor's parents objected to the individual's participation because of his or her sexual orientation.
- By Gordon J. Humphrey, R-N.H., condemning China for its suppression of pro-democracy demonstrations and its policy of forced family planning, 79-18. *(Vote 26, p. 8-S)*

Amendments rejected included:

- By Mitch McConnell, R-Ky., to abolish joint and several liability for nonprofit organizations, provide for alternative dispute resolution and give limited immunity from liability to unpaid volunteers, tabled 65-32. *(Vote 20, p. 7-S)*
- By McCain, to terminate the authorization as of Sept. 30, 1992, tabled 58-40. *(Vote 25, p. 8-S)*

Highlights of the Senate Bill

Other highlights of the bill and their authorization levels included:

- **School- and Community-Based Service,** $10 million in fiscal 1990 and $15 million in fiscal 1991. Priority would go to programs that involved senior citizens; focused on preventing drug and alcohol abuse, or school dropouts; and offered literacy training.
- **American Conservation and Youth Service Corps,** $14 million in fiscal 1990 and $21 million in 1991, for the creation or expansion of full-time or summer youth service corps programs. The programs could focus on outdoor projects such as the improvement of parks, wildlife habitats or urban areas; or on human services in nursing homes, hospitals, law enforcement agencies and the like.
- **National and Community Service,** $14 million in fiscal 1990 and $21 million in fiscal 1991 to set up demonstration projects in up to 10 states in which participants received post-service vouchers toward higher education or a first-home purchase.
- **Commission on National and Community Service,** $800,000 in fiscal 1990 and $1.2 million in fiscal 1991. The commission would administer the preceding programs and review grant applications from the states and Indian tribes. It would be run by a board of directors, with 21 members to be appointed by the president with the approval of the Senate.
- **Clearinghouses,** $800,000 in fiscal 1990 and $1.2 million in 1991 for three or more national or regional clearinghouses to help states and localities plan service programs and train administrators and participants.
- **Higher Education Programs.** Using funds authorized in other laws, would allow partial loan cancellation or deferral in Stafford student loan programs for people performing full-time community service and cancellation or deferral of Perkins student loans.

The bill would expand a demonstration program offering grants to institutions to run community service programs for postsecondary students and offer incentives for colleges to use work-study funds for community service.

- **Points of Light Initiative Foundation,** $10 million in fiscal 1990 and $15 million in 1991. The foundation would be responsible for encouraging volunteerism, identifying community service projects and disseminating information about them, and developing leadership among people who performed community service.

HOUSE COMMITTEE ACTION

The House Education and Labor Committee on July 19 approved HR 4330 by voice vote to establish school- and college-based community service programs.

HR 4330 would have authorized $183 million in fiscal 1991 for grants to states to promote volunteerism by students. One provision would have allowed college students to have their student loans forgiven or deferred if they provided volunteer service in their communities.

"This bill fits well into the president's thousands points of light, which have yet to be lit," committee Chairman Augustus F. Hawkins, D-Calif., said in his opening statement July 12.

But many Republicans, including ranking minority member Bill Goodling, Pa., said it would be impossible to fund the program fully during this time of fiscal austerity. Other GOP members argued, as the Bush administration had, that it was bad public policy to provide incentives to make people volunteer.

"What has the nation come to when Congress has to authorize money for volunteer programs?" said Marge Roukema, R-N.J.

The committee adopted by voice vote a Hawkins amendment that included compromise language making private schools eligible for the school-based community-service grants.

Roukema offered an amendment that would have removed a section of the bill allowing forgiveness of student loans for students helping tax-exempt organizations, drug counseling programs or the Indian Health Service. But she withdrew the amendment after Democrats protested that it was too broad to have been introduced at such a late date.

The committee rejected, 13-22, an amendment by Tom Tauke, R-Iowa, which would have required that, before a state could receive a grant, it would have to ensure that a volunteer of a nonprofit organization could not incur personal financial liability for injuries or damages that occurred while volunteering, unless they were caused by willful or wanton misconduct.

Tauke said people were becoming reluctant to volunteer for fear of being sued.

Pat Williams, D-Mont., objected to the amendment, saying it would force the bill to be referred to the Judiciary Committee, where similar legislation (HR 911) had been pending for more than a year.

The committee accepted an amendment by George Miller, D-Calif., stating that it was the sense of Congress that states should provide uniform standards to protect grocery chains and restaurants from liability for donating to food banks for the homeless.

A final amendment by Thomas C. Sawyer, D-Ohio, also approved by voice vote, suggested that states give special attention to projects that awarded students academic credit for volunteering.

HOUSE FLOOR ACTION

Despite stiff Republican opposition to paying volunteers and to creating new programs, the House passed a $193 million bill to spur national service — particularly among youth.

HR 4330 was passed by voice vote Sept. 13 and was sent to conference with S 1430 — the $125 million Senate measure.

Leading off the House debate, Robert S. Walker, R-Pa., complained that while budget negotiators met at Andrews Air Force Base outside Washington, looking to cut the deficit, the House was trying to add to it.

Hawkins said the bill was simply providing the means to back up President Bush's call for "a thousand points of light," the commitment to volunteerism.

"All we're doing is providing some fuel for those lights," Hawkins said.

But the administration continued to oppose the House bill strongly, and Bush's senior advisers planned to recommend a veto. "It is incompatible with the president's concept of voluntary service," a statement from the Office of Management and Budget said. "The reward for voluntary service should never be seen as financial."

That message was underscored by Steve Gunderson, R-Wis., with the help of a Webster's dictionary. "One who enters into or offers oneself to serve of his own free will," said Gunderson, reading the definition of volunteer.

Gunderson pointed out that the government was not meeting its commitment to fund other, more important programs. For example, only 20 percent of the Head Start program for preschoolers was funded. While student Pell grants were authorized at $2,900, the government gave out only $2,200. And while the federal government was authorized to pay 40 percent of the cost of educating every disabled child, only 7 percent was paid, he said.

"Do you know why?" he asked his colleagues. "Because we don't have any money."

Particularly controversial was a provision to expand the existing Perkins student loan cancellation program. For each year of full-time work in professional drug counseling, prevention, treatment or education programs or American Indian health care at public or nonprofit organizations, a portion of the Perkins loan principal and all interest would be canceled.

Goodling proposed striking the entire provision. His amendment was rejected in the only roll call vote on the measure, 200-212. *(Vote 330, p. 108-H)*

Other provisions included:

- **American Conservation Corps.** The secretary of Agriculture and the secretary of the Interior would be authorized to provide grants to states or local governments to create American Conservation Corps programs or to expand Youth Conservation Corps programs.

Projects to be carried out were to include wetlands protection, road and trail maintenance and conservation of rangelands and parks. Budget authority of $38 million would be provided in fiscal 1991.

- **Youth Service Corps.** $28 million would be authorized for grants to public and private nonprofit agencies for Youth Service Corps projects, including service in state, local and regional governmental agencies, nursing homes, day-care centers, law enforcement agencies and other social service agencies.
- **School-Based Service Projects.** $35 million would be authorized in fiscal 1991 for grants to states to finance partnership projects between school districts, local governments, community groups and colleges.

FINAL ACTION

Conferees on Oct. 12 agreed on the legislation, approving staff-drafted compromises and sending the measure to the floors of both chambers. The final version followed the structure set out in the Senate-passed bill.

It created a commission on national service to oversee and administer the variety of volunteer programs. These programs would give grants to the states or to public or private nonprofit organizations to encourage volunteerism.

Conferees, hoping to avoid the threatened Bush veto, agreed to drop the most contentious provision, the student-loan forgiveness proposal, and agreed to include Bush's Points of Light Foundation to help administer the volunteer programs.

The Senate then approved the conference report Oct. 16 and the House cleared the bill Oct. 24. ■

Medicare Beneficiaries To Pay More

Congress in 1990 agreed to trim $44.2 billion over five years from the fast-growing Medicare program, slashing payments to providers and raising out-of-pocket costs to beneficiaries by an estimated $10.1 billion.

The Medicare changes were included in the omnibus budget-reconciliation bill (HR 5835 — PL 101-508) cleared for President Bush on Oct. 27 and signed into law Nov. 5. *(Provisions, Title IV: Medicare, p. 143)*

While significant, the increase in costs to Medicare's 33 million elderly and disabled beneficiaries was only about a third of what it might have been. The White House-congressional budget-summit agreement of Sept. 30 proposed a $30 billion, five-year hit on beneficiaries. The backlash against that proposal helped doom the entire summit plan in the House on Oct. 5. *(Budget summit, p. 129)*

Ultimately, conferees on the budget-reconciliation bill approved only a modest increase in the costs borne by beneficiaries. They raised to $100, from $75, the annual deductible for Medicare's optional Part B insurance, which covered physician and other outpatient costs. That deductible had been unchanged since 1982.

The conferees also agreed to continue requiring the Part B premium, which in 1990 was $28.60 per month, to cover 25 percent of that program's costs. But instead of letting the amount float with actual costs each year, conferees fixed the premiums in advance to reflect what was estimated to be 25 percent of each future year's costs. Thus, the monthly premium for 1991 was fixed at $29.90; for 1992, $31.80; for 1993, $36.60; for 1994, $41.10; and for 1995, $46.10.

The purpose, said Rep. Pete Stark, D-Calif., chairman of the Ways and Means Subcommittee on Health, was to ensure that beneficiaries did not not have to pay for escalating program costs that were caused by inflation or increased prices by health-care providers.

"Chiseled in stone, at least for the next five years, we are going to have seniors participate, but not saddle them with runaway provider costs," Stark told reporters Oct. 29.

Members also wrangled over cuts in payments to doctors and hospitals. The most heated issue was how, and by how much, to shield hospitals in rural areas and inner cities, both of which suffered from Medicare's transition in the 1980s to a payment system based on each patient's diagnosis. In general, House negotiators wanted to provide more of a cushion to urban hospitals, while senators were most concerned about rural facilities.

In the end, the bill boosted payments to inner-city and rural hospitals by $1 billion each over five years. The provision amounted to a major win for rural interests, since far fewer Medicare patients were cared for in rural hospitals than in urban facilities. "That was a fight that left some scars," said Stark, noting that the final bill eliminated an additional $1.5 billion earmarked for inner-city hospitals. Senate conferees, he said, "felt there was something different and better about protecting rural hospitals."

Non-Budgetary Provisions

The bill provided one major expansion of Medicare coverage: For the first time, the program was to pay for routine screening mammograms to detect breast cancer. *(Mammograms, p. 564)*

Among the non-budget provisions in the final package was one — responding to so-called right-to-die cases — that required Medicare and Medicaid providers to inform patients about their rights under state law to execute "living wills" or other advance directives about their care should they become unable to communicate. *(Living wills, p. 566)*

The reconciliation bill also included a section tightening regulation of so-called Medigap insurance policies — private policies designed to fill some of the gaps in Medicare's coverage. *(Medigap, p. 572)*

Finally, the measure clarified provisions of past deficit-reduction bills that prohibited "patient dumping" by hospitals that participated in Medicare. Dumping occurred when a hospital either refused to treat uninsured patients needing emergency care or in active labor or transferred patients to another hospital before their condition had been medically stabilized.

Congress in the fiscal 1986 reconciliation bill (PL 99-272) barred hospitals that participated in Medicare from patient dumping. In the fiscal 1988 reconciliation bill (PL 100-203) Congress extended the ban on dumping to doctors. *(Fiscal 1988 bill, 1987 Almanac, p. 558; fiscal 1986 bill, 1986 Almanac, p. 252)*

HR 5835 changed the standard for what could be considered patient dumping to make it easier to assess civil penalties against hospitals and doctors. And it clarified standards for excluding offenders from the program. An unintended technical glitch in earlier laws had made it more difficult to impose fines, intended as the lesser punishment, than it was to expel a doctor or hospital from Medicare. The bill also reduced to $25,000 (from $50,000) the maximum penalty that could be assessed against small hospitals (those with fewer than 100 beds).

BACKGROUND

Medicare, the federal health-insurance program projected to serve 30 million elderly and 3 million disabled Americans in fiscal 1991, was actually two separate programs (Part A and Part B) with three distinct funding sources: general revenues, premiums paid by beneficiaries and the 1.45 percent payroll tax paid by workers and their employers.

Medicare covered far fewer health expenses than most employment-based insurance plans. With only a few exceptions, Medicare did not cover routine preventive care or most outpatient prescription drugs. It also did not cover most dental care or costs for eyeglasses or hearing aids.

With the repeal in 1989 of the 1988 Medicare Catastrophic Coverage Act, Medicare also did not contain "stop-loss" coverage, meaning that after benefit limits were reached, all additional costs had to be borne by patients. *(Catastrophic repeal, 1989 Almanac p. 149)*

Perhaps most significantly for senior citizens, Medicare did not cover most costs associated with long-term care. Medicare coverage of nursing home and home health care was very limited.

Program Structure: Parts A and B

Part A: Coverage. Part A, officially the Hospital Insurance (HI) program, covered certain expenses for in-

Medicare To Cover Mammograms

In a move hailed by women's groups, Congress in 1990 agreed to provide Medicare coverage for mammograms to detect breast cancer.

The mammography coverage was tucked into the final version of the fiscal 1991 budget-reconciliation bill (HR 5835 — PL 101-508) even though it was in neither the House nor the Senate bill. The federal government was to pay for biennial mammograms for women age 65 or over. Coverage for other women eligible for Medicare varied according to age and risk category.

Preventive Approach

Medicare, the federal health plan for 33 million elderly and disabled Americans, traditionally had not covered preventive services such as mammography, a special X-ray that can detect breast tumors at their earliest and most treatable stages.

Thus, the inclusion of a mammography benefit in the 1988 Medicare Catastrophic Coverage Act was hailed as a landmark change not only by women's groups but also by health analysts, who applauded the recognition that preventive health care could save lives and money.

The benefit, however, never took effect. It was repealed in 1989 along with most of the rest of the law, after beneficiaries rebelled at the prospect of paying for catastrophic coverage. *(1989 Almanac, p. 149)*

Advocates of the mammography coverage set out early in 1990 to restore the benefit. Despite widespread support on the committees that oversaw the program, however, the mammography benefit failed to make it into either the House or Senate reconciliation bill.

One problem was money; the benefit was estimated to cost $1.25 billion over its first five years.

"Mr. Panetta and Mr. Gephardt kept saying I had $2 billion to spend [on Medicare expansions], but I could never find it," complained Rep. Pete Stark, D-Calif., chairman of the Ways and Means Subcommittee on Health and a strong backer of the mammography benefit. Stark was referring to a $2 billion pot of money included in the failed White House-Congress budget summit agreement negotiated by, among others, House Budget Committee Chairman Leon E. Panetta, D-Calif., and Majority Leader Richard A. Gephardt, D-Mo.

Another problem was the decision by Ways and Means Chairman Dan Rostenkowski, D-Ill., to keep the initial House bill free of extraneous items. When Panetta and Rostenkowski wanted to add several items, including the mammography benefit, on the House floor, Republicans revolted, jeopardizing the budget bill.

Oakar's Crusade

Panetta and Rostenkowski relented, but that infuriated Rep. Mary Rose Oakar, D-Ohio, who had promoted the mammography benefit in the catastrophic coverage bill.

"When I found out they left it out, I just lost it," Oakar recounted after Congress adjourned.

Oakar went public, complaining loudly and repeatedly on the House floor. She also pursued the matter during Democratic Caucus and whip meetings.

"It was just day after day of badgering," she said. "Finally, Rostenkowski said to me, 'OK, Mary Rose, you've convinced me.' "

At that point, she said, Rostenkowski became "a zealot," and pushed relentlessly for the benefit in one-on-one meetings with Senate Finance Committee Chairman Lloyd Bentsen, D-Texas.

Sources said Bentsen finally accepted the benefit when Rostenkowski convinced him that its inclusion could bring the bill as many as 15 votes from wavering female members of the House.

But the ultimate credit, virtually everyone involved agreed, belonged to Oakar. Said Ways and Means Health Subcommittee member Sander M. Levin, D-Mich., "It shows that if you care enough around here, sometimes you prevail."

---

patient hospital care (60 days for each "spell of illness" after payment of a deductible, set at $592 in calendar 1990). It also provided limited coverage for nursing home stays (up to 100 days with coinsurance payments of $74 per day required from patients after the first 20 days), and home health and hospice care.

Eligibility. People age 65 who were eligible for Social Security benefits automatically qualified for Part A coverage, as did people who had been receiving Social Security disability payments for 24 months. Also eligible were most people with serious kidney failure (an estimated 160,000 people in fiscal 1991) through Medicare's End Stage Renal Disease program. People age 65 or older who were not eligible for Social Security could purchase Part A coverage for $175 per month.

Financing. Part A was financed by the HI portion of the Social Security payroll tax, which was 1.45 percent paid by employees and matched by employers on the employee's first $51,300 of income. Self-employed people paid the full 2.9 percent themselves.

Part B: Coverage. Part B, officially the Supplemental Medical Insurance program, paid 80 percent of certain physician and other non-hospital bills after patients paid an annual deductible ($75 in 1990). Covered services included outpatient laboratory and other diagnostic tests, certain durable medical equipment used in the home, and home health care and services provided by a variety of non-physician health professionals, such as physical therapists, psychologists or nurse-midwives.

Eligibility. Everyone eligible for Part A and all Americans age 65 or older, regardless of whether they qualified for Part A, could enroll in Part B, which was optional. About 97 percent of those eligible for Part A also bought Part B, which in 1990 cost $28.60 per month. Social Security recipients had Part B premiums deducted from their monthly checks.

Financing. The portion of Part B costs not covered by premiums was paid out of general Treasury revenues. As originally enacted in 1965, premiums were to cover 50 percent of program costs. However, when Part B costs began to skyrocket, Congress sought to ease the burden on beneficiaries by limiting premium increases to the same percentage as the Social Security cost of living increase. That sent the beneficiaries' share of costs plummeting. In 1982, when premiums covered only about 24 percent of program costs, Congress required that the premium be set to recoup 25 percent of program costs.

Although the provision, part of PL 97-248, was to be temporary, Congress renewed the 25 percent requirement each year thereafter. *(1982 Almanac, p. 471)*

Hospital, Doctor Payments

In 1983, as part of PL 98-21, Congress stopped paying hospitals according to what they charged for Medicare patients and instead put most of them under a Prospective Payment System, which paid a fixed rate based on the patient's ailment. Ailments were divided into nearly 500 "diagnosis-related groups," or DRGs, each of which had a fixed rate. The object was to encourage efficiency by allowing hospitals to keep the difference if a patient could be treated for less than the DRG rate, while requiring the hospital to absorb the loss if a patient cost more to treat.

Under the 1983 law, payments for each DRG (already adjusted for a variety of factors, including the hospital's region) were to be increased annually for inflation according to Medicare's measure of hospital inflation, the "market basket index." However, Congress tended to hold increases to less than the inflation rate to save money — a practice the hospital industry claimed was driving many hospitals to the brink of bankruptcy.

In 1989, as part of PL 101-239, Congress overhauled the way it paid physicians under Part B. The new system, to be phased in between 1992 and 1996, was to pay doctors according to a fee schedule based on the time, training and skill needed to perform a given service.

The system replaced Medicare's original reimbursement mechanism, which paid physicians essentially according to what they had charged in the past for the same service, adjusted for inflation. Under the old system, analysts determined that Medicare was paying too much for surgery or tests on patients, and not enough for services involving simple examinations or talking to patients. The new system also limited what doctors could charge Medicare beneficiaries above what Medicare would pay.

BUSH BUDGET

Congress began the 1990 debate by warning that it would not accept Bush's proposal to trim $5.5 billion from the Medicare program in fiscal 1991. *(Bush budget, p. 116)*

The first shots were fired the week of Feb. 19, when a majority of members in both chambers signed letters to their respective Budget committees urging rejection of Bush's proposed $3.4 billion spending reductions for Medicare's hospital program. Most of the remaining cuts sought by Bush were to come from payments to doctors and other providers of outpatient services.

"Many hospitals are already experiencing severe financial difficulties," said a letter sent by Nancy Landon Kassebaum, R-Kan., Carl Levin, D-Mich., and 49 other senators. "Cuts in the Medicare program of the magnitude that the president is proposing can only make the situation worse and will pose a real threat to health care for the elderly and disabled."

The House letter, written by Nita M. Lowey, D-N.Y., and Bob Whittaker, R-Kan., and signed by 225 of their colleagues, said, "Many consecutive years of Medicare spending reductions have compromised some hospitals' ability to meet our nation's obligation to seniors and the disabled, and the cuts proposed by the administration are unacceptable."

Also weighing in against the cuts was the House Ways and Means Committee, which shared jurisdiction over Medicare with the Energy and Commerce Committee. A Feb. 27 letter from Ways and Means Chairman Dan Rostenkowski, D-Ill., to House Budget Chairman Leon E. Panetta, D-Calif., said it was "not reasonable to expect providers or beneficiaries to absorb the level of reductions proposed by the administration."

Rostenkowski noted that Congress in 1989 had struggled mightily to "achieve somewhat less than $3 billion of Medicare reductions." *(1989 Almanac, p. 157)*

At a Feb. 28 hearing, Senate Finance Committee Chairman Lloyd Bentsen, D-Texas, expressed his disapproval directly to Health and Human Services Secretary Louis W. Sullivan. "The magnitude of these proposed Medicare cuts is astounding, given that the Medicare program has made substantial contributions to deficit reduction in past years," Bentsen told Sullivan. "You and I both know Medicare cuts as big as proposed in the administration's budget are not realistic this year."

THE BUDGET SUMMIT

Because Medicare cuts were a key to any budget agreement in 1990, the committees made no real attempt to address the problem until congressional and White House negotiators got to work on an overall budget accord.

The Sept. 30 budget-summit agreement called for Medicare savings of $4.6 billion for fiscal 1991 — more than Bush had sought at the beginning of the year — and $60 billion over five years. Of the total savings, the agreement assumed that half would be realized by requiring Medicare beneficiaries to pay higher premiums, deductibles and coinsurance payments, with the remainder to come from reducing payments to health-care providers.

Beneficiaries: The agreement assumed three specific beneficiary cost-sharing proposals that the Congressional Budget Office estimated would save the federal government $27.8 billion over five years.

The first would have gradually increased the $75 annual Part B deductible to $100 in 1991, $125 in 1992, and $150 thereafter.

The second proposal increased to 30 percent the share of Part B costs that premiums would have to cover. Under existing law (increasing the premium by the amount of the Social Security COLA) or another extension of the existing 25 percent policy, the 1991 premium was projected to rise from $28.60 per month to $29.90. With a 30 percent rule, the premium was projected at $33.50. By 1995, the 30 percent rule was expected to require a monthly premium of $54.30, while the 25 percent rule would render a premium of $47.

Finally, the plan assumed that beneficiaries would pay 20 percent of the costs of outpatient laboratory tests. Under existing law, laboratory fees were fully covered.

Providers: The agreement explicitly left to the committees that oversaw Medicare (Ways and Means and Energy and Commerce in the House; Finance in the Senate) decisions concerning how to apportion the cuts in payments to hospitals, doctors and other health providers.

The document included, however, a list of proposals that would produce the required savings.

Among the suggestions were several that had been

Health-Care Providers Told To Inform

In response to a controversial Supreme Court ruling, Congress in 1990 ordered health-care providers paid by Medicare and Medicaid to inform patients about their rights under state law to execute "living wills" or other advance directives about their care should they become unable to communicate.

The action came in the budget-reconciliation bill (HR 5835 — PL 101-508) cleared by Congress on Oct. 27, the final full day of the session. The provision was part of the Medicare section of the bill. *(Medicare, p. 563)*

"It's not an effort to tell people to exercise their rights, but to make sure they know what they are," said Sander M. Levin, D-Mich., primary sponsor of the House version of a living will bill (HR 5067).

John C. Danforth, R-Mo., sponsored a similar Senate bill (S 1766).

The point, Levin said, was "to make sure people can exercise their rights and to avoid situations like Nancy Cruzan's, where she probably wasn't aware."

Cruzan was a Missouri woman, comatose since January 1983 as a result of a car accident, whose parents were denied the right by the Supreme Court to remove the feeding tube keeping her alive. She died Dec. 26 at the age of 33 — 12 days after the Missouri courts, operating under the Supreme Court's guidelines, reconsidered the evidence in the case and decided to allow removal of the feeding tube.

The Cruzan Case

In its 5-4 ruling June 25, the Supreme Court held that a state could require clear and convincing evidence of a comatose patient's wish to be allowed to die under such circumstances before allowing family members to order life support systems to be removed.

The case, *Cruzan v. Director, Missouri Department of Health*, was the first in which the court had addressed the right-to-die issue.

Cruzan was being fed through a tube in her stomach that provided food and water. She was in what doctors called a persistent vegetative state, exhibiting motor reflexes but no cognitive function.

Her parents asked that the artificial feedings be stopped. When hospital officials refused, the Cruzans went to a Missouri trial court.

The lower court ruled that a person in Cruzan's condition had a fundamental right under state and federal constitutions to refuse "death prolonging procedures."

Based on evidence of conversations Cruzan had had with a housemate years earlier, the court concluded that "given her present condition she would not wish to continue on with her nutrition and hydration."

The Missouri Supreme Court reversed, however, saying Cruzan's statements were "unreliable for determining her intent" and stating that the Missouri Living Will statute favored the preservation of life.

The State's Interest

In its ruling, the Supreme Court accepted the Missouri requirement that evidence of the incompetent person's wishes for the withdrawal of treatment be clear and convincing.

"We believe Missouri may legitimately seek to safeguard the personal element of this choice through the imposition of heightened evidentiary requirements,"

adopted in the past, including limiting inflation increases for hospitals to less than inflation, reducing the amount Medicare paid to reimburse hospitals for capital expenses, and reducing payment for specific surgical procedures for which health analysts had determined Medicare was overpaying.

House Rejects Budget Deal

Unhappiness over the Medicare cuts was one of the major factors in the House's 179-254 rejection of the budget deal on Oct. 5 (session of Oct. 4). *(Vote 421, 136-H)*

Lawmakers objected not only to the magnitude of the cuts but also to the fact that half of them were to be realized by making the program's beneficiaries pay higher premiums and other fees.

"It's devastating," said John D. Rockefeller IV, D-W.Va., chairman of the Senate Finance subcommittee that oversaw Medicare.

Rockefeller noted that the 41 percent of the nation's senior citizens with incomes lower than 150 percent of the poverty threshold (about $9,420 in 1990) already were spending 19 percent of their incomes for health care.

But members were not worried just about the poor. They were also concerned about more affluent seniors, whose unwillingness to pay for catastrophic coverage torpedoed that 1988 law. With the congressional elections little more than a month away, few members were eager to antagonize such an important voting bloc.

According to a House Democratic leadership staff member, at the party caucus Oct. 3, the Medicare provisions of the agreement "weren't just one of the hardest parts of the package to sell. There was no second-hardest part."

The Medicare proposals were not the only problem for Republicans, but the provisions gave GOP members heartburn as well. "Our phone calls are fairly livid on this," said Sen. Dave Durenberger, R-Minn., who said he supported the plan nevertheless.

Backers of the plan from both parties struggled to sell the cuts.

"We're trying to contain the growth of medical care. We do not feel that these cuts are onerous to the elderly," Bush told a group of regional reporters Oct. 4. "But to get the deficit down, you have to deal with where the major growth in spending is."

House Speaker Thomas S. Foley, D-Wash., agreed. "Medicare has been the fastest rising cost of any government entitlement program."

Foley also noted that the agreement included an additional $2 billion to be used to offset the increased costs for Medicare beneficiaries with very low incomes.

Senior Citizens Revolt

Groups representing senior citizens wasted no time reminding lawmakers of their potential clout, calling a Capi-

Patients of Their 'Living Will' Rights

Chief Justice William H. Rehnquist wrote.

But Rehnquist also said that the Due Process Clause "protects an interest in life as well as an interest in refusing life-sustaining medical treatment." He stressed the need for a clear expression of the person's wishes on treatment and acknowledged that some persons' true desires would be frustrated because they were never put down in writing.

Rehnquist was joined by Justices Byron R. White, Anthony M. Kennedy, Sandra Day O'Connor and Antonin Scalia.

In a concurring decision, O'Connor wrote, "Procedures for surrogate decision-making, which appear to be rapidly gaining in acceptance, may be a valuable additional safeguard of the patient's interest in directing his medical care."

In a dissent, Justice William J. Brennan Jr. said that Cruzan was "entitled to choose to die with dignity" and that no state interest "could outweigh the rights of an individual in Nancy Cruzan's position."

Joining in Brennan's dissent were Justices Thurgood Marshall, Harry A. Blackmun and John Paul Stevens.

Living Will, Power of Attorney

There were two ways an individual could clearly indicate in advance how he or she wanted decisions about life-sustaining treatment to be made. The first was a living will — written directions spelling out what the person wanted to have done or not done. The second was by designating a family member or friend as a proxy to make the decisions if the patient was unable to.

By 1990, all but nine states had living will statutes. The exceptions were Massachusetts, Michigan, Nebraska, New Jersey, New York, Ohio, Pennsylvania, Rhode Island and South Dakota.

Many of the laws, however, had limitations. For instance, the statutes often applied only when the person was in a "terminal condition," which generally was defined as an irreversible condition that made death imminent. A person in a persistent vegetative state might not be covered. Also, some statutes did not permit doctors to follow an advance directive that called for the removal of a feeding tube.

Those problems could be overcome by appointing a health-care proxy through a "durable power of attorney." Whereas an ordinary power of attorney ceased to be effective when the principal became legally incompetent, the durable form remained in effect, or went into effect, in that event.

Because durable powers of attorney traditionally had been used in connection with the principal's property or financial affairs, it was not clear that courts would always recognize them as valid for making health-care decisions. Hence, some states enacted laws that permitted durable powers of attorney specifically for health care.

Some members of Congress had doubts about the living will provision included in the reconciliation bill. "We don't want anyone running around nursing homes with little right-to-die certificates," said Rep. Brian Donnelly, D-Mass.

Donnelly was particularly miffed because the final language eliminated a House provision exempting religious facilities from the requirements if they conflicted with their beliefs.

---

tol Hill news conference hours after the proposal was officially unveiled.

"This proposal is one that older persons throughout the country and disabled persons throughout the country aren't going to tolerate," warned Arthur S. Flemming, a former secretary of Health, Education and Welfare and chairman of the Save Our Security coalition of more than 100 groups that called the news conference.

"Senior citizens didn't cause the deficit," said Lawrence T. Smedley, executive director of the National Council of Senior Citizens. "They shouldn't be asked to pay more than their fair share."

The groups pointed out that seniors had seen their Medicare cost-sharing rise throughout the 1980s, because of previous congressional actions and skyrocketing medical inflation.

Between 1980 and 1990, the Part A and Part B deductibles rose from $180 and $60, respectively, to $592 and $75. At the same time, the Part B premium rose from $8.70 per month to $28.60. Overall, that represented an increase of 229 percent.

Adding projected medical inflation to the budget-summit agreement, by 1995 beneficiary costs for Medicare were projected to rise by 366 percent.

"Many beneficiaries are now paying a higher percentage of their income for out-of-pocket health-care costs than before Medicare was passed," said Flemming.

Almost drowned out by the din were complaints from health-care providers, who had borne the brunt of Medicare cost-cutting efforts over the preceding decade and would have seen their payments cut more if the budget deal had gone through. Among those complaining the loudest were the American Medical Association and the American Hospital Association.

Even groups representing patients worried about whether cutting payments to health-care providers could drive them away from Medicare altogether.

"This is a meat-ax approach to dealing with providers, and no one is sure what the impact might be on the quality of care," said Flemming.

BUDGET-RECONCILIATION BILL

Congressional negotiators went back to work after the defeat of the budget-summit deal. A compromise budget resolution (H Con Res 310) approved Oct. 9 permitted key committees to moderate the blow to Medicare envisioned by the summit agreement.

Members of the Ways and Means and Energy and Commerce committees in the House, and the Finance committee in the Senate, set to work drafting the final deal.

The Ways and Means Committee approved a barebones proposal Oct. 10 that sought to pare an estimated $50 billion over five years from Medicare, about $10 billion less than assumed in the budget-summit agreement. For fiscal 1991, Medicare was to be reduced by $4.2 billion.

The proposal called for saving $32.9 billion from reduced payments to health-care providers, including hospitals, doctors, medical equipment suppliers and laboratories. That was approximately the amount assumed in the budget summit.

The focus was on care with rapidly increasing costs, such as hospital outpatient procedures, which had been growing about 17 percent per year. The package cut payments for such services by $1.8 billion over five years.

The committee plan trimmed payments to hospitals by $13.8 billion, primarily by holding annual increases to less than the rate of inflation. Buried within the hospital cuts was $3.4 billion in new spending to help rural and inner-city hospitals that had been hard-hit by Medicare's payment-by-diagnosis system.

In Part B, the plan was aimed at saving an estimated $3.6 billion by reducing payments for procedures, mostly surgical, for which experts said Medicare paid too much and another $2.8 billion by limiting inflation increases in doctors' fees. Even with a one-year freeze on most fees in 1991, physician expenses under Medicare were expected to grow by 8.5 percent.

The plan reduced payments for durable medical equipment by $2 billion over five years and payments for laboratory services by another $1.2 billion. Medicare also was to recover another $5.7 billion over five years by requiring insurance companies that covered Medicare beneficiaries to pay their share of patient costs.

The major change from the budget-summit deal was in cost-sharing increases for Medicare beneficiaries. Under the summit, costs to patients would have risen by nearly $30 billion over five years. The Ways and Means proposal hiked premiums and deductibles by only $17.2 billion.

Under the Ways and Means plan, the annual Part B deductible, which had been $75 since 1982, was to rise to $100 in calendar 1991 and to $125 in calendar 1992-95. The budget-summit agreement would have hiked the deductible to $150. Beneficiaries also were to pay higher premiums — $32.40 in 1991, rising to $46.50 in 1995.

The Democratic alternative to the Ways and Means plan, unveiled Oct. 12 and approved by the House Oct. 16, left the provider cuts untouched but reduced the added beneficiary cost-sharing by $7 billion, mainly by imposing a smaller premium increase than in the committee package and raising the Part B deductible to $100 instead of $125.

Medicare Add-Ons

The packages contributed to the reconciliation bill by the Senate Finance Committee and the House Energy and Commerce Committee went well beyond what was required by the budget resolution, delving into some of the most arcane areas of Medicare payment policy and setting new requirements for so-called Medigap insurance policies sold to senior citizens to supplement their Medicare coverage.

The Ways and Means Subcommittee on Health had been working since June on its own package of miscellaneous health policy changes, including a proposed Medigap reform plan. But full committee Chairman Rostenkowski blocked inclusion of that package in HR 5835.

When it became clear that neither Energy and Commerce nor Finance was going to keep its package similarly "clean," House Budget Committee Chairman Panetta sought to put back some of the Ways and Means Medicare provisions on the floor.

But Republicans cried foul, noting that the Medicare provisions would cost an additional $1.8 billion and that they had not even seen the amendment until 10 minutes before it was offered. Panetta was forced to back down, and the bill passed without the Ways and Means miscellaneous Medicare provisions.

Ways and Means members did not give up. On Oct. 17, the day after the House passed HR 5835, the panel approved a measure including the miscellaneous Medicare items. And members were determined the items would somehow find their way into reconciliation.

Provider Payments

On the larger issues of deficit reduction, conferees had to resolve serious battles between the House and Senate over how, and how much, to cut payments to health-care providers. There were also disagreements over how much to increase costs to beneficiaries.

On the provider side, the overall savings targets were close. The Ways and Means proposal sought to trim payments by almost $33 billion over five years, the Finance plan by an estimated $34 billion over that period. The Energy and Commerce package, which included cuts only in Medicare's optional Part B program (the only portion over which that committee had jurisdiction), sought to trim spending by slightly more than $27 billion over five years.

Despite the similarities of the numbers, there were some major policy disagreements. The Finance Committee, for example, proposed to increase spending by phasing out the so-called urban-rural differential, under which rural hospitals received Medicare payments that averaged 7.6 percent less than those given their urban counterparts.

The Ways and Means package, on the other hand, expanded bonus payments to inner-city hospitals that served a disproportionate share of low-income patients, who tended to be sicker and whose care often cost more than average.

Beneficiary Blues

Both the Ways and Means and Energy and Commerce plans raised beneficiary costs by about $10 billion over five years, a third of the hit envisioned by summit negotiators.

The Senate Finance package was expected to cost beneficiaries about $17.6 billion over five years.

Not only did the Finance plan raise monthly Part B premiums (previously, $28.60) higher than either House proposal, the plan also raised the annual deductible (previously, $75) higher than either House plan and required beneficiaries to pay 20 percent of the cost of laboratory tests. Such tests were fully covered under existing law.

The full Senate on Oct. 18 rejected a plan to ease the beneficiary cost increases. The amendment, offered by Al Gore, D-Tenn., and Barbara A. Mikulski, D-Md., would have raised income tax rates for the wealthiest Americans and used that revenue to lower the added Medicare costs.

"I do not want to ask the Medicare patients to pay more so that the wealthiest in our society can pay less," Gore said in offering the amendment.

But backers of the Senate reconciliation bill objected strenuously, cautioning that adoption of the amendment could doom the entire budget process for the year. "Do you want to make a statement, or do you want to make a law?" asked Majority Leader George J. Mitchell, D-Maine.

The amendment failed when a motion to waive the budget act was rejected on a vote of 45-55 — 15 votes short of the 60 needed. *(Vote 280, p. 56-S)* ■

Medicaid Expands To Aid Poor Children

Following a pattern established in the 1980s, Congress in 1990 brushed aside protests from the states and mandated a phased expansion of Medicaid to cover all children in families at or below the federal poverty level.

As part of the budget-reconciliation bill (HR 5835 — PL 101-508) cleared Oct. 27, lawmakers approved a total of $1.1 billion over five years in child-related program expansions for Medicaid, the joint federal-state health program for the poor. *(Provisions, Title IV: Medicaid, p. 146)*

The most significant provision required all states, beginning on July 1, 1991, to provide Medicaid coverage to all children born after Sept. 30, 1983, in families with incomes at or below the federal poverty threshold. This meant that all poor children up to age 19 would be covered by 2002.

The legislation mandated outreach programs allowing eligible families to apply for Medicaid at places other than local welfare offices. Those included hospitals that served large numbers of low-income patients, plus community and migrant health centers.

The bill also sought to help low-income elderly Americans by requiring Medicaid to cover more cost-sharing requirements (premiums, deductibles and coinsurance) for indigent Medicare beneficiaries not quite poor enough to qualify for full Medicaid coverage.

The package also included two provisions pushed strongly by Senate Finance Committee members.

One initiative, the pet project of Sen. John D. Rockefeller IV, D-W.Va., made available an estimated $580 million over five years to provide home care to frail elderly people who might otherwise require costly institutional care.

This was the first significant long-term care proposal enacted by Congress, but it was a shadow of the home-care plan advanced in 1988 by Rep. Claude Pepper, D-Fla and rejected as too costly. *(Pepper bill, 1988 Almanac, p. 293)*

The other initiative, backed by Sen. John H. Chafee, R-R.I., provided $100 million over five years to pay for home- and community-based services for the mentally retarded and those with other developmental disabilities.

House-Senate conferees on the reconciliation bill also trimmed $2.9 billion from projected spending for Medicaid. Of that, $1.9 billion came from requiring pharmaceutical companies to give discounts on sales of drugs to Medicaid. The other $1 billion was to be gained by requiring states to pay the premiums of Medicaid beneficiaries eligible for private group health insurance if that would save Medicaid money. *(Prescription drug discounts, p. 570)*

BACKGROUND

The federal government paid about 55 percent of Medicaid costs nationwide. States had to match federal spending on a sliding scale ranging from 50 percent for wealthier states to slightly less than 20 percent for poorer states.

Medicaid required states to provide some services and cover certain populations and gave them the option to provide other services or to extend eligibility to certain groups. But Congress for years had shown a penchant for turning options into mandates.

In each of the past five budget-reconciliation bills, as well as in the 1988 Medicare Catastrophic Coverage Act and the 1988 Family Support Act, Congress required states to extend Medicaid coverage to more people, primarily pregnant women and young children. *(Medicaid mandates, 1989 Almanac, p. 174)*

In only one of those cases, the catastrophic-costs law, did Congress also provide a mechanism to help states pay their share of the cost. That mechanism disappeared, however, when Congress repealed most of the law in 1989. *(Catastrophic-costs repeal, 1989 Almanac, p. 149)*

One provision that was not repealed required states to use Medicaid funds to pay Medicare premiums, deductibles and copayments for beneficiaries with incomes below the poverty line (in 1990, $6,280 for a person over age 65).

The nation's governors were increasingly unhappy at the string of orders from Congress that forced states to spend a growing part of their budgets on health care for the poor. The governors' ire came to a head in 1989, when they voted 49-1 at their annual summer meeting to ask Congress for a two-year moratorium on new Medicaid mandates.

But Congress ignored the call, requiring in the fiscal 1990 reconciliation bill that states extend Medicaid coverage to pregnant women and to children up to age 6 in families with incomes below 133 percent of the federal poverty level. That was a smaller mandate than the one approved by the House, which wanted to require coverage of the same groups in families with incomes up to 185 percent of the poverty line. Congress could not come up with funds to pay the federal cost of that proposed expansion.

LEGISLATIVE ACTION

Picking up where Congress had left off in 1989, the House Budget Committee on April 19 approved a fiscal 1991 budget resolution that allowed more than $7 billion in new Medicaid spending over the next five years. The money would extend coverage to low-income members of several groups, including pregnant women, children, the elderly, the mentally retarded and AIDS patients.

The same day, a bipartisan group from the Senate Finance Committee, led by Chairman Lloyd Bentsen, D-Texas, introduced a less sweeping proposal (S 2459) to phase in mandatory Medicaid coverage of all children under age 19 in families with incomes at or below the federal poverty line, which was $12,675 for a family of four in 1990.

Predictably, the governors were unhappy. "More mandates without more money is just unrealistic for states who are already having trouble balancing their budgets," Gov. Edward D. DiPrete, R-R.I. testified before a Senate Finance subcommittee hearing on access to health insurance.

But Rep. Henry A. Waxman, D-Calif., chairman of the Energy and Commerce Subcommittee on Health, which had jurisdiction over Medicaid, had no intention of letting up. The Budget Committee approved funding for all six initiatives Waxman requested — five expansions passed by the House but dropped from 1989's reconciliation bill and a new proposal allowing states to pay for prescription drugs for low-income people infected with the human immunodeficiency virus, or HIV, which caused AIDS.

The proposals would have done the following:

- Required Medicaid coverage of children through age 18 in families with incomes below poverty, as well as of pregnant women and infants up to age 1 in families with incomes up to 185 percent of poverty.
- Allowed states to offer home- and community-based

Drug Discounts Mandated for Medicaid

Congress in 1990 took action to force drug manufacturers to give bulk-purchase discounts to Medicaid, the joint federal-state health-care program for the poor.

The fiscal 1991 budget-reconciliation bill (HR 5835 — PL 101-508) included a provision requiring pharmaceutical companies to give rebates to the states for Medicaid purchases. The requirement was expected to save the government $1.9 billion over five years. *(Reconciliation provisions, p. 146)*

The plan grew out of bills (S 2605, S 3029, HR 5589) introduced earlier in the year by David Pryor, D-Ark., chairman of the Senate Special Committee on Aging, and by Rep. Ron Wyden, D-Ore.

In studying prescription drug prices and the elderly, the Senate Aging Committee's staff discovered that the Department of Veterans Affairs (VA), groups of hospitals and health maintenance organizations often negotiated deep discounts from manufacturers on bulk purchases of drugs, but Medicaid programs did not.

"We simply cannot reduce Medicare payments to physicians and pharmacists and cut Medicaid drug benefits, while drug manufacturers continue to profit from an unreasonable pricing scheme," Pryor testified Sept. 14 before the House Energy and Commerce Subcommittee on Health and the Environment.

But the Pharmaceutical Manufacturers Association (PMA) said makers of brand-name prescription drugs had already been forced into price competition by the 1984 passage of legislation making it easier for generic copies to come to market. *(1984 Almanac, p. 451)*

At $3.3 billion in 1988, drugs represented a major expense for Medicaid. According to data compiled by the Senate Aging panel, Medicaid drug outlays for states that offered drug benefits rose 224 percent between 1980 and 1988 — faster than outlays for all other items except home health care and institutional care for the mentally retarded.

The primary reason, the committee said, was increased prescription drug prices, which grew by 88 percent between 1981 and 1988, a rate three times faster than inflation in the rest of the economy and significantly greater than other sectors of health care.

At the same time, Medicaid purchases accounted for a noteworthy portion of prescription drug sales overall — about 15 percent to 20 percent, according to the PMA. But given that the savings assumed by Pryor's more stringent bill, S 2605, amounted to less than 1 percent of annual drug company sales, the volume of PMA opposition caught lawmakers off guard.

Initially, the pharmaceutical industry said that the plan would not save money because drug therapy tended to be more cost-effective than other forms of medical treatment. The industry also insisted that price increases had been necessary to cover the rising research and development costs of bringing new drugs to market.

In April, individual companies, including Merck and Co. and Pfizer Inc., sought to derail the legislation by voluntarily offering rebates.

But when the Bush administration in June put forward a proposal based on Pryor's first bill as part of the budget-summit negotiations, the PMA stepped up its campaign. And it coordinated opposition by Medicaid beneficiaries to a portion of the Bush plan.

A July 9 letter to budget-summit negotiators was signed by, among others, Jesse Jackson, representing the National Rainbow Coalition; the presidents of the National Black Caucus of State Legislators and the National Coalition of Hispanic Health and Human Services Organizations; and representatives of groups such as the Epilepsy Foundation of America and the National Hemophilia Foundation.

The groups were most opposed to a provision of the Bush plan calling for "therapeutic substitution," under which Medicaid programs could decide to provide only certain drugs to treat various ailments. Under such a system, a drug different from what the doctor prescribed could be dispensed.

In the end, the industry both lost and won.

Although the proposal in the summit agreement — and the one ultimately adopted as part of the budget-reconciliation bill — required Medicaid discounts, the therapeutic-substitution provisions were dropped.

care to frail elderly, mentally retarded and other disabled people who might otherwise require institutionalization.

- Required states to offer hospice care to Medicaid patients with terminal illnesses.

Budget Resolution

The Sept. 30 budget agreement between congressional and White House negotiators left $2 billion over five years for Medicaid. That gave Congress the option to increase the threshold for using Medicaid to pay for Medicare beneficiaries' costs to about 115 percent of the poverty level.

That, however, raised problems of its own. Increased Medicare premiums alone were placing a new burden on state Medicaid programs that had to pay them for poor beneficiaries. Expanding the group of people who qualified for such help would only strain state budgets more.

One possible result, said Waxman, was that "states could end up cutting back services to poor women and children in order to pay for the poor elderly."

A compromise budget resolution (H Con Res 310) approved Oct. 9 allowed committees to ease the blow to Medicare recipients that had helped doom the budget-summit deal. *(Budget summit, p. 129; Medicare, p. 563)*

Three committees — Ways and Means and Energy and Commerce in the House and Finance in the Senate — set to work seeking five-year Medicare savings of between $40 billion and $45 billion in the budget-reconciliation bill. Members of the Energy and Commerce and Finance committees also struggled over whether to use the reconciliation bill as a vehicle to expand Medicaid.

In other years, the Medicaid expansions had been financed through larger-than-required cuts in Medicare. With Medicare scheduled to take such a large hit this time around, that option seemed foreclosed. But both the failed budget-summit agreement and the approved budget resolution assumed more than $2 billion in Medicaid savings over five years as a result of requiring pharmaceutical firms to offer bulk discounts to state Medicaid plans.

Committee Proposals

At a late-night markup Oct. 11, the Energy and Commerce Committee approved a package that would have reduced Medicaid spending by $3.24 billion over five years, including $2.1 billion from the drug-discount provision.

But the committee then spent all but $337 million of the savings on Medicaid initiatives, including requiring states to extend coverage to children up to age 12 in families with incomes below the federal poverty line. Existing law required coverage only for children up to age 7.

The Medicaid proposal also sought to moderate the effect of increased Medicare costs for low-income seniors.

The existing-law "buy-in" requirement that Medicaid pick up Medicare's premiums, deductibles and coinsurance for indigent elderly individuals was being phased in gradually. In 1991, states were scheduled to pay cost-sharing only for Medicare beneficiaries with incomes below 95 percent of the federal poverty line. But the added costs to Medicare beneficiaries envisioned under the reconciliation bill meant state Medicaid costs would climb.

The Energy and Commerce Committee plan called for Medicaid to cover the Medicare premiums of those with incomes up to 125 percent of poverty, instead of 95 percent. But under the proposal, the federal government was to foot the entire bill for those above the 95 percent level.

Republicans, led by William E. Dannemeyer, Calif., tried to strike the provisions extending coverage to children. But Democrats rose to defend the new spending.

"It's difficult to find a priority more urgent than that we have millions of kids in this country in need of basic health care," said Jim Slattery, D-Kan. Dannemeyer's amendment to strike the provision failed, 11-31.

Republicans, this time led by Joe L. Barton, Texas, also tried unsuccessfully to strike the provision extending the Medicaid buy-in for the low-income elderly. Barton called the provision "a terrible, terrible precedent."

Waxman, however, noted that even the failed budget-summit plan acknowledged the need for added federal spending to help poor Medicare beneficiaries cover their increased costs. The amendment was defeated on a straight party-line vote of 17-26.

The Senate Finance Committee's reconciliation proposal also extended Medicaid coverage for children, continuing to phase in the requirement for all children in poor families born after Sept. 30, 1983, until that cohort reached age 19 in 2002.

On the issue of Medicare costs, the Finance panel was less generous than the Energy and Commerce Committee.

The Finance panel's package moved up by one year (to 1991 instead of 1992) the requirement that states use Medicaid funds to help Medicare beneficiaries at or below the poverty line pay premiums, deductibles and copayments.

But it gave states an option on paying cost-sharing for those with incomes of up to 133 percent of the poverty line — rather than mandatory coverage for families up to 125 percent of the poverty line, as in the Energy and Commerce plan. And the Senate panel required the normal state-federal funding split rather than the full federal funding contained in the Energy and Commerce plan.

The Finance package also contained small versions of initiatives included by Energy and Commerce in the fiscal 1990 reconciliation bill but dropped in conference when the Senate balked. The proposals extended limited home health coverage under Medicaid to frail elderly people and created a program within Medicaid to provide home- and community-based services for those with developmental disabilities, such as mental retardation.

In the Energy and Commerce plan, but not the Finance package, was a mandate that states create outreach programs to find people potentially eligible for Medicaid.

Conference Accord

Conferees scrapped with each other and the administration over the Medicaid expansions until agreement was reached after an all-night session early Oct. 26.

The key problem was familiar: The White House Office of Management and Budget (OMB) maintained the Medicaid changes would cost more than the Congressional Budget Office had estimated. Waxman insisted the differences were an effort by the administration to block the changes.

In the end, conferees agreed to expand child-health programs by about $1.1 billion over five years, mostly by requiring states to provide coverage to all children in families with incomes at or below the federal poverty line.

Although the package was the largest expansion of Medicaid in several years, members vowed to come back for more the next year. Said Waxman, "I wanted more." ■

Medicaid Pay Suits OK'd

States and Congress faced potential new budget strains as a result of a June 14 Supreme Court ruling that allowed health-care providers to challenge the adequacy of Medicaid reimbursement rates. By 5-4, the court ruled in *Wilder v. Virginia Hospital Association* that hospitals, nursing homes and other providers could invoke a federal civil rights law, known as Section 1983, to seek higher reimbursement rates from the states.

The federal government paid a little over half of Medicaid costs — totaling $57.9 billion in fiscal 1989 — but states set the reimbursement rates for providers. If states had to pay more for each patient served, program costs were sure to climb.

Raymond C. Scheppach, executive director of the National Governors' Association, said: "Medicaid was built as an entitlement for individuals. Now we seem to be moving to an entitlement for hospitals."

At issue in the case was a 1980 amendment to the Medicaid legislation sponsored by Sen. David L. Boren, D-Okla., that required states to reimburse health-care providers at rates that "are reasonable and adequate to meet the costs which must be incurred by efficiently and economically operated facilities."

Writing for the court's majority, Justice William J. Brennan Jr. said that the amendment "creates a right, enforceable in a private cause of action pursuant to Section 1983, to have the state adopt rates" sufficient to "meet the costs of an efficient and economical health-care provider."

Brennan was joined by Justices Byron R. White, Thurgood Marshall, Harry A. Blackmun and John Paul Stevens. Dissenting were Chief Justice William H. Rehnquist and Justices Sandra Day O'Connor, Antonin Scalia and Anthony M. Kennedy. ■

Regulation of Medigap Plans Tightened

In a move hailed by consumer advocates, Congress greatly tightened federal regulation of so-called Medigap insurance, giving new protections to the millions of elderly Americans who relied on such policies to pay medical bills not fully covered by Medicare.

The provisions were part of the huge budget-reconciliation bill (HR 5835 — PL 101-508) cleared Oct. 27. *(Reconciliation provisions, Title IV: Medigap, p. 148)*

They had been debated and approved earlier by the House Energy and Commerce and Senate Finance committees when those panels submitted their Medicare recommendations for the reconciliation bill. The House Ways and Means Committee also considered Medigap reforms, although not as part of its reconciliation package. *(Medicare, p. 563)*

Among other things, the new rules required that Medicare beneficiaries be allowed to buy Medigap policies within the first six months they were eligible for Medicare, regardless of their health status.

The rules also imposed civil penalties for the sale of duplicative policies and required that insurers pay rebates if policies failed to return specified percentages of each premium dollar in benefits.

"If I had to pick one thing in this bill that is most important, that's it," Rep. Pete Stark, D-Calif., said of the Medigap reforms. Stark was chairman of the Ways and Means Subcommittee on Health and one of the authors of the new rules. "There is now federal control, and that was the issue. There will be federal penalties and federal enforcement."

Sen. John D. Rockefeller IV, D-W.Va., said, "It was high time we accomplished some degree of Medigap reform. It is vital to ensure our seniors are getting their money's worth when they buy a Medigap policy."

Rockefeller, one of several members of the Finance Committee who pushed for the changes, was chairman of that panel's Subcommittee on Medicare and Long-Term Care.

Gail Shearer, manager for policy analysis for the Consumers Union, which lobbied hard for the changes, said, "Consumers are confused and overwhelmed by Medigap insurance; they waste money on unnecessary coverage, cannot tell a good policy from a bad one and often have no one to turn to except the insurance agent for advice."

Highlights

Specifically, the Medigap provisions did the following:

- Required standardization of Medigap policies, thus permitting consumers to compare benefits and prices in a comprehensible manner.
- Required that for individual policies, companies return at least 65 cents of every premium dollar in benefits; and for group policies, 75 cents of every premium dollar. Insurers whose policies failed to meet the required loss ratios would have to provide customers with refunds or credits.
- Barred the sale of policies that duplicated Medicare or each other and barred the sale of Medigap policies to recipients of Medicaid, the federal-state health program for the poor, which paid all medical costs not covered by Medicare. Civil penalties of up to $25,000 would be imposed for violations.
- Required that every policy sold first be approved by insurance regulators at either the state or federal level. Civil penalties of up to $25,000 could be imposed on those who sold unapproved policies.
- Required insurance companies to sell Medigap policies to all seniors who sought them within six months of becoming eligible for Medicare.

This provision, one of the last issues resolved by House-Senate conferees and the one considered most important by many lawmakers, eliminated so-called medical underwriting for senior citizens. Insurers used such practices to deny coverage to people with chronic illnesses or other conditions that made them most likely to collect benefits.

In an era of tight budgets, lawmakers were looking more and more to the insurance industry to expand health coverage, and they saw the new Medigap law as an important first step.

Said Rep. Ron Wyden, D-Ore., a key architect of the new regulations, "Insurance reform is the future of health-care policy reform."

BACKGROUND

Medigap policies were designed to cover the gaps in Medicare coverage — primarily by paying the required hospital and physician-bill deductibles ($592 and $75, respectively, in 1990) and required coinsurance (20 percent of physician and outpatient bills, plus an increasing percentage for hospital stays longer than 60 days).

The 1988 Medicare Catastrophic Coverage Act capped the amount Medicare beneficiaries could be required to pay out-of-pocket for covered hospital, physician and prescription-drug bills. But Congress repealed the law in 1989, after senior citizens protested a new income surtax on middle- and upper-income seniors that would have helped finance the new benefits. *(1989 Almanac, p. 149)*

Repeal of the law "has once again made ownership of a Medigap policy an absolute necessity," Thomas Rice, a professor at the University of North Carolina School of Public Health, said at a Feb. 2 hearing of the Senate Finance Subcommittee on Medicare and Long-Term Care.

There was no central data base to determine exactly how many Medicare beneficiaries had what kind of policies to supplement their government coverage. Most analysts, however, estimated that from 70 percent to 80 percent of the Medicare population (about 20 million people) also had private health coverage, either through individually purchased policies or employment-based plans.

Not all of that coverage was technically Medigap. Some policies insured only against certain diseases (most often cancer), others paid cash for each day in the hospital (so-called hospital indemnity plans), while still others were comprehensive plans.

The Congressional Research Service estimated that 11 million Medicare beneficiaries (about 40 percent) had purchased supplemental insurance coverage, most of it Medigap. Another 8 million Medicare enrollees (about 30 percent) had coverage through an employer, less than half of which was Medigap.

About 2.5 million (8 percent) of Medicare beneficiaries had coverage under Medicaid, the joint state-federal health program for the poor. A survey by Market Facts Inc. for the American Association of Retired Persons (AARP), released in January, said that between 1.5 million and 2 million of these "dual eligibles" also owned Medigap policies, although they had virtually no need for them because Medicaid covered all health-care expenses not paid by Medicare. Several members of Congress were seeking to outlaw the sale of Medigap plans to Medicaid beneficiaries.

While most Medicare beneficiaries had supplemental protection, those who did not tended to need it the most. "A major problem with the Medigap market is that the people who are least able to afford large health-care expenses are exactly those groups who are least likely to have coverage: the poor, the very old and those in poor health," Rice testified.

The Federal Role

Federal intervention in the Medigap market began with the so-called Baucus amendment, officially part of the Social Security Disability Amendments of 1980 (PL 96-265). The law grew out of a major undercover investigation in 1978 by the House Select Committee on Aging that documented numerous abuses in the marketing and sale of Medigap policies. *(1980 Almanac, p. 435)*

Under the Baucus amendment, a voluntary certification program for policies was to be instituted in states that failed to implement Medigap standards equivalent to or stricter than those set forth in a model regulation the National Association of Insurance Commissioners (NAIC) adopted in 1979.

Under that model regulation, Medigap plans were required to cover all inpatient hospital (Part A) coinsurance charges, plus 90 percent of covered charges after a beneficiary exhausted Medicare hospital coverage. Plans also had to cover coinsurance required under Medicare's Part B (which paid 80 percent of approved costs for physician and outpatient care), subject to a $200 deductible and a $5,000 annual maximum.

In addition, insurers who sold policies through the mail had to offer purchasers a 10-day "free look" period during which they could return a policy for a full refund.

Finally, policies had to be designed to meet specific loss-ratio requirements (the percentage of each premium dollar paid out in benefits). For group policies, the target was 75 percent; for individual policies, which generally had higher marketing costs, the target was 60 percent.

Although 46 states were certified to meet or exceed the minimum standards, evidence of continuing abuses led Congress to beef up the requirements in 1988, as part of the catastrophic-costs law.

The new Medigap standards included a mandatory 30-day "free look" for all policies, required sellers of Medigap policies to submit their print, radio and television advertisements to the state insurance commissioner and required states to use actual instead of anticipated numbers in determining whether specific policies met loss-ratio requirements. These provisions were retained when Congress repealed the catastrophic-costs program. *(1988 Almanac, p. 281)*

In conjunction with the 1988 law, the NAIC also tightened its model regulation, specifically prohibiting Medigap policies from duplicating benefits offered by Medicare.

With repeal of catastrophic coverage, the NAIC again amended its model at a meeting Dec. 7, 1989. It required coverage of all or part of the Part A deductible, of all Part B coinsurance (subject only to the $75 annual deductible, thus eliminating the previous $5,000 maximum) and of Medicare's required deductibles for blood.

But it was unclear when — or whether — states would adopt the new standards.

Premium Increases

Renewed congressional interest in Medigap insurance was predictable. Medigap prices began to rise once Congress repealed the catastrophic-coverage law, which had subsumed much of the supplemental insurance market by dramatically increasing Medicare's coverage of hospital, physician and prescription-drug costs.

According to a General Accounting Office (GAO) survey presented at the Senate Medicare Subcommittee's Feb. 2 hearing, 1990 Medigap premiums were expected to increase by an average of 19.5 percent over 1989. As a result, many policyholders were paying more than they would have paid under the catastrophic-costs law.

According to the GAO, which surveyed 20 commercial Medigap insurers with about 2.6 million policyholders, 1990 premium increases were expected to range from 5 percent to 51.6 percent. One company anticipated no increase. The average increase was projected at $11.44 per month.

The average Medigap policy in 1989 carried an annual premium of $718, said the Health Insurance Association of America.

About half of the average Medigap premium increase was directly attributable to insurers' having to pick up coverage that Medicare provided under the 1988 law and to administrative costs associated with changing policies and notifying policyholders, according to the GAO survey. The other half, insurers told GAO, came from increased use of medical services, general inflation in health-care costs and "higher than expected claims experience in prior years."

Ironically, some of the largest increases were for what had traditionally been the highest-value policies.

Premiums for the nonprofit Blue Cross/Blue Shield plans, for example, were rising faster in 1990 (29 percent on average) than those for many commercial plans.

That was primarily because the "Blues" had far higher loss ratios. A 1987 GAO study found that six Blue Cross/Blue Shield plans had loss ratios of 104 percent, meaning they were paying out more money than they were taking in. In subsequent years, the plans had to seek increases to make up for the operating deficit — even before absorbing costs of the catastrophic-costs repeal.

"We have less wiggle room," explained Alan P. Spielman of the Blue Cross and Blue Shield Association. But even if many of the increases were justified, lawmakers worried about the potential for abuse. They noted that 28 states did not require prior approval for rate increases for group policies, and 12 did not require it for individual plans. "I am concerned that the repeal of catastrophic has provided the perfect opportunity for some of the less respectable insurers to jack their rates through the stratosphere," said Rep. Wyden.

Sen. David Pryor, D-Ark., chairman of the Special Committee on Aging, added, "I think we're about to see a very large increase in the fraud industry."

Indeed, the continuing presence in the market of plans that did not meet the loss-ratio targets provided strong evidence that the Baucus amendment needed strengthening, consumer advocates said.

Loss Ratios

The GAO study found that in 1988, one-third of commercial company plans failed to meet the 60 percent loss-ratio standard for individual policies, while two-thirds failed to meet the 75 percent minimum for group policies.

Most policyholders, however, were in plans that did meet the requirement, because the "Blues" and Prudential, which sponsored plans sold by the AARP, controlled two-thirds of the market.

According to GAO, only 2 percent of Blue Cross/Blue Shield plans failed to meet the 60 percent minimum for individual policies, while 24 percent failed to meet the 75 percent standard for group policies.

Most Medicare beneficiaries who paid for Medigap insurance would have been better off financially had the catastrophic-costs law remained in effect.

Medicare could provide benefits more cheaply than commercial carriers, GAO's Janet Shikles said at a Jan. 8 hearing of the Senate Aging Committee.

"Medicare has very low administrative costs, about 3 percent, and it doesn't do marketing, and you don't have the profits involved that you do under, say, commercial carriers," she said.

With 33 million elderly and disabled beneficiaries, Medicare spread the risk across a much larger population base than small insurance companies could. "And you see that in the rate increases," she said.

Abuses Continue

The problems with Medigap insurance went well beyond loss ratios, however.

"The state regulators just aren't doing their job," said Stark. "The old people are being gouged."

That was also the conclusion of Consumer Reports magazine, which surveyed state enforcement efforts as part of a major Medigap investigation published in the June 1989 issue. According to the article, "With few exceptions, we found, most states are regulating with a velvet glove."

Of the 37 states that responded to the survey, 23 were unable to provide information about how many complaints had been made to their departments in the preceding five years. Only nine reported any fines, license revocations or suspensions of agents who sold Medigap policies, and only eight reported penalties against companies for misleading advertising.

Another serious problem — one the insurance industry agreed should be addressed — was rampant confusion among consumers. The passage and subsequent repeal of the catastrophic-costs law increased that confusion, all agreed.

Confusion created an opportunity for unscrupulous operators to bilk the elderly.

"If consumers are misinformed about Medicare coverage, they are likely to be susceptible to sales pitches leading to more supplemental coverage than they need," testified Shearer, of Consumers Union, publisher of Consumer Reports.

The Industry's Model Standards

At its December 1989 meeting, the NAIC, in modifying its model regulation to account for repeal of the catastrophic-costs law, also adopted a series of "consumer protection" amendments. They included:

- Requiring that policies be renewable and prohibiting replacement policies from including new waiting periods for pre-existing conditions.
- Reducing the incentive for insurance agents to encourage policyholders to switch policies by reducing the difference between commissions paid for new policies and for renewals. Commissions for new policies could be no more than double those paid for renewals.

  Agents also were to be prohibited from receiving commissions on a replacement policy unless that policy contained benefits "clearly and substantially greater than the benefits under the replaced policy."
- Specifically prohibiting "twisting" (encouraging the purchase of a new policy instead of a renewal), high-pressure tactics and deceptive "cold-lead" advertising, in which the name and address of a prospective purchaser were obtained without that person's knowledge that someone would use that information to make a sales pitch.
- Prohibiting agents, in most cases, from selling more than one Medigap policy to a person and requiring agents to question prospective purchasers about other coverage they might own. Insurers were to report to state insurance regulators the names of individuals with more than one Medigap policy.

Virtually everyone agreed that states and volunteer groups should increase efforts to educate Medicare beneficiaries about their coverage needs.

At least a dozen states already operated counseling programs that helped seniors wade through complicated and sometimes contradictory information about Medicare, Medigap insurance and other types of health insurance coverage.

California's program had helped more than 5,000 seniors each year save an average of $900 apiece, according to the Senate Aging Committee.

HISTORY OF LEGISLATION

Omnibus Medigap overhaul bills (S 2050, HR 3959) were introduced in the Senate by Herb Kohl, D-Wis., and in the House by Edward R. Roybal, D-Calif., chairman of the Select Committee on Aging. Among other things, both sought to increase the required loss ratios for policies sold to individuals to 70 percent from 60 percent.

Other proposals severely restricted or barred the sale of hospital indemnity and "dread disease" policies. The former paid cash for hospital stays, while the latter paid when the policyholder suffered a specified disease, most often cancer.

Consumer advocates said that such policies tended to be of limited value. A 1989 GAO study of 62 hospital indemnity and dread-disease policies found that the indemnity policies had an average loss ratio of 52.7 percent, while the dread-disease policies had an average of 59.4 percent. For hospital policies, 25 of 37 (68 percent) had loss ratios below 50 percent; for dread-disease, 11 of 25 policies (44 percent) returned less than 50 cents in benefits for each premium dollar.

There were also various legislative efforts to "standardize" Medigap policies to make it easier for consumers to compare what they were buying. Most of these proposals set specific levels of coverage, stipulating what could and could not be covered.

But insurance regulators, as well as industry officials, warned that standardization had its downside. NAIC President Earl R. Pomeroy said, "When you standardize benefits, you restrict the consumers' ability to purchase coverage that uniquely suits their needs."

Blue Cross and Blue Shield Association's Spielman agreed, saying the organization had "serious concerns" about standardization. "We believe that rigid control of the contents of insurance policies would stifle, rather than enhance, market responses to changing consumer needs."

Indeed, the health insurance industry contended the situation did not warrant further federal efforts.

Medigap plans already were "clearly the most highly regulated form of health insurance," Linda Jenckes, Health Insurance Association of America vice president for federal affairs, told the Finance subcommittee Feb. 2.

"While numerous congressional hearings have shown that the problems addressed by the [Baucus amendment] have continued to a limited degree, we believe these problems have been adequately addressed by the NAIC."

Jenckes said, "One of the primary functions of state insurance departments is to protect the consumers from marketing abuse, and we think it appropriate that the occasional incidents of abuse that are reported be dealt with at that level."

But members of Congress said that was not enough.

Wyden said, "To say that there are only occasional instances of abuse is like saying foxes are only occasionally interested in chickens." ■

Standardized Food Labeling Ordered

Responding to consumer groups' calls for policing of advertising claims about the health benefits of food products, Congress cleared legislation that for the first time ordered manufacturers to display detailed nutritional information on most packaged food items and some seafood.

The legislation, supported by the Bush administration, required that specific, uniform labels detailing such things as caloric levels and the amount of fat and cholesterol in food items be included on product labels.

The bill (HR 3562), amending the Federal Food, Drug and Cosmetic Act of 1938, won approval in both chambers by voice vote. President Bush signed it into law Nov. 8.

> **BOXSCORE**
>
> **Legislation:** Nutrition Labeling and Education Act, PL 101-535 (HR 3562).
>
> **Major action:** Signed, Nov. 8. Cleared by House, Oct. 26; passed by Senate, amended, Oct. 24; passed by House, July 30.
>
> **Reports:** Energy and Commerce (H Rept 101-538).

The measure prohibited manufacturers from making certain nutritional claims about their products on the label — such as promoting a product as "high-fiber" or "low-sodium" — when other equally important nutritional information such as cholesterol level had not been mentioned.

Manufacturers were also barred from making health claims about their product — for example, saying that high-fiber diets prevented cancer — if the claim had not been fully tested or backed by the U.S. Food and Drug Administration (FDA).

The bill required the Department of Health and Human Services (HHS) to define terms such as "natural," "light" or "low-fat." Manufacturers could use the terms on labels or advertisements only if the product met the government's definition.

The legislation required that most processed food products have displayed on their labels specific nutritional information about a single portion of the product, including the amount of fat, saturated fat, cholesterol, sodium, sugars, dietary fiber, protein, total carbohydrates and complex carbohydrates.

Retailers also were required to provide similarly detailed information for the 20 most frequently consumed types of raw agricultural products as well as raw fish and shellfish.

The bill pre-empted a variety of state nutrition labeling laws, thus preventing manufacturers from having to market products with different labels for each state.

The measure did not, however, prohibit states from requiring their own labeled health warnings, such as those alerting consumers to potential toxins or the danger of allergic reactions to products.

BACKGROUND

With demand for healthier food on the rise, some health-conscious consumer groups found themselves at odds with certain advertisers pushing products that consumer groups and health officials claimed were advertised as being more healthful or beneficial than they were.

Under existing law, food labels had to list nutrition information only if a nutrition claim for the product (such as "low calorie") was made.

Even when information was provided voluntarily, there was no uniformity in labeling.

With increasing public awareness of nutrition issues, food producers began making nutritional claims about their products in the mid-1980s. Many companies began advertising campaigns proclaiming products to be valuable in preventing or treating various diseases.

Consumer groups pressured Congress to act to police the advertising claims, and congressional committees began considering bills in late 1989. *(1989 Almanac, p. 179)*

In 1990, the Bush administration embraced the issue as well, saying that it would exercise its existing regulatory authority to cut down on unsubstantiated health claims for foods and require more useful nutrition information on labels. In a speech to the National Food Policy Conference on March 7, HHS Secretary Louis W. Sullivan acknowledged that "unfounded health claims are being made in the marketplace."

LEGISLATIVE ACTION

Senate and House committees approved different versions of nutrition labeling legislation in the spring. A compromise version won approval by voice vote in the House July 30. The Senate passed an amended version on Oct. 24, which the House cleared for the president Oct. 26.

Senate Committee

The Senate Labor and Human Resources Committee, which had held a hearing on its bill (S 1425) on Nov. 13,

1989, approved the measure, 10-5, on April 25, 1990.

The bill's sponsor, Howard M. Metzenbaum, D-Ohio, said the measure would put an end to "despicable marketing practices appealing to consumers for all the wrong reasons."

Five Republicans voted against the bill: Orrin G. Hatch, Utah; Nancy Landon Kassebaum, Kan.; Daniel R. Coats, Ind.; Strom Thurmond, S.C.; and Thad Cochran, Miss.

The major debate at the markup came over a provision, included in the bill, to pre-empt state laws on nutrition labeling. The administration's proposed regulations would not pre-empt state laws.

Manufacturers and grocer groups lobbied hard for the pre-emption language in order to avoid the expense and hassle of having to provide different information for the same products sold in different states.

Having different laws in each state, said Hatch, "invites consumer confusion." Hatch, however, opposed the measure at the markup, claiming that the pre-emption language was not sweeping enough because it would permit states to obtain waivers in certain cases. He said the measure was "a call for higher food prices and more and more government intrusion in American lives."

On the other side, consumer groups opposed pre-emption altogether, because they wanted states to have the option of imposing standards even more stringent than those proposed at the federal level. "We believe federal legislation should provide a floor, not a ceiling," said Bruce Silverglade of the Washington-based Center for Science in the Public Interest.

Despite the bills' pre-emption language, Silverglade said his group preferred legislation to the regulations being put together by the executive branch, both because the deadlines were stricter and because the bills would give regulators explicit statutory authority to control labeling information and claims.

House Committee

The House Energy and Commerce Committee approved its bill (HR 3562) by voice vote on May 16. The measure, sponsored by Health and the Environment Subcommittee Chairman Henry A. Waxman, D-Calif., had been approved by that panel Oct. 25, 1989. He told the committee his measure would "make sense of the confusing array" of nutrition information facing consumers.

The pre-emption issue was again a point of contention. Amendments by Terry L. Bruce, D-Ill., and Edward Madigan, R-Ill., that would have pre-empted state food-safety labeling laws were barred after Waxman objected that they were not germane to the bill.

Bruce's amendment would have defined any food component, including carcinogens, as a nutrient. Madigan, the ranking Republican on the Health Subcommittee and a cosponsor of the bill, offered an amendment calling for warning labels on foods containing substances posing disease risks.

Members of the food industry supported the amendments, saying they would have provided needed uniformity lacking in food-safety labeling regulations. Consumer advocates, however, said the amendments would eliminate tough state regulations on food safety — such as a California law requiring disclosure of carcinogens — while failing to replace them with federal standards.

In committee, Waxman maintained the amendments would have greatly expanded the scope of his bill to include food safety and health warnings, rather than just nutrition information. His objection was reluctantly upheld by committee Chairman John D. Dingell, D-Mich., who said he supported the amendments.

An amendment offered by Thomas A. Luken, D-Ohio, that would have exempted fish, fresh fruit and vegetables from the labeling requirement was rejected, 19-24.

Several amendments were adopted by voice vote, including one to limit the amount of saturated fat information required on packages and another calling for a specific definition of what qualified as "light" butter.

House Floor

The House approved a revised HR 3562 by voice vote on July 30 after perfunctory debate. No one spoke in opposition.

Waxman said the bill's pre-emption provisions had been "substantially changed" since the committee's markup. The changes had helped win the support of a number of grocery and food marketing groups for the bill, he said.

The compromise bill slightly broadened the pre-emption provision so that state regulations regarding misleading containers and the prominence of labeling would also be pre-empted. A study of existing state and federal regulations in the area would be ordered to determine whether the federal rules should be strengthened.

But states would still be free, Waxman said, to adopt their own requirements for warnings about the ingredients or components of food.

Madigan joined Waxman in urging support for the bill.

"Neither federal regulation of nutrition labeling nor industry efforts have kept pace with scientific knowledge about diet and nutrition," Madigan said. "Consumers today are confronted with a variety of labels that provide them with disjointed and confusing information."

Senate Floor/Final Action

House and Senate staff members resolved minor differences in the House-passed and the Senate committee-approved bills. The result was taken to the Senate floor in the form of an amendment to HR 3562. The Senate passed the amended version of the House bill on Oct. 24.

The differences, resolved in the amendment by Metzenbaum and Hatch, provided for the nutritional labeling of certain vitamins and minerals if HHS determined that such information would assist consumers in maintaining a proper diet.

The amendment also gave HHS the right to require the use of boldface or highlighting on parts of the labels of certain products if it was thought that highlighting would help to better inform consumers of particular product information. Another provision in the amendment exempted the labeling requirement for food processed and prepared at a retail establishment, such as at a supermarket's prepared food section, and sold for consumption elsewhere.

A second amendment, sponsored by James M. Jeffords, R-Vt., and Herb Kohl, D-Wis., provided for a continuation of the existing FDA labeling requirements for dairy and maple products.

Hatch's earlier objection to S 1425 over the potential for some states to gain waivers under the pre-emption provisions was cleared up with language in the House bill requiring petitions to be submitted to HHS for exemption of products from label laws.

The House agreed to the Senate changes on HR 3562 on Oct. 26, thereby clearing the measure for Bush. ■

Bush Pocket-Vetoes Orphan Drug Measure

President Bush on Nov. 8 pocket-vetoed legislation to revise the Orphan Drug Act to allow marketing rights to be shared for certain drugs developed to combat rare diseases.

Bush's action marked the culmination of four years of Hill efforts to amend the law, which granted marketing monopolies and other incentives to companies that developed drugs to treat diseases afflicting a small fraction of the public.

The House on Oct. 23 had cleared the compromise legislation for Bush. By voice vote, the House approved HR 4638 for the second time, after having passed it earlier on July 30.

The Senate had passed the House bill — after changing only a single date — on Oct. 12.

In his veto statement, Bush said he had "serious concerns" that weakening the exclusivity language of the 1983 law would "certainly discourage development of desperately needed new orphan drugs." He also said the bill would lessen the appeal for investment in orphan drug research. *(Veto message, p. 578)*

The bill, a compromise between Congress and the drug industry, would have allowed the sharing of market exclusivity for orphan drugs developed within one year of each other by different firms. But it would have applied only to such drugs developed in the future.

The original bill in Congress would have revoked the exclusive marketing rights to profitable drugs already on the market. Trying to mollify the administration and drug companies, congressional sponsors watered down the bill, "grandfathering" companies that already held exclusive rights on an orphan drug from the new requirements.

The vetoed bill also would have ended market exclusivity once a drug was being used by more than 200,000 people, on grounds that it no longer qualified as an orphan drug. Existing law guaranteed a seven-year monopoly, even if the market turned out to be bigger than expected.

Promoters of the bill argued that drug companies were using the 1983 law to profit on some orphan drugs, either by charging high prices with no fear of competition or by seeing the market base expand vastly.

But drug companies argued that it was unfair to change the rules in the middle of the game. And Bush opposed any fundamental changes in the law.

> **BOXSCORE**
>
> **Legislation:** Orphan Drug Act revisions (HR 4638).
>
> **Major action:** Pocket-vetoed, Nov. 8. Cleared by House, Oct. 23. Passed by Senate, Oct. 12; by House, July 30.
>
> **Report:** Energy and Commerce (H Rept 101-635).

BACKGROUND

The Orphan Drug Act (PL 97-414) was designed to encourage the development and marketing of drugs to treat so-called orphan diseases, generally those afflicting fewer than 200,000 people. With such a limited potential market and no incentives, promising drugs were left to languish because it would cost companies more to bring drugs through the rigorous federal approval process than they could hope to earn back from sales.

The law — passed by Congress late in 1982 and signed Jan. 4, 1983 — provided a series of incentives, the most significant of which granted companies seven years of exclusive marketing rights for orphan drugs they developed. *(1982 Almanac, p. 490)*

By all accounts, the law had more than fulfilled its mission. The Food and Drug Administration (FDA) had granted orphan status to 417 drugs, 49 of which had reached the market by Jan. 18, 1991.

Drafters of the law became concerned, however, that some drugs were yielding windfall profits for the drug companies.

Such windfalls, particularly with some companies charging $30,000 or more per year for some of the drugs, drew the ire of Rep. Henry A. Waxman, D-Calif., chairman of the Energy and Commerce Subcommittee on Health and the Environment. "Drugs that are profitable are not orphans," said Waxman, one of the authors of the law. "Sponsors are very interested in claiming heritage."

Such profits, added Waxman, were "contrary to the purposes of the act."

In order to rectify the situation, which the market could not cure itself because of the government-granted monopoly, the original version of HR 4638 included provisions to permit "shared exclusivity" when two companies were developing the same drug at the same time. Under existing law, whichever company was the first to win approval from the FDA won exclusivity.

Such competition, Waxman reasoned, could help bring down the price of very profitable drugs for consumers.

But after an intensive lobbying effort by drug companies who objected to changing the rules, Waxman and Senate sponsor Howard M. Metzenbaum, D-Ohio, were forced to relent.

In the end, Waxman and Republicans who wanted the law left alone agreed to a compromise that would let market exclusivity be shared in the future but that would grandfather drugs on the market or in development.

"Those who wanted the Orphan Drug Act never envisioned it to create monopolies," Waxman said. "It has been heavily lobbied by groups looking at their own economic interests rather than the good of society. Those who favor the status quo as it exists were able to keep that status quo for themselves."

What the Bill Would Have Done

HR 4638 would have allowed for the sharing of market exclusivity for orphan drugs developed within one year of each other by different firms, though it would have grandfathered drugs on the market or in development.

The bill also would have paved the way for exclusive markets to be opened if a disease affected more than 200,000 people.

For future drugs, companies could have shared market exclusivity if the second company developing the drug did three things:

- Applied to the FDA to designate a drug orphan within six months of the first company.
- Showed that the drug was in clinical trials within 12 months after the first company began testing.

Bush Veto of Orphan Drug Act Revision

Following is the memorandum of disapproval issued by President Bush on Nov. 8 announcing that he would not sign a bill (HR 4638) revising the Orphan Drug Act.

I am withholding my approval of HR 4638, the "Orphan Drug Amendments of 1990." This legislation would make substantive changes to the orphan drug provisions of the Federal Food, Drug, and Cosmetic Act and the Orphan Drug Act.

Enacted in 1983, the Orphan Drug Act created economic incentives for drug companies to develop drugs for rare diseases and conditions — so-called orphan drugs. Typically, these drugs would not be profitable to develop because of their small patient populations.

By any measure, the Orphan Drug Act has been a tremendous success. A total of 49 new drugs for rare diseases have been approved under this program, and 370 others are in the development stage. These drugs have provided lifesaving treatments for such terrible diseases as enzyme deficiency, which affects adversely the immune system of about 40 children nationwide. Until the orphan drug was developed to treat these children, they had to spend their entire lives in the protection of an isolation bubble. One of the first orphan drugs is another example of a triumph. The most difficult form of leprosy affects only 4,000 people. A drug known for over 14 years to be effective in treating this condition was not being marketed by any drug company, because it was considered unprofitable — until the Orphan Drug Act provided the marketing incentive. In a similar manner, orphan drugs provide treatment for terrible diseases for which there is usually no alternative therapy.

I have serious concerns about the effect that HR 4638 would have upon the incentive of drug companies to develop orphan drugs. I believe we must not endanger the success of this program, which is due in large measure to the existence of the "market exclusivity" provision in the Orphan Drug Act that allows companies to have exclusive marketing rights to an orphan drug for seven years. Weakening the current seven-year exclusivity provision would certainly discourage development of desperately needed new orphan drugs.

Under current law, firms may apply to develop the same orphan drug, but only the first firm to have its drug approved receives market exclusivity. The certainty of this seven-year period is the basis of the economic incentive to attract drug firms to invest in orphan drugs.

The bill would make two major changes to the market exclusivity provisions of the Orphan Drug Act. First, the bill provides for "shared exclusivity." Firms that can demonstrate that they have developed the orphan drug simultaneously would be allowed to share the market with the firm initially awarded the market exclusivity. Second, the bill requires the Food and Drug Administration to withdraw the marketing exclusivity as soon as the patient population exceeds a 200,000 patient limit.

Both of these changes have the effect of weakening the marketing incentives provided by the Act. Under this bill, the length of the market exclusivity period will depend on how quickly the patient population grows and whether other firms file claims for simultaneous development.

In addition, as currently constructed, the 200,000 patient population limit would be applied to orphan drugs approved prior to the enactment of the bill as well as to those approved in the future. This retroactive rule change would send a troublesome signal to all those who might wish to develop orphan drugs that the Federal Government may change unilaterally the rules for firms that made investment decisions based on the expectation of seven years of market exclusivity.

I am aware that this bill was passed after a number of compromises among members of Congress. I am extremely concerned, however, that individuals with rare diseases may suffer because of changes that this bill would make in the incentives to develop new drug treatments. Accordingly, I am withholding my approval of HR 4638. ■

- Completed and filed its formal application for FDA approval within 12 months of the date on which the first company filed its application.

The bill also addressed the sudden growth of diseases such as AIDS. It would have shifted to companies the burden of proving that they were not capitalizing on a disease that was likely to boom. Under existing law, a company applying for orphan status for a drug had to show, at the time, that the disease the drug would treat "affects less than 200,000 persons in the United States." The bill would have required drug companies to make their determinations based on projections of how many people would be affected by the disease three years from the date that the designation was requested.

The legislation also would have authorized $20 million in grants in fiscal 1991, $25 million in fiscal 1992 and $30 million in fiscal 1993. The program had been authorized at $14 million in fiscal 1990.

HOUSE ACTION

The House on July 30 approved HR 4638 by voice vote. In passing the measure, members again pointed out that some orphan drugs had been so successful that companies had reaped huge profits — never the intent of the original legislation.

The Energy and Commerce Committee report accompanying the legislation cited three examples:

- EPO, used to treat anemia in kidney dialysis patients. It cost about $8,000 per year and was expected to have $200 million in annual sales, most of which was to come from purchases by the federal government through the Medicare program.
- Human Growth Hormone (HGH), used to treat dwarfism, cost between $10,000 and $30,000 a year for each patient and had annual sales of from $125 million to $150 million.
- Aerosol Pentamidine, used to treat and prevent a kind of pneumonia that was the most common complication of AIDS. It cost about $1,000 per year and had substantial annual sales, with the potential for more.

HR 4638 had sailed through the House Energy and Commerce Committee by voice vote on July 17. The Subcommittee on Health and the Environment on June 21 had approved the measure on a 6-4 show of hands. The routine markup and vote, however, belied the major revisions the bill underwent concerning the exclusivity question.

While Waxman had sought to revoke the exclusive marketing rights for some of drugs, drug firms lobbied heavily against his original bill. The Bush administration also opposed Waxman's approach.

"Despite concerns about anomalies in the operation of the act, we have concluded that the act should not be altered in any fundamental manner," Louis W. Sullivan, secretary of Health and Human Services, wrote Waxman on June 20.

Ultimately, Waxman and Thomas J. Bliley Jr., R-Va., worked out the compromise to permit exclusivity to be shared in certain future cases in which more than one company was developing the same drug at roughly the same time.

"The compromise allows all drugs currently in the pipeline to be grandfathered under the original market exclusivity provisions of the Orphan Drug Act," said Bliley. "For future orphan drugs, the market exclusivity provisions will be changed to enhance fairness for companies that truly develop the same drug simultaneously."

At the committee markup, members also adopted an amendment offered by Bliley extending to July 16 the date by which companies had to have applied for orphan drug designation in order to be grandfathered and thus not covered by the new requirements.

But while Waxman said he felt "honor bound" to abide by his compromise, on the other side of the Capitol, Metzenbaum was standing behind his version of the bill, S 2576. That bill was awaiting action in the Labor and Human Resources Committee and sought to revoke the exclusivity for the very profitable drugs.

SENATE ACTION

The Senate on Oct. 12 approved HR 4638 by voice vote.

Before passing the measure, the Senate by voice vote adopted an amendment to grandfather all drugs for which orphan-drug-status applications had been filed before enactment. As passed by the House, the grandfather provisions was to apply only if companies had filed for orphan drug status before July 16, 1990.

The legislation had moved a step closer to fruition on Sept. 26 when the Labor and Human Resources Committee approved a bill identical to the one passed by the House.

Members by voice vote approved S 2576, after substituting the text of HR 4638, which the House had passed July 30.

In the Senate, Metzenbaum shared Waxman's outrage about some of the very profitable drugs and had planned to try to press for revocation of their orphan status in that chamber.

With the 101st Congress winding down, however, Metzenbaum struck a deal with Orrin G. Hatch of Utah, the Labor Committee's ranking Republican, to accept the House version.

"Legislating has to do with the art of the possible," said Metzenbaum.

Indeed, that appeared to be why members declined to accept an amendment offered by Nancy Landon Kassebaum, R-Kan., even after a majority of members said they supported the idea.

Kassebaum's amendment would have revoked a company's market exclusivity three months after any orphan drug's cumulative net sales exceeded $200 million. Under the House-passed bill, companies could share exclusivity only if they were developing the same drug at roughly the same time.

Members generally agreed that Kassebaum's amendment would more directly address the problem of excess profits, but said they feared that it could end up scuttling the entire bill if the House did not agree. Kassebaum withdrew the amendment.

FINAL ACTION

The House on Oct. 23 cleared the measure for Bush, agreeing without controversy to the Senate's one change — the date for filing for orphan status.

Once Congress cleared the compromise, few observers expected a Bush veto. While the administration had expressed its objections to the legislation, Bush never issued a formal veto threat.

A Bush aide said that although a clear veto threat was not sent, "serious reservations" were made known through policy statements and the president's Council on Competitiveness.

Nevertheless, congressional backers of the bill professed surprise at Bush's Nov. 8 pocket veto. "Not a single person from the administration or the Department of Health and Human Services ever called and told us of any reservations on this bill," said Bill Corr, counsel to Metzenbaum.

The Pharmaceutical Manufacturers Association (PMA), the chief drug industry lobby, echoed Bush's opposition. PMA spokesman Jeffrey C. Warren said that, under the bill, a company "would theoretically have to consider losing 50 percent of the market" created by the introduction of its orphan drug.

The Association of Biotechnology Companies welcomed the veto but not for Bush's reasons. Small biotech companies wanted the law changed to allow more competition in orphan drugs that already were the exclusive domain of one company.

In the wake of a veto, congressional sponsors of the measures said they would try again in 1991 to enact similar legislation.

"We'll definitely come back to it. There was a lot of displeasure over this veto," said an aide to Waxman. ■

New Regulations for Medical Devices

Congress voted to overhaul federal regulation of medical devices, clearing legislation Oct. 27 that required the Food and Drug Administration (FDA) to upgrade its procedures for approving all such equipment — from tongue depressors to heart-lung machines. President Bush signed the bill (HR 3095 — PL 101-629) on Nov. 28.

The legislation — an update of a 1976 law (PL 94-295) governing medical devices — aimed to streamline the marketing approval process for new devices, improve the oversight of equipment already on the market and make it easier to recall defective products. *(1976 Almanac, p. 622)*

Lawmakers had been attempting for years to rewrite the law, which was intended to ensure the safety and effectiveness of medical devices before their approval by the FDA. In passing the law Congress required that devices be classified on the basis of their potential to cause serious injury or death. But it inadvertently created a large loophole through which most new products reached the market without undergoing the regular approval process.

Under the 1976 law, devices could be approved for market without a full FDA review if they were judged to be substantially equivalent to other products already in use.

A series of congressional hearings in the mid-1980s also revealed that the federal government was not receiving timely reports about faulty or dangerous devices that had reached the marketplace.

The 1990 law required the FDA to review the safety of the most risky medical devices — so-called Class III devices — by 1995 if they had not been previously screened. The earlier law had allowed Class III devices to stay on the market without review if they were in use prior to 1976.

BOXSCORE

Legislation: Safe Medical Devices Act of 1990, PL 101-629 (HR 3095).

Major action: Signed, Nov. 28. Conference report adopted by Senate, Oct. 27; by House, Oct. 26; passed by Senate, Oct. 12; by House, Oct. 10.

Reports: Conference report (H Rept 101-959); Labor and Human Resources (S Rept 101-513); Energy and Commerce (H Rept 101-808).

BACKGROUND

The 1990 legislative effort was not the first move by Congress to address concerns about the FDA's enforcement of the 1976 law.

The House in 1988 had passed a bill similar to HR 3095, but the Senate failed to act on it. The Reagan administration opposed the measure. *(1988 Almanac, p. 319)*

The 1976 law defined a medical device as any non-drug item used to achieve a medical purpose. It sought to give such items the same pre-market assurances of safety and efficacy required of prescription drugs.

The law classified devices in the following categories:

- Class I — those, such as tongue depressors, determined to pose no or minimal dangers to consumers.
- Class II — those deemed potentially more dangerous.
- Class III — potentially the most dangerous. The safety and efficacy of these had to be demonstrated before the FDA permitted them to be sold.

Because so many devices were already on the market, however, the law created an enormous loophole. If a manufacturer demonstrated that a new device was "substantially equivalent" to a Class III device already on the market in 1976, the company could bring the device to market without a full review.

In 1990, more than 90 percent of all new devices came to market under that procedure, officially known as 510(k).

Hearings conducted by the Energy and Commerce Committee's Oversight Subcommittee also revealed problems with identifying faulty or dangerous devices that had already reached the market.

A report by the General Accounting Office (GAO) in 1986 found that fewer than 1 percent of device problems in hospitals were being reported to the FDA.

In 1989, a GAO report concluded that while steps the FDA had taken to improve the reporting of problems had substantially increased the information the agency was receiving, "the resulting system is not adequate to handle the volume of reports currently received."

In addition, the FDA had never used its authority under the 1976 law for mandatory recall or notification, preferring instead to encourage voluntary recalls.

The FDA blamed too much paperwork and too little staff for its inability to enforce the existing law more strictly. In 1988, the agency said its Center for Devices and Radiological Health, with a staff of 850, needed 400 more people to cope with the 5,000 applications for approval of new devices and 18,000 recall reports each year.

What the Bill Would Do

The final bill called for a maximum penalty of $15,000 per violation, with a $1 million ceiling for all penalties combined.

Other provisions of the final bill, which amended the Federal Food, Drug and Cosmetic Act, included:

- A requirement that medical device user facilities, such as hospitals, report serious problems with medical devices. The FDA or product manufacturer was to be notified when a device caused a death or serious injury. Facilities were required to report to the FDA within 10 working days after becoming aware of the information in the case of a death and to the manufacturer in the case of serious illness or injury.
- A requirement that the secretary of Health and Human Services issue regulations mandating that distributors of devices keep records and report on possible problems.
- A requirement that manufacturers develop methods for tracking their products.
- Updated procedures for classifying devices. For example, the bill prohibited classifying a device used to support or sustain human life in the Class II category unless the secretary examined and identified the special controls necessary to adequately assure its safety and effectiveness. The special controls the secretary could place on Class II devices were expanded.
- A requirement that the secretary issue an order for the immediate cessation of use of a device deemed likely to cause serious injury or death. A formal hearing would follow within 10 days to help decide whether to reverse the order or to impose a recall. All individuals at risk from a recalled device had to be given notice.
- A provision allowing the secretary to temporarily suspend approval of applications when there was a reasonable probability that a device would cause serious injury, illness or death.
- A requirement that manufacturers, shortly after commercial distribution of a device, submit to the secretary a plan for any required postmarket surveillance.
- A provision calling on the secretary to place daily wear soft and daily wear nonhydrophilic plastic contact lenses into Class I or Class II within two years unless a lens was deemed to meet the Class III criteria. If the secretary made no decision within three years, the law directed him to define the lenses as Class II.
- A provision stating that a device could not be found to be substantially equivalent to an existing Class III product if it raised new questions of safety and effectiveness. That meant the new device would have to go through an FDA review rather than receiving the automatic approval previously afforded potentially dangerous devices that were substantially equivalent to products already on the market.

COMMITTEE ACTION

Committees in both chambers gave approval to their versions of the legislation on Sept. 26. The Senate Labor and Human Resources Committee approved its measure (S 3006) on a 16-0 vote.

The House Energy and Commerce Committee gave its approval by voice vote.

Both versions sought to streamline the approval process for bringing medical devices to market, create improved procedures for monitoring devices that failed to work as intended and make it easier for dangerous devices to be recalled.

The bill, said Sen. Christopher J. Dodd, D-Conn., author of the amended Senate version, was "intended to provide a balanced regulatory scheme which will protect the public against unsafe or ineffective new devices gaining entry to the market, assure that health practitioners can be confident about the medical equipment and devices they use or prescribe for their patients, and spur development of new medical technologies so that both our health-care system and our medical-device industry retain their status as world leaders."

The House and Senate committee bills sought to address the problems while taking into account that the FDA had been overworked and understaffed for years.

As in the 1988 House bill, both committee bills called for a requirement that only deaths associated with faulty medical devices be reported directly to the FDA.

Injuries were to be reported to device manufacturers, who in turn would have to file reports with the FDA.

That compromise was intended to prevent the agency from being inundated with information, while ensuring that it was made aware of serious medical-device problems.

Both committee bills also called for codifying the manner in which the FDA interpreted the substantial equivalence rule.

The bills still permitted devices to be brought to market under the abbreviated 510(k) process, but gave the agency authority to require evidence of safety and efficacy comparable to devices already on the market.

The bills also streamlined the administrative processes by which devices were reclassified and by which performance standards were to be written for Class II devices not deemed dangerous enough to require full safety and efficacy reviews.

Finally, both bills granted the FDA authority to recall devices deemed to "cause serious, adverse health consequences or death."

The major difference between the bills was the issue of enforcement.

The House bill provided that violators of the act be subject to civil penalties of $1 million for the most potentially dangerous devices, in addition to the criminal penalties already in existence.

During a Sept. 25 markup, House Energy and Commerce's Subcommittee on Health and the Environment had agreed to penalties of $5 million, but the figure was reduced after negotiations between bill sponsor and subcommittee Chairman Henry A. Waxman, D-Calif., and the subcommittee's ranking Republican, Edward Madigan of Illinois.

The Senate version included no provisions for civil penalties.

FINAL ACTION

The House passed its version of the bill by voice vote on Oct. 10, sending the measure to the Senate.

The Senate received the House bill on Oct. 12, inserting its own version — which excluded civil penalties — before passing the bill by voice vote and sending the measure to conference.

Among the many compromises embraced in the conference report, adopted by the House on Oct. 26 and cleared by the Senate on Oct. 27, was an agreement to impose civil penalties, with modifications to the penalty provisions contained in the original House version.

The final bill called for a maximum $15,000 per violation penalty, with a $1 million ceiling for all penalties combined.

The House version had sought a schedule for civil fines ranging from $1,000 to $20,000 per infraction, with a ceiling between $100,000 and $1 million, depending on the type of violation.

Edward M. Kennedy, D-Mass., chairman of the Labor and Human Resources Committee, spoke out in favor of the legislation before the Senate passed its version.

Kennedy said the bill sought to ensure that "all medical devices entering the market are safe and effective; second, that problems with devices are identified quickly; third, that defective devices are taken off the market as soon as possible; and fourth, that growth and innovation in the medical device field continue." ■

Automation, Consolidation Backed for FDA

The House on Oct. 27 cleared a bill to revitalize the Food and Drug Administration (FDA) by automating some activities and consolidating its 23 offices scattered throughout the Washington, D.C., area into one facility.

The bill (S 845), passed by the Senate on Oct. 24, authorized $100 million in fiscal 1991 for work leading to a new FDA administrative and laboratory complex. President Bush signed the bill Nov. 28 (PL 101-635).

The Senate Labor and Human Resources Committee had approved the bill, 16-0, on Nov. 1, 1989 (S Rept 101-242). *(1989 Almanac, p. 178)*

The measure also allowed the FDA commissioner to appoint technical and scientific review groups. The commissioner could pay the appointees, except for those already employed by the federal government.

In urging Senate approval of the bill Oct. 24, the committee's ranking Republican, Orrin G. Hatch, Utah, said the agency needed a new headquarters because at the time it was scattered among 23 different buildings at seven different sites in the Washington area. Hatch said the agency also needed to "enter the computer age by automating the application process, reducing the mountainous paper flow under which the agency is now laboring."

The Senate approved the bill by voice vote and sent it to the House, which debated it in the early morning hours of Oct. 27 (session of Oct. 26). The vote was postponed, however, until the Oct. 27 session; the bill was then cleared for the president by voice vote. ■

Bush Reluctantly Signs AIDS Measure

Congress on Aug. 4 cleared for President Bush fast-track legislation aimed at bolstering aid to areas hit by the AIDS epidemic.

Final action came when the Senate approved the conference agreement on the bill by voice vote, less than five months after it was introduced.

The legislation, passed by the House in the early morning hours of Aug. 4, was a compromise version of bills passed by both chambers (S 2240, HR 4785) aimed at helping state and local governments coordinate and pay for care for people with AIDS, acquired immune deficiency syndrome.

The bill authorized $875 million in fiscal 1991 for programs aimed at helping health and social service organizations cope with the mounting costs of the AIDS epidemic.

But Congress provided far less than that in the spending bill for the Departments of Labor, Health and Human Services, and Education — just over $220 million, a figure denounced by AIDS organizations and public health officials as inadequate. *(Labor-HHS appropriations, p. 847)*

Despite formal opposition to both chambers' bills and veiled veto threats, Bush signed the measure on Aug. 18.

Bush opposed the measures because of their "narrow, disease-specific approach." Similar complaints by conservative members of both chambers created some controversy on the bill's road to passage.

Jesse Helms, R-N.C., insisted during Senate debate that the crisis was being overstated by a too powerful AIDS lobby. House members spent much of their markup debating restrictive amendments offered by William E. Dannemeyer, R-Calif., an outspoken critic of homosexuality.

The primary intent of the legislation, according to its sponsors, was to increase the availability of non-institutional care for persons with AIDS and conditions arising from infection with HIV, the AIDS virus. One of the reasons the epidemic took such a heavy financial toll on many cities was that AIDS patients ended up in hospitals inappropriately. They did not always require such intensive care, but often had no other place to go.

To help provide those options, the bill created a series of grant programs. Some of the grants were to go exclusively to areas with the most confirmed cases of AIDS, some to states, and others directly to public or private nonprofit health-care and social service providers. *(Provisions, p. 584)*

"This legislation converts the millions of dollars of federal research into treatments that are available to the public," said Henry A. Waxman, D-Calif., sponsor of the House version. "It's not enough to develop drugs. We must also make sure that they are available to people regardless of their ability to pay, and we must be sure that they are available early enough in people's illnesses to make a real difference."

The bill authorized $275 million in fiscal 1991-92 and "such sums as necessary" for fiscal 1993-95 for emergency aid to cities that had more than 2,000 confirmed AIDS cases or where 25 people out of every 10,000 had AIDS.

At the time of passage, the 15 cities with more than 2,000 AIDS cases — Atlanta; Boston; Chicago; Dallas; Fort Lauderdale, Fla.; Houston; Los Angeles; Miami; New York; Newark, N.J.; Philadelphia; San Diego; San Francisco; San Juan, Puerto Rico; and Washington, D.C. — accounted for more than half the cases reported in the United States. Jersey City, N.J., also qualified for the emergency aid because of the high incidence of AIDS in that relatively small city.

The bill also authorized $275 million in each of fiscal 1991 and 1992 and "such sums as may be necessary" for fiscal 1993-95 for a grant program for states — which were required to match the federal funds — to help provide AIDS services.

The bill further authorized $305 million for fiscal 1991 — $230 million for state health departments and $75 million for public and private nonprofit clinics — for an initiative to provide funding for early intervention services for people with AIDS or HIV. It authorized "such sums as necessary" for the program for fiscal 1992-95.

Other provisions authorized $20 million in fiscal 1991 and "such sums as necessary" for fiscal 1992-95 for demonstration projects to develop treatments for and provide services to children with AIDS and HIV and to require a study of AIDS in rural areas.

BOXSCORE

Legislation: AIDS Resources Emergency Act, PL 101-381 (S 2240).

Major action: Signed, Aug. 18. Conference report adopted by Senate, Aug. 4; House, Aug. 4 (session of Aug. 3). HR 4785 passed by House, 408-14, June 13; S 2240 passed by Senate, 95-4, May 16.

Reports: Conference report (H Rept 101-652). Labor and Human Resources (S Rept 101-273).

BACKGROUND

"In terms of pain, suffering and cost, AIDS is a disaster as severe as any earthquake, hurricane or drought," said Edward M. Kennedy, D-Mass., sponsor of the Senate version of the bill.

Although AIDS was the No. 1 public health concern in the United States for much of the 1980s, Congress moved relatively slowly in dealing with the epidemic.

Lawmakers started pouring funds into research long before they addressed the policy questions involved in trying to slow the spread of the fatal disease, transmitted through bodily fluids and concentrated primarily among homosexuals and intravenous drug users.

As of July 30, 1990 — the most up-to-date numbers available to Congress before it passed the legislation — there were 143,286 reported cases of AIDS in the United States, and 87,644 of those people had died, according to the U.S. Public Health Service. About 1 million Americans were infected with HIV.

Congress cleared its first comprehensive AIDS bill in 1988. That legislation (PL 100-607) authorized significantly increased research, education and prevention activities. *(1988 Almanac, p. 296)*

Some controversial elements of a bill (HR 5142) passed overwhelmingly by the House in September 1988 failed to make it into that law, though, when Helms threatened to filibuster and block the entire package. Much of the 1990 bill was similar to, although not identical to, HR 5142.

Waxman said that the differences between the 1988 bill and the 1990 version reflected new scientific knowledge about the progression of the disease from infection with HIV to full-blown AIDS. "Now we know there's something we can do," he said, to prevent the uninfected from becoming infected and the infected from becoming ill.

Sponsors of the 1988 law said that funds were still needed to prop up hospitals, clinics and other health-care facilities — especially in urban areas — that were straining under the burden of caring for AIDS patients without health insurance.

"For nearly a decade, these urban centers have seen the numbers of diagnosed AIDS cases steadily increasing, the cost in human lives steadily mounting and the level of HIV health-care services provided increasingly incapable of meeting the growing demand," the Senate Labor and Human Resource Committee said in its report on the bill.

The committee noted that the percentage of AIDS victims with private health insurance had dropped to 29 percent from between 40 percent and 60 percent in the early years of the epidemic, leaving taxpayers and charity to cover the costs of treating most AIDS patients.

Helms, however, insisted during the Senate debate that the crisis was being exaggerated by a powerful AIDS lobby that was gobbling up funds needed to combat diseases that afflicted far larger numbers of people.

"I think one of the saddest things is that the taxpayers' money is being proposed to be used to proselytize a dangerous lifestyle," Helms said. "In the meantime, millions of other Americans, gravely ill with Alzheimer's or cancer or diabetes . . . are being cast aside, along with common sense, in the headlong rush to feed the appetite of a movement which will not be satisfied until the social fabric of the nation is irreparably changed."

Just as in 1987, when the Senate considered its first major AIDS bill, Helms was chastised by fellow conservative Orrin G. Hatch, Utah, ranking Republican on the Labor and Human Resources Committee and lead cosponsor of S 2240.

"Should we just let the disease run rampant because we do not agree with the morals of certain people?" asked Hatch. "I do not condone homosexual activity, but that does not have a thing to do with this bill. AIDS is a public health problem. . . . There are a lot of good people who are infected with the AIDS virus who make contributions to our society. We should provide them compassion and care."

SENATE ACTION

The Senate Labor and Human Resources Committee unanimously approved S 2240 on April 4. As approved by the committee, the measure authorized a total of $1.2 billion to help combat the AIDS epidemic.

The measure authorized $300 million annually in fiscal 1991-92 and "such sums as necessary" for fiscal 1993-95 for emergency grants to metropolitan areas hardest hit by the epidemic. According to the National Commission on AIDS, 5 percent of the nation's hospitals were treating half the nation's AIDS patients.

Half of the first installment of emergency funds was to be distributed within 60 days and the other half within five months. But Congress would first have to appropriate the funds.

Under the bill, funds could be used not only for hospital care, but also for clinics, community health centers, subacute care facilities that served a high percentage of low-income patients, and case-managed, community-based outpatient health and support services aimed at reducing hospitalization.

The measure also authorized $300 million for both fiscal 1991 and 1992 in grants to states to develop and operate cost-effective programs to provide comprehensive care for those with AIDS and HIV infection.

Among other things, states could use the funds to create and operate local consortia of public and private entities capable of delivering a comprehensive continuum of care to those with AIDS or HIV infection. States would have to set aside at least 15 percent of funds to provide care to children, women and families with HIV infection.

"The toll that AIDS is taking on many local communities and health-care systems is overwhelming, and federal assistance is essential," said Kennedy.

The bill also directed the new HHS Agency for Health Care Policy and Research to start a program to develop information on the effectiveness of various methods of financing and delivering care to those with AIDS and HIV infection.

Floor Debate

By 95-4, the Senate on May 16 approved S 2240, which authorized a total of $1.2 billion in grants for fiscal 1991-92, half for AIDS-riddled cities. *(Vote 97, p. 22-S)*

"There is a national crisis out there and without this, there is a very real chance the public health system in many parts of the country will collapse," said Kennedy.

The bill mirrored the legislation approved by the committee in April, with a few amendments. Sponsors fended off a number of other amendments, primarily from conservative Republicans concerned that too much money and attention were being devoted to AIDS.

Senate leaders tried for several weeks to work out a time agreement under which the measure could be considered, but a handful of Republicans refused to cooperate. When the negotiations failed, Majority Leader George J. Mitchell, D-Maine, filed for cloture on the motion to proceed to the bill.

The May 15 vote for cloture was 95-3, with Helms, Steve Symms, R-Idaho, and Gordon J. Humphrey, R-N.H., casting the "nay" votes. *(Vote 91, p. 22-S)*

Still, amendments from Helms and other members kept the Senate at work on the bill for two full days after the cloture vote.

The Senate adopted 10 amendments to S 2240, the most significant of which required states to have programs to enable public health officials to notify the sexual partners of those who tested positive for HIV. But the amendment left it to state officials to decide whether to put a notification program into effect.

"The specifics of this delicate policy issue ought to be resolved by the states and the public health officials of that state," said Kennedy, who offered the version of the amendment that was ultimately adopted.

In addition, the passage of the Americans with Disabilities Act, which prohibited discrimination against people with AIDS or HIV, was expected to ease the most significant fear that prevented people from seeking AIDS testing. *(Americans with Disabilities Act, p. 447)*

Other amendments adopted included the following:

- By Hatch, by voice vote, to change the bill's title to the

Continued on p. 586

AIDS Resources Act Provisions

Here are provisions of the Ryan White Comprehensive AIDS Resources Emergency Act of 1990 (S 2240 — PL 101-381):

Title I — HIV Emergency Relief Grants

Created a new grant program of emergency relief for areas with a "substantial need for services." For fiscal 1991, any metropolitan area in which more than 2,000 cases of AIDS had been reported to and confirmed by the Centers for Disease Control as of June 30, 1990, was eligible.

After fiscal 1991, the 2,000 or more cases had to be confirmed by March 31 of the most recent fiscal year. Areas with a per capita incidence of AIDS of 0.0025, based on the most recently available population data, were also eligible for emergency funds.

Funds were to flow to the top elected official in the metropolitan area who administered the public health agency serving the largest number of individuals with AIDS in the area.

In order to receive the grants, the elected official would be required to establish an administrative mechanism to allocate funds and services among each of the area's political subdivisions with at least 10 percent of the area's reported AIDS cases.

Allocations would be based on the number of AIDS cases, the severity of need for outpatient and ambulatory care, and the need for health and support services personnel.

• **HIV health services planning council.** In order to receive funds, the elected official would have to establish an HIV health services planning council. The official could also designate an existing entity with demonstrated experience in planning for HIV health-care service needs within the eligible area and implementing plans to address such needs.

The council would be responsible for establishing priorities for the allocation of funds, developing a comprehensive plan for the organization and delivery of health services to individuals with HIV disease, and assessing the efficiency of the administrative mechanism in rapidly allocating funds to the areas of greatest need within the eligible area.

The council would have to include providers of health care, social services, and mental health services; representatives of community-based and AIDS service organizations, local public health agencies, hospitals or health-care planning agencies; individuals with HIV disease, non-elected community leaders, state government officials, recipients of categorical grants for early intervention services (see Title III, below), and representatives of any federal adult and pediatric HIV-related care demonstration project operating in the area to be served.

• **Distribution of funds.** Required that half of the funds appropriated for emergency assistance be distributed to each metropolitan area eligible for assistance within 90 days after appropriations became available for fiscal 1991, and within 60 days after appropriations became available for each of fiscal 1992-95. The amount of each grant was to be based on the actual number of AIDS cases and the per capita incidence of AIDS.

• **Supplemental grants.** Required that the secretary of Health and Human Services (HHS) distribute the other half of appropriated emergency relief funds within 150 days after appropriations became available based on applications from areas eligible for emergency relief. Applications had to demonstrate at least the following:

— "Severe need" for supplemental funds.

— An existing commitment of local financial and in-kind resources.

— An ability to use the funds in an immediately responsive and cost-effective way.

— That funds would be allocated appropriately both among areas and among affected groups, including infants, children, women and families with HIV disease.

• **Use of grant funds.** Permitted grant funds to be awarded to public or private nonprofit entities, including hospitals (including Department of Veterans Affairs facilities), community-based organizations, hospices, ambulatory-care facilities, community health centers, migrant health centers and homeless health centers.

Funds were to be used to deliver or enhance HIV-related outpatient and ambulatory health and support services, including case-management and comprehensive treatment services, and inpatient case-management services that prevented unnecessary hospitalization or that expedited discharge, as medically appropriate, from inpatient facilities.

Required that priority be given in distributing funds to entities participating in HIV health-care demonstration projects under the auspices of HHS's Health Resources and Services Administration.

• **Personnel needs.** If the HIV health services planning council determined that a shortage of specific health, mental health or support service personnel existed and had resulted in inappropriate utilization of inpatient services, permitted up to 10 percent of emergency grant funds to be used to help pay for the training of personnel. Entities receiving such aid, however, had to provide assurances that the funds would not be used to supplant existing resources.

• **Other uses of emergency funds.** Allowed up to 5 percent of emergency funds to be used for administration, accounting, reporting and program oversight functions. Specifically prohibited use of funds to purchase or improve land; to purchase, construct or permanently improve any building or other facility; or to make cash payments to intended recipients of services.

• **Applications.** Required that applications for emergency funds include at least the following assurances:

— Funds would be used to supplement and not supplant state funds made available in that same year.

— Political subdivisions within the eligible area would maintain the level of expenditures on HIV-related services as in the preceding year.

— Entities within the eligible area would participate in an established HIV community-based continuum of care if such continuum existed.

— Services would be provided without regard to ability to pay or existing or past health condition.

— Services would be provided in settings accessible to low-income individuals with HIV disease, and outreach programs for such individuals would be provided to inform them of the availability of services.

Generally required that all applications be submitted within 45 days after appropriations became available, although the secretary could extend that deadline by an additional 60 days if he determined the eligible area had made a good-faith effort to comply.

• **Redistribution.** Authorized the secretary to redistribute funds appropriated but not granted to an eligible area because of the failure of that area to submit an application. The redistribution had to be in the same proportion as the original grants made to each of the areas.

• **Reduced charges for low-income patients.** Required that recipients pay for services in most cases. Services had to be provided free of charge to individuals with income below the federal poverty level ($5,980 for most individuals in 1989). For indivwith incomes between 100 percent and 200 percent of the poverty level, required that charges for services not exceed 5 percent of the individual's annual gross income. Charges for individuals with incomes between 200 percent and 300 percent of the poverty level could not exceed 7 percent of annual gross income, and charges for those with incomes higher than 300 percent of the poverty level could not exceed 10 percent.

• **Authorization.** Authorized $275 million for emergency relief grants in fiscal 1991-92, and "such sums as may be necessary" in each of fiscal 1993-95.

Title II — HIV-Care Grants

• **Authorization.** Authorized $275 million in fiscal 1991-92 and "such sums as may be necessary" in each of fiscal 1993-95 for grants to states to enable them to improve the quality, availability and organization of health and support services for individuals and families with HIV disease.

• **Use of grant funds.** States could use grant funds to:

— Establish and operate HIV-care consortia designed to provide a comprehensive continuum of care to those with HIV disease within areas most affected by the disease.

— Provide home- and community-based care for those with HIV disease.

— Provide assistance to assure the continuity of health insurance coverage of those with HIV disease.

— Provide treatments determined to prolong life or prevent serious deterioration of health to low-income individuals with HIV disease.

• **Set-aside for women and children.** Required states to use at least 15 percent of funds received under Title II to provide health and support services to infants, children, women and families with HIV disease.

• **Applications.** Applications from states for grant funds had to include the following:

— A detailed description of HIV-related services provided by the state in the preceding year, the number of persons served and methods used to finance such services;

— The number of persons to be served with grant funds, demographic data on the populations served, the average cost of providing each category of HIV-related health services and the extent to which costs were paid by third-party payers, as well as the aggregate amount to be spent on each category of services;

— A plan to organize and deliver HIV health-care and support services funded with the grant money;

— Assurances that the public health agency administering the grant would conduct public hearings concerning the proposed use and distribution of grant funds.

• **Reduced charges for low-income patients.** Required that services be free to people with income below the poverty level. For people with incomes between 100 percent and 200 percent of the poverty level, required that charges for services not exceed 5 percent of their annual gross income. Charges for individuals with incomes between 200 percent and 300 percent of the poverty level could not exceed 7 percent of annual gross income, and charges for those with incomes higher than 300 percent of the poverty level could not exceed 10 percent.

• **Matching funds.** Required that states with an AIDS caseload in excess of 1 percent of the nationwide total for the two preceding years match federal funds with the ratio of state funds to federal funds increasing progressively from 1 to 5 in the first year to 1 to 2 in the fourth and subsequent years.

Non-federal contributions had to be in cash or in-kind, and made directly by the state or through donations from public or private entities.

State expenditures for HIV-related services had to be included in calculating the match, whether or not those funds were being spent for programs to be funded by the grant money.

• **Special projects of national significance.** Required the secretary to set aside up to 10 percent of amounts appropriated for Title II to establish and administer special projects of national significance. Grants were to go to public and nonprofit private entities, including community-based organizations, to fund special programs for the care and treatment of individuals with HIV disease.

— Increase the number of health-care facilities willing and able to serve low-income individuals with HIV disease.

— Deliver drug-abuse treatment and HIV health-care services at a single location.

— Provide support and respite care for participants in family-based care networks critical to the delivery of comprehensive HIV care in the minority community.

— Deliver an enhanced spectrum of comprehensive health and support services to underserved hemophilia populations.

— Deliver HIV health and support services to Indians, the homeless, and those in prison who had HIV disease.

• **State allotments.** Grant funds were to be distributed according to a formula based on each state's number of AIDS cases and average per capita income.

• **State distribution of funds.** In states with 1 percent or more of AIDS cases nationwide, required that at least half of Title II grant funds be used for the creation and operation of comprehensive-care consortia in areas within the state in which the most individuals with HIV disease lived. States also were required to consider the unmet needs of areas not eligible for emergency relief under Title I. States could use up to 5 percent of funds for administration, accounting, reporting and program-oversight functions, but no grant funds could be used for construction or purchase or improvement of land.

• **Expedited distribution.** Required states to distribute at least 75 percent of grant funds within 150 days of receiving them in the first fiscal year and within 120 days in subsequent fiscal years.

Title III — Early Intervention Services

Subtitle 1: Formula Grants

Authorized $230 million for fiscal 1991 and "such sums as may be necessary" for fiscal 1992-95 for grants to states to provide early intervention services for persons with AIDS, persons who tested positive for HIV, and those at increased risk for contracting the virus.

• **Required services.** States had to provide at least the following services:

— Blood testing for exposure to HIV, including pre- and post-test counseling of persons whose blood was being tested. (See counseling requirements, below.)

— Testing to diagnose the extent of immune system deficiency and to provide information on appropriate therapeutic measures to prevent and treat deterioration of the immune system or conditions arising from HIV disease.

— Appropriate therapeutic measures.

— Referrals of individuals who tested positive for HIV to appropriate providers of health and support services.

— Other clinical and diagnostic services, and medical evaluations of persons with HIV disease.

• **Optional services.** States could spend up to 5 percent of their grant funds on hospitals that had treated at least 250 AIDS cases or for which AIDS patients accounted for 20 percent of their caseload for the most recent fiscal year for which data was available.

Hospitals had to agree to offer and encourage early intervention services to inpatients.

States could also use grant funds to:

— Provide outreach services to individuals who might have HIV disease or be at risk for HIV disease and who might be unaware of the availability and potential benefits of early treatment, as well as to health-care professionals who might be unaware of the availability and potential benefits of early intervention treatment.

— Provide case-management to coordinate provision of health-care services and review the extent of utilization of services by patients.

— Provide assistance to individuals to establish eligibility for federal, state or local financial assistance or service programs.

• **State distribution of funds.** States had to spend at least 35 percent of their grant funds for testing, counseling and referrals. Another 35 percent had to be spent on clinical and diagnostic services and treatments.

• **State matching funds.** Required states to provide matching funds for the federal grants in the same proportions as in Title II, above, and with the same stipulations.

• **Offering and encouraging early intervention services.** Required states to require certain health service providers receiving grant funds to agree to offer and encourage early intervention services, to the extent grant funds were adequate.

• **Notification of blood transfusion recipients.** Required states, as a condition of receiving grants, to establish public education and information programs. These programs were to notify persons who received blood transfusions or certain blood products between Jan. 1, 1978, and April 1, 1985, of the availability and need for early intervention services and of health facilities in their area providing such services.

• **Reporting and partner notification.** Required states, as a condition of receiving grants, to provide assurances that entities conducting HIV counseling and testing would report to the state public health officer "information sufficient to perform statistical and epidemiological analyses of the incidence of HIV infection in the state and demographic characteristics of populations who have the disease, and to assess the adequacy of early intervention services in the state."

To receive grants, states also had to require the public health officer to carry out, "to the extent appropriate in the determination of the officer," a program to notify the partners of those with HIV disease.

[Sen. Edward M. Kennedy, D-Mass., the bill's sponsor and author of the amendment adopted on the notification issue, described the provision as leaving it up to the states as to what the procedure would be.]

The act specifically did not require nor prohibit any state from requiring that identifying information concerning individuals with HIV infection be reported to state health authorities, nor did it require states to establish a requirement that anyone other than the state's public health officer perform partner notification.

The act specifically did not mandate nor prohibit any state from requiring that information concerning individuals with HIV infection be reported to state health authorities.

The act also did not require states to establish a requirement that anyone other than the state's public health officer perform partner notification.

• **Laws regarding intentional transmission.** Required states, as a condition of receiving grants, to assure the secretary that the state's criminal laws were adequate to prosecute any person who knew he or she was HIV-infected and who:

— Donated blood, semen or breast milk with the specific intention of exposing another to HIV.

— Engaged in sexual activity with the specific intention of exposing another to HIV.

— Shared a hypodermic needle with another person with the specific intention of having the needle expose that person to HIV infection.

Laws would not be required to apply in cases in which the individual who was subjected to the activity involved knew that the other individual was HIV-infected and provided prior informed consent for the activity.

For fiscal years 1991-92, the secretary could make grants in the absence of such laws if the state provided satisfactory assurances that prohibitions would be in place by Oct. 1, 1992.

[Conferees made clear that most states already had requisite criminal laws that could be applied to intentional HIV transmission and that the provision did not require states to pass new, HIV-specific laws.]

Subtitle 2: Categorical Grants

Authorized $75 million in fiscal 1991, and such sums as necessary in fiscal 1992-95, for grants to be made directly to public and private nonprofit entities that delivered primary health care to help them provide early intervention services on an outpatient basis. Required and optional services to be provided by recipients of these grants would be essentially the same as for the formula grants, above.

• **Participation in consortia.** Required that entities receiving grants make "reasonable efforts" to participate in HIV-care consortia.

• **Eligible recipients.** Defined as eligible to receive categorical grants community and migrant health centers, health centers for the homeless, comprehensive hemophilia diagnostic and treatment centers, family planning, and private nonprofit AIDS health service facilities.

• **Services for hemophiliacs.** Required the secretary, in making grants, to ensure that grants to provide early intervention services for hemophiliacs were made through the network of comprehensive hemophilia diagnostic and treatment centers.

Subtitle 3: General Provisions

• **Confidentiality and informed consent.** Required states, as a condition of receiving grant funds under Title III, to maintain confidentiality for all information regarding preventive health services (including counseling, testing and treatment), in a manner "not inconsistent with any applicable local, state or federal law." Categorical grant recipients had to agree to maintain confidentiality for all information regarding receipt of services in a manner not inconsistent with applicable law. AIDS tests could not be conducted unless the person to be tested had signed a written statement that he or she had received pretest counseling and that the test had been undertaken voluntarily.

Specified that individuals wishing to undergo anonymous testing be permitted to do so to the extent permitted under state law, regulation or rule, and in such a case to use a pseudonym.

• **Counseling.** Required that all grantees providing testing also provide specific counseling services appropriate to the individual being tested and based on the most recently available scientific information. Pretest counseling had to include all of the following:

1) methods of preventing exposure to and transmission of HIV;

2) the accuracy and reliability of AIDS test results;

3) the significance of test results, including the potential for developing AIDS;

4) encouragement, as appropriate, for the individual to undergo testing;

5) benefits of such testing, including the medical benefits of diagnosing HIV disease in its early stages and of receiving early intervention services.

6) laws relating to confidentiality of the process or receiving testing services, including what information would and would not be reported to state public health authorities; and

7) laws relating to discrimination against individuals with HIV disease.

Those who tested negative had to be counseled further regarding items 1 through 3 above, as well as about the appropriateness of further counseling, testing and education.

Post-test counseling for those who tested positive had to include the same requirements as for those who tested negative, as well as information and referrals regarding early intervention services; the benefits of locating and counseling any individual who might have been exposed to HIV by the person who tested positive; and the availability of services of public health officials in locating and counseling any such exposed individuals.

Counseling programs "shall not be designed to promote or

Continued from p. 583

"Ryan White Comprehensive AIDS Resources Emergency Act of 1990." White was an Indiana youth barred from attending school after he contracted AIDS from a blood transfusion. He died April 8 at age 18.

• By Kennedy, by 98-0, to prohibit use of funds in the bill to provide clean needles for intravenous drug users. The vote followed the defeat, by 28-70, of a Helms amendment that would have barred the use of funds for either needles or bleach. Bleach was often used to cleanse needles to prevent transmission of AIDS and other blood-borne diseases. *(Votes 94, 93, p. 22-S)*

• By Kennedy, by 99-0, to condition grant funds on certification that state law made it a criminal offense for anyone who was aware that he or she had AIDS or HIV infection to donate or sell blood or other tissues or fluids. The Senate first rejected, 47-52, a Helms amendment that would have made such activity a federal crime. *(Votes 96, 95, p. 22-S)*

• By Hatch and Kennedy, by voice vote, to authorize $1.5 million for fiscal 1991 and "such sums as necessary" for fiscal 1992-95 for the Food and Drug Administration to hire up to 150 people to inspect blood and blood products.

• By Don Nickles, R-Okla., by voice vote, to extend through 1995 a program to provide federal assistance for states to test convicted sex offenders or users of illegal intravenous drugs in state penal facilities for exposure to HIV. The program originally was authorized in the 1988 AIDS bill.

In addition to the two Helms amendments, members also rejected, by 33-65, an amendment by Malcolm Wallop, R-Wyo., that would have permitted states with fewer than 100 reported cases of AIDS to use grant funds to care for

encourage, directly, intravenous drug abuse or sexual activity, homosexual or heterosexual; shall be designed to reduce exposure to and transmission of HIV disease by providing accurate information; and shall provide information on the health risks of promiscuous sexual activity and intravenous drug abuse."

• **Prohibition against testing as a condition for receiving other services.** Required that recipients of grant funds not require any person to undergo HIV testing as a condition of receiving any health services, unless such testing was medically indicated in the provision of health services that person was seeking.

• **Maintenance of effort.** Required grant recipients to maintain expenditures for early intervention services at a level equal to that spent in the preceding fiscal year.

• **Reduced charges for low-income patients.** Required that services be provided free to individuals with income below the federal poverty threshold. For individuals with incomes between 100 percent and 200 percent of the poverty level, required that charges for services not exceed 5 percent of the individual's annual gross income.

Charges for individuals with incomes between 200 percent and 300 percent of the poverty level could not exceed 7 percent of annual gross income, and charges for those with incomes higher than 300 percent of the poverty level could not exceed 10 percent.

• **Supplies and services in lieu of grant funds.** At the request of the grant recipient, permitted the secretary to provide supplies, equipment or services in lieu of funds, and to detail any officer or employee of the department.

• **Reauthorization of the Prison Testing Act of 1988.** Reauthorized, through fiscal 1995, and revised the program of grants to states to help pay for mandatory HIV testing for individuals incarcerated in state penal facilities.

The new program authorized states to provide appropriate early intervention services. The program would continue to be authorized at "such sums as necessary." [Although this program was first authorized in 1988 as the Prison Testing Act of 1988, part of an omnibus health bill (PL 100-607), it had not been funded as of fiscal 1990. *(1988 Almanac, p. 296)*]

Title IV: General Provisions, Reports and Evaluations

• **Demonstration grants for research and services for infants and children with HIV disease.** Authorized $20 million in fiscal 1991 and "such sums as necessary" for demonstration grants to develop therapeutic drugs and provide services to pediatric AIDS patients.

Grants could go to community health centers and other public or private nonprofit entities providing primary health care to significant numbers of HIV-infected children or pregnant women. Funds were to be used to conduct clinical research on therapies for pediatric HIV patients and provide outpatient health care for such patients and their families. Entities that received grants had to establish cooperative agreements with biomedical research establishments to assist in the design and conduct of the research protocol.

• **Blood banks.** Authorized $1.5 million in fiscal 1991 and "such sums as necessary" in each of fiscal 1992-95 for the secretary to develop and make available to personnel in blood banks and blood products production facilities materials and information on diagnostic, testing, and quality assurance procedures to protect the safety of the blood supply. Also required the secretary to develop and implement a training program to increase the number of HHS employees qualified to inspect blood banks and facilities that produced blood products.

• **Research, evaluation, and assessment program.** Authorized "such sums as necessary" for fiscal 1991-95 for the HHS Agency for Health Care Policy and Research to conduct research comparing the impact and cost-effectiveness of major models for organizing and delivering HIV-related health care, mental health care, early intervention, and support services. The agency was also charged with conducting a review of private-sector financing for the delivery of HIV-related health and support services, an assessment of strategies for maintaining private health insurance benefits for those with HIV disease, and an assessment of specific business practices or regulatory barriers that reduced access to private-sector benefits programs.

Findings were required to be included in a report to applicable congressional committees within two years after enactment.

• **Partner-notification study.** Required the secretary to study and report within one year on programs to notify the partners of those who tested positive for HIV. The study had to determine how many individuals who were notified of possible exposure underwent counseling and testing as a result; the number of those who were tested and who tested positive; the extent to which such programs had resulted in behavior changes that would help prevent exposure to and transmission of HIV; and the extent to which such programs represented a cost-effective use of HIV-related resources.

• **Study of HIV disease in rural areas.** Authorized "such sums as necessary" and required the secretary to study and report within one year on the incidence and prevalence of AIDS and HIV in rural areas and to assess the adequacy of services for diagnosis and early intervention in rural areas.

• **Prohibition on use of funds for hypodermic needles or syringes.** Prohibited the use of funds authorized under any title of the act to provide anyone with hypodermic needles or syringes so that such person might use illegal drugs.

Subtitle B: Emergency Response Employees

• **Grants for putting emergency-worker protection guidelines into effect.** Authorized $5 million in each of fiscal 1991-95 for grants to states to put into effect recommendations (whose development was required by provisions of PL 100-607) for protecting police officers, firefighters, paramedics and other emergency workers from exposure to HIV.

• **Notification requirements.** Required that medical facilities routinely inform emergency workers (in most cases not later than 48 hours after a determination was made) if a patient they transported had an airborne infectious disease; created a system to notify emergency response employees who might have been exposed to any infectious disease. ■

people with other chronic diseases. *(Vote 92, p. 22-S)*

HOUSE ACTION

On May 3, the House Energy and Commerce Subcommittee on Health and the Environment approved its version of an AIDS-relief bill (HR 4470). The measure authorized $500 million annually in fiscal 1991-95 for grants to provide AIDS-prevention services, including confidential testing and counseling.

A new title paralleled the Senate legislation by authorizing $300 million annually in fiscal 1991-92 and "such sums as necessary" thereafter for areas hardest hit.

The legislation also authorized $30 million for fiscal 1991 and "such sums as necessary" through fiscal 1995 for demonstration projects to provide comprehensive treatment services for those with AIDS or HIV, and the same amounts to help states pay for AIDS drugs for the poor.

The subcommittee dropped provisions that would have permitted states to provide special benefits to those with AIDS or HIV through the state-federal Medicaid program.

Just as they did two years earlier, members spent much of the markup debating restrictive amendments offered by Dannemeyer.

Dannemeyer was successful, as he was in 1988, in attaching a requirement that states, in order to receive grant funds, make knowing transmission of AIDS or HIV a crime.

But he was unsuccessful — just as he had been in 1988 — with amendments that would have required hospitals to offer AIDS tests routinely to patients, required states to encourage testing of marriage license applicants in high-risk areas, mandated testing of prisoners, struck requirements that informed consent for AIDS tests be in writing, and ordered states to require that positive test results be reported to state health authorities.

Full Committee

On May 15, the full committee by voice vote approved HR 4785 — a clean version of HR 4470 — to authorize more than $1.6 billion for fiscal 1991-92. The measure also explicitly authorized funds for confidential AIDS testing and counseling.

In contrast to the Senate debate a month earlier and some of its own prior experiences considering legislation to address AIDS, Energy and Commerce's markup was relatively tame.

As it had done in the past, the committee rejected an amendment by Dannemeyer to require states to report to public health authorities names or other identifying information of those who tested positive for HIV.

Among amendments the panel approved was one by ranking Republican Norman F. Lent, N.Y., to authorize $20 million for fiscal 1991 and "such sums as necessary" for fiscal 1992-95 for demonstration grants to address the needs of children with AIDS.

Although AIDS was projected to become the fifth leading cause of death for children in the 1990s, Lent said, "research and services for children with AIDS have lagged behind those of adults."

Other amendments adopted included the following:

- By Dannemeyer, by voice vote, to authorize "such sums as necessary" in fiscal 1991-95 for grants to permit hospitals that treated more than 250 AIDS patients per year to provide voluntary AIDS blood tests.
- By Dannemeyer, by voice vote, to require grantees to report the number of patients treated with grant funds, as well as epidemiological and demographic data about them. The amendment also required the Department of Health and Human Services to study and report the extent to which state partner-notification programs had resulted in behavioral changes that stemmed the spread of the virus.

Floor Debate

The House passed HR 4785 on June 13 by a vote of 408-14. Members immediately substituted the text of their measure for that of S 2240 and asked for a conference. *(Vote 168, p. 58-H)*

The differences in funding levels and approaches to certain programs set the stage for a conference.

The House bill authorized $275 million annually for fiscal 1991 and 1992 in aid to cities with major AIDS crises; the Senate bill authorized $300 million each year. Both authorized "such sums as necessary" through fiscal 1995.

Both bills required that half of the funds, to be distributed according to a formula, be made available quickly. The House bill required disbursement of the funds within 90 days of when appropriations became available; the Senate bill required distribution within 60 days. Both bills required the remainder of the emergency funds to be made available within five months. The money would be dispensed upon application from the cities.

From there, however, the bills diverged markedly. While the Senate version authorized millions of dollars for block grants to states, the House measure envisioned several different programs.

The largest authorized $400 million annually in fiscal 1991-95 to pay for preventive services for people with AIDS or HIV. Among other things, the funds could be used for confidential AIDS blood testing and counseling. They could also pay for drugs such as AZT, which slowed the course of the disease, and for other medical services for those who tested positive for HIV but were not yet ill.

Other major provisions of the House-passed bill:

- Authorized $50 million in fiscal 1991 and "such sums as necessary" in fiscal 1992-95 for demonstration projects to provide comprehensive treatment services to people with AIDS or HIV.
- Authorized $30 million annually in fiscal 1991-95 for grants to states to help pay for AZT and other drugs to fight AIDS and medical complications from the infection.
- Authorized $20 million in fiscal 1991 and "such sums" in fiscal 1992-95 for demonstration projects to develop treatments for and provide services to children with AIDS or HIV.
- Authorized $5 million per year in fiscal 1991-95 for grants to help state and local governments put into effect guidelines to shield emergency-response workers from exposure to HIV in the course of their duties.

Members rejected proposals by Republicans to mandate AIDS blood testing for all Americans and to require states to collect names of those who tested positive for HIV. Both issues were also raised during consideration of the 1988 bill.

First, by voice vote, the House rejected an amendment by Dan Burton, R-Ind., requiring universal annual blood testing for AIDS. "In my view we will have testing," Burton said. "The only question is do we wait until we have 20 to 30 million people dead or dying . . . or do we do it now?"

But opponents argued that such testing, which the Centers for Disease Control estimated would cost more than $11 billion, would be unnecessary and potentially counterproductive. Bill Green, R-N.Y., said groups at low risk for AIDS had a high rate of false-positive test results.

"When you test everyone, you get more than four times as many false positives as true positives," Green said. "That is an absurd way to spend your money trying to fight AIDS."

More contentious was a perennial amendment by Dannemeyer that would have required that the names and addresses of those who tested positive for HIV be reported to state health officials.

Despite the rejection of his amendment in subcommittee and full committee, Dannemeyer pressed on. "I happen to believe as a matter of principle that the civil rights of the uninfected take precedence over the civil rights of the infected," he said.

Some said the issue of whether to identify those who tested positive should be left to the states. Others said that mandatory reporting of names would frighten away from being tested those at risk for contracting HIV.

Members ultimately approved, 312-113, a substitute by J. Roy Rowland, D-Ga., that left to the states the choice of whether to require name reporting. Then they approved Dannemeyer's amendment, as amended, by a vote of 422-1. *(Votes 166, 167, p. 58-H)*

Members also adopted two amendments, both by voice vote.

They were:

- By Lent, to increase from $30 million to $50 million the fiscal 1991 authorization for the comprehensive care demonstration projects, and to include among projects that could be funded those to children with AIDS or HIV.
- By Edward Madigan, R-Ill., to reduce the authorization for preventive services grants from $500 million to $400 million per year; to reduce the authorization for

emergency grants from $300 million to $275 million per year; and to require state matching payments for the preventive service and drug grant programs as well as sliding-scale fees from patients for services provided under the bill.

CONFERENCE AGREEMENT

House passage of the AIDS bill sent the legislation to conference, where negotiators expected to have little difficulty resolving their differences. However, they faced the task of making the bill more palatable to the administration, which expressed opposition to both versions.

"The bill's narrow, disease-specific approach sets a dangerous precedent, inviting treatment of other diseases through similar ad hoc arrangements," said an official statement of administration policy.

Congressional sponsors of the bill stood firm. "There's an epidemic out there," said Waxman, chairman of the House Energy and Commerce Subcommittee on Health and the Environment. "We need specific provisions."

Said Susan Molinari, R-N.Y., in response to the White House complaint about disease-specific bills, "We responded as a nation ... to the polio epidemic, and we contribute on an annual basis to research and preventive measures for cancer. We can no longer ignore this national tragedy."

Conferees completed work on the AIDS bill the week of July 30. Negotiators combined the chambers' bills instead of splitting the differences. "I think we merged the bills in a way satisfactory to both houses," said Waxman.

In authorizing funds for hard-hit metropolitan areas, conferees went with the House bill's total of $275 million.

Cities were to use the emergency funds to increase and improve outpatient services for low-income AIDS patients and their families, hire and train health and support personnel, and expedite the provision of medical care.

Conferees also opted for the House provision in requiring half the emergency funds to be distributed within 90 days of when appropriations became available, with the other half to be allocated on the basis of applications from the cities. The compromise also included the Senate block grant program for states and the House initiative to provide funding for early intervention services. ■

Disabilities Prevention Bill

The House on July 23 passed by voice vote a bill (HR 4039) aimed at combating disability by formally authorizing an existing program within the Centers for Disease Control (CDC) that sought to reduce the incidence of disability in the general population and to prevent further impairment in the disabled.

The bill was never considered by the Senate. A similar Senate bill (S 2153) was referred to the Senate Labor and Human Resources Committee, which did not take action on the legislation.

The House bill would have authorized, over three years, $10 million for fiscal 1991, with the level rising to $20 million in fiscal 1993.

The CDC could have used the funds to coordinate existing programs, conduct demonstration programs, and educate the public and health professionals about preventing disability. ■

Nursing Home Regulations Modified

Congress responded to complaints by states and the nursing home industry about delays in promulgating regulations to implement the 1987 nursing home reform law by limiting financial penalties against states that had made good-faith efforts to comply prior to the issuance of two principal sets of rules in May 1989.

The provisions were rolled into the fiscal 1991 budget reconciliation bill (HR 5835 — PL 101-508). *(Budget reconciliation, p. 138; provisions: Nursing Home Reform Amendments, p. 148)*

The 1987 law, part of that year's omnibus budget-reconciliation act (PL 100-203), tightened regulation of nursing homes certified to participate in the Medicare and Medicaid programs.

Among other things, the law imposed training requirements for nurses' aides, mandated pre-admission screening to guard against "inappropriate" placement of patients in facilities not equipped to provide needed care, and required annual review of nursing home residents to devise individual plans for care. *(1987 Almanac, p. 540)*

But the Department of Health and Human Services (HHS) and its Health Care Financing Administration (HCFA) had been slow to issue rules implementing the law. As a result, Congress delayed some of the act's deadlines and altered some of its requirements in the 1989 budget-reconciliation act (PL 101-239). *(1989 Almanac, p. 100)*

States, through the National Governors' Association, continued to complain in 1990 about the high costs of complying with the act, the limited flexibility allowed the states, and the uncertainty resulting from delays in writing guidelines.

The provisions rolled into the 1990 budget-reconciliation act responded to those complaints by barring compliance actions — chiefly, reduced aid under Medicare or Medicaid — against states that had made good-faith attempts to comply with the nurses' aide training and pre-admission screening provisions prior to HCFA's issuance of regulations in May 1989.

States were similarly protected against compliance actions regarding their enforcement of the act until the HCFA published rules on the issue.

The amendments also extended through Oct. 1, 1990, a provision for 90 percent reimbursement (rather than 50 percent) of the cost of nurses' aide training; the enhanced matching rate had expired July 1. The governors' group, however, had asked for the higher match to be extended through Oct. 1, 1991.

In addition, the provisions modified the definition of mental illness to target pre-admission screening rules on patients with serious disorders and extended from four to 14 days the time for a nursing home to complete the initial assessment of a newly admitted resident. ■

Radiation Victims Given Compensation

Congress on Sept. 27 voted to compensate the forgotten victims of the Cold War — Americans who developed cancer because they lived downwind from open-air nuclear tests in the 1950s or mined the uranium used in nuclear weapons.

By voice vote, the House sent to President Bush a bill (HR 2372 — PL 101-426) authorizing compensation of $50,000 per person for fallout victims in three Western states and $100,000 per person for uranium miners in five states who developed cancer or respiratory diseases. Family members could collect compensation for those who had died of radiation-induced illnesses.

The money would come from a $100 million special Radiation Exposure Trust Fund authorized under the bill.

"The downwinders are no different from the veterans of World War II, Korea or Vietnam — they are veterans of the Cold War," said Rep. James Bilbray, D-Nev.

Despite voicing early reservations about the measure, Bush signed it Oct. 15. "These payments fairly resolve the claims of persons present at the test site and of downwind residents, as well as claims of uranium miners," Bush said in a statement.

The legislation was approved by the House on June 5. The Senate subsequently approved its bill by voice vote in the early hours of Aug. 2 (session of Aug. 1). The House vote Sept. 27 cleared the measure for the president's signature.

The "downwinders" eligible for compensation under the legislation included people who lived in specified counties of Nevada, Utah and Arizona for at least two years in the period from Jan. 21, 1951, to Oct. 31, 1958, or during July 1962. Those were periods when the United States conducted above-ground nuclear tests in Nevada without warning the civilian population about the known dangers of radioactive fallout.

Eligible miners, many of them Navajo Indians, included those who worked in uranium mines in Colorado, New Mexico, Arizona, Wyoming or Utah any time between Jan. 1, 1947, and Dec. 31, 1971, and who were exposed to unsafe levels of radiation.

BACKGROUND

The radiation compensation issue had been before Congress for more than a decade. Passage of HR 2372 marked the third time the government offered compensation to victims of the government's own atomic weapons program.

In 1954, the United States conducted a nuclear test in the South Pacific that contaminated the Marshall Islands. The United States paid $2 million to the families of fishermen whose catches were affected. In 1985, Congress passed legislation (PL 99-239) establishing a $150 million trust fund to compensate residents of the Marshall Islands whose homes were destroyed and whose health was impaired by tests in the South Pacific in the 1950s. *(1985 Almanac, p. 99)*

Approval of the downwinders legislation also marked the second time in recent years that Congress ordered restitution to Americans wronged in the name of national security.

In 1988, lawmakers authorized $1.25 billion to provide compensation of $20,000 per person to Japanese-Americans interned during World War II. *(1988 Almanac, p. 80)*

With the discovery of high incidences of cancer in the Western test regions during the 1970s, a number of individuals unsuccessfully sued the government. Former Interior Secretary Stewart L. Udall and bill sponsor Rep. Wayne Owens, D-Utah, were among more than a dozen attorneys who represented them.

Udall, who had spent 12 years representing the Navajos, said the Public Health Service "used the miners as guinea pigs to study the effects of radiation" but did not warn them of the danger.

From 350 to 500 miners or their survivors would be eligible for compensation under the bill, according to an aide to Sen. Orrin G. Hatch, R-Utah. About 17 percent were Navajo Indians. From 900 to 1,100 downwinders would be eligible, the aide said.

(The Office of Management and Budget said that under the House bill, 250 to 450 miners and 600 to 800 downwinders would have been eligible for compensation.)

Owens, who said his brother-in-law had died from cancer linked to radiation exposure, said the government should be held accountable because it purposely neglected to tell people of the dangers of radiation exposure. The policy led to "the death of hundreds of Americans who trusted their government," he said.

"The case of the Navajo uranium miners is one of egregious government malfeasance," Udall said, because of the federal government's "special trust relationship with respect to Indian tribes."

During Senate debate, Hatch said victims had tried to obtain relief through the courts but to no avail. Although the courts often agreed that the government was responsible, most decided in its favor under the federal doctrine of "sovereign immunity," under which the government could not be held liable for its policies.

In 1985, the 9th U.S. Circuit Court of Appeals said, "This is the type of case that cries out for redress, but the courts are not able to give it. Congress is the appropriate source."

ACTION BY CONGRESS

A key reason for Congress' failure to act, Hatch said, had been steadfast opposition from both Democratic and Republican administrations. The Bush administration opposed both the House and Senate bills, and officials said early in the process that they would advise the president to veto the legislation.

Hatch said the Bush administration, like those before it, "doesn't want any precedents set, but that's not the moral high ground position. I just want justice done."

The Justice Department argued in a March letter to House Judiciary Committee Chairman Jack Brooks, D-Texas, that no scientific evidence proved that the illnesses suffered by miners and downwinders were the result of radiation exposure from the government's nuclear weapons program. It also said the legislation would pay workers who could otherwise file for worker's compensation.

The Justice and Energy departments finally backed away from positions they had held for more than a decade. They had previously opposed congressional plans to compensate nuclear weapons industry workers or their families. However, after HR 2372 cleared Congress, they decided it would be cheaper to have the compensation fund than to pay injury and liability claims directed by the courts.

Committee Action

The Senate Labor and Human Resources Committee approved its version of the bill (S 2466 — S Rept 101-264) on Feb. 28 by voice vote.

The Senate bill was modeled on the compensation system created in 1986 for families of children injured or killed as a result of adverse reactions to vaccines to prevent childhood diseases. It required the Department of Health and Human Services (HHS) to administer the program. *(1986 Almanac, p. 238)*

Eligibility for the awards would be determined by "special masters" of the U.S. Court of Claims, who would be charged with determining whether a claimant lived or worked in the specified area for a specified period of time, and contracted one of the cancers, set forth in the bill, that had the highest probability of having been caused by exposure to low levels of ionizing radiation. That list included cancers of the thyroid, lung, breast (in women), stomach, colon and esophagus.

Hatch first drafted the bill to give the attorney general jurisdiction over the program. But Alan K. Simpson, R-Wyo., and other Republican opponents bottled it up in the Judiciary Committee. Hatch then rewrote the bill with the HHS provision so that it would go to the Labor and Human Resources Committee.

Simpson opposed the downwinder provision, according to a spokesman, because "the whole world" could claim to be downwind of the test sites. Simpson said the bill should compensate those who proved their cases in court.

Simpson, in a letter to Hatch, also asked the Utah senator to include affected Wyoming residents since Wyoming had also been a site of uranium mining.

The House Judiciary Committee meanwhile approved HR 2372, 27-6, on March 28 (H Rept 101-463). A recorded vote was taken at the insistence of William E. Dannemeyer, R-Calif., who objected to the cost of the compensation fund.

The bill had been approved Feb. 7 by the Subcommittee on Administrative Law and Governmental Relations.

Under the House version of HR 2372, the attorney general, in consultation with the surgeon general, was to set up guidelines to determine what medical proof was necessary to claim compensation. The provisions of the bill were similar to those Congress established in 1988 for the program compensating the Japanese-American internees.

Floor Action

The House passed HR 2372 on June 5. The Senate followed suit on Aug. 2 (session of Aug. 1) after accepting an amendment that brought the bill into line with the House approach.

At the request of Craig Thomas, R-Wyo., supporters of the bill agreed to ask that Wyoming residents be included in the bill during the conference with the Senate — echoing Simpson's request in the Senate. The final version of the bill did include Wyoming.

When the legislation finally passed, floor manager Barney Frank, D-Mass., was especially pleased that the bill contained an apology to the victims "to the individuals . . . and their families for the hardships they have endured."

"This is an example of something we do from time to time, and I think it is something of which we should be proud," said Frank. "We admit mistakes." ■

Childhood Vaccine Programs Reauthorized

The House on Oct. 15 cleared legislation to reauthorize the federal program that helped pay for childhood vaccines and to alter a 1986 law providing compensation to families of children injured or killed as a result of adverse vaccine reactions.

The House by voice vote approved a compromise version of HR 4238, which the Senate had approved by voice vote late Oct. 12. The House originally passed the bill July 23. President Bush signed the measure (PL 101-502) on Nov. 3.

The legislation authorized $205 million in fiscal 1991 and "such sums as necessary" for fiscal 1992-95 for the Centers for Disease Control (CDC) program that paid for vaccines. The amount was intended to pay for a double dose of measles vaccine recommended by health officials, as well as to operate outreach programs to find children who were not being immunized against significant preventable childhood diseases.

The measure also authorized an additional $5 million in fiscal 1991 and "such sums" in fiscal 1992-93 to acquire and maintain a six-month supply of vaccine and $30 million in fiscal 1991 for the National Vaccine Program, which coordinated federal research, licensing and distribution of vaccines.

Finally, the measure extended by four months the deadline to apply for benefits under the vaccine compensation program — originally Oct. 1, 1990 — for families of children injured or killed by adverse vaccine reactions prior to enactment Oct. 1, 1988.

Sen. Edward M. Kennedy, D-Mass., noted that the Department of Health and Human Services (HHS) did not even publicize the existence of the program until July 1990.

"With the deadline for filing pre-act claims having expired Oct. 1, 1990, families just learning about the program this summer had little time to put together the documentation necessary for filing a complete claim," Kennedy said. "The extension will enable these families to have full access to the program."

Legislative Action

The House approved HR 4238 by voice vote July 23. The bill, sponsored by Henry A. Waxman, D-Calif., chairman of the Energy and Commerce Health Subcommittee, extended the federal Childhood Immunization Program and the National Vaccine Program through fiscal 1995 and authorized funds for maintaining a six-month vaccine stockpile.

It authorized $185 million for the Childhood Immunization Program in fiscal 1991, $34 million for the National Vaccine Program and $5 million for the stockpile.

The Energy and Commerce Committee had approved HR 4238 on May 15.

The Senate Labor and Human Resources Committee had approved companion legislation (S 2629) on May 16 to authorize $200 million in fiscal 1991 to pay for immunizations for preventable diseases, as well as "such sums as necessary" each year for fiscal 1992-95.

Congress appropriated $133.2 million for the program for fiscal 1990, which health officials said was not enough to meet existing needs, particularly given recurrent outbreaks of measles over the past year. The extra money could pay for a second measles shot for middle-school-age children, as health authorities recommended in the fall of 1989.

Both measures also authorized $34 million in fiscal 1991 and "such sums" through fiscal 1995 for the National Vaccine Program, which coordinated federal research, licensing and distribution of vaccines.

The Labor-HHS spending bill appropriated $182 million in CDC grants for immunization programs, $2.9 million for the stockpile and $9.8 million for the National Vaccine Program. *(Labor-HHS appropriations, p. 847)* ■

Antismoking Bills Fail To Reach Floor

House and Senate panels in 1990, over the objections of the powerful tobacco industry, approved omnibus antismoking bills. Though the measures did not reach the floor of either chamber, the progress during the session boosted the hopes of backers of stronger tobacco restrictions.

The Senate Labor and Human Resources Committee on May 16 approved a bill to authorize $110 million in fiscal 1991 to publicize the health risks of tobacco.

Among other things, the measure would have created a Center for Tobacco Products in the Department of Health and Human Services (HHS) to administer a $50 million-a-year information program featuring public service and paid advertisements that would point out the dangers of using tobacco.

The House Energy and Commerce Subcommittee on Health and the Environment on Sept. 11 approved legislation (HR 5041) to impose new restrictions on cigarette promotion.

HR 5041 would have banned most cigarette sales by vending machine, ended public distribution of free tobacco samples, and forbidden the sale of candy and gum in packages designed to resemble tobacco products.

The original version introduced by subcommittee Chairman Henry A. Waxman, D-Calif., included a ban on tobacco company sponsorship of sports and entertainment events and would have permitted print advertisements only in what was known as the "tombstone" format — black and white print with no photographs or graphics allowed.

The substitute measure dropped the controversial advertising and promotion provisions.

The antismoking lobby also took the offensive against the tobacco industry on another issue: efforts to open up markets for U.S. tobacco products abroad.

Antismoking forces acted after the tobacco industry, with the support of the Bush administration, sought to break down trade barriers against U.S. cigarettes and other tobacco products, especially in Asian countries.

No legislation passed on the topic in 1990, however.

Meanwhile, Congress did enact an 8 cents per pack increase by 1993 in the cigarette excise tax as part of the deficit-reduction bill (HR 5835 — PL 101-508).

But the increased tax was principally aimed at raising revenue, not decreasing consumption. *(New taxes, p. 167)*

In addition, Congress enacted legislation (HR 293 — PL 101-352) directing the Consumer Product Safety Commission (CPSC) to supervise a study of cigarette safety and the technical feasibility of devising self-extinguishing cigarettes. *(Fire-safe cigarettes, p. 402)*

BACKGROUND

In previous years, tobacco companies had supported compromise antismoking initiatives in Congress, such as barring television advertisements and requiring health warning labels, as a means of fending off restrictions that the industry considered more extreme. *(Warning labels, 1984 Almanac, p. 478; 1965 Almanac, p. 344; broadcast commercials ban, 1970 Almanac, p. 145)*

Growing public awareness of the health risks of smoking as well as a greater willingness on the part of non-smokers to assert their "right" not to have to breathe unhealthful air persuaded some key members to consider stricter rules on smoking and tobacco promotion in the late 1980s.

A major victory was declared when Congress cleared a transportation spending package for fiscal 1988 that included a two-year ban on smoking on domestic flights scheduled to last no more than two hours. Pro-ban forces defeated a last-ditch effort by the tobacco industry and tobacco-state lawmakers to kill the proposals in conference. *(1987 Almanac, p. 438)*

Congress had begun warming up for a repeat of the bitter 1987 fight between the tobacco and health interests as the two-year ban neared expiration. The House Public Works and Transportation Committee in 1989 approved a permanent ban on smoking on flights of two hours or less. Proponents of a tougher ban had lined up in support of a weaker, temporary proposal; tobacco interests realized a temporary ban would give antismoking advocates an opportunity to come at them again.

The antismoking forces gained considerable ground when the House-Senate appropriations conference on Oct. 16, 1989, included a permanent smoking ban on all but a handful of U.S. airline flights in the 1990 transportation spending bill that was eventually signed into law (HR 3015 — PL 101-164). Opponents of the ban did manage to exempt flights to Alaska and Hawaii. But conferees added report language urging airlines to be mindful of the health of attendants on the few remaining flights where smoking was permitted. *(1989 Almanac, p. 749)*

Administration's Stance

The antitobacco groups had gained considerable clout on Capitol Hill by 1990, but they received mixed signals from the administration.

HHS Secretary Louis W. Sullivan had levied strongly worded, highly publicized attacks on smoking and the tobacco industry.

But Sullivan had repeatedly declined to endorse federal action to reduce tobacco consumption at home or abroad. He would not endorse any of the major bills before Congress decided to accomplish that objective.

"He's a perfect fit for this administration," said Matthew Myers of the Coalition on Smoking OR Health, comprising the American Lung Association, the American Heart Association and the American Cancer Society. "He says we've got a big problem out there, and somebody else should solve it."

Sullivan unveiled his department's weapon in its war on smoking — a proposed model law for the states.

The model law would require licensing of retail establishments that sold tobacco products and a phaseout of vending machine sales of cigarettes, except in bars or other establishments where minors were not allowed.

Sen. Edward M. Kennedy, D-Mass., chairman of the Labor and Human Resources Committee, called Sullivan's plan "halfhearted."

"The White House tactic of paying lip service to important national goals while rejecting federal action is irresponsible," said Kennedy.

Pushing Tobacco Overseas

Even as tobacco lost its luster — and many of its customers — at home, it found a growing market overseas, particularly among Third World countries. Sales in Thailand were increasing by about 8 percent a year, and South Korea was close behind at 7 percent.

Tobacco played a growing role in U.S. trade: In 1989, exports of tobacco leaf and cigarettes contributed more than $1 billion to the U.S.-Japanese trade balance.

The industry "has got to go overseas," said Rep. Chester G. Atkins, D-Mass. "That's the main source of their profits now."

Antismoking advocates predicted continued leaps in cigarette exports, and they pointed to the government's promotion activities abroad as a principal cause. For example, during the Reagan administration, U.S. Trade Representative Clayton Yeutter won the right to advertise U.S. cigarettes in Korean and Taiwanese publications without the surgeon general's health warning, even though those countries had almost total bans on cigarette advertising.

Tobacco lobbyists said cigarette exports were a trade issue, not a health concern. "It's not as if cigarettes don't exist there," said Brennan Dawson, spokeswoman for the Tobacco Institute, the industry's Washington outpost.

"To call it a trade issue and not a health issue is a copout," former Surgeon General C. Everett Koop said May 21.

"That's using the same kind of doublespeak that the tobacco companies use."

Even members who had not been associated with the antismoking cause had begun attacking the administration's mixed position.

"I'm concerned that what I'm hearing from the administration is an attempt in fact to have it both ways," Sen. John B. Breaux, D-La., said at a Finance Committee hearing on May 24. "We have a Department of Agriculture which aggressively supports and defends a price-support program for tobacco products; we have trade representatives who have fought for the right to advertise tobacco products in other countries which were prohibiting our advertising those products.... It seems like we ought to get a consistent policy."

LEGISLATIVE ACTION

Senate and House panels broke ground in 1990 with tough new affronts to the tobacco lobby. While the House Energy and Commerce Subcommittee on Health and the Environment looked to curb cigarette promotion, the Senate Labor and Human Resources Committee considered more educational efforts on the dangers of smoking.

Senate

The Senate Labor Committee, chaired by Kennedy, fired the year's first legislative shot in the stepped-up war on smoking, approving on May 16 the measure to authorize $110 million in fiscal 1991 to publicize the health risks of tobacco.

The measure, a clean version of S 1883, was approved 10-4 and would have created the Center for Tobacco Products to publicize the dangers of tobacco.

The bill also would have required public disclosure of additives in cigarettes and would have authorized the HHS secretary to restrict additives that increased health risks. And it would have authorized grants to states, schools and public health organizations to reduce tobacco use.

Although Sullivan had been outspoken in opposing tobacco use, the administration officially opposed the bill. Sullivan told the committee Feb. 20: "We do not believe ... that the additional authorizations and requirements contained in S 1883 would measurably add to our current or planned efforts." Others opposed the legislation on budget grounds.

"When we have a whole series of public interest groups raising funds and sponsoring ads, it seems to me, when federal dollars are so squeezed, there are other areas where we can put our emphasis that would be more important," said Sen. Daniel R. Coats, R-Ind.

But Kennedy, the bill's sponsor, was vehement about the need for the measure. "This addresses something that is public health enemy No. 1," he said.

He called the proposal "an extremely modest program," noting that the authorization had already been reduced to $110 million from $185 million and that several provisions were dropped to avoid jurisdictional poaching.

Among those provisions were proposals to repeal a federal pre-emption on states' regulating tobacco advertising and to add a new label to cigarette packages warning that smoking was addictive.

House

The House Energy and Commerce Health Subcommittee approved HR 5041 on Sept. 11. The markup was the first time any Energy and Commerce subcommittee approved a major antitobacco measure over the objections of the tobacco industry.

Among other things, HR 5041 would have ended most cigarette vending machine sales, barred distribution of free tobacco samples in public, and banned the sale of candy and gum in packages resembling tobacco products.

The measure was watered down substantially during the markup from the original version introduced by subcommittee Chairman Waxman. His original bill included a ban on tobacco company sponsorship of sports and entertainment events and would have permitted only tombstone print advertisements.

The substitute measure, sponsored by Bob Whittaker, R-Kan., and adopted by the subcommittee by voice vote, dropped the controversial advertising and promotion provisions.

But what was left was still too much for the tobacco industry. "We're pleased that the advertising restrictions were taken out, but we are still opposed to many of the provisions of the bill," said Dawson of the Tobacco Institute. "It's better, but still not something we like."

Waxman and the leading proponent of the advertising and promotion restrictions, Mike Synar, D-Okla., finally lined up behind the Whittaker substitute in an effort to defuse the controversy over what had been by far the most contested portion of the bill.

Although Whittaker said he continued to support advertising and promotion restrictions, he said dropping them was "pragmatic." Even without the advertising and promotion restrictions, the subcommittee's bill was one of the most sweeping antitobacco bills ever.

Among other things, the substitute also would have:

- Required new, shorter warning labels on tobacco products and print ads, including billboards. The shorter labels were designed to drive home more forcefully the dangers of tobacco use.
- Enhanced the visibility of the cigarette labels by requiring the words "Surgeon General's Warning" to be printed in red and requiring the warnings to be large enough to cover an entire side of the product's package.
- Required states, as a condition of receipt of funds under the federal Alcohol, Drug Abuse, and Mental Health block grant program, to make it illegal for anyone under age 18 to purchase or possess any tobacco product.
- Barred tobacco product ads within 750 feet of elementary or secondary schools, churches or hospitals.
- Prohibited the paid placement of tobacco products or their trademarks in movies, television shows, plays or video arcade games. Tobacco ads would also be barred from appearing before movies or on rented videotapes.
- Required the HHS secretary to issue guidelines for the advertisement of tobacco products as "low tar" or "low nicotine."

In an important test vote, members by a 13-9 vote approved an amendment to strike advertising restrictions from the underlying Waxman bill. The amendment was offered despite the fact that both Waxman and Synar had said they planned to vote for the Whittaker substitute — a vote that would have wiped out the restrictions anyway.

Synar failed to add to the Whittaker substitute his fallback position: codifying the tobacco industry's own advertising guidelines. Among other things, the guidelines stipulated that ads not picture people who were or appeared to be under age 25, nor show people smoking during or directly after strenuous exercise.

"It doesn't take a rocket scientist . . . to figure out this industry does not meet its own code of ethics," said Synar, who held up clippings of magazine ads he said obviously violated the guidelines.

But other members said the difficulty of enforcing the code would make the amendment more unwieldy than even an outright ban. "You're setting up the Federal Trade Commission as some giant censor in the sky," said Tom Tauke, R-Iowa.

Cigarette Exports, Taxes

Using U.S. trade leverage to promote cigarette sales overseas was under growing attack throughout the year, even within the administration. On April 5, James O. Mason, assistant secretary for health at HHS, criticized the policy, saying cigarette companies "play our free-trade laws and export policies like a Stradivarius violin."

Reps. Mel Levine, D-Calif., and Atkins introduced legislation (HR 1249) to require the same health warnings on exported tobacco products as required on cigarettes sold in the United States.

The idea, antismoking lawmakers said, was to force the government to bring federal policy in line with the indisputable health toll of tobacco — regardless of the economic price. "For too long, there has been a conspiracy of silence among people in government," Kennedy said. "Certainly, public outrage is far ahead of federal policy." Supporters of the legislation, though, failed to move it during the session.

Meanwhile, when the Senate finally cleared the massive budget-reconciliation bill just after dusk Oct. 27, it included a substantial levy on tobacco products. The bill increased excise taxes on cigarettes, cigarette papers, cigarette tubes, chewing tobacco, snuff and pipe tobacco by 25 percent on Jan. 1, 1991, and the identical dollar amount on Jan. 1, 1993. For smokers, the additional tax translated into an extra 4 cents on a pack of 20 cigarettes in 1991, rising to 8 cents, or a total of 24 cents tax, two years later. ■

TB Prevention Program

The Senate on Aug. 4 cleared a bill to extend the Centers for Disease Control (CDC) program of grants for health services to prevent tuberculosis. The House had passed the bill on June 18. President Bush signed the measure (HR 4273 — PL 101-368) on Aug. 15.

The Energy and Commerce Committee approved the bill (H Rept 101-542) on May 16, the same day the Senate Labor and Human Resources Committee approved a similar measure (S 2630).

The bill authorized $36 million in fiscal 1991 and "such sums as necessary" for fiscal 1992-95, and established an advisory council to provide advice and recommendations on eliminating tuberculosis (TB), which health officials reported was on the rise in the United States.

The CDC program aimed to eliminate the disease, which afflicted 20,000 Americans and killed 2,000 a year, by 2010.

An estimated 10 million Americans were infected with TB, which killed about half of its victims within two years if untreated, according to Senate bill sponsor Edward M. Kennedy, D-Mass., chairman of the Senate Labor and Human Resources Committee.

TB rates remained high, he said, in part because of its occurrence among AIDS victims. It also hit low-income, medically underserved individuals, especially the elderly, children, minorities and foreign-born.

"TB is a disease that should have been eradicated in our country, but it continues to infect and kill Americans," said bill sponsor Henry A. Waxman, D-Calif., chairman of the House Energy and Commerce Subcommittee on Health and the Environment, when the bill was in the House. "With the aid of this legislation, there is hope of eliminating this 19th-century plague from our nation."

The HHS spending bill (HR 5257 — PL 101-517) appropriated $9.1 million for the TB grants in fiscal 1991 *(Labor-HHS Appropriations, p. 847)*

Health Service Corps Measure Enacted

The Senate cleared for the president Oct. 26 a compromise bill to reauthorize the National Health Service Corps (NHSC), which offered incentives to doctors and other health professionals to practice in medically underserved areas, such as rural regions, inner-city neighborhoods and Indian reservations.

The legislation (HR 4487) authorized $63.9 million in fiscal 1991 for the corps, which provided scholarships to medical students and repaid the loans of doctors and other health-care providers who agreed to serve in areas with few or no medical personnel.

The program was authorized at "such sums as necessary" through fiscal 1993.

The House approved the conference report on the bill by voice vote Oct. 26.

President Bush signed the measure (PL 101-597) on Nov. 16.

The bill increased from $20,000 to $35,000 the annual amount that could be repaid through the loan program. It also required that at least 30 percent of funds appropriated be used for scholarships rather than loan repayments. A total of 10 percent would have to be used for scholarships to those studying to become nurse practitioners, nurse midwives or physician assistants.

The corps was funded at just $11.3 million in fiscal 1990.

BACKGROUND

When it was created in 1970, the NHSC was to provide scholarships to medical students who agreed, upon graduation, to serve for a time in medically underserved areas, primarily in rural America and on Indian reservations. Later, Congress expanded the program to include inner cities and added incentives to entice health professionals other than physicians.

But the Reagan administration did not like the corps and all but stopped giving out scholarships. As a result, by the late 1980s, when corps members finished their tours, no one was in the pipeline to take their place.

"The corps has been decimated," Rep. Henry A. Waxman, D-Calif., chairman of the Energy and Commerce Subcommittee on Health and the Environment, said. According to Waxman, only 123 new scholarship recipients began serving in the program in 1990.

The Reagan administration preferred a different approach.

In 1987, at the administration's urging, Congress created a loan-repayment program, under which health professionals in training or who had already completed their education could agree to serve in the corps in exchange for the federal government's repaying up to $20,000 per year of their student loans. *(1987 Almanac, p. 515)*

But with only 123 scholarship recipients and 74 loan-repayment recipients in line to replace retiring members of the corps, members of Congress were trying in 1990 to bolster the program in HR 4487, which originally reauthorized the corps through the year 2000.

Decrying the "crisis in rural health care," Rep. Bill Richardson, D-N.M., said: "Today, people living in rural areas continue to be in poorer health, travel farther for health care, report chronic or serious illness more frequently, are more likely to die from injury and are older than their urban counterparts."

HOUSE ACTION

The House on July 30 gave voice-vote approval to its version of HR 4487. The House bill authorized a total of $63.9 million — the figure requested by the Bush administration — for scholarships and loan repayments, rather than an open-ended authorization favored by Democrats on the House Energy and Commerce Committee.

Among other things, the bill sought to increase the maximum loan-repayment amount, from $20,000 per year per corps member to $35,000 per year.

The House Energy and Commerce Committee had approved the measure by voice vote on June 28, after adopting an amendment by Edward Madigan, R-Ill., to set the fiscal 1991 figure at $63.9 million instead of "such sums as may be necessary."

The amendment also effectively lowered the percentage of funds set aside for medical school scholarships. Committee Democrats preferred the scholarship approach, while the administration preferred repaying the medical school loans of doctors who served in the corps.

The House Energy and Commerce Subcommittee on Health and the Environment had approved HR 4487 on June 20. That version reauthorized the NHSC through the year 2000.

Subcommittee members by voice vote approved a substitute to HR 4487, which sponsor Richardson said would help the corps meet both the long- and short-term needs of areas with shortages of health professionals.

The existing reauthorization would continue the loan-repayment program and would increase the annual maximum repayment to $35,000. But it would also, in Richardson's words, "rejuvenate the scholarship program" by requiring that at least 10 percent of each year's funds be spent on scholarships.

Speaking for the administration, Madigan, the panel's ranking Republican, complained that the measure "would lead to micromanagement of the program." He did not, however, vote against the measure.

SENATE ACTION

The Senate on Aug. 4 passed a bill (S 2617) by Edward M. Kennedy, D-Mass., aimed at revitalizing the NHSC.

Senate Majority Leader George J. Mitchell, D-Maine, said the NHSC was nearly eliminated over the last decade. This made it difficult for the corps to serve rural and poor urban areas, he said.

The program had lost hundreds of health-care professionals because of funding reductions and planned to phase out the scholarship program, bill sponsors said.

The legislation would halt plans to end the scholarships and instead would increase the number of scholarships and loan-repayment assistance.

Members adopted Mitchell's amendment to establish a three-year demonstration program to allow rural areas to finance the medical education of a future physician, who would in turn serve the community. The federal government would pay 25 percent of the costs for any community that put up at least half the schooling costs. States would have to pay between 15 percent and 25 percent. The program would be authorized at $5 million in fiscal 1991 and $10 million in fiscal 1992.

The Senate inserted the text of S 2617 into HR 4487, the House companion bill, and approved that measure, asking for a conference with the House.

The Senate Labor and Human Resources Committee on May 16 had approved S 2617 by voice vote. The committee measure authorized $65 million for the corps for fiscal 1991 and "such sums as necessary" for fiscal 1992 through 1994. At least 8 percent of the money was to be spent for nurses, certified nurse-midwives and physicians' assistants, among other non-physicians. ■

Health Programs for Minorities Enacted

The Senate on Oct. 16 cleared legislation to expand programs aimed at improving the health status of disadvantaged members of minority groups and increasing their role in the health professions.

President Bush signed the bill (HR 5702 — PL 101-527) on Nov. 6.

The measure incorporated a number of proposals contained in the administration's minority health initiative, including a provision to give communities federal funding to underwrite the health-professions training of local residents in exchange for a service commitment.

The bill authorized roughly $112 million in fiscal 1991 for the new programs, including one to make health care and health education more accessible to residents of public housing. It also reauthorized through fiscal 1994 the Public Health Service's community and migrant health centers.

Louis W. Sullivan, secretary of Health and Human Services (HHS), had requested $117 million in the fiscal 1991 budget for programs to improve minorities' access to health care and medical education.

The bill also:

- Established Hispanic and Native American centers of excellence in the health professions, to encourage members of those groups to enter the health field.
- Broadened and strengthened the Office of Minority Health within HHS, which was to be headed by a deputy assistant secretary for minority health.

The measure authorized $25 million annually in fiscal 1991-93 for the office to conduct research, set up a minority health resource center and provide grants for projects to promote the health of such Americans.

- Called for health-care institutions to be provided with bilingual professionals or translators to make services more accessible to Hispanics.
- Authorized $35 million in fiscal 1991 and "such sums as may be necessary" in fiscal 1992-93 for health-services grants aimed at helping residents of public housing, and $32 million in fiscal 1991 and more funds in fiscal 1992-93 in loans and scholarships for low-income students of the health professions.

The measure also authorized millions of dollars for other grant programs.

Members of racial and ethnic minority groups suffered disproportionately high rates of cancer, stroke, heart diseases, diabetes, substance abuse, AIDS and infant mortality, bill sponsors noted.

While blacks, Hispanics and Native Americans constituted 12 percent, 7.9 percent and .01 percent of the population, respectively, they made up 3 percent, 4 percent and fewer than .01 percent of physicians, the sponsors said.

Minorities' access to health services could be substantially improved if more of their numbers were members of the professions, they said.

The House Energy and Commerce Committee approved HR 5702 on Sept. 26 (H Rept 101-804). The bill passed the House by voice vote, with amendment, on Oct. 10. The Senate adopted the measure by voice vote Oct. 16, sending the bill to the president.

The Senate had passed a more sweeping bill (S 1606 — S Rept 101-211) on Nov. 20, 1989. That version received no action after being referred to the House Energy and Commerce Committee. *(1989 Almanac, p. 177)* ■

Organ and Bone Marrow Programs Aided

The House on Oct. 26 cleared legislation (S 2946) to renew and improve programs to match organ and bone marrow donors with patients in need. President Bush signed the bill into law (PL 101-616) on Nov. 16.

The measure aimed to strengthen the National Bone Marrow Donor Registry with new initiatives and extra money in hope of building the list to 250,000 potential donors. The registry was a file of potential volunteers whose marrow could save a leukemia patient or another extremely sick person with matching marrow type.

In an effort to increase organ donations, the bill also expanded an organ procurement grants program.

As signed into law, S 2946:

- Authorized $15 million in fiscal 1991 for the National Bone Marrow Donor Registry and $8 million in fiscal 1991 and "such sums as may be necessary" in fiscal 1992 and 1993 for activities of the Department of Health and Human Services Division of Organ Transplantation. The organ transplantation authorization included funds for grants and contracts for organ procurement organizations and a procurement and transplantation computer network.
- Required the Department of Health and Human Services to establish quality standards for registries participating in the national bone marrow registry program and required the national registry to give patients information on private registries that met the standards. The provision was aimed at fostering better coordination among the bone marrow registries.

• Established an advocacy system to help patients, their families and doctors find an unrelated marrow donor, and called for increasing the number of ethnic and racial minority members in the registry's pool of potential donors.

Background

Congress had passed two earlier laws to encourage organ and marrow donations. The 1984 Organ Procurement and Transplantation Act (PL 98-507) established a computerized network to match patients with organs. A 1988 omnibus health bill (PL 100-607) required the secretary of the Department of Health and Human Services to establish a national registry of volunteer bone marrow donors, administered through the National Heart, Lung and Blood Institute. *(1988 Almanac, p. 299; 1984 Almanac, p. 476)*

But, according to Rep. Henry A. Waxman, D-Calif., chairman of the Health Subcommittee of the House Energy and Commerce Committee, and other key health lawmakers in both chambers, more steps were needed to increase the number of potential donors, especially those in ethnic and racial minority groups.

About 9,000 Americans were waiting for a bone marrow transplant at the time of enactment. The bill aimed to add significantly to the list of potential donors.

Bone marrow, which offered hope to those suffering from certain deadly forms of leukemia and anemia, was extremely difficult to match. Research showed that matches among donors not related by blood were most likely within a person's own racial or ethnic group.

Legislative Action

Waxman's Health Subcommittee approved his bill (HR 5146) calling for $5 million in fiscal 1991 for the National Organ Transplant Program and $15 million for the National Bone Marrow Donor Program on June 21.

The measure then won voice-vote approval from the full Energy and Commerce Committee on June 27 (H Rept 101-614). The House passed the measure by voice vote on July 23. The bill was sent to the Senate Labor and Human Resources Committee, which took up its own version instead.

The bill approved by the Labor Committee on Aug. 1 (S 2946 — S Rept 101-530) included a provision — not contained in the House version — to authorize funds to help organ recipients buy expensive antirejection drugs.

The committee bill, approved by voice vote, authorized $17 million in fiscal 1991 and "such sums as necessary" in fiscal 1992 and 1993 for the National Bone Marrow Donor Registry. It also authorized an additional $5 million a year through fiscal 1995 for grants to organ procurement organizations.

In addition, the legislation included an authorization of $5 million per year through fiscal 1993 for a state block grant program intended to help transplant patients without insurance coverage pay the cost of antirejection immunosuppressive drugs. The most common of such drugs, cyclosporine, cost about $5,000 per year.

Senators and House members worked out a compromise between the two bills without a conference. The Senate provision to authorize money to help pay for antirejection immunosuppressive drugs was dropped.

The Senate passed the compromise version of S 2946 by voice vote on Oct. 25, and the House cleared the measure by voice vote the next day.

Emergency Services, Trauma Care Improved

The Senate on Oct. 27 approved the conference report on a measure (HR 1602) calling for improvements in emergency medical services and trauma care, clearing the bill for the president. The House had passed the legislation the previous day.

President Bush signed the bill Nov. 16 (PL 101-590).

The measure authorized $60 million in fiscal 1991 and "such sums as may be necessary" in fiscal 1992-93 for states to develop and implement regional trauma care and emergency medical networks, following nationally recognized standards and a model plan provided by the secretary of Health and Human Services (HHS).

Background

The House had passed HR 1602 (H Rept 101-346) by voice vote Nov. 14, 1989, shortly after its Energy and Commerce Committee approved it.

Similar legislation was passed by the House in 1988 but died in the Senate. *(1989 Almanac, p. 178; 1988 Almanac, p. 323)*

Although immediate emergency care of the type provided through trauma systems could reduce dramatically the rates of death and disability for injured people, trauma care was very expensive and trauma patients were less likely than other patients to have health insurance.

As a result of chronic financial losses from providing uncompensated care, noted the sponsor of the Senate version (S 15), Alan Cranston, D-Calif., many hospitals were withdrawing from existing trauma-care systems.

In Los Angeles alone, 11 of the city's 23 trauma centers had dropped out of the system because of financial losses. The compromise bill, however, did not permit states to spend grant money on uncompensated care until trauma-care systems were in place statewide.

Sen. Edward M. Kennedy, chairman of the Labor and Human Resources Committee, said that 40 percent of the nation was not covered by 911 emergency response systems and that 29 states had not started to designate trauma centers.

He also said that most rural areas still relied on basic life support systems in emergency transport, while suburban areas employed advanced life support.

Physical trauma in the United States cost $180 billion a year in medical expenses, insurance, lost wages and property damage, according to the legislation's authors.

Legislative Action

House and Senate conferees Oct. 25 agreed on compromise trauma-care legislation (HR 1602 — H Rept 101-956). The House ratified the agreement Oct. 26, and the Senate cleared the measure the following day.

The Senate had passed S 15 on Oct. 18; the next day, it substituted the text of its bill for that of HR 1602 and passed that bill.

The Labor and Human Resources Committee had agreed to S 15 (S Rept 101-292) on Feb. 28.

In the final bill, grants to states were to be determined by a formula using population and land size — a provision taken from the earlier Senate version. A state's grant would be the greater of $250,000 or an allotment based on the population and size formula.

The measure also authorized new trauma-care research and pilot project grants to improve emergency medical service in rural areas.

States were prohibited from using the funds to pay for uncompensated trauma care — that provided to uninsured patients who could not afford the costly services — until their emergency medical systems, including emergency medical service systems in rural areas, were in place. (The Senate bill would have permitted up to 35 percent of grant funds to be spent to reimburse trauma centers for unpaid patient bills).

The legislation called on the HHS secretary to form an advisory council on trauma-care systems to assess the needs of the nation and the states' response with regard to trauma care.

The measure also included a provision to authorize a maximum $50 million grant for fiscal 1992 and 1995 to modernize the George Washington University Hospital in Washington if the hospital matched the grant dollar for dollar and agreed to provide substantial medical services to the poor. ■

Bill Authorizes Grants For Injuries Research

The House on Oct. 26 cleared a bill (HR 5113) to renew through fiscal 1993 programs that provided grants for research on the prevention and treatment of injuries, accepting minor Senate amendments to the measure.

President Bush signed the bill into law (PL 101-558) on Nov. 15.

The bill authorized $30 million in fiscal 1991 and "such sums as necessary" in fiscal 1992-93 for the grants, awarded by the Centers for Disease Control (CDC).

It authorized grants for contracts with academic institutions to provide training on the causes, prevention, diagnosis and treatment of injuries. The measure also called for the government to promote injury control.

The Senate passed the bill by voice vote on Oct. 24, adding minor amendments from an earlier bill (S 2631) to the version the House originally had passed July 23.

The Energy and Commerce Committee had approved HR 5113 (H Rept 101-613) on June 27.

The CDC's injury control program provided grants to state and local health departments and to academic facilities for research and programs on the prevention and control of injuries, trauma care and spinal cord injury, said bill sponsor Henry A. Waxman, D-Calif.

"Tragically, one in four Americans will be seriously injured this year and these injuries will be costly," said Edward Madigan, R-Ill.

"The total lifetime costs of injuries sustained in 1985 was estimated at $185 billion."

The HHS spending bill (HR 5257) appropriated $24.1 million for injury prevention in fiscal 1991 *(Labor-HHS appropriations, p. 847)*

Elderly, Alzheimer's Programs Renewed

Legislation to renew pilot programs providing medical services for people with Alzheimer's disease and home health care for low-income people was cleared by the House on Oct. 25.

President Bush signed the bill (HR 5112 — PL 101-557) on Nov. 15.

The measure, a hybrid of earlier House versions and a related Senate bill (S 2602), reauthorized through fiscal 1993 separate demonstration programs to provide community-based services to those suffering from Alzheimer's disease and home health care to low-income people.

A total of $7.5 million was authorized for each of the programs in fiscal 1991, with "such sums as necessary" in fiscal 1992-93.

The measure, passed by the House on a 417-1 vote, also expanded the government's Alzheimer's disease research program to incorporate such facilities as diagnostic and treatment clinics to serve minority and rural populations. *(Vote 521, p. 164-H)*

The home health-care program provided services to low-income people who otherwise might have needed to go to an institution or a hospital.

The other program provided similar services to patients with Alzheimer's disease.

Both projects provided grants to states.

The bill set aside at least 25 percent of home health-care grant money for people over 65. At least 10 percent of those funds was to be reserved for individuals 85 or older.

The bill also:

- Established within the Department of Health and Human Services a task force to coordinate ongoing federal efforts on aging research.
- Named a series of federally backed centers devoted to aging research after the late Rep. Claude Pepper, D-Fla. (House 1963-89; Senate 1936-51).

House Action

The House approved legislation (HR 5112 — H Rept 101-612) sponsored by Terry L. Bruce, D-Ill., by voice vote on July 23.

Portions of two other related measures were incorporated into the bill before its adoption.

Edward R. Roybal, D-Calif., chairman of the House Select Committee on Aging, and a bipartisan group of cosponsors introduced their first piece of legislation (HR 4770) on May 9 to fund research on Alzheimer's disease and related disorders involving dementias.

Roybal and his cosponsors said the "aging of America"

had made it urgent that researchers find ways to prevent or treat Alzheimer's, which primarily affected the elderly.

The degenerative disease gradually sapped the memory of its victims, altering their behavior and eventually killing them.

Sponsors said Alzheimer's research was underfunded compared with research on other major diseases such as heart disease, cancer and AIDS, which received funding of between $700 million and $1.69 billion annually.

On June 20, the House Energy and Commerce Subcommittee on Health approved HR 5042 to reauthorize demonstration programs to provide home health-care services to the frail elderly and home health and other services to people with Alzheimer's disease.

Both programs would have been authorized at $7.5 million in fiscal 1991 and "such sums as necessary" for fiscal 1992-93.

The full committee later approved HR 5112, allowing HR 5042 to die.

One week later, on June 27, the House Energy and Commerce Committee amended and approved an earlier version of HR 5112 (H Rept 101-612). Like the final version, it called for $7.5 million each in fiscal 1991 for the two home health-care demonstration programs. The committee adopted an amendment by Michael Bilirakis, R-Fla., to set aside 10 percent of program funds for the very elderly.

Senate Action

During Senate debate on HR 5112, Howard M. Metzenbaum, D-Ohio, sponsor of the earlier Senate version, said that Alzheimer's disease was draining $90 billion a year from the Treasury.

Unless a prevention method or cure was found, the number of people with the disease would double to 8 million by the following decade and grow to 14 million by the middle of the 21st century, Metzenbaum warned.

Edward M. Kennedy, D-Mass., chairman of the Labor and Human Resources Committee, cited a report by the Alliance for Aging Research stating that while older Americans accounted for roughly $215 billion in health care costs in 1990, the federal government would spend only $425 million on research into human aging. Billions of dollars could be saved by prolonging the independence of senior citizens, he told his colleagues.

"This bill offers a crucial strengthening of research concerning Alzheimer's disease and other research efforts necessary to increase the independence of the elderly and an improvement in the long-term care services for those patients needing health-care services in the home," Kennedy said on the floor Oct. 23.

Kennedy's committee on Sept. 26 approved S 2602 (S Rept 101-512) to authorize $80 million in fiscal 1991 for a variety of elderly health-care programs, including $40 million in grants to university medical centers for multidisciplinary research into Alzheimer's disease and $20 million to reauthorize an existing program to coordinate health services for people with the disease.

The Senate bill also called for $20 million to be spent to create centers — to be named after Pepper — to research, train and provide information on ways to enhance the independence of older Americans. Like the final bill, the Senate version called for a task force in the Department of Health and Human Services to coordinate federal research on aging. That research took place in various agencies and offices within the department.

The full Senate never considered its own version of the bill.

Final Action

House and Senate lawmakers reached a compromise on HR 5112, incorporating some of S 2602's provisions into the House measure.

The compromise version did not include the Senate bill's authorization levels, but did contain its provisions to expand authority for Alzheimer's disease centers, to focus the work at at least 10 geriatric research and training centers on prolonging the independence of the elderly, and to name the centers after Pepper.

The Senate passed the revised version Oct. 23. The House agreed to the Senate amendment Oct. 25, clearing the bill for the president. ■

Mental Health Projects

The Senate on Oct. 24 cleared a bill (S 2628) to renew for three years certain demonstration projects within the National Institute of Mental Health. President Bush signed it into law (PL 101-639) on Nov. 28.

The Senate first passed the bill on Aug. 4. The House passed an amended measure by voice vote Oct. 23, and the Senate agreed to the House amendments Oct. 24, clearing the legislation. The measure aimed to improve the delivery of mental health services to a variety of people, including those with severe emotional problems.

Passed by voice vote, the legislation authorized "innovative" mental health projects for fiscal 1991, 1992 and 1993, including those that provided community-based services for seriously ill patients and their families, for victims of family violence and to prevent suicide among youths.

George Miller, D-Calif., said that his House Select Committee on Children, Youth and Families had documented "the significantly increasing risk of emotional problems faced by the nation's young people and their families." About 7.5 million, or 12 percent of the nation's children had a diagnosable emotional disorder, he said.

Miller noted that S 2628 renewed the Child and Adolescent Service System Program, a demonstration project operated under the National Institute of Mental Health aimed at serving youth with severe emotional problems.

The major change made in the House amendment was a lower authorization level and a one-year delay in the requirement that states implement most activities mandated under a 1986 law. (Many states were not expected to meet the law's deadlines and would have been fined a potential 10 percent of their federal block grant funds). *(1986 Almanac, p. 240)*

The final bill sought $40 million in fiscal 1991 and "such sums as necessary" in 1992-93 for grants to states for a variety of services, including those for the seriously mentally ill and for children and adolescents with severe emotional and mental disturbances.

It also called for $5 million a year for states to develop comprehensive mental health services plans to provide community-based programs that helped mentally ill people function without being institutionalized. ■

Stripped-Down NIH Authorization Passed

Legislation to authorize certain programs at the National Institutes of Health (NIH) was cleared for President Bush on Oct. 27, but only after the bill (S 2857) was stripped of all controversial provisions.

Jettisoned were provisions in the House version (HR 5661) to overturn an NIH ban on certain types of fetal research and provisions in both versions to authorize new research centers to study infertility and contraception. The Bush administration and other critics objected to the provisions on grounds that they might encourage abortions.

Also dumped were provisions intended to eliminate sex and race bias in NIH-funded research studies and to provide new research attention to women's health concerns.

BOXSCORE

Legislation: National Institutes of Health reauthorization, PL 101-613 (S 2857, HR 5661).

Major action: Signed, Nov. 16. Cleared by Senate, Oct. 27; passed by House, Oct. 26.

Reports: Energy and Commerce (H Rept 101-869); Labor and Human Resources (S Rept 101-459).

In fact, the bill as cleared lacked even its primary provisions — language reauthorizing NIH's two largest entities, the National Cancer Institute and the National Heart, Lung and Blood Institute. Sponsors decided to wait until 1991 to reauthorize the institutes, knowing they would be kept alive through funding in the Labor-HHS appropriations bill. *(Labor-HHS bill, p. 847)*

As cleared, S 2857 authorized creation of a non-governmental, nonprofit National Foundation for Biomedical Research to establish an endowment that could support the work of senior scientists at NIH and attract visiting scientists in mid-career who could not otherwise afford to work there.

The bill also established a National Center for Medical Rehabilitation Research within the National Institute on Child Health and Human Development.

Sen. Edward M. Kennedy, D-Mass., chairman of the Labor and Human Resources Committee, said that a full NIH reauthorization bill, including the provisions aimed at focusing new attention on women's health concerns, would be a top priority for his committee in 1991.

BACKGROUND

The NIH reauthorization bill was no stranger to abortion-related controversies. All during the 1980s, NIH was at the center of a storm over whether the federal government should fund research on or use tissue from human fetuses. The last NIH reauthorization cleared by Congress was rolled into an omnibus health bill (PL 100-607) in 1988. *(1988 Almanac, p. 297)*

Since then, however, abortion-related issues had stalled an NIH reauthorization as well as the appointment of a new director for the multibillion-dollar federal research complex.

The abortion issue led to a year's delay in President Bush's search for a scientist willing to accept the post. *(NIH director, p. 602; background, 1989 Almanac, p. 305)*

Fetal Tissue Research

At issue was research ranging from studies on living fetuses in the womb to transplants of tissue from aborted fetuses into people suffering from a variety of ailments.

Scientists had used fetal tissue for decades. Cell lines derived from fetuses, for example, were instrumental in developing vaccines, among them that for polio.

By 1990, many scientists had hopes that fetal tissue transplants could successfully treat such diseases as juvenile diabetes and Parkinson's. Fetal tissue, researchers said, grew much faster than other human tissue, was more adaptable and was less likely to be rejected by a transplant recipient's immune system.

Debate over abortion, however, had virtually halted federal regulation and funding of most types of fetal research. Over the preceding decade and a half, the Department of Health and Human Services (HHS) and Congress had imposed a multitude of funding bans and moratoriums on fetal research. Advisory committees had issued volumes of reports, but disputes over the bottom-line issue — whether such research encouraged abortions — had prevented officials from agreeing on a policy.

In the meantime, as research in other countries began to outpace that in the United States, many scientists and some lawmakers wanted to end the funding bans, saying it was immoral to restrict research that could benefit so many people — including other fetuses.

Early Guidelines

Congress first addressed the issue in 1974, in response to horror stories about unregulated and ethically questionable research on fetuses dead and alive and on other living human subjects.

As part of that year's NIH reauthorization, Congress imposed a moratorium on, among other things, federally funded research on the "living human fetus, before or after abortion," unless the purpose of the research was to assure the fetus' survival.

That same law (PL 93-348) called for the creation of a National Commission for the Protection of Human Subjects of Biomedical and Behavioral Research to recommend whether and how such research should proceed.

The commission concluded that fetal research could be ethical if proper safeguards were imposed. Regulations stemming from the commission's findings stipulated the following:

- Research on fetuses that would pose more than a "minimal risk" to the woman or fetus was permitted only if performed to meet the health needs of that specific fetus or pregnant woman.
- Research could not delay or change the method for a planned abortion.
- In research using aborted fetuses, researchers could neither artificially maintain nor terminate vital signs.
- Research using fetal tissue was permitted if it was in accordance with state or local law.

The regulations also permitted the HHS secretary to waive the minimal risk standard case by case, but only if the research project was approved by the department's Ethics Advisory Board (EAB). The EAB also had to approve any application for federal funding for in vitro fertilization research.

HHS, however, had not had an EAB since the first one was disbanded in 1980. The absence of the board in effect banned in vitro fertilization research funding. All such research in the United States had since been conducted with private funds.

The secretary's authority to waive the "minimal risk" standard, on the other hand, was placed on hold by Congress in 1985 and again in 1988 NIH reauthorization bills, pending a study of the subject by a Congressional Biomedical Ethics Board. That board, split by abortion controversies, acted on nothing.

Transplant Moratorium

By far the most publicized of the fetal research bans was a 1988 moratorium on fetal tissue transplants imposed by HHS Assistant Secretary for Health Robert E. Windom.

In denying an NIH request to fund a fetal tissue transplant for a patient with Parkinson's disease, Windom in March placed a moratorium on transplantation of human tissue from induced abortion and appointed an advisory panel to study the question.

That September, the advisory panel concluded overwhelmingly that because abortion was legal and the research was designed to achieve significant medical goals, the "use of such tissue is acceptable public policy," as long as safeguards prevented commercial profit from the tissue and did not encourage women to have abortions.

In December the NIH director's standing advisory committee unanimously endorsed the Windom panel's conclusions. NIH in January 1989 formally recommended lifting the moratorium.

With the Bush administration taking over, however, the decision languished until November 1989, when HHS Secretary Louis W. Sullivan opted to leave the final decision to Windom's successor, James O. Mason.

Mason, one of the administration's leading anti-abortion voices, concluded that the moratorium shoudl be continued.

"I do not believe that a practice which to succeed must have a continuous supply of aborted fetuses is one that this nation wants or needs," Mason testified before the House Energy and Commerce Subcommittee on Health and the Environment in April 1990. "We must find other ways that do not require the destruction of one or more fetal lives in order to relieve the suffering of one person with Parkinson's disease or diabetes."

At the same hearing, members of the advisory panel protested that decision.

The panel's chairman, retired U.S. appeals court Judge Arlin Adams, said he opposed abortion but was nevertheless convinced that fetal tissue transplants should be permitted. Without government funding, he warned, there might be more fetal tissue research that would be "completely unsupervised and not governed by any reasonable guidelines."

SENATE ACTION

Women's health concerns — including the politically sensitive abortion issue — took center stage when the Senate Labor and Human Resources Committee turned to the NIH reauthorization on Aug. 1.

Responding to studies showing that women had been systematically excluded from much of the research funded by the NIH, members approved a four-year reauthorization measure that included a half-dozen initiatives aimed at increasing scientific attention to the health needs of women.

Before approving the bill by 16-0, members also agreed by 10-6 to add to the measure the text of S 2215, which was designed to encourage research into infertility and methods of contraception.

The amendment, offered by S 2215 sponsor Tom Harkin, D-Iowa, proved controversial when abortion opponents alleged that it could open the door to federal funding of research on RU 486, an abortion-inducing drug widely used in France.

The committee, however, rejected on a 4-12 vote an amendment offered by Daniel R. Coats, R-Ind., that would have barred all research on drugs or devices, including RU 486, known to terminate pregnancy after implantation of a fertilized ovum into a women's uterus.

Funding, Scientists' Pay

The underlying bill sought to extend through 1994 the portions of NIH requiring periodic reauthorization. Among those were the two largest of NIH's 13 institutes, one to study cancer and one to examine ailments affecting the heart, lungs and blood systems.

Under the measure, $2.25 billion was authorized in fiscal 1991 for the National Cancer Institute and $1.65 billion for the National Heart, Lung and Blood Institute (NHLBI). Fiscal 1990 appropriations for the cancer institute totaled $1.7 billion; NHLBI received $1.1 billion.

Overall appropriations for NIH, which supported medical research performed in universities, hospitals and other facilities as well as that by its own researchers, totaled $7.7 billion in fiscal 1990.

In past years, the NIH reauthorization had frequently served as a vehicle to impose policy changes on the nation's premier biomedical research establishment, and S 2857 was no exception.

In an effort to help recruit top-level scientists who were loath to accept NIH salaries and working conditions far below those available in the private sector, the bill created a non-governmental, nonprofit foundation for biomedical research. The foundation in turn would be able to help fund research conducted by NIH's scientists.

The bill also officially created a National Center for Human Genome Research to coordinate activities designed to map all the human genes.

Abortion, Again

As approved by the committee, S 2857 maintained the ban on fetal research that did not directly benefit the fetus or that posed more than an "insignificant risk."

Harkin professed surprise that his amendment, which sought to create five new research centers — three to study contraceptives and two to look into infertility treatments — became so controversial.

He noted that among the cosponsors were the two senators from Oregon, Republicans Mark O. Hatfield and Bob Packwood, who were on opposite sides of the abortion debate. (Hatfield opposed legalized abortion, while Packwood was a leading abortion-rights advocate.)

"I think we can all agree that the high rate of unintended pregnancy should be reduced," said Harkin, further asserting that the amendment would "take an affirmative

NIH Director Selected After Yearlong Search

After a yearlong search complicated by abortion-related issues, the administration disclosed Sept. 9 that it had selected Dr. Bernardine P. Healy to be director of the National Institutes of Health (NIH).

President Bush formally announced his intention to nominate Healy, a Cleveland cardiologist, to the position on Jan. 9, 1991.

The prestigious post as head of the huge federal research complex had gone unfilled since the resignation of Dr. James Wyngaarden in August 1989. Several candidates — including William H. Danforth, chancellor of Washington University in St. Louis and brother of Sen. John C. Danforth, R-Mo. — had backed away from the job complaining about White House questioning of their views on abortion.

Anti-abortion groups had raised a number of concerns about NIH funding policies, chiefly the question of support for medical research that used tissue from aborted fetuses. Healy had served on an NIH advisory panel that recommended approval of fetal tissue research. The recommendation had been overruled by the Reagan and Bush administrations.

A graduate of Harvard Medical School, Healy had been head of research at the Cleveland Clinic Foundation since 1985 and for two years before that had been deputy director of the White House Office of Science and Technology. A former president of the American Heart Association, she had also worked as a pathology fellow at the National Heart, Lung and Blood Institute, an NIH entity, in the 1970s.

If confirmed by the Senate, Healy would become the first woman to head the NIH, which came under fire in 1990 from women's groups to increase research on women's diseases and include more women in studies in which experimental therapies were tested.

Administration officials leaked news of Healy's selection in September, less than a month after Danforth had finally withdrawn from consideration after a second and third round of negotiations over the post.

A White House official told The Washington Post that the administration had renewed talks with Danforth after he initially complained of questioning about his views on abortion and fetal research in the fall of 1989.

But efforts to persuade him finally failed because of government ethics rules that would have required him to dissociate himself from a large charitable family trust that he administered, the official said.

After word of Healy's selection was disclosed, a spokesman for the anti-abortion National Right to Life Committee said the group could not support her confirmation but would not oppose it.

---

step in reducing the number of abortions in this country."

Barbara A. Mikulski, D-Md., noting that Harkin's bill was also part of a broader package of women's health initiatives she had unveiled the day before, argued that the new research authority was badly needed. "No new contraceptive method has been developed since 1960," when the birth control pill was approved, she said.

But Coats disagreed. "It's very nice to talk about contraception and infertility, but the real issue is the whole question of abortion," he said. "In some segments of the research community there's only one item on the agenda . . . and that's RU 486."

Coats said that without his amendment, which would have barred research on any drug, device or contraceptive method which, "as one of its known effects" terminates pregnancy after implantation, the bill "is going to be perceived as permission to fund research into RU 486."

Harkin argued that Coats' amendment was so broad that it would have a chilling effect on researchers worried about accidentally running afoul of the law. "This would inhibit, if not close down, any research on contraception or infertility," he said.

Women's Health Initiatives

While reproductive issues dominated the committee's debate over the NIH bill, more than half of the legislation was aimed at research into women's health overall.

These provisions were added at Mikulski's insistence. They were among the nearly 20 initiatives included in the Senate version of the Women's Health Equity Act, which Mikulski unveiled at a July 31 news conference.

Reps. Patricia Schroeder, D-Colo., and Olympia J. Snowe, R-Maine, co-chairs of the Congressional Caucus for Women's Issues, introduced the House version of the Women's Health Equity package (HR 5397) July 27.

"NIH has let us down and we're asking for a new prescription," said Mikulski.

She noted that in 1987 less than 14 percent of the agency's research funds were spent on women's health projects.

The most significant change sought to codify an existing NIH policy encouraging the use of women and minorities in clinical studies of drugs and other medical treatments.

In June the General Accounting Office found that enforcement of the policy, first announced in 1986, had been virtually non-existent.

Indeed, a famous study demonstrating that taking an aspirin each day could help prevent heart attacks was conducted using 22,000 subjects — all men.

"We have no idea whether that technique will help women or not," said Mikulski. "This is blatant discrimination. It is inexcusable, unforgivable, and we will not allow it to continue."

The bill also sought to do the following:

- Create within NIH an Office for Women's Health Research and Development.
- Require NIH to establish an in-house research program in gynecology.
- Require the establishment, by Jan. 1, 1993, of a Center for Women's Health Research to support research pertaining to women's health conditions.
- Require, beginning Jan. 1, 1992, that the NIH director submit to Congress an annual report detailing expenditures and progress made concerning women's health.
- Require the creation of a data bank to compile information concerning the results of research with respect to

women's health and gender differences that affected women's health.

- Impose the same requirements for inclusion of women and minorities in NIH clinical trials as for those conducted by or under the auspices of the Alcohol, Drug Abuse, and Mental Health Administration, NIH's sister research entity.

NIH Director

Some committee members took the opportunity to chastise the Bush administration for its inability to find a permanent director for NIH since the resignation of Dr. James Wyngaarden in August 1989.

Several candidates dropped out of the running for the prestigious post because they believed they would be judged by a "litmus test" concerning their opinions on abortion and fetal research.

"If we can fill a Supreme Court vacancy in 72 hours, then surely we can find an NIH director in 14 months," said Mikulski.

"And just as Bush is saying there should be no litmus test for the Supreme Court, there should be no litmus test for a director of NIH."

By mid-September, however, the administration had found a candidate: Dr. Bernardine P. Healy, a Cleveland cardiologist.

Senate Approval

The Senate on Oct. 19 approved S 2857, but only after striking some of the most sensitive provisions from the bill. Members ultimately passed the measure by voice vote.

As passed, the bill included several provisions aimed at making the nation's largest biomedical research establishment more attentive to women's health needs.

Stripped out, however, were provisions approved by the Senate Labor and Human Resources Committee on Aug. 1 that would have authorized new research centers to study contraception and infertility.

Abortion opponents had complained that the centers could end up providing federal support for study of RU 486.

During a colloquy on the Senate floor, committee Chairman Kennedy told Harkin, sponsor of the contraception and infertility center provisions, that the language was dropped after Republican abortion opponents threatened to prevent the bill from being brought up for debate.

Similar provisions were included in a bill (HR 5661) ordered reported by the House Energy and Commerce Committee on Sept. 26, but that measure had yet to come before the full House, and it was unclear whether action could be completed before Congress adjourned.

HOUSE ACTION

Action on an NIH reauthorization did not get under way in the House until Sept. 18, when the Energy and Commerce Subcommittee on Health and the Environment approved its own version of a reauthorization bill by voice vote.

Like the Senate committee bill, the measure carried a number of controversial riders. Among other things, the bill, written by subcommittee Chairman Henry A. Waxman, D-Calif., sought to lift the existing ban on research involving transplants of tissue from aborted fetuses, order the creation of research centers to study infertility and contraception, and create federal civil and criminal penalties for animal-rights activists who broke into federally funded animal research facilities. *(Animal rights dispute, p. 441)*

Subcommittee Republicans complained that the bill was yet another in a long string of attempts by congressional Democrats to micromanage the executive branch.

"This undermines the secretary of Health's authority to run NIH," said Howard C. Nielson, R-Utah.

But Republicans declined to offer amendments at the brief markup. With Waxman confident he had enough Democratic votes to keep the bill intact, Republicans decided to hold their fire until full committee markup.

At $1.8 billion and $1.2 billion, respectively, for fiscal 1991, the House subcommittee bill authorized considerably less for the cancer and heart, lung and blood institutes than the bill approved by the Senate committee.

Both bills, however, sought to increase NIH's attention to women's health concerns. Both specifically required that women and minorities be included in clinical studies of drugs and other treatments, and both required the creation of an office to identify research needs within NIH related to women's health.

NIH officials Sept. 10 announced they would create such an office, and in August the agency had issued guidelines for the inclusion of women and minorities as research subjects.

Among areas of controversy, both bills also called for the creation of research centers to study contraception and infertility. Sponsors touted this proposal as a potential middle ground in the bitter abortion debate, but abortion opponents asserted that the language could open the door to federal funding of research on RU 486.

The House bill went considerably further into politically sensitive areas than its Senate counterpart.

Probably the single most controversial provision of the 77-page bill sought to overturn the HHS moratorium on funding of fetal-tissue transplant research. And it would have limited the HHS secretary's authority to impose bans and restrictions on any research approved through NIH's peer-review process.

Other New Programs

The subcommittee bill authorized creation of a Senior Biomedical Research Service within NIH. The service, aimed at helping recruit senior scientists who could earn more in the private sector, permitted a limited number of top NIH researchers to earn up to about $190,000, more than twice as much as most senior NIH personnel received in 1990.

The provisions were based on HR 3752, sponsored by Rep. Silvio O. Conte, Mass., ranking Republican on the Appropriations Committee. In introducing the bill in November 1989, Conte noted that the NIH "brain drain" was so severe that not a single senior researcher had been hired into the agency from the private sector in more than 10 years.

The subcommittee bill also included a variety of less controversial changes to NIH policy:

- Authorized $40 million in fiscal 1991 for the establishment of a research program to study osteoporosis and related bone disorders.
- Called for the development and creation of research centers to study chronic fatigue syndrome, also known as "yuppie flu."
- Established within the National Institute of Child Health and Human Development a National Center for

Medical Rehabilitation Research. The center was to support research and training regarding the rehabilitation of people with physical disabilities.

House Committee Approval

The House Energy and Commerce Committee approved HR 5661 on Sept. 26. The bill contained so many contentious provisions that it took HHS Secretary Sullivan more than five single-spaced pages to outline all of the administration's objections in a Sept. 25 letter to Energy and Commerce Chairman John D. Dingell, D-Mich. Sullivan especially disliked the provision to overturn the ban on use of fetal tissue for medical research.

But Republicans again declined to try to strike or alter any of the contested provisions, including several abortion-related matters.

Instead, after a brief debate and adoption of three minor amendments offered by Democrats, the committee approved the bill by voice vote.

"We haven't gotten everything sorted out yet, and we didn't want to waste the time of the committee," said Edward Madigan of Illinois, the Health Subcommittee's ranking Republican, in explaining why his colleagues did not offer amendments.

Madigan said he hoped that continued negotiations with Waxman, the bill's sponsor and chairman of the Health Subcommittee, could yield an acceptable bill. "We want to see if it can be worked out," said Madigan. "If it can't be, we'll continue to oppose it."

Sullivan also reiterated the administration's opposition. "If the bill were presented in its present form, the president's advisers would recommend that he veto the bill," Sullivan wrote to Dingell.

Although Sullivan took issue with what he termed "excessive authorization levels," and attempts to "allow unwarranted and unwise intrusions into my authority" as HHS secretary, the most vociferous complaints were reserved for provisions deemed related to abortion.

The bill's overturning of an administration ban on research using tissue from aborted fetuses, wrote Sullivan, could "create a demand cycle, dependent upon maintaining the legality of induced abortions."

Sullivan also objected to provisions in both the House bill and the NIH bill approved by the Senate Labor Committee that called for the creation of research programs to study contraception and infertility.

FINAL ACTION

With time running out in the 101st Congress and the administration opposed to most provisions of the legislation, sponsors decided to strip the NIH bill of all but a couple of non-controversial sections.

On Oct. 26, the House suspended the rules and passed the final, bare-bones version by voice vote.

The Senate took up the bill on Oct. 27, the last full day of the session, and approved it by voice vote.

Bush signed the bill into law Nov. 16. ■

Family Planning Program Sinks in Senate

Family planning advocates won some major battles on both sides of Capitol Hill in 1990, but anti-abortion forces won the war.

Seesawing votes on abortion combined with unrelated end-of-session disputes doomed efforts to reauthorize the federal family planning program, Title X of the Public Health Service Act.

A bill (S 110) to reauthorize Title X was pulled from the Senate floor Sept. 26 by its sponsor, Edward M. Kennedy, D-Mass., after supporters failed to muster enough votes to choke off a filibuster. A motion to invoke cloture on the measure won a majortiy, 50-46, but fell 10 votes short of the 60 needed to limit debate. *(Vote 256, p. 51-S)*

BOXSCORE

Legislation: Family planning — reauthorization of Title X of the Public Health Service Act (S 110, HR 5693).

Major action: S 110 withdrawn from floor after cloture motion failed, 50-46, Sept. 26; HR 5693 approved by Energy and Commerce Committee Sept. 26.

Reports: Energy and Commerce (H Rept 101-870); Labor and Human Resources (S Rept 101-95).

The House Energy and Commerce Committee approved its own Title X bill (HR 5693) on the same day but made no attempt to bring the measure to the floor after the Senate version had stalled.

Although Title X, since its inception in 1970, had forbidden the use of federal funds to pay for abortions, critics argued that the program was tainted by its close association with facilities that did perform abortions.

With congressional support for abortion rights on the upswing in the wake of the 1989 Supreme Court decision giving states broader authority to restrict abortions, family planning advocates were optimistic that 1990 would be the year they could break the stalemate that had prevented Title X from being reauthorized since its last renewal expired in 1985. *(Abortion, p. 528)*

But it was not to be. In the absence of a reauthorization, Title X survived as it had since its last authorization expired at the end of fiscal 1985 — as a stepchild in the appropriations process.

Funding levels had declined, however, from a peak of $162 million in 1980 to $138 million in fiscal 1989. In fiscal 1990 the program received a slight increase to $139 million.

"Today, more than 31 million women are at risk of unintended pregnancy in the United States," said Kennedy. "Yet Title X is serving fewer people than it was serving in 1981 — and I regard that as unacceptable."

BACKGROUND

Since it was first passed in 1970, the federal family planning program had barred use of federal funds for abortions. From 1981 to 1988, however, program guidelines required that pregnant women be advised of all options, including pregnancy termination.

In 1988, at the urging of anti-abortion groups, the Reagan administration issued new regulations barring recipients of Title X grants from giving abortion counseling. Grant recipients challenged those regulations, and the Supreme Court on May 29 announced that it would hear the case in its next term.

In the meantime, two House members July 9 introduced legislation (HR 5231) that sought to overturn the regulations by statute; supporters planned to try to attach it as an amendment to the reauthorization bill.

The Senate version of the reauthorization bill (S 110) was approved by the Labor and Human Resources Committee in 1989. *(1989 Almanac, p. 180)*

LEGISLATIVE ACTION

Family planning backers — who in many but not all cases also supported abortion rights — did win important test votes in both chambers.

In the Senate, members on Sept. 25 voted 62-36 for an amendment that, in effect, would have overturned administration regulations on abortion counseling.

Both the Reagan and Bush administrations had tried to bar Title X grant recipients from informing pregnant women about abortion as an option. But the Senate voted to require that such counseling be available. *(Vote 252, p. 50-S)*

The Supreme Court took up the constitutionality of those rules in the term that began Oct. 1. But it had made no decision on the case by year's end.

However, abortion opponents chalked up a win of their own in the Senate, as members agreed to an amendment that would have required Title X facilities that performed abortions to notify the parents of minors 48 hours before an abortion could be performed.

The House Energy and Commerce committee rejected an amendment to that chamber's three-year Title X reauthorization bill, HR 5693, that would have required parents to be notified before teenagers could receive Title X services.

Avoiding Abortion

Proponents of S 110 argued that it deserved support even from those who opposed abortion.

"There is one connection and one connection only between Title X family planning services and abortion: Adequate funding for Title X helps prevent abortion," said Bob Packwood, R-Ore.

Backers also maintained that Title X facilities served important health needs other than family planning.

For many poor women, said Brock Adams, D-Wash., "family planning clinics are not only a critical resource for contraceptive information and services, but are the entry point for very basic health-care services.... The clinic is often the only access to health and medical care for millions of American women."

Critics, however, said that the program was already too intertwined with abortion and that S 110, which included provisions to fund research into new contraceptive technologies and to authorize community-based education programs, made matters worse.

S 110, complained Orrin G. Hatch, R-Utah, "only exacerbates the connection between family planning and abortion.... S 110 further mires Title X in the abortion controversy by expanding research and education efforts without providing assurances that no funds will be used" for abortion research or education.

Specifically, abortion opponents — including the Bush administration, which threatened to veto the bill — expressed concern that the research provisions could authorize funding of RU 486, an abortion-inducing pill that had been on the market in France since 1989.

They also worried that the community-based education programs could open the way for school-based clinics that would dispense contraceptives to students without parental permission.

"To distribute contraceptives in school settings is to give a strong message that premarital sex in adolescence is acceptable and may further perpetuate the problem of teen pregnancy," said Daniel R. Coats, R-Ind.

Abortion Counseling

The abortion counseling amendment, offered by John H. Chafee, R-R.I., would have codified the guidelines under which women with unintended pregnancies were counseled between 1981 and 1988, when the Reagan administration issued the regulations barring Title X recipients from mentioning abortion as an option.

Under those rules, women with unintended pregnancies were to get "non-directive counseling, and referral on request" about alternatives that had to include prenatal care and delivery, infant foster care or adoption, and pregnancy termination.

"The subject before us is solely whether the woman, when she asks, can be given the full range of options before her," said Chafee.

"Nobody is funneling money into these clinics for abortion," he added.

Other members complained that under the Reagan regulations, doctors could expose themselves to malpractice suits for failing to provide information about a legal medical procedure.

But opponents argued that requiring abortion counseling and referral on request was tantamount to encouraging abortion.

"This is not a bill about family planning, exclusively, as some might suggest," said Gordon J. Humphrey, R-N.H., a leading anti-abortion lawmaker.

"This is a bill that would use federal funds to counsel women with respect to the killing of their unborn children."

Parental Involvement

In the House Energy and Commerce Committee, family planning advocates managed to beat back an amendment by Joe L. Barton, R-Texas, that would have required that parents be notified before minors could obtain services, such as contraceptives, at a Title X clinic.

"In most cases, parents can and should know best about their children," said W. J. "Billy" Tauzin, D-La., who supported the amendment.

Opponents, led by Henry A. Waxman, D-Calif., chairman of the Commerce Subcommittee on Health and the Environment, said such a rule would be counterproductive. "Rather than seek parental permission," Waxman said, "teenagers will simply stop going to family planning clinics, but they will not stop having sex ... and the result will be more teen pregnancies."

Madigan said that while he backed parental-involvement laws for abortion, he did not support notification "for someone seeking advice.... I think it's a mistake to put this provision in this law."

The amendment failed, 17-24.

But the vote went the other way in the Senate, where the issue was framed as parental notification for abortion.

William L. Armstrong, R-Colo., was procedurally blocked by Kennedy late Sept. 25 from getting an up-or-down vote on his amendment to require that Title X recipients who also performed abortions notify parents of minors seeking an abortion 48 hours before the procedure could be performed.

But the next day, after procedural wrangling, Armstrong appended the language to a totally unrelated amendment by Joseph I. Lieberman, D-Conn., dealing with the Strategic Petroleum Reserve.

Lieberman, at Kennedy's request, found himself in the awkward position of sponsoring a motion to kill his own proposal.

Armstrong, however, turned the vote on the Lieberman amendment into a vote on parental notification.

"You have to get parental consent to make a blood donation," said Armstrong.

"You have to get parental consent to get your ears pierced. What this amendment says is you ought to at least have parental notification before an abortion is performed on a minor child."

Tim Wirth, D-Colo., opposed Armstrong's amendment.

"This amendment could cause great pain for many unstable, troubled families," said Wirth.

"Passing this today cannot transform abusive families into supportive ones, nor will it reduce the alarmingly high rate of teenage pregnancy. Instead, this amendment will only add to the crushing problems faced by pregnant, low-income teenagers."

After the debate, members voted 43-54 against tabling the Lieberman amendment, and then adopted the Armstrong amendment by voice vote. *(Vote 255, p. 51-S)*

It was unclear, however, which amendment individual senators thought they were voting on.

Chafee, for example, voted against tabling the amendment, but said later that he opposed the Armstrong amendment, and voted the way he did to give Armstrong an up-or-down vote.

The 50-46 cloture vote was similarly unrevealing. Among those voting against cloture were five of the nine Republican cosponsors of the measure, including Chafee, who worked hard to get his counseling amendment added. *(Vote 256, p. 51-S)* ■

Congress OKs Cancer-Screening Grants

Legislation (HR 4790 — PL 101-354) aimed at preventing cervical and breast cancer deaths by providing grants to states for early-detection programs was cleared by Congress Aug. 3 after both chambers approved the non-controversial measure by voice vote.

Final action on the bill came when the House concurred in a minor amendment adopted by the Senate before it passed the measure.

The bill, signed by President Bush Aug. 10, gave low-income women top priority for the cancer screenings in the newly authorized programs and also called for the states to provide referrals and follow-up care for women who have Pap smears and mammograms.

The states were authorized to use some of the funds to develop public education materials and improve the training of health professionals in detecting and controlling the sometimes fatal diseases.

The measure by Rep. Henry A. Waxman, D-Calif., and Sen. Barbara A. Mikulski, D-Md., authorized $50 million in grants to states in fiscal 1991 to conduct the screenings and provide other services, and authorized unspecified amounts in fiscal 1992 and 1993.

States with unusually high death rates from breast and cervical cancer were given preferences for the grants, as were those with inadequate services for early detection and care.

"It is an aggressive program that combines health care, education, payment for services and proper follow-up in a single package, and it delivers these services to low-income women, who need it most," Mikulski said in a statement.

Supporters of the legislation in the House said that 43,000 women died from breast cancer and 6,000 from cervical cancer in 1989.

"This is one of the best pieces of legislation I've seen since I've been in the Congress," said J. Roy Rowland, D-Ga., one of the two physicians serving in the House. Rowland noted that cervical cancer, in particular, was highly treatable if detected early.

States participating in the program were required to provide $1 for every $3 in federal grants — either from public or private funding. States receiving the grants had to agree to give low-income women priority for the screening services.

They also had to use the grants to subsidize all or part of the tests' costs, with women whose incomes fall below the poverty line receiving the screening services free.

When treated early, breast and cervical cancer patients had a 90 percent-to-100 percent, five-year survival rate.

Impoverished women had the lowest survival rates because they had less access to early screening and detection services, bill sponsors said.

Legislative History

The House Energy and Commerce Health Subcommittee approved HR 4790 on May 10, and the full committee approved the measure (H Rept 101-543) on May 16. The full House passed the bill by voice vote on June 18.

The Senate Labor and Human Resources Committee on June 27 approved a virtually identical bill (S 2283 — S Rept 101-380). The full Senate then passed HR 4790 on Aug. 3 after making minor amendments generally having to do with the distribution of grants among the states.

Later that day, the House cleared the measure.

Present at the president's signing of the legislation was Marilyn Quayle, wife of the vice president, who had lobbied for the bill. Mrs. Quayle, whose mother died of breast cancer, testified in favor of the measure several weeks before undergoing surgery for a precancerous condition detected by one of the very tests the measure made more widely available. ■

Bipartisan Health-Care Group Divided

A bipartisan 15-member commission, which struggled for a year to devise improvements in the nation's health-care system, on March 2 approved two far-reaching proposals. But its recommendations had no discernible impact because the commission was sundered by partisan and philosophical divisions.

The panel, made up primarily of members of Congress, was named for its first chairman and creator, Rep. Claude Pepper, D-Fla., who died in 1989. The commission proposed two programs: one to provide basic health insurance to those lacking it and a second to underwrite long-term care.

The cost of both to the federal government was estimated at $66.2 billion per year, but the commission made no recommendation on how that might be covered.

"The question is not whether America can afford the Pepper Commission's recommendations," insisted Sen. John D. Rockefeller IV, D-W.Va., the panel's chairman. "The question is whether Americans can afford not to do what the Pepper Commission recommends, to continue to do nothing, which is what we've been doing."

At the last of a series of closed meetings, members voted 11-4 for a $42.8 billion plan to create a largely federal program to provide long-term health care for all Americans, regardless of age. The program would help pay for home care for all severely disabled individuals and would pay for three months of care in a nursing home.

Members were more divided over a $23.4 billion plan to assist the estimated 31 million Americans who lacked health insurance coverage. The vote on that portion of the proposal was 8-7.

The plan called for various tax incentives and subsidies over the following five years to encourage businesses to provide health insurance to their workers. It also called for changes in private insurance to prevent companies from refusing to cover those most likely to need it. And it urged expanded federal health coverage of the poorest Americans.

If, after five years, at least 80 percent of small-business employees still lacked health insurance coverage, the plan called for a "pay or play" system requiring employers either to provide workers with health insurance or to pay into a special fund from which insurance would be provided. Rep. Pete Stark, D-Calif., Sen. Max Baucus, D-Mont., and John Cogan, a former Office of Management and Budget (OMB) official, joined all four congressional Republicans on the panel in opposition.

Despite their differences, members took pains to point out that they had reached consensus on several issues. Sen. John Heinz, R-Pa., said, "We reached agreement on eliminating the current two-tiered system of Medicaid for the poor only.... We've reached agreement, perhaps less so, for building upon the present employer-based system for acute health care.... And we rejected the philosophy of the current health-care system that access should be rationed by the size of one's wallet."

BACKGROUND

The commission had been ensnared in controversy since its inception.

Language to create the panel was appended in 1987 to Medicare catastrophic-coverage legislation then moving through the House. Sponsors of that bill agreed to order the commission study to appease Pepper, who at the time was threatening to use his power as Rules Committee chairman to add to the catastrophic-costs bill costly amendments to cover long-term home health care.

As envisioned by Pepper, the commission was to have six months to come up with a proposal to create a long-term care program for Medicare beneficiaries, then an additional six months to recommend how to provide "comprehensive health care services for all individuals in the United States." *(1987 Almanac, p. 493)*

By the time the catastrophic-costs law was enacted in 1988, however, many members had concluded that access to health care for the estimated 31 million to 37 million Americans without health insurance was at least as important as the lack of affordable long-term care for the elderly, which was Pepper's top priority.

A key concern was that if the commission were to recommend a plan for long-term care first, funds needed to cope with the uninsured would be used up. "It shouldn't be like a joint account, that the first person to get at the funds gets to keep them," said Rep. Bill Gradison, R-Ohio, in 1988.

Sparring over how to proceed kept the commission from even meeting until February 1989, when Pepper was unanimously elected chairman. The struggles continued, however, even extending to the selection of staff director, since Pepper's choice was considered by many to be more interested in the long-term care issue than the uninsured.

Pepper finally agreed to issue both reports simultaneously in November 1989. Some members had wanted to take until March 1, 1990, but Pepper opposed that as an unwise delay.

The commission's work was set back by Pepper's death May 30, 1989. Rockefeller, originally named to a seat that George J. Mitchell, D-Maine, vacated when he was elected majority leader, was elected chairman June 15.

The commission was officially renamed the Pepper Commission and had its deadline extended to March 1 in the fiscal 1990 budget-reconciliation bill (PL 101-239). Even though Congress on Nov. 22 repealed most of the 1988 Medicare Catastrophic Coverage Act, the authorization for the Pepper Commission was left undisturbed. *(Catastrophic repeal, 1989 Almanac, p. 149)*

COMMISSION RECOMMENDATIONS

The commission's final recommendations were divided into two parts, one dealing with the problem of health insurance coverage for all Americans and the other focusing on long-term care for the disabled.

Health Insurance

The panel called for creation of a new public health plan to replace the state-federal Medicaid program for basic health care, including hospital treatment, doctor bills and preventive care.

The program was to be financed primarily by the federal government. Other payers included states (to the extent, adjusted for inflation, they already paid for Medicaid for the services), employers who used it to purchase coverage for their workers and individuals with sufficient income and with no other access to health insurance.

The plan was to be administered primarily by the federal government, paying providers under the rules used for Medicare. Those not enrolled through their employers would have to pay premiums based on their wages. Coverage would have a deductible of $250 for an individual or $500 for a family, coinsurance of 20 percent for most services and an out-of-pocket cap of $3,000 per year. Costs for those with incomes of less than 200 percent of the federal poverty line would be subsidized on a sliding scale by the federal government.

Employers with more than 100 workers would be required to provide employees and their non-working dependents with private health insurance or to contribute to the public plan in their behalf. Workers could be required to pay up to 20 percent of private insurance premiums.

Employers with 100 or fewer workers would be encouraged to provide coverage, and those with fewer than 25 workers would be given tax incentives and subsidies to make insurance more affordable.

If, after five years, 80 percent of previously uninsured workers and dependents in these small businesses were not covered by insurance, those employers would be required either to purchase private insurance for employees or to contribute to the public plan.

The panel proposed that private insurance companies be barred from refusing to cover people with pre-existing conditions and from refusing coverage for any individual within a covered group. Insurers could not refuse any group wishing to purchase insurance and would have to set rates on the same terms to all groups in a particular area.

Long-Term Care

In the area of long-term care, the Pepper Commission called for federal coverage of up to three months of care in a nursing home, regardless of age or ability to pay.

However, a 20 percent copayment would be required from those with incomes at least double the federal poverty level. Both skilled and custodial care would be covered.

The panel called for federal coverage of both home- and community-based care for severely disabled individuals of all ages.

As with nursing-home care, a 20 percent copayment would be required of those with incomes at least double the poverty level. Eligibility would be determined by local assessment agencies, and specific services would be determined and supervised by case managers.

The panel called for a state-federal program to prevent those who required nursing-home stays of longer than three months from having to deplete all of their assets.

Under the program, individuals would be permitted to keep their home and up to $30,000 worth of assets; couples could keep their home and up to $60,000 worth of assets. Both the person in the nursing home and a spouse living in the community would be permitted to keep more income than was allowed in 1990; all remaining income would go to the cost of nursing-home care.

The panel called for expanded research aimed at reducing the need for long-term care through better understanding of the ailments that resulted in long-term illness and disability.

Revenues

For both the insurance access and long-term care programs, the commission recommended that taxes be progressive, "requiring a higher contribution from those most able to bear increased tax burdens."

The panel urged that taxes be assessed regardless of age, in contrast to the ill-fated tax to finance the 1988 Medicare Catastrophic Coverage Act, which was leveled only on the Medicare-eligible population, 90 percent of whom were over age 65.

That law was repealed in 1989 primarily because of complaints about the financing mechanism.

The Pepper Commission also recommended choosing taxes that could be expected to keep pace with health care inflation.

POLITICS AND AFTERMATH

As always in the health-care debate, the dissension within the commission centered on the question of how to pay for needed care. The divide was largely, but not completely, along party lines.

"It's easy to figure out how to spend the money," said Rep. Tom Tauke, R-Iowa. "The hard part is figuring out how to raise it."

"I don't think we've done our job," said Stark, one of two members from the revenue-raising House Ways and Means Committee. "We didn't figure out how to pay for it. There is no tax fairy out there who's going to pull it out from under a pillow."

Stark said, "The fact is there are too many philosophical differences on the commission, and there wasn't enough pressure to bring us together."

Administration Pressure

Adding to the ire for several days leading up to the pivotal March 2 meeting were charges by commission Democrats that the Bush administration was tampering with the commission by urging Republican members to vote against the proposals.

"They're saying that they don't want a bipartisan agreement on a program that involves a major revenue component because they're afraid the Democrats will use it against them in an election year," said Stark of the administration efforts.

Thomas Scully, who oversaw health policy at OMB, confirmed March 2 that he had called two of the three Reagan administration appointees "who are not creatures of the ways of Washington." But he said he did not seek to influence their votes.

"I did not tell them we wanted them to vote 'no,'" Scully said. "I just wanted them to be aware of the broader political ramifications.... $65 billion in new taxes is not what this administration is interested in."

In the end, however, both appointees in question — James Balog, who headed the Public-Private Sector Advisory Committee on Catastrophic Illness during the Reagan administration, and James Davis, immediate past president of the American Medical Association — voted for both the universal insurance and long-term care plans.

Cost Calculations

Commission members said that Rockefeller had wanted to specify sources of new revenues to pay for the plans, but a questionnaire on the subject distributed to members in January showed a lack of consensus, and it was dropped.

Publicly, Rockefeller defended the commission's decision not to specify revenue sources. "We have established a cost. Nobody's ever done that before," he said.

According to commission staff, when fully put into effect, the health insurance-access proposal would result in net new health-care costs of about $14 billion per year (on top of a total national health bill already more than half a trillion dollars).

The federal government would pay an additional $23 billion, primarily for subsidies to small businesses and a new public health insurance plan for those who were too poor to afford or had no other access to insurance.

States would save about $5 billion per year in money they were spending largely on care for the uninsured who were unable to pay their bills.

Businesses and individuals together would also save about $4 billion annually. That was because the additional $27.4 billion cost to employers not providing insurance would be more than offset by the $10.6 billion savings for employers that did provide insurance (and indirectly subsidized those that did not) and the $20.6 billion saved by individuals in out-of-pocket expenses for insurance premiums, deductibles and copayments. But that savings did not take into account the likelihood of increased taxes to help pay the federal share.

The cost of the long-term care proposal was considerably higher because, unlike the case with the uninsured in which most people were getting care with someone paying the bill, many of those who needed long-term care were not receiving it or were receiving it free from family members and friends.

According to commission figures, the portion of the plan guaranteeing federal coverage of three months in a nursing home regardless of ability to pay would cost the federal government about $18.8 billion per year, while home care for the severely disabled would cost $24 billion.

Up to Administration

One of the few things on which commission members did seem to agree was that administration backing was essential for any progress on health-care financing.

"This issue requires the contributions and leadership of the executive branch," said Sen. Dave Durenberger, R-Minn, the commission vice chairman. "By this, I mean the president of the United States."

Working groups within both Health and Human Services and the White House Domestic Policy Office were looking at health care.

At the same time, the quadrennial Advisory Council on Social Security was also developing recommendations. That panel, chaired by Deborah L. Steelman, the Bush campaign domestic policy chief and a Reagan administration OMB official, included neither members of Congress nor executive branch officials, but its recommendations on other topics carried weight in the past. ■

Health Planning Grants

The Senate on Oct. 27 cleared a bill (S 2056) that authorized $10 million in public health planning grants to states to work on state health objective plans. The plans would plot ways to meet health goals set by the secretary of Health and Human Services (HHS). President Bush signed the bill into law (PL 101-582) on Nov. 15.

The Senate passed the bill Oct. 20, and the House amended the measure and passed it Oct. 26. The Senate Labor and Human Resources Committee had approved the bill (S Rept 101-417) on Aug. 3.

In September, HHS Secretary Louis W. Sullivan had announced health promotion and disease prevention objectives for the nation to achieve by 2000.

Bill supporters said the legislation would reduce astronomical health-care costs by encouraging steps to promote health and prevent disease and disability.

Sen. Tom Harkin, D-Iowa, tried to get the $10 million grant attached to the HHS appropriations bill (HR 5257), but the House removed the provision, leaving the program unfunded. ■

Developmental Disabilities

The Senate on Oct. 12 cleared a bill to reauthorize for three years programs aimed at protecting the rights and promoting the independence of people with developmental disabilities, such as mental retardation or cerebral palsy.

President Bush signed the measure (S 2753 — PL 101-496) on Oct. 31.

The legislation:

- Authorized $77.4 million in fiscal 1991 and "such sums as may be necessary" in fiscal 1992-93 for grants to states for developmental disabilities councils.

The councils planned, monitored, evaluated and coordinated services to those with developmental disabilities and their families.

- Authorized $24 million in fiscal 1991 and "such sums" in fiscal 1992-93 for protection and advocacy services for the developmentally disabled.
- Authorized $16.5 million in fiscal 1991 and "such sums" in fiscal 1992-93 for university-affiliated programs that provided interdisciplinary training, information dissemination and technical assistance.
- Authorized $3.65 million in fiscal 1991 and "such sums" in fiscal 1992-93 for "projects of national significance," which developed new technologies and applied and demonstrated methods to promote the independence of those with developmental disabilities.

The Senate Labor and Human Resources Committee approved the bill June 27 (S Rept 101-376) and the full Senate passed it by voice vote Aug. 2.

The early Senate version sought a four-year reauthorization and included higher funding levels. For example, it would have authorized $81.27 million in fiscal 1991 for state planning councils, compared with $77.4 million in the House measure.

The House Energy and Commerce Committee approved a companion bill (HR 5679 — H Rept 101-803) on Sept. 26, and the House passed it by voice vote Oct. 10, incorporating the text of its bill into S 2753.

The House measure also called for $122 million in fiscal 1991 for developmental-disabilities block grants, protection and advocacy grants, and other monetary awards targeted at universities and other facilities to help finance their efforts to improve conditions for those with developmental disabilities.

The Senate agreed to the House amendment Oct. 12, clearing the measure for the president. ■

Bush's Education Proposals Unfulfilled

Halfway through his first term, George Bush remained a long way from fulfilling his 1988 campaign pledge to be "the education president."

The only education initiative that Bush had presented to Congress since he entered the White House died at the end of the session Oct. 27, the victim of a threatened Senate filibuster by members of the president's own party.

The final bill (HR 5932) included Bush's proposals to authorize cash awards for excellent schools and teachers, math and science scholarships, and alternative methods for certifying teachers. It also sought to coordinate literacy programs on a regional and local level and included provisions on teacher recruitment and training.

Congress cleared and Bush signed a separate measure (HR 996 — PL 101-589) creating new math and science scholarships. *(Math-science bill, p. 612)*

But the rest of the Bush package died at adjournment.

Democrats said that Republican Sens. Jesse Helms, N.C., Daniel R. Coats, Ind., and Charles E. Grassley, Iowa, among others, blocked action on the bill because they philosophically opposed federal involvement in educational issues.

But Republicans said they had legitimate concerns that Democrats refused to address, including objections to an authorization of $10 million for the National Board for Professional Teaching Standards, which was developing a voluntary certification process for teachers nationwide.

BOXSCORE

Legislation: Educational Excellence and Equity Act (HR 5932) [earlier versions: HR 5115, S 695, S 1310, S 1676].

Major action: HR 5932 died in Senate, Oct. 27; passed by House, Oct. 26. HR 5115 passed by House, 350-25, July 20; S 695 passed by Senate, 92-8, Feb. 7; S 1310 passed by Senate, 99-0, Feb. 6.

Reports: Education and Labor (HR 5115 — H Rept 101-570); Labor and Human Resources (S 1676: S Rept 101-360; S 1310: S Rept 101-196; S 695: S Rept 101-136).

BACKGROUND

Bush followed up his campaign pledge with a September 1989 "summit" meeting with the nation's governors that led to the joint adoption of seven vaguely phrased goals for improving the education system. *(Education summit, 1989 Almanac, p. 191)*

But the president never offered legislation expressly related to those goals.

Instead, Bush sent Congress a proposed "Educational Excellence Act" in April 1989, asking lawmakers to authorize $423 million for cash awards to excellent schools and teachers, math and science scholarships, and alternative methods for certifying teachers.

The Senate Labor and Human Resources Committee approved a revised version of the package (S 695) on July 20, 1989, but the bill went no further that year.

Bush's proposals focused primarily on elementary and secondary education. Senate committee members pared the Bush plan from more than $400 million to just over $300 million, then added proposals of their own costing nearly $200 million. Most sought to expand postsecondary student aid by relaxing eligibility requirements. *(1989 Almanac, p. 193)*

Later in 1989, on Nov. 1, the Senate committee also approved legislation (S 1310 — S Rept 101-196) authorizing more than $200 million in new funding to combat adult illiteracy and coordinate existing governmental and private-sector programs. *(1989 Almanac, p. 198)*

This bill later was rolled into the legislation carrying Bush's proposals.

ACTION IN SENATE

The Senate passed S 1310, the literacy bill, on Feb. 6, 1990. It approved S 695 a day later.

And on June 27, the Senate Labor and Human Resources Committee approved, 15-1, a bill (S 1676) aimed at recruiting more teachers and improving the skills of those already in the classroom.

S 1676, which authorized $215 million in fiscal 1991 and such sums as necessary in fiscal 1992-95, was the third bill in the package. But Republicans blocked its consideration by the full Senate.

Literacy Bill: S 1310

Embracing a cause long championed by first lady Barbara Bush, the Senate on Feb. 6 voted to launch a comprehensive and coordinated campaign to erase adult illiteracy.

By 99-0, the Senate passed S 1310, which authorized $229 million in budget authority ($50 million in outlays) in fiscal 1991 for new and existing programs to promote adult literacy. *(Vote 4, p. 4-S)*

Paul Simon, D-Ill., chief sponsor of S 1310, said he spoke to Bush about the literacy initiative, but received no commitment of support.

"I told him I expected he would be lobbied at home on this one," Simon said.

Simon told his colleagues that 23 million Americans were functionally illiterate — unable to read or write above a fourth-grade level — and that 4 million of them were completely unable to read or write.

"It holds back the growth of our economy when we have people who do not read and write," Simon said.

He said the average worker in 1990 needed literacy skills at the ninth- through 12th-grade level, compared with the fourth-grade level necessary after World War II.

Lending urgency to the problem, Simon said, was the fact that the U.S. work force in the future would rely increasingly on minorities and immigrants, who had disproportionately high rates of illiteracy.

"Our nation's economic security is directly tied to the quality of the nation's work force," he said.

Although no senator voted against the bill, Christopher S. Bond, R-Mo., expressed reservations.

"It seems to me the question we should be asking is why our schools are graduating so many illiterates," he said. "They are failing in their basic mission, which is to equip our children with the basic skills they need to be productive citizens. We will not solve this problem by setting up the duplicative structures provided for in this bill."

Commercial Drivers. Perhaps in testament to the severity of the illiteracy problem, the Senate adopted an amendment to S 1310 authorizing $5 million annually for fiscal 1991-92 to help truckers and other commercial drivers improve their literacy skills enough to pass written driving tests required under the 1986 Commercial Motor Vehicle Safety Act.

John Heinz, R-Pa., who wrote the amendment, said that in the first months after the new licensing requirements took effect in California, more than 50 percent of the driver applicants failed the written portion of their exams.

"The commercial drivers who need literacy training earn a good living. They are making substantial contributions to the American economy. It is not right for them to lose their jobs or their rigs . . . because they could not pass a written test," Heinz said.

Several existing federal programs sought to combat illiteracy, including the Adult Basic Education grant program, Library Literacy Programs and the VISTA Literacy Corps.

Major Provisions. S 1310 authorized the following initiatives:

- Creation of a National Literacy 2000 Federal Interagency Council to coordinate and monitor existing programs.
- Coordination of all literacy-related programs in the Department of Education by the assistant secretary for vocational and adult education.
- Creation of a National Center for Literacy, with authorization for $10 million in 1991, to provide a "national focal point" for research, technical assistance, policy analysis and information dissemination in the literacy area.
- $15 million in fiscal 1991 for literacy resource center grants to states. Grants were to be awarded for no more than three-year periods with a cap of $500,000.
- Expansion of adult education teacher-training programs and an increase in the number of full-time professional adult educators.
- $100 million in fiscal 1991 on top of the existing appropriation of $160 million for basic adult education. In fiscal 1992-93, the authorization was to go up by $100 million over the preceding year's actual appropriation.

The Bush administration was proposing $200 million for 1991.

- $60 million in fiscal 1991, an increase of $10 million, for the existing Even Start program, which helped preschoolers and their parents in order to give the children a good educational start.
- $10 million for 50 to 100 demonstration grants to nonprofit groups to develop "intergenerational learning programs" for children age 3 and under and their low-income, illiterate parents.
- $2 million in grants during fiscal 1991 to libraries to acquire books, tapes and computer software.
- Provision for college students to become literacy tutors under the Work-Study program of the Higher Education Act of 1965.
- $5 million for literacy challenge grants under the VISTA program to encourage partnerships among volunteers, business, nonprofits and government to provide community literacy programs.

S 695: Bush Initiative

After nearly two days of fighting over a relatively minor provision, the Senate on Feb. 7 passed, 92-8, its revised, $414 million version of Bush's initiative. *(Vote 10, p. 5-S)*

Senators of both parties praised the initiatives in the "Educational Excellence Act," but Democrats noted pointedly that the bill was merely an authorization for new spending.

Brock Adams, D-Wash., reminded his colleagues that Bush's education budget called for only a 2 percent funding increase overall, while inflation was expected to run at more than 4 percent in fiscal 1991. "In other words, if we are to fund this $414 million in new initiatives, we are going to have to cut other education programs to do it," he said.

As approved by the Labor and Human Resources Committee on July 20, 1989, the package authorized about $414 million in 1991 and $1.5 billion over five years (S Rept 101-136). Floor amendments added about $23 million.

The bill authorized several new programs, including college scholarships for outstanding science students, a new magnet schools program, rewards for excellence in teaching, and endowment grants to historically black colleges and universities. It also contained provisions to crack down on student loan defaults.

Among the most expensive components of the bill was Bush's $200 million "Presidential Schools of Distinction" plan to reward schools beginning to overcome problems such as drugs and dropouts.

Also likely to prove costly was a provision to exclude a family's home or farm in calculating a student's eligibility for Pell grants and Stafford guaranteed student loans if the family earned $30,000 or less annually. Staff members estimated that would add $187 million to Pell grant outlays.

Teacher Standards Board. Jesse Helms, R-N.C., led a fight to delete Title X, a provision added to S 695 by the Labor Committee. It authorized $25 million in federal funds, to match an equal sum in private donations, for research and development activities of the National Board for Professional Teaching Standards.

The board, created in 1987 with funding from the Carnegie Corporation of New York and a number of other foundations, was drawing up guidelines for voluntary certification of teachers nationwide.

Helms claimed the board was dominated by teachers' unions, and he predicted that its certification guidelines would soon turn into licensing standards for teachers. "What this board wants is to be the sole standard-bearer on deciding who can and can't teach," Helms said. "And I think that's an outrage. ... The labor unions want to control education in America. No one else need apply."

The Bush administration also opposed the provision, saying federal funds should not be used for a program over which the government had no control.

Christopher J. Dodd, D-Conn., fended off Helms' attack, pointing out that the board was not controlled by the National Education Association (NEA) or the American Federation of Teachers (AFT).

Dodd said the independent 63-member board allotted seven seats to the NEA and seven seats to the AFT. The remainder included teachers, business executives, school board members and other education professionals.

"To suggest somehow that it is a cabal that has met somewhere secretly and privately to come up with some standards which will only guarantee that the National Education Association teachers are going to be allowed to serve as members of the teaching profession is just ridiculous," Dodd said.

Math, Science, Engineering Education

Legislation designed to spur students to study and work in mathematics, science and engineering cleared the Senate on Oct. 26 and was signed by President Bush on Nov. 16 (HR 996 — PL 101-589).

Growing concerns about the tenuous U.S. position in the global technology marketplace had influenced educational priorities. Several studies painted a bleak picture of U.S. mathematics and science education.

The three-year bill authorized $149.1 million in fiscal 1991, but only $26.2 million was new authorization. The remaining $122.9 million was carved out of existing authority in the National Science Foundation (NSF) act (PL 100-570).

The lion's share of the new money — $23.7 million — was directed toward the Department of Education, with the remaining $2.5 million earmarked for teaching scholarships at the NSF.

The legislation established 10 regional consortia on mathematics, science and engineering education. It also established a clearinghouse at the Department of Education to be a depository for information on teaching methods for math and science.

The bill also provided for a congressional scholarship program to be established at the NSF for undergraduate scholarships in math, science, and engineering. This program was aimed at encouraging greater participation in science and technology by women, minorities and individuals with disabilities.

Legislative Action

The House had approved legislation (HR 996) Sept. 12, 1989, creating three merit-based congressional scholarship programs aimed at encouraging more college students to pursue careers in science, mathematics and engineering.

The bill authorized $13 million in fiscal 1990, rising to $40.75 million in fiscal 1993, for the scholarship programs. All three were to be administered by the NSF. However, the measure did not move in the Senate. *(1989 Almanac, p. 199)*

Attention was again directed toward the issue on July 17 when the House approved, 347-19, a bill (HR 4982) to authorize $250 million for programs aimed at making U.S. students first in the world in science and mathematics achievement by the year 2000. *(Vote 234, p. 80-H)*

The Bush administration opposed the bill, saying it was not focused properly and was too expensive — $10 million more than the president's request.

A component of the legislation would have substantially boosted budget authority for the Dwight D. Eisenhower Mathematics and Science Education Act (PL 98-377), since 1984 the main federal conduit for grants to local education agencies for math and science instruction.

The administration issued a statement opposing the bill, citing its "excessive authorizations," reduced discretion for local education agencies and duplication of existing activities by the regional consortia.

Both Democrats and Republicans said they were dismayed by the administration's stance.

The next day, July 18, the Senate Labor and Human Resources Committee without opposition approved legislation (S 2114) that included a substantially smaller authorization, $125 million.

S 2114 would have authorized a scholarship and grant program to encourage female and minority students to choose careers in mathematics, science and engineering. The measure would have also authorized a math-science teacher corps, a national science scholars program and a doubling of the NSF graduate fellowship program.

The Senate passed HR 996 on Aug. 3 after amending it to include the provisions outlined in S 2114.

The Senate insisted on the amendment and requested a conference with the House.

On Oct. 19, the House disagreed to the amendment and also asked for a conference.

The amended bill was sent to conference with the two House-passed bills: the House Science Committee version of HR 996, the scholarship bill; and HR 4982, the Eisenhower Act expansion.

The conference report (H Rept 101-36) contained provisions from HR 4982 and the Senate amendment.

The Eisenhower provisions required that funds be focused on training teachers in the elementary grades; allowed the secretary of Education to carry out a model program for training and instruction in the use of computers; and allowed the secretary to establish a National Clearinghouse for Science, Mathematics, and Technology Education. The Eisenhower amendments also authorized funds to establish regional science, mathematics, and technology education consortia.

The bill also included the National Science Scholars Program proposed by the president and two other smaller scholarship programs to encourage students to major in the sciences.

The House approved the conference report by voice vote on Oct. 25; Senate approval by voice vote on Oct. 26 cleared the measure for the president.

In addition, he said, giving public funds to private organizations was not a radical concept.

Dodd pointed to the Corporation for Public Broadcasting and the American Red Cross as recipients of federal tax dollars.

Proponents of the plan stressed that certification was not designed to take the place of state and local standards for teachers.

The Senate rejected Helms' amendment, 35-64, with 10 Republicans joining the Democratic majority to defeat it. *(Vote 6, p. 4-S)*

Nancy Landon Kassebaum, R-Kan., followed with an amendment to cut the grant from $25 million to $6 million and to force the board to compete for the money.

Helms contributed a second-degree amendment that would have taken $10 million from the grant and given it to an alternative teacher certification program to help retired people and other professionals become teachers without having to obtain teaching degrees.

The remaining $15 million, Helms proposed, would go to states to develop minimum competency standards for teachers.

Pell moved to table, or kill, Helms' amendment, and the Senate agreed, 60-37. *(Vote 7, p. 4-S)*

The Senate then rejected Kassebaum's amendment, 40-57. *(Vote 8, p. 4-S)*

Before passing the bill, the Senate by voice vote adopted a modified Helms amendment clarifying that "nothing in this act shall be construed to infringe upon the practice or accreditation of home school or private school teaching."

Despite two days of debate, some staff members suggested that Title X would not have become such a lightning rod were it not for Helms' hostility toward former North Carolina Gov. James B. Hunt Jr., whom Helms defeated in winning re-election in 1984 after a rancorous campaign. Hunt chaired the teacher-standards board.

Other Amendments. The closest vote during debate on the bill came on an amendment by Pete Wilson, R-Calif., that would have authorized $10 million for a "Healthy Start" demonstration program for school districts receiving money under Chapter 1, the federal compensatory aid program for disadvantaged students.

To qualify for funds, school districts would have to set up local councils to coordinate social support services for students.

Although authors of S 695 praised the intent, Dodd said the five-page proposal should not be adopted without study by the relevant committees and testimony by the kinds of social agencies the amendment would affect.

Wilson's amendment was tabled on a largely party-line vote of 51-49. *(Vote 9, p. 5-S)*

Amendments adopted by the Senate, all by voice vote, included:

- By Sen. Bill Bradley, D-N.J., to require colleges and universities that offered athletic scholarships to inform prospective student-athletes of the school's overall graduation rates, by race and sex, and of the graduation rates of student-athletes by race, sex, and sport. Congress later cleared separate legislation (S 580 — PL 101-542) to this end. *(Student right-to-know, p. 624)*
- By Wilson, to authorize $10 million for an antidrug education program called DARE.
- By Daniel R. Coats, R-Ind., to authorize a supplemental grant of $5 million over three years for random drug testing of high school student-athletes.
- By Mitch McConnell, R-Ky., to authorize $7.6 million for excellence awards to at least one educator per congressional district. The provision had been part of the president's initiative, but the Labor Committee had shifted it to pending teachers' bills (S 1675 and S 1676).
- By Claiborne Pell, D-R.I., to change the name of Presidential Merit Schools to Presidential Schools of Distinction in order to avoid confusion with the National Merit Scholars program.

Other Provisions. Provisions of the bill not previously mentioned included:

- $50 million to extend an existing dropout-prevention program.
- $5 million to educate people about the Constitution.
- $25 million to create a grant program for colleges and universities to train middle-school teachers about the needs of adolescents.
- A reduction in the amount of earnings a dependent student would have to contribute to educational expenses to 50 percent from 70 percent.
- A prohibition on payments by postsecondary schools to recruiters, a practice used by many trade schools.
- Authorization for the Department of Education to bar from student aid programs schools that had lost their accreditation.
- Authorization for the use of records from various state licensing agencies to track down those who default on student loans.
- Requirements that lenders report to credit bureaus any borrower more than 90 days delinquent in repaying a student loan.

ACTION IN HOUSE

In the House, Democrats derided the president's package (HR 1675), saying it was little more than a vehicle to hand out ribbons and awards.

The Elementary, Secondary and Vocational Education Subcommittee on March 7 erupted into partisan bickering about the package, with Republicans demanding action and Democrats led by Chairman Augustus F. Hawkins, D-Calif., refusing to move.

Major R. Owens, D-N.Y., successfully offered a motion to postpone action on the bill. He said he did not see how Bush's initiative would help the nation's governors and the president carry out the lofty goals they had announced for eliminating illiteracy and making U.S. students first in the world in math and science by the year 2000.

"We need a master plan," Owens said. "This bill doesn't do that."

Republicans conceded the bill was not perfect, but said the committee should "get on with it."

Full Committee Action

Hawkins and the full Education and Labor Committee did just that a few weeks later. In a direct challenge to Bush, Hawkins fashioned a bill purporting to implement the education goals Bush and the governors had embraced.

The legislation (HR 4379) was patched together from portions of six pending bills — including the president's education initiative (HR 1675).

"Having a set of goals for achievement in education is quite laudable," Hawkins said. "But, as most first-year management students know, having goals without a plan to achieve them is not very useful — particularly to teachers, principals and others expected to reach the imposed targets."

Each title in Hawkins' bill shadowed the national goals and listed programs to achieve them. In addition, Hawkins added two titles dealing with teaching and with postsecondary education.

The bill primarily focused on raising the amount of money that Congress could appropriate for existing, proven programs, such as Head Start and the Women, Infants and Children (WIC) food program; the Education of the Handicapped Act; and the Chapter 1 program of compensatory education for disadvantaged children.

Altogether, the bill authorized $3.7 billion in new spending in fiscal 1991.

Republicans dismissed Hawkins' bill as a partisan ploy.

"The whole thing's a tragedy," said ranking Republican Bill Goodling, Pa.

"You don't put together a comprehensive bill unless you do it in a bipartisan fashion. And you don't put together a

Alexander Named To Education Job

President Bush announced Dec. 17 his intention to nominate Lamar Alexander, president of the University of Tennessee and a former governor of the state, to succeed fired Education Secretary Lauro F. Cavazos.

Cavazos announced his resignation Dec. 12, the day after White House Chief of Staff John H. Sununu called him in and asked him to step down.

Cavazos, the former president of Texas Tech University and the first Hispanic Cabinet member, was viewed as ineffective by members of Congress, White House officials and the education community.

Alexander, a Republican, gained wide attention in the middle of his eight years as governor from 1979 through 1986 for pushing a major education package through a Democratic-controlled legislature.

His selection to succeed Cavazos appeared to be an attempt by Bush to make good on his 1988 campaign promise to be the "education president" after two disappointing years that ended with Senate Republicans torpedoing his education proposals in the final days of the 101st Congress.

Cavazos' performance in office had also been a source of disappointment.

Appointed by President Ronald Reagan in 1988 and kept in office by Bush, Cavazos did get credit from education groups for reopening lines of communication shut by William J. Bennett, his combative predecessor. *(Cavazos appointment, 1988 Almanac, p. 344)*

During most of Cavazos' tenure, however, many observers said education policy decisions appeared to have been made by the White House.

comprehensive bill in a two-week period. The whole thing boils down to the fact that they can't stand the popularity of the president."

Nonetheless, the Education Committee voted 29-5 on June 27 to approve a somewhat scaled-down omnibus education measure (HR 5115) that combined Bush's proposals with the broader Democratic alternative.

Although the new bill reflected a bipartisan agreement, there was still some GOP grumbling about its $1.1 billion funding level. Marge Roukema, R-N.J., called the debate "Kafkaesque" and said that HR 5115 "is a bill for an unreal world."

House Floor Action

The House passed HR 5115 by 350-25 on July 20, ignoring a Bush veto threat against the $1 billion bill. *(Vote 256, p. 86-H)*

Members agreed to drop four contentious amendments, water down others, and bundle yet others in an en bloc amendment, ensuring smooth floor passage.

Behind the comity lay cold reality. The bill authorized nearly $1.1 billion in new programs — almost $700 million more than Bush requested.

The administration opposed HR 5115 as "a complex and costly amalgam" of new programs that called for funding boosts that were "totally unrealistic in the current fiscal environment," according to a statement by the Office of Management and Budget.

Democrats and Republicans alike discounted the veto threat. But the bill still faced an enormous hurdle: finding the money.

The House, in approving its annual Labor-HHS appropriations bill, which funded education programs, set aside only $2.7 billion for new programs. The $170.7 billion spending bill (HR 5257) was approved July 19. *(Labor-HHS funding bill, p. 847)*

With both sides finally working together, floor action was quick. Republicans agreed to drop a substitute that would have slashed the bill's budget authority to $680 million. Democrats dropped three of their amendments.

And they accepted two watered-down GOP proposals, including one from Minority Whip Newt Gingrich of Georgia, to require states to provide literacy programs in all prisons. Originally, Gingrich would have kept states from allowing parole for prisoners who did not participate in the literacy training.

Democrats agreed to approve $40 million in planning grants for school districts to develop "open enrollment" plans, to encourage businesses and parents to get involved in schools and to study school finance equity. In exchange, Steve Bartlett, R-Texas, dropped his amendment to require Chapter 1 funds to follow students to the schools of their choice.

Finally, the Democrats accepted a proposal from Peter Smith, R-Vt., to permit states to cut red tape, allowing them to pool local, state and federal funds to improve their education programs.

The House agreed to the en bloc amendment by a vote of 387-0. *(Vote 253, p. 86-H)*

A handful of amendments were considered separately, including one to halt financial aid to students convicted of drug possession. Offered by Gerald B. H. Solomon, R-N.Y., it would have suspended financial aid for possession of a controlled substance for one year for the first offense, two years for the second conviction and indefinitely for the third. Students convicted of selling drugs would lose their aid for two years the first time and indefinitely the second time.

Pat Williams, D-Mont., opposed the plan, pointing out that the law already allowed the courts to suspend a student's eligibility for financial aid. But Solomon said not one judge had done so. "If you become a drug pusher, don't expect the American public to help pay for your college education," Solomon said.

Although the House agreed to the amendment on a voice vote, Robert S. Walker, R-Pa., insisted on a recorded vote. The amendment carried, 315-59. *(Vote 255, p. 86-H)*

Members of the Education and Labor Committee beat back an amendment by Marge Roukema, R-N.J., that sought to reduce the default rate for guaranteed student loans.

"We need to address this problem or we'll have another S&L crisis on our hands," she said.

But committee Democrats and Republicans ganged up on her, complaining that the issue had not had a hearing and pointing out that Congress was due to reauthorize the Higher Education Act in 1991. The House rejected the amendment by 122-264. *(Vote 254, p. 86-H)*

Essentially, HR 5115 combined three bills: the president's "excellence" initiatives, a literacy bill (HR 3123) sponsored by Thomas C. Sawyer, D-Ohio, and a teacher training and recruitment measure (HR 4130), introduced by Hawkins, Goodling and Williams.

Besides including provisions and programs to carry out Bush's education goals for the year 2000, the measure urged full funding for a number of existing programs. The goals and the bill provisions follow:

- *All children in America will start school ready to learn.* The legislation called for full funding by 1994 of Head Start, which provided child care and education to low-income preschoolers, and the Special Supplemental Food Program for Women, Infants and Children, and expanded funding by 1995 for Even Start, which aided disadvantaged children ages 1 to 7 and their parents.
- *The high school graduation rate will increase to at least 90 percent.* The bill called for expanded funding for existing federal dropout-prevention programs, including the Secondary Schools Basic Skills program and the Dropout Prevention and Re-entry Act of 1988.
- *Students will leave grades four, eight and 12 having demonstrated competency in English, math, science, history and geography.* The bill called for full funding of Chapter 1, and restoration of the federal commitment to provide 40 percent of the cost of educating children with disabilities. This section replaced Bush's proposed merit schools program with the President's Schools of Distinction program.
- *Students will be first in the world in mathematics and science.* The legislation called for expansion of the Dwight D. Eisenhower Mathematics and Science Education Act. And it included a more expensive substitute to Bush's National Science Scholars program for college scholarships.
- *Every adult American will be literate and will possess the knowledge and skills necessary to compete in a global economy.* Among other things, the measure increased authorization for grants to states for adult literacy programs to $320 million.

The legislation authorized $15 million for the creation of a National Institute for Literacy to conduct research into literacy instruction, help federal, state and local agencies develop and evaluate literacy policies, provide program assistance and training, and collect and disseminate information on quality literacy programs.

- *Every school in America will be free of drugs and violence and will offer a disciplined environment conducive to learning.* The legislation called for expanded funding of student antidrug programs.
- *There will be a well-qualified teacher in every classroom in the nation, and these teachers will reflect the demographic makeup of the general population of the United States.* This was one of two goals added to the president's list by the committee. The legislation authorized a new college loan program for students willing to go into teaching.

It also offered loan forgiveness for students who agreed to teach in inner cities or rural school districts with teacher shortages.

CONFERENCE/FINAL

Once the House had acted, the education package languished for almost three months. The administration disliked the add-ons from the House and Senate. Lawmakers were preoccupied with other business, including the budget battles.

And Republicans were blocking Senate efforts to pass a teacher training measure that needed to be in the package for House-Senate conference consideration.

Finally, on Oct. 9, key House members and senators got together informally to work out a compromise.

"We are in an intolerable situation," said Sen. Edward M. Kennedy, D-Mass., chairman of the Labor and Human Resources Committee. "We're basically being stymied."

Kennedy accused the White House of orchestrating an effort by Republican senators to hold up passage of the teacher recruitment and training bill (S 1676) to prevent Congress from sending Bush a package he would veto.

Kennedy had been trying to bring the teacher bill up on the floor since July, but Helms, Gordon J. Humphrey, R-N.H., and possibly others put holds on it.

"We regret that situation and we apologize to House members," Kennedy said at the meeting.

Victor F. Klatt, director of legislation and congressional affairs for the Department of Education, said the administration was not trying to stall and denied that administration officials had been working with Helms or Humphrey to prevent the bill from moving along.

"We haven't requested them to delay things," Klatt said. "We haven't requested they not delay things, either."

Thirty minutes before the members got together, Hawkins received a letter from Education Secretary Lauro F. Cavazos threatening a veto.

In his letter, Cavazos said major objections stemmed from the House version.

"The House bill, especially, is a disappointment: a complex, unwieldy array of new programs, most of which are not needed, and undesirable amendments to current program statutes," he wrote.

White House officials finally asked to join the discussions, and Roger B. Porter, assistant to the president for economic and domestic policy, participated in the negotiations. In a closed-door meeting Oct. 18, a final, compromise version was approved.

The House passed the new bill (HR 5932) by voice vote on Oct. 26, with Hawkins calling it "the final product of two strong bipartisan measures."

But when Senate Majority Leader George J. Mitchell, D-Maine, tried to call the measure up on Oct. 27, Helms and a number of other conservative Republicans objected.

Congress adjourned a few hours later, and the education bill died. ■

Compensatory Education

Congress on May 14 cleared legislation (HR 3910 — PL 101-305) authorizing a detailed nationwide assessment of the Chapter 1 program of compensatory education for educationally disadvantaged children.

Chapter 1, the biggest program of federal aid to elementary and secondary education, served more than 5 million children. It would be up for reauthorization in 1993, and Congress wanted a fresh assessment of the program by that time.

HR 3910, authorizing $6 million for the assessment from existing appropriations, was passed by the House on Feb. 27. The Senate approved the bill May 7, with minor amendments. The House accepted most of those May 10, and the Senate gave final approval to the bill May 14. President Bush signed the measure May 30. ■

Education for Disabled Reauthorized

In the rush to adjournment, House members on Oct. 15 cleared the conference report on legislation to reauthorize some of the programs under the Education of the Handicapped Act (EHA), the landmark 1975 act that mandated free education for children with disabilities and created a permanent federal grant program to states.

President Bush signed the bill (S 1824) on Oct. 30. The Senate approved the conference report on Oct. 2.

The bill authorized $321 million in fiscal 1991, rising to $409 million in fiscal 1994, for the discretionary programs under the 1975 law. Congress appropriated $182 million for these programs in fiscal 1990 and $203 million in fiscal 1991.

The legislation also renamed the act the Individuals with Disabilities Act and substituted the word "disabilities" for "handicapped" throughout the law. In keeping with this, the Senate Labor Committee in 1989 changed the name of its subcommittee from Handicapped to Disability Policy. *(1989 Almanac, p. 198)*

BOXSCORE

Legislation: Individuals with Disabilities Act, PL 101-476 (S 1824, HR 1013).

Major action: Signed, Oct. 30. Conference report adopted by House, Oct. 15; by Senate, Oct. 2. Passed by House, June 18; by Senate, Nov. 16, 1989.

Reports: Conference report (H Rept 101-787). Education and Labor (H Rept 101-544). Labor and Human Resources (S Rept 101-204).

BACKGROUND

The landmark 1975 EHA (PL 94-142) helped states pay for the added expense involved in educating children with disabilities. While the basic grant program under the act was permanently authorized, smaller discretionary programs under the law needed periodic renewal. *(1975 Almanac, p. 651)*

The most recent reauthorizations, in 1983 and 1986, created sizable programs aimed at disabled infants and toddlers. *(1986 Almanac, p. 270)*

The new bill focused on "fine-tuning the discretionary programs," said Sen. Tom Harkin, D-Iowa, chairman of the Subcommittee on Disability Policy. S 1824 authorized money for a wide array of the discretionary programs, including those to provide early education to children with disabilities, to provide postsecondary educational opportunities, to train personnel to teach the disabled, to fund research into ways to educate the disabled and to advance the use of new technology, educational media and materials for those with disabilities.

Harkin said his committee was especially eager to address a shortage of trained special education teachers. The Department of Education had estimated the shortfall at 27,474 teachers in the 1985-86 school year.

By voice vote, the Senate on Nov. 16, 1989, approved S 1824 to reauthorize through fiscal 1994 discretionary programs under the Education of the Handicapped Act.

The measure had been approved unanimously Nov. 1, 1989, by the Labor and Human Resources Committee.

One provision of S 1824 had the effect of reversing a Supreme Court decision. In June 1989, the Supreme Court ruled 5-4 in *Dellmuth v. Muth* that children with disabilities who were denied an appropriate, free public education by a state were not entitled to be reimbursed for tuition paid by their parents for their education in an alternative program.

The court held that the state was immune, under the 11th Amendment, from suits in federal court arising out of the handicapped education act.

S 1824 clarified that it was the intention of Congress to allow litigants the right to sue in federal court to enforce their rights under the act.

The measure also created several new programs, among them:

- $27.5 million for programs to help disabled youths make the transition from school to the outside world.

At hearings in 1989, experts testified that disabled children often did not learn essential, routine tasks such as doing laundry, balancing a checkbook or using public transportation. According to the Senate Labor and Human Resources Committee's report, more than 200,000 students left the nation's school systems every year, many lacking these fundamental skills.

This transitional assistance could also include vocational training, as well as postsecondary education.

- $19.25 million for historically black colleges and universities, to encourage more minority students to get special-education degrees. According to the House Education and Labor Committee report, while 28 percent of the children enrolled in special-education classes were black, only 11.2 percent of their teachers were black. The bill directed special-education grants to colleges or universities with at least 25 percent minority enrollment.
- $6.5 million to improve research and information on teaching emotionally disturbed children. Part of the money would go for state grants — to colleges, for example — to develop curricula for disturbed children.

COMMITTEE ACTION

The House Education and Labor Committee approved legislation (HR 1013) May 16 to reauthorize discretionary programs under the EHA. The Subcommittee on Select Education had approved the legislation May 3.

HR 1013 set funding levels for smaller discretionary programs, including those to help preschoolers, train personnel to teach the disabled and advance the use of new technologies that could help the disabled. Specifically, the bill authorized two new programs — one to encourage blacks to become special-education teachers and another to help disabled people make the transition from classrooms to jobs or from dependent to independent living situations.

HR 1013 authorized $319 million in fiscal 1991 for a variety of smaller programs to help preschoolers, to train people to teach the disabled and to develop technologies to help the disabled. The amount was 10.8 percent more than the 1990 authorization.

S 1894, the Senate measure passed in 1989, authorized $259 million in fiscal 1991.

Under the House bill, historically black colleges and universities could have received up to $17.5 million to begin programs to train students to teach special education. The bill authorized $25 million for one-time, five-year grants for a transition demonstration program to coordinate existing services for the disabled.

Like the Senate-passed measure, the House bill also provided for reversing the 1989 Supreme Court ruling in *Dellmuth v. Muth.*

On a motion by Steve Bartlett, R-Texas, the committee agreed, 16-12, to strike from the bill any mention of corporal punishment, settling a contentious issue that had emerged in subcommittee. Some of the bill's supporters, led by subcommittee Chairman Major R. Owens, D-N.Y., sought to restrict corporal punishment. During subcommittee markup, Owens pushed through an amendment to ban corporal punishment of students with disabilities.

The panel rejected a substitute offered by Bartlett that would have allowed the teacher and parents of a disabled student to meet before each school year to determine whether corporal punishment should be used.

But in full committee, Bartlett recovered and prevailed. When Owens amended the provision to exclude "aversive therapy" from the ban, Bartlett and committee Chairman Augustus F. Hawkins, D-Calif., protested that the distinction between punishment and therapy was not clear. They ushered through the amendment ridding the bill of any mention of corporal punishment.

FLOOR, FINAL ACTION

The House on June 18, after a year of hearings in the Education and Labor Committee, passed its version of the bill and inserted it into S 1824. The bill authorized a 10 percent annual increase in budget authority for fiscal years 1990-94, beginning at $282.1 million in fiscal 1990. Also included was a new $25 million transition program to help disabled students move from school to the workplace.

In addition, the measure placed greater emphasis on the need to work with minority children with disabilities.

The bill included $17.5 million for historically black colleges and universities to recruit and train students to become special-education teachers.

The legislation did not affect a state grant program, which was permanently authorized to provide money to state education agencies to support educational programs for children with disabilities.

After convening for only minutes, House-Senate conferees on Sept. 27 reached agreement on S 1824.

Action on the bill, which conferee Harkin called "responsive to the changing needs of students and parents," was smooth because the differences were largely technical. Staff members quickly compromised on the one substantive area of disagreement: whether students with "attention deficit disorder" should get benefits. The House bill included the problem as a covered disability; the Senate version did not. The compromise mandated a six-month study of the issue.

Once the measure made its way back to the House and Senate, it faced little difficulty.

Both chambers approved the conference report by voice vote, as they were concerned with more controversial issues that threatened to delay further their already late adjournment. ■

Library Programs Funded

Congress early in 1990 cleared legislation (HR 2742 — PL 101-254) reauthorizing federal support for libraries for five years.

The House on Feb. 27 approved the conference report (H Rept 101-407) on the measure by a vote of 401-4. *(Vote 16, p. 10-H)*

The Senate followed suit by voice vote on March 1, sending the bill to President Bush, who signed it March 15.

Rep. Pat Williams, D-Mont., said the bill made few substantive changes in the existing law because lawmakers wanted to wait for an assessment of the nation's libraries from an upcoming White House Conference on Libraries as the basis for future changes.

The conference on the bill was completed Feb. 20. The Senate's version (S 1291) had been approved Oct. 12, 1989; the House passed its bill Sept. 12. *(1989 Almanac, p. 194)*

Major Provisions

As cleared, the bill authorized $207.5 million in fiscal 1990, up from actual 1989 spending of $127.2 million. The Senate had voted $201.5 million, while the House had approved $213.5 million. However, actual appropriations for the year were only $126.3 million.

Conferees accepted a House proposal authorizing funds for family learning centers and a Senate plan for literacy centers at local libraries. But no funds could be spent for these purposes until the regular library services, construction and interlibrary cooperation programs were funded at 1989 appropriations levels plus 4 percent.

The legislation sought to encourage libraries to remain open on weekday evenings, Saturdays and some Sundays, plus legal holidays, in order for families to use the library together. The bill authorized $3 million for fiscal 1990 for the family program.

The second half of the new title was supplied by Sens. Thad Cochran, R-Miss., and Paul Simon, D-Ill., for adult literacy centers at libraries. The bill authorized $3 million in fiscal 1991 for grants not to exceed $350,000 per state.

In other conference changes:

- The Senate accepted a House provision authorizing use of library act funds to reimburse school libraries that stayed open to the public when school was out of session.
- The House accepted a Senate provision by Jesse Helms, R-N.C., to prohibit libraries receiving funds under the act from discriminating against groups on the basis of race, religion, age, gender, national origin or handicap when providing space for public meetings.
- The Senate agreed to a House proposal for libraries to participate in drug-abuse prevention programs.

Before conference, both the House and Senate decided to change the bill by allowing federal funds to be used to buy state-of-the-art technological equipment and to preserve aging books.

The bill also allowed funding to bring mobile library services to child-care centers. And it authorized $500,000 for the Department of Education to study the effectiveness of the federal library programs.

A portion of the law authorizing funding for library services to American Indians and Native Hawaiians was to receive 1.5 percent of the amount spent on the main programs. ■

Student Religious Groups' Rights Upheld

The Supreme Court on June 4 upheld the constitutionality of a 1984 federal statute that allowed student religious groups to meet in public high schools on the same basis as other extracurricular clubs.

By 8-1, the court in *Board of Education of Westside Community Schools v. Mergens* affirmed an appeals court ruling that a student who wanted to start a Bible study group at her high school in Omaha, Neb., should have been permitted to do so.

The Equal Access Act (PL 98-377) barred secondary schools that received federal funds and allowed extracurricular student groups to meet on school grounds before or after classes from discriminating against any group because of the subject it wished to discuss. *(1984 Almanac, p. 488)*

The bill was passed after the Senate had rejected a proposed constitutional amendment to permit organized, recited prayer in the public schools.

The access bill was seen as a political safety net that might protect members from constituent anger over the defeat of the school prayer amendment, which the Senate rejected in March 1984. Opponents complained that the law was a "backdoor" effort to slip religion into the public schools.

Justices' Opinions

Justice Sandra Day O'Connor, writing the lead opinion in the court's decision to uphold the law, however, said that Congress' purpose in passing the law was "undeniably secular."

"Because the act on its face grants equal access to both secular and religious speech, we think it clear that the act's purpose was not to endorse or disapprove of religion," O'Connor wrote. She was joined in her analysis by Chief Justice William H. Rehnquist and Justices Byron R. White and Harry A. Blackmun.

Justice Anthony M. Kennedy, joined by Justice Antonin Scalia, wrote a separate opinion that took a more relaxed view of permissible mixing of religion in the schools.

In another concurrence, Justices Thurgood Marshall and William J. Brennan Jr. leaned the opposite way, saying schools that allowed a Bible study club had to take steps to fully dissociate themselves from the club's religious speech.

Justice John Paul Stevens dissented, saying the act should have been more narrowly construed so that the school would not be required to open its doors "to every religious, political, or social organization, no matter how controversial or distasteful its views may be."

Background of Case

The case had begun with an effort by Bridget Mergens to gain formal club status for a Christian Bible club at Westside High School in Omaha.

The principal and the school board turned her down, saying that official sponsorship would violate the Establishment Clause of the Constitution.

A federal district court ruled for the school officials, saying that Westside did not have a limited open forum because all of the student clubs were curriculum-related. But the 8th U.S. Circuit Court of Appeals reversed the decision, saying that interpretation of the act would render it "meaningless."

Dropout Program Cleared

The Senate on Feb. 20 approved, 94-0, legislation (HR 2281) to reauthorize a nationwide program of demonstration projects designed to reduce school dropout rates, clearing the bill for President Bush. *(Vote 15, p. 6-S)*

Bush signed the bill March 6 (PL 101-150). The House had passed the bill June 13, 1989. *(1989 Almanac, p. 198)*

Since the dropout-prevention program was created in 1988 (PL 100-297), the federal government had spent more than $45 million on 89 projects affecting 50,000 students in 32 states. Most of the projects targeted educationally or economically disadvantaged students. About one-third focused on pregnant teenagers.

HR 2281 authorized $50 million annually for fiscal 1990-91. The program's authorization had lapsed at the end of fiscal 1989; that year, Congress appropriated $21.7 million for it.

The Senate included provisions reauthorizing the dropout-prevention program in two broader bills — S 1939, a reauthorization of the Taft Institute, and S 695, its version of the Bush education initiative — that it passed during the 101st Congress. But when the House had failed to approve either of those bills, senators decided it was time to move the reauthorization separately. *(Bush education initiative, p. 610; Taft Institute, p. 628)*

In floor debate Feb. 20, senators lined up to explain the benefits of keeping students in school and to offer praise for the demonstration projects. Claiborne Pell, D-R.I., chairman of the Labor and Human Resources Subcommittee on Education, said the annual dropout rate in the United States averaged 25 percent and that dropout rates in urban areas often reached 50 percent or higher.

"While dropping out of school holds severe repercussions for the individual student, and while it means an immediate cost to us in welfare and other social costs, it is the loss in productivity and output which poses the greatest danger," Pell said.

Nancy Landon Kassebaum, R-Kan., concurred: "Failure to receive a high school diploma spells tragedy for the individual dropout, who operates at a permanent disadvantage in job prospects and lifetime earnings. It is a tragedy as well for our nation, which loses the productive capacity we so badly need from all our workers."

Edward M. Kennedy, D-Mass., reminded lawmakers that despite the positive impact of many pilot programs, Congress had not provided nearly enough money to reach the 700,000 or more students who dropped out each year. He noted that the Department of Education had received more than 800 proposals for funding under the dropout-prevention program — nine times more than it could fill. ■

Overhaul of Vocational Education Aid

Congress on Sept. 13 cleared legislation authorizing a fresh infusion of funds for vocational education programs and somewhat relaxing federal strings on the money.

Final action on the bill (HR 7) to reauthorize and redirect federal support for vocational education came when the House adopted the conference report by voice vote Sept. 13. The Senate had approved the measure Aug. 2, also by voice vote.

The bill authorized $1.6 billion in fiscal 1991 for programs designed to serve students unlikely to pursue a traditional college education.

Rep. Augustus F. Hawkins, D-Calif., chairman of the House Education and Labor Committee, called it a comprehensive measure to revamp vocational education programs "for the modern era and the changing workplace."

BOXSCORE

Legislation: Carl D. Perkins Vocational and Applied Technology Education Act, PL 101-392 (HR 7, S 1109).

Major action: Signed, Sept. 25. Conference report adopted by House, Sept. 13; by Senate, Aug. 2. Passed by Senate, 96-0, April 5; by House, 402-3, May 9, 1989.

Reports: Conference report (H Rept 101-660). Labor and Human Resources (S Rept 101-221). Education and Labor (H Rept 101-41).

The Senate version had emphasized high school programs, rather than postsecondary education. The House version and the final bill retained existing law, which allowed states to decide where to focus their money.

The money was targeted by formula, however, to students with disabilities, students who did not speak English well, students who were economically disadvantaged and programs serving men and women in non-traditional occupations.

The measure also relaxed some of the rigid set-asides that had splintered the available federal aid into fragments too small to be of much help to anybody.

And it authorized $125 million in fiscal 1991 for new "tech-prep" programs, in which students would start a vocational training program in their last two years of high school and complete it during two years at a community college or postsecondary technical school.

The bill boosted to 75 percent the federal aid states would have to direct toward improving programs and lowered to 25 percent the amount to be carved up for special groups such as the disabled or displaced homemakers.

The legislation also required states to make grants of at least $15,000 to secondary schools and at least $50,000 to postsecondary institutions, although waivers could be obtained for rural areas.

President Bush signed the bill Sept. 25, saying the measure "creates a more effective vocational education program through its emphasis on accountability and program improvement."

BACKGROUND

Vocational education had long been the neglected stepchild of the education world — fending for itself with only the bare essentials of survival. Vocational education's slice of the federal education budget had declined significantly since the 1960s. So had the federal share of total vocational education spending — from about 20 percent to less than 10 percent.

Persistent attacks during the Reagan years — culminating in 1988 with an attempt to abolish the Carl D. Perkins Vocational Education Act's grant program (PL 98-524) — left the vocational education budget with nearly one-third less purchasing power than it had in 1980, according to the Congressional Research Service.

The result was a program dominated by relatively tiny grants — some as small as $100 — that paid primarily for equipment instead of teachers.

With all that in mind, Congress set out in 1989 to extend and rewrite the Perkins Act in the first major look at the programs since 1984. *(1989 Almanac, p. 182)*

The curtain raiser for congressional debate on vocational education was a November 1988 report called "The Forgotten Half," produced by the nonprofit William T. Grant Foundation's Commission on Work, Family and Citizenship.

The report said that the U.S. education system unfairly favored college-bound students over those unlikely to attend a traditional college. It concluded that federal, state and local governments and private entities spent $45 billion a year subsidizing college students but no more than $7 billion annually on postsecondary training for those who did not go to traditional colleges. According to the study's rough estimates, 20 million 16-to-24-year-olds were not likely to attend college, while an equal number would attend or already had attended.

"Educators have become so preoccupied with those who go on to college that they have lost sight of those who do not," the report concluded. "And more and more of the non-college-bound now fall between the cracks when they are in school, drop out or graduate inadequately prepared for the requirements of society and the work place.... The loss of The Forgotten Half's potential is unfair to them and wasteful to the nation."

The House passed its version of HR 7, reauthorizing programs at $1.4 billion, on May 9, 1989, by a vote of 402-3. The House Education and Labor Committee had given its approval to the measure on April 25.

Meanwhile, the Senate Labor and Human Resources Committee approved its own $1.5 billion reauthorization (S 1109) on Nov. 1 by a 16-0 vote.

Full Senate action and the House-Senate conference were expected early in 1990 since differences between the chambers' bills were relatively minor.

SENATE ACTION

The Senate approved its five-year reauthorization bill with major funding increases 96-0 on April 5. The bill set fiscal 1991 funding at $1.5 billion and permitted spending of "such sums as may be necessary" over the other four years. *(Vote 57, p. 14-S)*

Continued on p. 622

Vocational Education Act Provisions

Following are provisions of the Carl D. Perkins Vocational and Applied Technology Education Act (PL 101-392 — HR 7):

• **Purpose.** Attempted to make the United States more competitive in the world economy by developing more fully the academic and occupational skills of all segments of the population. That included concentrating resources on improving educational programs leading to academic and occupational skills needed to work in a technologically advanced society.

• **Appropriations.** Authorized $1.6 billion in fiscal 1991 and such sums as might be necessary through fiscal 1995.

• **Coordination of vocational education programs.** Established the Interdepartmental Task Force on Vocational Education and Related Programs. Membership would include the secretaries of Education, Labor, and Health and Human Services.

Required the task force to examine common objectives, definitions, measures and standards for the Adult Education Act, the Carl D. Perkins Vocational and Applied Technology Education Act, the Job Training Partnership Act, the Rehabilitation Act of 1973 and the Wagner-Peyser Act.

Required the task force to report to Congress every two years on its findings.

Assistance to States

• **Allotment.** Limited states to receiving no more than an amount calculated by multiplying the number of individuals in the state counted in the formula for vocational education funds by 150 percent of the national average per student payment. No state would receive less than it received in fiscal 1989.

Reserved 1.25 percent of appropriations for Indian programs and 0.25 percent for native Hawaiians.

Required that 0.2 percent of appropriations be reserved for the territories, except for the Virgin Islands.

Required states to match federal funds on a dollar-for-dollar basis, using non-federal funds.

Required 10.5 percent of the Basic State Grants to go to programs for single parents, displaced homemakers, single pregnant women and sex equity. Sex equity programs were designed to encourage women to go into traditionally male occupations and vice versa.

Minimum grants to Bureau of Indian Affairs' schools for vocational education programs would be $35,000.

• **State organizational and planning responsibilities.** Required the state board for vocational education, which governed the federal funds for vocational programs, to consult not only with the state council, which was an advisory body to the board appointed by the governor, but also with business, industry and labor in planning, administering, evaluating and coordinating programs.

Required the state board to review and comment upon plans of local educational agencies, area vocational education schools, intermediate educational agencies and postsecondary education institutions to ensure that the needs of those training in non-traditional jobs were met.

Required states to ensure access to programs for students with disabilities.

• **State council on vocational education.** Required that no state council receive more than $250,000 for each fiscal year, no less than $150,000 for each fiscal year and no less than was allotted in fiscal 1990.

• **State plan.** Required any state that wanted to receive federal vocational education funds to submit to the secretary of Education a three-year plan.

Required the state board to conduct public hearings to receive recommendations about the plan.

Required that the state plan be submitted to the secretary by May 1. The secretary would have to approve qualifying plans within 60 days.

• **Standards and measures.** Required each state board receiving funds to develop and put into effect a statewide system of core standards and measures of performance for secondary and postsecondary vocational education programs.

• **Assessment.** Required each state board receiving assistance to conduct an assessment using measurable objective criteria developed by the state board to assess program quality.

• **Criteria for services for special populations.** Required the state board in its state plan to provide assurances that people who were members of special populations, such as people who were disabled or had limited English proficiency, be provided with equal access to recruitment, enrollment and placement activities. And those people would be provided equal access to the full range of vocational education programs available to people who were not members of special populations.

Basic State Grants

• **State programs.** Required each state to conduct programs and leadership activities such as professional development for vocational teachers and academic teachers working with vocational education students, as well as corrections educators and counselors and educators in community-based organizations. The programs could also include the promotion of partnerships among business, education, industry, labor, community-based organizations and government agencies.

• **Programs for single parents.** Required states to provide, subsidize, reimburse or pay for preparatory services, including instruction in basic academic and occupational skills, in preparing for vocational education and training that would provide single parents, displaced homemakers and single pregnant women with marketable skills.

Required states to make grants to community-based organizations for providing preparatory and vocational education services to single parents, displaced homemakers and single pregnant women if the state determined that the community-based organization was more effective in providing these services.

• **Sex-equity programs.** Required states to provide programs, services, career guidance and counseling to eliminate sex bias and stereotyping in secondary and postsecondary vocational education. Required states to provide preparatory services and vocational education programs for girls and women, ages 14-25, to enable them to support themselves and their families.

• **Programs for criminal offenders.** Required each state board to designate one or more state corrections agencies as the state corrections education agency to administer vocational education programs for juvenile and adult criminal offenders in correctional institutions.

• **Distribution of funds to secondary school programs.** Required each state to distribute Basic State Grant funds in any fiscal year for secondary school vocational education programs to local education agencies as follows:

• 70 percent of the allocation based on a local education agency's share of Chapter 1 basic grants, serving economically disadvantaged students.

• 20 percent based on disabled students.

• 10 percent based on adults enrolled in training programs and general enrollment.

Set the minimum grant to local education agencies at $15,000. Allowed local education agencies to enter into a consortium with other agencies in order to qualify for the minimum grant.

• **Distribution of funds to postsecondary and adult programs.** Required each state to distribute funds available in any fiscal year for postsecondary and adult vocational education programs to eligible institutions. Those institutions would receive their allocations on the following basis:

• 70 percent on the number of Pell grant recipients and the number of students receiving aid from the Bureau of Indian Affairs.

• 20 percent based on vocational rehabilitation enrollment.

• 10 percent based on general enrollment.

Set the minimum grant at $50,000.

• **Uses of funds.** Each local education agency and postsecondary institution would have to use its funds only to:

• Serve schools with the most special-needs students.

• Provide programs that integrated academic and occupational disciplines, offered coherent sequences of courses leading to a job skill, offered counseling, assisted special needs students through supportive services, upgraded curricula, and gave in-service training of vocational and academic instructors, among other things.

Special Programs

• **Use of funds.** Permited community-based organizations to use vocational funds for model programs for school dropouts.

• **Business-labor-education partnership for training.** Required the secretary of Education to make grants to states to enable states to award grants to partnerships among: an area vocational education school, a state agency, a local educational agency, a secondary school funded by the Bureau of Indian Affairs, an institution of higher education, a state corrections educational agency or an adult learning center and business, industry, labor organizations or apprenticeship programs.

The partnerships would carry out business-labor-education training programs. Funds were to include incentives for coordinating programs with other programs under the Job Training Partnership Act.

Funds were to be awarded on a competitive basis for vocational education programs, including programs to:

• Provide apprenticeships and internships in industry.

• Provide new equipment.

• Provide teacher internships or training.

• Bring representatives of business and organized labor into the classroom.

• Increase the access to programs for people who were members of special populations.

• **Tech-prep education.** Provideed planning and demonstration grants to consortia of local educational agencies and postsecondary education institutions to develop and operate four-year programs to provide a technical-preparation program leading to a two-year associate degree or a two-year certificate; and to provide strong, comprehensive links between secondary schools and postsecondary education institutions.

The program was to consist of two years of secondary school prior to graduation and two years of higher education or an apprenticeship program of at least two years following secondary school with a common core of math, science, communications and technologies.

Authorized $125 million in fiscal 1991 and such sums through fiscal 1995.

• **Supplementary state grants for facilities and equipment.** Provided funding to local educational agencies in economically depressed areas for program-improvement activities, especially the improvement of facilities and acquisition or leasing of equipment to be used to carry out vocational education programs.

Required each local education agency or consortium of agencies to use these grants to first improve facilities and equipment and then for curriculum development or teacher training.

• **Community education employment centers.** Provided grants to enable schools to establish community education employment centers to provide students with the education, skills, support services and enrichment to ensure:

• Graduation from secondary school.

• Successful transition from secondary schools to a broad range of postsecondary institutions.

• Employment, including military service.

Authorized 10 centers to be established nationwide. Grants awarded were to be provided for a five-year period. Authorized $10 million in fiscal 1991-92 to be divided between community education centers (75 percent) and lighthouse schools (25 percent).

• **Vocational education "lighthouse" schools.** Authorized the secretary to make grants to secondary schools and area vocational education schools to enable them to establish and operate vocational education lighthouse schools.

Lighthouse schools would:

• Serve as a model vocational education program.

• Provide information and assistance to other grant recipients, vocational programs, vocational education personnel, parents, students, other educators, community members and community organizations throughout the state.

• Develop comprehensive links with other local schools, community colleges, four-year colleges, private vocational schools, community-based organizations, labor unions, employers and other business groups.

• Develop and disseminate model approaches to meet the education training needs and career counseling needs for minority students, disadvantaged students, students with disabilities and students of limited English proficiency and to reduce and eliminate sex bias and stereotyping.

• **Tribally controlled postsecondary vocational institutions.** Provided grants to operate and improve tribally controlled postsecondary vocational institutions to ensure continued and expanded educational opportunities for Indian students and to allow for the improvement and expansion of the physical resources of those institutions. Grants were to be used for training, education, equipment and administrative costs.

• **Tribal economic development.** Authorized the secretary to make grants to tribally controlled community colleges that received grants for vocational education or from the Navajo Community College Act to support tribal economic development and education institutes.

Each program would:

• Determine the economic development needs and potential of the Indian tribes involved in the program, including agriculture and natural resources needs.

• Develop courses to prepare postsecondary students, tribal officials and others to meet those economic development, agriculture and natural resources needs.

• Provide technical assistance and training to federal, tribal and community officials and business managers and planners deemed necessary by the institution to enable tribal economic development.

• Provide clearinghouse activities to coordinate all vocational activities serving all students of the Indian tribe.

Authorized $2 million in fiscal 1991.

National Programs

• **Research and development.** Required the secretary of Education to research developing performance standards and measures. Required the secretary to evaluate the use of performance standards, including their effect on students.

Authorized the secretary to establish a national network for curriculum coordination, including six regional curriculum coordination centers. Required the network, among other things, to:

• Disseminate information of effective vocational education programs and materials.

• Be accessible electronically.

• Provide leadership and technical assistance in the design and development of curricula for vocational education.

• Promote the use of research findings to vocational education curricula.

Required a national assessment of vocational education to be conducted through the Office of Education Research and Improvement by an independent assessment group. Required a final report to Congress by July 1, 1994.

Authorized the secretary to award a grant or grants to establish one or two national centers to study applied research and development, and dissemination and training of vocational education issues. Those issues included:

• Economic changes that affected the skills that employers sought and entrepreneurs needed.

• Integration of academic and vocational education.

• Teacher and administrator training and leadership development.

• **Demonstration programs.** Authorized the secretary to make grants to nonprofit educational telecommunications entities to pay the federal share of the costs of the development, production and distribution of instructional telecommunications materials and services for use in local vocational and technical schools and colleges.

The federal share of each project was 50 percent. The rest of the funds were to have to come from non-federal sources.

Authorized the secretary to establish one or more demonstration centers to retrain dislocated workers.

The center or centers were to recruit unemployed workers and provide vocational evaluation, assessment and counseling services, vocational and technical training, support services and job-place ment assistance. Eligible groups to run a center included any private, nonprofit organization that was eligible to receive funding under the Job Training Partnership Act.

Authorized the secretary to provide grants to institutions of higher education, state educational agencies or state correctional education agencies to provide grants, awards or stipends for:

- People entering the vocational education field.
- Graduate training in vocational education.
- Vocational teacher education.
- Attracting gifted and talented students in vocational programs into further study and professional development.

Authorized the secretary to provide grants to institutions for stipends to individuals not to exceed $9,000 per individual per academic year and $3,000 per individual per summer session.

Authorized the secretary to provide awards to secondary and postsecondary schools or programs that had established a high level of quality.

The schools and programs would be known as "Blue Ribbon Vocational Programs."

Authorized the secretary of Education, in consultation with the secretary of Labor, to provide grants to industrial trade associations, labor organizations or comparable national organizations to organize and operate business-labor-education technical committees.

The committees were to propose national standards for competency levels in different industries and trades, including standards for minimum hours of study to be competent in a specialty, minimum qualifications for instructional staff, and minimum tools and equipment required in a specialty.

Authorized the secretary of Education to make grants to federal correctional institutions in consortia with educational institutions, community-based organizations or business and industry to provide education and training for criminal offenders.

Authorized the secretary to make grants to partnerships between local education agencies or area vocational education schools; and institutions of higher education or public or private nonprofit groups. The partnerships were to develop and operate vocational education programs to prevent students from dropping out of school.

General Provisions

- **Federal regulations.** Require the secretary of Education to convene regional meetings in developing proposed regulations. Required the secretary to include tribal administrators and members of special populations, such as the disabled, in regional meetings to help develop proposed regulations.

Permited regional meeting and negotiated rulemaking requirements to be waived in cases in which a regulation would have to be issued quickly to assist state and local programs operate. Required the secretary to immediately convene regional meetings to review the regulation before it became final.

Requireed that states provide non-federal funds for program administration in an amount no less than that provided in the previous fiscal year.

Renamed vocational education as vocational and applied technology education.

Limited the term "disadvantaged" to only those who were economically disadvantaged and ensured that any individual considered economically disadvantaged under the Job Training Partnership Act would be considered economically disadvantaged under this act.

Defined special populations to include people with disabilities, disadvantaged individuals, people with limited English proficiency, foster children and people in correctional institutions.

Required an effective date for the act of July 1, 1991. ■

Continued from p. 619

Both the Senate bill and the House bill, passed in 1989, recommended much more money for the Perkins program than the $929.7 million requested by the Bush administration in 1991, the same as the 1990 level.

Senators said a strong program of vocational education was essential to maintain U.S. economic competitiveness in a world marketplace.

"Where we eventually stand in that competition will depend directly upon the quality of the education and training provided our citizens," said Claiborne Pell, D-R.I., chairman of the Labor and Human Resources Subcommittee on Education, Arts and the Humanities.

Nancy Landon Kassebaum, Kan., the subcommittee's ranking Republican, said, "Strong vocational programs are a critical component of the economic machinery which will assure our continued world leadership and prosperity."

The legislation sought to address problems arising from the 1984 reauthorization of the Perkins Act. That law created so many set-asides for various population subgroups that money was spread too thinly and few were served adequately, the committee found. *(1984 Almanac, p. 455)*

The 1990 legislation required the federal government to bypass the states and distribute funds directly to local school districts using the formula of the Chapter 1 program of compensatory education, serving areas with high concentrations of economically disadvantaged students.

The money had to be targeted to students who were economically disadvantaged or disabled, had limited proficiency in English or were learning a non-traditional occupation for their gender. To have an impact, grants had to be at least $25,000.

The Senate bill, but not the House version, required 65 percent to 75 percent of federal vocational education aid to go to secondary schools.

"That is where the majority of our students are, and that should be the primary thrust of the federal dollar," Pell said. "It is also the area where quality vocational education programs are most necessary in terms of combating the dropout rate, overcoming the wrenching effect poverty can have on the pursuit of an education and preparing young people either for the workplace or for additional education."

Existing law gave states total discretion over distribution of the federal funds, and Dave Durenberger, R-Minn., protested elimination of that flexibility. In Minnesota, he said, state officials had long ago decided to direct federal vocational education funds to postsecondary programs and to supplement secondary school programs with state money.

In a compromise between Durenberger and the Labor and Human Resources Committee, the bill allowed states to seek a waiver, which would allow them to direct 50 percent of the federal funds to postsecondary and adult vocational programs.

Up to 15 percent of the money received by postsecondary programs would have to be used only for the neediest students, including high school dropouts and adults without a high school diploma, according to the compromise.

The bill contained a partial "hold-harmless" clause for a three-year period, to ease the shift of money away from postsecondary schools.

One widely praised provision of the bill authorized 5 percent of all funds authorized under the bill to establish the tech-prep programs in each state. Also known as 2 + 2 programs, these would offer grants to local schools to link secondary and postsecondary schools, including community colleges and apprenticeship programs.

The schools would then develop curricula to ensure that students progressed smoothly from one level to the next without repetitive coursework. The grants could also be used for training teachers and buying equipment.

The Senate adopted a proposal by Frank R. Lautenberg, D-N.J., to establish a Community Education Employment Centers demonstration program, authorizing $16 million in 1991 and in each year through 1995.

The centers would not only teach vocational and academic courses, but also provide counseling, day care and other social services to help students graduate from high school, enroll in postsecondary schools and find jobs.

"We cannot let there become a permanent urban and rural underclass," Lautenberg said. "We must assume a greater responsibility for the education of low-income youth."

CONFERENCE ACTION

After a daylong meeting July 23, staff members found a solution to the most contentious issue conferees had left hanging: whether to target money to secondary or to postsecondary students.

The Senate bill targeted high school programs, rather than community college or postsecondary technical schools, in an effort to reduce the high school dropout rate. The House retained existing law, which allowed states to decide where to focus their money.

Vocational education programs "don't exist to catch dropouts," said Rep. Peter Smith, R-Vt. Instead, House members argued that vocational training was crucial for developing a skilled work force.

The House prevailed under the agreement, which let states continue to decide where the money was needed most. If a state wanted to spend up to 15 percent of its federal grant on either postsecondary or secondary vocational education, those funds did not have to be distributed under a formula. Opponents argued that the formula process would spread the money too thin.

At their first meeting July 19, House and Senate conferees had been sharply divided over the thrust of the bill and failed to resolve the targeting issue. Kassebaum offered a compromise that would have rewarded states for putting 70 percent of their federal funds into secondary schools by allowing them to distribute the balance of the money through grants to trade schools and community colleges rather than allocating funds by strict formulas.

But House conferees had just yielded on another issue, allowing the Senate to keep its language on state oversight boards. It was the senators' turn to give in, House members insisted. In the end, the conferees moved on to other issues, leaving the Kassebaum compromise hanging.

Compromises Reached

A week later, staff members reached the final compromise on targeting funds and also settled a host of smaller issues. They agreed to include a modified version of negotiated rulemaking in the final bill. The House had included a provision to require the secretary of Education to submit potential regulations for review by public panels. The Senate had no such provision. Conference staffers agreed to narrow the process: Ten people from throughout the country would negotiate no fewer than two issues affecting vocational education with officials from the Department of Education.

And a complicated formula for states distributing federal dollars to secondary schools was revised.

"Area schools" that offered only vocational classes could receive funds directly from the state, rather than the school district, if they participated in a consortium with other secondary schools and school districts, served the same proportion of poor or disabled students as the school districts they served, and divided the funds in proportion to the number of poor and disabled students.

For example, if the area school served half the poor and disabled students in a school district, the area school could receive half the district's vocational education funds. The school district would receive the other half.

Both sides also agreed to boost to 75 percent the aid states direct toward improving programs and lower to 25 percent amounts set aside for displaced homemakers and other special groups.

Sen. Strom Thurmond, R-S.C., protested that his state would be hurt by the change, requiring it to put more of its own money into administration. But he did not press the issue.

Both versions of the measure sought to prevent states from spreading grants too thin.

Under the Senate bill, the minimum a state could give a school was $25,000, while the House set the minimum at $5,000. Conferees split the difference, settling on $15,000 as the minimum, except when waivers were obtained for rural areas.

House members agreed to a Senate request to drop a school prayer amendment tacked onto their bill on the floor.

The amendment, sponsored by William E. Dannemeyer, R-Calif., said no money from the bill could go to states or school districts that prevented students from voluntarily praying in public schools.

On a symbolic note, conferees compromised on the bill's title.

The House had wanted a forward-looking "applied technology" act; the Senate preferred the traditional "vocational education."

The compromise: the Carl D. Perkins Vocational and Applied Technology Education Act.

Bush issued a statement Sept. 25 saying the bill "excludes many of the changes proposed by my administration." But he signed the measure because it still reflected "progress over current law," said the statement. ■

Court Backs Tenure Inquiry

The Supreme Court on Jan. 9 rejected a university's plea on grounds of academic freedom to limit an investigation by the Equal Employment Opportunity Commission (EEOC) of its faculty tenure decisions for possible violations of federal anti-job discrimination laws.

The court's 9-0 ruling in *University of Pennsylvania v. EEOC* held that colleges and universities had no special privilege that would require judicial review of EEOC requests for so-called peer review materials used in granting or denying tenure to prospective faculty members.

Justice Harry A. Blackmun, writing for the court, dismissed as "remote and attenuated" the warning by higher education groups that the tenure evaluation process would be compromised by EEOC inquiry without a specific finding that the requested information was needed. ■

Student 'Right-to-Know' Bill Enacted

College students and applicants became entitled to detailed information about graduation rates and campus crime statistics under legislation passed by the 101st Congress.

The Senate cleared the legislation on Oct. 24, two days after the House had adopted the conference report. President Bush signed the measure into law Nov. 8.

Conferees had agreed Oct. 9 on the landmark student "right-to-know" legislation (S 580) that, among other things, made it easier for athletes and scholars alike to gauge their prospects for obtaining a degree at any given school. Colleges and universities that failed to comply adequately with the new provisions could lose some of their federal funding.

Pat Williams, D-Mont., chairman of the House Subcommittee on Postsecondary Education, acknowledged before passage that the legislation would place "additional burdens" on institutions. "But parents and students have the right to know. This will provide students and their parents with consumer information when choosing a college."

The Senate passed its version of S 580 on Feb. 22. The House passed similar legislation (HR 1454) on June 5, under the Senate bill's number. On Sept. 13, the Senate passed an amended version of the House bill.

Two key differences were the Senate's refusal to include a House provision that would have required colleges to break down expenditures and revenues by sport and another provision to require schools to report information on crime rates and security policies to the Department of Education.

In conference, the House yielded on the first point. Although Rep. Paul B. Henry, R-Mich., had insisted on requiring colleges to show what they spent and what they took in for each sport, the House agreed to allow the General Accounting Office to study whether that information would be desirable.

Conferees compromised over requiring schools to distribute campus crime information. The House had wanted crime rates sent to the Education secretary; the Senate wanted them given to students. Under the compromise, schools would have to distribute crime information to students and, upon request, to the secretary.

The final compromise also amended federal privacy laws to allow colleges to tell student victims of crime what punishment, if any, had been meted out to a suspect.

BOXSCORE

Legislation: Student Right-to-Know and Campus Security Act, PL 101-542 (S 580, HR 1454).

Major action: Signed, Nov. 8. Conference report adopted by Senate, Oct. 24; by House, Oct. 22. Passed by Senate, Sept. 13; by House, June 5; earlier version of S 580 passed by Senate, Feb. 22.

Reports: Conference report (H Rept 101-883). Education and Labor (H Rept 101-518). Labor and Human Resources (S Rept 101-209).

BACKGROUND

The right-to-know legislation grew out of public and congressional concern about colleges and universities that recruited star athletes with scholarships but made little effort to see that the students learned enough to earn a degree.

The final version of S 580 combined portions and versions of a number of other measures.

On Feb. 22, the Senate passed on a voice vote an early version of S 580 dealing only with the graduation rates of college athletes. Its provisions were also adopted as an amendment to a bill (S 695) incorporating President Bush's education initiatives.

The measure was sponsored by the Senate's most famous former athlete, Bill Bradley, D-N.J., who was a star basketball player for Princeton University and for the professional New York Knicks.

The crime sections of the bill also came from other legislation. When a House subcommittee approved HR 1454 in May, it incorporated the crime provisions offered in two other measures, HR 3344 and HR 4570.

Provisions drawn from HR 3344, sponsored by Bill Goodling, R-Pa., required colleges and universities to collect and report statistics about campus crime. The key provision of HR 4570, sponsored by Mel Levine, D-Calif., amended the Family Educational Rights and Privacy Act to allow colleges and universities to inform a student victim of violent crime of the outcome of disciplinary proceedings against the suspect.

Meanwhile, S 1930, to require disclosure of campus crime statistics, was pending before the Labor and Human Resources Subcommittee on Education, Arts and Humanities.

The Senate Labor and Human Resources Committee first approved S 580 in November 1989. That version would have required colleges and universities to report annually the graduation rates of student-athletes.

The secretary of Education would have been required to make the information available to anyone who requested it, whether a school or individual, and the colleges or universities involved would have been required to give the information to potential student-athletes.

"Too many student-athletes sacrifice academic achievement to the fantasy of professional sports. It is a national shame," Bradley said in introducing the measure in March 1989. He said that only one in 10,000 high school athletes ever became a professional.

"Hopefully, an informed choice will lead to a real education and a college degree. For most students, that is a more realistic and valuable reward than dreams of a professional sport career."

What the Bill Would Do

The final bill, as cleared by Congress on Oct. 24, contained three main sections.

First, it required colleges and universities that awarded athletic scholarships to disclose annually the graduation rate, broken down by race and sex, of students who had received such aid. The rates were to be reported separately for football, basketball, baseball, cross-country and track, and all other sports combined.

Schools were to start collecting the information

as of July 1, 1991, and provide it to prospective student-athletes, their parents and coaches beginning July 1, 1993.

The National Collegiate Athletic Association (NCAA) agreed in 1990 to require such reports by its Division I and II schools.

Second, the federal legislation required colleges and universities to disclose the graduation rates of all full-time, degree-seeking students on a similar timetable. This provision specified that colleges could report as graduating only students who earned a degree within "150 percent of the standard time."

A study by the National Institute of Independent Colleges and Universities found that 43 percent of students attending four-year public institutions and 54 percent of students entering private colleges and universities graduated within six years of enrolling.

Finally, the bill required that colleges and universities provide to students and applicants an annual security report on all violent crimes against students in the most recent school year, on or off campus. The information was to be collected beginning July 1, 1991, and made available starting Sept. 1, 1992.

This provision received added impetus from a surge of public attention and concern about campus crime after the late August slayings of five university students in Gainesville, Fla.

The bill required schools to provide information about campus security practices and law enforcement, crime prevention, and the policy of local police on monitoring of criminal activity at off-campus housing.

Goodling had introduced this part of the bill as separate legislation at the behest of two constituents whose daughter was slain in 1988 on the campus of Lehigh University in Pennsylvania. "We can ensure that [college] students are as aware of crime as you and I are about crime in our neighborhoods or in the cities we work in. We think of college campuses as quiet and idyllic. But that's a false image," Goodling said.

The bill also amended the Family Educational Rights and Privacy Act to allow colleges and universities to tell a student victim of violent crime of the outcome of any disciplinary proceedings against an accused assailant.

Because college disciplinary hearings were considered part of a student's record, existing outcomes were confidential. "Under existing law, a rape victim, for example, has no way of knowing if her attacker is still on campus," said Rep. Levine. "This lack of crucial information dramatically increases the victim's trauma."

COMMITTEE ACTION

The House Education and Labor Committee on May 22 approved HR 1454 to require colleges to disclose athletes' graduation rates and campus crime statistics and to amend federal privacy laws to allow colleges to tell student victims of crime what action, if any, had been taken against suspects.

The full committee acted a week after the subcommittee had approved the measure.

Subcommittee Action: Crime

HR 1454 won voice-vote approval May 15 from the House Education and Labor Subcommittee on Postsecondary Education. The Senate Labor and Human Resources Committee had approved S 580 on Nov. 1, 1989.

In approving HR 1454, the subcommittee combined the right-to-know provisions with the crime statistics provisions. The bill actually incorporated the crime provisions offered in two other measures, HR 3344 and HR 4570.

The provisions drawn from HR 3344 required colleges and universities to collect and report statistics about campus crime and established uniform federal standards for collecting and disseminating the statistics.

Four states had passed such legislation, and at least 12 others were considering such measures. But their standards varied widely.

The subcommittee deleted a provision that would have ordered colleges and universities to make crime statistics available to the FBI Uniform Crime Reports, Goodling said, because the FBI was changing that program.

The key provision of HR 4570, sponsored by Levine, was the amendment of the privacy act to allow schools to reveal the outcome of disciplinary proceedings against a crime suspect.

Levine introduced the bill in response to growing public awareness and concern about campus rapes. Recent studies had indicated that one in six female students was the victim of rape or attempted rape each year, according to Levine's staff.

Subcommittee Action: Athletes

The student-athlete provisions of the bill sought to accelerate action that was being undertaken voluntarily by some institutions.

The NCAA had taken some recent steps designed to improve athletes' graduation rates. But Williams, the subcommittee chairman, said the annual reporting requirements would give schools the push they needed to significantly improve the rates.

The panel adopted an amendment by Carl C. Perkins, D-Ky., to order the Education Department to develop a formula that would make schools responsible for reporting the graduation rates of all students, not just athletes, according to the program in which they were enrolled.

Perkins said higher education groups opposed his "goose and gander amendment." He said the study should also focus on the success of schools' individual academic programs.

"If it is important to the student-athlete, then it is important to all other students and their parents. This is a right-to-know provision," he said.

The amendment specified that colleges could report as graduating only those students who earned a degree within "150 percent of the normal time."

One reason for his amendment, Perkins said, was to encourage colleges and universities to help students "once they get them in the door." Goodling, however, said that community colleges might require a different standard because students who attended those institutions usually were employed.

The subcommittee also adopted an amendment by Henry to require schools to disclose each sport's revenues and spending.

Henry said his amendment would not require the institutions to list contributions to athletic programs or to specify how much they spent on each student-athlete. However, he said, schools should be required to show how they spent their revenues from athletics.

Committee Markup

The Education and Labor Committee gave voice-vote approval to HR 1454 on May 22.

Institutions With High Default Rates

Prompted by bipartisan concern about the soaring cost of student loan defaults, Congress in 1990 moved to cut off federally guaranteed loans to students at colleges and trade schools with high default rates.

As part of the omnibus budget-reconciliation bill (HR 5835 — PL 101-508), Congress barred participation in the student loan program by colleges or trade schools with a default rate of 35 percent or greater. The cutoff level was to fall to 30 percent in 1993.

The ban, along with other provisions of the Student Loan Default Act, was projected to save $1.7 billion over five years. The cost of student loan defaults had risen from $224 million in 1978 to nearly $2 billion in 1987 and just under $2.4 billion in fiscal 1990.

Other provisions authorized schools to refuse to certify certain students for loans; required a 30-day delay in the disbursement of loans to first-time, first-year undergraduate borrowers; and required students who had not graduated from high school to pass an independently administered test. *(Budget reconciliation provisions: Student Loans, Title III, p. 143)*

The cutoff plan had first been proposed in 1987 by the Reagan administration's combative secretary of Education, William J. Bennett, but rejected by Congress in the face of strong opposition from trade school groups. The proposal was revived in 1990 when lawmakers saw no other way to achieve the goal of cutting defaults by $2 billion over five years.

As of 1988, the overall default rate on student loans was 16 percent, but the rate was significantly higher — 27 percent — at trade schools.

The Bush administration had its own proposal, an omnibus plan that included attaching the wages of people who defaulted on student loans.

The proposal, introduced Jan. 29 as S 2029 by Sens. Phil Gramm, R-Texas, and Bob Dole, R-Kan., also would have barred schools from employing commissioned sales representatives to recruit students and required lenders to offer graduated repayment plans to borrowers.

Under the Gramm-Dole proposal, schools with default rates higher than 30 percent would have to refund tuition to aid recipients who dropped out early. And students lacking a high school diploma or its equivalent would have had to pass a test before enrolling in postgraduate training.

The proposal was referred to the Labor and Human Resources Subcommittee on Education, but was never considered by the full committee.

Background

As default costs for all student-loan programs started to approach $2 billion in 1987, Congress began taking a closer look at how to clamp down on the offenders.

Contributing to the high level of defaults were significant increases in the Guaranteed Student Loan (GSL) annual loan volume and the amount of loans in repayment and a shift to borrowing by a greater proportion of higher financial risk, low-income students.

Trade school students and freshmen were traditionally the most likely defaulters. Some members believed that abusive practices by for-profit trade schools resulted in particularly high default rates among borrowers attending these institutions. Other lawmakers, however, contended that defaults at such schools were simply a function of the large proportion of low-income students they served.

Compounding the problem was the dramatic Reagan-era shift from grants to loans.

This switch had turned the Supplemental Loans for Students (SLS) program from a program of last resort into the primary source of funds for hundreds of thousands of students.

More students, including freshmen and those seeking to learn trade skills, turned to the SLS program for cash as Congress tightened eligibility requirements for other grant and loan programs. Consequently, defaults in that program skyrocketed — from $14 million in 1987 to $247 million in 1989, according to a General Accounting Office sampling.

Bennett viewed trade schools as a primary source of the problem, depicting them as diploma mills designed to trick the poor into taking on federally backed debt, milk them for their loan money and then wash them out or graduate them with inadequate preparation to enter the

---

Members of the NCAA had decided in January to begin reporting graduation rates of athletes after the 1990-91 academic year. But lawmakers said that such reporting should be required of all schools that awarded athletic scholarships.

An amendment adopted in subcommittee would have required schools that offered such scholarships to disclose each sport's revenues and spending.

William D. Ford, D-Mich., said he saw no need for that requirement. But instead of trying to kill it outright in full committee, as he said he would have liked to do, Ford offered an amendment that would have required schools to report separately only on football and basketball, lumping together all other sports. His amendment was rejected by 16-17.

A second Ford amendment, which failed by voice vote, would have required all schools — rather than just those providing athletic scholarships in Divisions I and II of the NCAA — to report the required information.

"Let's just have everybody report, and we'll find out how popular it is," said Ford.

Henry argued that the financial reporting was necessary only in large schools because "that's where the problem is," not in schools that did not give athletic scholarships.

Williams sided with Henry on both of Ford's amendments. He said he was concerned that if Congress limited the disclosure requirement, it would be impossible to compare spending on women's sports teams with that on men's teams.

Education groups said they were concerned about the Perkins amendment to order the Education Department to develop a formula that would make schools responsible for reporting all students' graduation rates.

"The Perkins amendment asks for data that colleges

Denied Participation in Loan Program

job market or earn the money needed to pay off their loans.

But strong lobbying by groups representing the predominantly for-profit trade schools blocked Bennett's plan in Congress in 1988 after it had passed the Senate in 1987. Instead, relatively mild regulations tightening the SLS program were enacted. *(1988 Almanac, pp. 337, 343)*

With loan defaults continuing to increase, Congress took stronger action in 1989 with provisions — titled the Student Loan Reconciliation Amendments of 1989 — inserted in the 1990 budget-reconciliation bill (HR 3299 — PL 101-239).

Many of these amendments were aimed at reducing defaults, particularly in the SLS program. One provision curtailed trade schools' ability to enroll high school dropouts by mandating that all SLS borrowers have a diploma or an equivalency certificate. Other provisions required the multiple disbursement of any GSL or SLS loan regardless of size or the term of the educational program; required a 30-day delay in the disbursement of SLS loans to students lacking a year of successfully completed undergraduate study; and limited SLS eligibility to students with a high school diploma or equivalency. *(1989 Almanac, p. 189)*

Legislative Action

In 1990, the budget-reconciliation measure again served as the legislative vehicle for further efforts to tighten the student loan rules. The measure cleared the Senate on Oct. 27 after having passed the House in the early morning hours the same day (session of Oct. 26); President Bush signed it into law Nov. 5.

The centerpiece of the student loan default provisions was the plan to cut off loans for students at schools with default rates of 35 percent or higher (30 percent in 1993) for the three most recent fiscal years. The school would be ineligible in the fiscal year in which the determination was made and for the following two fiscal years.

Schools could appeal the ineligibility ruling within 30 days of notification from the secretary of Education, who was required to rule on the appeal within 45 days.

The school could continue to participate in the student loan program if the secretary decided that the calculation of the default rate was inaccurate and recalculation would reduce it for any of the three fiscal years. Or the school could continue to participate in the student loan program if the secretary decided there were exceptional mitigating circumstances. During the appeal, the secretary could permit the institution to continue to participate in the program.

After enactment of the measure, Education Department officials estimated that 268 private trade schools would be subject to the ban, along with 57 two-year colleges and fewer than 20 four-year colleges.

Two categories of schools were exempted from the cutoff until July 1, 1994: about two dozen colleges controlled by Native American tribes and 117 historically black colleges and universities.

In other efforts to control defaults, schools were prohibited from giving first-year students the first installment of any loan until 30 days after the student enrolled in the institution. The loans, however, could be delivered to the school before the end of that 30-day period.

To deal with the problem of loans to unqualified students, the bill required that students without high school diplomas had to pass an independently administered examination before enrollment.

Financial aid administrators were also authorized to certify students for loans. Even if a student had been ruled eligible for the loan by a bank, schools could determine whether a student's expenses could be met from other sources, such as the institution or the student. Schools had wanted a say in determining eligibility because the schools were to be held accountable for their students' defaults.

In addition, the bill provided for paying collection agencies for their work in getting students to repay loans. Under existing law, guarantee agencies trying to collect on loans for banks were paid by the government for their work only after the loans went into default. The fiscal 1991 reconciliation provision required the secretary of Education to pay the guarantee agency $50 for each loan on which students did not default.

---

just don't have," said Becky H. Timmons, vice president of the American Council on Education.

FLOOR, FINAL ACTION

The House on June 5 approved HR 1454 by voice vote. The House then called up the simpler Senate-passed version and substituted its own provisions before approving the bill and readying the measure for conference. Goodling, who pressed for the campus crime-reporting provisions, called the measure a "consumer rights bill for students."

The Senate on Sept. 13 passed the bill again by voice vote and sent it back to the House. Four days later, the House requested a conference and the Senate agreed on Oct. 3.

Conferees settled a number of relatively minor disputes between the chambers, with both sides compromising to get the legislation passed. Among the issues settled was the Perkins amendment ordering the Education Department to develop a formula that would make schools responsible for reporting graduation rates of all students according to the program in which they were enrolled.

The final bill commissioned the secretary of Education to study the feasibility of making available schools' graduation rates by academic major, graduates' rates of passage of applicable licensure or certification exams, and the employment prospects and the rate at which individuals who graduate from a particular program and enter the job market obtain employment in the occupation for which they were trained.

Once conferees on the bill reached their agreement on Oct. 9, final passage became a formality. Both chambers approved the compromise quickly, sending the bill to Bush — the House on Oct. 22, the Senate on Oct. 24. ■

Taft Institute Seminars Program Funded

With passage of the 1990 authorization, Congress gave the Taft Institute, a quasi-governmental institute that conducted seminars on American government for educators, its final four years of federal funding.

Unlike previous years, the bill (S 1939 — PL 101-638) cleared by the Senate on Oct. 27 by voice vote had no extraneous amendments, only language to reauthorize the institute through fiscal 1994 for $1.8 million.

The bill mandated that after fiscal 1994, funding for the institute would have to come from private donations.

The bill sailed through Congress after a provision in the original Senate measure to extend a $50 million-a-year program to a high school dropout-prevention program was dropped.

The House passed the program extension as a separate bill (HR 2281), and Senate conferees agreed to drop the amendment in conference in late October. *(Dropout prevention, p. 618)*

The House then quickly passed the Taft Institute measure by voice vote Oct. 22, and President Bush signed the bill Nov. 28.

BACKGROUND

The Taft Institute for Two-Party Government was founded in 1961 under a charter from the New York State Board of Regents. The nonpartisan, nonprofit tax-exempt corporation, named as a memorial to the late Sen. Robert A. Taft, R-Ohio (1939-53), did not receive federal funds until 1980.

The goals of the institute were to stimulate an understanding of the principles and the process of government; to inspire a more active interest and participation in government at all levels; and to advance the science of government and help citizens meet more effectively the problems confronting the nation.

The federal government began giving funds to the Taft Institute under the Higher Education Act Amendments in 1980. That year, $750,000 was authorized for the institute. *(1980 Almanac, p. 422)*

The Taft Institute was reauthorized at that same amount through 1988. In that year, reauthorizing legislation died because of arguments over the many costly extraneous programs in amendments attached to the bill. *(1988 Almanac, p. 348)*.

Because of this failure in 1988, lawmakers worked hard in 1990 to keep the measure "clean" — free of amendments. Members also made clear their intention that this was to be the final authorization for the institute because they believed it could function using private funds only.

COMMITTEE ACTION

The House Education and Labor Subcommittee on Postsecondary Education on Nov. 14, 1989, approved, by voice vote, what was expected to be the institute's final reauthorization. *(1989 Almanac, p. 197)*

As approved by the subcommittee, HR 3315 would have authorized $750,000 in fiscal 1990, $500,000 in fiscal 1991 and $250,000 in fiscal 1992; the institute was supposed to be fully supported by private donations by fiscal 1993.

Before approving the bill, the subcommittee defeated an amendment offered by ranking Republican E. Thomas Coleman of Missouri that would have cut off federal funding one year earlier.

Coleman said institute staffers had told him they could meet that target. But subcommittee Chairman Pat Williams, D-Mont., said he was not as confident as the staff that private funds would be readily available.

The full Education Committee ratified the subcommittee work, approving the bill by voice vote on Feb. 6 (H Rept 101-406).

FLOOR ACTION

The Senate approved by voice vote its version of the bill (S 1939) to authorize the Taft Institute through fiscal 1994 on Nov. 20, 1989. But senators attached to the measure a provision to reauthorize a popular $50 million-a-year high school dropout prevention program.

The House passed S 1939 by voice vote on June 7 after deleting its text and inserting the provisions of HR 3315. The Senate stood by its provisions, and both chambers requested a conference.

During the conference, the two chambers compromised. While the Senate negotiators agreed to drop all the extraneous provisions, their House counterparts allowed the Taft Institute another year of federal funding.

The conference report provided $750,000 for fiscal 1991, $550,000 for fiscal 1992, $325,000 for fiscal 1993 and $150,000 for fiscal 1994 (H Rept 101-884). The report also explicitly stated that this was to be the last authorization for the institute.

The House adopted the conference report by voice vote Oct. 22. The Senate followed suit on Oct. 27, clearing the measure for the president. ■

Chapter 9

HOUSING & COMMUNITY DEVELOPMENT

National Affordable Housing Act 631
Housing Act Provisions 644
FHA Insurance Fund 657
Housing Benefit Plans 659
Mortgage 'Prepayment' Compromise 661
Homeless Assistance Act 665
HUD Scandal Investigation 666

U.S. Housing Programs Overhauled

Bill Aimed To Increase Stock of Affordable Homes

BOXSCORE

Legislation: Cranston-Gonzalez National Affordable Housing Act, PL 101-625 (S 566).

Major action: Signed, Nov. 28. Conference report adopted by Senate, 93-6, Oct. 27; by House, Oct. 25. HR 1180 passed by House, 378-43, Aug. 1. S 566 passed by Senate, 96-1, June 27.

Reports: Conference report (H Rept 101-943). Banking, Housing and Urban Affairs (S Rept 101-316); Banking, Finance and Urban Affairs (H Rept 101-559).

After lengthy negotiations with the Bush administration, Congress enacted the first major overhaul of federal housing programs since 1974 with the goal of increasing the nation's stock of affordable housing and helping public housing tenants become homeowners.

Passage of the Cranston-Gonzalez National Affordable Housing Act was spurred by congressional dissatisfaction with the Reagan administration's deep cuts in federal housing programs and the desire of the Bush administration's activist secretary of Housing and Urban Development (HUD), Jack F. Kemp, to make his imprint on national housing policy.

The legislation authorized $27.5 billion in fiscal 1991 and $29.9 billion in fiscal 1992 to continue existing housing programs — such as rent subsidies, public housing and housing for the elderly and disabled — and to create a number of programs.

The authorization was about $3.3 billion more than existing spending levels and was aimed at providing as many as 360,000 additional units over two years.

The legislation represented a marked change in direction for federal policy. Its centerpiece was the HOME (Homeownership Made Easy) Investment Partnerships, to provide block grants to state and local governments to meet local housing needs.

Included in that program was a set-aside for construction of affordable housing — 10 percent the first year and 15 percent the second year. Administration officials had staunchly opposed new programs to build housing, preferring to renovate existing property for low-income tenants.

The measure also contained a Bush administration initiative that had a contradictory aim: getting the federal government out of the business of subsidized housing. The program — called HOPE, an acronym for Home Ownership and opportunity for People Everywhere — was designed to sell off public housing projects to tenants.

The 1990 housing bill included another Kemp initiative, Shelter Plus Care, combining housing assistance with social services. For Kemp, passage of the act gave him a concrete legislative accomplishment to add to his work in 1989 in cleaning up HUD in the wake of Reagan-era scandals. *(HUD scandals, p. 666; 1989 Almanac, p. 639)*

Congress provided no funds for either the HOME or HOPE programs in the fiscal 1991 spending bill, however. *(HUD appropriations, p. 854)*

In early 1991, Bush requested $165 million for HOPE and $500 million for the HOME block grant program in the supplemental fiscal 1991 appropriations bill.

Also new was a program by House Banking Committee Chairman Henry B. Gonzalez, D-Texas, to help first-time home buyers meet down payment costs and afford mortgage interest rates. Called the National Housing Trust, it was authorized at $250 million in fiscal 1991 and $521.5 million in fiscal 1992.

Lawmakers also resolved a couple of longstanding problems. With the Federal Housing Administration (FHA) mortgage insurance fund losing money, the new law required buyers to pay additional costs upfront and annual insurance fees when purchasing a home. On a $65,000 house, buyers would have to pay an additional $833 in cash upfront. New "risk-based" requirements were expected to weed out people more likely to default on the mortgages. Members of the real estate industry predicted that as many as 60,000 families each year would be unable to afford a house under the new FHA rules. *(FHA, p. 657)*

The law also attempted a permanent solution to the problem of building owners who wanted to pay off their federally subsidized mortgages. Offered in the 1960s and '70s, these mortgages required owners to rent to low-income families but gave owners the option of paying off their loans after 20 years and doing whatever they wanted with their properties. Since 1987, Congress had maintained a moratorium on prepayments. *(Prepayments, p. 661)*

The new law required HUD to offer incentives to owners to continue renting to low-income families or to people who bought the property and promised to continue the affordable rents.

Owners would be allowed to receive fair market values for their property, which would then have to be used for low-income tenants until the building was no longer livable. In limited circumstances, owners could pay off their mortgages and continue to own the property.

The legislation passed the Senate and House in the summer by overwhelming margins that masked the difficulties and disagreements in committee markups and in negotiations between lawmakers and administration officials.

Resolving the differences between the House and Senate versions led to more tense negotiations. But once an agreement was reached Oct. 15, the legislation again won overwhelming approval in each chamber. *(Provisions, p. 644)*

The House adopted the conference report by voice vote Oct. 25. The Senate cleared the legislation Oct. 27 by 93-6. *(Vote 325, p. 63-S)*

In a statement issued as he signed the bill Nov. 28, President Bush called the measure "an exciting bipartisan initiative to break down the walls separating low-income people from the American dream of opportunity and homeownership." He said the FHA reforms would ensure that the agency remain "actuarially safe and financially sound." Bush also said he was pleased by the compromise solution on the prepayment issue but concerned that the incentives were "more generous than necessary."

BACKGROUND

In 1990, members of Congress were determined to regain the initiative in coping with the country's housing problems. Not since 1974, when President Gerald R. Ford signed a law to fight urban blight and institute Community Development Block Grants (CDBGs), had Washington launched a major housing program.

History of Federal Role

The major federal role in housing dated to the founding of the FHA in 1934 to insure home mortgages and expanded after World War II with passage of the 1949 National Housing Act, a broad slum clearance and public housing bill. *(Congress and the Nation Vol. I, p. 459)*

Insuring home mortgages, effectively a middle-class subsidy, remained as the most important federal housing program and stirred little controversy. But urban renewal — construction of central city public housing units to replace slums — was very controversial.

Public housing drew criticism from political conservatives, real estate dealers and landlords from the right. Even some supporters of the concept of public housing found the "projects" to be sterile and institutional and local public housing authorities intrusive and insensitive in dealing with tenants.

Republican President Dwight D. Eisenhower maintained federal support for urban renewal but fought with the Democratic-controlled Congress to reduce the commitment, vetoing two omnibus housing bills in 1959 before an acceptable compromise was worked out.

In the 1960s, two Democratic presidents expanded federal housing programs. President John F. Kennedy won passage of an omnibus act in 1961 authorizing new low-interest FHA loans for housing for low- and moderate-income families and increasing federal support for urban renewal.

In 1965, President Lyndon B. Johnson, as part of his Great Society program, won enactment of a $7.8 billion housing bill that included a controversial rent supplement program. The program — which House Republicans and conservative Democrats fell six votes short of defeating — provided that an individual was to pay 25 percent of his or her income for rent in private, nonprofit housing and the government would make up the balance.

Separate legislation in 1965 also established HUD, consolidating the variety of federal housing programs into a single, Cabinet-level department. *(1965 Almanac, pp. 358, 382)*

A 1968 housing act passed with bipartisan support, but in the Nixon administration housing programs again became a focus of partisan debate. In 1973, President Richard M. Nixon declared a moratorium on new commitments for subsidized housing projects. The administration followed with a proposal that became the centerpiece of legislation in 1974: supplanting previous home-ownership and rental subsidy programs with a new rental assistance plan providing for public housing authorities to subsidize rents in privately owned leased units.

Lawmakers and administration officials negotiated the details of the bill, including the new CDBGs, in the shadow of the Nixon impeachment hearings. Conferees reached agreement in August 1974 just two days before Nixon announced his resignation, and Ford signed the measure into law (PL 93-383) later that month. *(1974 Almanac, p. 345)*

Congress in 1976 ordered HUD to resume spending on new public housing. In 1977, the first year of the Carter administration, Congress appropriated funds for about 374,000 additional subsidized units. Under budget pressure, that number dipped by a third in 1979 and rose again in 1980 to a total of 282,000 units, half new and half rehabilitated. *(Congress and the Nation Vol. V, p. 429)*

In the 1980s, President Ronald Reagan directed a fundamental shift in federal housing policies by cutting funds for new construction and pushing vouchers, which poor people could use like cash toward rent for housing they found on their own.

Immediately upon taking office, Reagan reduced the number of additional subsidized units for fiscal 1982 to 175,000. The number would drop below 35,000 units — mostly for the elderly and the disabled — in 1988, his last year in office. Spending, which had peaked at $30.1 billion in the last year of the Carter administration, totaled barely more than that — $33.2 billion — for Reagan's entire second term. *(Congress and the Nation Vol. VI, p. 667)*

Administration critics blamed the cuts for growing homelessness, which became a major national concern in Reagan's final years in office. In 1987, Congress reauthorized existing housing programs and added a couple, but members decided to wait for a new administration before undertaking an overhaul. *(1987 Almanac, p. 682)*

Bush came to office promising to work with lawmakers in restructuring housing programs. Kemp, too, wanted to make a mark. The one-time presidential hopeful saw the Republican Party's future in increasing economic opportunities for the poor.

Housing advocates said the need was great. Some 800,000 to 1 million families were on waiting lists for public housing across the country, and another 1 million were waiting for federal vouchers and certificates to subsidize their rents, according to Richard Y. Nelson Jr., executive director of the National Association of Housing and Redevelopment Officials. In many cases, public housing authorities had closed their waiting lists to new names.

But fiscal constraints made it difficult to increase housing opportunities for the poor. Housing advocates in Congress conceded that as long as Congress was under pressure to reduce the deficit and Bush refused to endorse higher taxes, no big-dollar attack on housing problems would be possible.

Old Argument: Build or Rent?

The key issue as housing bills moved through Congress in 1989 and 1990 was the same one that led to a stalemate between Congress and the White House throughout the Reagan administration: whether the government should subsidize the construction of more housing for low-income families or help the poor pay rent on the private market.

Pending before the House and Senate were bills authorizing new spending for construction.

The Senate bill — S 566, cosponsored by Banking Subcommittee on Housing Chairman Alan Cranston, D-Calif., and ranking Republican Alfonse M. D'Amato, N.Y. — included a $3 billion development subsidy program. The House version — HR 1180, sponsored by Banking Chairman Gonzalez — would have boosted funding for the construction of public and Indian housing, in addition to authorizing $300 million in grants to spur production of rental housing. *(Background, 1989 Almanac, p. 653)*

The administration, however, proposed cutting back the few construction programs still in operation. Kemp proposed his package, the so-called HOPE proposal (HR 4245, S 2304), which focused on helping residents of public housing buy their units and on assisting other low-income families to become homeowners. It offered no new construction initiatives.

In fact, the only HUD construction program that was receiving new funding was for the elderly and disabled. HUD provided direct loans and below-market interest rates to nonprofit corporations, which could then charge lower rents for units. The Farmers Home Administration (FmHA) also provided direct loans to public, nonprofit and private developers to build rental housing projects in rural areas.

HUD proposed slashing the number of units constructed for the elderly and disabled from 7,689 in 1990 at a cost of about $473 million to 3,967 in 1991 at a cost of about $283 million.

The FmHA proposed cutting back its construction programs as well. In 1990, the FmHA made or insured loans for construction of about 41,885 units at a cost of about $1.9 billion. For 1991, the administration wanted to scale that back to about 28,785 new units.

Vacancy Rates

The policy debate turned in part on a debate over the nation's housing supply. Administration officials opposed to construction programs pointed to a 7.3 percent vacancy rate for all rental units during the first three quarters of 1989 and a 35 percent vacancy rate for new apartments during much of the 1980s as proof that the federal government should help make the market work better rather than finance expensive construction.

"There is housing nationally," said HUD Under Secretary Alfred A. DelliBovi. "If you look across the nation, there's about 105 million housing units with 500 million rooms, and that's about a bedroom for every person in the United States."

DelliBovi conceded that not everyone who wanted a room had one, because some people owned two or three homes and because others could not afford even one.

Housing advocates, however, insisted that the national vacancy rate was meaningless. "It's not like being a regional grocery store manager and noticing that more people eat Wheaties in Baltimore than Washington, and so shipping more Wheaties to Baltimore from Washington will solve the problem," explained Barry Zigas, president of the National Low Income Housing Coalition.

Besides ignoring regional differences, an overall vacancy rate obscured the lack of usable low-cost housing by including vacancies in top-dollar luxury units and in uninhabitable buildings, housing advocates maintained.

William C. Apgar, associate director of the Joint Center for Housing Studies at Harvard University, acknowledged that vacancy rates for apartments renting for $150 to $300 a month had increased from 4.7 percent in 1981 to 8 percent in 1987. But he said the actual number of those apartments had dropped — from 10.1 million in 1974 to 8.5 million in 1985. And the empty units, Apgar said, typically were in extremely poor condition or were in declining neighborhoods.

Affordability, Availability

For their part, housing advocates emphasized that most people eligible for federal help were not getting it even though the number of people served had increased slowly since creation of the new rental assistance program.

In 1974, 19 percent of poverty-level renters received housing subsidies from the government. In 1980, 23 percent received help, and in 1985, 31 percent did, according to the Joint Center. As of 1988, the Congressional Budget Office (CBO) said that, depending on the factors considered, the percentage of eligible households receiving assistance varied from a low of 25 percent to a high of 44 percent.

"The point is that you can either look at the fact that we added all these subsidized units or you can look at the number of poverty families still in need of assistance," said Apgar.

While low-rent units had declined, the number of households living in poverty increased from 9.5 million in 1974 to 13.9 million in 1985. In terms of people, that translated to a jump from 23 million to 33 million. In 1985, the poverty threshold for a family of four was $10,989, according to the Bureau of Labor Statistics.

HUD recommended that a household spend no more than 30 percent of its income for a place to live.

But housing advocates said the poor often spent much more, indicating that not enough low-cost housing was available.

"Most people who are in desperate need of housing are paying huge amounts of income for it," Zigas said.

According to the Joint Center, the total number of poverty-level households spending more than 50 percent of their monthly income on rent jumped from 57 percent in 1974 to 70 percent in 1985.

A study by the Low Income Housing Information Service showed that 45 percent of all poor renters in 1985 paid more than 70 percent of their monthly income for housing.

The Debate Over Vouchers

The Reagan administration — and later the Bush administration — advocated rent-subsidy vouchers for the poor as the alternative to expensive construction programs for low-income people.

HUD vouchers were set at a figure designed to reflect a "fair market rent standard." Under this program, families could choose where they lived as long as they paid the difference between the voucher and the actual rent.

Housing certificates were like vouchers, except that families could not spend more than 30 percent of their monthly income to make up the difference between HUD's contribution and the rent.

John Scanlon, housing and urban affairs policy analyst with the Heritage Foundation, a conservative think tank in Washington, recommended shifting HUD's entire assistance budget to vouchers.

"It gives people the opportunity to climb out of the poverty trap," Scanlon said. He predicted that the market would respond to the vouchers by producing more housing.

Rep. Steve Bartlett, R-Texas, a member of the Banking Subcommittee on Housing, agreed.

"The housing issue is not a physical issue of sticks and bricks," he said.

The real solution to the housing problem was to spur private construction by increasing demand, Bartlett said. If the government provided people with vouchers to pay for housing, the market would respond, he said.

"I'm not ideological about it. I just want to help people," he said. "By and large, government-built housing is not the best way to do it."

Warming to his theme, Bartlett asked, "What is the

worst housing in the country? What is the most segregated housing? What keeps people from living where they want to?" The answer, he said, was public housing.

Housing advocates, however, said the market probably would not respond to a big increase in vouchers because vouchers were not worth enough to guarantee developers a return on their investment.

"Vouchers would have to get up to about $1,000 a month to induce new construction," said Cushing N. Dolbeare, founder of the Low Income Housing Information Service and the National Low Income Housing Coalition. "Theoretically, you could do it that way, [but] I think you'd be out of your mind to try it."

Despite Republican praise for vouchers, the voucher and certificate program did not grow during the Reagan years. At its peak during the Carter era, 127,581 new families were given vouchers or certificates in fiscal 1977. That number hit a low of 38,372 in 1982, climbing to 85,741 in 1985. In fiscal 1990, the government was funding approximately 72,572 vouchers and certificates.

Kemp said repeatedly that he wanted to be secretary of Housing, not secretary of vouchers, and that he would not abandon other housing programs. But DelliBovi said he preferred vouchers over new construction and criticized the housing construction Democrats favored as "tools of segregation."

"The Reagan and Bush administrations want to give people the voucher to choose where to live and to reject the building where there's no heat in the winter and where the elevator is not consistently repaired," DelliBovi said. "The slumlord lobby wants these people to be prisoners in their buildings. That is the essential difference between the conservative Republican approach and the liberal Democrat slumlord."

Democrats took strong exception to DelliBovi's characterization of the housing debate. Gonzalez called the remarks "outlandish," and another key Banking Committee Democrat, Charles E. Schumer, N.Y., called the analysis "one of the most appalling comments" he had heard.

W. Donald Campbell, staff director of the Senate Banking Subcommittee on Housing, said many of the problems plaguing public housing were created by a hostile Reagan administration unwilling to provide funds for repairs and uninterested in managing programs well.

Campbell added that the Bush administration was taking a shrewd tack by promoting vouchers while actually retrenching the federal commitment to housing. "Obviously you can't attack something with nothing, so they come in saying, 'We want to help the poor with vouchers,' " he said.

Some experts, however, avoided defining the debate as a case of either construction or rental subsidies.

"Trying to decide whether you need one or the other is a little like trying to decide whether your left foot or your right foot is more important if you're going to run a marathon," said Dolbeare, of the Low Income Housing Information Service. "They're both going to be necessary except in a small number of markets where you have an adequate supply of inexpensive housing."

COMPETING PROPOSALS

Each of the three omnibus housing bills weighed by Congress took a different approach to reworking federal housing programs.

The House version (HR 1180) was aimed at significantly expanding existing programs. The Senate measure (S 566) took the approach of reorganizing existing programs and creating new ones. The Bush administration's proposal (HR 4245, S 2304) did not address most existing programs. Instead, the HOPE proposal focused on creating programs to help low-income people buy homes.

The House bill would have authorized spending $27.8 billion in fiscal 1991, an increase of roughly $11 billion over spending in fiscal 1990.

The House Budget Committee, by contrast, had only approved a $3.3 billion increase in housing budget authority for the following year.

The House legislation sought to add about 183,357 households to the overall assistance rolls in fiscal 1991.

When the Cranston-D'Amato bill was introduced, it proposed spending $15.1 billion in fiscal 1990, or $4.1 billion more than the amount then being spent on programs addressed in the legislation. In fiscal 1991, the bill would have authorized spending $15.7 billion. In the spring of 1990, 29 senators, including all Democratic members of the Banking Committee, wrote to the Budget Committee requesting an increase of between $3.6 billion and $4 billion in the baseline for housing programs.

As introduced, the legislation would provide rental assistance to about 30,000 new households in fiscal 1991.

For the HOPE initiative, Bush urged $1.2 billion in new budget authority for fiscal 1991, plus $187 million in tax expenditures. But the proposed fiscal 1991 budget for HUD sought only $80 million in new budget authority, about a 1 percent increase over existing spending. Under the HOPE proposal, about 35,900 new households would receive housing assistance in 1991.

HR 1180: The Gonzalez Bill

The Gonzalez bill would primarily boost funding ceilings of existing programs, although it would also create two new programs.

For first-time home buyers, the bill would authorize a new $5 million National Housing Trust, offering a maximum 6 percent interest rate on mortgages.

To qualify, a home buyer would have to have a total family income that did not exceed 115 percent of the median income for a family of four in the metropolitan area in question.

Also new — and controversial among some Republicans — was a Community Housing Partnership program that would provide grants to local governments and nonprofit sponsors for the production of housing and for assistance to low- and moderate-income families in buying a home. The partnership was designed to encourage nonprofit groups to develop and manage housing projects as well as to build and rehabilitate units for sale to low- and moderate-income families.

Additional budget authority would be provided for construction and operating subsidies of public and Indian housing, for construction of housing for the elderly and disabled, for rental certificates, and for Section 8 moderate rehabilitation assistance. The legislation would authorize $300 million in grants for rental housing development.

The bill set aside about $8 billion in fiscal 1991 to extend for five years contracts with owners of low-rent subsidized units covered by the congressional moratorium on mortgage prepayments due to expire on Sept. 30. Without the extensions, landlords could pay off their mortgages and convert their buildings to condominiums or rent the apartments at market rates.

S 566: Cranston-D'Amato Bill

The Cranston-D'Amato bill attempted to give more flexibility to federal housing programs so they could respond to local housing needs.

Its centerpiece was a new $3 billion-a-year subsidy program — Housing Opportunity Partnerships (HOP) — to encourage development of rental apartments for low-income families.

State and local governments would be required to match federal grants by at least 25 percent. They could use the funds to buy, build or rehabilitate housing. And at least 10 percent of a local jurisdiction's funds would have to go to housing developed, sponsored or owned by nonprofit community housing groups. The HOP program would be administered by a new agency within HUD, called the HOME Corporation.

For first-time home buyers, the bill would have required people to save money in a federally insured institution for at least three years to receive an FHA-insured mortgage. The FHA mortgage could be as much as $125,000 or 90 percent of the median sales price for the state.

The bill would have done away with the certificates and vouchers that tenants received to help pay their rent. Instead, it would have created a "rent credit" program, a new form of assistance that would be either tenant-based or project-based, depending on local need. Rent credits would be used to renew expiring Section 8 assistance contracts, to help tenants displaced by owners who refused to renew project-based contracts and to increase the number of very-low-income families receiving housing aid.

HR 4245: Kemp's HOPE

HUD Secretary Kemp detailed the Bush administration's proposal before the House Banking Subcommittee on Housing on March 13.

The HOPE bill consisted of four parts. Title I would authorize HUD to distribute grants to public housing tenants to purchase their apartments. HUD could also make grants to low-income people to purchase homes from HUD in multifamily projects with mortgages that were insured by the FHA and later foreclosed upon. And grants could be awarded to nonprofit groups to develop programs for the transfer of publicly held, vacant, single-family homes to low-income people.

Title II sought to shield from sudden rent increases low-income tenants of thousands of housing units covered by the moratorium on mortgage prepayments for federally subsidized housing. The moratorium was to expire Sept. 30, 1990.

At that point, owners of the low-rent apartments could pay off their subsidized mortgages and convert their buildings to higher-priced housing, which could result in a surge of homelessness.

Under Kemp's proposal, building owners had to file notice of whether they intended to prepay their mortgages.

If so, tenants would be given a two-year right of first refusal to purchase their building with grants from HUD.

Furthermore, if owners decided to prepay a mortgage and tenants did not buy the building, the owners would have to underwrite moving expenses, security deposits and the cost of six months' housing for each tenant. HUD could approve a building owner's prepayment plan only if the agency had enough money to provide rent-assistance vouchers or certificates to tenants who had to move.

Title III included a Shelter Plus Care program to provide both rental assistance and support services to homeless people who were seriously mentally ill or had alcohol and drug problems; a demonstration program to test whether combining housing vouchers with support services would help elderly people continue to live independently; and Operation Bootstrap, which would require public housing agencies to develop local programs to help families become economically independent.

Finally, under Title IV, Kemp would designate 50 Housing Opportunity Zones and encourage them to design "barrier removal plans" that scrapped restrictive zoning laws, outdated building codes and other regulations to spur building affordable housing.

Democrats acknowledged Kemp's initiatives, but found them lacking. Schumer said the proposal "is often more hype than hope." Gonzalez said the proposals addressed "only a small segment of this nation's housing needs" and the emphasis on promoting home ownership could be interpreted as "a thinly veiled effort to abdicate the federal government's responsibility for affordable housing in the long run."

Republican Bartlett, however, praised Kemp's plan, saying that "the HOPE proposal signifies a revolution in housing policy." But he did criticize a section setting resale restrictions on people who bought their homes under the program.

Under Kemp's bill, people who bought apartments in their public housing projects would have to sell them back to the tenant organization overseeing the project for the amount of their initial down payment, plus the cost of improvements and inflation, so that another low-income person could buy into the project.

Kemp told Bartlett that he was "preaching to the choir." But he said a bill that did not have resale restrictions would not get through Congress.

Furor Over Consolidating Programs

In an attempt to rein in and revive what they saw as a runaway, floundering housing bill, D'Amato and Sen. Christopher J. Dodd, D-Conn., introduced legislation April 24 to consolidate nine federal housing programs into a single block grant to states and local governments.

The proposal (S 2504) blindsided Banking Committee Democrats and sparked near-hysteria among housing interest groups that had been waiting anxiously for the scheduled May 2 markup of the Cranston-D'Amato omnibus housing measure.

As introduced, the D'Amato-Dodd bill would have circumvented the scandal-scarred HUD and given away $7 billion from public housing, construction programs for the elderly and disabled, rehabilitation programs, Indian housing and Housing Development Action Grants.

But after a barrage of criticism from housing groups and no support from other committee members, D'Amato and Dodd — both longtime supporters of low-income housing — retreated, conceding that public housing should not be included in a block grant.

Christopher S. Bond, R-Mo., and John Heinz, R-Pa., who served on the full committee but not on the Housing Subcommittee, worked on a compromise amendment to consolidate some smaller housing programs into a block grant while excluding public housing and housing construction for the elderly and disabled.

Their plan also included some reform provisions for public housing agencies from an earlier bill (S 2304).

Public housing officials were particularly upset by the

D'Amato-Dodd measure. They warned that public housing could die if its money was spread to other programs. And housing groups warned that Congress would find it easier to shift the burden for paying for housing programs to the states if the programs were lumped together.

Equally disturbed by the proposal was the National Governors' Association (NGA). "We don't want people coming to the state capitals because there's not enough money for public housing. That's a federal responsibility," said Tim Masanz, NGA director for economic development and technological innovation.

Only the National League of Cities, with a longtime policy favoring block grants, backed the measure.

In a floor speech to introduce his new bill, D'Amato said it was intended to supplement, not gut, his original S 566. D'Amato said that when S 566 was being developed, "no one knew that [HUD's] effectiveness had been so seriously eroded. No one was aware of the rampant abuses occurring with housing programs. No one knew that HUD had fallen under the undue influence of lobbyists and interest groups."

Even though Congress had enacted legislation to reform HUD, D'Amato said that it takes time to turn around a 14,000-person bureaucracy and that state and local officials could more efficiently see to housing needs. *(HUD reform, 1989 Almanac, p. 631)*

However, Mary Brunette, Kemp's policy and communication assistant, said the proposal would mean an "abdication of responsibility and leadership" by the federal government. "The secretary opposes new construction block grants because they institutionalize the failures of the past at the state and local levels," she added.

SENATE COMMITTEE MARKUP

After scuttling 10 existing programs and cutting back new spending, the Senate Banking, Housing and Urban Affairs Committee on May 2 approved the Cranston-D'Amato bill by 16-4. As approved, S 566 would authorize $17.6 billion for housing programs in fiscal 1991.

Although a Cranston compromise amendment picked up enough GOP votes to give the final bill a bipartisan imprint, the measure's cost remained a sticking point.

Four Republicans voted against the bill: Utah's Jake Garn, the committee's ranking minority member; William V. Roth Jr., Del.; Connie Mack, Fla.; and Nancy Landon Kassebaum, Kan.

Immediately after the Senate vote, Cranston met with Richard G. Darman, director of the Office of Management and Budget (OMB), and Kemp to discuss the administration's position on the bill.

"Darman and Kemp told me they would take a fresh look at our revised bill," Cranston said. "Darman said he did not want to make any threats about a possible veto. In fact, he said he didn't even want to discuss a veto."

The compromise, brokered by Bond, would cut the new fiscal 1991 spending authorized in the bill from $3.7 billion to $3.1 billion. The rest of the money authorized in the legislation would go to maintain rent subsidies and other programs at their existing levels.

HUD had asked for only an $80 million increase in new budget authority in fiscal 1991, about 1 percent more than fiscal 1990 spending.

Killing Old Programs

D'Amato emerged somewhat vindicated by the compromise. He and Dodd had surprised and angered their fellow committee members with their plan to consolidate existing housing programs into a block grant.

The compromise approved by the committee left the bulk of public housing alone but would kill 10 smaller programs worth $551 million. The funds would be shifted to the new Housing Opportunity Partnership envisioned under the bill to supply funds to cities and states for development and rehabilitation of affordable housing.

Cities and states would split the money 60-40, respectively, rather than 50-50 as the original bill provided. Recipients would have to put up a 25 percent match to the federal funds.

The programs slated to be killed were:

- Urban homesteading — a program under which the federal government transferred ownership of housing to local communities for resale to low-income people whose existing housing was substandard.
- Nehemiah grants — loans for the construction of single-family homes for moderate-income families.
- Home ownership counseling — financial and maintenance counseling to potential low-income buyers.
- Rental rehabilitation — grants to local governments for the renovation of rental property.
- Public housing development — financing for construction and acquisition of low-income housing.
- Rehabilitation loans — low-interest loans to bring housing and commercial property to local housing code standards.
- Housing development action grants (HoDAG) — aid to developers to help cut the cost of building low-income housing.
- Moderate rehabilitation — Section 8 housing aid to finance the modernization of substandard housing.
- Congregate housing services — meals, health care and other services to allow the elderly to remain in existing housing and avoid institutions.
- Public housing sales.

In cutting costs, the committee reduced the price of the HOP program to $2 billion from $3 billion.

In addition, the compromise called for eliminating several proposed structural changes to HUD, such as creating a HOME Corporation to administer the HOP program. Also eliminated were a proposed new Office of Affordable Housing Preservation and the post of assistant secretary for supportive housing.

Also, the bill would simply extend existing law regarding the FHA mortgage-insurance program for two years, rather than increasing ceilings for mortgages for first-time home buyers. In the HUD spending bill (HR 2916 — PL 101-144) for fiscal 1990, Congress raised the ceiling for FHA-insured mortgages to $124,875 in most high-cost areas, up from $101,250.

Public Housing Loses

Most unhappy about the agreement were advocates of public housing, which would lose $369 million of the development funding proposed under the original version of the bill. That money was being used to acquire, rehabilitate and build public housing; to replace demolished housing; and to undertake major reconstruction of public housing.

"We were just stunned, shocked and dismayed that we ended up being the chip to buy a few Republican sponsors," said Gordon Cavanaugh, general counsel to the Council of Large Public Housing Authorities.

But Housing Subcommittee Staff Director W. Donald

Campbell said the bill said the bill could not pass the Senate if it was voted out of committee on a straight party-line vote. The compromise was an effort to win broader support for the bill — including the support of D'Amato, Cranston's original cosponsor.

"That was the best we could do," Campbell said. The compromise did not affect $2 billion that would be authorized for public housing modernization and $1.9 billion in operating subsidies for fiscal 1991.

D'Amato, still smarting from the criticism that greeted the block-grant proposal, kept the committee on tenterhooks until the afternoon of May 2, when he finally decided to vote for the bill. Though he said he liked the bill's thrust in giving flexibility to local governments, D'Amato said he was still concerned about the total cost.

Unlike the big compromise, which was clinched during a break in the markup, other changes were agreed upon before the senators even sat down to offer amendments.

One key provision dropped from the original bill would have merged rental vouchers and certificates into a new program called rental credits.

Instead, the legislation would modify the existing programs, which provided rental assistance based upon a fair market rent standard. The changes would allow the HUD secretary to approve locally developed fair market rent standards rather than impose a regional standard set by HUD.

The amendments also would allow tenants to use HUD certificates to rent apartments that cost more than 30 percent of their monthly income. Under existing law, that was possible only with vouchers.

Public housing authorities would be required to make sure that tenants were not forced to pay exorbitant amounts of their total income for rent because of inadequate supplements by HUD. They would have to check whether the rents paid by voucher holders were reasonable and would be required to tell HUD if more than 10 percent of households using vouchers spent more than 30 percent of their monthly income on rent.

Other Senate Amendments

Other amendments adopted by the Senate committee, by voice vote unless otherwise indicated, included:

- By D'Amato, 15-5, to expedite construction of supportive housing for the elderly when the HUD secretary determined that cost-containment rules and regulations had been satisfied.
- By Larry Pressler, R-S.D., to ensure a minimum state share of 0.5 percent of funds for certain housing programs, including Section 202 loans for the construction of housing for elderly and disabled people, public housing modernization, public housing operating subsidies and Indian housing development.
- By Roth and John Kerry, D-Mass., to exclude individuals or families evicted from subsidized housing for drug-related criminal activity from receiving preference for publicly assisted housing for five years, unless they successfully completed a rehabilitation program.
- By Bond, to make an exception to the existing rule requiring one-for-one replacement of public housing that was demolished. Units could be replaced on a one-for-two basis when the project to be demolished had vacancies exceeding 35 percent for the previous five years; the project was located in an area with a vacancy rate for standard rental units that exceeded 10 percent; and the project was located in an area experiencing severe economic distress.
- By Bond, to direct the HUD secretary to assess annually and report to Congress which public housing agencies had experienced serious management problems.
- By Bond, to require local jurisdictions to assess the public housing within their boundaries as part of their local housing strategy.

HOUSE COMMITTEE MARKUP

While the Senate panel moved quickly to work out its differences and vote out the bill, the House Banking Subcommittee on Housing and Community Development laboriously picked through 147 amendments. The panel eventually approved the bill by voice vote on May 10 after five days of markups, but it bucked decisions on some of the thorniest issues to the full committee.

The full committee approved the bill on June 13, after three days of markups.

The House legislation would reauthorize federal housing programs for one year and would authorize about $28 billion — an increase of about $11 billion over spending in fiscal 1990. Essentially, the bill would renew existing programs and add a little something for everybody — Democrats, Republicans and the administration.

The House committee also duplicated the bill's provisions to help the homeless under the Stewart B. McKinney Homeless Assistance Act, reporting them out separately in HR 3789. The precaution was taken in case the omnibus housing bill bogged down. *(Aid for homeless, p. XXX)*

Despite perfunctory arguments over key philosophical issues, roll call votes in the subcommittee were relatively few and, as Schumer put it, a "spirit of comity" prevailed. The issues that drew the most fire were new construction, replacement of public housing and the amount of profit low-income families should be able to reap from selling homes bought with government assistance.

New Construction

In the House, what could have become a nasty, protracted battle over funding authorizations for new construction was instead a serious but good-humored debate.

Saying that the bill's $300 million rental-housing production program caused him and every other Republican "considerable heartburn," Tom Ridge, Pa., proposed killing the entire program.

The bill would establish a revolving loan fund to provide advances to developers, nonprofit groups and public housing agencies to construct or rehabilitate affordable rental housing. Loans could cover up to 50 percent of the cost, and interest rates could not be more than 3 percent.

"I look at this program as a scandal waiting to happen," Ridge said. "This does not advance the cause of low- and moderate-income people; it advances the cause of fat-cat developers."

Also troubled by the program was Democrat Floyd H. Flake of New York, who proposed increasing the percentage of low- and lower-income families who would live in the rental projects from 15 percent to 35 percent.

"We ought to be doing the most for the people who need the most," Flake said. As the program stood, he said, it appeared to work for the rich, not the poor.

But Schumer, who proposed the new program, said he designed it to avoid scandals by including rigid guidelines and limited discretion for developers.

And he said the percentage of poor people in each project was set so that market-rate apartments in each building would subsidize the low-cost units. Besides, he said, the percentage was not a maximum, but a minimum.

The subcommittee rejected Ridge's amendment on a straight party-line vote, 15-25, and Flake's amendment by voice vote.

The subcommittee also rejected a Bartlett amendment to allow people who bought homes through the bill's proposed Community Housing Partnership program to reap a profit if they sold the home after five years.

The partnership program was similar to the Senate's proposed HOP program, but smaller, with an authorization level of $300 million in fiscal 1991. Grants would be provided to cities, states and nonprofit groups to rehabilitate, construct and acquire low- and moderate-income housing. Grants could also be used to buy and manage rental-housing projects, as well as to help families buy their own homes.

The vote against Bartlett's amendment was 16-23, with Marge Roukema, R-N.J., voting with the Democrats, and Thomas R. Carper, D-Del., voting with the Republicans. Bartlett had initially proposed dropping the entire partnership program before modifying his amendment.

Poor people should not have to bear the risks of home ownership without being able to earn the rewards, Bartlett told the other members. But Joseph P. Kennedy II, D-Mass., who proposed the partnership program, said sellers could receive the price they paid, plus an adjustment for inflation and improvements to the home. Kennedy said that if the homes were sold at the market rate, they would be lost from the stock of affordable housing for low-income families.

During full committee action the following month, Bartlett proposed an amendment that would allow families to retain any increase in value minus the public subsidy after the fifth year of ownership. By the 10th year, the family would keep all the equity in the home. But under a substitute amendment by Kennedy, a family could keep 5 percent of the profits for each year the family lived in the home until the 10th year. From then on, the family could keep 50 percent of the profits. The full committee adopted the Kennedy amendment 27-20 on a party-line vote.

Another Bartlett amendment offered in subcommittee would have changed the requirement that one unit of new public housing be built to replace every unit demolished with a one-for-two requirement. The amendment was rejected on an 18-23 party-line vote after Democrats argued that the change would encourage public housing authorities to allow their units to remain vacant and in disrepair.

One amendment, which was approved by voice vote, ended up pitting Chairman Gonzalez against Republicans and Democrats.

David E. Price, D-N.C., proposed reducing the percentage of spots reserved in public housing for "preference" families from 90 percent to 70 percent.

Preference families qualified for public housing because they were paying more than 50 percent of their monthly income for rent, lived in substandard housing or had been involuntarily displaced from their homes.

Gonzalez said he opposed the amendment because it would harm the neediest families. But Schumer and Bartlett said the change would increase the income mix of families living in public housing.

"We never do anything for the struggling poor," said Schumer. "These are people who are just hanging on."

The subcommittee also agreed to three amendments making slight changes in the proposed $500 million National Housing Trust, which would help first-time home buyers by providing interest rates no higher than 6 percent and helping to cover the cost of down payments and closing costs.

The home buyer's annual family income could not exceed 115 percent of the median income for a family of four in the metropolitan area in which they lived.

As amended, the program would also provide grants for second mortgages. First-time home buyers would be required to certify that they could not find credit commercially and would have to make a minimum down payment of 1 percent of the purchase price. And home buyers would have to repay the assistance they received from the government if their home was no longer their principal residence.

Manufactured Homes

One contentious issue was an amendment by John Hiler, R-Ind., to relax the National Manufactured Housing Construction and Safety Standards Act of 1974 and give the HUD secretary discretion to set standards for such homes.

Even before the amendment was raised, Gonzalez issued a news release calling Hiler's proposal the "Fire-Trap Act of 1990."

Gonzalez called the plan "an open invitation for irresponsible manufacturers to turn out sleazy, unsafe products, forcing legitimate companies to the sidelines and placing thousands of homeowners at great risk."

Hiler, however, said the existing law was based on the National Traffic and Motor Vehicle Safety Act because manufactured homes had formerly been primarily mobile homes rather than homes equipped with a chassis and wheels mostly for shipping purposes. "Manufactured homes are just that — homes. They are things people live in, not drive," Hiler said.

Gonzalez objected to removing from the law's statement of purpose the "reduction of deaths and injuries." He also said HUD's power to test homes for safety defects would be sharply curtailed by Hiler's amendment.

Gonzalez repeatedly tried to beat back Hiler's amendment by urging hearings on the subject. But six Democrats defected, allowing Hiler to win approval for his amendment, 24-20.

A replay of the controversy in full committee was averted in June when Gonzalez and ranking Republican Chalmers P. Wylie, Ohio, offered a compromise leadership amendment.

Under the compromise, language that Hiler wanted to strike from existing law was reinserted. The full committee's measure stated that manufactured home standards should meet the highest standards of quality, safety and affordability. Instead of a one-year warranty to consumers who purchased a mobile home — as Hiler had wanted — manufacturers would be required to provide a two-year warranty and to notify purchasers of all serious defects and correct them for the life of the home.

Public Housing

Public housing received substantial attention, as well, with the subcommittee agreeing by voice vote to allow police officers to live free in public housing. Under the existing law, officers had to pay 30 percent of their monthly income toward rent. The change, proposed by Bartlett, would encourage police officers to live in public housing and help security by patrolling the area and leaving their police cars in front of the building.

The subcommittee also agreed to a plan by Kweisi Mfume, D-Md., to change how public housing tenants calculated their rents. Under the existing system, tenants had to estimate their income and then pay 30 percent of that toward rent. Mfume said he wanted to protect people from being evicted when they did not receive wages, tips, alimony or child support as expected. His amendment would exclude money not actually received from the rent calculation. If the money came in later, the rent would be recalculated.

Another Mfume proposal to prevent families from being evicted from public housing when a family member committed a crime was rejected, 11-24. The amendment would have allowed the family to stay in its apartment, while evicting the person who committed the crime. If the family allowed that person to return, then the housing authority could evict the entire family.

Schumer and other members said it was already too difficult for a housing authority to evict people from public housing. He asked: "What if 16-year-old, 6-foot Johnny comes back, and his mom and two young sisters don't want him, but there he is?"

Other changes, agreed upon by voice vote unless otherwise noted, included:

- By Doug Bereuter, R-Neb., to increase the town population limit to qualify for FmHA subsidies to 25,000 from 20,000.
- By Wylie, by 31-9, to increase low- and moderate-income targeting in the CDBG program to 75 percent from 60 percent.
- By Bartlett and Flake to enable HUD to buy properties from the Resolution Trust Corporation for affordable housing.

Divisions and Delays

Sharp divisions among members of the full House Banking, Finance and Urban Affairs Committee led to delays in markup of the omnibus housing bill.

Fearing Republicans had the votes to quash a proposed $300 million rental housing production program, Chairman Gonzalez canceled a markup of HR 1180 scheduled for June 6 and introduced a second bill (HR 4971) reordering the titles.

His purpose was to force the committee to act on the rental housing program before it decided whether to approve a title incorporating the Bush administration's proposals to spur home ownership.

Gonzalez was concerned that some Democrats might join committee Republicans in opposing the rental housing program, particularly if Flake did so first. The New York Democrat had expressed serious reservations about the program in subcommittee meetings, saying it did not do enough for the very poor.

But Flake finally agreed to return to the fold after meeting late June 6 with Schumer, who had proposed the program, and extracting promises that it would be modified.

Gonzalez held a brief markup June 7 but allowed only technical and non-controversial amendments to be offered.

Kemp's Objections

Also helping to delay consideration of the legislation was a nine-page letter from Kemp on June 6 outlining the administration's opposition to a number of provisions in the bill.

In particular, Kemp complained about new construction programs, such as Schumer's, which he said had never worked. "These programs didn't empower the poor or create a ladder of opportunity out of poverty, they entrapped the poor into squalor and dependency — the epitome of hopelessness and despair," Kemp wrote.

Construction programs long had been anathema to conservatives, who phased out most of them during the Reagan years. Kemp preferred vouchers that recipients could use to help pay rent on a house or apartment of their choice.

The Schumer Program

Schumer's program would establish a revolving loan fund to provide advances to developers, nonprofit groups and public housing agencies for up to 50 percent of the costs of construction, acquisition or rehabilitation of affordable rental housing.

Interest payments, at no more than 3 percent, would begin one year after completion of a project. If not enough cash flow was generated to provide a minimum return on the equity, no interest would be paid. If the cash flow was greater than the interest due, HUD would receive 50 percent of the additional money.

The principal and remaining interest would be due 25 years after construction was completed, but if the developer agreed to continue renting to low-income families, the balance would be forgiven at a rate of 6.7 percent a year.

During the 25-year period, at least 15 percent of the units would have to be rented to low-income families and another 15 percent to lower-income families. Low-income families were defined as earning 60 percent or less of area median income, and lower-income families as those who 80 percent of area median income. Rents would be 30 percent of the family's income.

Flake said that the program would not provide enough units to the very poor and ultimately would subsidize people who were not poor. In addition, he said developers should be required to share the risk by putting their own money into the projects.

After Schumer met with Flake, Schumer agreed to modify the program to require that either 40 percent of a building's tenants would be low-income or 20 percent would be lower-income. In addition, developers would have to put equity into the projects so that the government's loan would not effectively subsidize construction of units going to middle- or upper-income people.

HOPE vs. New Construction

GOP lawmakers and the administration continued to strongly oppose Schumer's program, saying developer subsidies for construction of low-income housing never worked in the past and would only lead to influence-peddling and scandals.

With Republicans threatening to kill Schumer's plan in the full committee markup, Democrats mobilized to retaliate against the administration's HOPE provisions. But when the committee finally convened June 12, Republican Ridge quietly agreed not to put up a fight. Democrats then promised to leave HOPE alone, and Gonzalez said he would seek an open rule governing the floor debate to give Ridge a chance to offer his amendment there.

Schumer's plan was altered, however, as he had agreed with Flake: The committee adopted a Flake amendment to change the targeting in the rental housing production program. Flake's amendment would allow developers to rent either 20 percent of their units to very-low-income people or 40 percent to low-income people.

Flake's amendment would instruct HUD to give preference, in deciding which developers should have subsidies, to those who put the most of their own money into a project. Ridge, however, said the changes were "like putting on deodorant after running a marathon."

Expiring Prepayment Moratorium

Before approving the bill, the committee also resolved the pressing issue of what to do about the soon-to-expire, congressionally imposed moratorium on mortgage prepayments by landlords with federally subsidized mortgages.

On a 29-19 vote, the committee adopted a proposal by Bartlett to lift the moratorium while providing incentives to building owners to continue renting to low-income families for the full 40 years of their mortgages rather than paying off the loans at the 20-year mark.

Nine Democrats joined the committee's 20 Republicans in the plan, which was backed by building owners and the housing industry. The Democrats were Stephen L. Neal, N.C.; Carroll Hubbard Jr., Ky.; Doug Barnard Jr., Ga.; Ben Erdreich, Ala.; Thomas R. Carper, Del.; Gerald D. Kleczka, Wis.; Liz J. Patterson, S.C.; David E. Price, N.C.; and Peter Hoagland, Neb.

Housing for AIDS Victims

The final fight of the markup resulted in a new provision to authorize $150 million in housing assistance for people with AIDS. Roukema and most other committee Republicans objected to the proposal.

Roukema failed to kill the plan, however, losing 17-31. Republicans Bereuter and Patricia Saiki, Hawaii, voted with committee Democrats not to strike the program.

"HUD should not be put in the business of providing AIDS-related medical care," Roukema said. She suggested shifting $50 million of the $150 million to the HOPE Shelter Plus Care program, which would coordinate housing, medical and social services with other agencies. She said AIDS patients would be better served in that program.

Led by Jim McDermott, Wash., Democrats fought hard to retain the set-aside. "Providing housing assistance for people with AIDS is not only more humane, it is cost-effective," McDermott said. He said hospitals would often keep AIDS patients when they had nowhere else to go. "Hospitalization may cost $650 a day, while assisted housing can be provided for as little as $60 a day."

The bill called for $8 million for emergency assistance to prevent homelessness among AIDS patients, $53 million for Section 8 rental certificates, $18 million for renovation of single-room units and $68 million for community residential facilities. Another $3 million would be spent on information and counseling.

With final approval of the bill June 13, attention turned to the Senate.

SENATE FLOOR ACTION

After a week of veto threats and uncertainty, Democrats, Republicans and administration officials worked out their differences — largely when Democrats gave the administration what it wanted — and passed S 566 on June 27, 96-1. Republican Roth, casting the lone "no" vote, said the cost was prohibitive. *(Vote 132, p. 31-S)*

The Senate bill would have authorized about $25 billion in spending in fiscal 1991 to add 213,844 subsidized housing units to the market. The bill's goal was to provide housing for the elderly and disabled, to help low-income tenants buy their public-housing units, to preserve older subsidized housing projects threatened by condominium conversion and to provide shelter and services to the homeless.

The Senate bill would have exceeded existing spending by $3 billion, the House bill by $6 billion. (The Senate would authorize programs for three years, the House for one.)

OMB Director Darman had promised senators that if they met administration policy objections, Bush would not veto S 566 because of its cost.

But at a June 27 news conference, Kemp warned reporters not to confuse authorization levels with appropriations, the actual money spent on a program. "It is obvious the budget summit will have an impact upon the final — not only authorization — but the final appropriation of housing monies," he said.

Long Negotiations

Senators had begun action on the bill June 18, while staff members for the two prime sponsors, Cranston and D'Amato, started negotiating with administration officials.

The administration had said that the bill put too much emphasis on building rental housing, did not target the very poor, did not include the administration's plan to bring the FHA back to financial health and cost too much.

In addition, Kemp had strenuously objected that his HOPE program, which would help public-housing tenants and other low-income people buy homes, was not fully funded.

After an all-day meeting June 22 involving Kemp, Cranston, D'Amato and the deputy director of OMB, staff members spent the weekend and Monday in negotiations. On June 26, the principals got back together and ironed out the last wrinkles.

In the end, Kemp got almost everything he wanted.

An administration proposal to shore up the FHA Mutual Mortgage Insurance Fund was agreed to by both Democrats and Republicans. The fund had been suffering from a high default rate and low capital reserves, but Cranston had protested that the administration's plan would shut out potential first-time home buyers. D'Amato, on the other hand, complained that it did not go far enough in protecting the fund from further defaults.

The administration prevailed in the final agreement, which called for higher premiums, two-thirds of closing costs to be paid with the down payment and increased capital requirements for the insurance fund. In addition, the FHA would continue to insure homes up to $124,875, the existing mortgage limit in high-priced areas of the country.

Housing Opportunity Partnerships

The Senate bill's centerpiece was the $2 billion HOP program, designed to increase affordable housing by giving matching grants to state and local governments.

The program was supposed to simplify the way HUD worked by creating a "one-stop shop" in which local governments could deal for all their housing programs.

State and local governments would be required to design a housing plan, including the types of programs needed for their area. The HOP program would provide grants to the local governments to put the plan into effect, and it would encourage them to form partnerships with private industry and nonprofit groups to help match the funds.

The funding would be used to develop mixed-income housing, rehabilitate substandard housing and resell homes to low- and moderate-income families. For every $4 of federal money, states and municipalities would be required to kick in $1, in addition to money from private-sector sources.

During floor action June 21, the Senate voted 52-45 to kill an amendment by Florida's Mack that would have refocused the HOP program to allow its funds to be used for rental assistance for a community's poorest residents. *(Vote 123, p. 29-S)*

The program was intended to increase affordable housing, Democrats argued. Helping tenants pay their rent does nothing to increase affordable housing, they said.

The administration, however, strongly opposed new construction programs and feared that HOP money would be used primarily for that purpose. "I am convinced that flawed programs were as much to blame for HUD scandals as political appointees who tolerated or encouraged abuses," Kemp said in his letter to Cranston.

In the end, only two Democrats, Bob Graham of Florida and Sam Nunn of Georgia, joined Republicans in supporting Mack's amendment.

In his compromise agreement with Senate sponsors of the bill, however, Kemp succeeded in curtailing construction under HOP.

The agreement would impose criteria for communities to meet to qualify to build housing. HUD would allow new construction if an area had a low vacancy rate, a low turnover of units renting below the existing fair market rent levels and a high ratio of substandard housing. HUD would be required to approve at least 30 percent of all localities in the HOP program for construction.

Before the funds could be used for construction, however, state and local governments would also have to show that there was a severe shortage of buildings that could be renovated and used as rental housing.

The criteria would not have to be met if the construction was intended for large families, people with disabilities, single-room occupancy units or other special housing needs. Also excluded from the restrictions would be neighborhood revitalization efforts.

And despite protests that tenant-based rental assistance did nothing to expand the supply of affordable housing, Democrats gave in and agreed to let local governments spend HOP funds on rental assistance. But they included restrictions of their own — for example, requiring local governments to certify that rental assistance was an essential element of their overall housing strategy.

Other Agreements

Democrats also gave in to Kemp's insistence that rental and home-ownership programs target very-low-income people. Democrats had wanted to primarily help a mix of moderate-, low- and very-low-income families.

Under the agreement, 90 percent of the rental units were to be aimed at very-low-income families and 10 percent allotted for low-income households. The administration had originally proposed that 95 percent of the units go to very-low-income families; Democrats wanted 50 percent.

For home-ownership programs, both sides shifted considerably. The agreement called for 100 percent of the home-ownership programs to be targeted to low-income families. The administration originally wanted a 50-50 split between very-low- and low-income households. Democrats had planned to aim the program at low- and moderate-income families, 51-49 percent.

Finally, negotiators agreed to provide full authorization for Kemp's brainchild, the HOPE program, at $240 million in fiscal 1991, $650 million in fiscal 1992 and $1 billion in fiscal 1993. The bill originally called for $435 million in authorizations over three years, less than a quarter of what Kemp finally got.

Although Kemp previously had said he preferred the House bill to the Senate bill, he reversed himself after the agreement was reached. In an interview, Kemp said the Senate's housing legislation was "immensely superior" to the House bill.

Gramm Objects

Despite glowing words for the compromise from the administration and lawmakers on both sides of the aisle, debate over the housing bill still faced a major hurdle. A "killer" amendment from Phil Gramm, R-Texas, snarled the proceedings with histrionics and filibustering for more than four hours on the day of passage.

The Gramm amendment, which was ultimately defeated, would have allocated the $3 billion in CDBG funds to states by population, rather than through the existing formula. The result would be that 36 states, including Texas, would receive more money and 14 states would receive less.

Gramm complained that the existing formula used — with its heavy emphasis on older housing — was designed to favor the Northeast. The formula also weighted population, poverty and housing overcrowding.

By concentrating funds to areas with older housing, Gramm argued, the formula ignored areas such as Texas that had inadequate new housing. "There is not a relationship between age of housing and poverty. There is a relationship between quality of housing and poverty," he said.

Gramm said 10 of the 14 states that would lose money if his amendment were adopted ranked in the top half of per-capita income. And six of the 14 were among the 15 richest states in the union, he said.

New York, which had the third highest per-capita income in the country, would have lost $95 million in 1991 under the plan. Other losers would have included Massachusetts, Michigan, Pennsylvania and Illinois.

The big winners would have been California, with a gain of $31 million; Florida, at $26 million; North Carolina, at $22 million; Texas, at $22 million; and Virginia, at $21 million.

Lloyd Bentsen, D-Texas, joined Gramm in pushing the amendment.

D'Amato complained bitterly that Gramm was thinking solely of parochial interests and countered that taxpayers in the Northeast were bearing the cost of the savings and loan bailout even though thrift collapses were concentrated in Texas.

"If we're going to get down to parochialism," D'Amato said, "then let's get down to it. Why should my taxpayers bail out Texas S&L victims?"

D'Amato offered a second-degree amendment to cap the amount of block grant funds a state could receive if that state also received more than a per-capita proportion of savings and loan bailout funds. He acknowledged that the amendment was ludicrous but said Gramm's was even more outrageous.

The Gramm amendment was killed, 65-35, although some longtime supporters of the bill, including both Florida senators, voted with Gramm. *(Vote 129, p. 30-S)*

Before passage, the Senate agreed to instruct HUD to study the formula used to distribute block grant funds.

HOUSE FLOOR ACTION

The House passed its version of the housing legislation, 378-43, on Aug. 1. With many contentious issues worked out in advance, HR 1180 moved swiftly despite an open rule lifting customary restrictions on amendments to complex bills. *(Vote 294, p. 96-H)*

Approval came despite strong opposition from Kemp to the FHA overhaul plan included in the bill. Kemp said the plan did not go far enough to prop up the FHA's faltering single-family insurance fund. But concerned about hitting voters in the wallet, even the Republican leadership rejected Kemp's plan, and it was never offered on the floor.

Before the measure reached the floor, OMB had weighed in with a veto threat contained in a five-page, single-spaced statement spelling out objections to the bill.

The OMB statement protested that both the rental production program and the Community Housing Partnership program, which would provide grants to state and local governments to renovate or build low- and moderate-income housing, would "encourage costly, developer-driven new construction in lieu of more efficient tenant-based housing assistance."

Banking Chairman Gonzalez said the complaints were nothing new. "They have all along resisted the new construction, new production [programs]. That is the basic point of difference. We're not going to give in on that," he said.

In contrast to the Senate bill's focus on a new block grant program to encourage state and local housing initiatives, the House bill emphasized traditional programs at HUD. It also created a number of programs, including one similar to the Senate's HOP program.

Finding the Funds

Despite the intention of each chamber to craft effective measures to prevent homelessness and expand the supply of affordable housing, both bills faced budget cuts.

Wylie, ranking Republican on the Banking Committee, insisted that members of the House recognize that fact by offering an amendment to require the legislation to conform to the House budget resolution. The amendment was agreed to by voice vote after no discussion.

The budget resolution assumed that housing authorizations would grow by $3.3 billion over CBO's baseline estimate of current-level funding, but the House bill authorized $27.877 billion, about $4 billion more than the baseline, according to CBO.

Besides the $700 million cut needed to comply with the budget resolution, the bill was likely to face further reductions once administration and Hill negotiators concluded their budget summit.

William E. Dannemeyer, R-Calif., proposed a more stringent amendment to limit the increase in housing authorizations to 4.8 percent of the fiscal 1990 level. He complained that the bill would increase budget authority by 65 percent because housing programs received $17 billion in appropriations during fiscal 1990, a far cry from the $28 billion proposed for fiscal 1991.

Dannemeyer's figures, however, did not account for $7 billion included in the CBO baseline to renew expiring rental assistance contracts.

"You can't argue with bad facts," Gonzalez said, arguing against the amendment. "Mr. Dannemeyer is just way off." With Gonzalez and Wylie teaming to oppose it, the amendment was rejected 62-354. *(Vote 293, p. 96-H)*

The Senate's legislation called for spending about $17 billion in fiscal 1991 for existing and new programs. But unlike the House version, it did not include $9 billion for the expiring contracts and other costs, to be handled in the appropriations process.

In the House, one controversial item, to create the first housing entitlement program ever, survived floor action but faced a battle over its cost in conference.

Schumer had inserted a provision that would require HUD to provide rental aid to families when their lack of adequate housing would cause their children to be placed in foster care. CBO estimated that the program would require more than $1 billion in budget authority over the following five years.

The administration opposed the entitlement, saying that it would put pressure on local welfare agencies to certify that a family was about to be broken up in order to get housing assistance for the family. Republicans, not wanting to be seen voting against children just before an election, never mentioned it on the floor.

Neither did members of the Appropriations Subcommittee on VA, HUD and Independent Agencies, who could have called a "point of order" objecting to the provision. However, Bob Traxler, D-Mich., chairman of the subcommittee, sent a letter to Gonzalez asking him to delete it in conference. Schumer, however, vowed to fight for the provision.

Despite the specter of budget cuts and the daunting task of obtaining real money from appropriators, lawmakers said it was important just to get the programs into place — with or without the funds. "We believe we've got to put the programs on the books and fund them more radically in later years," said Barney Frank, D-Mass.

FHA, Prepayment Issues

The cause célèbre of the housing debate was not over providing shelter for those who needed it most, but over how to protect the solvency of the FHA fund used to help middle-income families buy homes.

After the Senate had voted to shore up the agency's Mutual Mortgage Insurance Fund by tightening lending conditions, interest groups — including state housing finance agencies, housing industry groups and activist organizations — teamed to back a plan developed by Republican Ridge and Democrat Bruce F. Vento, Minn., that would avoid increased upfront costs for home buyers but charge an annual 0.6 percent premium over the life of the 30-year loan.

The administration opposed the plan, saying that it was not strong enough to revive the fund. Kemp said Bush would veto any legislation that did not include his plan to fix the insurance fund.

But Kemp found few allies on the Hill, even among Republicans. Gonzalez rejected a compromise, and Republicans deserted him. A few hours before the scheduled vote the Republican Leadership Conference decided to back it over the administration's plan.

On the floor, Vento-Ridge was adopted by an overwhelming 418-2 vote. *(Vote 290, p. 94-H)*

Before Kemp put the FHA fund on the front burner, members had been preoccupied with what to do about several hundred thousand tenants at risk of eviction under a federally subsidized mortgage program.

On that issue, the House built on the amendment approved in the Banking Committee by approving a Democrat-sponsored refinement containing additional incentives and requirements to persuade owners to continue renting to low-income tenants.

The House agreed to the amendment by 400-12. *(Vote 292, p. 96-H)*

Resolution of the FHA and prepayment issues allowed the House to complete action on the bill, approving it with only 43 lawmakers — 42 Republicans and Democrat Timothy J. Penny, Minn. — voting against it.

HOUSE-SENATE CONFERENCE

Conferees needed nearly three weeks of painstaking negotiations to complete work on the housing bill, but the agreement reached Oct. 15 had something for everyone.

The Bush administration's home-ownership programs were included in the final product, in addition to the House's and the Senate's priority programs. Bipartisan compromises were crafted to fix the FHA's single-family insurance fund and to restrict prepayments on low-income housing.

State and local governments appeared in line for the biggest victory. Using a block grant, state and local governments would have more say when putting together housing programs with federal dollars. Nonprofit community development groups, for the first time, would share a piece of the money pie. And the federal government would get back in the business of subsidizing the construction of affordable housing.

"It's a great step forward," said Zigas of the National Low Income Housing Coalition. "It's far less than is needed, but it's also a major reversal of 10 years of neglect and retreat."

Altogether, the bill authorized housing programs for two years to fund existing programs plus an estimated 360,000 additional units of affordable housing. In fiscal 1991, the legislation authorized $17.9 billion in spending, about $3.36 billion over existing levels. In fiscal 1992, it authorized $20.6 billion — about $5.5 billion above existing spending. Those figures did not include close to $9 billion required to renew expiring rental assistance contracts and to fulfill existing contracts.

Heated Negotiations

During the long Columbus Day weekend, staff members reached an impasse and the talks often erupted into shouting matches.

At more than one meeting, Campbell, staff director of the Senate's Housing Subcommittee, pleaded with House staff to be realistic in demands for building programs. He said it would be hard enough to move a housing conference report through the Senate floor.

Senate staff members also felt constrained to stick with agreements that they made with the administration during floor passage of the legislation limiting construction and increasing targeting to the very poor.

Given the snail's pace of progress, at least one GOP staff member began the week of Oct. 8 by drafting an alternative, bare-bones measure in case the omnibus bill failed.

"The staffs did meet and the enemy is us," Gonzalez joked as members returned to the conference table Oct. 9. There, the clash continued.

Senators tried to tone down the House members' penchant for new buildings. But the House clung to two pet programs: public housing construction and rental housing. Together, the programs would authorize more than $800 million in spending.

Kemp spent Oct. 11 on Capitol Hill, first meeting with GOP conferees in the House's Rayburn Office Building, then privately with Gonzalez. His approach was low-key — in stark contrast to his testy threat in August to quit when the House went against him on the FHA issue.

The next day, Oct. 12, conferees agreed on compromises on two of the thorniest issues: the FHA mortgage insurance fix and the landlord prepayment question.

Construction Programs

The administration continued to hammer at the new construction programs included in both the House and Senate bills.

The Senate's showpiece was the $2 billion block-grant program to states and local governments to help them build and rehabilitate housing. But the administration argued there was already enough housing in the country and wanted funds shifted to rental assistance.

In negotiations with HUD and OMB officials, the senators backed down, agreeing that block-grant money could also be used for rental assistance, duplicating the Section 8 rent subsidy program.

Senators also accepted limits on the number of communities that could use the money for construction, and they agreed to structure federal matching funds to make it more expensive for a community to build housing rather than to provide rent subsidies.

The House, however, was not so easily swayed. Conferees insisted on retaining public housing construction, a longstanding program that had been killed by the Senate, as well as Schumer's rental construction program. The administration opposed both.

To gain concessions on the Schumer program, the administration held public housing hostage. Backed by Senate Republicans, the administration insisted on killing construction of public housing, a $500 million-a-year program. The House was unable to roll over the GOP objections because with Democrat Dodd's support, Republican senators had a majority on the issue.

For Gonzalez, who had lived and worked in public housing in San Antonio in the 1950s, the program was a must. Senate Democrats had promised public housing advocates that the program would be restored in conference, after they had killed the program to gain votes in the Banking Committee and on the floor.

No one made a sound as Gonzalez described how a public housing project replaced an area in the city known as "Death Triangle" that had an unusually high infant mortality rate.

"I have seen what public housing can do," he said. "I would hope we'd not [kill] this — not just out of respect for me — but out of responsiveness to the poor."

Public housing advocates were puzzled by Dodd's refusal to discuss his reasons for opposing the program. But Gonzalez said Dodd held out to extract a concession from the Banking chairman on an unrelated matter. Dodd wanted Banking conferees on the Export Administration Act (HR 4653) to support his provision requiring the Export-Import Bank to finance defense sales to NATO and Japan. This would enable Sikorsky helicopters, which were made in Connecticut, to be sold to Turkey, bringing in millions of dollars.

Continued on p. 656

Housing Program Authorizations

President Bush signed the Cranston-Gonzalez National Affordable Housing Act into law on Nov. 28 (S 566 — PL 101-625). Following are major provisions:

General Provisions and Policies

• **National housing goal**. Affirmed that every American family be able to afford a decent home in a suitable environment.

• **National housing policy**. Set the following objectives:

• To forge a nationwide partnership of public and private institutions to ensure that every U.S. resident has access to decent shelter or assistance in avoiding homelessness.

• To increase the supply of decent housing affordable to low- and moderate-income families and accessible to jobs.

• To improve housing opportunities for all U.S. residents, particularly members of disadvantaged minorities.

• To help make neighborhoods safe and livable.

• To expand opportunities for home ownership.

• To provide every community with a reliable, readily available supply of mortgage financing at the lowest possible interest rate.

• And to encourage tenant empowerment and reduce generational poverty in federally assisted housing and public housing by improving the means by which self-sufficiency may be achieved.

• **Purposes of the Cranston-Gonzalez Act**. To help families save money for a down payment on a house.

• To retain, wherever feasible, affordable housing for low-income families that were produced with federal assistance.

• To extend and strengthen partnerships among all levels of government and the private sector, including for-profit and nonprofit organizations, in the production and operation of affordable housing.

• To expand and improve federal rental assistance for very-low-income families.

• And to increase the supply of supportive housing, which combines structural features and services needed to enable people with special needs to live with dignity and independence.

• **State and local housing strategies**. Required the HUD secretary to provide assistance directly to a state or local government if the jurisdiction submitted a comprehensive housing affordability strategy, if the jurisdiction submitted annual updates of the housing strategy and if the strategy was approved by the secretary.

• **Citizen participation**. Required state and local governments to publish a proposed housing strategy and to hold at least one public hearing before submitting the strategy to the secretary.

• **Energy-efficiency standards**. Required the secretary to write energy-efficiency standards for construction of public and assisted housing, as well as for single-family and multifamily housing subject to FHA mortgages. The standards would have to be produced no later than one year after enactment.

• **Capacity study**. Required the secretary to ensure that HUD had the capacity and resources, including staff and training programs, to carry out its mission and responsibilities, and to carry out the provisions of the act, including the multifamily mortgage insurance program. No more than 60 days after enactment, the secretary would have to submit to Congress a study detailing plans to maintain the department's capacity for carrying out the law.

• **Protection of state and local authority**. Prevented the secretary from denying federal funds to any state or local government based on a jurisdiction's policy or law that did not violate any federal law.

HOME Investment Partnerships Act

• **Funds**. Authorized $1 billion in fiscal 1991 and $2.1 billion in fiscal 1992 to be appropriated for the HOME Investment Partnerships Act. Considered the cornerstone of the entire bill, this program would provide federal block grants to state and local governments, which would be responsible for matching the money and using it to solve local housing needs.

• **Eligible uses**. Funds could be used to provide incentives to develop and support affordable rental housing and home-ownership programs through the acquisition, construction and moderate or substantial rehabilitation of affordable housing. Eligible activities also included financing costs, relocation expenses of displaced people and rental assistance.

Jurisdictions would have to give preference to using their federal funds for the rehabilitation of substandard housing unless that was not the most cost-effective way to expand the affordable housing supply.

• **Conditions for construction**. Funds would be used for housing construction only if there were an inadequate supply of housing at rentals below the fair market value set for the area by HUD and if there were a severe shortage of substandard residential buildings in the area that were suitable for rehabilitation as affordable rental housing.

• **Criteria**. Required the HUD secretary to publish objective criteria for determining whether a jurisdiction's housing supply was inadequate, to permit federal funds to be used for construction. Also required the secretary to publish a list of jurisdictions that met those criteria.

Required the secretary to give jurisdictions that did not meet the criteria a reasonable opportunity to provide additional information showing that they did qualify. Required that the criteria include objective data on housing market conditions such as low vacancy rates, low turnover of units with rents below market levels and a high proportion of substandard housing.

Required that at least 30 percent of the jurisdictions receiving HOME block grants met the criteria to be allowed to use the money for construction. [This provision was aimed at forcing HUD to approve plans that included construction, an approach the administration had opposed.]

• **Neighborhood revitalization**. Authorized jurisdictions to use federal funds for construction if they certified that:

• Construction was needed to help a neighborhood revitalization program that emphasized rehabilitation of substandard housing for rent or home ownership by low- and moderate-income families.

• Housing would be built in a low- or moderate-income neighborhood.

• The number of units to be built did not exceed 20 percent of the total number of units in the neighborhood revitalization program.

• And the housing would be built by a community housing development organization or by a public agency.

• **Exemptions**. Eliminated the 20 percent cap on units to be built out of the total neighborhood revitalization program when the housing was to be in a severely distressed area with large tracts of vacant land and abandoned buildings; the housing was to be in an area with an inadequate supply of existing housing that could economically be rehabilitated to meet the area's housing needs; or, the construction was required to finish the neighborhood revitalization program.

• **Special needs housing**. Allowed jurisdictions to use funds for construction in certain cases without meeting the criteria for construction. For example, the money could be used to build affordable housing for large families, affordable housing for people with disabilities, single-room occupancy housing and other categories designated by the secretary.

• **Tenant-based rental assistance**. Authorized jurisdictions to use HOME block grant funds for rental assistance that was provided directly to the tenant to be used for the apartment or home of the tenant's choice under certain circumstances.

For example, tenant-based rental assistance could be provided if it was an essential element of the jurisdiction's annual housing strategy to expand the supply of affordable housing. And, it could be used if it was given to people on waiting lists for Section 8 rental assistance.

Required that a jurisdiction's Section 8 rental assistance allocation not be affected by the use of HOME block grants for rental assistance.

• **Investments**. Required that jurisdictions participating in the HOME block grant program be allowed to invest funds as equity investments, interest-bearing loans or advances, non-interest-bearing loans or advances, interest subsidies, or other forms of assistance that the secretary had agreed to.

• **Prohibited uses**. Forbade the use of federal HOME funds for the following purposes:

• To defray a jurisdiction's administrative costs.

• To provide tenant-based rental assistance to replace public housing that was demolished; to preserve federally assisted housing; to help dispose of housing held by the secretary; to prevent displacement from rental rehabilitation projects; or to extend or renew tenant-based Section 8 rental assistance contracts.

• To provide non-federal matching contributions required under any other federal program.

• For public housing operating subsidies.

• To modernize public housing.

• To solve the prepayment problem.

• **Cost limits**. Required the secretary to establish limits on the amounts of funds that could be invested per unit of housing. Required that the limits be established on a market-by-market basis, with adjustments made for the number of bedrooms. Required that the cost reflect the actual cost of the construction or renovation with adjustments made annually for inflation.

• **Model programs**. Required the secretary to develop a variety of model housing programs designed to address local market conditions and housing problems. The programs, including guidelines, procedures, forms and legal documents, would be available to participating jurisdictions.

Allowed jurisdictions discretion to adopt one or more model programs according to their own needs.

• **Income targeting**. Required jurisdictions to invest federal HOME funds each fiscal year. For rental assistance and rental units, no less than 90 percent of the money invested would have to go to families whose incomes did not exceed 60 percent of the median family income for the area. The remainder of the money invested would have to benefit families that qualified as low-income.

For home-ownership assistance, 100 percent of the funds invested would have to benefit low-income families. All funds invested would have to be used for affordable housing.

• **Affordable housing**. Required that housing qualify as affordable only under certain conditions.

For example, if the rent was not greater than the existing fair market rent for comparable housing in the area or did not exceed 30 percent of the income of a family that earned 65 percent of the median income for the area.

Housing would also qualify as affordable if no less than 20 percent of the units were occupied by very-low-income families; if the building were occupied only by low-income households; and if the building were to continue to be affordable for the remaining useful life of the property.

Housing that was sold to people under home-ownership programs would be considered affordable if the initial purchase price did not exceed 95 percent of the median purchase price for the area; if it was the principal residence of an owner whose family qualified as low-income at the time of purchase; and if it was available only to first-time home buyers.

Families that bought affordable housing with government assistance and subsequently sold such housing would have to be provided with a fair return on their investment, including any improvements, and the housing would have to remain affordable to low-income home buyers.

• **Participation by state and local governments**. Required the secretary to designate a state or local government to be a participating jurisdiction when it complied with procedures set out by the secretary.

No later than 20 days after funds become available to carry out the HOME Investment Partnerships program, required the secretary to allocate funds to each jurisdiction.

Required the secretary to deem a consortium of geographically contiguous units of local government as one local government if the consortium had the ability and authority to carry out the program.

A jurisdiction would become eligible to participate if its formula allocation was $750,000 or more.

No later than 90 days after notifying the secretary that it wished to participate, the jurisdiction would have to submit a comprehensive housing affordability strategy to HUD.

• **Allocation of resources.** Required the secretary to allocate 60 percent of federal funds to local governments and 40 percent to states. Required the secretary to reserve 1 percent of the total amount appropriated by Congress for Indian tribes.

Of the total amount appropriated, required the secretary to spend 10 percent in fiscal 1991 and 15 percent in fiscal 1992 only for building affordable rental housing. If any funds were not committed for construction within 12 months, the money would remain available for construction only for another 12 months. After two years, the money could be used for other housing programs.

Required the secretary to establish regulations for an allocation formula reflecting each jurisdiction's share of the total need among eligible jurisdictions for an increased supply of affordable housing for very-low- and low-income families.

Required the secretary to apply the formula giving 20 percent weight to measuring states' needs and 80 percent weight to measuring the local governments' needs.

Required the secretary to avoid allocating an excessively large share of money to any one state or unit of local government and to take into account the need for a geographic distribution of federal funds.

Required the secretary to develop a formula for allocating funds in consultation with the House and Senate housing subcommittees and organizations representing state and local governments.

Required that the minimum state allocation be $3 million under the HOME Investment Partnerships program. If no unit of local government within a state received any funds under the program, the state's allocation would be increased by $500,000.

Required that only local governments that qualified for at least $500,000 under the formula would receive their allocation.

• **Home investment trust funds**. Required the secretary to establish a trust fund for each jurisdiction participating in the HOME Investment Partnerships program. The trust fund would be used only to invest in affordable housing. Each trust fund would have a line of credit set by the secretary. Jurisdictions that drew money from the trust funds would have to invest that money in affordable housing within 15 days. If the money was not used within two years of deposit in the trust fund, the secretary would have to reduce the line of credit and reallocate the money.

• **Repayment of investment**. Required each jurisidiction to repay the federal funds invested in affordable housing when the housing no longer qualified as affordable. Any money that was paid back would be placed in the jurisdiction's trust fund.

• **Matching requirements**. Required each jurisdiction to contribute money to its affordable housing plans during each fiscal year. For rental assistance and housing rehabilitation, the jurisdiction would have to contribute 25 percent of the total amount of money drawn from its trust fund. For substantial rehabilitation, the state or local government would have to provide 33 percent of the total amount drawn from the trust fund. And for construction, the jurisdiction would have to provide 50 percent of the total amount coming from its trust fund.

State and local contributions could include cash contributions from non-federal sources; payment of administrative expenses from non-federal sources; the waiver of the value of taxes, fees or other charges that were normally imposed; the value of the land; and the value of investment in on-site and off-site infrastructure, such as roads or sewers, required for the affordable housing.

Authorized the secretary to reduce the matching requirement if a jurisdiction demonstrated that it was necessary to carry out the program. The matching requirements could be reduced for no more than three years. The reduction could not exceed 75 percent the first year, 50 percent the second year and 25 percent the third year.

• **Private-public partnership**. Required each jurisdiction to make all reasonable efforts to involve the private sector, including nonprofit and for-profit groups, in carrying out the housing strategy.

• **Distribution of assistance**. Required each jurisdiction to distribute its housing funds throughout the state or throughout the locality. Required states to distribute money by taking into account the non-metropolitan share of the state's total population and objective measures of rural housing needs.

• **Penalties for misuse of funds**. Required the secretary to reduce a jurisdiction's trust fund credit line if the jurisdiction had failed to comply with any provision under the HOME Investment Partnerships program. The secretary could prevent withdrawals from the trust fund, restrict the jurisdiction's activities to one or more model programs or remove the jurisdiction from participation in the HOME program.

• **Limitation of jurisdictions under court order**. Required the secretary to ensure that no federal funds under the HOME program went to carry out housing remedies or to pay fines, penalties or costs ordered by a federal, state or local court. Funds could be used to carry out court settlements in some cases.

• **Tenant and participant protections**. Required that a lease between a tenant and a landlord last for at least one year, unless the tenant and owner agreed otherwise.

Prohibited owners from ending the tenancy or refusing to renew the lease of a tenant in rental housing assisted under the HOME program except for serious or repeated violation of the terms of the lease or for violation of federal, state or local laws. Any termination of a lease would have to be preceded by 30 days' notice.

Required owners of rental housing assisted under the HOME program to maintain the property according to all housing standards and local code requirements.

Required the owners of rental housing to adopt written tenant selection policies that were consistent with providing housing for very-low- and low-income families.

• **Monitoring**. Required each jurisdiction annually to review the activities of owners of rental housing assisted under the HOME program, including on-siteinspections to determine housing code compliance.

• **Community Housing Partnership**. Required jurisdictions to reserve no less than 15 percent of their HOME funds for investment in housing to be developed, sponsored or owned by community housing development organizations.

• **Technical assistance**. Money set aside for Community Housing Partnerships could be used to provide technical assistance and loans for sites to community housing development organizations in the early stages of developing an eligible project.

A community housing group that received a loan would have to repay it to the jurisdiction's HOME Investment Trust Fund. The jurisdiction, however, could waive repayment of the loan.

• **Housing education and organizational support**. Authorized the secretary to provide funds for educational activities and organizational support to community housing groups.

Organizational support would include covering expenses for training and technical help, or legal and engineering assistance.

Housing education assistance would include covering expenses for providing programs to educate, counsel or organize homeowners and tenants eligible to receive assistance under the HOME program.

Technical assistance funds could be used to establish privately owned, local community development banks and credit unions to finance affordable housing.

Contracts between HUD and local housing groups could not exceed 20 percent of the amount appropriated for the Community Housing Partnership program and could not provide more than 20 percent of the operating budget of the contracting group for any one year.

• **Other support for state and local housing strategies**. Required the secretary to contract with organizations to develop the capacity of state and local governments, housing finance agencies, nonprofit and for-profit groups to meet the needs for affordable housing.

Funds would be used to help exchange information on housing finance, land use and building construction techniques; to help state and local governments design and carry out their housing affordability strategies; to encourage public-private partnerships; and to improve energy efficiency in affordable housing.

Contracts could last no more than three years and could not provide more than 20 percent of the operating budget of the organization in any one year.

• **Research in housing affordability**. Authorized the secretary to support research and to publish research reports that would help expand the supply of affordable housing.

• **Asset recycling**. Upon request, required the secretary to provide jurisdictions with a list of properties within that jurisdiction owned or controlled by HUD. The purpose was to encourage the jurisdiction to develop or rehabilitate the properties under the HOME program.

• **Specific model programs**. Required the secretary to include the following model programs for jurisdictions to follow under the HOME Investment Partnerships program:

• **Rental housing production model**. This program would allow repayable advances to be made to public and private project sponsors in building, acquiring or substantially rehabilitating projects for affordable rental housing. An advance under this program could not exceed 50 percent of the project's costs.

Required advances to be repaid with interest calculated at no more than 3 percent per year. Interest would begin to accrue one year after completion of the project and would be paid in annual installments.

Interest would be paid only from the surplus cash flow of the project, after a minimum return on the equity, which the jurisdiction would determine.

Required that the principal amount of an advance and any unpaid interest would have to be repaid when the housing no longer qualified as affordable. [Rep. Charles E. Schumer, D-N.Y., pushed for this program throughout the housing bill's development and threatened to kill the administration's pet program for home ownership if his program was not included.]

• **Rental rehabilitation model**. Required the secretary to design a model program to support the rehabilitation of privately owned rental housing in neighborhoods in which the median income did not exceed 80 percent of the area median income. Required that the rehabilitation subsidy not exceed 50 percent of the total cost of the project.

• **Rehabilitation loans model**. Required the secretary to design a model program to provide direct loans to finance the rehabilitation of low- and moderate-income single-family and multifamily residential buildings. The secretary could establish the interest rate for loans, which would include special rates to borrowers with incomes below 80 percent of the area median income.

The property would have to be in an area that contained a substantial number of buildings needing rehabilitation. The property would have to be residential and occupied by the owner. And the property would have to be in need of rehabilitation.

• **Sweat equity model**. Required the secretary to design a model program to provide grants to public and private nonprofit groups to provide technical and supervisory help to low- and very-low-income families, including the homeless. The help should include how to acquire, rehabilitate and build housing.

• **Home repair grants model**. Required the secretary to design a model program to provide home repair services for older and disabled homeowners. Those services should include home examination, repairs and follow-up help.

• **Conservation and efficiency grants model**. Required the secretary to develop a model program to provide safe, energy-efficient affordable housing for low-income people. The program would have to help identify housing that was owned and occupied by low-income families who had received money under the weatherization assistance program; was in danger of becoming uninhabitable within five years due to structural problems; and would benefit from repairs such as roofing, electrical, plumbing, furnace and foundation work.

• **Second mortgage assistance for first-time buyers**. Required the secretary to design a model program in which local governments provided loans, secured by second mortgages, with deferred payments of interest and principal to first-time home buyers.

Required that first-time home buyers receive home ownership counseling.

The property secured by the second mortgage would have to be a single-family home and the buyer's principal residence. The principal obligation of the deferred payment loan secured by the second mortgage could not exceed 30 percent of the home's cost.

The payment of the principal and interest on the loan could be deferred for no less than five years beginning on the purchase date.

The interest rate on the unpaid balance of the loan would have to be at least 4 percent.

A deferred-payment loan secured by a second mortgage would have to be repayable over the 15-year period beginning at the end of the deferral period.

• **Rehabilitation of state and local government properties model**. Required the secretary to design a model program in which state and local governments could convert vacant properties to provide affordable permanent housing for the homeless by leasing those properties to nonprofit groups and allowing those groups to rehabilitate the properties.

• **Mortgage credit enhancement**. Required the comptroller general to study the ways in which financing for affordable housing may be made available to help expand the housing supply. Required the comptroller general to submit the report to Congress and the secretary no later than one year after enactment.

• **Equal opportunity**. Required each jurisdiction in the HOME program to ensure that minorities, women and companies owned by minorities and women were included in the effort to provide affordable housing.

Required the secretary to submit a report to Congress on each jurisdiction's effort to work with minorities and women within 180 days after the first allocation of federal funds.

• **Annual audits**. Required the secretary to contract annually with an independent accounting firm to provide a full financial audit of the records of the HOME Investment Partnerships program.

• **Labor**. Required that any contract for the construction of affordable housing with 12 or more units contain a provision to pay no less than the wages prevailing in the locality, according to the Labor secretary. Exempted volunteer workers who received no compensation or only received money for expenses.

• **Termination of existing housing programs**. Prohibited new grants or loans after Oct. 1, 1991, under the following programs:

• Housing Development Action Grants (HoDAG), which provided aid to developers to help reduce the cost of building low-income housing.

• Rehabilitation Loans, which provided low-interest loans to bring housing and commercial property to local housing code standards.

• Rental Rehabilitation, which provided grants to local governments for the rehabilitation of rental property.

• Nehemiah Grants, which provided financing for the construction of single-family homes for moderate-income families.

• Moderate Rehabilitation, which provided Section 8 housing aid to finance the modernization of substandard housing.

• Urban Homesteading, which allowed the federal government to transfer ownership of housing to local communities for resale to low-income people whose current housing is substandard.

National Homeownership Trust

• **Establishment**. Authorized the establishment of a new program called the National Homeownership Trust, within HUD, providing financial aid to first-time home buyers. [This program was the brainchild of Henry B. Gonzalez, chairman of the House Banking Committee.]

A board of directors would govern the trust, including the HUD secretary and the secretary of the Treasury.

• **Assistance for first-time home buyers.** Required the trust to provide interest-rate subsidies and down payment assistance to first-time home buyers. The interest-rate subsidies would ensure that the rate paid by home buyers did not exceed 6 percent.

Assistance payments could only be made to first-time buyers. The buyers must not have owned a residence during the three years before purchasing the property with help from the trust.

The buyer could be a displaced homemaker or a single parent who might have owned a home with his or her spouse but had not owned a home in the three years before buying one with help from the trust.

• **Maximum income of home buyer.** During the 12 months before buying a home, the annual income of the buyer and members of the buyer's family could not exceed 95 percent of the median income for a family of four; or the annual income could not exceed 115 percent of the median income in an area that was subject to a high-cost-area mortgage limit, according to HUD.

• **Certification**. Required the buyer to certify that he or she had made a good-faith effort to obtain a market rate mortgage but was denied due to insufficient income.

• **Principal residence**. Required that the property securing the mortgage must be a single-family home and must be the principal residence of the buyer.

• **Maximum mortgage amount.** Required that the principal obligation of the mortgage not exceed $124,875.

• **Maximum interest rate**. Required the interest payable on the mortgage to be set at a fixed rate that did not exceed a maximum interest rate set by the trust.

• **Mortgagee**. Required that the mortgage be held by a federally insured mortgagee or a mortgagee who had been approved by the trust.

• **Minimum down payment**. Required buyers to pay no less than 1 percent of the cost of buying the property in order to receive down-payment assistance from the trust.

• **Repayment upon sale**. Required that homeowners repay the trust when selling their homes. No interest was required when repaying the original assistance. If there were no net proceeds when the sale was completed, the board of the trust was required to release the lien on the homeowner's property.

• **Repayment due to increased income**. Authorized the board of the trust to ask a homeowner to repay all or some of the original aid on a monthly basis if the annual income of the homeowner and the homeowner's family exceeded the maximum annual income allowed during any two-year period after the financial assistance was provided.

• **Repayment if property is no longer primary residence**. Authorized the board of the trust to ask a homeowner to repay all or some of the original aid if the property was no longer the owner's principal residence.

• **Demonstration programs**. Required the HUD secretary to use no more than $20 million of any amount appropriated for the National Housing Trust in order to carry out the following demonstration programs:

• $4.2 million in Milwaukee, to develop and renovate two vacant structures in a blighted minority neighborhood.

• $10 million in Washington, D.C., for nonprofit neighborhood groups to buy and renovate vacant public and private housing for resale or rent to low- and moderate-income families.

• $1 million in Philadelphia, to provide technical assistance and organizational support for a community development corporation.

• The remaining funds could be spent however the secretary decided.

• **Authorization**. Authorized appropriations to carry out the trust of $250 million in fiscal 1991 and $521.5 million for fiscal 1992.

• **Termination**. Required that the trust end Sept. 30, 1993.

FHA and Secondary Mortgage Market

• **Limitation on FHA insurance authority**. Required the HUD secretary to insure mortgages with a total principal amount of $76.8 billion in fiscal 1991 and $79.8 billion in fiscal 1992.

• **Increase in mortgage limit**. Removed the termination date of fiscal 1990 from the $124,875 FHA mortgage limit.

• **Mortgagor equity**. Prevented homeowners from borrowing more than the value of their home when other fees were financed into the mortgage.

Limited the insured principal to 98.75 percent of the appraised value of the property, plus the amount of the mortgage insurance premium paid at the time the mortgage was insured. For properties with an appraised value of more than $50,000, the insured principal obligation was limited to 97.75 percent.

• **Mortgage insurance premiums**. Required the secretary to institute a new premium structure to shore up the financially shaky FHA insurance fund for single-family homes. The plan, which used a risk-based premium based on how much money a buyer put into the down payment, was designed to prevent people who were likely to default on loans from receiving them.

For mortgages on single- to four-family homes executed on or after Oct. 1, 1994, required the secretary, at the time of insurance, to collect a single payment equal to 2.25 percent of the amount of the original insured principal of the mortgage.

Required the secretary to refund a portion of the initial premium charge paid on payment in full of the principal obligation before the maturity date of the mortgage.

Allowed HUD to devise a refund schedule laying out how long it would have to handle the insurance on a loan before the homeowner no longer qualified for the return on the initial premium. The purpose of this was to allow homeowners to recoup some of their initial costs when HUD did not insure the loan for a long period.

Authorized the secretary to collect annual premium payments equal to 0.5 percent of the remaining insured principal balance. For any mortgage involving an original principal obligation that was less than 90 percent of the appraised value of the property, the premium would have to be paid for the first 11 years of the 30-year loan. For mortgages greater than or equal to 90 percent of the value, premiums would have to be paid for the entire 30-year life of the loan.

For mortgages involving an original principal obligation that was greater than 95 percent of the appraised value of the property, the secretary was authorized to collect an annual premium of 0.55 percent of the remaining insured principal balance during the 30-year loan.

• **Transition premiums**. Until Oct. 1, 1994, when the new risk-based insurance program was to be instituted, the act provided for a transition period to change the premium structure. For mortgages executed during fiscal 1991 and 1992, the secretary was authorized to collect at the time of insurance a single premium payment equal to 3.8 percent, the prevailing upfront premium.

In addition, the secretary was authorized to collect annual premium payments equal to 0.5 percent of the remaining insured principal balance. For any mortgage involving an original principal obligation that was less than 90 percent of the appraised value of the property, the annual premium would have to be paid for the first five years of the loan. For any mortgage that was originally from 90 percent to 95 percent of the value of the property, the annual premium would have to be paid for the first eight years of the loan. And for mortgages greater than 95 percent of the value, annual premiums would have to be paid for 10 years.

For mortgages executed during fiscal 1993 and 1994, the secretary was authorized to collect at the time of insurance a single premium payment equal to 3 percent of the amount of the original insured principal obligation.

In addition, the secretary was authorized to collect annual premium payments equal to 0.5 percent of the remaining insured principal balance. For mortgages involving an original principal obligation less than 90 percent of the appraised value of the property, the premium would have to be paid for the first seven years of the loan. For mortgages from 90 percent to 95 percent of the value, premiums would have to be paid for the first 12 years. And for mortgages in which the principal obligation was more than 95 percent of the value, premiums would have to be paid for the full 30 years of the loan.

Required the secretary to refund all of the unearned premium charges paid during fiscal 1991-1994 on payment in full of the principal obligation of the mortgage before maturity.

Required the secretary to issue regulations to carry out this section no later than 90 days after enactment.

• **Mutual Mortgage Insurance Fund distributions**. Required the secretary to consider the actuarial status of the fund in determining whether there was a surplus of funds to distribute to mortgagors.

• **Actuarial soundness of Mutual Mortgage Insurance Fund**. Required the secretary to ensure that the fund attained a capital ratio of no less than 1.25 percent within 24 months after enactment. The capital ratio was the percentage of the amount of cash on hand out of the total amount of outstanding mortgages. [During a 10-year period, the capital ratio had steadily declined, with cash on hand dropping from $3.4 billion in 1979 to $2.6 billion in 1989. Had it been sound, the fund would have grown to $8 billion during that decade, according to a report by the accounting firm of Price Waterhouse.]

Required the secretary to ensure that the fund attained a capital ratio of no less than 2.0 percent within 10 years of the date of enactment and to ensure that the fund maintained that ratio at all times thereafter.

Required the secretary to submit a report to Congress 24 months after enactment describing the actions that would be taken to ensure that the fund attained the required capital ratio.

Required the secretary to conduct an annual independent actuarial study of the fund and to report annually to Congress on its financial status.

Prohibited the secretary from sending mortgagors distributive shares, or excess premiums, if the insurance fund was not meeting operational goals. For example, during the 1970s, FHA-insured loans had a low default rate and HUD returned some premiums when owners paid off their loans. Operational goals included:

• Maintaining the required capital ratio.

• Meeting the needs of home buyers with low down payments and first-time buyers by providing access to mortgage credit.

• Minimizing the risk to the fund and to homeowners from defaults.

• Avoiding policies that caused low-risk borrowers to go instead to commercial lenders, a phenomenon called "adverse selection."

Also authorized the secretary to adjust the insurance premiums if the fund was not meeting its operational goals. Required the secretary to notify Congress of the proposed change and the reasons for the change. Changes in premiums would take effect no earlier than 90 days after Congress was notified unless Congress acted during that time to increase, prevent or modify the change.

• **Home equity conversion mortgage insurance demonstration**. Extended the termination date to Sept. 30, 1995, from Sept. 30, 1991. Limited the number of mortgages insured under the program to no more than 25,000.

• **Auction of federally insured mortgages**. Required HUD to arrange for the sale of interests in mortgage loans through an auction rather than accepting the multifamily mortgages from the original holders and giving a 10-year market-rate bond. [To entice people to invest in multifamily housing during the late 1960s and early '70s, HUD offered to take over mortgages after 20 years in exchange for an interest-bearing bond. HUD now wanted to buy out these mortgage agreements in order to save money.]

Required HUD to arrange the auction at a price, to be paid to the mortgagee, of the base amount plus accrued interest to the date of sale. Provided that the sale price also included the right to a subsidy payment to the mortgagee that would make up for any improvements on the property.

Required HUD to conduct a public auction to determine the lowest interest rate necessary to accomplish a sale of the mortgage and any benefits accrued to it on the property and insurance.

Required a mortgagee who decided to assign a mortgage to HUD to provide the department and bidders at auction a description of the property and mortgage, including the principal mortgage balance, original stated interest rate, service fees, real estate and tenant characteristics, level and duration of federal subsidies and any other information HUD said was appropriate.

Required HUD to provide information regarding the status of the property relating to the Emergency Low-Income Housing Preservation Act of 1989 that had to do with prepayment provisions. (This was to ensure that affordable housing for low-income people was not lost to the market as owners paid off their federally subsidized mortgages.)

Required HUD, after receiving the description of the property, to advertise for auction and publish mortgage descriptions in advance of the auction. Authorized HUD to wait up to six months to conduct the auction but prohibited HUD from holding the auction sooner than two months after receiving the mortgagee's written notice of intent to assign its mortgage to HUD.

Required HUD to accept the interest rate bid for purchase that HUD determined to be acceptable and required HUD to publish the accepted bid in the Federal Register.

Required settlement to occur no later than 30 business days after the winning bidders were selected in the auction, unless HUD determined that extraordinary circumstances required an extension.

Authorized mortgagees to retain all rights to assign the mortgage loan to HUD if no acceptable bids were received or settlement did not occur within the required time period.

Required HUD, as part of the auction, to agree to provide a monthly interest subsidy payment from the General Insurance Fund to the purchaser of the original property and mortgage securing that property. This was part of the buyout of the mortgagee's right to an interest-bearing bond.

Required HUD to encourage state housing finance agencies, nonprofit organizations, tenant organizations and mortgagees participating under an Emergency Low-Income Housing Preservation plan of action to participate in the auction.

Required HUD to put the requirements under this section into effect within 30 days from enactment and not subject them to the requirement of prior issuance of regulations in the Federal Register. Required HUD to issue implementing regulations within six months of enactment.

Prohibited any of these provisions from diminishing or impairing the low-income use restrictions applicable to the project under the original regulatory agreement or the revised agreement entered into under the Emergency Low-Income Housing Preservation Act or other agreements to provide federal assistance to the housing or its tenants.

Provided that these provisions did not apply after Sept. 30, 1995, and required HUD, beginning in 1992, to report to Congress on these provisions no later than Jan. 31 of each year.

- **Limitation on secondary residences**. Prohibited the secretary from insuring mortgages on second homes, except when a second home was necessary to avoid hardship. For example, seasonal employment in different areas might require a second home.
- **Mortgage counseling**. Authorized FHA funds to be used for mortgage counseling to people who were delinquent in paying off their FHA-insured mortgages.
- **Delegation of processing**. Required the secretary, within 60 days of enactment, to begin delegating the job of processing FHA loans for low- and moderate-income multifamily housing to private lenders to replace HUD's coinsurance program. Under the coinsurance program, which the secretary killed, HUD delegated underwriting authority to approved private lenders in exchange for the lender sharing with HUD a portion of the risk of loss.
- **Disclosure regarding interest due**. Required FHA mortgagors such as banks to notify homeowners annually of possible interest that would be due if the owner paid off the mortgage early.
- **Neighborhood accountability**. Prohibited banks that provided FHA mortgages from varying mortgage interest rates, the level of discount points, loan origination fees or any other amount charged based on the neighborhood and the loan amount.
- **Property disposition**. Authorized groups that assisted the homeless to obtain HUD-held property for use under a $1 lease program without a 30-day waiting period.
- **Foreclosed properties**. Required the secretary to report to Congress on the strategies and plans for disposing of HUD-foreclosed properties. The report was due 60 days after enactment.
- **GNMA guarantees of mortgage-backed securities**. Authorized the Government National Mortgage Association (Ginnie Mae) to guarantee securities issued by private lenders of $85 billion in fiscal 1991 and $88.3 billion in fiscal 1992. GNMA sells securities backed by mortgages insured by the FHA and the Department of Veterans Affairs.
- **Property improvement insurance**. Increased the maximum loan available from $17,500 to $25,000 for single-family homes and from $43,750 to $60,000 for multifamily buildings.

Homeownership and Opportunity for People Everywhere (HOPE)

- **Home ownership of public and Indian housing.** Authorized $68 million in fiscal 1991 and $380 million in fiscal 1992 to be appropriated. [The HOPE programs were brought to the table by Bush administration officials who would have preferred that they be the only new programs authorized by Congress. House Democrats, in particular, used HOPE to gain concessions in other areas, such as construction, from the administration.]
- **Planning grants**. Authorized the HUD secretary to award planning grants of up to $200,000 to applicants to develop home-ownership programs for public and Indian housing. Applicants could include public housing authorities, cooperative associations, and public or private nonprofit groups.

Grants could be used to develop resident management corporations and resident councils; to provide training and technical assistance; to study the feasibility of home-ownership programs; to develop preliminary architectural and engineering work; and to provide tenant and buyer counseling, among other things.

- **Implementation grants**. Authorized the secretary to award grants to carry out the public and Indian housing ownership program.

Grants could be used for architectural and engineering work; acquisition of a public housing project; rehabilitation of public housing projects; administrative costs; and temporary relocation of tenants, among other things.

Required grant recipients to match 25 percent of the federal funds with money from non-federal sources.

Required the secretary to develop criteria for awarding the grants through a national competition.

- **Affordability**. Required that home-ownership programs provide sale prices that did not force eligible families to spend more than 30 percent of their income to complete the sale.
- **Home-ownership plans**. Required that home-ownership programs include a plan to identify and pick eligible families to participate.

Required a plan to provide relocation help to families who decided to move.

Required a plan to ensure continued affordability by tenants, home buyers and homeowners in the housing project.

- **Replacement plan**. Prohibited public housing from being transferred to the home-ownership program unless the secretary had entered into a binding agreement with the local public housing agency to replace each unit of public housing with additional affordable housing.

Replacement housing could include the development of new public housing units; the rehabilitation of vacant public housing units; and the use of five-year, tenant-based rental assistance.

- **Protection of non-purchasing families**. Prohibited tenants who chose not to participate in home-ownership programs from being evicted.
- **Resale restrictions**. Authorized home-ownership programs to establish restrictions on resale of units. Required that resident management corporations, resident councils or cooperatives have the right to purchase the unit or shares representing the unit from the homeowner for the same amount offered by a prospective buyer. If the resident management corporation, resident council or cooperative did not want to purchase the unit and the prospective buyer was not a low-income family, then the public housing agency would have the right to purchase the unit for the same amount offered by the prospective buyer.

If a homeowner wished to sell the unit within six years of the original purchase, the program would have to provide restrictions to assure that the owner did not receive an undue profit. Required the program to consider the original amount paid by the family; the value of the home and any improvements made by the family; and the appreciated value of the home due to inflation and other factors.

If a homeowner wished to sell the unit in the period between six and 20 years after the purchase, the home-ownership program would have to recapture a portion of the difference between the original market value and the original purchase price. Of the profits not kept by the seller, 50 percent would have to go to the secretary and 50 percent to the organization that processed the sale.

- **Annual report**. Required the secretary to submit a report to Congress each year describing the number of public housing units sold under this program; the characteristics of families participating in the program, such as income, race and gender; the amount and type of financial assistance provided under this program; and recommendations of the secretary.

• **Home ownership of multifamily units.** Authorized the secretary to make planning grants and grants to carry out home-ownership programs for multifamily housing, such as buildings owned or insured by HUD, the Department of Agriculture, the Resolution Trust Corporation (RTC) or a state or local government. Authorized $51 million in fiscal 1991 and $280 million in fiscal 1992 to be appropriated.

• **Home ownership of single-family homes.** Authorized the secretary to make planning grants and grants to carry out home-ownership programs for single-family homes, such as those owned or held by HUD, Veterans Affairs, Agriculture, RTC, state or local governments and public housing authorities. Authorized $36 million in fiscal 1991 and $195 million in fiscal 1992 to be appropriated.

Public and Indian Housing

• **Public housing preferences.** Reduced from 90 percent to 70 percent the amount of public housing that was set aside specifically for "preference" families. Preference families were those who lived in substandard housing, including families who were homeless, families who paid more than 50 percent of their monthly income for rent or families who were involuntarily displaced from their homes.

Allowed the remaining units to be available according to a preference system established by the local public housing agency, according to local needs and priorities.

Prohibited individuals or families who had been evicted from federally assisted housing for drug-related criminal activities from being considered a "preference" family for three years. If the evicted tenant successfully completed a rehabilitation program approved by the public housing agency, the three-year period could be dropped.

Suggested that public housing projects include families with a broad range of incomes and avoid concentrations of low-income and deprived families with serious social problems.

• **Public housing management reforms.** Required the HUD secretary to develop and publish indicators to assess the management performance of public housing agencies. Indicators should include the number and percentage of vacancies and the percentage of rents uncollected.

Required the secretary to designate troubled public housing agencies by their failure to perform according to the indicators. Authorized the secretary to identify and commend public housing agencies that met and exceeded the performance standards. Required the secretary to establish procedures for public housing agencies to appeal their designation as a troubled agency.

Required the secretary to enter into an agreement with each troubled public housing agency setting targets for improving performance, strategies for meeting those targets and incentives for putting those strategies into place.

Authorized the secretary, if a public housing agency was not able to meet the conditions of the agreement, to solicit competitive proposals from other public housing agencies to manage the troubled agency, petition for the appointment of a receiver for the agency and require the agency to follow other requirements set out by the secretary.

Required the secretary to submit an annual report to Congress that identified the troubled public housing agencies and described the efforts that had been taken to improve the agencies.

• **Accounting systems.** Required public housing agencies to establish an accounting system for rental collections and costs for each housing project.

• **Buffalo housing authority.** Required the secretary to submit to Congress a report on the operation and efficiency of the Buffalo Municipal Housing Authority within 180 days of enactment. Authorized the secretary to determine whether to petition for a receiver for the housing authority or to reduce the operating subsidies for the authority.

• **Eviction procedures.** Authorized the public housing agency to establish an expedited grievance procedure concerning an eviction that involved any criminal activity threatening the health, safety or right to peaceful enjoyment of the premises by other tenants.

• **Public housing and foster care children.** Authorized agencies administering public housing and Section 8 rental assistance to coordinate with local child-welfare agencies in providing units to families whose children had been placed or could be placed in foster care due to poor housing conditions, families whose child was prevented from rejoining them from foster care due to inadequate housing, and youngsters who had been released from foster care and could not rejoin their families or extended families and for whom adoption was not possible.

• **Public housing operating subsidies.** Authorized $2 billion in fiscal 1991 and $2.1 billion in fiscal 1992 to be appropriated.

• **Utility subsidy.** Required the secretary, in determining how much money to give public housing agencies for utility subsidies, to consider extremely hot and extremely cold weather conditions. Under existing law, the secretary only considered extremely cold weather.

• **Modernization.** Required the secretary, in fiscal 1992, to reserve no more than $75 million for modernization needs resulting from natural and other disasters. The money provided for emergencies would be repaid by agencies from future funds.

Required the secretary to distribute the remaining funds by comparing needs of public housing agencies and by examining the backlog of needs by public housing agencies.

Required the secretary to limit the total amount of money for troubled public housing agencies in fiscal 1992 and in years after that, but allowed for a credit system so that agencies that overcame their "troubled" designation could regain the money denied to them previously.

• **Vacancy reduction.** Required any public housing agency that had a vacancy rate that twice exceeded the average rate among all agencies or that was designated as a troubled agency to participate in a vacancy-reduction program.

Required agencies to develop and submit a vacancy-reduction plan to the secretary. The plan would have to identify the vacant units and explain why they were vacant, describe what the agency would do over the next five years to eliminate the vacancies and identify barriers to eliminating the vacancies.

Required the secretary to provide an assessment team of experts to examine the public housing agencies' vacancy problems and to submit recommendations to HUD.

Authorized $105 million in fiscal 1991 and $220 million in fiscal 1992 to be appropriated from modernization funds for large public housing agencies.

• **Income eligibility.** Authorized public housing agencies to raise from 5 percent to 15 percent the number of units that could be leased to low-income families, not including very-low-income families. The number of low-income families in any project was limited to 25 percent, except for projects that exceeded this limit before enactment.

• **Replacement housing.** Required the secretary to demonstrate the effectiveness of replacing public housing units eligible for demolition with five-year rental certificates. This demonstration requirement applied only to the public housing authority in St. Louis.

• **Resident management.** Authorized up to $5 million out of modernization funds in fiscal 1991 and 1992 to be used for public housing resident management programs.

• **Family investment centers.** Provided families living in public housing with better access to educational and employment opportunities to help them become independent. Developed facilities in or near public housing for training and support services such as child care, job training, literacy training and computer training. Mobilized public and private resources to expand and improve the delivery of services.

Authorized the secretary to make grants to public housing agencies to provide family investment centers in or near public housing. Authorized $25 million in fiscal 1991 and $26.1 million in fiscal 1992 to be appropriated.

• **Early childhood development grants.** Authorized $15 million in fiscal 1991 and $15.7 million in fiscal 1992 to be appropriated. Changed the name of "child care services" program to "early childhood development services."

Authorized a set-aside from Indian housing development funds for an Indian public housing early childhood development demonstration program. Authorized $5 million in fiscal 1991 and $5.2

million in fiscal 1992.

• **Rent waiver for police.** Authorized the secretary to permit public housing agencies to allow police officers and other security officers to live in public housing units even if they were not otherwise eligible for public housing. Housing agencies could set special rents for the officers.

• **Youth sports program.** Authorized the secretary to make grants to carry out youth sports programs in public housing projects with substantial drug problems. Required matching grants of 50 percent or more from non-federal sources.

Limited grants to $125,000 per project. Authorized 5 percent of public and assisted housing drug-elimination grant funds to be used for the youth sports grants.

• **One-stop perinatal services demonstration.** Required the secretary, in consultation with the secretary of Health and Human Services, to provide grants to public housing agencies so that they could provide space for a one-stop services program for pregnant women living in public housing. Required the secretary to make no more than 10 grants to 10 public housing agencies. Grants could not exceed $15,000 for any one housing project. The program could provide information and education, health-care services, referrals, follow-up care for women and infants, and assistance from social workers. Authorized $150,000 to be appropriated from the fiscal 1991 family investment center funds.

• **Mixed-income communities.** Required the secretary to conduct a program demonstrating the effectiveness of promoting the revitalization of troubled urban communities through public housing in socioeconomically mixed settings combined with public housing operating subsidies to stimulate new affordable housing in those communities. Provided supportive services in conjunction with housing. Authorized the programs to be conducted with the Chicago Housing Authority and three other public housing agencies chosen by the secretary.

• **Energy efficiency demonstration.** Required the secretary to conduct a demonstration program to encourage public housing agencies to use private energy service companies to reduce energy costs.

Low-Income Rental Assistance

• **Drug-related rent adjustments.** Authorized HUD to approve rent increases of no more than 20 percent in communities in which drug-related criminal activity was prevalent and had caused the housing project's operating expenses to rise.

• **Tenant rent contributions.** Authorized families receiving tenant-based rental assistance to pay more than 30 percent of their monthly income toward rent if the family notified its public housing agency and the agency determined that the rent was reasonable and that the family could handle it. Required that public housing agencies not approve more than 10 percent of the number of new families in a year receiving rental assistance to pay the higher rent. Required any public housing agency that approved more than 5 percent of those new families to pay the higher rent to submit a report to the secretary.

• **Preference rules.** Required that 70 percent of project-based rental assistance for families go to people living in substandard housing, paying more than 50 percent of their monthly income toward rent or who were involuntarily displaced from their homes.

Required that 90 percent of the rental assistance to families that was not tied to a specific housing project go to people living in substandard housing, paying more than 50 percent of their monthly income toward rent or who were involuntarily displaced from their homes. Required that the remaining spots for housing assistance during any one-year period go to families who qualified under a system of local preferences, determined by local need.

Prohibited any person or family evicted from assisted housing due to drug-related criminal activity from receiving a preference for rental assistance for three years unless they had successfully completed a drug-rehabilitation program. The public housing agency could waive the prohibition for innocent family members.

• **Tenant protections.** Authorized project-based rental assistance to be terminated due to any criminal activity that threatened the health, safety or right of peaceful enjoyment of the premises by other tenants or any drug-related criminal activity on or near the premises by any tenant or guest of any tenant.

• **Project-based assistance.** Required owners of buildings with contracts for rental assistance to adopt written tenant selection procedures that met with the secretary's approval.

• **Manufactured home rentals.** Authorized rental vouchers to be used for people who rented mobile homes.

• **Portability rights.** Authorized holders of rental vouchers or certificates to use them within the same state as the public housing agency that issued them or within the same metropolitan area.

• **Short-term contracts.** Required the HUD secretary to permit public housing agencies to enter into contracts for rental assistance payments of less than 12 months to avoid disrupting families receiving assistance under a contract within one year of expiring.

• **Assistance to avoid foster care.** Authorized an increase in Section 8 rental assistance by $35 million in fiscal 1991 and fiscal 1992 to aid families who were eligible for rental assistance and were on the verge of losing their children to foster care due to inadequate housing. Families could also receive the rental assistance if their children were delayed from leaving foster care because the families were living in inadequate housing. A public child-welfare agency would have to certify each family's situation.

The secretary was required to allocate these funds through a national competition based on need.

• **Family self-sufficiency.** Authorized a new program to coordinate the use of public housing and rental assistance with other public and private resources to promote economic independence.

Required the program to be carried out by each public housing agency beginning in fiscal 1993 except when supportive services were not available at the local level.

Required the secretary to consult with heads of other federal agencies to provide for funding agreements and cooperation in carrying out the services to public housing tenants and rental assistance recipients.

Required each public housing agency to enter into a contract with tenants who agreed to participate in the program. Required the contract to list the responsibilities of the family, to specify the services available and to say that the agency could terminate rental assistance and services if the family failed to meet the requirements of the program.

Supportive services in the program could include child care, transportation to receive services, remedial education, education to complete high school, job training, drug and alcohol abuse treatment and counseling, parenting training, money-management training and any other services to help families achieve self-sufficiency.

Required participating families to fulfill their obligations under the contract within five years unless the public housing agency granted an extension.

Required the head of any participating family to seek employment during the program.

Prohibited rent increases for any family participating in the program if the family's income increased, unless the income exceeded 50 percent of the area median income. Families with incomes between 50 percent and 80 percent of median income would have rents raised as incomes increased so that families paid 30 percent of their income toward rent.

Authorized $25 million out of the public housing operating subsidies to be used for administrative costs incurred by the family self-sufficiency program.

• **Income eligibility.** Required that any new housing or housing that had been substantially rehabilitated be reserved for low- and very-low-income families.

• **Settlement agreement.** Required the secretary to provide 186 rental certificates to Norfolk, Va., to satisfy an Oct. 6, 1981, court settlement.

• **GAO study.** Required the General Accounting Office to study the feasibility of establishing fair market rents for areas smaller than the existing market areas.

• **Vouchers for Indian tribes.** Required the secretary to study the feasibility of entering into contracts with Indian housing authorities to provide rental vouchers.

• **Low-income housing.** Authorized an additional $16.2 billion in fiscal 1991 and $14.7 billion in fiscal 1992 to be spent for assisted housing programs.

In fiscal 1991 that included:

- $742.1 million for public housing grants, of which no more than $228 million could be spent for Indian housing;
- $1.88 billion for Section 8 rental vouchers and certificates;
- $1.2 billion for Section 8 rental assistance for tenants in Section 202 housing for the elderly and disabled;
- $2.15 billion for public housing modernization, of which no more than $3 million may be used for resident home-ownership financial assistance;
- $420 million for Section 8 property disposition;
- 160 million for Section 8 loan management;
- $7.7 billion to extend expiring Section 8 rental assistance contracts;
- $1.6 billion to shore up existing Section 8 rental assistance contracts that had run out of money;
- $207 million for public housing lease adjustments; and
- $79 million for public housing replacement activities.

• **Family.** Amended the definition of family to include single people but did not entitle them to housing with two bedrooms or more.

• **Income.** Amended the definition of income so that it excluded amounts not actually received by the family, such as alimony and child support payments that are owed but not paid.

This change would go into effect if included in future appropriations measures.

• **Adjusted income.** Amended the definition of adjusted income by increasing the allowance for each dependent from $450 to $550 and allowing medical expense deductions for non-elderly people. This change would go into effect if included in future appropriations measures.

• **Determination of income limits.** Required HUD to determine separate median incomes and income ceilings for Westchester County, a wealthy suburb of New York, as if it were not within the metropolitan statistical area in which it was located and calculated.

• **Foster care.** Required that the absence of a child due to foster care not be considered in counting the size of a family.

• **Housing counseling.** Authorized $3.6 million in fiscal 1991 and $3.7 million in fiscal 1992 for housing counseling services. Authorized $6.7 million in fiscal 1991 and $7 million in fiscal 1992 for emergency home ownership counseling, including $2 million each year to set up a toll-free telephone number for information on counseling agencies. Authorized $350,000 in fiscal 1991 and $365,000 in fiscal 1992 to be spent on a foreclosure-prevention demonstration counseling program to reduce defaults and foreclosures on FHA-insured single-family loans.

• **Flexible subsidy fund.** Authorized $50 million in fiscal 1991 and $52.2 million in fiscal 1992 to be spent on the flexible subsidy fund, which was used to make capital improvements to multifamily housing to prevent prepayments of federally subsidized mortgages.

• **Public housing drug-elimination grants.** Authorized the secretary to make grants to public housing authorities to help eliminate drug-related crime. Grants could be used to hire security officers, reimburse local law enforcement agencies, make physical improvements to the property to enhance security and to hire people to investigate drug-related crime, among other things.

Authorized $160 million in fiscal 1991 and $166.9 million in fiscal 1992 to be spent on drug-elimination grants.

Preservation of Affordable Rental Housing

• **Prepayment of mortgages.** Under the terms of federally subsidized mortgages signed with private building owners in the late 1960s and early '70s, owners were to be allowed to pay off their loans after 20 years and do whatever they wished with their property. About 350,000 low-income households would have been at risk of eviction due to the resulting increased rents when a congressionally imposed moratorium on prepayments was set to expire in the fall of 1990.

The following new provisions, called the Low-Income Housing Preservation and Resident Home Ownership Act of 1990, provided owners with incentives to continue renting to low-income tenants for the remaining useful life of the property or with fair-market value to owners who wished to sell their property to others who would continue to rent to low-income families. If no one were willing or able to purchase the property, the owner would be allowed to prepay the mortgage.

• **Notice of intent.** Required owners of eligible low-income housing to file a notice with HUD indicating whether they intended to follow one of three options. Owners could seek to prepay their mortgage and no longer rent to low-income tenants, they could seek incentives to help them continue renting to low-income tenants, or they could seek to sell the housing to a qualified purchaser.

Required owners to file the notice up to 24 months before they were eligible to pay off their mortgages. Owners would have to also file the notice with the state and local governments in which the housing was located, and they would have to notify the tenants living on the property.

• **Termination of low-income restrictions.** Required the HUD secretary, within six months of receiving a notice seeking to prepay, to provide the owner with information for the owner to prepare a plan of action.

In order for the secretary to approve a plan seeking to prepay, the secretary would have to find that the plan would neither create hardship for current tenants nor displace them if comparable and affordable housing was not available, nor materially affect the general supply of low-income housing in the market area, lessen the ability of low-income people to find housing near job opportunities nor reduce housing opportunities for minorities.

If the secretary rejected the plan, the owner could seek incentives from HUD to continue renting to low-income families, or the owner could sell the housing to a buyer who would continue renting to low-income families.

• **Receipt of notice.** Required HUD, within nine months of receiving a notice from an owner who wished to continue renting to low-income people or who wanted to sell the housing to an owner who would rent to low-income people, to do three things:

1) establish the value of the property through an appraisal;

2) estimate the cost of preserving the housing for low-income use; and

3) determine whether these costs could be paid for by the rents allowed through the federal cost limits.

• **Valuation.** Required two appraisals for each property. The first would equal the appraised fair market value of the housing as multifamily rental housing. The second would equal the appraised "highest and best use" value of the property. If the two appraisals conflicted, then a third appraisal would be used to resolve the difference.

• **Assessing rents.** Required HUD to assess the costs of preserving the property for low-income use against the total rent. If an owner decided to continue renting to low-income families, the total rent would be required to cover an 8 percent return to the owner, debt service on any rehabilitation loan, debt service on the federally assisted mortgage, project operating expenses and adequate reserves. The 8 percent return would come from the preservation value of the property minus the debt on the property and the rent in the preserved property.

If the owner sold, the total rent would have to cover the debt service on the loan to buy the housing, debt service on any rehabilitation loan, debt service on the federally assisted mortgage, project operating expenses and adequate reserves.

• **Federal cost limits.** Required HUD to compare the total rent required to preserve the property for low-income use against 120 percent of the area's fair market rent under the Section 8 program. If the rent required to preserve the property was equal to or less than the fair market rent, the cost of preserving the project would be considered within federal cost limits.

If the preservation cost did not meet that test, HUD would have to compare the total rent required to preserve the property against 120 percent of the local market rent for the area in which the building was located. If it was equal to or less than 120 percent of the local market rent, the preservation cost would be considered within federal cost limits.

• **Preservation rents within cost limits.** Required owners of housing that met the federal cost limits to choose incentives to continue renting to low-income families or to sell the housing to a purchaser who would do so.

Owners who decided to continue renting to low-income families would have to file a plan of action within six months of receiving information from HUD about the federal cost limits.

Required HUD to then offer incentives to owners that enabled owners to receive an 8 percent return on their preservation costs, pay debt service on the existing HUD mortgage, pay debt service on any loan for rehabilitation approved by HUD, meet project operating expenses and establish adequate reserves.

Owners who decided to sell the property would be required to file a second notice of intent with HUD.

Owners would have to give "priority purchasers" 12 months from the date of the second notice to make an offer for the property and negotiate a purchase price with the owner. Priority purchasers included resident councils, nonprofit organizations, and state and local housing agencies.

If no acceptable offer was made within the 12-month period, owners would have to give "qualified purchasers" another three months to make an offer for the property and negotiate a purchase agreement. Qualified purchasers included priority purchasers and any other group, such as for-profit organizations, that agreed to continue renting to low-income families for the remaining useful life of the property.

Once an agreement was reached with a purchaser, the parties would have to file a plan of action requesting incentives from HUD. Once HUD approved these plans, the agency would have to provide subsidies to the purchaser to acquire the property at a price no greater than the preservation value, pay the debt service on any loan approved by HUD to rehabilitate the housing, pay debt service on the existing HUD loan and establish sufficient operating and replacement reserves.

• **Preservation rents exceeding cost limits.** Offered two choices to owners of housing that could not be preserved for low-income tenants within the federal cost limits. Owners could decide to seek incentives within the federal cost limits, or they could seek to prepay the mortgage, after offering the property for sale.

• **Safeguards.** Offered six protections to tenants if an owner was able to prepay the mortgage:

• Provided Section 8 rental certificates or vouchers to tenants with incomes below 80 percent of the area median income.

• Required owners who prepaid to continue renting to existing tenants at the existing rent for three years. Applied to housing located in low-vacancy areas.

• Required owners in all areas who prepaaid to continue renting to tenants with special needs, such as the elderly and people with disabilities, for three years.

• Required owners to pay 50 percent of moving expenses to displaced tenants. State or local laws would apply if they required a higher level of assistance to tenants.

• Required owners who prepaaid but continued renting to accept tenants with rental certificates or vouchers.

• Required HUD to set aside from appropriations for preservation the amount of money necessary to help tenants displaced from prepaid projects.

• **Resident home-ownership program.** Required tenants who wished to purchase eligible low-income housing to organize a resident council to develop a resident home-ownership program. Required the resident council to work with a public or private nonprofit organization to develop the ability to own and manage the housing.

Required the resident council to develop a plan identifying the price of the units, a comparison of the price to the appraised value, underwriting standards for prospective purchasers, financing arrangements and a sales schedule.

Required the secretary to approve the plan to convert the housing to home ownership.

Required the secretary to impose certain conditions for home ownership to assure that the number of initial owners were very-low-income, low-income or moderate-income people; incomes of initial and subsequent owners would cover occupancy charges to cover the full operating costs of the housing and any debt service; and each initial owner occupied the unit he or she bought.

Authorized homeowners under a home-ownership program to sell their interest in a unit but allowed the program to restrict resale of units. For example, resident councils could require the owner to sell the unit to the council.

If an owner sold a unit within six years, the home-ownership program would have to restrict the sale so that the owner did not receive any undue profit. For example, the price could be limited to the original equity paid by the family, the value of any improvements and any appreciation gained by the property.

If an owner sold a unit between six and 20 years, the home-ownership program would have to restrict the sale so that the secretary recaptured the amount of money left on an initial promissory note signed by the original owner at purchase. The promissory note would be equal to the difference between the market value and the purchase price of the property.

Required that no tenant living in a unit of a property that had been approved for a home-ownership program would be evicted. Non-purchasing tenants would receive Section 8 rental assistance to be used in the existing project or in other housing. If the tenant moved, relocation assistance would be provided by the owner.

• **Pre-emption of state and local laws.** Required that no state or local government could establish, continue or enforce any law that restricted the prepayment of any mortgage on eligible low-income housing, restricted owners from receiving the authorized 8 percent annual return and was not consistent with federal law.

The pre-emption of state and local laws would not apply to building standards, zoning limitations, health or safety standards, rent control or conversion of rental housing to condominiums or cooperatives.

• **Remaining useful life.** Required that owners and purchasers accepting incentives from HUD maintain the housing for low-income tenants for its remaining useful life — as long as the building was physically viable.

• **Consultation.** Required HUD to consult with interested parties, such as national and regional nonprofit groups, in developing a plan of action for preservation properties.

• **'Windfall profits' test.** Authorized the secretary to develop and apply a "windfall profits" test in limited cases. The test would be used to ensure that owners did not reap unusually high profits from HUD incentives.

• **Income.** Defined income to exclude amounts not actually received by a family, such as alimony or child support.

• **Advances for capital improvements.** Authorized HUD to repay owners for advances for capital improvements by phasing in rent increases.

• **Management of federally assisted housing.** Required tenants whose incomes exceeded 80 percent of area median income and who were living in federally assisted housing to pay either 30 percent of their monthly income or the fair market rent standard for the area in which the housing was located.

• **State mortgage programs.** Authorized HUD to assist states in preserving state-subsidized affordable housing that could be lost due to mortgage prepayments.

• **Funding.** Authorized $425 million to be spent in fiscal 1991 and $858 million in fiscal 1992, including $100 million in each year for grants in mandatory sales of housing.

Rural Housing

• **Funds.** Authorized the Farmers Home Administration (FmHA) to insure and guarantee loans during fiscal 1991 and 1992 not to exceed a total of $2.1 billion and $2.2 billion, respectively. That included:

• $1.4 billion in fiscal 1991 and $1.5 billion in fiscal 1992 for the Section 502 single-family loan program;

• $11.9 million in fiscal 1991 and $12.4 million in fiscal 1992 for Section 504 home repair loans;

• $12 million in fiscal 1991 and $12.5 million in fiscal 1992 for Section 514 loans to provide housing for farm laborers;

• $709 million in fiscal 1991 and $739.5 million in fiscal 1992 for Section 515 loans to finance rural rental housing projects;

• $800,000 in fiscal 1991 and $800,000 in fiscal 1992 for Section 523 self-help loans;

• $800,000 in fiscal 1991 and $850,000 in fiscal 1992 for Section 524 site loans.

• **Funds.** Authorized appropriations for fiscal 1991 and 1992, including:

• $1 million in fiscal 1991 and $1.1 million in fiscal 1992 to supplement Section 502 loans in remote rural areas;

• $20.2 million in fiscal 1991 and $21.1 million in fiscal 1992 in Section 504 home repairs;

• $550,000 in fiscal 1991 and $600,000 in fiscal 1992 for construction defects;

• $5 million in fiscal 1991 and $5.3 million in fiscal 1992 for assistance in preparing applications for housing loans in underserved areas;

• $20.9 million in fiscal 1991 and $21.7 million in fiscal 1992 for Section 516 farm labor housing;

• $10 million in fiscal 1991 and $10.5 million in fiscal 1992 for Section 516 assistance for rural housing and migrant workers;

• $13.4 million in fiscal 1991 and $13.9 million in fiscal 1992 for self-help housing;

• $29.6 million in fiscal 1991 and $30.8 million in fiscal 1992 for Section 533 housing preservation.

• **Funds.** Authorized appropriations for rural rental assistance contracts of $397 million in fiscal 1991 and $414.1 million in fiscal 1992.

Authorized appropriations for supplemental contracts of $5.2 million in fiscal 1991 and $5.5 million in fiscal 1992.

• **Remote rural areas.** Required the Agriculture secretary to consider the actual cost of the land and structure to be financed as adequate security for loan applicants who lived in remote rural areas. This would allow the FmHA to make loans without considering the value of surrounding property. Also authorized the secretary to provide grants to make up the difference between the appraised value and the costs of the land and building.

• **Deferred mortgage demonstration.** Authorized the Agriculture secretary to defer mortgage payments on single-family Section 502 loans. This loan program was the largest housing program operated by the FmHA. It consisted of subsidized and unsubsidized direct loans and unsubsidized guaranteed loans to finance the construction or acquisition of a new or existing home. Up to 25 percent of Section 502 mortgage payments could be deferred at 1 percent interest for very-low-income families or people otherwise unable to afford the regular payment.

• **Rural housing loan guarantees.** Required the Agriculture secretary to establish a program guaranteeing 90 percent of single-family housing loans. Required that the loans guaranteed go to low- and moderate-income borrowers to buy or build homes in rural areas more than 25 miles from any urban area.

• **Foreclosure procedures.** Required the Agriculture secretary to follow foreclosure procedures of a state when those procedures were more favorable to the borrower than were FmHA procedures.

• **Indian trust land.** Required the Agriculture secretary, in the event of defaults on Indian trust land, to offer to transfer the account to any eligible tribal member, the tribe or the Indian housing authority.

• **Underserved areas.** Required the Agriculture secretary to designate 100 counties with severe, unmet housing needs as underserved areas in fiscal 1991, including areas in the Lower Mississippi Delta. Those areas would have to have 20 percent or more of their population earning income at or below the poverty level and 10 percent or more of its population living in substandard housing.

Required the secretary to set aside 3.5 percent of its appropriations from fiscal 1991 and 5 percent in fiscal 1992 from five of its rural housing programs to be targeted to the designated areas.

In addition to the designated areas, set-aside funds could be used in "colonias," areas within 150 miles of the Mexican border in Arizona, California, New Mexico or Texas that lacked adequate housing, water and sewerage systems.

• **Section 515 rental housing loans.** Required that equity takeout loans be limited by the appraised value of the property, not the original mortgage amount, for loans made after Dec. 15, 1989.

Reserved 7 percent in fiscal 1991 and 9 percent in fiscal 1992 of Section 515 funds for nonprofit sponsors.

• **Rural homeless and migrant farmworkers.** Authorized $10 million in fiscal 1991 to provide assistance to groups providing affordable rental housing for migrant farmworkers. Permitted housing the homeless who were not migrant workers on an emergency basis in the off-season. Required FmHA to complete a study regarding the extent of the problem of homelessness in rural areas with recommendations for future legislation and programs.

• **Rural area definition.** Redefined a rural area as any open country or place, town, village or city that was not part of an urban area and had a population of no more than 10,000 if it was rural in character. Or, the population could be more than 10,000 but no greater than 25,000 that was rural in character and not part of a standard metropolitan statistical area. In addition, the areas would have to lack mortgage credit for lower- and moderate-income households.

Grandfathered all existing eligible communities under 20,000 population that did not exceed 25,000 in population according to the 1990 census and were rural in character and had a serious lack of mortgage credit.

Housing for People With Special Needs

• **Supportive housing for the elderly.** Changed the Section 202 housing program for the elderly and disabled by creating two separate programs, one for the elderly and one for the disabled. Instead of providing direct loans to build housing, HUD would now provide capital advances and rental assistance to build housing for the elderly. [These financing changes were incorporated into the fiscal 1991 VA-HUD appropriations measure.]

The housing for the elderly would be combined with services to enable the tenants to continue to live independently. Services included meals, housekeeping, transportation, personal care and health services.

Capital advances were defined as no-interest loans to be repaid only if the housing was no longer available for very-low-income elderly people.

Required the HUD secretary to provide rental assistance to projects in which the operating costs were not covered by rental income.

Tenant rents would be the highest of the following: 30 percent of a person's adjusted monthly income, which took into account costs such as food; 10 percent of a person's total monthly income; or the amount of money designated for housing out of welfare assistance if the person was receiving welfare.

Required that all units built with funds from the program be available to very-low-income people for at least 40 years.

Funds could be used to finance construction or rehabilitation of a project or acquisition of a building from the RTC, the lead agency charged with salvaging failed thrifts.

Authorized the revised Section 202 program to go into effect in fiscal 1992. Authorized $659 million for capital advances and $363 million for rental assistance in fiscal 1992. Required 20 percent of funds to be allocated to non-metropolitan areas. Authorized $714.2 million in loans for the existing Section 202 program in fiscal 1991.

• **Congregate housing services.** Authorized HUD and the FmHA to administer a revised congregate housing services program providing meals and other services to residents of federally assisted housing. Residents would have to be elderly or disabled. To better accommodate the physical needs of residents, the program would also adapt housing, such as installing grab bars in bathrooms.

Required HUD and the FmHA to enter into contracts with states, Indian tribes, local governments and local nonprofit housing groups to provide services to residents and to adapt the housing to the residents' needs.

Required contract recipients to supplement federal funds with 50 percent of the cost of providing the congregate services program. Federal funds would cover 40 percent and fee charges to residents would cover 10 percent. Fees could be waived for tenants who were unable to pay.

Authorized $25 million in fiscal 1991 and $26.1 million in fiscal 1992. Required HUD and the FmHA to split the cost proportionately according to the number of units participating in the program under their jurisdiction.

• **HOPE for elderly independence.** Authorized a five-year demonstration program to combine rental certificates and vouchers with supportive services for frail elderly people. The purpose was to enable elderly people to continue to live independently.

Authorized HUD to provide no more than 1,500 new rental vouchers and certificates to public housing authorities to carry out this program. Public housing agencies could not require that a frail elderly person live in a particular building, but the agency could restrict them to living in a certain geographic area so that services could be provided more easily.

Of the amount required to carry out the program, HUD would provide 40 percent, the public housing agency would provide 50 percent and the frail elderly participants would pay 10 percent. However, the tenants could not be required to pay more than 20 percent of their adjusted income. If the public housing agency collected less than the 10 percent required from the tenants, HUD and the agency would equally split the remaining costs.

Required the secretary to distribute funds through a national competition.

Supportive services included personal care, transportation, meals, counseling and supervision.

Authorized $34 million in fiscal 1991 and $35.5 million in fiscal 1992 for Section 8 rental assistance. Authorized $10 million in fiscal 1991 and $10.4 million in fiscal 1992 for supportive services.

• **RTC properties.** Authorized Section 202 funds to be used to acquire and rehabilitate housing for the elderly from the RTC.

• **Centralized applications.** Designated a central location in each area to be used for the elderly to apply for admission to all Section 202 housing for the elderly. HUD area offices would be required to provide a listing of available projects for the elderly to local agencies serving the elderly.

• **ECHO units.** Authorized a demonstration program expanding the definition of housing in the Section 202 elderly housing program to include elder cottage housing opportunity (ECHO) units. ECHO units were designed to be installed next to existing homes and were typically used for elderly parents.

• **Supportive housing for people with disabilities.** Authorized HUD to provide capital advances and project rental assistance to private nonprofit groups to finance, acquire, build and rehabilitate buildings for people with disabilities and to provide supportive services to enable them to live independently. Also authorized funds to be used to acquire properties from the RTC.

The program would become effective in fiscal 1992.

Authorized $271 million for capital advances in fiscal 1992 and $246 million for rental assistance in fiscal 1992.

• **Supportive housing for the homeless.** Revised the Stewart B. McKinney Homeless Assistance Act (PL 100-77) to combine existing McKinney Act emergency shelter grants program, supportive housing demonstration program and permanent housing for the homeless disabled program. Other existing programs would be considered eligible activities.

• **Funds.** For fiscal years 1991 and 1992, authorized:

Emergency Shelter Grants program, $125 million and $138 million, respectively.

Supportive Housing Demonstration Program, $125 million and $150 million.

Supplemental Assistance for Facilities to Assist the Homeless (SAFAH) program, $30 million and $30 million.

Section 8 Moderate Rehabilitation for Single Room Occupancy (SRO) Dwelling Program, $79 million and $82.4 million.

Shelter Plus Care Rental Housing Assistance Programs, $80.4 million and $167.2 million.

Shelter Plus Care Single Room Occupancy Dwelling Program, $24.8 million and $54.2 million.

Shelter Plus Care Section 202 Program, $18 million and $37.2 million.

Also authorized such sums as may be necessary to restructure the McKinney Act programs.

• **Shelter Plus Care Program.** Authorized rental housing assistance to be used in conjunction with supportive services paid for by other sources for homeless people with disabilities. In particular, this program was aimed at people who were seriously mentally ill or had chronic problems with alcohol, drugs or both, or had AIDS.

• **Comprehensive Homeless Assistance Plan (CHAP).** Required state and local governments to report to HUD on how they were using their McKinney funds and what their strategy was to address homelessness. Amended the plan to require state and local governments to include child-care and food-donation strategies. Required the plan to be submitted biennially, rather than annually. Beginning Oct. 1, 1991, state and local governments could receive McKinney Act funds only if they certified that they were following a housing affordability strategy approved under the HOME Investment Partnerships program or a CHAP approved during the 180-day period following the date of enactment.

• **Housing opportunities for people with AIDS.** Required the secretary to make grants to state and local governments to meet the long-term housing needs of people with acquired immune deficiency syndrome (AIDS). Ninety percent of the funds appropriated were to be allocated on the basis of the incidence of AIDS, with 75 percent going to local governments with populations above 500,000 and more than 1,500 AIDS cases or to states with more than 1,500 AIDS cases. Twenty-five percent would go to local governments with populations over 500,000 and more than 1,500 AIDS cases that had a higher than average per capita incidence of AIDS.

Required the secretary to allocate 10 percent of the funds to meet housing needs in states and localities that did not meet the previous requirements, and to fund special projects of national significance.

• **Eligible activities.** Required that grant recipients use federal funds only for approved activities to prevent homelessness among people with AIDS. Those activities included:

• Enabling public and nonprofit groups to provide housing information to people and to coordinate efforts to expand housing assistance resources.

• Developing and operating shelters and services.

• Providing short-term rental assistance.

• Rehabilitating single-room occupancy dwellings.

• Developing community residences.

• **Funds.** Authorized $75 million in fiscal 1991 and $156.5 million in fiscal 1992 to be spent on housing for people with AIDS.

Community Development, Miscellaneous

• **Funds.** Authorized $3.1 billion to be appropriated in fiscal 1991 and $3.3 billion in fiscal 1992 for Community Development Block Grants (CDBGs).

Of those amounts, the HUD secretary was required to provide:

• No less than $3 million in fiscal 1991 and 1992 in grants to institutions of higher education to provide assistance to economically disadvantaged and minority students who participated in community development work-study programs.

• No less than $6.5 million in fiscal 1991 and $6.5 million in fiscal 1992 in grants to historically black colleges.

• No less than $7 million in fiscal 1991 and $7 million in fiscal 1992 for grants in Guam, the Virgin Islands, American Samoa, the Northern Mariana Islands and the Trust Territory of the Pacific Islands.

• No less than $500,000 in fiscal 1991 for grants to demonstrate the feasibility of developing an integrated database system and computer mapping tool to evaluate CDBGs.

• **Targeting.** Changed the low- and moderate-income targeting requirement in the block grant program from 60 percent to 70 percent.

• **City and county classifications.** Allowed any city classified as a metropolitan city for at least two years to remain classified as a metropolitan city.

Allowed any county classified as urban for at least two years to remain classified as such unless it failed to meet the basic population requirements because of the election of a new local government that would exclude a portion of its population.

• **Eligible activities.** Authorized funds to private, for-profit groups in order to carry out economic development projects that created or retained jobs for low- and moderate-income people, prevented or eliminated slums and blight, met urgent needs, created or retained businesses owned by community residents, and assisted businesses that provided goods or services needed by and affordable to low- and moderate-income residents.

Also authorized funds to be used to provide assistance to low- and moderate-income families that wanted to buy their own houses by subsidizing mortgage rates and principal amounts.

• **Community development loan guarantees.** Allowed non-entitlement communities to receive Section 108 loan guarantees.

Expanded the Section 108 authority to include guarantees for construction of low- and moderate-income housing for home ownership by nonprofit housing groups also receiving a HoDAG or Nehemiah grant.

Authorized HUD to assist communities in paying its debt service in cases of extreme hardship.

• **Urban homesteading.** Authorized the HUD secretary to acquire single-family homes from the RTC for use in urban homesteading programs.

• **Neighborhood Reinvestment Corporation.** Authorized appropriations of $35 million in fiscal 1991 and $36.5 million in fiscal 1992.

• **Disaster relief.** Authorized assistance to areas affected by disasters without appropriations limits under the Section 8 certificate, voucher and moderate rehabilitation programs and the CDBG program.

• **Regulatory programs.** Amended the Real Estate Settlement Procedures Act of 1974 to require disclosure of transfer of mortgage servicing. Also required lenders to notify borrowers of escrow account shortages annually and to provide annual escrow account statements.

Established a national commission on manufactured housing to develop recommendations for modernizing the National Manufactured Housing Construction and Safety Standards Act of 1974. Authorized $500,000 to be appropriated for the commission in fiscal 1991.

Required the HUD secretary to write a five-year plan to encourage and improve energy efficiency in new, rehabilitated and existing housing. Required the secretary, in consultation with the Energy secretary, to create a uniform plan to make housing more affordable through mortgage financing incentives for energy efficiency.

• **Miscellaneous programs.** Authorized $21.2 million in fiscal 1991 and $22.1 million in fiscal 1992 for HUD policy development and research. Up to $500,000 in fiscal 1991 was to be used for a demonstration project to test affordable housing technologies.

Authorized $512,000 in fiscal 1991 and $534,000 in fiscal 1992 for the Advanced Building Technology Council to be established within the National Institute of Building Sciences.

Authorized $6 million in fiscal 1991 and $6.3 million in fiscal 1992 for the fair housing initiatives program. Of those amounts, no more than $3 million annually could be used for the private enforcement initiative demonstration program.

Exempted Davis-Bacon wage requirements under the CDBG program, Section 8 rental assistance program, public housing and Section 202 housing for the elderly and disabled for work performed by volunteers who did not receive compensation or who wewe paid expenses, reasonable benefits or a nominal fee and who were not generally employed in construction work.

• **Expedited Funds Availability.** Extended the Expedited Funds Availability Act for two years after enactment of the housing bill. ■

Continued from p. 643

The Ex-Im Bank was not allowed to finance military sales for developing countries and its policy was not to finance them at all. Conferees were divided over that issue. *(Export Administration Act, p. 198)*

Gonzalez said Dodd made the request Oct. 10, but Gonzalez sent him a note the next day, refusing to intervene. "I think issues should stand on their own," said Gonzalez.

Finally, Kemp told Gonzalez that he would free public housing if conferees agreed to limit Schumer's program. That left Dodd out in the cold.

Although Schumer had been negotiating with Cranston all along to combine his program with the Senate's block grant, the administration's action forced some last-minute tinkering.

Schumer intended for the program to be run by HUD with exact guidelines on financing loans for developers and nonprofit groups. Instead, his program was added to the Senate's block grant, with construction funds making up 10 percent of the total the first year and 15 percent the second year.

Under the bill, communities would have to show HUD that they had low vacancy rates before they could qualify to build.

Then they could use the construction money as loans or grants, depending on their preference. Finally, if a community kept its construction money for two years without using it, the money could then be used for other housing activities.

New Programs

Though they did not receive much attention in conference, a number of significant new programs were added to the final bill.

For people with AIDS, the conference authorized $150 million in housing programs.

For the elderly, programs would emphasize combining housing with social services to help people live independently. Those services included personal care, transportation, meals and counseling.

A National Housing Trust, created by Gonzalez, would subsidize down payments and mortgages for first-time, moderate-income home buyers.

The conference authorized $30 million for housing to keep together families whose children otherwise would be placed in foster care because of inadequate housing.

Schumer tried to establish the program as an entitlement for anyone who needed it, but the administration said that the $1 billion in budget authority required over five years was too expensive.

Floor Action, Signing

With the conference over, lawmakers and administration officials adopted a tone of mutual self-congratulation on the final product.

Gonzalez presented the conference report to House members Oct. 25 by recalling Wylie's help in setting up a White House meeting with Bush and Kemp in February to try to forge common objectives.

"We have a president that is sympathetic to housing needs," Gonzalez said. "... And then Secretary Kemp followed through."

Voice vote approval in the House was followed by overwhelming passage in the Senate. Only six Republicans voted against the final bill Oct. 27: William L. Armstrong, Colo.; Jesse Helms, N.C.; Gordon J. Humphrey, N.H.; Roth; Steve Symms, Idaho; and Malcolm Wallop, Wyo.

When Bush signed the bill Nov. 28, he had praise for Kemp and the key lawmakers — Cranston and D'Amato in the Senate and Gonzalez and Wylie in the House.

Bush pointed to his administration's role in proposing the HOPE initiative on home ownership, though without noting that the HUD spending bill he had signed Nov. 5 omitted any funds for it.

The president also had praise for the block grant HOME program, but he voiced regret that the final bill contained a provision that earmarked 15 percent of the funds in fiscal 1992 for construction.

"I do not believe that the earmarking of funds for new construction is consistent with the goal of providing states and localities with maximum flexibility to meet their specific affordable housing needs," he said. ■

FHA's Insurance Fund Shored Up

Amid warnings of a repeat — albeit on a much smaller scale — of the nation's savings and loans debacle, Congress took steps in 1990 to shore up the Federal Housing Administration (FHA) mortgage insurance fund.

As part of the Cranston-Gonzalez omnibus housing bill (S 566 — PL 101-625), lawmakers required buyers to pay additional costs upfront and annual insurance fees when purchasing a home.

Since Congress first authorized the FHA in 1934, the agency's single-family insurance program had backed loans for about 15 million homes worth more than $374 billion. The program was intended to spur home ownership and stimulate the housing industry by encouraging banks to make loans to people who did not have the money for a traditional 10 percent to 20 percent down payment. FHA loans required down payments of 3 percent on the first $25,000 and 5 percent on the remainder.

As lawmakers worked on the omnibus housing bill in 1990, little was planned for the FHA beyond extending the maximum loan amount of $124,875. But on June 6, the Bush administration released a report from the accounting firm of Price Waterhouse that showed the program was heading for insolvency.

The House and Senate approached the problem in vastly different ways. The Senate modified an administration plan, which would have cost home buyers an additional $1,300 in cash on the average $65,000 home.

Under existing law, buyers could finance a 3.8 percent upfront mortgage insurance premium as well as their closing costs. The Senate voted to continue to allow buyers to finance the 3.8 percent premium, but it would have had them pay two-thirds of their closing costs in cash; in addition, people who could not come up with at least a 10 percent down payment on the price of their home would be required to pay a 0.5 percent annual premium for up to 15 years.

The House bill would have restructured the insurance premiums to a "pay as you go" plan, eliminating additional upfront costs.

The House proposal would have continued to allow buyers to finance all of their closing costs as well as a reduced upfront premium of 1.35 percent. Each owner, however, would have been required to pay an annual 0.6 percent premium over the life of the 30-year loan.

In House-Senate conference, Jack F. Kemp, secretary of Housing and Urban Development (HUD), dug in against the House plan, which he considered irresponsible.

It was the congressional-White House budget summit agreement, however, requiring $2.5 billion in revenues from FHA premiums over the next five years, that dealt the final blow to the House plan.

Conferees approved a plan close to the administration's proposal. On a $65,000 house, buyers would have to pay an additional $833 in cash upfront, in contrast to the $1,300 they would have to pay under the Senate plan.

In addition, new "risk-based" requirements were adopted to weed out people more likely to default on the mortgages.

Buyers would pay an annual premium of 0.5 percent for the life of the loan if their down payment was between 5 percent and 10 percent or for 11 years if their down payment was more than 10 percent.

Buyers who put down less than 5 percent of their loan would pay a 0.55 percent annual premium for the 30-year life of the loan. *(Provisions: FHA and Secondary Mortgage Market, p. 647)*

Members of the real estate industry predicted that as many as 60,000 families each year would be unable to afford a house under the new FHA rules.

WARNINGS FROM STUDY, KEMP

Neither chamber had included provisions in its housing bill to change the FHA Mutual Mortgage Insurance (MMI) Fund. Both Banking committees had already marked up their legislation when HUD released the Price Waterhouse report June 6.

The long-awaited independent study confirmed suspicions that the FHA was losing money and could be insolvent by the end of the century. The study became a rallying cry for Kemp, who insisted that if Congress wanted a housing bill, it would have to include his plan for shoring up the fund.

Kemp told the Senate Banking Subcommittee on Housing and Urban Affairs on June 6 that Price Waterhouse determined that the FHA's single-family loan program, although solvent, was losing about $350 million a year.

The Price Waterhouse study found that the MMI had a net worth of $2.6 billion, down sharply from a high of $8 billion in 1979. "It is not now actuarially sound. The good news is that we can take steps to make FHA sound," Kemp said.

Subcommittee members, led by Chairman Alan Cranston, D-Calif., said Congress would have to move fast to rescue the FHA program. Ranking Republican Alfonse M. D'Amato of New York said the administration needed to reveal quickly all problems associated with the FHA program to avoid "the debacle that we have seen relating to the S&Ls."

Kemp assured the members that the administration was not trying to deceive Congress, but he acknowledged that HUD and the Office of Management and Budget (OMB) still had not resolved key elements of the Bush administration's recommendations.

Kemp said the independent advisers recommended that the MMI fund's capital be increased immediately to a minimum of 1.25 percent of its total insurance exposure — $271 billion at the time — and to 2 percent by the end of the 1990s.

Administration Recommendations

Kemp said the administration recommended a five-part strategy to improve the FHA's financial standing.

Key elements of those recommendations would require Congress to impose an additional 0.5 percent loan assessment on FHA home buyers who provided less than a 10 percent down payment and would require borrowers to pay at least two-thirds of closing costs in cash.

The 0.5 percent mortgage premium for buyers would be financed as part of the overall mortgage. It would be paid over a period of from four to 15 years, depending on the amount of the down payment.

Under the existing system, the FHA allowed buyers to finance closing costs, which usually ran to several thousand dollars. Kemp said requiring the borrowers to pay the closing costs upfront would provide them with more equity and decrease the risk of default.

Cranston, however, voiced concern that the recommendations could decrease the number of low- and moderate-income home buyers able to use the FHA program.

The administration's proposals also would hold the FHA mortgage loan limits at $124,875 in order to keep high-income families from qualifying for loans. Kemp said he also opposed any move to allow FHA mortgages on second homes.

The fourth recommendation would have discontinued the system of paying distributive shares to buyers at the end of their 30-year loans. The shares were the excess of premiums paid over losses. HUD, however, would continue to pay the distributive shares for home buyers who purchased their homes prior to 1980.

Kemp said he wanted further reforms in the FHA's administrative and accounting procedures to cut costs. According to the Price Waterhouse study, the FHA was losing 37 cents on the dollar on foreclosures. Kemp said the FHA needed to cut losses in foreclosures by reselling those homes faster. The FHA was spending $500 million a year in carrying costs of 80,000 homes it had foreclosed on, Kemp said.

SENATE ACTION

Two weeks after the study was released, the Senate heeded the warnings and voted to toughen FHA lending requirements.

On June 18, as the chamber began debating the housing bill, Cranston and four other senators (Christopher S. Bond, R-Mo.; Connie Mack, R-Fla.; Donald W. Riegle Jr., D-Mich.; and Paul S. Sarbanes, D-Md.) met with Kemp and budget director Richard G. Darman to negotiate provisions of S 566. The disagreement over how to make the FHA actuarilly sound was one of four primary issues dividing Capitol Hill and the administration.

On June 19, Darman's OMB released a blunt statement criticizing the bill: "If S 566 were presented to the president in its current form, his senior advisers would recommend that the bill be vetoed."

D'Amato, an original cosponsor of the bill, who was working with the administration, sought to drive home the point: "Unless these issues are resolved, a veto is not only a possibility, but a certainty."

With negotiations continuing, Cranston voiced optimism, saying everyone wanted to strengthen the FHA. Although the Democrats had a slightly different approach, Cranston said, "we believe it is just as sound."

D'Amato's Proposed Fix

On June 20, D'Amato offered an FHA-reform amendment even tougher than the administration's proposal.

D'Amato's amendment would have:

- Increased FHA down payment requirements to 5 percent of the total purchase price. Under the existing system, a buyer paid 3 percent on the first $25,000 and 5 percent on the rest. The administration had not recommended increasing the down payment.
- Established a risk-based premium, requiring higher premiums on smaller down payments, as recommended by the administration.
- Required buyers to pay all closing costs upfront in cash, in contrast to the administration's recommendation of allowing one-third of those costs to be financed.
- Made the existing mortgage limit permanent at $124,875. The administration had also proposed doing this.

Housing industry groups lined up in opposition to D'Amato's amendment and the administration's proposal. They included the National Association of Realtors, the National Association of Home Builders, the Mortgage Bankers Association of America and Consumers Union.

D'Amato said it was better to institute tougher requirements that might shut out potential home buyers than to lead them into a situation in which they would end up defaulting on their mortgages.

Cranston's Proposed Solution

Cranston, however, said he wanted to restore the FHA's health "without placing a draconian burden on millions of middle-income families who are trying to buy a home."

Under the administration's proposal, more than 40 percent of families who were FHA homeowners would not have been able to buy, Cranston contended. In a letter to his colleagues, Cranston said the administration's plan would mean that a typical family using FHA insurance would need to pay $900 more at closing, in addition to the $3,550 it would pay under the existing rules.

Cranston offered a plan that he said would restore the FHA to full financial health without hurting potential home buyers. It would have:

- Increased the FHA premium to equal to or higher than the level the administration proposed.
- Required the HUD secretary to set an annual premium to reach goals for actuarial soundness, using a small upfront fee and annual premium payments through the life of the mortgage.
- Ended the practice of allowing the mortgage loan to exceed the value of the home.
- Required the secretary to work with independent actuaries to recommend ways to base the premium on the equity the home buyer invested in his home.

Kemp Prevails

After an all-day meeting June 22 involving Kemp, Cranston, D'Amato and the deputy director of the OMB, staff members spent the weekend and Monday in negotiations. On June 26, the principals got back together and ironed out the last wrinkles.

In the end, Senate Democrats and Republicans agreed to the administration's proposal, which would establish higher premiums, require two-thirds of closing costs to be paid with the down payment and increase capital requirements for the insurance fund. In addition, the FHA would continue to insure homes up to $124,875, the existing mortgage limit in high-priced areas of the country.

The Senate accepted the compromise by voice vote on June 27. "I believe this is a sound decision, although I remain concerned about the impact on home buyers, particularly young families who are struggling to buy their first home," Cranston said. He said he would try to modify the provision in conference.

HOUSE ACTION

A month later, the House handed Kemp a stunning defeat on the issue. Ignoring his warnings of a veto and a thrifts-type crisis, members overwhelmingly passed a $28 billion housing authorization bill (HR 1180) that included an FHA overhaul plan that Kemp vehemently opposed.

Kemp said the plan did not go far enough to prop up the faltering single-family insurance fund. He had lobbied hard for a more stringent proposal that would have required first-time home buyers to pay another $1,000 in cash. But concerned about hitting voters in the wallet, even the Republican leadership rejected that idea, and it was never offered on the floor.

Interest groups had been caught off guard on the FHA issue. But immediately following Senate passage of the housing bill June 27, an unusual coalition of housing industry groups and activist organizations joined forces to lobby House members.

By the time the House began debating HR 1180 on July 27, two proposals had been put on the table early, one pushed by administration officials and the other proposed by Bruce F. Vento, D-Minn., and Tom Ridge, R-Pa. Banking Committee Chairman Henry B. Gonzalez offered a third compromise proposal, but Kemp rejected it.

Under the existing system, home buyers were required to pay a 3.8 percent mortgage insurance premium upfront that could be financed; their total closing costs could be financed; and their down payment was 3 percent on the first $25,000 and 5 percent on anything on top of that.

The three proposals would have made the following changes:

- The administration plan would have forced buyers to come up with more cash upfront and pay a premium based on the amount of their down payment. The administration would switch to a risk-based premium program, retaining the 3.8 percent premium upfront, adding a 0.5 percent annual premium when the loan was greater than 90 percent of the value of the home, and requiring that at least two-thirds of the closing costs be paid upfront in cash and that no more than one-third be financed. There would be no change in the basic down-payment requirement.
- The Vento-Ridge proposal would have spread the insurance premium out and left intact the amount of money people paid upfront. It would have required a 1.35 percent mortgage insurance premium upfront, though it could be financed. In addition, the owner would have to pay a 0.6 percent annual premium over the life of the loan; closing costs could be financed.
- The Gonzalez proposal would have used a 2.6 percent upfront premium, with annual premium levels as necessary, and two-thirds of the closing costs could be financed. The secretary would have to report to Congress every six months on the soundness of the mortgage insurance fund; and with Congress' approval, the secretary could change the annual premium level.

Industry, Advocacy Lobbying

In an unusual alliance, housing industry as well as advocacy groups backed the Vento-Ridge proposal. They included the National Association of Realtors, the National Association of Home Builders, the Mortgage Bankers Association of America, the Consumer Federation of America, Consumers Union, the National Council of State Housing Agencies and ACORN, an activist group.

Directors of state housing finance agencies, which issued tax-exempt mortgage revenue bonds to help low-income families buy homes, wrote letters and met with members of their states' delegations. They pointed out that 60 percent of the mortgages they wrote relied on FHA insurance. They feared that if FHA insurance were harder to get, their mortgages would be available only to middle-income people.

The Realtors group said 100,000 families a year would be unable to afford a home if they had to pay more upfront. The Mortgage Bankers Association put the figure at 250,000. The administration said the number was closer to 35,000. The FHA program insured about 900,000 to 1 million homes a year.

The National Association of Home Builders said the administration plan would cost people about $1,300 more than they already paid upfront on a $70,000 home.

Mary S. Brunette, spokeswoman for Kemp, said that those families might have to defer home ownership but that eventually they could save the money they needed.

But Ridge argued that young families often faced unanticipated medical or repair bills with little excess cash. To wait a little longer, he said, "sounds good, but in the real world I don't think it works."

And Norman D. Flynn, president of the National Association of Realtors, called the increased upfront costs under both the HUD and Gonzalez plans a "fatal flaw," taking the bulk of the people out of the market.

Brunette, however, said people were less likely to default on a mortgage when they invested more of their own money. Under Vento-Ridge, she said, "you may make some short-term money for people in the real estate industry, but you don't do homeowners any favors if they default."

She argued that the Vento-Ridge proposal would lead to a default rate higher than 12 percent, compared with the existing rate of 11.6 percent.

The National Training and Information Center, an advocacy and resource agency for grass-roots housing groups, maintained, however, that defaults often occurred when a family took on more debt than the home was worth. Exist-

Housing Benefit Plans

Legislation that for the first time allowed collective-bargaining agreements to include provisions for employers to help pay employees' housing costs cleared Congress on April 3 and was signed into law by President Bush April 18 (S 1949 — PL 101-273).

The measure amended the Taft-Hartley Labor Management Relations Act of 1947 (PL 80-101) to permit — but not require — employers to establish housing trust funds in order to give employees money for down payments, closing costs, bank fees and mortgage interest buy-downs to buy homes. The trust fund could also help pay initial rental costs such as security deposits and the first month's rent.

Previously, employers were prohibited from making payments into jointly administered trust funds for anything other than a limited number of benefits, including health, life insurance and retirement.

"This legislation promotes a private-sector solution to the increasing difficulties workers face in obtaining affordable, decent housing," said William L. Clay, D-Mo., chairman of the House Education and Labor Subcommittee on Labor-Management Relations.

The House cleared the bill (S 1949) April 3 by voice vote, after first approving an identical version (HR 4073 — H Rept 101-441) of its own. The Senate had passed the measure Nov. 22, 1989, also by voice vote.

ing policy allowed financing of many costs on top of the actual mortgage, driving up the monthly payments.

Nicole Kemeny, the center's housing organizer, said her group preferred most of the Vento-Ridge provisions because the plan would not allow a person's debt to exceed 100 percent of the value of his home. The administration plan would not cap the debt.

"Foreclosures are just devastating neighborhoods," Kemeny said. "And an abandoned house pulls down everyone else's real estate values."

Other critics said that the "risk-based premium" for families that could not afford to put 10 percent down on a home circumvented FHA's mission. "There is a public policy purpose behind the FHA," Ridge said. "That's to assist first-time home buyers, some of whom might admittedly be at risk.... You can make FHA so sound that those for whom the program was designed can't use it."

Vento-Ridge Passed

In a letter to key housing lawmakers that was also sent to every member of the House, Kemp said President Bush would veto any legislation that did not include his plan to fix the insurance fund.

And in the two weeks before the housing bill reached the floor, Kemp came to Capitol Hill three times to meet with Gonzalez, the committee's ranking Republican, Chalmers P. Wylie of Ohio, and Marge Roukema, N.J., ranking Republican on the Housing Subcommittee, to try to reach a compromise.

The day before the bill was to go to the floor, they met one last time in Gonzalez's office. "I'm like you; I have a social conscience," Kemp reportedly told Gonzalez, explaining that he could not support a plan that would increase the number of families who defaulted on their loans.

At the meeting, Kemp offered to modify an earlier Gonzalez plan by requiring buyers to pay 50 percent of closing costs upfront. But late that night, Gonzalez rejected the idea, saying it would cost buyers too much.

Without a compromise, Wylie and Roukema decided to offer Kemp's plan as an amendment.

Support for the Vento-Ridge proposal had been growing steadily, however, and nose counts showed a sure win. A few hours before the vote, the dam broke. The Republican Leadership Conference decided to back the Vento-Ridge proposal despite pleas from Kemp, who underscored his point by threatening to resign if the Vento-Ridge proposal reached Bush's desk.

On the floor, Minority Whip Newt Gingrich, R-Ga., said that Vento-Ridge "is a good plan," and that members should vote for it and then work with Kemp in conference to avoid a veto.

Wylie, saying he could read the tea leaves, did not bother to offer the Kemp amendment. Roukema, who had to leave for New Jersey to care for her sick husband, complained: "The Republican leadership has got to share the blame for not being successful. Without Bob Michel and Newt Gingrich aboard, there was no point" in offering her amendment.

The vote on Vento-Ridge was an overwhelming 418-2, with only Jim Cooper, D-Tenn., and Thomas E. Petri, R-Wis., voting nay. *(Vote 290, p. 72-H)*

Alfred DelliBovi, HUD under secretary, said that while the money involved would not come close to the $100 billion-plus thrifts crisis, "it will certainly win second place when it comes to bailouts."

"This Band-Aid is not going to stop the hemorrhaging," he said. "This is the same lullaby that we heard about the S&L crisis in 1986, that it wasn't as bad."

In an interview days later, Kemp said he did not mean for his threat to resign over the Vento-Ridge plan to be taken literally. "I said it in a way that conveyed to anybody who was listening that I didn't think, that I don't believe it will come to that," he said. "I just wanted them to know how strongly I felt."

HOUSE-SENATE CONFERENCE

The financial health of the FHA mortgage insurance program emerged as a major sticking point in the House-Senate conference on the housing bill.

Kemp reiterated that if House members insisted on their plan, he would recommend that Bush veto the legislation, even if it meant sacrificing the administration's home ownership initiatives.

The HUD secretary's veto threats, however, angered Gonzalez. He wrote Kemp that he was "very disappointed" to learn that FHA "had been made a quid pro quo for passage of an omnibus housing authorizations bill this year." He added that he considered the threats a breach of Kemp's agreement to cooperate with Congress to move a housing bill.

Responding to Gonzalez in an Aug. 17 letter, Kemp said that when he promised to cooperate with Congress, no one knew the FHA required major surgery. The secretary said he was "taken aback" that Gonzalez thought he was being bludgeoned, when the Bush administration had been trying to negotiate a compromise.

Administration officials said that despite the flaws in the FHA program, they would prefer to retain existing law rather than adopt the Vento-Ridge proposal. The reason, they said, was that defaults would increase under the Vento-Ridge plan.

Also, administration officials insisted that a risk-based premium was essential to reduce the default rate.

"There is a very positive correlation between the amount of equity someone has in a home and the willingness not to walk away from that mortgage," Kemp said.

Real estate agents, mortgage bankers and home builders continued to oppose the changes. "That's not what FHA is all about," said Stephen Driesler, senior vice president of government affairs at the National Association of Realtors. "It is a mutual insurance fund, a mutual sharing of the risk."

By spreading the risk among all FHA home buyers, people with good credit ratings essentially subsidized people with poor credit ratings, Driesler said.

And home buyers in economically unstable areas of the country subsidized buyers in economically secure areas, he said.

In unsuccessful negotiations with Gonzalez before the House debated the bill, Kemp moved only slightly from his position.

He stuck to risk-based premiums while offering to reduce the amount of cash a buyer must pay in closing costs from two-thirds to one-half.

However, both Cranston and Gonzalez signaled willingness to accept a risk-based premium despite the objections of interest groups.

Driesler argued that the situation was not nearly as bleak as the administration would have everyone believe. Price Waterhouse was saying the insurance fund had a net worth of $3.2 billion, rather than the $2.6 billion it originally reported. In addition, it was operating at an $80 million surplus for the first half of fiscal 1990; it had been estimated to lose $40 million to $50 million in 1990.

Reaching Agreement

After days of wrangling in October, Kemp traveled to Capitol Hill on Oct. 11 to jump-start the bill.

The next day, conferees agreed on an FHA compromise under which first-time home buyers would have to pay an average of about $833 in cash upfront. The aim was to meet the budget summit's stipulation for the FHA insurance program to provide $2.5 billion in revenue from premiums paid by home buyers over the next five years.

Discussions, carried out only behind closed doors, were more technical than philosophical. Kemp offered Vento and Ridge three FHA proposals. Vento and Ridge did not like any of them.

D'Amato tried another approach that would have cost home buyers $975 upfront in cash on the average home. Ridge countered with Gonzalez's old proposal that would cost $833 in cash. Vento said he was still not pleased with the plan, which also would add a 0.5 percent annual premium to buyers' mortgages, but the conference approved it.

"I just unhappily disagree with this," Vento said.

Vento and Ridge zeroed in on one proposal that would have reduced the amount of cash home buyers would need for closing costs on a $65,000 home from the $1,300 in the Senate plan to about $800. Under Vento-Ridge, a home buyer could finance all closing costs, without putting down cash. The Kemp proposal would also have required buyers to pay an annual premium of 0.5 percent compared with the 0.6 percent of the Vento-Ridge plan.

But the budget-summit requirement for $2.5 billion in revenues from FHA premiums over the next five years doomed the House plan.

In meeting the administration's demands to cut default rates and shore up the amount of money on hand to cover defaults, the plan could not also come up with the additional revenue for the U.S. Treasury.

"American homeowners have become the first victims of this budget chaos," said Realtors' lobbyist Driesler.

Ridge eventually offered a compromise plan that would cost home buyers $833 more than what they had been required to put down on a $65,000 home. The plan was similar to the administration's in every respect except that it would allow 57 percent of the closing costs on a home to be financed, rather than 33 percent.

Although Vento did not support the plan, he and Ridge played key roles in bringing down costs for home buyers.

Driesler said the Realtors estimated that the changes would put home ownership out of reach for at least 60,000 families each year. He predicted a ripple effect in lost sales for furniture companies, movers and house painters.

And he complained that the administration was trying to lower default rates by tenths of a percent — not enough to make a difference. "One household out of 10 goes into default," he said. "We have a much higher divorce rate than that. Should we discourage people from getting married because one in three will get divorced?"

But John C. Weicher, assistant secretary for policy development and research at HUD, said that with 80,000 to 90,000 families defaulting on their loans, losing their homes and ruining their credit each year, those percentages had a high human significance. "It's no great social policy to help families buy a home in order to default," he said. "Each of those tenths of percentages is real people."

Nevertheless, the Realtors withdrew their support for the entire housing bill. They said they would not work to defeat the legislation but would sit out the final hurdles as the House and Senate took up the conference report. ■

Mortgage 'Prepayment' Compromise

Congress crafted a complex compromise to a conflict between landlords who wanted to pay off their federally subsidized mortgages early and their low-income tenants who faced possible eviction if landlords converted the properties to more profitable use.

The solution — part of the 1990 omnibus housing authorization legislation (S 566 — PL 101-625) — lifted a moratorium on landlords' paying off the mortgages while imposing procedures that guaranteed landlords an 8 percent return on their investments and also gave tenants the chance to buy the property if the landlord wanted to sell.

The subsidized mortgages, offered in the 1960s and '70s, required building owners to rent to low-income families but gave owners the option to pay off their loans after 20 years and do whatever they wanted with their properties. Since 1987, Congress had maintained a de facto moratorium on such "prepayments."

With the moratorium set to expire Sept. 30, 1990, and tenants in about 300,000 units at risk of eviction and homelessness, members of the House and Senate tried to find a way to prevent landlords from prepaying their loans and converting their buildings to more lucrative condominiums or high-priced apartments.

In its version of the omnibus housing bill, the Senate sought to leave little room for owners to prepay unless the secretary of Housing and Urban Development (HUD) gave permission.

The House, however, with Bush administration backing, approved a plan that would offer incentives to owners not to pay off the loans but would still allow them the option of getting out of the program and doing what they wanted with their property.

With House-Senate conferees still negotiating over the prepayment provisions as the Sept. 30 deadline neared, Congress cleared a one-month extension of the deadline on Sept. 28 (HR 5747 — PL 101-402).

The prepayment question was one of the contentious issues settled by conferees on Oct. 12. Under the compromise, the moratorium was lifted. But lawmakers did so only after establishing procedures to protect low-income tenants from being evicted and to provide a fair market return of 8 percent on the owners' investment.

HUD would be required to offer incentives to owners to continue renting to low-income families or to people who bought the property and promised to continue the affordable rents.

Owners would be allowed to receive the fair market value for their property, which would then have to be used for low-income tenants until the building was no longer livable. In limited circumstances, owners could pay off their mortgages and continue to own the property. *(Provisions: Preservation of affordable rental housing, p. 652)*

BACKGROUND

The prepayment dispute pitted owners' rights against tenants' needs and set congressional liberals against conservatives and the Bush administration. *(Background, 1989 Almanac, p. 656)*

The mortgages stemmed from the government's decision beginning in 1961 to entice private entrepreneurs and nonprofit developers to build housing for low-income tenants by offering mortgage insurance and interest-rate subsidies in return for a commitment to keep the housing available for low-income persons for the life of the mortgage, usually 40 years.

As an additional incentive, the government promised that owners could prepay the mortgages after 20 years. By the 1980s, prepayment offered a financial opportunity to the landlords to convert their properties to more lucrative uses — and thus threatened the tenants' interests and the government's goal.

Congress responded with provisions in the 1987 omnibus housing act that came to be viewed as an effective moratorium on prepayments. A provision set to expire in 1990 forbade prepayments unless owners could prove that their tenants' "economic hardship" would not be increased and that any shortage of low-rent housing in the area would not be exacerbated.

Kemp's Proposal

With the moratorium due to expire, the Bush administration and the housing committees in both chambers turned in 1990 to crafting a solution that could protect tenants as well as landlords without undue cost to the federal government. The solution would also have to pass muster in the courts — which had started to review with skepticism regulations limiting property owners' rights.

In unveiling Project HOPE, his omnibus housing initiative, on March 13, HUD Secretary Jack F. Kemp proposed lifting the moratorium, but softening the blow somewhat to low-income tenants by shielding them from sudden rent increases.

Under Title II of Project HOPE, building owners would have to file notice of whether they intended to prepay their mortgages.

If so, tenants would be given a two-year right of first refusal to purchase their building with grants from HUD.

Furthermore, if owners decided to prepay a mortgage and tenants did not buy the building, the owners would have to underwrite moving expenses, security deposits and the cost of six months' housing for each tenant.

HUD could approve a building owner's prepayment plan only if the agency had enough money to provide rent-assistance vouchers or certificates to tenants who had to move.

Nancy Pelosi, D-Calif., and Joseph P. Kennedy II, D-Mass., criticized Kemp's plan on mortgage prepayments. Both represented areas (in San Francisco and Boston) with shortages of low-cost rental housing.

Pelosi told Kemp that the option allowing owners to prepay if they underwrote six months' rent and moving expenses for tenants should be called "Happy Days Are Here Again for Developers." In a tight housing market like her district, Pelosi said, "they would jump for joy" at the plan.

ACTION IN CONGRESS

The House and Senate both included prepayment restrictions in their versions of the omnibus housing legislation being worked on during the summer, but the plans differed sharply. The Senate's version favored tenants, while the House's leaned toward landlords.

Senate Provisions

Prepayment did not emerge as a contentious issue in the Senate. Alan Cranston, D-Calif., chairman of the Banking Subcommittee on Housing and Urban Affairs, had the votes in his panel for his plan, which would have made it very difficult for landlords to prepay and essentially would have protected tenants.

The Senate version of the housing bill, approved by Cranston's committee May 2 and on the floor June 27, would have allowed owners to prepay their mortgages only if they informed HUD 18 months in advance and the secretary approved a plan of action for the project and its tenants.

If owners decided to continue renting to low-income tenants, they could take advantage of incentives giving them an annual return of 8 percent on their equity in the housing. In addition, some rents could be increased, and owners could finance capital improvements to their buildings through HUD loans.

Under the specifics of Cranston's plan:

- Owners of eligible low-income housing would have been allowed to prepay their mortgages only according to a plan approved by the HUD secretary. The bill would have authorized $412.5 million in fiscal 1991 for assistance and incentives to deter prepayment.
- Owners who wanted to prepay their mortgages and stop renting to low-income families or wanted to sell the housing would have been required to file a notice of intent with the HUD secretary. The owner also would have been required to notify appropriate state or local government officials and to advise the tenants.
- The HUD secretary would have been required to provide owners with information to prepare a plan of action.

The secretary would have been required to provide the information within six months of receiving an owner's notice of intent.

That information would have to include a notice of the housing's preservation value, which equaled the appraised fair market value of the housing as rental housing minus costs that would have been incurred for conversion to market rate housing.

In addition, the information would have to include authorized federal incentives to maintain the property for low-income tenants.

The secretary would have been required to provide the same information to the building's tenants.

The owner would have been required to return a plan of action to the secretary, tenants and state or local government officials within six months of receiving the information from the secretary.

Owners who failed to turn in a plan of action in six months would have to wait another six months to file a notice of intent.

The HUD secretary would have been allowed to approve plans to pay off the mortgage and stop renting to low-income tenants if the secretary found the following:

- That the action would not "materially" increase economic hardship for current tenants.
- And that the supply of vacant, comparable housing was sufficient and prepayment would not affect the availability of that housing.

The Senate plan also would have required the HUD secretary to offer owners incentives that would provide an annual return equal to 8 percent of the owner's equity in the housing in order to persuade them not to pay off their mortgages, including an increase in the rents permitted under existing Section 8 rental assistance contracts and financing of capital improvements.

The plan would have required a right of first offer to buy the housing to "priority purchasers," such as resident councils, nonprofit organizations and state and local agencies.

It also would have required the HUD secretary to provide potential buyers with information on the types of assistance available to new owners.

It would have given buyers nine months from receiving the information from the secretary to negotiate the sale with the existing owners.

Residents in at least 50 percent of the housing units would have to support the sale for the secretary to approve it.

The plan would have required the secretary to provide money to pay for training for a resident council, home ownership counseling, fees for the nonprofit agency or public agency working with the resident council and the cost of relocating tenants who wanted to move when residents purchased their building.

The Cranston plan would have required the HUD secretary, before approving a plan that used federal incentives to ensure owners continued renting to low-income tenants, to find:

- The incentives were the least costly alternative in preserving low-income housing.
- The housing would be rented to very-low-, low- and moderate-income families.
- Enough money would be spent to maintain and operate the housing.
- Existing tenants would not be involuntarily displaced.
- And any increase in rent would not exceed 30 percent of the tenant's income.

House Committee Action

Landlords had been relying on Rep. Steve Bartlett, R-Texas, who knew the issue well, to carry the prepayment issue for them in the House and in conference.

By the time the House Banking Committee approved its version of the housing bill (HR 1180) on June 13, Bartlett had spent days huddling with Massachusetts Democrats Kennedy and Barney Frank, trying in vain to work out a compromise House proposal.

"What the committee did in '87 was dead wrong," Bartlett said of the moratorium. He passionately called for the government to honor its contracts with building owners, using incentives to encourage them to continue renting to low-income tenants rather than requiring them to do so.

But Frank and other members from low-vacancy, high-cost areas, such as Boston, were equally passionate. Both sides spent months talking to special-interest groups and negotiating with each other and with the administration — to no avail.

In the markup, Bartlett scored a coup. His amendment, backed by building owners and the housing industry, was adopted, 29-19, after a lengthy debate with Frank, whose alternative proposal went nowhere despite support by committee Chairman Henry B. Gonzalez, D-Texas.

Nine Democrats joined the committee's 20 Republicans in support of Bartlett's plan, which sought to provide incentives to building owners to continue renting to low-income families for the full 40 years of their mortgages rather than paying off the loans at the 20-year mark.

Joining GOP members in supporting the amendment were Democrats Stephen L. Neal, N.C.; Carroll Hubbard Jr., Ky.; Doug Barnard Jr., Ga.; Ben Erdreich, Ala.; Thomas R. Carper, Del.; Gerald D. Kleczka, Wis.; Liz J. Patterson, S.C.; David E. Price, N.C.; and Peter Hoagland, Neb.

The key difference between the two proposals was that owners could prepay their mortgages for any reason under the Bartlett plan, but Frank's amendment would have made the existing moratorium permanent, allowing owners to prepay in only limited cases.

In addition, the Frank plan would have required owners to continue renting to low- and moderate-income families for the remaining "useful life of the property," rather than for the remainder of the mortgage, as under the Bartlett plan.

Bartlett argued that the government had a moral obligation to honor its contracts with building owners. If it did not, he said, people would not be interested in doing business with the government in the future.

Tenants' advocates said the lawmakers' decision cast a cloud over the bill. "The Bartlett proposal in fact plays Russian roulette, and the gun is being held to the tenants' heads," said Barry Zigas, president of the National Low Income Housing Coalition.

Bartlett, however, said, "We protected both the tenants' and the owners' rights." And Frank said that while he was disappointed that Bartlett's proposal won, "it's not a disaster. It will protect a majority of the tenants."

Details of Bartlett Plan

At the annual meeting of the National Leased Housing Association on June 14, Bartlett conceded to the owners that under his plan the issue would return to haunt Congress. He told them that it was a problem he would have to address.

The plan would require owners to file a notice with HUD two years before they intended to prepay their mortgages. In low-vacancy areas, tenants could stay in their units at existing rents for three more years. Displaced tenants would receive rental vouchers or certificates.

If owners decided to sell their buildings during the two-year notice period, they would have to do so to a nonprofit or other group that agreed to maintain the property for low-income tenants. Grant assistance would also be provided to help tenants' groups buy their housing projects.

Incentives to keep the owners renting to low-income tenants included increased rents, project-based Section 8 rental assistance to all tenants earning below 80 percent of the area median income, financing of capital improvements under HUD's Section 201 program, and equity take-out loans insured by the FHA.

To help displaced tenants, the plan would have authorized $250 million in fiscal 1991 and $250 million in fiscal 1992.

An amendment by Price and Carper, agreed to by voice vote, would have required owners to pay at least 50 percent of a tenant's moving expenses. And it would have authorized $200 million in fiscal 1991 for HUD to provide grants to nonprofit organizations purchasing housing.

House Floor Action

During House floor action on the housing bill July 31, four Democrats who had backed Bartlett's proposal in committee — Carper, Price, Hoagland and Patterson — proposed an amendment to build on that plan. Their amendment — adopted by an overwhelming vote of 400-12 — offered new incentives and requirements to persuade owners to continue renting to low-income families. *(Vote 292, p. 96-H)*

Under the plan, owners would have to give tenants and HUD a two-year notice that they planned to pay off the mortgage. HUD then would appraise the property and offer incentives to the owner to stay in the program. If the owner still wanted to pay off the mortgage, then any group willing to buy the property and maintain it for low-income tenants would have a right of first refusal. The owner would be required to sell to the group if it offered to pay the appraised value set by HUD.

If no one offered to buy the property, the owner could pay off the mortgage and do whatever he wanted with the building.

In areas with very low vacancy rates, owners would have to give tenants an additional three years' notice on top of the two years to find a new place to live. The owner would be required to pay up to half of the tenants' moving expenses, and tenants would receive Section 8 rent-subsidy certificates or vouchers to pay for their next home.

The Carper-Price plan was supported by building owners who did not want to be forced to continue renting to low-income families. Tenant advocacy groups, such as the National Low Income Housing Coalition, opposed the plan, saying it gave too much to landlords.

"Members were torn," Carper said. "On the one hand, they don't feel comfortable in reneging on contracts. On the other hand, they don't want to throw tenants out in the cold."

Kennedy and others argued that the plan was too lenient and should not allow owners to leave the program at all. When Bartlett said the plan would guarantee every tenant the right to receive rental assistance, Kennedy shot back: "That is a complete crock of baloney, and the gentleman from Texas knows it. The reality is that you are going to throw those people out on the street. I do not care what that piece of paper says."

After seeing the overwhelming support for the Carper-Price plan, Frank withdrew an amendment he had planned to offer that would have required owners to continue renting to low-income tenants if the government offered incentives equaling an 8 percent return on the owners' equity. But the Frank plan remained a live option in House-Senate conference as a midpoint between the House's pro-landlord plan and the Senate's pro-tenant plan.

FINAL ACTION

The House and Senate plans had to be reconciled in conference. But first Congress had to give itself more time on the issue by extending the Sept. 30 deadline on the moratorium.

One-Month Extension

The Senate on Sept. 27 passed a bill (HR 5558) to extend the moratorium for a month, but only after criticism from William L. Armstrong, R-Colo., who said he was concerned that conferees would favor tenants over landlords.

In addition, the extension bill was complicated by an amendment by Larry Pressler, R-S.D., adopted by voice vote, that would have required Congress to take a pay cut if automatic spending cuts kicked in for federal civil servants. *(Pay issue, p. 73)*

The Senate asked for a conference with the House. But the House instead passed an identical bill (HR 5747) without the Pressler amendment. The Senate approved HR 5747 by voice vote Sept. 28. That bill went to President Bush, who signed it Oct. 1.

Conference

Mortgage prepayment was one of a handful of controversies delaying conferees' agreement on the big housing bill in October.

The House and Senate came at the tough issue from diametrically opposite positions. The Senate's pro-tenant approach would have essentially continued the moratorium, while the House would have allowed many owners to pay off the mortgage and get out of the program.

Frank, an advocate for the tenants, said the Senate's approach would have caused too many lawsuits from owners. With a conservative majority on the Supreme Court, he said, they were likely to win. But the House plan, he said, was likely to have caused too many evictions.

Talks moved from the table to the hallway to side rooms and back again as the House and Senate positions inched closer together.

On Oct. 11, Kemp arrived on Capitol Hill to accelerate the conference negotiations on the overall bill. By then, however, an agreement had been reached outside the conference room.

Most important to tenants' groups, the deal would be through the "useful life of the property," rather than through the 40-year contract. Conferees gave their final approval of the plan Oct. 12.

Under the compromise, worked out between Frank, Bartlett and Cranston's staff, owners would be compensated at fair market values in exchange for preserving the housing for low-income tenants for the remaining useful life of the property. In some cases, the owners could still pay off their loans if the community had high vacancy rates for affordable housing.

Both sides agreed that the solution was likely to withstand court challenges.

The plan would also allow owners to sell their properties to residents or nonprofit groups committed to maintaining the buildings for low-income families.

Though conferees approved the compromise, OMB and HUD officials worried that it would cost too much.

Even after the conference ended Oct. 15, members worked to cut costs. The plan was estimated to cost $30 billion over 20 years. The administration complained that it was $4 billion too high.

Armstrong, who had previously threatened to stop the housing bill if the prepayment question was not resolved fairly for the owners, acceded in the end. The conferees' plan, he said, "sounds to me, if not absolutely completely fair, it's close to fair."

On the House floor Oct. 25, Gonzalez said the conferees had come to "an acceptable solution of the difficult issue." Banking Committee ranking Republican Chalmers P. Wylie, Ohio, was more upbeat. He called the accord a "permanent solution" to the issue and depicted the provisions giving tenants' groups right of first refusal as in line with "the administration's goal of empowerment of low-income [families]."

The House adopted the conference report by voice vote; the Senate followed on Oct. 27 with a 93-6 vote that cleared the measure for the president. *(Vote 325, p. 63-S)*

Bush Statement

In signing the bill Nov. 28, Bush said he was pleased that the prepayment provisions protected project residents while honoring the government's contracts with the owners and crafting alternative prepayment strategies that emphasized home-ownership opportunities.

Bush noted his concern, however, that the incentives for landlords to keep their properties in use for low-income tenants were "more generous than are necessary, providing excessive benefits over the long term that will be paid by all taxpayers."

But he said he recognized that the proposal was a compromise and represented "a good-faith effort" by Congress to meet the administration's fiscal concerns. ■

McKinney Homeless Act Reauthorized

Congress cleared on Oct. 26 a reauthorization of the Stewart B. McKinney Homeless Assistance Act, the principal source of federal aid for the homeless, even though similar provisions were included in the larger 1990 bill that overhauled federal housing programs.

The Senate cleared the measure after the House had adopted the conference report earlier that day. President Bush signed the measure (HR 3789 — PL 101-645) on Nov. 29.

The law, enacted in 1987, authorized grants to local governments to provide emergency food and shelter to the homeless, develop transitional housing to help homeless people move toward permanent homes and convert federal surplus property to shelter the homeless.

The 1990 bill included an initiative by Sen. Pete V. Domenici, R-N.M., to expand services for homeless people who were mentally ill or substance abusers. It authorized $75 million in grants in fiscal 1991 to underwrite screening and diagnostic services, rehabilitation, mental health counseling, and alcohol and drug treatment.

Altogether, the legislation authorized $937 million in fiscal 1991 and $941 million in fiscal 1992.

The original act (PL 100-77) provided shelter, health programs, job training and food for the homeless. The measure was named for Rep. Stewart B. McKinney, R-Conn. (1971-87), who died several months before the law was enacted.

President Ronald Reagan signed the bill into law despite reservations that the measure was costly and contained "duplicative programs." *(1987 Almanac, p. 506)*

The 1988 reauthorization of the act had only token opposition. The bill received a great boost when then-Vice President Bush, in his Sept. 25 presidential debate with Democratic rival Michael S. Dukakis, broke with the Reagan administration by saying he supported "fully funding" the McKinney Act. *(1988 Almanac, p. 371)*

Committee Action

The House Banking, Finance and Urban Affairs Committee on June 13 approved its version of legislation (HR 1180) to overhaul federal housing programs. At that time, the committee duplicated the bill's provisions to help the homeless under the McKinney Act, reporting them out separately in HR 3789 (H Rept 101-583, Part I).

The precaution was taken in case the omnibus housing bill bogged down. The McKinney Act had become a very popular program that few members opposed. *(Housing bill, p. 631)*

The House Energy and Commerce Committee approved June 27 the health care for the homeless provisions of HR 3789 (H Rept 101-583, Part II).

The measure was adopted over Republican objections that the funding levels in the bill were too high. The bill would have authorized $289.4 million over three years as well as $33 million in fiscal 1992 for a block grant to provide community mental health services. The Subcommittee on Health and the Environment had approved the bill on June 20.

The Senate Labor and Human Resources Committee then approved its reauthorization of the McKinney Act (S 2863 — S Rept 101-436) on July 18 by a vote of 16-0. That version sought to extend all programs under the McKinney Act for three years. For fiscal 1991, the measure would have authorized $253 million, including:

- $69 million to expand and improve the Health Care for the Homeless program.
- $28.5 million to continue demonstration grants dealing with substance abuse and mental health.
- $50 million for the Emergency Community Services program for the homeless.
- $15 million for job training.
- $50 million for educational and special services for homeless children.
- $25 million for a new demonstration program to provide grants to prevent separation of children from their families and to prevent abuse and neglect of those children.

Chamber Action

The Senate passed S 2863 on Sept. 26 by voice vote and the House gave voice vote approval to HR 3789 on Oct. 10, after little debate and over no opposition. The Senate passed an amended version of HR 3789 on Oct. 12 by voice vote and requested a conference with the House.

Before those October votes, though, conferees on the major housing bill had already agreed to reauthorize the McKinney Act programs for two more years, even as the separate measures were still being considered in each chamber. By Oct. 5, negotiators had agreed on the homeless provisions, even as they bogged down on several issues, sending staff members back to work them out.

Negotiators had little trouble producing an acceptable conference report on the politically sacrosanct McKinney Act.

Both chambers then quickly adopted the conference report (H Rept 101-951) on Oct. 26, shortly before the 101st Congress adjourned. ■

HUD Scandal Investigation Continues

Nearly two years after President Ronald Reagan left office, a special prosecutor was still investigating alleged influence-peddling at the Department of Housing and Urban Development (HUD) during his administration.

Arlin M. Adams was appointed in March to investigate whether former HUD Secretary Samuel R. Pierce Jr. and other HUD officials conspired to defraud the United States or committed any other federal crimes during the Reagan administration.

The investigation was originally limited to crimes within the Section 8 moderate rehabilitation program, designed to make relatively small repairs on government-assisted housing.

But the investigation was expanded to scrutinize the special projects, technical assistance and Urban Development Action Grant (UDAG) programs as a result of testimony by former HUD official DuBois L. Gilliam to the House Government Operations Subcommittee on Employment and Housing.

By midsummer, the subcommittee, led by Tom Lantos, D-Calif., had concluded 27 hearings on the scandals and influence-peddling.

Subcommittee members sent Adams a letter July 24 requesting that he expand his investigation into the coinsurance mortgage program and possible perjury by Pierce. Pierce testified under oath on May 25, 1989, that he did not get involved in selecting grant recipients.

In a prepared statement, Adams called the 27-page letter "thoughtful" and said he would review it "promptly and thoroughly" before making a recommendation to Attorney General Dick Thornburgh. Under the law, the attorney general was responsible for making any requests to expand the investigation to a special three-judge panel. The panel's request to broaden the investigation was still pending at the end of 1990.

In their letter, the five Democrats and three Republicans said it "defies logic" that without Pierce's urging, his assistant, Deborah Gore Dean, would have helped lawyers in Pierce's former law firm — Battle, Fowler, Jaffin and Kheel — to the extent that she did.

The letter said the New York firm sought out Pierce to meet with a client, to discuss a UDAG application, to receive rental rehabilitation vouchers and to obtain Section 8 mod-rehab units. The members asked Adams to probe whether Pierce and others violated federal bribery, conspiracy and conflict of interest laws.

Pierce's attorney, Paul L. Perito, said, "There is nothing new, different or truly worthy of attention" in the panel's letter. "I believe that it appears to be a rehash of stale allegations or the stacking of faulty conclusions based upon surmise, innuendo or conjecture, but not upon hard testimonial evidence."

A 271-page report released Nov. 1 by the panel concluded that Pierce had directed federal grants to political friends and later misled Congress about his involvement. "At best, Secretary Pierce was less than honest and misled the subcommittee," the report said. "At worst, Secretary Pierce knowingly lied and committed perjury during his testimony."

Perito criticized the panel's final report, calling it "a rehash of stale and unfounded allegations."

By year's end, Adams' investigation was continuing, with no indication of whether or when indictments would be handed up.

Background

The biggest scandal to rock the federal government since the Iran-contra affair of 1986-87 unfolded on Capitol Hill during 1989, as lawmakers investigated influence-peddling and political favoritism at the Reagan-era HUD.

Beginning in April 1989 with the release of a critical report by HUD's inspector general, the congressional probe of the HUD scandal lasted through the year and included some 18 hearings with testimony from 39 witnesses before three different committees.

Responding to the months of revelations, Congress on Nov. 22, 1989, cleared legislation (PL 101-235) designed to clean up the mess. The legislation subjected HUD's management to a great deal more scrutiny, limited its discretion, threatened violators with big penalties and curtailed private firms' ability to make huge profits from HUD.

Before the end of 1990, the Justice Department was also preparing to request appointment of an independent counsel to investigate the activities of Pierce, Reagan's longest-serving Cabinet member. *(HUD scandal, 1989 Almanac, p. 639; HUD reform, p. 631; Pierce, p. 636)*

PIERCE INVESTIGATED

Thornburgh on Feb. 1 sought appointment of an independent counsel to investigate charges of criminal fraud against Pierce and other Reagan-era HUD officials.

Thornburgh waited until late Feb. 1 — his 60-day deadline — before asking a panel of the U.S. Court of Appeals for the District of Columbia Circuit to select a special prosecutor. Members of the House Judiciary Committee on Nov. 2, 1989, had demanded that Thornburgh seek an independent prosecutor to investigate possible criminal conduct by Pierce and other HUD officials implicated in alleged influence-peddling and other wrongdoing at the department.

"At this point, Secretary Pierce is presumed innocent," said Rep. Charles E. Schumer, D-N.Y., chairman of the Subcommittee on Criminal Justice. "But because of the attorney general's action, the American people can rest assured we will get to the bottom of the mess at HUD."

Thornburgh asked that an independent counsel investigate allegations that Pierce and others engaged in a conspiracy to defraud the U.S. government through HUD's mod-rehab program. But he said the evidence did not warrant investigating Pierce for perjury, as the Judiciary Committee had asked.

Thornburgh said "voluminous information" compiled by HUD's inspector general and by the House Government Operations Subcommittee on Employment and Housing forced him to conclude that an investigation should be conducted.

"Under the terms of the Independent Counsel Act, I have very little latitude in making this determination," Thornburgh wrote in his recommendation to the court. "I must apply to the court for appointment of an independent counsel unless I can determine that there are no reasonable grounds to believe that further investigation is warranted."

Pierce's attorney at the time, Robert Plotkin, said

Pierce was "disappointed, but not totally shocked or surprised." Plotkin said Thornburgh's refusal to ask for an investigation into the perjury charges was significant. "We're pleased that the perjury charges have been thrown out, and I think that reflects that he hasn't done anything wrong."

A three-judge panel on March 2 chose Adams, a member of the 3rd U.S. Circuit Court of Appeals from 1969 to 1986, as independent counsel in the case.

Former Aide Testifies

A former Pierce aide told a House subcommittee during three days of testimony the week of April 30 that Pierce funded housing and community development projects based on personal relationships and political favoritism.

The testimony by Gilliam, who served under Pierce as deputy assistant secretary for program policy development and evaluation, directly contradicted Pierce's sworn statements from 1989 that he did not make decisions on who got HUD grants. Both men appeared before Lantos' Government Operations subcommittee.

"I know for a fact that the secretary made decisions," said Gilliam, who was serving an 18-month prison sentence for taking bribes during his HUD tenure from 1984 to 1987. Gilliam said he received about $100,000 in gifts, trips and money from developers and consultants while at HUD.

During the first of three days of testimony, Gilliam called HUD "a domestic political machine," saying, "If you were well-connected in political circles, then your applications were given strong, favorable consideration."

While at HUD, Gilliam was responsible for overseeing the UDAG program and the secretary's discretionary fund. Action grants were intended to boost development in blighted areas.

Gilliam said Pierce asked him to provide a grant to a project at Hampton University, a predominantly black college in Virginia, before the school had even filled out an application or lined up financing.

And Gilliam said that when Lance Wilson, Pierce's former executive assistant, applied for a grant with a developer for a project in Belle Glade, Fla., the secretary dropped the cutoff line for funding projects in order to include Belle Glade, which had not qualified. In March 1987 HUD awarded the project a $5.6 million grant.

Gilliam said he, Pierce and Dean, Pierce's executive assistant, decided to transfer David Sowell, a career HUD official who became suspicious of the arrangement. He said they feared Sowell would call HUD's inspector general, who might investigate the deal. Ultimately, Sowell was placed in Gilliam's office, where Gilliam "kept him traveling."

Lantos said, "What you are telling us under oath, Mr. Gilliam, is that ... when you advised the secretary of Housing and Urban Development that an honest HUD career employee was about to blow the whistle on another scandal, the secretary wanted him physically transferred out of Washington so he would not be able to detect similar fraudulent schemes?"

Gilliam said that was the case.

Pierce not only ordered that certain projects receive funding, he also told Gilliam not to fund a project in San Antonio, Texas, the district of Democrat Henry B. Gonzalez, chairman of the House Banking Committee and its Subcommittee on Housing and Community Development.

Pierce had long held a grudge against Gonzalez, said Gilliam, because the representative had once called the HUD secretary a "Stepin Fetchit" for the Reagan administration.

Other Testimony, Action

In his third appearance before the subcommittee, former Assistant Secretary for Housing Thomas T. Demery on May 23 told of a meeting in which Pierce wanted to know "who was behind" each request for Section 8 mod-rehab grants.

Demery said that during his first couple of months on the job, Dean would hand him scraps of paper listing various public housing authorities, saying, "The secretary wants these requests funded."

After he had insisted on meeting with Pierce in January 1987, Demery said, Pierce told him he wanted to know which consultants and lawyers were behind each request. "At that time, I realized that political considerations were to be a factor in the award of mod-rehab units as viewed by Secretary Pierce," Demery said.

In a letter released May 29, Thornburgh asked Adams to broaden his inquiry beyond allegations of wrongdoing in the mod-rehab program. Thornburgh wrote to Adams, calling his attention to testimony by Gilliam before the subcommittee regarding the UDAG program and the secretary's discretionary fund. That testimony, he said, was "related to allegations you are already investigating."

HUD INVESTIGATED

While much of the focus of the HUD investigations in 1989 and 1990 focused on Pierce, other officials also came under scrutiny. Critical reports and views also came from independent sources during the year that offered further damaging testimony about Pierce's tenure as secretary and the troubled status of the housing agency.

Congressional Investigation

California businessman A. Bruce Rozet appeared before the House Banking Subcommittee on Housing and Community Development on Feb. 27 to answer questions about his operation of nearly 45,000 units of subsidized housing. Rozet was temporarily barred Jan. 26 from taking on any new federally subsidized projects after Kemp expressed dismay at the condition of some of his companies' projects.

At the hearing, Chairman Gonzalez said he was concerned not only about Rozet's business practices, but also about HUD's policies, procedures and monitoring.

Rozet, a major Democratic fundraiser, was the second-largest owner and operator of government-subsidized housing projects through his company, Associated Financial Corp., and its subsidiaries.

In barring Rozet and his companies from taking on any new HUD projects, Kemp said Feb. 1 that he wanted to know "why, after very significant economic benefits to the ownership and management, tenants are still required to live like rats?"

At the hearing, however, Rozet went on the attack, accusing HUD of ignoring his companies' pleas during the Reagan years for help in cleaning up several drug-infested and deteriorating projects that they managed. Perhaps, Rozet suggested, he would not be sitting before the committee had he retained Republican consultants.

Upon hearing of Rozet's remarks, HUD Under Secretary Alfred DelliBovi said: "His public relations firm wrote a good statement. But I think they neglected the fact that Mr. Rozet made huge amounts of money making tax shelters and did not plow any of those obscene profits back into the projects."

Meanwhile, in the Senate, also on Feb. 27, a special Banking Committee panel headed by Bob Graham, D-Fla., began looking into "the anatomy of a deal," or how two redevelopment projects in the now-suspended Section 8 mod-rehab program came to fruition.

With the HUD reform bill long gone and a major housing reauthorization looming, some in Congress wondered what the point was of new hearings. Those responsible for continuing the hearings insisted they were serving a useful purpose.

"They don't seem to me to be leading anywhere," said Rep. Steve Bartlett, R-Texas, who skipped the Rozet hearing in favor of another. Bartlett said he did not expect any new reform legislation to grow out of the hearings.

Lantos disagreed, maintaining that the committee had found "extremely important and new and relevant information" and that "some additional arenas will need to be addressed in future legislation."

Critical Report

A report highly critical of the ethics program at HUD, released in mid-March, also placed the blame for that program's failure squarely on Pierce.

The study of financial disclosure forms for HUD officials and experts or consultants hired by HUD was conducted by the General Accounting Office (GAO) at the request of a Senate Governmental Affairs subcommittee. It found that:

- Of 62 consultants hired from 1986 to 1989, no disclosure statements were filed for 52.
- Of 111 HUD employees required to file a public disclosure statement by May 15, 1989, 44 percent missed the deadline.
- Of the statements filed on time, none had been reviewed more than 100 days later. The Ethics in Government Act required the statements to be reviewed and approved within 60 days of filing.

The report was the third such critical analysis since 1982. In 1986, a scathing review by the Office of Government Ethics concluded, "HUD's ethics program is one of the most ill-managed this team has ever seen in a major department." Furthermore, the 1986 report said, little had been done "to save what appears to be a deteriorating program" since a similar review in 1982.

The 1990 report concluded that "the fact that the problems we are reporting existed for so long demonstrates to us that the HUD secretary did not hold the [designated agency ethics official] and his alternate sufficiently accountable for developing and administering an effective financial disclosure system."

And without that system, "HUD was not in a position to address actual or potential conflicts of interest," the report said.

Although GAO found that some of the lapses continued under Kemp, the new HUD secretary said in a letter to the comptroller general that "under my leadership, ethical conduct is the only way of 'doing business' at, or with, HUD." He cited a number of changes he had made to prevent such problems from recurring, including creating a special office to improve HUD's ethics program.

Critical Testimony

Despite the intense scrutiny Congress gave since 1989 to fraud and abuse at HUD, it generally failed in its oversight of the agency, the current and former HUD inspectors general told a special Senate panel May 8.

Paul A. Adams, HUD's inspector general since 1985, told the Senate Banking Subcommittee on HUD Investigations that his office wrote reports at least twice a year that frequently went unread by Congress.

"Congress, when it enacts legislation and mandates reporting requirements, should at a minimum read the reports and provide some oversight," Adams said. "Without such oversight, there is no accountability or follow-up. Without oversight, report preparation becomes a staff-intensive paperwork exercise that benefits no one."

It was an Adams report that precipitated the congressional investigation into mismanagement and political influence-peddling at HUD.

Charles L. Dempsey, who served in 1978-85 and was HUD's first inspector general, echoed Adams' view. When asked whether members of Congress or their staffs had ever called him about the agency, he replied, "Never, sir. I never received so much as a phone call."

Dempsey said his office investigated HUD's under secretary, assistant secretary and deputy assistant secretary and three regional administrators. All eventually left the department. ■

Chapter 10

DEFENSE

National Defense Authorization Act 671
  Cheney Defense Programs 673
  Pentagon Pay Deadlock 676
  Staten Island Home Port 681
  Defense Act Provisions 684
B-2 'Stealth' Bomber 687
Strategic Defense Initiative 691
Base Closings Commission 693
National Guard Ruling 694
Reserves Call-Up for Persian Gulf Crisis 695
Conventional Forces in Europe Treaty 696
  CFE Limits 697
Strategic Arms Reduction Treaty 704
  Bush-Gorbachev Statement on START 708
U.S.-Soviet Chemical Weapons 709
Nuclear Testing Limits Treaties 711

Congress Cuts Bush Defense Request

Measure trims SDI, troop levels; spares B-2

BOXSCORE

Legislation: National Defense Authorization Act, PL 101-510 (HR 4739, S 2884).

Major action: Signed, Nov. 5. Conference report adopted by Senate, 80-17, Oct. 26; by House, 271-156, Oct. 24. Passed by House, 256-155, Sept. 19; by Senate, 79-16, Aug. 4.

Reports: Conference report (H Rept 101-923); Armed Services (H Rept 101-665); Armed Services (S Rept 101-384).

Facing a budget crunch and remarkable changes abroad, Congress authorized $288.3 billion in defense spending for fiscal 1991 — $14 billion less than the previous year and $18 billion less than President Bush had requested.

The annual defense bill (HR 4739), which also cut and sought to refocus the strategic defense initiative (SDI), cleared the Senate on Oct. 26. Despite some reservations, Bush signed the bill Nov. 5 (PL 101-510).

From the beginning of debate over the measure, the federal deficit created dollars-and-cents pressures to hold down defense spending. At the same time, the warming of U.S.-Soviet relations and the crumbling of communist regimes in Eastern Europe added a strategic rationale for ending the massive defense buildup that had been a centerpiece of the Reagan administration.

The bill represented a tightening of defense authorizations from the $302.9 billion approved a year earlier for fiscal 1990. *(1989 Almanac, p. 436)*

For fiscal 1991, Bush initially proposed a $307 billion authorization bill, which represented a 2 percent decline in purchasing power, after inflation. There was considerable sentiment in Congress to cut more deeply.

The defense authorization bill (S 2884) passed by the Senate on Aug. 4 trimmed $18 billion from Bush's request. In the same week, the House Armed Services Committee completed work on a bill (HR 4739) reducing Bush's request by $24 billion. As lawmakers left Washington for their August recess, the conventional wisdom was that the deeper cuts sought by the House would prevail.

Iraq Changes Equation

The political calculus changed abruptly on Aug. 2, however, when Iraq invaded neighboring Kuwait. In the weeks that followed, Bush authorized a massive mobilization of U.S. forces to the Persian Gulf to defend Saudi Arabia and confront Iraq's President Saddam Hussein. *(Gulf crisis, p. 717)*

Although U.S. allies, including Saudi Arabia and Kuwait's ousted rulers, were expected to foot much of the direct cost of the gulf deployment, Saddam's aggression was cited as a vivid example of the enduring threats to world peace that would justify a robust defense in the aftermath of the Cold War.

"These are the threats we face today, and they [will] profoundly shape our defense tomorrow when we are no longer completely preoccupied with the Soviet Union," House Armed Services Committee Chairman Les Aspin, D-Wis., said in September.

Although leaders of the Armed Services committees boasted that the authorization bill began the reshaping of U.S. defenses for the post-Cold War era, Congress finessed many of the hard choices.

The Armed Services conferees constrained development of some of the more costly weapons systems but stopped short of eliminating any of them. For the second straight year, for example, Congress rejected Defense Secretary Dick Cheney's efforts to terminate work on the V-22 Osprey, a hybrid airplane/helicopter sought by the Marine Corps as a troop transport.

The authorization measure provided $2.89 billion of Bush's $4.69 billion request for SDI and set the stage for battles over plans to deploy a first-phase antimissile defense, of limited effectiveness, by the end of the decade. *(SDI, p. 691)*

Members hammering out the defense authorization bill simply sidestepped the conflict over the future of the B-2 "stealth" bomber. They approved $2.3 billion for B-2 procurement but were deliberately vague about whether the funds could be spent only to pay cost-overruns on the 15 bombers previously authorized (as House members asserted) or could be used to buy additional B-2s (as senators maintained). *(Stealth bomber, p. 687)*

The final version of the measure provided for a cut of 80,000 military personnel, from the 2,076,405 authorized for fiscal 1990. Cheney had warned that he would recommend a veto of the authorization measure if it came to the president's desk with the 100,000-person cut initially accepted by House-Senate conferees. *(Provisions, p. 684)*

In signing the bill, Bush said it reflected "most of the administration's major defense priorities," but he voiced concern about congressional efforts to dictate restrictions on SDI and burden-sharing moves toward U.S. allies.

As usual, the defense appropriations bill (HR 5803 — PL 101-511) roughly paralleled the authorization measure in its treatment of most major issues. The spending bill, also signed by Bush on Nov. 5, provided $269 billion for fiscal 1991. *(Defense appropriations, p. 812)*

BACKGROUND

Compared with the boom defense budgets of the Reagan years, Bush's no-growth budget proposal in January was part of a significant retrenchment.

Although the defense buildup actually began during the administration of President Jimmy Carter, it was Ronald Reagan who made "peace through strength" a central slogan of his campaign for the White House and a central theme as president. Defense spending, which had totaled $160 billion in Carter's last year, rose sharply in Reagan's first term — from $200 billion for fiscal 1982 to $270 billion for fiscal 1985.

Even in his first term, though, Congress had begun to cut Reagan's defense budget requests. As budget pressures increased during Reagan's second term, the defense buildup essentially ran out of money and the Pentagon budget began declining in "real" terms after taking account for inflation. *(Congress and the Nation Vol. VI, p. 273)*

Before leaving office in January 1989, Reagan sent Congress an overall defense budget for fiscal 1990 that called for $315.2 billion, a 2 percent increase in constant dollars over the fiscal 1989 appropriation.

But in April 1989, Bush cut an overall budget deal with congressional leaders that led to the $302.9 billion defense bill for fiscal 1990 — the fifth consecutive year of declining purchasing power for the Pentagon.

Although Bush's initial $307 billion request for fiscal 1991 would have continued the downward trend in real defense spending — after inflation was factored in — even deeper cuts were demanded on Capitol Hill.

Equally significant, there were demands for fundamental changes in defense strategy to reflect the fading of East-West tensions and the functional demise of the Soviet-led Warsaw Pact.

"Without any doubt, fundamental changes and fundamental rethinking are going to have to occur," Senate Armed Services Committee Chairman Sam Nunn, D-Ga., told Cheney at a Feb. 1 hearing on Bush's $306.9 billion defense budget proposal.

The Bush budget would have achieved much of the $22 billion in savings over the request from the prior April through personnel cuts, management reforms and cancellation of some conventional weapons programs. But it would have maintained full-scale development of big-ticket strategic programs, including the B-2 bomber, the MX missile and SDI.

This approach produced doubts not only about the price tag for the defense budget but also about the mix of weapons it would buy.

"The question that Congress faces is that, in this period of change and uncertainty in the Soviet Union, are we buying the right stuff?" said Aspin, the House Armed Services Committee chairman. "We will debate it. And some people will emphasize change, and other people will emphasize uncertainty."

The defense debate also began with raw feelings because of Cheney's announcement that he would seek to close 47 military bases, including 35 in the United States and 12 overseas. Democrats accused the Pentagon of drawing up a politically tilted "hit list" that targeted bases in their districts.

Administration officials denied that but undercut the denials by saying that liberals who demanded deeper defense cuts should start by sacrificing obsolete bases in their hometowns. "Since that list has come out, all hell has broken loose," said Aspin. *(Base closings, p. 693)*

Defending an Unfinished Product

Cheney gamely defended the administration's defense budget, but he acknowledged that it was not "a final finished product." He conceded it would be revised as the Pentagon crafted a new long-range defense plan to catch up with dramatic changes in the world. Urging Congress not to impose hasty cutbacks, Cheney added, "We're willing to cut the defense budget, but please, let's do it in an intelligent, orderly fashion."

The Defense secretary argued that the Soviet Union had not slowed its modernization of strategic weapons, despite the warm new atmosphere in U.S.-Soviet relations, and that changes wrought by Soviet President Mikhail S. Gorbachev were not yet irreversible. "There is enormous uncertainty about the likely political developments in the Soviet Union in the months and years immediately ahead," Cheney said Jan. 29.

Cheney also acknowledged that cutbacks would be warranted, even required, by terms of treaties under negotiation between the United States and the Soviet Union to reduce conventional and strategic arms. But he added, "I do believe caution is still in order until these agreements are signed, sealed and delivered."

Some members of Congress, especially conservatives, shared Cheney's sense of caution. "You don't know who is going to be in command" in the Soviet Union in the coming months or years, argued Sen. Malcolm Wallop, R-Wyo. "Gorbachev is mortal. We have to have insurance."

BUSH BUDGET

Under the president's budget, the Pentagon would have reduced active military personnel by 38,000, to just more than 2 million by the end of fiscal 1991. The Army would have taken the biggest hit, losing 17,000 active-duty military personnel. Navy forces would have fallen by 6,000 and the Air Force by 15,000.

Selected reserves would have fallen by 3,000 to 1.2 million; the Pentagon's civilian work force would have dropped by 5,000 to 1.1 million.

Long range, the Pentagon planned to reduce its work force by 300,000, including about 200,000 military personnel and 100,000 civilians.

The fiscal 1991 plan also called for a 3.5 percent pay raise for military and civilian personnel — the same requested for the entire federal government — and retaining several bonuses and incentives instituted in recent years to attract workers.

Force Structure

The administration proposed a fiscal 1991 savings of $1.7 billion and a five-year savings of $7.5 billion through changes in overall military force structure.

These included deactivating two of the Army's 18 divisions — the 9th Infantry Division at Fort Lewis, Wash., and the 2nd Armored Division at Fort Hood, Texas.

The Pentagon would also begin to retire two battleships, the USS *Iowa* and the USS *New Jersey*, and two nuclear cruisers. It would also deactivate eight attack submarines and 14 B-52 bombers.

Planned changes in the Minuteman II intercontinental ballistic missile (ICBM) also would not be made, in anticipation of a U.S.-Soviet strategic arms reduction treaty (START).

If arms control talks proved successful, Cheney said, the Pentagon's long-range plan included possibly reducing three more Army divisions and eliminating five Air Force tactical air wings.

The fiscal 1991 plan did not seek to kill any aircraft carriers, and Cheney made clear that, even with worldwide changes, the United States would want to preserve its naval superiority.

Carriers are "an important peacetime asset," he said. "Every time we get into a scrape someplace, the first thing I'm asked is, 'Where's the nearest aircraft carrier?' "

Strategic Defense

The administration proposed $4.5 billion for the Pentagon's share of the SDI antimissile research program,

Cheney Outlines Plans for Leaner Programs

Defense Secretary Dick Cheney announced Jan. 11 a series of bureaucratic steps that he said would reduce Pentagon overhead costs by $2.3 billion in fiscal 1991 and $39 billion through fiscal 1995.

Most of the changes, a part of Cheney's continuing Defense Management Review project, were aimed at streamlining the Pentagon's weapons procurement, maintenance and supply systems.

The 580,000 military and civilian personnel working on those jobs would be reduced by 16,000 in fiscal 1991 and by 42,000 by fiscal 1995, mostly by attrition.

"Our defense budgets are going to be leaner in the years ahead," Cheney said, "so every dollar we can cut from the cost of running the department is a dollar we don't have to cut out of force structure or readiness or the quality of life for our men and women in uniform."

Several of the procedural changes would have reduced the number of bureaucratic layers above the officers who managed major new weapons programs. Under the existing system, Defense Under Secretary John Betti told reporters, program managers spent an exorbitant amount of time briefing their numerous bureaucratic overseers. "They spend more time in working the system than they do in managing the program, and that's just got to be wrong," he said.

Some critics had insisted that to improve the efficiency of the weapons procurement process significantly, Cheney would have to amputate some of the military services' main administrative agencies, such as the Air Force Systems Command. But the Systems Command and similar bureaus in the other services survived in a slimmed-down form under the new system, although they would have no control over the big weapons programs.

In a statement released the same day as Cheney's announcement, House Armed Services Committee Chairman Les Aspin, D-Wis., announced that Cheney and his top aides would meet with Aspin and other senior congressional defense specialists to agree on a detailed timetable for specific improvements in the weapons purchasing system. "The Defense Management Review ... offers no blueprint for implementation," he said. "That's where reform efforts have failed in the past."

Nuts and Bolts

In addition to streamlining the management of weapons procurement, Cheney said, other changes were intended to reduce duplication and to make supply and maintenance operations more cost-effective by making more visible to the separate services the cost of alternative ways of doing business.

For example, among the changes announced Jan. 11 were the following:

- The military services would begin absorbing in their own budgets the cost of operating certain supply systems that were covered by another part of the Pentagon budget. The services also would begin absorbing the cost of certain kinds of replacement parts, which might encourage them to repair old parts rather than requisitioning new ones.
- The ratio of personnel managers to civilian employees, lower in the Defense Department than in federal government as a whole, would be increased to a ratio of 1 manager per 61 employees, thus reducing the number of civilian personnel managers. On the other hand, some military personnel assigned to administrative jobs that did not require military training would be replaced by civilians. As a rule, civilian federal employees cost less than military personnel of a comparable grade.
- Gradually, the Pentagon's $4 billion annual investment in developing new data processing systems would be used in departmentwide systems to replace the duplicative systems used by the separate services for payroll, warehouse management and accounting.
- The Navy announced a bevy of changes in its program to train some of its officers as procurement management specialists. Under the new rules, officers would specialize in procurement management earlier in their careers and would be given more formal training.

$900 million more than Congress agreed to the previous year but about the same as Bush had requested in April 1989. The fiscal 1991 budget also called for $192 million for SDI research by the Energy Department.

The Pentagon's SDI proposal continued to emphasize the so-called brilliant pebbles technology that envisioned tens of thousands of relatively small missiles orbiting the Earth, each able to destroy a Soviet ICBM in the first few minutes after its launch. Earlier SDI plans featured a more intricate network of ground- and space-based detectors and antimissile missiles.

The budget called for $280 million for an antisatellite (ASAT) weapons-development program, more than three times the prior year's request and about $125 million more than the fiscal 1990 amount.

For research on the air defense initiative, intended as an antibomber counterpart to the antimissile SDI program, the administration requested $247 million.

This was similar to the prior year's request, which Congress cut to $150 million.

As part of its $1.2 billion involvement in the war against drugs, the Pentagon requested $209 million to continue deployment of the very-long-range OTH-B radar. The radar was intended to detect bomber and air-to-surface missile attacks but could also enhance the Pentagon's drug-fighting efforts.

Strategic Offense

The administration sought $2.8 billion for the MX program that would include buying 12 missiles and rail-garrison trains on which the 10-warhead ICBM could be deployed. That included $674 million for the missiles, $1.3 billion to procure rail garrisons, including seven trains, and $548 million to continue research and development. The budget also called for $202 million to develop the smaller, single-warhead "Midgetman" ICBM.

The budget proposed $2.5 billion to buy five B-2 stealth bombers and $710 million for components to buy an unspecified number of additional bombers in the future. The previous year, Congress approved funding to buy two of the radar-evading planes in fiscal 1990 and components for the five bombers in the fiscal 1991 budget envisioned. The Pentagon also requested $1.6 billion to continue research and development of the plane.

The budget included $473 million to buy 100 advanced cruise missiles and a stealth missile with a range of more than 1,000 miles, and $157 million to continue developing a smaller bomber missile called SRAM II. It also requested $447 million to modify 24 KC-135 aircraft.

Funding of $1.4 billion was requested to procure the Navy's 18th missile-launching Trident submarine and to buy components to build the next two Trident submarines. It also included $1.3 billion to buy 52 Trident II missiles. The Trident was one of the strategic programs Cheney said the Pentagon would have to reassess if a strategic arms reduction agreement was reached with the Soviet Union.

Ground Combat

The Pentagon wanted to stop production of the Army's M-1 tank after producing 225 tanks in fiscal 1991. The proposal called for mothballing a production plant in Warren, Mich., in September 1991 and closing a plant in Lima, Ohio, in March 1993, unless the tank was sold overseas. Egypt and Saudi Arabia had planned to buy M-1s, but those deals were in doubt.

The administration projected saving $1.1 billion in fiscal 1991 and $6.2 billion through fiscal 1994 from ending the program.

Cheney cited the M-1 as an example of his strategy of shutting down older programs to concentrate on developing the "next generation" of equipment.

The administration requested $688 million to buy 600 Bradley armored troop carriers, tanklike vehicles carrying small cannon and antitank missiles in addition to infantrymen. Congress approved buying 600 carriers in fiscal 1990.

The budget proposed eliminating the Apache antitank helicopter, for a one-year savings of $682 million and a four-year savings of $2.5 billion. Congress had agreed to stop buying Apaches after fiscal 1991.

Also slated for elimination was the Army Helicopter Improvement Program (AHIP), for an estimated one-year savings of $328 million and a $1.4 billion four-year savings. Cheney proposed killing the program in fiscal 1990, but Congress approved $192 million to install the sophisticated radar-evading equipment on 36 "scout" helicopters and then to end the program in fiscal 1991.

To continue developing a small armored helicopter called the LHX, the budget requested $465 million, almost $200 million more than Congress provided in fiscal 1990. The LHX would replace the Apache and AHIP helicopters.

To buy 4,200 laser-guided Hellfire missiles, the budget requested $165 million in fiscal 1991. Another $230 million was requested for 13,946 of the smaller TOW II missiles.

The administration also proposed $77 million for the AAWS-M, which was being developed to replace the TOW. In fiscal 1990, Congress appropriated $138 million.

The administration proposed continued development of a long-range replacement for the 70-mile-range Lance nuclear-armed missile, deployed in Europe. It sought $112 million, up from $32 million in fiscal 1990. It requested $119 million more to continue developing the SRAM-T air-to-ground missile.

It also proposed increasing funding to build the ATACMS missile — designed to shower armor-piercing grenades on enemy road convoys up to 100 miles away — from $94 million in fiscal 1990 to $187 million. The funds would provide 377 such missiles.

The budget also included $233 million to continue developing a radar, called Joint STARS, that would find tank columns and guide ATACMS missiles toward them.

To buy 24,000 more 20-mile-range MLRS artillery rockets, the budget included $374 million. In fiscal 1990, Congress doubled a similar request to provide 48,000 such rockets.

The budget included $883 million for 817 long-range Patriot anti-aircraft missiles and $252 million for 7,203 short-range, shoulder-fired Stinger anti-aircraft weapons. It also requested $123 million to equip jeeps with multiple Stinger launchers.

For the ADATS, an armored anti-aircraft missile launcher to escort tank columns, the administration requested $236 million. It proposed eliminating the "non-line-of-sight missile," a short-range anti-aircraft missile, for a one-year savings of $131 million and a four-year savings of $1.2 billion.

The budget included $67 million to begin producing the Bigeye chemical bomb and $74 million to continue producing artillery shells that dispensed lethal nerve gas. Bush had promised to end production of modern "binary" chemical bombs as soon as an international treaty banning such weapons was put into effect, provided that the Soviets agreed to interim steps to slash each superpower's stockpile. *(Chemical weapons, p. xxxx)*

Tactical Air Combat

As it did in fiscal 1990, the administration proposed ending production of the F-14D carrier-based fighter for the Navy, although it included $780 million to modernize 12 older F-14As. After a considerable battle, Congress had agreed to end production of the F-14D when work on 18 new planes was finished.

The administration once again proposed ending the F-15E program after production of 36 additional aircraft, for which the budget requested $1.7 billion. The F-15E was designed to attack ground targets at night and in bad weather, and many in Congress were reluctant to end production years before the first flight of its planned replacement, the ATA aircraft.

The administration estimated savings from ending the program at $3.3 billion through fiscal 1994.

The budget request included $2.4 billion to procure 150 of the smaller F-16s, the same as fiscal 1990.

To produce 66 F/A-18 fighters, the administration requested $1.9 billion.

For 24 Harrier vertical-takeoff jets, used by the Marines, the budget requested $457 million.

The budget included more than $1 billion to continue developing a new fighter plane, the Advanced Tactical Fighter, which was supposed to replace the F-15 and the F-14 in the late 1990s. This was similar to what Congress appropriated in fiscal 1990 but about $340 million less than what the administration projected that it would be seeking for fiscal 1991.

The budget also included secret amounts for the Navy's ATA attack plane. The figure was estimated to be more than $1 billion, possibly to produce up to eight planes.

The administration proposed eliminating the 100-mile-range Phoenix missile carried only by the F-14. It projected a savings of $333 million in fiscal 1991 and a four-year savings of $614 million.

The Pentagon sought to double to 1,800 the number of AMRAAM missiles produced, for a cost of $1.3 billion. In fiscal 1990, the administration projected that it would request funds for 3,000 of the long-range missiles in the following budget.

It also requested $84 million to continue developing an advanced air-to-air missile, or AAAM.

Naval Warfare

To build five destroyers, equipped with the Aegis anti-missile radar system to protect carrier task forces, the administration requested $3.6 billion. Congress had approved a similar request for fiscal 1990.

The administration wanted $608 million to produce 900 Standard anti-aircraft missiles and $70 million to produce 405 of the smaller RAM missiles, designed as a short-range, last-ditch defense against antiship missiles.

The budget included an increase in funding for the Tomahawk cruise missile from $572 million for 400 missiles in fiscal 1990 to $809 million for 600 missiles. Production of the shorter-range Harpoon cruise missile would increase slightly to 215 missiles, for a cost of $241 million.

The budget included $2.3 billion for two *Seawolf*-class sub-hunting submarines and $1.1 billion for components for future production.

It also requested $350 million to produce 240 Mark 48 long-range antisub torpedoes, a program plagued by test failures. In fiscal 1990, the administration projected that it would request funding for 320 of the torpedoes. The budget included $328 million to produce 265 smaller Mark 50 torpedoes, which aircraft and surface ships carried.

Also requested was $255 million for continued development and advance procurement of the P-7 patrol plane and $416 million to produce 24 sub-hunting SH-60 helicopters.

The administration sought no funds for oceangoing minesweepers, but it did ask for $268 million for three smaller coastal minesweepers. The budget included $398 million to produce a combat-support ship.

Air and Sea Transport

The administration lowered its planned production of the C-17 wide-body cargo jet from 10 to six in fiscal 1991. In fiscal 1990, Congress cut the program, contending that it had fallen behind schedule, and the administration said its planned rate of production was impossible because of the cuts. The budget included $1.7 billion to produce the six jets, $204 million to buy components for future production and $541 million to continue development.

The budget included $272 million to buy 72 Blackhawk troop carriers, with $197 million for advance purchase of components for future production of the transport helicopter. The Pentagon also asked for $294 million to modernize the CH-47 helicopter.

To produce one LHD, a helicopter carrier the size of a World War II aircraft carrier that could carry 1,800 Marines and up to 30 helicopters, the administration requested $960 million. It asked for $240 million for an LSD-41 amphibious landing ship and $268 million for 12 LCAC air-cushion landing barges to haul heavy combat gear ashore from an amphibious fleet.

As in fiscal 1990, the administration wanted to end the V-22 Osprey, the hybrid airplane/helicopter to haul Marines ashore, for a fiscal 1991 savings of $1.4 billion and a four-year savings of $6.5 billion. Congress refused to stop production in the prior year, but defense authorization conferees warned that the program might be too expensive unless more uses and a commercial market were found.

The administration again requested funding for 23 Super Stallion helicopters, at a fiscal 1991 cost of $435 million, which Cheney proposed as a cheaper alternative to the Osprey. In fiscal 1990, Congress had cut that request by more than half.

Satellite Launchers

The budget included $209 million to produce two Titan IVs and $270 million for five smaller Atlas boosters. These were the Pentagon's major satellite launch vehicles.

The Pentagon requested $60 million more for research and development of the Advanced Launch System and sought $158 million for the Pentagon's share of a project to develop a National Aerospace Plane, designed to fly into orbit at 25 times the speed of sound.

Other Programs

The administration attributed fiscal 1991 savings of about $2.3 billion to management initiatives in its Defense Management Report, but it was unclear how it planned to achieve all of the savings. In part, the initiatives were expected to cut civilian employment by about 7,800 and military personnel by 8,600.

The budget assumed $2.7 billion more in savings by financing the purchase of spare parts for the Army and the Air Force through stock funds rather than through procurement accounts. But an analysis by the Defense Budget Project, a nonpartisan research group estimated that long-term savings would be significantly less than $2.7 billion.

The budget included $817 million for the Pentagon's environmental restoration fund, used to clean up toxic waste and debris at current and former military installations. About $700 million more was requested for Pentagon efforts to upgrade facilities to limit environmental damage. The requests represented an increase of $118 million over fiscal 1990.

The Pentagon budget included $1.2 billion, up from $800 million in fiscal 1990, to pay for activities related to Bush's national drug-control strategy. Planned activities included detecting and monitoring drug trafficking activity, as well as counternarcotics assistance to law enforcement agencies.

Seeking a Peace Dividend

In the weeks after the president's budget was introduced, critics of big defense budgets pursued their quest for deeper cuts. They insisted that eased international tensions could provide a "peace dividend" of funds that could be shifted from defense to other purposes.

"We have to have a [defense] modernization program, but does it have to be at the madcap pace of the 1980s?" asked Sen. Edward M. Kennedy, D-Mass., who proposed cutting defense spending by $169 billion over five years to help pay for more domestic programs, tax relief and deficit reduction. By March, even the relatively conservative Nunn was openly denouncing what he called Cheney's "1991 budget based on a 1988 threat and a 1988 strategy."

In April, Cheney made some concessions to the new budgetary and international realities.

He proposed slashing the number of radar-evading B-2 bombers (from 132 to 75) and C-17 long-range transport planes (from 210 to 120) while delaying production of new fighters and ground-attack planes for the Navy and Air

Pay Deadlock Broken

Defense Secretary Dick Cheney announced June 7 that he and House Speaker Thomas S. Foley, D-Wash., had broken a three-month deadlock over Pentagon funding that had threatened tens of thousands of military personnel with early discharges or delayed promotions and transfers.

The agreement allowed the Pentagon to shift (or "reprogram") $1.4 billion from various parts of the Pentagon budget to cover shortfalls in the accounts for military pay and fringe benefits.

Since late February, the Pentagon's reprogramming request — requiring the concurrence of both chambers' Armed Services and Appropriations committees — had been hostage to a power struggle between Cheney and House Armed Services Committee Chairman Les Aspin, D-Wis. At stake, according to Aspin, was Democratic leverage in future budget battles with the White House.

The reprogramming would offset the impact on the military personnel accounts of an across-the-board budget cut imposed on all federal agencies for part of fiscal 1990 under the Gramm-Rudman antideficit law.

If the Bush administration thus could shield the Pentagon against the most painful consequences of such an automatic cut (or "sequestration"), which would slash domestic programs, then Republicans would have a leg up in future budget battles with the Democrats, Aspin said.

To ensure that the fiscal 1990 sequestration stung the Pentagon, Aspin insisted that the offsetting reprogramming take some money from major weapons programs of interest to the military services and the Bush administration, such as the B-2 "stealth" bomber, the strategic defense initiative (SDI) and the *Seawolf*-class nuclear submarine.

On May 24, Aspin put the negotiations in Foley's hands, and the Speaker proposed a deal drawing $235 million from major weapons. But Cheney hung tough, and Foley gave ground.

The deal reached June 7 would draw $58 million from major weapons, but none of it would come from the B-2 or SDI.

Force. "We can afford to slow down the pace of developing and fielding our next generation of aircraft," he said.

Although the cutbacks would have reduced planned budget requests through 1997 by a total of $35 billion, the reduction from Bush's original request for fiscal 1991 would have been only $2.4 billion in budget authority and $109 million in actual outlays.

Nunn complimented Cheney on his "more sensible approach." But John R. Kasich, R-Ohio, a member of the House Armed Services Committee opposed to the B-2, scoffed, "We are cutting a little bit and stretching a lot, and when you cut and stretch you drive up the cost."

SENATE COMMITTEE

The reshaping of Cheney's defense budget began in earnest in the Senate Armed Services Committee, where members crafted a scaled-down budget with a prophetic price tag of $289 billion, essentially the amount that was eventually enacted. They completed marking up the bill in the early morning hours of July 13.

Committee Chairman Nunn told reporters that the bill would put the Pentagon on "a responsible and manageable glidepath toward a major restructuring."

The committee agreed to pull the plug on most of the 13 weapons programs that Cheney proposed eliminating. A notable exception was the V-22 Osprey, which was a joint project of contractors in Fort Worth and Philadelphia and, not coincidentally, enjoyed vigorous support in the Texas and Pennsylvania congressional delegations.

The committee also voted to eliminate 15 other weapons to reduce the budget by $2.35 billion in fiscal 1991 and $45 billion over the life of the programs.

The committee approved Cheney's revised April proposal for the B-2, agreeing to authorize $4.6 billion to develop the aircraft. The panel cut $972 million from Bush's $4.65 billion request for SDI.

Cutting Personnel

Beyond weaponry, the Senate committee's bill called for a military that would be leaner in personnel. It would have required a reduction of 100,000 active-duty personnel, compared with the 38,000 that Cheney had recommended trimming.

Over the longer term, the bill called for reducing active-duty personnel by 385,000 by fiscal 1995. The Army was to take the brunt of the cutbacks because its traditional duty of guarding Western Europe had become less relevant with the fall of the Iron Curtain.

On the other hand, the Senate panel rejected Cheney's call to cut the National Guard and reserves, anticipating a greater reliance on the backup forces.

Administration Goes Along

Although the Bush administration had threatened a veto if the authorization bill made significant cuts in strategic weapons or troop levels, Cheney's spokesman, Pete Williams, said the Defense secretary accepted the Senate committee bill as "reasonable."

"We have frankly avoided drawing the line in the sand," Williams told reporters July 26. "There's no point in doing that at this point in the process."

In fact, the administration had ample reason to embrace the Senate committee bill as the best it was likely to get. Deeper spending cuts were being demanded by Senate Budget Committee Chairman Jim Sasser, D-Tenn., and by many House Democrats. And stiff challenges were developing as the measure headed to the Senate floor.

HOUSE COMMITTEE

The shaping of the House defense bill had begun not in the Armed Services Committee but in the House Democratic Caucus, where members engaged in a series of closed-door debates over the budgetary, military and political implications of cutting Pentagon spending more deeply than the administration wanted.

In sessions in early March, Speaker Thomas S. Foley, D-Wash., sternly warned a group of Budget Committee liberals, including Marty Russo, D-Ill., and Howard L. Berman, D-Calif., that the deep cuts they sought were politically unrealistic.

Gradually, the caucus moved toward a consensus on

how deeply Democrats would seek to cut defense spending and on the practical reality that deep reductions in defense outlays could be achieved only by phasing them in over five or more years.

Equally significant, by summer, Aspin, the influential and relatively hawkish Armed Services Committee chairman, was ready to step forward and offer his own scenario for a scaled-down defense budget. On July 20, Aspin announced that his panel would come down hard on weapons procurement programs in order to cut the fiscal 1991 defense budget to $283 billion, $24 billion less than requested by Bush in January and $6 billion less than marked up by the Senate Armed Services Committee on July 13.

Aspin said the committee would make only a minor reduction in Bush's request for military personnel funding because "the real strength of the United States armed force right now is the quality of the people in the force."

But Aspin made it clear that something had to give in spending on weapons. Citing a series of costly new aircraft being developed by the Pentagon, Aspin warned that they "won't all fit in the reduced budgets of coming years."

Aspin revealed what he had in mind on July 23, when he dropped his longtime support for the B-2 bomber. He announced he would join liberal Democrat Ronald V. Dellums of California and conservative Republican Kasich in trying to bar production of any B-2s beyond the 15 already built or under construction.

Cordial 'Heavy Lifting'

The Armed Services Committee followed its chairman's lead, as usual. On July 31, the panel voted, 34-20, to cut off B-2 production. It then adopted the $283 billion defense authorization bill by a vote of 40-12. Although senior committee Republican Bill Dickinson, Ala., warned that Bush would veto the measure in that form, nine of the panel's 21 Republicans voted "aye."

The session was notable for its lack of rancor compared with past conflicts between committee members and their sometimes abrasive chairman. "It was cordial," said Dave McCurdy, D-Okla. "For the heavy lifting that had to be done, it was amazing."

Much of the difference was a new willingness by Aspin to work cooperatively. "Instead of carrying all the load himself, he kind of spread it around," said G. V. "Sonny" Montgomery, D-Miss., a senior committee member.

The cooperative mood did not eliminate partisan finger-pointing, however. Dickinson complained that Aspin assembled his majority the old-fashioned way — he bought it.

"I used to wonder how much pork it took to buy enough votes to pass a bad defense bill, and now I know," Dickinson said. He charged that Aspin "got $2.7 billion worth of chits" by canceling the B-2.

Among the pork that Dickinson objected to was a ban on closing any additional military bases in fiscal 1991, a $437 million increase for F/A-18 Navy jets and $403 million to move toward production of the V-22 Osprey.

Aspin had supported Cheney's effort to cut the tilt-rotor Osprey the year before. But he argued that he changed his mind because it was well-suited to the new international environment.

Noting its capability to move a small number of troops a great distance and land them in small clearings, Aspin reasoned, "You're looking beyond the Soviet threat to other threats — terrorism, drugs, other kinds of things that you're going to call upon your military to do."

The committee version of the bill called for reducing U.S. troops in Europe by 50,000, as part of an overall reduction of 129,500 active-duty personnel. It also called for slowing — but not canceling — development of weapons including the ATF fighter plane and the Army's LH armed helicopter.

It also called for reducing spending on SDI to $2.9 billion, compared with the $4.6 billion requested by Bush and the $3.6 billion supported by the Senate.

SENATE FLOOR

Sentiment was building against the B-2, as a high-priced weapon and as a symbol of the fading Cold War. When the Senate version of the (S 2884) defense measure went to the floor, Nunn successfully fended off amendments to kill the program or phase it out, although opposition to the B-2 had increased over the previous year.

Conservative defenders of the plane, and of large defense budgets more generally, were helped by the coincidental timing of the brutal events in the Persian Gulf. On Aug. 2, the day the Senate debate began, Iraq invaded Kuwait.

On the Senate floor Aug. 3, Minority Leader Bob Dole, R-Kan., called the invasion "a wake-up call."

"This is a very important debate," Dole said, "more important this morning than it was last night.... If we err, let us err on the side of being ready."

Wallop added, "Saddam Hussein, whether we like it or not, represents one wave of the future."

Reining In SDI

Nonetheless, the Bush administration's defense policies did not emerge from the Senate unscathed.

Splitting almost exactly along party lines, the Democratic-controlled Senate moved to reshape the strategic defense initiative by blocking development of a partial antimissile defense in the late 1990s.

The commitment to begin deploying a first-stage SDI system as soon as possible was an article of faith among some conservatives, and a touchstone of their support for Bush.

By a vote of 54-44, the Senate adopted the amendment by Democrats Jeff Bingaman, N.M., and Richard C. Shelby, Ala., to slow development of brilliant pebbles, the array of tiny heat-seeking guided missiles that was embraced by Bush as the most promising first-stage method to destroy Soviet missiles as they were blasting into space. Imposing spending ceilings on different categories within the wide-ranging SDI program, the Bingaman-Shelby amendment called for limiting research on brilliant pebbles to $129 million, the same amount spent in fiscal 1990. *(Vote 223, p. 46-S)*

In a letter to Republican senators two days before the vote, Bush had warned that the SDI overhaul was "more serious than a funding cut."

Just two Republicans deserted the president to vote for the amendment — Mark O. Hatfield, Ore., and Pete V. Domenici, N.M.

The bill approved by the Senate also called for killing several major weapons systems, including the proposed multibillion-dollar system of Milstar communications satellites and a new battlefield anti-aircraft missile for the Army. It also called for slowing development or production of several other costly programs, including the ATF fighter plane, the A-12 ground attack plane, the *Seawolf*-class submarine, and the Army LH helicopter.

Battle Over Battleships

In other action, the Senate turned back an amendment that would have retired one of the Navy's two remaining battleships. The amendment by Dale Bumpers, D-Ark., was tabled (killed), 55-44. *(Vote 215, p. 44-S)*

Bumpers had opposed refurbishing old battleships since the Reagan administration's decision to take four of them out of mothballs a decade earlier. But he was not satisfied with Cheney's proposal to retire two of the four ships, including the *Iowa*, which was damaged in 1989 by an explosion in one of its three main gun turrets that killed 47 sailors.

The fight over the battleships also was affected by the determination to counter Iraq's invasion of Kuwait. "Saddam Hussein has made the case for the battleships," argued John McCain, R-Ariz. "In most parts of the world, the key capability we have to counter thugs of Saddam Hussein's ilk is by deploying significant naval capability."

Bumpers countered that the Navy had hundreds of ships and planes able to carry cruise missiles, and he emphasized that the battleships' big guns were not being fired as a precaution after the *Iowa* disaster. "If you want to steam into the Persian Gulf," he said, "for God's sake do it with something that works."

Nunn supported Bumpers, complaining that the Navy had made no effort to exploit the potential of the refurbished battleships. Nunn cited the lament of the *Iowa's* former captain that Navy personnel officers had accorded his ship a low priority in assigning top-notch crew members.

But the battlewagons drew powerful support from Texans Lloyd Bentsen, D, and Phil Gramm, R, and from Defense Appropriations Subcommittee Chairman Daniel K. Inouye, D-Hawaii. Of the two ships still in service, the Navy planned to station the *Missouri* at Pearl Harbor and the *Wisconsin* at Ingleside, Texas, near Corpus Christi.

Air Base Feud

The Senate also rejected an amendment that would have prohibited U.S. contributions to the construction of a new NATO air base at Crotone, Italy, intended to house a wing of 72 U.S. Air Force F-16s.

The amendment against the air base was sponsored by Alan J. Dixon, D-Ill., who was enraged that the Pentagon planned to back a new NATO base, with all the amenities, after closing Rantoul Air Force Base in his state.

"I want the folks back home to know how good we do it overseas when we give up a hometown in Illinois," Dixon said, his voice dripping with sarcasm as he gestured at a map of the proposed facility at Crotone. "Can they see the boulevards and the beautiful trees? Oh, Mr. President, a nice shopping center. . . . Hot dog! Oh boy! A base theater. Wonderful! A bookstore. Nice!"

John W. Warner, R-Va., retorted that Crotone's location on NATO's southern flank made it a splendid fulcrum from which U.S. fighters could exert military and diplomatic leverage. On Warner's motion, Dixon's anti-Crotone amendment was tabled, 51-47. *(Vote 210, p. 44-S)*

But the base at Crotone became something of a symbol of congressional resistance to military spending overseas. Language limiting spending on the facility was attached to the annual appropriations bill for military construction. *(Military construction appropriations, p. 826)*

By a vote of 59-40, the Senate also tabled an amendment by Kent Conrad, D-N.D., that would have cut the force of 311,000 Army and Air Force personnel in Europe by 80,000 instead of the 50,000-person reduction written into the measure by the Armed Services Committee. *(Vote 213, p. 44-S)*

By voice vote the Senate also adopted two amendments, by William V. Roth Jr., R-Del., and Richard H. Bryan, D-Nev., each of which promoted the idea of encouraging NATO to rent as a training site some domestic U.S. base that otherwise would be closed.

Domestic Base Closings

As reported by the Armed Services Committee, the bill would have made it easier for the Pentagon to shut down domestic bases, removing some of the procedural hurdles Congress created since the mid-1970s to give it leverage to protect constituents' jobs.

But Bumpers and many other members were of an opposite mind, because of Cheney's announcement that 21 bases — including Eaker Air Force Base in Blytheville, Ark. — were candidates for being shut down in fiscal 1991.

Cheney's proposal would have wiped out 44,000 jobs, and 99 percent of them were in House districts represented by Democrats, Bumpers said.

So he offered an amendment that would have nullified Cheney's hit list, barred domestic base closures through fiscal 1991 and ordered Cheney to send Congress a report on the size and organization of U.S. forces through fiscal 1996.

But Nunn objected that the amendment would "send a signal to the American people that the Congress has a lot of rhetoric in terms of cutting defense expeditures, but . . . we are not willing to [close bases]."

A motion to table Bumpers' amendment was rejected 43-54, but immediately thereafter, the Senate rejected the amendment 43-54. *(Votes 220-221, p. 45-S)*

The Senate rejected an amendment by Roth that would have gone further than the Armed Services Committee in giving the Defense secretary more leeway to shut down domestic bases. By a vote of 81-18, the Senate tabled the amendment that would have let the Pentagon close a base without waiting for congressional approval if fewer than 1,000 civilian employees would lose their jobs. The bill would allow the Pentagon to act unilaterally to close bases with fewer than 300 civilian workers. *(Vote 218, p. 45-S)*

Also rejected was a Roth amendment that would have barred the Defense Department from acquiring any parcels of land larger than 25 acres. The amendment, intended to block for one year plans to expand several training areas, was tabled 93-6. *(Vote 217, p. 45-S)*

And the Senate upheld a provision recommended by the Armed Services Committee that the funds from the sale or lease of unneeded land controlled by the Pentagon would go to the department. The committee insisted the provision would give department managers an incentive to dispose of unneeded land. John Glenn, D-Ohio, objected that the officials should not need a special incentive just to do their jobs, but his amendment providing that sale and lease proceeds would revert to the Treasury Department was rejected 29-67. *(Vote 222, p. 46-S)*

Procurement Policy

Congress had added to previous defense bills provisions to prod the Pentagon to buy more commercially available items, permitting extraordinary specifications only when essential. By voice vote, the Senate added to the bill an amendment by Carl Levin, D-Mich., that, in effect, would extend to all other government agencies those provisions aimed at promoting more "off-the-shelf" buying.

It also approved by voice vote two amendments:

- By Roth, to make it easier for Pentagon contracting officers to withhold progress payments to companies if there was "substantial evidence" that the request for payment was fraudulent.
- By Strom Thurmond, R-S.C., to prohibit payment to any person who lobbied the Pentagon for a so-called contingency fee — a fee that increased if the agency bought whatever the lobbyist was promoting. According to Levin, 35 states prohibited the payment of lobbyists on a contingency basis. Thurmond denounced the practice as "an incentive to gouge the government."

Warner cautioned that the provision would ban a relatively widespread practice, referred to as "value billing."

In fiscal 1990, the Senate version of the annual defense bill included several provisions that were intended to give Pentagon managers more flexibility in managing scientists, engineers and other technically trained specialists — including paying them salaries higher than those provided by the federal civil service system. Those provisions were dropped for that year in conference.

But committee members led by Bingaman — who chaired the subcommittee dealing with technology — included them in S 2884.

This time, Bingaman worked out compromises with committee member Glenn, who was also chairman of the Governmental Affairs Committee.

Noting that low federal salaries made it difficult for many agencies to hire technical specialists, Glenn had objected previously to singling out the defense-related agencies for special treatment.

By voice vote, the Senate approved the following amendments:

- By Glenn, to allow for up to 800 people in all agencies occupying critical positions special salaries as high as those paid to the most senior executive branch officials.
- By Glenn, to allow federal laboratories to experiment with more flexible pay scales for scientists and engineers.
- By Levin, to apply to the entire executive branch, certain provisions that, as reported by the committee, had applied only to defense agencies. Among them was a provision that would waive for up to 1,250 people the so-called double-dipper law, which required military retirees in federal jobs to forgo an amount of their salary equal to their military pension.

Drug Wars

The Senate tabled 51-48 an amendment by Dennis DeConcini, D-Ariz., that would have earmarked for the treatment of drug-addicted mothers $100 million in unspent funds left over in Pentagon accounts at the end of fiscal 1990. *(Vote 216, p. 45-S)*

The funds would have been used to enable children to stay with mothers who were enrolled in residential treatment programs. "Why should the defense budget not participate in a problem that is devastating to this country?" DeConcini asked.

Wallop decried the amendment as "one of the most dreadful," since opponents risked appearing insensitive to the problem of so-called crack babies. "The defense authorization bill is becoming a cash cow to be milked for every social ill in the country," Wallop said.

Aside from that amendment, however, the Senate approved by voice vote several proposals intended to boost the war on drug smuggling, including these amendments:

- By McCain, to authorize the administration's "drug czar" to establish a small office to develop technologies that might be useful in the war on narcotics traffickers, such as drug-detection gear and computer methods for tracing laundered money.
- By Mitch McConnell, R-Ky., to direct the Defense secretary to comb the inventory of equipment brought back from overseas by returning U.S. forces in search of items that could assist state or local drug enforcement agencies.
- By Orrin G. Hatch, R-Utah, to order the Pentagon to study the value of turning over to National Guard units modern "scout" helicopters with night-viewing equipment, for use in antidrug patrols of the Mexican border.

Also adopted by voice vote was an amendment by Alfonse M. D'Amato, R-N.Y., to order a report by the General Accounting Office (GAO) on the Pentagon's expenditure of funds appropriated in fiscal 1989-90 for antinarcotics operations. D'Amato complained that the Pentagon was not spending the money Congress gave it.

An amendment by Alan Cranston, D-Calif., also adopted by voice vote, demanded an interdepartmental report to Congress on the impact on democratic institutions in the Andean countries of the role played by their respective militaries in counternarcotics operations.

Nuclear, Toxic Cleanup

An amendment by Tim Wirth, D-Colo., to shift $45 million from the Energy Department's defense nuclear program to the Pentagon's environmental cleanup account was approved by voice vote.

Because the funds were in excess of the amounts appropriated for the Energy defense program, they would have been wasted if they had not been transferred into another account.

To authorize $5 million for tracking down people who might have been exposed to radioactive material released from the Energy Department's nuclear material production facilities at Hanford, Wash., the Senate approved by voice vote an amendment by Brock Adams, D-Wash.

Also adopted by voice vote — despite vigorous opposition — was an amendment by Harry Reid, D-Nev., to repeal a law barring damage suits against contractors associated with nuclear weapons tests in the atmosphere in 1946-62. Opposing the Reid amendment, Domenici predicted a barrage of lawsuits from antinuclear activists, not to win compensation for radiation victims but to ferret out by court order documents on the conduct of the nuclear testing program.

Before the Reid amendment was approved, the Senate approved, by voice vote, two amendments by Alan K. Simpson, R-Wyo., to limit attorneys' fees in such suits to 10 percent of the damage award and to oblige the government to reimburse contractors for all reasonable costs arising from such suits.

An amendment by Pete Wilson, R-Calif., adopted by voice vote, called for the Defense Department to enter into an agreement with the Environmental Protection Agency (EPA) to clean up toxic waste on a miltary base within a year after the base had been cited as a problem site under the so-called Superfund Act.

Also adopted by voice vote was an amendment by Al Gore, D-Tenn., and Warner, to require the Defense and Energy departments to reimburse EPA for the cost of their oversight activities at superfund sites owned by those two agencies.

Arms Control Policy

An effort by John Kerry, D-Mass., to slow the development of an antisatellite (ASAT) missile was tabled 52-45. Kerry's amendment would have sliced funding to develop a ground-launched ASAT missile from $208 million to $77 million — slightly more than was appropriated in fiscal 1990. *(Vote 219, p. 45-S)*

Arms control advocates long had pressed for a negotiated ban on antisatellite weapons since the United States — which relied on satellite communications more heavily than the Soviet Union — would have more to lose in an ASAT arms race. However, while concurring in the desirability of an ASAT ban, Nunn and other committee members argued for going ahead with the U.S. program pending such an agreement.

The committee's ASAT funding recommendation was reduced by $55 million, though, by a Nunn-Warner amendment, adopted by voice vote, that made a number of minor changes in the committee bill. The ASAT cut reflected a change in Pentagon plans for the program.

Also adopted by voice vote was an amendment by Jesse Helms, R-N.C., to require the president to report on whether the Soviet Union had circumvented the 1988 intermediate-range nuclear forces treaty by transferring SS-23 missiles to some of its Warsaw Pact allies. It also demanded a report on the demolition of a Soviet antimissile radar near Krasnoyarsk, in Sibera, which violated the 1972 U.S.-Soviet ABM treaty. Conservatives had cited both cases as reasons why the Senate should scrutinize any START treaty with the Soviet Union.

Missile Technology Controls

The Senate approved by voice vote a non-binding amendment by Edward M. Kennedy, D-Mass., recommending creation of a committee of U.S. and Soviet technical experts to study methods that might be used to verify a future arms control agreement that banned the production of nuclear weapons material and required the dismantling of nuclear warheads. Kennedy was a leading proponent of a nuclear material production cutoff, something the Bush administration adamantly opposed.

Also agreed to by voice vote was a Bingaman amendment intended to penalize corporations that sold to other countries technologies essential to the production of long-range ballistic missiles. Among other things, the amendment called for a ban on such companies from doing business with the U.S. government and for public reports on their activities, though the president would have authority to modify or waive some of the penalties.

Because the amendment would impose such sanctions unilaterally, however, Senate Foreign Relations Committee member Richard G. Lugar, R-Ind., warned that it might undermine longstanding U.S. efforts to negotiate multilateral controls on the export of missile-related technology.

But amendment proponents contended that proliferation was outrunning the U.S. negotiating strategy: "The very gradual diplomatic processes that have been under way among potential suppliers . . . are too slow," said Gore.

Other Amendments

An effort by Glenn to boost from 3.5 percent to 4.1 percent the military pay raise authorized in the bill was tabled, 67-32. The higher rate, which was included in the House Armed Services Committee version of the defense bill, would have cost $314 million more than the raise recommended by the Senate panel. *(Vote 214, p. 44-S)*

Because annual military pay raises had lagged behind inflation since 1983, Glenn contended, the purchasing power of military pay had dropped by more than 11 percent. But Nunn countered that, because of the budget crunch, higher pay would have to be linked with deeper cuts in the size of the force.

A Levin amendment reducing by $180 million the amount authorized to buy spare parts and supplies was adopted by voice vote. Levin cited GAO reports concluding that the Pentagon routinely overestimated its inventory requirements for such items.

Also approved by voice vote were the following amendments:

- By David Pryor, D-Ark., to bar use of any funds in the bill for production of the ASPJ airborne radar jammer, which had failed various tests.
- By Dixon, to authorize $8 million to modify the V-22 Osprey for guerrilla operations.
- By Ted Stevens, R-Alaska, to slow the Armed Services Committee's effort to meld active-duty military personnel into National Guard and reserve units. Stevens' amendment would have guaranteed that a certain number of Guard and reserve personnel could serve on active duty.
- By Dixon, to extend the Pentagon's hospitalization program for military dependents (CHAMPUS) to cover routine mammograms and Pap tests.

The final day of debate on the bill was marked by arguments not about defense policy but about abortions. Wirth offered an amendment that would have overturned the Pentagon's policy banning elective abortions in military hospitals, even when paid for by private funds. But the amendment was withdrawn after the Senate refused to invoke cloture on the amendment (thereby cutting off debate). The cloture motion would have required 60 votes but was rejected 58-41. *(Vote 212, p. 44-S)*

The Senate's final approval of the defense authorization measure (S 2884) came Aug. 4, on a vote of 79-16. Senators voting against the bill on final passage included 12 Democrats and one Republican — Hatfield — who had sought to lower defense spending, and three conservative Republicans — Colorado's William L. Armstrong, Roth and Wallop — who favored higher spending. *(Vote 227, p. 46-S)*

HOUSE FLOOR

On Sept. 11, the day the full House began debate on the defense authorization bill, Defense Secretary Cheney told House Republicans that he would urge Bush to veto the bill if it were not significantly modified.

Cheney's spokesman cited as particularly objectionable the bill's cuts in strategic weapons; its ban on closing domestic military bases; and its reduction of almost 130,000 active-duty personnel, more than three times the 37,600-person cutback supported by the administration.

In the weeks after the Armed Services Committee marked up the bill, the political climate had also changed because of Iraq's invasion of Kuwait on Aug. 2.

Yet, not even conservative Democrats seemed to be having second thoughts about the cutbacks called for by the Armed Services Committee.

"We tended to emphasize conventional forces as opposed to strategic forces," said committee member Norman

Continued on p. 682

House Vote Spares Staten Island Home Port

The youngest and most junior member of the House, New York Republican Susan Molinari, blindsided senior members of the Armed Services Committee on Sept. 11, with appeals to a number of her colleagues' bedrock instincts: party loyalty, turf consciousness and a sense of fair play.

By a 230-188 vote, the House gutted a proposal by Armed Services subcommittee Chairmen Charles E. Bennett, D-Fla., and Patricia Schroeder, D-Colo., that would have shut down a naval base in Molinari's Staten Island district. *(Vote 322, p. 106-H)*

"It's a real David and Goliath story," exulted Molinari aide Daniel Leonard.

But Aesop's tale of the grasshopper and the ant might be as good a metaphor for the duel. As Bennett and Schroeder coasted toward the showdown, Molinari, 32, pulled out the stops to save the installation. She was aided in the effort by her father, Staten Island Borough President Guy V. Molinari, from whom she inherited the House seat after a special election March 20. The elder Molinari, who served in the House from 1981-90, flew to Washington for personal lobbying of his former colleagues on the day of the showdown vote.

Controversial Plans

The Staten Island base was one of several new Navy "home ports" proposed in the mid-1980s to accommodate the Reagan administration's naval expansion. *(1985 Almanac, p. 392)*

Among the other planned sites were Everett, Wash.; Ingleside, Texas; Mobile, Ala.; Pascagoula, Miss.; and Pensacola, Fla.

The bases were opposed by members of Congress with established bases that would lose jobs to the new sites, such as San Diego Republican Duncan Hunter. The New York City base also became a lightning rod for antinuclear activists, because the battleship *Iowa* earmarked for Staten Island carried nuclear-armed cruise missiles.

Though the House opposed the home ports, the project survived. By 1990, $240 million had been spent at Staten Island. The Aegis cruiser *Normandy* replaced the mothballed *Iowa* as queen of the new facility.

Early in the year, however, Defense Secretary Dick Cheney froze construction on the Staten Island, Ingleside, Pascagoula, and Mobile home ports as part of a budget-cutting move affecting 207 military installations altogether. The freeze, announced Jan. 24, was originally to last three months, but Cheney extended it in May through June 15.

In doing so, Cheney pointedly suggested that many members of Congress were willing to support defense spending cuts except in their own back yards. "Some of these actions may not be popular with members of Congress who want to cut the defense budget even as they plead to save the projects in their own states and districts," he said.

Opponents of the home ports also noted that with the Navy shrinking in the Bush administration rather than expanding, the rationale for the new facilities was more questionable. The General Accounting Office told two House Armed Services subcommittees April 24 that any additional funds for new home ports should be held up pending a later report by the Navy defining its base needs.

When House Armed Services marked up the fiscal 1991 defense authorization bill (HR 4739) in July, however, Bennett's Seapower Subcommittee rejected an effort to kill both the Staten Island home port and the one at Everett, Wash., which had not been included in Cheney's construction freeze.

After the committee completed work on the bill, home port opponents decided to concentrate on Staten Island, knowing that 11 of the 14 members of New York City's overwhelmingly liberal, Democratic House delegation opposed the base, as did Democratic Mayor David N. Dinkins.

A Textbook Counterattack

So the amendment by Bennett and Schroeder, who chaired the Military Installations Subcommittee, called for closing the Staten Island home port and putting on hold construction at five other home ports: Everett, Ingleside, Mobile, Pascagoula and Pensacola.

Molinari responded with a textbook counterattack:

- She lined up fellow Republicans, even taking advantage of Cheney's meeting with the House GOP caucus to issue a tub-thumping appeal for support.
- She trumped the opposition of most of New York City's House members by noting that the base was backed by New York's Democratic governor, Mario M. Cuomo; most of the state's House members; four of the city's five borough presidents — and by the House member with the most at stake: herself.
- She warned members with their own districts that the Bennett-Schroeder run at Staten Island was a dangerous precedent: "Your military installation could be next," she said Sept. 11.
- Finally, she argued that her base had been unfairly singled out, an argument that won over not only San Diego's Hunter but also several prominent liberal Democrats, such as Nicholas Mavroules of Massachusetts and Mel Levine of California.

"We didn't do any of that kind of organizing," conceded an aide to Bennett, "and it showed."

Molinari's substitute for the Bennett-Schroeder amendment was supported by 163 Republicans (of 171 voting) and by 67 Democrats. Under her amendment, no funds could be used to close the Staten Island facility until 30 days after the Defense Department sent Congress an overall plan to close and realign Navy installations within the United States.

That left the port's long-term survival yet to be determined. But Molinari's aide Leonard insisted that the strong House vote would discourage renewed efforts by the Pentagon to close the port. In addition, he noted early in 1991, the new head of the base-closing commission was former Rep. Jim Courter, R-N.J. (1979-91), who had spoken on the floor in support of Molinari's amendment to protect the Staten Island facility.

Continued from p. 680
Sisisky, D-Va. "The events of the last few weeks prove us right."

Aspin insisted that the gulf crisis vindicated his strategic premise. "Because the Soviets are being so cooperative [in supporting U.S. policy toward Iraq], the core philosophy of the bill stands," he said. "The guys who want to use it to reverse [cuts in] SDI or B-2 are not finding much resonance."

Republicans, however, scoffed that the bill's chief strength remained its pork-barrel appeal. Armed Services member Jim Courter, R-N.J., called it "a collection of deep cuts, of some questionable add-ons, all sprinkled with a heavy dose of politics as usual."

Champions of the B-2 bomber decided not to try to resuscitate that program on the House floor, biding their time for the Senate-House conference committee.

Much of the House debate concerned "burden-sharing," the growing demand that allies pay more of the cost of collective defense. Critics argued that, in effect, the United States was subsidizing the economies of commercial competitors — including Japan and Germany — by spending a substantially larger share of its national income on defenses that provided for their security as well.

This sentiment was reflected in some provisions of the defense bill that came to the House floor from the Armed Services Committee, including a ban on stationing U.S. units at the planned NATO air base at Crotone, Italy.

By a largely party-line vote of 174-249, the House on Sept. 12 rejected an effort by David O'B. Martin, R-N.Y., to drop the committee's restrictions on the Crotone base. *(Vote 324, p. 106-H)*

Another twist on the burden-sharing theme had been drafted by David E. Bonior, D-Mich., in July as a floor amendment. It called for reducing the 50,000 U.S. military personnel stationed in Japan by 5,000 a year unless the Japanese government began paying all costs associated with the deployment.

In the politically charged atmosphere created by the Iraq crisis, Bonior's amendment became a lightning rod for festering congressional anger at Japan.

Debating the amendment Sept. 12, Bonior argued that Japan, which "gets almost 70 percent of its oil from the Middle East," had offered to pay only a fraction of the costs of the U.S.-led deployment of forces in the Persian Gulf. Other members vented broader resentments against the Japanese. "While they open their arms to our sailors and soldiers, they close their markets to our telephones and TVs," said Byron L. Dorgan, D-N.D. "That's why we have a $45 billion trade deficit with Japan."

Opposing the amendment, Stephen J. Solarz, D-N.Y., argued that U.S. troops in Japan defended U.S. interests and that, by requiring Japan to pay their salaries, Bonior's amendment would turn them into mercenaries — as Solarz put it, "latter-day Hessians."

But many lawmakers wanted to send a strong signal to Japan, perhaps knowing that Bonior's amendment would not make it into the final defense bill. (Ultimately, the version sent to the president called for capping the number of U.S. personnel in Japan at 50,000 but dropped the 5,000-a-year automatic reduction.) The House adopted Bonior's amendment, 370-53. *(Vote 325, p. 106-H)*

Weapons Procurement

By a vote of 413-1, the House adopted an amendment by Nicholas Mavroules, D-Mass., aimed at setting higher standards of education and experience for those who served as weapons procurement officers. It was the latest in a series of congressional efforts to bolster the standing of the Pentagon's purchasers in the hope of making them better able to deal both with contractors and the military brass. *(Vote 321, p. 106-H)*

Over the previous decade, Congress had tacked onto annual defense bills a series of provisions intended to professionalize the Pentagon's purchasers, setting minimum standards of training and experience.

The omnibus amendment that was hammered out by Mavroules' Armed Services Investigations Subcommittee reflected the panel's conclusion that the Defense Department had not yet accepted the premise that procurement management was a job for specialists.

"You'd never send a great military commander to perform heart surgery or defend your case in court," said Mavroules. "Why on Earth do we send them to handle immensely intricate acquisition programs?"

The amendment called for the Pentagon to designate critical weapons acquisition jobs that could be held only by military officers and civilians who were career specialists in that process. It demanded minimum education and experience requirements for people holding those key jobs. It also called for increasing the number of civilians in key acquisition jobs and the length of time officials assigned to those posts would stay in them.

Before its adoption, Mavroules' proposal was amended by voice vote to include a proposal sponsored by Benjamin A. Gilman, R-N.Y. Gilman's amendment would have authorized federal agencies to reimburse employees for the cost of getting a degree in a critical skill and to repay federal student loans in return for a commitment to work for the federal government for a specified period.

The House also approved 287-134 an amendment by Glen Browder, D-Ala., which reaffirmed provisions in the committee's bill barring closure of any domestic bases until Cheney proposed legislation to establish a nonpartisan basis for deciding which bases to close. *(Vote 327, p. 106-H)*

Shifting Funds

When House debate on the defense bill resumed on Sept. 18, Democrats found an opportunity to hone their political message that they were sharpening U.S. defenses for the future.

They pushed through an amendment by Charles E. Bennett, D-Fla., and Tom Ridge, R-Pa., that cut another $600 million from the $2.9 billion that the Armed Services Committee had recommended authorizing for SDI. Rejecting several amendments to cut SDI more or less deeply, the House adopted the Bennett-Ridge amendment, 225-189. *(Vote 339, p. 110-H)*

Using the money cut from SDI and other funds, Aspin fashioned a $948 million package for equipment and personnel associated with Operation Desert Shield, the deployment against Iraq. The package included new minesweepers, fast cargo ships and protective clothing to deal with attacks by chemical and biological weapons. It also provided benefits for forces stationed in the Persian Gulf, including "imminent danger pay" of $110 a month.

Aspin's Persian Gulf package was adopted, 413-10. *(Vote 350, p. 114-H)*

In a final effort to portray the Democratic-backed bill as a pork-barrel package, Dickinson proposed an amendment that, in effect, would have deleted $428 million that the committee had added to the budget request for F/A-18 fighter planes and used the money to restore 28,500 of the 129,000 personnel the bill would have cut from the Army. The pork-barrel connection was that the F/A-18 was manufactured in St. Louis, hometown of Majority Leader Richard A. Gephardt, D.

Minority Whip Newt Gingrich, R-Ga., said the amendment was needed to avoid sending U.S. troops in the Persian Gulf "the message that pork barrel, in the form of F/A-18s, is more important than human beings." But the amendment was rejected, 156-254. *(Vote 351, p. 114-H)*

Displaced Workers

The House voted 288-128 to siphon $200 million from the Pentagon budget to help workers and communities adjust to the loss of defense contracts. *(Vote 341, p. 112-H)*

The amendment, sponsored by Mavroules, earmarked $100 million for existing programs in the Commerce and Defense departments to help communities plan how to take up the economic slack when a local business lost a large defense contract or a local base was closed.

The remaining $100 million was for aid to displaced defense workers. It could be used to fund job retraining programs and grants to individuals to defray the cost of looking for work and relocating to take a new job.

"We simply cannot afford to do nothing in the face of layoffs of tens of thousands," Mavroules said. "We simply cannot afford to delay economic assistance to communities devastated by defense cuts."

Through months of negotiation, Gephardt fostered creation of the adjustment package as a key element of the Democratic leadership's long-term strategy for slicing the Pentagon budget.

By promising help for affected constituencies, Gephardt said, the adjustment program would make it easier for members to support defense cuts.

To avert a clash with Ways and Means Committee Chairman Dan Rostenkowski, D-Ill., the Democrats dropped from the package a provision that would have doubled, to 52 weeks, the period during which displaced defense workers could draw unemployment compensation.

Larry J. Hopkins, R-Ky., complained that Mavroules' package was inequitable.

"It grants special status and benefits to a limited category of our work force without regard to the millions of other civilian employees who perform similar work," he said.

Hopkins proposed a GOP alternative that would have required the executive branch to provide early warnings to localities of planned defense cuts. His amendment also would have authorized $6 million for the Pentagon's economic impact assistance program.

Hopkins' substitute was rejected, 161-253. *(Vote 340, p. 112-H)*

MX Missile

Some of the great ideological brouhahas of the Reagan years were dealt with in an almost perfunctory way during House debate on HR 4739.

For example, opposition to the MX missile was a banner issue for the liberal arms control community during the mid-1980s.

In 1990, however, the Armed Services Committee denied funds to begin production of a rail-mobile version of the controversial MX missile and sliced the total amount available for development of both the rail-based MX and the smaller Midgetman mobile missile.

While contending that the country could afford to develop both mobile missiles, the committee left to Bush the choice between the MX and Midgetman.

Barney Frank, D-Mass., offered a floor amendment that would have cut an additional $200 million from the rail-MX program, but it was rejected 153-264, drawing only nine more ayes than nays among Democrats. *(Vote 345, p. 112-H)*

The House did adopt by voice vote a Mavroules amendment to transfer $46 million in unobligated rail-MX funds to environmental restoration activities, bringing that program's total funding to $1.05 billion.

Other Amendments

The House adopted the following additional amendments:

- By Douglas H. Bosco, D-Calif., 234-182, expressing the sense of Congress that the president should, "at the earliest possible date," seek a comprehensive, verifiable ban on nuclear weapons testing. *(Vote 343, p. 112-H)*
- By Barbara Boxer, D-Calif., by voice vote, requiring the Pentagon to suspend progress payments to a contractor against whom there is "substantial evidence" of fraud.
- By Boxer, 334-83, barring the use of psychiatric examinations or involuntary hospitalizations to harass so-called whistleblowers who informed their superiors or members of Congress of allegedly improper activities within their agency. *(Vote 344, p. 112-H)*

Among the amendments rejected by the House were the following:

- By James A. Traficant Jr., D-Ohio, 133-284, to reduce by 2 percent all amounts authorized by the bill. *(Vote 347, p. 112-H)*
- By Vic Fazio, D-Calif., 200-216, to permit U.S. military personnel or their dependents living overseas to obtain abortions in U.S. military hospitals, provided the costs were privately covered. *(Vote 342, p. 112-H)*
- By Denny Smith, R-Ore., by voice vote, requiring the Pentagon to test cheaper alternatives to the F-16 fighter plane, which the Air Force intended to buy to provide aerial support for ground-combat troops.

Paying Dues

Aspin's politicization of the defense bill extended to the decisions about whose amendments would be incorporated into an omnibus package of non-controversial proposals that could be expected to be approved routinely.

As adopted 373-45, the en bloc amendments included 21 provisions. Among the most significant were ones to impose economic sanctions on companies exporting ballistic-missile technology and to sharply reduce, over several years, the amount that the United States would pay toward the salaries of foreign civilians employed at U.S. bases abroad. *(Vote 349, p. 114-H)*

Only four of the 21 amendments rolled into the en bloc package came from Republicans, however. Dickinson complained that some GOP proposals had been shelved for no reason. "Some of our members feel aggrieved," he said.

Dickinson ended by urging colleagues to vote against the measure.

"It's a bad bill," he said. "It should be voted down, and the president is going to veto it."

Most Republicans followed Dickinson's lead in the 256-155 vote to pass the bill. GOP lawmakers split 33-135 against the bill.

Continued on p. 686

Defense Authorization Act Provisions

Following are major provisions of the National Defense Authorization Act for Fiscal 1991 (HR 4739 — PL 101-510):

Force Cuts

• Authorized a reduction of 100,000 active-duty personnel. To meet objections from Secretary of Defense Dick Cheney, however, the bill permitted him to exceed the annual personnel cap by 1 percent, thereby cutting the force by only about 80,000. Prior law gave the Defense secretary authority to exceed the annual cap by 0.5 percent.

The House had authorized a reduction of 129,500 in the active-duty force, which had been capped at 1,976,405. The conferees initially had agreed to the reduction of 100,000 authorized by the Senate.

Pentagon officials objected that making a cut of that size in one year would force thousands of careerists out of the service, undermining the morale of those who remained and discouraging talented people from signing up.

The cut would be particularly disruptive, Cheney and his aides contended, when the department had hundreds of thousands of service members deployed in and around Saudi Arabia in response to the Iraqi invasion of Kuwait.

• Required the Pentagon to reduce active-duty manpower by 22 percent by fiscal 1995.

Strategic Arms

• Authorized $2.35 billion in additional spending for procurement of the B-2 "stealth" bomber. But the bill skirted a debate over how many more to build, giving no indication whether the money could be used only to pay for cost-overruns on the 15 planes previously authorized or whether some funds could be used to begin work on additional aircraft.

• Called for spending $2.89 billion on the strategic defense initiative (SDI), a reduction of almost $1.7 billion from President Bush's budget request.

• Divided the SDI funds into five programs, limiting the amount available to each one, but permitting Cheney to increase any category by as much as 10 percent as long as the total SDI budget stayed within the authorized limit.

Based on a Senate-passed provision, the conferees had divided the SDI funds into five programs as a technique to reduce the amount that could be spent on a partially effective, "phase-one" defense, which proponents said could be deployed by the end of the decade.

The final version of the measure retained the division of SDI's budget into five categories but permitted Cheney the 10 percent increase in any one category.

• Authorized $64 million for components of 100 advanced cruise missiles — bomber-launched nuclear weapons with a range of 2,000 miles and "stealthy" radar-evading design. It specified that an additional $43 million would become available if missile flight tests were successful.

With a minor funding difference, both houses had approved the request for 100 of the high-tech missiles. But conferees tangled over Air Force plans to buy another 250 in fiscal 1992: The Senate approved, as requested, $107 million for enough components for the planned production speedup. The House approved only $64 million to buy enough components to build 100 missiles in fiscal 1992.

• Authorized $10 million to continue slowed-down development of the bomber-launched SRAM II, a short-range attack missile.

Both houses had approved the $156 million requested to continue development of SRAM II and $21 million to gear up for SRAM II production. But the Air Force later informed conferees that technical problems had so slowed the program that only $10 million would be needed to prepare for production; that amount was included in the final version.

• Authorized $35 million for SRAM-T, a "tactical version" of the SRAM II that could be carried by fighter planes.

The Senate had approved $119 million, as requested, to develop SRAM-T. The House had approved only $2 million, contending that the weapon had become superfluous because it had been designed to beef up the European-based U.S. nuclear deterrent against a Soviet-led Warsaw Pact attack on NATO.

• Apportioned $680 million between two projects to develop a new intercontinental ballistic missile (ICBM): one to develop a rail-mobile version of the 10-warhead MX; the other to develop the much smaller, single-warhead Midgetman.

The House had approved $610 million for both programs, while the Senate authorized separate amounts for each, totaling $750 million.

But the conferees also adopted language declaring the sense of Congress that the country would not be able to buy both kinds of mobile missiles, assuming peaceful trends in the Soviet Union permitted declining U.S. defense budgets.

The non-binding provision, similar to House-passed language, also declared that the Pentagon should plan to deploy Midgetman in existing missile silos to save money "while preserving a realistic option for subsequent mobile basing."

The provision further declared that the rail-mobile MX program should be directed only toward completing development of key technologies in the expectation that they then would be mothballed. Both houses had rejected the $1.6 billion requested to begin buying rail-mobile MX launchers and building sites for them.

• Authorized $1.34 billion, as requested, for Trident II sub-launched missiles.

The Senate had approved $1.34 billion, as requested, for 52 of the missiles. The House approved $1.14 billion for 42 Trident IIs. The final version authorized the Senate-passed amount, but noted that it might buy fewer than 52 missiles because the British government's delay in placing an anticipated order for 14 of the missiles would boost the cost per copy in fiscal 1991.

• Authorized $210 million for a new attack warning satellite for the Air Force as a replacement for its fleet of DSP satellites. But conferees insisted that the contract for the new satellite be awarded competitively rather than simply choosing a system known as BSTS.

The administration's original budget proposal called for $402 million to develop the BSTS satellite as part of SDI's network of weapons and detection devices. Subsequently, the project was dropped from SDI and transferred to the Air Force.

The House approved $230 million, the Senate $242 million, to develop a new attack warning satellite, but both insisted the Pentagon consider competing satellites for the early warning mission.

• Approved $126 million to develop an antisatellite (ASAT) missile. The House had authorized $100 million and the Senate $152 million of the $208 million requested.

The bill also included two House-passed provisions intended to boost the prospects of an arms control agreement limiting ASAT weapons. One banned tests of a ground-based laser designated MIRACL against an object in space; the other added to the bill $8 million to develop techniques for verifying a ban on ASAT lasers.

• Authorized $15 million to design a plant to recover plutonium from obsolete bombs, provided that the design work not be oriented toward building the plant at any specific site.

The House had approved the $15 million. But the Senate had rejected the entire $65 million requested to begin designing a plant for construction at Rocky Flats, near Denver, home of a nuclear weapons plant that was contaminated with radioactivity.

Ground Combat

• Authorized $747 million to buy some combination of two versions of the M-1 tank. It called for either 225 tanks of the two versions or the larger number of the current "A1" model tanks that could be afforded if the new and untested "A2" model was deemed not yet ready for production.

It also authorized $64 million to begin converting the earliest model M-1s to A2 version tanks and an additional $150 million that could be used either for such modifications or to buy more new A2 model tanks.

Though they differed in detail, both houses had challenged the Army's plan to buy 163 of the existing model M-1A1 tanks, then 62 of the improved — but untested — M-1A2 model, after which the two U.S. tank plants would be mothballed.

- Approved $430 million for 300 Bradley armored troop carriers.

Report language attached to the legislation echoed the Senate's skepticism of Army plans to use jeeplike HMMWV trucks for scouting missions, instead of the armor-plated, missile-carrying Bradleys.

The House had approved the Army's plan to buy 1,200 additional Bradley armored troop carriers; but to keep the production line running longer, it approved only 300 in fiscal 1991, rather than the 600 requested. The Senate approved the purchase of 600 Bradleys, but complained that the Army was cutting off production prematurely.

- Authorized the $176 million requested to develop a "family" of future armored vehicles, including a new tank to replace the M-1, a new troop carrier to replace the Bradley and a new mobile artillery piece, that would share some components, including a chassis.

Report language, however, ordered the Army to give development of the new artillery piece "substantially higher priority" than the new tank, which was the pacesetter at the time.

- Authorized $10 million to help the Army select a relatively lightweight mobile artillery piece for units intended to be flown quickly from U.S. bases to distant trouble spots.

But conferees urged the Army to select one of five weapons that were already available "off the shelf," rather than develop a new one. And they complained that the Army was putting too much emphasis on being able to drop the new vehicle by parachute, and too little on crew-protecting armor, which might make the weapon too heavy to airdrop.

- Authorized $169 million for the 100-mile-range ATACMS missile and $298 million for the JSTARS airborne radar, intended to steer the missile to its target.

Those were the amounts requested and approved by the Senate for the two systems. The House had proposed canceling both programs, which had been designed with an eye toward stopping a Soviet tank blitz against NATO.

- Approved $77 million for modifications of missile-armed Apache helicopters — including $20 million toward fixing their reliability problems — and $159 million to outfit them with new target-finding radar.

Conferees ordered the Army to draw up a long-term plan to modernize the Apache and make it more reliable.

The Army had requested $86 million to modernize Apache helicopters and $159 million to continue developing a new target-finding radar for these aerial tank-hunters. But Congress focused on chronic breakdowns afflicting the Apache.

The House approved the radar request, but cut modernization funding to $20 million, to be used to make the Apache more reliable. The Senate approved both amounts requested, but set aside $30 million of the radar budget to fix the Apache's problems.

- Authorized $291 million to develop a new armed "scout" helicopter under a new name: "scout/attack."

Both houses had cut the $411 million requested to develop a new helicopter designated LH. Both ordered the Army to slow the program and to flight-test some prototypes before making a commitment to buy the new craft. Cheney reorganized the project along these lines and gave it the new name as well.

- Authorized $92 million for trouble-shooting of the ADATS anti-aircraft missile — designed to protect front-line combat units — plus $30 million for the Army to test other mobile anti-aircraft weapons that might replace the ADATS.

Citing test failures of the ADATS, both houses had rejected the $235 million requested to begin production of the weapon. The Senate canceled it outright, arguing that it was too heavily oriented toward the now defunct Warsaw Pact threat; the House approved the $92 million that was later adopted in the final version of the bill for Army researchers to fix the problems.

Tactical Air Combat

- Approved $1.54 billion for 36 Air Force F-15Es and $781 million to modernize a dozen existing Navy F-14s.

Both houses essentially had approved the administration requests for the two heavyweights of the Pentagon's fighter plane fleet, and the conferees ironed out minor differences in funding.

- Authorized $1.5 billion for 48 copies of the F/A-18, used by the Navy and Marines as both a fighter and a bomber.

The administration had requested 66 F/A-18s. The House boosted that number to 84 and the Senate cut it to 42.

- Authorized $1.92 billion for 108 Air Force F-16s, and an additional $225 million for components to be used in future production runs.

Both houses approved the purchase of 108 Air Force F-16s, instead of the 150 planes requested. Declining defense budgets would require the Air Force to break its current multi-year contract for F-16 production, conferees on the bill acknowledged.

- Authorized $964 million for development of the advanced tactical fighter (ATF).

Both houses had approved most of the $1.05 billion sought for development of the ATF, intended to replace the F-14 and F-15. But both also had ordered the Air Force to spend more time flight-testing prototype airplanes before committing to production.

- Provided $592 million to permit a resumption of production of the A-12 ground-attack plane if problems with it were eventually solved. (Cheney canceled the plane early in 1991.)

Both houses had turned down the $1.21 billion requested for eight A-12s, intended for use by the Navy and Air Force as the next generation of ground-attack plane. The Senate approved no A-12 production money, while the House authorized $352 million to keep the production line intact while bugs were worked out. The conferees complained that the futuristic, delta-wing plane was "seriously overweight, far behind schedule, increasingly complex in design and more difficult to manufacture."

- Authorized $815 million to buy 900 AMRAAM air-to-air missiles, the same number as was funded in fiscal 1990.

The House denied the $1.32 billion request for 1,800 AMRAAMs, citing a long history of test failures and production problems. The Senate proposed the amount that was adopted.

The conferees expressed their "frustration" with the program, noting that the Air Force had accepted delivery of only 200 AMRAAMS, though Congress had authorized $3 billion for a total of 2,300 missiles. Their dilemma, they said, was that continued production in fiscal 1991 would be needed to avoid a costly break in the production line, if efforts to debug the missiles proved successful.

- Approved $64 million to upgrade the long-range, half-ton Phoenix missiles carried by the Navy's F-14s.

The final version followed the Senate's lead in increasing the funds for modernization from the $4 million requested.

- Authorized the $84 million requested to develop a lightweight replacement for Phoenix, designated AAAM. However, noting that the new missile would not enter service for a decade, the conferees told the Navy to reconsider its plan to end Phoenix production.
- Approved $48 million for continued development of the ASPJ radar jammer to protect combat planes, which began as a joint project with the Air Force but was later supported only by the Navy. It authorized in addition: $15 million to keep the Air Force involved with ASPJ development, $6.5 million for more testing, and $39 million to buy Air Force jammers.

It also authorized $162 million for a consolidated electronic warfare program. This money was to be allocated among radar-jammer programs under a long-term plan aimed at reducing the types of equipment the services were buying.

The conferees criticized the Pentagon's weapons managers for allowing the Navy and Air Force to go their separate ways in developing radar jammers. The administration asked for $162 million for the Navy to continue development of the ASPJ jammer, initially intended as a joint project. It also requested $301 million to buy two other kinds of radar jammers for Air Force planes.

"We cannot afford redundant and duplicative development and procurement programs in a period of stringent budgets," the conferees declared. The House had slashed the Air Force jammer request, while the Senate had slashed the request for the ASPJ.

Naval Warfare

- Authorized $1.46 billion for one *Seawolf*-class submarine and

$3.2 billion for four *Arleigh Burke*-class destroyers, equipped with the Aegis anti-aircraft system.

Initially, Cheney had requested another new ship of each type. Early in August 1990, Cheney pared back his fiscal 1991 shipbuilding request, and the final version of the defense bill endorsed the revision.

- Authorized $55 million for the Sea Lance missile, intended to be fired from warships at submerged submarines up to 30 miles away, and $5 million to develop a new version of the existing ASROC antisub missile, which had a much shorter range.

The Senate and House Armed Services committees each had challenged the Navy's decision to cancel development of the Sea Lance. The Navy had requested instead $30 million to develop the new version of the ASROC missile.

The House had added $50 million and the Senate $71 million to continue the Sea Lance program, and the House also denied all funds for ASROC.

- Approved $398 million for a high-speed supply ship intended to serve as a mid-ocean, one-stop shopping center supplying a fleet with fuel, food and ammunition.

Air and Sea Transport

- Authorized the production of two additional C-17 cargo planes, but provided only $400 million for procurement.

Because of delays in the production of C-17s, both houses had slashed funding to build additional planes in fiscal 1991, while providing funds to keep the production line intact.

As a practical matter, the Air Force would be unable to build the planes without gaining the approval of the Armed Services and Appropriations committees to reprogram additional funds to the C-17 account from other parts of the defense budget. In addition, the conference report barred the use of any fiscal 1991 C-17 procurement money until after the first plane's initial test flight.

- Authorized $803 million for the V-22 Osprey.

The final version followed the amount approved by the House for the hybrid airplane/helicopter the Marine Corps wanted to use as a troop transport, but which Cheney had tried to kill several times. That total included $238 million to continue development of the plane, $200 million appropriated for procurement in fiscal 1989 but not previously available, and an additional $165 million for procurement.

The conferees emphasized that the procurement funds were to be used only to build enough production-line aircraft for testing.

According to various analyses, the V-22's higher speed made it superior to the conventional helicopters Cheney wanted to buy instead. But before Congress would commit to buying the Osprey, conferees declared, the V-22 would have to demonstrate that it could carry heavy cargo — such as an artillery piece — slung under its belly while flying more than 200 miles per hour.

- Approved $250 million to buy more fast cargo ships to haul tanks and other heavy combat equipment from U.S. ports to trouble spots abroad.

Burden-Sharing

- Required a reduction of 50,000 in the number of U.S. personnel stationed in Europe, reducing the number to 261,855.

The conferees also put in the final version several other restrictions intended to reduce the cost of stationing U.S. forces overseas, but they softened initial provisions.

One such restriction was intended to force the Pentagon to cut the payroll for foreign civilians employed on U.S. bases abroad by 25 percent.

But the final language in the bill permitted the secretary of Defense to waive that limit, if the national interest required it, simply by notifying Congress.

- Imposed a cap of 50,000 on the number of U.S. forces stationed in Japan unless the Japanese government shouldered the cost of keeping them there.

The conferees greatly diluted a House provision that not only would have capped the U.S. personnel level at 50,000 but also would have reduced that number by 5,000 annually.

Base Closings

- Established an eight-member, bipartisan commission for each of the next three Congresses to recommend a list of unneeded military bases that should be closed. The president and Congress each would have to accept or reject each list in toto. Congress, acting under fast-track procedures, could reject a list only by a joint resolution, which could be vetoed.

Personnel Issues

- Provided a 4.1 percent military pay raise, which took effect on Jan 1, 1991.
- Offered more liberal severance payments to personnel discharged before they qualified for retirement. The measure called for removing the current $30,000 cap on the payment and for making enlisted personnel eligible for the first time.
- Continued eligibility for military medical care for 60 days after discharge (for personnel with less than six years' service) or 120 days (for personnel who had served six years or more).
- Created an option for personnel to buy into contributory veterans' education benefit programs, even if the member previously had elected not to join the program.
- Authorized $1.9 billion for equipment earmarked for use by the National Guard and reserves, $1.4 billion more than requested.

Both houses had rejected Cheney's proposals to reduce the number of personnel in the National Guard and reserves and to disband some Guard and reserve units.

Continued from p. 683

Also voting no were 20 liberal Democrats, most of them black or Hispanic members. *(Vote 352, p. 114-H)*

FINAL ACTION

As a House-Senate conference committee on the defense bill went to work Oct. 2, it labored in the shadow of a tentative agreement between the administration and Democratic congressional leaders on the overall federal budget.

Although the agreement would later collapse and have to be pieced together again, the deficit-cutting pact ironically created pressure to spend more for defense. The accord allowed $289 billion in budget authority for defense in fiscal 1991, the higher figure approved by the Senate.

Senate Armed Services Chairman Nunn and Defense Secretary Cheney maintained that the deal obliged Congress to appropriate no less than that amount. This brought protests from House liberals. "Here we are with a big deficit, and they drop $6 billion on the table and say, 'Spend it,' " complained Rep. Patricia Schroeder, D-Colo.

The more conservative Dave McCurdy, D-Okla., also took a wary stance: To give the Pentagon the entire $289 billion in budget authority in fiscal 1991, he said, would simply compound the difficulty of meeting the steadily declining caps on defense outlays set by the summit agreement for fiscal 1992 and 1993.

"If you give in to the temptation to just fill up budget authority," McCurdy said, "you make that problem much worse next year."

Sidestepping the B-2 Conflict

On Oct. 17, the negotiators reached agreement on a $288.3 billion defense budget. But they arrived at a deal only by remaining calculatedly silent on the touchiest single issue before them — the fate of the B-2 bomber.

They agreed to provide $2.35 billion in additional spending for procurement of the stealth plane but gave no indication whether the money could be used only to pay for cost-overruns on the 15 planes previously authorized or whether some of it could be used to begin work on additional aircraft. Members stepped into the vacuum with conflicting opinions as to what the conferees really had in mind.

"As far as we're concerned, the B-2 is dead," said Dellums, a leading opponent. "The B-2 program is alive and well," countered Nunn, a leading supporter.

Fundamentally the conference report's B-2 provision was just one more compromise — "a way to get by this year," according to Aspin. "The Senate will probably come back with whatever the administration requests [by way of building additional B-2s in fiscal 1992] . . . and we will have another fight," he said.

Aspin and Nunn did their best to portray the defense budget compromise as a significant first step toward a post-Cold War military strategy. "It's a sound bill that begins to make the difficult transition of implementing a new military strategy in response to a changing threat in the world, and in reponse to a very tough and austere fiscal environment," Nunn said.

But the shift of focus had more impact on the rhetoric than the outcome of the defense debate. In salvaging the big-ticket defense systems initiated in past years, the conferees simply came up with new rationales.

"You'd be surprised," Aspin said wryly, "at how many weapons systems [that] were designed long ago, when we had the threat of the Soviet Union, turned out to be just perfectly suitable for this new situation with Iraq."

Reopening the Deal

After the conferees thought they had completed their grueling work, they received a disconcerting call back to session. Cheney announced he would recommend a veto of their handiwork. In particular, he cited the provision that would have cut 100,000 personnel from the military payroll.

So negotiations between Cheney and the House and Senate Armed Services committees continued through the following Sunday, Oct. 21, when a provision was added to the bill allowing a more modest troop cut of 80,000.

Although Cheney had sought a reduction of 37,605, he deemed the 80,000-man cut tolerable because it could be carried out without forcing thousands of people out of the armed services involuntarily. "That's what the secretary thinks the department can manage as a reduction in active-duty personnel without . . . firing people," Pentagon spokesman Williams said Oct. 24.

Cheney reluctantly accepted the conferees' scaled-down funding of $2.89 billion for the strategic defense intiative, but he demanded more flexibility in allocating SDI funds.

Based on a Senate-passed provision, the conferees had divided the SDI funds into five programs, limiting the amount available for each one. The point was to reduce the amount that could be spent on a partially effective, "phase-one" defense, which proponents said could be deployed by the end of the decade.

Williams said Oct. 24 that last-minute changes in the SDI provisions "substantially improved the bill" by removing some of the limits on Cheney's flexibility to manage the program. The revised conference report retained the division of SDI's budget into five categories but permitted Cheney to increase any one by up to 10 percent, provided that the total SDI budget did not exceed $2.89 billion.

Cheney was also unhappy with the conferees' decision to establish an eight-member, bipartisan commission in each of the next three Congresses to recommend a list of military bases that should be closed. The president and Congress each would have to accept or reject each list in toto. Congress, acting under fast-track procedures, could reject a list only by a joint resolution, which could be vetoed.

According to congressional sources, Pentagon officials had objected to the fact that the commission would be subject to Senate confirmation at the start of each Congress. But the provision remained in the conference report.

The 912-page compromise version of the defense authorization bill, accompanied by 765 pages of explanation, was filed Oct. 23.

It was adopted by the House, 271-156, on Oct. 24 and approved by the Senate, 80-17, on Oct. 26. *(House vote 517, p. 162-H; Senate vote 320, p. 62-S)*

Bush Signing

In signing the bill Nov. 5, Bush reiterated his concern about the restrictions on SDI, saying the curbs would direct funds "away from the most promising technologies."

He also complained — as he frequently did in signing bills — about intrusions on presidential prerogatives, specifically citing provisions that sought to require him to begin negotiations with Japan on funds to offset the costs of stationing U.S. troops in that country and to consult with NATO about the future of the proposed Crotone air base in Italy.

"I will construe all these provisions to be precatory rather than mandatory," Bush said.

With those reservations, Bush said the authorization bill reflected "most of the administration's major defense priorities" and "will provide for a strong national defense during fiscal year 1991." ■

Fate of 'Stealth' Bomber Left Uncertain

When 1990 began, supporters and opponents of the B-2 "stealth" bomber expected the year would decide the fate of the controversial aircraft. By year's end, Congress had resolutely sidestepped the issue.

The defense authorization bill for fiscal 1991 (HR 4739 — PL 101-510) called for $2.3 billion for B-2 procurement. But in the accompanying report (H Rept 101-938), conferees were intentionally vague about whether the funds could be spent only to pay cost overruns on the 15 bombers previously authorized (as House members asserted) or used to buy additional B-2s (as senators maintained).

House Armed Services Committee Chairman Les Aspin, D-Wis., who turned from a supporter of the B-2 to its most influential opponent in 1990, called the defense bill's calculated silence "a way to get by this year." He predicted, "We will have another fight" in 1991.

BACKGROUND

Built of ultramodern lightweight materials and with its

angles rounded off, the sleek B-2 was the standard-bearer for a new generation of "stealth" aircraft engineered to slip through Soviet defenses without radar detection. But the B-2's costs escalated even as superpower tensions faded. The result was increasing opposition in Congress.

Most Americans first learned of the effort to develop the "stealth bomber" in August 1980, when Harold Brown, President Jimmy Carter's Defense secretary, confirmed press reports of the top-secret project.

Ronald Reagan, Carter's opponent in the presidential campaign that year, charged that the existence of stealth was leaked by the administration to conceal Carter's "dismal defense record." Reagan charged that the disclosure gave the Soviet Union a "10-year head start" in countering the new technology.

The details of the project and its cost remained top-secret for several years. The only congressional debate about the stealth focused on whether the United States needed to build the B-1 bomber to maintain U.S. deterrence against the Soviet Union while the B-2 was being developed. Carter canceled the B-1, but Reagan, as president, later revived it. *(B-1 dispute, 1980 Almanac, p. 48; 1981 Almanac, p. 226)*

The defense authorization bill for fiscal 1990 slowed the planned production rate for the B-2, largely because of debate over the project's escalating cost. That year's budget provided $2.09 billion for two planes in fiscal 1990 and components for five in fiscal 1991. The Senate rebuffed efforts to stop B-2 production outright. *(1989 Almanac, p. 414)*

The B-2 prototype began flying in 1989, but tests of the plane's "stealth" qualities were yet to be conducted when Congress took up the issue of its future in 1990.

The Bush administration had defended the B-2 as fundamental to U.S. strategic defenses. On April 26, however, Defense Secretary Dick Cheney cut the number of B-2s to be produced from 132 to 75, trimming the total cost of developing and purchasing the fleet from $72 billion to $61 billion.

Scaled-Down Request

Cheney originally requested $4.77 billion for fiscal 1991 to continue development of the B-2 while buying five planes and the components that would be used in fiscal 1992 to build 10 more. His scaled-down April request called for $4.51 billion — including $1.57 billion to continue development of the plane, $1.99 billion to buy two additional planes (the 16th and 17th) and $767 million for components that would be used to build six additional planes to be funded in the fiscal 1992 budget.

Through fiscal 1990, Congress had appropriated $27 billion for the B-2. According to the Pentagon, completing Cheney's slimmed-down program would cost an additional $34 billion from fiscal 1991 onward.

Cheney told the Senate and House Armed Services committees that the budget crunch required the kinds of reductions he was proposing in the B-2 and several other weapons while the decline of the Soviet military threat made the cutbacks tolerable. "We can afford to slow down the pace of developing and fielding our next generation of aircraft," he said.

Supporters of the B-2 felt Cheney's cutback improved the bomber's political stock. "You have probably made it a little easier for us to sell," House Armed Services member Robert W. Davis, R-Mich., told the Defense secretary.

Senate Armed Services Chairman Sam Nunn, D-Ga., who also remained firmly committed to the B-2, concurred. "It's a more sensible approach," he said of Cheney's new package, "and that helps."

But B-2 critics, among them House committee member John R. Kasich, R-Ohio, rejected the proposal, contending that Cheney would simply compound the Pentagon's budgetary dilemmas. "We are cutting a little bit, and we are stretching a lot," Kasich complained, "and when you cut and stretch you drive up the cost."

Cost Per Plane

Because the cost of developing the plane and setting up a manufacturing line to handle its exotic materials would be amortized over fewer planes under Cheney's new plan, the cost per copy was projected to rise from $530 million to about $815 million. A B-2 critic, Sen. Carl Levin, D-Mich., called that "an astronomical figure."

Cheney built his case for continuing B-2 production on the longstanding U.S. policy of maintaining a diverse arsenal of strategic weapons able to strike the Soviet Union.

The traditional argument had been that a "triad" of weapons — land-based missiles, submarine-launched missiles and manned bombers — provided an ample hedge against the possibility of a technological breakthrough that might suddenly give Moscow a defense against any one type of weapon.

In addition, Cheney concurred in the view long held by senior Air Force officers that deterrence was further enhanced by a bomber fleet that included both "manned penetrators" and planes launching long-range cruise missiles from far beyond the reach of Soviet air defenses.

"If you believe in the triad," Cheney told the House committee, "the B-2 is important."

Cheney's scaled-down fleet of 75 planes would equip two wings of 30 planes each with enough left over for training. Fielding a force any smaller than that would incur overhead costs that could be nearly as high as the larger force, but would be militarily useless, he said.

One reason the Pentagon could live with a smaller B-2 force, Cheney said, was that its list of potential nuclear targets was shrinking, partly because of Eastern Europe's growing independence from Moscow. "The target base in shrinking," he said. "The Warsaw Pact no longer is a target-rich environment."

COMMITTEE ACTION

Despite some restiveness over the B-2's escalating price tag, the Senate Armed Services Committee stuck to its solid support for the aircraft. But in the House Armed Services Committee, where opponents had failed 16-36 in trying to kill the stealth in 1989, Aspin's decision to oppose the B-2 led to a different result.

Senate Committee

The Senate Armed Services Committee had been a bastion of support for the B-2 under Nunn's leadership. When the committee approved its version of the defense authorization bill (S 2884) on July 13, it included Cheney's revised request for the B-2 without alteration.

The committee did weigh in on a side issue, however, deleting $96.4 million requested for hangars and other facilities at Whiteman Air Force Base in Missouri, where the first operational B-2s were to be based.

For more than a year, Strategic Forces Subcommittee Chairman Jim Exon, D-Neb., had complained that the Air

Force was being extravagant in planning to custom-build a hangar for each B-2, a decision the Air Force claimed would simplify maintenance.

House Committee

Despite the Senate panel's vote, opposition to the B-2 was growing. Anticipating a bruising congressional battle, President Bush made a pitch for the plane and other efforts to modernize the U.S. nuclear arsenal. Visiting an MX missile base on July 20, the president said such improvements were the only way to maintain deterrence "in the face of continuing, across-the-board modernization of Soviet strategic forces."

But the House Armed Services Committee was in no mood to rubber-stamp Cheney's proposal on the B-2. The influential Aspin guaranteed that when he announced on July 23 that he would switch from a supporter to an opponent of the plane.

The Armed Services chairman said he would join with two committee members, liberal Democrat Ronald V. Dellums of California and conservative Republican Kasich, in attempting to bar production of any B-2s beyond the 15 already built or under construction. Aspin said his decision was based on the high cost of the plane in an era of sharply declining defense budgets and the availability of cheaper alternatives for various missions.

In approving its version of the defense authorization bill (HR 4739) on July 31, the committee voted 34-20 to block further B-2 production.

The committee's senior Republican, Bill Dickinson of Alabama, complained that Aspin had used the savings reaped from elimination of the B-2 to provide pork-barrel benefits to committee members in exchange for their support for the authorization measure.

"When he canceled the B-2, he automatically got $2.7 billion worth of chits," Dickinson told a reporter Aug. 1. "He and his staff have been all over working on my [Republican] guys."

The panel also sliced $25 million from the $96 million requested to continue building B-2 facilities at Whiteman Air Force Base in Missouri. The installations already funded at Whiteman would suffice for the 15-plane fleet envisaged by the committee.

The Air Force case for the B-2 rested primarily on the assumption that Soviet air defenses would become impervious to existing B-1B and B-52 bombers. But pointing to the troubled Soviet economy, the committee was skeptical that Moscow could afford the necessary improvements.

To lay the groundwork for deciding how much to spend beefing up the B-1B's radar-jamming gear, Congress in fiscal 1990 ordered an independent panel of experts to evaluate the plane's ability to penetrate Soviet defenses through the late 1990s. For the fiscal 1991 bill, Armed Services included a provision asking that the study's scope be extended to cover the B-1B's effectiveness through the year 2010.

Unlikely Alliance

The unlikely team of liberal Dellums and conservative Kasich was joined in opposing the B-2 by liberal arms control lobby groups, most of which had embraced the campaign to stop B-2 production as their top legislative priority for 1990.

But according to Kasich, the key effort came from members lobbying their own colleagues. Kasich presented his case against the bomber to about 40 members in their offices, he estimated, leaving aside others he had buttonholed in corridors or on the House floor.

Even before Aspin's announcement on July 23 that he would incorporate their provision into the Armed Services bill, the B-2 opponents claimed that 207 members would support their position on the House floor.

FLOOR ACTION

With their victory in the House Armed Services Committee, opponents of the B-2 focused on the Senate, where the debate over the aircraft became the highlight of action on the defense authorization bill.

Senate Floor

Taking up its version of the defense authorization bill (S 2884), the Senate voted on Aug. 3 to continue production of the B-2 by turning back two amendments devised by the plane's opponents. But opposition had grown over the year before, when an amendment to kill the B-2 attracted only 29 votes.

An amendment by Patrick J. Leahy, D-Vt., which would have killed the program outright after completing six test planes under construction, was rejected, 43-56. *(Vote 208, p. 43-S)*

An amendment by William S. Cohen, R-Maine, which would have denied funding for two additional B-2s authorized in the bill, was rejected, 45-53. *(Vote 209, p. 43-S)*

Both votes were largely, though not completely, along party lines. Eight Republicans voted to kill the B-2, and nine backed Cohen's amendment to bar funding for the additional aircraft. Twenty Democrats backed the B-2 by voting against Leahy's amendment, and 19 opposed Cohen's amendment.

Opponents were particularly encouraged that 15 of 29 Appropriations Committee members voted for Leahy's amendment, leading to hopes that they still might win a vote to bar or limit funds for the B-2.

'Sticker Shock'

During the Senate debate, Nunn conceded that the price tag was an attention-getter: "All of us are suffering from sticker shock," he said. But he insisted that the plane would be worth the money.

The Soviet Union was continuing to modernize its vast nuclear arsenal, Nunn said. By confronting Moscow with the threat of a retaliatory strike that could not be stopped, he argued, the B-2 would enhance nuclear deterrence.

"The pilot of the most modern Soviet . . . interceptor has a better chance of detecting a B-2 if he looks out of his cockpit with his naked eyeballs than if he concentrates on his radar scope," Nunn said. "Stealth works."

Moreover, he insisted the plane could carry powerful nuclear weapons to attack targets that could not be reached with other weapons. B-2 proponents also emphasized that the plane's long range would give it great flexibility for striking targets other than the Soviet Union. It was a timely issue, because Iraq had invaded Kuwait only the day before the Senate debate. *(Gulf crisis, p. 717)*

If it became necessary for the United States to weigh in against Iraq, Nunn argued, a B-2 squadron would be a far less risky instrument than an aircraft carrier sent into the narrow confines of the Persian Gulf.

"Saddam Hussein, whether we like it or not, represents one wave of the future," warned B-2 backer Malcolm Wallop, R-Wyo.

But some past supporters had turned to doubters. John Glenn, D-Ohio — a test pilot before he gained fame as an astronaut — had supported the B-2 in previous years, but told the Senate that, in the current budgetary environment, the plane "has gotten too expensive to permit us to do some of the things in conventional [weaponry] and manpower that we need to do."

Glenn called for greater reliance on very accurate, long-range cruise missiles launched from existing B-52 and B-1 bombers to keep the U.S. deterrent force in fighting trim. He described as "almost miraculous" a new type of cruise missile — itself designed to be "stealthy."

In addition to complaining that the B-2's cost was rising as its rationale was shifting, Cohen argued that its stealthiness had not yet been tested: "The costs are elusive; the mission, at this point, is at least questionable, and the capability is, as yet, unproven."

Before rejecting the Leahy and Cohen amendments, the Senate adopted 97-2 an amendment by Nunn and Armed Services ranking Republican John W. Warner, Va., barring expenditure of funds until the B-2 program successfully completed certain tests. Cohen dismissed the Nunn-Warner limitations as "a fig leaf." *(Vote 207, p. 43-S)*

Leahy, the Senate's leading B-2 opponent, made one more attempt to kill the weapon on Oct. 11, as the Senate Appropriations Committee considered the defense appropriations measure. But his motion to stop B-2 production was defeated, 15-14. *(Defense appropriations, p. 812)*

House Floor

The B-2 never came up as an issue when the House debated the defense authorization bill in September.

Opponents of the stealth plane were delighted with their Armed Services Committee for its vote to end production. Supporters decided to bide their time and depend on the pro-B-2 Senate Armed Services Committee to defend the plane in the House-Senate conference committee on the defense bill.

On Sept. 19, the House passed the defense authorization bill (HR 4739), 256-155. *(Vote 352, p. 114-H)*

CONFERENCE/FINAL ACTION

As the conference committee on the defense authorization bill worked its way through the voluminous measure, the House-Senate conflict over the B-2 loomed over the talks.

Opponents were bolstered by new disclosures of trouble for the B-2 and its prime contractor, the Northrop Corp. On Oct. 11, Air Force Secretary Donald Rice told the Senate Armed Services Committee that the first test flight of the second B-2 in production would be delayed by nine months because of problems at Northrop and funding cuts.

That setback followed testimony to House members by Air Force investigators about serious cost accounting and production problems they had found at Northrop. Even Exon, one of the plane's leading supporters, conceded at the Armed Services hearing that "the B-2 program is in big, big trouble."

During a break in the conference negotiations, Nunn, the plane's most important advocate, quipped, "We're hanging on by stealthy fingers."

Making a Deal

On Oct. 17, the conference committee reached its deal: Splitting the difference between the Senate's yes and the House's no, conferees approved $2.35 billion in additional spending for procurement of the B-2 stealth bomber. The deal was part of an overall agreement on a $288.3 billion defense budget.

The conferees were calculatedly silent, however, as to whether the B-2 money could be used only to pay for cost-overruns on the 15 planes previously authorized or whether some of it could be used to begin work on additional aircraft.

Proponents and opponents of the controversial bomber promptly stepped into that informational vacuum with explanations of the deal that were as unconditional as they were contradictory:

"As far as we're concerned, the B-2 is dead," Dellums declared.

"The B-2 program is alive and well," contended Nunn.

Technically, the competing sides were quibbling over how much leeway the conference committee agreement gave the Pentagon.

"The Air Force cannot build more planes than [Congress] authorizes," insisted Aspin.

"They can begin producing planes according to the money they have available," Nunn maintained. "There are no restrictions in law."

Fundamentally, the conference report's B-2 provision was just one more compromise — "a way to get by this year," according to Aspin.

"The Senate will probably come back with whatever the administration requests [by way of building additional B-2s in fiscal 1992] . . . and we will have another fight," he said.

B-2 opponents professed confidence that they had the political momentum and would be in a stronger position next year to kill the program. "Time is on the side of the people who want to limit the B-2 buy," said Aspin. "We may end up buying more than 15, but we're not going to buy many more."

While not conceding that the bomber's prospects were dimming, Nunn said that the plane would have to begin delivering on the promise of the radar-evading qualities that made it so costly.

"It's got to prove itself this year," he said. "If this is not a revolutionary development in strategic weapons and in conventional capability, then it will not be built in the long run."

Those on both sides also continued to argue about whether the B-2 was no longer needed — or more crucial than ever.

Proponents contended that the plane still was needed for strategic deterrence, since the retrenchment in Soviet conventional forces had not yet been matched in the Soviet nuclear arsenal.

But backers of the airplane also touted its long range with a heavy conventional bombload.

"As we bring our forces back home," said Nunn, "our long-range strike aircraft are going to be more and more important."

Aspin disagreed. While the Iraq crisis made some controversial weapons look more worthwhile, "it didn't improve the case for the B-2," he said.

Floor Debate

When the House took up the authorization conference report Oct. 24, opponents of the B-2 tried to win more ground in their battle against the costly plane than Senate conferees would concede.

Dellums, Kasich and Aspin warned the Pentagon of dire political consequences if the agency exploited the conference report's ambiguity by contracting for more B-2s than the 15 previously authorized.

On the Senate side, proponents of the bomber, led by Nunn and Warner, insisted just as adamantly that nothing would prohibit the Air Force from buying additional bombers, if the money were available.

Cheney took the latter view, according to Dickinson, the ranking Republican on House Armed Services. In Cheney's view, "there's no prohibition here; we've got the money and we're going to build them," Dickinson told the House on Oct. 24.

"Somebody's being lied to," Dickinson commented.

If the Air Force tried to contract for additional planes, Dellums declared, "we will go into court to file an injunction against them."

But the critics felt they had more potent leverage in the Air Force's need for additional appropriations to complete work on the 15 B-2s already on the books. Kasich said the funds authorized so far would pay for only about 12 planes.

If the Air Force defied the House by signing up for additional B-2s, Aspin warned, he would join Dellums and Kasich in trying to block future B-2 funding — even the funds needed for the planes already approved. "If they jack around," Aspin said, "we cut off all B-2 money, and we don't care whether they get 15 operational planes or a lot of boxes full of spare parts."

The defense authorization conference report, including the funds to keep the B-2 program going, was adopted by the House, 271-156, on Oct. 24 and cleared by the Senate, 80-17, on Oct. 26. *(House vote 517, p. 162-H; Senate vote 320, p. 62-S)*

Bush signed the measure Nov. 5. ■

SDI Budget Slashed, Funds Earmarked

Former President Ronald Reagan's grand dream of an impregnable defense against nuclear attack survived in fiscal 1991, but with its ambitions scaled down to match changing times and limited funding.

The defense authorization bill (HR 4739 — PL 101-510) called for $2.89 billion of the $4.69 billion that President Bush requested for the strategic defense initiative (SDI). In addition to sharply reducing Bush's funding request, Congress also imposed — over the president's objections — significant restrictions on how to spend the money.

In an effort to impose more control on SDI, Congress divided the funding into categories — and, in the process, limited the Pentagon's flexibility to pour resources into a first-phase antimissile defense of limited effectiveness. Bush had promised to make a decision by late 1992 on deployment of such an initial system.

Before agreeing to accept the defense authorization bill, Defense Secretary Dick Cheney demanded that Senate-House conferees modify it to loosen the restrictions on SDI. The conferees granted the Pentagon slightly more flexibility to manage the program but retained the new categories of funds. *(Defense authorization bill, p. 671; provisions: strategic arms, p. 684)*

BACKGROUND

When Reagan launched SDI in 1983, he linked it with a visionary goal of transcending the balance of nuclear terror — rendering nuclear missiles "impotent and obsolete," in Reagan's words.

The idea of a space-based umbrella of antimissile defenses was sold to Reagan by a group of conservatives including Edward Teller, the physicist known as "the father of the hydrogen bomb."

Critics, including some scientists and many arms control advocates, derided the idea as a fantasy that they nicknamed "star wars." They also argued its development would require the United States to abrogate the 1972 U.S.-Soviet antiballistic missile (ABM) treaty.

In the years that followed, Soviet negotiators persistently but unsuccessfully sought a ban on strategic defense programs in arms control talks.

Even before Reagan left office, SDI backers were oriented toward a more technically realistic goal: a defense that would disrupt the kind of meticulously timed attack in which Moscow could use a fraction of its intercontinental ballistic missiles to obliterate the U.S. missile force.

Congress funded research into the strategic defense concept but consistently reduced Reagan's budget requests.

The first installment was trimmed from $1.8 billion that Reagan requested for fiscal 1985 to the $1.4 billion that was endorsed by Congress in that year's defense authorization bill. *(1984 Almanac, p. 35)*

The requests grew larger — and the cuts deeper — in later years. In fiscal 1987, Reagan requested $5.3 billion. Congress trimmed the program to $3.5 billion, and the Senate fell one vote short of cutting it even further. *(1986 Almanac, p. 16)*

Beginning in 1985, the Reagan administration asserted a new and controversial interpretation of the 1972 ABM treaty, maintaining that certain antimissile tests in space could be conducted without violating the pact. In 1987, the House and Senate added amendments to the fiscal 1988 defense authorization bill intended to bar any such space testing of SDI weapons.

Under a compromise reached with the administration, the final version of the bill provided that no SDI tests would be conducted in fiscal 1988 other than those officially proposed — all of which were to be consistent with the traditional, restrictive interpretation of the treaty. In return, congressional negotiators agreed to provide slightly more money for SDI ($3.9 billion) than they had originally intended. *(1987 Almanac, p. 195)*

In 1988, a provision of the fiscal 1989 authorization bill that took a mild swipe at SDI was the principal reason why Reagan vetoed the measure. The provision was dropped in a second version of the bill. *(1988 Almanac, p. 399)*

When Bush became president, he maintained support for SDI but shifted attention to a less expansive system known as "brilliant pebbles" that would rely on thousands of small, heat-seeking guided missiles to be placed in Earth orbit. This system became the leading contender for a first-phase SDI deployment.

In 1989, Bush's revised budget requested $4.9 billion for SDI — a $1 billion cutback from Reagan's initial proposal for fiscal 1990. After four years of permitting annual increases, Congress approved $3.8 billion, a $279 million reduction from the year before. *(1989 Almanac, p. 18)*

SENATE ACTION

Compared with the $4.06 billion Bush requested for the Pentagon's share of SDI research in fiscal 1991, the Armed Services Committee recommended $3.57 billion when it marked up its version of the defense authorization bill (S 2884) in July.

During three days of debate on the Senate floor, ending Aug. 4, members approved a defense authorization bill that called for a radical reshaping of SDI.

Voting almost exactly along party lines, the Democratic-controlled Senate adopted a Democratic amendment to block development of a partial antimissile defense in the late 1990s, a project that had become a touchstone of support for Bush among some foreign policy conservatives.

The SDI revamping was the only major change the full Senate made in the defense bill that came to it from the Armed Services Committee.

Changing Focus

By a vote of 54-44, the Senate adopted the amendment by Democrats Jeff Bingaman, N.M., and Richard C. Shelby, Ala., that was intended to derail the administration's plan to make an early decision on deploying the first phase of SDI. *(Vote 223, p. 46-S)*

While designed to slow development of brilliant pebbles, the Bingaman-Shelby amendment also called for increasing the emphasis within SDI on developing two other kinds of antimissile defenses:

- Small networks of ground-based interceptor missiles that could stop a small number of missiles launched by accident or by a Third World country. The 1972 U.S.-Soviet treaty limiting ABM systems would permit deployment of up to 100 such interceptor missiles.
- Laser-armed satellites and other exotic weaponry, which could not be deployed for decades but might offer a far more robust shield against a large-scale missile attack than the brilliant pebbles network.

The Bingaman-Shelby amendment called for subdividing the $3.57 billion that the Armed Services Committee approved for SDI in fiscal 1991 into 11 components, setting a spending ceiling on each.

In a letter to GOP senators two days before the vote on the amendment, Bush warned that the SDI overhaul was "more serious than a funding cut."

While Bush planned to spend $329 million on brilliant pebbles, the amendment allowed only $129 million, the amount spent on that part of the program in fiscal 1990.

Including brilliant pebbles, Bush's budget request had $1.95 billion earmarked for development of a Phase I system. The amendment would have reduced that to $1.51 billion.

Defenders of SDI argued that even a limited first-phase system would "generate the necessary doubt in the mind if the attacker" to deter attack, as Malcolm Wallop, R-Wyo., told the Senate on Aug. 4.

Aside from its strategic merits, some SDI backers also saw a political advantage to planning for a system that could be deployed in the relatively near-term. By promising some return on the investment in SDI before the turn of the century, they reasoned, the Phase I approach should make the costly program more politically attractive.

Two Types of Opponents

The Phase I approach drew vigorous opposition, however, on two fronts, mostly from Democrats:

- For practical purposes, most liberal arms control activists opposed any effort to develop antimissile defenses, deeming them superfluous at best and possibly an incitement to a new and dangerous phase in the U.S.-Soviet arms race. But rather than challenge the politically attractive notion of trying to defend the country against attack, many of the liberals seized on Reagan's expansive rhetoric to insist that the SDI effort focus on development of futuristic weapons that could weave a nearly impervious shield over the country.
- On the other hand, some more conservative Democrats, such as Armed Services Committee Chairman Sam Nunn, D-Ga., favored trying to develop a ground-based, treaty-compliant ABM system, if only to pressure Moscow into reaching arms control agreements.

But Nunn opposed junking the ABM treaty to deploy a system of limited effectiveness, which, he insisted, would be unaffordable.

To those two strains of opposition to the Bush administration's Phase I focus for SDI, the Bingaman-Shelby amendment added the all-purpose political lubricant of constituent interest: Much of the research on Nunn's favored ground-based approach was being performed in Huntsville, Ala.; and Energy Department laboratories in New Mexico were the site of much research on antimissile lasers. New Mexico's Pete V. Domenici was one of only two Republicans — the other was Oregon's Mark O. Hatfield — to support the amendment.

Wallop, for more than a decade the Senate's most prominent advocate of an antimissile program, fumed that the amendment turned SDI into "a technological welfare program" for constituents of Bingaman and Shelby.

The Senate also tabled (killed) amendments:

- By Dale Bumpers, D-Ark., to reduce funding for SDI by $600 million. In the 56-41 vote, four Republicans voted against Nunn's motion to table the amendment while 16 Democrats followed Nunn in voting to kill the amendment. *(Vote 225, p. 46-S)*
- By John Kerry, D-Mass., to shift $400 million from SDI to programs for drug treatment, and health care for veterans and pregnant women. In the 54-43 vote, six Republicans crossed party lines to vote against the tabling motion, while 17 Democrats again joined in the vote to kill the amendment. *(Vote 226, p. 46-S)*

HOUSE ACTION

The defense authorization bill passed Sept. 19 by the House (HR 4739) cut even more deeply into the strategic defense initiative than the Senate-passed version, calling for only $2.3 billion for SDI in fiscal 1991.

On Sept. 18, House Democrats pushed through, 225-189, an amendment by Charles E. Bennett, D-Fla., and Tom Ridge, R-Pa., that cut $600 million from the $2.9 billion SDI authorization recommended by the Armed Services Committee. *(Vote 339, p. 110-H)*

Then, using that money and other funds, Aspin put together his own package of hardware and personnel funding to back up troops deployed in the Persian Gulf to confront Iraq.

The House on Sept. 18 had rejected three other SDI amendments:

- By Robert K. Dornan, R-Calif., to raise SDI funding to $4.2 billion, rejected 83-338. *(Vote 336, p. 110-H)*
- By Ronald V. Dellums, D-Calif., to authorize $1.5 billion, rejected 135-286. *(Vote 337, p. 110-H)*
- By Jon Kyl, R-Ariz., to increase the authorization to $3.6 billion, rejected 141-273. *(Vote 338, p. 110-H)*

FINAL ACTION

As expected, the conference committee on the defense authorization measure essentially split the difference between the $3.57 billion approved by the Senate and the $2.3 billion approved by the House for SDI in fiscal 1991.

The conferees agreed to a funding level of $2.89 billion for SDI, a reduction of almost $1.7 billion from President Bush's budget request and $700 million less than Congress authorized in fiscal 1990.

Based on the Senate-passed provision, the conferees divided the SDI funds into five programs, limiting the amount available for each one — including the controversial "phase-one" defense.

John W. Warner of Virginia, the Senate Armed Services Committee's senior Republican, criticized the SDI provision as "the largest incursion we've seen to date by the legislative branch into the authority of the executive branch to manage a program." Ultimately, the restrictions on SDI contributed to a threat to veto the defense measure.

Conferees had announced agreement on the authorization bill in the early hours of Oct. 17. But Cheney threatened to recommend a veto of the compromise. The level of troop cuts it demanded was the main reason, but his list of objections also included the restrictions on SDI.

Cheney's efforts to modify the deal focused on obtaining more flexibility in allocating the SDI funds rather than increasing the amount.

So negotiations between Cheney and the House and Senate Armed Services committees continued through the following Sunday, Oct. 21, when a revised version of the defense bill was nailed down.

Pentagon spokesman Pete Williams said Oct. 24 that last-minute changes in the SDI provisions "substantially improved the bill" by removing some of the limits on Cheney's flexibility to manage the program. Congressional sources dismissed the revisions as face-saving changes.

The final bill retained the division of SDI's budget into five categories but permitted Cheney to increase any one by up to 10 percent, provided that the total SDI budget not exceed $2.89 billion.

Arizona Republican Kyl, a leading House proponent of SDI, complained that the deal "will cost us at least two years" in trying to field an antimissile defense. Referring to Bush's plan to decide in late 1992 whether the phase-one system was ready for deployment, SDI chief Henry Cooper predicted that the decision would have to be postponed until 1994.

The conference reports on the annual defense authorization bill (H Rept 101-923) and the companion appropriations measure (HR 5803 — H Rept 101-938) were cleared for the president Oct. 26.

President's Message

In his message upon signing the defense authorization bill on Nov. 5 (PL 101-510), Bush registered his protest at the restrictions on SDI.

"The earmarking of funds, in combination with a funding level that is $1.8 billion below the amount requested, unduly restricts the flexibility necessary for sound management and virtually guarantees that funds will be redirected away from promising technologies," he said.

Objecting as well to congressional language intended to prohibit any potential violation of the ABM treaty, Bush said he took the position that "Congress did not intend that obligation of funds for the ground-based interceptors and sensor identified in HR 4739 be dependent on a determination at this time that these systems are deployable under the ABM treaty." ■

Base Closings Commission Established

Congress, in the fiscal 1991 defense authorization bill, established a blue-ribbon commission to make recommendations about possible military base closings into the mid-1990s. The procedure would resemble the one established by Congress on a one-shot basis in 1988.

The 1990 defense debate began with raw feelings because of Defense Secretary Dick Cheney's announcement that he would seek to close 47 military bases. Democrats accused the Pentagon of drawing up a politically tilted "hit list" that targeted bases in their districts; administration officials denied the charges.

The final defense bill (HR 4739 — PL 101-510) established an eight-member, bipartisan commission for each of the next three Congresses to recommend a list of unneeded military bases that should be closed. The president and Congress each would have to accept or reject each list in toto. Congress, acting under fast-track procedures, could reject a list only by a joint resolution, which could be vetoed.

According to congressional sources, Pentagon officials had objected to the fact that the commission would be subject to Senate confirmation at the start of each Congress; however, that remained in the conference report.

BACKGROUND

Congress enacted legislation in 1988 to set up a blue-ribbon commission that would identify military bases to be closed as a money-saving move. It designed the process to thwart efforts by members to block closure of individual bases, an effort that succeeded during 1989.

A 12-member Commission on Base Realignment and Closure, established by the legislation, made its recommendations Dec. 29, 1988. The panel targeted 91 bases for closure or partial closure, and it estimated savings of some $700 million annually. *(Background, 1988 Almanac p. 439; list of bases, p. 442)*

In a procedure designed to shield the commission's recommendations from congressional meddling, the list could not be amended. The 1988 law (PL 100-526) gave

National Guard Ruling

The Supreme Court on June 11 unanimously upheld a 1986 law that barred any governor from overriding federal orders to send a state's National Guard units on training exercises outside the United States.

Congress had enacted the law as part of the fiscal 1987 defense authorization act (PL 99-661) after several governors had objected on political grounds to sending state National Guard units to Pentagon-sponsored training exercises in Central America.

The provision — called the Montgomery amendment after its sponsor, Rep. G. V. "Sonny" Montgomery, D-Miss. — amended the Armed Forces Reserve Act of 1952, which had required a governor's consent before a National Guard unit could be called to active duty. *(1986 Almanac, p. 464)*

The 1986 law was challenged by Minnesota Gov. Rudy Perpich, a Democrat, who objected to members of the Minnesota National Guard being placed in active service and sent to Honduras for joint exercises with that country's military forces. He contended that the law intruded on states' control over the National Guard under the Constitution's so-called militia clauses.

Under Article I, Section 8, Congress had the power to "provide for calling forth the Militia to execute the Laws of the Union, suppress Insurrections and repel Invasions." A second clause gave Congress power to govern the militia while "employed in the Service of the United States, reserving to the States respectively, the Appointment of the Officers, and the Authority of training the Militia according to the discipline prescribed by Congress."

Writing for a unanimous court in *Perpich v. Department of Defense*, however, Justice John Paul Stevens said the 1986 law was valid under the National Guard's dual-enlistment system and did not infringe on state powers under the militia clauses.

" ... [T]he members of the National Guard of Minnesota who are ordered into federal service with the National Guard of the United States lose their status as members of the state militia during their period of active duty," Stevens wrote.

"If the discipline required for effective services in the Armed Forces of a global power requires training in distant lands, or distant skies, Congress has the authority to provide it," he added.

Stevens rejected Perpich's argument that the broad interpretation of Congress' power nullified the states' role under the militia clauses. "It merely recognizes the supremacy of federal power in the area of military affairs," Stevens concluded.

each chamber 45 working days from March 1, 1989, to vote to kill the list in toto. If Congress did not act, the closings would proceed.

Both chambers in 1989 voted overwhelmingly not to block or delay the closure process. *(1989 Almanac, p. 470)*

Cheney's Plan

Cheney on Jan. 29 released his list of military installations slated for closure or realignment. The proposed base reductions immediately became the most contested issue in President Bush's budget request, even though no fiscal 1991 funds were involved.

"Since that list has come out all hell has broken loose," said House Armed Services Chairman Les Aspin, D-Wis. "All over Capitol Hill there are groups — bipartisan groups — forming up to fight the closing of one base or another."

Cheney targeted 35 domestic bases and 12 overseas bases for closure, mostly in Democratic congressional districts. Cheney's bid came as the Pentagon began the actual process of closing 86 other domestic bases — the fruits of the successful 1988 base-closing package crafted by Rep. Dick Armey, R-Texas, and the Armed Services committees.

Members with hometown bases on Cheney's list did not have to worry about actual closures for at least a couple of years. Cheney had not made his formal announcement to close any new bases, and could not by law until he submitted his next budget a year later.

Under a 1977 law, a Defense secretary was required to announce all final decisions to close bases during a budget request and at that time also supply Congress with evaluations of the targeted bases' physical, environmental, strategic and operational impact.

Democratic lawmakers complained loudly about Cheney's list, arguing that their party was hit hardest and saying the list was drawn up before any announcement of reductions in force structure.

"Instead of producing a comprehensive force-structure plan, which included base closures, Secretary Cheney has produced an unbalanced, partisan hit list," said Rep. Patricia Schroeder, D-Colo., who chaired the Armed Services Military Installations and Facilities Subcommittee. "Democratic districts are hit and Republican districts get off scot free."

While 29 of the 35 major closures Cheney recommended were in Democratic congressional districts, Cheney denied political gamesmanship.

"My former colleagues need to know — and I think most of them do in fact believe — that ... I didn't come down and say hit Democrats or hit liberal Democrats, not conservative Democrats," said Cheney, a House member for 10 years before assuming the Pentagon post in 1989. "I think if you look at the list, you'll find that it is in fact the best judgment of the services of what their requirements are."

Cheney reiterated that the list was drawn up by the four services and that he neither added nor subtracted bases from it.

Aspin, though, proposed the creation of another independent base-closing commission that would come up with a new list of bases and force Congress to vote up or down on the entire package.

"I'm certainly willing to consider it," Cheney said Jan. 30. "[But] I think the intelligent way to proceed is to let me manage the department. ..."

LEGISLATIVE ACTION

The House Armed Services Committee on July 31 adopted the $283 billion defense authorization bill that contained a ban on closing any additional military bases in fiscal 1991.

On Sept. 11, the day the full House began debate on the defense authorization bill, Cheney told House Republicans that he would urge Bush to veto the bill if it were not significantly modified. Cheney's spokesman cited as particularly objectionable the bill's ban on closing domestic military bases.

The full House, when it passed the defense bill on Sept. 19, approved the amendment that reaffirmed the committee's provisions barring closure of any domestic bases until Cheney proposed legislation to establish a nonpartisan basis for deciding which bases to close.

As first reported by the Senate Armed Services Committee, though, the defense authorization bill would have made it easier for the Pentagon to shut down domestic bases, removing some of the procedural hurdles Congress created since the mid-1970s to give it leverage to protect constituents' jobs.

But Dale Bumpers, D-Ark., and many other members were of an opposite mind, because of Cheney's earlier announcement on his proposed base closings. In response, Bumpers offered an amendment to nullify Cheney's list, bar domestic base closures through fiscal 1991 and order Cheney to send Congress a report on the size and organization of U.S. forces through fiscal 1996.

Nunn objected that the amendment would "send a signal to the American people that the Congress has a lot of rhetoric in terms of cutting defense expenditures, but . . . we are not willing to [close bases]."

A motion to table Bumpers' amendment was rejected 43-54, but immediately thereafter the Senate rejected the amendment 43-54. *(Votes 220-221, p. 45-S)*

The Senate also rejected an amendment by William V. Roth Jr., R-Del., that would have gone further than the Armed Services Committee in giving the Defense secretary more leeway to shut down domestic bases. By a vote of 81-18, the Senate tabled the amendment that would have let the Pentagon close a base without waiting for congressional approval if fewer than 1,000 civilian employees would lose their jobs. The bill would have allowed the Pentagon to act unilaterally to close bases with fewer than 300 civilian employees. *(Vote 218, p. 45-S)*

In conference, negotiators agreed to a provision establishing the bipartisan commission to draw up lists of superfluous military bases that could be closed.

Pentagon spokesman Bob Hall dismissed the new commission as "a cumbersome process that appears to be designed to delay and deter and prevent management decisions. . . . The secretary of Defense has to have some management flexibility to make decisions on base closures."

According to congressional sources, Pentagon officials had objected to the fact that the commission would be subject to Senate confirmation at the start of each Congress. But the provision remained in the conference report filed Oct. 23.

The conference report was adopted by the House, 271-156, on Oct. 24 and approved by the Senate, 80-17, on Oct. 26. *(House vote 517, p. 162-H; Senate vote 320, p. 62-S)* ■

50,000 Reservists Called Up for Gulf Crisis

President Bush's decision Aug. 22 to call to active duty nearly 50,000 military reservists to back up U.S. forces in Saudi Arabia provided the first real test of the congressionally backed policy of heavy reliance on National Guard and reserve units.

The most visible evidence of this "total force" policy had been the issuing of front-line equipment, such as M-1 tanks and F-16 fighter planes, to reserve combat units. Earlier, reservists had typically been given superannuated hand-me-downs from active-duty units.

A more radical consequence was the Pentagon's delegation to the reserves of essential support missions, including airlift, cargo handling and medical care.

"The capability to perform certain critical military activities has been concentrated in the reserve component," Bush said. "Activating reservists to support operations such as those now under way has been a central feature of this approach."

The decision to call up the reserves was a victory for congressional backers such as House Armed Services Committee member G. V. "Sonny" Montgomery, D-Miss. Since 1984, Congress had increased funding for National Guard and reserve equipment by more than $26 billion above the amounts the Pentagon requested.

Bush activated the reserves under a law, initially passed in 1976, that permitted him to order to active duty as many as 200,000 reservists for up to 90 days, with the option of a 90-day extension. *(1976 Almanac, p. 321; 1986 Almanac, p. 464)*

According to Pentagon spokesman Pete Williams, most of the mobilized reservists were to be sent overseas — some to Saudi Arabia and others to Europe, where they would fill in for units shipped to the Persian Gulf.

Bush's activation of the reserves was applauded by Senate Armed Services Chairman Sam Nunn, D-Ga., a prime mover behind the 1976 law giving the president authority for a limited reserve mobilization.

"The president's action . . . will enable military planners to have greater confidence in the availability of the reserves for future military contingencies," Nunn said Aug. 22. "It sends a signal to active and reserve personnel alike that the total force is a reality."

Kept From Combat

By mid-December, roughly one-fourth of the 280,000 U.S. personnel deployed in Desert Shield were National Guard members or reservists serving on active duty. An additional 57,000 already activated were either preparing for deployment or filling in for active-duty troops sent to the gulf. *(Gulf crisis, p. 717)*

The call-up stopped short, however, of the total integration of active-duty forces and reserves that congressional advocates had long urged. The Pentagon called up reserve units mostly in supporting roles.

When the Army's 24th Infantry Division shipped out in August, the Georgia National Guard's 48th Infantry Brigade, one of the division's three brigades, was replaced by an active-duty unit.

The 48th Brigade was sent to the National Training Center at Fort Irwin in California's Mojave Desert — and remained there, ostensibly getting in shape for combat, throughout the war. The experience left the reservists bitter and the future of the "total force" concept unresolved.

Treaty To Cut Forces in Europe Signed

President Bush and the leaders of 21 other countries signed a treaty Nov. 19 that would dismantle the massive Soviet army that fostered Europe's Cold War division and militarization for four decades. But at year's end, questions about Soviet compliance with the pact and concerns about political retrenchment in Moscow kept the Bush administration from submitting it to the Senate for approval.

The treaty limiting conventional forces in Europe (CFE) provided for the scrapping or removal from the continent of roughly 100,000 of the 250,000 tanks, cannons and other weapons deployed, with the Soviet arsenal taking by far the largest hit. *(Chart, p. 697)*

Calling it "the farthest-reaching arms agreement in history," Bush said at the treaty-signing ceremony in Paris that the CFE treaty "signals the new world order that is emerging."

The signing marked a high point in relations between Washington and Moscow. Earlier, in talks May 31-June 3, Bush and Soviet President Mikhail S. Gorbachev moved to codify the transformation of U.S.-Soviet relations in the past year resulting from fundamental changes in the Soviet Union and in the states of Eastern Europe: the easing of the military confrontation, the disintegration of the Warsaw Pact as a military alliance, and the growth of political pluralism and regional separatism in the Soviet Union.

The centerpiece of the Washington summit was the two leaders' agreement on trade; in addition, the two countries reached a host of other, minor agreements. *(Trade pact, p. 205; U.S.-Soviet relations, p. 757)*

On the arms control front:

- A few relatively technical issues blocked conclusion of a strategic arms reduction treaty (START) that would reduce by nearly one-third the two countries' strategic nuclear stockpiles. However, the two leaders signed one joint statement nailing down the major elements of the pact, and a second statement setting goals for further reductions. Both sides hoped that a START deal would be ready for signing at the next Bush-Gorbachev summit in Moscow. *(START, p. 704)*
- Early Senate action on two treaties to limit the size of underground nuclear test explosions was guaranteed by the presidents' approval of an appendix (or "protocol") to each treaty intended to tighten up verification procedures. The Senate approved both of these treaties Sept. 25. *(Testing treaties, p. 711)*
- Both countries agreed to slash stockpiles of lethal chemical munitions. *(Chemical weapons, p. 709)*

Agreement on the CFE treaty proved elusive until October, when Secretary of State James A. Baker III and Soviet Foreign Minister Eduard A. Shevardnadze agreed on ceilings on the number of tanks, artillery pieces, armored troop carriers, armed helicopters and combat planes that could be fielded by NATO and the rapidly crumbling Soviet bloc.

Their negotiating breakthrough paved the way for the Nov. 19 signing — one of the year's most tangible symbols of eased East-West tensions. And the CFE breakthrough coincided with another powerful event in the changing European order: that very day, Oct. 3, East and West Germany were merging. *(German unification, p. 762)*

Most observers had predicted that as one of the first orders of business in 1991, the CFE pact would receive approval by the required two-thirds majority of the Senate.

At the end of 1990, however, the treaty's future was clouded. First, U.S. officials were dissatisfied with the Soviets' accounting of forces and weapons covered by the agreement. (Under the treaty, officials would have 90 days from the signing to review and correct the data.) The Soviet army reportedly was dug in against the treaty, stoking U.S. concerns about a Soviet end-run.

Those fears were exacerbated by continuing political turmoil in the Soviet Union, dramatically illustrated on Dec. 20 when Shevardnadze resigned abruptly. Shevardnadze, whom U.S. officials viewed as a trusted negotiator and an architect of improved relations, denounced the hard-liners who had been attacking Gorbachev, but also warned that the Soviet president's drive for increased powers could lead to a "dictatorship."

Relations between the two superpowers were cooled further by Moscow's crackdown in January 1991 against its breakaway Baltic republics. In the wake of the Soviets' armed intervention in Lithuania and Latvia, the White House announced later that month that the Moscow summit, scheduled for mid-February, would be indefinitely postponed.

Left in limbo was further action on the CFE, START, and chemical weapons treaties.

Significance of the Treaty

In large measure, the CFE pact merely ratified an unraveling of Soviet military power that had outstripped the arms control negotiating process. Since late 1988, the Soviet government had dramatically retrenched militarily, as it faced political tensions and economic stagnation at home. Meanwhile, largely peaceful revolutions in the former Soviet satellites had supplanted communist regimes with popularly elected governments less pliant to Kremlin wishes.

The contraction had gone so far and so fast that once-major provisions were dropped from the treaty, such as a limit on troop levels in Europe.

Nevertheless, administration officials insisted that the treaty remained significant. By formalizing the reduction of Soviet forces and their withdrawal from central Europe, negotiator R. James Woolsey said, the treaty was intended "to establish a structure that would make those remarkable gains into something lasting."

In a televised interview, national security adviser Brent Scowcroft said the treaty "makes virtually impossible the kind of surprise attack that NATO has been worried about."

A small but vigorous band of conservative critics, however, warned that the pact would arrest the retrenchment of Soviet military power by legitimizing continued deployments that otherwise would be withdrawn under political pressures in the Soviet Union and Eastern Europe.

"It is trying to freeze-frame a motion picture that we want to see progress," argued Frank J. Gaffney, a Pentagon official in the Reagan administration.

BACKGROUND

Bush had eased international pressure on his administration in May 1989, by proposing that Washington and Moscow each be limited to 275,000 troops in Europe.

Conventional Forces in Europe

The basic structure of the treaty limiting conventional forces in Europe (CFE) was settled in May 1989, only two months after negotiations began. The Soviet Union accepted NATO's proposal to apply equal ceilings to NATO and the Warsaw Pact for certain types of weapons deployed between the Atlantic Ocean and the Ural Mountains. *(1989 Almanac, pp. 478, 483)*

It was also agreed that the limits would be lower than the number of weapons then in NATO's inventory. Because the Eastern bloc's holdings were far larger than NATO's, this ensured that the Soviet Union and its allies would have to dispose of far more weapons.

The Warsaw Pact agreed to NATO's proposal to limit tanks, armored troop carriers and artillery, but insisted that limits also be applied to combat airplanes, helicopters and troops. Both sides also agreed on a sublimit on the percentage of each category that could belong to the United States or the Soviet Union.

As signed in Paris on Nov. 19, the treaty set alliance-wide limits on the five types of weapons with sublimits for any one country of 60 percent to 70 percent.

By the time the pact was signed, it had been partly overtaken by the Warsaw Pact's disintegration and by Moscow's withdrawal of forces from the territory of its former allies. So the treaty did not include earlier proposals to limit troops and to restrict the number of weapons stationed outside a country's territory.

The numbers of weapons held by each signatory remained in dispute even after the treaty was signed. The following chart on the impact of CFE was based on estimates provided by the Arms Control Association and the British American Security Information Council:

	NATO [1]	Warsaw Pact	CFE Limit	Comments
Tanks				Category included wheeled or tracked vehicles carrying a gun of 75mm or larger and weighing at least 16.5 metric tons (excluding the weight of crew, ammunition, fuel and removable armor).
Per alliance	22,230	36,798	20,000	
Largest nation	5,100	24,898	13,300 [2]	
Armored Combat Vehicles				Of the 30,000 permitted, no more than 18,000 could carry a gun of 20mm or larger. Of those 18,000, no more than 1,500 could weigh more than 6 metric tons or more and carry a gun of 75mm or larger.
Per alliance	30,000	47,220	30,000	
Largest nation	5,500	32,320	20,000	
Artillery				Category included both guns and rocket launchers firing projectiles of 100mm caliber or larger.
Per alliance	18,500	32,000	20,000	
Largest nation	2,700	18,300	13,700 [3]	
Airplanes				Category included "combat-capable" aircraft, excluding basic trainers and carrier-based planes. Each alliance would be permitted an additional 430 land-based naval aircraft.
Per alliance	5,700	9,790	6,800	
Largest nation	700	8,190	5,150	
Helicopters				Category included armed helicopters, but not land-based naval helicopters.
Per alliance	2,235	3,550	2,000	
Largest nation	600	2,850	1,500	

[1] *Excluded holdings of former East German forces, which would be counted against NATO limits as part of the forces of unified Germany.*

[2] *Because of negotiations among Warsaw Pact members, the limit on Soviet tanks would be 13,150.*

[3] *Because of negotiations among Warsaw Pact members, the limit on Soviet artillery would be 13,175.*

NATO adopted that figure in its negotiating strategy in the international CFE negotiations. *(1989 Almanac, pp. 477, 478, 483)*

The Soviet Union and its increasingly fractious allies were pressing for a limit on military personnel in either NATO or the Warsaw Pact who were stationed in central Europe outside their home country.

NATO, by contrast, would agree only to a limit on the number of U.S. and Soviet personnel in the central region — East and West Germany, the Low Countries, Poland, Hungary and Czechoslovakia.

As Soviet influence over other Warsaw Pact countries waned, Bush's CFE position came under fire:

- The proposed limit of 275,000 men apiece for the United States and the Soviet Union was criticized as so high as to be meaningless. Compared with existing deployments, it would force U.S. cuts of only about 30,000 — far fewer than likely to be withdrawn from Europe because of tightening Pentagon budgets. The limit would require a far deeper reduction in Soviet personnel — on the order of 370,000 — but many believed that Soviet budget constraints and pressure from the newly independent governments of Eastern Europe would force Soviet troops far below the ceiling.

• Some GOP conservatives also objected to equal ceilings, contending that this implied that the Soviets had the same "moral" right to impose forces on Eastern Europe as the United States had to station forces in Western Europe with the host countries' consent.

Scrambling to keep up with the developments overseas and to maintain the political initiative at home, Bush early in 1990 revised his CFE position, proposing faster superpower troop cutbacks in Europe.

As a centerpiece to his State of the Union address Jan. 31, Bush revised his troop-cut proposal to deal with both objections: The CFE treaty would limit each superpower to no more than 195,000 personnel in the central region, there would be no additional Soviet personnel in Europe outside Soviet territory, and U.S. personnel in the peripheral countries (principally Britain, Italy and Turkey) would not exceed 30,000. *(State of the Union text, p. 18)*

The ceiling on U.S. troops outside the central region, however, was proposed as a unilateral statement of U.S. intentions.

Under the proposal, the United States would have to withdraw about 80,000 troops from Europe, and the Soviet Union would have to pull out more than 370,000.

The new troop limit, Bush told Congress, was "designed to protect American and European interests — and sustain NATO's defense strategy." Bush said a continued U.S. military presence on the continent was "essential" and must not be linked to the Soviet presence. He cited only the 195,000 limit for Central Europe and did not mention his plan to keep another 30,000 U.S. troops elsewhere in Europe.

Praise, but Questions Remain

Bush's proposal won praise on Capitol Hill, where members of both parties said the rapid collapse of the Soviet empire in Eastern Europe was rendering obsolete NATO's positions in the conventional arms control talks in Vienna.

Moscow already was talking with Czechoslovakia and Hungary about withdrawing its forces; key Polish leaders also had demanded a rapid pullout of Soviet troops. In that context, some Western leaders worried that a Soviet retreat from Eastern Europe would create political pressure for a hasty, and possibly destabilizing, U.S. departure from the continent.

That kind of pressure was seen in Washington as well, despite Bush's proposal.

Key Democrats had resumed criticism of Bush for not moving quickly enough to take advantage of the collapse of communism in Eastern Europe. Hoping for Pentagon budget cuts, some Democrats suggested pulling most U.S. troops from Europe. And several members of the Senate Armed Services Committee said on Feb. 1 that Bush's proposal did not go far enough. Democrats challenged Pentagon assertions that the Bush numbers should be a "floor" on U.S. troop strength in Europe as well as the "ceiling."

However, committee Chairman Sam Nunn, D-Ga., said the proposal "makes the conventional arms control proposal that we now have tabled in Vienna much more relevant both to the changes in Eastern Europe and to the budget reality here at home."

Sen. Richard G. Lugar, R-Ind., called the proposal "tremendously significant" because it addressed concerns in the West about unilateral Soviet troop pullouts. Lugar, an influential member and former chairman of the Foreign Relations Committee, also expressed hope that Bush had gained the upper hand against those in Congress who would cut the defense budget so deeply that "we might undercut our own negotiating position prior to getting an agreement" in the conventional arms talks.

Bush sought, and apparently got, approval of his proposal from key allies in advance of his Jan. 31 speech. Several NATO governments praised the plan.

Bush discussed the proposal by telephone with Gorbachev. Kremlin spokesman Gennadi I. Gerasimov said Feb. 1 that the Soviet Union welcomed the plan.

Because Moscow had nearly twice as many troops in Europe as did the United States, all CFE proposals under study would have required substantially greater cuts by the Soviets.

A senior Bush administration official said Moscow had 565,000 to 570,000 troops in central Europe, including about 355,000 in East Germany. Washington had about 305,000 troops in Europe, including 255,000 to 260,000 in West Germany, the official said. Most of the rest were in Italy, Britain and Turkey. Other NATO nations kept 160,000 foreign troops in West Germany, according to the International Institute for Strategic Studies in London.

THE GERMAN EQUATION

While the superpowers were looking to reduce their troops in Europe, the dramatic process of unifying East and West Germany was about to begin in earnest. It had taken less than four months for the East German regime to make the transition from hard-line anchor of the Soviet bloc to political basket case.

In October 1989, it became clear that Soviet President Gorbachev would not use his troops in East Germany to bolster the government of East German Communist Party boss Erich Honecker against massive public demonstrations in Leipzig and other cities calling for political and economic liberalization.

By some accounts, Gorbachev collaborated with some top East German officials to push aside the elderly and ailing Honecker in mid-October.

In any case, the new government in East Berlin fared no better than Honecker's. Popular pressure for further liberalization increased, and the East German economy began to slow down, partly because East Germans were emigrating across the virtually open border into West Germany.

On Nov. 28, West German Chancellor Helmut Kohl unveiled a 10-point plan for German reunification under which the two German governments would go through an interim stage of confederation.

Early in December, the East German government, including by then a substantial minority of non-Communists, set parliamentary elections for May 6. But by late January 1990, the country was in a critical state, with as many as 3,000 of its citizens decamping for the West daily.

By then, it had become generally accepted in West Germany that the long-held goal of unification was at hand, willy-nilly. Moreover, there was a consensus in Bonn that the East German population quickly had to be given credible assurances that their lot would improve fast, lest the government and economic system in East Germany simply collapse.

Under pressure from Bonn, the East German government advanced parliamentary elections from May 6 to March 18. And by early February, the Bonn government was pushing for a rapid monetary and economic union between the two German states.

On Feb. 9, West German Foreign Minister Hans-Dietrich Genscher called such an economic union a top priority. Coupled with West German economic aid, he said, the currency union would help to stabilize East German industry, stop the exodus to the West and help guarantee stability in Europe.

The impending union raised several strategic questions:

- What would the relationship be between a unified Germany and NATO on the one hand and the Soviet Union on the other?
- If Germany remained in NATO, as was the policy of the right-of-center coalition in Bonn, what would its military strategy be? In particular, how would NATO's military planners deal with the presence of more than 300,000 Soviet troops in enclaves throughout the country's eastern third?
- What would be the mission of U.S. military forces in Europe if the East-West military standoff centered in Germany evaporated quickly?

East German Prime Minister Hans Modrow had conceded Jan. 30 that rapid amalgamation of the two Germanys was inevitable. Modrow insisted that the new unified Germany would have to be neutral. Bonn and the other NATO governments rejected that demand out of hand.

Bonn's center-right coalition of Kohl's Christian Democrats and Genscher's Free Democrats proposed a different solution to the question of the unified Germany's international status: The country would remain a part of NATO, the government maintained; however, non-German NATO military forces would stay out of the territory that had comprised East Germany.

The Soviet government, which had ruled out any discussion of rapid German unification as recently as late January, announced Feb. 8 that Gorbachev would meet Feb. 10 with Kohl and Genscher. Soviet Foreign Minister Shevardnadze called Genscher's plan for German membership in NATO "interesting" and said it would be discussed in the meeting.

Moscow's main concern regarding German unification, Shevardnadze said, was preserving the stability of Europe — a goal that, he implied, required that Germany's economic power and military potential be counterbalanced in the new European order. "We are in favor of a European Germany," he said, "not a German Europe."

Where To Put the Troops?

The impact of events on West German politics, and their potential impact on NATO, was vividly apparent at a conference of national legislators, government officials and defense analysts from NATO countries held Feb. 2-4 in Munich.

The conference, an annual affair sponsored by the West German defense journal *Wehrkunde*, was a venue for informal and frank, though public, discussion of issues facing the Western alliance. In 1990, unification was the big issue, with West German participants debating the implications for West Germany's membership in NATO.

West German Defense Minister Gerhard Stoltenberg outlined his government's notion of a unified Germany in NATO but with non-German troops remaining in what was West Germany.

Stoltenberg did not discuss the status under that proposed arrangement of the 355,000 personnel in East Germany. But several U.S. and German officials at the conference speculated that all parties concerned would have an incentive to simply accept their continued presence for the time being.

The Bonn government's view was challenged by Egon Bahr and Karsten Voigt, leaders of the opposition Social Democratic Party. Both men brushed aside as impossible the Bonn government's notion of continued NATO membership with some kind of special status for the territory formerly making up East Germany.

With democratization sweeping Eastern Europe and the CFE treaty nearing completion, Voigt said, no country or alliance would have the physical ability to threaten a significant military offensive. "The capability of surprise attack [will be] done away with," he said.

And How Many To Keep?

On Feb. 3, White House national security adviser Scowcroft assured the *Wehrkunde* participants that Bush's proposal to limit U.S. and Soviet troops in central Europe to 195,000 was intended to set a floor below which U.S. troop strength in Europe would not decline for the time being, whether or not the Soviets made additional reductions.

"The United States has an enduring responsibility to remain here," Scowcroft said, "as a counterweight to the Soviet Union's permanent geographical advantage on this continent."

But several members of the predominantly Republican congressional contingent at Munich expressed doubts that Bush could hold the line at 195,000.

Noting that West Germany had announced plans to trim its military by about 20 percent, Senate Armed Services Committee member Alan J. Dixon, D-Ill., had vowed to push for a proportional U.S. troop cut in fiscal 1991 — a reduction of about 60,000. That would be "a modest number," he said, that took due account of the changes sweeping Eastern Europe.

Bush's proposal to stand pat pending a negotiated reduction to 195,000, Dixon said, was "way behind the curve. The American people are very unhappy with that."

Notwithstanding budget pressures at home and developments abroad, several members of Congress predicted that Bush's proposal for a negotiated cut to 195,000 might help him fend off Hill suggestions of a smaller immediate reduction.

But Rep. Patricia Schroeder, D-Colo., disagreed, contending that the apparent ease with which Bush revised the U.S. negotiating position would make it easier for Congress to impose its own judgment. "He can't come and plead with us to be cautious when he can pick up the phone [and] go down to 195,000 that easily," she said.

Schroeder did not commit herself to pushing for a fiscal 1991 reduction of a particular size.

NEGOTIATING PROGRESS

In mid-February, Soviet President Gorbachev essentially accepted Bush's troop-level proposal, agreeing to let the United States keep a larger military force in Europe than would the Soviet Union.

The superpowers also took significant steps toward agreement on other CFE provisions.

The scope of progress reflected some give on all sides. But by far the most far-reaching of the compromises seemed to come from Moscow.

Since Bush unveiled his new proposal to cut U.S. and Soviet troop strength in Europe, CFE negotiator Woolsey and other administration officials had touted the political significance of establishing the principle that U.S. and Soviet troops remaining in Europe under the CFE pact would not have an equal moral footing.

As Bush and his aides argued for enshrining in the treaty a 30,000-man advantage over the Soviet Union, political symbolism weighed as heavily as concrete military requirements: NATO countries and some nominal Soviet allies wanted U.S. troops in Western Europe, while the non-Soviet Warsaw Pact countries were pressing Moscow to withdraw some or all of its troops.

"The U.S. troops are there as a stabilizing factor," Bush told reporters Feb. 12, adding that "European allies want us there [and] I have a feeling that some of the Eastern Europeans want us there."

The Soviets conceded in two stages. On Feb. 9, when Baker presented Bush's new troop proposal in Moscow, Gorbachev rejected the idea of allowing the United States an advantage and countered that he would agree to a common ceiling on U.S. and Soviet forces of 195,000 or 225,000.

This marked a departure from Moscow's earlier demand that a CFE troop ceiling cover all forces in central Europe outside their home countries. In effect, Gorbachev thus appeared to abandon any effort to limit in this treaty about 180,000 British, Dutch, Belgian and French NATO troops, most stationed in Germany.

But Bush stood firm, and the Soviets moved again. On Feb. 13, Baker and Soviet Foreign Minister Shevardnadze, along with 21 other foreign ministers from NATO and the Warsaw Pact, concluded a meeting in Ottawa to discuss an "Open Skies" aerial reconnaissance plan. Shevardnadze told Baker that Moscow would accept the U.S. proposal, with the significant difference that the limit of 30,000 U.S. personnel outside the central region would be legally binding. The United States quickly agreed.

Arms Control and Disarmament Agency Director Ronald F. Lehman II later told the House Foreign Affairs Committee that the administration decided it could accept the revision "if that would conclude the manpower issue," and thus put an end to Soviet demands for a limit on the manpower of countries other than the United States and Soviet Union. "It was a compromise with which we could work," Lehman said on March 1.

Conventional Weaponry

On Feb. 8, NATO formally proposed at the CFE talks in Geneva compromises that seemed to narrow differences with the Warsaw Pact over limits on certain kinds of weaponry particularly useful in a massive conventional invasion.

The most important of these shifts was on an issue in which there remained the broadest disagreement between the two sides: combat aircraft.

For months, NATO proposed limiting to 5,700 "combat-capable" planes, including trainers that might be armed. The Warsaw Pact had proposed a limit of 4,700 planes but would exclude several categories, including trainers, interceptors — designed to attack other planes, instead of ground targets — land-based naval planes and medium-sized bombers.

In its new proposal, NATO agreed to allow each side 500 interceptors, in addition to the 5,700 combat planes. The Soviets had proposed an allowance of 1,500 to 1,800 interceptors.

The new NATO offer also would exempt from the ceiling some 2,000 to 2,200 "primary trainers" — relatively unsophisticated, slow-flying aircraft of limited combat capability.

But there remained at issue more than 3,000 other Warsaw Pact trainers, two-seat versions of front-line fighters and ground-attack planes, having nearly the same firepower as the non-training models.

The dilemma posed by these advanced craft was that while most U.S. flight training was done outside the region covered by the CFE treaty, practically all of the Soviet air force's training establishment was west of the Ural Mountains — in the part of Soviet territory covered by CFE.

The two alliances also were at odds over the Soviet demand to exempt from the ceiling land-based naval planes and medium bombers.

NATO's Feb. 8 proposals moved toward the Soviets' on two other issues:

- For tanks, armored troop carriers and other armored combat vehicles, NATO proposed an elaborate set of subcategories intended to limit certain kinds of weapons that were less powerful than front-line tanks, such as the U.S. Army's 60-ton M-1, but were of concern to one side or the other. The new NATO position would impose limits on "light tanks" weighing less than 20 tons and on wheeled armored cars with large, tank-sized cannons.

In particular, according to Lee Feinstein of the Arms Control Association, a Washington think tank, the new categories would meet Soviet demands for limits on the French AMX-10RC, a huge, six-wheeled armored car carrying the same 105mm cannon used by many modern tanks.

- For armed helicopters, on the other hand, NATO shifted its position in the opposite direction, proposing to exempt from the treaty's limit of 1,900 craft all but a narrowly defined category of attack helicopters carrying air-to-air missiles or antitank missiles.

Moreover, the provision would allow either alliance to redefine out of the limited class any already armed helicopter, except for four types, designed as tank-busters, that would be of very limited use in any other role: The U.S. Apache and Cobra, the Italian Mangusta and the Soviet Mi-24.

CAPITOL HILL REACTION

Bush's deal with the Soviets on troop strengths in Europe came under heavy fire from Senate Armed Services Chairman Nunn. The agreement would unduly limit U.S. flexibility, Nunn complained.

For one thing, he argued, a cap of 30,000 U.S. personnel in the peripheral countries would prevent a compensatory buildup of U.S. forces on the rim of Europe in case political pressures in Germany forced a reduction of U.S. personnel below the 195,000 allowed under the CFE pact. "I think the trend is going to be to get forces out of the central region," he warned during a Feb. 27 hearing.

Air Force Secretary Donald Rice told Nunn that the top military leadership "would certainly prefer" to be able to offset any reduction below 195,000 men in the central region with an increase above 30,000 in the periphery.

"There's still discussion within our government," Rice told the Senate panel, a statement echoed by Gen. Larry D. Welch, Air Force chief of staff, the next day.

Welch and the chiefs of the three other services insisted to the Senate panel that the emerging CFE pact would not prohibit a U.S. military buildup on the periphery of Europe in an emergency. "Nothing limits our right to reinforce in a contingency," said Welch. However, that interpretation was not shared by most observers of the CFE talks.

Nunn's objection to the Ottawa formula was echoed by some other Senate Democrats, among them Tim Wirth, Colo., and Wyche Fowler Jr., Ga., and by senior Armed Services Republican John W. Warner, Va.

Meanwhile, Secretary of State Baker and other administration officials vigorously defended the Ottawa formula. "We came out with exactly the policy that we intended to come out with," Baker told the Senate Budget Committee on Feb. 28.

Nunn broached his concern about the rigidity of the 30,000-man ceiling at a White House meeting with Bush and other Hill leaders Feb. 27. "That was the first time people began to focus on the military implications," Warner later said.

Nunn, Warner and other critics eyed two scenarios under which the United States might want to boost its manpower in the peripheral states while respecting a Europe-wide ceiling of 225,000:

- The government of a united Germany might request a sharp reduction in the 195,000 U.S. troops in the central region, most of whom would be on German territory. If unification proceeded so quickly that the national elections scheduled in West Germany for December covered both West and East Germany, the opposition Social Democratic Party — historically strong in East Germany — might win control of a unified German government. Many party leaders favored a neutral Germany.

But Nunn speculated that even if Chancellor Kohl's right-of-center coalition retained power, internal forces within Germany might push him to demand a substantial U.S. troop cut "within two or three years."

- Washington might want to beef up its forces on the European periphery, not with an eye on the East-West military confrontation in Germany but to boost its leverage in dealing with potential conflicts in the Middle East.

In the new political environment caused by massive Soviet retrenchment and German unification, Nunn contended, Britain, Turkey or other NATO members outside the central region may allow an increase of U.S. forces under some circumstances. Nunn said he would welcome establishing the principle that the United States could keep more forces in Europe than could the Soviet Union, but added that the binding ceiling on U.S. forces outside the central region was "too high a price."

But some other Democratic heavyweights — including Sen. Joseph R. Biden Jr., Del., and House Armed Services Committee Chairman Les Aspin, Wis. — discounted Nunn's argument.

In a sharp counterattack March 1 that conspicuously avoided naming Nunn as his target, Biden, chairman of the Foreign Relations Subcommittee on Europe, dismissed as "fanciful" the notion that Turkey, Italy or other NATO countries outside the central region would accept a U.S. military buildup if Soviet troops were withdrawn from Eastern Europe.

Budgeting Fallout

While the Democrats debated the strategic impact of the troop cutbacks, they also weighed the potential for defense budget savings.

Aspin tried to lay the political groundwork for cuts by undermining Defense Secretary Dick Cheney's call for a more cautious approach. Cheney reprised his case in a March 13 speech to the United Jewish Appeal, warning against "slash-and-burn budgeting."

Cheney conceded that the threat of a sudden Soviet invasion of Western Europe had faded, but added: "We must never forget that whatever other changes they may have made, the Soviets retain enormous military capabilities, including a massive inventory of modern nuclear weapons. . . .

"It is hard for me to look at that capability, to consider the possibilities for upheaval within the Soviet Union, and to remain peacefully sanguine as if we no longer need to be concerned about our own defense."

Shortly before Cheney's speech, however, Aspin conducted another in a series of hearings in which he highlighted assessments by U.S. intelligence agencies and top military brass that were far more sanguine than Cheney's in judging how far the Soviet military threat had declined.

Presenting the panel with the Pentagon's most recent "net assessment" of U.S. and Soviet power, Maj. Gen. John D. Robinson, an intelligence analyst with the Pentagon's Joint Staff, endorsed the cautious approach embodied in Cheney's budget, saying it would provide "a hedge against a sudden reversal of events."

But Robinson also told the panel that NATO now would have much longer advance warning of a pending attack by the Soviet Union. Because of Soviet troop cuts, he said, U.S. officials now had multiplied by a factor of four or five their previous estimate of the warning time. Though secret, the previous estimate was generally believed to have been 14 days of warning.

Aspin later told reporters that, based on his reading of Robinson's secret testimony, the Pentagon believed that it would be possible for NATO to fend off a Soviet attack without using nuclear weapons, assuming completion of the CFE treaty.

On top of that, Aspin argued, the virtual defection of Moscow's erstwhile allies in the Warsaw Pact made it likely that in case of war, NATO forces could go on the offensive: "We can go the other way; NATO wins."

WASHINGTON SUMMIT

The timetable for the second summit meeting between Bush and Gorbachev was speeded up by nearly a month. During meetings April 4-6 between Secretary of State Baker and Soviet Foreign Minister Shevardnadze, the Washington summit was set for May 31-June 3.

The shift was aimed at giving the Soviet chief more time to mend political fences in Moscow between the end of his U.S. trip and an important meeting of the Soviet Communist Party scheduled for early July.

But it also reduced the time remaining before the summit in which negotiators could try to iron out the details of the CFE and START treaties.

Meanwhile, conservative critics, such as Richard N. Perle, the Reagan administration's most prominent anti-Soviet hard-liner, complained that Baker had not pressed the Soviets hard enough on CFE, START or other matters.

With the summit nearing, negotiations on CFE seemed to slow to a crawl. In a May 24 news conference, Bush called that development troublesome.

Some observers attributed the stall to a growing sense of diplomatic and strategic isolation as Moscow watched its erstwhile allies test their independence. "It's a question of whether you can get this treaty [CFE] done before the

Warsaw Pact disintegrates and you've got nobody to negotiate with," said Thomas K. Longstreth of the pro-arms control Federation of American Scientists.

Other observers speculated that Moscow had slowed its military retrenchment in hope of getting West Germany and its Western allies to accept substantial limits on the military power of a unified Germany. "They want to be sure there are limits on the Bundeswehr [German army] and on nuclear deployments," said Sovietologist Dimitri K. Simes of the Carnegie Endowment for International Peace. In hope of jump-starting the CFE agreement and making more progress on START, Soviet negotiators scheduled new meetings with their U.S. counterparts in Washington on May 26.

CFE Treaty Eludes Leaders

In four days of talks in Washington May 31-June 3, Bush and Gorbachev picked up arms control trophies:

- While a few unsettled issues blocked conclusion of the START treaty, the two leaders signed one joint statement nailing down the major elements of the pact, and a second statement setting goals for further reductions.
- Capitol Hill approval of the two treaties to limit the size of underground nuclear test explosions was virtually guaranteed by the presidents' approval of an appendix (or "protocol") to each treaty intended to tighten up verification procedures.
- The U.S.-Soviet agreement to slash stockpiles of lethal chemical munitions was completed.

But the summit's most significant arms-related outcome was the prize that proved elusive. Moscow refused to wrap up the CFE treaty without additional political and military constraints on a rapidly unifying Germany. The positive and businesslike tone of the summit, however, left congressional defense budget intentions unchanged.

"If the atmospherics [of the summit] had come out sour, it might have affected the defense bill," speculated House Armed Services Chairman Aspin, who said that a clearly hostile Gorbachev might have induced some members to support a higher budget than they would otherwise. Conversely, Aspin said: "If it had come out euphoric, it might have affected the bill," by encouraging members to seek even larger reductions.

NATO Endorses Bush Plan

Meeting in London July 5-6, NATO leaders recast long-established elements of the alliance's military strategy, including plans for using short-range nuclear weapons, in hope that the Soviets would acquiesce in German membership in the Western alliance.

With Gorbachev insisting that Germany be neutral once East and West Germany were politically unified, Soviet negotiators apparently sought to reinforce that demand by dragging their feet on the CFE treaty.

Bush said after the London meeting that he hoped the Soviets would "look at the changes that have taken place in NATO and say, 'Well, if NATO had been a threat to us, it no longer is a threat to us.' "

Bush had proposed several of the moves adopted by the NATO summit, including the decision to invite Gorbachev to address a future meeting of the North Atlantic Assembly, NATO's top decision-making body. The alliance also invited members of the disintegrating Warsaw Pact to assign diplomatic observers to NATO.

Among other policy shifts:

- NATO would plan to use nuclear weapons against an attacker only as a last resort, moving away from the more permissive doctrine of "flexible response," adopted in the late 1960s to deter any massive Soviet conventional attack.
- The United States would remove from Europe an estimated 1,400 short-range nuclear artillery shells on the continent, provided the Soviet Union removed its nuclear artillery stockpile.
- The 35-nation Conference on Security and Cooperation in Europe (CSCE), which met occasionally, would get a permanent staff and meet regularly to provide the Soviets with membership in a major European political forum.
- When the CFE treaty was signed, NATO would announce an unspecified limit on the number of military personnel allowed to a unified Germany. The Soviets had talked about a ceiling of 200,000 to 250,000, while the Germans reportedly were considering 300,000 to 400,000.

TREATY SIGNING

Presidents Bush and Gorbachev and the leaders of 20 other countries signed the CFE treaty, effectively codifying the end of the Cold War, in Paris on Nov. 19. Bush hailed the pact as "the most far-reaching arms agreement" ever negotiated.

Signing of the treaty followed an agreement reached by Secretary of State Baker and Soviet Foreign Minister Shevardnadze on ceilings for U.S. and Soviet weapons and aircraft in Europe.

But after the treaty was signed, a dispute arose over planned Soviet steps to comply with the limits, holding up Bush's formal submission of the pact to the Senate for ratification.

Limits on Weapons, Aircraft

The months of diplomatic deadlock ended Oct. 3, when Secretary of State Baker and Soviet Foreign Minister Shevardnadze agreed on a limit for Soviet combat aircraft deployed in Europe.

The compromise ensured that the CFE treaty would be signed in Paris at the summit meeting of 34 European and North American countries Nov. 19-21.

The agreement would impose equal ceilings on NATO and the fading Warsaw Pact for the number of tanks, artillery pieces, armored troop carriers, armed helicopters and combat planes deployed between the Atlantic Ocean and the Ural Mountains.

The treaty also would limit the number of such weapons that could be deployed in that area by any one country. While it would require the destruction of thousands of items of NATO equipment, the agreement's most dramatic practical impact would be to erase the Soviet Union's huge advantage in numbers of weapons, forcing the destruction of some 75,000 tanks, troop carriers and aircraft.

Final agreement on alliancewide limits on aircraft remained to be worked out, but Baker and Shevardnadze had broken the back of the problem by finessing Moscow's insistence on exempting from CFE hundreds of its land-based planes that were armed for antiship missions. Baker and Shevardnadze agreed that the number of such aircraft would be limited, in a separate deal.

Moscow's argument for exempting land-based planes aimed at naval targets was that they were its counterpart to the U.S. Navy's hundreds of carrier-based planes, which were not covered by CFE.

Under the compromise, no country could have more than 5,150 land-based combat planes, not counting naval aircraft. The separate agreement would permit any country to have 400 land-based naval aircraft, slightly fewer than Moscow had at the time.

Bush said Oct. 4 that the treaty would "decisively improve the balance of military power" in Europe.

Despite the collapse of Communist regimes in Eastern Europe and the large-scale retrenchment of Soviet forces from the territory of erstwhile allies, Bush said, Europe remained "the site of the greatest concentration of armed strength in the world."

"As Europe is transformed politically, we must also redraw the military map of the continent and lift some of the shadows and fears that we and our allies have lived with for nearly half a century," Bush said.

Applauding the progress toward a CFE agreement, Senate Majority Leader George J. Mitchell, D-Maine, said he hoped the Senate would give the pact "early and enthusiastic approval."

CFE negotiators abandoned earlier plans to include in the treaty limits on the number of military personnel.

In part, that effort bogged down over substantive disagreements. For the most part, though, the provision simply was overrun by events: A tentative agreement capping the number of U.S. and Soviet troops in Europe at 225,000 for each side became pointless as Moscow concluded a series of agreements to withdraw its forces from the territory of its former satellites.

The Soviet Union agreed to remove all of its troops from Hungary, Czechoslovakia and the former territory of East Germany. At midnight Oct. 3, East Germany was absorbed into a unified German state, which retained West Germany's membership in NATO.

Pressure to reduce the Pentagon budget also sharply eroded the significance of an agreement that would have allowed 225,000 U.S. troops in Europe.

Even some of the Defense Department's staunchest political allies, such as Senate Armed Services Chairman Nunn, had called for reducing the number of U.S. personnel stationed in Europe to between 50,000 and 100,000 by the mid-1990s.

Even though political and budgetary realities had outpaced the arms negotiators, Baker insisted that CFE remained tremendously significant.

Aside from formalizing reductions that might occur for other reasons, the treaty would lock them in by requiring the destruction of excess weapons.

Moreover, he said Oct. 4, the treaty's provisions for very intrusive monitoring of each side's compliance would bar any covert military buildup even if Soviet politics took a hard-line bounce:

"Where tens of thousands of Soviet tanks previously were poised for an offensive, now hundreds of inspectors will stand, and this will help insure stability and provide warning, even if political conditions change," Baker said.

The Numbers

Under the Baker-Shevardnadze agreement, CFE would provide that neither NATO nor the Warsaw Pact could deploy in the region covered by the treaty more than 20,000 tanks, 30,000 armored troop carriers, 20,000 artillery pieces, or 2,000 armed helicopters.

In each category, any single country would be allowed no more than about two-thirds of the number of weapons permitted for its alliance.

Since the Warsaw Pact had fallen apart as a military alliance, for all practical purposes, Moscow had demanded a higher ceiling on its holdings — 80 percent of the alliance total — than the 60 percent ceiling pushed by Washington.

In the end, separate single-country limits were negotiated for each category of weapons, averaging 67.2 percent of the alliancewide totals.

Paris Summit

The signing of the CFE pact in Paris on Nov. 19 was the highlight of the three-day summit meeting of the CSCE, the loosely knit association of now 34 countries with the unification Oct. 3 of the two Germanys.

Proponents of the CSCE touted it as the embryo of Europe's new political framework, destined to supplant the old, bipolar confrontation.

Others, including the Bush administration, had been more skeptical about permitting it to expand its mandate at the risk of the NATO alliance and other established alliances.

Members of the CSCE included the United States, Canada and every state in Europe except Albania. Even Lichtenstein, Monaco, San Marino and Vatican City had seats at its deliberations.

Before adjourning Nov. 21, the CSCE members signed the Charter of Paris for a New Europe, a 19-page agreement proclaiming a new order of peaceful relations among multiparty democracies with market economies.

"The era of confrontation and division of Europe has ended," it proclaimed. "We declare that henceforth our relations will be founded on respect and cooperation."

The charter established a permanent CSCE secretariat in Prague, a center for conflict prevention in Vienna and an office for free elections in Warsaw. It also called for creation of a CSCE parliamentary assembly.

Amid the euphoria surrounding the Cold War's demise, however, there were harbingers of a potentially disruptive side of Europe's new order.

At the French government's invitation, the foreign ministers of the Soviet republics of Estonia, Latvia and Lithuania, all of which had declared their intention to seek independence from Moscow, came to Paris as unofficial observers of the CSCE meeting.

But the Soviet government vetoed their participation, and Gorbachev warned that ethnic unrest could arrest progress toward European cooperation.

"Militant nationalism and mindless separatism can easily bring conflict and enmity, Balkanization and even, what is worse, the Lebanonization of different regions," Gorbachev said.

Several Western European governments, facing actual or potential separatist movements within their own borders, stymied discussion of a Swiss proposal to protect minorities.

Conservatives' Criticism

In the wake of the signing, conservative critics continued to voice misgivings.

One such critic was Gaffney, the former Pentagon official who was directing the Center for Security Policy, an organization that was highly skeptical of Soviet good faith in carrying out arms control agreements.

In addition to challenging the treaty's overall premise, Gaffney and others complained that CFE would eliminate far fewer Soviet weapons than had been predicted only a few months earlier. The principal reason was that the Soviet government shipped 17,000 tanks and tens of thousands of other heavy weapons to storage dumps east of the

Ural Mountains, outside the region covered by the CFE limits.

Soviet officials had outlined the weapons shifts to U.S. counterparts in October, pledging that much of the equipment would be destroyed and that it would be stored in the open, where it would deteriorate.

But U.S. officials were taken aback Nov. 19 when the Soviet Union submitted an inventory of weapons subject to the CFE limits that listed considerably fewer artillery pieces and military installations than had been anticipated. Under the treaty, fewer military facilities would mean fewer opportunities for Western officials to inspect Soviet sites to verify compliance.

"It looks like there may be some problems there," national security adviser Scowcroft said.

However, other administration officials insisted that U.S. intelligence agencies could keep an eye on the trans-Ural storage dumps to be sure they did not become staging areas for military operations.

"We're getting on the inside of the Soviet Union in ways that were never anticipated years ago," a senior administration official told reporters Nov. 15. "You are beginning to see internal discussions [and] whistleblowers. . . . We will have far more information than we ever had before on what the Soviet Union is doing even east of the Urals."

A month after the CFE pact was signed, Secretary of State Baker acknowledged that "serious" concerns had been raised with the Soviets about data they had provided on weapons to be scrapped under the new treaty on conventional forces in Europe.

"We have furnished them with evidence," Baker told reporters during a Dec. 18 NATO meeting in Brussels. "They have agreed to look at that evidence and get back to us."

He said the United States had questioned the expansive Soviet definition of "naval infantry," whose equipment was exempt from the treaty.

He said the United States also doubted the accuracy of the Soviet inventory of military equipment that had been moved east of the Ural Mountains, outside the area covered by the treaty.

State Department officials emphasized that the treaty provided for a 90-day period to review and correct data submitted once the document was signed by Bush and the leaders of 21 other countries in Paris on Nov. 19.

At year's end, the dispute had not been resolved, and Bush had yet to submit the treaty to the Senate for ratification. ■

U.S.-Soviet Strategic Arms Agreement Stalls

The United States and the Soviet Union came close in 1990 to wrapping up a strategic arms reduction treaty (START) that would reduce by nearly one-third the two superpowers' stockpiles of strategic nuclear weapons.

At a May 31-June 2 summit in Washington, President Bush and Soviet leader Mikhail S. Gorbachev signed one joint statement nailing down the major elements of the pact and a second statement pledging to wrap up the treaty by year's end and set goals for further reductions.

By the end of 1990, both sides had hoped to produce a final START agreement that had been eight years in the making. It was to be signed at a Moscow summit, scheduled for February 1991. But the pact stalled as a result of a few unsettled technical issues and high-level inattention by both countries' governments. Washington was preoccupied with the march toward war in the Persian Gulf while Moscow was grappling with a host of domestic political problems, including the independence efforts in the Baltic states and hard-liners' criticisms of Gorbachev's policies.

As 1991 began, negotiators remained stumped on the technical issues and the superpowers' relations were complicated by the politics of the gulf war and Baltic crackdown. With those difficulties continuing, and Bush reluctant to go to Moscow during the gulf war, the administration postponed the Moscow summit until later in the year. *(U.S.-Soviet relations, p. 757; gulf crisis, p. 717; background, 1989 Almanac, p. 477)*

Major Areas of Agreement

The Bush-Gorbachev June 1 joint statement on START outlined agreements that would have the practical effect of reducing the number of ballistic missile warheads and strategic-bomber weapons deployed by the two sides from about 22,000 to about 16,000. These provisions would:

- Limit to 4,900 the number of warheads on land-based intercontinental ballistic missiles (ICBMs) and submarine-launched ballistic missiles.
- Cut in half (to 154) the Soviet fleet of large, 10-warhead SS-18 missiles.
- Permit 150 U.S. bombers carrying long-range cruise missiles (ALCMs) and 210 Soviet bombers, carrying fewer ALCMs apiece.
- Limit to 1,100 the number of warheads on mobile ICBMs.
- Bar each country, by a separate, "politically binding" agreement, from deploying more than 880 nuclear-armed sea-launched cruise missiles (SLCMs). *(Provisions, p. 708)*

But the two sides remained at odds over U.S. demands that the Soviet Union choke off modernization of the SS-18 force and limit deployment of the Backfire bomber.

In their companion joint statement on future strategic arms negotiations, Bush and Gorbachev pledged completion of the START treaty "this year," and promised "consultations without delay," immediately after that agreement was signed, on future strategic arms reduction talks. Among other goals, those follow-on talks would emphasize "reducing the concentration of warheads on strategic delivery vehicles," according to the statement.

Some administration officials cited that as support for the earlier U.S. effort — rejected by Gorbachev — to ban mobile, multiwarhead ICBMs, such as the Soviet SS-24 and the U.S. MX.

However, the statement also would apply to multiwarhead submarine-launched missiles, which Gorbachev insisted be banned along with land-based weapons, a position rejected by the Bush administration.

For 15 years, conservative defense specialists had vehemently opposed any strategic arms agreement that did not impose stringent limits on the SS-18 and the Backfire. Frank J. Gaffney Jr., a former Reagan Pentagon official who headed the hard-line Center for Security Policy, was representative of these critics, who insisted that START's 50 percent reduction in the SS-18 fleet was nullified by the improvements that had doubled the military effectiveness of the remaining missiles.

Secretary of State James A. Baker III said June 1 that U.S. negotiators were pressing for a limit on the number of SS-18 test flights that would have the effect of preventing further improvements in the big Soviet missiles.

Many Senate defense specialists from the right and center of the political spectrum worried that START would be concluded while another arms control treaty, limiting conventional forces in Europe (CFE), was stalled. The Bush administration had indicated that the conventional-arms reduction treaty had a higher priority.

"The aspect of it that concerns most of us is the reversal of policy without adequate explanation," said Senate Armed Services Committee member John McCain, R-Ariz.

U.S. and Soviet negotiators subsequently did reach agreement on the CFE pact, which was signed in Paris on Nov. 21. *(CFE treaty, p. 696)*

BACKGROUND

Since 1982, U.S. and Soviet negotiators had been closing in on a START agreement largely shaped by two of President Ronald Reagan's basic arms control goals. *(Reagan's goals, 1982 Almanac, p. 21-E)*

First, the treaty would reduce the number of weapons in the U.S. and Soviet arsenals by a significant fraction, although it also would allow the deployment of new, more lethal weapons within those numerical ceilings.

"As with many past treaties, this will be arms control without pain or sacrifice," said Robert S. Norris of the Natural Resources Defense Council, an organization demanding more comprehensive nuclear arms cuts in a follow-on START negotiation.

Second, START also would require hefty reductions in the number of ballistic missile warheads — particularly those on the Soviet Union's fleet of massive, multiwarhead intercontinental ballistic missiles (ICBMs), designated SS-18s. For two decades, conservative nuclear strategists had contended that this force was particularly dangerous because of its potential for wiping out most of the U.S. retaliatory arsenal with very little warning.

The treaty's limit of no more than 6,000 strategic warheads for each superpower on a total of no more than 1,600 missiles and bombers frequently was described as a 50 percent reduction in forces.

In fact, it would reduce the number of strategic warheads by less than one-third, because its counting rules — biased against ICBM warheads — discounted thousands of missiles and bombs that could be carried by long-range bombers. Because an adversary would have several hours' notice of a bomber attack, the U.S. government maintained, bomber weapons were inherently less destabilizing than the lightning-quick ICBMs.

START would, however, reduce by 50 percent the SS-18 fleet and the total "throw-weight" of the Soviet ballistic missile force. *(Scoresheet on START talks, 1989 Almanac, p. 494)*

FEBRUARY AGREEMENTS

Meeting in Malta in December 1989, Bush and Gorbachev agreed to settle the major START issues in time for their next meeting while aiming to complete the treaty by the end of 1990. So the superpowers stepped up their efforts for START in February 1990.

Gorbachev and Secretary Baker, meeting in Moscow on Feb. 9, settled several disputed provisions.

U.S. START negotiators had demanded from the beginning that any limit on strategic warheads discount bomber-carried weapons, by comparison with ballistic missile warheads, both because they were less suited to a surprise attack and because they were vulnerable to enemy air defenses.

Regardless of how many bombs and short-range missiles a strategic bomber carried, the Bush administration proposed, it should be counted as carrying only a single warhead against the overall START limit of 6,000 warheads, unless it carried air-launched cruise missiles (ALCMs) with a range of more than 1,500 kilometers.

ALCM-armed bombers would be counted as having 10 warheads, regardless of either the actual number of ALCMs carried or the maximum the plane could carry. U.S. B-1 and B-52 bombers could carry up to 20 ALCMs.

The Soviets called for inspection of all bombers to count the actual number of long-range ALCMs carried, and they would have counted all missiles with a range of more than 600 kilometers.

The practical effect of the U.S. proposal would be to allow a huge "bonus" of ALCMs, short-range missiles and gravity bombs that were nearly immune to the START warhead limit.

The Air Force used this fact as an argument for the B-2 bomber, which would carry no ALCMs. However, House Armed Services Committee Chairman Les Aspin, D-Wis., warned that that argument would not save the costly plane in the existing stringent budgetary environment. *(Stealth bomber, p. 687)*

The ALCM counting rule agreed on by Baker in Moscow marked practically total Soviet capitulation on the issue.

Both sides agreed that each ALCM-armed U.S. bomber would be counted as having 10 warheads and would be prohibited from carrying more than 20 missiles. Soviet ALCM carriers, which had smaller payloads, would be counted as having eight missiles and could carry no more than 12.

Consistent with the U.S. position, neither side's ALCM-armed bombers could be inspected by the other.

The two sides remained at odds over the minimum range above which a missile should be counted as an ALCM for START purposes.

Moscow also accepted, in the main, the U.S. position on long-range, sea-launched cruise missiles (SLCMs). Insisting that no ceiling on such small weapons could be verified, the Reagan and Bush administrations insisted that each country declare the number of nuclear-armed SLCMs it would deploy.

The Soviet Union called for binding limits on the number of nuclear and non-nuclear SLCMs deployed by each side.

But at Moscow, it accepted the U.S. position that each side simply inform the other of the number of SLCMS deployed and planned, with the proviso that these declarations be "politically binding."

The U.S. continued to oppose the Soviet demand for a limit on non-nuclear SLCMs, and the two sides also differed over the minimum range below which SLCMs would be exempt from limits.

Baker and Gorbachev also nailed down other START issues, agreeing to:

- Allow each side to deploy long-range, non-nuclear ALCMs on designated bombers.
- Require each side to broadcast all data from test launches of missiles that were covered by START, while exempting from the requirement types of missiles not counted by START and missiles test-fired from operational silos, a practice used by the Soviets.
- Limit the number of missiles of types deployed on mobile launchers that could be kept in storage, a provision intended to inhibit either side's ability to use "non-deployed" missiles in the second wave of a nuclear attack.

PREPARING FOR THE SUMMIT

The pressure on START negotiators to iron out details of the pact intensified in the spring, when the superpowers decided to move up the second Bush-Gorbachev summit by a month.

The speeded-up timetable was announced during meetings April 4-6 between Secretary of State Baker and Soviet Foreign Minister Eduard A. Shevardnadze.

Shifting the Bush-Gorbachev U.S. meeting to May 31-June 3 gave the Soviet chief more time to mend political fences in Moscow between the end of his U.S. trip and an important meeting of the Soviet Communist Party in early July.

But it also reduced the time remaining before the summit in which negotiators could work out the main features of their arms control deals.

Cruise Missile Agreements

In hope of making more progress on START, Baker went to Moscow May 16-19. During that trip, both sides settled two issues, involving long-range cruise missiles — tiny, nuclear-tipped, robot jet planes that could be launched from ships or larger aircraft.

The Soviet Union had wanted air-launched cruise missiles (ALCMs) to be counted against the treaty limits if they had a range of more than 600 kilometers. The United States insisted that they be exempt unless they had a range of 800 kilometers or more. Baker accepted the lower Soviet range after the Soviets agreed to exempt from coverage a conventionally armed U.S. missile, dubbed Tacit Rainbow, intended to protect U.S. bombers by homing in on enemy anti-aircraft radars.

The second Moscow agreement involved SLCMs. Since the 1960s, the Soviet navy had based its surface fleet on an arsenal of such weapons with ranges of a few hundred miles and capable of carrying either nuclear or conventional warheads.

Since the early 1980s, the U.S. Navy had been deploying on dozens of surface ships and submarines both nuclear-armed and conventionally armed versions of the Tomahawk SLCM. Though only the size of a torpedo, the nuclear-armed version had a range of 1,500 miles.

Though willing to exempt SLCMs from START, the Soviet Union had insisted that the treaty be accompanied by the separate, legally binding agreement that would set a firm limit on the number of SLCMs with a range of more than 600 kilometers, whatever their armament.

The U.S. government had insisted that an SLCM limit could not be verified without intrusive inspections that would hamstring naval operations, partly because the missiles were so small. But it proposed that each side make a "politically binding" statement of its nuclear SLCM production plans for the following five years, a projection that would be updated — and could be increased — annually.

U.S. negotiators also wanted any SLCM deal to cover nuclear missiles with a range of 300 kilometers or more because relatively few Soviet weapons would be covered under the 600-kilometer ceiling.

The deal struck in Moscow would have required both sides to make politically binding agreements to deploy no more than 880 nuclear-armed SLCMs with a range of 600 kilometers or more. The U.S. Navy had planned to deploy only 758 nuclear-armed Tomahawks, and that number faced reductions because of the budget crunch.

Conservatives Unhappy

Conservative critics, among them Richard N. Perle, the Reagan administration's most prominent anti-Soviet hard-liner, complained that Baker had given too much ground on START. In particular, they objected to Baker's acceptance of the cruise-missile limits and warned that he was weakening longstanding U.S. efforts to limit the Soviet fleet of *Backfire* bombers and its huge, multiwarhead SS-18 missiles.

In a May 23 letter to Bush, nine Senate GOP conservatives, led by Jesse Helms, R-N.C., objected to aspects of the cruise missile arrangement.

Baker lashed out at the START critics May 23, contending that the emerging treaty largely reflected U.S. positions and that the Soviets had made most of the concessions in recent negotiating rounds. "I don't think you should look just at one negotiating session," he said at a news conference.

Noting that the pact had the support of top U.S. military officials, Baker dismissed most of his critics as people "who, in the past . . . have simply rejected the concept of arms control, generally."

Even as he was rebutting conservative critics of START, however, Baker acknowledged that U.S.-Soviet relations would turn on much more than strategic arms control in the years to come: "Over the long term, sustained improvement in our relations is going to depend substantially upon a deepening and a widening of democratic values throughout Soviet society."

The conservatives' unhappiness with START was rooted, to some degree, in the treaty's fundamentals rather than its fine print.

Many conservative critics of the arms control process, among them Kenneth L. Adelman, who was Reagan's arms control chief, were skeptical of the treaty's emphasis on "deep cuts" in existing arsenals, even though that was Reagan's cardinal goal.

Smaller strategic arsenals would not necessarily make for a safer world, the skeptics argued. During the Reagan years, that view was shared by some less conservative national security specialists, including Brent Scowcroft, who later became Bush's national security adviser.

Early in Bush's term, administration aides indicated that nailing down CFE to get Soviet troops out of Eastern Europe would take precedence over START. But while Bush and Baker worked hard to wrap up START, the CFE pact was bogging down. "There's been a little bit of a somersault to put strategic arms control in the forefront," Adelman said to reporters May 22.

Another sore point with some early START critics was the treaty's limits on cruise missiles, which were seen by many as offering a relatively inexpensive means of delivering not only nuclear weapons but also conventional explosives with great accuracy.

One of the most hotly contested issues in the 1988 Senate debate on the treaty banning ground-launched, intermediate-range nuclear-force (INF) missiles was an effort to exempt from that ban long-range conventionally armed cruise missiles. *(INF treaty, 1988 Almanac, p. 379)*

In their May 23 letter to Bush, Helms and his allies objected to Baker's assurance to Gorbachev that the United States would not equip Tacit Rainbow antiradar missiles with nuclear weapons. The Pentagon had announced no plans for such a modification.

The treaty placed no limits on the development or deployment of conventionally armed ALCMs, as long as they were observably distinct from nuclear-armed weapons. Several conventionally armed ALCMS were under development, including at least one with a range of more than 600 kilometers.

START critics also singled out three elements of the treaty that, they contended, might accord the Soviet Union an advantage over the United States.

One provision, already agreed to, would have allowed 210 ALCM-equipped Soviet bombers but only 150 such U.S. planes. "That's a 40 percent advantage," said a Senate conservative source.

Helms suggested that this might violate the so-called Jackson amendment adopted by the Senate in 1972, requiring that any strategic arms treaty allow "equal forces" to each party. The basis of the proposed START provision was that it would give each side roughly equal numbers of ALCMs, because the U.S. planes carried more missiles apiece.

Remaining unsettled were two other issues the conservatives feared might be resolved in the Soviets' favor:

- To what degree could the Soviets continue improving their SS-18 missile? The critics warned that the START-limited force of 154 improved versions would be as powerful as the pre-START force of 308 missiles.

The Bush administration was pressing for a ban on further SS-18 production after 1992 and a prohibition on more than two SS-18 test launches per year. Eventually, the reasoning went, Soviet military planners would lose confidence in the reliability of the aging missiles.

- What limits would be placed on the Soviet *Backfire* bomber? Since the mid-1970s, hard-liners had insisted that this plane be covered by any strategic arms agreement, since it could reach U.S. targets from Soviet bases. Insisting that the plane was used for regional and naval missions, the Soviets refused.

In a letter appended to the unratified 1979 SALT II accord, Soviet leader Leonid I. Brezhnev promised to produce no more than 30 *Backfires* annually and to abstain from certain kinds of improvements to the plane.

The Bush administration insisted that the plane either be counted as a strategic bomber under START or else be limited in CFE as a regional weapon.

Verification

Several aspects of the routine for verifying compliance with START limits also were unsettled. Particularly touchy politically was the question of how to verify limits on mobile ICBMs.

The Soviet Union was deploying several dozen multi-warhead, rail-mobile SS-24s and about 200 single-warhead, road-mobile SS-25s. Neither of the corresponding U.S. weapons — rail-MX and Midgetman — was in production, and both faced strong political opposition. *(MX-Midgetman, 1989 Almanac, p. 423)*

The United States wanted an expanded version of the system set up under the INF treaty, under which each country's inspectors continually monitored factories in the other country that built key parts and assembled the missile types at issue. But Moscow rejected that idea.

Gaffney, of the Center for Security Policy, was one of many START critics who contended that limits on mobile missiles were hopelessly unverifiable. And verification concerns were voiced by centrists as well.

Soviet-built SS-23 missiles, banned by the INF pact, had turned up in East Germany, Czechoslovakia and Bulgaria.

Soviet Foreign Minister Shevardnadze insisted that he and other top Soviet leaders were unaware that the missiles had been transferred to other countries.

But in a Senate Foreign Relations Committee hearing on May 3, the SS-23 incident drew a sharp protest from Richard G. Lugar, R-Ind., a political centrist who was a strong supporter of INF and other arms control efforts.

"The whole purpose of this [INF] treaty was to eliminate intermediate weapons in Europe," Lugar said, demanding that the Bush administration secure the destruction of the weapons. "It is imperative that we solve this one prior to coming into [the debate on] START and CFE."

WASHINGTON SUMMIT

The joint statements on the START pact were just a part of the Bush-Gorbachev arms-control agenda at the May 31-June 3 summit in Washington. The two leaders also agreed to slash their chemical weapons stockpiles and to accept verification protocols that would pave the way for Senate approval of two nuclear-testing treaties. *(Testing treaties, p. 711; chemical weapons pact, p. 709)*

While such arms control issues had dominated U.S.-Soviet summits — and correspondingly the interest of Congress — for more than two decades, the latest meeting dealt with a broader agenda of Soviet political transformation and change in the military and political arrangement of Europe.

And progress on arms control debates drew little attention on Capitol Hill compared with Congress' strong interest in a U.S.-Soviet trade agreement signed by Bush and Gorbachev. *(Trade agreeement, p. 205)*

Still, the two presidents did nail down the major elements of START and sign a second statement setting goals for further reductions. Even though the talks had failed to overcome the disputes between the two sides, both leaders voiced a historic sense of optimism as the summit ended with a White House ceremony signing the trade treaty and a number of other agreements.

In their June 1 statement on strategic arms, Bush and Gorbachev said the START treaty would be "a major landmark in both arms control and in the relationship" between the two countries. They glossed over the remaining problems, expressing "great satisfaction with the great progress that has been made" and saying that the negotiating teams in Geneva had been "instructed . . . to accelerate their work."

Earlier in the day, at a breakfast meeting with congressional leaders, Gorbachev had similarly treated the remaining disagreements as easily solved.

"We have done a lot of difficult — I am frank with you, very difficult work — and we feel that the U.S. side has

Strategic Arms: Bush-Gorbachev Statement

Following are major provisions of the joint statement signed by President Bush and Soviet President Mikhail S. Gorbachev at their May 31-June 3 summit in Washington regarding a strategic arms reduction treaty (START). The statement covered major elements of the pact, while a second statement set goals for further reductions.

• **Overall Ceilings.** No more than 6,000 strategic warheads could be carried on no more than 1,600 ballistic missiles and heavy bombers of strategic range. No more than 4,900 warheads on land-based intercontinental ballistic missiles (ICBMs) and submarine-launched ballistic missiles (SLBMs).

• **Basic Counting Rules.** Each ICBM and SLBM of a given model would be counted as carrying a stipulated number of warheads (for example, 10 warheads each for the U.S. MX missile and the Soviet SS-18). Each bomber that did not carry long-range air-launched cruise missiles (ALCMs) would be counted as carrying only one warhead, no matter how many bombs and short-range missiles it carried.

• **'Heavy' ICBMs.** Neither side would deploy more than 1,540 warheads on ICBMs larger than the U.S. MX and the Soviet SS-19. Neither side would deploy more than 154 such "heavy" ICBMs. (The only such missile was the Soviet SS-18, a more powerful version of which was being deployed.) The agreement would cut in half the Soviets' fleet of SS-18s.

• **Mobile ICBMs.** No more than 1,100 warheads on ICBMs carried on mobile launchers. Mobile ICBMs would be limited by restricting the size of the areas in which they were routinely deployed and permitting deployment outside those areas only with prior notice to the other side. There would be limits on the location of "spare" missiles to prevent their rapid co-location with mobile launchers.

• **ALCM Counting Rules.** All existing types of ALCMs with a range of more than 600 kilometers would be counted under the limit, except the conventionally armed U.S. "Tacit Rainbow." To be exempt, conventionally armed ALCMs developed in the future would have to be observably different from nuclear ALCMs. The U.S. could deploy up to 150 ALCM-carrying bombers able to carry up to 20 missiles each, to be counted as carrying 10 missiles each. The Soviets could deploy up to 210 ALCM-carriers able to hold up to 12 missiles and counted as carrying eight.

• **Sea-Launched Cruise Missiles (SLCMs).** Sea-launched cruise missiles (SLCMs) would not be covered by START. But in a separate, "politically binding" agreement covering missiles with a range of more than 600 kilometers, the two sides agreed June 1 to deploy no more than 880 nuclear-armed SLCMs each. ■

done a lot of difficult work, too," Gorbachev told the lawmakers. " . . . And I think that as a result, we can say now that the document, and that is the statement on the main provisions of the future treaty, can be signed. And the remaining issues will be worked on by our negotiators."

THE NEXT PHASE

In the wake of the June summit, the superpowers concentrated their efforts on wrapping up the conventional forces in Europe treaty. Baker and Shevardnadze reached a breakthrough on that accord Oct. 3, agreeing on aircraft and weapons limits.

Two days later, Baker and Shevardnadze met Oct. 5 in New York in an effort to solve the remaining obstacles to concluding the START pact.

Technical disputes continued to dog the negotiations, but by Dec. 12, both sides were optimistic enough to schedule a summit in Moscow for Feb. 11-13, 1991.

That decision came as the United States took steps to show support for Gorbachev, who was facing increasing criticism as his country's economy was crumbling and food was running short.

After meeting with Shevardnadze at the White House, Bush announced that the United States would suspend its 15-year ban on extension of commercial credits to the Soviets. The trade break would help the Soviets buy up to $1 billion in U.S. agricultural goods.

Although Shevardnadze and Baker insisted that significant progress had been made toward completion of the START pact, they were not eager to get into the vexing details.

Sounding more like old fishing buddies than foreign ministers, they literally laughed off efforts by reporters to inquire about the technical disagreements.

"I'm sure you're quite familiar with the perimeter-portal monitoring concept," Baker teased. "It's those kind of issues that we're still struggling with, and we still have quite a few of those to deal with."

At least three START issues remained open:

• U.S. negotiators were resisting Soviet demands to inspect the B-2 "stealth" bomber to verify claims that the plane was not equipped to carry long-range cruise missles.

• Although the two sides agreed that each could observe the other's production of mobile intercontinental missiles, there was a dispute over which of several plants should be the monitored site.

• The two sides also differed over how much data from missile test flights each would have to make available to the other.

Bush's announcement of the plans for the February summit marked an apparent departure from the administration's previous insistence that it would not schedule another Bush-Gorbachev meeting until the treaty's terms were nailed down.

While Baker was belittling the jargon of the nuts and bolts of arms control agreements, other administration officials expressed anxiety over the unresolved issues.

"Things can always come up," said one. "The assumption is we have made progress and are very hopeful we will have a treaty to sign. There are no guarantees."

By early 1991, what came up was the Persian Gulf War and the Soviets' crackdown on the breakaway Baltic republics.

The Bush administration found itself in a delicate balancing act: maintaining good relations with the Soviet Union while signaling displeasure with the Soviet army's violent suppression of the democracy movements in the Baltics.

Complicating matters further, the Kremlin was proving an essential, if reluctant, ally against Iraq. *(Persian Gulf War, p. 717)*

With the technical issues on START remaining to be settled, and Bush reluctant to go to Moscow while the United States was fighting a war in the gulf, Washington and Moscow announced Jan. 28 what both countries depicted as a mutual decision to postpone the summit "to a date later in the first half of this year." ■

U.S., Soviets To Cut Chemical Weapons

Throughout the Cold War, the United States and the Soviet Union each stockpiled huge quantities of deadly chemical weapons that — just like nuclear weapons — were supposed to deter an attack. During a summit meeting in Washington, President Bush and Soviet President Mikhail S. Gorbachev on June 1 signed an agreement to begin a unique cooperation program to destroy those chemical weapons and to persuade other countries to do the same.

By year's end, however, the Bush administration had not sent the accord to Capitol Hill. U.S. and Soviet negotiators were still working on some of the final protocols, the most difficult of which was how each country would ensure the other's destruction of chemical weapons. And the Kremlin's increasingly hard-line political stance and crackdown on its breakaway Baltic States cast doubt on the accord's future in Congress. *(U.S.-Soviet relations, p. 757)*

Just how the pact would be ratified also provoked a dispute with implications for both political strategy and congressional prerogatives.

Some House leaders asked Bush to submit the agreement to both chambers, to be approved by a simple majority vote in each.

But key senators, including most members of the Foreign Relations Committee, wrote Bush insisting that the Constitution required the agreement to be in "treaty form," and thus subject to approval by a two-thirds vote only of the Senate.

Bush had been expected to send the accord to both chambers and avoid the need to muster the two-thirds vote. However, with the Senate eager to maintain its unique role in approving arms control pacts, Bush administration officials said they were considering the senators' demand. By fall, though, Secretary of State James A. Baker III said the Bush team would send it to both chambers.

In June, Bush announced that as a major first step toward the treaty's goals, the United States would stop making chemical weapons — matching a move that Gorbachev said the Soviet Union made in 1987.

The progress toward a U.S.-Soviet accord on chemical weapons came as lawmakers were working on mandatory sanctions bills largely inspired by Iraq's use of chemical weapons during the 1980s in its war with Iran and its suppression of a domestic rebellion by separatist Kurds.

The administration resisted imposing sanctions against Iraq, however, until after its invasion of Kuwait on Aug. 2. And Bush vetoed an export controls measure (HR 4653) that would have required sanctions against countries that used chemical weapons or aided other countries in manufacturing them. *(Gulf crisis, p. 717; export controls, p. 198)*

BACKGROUND

In 1989, Bush had said that the United States would dismantle 80 percent of its stockpile if the Soviet Union agreed to cut its larger arsenal to an equal level.

The Pentagon was continuing to request funding for a new generation of chemical weapons. In the wake of his pledge, however, Bush canceled the request for $169 million in fiscal 1991 for more new chemical weapons.

The United States already had about 25,000 to 30,000 metric tons of chemical weapons; the Soviet Union was estimated to have from 50,000 to 75,000 tons. The superpowers exchanged data about their supplies Dec. 29, but the information was not immediately made public.

The chemical weapons accord followed the 1987 intermediate-range nuclear forces (INF) treaty in calling for destruction of an entire class of weapons, with each superpower monitoring the other's compliance. *(1987 Almanac, p. 135)*

But the new accord went beyond the INF treaty in providing for active U.S.-Soviet cooperation in developing and using techniques to destroy the weapons. It also allowed for "systematic on-site inspections" of all facilities used for storing and producing chemical weapons.

Having built thousands of tons of deadly poison weapons, Washington and Moscow struggled with the question of how to get rid of them. The Pentagon had hoped to have the first of eight facilities to dismantle and destroy chemical weapons by incineration in operation by the end of 1990, but that fell behind schedule.

Seven other U.S. chemical weapons destruction facilities were in various stages of planning. Congress, however, in 1986 had ordered the Pentagon to destroy 90 percent of its chemical weapons by Sept. 30, 1994 — a deadline later extended to Sept. 30, 1997. *(1986 Almanac, p. 464)*

The Soviet Union in 1989 closed down its only chemical weapons destruction plant because of environmental concerns. U.S. officials said Moscow would rely heavily on the Pentagon and private contractors for advice in developing new facilities.

Pact's Provisions

Under the June 1 agreement, the superpowers were to begin destroying their chemical weapons by the end of 1992. By the end of 1999, each had to destroy at least 50 percent of its declared stockpile and, by the end of 2002, destroy all but 5,000 tons — equal to 20 percent of the existing holdings declared by the United States.

In the meantime, the superpowers pledged to press for progress in Geneva, where 40 nations were negotiating for an international treaty banning such weapons.

If an international treaty was signed and ratified, the United States and the Soviet Union would accelerate the destruction of their poison gas supplies. Eight years after the Geneva treaty entered into force, the superpowers pledged to eliminate all but 500 tons of chemical weapons each — equal to 2 percent of the existing U.S. stockpile.

TREATY NEGOTIATIONS

Meeting in Moscow on Feb. 7-9, Baker and Soviet Foreign Minister Eduard A. Shevardnadze pledged in a joint statement to complete work soon on the bilateral chemical weapons agreement. They predicted the pact would be ready for signature at the Bush-Gorbachev summit scheduled to begin at the end of May.

The Baker-Shevardnadze statement contained no specifics, but the bilateral pact would require the superpowers to destroy the bulk of their chemical arms, putting their arsenals at "equal low levels" for the first time.

Elisa D. Harris, a senior research analyst at the Brookings Institution, said the U.S.-Soviet accord was not "terribly relevant" because neither country had adequate facilities to disarm the deadly weapons. At Moscow's request, Baker and Shevardnadze agreed to share information on how to dismantle the weapons.

The Baker-Shevardnadze meetings left open several questions about the worldwide nerve-gas treaty under negotiation in Geneva. That treaty called on all countries to stop producing chemical weapons and to eliminate their stockpiles within 10 years.

A potential obstacle was a Bush position that some critics — and reportedly negotiators for most other nations — viewed as holding out the option that Washington might not dismantle all its weapons within 10 years.

At the United Nations Sept. 25, 1989, Bush said the United States would destroy 98 percent of its nerve gas within eight years of signing the Geneva pact, provided the Soviet Union also signed. *(1989 Almanac, p. 500)*

Under his timetable, the United States and the Soviet Union immediately would begin destroying all but about 5,000 metric tons of their existing stockpiles. That figure equaled about 20 percent of the U.S. holdings of chemical weapons, estimated at 25,000 tons. Most estimates put the Soviet holdings at 50,000 to 75,000 tons.

Under existing U.S. law, the Army had to destroy 90 percent of its chemical weapons stockpiles by 1997.

But Bush said the United States would destroy its remaining 2 percent only "once all nations capable of building chemical weapons" signed.

Some critics said Bush's condition could mean that Washington indefinitely retained a small weapons reserve. "Any country, even Upper Slobbovia, is capable of producing chemical weapons," said John Isaacs, legislative director of the Council for a Livable World.

The Baker-Shevardnadze statement in February was ambiguous on the 2 percent issue, apparently reflecting Moscow's refusal to accept it. The statement noted that during the first eight years of the Geneva treaty the superpowers would reduce their chemical weapons to a "very small fraction" of existing stocks. It added: "All remaining CW [chemical weapon] stocks should be eliminated over the subsequent two years. Of course, all CW capable states must adhere" to the treaty.

Lee Feinstein of the private Arms Control Association said that statement left unclear just how explicit the link was between U.S. dismantling of its remaining 2 percent and the adherence of other countries to the treaty.

Harris said the statement was "designed to paper over fundamentally different positions" on the 2 percent issue.

The statement also created uncertainty about the status of another controversial Bush position. The wording of the treaty demanded that all countries halt production upon signing it, but the Bush administration in 1989 held out the prospect that Washington might keep the option of continuing production even after signing. That created a small furor among arms control specialists in Washington and at the Geneva negotiations. After meeting with Gorbachev at Malta in December 1989, Bush said he would drop his position if the Soviet Union accepted other U.S. proposals at the Geneva talks.

The Baker-Shevardnadze statement noted that the treaty "shall contain the provision that all production of chemical weapons will halt upon its entry into force."

Isaacs said he read the statement as a retreat by Bush. But some experts said the continued U.S.-Soviet disagreement on the 2 percent issue raised a question about whether Bush had backed down on continued production. "It would be nice to get some clarity on some of these issues," Harris said.

Breakthrough in May

Baker and Shevardnadze completed the essential details of the chemical weapons pact in May, during Baker's trip to Moscow weeks before the summit.

Baker called the agreement a "trailblazing agreement" that "provides a real pathway toward a global ban on horrific weapons that we already know from bitter experience actually get used."

In their Moscow talks, Baker and Shevardnadze resolved a key sticking point: Bush's insistence on retaining the right to continue producing chemical weapons. Baker accepted a Soviet proposal for an immediate halt to chemical arms production once the U.S.-Soviet pact entered into force.

Subsequently, Bush scrubbed his request for $169 million in fiscal 1991 authorization for binary munitions — weapons containing two chemicals mixed together to produce toxic gas when fired.

In exchange for the U.S. concession on production, the Soviet Union appeared to accept the essential elements of Bush's September 1990 timetable for the superpowers to destroy their stockpiles.

Within eight years of signing the agreement, each superpower would scrap all but 500 tons of chemical weapons — or about 2 percent of of the existing U.S. stockpile.

Baker said in Moscow that the superpowers would destroy the remaining 2 percent "at such time as all chemical weapons-capable states had indicated a willingness to come on board and, in effect, accomplish a global ban." Officials said Baker was referring to an agreement by other countries to sign the Geneva treaty barring possession of chemical weapons.

The provision allowing the superpowers to keep 500 tons of weapons was controversial, particularly among those who wanted speedy negotiations toward the Geneva pact.

Charles Flowerlee, a consultant on chemical weapons for the Arms Control Association, argued that the U.S. insistence on keeping some chemical weapons posed a serious obstacle to the Geneva treaty. That treaty called on each signing nation to destroy all its chemical weapons within 10 years — without regard to whether the treaty had been signed by every nation with the capability of producing poison gas.

Flowerlee said nations such as Iraq would argue: "Why shouldn't all countries have the right to retain residual stockpiles" if the superpowers did?

Flowerlee and Harris said the U.S.-Soviet pact made a significant advance by providing for the superpowers to share information about their stockpiles and the technology of eliminating chemical weapons.

The Soviet Union had no environmentally safe means of destroying its weapons, but Washington said it would give it access to new technologies under development in the United States.

By the time of the summit, the two countries had negotiated a provision stating that after the treaty had been in effect for eight years, the superpowers would propose a conference to determine whether enough nations had signed the pact to justify destruction of the final 2 percent.

That paved the way for Bush and Gorbachev to sign the chemical weapons pact in Washington on June 1.

Dante B. Fascell, D-Fla., chairman of the House Foreign Affairs Committee, praised the agreement as representing "real disarmament" and said congressional reluctance to fund chemical weapons production pressured the Bush administration into negotiating with the Soviets.

But Frank J. Gaffney, a former Pentagon official in the Reagan administration who headed the private Center for Security Policy in Washington, led criticism of the agreement. He said the United States had no way of determining exactly how many chemical weapons the Soviets had or whether the Kremlin would follow through on its pledge to destroy them.

Treaty or Executive Agreement?

With the agreement signed, attention turned to how it would be approved on Capitol Hill.

Earlier in the year, Gaffney said he had been told the administration wanted to avoid submitting it as a treaty because of concerns about getting the necessary two-thirds vote in the Senate.

Bush instead would send Congress the accord as an executive agreement, which would need endorsement by a simple majority in each chamber, Gaffney and other conservatives predicted.

Administration officials indeed were expected to seek Congress to approve it by a joint resolution of approval. But they rejected the conservatives' reasoning, saying the president preferred to get the broader backing of both houses of Congress.

But the Senate jealously guarded its prerogative to approve treaties. Senators periodically accused presidents of undermining the Constitution by refusing to put agreements with foreign governments in treaty form.

Senior Senate leaders lobbied Baker and Bush to submit the agreement as a formal treaty, requiring approval by a two-thirds vote only of the Senate.

Nevertheless, Baker told the Senate Foreign Relations and House Foreign Affairs committees on June 12-13, that the administration's "tentative and initial decision" was to send the chemical weapons accord to Congress as an executive agreement, to be approved by majority votes in both chambers.

Baker told both committees that the administration always had planned to make the chemical weapons accord an executive agreement. The administration considered the senators' request but decided to stand by the initial decision, he said. ■

Senate OKs Treaties To Limit Nuclear Tests

Ending 14 years of controversy and delay, the Senate engaged in only perfunctory debate Sept. 25 before approving two treaties with the Soviet Union aimed at limiting the power of nuclear test explosions.

A handful of members offered speeches consuming slightly more than half the allotted two hours before the 98-0 vote approving the agreements to bar underground nuclear blasts with an explosive force greater than 150,000 tons of TNT (150 kilotons). *(Votes 249, 250, p. 50-S)*

The Threshold Test Ban Treaty, signed July 3, 1974, applied to underground nuclear weapons tests. On May 28, 1976, the companion Peaceful Nuclear Explosions Treaty was signed to cover underground nuclear explosions for peaceful purposes, such as large-scale excavation for dams or canals. The agreements followed the partial test-ban treaty signed in 1963, which banned nuclear test explosions except those conducted underground.

President Bush signed the document formally ratifying the treaties Dec. 11.

Various political factors had stalled Senate action on the agreements since they were negotiated under the administrations of Richard M. Nixon and Gerald R. Ford.

President Jimmy Carter shelved the pacts and sought instead to negotiate a comprehensive test ban treaty with the Soviets. But those negotiations ended without success in late 1980.

From 1982 on, the obstacle was President Ronald Reagan's insistence that the networks of seismometers provided for in the treaties could not adequately verify Soviet compliance with the 150-kiloton limits.

Bush requested Senate approval of the two treaties four weeks after he and Soviet President Mikhail S. Gorbachev signed, at their summit meeting in Washington on June 1, 1990, detailed appendixes (or "protocols") tightening verification procedures. *(U.S.-Soviet relations, p. 757)*

These new agreements would allow each country to use not only seismic measurements but also a U.S.-backed method called CORRTEX to measure the size of any explosion expected to have a force of more than 50 kilotons. This new technique would use instruments located practically adjacent to the explosive device being monitored.

The unanimous vote for the two treaties, and the desultory debate preceding it, reflected in part the dramatic decline in U.S.-Soviet tensions as Gorbachev retrenched abroad while grappling at home with economic chaos and ethnic separatism.

But the Senate's low-key approval of two treaties that dealt, although peripherally, with the U.S. nuclear arsenal also attested to the blandness of the agreements. The U.S. nuclear testing program had lived with the 150-kiloton limit since 1976, when both countries agreed to abide by the ceiling, pending ratification of the two pacts.

Citing seismic measurements, the Reagan administration contended that the Soviet Union had violated that limit many times. But many prominent specialists in seismic measurement sharply contested that claim.

The duel over Soviet compliance was one of many controversies that had kept the two treaties languishing. Policy-makers continued to debate whether the United States should maintain an aggressive testing program or press for a comprehensive ban on testing.

Some issues resurfaced during Senate deliberations on the pacts, but all were finessed.

Checking Up: Treaty Protocols

The new verification protocols were extremely long, largely because they spelled out in exquisite detail the procedures for using the CORRTEX method. The two-page text of the Threshold Test Ban Treaty was followed by a 107-page protocol.

For each treaty, the protocols provided that:

- When one country planned an explosion with a yield

greater than 50 kilotons, the other could monitor its strength using CORRTEX, seismic methods, or both.

To monitor such explosions seismically, the verifying country could temporarily install its own equipment at three existing seismic stations in the territory of the testing country. The Soviet Union could use stations at Tulsa, Okla.; Black Hills, S.D.; and Newport, Wash. The United States could use stations at Arti, Novosibirsk and Obninsk in the Soviet Union.

- When one country planned an explosion with a yield of 35 to 50 kilotons, the other could inspect the test site and collect samples of the rock and soil to better interpret its seismic measurements of the blast.
- If one country conducted no explosions larger than 50 kilotons in a year, the other could use CORRTEX to measure two smaller blasts in each of the first five years the treaty was in effect and one blast annually thereafter.
- Explosions could not be conducted in caverns larger than 20,000 cubic meters, because an extremely large hole might muffle the seismic shock of the blast, thus deceiving distant seismic equipment.

Advance estimates of how big a bang to expect from a given nuclear device were inherently uncertain, as were measurements of the actual blast. So the U.S. and Soviet governments agreed that the occurrence of one or two blasts measured as being slightly over the 150-kiloton limit would not be interpreted as a violation of these treaties. Aficionados called this the treaties' "whoops!" clause.

Proponents of a comprehensive test ban viewed the long duel over new verification methods as just another skirmish within a larger battle over eliminating underground nuclear blasts.

Seismic experts aligned with these arms control advocates contended that officials of the Reagan and Bush administrations exaggerated the uncertainties in seismic measurement of nuclear blasts while playing down potential weak spots in CORRTEX.

Ray E. Kidder, a physicist at the Energy Department's Lawrence Livermore Laboratory, summarized one widely held suspicion in a letter to Senate Intelligence Committee Chairman David L. Boren, D-Okla.: "The primary reason for U.S. insistence on [CORRTEX] was a mistaken belief that its intrusiveness would result in its unacceptability [to] the Soviets."

Senate Debate

The Foreign Relations Committee, which had favorably reported the two treaties in 1987, held hearings July 17, July 31 and Sept. 13. It marked up the resolution of ratification Sept. 14 (Exec N 94-2, Treaty Doc 101-19 — Exec Rept 101-31).

Some GOP conservatives, among them Malcolm Wallop of Wyoming and Steve Symms of Idaho, had contended that Soviet explosions had violated the 150-kiloton ceiling many times.

But the new, intricately detailed verification arrangements apparently satisfied conservatives' contentions that Soviet violations might not be detected using the verification techniques first provided for in the treaties.

The only potential controversy facing the Senate's debate over the treaties was whether liberal arms control advocates would try to press Bush to try to negotiate more far-reaching nuclear testing constraints with the Soviets, possibly including a comprehensive nuclear test ban.

Both chambers went on record during the year in favor of moving toward a comprehensive test ban while working on the fiscal 1991 Department of Defense authorization bill (S 2884 — PL 101-510).

The Senate on Aug. 2 approved by voice vote a nonbinding amendment by Edward M. Kennedy, D-Mass., recommending creation of a committee of U.S. and Soviet technical experts to study methods that might be used to verify a future arms control agreement that banned the production of nuclear weapons material and required the dismantling of nuclear warheads. Working on its version of the legislation (HR 4739), the House on Sept. 28 voted 234-182 in favor of an amendment by Douglas H. Bosco, D-Calif., expressing the sense of Congress that the president should, "at the earliest possible date," seek a comprehensive, verifiable ban on nuclear weapons testing. *(Vote 343, p. 112-H; Defense authorization, p. 671)*

The Reagan and Bush administrations had rejected any move toward a total test ban in the near future while insisting that a comprehensive ban remained the ultimate U.S. goal: "As long as we must rely on nuclear weapons for our deterrent, we have to maintain a reasonable test program," Ronald F. Lehman II, director of the Arms Control and Disarmament Agency, told the Foreign Relations panel at its July 17 hearing.

Reagan promised Congress in October 1986 that once the two 150-kiloton treaties were approved, he would propose that U.S. and Soviet officials "immediately engage in negotiations" aimed at a step-by-step program of limiting and ultimately abolishing nuclear weapons — a process that would, however, be linked with the gradual abolition of nuclear weapons.

But early in 1990, apparently breaking with Reagan's pledge to begin negotiations for a next step "immediately" after tying up the 150-kiloton pacts, the Bush administration said it would have to evaluate the operation of the new treaties before deciding whether more test limits would be tolerable.

The Energy Department said the evaluation period could last up to 10 years.

Looking at the Next Steps

One argument for a comprehensive test ban (CTB) was that continued testing would only rekindle superpower tensions by fostering new, more lethal weapons.

CTB advocates, among them Senate Foreign Relations Committee Chairman Claiborne Pell, D-R.I., also sounded another theme: Continued testing by the superpowers undermined the nuclear non-proliferation treaty signed in 1968, under which 140 countries renounced efforts to develop nuclear weapons.

Pell pointed to a provision of the non-proliferation pact that bound signatories with nuclear arms, including the United States and the Soviet Union, to seek abolition of the weapons.

"While we may not treat these commitments seriously," Pell told the Senate on Sept. 25, "others do." If the United States refused to seek a nuclear ban, he said, other signatories might allow that treaty to expire in 1995, "and thus wreak havoc on efforts to control the spread of nuclear weapons."

While endorsing a comprehensive test ban as an ultimate goal, the Reagan and Bush administrations had insisted that it would be feasible only in conjunction with the abolition of nuclear weapons. "As long as we must rely upon nuclear weapons for our deterrent," Lehman told Pell's committee July 17, "we have to maintain a reasonable test program."

Slade Gorton, R-Wash., echoed that view during the Senate debate. "A CTB can only be the result of a new strategic environment in which nuclear deterrence has become irrelevant," he said.

Straddling the controversy, the Foreign Relations Committee on Sept. 14 included in the resolution approving ratification of the Threshold Test Ban Treaty two declarations, one sought by advocates for speedy completion of a comprehensive test ban and another, sought by the administration, intended to forestall such haste.

Once the panel finished massaging the declarations for the sake of consensus, both were so innocuous that the panel approved the resolutions of approval for both treaties by unanimous votes of 19-0:

- The "pro-CTB" declaration cited a provision in the treaty stating that the two countries "shall continue their negotiations with a view toward achieving a solution to the problem of the cessation of all underground nuclear tests."

The provision would be "legally binding" once the treaty was ratified, according to the declaration, placing the United States and the Soviet Union under a special obligation "to achieve further limitations on nuclear testing, including the achievement of a verifiable comprehensive test ban."

But Republicans Richard G. Lugar, Ind., and John W. Warner, Va., dismissed the declaration as virtually meaningless. Taken in context, they maintained, the provisions cited in the declaration were consistent with the Bush administration's position that a comprehensive ban was a distant goal, to be sought only in a much kinder and gentler world.

"This resolution would not have been voted out of committee by a vote of 19-0 if it had been intended to change or undermine existing U.S. policy," Lugar said.

- For its part, the Pentagon requested a declaration committing the country to certain "safeguards," intended to ensure that the nuclear weapons complex would remain intact and ready to respond to any international challenge. Among these were a continuing test program, consistent with the limits of the test-ban treaty, and preparedness to resume testing forbidden by this or other treaties, should national security require it.

Foreign Relations approved the safeguards but only after watering them down. For example, the Pentagon requested a commitment to an "aggressive" underground test program, but the committee changed that to an "effective" program.

In a letter to Jesse Helms, N.C., the senior Republican member of Foreign Relations, Robert B. Barker, the Pentagon's nuclear weapons chief, said the committee's version was "acceptable" because it did not change the meaning of the safeguards.

But in its report on the resolutions of approval, the Foreign Relations panel emphasized that it saw the revised safeguards as no warrant for expanding the test program: "The standards . . . are being essentially met now, so far as is practicable, and . . . no major new programs or expenditures would be required."

Small Tests

The chances for a total test ban — or a treaty limiting tests to blasts of only a few kilotons — would vanish if the CORRTEX method acquired the patina of sole reliable measurement technique. Since CORRTEX equipment had to be placed within yards of the blast it was measuring, it would be useless as a check on small tests that a country tried to conceal.

But a prominent CTB backer, Columbia University geologist Paul G. Richards, took an optimistic view. Citing U.S. and Soviet test explosions conducted in 1988, which were monitored using both methods, Richards told Boren's Intelligence panel that the comparison vindicated the seismic approach.

"A principal outcome of CORRTEX turns out to be restoration of confidence in seismic methods," he said, "which can, in turn, be applied to the verification of more stringent treaties."

One issue resolved during deliberations on the threshold test-ban treaty involved technical changes in verification procedures. The verification protocol provided that the two sides could make such changes, but the administration assured senators that they would be notified before any changes took effect.

Arms control chief Lehman also assured worried members that his explanations of the treaties could be considered "authoritative." The Reagan administration created an uproar by challenging well-established interpretations of the ABM (Anti-ballistic Missile) Treaty under the argument that testimony by Nixon administration officials had not been authoritative. ■

Chapter 11

FOREIGN POLICY

Persian Gulf Crisis 717
Map of Mideast Region 718
Chronology 719
Map of Kuwait 725
Operation Desert Shield 726
Bush Aug. 8 Address 726
Bush Aug. 28 Briefing 729
Bush Address to Congress 731
U.S. Arms Sales to Allies 734
The Offensive Option 737
U.N. Resolution 678 737
War Powers Suit 739
Choice of Allies Questioned 740
Bush News Conference 741
Rationales, Objectives 744
Operation Desert Storm 747
Bush Letter to Congress 747
Use of Force Resolution 748
Senate Vote on Use of Force 749
House Vote on Use of Force 750
Congressional Debate 752
Bush Jan. 16 Address 754
U.S.-Soviet Relations 757
Moscow Embassy 760
German Unification 762
U.S.-China Relations 764
Chinese Students Veto Sustained 767
Pakistan Aid 768
U.S.-Nicaragua Relations 770
Credit-Taking for Chamorro's Win 772
Panama Aid 774
El Salvador Aid 779
U.S. South Africa Policy 787
Kenya Aid 790
Zaire Aid 790
Intelligence Bill 791
Veto Message 798
State Department Authorization 799
State Department Nominations 801
United Nations Funding 802
Food for Peace Program 803
Andean Initiative Drug Strategy 805
Torture Treaty Ratification 806
'Armenian Genocide' Resolution 807
Palau 'Compact of Free Association' 808

Gulf Crisis Grows Into War With Iraq

Arab states, European allies join U.S. to free Kuwait

The United States engaged in a tense diplomatic and military confrontation with Iraq during the last five months of 1990, a crisis that turned into war in January 1991. The war ended in a quick and smashing success for a U.S.-led coalition.

President Bush sent U.S. troops into battle to enforce the demand that Iraq withdraw its troops from Kuwait, the small neighbor that Iraqi forces invaded in a sudden and largely unexpected strike Aug. 2.

Bush won wide praise for his diplomatic efforts in building and maintaining a coalition of Arab countries, European allies and others to confront Iraq's belligerent president, Saddam Hussein. While Bush's political handling of the Persian Gulf crisis drew both praise and criticism, he won a rare congressional vote specifically authorizing his use of military force to oust Iraq from Kuwait. And with the war ended, his popularity soared to record levels.

Congress supported the president's actions from the start of the crisis, but at times the support was wary or questioning.

Lawmakers generally endorsed Bush's imposition of an economic embargo against Iraq and his immediate move to deploy 100,000 U.S. troops to Saudi Arabia, a key U.S. ally, in order to ward off a possible Iraqi invasion of that country. Members joined with Bush in warning of the dangers to world oil supplies and regional security in the Middle East if the Iraqi invasion of Kuwait was allowed to stand.

On the other hand, lawmakers in both parties pressed Bush to do more to get Arab nations and U.S. allies such as Germany and Japan to help pay for the costs of what the Pentagon dubbed Operation Desert Shield. And many members, especially Democrats, warned that Bush should not send U.S. troops into combat without prior congressional approval.

The House and Senate passed non-binding resolutions on Oct. 1 and Oct. 2, respectively, that endorsed Bush's actions but did not provide any explicit authority to go to war. The resolutions differed in some details, and neither chamber acted on the measure approved by the other.

After the 101st Congress had adjourned and the midterm elections had passed, Bush jolted lawmakers and the public with an announcement Nov. 8 of a substantial troop buildup with the aim of giving U.S. forces an offensive capability. The sudden move — which brought U.S. troop strength to 430,000, nearly double the pre-election level — provoked a firestorm of criticism from lawmakers. Bush's approval rating in the polls dipped.

Congressional leaders who met with Bush on Nov. 14, however, said they were satisfied that he still intended to give economic sanctions time to work.

PERSIAN GULF CRISIS

Background .... p. 717
- Map of Mideast region..... p. 718
- Chronology............... p. 719
- Map of Kuwait............ p. 725

Operation Desert Shield .... p. 726
- Bush Aug. 8 address ...... p. 726
- Bush Aug. 28 briefing ..... p. 729
- Bush address to Congress . p. 731
- U.S. arms sales to allies ... p. 734

The offensive option........ p. 737
- U.N. Resolution 678 .... p. 737
- War powers suit .... p. 739
- Choice of allies questioned. p. 740
- Bush news conference..... p. 741
- Rationales, objectives...... p. 744

Operation Desert Storm .... p. 747
- Bush letter to Congress.... p. 747
- Use of force resolution .... p. 748
- Senate vote .... p. 749
- House vote............... p. 750
- Anguished debate......... p. 752
- Bush Jan. 16 address ..... p. 754

Bush and Secretary of State James A. Baker III directed a major diplomatic initiative aimed at passage by the U.N. Security Council of a resolution to authorize the use of force against Iraq if it had not withdrawn from Kuwait by a stated deadline. Key to the effort was the cooperation of the Soviet Union, which had formerly supported Iraq but was more interested, with the end of the Cold War, in building good relations with the United States.

The diplomatic campaign culminated in the Security Council's adoption of Resolution 678 on Nov. 29 setting Jan. 15, 1991, as the deadline for Iraq to pull out of Kuwait. After that, the resolution authorized all member states to use "all necessary means" to enforce previous U.N. resolutions demanding the withdrawal.

In Washington, lawmakers continued to debate the use of force vs. reliance on sanctions, with most Democrats coalescing around a position favoring sanctions and most Republicans backing discretion for the president to go to war if he chose. After the 102nd Congress convened on Jan. 3, Bush decided to formally request congressional authorization to use force, and his letter of Jan. 8 prompted the most serious and solemn of congressional debates.

The debate concluded Jan. 12 with the passage of identical resolutions (S J Res 2, H J Res 77) authorizing Bush "to use United States armed forces" to end Iraq's "illegal occupation of, and brutal aggression against, Kuwait." The Senate voted 52-47 to approve the resolution; the House vote was 250-183. Republicans in both chambers were virtually unanimous in voting for the resolutions; Democrats voted against the resolutions by substantial majorities.

Once the U.N. deadline had passed, President Bush acted swiftly. On Jan. 16, he ordered the beginning of an intense air war against Iraq. On Feb. 22, Bush gave Iraq an ultimatum: withdraw by noon the next day or face a ground war. When that deadline, too, passed without Iraqi compliance, U.S. commanders led a massive invasion by allied forces into Kuwait and southern Iraq.

The Iraqi army's collapse was astonishingly quick, and U.S. casualties unexpectedly light. On Feb. 27, Bush announced a cease-fire and declared Kuwait liberated.

BACKGROUND

For most of the 1980s, the United States sought to improve and expand its relations with Iraq.

The policies initiated under President Ronald Reagan and continued by President Bush had geopolitical motivations: to maintain Iraq as a counterweight to the anti-American government in Iran and to wean Iraq away from the Soviet sphere of influence. The United States also had

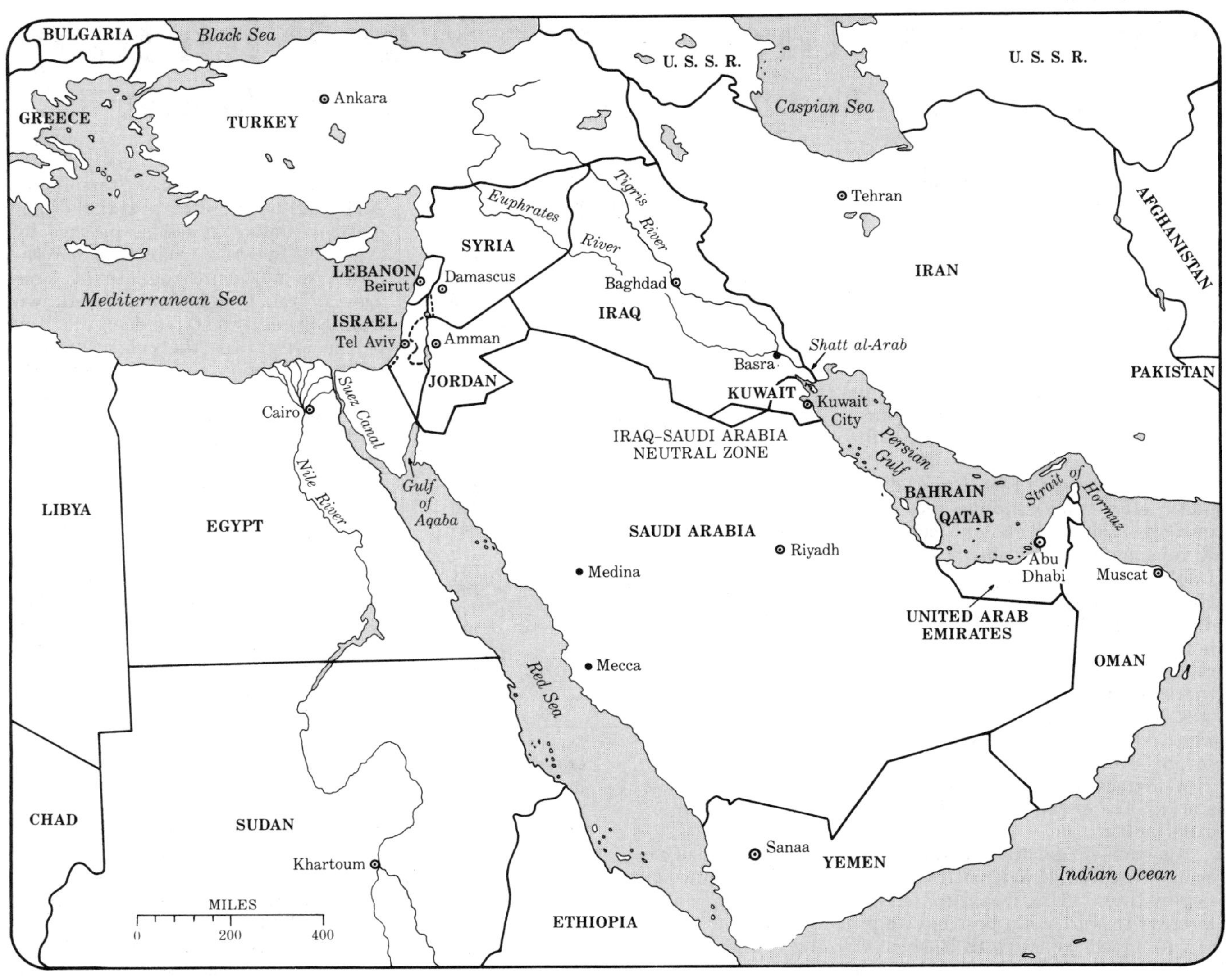

economic interests: to establish markets for U.S. goods, especially food, and to keep Iraqi oil flowing to the United States as well as to Western Europe and Japan.

The policies aligned the United States with a government that sharply restricted civil and political rights at home and pursued bellicose policies abroad. But many in Washington were impressed with Iraqi President Saddam Hussein's stated intent to modernize his country, saw evidence of moderation in his foreign policies, and preferred Iraqi secularism to the Islamic fundamentalism of Iran.

Until the end of the decade, the U.S. tilt toward Iraq drew little critical attention except among Mideast specialists, the Israeli lobby, human rights groups and a handful of members of Congress. But Saddam's use of chemical weapons — first in the war with Iran (1980-88) and then in a "final offensive" against the separatist Kurdish population in northern Iraq — led to congressional scrutiny of the policies and efforts to impose sanctions against Iraq.

The debate over sanctions intensified on Capitol Hill in 1989 and 1990, but the Bush administration decided to continue the rapprochement toward Iraq. Broad sanctions measures were progressing in early 1990. And in late July, both the House and Senate added amendments to the omnibus farm bill to cut off food sale credits to Iraq.

The Nature of Saddam's Rule

Iraq's pan-Arab Baath Socialist Party overthrew the country's pro-Western monarchy in 1958, was ousted in 1963, and returned to power in a second coup in 1968. Saddam, drawn to the party as a young man by its Arab nationalism, emerged as the strongman of the regime in the 1970s and in 1979 became president of the state and the ruling Revolutionary Command Council.

Saddam built up a cult of personality tied to the Baath Party and its distinctive Arab nationalism. He dedicated himself to restoring his country's former glories and forging a single Arab nation, and he built the Baath Party into a mass organization that helped sustain him in power.

In his 1990 book "Human Rights in Iraq," former foreign service officer David Korn wrote that political killings had been "a hallmark of the Baath regime in Iraq from the beginning." Legends linked Saddam personally to assassinations or attempted assassinations as early as 1959.

In its annual human rights report in 1989, the U.S. State Department said that Iraq's human rights record was

Continued on p. 722

Key Dates in Persian Gulf Crisis

Aug. 2 — Iraq invades Kuwait. Kuwait's ruling emir flees to Saudi Arabia. President Bush freezes Iraqi and Kuwaiti assets in the United States, bans trade and transactions with Iraq, and bans air and sea travel to Iraqi ports. The U.N. Security Council unanimously calls for Iraq's unconditional withdrawal from Kuwait (Resolution 660).

Aug. 3 — The United States and the Soviet Union jointly call for a halt to international arms exports to Iraq. The United States also proposes an international economic boycott of Iraq. The Arab League condemns the invasion and calls for the immediate withdrawal of Iraqi troops.

Aug. 4 — The European Community imposes a boycott on Iraqi and Kuwaiti oil and prohibits the sale of arms to those countries; Japan follows suit the next day. Iraqi troops reported near Saudi Arabian border.

Aug. 5 — Bush declares that the invasion "will not stand" and announces that the United States will not recognize the new Iraqi-installed government in Kuwait.

Aug. 6 — U.N. Security Council votes to prohibit U.N. members from importing or exporting either Iraqi or Kuwaiti products (Resolution 661).

Aug. 7 — Bush dispatches U.S. forces to Saudi Arabia to prevent an Iraqi invasion of that country and calls on other nations to send forces. The Gulf Cooperation Council calls on Iraq to withdraw from Kuwait.

Aug. 8 — Iraq declares that it has annexed Kuwait in a "comprehensive and eternal merger." Bush waives a congressional amendment limiting the number of F-15s that Saudi Arabia could possess. Britain agrees to send forces to Saudi Arabia. Iraq says it will respect its non-aggression pact with Saudi Arabia. U.S. officials say that U.S. forces sent to Saudi Arabia will reach 50,000 within a month's time.

Aug. 9 — Bush officially notifies Congress of the deployment of troops but says he does not believe involvement in hostilities is imminent, sidestepping a triggering of the War Powers Resolution. Iraq seals off its borders to all foreigners except diplomats, trapping an estimated 550 Americans in Iraq and 3,000 in Kuwait. The Security Council unanimously declares Iraq's annexation of Kuwait "null and void" (Resolution 662).

Aug. 10 — Iraqi President Saddam Hussein calls for "holy war" against foreign troops. Arab leaders agree to dispatch troops to Saudi Arabia to support the U.S.-led deployment.

Aug. 12 — Bush orders Navy to halt all Iraqi imports and exports but refuses to call such action a "blockade." Saddam links a pullout from Kuwait to an Israeli withdrawal from the West Bank.

Aug. 15 — Iraq proposes a peace initiative to Iran that includes recognizing borders before their war. Iran accepts, officially ending the conflict that began in 1980.

Aug. 18 — U.S. ships fire warning shots across bows of two Iraqi tankers in the Persian Gulf and Gulf of Oman. The Security Council unanimously demands the release of all foreign nationals from Iraq and Kuwait.

Aug. 19 — Iraq orders all Westerners to report for relocation to strategic military sites to be used as "human shields" against U.S. attack.

Aug. 20 — Bush refers to Americans trapped in Iraq as "hostages" for the first time.

Aug. 22 — Bush calls up more than 40,000 reserves. Oil prices rise to $31.22 a barrel, highest price in five years.

Aug. 23 — Saddam visits British hostages; the meeting is broadcast on Iraqi TV. Britain calls broadcast a "repulsive charade."

Aug. 24 — Iraqi troops surround U.S. and European embassies in Kuwait after their governments refuse to close them.

Aug. 25 — The Security Council votes to authorize the multilateral naval force to uphold the anti-Iraq embargo.

Aug. 28 — Saddam announces that he will allow all detained women and children to leave Iraq and Kuwait.

Aug. 29 — Bush approves a $2.2 billion Saudi purchase of advanced weapons.

Sept. 6 — Saudis agree to help defray the cost of Operation Desert Shield and to aid other Arab nations affected by the trade embargo against Iraq.

Sept. 8 — Secretary of State James A. Baker III completes three days of talks with Egyptian President Hosni Mubarak and Saudi King Fahd. All agree that there will be no negotiations with Iraq until its troops withdraw from Kuwait.

Sept. 10 — After meeting in Helsinki, Finland, Bush and Soviet President Mikhail S. Gorbachev reiterate their united stand on the Persian Gulf crisis. Iraq offers free oil to Third World countries that can arrange their own shipping.

Sept. 11 — In a speech to a joint session of Congress, Bush says: "Iraq will not be permitted to annex Kuwait. And that's not a threat; it's not a boast — it's just the way it's going to be."

Sept. 14 — Iraqi soldiers raid Canadian and European diplomatic compounds and briefly take three French diplomats hostage.

Sept. 17 — Defense Secretary Dick Cheney fires Air Force Chief of Staff Michael J. Dugan for saying Baghdad would be "flattened" after an air attack on Iraq.

Sept. 19 — Bush administration announces it will scale down its plan to sell Saudi Arabia a $20 billion package of military weapons after key members of Congress say it would not be approved as written.

Sept. 22 — The last chartered flight evacuating Westerners from Iraq and Kuwait lands in London, but about 1,000 Westerners remain in the region.

Sept. 23 — Saddam threatens to destroy Middle East oil fields if Iraq is "strangled" by U.N. sanctions.

Sept. 24 — Oil prices hit $38.35 a barrel.

Sept. 25 — The United Nations votes to extend the anti-Iraq boycott to aircraft. Soviet Foreign Minister Eduard A. Shevardnadze warns Iraq that "war may break out . . . any moment."

Oct. 1 — The House votes 380-29 for a resolution (H J Res 658) supporting U.S. military deployment in the gulf. The Senate votes 96-3 to approve a similar resolution (S Con Res 147) the next day. Members in both chambers emphasize that the measures do not authorize future use of force.

Oct. 3 — Gorbachev sends envoy to meet with Arab leaders. Saddam visits Kuwait and declares, "There will be no compromise. Iraq will never give up one inch of this land now called Province 19."

Oct. 8 — Israeli police fire on stone-throwing Palestinians, killing 17 Arabs.

Oct. 11 — The price of crude oil tops $40 a barrel.

Oct. 16 — U.S. forces in the Persian Gulf reach 200,000.

Oct. 17 — Baker, in testimony before the Senate Foreign Relations Committee, refuses to promise that the administration will seek congressional approval before any attack on Iraq.

Oct. 18 — Oil prices drop to $37 a barrel. Iraq offers to sell oil at the pre-crisis price of $21 a barrel.

Oct. 20 — Antiwar marches are staged in about 20 cities across the United States. Largest demonstration, in New York, draws crowd estimated between 5,000 and 20,000; most other rallies attract only hundreds of people.

Oct. 22 — Senate Majority Leader George J. Mitchell of Maine insists that under the Constitution, Congress, not the administration, has the power to declare war.

Oct. 30 — Bush tells congressional leaders that he is growing impatient with the "barbarous" treatment of Western hostages in Iraq. Saddam puts troops on "extreme alert."

Nov. 1 — Bush compares Saddam to Adolf Hitler, saying Hitler did not respect much but at least he "did respect the legitimacy of the embassies."

Nov. 8 — Bush orders near doubling of U.S. forces, stating that the United States must have an "adequate offensive option." U.S. officials later indicate that plans to rotate U.S. troops out of Persian Gulf have been scrapped.

Nov. 11 — Senate Armed Services Committee Chairman Sam Nunn, D-Ga., criticizes the massive troop buildup and the decision to drop troop rotations, calling them mistakes.

Nov. 13 — Leading Senate Republicans call for a special session of Congress to discuss troop deployments. Minority Leader Bob Dole, Kan., calls it a chance for Congress to "put up or shut up." Baker says the buildup in the gulf is to protect jobs.

Nov. 15 — Saddam says he wants to negotiate with the United States but will not withdraw from Kuwait first.

Nov. 18 — Iraq vows to gradually release all remaining hostages over three months, providing there is no war.

Nov. 19 — Iraq announces it will add 250,000 troops to its 430,000 troops already in or near Kuwait.

Nov. 20 — Forty-five Democratic congressmen file suit to force Bush to seek congressional approval before launching an attack against Iraq. Later, additional members join the lawsuit.

Nov. 21-22 — Bush and congressional leaders visit troops in Saudi Arabia. In remarks to troops, Bush emphasizes the dangers of Iraq's development of nuclear weapons.

Nov. 27-29 — At Senate Armed Services hearings, ex-Defense Secretary James R. Schlesinger and former Joint Chiefs of Staff chairmen David Jones and William J. Crowe urge that sanctions be given more time. Former Secretary of State Henry A. Kissinger says, "I think sanctions will get us eventually to a negotiation, but they will not get us to our objectives."

Nov. 29 — Security Council votes 12-2 to authorize "all means necessary" to remove Iraq from Kuwait if it does not withdraw by Jan. 15 (Resolution 678). It is the first time since the Korean War began in 1950 that the United Nations has authorized force against a member nation.

Nov. 30 — Bush says he wants to "go the extra mile for peace" and proposes meetings between the United States and Iraq. Congressional leaders meet with Bush and agree not to call a special session of Congress.

Dec. 1 — Iraq accepts the idea of meetings, but the country's ruling Revolutionary Command Council condemns Bush as contemptuous of Arabs and Muslims and "an enemy of God."

Dec. 6 — Saddam says all hostages may leave.

Dec. 7 — Bush announces that he will evacuate all U.S. Embassy personnel in Kuwait after all Americans seeking to leave are out. The embassy, however, officially will remain open.

Dec. 9 — Baker reports deadlock on when talks can take place, with Saddam suggesting Baker visit Baghdad on Jan. 12 and Bush insisting it be no later than Jan. 3.

Dec. 11 — The State Department says about 500 Americans choose to stay in Iraq or Kuwait because of dual citizenship or other reasons rather than leave on evacuation flights.

Dec. 13 — Federal Judge Harold H. Greene declines to rule on a lawsuit by members of Congress challenging the president's right to attack Iraq without a declaration of war because the full Congress has not yet taken a stand on the issue. But Greene says authority to declare war belongs "to the Congress, and to it alone."

Dec. 17 — NATO foreign ministers formally commit themselves to the U.N. resolution to use force if Iraq does not leave Kuwait by Jan. 15.

Dec. 19 — Lt. Gen. Calvin A. H. Waller, deputy commander of U.S. forces in the gulf, says there is a "distinct possibility" that U.S. troops will not be ready for war until after Feb. 1.

Dec. 25 — Six Arab nations of the Gulf Cooperation Council end a summit, warning Iraq that war is the only alternative to withdrawal from Kuwait.

Dec. 26 — White House officials say Bush will not hold back attack orders despite the fear of some commanders that they will not be ready to fight by Jan. 15. American and Australian troops seize a cargo ship bearing 50 pacifists and tons of food bound for Iraq.

Dec. 27 — According to media reports, the Pentagon plans to vaccinate gulf troops against possible Iraqi use of biological weapons. Iraq says it is ready for a "serious and constructive" dialogue with the United States but again links any pullout to the Palestinian issue.

Jan. 3, 1991 — Bush proposes talks in Geneva between Baker and Iraqi Foreign Minister Tariq Aziz. 102nd Congress convenes.

Jan. 4 — Senate begins debate on gulf situation. Iraq accepts offer of Baker-Aziz talks, and they are scheduled for Jan. 9.

Jan. 8 — Bush sends a letter to leaders of Congress requesting for the first time congressional approval on actions being taken in the Persian Gulf. It is the first such request by a president since the 1964 Gulf of Tonkin Resolution that authorized use of force in Vietnam.

Jan. 9 — Baker meets with Aziz in Geneva. Baker brings with him a letter from Bush to Saddam reiterating demands for Iraqi forces to leave Kuwait. After reading the letter, Aziz refuses to take it to Saddam because Bush did not use "polite language."

Jan. 12 — The Senate votes 52-47 for a resolution (S J Res 2) to authorize the use of military force if Iraq has not withdrawn from Kuwait and complied with U.N. resolutions by Jan. 15. The House votes 250-183 to approve a similar resolution (H J Res 77).

Jan. 15 — U.N. deadline for Iraqi forces to withdraw from Kuwait.

Jan. 16 — Bush gives the go-ahead for aerial bombing to begin in the gulf and notifies certain congressional leaders about one hour before the information is released to the public. CNN correspondents broadcast eyewitness accounts of damage from the Al-Rashid Hotel in downtown Baghdad.

Jan. 17 — Israel is struck by at least seven Iraqi Scud missles. Commander in chief of the operation, U.S. Army Gen. H. Norman Schwarzkopf, reports 80 percent of allied attacking planes have reached their targets.

Jan. 18 — Attacks continue around the clock at a rate of more than 1,000 sorties a day, with 159 separate targets hit in the first wave of attacks against Iraq.

Jan. 21 — Bush states Saddam's parading of allied POW pilots on television violates the Geneva Convention governing treatment of prisoners. Two days later, House votes 418-0 for resolution (H Con Res 48) condemning Iraq for treatment of POWs. Senate votes 99-0 on companion measure (S Con Res 5) the next day.

Jan. 26 — U.S. forces bomb two Kuwaiti pipelines in an effort to cut off the flow of oil being dumped into the Persian Gulf since Jan. 19. The situation is called an environmental catastrophe and threatens marine life and Saudi Arabian water supplies. U.S. blames Saddam for "environmental terrorism."

Jan. 27 — The 2nd Battalion of the 7th Air Defense Artillery tallies destruction of 10 Iraqi Scud missiles during previous eight days.

Jan. 29 — Iraqi troops launch attacks across the Saudi border and 11 U.S. Marines are killed — more than have died in the air war up to this point. Iraq takes over Khafji, an abandoned port city in Saudi Arabia.

Jan. 31 — Saudi forces proclaim the recapture of Khafji. Reports from the front line say that Iraqi tanks and other vehicles are moving into southern Kuwait. The Iraqi forces come under massive strikes by B-52 bombers and other allied aircraft.

Feb. 1 — The Pentagon confirms that an AC-130 gunship with 14 airmen aboard is lost over Kuwait.

Feb. 5 — During a news conference, Bush says he is "somewhat skeptical" that "air power alone [will] get the job done," and that he will not go against sound military doctrine in order to "just delay for the sake of delay, hoping that it would save lives."

Feb. 13 — U.S. bombing kills hundreds of Iraqi civilians. U.S. officials report the target to have been a hardened bunker used as a military command center, while Iraqi authorities claim it was an air raid shelter.

Feb. 15 — Saddam sends message by Baghdad radio announcing "Iraq's readiness to deal with Security Council Resolution No. 660 of 1990 with the aim of reaching an honorable and acceptable political solution, including withdrawal" from Kuwait. The United States rejects the proposal, saying it is filled with demands and conditions for withdrawal.

Feb. 18 — Soviets offer peace proposal assuring Saddam of his security as well as promises to deal with other Middle East issues such as the future of Palestinians in Israel's occupied territories.

Feb. 22 — Bush gives Saddam an ultimatum to begin withdrawal of Iraqi troops from Kuwait by noon Feb. 23 or risk the brutal combat of a ground war. Soviets announce a revised peace proposal excluding many of the promises in the earlier proposal.

Feb. 24 — A massive ground invasion of Kuwait begins hours after Iraq rejects ultimatum. Iraqi troops fold at first contact with allied forces and thousands of POWs are taken into captivity.

Feb. 25 — Saddam agrees to withdraw his troops from Kuwait in compliance with U.N. Security Council Resolution 660, according to a Baghdad radio announcement.

Feb. 27 — Bush announces a cease-fire and declares Kuwait free.

Continued from p. 718
"abysmal" and that executions had been "an established Iraqi method for dealing with perceived political and military opponents" for years.

Saddam also built up Iraq's military might. By the end of the decade, the Iraqi army numbered more than 1 million men — the largest military force of any country in the Middle East. While Iraq was a signatory to the 1925 Geneva Protocol banning the use of chemical weapons, Saddam directed the development of a chemical weapons storehouse that was used against Iran and against Iraqi Kurds. He also appeared to be seeking to develop a nuclear weapons capability — plans that prompted Israel to launch a pre-emptive air strike in 1981 against an Iraqi nuclear reactor under construction.

U.S.-Iraq Relations

Through the 1970s, the United States was closely allied with Iran, under Shah Mohammed Reza Pahlavi. Iraq aligned itself with the Soviet Union and broke off diplomatic relations with the United States in 1967 after the Israeli victory in the Six-Day War. *(U.S.-Iran relations, Congress & the Nation Vol. V, p. 111)*

The Iranian revolution of 1979 deprived the United States of an ally, but Saddam made no immediate move to step into the void. As author Korn relates, as late as February 1980 Saddam was denouncing the United States as "an enemy of the Arabs" because of its support for Israel.

By 1982, however, having suffered reverses in the war with Iran and having been cut off from arms from the Soviets, Saddam began putting out feelers to the United States. The Reagan administration responded positively, and U.S. relations with Iraq expanded and U.S.-Iraqi trade grew until 1990.

In 1982, the United States removed Iraq from an official list of nations found to be sponsoring terrorism. The move, which some pro-Israel members of Congress sought unsuccessfully to overturn by legislation, made Iraq eligible for some forms of credit and trade. Formal diplomatic relations were restored in November 1984.

Short of cash and its domestic economy devastated by the war with Iran, Iraq turned to the United States for food and other trade. Beginning in 1983, Iraq bought $230 million worth of feed grains, rice and wheat using the Agriculture Department's GSM-102 program, which provided short-term credit guarantees to foreign countries.

By 1988, U.S. farmers were doing about $1 billion in sales with Iraq. Almost all the sales came on loans backed by the U.S. government through the Commodity Credit Corporation (CCC). Iraq was the second-largest user of the program; in August 1990 its indebtedness to the CCC stood at $2 billion.

In 1989, though, Iraq's line of credit was cut in half — from $1 billion to $500 million — and then suspended in November, ostensibly because of an investigation into improprieties by the Atlanta-based bank that handled the transactions. Despite the suspension, John H. Kelly, assistant secretary of State, defended the credits during a hearing by the House Foreign Affairs Middle East Subcommittee in April 1990.

"The Iraqis have not defaulted on any of these [credits]," Kelly told lawmakers April 24. "It is very simple. We can cut this off and then the Iraqis can buy the same wheat or rice from the Australians, Europeans or any other supplier in the world."

Overall U.S. trade with Iraq increased more than sevenfold from 1983 to 1989 — from $571 million to $3.6 billion, according to the Commerce Department. Besides food, Iraq bought other goods, including high-technology items, with $270 million in government-guaranteed credit from the Export-Import Bank.

For its part, the United States bought oil — about $5.5 billion worth over the period, according to the Commerce Department. Kelly told the House subcommittee in April 1990 that U.S. purchases in 1989 amounted to 675,000 barrels, or 8 percent of total U.S. imports that year.

The Iran-Iraq War

As the eastern flank of the Arab world, Iraq inherited a history of border disputes with Persia and its modern incarnation, Iran. While the border between the Arab and Persian worlds had stabilized in the 17th century, there was lingering tension over a British-imposed border settlement in 1913 along the waterway called the Shatt-al-Arab.

Algeria brokered a border agreement between Iran and Iraq in 1975, but the truce dissolved in 1979 with the revolution that brought the Ayatollah Ruhollah Khomeini to power in Iran. Growing tensions broke out in warfare in September 1980 — with Iranian shelling of Iraqi cities on Sept. 4 and Iraq's decision to invade Iran on Sept. 22.

The eight-year war that followed was bloody for both sides. Casualty estimates ran as high as 1 million dead and 1.7 million wounded; and an estimated 1.5 million refugees had to neighboring countries. Fighting ended with a United Nations-negotiated cease-fire in August 1988.

As the war progressed, a clear U.S. tilt toward Iraq developed. "We were terrified Iraq was going to lose the war," Geoffrey Kemp, head of the National Security Council's Middle East section in the early 1980s, remarked to The Washington Post in late 1990.

The tilt toward Iraq culminated in President Reagan's decision in 1987 to reflag Kuwaiti oil tankers in the Persian Gulf as U.S. vessels to ward off attacks by Iran. The ostensible purpose was to protect neutral shipping, but the policy was pro-Iraqi in perception and reality since Kuwait was allied with its bigger neighbor, Iraq, in the war.

Reagan's decision drew fire in Congress, and the House and Senate both cast votes in 1987 to delay the policy. But legislative efforts to block the move fell short, and by 1988 the political challenge to Reagan's policies had faded. *(1988 Almanac, p. 434; 1987 Almanac, p. 252)*

While neither Iran nor Iraq could claim an outright victory in the war, the outcome was a setback for Khomeini, who had set the goal of exporting Iran's fundamentalist revolution to other countries. For Saddam, the cease-fire meant that he was free to turn to his own goal: establishing his supremacy as a leader of the Arab world.

Chemical Weapons

Iraq's use of chemical weapons against separatist Kurds in 1988 led to the first direct congressional challenge to the Reagan administration's moves to open up relations with Baghdad.

Beginning in 1983, Iraq used chemical weapons "extensively and effectively" in its war against Iran, according to a Senate Foreign Relations Committee staff report published in October 1988. Iran first complained to the United Nations in November 1983 and in February 1984 sent soldier victims of poison gas attacks abroad for treatment that would document its accusations

The United States, engaged at the time in a diplomatic initiative with the Soviet Union to reduce chemical weapons stockpiles, protested Iraq's resort to chemical warfare. But the Reagan administration took no punitive action toward Iraq.

Many observers credited Iraq's victory in the war to its use of chemical weapons.

In 1988, as the cease-fire with Iran was taking effect, Iraq turned its chemical weapons on its own citizens — minority Kurds in the country's northeastern region. Kurds constituted about one-fifth of Iraq's population.

As described in the Senate Foreign Relations Committee staff report written by Peter W. Galbraith and Christopher Van Hollen Jr., Saddam undertook a "final offensive" against the Kurdish insurgency as soon as the fighting with Iran had stopped on Aug. 20, 1988. "Some of Iraq's most battle-tested forces were dispatched to wrest control of the area from Kurdish fighters, drop poison gas on Kurdish villagers, and destroy Kurdish villages," they wrote.

Dramatic press accounts of the attacks began appearing almost immediately. On Sept. 8, Secretary of State George P. Shultz publicly condemned the attacks as "unjustified and abhorrent" and delivered a strong protest to Iraq's visiting foreign minister.

In Congress, Senate Foreign Relations Chairman Claiborne Pell, D-R.I., and the committee's ranking Republican, Jesse Helms of North Carolina, introduced a bill to cut off all forms of U.S. aid to Iraq, including the CCC and Export-Import Bank credit guarantees. The Senate passed the measure by voice vote Sept. 9.

The State Department called the Senate bill premature and urged the House to soften it. The House responded with a milder bill — passed Sept. 27 by a 388-16 vote — that would have banned the export of military-related items, computers and oil-drilling equipment but left farm exports untouched. The State Department continued to oppose any mandated sanctions, and lawmakers' efforts to get a compromise passed by both chambers fell victim to end-of-session maneuvering. *(1988 Almanac, p. 510)*

RISING TENSIONS: 1989-90

The fight between Congress and the White House over chemical warfare sanctions resumed in the 101st Congress and broadened into wide questioning of the rationale for the U.S. rapprochement with Iraq.

Chemical Weapons Sanctions

Senate Foreign Relations Committee Chairman Pell renewed the push for sanctions when the 101st Congress convened in 1989, introducing a broad measure (S 195) to require sanctions against any country that used chemical or biological weapons in violation of international law and against any company that helped those nations develop such weapons.

The proposal to penalize companies that aided in the development of chemical weapons responded to evidence that European firms had supplied materials needed for chemical-weapon production facilities to Iraq and to Libya.

The Foreign Relations Committee approved the bill on Oct. 6, 1989 (S Rept 101-166). But the export controls provision fell under the jurisdiction of the Senate Banking Committee, which held up floor action on the bill in 1989.

Meanwhile, the House was moving on a milder sanctions bill (HR 3033) that gave the president discretion to waive sanctions if he determined they would not be in the interest of national security. That bill won approval from the House Foreign Affairs Committee on Nov. 1, 1989, and from the Ways and Means Committee one week later (H Rept 101-334, Part I; Part II). The House approved the bill by voice vote on Nov. 13, 1989. *(1989 Almanac, p. 501)*

The Bush administration continued to oppose mandatory sanctions, but in negotiations over the House bill it indicated it could accept a package that gave the president broad discretion in determining when to impose sanctions.

President Reaffirms Policy

The Bush administration inherited the policy of rapprochement with Iraq from the Reagan administration.

It was only well after the fact that news accounts disclosed that Bush had specifically reaffirmed U.S. policies toward Iraq after a behind-the-scenes review of Mideast issues in the fall of 1989. According to an account in The Washington Post in March 1991, Bush signed National Security Directive 26 on Oct. 6, 1989, reaffirming that normal relations with Iraq would serve U.S. interests and that U.S. companies were to be encouraged to help rebuild its war-shattered economy.

In furtherance of that policy, Bush signed an order on Jan. 17, 1990, overriding congressional objections to continuing U.S. Export-Import Bank financing for commercial transactions with Iraq. The order stated that to halt the Ex-Im guarantees would be "not in the national interest of the United States."

Saddam's actions in early 1990 put the U.S. policies to a test. In March, the State Department learned that Iraq had placed missile launchers at an air base near the Jordanian border — within range of Israel and other countries in the region. Also in March, Iraq executed an Iranian-born journalist working for a British newspaper after accusing him of spying. And in April, U.S. and British customs thwarted an apparent attempt to smuggle electrical components for nuclear weapons; five Iraqis were arrested.

Most dramatically, Hussein gave a speech on official Baghdad radio on April 2 that threatened Israel in the strongest terms. Boasting of Iraq's chemical weapons capacity, Saddam said that "we will make the fire eat up half of Israel if it tries to do anything against Iraq."

According to an account in The Wall Street Journal in October 1990, Saddam's speech prompted a re-examination of U.S. policy by Kelly and other State Department officials, concluding in a recommendation approved by Secretary of State James A. Baker III to impose economic sanctions. But, according to that account, the recommendation fell victim to interdepartmental opposition and Baker's inattentiveness due to other foreign policy priorities.

As a result, when Kelly appeared before the House Foreign Affairs Middle East Subcommittee on April 24, he defended the existing policy toward Iraq under skeptical questioning by several lawmakers, including Tom Lantos, D-Calif.

Saying the administration's policy had "an Alice in Wonderland quality," Lantos asked: "At what point will the administration recognize that this is not a nice guy and that conceivably sanctions are appropriate?"

"We believe there is still a potentiality for positive alterations in Iraqi behavior," Kelly answered. "We do not believe that the imposition of economic sanctions now would leave that possibility open. So we are still opposed to the imposition of economic sanctions."

Debate Over Food Credits

Three months later, in the most sustained congressional floor debate over U.S.-Iraqi relations to date, both the

House and Senate rejected the administration's rationale and voted to impose economic sanctions — specifically, a cutoff of U.S. guarantees for food sales.

The July 27 debates came while the House and Senate were working on parallel bills (S 2830, HR 3950) reauthorizing U.S. farm programs, including provisions for CCC sales abroad.

In the Senate, Alfonse M. D'Amato, R-N.Y., proposed to bar Iraq from loans guaranteed by the CCC or the Export-Import Bank until the president certified that it was in compliance with international law.

In the House, Dan Glickman, D-Kan., aimed at Iraq with an amendment to bar food credits to any country that had shown a consistent lack of respect for human rights, used chemical weapons or provided support for international terrorism. Glickman's amendment would have allowed the president to waive the sanctions upon a written certification that such a step was "essential to the national interest of the United States."

Glickman, representing a wheat-growing district, reeled off a list of Iraqi human rights violations and urged "as a matter of principle" that the taxpayer-supported credit guarantees be cut off. But he was challenged by other farm-state lawmakers, including Republicans Pat Roberts of Kansas, Bill Emerson of Missouri and Fred Grandy of Iowa and Arkansas Democrat Bill Alexander.

"I wonder who we are hurting here? The people of Iraq or the farmers, as opposed to the leaders of that country?" Roberts asked.

Glickman's amendment was adopted 234-175, with Republicans dividing evenly on it (84-84) and Democrats splitting for the sanctions (150-91). *(Vote 276, p. 92-H)*

But Nebraska Republican Doug Bereuter followed with a softening amendment that gave the secretary of Agriculture authority to lift the restrictions if they would have "a negative impact greater upon American farmers" than upon the foreign country. With greater Republican support (109-56), the amendment was adopted 208-191. *(Vote 277, p. 92-H)*

In the Senate, meanwhile, the attack on the administration's policy was being directed by Republicans D'Amato and William S. Cohen of Maine while farm-state Republicans Phil Gramm of Texas and Rudy Boschwitz of Minnesota led a move to deflect the amendment.

Urging the credit cutoff, Cohen listed Iraq's past use of chemical weapons in Iran and in Kurdistan, but he also cited the looming crisis: Iraq's threatening moves toward Kuwait over the previous month in a dispute over borders and oil production policies.

"When are we going to start exercising some moral leadership in this country," Cohen asked, "saying we are not going to support nations like Iraq that engage in acts of terrorism, that engage in the use of chemical weapons, that engage in the attempt to intimidate their neighbors who supported them during their war against Iran?"

But Gramm said the restrictions would only hurt U.S. farmers and manufacturers and offered an amendment to require the secretaries of Agriculture and Commerce to weigh the domestic impact before putting them into effect. Gramm's amendment was killed on a tabling motion, 57-38; the Senate then adopted D'Amato's amendment, 83-12. *(Votes 180, 181, p. 40-S)*

After the Iraqi invasion of Kuwait, the credit restrictions became moot, as Bush imposed a broad U.S. trade embargo against Iraq and Congress rolled a sanctions package into the foreign aid appropriations bill (HR 5114 — PL 101-513). So conferees on the farm bill dropped the Iraq sanctions from that measure.

KUWAIT

The tiny, oil-rich emirate of Kuwait had been of little diplomatic importance to the United States until the reflagging of Kuwaiti vessels in 1987 as part of the tilt toward Iraq in the Iran-Iraq War.

Independent only since 1961, Kuwait's boundaries were drawn by the British in 1922 as they and their French allies carved up the defeated Ottoman Empire after World War I. While still claimed by the Ottoman Empire, Kuwait had been a British protectorate since 1899 and had been governed as a sort of fiefdom by the Sabah family since the mid-18th century.

Iraq was not reconciled to the boundary, which left it only limited access to the Persian Gulf. When Kuwait declared its independence in 1961, Iraq made menacing gestures, which were countered by a British show of force. But in 1963, Iraq's Baath Party, in its first time in power, recognized Kuwait's independence and generally acknowledged its frontiers.

Just as Kuwaiti rulers had once played the British against the Turks, Kuwait had a reputation for playing the United States against the Soviet Union after World War II. But by the late 1980s, it was counted as a moderate Arab state, and it had assiduously invested billions of petrodollars in businesses in Europe and the United States.

Domestically, the latest Sabah sheik, Jaber al Ahmed al-Sabah, was clamping down on a pro-democracy movement that was protesting plans for a new National Assembly to replace the National Parliament that had been dissolved in 1986. Twelve prominent pro-democracy advocates were arrested in May 1990.

The Dispute With Iraq

Kuwait sided with Iraq in its war with Iran, providing Iraq massive financing during the long conflict. After the war ended, Kuwait demanded repayment of the estimated $10 billion debt, which Iraq, its economy devastated, could repay, if at all, only from oil revenues.

As Kuwait stepped up demands for payment of the debt, Iraq accused Kuwait, along with the United Arab Emirates (UAE), of exceeding quotas set by the Organization of Petroleum Exporting Countries (OPEC), keeping the world price of oil down, and, consequently, depriving Iraq of much-needed revenue. In addition, Iraq claimed that Kuwait was stealing billions of dollars' worth of oil from disputed oil fields along their border.

Tension between the two countries rose during the summer. In late July, Iraq began massing troops in its southern region near the Kuwaiti border. At the same time, it pursued its case in OPEC and, at a meeting of OPEC oil ministers in Geneva on July 25-27, appeared to win agreement from Kuwait and the United Arab Emirates to cut back on production.

Iraq's victory at the OPEC meeting left the border dispute with Kuwait unsetttled, and the massing of troops continued — rising to 100,000 by the end of the month. To mediate the dispute, Saudi Arabia's King Fahd hosted talks between the two countries on July 31 in Jiddah.

The U.S. Stance

The United States had been watching the growing tensions in the gulf with anxiety. But the administration was sending mixed signals on its stance.

On July 24, the administration announced "a short-notice" military exercise with the UAE, deploying combat ships and aerial refueling planes to the southern Persian Gulf nation. Officials quoted in news accounts made clear the maneuvers were designed to demonstrate U.S. support for the UAE and Kuwait in their confrontation with Iraq.

On the same day, however, State Department spokeswoman Margaret D. Tutwiler, told reporters: "We do not have any defense treaties with Kuwait, and there are no special defense or security commitments to Kuwait."

In Baghdad the next day, Saddam summoned the U.S. ambassador, career diplomat April C. Glaspie, for an audience. A purported transcript of the session, disclosed by the Iraqis in September, depicted Glaspie as giving Saddam little reason to expect a strong response if Iraq moved against Kuwait.

"We have no opinion on the Arab-Arab conflicts, like your border disagreements with Kuwait," Glaspie was quoted as saying.

On July 30, Glaspie left Baghdad, as scheduled, to return to the United States for consultations and home leave. (On March 20, 1991, appearing before the Senate Foreign Relations Committee, Glaspie described the Iraqi transcript of the meeting with Saddam as "disinformation" and said she had warned him clearly that the United States would not tolerate aggression against Kuwait.)

On July 31, Kelly returned to the House Foreign Affairs Mideast Subcommittee and repeated the State Department line that the United States had no treaty obligation to come to Kuwait's defense.

Subcommittee Chairman Lee H. Hamilton, D-Ind., asked Kelly about a statement that Defense Secretary Dick Cheney had made to reporters July 19 promising that the United States would come to Kuwait's defense if attacked.

"We have no defense treaty relationship with any gulf country. That is clear," Kelly responded.

When Hamilton asked specifically what would happen if Iraq charged across the Kuwaiti border, Kelly was noncommittal: "That, Mr. Chairman, is a hypothetical or a contingency question.... Suffice it to say we would be extremely concerned, but I cannot get into the realm of 'what if' answers."

The Invasion

Despite the weeks of rising tensions, the Bush administration and most members of Congress were equally surprised by Iraq's invasion of Kuwait in the early morning hours of Aug. 2.

After two weeks of threatening Kuwait, Saddam moved with intensity and machinelike efficiency. He ordered more than 100,000 troops and several hundred tanks to attack the lightly armed Arab emirate.

Within a few hours, Iraq completely controlled the country and its power of resistance was effectively eliminated. "The military situation is in essence over," David L. Boren, D-Okla., chairman of the Senate Intelligence Committee, said following a briefing by officials.

Bush denounced the invasion and ordered economic sanctions against Iraq, but he initially said that he was not planning to intervene militarily. Following a previously scheduled meeting with British Prime Minister Margaret Thatcher in Aspen, Colo., later in the day, however, Bush said, "We're not ruling any options in, but we're not ruling any options out."

On Capitol Hill, lawmakers scrambled to issue the

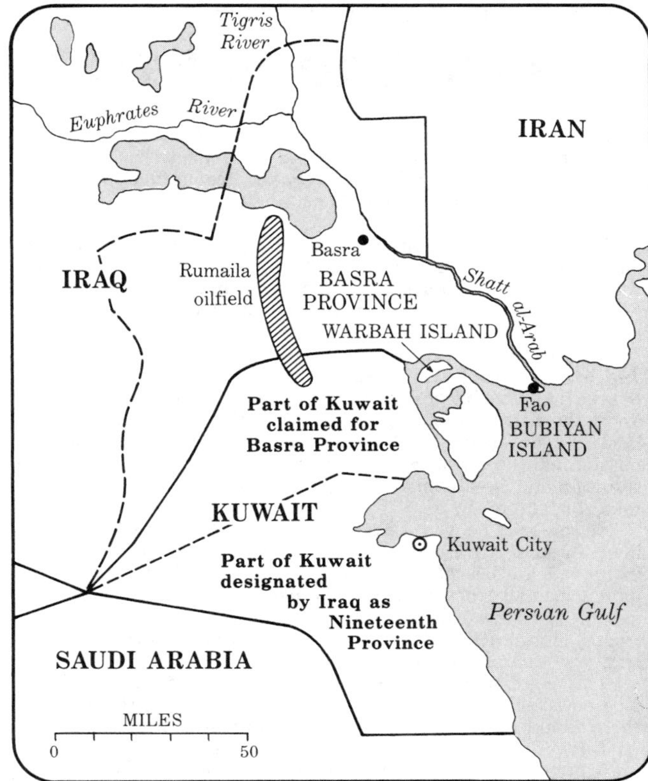

harshest possible denunciations of Saddam. Several hinted at the possible need to use military force.

"Saddam Hussein is a cancer on the world body politic, and we must excise that cancer now lest it engulf the Middle East," Pell declared.

"My own view is that at some point military action is probably going to be necessary," said Sen. Christopher J. Dodd, D-Conn.

Aside from the immediate threat of a wider regional war, the invasion quickly triggered a sharp rise in the world price of oil. "What [the invasion] means is that OPEC discipline now has been ensured by the point of a gun," said Sen. J. Bennett Johnston, D-La.

With Kuwait already conquered, administration officials turned their attention to the possibility that Saddam's forces might attempt to move on Saudi Arabia, which shared a long border with Iraq. Iraqi troops were only 250 miles away from the main Saudi Arabian oil fields. The fields provided 15 percent of oil imports to the United States, Boren said.

Blocking Trade

Presented with a fait accompli in Kuwait and what was perceived as a potential threat to a second key ally and source of imported oil, Bush immediately imposed what amounted to a total ban on economic relations with Iraq.

The president's executive order blocked Iraqi access to assets in the United States and prohibited all trade — including trade in oil — with Iraq. Bush also barred most travel to Iraq.

Congress also acted quickly. The House passed an economic sanctions bill on Aug. 2 aimed at writing the executive order into law. While the bill (HR 5431) was new, it incorporated language approved by the Foreign Affairs Committee the previous day (HR 4585). In addition, the

Bush Announces U.S. Troop Deployment

Following is President Bush's address to the nation from the Oval Office of the White House on Aug. 8, 1990, on his decision to send U.S. air and ground forces to Saudi Arabia to help it defend against possible aggressive actions by Iraq:

In the life of a nation, we're called upon to define who we are and what we believe. Sometimes, these choices are not easy. But today, as president, I ask for your support in a decision I've made to stand up for what's right and condemn what's wrong, all in the cause of peace.

At my direction, elements of the 82nd Airborne Division, as well as key units of the United States Air Force, are arriving today to take up defensive positions in Saudi Arabia. I took this action to assist the Saudi Arabian government in the defense of its homeland. No one commits American armed forces to a dangerous mission lightly, but after perhaps unparalleled international consultation and exhausting every alternative, it became necessary to take this action.

Let me tell you why. Less than a week ago in the early morning hours of Aug. 2, Iraqi armed forces, without provocation or warning, invaded a peaceful Kuwait. Facing negligible resistance from its much smaller neighbor, Iraq's tanks stormed in blitzkrieg fashion through Kuwait in a few short hours. With more than 100,000 troops, along with tanks, artillery and surface-to-surface missiles, Iraq now occupies Kuwait.

This aggression came just hours after [Iraqi President] Saddam Hussein specifically assured numerous countries in the area that there would be no invasion. There is no justification whatsoever for this outrageous and brutal act of aggression.

A puppet regime, imposed from the outside, is unacceptable. The acquisition of territory by force is unacceptable.

No one, friend or foe, should doubt our desire for peace, and no one should underestimate our determination to confront aggression.

Four simple principles guide our policy.

First, we seek the immediate, unconditional and complete withdrawal of all Iraqi forces from Kuwait.

Second, Kuwait's legitimate government must be restored to replace the puppet regime.

And third, my administration, as has been the case with every president from President [Franklin D.] Roosevelt to President [Ronald] Reagan, is committed to the security and stability of the Persian Gulf.

And fourth, I am determined to protect the lives of American citizens abroad.

Immediately after the Iraqi invasion, I ordered an embargo of all trade with Iraq, and together with many other nations, announced sanctions that both froze all Iraqi assets in this country and protected Kuwait's assets.

The stakes are high. Iraq is already a rich and powerful country that possesses the world's second-largest reserves of oil and over a million men under arms. It's the fourth-largest military in the world.

Our country now imports nearly half the oil it consumes and could face a major threat to its economic independence. Much of the world is even more dependent on imported oil and is even more vulnerable to Iraqi threats.

We succeeded in the struggle for freedom in Europe because we and our allies remain stalwart. Keeping the peace in the Middle East will require no less.

We're beginning a new era. This new era can be full of promise, an age of freedom, a time of peace for all peoples. But if history teaches us anything, it is that we must resist aggression, or it will destroy our freedoms.

Appeasement does not work. As was the case in the 1930s, we see in Saddam Hussein an aggressive dictator threatening his neighbors. Only 14 days ago, Saddam Hussein promised his friends he would not invade Kuwait. And four days ago, he promised the world he would withdraw. And twice we have seen what his promises mean. His promises mean nothing.

In the last few days I've spoken with political leaders from the Middle East, Europe, Asia, the Americas, and I've met with [British] Prime Minister [Margaret] Thatcher, [Canadian] Prime Minister [Brian] Mulroney, and NATO Secretary General [Manfred]

---

bill included language requiring the president to notify Congress before lifting the executive order.

The measure was rushed through two committees and onto the House floor with virtually no debate. The bill passed 416-0; an amendment offered by Sam M. Gibbons, D-Fla., to grant the president authority to cut off imports from nations that traded with Iraq was agreed to by unanimous consent. *(Vote 303, p. 98-H)*

The Senate also endorsed the executive order Aug. 2 but chose not to put it in statutory form. The Senate resolution (S Res 318) urged the president to use diplomacy, but it added that a multilateral military effort "may be needed to maintain or restore" stability in the region. The measure passed 97-0. *(Vote 211, p. 44-S)*

Despite the near-unanimous support for the president's action, there was criticism of the administration's previous opposition to sanctions legislation. "The State Department has been mollycoddling Hussein for a long time," said D'Amato, sponsor of the credit cutoff voted by the Senate on July 27.

Because of the gravity of the situation, the recriminations and political posturing were relatively short-lived. Members in both houses focused on the possible military and economic ramifications of the invasion.

The Navy had a task force of eight warships in the Persian Gulf at the time of the invasion and subsequently ordered an aircraft carrier battle group to steam to the northern Arabian Sea near the mouth of the gulf.

But U.S. naval forces alone were clearly no match for the enormous contingent of troops Iraq sent into Kuwait.

Even lawmakers who believed that a confrontation was inevitable acknowledged the weakness of the U.S position in those first days after the invasion. Military action should only be taken "in conjunction with our allies," Dodd said.

Still, the initial mood in Congress was that any Iraqi move against Saudi Arabia would force a U.S. military response. Such an attack would represent "a direct threat to the national security of this country," said Boren.

"We need to tell Hussein that an invasion of Saudi Arabia means war," said Les Aspin, D-Wis., chairman of the House Armed Services Committee.

OPERATION DESERT SHIELD

Within days of the Iraqi invasion of Kuwait, Bush stiffened the U.S. response, vowing Aug. 5 that the invasion "will not stand" and two days later ordering U.S. forces to Saudi Arabia to defend it against possible Iraqi attack.

The mobilization — dubbed Operation Desert Shield — won wide support on Capitol Hill, and a Gallup Poll taken Aug. 9-10 registered 77 percent approval for Bush's actions. But lawmakers immediately began raising questions of strategy and of institutional prerogatives

Lawmakers pressed the administration to secure more active support from Arab nations for the U.S. efforts. They offered conflicting views on whether economic sanctions

Wöerner. And all agree that Iraq cannot be allowed to benefit from its invasion of Kuwait.

We agree that this is not an American problem or a European problem or a Middle East problem. It is the world's problem, and that's why soon after the Iraqi invasion, the United Nations Security Council, without dissent, condemned Iraq, calling for the immediate and unconditional withdrawal of its troops from Kuwait.

The Arab world, through both the Arab League and the Gulf Cooperation Council, courageously announced its opposition to Iraqi aggression. Japan, the United Kingdom and France, and other governments around the world have imposed severe sanctions. The Soviet Union and China ended all arms sales to Iraq, and this past Monday, the United Nations Security Council approved for the first time in 23 years mandatory sanctions under Chapter 7 of the United Nations Charter.

These sanctions, now enshrined in international law, have the potential to deny Iraq the fruits of aggression, while sharply limiting its ability to either import or export anything of value, especially oil.

I pledge here today that the United States will do its part to see that these sanctions are effective and to induce Iraq to withdraw without delay from Kuwait. But we must recognize that Iraq may not stop using force to advance its ambitions.

Iraq has massed an enormous war machine on the Saudi border, capable of initiating hostilities with little or no additional preparation. Given the Iraqi government's history of aggression against its own citizens as well as its neighbors, to assume Iraq will not attack again would be unwise and unrealistic. And therefore, after consulting with [Saudi] King Fahd, I sent Secretary of Defense Dick Cheney to discuss cooperative measures we could take.

Following those meetings, the Saudi government requested our help and I responded to that request by ordering U.S. air and ground forces to deploy to the kingdom of Saudi Arabia.

Let me be clear: The sovereign independence of Saudi Arabia is of vital interest to the United States. This decision, which I shared with the congressional leadership, grows out of the longstanding friendship and security relationship between the United States and Saudi Arabia. U.S. forces will work together with those of Saudi Arabia and other nations to preserve the integrity of Saudi Arabia and to deter further Iraqi aggression.

Through their presence, as well as through their training and exercises, these multinational forces will enhance the overall capability of Saudi armed forces to defend the kingdom.

I want to be clear about what we are doing and why. America does not seek conflict, nor do we seek to chart the destiny of other nations. But America will stand by her friends. The mission of our troops is wholly defensive. Hopefully, they will not be needed long.

They will not initiate hostilities, but they will defend themselves, the kingdom of Saudi Arabia and other friends in the Persian Gulf.

We are working around the clock to deter Iraqi aggression and to enforce U.N. sanctions. I'm continuing my conversations with world leaders. Secretary of Defense Cheney has just returned from valuable consultations with President [Hosni] Mubarak of Egypt and King Hassan of Morocco. Secretary of State [James A.] Baker [III] has consulted with his counterparts in many nations, including the Soviet Union. And today he heads for Europe to consult with President [Turgut] Ozal of Turkey, a staunch friend of the United States. And he'll then consult with the NATO foreign ministers.

I will ask oil-producing nations to do what they can to increase production in order to minimize any impact that oil-flow reductions will have on the world economy. And I will explore whether we and our allies should draw down our strategic petroleum reserves. Conservation measures can also help. Americans everywhere must do their part.

And one more thing: I'm asking the oil companies to do their fair share. They should show restraint and not abuse today's uncertainties to raise prices. Standing up for our principles will not come easy. It may take time and possibly cost a great deal, but we are asking no more of anyone than of the brave young men and women of our armed forces and their families, and I ask that in the churches around the country prayers be said for those who are committed to protect and defend America's interests.

Standing up for our principles is an American tradition. As it has so many times before, it may take time and tremendous effort, but most of all, it will take unity of purpose. As I've witnessed throughout my life in both war and peace, America has never wavered when her purpose is driven by principle, and on this August day, at home and abroad, I know she will do no less.

Thank you, and God bless the United States of America. ■

would succeed in forcing Iraq out of Kuwait. Many warned against precipitate military action, but several also questioned whether the public had the patience to support a protracted U.S. commitment in the gulf.

Above all, lawmakers warned that Bush should not send U.S. troops into action without congressional approval. At the same time, though, they shrank from confronting the issue directly.

As a result, resolutions passed by the House and Senate in October endorsed Bush's actions without any mention of possible use of force in the future.

Notifying Congress

Bush announced his decision to dispatch U.S. troops to Saudi Arabia on Aug. 7 with Congress in recess. As a result, some key lawmakers learned about the move at the same time as the public.

Senate Majority Leader George J. Mitchell, D-Maine, said the president failed in an effort to track him down to inform him personally. "The president attempted to call me a couple of times yesterday, but we weren't able to make contact," Mitchell said at a press briefing on Aug. 8.

Senate Armed Services Committee Chairman Sam Nunn, D-Ga., said he too had found out about the deployment "after the fact" but added that he had "no complaint" about the process. "The president has to be the one to make these decisions, and I think that in this case things have moved so fast that he had to do it," Nunn said.

On Aug. 8, the president addressed the nation via television from the Oval Office. "If history teaches us anything, it is that we must resist aggression, or it will destroy our freedoms," he said. *(Bush address, p. 726)*

Later that week, Bush formally notified Congress of the deployment to the Persian Gulf. He indicated that while the forces sent to Saudi Arabia "are equipped for combat, their mission is defensive." Bush said that "this deployment will facilitate a peaceful resolution of the crisis."

Significantly, the president did not acknowledge that the troops faced "imminent" danger, language that would have triggered the War Powers Resolution of 1973 (PL 93-148). Bush, like his predecessors in the White House, did not recognize the constitutionality of the measure, which imposed a 60-day limit on deployments into areas of existing or likely hostilities unless Congress voted its approval. *(Congress and the Nation, Volume IV, p. 849)*

Senate Foreign Relations Committee Chairman Pell issued a reminder to the administration that if a situation of "imminent hostilities" were to develop, Congress had a right under the resolution to authorize continued troop deployments.

Lawmakers' immediate reaction, however, was to put partisan interests and difficult questions aside. Every member who issued a statement on the U.S. military buildup in the Persian Gulf praised the president's actions, and several interrupted their August recess to return to the capital for briefings and consultation.

The administration combined the U.S. military response with diplomatic moves at the United Nations and with other Arab nations — actions that helped shore up public support but also raised questions about how long the crisis would last.

On Aug. 6, the U.N. Security Council voted to prohibit U.N. members from import or export trade with Kuwait or Iraq — the first of a dozen Security Council resolutions that gave the international organization's imprimatur to the U.S.-led coalition confronting Saddam.

Britain agreed Aug. 8 to send forces to the gulf, and on Aug. 10 the Arab League decided to send a multinational force to assist the kingdom. Several key members of Congress had warned the administration of the dangers of proceeding without Arab participation.

The immediate goal of the military and diplomatic moves was to prevent a quick Iraqi strike against Saudi Arabia. But, according to many members, the danger was relatively short-lived, since it would have been to Saddam's advantage to invade only before U.S. forces had the opportunity to fully deploy in the region.

"I think in the next three or four days, if there is not an attack on the American military, that's probably past," House Armed Services Committee Chairman Aspin said on Aug. 8.

The other goal set by the administration, the removal of Iraqi forces from Kuwait, would clearly take longer to achieve — and the administration did not initially hold out force as the likely means to achieve it.

Bush played down the possibility that U.S. forces would be used to roll back the occupation. "We have economic sanctions that I hope will be effective to that end," he said.

Reliance on sanctions suggested, however, that the crisis would not be quickly resolved. Aspin, for example, predicted that it would be three to five months before the economic sanctions might lead to the withdrawal of Iraqi troops from Kuwait. Other experts predicted longer.

Aspin was one of several lawmakers who openly wondered whether the American people — as well as the government — were prepared for a long haul.

House Mideast Subcommittee Chairman Hamilton was another. He noted the public opinion polls showing approval of Bush's actions, but questioned the depth of the support. "What they are supporting is a rather sterile action that would not bring about combat casualties," Hamilton said. "If we began to experience heavy casualties, I am sure that percentage would drop."

The administration was reluctant to speculate how long U.S. forces would be needed in the region. At a Pentagon briefing on the military operations, Defense Secretary Dick Cheney said, "We don't know how long it will last; we don't know when it will end."

The formal notification that Bush sent to Congress was similarly vague on the subject, saying only that "our armed forces will remain so long as their presence is required to contribute to the security of the region and desired by the Saudi government."

But Nunn forecast extended U.S. involvement in the region.

"I'd say we're going to be there several months with whatever ground forces we have and we're going to be there a long time with our Air Force," Nunn said.

U.S. Hostages

An early concern was the potential for a hostage situation. The State Department estimated that there were 3,000 Americans in Kuwait and 500 in Iraq. Within days of the U.S. buildup, Iraqi authorities began to prevent Westerners from leaving either country.

The administration was initially reluctant to heighten the crisis atmosphere by characterizing the trapped Americans as hostages.

"We are not calling them hostages because discussions are ongoing about obtaining permission for them to leave," said Secretary of State Baker, after a meeting of NATO ministers on Aug. 10.

Most lawmakers, citing the sensitivity of the subject, felt constrained from commenting on the trapped Americans. But there were fears that a continuing hostage crisis could erode the substantial backing the administration had drawn from Congress.

Saddam added to the concerns Aug. 19 when he ordered all Westerners in Iraq to report for relocation to military sites to be used as "human shields" against U.S. attack. The next day, in a speech to the Veterans of Foreign Wars (VFW) in Baltimore, Bush dropped the administration's semantic sensitivities and referred to the detained Americans as hostages. "I will hold the government of Iraq responsible for the safety and well-being of American citizens held against their will," he declared.

Lawmakers' Uncertainties

As lawmakers became convinced that the U.S. involvement in the Persian Gulf would be a massive and lengthy one, they pondered whether they would have to go on the record supporting or opposing the operation.

"We're going to have to be in some form of ratifying mode if this thing goes over 60 days, whether or not we invoke the War Powers act," said Kansas Democrat Glickman, who served on the House Intelligence Committee. "People are going to start getting impatient if there is no action" by Congress, he said.

Senate Armed Services Committee member John McCain, R-Ariz., said while he "would hate to see us get into War Powers, it's very important for us to state what so many Americans feel about the operation."

Maine Republican Cohen, co-chairman of the Senate Intelligence Committee, used stronger language to express that sentiment. In a speech Aug. 12, Cohen said that the president should "put Congress on record" in backing the deployment of forces.

"It's easy to support the president when the polls show 75 percent of the American public supports" the operation, Cohen said. "But what happens if chemical weapons are used, or if hostages are taken? That's when America runs the risk of being divided."

Adding to the uncertainty were the first rumblings of opposition to U.S. military action, which came, surprisingly, from conservative lawmakers and commentators.

"Americans don't die for princes, sultans and emirs," said Rep. Robert K. Dornan, R-Calif. "It will only be a matter of time before Republicans ask why American boys are fighting to defend one monarchy and restore another."

Even lawmakers who supported the moves agreed that U.S. financial interests — securing a steady flow of oil from the Middle East to the industrialized world — were driving U.S. policies more than grander principles. "Let's have no illusions; if this were another part of the world, we would not see this kind of response," McCain said.

For the administration to depend on such a cold-blooded economic rationale for military action, however, would have been a new development in U.S. foreign policy.

Bush Briefs Members on Gulf Policy

Following are President Bush's public comments to about 150 members of Congress on Aug. 28 preceding an executive session to brief the lawmakers on the situation in the Middle East:

Meeting the challenge in the Persian Gulf is not something that I or this administration can do by ourselves. We can only succeed if all of us, executive and legislative, Republican and Democrat, work together. And that was one of the reasons I wanted you to come here today.

Let no one at home doubt that my commitment to work with the Congress — and let no one abroad doubt our national unity or our staying power.

Let me begin by providing some background to the unfolding drama in the gulf, and then later, I want to hear from you, and as I say, respond to — respond to questions.

First, the background. When this administration began, we sought to strengthen the cease-fire between Iran and Iraq, and to improve relations with Iraq. While we held no illusions about that, we hoped, along with many in the Congress, that Iraqi behavior might be moderated.

But even before the current crisis, though, Iraq was moving at odds to our interest, and to the interests of many around the world. And so we suspended the provisions of the CCC [Commodity Credit Corporation] agricultural credits; stopped the export of furnaces that had the potential to contribute to Iraq's nuclear capabilities.

And you all know the events of the last several weeks. Iraq threatened Kuwait, lied about its intentions and, finally, invaded.

And in three days Iraq had 120,000 troops and 850 tanks in Kuwait moving south toward the Saudi border. And it was this clear and rapidly escalating threat that led King Fahd of Saudi Arabia to ask for our assistance. And we knew that an Iraq that had the most powerful military machine in the gulf and controlled 20 percent of the world's proven reserves of oil would pose a threat to the Persian Gulf, to the Middle East and to the entire world.

We responded to this quickly, without hesitation. And our objectives were obvious from the start: the immediate, complete and unconditional withdrawal of all Iraqi forces from Kuwait, the restoration of Kuwait's legitimate government, security and stability of Saudi Arabia and the Persian Gulf, and the protection of American citizens abroad. Our actions to achieve these objectives have been equally clear.

Within hours of the assault, the United States moved to freeze Iraq's assets in this country and to protect those of Kuwait. I asked Dick Cheney, [Defense] Secretary Cheney, to go to Saudi Arabia, Egypt and Morocco to arrange for military cooperation between us and key Arab states. And I asked Jim Baker, Secretary [of State James A.] Baker [III], to go to Turkey and to Brussels to rally the support of our NATO allies. Both of these missions were extraordinarily successful.

The world response to Iraq was a near-unanimous chorus of condemnation, and with great speed the United Nations Security Council passed five resolutions. These resolutions condemned Iraq's invasion of Kuwait, demanded Iraq's immediate and unconditional withdrawal and rejected Iraq's annexation of Kuwait. The U.N. has also mandated sanctions against Iraq — those Chapter 7 sanctions — and endorsed all measures that may be necessary to enforce these sanctions. And the United Nations has demanded that Iraq release all foreign nationals being held against their will without delay.

The United Nations sanctions are in effect and have been working remarkably well, even on a voluntary basis. Iraqi oil no longer flows through pipelines to ports in Turkey and Saudi Arabia, and again I want to thank both the Saudis and the Turks for their lead role in all of this.

And today, reports indicate that traffic through Aqaba [Jordanian port] has come virtually to a halt. U.S. military forces stand shoulder to shoulder with forces of many Arab and European states to deter, and, if need be, defend Saudi Arabia against attack, and U.S. naval forces sail with the navies of many other states to make the sanctions as watertight as possible.

This is not, as [Iraqi President] Saddam Hussein claims, the United States against Iraq. It is truly Iraq against a majority in the Arab world, Iraq against the rest of the world.

And so the basic elements of our strategy are now in place, and where do we want to go? Well, our intention, and indeed the intention of almost every country in the world is to persuade Iraq to withdraw, that it cannot benefit from this illegal occupation, that it will pay a stiff price by trying to hold on, and an even stiffer price by widening the conflict.

And of course we seek to achieve these goals without further violence. The United States supports the U.N. secretary-general [Javier Pérez de Cuéllar] and other leaders working to promote a peaceful resolution of this crisis on the basis of Security Council Resolution 660.

I also remain deeply concerned about the American and other foreign nationals held hostage by Iraq. As I've said before, when it comes to the safety and well-being of American citizens held against their will, I will hold Baghdad responsible. ■

"The public, and Congress, are used to seeing international expeditions discussed in grander, more apocalyptic terms," said Robert Tucker, professor emeritus from Johns Hopkins University.

Sensing the need to define U.S. stakes more broadly, Bush repeated the comparison — first made in his Aug. 8 Oval Office address — of the Iraqi invasion to the expansionist moves by Nazi Germany that led to World War II.

"Half a century ago, the world had the chance to stop a ruthless aggressor and missed it," Bush told the VFW on Aug. 20. "And I pledge to you we will not make that mistake again."

On Aug. 22, Bush signed an order calling to active duty nearly 50,000 military reservists to back up U.S. forces in Saudi Arabia. It was the first mobilization in connection with potential hostile action since President Lyndon B. Johnson called up 35,000 reservists during the Vietnam War in January 1968. *(Reserves call-up, p. 695)*

'Burden Sharing'

A briefing for members of Congress on Aug. 28 focused the administration's attention on the need to show that Arab countries whose security was at stake and U.S. allies who depended on Mideast oil were sharing the burden of confronting Saddam.

More than 150 members returned to Washington for the session, which began with public remarks by Bush and then went behind closed doors for a question-and-answer session with the president, Defense Secretary Cheney and Gen. Colin L. Powell Jr., chairman of the Joints Chief of Staff. *(Bush's remarks at briefing, this page)*

Besides reviewing the post-invasion U.S. military and diplomatic moves, Bush claimed the administration had begun efforts against Iraq even earlier, noting the suspension of CCC food credits and an action in July blocking the export of high-temperature furnances "that had the potential to contribute to Iraq's nuclear capabilities." Left unmentioned, however, was the administration's opposition to mandatory food credit sanctions or the Commerce Department's efforts up until June to secure an export license for the furnace.

After the session, House Speaker Thomas S. Foley, D-Wash., told reporters the president had "strong across-the-board support from members of Congress, both the Senate and House, Democrats and Republicans alike." But he said there were "expressions of concern about burden-sharing."

Other lawmakers were more pointed. "I have real questions obviously about what we're doing to get some real substantial support from our allies besides votes in the United Nations," Rep. Patricia Schroeder, D-Colo.

Bush moved to defuse the issue two days later, announcing a program to press U.S. allies to step up their contributions to the multinational effort.

At a news conference Aug. 30, Bush said that he was asking wealthy U.S. allies — including Japan and West Germany — to step up their contribution to the military deployment in the gulf and to aid the countries that had been hardest hit as a result of the global trade embargo against Iraq.

"It is important to get the priorities right and make sure that those most deserving of assistance receive it, and those most able to contribute do so," the president said.

Some in Congress remained skeptical about how much Japan and other allies would contribute. "They have a reputation for offering things, but when you get beyond the wrapping paper, there's not a lot there," said Rep. David E. Bonior, D-Mich.

As the congressional recess was about to end, however, Bush had managed to keep Congress largely pacified. Senate Foreign Relations Chairman Pell abandoned his previous insistence that the administration would have to invoke the restrictions of the War Powers Resolution. After meeting with Bush, the senator said an immediate debate over its requirements would "upset the apple cart."

But many members did urge the president to provide a clearer rationale for the gulf military buildup. "One of the suggestions made was the importance of the president talking directly to the American people soon to try to articulate these goals," said House Majority Leader Richard A. Gephardt, D-Mo.

Baker Goes to the Hill

Soon after, Secretary of State Baker took the administration's campaign for congressional support to Capitol Hill, testifying before the House Foreign Affairs Committee on Sept. 4 and the Senate Foreign Relations Committee the next day.

During both sessions, he repeatedly stated that it was impossible to put a time limit on U.S. military operations in the gulf. "I can't tell you how long we might be there; it will depend on a whole host of factors," Baker said.

Baker said the administration was asking the American people — and by extension Congress — to "stand firm" and "be patient."

Moreover, the secretary left open the possibility that U.S. forces could remain in the Middle East as part of a new "regional security structure," even if Iraq withdrew from Kuwait. Such an arrangement could "contain and roll back" the nuclear and chemical weapons capability of Iraq, he said. Baker gave no specifics.

He was equally vague about whether the administration would ever launch a military strike at Saddam's weapons arsenals. "The president has made it clear: We're not going to rule anything in; we're not going to rule anything out," Baker said.

The administration did publicly release, for the first time, estimates of the numbers of troops that had been deployed to the region. Defense Secretary Cheney told the International Institute for Strategic Studies on Sept. 6 that the United States had dispatched more than 100,000 troops to Saudi Arabia, the Persian Gulf and the Red Sea.

Help for Egypt

The first sharp dispute between the administration and Congress emerged over Bush's plan — which was ultimately approved as part of the foreign aid appropriations bill (HR 5114 — PL 101-513) — to forgive Egypt's debt of approximately $6.7 billion for previously delivered military equipment. *(Foreign aid appropriations, p. 830)*

Many lawmakers questioned the debt relief plan, which was aimed at shoring up Egypt's President Hosni Mubarak against domestic political opposition over his support for U.S. policy in the crisis.

At the Foreign Relations hearing on Sept. 5, Connecticut Democrat Dodd said that while he did not reject the idea of providing relief to Egypt, he did not like the feeling that Cairo's backing for the United States had a "price attached to it." Baker responded that "this was not something that was bargained, [and] it was not a quid pro quo for the very courageous stand that President Mubarak has taken."

The administration included the debt relief plan in an emergency request sent to Congress on Sept. 14. The package also sought a $1.9 billion supplemental appropriation to pay for costs of Operation Desert Shield during the remainder of the 1990 fiscal year.

Mickey Edwards, Okla., the ranking Republican on the House Appropriations Subcommittee on Foreign Operations, said on Sept. 11, before the package was presented to Congress, that he opposed debt relief for Egypt. "I would be in favor of doing something, possibly restructuring the loan, but I'm not for [forgiving] it," he said.

Many members, such as Patrick J. Leahy, D-Vt., chairman of the Senate Appropriations Subcommittee on Foreign Operations, were concerned about the precedent that could be set by the action. Leahy acknowledged that Egypt deserved special consideration because of its role in the crisis, but said the move could trigger requests for debt relief from other nations.

At private meetings on Capitol Hill, Deputy Secretary of State Lawrence S. Eagleburger responded to such concerns, according to congressional sources. He said that the department was making a one-time exception for Egypt and would not grant similar concessions to any other debtor nations, the sources said.

Other nations with large and powerful constituencies in the United States, notably Poland and Israel, also owed huge official debts to the United States.

At the end of 1989, Israel had an official debt to the United States of $4.6 billion — most of it owed for previous deliveries of military equipment. The government of Poland owed the United States $2.85 billion in official debt at the end of 1989, according to Treasury Department data.

A White House official, asked on the day Congress was officially notified of the debt forgiveness plan whether other nations could anticipate similar treatment, said, "No, but we've heard from a few that would like to get it."

But Howard L. Berman, D-Calif., a member of the House Foreign Affairs Committee, said in an interview Sept. 13, "A lot of us are starting to ask, why shouldn't Israel receive debt forgiveness also?"

On Sept. 19, the chairman of the House Appropriations Subcommittee on Foreign Operations, David R. Obey, D-Wis., warned a panel of administration witnesses that the proposal could "go down in flames on the [House] floor."

Continued on p. 732

New 'Partnership' Answers Gulf Crisis

Following is President Bush's address to a joint session of Congress on Sept. 11 on the U.S. response to Iraq's invasion of Kuwait. (The president's remarks concerning the budget deficit and the budget process, which followed his comments on the Persian Gulf crisis, have been omitted here; see p. 133.)

Mr. President, Mr. Speaker, members of the Congress, distinguished guests, fellow Americans, thank you very much for that warm welcome.

We gather tonight witness to events in the Persian Gulf as significant as they are tragic. In the early morning hours of Aug. 2, following negotiations and promises by Iraq's dictator Saddam Hussein not to use force, a powerful Iraqi army invaded its trusting and much weaker neighbor, Kuwait. Within three days, 120,000 Iraqi troops with 850 tanks had poured into Kuwait and moved south to threaten Saudi Arabia. It was then I decided to act to check that aggression.

At this moment, our brave servicemen and women stand watch in that distant desert and on distant seas, side by side with the forces of more than 20 other nations. They are some of the finest men and women of the United States of America, and they're doing one terrific job.

These valiant Americans were ready at a moment's notice to leave their spouses, their children, to serve on the front line halfway around the world. And they remind us who keeps America strong — they do.

In the trying circumstances of the gulf, the morale of our servicemen and women is excellent. In the face of danger, they are brave, they're well-trained and dedicated.

A soldier, Pfc. Wade Merritt of Knoxville, Tenn., now stationed in Saudi Arabia, wrote his parents of his worries, his love of family, and his hopes for peace. But Wade also wrote: "I am proud of my country and its firm stand against inhumane aggression. I am proud of my army and its men. I am proud to serve my country."

Well, let me just say, Wade, America is proud of you and is grateful to every soldier, sailor, marine, and airman serving the cause of peace in the Persian Gulf.

I also want to thank the chairman of the Joint Chiefs of Staff, Gen. [Colin L.] Powell [Jr.], the chiefs here tonight, our commander in the Persian Gulf, Gen. [H. Norman] Schwarzkopf, and the men and women of the Department of Defense.

What a magnificent job you all are doing, and thank you very, very much from a grateful country.

I wish I could say that their work is done, but we all know it is not.

So if ever there was a time to put country before self and patriotism before party, the time is now. And let me thank all Americans, especially those here in this chamber tonight, for your support for our armed forces and their mission. That support will be even more important in the days to come.

So tonight, I want to talk to you about what's at stake, what we must do together to defend civilized values around the world and maintain our economic strength at home. Our objectives in the Persian Gulf are clear, our goals defined and familiar:

Iraq must withdraw from Kuwait completely, immediately and without condition. Kuwait's legitimate government must be restored. The security and stability of the Persian Gulf must be assured, and American citizens abroad must be protected.

These goals are not ours alone. They've been endorsed by the United Nations Security Council five times in as many weeks. Most countries share our concern for principle. And many have a stake in the stability of the Persian Gulf. This is not, as Saddam Hussein would have it, the United States against Iraq. It is Iraq against the world.

As you know, I've just returned from a very productive meeting with Soviet President [Mikhail S.] Gorbachev. And I am pleased that we are working together to build a new relationship. In Helsinki, [Finland], our joint statement affirmed to the world our shared resolve to counter Iraq's threat to peace. Let me quote: "We are united in the belief that Iraq's aggression must not be tolerated. No peaceful international order is possible if larger states can devour their smaller neighbors. Clearly, no longer can a dictator count on East-West confrontation to stymie concerted United Nations action against aggression."

A new partnership of nations has begun, and we stand today at a unique and extraordinary moment. The crisis in the Persian Gulf, as grave as it is, also offers a rare opportunity to move toward an historic period of cooperation. Out of these troubled times, our fifth objective — a new world order — can emerge: a new era — freer from the threat of terror, stronger in the pursuit of justice, and more secure in the quest for peace, an era in which the nations of the world, East and West, North and South, can prosper and live in harmony.

A hundred generations have searched for this elusive path to peace, while a thousand wars raged across the span of human endeavor. And today that new world is struggling to be born, a world quite different from the one we've known, a world where the rule of law supplants the rule of the jungle, a world in which nations recognize the shared responsibility for freedom and justice, a world where the strong respect the rights of the weak. This is the vision I shared with President Gorbachev in Helsinki. He, and other leaders from Europe, the gulf and around the world, understand that how we manage this crisis today could shape the future for generations to come.

The test we face is great and so are the stakes. This is the first assault on the new world that we seek, the first test of our mettle. Had we not responded to this first provocation with clarity of purpose, if we do not continue to demonstrate our determination, it would be a signal to actual and potential despots around the world.

America and the world must defend common vital interests, and we will.

America and the world must support the rule of law, and we will.

America and the world must stand up to aggression. And we will.

And one thing more — in the pursuit of these goals — America will not be intimidated.

Vital issues of principle are at stake. Saddam Hussein is literally trying to wipe a country off the face of the Earth. We do not exaggerate. Nor do we exaggerate when we say Saddam Hussein will fail.

Vital economic interests are at risk as well. Iraq itself controls some 10 percent of the world's proven oil reserves. Iraq plus Kuwait controls twice that.

An Iraq permitted to swallow Kuwait would have the economic and military power, as well as the arrogance, to intimidate and coerce its neighbors, neighbors who control the lion's share of the world's remaining oil reserves. We cannot permit a resource so vital to be dominated by one so ruthless — and we won't.

Recent events have surely proven that there is no substitute for American leadership. In the face of tyranny, let no one doubt American credibility and reliability.

Let no one doubt our staying power. We will stand by our friends. One way or another, the leader of Iraq must learn this fundamental truth.

From the outset, acting hand in hand with others, we've sought to fashion the broadest possible international response to Iraq's aggression. The level of world cooperation and condemnation of Iraq is unprecedented. Armed forces from countries spanning four continents are there at the request of King Fahd of Saudi Arabia to deter and, if need be, to defend against attack. Muslims and non-Muslims, Arabs and non-Arabs, soldiers from many nations stand shoulder to shoulder, resolute against Saddam Hussein's ambitions.

And we can now point to five United Nations Security Council resolutions that condemn Iraq's aggression. They call for Iraq's immediate and unconditional withdrawal, the restoration of Kuwait's legitimate government, and categorically reject Iraq's cynical and self-serving attempt to annex Kuwait.

Finally, the United Nations has demanded the release of all foreign nationals held hostage against their will and in contravention of international law. It is a mockery of human decency to call these people "guests." They are hostages, and the whole world knows it.

[British] Prime Minister Margaret Thatcher, our dependable ally, said it all: "We do not bargain over hostages. We will not stoop to the level of using human beings as bargaining chips — ever."

Of course — of course our hearts go out to the hostages and their families. But our policy cannot change. And it will not change. America and the world will not be blackmailed by this ruthless policy.

We're now in sight of a United Nations that performs as envisioned by its founders. We owe much to the outstanding leadership of Secretary-General Javier Pérez de Cuéllar. The United Nations is backing up its words with action. The Security Council has imposed mandatory economic sanctions on Iraq, designed to force Iraq to relinquish the spoils of its illegal conquest. The Security Council has also taken the decisive step of authorizing the use of all means necessary to ensure compliance with these sanctions.

Together with our friends and allies, ships of the United States Navy are today patrolling Mideast waters, and they've already intercepted more than 700 ships to enforce the sanctions.

Three regional leaders I spoke with just yesterday told me that these sanctions are working. Iraq is feeling the heat. We continue to hope that Iraq's leaders will recalculate just what their aggression has cost them. They are cut off from world trade, unable to sell their oil, and only a tiny fraction of goods gets through.

The communiqué with President Gorbachev made mention of what happens when the embargo is so effective that children of Iraq literally need milk or the sick truly need medicine. Then, under strict international supervision that guarantees the proper destination, then food will be permitted.

At home, the material cost of our leadership can be steep. And that's why Secretary of State [James A.] Baker [III] and Treasury Secretary [Nicholas F.] Brady have met with many world leaders to underscore that the burden of this collective effort must be shared.

We are prepared to do our share and more to help carry the load; we insist others do their share as well.

The response of most of our friends and allies has been good. To help defray costs, the leaders of Saudi Arabia, Kuwait and the UAE, the United Arab Emirates, have pledged to provide our deployed troops with all the food and fuel they need. And generous assistance will also be provided to stalwart front-line nations, such as Turkey and Egypt.

And I'm also heartened to report that this international response extends to the neediest victims of this conflict — those refugees. For our part, we have contributed $28 million for relief efforts. And this is but a portion of what is needed. I commend, in particular, Saudi Arabia, Japan, and several European nations who have joined us in this purely humanitarian effort.

There's an energy-related cost to be borne as well. Oil-producing nations are already replacing lost Iraqi and Kuwaiti output. More than half of what was lost has been made up, and we're getting superb cooperation.

If producers, including the United States, continue steps to expand oil and gas production, we can stabilize prices and guarantee against hardship. Additionally, we and several of our allies always have the option to extract oil from our Strategic Petroleum Reserves, if conditions warrant. As I've pointed out before, conservation efforts are essential to keep our energy needs as low as possible.

And we must then take advantage of our energy sources across the board: coal, natural gas, hydro and nuclear. Our failure to do these things has made us more dependent on foreign oil than ever before.

And finally, let no one even contemplate profiteering from this crisis. We will not have it.

And I cannot predict just how long it will take to convince Iraq to withdraw from Kuwait. Sanctions will take time to have their full intended effect. We will continue to review all options with our allies, but let it be clear: We will not let this aggression stand.

Our interest, our involvement in the gulf, is not transitory. It predated Saddam Hussein's aggression and will survive it. Long after all our troops come home — and we all hope it's soon, very soon — there will be a lasting role for the United States in assisting the nations of the Persian Gulf. Our role then, is to deter future aggression. Our role is to help our friends in their own self-defense and something else: to curb the proliferation of chemical, biological, ballistic missiles and, above all, nuclear technologies.

And let me also make clear that the United States has no quarrel with the Iraqi people. Our quarrel is with Iraq's dictator and with his aggression. Iraq will not be permitted to annex Kuwait. And that's not a threat, it's not a boast — it's just the way it's going to be. . . . ■

Continued from p. 730

Lawmakers from both parties were particularly dubious about claims by William M. Diefenderfer III, deputy director of the Office of Management and Budget (OMB), that writing off the debt would have no negative budgetary impact during the next five years.

Initially, the administration took the position expressed publicly by Diefenderfer — that the action would not add to the deficit. But the officials reportedly reversed that view a few days later, saying that forgiveness could cost from $1 billion to $2 billion over five years. Then Diefenderfer, at the hearing, went back to the original position.

The Congressional Budget Office (CBO) set a preliminary estimate of the cost at $2.4 billion over five years. Diefenderfer questioned the CBO estimate. "As you know, there are a number of CBO estimates that we don't agree with," he said.

Points of Contention

The controversy over the Egyptian debt issue was one of several points of contention as Congress addressed the nuts and bolts of the administration's policies.

Some pro-Israel lawmakers, for example, were critical of administration proposals to bolster the military capabilities of Saudi Arabia and other Arab allies in the region as part of its overall effort to contain Iraq. Rep. Mel Levine, D-Calif., questioned whether the sale of additional, more sophisticated attack aircraft could pose a threat to Israel's security. *(Saudi arms sales, p. 734)*

Members from across the political spectrum challenged an administration plan that would have shielded foreign government contributions to support the U.S. military deployment from congressional oversight. The full House included language in the fiscal 1991 defense authorization bill (HR 4739) barring expenditure of the contributions from allied governments unless the spending was specifically authorized by Congress.

The week of Sept. 17 also marked the first time lawmakers seriously posed the question: "Who lost Kuwait?" At a Sept. 18 hearing of the House Foreign Affairs Subcommittee on Europe and the Middle East, Democrats lambasted Assistant Secretary of State Kelly, the department's point man for the gulf, for the administration's failure to recognize the threat created by Saddam earlier.

Edging Toward a Stand

Despite the controversies, Congress began edging toward a formal stand in support of the U.S. military deployment in the gulf. Resolutions supporting the president's gulf policy began moving through both chambers during the week of Sept. 24, but they conspicuously avoided confronting the question of future actions.

The House Foreign Affairs Committee on Sept. 27 approved, by voice vote, legislation (H J Res 658) supporting the actions "taken by the president with respect to the Iraqi aggression in Kuwait."

The Senate opened debate Sept. 28 on a similarly worded concurrent resolution (S Con Res 147) that backed continued action by the United States and the United Nations "to deter Iraqi aggression and to protect American lives and vital interests."

The resolutions were non-binding, and neither mentioned future military action. A House leader said that body's resolution merely "ratifies what has been done to this point."

The resolutions' highly nuanced language and the sluggish pace of action on them underscored the widespread reluctance in Congress to become locked into a position. "There was nobody pounding on our door to get this thing on the floor," said Richard G. Lugar, R-Ind., an influential member of the Senate Foreign Relations Committee.

Foreign Relations Chairman Pell said that ideally there should be a broader authorization of the president's actions. But, he added, "there is no consensus on the nature of authorization."

In a floor speech Sept. 24, Daniel Patrick Moynihan, D-N.Y., also a Foreign Relations Committee member, described the pitfalls created by the resolutions.

"Some [members] are concerned that any resolution on the Persian Gulf crisis would turn into a Tonkin Gulf resolution for the 1990s," he said, referring to the 1964 congressional resolution that President Lyndon B. Johnson repeatedly invoked to justify expanded involvement in the Vietnam War. *(1964 Almanac, p. 331)*

"At the opposite end of the spectrum," Moynihan continued, "are those senators who fear that they are somehow being lured into endorsing a resolution that will be amended to include War Powers restrictions."

The two resolutions had in fact been crafted to sidestep a direct confrontation over the 1973 War Powers Resolution. The document drafted by the House panel, for example, reiterated the objectives the president set for Operation Desert Shield and offered support for the deployment of forces: "The Congress declares its support for [U.S. Armed Forces] as they perform their vital role in the achievement of United States objectives."

But members clearly were concerned that Bush might interpreting any ambiguity in the document as authorizing an unprovoked military action against Iraq. Democrats drafting the resolution temporarily were stalemated over a phrase stating that the United States would achieve its objectives in the gulf through peaceful means "to the extent possible."

That language was deemed too controversial by Rep. Ted Weiss, D-N.Y., and some other members, who believed it created the perception that Congress was providing advance approval for military action if a peaceful resolution proved not to be achievable. The offending phrase was rewritten; the document that passed the committee asserted that the United States "will continue to emphasize" non-military means in pursuing its goals.

Yet even with such "artful phrasing," as one member characterized it, questions remained over whether the document gave implicit authorization for a military strike. Rep. Stephen J. Solarz, D-N.Y., who said he would have preferred "much stronger language" in the resolution, argued "the word 'emphasize' does not preclude other methods for achieving objectives."

The Foreign Affairs Committee had initially used the same language Bush had employed when he made his initial report on the crisis to Capitol Hill. Its resolution took note of Bush's own statement that he was consulting with Congress in a manner "consistent with the War Powers Resolution."

But in response to the extreme sensitivity demonstrated by the White House over the War Powers question, language confirming that Bush's actions were, in fact, "consistent with" the 1973 law was removed from the final version of the legislation.

In the Senate, meanwhile, lawmakers also agonized over language, although they had the luxury of marking up the resolution in private. The Senate resolution was not markedly different from the document passed by the Foreign Affairs Committee. It too originally contained a reference to the War Powers Resolution that was deleted before the measure was debated on the floor.

Paying for the Deployment

While the authorizing panels in both bodies tried to make a comprehensive statement about Operation Desert Shield, the appropriating committees faced the issue of how to pay for the deployment.

The price tag of the $2 billion Desert Shield supplemental appropriation drew virtually no opposition when the House Appropriations Committee marked up the bill on Sept. 25. The funds were included in a fiscal 1991 continuing resolution (H J Res 655 — PL 101-403) that also temporarily waived Gramm-Rudman spending ceilings. Republicans on the committee were unable to strip the funds out for consideration as a separate measure. *(Continuing resolutions, p. 895)*

The Egyptian debt forgiveness plan was also attached to the original supplemental request, but the panel scrapped it and substituted a three-month waiver of payments. As a result of the action, Egypt would still be eligible to receive security-related assistance despite its failure to meet requirements of the Brooke Amendment, which barred aid to nations that were more than one year in arrears on debt repayments.

The committee also altered the administration request for a special fund, to be controlled by the Secretary of Defense, for receiving contributions from foreign governments to Operation Desert Shield. The committee provided that the contributions would be subject to the usual appropriations process.

On Sept. 27, the Senate Armed Services Committee followed suit, authorizing the fiscal 1990 supplemental and providing for the establishment of a Defense Cooperation Fund to accept contributions from other governments.

Floor Action on Resolutions

During the week of Oct. 1, both the House and Senate overwhelmingly backed the resolutions offering support for the actions Bush took in the first weeks of the crisis but not authorizing any future military operations against Iraq.

Before acting, lawmakers agonized over whether the administration would see the resolutions as a "blank check" for future actions. House Foreign Affairs Committee Chairman Dante B. Fascell, D-Fla., entered into the record a chart delineating the differences between the open-ended Tonkin Gulf Resolution of 1964 (PL 88-408) and the narrowly defined House resolution (H J Res 658).

U.S. Arms Sales to Gulf Crisis Allies . . .

From the beginning of the Bush administration's massive buildup of forces in the Persian Gulf, members of Congress stressed the need to gain Arab backing for the policy.

But one means of ensuring continued Arab support — increasing U.S. arms sales to Saudi Arabia and other key allies — created anxiety for some of Israel's longtime supporters in Washington.

Prodded by congressional questioning, the administration proceeded to sell the Saudis $7 billion worth of tanks, antimissile batteries and other high-tech weapons, but put off plans for a larger package until 1991.

Secretary of Defense Dick Cheney said Aug. 22 that it was U.S. policy to help "our friends in the region, including the Saudis, satisfy their legitimate security needs." And Iraq's massing of troops and tanks on the northern border of Saudi Arabia qualified as a "legitimate security need," Cheney said.

In addition to helping Saudi Arabia meet the immediate threat from Iraq, "the administration obviously feels a certain sense of obligation to those Arab states that have stood with us," said William Quandt, a former National Security Council analyst who was with the Brookings Institution.

No one in Washington's pro-Israel community disputed Cheney's characterization of the threat posed by Iraq. But concerns emerged over whether the sophisticated hardware that the United States was transferring to Saudi Arabia, and to other allies in the Arab world, might eventually constitute a threat to Israel.

Lawmakers and lobbyists focused on the possibility that the kingdom could receive state-of-the-art F-15E attack fighters.

The F-15s sold to Saudi Arabia previously were air-to-air fighters, but the E model was a ground-attack plane, with a 12-ton bombload and high-tech electronic gear for finding targets at night.

Cheney left the door open for such an action in August. While he denied that the United States was about to provide the F-15Es, he added, "That's the kind of thing we'd work into a longer-term package."

The talk of bolstering Saudi Arabia's future offensive capability worried lawmakers such as Mel Levine, D-Calif., a member of the House Foreign Affairs Committee. Levine said Congress probably would not oppose an emergency, short-term transfer of the F-15Es. But, in an Aug. 23 interview, he predicted that members would "scrutinize very carefully" any plan to make the arrangement permanent. Levine said he would be "very concerned if this crisis were used as a vehicle for transferring any sophisticated weapons to the region."

In addition to possible sales of F-15Es, the administration was also reported to be considering the transfer of Stinger ground-to-air missiles to Saudi Arabia. Pro-Israel lawmakers had previously opposed such sales, in part because of fears that they could fall into the hands of terrorists. "If diversion to terrorists was a threat three weeks ago, it remains that today," Levine said.

Supporters of Israel emphasized the longstanding commitment to maintain Israel's qualitative edge in weaponry over its neighbors, which Levine termed the "cornerstone of U.S. policy."

$20 Billion Proposal

By mid-September, the administration had put together a $20 billion arms deal for Saudi Arabia. On Sept. 19, senior State Department officials tried to sell skeptical members of Congress on the package.

But during a closed briefing, the officials bowed to intense opposition from a large group of lawmakers and signaled that they would make substantial changes to the package. Levine, part of a group that opposed the sale, said after the briefing, "There is no deal, as it was originally constituted, now on the table."

Lawmakers were particularly disturbed that the timing of the deal would have eliminated the informal, 20-day pre-notification period that was normally extended as a courtesy to Congress on controversial weapons deals.

The sale was leaked to the press before lawmakers learned about it directly from administration officials.

One Democratic member of Congress, who was sympathetic to the administration's view on the arms sale, said the White House knew precisely what it was doing when it put together the $20 billion deal, one of the largest arms transactions in history.

"They tried it because they wanted to see how much Congress would accept in the current environment. In effect, they overreached," he said.

The American Israel Public Affairs Committee, which had assumed a relatively low profile during the Middle East turmoil, was particularly active in trying to persuade Congress to change the terms of the sale.

Pro-Israel lawmakers and lobbyists, who acknowledged that further sales to the kingdom were inevitable, floated what amounted to a compromise position calling for dividing the sale into two stages and reducing the sophisticated weaponry that would comprise the second part.

Edward M. Kennedy, D-Mass., one of three members to vote against the Senate measure (S Con Res 147), disagreed, saying, "It is, in effect, a Tonkin Gulf resolution for the Persian Gulf." But most lawmakers went along with Fascell and Senate Majority Leader Mitchell, who in supporting the Senate measure said, "This resolution is not an authorization for the use of forces, now or in the future."

The House approved its legislation Oct. 1 by 380-29. The Senate passed its resolution Oct. 2 by 96-3. *(House vote 394, p. 128-H; Senate vote 258, p. 52-S)*

Although the two resolutions expressed similar sentiments, they differed in form and some details, and neither chamber ever acted on the handiwork of the other. The effect was to leave the two non-binding statements on the record as reflections of the mood in Congress.

Hit-and-Miss Consulting

Despite early praise for the administration's efforts to consult with Congress, strains began to develop by October.

In floor debate on Oct. 5, several leading senators com-

. . . Deeply Concern Israel's Supporters

On Sept. 27, President Bush announced a scaled-down proposal to sell $7 billion worth of tanks and other high-tech weapons to Saudi Arabia. The administration split its original package in two, seeking immediate action only on items that were supposedly essential to respond to Iraq's Aug. 2 invasion of Kuwait.

Pentagon spokesman Pete Williams described the slimmed-down package as "material that [the Saudis] urgently need for their defense."

The move appeared to mollify some of the congressional objections to Bush's earlier proposal for a sale three times as large. Nonetheless, some critics challenged the need for immediate action on some of the most lethal items in the revised package which, they noted, could not be delivered to the Saudis for months or even years.

In particular, members questioned the proposal to sell 150 copies of a version of the M-1 tank that had not yet gone into production and could not be delivered to Saudi Arabia for three years.

Levine called the cut-down version "a significant improvement." But he said two of the most lethal weapons in the package — the tanks and Patriot long-range anti-aircraft missiles — would receive closer scrutiny because neither would soon be available to the Saudis.

The tanks were to be the "A2" model of the M-1. Compared with earlier models that were already in U.S. service, they would include improved optical equipment for driving and fighting at night. The 150 tanks proposed for sale to Riyadh cost $1.3 billion.

The sale would include 384 Patriot missiles and 48 launchers, for $948 million. Designed to hit high-speed airplanes, the Patriot also could shoot down short-range ballistic missiles, such as those deployed by Iraq.

Senate Majority Whip Alan Cranston, D-Calif., also questioned the tank sale: "What's going to happen to sophisticated weapons we're proposing to sell the Saudis after [Iraqi President] Saddam Hussein withdraws? How do we know, for example, that they won't ultimately be turned against Israel?" he asked.

Selling the Deal

A pair of key administration officials — Under Secretary of State for Security Assistance, Science and Technology Reginald Bartholomew and Under Secretary of Defense for Policy Paul Wolfowitz — testified before two House Foreign Affairs subcommittees Oct. 3 in an effort to sell the proposed $7.3 billion arms sale.

Rather than focusing solely on the immediate needs of the Saudis, the officials outlined a long-term strategy to provide a steady stream of arms to a group of moderate gulf states.

The Saudi sale was just "one of a series of steps in assisting nations in the area, not only in the current crisis, but in building lasting stability in the region," said Bartholomew.

With the expanded arms sales, said Wolfowitz, the administration hoped to increase deterrence against a possible attack by either Iraq or Iran. "If deterrence fails, we would expect Saudi forces to slow and perhaps stop an attacking army long enough for reinforcements to arrive."

Wolfowitz and Bartholomew reiterated the oft-stated administration pledge to maintain Israel's qualitative advantage in weapons over its neighbors. "We firmly believe that the risks [the Saudi] sale poses to Israel are minimal," Wolfowitz said.

But skepticism persisted on Capitol Hill. Levine complained to the officials of the "boilerplate administration response that no matter what weapons get injected into this region of the world, it doesn't affect the qualitative balance."

Members Attack Sale

On Oct. 11, four senators introduced a resolution of disapproval to strip advanced weapons from the $7 billion arms package.

"We must not become the unwitting arms supplier for a new Arab war of annihilation against Israel," said Cranston, who sponsored the resolution along with Democrat Paul Simon of Illinois and Republicans Bob Packwood of Oregon and Arlen Specter of Pennsylvania.

The resolution called for stripping from the sale M-1A2 tanks, TOW 2 missile launchers, multiple-launch rocket systems and Apache attack helicopters.

The sale of other equipment, including Bradley fighting vehicles and Patriot antimissile batteries, would not be blocked.

But the resolution of disapproval never progressed beyond its introduction, and some of the opposition to the sale was mollified by the administration's agreement to provide additional aid to Israel in the annual foreign aid appropriations bill. *(Foreign aid appropriations, p. 830)*

Rather than provoke renewed controversy during the war against Iraq, however, the administration ultimately postponed introduction of the more sensitive second stage of the Saudi arms sale that had been expected early in 1991.

plained about the lack of recent consultations with the administration.

"There was a meeting that took place a couple of weeks ago, a general leadership meeting at the White House," Maine Republican Cohen said.

A handful of other senators, including Moynihan and Pell, agreed that the session described by Cohen was the most recent they could remember.

Armed Services Chairman Nunn added: "That was the only meeting in which I met with the president."

The exchanges underscored the hit-or-miss nature of the administration's efforts to keep Congress in the decision-making loop.

Moreover, there was a widespread fear among lawmakers that if war broke out in the Middle East, the administration could present Congress with a fait accompli: a major military engagement that would result in significant casualties before the administration sat down with members to review the situation.

Few lawmakers had the appetite to demand more in the

way of notification from the administration. Nunn proposed the establishment of a consultative group that would receive regular briefings from the administration on the gulf crisis; it was one of several plans for expanding the process being floated on Capitol Hill.

But many members had reservations about legislating a requirement for regular briefings.

"I'm not too keen on legislation," said Fascell, who for several years had pressed for greater consultation on military operations. "You have to preserve the flexibility of the president."

The official view from the White House, according to a spokesman, was that it consulted with Congress on the gulf crisis as it did "on any other issue."

The administration "tries to keep appropriate members informed of anything that happens," the spokesman said.

But Defense Secretary Cheney told The Washington Post that "it was an advantage that Congress was out of town" when the initial forces were dispatched. "We could spend August doing what needed to be done rather than explaining it" to Congress, said Cheney, a former House member.

Baker's Refusal

In appearances before the two foreign policy committees Oct. 17 and 18, Secretary of State Baker emphatically told lawmakers that the power to authorize the use of military force in the Persian Gulf remained firmly in the hands of the administration.

Testifying before the House Foreign Affairs Committee on Oct. 18, Baker rejected a suggestion that the administration promise Congress the opportunity to consider, in advance, the use of force in the gulf. "I really think it would be self-defeating," he said.

With adjournment scheduled within days, the question of how an absent Congress would be able to monitor the crisis took on increased urgency. Lawmakers expressed concern over the possibility that they would be hundreds of miles from Washington if a war broke out.

A number of proposals for dealing with that contingency circulated on Capitol Hill during the week of Oct. 15. Speaker Foley endorsed a suggestion by some House members that Congress plan to return for a special session if hostilities erupted. Both houses of Congress considered the establishment of a special consultative group — consisting of congressional leaders and members of key committees — to meet regularly with the president on the gulf crisis.

But Baker, in the administration's first detailed response to such proposals, insisted that the existing, ad hoc consultative procedures were adequate. Testifying before the Senate Foreign Relations Committee on Oct. 17, Baker said he had reservations about a "formal mechanism" for presidential consultation with Congress.

Baker was caustic in rejecting requests for advance congressional authorization of military action. He raised the possibility that Congress and the administration would become mired in a time-consuming debate over military options, ruling out a fast response and eliminating the element of surprise in any operation. He sarcastically envisioned how such congressional advice could turn to micromanagement: "No, don't use this air wing, use this one over here. Or, don't use that division, use this one over here."

Baker said the administration would have no difficulty with a formal declaration of war by Congress, but only if Iraq were to launch an all-out attack on U.S. forces. The administration wished to retain all options under any other circumstances — including a possible retaliatory strike if U.S. hostages in the region were harmed, Baker said.

"You're not going to bless our action in advance, and I don't think you should ask us to give you carte blanche in advance," he said.

In his testimony before the two panels, Baker did not dissuade lawmakers of plans to press for wider consultation over the gulf issue. There was strong support, especially in the Senate Foreign Relations Committee, for ensuring that Congress acted in some way to provide authorization before military action ensued.

Paul S. Sarbanes, D-Md., agreed with Baker that such a step could eliminate the possibility of a surprise attack. But he told Baker of his "strongly held view" that "the commitment of American forces by the president in a major assault to drive Saddam Hussein out of Kuwait would require an authorization from Congress."

Other panel members, including Republicans, at least tacitly agreed. Lugar said that if further military steps were needed, "Congress ought to come back into session to entertain a declaration of war."

Despite the support in both houses for requiring advance authorization of a military strike, time and circumstance were working in favor of the administration. Bush's actions in the gulf crisis still enjoyed wide public support, although the latest Gallup Poll showed it had dropped to 61 percent. Moreover, members were far from united about what course to take.

Finally, even if Foley's proposal to return to session was adopted, members would be summoned to the Capitol only if U.S. troops "attack Iraqi forces or come under fire from them," according to a letter to Foley from a group of House members. By then, the issues of advance authorization and consultation would be moot.

For his part, Baker made clear that Congress should not expect a more intense level of consultation. "I cannot give you a blank-check commitment," Baker said, "that we will, in every case, do nothing until we consult with all 535 members of Congress."

Mitchell's Response

Senate Majority Leader Mitchell responded equally emphatically Oct. 21, insisting in a television inteview that a decision to go to war required congressional approval.

"Under the American Constitution, the president has no legal authority — none whatsoever — to commit the United States to war," Mitchell declared. "Only Congress can make that grave decision."

Asked what would happen if the administration went to war without congressional approval, he said flatly, "Well, that will not be consistent with the Constitution, and we strongly urge the president to obey the Constitution."

Mitchell, and other members who addressed the subject, appeared to have more on their minds than scoring rhetorical points on the administration.

There was a real sense on Capitol Hill that "we are going to have a major problem" in the Persian Gulf relatively soon, as Rep. Lawrence J. Smith, D-Fla., a member of the Foreign Affairs Committee, put it.

Smith made his remarks Oct. 24, after mass briefings for members of each house on Operation Desert Shield by Baker and Defense Secretary Cheney.

The same day, Mitchell and Foley designated a group of lawmakers to be available for consultation while Congress was out of session. The group consisted of the congressional leaders and the chairmen and ranking members from the national security committees along with one surprise selection — Robert C. Byrd, D-W.Va., chairman of the Senate Appropriations Committee, who was apparently included in deference to his seniority and influence.

Mitchell and Foley also wrote language for the concurrent adjournment resolution to ensure that the leadership would have the authority to recall Congress to Washington "as necessary."

As Cheney informed the members he briefed, U.S. military personnel in the region would soon exceed 240,000 — more troops than the United States had in Vietnam in early 1966.

After the briefing, Cheney left open the possibility of further deployments, telling reporters, "We have never put an upper limit on numbers" of personnel. In television interviews, he conceded that as many as 100,000 more troops might be dispatched.

The 101st Congress adjourned in the early hours of Oct. 28. The midterm elections were nine days away.

THE OFFENSIVE OPTION

Tension and apprehension over the prospect of war in the gulf grew rapidly in November, after Bush stunned Congress with plans to nearly double the U.S. deployment in the region.

The ante was raised once again on Nov. 29, when the U.N. Security Council approved a U.S.-crafted resolution setting a deadline of Jan. 15 for Iraq to pull out of Kuwait or be forced out.

On Dec. 6, Saddam announced he would free the hostages he was holding, but that move did little to defuse the tension. On Dec. 13, a federal judge rejected a lawsuit filed by 54 members of Congress challenging Bush's authority to initiate an offensive attack against Iraq without congressional approval.

By the end of the year, war seemed increasingly likely, and members of Congress began to move, fitfully but inexorably, toward a full-scale debate on the prospect of war with Iraq.

Post-Election Surprise

The Nov. 6 elections came and went with few dramatic changes in the congressional landscape — and little debate by incumbents or challengers over the U.S. deployment in the Persian Gulf.

Two days later, however, Bush jolted Congress and the country with a dramatic announcement that he apparently withheld until after Election Day. The president disclosed that he had ordered a massive new buildup of U.S. forces and that the purpose was to develop an "adequate offensive military option should that be necessary to achieve our common goals."

Neither Bush nor Cheney would say how many more troops were to be sent, but reports indicated the number would be close to 200,000 — which would raise U.S. forces in the region to 430,000 by early 1991.

In ordering a deployment intended to shock Iraq into retreat, the White House apparently failed to anticipate that Congress would be equally shaken.

During the week of Nov. 12, Bush was caught in what one member of Congress called a "mini-firestorm" of criticism. By midweek, the president managed to quell demands for a special session of Congress by assuring congressional leaders — according to members who recounted a session at the White House on Nov. 14 — that "no Rubicon was crossed" in the movement toward war.

The idea of calling back Congress for a special session was initially floated by two Republican senators who supported the president — Minority Leader Dole and Foreign Relations member Lugar. Their goal was to provide the president with standing authorization for military action.

After abandoning the plan for an immediate session, congressional committees scheduled post-Thanksgiving hearings on developments in the gulf crisis. And some Republicans joined Democratic leaders in strongly asserting that only Congress could declare war.

"If there is to be a war in the Persian Gulf or anywhere else," Senate Majority Leader Mitchell stated repeatedly, "it requires a formal act of Congress to commit to it."

The uneasy bipartisanship of summer gave way to increasingly partisan rhetorical skirmishing. "The president's announcement suddenly brought into focus some of the differences that were lying beneath the surface," House Armed Services Chairman Aspin observed.

Even Rep. John P. Murtha, D-Pa., who consistently backed the president's gulf policy, said he found the size of the buildup "shocking." Aspin, who had also been a supporter of the administration policy, said the number of troops involved was more than double what he anticipated.

Despite his support, Aspin said he found disturbing the indications that Defense Secretary Cheney had abandoned plans to rotate the troops already deployed to defend Saudi Arabia. "What that means is you eliminate the option to wait for the [economic] embargo to work," he said.

U.N. Resolution 678

Following is the text of the resolution the U.N. Security Council adopted Nov. 29:

THE SECURITY COUNCIL, RECALLING, AND REAFFIRMING its resolutions 660 (1990) of 2 August, 661 (1990) of 6 August, 662 (1990) of 9 August, 664 (1990) of 18 August, 665 (1990) of 25 August, 666 (1990) of 13 September, 667 (1990) of 16 September, 669 (1990) of 24 September, 670 (1990) of 25 September, 674 (1990) of 29 October, and 677 (1990) of 28 November,

NOTING THAT, despite all efforts by the United Nations, Iraq refuses to comply with its obligation to implement resolution 660 (1990) and the above-mentioned subsequent relevant resolutions, in flagrant contempt of the Security Council,

MINDFUL of its duties and responsibilities under the Charter of the United Nations for the maintenance and preservation of international peace and security,

DETERMINED to secure full compliance with its decisions,

ACTING under Chapter VII of the Charter,

1. DEMANDS that Iraq comply fully with resolution 660 (1990) and all subsequent relevant resolutions, and decides, while maintaining all its decisions, to allow Iraq one final opportunity, as a pause of good will, to do so;
2. AUTHORIZES Member States cooperating with the Government of Kuwait, unless Iraq on or before 15 January 1991 fully implements, as set forth in paragraph 1 above, the foregoing resolutions, to use all necessary means to uphold and implement resolution 660 (1990) and all subsequent relevant resolutions and to restore international peace and security in the area;
3. REQUESTS all States to provide appropriate support for the actions undertaken in pursuance of paragraph 2 of the present resolution;
4. REQUESTS the States concerned to keep the Security Council regularly informed on the progress of actions undertaken pursuant to paragraphs 2 and 3 of the present resolution;
5. DECIDES to remain seized of the matter. ■

Senate Democrats, including Kennedy and Colorado's Tim Wirth, were especially sharp in their criticism of the new deployment. Kennedy said the buildup made war "inevitable." In an interview, Wirth said of administration officials: "I am increasingly wondering if they know what they're doing."

But complaints came as well from Republicans, such as Wyoming Sen. Malcolm Wallop and Michigan Rep. William S. Broomfield, the senior minority member of the House Foreign Affairs Committee.

The avuncular Broomfield, who said he had not been informed in advance of the second-stage buildup, angrily charged that the administration's failure to consult more closely with key lawmakers "is the main reason support for the policy is eroding."

At week's end, in a gesture to bolster sagging congressional support for the buildup, Bush invited House and Senate leaders to join him for Thanksgiving Day with the troops in Saudi Arabia.

Maintaining Sanctions

The troop buildup caught the administration in a debate over whether the economic sanctions that it had helped put in place and loudly trumpeted for three months were being jettisoned without being given time to work.

Senate Armed Services Chairman Nunn, who called the troop buildup and the decision to drop troop rotations mistakes, said that the actions indicated a decision to deemphasize, if not abandon, economic sanctions.

In the House, Wisconsin Democrat Obey said of the sanctions, "How long are you willing to wait it out to save lives? My answer is, a fair amount of time."

Bush himself had repeatedly said the sanctions were working. "The sanctions are beginning to take hold," he told lawmakers in the Aug. 28 briefing. In his Sept. 11 address to Congress, he declared: "Three regional leaders I spoke with just yesterday told me that these sanctions are working." And on Nov. 1, he said in an interview that he was "prepared to give sanctions time to work."

The administration was still setting no deadline for sanctions, but in an interview with Cable News Network (CNN) on Nov. 15, Bush said that there was "a ticking of the clock" in terms of how long support for the effort could be maintained domestically or internationally.

The effects of the sanctions could not be gauged fully, but by most accounts the U.N.-backed embargo was being widely observed and was having an impact inside Iraq. CIA Director William H. Webster, testifying before the House Armed Services Committee on Dec. 5, said the blockade had cut off more than 90 percent of Iraq's imports and 97 percent of its exports.

"All sectors of the Iraq economy are feeling the pinch of sanctions, and many industries have largely shut down," Webster said. "Most importantly, the blockade has eliminated any hope Baghdad had of cashing in on higher oil prices or its seizure of Kuwaiti oil fields."

Iraqi efforts to break sanctions had been "largely unsuccessful," Webster added. But he told the lawmakers that there was "no assurance or guarantee that economic hardships will compel Saddam to change his policies or lead to internal unrest that would threaten his regime."

In his meeting with congressional leaders on Nov. 14, however, Bush took a conciliatory tone and assured lawmakers that his intentions had not changed. Afterward, Mitchell and Foley both explained, in measured terms, that they were convinced the administration had not abandoned economic sanctions and become committed to war.

"At the moment," said Foley, "our forces are there for defensive purposes and to enforce the embargo authorized by the U.N."

The Perils of Debate

The widening debate over U.S. policy discomforted the administration and its supporters.

The mood was captured by Sen. Trent Lott, R-Miss. He said Congress needed to debate military action in the gulf but added: "If we start allowing this to be a backing away from the [administration's] policy, it could be giving aid and comfort to Saddam Hussein."

Bush made the same point in his meeting with congressional leaders Nov. 14 by pulling out a clip from an Iraqi newspaper that purportedly described dissent among lawmakers on the question of whether the United States should go to war. The message behind the visual aid was clear, members who attended the meeting said: A cacophonous debate over the issue could only serve to undercut U.S. strategy.

Republicans picked up the theme during congressional hearings on U.S. policy in the gulf, which began Nov. 27. "I am concerned that our debating in public what our strategy is going to be simply plays into Saddam Hussein's strategy," said Sen. Daniel R. Coats of Indiana.

Some Democrats protested that the administration was exaggerating the need for a common front against Saddam in order to stem the widening opposition to the administration's gulf policy. "The fact of the matter is this country is divided and divided deeply," Kennedy said on Nov. 29.

The complexities of the gulf crisis, combined with the omnipresence of television, placed Congress in a peculiar position. Saddam could follow any congressional debate.

"CNN is on, and CNN is being watched in Baghdad," Gen. David C. Jones, former chairman of the Joint Chiefs of Staff, told the Senate Armed Services Committee on Nov. 28.

In addition, said Nancy Landon Kassebaum, R-Kan., a member of the Foreign Relations Committee, a certain level of congressional skittishness was understandable, given the stakes involved. "We've argued endlessly about Nicaragua and El Salvador," she said, "but we didn't have 400,000 people poised on the border."

Divisions over U.S. policy had been emphasized when a group of Democratic congressmen filed suit Nov. 20 in U.S. District Court in Washington to block Bush from launching an attack against Iraq without congressional approval. U.S. District Judge Harold H. Greene's decision Dec. 13 denying a preliminary injunction merely left the divisions unchanged: it was up to a majority of Congress, he said, to adopt a position on war or peace, not just a group of members. *(War powers suit, p. 739)*

Bush had been equivocal on the issue of seeking congressional approval when asked about it in the CNN interview. "The question is too hypothetical," he said, adding in the next breath, "I want Congress to be a partner."

Meanwhile, Defense Secretary Cheney, a former House GOP whip, offered a critical view of lawmakers' ability to confront the question of going to war.

Appearing on the NBC News program "Meet the Press" on Nov. 18, Cheney noted that in 1941, two months before Pearl Harbor, Congress had agreed to extend the draft by only a one-vote margin.

"It's a difficult proposition for Congress to come together and do that [conduct a full debate on military

War Powers Suit Premature, Judge Rules

As the Bush administration and Congress braced for a possible war in the Persian Gulf, their debate turned in part on one of the great unresolved questions of U.S. constitutional law: Who controls the power to wage war?

Presidents and Congresses had asserted their conflicting prerogatives for most of the nation's 200-year history — with no definitive conclusion — and the courts had been conspicuously reluctant to intervene.

On Nov. 20, a group of 45 House members filed suit *(Dellums v. Bush)* in U.S. District Court in Washington, seeking a preliminary injunction to prevent President Bush from ordering U.S. troops in the gulf into offensive combat without prior authorization from Congress.

The plaintiffs, who eventually numbered 53 House members and one senator, relied on the Constitution's provision in Article I that Congress "shall have the power . . . to declare war. . . ."

"The power to declare war is synonymous with the power to initiate it," the lawmakers argued.

In its response to the suit, the Justice Department said Article II dictated that the president was the ultimate authority in foreign affairs as "commander in chief."

The president acts "as the sole organ of the federal government in the field of international relations," the department said, quoting the Supreme Court's decision in *United States v. Curtiss-Wright Export Corp.* In that 1936 case, the court upheld a grant of authority to the president allowing him to bar the sale of arms to warring countries in South America.

In arguments before U.S. District Judge Harold H. Greene on Dec. 4, the members said the Constitution's war powers clause dictated that Congress debate and vote in favor of a formal declaration of war before U.S. troops could be used to drive Iraqi forces from Kuwait.

"If the president takes it upon himself, as he may at any moment, to initiate such a war without the unequivocal consent of Congress," they said, "the victim of Iraqi aggression will be, not just Kuwait, but the Constitution of the United States."

Stuart M. Gerson, assistant attorney general, who argued the administration's position, said that if Congress did not like what the administration was doing, it should take legislative rather than legal action.

In his brief, Gerson argued, "While . . . the president has the right and power to deploy our military forces, the ultimate check on such action is not with the courts, which are ill-equipped to deal with the matter, but with the Congress itself. . . ."

In his Dec. 13 ruling, Greene refused to issue an injunction, saying that the case was not ripe because only 10 percent of Congress was seeking relief rather than a majority.

"It would be both premature and presumptuous for the court to render a decision on the issue of whether a declaration of war is required at this time or in the near future when the Congress itself has provided no indication whether it deems such a declaration either necessary, on the one hand, or imprudent, on the other," Greene said.

But Greene also rejected the Justice Department's position, holding that the courts had the authority to decide a dispute between Congress and the president over war powers if it was squarely joined.

"The Court is not prepared," Greene wrote, "to read out of the Constitution the clause granting to the Congress, and to it alone, the authority 'to declare war.' "

The plaintiffs, led by Rep. Ronald V. Dellums, D-Calif., said Greene's holding amounted to a partial victory for their position.

On the same day, another federal judge, Royce C. Lamberth, issued a decision more in keeping with the courts' traditional reluctance to become embroiled in war-making disputes. He held that the courts could not decide whether Bush needed congressional permission to go to war because it was a political question beyond the judicial realm.

Lamberth dismissed a complaint by a member of the National Guard who protested serving in the gulf until Bush received congressional authorization.

In January 1991, the legal issue became moot when Bush decided to request — and Congress approved — a resolution (H J Res 77 — PL 102-1) authorizing use of U.S. armed forces to force Iraq out of Kuwait.

Bush did his best to avoid setting a precedent, however, linking his request not to constitutional necessity but to political efficacy. He said a vote from Congress backing his policies would "send the clearest possible message to Saddam Hussein that he must withdraw without condition or delay from Kuwait."

action]," Cheney said. "It's been done only a very few times in our history. I don't know whether or not it would be appropriate in this instance."

For many Democrats, however, the appropriate historical precedent came not from the 1940s but from the 1960s. "One of the lessons of Vietnam," said a Democratic aide, "was that if you want us in for the landing, we'd better be in for the takeoff."

The Diplomatic Front

The Bush administration was having greater success with its diplomatic game-plan. Its efforts culminated Nov. 29 with the U.N. Security Council's adoption of a resolution that authorized member nations to "use all necessary means" to eject Iraq from Kuwait unless it had obeyed all previous U.N. resolutions by Jan. 15, 1991.

The Security Council vote approving Resolution 678 — universally understood to authorize the use of force against Iraq — was 12-2, with Cuba and Yemen opposed and China abstaining. *(U.N. resolution text, p. 737)*

The next day, Bush offered to send Secretary of State Baker to Baghdad sometime between Dec. 15 and Jan. 15 in what he called an effort "to go the extra mile for peace." He tied the offer to an invitation for Iraq's Foreign Minister Tariq Aziz to visit Washington "at a mutually convenient time during the latter part of the week Dec. 10 to meet with me." *(Bush news conference, p. 741)*

Administration officials had lobbied for six weeks to

Choice of Gulf Partners Questioned

The U.S. alliance in the Persian Gulf produced new evidence for the adage that international alliances, like politics, can make strange bedfellows.

During November, some members of Congress became concerned with the less than savory reputations of the partners the Bush administration had recruited in the effort to dislodge Iraq from Kuwait.

At the top of the list was Syria, which deployed 7,500 troops to the multilateral force in Saudi Arabia. Sharp criticism followed a meeting between President Bush and Syrian President Hafez al-Assad in Geneva on Nov. 23.

It was the same Assad, administration officials acknowledged, who was responsible for countless acts of terrorism in the Middle East. Syria had been identified as a terrorist nation each year since the State Department began making such designations in 1979, and it had been linked to the December 1988 bombing of a Pan Am jetliner over Lockerbie, Scotland, that killed 270 people.

Senate Majority Leader George J. Mitchell, D-Maine, called Bush's session with Assad "an unneeded and gratuitous gesture that sent a chilling message throughout the Arab world."

Mitchell compared the new relations with Assad to efforts by the Bush and Reagan administrations to "cozy up to Saddam Hussein of Iraq because he was opposed to Iran." Mitchell said, "Now here is the president dignifying him [Assad] with a meeting of this type."

But Bush, the first U.S. president to meet with Assad since 1977, seemed prepared for the criticism. After his three-hour meeting with Assad, Bush acknowledged that "we've got big differences on certain categories" with the Syrian regime, although he did not specifically address the terrorism allegations. Nevertheless, he said Syrian troops were "on the front line, or will be, standing up against this aggression."

Rep. Sam Gejdenson, D-Conn., renewed the criticism at a House Foreign Affairs Committee hearing Dec. 6, with Secretary of State James A. Baker III in the witness chair.

"Your description of Saddam Hussein today, with the exception of one or two small details, could easily be laid at the feet of Mr. Assad, President Assad," Gejdenson said.

Baker answered first by stating that "the foreign policy of the United States can never be and will never be immoral."

But, he said, "we're going to talk to countries, though, where we think it is important to our goals in the gulf." He added that the administration had "made no decision" to remove Syria from the list of terrorist nations.

---

win support for the U.N. resolution and timed its consideration to the last day of the United States' month of presiding over the Security Council. An early version of the resolution set a deadline of Jan. 1, but the time was extended at the behest of the Soviet Union.

Bush and Secretary of State Baker both devoted much of their time in November to lining up the votes needed for approval of the resolution. Baker met for 13 hours with Soviet President Mikhail S. Gorbachev and Foreign Minister Eduard A. Shevardnadze in Moscow on Nov. 8. He stopped over in London and Paris for meetings with British and French officials before returning to Washington.

According to an account in The New York Times, the president's meeting with congressional leaders on Nov. 14 convinced Bush, Baker and national security adviser Brent Scowcroft that an international resolution was needed to allay complaints that the United States was "going it alone." So Baker resumed the lobbying effort, hoping to win China's support or at least neutrality and courting the other countries that held rotating seats on the council: Canada, Colombia, Cuba, Ethiopia, Finland, Ivory Coast, Malaysia, Romania, Yemen and Zaire.

By abstaining rather than using its veto power to block the resolution, China won a tangible reward: Bush met with Foreign Minister Qian Qichen in Washington on Nov. 30. It marked the first visit by the Chinese foreign minister since the massacre of pro-democracy protesters in June 1989 at Tiananmen Square. *(U.S.-China relations, p. 764; background, 1989 Almanac, p. 528)*

On the other hand, Yemen, the only Arab country on the council, resisted Baker's lobbying. The secretary had gone to Yemen after a visit to Saudi Arabia and, according to several accounts, offered U.S. aid as an inducement. After Yemen cast its no vote, the Times reported, a U.S. diplomat was instructed to tell the Yemeni delegate: "That was the most expensive no vote you ever cast."

With the successful diplomatic effort, members of Congress, who had become increasingly divided over the administration's seeming march toward war, rallied around the president yet again.

"There's obviously strong support for the continued efforts of the president and the United Nations to convince Saddam Hussein that an immediate withdrawal from Kuwait must occur," House Speaker Foley said.

Some members, however, took umbrage at the administration's intensive effort to round up international support for the use of force before coming to Congress. "The countries that are voting today are not the countries that are going to have their young people dying," House Majority Leader Gephardt said shortly after the U.N. vote.

The question remained, however, whether Bush's decision to try diplomacy would do more than delay a contentious congressional debate.

"The Jan. 15 fuse for war is still lit, and the current peace initiative must not be permitted to divert the nation's attention from that fact," said Kennedy.

Bush remained concerned about the possibility of a fractious congressional debate.

"What I don't want to do," he told reporters Nov. 30, "is have [Congress] come back and end up where you have 435 voices in one house, and 100 in the other, saying what not to do . . . kind of a hand-wringing operation that would send bad signals."

Continued on p. 742

Bush Defends Buildup, Sends Baker to Iraq

Following is President Bush's opening statement at a White House news conference on Nov. 30, along with answers to the first two questions dealing with the Persian Gulf crisis:

PRESIDENT BUSH: We're in the gulf because the world must not and cannot reward aggression. And we're there because our vital interests are at stake. And we're in the gulf because of the brutality of Saddam Hussein.

We're dealing with a dangerous dictator all too willing to use force, who has weapons of mass destruction and is seeking new ones and desires to control one of the world's key resources, all at a time in history when the rules of the post-Cold War world are being written.

Our objectives remain what they were at the outset. We seek Iraq's immediate and unconditional withdrawal from Kuwait. We seek the restoration of Kuwait's legitimate government. We seek the release of all hostages, and the free functioning of all embassies. And we seek the stability and security of this critical region of the world.

We are not alone in these goals and objectives. The United Nations, invigorated with a new sense of purpose, is in full agreement. The United Nations Security Council has endorsed 12 resolutions to condemn Iraq's unprovoked invasion and occupation of Kuwait; implement tough economic sanctions to stop all trade in and out of Iraq; and authorize the use of force to compel Saddam to comply.

Saddam Hussein has tried every way he knows how to make this a fight between Iraq and the United States, and clearly he has failed. Forces of 26 other nations are standing shoulder to shoulder with our troops in the gulf. The fact is that it is not the United States against Iraq; it is Iraq against the world. And there's never been a clearer demonstration of a world united against appeasement and aggression. Yesterday's United Nations Security Council resolution was historic. Once again, the Security Council has enhanced the legitimate peacekeeping function of the United Nations.

Until yesterday, Saddam may not have understood what he's up against in terms of world opinion, and I'm hopeful that now he will realize that he must leave Kuwait immediately.

I am continually asked how effective are the U.N. sanctions, those put into effect on Aug. 6. I don't know the answer to that question. Clearly, the sanctions are having some effect, but I can't tell you that the sanctions alone will get the job done, and thus, I welcome yesterday's United Nations action. The fledgling democracies in Eastern Europe are being severely damaged by the economic effects of Saddam's actions. The developing countries of Africa and in our hemisphere are being victimized by this dictator's rape of his neighbor, Kuwait.

Those who feel that there is no downside to waiting months and months must consider the devastating damage being done every day to the fragile economies of those countries that can afford it the least.

As [Federal Reserve] Chairman Alan Greenspan testified just the other day, the increase in oil prices resulting directly from Saddam's invasion is hurting our country, too, and our economy, as I said the other day, is at best in a serious slowdown, and if uncertainty remains in the energy markets the slowdown will get worse.

I've spelled out, once again, our reasons for sending troops to the gulf. Let me tell you the things that concern me most.

First, I put the immorality of the invasion of Kuwait itself. No nation should rape, pillage and brutalize its neighbor. No nation should be able to wipe a member state of the United Nations and the Arab League off the face of the Earth.

And I'm deeply concerned about all the hostages — innocent people held against their will in direct contravention of international law. And then there's this cynical and brutal policy of forcing people to beg for their release, parceling out human lives to families and traveling emissaries like so much chattel.

I'm deeply concerned about our own embassy in Kuwait. The flag is still flying there. A handful of beleaguered Americans remain inside the embassy, unable to come and go. . . .

This treatment of our embassy violates every civilized principle of diplomacy and it demeans our people. It demeans our country. And I am determined that this embassy, as called for under Security Council resolution 674, be fully replenished and our people free to come home. . . .

I'm deeply concerned about Saddam's efforts to acquire nuclear weapons. Imagine his ability to blackmail his neighbors should he possess a nuclear device. We've seen him use chemical weapons on his own people. We've seen him take his own country, one that should be wealthy and prosperous, and turn it into a poor country, all because of an insatiable appetite for military equipment and conquest. . . .

In our country I know that there are fears about another Vietnam. Let me assure you, should military action be required, this will not be another Vietnam. This will not be a protracted, drawn-out war.

The forces arrayed are different. The opposition is different. The resupply of Saddam's military would be very different. The countries united against him in the United Nations are different. The topography of Kuwait is different. And the motivation of our all-volunteer force is superb.

I want peace. I want peace, not war. But if there must be war, we will not permit our troops to have their hands tied behind their backs, and I pledge to you there will not be any murky ending. If one American soldier has to go into battle, that soldier will have enough force behind him to win and then get out as soon as possible, as soon as the U.N. objectives have been achieved. . . .

Many people have talked directly to Saddam Hussein and to his foreign minister, Tariq Aziz. All have been frustrated by Iraq's ironclad insistence that it will not leave Kuwait.

However, to go the extra mile for peace, I will issue an invitation to Foreign Minister Tariq Aziz to come to Washington at a mutually convenient time during the latter part of the week of Dec. 10 to meet with me. And I'll invite ambassadors of several of our coalition partners in the gulf to join me at that meeting.

In addition, I'm asking Secretary [of State] Jim [James A.] Baker [III] to go to Baghdad to see Saddam Hussein, and I will suggest to Iraq's president that he receive the secretary of State at a mutually convenient time between Dec. 15 and Jan. 15 of next year.

Within the mandate — within the mandate of the United Nations resolutions, I will be prepared, and so will Secretary Baker, to discuss all aspects of the gulf crisis. However, to be very clear about these efforts to exhaust all means for achieving, all means for a diplomatic and political solution, I am not suggesting discussions that will result in anything less than Iraq's complete withdrawal from Kuwait, restoration of Kuwait's legitimate government, and freedom for all hostages.

Q: Mr. President, now that you have a clear-cut U.N. resolution on use of force . . . doesn't this force you into the position of having to use force on Jan. 15 if Saddam Hussein hasn't left?

P: No, the date was not a date that — at which point force had to be used.

Q: Are you going to ask Congress for approval of this resolution? Would you like to see Congress pass the same kind of resolution as the U.N.?

P: I'd love to see Congress pass a resolution enthusiastically endorsing what the United Nations has done, yes. But we're in consultation on that, and I have no plans to call a special session. I'm not opposed to it, but we're involved in consultations right now.

I've talked to several members of Congress. I've talked to the leaders in the House. I've talked to several on the Republican side and Democratic side in the Senate. And I want to be sure that these consultations are complete.

Some feel a lame-duck session is not good, that the new members should have a right to have a say. Others feel that we ought to move right now.

The Congress, as you know, in their adjournment resolution, had a provision in there that they could come back and take this up; they are a coequal branch of government. They can do that if they want to. . . . ■

Continued from p. 740

Committee Hearings

The U.N. vote had come in the same week that a manifestly skeptical Nunn presided over two days of Armed Services Committee hearings marked by similarly skeptical testimony from a trio of former Pentagon officials.

Nunn opened the sessions Nov. 27 by saying that if the president wanted carte blanche authority to wage a war, "then I think he has to make the corresponding case the current policy is not working.... That case has not yet been made."

The former Pentagon officials — James R. Schlesinger, Defense secretary under President Gerald R. Ford, and two former chairmen of the Joint Chiefs of Staff, Admiral William J. Crowe Jr. and Gen. David C. Jones — all counseled that if the United States' main intention was to force Saddam out of Kuwait, sanctions would succeed.

"The issue is not whether an embargo will work but whether we have the patience to let it work," said Crowe.

The testimony urging a continued reliance on economic sanctions received added attention because the administration delayed sending Baker and other top officials to appear before congressional committees until after the U.N. Security Council vote.

In their absence, however, other witnesses, including former Secretary of State Henry A. Kissinger and former Assistant Secretary of Defense Richard N. Perle, questioned whether the United States could maintain a military presence in the Middle East for that long, especially once Bush made the commitment to double the deployment.

Kissinger and Perle also said there was a good chance the international coalition behind the United States would begin to erode as time passed.

Perle also questioned whether international sanctions would work, noting that Saddam had withstood the hardships of an eight-year war with Iran. "I do not believe time is on our side," he said. "Iraq's capacity to absorb pain is very great."

However, other witnesses said they were concerned that the military buildup proposed by Bush might itself lead to war.

"My main concern with this latest scheduled reinforcement isn't that we might choose to fight but rather that the deployment might cause us to fight," Jones said.

When he came before the committee on Dec. 3, however, Defense Secretary Cheney was pessimistic about relying on sanctions and concerned about the United States' ability to maintain an anti-Iraq coalition for the time needed for sanctions to work.

"I think we always have to come back and remind ourselves that there is no guarantee, even in five years, that sanctions will force him [Saddam] out of Kuwait," Cheney said. "It might. But there is no certainty there."

"My own personal view," he added, "is that it is far better for us to deal with him now, while the coalition is intact, while we have the United Nations behind us, while we have some 26 other nations assembled with military forces in the gulf, than it will be for us to deal with him five or 10 years from now, when the members of the coalition have gone their disparate ways and when Saddam has become an even better armed and more threatening regional superpower than he is at present."

Nunn replied curtly: "If we have a war, we're never going to know whether they would work, are we? That's the point."

Secretary of State Baker presented the administration's case to the two congressional foreign policy committees the week of Dec. 3, appealing for the "fullest support of Congress" for the administration's policy to work. But his testimony and Cheney's appearance before Senate Armed Services did not quiet the increasingly contentious tone of the debate on Capitol Hill.

What the administration was seeking, Baker said, was for Congress to send an unmistakable message to Saddam: "Get out of Kuwait now, or risk all."

What it got, during exhaustive sessions held by several committees, was a plea from Democrats in both chambers that economic sanctions be given more time to work. Perhaps as important, some members of the party accused the administration of rushing toward war — a fear heightened when Baker told the Senate Foreign Relations panel Dec. 5 that if necessary, the United States was prepared to launch an attack "suddenly, massively, and decisively."

"You had a policy that was working," Maryland's Sarbanes countered. "Instead, we've abandoned that policy, and we've shifted off to a course now which I think is going to take us into conflict."

Earlier, before the House Foreign Affairs Committee on Dec. 3, Baker had challenged the testimony that the former Joints Chiefs chairmen, Crowe and Jones, had given to the Senate panel the week before.

"I think the reality is that from what we've seen so far, we have to be very pessimistic about whether economic sanctions alone could do the job," Baker said.

He praised Crowe and Jones as "superb military men," but said, "they are not experts with respect to political questions."

CIA Director Webster's assessment of sanctions — pointing to hardships within Iraq but doubting their effectiveness at reversing Saddam's policies — came in the same week, before the House Armed Services Committee. House Middle East Subcommittee Chairman Hamilton picked up on Webster's points when Baker appeared before the Foreign Affairs Committee.

"He said that Iraq can maintain its military readiness no more than nine months. He said that the air force is going to decline its capabilities within three months," Hamilton said. Why then, the lawmaker asked, should the administration not continue a policy of restraint?

Because, answered Baker, "there are significant costs that will be imposed upon us if we wait too long. How long is too long? I don't have an answer for that."

Democratic Caucus Resolution

Lawmakers, including many Republicans, also reiterated their demand to play a role in deciding if and when military action should be taken. The issue was touched off when Cheney told the Senate Armed Services panel Dec. 3 that the president could launch a military strike without prior congressional authorization.

"I do not believe the president requires any additional authorization from the Congress before committing U.S. forces to achieve our objectives in the gulf," Cheney said.

Reacting to the statement, the House Democratic Caucus on Dec. 4 approved a resolution explicitly stating that the president should first seek such authorization, unless American lives were in danger.

The caucus voted 177-37 in favor of the non-binding policy statement. But the closed-door debate over the issue revealed some differences within the Democratic Party.

The original statement, drafted by Richard J. Durbin,

D-Ill., one of the plaintiffs in the war powers suit, was a simple reaffirmation of the congressional power to declare war. Southern conservatives and those fearful of sending mixed signals to Iraq — as well as being seen as undercutting the president in a crisis — added language allowing for quick presidential action if lives were in jeopardy.

The caucus discussion was also shaped by a Washington Post-ABC News poll that showed that nearly two-thirds of those surveyed said the United States should go to war to oust Iraqi forces "at some point after Jan. 15."

Rep. Norm Dicks, D-Wash., said the Post-ABC poll was one factor behind his move in the Democratic Caucus to amend (with Rep. W. J. "Billy" Tauzin, D-La.) the Durbin resolution.

"Frankly, a lot of people were a little surprised about the Post-ABC poll, and that tempered some views," said Dicks, adding, "there would have been more 'no' votes if Durbin had remained unchanged."

Durbin, on the other hand, said the amendment did not undermine the primary purpose of his resolution.

Republicans also had varying views. Maine's Cohen warned Cheney against overly optimistic assumptions about the course of possible military action against Saddam. "History is littered with the bones of optimists and generals who thought they were headed for a short war," Cohen said.

But Senate GOP leader Dole said too many members were trying to "tie the president's hands behind his back."

"The president's policy is working," he declared. "The last thing we need are more timid signals from Congress."

Hostages Released

Bush achieved one of the major objectives of his Persian Gulf policy Dec. 6 when Saddam agreed to release all foreign hostages. But the success had no immediate impact on the policy debate in the United States.

Each side seized on the development as reinforcement for its position.

The president asserted that the hostage release was a sign that the tough line his administration had taken with Saddam was having an effect. The threat of war "is working," Bush said. "We've got to keep the pressure on."

During testimony before the House Foreign Affairs Committee, Secretary of State Baker said, "It seems no coincidence that this announcement comes just one week, just one week after the international community has authorized the use of force."

But the release undercut one of the principal justifications for the use of force and bolstered Democrats who had been calling for more patience.

Sen. Alan J. Dixon, D-Ill., called the planned release "further evidence" that a resolution to the crisis could be reached without resorting to military action. Maryland Democrat Sarbanes said the move could "represent the achievement of one of our major goals without the expenditure of any lives."

The Israel Factor

Bush shored up the multinational coalition against Iraq the week of Dec. 10, as the visiting prime minister of Israel agreed to maintain his country's role as a silent partner.

Israeli officials had expressed strong doubts about Bush's offer of direct talks between Baker and Saddam. But in two days of meetings with administration officials and congressional leaders, Prime Minister Yitzhak Shamir spoke in general terms of his support for Bush's efforts to force Iraq to abandon its conquest of neighboring Kuwait.

The United States had urged Israel to maintain a low profile in the crisis in the conviction that any visible role for Israel could jeopardize the Arab coalition against Iraq.

Apparently accepting that strategy, Shamir said that Israel should not be thought of as part of the "anti-Iraq coalition."

"We are not part of the decision-making — or the decision-makers," he told a forum of the American Enterprise Institute on Dec. 12.

Relations between the United States and Israel had been strained by the U.S. support of two Security Council resolutions in October criticizing Israel for excessive force in an Oct. 8 confrontation with Palestinian stone-throwers in Jerusalem that left 17 Palestinians dead and for the Shamir government's refusal to cooperate with a U.N. fact-finding mission on the incident. No substantive progress was announced on bilateral issues during Shamir's visit, but the Israeli leader and his U.S. hosts seemed relieved that, at least in appearance, the "special relationship" between Israel and the United States still held.

Shamir also left with something slightly more tangible: strong hints from lawmakers that they would consider new housing loan guarantees to help the government cope with its influx of Soviet immigrants.

"He clearly laid a foundation for Israel's economic plight," said Sen. John W. Warner, R-Va., after a meeting with Shamir. Sen. Joseph R. Biden Jr., D-Del., who hosted a coffee for the Israeli leader, said new loan guarantees "were raised as a possibility" during the session.

For its part, administration officials said they provided assurances that no solution to the gulf crisis would be pursued at Israel's expense. And Assistant Secretary of State Kelly told reporters, "The president did express appreciation for the low profile that the government of Israel has taken during the crisis."

Talks on Hold

The prospects for high-level talks between Washington and Baghdad remained in doubt throughout December as the United States and Iraq bickered over meeting dates.

When Bush publicly called for U.S.-Iraqi meetings, he invited Iraqi Foreign Minister Aziz to the White House on Dec. 17. He said a reciprocal visit by Baker to Saddam in Baghdad could come any time before Jan. 15.

However, the administration rejected Baghdad's counterproposal for a meeting Jan. 12 as being too close to the deadline for possible military action. The administration viewed the Iraqi proposal as an effort to corner the United States into extending the U.N. deadline.

Bush said Dec. 14 that he would stand firm on his revised proposal that a Saddam-Baker meeting had to take place before Jan. 3.

"To show flexibility, I have offered any one of 15 dates for Secretary Baker to go to Baghdad, and the Iraqis have offered only one date," Bush told reporters. "It simply is not credible that he cannot over a two-week period make a couple of hours available . . . unless, of course, he is seeking to circumvent the United Nations deadline."

Neither the duel over the meeting dates nor the broader state of U.S.-Iraqi relations was much affected by a surprise decision by Saddam to allow all foreigners, including U.S. citizens, to leave Iraq and Kuwait.

The last of several evacuation flights left Baghdad on Dec. 13 carrying Ambassador Nathaniel Howell and four

Continued on p. 746

Persian Gulf Crisis Brings Forth . . .

During the United States' 5½-month confrontation and six-week war with Iraq in late 1990 and early 1991, President Bush and officials of his administration put forth a variety of rationales and goals for their actions.

In the early days of the crisis, critics in Congress and elsewhere accused the administration of failing to define U.S. goals or to give the American people a convincing explanation of U.S. stakes in the Persian Gulf.

Later, as war appeared to be more and more likely, the administration found itself criticized from opposing perspectives. Some found the administration too eager to launch an attack against Iraq, while others faulted Bush for failing to adopt the explicit goal of dismantling Iraq's military capability and dislodging Iraqi President Saddam Hussein from power.

That debate continued even after Congress had voted on Jan. 12, 1991, to authorize the use of U.S. armed forces to oust Iraq from Kuwait and the U.S.-led forces began the air war on Jan. 16. And it remained unresolved when Bush declared a cease-fire Feb. 27 with Kuwait freed but Saddam still in power in Baghdad.

Following are some of the rationales and goals that the administration gave for its policy during the crisis:

Oil. The administration's most concrete immediate concern — and the public's — was the threat to oil supplies and stable oil prices.

"Iraq itself controls some 10 percent of the world's proven oil reserves," Bush told Congress on Sept. 11. "Iraq plus Kuwait controls twice that.

" . . . We cannot permit a resource so vital to be dominated by one so ruthless — and we won't."

The immediate effect of the invasion was a sharp rise in the world price of oil — from around $20 per barrel just before the invasion past $35 in October, the highest level since 1980. U.S. motorists saw gasoline prices rise in August by as much as 20 cents per gallon.

The pressure on prices was eased, however, when the Organization of Petroleum Exporting Countries (OPEC) voted Aug. 29 to let members increase production. By mid-January, the price was back below $20 per barrel.

Most members of Congress seconded the administration's concern about limiting Saddam's leverage over oil markets. But a few endorsed the criticism of protest groups that it was beneath the nation's loftier ideals to shed "blood for oil." Others said the crisis showed the need to turn to conservation and alternative energy sources in order to reduce the growing dependence on imported oil.

"Conservation is the key to an energy policy that will reduce our dependence on foreign oil and make the Saddam Husseins of the world as irrelevant to U.S. interests as they are hostile to American ideals," Rep. Gerry E. Studds, D-Mass., said in September.

Jobs. Attaching a lunch-bucket economic rationale to the threat to oil supplies, the administration on occasion argued that American jobs were at stake in the sands of Kuwait.

Bush in August told a group of Pentagon employees: "Our jobs, our way of life, our own freedom and the freedom of friendly countries around the world would all suffer if control of the world's great oil reserves fell into the hands of that one man, Saddam Hussein."

Secretary of State James A. Baker III hit harder on an economic rationale in comments to reporters Nov. 13 that drew a sharp negative reception.

"If you want to sum it up in one word," Baker said, "it's jobs. Because an economic recession, worldwide, caused by the control of one nation, one dictator, of the West's economic lifeline will result in the loss of jobs on the part of American citizens."

Economists generally agreed that the gulf crisis had the more immediate effect of contributing to the U.S. recession by feeding uncertainty and doubts among businesses and consumers. "The interaction of rising oil prices, Persian Gulf uncertainties and credit tightening is apparently creating a greater suppression of economic activity than the sum of the forces individually," Federal Reserve Chairman Alan Greenspan told the Senate House Banking Committee on Nov. 28.

The negative reaction accorded Baker's comments did not prevent him from returning to the point, warning the Senate Foreign Relations Committee on Dec. 5 of a possible "recession and depression, here and abroad" if Iraq did not withdraw from Kuwait. But neither lawmakers nor the American public appeared to rely on U.S. economic conditions for determining the best diplomatic or military course in the gulf.

Security of U.S. allies. A second immediate concern for the administration was Saudi Arabia's security.

"The sovereign independence of Saudi Arabia is of vital interest to the United States," Bush said Aug. 8 in announcing the first deployment of U.S. troops.

This goal, too, won virtually unanimous endorsement in Congress. But when the administration developed plans to sell Saudi Arabia sophisticated attack fighter planes, some pro-Israeli lawmakers questioned whether Israel's future security was being jeopardized. Despite its pro-American policy on most issues, Saudi Arabia lined up with other Arab states in refusing to recognize Israel and calling for a Palestinian homeland.

Once U.S. troops were stationed in Saudi Arabia, a new issue arose: the limited political and human rights that its citizens enjoyed. Saudi women were not permitted to drive, Americans learned. Religious freedom was not permitted, nor was there a free press.

Saudi King Fahd, sensitive to the criticism, announced plans in November to set up a consultative assembly. But when Sen. Joseph R. Biden Jr., D-Del., explained his reasons for voting against the use of force resolution in January, he complained that the "Saudi royal family" was "quite eager to witness the expenditure of American blood to rescue" its "lucrative and undemocratic" regime.

Restoring the Kuwaiti government. From the start of the crisis, Bush had coupled the goal of forcing Iraqi withdrawal from Kuwait with a demand that "Kuwait's legitimate government must be restored."

The exiled Kuwaiti government sought to keep its plight before the American public, helping finance a $5.7 million lobbying campaign, complete with U.S. pub-

... A Variety of Rationales, Objectives

lic relations and polling firms. "Kuwait has always been an oasis of peace and stability," Citizens for a Free Kuwait wrote in an open letter "to the American people" on Oct. 17. "Our country has long enjoyed a climate of freedom and respect for democracy under our constitution of 1962."

But the same questions raised about Saudi Arabia's internal policies were asked more pointedly about Kuwait, a country that had no great strategic importance to or history of close relations with the United States.

"Is Kuwait worth the life of a GI?" Sen. Ernest F. Hollings, D-S.C., asked in January. "Not really. . . . They haven't been our friend. They're certainly not a friend of democracy and human rights."

Hostages. Saddam's decision to prevent Americans and other Westerners from leaving Iraq or Kuwait after the Aug. 2 invasion, followed by his announcement that they would be relocated to military installations to be used as "human shields" against a U.S. attack, enraged Bush and Congress alike. But the administration, concerned about being pressured to stand down from the confrontation to secure their release, initially declined to characterize the detained Americans as hostages.

Even after Bush, on Aug. 20, declared the Americans hostages and vowed to hold Saddam responsible for their safety, he and others in the administration tried to avoid dramatizing the issue. For example, the administration declined to release a complete list of Americans held.

Saddam defused the issue Dec. 6 when he announced the release of all Americans and other Westerners.

Iraqi nuclear weapons. Bush abruptly injected the issue of Iraq's potential nuclear capability as he visited U.S. troops in Saudi Arabia over Thanksgiving. Defense Secretary Dick Cheney and national security adviser Brent Scowcroft elaborated on the issue during television interviews Nov. 25.

Cheney said that Iraq could have a crude nuclear device in as little as a year. Scowcroft described a wider time-range — "from months to as much as 10 years" — but said the risk made reliance on sanctions untenable.

Waiting a year or two, Scowcroft said, "raises the possibility that we could face an Iraq armed with nuclear weapons, which would dramatically change the character of any conflict."

But several Democratic senators, including Armed Services Committee Chairman Sam Nunn, D-Ga., and committee member Al Gore, D-Tenn., found the administration's warnings exaggerated and sided with independent experts who said Iraq was many years away from being able to make a reliable nuclear weapon.

Gore, who voted for the use of force resolution in January, simultaneously chided the administration for mishandling the nuclear issue, calling it "not helpful."

Deterring aggression. When he addressed the nation Aug. 8, Bush called the Iraqi invasion of Kuwait an "outrageous and brutal act of aggression" that had to be resisted. "Appeasement does not work," he warned, pointing to the diplomatic policies of the 1930s that failed to prevent World War II.

The administration returned time and again to the theme of deterring aggression. In a speech to the United Nations General Assembly on Oct. 1, Bush spoke of his goal for the post-Cold War world: a "new world order" that would be marked by a "new partnership of nations . . . based on consultation, cooperation and collective action."

Members on both sides of the aisle agreed on the goal of deterring aggression, but some Democrats chided the administration for applying its anti-aggression policies selectively.

"Naked aggression? Pick up the morning paper," Hollings said Jan. 12, pointing to Soviet military intervention in Lithuania. "Are we going to intervene to rescue Lithuania? Not a chance. Oh, Lithuania does not have oil."

More broadly, many Democrats and independent experts questioned whether the administration had any concrete plan for establishing security in the Mideast.

Ousting Saddam. Bush personalized the conflict with Saddam from the start of the crisis, likening him to Adolf Hitler, first by implication and then by name.

"We're dealing with Hitler revisited, a totalitarianism and brutality that is naked and unprecedented in modern times," Bush said at a political rally in Manchester, N.H., on Oct. 23.

Only after the war was under way, however, did the administration take the next step of calling for Saddam's ouster. But Bush and other officials were tentative on the point, insisting that Saddam's removal from power was not a U.S. objective in the war.

"We haven't shifted our objectives on this," Bush told a news conference Feb. 5.

"Now would I weep? Would I mourn, if somehow Saddam Hussein did not remain as head of his country?" Bush continued. " . . . I would like to think that somehow, some way that would happen, but I have no evidence that it will."

Bush's statements drew criticism from both sides. Some said he was, implicitly, going beyond forcing Iraq from Kuwait — the stated purpose of the Nov. 29 U.N. Security Council resolution. Others said he was failing to confront directly the question of whether a lasting peace was possible if the war left Saddam in power.

The administration's efforts to articulate the rationale for its policies came at the same time it was dealing with the nuts and bolts of a high-stakes international diplomatic initiative and a massive, long-distance deployment of U.S. troops.

In an interview with Cable News Network on Nov. 15, Bush acknowledged the criticisms of his administration's salesmanship on the crisis: "If I haven't done as clear a job as I might have on explaining this, then I've got to do better, because I know in my heart of hearts that what we are doing is right."

Despite the criticisms, however, public opinion polls measured consistently solid approval of Bush's actions — never falling below 55 percent. And shortly after the end of the war, Bush's overall approval rating — as measured by the Gallup Poll — stood at 89 percent, the highest of any post-World War II president.

Continued from p. 743
other diplomats who had kept open the U.S. Embassy in Kuwait for 13 weeks in defiance of Iraqi orders.

But Bush, meeting former hostages at the White House, rejected any suggestion of rewarding Saddam for freeing the foreign hostages. "Hell, no!... You don't reward a kidnapper," Bush said.

The Public's Views

The policy debate in Washington in November and December was conducted against a backdrop of continuing popular approval of the president's handling of the crisis but ambivalence about possible military action.

The Gallup Poll, which had measured 75 percent approval for Bush's actions in late August, recorded a drop to 57 percent by November — after the offensive buildup. But in December, the drop had been reversed. Gallup showed the public endorsing Bush's actions by 60 percent to 32 percent.

Significantly, the dip in Bush's approval rating in November was accompanied by a marked increase in the number of people who thought U.S. forces would become engaged in combat. In October, only 29 percent of those surveyed thought war was "very likely." The figure rose to 41 percent in November, then dipped again to 31 percent in December.

ABC News found a similar trend when it asked, "Just your best guess, do you think the United States is going to get involved in a war with Iraq, or not?" The percentage of those surveyed saying yes rose from 65 percent in September to 71 percent in mid-November and to 75 percent Nov. 30-Dec. 2 before dipping to 61 percent Dec. 9.

Poll results were ambiguous on whether the public favored going to war or sticking with sanctions. ABC News found a declining percentage of respondents who believed that the economic boycott would make Iraq withdraw from Kuwait: 53 percent in August, down to 38 percent Dec. 9. Solid majorities said the United States should take "all action necessary, including the use of military force," to make Iraq withdraw: 75 percent in September, 65 percent in December. And when the ABC poll specifically asked Dec. 9 whether the United States should go to war if Iraq had not withdrawn from Kuwait by Jan. 15, it recorded 58 percent saying yes, 38 percent saying no.

The Gallup Poll, however, recorded a different result Dec. 6-7 when it asked whether Bush "should begin military action" after Jan. 15 or "wait longer to see if economic and diplomatic sanctions are effective." Offered these alternatives, 41 percent of those surveyed favored military action, but 53 percent wanted to wait longer.

An ideologically disparate group weighed in to the debate in December to try to build support for a harder line against Iraq: not just forcing Iraq out of Kuwait but dismantling its military arsenal as well.

The Committee for Peace and Security in the Gulf included such conservative hard-liners as Perle, the hard-line former assistant secretary of Defense, and his Reagan administration colleague, former U.N. Ambassador Jeane J. Kirkpatrick. But Perle's co-chair was Ann F. Lewis, former political adviser to Democratic presidential candidate Jesse Jackson and a persistent critic of the Reagan administration's hawkish military policies.

"It's a very different set of people than I'm used to working with," said Lewis, who was joined by such liberal Democrats as New York Rep. Solarz and former House Majority Whip Tony Coelho of California. The committee made its debut at a Washington news conference Dec. 10.

From the opposite perspective, the Coalition to Stop U.S. Intervention in the Middle East, organized by former Attorney General Ramsey Clark, opposed the military deployment and sanctions against Iraq, arguing that the Iraq-Kuwait conflict should be left to Arabs.

Daring To Move First

As 1990 ended, it was often said that Bush and Saddam were engaged in a high-stakes game of chicken over whether to go to war. But Bush and Congress were also playing chicken, daring each other to make the first move to give lawmakers a decision-making role in the crisis.

Congressional leaders were maintaining it was up to Bush to seek congressional approval before launching a war. At the same time, the Bush administration began inviting Congress to take the initiative — provided, that is, that members were prepared unreservedly to endorse the U.N. resolution authorizing military force if Iraq did not reverse its invasion of Kuwait by Jan. 15.

"If the Congress would pass a resolution that mirrors the U.N. resolution, that would be very helpful," White House spokesman Marlin Fitzwater said Dec. 19. "But if we get a long, strung-out debate, that would not be helpful... Within the Congress itself, there is no clear consensus on whether or not they want a session, whether they want a resolution, whether they want a debate, whether they want to wait and see what happens. They don't know what they want to do."

By year's end, the mood in Congress had changed from fretful to anguished, not only over the best course for the nation to follow but also over the institutional responsibility to take a stand.

"To cast the vote to place other Americans in the line of fire is the most humbling, painful decision I can imagine," said Sen. Joseph I. Lieberman, D-Conn.

"This is the kind of issue that makes knees tremble in Congress," said Nebraska GOP Rep. Bereuter.

The anxiety appeared justified. Despite a spate of diplomatic initiatives, the elements for a major war were all in place. Nearly 1 million troops were poised along both sides of Kuwait's border with Saudi Arabia. One of the few missing pieces was a firm and formal stand by Congress.

Many lawmakers were determined to erase the stigma of Vietnam, when Congress effectively acquiesced while two successive administrations waged a costly and bloody war in Southeast Asia. "Congress simply ducked its responsibility in Vietnam," said Vermont Democrat Leahy.

But for all of the preoccupation with the legacy of that war, congressional opinion on the gulf crisis did not divide along the stark fault lines of the Vietnam debate.

This time there were not simply "hawks" who supported U.S. intervention and "doves" who opposed it. Instead, there was nearly universal agreement on the fundamentals — that Saddam was a dangerous enemy of U.S. interests and that strong action had to be taken to counter his invasion of Kuwait — but conflict and confusion in Congress over what to do next.

In spite of the seismic importance of the crisis, many members from both parties still had not developed well-defined views. "They won't admit it, but there are a lot of people here [in Congress] who would like the president to do something, and then they could take credit or place blame," said Rep. Wayne Owens, D-Utah.

Most Republicans appeared ready to back legislation patterned on the U.N. resolution authorizing the use of force to remove Iraqi troops from Kuwait. At the same time, members of the president's party did not hesitate to question, sometimes harshly, key aspects of the administration's policy and tactics.

Senate Minority Leader Dole was skeptical about one of the primary objectives set by the administration for Operation Desert Shield: the restoration of the legitimate government of Kuwait. Appearing on NBC's "Meet the Press" on Dec. 30, Dole said that returning the emir to power "wasn't worth one American life, as far as I'm concerned."

For Indiana Republican Lugar, the administration's goals were too limited. Perhaps more forcefully than any other Republican, he stressed the goal of eliminating Saddam's arsenal of chemical and biological weapons — a goal he had advocated as early as August.

The administration had left itself open to such questioning even from supporters of its policies by failing, in the view of many lawmakers, to precisely define U.S. goals in the crisis and the rationale underlying U.S. actions. *(U.S. policy rationales, objectives, p. 744)*

Republicans were far less divided or ambivalent, however, than Democrats.

On the surface, Democratic leaders presented a united front, partly because they dwelled more heavily on the policy-making process — the need for a congressional vote before force was used — than on the policy itself.

On matters of policy, Democratic leaders were somewhat elusive. They emphasized that they did not rule out the option of force but urged that it be used as a "last resort," as Senate Majority Leader Mitchell put it.

The most prominent, and perhaps most unexpected, voice of restraint was Nunn, the conservative chairman of the Armed Services Committee. He became the party's point man in arguing for continuing tough economic sanctions against Iraq rather than resorting to a quick use of military force.

The go-slow approach was tentatively endorsed by most, but not all, Democrats. House Majority Leader Richard A. Gephardt told a CNN interviewer that "probably a majority of Democrats would be for staying the course with sanctions."

Many Democrats were wary of establishing even a vague deadline for the possible use of force. A group of 110 Democrats, most from the liberal wing of the party, sent a letter to Bush on Dec. 27 urging continued restraint.

"So long as neither the lives of American citizens nor our troops are subjected to immediate danger and the international economic embargo continues to exert substantial pressure against Iraq," military action should not be initiated, said the letter, circulated by California Rep. George Miller, a lead plaintiff in the unsuccessful war powers suit.

At the same time, equally prominent Democrats wanted the party to move beyond the "force as last resort" stance adopted by their leadership.

Solarz, a House Foreign Affairs subcommittee chairman, emerged as the leading proponent of this view. But he too was less than explicit about when he would favor pulling the trigger on war. Instead, he emphasized his belief that "there isn't a reasonable chance that sanctions will do the job."

OPERATION DESERT STORM

Congress capped months of debate and indecision on Jan. 12, 1991, by authorizing Bush to use force against Iraq if it did not end its occupation of Kuwait. The measure passed with a wide margin of support in the House and more narrowly in the Senate.

Three days later, the U.N. Security Council deadline for Iraq to withdraw from Kuwait passed, with no Iraqi withdrawal. The next day, Jan. 16, Bush ordered the war (code-named Operation Desert Storm) to begin, sending waves of American fighters and missiles to attack Iraq in a devastating 38-day air attack.

On Feb. 23, after last-ditch efforts by the Soviet Union to broker a peace, Bush ordered a massive ground assault that ended the combat 100 hours later in a smashing victory for U.S. and allied forces.

Despite continued partisan bickering in Congress over the many Democrats who had opposed authorizing the use of force, there were bipartisan ovations when Bush appeared at the Capitol on March 6 to announce, "Aggression is defeated. The war is over."

The President's Letter

On Jan. 8, after months of hesitation at the White House, Bush sent congressional leaders a letter formally asking for the first time that Congress take action to approve a potential war in the gulf.

Bush's letter was crafted to avoid any suggestion that he was constitutionally required to obtain congressional approval.

Instead, he described the issue as one of sending Saddam a strong signal of U.S. determination.

Letter to Congress

Following is the text of President Bush's letter to Congress on Jan. 8, 1991, requesting passage of a resolution authorizing the use of force in the Persian Gulf:

The current situation in the Persian Gulf, brought about by Iraq's unprovoked invasion and subsequent brutal occupation of Kuwait, threatens vital U.S. interests. The situation also threatens the peace. It would, however, greatly enhance the chances for peace if Congress were now to go on record supporting the position adopted by the U.N. Security Council on twelve separate occasions. Such an action would underline that the United States stands with the international community and on the side of law and decency; it also would help dispel any belief that may exist in the minds of Iraq's leaders that the United States lacks the necessary unity to act decisively in response to Iraq's continued aggression against Kuwait.

Secretary of State [James A. Baker] Baker [III] is meeting with Iraq's Foreign Minister [Tariq Aziz]] on January 9. It would have been most constructive if he could have presented the Iraqi government a Resolution passed by both houses of Congress supporting the U.N. position and in particular Security Council Resolution 678. As you know, I have frequently stated my desire for such a Resolution. Nevertheless, there is still opportunity for Congress to act to strengthen the prospects for peace and safeguard this country's vital interests.

I therefore request that the House of Representatives and the Senate adopt a Resolution stating that Congress supports the use of all necessary means to implement U.N. Security Council Resolution 678. Such action would send the clearest possible message to Saddam Hussein that he must withdraw without condition or delay from Kuwait. Anything less would only encourage Iraqi intransigence; anything else would risk detracting from the international coalition arrayed against Iraq's aggression.

I am determined to do whatever is necessary to protect America's security. I ask Congress to join with me in this task. I can think of no better way than for Congress to express its support for the President at this critical time. This truly is the last best chance for peace. ■

Resolution Authorizing Use of Force

Following is the text of the Authorization for Use of Military Force Against Iraq Resolution (H J Res 77 — PL 102-1) passed by Congress on Jan. 12, 1991, and signed by President Bush on Jan. 14. The House approved the resolution by a vote of 250-183; the Senate passed the measure (originally introduced as S J Res 2) by a vote of 52-47.

To authorize the use of United States Armed Forces pursuant to United Nations Security Council resolution 678.

Whereas the Government of Iraq without provocation invaded and occupied the territory of Kuwait on August 2, 1990; and

Whereas both the House of Representatives (in H J Res 658 of the 101st Congress) and the Senate (in S Con Res 147 of the 101st Congress) have condemned Iraq's invasion of Kuwait and declared their support for international action to reverse Iraq's aggression; and

Whereas, Iraq's conventional, chemical, biological, and nuclear weapons and ballistic missile programs and its demonstrated willingness to use weapons of mass destruction pose a grave threat to world peace; and

Whereas the international community has demanded that Iraq withdraw unconditionally and immediately from Kuwait and that Kuwait's independence and legitimate government be restored; and

Whereas the U.N. Security Council repeatedly affirmed the inherent right of individual or collective self-defense in response to the armed attack by Iraq against Kuwait in accordance with Article 51 of the U.N. Charter; and

Whereas, in the absence of full compliance by Iraq with its resolutions, the U.N. Security Council in Resolution 678 has authorized member states of the United Nations to use all necessary means, after January 15, 1991, to uphold and implement all relevant Security Council resolutions and to restore international peace and security in the area; and

Whereas Iraq has persisted in its illegal occupation of, and brutal aggression against, Kuwait: Now, therefore be it

Resolved by the Senate and House of Representatives of the United States of America in Congress assembled,

Section 1. Short Title. This joint resolution may be cited as the "Authorization for Use of Military Force Against Iraq Resolution."

Section 2. Authorization for Use of United States Armed Forces

(a) AUTHORIZATION. — The President is authorized, subject to subsection (b), to use United States Armed Forces pursuant to United Nations Security Council Resolution 678 (1990) in order to achieve implementation of Security Council Resolutions 660, 661, 662, 664, 665, 666, 667, 669, 670, 674, and 677.

(b) REQUIREMENT FOR DETERMINATION THAT USE OF MILITARY FORCE IS NECESSARY. — Before exercising the authority granted in subsection (a), the President shall make available to the Speaker of the House of Representatives and the President pro tempore of the Senate his determination that —

(1) the United States has used all appropriate diplomatic and other peaceful means to obtain compliance by Iraq with the United Nations Security Council resolutions cited in subsection (a); and

(2) that those efforts have not been successful in obtaining such compliance.

(c) WAR POWERS RESOLUTION REQUIREMENTS. —

(1) SPECIFIC STATUTORY AUTHORIZATION. — Consistent with section 8(a)(1) of the War Powers Resolution, the Congress declares that this section is intended to constitute specific statutory authorization within the meaning of section 5(b) of the War Powers Resolution.

(2) APPLICABILITY OF OTHER REQUIREMENTS. — Nothing in this resolution supersedes any requirement of the War Powers Resolution.

Section 4. REPORTS TO CONGRESS.

At least once every 60 days, the President shall submit to the Congress a summary on the status of efforts to obtain compliance by Iraq with the resolutions adopted by the United Nations Security Council in response to Iraq's aggression. ■

"I therefore request that the House of Representatives and the Senate adopt a Resolution stating that Congress supports the use of all necessary means to implement U.N. Security Council Resolution 678," Bush wrote.

"Such action would send the clearest possible message to Saddam Hussein that he must withdraw without condition or delay from Kuwait. Anything less would only encourage Iraqi intransigence; anything else would risk detracting from the international coalition arrayed against Iraq's aggression."

The letter made history in itself: It was the first such request by a president since the 1964 Gulf of Tonkin Resolution that authorized the use of force in Vietnam. *(Bush letter, p. 747)*

A Letter to Saddam

A second letter also contributed to the mood as Congress prepared for its debate over war. A letter from Bush to Saddam, it was to have been delivered by Baker to Iraqi Foreign Minister Aziz when the two men held their much delayed meeting in Geneva on Jan. 9.

Bush had suggested the session in Geneva on Jan. 3, after weeks of diplomatic stalemate on his original proposal for sequential visits by Aziz to Washington and Baker to Baghdad. Iraq agreed to the Geneva meeting on Jan. 4.

Baker opened the meeting by handing Aziz the letter from Bush.

After reading it, the Iraqi minister said he would not take it to Saddam, complaining that Bush had not used "polite language."

The letter, which Bush subsequently released, largely reiterated his demand that Saddam pull his forces out of Kuwait. While insisting that the administration would never negotiate with Baghdad, the president said that "Iraq will gain the opportunity to rejoin the international community," if it complied with the U.N. resolutions.

While the letter contained little new material, Aziz's rejection came to symbolize the unyielding stance he took in his meeting with Baker and provided yet another argument for lawmakers advocating a tough line against Iraq.

"He stiffed us," said Pennsylvania Democrat Murtha. "We got an excellent illustration of Iraqi intransigence" at the meeting, said Sen. Christopher S. Bond, R-Mo.

Congress Acts

On Jan. 12, Congress gave the president what he sought, voting to authorize the use of force unless Iraq withdrew from Kuwait.

The Senate voted 52-47 for the "Authorization for Use of Military Force Against Iraq Resolution." Ten Democrats joined with virtually unanimous Republicans in support of the resolution (S J Res 2). *(Senate vote, p. 749)*

Minutes later, the House approved identical legislation (H J Res 77) by a vote of 250-183. An unusual alliance of Republicans, Northeastern liberals and conservative Democrats gave Bush a solid victory. *(House vote, p. 750)*

The vote came just three days before the expiration of the U.N. deadline, after which member nations were authorized to "use all necessary means" to force Iraq to withdraw from Kuwait.

The joint congressional resolution authorized the president "to use United States Armed Forces" to enforce the ultimatum set by the U.N. Security Council. *(Use of force resolution, p. 748)*

"This sends the clearest message to Iraq that it cannot scorn the Jan. 15 deadline," Bush said after Congress acted. He signed the measure (PL 102-1) on Jan. 14.

The decision was taken in an atmosphere of almost mournful solemnity. It marked the first time since World War II that Congress had directly confronted the issue of sending large numbers of American forces into combat.

Passage of the resolution put the political and constitutional weight of the legislative branch behind Bush as he prepared the nation for potential battle. But the divided vote showed continuing doubts in Congress over the wisdom of going to war. *(Members' anguished debate, p. 752)*

Underscoring much of the debate was a sense that the legislative branch had acted too late to have any real choice except to back Bush in his showdown with Iraq. Sen. Charles S. Robb, D-Va., a key administration supporter, said it would be a "fundamental mistake to give even the appearance of withdrawing our trust and support."

During the dignified, often moving, congressional debate, some members offered prayers for the country, the president and the nearly 400,000 U.S. troops arrayed against Iraqi forces in the Persian Gulf.

Even though lawmakers differed significantly over U.S. gulf policy, they said they would close ranks behind the president after the debate and vote.

House Majority Leader Gephardt said before the final vote, "Whatever our decision, we will leave this room one again and whole again."

After the vote, even the winners spoke in subdued tones. "Normally, after a bipartisan victory, for me there's jubilation," said House Republican leader Robert H. Michel, Ill. "This is different."

Conflicts Lingered

The expressions of unity could not hide the conflicts that remained in Congress, especially the Senate, over gulf policy. Even after the outcome was no longer in doubt, senators rejected calls to back the president and voted largely along party lines.

When it became clear that Bush's position would prevail by a small margin in the Senate, Paul Simon, D-Ill., said the vote "shows a deeply divided Congress and a deeply divided American people."

"There is no consensus in America for war," said Sen. John Kerry, D-Mass.

Most Democrats in both chambers supported alternative resolutions sponsored by their leaders (S J Res 1, H Con Res 33) that called for maintaining economic sanctions against Iraq while deferring the decision to use military action.

Majority Leader Mitchell, who led the Senate effort to block authorization for war, passionately pleaded against the administration's contention that relying on economic sanctions was too risky.

"Prematurely abandoning the sanctions and immediately going to war also involves risk," Mitchell said as he opened debate Jan. 10. "The risk there is foremost in human life. How many people will die? How many young Americans will die? That's a risk, a terrible risk.

"Just this morning I heard it said that there may be only a few thousand American casualties. For the families of those few thousand — the fathers and mothers, husbands and wives, daughters and sons — the word 'only' will have no meaning," he said. "And the truly haunting question, which no one will ever be able to answer, will be: Did they die unnecessarily? For if we go to war now, no one will ever know if sanctions would have worked if given a full and fair chance."

In the end, a bare majority of senators found the administration's arguments compelling. Minority Leader Dole argued Bush's case that only the credible threat of force would cause Saddam to relent: "The best chance for peace

Use of Force Resolution: Senate Vote

Following is the 52-to-47 roll call by which the Senate passed a resolution (S J Res 2) authorizing authorizing President Bush to use military force against Iraq pursuant to U.N. Security Council Resolution 678. Voting yes were 9 Democrats and 43 Republicans; voting no were 45 Democrats and 2 Republicans; xxx denotes senators not voting.

Adams, D-Wash., no; Akaka, D-Hawaii, no; Baucus, D-Mont., no; Bentsen, D-Texas, no.

Biden, D-Del., no; Bingaman, D-N.M., no; Bond, R-Mo., yes; Boren, D-Okla., no;

Bradley, D-N.J., no; Breaux, D-La., yes; Brown, R-Colo., yes; Bryan, D-Nev., yes; Bumpers, D-Ark., no; Burdick, D-N.D., no.

Burns, R-Mont., yes; Byrd, D-W.Va., no; Chafee, R-R.I., yes; Coats, R-Ind., yes; Cochran, R-Miss., yes.

Cohen, R-Maine, yes; Conrad, D-N.D., no; Craig, R-Idaho, yes; Cranston, D-Calif., xxx; D'Amato, R-N.Y., yes; Danforth, R-Mo., yes.

Daschle, D-S.D., no; DeConcini, D-Ariz., no; Dixon, D-Ill., no; Dodd, D-Conn., no; Dole, R-Kan., yes.

Domenici, R-N.M., yes; Durenberger, R-Minn., yes; Exon, D-Neb., no; Ford, D-Ky., no; Fowler, D-Ga., no.

Garn, R-Utah, yes; Glenn, D-Ohio, no; Gore, D-Tenn., yes; Gorton, R-Wash., yes; Graham, D-Fla., yes.

Gramm, R-Texas, yes; Grassley, R-Iowa, no; Harkin, D-Iowa, no; Hatch, R-Utah, yes; Hatfield, R- Ore., no.

Heflin, D-Ala., yes; Heinz, R-Pa., yes; Helms, R-N.C., yes; Hollings, D-S.C., no;

Inouye, D-Hawaii, no; Jeffords, R-Vt., yes; Johnston, D-La., yes; Kassebaum, R-Kan., yes; Kasten, R-Wis., yes

Kennedy, D-Mass., no; Kerrey, D-Neb., no; Kerry, D-Mass., no; Kohl, D-Wis., no; Lautenberg, D- N.J., no.

Leahy, D-Vt., no; Levin, D-Mich., no; Lieberman, D-Conn, yes; Lott, R-Miss., yes; Lugar, R-Ind., yes.

Mack, R-Fla., yes; McCain, R-Ariz., yes; McConnell, R-Ky., yes; Metzenbaum, D-Ohio, no.

Mikulski, D-Md., no; Mitchell, D-Maine, no; Moynihan, D-N.Y., no; Murkowski, R-Alaska, yes; Nickles, R-Okla., yes.

Nunn, D-Ga., no; Packwood, R-Ore., yes; Pell, D-R.I., no; Pressler, R-S.D., yes; Pryor, D-Ark., no,

Reid, D-Nev., yes; Riegle, D-Mich., no; Robb, D-Va., yes; Rockefeller, D-W.Va., no; Roth, R-Del., yes.

Rudman, R-N.H., yes; Sanford, D-N.C., no; Sarbanes, D-Md., no; Sasser, D-Tenn., no; Seymour, Calif., yes; Shelby, D-Ala., yes.

Simon, D-Ill., no; Simpson, R-Wyo., yes; Smith, R-N.H., yes; Specter, R-Pa., yes; Stevens, R-Alaska, yes; Symms, R-Idaho, yes.

Thurmond, R-S.C., yes; Wallop, R-Wyo., yes; Warner, R-Va., yes; Wellstone, Minn., no; Wirth, D-Colo., no.

Use of Force Resolution: House Vote

Following is the 250-183 roll call by which the House passed a resolution (H J Res 77) authorizing President Bush to use military force against Iraq pursuant to U.N. Security Council Resolution 678. Voting yes were 86 Democrats and 164 Republicans. Voting no were 179 Democrats and 3 Republicans. Also voting no was 1 Independent. (X denotes those not voting.)

ALABAMA
Democrats — Bevill, yes; Browder, yes; Cramer, yes; Erdreich, yes; Harris, yes.
Republicans — Callahan, yes; Dickinson, yes.
ALASKA
Republican — Young, yes.
ARIZONA
Democrat — Udall, X.
Republicans — Kolbe, yes; Kyl, yes; Rhodes, yes; Stump, yes.
ARKANSAS
Democrats — Alexander, no; Anthony, no; Thornton, yes.
Republican — Hammerschmidt, yes.
CALIFORNIA
Democrats — Anderson, yes; Beilenson, no; Berman, yes; Boxer, no; Brown, no; Condit, yes; Dellums, no; Dixon, no; Dooley, no; Dymally, X; Edwards, no; Fazio, no; Lantos, yes; Lehman, yes; Levine, yes; Martinez, no; Matsui, no; Miller, no; Mineta, no; Panetta, no; Pelosi, no; Roybal, no; Stark, no; Torres, no; Waters, no; Waxman, no.
Republicans — Campbell, yes; Cox, yes; Cunningham, yes; Dannemeyer, yes; Doolittle, yes; Dornan, yes; Dreier, yes; Gallegly, yes; Herger, yes; Hunter, yes; Lagomarsino, yes; Lewis, yes; Lowery, yes; McCandless, yes; Moorhead, yes; Packard, yes; Riggs, no; Rohrabacher, yes; Thomas, yes.
COLORADO
Democrats — Campbell, yes; Schroeder, no; Skaggs, no.
Republicans — Allard, yes; Hefley, yes; Schaefer, yes.
CONNECTICUT
Democrats — DeLauro, no; Gejdenson, no; Kennelly, no.
Republicans — Franks, yes; Johnson, yes; Shays, yes.
DELAWARE
Democrat — Carper, yes.
FLORIDA
Democrats — Bacchus, yes; Bennett, no; Fascell, yes; Gibbons, no; Hutto, yes; Johnston, no; Lehman, no; Peterson, no; Smith, no.
Republicans — Bilirakis, yes; Goss, yes; Ireland, yes; James, yes; Lewis, yes; McCollum, yes; Ros-Lehtinen, yes; Shaw, yes; Stearns, yes; Young, yes.
GEORGIA
Democrats — Barnard, yes; Darden, yes; Hatcher, yes; Jen kins, no; Jones, yes; Lewis, no; Ray, yes; Rowland, yes; Thomas, yes.
Republican — Gingrich, yes.
HAWAII
Democrats — Abercrombie, no; Mink, no.
IDAHO
Democrat — LaRocco, no; Stallings, no.
ILLINOIS
Democrats — Annunzio, no; Bruce, no; Collins, no; Costello, no; Cox, no; Durbin, no; Evans, no; Hayes, no; Lipinski, no; Poshard, no; Rostenkowski, yes; Russo, no; Sangmeister, no; Savage, no; Yates, no.
Republicans — Crane, yes; Fawell, yes; Hastert, yes; Hyde, yes; Madigan, yes; Michel, yes; Porter, yes.
INDIANA
Democrats — Hamilton, no; Jacobs, no; Jontz, no; Long, no; McCloskey, no; Roemer, no; Sharp, no; Visclosky, no.
Republicans — Burton, yes; Myers, yes.
IOWA
Democrats — Nagle, no; Smith, no.
Republicans — Grandy, yes; Leach, yes; Lightfoot, yes; Nussle, yes.
KANSAS
Democrats — Glickman, yes; Slattery, yes.
Republicans — Meyers, yes; Nichols, yes; Roberts, yes.
KENTUCKY
Democrats — Hubbard, yes; Mazzoli, no; Natcher, no; Perkins, no.
Republicans — Bunning, yes; Hopkins, yes; Rogers, yes.
LOUISIANA
Democrats — Hayes, yes; Huckaby, yes; Jefferson, no; Tauzin, yes.
Republicans — Baker, yes; Holloway, yes; Livingston, yes; McCrery, yes.
MAINE
Democrat — Andrews, no
Republican — Snowe, yes
MARYLAND
Democrats — Byron, yes; Cardin, no; Hoyer, no; McMillen, yes; Mfume, no.
Republicans — Bentley, yes; Gilchrest, yes; Morella, no.
MASSACHUSETTS
Democrats — Atkins, no; Donnelly, no; Early, no; Frank, no; Kennedy, no; Markey, no; Mavroules, no; Moakley, no; Neal, no; Studds, no.
Republican — Conte, no.
MICHIGAN
Democrats — Bonior, no; Carr, no; Collins, no; Conyers, no; Dingell, yes; Ford, no; Hertel, no; Kildee, no; Levin, no; Traxler, no; Wolpe, no.
Republicans — Broomfield, yes; Camp, yes; Davis, yes; Henry, yes; Pursell, yes; Upton, yes; Vander Jagt, yes.
MINNESOTA
Democrats — Oberstar, no; Penny, no; Peterson, no; Sabo, no; Sikorski, no; Vento, no.
Republicans — Ramstad, yes; Weber, yes.

and the best hope for peace is to strengthen the president's hand any way we can," Dole said.

Senate Vote

As Congress opened debate, the administration could count on virtually unanimous support from Republicans but had to win over enough votes from divided Democrats.

Mitchell put his prestige on the line to lead the Senate opposition. Nunn played a pivotal role because his opposition to the early use of force deprived the administration of the united support it usually received on defense issues from conservative Southern Democrats.

The administration and its supporters delayed introducing a resolution supporting force until the second day of Senate debate, Jan. 11, when they became increasingly confident that they would prevail.

Gradually, a contingent of Senate Democrats supporting Bush began to take shape. Four Democrats joined in cosponsoring the resolution: Lieberman, Robb, and Alabama's Howell Heflin and Richard C. Shelby.

But the process of lining up Democrats and keeping Republicans on board was difficult. Key conservative Democrats, such as Intelligence Committee Chairman Boren, joined Nunn instead. And Charles E. Grassley of Iowa became a surprise Republican defector, joining Oregon's Mark O. Hatfield.

In the end, the administration cobbled together a group of 10 Senate Democrats, three more than needed: Heflin,

MISSISSIPPI
Democrats — Espy, no; Montgomery, yes; Parker, yes; Taylor, no; Whitten, yes.
MISSOURI
Democrats — Clay, no; Gephardt, no; Horn, no; Skelton, yes; Volkmer, yes; Wheat, no.
Republicans — Coleman, yes; Emerson, yes; Hancock, yes.
MONTANA
Democrat — Williams, no.
Republican — Marlenee, yes.
NEBRASKA
Democrat — Hoagland, yes.
Republicans — Barrett, yes; Bereuter, yes.
NEVADA
Democrat — Bilbray, yes.
Republican — Vucanovich, yes.
NEW HAMPSHIRE
Democrat — Swett, yes.
Republicans — Zeliff, yes.
NEW JERSEY
Democrats — Andrews, no; Dwyer, no; Guarini, no; Hughes, yes; Pallone, yes; Payne, no; Roe, no; Torricelli, yes.
Republicans — Gallo, yes; Rinaldo, yes; Roukema, yes; Saxton, yes; Smith, yes; Zimmer, yes.
NEW MEXICO
Democrat — Richardson, no.
Republicans — Schiff, yes; Skeen, yes.
NEW YORK
Democrats — Ackerman, yes; Downey, no; Engel, yes; Flake, no; Hochbrueckner, no; LaFalce, no; Lowey, no; Manton, no; McHugh, no; McNulty, yes; Mrazek, no; Nowak, no; Owens, no; Rangel, no; Scheuer, no; Schumer, no; Serrano, no; Slaughter, no; Solarz, yes; Towns, no; Weiss, no.
Republicans — Boehlert, yes; Fish, yes; Gilman, yes; Green, yes; Horton, yes; Houghton, yes; Lent, yes; Martin, yes; McGrath, yes; Molinari, yes; Paxon, yes; Solomon, yes; Walsh, yes.
NORTH CAROLINA
Democrats — Hefner, no; Jones, yes; Lancaster, yes; Neal, no; Price, no; Rose, no; Valentine, yes.
Republicans — Ballenger, yes; Coble, yes; McMillan, yes, Taylor, yes.
NORTH DAKOTA
Democrat — Dorgan, no.
OHIO
Democrats — Applegate, no; Eckart, no; Feighan, no; Hall, no; Kaptur, no; Luken, yes; Oakar, no; Pease, no; Sawyer, no; Stokes, no; Traficant, no.
Republicans — Boehner, yes; Gillmor, yes; Gradison, yes; Hobson, yes; Kasich, yes; McEwen, yes; Miller, yes; Oxley, yes; Regula, yes; Wylie, yes.
OKLAHOMA
Democrats — Brewster, yes; English, no; McCurdy, yes; Synar, no.
Republicans — Edwards, yes; Inhofe, yes.
OREGON
Democrats — AuCoin, no; DeFazio, no; Kopetski, no; Wyden, no.
Republicans — Smith, yes.
PENNSYLVANIA
Democrats — Borski, yes; Coyne, no; Foglietta, no; Gaydos, no; Gray, no; Kanjorski, no; Kolter, no; Kostmayer, no; Murphy, no; Murtha, yes; Yatron, no.
Republicans — Clinger, yes; Coughlin, yes; Gekas, yes; Goodling, yes; McDade, yes; Ridge, yes; Ritter, yes; Santorum, yes; Schulze, yes; Shuster, yes; Walker, yes; Weldon, yes.
RHODE ISLAND
Democrat — Reed, no.
Republican — Machtley, yes.
SOUTH CAROLINA
Democrats — Derrick, yes; Patterson, yes; Spratt, yes; Tallon, yes.
Republicans — Ravenel, yes; Spence, yes.
SOUTH DAKOTA
Democrat — Johnson, no.
TENNESSEE
Democrats — Clement, yes; Cooper, yes; Ford, no; Gordon, yes; Lloyd, yes; Tanner, yes.
Republicans — Duncan, yes; Quillen, yes; Sundquist, yes.
TEXAS
Democrats — Andrews, yes; Brooks, yes; Bryant, no; Bustamante, no; Chapman, yes; Coleman, no; de la Garza, yes; Edwards, yes; Frost, yes; Geren, yes; Gonzalez, no; Hall, yes; Laughlin, yes; Ortiz, yes; Pickle, no; Sarpalius, yes; Stenholm, yes; Washington, no; Wilson, yes.
Republicans — Archer, yes; Armey, yes; Bartlett, yes; Barton, yes; Combest, yes; DeLay, yes; Fields, yes; Smith, yes.
UTAH
Democrats — Orton, yes; Owens, no.
Republican — Hansen, yes.
VERMONT
Independent — Sanders, no.
VIRGINIA
Democrats — Boucher, no; Moran, no; Olin, no; Payne, yes; Pickett, yes; Sisisky, yes.
Republicans — Bateman, yes; Bliley, yes; Slaughter, yes; Wolf, yes.
WASHINGTON
Democrats — Dicks, no; Foley, no; McDermott, no; Swift, no; Unsoeld, no.
Republicans — Chandler, yes; Miller, yes; Morrison, yes.
WEST VIRGINIA
Democrats — Mollohan, yes; Rahall, yes; Staggers, no; Wise, no.
WISCONSIN
Democrats — Aspin, yes; Kleczka, no; Moody, no; Obey, no.
Republicans — Gunderson, yes; Klug, yes; Petri, yes; Roth, yes; Sensenbrenner, yes.
WYOMING
Republican — Thomas, yes.

Lieberman, Robb, Shelby, Louisiana's John B. Breaux and J. Bennett Johnston, Nevada's Richard H. Bryan and Harry Reid, and Tennessee's Al Gore.

With the exception of Hatfield, who voted against both resolutions, senators split the same way on a resolution offered by Mitchell and Nunn that demanded a continued reliance on economic sanctions. That measure (S J Res 1) was defeated, 46-53.

The only absentee — liberal Democrat Alan Cranston, who was undergoing cancer treatment in his home state of California — did not say how he would have voted.

House Vote

In the House, the administration had a much more comfortable margin entering the debate. The opponents of the resolution authorizing force, led by Speaker Foley, faced what both sides agreed was an uphill battle.

Nunn's counterpart on the House Armed Services Committee, Aspin, weeks before had voiced his skepticism that sanctions would work and predicted as the debate began that war would produce a quick U.S. victory.

Liberal Democrat Solarz, who cosponsored the winning resolution with House GOP leader Michel, worked to bring together disparate Democrats to support the president.

Foley remained relatively silent through much of the debate but emerged in the closing hours as his chamber's most eloquent opponent of a resolution authorizing force.

For Foley, the administration's central claim — that it

Members' Anguish: The Passionate Debate

Members said it over and over and over again. Whether they had been in Congress two days or 22 years, in all their time they had never seen a debate quite like the one that began Jan. 10 at 11:40 a.m. in the Senate and 4:10 p.m. in the House.

Over three days, hundreds of legislators went to the wells of their respective chambers and poured their hearts out.

For the first time in anyone's memory, the U.S. Congress was debating openly and extensively whether the president should be authorized to take the country, unprovoked by direct attack, into war.

It was a decision many members considered a gamble, and their fears and anguish were clear to the hundreds who listened from the chambers and the thousands or even millions who watched on television. It was a rare look at passion in the legislative process.

"In 26 years in the House of Representatives, I have never seen this House more serious nor more determined to speak its heart and mind on a question than they are at this time on this day," Speaker Thomas S. Foley, D-Wash., said the day of the final vote, which concluded one of the longest single debates in House history.

In a place where members had been known to wear pig masks to ridicule pork-barrel spending and where each party had booed and hissed the other, discourse was somber, thoughtful and nonpartisan. This, despite a final vote that reflected deep divisions and found party leaders on opposing sides.

Instead, members talked of the awesome responsibility they felt and of their distress at having to choose between what many saw as two equally uncertain courses of action.

Sen. Robert C. Byrd, D-W.Va., said that of the 12,822 votes he had cast during his 38 years in Congress, this was the most important and also one of the most troubling: "My natural instincts are to support the president today. . . . But the question before the Senate is too grave to be decided by gut feelings. . . . I think it is better to be wise than simply tough."

Sens. Charles E. Grassley, R-Iowa, John C. Danforth, R-Mo., and others spoke of agonizing internal struggles as they tried to choose between using force or economic sanctions against Iraqi President Saddam Hussein. "I was hoping for a miracle, hoping for an answer to my prayers, but of course it did not happen," said Grassley, who ultimately opposed his party's president.

On the other side of the Capitol, House Minority Leader Robert H. Michel, R-Ill., a veteran of World War II, made an emotional plea to members not to forget the lessons of the past: "Those of our generation know from bloody experience that unchecked aggression against a small nation is a prelude to international disaster. . . . Patience at any price is not a policy. It is a cop-out."

But others said history had taught them something different. Newly elected Florida Democrat Pete Peterson, a former Vietnam prisoner of war, told colleagues: "I vowed when I sat in Hanoi that I would never commit troops to battle without the support of the American people."

History hung heavily over the debate, as members invoked not only the lessons of past wars but the words of Socrates, Abraham Lincoln, James Madison and Winston Churchill. Byrd quoted from the Bible, Sen. Edward M. Kennedy, D-Mass., read Robert Frost, and Sen. Wyche Fowler Jr., D-Ga., quoted Thucydides. On a more contemporary note, Rep. Barbara Boxer, D-Calif., read the lyrics of a Bette Midler song.

When Rep. Joseph P. Kennedy II, D-Mass., implored members to think about facing the mothers and fathers of those who might be killed in the Persian Gulf, Rep. Gerald B. H. Solomon, R-N.Y., responded with the words of Kennedy's late uncle, President John F. Kennedy, during the 1962 Cuban missile crisis: "The greatest danger of all would be to do nothing."

Perhaps most moving were the personal histories.

---

was seeking to threaten war to avoid war — was badly flawed. Making a rare speech from the well, he told his colleagues that they should have no illusions that supporting the resolution authorizing the use of force would simply help Bush make a show of U.S. determination.

"Do not do it under the notion that you merely hand him another diplomatic tool, another arrow in the quiver of economic leverage or international leverage," Foley said. "The president has signaled no doubt about this. He has said again and again that if given the power, he may well use it, perhaps sooner than we realize."

Yet those who backed the administration gave no ground. "Saddam Hussein has a choice," said Solarz, "between leaving [Kuwait] and living, and staying and dying."

Stating the choice in stark terms "offers the best chance for peace," said Solarz, who closed the debate on the resolution.

Among the 86 Democrats who backed the House resolution authorizing force were several committee chairmen, including Dan Rostenkowski, Ill., and John D. Dingell, Mich. Because the issue was deemed "a conscience vote" by the leadership, there were promises of no recriminations against those who voted with the administration.

Three Republicans voted against the administration: Silvio O. Conte, Mass.; Constance A. Morella, Md.; and Frank Riggs, Calif.

The resolution urging continued reliance on sanctions (H Con Res 33), cosponsored by Gephardt and Hamilton, fell by the same 183-250 margin that produced victory for the authorization to use force.

'The Constitution Prevailed'

By the time Congress finally debated an authorization for war, months of feuding with the White House over the constitutional role of the two branches was beside the point. But House leaders scheduled a debate and vote first on a concurrent resolution (H Con Res 32) asserting congressional war-making powers.

The resolution — cosponsored by Democrats Durbin of Illinois and Charles E. Bennett of Florida — was adopted 302-131, with five Democrats and 126 Republicans voting against it.

Over Authorizing Use of Force in the Gulf

Florida Democratic Reps. Charles E. Bennett and Sam M. Gibbons, both World War II veterans, spoke of the deep burden they felt for their votes supporting a resolution in 1964 authorizing the use of force in Vietnam. They urged colleagues not to repeat what they said was their mistake.

But Republican Rep. Barbara F. Vucanovich of Nevada, recalling a brother who died in military action, said sometimes sacrifices were required: "If we do nothing, and Saddam Hussein pays no price for swallowing up the country of Kuwait, destroying people's property, torturing, raping and killing innocent men and women and children, we are as guilty as he is."

Speaking on the Senate floor, Hawaii Democrat Daniel K. Inouye, who lost his right arm in World War II, cautioned against hasty military action. He was followed by Minority Leader Bob Dole of Kansas, who lost the use of his right hand in the same war but asked members not to give Saddam a "holiday" by failing to authorize force.

Republican Sen. William S. Cohen of Maine remarked that he was struck by the very different conclusions that members drew from such experiences of war: "They remind us that there are no absolutes, no blueprints from the past that will provide a clear guide to the right decision. So we are left to make judgments while doubt sits like a raven on our shoulders and taunts us."

It was the gravity of the choice before them and the uncertainty of its results that made the deliberations unlike most others that members had seen. Leaders repeatedly said the decision was one of conscience and that, while they would count votes, they would not "whip," or try to sway, them. Members reported none of the arm-twisting, threats or promises that routinely accompanied difficult votes.

Although President Bush and Cabinet members called wavering legislators, the members said they felt no pressure. White House officials did not threaten to take Kennedy Center tickets from Republicans who failed to toe the party line, as happened during 1990's chaotic budget battle.

Instead, the debate reflected an almost idealized image of how Congress should work, with all eyes focused on chamber floors rather than on the halls and back rooms where congressional decisions were most often made.

At times, both the House and Senate floors were filled with members sitting in unusual silence, listening to colleagues speak. More than 300 speeches were given in the House, where some members waited six or more hours for a turn at the podium; in the Senate, 94 senators took the floor during the three-day debate.

The mood was perhaps most solemn during the votes in the Senate, over which Vice President Dan Quayle presided. In a procedure reserved for occasions such as impeachments, members rose one by one from their chairs as the roll was called to cast their "yea" or "nay."

During most of the debate, the galleries were packed with onlookers, many of them young men and women the same age as the U.S. troops in the Persian Gulf whose fate was being discussed.

The pensive mood was pierced only once in the Senate, on Jan. 11, when about a dozen scattered antiwar protesters began to shout "No war for Bush" and "No blood for oil." They were quickly dragged from the chamber by Capitol Hill security guards, who were out in full force during the entire Persian Gulf debate.

Although brief, the outburst appeared to unsettle members, some of whom had questioned earlier whether the nation would again be torn apart as it had been by Vietnam.

Senate Armed Services Committee Chairman Sam Nunn, D-Ga., whose floor speech against authorizing force was interrupted by the protests, resumed with words intended as much for Saddam Hussein as for anyone: "We may disagree in this chamber, but when this vote is over . . . we are going to stand united."

The Senate took no similar action.

Durbin said the action demonstrated that "the Constitution had prevailed."

The use of force resolution itself affirmed Congress' powers. The legislation stated that the 1973 War Powers Resolution granted Congress specific statutory authority for using force.

The War Begins

On the evening of Jan. 16, a resolute Bush informed the nation of his decision to transform Operation Desert Shield into Operation Desert Storm. "Tonight, the battle has been joined," he said. *(Bush address, p. 754)*

As the president spoke, waves of fighters, bombers and missiles had already been crushing strategic targets throughout Iraq for several hours. At 7 p.m. Eastern Standard Time, administration officials began calling leading members of Congress to inform them that the war had begun. In the days that followed, the relentless air bombardment continued.

In Washington, the Senate approved a resolution on Jan. 17 backing Bush by a vote of 98-0. S Con Res 2 affirmed that Congress "commends and supports the efforts and leadership of the president as Commander in Chief in the Persian Gulf hostilities" and "unequivocally supports the men and women of our Armed Forces."

The House approved the resolution 399-6 the next day, with six members voting "present."

Yet lawmakers sensed that all of their resolutions and statements would make little difference in the end. Having already authorized Bush to begin a war, members were well aware that they were reduced — politically and even constitutionally — to the role of bystanders.

"We voted and gave the president our power of attorney," said Rep. Gary L. Ackerman, D-N.Y.

Some Democrats continued to balk at voting Bush their unconditional support.

Despite the overwhelming margins, the sense of Congress resolutions were approved only after hours of bickering over precise language.

Democratic leaders, led by House Speaker Foley and Senate Majority Leader Mitchell, initially proposed a reso-

The President Announces War on Iraq

On Jan. 16, President Bush addressed the nation from the Oval Office in the White House shortly after the beginning of a multinational military effort to force Iraq to withdraw from Kuwait. Following is the official White House transcript of the address:

Just two hours ago, allied air forces began an attack on military targets in Iraq and Kuwait. These attacks continue as I speak. Ground forces are not engaged.

This conflict started Aug. 2 when the dictator of Iraq invaded a small and helpless neighbor. Kuwait, a member of the Arab League and a member of the United Nations, was crushed, its people brutalized.

Five months ago, Saddam Hussein started this cruel war against Kuwait. Tonight the battle has been joined.

This military action, taken in accord with United Nations resolutions and with the consent of the United States Congress, follows months of constant and virtually endless diplomatic activity on the part of the United Nations, the United States and many, many other countries.

Arab leaders sought what became known as an Arab solution, only to conclude that Saddam Hussein was unwilling to leave Kuwait. Others traveled to Baghdad in a variety of efforts to restore peace and justice.

Our Secretary of State James [A.] Baker [III] held an historic meeting in Geneva, only to be totally rebuffed.

This past weekend, in a last-ditch effort, the secretary-general of the United Nations went to the Middle East with peace in his heart — his second such mission. And he came back from Baghdad with no progress at all in getting Saddam Hussein to withdraw from Kuwait.

Now, the 28 countries with forces in the gulf area have exhausted all reasonable efforts to reach a peaceful resolution [and] have no choice but to drive Saddam from Kuwait by force. We will not fail.

As I report to you, air attacks are under way against military targets in Iraq. We are determined to knock out Saddam Hussein's nuclear bomb potential. We will also destroy his chemical weapons facilities. Much of Saddam's artillery and tanks will be destroyed. Our operations are designed to best protect the lives of all the coalition forces by targeting Saddam's vast military arsenal.

Initial reports from Gen. [H. Norman] Schwarzkopf are that our operations are proceeding according to plan. Our objectives are clear: Saddam Hussein's forces will leave Kuwait, the legitimate government of Kuwait will be restored to its rightful place, and Kuwait will once again be free.

Iraq will eventually comply with all relevant United Nations resolutions, and then, when peace is restored, it is our hope that Iraq will live as a peaceful and cooperative member of the family of nations, thus enhancing the security and stability of the gulf.

Some may ask, why act now? Why not wait? The answer is clear. The world could wait no longer. Sanctions, though having some effect, showed no signs of accomplishing their objective. Sanctions were tried for well over five months, and we and our allies concluded that sanctions alone would not force Saddam from Kuwait.

While the world waited, Saddam Hussein systematically raped, pillaged and plundered a tiny nation, no threat to his own. He subjected the people of Kuwait to unspeakable atrocities, and among those maimed and murdered, innocent children.

While the world waited, Saddam sought to add to the chemical weapons arsenal he now possesses an infinitely more dangerous weapon of mass destruction, a nuclear weapon. And while the world waited, while the world talked peace and withdrawal, Saddam Hussein dug in and moved massive forces into Kuwait.

While the world waited, while Saddam stalled, more damage was being done to the fragile economies of the Third World, the emerging democracies of Eastern Europe, to the entire world, including to our own economy. The United States, together with the United Nations, exhausted every means at our disposal to bring this crisis to a peaceful end. However, Saddam clearly felt that by stalling and threatening and defying the United Nations, he could weaken the forces arrayed against him.

While the world waited, Saddam Hussein met every overture of

---

lution that would have commended U.S. troops in their efforts against Iraq without ever mentioning the president.

House Minority Leader Michel termed one of several Democratic draft resolutions "pretty wishy-washy and mealy-mouthed, to say the least."

But the Democrats accepted the compromise commending Bush, and even vocal opponents of administration policy, such as Democratic Sens. Kennedy and freshman Paul Wellstone of Minnesota, voted for the resolutions.

Noting the token resistance of the Iraqi air force to the initial U.S. onslaught, Senate Minority Leader Dole said he wondered, "Where was this guy, where was Saddam Hussein? He must have been on vacation or asleep because nothing — there was no response."

The administration attempted to dampen the early expectations of a quick and virtually painless victory.

"We must be realistic," Bush said at a Jan. 18 news conference. "There will be losses. There will be obstacles along the way. And war is never cheap."

Israel Under Attack

The war took a dangerous turn when Iraq bombarded two heavily populated Israeli cities, Tel Aviv and Haifa, with crude Soviet-made missiles called Scuds.

The United States rushed Patriot missile batteries, and U.S. operators, to Israel to deflect the Scuds. Allied bombers concentrated on a partially successful effort to hunt down and destroy the Scud launchers in Iraq.

Israel earned admiration and appreciation in Washington for enduring the attacks without hitting back at Saddam's forces. By withholding a response, Israel avoided being drawn into the war, a step that would have embarrassed moderate Arab states and risked fracturing the anti-Saddam coalition.

Secretary of State Baker said the coalition "might not" collapse if Israel retaliated. "But the point is, it is something very much appreciated by the United States — the restraint that has been shown," he said.

Administration officials, after largely eschewing contact with the Shamir government, became conspicuously available. Bush stayed in close telephone contact with Shamir, as did Baker. Deputy Secretary of State Eagleburger was dispatched on an emergency mission to Israel.

The House and the Senate also weighed in on Israel's behalf, passing resolutions that commended Israel's performance during the crisis. Support for the non-binding resolutions was unanimous in both chambers.

The House resolution (H Con Res 41) "condemns the unprovoked attack by Iraq on Israel," and "commends Israel for its restraint." The concurrent resolution passed the House, 416-0, on Jan. 23.

The Senate acted the next day, approving a similar resolution (S Con Res 4), 99-0.

Iraq jolted allies by producing videotapes of allied pris-

peace with open contempt.

While the world prayed for peace, Saddam prepared for war.

I had hoped that when the United States Congress, in historic debate, took its resolute action, Saddam would realize he could not prevail and would move out of Kuwait in accord with the United Nations resolutions. He did not do that. Instead, he remained intransigent, certain that time was on his side. Saddam was warned over and over again to comply with the will of the United Nations, leave Kuwait or be driven out. Saddam has arrogantly rejected all warnings. Instead he tried to make this a dispute between Iraq and the United States of America. Well, he failed.

Tonight 28 nations, countries from five continents — Europe and Asia, Africa and the Arab League — have forces in the gulf area, standing shoulder to shoulder against Saddam Hussein. These countries had hoped the use of force could be avoided. Regrettably, we now believe that only force will make him leave.

Prior to ordering our forces into battle, I instructed our military commanders to take every necessary step to prevail as quickly as possible and with the greatest degree of protection possible for American and allied servicemen and women.

I've told the American people before that this will not be another Vietnam, and I repeat this here tonight. Our troops will have the best possible support in the entire world, and they will not be asked to fight with one hand tied behind their back.

I'm hopeful that this fighting will not go on for long and that casualties will be held to an absolute minimum. This is an historic moment. We have in this past year made great progress in ending the long era of conflict and cold war. We have before us the opportunity to forge for ourselves and for future generations a new world order, a world where the rule of law, not the law of the jungle, governs the conduct of nations.

When we are successful — and we will be — we have a real chance at this new world order, an order in which a credible United Nations can use its peacekeeping role to fulfill the promise envisioned of the U.N.'s founders. We have no argument with the people of Iraq; indeed, for the innocents caught in this conflict, I pray for their safety.

Our goal is not the conquest of Iraq; it is the liberation of Kuwait. It is my hope that somehow the Iraqi people can even now convince their dictator that he must lay down his arms, leave Kuwait and let Iraq itself rejoin the family of peace-loving nations.

Thomas Paine wrote many years ago, "These are the times that try men's souls." Those well-known words are so very true today, but even as planes of the multinational forces attack Iraq, I prefer to think of peace, not war.

I am convinced not only that we will prevail, but that out of the horror of combat will come the recognition that no nation can stand against a world united, no nation will be permitted to brutally assault its neighbor.

No president can easily commit our sons and daughters to war. They are the nation's finest. Ours is an all-volunteer force, magnificently trained, highly motivated. The troops know why they're there, and listen to what they say, for they've said it better than any president or prime minister ever could.

Listen to Hollywood Huddleston, Marine lance corporal. He says: "Let's free these people so we can go home and be free again." He's right. The terrible crimes and tortures committed by Saddam's henchmen against the innocent people of Kuwait are an affront to mankind and a challenge to the freedom of all.

Listen to one of our great officers out there, Marine Lt. Gen. Walter Boomer. He said: "There are things worth fighting for. A world in which brutality and lawlessness are allowed to go unchecked isn't the kind of world we're going to want to live in."

Listen to Master Sgt. J. P. Kendall of the 82nd Airborne: "We're here for more than just the price of a gallon of gas. What we're doing is going to chart the future of the world for the next 100 years. It's better to deal with this guy now than five years from now."

And finally we should all sit up and listen to Jackie Jones, an Army lieutenant, when she says: "If we let him get away with this, who knows what's going to be next."

I have called upon Hollywood and Walter and J. P. and Jackie and all their courageous comrades in arms to do what must be done. Tonight, America and the world are deeply grateful to them and to their families.

And let me say to everyone listening or watching tonight, when the troops we've sent in finish their work, I am determined to bring them home as soon as possible.

Tonight, as our forces fight, they and their families are in our prayers. May God bless each and every one of them, and the coalition forces at our side in the gulf, and may He continue to bless our nation, the United States of America. ■

oners of war (POWs), some of whom appeared battered and dazed as they denounced the U.S. attacks on Iraq in stilted tones.

Congress responded by approving companion unanimous resolutions (H Con Res 48, S Con Res 5) condemning Iraq's treatment of the POWs. The resolutions, passed 418-0 by the House on Jan. 23 and 99-0 by the Senate the next day, declared Iraq's actions in violation of the Geneva Conventions governing treatment of prisoners.

The attacks on Israel and the videotapes of allied prisoners combined to puncture the early giddy optimism in Congress. "Some euphoria early on . . . is turning pragmatic now," said Florida Democratic Sen. Graham. "We're facing a very large and experienced adversary."

Members also introduced the first in a long series of bills to provide new benefits and protections to troops serving in the gulf.

Awaiting Ground Combat

Two weeks into a bombing campaign against Iraq that seemed an antiseptic montage of high-tech wizardry, 11 U.S. Marines died Jan. 29 in the first sustained land battle of the Persian Gulf War.

As combat goes, it was hardly an epic battle. The U.S. commanding general, H. Norman Schwarzkopf, belittled the Iraqi attacks as "no more significant than a mosquito to an elephant."

U.S. commanders acknowledged later that seven of the 11 Marines were killed by "friendly fire" from a misaimed U.S. Maverick missile.

But the engagement set off political ripples in Washington because more Americans died in the fighting on the ground Jan. 29 than had been killed in the air war up to that date. Members of Congress from both parties urged Bush to rely on air power as long as possible for fear of the heavy casualties a ground war could bring.

House Minority Whip Gingrich, a vigorous advocate for Bush's move to war, nonetheless predicted that public opinion would soon recoil from large numbers of fatalities that would be reported almost instantaneously in this "television war."

"My concern is that once we get into the ground phase that the level of violence is so intense that even if we're winning decisively, we simply can't in a decent society sustain the shock levels for months," Gingrich said in a speech to the conservative Federalist Society on Jan. 25. "I think it's got to occur relatively rapidly, six to eight weeks, once the ground campaign starts."

U.S. boasts of precision-bombing of strategic targets in Iraq were undercut by a tragedy of war on Feb. 13. A bomb slammed into an underground bunker in Baghdad that proved to be sheltering Iraqi civilians. Hundreds were killed.

White House spokesman Fitzwater suggested that Saddam might have intentionally located civilians in a military "command-and-control center."

"We don't know why civilians were there," Fitzwater said. "But we do know that Saddam Hussein does not share our value in the sanctity of life.... He kills civilians intentionally and with purpose."

Diplomatic Endgame

On Feb. 9, Soviet President Gorbachev warned that the war was taking on "an ever more alarming and dramatic scope" and that the U.S.-led alliance was in "danger of exceeding the mandate" of the Security Council resolutions, which set the goal of ousting Iraq from Kuwait.

The Soviet Union had supported the U.N. resolutions but declined to take part in the gulf combat. Gorbachev's caution that the war was getting out of hand proved to be the opening gambit in an effort to broker a settlement.

A communiqué issued by Iraq's Revolutionary Command Council on Feb. 15 briefly raised hopes in Washington that Saddam had agreed to an unconditional pullout of his forces from Kuwait. But the statement premised the action on an exhaustive list of demands — including an Israeli withdrawal from occupied territories — that the White House promptly labeled unacceptable.

"There is nothing new here," Bush told a group of scientists meeting in the Old Executive Office Building. "It is a hoax. There are new demands added."

Again demonstrating his firm opposition to offering any concessions to Saddam, Bush for the first time issued a direct call for Iraqis to oust their president. "There is another way for the bloodshed to stop and that is for the Iraqi military and the Iraqi people to take matters into their own hands to force Saddam Hussein, the dictator, to step aside," he said.

Although many members of Congress joined Bush in criticizing the Iraqi communiqué, some said the statement might offer at least a glimmer of hope for a diplomatic resolution of the war. "I do think there is something new here," Rep. Hamilton said. "Iraq is blinking and may be rethinking its policies."

The message from Baghdad was timed to lead up to the dispatch of Foreign Minister Aziz to Moscow for meetings with Gorbachev that produced a series of Soviet peace proposals over the next week. Each of the proposals was tentatively endorsed by Aziz in Moscow but rejected by Bush in Washington.

On the evening of Feb. 21, the Soviets proposed an Iraqi withdrawal that would have begun two days after a cease-fire and would have been weighted with several other conditions. These included ending U.N. economic sanctions against Iraq after two-thirds of its troops had been withdrawn. Although the administration said it "appreciated" the Soviet efforts, it clearly preferred to take matters into its own hands.

The following day, Kremlin officials announced that their plan had been revised to require a 21-day withdrawal from Kuwait, starting one day after a cease-fire. Economic sanctions would not have been lifted until the withdrawal was complete.

U.S. officials, however, had said repeatedly that they would not cease military operations without concrete evidence that Saddam's troops were making a massive, rapid withdrawal from Kuwait. That would have required them to leave many of their heavy tanks and weapons behind.

Prodded by the Soviet peace initiative, Bush gave Saddam an ultimatum Feb. 22 to begin withdrawing his troops from Kuwait by noon the next day or risk the brutal combat of a ground war. The president called for Saddam's "immediate and unconditional withdrawal from Kuwait" and said that coalition forces would need to hear "publicly and authoritatively his acceptance of these terms."

"I have decided that the time has come to make public, with specificity, just exactly what is required of Iraq if a ground war is to be avoided," Bush said. Later, the White House elaborated, insisting that the withdrawal be completed within seven days and that troops leave Kuwait City within 48 hours.

It was revealed later that Bush and U.S. commanders had planned to begin the climactic ground war on Feb. 23 even before the Soviet efforts at peacemaking had inspired the president's ultimatum.

The 100-Hour Ground War

On the evening of Feb. 23, hours after the president's noon deadline had passed, the president went on television to announce the start of the allied ground offensive.

"Saddam Hussein was given one last chance . . . ," Bush said. "Regrettably, the noon deadline passed without the agreement of the government of Iraq to meet demands of United Nations Security Council Resolution 660, as set forth in the specific terms spelled out by the coalition....

"To the contrary, what we have seen is a redoubling of Saddam Hussein's efforts to destroy completely Kuwait and its people. I have therefore directed Gen. Norman Schwarzkopf, in conjunction with coalition forces, to use all forces available, including ground forces, to eject the Iraqi army from Kuwait."

In the next 100 hours, the allies swept to triumph. They recaptured Kuwait and dismembered the occupying Iraqi army in a blitzkrieg of breathtaking scope and dizzying tempo.

Having already grounded Iraq's air force, blinded its electronic surveillance and destroyed much of its communications system in 38 days of aerial bombardment, allied forces were able to sweep unchallenged around the western flank of Iraq's supposedly formidable dug-in defenses.

Iraq floated increasingly desperate cease-fire offers, but Bush scoffed that Saddam was still "trying to claim victory in the midst of a rout."

On Feb. 27, Bush announced a cease-fire in place on allied terms: "Kuwait is liberated. Iraq's army is defeated. Our military objectives are met."

The Pentagon said 304 Americans died in the war. Iraqi casualties were estimated in the tens of thousands, but the Pentagon refused to give out a figure, saying it wanted to avoid criticism for inflating enemy losses like that directed against the Defense Department during the Vietnam War.

Although Democrats and Republicans would soon revert to squabbling over the significance of the Democratic votes against authorizing the war, the enthusiasm at the outcome was buoyant and bipartisan.

At the invitation of congressional leaders, Bush addressed a joint session of Congress on March 6. He received exuberant ovations from members waving tiny U.S. flags.

Bush spoke of the need to address difficult challenges in the Mideast, including the proliferation of chemical and nuclear weapons capabilities and the conflict between Israel and its neighbors. But the members cheered most lustily for the declaration of victory over Iraq that was the centerpiece of the president's appearance.

"As president," Bush said, "I can report to the nation: Aggression is defeated. The war is over." ■

U.S.-Soviet Relations Chill by Year's End

A year that began on an optimistic note for U.S.-Soviet relations — with President Bush publicly expressing support for the continued strength of Soviet President Mikhail S. Gorbachev — turned sour by early 1991. The Soviet Union's violent crackdown in Lithuania and the other Baltic States in January 1991 threatened the improving status of relations between the two superpowers.

The United States and the Soviet Union signed a major trade agreement in June granting the Soviets normal trade status. In November, Bush and the leaders of 21 other countries signed the conventional forces in Europe (CFE) treaty, providing for the scrapping or removal from the continent of roughly 100,000 tanks, cannons and other weapons deployed, with the Soviet arsenal taking by far the largest hit.

By the end of 1990, however, both agreements had stalled. Bush said repeatedly that he would not send the trade pact to Congress for approval until the Soviet parliament had codified more open Soviet emigration policies.

Meanwhile, concerns about political retrenchment in Moscow and questions about Soviet compliance with the arms pact kept the Bush administration from submitting it to the Senate for approval. U.S. officials were dissatisfied with the Soviets' accounting of forces and weapons covered by the agreement. The Soviet army reportedly was dug in against the treaty, stoking U.S. concerns about a Soviet end-run.

Those fears were exacerbated by continuing political turmoil in the Soviet Union, dramatized on Dec. 20 when Soviet Foreign Minister Eduard A. Shevardnadze resigned abruptly. Shevardnadze, regarded by U.S. officials as a trusted negotiator and an architect of improved relations, denounced the hard-liners who had been attacking Gorbachev, but also warned that the Soviet president's drive for increased powers could lead to a "dictatorship."

Despite the Soviet Union's role as an essential, if at times reluctant, ally against Iraq in the Middle East crisis, relations between the two superpowers cooled — especially in light of Moscow's crackdown against its breakaway Baltic republics.

In the wake of the Soviets' armed intervention in Lithuania and Latvia, the White House announced Jan. 28, 1991, that the Moscow summit, scheduled for mid-February, would be indefinitely postponed.

Also left in limbo at year's end was further action on the CFE treaty, the strategic arms reduction treaty (START) to reduce by nearly one-third the two countries' strategic nuclear stockpiles, and a chemical weapons pact designed to get both countries to slash stockpiles of lethal chemical munitions.

BACKGROUND

At the end of 1989, Bush and Gorbachev had cleared away much of the ideological debris left over from the Cold War and moved to put relations between the superpowers on a businesslike footing.

Meeting at a Dec. 2-3 shipboard summit off Malta, against a backdrop of political revolutions in Eastern Europe, the two leaders scheduled an ambitious diplomatic agenda to be completed in time for a full-scale summit in June 1990. Major items included accelerated negotiations on the entire range of arms control issues and normalizing U.S.-Soviet trade.

At a joint news conference closing the Malta meetings, Bush said: "We stand at the threshold of a brand new era of U.S.-Soviet relations."

Gorbachev declared that the Cold War "epoch" had ended: "We are just at the very beginning of our road, a long road, to a long-lasting peaceful period."

By the December summit, Bush had decided it was in the interests of the United States to support Gorbachev's uphill efforts to reform the Soviet economic and political systems. Bush offered more than rhetoric by pledging trade concessions and offering to help the Soviet Union fully enter the world economy.

Bush said he made up his mind after watching Gorbachev allow, and even encourage, the breakup of the Soviet empire. As Bush and Gorbachev were meeting, the collapse of communist governments in East Germany and Czechoslovakia accelerated. *(1989 Almanac, p. 477)*

By 1990, Gorbachev was preparing to face a number of domestic crises stemming from ethnic unrest in the Azerbaijan region and separatist movements in the Baltic republics. President Bush said on Jan. 24, 1990, that he hoped Gorbachev would overcome these challenges. "I hope that he not only survives but stays strong, because I think it is in our interest that *perestroika* [reform] succeed and go forward," Bush said.

Testifying before the Senate Armed Services Committee on Jan. 23, CIA Director William H. Webster said that while Moscow retained enormous power, the threat of a Soviet attack on the West was diminishing. The Warsaw Pact's "strength and capabilities have declined" and likely would continue to do so, Webster said, largely because of the collapse of East-bloc communist regimes.

Soviet leaders were preoccupied with domestic unrest and economic decline, Webster testified. Despite those problems, he said, Gorbachev's removal by hard-line factions in the Kremlin "does not seem likely now."

Events in Baltics

Events in the Soviet Baltic States throughout the year, however, served as a constant reminder of how frail the U.S.-Soviet détente was. From the moment the new government of Lithuania declared independence on March 11, Lithuania's assertion of freedom created a dilemma for the United States.

U.S. politicians had demanded freedom for the Baltic States of Lithuania, Latvia and Estonia ever since Soviet leader Josef Stalin absorbed them into the Soviet Union in 1940. Resolutions condemning Soviet occupation of the "captive nations" were rituals in Congress.

Lithuania's bold dash to independence seemed to satisfy those demands, even as it fit into the pattern of what many saw as the historically inevitable disintegration of the Soviet empire.

But Lithuania's action also came at an embarrassingly inconvenient time for the Soviets and the West. By insisting on immediate secession before Gorbachev was prepared to deal with it, the Lithuanians exposed anew Gorbachev's domestic difficulties, particularly his political need to court the hard-line constituencies that opposed his economic and political reforms.

Senate Majority Leader George J. Mitchell, D-Maine, and Minority Leader Bob Dole, R-Kan., said Shevardnadze, in an April 4 meeting in Washington, acknowledged that Gorbachev was under intense pressure to crack down on Lithuania and prevent the dismembering of the Soviet Union. Shevardnadze said publicly that the Kremlin wanted a peaceful, "wise and fair" outcome.

Bush's initial reaction to the events in Lithuania was to warn Gorbachev not to intervene. But as the situation alternately tensed and eased, Bush kept his silence and ordered what amounted to a hands-off approach.

The Lithuanian government itself raised a central issue by calling on "democratic nations" to recognize its independence. The Bush administration refused to do so on two grounds: The United States never officially acknowledged the Soviet Union's authority over the Baltic republics — treating them instead as "captive nations" — and so no change in U.S. policy was in order; and, in any event, the new regime in Vilnius did not control the territory it claimed to rule.

Thus, the furor caused by Lithuania's declaration of independence from the Soviet Union showed that the United States and the Soviets were coming to have as many interests in common as in dispute.

From the day that the new government of Lithuania declared independence, most of Washington's policy-makers and politicians exercised a rhetorical restraint inconceivable in times past.

The Bush administration gathered broad political support for sympathizing with the Soviet Union's dilemma and pressing for a settlement by negotiation, not by force or capitulation. Even after Gorbachev ordered tanks into Vilnius to intimidate Lithuania's parliament, Congress responded by passing resolutions condemning his action in surprisingly mild terms and avoiding specific threats of retaliation.

Congress seriously debated only one issue: whether to insist that Bush heed the Lithuanian government's appeal for official recognition by Western nations. In their resolutions, both chambers said Bush should do so soon, but they did not demand it or set deadlines.

"I don't think that keeping Gorbachev credible in his own country is the dumbest idea we've ever had," said Rep. Henry J. Hyde, R-Ill., one of the prominent conservative spokesmen advocating caution and some understanding of the Soviet leader's political problems at home.

There was little negative reaction on Capitol Hill to the April 5 announcement that Bush and Gorbachev would hold summit meetings in the United States May 31-June 3, despite the Kremlin's confrontation with Lithuania.

ARMS CONTROL

Bush and the leaders of 21 other countries signed a treaty Nov. 19 to begin the dismantling of the huge Soviet army that fostered Europe's Cold War division and militarization for more than 40 years. But at year's end, questions about Soviet compliance with the pact and concerns about political retrenchment in Moscow kept the Bush administration from submitting it to the Senate for approval. *(Arms control, p. 696)*

The CFE treaty provided for the scrapping or removal from the continent of roughly 100,000 of the 250,000 tanks, cannons and other weapons deployed, much from the Soviet arsenal.

Calling it "the farthest-reaching arms agreement in history," Bush said at the treaty-signing ceremony in Paris that the CFE treaty "signals the new world order that is emerging."

Agreement on the CFE treaty proved elusive until October, when Secretary of State James A. Baker III and Shevardnadze agreed on ceilings on the number of tanks, artillery pieces, armored troop carriers, armed helicopters and combat planes that could be fielded by the West's NATO and the rapidly crumbling Soviet bloc.

Their negotiating breakthrough paved the way for the Nov. 19 signing — one of the year's most tangible symbols of eased East-West tensions.

Also on the arms control front:

- A few relatively technical issues blocked conclusion of the START treaty to drastically reduce the two nations' nuclear stockpiles. *(START, p. 704)*
- Early Senate action on two treaties to limit the size of underground nuclear test explosions was guaranteed by the presidents' approval of an appendix (or "protocol") to each treaty intended to tighten up verification procedures. The Senate ratified both of these treaties Sept. 25. *(Testing treaties, p. 711)*
- Both countries agreed to slash stockpiles of lethal chemical munitions. *(Chemical weapons, p. 709)*

TRADE AND COMMERCIAL AGREEMENTS

The United States and the Soviet Union signed a trade agreement June 1 granting the Soviets most-favored-nation trade status, enabling them to pay lower tariffs on goods imported into the United States. But Bush said he would not send the pact to Congress for approval until the Soviet parliament had codified more open Soviet emigration policies. *(Trade agreement, p. 205)*

Soviet leaders said many times that an emigration law was about to be passed, but it had not been adopted by the end of 1990. "This agreement will not be sent to the Congress until after such legislation has been enacted," said Secretary of State Baker.

Before the summit, Bush had linked his willingness to sign the trade agreement to two actions by Moscow: passage of legislation codifying the right of Soviet citizens to emigrate and a lessening of pressure on Lithuania and the other Baltic States.

"Lithuania by itself might not be enough to stop [the agreement]," said Sen. Lloyd Bentsen, D-Texas. "But if the Soviets have not passed that [emigration] law by the time we see the agreement, that agreement will be in very, very serious trouble."

Bush appeared with Shevardnadze at the White House on Dec. 12 and announced that, despite continued disagreement over the June trade agreement, he was suspending a 15-year-old ban on extending commercial credits to the Soviets, enabling them to buy up to $1 billion worth of U.S. agricultural goods.

Secretary of Commerce Robert A. Mosbacher said, "This administration doesn't want to take the chance of having people starve in the Soviet Union when we can be helpful. And it is real help."

Members of Congress were generally supportive of the new administration overtures, although some saw the offer of agricultural credits as long overdue.

Most analysts of Soviet affairs viewed the president's offer of credits as further evidence of the administration's commitment to buttress Gorbachev's increasingly shaky leadership.

Key Republicans, including Dole, had joined with Democrats in urging the administration to lift the 1974 Jackson-Vanik amendment, which prohibited the extension of credits to the Soviet Union.

Bush waived the law, originally aimed at pressuring communist nations to allow free emigration of their citizens, until June 1991. The president praised the Gorbachev government for its "generally excellent [emigration] practices of the past year."

Following the announcement, Dole issued a statement saying, "Let's just hope that this is the beginning," adding that he "would like to see additional credits, substantial enough to have a market impact."

More substantive criticism came from conservatives who worried that the United States was moving too quickly to assist its old rival. New Jersey Sen. Bill Bradley, a moderate Democrat, voiced similar concerns, calling the economic aid "ill-advised."

Bradley said he was especially troubled by reports that the KGB, the Soviet security police and intelligence agency, would be overseeing the distribution of foreign assistance and that the Soviet military had denied a request from the mayor of Leningrad to release food stocks.

"At the least," said Bradley, "we should insist that the Soviet military do as much to feed the Soviet Union as the U.S. or the Germans."

Economic Aid

Sending more direct economic aid to the Soviet Union was not much of an issue for Congress. Few lawmakers saw any value in it or were willing to take the political heat for advocating help to an "enemy."

House Majority Leader Richard A. Gephardt, D-Mo., sparked a debate, though, with a proposal March 6 for broader forms of aid to the Soviets. The proposal was part of his speech blasting Bush for having a "lack of vision" in responding to communism's collapse in Eastern Europe.

"I believe that support of the process of democratization in the U.S.S.R. is in America's self-interest," Gephardt said. "A stronger Soviet economy will facilitate the process of peace. How can the Soviets pull Red Army troops out of Eastern Europe if they have no jobs and no homes for them to return to in Russia?"

In particular, Gephardt suggested providing the Soviets with food aid, Export-Import Bank export subsidies and private investment guarantees by the Overseas Private Investment Corporation (OPIC).

Gephardt got little outright support for his Soviet-aid idea, even from fellow Democrats. One of the few endorsing his plan was David R. Obey, D-Wis., chairman of the House Appropriations Subcommittee on Foreign Operations, who said the United States had to respond to the "political earthquake" in Eastern Europe just as it did to the 1988 geological earthquake in Soviet Armenia.

But most other Democrats sidestepped the question or denounced any suggestion of aiding the Soviet Union. Unless the Soviets drastically reformed their economy, said Sen. Bradley, aid would be "going down a rathole."

Some Republicans gleefully said Gephardt — a 1988 presidential aspirant — had blundered, first by attacking a popular president and then by proposing to send taxpayer dollars to the Soviet Union.

"If you're going to start giving foreign aid to the hated commies . . . you've got a real sales job to do in the United States," said Alan K. Simpson, R-Wyo., the Senate minority whip.

The day after Gephardt's speech, Secretary of State Baker appeared before a House Appropriations subcommittee and advocated expanded commercial relations with the Soviet Union — including trade agreements that would benefit the Soviet economy. But Baker rejected the idea of direct aid for Moscow, and he was joined by other administration officials.

White House spokesman Marlin Fitzwater called Gephardt "the Maxwell Smart of politics. Can you believe he wants to raise taxes on the American people to give money to the Soviet Union?"

Congress included $369.7 million in the fiscal 1991 foreign aid appropriations bill to help former East-bloc countries develop market-based economies. But lawmakers and the administration failed to reconcile differences over broader aid programs. And the dispute doomed passage of legislation to authorize U.S. contributions to the lending arm of the World Bank, the International Development Agency. *(Bank aid to Eastern Europe, p. 206)*

In the Senate, a bill (S 2944) that would have authorized $535 million in aid for emerging Eastern and Central European democracies never reached the floor. The measure did not have the support of GOP senators because of language that would have given technical and business advice to the Soviet Union.

A broad aid measure (HR 5153) died in the House without being considered on the floor or in the Senate. The measure would have authorized U.S. contributions totaling $1.2 billion to the European Bank for Reconstruction and Development (EBRD).

The foreign aid appropriations bill, however, did provide a $70 million contribution to the EBRD.

Other Agreements

Also on June 1, when the trade agreement was signed, U.S. and Soviet officials signed agreements aimed at improving commercial, cultural and other relations. Among them:

- **Civil aviation.** Baker and Shevardnadze signed an aviation agreement expected to more than triple the allowed number of commercial air flights between the United States and the Soviet Union. The agreement also would allow airlines other than Pan Am and Aeroflot to service U.S.-Soviet routes.

Under it, U.S. airlines could increase the number of flights to Moscow and Leningrad and could open up service over the Atlantic Ocean to Kiev, Riga, Minsk and Tblisi. Magadan and Khabarosk would be served on Pacific Ocean routes. The Soviet airline Aeroflot would be able to increase its service to New York and Washington and would be allowed to open new service to Chicago; San Francisco; Anchorage, Alaska; and Miami.

For the first time, Soviets traveling to the United States would be able to use rubles to buy a limited number of tickets on U.S. carriers. They would have to buy them through Soviet airlines, which would pay dollars to U.S. carriers.

- **Nuclear energy.** A five-year agreement provided for new U.S.-Soviet cooperation in nuclear energy, including reactor safety, fusion energy and basic nuclear science. This agreement sprang, in part, from international concern about the Soviet Union's lack of safety standards, as demonstrated by the 1986 accident at the Chernobyl plant in the Ukraine. Bush and Gorbachev signed this agreement.
- **Ocean studies.** Baker and Shevardnadze signed an extension of a 1973 agreement providing for cooperation

Plan To Raze Moscow Embassy Blocked

The Bush administration tried to move ahead in 1990 with a plan to tear down and rebuild the bug-riddled U.S. Embassy in Moscow, but was blocked by Congress.

Acting in large part because of budget constraints, Congress refused to provide money to raze the building in fiscal 1991 and instead allowed a reprogramming request to begin a design study.

Even just to win authority from Congress to reprogram $3.8 million for the study, the administration was forced to agree that the architects also would study and design a separate structure for another site. "In order to avoid further delay, we agreed to do design work on the things we'd prefer not to," said one administration source.

Construction of the embassy began in 1979, but the discovery of listening devices throughout the building halted work in August 1985. After that, the building was in limbo while Congress and the administrations of Ronald Reagan and George Bush debated what to do.

Betweeen 1980 and 1984, three proposed solutions surfaced: razing the building and rebuilding it from its foundation, replacing only the top four floors or building a secure annex next to the structure and using the current building for non-classified purposes.

President Bush in December 1989 opted for razing the structure and rebuilding it, and he requested $270 million in his fiscal 1991 budget to do so. *(1989 Almanac, p. 536)*

But the high cost of this proposal provoked opposition in Congress far beyond what the State Department had expected. Officials said they had anticipated adamant opposition from Rep. Neal Smith, D-Iowa, chairman of the Appropriations Subcommittee on Commerce, Justice, State and the Judiciary but had expected overwhelming support from others in Congress for razing the facility.

The administration did get strong endorsements for the tear-down option from Senate Intelligence Chairman David L. Boren, D-Okla., and Ernest F. Hollings, D-S.C., Smith's counterpart in the Senate. But others who had not previously taken a position spoke out in opposition.

"I can't think of a more terrible waste of public money," Sen. Terry Sanford, D-N.C., said of the administration's request.

Frank H. Murkowski, R-Alaska, a member of the Senate Intelligence Committee, which wanted the structure torn down, said the building did "have value as is for office space."

The congressional opposition led to an impasse with no two committees agreeing on how the situation should be handled.

The House Foreign Affairs Committee approved Bush's $270 million request in a supplemental fiscal 1991 State Department authorization bill (HR 4610). But it voted 22-17 to require that Bush get the committee's approval before spending any of it.

In its version (S 2749) of the authorization bill, the Senate Foreign Relations Committee voted 16-0 to slash the request to $50 million and instructed that it be used only to complete construction of the existing building.

Neither of those bills saw further action in the 101st Congress. A standard two-year State Department authorization bill had been cleared in January. *(State Department authorization, p. 799)*

The Senate Appropriations Subcommittee on Commerce, Justice, State and the Judiciary included in its version of the State Department spending bill (HR 5021 — PL 101-515) a proposal to reprogram $10 million to begin tearing down the building. That provision had not been included in the House version and was dropped in conference. As enacted, however, the appropriation measure did include authority to reprogram funds for a design study. *(Commerce, Justice, State appropriations, p. 881)*

After a plan was agreed upon, it was expected to take at least four years to finish action on the embassy at a cost of at least $270 million, the administration estimated.

between the superpowers on oceanographic research. The previous agreement was to expire June 14.

- **Maritime.** A maritime agreement would allow U.S. ships to call at 42 Soviet ports, and vice versa, with only two days' notice.
- **Student exchanges.** This agreement established a goal of 1,500 students from each country annually by 1995. Bush and Gorbachev signed it.
- **Arctic islands.** A maritime boundary treaty would give the Soviets official recognition of their jurisdiction over four Arctic islands. The two nations for years had disputed sovereignty over the islands, the largest of which was Wrangel Island in the East Siberian Sea. Baker and Shevardnadze signed this agreement.

ACTION IN THE BALTICS

From the day that the Lithuanian government declared independence from the Soviet Union on March 11, Congress was eager to express support for the cause of freedom for Lithuania.

Sen. Jesse Helms, R-N.C., first sought to force Bush's hand by offering a resolution on March 21 — as an amendment to clean air legislation (S 1630) — demanding recognition of Lithuania's new government and "direct relations" with it.

A vehement anticommunist, Helms wanted to slam Bush for not reacting enthusiastically enough to Lithuania's March 11 declaration of independence. "Is the United States going to sit back now and allow the Soviet Union to recapture Lithuania once again?" he asked.

Caught by surprise, senior Bush administration officials lobbied against Helms' resolution and persuaded the Senate to reject it, 36-59. *(Vote 39, p. 11-S)*

During debate on the amendment, the administration told GOP leader Dole that Bush wanted the Soviets and Lithuanians to negotiate their problems. "We should not do anything that might upset those discussions or in any way indicate that we want to meddle in their affairs," Dole said. Especially troubling, he added, were Helms' calls for formal recognition and appointment of an ambassador.

Helms called the vote a "disgrace." Dole fretted that the vote might cause some "misunderstanding" about the Senate's attitude toward Lithuania. Paul Simon, D-Ill., facing a tough re-election in the home state of many Lithuanian-Americans, said, "I do not want anyone misinterpreting a negative vote as believing I am not for freedom for Lithuania."

The next day, the Senate adopted, 93-0, a much milder resolution (S Con Res 108) urging Bush to "consider" Lithuania's appeal for recognition. *(Vote 42, p. 11-S)*

The House followed suit on April 4, when it adopted H Con Res 289 by a vote of 416-3, urging the president to "plan for and take those steps, at the earliest possible time," that would create normal diplomatic relations with Lithuania. *(Vote 67, p. 26-H)*

In their resolutions, the House and Senate issued identical warnings to Gorbachev that using force against Lithuania would cause "severe repercussions" in U.S.-Soviet relations. But at the administration's request, the resolutions mentioned no specifics.

Impact on Trade

Congress laid down its next marker on Lithuania in May for both the Bush administration and the Soviet Union: There would be no U.S.-Soviet trade agreement unless the Kremlin negotiated in good faith with the Lithuanian government and lifted its economic embargo.

The Senate took that position on May 1 with a 73-24 vote; the House followed suit June 6, just five days after Bush and Gorbachev signed the historic trade agreement. The House vote was 390-24. *(Senate vote 75, p. 18-S; House vote 149, p. 52-H)*

Virtually without exception, members of Congress called for complete independence for the Baltic States. But as a practical matter, most recognized that it would take some time, perhaps years, to untangle the political, economic and other links between Moscow and the Baltics.

As a compromise, members who had been most active in promoting the Lithuanian cause settled on two more immediate demands as the price for the Soviet trade agreement.

The first was the lifting of several economic sanctions that Moscow had imposed since mid-April, including the cutting off of oil and gas supplies to Lithuania.

In its resolution on the issue, offered as an amendment that was later dropped from the fiscal 1990 supplemental spending bill (HR 4404 — PL 101-302), the Senate demanded that the Soviet Union lift "its economic embargo against Lithuania."

The House, acting on an export administration bill (HR 4653), adopted somewhat more general language, insisting that Moscow not apply "economic coercion" to Lithuania.

Both chambers also called on Gorbachev to negotiate with the Lithuanians.

The Senate's resolution said those negotiations should be aimed at producing "the Soviet recognition of the independence of the government of the Republic of Lithuania in an orderly and expeditious manner."

The House language called for "serious negotiations with the elected government of Lithuania for the purpose of allowing the self-determination" of that country.

Some members wanted to add other conditions on Soviet behavior toward the Baltics, but most leaders on Capitol Hill said the demands for negotiating and ending the embargo were enough for the moment.

"Those are the essential elements of the situation, the ones which have been recognized by all concerned for some time," said Senate Majority Leader Mitchell.

A small minority argued against immediate congressional action, saying that Gorbachev clearly understood U.S. concerns and that Bush should have room to maneuver on his own.

Calling the House action a "gratuitous slap at the president," Rep. Lee H. Hamilton, D-Ind., a senior member of the Foreign Affairs Committee, warned against putting explicit conditions in the law.

"It is one thing to tie two events together rhetorically," he said. "It's quite another to tie things together by statute, which is difficult to get around or to adjust to meet the circumstances."

Crackdown in the Baltics

Tensions heightened by year's end as the Persian Gulf crisis heated up and events in Lithuania approached a boiling point.

Shevardnadze's abrupt resignation on Dec. 20 was a precursor of the instability ahead. Shevardnadze shocked Gorbachev by announcing his resignation to the Congress of People's Deputies, and the move stunned U.S. officials as well.

"We would obviously be foolish not to take the warning in Minister Shevardnadze's resignation statement seriously," Secretary of State Baker told reporters, although he noted that Gorbachev had promised continuity in Soviet foreign policy.

Three weeks later, on Jan. 13, 1991, Soviet tanks rumbled into Lithuania, leading to the deaths of 15 resisters and challenging improved relations with the United States.

Democrats and Republicans in both chambers called during the week of Jan. 14 for the administration to send a strong signal to Gorbachev that continued use of such force would seriously impair future U.S.-Soviet relations.

"It would be a travesty to concentrate so much of our nation's energy on stopping Iraqi aggression and freeing Kuwait [referring to the Iraqi invasion of that country on Aug. 2, 1990, and and the Persian Gulf War, which began on Jan. 16], while ignoring Soviet aggression in the captive Baltic nations," said Sen. Robert C. Byrd, D-W.Va. "There should be no confusion in our response to this latest brutal crackdown by the Soviet Union in Lithuania. It is wrong."

By voice vote Jan. 16, the Senate approved a non-binding resolution (S Res 14), sponsored by Byrd and others, that called on the administration to review and possibly cut off economic and other aid to the Soviet Union until Moscow withdrew its troops from the Baltic States and undertook good-faith negotiations with the republics of Lithuania, Latvia and Estonia.

The House on Jan. 23 passed a concurrent resolution (H Con Res 40), 417-0, condemning the violence and asking Bush to work with allies in Europe toward a "coordinated approach" to sanctions if the Soviets continued to use force to suppress the movements for independence by the Baltic States of Lithuania, Latvia and Estonia.

The Senate passed a similar non-binding resolution (S Con Res 6) on Jan. 24.

Noting warming relations between the United States and China despite U.S. outrage over that government's massacre in 1989 of students in Tiananmen Square, Sen. Connie Mack, R-Fla., called for some tangible response to the Soviet actions. "The Soviets correctly could have concluded as a result of what occurred after Tiananmen Square ... that while there may be some condemnation, the bottom line [is that] things will work out fine."

While a number of lawmakers called on the United States to impose sanctions against the Soviet Union, some leaders, including House Speaker Thomas S. Foley, D-Wash., cautioned against hasty action that might aggravate the deteriorating situation in the Soviet Union.

The trouble with sanctions, Foley said, "is that they tend to create the very circumstance in which those who oppose economic and political reform can claim that they have failed and argue for the return to old methods and attitudes."

Both chambers backed away from asking Bush to cancel the program, offered in December, to ease the Soviet Union's food shortage with up to $1 billion in export credit guarantees to buy U.S. grains, oilseeds and meat. Moscow had used more than $750 million of the credit.

U.S., Soviet Actions

Secretary of State Baker juggled conflicting U.S. concerns during talks in Washington with Aleksandr A. Bessmertnykh, the new Soviet foreign minister.

The week of Jan. 28 began with the expected announcement from the White House of an indefinite postponement of the U.S.-Soviet summit, originally set to take place in Moscow Feb. 11-13. But administration officials took pains to state that the crisis in the Baltics had not caused the delay.

"If the war was not going on, we'd go" to the summit, said presidential spokesman Fitzwater.

The only other impediment to a summit that Fitzwater cited was the slow progress toward reaching a bilateral agreement to limit strategic arms.

In going to considerable lengths to avoid a confrontation over the Baltics, the administration also reaped some unexpected benefits.

During his State of the Union address Jan. 29, Bush announced that Gorbachev had provided "representations" that his government would "move away from violence" in the Baltic States. Kremlin officials announced Jan. 30 that a tentative troop withdrawal had begun in Lithuania.

The reports of a pullout were welcomed by members of Congress, who had been urging, with rhetoric and resolutions, that the White House more forcefully oppose Moscow's reversion to hard-line tactics.

Some lawmakers had speculated that Bush was restrained in his criticism because of his desire to hold together the anti-Iraq alliance, which included the Soviet Union.

They said they believed it was no coincidence that the Soviet government undertook the attacks when the attention of the world was focused on the Persian Gulf.

"It would be a sad irony if the price of Soviet support for freeing Kuwait turns out to be American acquiescence in Soviet aggression against other small illegally annexed nations," Sen. Bradley said shortly before the confrontation in Lithuania.

Sen. Mitch McConnell, R-Ky., said it appeared that the administration's "quiet diplomacy" was "getting our message across without fracturing [the U.S.-Soviet] relationship."

Despite denials by both governments, some observers said the week's developments indicated that the two countries had reached a tacit compromise: The United States would soften its rhetoric on the Baltics in return for a troop withdrawal and the statement of support on the gulf.

"There certainly seems to be a compromise possible," said Marshall Goldman, associate director of the Russian Research Center at Harvard University. If so, he said, it would be a "masterful stroke" by the administration. ■

German Unification Treaty Approved

President Bush signed ratification documents Oct. 18 for the treaty approving Germany's unification. The treaty was signed by the former East and West Germany and the four Allies that had exercised jurisdiction over the divided Germany since World War II.

The Senate voted 98-0 on Oct. 10 to approve the Treaty on the Final Settlement with Respect to Germany (Treaty Doc. 101-20) to return full sovereignty to a unified Germany, formally ending the division of Germany that followed World War II. The action was a footnote to the merger of East and West Germany that proceeded with international approval Oct. 3. *(Vote 263, p. 53-S)*

Presenting the treaty on the Senate floor, Foreign Relations Committee Chairman Claiborne Pell, D-R.I., underscored the historic import of the document, which was signed Sept. 12 in Moscow by the two German states and the four World War II allies: the United States, France, Great Britain and the Soviet Union.

"History in our century has been dominated by two overarching events — successive world wars in the first half, and throughout the second half, a great geopolitical rift which has threatened civilization on our planet," Pell said. "The treaty before us today marks an end to both of these major events of the 20th century."

The Senate Foreign Relations Committee quickly and unanimously approved the treaty Oct. 2 that marked the close of a 45-year chapter in U.S. foreign policy. Members of the committee approved the treaty 19-0. Their comments reflected the gravity of the historic moment, both in the prospects for a vibrant democratic state and the heavy weight of Germany's fearsome past.

Pell emphasized Germany's importance to the United States' Cold War doctrine of "containment" of communism. He called unification the closing of a "geopolitical rift" that had shaped world politics since 1945.

"The treaty now before us provides not only for German unification, but also for the steps needed to end that East-West divide," he concluded.

President Bush invoked the same theme in a Rose Garden ceremony Oct. 3 honoring the new German nation: "For 45 years at the heart of a divided continent lived a divided people.

"Dreams sometimes do come true," Bush said. "Germany is united. Germany is free."

The treaty required Germany to reduce its military from 600,000 to 370,000 troops and to renounce the manufacture and use of nuclear, biological and chemical weapons. Germany would remain in the NATO alliance, a triumph for Bush and the West, and Soviet troops would have to leave the country by the end of 1994.

Background

In October 1989, it became clear that Soviet President Mikhail S. Gorbachev would not use his troops in East Germany to bolster the government of East German leader Erich Honecker against massive public demonstrations in Leipzig and other cities calling for political and economic liberalization.

By some accounts, Gorbachev collaborated with some top East German officials to push aside the elderly and ailing Honecker in mid-October.

The East German government's decision on Nov. 9, 1989, to open its borders to the West, followed by the collapse of the communist leadership less than a month later, suddenly revived interest in the possibility of some sort of merger of the two Germanys.

West German Chancellor Helmut Kohl seized the initiative on Nov. 28, 1989, proposing a 10-point plan leading first to a confederation of East and West Germany and then to a united nation.

Voicing historic Russian fears of German military power, Gorbachev initially rejected Kohl's plan outright, saying it was "the bidding of history" that there be two German states.

In a Dec. 4, 1989, news conference in Brussels, Bush said it was a major point of U.S. policy that unification occur in the context of West Germany's "continued commitment to NATO" and the move toward economic integration of the European community, and "with due regard for the legal role and responsibilities of the allied powers." The last phrase was a reference to the fact that Britain, France, the Soviet Union and the United States since World War II had been Berlin's legal protectors.

Baker said the reference to NATO meant that the United States opposed transforming West Germany into a neutral state as part of any unification bargain. "There should be no trade of neutralism for unity," he said. There had been widespread speculation that a possible outcome would be a united Germany aligned with neither superpower, like Austria.

Under pressure from Bonn, the East German government advanced parliamentary elections in 1990 from May 6 to March 18. And by early February, the Bonn government was pushing for a rapid monetary and economic union between the two German states.

Finally, amid worldwide attention and excitement, at midnight Oct. 3, East Germany was absorbed into a unified German state, which retained West Germany's membership in NATO.

Remaining Questions

During the Foreign Relations Committee's deliberations on the treaty, Rudy Boschwitz, R-Minn., expressed concern that the monstrous legacy of Nazi rule might be glossed over in the enthusiasm for Germany's future. "Their history as a unified country leaves something to be desired," he said.

Boschwitz, whose family fled Berlin when he was 2 years old and who lost many relatives in the Holocaust, added that he had "mixed emotions about seeing them get back together. Hopefully, it's for the good." But he warned, "We shall have to watch Germany."

Daniel Patrick Moynihan, D-N.Y., emphasized the ideological significance of East Germany's demise. After the defeat of Adolf Hitler in 1945, the carving of Germany into a democratic West and communist East provided the best test case for the theories of Karl Marx, Moynihan noted at a Foreign Relations hearing Sept. 28.

"At long last Marx would have his chance," Moynihan said, with the establishment of a Marxist regime in "an advanced industrial society."

"It did not work," Moynihan said. "It did not work at all, . . . that whole set of 19th-century expectations, for which people gave their lives and oceans of blood were spilt."

Some of the provisions of the unification treaty were directed at the concerns of other European nations over a unified Germany. Article I of the pact stated that the existing German-Polish border, drawn after World War II along the Oder and Neisse rivers, was the recognized, legitimate border.

In giving reassurance to Poland, however, this provision had unexpected consequences.

Representatives of the Baltic States — Estonia, Latvia and Lithuania, the three republics taken over by the Soviet Union during World War II — worried that the treaty could undercut their campaign for independence by legitimizing postwar borders.

Jesse Helms of North Carolina, Foreign Relations' ranking Republican, said the world was "still waiting to celebrate the Baltic States' freedom."

The Foreign Relations Committee on Oct. 2 approved a separate draft resolution stating that U.S. approval of the German borders should not "imply any diminution or compromise of the U.S. determination not to recognize the forceful incorporation of the Baltic States by the U.S.S.R."

Another issue raised before the Foreign Relations Committee was the fate of unresolved claims against East Germany by U.S. citizens.

Although the issue was not addressed in the treaty, the German government pledged to be responsible for resolution of the claims in a letter Sept. 18 from Foreign Minister Hans Genscher to the administration.

Robert B. Zoellick, counselor for the State Department, said that the United States was pursuing about 1,900 claims that had a value, as of 1981, of $77.8 million. He said these did not include claims by Jewish victims of the Holocaust who were pursuing their demands for restitution separately.

The NATO Issue

In requiring Soviet troops to leave Germany by the end of 1994 and providing for Germany to remain in NATO, the treaty marked a major triumph for Bush and the West.

NATO leaders meeting in London July 5-6 had recast long-established elements of the alliance's military strategy in hopes that the Soviets would acquiesce in German membership in the Western alliance.

Soviet President Gorbachev had originally insisted that Germany be neutral once East and West Germany were politically unified.

Apparently to reinforce that demand, Soviet negotiators slowed progress toward a treaty that would slash the number of conventional forces in Europe (CFE). Bush said after the meeting that he hoped the Soviets "will look at the changes that have taken place in NATO and say, 'Well, if NATO had been a threat to us, it no longer is a threat to us.' " *(CFE treaty, p. 696)* ■

Efforts at Hard Line on China Thwarted

President Bush deflected a number of efforts on Capitol Hill in 1990 to force the administration to take a harder line toward China because of Beijing's suppression of pro-democracy movements in June 1989 and other alleged human rights abuses by the communist regime.

Members of Congress had been agitating to impose sanctions on the Chinese government since the massacre of pro-democracy demonstrators near Tiananmen Square in Beijing in June 1989.

In 1990, those efforts took the shape of a number of legislative proposals dealing with issues such as trade, immigration and arms exports. But in a series of foreign policy victories for Bush, the measures were either defeated or amended to his liking.

Some lawmakers wanted to withdraw China's most-favored-nation (MFN) trading status, first granted in 1980. Withdrawal of MFN would have resulted in dramatically higher tariffs on Chinese goods sold in the United States.

Efforts to withdraw MFN status or to put restrictions on a further extension of MFN to China in 1991 failed when the Senate did not act on two House-passed bills or its own measures.

The White House had threatened to veto both House-passed bills.

Senate Majority Leader George J. Mitchell, D-Maine, introduced a bill (S 2836) to withdraw MFN immediately. Under expedited rules governing some trade bills in Congress, H J Res 647 was introduced to disapprove Bush's May decision to renew MFN for another year. And Rep. Don J. Pease, D-Ohio, offered a bill (HR 4939) that would have put new human rights conditions on a further one-year extension of MFN to China in 1991.

The House passed HR 4939 by a 384-30 vote Oct. 18, after adopting amendments that were said by opponents to be veto-bait. The House had passed H J Res 647 by a 247-174 vote earlier the same day.

Neither the Senate Finance Committee nor the full Senate acted on any of the bills.

In other action related to China in 1990, the Senate in January narrowly sustained a Bush veto of legislation (HR 2712) that would have permitted Chinese students who were in the United States at the time of the Tiananmen Square massacre to remain for an indeterminate period and to seek permanent resident status without returning to China. *(Chinese students, p. 767)*

Also in January, lawmakers included a number of sanctions on China in the State Department authorization bill including a ban on arms exports to China, a suspension of guarantees of U.S. private investments in China by the Overseas Private Investment Corporation, a suspension of nuclear cooperation agreements between the United States and China, and a suspension of U.S. participation in international moves to ease restrictions on exports to China of sophisticated technology. *(State Department authorization, p. 799)*

And the House Banking Committee in June approved a broad foreign economic aid measure (HR 5153) that contained language critical of China's human rights practices and that was intended to pressure the administration to hold firm on a policy severely restricting World Bank loans to China.

Though the bill died, the China provisions were included in the fiscal 1991 foreign aid appropriations bill. *(Eastern Europe bank aid, p. 206; foreign aid appropriations, p. 830)*

BACKGROUND

Two decades of progress toward improving relations between the United States and China froze June 3-4, 1989. The slaughter of hundreds of students and other protesters in Tiananmen Square by the Chinese army appeared aimed at ending seven weeks of peaceful demonstrations in China's main cities. *(1989 Almanac, p. 518)*

With Beijing surrounded by a massive military force and hard-line factions of the government in control, China seemed to be entering a new period of repression. China's senior leaders called on protest leaders to turn themselves in — the latest sign that they were no longer willing to tolerate mass public opposition.

Washington led the international chorus of condemnation of the Chinese massacre, taking steps intended to isolate the government leaders and to express moral support for the opposition. Bush on June 5 effectively froze relations between the two countries, particularly at the military level.

But Bush also said the United States did not want to undermine long-term relations between the two countries, which had progressed on a step-by-step basis since President Richard M. Nixon went to China in 1972. *(Congress & the Nation Vol. III, p. 893)*

Legislative Events in 1989

Both chambers of Congress passed legislation in 1989 imposing economic and political sanctions against China to protest the Beijing government's slaughter of hundreds of antigovernment protesters.

Bush imposed sanctions of his own in the wake of the Beijing massacre, but members of Congress felt they did not go far enough. Both chambers put sanctions on separate bills, and while Congress was moving to impose the sanctions, the Bush administration tried to patch up relations with Beijing.

A new diplomatic overture at the end of 1989 rekindled congressional and public anger at the Chinese government and put Bush on the defensive. Brent L. Scowcroft, Bush's national security adviser, led a high-level U.S. delegation on a surprise trip to China, ostensibly to brief leaders there on the outcome of the U.S.-Soviet summit meeting the week before. Other administration officials later acknowledged that the more important purpose of the trip was to begin repairing U.S. relations with China.

Democrats and Republicans in Congress questioned Bush's judgment in sending senior aides to China. They said the step had the appearance of relaxing the sanctions imposed to punish China for its slaughter of protesters and continuing repression of dissent.

Majority Leader Mitchell said Bush "kowtowed to the Chinese government."

Trade With China

In 1990, the main issue confronting lawmakers over U.S.-China relations dealt with trade relations with the expiration of China's MFN trading status on June 3.

The consequences of denying MFN status to China would have been to increase tariffs on imported Chinese goods by tenfold, perhaps doubling the domestic prices of some Chinese-made products.

China was the 10th-largest U.S. trading partner, and trade between the two countries was growing rapidly.

The country was a major supplier to the United States of clothing produced from silk, man-made fibers and cotton, and of certain categories of toys. The tariff on knitted sweaters, the largest single item imported from China, was 6 percent of customs value; it would increase to 60 percent if MFN were revoked. For most toys, the existing tariff was 6.8 percent and would increase to 70 percent.

If tariffs were to increase dramatically through loss of MFN status, the total value of Chinese imports would be expected to plummet. Imports from Romania fell by more than half when that country lost MFN status in 1988. Also, the Chinese government announced in May that if Congress denied continued MFN status, it would reciprocate by cutting off purchases of U.S. goods.

The United States imported goods worth $12 billion from China in 1989, up from $6.2 billion in 1987 and $8.4 billion in 1988. U.S. exports to China increased from $3.5 billion in 1987 to $5.8 billion in 1989.

Trade Status Renewal

President Bush on May 24 — just shy of the one-year anniversary of the Tiananmen Square massacre — announced his decision to renew normal trade status for China. The move was broadly denounced in Congress as yet another signal that the administration had turned its cheek to the country's human rights abuses.

"The president's repeated concessions to the Chinese government have been met with intransigence," Senate Majority Leader Mitchell said in a news conference shortly after Bush's announcement. "The answer is not more concessions."

By acting before the June 3 expiration of China's MFN status, Bush avoided making the announcement on the eve of the June 4 anniversary of the killings of Chinese student demonstrators.

Earlier in the week, after a Republican meeting at the White House, Sens. John H. Chafee, R.I., and Alan K. Simpson, Wyo., and House Minority Leader Robert H. Michel, Ill., backed Bush's move as the best way to keep U.S. leverage in China and to encourage human rights improvements.

But after Bush's announcement, legislation was quickly introduced in both chambers to overturn the order.

Among the Republicans denouncing the president's decision was Sen. Alfonse M. D'Amato of New York, who called it a "a shortsighted accommodation with a blood-stained and discredited regime."

Stephen J. Solarz, D-N.Y., chairman of the House Foreign Affairs Subcommittee on Asian and Pacific Affairs, offered the administration a middle road: less far-reaching legislation to tie 1991's decision on MFN status to the release of political prisoners and other human rights gains.

If the administration did not support this approach, Solarz warned at a hearing before three House Foreign Affairs subcommittees May 24, it could "run the risk of immediate termination" of MFN. "I assure you, Congress will move forward," he said.

The administration, though, showed no interest in tying China's trade status to human rights conditions.

"Let me emphasize that granting MFN is in no sense an act of approval of a given country's policies," Richard H. Solomon, assistant secretary of State for East Asian and Pacific affairs, said at the May 24 hearing. "It does not mean that the country in question is our most favorite nation."

There was also a fundamental division between the administration and a large bloc of critics in Congress over whether trade restrictions would improve, or worsen, the human rights situation in China.

Bush said renewing MFN status would further democratic reforms by keeping open channels of commerce and communication. "The people in China who trade with us are the engine of reform, an opening to the outside world," he said.

Revoking the trade treatment, he said, would mean lost jobs and revenue in China, Hong Kong and the United States. He said the price in Hong Kong, which had considerable investments in China and served as a conduit in many trade and manufacturing ventures, could be as high as 20,000 jobs and $10 billion in revenue.

But critics, including Democrats Tom Lantos, Calif., Nancy Pelosi, Calif., and Sam Gejdenson, Conn., said there was ample evidence that the administration's conciliatory approach had failed. They cited testimony by human rights groups that 10,000 to 30,000 political prisoners were in custody and that torture and executions were continuing.

HOUSE COMMITTEE ACTION

Legislative activity on U.S.-China trade relations began in the House when Sam M. Gibbons, D-Fla., chairman of the Ways and Means Trade Subcommittee, held hearings June 19 and June 21.

Deputy Secretary of State Lawrence S. Eagleburger presented the administration's case in favor of extending MFN status.

"The withdrawal of MFN would hurt those segments of the Chinese economy that are the most dynamic, the most Western-oriented and the most committed to the marketplace," Eagleburger told the subcommittee June 21. "It would severely damage the economic base of those forces generating pressure for further reform."

Subcommittee Action

Despite administration warnings, the subcommittee approved a bill July 12 to make renewal of China's MFN trade status in 1991 contingent upon improvements in human rights conditions. The bill (HR 4939), approved by voice vote, would have allowed China another year of normal U.S. tariffs under MFN status.

But before renewing that status in June 1991, the president would be required to certify that China had made "significant progress" toward meeting a list of human rights objectives.

These would include releasing political prisoners, accounting for those arrested since the June 1989 massacre in Tiananmen Square, ending martial law in all of China (including Tibet), easing restrictions on the news media and ending the intimidation of Chinese citizens abroad.

Without a presidential certification of progress on these fronts, Congress would disapprove any further extension of MFN status, which was renewed annually for China since it was granted in 1980.

"Our aim as a nation should not be to cut off MFN but to use the leverage of annual renewal to make progress," said Ohio's Pease, the bill's chief sponsor. "If we hold up absolute standards, why should they even try to meet them?"

Before adopting Pease's amended bill, the committee rejected, on a 3-10 vote, a tougher substitute offered by Thomas J. Downey, D-N.Y. Downey's bill would have required the Chinese to meet — not merely make progress toward — specified standards of behavior.

The subcommittee began July 12 with a version of HR 4939 that Pease had reworked. Gone was an earlier requirement that the Chinese stop supporting the Khmer Rouge in Cambodia.

Gone, too, was a provision under which the withdrawal of MFN would also prompt a U.S. proposal that China be stripped of its observer status in the General Agreement on Tariffs and Trade (GATT).

New in the revised Pease bill was a requirement that the president, in deciding whether to renew MFN for China, consider the effect his decision would have on the economy of Hong Kong.

Hong Kong's exposure was an often-mentioned issue in hearings held by both the Ways and Means and Senate Finance committees the week of June 18.

Frank J. Guarini, D-N.J., called Pease's modified bill a "solid middle-ground approach." Beryl Anthony Jr., D-Ark., said it would "send a strong signal, yet not impair the opportunity for trade to continue."

Despite Pease's changes, the administration continued to express opposition to the bill on July 12.

In a letter to subcommittee Chairman Gibbons, Deputy Secretary of State Eagleburger said making MFN contingent on reforms in human rights could backfire and cause conditions in China to worsen.

The one major amendment approved in subcommittee was offered by ranking member Philip M. Crane, R-Ill. It required that, to win 1991 renewal of MFN status, the Chinese be certified as having moderated their longstanding opposition to Taiwan's participation in GATT.

Although China enjoyed only observer status in GATT, its opposition had been a major obstacle to participation by Taiwan.

Full Committee Action

The House Ways and Means Committee voted July 18 to continue normalized trade relations with China for another year but tied extension of the low tariffs on Chinese imports beyond June 1991 to "significant" improvements in that nation's human rights behavior.

By voice vote, the committee sent HR 4939 to the House floor. The bill as approved was unchanged from the subcommittee version, despite efforts by several members to stiffen its provisions.

The committee turned back three amendments sponsored by Richard T. Schulze, R-Pa. One would have canceled immediately China's eligibility for MFN status. That amendment would have left intact the bill's proposed new restrictions for extending MFN status to China in 1991. It was defeated on a 7-12 show-of-hands vote.

Two other defeated amendments would have stiffened the procedures for granting MFN to China in 1991.

Schulze and a handful of others on the committee complained that the Pease bill was tantamount to telling the Chinese government: "You've got one more year, but please do a little bit better."

The administration strongly opposed a cutoff of MFN, and supporters of Pease's approach called it a good compromise. Committee Chairman Dan Rostenkowski, D-Ill., said withdrawal of MFN would be "counterproductive."

Schulze and his allies were further rebuffed in their effort to seek the committee's endorsement — and Rostenkowski's in particular — of a House floor vote on terminating MFN for China. The committee voted instead to ask the Rules Committee to permit no amendments during floor debate.

Provisions

The bill's provisions were fairly straightforward. The measure would change the so-called Jackson-Vanik amendment to the 1974 Trade Act to require that, to grant MFN to China, the president would have to report to Congress that prior to June 4, 1991, China had made "significant progress" toward achieving seven human rights goals listed in the bill.

Jackson-Vanik specified that MFN could be extended to non-market-economy countries only when they guaranteed their citizens free emigration. The president could waive that requirement annually, provided that he reported that the country was making progress on improving its emigration policies.

It was under such an annual waiver that China had been granted MFN status since 1980.

The provisions of HR 4939 would have extended Jackson-Vanik requirements beyond emigration for the first time. The human rights goals set out in the bill included the following:

- Terminating martial law throughout China and Tibet.
- Accounting for people detained or accused of crimes in the aftermath of the 1990 crackdown on dissenters and their release from prison.
- Easing press freedom restrictions.
- Terminating harassment of Chinese citizens in the United States.
- Eliminating fees imposed since June 1989 on Chinese citizens seeking to travel abroad.

The provisions would have been in effect only for 1991. Extension of MFN status beyond 1991 would not have been tied to human rights progress beyond the Jackson-Vanik emigration requirements.

HOUSE FLOOR ACTION

HR 4939 had been expected to come to the floor the first week of October, but it was delayed after the Rules Committee first approved and later withdrew procedures for floor debate and amendments.

The Rules Committee originally voted to allow four floor amendments — two of which were controversial and would have toughened the standards against which China's human rights progress would be measured. But it later reversed itself. Ways and Means Chairman Rostenkowski had asked the committee to allow no floor amendments.

Nancy Pelosi, D-Calif., one of a group of congressional hard-liners on China's human rights record, had been given permission to offer an amendment that she said would merely "tighten" the Pease language. Among other things, she wanted to require that dissidents jailed during and after 1989 pro-democracy demonstrations be freed.

She said the Rules Committee indicated that the amendment's sponsors would have to make their case again for the reason changes were needed.

When the measure finally reached the floor on Oct. 18, the House voted first to deny normalized trade status to China and then to put severe restrictions on resuming

Veto on Chinese Students in U.S. Sustained

The Senate on Jan. 25 narrowly sustained President Bush's veto of legislation (HR 2712) to protect Chinese students in the United States. During and after the debate, Republican senators, who provided the margin of victory, framed the vote in partisan rather than substantive terms.

The bill would have permitted Chinese students who were in the United States at the time of the Tiananmen Square massacre in June 1989 to remain for an indeterminate period and to seek permanent resident status without returning to China. It also would have waived for four years a requirement that Chinese exchange students on "J" visas return home for at least two years before applying for permanent U.S. residency.

The House had passed HR 2712 by a vote of 403-0 and the Senate by voice vote in 1989. Bush vetoed the legislation Nov. 30, 1989, while Congress was in recess. The action was part of the administration's effort to restore cordial relations with China despite that country's repression of pro-democracy forces. *(1989 Almanac, p. 279; veto message, 1989 Almanac, p. 42-C)*

Before the Senate's 62-37 vote, which fell four short of the number needed to override the veto, Minority Leader Bob Dole, R-Kan., referred to the fact that 1990 was an election year and said, "It's not about China policy. It's American politics. It is not freedom or morality or human rights — it is bash Bush." *(Vote 1, p. 2-S)*

Bush's overtures to China since the June 1989 crackdown had enraged many in Congress, and Republicans in both chambers were among those criticizing his policies during the veto debate. Nonetheless, most GOP senators swallowed their reservations and stuck with Bush. All of those voting to sustain the veto were Republicans; eight GOP members joined 54 Democrats in voting to override.

A day earlier, the House voted 390-25 to nullify the veto. Again, all of those supporting the president were Republican. *(Vote 4, p. 2-H)*

"Today was a victory for President Bush and for the Chinese leadership that was responsible for Tiananmen Square," Edward M. Kennedy, D-Mass., said after the Senate vote.

Alfonse M. D'Amato, R-N.Y., who decided to oppose the override after a personal meeting with Bush the day before, called the vote "a great victory." During the debate, D'Amato said, "I don't know what we gain by embarrassing him [Bush]. If this isn't politics, I don't know what is."

Bush interpreted the vote as an endorsement of his China policy. He said at a news conference, "The thing I like about it, given the mournful predictions of some a couple of weeks ago, is that it gives me the confidence that I'm going to go forward the way that I think is correct here [on China policy]."

Bush reiterated his pledge that no students would be sent back to China while it was unsafe for such a return. Immediately after his veto, Bush ordered the Justice Department to put protections into effect for Chinese nationals who were in the United States at the time of Beijing's crackdown.

The president and his allies had argued strenuously that Bush's administrative action would protect the students and that he should be free to handle foreign policy with China.

Before the veto, 48 Democratic and 26 Republican senators wrote to Bush asking that he let the legislation stand. The senators said the students needed the security of a statute rather than the uncertainty of a presidential directive that could be withdrawn at any time. Of those 26 Republicans, however, 18 voted to sustain the veto.

If the legislation had passed, the government in Beijing threatened to abandon participation in the Fulbright scholarship program and other educational exchanges. It also had signaled that passage of HR 2712 would hurt its already strained relations with the United States.

Bush chose to be conciliatory. He insisted that by giving relief to the students through a less formal means he would gain additional leverage to persuade the Chinese government to adopt reforms.

To the dismay of many in Congress, the administration had taken a number of other steps to lessen U.S.-Chinese tensions resulting from the massacre in Tiananmen Square.

Those actions in 1989 included sending a secret delegation to China in July and a public visit in December by national security adviser Brent Scowcroft. On Dec. 19, Bush lifted a ban on exporting three communications satellites to China.

Administration officials had said they were trying privately to persuade the Beijing government to ease oppression and that they believed the Jan. 10, 1990, lifting of martial law in the capital was a sign of progress. In addition, the Chinese government announced Jan. 18 that it had released 573 people who had been detained for involvement in pro-democracy protests.

Bush Issues Order

Responding to the criticism from lawmakers, Bush on April 11 issued a promised executive order shielding from deportation Chinese students who had been in the United States since the Chinese government crackdown in 1989. The order directed the attorney general to "take any steps necessary to defer until Jan. 1, 1994, the enforced departure of all nationals of the People's Republic of China and their dependents."

Bush had promised he would issue an executive order to accomplish the same goal, but he had not done so until April 11, relying instead on a directive to the Justice Department. His inaction had drawn complaints from many members of Congress.

Congress had one final word on the matter when lawmakers included a non-binding provision in the conference report on legislation (S 358 — PL 101-649) overhauling the U.S. immigration system. The conference report, cleared on Oct. 27, stated that Congress intended that the president's executive order barring the return of Chinese nationals remain in effect as Bush had indicated until 1994. *(Immigration overhaul, p. 474)*

normal relations in June 1991. Even supporters of the legislation (H J Res 647, HR 4939), though, conceded the votes were a more symbolic than substantive act.

The House Ways and Means Committee had sent H J Res 647 to the House floor Sept. 25 without recommendation. Rep. Gerald B. H. Solomon, R-N.Y., had introduced H J Res 647 to disapprove Bush's Jackson-Vanik waiver for China.

Pease, chief sponsor of HR 4939, had worked with the administration and those in Congress opposed to denying MFN to China, to make his bill acceptable. But Pelosi, like Solomon a hard-line opponent of the existing Chinese regime's treatment of its own people, worked to stiffen the requirements of the Pease bill.

On Oct. 18, when the Pease bill reached the House floor, Pelosi and others succeeded in adding amendments to make it more difficult for the president to rule that China was reforming its human rights record.

Congressional antipathy toward the Chinese government was loud: Solomon said Congress should act "to send a message to the angry old men who are hiding out in the so-called Great Hall of the People" in Beijing. And more than one member referred to the "butchers of Beijing."

The administration signaled its intention to veto the Solomon bill and also the Pease bill, if it were amended.

As it came to the floor, Pease's bill required the president to find that China was making "significant progress" toward meeting seven specific human rights goals. By a 347-74 vote, however, the House stiffened the definition of significant progress and added new requirements — including a condition that the Chinese government release political prisoners detained after the Tiananmen massacre. *(Vote 484, p. 154-H)*

After the House adopted other amendments affecting U.S. companies doing business in China and China's treatment of Hong Kong, it passed the Pease bill by a 384-30 vote. The House previously passed Solomon's disapproval resolution by a smaller, but still bipartisan, 247-174 vote. *(Votes 486, 483, p. 154-H)*

SENATE ACTION

The Senate never acted on its own legislation or any of the House-passed bills or resolutions dealing with trade with China. The Senate's inaction prevented any measures from becoming law in 1991.

In the only legislative activity on the Senate side, Finance Chairman Lloyd Bentsen, D-Texas, held a full committee hearing June 20.

Afterward, Bentsen would say only that he was still reviewing Congress' options on China. But in his opening remarks at the hearing, he said he thought sanctions would hurt China only if enough countries joined in to make them stick. "Embargoes are effective only so far as you hurt [the sanctioned country] more than you hurt yourself," he said.

That set Bentsen apart from the strict non-renewal posture struck in May by Mitchell, who had been the most outspoken member of the Democratic leadership in either body. "Waiting and hoping has not changed the policies of the Chinese government," Mitchell said.

Awarding MFN status, the majority leader added, "rewards the Chinese government for a year of political arrests and executions, a year of intensive public security controls, a year of continued arms sales to the Mideast, a year of restrictions on foreign journalists in China and harassment of Chinese students residing in the United States."

John D. Rockefeller IV, D-W.Va., a student of Chinese history, said June 20 that he feared that Chinese leaders would not respond as hoped to U.S. pressure. He said cutting off MFN would, "in classic fashion, be hurting precisely those we were trying most to help."

Minority Leader Bob Dole, R-Kan., while acknowledging his own state's interest in grain sales to China, said he was convinced that sanctions would cost jobs in China's southern and coastal provinces where free-market and partly private ventures had flourished.

Dole also pointed to Hong Kong, which he said he hoped would be a "highly contagious center of capitalism," and said this was "precisely not the time to deliver a body blow to the Hong Kong economy."

Daniel Patrick Moynihan, D-N.Y., was alone among senators at the June 20 hearing in supporting a denial of MFN status for China. Moynihan, who introduced a bill to that effect shortly after Tiananmen, contrasted trends in China with those in Eastern Europe and the Soviet Union.

He criticized Bush for denying MFN to the Soviets because they had not fully codified their liberalized emigration practices while granting it to China, where "the desperation of totalitarianism lives on."

Moynihan cast the argument in explicit moral terms: "Either we believe in human rights or we don't."

But the preponderance of testimony over the three days addressed itself not to ends — all the witnesses made clear their support for a freer China — but to means. ■

U.S.-Pakistan Relations Strained; Aid Frozen

The future of the U.S.-Pakistan alliance came into question in 1990 because of that nation's emerging nuclear potential, as well as antidemocratic moves by Pakistan's military rulers. President Bush declined to certify that Pakistan had refrained from developing nuclear weapons, a step that was required under a 1985 law for the continuation of the more than $560 million a year in U.S. assistance to Islamabad.

Suspension of the aid, which took effect Oct. 1, was unpopular in Pakistan, where all political parties had backed a nuclear arms program. Pakistani President Ghulam Ishaq Khan, elected Oct. 24, pledged to resist bowing to U.S. demands to halt the program.

But U.S. Ambassador Robert Oakley responded with a letter to a leading Pakistani newspaper the next month, stating that for aid to be resumed, Pakistan would have to prove that it had not assembled a nuclear weapon or its components.

By early 1991, the Bush administration indicated that it was going to seek more than $100 million in security assistance for Pakistan in fiscal 1992, even though the country remained barred from receiving U.S. aid.

Robert Bauerlein, an aide to Deputy Secretary of State Lawrence S. Eagleburger, said, "It is still the intention and the policy of the administration to have an assistance program with Pakistan."

Background

A 1985 amendment to the Foreign Assistance Act, sponsored by Sen. Larry Pressler, R-S.D., stated that aid must be cut off automatically unless the president certified before the start of each fiscal year that Pakistan "does not possess a nuclear explosive device." *(1985 Almanac, p. 61)*

In recent years, the Reagan and Bush administrations provided the certification despite serious reservations about Pakistan's emerging nuclear potential. In 1989, CIA Director William H. Webster told the Senate Governmental Affairs Committee that "clearly, Pakistan is engaged in developing a nuclear capability." But such concerns were set aside — until 1990 — largely because of Islamabad's activities in support of the U.S.-backed Afghan rebels.

With Soviet troops being withdrawn from Afghanistan, though, Pakistan's role in that conflict became less important. At the same time, experts said that Pakistan had developed the ability to launch a nuclear strike, despite pledges to slow its weapons program.

Leonard S. Spector, a senior associate at the Carnegie Endowment For International Peace, said Pakistan was able to deploy 10 to 12 nuclear bombs, probably by aircraft. "As a result of the crisis this year over Kashmir, [territory along the Indian border that was claimed by both countries], any restraints that were on the program have been removed," he said.

Foreign Aid Questions

With the passing of the Cold War, Congress had grown increasingly dubious of the need for foreign military grants, aside from those provided to allies in the Middle East. Excluding the $3.1 billion specified for Israel and Egypt, the $15.4 billion fiscal 1991 foreign aid bill (HR 5114 — PL 101-513) cut the administration request for grants by nearly 25 percent. The bill, cleared by the Senate on Oct. 27, replaced some of the grants with low-interest loans.

Perhaps more important, the legislation reduced by $400 million the administration request for Economic Support Fund (ESF) aid. Such aid was widely used, especially by the Reagan and Bush administrations, to bolster the economies of U.S. military allies.

Aside from the slightly more than $2 billion in ESF funds earmarked for Israel and Egypt, the State Department would have only about $1 billion to spread among other countries.

"It's clear that ESF has been hit the hardest," said one administration official.

The official pointed out that the existing prohibition on aid to Pakistan could work to the advantage of other ESF recipients, who could otherwise face a reduction. (The administration had requested $210 million in ESF aid for Pakistan, along with $228 million in military grants.)

Demonstrating the zero-sum nature of foreign aid in 1990, the official added that ESF aid for countries such as Nicaragua could be jeopardized if the administration certified that Pakistan was again eligible for assistance.

Short-Term Waiver

Before the foreign aid bill cleared Congress, the administration initiated an intensive lobbying campaign on Capitol Hill for a temporary waiver of the Pressler amendment, even though officials indirectly acknowledged Pakistan's nuclear capability.

The idea of a short-term waiver that would allow aid to flow to Pakistan received a cool response in Congress at the time. Stephen J. Solarz, D-N.Y., chairman of the House Foreign Affairs Subcommittee on Asian and Pacific Affairs, told a hearing of his panel Oct. 2, "We cannot continue to warn Pakistan of adverse consequences if it takes certain actions and then fail to follow through on our warnings when Pakistan persists in taking these actions."

In the Senate, where the foreign aid appropriations bill would have been an appropriate vehicle for such a waiver, there also was little support for the proposal. Patrick J. Leahy, D-Vt., chairman of the Senate Appropriations Subcommittee on Foreign Operations, did not include language authorizing a waiver in the bill his subcommittee considered. Nor was the bill amended for that purpose, either in the full committee or on the Senate floor.

The administration asked for the waiver, said one official, in order to leave all of its options open at least until Pakistan held elections Oct. 24. Prime Minister Benazir Bhutto was dismissed from office in August, and there was widespread concern throughout official Washington that the caretaker military government could delay the balloting or, even worse, hold sham elections.

If the military had been defeated in free elections, the administration was expected to try to exert influence on the new government, the official said. But if the elections were tainted, he added, "it is difficult to see how the aid program can be rescued."

Bhutto was routed in the election, though a U.S.-led observer team initially raised some questions about the conduct of the election. The team soon concluded, however, that it found no evidence of rigging in the election that would have significantly changed the results of the vote.

Early Committee Action

Earlier in the year, Congress was more receptive to a waiver for Pakistan. Tension and instability in the Middle East, though, also heightened concerns over any nuclear threats in the volatile region.

On June 13, the House Appropriations Foreign Operations Subcommittee included in its fiscal 1991 foreign aid appropriations bill a provision to extend the waiver for Pakistan for one year. Because of Pakistan's strategic location, Congress had allowed aid there until April 1, 1991 — despite strong evidence that Pakistan was developing nuclear bombs.

The panel's draft bill, sponsored by David R. Obey, D-Wis., was silent on the issue, thus allowing the existing waiver to expire and requiring an aid cutoff halfway through fiscal 1991. Charles Wilson, D-Texas, a longtime advocate of aid to Pakistan, said the government in Islamabad would consider that a "hostile act," and pushed for the waiver. Obey eventually relented and agreed to insert in the bill another waiver for Pakistan until April 1992.

The administration's stance on aid suspension apparently shifted in response to new intelligence that cast doubt on Pakistan's previous assurances that it was keeping the components of any nuclear bomb separated. After the aid suspension, The Washington Post quoted unidentified sources as saying that the United States had learned that Pakistan had resumed its enrichment of uranium to the quality required for nuclear weapons and had taken steps interpreted as potential preparations for the deployment of nuclear bombs aboard U.S.-made F-16 fighter aircraft. ■

Chamorro Win Ensures Aid to Nicaragua

The upset victory of opposition leader Violeta Chamorro in Nicaragua's presidential election Feb. 25 paved the way for Congress and the Bush administration to all but end more than eight years of partisan conflict over U.S. policy toward the Central American nation.

President Bush and lawmakers in both parties hailed the election of the U.S.-backed Chamorro over leftist President Daniel Ortega. Bush requested, and Congress approved, an infusion of $300 million in U.S. aid to help the former newspaper publisher's new government grapple with excrutiating economic problems caused in part by U.S. economic sanctions imposed in 1985.

By defeating the Sandinista leader at the ballot box, Chamorro achieved what the United States had been unable to accomplish with $311.7 million in aid from 1982 through 1989 to the antigovernment rebels known as the contras. The Reagan administration had clashed repeatedly with Congress over its efforts to topple the Marxist regime. The Bush administration tried a different tack, crafting a bipartisan policy that emphasized regional peacekeeping efforts and pressure on Ortega to allow a free and fair election. *(1989 Almanac, p. 569)*

Even after Chamorro's election, a residue of bitterness, and some policy disagreements, persisted in Washington. The administration and its critics predictably disagreed on who deserved credit for the outcome, and they differed on the terms for repatriation of the contras in Nicaragua. *(Policy debate, p. 772)*

The overwhelming reaction, however, was one of jubilation and relief. "It's almost as if a dark cloud has passed us by," said Sen. Christopher J. Dodd, D-Conn., a leading critic of U.S. policy in Central America.

While Congress raised few concerns about Bush's March 13 request for aid to Nicaragua, final approval came slower than the president had hoped. The funds were added to a previously introduced supplemental appropriations bill (HR 4404) to provide aid to the new government of Panama. *(Aid to Panama, p. 774)*

Parliamentary delays largely unrelated to foreign aid issues held up the bill despite Bush's repeated pleas for speedy action. The measure finally cleared Congress on May 25, one month after Chamorro had been inaugurated in Managua. Bush signed it into law the same day.

BOXSCORE

Legislation: Aid to Nicaragua, contained in Dire Emergency Supplemental Appropriations Act, PL 101-302 (HR 4404).

Major action: Signed, May 25. Conference report adopted by Senate, May 25 (session of May 24); by House, 308-108, May 24. Passed by Senate, May 1; by House, 362-59, April 3.

Reports: Conference report (H Rept 101-493); Appropriations (S Rept 101-272); Appropriations (H Rept 101-434).

BACKGROUND

The United States played a major role in Nicaragua's presidential election, its first since 1984. At that time, the Reagan administration had tried to discredit the balloting in advance and persuaded the main opposition candidate, former contra leader Arturo Cruz, to withdraw.

The Bush administration instead centered its policy on the presidential balloting, fashioning a combination of "incentives and disincentives" to encourage the Sandinistas to keep their promises of reform. Ortega had agreed to the election at the February 1989 conference of presidents of five Central American countries (Costa Rica, El Salvador, Guatemala, Honduras and Nicaragua). In exchange, Ortega received international support for a call on the contras to demobilize.

The administration's commitment to the Central American leaders' peace process helped persuade Congress to approve non-military aid to the contras until after the Nicaraguan election. The administration then concentrated its efforts on pressuring the Sandinistas to open their political system and allow the election to be conducted freely.

In October 1989, Congress passed legislation sought by Bush (HR 3385 — PL 101-119) authorizing $9 million in U.S. aid for the Nicaraguan election. The funds included $1.8 million in direct aid to the major opposition group, the loosely knit National Opposition Union (UNO) headed by Chamorro, and $1.5 million for a related poll-watching institute.

Conditions in Nicaragua

For Nicaragua, the election offered the prospect of ending a conflict that had cost thousands of lives, devastated its economy and produced a desperate longing for peace among Nicaraguans of all stripes.

Moreover, the Sandinistas were being pressed by their primary benefactor — the Soviet Union — to end the confrontation with the United States. Soviet President Mikhail S. Gorbachev cut off direct arms shipments to the Sandinistas, and the Soviets also curtailed their economic subsidies.

Nonetheless, the election process was not easy for anti-Sandinista groups. Accustomed to dominating local politics, the Sandinistas resisted moves that the opposition said were necessary for a free election.

Strong outside pressures were needed, for example, to get opposition parties fair access to the major government-owned television station. The government resisted election-law reforms, and it released U.S.-supplied aid to UNO only after a strong demand by former U.S. President Jimmy Carter, who headed an independent election monitoring group.

The Sandinistas eventually bowed to most outside demands, however, and satisfied most observers, including many skeptics, that the election would be untainted. Joao Baena Soares, secretary general of the Organization of American States (OAS), said Feb. 8 that the election process appeared "normal" for Latin America.

Rep. Doug Bereuter, R-Neb., a member of Carter's delegation, said that until early February, "the opposition did not have a fair opportunity to get its message across." But belated concessions by the Sandinistas "may be sufficient to suggest that there will be a fair opportunity" for the opposition to win, he said.

The Bush administration complained about alleged Sandinista intimidation of the opposition and also objected to the government's refusal to allow an official U.S. delegation to monitor the election. White House spokesman Marlin Fitzwater on Feb. 7 said Ortega's refusal to admit Bush's observers, coupled with previous moves against the opposition, "bring into question the Sandinista commitment" to a free and fair election.

At the same time, though, the administration was signaling that it would abide by the results of untainted balloting. Secretary of State James A. Baker III said on Feb. 1 that "we would be prepared to improve relations with any government that wins a certifiably free and fair election in Nicaragua." Baker added, though, that Washington would first insist that Nicaragua keep its past pledges to stop shipping weapons to rebels in neighboring El Salvador.

Decisive Victory for Chamorro

Polls in advance of the Feb. 25 election showed Ortega, who had led the Sandinista government since it came to power in 1979, well ahead of Chamorro, who had been publisher of the main opposition newspaper *La Prensa*. In the actual balloting, however, Chamorro scored a decisive victory: 55 percent to 41 percent.

The balloting was witnessed by thousands of observers and journalists and universally regarded as free and fair. Public opinion experts in the United States suggested afterward that the pre-election polls may have been skewed by Nicaraguans' fears of openly stating their preference for the opposition.

Bush promptly congratulated Chamorro, promised U.S. help in a "peaceful reconciliation and transition," and called for re-establishment of the cease-fire between the government and the contras. "Given the election's clear mandate for peace and democracy, there is no reason at all for further military activity from any quarter," Bush said in a statement Feb. 26.

On Capitol Hill, lawmakers on both sides of the contra debate claimed credit for the outcome. Conservatives stressed the military pressure from the rebels, while liberals discounted the contras' importance and emphasized instead the Central American leaders' peace process.

The disagreements were in view March 1 as the Senate argued over several proposed resolutions congratulating Nicaragua on the election. Unable to agree on who should be commended for the outcome, senators withdrew their proposals and left everyone in Nicaragua without official praise from Congress.

There was general agreement, however, on the need for the United States to provide aid to the new government and to move quickly to normalize trade and diplomatic relations with Nicaragua for the first time since 1985. Some on Capitol Hill spoke of an aid package matching or exceeding the $500 million that Bush had requested for Panama following the U.S. invasion and ouster of strongman Gen. Manuel Antonio Noriega. Administration officials, however, held off any specific figure to await a visit by Francisco Mayorga, Chamorro's senior economic adviser, to Washington during the week of March 5.

Both Bush and Chamorro called on the estimated 10,000 contras to lay down their arms immediately. The issue remained, however, of what the United States would do to assist resettlement of the rebels and their 50,000 family members, most of whom were camped in neighboring Honduras. Bush on March 2 sent diplomat Harry Schlaudeman — later to be named U.S. ambassador to Nicaragua — to discuss the issue with contra leaders.

Aid Package Proposed

In his meetings with Bush officials and members of Congress, Mayorga requested $300 million in emergency aid. Bush asked for a $300 million package March 13 and urged Congress to act on it promptly.

Bush's package included about $60 million for major agricultural supplies and oil; about $60 million for development projects such as infrastructure repair, health and education, and support for democratic institutions; and $75 million in balance-of-payments support to rebuild the economy. Other elements included $32 million to repatriate the contras and $15 million for other Nicaraguan refugees; $10 million for emergency employment programs; and $50 million to help pay off Nicaragua's $234 million debt to international financial institutions.

Bush also said he would submit a fiscal 1991 funding request for $200 million for Nicaragua.

Sanctions Lifted

At the same time, Bush lifted the economic sanctions and trade embargo imposed in 1985 and took other preliminary steps to restore trade with Nicaragua. According to Commerce Department figures, U.S.-Nicaragua trade had dropped from $181 million in 1984 to $7 million in 1988.

One immediate action was to restore Nicaragua's sugar quota, which the State Department estimated could bring $33 million to Nicaragua by the end of the year. Other steps included helping Nicaragua qualify for trade benefits under the Generalized System of Preferences, the Caribbean Basin Initiative, the Export-Import Bank and the Overseas Private Investment Corporation.

The lifted sanctions also had included a ban on flights between Nicaragua and the United States and the barring of Nicaraguan ships from U.S. ports.

HOUSE ACTION

Bush's aid request appeared to have broad support on Capitol Hill.

Senate Minority Leader Bob Dole, R-Kan., seconded the president's call for quick action. "The people of Nicaragua and Panama have courageously opted for freedom and democracy," Dole said. "We can't let them down now."

Rep. David E. Bonior, D-Mich., a longtime opponent of contra aid, said Bush's plan "seems at the outset to be reasonable."

Some Democrats, however, grumbled about the amount requested and the lack of specifics. David R. Obey, D-Wis., chairman of the House Appropriations Foreign Operations Subcommittee, called the Bush proposal "a press release." His counterpart on the Senate Appropriations Foreign Operations Subcommittee, Patrick J. Leahy, D-Vt., echoed Obey's concerns: "Every day something new happens, we send a delegation out quickly to say 'the check's in the mail,' but no one's looked at the balance in the checkbook, which is zero."

The administration was asking for more money for Panama and Nicaragua "than the state of Vermont will use in two years," Leahy complained.

Subcommittee Hearing

Lawmakers got a chance to air their complaints formally at a joint hearing of two House Foreign Affairs

Both Sides Claim Credit for Chamorro's Win

Both sides in the decade-long debate over U.S. policy in Nicaragua rushed to claim credit for the Feb. 25 victory of the U.S.-backed opposition candidate in Nicaragua's presidential election.

Longtime supporters of the contras argued with passion that the leftist Sandinistas agreed to hold free elections only because of military "pressure" from the rebels. According to this view, President Ronald Reagan forced the Nicaraguan elections by supporting the contras with arms aid and demanding at every opportunity that the Sandinistas yield power at the ballot box.

"When President Reagan recognized what was taking place down there and confronted the Sandinista government with American purpose, and with the contras, and with the sometimes-cooperation of the Congress, it was an act that brought into place that which culminated in the election," said Sen. Malcolm Wallop, R-Wyo.

Liberal Democrats who consistently opposed contra aid insisted instead that Reagan and the guerrillas had little to do with the election outcome. It was the Central American "peace process" created by Oscar Arias, president of Costa Rica, that did most to persuade the Sandinistas to risk their power at the ballot box, the liberals maintained. These Democrats noted that the contras had received no U.S. military aid for nearly two years — during which time the Sandinistas signed agreements that led to the elections.

"This election was the fruit of the labors by Oscar Arias and those who supported his efforts," said Sen. Christopher J. Dodd, D-Conn. "The view that the contra war created Sunday's election is absolutely false."

The Bush administration offered a third perspective, melding arguments from each of the other two.

The United States' diplomacy over the previous year helped lay the groundwork for the election in Nicaragua, a senior State Department official told reporters Feb. 27. The administration early in 1989 developed a multipronged policy, this official said, including avidly supporting the elections and the Central American peace process and encouraging Europe and the Soviet Union to condition aid to Nicaragua on free elections.

Another element, he said, was keeping the contras intact as a military force, ready for a return to action if the Sandinistas failed to carry out their promises.

That policy, which gained broad bipartisan support on Capitol Hill, was designed to "create" the opportunity for free elections in Nicaragua, the official said.

Members of Congress said the administration deserved credit, but few gave it the major share. "I'm a little skeptical that somebody sat down and figured out how to orchestrate all this," said Rep. Porter J. Goss, R-Fla.

Nearly all members of Congress who went to Nicaragua to watch the elections said much of the credit for the outcome went to former President Jimmy Carter, who headed his own delegation and was the de facto leader of 3,000 observers.

Republicans and Democrats alike praised Carter for intervening at delicate moments to persuade the Sandinistas to allow free voting. On election night, Carter persuaded both the Sandinistas and the opposition to respect the results and to honor the election by avoiding violence and retribution.

"President Carter played a crucial role in all of this," said Rep. Doug Bereuter, R-Neb.

Another election observer, Republican Sen. John C. Danforth of Missouri, said valid arguments could be made supporting all the claims for credit. But events in Nicaragua were more important than what happened in Washington, he said.

"My guess is that in the real world, the [Sandinistas'] system didn't work and it just fell of its own weight," Danforth said. "All over the world, people are assuming control of government rather than the other way around."

subcommittees March 14. Sam Gejdenson, D-Conn., chairman of the International Economic Policy Subcommittee, and others told two State Department officials that they did not appreciate waiting for Bush's plan and then being given just three weeks to consider it. And Gejdenson said Americans should not be excluded from the peace dividend. "We can't ask Americans to get in line behind Panamanians and Nicaraguans and Romanians and East Germans," Gejdenson said.

Michael Kozak, principal deputy assistant secretary of State at the Bureau of Inter-American Affairs, responded: "We need to look at this package as an investment in peace and stability. We have peace breaking out all over, but I think we need to solidify it before we declare a dividend."

Contra Resettlement

Gejdenson and others also pressed for details on the administration's plans for resettling the contras.

Joseph G. Sullivan, director of the State Department's Office of Central American Affairs, said the administration wanted to spend $500 per contra family member on transportation, shelter, food, seeds and other agricultural implements and, if necessary, a United Nations observer force. Kozak told the hearing that the U.S. government was not buying back weapons from the rebels.

Gerry E. Studds, D-Mass., noted reports that contras with weapons were returning from Honduras and asked Sullivan, "How can we justify continuing aid to armed contras inside Nicaragua?" Sullivan said the aid would help the contras reintegrate into society.

The State Department's highest ranking Latin American expert repeated that message to a skeptical Matthew F. McHugh, D-N.Y., in a hearing before the Foreign Operations Appropriations Subcommittee on March 19.

"The purpose is to allow [the contras] to return to civilian life unarmed," said Bernard W. Aronson, assistant secretary of State for inter-American affairs. The prospect of aid will be a "genuine economic incentive" for the contras to surrender their arms, he said.

Skepticism about the contras persisted, however, leading the House Appropriations subcommittee to attach a provision that would allow resettlement aid only for contras who agreed to lay down their arms. Over administration objections, the bill also stipulated that the resettlement funds be channeled through a "verification commission" run by the United Nations and the OAS.

Opponents of the contras feared that the administration might use the money merely to extend a current program to keep the guerrillas intact. The State Department had wanted no strings on how the $30 million would be spent. In a concession to that view, the bill allowed the president flexibility to spend the money as he saw fit if he notified Congress 15 days in advance.

While Congress and the administration wrangled over contra demobilization, however, the issue largely passed into the hands of the former combatants in Nicaragua. A major contra faction on March 23 signed an agreement with Chamorro's representatives promising to demobilize by April 20.

On March 28, the incoming Chamorro government and the outgoing Sandinista government signed a broader accord, providing for complete transfer of political and military power once Chamorro took office.

On March 27, the House Appropriations Committee approved the $300 million as Bush had requested just two weeks earlier, but with the restrictions on contra aid. At that point, though, the administration's pleas for prompt action fell victim to a combination of scheduling difficulties, clashes over institutional prerogatives and controversial add-ons from lawmakers and the administration.

Delays and Complications

First, the Panama-Nicaragua legislation became the vehicle for an attempt by the House Foreign Affairs and Senate Foreign Relations committees to regain some of their lost influence over foreign aid issues.

Congress had not enacted an omnibus foreign aid authorization bill since 1985. Instead, foreign aid programs received funding from appropriations bills, bypassing the two authorizing committees.

In the House, members facing election every two years were often reluctant to vote for politically unpopular foreign aid. In the Senate, foreign aid bills faced an added difficulty: Jesse Helms of North Carolina, the staunch anti-communist and ranking Republican on the Foreign Relations Committee, used foreign policy legislation to offer controversial amendments that vexed not just Democrats but the Republican-controlled State Department as well.

House Foreign Affairs Chairman Dante B. Fascell, D-Fla., led his committee in fashioning an omnibus 1990-91 authorization measure (HR 4636) that included authority for $470 million in aid to Panama and $340 million — more than Bush requested — for Nicaragua. The legislation cleared the committee March 28. On the same day, a straightforward supplemental authorization bill won approval from Senate Foreign Relations (S 2364).

The Senate approved its bill April 3; but when the Foreign Affairs Committee's bill reached the House floor in May, it became snarled in a third controversy over U.S. policy in Central America: aid to El Salvador.

Eventually, the bill died, but not before it had served to divert attention from the Panama and Nicaragua funding bill. *(El Salvador aid, p. 779)*

Still, House Speaker Thomas S. Foley, D-Wash., lived up to his word to push the House on the aid package. But when he readied the bill for floor consideration on March 29, he encountered a scheduling problem. Other legislation took longer than expected, and House members wanted to adjourn in time for a dinner event.

With that, consideration of the bill moved into the next week — the final week before Congress' scheduled Easter recess, making final congressional action impossible before lawmakers left Washington for a week.

There was little controversy when the House debated the measure April 3. Members decisively rejected several amendments to delete or cut the foreign aid funding before approving the measure 362-59. *(Votes 61-65, p. 26-H)*

In the process, however, House appropriators added some $1.5 billion for a raft of domestic programs. The White House said it wanted to pare the cost of some of the add-ons, but lax Senate rules on attaching new funding provisions suggested the bill's price tag was likely to grow rather than get smaller as it progressed.

SENATE ACTION

The Senate also was concerned with institutional prerogatives.

Majority Leader George J. Mitchell, D-Maine, said on April 2 that the Senate would not take up the supplemental appropriations until after it had passed Foreign Relations' bill. Mitchell also insisted that the administration first provide Congress with a "long-range plan" showing how aiding Nicaragua and Panama fit into broader foreign aid plans in future years.

Senate passage of the authorizing measure April 5 resolved one of Mitchell's issues. And Secretary of State Baker promised a plan to meet Mitchell's other request.

Approved After Delays

As Chamorro's scheduled inauguration on April 25 neared, Bush pressed for action on the aid package before the ceremony. Despite the pleas, the Senate Appropriations Committee succeeded in acting on the aid package only one day earlier. Vice President Dan Quayle was able to go to Managua, however, with $2.5 million in medical aid authorized under a seldom-exercised emergency authority and $24 million in food assistance transferred from other foreign aid programs. He also certified Nicaragua's eligibility for U.S. Export-Import Bank credits and guarantees and restored Nicaragua's allocation of the U.S. global sugar quota.

In its action April 24, the Appropriations Committee approved the $300 million in aid for Nicaragua intact. But Mitchell and his Republican counterpart, Dole, both noted the difficulties of keeping a supplemental funding measure free of extraneous items.

"Mrs. Chamorro's first term may expire before we get the aid down there," said Dole. For his part, Mitchell observed, "The lure of an important bill has proved irresistible."

As the bill reached the Senate floor April 25, it contained $1 billion more than the House had approved. It took another week — and a visit to the Hill by Panama's new president, Guillermo Endara, April 30 — to resolve a host of issues unrelated to the foreign aid provisions. Nicaragua was debated only briefly; the only provision added on the floor was an Appropriations Committee amendment, approved 96-0, to earmark $8 million of the package for environmental activities, including preservation of rain forests. *(Vote 67, p. 17-S)*

Final Senate approval came May 1. But action on the bill was then delayed by the moves of House Democrats to use the measure as leverage in their effort to cut U.S. military aid to El Salvador.

El Salvador Dispute

House Democrats for weeks had linked the El Salvador conditions to the Nicaragua-Panama aid package by refusing to put on the spending bill technical "waivers" that would be required for the aid money to be spent. One of the waivers was to eliminate the need for enactment of the authorization bill; another was to exempt Nicaragua and Panama from a law barring aid to nations that were more than a year behind on their official debt payments to the U.S. government.

The administration vehemently objected to linkage between the El Salvador issue and the Nicaragua-Panama bill. Bush said Democrats were holding aid for the new democracies in Central America "hostage."

After firming up plans for House action on the authorization bill — complete with the El Salvador amendment — Foley said on May 17 that the Democrats would drop the linkage. On his instructions, House negotiators agreed to put the necessary waivers in the conference version of the supplemental spending bill. But after the House rejected the aid authorization bill on May 22, some liberal Democrats argued in favor of pulling the Nicaragua-Panama waivers out of the spending bill. Foley vetoed the idea, however, reportedly telling fellow Democrats that they should no longer give Bush grounds to attack Congress for holding up the Nicaragua-Panama aid.

FINAL APPROVAL

While the El Salvador dispute simmered, House and Senate negotiators were working to resolve other issues in the supplemental appropriations bill. Once the El Salvador dispute was shelved, the conference report was completed and sent first to the House. Members gave their final assent to the legislation, 308-108, on May 24; the Senate followed suit with voice vote approval shortly after midnight. *(House vote 138, p. 48-H)*

A White House spokesman said Bush called Chamorro in the morning to inform her of passage of the legislation. After a decade of unremitting hostility between the United States and Nicaragua, Bush was now quoted as having told Chamorro of "the continued U.S. desire for close relations and for the continued partnership" with Nicaragua. ■

Panama Given Aid After U.S. Invasion

Congress approved $462 million in emergency aid to the new government of Panama to help rebuild its economy after the devastation of the dictatorship of Gen. Manuel Antonio Noriega and the U.S. economic sanctions and military invasion that ousted him.

Congress and President Bush largely agreed on the need for financial assistance after Noriega's ouster in the U.S. invasion Dec. 20, 1989, and his surrender to U.S. authorities Jan. 3, 1990, to face federal drug trafficking charges. Bush outlined an aid package Jan. 25 that included $500 million in cash and a longer-term request for loans, credits and loan guarantees "valued" at $500 million.

Congress acted quickly to approve an appropriation of $42 million in emergency humanitarian aid, most of it coming from 1989 foreign aid funds. The bill (HR 3952) cleared both chambers by voice vote Feb. 7, and Bush signed it into law Feb. 14.

The supplemental appropriations bill containing the larger request (HR 4404) moved more slowly, however, despite repeated pleas by Bush for Congress to expedite it.

The president himself expanded the request to include $300 million in emergency assistance for the new government of President Violeta Chamorro in Nicaragua after the anti-Sandinista leader's election Feb. 25. The measure was then delayed further by political clashes over foreign aid and unrelated funding provisions added by the administration and lawmakers. *(Aid to Nicaragua, p. 770; supplemental appropriations, p. 844)*

The House approved the bill 362-59 on April 3 after the Appropriations Committee trimmed the request for Panama to $420 million. The Senate approved the bill with the same level of funding by voice vote May 1. After conference, the bill was cleared for the president May 25, shortly after midnight, and he signed it into law later that day.

The aid was substantially less than the leaders of Panama's new government, headed by President Guillermo Endara, had wanted from Washington. Panamanian officials had said they needed up to $2 billion in outside aid to revive the battered economy and repair the physical damage from the U.S. invasion.

BACKGROUND

The United States succeeded in removing Noriega from power after two years of legal, diplomatic and finally military action. But the ouster left the Bush administration with the question of how to repair the damage from the anti-Noriega campaign and shore up the Endara government. *(1989 Almanac, p. 595)*

BOXSCORE

Legislation: Aid to Panama, contained in Dire Emergency Supplemental Appropriations Act, PL 101-302 (HR 4404); Urgent Assistance for Democracy in Panama Act of 1990, PL 101-243 (HR 3952).

Major action: Supplemental Appropriations: Signed, May 25. Conference report adopted by Senate, May 25 (session of May 24); by House, May 24. Passed by Senate, May 1; by House, 362-59, April 3.

Emergency Assistance: Signed, Feb. 14; approved, both chambers, Feb. 7.

Reports: Supplemental Appropriations: Conf Rept, H Rept 101-493; Appropriations (S Rept 101-272); Appropriations (H Rept 101-434).

Emergency Assistance: Foreign Affairs (H Rept 101-401, Part I); Ways and Means (Part II).

Federal grand juries in Florida had indicted Noriega on Feb. 4, 1988, on multiple drug charges. To try to force Noriega from office, President Ronald Reagan imposed economic sanctions April 8, 1988. But Noriega stood firm, refusing U.S. efforts to negotiate his withdrawal.

The Bush administration inherited the impasse when it took office in 1989. The administration reportedly provided covert assistance to opposition groups prior to elections May 7, 1989. The anti-Noriega coalition headed by Endara appeared to have been victorious, but the Noriega regime nullified the elections May 10.

Bush responded the next day by ordering 1,881 additional U.S. troops to Panama. He continued through the remainder of the year to step up diplomatic efforts, unilaterally and through the Organization of American States, to force Noriega to yield to the election results.

When those efforts failed, Bush launched the massive invasion Dec. 20 that deposed Noriega and crushed military resistance by his forces. Endara had been sworn into office at a U.S. base in Panama City shortly before the attacks started.

Bush immediately moved to lift the economic sanctions against Panama and began the withdrawal of U.S. troops once Noriega had surrendered Jan. 3. Announcing Noriega's surrender in a televised address, Bush said the United States was "engaged in the final stages of a process that includes the economic and political revitalization of this important friend and neighbor, Panama."

Bush noted that an economic team headed by Deputy Secretary of State Lawrence S. Eagleburger and Deputy Treasury Secretary John E. Robson had already visited Panama, and a team of experts remained behind to assess the country's needs. But administration officials were cautious about making firm commitments and asked members of Congress visiting Panama not to discuss specific figures or make promises that the United States might not be able to keep.

History of U.S. Aid

Congress and the Reagan administration suspended most direct aid to Panama between 1987 and 1988. Before that, annual levels of U.S. economic and military aid ranged from $25.5 million in fiscal 1984 to $85.1 million in fiscal 1985.

On Capitol Hill, leaders said Congress would want to help Panama, but warned that meeting Panama's needs would not be easy. Senate Minority Leader Bob Dole, R-Kan., said that aiding Panama was a high priority "because of our intervention there. We caused some of the damage. We certainly are in part responsible for some of the economic problems because of sanctions."

But David R. Obey, D-Wis., chairman of the House Appropriations Subcommittee on Foreign Operations, said aid to Panama would be no more popular than any other kind of foreign aid. "The American public likes what happened to Noriega, but they aren't going to like the fact that they have to pay for it," Obey said.

Panamanian Vice President Ricardo Arias Calderon said he had seen studies, prior to the invasion, putting his country's need for outside economic help at "something between $1 billion and $2 billion." Such amounts, he told NBC News, "will be huge by our accounts and peanuts by yours."

Administration officials began working after the invasion on the legal procedures necessary to restore aid.

Congress in 1988 and again in 1989 barred all U.S. aid to Panama — except for emergency food and other humanitarian supplies — unless the president certified to Congress that a number of actions were under way. Among the requirements were that the Panamanian government had demonstrated "substantial progress" in putting the military under civilian control, that an impartial inquiry was under way into illegal actions by Panamanian soldiers, that the government and opposition forces had agreed on procedures for free elections, and that freedom of the press and other liberties were being restored.

In ordering the end to U.S. economic sanctions, Bush also allowed the Treasury Department to begin releasing about $370 million in Panamanian assets frozen subsequent to an executive order signed by President Reagan on April 8, 1988. More than half the total available, about $188 million, was owed directly by the U.S. government to Panama. The bulk of it was for fees generated by the Panama Canal. The remainder of the blocked money was for such things as taxes and other fees owed by U.S. firms.

After the invasion, the Pentagon moved to provide millions of dollars in emergency aid for civilians made homeless during the fighting. That aid included medical supplies, food, tents and sleeping bags.

Assessment of Invasion

For Bush, Noriega's ouster was a significant foreign policy achievement. He at once erased politically harmful doubts about his willingness to act decisively and reached a goal that had eluded his predecessor.

The House Armed Services Committee, however, warned against thinking that the military success of the invasion could be duplicated if the United States decided to intervene elsewhere in the world.

Releasing the committee's report on the invasion, Chairman Les Aspin, D-Wis., said Jan. 12 that U.S. forces "had some advantages that are unlikely to be repeated" elsewhere. For example, he said, the United States already had 13,000 troops stationed in Panama and American military planners had detailed information about the capabilities of the Panamanian Defense Forces.

"If Panama has made anyone think that military intervention in the Third World is easy, they should think again," Aspin said, adding that the U.S. forces also were "lucky" because the Panamanian military put up little resistance and because Noriega loyalists did not seize American citizens as hostages.

Endara Government's Problems

In Panama, the Endara government faced intertwined economic problems: the need to restore local and world confidence in the country's stability and the need to do something about the large foreign debt built up during the Noriega regime.

The U.S. sanctions devastated Panama's economy, contributing to a 25 percent drop in its gross national product and a 25 percent unemployment rate.

Additionally, banking was tied up with the freezing of deposits, and the government owed nearly $1 billion in overdue debts to international and commercial banks, according to former Panamanian President Nicolas Barletta, who testified on Feb. 5 before the House Foreign Affairs Subcommittee on International Economic Policy and Trade.

According to State Department and World Bank figures, Panama owed about $1.6 billion immediately to overseas sources and had a long-term foreign debt of up to

$4 billion. The bulk of Panama's debts was owed to private commercial banks; other creditors included multilateral institutions — such as the World Bank, the International Monetary Fund and the Inter-American Development Bank — and the United States and other countries. Panama had paid virtually nothing on its overseas debts for nearly two years.

A second immediate problem for Endara and the Bush administration was how to turn Panama over to the new government. In the days after Noriega's surrender, administration officials insisted that Endara and his aides were making the important decisions and that U.S. combat forces were merely playing a supportive role.

Treasury's Robson, in discussing plans for aid, said, "We did not go down there to shove some preconceived plan in their face. They're a sovereign nation."

But one visiting lawmaker, Rep. Don Edwards, D-Calif., said he left Panama on Jan. 5 concerned that "to a large extent we are continuing to run things because we are choosing to do that and that we will set the timetable for turning those functions over to the Panamanians."

As an example, Edwards said that the U.S. military was making the major decisions on public security and that the government's new "Public Force" — the successor to the military — was waiting for U.S. permission to take over some security functions.

"To a large extent, what's taking place in Panama is being directed" by the U.S. military, Edwards said.

EMERGENCY HUMANITARIAN AID

Bush announced his proposal for aid to Panama at the opening of a news conference Jan. 25. Earlier, the administration had warned Panama not to expect a massive aid program and had called on other countries, principally Japan, to join an international effort to provide aid.

Bush said his total plan was valued at about $1 billion and included $500 million in humanitarian assistance for housing, emergency public works, business assistance, loans, guarantees and export opportunities, and an additional $500 million in additional assistance for balance of payments support, public investment and economic restructuring.

Bush acknowledged that Panama probably would need more outside aid than his proposal would allow, but he insisted that "this is what we think is a good and full program to give them the help they need right now."

Christopher J. Dodd, D-Conn., chairman of the Senate Foreign Relations Subcommittee on the Western Hemisphere, agreed, calling the proposal "a very responsible package, a very realistic package."

Lawmakers immediately began to press the administration for conditions on the aid.

At a Foreign Relations hearing Jan. 25, Dodd sought assurances that the United States would not support re-establishing the Panamanian Defense Forces, which had been Noriega's support base. Bernard W. Aronson, assistant secretary of State for inter-American affairs, told Dodd the administration opposed creating "another monster" military force in Panama and that Panamanians did not want "to be ruled by the same old gang" that was ousted by the U.S. invasion.

Aronson gave similar assurances Feb. 6 to House Foreign Affairs Committee members who raised concerns that the new Panamanian police force might evolve into the kind of group Noriega had used to maintain control over the country. "They've already weeded out the bulk of officers loyal to Noriega," Aronson said.

Dodd and several other members also called for Panama to repeal its bank secrecy laws, which for years had attracted billions of dollars from drug cartels. Dodd said he planned amendments on the question when Bush's bill reached the Senate, and in the House Rep. Peter H. Kostmayer, D-Pa., also readied an amendment on the issue.

Details of Package

Congress hastened to meet Panama's needs and its own recess deadline by approving an initial $42 million in emergency aid on Feb. 7 while putting off action on the larger package.

Approval of HR 3952 by voice vote in both chambers came just one day after the measure had cleared the House Foreign Affairs and Senate Foreign Relations committees.

The legislation was aimed at helping rebuild Panama after years of internal corruption and mismanagement, the U.S. economic sanctions and invasion. The economic aid was for housing, public works, small business loans, and training and equipment for a new Panamanian police force.

The bill also lifted numerous U.S. economic and aid sanctions. Removal of those sanctions allowed the administration to speed the $42 million and to begin separate programs of loans and investment credits, estimated by the administration to be worth up to $500 million.

Most of the $42 million was transferred from unspent foreign aid funds from previous years. Specifically, the bill provided:

- $22.5 million for housing. Of this total, $12.5 million was for the poverty-stricken Chorillo district in Panama City, which was partially destroyed by rioting that followed the U.S. invasion. A program that provided housing loans to foreign countries also received $10 million.
- $7 million earmarked for public works projects, principally in the Panama City and Colon areas but also in some rural areas.
- $5.5 million for technical assistance, training programs and help in creating a national budget.
- $5 million in rehabilitation funds for small businesses, especially those that lost inventories in the looting that followed the invasion.
- $2 million to help re-establish a Panamanian police force. The money was taken from a U.S. program to improve police departments and judicial systems, primarily in Central America. The authorization set aside up to $1.2 million for administering the program and for training law enforcement officers in "human rights, civil law, and investigative and civilian law enforcement techniques." The bill also set a limit of $500,000 for purchases of "lethal equipment" — shotguns and .38-caliber handguns, according to State Department officials.

About $30 million of the $42 million in the Panama bill came from foreign aid funds withheld from the African countries of Sudan and Somalia because of human rights violations in 1985-86. Some members, among them Sen. Paul Simon, D-Ill., and Reps. Howard Wolpe, D-Mich., and George W. Crockett Jr., D-Mich., opposed the move as unfairly targeting an economically strapped region. But Wolpe and Simon worked out an agreement with the administration and congressional leaders to restore the money later, by taking $30 million from the $500 million supplemental Panama aid bill and giving it to Africa.

The bill also contained a provision allowing the administration to shift, or reprogram, up to $10 million in already appropriated fiscal 1990 funds to support democratic elections in Eastern Europe and Yugoslavia.

Several Laws Waived

Several laws had to be waived to permit the aid to flow to Panama. The bill allowed a waiver of the Brooke-Alexander amendment, which prohibited aid to countries that had fallen behind in their debt payments to the United States. It also waived Section 660 of foreign aid law, which prohibited funding for training and support of foreign police forces, and another requirement in foreign aid law aimed at curbing assistance to countries that did not "fully cooperate" in international efforts to combat drug trafficking.

Bush on Jan. 26 certified to Congress that the new Endara government was willing to cooperate in antidrug efforts, but under the law Congress had 45 days to disapprove that finding. The bill waived that 45-day period.

The bill also allowed Panama to resume receiving substantial trade benefits under the Generalized System of Preferences and the Caribbean Basin Initiative. The 45-day waiting period to receive those concessions also was waived. Reagan had suspended Panama's right to receive those benefits because of widespread allegations of Noriega's involvement in drug-trafficking.

The legislation asked the president to submit a report by April 15 on specific steps that Panama was taking to change its bank secrecy laws, which in the past had been taken advantage of for money laundering by international drug cartels..

"This country is a cesspool of money laundering, and it needs to be cleaned up," said Aronson, testifying before the Senate Appropriations Foreign Operations Subcommittee on Feb. 8.

Kostmayer withdrew an amendment during House Foreign Affairs Committee markup of the emergency aid bill that would have delayed the bill's taking effect until the U.S. secretary of State and the government of Panama had come to an agreement on enacting bank secrecy reform. Kostmayer was persuaded by fellow committee members to save his amendment for the supplemental aid bill.

Alfonse M. D'Amato, R-N.Y., echoed the concern over banking reform at the Feb. 8 Senate Appropriations Foreign Operations hearing on aid to Panama and El Salvador. "At a time when they need our aid, we'd better lay it on the line."

SUPPLEMENTAL APPROPRIATION

Bush asked Congress to approve the larger aid package in a supplemental appropriations bill for fiscal 1990. Bush told reporters Jan. 25 he did not know where the money would be found, but his formal request to Congress on Feb. 6 outlined a series of cuts in Defense Department spending to pay for the aid.

The aid package was aimed at boosting the Panamanian economy by providing public works jobs and loans and grants to get private businesses operating again and easing its international debt burdens. Specifically, it called for $140 million for public works jobs, $185 million for loans and grants to businesses and $130 million to help Panama pay its debts to international development banks.

Panama had fallen about $540 million behind on its payments to the International Monetary Fund, the World Bank and the Inter-American Development Bank. Clearing up those debts, officials said, would help make the country creditworthy and able to attract loans and investments.

The Bush proposal also called for about $500 million in loans, credits and other off-budget programs. The major item was $415 million in loan guarantees by the Export-Import Bank to finance potential exports to Panama of U.S. products. Also included were $30 million in credits for food aid and $50 million for guarantees by the Overseas Private Investment Corporation of U.S. business investments in Panama.

Bush's proposal drew generally favorable reaction on Capitol Hill, but one key member, Sen. Patrick J. Leahy, D-Vt., chairman of the Senate Appropriations Subcommittee on Foreign Operations, said, "I won't bring a bill out of my subcommittee with $500 million in it."

In a report to the Senate on Feb. 28, Leahy said he found during a trip to Panama earlier in the month that the country needed aid but probably could not absorb all of what Bush proposed.

Delays and Complications

Bush wanted speedy action on the proposal, and after some initial delays Secretary of State James A. Baker III on March 7 appealed for Congress to move more quickly. But several factors combined to delay congressional action.

First, Bush expanded the request on March 13 to include $300 million in aid for Nicaragua to help the new government of Violeta Chamorro, the U.S.-backed opposition candidate who won Nicaragua's Feb. 25 election and was scheduled to take office on April 25.

That caused some lawmakers, including Dodd, to suggest transferring some of the money for Panama to Nicaragua. Other Senate Democrats, including Leahy, called for providing aid for Eastern Europe by taking money away from Nicaragua and Panama. In the House, some Democrats also wanted to use the bill as a platform to debate U.S. policy toward El Salvador. They later backed off, however, after Secretary Baker requested time to try to fashion a bipartisan compromise on the issue.

Procedural matters also intervened. Bush requested a straightforward supplemental appropriations measure, but the two foreign policy authorizing committees — House Foreign Affairs and Senate Foreign Relations — both insisted on having a role. The upshot was that committees were working on authorization bills at about the same time they were working on appropriations — adding substantial complications to the simple process Bush had envisioned.

One example of the complications was the first legislative session scheduled for action on the request. The Foreign Affairs Committee sat down on March 22 to work on its authorization bill, planning to approve it quickly. But the panel spent more than two hours arguing over details, particularly over a provision conditioning aid for Panama on that country's actions to prevent narcotics traffickers from using its banking system for money laundering.

A frustrated Chairman Dante B. Fascell, D-Fla., said Panama might solve the money-laundering problem "before we ever get around to the bill."

The panel failed to take formal action on the bill, prompting Fascell to schedule markups for the week of March 26 on it and a full-scale foreign aid authorization bill for fiscal 1991.

The failure of Foreign Affairs to act pushed back the entire schedule. The House Appropriations Subcommittee on Foreign Operations had set its markup for the afternoon of March 22, but postponed that meeting out of courtesy to Foreign Affairs. That meant the House could not consider the bill during the week of March 26, as had been planned.

Noting the delays, Senate Majority Leader George J. Mitchell, D-Maine, said on March 21 that Bush's request for speedy action on the supplemental "is not going to be able to be met."

Later the same day, Speaker Thomas S. Foley, D-Wash., said the House would cooperate with Bush but would not rush to meet "artificial deadlines." The president's request is "something we consider, but it's not a primary concern," Foley said. "The primary concern is over the substance of the legislation."

Finally, the supplemental, as a must-pass bill, attracted a variety of add-ons from both the administration and Congress. The new provisions eventually pushed the total cost of the measure to more than $4 billion, only $885 million of it for foreign affairs items.

Need for Urgency Debated

Despite Bush's repeated calls for urgent action, even some supporters said the administration had failed to demonstrate the need for fast congressional action. Sen. Bob Kasten, R-Wis., said he supported the request, but he demanded that the administration show more proof of its urgency. "Right now there is not enough of an emergency nature" to the request, he said.

Senior administration officials responded that much of the urgency stemmed from the fact that Nicaraguans and Panamanians were counting on U.S. aid to correct economic problems that Washington's policies helped create.

"In both Panama and Nicaragua there is now a revolution of rising expectations brought on by democracy and the chance for economic opportunity that the citizens of those countries have not felt for many years," Aronson told the House Appropriations Subcommittee on Foreign Operations on March 19.

Juggling the Numbers

Besides delaying Bush's request, Congress also changed the amount.

Eagleburger had already agreed to shift $30 million of the requested aid to Africa in order to speed action on the initial $42 million package. In the week before committee markups, he denied rumors that the administration was willing to settle for a far bigger cut — as little as half of the $800 million sought for Panama and Nicaragua together.

A substantial cut by Congress in the aid request, Eagleburger told a Senate Appropriations subcommittee March 20, "would send wrong messages" to the people in Panama and Nicaragua.

In contrast to the rumblings in the Senate, Speaker Foley expressed confidence the House would approve the bulk of Bush's request. On March 27, the House Appropriations Committee did so, voting to approve the supplemental funding bill after trimming the Panama request by $80 million.

In addition to the funds shifted to Africa, $50 million was transferred to other Hill priorities: $30 million to aid refugees outside the United States, including $5 million for Soviet Jews in Israel; and $20 million to the countries of the eastern Caribbean, including $5 million to deal with the effects of Hurricane Hugo in 1989.

The same day, House Foreign Affairs endorsed an authorization bill that approved all of the Panama aid except for the $30 million shifted to Africa. The Senate Foreign Relations Committee approved a similar measure the next day.

Foley wanted the House to act on the supplemental March 29, but lawmakers adjourned that evening before acting on the bill because members wanted to attend a dinner sponsored by broadcasters. Instead, the House considered the bill April 3, approving it by a vote of 362-59 after a desultory debate that only occasionally focused on Panama. *(Vote 65, p. 26-H)*

By that time, it was too late for the Senate to take up the funding bill before its Easter recess.

Paying Off Bad Debts

Bush's request to use U.S. tax dollars to help Panama and Nicaragua pay off their past debts to the international development banks encountered some resistance.

Panama owed the World Bank, the International Monetary Fund and the Inter-American Development Bank $540 million on past loans, and another $265 million was to fall due in 1990. Under Bush's proposal, Panama would repay about half its debts to the banks with the United States' $130 million contribution, an identical contribution of its own from bank accounts that had been frozen in the United States, and another $130 million to be donated by Japan and other countries.

The chairmen of both Foreign Operations Appropriations subcommittees, however, challenged the idea.

"I can't think of anything that makes less sense," Leahy said, noting that Panama, the United States and other countries would pay the banks nearly as much money on bad debts as Panama would receive in new loans. His House counterpart, Obey, called the proposal part of a "funny-money game."

Few Restrictions Imposed

Despite the complaints, the House and Senate Appropriations panels attached relatively few conditions on the aid. The House committee earmarked $15 million for environmental protection, including a so-called debt-for-nature swap (reducing external debt in return for using freed funds for conservation). The Senate committee stipulated that the Agency for International Development (AID) and the General Accounting Office (GAO) closely monitor the aid and report findings to the panel "regularly."

More specific conditions were left to the foreign aid authorization measures being crafted by the Senate Foreign Relations and House Foreign Affairs committees. And before Congress left for the Easter recess, the Senate did take up the authorization bill (S 2364), approving it by voice vote April 3.

When Congress returned, the supplemental appropriations measure encountered further delays and pitfalls. So did the House's foreign aid authorization bill — being left in limbo after a heated debate over aid to El Salvador. *(El Salvador, p. 779)*

In the Senate, the $420 million Panama aid package barely survived two attempts to slash it to $300 million. The effort to cut the funds, led by Appropriations Committee Chairman Robert C. Byrd, D-W.Va., and Foreign Operations Appropriations Subcommittee Chairman Leahy, was rejected 14-15 in committee and then killed on a tabling motion in the full Senate by a largely party-line vote of 51-48 on April 26. *(Vote 64, p. 17-S)*.

Byrd said he was not convinced that all the funds were justified. "I don't think it's an emergency to send $30 million to stimulate tourism in Panama.... I'll have some words to say about tourism in West Virginia."

Byrd also objected to the inclusion of $130 million to

pay Panamanian debts to multinational banks. "I don't think that's an emergency," Byrd charged during floor debate April 26. "I think paying our debts is more important."

Byrd's amendment would have spent the money taken from Panama on Indian health care, Energy Department waste cleanup, agriculture conservation programs, and the Women, Infants and Children nutrition program.

Meanwhile, the committee had been busy adding a variety of unrelated domestic spending provisions to the bill, and on the Senate floor the measure became a target for flash-point controversies including abortion and the death penalty.

In the midst of the delay, President Endara visited Washington, and Bush used the occasion to pressure Congress to move on the bill.

"It's embarrassing," Bush said of the stalled bill April 30. "I've asked the Senate and the House to move on that legislation over a month ago."

Endara's visit, which included a trip to Capitol Hill, did the trick. Unrelated disputes that had been holding up final action quickly evaporated, and the Senate approved the bill by voice vote May 1.

Endara graciously said Bush had no reason to be embarrassed. "One of the prices we pay for democracy," Endara said May 2, "is that it takes longer, and it's a little bit more complex."

FINAL APPROVAL

Bush prodded Congress one more time to hurry final approval. "Panama is also in dire need of the jump-start that our assistance will give to enable it to recover from the economic devastation of the Noriega dictatorship," he told reporters May 16.

Conferees, who began work on the bill that day, settled most of the issues by May 18 and finally completed agreement May 21. In their report, conferees did "strongly urge" the administration to condition 80 percent of Panama's aid on such steps as that government's reaching agreement to disclose to U.S. narcotics agencies information on current international currency transactions. But the conferees dropped Senate-added conditions for close monitoring of the funds by AID and the GAO, with regular reports to the Appropriations Committee.

The final bill provided that up to $15 million could be used for a debt-for-nature swap or immediate environmental needs. And it also barred use of U.S. aid projects that would result in the "significant loss" of tropical forests in Nicaragua or Panama.

The bill also included $7.4 million for added salaries for the U.S. Marshals Service to meet expenses associated with Noriega's court appearances in Florida and other drug extraditions from South America. The funds were transferred from the Bureau of Prisons. (The Noriega trial was pending at the end of 1990.)

Final agreement on other issues in the bill allowed both chambers to take up the conference report in the session of May 24.

The House approved the measure 308-108; Senate approval followed by voice vote shortly after midnight. *(Vote 138, p. 48-H)*

Bush signed the measure May 25 and called Endara to inform him of the passage of the legislation. A spokesman said Bush expressed "the continued U.S. desire for close relations" with Panama.

At year's end, however, the two countries remained in disagreement over the bank secrecy issue. A U.S.-drafted Mutual Legal Assistance Agreement initialed by the two governments in August became the subject of bitter debate in Panama that forced the Endara government to repudiate it in October. Opposition to the agreement was fueled by the aid bill's provision to hold back 20 percent of the funds unless an agreement was reached. ■

U.S. Aid to El Salvador Slashed, Restored

Aid to El Salvador, an issue that re-emerged in 1989, received more attention in 1990 as Congress grew increasingly frustrated with the slow pace of negotiations to end the conflict and the continuing pattern of human rights violations by the Salvadoran military. A badly flawed investigation into the 1989 murders of six Jesuit priests was particularly galling to lawmakers.

In approving the fiscal 1991 foreign aid appropriations bill (HR 5114 — PL 101-513), Congress voted to withhold half of the $85 million military assistance package for El Salvador. The government in San Salvador was to receive the money being withheld only if President Bush determined that the country's leftist guerrillas were failing to meet certain conditions outlined in the legislation.

Over strenuous administration objections, Congress attached a complex set of conditions to future aid: Aid would be fully funded only if the president determined that the rebel Farabundo Marti National Liberation Front (FMLN) had failed to participate in "good faith" negotiations to end the conflict or that it had launched a "substantial and sustained" offensive against the government. No aid would be provided unless the president determined that the government of El Salvador was willing to engage in negotiations and that it had conducted a "thorough and professional" inquiry into the Jesuit murders.

For Rep. Joe Moakley, D-Mass., chairman of the powerful Rules Committee and head of a House task force on El Salvador, tolerance for rights abuses perpetrated by the Salvadoran military reached a breaking point in 1990. "Enough is enough," said Moakley during the House debate on the fiscal 1990 foreign aid supplemental authorization bill (HR 4636).

It was during debate on that measure that lawmakers in 1990 first tackled the El Salvador aid issue. Moakley's colleagues agreed and on May 22 approved a 50 percent cut in military aid to the government in San Salvador by adopting a Moakley amendment.

The May 22 vote was the first of several defeats for the administration on the issue, culminating in Senate passage Oct. 19 of an amendment to the foreign aid spending measure that also required a 50 percent aid cut. *(Foreign aid appropriations, p. 830)*

In a pattern later repeated in the Senate, liberal House opponents of the aid to El Salvador were able to enlist more moderate members — such as John P. Murtha, D-Pa., chairman of the Defense Appropriations Subcommittee — who in the past had strongly backed the Salvadoran military. Murtha, a member of the Moakley task force, which traveled to El Salvador to investigate the priests' slayings, cosponsored the measure to reduce the aid.

Still, it took some time for a consistent House position on the issue to jell. On May 24, with the El Salvador aid as only one of the issues in dispute, the House voted down the foreign aid bill to which the language sponsored by Moakley and Murtha was attached.

But by June, when the House considered HR 5114, support for a 50 percent aid cut had solidified. The bill including the aid cut passed the House, and eventually the Senate, by a wide margin.

The House adopted the conference report on HR 5114, 188-162, on Oct. 27. The Senate cleared the conference report by voice vote later that day. *(Vote 531, p. 168-H)*

In January 1991, reacting to the apparent execution of two U.S. servicemen by guerrillas in El Salvador two weeks earlier, Bush announced that he would release the full allotment of fiscal 1991 U.S. military aid to that Central American nation. The White House said Bush's decision was based on the FMLN's violations of the congressional conditions against attacking civilian targets and receiving military assistance from outside El Salvador.

BACKGROUND

Few foreign policy issues were more contentious during the 1980s than military aid for El Salvador. Conservatives argued that the support was essential to prevent left-wing guerrillas from taking over; liberals objected to the assistance because of the poor human rights record of the government in San Salvador.

The United States provided more than $3.4 billion in economic, development and military aid to El Salvador from 1981 through 1989, making the tiny Central American country one of the biggest recipients of U.S. foreign aid.

President Ronald Reagan stepped up aid to El Salvador shortly after taking office, winning reluctant support for $140 million in fiscal 1981. Congress gradually boosted the aid in subsequent years but showed no enthusiasm for Reagan's policy of backing the Salvadoran government until José Napoleón Duarte won the presidency there in 1984. A longtime foe of Salvadoran military regimes and an advocate of social reform, Duarte won almost universal respect on Capitol Hill.

In subsequent years, Congress voted hundreds of millions of dollars in aid to El Salvador based largely on Duarte's personal appeal. Throughout the latter part of the 1980s, U.S. aid averaged more than $400 million annually. *(1985 Almanac, p. 80; 1984 Almanac, p. 80)*

Congress had imposed conditions on the aid since 1981; they were stringent in the early 1980s, but most were relaxed after Duarte's election.

Early in 1989, another round of controversy in Washington over El Salvador loomed.

The circumstances seemed ripe: renewed reports of human rights abuses, an economy in shambles, and political instability surrounding Duarte's fragile government. Duarte was dying of cancer and had lost most of his physical stamina and political clout.

After a few years out of the limelight, El Salvador re-emerged in 1989 as a major foreign policy topic on Capitol Hill. The rightist National Republican Alliance (ARENA) party's victory in the March presidential elections, coupled with human rights abuses by both the right and the left, raised new concerns. Those concerns intensified in November with urban warfare and the murder of the six Jesuit priests in San Salvador.

But despite controversy over military aid to the Salvadoran government, Congress approved most of the money Bush had asked for. Bush requested $97 million; the foreign aid appropriations bill (HR 3743 — PL 101-167) limited this aid to $85 million, the fiscal 1989 amount. In the wake of the November violence, Hill liberals tried to withhold some of the aid, but strong majorities in both chambers rebuffed the effort. The stage, though, was set for major legislative battles in 1990. *(1989 Almanac, p. 585)*

Murders and Their Aftermath

Lawmakers from both parties agreed that the character of the issue changed substantially on Nov. 16, 1989, when six Jesuit priests and their two housekeepers were murdered. Eight soldiers were arrested after the execution-style slayings, and there were suspicions that high-ranking officers — including the head of military forces — had prior knowledge of the murders.

House Speaker Thomas S. Foley, D-Wash., appointed the 19-member task force Dec. 5, 1989, with a mandate to monitor the Salvadoran government's response to the killings.

The murders caused an international outcry — largely by serving as a reminder of numerous human rights abuses in El Salvador that were never prosecuted. Several of the priests were well-known outside El Salvador because of their outspoken criticism of the government and military.

Salvadoran President Alfredo Cristiani said on Jan. 7 that investigators had determined that "some elements of the armed forces" were responsible for the killings and Cristiani said he had formed a special investigating panel.

On Capitol Hill, there was broad praise for Cristiani's statement and general agreement that the United States should keep up pressure on his government to bring to justice those responsible for the killings.

As in the past, liberals were the most critical of the Salvadoran government, skeptical that Cristiani had the political clout to prosecute any high-level military officers.

"I want to see what finally comes out of the case, who is identified, who is prosecuted, who has to pay the price," said David R. Obey, D-Wis., chairman of the House Appropriations Subcommittee on Foreign Operations. "I'm talking about the planners, not just the triggermen."

Moakley, head of the House task force, said Jan. 12 that he still feared a "coverup" and warned that a failed investigation "would seriously endanger" congressional backing of the Cristiani government.

Conservatives and moderates were more sanguine. Rep. Dave McCurdy, D-Okla., a key Cristiani supporter, said Congress should not, and probably would not, curtail aid as long as El Salvador made progress on the case.

Concluding a four-day visit to El Salvador, a bipartisan delegation of 14 members on Feb. 14 demanded a continued inquiry into the November murders. Headed by Moakley and Bud Shuster, R-Pa., the delegation said that key leads and allegations had yet to be investigated, including the possibility that some members of the armed forces might have engaged in a coverup or that the "intellectual authors" of the killings had not yet been identified.

The members also voiced concern that, because of technicalities in Salvadoran law, the evidence then available "may be insufficient to bring all the murderers to justice."

Salvadoran authorities had indicted nine military personnel in connection with the murders. Those charged included Col. Guillermo Alfredo Benavides, the highest-ranking military officer ever brought to justice in a major human rights case in El Salvador.

While in El Salvador, the House members met with Cristiani and other senior government officials, religious leaders, politicians and others.

In early March, Moakley said that his task force had information that "somebody high up" in the government or military of El Salvador was involved in the November 1989 murders. While refusing to name individuals, Moakley said the task force had uncovered "information, as opposed to evidence," that a high-ranking official might have ordered the murder of the six priests.

Moakley also noted that, under Salvadoran law, an accused colonel, Benavides, could not be tried solely on the basis of available evidence — the testimony of two lieutenants. Cristiani said there was no evidence that anyone higher than Benavides was involved in the murder.

Task Force Report Released

The task force of House Democrats released its report on April 30, and the report painted a grim picture of Salvadoran affairs. The group — including supporters and critics of official policy toward El Salvador — found that an investigation there into the brutal murders had come to a "virtual standstill."

In a 56-page report, the task force expressed doubt that military personnel charged with the crime would be punished and complained that Salvadoran authorities had not seriously investigated the possibility that senior military officials were involved.

U.S. and Salvadoran officials said the murders were "committed by individuals, and not an indictment of the armed forces as an institution," the task force noted. "Unfortunately, the task force believes it is both."

Bush administration officials generally praised the task force report, although not all its conclusions. Secretary of State James A. Baker III said on May 1 that the task force had conducted its inquiry "in a balanced and professional manner" and said he would ask Cristiani to respond to it.

Shuster, head of a counterpart GOP effort to monitor the Jesuits' case, challenged some parts of the Moakley report but said most of it was "fair."

Cristiani acknowledged on May 1 that El Salvador's judicial system "might be a little bit slow" but said that those charged with the murders would be tried. Cristiani insisted that military commanders had supported the inquiry into the case.

The Investigation

The Moakley task force praised the early stages of the Salvadoran government's inquiry. A military investigative unit handled the initial probe, working with experts sent by the FBI, Britain's Scotland Yard and other foreign agencies. Cristiani, the report said, had made "a sincere effort to encourage a professional investigation."

The investigation was then under the control of a local judge, Ricardo Zamora. In El Salvador, judges handled much of the investigative work before criminal cases reached trial.

The task force said the investigation had stalled. Investigators were making no serious attempt to examine allegations that senior military officers other than Benavides might have been involved and were not actively collecting more evidence against the nine military personnel charged.

Shuster disputed what he said was an implication by the task force that senior Salvadoran officials had tried to cover up the case. "There's no evidence to support that assertion," he said.

The task force report said that military investigators and Judge Zamora also had failed to act on suggestions from the U.S. Embassy and others that certain people with possible knowledge of the case be questioned.

Moakley's group noted several obstacles facing investigators. Among them were: The military's inquiry unit was headed by a lieutenant colonel whose task had been "gravely complicated" by the fact that he was investigating officers of higher rank; and Zamora, like all other Salvadoran judges, lacked the staff, training and technical support for such a complex investigation.

Shuster primarily criticized Zamora, saying he had failed to follow through on leads and to order interrogations of those who might have had evidence.

Failures of the System

While focusing on the Jesuits' case, the Moakley task force used its report to denounce what it said were the failures of the Salvadoran judicial and military systems — both of which had been heavily subsidized by U.S. aid.

In general, the task force said, El Salvador's judicial system did not work.

The investigation into the Jesuits' case had proceeded as far as it had only because of enormous international pressure, the Moakley group said. For example, the task force expressed doubt that the nine military personnel would have been arrested if a U.S. military officer (Maj. Eric Buckland, who was not named in the report) had not gone to the U.S. Embassy with information implicating Benavides.

The task force noted that judges and criminal investigators lacked local technical and political support. Thousands of crimes never had been investigated.

"Despite a decade of promises, tens of millions of dollars in U.S. aid and repeated statements that progress is just around the corner, the Salvadoran justice system remains essentially an oxymoron — neither systematic nor just," the report said.

Moakley's group also said that the case was an indictment of the Salvadoran military — even though many officers and enlisted personnel were honest and had nothing to do with rights abuses.

"The murder of the Jesuits was a symptom of a too-frequent failure within the military to accept civilian authority and to pattern its own actions on the requirements of law," the Moakley report said.

Moakley himself noted that, during his group's trip to El Salvador in February, no senior military officer expressed remorse about the murders. "They said it was a stupid thing to do, but no one had any sorrow in their hearts," Moakley said.

The task force included in its report several Pentagon documents revealing that all of the soldiers charged in the case had received U.S. military training. Several members of the unit allegedly responsible for the crime had attended U.S. training sessions just two days before the murders.

U.S. officials said that all Salvadoran military personnel received human rights instruction as part of their training.

Miguel Salaverria, El Salvador's new ambassador to the United States, insisted that the case did not demonstrate a failure of training, because nearly all Salvadoran military personnel received some U.S. instruction.

SUPPLEMENTAL APPROPRIATIONS: HOUSE COMMITTEE ACTION

Early in 1990, Congress decided to take up aid to El Salvador on a number of related foreign aid authorization and appropriations measures. The timing of the legislative maneuvers, though, depended on negotiations between the warring factions in the Central American nation and occasionally the Bush administration.

Looking for Leverage

House Democratic leaders agreed on March 27 to delay action on the issue until Secretary of State Baker could present his case for an agreement to avoid what administration officials feared would be a precipitous aid cutoff.

Democrats on the House Foreign Affairs Committee for weeks had been hoping to attach an El Salvador amendment to whatever foreign aid legislation emerged. But as the committee wrapped up its work on an omnibus bill to authorize the fiscal 1990 supplemental and regular fiscal 1991 programs, Baker appealed for a delay in action on the El Salvador aid.

Meeting with House Democrats on April 3, Baker said he wanted to negotiate a bipartisan agreement on aid to El Salvador. Foley and other Democrats accepted the appeal and agreed to begin talks on the El Salvador issue after the Easter recess. Any legislation on El Salvador, the House Democrats said, would be offered on the authorization bill pending in Foreign Affairs.

While that accord averted an El Salvador aid battle during House action on the Nicaragua-Panama supplemental bill, it did postpone the Foreign Affairs Committee's conclusion of the companion authorization bill (HR 4445). Chairman Dante B. Fascell, D-Fla., said he agreed to delay his bill because Baker had expressed a "sincere willingness" to negotiate with Congress over El Salvador.

But to maintain some negotiating leverage over Baker — and to help preserve the Foreign Affairs Committee's jurisdiction — committee Democrats agreed to try to block the actual expenditure of money in the Nicaragua-Panama supplemental appropriations bill unless Congress also passed an authorization bill.

Rep. Peter H. Kostmayer, D-Pa., said he would try to do that by opposing what in recent years had been a routine provision on appropriations bills to waive the requirement for an authorization. The House did not include such a waiver in its supplemental spending bill, but the Senate normally did. If the bill returned from conference committee with such a waiver, Kostmayer said, he would move to strike that provision.

Kostmayer later acknowledged that such a step also was intended to strengthen the hand of Democrats in their negotiations with Baker over El Salvador. If the authorizing requirement was not waived, Congress would have to pass two bills before the Nicaragua and Panama money could be spent, doubling the opportunity for El Salvador amendments to be offered and passed. *(Nicaragua aid, p. 770; Panama aid, p. 774; supplemental appropriations bill, p. 844)*

Meeting under United Nations auspices the day after Baker met with congressional leaders, representatives of the Salvadoran government and the leftist guerrillas agreed April 4 in Geneva to negotiate an end to the civil war. The sides signed an accord, along with U.N. Secretary-General Javier Pérez de Cuéllar, pledging to "end the armed conflict through political means as speedily as possible" and to "reunify Salvadoran society."

The remaining question in Washington was how to use aid to influence future events in El Salvador. Key liberal Democrats in both chambers still agreed generally on a proposal, advanced by Sen. Christopher J. Dodd, D-Conn., to suspend 50 percent of fiscal 1990 military aid unless the rebels refused to negotiate or the Salvadoran government was endangered by a rebel offensive.

The administration opposed an aid restriction. However, some officials reportedly voiced willingness to consider suspending a much smaller portion of El Salvador's $85 million in military aid in fiscal 1991. Congress already was withholding $5 million pending successful prosecution of those responsible for previous human rights abuses.

The Committee Acts

Sending a message to Secretary of State Baker — as well as to the government of El Salvador — the House Foreign Affairs Committee on April 26 voted to cut half of U.S. aid to the Salvadoran military.

The cut was included in a fiscal 1990 foreign aid supplemental authorization bill (HR 4636), the companion to a supplemental appropriations bill (HR 4404) debated by the Senate the week of April 23. Both supplementals contained aid for Nicaragua, Panama and other countries.

Foreign Affairs also approved a full-scale aid authorization bill (HR 4610) for fiscal 1991. All committee actions were by voice vote.

Committee Democrats forced the action on El Salvador in part because Baker did not follow through on his pledge to negotiate with Congress for a bipartisan agreement on U.S. policy. Foreign Affairs finished most of the work in late March on its foreign aid authorizing legislation for fiscal 1990 and '91. But the panel held up final action pending the Baker negotiations.

Chairman Fascell said he became nervous about the legislation April 24 when the Senate Appropriations Committee approved the companion fiscal 1990 supplemental appropriations bill containing aid for Nicaragua, Panama and other countries. Fascell said he worried that his authorization measure might be "left behind" as Congress completed its business for the year. Congress had not enacted a full-scale foreign aid authorization bill since 1985.

Fascell decided to complete work on the authorizing bill April 26 and to include a Democratic amendment slashing El Salvador's military aid. Fascell was backed by Speaker Foley, who earlier had argued against legislating on El Salvador until Baker had time to negotiate with Congress.

William S. Broomfield, Mich., the panel's ranking Republican, objected on the administration's behalf to including the controversial El Salvador language in the fiscal 1990 bill — which was supposed to be emergency legislation. Broomfield said Bush would veto any legislation sharply curtailing Salvadoran aid.

Fascell said he decided to allow the El Salvador amendment on the fiscal 1990 bill, rather than the follow-up fiscal 1991 measure, because "there is no assurance the '91 bill will be considered" in the Senate.

The amendment adopted by the committee April 26 was sponsored by Gerry E. Studds, D-Mass., and most of the panel's Democrats. It was based on a proposal offered earlier in the year by Dodd.

The Studds amendment would have set up complex

conditions for cutting or restoring El Salvador's military aid. If enacted, the amendment immediately would suspend half the remaining unspent military aid for El Salvador in fiscal 1990. The amendment would limit fiscal 1991 arms aid to $85 million but suspend half of that amount. All military aid would be suspended if the president reported to Congress that the Salvadoran government refused to participate in good faith in negotiations with the rebels or failed to conduct a serious inquiry into the priests' murder.

All of the military aid would be restored if the president reported to Congress that the guerrillas refused to negotiate in good faith, there was proof that the guerrillas continued to receive significant shipments of military supplies from outside El Salvador or the Salvadoran government was imperiled by a major guerrilla offensive.

Studds said the amendment was crafted to "provide an incentive for both sides" in the Salvadoran war to negotiate a peace settlement.

Republicans heatedly denounced the amendment, with Henry J. Hyde, R-Ill., calling it "'an effort to sabotage the government" of El Salvador.

Negotiations

Baker told leaders in both chambers on May 1 that the administration wanted a negotiated end to the Salvadoran war and was willing to use aid as leverage. Baker's approach represented a significant shift of position for the administration, which — like its predecessor — previously had resisted serious conditions on aid to El Salvador.

In separate meetings at the Capitol on May 1, Baker and key members of both parties reached general agreement on the desirability of working out an aid proposal that would provide incentives for both the government and the guerrillas to negotiate.

Baker reportedly told congressional leaders that the Democratic approach remained too "one-sided" in punishing El Salvador's government. He proposed including more conditions putting pressure on the guerrillas to negotiate in good faith and to end attacks on civilian targets.

Procedural matters posed a hurdle to Baker's quest for a deal on El Salvador. He asked Hill leaders not to hold the fiscal 1990 supplemental spending bill (HR 4404) hostage to the talks on El Salvador. But that bill — a high priority for Bush because of its aid for Nicaragua and Panama — represented political leverage for Democrats, and they appeared reluctant to cede it.

Confident of a House vote rebuffing Bush's policy toward El Salvador, House Democrats agreed on May 17 to remove the link between that issue and the Nicaragua-Panama aid. With Foley's approval, conferees on the aid supplemental bill inserted language to allow the money to be spent without the authorization legislation.

When taking up HR 4636, the foreign aid supplemental authorization bill, the House essentially was to be faced with two competing proposals on aid to El Salvador:

- A GOP-backed amendment, sponsored by Broomfield, senior Republican on the Foreign Affairs Committee. The Broomfield amendment would require the president in November 1990 to withhold one-fourth of El Salvador's military aid if he reported to Congress that the Salvadoran government was not making progress in respecting human rights, was not conducting a serious investigation into the Jesuits' murder, was not moving to separate police forces from the military, was not reforming its judicial system or was not making plans to reduce the military's role after the war ended. Under this proposal, the president could restore El Salvador's aid if the guerrillas took any one of four steps, such as refusing to negotiate in good faith or continuing to receive military aid from outside El Salvador.

Mickey Edwards, R-Okla., said that the Broomfield proposal would impose more conditions on El Salvador than many Republicans would like but that it was crafted in an attempt to win some Democratic votes.

- The provision, endorsed by the Democratic leadership, to suspend half of El Salvador's military aid in fiscal 1990 and '91. That provision was based on an amendment to HR 4636 adopted by the Foreign Affairs Committee.

The efforts to negotiate a bipartisan compromise, however, collapsed in mid-May, setting the stage for a partisan floor battle the week of May 21.

The collapse of the talks made it likely that the House would just adopt a modified version of the Democratic-sponsored plan to suspend 50 percent of El Salvador's military aid in fiscal 1990 and '91.

SUPPLEMENTAL APPROPRIATIONS: FLOOR ACTION

Congress — wanting to crack down on the government of El Salvador but not yet ready to do it — demonstrated this apparent ambivalence in a set of contradictory actions by the House on May 22. The House approved a proposal by the Democratic leadership to cut in half El Salvador's military aid as a signal of dissatisfaction with the government and armed forces there.

However, responding to lobbying by the administration and some moderate Democrats, the House then rejected the underlying foreign aid authorization bill (HR 4636) to which the El Salvador aid cut was attached. Two days later, the chamber turned around and approved another version of the bill (S 2364) without the Salvadoran aid cut.

'The Position of the House'

The net effect was to send back to the drawing board efforts by Congress and the Bush administration to craft a new, broadly supported policy toward El Salvador. Members said negotiations toward a bipartisan policy were still possible, but only after a cooling-off period.

Although El Salvador's government and rebels were engaged in their most serious peace negotiations ever, Congress was reacting to continuing human rights abuses.

Even the most conservative approach presented to the House would have allowed for a suspension, starting in the fall, of up to 25 percent of the $85 million in military aid that Washington provided annually to El Salvador. The Democratic proposal, backed at first by a strong majority in the House, would have doubled the aid suspension and made it mandatory, effective immediately.

By rejecting the foreign aid bill, however, the House stepped back from an immediate confrontation with Bush. The administration had signaled its readiness to shift to a more assertive policy toward the Salvadoran government but had resisted House Democrats' abrupt approach.

Although officials privately had said that the administration eventually might accept some form of a 50 percent aid cut, they warned publicly that Bush would veto any legislation containing the Democrats' plan for an immediate halving of the aid.

Despite the rejection of the foreign aid bill May 22, Foley insisted that the House had demonstrated its determination to restrict aid to El Salvador.

The effort to make the 50 percent cut "was a watershed amendment in the House with respect to military aid to El Salvador," he said the day after the House acted. "I think almost certainly in some form military aid will be curtailed in the future."

Giving Up Linkage

After the rejection of the bill, House Democrats officially gave up the main lever that they had to encourage concessions on El Salvador by the administration. That leverage was a $720 million aid package requested by Bush for the new governments of Nicaragua and Panama. The money was to be authorized in HR 4636 (the bill defeated by the House) and actually appropriated in a companion fiscal 1990 supplemental spending bill (HR 4404).

The administration vehemently objected to linkage between the El Salvador issue and the Nicaragua-Panama bill. Bush said Democrats were holding aid for the new democracies in Central America "hostage."

After firming up plans for House action on the authorization bill — complete with the El Salvador amendment — Foley had said on May 17 that the Democrats would drop the linkage. On his instructions, House negotiators agreed to put the necessary waivers in the conference version of the supplemental spending bill.

But after the House rejected the aid authorization bill on May 22, some liberal Democrats argued in favor of pulling the Nicaragua-Panama waivers out of the spending bill. Doing that would have restored the link between Nicaragua-Panama aid and El Salvador aid conditions, in hope of forcing concessions by the administration.

Foley vetoed that idea, however, reportedly telling his fellow Democrats that they should no longer give Bush grounds to attack Congress for holding up the Nicaragua-Panama aid.

With the linkage question cleared away, the House on May 24 passed the authorization bill by inserting it in a companion Senate measure. That move was aimed at bolstering the role of the House Foreign Affairs Committee, which had seen its regular aid authorization bills die in the Senate while foreign assistance programs were folded into appropriations bills.

Conflicting Votes

The House's May 22 debate and voting on El Salvador strongly resembled debates over Nicaraguan contra aid in the 1980s, with conservative and moderate Democrats holding the balance of power.

The end result left no one happy, but both sides claimed victory. Republicans said they had achieved a strategic win over the Democratic leadership; Democrats insisted they had shown the strong desire of Congress for a change of policy.

As approved by the Foreign Affairs Committee, HR 4636 included a Democratic-sponsored provision conditionally suspending half of El Salvador's military aid in fiscal 1990 and '91.

Republicans offered a substitute, sponsored by Broomfield, to allow Bush to suspend up to 25 percent of El Salvador's aid if the government refused to take certain actions, such as fully investigating the Jesuits' murders.

Broomfield called that proposal a "measured response" to events in El Salvador. By endorsing it, the administration effectively conceded a need for a policy change. However, Democrats insisted that the Broomfield approach did not represent a big enough break with past policy. The House rejected Broomfield's amendment 175-243, with only 23 Democrats supporting it. *(Vote 126, p. 44-H)*

By an almost mirror-image vote of 250-163, the House then adopted the proposal backed by the House Democratic leadership for a 50 percent cut in El Salvador's arms aid. That proposal was sponsored by Moakley and Murtha. *(Vote 127, p. 46-H)*

"Enough is enough," Moakley said in an impassioned speech. "The time to act has come. They killed six priests in cold blood. I stood on the ground where my friends were blown away by men to whom the sanctity of human life bears no meaning — and men who will probably never be brought to justice."

Republicans said they, too, were disgusted by continued human rights abuses in El Salvador. But they insisted that the Cristiani government was trying to curb the military. GOP Whip Newt Gingrich, Ga., also said an aid suspension would encourage the rightist elements of the Salvadoran military to take matters into their own hands.

"I know my friends mean well," Gingrich said of the Democrats. "But the effect of what they are doing is to say to the hard-line elements in the army: 'You had better slaughter everyone now before the American aid ends.'"

Moments after approving Moakley's amendment, the House rejected the underlying foreign aid bill 171-244, with 94 Democrats joining all but 16 Republicans in opposing final passage. *(Vote 128, p. 46-H)*

Once the House acted, the members disputed the meaning of the vote.

Republicans maintained that this vote — not the one on the Moakley amendment — was the truly important one of the evening because it showed that the House was unwilling to take the step of cutting El Salvador's aid in half.

Most Democratic leaders, however, insisted that the vote killing the underlying bill was in large part a protest against foreign aid in general — and not just a rejection of the El Salvador aid cut.

The issue was due to arise again in June, when a House Appropriations panel was to begin writing the foreign aid spending bill for fiscal 1991.

Chairman Obey said the 50 percent aid cutback would be included in his subcommittee's bill. "That's the position of the House," Obey said, referring to the 250-163 vote by which the House tentatively backed the 50 percent cut.

FOREIGN AID APPROPRIATIONS: HOUSE ACTION

The House on June 27 passed a $15.6 billion foreign assistance appropriations bill (HR 5114) that would have cut in half the U.S. military aid to the Cristiani government. The cut, written into the bill by the Appropriations Committee, was identical to the amendment to HR 4636 adopted in May.

Bush vowed to veto the foreign aid appropriations bill if it reached his desk containing that El Salvador provision. But administration allies made no attempt to amend it on the House floor. Administration officials and Democratic leaders were trying to work out compromise language that could be incorporated in the conference report on the bill.

Details of Bill

The bill would limit military aid to El Salvador to $85 million. However, to provide incentives for both the El Salvador government and the country's leftist guerrillas (the FMLN) to negotiate a peace settlement, the bill would withhold half that amount from the government.

The withheld funds would be turned over if the president reported any of the following to Congress:

- The FMLN declined to negotiate in good faith for a cease-fire and permanent settlement of the war.
- The guerrillas were receiving lethal military equipment from outside El Salvador. Congress would have to be shown proof of this.
- The survival of the El Salvadoran government was jeopardized by "substantial and sustained military actions" by the FMLN.
- The FMLN was engaging in acts of violence against civilian targets.

On the other hand, military aid to El Salvador would be cut off entirely if:

- The elected government were overthrown by a coup.
- The government declined to participate in good-faith negotiations aimed at a cease-fire and settlement.
- The government was "failing to conduct a thorough and professional investigation" of the November 1989 murders.
- Salvadoran military or security forces were engaging in acts of violence against civilians.

The administration agreed in principle to withhold conditionally some aid as a means of pressuring the Salvadoran government to seek a negotiated settlement with the FMLN, but it argued that 50 percent was too large a cut.

New Administration Deal

After the House passed the foreign aid bill, complete with the aid cut, the State Department offered a new proposal to conditionally reduce military aid to El Salvador by 30 percent during fiscal 1991. The plan got a lukewarm reception from House Democrats.

Under the proposal, which Assistant Secretary of State Bernard W. Aronson presented to a group of House Democrats on July 12, 15 percent of the $85 million military aid program for El Salvador in fiscal 1991 would be withheld for six months. An additional 15 percent could also be withheld if leftist FMLN guerrillas moved to end the conflict in the country. Aronson offered the new strings to restart negotiations with key Democrats.

House Deputy Majority Whip David E. Bonior, D-Mich., termed the plan "obviously inadequate. A flat 30 percent withholding would have been a much better starting point."

Moakley said Aronson's trip to Capitol Hill showed the administration's good faith. But, he added, "the cuts being offered simply aren't deep enough. We want to see some action" in El Salvador.

In addition to differences in the percentage of aid to be withheld, the new administration approach differed markedly from the Democratic plan (as reflected in HR 5114) in the conditions placed on the two sides in the conflict.

The only conditions that would trigger an end to all military aid in the new administration proposal would be a refusal by the government to negotiate in good faith, "despite the willingness of the FMLN to do so," or a military coup. In the former instance, the president could reverse his position and restore aid if he found "that the facts giving rise to that determination no longer prevail."

Also unlike the foreign aid bill, Aronson's proposal included $2 million to train El Salvador's security forces. The police training, which would be linked to human rights progress, would be provided by U.S. civilians.

While lawmakers negotiated among themselves and with the administration over aid proposals, Salvadoran President Cristiani came to Washington to do a little lobbying for himself. Skepticism ran strong the week of Sept. 25 toward Cristiani's assertion, though, that his government would improve its poor human rights record.

Cristiani came to Washington armed with two new proposals aimed at obtaining the full $85 million in military aid proposed for the next fiscal year.

Cristiani reiterated that his government would proceed vigorously with the investigation of the priests' slayings and, to try to convince skeptics, said he had invited a three-member panel of distinguished U.S. jurists to advise his government on how to adjudicate the Jesuit case.

More significantly, he suggested that any reduction in military aid would take effect only if El Salvador's leftist rebels agreed to a cease-fire.

Moakley dismissed the notion of a blue-ribbon panel. "It is our view that all the jurists in the world won't solve the Jesuit killings. We want to see results," he said.

Moakley also said reform of the military should take place before a cease-fire. But other Democrats said the idea of tying an aid reduction to a cease-fire could have appeal. "It could be the basis for a compromise," said Rep. McCurdy, a member of Moakley's task force.

FOREIGN AID APPROPRIATIONS: SENATE ACTION

The Senate Appropriations Committee approved its version of HR 5114 on Oct. 10. Its Foreign Operations Subcommittee approved the bill Oct. 2, following the lead of the House and placing heavy conditions on the $85 million military-assistance program for El Salvador.

A turning point in the Senate's consideration of the issue came in August, when Dodd agreed to back a plan by Patrick J. Leahy, D-Vt., which was similar in intent to House-passed language, for restrictions on fiscal 1991 military aid to El Salvador.

The Dodd-Leahy proposal would tie military assistance to a U.N.-drafted plan for settling the conflict in El Salvador. The $85 million in aid would depend on three major conditions:

- Aid would be cut off completely if the president determined that El Salvador's government had rejected the peace plan but the FMLN had accepted it.
- It would also be eliminated if the president reported that El Salvador's government "has failed to conduct a thorough and professional" investigation into the November 1989 murders. Leahy described the progress in the case as a "fiasco."
- It would be cut in half if the leftists cooperated in peace talks. The full $85 million would be provided if the president determined that the FMLN had rejected a U.N.-drafted peace settlement that the government accepted, or if the rebels began a major offensive.

But Republicans held fire on the proposal in the subcommittee and full committee, preferring to take their chances with an amendment to the Dodd-Leahy proposal on the floor.

The Republican strategy appeared to be to tie full funding of the program to the government's acceptance of a U.N.-monitored, but not necessarily U.N.-drafted, peace plan, which the FMLN rejected.

Senate Floor Votes

On Oct. 19, the Senate agreed to the Dodd-Leahy amendment by a wide margin (74-25) and rejected (39-58) a milder, administration-backed amendment by Bob Graham, D-Fla. *(Votes 293, 295, p. 58-S)*

"The murders certainly provided aid opponents with easier ground to plow," said Dave Durenberger, R-Minn., who reluctantly supported the Dodd-Leahy language.

Salvadoran military personnel had been charged with the murders. But nearly a year after the slayings, the government had still brought none of the suspects to trial. And key evidence in the case that could point to the involvement of high military officers in the murders had been destroyed.

The Dodd-Leahy language demonstrated — just as the House vote in June had — that the congressional mood on El Salvador had changed. After the House action, the administration had undertaken negotiations with lawmakers of both parties in an effort to obtain less stringent terms for aid.

The negotiations never gained momentum, in part because the administration was diverted by the crisis in the Persian Gulf. State Department officials never engaged in serious talks with key members. When the administration finally focused on the issue, a surprising majority in the Senate had already made up their minds.

In lining up votes for their amendment, Leahy and Dodd said they noticed that many senators had grown tired of dealing with the war in El Salvador, particularly in light of reduced superpower tensions. According to both men, the government's long record of human rights violations, climaxed by the Jesuit case, also soured many lawmakers.

Dodd said the wide margin of victory illustrated how "fed up" senators were with the ongoing violence. Leahy added that, in spite of the vote, there was no sympathy for the left-wing FMLN guerrillas. "The feeling is 'a pox on both your houses,'" Leahy said.

As sentiment tilted against military aid to El Salvador, Jesuits and members of other religious orders tried to solidify the opposition. The religious orders, especially Catholics, had long been in the forefront of opposition to military aid, but the killings of the Jesuits lent their message urgency.

The Jesuits also demonstrated political savvy, enlisting the president of Fordham University to lobby Sen. Alfonse M. D'Amato, R-N.Y., and the president of Loyola University in New Orleans to contact Sen. J. Bennett Johnston, D-La. Both universities were Jesuit institutions. The two conservatives supported the Dodd-Leahy amendment and opposed Graham's.

While supporters of the Dodd-Leahy amendment believed that it would send a signal to the Salvadoran military, they had no illusions that the legislation alone would halt the cycle of violence. "I don't believe I affected the outcome in El Salvador," said a pessimistic Durenberger. "The violence will continue regardless of the vote [on Dodd-Leahy]."

FINAL ACTION . . . AND BEYOND

The Bush administration had to accept restrictions on aid to El Salvador in order to win debt relief for Egypt, a key ally in the Persian Gulf crisis, in the final shaping of the foreign aid appropriations bill (HR 5114) for fiscal 1991. Politically, the items counterbalanced each other.

The White House, which found the El Salvador aid restrictions onerous, was constrained from making good on a threatened veto because of the crucial importance of the debt relief for Egypt, according to administration sources.

Republicans, led by Edwards, the ranking member of the House Foreign Operations Subcommittee, tried to weaken the Dodd-Leahy amendment in conference.

The key change urged by Edwards would have given the president complete authority to restore military aid to the government of El Salvador, if he determined that it was in full compliance with a complex set of provisions included in the amendment. Under the Dodd-Leahy measure, aid could be restored only with congressional approval.

Both Leahy and Obey rejected the proposal, with the House chairman asserting, "I would be eaten for lunch if I acceded" to the amendment. But Edwards pressed on, restating the administration's veto threat.

Finally, Edwards and Sen. Bob Kasten, Wis., Leahy's Republican counterpart on the Senate committee, crafted a compromise under which Leahy promised to request special procedures for restoring the aid, should the circumstance arise. The compromise also would exclude all military assistance "in the pipeline" — appropriated but not yet delivered — from the Dodd-Leahy restrictions.

House adoption of the conference report on HR 5114 came Oct. 27 on an 188-162 vote — a relatively narrow margin that was blamed on opposition to provisions for forgiving Egyptian debts as part of U.S. policy in the Persian Gulf crisis. The Senate cleared the measure by voice vote the same day. *(Persian Gulf crisis, p. 717)*

New Developments

The Bush administration announced Dec. 6 that it was rushing $48.1 million in military aid to El Salvador to help it counter a widening offensive by left-wing guerrillas. The emergency aid included $37.5 million of the $42.5 million that was readily available for El Salvador in fiscal 1991.

The next month, reacting to the apparent execution of two U.S. servicemen by guerrillas, Bush announced Jan. 15, 1991, that he would release the full allotment of fiscal 1991 U.S. military aid to El Salvador.

Bush froze delivery of the funds for 60 days, saying he hoped the pause would encourage peace talks between the Salvadoran government and the FMLN guerrillas.

The FMLN claimed responsibility for downing a helicopter carrying three U.S. servicemen Jan. 2; one died in the crash, and U.S. officials said the other two appeared to have been executed.

Congressional Democrats, who pressed hard for the aid restrictions, shared the administration's disgust with the alleged executions. Leahy, co-author of the Senate version of the legislation that restricted aid, said the rebels "should probably get a retainer from the Salvadoran government for lobbying for increased military aid."

But Leahy and some other Democrats were not convinced that the incident justified providing more aid.

In a letter to Cristiani, Leahy wrote that, even if Bush released the assistance, "efforts in Congress to terminate American involvement in the war will continue."

The White House said Bush's decision "was based on the FMLN's violation of the [congressional] conditions against 'engaging in acts of violence directed at civilian targets' and acquiring or receiving 'significant shipments of lethal military assistance from outside El Salvador.'"

The statement said the funds would be delayed "in the interest of promoting a peaceful settlement to El Salvador's tragic conflict." But, it added, "the United States will monitor carefully security conditions in El Salvador, and the president may release military assistance sooner than 60 days in case of a compelling security need." ■

Mandela, de Klerk Vie for U.S. Support

The dramatic release by the South African government of imprisoned black leader Nelson Mandela on Feb. 11 won broad praise around the world, but the United States retained congressionally enacted economic sanctions against the white-minority regime.

Congress and President Bush both hosted Mandela in June and South African President F. W. de Klerk in September as the two leaders sought to gain support and good will from lawmakers and from the administration.

Mandela, deputy president of the African National Congress (ANC), met with Bush on June 25 and received a warm welcome as he visited Capitol Hill on June 26 to address a joint session of Congress — an honor customarily reserved for government leaders. He then continued a 12-city, cross-country tour to raise funds for the ANC.

De Klerk's visit — the first by a South African state leader to the United States since 1945 — was lower key, but his reception at the White House and on Capitol Hill marked an important step in his efforts to regain international standing for his country.

Mandela's release after 27 years in prison and the legalization of the ANC, the leading black organization in South Africa, were among several moves orchestrated by de Klerk aimed at starting talks with black leaders.

To pressure the Pretoria government to dismantle its system of racial separatism called apartheid and bring the country's majority-black population into the political system, Congress had enacted broad trade sanctions against South Africa in 1986 (PL 99-440). The law, enacted over President Ronald Reagan's veto, demanded a series of steps by the South African government before the sanctions could be lifted.

Mandela's visit helped cement support on Capitol Hill for keeping the U.S. sanctions in place. "We have yet to arrive at the point when we can say that South Africa is set on an irreversible course" toward democracy, Mandela told the lawmakers. Sanctions should continue, he added, because "the purpose for which they were imposed has not yet been achieved."

In his visit, de Klerk did not press to have the sanctions lifted, but repeatedly said that the reforms his Nationalist Party government had instituted would not be reversed. "My government's commitment to remove the last pillars of apartheid is final and irreversible," he said in a speech at the National Press Club on Sept. 25.

Bush made no immediate move to lift sanctions. Speaking with reporters the day after Mandela's release, Bush said, "We can't do that. I am bound by the law."

When he met with de Klerk on Sept. 24, however, Bush indicated the administration would try to persuade Congress to modify or suspend the sanctions if the congressionally established conditions were met.

Echoing de Klerk's assurances, Bush said, "We believe the process of change in South Africa is irreversible, a fact that we'll bear squarely in mind as we consider specific issues in the future."

BACKGROUND

South Africa's apartheid system, established by the Nationalist Party after a 1948 election victory, was a uniquely pervasive legal system for separating the country's white, black, Asian and mixed-race populations. All South Africans were classified by race, and government facilities and public accommodations were segregated.

The country's 26 million blacks, who outnumbered whites 5-to-1, had no right to vote in national elections.

The apartheid system — and the police state measures used to keep it in place — had made South Africa an international pariah, the target of worldwide criticism and economic sanctions voted by the United Nations.

But the country's value to the United States as an anticommunist ally and a source of strategic minerals created a tension between liberal opponents of apartheid in the United States and political conservatives who favored maintaining some ties to the Pretoria regime.

Constructive Engagement, Sanctions

In the 1980s, the Reagan administration sought to bridge that political gap with a policy it called constructive engagement — diplomatic negotiations aimed at bringing about reform in South Africa and settling regional disputes involving South Africa and neighboring Angola, Mozambique and Namibia.

The policy made some progress on the regional issues, but it did not satisfy the increasingly active U.S. anti-apartheid movement or its supporters on Capitol Hill. *(Reagan policies, 1985 Almanac, p. 360)*

The result was the 1986 sanctions law, enacted by Congress over Reagan's veto by votes of 313-83 in the House and 78-21 in the then majority-Republican Senate. Among those instrumental in shaping the legislation was Indiana Republican Richard G. Lugar, then chairman of the Senate Foreign Relations Committee.

Among other things, the sanctions barred importation of South African coal, steel and agricultural products and prohibited air travel between the United States and South Africa. The sanctions also banned exports of oil, arms, computers and nuclear items to agencies enforcing apartheid and forbade U.S. firms to extend new loans to South Africa or to make new investments there.

The 1986 law said the sanctions could be lifted if South Africa freed Mandela and all other political prisoners, repealed the state of emergency and release all people detained under it, legalized democratic political parties and incorporated all South Africans into the political process, repealed the Group Areas Act and the Population Registration Act, and agreed to enter into good-faith talks with "truly representative" black leaders.

But the act also permitted the president to suspend sanctions, subject to a congressional veto, if political prisoners were freed and three of the other four conditions were met. *(1986 Almanac, p. 359)*

Bush Administration Shifts

Breaking with Reagan's confrontational approach, Bush had tried to work with Congress in developing a bipartisan policy toward South Africa.

When some lawmakers were calling for additional sanctions against South Africa in 1989, Bush persuaded leaders to hold off until de Klerk's new government had a chance to deliver on its promise to move the country toward multiracial democracy. De Klerk was elected state president on Sept. 14, 1989, succeeding P. W. Botha, whose 11 years in power had seen only limited moves away from apartheid.

Meeting a requirement in the 1986 sanctions law for the administration to report annually on its policy toward South Africa, Bush reported to Congress on Oct. 2, 1989, that the South African government had taken no fundamental steps to dismantle apartheid. The administration urged against further economic or political sanctions, instead requesting that de Klerk's government be given "reasonable time to demonstrate" whether it intended to begin abolishing apartheid.

Some advocates of more sanctions complained that the administration was allowing Pretoria too much of a "grace period." Even so, they did not push for more sanctions by legislation. *(1989 Almanac, p. 625)*

CHANGE IN SOUTH AFRICA

South Africa's announcement the week of Feb. 5, 1990, that it would legalize the ANC and release Mandela from prison was greeted warmly on Capitol Hill, but members stressed that reforms were only a first step toward ending apartheid.

Republicans and Democrats alike commended de Klerk, who in a Feb. 2 speech at the opening of Parliament unveiled the most far-reaching revisions of apartheid since its inception 42 years earlier.

But U.S. lawmakers also called for more change, and most indicated it was premature to suspend the 1986 sanctions. Sanctions had to remain in effect, many said, because de Klerk's announced reforms did not go far enough.

The reforms, however, deflated efforts for tougher sanctions, and the Bush administration gained more time to negotiate a bipartisan policy with Congress.

"The unbanning of the ANC, the release of political prisoners . . . are very positive steps toward reconciliation," said Sen. Nancy Landon Kassebaum, R-Kan. But "much more needs to be done."

In addition to revoking the 30-year ban on the ANC and promising the release of Mandela, jailed on treason-related charges since 1962, de Klerk announced other changes in February. Among them were:

- The repeal of emergency regulations restricting freedom of the press, except for those governing television coverage of scenes of unrest.
- A more limited application of the death penalty, which had been used against political prisoners.
- The removal of curbs on the activities of 32 other organizations.
- The lifting of restrictions on the movements and contacts of 374 people who had been under government surveillance for political agitation.
- The provision of a doctor and lawyer to political detainees and the limiting of their detention to six months.

On Feb. 11, Mandela walked out of Victor Verster prison near Cape Town. Television cameras beamed his image around the world as he strode to freedom, returning a clenched-fist salute to the cheering crowds.

Apartheid Continues

Dramatic as they were, however, de Klerk's reforms left untouched the basic structure of apartheid. The Population Registration Act, which classified every South African by race, and the Group Areas Act, which enforced the segregation of neighborhoods, remained in place. Also remaining were the national state of emergency laws, except for those curtailing radio and newspaper coverage. Thousands of dissidents had been jailed since the state of emergency was imposed in June 1986.

Rep. Ronald V. Dellums, D-Calif., chair of the Congressional Black Caucus and one of the most vociferous critics of apartheid in Congress, said of the new reforms: "It is imperative to clearly understand that even these measures, laudable as they are, do not constitute the establishment of freedom or true democracy for the black majority."

Dellums and other members dismissed speculation that de Klerk's announced reforms might warrant a review of the U.S. policy of economic sanctions against South Africa.

"The sanctions should be maintained in full force. This is no time to relax them," said Sen. Edward M. Kennedy, D-Mass. Kennedy credited the sanctions with helping force the reforms unveiled by de Klerk.

A study cited in The Washington Post Jan. 14 indicated that U.S. sanctions, along with those of other countries, had cost South Africa between $32 billion and $40 billion in 1986-90, including $11 billion in net capital outflows and $4 billion in lost export earnings.

Coenraad Bezuidenhout, a South African spokesman, said that sanctions had hurt his country's economy. In order to help de Klerk along the path toward reform, he said, the United States should "encourage the moderates in South Africa by assisting the economy."

As of Feb. 8, de Klerk had gone part of the way toward meeting the first three of the five conditions outlined under the U.S. anti-apartheid law.

"These actions clearly fail to satisfy the conditions for repeal of the Comprehensive Anti-Apartheid Act," said Senate Majority Leader George J. Mitchell, D-Maine.

Terms for Ending Sanctions

On Feb. 2, Howard Wolpe, D-Mich., who chaired the House Foreign Affairs Africa Subcommittee as well as a bipartisan task force on South Africa, ticked off a list of changes that Pretoria needed to make before the United States could consider ending sanctions.

Wolpe said de Klerk had to follow through on the partial lifting of the state of emergency and release some 1,000 political prisoners held under the nation's strict security laws.

In addition, Wolpe said de Klerk should "establish a specific timetable" for negotiations with black leaders. He dismissed as unacceptable de Klerk's "group rights" proposal, a formula that many said would grant political representation to blacks while preserving white-minority rule.

While Wolpe's tough stance reflected prevailing sentiment on the Hill, some members backed more flexibility. The ranking Republican on Wolpe's Africa Subcommittee, Dan Burton, Ind., favored a "carrot and stick" policy, one in which the United States would ease sanctions one by one as new reforms were instituted.

"If the South African government continues to move toward democracy . . . I will be happy to lead the charge to start ending the sanctions," said Burton, a longtime sanctions foe.

Speaking of the Pretoria government, Bush told reporters Feb. 2: "I think when people move in the right direction, it's certainly timely to review all policy." But the president refused to commit to a timetable or a quid pro quo on sanctions.

The administration's reluctance to act unilaterally also may have reflected the importance of the apartheid issue to U.S. civil rights groups.

Some political analysts suggested Bush would not risk a

fight on the South Africa issue at a time when the Republican Party was courting black voters. Other observers said de Klerk's announcement took the wind out of the sails of those pushing for added sanctions against South Africa.

A Democratic staff member at the Africa Subcommittee said that de Klerk's reforms could delay the negotiations between Wolpe's task force and administration officials over a new, bipartisan approach toward South Africa and any additional sanctions. The aide said that de Klerk's speech had bought the South African government more time, but "how much more time is unclear."

MANDELA'S VISIT

Mandela received the welcome of a visiting dignitary in his visit to Washington.

At the White House on June 25, Bush praised Mandela as "a man who embodies the hopes of millions" and pledged U.S. support in the struggle against apartheid. But Bush also called on "all elements in South African society to renounce the use of violence in armed struggle."

Mandela responded pointedly. "The methods of political action which are used by the black people of South Africa were determined by the South African government," he said. "... [W]hen a government decides to ban political organizations of the oppressed, intensifies oppression, and does not allow any free political activity, no matter how peaceful and nonviolent, then the people have no alternative but to resort to violence."

On Capitol Hill the next day, Mandela's antiapartheid message was greeted with roaring applause, giving a boost to his efforts to keep trade sanctions, and political heat, on the South African government.

Recognizing Congress' support, Mandela thanked members "for the principled struggle you waged" in pressing for a law that made a "decisive contribution" to the negotiating process. Speaking to a packed House chamber, Mandela was applauded on both sides of the aisle when he told lawmakers that sanctions should be maintained.

"I think we ought to keep the sanctions on that we have," Sen. Paul Simon, D-Ill., chairman of the Foreign Relations Subcommittee on Africa, said afterward.

Rep. Constance A. Morella, R-Md., who had visited South Africa in January, agreed. "I don't think it's time yet" to lift sanctions, she said.

Mandela's speech was marred only slightly by a controversy over remarks he had made before arriving in Washington that embraced Palestine Liberation Organization leader Yasir Arafat, Libyan leader Muammar el-Qaddafi and Cuban President Fidel Castro. A few lawmakers boycotted the speech as a result. More commonly, however, members mildly criticized the comments but discounted their importance to U.S. policy toward South Africa.

Aid Issue

One purpose of Mandela's visit to the United States was to raise money the ANC needed to build a party infrastructure and to repatriate about 20,000 exiled members. After the tour ended, organizers reported raising $7 million.

For its part, Congress had included a $10 million allocation to South African political organizations in the fiscal 1990 supplemental appropriations (HR 4404 — PL 101-302) that Bush signed on May 25. The earmarking — crafted by Reps. William H. Gray III, D-Pa., the majority whip, and Stephen J. Solarz, D-N.Y. — provided that the funds go to organizations "committed to a suspension of violence in the context of negotiations to build a democratic system of government in South Africa."

The clause spawned differing views on whether funds could be provided to the ANC. Herman J. Cohen, assistant secretary of State for foreign affairs, said the ANC had to "renounce violence," something Mandela refused to do during his visit, to qualify for any of the money.

But Chairman Wolpe of the House Subcommittee on Africa said the ANC qualified for the money. "That's wrong," he said of Cohen's reading of the law. To get any of the $10 million, Wolpe said, the ANC had to be willing to suspend violence, a standard he said had been met.

Meeting with Bush at the White House on June 25, Mandela said the ANC would suspend hostilities once the obstacles to negotiation were overcome.

In addition to the $10 million approved in the supplemental, Congress annually provided $32 million in humanitarian aid to disadvantaged South Africans. This money did not go to political groups.

When Mandela visited the White House, Cohen backed away from his earlier statements. Asked whether the ANC was eligible for any of the $10 million, Cohen first responded "no," then said: "I don't know. We'll have to consult the lawyers on that." He added, "The president says that the moneys we have appropriated are not for the purpose of helping any particular political organization."

The issue remained unsettled at the end of 1990. In March 1991, The Washington Post reported that the Agency for International Development had formally notified Congress that it intended to allocate $3.7 million to the ANC; $1 million to the rival black political organization Inkatha; and $1.2 million each to Republican and Democratic Party institutes that conducted training programs in emerging democracies. But the Post said some conservative lawmakers, including Sen. Jesse Helms, R-N.C., were seeking to block the funds for the ANC.

DE KLERK'S VISIT

Three months after Mandela's visit to the United States, de Klerk traced a similar path, meeting with Bush at the White House and with congressional leaders.

The South African president did not ask for an easing of U.S. economic sanctions against South Africa, hoping instead to pick up statements of support for his efforts to change apartheid. But when the two presidents met at the White House on Sept. 24, Bush was effusive in his praise for de Klerk's policies.

"I think all Americans recognize that President de Klerk is courageously trying to change things," Bush said.

Under the 1986 sanctions law, the president could seek a revision or suspension of the sanctions if four of the five conditions were met. Bush acknowledged that Pretoria had not met those conditions yet, but his hint that he might be considering such a request drew fire from some lawmakers.

"I am concerned about the voices within the administration that seem to be rushing to lift sanctions," said Gray. The Democratic whip said he was dubious that de Klerk's movement away from apartheid was irreversible, but acknowledged that de Klerk's visit could "be counted as a diplomatic success back home."

To blunt that success somewhat, Congressional Black Caucus Chairman Dellums decided to cancel the group's scheduled meeting with the South African president. "I thought the meeting could be misused, especially by the media," Dellums said. ■

Kenya Aid Under Scrutiny After Turmoil

Responding to congressional pressure, the Bush administration suspended military aid to Kenya in July 1990 to protest a crackdown on dissent by the one-party government of President Daniel arap Moi. But the administration lifted the freeze in February 1991.

Citing violent clashes between police and antigovernment rioters and the detention of prominent government opponents, Howard Wolpe, D-Mich., chairman of the House Foreign Affairs Subcommittee on Africa, spearheaded an effort in July to cut development and military aid to the east African nation.

Wolpe and four other members active in international affairs wrote Secretary of State James A. Baker III on July 12 to urge the administration to suspend aid to Kenya "until there is a marked improvement in the human rights situation in that country, including the unconditional release of all persons detained for their political beliefs."

Paul Simon, D-Ill., Wolpe's counterpart in the Senate, also called for cuts, and Senate Foreign Relations Chairman Claiborne Pell, D-R.I., said aid to Kenya needed to be re-examined.

Wolpe's letter was also signed by Dante B. Fascell, D-Fla., chairman of the House Foreign Affairs Committee; Gus Yatron, D-Pa., chairman of the House Foreign Affairs Subcommittee on Human Rights and International Organizations; House Majority Whip William H. Gray III, D-Pa.; and Simon.

Dan Burton of Indiana, ranking Republican on the House Africa Subcommittee, also wrote Moi on July 18 to urge him to end the crackdown.

"The crackdown by the Kenyan government can only help those who would like to see our aid level to Kenya cut, and our relations with Kenya harmed," he wrote. His letter was cosigned by the ranking Republican on the Foreign Affairs Committee, William S. Broomfield of Michigan, and seven other House Republicans.

The Bush administration said it was distressed by the detention of political opponents and regretted the violence. Late in July, it put a freeze on $5 million in military aid that Kenya had not yet received in fiscal 1990 funds.

Kenya had been one of the largest recipients of U.S. aid in sub-Saharan Africa. Excluding food aid, its total allocation for fiscal 1990 was $10 million in military assistance and $35 million for economic development.

Background

The moves to hold up U.S. aid followed turmoil that began in Kenya in late June when the government arrested six dissidents and their aides who had advocated an end to one-party rule. Among those detained were two Cabinet ministers who had been unofficial leaders of the movement for multiparty government.

Calls for a multiparty system to replace the one-party rule that Moi had instituted in 1982 erupted into four days of violence that began July 7. At least 20 people died as riot police battled antigovernment protesters, looters and vandals.

Kenya's relative stability had made it attractive for investment, and the country was one of the largest sub-Saharan importers of U.S. products. Its pro-Western government and its strategic Indian Ocean port of Mombassa added to Kenya's importance to the United States.

But after surviving a coup attempt in 1982, Moi pushed through the National Assembly a ban on rival political parties. U.S. ties to the nation became strained in 1989 and 1990 as Moi stepped up his opposition to multiparty politics, which he claimed would fuel tribal factionalism.

Human Rights Proviso

After the summer violence, members of Congress working on the annual foreign aid appropriations bill (HR 5114 — PL 101-513) attached a human rights proviso to the $15 million allocation in military aid for Kenya and its share of $800 million in economic aid for sub-Saharan Africa.

The proviso specified that before Kenya could get the money, President Bush had to certify a number of human rights improvements — including that Moi's regime had charged and tried or released all prisoners; stopped physical abuse of prisoners; restored the independence of the judiciary; and permitted freedom of expression. *(Foreign aid appropriations, p. 830)*

After Congress adjourned, a three-member Senate delegation visited Kenya in November and warned that Moi's refusal to permit political pluralism was jeopardizing both its military aid and its share of the increased U.S. economic development aid for Africa. The delegation was headed by Foreign Operations Appropriations Subcommittee Chairman Patrick J. Leahy, D-Vt.

In February 1991, however, the Bush administration lifted the freeze on the $5 million in fiscal 1990 funds. The New York Times, reporting the action from the Kenyan capital of Nairobi, said that U.S. Ambassador Smith Hempstone described the step as "appreciation" for a number of actions by Kenya in the previous month, including support for U.S. policies in the Persian Gulf crisis and the stepping-up of antiterrorist activities.

In a later report from Washington, the Times quoted unnamed administration officials as saying the release of the aid was an expression of gratitude to Moi's government for granting refuge to Libyan dissidents who had taken part in a failed U.S.-backed effort to destabilize the government of Col. Muammar el-Qaddafi. ■

Aid to Zaire Restricted

To protest human rights conditions and corruption in Zaire, Congress provided that fiscal 1991 foreign aid be channeled only through non-governmental organizations, not through the government of the central African nation.

The restriction approved by House-Senate conference committee on the foreign operations appropriations bill (HR 5114 — PL 101-513) softened outright prohibitions on U.S. aid approved by both the House and Senate. *(Foreign aid appropriations, p. 830)*

Conferees said allowing aid through non-governmental organizations, private groups and universities would permit a continuation of humanitarian programs and child-survival activities in Zaire (H Rept 101-968).

In its report on the bill (H Rept 101-553), the House Appropriations Committee said Zaire had "one of the most mismanaged and corrupt economies in the world today." ■

Bush Pocket-Vetoes Intelligence Bill

After the Iran-contra scandal, congressional Intelligence panel members assigned themselves a daunting task: to rewrite the rules for executive branch reporting of covert actions, with an eye toward preventing a recurrence of that debacle. The Senate panel drafted new rules in 1990 and, while criticized by House Democrats for being too weak, they were approved by both chambers of Congress.

But on Nov. 30, in a surprise action, President Bush announced that he was pocket-vetoing the intelligence authorization bill (S 2834) to which they were attached. As a result, Congress and the administration were expected to renew their battle over the requirements for the White House to report to the Intelligence committees when secret operations were undertaken.

Bush said he was particularly disturbed by a section requiring that Congress be notified of requests by U.S. government agencies "to a foreign government or a private citizen to conduct a covert action on behalf of the United States."

In his veto message, Bush complained that the provision "purports to regulate diplomacy . . . by forbidding the expression of certain views to foreign governments and private citizens." *(Veto message, p. 798)*

The authors of the bill insisted that the provision was intended only to curtail unchecked covert operations conducted by third countries at the behest of the United States — of the type that occurred during the Iran-contra affair — and was not an attempt to hamper diplomacy.

In addition, the bill would have placed new restrictions on covert aid to guerrilla forces in Angola and Afghanistan, and terminated secret aid to the Cambodian rebels. The large-scale covert aid programs of the Reagan era had been losing favor with Congress because of the reduction in tensions between the United States and the Soviet Union. The administration had been working toward a diplomatic resolution of conflicts in all three countries.

But Congress, impatient with the pace of diplomacy, altered terms of the covert aid programs. For Cambodia, the $13 million covert package for the non-communist resistance would be provided openly beginning early in 1991, along with $7 million in previously approved overt aid. For Angola, Congress placed conditions on $25 million to $30 million in lethal aid to the National Union for the Total Independence of Angola (UNITA), aimed at inducing the rebels and the Luanda government to reach a settlement.

For Afghanistan, lawmakers reportedly slashed assistance for rebel forces from approximately $300 million to $250 million in fiscal 1991. In addition, Congress established new rules for the reporting of covert operations, although the president was not required, in all cases, to inform Congress immediately of such actions.

The Senate cleared the conference report on Oct. 25 by voice vote. The House adopted the conference report Oct. 24, also by voice vote.

David L. Boren, D-Okla., chairman of the Senate Intelligence Committee, vowed to draft a new bill to replace the one that was vetoed and to move it to the floor early in the 102nd Congress.

But any plan not acceptable to the administration would again be vetoed with no certainty that a veto could be overridden. In addition, some key advocates for imposing tighter requirements on covert actions departed the committees. William S. Cohen, R-Maine, a driving force for the new rules, concluded his term as vice chairman of the Senate committee. In the House, Intelligence Committee Chairman Anthony C. Beilenson, D-Calif., also left.

BOXSCORE

Legislation: Fiscal 1991 Intelligence Authorization Act (S 2834).

Major action: Pocket-vetoed, Nov. 30. Conference report cleared by Senate, Oct. 25; adopted by House, Oct. 24. S 2834 passed by House, Oct. 17; by Senate, Aug. 4. HR 5422 passed by House, Oct. 17.

Reports: Conference report (H Rept 101-928). S 2834: Armed Services (S Rept 101-394); Intelligence (S Rept 101-358). HR 5422: Intelligence (H Rept 101-725, Part I); Armed Services (Part II).

BACKGROUND

Covert action had been used in one form or another since the beginning of warfare, but for the United States, it took on unprecedented importance with the arrival of the Cold War. Successive administrations embraced covert action as a useful tool in fighting Soviet expansionism and other threats to U.S. national security.

Between 1951 and 1975, according to a 1976 Senate Select Intelligence Committee investigation, the Central Intelligence Agency (CIA) was involved in about 900 major projects in foreign countries, including dozens in Vietnam. Although most of the operations were designed to affect foreign politics at the margin, several were intended to overturn governments. *(1976 Almanac, p. 303; background, Congress & the Nation Vol. IV, p. 182)*

The number of covert operations increased dramatically when President Ronald Reagan took office in 1981 and nominated William J. Casey as the director of central intelligence. Casey had served in the Office of Strategic Services (OSS), the forerunner of the CIA, during World War II. The Reagan administration employed the CIA to assist those seeking to overthrow, or at least harassing, regimes backed by the Soviet Union or its surrogates.

According to Gregory F. Treverton, a former staff member on the Senate Intelligence Committee and author of a study of covert action in the postwar era, the number of actions roughly tripled in number during the Reagan years.

Iran-Contra Legacy

Much of the furor over covert operations stemmed from the so-called Iran-contra affair during the Reagan administration. Late in 1986, the administration made the startling revelation that it had contradicted its own public policy and secretly sold arms to Iran, whose government it had branded as terrorist. The administration also revealed that it might have diverted some of the profits from the arms sales to secretly supply the Nicaraguan contra guerrillas. *(Background, 1987 Almanac, p. 67; 1986 Almanac, p. 415)*

The Iran-contra affair might have faded into memory as the Reagan era's least praised foreign policy venture, but Congress' Intelligence committees tried for years to enact legislation aimed at preventing a similar scandal from recurring.

In the wake of the Iran-contra affair, Reagan administration officials feared that Congress would rush to load up the statute books with hastily drafted, ill-considered "reforms" limiting the president's foreign policy powers.

However, it took Congress two years, and much compromising, to agree on major legislative changes intended to prevent a repeat of some of the most controversial actions of the Reagan team's dealings with Iran and the Nicaraguan contras.

One of the most significant unresolved legislative issues from the Iran-contra affair concerned the procedure for Congress to be told about CIA covert operations.

Existing law, dating from 1980, required the president to tell the House and Senate Intelligence committees in advance about all covert operations. Under exceptional circumstances, the president could delay notice until after a covert action had begun — but he would then have to give notice in a "timely manner."

In their report, the Iran-contra committees recommended legislation putting a limit of 48 hours on the time the president could wait before telling Congress about covert actions.

The Senate in 1988 passed a 48-hour notice bill (S 1721) by a broad bipartisan majority. The bill also mandated broader changes in procedures governing covert actions, including the first-ever formal definition of what they were. The bill never reached the House floor because of partisan disputes. *(1988 Almanac, p. 498)*

In 1989, leaders of the Senate Intelligence Committee tried to get Bush to agree to strict guidelines for notifying Congress of covert actions. The panel was blocked for months by legal objections from White House lawyers. That angered the committee leaders, who resurrected the 48-hour bill in October and attached it to their version of the intelligence authorization bill.

As it was intended to do, that move got the attention of the president, who agreed to some of the guidelines the committee had wanted. In an Oct. 30 letter to the two Intelligence committees, Bush agreed to respect the 1980 law requiring him to tell Congress about covert operations in advance. Under special emergency circumstances, Bush said, he might have to wait for "a few days."

Because each branch saw its rights and responsibilities at issue, Lee H. Hamilton, D-Ind. — who had once chaired House Intelligence as well as the Iran-contra panel — added, the covert-notice question "is probably one of those constitutional issues that is not going to be resolved. And it may be one of those issues that is better off not resolved." *(1989 Almanac, p. 543)*

Three Major Cases

With the easing of tensions between the United States and the Soviet Union during 1990, many in Congress had grown increasingly skeptical about large-scale covert-assistance operations that the United States supported in Afghanistan, Angola and Cambodia.

"There is no doubt that the level of dissatisfaction [over the programs] is rising," said Hamilton.

• **Afghanistan.** Less than a month after the Soviet Union invaded Afghanistan in December 1979, President Jimmy Carter declared that the United States had a "moral obligation" to arm the Afghan resistance. Carter reportedly allocated $30 million for covert military assistance in a plan that included sending old Soviet weapons from Egypt.

By the winter of 1982, over 100,000 Soviet troops had occupied Afghanistan, leaving the resistance comparatively underarmed, and in December, the Senate Foreign Relations Committee called on the administration to provide "effective material assistance."

That same month, Reagan directed the CIA to provide more sophisticated weapons, including mortars and grenade launchers. By September 1986 rebel forces were receiving Stinger anti-aircraft missiles, and total covert military aid to the Afghan resistance had climbed to roughly $300 million.

The Soviet Union withdrew the last of its 100,000-plus troops from Afghanistan in February 1989, but it still provided the Kabul government with an estimated $300 million a month in assistance and left behind a cadre of advisers. The United States, meanwhile, reportedly continued to aid rebel groups fighting the Soviet-backed government. U.S. covert aid for the *Mujahedeen* totaled about $280 million in 1989, according to congressional sources.

In 1990, though, the United States and the Soviet Union appeared to be close to an agreement to enable both superpowers to exit gracefully. Secretary of State James A. Baker III and Soviet Foreign Minister Eduard A. Shevardnadze, meeting in Irkutsk in Siberia on Aug. 1, discussed a proposal for Afghan elections that was seen as a possible phasing out of outside assistance.

Despite the momentum toward a settlement and Congress' reluctance to tie the hands of the administration during negotiations, and even though the Afghan program was traditionally popular on Capitol Hill, aid for the rebels drew widespread criticism in 1990. Members of the Senate Intelligence Committee, including Boren, the panel's chairman, and Sam Nunn, D-Ga., called for a full-scale review of U.S. policy toward Afghanistan.

Hamilton and others expressed concerns over the Islamic fundamentalist character of the rebels being backed by the United States. "We've been supplying enormous amounts of money to these groups, some of whom have little in common with the United States," said Hamilton.

Even Rep. Charles Wilson, D-Texas, perhaps the most passionate congressional advocate for the rebels, questioned the capability of the resistance to absorb more U.S. weapons, although he added that "the reality is that the Soviets provide 10 times what we send."

By the end of 1990, the United States and the Soviet Union still disagreed on what role the existing Soviet-backed Afghan president should play in an interim government before elections could be set up.

• **Angola.** Even in the post-Cold War era, U.S. support for rebels in Angola — the operation in support of the Jonas Savimbi-led UNITA forces — still managed to evoke some familiar sentiments and raise ideological hackles.

Rep. Ronald V. Dellums, D-Calif., called military aid for UNITA "morally indefensible," while an analyst for the conservative Heritage Foundation said continued Soviet support for the government of President José Eduardo dos Santos was an indication "that Moscow has not yet abandoned the use of military force in pursuit of its global objectives."

The CIA first became involved in Angola in 1975 when it provided money and arms to the pro-Western UNITA faction in the Angolan civil war. UNITA lost that battle to the leftist Popular Movement for the Liberation of Angola, which received aid from Cuba and the Soviet Union, but UNITA continued to use its base in southern Angola to fight the new Marxist government.

But because UNITA had relied for years on military and financial support from South Africa, members of Congress were reluctant to support it, and in 1976 approved an amendment to the defense appropriations bill (PL 94-212) by Sen. Dick Clark (D-Iowa, 1973-79) effectively barring CIA intervention in Angola.

In June 1980, in light of State Department estimates that about 20,000 Cuban troops remained in Angola at the time, Congress weakened the Clark amendment allowing military support of UNITA if the president openly requested it and Congress approved.

In July 1985, after receiving assurances that the Reagan administration had no immediate plans to aid UNITA, Congress repealed the Clark amendment.

Early in 1986, Savimbi visited Washington to appeal for U.S. assistance. Reagan enthusiastically backed Savimbi and in February ordered the CIA to provide up to $15 million worth of arms and ammunition to UNITA.

In spite of regional peace efforts, the United States continued to arm UNITA, providing by some estimates up to $60 million in fiscal 1990.

Congressional opponents questioned whether the administration would be willing to wind down the covert program even if a cease-fire could be negotiated, given Bush's previous statements of support for Savimbi. In January 1989, Bush sent the UNITA leader a letter saying he would continue "all appropriate and effective assistance" until "national reconciliation" was achieved in the country.

"National reconciliation" was usually taken to mean a process leading to multiparty elections, which would include participation by members of UNITA. Thus far, the two sides had been unable to agree on a formula that would lead to elections, or a cease-fire.

While the administration wanted to see democratization in Angola, many members of Congress apparently would be satisfied with the elimination of all outside military assistance — from the Soviet Union and the United States — to the country.

The administration, however, was concerned about the wide discrepancy in the military stockpiles held by each side. The State Department estimated that the Soviet Union would send the dos Santos government $800 million in military aid in 1990 — more than 10 times what the U.S. would provide for Savimbi forces.

In addition, although the geopolitical situation had changed a great deal since he first burst upon the scene, Savimbi remained an extremely popular figure with American conservatives. For a president concerned about his right flank, it could prove politically risky to endorse any peace settlement for Angola that was perceived as containing less than favorable terms for Savimbi.

• **Cambodia.** Of the three regional conflicts, all sides agreed that the civil war in Cambodia would be the most difficult to resolve. "It's a conundrum," said House Intelligence Committee member Dave McCurdy, D-Okla.

Vietnamese forces invaded Cambodia in 1979, and in 1982 the United States began trying to force them out, providing covert aid to two small non-communist guerrilla groups allied in a loose coalition with the Khmer Rouge against the Vietnamese-backed government.

The United States supported the groups led by former Cambodian leader Prince Norodom Sihanouk and Sonn Sann, a former prime minister. But the two forces were part of a loose coalition with the infamous Khmer Rouge — and that connection formed the basis for congressional opposition to the program.

By 1990, the United States was reportedly sending the non-communist resistance $10 million a year in covert assistance, although diplomatic sources in the region cited a much higher figure — as much as $24 million annually.

Though foreign aid legislation — including that moving in 1990 — prohibited any assistance for the Khmer Rouge and although the money was only a tiny part of the foreign aid budget, the issue was fraught with controversy. Human rights groups charged that the rebels, rulers of Cambodia from 1975 to 1979, killed more than 1 million Cambodians. The assistance program also represented the first active U.S. role in the region since the Vietnam War.

For years, concern about Vietnamese expansionism outweighed that of the Khmer Rouge returning to power. But reports in 1990 that the Khmer Rouge was gaining in strength vis-à-vis the non-communist resistance, as well as reports that the Khmer Rouge was indirectly receiving American aid, sparked congressional concern and led to an administration re-evaluation of its policy.

Speculating on the likelihood of a Khmer Rouge victory, Secretary of State Baker said, "It would appear that the risks are greater that that might, in fact, occur." As a result, on July 18 Baker announced a series of steps he said were aimed at preventing a Khmer Rouge takeover.

The secretary outlined three areas in which U.S. policy would change. The most important shift was the withdrawal of diplomatic support for the antigovernment coalition that included the Khmer Rouge and the two U.S.-backed factions. In that regard, Baker said, the United States would no longer back the coalition's claim to a seat in the United Nations.

In addition, Baker said the United States would open a dialogue with Vietnam about Cambodia, although he emphasized that the move "does not constitute a decision to normalize relations with Vietnam."

Finally, Baker said the United States would "enhance our humanitarian assistance to Cambodia."

Baker stressed that the United States would continue to provide aid to the non-communist resistance, despite the Khmer Rouge's presence in the coalition. Significantly, flagging congressional support for the program was given as a key factor behind the decision to withdraw diplomatic — but not financial — support for the coalition.

Most members of Congress welcomed the revisions, but said that they would be insufficient to prevent the return to power of the Khmer Rouge. A congressional letter recommending further changes, circulated by Senate Majority Leader George J. Mitchell, D-Maine, attracted 66 signatures.

And to the administration's chagrin, as the House Intelligence Committee deferred consideration of aid measures in mid-1990, undecided members were clearly influenced by reports indicating that the Khmer Rouge had made substantial gains on the battlefield.

The administration, aware of the mood on Capitol Hill, indicated that it might make further policy revisions — including possibly initiating direct talks with the Cambodian government. But the administration said it was committed, in the short run at least, to continuing aid for the non-communist resistance.

In July, a senior administration official said that without the program, "there might be the very real likelihood that they [the resistance] would turn elsewhere for support, and that turn might be to the KR [Khmer Rouge]."

SENATE ACTION

In the most significant legislative action to date on the intelligence authorization bill, the Senate Intelligence Committee voted June 28 to cut off the estimated $10 million in covert aid to the Cambodian resistance, according to congressional sources.

The panel also voted to cut approximately $100 million from the $280 million covert aid program for the *Mujahedeen* in Afghanistan but left the Angola program intact.

The action came as part of the committee's markup of the Senate version of the legislation (S 2834).

After the markup, the Bush administration began to reconsider its policy of providing assistance for the non-communist resistance in Cambodia, partly in response to growing congressional restiveness over the issue.

"I think it's fair to say that we are rethinking the question of assistance to the non-communist resistance," Secretary of State Baker said July 8.

A department spokesman said subsequently that the administration was undertaking a review of its entire Cambodia policy. The review came at a time when pockets of opposition to the administration's policy were emerging on Capitol Hill.

Members of the Intelligence Committee, whose proceedings were classified, and others in the House and Senate expressed concerns about news reports that the resistance groups backed by the United States were coordinating their military actions with the Khmer Rouge.

Boren declined to discuss the committee action but said, "For me to favor any aid to the resistance, none of it should help the Khmer Rouge."

He also rejected the notion of aiding the resistance secretly, which precluded open discussion of the issue.

"It is a policy question that should be publicly debated," he said.

Similar sentiments were expressed by other members, including many in the House. But after a floor debate about the issue, the House in June adopted, 260-163, an amendment to the fiscal 1991 foreign aid appropriations bill (HR 5114), to allow the administration to provide up to $7 million in non-lethal aid to the resistance.

Despite the comfortable margin of the House vote, the Bush administration appeared less than sanguine about prospects for final approval of the total aid package, including its covert component.

"We were worried even before the [Senate] Intelligence Committee action," said one official. In part, that was because of the highly emotional nature of the Cambodian aid issue.

Even aid supporters, such as Stephen J. Solarz, D-N.Y., chairman of the House Foreign Affairs Subcommittee on Asian and Pacific Affairs and sponsor of the aid amendment, agreed that it was crucial to avoid strengthening the Khmer Rouge.

"Everyone agree that our goal should be to prevent a Khmer Rouge victory," Solarz said. "The disagreements are over how best to achieve the goal." *(Foreign aid appropriations, p. 830)*

Opponents of U.S. policy in Cambodia, among them Sen. Mitchell, voiced skepticism that a political settlement could be achieved, and said the sole U.S. interest in Cambodia should be in keeping the Khmer Rouge out of power.

Mitchell became involved in the debate in June, issuing a statement highly critical of U.S. policy in Cambodia.

While his statement stopped short of calling for an aid cutoff, Mitchell advocated withdrawing U.S. diplomatic support for the antigovernment coalition's seat in the United Nations. "This U.S.-engineered coalition gives the Khmer Rouge international legitimacy it does not deserve," he said.

"In the literal sense of the word," Mitchell's statement said, "the administration's Cambodia policy is incredible. It is unsupportable. It must be changed."

Patrick J. Leahy, D-Vt., chairman of the Senate Appropriations Subcommittee on Foreign Operations, also expressed reservations about the aid program, although he, like Mitchell, did not call for an aid cutoff.

Leahy said he was "troubled" by reports that aid was benefiting the Khmer Rouge. "I can't support anything that would allow that to happen," he said.

The Senate Armed Services Committee approved S 2834, with some technical and conforming amendments, on July 12.

The full Senate in the early morning hours of Aug. 4 approved S 2834 by voice vote after agreeing to adopt the committee's en bloc amendments. Unlike during House action on the measure, there was no controversy over the bill.

HOUSE COMMITTEE ACTION

After the Senate Intelligence Committee voted in June to cut off funding for the U.S. covert aid program in Cambodia, opponents and supporters of the administration's Cambodia policy anxiously awaited the House Intelligence Committee's consideration of the program.

The House panel was supposed to take up the covert-assistance question in July as part of the fiscal 1991 intelligence authorization (HR 5422), but voted to defer consideration of the programs for two months. One factor was that members wanted to give the diplomatic process more time to work.

The committee's decision gave the administration breathing space, but it also raised expectations for tangible progress on the diplomatic front.

Said one congressional critic of assistance to the Angolan rebels, "Unless there is a real prospect for a peace settlement that could be achieved quickly, there is a real question over whether we should continue the aid."

Members of the Intelligence panel, whose proceedings were classified, declined to discuss the move to delay the vote.

But it appeared to have been motivated, at least in part, by a desire to see how far the administration was prepared to go in further altering its Cambodia policy.

In response to congressional pressure, Secretary of State Baker on July 18 announced policy changes. Baker said the United States would withdraw diplomatic support for the coalition, initiate talks with Vietnam and ease restrictions on humanitarian aid.

"In the absence of the bipartisan policy approach, I think it will be more difficult to continue to generate the funds that we need from the Congress" for the resistance, said Baker. "And as you know, we've recently had an adverse vote in that connection."

The secretary was referring to the Senate Intelligence Committee's June 28 vote on Cambodia.

But given the similar reluctance by the House Intelligence Committee to fund the program, at least for the following two months, the strategy apparently had not won the policy any significant new congressional backing.

Meanwhile, as lawmakers awaited the panel's debate, Beilenson joined his Senate counterpart Boren in calling for an open debate of all foreign assistance programs. "Given the changes that have taken place in the world, there is no reason why these things should not be openly considered," said Beilenson.

Committee Action — Finally

Apparently swayed by administration diplomatic efforts aimed at resolving the regional conflicts, the House Intelligence Committee voted Sept. 12 to continue funding for the three controversial covert-assistance programs, according to sources familiar with the committee's action.

The committee approved aid for antigovernment rebels in Cambodia, Afghanistan and Angola. The action came as the panel was completing its markup of its fiscal 1991 intelligence authorization bill (HR 5422).

While the Senate panel voted to eliminate and scale back assistance, the House committee restored the aid to rebels in Afghanistan and Cambodia, which set the stage for a conference fight over the programs.

The State Department had been able to demonstrate progress toward settlement of the wars in Afghanistan and Cambodia.

As a result, the administration apparently was able to convince the House panel that withdrawing support for the rebels would undercut ongoing negotiations.

But progress toward a peaceful conclusion of the war in Angola was slow. As one member of the committee said before the vote, "It is the only case where no solution is on the horizon."

The committee voted to continue funding for the Angola program, but only after a contentious debate, said one source.

An amendment offered by Solarz that would have placed tight conditions on future aid to the UNITA rebels was narrowly defeated, the source said.

The United States provided the guerrillas with more than $60 million in military aid during fiscal 1990; the panel reportedly voted to fund the program in fiscal 1991 at roughly the same level.

In the case of Cambodia and Afghanistan, the administration had an easier time convincing the committee that diplomatic progress had been achieved.

The five permanent members of the U.N. Security Council had agreed on a plan that could eventually lead to a cease-fire and elections in Cambodia. The various factions in the conflict had tentatively endorsed the plan.

In the 11-year-old Afghanistan war, the United States and the Soviet Union had been moving closer to an agreement, under which both sides would wind down support for their surrogates. The committee apparently did not want to undercut the administration's position in the ongoing negotiations by reducing aid to the *Mujahedeen.*

Members of the House committee, contacted after the markup, declined to discuss their deliberations. Several lawmakers said they had been threatened with expulsion from the committee if they talked about the covert programs.

But in character with the unusual conventions governing the so-called covert-overt programs, the members were lobbied intensively prior to the vote, particularly by representatives of the two sides in the Angola conflict.

Said Dan Glickman, D-Kan., "I resent being lobbied on programs that are supposed to be secret."

The House Armed Services Committee approved HR 5422 on Sept. 27.

HOUSE FLOOR ACTION

In another sign of congressional disenchantment with the large-scale covert operations, the House voted by the narrowest of margins Oct. 17 to place new conditions on military aid to the rebels in Angola.

By 207-206 — with Speaker Thomas S. Foley, D-Wash., called on to cast the deciding vote — the House approved an amendment on Angola aid offered by Solarz to HR 5422. The House approved the amended bill by voice vote. *(Vote 482, p. 152-H)*

The Solarz amendment, which was altered on the floor, was aimed at inducing both sides in the Angolan civil war to seek a diplomatic resolution of the conflict.

Henry J. Hyde, R-Ill., ranking minority member of the Intelligence Committee, complained that one needed "a Ph.D. in astrophysics to understand" Solarz's amendment, which would provide for lethal aid to be funneled to UNITA in four installments.

If the president certified that the government in Luanda had established a timetable for elections and was willing to abide by a cease-fire, assistance would be suspended for a three-month period. If, on the other hand, the president found evidence that the government was preparing for a military offensive or was otherwise not working toward peace, he could restore the aid. Non-lethal aid would not be affected by the provision.

Administration officials, who lobbied aggressively against the measure, said they were surprised by the outcome. But they were confident that the House-Senate conference to craft a final intelligence bill would scrap the amendment.

"Since it only won by one vote on the floor and was opposed in the [House Intelligence] Committee, it would seem unlikely that the conference would accept the amendment," said one official.

Despite administration efforts to minimize the significance of the Solarz amendment, its supporters believed that the House action would, at the least, force the administration to redouble diplomatic efforts in southern Africa.

Solarz characterized the action in more dramatic terms. The congressman, a member of the Intelligence panel, said the House voted for a "fundamental change" from "a policy of continued war to a policy of a creative search for peace."

After losing in the Intelligence Committee by three votes, the Solarz amendment initially was adopted by the House, 213-200. *(Vote 480, p. 152-H)*

But Hyde invoked an infrequently used parliamentary maneuver to request a separate ballot on the measure.

After a flurry of last-minute calls to members, the White House persuaded eight Republicans to withdraw their backing for the measure. Even with that, the administration still only earned itself a stalemate.

With the vote tied, the Speaker, who had been napping in his office, entered the tumultuous chamber to break the deadlock.

Under terms of the provision, the lethal portion of the covert aid to UNITA — which reportedly was close to half of the total aid — would be suspended for three months if the president determined that the Luanda government was engaging in good-faith negotiations and was taking steps toward democratization.

Amendments Considered

Because the Rules Committee granted an open rule governing debate on the bill, members were free to discuss operations that were officially classified. While continued aid for UNITA was expected to be the most contentious issue facing the House, the open rule permitted additional floor amendments, an invitation that other members were expected to accept. A prevailing theme ran through all the proposals: Lawmakers were sharply questioning the need for covert-assistance programs, a staple of foreign policy during the 1980s.

Language added on the floor by Rep. John Miller, R-Wash., would require that the Soviet Union cease arms shipments to Angola before the conditions could take effect. The Miller amendment would put into law the "zero-zero" option, under which both the United States and the Soviet Union would terminate military aid to their surrogates. Conditions on aid to UNITA would be triggered only if the president certified that the government was "no longer receiving aid from the Soviet Union."

Backers of the covert program were encouraged by the House's rejection — by a substantial margin (175-246) — of an amendment by California Democrats Dellums and Mervyn M. Dymally that would have required the president to openly request continued aid to the rebels. *(Vote 479, p. 152-H)*

Beyond removing the last vestige of secrecy from the aid, the Dellums amendment probably would have had the practical effect of terminating the program at least temporarily because of the approaching end of the session.

Dymally and Dellums opposed assistance for UNITA no matter how it was provided. Dymally displayed photographs of children he said had been maimed by rebel land mines. "Let's stop the bombing," he pleaded. "Let's save the children." Dellums argued that with the Cold War winding down elsewhere, the UNITA program represented "an anachronism." As the world was "rushing toward democracy," he said, "covert actions undermine those ideals."

But the emotional entreaties failed to win significant support. In fact, Hamilton, former Intelligence Committee chairman, had gained more backing when he offered a similar amendment to the intelligence authorization bill in 1986, when public popularity for such programs was much higher.

The administration was able to sway House members, not by resorting to Cold War rhetoric, but by promising progress on the diplomatic front. In a letter to House members, Secretary of State Baker promised that "political settlements are within reach" in the "three centers of conflict," Angola, Afghanistan and Cambodia.

The House passed another amendment, by Bill Richardson, D-N.M., aimed at removing the secrecy surrounding the U.S. aid program for the non-communist resistance in Cambodia. The measure would require that the administration terminate covert assistance for the resistance within 30 days after the warring factions in Cambodia agreed to a settlement in the country's civil war.

All unexpended funds would then be provided openly by the United States, according to the amendment, which passed by a voice vote.

Secrecy Under Fire

Maneuvering over covert aid was not confined to the intelligence measure. During the week of Oct. 15, Sen. Edward M. Kennedy, D-Mass., weighed an attempt to amend the foreign aid appropriations bill on the Senate floor to require that any aid to the Angola rebels be provided openly.

Simply by subjecting the intelligence legislation to detailed, open discussion, the House eliminated some of the secrecy associated with the ostensibly covert operations.

With the open rule, members discussed various aspects of the Angola program, including the amount of U.S. aid annually provided for UNITA, and the country — Zaire — which served as a transshipment point for the aid. At one point, Hyde inadvertently confirmed that the administration covertly supported forces in Angola, Cambodia and Afghanistan.

All the details mentioned during the debate had been reported by the media. But lawmakers, particularly members of the Intelligence panels, chafed under rules that prevented them from talking about the widely publicized operations.

"The president discusses [aid to UNITA]; the press discusses it," Hamilton complained. "The only place we cannot discuss it is in the Congress of the United States."

Other Issues

While consideration of covert operations occupied most of the floor debate on the intelligence authorization bill, the House also passed a budget for the intelligence community for fiscal 1991. Despite the extraordinarily open discussion of intelligence matters, the classified budget — which outside experts estimated at $30 billion annually — remained just that.

Nevertheless, both in their unclassified report and in comments during the floor debate, members of the Intelligence panel gave some clues about current spending and future intelligence needs.

"Overall, the committee has recommended a funding level for intelligence in FY 1991 lower than that requested by the president," said the report. Matthew F. McHugh, D-N.Y., a member of the Intelligence Committee, added, "The budget figures, while less than last year, are still significant."

During the floor debate, many members offered views about how the priorities of the intelligence community should change in light of the thaw in superpower relations. Committee members concerned about the erosion of U.S. economic competitiveness, such as Glickman, wanted to see intelligence agencies move more heavily into the economic arena. "We must focus as much as possible to ensure that intelligence agencies provide that [economic] information," he said.

But the committee report noted concern about the possible misuse of such data. Neither the intelligence nor policy-making communities "addressed the implications of disseminating that intelligence either directly or indirectly in the private sector," the report said.

The House turned back an effort by Barbara Boxer, D-Calif., to respond to language in the Senate version of the intelligence bill regarding congressional oversight of covert operations.

Boxer objected to the new language, charging that the Senate legislation would usurp congressional authority by tacitly legitimizing covert operations. But Intelligence Committee Chairman Beilenson, who vowed to work with the Senate to alter certain provisions, angrily disputed Boxer's charges.

"I can assure members" that any provision agreed to in

the House-Senate conference would "strengthen oversight," Beilenson said. With the chairman leading the floor debate against the amendment, the provision was defeated 70-341. *(Vote 481, p. 152-H)*

Passage of the final bill sent both chambers' authorization measures to conference, which began Oct. 18. A week later, the conference report cleared the 101st Congress.

CONFERENCE/FINAL ACTION

There was a new element of openness in the conference report and the legislative debate that accompanied passage of the fiscal 1991 intelligence authorization measure (S 2834). Some key provisions in the bill were openly explained in a House-Senate conference report that broke with secretive precedent.

"The conferees also agree," read one such statement, "that any non-lethal assistance being provided the non-communist resistance [in Cambodia] should transition to an overt, acknowledged program of U.S. assistance."

The House passed the conference report on Oct. 24 and the Senate gave the legislation final approval in the early morning of Oct. 25, both by voice vote. House Republicans, while vehemently expressing their unhappiness with the measure, did not even ask for a recorded vote.

In addition to requiring a transition to overt aid for the resistance in Cambodia, the bill attached conditions on future assistance to antigovernment rebels in Angola, and it reportedly cut aid for the Afghan rebels by more than 10 percent.

In an attempt to require more executive branch disclosure to Congress in the aftermath of the Iran-contra scandal, the legislation also included new ground rules for notification of covert actions. The revised rules would require the president to make written reports to Congress on all such operations, although in some cases he could do so after action had begun.

The vast secrets still protected in the intelligence authorization measure included the budgets for individual intelligence agencies and the number of personnel performing such functions.

Hyde, the ranking minority member of the Intelligence panel, said the bill represented another attempt by Democrats at "micro-managing foreign policy."

Many Democrats who worked on drafting the conference report wondered what all the fuss was about. Solarz, perhaps the most ardent congressional supporter of the Cambodian resistance, said he was "completely satisfied" by the provision calling for a transition to overt aid.

McHugh, chairman of the Intelligence panel's Subcommittee on Legislation, insisted that the new language on covert operations was far less restrictive on the president than 48-hour provisions approved by the Senate two years earlier.

The rules in the 1990 bill did not include such a deadline. Yet they were "the best we could get," said McHugh, in the face of Bush's threat to veto any tougher limit.

From Covert to Overt

The compromise on aid to the Cambodian resistance involved the Senate Democratic leadership in addition to the two Intelligence panels.

While there was widespread opposition to the covert aid program in both bodies, there also was reluctance to end all support for the rebels. The administration had urged Congress not to eliminate the program as combatants in the Cambodian civil war appeared to be making progress toward peace.

The Senate had not authorized any funds for covert aid to the non-communist resistance. The House had approved an amendment providing for the administration to provide aid — but only within an openly acknowledged program — after a final peace agreement was reached.

The only point left unstated publicly was when the transition from covert aid to overt aid would take place. But Hyde, in arguing against the amendment, said that the conferees set a specific deadline for phasing out the secret operation. Sources confirmed that the transition was to take place early in 1991.

The program to support the *Mujahedeen* rebels in Afghanistan was also officially classified and therefore not mentioned in the conference report. But the conferees reportedly agreed to reduce the assistance from approximately $300 million to $250 million for fiscal 1991. According to published reports, the conferees followed the lead of the Defense Appropriations Committee, dividing the program in two parts and requiring further congressional approval for the release of the second half.

Compromise on Angola

The conference committee also divided military assistance for antigovernment rebels in Angola into two sections, with a portion of the aid "placed in a restricted account and its release subject to the approval of the Intelligence committees," according to the statement issued by the conferees.

The committee took much of the House-passed language placing conditions on the annual $60 million covert aid program for UNITA. Solarz, who drafted the House restrictions, said the provision in the final bill represented "a remarkable victory."

As in the House version, lethal aid to the rebels was to be suspended if the president certified that the Luanda government was willing to accept what was termed a "realistic" cease-fire and proposed a timetable for free elections, and if the Soviet Union terminated military aid to the government.

But many Democrats, including Beilenson, said that the president's latitude for disbursing military aid remained largely unchanged. The Solarz amendment had provided for Congress to suspend aid through a joint resolution even if the president did not make the certification. The conference committee dropped that provision. According to Beilenson, "Only the president is involved here [in the final version of the legislation]."

In addition, said McCurdy, a longtime UNITA supporter, the legislation provided for the president to verify, through intelligence reports, that the Soviet Union had in fact halted military aid to the Angolan government. The president would not have to rely solely on Angolan and Soviet assurances, said McCurdy.

But while the president would retain most of his prerogatives, members who advocated terminating the aid to UNITA were cheered by at least one section added by the conferees. If the president did not certify that the conditions for a military aid cutoff existed by March 31, 1991, he was required to report to the Intelligence panels on why he had not made such a determination.

Conferees also approved Senate language repealing a 1980 law that governed covert action. Under the new legislation, the president would be required to provide a written "finding" reporting a covert action to the Intelligence com-

'Covert Action' Cited in Intelligence Veto

Following is the memorandum of disapproval President Bush issued Nov. 30 announcing that he would not sign the fiscal 1991 intelligence authorization bill (S 2834).

I have withheld my signature from S 2834, the proposed "Intelligence Authorization Act, Fiscal Year 1991," thereby preventing it from becoming law. I am compelled to take this action due to the bill's treatment of one highly sensitive and important issue that directly affects the nation's security, although there also are several objectionable elements of the bill that trouble me.

I cannot accept the broad language that was added in conference to the definition of covert action. Section 602 of the bill defines "covert action" to include any "request" by the United States to a foreign government or a private citizen to conduct a covert action on behalf of the United States. This provision purports to regulate diplomacy by the president and other members of the executive branch by forbidding the expression of certain views to foreign governments and private citizens absent compliance with specified procedures; this could require, in most instances, prior reporting to the Congress of the intent to express those views.

I am particularly concerned that the vagueness of this provision could seriously impair the effective conduct of our nation's foreign relations. It is unclear exactly what sort of discussions with foreign governments would constitute reportable "requests" under this provision, and the very possibility of a broad construction of this term could have a chilling effect on the ability of our diplomats to conduct highly sensitive discussions concerning projects that are vital to our national security. Furthermore, the mere existence of this provision could deter foreign governments from discussing certain topics with the United States at all. Such a provision could result in frequent and divisive disputes on whether an activity is covered by the definition and whether individuals in the executive branch have complied with a statutory requirement.

My objections to this provision should not be misinterpreted to mean that executive branch officials can somehow conduct activities otherwise prohibited by law or executive order. Quite the contrary. It remains administration policy that our intelligence services will not ask third parties to carry out activities that they are themselves forbidden to undertake under Executive Order No. 12333 on U.S. intelligence activities. I have also directed that the notice to the Congress of covert actions indicate whether a foreign government will participate significantly.

Beyond this issue, I am also concerned by the treatment in the joint explanatory statement accompanying the conference report of notification to the Congress of covert actions. I reached an accommodation with the Intelligence committees on the issue of notifying the Congress of covert actions "in a timely fashion," as required by current law, and have provided letters to the Intelligence committees outlining how I intend to provide such notice. I was consequently dismayed by the fact that language was inserted in the joint explanatory statement accompanying the conference report that could be construed to undercut the agreement reached with the committees. This language asserts that prior notice may be withheld only in "exigent circumstances" and that notice "in a timely fashion" should now be interpreted to mean "within a few days" without exception. Such an interpretation would unconstitutionally infringe on the authority of the president and impair any administration's effective implementation of covert action programs. I deeply regret this action.

Additionally, I am concerned that there are several legislatively directed policy determinations restricting programs of vital importance to the United States that I do not believe are helpful to U.S. foreign policy.

This bill, like its predecessor last year, also contains language that purports to condition specified actions on the president's obtaining the prior approval of committees of the Congress. This language is clearly unconstitutional under the presentment clause of the Constitution and the Supreme Court's decision in *INS v. Chadha,* 462 U.S. 919 (1983). I again urge the Congress to cease including such unconstitutional provisions in bills presented to me for signature.

This administration has had a good relationship with the Intelligence committees. I am willing to work with the Congress to address the primary issue that has prompted my veto as well as other difficulties with the bill. I will also continue to work with the Congress to ensure there is no change in our shared understanding of what constitutes a covert action, particularly with respect to the historic missions of the armed forces. I am confident that these issues can be resolved quickly in the next Congress through mutual trust and a good-faith effort on the part of the administration and the Congress. ■

mittees — except in "extraordinary circumstances," when only key leaders would have to be informed.

Most of this was not a marked departure from existing law, said many Democrats. Indeed, one title of the National Security Act of 1947 (50 U.S.C. 413) already required that the president inform the committees of covert operations, at the very least, in a "timely fashion."

The new law would generally require prior notification of such operations but would permit the president to delay informing the committees "on rare occasions." On such occasions, the president would have to report "in timely fashion," just as he was required to do already.

But in language that was a direct response to the Iran-contra affair, the conference report specified that all covert actions would have to be taken to support "identifiable foreign policy objectives of the United States."

The congressional report on the Iran-contra affair concluded that the "findings process was circumvented." Most members of the Intelligence panels felt the provisions in the authorization measure would discourage future abuses.

VETO AND AFTERMATH

When the Intelligence measure passed in October, lawmakers were aware that the White House was less than enthusiastic over the final version of S 2834. Yet there was wide expectation among lawmakers from both parties that the administration would, in the end, "hold its nose and let it become law," as Rep. Gerald B. H. Solomon, R-N.Y., said Oct. 24.

When Bush announced Nov. 30 that he was pocket-vetoing the bill, the action surprised even opponents of the legislation.

Because the bill did not specify what constituted a covert-action request, said Bush, the notification requirement "could have a chilling effect on the ability of our diplomats to conduct highly sensitive discussions."

When they learned of Bush's concern, three members — Beilenson, Boren and Cohen — wrote to assure him that the provision was not intended to preclude "informal contacts and consultations."

In his veto message, Bush referred to his "good relationship" with the Intelligence panels, but that could very well have been put in jeopardy.

Both Beilenson and Boren issued statements noting their disappointment with the veto. Beilenson said flatly that Bush "received bad advice."

Boren, a promoter of cooperation between the White House and Congress on intelligence matters, said, "It is very clear that some members of the White House staff do not adequately understand this bipartisan partnership."

Many members of the Intelligence panels expressed confusion over the veto, because administration officials, including CIA officials, had provided assurances that the president would sign the bill.

While the CIA apparently could have lived with the third-country provision, White House counsel C. Boyden Gray could not, and he pressed hardest for the veto, according to a number of sources.

Gray described by one Republican as a "jealous protector of the president's constitutional prerogatives," reportedly also persuaded Bush to veto the Export Amendments Act (HR 4653) the month before. In both cases, Bush objected to what he termed congressional encroachments on executive branch authority in foreign policy. *(Export controls, p. 198)*

Temporary Setback

For Republican Cohen and a handful of Democrats, the veto represented at least a temporary setback in efforts to draft new rules for the reporting of covert operations to Congress.

In his veto message, Bush took the unusual step of criticizing the legislative report, even though it did not have the weight of law.

The report's definition of what was timely "would unconstitutionally infringe on the authority of the president and impair any administration's effective implementation of covert actions," he said.

Because of the veto, there was no specific authorization for the intelligence community's estimated $30 billion budget for fiscal 1991; under a section of the National Security Act, appropriations for intelligence activities must be authorized.

McHugh, for one, said he was so angry over the affair that he wanted to see the provision enforced, which would have required the administration to seek quick authorization from the committees.

"It's my instinctive reaction" to trigger the provision, McHugh said. "The veto was totally unjustified."

Administration officials said the bulk of intelligence programs were included in the Defense Department authorization bill (HR 4739 — PL 101-510). Most Democrats on the committees apparently disagreed, although few seemed willing to force a confrontation.

The veto and authorization flap came at a time when the membership on the Intelligence committees was about to change. Cohen's term as vice chairman of the Senate panel was expiring, and several members were due to rotate off the House committee.

The House Democratic Caucus, meeting Dec. 3-5, declined to take up a rule change that would have lengthened the tenure of Intelligence Committee members. That meant that the terms of Beilenson, Hyde and other panel members expired.

Speaker Foley appointed McCurdy to replace Beilenson and four liberals and one moderate to fill Democratic vacancies on the panel. In redrafting the measure, McCurdy said, he hoped to "preserve the intent of that original bill." ■

State Department Authorization Cleared

After two committees reached a truce in a jurisdictional dispute, the Senate on Jan. 30 cleared for President Bush a bill (HR 3792) making authorizations for the State Department and related agencies in fiscal 1990-91.

But in a sweeping challenge to congressional intervention in foreign policy-making, the president said he might ignore at least nine provisions of the otherwise routine authorization bill. Bush signed the bill on Feb. 16 (PL 101-246), but he declared that nine provisions represented unconstitutional intrusions into his power to conduct foreign policy. Bush said he was reserving the right to interpret those provisions as he saw fit.

He said several other parts of the bill were improper and would be enforced according to the views of the executive branch.

The bill also put into law several sanctions that Bush had imposed on China as a protest against the Beijing government's brutal crackdown on dissent June 1989. However, the measure gave the president broad discretion to lift those sanctions. *(U.S.-China relations, p. 764)*

The State Department bill traveled a complicated path to enactment — suffering lengthy delays in conference and then a veto and a last-minute holdup at the close of the 1989 session before the Senate finally took it up on Jan. 29-30.

The Senate passed the bill 98-0. *(Vote 2, p. 3-S)*

The bill authorized $4.7 billion in fiscal 1990 and $5 billion in fiscal 1991. The largest share was for the State Department ($2 billion in 1990 and $2.2 billion in 1991).

Other major items included U.S. contributions to the United Nations and other international agencies and operations of the United States Information Agency and the Board for International Broadcasting (BIB).

The legislation also in effect nullified key provisions of the McCarran-Walter Act, under which foreigners had been barred from the United States because of their political beliefs.

HR 3792 was the second complete version of the biennial State Department bill. Bush vetoed an earlier version (HR 1487) because it contained a provision, stemming from the Iran-contra affair, that he claimed violated his presidential powers over foreign affairs. The House then produced HR 3792, which excluded the provision. *(1989 Almanac, p. 526)*

China Sanctions

The State Department bill embodied Congress' most sweeping response to the Chinese government's crackdown. It denounced the "unprovoked, brutal and indiscriminate" attack on thousands of protesters in Beijing on June 3-4. Adding teeth to the rhetoric, the bill put into law a number of sanctions that Bush had imposed during the summer of 1989 under his own authority.

Among the sanctions included in the bill were a ban on arms exports to China, a suspension of guarantees of U.S. private investments in China by the Overseas Private Investment Corporation, a ban on exports to China of crime-control and detection equipment, a suspension of nuclear cooperation agreements between the United States and China, and a suspension of U.S. participation in international moves to ease restrictions on exports to China of sophisticated technology.

The president could lift any or all of the sanctions by reporting to Congress that the Chinese government had made "progress on a program of political reform." Under a broader waiver, the president could lift the sanctions by reporting that doing so was in the national interest.

Bush already had demonstrated his readiness to ease sanctions voted by Congress. On Dec. 19, 1989, he waived a ban on loans to China by the Export-Import Bank. Congress had put the prohibition in an authorization bill for Ex-Im and other matters (HR 2494 — PL 101-240). Bush also allowed an exemption to his ban on exports to China of U.S.-made satellites.

Committee Turf Battle

Final passage of HR 3792 resolved, at least for the moment, a jurisdictional dispute between the Senate Foreign Relations and Appropriations committees. Foreign Relations produced the biennial State Department authorization bill. Appropriations wrote an annual spending bill covering the same programs.

Leaders of each of the committees charged in the fall of 1989 that the other panel was invading its jurisdiction. Foreign Relations won a significant victory on Oct. 31, 1989, when it got the Senate to side with it on one turf issue.

At the very end of the session Nov. 21, 1989, however, Ernest F. Hollings, D-S.C., chairman of the Appropriations Subcommittee on Commerce, Justice and State, blocked final action on HR 3792. Hollings objected to a House-initiated provision in the bill putting into permanent law a requirement that Congress pass authorizing legislation for the BIB, which ran Radio Free Europe and Radio Liberty.

After Congress returned to work in 1990, Hollings and Foreign Relations Chairman Claiborne Pell, D-R.I., worked out a deal: Foreign Relations would drop the BIB authorizing requirement if Hollings would lift his objections to the State Department bill. That deal led to final passage of the bill Jan. 30.

Two Powers at Issue

Bush said various provisions of the State Department bill violated two of the president's powers under the Constitution: the right to appoint and receive ambassadors, and the right to "make" treaties. The latter power was not spelled out in the Constitution, but presidents generally interpreted it to mean that the executive branch had exclusive control over negotiations with foreign countries.

Because he had those powers under the Constitution, Bush said in a three-page statement, "the president is entrusted with control over the conduct of diplomacy." But several provisions of the State bill "could be read to violate these fundamental constitutional principles by using legislation to direct, in various ways, the conduct of negotiations with foreign nations."

Members of Congress generally acknowledged that the president was responsible for negotiating with other countries. But most members insisted that Congress could use its control over spending to try to influence foreign policy, for example, by determining how much aid the president could give to other countries.

Besides the constitutional issues, Bush complained that Congress included in the State bill trade sanctions against China to protest its crackdown on political protesters. Those sanctions represented "an unwise constraint" on presidential powers, he said, but conceded that Congress gave him broad discretion to lift the sanctions.

The Disputed Provisions

In his statement, Bush objected to nine specific provisions and several general provisions. Among them:

- **'Helsinki commission.'** Administration officials and Hill aides said the most contentious issue was a provision by Rep. Bill Richardson, D-N.M., aimed at requiring the administration to accept Hill observers at conventional arms negotiations in Vienna among 23 nations on a treaty to reduce conventional military forces in Europe (CFE). *(CFE treaty, p. 696)*

The CFE negotiations were under the aegis of broader diplomatic talks on human rights, arms control and other issues that had been under way since a conference in Helsinki in 1975. Those talks were referred to as the Conference on Security and Cooperation in Europe or the "Helsinki process."

The Richardson provision said the president could make no contributions to any international organizations unless he included in any U.S. delegations to Helsinki meetings representatives of a congressionally controlled commission.

That body, known as the "Helsinki commission," monitored the Helsinki process, particularly compliance by communist countries with their pledges to respect human rights. The commission included 18 members of Congress and three administration officials.

Richardson said he offered the provision because an administration official said that members of the Helsinki panel would not get official status at the CFE talks. Commission members had served on official U.S. delegations to all previous meetings related to the Helsinki process — including those at which agreements were negotiated.

Bush said the provision, by specifying the makeup of a diplomatic delegation, "impermissibly intrudes upon my constitutional authority to conduct our foreign relations and to appoint our nation's envoys."

As a result, Bush said he would construe the provision as declaring the sense of Congress but not as imposing a "binding legal obligation." Administration officials said that comment meant that Bush would not give the Helsinki commission official access to the CFE talks.

Richardson called on Bush to change his mind, saying, "We're not talking about [members of Congress] negotiating. We're talking about observing."

- **PLO talks.** Bush objected to two provisions that arose out of Hill concerns about the continued dialogue between U.S. diplomats and representatives of the Palestine Liberation Organization (PLO).

One provision was aimed at prohibiting U.S. negotiations with any PLO representatives who were known terrorists. It barred expenditure of U.S. funds to negotiate with any PLO representative who was involved in any terrorist activity that resulted in the death or kidnapping of a U.S. citizen.

The sponsor, Sen. Jesse Helms, R-N.C., said he had in mind a PLO official known as Abu Iyad.

Congressional aides noted that the provision was a compromise worked out in July 1989 between Senate leaders and Deputy Secretary of State Lawrence S. Eagleburger.

In his statement, Bush said he had "no intention of

Continued on p. 802

23 Envoys OK'd; Others Derailed, Assailed

Prodded to action by the threat of an all-night session, the Senate approved 23 of President Bush's diplomatic nominees en masse in the early hours of Oct. 19. Earlier in the year, though, the administration had been forced to give in on a number of controversial nominees.

Sen. Jesse Helms, R-N.C., successfully opposed the appointment of George Fleming Jones as ambassador to Guyana, even as the Senate was confirming the other 23 nominees on Oct. 19.

At the beginning of the year, Bush dropped the nomination of Joy A. Silverman to be ambassador to Barbados. She had drawn criticism because she had no experience in foreign policy.

On Oct. 4, the State Department said the nomination of Frederick Vreeland to be U.S. ambassador to Myanmar (formerly Burma) would be withdrawn by the president, citing a decision by that country not to accept him.

Bush also failed at the end of the session when he submitted the nomination of John Bushnell to be ambassador to Costa Rica hours before Congress adjourned; Congress did not act on the nomination.

The Senate, meanwhile, did confirm Harry M. Shlaudeman to serve as ambassador to Nicaragua, the first U.S. envoy to that country since 1988.

One Nomination Held Up, 23 Others Confirmed

As the Senate was approving the 23 diplomats on Oct. 19, it failed to act on one other.

Helms, ranking Republican on the Foreign Relations Committeee, frequently blocked State Department candidates whose conservate credentials he doubted. He opposed Jones' appointment as ambassador to Guyana and succeeded in derailing it.

Sources told The Associated Press that Helms suspected Jones, a career foreign service officer, was involved in the 1986 leak of a secret Chilean report about the death of an American in Santiago. Helms reportedly was angered that his office was blamed for the leak.

Jones' appointment remained pending before the Foreign Relations Committee and was not acted upon again before Congress adjourned.

The Senate pushed through the other nominees after Minority Leader Bob Dole, R-Kan., suggested the members remain on duty all night to resolve the impasse. "These people have families and have made plans," he said. "It's unfair to keep them twisting in the wind."

Envoys to Central America

On Oct. 26, less than two days before the 101st Congress adjourned, Bush submitted the nomination of Bushnell to be ambassador to Costa Rica. Congress did not take up the nomination in its waning hours.

Bushnell's nomination had been stalled for months by Helms, who apparently had concerns about Bushnell's performance as deputy chief of the U.S. Embassy in Panama when the United States invaded in December 1989 and about Bushnell's role in the State Department 10 years earlier when the leftist Sandinistas came to power in Nicaragua.

In a less controversial move, the Senate on May 25 confirmed Shlaudeman to serve as ambassador to Nicaragua. In assuming the post, Shlaudeman became the first U.S. ambassador to Nicaragua since July 1988 when that country expelled Richard Melton and seven other U.S. officials for allegedly planning to incite revolt against the Sandinista government.

Shlaudeman was a former ambassador to Argentina, Peru, Brazil and Venezuela and a Latin America aide under President Gerald R. Ford. He also served as a liaison to the Nicaraguan contras under President Ronald Reagan.

U.S.-backed Violeta Chamorro scored an upset victory over Sandinista President Daniel Ortega in Nicaragua's presidential election Feb. 25, setting the stage for the resumption of normal relations between the two countries. *(Nicaragua, p. 770)*

Controversy Over Barbados, Myanmar

During 1990, the White House dropped its nominations of ambassadors to Barbados and Myanmar. The nominees had come under attack for different reasons.

At the end of January, the White House dropped its nomination of Silverman to be ambassador to Barbados. She had been criticized because she had no experience in foreign policy and had had little paid employment.

After hearings in the fall of 1989, the Senate sent the nomination back to the White House as Congress was ending its session in late November.

Several members of Congress had criticized this and other nominations, complaining that Bush was handing out ambassadorships to his major campaign donors.

Silverman, of New York City, had given $299,360 to GOP causes from 1987 to 1989, according to the Senate Foreign Relations Committee. As a qualification for the ambassadorship, she wrote that she had "assisted husband ... by planning and hosting corporate functions."

Foreign Relations member Paul S. Sarbanes, D-Md., who worked to derail the nomination, called its withdrawal "a wise move." In 1989, Sarbanes led the charges against a number of political appointees. *(1989 Almanac, p. 541)*

On Oct. 4, the State Department said that Bush would withdraw the Vreeland nomination to be U.S. ambassador to Myanmar. The State Department cited the decision of the Myanmar government to reject Vreeland because of his criticisms of human rights violations in that country.

Vreeland's nomination had also run into difficulty in the Senate. The Foreign Relations Committee was upset that Vreeland had misrepresented his career by submitting to the panel a biography that listed him as a career Foreign Service officer rather than a career CIA official.

Sen. Alfonse M. D'Amato, R-N.Y., was not a member of the committee but wrote Helms to voice concerns about allegations that Vreeland, while serving in Rome, had sought to play down suspicions that the Soviets and Bulgarians had a connection to the 1981 assassination attempt against Pope John Paul II. Helms agreed to hold up a vote on the nomination. Before the panel acted again, the nomination was withdrawn.

Continued from p. 800
negotiating with terrorists." But the provision would "impermissibly limit" his constitutional authority if it was aimed at barring talks "with particular individuals under certain circumstances," Bush said. As a result, Bush said that he would construe the provision in a way to "preserve my constitutional discretion for the conduct of foreign negotiations."

Bush also cited as unconstitutional a provision called the "PLO Commitments Compliance Act" by its sponsors. That provision required the president to submit regular reports to Congress on 10 specific issues involving past promises by PLO leaders no longer to engage in terrorism.

Bush said the provision was unconstitutional because it could be read to compel him to disclose "the contents of sensitive ongoing negotiations" between the United States and the PLO.

• **Kiev consulate.** The State Department bill allowed the Soviet Union to open a consulate at the United Nations in New York City only if the secretary of State certified that the United States was able to begin work at its new consulate in the Ukrainian capital of Kiev.

This provision was the latest of numerous Hill attempts to enforce equal treatment of U.S. and Soviet diplomatic missions.

Saying the provision would infringe on his constitutional authority, Bush insisted he would treat it as "advisory" rather than mandatory.

• **Soviets at the U.N.** Another provision was aimed at curtailing the use of the United Nations as a base for espionage in the United States by the Soviet Union and other countries. The provision said that no one could be admitted as a U.N. representative if he had been found to have engaged in anti-U.S. spying and could pose a threat to U.S. security.

Bush said that provision violated his authority to receive foreign ambassadors, and he warned that he would consider it only as "advisory." ■

Overdue United Nations Funding Approved

In approving the fiscal 1991 Commerce, Justice, State and the judiciary spending measure, Congress voted to end what Secretary of State James A. Baker III described as the "deadbeat" status of the United States in paying its dues to the United Nations.

As part of the appropriations bill (HR 5021 — PL 101-515), lawmakers approved $92.7 million — roughly 20 percent of the total requested — to pay the first installment of overdue contributions to the international body. *(Commerce, Justice, State appropriations, p. 881)*

In recent years, Congress had withheld portions of U.S. dues because of congressional objections to various U.N. policies and management practices. But in 1990 President Bush requested $463.6 million to pay the past-due U.S. contributions, called "arrearages," over five years.

Background

As part of a two-year State Department authorization measure passed in 1985 (PL 99-93), Congress had voted to limit U.S. contributions to the United Nations unless it shifted to a system under which voting strength on budget matters was proportional to each member state's financial contributions. The State Department opposed the provision, and President Reagan warned in signing the bill that the restriction would create "serious problems" for the United States. *(1985 Almanac, p. 104)*

Antipathy toward the United Nations began to recede after Secretary-General Javier Pérez de Cuéllar negotiated a cease-fire between Iran and Iraq in 1988. Both Bush and his Democratic opponent in the 1988 presidential campaign, Michael S. Dukakis, said they favored resuming payments to the United Nations. On Sept. 13, President Ronald Reagan announced that he was releasing $188 million in withheld dues. *(1988 Almanac, p. 519)*

The United Nations gained further support on Capitol Hill and within the administration in 1990 as it took a high-profile role in putting together the trade embargo against Iraq after its invasin of Kuwait on Aug. 2. *(Persian Gulf crisis, p. 717)*

But Sen. Jesse Helms, R-N.C., one of seven members to oppose the State Department spending bill when the Senate first passed it Oct. 11, still had doubts about U.S. participation with the United Nations, especially in the context of the Persian Gulf crisis. Helms suggested the State Department pay the U.N. dues from existing accounts.

The Senate Commerce, Justice and State Appropriations Subcommittee approved the spending bill by voice vote Sept. 12 after members accepted an amendment that included $203 million for U.S. payments to international organizations. The committee bill also allocated $615 million to pay U.S. dues for fiscal 1991 — nearly $80 million less than the administration requested.

The subcommittee bill initially included no funds for arrearages. The House cleared the final measure for the president Oct. 24. The Senate had approved the conference report (H Rept 101-909) earlier that day. Bush signed the measure into law on Nov. 5.

The Senate Foreign Relations Committee on June 7 voted 12-5 to approve legislation (S 2749 — S Rept 101-334) to authorize supplemental appropriations of nearly $619 million for a variety of programs under the State Department's jurisdiction. The largest item in the bill was $475 million to make up for overdue U.S. contributions to the United Nations and other international organizations.

Neither S 2749 nor its House counterpart (HR 4610 — H Rept 101-472, Part I) saw further action in the 101st Congress. A standard two-year State Department authorization bill had been cleared in January. For the first time in many years, that legislation inculded full funding for assessed and voluntary contributions to the United Nations with the exception of a few programs. *(State Department authorization, p. 799)*

When the Foreign Relations panel approved the U.N. funding in June, Helms objected, saying that compensating the U.N. in the manner proposed sent the message that the United States was wrong to withhold the funds in the first place. "The United States should not apologize for opposing inept U.N. management policies and nor should it apologize for refusing to fund U.N. programs with which the American people do not agree," he said. ■

Food for Peace Program Overhauled

Congress in 1990 overhauled the nation's principal program for distributing the bounty of its farmland to famine-stricken, less productive regions of the world, and insulated it from being used as a foreign policy tool.

Lawmakers made wholesale changes to the so-called Food for Peace program — also called PL 480, after its 1954 public law number — as part of the omnibus farm bill that cleared the Senate on Oct. 25 and was signed by President Bush on Nov. 27 (S 2830 — PL 101-624).

The PL 480 overhaul trimmed the president's discretion to dole out the food in the bill. It was expected to result in a modest shift in U.S. food aid dollars away from Central America and the Middle East to the poor countries of sub-Saharan Africa, where there was the greatest need for food donations, and Asia, where there was the greatest market potential.

This was the first time the program had been restructured since 1966, when Congress replaced the program's original mandate for commodity disposal with more humanitarian and market-development missions. *(Background, 1966 Almanac, p. 118; 1954 Almanac, p. 120)*

The Bush administration viewed the 1990 effort to restructure PL 480 as a power play by Congress. "We think it's really inappropriate for the legislative branch to dictate to the administration to quite such a degree," Christopher E. Goldthwait, the Agriculture Department administrator who oversaw PL 480, said of the changes after slightly different versions were folded into the farm bills passed by the House (HR 3950) and Senate (S 2830) in the summer.

There was also pressure to streamline PL 480 from those who relied on it — farm groups and international relief organizations.

In 1990, less than 5 percent of U.S. agricultural commercial exports were subsidized under PL 480, but farmers and grain traders saw the program as an important mechanism for nurturing the Third World's taste for U.S. farm products. They hoped the cash-poor recipients would eventually "graduate" into full-fledged commercial customers.

World hunger organizations had a different reason for wanting changes to PL 480. Malnutrition and hunger were on the rise. The National Research Council had estimated that the world would need 20 million metric tons of food aid a year from all sources during the 1990s. Only 10 million metric tons were supplied most years, roughly half of which came from the United States.

As enacted, the PL 480 provisions continued to allow the program to be used to advance U.S. foreign policy goals, but narrowed the definition of foreign policy to include only improving the food security of recipient nations. A requirement that countries be termed "friendly" before they could receive PL 480 aid was removed.

The overhaul also sought to clarify lines of authority by specifying that the Agriculture Department was to be designated to carry out PL 480 credit sales programs while the Agency for International Development (AID) was to carry out the grants program. *(Farm bill, p. 323; provisions: Food for Peace, p. 344)*

BACKGROUND

Food for Peace had always had a chameleonlike quality, taking on whatever hue politicians wanted at the time.

Most U.S. food aid was sold to foreign governments on easy credit (loans of up to 40 years at 2 percent to 4 percent interest).

The government also donated food overseas for disaster relief, economic development and feeding programs. By law, at least 1.9 million metric tons of grain (or the equivalent amount of other commodities) had to be donated each year, of which 1.4 million tons had to go to humanitarian feeding organizations.

In 1954, the program had been sold to Congress as a surplus commodity distribution plan. Lawmakers pushing the legislation, including Sen. Hubert H. Humphrey, D-Minn., stressed that the bill — enacted as PL 83-480 — did not call for a "giveaway" program.

Successive administrations had discovered the value of sprinkling PL 480 commodities among strategic allies. Among the first recipients were the war-ravaged countries of Europe — Germany, France, Italy and Poland. Over the years, Congress added restrictions on distribution of food to communist countries.

By 1966, the United States had succeeded in controlling its longstanding problem of farm surpluses, and the foreign policy component of the program became pre-eminent.

The 1966 reauthorization of the program (PL 89-908) reoriented its goals toward combating world hunger and emphasized the need for recipient countries to adopt self-help measures to improve their own agricultural production.

Despite the stated goal of combating world hunger, aid priorities continued to reflect U.S. foreign policy goals. In the early 1970s, almost half of the aid shipments — more than $400 million a year — went to South Vietnam and Cambodia, while regions of severe famine in Africa received only $61.5 million worth.

Over the years, Congress also had periodically accused the executive branch of mismanaging food aid and running the program as if it were a private kitty.

The attacks on the program were renewed in 1990, as lawmakers grappled with the scarcity of foreign aid dollars and searched for an economic strategy in the post-Cold War era.

When it was needed most, said numerous critics in the Agriculture and foreign affairs committees of Congress, Food for Peace was in disarray.

Washington bureaucrats spent countless hours haggling over shipments to minor markets, many critics said, yet the federal government did not have the cash — and sometimes not even the grain — to send more than a fraction of what was shipped overseas during the heyday of the program.

"No one is in charge. No goals are clearly achieved because no agency is responsible for the final outcome," Sens. Patrick J. Leahy, D-Vt., and Richard G. Lugar, R-Ind., chairman and ranking Republican of the Senate Agriculture Committee, respectively, wrote in a letter to administration officials.

Alarmed over the use of the program as a foreign policy weapon, Congress had repeatedly revised the objectives of the program to try to limit the president's options.

"The Food for Peace program is being used as walking-around money by presidents," said Doug Bereuter, R-Neb., a member of the House Foreign Affairs Committee.

It was also difficult to say who ran the program. The Agriculture Department bought the commodities, arranged the financing and sometimes the shipping. The Agency for International Development (AID), an independent federal agency, handled the food after it left the dock.

But the real power — the power to decide which countries received food aid — was vested in an obscure body called the Development Coordination Committee (DCC), composed of midlevel officials from the Agriculture Department, AID, the State Department, the Treasury Department, the Office of Management and Budget (OMB) and occasionally the National Security Council (NSC). They held weekly meetings to discuss PL 480.

Early in 1990, the Bush administration had to scramble to put together an aid package for the government of Nicaragua after the unexpected victory of Violeta Chamorro in the presidential election turned the leftist Sandinistas out of power.

Initially, the Agriculture Department insisted in DCC meetings that very little wheat was available. Several weeks later, the Agriculture Department revised its estimates and added 800,000 tons of wheat to the docket. Nicaragua subsequently was promised 26,000 tons.

Before the Agriculture Department found more wheat, though, the Bush administration found itself in an embarrassing position, unable to assure delivery of an aid package it had ready promised to Chamorro.

In Congress, the Nicaraguan case was cited as an example of what was wrong with PL 480. Administration officials countered that the episode showed how important it was for the president to have the flexibility to respond to changing international circumstances.

LEGISLATIVE ACTION

House and Senate committees fashioned similar provisions overhauling the PL 480 program that were included in the farm bills the two chambers considered in late July and early August.

Committee Action

In its report on S 2830, the Senate Agriculture Committee said the overhaul aimed at "cleaning up the bureaucratic morass" in the program and focusing aid on countries that needed it most (S Rept 101-357). A new Food for Freedom program was to be established to funnel food aid to the "emerging democracies" in Eastern Europe, and a mechanism was to be provided for poor countries to receive debt forgiveness for previous food purchases.

The Senate bill also included a provision to bar the use of overseas shipping agents — a controversial practice that had raised complaints about commissions paid to the agents and accusations of conflicts of interest. Instead, it would have required that the Agriculture Department act as agent or allow the recipient country to purchase commodities on a cost and freight basis.

The provisions in the House bill (HR 3950) were a compromise between the Agriculture Committee and the Foreign Affairs Committee, which shared jurisdiction over the PL 480 program (H Rept 101-569, Part I [Agriculture]; Part II [Foreign Affairs]).

Like the Senate bill, the House measure divided authority for the program between the Agriculture Department and AID and set improving food security of recipient nations as the overriding foreign policy goal for the program. It also contained Eastern Europe and aid forgiveness provisions like those in the Senate bill. Unlike the Senate measure, however, the House bill sought to tighten regulation of overseas shipping agents rather than barring their use.

Neither chamber debated the bulk of the PL 480 overhaul proposals, but the food aid provisions served as the backdrop for contentious arguments on one domestic concern and one urgent foreign policy issue.

Amendments that came to a vote in both chambers on July 27 were aimed at cutting off credit sales to Iraq, whose bellicose policies and use of chemical weapons against its separatist Kurdish population had prompted a number of efforts on Capitol Hill to reverse the Reagan and Bush administrations' policy tilt toward Iraq.

By substantial margins, mandated credit cutoffs were added to the food aid provisions in both the House and Senate farm bills. But they became moot after Iraq invaded Kuwait on Aug. 2 and President Bush imposed a total U.S. embargo against Iraq. *(Persian Gulf crisis, p. 717)*

The domestic issue was a perennial regional concern: cargo preference provisions to force transport of a specified percentage of PL 480 foodstuffs through dying Great Lake ports. A Senate floor clash on the issue ended in a compromise between Great Lakes senators and senators representing states along the Gulf of Mexico. Combined with a stronger House position, the compromise allowed Great Lakes states to preserve what they had won in the 1985 farm bill: a provision guaranteeing Great Lakes ports the same percentage of cargo they had had in 1984. *(Cargo preference, p. 338)*

Final Action

The Senate passed S 2830 on July 27, while the House completed work on HR 3950 on Aug. 1. House and Senate negotiators reached agreement on the final version of the 1990 farm bill on Oct. 16 (H Rept 101-916).

The final agreement incorporated the program management change. Instead of six agencies with veto power over food shipments, the bill said the Agriculture Department was to decide which countries to sell to and AID was to determine which countries should receive food donations.

Most food donations were made through humanitarian organizations. The new program would expand donations between the U.S. government and those of nations that could not feed their own people, many of which were in sub-Saharan Africa.

Funding for this program was to be taken out of concessional PL 480 sales. The Senate bill provided that at least 40 percent of the funds appropriated for sales was to be transferred to grants; the House bill put the figure at 33 percent. The final measure set the funds transferred to grants at not less than 40 percent.

However, there was not likely to be much additional money for food aid in coming years. In 1985, Congress increased the annual authorization for PL 480 grants from $1 billion to $1.2 billion, but appropriations had not matched that level.

The 1990 bill limited appropriations to no more than $1 billion, unless the president determined that more was necessary to meet urgent humanitarian needs.

In the fiscal 1991 Agriculture spending bill (HR 5268 — PL 101-506), Congress appropriated $1.01 billion for the PL 480 program — a slight increase over the fiscal 1990 appropriation of $992 million. The bill fixed the program level — including contributions from other sources — at $1.6 billion, $54 million more than in fiscal 1990. *(Agriculture appropriations, p. 867; 1989 Almanac, p. 741)* ■

Andean Initiative Drug Strategy Prevails

President Bush's international drug war strategy stayed the course in 1990, with Congress clearing legislation (HR 5567 — PL 101-623) to authorize funding for military and economic aid to Colombia, Peru and Bolivia.

The strategy, called the Andean Initiative, was aimed at giving those drug-exporting countries funds in return for their promises to crack down on the illicit drug trade in their countries.

Controversy over how much funding the U.S. should provide for military aid to the countries, though, nearly derailed the bill. The Bush administration had requested about $137 million in foreign military aid for fiscal 1991 for the three countries.

Members of Congress were reluctant to accede to the Bush proposal because of problems in distributing the aid for fiscal 1990 and because of concerns over the level of military aid in the package. Members of the House Foreign Affairs Committee put a $100 million cap on total military aid to the three nations; Bush responded with a threat to veto the bill.

Eventually, Congress and the administration reached a compromise: military aid for the Andean countries was authorized for fiscal 1991 at $118 million with a cap of $250 million in military aid from all U.S. sources.

The final bill did not completely please anyone: Democrats disliked the high cap level, while the administration disapproved of the reporting and human rights requirements put on the aid. The measure slid through at the end of the session, clearing the House on Oct. 27 by voice vote. The president signed the bill Nov. 21.

BACKGROUND

President Bush's Andean Initiative was based on a rapid infusion of aid to the armed forces in the three major cocaine-producing countries of South America.

Bush first announced his initiative in 1989 and proposed giving the three countries an additional $129 million in military aid for fiscal 1990. This was in addition to the $119.1 million in narcotics-related economic, military and law enforcement aid already authorized for Andean nations in fiscal 1990.

Congress eventually approved $125 million in aid, which was to come from the Pentagon's fiscal 1990 budget. *(1989 Almanac, pp. 253, 760, 780)*

Bush met with the leaders of the Andean countries in Cartagena, Colombia, on Feb. 15, 1990, and reiterated earlier administration proposals to give the three nations $2.2 billion in unspecified military and economic assistance over the following five years.

A joint communiqué signed by Bush, Colombian President Virgilio Barco, Bolivian President Jaime Paz Zamora and Peruvian President Alan García also called, in general terms, for more cooperation in interdiction of drug-trafficking, greater trade incentives for the Andean region, increased efforts to limit the sale of automatic weapons and chemicals needed for cocaine production, the sharing of drug-related forfeitures and new resolve in seeking alternative work for people employed in growing coca and producing cocaine.

But changes in the region in 1990 led some members of Congress to move to cut back the three nations' military aid for fiscal 1991. The newly elected president of Peru, Alberto Fujimori, refused to accept the fiscal 1990 military aid, and the Bush administration acknowledged that none of the $125 million in aid approved earlier had been distributed to the countries.

House Foreign Affairs Republicans, however, argued that the international war on drugs was progressing well and pleaded with other members of Congress not to cut off the aid precipitously.

Provisions

As cleared Oct. 27, HR 5567:

- Authorized $300 million in economic aid for the Andean countries in fiscal 1991.
- Authorized $118 million in military aid for fiscal 1991. Military aid from all sources was capped at $250 million. A subcap of $175 million was placed on aid to law enforcement agencies and the armed forces.
- Allowed the president to provide such aid only after he had determined that 1) the country had implemented programs to reduce the flow of cocaine to the United States in accordance with a bilateral treaty (to be negotiated) that contained specific quantitative and qualitative performance measures and 2) the armed forces of the country were not engaged in a consistent pattern of human rights violations and the government of that country had made significant progress in protecting internationally recognized human rights. As a part of this requirement, the president would have to notify Congress not less than 15 days before the funds were obligated with details on the aid to be transmitted.

HOUSE COMMITTEE ACTION

The only committee to consider HR 5567, the Foreign Affairs panel, approved it easily Sept. 11 by voice vote. During the markup, committee Democrats, led by Chairman Dante B. Fascell and International Narcotics Control Task Force Chairman Lawrence J. Smith (both from Florida), amended the draft legislation by capping at $100 million the total amount of military aid the U.S. could provide to the three nations. The original draft measure did not impose a cap on military aid.

There were five outlets through which the U.S. could have provided military aid to the Andean countries: Foreign Military Sales (FMS), the most well-known and the only one to require explicit congressional approval; excess defense articles, where the Pentagon in essence donated military hardware it no longer needed; two types of drawdown authority for the president to provide aid in case of emergency or narcotics or refugee reasons; and Export-Import Bank loans.

The cap applied to all forms of military assistance except the Ex-Im loans. Democrats argued that the ceiling was necessary because they needed to see how well the aid was working before approving any more.

At that time, none of the fiscal 1990 aid — $125 million — had been spent, or even given to the countries for which it was earmarked.

Floor action on HR 5567 was delayed for several weeks while supporters and administration officials negotiated behind the scenes, finally compromising on language that placed a cap on the aid but at a much higher level than the Foreign Affairs-approved bill.

FLOOR ACTION

HR 5567 first appeared on the House floor as an amendment to the crime bill (HR 5269). Some of the provisions of the measure were changed after the Sept. 11 markup because of negotiations with the Bush administration. *(Crime bill, p. 486)*

The amendment reflected several changes agreed to by the negotiators.

In the compromise version of the bill attached to the anticrime measure by the House on a voice vote Oct. 4, military aid to the Andean countries was to be capped at $250 million. Within that amount, the measure further restricted aid to both the armed forces of the countries and the law enforcement agencies to $175 million each.

Because Fascell and others were worried that HR 5269 would not become law, the House took up the amended version of HR 5567 on Oct. 22 as a separate bill and passed it easily by voice vote. There was little floor debate on the measure, though Fascell inserted in the Congressional Record a lengthy explanation of the bill's background and the eventual agreement with the White House.

The Senate passed the bill by voice vote Oct. 26 after approving two amendments, also by voice vote.

The first struck the word "strongly" from a phrase in the legislation stating that Congress strongly urged the president to use authority under existing law to provide debt relief to the Andean countries if certain conditions had been met. The second amendment deleted a provision in the bill that would have capped at 12 the number of military advisers the U.S. could have in any of the three nations.

Members of the House Foreign Affairs panel had added the limit to address a portion of existing law regarding ceilings on the number of U.S. military advisers in foreign countries. Under that provision, there was a six-person ceiling on the number of U.S. military advisers in any one country. That ceiling could be waived either by the president, or by legislative action; once the six-person ceiling was waived, however, there was no further limit to the number of U.S. military personnel who could be assigned to that country.

Fascell and others were concerned that in the Andean countries the absence of any ceiling — which, in the case of Colombia was legislatively waived, and in the case of Bolivia and Peru was waived by the president — might encourage excessive deployment of U.S. military personnel.

The Foreign Affairs Committee, therefore, adopted language in HR 5567 that would have established a new ceiling of 12 if the six-person ceiling were waived. As in existing law, the 12-person ceiling could have been waived by the president.

This provision was deleted by the Senate. Though Fascell disliked the amendment, he agreed to it after putting the administration on notice that the issue would come up again in the future.

Finally, on Oct. 27, the House agreed to the Senate amendments by voice vote, clearing the measure for the president. ■

Senate OKs Ratification of Torture Treaty

Six years after it was originally passed by the United Nations, the Senate on Oct. 27 approved a treaty that made torture a criminally punishable offense under international law.

Senate passage by division vote of a resolution to ratify the Convention Against Torture and Other Cruel, Inhuman or Degrading Treatment or Punishment (Treaty Doc. 100-20) came after supporters of the pact and a key critic, Jesse Helms, R-N.C., compromised on reservations to be attached to the pact.

BACKGROUND

The General Assembly of the United Nations unanimously approved the torture treaty on Dec. 10, 1984.

The pact made torture a criminal offense and required member nations to prosecute those accused of torture or extradite them for prosecution elsewhere. Signatories to the pact also had to include torture as an extraditable offense in their bilateral treaties.

The treaty defined torture as "any act by which severe pain or suffering, whether physical or mental, is intentionally inflicted on a person . . . when such pain or suffering is inflicted by or at the instigation of or with the consent or acquiescence of a public official or other person acting in an official capacity."

The definition did not include any action, resulting in pain or suffering, that arose from lawful sanctions.

Another provision of the treaty stated that "no exceptional circumstances," such as war or political instability, were justifications for the use of torture.

The treaty mandated that member states take legislative, administrative or judicial action to prevent torture in any territory under their jurisdiction. To monitor compliance with the treaty's provisions, it created a Committee Against Torture, organized under U.N. auspices, made up of 10 experts in the human rights field. They investigated any allegations of the use of torture.

By 1990, the treaty had been ratified by 51 nations and signed by 21 others.

U.S. Action

The United States signed the pact April 18, 1988, and President Ronald Reagan submitted it to the Senate for ratification the next month. But Reagan included 19 proposed conditions, many of which concerned treaty supporters, including human rights groups and the American Bar Asssociation.

The Bush administration reconsidered the reservations and agreed to remove most of them. Approval of the measure was then held up by senators concerned that some of the requirements of the treaty would have superseded the U.S. Constitution.

Somewhat similar concerns had held up for nearly 40 years Senate ratification of a 1948 treaty against genocide. When the Senate finally approved that pact in 1986, it included several controversial reservations, including a so-called sovereignty proviso that nothing in the treaty required the United States to take any action that would be prohibited by the Constitution. *(1986 Almanac, p. 381)*

SENATE ACTION

The Senate Foreign Relations Committee held a hearing on the torture treaty Jan. 30 and voted 10-0 to approve the measure July 19 (S Exec Comm Rpt 101-30).

In the intervening time, Foreign Relations Chairman Claiborne Pell, D-R.I., and Helms, the committee's ranking Republican, along with the Bush administration, worked to fashion a package of reservations to the treaty that addressed Helms' constitutional concerns.

Helms again wanted to attach a sovereignty proviso to the torture treaty as had been done in the case of the genocide pact. But he agreed with Pell that the reservation would be attached to the resolution of ratification, not to the instrument of ratification itself — the legal document notifying the United Nations of U.S. assent to the treaty.

Although several senators, including Daniel Patrick Moynihan, D-N.Y., argued the proviso was unnecessary and harmful in the eyes of other countries, the Senate adopted Helms' amendment along with three other reservations as an en bloc amendment by division vote.

The three other reservations, also crafted with the help and approval of the Bush administration, did the following:

- Limited the definition of "cruel, inhuman or degrading" treatment to cruel and unusual punishment as defined under the Fifth, Eighth and 14th Amendments to the Constitution;
- Clarified the restrictions on application of the treaty in cases of lawful sanctions; and
- Required reciprocity on the part of any nation that filed a complaint with the Committee Against Torture.

Though the Senate often approved reservations for treaties, those reservations did not amend the treaty itself. Rather, the reservations expressed the Senate's understanding of how the pact was to be implemented. ■

'Armenian Genocide' Commemorative Fails

With two failed cloture votes behind him and support waning, Sen. Bob Dole, R-Kan., on Feb. 27 abandoned his effort to break a weeklong filibuster on a joint resolution commemorating the "Armenian genocide of 1915-1923."

A vote of 48-51, down from the previous 49-49, convinced Dole that he was not going to get the 60 votes needed to shut off debate on S J Res 212. But he said the idea behind his resolution would not die. *(Vote 17, p. 7-S; vote 16, p. 6-S)*

The resolution would have marked April 24 as a National Day of Remembrance for the Armenian Genocide for the estimated 1.5 million Armenians killed under the Turkish Ottoman Empire between 1915 and 1923.

The resolution appeared to have widespread support until Turkey, a key NATO ally, raised strong objections. In a letter from its ambassador, the government of Turkey argued the resolution could "inflame nationalist passions and historic grievances and incite further violence."

Background

Dole had 54 cosponsors when he introduced the measure in the 101st Congress. Within a month, seven other senators signed on to what seemed to be a routine commemorative.

But then Turkey raised its objections. And the administration, brushing aside a Bush presidential campaign promise, came out against the resolution.

"I considered it a commemorative resolution, which most of us around here sign without giving much thought to it," said Dale Bumpers, D-Ark., one of the dropout cosponsors.

"There is not any question," he said, "but that we are imposing a gross insult on the Turks."

The Senate Judiciary Committee had approved the resolution 8-6 in October 1989 after rejecting an attempt to water it down in response to administration objections.

On Nov. 20, 1989, Dole announced that he was dropping his effort to gain passage of the measure for the year. He vowed to resume his efforts in early 1990, though.

In August 1987, the House had failed to approve a similar resolution, after the Reagan administration lobbied hard to kill it.

Dole had long had a special feeling for Armenia, a kingdom since divided between the Soviet Union, Turkey and Iran. He credited an Armenian doctor in Chicago with saving his life after he was severely wounded in World War II.

While Dole said he hoped a watered-down version, "either in concurrent resolution form or as a sense of the Congress amendment, might garner a better vote," others wanted to put the issue behind them.

"I think we've wasted enough time on this," said Jim Exon, D-Neb.

Senate Action

Leading the opposition to the resolution was Robert C. Byrd, D-W.Va., who had vowed to continue the filibuster. Byrd rejected Dole's attempt to get cloture by offering amendments to change the event to "Armenian Martyrs Day" and to rework language to clearly absolve the current Republic of Turkey of any wrongdoing. "Turkey is still on trial on this floor," Byrd said. "There is no use in fooling ourselves with such cosmetic surgery."

Byrd also took exception to Dole's last-minute offer to change the legislation from a joint resolution to a concurrent resolution that would not require the president's signature. Byrd said that would only have been "a way for the White House to wash its hands" of the matter.

President Bush was in a difficult spot because his opposition to the resolution appeared to conflict with a 1988 campaign response to a questionnaire from the Armenian Assembly of America. Bush said then, "I would join Congress in commemorating the victims of that period."

Unable to persuade Dole to drop the matter, Bush sent Chief of Staff John H. Sununu and national security adviser Brent L. Scowcroft to negotiate a compromise that would satisfy Turkey. But their efforts were to no avail.

The entire matter evoked intense lobbying by both

sides. The Turkish government sent its letter critical of the resolution. On the day of the second cloture vote, about 40 Armenians who survived the Ottoman Empire, ranging in age from 76 to 99, lobbied senators to pass the resolution and sat in the gallery during the vote.

Proponents of the resolution said they would not give up. "We'll start offering it as an amendment to every bill that comes up," Dole cautioned before the first cloture vote Feb. 22.

But neither that threat nor the promise to water down the resolution had much effect. Sixteen former cosponsors voted against cloture in the first vote. For the second vote, two Republicans — John W. Warner, Va., and Conrad Burns, Mont. — also changed their votes to "no."

In the floor debate Feb. 21-22, Sam Nunn, D-Ga., chairman of the Armed Services Committee, expressed the concerns of the defense establishment.

"The Republic of Turkey today makes an important contribution to the success of the NATO alliance and is a key country for the support of United States strategic interests," he said.

Joining Nunn was David L. Boren, D-Okla., who raised concern over the word "genocide." The word became the rallying cry for opponents, who argued that historians have not done enough research to determine whether an actual genocide occurred between 1915 and 1923.

Dole refuted that claim, citing newspaper accounts, testimony and telegrams dating back to the Ottoman Empire that he said proved the events constituted a genocide. "This is a book on the Armenian genocide," Dole said, holding up a volume the size of a telephone directory.

Nancy Landon Kassebaum, R-Kan., said Turkey should not let the resolution hurt relations. "I knew from a foreign policy standpoint there would be complications," she said after voting for cloture. "But it's important for Turkey to realize we can still be allies."

In the end, however, too many senators backed off from their original support for the measure. "I've come to realize that this is not only a statement of what went on 75 years ago," said Bob Graham, D-Fla. "In the general area of foreign policy we have been too casual. What we do up here is taken very seriously." ■

Palauans Reject Charter on Autonomy

Voters in the trust territory of Palau failed on Feb. 6 to approve a proposed charter granting autonomy to the sprawling Pacific archipelago while reserving U.S. base rights.

U.S. lawmakers who designed the "Compact of Free Association" were frustrated by the measure's failure to win the 75 percent majority required under the Palauan Constitution — the seventh failure since 1983 to ratify a new charter.

The compact, which would have granted Palau autonomy but allowed for the United States to retain defense rights on the archipelago for 50 years and to take over key lands for military purposes, won approval from just more than 60 percent of the voters.

"I was disappointed, but it was their decision," said Del. Ron de Lugo, D-Virgin Islands, chairman of the House Interior Subcommittee on Insular and International Affairs, after the referendum. There was talk of an eighth referendum in Palau in October, but none materialized.

Made up of more than 200 islands in the western Pacific Ocean, Palau was the last remaining component of the U.N.-sanctioned Trust Territory of the Pacific Islands, administered by the United States since 1947. Other members of the trust territory, such as the Federated States of Micronesia and the Marshall Islands, gained autonomy in 1986.

The United States cleared the way for Palau to follow suit when President Bush signed legislation (H J Res 175 — PL 101-219) on Dec. 12, 1989, that would have provided Palau with autonomy and $478 million in aid over 15 years — if residents of Palau approved the compact. *(1989 Almanac, p. 627)*

The base rights issue was one of the points of the controversy in the campaign leading up to the Feb. 6 vote.

Bonifacio Basilius, a spokesman for Palau President Ngiratkel Etpison, said the base rights defense provision was "one that generated . . . a very emotional response."

But, Basilius added, "there are a large number of people who look at the defense provision of the compact very favorably."

A number of Palauans also wanted to continue their relationship with the United States.

The supermajority requirement had frustrated every attempt to pass the compact to date. Each time the referendum received a simple majority, and a few results had been just under the 75 percent minimum.

One referendum passed in 1987 following an amendment to the constitution that provided for simple-majority passage. But the referendum result and the constitutional amendment were challenged by compact opponents, and both were invalidated by the Supreme Court of Palau.

"Politically, Palau is a society in which you almost never get a simple majority, let alone a supermajority," said Allen Stayman, an aide to Sen. J. Bennett Johnston, D-La., who as chairman of the Energy and Natural Resources Committee was a key player in steering H J Res 175 through Congress in 1989.

Basilius said it was "humanly impossible" to get a supermajority among the many rival Palauan clans.

Results of the 1990 referendum changed the way some in Washington were viewing Palau.

"Before February we were always dealing in anticipation of the compact," said an official in the Department of the Interior's Territorial and International Affairs division. "We are no longer acting as if it will be implemented."

Aid to Palau in fiscal 1991 amounted to about $16 million. In its role as trustee, the United States specified exactly how the money was to be used, with emphasis placed on health and education programs.

If the compact had been adopted, the aid would have been in a block grant form without any specific instructions on its use.

"The ball is in the Palauans' court, as it has been. And the compact remains on the table," the Interior Department official said. "But it's sort of like beating a dead horse." ■

Chapter 12

APPROPRIATIONS

Fiscal 1991 Appropriations 811
  Fiscal 1991 Spending 811
Defense 812
  Defense Appropriations 813
  Funding for Major Weapons 815
  Major Provisions 824
Military Construction 826
  Military Construction Appropriations 828
Foreign Aid 830
  Foreign Aid Appropriations 832
  U.N. Family Planning Agency 838
Fiscal 1990 Supplemental 844
Labor/HHS/Education 847
  Labor/HHS/Education Appropriations 848
VA/HUD/Independent Agencies 854
  VA/HUD Appropriations 855
  The Archenemy of Pork 857
Energy, Water 861
  Energy/Water Appropriations 862
Agriculture 867
  Agriculture Appropriations 869
Interior 870
  Interior Appropriations 873
Transportation 876
  Transportation Appropriations 879
Commerce/Justice/State 881
  Commerce/Justice/State Appropriations 882
Treasury/Postal Service 886
  Treasury/Postal Service Appropriations 887
District of Columbia 891
  D.C. Appropriations 892
Legislative Branch 894
  Legislative Branch Appropriations 895
Continuing Resolutions 896

13 Spending Bills OK'd in Final Days

Budget deal forces few changes; no Bush vetoes

For the House and Senate Appropriations committees, it was the most productive week of the session. Not coincidentally, it was also the last.

Twelve of the 13 regular appropriations bills for fiscal 1991 cleared Congress during the week of Oct. 22 and were sent to President Bush, who signed all of them on Nov. 5. The other — a spending bill for energy and water development — cleared the week before, on Oct. 19.

The budget standoff between the Bush administration and Congress had precipitated the end-of-the-year appropriations logjam. But, in the end, the budget deal forced few changes in the so-called discretionary accounts funded in the annual spending bills.

Defense spending still took a relatively big cut. Foreign aid was nicked for several million dollars. However, many domestic programs, particularly those involving education, child care, housing, public works and environmental protection, were given modest increases — in spite of the intense pressure to reduce the deficit.

For the third year in a row, Congress managed to pass all of the 13 spending bills separately, instead of rolling them into the sort of massive "must-pass" appropriations measure that President Ronald Reagan lampooned so effectively in 1988. *(State of the Union address, 1988 Almanac, p. 4-C)*

But none of the fiscal 1991 bills had cleared by the beginning of the fiscal year, Oct. 1, the ostensible deadline. So Congress had to pass five short-term appropriations measures (called "continuing resolutions") in order to keep the government running during the prolonged budget fight. *(Continuing resolutions, p. 896)*

In most cases, the spending levels in the regular spending bills were relatively non-controversial. Repeated attempts at making across-the-board spending cuts were rejected, except in the case of foreign aid and legislative branch funding bills.

Several of the bills had been the target of veto threats. But in the waning days of the session, Congress went a long way toward satisfying the administration's objections.

A provision permitting the use of federal funds for abortion was removed from the District of Columbia bill.

Lawmakers also agreed with an administration proposal to forgive Egypt's $6.7 billion military debt.

On the bill funding the Labor and Health and Human Services (HHS) departments, an expected fight with the Bush administration over abortion never materialized.

Abortion opponents in the Senate managed to attach a provision requiring parental notification to another amendment that would have allowed HHS funding of abortions in cases of rape or incest. Dropping the notification requirement was more important to abortion rights supporters than was keeping the rape and incest provisions.

Floor debates often focused on small pork-barrel provisions, such as the $500,000 Farmers Home Administration grant earmarked in the Agriculture bill by Senate Agriculture Appropriations Subcommittee Chairman Quentin N. Burdick, D-N.D, for a museum at the North Dakota birthplace of bandleader Lawrence Welk. Rep. Silvio O. Conte of Massachusetts, ranking Republican on the House Appropriations Committee, mocked the project on the House floor.

Some bills still contained major provisions that the administration had staunchly opposed, including military construction and Veterans Affairs/Housing and Urban Development (VA/HUD). But a veto so late in the year would either have forced Bush to call Congress back for a lame-duck session or have left part of the government unfunded until Congress returned in January 1991.

Seven appropriations bills cleared on or before Oct. 26: Agriculture; Commerce-Justice-State; Defense; energy and water; Treasury-Postal Service; VA/HUD; and District of Columbia. The other six cleared in the session of Oct. 27: foreign operations; Interior; Labor/HHS; legislative branch; military construction; and Transportation.

In signing the spending bills Nov. 5, Bush issued statements on eight of them voicing various reservations about specific budget priorities or congressional intrusions on presidential powers. ■

Fiscal 1991 Spending

(In billions of dollars)

	Fiscal 1990 Appropriation	President's Request	House Bill	Senate Bill	Final Bill
Agriculture	$ 45.18	$ 52.25	$ 50.35	$ 52.26	$ 52.16
Commerce, State	19.86	20.01	10.59 *	19.31	19.32
Defense‡	285.29	287.28	269.28	268.24	268.98
District of Columbia	0.56	0.52	0.53	0.55	0.55
Energy	18.42	20.21	20.78	20.78	20.16
Foreign Operations	15.52	15.52	15.64	15.53	15.39
Interior	11.41	9.86	11.78	11.70	11.74
Labor/HHS/Education	157.17	174.89	170.67 *	183.54	182.18
Legislative†	1.94	2.41	1.67	2.07	2.16
Military Construction	8.49	9.13	8.31	7.98	8.36
Transportation	13.06	11.88	13.09	13.19	12.99
Treasury/Postal	18.45	20.71	20.72	20.96	20.72
VA/HUD/Ind. Agencies	66.32	76.18	80.66	78.59	78.01
TOTAL	**$661.67**	**$700.85**	**$674.07**	**$694.71**	**$692.72**

* *The House did not consider requests for programs not authorized.*

† *The House figure does not include amounts for the Senate. The administration does not propose legislative spending; it merely includes numbers from the congressional branch.*

‡ *Congress also approved additional funding of $2.04 billion for Operation Desert Shield not counted within the Defense bill.*

SOURCE: House Appropriations Committee

Defense Spending Held to $288 Billion

The big defense issues had already been settled by the time Congress gave its final approval to the $269 billion defense appropriations bill for fiscal 1991.

As usual, the annual appropriations bill (HR 5803) closely paralleled the companion defense authorization measure (HR 4739) in its treatment of most major issues. The Senate adopted both bills Oct. 26 by identical votes of 80-17, clearing them for President Bush's signature. *(Votes 319, 320, p. 62-S; defense authorization bill, p. 671)*

As part of the fiscal 1991 budget package, Congress and the White House agreed to reduce total spending for the Defense Department and defense-related programs to $288 billion from Bush's initial budget request of $307 billion. *(Bush budget, p. 122)*

BOXSCORE

Legislation: Fiscal 1991 Defense Department appropriations, PL 101-511 (HR 5803).

Major action: Signed, Nov. 5. Conference report adopted by Senate, 80-17, Oct. 26; by House, Oct. 25. Passed by Senate, 79-16, Oct. 15; by House, 322-97, Oct. 12.

Reports: Conference report (H Rept 101-938). Appropriations (S Rept 101-521); Appropriations (H Rept 101-822).

The president's fiscal 1991 budget request for defense amounted to a 2 percent decline in purchasing power, after allowing for inflation. But the reduced threat of the Soviet conventional military threat to Western Europe initially fueled congressional demands for larger cuts.

When Congress began its August recess, the prevailing wisdom was that the deeper cuts in defense spending sought by the House would prevail. But the political dynamics changed when Iraq marched into Kuwait on Aug. 2, and the administration deployed more than 200,000 U.S. troops to the Persian Gulf. The prospect that U.S. military personnel could wind up engaged in a large-scale combat operation made members more cautious of cutting the defense budget too dramatically.

Combined with funds provided in separate legislation for military construction and for defense-related projects of the Energy Department, HR 5803 brought the total defense-related appropriation for fiscal 1991 to $288.3 billion — the ceiling set by the congressional budget resolution. *(Major provisions, p. 824; funding for major weapons, p. 815; military construction spending bill, p. 826)*

For programs covered by HR 5803 alone, Bush requested $287.3 billion in January. The $18.3 billion reduction in the final bill brought funding to a level $15.4 billion less than was appropriated for fiscal 1990. *(1989 Almanac, p. 760)*

In addition to the $269 billion appropriated by the conference report, the bill also authorized transfer to the Pentagon of $1 billion from contributions made by other countries to defray the cost of U.S. deployments in and around Saudi Arabia. *(Persian Gulf crisis, p. 717)*

The vast majority of funding limits set by the bill or described in the conferees' explanatory statement echoed the decisions embodied in the authorization bill. For example, the final version of the appropriations bill provided:

- $2.35 billion for procurement of the B-2 "stealth" bomber without addressing the controversy between the Senate and House as to whether the money could be used to begin building additional copies of the controversial plane. *(Stealth bomber, p. 687)*
- $403 million to continue development and slowly begin production of the V-22 Osprey, a hybrid airplane/helicopter wanted by the Marine Corps as a troop transport. Thus, for the second year running, Congress rejected the effort by Defense Secretary Dick Cheney to terminate the Osprey program.
- $2.89 billion for the strategic defense initiative (SDI). The bill provided an additional $218 million for work on so-called antitactical missiles, intended to shoot down missiles with ranges measured in the hundreds of miles. Some missiles in that range were deployed by Iraq. *(SDI, p. 691)*

As always, the bill appropriated tens of billions of dollars for secret programs described only in a secret appendix to the bill, called an annex. But in 1990, the measure incorporated a Senate-passed provision stipulating that the detailed provisions of the annex "shall have the force and effect of law as if enacted into law."

In a letter, Senate Appropriations Chairman Robert C. Byrd, D-W.Va., complained that defense and intelligence agencies had "ignored or challenged" congressional directions regarding funds appropriated for some secret programs.

When he signed the appropriations bill Nov. 5, however, Bush construed the proviso as non-binding.

"I will certainly take into account Congress' wishes in this regard," Bush said, "but will do so mindful of the fact that, according to the terms of the statute, the provisions of the annex are not law."

Touchy Issues

During the conference on the defense spending bill, the chronic tension between the Armed Services and Appropriations panels flared over three elements of the bill:

- A provision expressly nullifying language in the authorization bill intended to slow moves toward production of a new Air Force fighter plane, designated ATF.
- A series of "earmarks" awarding funds to specific colleges and universities, bypassing the Pentagon's procedures for awarding university research funds on a competitive basis.
- A provision doubling to 360 days the period for which the president could order members of the National Guard and reserves to active duty, except under a declaration of war or in a national emergency.

As a result of Iraq's invasion of Kuwait, the Defense Department wanted to be able to call on the reserves or National Guard to bolster the U.S. troops already sent to the region. But according to Pentagon officials, one reason they had delayed in mobilizing ground-combat units from the reserves or National Guard for deployment to Saudi Arabia was that existing law permitted them to be called up for only 180 days. After refresher training, the Pentagon contended, there was too little time left to make it worthwhile to ship the units overseas.

So congressional proponents of a greater role for Guard and reserve forces proposed extending how long they could be called to active duty.

But Senate Armed Services Committee Chairman Sam Nunn, D-Ga., objected that this potentially far-reaching change was being enacted without proper review. "We need to determine whether changing the rules on National Guard and reserve [members] — and also on employers — in the middle of the game would have an adverse impact," Nunn said.

Nunn complained that all three disputed elements of the appropriations bill were "invented in a conference committee.... The Senate has never had an opportunity to consider these items," he said.

But Alaska's Ted Stevens, the senior Republican on the Defense Appropriations Subcommittee, insisted that Senate conferees on the appropriations bill had been forced to cut their own deals with the House because of political controversies swirling around the authorization bill.

According to Stevens, the appropriations conference report "made some concessions to members of the House ... to get a bill that could go to the president," regardless of whether the authorization measure ever became law.

Air Force Fighter Plane

In the case of the so-called advanced tactical fighter (ATF), the authorizers and appropriators differed not so much on the amount of money to be spent in fiscal 1991 as on the pace of the program.

Two prototype designs, each backed by a team of contractors, were being tested against demanding performance requirements, with the Air Force due to select the winner in the fall of 1991.

The fiscal 1991 budget request earmarked $764 million to continue the competition and an additional $283 million to move into "full-scale development" with the winning design.

Full-scale development was the transition from hand-built prototypes to the detailed specifications that would be needed to put a particular design into production.

Conferees from the Senate and House Armed Services committees approved $964 million to continue the ATF program, but they added to the authorization bill a flat prohibition on beginning full-scale development.

The appropriations bill, on the other hand, provided a total of $964 million for the ATF but earmarked $200 million for full-scale development.

Senate Defense Appropriations Chairman Daniel K. Inouye, D-Hawaii, minimized the difference. "The authorizers wanted us to delay this by three months," he told the Senate. "This is speeding up the process by three months."

But Nunn and other authorizers protested what they said would be a premature commitment to building the plane.

"There are too many unanswered questions to justify launching a $75 billion aircraft," Nunn said.

Aside from the question of whether the prototypes met the ATF specifications, Armed Services Committee member William S. Cohen, R-Maine, wondered whether those specifications were unreasonably demanding because the threat of a high-tech Soviet blitz against Western Europe seemed more remote.

Research Policy

The debate over earmarking research funds for specific colleges and universities reprised a battle that had occupied the Senate intermittently.

Nunn and others complained that the earmarks short-circuited the "peer review" process through which federal research funds were awarded to competing institutions by a panel of established experts in a given field.

"If these programs have merit, they will succeed in a fair and competent review and competition," Nunn told the Senate.

"It is a matter of diverting research funds from high-quality research to lesser quality research," declared John C. Danforth, R-Mo.

Stevens countered that the earmarks had been paid for by trimming 10 percent from large increases requested for 10 research centers operated under contract to the government. He offered a more critical view of the peer review process as one in which "the people from the 'good old boy league' continue to pull one another up by their bootstraps."

Inouye, too, defended the earmarks as a matter of equity to the students who would benefit as a byproduct of spreading the federal wealth.

"Do we make a big university bigger," he demanded, "or

Defense Appropriations

Following are the budget authority totals in the fiscal 1991 appropriations bill (HR 5803 — PL 101-511) for the Department of Defense and related agencies.

(Figures, in thousands of dollars, may not add due to rounding.)

	Bush Request	House Passed	Senate Passed	Final Bill
Military Personnel	$ 79,053,700	$ 78,553,202	$ 77,753,700	$ 78,080,467
Operations and Maintenance	88,764,624	86,026,480	83,238,227	83,452,560
Procurement	77,288,050	67,021,045	65,489,817	67,176,648
Research and Development	38,092,800	34,937,611	34,140,306	35,974,792
Revolving Funds	2,228,200	1,730,950	3,939,200	1,984,200
Miscellaneous	1,661,800	818,610	3,486,100	2,119,300
Other Agencies	193,500	193,500	193,500	193,500
Total, new budget authority	**$ 287,282,674**	**$ 269,281,398**	**$ 268,240,850**	**$ 268,981,467**
Transfers from:				
Desert Shield gift fund	—	—	—	1,000,000
Prior year budgets	1,359,050	—	—	—
TOTAL	**$ 288,641,724**	**$ 269,281,398**	**$ 268,240,850**	**$ 269,981,467**

do we provide ... the sons and daughters of coal miners [and] farmers an equal break?"

HOUSE COMMITTEE ACTION

The U.S. military commitment in the Persian Gulf left its imprint on the Pentagon funding bill reported Oct. 9 by the House Appropriations Committee. The measure slowed the cutback of military manpower and provided for the purchase of more high-speed cargo ships.

On most issues, the defense appropriations bill conformed to the House-passed version of the companion defense authorization measure (HR 4739).

As drafted by the Defense Appropriations Subcommittee, the bill presumed a total defense budget for fiscal 1991 of $283 billion, the ceiling set by the House in its budget resolution.

The Defense Subcommittee's bill reduced by about 80,000 the 2.1 million members of the armed forces on active duty. The House-passed version of the companion defense authorization bill cut manpower by 129,500.

While concurring that Pentagon manpower should be reduced substantially over the next several years, members of the Appropriations subcommittee warned that the larger cut could complicate efforts to reinforce units in Saudi Arabia and efforts to work out a schedule for bringing those units home periodically while replacing them with others.

'Ro-Ro' Ships

The subcommittee's $1 billion allowance for cargo ships, combined with $375 million appropriated in fiscal 1990 but not spent by the Pentagon, was earmarked to buy at least eight "Ro-Ro ships," equipped with large loading ramps so that vehicles could quickly "roll-on" and "roll-off," reducing the time needed to load and unload.

The full Appropriations Committee, when marking up its bill, agreed with the subcommittee that more cargo ships were needed for the Navy. The House Armed Services Committee also saw that need.

But the Appropriations and Armed Services panels disagreed over how to design and operate these new "fast sealift ships."

Essentially, both committees wanted to replicate the Navy's eight fast cargo liners of the "SL-7" class.

Built in the early 1970s as commercial container ships for the SeaLand Corp., they were the fastest cargo ships ever to sail under the U.S. flag. But when fuel prices skyrocketed in 1973, the gas-guzzling turbine engines that drove them at 33 knots (38 mph) made them prohibitively expensive for commercial use.

The Navy bought them and built loading ramps and vehicle decks to make them Ro-Ro ships.

Named after stars and constellations, as was traditional for Navy cargo ships, the eight were moored in East Coast ports, under orders to be ready to sail on very short notice.

Mobilized Aug. 7, five days after Iraq invaded Kuwait, the eight ships took aboard the tanks, trucks and combat supplies of the Army's 24th Division near Savannah, Ga., and most arrived in Saudi Arabia within three weeks. (One ship broke down and was towed to Spain.)

House Armed Services included in the fiscal 1991 defense authorization bill a provision ordering the Navy to design new cargo vessels that could carry either heavy Army combat gear or commercial loads at competitive rates. Rather than sitting alongside wharves waiting for a war, these ships would be chartered to commercial operators subject to recall by the Navy in time of need.

Armed Services told the Navy to launch this program using $375 million that was appropriated for sealift in fiscal 1990 but was not spent.

The Appropriations panel saw that approach as self-defeating: Just as important as the SL-7s' high speed and their efficiency in loading and unloading was their immediate availability. They were sitting there, ready to go, when the Pentagon needed them.

"If the ship's out being used someplace," by a commercial charterer, "you can't use it in a crisis like this," argued Appropriations member Norm Dicks, D-Wash.

Appropriations added to its defense spending bill $1.5 billion for ships similar to the SL-7s. The Appropriations Committee decided that the new ships could make do at lower speeds than their predecessors.

"That really drives the cost up," said Dicks, suggesting that 23 knots could be an acceptable speed. But the Appropriations panel wanted the new ships to be operated fire brigade-style, like the SL-7s: sitting in port, manned and ready.

House Appropriations also included in its defense bill two other sealift initiatives, appropriating:

- $900 million to build "prepositioning" ships: floating warehouses, packed with combat equipment and supplies, that could loiter unobtrusively near potential trouble spots, as did 13 such vessels the Navy already had in service. A few weeks after Bush gave the word, prepositioning ships based at Guam and Diego Garcia had disgorged in Saudi Arabia enough materiel for 30,000 Marines to fight for a month. "That was a major success story out of the Persian Gulf," Dicks said.
- $38 million for more frequent practice mobilization of some of the nearly 100 laid-up cargo ships, maintained by the Maritime Administration as the "ready reserve fleet." Of the first 41 ships mobilized for the gulf crisis, 10 were six to 20 days late in loading.

HOUSE FLOOR ACTION

The $268 billion defense appropriations bill passed by the House on Oct. 12 showed that the Pentagon still had a lot of the political top-spin it picked up from the crisis in the Persian Gulf.

But even with the 200,000 U.S. troops deployed against Iraq in October, the House rejected a 2 percent across-the-board cut by only a narrow margin. The close vote demonstrated a strong undercurrent of support for further cuts in defense when official Washington was in a paroxysm of budget maneuvering and the Soviet threat was receding.

The defense bill, passed 322-97, pared down the Pentagon's money and manpower — but by far smaller amounts than had seemed likely prior to Iraq's invasion of Kuwait on Aug. 2. *(Vote 455, p. 146-H)*

- The bill brought the total defense-related budget for fiscal 1991 to $288.3 billion, an amount approved by the Senate but $5.3 billion higher than the original House-passed defense ceiling. President Bush had requested $306.9 billion in his proposed budget in January.
- The bill also reduced the 2.1 million-member military payroll by 77,100 — less than either the 129,000 that would be cut by the House-passed version of the companion defense authorization bill or the 100,000 cutback called for in the Senate version of the authorization bill.

Some provisions of the appropriations bill responded to problems highlighted by the deployment of U.S. personnel

Continued on p. 816

Funding for Major Weapons

Following is a comparison of President Bush's request for major weapons programs in fiscal 1991, the amounts approved by the Senate and House, and the amounts provided in the final version of the defense appropriations bill (HR 5803 — PL 101-511).

Some amounts include money for spare parts or for components to be included in weapons to be funded in subsequent budgets.

The amounts are for procurement, except that lines labeled R&D indicate funds exclusively for research and development, and lines with an asterisk (*) include both procurement and R&D.

(Amounts in millions of dollars)

PROGRAM	Bush Request		Senate (S 3189)		House (HR 5803)		Final passage (HR 5803)	
	Number	Amount	Number	Amount	Number	Amount	Number	Amount
Strategic weapons								
B-2 bomber	5 [1]	$3,206	2	$2,756	0	$0	--	$2,349
Advanced cruise missile	100	366	100	366	100	314	100	366
Trident submarine	1	1,245	1	1,331	1	1,245	1	1,331
Trident II missile	52	1,536	52	1,536	52	1,536	52	1,536
MX rail procurement		1,346		0		0		0
MX rail R&D		548		548		445		688 [2]
Midgetman R&D		202		202		165		
Strategic defense initiative R&D [3]		4,460		3,573		2,300		2,890
SRAM-T air-launched nuclear missile R&D		119		119		119		119
Ground combat								
M-1 tank [4]	225	0	225	891	225	1,003	225	1,041
Bradley fighting vehicle	600	688	600	688	600	688	600	688
MLRS artillery rocket	24,000	314	24,000	314	36,000	403	36,000	403
ATACMS long-range conventional missile	318	187	318	187	318	187	318	187
LH armed helicopter R&D		411		261		300		291
Patriot anti-air missile	817	883	817	705	817	829	817	736
ADATS anti-air missile *	220	272		0		92		92
Transportation								
C-17 cargo plane *	6 [1]	1,909	0	300	2	1,004		460
V-22 Osprey *		0		38		403		403
CH-53E helicopter	23	435	12	282	15	299	12	315
Blackhawk helicopter	72	469	72	320	72	388	72	308
LHD helicopter carrier	1	960	1	960	1	934	1	960
LSD-41 amphibious ship	1	240	1	240	1	240	1	240
Naval warfare								
Aegis destroyer	5 [1]	3,566	4	3,109	4	3,109	4	3,209
Tomahawk cruise missiles	600	809	400	662	400	659	400	659
Seawolf-class sub	2 [1]	3,482	1	1,382	1	2,106	1	1,783
Tactical air combat								
F-15 Air Force fighter	36	1,201	36	1,700	36	1,474	36	1,544
F-16 Air Force fighter	150	2,357	88	1,672	108	1,857	108	1,857
F/A-18 Navy fighter	66	1,894	42	1,310	48	1,525	48	1,450
ATF fighter R&D		1,047		870		964		964
A-12 ground-attack plane [1]		1,502		592		592		592

[1] *Request subsequently was reduced.*

[2] *Includes R&D for both MX and Midgetman.*

[3] *Defense Department share of program.*

[4] *Includes modification program for existing tanks; administration request called for using $827 million left from prior years.*

Continued from p. 814
in and around Saudi Arabia after the Iraqi invasion. For instance, the measure earmarked nearly $2.5 billion to buy more cargo ships to haul the tanks and other heavy weapons of U.S. combat units to distant trouble spots.

More generally, however, the bill's pro-Pentagon tilt reflected members' reluctance to appear soft on defense at a time when U.S. interests faced a challenge from Iraq and U.S. troops were in the field.

"The Iraq thing obviously has changed the climate," said Matthew F. McHugh, D-N.Y.

But the House also had demonstrated a strong desire to restrain defense spending, McHugh added, citing the close vote on the 2-percent-cut amendment. That amendment, offered by Democrats Timothy J. Penny, Minn., and Charles E. Schumer, N.Y., was rejected 201-215. Republicans opposed it in a ratio of 2-to-1, but Democrats backed it by about 7-to-5. *(Vote 454, p. 146-H)*

The House also defeated two budget-reduction amendments by James A. Traficant Jr., D-Ohio: A 10 percent reduction was rejected by voice vote, and a 5 percent cut was defeated 97-319. *(Vote 453, p. 146-H)*

By voice vote, the House agreed to a third Traficant amendment cutting $400 million to reduce Pentagon parts inventories.

The Defense Appropriations Subcommittee initially drafted the Pentagon spending bill at $262.9 billion, the amount allowed by the House-passed version of the budget resolution. But the final version of the resolution adopted Oct. 9 set a ceiling of $288.3 billion on all defense-related appropriations. Counting defense funds in bills already passed, that left room for an additional $5.3 billion in the defense appropriations bill.

When the Appropriations Committee reviewed the defense bill Oct. 9, it adopted by voice vote an amendment by Defense Subcommittee Chairman John P. Murtha, D-Pa. to spend the entire $5.3 billion for assorted other projects.

On most contentious issues, the House appropriations bill conformed with positions embodied in the House-passed defense authorization bill. For instance, HR 5803 provided no funds for production of the B-2 stealth bomber and sliced $2.4 billion from Bush's request for SDI.

One exception was an air-launched, nuclear-armed missile designated SRAM-T. The authorization bill approved no funds for the missile, but the House spending bill included $119 million, as requested by the administration.

The House approved a compromise to appropriate funds for SRAM-T but permitted it to be spent only if the missile survived the authorization conference committee.

The key elements of the House-passed defense spending bill included:

Personnel Issues

Manpower levels. The administration budget called for reducing active-duty military manpower by 37,600. The cut of 77,100 imposed by the House bill would trim the administration's payroll request by $455 million.

To ensure that the Pentagon's civilian work force would be cut back in proportion with the uniformed services, the bill also cut $357 million from accounts that covered civilian pay.

And, to reflect a civilian hiring freeze that had been in effect at the Pentagon since early in the year, the House cut an additional $178 million from the budget request.

Pay. The House approved the 3.5 percent military pay raise proposed by the administration.

In its report on the bill, the Appropriations Committee ordered the Pentagon to propose legislation to reduce the plethora of bonuses and fringe benefits built into the military compensation system.

Medical programs. The bill approved $7.39 billion, as requested, for the Pentagon's medical programs. And it added to the budget $1.25 billion to cover an anticipated funding shortfall in CHAMPUS, a hospitalization insurance program for military dependents and retirees.

Reserves. In keeping with the strong support Congress typically accorded the National Guard and the reserve branches of the armed services, the bill rejected the administration's proposal to trim the number of reservists who drilled regularly from 1.18 million to 1.15 million.

The bill set a ceiling of 1,205,158 reservists, 23,000 higher than the fiscal 1990 ceiling. To fund the additional personnel, the bill added $184 million to the reserve components' budget accounts, most of which was offset by reductions in the amounts requested for active-duty forces.

Reserves' equipment. The administration had requested $455 million for equipment specifically earmarked for Guard and reserve units. But the House bill increased that amount to $1.57 billion. Nearly half the increase was accounted for by various cargo planes, helicopters and executive jets. That House-passed total did not include the value of additional items funded in the services' budget accounts but earmarked by the Appropriations panel for the Guard or reserves.

In its report, the Appropriations Committee ordered the Pentagon to draw up a plan to replace some active-duty units stationed in Europe with Guard and reserve units serving for a few weeks at a time.

Operations and Maintenance

Reflecting the growing congressional demands that allied governments pick up more of the cost of stationing U.S. forces on their territory, the bill cut a total of $1.46 billion from the amounts requested for the operation and maintenance of overseas bases and the pay of foreign nationals employed at those sites.

The House bill also nearly doubled, to $1.55 billion, the amount requested to clean up toxic waste on military bases and former bases. The administration had asked for $817 million.

But the bill trimmed $198 million from the amount requested for drug-interdiction activities, approving $1.01 billion.

Strategic and Nuclear Systems

B-2 bomber. Echoing the action taken by the House on the defense authorization bill, the appropriations measure eliminated the entire $3.83 billion requested for production of the B-2 bomber, while approving the $1.57 billion requested to continue development of the plane.

ACM. The House also approved $383 million of the $473 million requested for production of the so-called advanced cruise missile (ACM). It flew farther and faster and was harder for radars to detect than the cruise missiles deployed in the mid-1980s.

The appropriations measure would pay for 100 missiles in fiscal 1991, as requested. But the Appropriations Committee ordered the Air Force to slow the planned pace of production and drop one of the two contractors building the weapon.

The committee acknowledged that the Pentagon had saved money on several weapons by making two firms bid against each other for production contracts. But with defense budgets shrinking, the number of weapons of a given type purchased in one year might be too small to justify keeping two firms in business, the committee warned.

Submarine-launched missiles. The House also approved $1.34 billion for 52 Trident II submarine-launched missiles and $1.24 billion for the 18th and last of the big submarines designed to carry those weapons. In each case, it was the full amount requested.

ICBM. For intercontinental ballistic missile (ICBM) programs, the House recommended essentially the amounts included in the House-passed defense authorization bill:

- $618 million of the $758 million requested to develop two mobile intercontinental ballistic missiles — a rail-launched version of the 10-warhead MX and the much smaller, single-warhead Midgetman.
- None of the $1.1 billion requested to begin procurement of the rail-mobile launching system for the MX.
- $655 million of the $672 million requested for 12 MX missiles to be used in test launches.

BSTS. For the Defense Department's share of the SDI antimissile research program, the administration initially requested $4.46 billion.

The Pentagon later shifted $265 million of that total to the Air Force for a satellite designated BSTS. The satellite had been intended to detect and track Soviet missiles, but after SDI managers dropped it, the Air Force picked it up as a replacement for its fleet of early-warning satellites.

SDI. Reflecting earlier House action on the defense authorization bill, the spending bill sliced SDI funding to $2.3 billion. It also included a provision that would boost from $22 million to $50 million the amount spent on a so-called red team — a group of technical experts charged with trying to anticipate enemy countermoves that could thwart the planned antimissile defense.

The provision, sponsored by SDI critic Les AuCoin, D-Ore., also would make the red team bureaucratically independent of the SDI development organization, placing it under a committee of technical experts drawn from outside government and from the Energy Department's national weapons laboratories.

Separate from the SDI funds, the House included in the bill $260 million to wrap up the existing BSTS contract and stage a competition among satellite builders to select a new early-warning satellite.

Also separate from the SDI total was $250 million the House appropriated to develop defenses against short-range missiles, such as those deployed by Iraq and several Asian countries.

Long-range radar. On the basis of fiscal constraints, the House approved only $148 million of the $247 million requested to develop systems intended to protect North America against bombers and cruise missiles. Of the amount appropriated, at least $53 million would go to develop a fleet of blimps toting long-range radars to detect aerial intruders.

The administration included in its antidrug-smuggling program $241 million to continue building a network of long-range, ground-based radars previously justified as a bomber detection screen. Dismissing that proposal as a "budget ploy," the Appropriations Committee declared that it would not even consider using drug war money to build the radars.

But the House did include in the bill $25 million to test whether the radars, designed to detect high-speed bombers and cruise missiles, also could detect drug smuggling aircraft, which typically were small and much slower. And it added $6 million to adapt the prototype radar for anti-smuggling operations.

Ground Combat

The House recommended a much more ambitious tank production program than the administration requested and added more than $1.1 billion to pay for it.

M-1 tank. The administration's plan would have used $747 million left from previous budgets to buy 225 M-1 tanks: 162 of the A1 version that was already in service, followed by the first 63 of the new A2 version, with improved optical equipment for driving and fighting at night. After that, the M-1 production line would be mothballed.

The plan was doomed from a budgetary standpoint because Congress had allocated the leftover money for other purposes.

Aside from that, the Appropriations Committee objected to cutting off tank production and complained that the Pentagon's timetable would rush the A2 version, with its complex new electronic equipment and associated computer software, into production prematurely.

Instead, the House added to the bill $808 million to buy 300 A1 model tanks in fiscal 1991 and $150 million to buy components that could be used in fiscal 1992 to begin building the A2 model.

The House also added $144 million to begin upgrading the 3,000 tanks of the first-generation model M1, giving some the larger cannon and other improvements included in the A1 version.

Rockets. The measure provided for $403 million for 36,000 bombardment rockets, instead of the $314 million requested for 24,000 rockets.

However, it recommended only $181 million of the $207 million requested to rebuild existing mobile artillery pieces to shoot farther and more accurately. Rising costs had brought the program "to the brink of unaffordability," the Appropriations Committee complained.

Contending that the price of modifying each gun had quadrupled, Army officials warned that they might take the project away from BMY Corp., in York, Pa., and award it to another contractor or to the nearby Letterkenny Army Depot.

New combat vehicles. The Army asked for $176 million for a broad-gauged program to develop a new generation of combat vehicles — including a tank, a troop carrier and a mobile artillery piece — intended to save money by sharing components such as the engine and suspension.

The Appropriations Committee approved the general approach. Like the Senate and House Armed Services panels, however, it ordered the Army to place a higher priority on the new artillery piece.

Mobile cannons, antitank missiles. The committee also added to the bill $40 million to buy lightly armored mobile cannons — with perhaps half the weight and twice the speed of the Army's existing artillery. These would equip units intended for rapid overseas deployment by aircraft.

Pointing to recent bids that came in lower than anticipated, the Appropriations Committee trimmed $20 million from the amount requested for Hellfire antitank missiles — $145 million would suffice to buy the 4,200 missiles, it concluded.

Despite Pentagon objections, the Appropriations Committee added to the budget $200 million to continue equipping small "scout" helicopters with sophisticated target-finding equipment and lasers to steer Hellfire missiles into enemy tanks.

But the panel also approved $195 million of the $219 million requested to develop a new radar guidance system for the Hellfire, which would be added onto existing antitank helicopters.

Joint STARS. In one of the most significant departures from the authorization bill, which would cancel the program, the appropriations bill included the $419 million requested to continue development and begin production of a system intended to knock out tank columns up to 100 miles behind enemy lines. The project used airborne radars (designated Joint STARS) to steer ground-launched ATACMS missiles toward such targets.

But the House approved only $24 million of the $177 million requested to develop three other antitank weapons intended to knock out tanks at long range using aerial bombs, artillery and bombardment rockets. In each case, the Appropriations Committee complained of rising costs, slipping deadlines and uncertain Army plans.

On the other hand, the House approved the requests for $73 million to develop a replacement for the TOW missile, the Army's mainline antitank weapon. It also approved $93 million to continue development and prepare for production of a smaller, more portable antitank missile designated AAWS-M.

Anti-aircraft missiles. In general, the House supported the requests to continue production of anti-aircraft missiles already in service, approving:

- $252 million, as requested, for nearly 7,000 shoulder-fired, short-range Stingers.
- $92 million, of $97 million requested, for 88 Avengers — basically pickup trucks rigged to carry a battery of Stinger launchers.
- $829 million of $883 million requested for 817 long-range Patriot missiles. This included $248 million to buy missiles that would be used by Italian forces to protect U.S. installations in Italy. But the measure barred use of the funds earmarked for Italy until that country's parliament appropriated funds for its share of the joint project.

The ADATS anti-aircraft missile, intended to protect armored units on the front lines, was not ready for production, the Appropriations Committee concluded. So the measure denied the $272 million requested to begin production, instead adding $92 million to the Army's research budget for additional ADATS testing.

The Defense Appropriations Subcommittee had denied the $99 million requested for another anti-aircraft missile, designated FOG-M, intended to strike helicopters lurking out of sight, behind ridgelines or trees. But when Defense Subcommittee Chairman Murtha was deciding which programs to include in the $5.3 billion add-on, Interior Subcommittee Chairman Tom Bevill, D-Ala., put in a plug for FOG-M, which would be built in his district. The House bill included the full $99 million.

Tactical Air Combat

Fighter planes. The administration budgeted $1.7 billion to buy 36 F-15Es, used by the Air Force for long-range ground-attack missions. But it assumed that $500 million of that amount could be drawn from funds previously appropriated for other projects. Because Congress had rejected that approach, the House approved $1.47 billion to cover the cost of the planes.

To slow production of the Air Force's F-16 fighter, the House recommended $1.86 billion for 108 planes instead of the $2.36 billion requested for 150 aircraft.

It approved the request for $780 million to equip a dozen of the Navy's F-14 fighters with new engines and radars. But the Appropriations panel contended that the Navy and Marine Corps had nearly as many F/A-18 fighters as would be needed given the force cuts in prospect. The bill provided for 48 planes ($1.52 billion) instead of the 66 requested ($1.89 billion).

To continue production of the Navy's new A-12 carrier-based ground-attack plane (formerly designated ATA), the House approved $610 million of the $1.60 billion requested. In April, Cheney announced unspecified reductions in the program because of budget limits and a projected reduction in the number of aircraft carriers.

Because a slowdown in A-12 production would keep the Vietnam War-era A-6Es in service longer than planned, the House boosted from $84 million to $184 million the amount appropriated to modernize those planes.

On Jan 7, 1991, Cheney announced cancellation of the troubled A-120.

To continue development of the Air Force's new ATF fighter, the House approved $964 million of the $1.05 billion requested.

Air-to-air missiles. The House approved only 900 AMRAAM air-to-air missiles (at $815 million) instead of the 1,800 requested (at $1.31 billion). The production rate was not to be stepped up until the two contractors had demonstrated "irrefutably" that they had solved the problems that plagued the program, the Appropriations Committee declared.

Antiradar missiles. Test failures also were behind the decision to deny $227 million requested for production of an antiradar missile designated Tacit Rainbow. The House measure provided $27 million for additional tests.

The House approved the $370 million requested to buy 1,440 HARM antiradar missiles. But this was another case in which the Appropriations Committee concluded that declining budgets barred the Pentagon from buying enough copies of a weapon to reap the benefits of playing two contractors against one another. It ordered the Navy to drop one of the two HARM contractors.

Naval Combat

Like many other Pennsylvania-based projects, the Navy's so-called SLEP program to rebuild aircraft carriers at the Philadelphia Navy Yard fared well at the hands of the Defense Subcommittee; subcommittee Chairman Murtha and ranking Republican Joseph M. McDade were both from Pennsylvania.

Initially, the subcommittee approved the request for $113 million to begin stockpiling components for work on the *John F. Kennedy*, scheduled to begin in 1993. But when the defense budget was allocated the additional $5.3 billion by budget negotiators, the subcommittee boosted the SLEP account to $963 million.

Tomahawk cruise missiles. The House approved $659 million for 400 Tomahawk cruise missiles, which were carried by more than 100 warships and submarines. The budget requested $809 million for 600 missiles.

Surface-to-surface missiles. The Defense Subcommittee had turned down the $44 million request for Penguin surface-to-surface missiles — small weapons of Norwegian design to be carried by helicopters and patrol boats. But the funds were included in the full committee's last-minute add-on amendment.

Aegis anti-aircraft system. The president's budget

requested five destroyers equipped with the powerful Aegis anti-aircraft system ($3.57 billion). But in August, Defense Secretary Cheney pared back that request to four ships ($3.11 billion), the number approved by the House.

Initial production of a new version of the Standard anti-aircraft missile had been delayed so the House approved $346 million for 600 missiles instead of the $608 million requested for 900 missiles.

RAM. The House bill called for canceling the RAM short-range anti-aircraft missile — a joint U.S.-German project under development since 1976. The General Accounting Office and its counterpart agency in the German government had blasted the program for rising costs, incomplete tests and inadequate performance.

Submarines. Again reflecting Cheney's revision of the shipbuilding budget in August, the House approved one *Seawolf*-class submarine ($1.46 billion), instead of the two ships requested in January ($2.34 billion).

In light of the Navy's cancellation of a program to develop the P-7 long-range antisubmarine plane, the House dropped $256 million that had been requested for the project. It boosted from $294 million to $328 million the funds for modernization of the fleet of P-3C patrol planes, which the P-7s were to replace.

Sonobouys. The Appropriations Committee accused the Navy of budgetary gamesmanship in requesting only $71 million for sonobouys — small listening devices dropped from planes and helicopters to detect submarines. In each of the past several years, Congress had boosted the sonobouy budget because the Navy's request would have forced the service to dip into wartime stocks for routine training. Once again, the committee said, the Navy was relying on Congress to provide extra money for the account.

"To encourage the Navy to budget responsibly," the committee declared, it included only the $71 million requested but added a provision requiring the Navy to scrape up from within its budget an additional $89 million to bring the sonobouy total to $160 million.

Minesweepers. Because of production delays and cost increases in the production of small minesweepers, the House approved only two of the ships ($204 million) instead of the three requested ($268 million). But the Appropriations Committee emphasized that this slowdown would not affect the Navy's decision to base two of the minesweepers at Astoria, Ore., which was represented by Defense Subcommittee member AuCoin.

Cargo Planes, Landing Ships

Amphibious landing ships. The House approved virtually without change the amounts requested for amphibious landing ships, designed to launch Marine Corps assaults against defended beaches:

- $934 million (of $960 million requested) for a helicopter carrier able to haul 2,000 Marines.
- $240 million, as requested, for an LSD-type cargo ship to carry tanks and other heavy equipment along with barges to haul them ashore.
- $245 million for a dozen air-cushion landing barges, able to carry a 60-ton tank to the beach at 50 mph.

V-22 Osprey. Overruling Cheney, the House kept alive the hybrid airplane/helicopter the Marine Corps wanted as a troop transport. The House added to the bill $403 million to continue development and set up a production line.

As an alternative to the Osprey for the Marine mission, Cheney had requested $377 million for 23 big CH-53E helicopters ($377 million). The House approved 15 of the helicopters ($241 million) for assignment to the Naval Reserve.

C-17 cargo plane. Consistent with Cheney's decision in April to slow down several aircraft programs, the House also reduced the budget for the C-17 wide-body, intercontinental cargo plane. It approved $1.54 billion for C-17 production instead of the $2.45 billion requested in January. However, the Appropriations Committee warned that any deeper funding cuts might disrupt the program, resulting in thousands of layoffs.

SENATE COMMITTEE ACTION

The B-2 survived another attack on its funding Oct. 11, as the Senate Appropriations Committee narrowly defeated a motion to slash money for the stealth bomber.

The action came as the committee approved its $268.8 billion defense appropriations bill for fiscal 1991.

Not only did amendment sponsor Patrick J. Leahy, D-Vt., lose the vote, he suffered his defeat at the hands of a fellow Democrat who agreed that funding for the B-2 ought to be cut.

B-2 Survives

The markup of the defense spending measure had been relatively routine until Leahy offered his amendment to cut $2.75 billion from the B-2 program, which would kill the program outright after the six test planes under construction were completed.

Both Appropriations Committee Chairman Byrd and Defense Subcommittee Chairman Inouye had implored members not to offer amendments on controversial subjects that would also be debated on the Senate floor.

But supporters of the bomber program had been winning their cause by fewer votes each year. On Aug. 3, an amendment Leahy offered on the Senate floor to the defense authorization bill to cut the B-2 program managed to get the support of 43 senators. *(Vote 208, p. 72-H)*

Going into the Appropriations Committee session, Leahy knew that a majority of the panel's 29 members had voted for his amendment on the floor in August.

Leahy's confidence also was bolstered by the latest revelations of trouble for the B-2 and its prime contractor, the Northrop Corp. On the morning of Oct. 11, Donald Rice, secretary of the Air Force, told the Senate Armed Services Committee that the first flight of the second B-2 in production would be delayed by nine months because of problems at Northrop and funding cuts.

That setback followed testimony to House members by Air Force investigators about serious cost accounting and production problems they had found at Northrop.

Even one of the plane's foremost supporters, Jim Exon, D-Neb., conceded at the Armed Services hearing, "The B-2 program is in big, big trouble."

While the Appropriations panel was considering its bill, Senate-House conferees on the companion defense authorization bill remained deadlocked over the B-2, with Senate Armed Services Chairman Nunn determined to save the program and House Armed Services Chairman Les Aspin, D-Wis., just as vigorously opposed to further production.

"We're hanging on by stealthy fingers," Nunn said.

During the appropriations meeting, Leahy argued that the B-2 was costly and unnecessary: "Our greatest threat to national security is not the Soviet Union, but our spiraling national deficit."

Inouye countered that it was premature to assert that

the Soviet Union had changed. Referring to Soviet President Mikhail S. Gorbachev, Inouye said: "With all the pleasant speeches we've heard from Mr. Gorbachev, the facts just don't support it."

President Bush also added his muscle to the debate.

Inouye's staff passed out an Oct. 11 letter from Bush warning that he would veto the entire defense spending bill if senators cut the $2.75 billion from the B-2.

After his defense of the bomber, Inouye made a motion to table, or kill, Leahy's amendment. That was when Leahy's plan began to fall apart.

Harry Reid, D-Nev., voted against the Leahy amendment, which went down to defeat 15-14. Reid said that he felt the proper place to debate funding for the B-2 was on the Senate floor.

Leahy was clearly taken aback by the vote. He had Reid's proxy in his pocket, although Reid later blamed an aide for providing it without permission. As the meeting ended, Leahy turned to Reid and said angrily, "I never would have offered it if I knew you were going to do that."

Leahy also lost the support of Byrd, who had voted for his amendment earlier in the year. But Byrd's loss, while a surprise for Leahy, was balanced by Wyche Fowler Jr., D-Ga., who had changed his position and decided to oppose the bomber.

Other Provisions

The Defense appropriations bill unanimously approved by the Senate Appropriations Committee would provide defense programs under its jurisdiction about $20 billion less than those programs received in fiscal 1990 and nearly $14 billion less than Bush requested. Inouye said it reflected the "fact-of-life changes" in the world.

SDI would receive $3.5 billion in fiscal 1991, a cut of more than $1 billion from Bush's request but $1.3 billion more than the House included in its spending bill.

Inouye touted the SDI funding as a bargaining chip that would "protect the Senate position on many other items in conference with the House."

The committee also approved a motion by Dale Bumpers, D-Ark., to slow development of the SDI program "brilliant pebbles," miniature heat-seeking missiles intended to destroy Soviet missiles as they blasted into space. Bush had embraced brilliant pebbles as the key to any development of SDI in the next decade.

Language to slow brilliant pebbles was also part of the Senate-passed defense authorization bill. But Bumpers offered the amendment, crafted by Jeff Bingaman, D-N.M., and Richard C. Shelby, D-Ala., to ensure that the language remained in defense spending legislation, should the authorization conferees decide to take it out.

SENATE FLOOR ACTION

The Senate approved a $268.2 billion defense appropriations measure (S 3189), 79-16, on Oct. 15, but only after many members voiced frustration that U.S. allies were not paying more of the defense burden. *(Vote 273, p. 55-S)*

Compared with Bush's January budget request, the bill reduced Pentagon appropriations by $19 billion. It provided $16.2 billion less than had been appropriated in the corresponding bill for fiscal 1990.

The Senate rejected by only four votes, 46-50, an amendment that would have sliced the number of U.S. troops stationed in Europe by 80,000 instead of the 50,000-person reduction imposed by the bill. *(Vote 271, p. 54-S)*

Complaints that allied governments were sponging off the U.S. defense effort had festered on Capitol Hill since the mid-1970s.

Kent Conrad, D-N.D., author of the troop-cut amendment, contended that sentiment was swinging his way because of the severity of the U.S. budget crunch and because of dissatisfaction with shouldering the load of protecting U.S. allies' economic interests in the Persian Gulf.

"It is time to send a clear and unmistakable message to our allies that they must take on a greater share of this common defense burden," he said.

Conrad's amendment was rejected for the second time, but also by a narrower margin. It had been killed on a tabling motion, 59-40, when he offered it to the defense authorization bill Aug. 3. *(Vote 213, p. 44-S)*

On most issues, the Senate appropriations bill reprised the positions taken by the Senate in the authorization bill it passed Aug. 4.

The Senate remained unmoved from its position of early August on the B-2 stealth bomber. It continued to back the controversial and costly plane, although an amendment by Leahy to cut off B-2 production failed by a narrower margin than in August.

Backers of the B-2 had hoped that Iraq's seizure of Kuwait and its threat to the oil fields of Saudi Arabia and neighboring sheikdoms would dramatize the new plane's value for long-range attacks with conventional bombs.

The Senate appropriations bill provided $268.2 billion for Pentagon programs in fiscal 1991, exclusive of military construction projects funded in the separate bill.

'Burden-Sharing'

The Senate bill reduced the number of active-duty military personnel by 100,000 and required a reduction of 50,000 in the number deployed in Europe.

Conrad's amendment would have reduced the ceiling on U.S. personnel stationed in Europe by 80,000, to 231,000. It also would have reduced total military manpower by the same number, to a ceiling of 1,946,000.

Both limits would have been waived in case of a declaration of war or national emergency. And U.S. personnel in Europe whose costs were paid by NATO countries would not have counted against the ceiling on troops in Europe.

The Bush administration's budget request would have reduced total military manpower by 37,600 to 2,038,800. In August, the administration announced that the number of U.S. troops in Europe alone would be reduced by 40,000.

During the brief and sparsely attended debate, Conrad hammered at the argument that U.S. deployments in Europe and the Pacific were protecting German and Japanese interests, which those countries now could better afford to protect themselves.

"Germany says they cannot send troops to the [Persian] Gulf because of their constitution; Japan says the same thing," Conrad declared. "There is nothing in their constitutions that prevents them from paying for their own defense."

Defense Subcommittee Chairman Inouye warned against too sanguine an assessment of the Soviet military threat. But he concentrated mostly on the tangible effects of Conrad's amendment in cutting the military payroll by 150,000 instead of 100,000, as recommended by his panel.

That large a reduction in one year would require the government to break enlistment contracts with tens of thousands of service personnel, Inouye said, harming the morale of those who remained and making a military career less attractive. "You do not entice men and women to serve in uniform if we do not provide them stability," he warned.

Seven senators who opposed Conrad's amendment in August supported it this time. The switchers included conservatives Gordon J. Humphrey, R-N.H., and Richard C. Shelby, D-Ala., as well as liberals Dale Bumpers, D-Ark., and Bob Kerrey, D-Neb. Other senators who switched to support Conrad were Republicans William S. Cohen of Maine, Bob Packwood of Oregon and Alfonse M. D'Amato of New York.

The Senate also adopted by voice vote several other amendments reflecting the "burden-sharing" theme:

- By Conrad, reducing the number of U.S. military personnel stationed in Japan by 10,000 per year, except for those whose costs were paid in full by Japan.
- By John McCain, R-Ariz., requiring a quarterly report by the president to Congress on contributions made by other countries to Operation Desert Shield, the military deployment against Iraq.
- By Donald W. Riegle Jr., D-Mich., expressing the sense of Congress that the president should negotiate with the principal U.S. allies a formula for more equitable distribution of the burden of "common security objectives."

The Senate also adopted by voice vote an amendment by Alan J. Dixon, D-Ill., that would put a hold on a pending deal under which South Korea would build F/A-18 fighter planes for its own use, until 15 days after the agreement had been sent to Congress.

B-2 Bomber

The debate on Leahy's B-2 amendment was essentially a rerun of the authorization battle in August.

The amendment would have deleted from the bill $2.7 billion for B-2 procurement. It would have allowed the Pentagon to finish building six planes in order to test the new technologies embodied in the design.

A combination of the plane's shape and its exotic materials were supposed to make it impossible for an enemy to locate it with sufficient precision to shoot it down. But those factors also drove its high cost — between $450 million and $850 million per copy, according to competing estimates. Leahy and his allies argued that the plane's cost was unbearable and that its mission had been overtaken by history: The budget deficit, Bumpers warned, was "a greater threat to this country than the Soviet air defense system," which the bomber was designed to penetrate.

But supporters of the plane mounted a vigorous defense, none more strongly than Nunn. He insisted that the B-2 was "a revolutionary airplane that's going to change the nature of warfare . . . in our favor."

While arguing that the plane would be valuable in nonnuclear conflicts, Nunn also contended that it was so essential to U.S. strategic planning that the U.S.-Soviet strategic arms reduction treaty (START), nearing completion, would have to be renegotiated if the B-2 were canceled.

That brought a retort from Armed Services Committee member Tim Wirth, D-Colo. "We don't have to be blackmailed to spend $35 billion [on B-2 production] to get an arms control agreement," he said.

Leahy's amendment, rejected 43-56 on Aug. 2, was rejected 44-50 on Oct. 15. *(Vote 272, p. 54-S)*

When account was taken of absences and votes on a related amendment in August, only two senators switched unambiguously from support for the B-2 in August to opposition in October:

- James A. McClure, R-Idaho, who told reporters that his vote was intended as a protest against the way the Air Force had treated an Idaho firm in a long-running dispute.
- Bob Graham, D-Fla., who attributed his change of mind to "the new security priorities which the gulf crisis have dramatized at a time when budgets are constrained."

Personnel Issues

Manpower, pay. Because the Senate bill trimmed the Pentagon payroll by 100,000 active-duty service personnel, it reduced the personnel accounts by $1.10 billion and the operating accounts by an additional $250 million.

An additional cut of $3 million from the payroll request was intended to ensure that the number of generals and admirals was cut back in proportion to the overall force reduction.

On the assumption that a civilian hiring freeze inaugurated by Defense Secretary Cheney in January would remain partly in effect, the bill reduced the Pentagon's civilian payroll by $1.11 billion.

Medical benefits. The bill included $2.87 billion for CHAMPUS, a hospitalization program for military dependents. However, the bill also included provisions aimed at restraining that program's ballooning costs. For example, it tripled the annual deductible paid by CHAMPUS beneficiaries from $50 per individual ($100 per family) to $150 per individual ($300 per family). Dependents of enlisted personnel in the lowest ranks were exempt from the deductible payments.

Reserves, National Guard, equipment. The bill trimmed by about 1,800 the 1.15 million National Guard and reserve personnel who drilled regularly. However, it rejected the Pentagon's proposal to disband 14 Air Force Reserve and Air National Guard units.

The bill included $2.5 billion for equipment earmarked for Guard and reserve units, an increase of $2 billion over the amount requested. Of the amount added, $390 million was for 14 Hercules cargo planes; an additional $511 million was earmarked for smaller airplanes and helicopters.

Operations and Maintenance

To cover operating expenses other than the military payroll, the Senate gave the Pentagon $83.2 billion, amounting to a net reduction of $5.53 billion from the budget request.

Reflecting changes in the economic facts of life, the Senate made two large additions to the budget request: $2.36 billion to pay oil prices $16 per barrel higher than had been projected when the budget was drawn up and $248 million to cover the rise in the cost of overseas operations because of the dollar's declining value relative to the German mark and the Japanese yen.

The bill also made "green eyeshade" cuts that reflected the Appropriations Committee's routine scrutiny of the budget request in search of waste. For instance, the Senate cut the following:

- $560 million from the request for spare parts. The committee cited various objections by the General Accounting Office about the services' management of their parts inventories.
- $550 million from the request for purchasing and operating data processing systems. The Appropriations panel complained that the services were duplicating efforts to develop Pentagon-wide information systems.
- $100 million from the request for overhauls of Air Force planes. The committee ordered that service to follow the Navy's lead by overhauling aircraft only after an in-

spection showed they needed it, rather than performing the work routinely at set intervals.

Some Senate reductions reflected the mounting congressional sentiment for cutting the cost of overseas deployments. The bill cut $200 million from the amount requested to transfer military personnel between assignments. And it cut an additional $207 million from the payroll for foreign nationals employed at U.S. bases overseas.

Other reductions in the operations and maintenance budget were linked to the easing of tensions with the Soviet Union and anticipated reductions in the size of the U.S. military. For example, the bill included none of the $565 million requested to boost the stockpiles of fuel and parts held for wartime use. It also cut:

- $119 million from the request for recruiting costs, including advertising.
- $100 million, on the assumption that older weapons that needed to be maintained and kept in service when the military balance with the Soviets was less favorable would quickly be retired.
- $600 million from the request for facility maintenance.
- $262 million from the request for routine base operating costs.

Aid to Israel

The bill included several provisions beneficial to Israel, reflecting the determination of some key members to bolster that country at a time when it faced the threat of attack from Iraq and international criticism for its treatment of Palestinians.

One such provision made Israeli firms eligible to bid for contracts to overhaul U.S. weaponry located in Europe. The Appropriations Committee urged the Pentagon, and particularly the Air Force, to foster new maintenance and repair capabilities in Israel.

Another provision permitted the transfer of surplus U.S. military equipment to "NATO allies which are contiguous to Iraq" — in other words, Turkey — "and to major, non-NATO allies on the southern and southeastern flank of NATO which do not receive financial assistance from any country in the Near East region" — namely Israel.

The Senate earmarked $15 million of the Navy's operations and maintenance appropriation as the minimum that would be spent to upgrade port facilities in Israel used by ships of the Mediterranean-based Sixth Fleet.

The Appropriations Committee urged the Navy to consider using Ashdod, in southern Israel, as a routine port of call on the Mediterranean Sea in addition to Haifa, farther north.

The bill also mandated establishment in Israel of a large fuel depot, for wartime use.

The committee urged the Pentagon to buy an Israeli-designed gunboat for commando missions.

Within the $3.57 billion appropriation for the SDI anti-missile program, the bill earmarked $42 million to continue support of the Israeli Arrow missile, designed to deal with short-range missiles such as those deployed by Iraq.

Strategic Arms

The bill's treatment of long-range bomber programs illustrated the Appropriations Committee's decision to curb spending on existing weapons in order to free up money for new technologies.

B-2 bomber. Like the companion authorization measure, the appropriations bill approved the pared-back B-2 program Cheney unveiled in April: $1.75 billion to continue development of the plane and $2.76 billion to continue production at a slow pace.

Bomber modification. The bill provided only $69 million of the $110 million requested to modify the fleet of 30-year-old B-52Gs and B-52Hs. More than half the 254 planes still in service were "G" models with old engines, which the Appropriations Committee predicted would not remain in service for very long.

The bill also sliced by $13 million, to $122 million, the appropriation for modifying 97 B-1Bs built in the mid-1980s. With billions of dollars earmarked for the B-2, it was "inappropriate" to spend money to boost the capability of existing bombers, the committee said.

On the other hand, a few hundred 1960s-vintage aerial tankers used to refuel bombers and other craft in midair would continue in service for another three decades, under existing plans. So the bill increased by $100 million, to $732 million, the amount appropriated to renovate tanker planes with new, more powerful engines.

Cruise missiles. For 100 advanced cruise missiles — bomber-launched weapons with a range of about 2,000 miles — the bill included $473 million, as requested, including funds for components to be used to build more missiles in future years.

However, the bill provided only $10 million of the $21 million requested to prepare for production of a shorter-range bomber missile designated SRAM II. According to the committee, the program was being delayed by one of the software design problems that plagued many new weapons programs.

ICBMs. For intercontinental ballistic missiles, the Senate appropriated essentially the amounts it had authorized:

- $758 million to develop two mobile weapons — a rail-launched version of the 10-warhead MX and the much smaller, single-warhead Midgetman.
- None of the $1.1 billion requested to begin production of the rail-mobile MX launchers.
- $580 million for 12 MXs to be used in test launches, a reduction of $94 million compared with the Senate-passed authorization bill. The $94 million was left over from prior appropriations because competitive bidding yielded lower-than-anticipated prices for MX guidance equipment, the Appropriations Committee said.

Trident. Like the other congressional committees dealing with defense, Senate Appropriations decided that the huge Trident missile-launching submarine requested — the 18th of the class — should be the last. So the bill included none of the $143 million requested for components to build more ships. But it boosted the Trident sub appropriation by $87 million, to $1.33 billion, with the increase intended to cover some of the costs of wrapping up production of the subs.

As requested, the bill included $1.54 billion to build Trident II sub-launched missiles. But it included only $71 million of the $92 million requested for further development of the Trident II: Since the missile had been operational only since March and since it already was accurate enough to deal with most targets, the committee saw no need to try to improve it.

SDI. For the Pentagon's share of SDI, the bill included $3.57 billion of the $4.46 billion requested.

But of the $887 million cut from the request, $137 million had been earmarked for the BSTS missile-detection satellite. The bill shifted the BSTS funds to the Air Force budget, increased it to a total of $152 million, and earmarked the funds for a competition among satellite builders to select a new attack warning satellite.

ASAT. The amounts requested to develop antisatellite weapons, totaling nearly a quarter of a billion dollars, were trimmed by about one-fourth in the Senate bill. The $208 million requested for ground-launched ASAT missiles could be cut to $158 million, the committee said, because of lower-than-anticipated contract prices. The $41 million requested for ground-based ASAT lasers was reduced to $25 million because the Pentagon had slowed down the laser program.

Ground Combat

M-1 tanks. The bill included $747 million to buy M-1 tanks for the Army. The administration had planned to spend the same amount for tanks, but using funds left over from prior budgets. However, that money subsequently was used for other programs, so the Appropriations Committee added new budget authority to cover the tanks.

Tanks, artillery. The committee objected to the administration's plan to use the money to build 163 "A1" models of the tank, and then build the first 62 of an improved "A2" model, before shutting down the production line. Insisting that the new model needed more testing, the committee ordered the Army to use all of the money to build A1 model tanks. It also included $64 million to begin upgrading the earliest model M-1s to the A2 version, after the new model had been tested.

The bill included none of the $207 million requested to begin rebuilding existing mobile howitzers. Observing that the program was six years old and still had not produced a modernized cannon at an acceptable cost, the Appropriations panel warned that future funding for the project was "in serious jeopardy."

The committee also ordered far-reaching changes in the Army's programs to develop a new generation of tanks and artillery, and it amended the bill accordingly.

The budget request included $177 million to develop a so-called Block III tank to replace the M-1, plus $46 million to develop a 140mm gun for the new vehicle. But the Senate bill included only $64 million for the new tank and none of the funds requested for the big cannon.

In its report, the Appropriations Committee contended that the new tank program could be deferred because the Soviet military threat was receding and existing M-1s could be upgraded to the A2 model.

More fundamentally, however, the committee challenged the thrust of the Army's thinking about a new tank: "The Army needs to develop lighter, lethal, more deployable tanks rather than building yet another main battle tank weighing 60 to 70 tons," the panel said. "Realistically, the Block III tank will be a 70-ton tank that will take weeks or months to reach any potential battlefield."

Ammunition. The Senate bill also added to the budget $15 million for research on a more powerful kind of ammunition for the 120mm guns carried by late-model M-1s and $12 million for a new cannon technology.

To encourage development of a new mobile artillery piece, the Senate bill included $22 million, rather than the $4 million requested for the artillery project.

On the other hand, the panel rejected the Army's plan to hold a competition to select what type of armored car equipped with 105mm cannon it should buy "off-the-shelf" to equip the 82nd Airborne Division. The committee ordered the Army to buy the cannon-equipped version of the so-called Light Armored Vehicle used by the Marine Corps.

Antitank missiles. The bill included $185 million to buy nearly 11,000 TOW antitank missiles, omitting an additional $44 million that the administration had initially requested to buy 3,000 more missiles from a second contractor. After the budget was submitted in January, the Army decided that it could not afford to buy enough TOW missiles in future years to keep two contractors in business bidding against each other.

The program to develop the so-called LOSAT antitank missile launcher, a proposed replacement for TOW, had fallen behind schedule, so the Senate bill included only $31 million of the $73 million requested.

But the bill included the amounts requested for three other future tank-killers:

- $99 million to develop a missile intended to hunt out hidden tanks with a TV camera in its nose that would be linked to the launcher by six miles of fiber-optic cable.
- $106 million to develop antitank warheads that could be dispensed from artillery shells or rockets at a distance of 10-20 miles.
- $187 million to begin production of the so-called ATACMS missile, intended to scatter antitank warheads over enemy tank columns up to 100 miles away. However, the bill included only $176 million of the $278 million requested to continue development of the JSTARS airborne radar, intended to steer ATACMS missiles toward their targets.

The bill included $172 million of the $220 million requested to test a new radar on Apache attack helicopters to find tanks and guide missiles into them.

It included $315 million of the $465 million requested to develop a new, smaller armed helicopter, designated LH. But the Senate rejected the request for $26 million to hang antitank missiles on existing "scout" helicopters.

Anti-aircraft missiles. The bill included $705 million of the $883 million requested for Patriot long-range anti-aircraft missiles: The balance of $178 million could be made up from funds left over from prior appropriations, the Appropriations Committee said.

In addition, the Senate bill omitted the $272 million requested to begin production of the ADATS short-range anti-aircraft missile. Like Senate Armed Services, the Appropriations panel cited test failures, rising costs and the decline of the military threat from Eastern Europe as reasons to pull the plug on ADATS.

Tactical Air Combat

In general, the Senate bill supported the Pentagon's plan to phase down spending on existing types of combat planes and weaponry, in order to pay for their high-tech replacements. But the bill also included a few wrinkles intended to hedge against the possibility that the new hardware might be delayed.

The bill included $870 million of the $947 million requested to develop the Air Force's new ATF fighter plane and an additional $66 million, as requested, to develop a Navy version equipped to land on aircraft carriers.

For planes in production, the bill included:

- $1.7 billion for 36 F-15Es, $499 million more than the administration had requested. The budget request anticipated that leftover funds from prior appropriations could be used to cover that difference, but those funds subsequently were put to other purposes.
- $1.67 billion for 88 smaller F-16s. The reduction of 62 planes and $685 million from the budget request antici-

Continued on p. 826

Defense Appropriations: Major Provisions

Following are major provisions of the fiscal 1991 Department of Defense appropriations act (HR 5803 — PL 101-511):

Strategic Weaponry

Aside from the B-2, the major strategic weapons programs engendered little controversy in 1990 on Capitol Hill, and, in most cases, the appropriations conferees had to settle only relatively minor differences in funding.

Trident submarine. All four congressional defense committees had agreed that only one more Trident missile-firing submarine should be built, a view the Pentagon shared. The conference report appropriated $1.33 billion for that 18th Trident submarine. Both houses had agreed to appropriate $1.54 billion for 52 of the Trident II missiles carried by the big submarines.

ICBMs. Similarly, the appropriations conferees' action on mobile intercontinental ballistic missiles (ICBMs) fell squarely within the congressional consensus that was apparent for months.

The bill provided $688 million to be allocated by the Pentagon between two programs: One to develop a version of the existing MX missile that could move by rail, and another to develop the much smaller Midgetman ICBM. Both houses had denied the $1.35 billion requested to begin production of the MX rail launchers.

Bomber modification. The bill included only $70 million of the $134 million requested to upgrade the B-1B bombers built in the mid-1980s. Equipping the planes with the SRAM II ground-attack missile would be delayed by problems with that weapon, the conferees said.

It provided $59 million of the $110 million requested to upgrade the remaining 30-year-old B-52 bombers. The conferees asked the Air Force for a detailed report on the cost and effectiveness of major improvements of the big planes.

Reportedly, some Air Force officials believed that B-52s could remain in service for an additional three decades, with certain modifications. Some B-2 critics contended that upgraded B-52s could substitute for the much more expensive stealth planes on certain missions.

Cruise missiles. The conference report included the $157 million requested to continue development of the SRAM II missile, which had a range of a few hundred miles. It also approved the $366 million requested for 100 bomber-launched cruise missiles with a range of nearly 2,000 miles. But the conferees endorsed the House Appropriations Committee's warning that tight budgets would keep the annual funding for this missile too low to keep two manufacturers in business.

The appropriations bill flatly contradicted the companion authorization measure by approving the full $119 million requested to develop a "tactical" version of SRAM II.

The weapon, designated SRAM-T, was designed to be carried by fighter planes to beef up the U.S. nuclear deterrent in Europe against a Soviet-led Warsaw Pact attack. Citing the pact's collapse, some political centrists had joined liberal arms control activists to oppose the weapon. The authorization bill approved only $35 million for SRAM-T.

Loath to step into the jurisdictional cross-fire between congressional committees, the Pentagon often declined to spend appropriations in excess of the amount specifically authorized.

BSTS. After submitting its January budget request, the Pentagon cut from the SDI program $265 million for a satellite designated BSTS, designed to detect and track attacking missiles. But the Air Force picked up BSTS as a replacement for its fleet of early-warning satellites. The conference report included $210 million to develop a new warning satellite, but the conferees ordered the Air Force to award the contract on the basis of a competition open to other satellite manufacturers as well as to the builders of BSTS.

ASAT missile. For development of a ground-launched antisatellite (ASAT) missile, the conference report approved $126 million of the $208 million requested.

Both houses had approved $25 million of the $41 million requested for work on an antisatellite laser.

Ground Combat

Tanks, artillery. The administration's budget request anticipated using $747 million left over from previous budgets to build 163 M-1A1 tanks, followed by 62 copies of an improved model — the M-1A2, equipped with electronic gear for driving and fighting in the dark.

The bill appropriated $747 million in new budget authority for M-1 production in fiscal 1991. However, to provide more time to thoroughly test the A2 design, the conferees insisted that the money be used to buy A1 model tanks. The bill also provided:

- $150 million to gear up for A2 production beginning in fiscal 1992.
- $80 million to upgrade existing tanks.
- $64 million to begin a program to convert into A1 model tanks the 3,000 oldest M-1s, which had a smaller cannon and thinner armor.

The bill included $181 million of the $207 million requested to modernize existing mobile artillery pieces. The Senate had denied the entire request because of cost increases and delays in the program.

For development of a new "family" of armored vehicles — including the Block III tank, a new armored troop carrier and several others — the bill included $144 million of the $177 million requested. But the conferees ordered the Army to de-emphasize the tank, giving higher priority to developing a new mobile artillery piece.

The bill added $30 million to the budget request to speed up work on the new artillery piece and $15 million to develop more powerful ammunition for the 120mm gun carried by M-1A1 and A2 tanks.

Mobile cannon. The bill also included $5 million to speed the Army's search for a lightly armored mobile cannon to equip its "light" divisions, intended for rapid aerial deployment to distant trouble spots. But the conferees warned the Army that it would have to show "clear and convincing evidence" why it should not simply buy a mobile gun that was being developed for the Marine Corps.

Antitank missiles. Both houses had approved the $187 million requested for production of the 100-mile-range ATACMS missile, designed to strike tank columns behind enemy lines. The conferees appropriated $226 million of the $278 million requested to develop an airborne radar, designated Joint STARS, intended to guide ATACMS to its target.

The prospect of declining budgets led the Army to abandon plans to bring a second contractor online to build TOW antitank missiles. The conferees approved $186 million of the $230 million requested, deleting the $44 million earmarked to set up a second production line.

Both houses had approved the $92 million requested to gear up for full-scale production of a more portable antitank missile, designated AAWS-M. Noting that the AAWS-M might be useful against the tank-heavy Iraqi forces, the conferees asked the Army for a report by March 1, 1991, on the feasibility of accelerating the weapon's production schedule — possibly fielding the weapon by the fall of 1991.

Missile-guidance radar. The bill included $196 million of the $220 million requested to develop a missile-guidance radar called Longbow, to be added to the Army's Apache antitank helicopter. The Apache's Hellfire missiles homed in on the reflection of a laser aimed at their target. If equipped with radar, the Hellfires would become "fire-and-forget" weapons, flying to their targets without external guidance.

As part of a $2.46 billion package of equipment for the National Guard and reserve components, the bill appropriated $200 million to equip three dozen "scout" helicopters with sophisticated electronic equipment to find ground targets at night and steer laser-guided missiles into them. The conferees said that the equipment could also be assigned to active-duty forces.

The bill also included $26 million requested to begin arming the scout copters with antitank missiles.

ADATS. Both houses had denied the request to begin production of an anti-aircraft missile launcher designated ADATS, intended to protect front-line combat units. The Senate recommended killing the project, but the conference committee followed the lead of the House, adding to the bill $92 million for additional development work on ADATS.

However, the conferees also told the Army to report by April 1, 1991, on the potential use of a less expensive anti-aircraft vehicle used by the Marines, equipped with a small cannon and short-range Stinger missiles.

Tactical Air Combat

F-14, F-15. Both houses had essentially concurred in the Pentagon's plans for the two aerial heavyweights in service: the Navy's F-14 and the Air Force's F-15.

The conference report provided $771 million of the $780 million requested to equip 12 existing F-14s with more powerful engines and radars. It also appropriated $1.54 billion for 36 F-15s instead of the $1.20 billion requested. The increase was necessary because the Air Force had assumed that it could cover part of the F-15 price with prior-year funds that Congress used for other purposes.

F-16, F/A-18. Both houses had voted to slow down production of the two smaller fighter planes in service: the Air Force F-16 and the F/A-18, used by the Navy and Marine Corps. The conference report included funds for 108 F-16s ($1.86 billion) and 48 F/A-18s ($1.45 billion). Together, the two programs were cut by 60 planes and $868 million.

Radar jammers. The appropriations conferees endorsed the demand by the defense authorization conferees that Pentagon managers make the Navy and Air Force work out a common plan for buying radar jammers to protect combat planes against guided missiles. The appropriations bill denied $422 million requested for various jammer programs. But it also added to the budget $162 million to be parceled out under a new joint procurement plan.

Naval Warfare

The House version of the bill included several add-ons earmarked for Pennsylvania, home state of Democrat John P. Murtha, who chaired the House Defense Appropriations Subcommittee, and Joseph M. McDade, the panel's senior Republican.

The largest single element of the Pennsylvania bonanza was $963 million the House bill provided for a keel-to-masthead modernization of the aircraft carrier *John F. Kennedy,* launched in 1967. This was part of the "service-life extension program" (SLEP) at the Philadelphia Navy Yard, intended to update the Navy's older, non-nuclear-powered carriers for 15 more years of service.

The Senate bill included only the $113 million requested by the Navy for components that would be used in the overhaul, scheduled to begin in fiscal 1993.

The conferees approved $401 million for the *Kennedy* SLEP.

Destroyers, submarines. Both houses accepted Defense Secretary Dick Cheney's decision in August to scale back the planned production of the Navy's two most high-tech warships.

The conference report provided $3.21 billion for four destroyers equipped with the Aegis anti-aircraft system. Adjusting for the most recent price estimates, the conferees provided $100 million more than the House and Senate bills.

The conference report also included $1.78 billion for the second *Seawolf*-class submarine and components to be used in future subs of this type. The January budget had requested five destroyers and two subs.

Overriding a House proposal to slow down production of the Navy's Standard anti-aircraft missile, the conference report included the $608 million requested for 900 of them.

But the bill concurred in the decision of the House to deny the $70 million requested for the RAM, a short-range anti-aircraft missile that was a joint project with Germany.

Sea Lance missile. Like the authorization bill, HR 5803 rejected the Navy's decision to abandon development of the Sea Lance ship-launched antisubmarine missile. It earmarked $71 million to continue Sea Lance development and cut in half the $30 million that the Navy requested to develop a short-range alternative.

Minesweepers. The Senate had denied in toto the $268 million request for three coastal minesweepers, citing delays in constructing the ships previously ordered. But the conference report, like the House bill, provided $204 million for two of the ships.

Air and Sea Transport

Cargo planes. As part of his review of major aircraft programs, Cheney announced in April a cutback in production of the C-17 wide-body, intercontinental cargo plane. The House approved his revised fiscal 1991 request: $1 billion for two planes and components to be used to build six more in fiscal 1992.

Citing a backlog of 10 planes previously funded, the Senate provided only $300 million, to be used to keep in place the network of C-17 subcontractors.

Without elaboration, the conference report provided $460 million for C-17 procurement.

Cargo ships. To expand the Navy's fleet of fast cargo ships able to haul U.S.-based Army units overseas, the conference report appropriated $900 million. The House bill had provided $1.5 billion for sealift, but House members conceded that was simply a ploy to use up the full amount of budget authority allowed for defense under the congressional budget resolution.

Transport helicopters. Cheney's budget request included $435 million for 23 CH-53E transport helicopters, to be used by the Marines in lieu of the Osprey, a troop-carrying hybrid airplane/helicopter, which Cheney was trying to cancel. Congressional supporters of the Osprey rejected the CH-53E funding and used the money instead as one source of funds for their program.

But the package of National Guard and reserve equipment added to the bill included $282 million for a dozen copies of a different version of the CH-53E, modified to serve as an aerial minesweeper.

Personnel Issues

The bill reduced the request for military personnel funds by $1.33 billion to cover the direct and indirect savings from cutting the military payroll by 78,600 from its fiscal 1990 ceiling of 2.08 million personnel.

It also included $169 million to reverse Cheney's proposal to reduce reserve personnel and disband some reserve units. The conferees increased the reserve accounts by an additional $81 million to cover the cost of taking over more missions from active-duty forces. Both increases were largely offset by cuts in the budget request for active-duty personnel and operating costs.

Sharing Burdens

The bill included several provisions aimed at reducing the cost of U.S. deployments overseas. One capped the number of U.S. personnel stationed in Japan at 50,000.

It also reduced the cap by 5,000 annually unless the Japanese government paid all direct costs of U.S. deployments in Japan, except for the pay and fringe benefits of service members. The president could waive this provision if he deemed it in the national interest to do so.

The bill also cut from the budget request:

- $500 million of the amount requested for maintenance of overseas facilities.
- $408 million — 25 percent of the amount requested to pay foreign nationals employed on U.S. bases.
- $96 million of the amount requested for overseas base operating costs.

On the other hand, the bill included provisions helpful to Israel.

One, initially adopted by the Senate, established in Israel a 4.5 million-barrel petroleum reserve "to meet the wartime needs and combined military training requirements of the United States and Israel."

Another provision earmarked $15 million of the Navy's operations and maintenance budget to upgrade port facilities in Israel for U.S. use. ■

Continued from p. 823
pated reductions in the size of the Air Force, the committee said.

- $1.31 billion for 42 F/A-18s, used by the Navy and Marine Corps as both fighters and bombers. As with the F-16s, the committee cited anticipated cutbacks to justify the reduction — in this case, a cut of 24 planes and $585 million from the request.
- $781 million to equip a dozen F-14 Navy fighters with new engines and radars. This included $10 million added to the bill by the Appropriations Committee to speed up tests of how long the 1970s-vintage planes could be kept in service if the Navy's version of the ATF could not be brought online.

AMRAAM. The bill included $865 million for 900 AMRAAM air-to-air missiles instead of the $1.32 billion requested for 1,800, thus continuing the existing limited production rate while the engineers worked out bugs uncovered in flight tests.

Also included was the $84 million requested to develop a new long-range missile, designated AAAM, as a lightweight replacement for the half-ton Phoenix, carried by the Navy's F-14s. But the bill included an additional $73 million to start upgrading the target-finding radars on Phoenix missiles in case AAAM development took longer than planned.

Naval Warfare

The bill included $113 million, as requested, for components to be used in a major reconstruction (called a SLEP) of the aircraft carrier *John F. Kennedy*, slated to be done at the Philadelphia Navy Yard. But the Appropriations Committee ordered the Pentagon to submit a broad report on its plans for the future of the carrier fleet. The subject was touchy because Cheney said he might try to trim the number of ships in service from 14 to 12.

The bill included $3.1 billion for four destroyers equipped with the Aegis anti-aircraft system, reflecting Cheney's decision in August to slow production of these vessels. Similarly, the bill reflected his decision to fund one *Seawolf*-class submarine in fiscal 1991, instead of the two initially requested. The bill provided $1.38 billion for the sub, but none of the $1.14 billion requested for components that would be used to build more subs in the future.

Since the first ship of this type was funded in fiscal 1989 and was only 5 percent complete, the Appropriations Committee said, the Navy should wait for more progress on that vessel before starting on additional ships.

However, the bill included $534 million, as requested, to continue development of the sub and its electronic target-finding equipment.

Sea Lance missile. The Navy had abandoned development of the Sea Lance guided missile, intended to be fired from surface ships at submerged submarines up to 35 miles away, instead requesting $30 million to develop a shorter-range replacement. But the Senate bill knocked out the money for the substitute and added $71 million to put the Sea Lance project back on track.

Minesweepers. The bill included none of the $268 million requested for three minesweepers. The committee insisted that no more of the ships should be funded until the contractor made more progress on its backlog of previously funded ships of the same class.

Air and Sea Transport

The bill included $1 billion not requested by the Pentagon for "sealift": cargo ships to haul U.S.-based combat units to the territory of threatened allies abroad. The committee recommended that the money be used for a squadron of four or five "prepositioning" ships — floating warehouses anchored in out-of-the-way harbors like the 13 ships based at Guam, Diego Garcia and in the Atlantic.

Amphibious landing ships. The Senate also approved without change the $1.44 billion requested for amphibious landing ships designed to help a Marine Corps unit fight its way onto a hostile shore. The bill included:

- $960 million for a helicopter carrier able to carry 2,000 Marines and 30 helicopters.
- $240 million for a cargo ship to carry tanks and other heavy gear.
- $245 million for a dozen air-cushion landing barges.

The bill included only $26 million of the $43 million requested, however, to develop a new amphibious personnel carrier for the Marines that would have a water speed appreciably faster than the 8 miles per hour of the vehicle in service.

The bill also added to the budget $40 million to modify two old missile-launching subs for use as commando transports.

Cargo planes. To continue development of the C-17 wide-body intercontinental cargo plane, the bill included $541 million, as requested. But it included only $300 million of the $1.91 billion requested to continue production of the plane. Because of production delays, the committee said, the funds requested for fiscal 1991 would not have been spent until very late in the year. The $300 million allowed was intended to be used only to keep intact the network of firms working on the project. ■

Hefty Cuts in Spending for Overseas Bases

Budget pressures and reduced international tensions led Congress to cut spending for U.S. military facilities and housing around the world in the fiscal 1991 military construction appropriations bill (HR 5313).

The $8.36 billion measure was cleared by the Senate on Oct. 28 — just after midnight in the session of Oct. 27 — by voice vote. The House had adopted the conference report on the bill, also by voice vote, on Oct. 19.

HR 5313 reduced President Bush's original budget request by $764 million. It also shifted priorities from overseas projects, including cooperative efforts with NATO, to domestic facilities.

Lawmakers went ahead with the spending bill even though the administration had threatened to veto it over a dispute affecting a proposed air base in Italy. The Pentagon backed away from a recommendation that Bush veto the bill, however, and Bush signed it into law Nov. 5.

A spokesman for Defense Secretary Dick Cheney had warned on Oct. 23 that the secretary would recommend a veto of the construction bill because of the provision opposing NATO's plans for a new $800 million base at Crotone, Italy. The base would have housed the United States' 401st Tactical Fighter Wing with its 72 F-16 aircraft.

The Spanish government had insisted that the unit vacate its base at Torrejon, near Madrid.

Senior defense officials had touted the proposed base at Crotone as a fulcrum for U.S. military leverage in southern Europe and the Mediterranean.

While slamming the planned facility as unduly lavish, congressional critics hinted for months that they would consider approving a less elaborate installation at Crotone.

But when the Air Force did not propose a sufficiently austere alternative, the conferees included in the final version of the construction appropriations bill a provision barring the use of any U.S. funds for the project.

The ban included funds that made up 28 percent of NATO's so-called Infrastructure program — its kitty for construction projects, which would have funded the proposed $800 million Crotone base.

"We have seen amazing changes occur in Europe over the last year," Military Construction Appropriations Subcommittee Chairman W. G. "Bill" Hefner, D-N.C., told the House on Oct. 19. "There is a need for NATO to re-examine the need for the Italian base, as well as whether there are other, more cost-effective alternatives."

Backing away from the veto threat, Pentagon spokesman Robert Hall said Nov. 1 that "the intent of the appropriators as expressed is not to kill the base but put a moratorium on U.S. funding while NATO re-evaluates the need for the base and also while [the Defense Department] comes up with what they call a 'more austere' program."

In signing the bill, Bush said he was "deeply disappointed" with several provisions of the bill, including the ban on funding for the base at Crotone. "Moving the 401st [Tactical Fighter Wing] to this strategic location remains a crucial element of NATO defense strategy and a top priority for the United States," Bush said. He said the administration would "continue to work with the Congress" to resume work on the base and hoped that NATO would continue construction in the meantime.

BOXSCORE

Legislation: Fiscal 1991 military construction appropriations, PL 101-519 (HR 5313).

Major action: Signed, Nov. 5. Conference report adopted by Senate, Oct. 28 (session of Oct. 27); by House, Oct. 19. Passed by Senate, Oct. 1; by House, 312-82, July 30.

Reports: Conference report (H Rept 101-888). Appropriations (S Rept 101-410); Appropriations (H Rept 101-608).

Bush Request Trimmed

As reported by House-Senate conferees, the compromise bill not only reduced Bush's fiscal 1991 budget request by $764 million but also, as requested by the administration, rescinded $286 million previously appropriated for construction overseas. It applied those leftover funds to the fiscal 1991 program, thus reducing by that amount the new budget authority required.

The bill included only one-third of the $955 million Bush had requested for projects in foreign territory.

By far the largest single component of the $624 million reduction in foreign-oriented funding came from the annual U.S. contribution to the NATO Infrastructure fund: The bill provided $193 million of the $420 million requested.

Most of the remaining cuts in overseas spending came from five projects planned in five countries: Germany, Britain, South Korea, Japan and Italy. Of a total of $347 million requested for projects in those countries, the bill provided only $20 million.

The hefty cuts in overseas spending reflected some of the thinking behind the Hill's widespread, bipartisan opposition to the proposed air base at Crotone.

For one thing, with Soviet military power retrenching on most fronts, members questioned the need for programs oriented toward the threat of a Soviet-led attack on NATO.

That belief, spawned by the collapse of the Soviet-led Warsaw Pact, meshed with longstanding and growing congressional demands that U.S. allies pay a larger share of the cost of mutual defense efforts.

HOUSE ACTION

The House Appropriations Committee approved a fiscal 1991 spending bill for military construction on July 19 that clearly reflected Congress' desire to cut defense spending.

"This is a good bill and considerably below budget. It is a reflection of the changes that are taking place in the world today," said Californian Bill Lowery, the ranking Republican on the Military Construction Subcommittee.

The draft legislation called for $8.3 billion for new military facilities and military family housing, $700 million below the appropriation for fiscal 1990.

The spending bill would appropriate $220 million less than the subcommittee was allowed to spend under the so-called 302(b) allocation resolution.

The $8.3 billion total appropriation was also $850 million less than what President Bush had requested.

In a year of a burgeoning budget deficit and contentious debate to get spending under control, the low spending bill won easy approval.

The committee's spending measure provided $450 million for construction at overseas military installations, a 60 percent reduction from 1990.

Subcommittee Chairman Hefner said $300 million allocated for 1990 would be rescinded. Those figures reflected U.S. plans to reduce troop strength in Europe and other foreign sites.

The bill appropriated $998 million more for closing and cleaning up domestic bases targeted for closure. The 1989 appropriation bill had included $500 million for the Pentagon to activate a revolving fund to clean up bases ordered closed. Congress later decided that was not enough. *(1989 Almanac, p. 776)*

The appropriation for the environmental cleanup for fiscal 1991, however, was still $82 million more than Bush requested.

The military construction bill also required the Defense secretary to report to the Appropriations Committee on plans for the environmental cleanup of military facilities outside the United States that were to be closed.

The Pentagon was told to submit an analysis of the costs for the anticipated cleanups, including financial assistance that might have to be provided to the host countries.

An amendment by Jerry Lewis, R-Calif., stopping an Air Force plan to move the Ballistic Missile Organization at

Norton Air Force Base in California, was given quick approval by the committee.

Norton was scheduled to be closed. But the Ballistic Missile Organization, which was independent of the rest of the facility and employed 2,000 workers, was not included in the closure plan.

Lewis said he introduced the amendment on behalf of Democrat George E. Brown Jr., whose district included the air base in Riverside.

A Brown aide said the Defense Secretary's Commission on Base Realignments and Closures had recommended that the program stay at Norton even after the base was closed. But the Air Force wanted to rename it and move it.

Hefner, in calling for adoption of the amendment, said the Air Force "was trying to make an end run" by trying to move the program away from Norton.

Floor Action

House passage of HR 5313 on July 30, with its 9 percent cut in Bush's funding request for military construction, was its first real step toward paring the Pentagon budget. Overseas projects accounted for the lion's share of the reductions. The vote was 312-82. *(Vote 283, p. 94-H)*

As approved, the bill appropriated $8.6 billion for construction of facilities and family housing, a reduction of $528 million from Bush's January budget request.

The measure also included Defense Secretary Cheney's subsequent request to rescind $286 million appropriated in prior years for construction projects abroad. Since those rescinded funds were used to offset the cost of the programs approved, the House was able to reduce the total new budget authority in the bill to $8.31 billion, a total reduction of $815 million from the January budget request.

The House rejected Cheney's proposal to rescind an additional $41 million that had been appropriated for three domestic construction projects, including $39 million for an Army supply depot in Texarkana, Texas. Texarkana was represented by Appropriations Committee Democrat Jim Chapman.

The House passed the bill after rejecting amendments:

- By Timothy J. Penny, D-Minn., to reduce funding for each account in the bill by 2 percent, for a total cut of $166 million; rejected 164-239. *(Vote 281, p. 92-H)*
- By Bill Frenzel, R-Minn., to reduce funding in each account by 0.8 percent, for a total cut of $70 million; rejected 180-214. *(Vote 282, p. 92-H)*

By voice vote, the House adopted an amendment by Bill Alexander, D-Ark., that barred through the end of fiscal 1991 the use of any U.S. funds to construct the NATO air base at Crotone.

As reported by the House Appropriations Committee, the bill would have barred use of funds at Crotone only through the end of December 1990.

Overseas Cutbacks

The House bill included barely 50 percent of the amount Bush requested for overseas construction — $463 million of $920 million requested.

Since the mid-1970s, the House Appropriations Military Construction Subcommittee had demanded that Japan, South Korea and U.S. allies in NATO pay a larger share of the cost of mutual defense efforts.

In its report accompanying HR 5313, the Appropriations Committee acknowledged that the allies were bearing an increased share, but said it still was not enough.

More than one-third of the amount the House cut from the overseas construction budget came from the annual U.S. contribution to NATO's so-called Infrastructure fund — the alliance's kitty for funding common-use projects, of which the United States contributed 28 percent. The bill provided $250 million of the $420 million requested.

The Pentagon touted the proposed F-16 base at Crotone as a prime example of burden-sharing: Except for the housing for U.S. personnel and their families, the base was being paid for with NATO Infrastructure funding. In a June 30 letter to the chairmen and senior Republicans on the Senate and House Armed Services committees, U.S. Army Gen. John Galvin, NATO's military commander in chief, said the new base was "absolutely necessary for stability and deterrence in the southern region.... If I had only two U.S. Air Force wings remaining in Europe, I would place one of them at Crotone."

But Alexander and other critics challenged the need for a new base, at an estimated total cost of some $700 million, when the Soviet threat to Western Europe was fading.

Under the Pentagon's plan, the 72 fighters would be based in the United States for a few years, pending completion of the base at Crotone, periodically moving to austere combat bases in Europe.

Patricia Schroeder, D-Colo., suggested that as a permanent arrangement, the unit be based in the United States and moved periodically to

Military Construction

Following are the budget authority totals in the fiscal 1991 military construction appropriations bill (HR 5313 — PL 101-519).

(Figures, in thousands of dollars, may not add due to rounding.)

	President's Request	House Bill	Senate Bill	Final Bill
Army	$ 774,900	$ 747,067	$ 697,967	$ 746,137
Navy	1,113,300	1,137,278	1,083,826	1,132,606
Air Force	1,376,200	949,446	891,784	949,094
Defense agencies	787,500	625,326	600,113	601,288
NATO Infrastructure	420,400	250,000	210,400	192,700
National Guard and reserves	280,378	506,095	573,451	690,117
Family housing	3,457,050	3,384,524	3,291,919	3,364,798
Base realignment and closure	916,500	998,100	916,500	998,100
Subtotal: Appropriation	9,126,228	8,597,836	8,265,960	8,674,840
Rescission	—	−286,419	−286,419	−312,419
Debt reduction	−250	−250	−250	−250
Net New Budget Authority	**$ 9,125,978**	**$ 8,311,167**	**$ 7,979,291**	**$ 8,362,171**

bases in Europe, thus obviating the need for the base at Crotone. Schroeder chaired the Armed Services Subcommittee on Military Installations, which also moved to block construction of Crotone in the companion defense authorization bill. *(Defense authorization, p. 671)*

Schroeder, Alexander and other Crotone critics also complained about building a new base overseas while the Pentagon was shutting down dozens of bases in the United States.

"What are you going to say in your district when a constituent asks you, 'Why did you vote to build a new base in Italy at the same time that the Defense Department is closing Camp Swampy, right here?' " Schroeder asked.

Domestic Projects

The construction bill also reflected the widespread belief on Capitol Hill that a larger share of the U.S. defense structure could be shifted to the politically potent National Guard and reserve components.

With Soviet military retrenchment — the argument went — a large-scale military threat would take so long to develop that there would be ample time to mobilize the reserves.

The measure increased by $226 million (to $506 million) the amount earmarked for National Guard and reserve facilities.

In its report, the Appropriations Committee ordered Cheney to lift a construction moratorium established in January and extended through Nov. 15. The construction hold was required, Cheney said, to allow time for a re-evaluation of future defense needs in the light of the rapid decline of the Soviet threat.

But the committee objected that the sweeping ban on new construction starts was delaying work and running up costs on projects that were certain to pass muster in the review.

The committee warned against prematurely closing domestic bases that could be needed to house units deployed overseas. And it ordered the Pentagon to report by Feb. 1, 1991, on the implications for future military construction budgets of a decision to station domestically 85 percent, 90 percent or 95 percent of all U.S. forces. In 1990, about 25 percent of U.S. forces were stationed domestically.

The House bill appropriated $998 million to cover the cost of cleaning up and shutting down superfluous bases. That included $82 million earmarked for environmental cleanup that Bush had included in another part of his request.

The bill also made sizable reductions in the construction budgets associated with two controversial strategic weapons. It provided:

- None of the $254 million requested to deploy a rail-mobile version of the MX intercontinental ballistic missile.
- $55 million of the $92 million requested for facilities to house the B-2 "stealth" bomber at Whiteman Air Force Base in Missouri.

SENATE ACTION

The Senate Appropriations Committee on Aug. 1 approved its version of the military construction bill, which appropriated $8.3 billion, partly offset by the $286 million rescission that also was part of the House bill.

Accordingly, the new budget authority provided by the Senate committee's bill would be $7.98 billion — $332 million less than the House bill and $1.15 billion less than Bush's request. Like the House, the Senate panel targeted overseas projects for most of its cuts.

The bill approved by Senate Appropriations closely tracked several provisions of the House-passed bill intended to force U.S. allies to pay more of the cost of U.S. operations abroad.

The panel approved only $89 million of the $516 million requested for specific construction projects abroad. And, like the House, it approved only $170 million of the $420 million requested for the annual contribution to NATO's Infrastructure fund.

It barred use of any funds for the base at Crotone. But in its report on the bill, the Senate committee also urged the Pentagon to redesign the proposed air base in Italy as a "minimum cost, bare-base."

Under this approach, fighter squadrons that were permanently based in the United States would briefly deploy to the new facility periodically to perform training exercises and to show the flag. Since the squadron personnel would not be accompanied by their dependents, there would be no need for schools, day-care centers or other accoutrements of a full-scale air base, proponents of this approach contended.

Those promoting this bare-base idea included Senate Military Construction Appropriations Subcommittee Chairman Jim Sasser, D-Tenn.; Senate Armed Services Committee Chairman Sam Nunn, D-Ga.; and Schroeder.

As the Pentagon planned to close upwards of 100 overseas bases, the Senate Appropriations panel also directed the agency to press host countries to cover the cost of cleaning up toxic waste on those sites.

The Senate panel was even more generous to the National Guard and reserve component forces than was the House: It boosted funds for Guard and reserve facilities to $572 million, more than double the amount Bush requested and $66 million more than the House appropriated.

The Senate committee also approved the following:

- $916 million — the amount requested by Bush — to cover the cost of shutting down and cleaning up bases in the United States closed pursuant to the 1988 legislation. *(1988 Almanac, p. 439)*
- $55 million of the $92 million requested for facilities at Whiteman Air Force Base in Missouri, which was to be used by the B-2 stealth bomber.
- None of the $238 million requested for facilities associated with the controversial plan to deploy MX missiles on rail-mobile launchers.

Floor Action

The Senate used the annual appropriations bill for military construction to take swipes at international terrorists and the government of Iraq.

Before approving the $7.98 billion appropriations measure by a voice vote Oct. 1, the Senate added an amendment permitting U.S. citizens victimized by terrorists abroad to sue for damages in U.S. courts. It also adopted an amendment authorizing the president to use Iraqi assets in this country to pay claims against Iraq by U.S. citizens.

The Senate bill appropriated $8.3 billion for military construction projects but would offset part of the cost by approving the administration's request to rescind $286 million in unused funds appropriated in prior years for construction projects overseas.

So the Senate version of the bill provided the Pentagon with $7.98 billion in new budget authority — $1.15 billion less than Bush requested and $332 million less than the version the House passed July 30.

Like the House-passed version, the Senate bill made a substantial cut in the amount requested for construction overseas while boosting the amount earmarked for domestic facilities to be used by National Guard and reserve units.

The shift in priorities from the administration's budget reflected congressional sentiment that allies should bear a greater burden of U.S. operations abroad, combined with the tendency to protect and improve domestic facilities.

The Senate measure appropriated only $89 million of the $516 million requested for projects at specific overseas locations and only $210 million of the $420 million requested for NATO's Infrastructure fund.

On the other hand, the Senate bill provided $572 million for National Guard and reserve facilities, more than double the amount Bush requested and $66 million more than was provided by the House.

Floor Amendments

The amendment permitting civil suits against terrorists was identical to S 2465, introduced in April by Sens. Howell Heflin, D-Ala., and Charles E. Grassley, R-Iowa, members of the Judiciary Committee, and supported by eight other members of the committee.

As introduced, the measure would have codified a June 7 ruling by a federal district court in New York that allowed a civil damage suit against the Palestine Liberation Organization (PLO) by the family of Leon Klinghoffer, who was murdered on the cruise ship *Achille Lauro* by agents for a faction of the PLO in 1985. PLO assets could be seized to pay fines levied by a court in such a case.

Offered by Grassley as an amendment to the military construction bill, the proposal was adopted by voice vote.

The provision was removed in conference, however, after House Judiciary Chairman Jack Brooks, D-Texas, objected to dealing with the issue on an appropriations bill and bypassing his committee. In commenting on the conference report to the Senate on Oct. 27, Grassley said that Brooks had promised to hold hearings on the issue in the 102nd Congress.

Other amendments the Senate adopted Oct. 1, both by voice vote, were as follows:

- By Max Baucus, D-Mont., authorizing the president to liquidate Iraqi assets in the United States to pay claims by U.S. citizens against the Iraqi government.

In particular, Baucus wanted Iraqi funds to pay back some of the nearly $2 billion in loans to Iraq, guaranteed by the Agriculture Department, for the purchase of U.S. agricultural commodities.

- By Frank H. Murkowski, R-Alaska, barring any company from working on projects funded by the bill if the firm was based in a country where U.S. firms were discriminated against in awarding government construction contracts. Murkowski made clear that the provision was aimed at Japan. ■

Reluctant Approval for $15.4 Billion Aid Bill

For a brief period in 1990, foreign aid became popular on Capitol Hill. As the Soviet bloc began to break apart, lawmakers scrambled to support new assistance for the fledgling democracies in Eastern Europe.

But that popularity lasted only until the summer budget crunch, which renewed the customary skepticism toward spending abroad the dollars of U.S. taxpayers. With a conspicuous lack of enthusiasm, both houses of Congress on Oct. 27 approved the conference report accompanying the $15.4 billion fiscal 1991 foreign aid appropriations bill (HR 5114).

As enacted, the spending bill included $369.7 million in aid for Eastern Europe, along with new help for Israel and other favored aid recipients. Most lawmakers welcomed those provisions. But the overall mood was perhaps best expressed by Rep. Clarence E. Miller, R-Ohio, who said during the House floor debate on the bill, "We simply do not have the resources to devote to other nations to the extent we have in the past."

That attitude was reflected in the total amount of aid provided in the bill, which was $129 million less than the administration request for fiscal 1991 and nearly $300 million below the figure approved by the House.

It also was demonstrated by the approval of an amendment offered by Senate Appropriations Committee Chairman Robert C. Byrd, D-W.Va., raising the amount of tied-aid credits — funds that, if used, had to be spent on U.S. goods and services — from $50 million to $300 million.

> **BOXSCORE**
>
> **Legislation:** Fiscal 1991 foreign aid appropriations, PL 101-513 (HR 5114).
>
> **Major action:** Signed, Nov. 5. Conference report adopted by Senate, Oct. 27; by House, 188-162, Oct. 27. Passed by Senate, 76-23, Oct. 24; by House, 308-117, June 27.
>
> **Reports:** Conference report (H Rept 101-968). Appropriations (S Rept 101-519); Appropriations (H Rept 101-553).

Rep. Matthew F. McHugh, D-N.Y., noted that the legislation was "substantially less" than the 1985 bill, which allocated $20.9 billion for foreign aid. Yet even a 20 percent reduction over the preceding five years was not enough for many lawmakers. *(1985 Almanac, p. 367)*

The real threats to the measure in 1990, however, were the administration's proposals to secure loan forgiveness for Egypt, a key ally in the Persian Gulf crisis, and to maintain aid for El Salvador despite new concerns about human rights conditions in the Central American country.

Egyptian Debt Forgiveness

The White House underestimated the depth of congressional opposition to generosity abroad when it pressed for an amendment to forgive Egypt's $6.7 billion military debt. Although the amendment was moderated in conference, many lawmakers said it accounted for the relatively narrow margin by which the House passed the conference report (188-162) on Oct. 27. *(Vote 531, p. 168-H)*

The Senate cleared the report the same day without a recorded vote. President Bush signed the bill Nov. 5.

Bush had argued that a grant of debt relief was needed to reward Egypt's President Hosni Mubarak, who was a linchpin of Arab support for the U.S. response to Iraq's invasion of Kuwait. *(Persian Gulf crisis, p. 717)*

But lawmakers, especially in the House, strongly objected to forgiving the debt outright, rather than restructuring payment terms.

Rep. David R. Obey, D-Wis., who chaired the House-Senate conference on the bill and fought hard to alter the terms of the forgiveness plan, said after the vote, "If this bill had come up any other day than the last day [of the session], it would have been defeated."

In the conference, Obey, chairman of the House Appropriations Subcommittee on Foreign Operations, added language that provided for a six-month payment moratorium, although the president also would get the power he sought to forgive the debt.

In addition, Obey won approval for a provision granting similar presidential authority to adjust Poland's debt, which he called the most important provision in the bill. It is authority that "I am certain that the president will use," said Obey.

Rep. Mickey Edwards, Okla., the senior Republican on Obey's subcommittee, was also exercised over the Egyptian debt proposal, especially over its timing. Speaking just hours after the House approved the conference report on the budget-reconcilation bill (HR 5835), he said it was difficult to justify debt forgiveness "when we have just made a substantial increase in the taxes on the American people."

Aid to El Salvador

A second controversial provision, withholding half of the $85 million military aid package to El Salvador in fiscal 1991, triggered broad Republican opposition. Edwards also was concerned over a section in the bill that would have barred all military aid if the government failed to prosecute the 1989 murders of eight Jesuit priests or did not participate in talks aimed at ending the country's civil war.

Edwards complained that the measure did not allow the president to restore the aid. But the House-Senate conference ensured that Congress would have final say about resuming the assistance. *(EL Salvador, p. 779)*

The White House, which found the El Salvador aid restrictions onerous, was constrained from making good on a threatened veto because of the crucial importance of the debt relief for Egypt. Congressional opponents of the Egypt provision were likewise limited in fighting the measure because of a range of popular items that were in the bill — including the El Salvador restrictions and important new programs for Israel.

HOUSE COMMITTEE ACTION

The House Appropriations Foreign Operations Subcommittee approved a $15.8 billion foreign operations spending bill (HR 5114) on June 13.

Obey, chairman of the subcommittee, drafted the bill to start shifting priorities to reflect what he called "the new realities" following the collapse of communism in Eastern Europe. The subcommittee-approved bill cut $526 million from President Bush's request for military aid to U.S. allies and allocated the money instead for development in Eastern Europe, Africa and elsewhere.

Republicans and the administration opposed Obey's bill, and it was approved on a party-line vote of 8-4. But the vote disguised the disagreements on foreign aid that crossed party lines. One conservative Democrat, Charles Wilson of Texas, reserved the right to vote with Republicans when the bill reached the floor. And one Republican, John Porter of Illinois, said he voted with his colleagues only out of party loyalty.

The subcommittee included in the bill a provision to suspend half of U.S. military aid to El Salvador in fiscal 1991. The House on May 22 had voted to include that provision in a foreign aid authorization bill, but the bill subsequently was defeated.

Edwards, the subcommittee's ranking Republican, said the administration would wage an all-out fight on the House floor to kill the Salvadoran aid provision. Bush sought $85 million for military aid to El Salvador in fiscal 1991.

Panel members said another floor battle would occur over a proposal by Porter and others to ease restrictions on U.S. support for international organizations that provided family planning services overseas. Existing law barred support for the U.N. Fund for Population Activities (UNFPA) because of its activities in China and for the International Planned Parenthood Federation (IPPF) because some of its affiliates offered abortion services. *(Family planning, p. 604)*

While reducing the president's overall request for military aid, the subcommittee bill gave the administration unusually broad discretion to determine how much to give to individual countries.

Obey said he tried to avoid the popular congressional practice of earmarking precise amounts of aid for particular countries — a practice that the Bush administration staunchly opposed.

The subcommittee's bill included full-scale earmarks for only four countries: Israel ($3 billion in economic and military aid); Egypt ($2.1 billion in economic and military aid); Jordan ($35 million in economic aid); and Cyprus ($15 million in economic aid).

Shifting Priorities

As a symbolic step away from Cold War priorities — and also to find money for programs favored by most Democrats on the subcommittee — Obey reduced Bush's request for the main military aid program by $526 million.

Foreign Military Financing (formerly Foreign Military Sales) helped allies buy U.S. weapons and defense services. It was budgeted for $4.7 billion in fiscal 1990, and Bush sought $5 billion for fiscal 1991. Obey proposed just less than $4.5 billion.

Obey also proposed limits on military aid to three NATO countries that hosted U.S. bases.

Portugal would be limited to $90 million (a slight boost over the $84.6 million budgeted for fiscal 1990), Greece would be limited to $280 million (a cut from $348.5 million in fiscal 1990) and Turkey's aid would be capped at $400 million (reduced from $497.9 million in fiscal 1990). The figures for Greece and Turkey represented the traditional 7-10 aid ratio, intended by Congress to hold down Turkey's aid in comparison with that given Greece.

Obey found three uses for the money he suggested trimming from military aid. Eastern Europe programs were to get $200 million above Bush's request, development efforts in sub-Saharan Africa were to get another $200 mil-

Foreign Aid Appropriations

Following are the budget authority totals in the fiscal 1991 foreign operations appropriations bill (HR 5114 — PL 101-513). Figures in parentheses show program limitations that do not count as new budget authority. The figures for individual development banks include only paid-in capital and direct contributions.

(Figures, in thousands of dollars, may not add due to rounding.)

Program	Bush Request	House Bill	Senate Bill	Final Bill
Inter-American Development Bank	$ 78,299	$ 78,299	$ 78,299	$ 78,299
Inter-American Investment Corporation	25,500	13,000	0	13,000
World Bank	110,592	50,001	110,592	110,592
International Development Association	1,064,150	1,064,150	1,064,150	1,064,150
International Finance Corporation	40,331	40,331	40,331	40,331
Enhanced Structural Adjustment Facility (International Monetary Fund)	10,602	10,602	10,602	10,602
Asian Development Fund	301,809	243,900	187,882	126,854
African Development Fund	105,452	105,452	105,452	105,452
African Development Bank	10,136	10,136	10,136	10,136
European Development Bank	70,021	70,021	56,820	70,021
Total callable capital for development banks	(5,433,457)	(4,153,540)	(5,433,457)	(5,433,457)
International organizations and programs	218,750	248,750	254,730	254,730
International Fund for Agricultural Development	6,250	20,000	30,000	30,000
Montreal Protocol Facilitation Funds (Aid to Reduce Ozone Depletion)	0	0	10,000	10,000
Subtotal, multilateral aid	**2,041,891**	**1,954,640**	**1,958,994**	**1,924,166**
Agriculture aid	424,520	481,635	481,635	481,635
Population aid	193,191	250,000	250,000	250,000
Health aid	115,465	135,000	135,000	135,000
AIDS prevention	38,200	52,000	52,000	52,000
Child Survival Fund	74,538	100,000	100,000	100,000
Education, human resources aid	134,201	134,201	134,201	134,201
Private sector, energy selected development aid	144,223	152,223	152,223	152,223
Science and technology aid	8,662	8,624	8,624	8,624
Private sector revolving fund, limitation on guaranteed loans	(125,000)	(12,500)	(62,500)	(57,000)
Reappropriation authority	23,000	23,000	23,000	23,000
Section 557 (reallocation of development assistance to other accounts)	0	0	−70,500	−40,000
Sub-Saharan Africa development aid	560,500	800,000	800,000	800,000
American Schools and Hospitals Abroad	23,000	23,000	35,000	29,000
International disaster aid	40,000	40,000	40,000	40,000
Foreign service retirement and disability fund	40,341	40,341	40,341	40,341
Agency for International Development (AID) operating expenses	447,794	435,000	435,000	435,000
AID inspector general	33,884	31,384	33,884	33,884

lion, and programs aiding refugees and children in the Third World were to be boosted by $150 million.

When Edwards offered an amendment that would have restored $270 million of the military aid that Obey wanted to cut, Obey noted that his bill would reduce military aid spending by less than 5 percent.

"If we can't do that much, we might as well all quit," Obey said.

Edwards said he, too, would like to see more aid in the bill for the countries of Eastern Europe and Africa. But Obey's proposal for shifting money directly to those countries from the military aid program "is so far off base" that it made the bill unacceptable to most Republicans and to the Bush administration, he said.

Even so, Edwards voiced frustration with the administration, saying he found "no one at home" when he tried to

Foreign Aid Appropriations

Program	Bush Request	House Bill	Senate Bill	Final Bill
African Development Foundation	11,500	13,000	13,000	13,000
Inter-American Foundation	16,941	25,000	25,000	25,000
Peace Corps	181,061	186,000	186,000	186,000
International narcotics control	150,000	150,000	150,000	150,000
Migration and refugee aid	450,648	485,648	485,648	485,648
Emergency migration aid	25,000	35,000	35,000	35,000
Antiterrorism aid	12,026	12,026	12,026	12,026
Economic Support Fund (ESF)	3,544,000	3,460,000	3,141,000	3,141,000
ESF reappropriation authority	14,000	14,000	14,000	14,000
ESF rescission	0	0	0	0
ESF transfer to Multilateral Assistance initiative (MAI) for Philippines	0	0	0	−30,000
International Fund for Ireland	0	20,000	0	20,000
Multilateral assistance initiative (Philippines)	200,000	160,000	160,000	160,000
Other Special Assistance (Eastern Europe)	229,979	418,675	320,000	369,675
Development Policy Reform	75,000	0	0	0
Housing Guaranty Program, reserve	48,000	48,000	48,000	48,000
Subtotal, bilateral aid	**7,259,674**	**7,733,757**	**7,241,082**	**7,304,757**
Military aid operating expenses	28,000	27,920	27,920	27,920
Foreign Military Financing (FMF) program grants	4,988,900	4,202,000	4,664,347	4,232,000
FMF concessional loans	0	405,000	0	403,500
FMF deobligation-reobligation authority	0	0	45,000	45,000
International Military Education and Training	50,500	47,196	47,196	47,196
Guarantee Reserve Fund	587,061	587,061	587,061	587,061
Special defense acquisition fund (limitation on obligations)	(325,000)	(278,796)	(350,000)	(350,000)
Peacekeeping operations	32,800	32,800	32,800	32,800
Subtotal, bilateral military aid	**$ 5,687,261**	**$ 5,301,978**	**$ 5,404,325**	**$ 5,375,478**
Housing Guaranty Program, limitation	(100,000)	(150,000)	(150,000)	(100,000)
Overseas Private Investment Corporation (loan limitations)	(208,000)	(290,000)	(290,000)	(290,000)
Export-Import Bank direct loans	500,000	750,000	750,000	750,000
Export-Import Bank total limitations	(11,236,235)	(11,522,235)	(11,522,235)	(11,522,235)
Trade and development	30,000	35,000	35,000	35,000
Central fiscal operations	0	0	-852,000	-852,000
Guarantee reserve fund	0	0	382,639	382,639
Interest payments, foreign military aid	0	0	569,000	569,000
Polish debt restructuring	0	0	44,000	44,000
Benefits for U.S. hostages in Middle East	0	0	(10,000)	(10,000)
General reduction	0	-138,282	0	0
Reconciliation agreement adjustment	0	0	-143,639	-143,639
GRAND TOTAL	**$ 15,518,827**	**$ 15,637,093**	**$ 15,389,411**	**$ 15,389,401**

get a clear position from the White House on how much military aid it would demand.

Jerry Lewis, R-Calif., and Wilson noted that Obey's proposal would have an impact greater than the nominal 5 percent the chairman claimed. That was because the bill also protected the military aid budgets for Israel ($1.8 billion) and Egypt ($1.3 billion). After the $3.1 billion for those two countries was set aside, Obey's bill would leave about $1.4 billion for all other countries — a cut of about 27 percent from what Bush had budgeted.

Edwards' amendment to restore some of the military aid failed on a voice vote, with Wilson joining the Republicans in voting "yes." The subcommittee also rejected, by voice vote, an Edwards amendment to repeal the limits that Obey placed on military aid to Greece, Turkey and Portugal.

As a signal of continuing unhappiness with Bush's policy toward China, the subcommittee approved a provision to withhold some contributions to the World Bank's International Development Association (IDA) if that agency made new loans to China other than for "basic human needs." But the provision gave the president broad discretion to provide the money anyway. *(U.S.-China relations, p. 764)*

IDA, which aided the world's poorest countries, approved a $300 million loan for the reforestation of rural areas in China on May 29. The United States had joined other industrialized countries in supporting the loan on the grounds that it would help China meet basic needs, such as jobs and housing.

Pressured by Congress to protest Beijing's June 1989 crackdown on political dissent, the Bush administration had opposed international financial aid for China except for humanitarian needs. *(1989 Almanac, p. 518)*

Protesting the administration's support of the China loan, Obey included in his draft of the bill a provision to curtail the fiscal 1991 U.S. contribution of $1.06 billion to IDA. Obey's draft would have withheld from IDA the amount of any loans that it made to China for projects that did not meet U.S. criteria for "basic human needs." However, Obey's draft gave the president the authority to give IDA the money anyway by certifying to Congress that it was in the U.S. national interest to do so.

At McHugh's suggestion, the subcommittee adopted a milder proposal to withhold from IDA only the proportionate U.S. share of any loans to China not for basic human needs. The United States provided about 20 percent of IDA's funds overall, so the amendment would restrict that percentage of the value of some IDA loans to China.

As with Obey's original proposal, the McHugh amendment allowed the president to give the money if he found that it was in the national interest.

Poland Debt

Obey insisted on withholding the entire U.S. contribution for the International Bank for Reconstruction and Development (IBRD), the World Bank's main lending arm.

Bush had requested $110.6 million in direct contributions and $2.9 billion in "callable capital" for the IBRD, which made loans to middle-income developing countries. Callable capital could be used by the bank as collateral for borrowing on world markets but would not actually be spent unless the bank faced default.

Obey for several years had used U.S. support for the World Bank as his lever to protest the refusal of large commercial banks to write off bad loans they made in the 1970s to developing countries. He had accused the World Bank and its sister institution, the International Monetary Fund, of making loans to those countries that essentially were used to repay commercial banks.

In 1990, Obey focused on Poland, which owed about $40 billion to commercial banks and foreign governments. The refusal of those banks and governments to forgive that debt "is a very big example of unreality" and was hampering the efforts of the Solidarity-led government to make the difficult transformation from communism to a free-market economy, Obey said.

Obey said he was withholding the contribution to the World Bank in hope of pressuring the administration into negotiating an agreement with other industrialized countries to reduce Poland's debt burden. Obey also linked the initial $70 million U.S. contribution to the proposed new European Bank for Reconstruction and Development to the Polish debt issue. The money was in the bill but could not be given to the bank until the administration had made progress in international negotiations to ease Poland's debt burden. *(Eastern Europe development bank, p. 206)*

During the subcommittee markup, Dean A. Gallo, R-N.J., offered an amendment to provide the full World Bank funding requested by Bush. The subcommittee rejected that amendment 3-9, however, with only Lewis and Porter supporting Gallo.

The panel approved nearly all of Bush's requests for other international development banks.

Eastern Europe

Repeating another political battle from 1989, Congress was moving to provide more aid money for Eastern Europe's emerging democracies than Bush sought. *(Eastern Europe aid, 1989 Almanac, p. 503)*

Obey's panel voted $500 million for programs in Eastern Europe; Bush had requested only $300 million.

The bulk of the money in the subcommittee's bill — $430 million — was to go to bilateral aid programs directly run by, or funded by, the U.S. government. The remaining $70 million would be the first U.S. contribution to the new European development bank.

In one significant change from 1989 legislation providing aid to Poland and Hungary, the Obey subcommittee bill gave the administration broad discretion to determine which Eastern European countries would get U.S. aid. Congress in 1989 had earmarked precise amounts for specific programs in Poland and Hungary, prompting complaints from the administration.

The House subcommittee bill divided the $430 million by category but generally allowed Bush to determine which countries received which types of aid. One exception was a $125 million earmark for quasi-governmental "enterprise funds" that invested in private businesses in Poland and Hungary.

Other aid categories in the bill were $100 million for private enterprise investments other than the funds for Poland and Hungary, $80 million for scholarships and technical training, $75 million for environmental cleanup, $30 million for technical advice on housing, and $20 million to bolster labor unions, political parties and other "democratic" institutions.

The subcommittee also called for increased activity in Eastern Europe by the Export-Import Bank, which provided loans and guarantees to finance exports of U.S. products. The subcommittee added $250 million to Bush's $500 million request for direct loans by the bank, and Obey urged the bank to use much of the extra money for exports to Eastern Europe.

Other Issues

Other major issues in the subcommittee's foreign aid spending bill were:

- **Nicaragua.** As part of Obey's campaign to avoid earmarks, the subcommittee took no position on Bush's request for $200 million in economic aid for Nicaragua. That would would have been in addition to the $300 million that Congress had just approved in a supplemental appropriation for fiscal 1990. *(Nicaragua aid, p. 770)*
- **Philippines.** Despite Obey's skepticism of the program, the panel approved $160 million in fiscal 1991 as the second U.S. contribution to an international aid program for the Philippines. Bush had requested $200 million.

Obey had criticized the program as wasteful, noting that Manila had not spent millions of dollars in previous aid.

The subcommittee took no stand on Bush's request for $200 million in military aid and $160 million in the regular U.S. bilateral economic aid program for the Philippines.

- **Cyprus.** The subcommittee directly rebuffed Obey only once during its June 13 markup. The issue was a perennial one: assistance to Cyprus.

As part of his campaign to avoid earmarks, Obey's draft of the bill recommended, but did not require, that the administration give Cyprus $15 million in economic aid — the amount approved routinely by Congress.

On a 7-5 vote, the subcommittee accepted an amendment by Porter to earmark the customary $15 million. Obey at first resisted the amendment but relented when it became clear that a majority favored it.

- **Pakistan.** At Wilson's request, the panel included a provision to extend for one year a waiver for Pakistan from a law barring aid to countries that appeared to be trying to develop atomic weapons. Because of Pakistan's strategic location, Congress had allowed aid there until April 1, 1991 — despite strong evidence that Pakistan was developing nuclear bombs.

Obey's draft bill was silent on the issue, thus allowing the existing waiver to expire and requiring an aid cutoff halfway through fiscal 1991. Wilson, a longtime advocate of aid to Pakistan, said the government in Islamabad would consider that a "hostile act." Obey eventually relented and agreed to insert in the bill another waiver for Pakistan until April 1992.

Full Committee Acts

The House Appropriations Committee approved HR 5114 on June 21 after amending the $15.8 billion bill to defer a battle between the administration and House Democrats over the balance of military and economic aid programs.

As approved by the committee, the bill contained the subcommittee's provision to suspend half the $85 million in military assistance earmarked for El Salvador.

It also contained a flat ban on aid to Cambodian insurgents — a substitute for a provision worked out earlier between Obey and Stephen J. Solarz, D-N.Y., to permit aid to non-communist insurgent movements as long as it in no way benefited the communist Khmer Rouge in Cambodia.

Committee Report Provisions

"The West has won the Cold War, and we have a right to say so," the committee stated in its report on HR 5114. But the administration's budget request ignored the decline of military threats to U.S. interests, reflecting "a lack of creativity and a hesitancy to move away from habitual and outmoded thinking," the committee said.

For development programs, the panel's bill provided $6.21 billion, $471 million more than Bush's request. It included an additional $785 million for programs intended to encourage U.S. exports, an increase of $255 million over the administration request.

To cover those increases, the committee pared Bush's budget for military aid to $5.3 billion, a reduction of $385 million. And, for the Economic Support Fund, used to bolster the economies of U.S. military allies, the panel provided $3.47 billion, a reduction of $84 million from Bush's request.

In another effort to reduce the military component of the foreign aid program, the committee cut the amounts requested for aid to Turkey, Greece and Portugal, all of which hosted important U.S. military bases. The panel's bill limited military aid to the three countries to $430 million for Turkey, $301 million for Greece and $95 million for Portugal.

In sum, the caps allowed the three countries $189 million less in military aid than the Bush administration requested and $109 million less than had been provided in fiscal 1990. The bill also required that military aid to Greece and Turkey be in the same 7-10 ratio that Congress had mandated for years. Neither this ratio nor the caps applied to economic aid. Greece received no economic aid; Turkey was slated to get $50 million.

Multilateral programs. The committee approved appropriating $1.69 billion for contributions to multinational banks and development funds, $161 million less than Bush's request. It also approved pledges to those institutions of $4.15 billion in callable capital.

The committee added $50 million for the IBRD, about half what Bush had requested.

Amounts appropriated for the multilateral agencies included $1.06 billion, as requested, for the International Development Agency. But the bill included a requirement that the administration withhold from that payment the U.S. share of any loan made to China that was not intended to meet basic human needs. The president could waive the requirement if he determined that doing so would be in the national interest.

But the Appropriations Committee strongly urged him not to use that authority unless the Chinese government stopped its repression of domestic dissent. And the committee warned the World Bank that it would face "increasingly severe sanctions . . . if it chooses to ignore the wishes of civilized people and engages in business as usual with a cruel and tyrannical regime."

The Appropriations Committee also approved the requested $70 million for a new development bank for Eastern Europe. The panel urged the administration to permit the Soviet Union to join the bank, since Moscow had agreed to severely limit the amount it would borrow in the first three years after joining. The rules of the bank made it easy for the United States to block any subsequent increase in Moscow's right to borrow from the agency. Soviet membership would promote private enterprise and democratization in that country, the committee argued.

The panel also appropriated $269 million for U.S. contributions to international agencies, most of them agencies of the United Nations working on development, health and environmental issues.

Bilateral developmental aid. For U.S. aid that was channeled neither through multilateral agencies nor through the security-oriented Economic Support Fund, the panel approved $4.26 billion. Among the major components of that amount were $482 million for agriculture and nutrition, $135 million for health, $134 million for education and human resources development and $435 million for the operating expenses of the Agency for International Development (AID).

The committee-approved bilateral aid program also included $186 million for the Peace Corps, $40 million for global disaster relief and $23 million for U.S. hospitals and schools abroad, such as the American University in Beirut.

El Salvador Aid Cut

The bill limited military aid to El Salvador to $85 million and, to provide incentives for both the Salvadoran government and the country's leftist guerrillas (the FMLN) to negotiate a peace settlement, withheld half that amount from the government.

The withheld funds would be turned over if the president reported any of the following to Congress:

- The FMLN declined to negotiate in good faith for a cease-fire and permanent settlement of the war.
- The guerrillas were receiving lethal military equipment from outside El Salvador. Congress would have to be shown proof of this.
- The survival of the Salvadoran government was jeopardized by "substantial and sustained military actions" by the FMLN.
- The FMLN was engaging in acts of violence against civilian targets.

On the other hand, military aid to El Salvador would be cut off entirely if:

- The elected government were overthrown by a coup.
- The government declined to participate in good-faith negotiations aimed at a cease-fire and settlement.
- The government were "failing to conduct a thorough and professional investigation" of the murder of six Jesuit priests, their housekeeper and her daughter at the University of Central America in San Salvador in November 1989.
- Salvadoran military or security forces were engaging in acts of violence against civilians.

The administration agreed in principle to withhold conditionally some aid as a means of pressuring the Salvadoran government to seek a negotiated settlement with the FMLN, though it insisted that 50 percent was too large a reduction.

In discussions with Democratic critics of the Salvadoran regime, Assistant Secretary of State Bernard W. Aronson reportedly proposed withholding 15 percent to 30 percent of the fiscal 1991 military aid allotment. But, aside from the percentage, there were other issues under negotiation. For instance, some liberals worried that the administration would demand such strict limits on the guerrillas that it would be able to release the withheld funds in case of a relatively minor military operation.

Sub-Saharan Africa

The House committee approved $800 million for bilateral economic aid to the states of sub-Saharan Africa, an increase of more than 40 percent over the Bush administration's request of $560.5 million. In addition, its bill provided the amounts requested for two multilateral funding agencies oriented toward those countries: the African Development Fund ($105.4 million) and the African Development Bank ($10.1 million).

"No other region of the world faces a development crisis as severe" as that confronting Africa, the Appropriations panel said.

In its report, the committee ordered AID to allocate funds from the African assistance package on the basis of two criteria: countries' need for assistance and their commitment to alleviating poverty.

By contrast, the committee complained, AID wanted to give a large slice of aid to Zaire, which, it said, had "one of the most mismanaged and corrupt economies in the world today." The bill barred military assistance to Zaire as well as payments to that government from the Economic Support Fund. It required that any development assistance to Zaire be channeled through private organizations, rather than the government.

The bill also barred military assistance to Somalia and the Sudan because of human rights abuses by those governments. In its report, the committee applauded AID's decision to cut off aid to Liberia because of human rights abuses, but argued against plans to resume assistance to that country and the Sudan in fiscal 1992, unless there were domestic reforms.

On the other hand, the committee cited Ghana as an example of a country that was trying to solve its economic problems and chided AID for not rewarding those efforts. It "strongly suggested" that aid to Ghana be increased by the proportion that the committee increased aid to Africa.

Eastern Europe

For bilateral assistance to Eastern European countries moving toward democratic political systems and private-sector economies, the panel approved $418.7 million, an increase of $188.7 million over the administration request.

More than half that amount ($213.7 million) was earmarked for programs to foster private enterprise, with the remainder parceled out for technical training ($80 million), environmental programs ($75 million), housing ($30 million) and "democratic activities" ($20 million).

As requested, the committee also approved $70 million for the European Bank for Reconstruction and Development and approved a limit of $163.4 million in callable capital.

The panel also included other kinds of guarantees intended to stimulate U.S. trade and investment in Eastern Europe: $200 million in short-term trade credit insurance, to encourage U.S. banks to provide trade credits, and $82 million in loans by the Overseas Private Investment Corporation (OPIC).

The panel also added Czechoslovakia to the list of countries where U.S. investments would be eligible for OPIC coverage.

Narcotics Control

The committee earmarked $574.9 million to combat international drug traffic, most of it by encouraging crackdowns by governments of countries where narcotics were produced or transshipped.

Of that amount, $372.9 million was military assistance or security-related economic aid divided among Peru, Bolivia, Colombia, Ecuador and Jamaica, provided they met certain goals in combating drug traffic.

An additional $150 million, the amount requested, was appropriated in the measure for the State Department's international narcotics control program.

To help wean countries from economic dependence on the drug trade, the panel included $40 million for development projects. It also included a provision allowing countries to use development assistance and Economic Support Fund money to promote the production, processing and distribution of crops that could serve as economic alternatives to coca and other plants used to produce narcotics.

In its report, the committee particularly commended a project aimed at encouraging silkworm cultivation in parts of Colombia, to replace coca.

The panel also earmarked $10 million for narcotics awareness education and $2 million to train foreign military personnel in narcotics control.

Environmental Programs

The committee provided $145 million for bilateral programs and $31.3 million for international organizations aimed at long-term environmental protection, particularly through protecting tropical forests as a means of combating global warming.

The bilateral amount included $30 million for projects to fight global warming, $15 million to maintain the diversity of animal and plant life, and $5 million for the conservation of African elephants, then estimated to number some 700,000 — 50 percent lower than in 1980.

The Appropriations panel approved none of the $500,000 requested for the tropical forestry action plan because, the report said, the program was oriented to encouraging commercial logging of tropical forests.

"Tropical-forest preservation will be a critical element of two of AID's leading environmental initiatives: biodiversity and global warming," the committee said. Accordingly, it directed the agency to support no project for industrial logging of primary tropical forests.

The committee specifically blasted AID programs in the Philippines that encouraged logging there and the export of raw logs from other Southeast Asian nations to the Philippines.

Included in the $31.3 million for environmentally oriented contributions to multilateral agencies was $10 million to implement the 1987 Montreal Protocol, intended to encourage developing countries to stop using chemicals that destroyed the Earthy's ozone layer, such as chlorofluorocarbons. The funds would provide credits, loans or insurance guarantees for developing alternative technologies and substitute products.

Aid to Refugees, Children

For aid to refugees, the panel approved $520.6 million, $45 million more than the administration's request. The committee said the boost was needed to cover the cost of the larger-than-anticipated number of refugees admitted.

That total included $35 million for emergency assistance and $45 million to resettle refugees — mostly Soviet Jews — in Israel.

The committee recommended that $67 million of the total be allocated to the U.N. refugee program for Palestinians to cover the increased cost of operating medical clinics as a result of the ongoing Palestinian *intifada* or uprising against Israeli occupation of the West Bank of the Jordan River and Gaza, launched in December 1987.

The Appropriations Committee recommended that $225 million in the bill go to programs aimed at the health and welfare of children.

That amount included $100 million for AID's Child Survival Fund, which paid for immunization and nutrition programs, and $75 million for UNICEF, the United Nations Children's Fund. In each case, the bill provided $25 million more than the administration's request.

The panel also earmarked $5 million in development assistance for children orphaned or displaced by man-made or natural disasters. Another $5 million was earmarked for humanitarian aid to children in Cambodia, with the proviso that none of the funds go directly or indirectly to the Khmer Rouge.

HOUSE ACTION

The House passed a $15.6 billion foreign assistance appropriations bill, 308-117, on June 27. *(Vote 204, p. 70-H)*

HR 5114 cut Bush's fiscal 1991 request for military aid to countries outside the Middle East by 13 percent, but the overall appropriation for foreign assistance was $117 million more than Bush requested and $112 million more than was appropriated for fiscal 1990.

In effect, the measure shifted more than $400 million that Bush budgeted for security-oriented programs to fund economic development.

As usual, the bulk of the bilateral military and economic aid was earmarked for countries in the Middle East and for nations that hosted major U.S. military bases. The bill earmarked amounts for Israel ($3 billion), Egypt ($2.1 billion), Jordan ($85 million), Lebanon ($7.5 million) and Israeli-occupied territories in the Gaza Strip and the West Bank of the Jordan River ($12 million).

Before passage, members debated amendments on two controversial issues: aid for family planning overseas and for non-communist rebels in Cambodia.

Members argued over the White House policy of denying funds for family planning programs from public or private agencies that promoted either abortion or coercive family planning policies.

Citing a critical need for large-scale family planning in Romania, critics of the policy tried to channel $3 million for such activity through the U.N. population fund and the London-based affiliate of the International Planned Parenthood Federation. Both agencies had been blacklisted since the Reagan administration. But facing a White House veto threat, the House voted instead to have other organizations administer the aid.

Cambodia: Democrats Split

The House also voted to uphold existing policy in the Cambodia vote. Overriding the Appropriations Committee, the House adopted by 260-163 an amendment by Solarz that would allow up to $7 million to be given to the non-communist rebels fighting the government of Cambodia, provided that none of the funds reached the Khmer Rouge, which also was fighting the Cambodian government. *(Vote 203, p. 70-H)*

Solarz, chairman of the House Foreign Affairs Subcommittee on Asian and Pacific Affairs, had been the leading political patron since 1985 of aid to the non-communist forces, headed by Cambodia's former leader Prince Norodom Sihanouk and by Son Sann, a former prime minister. The goal, said Solarz, was to prevent the Khmer Rouge, which had killed more than a million Cambodians when it ruled in 1975-79, from regaining control.

But that approach was challenged by Chester G. Atkins, D-Mass. He contended that aiding Sihanouk would have the effect of strengthening the Khmer Rouge, with which Sihanouk was allied. Atkins' district near Boston was home to many refugees from Cambodia's civil war.

That war was more than a Cambodian fight. The Phnom Penh government in 1990 was headed by Hun Sen, installed in 1979 by Vietnam. Then, Hanoi's forces, with Soviet backing, had invaded Cambodia to oust the Khmer Rouge and their leader, Pol Pot.

China, historically hostile to any expansion of Vietnamese power, supplied arms aid through Thailand to the Khmer Rouge, which had 45,000 troops. In addition, China, the United States, North Korea and the Association of South East Asian Nations had supported Sihanouk's force of 15,000 and Son Sann's National Liberation Armed Forces (NLAF), numbering about 10,000.

Vietnam announced in 1989 that it was withdrawing its 60,000 troops. But talks among the Cambodian factions — including the Hun Sen government — yielded no apparent movement toward a political settlement.

When the House Appropriations Committee marked up

U.N. Family Planning Agency . . .

Members of Congress who sparred regularly over abortion and family planning during debate on domestic legislation held a similar skirmish in the foreign policy arena in 1990.

When the House debated the fiscal 1991 foreign aid appropriations bill (HR 5114) on June 27, it replayed the 1989 fight over resuming support for the United Nations population fund (UNFPA), the largest multilateral agency aiding family planning. The agency gave assistance to 140 developing nations. *(1989 Almanac, p. 780)*

Like his predecessor, Ronald Reagan, President Bush opposed federal aid for abortions, at home or abroad. The administration opposed funding the UNFPA, which operated in China, where the government was criticized for allegedly supporting forced abortions and other coercive population-control policies. And the Bush team opposed funding the private International Planned Parenthood Federation (IPPF) because some of its affiliates offered abortion-related services.

Bush had vetoed the fiscal 1990 foreign aid appropriations bill over a provision mandating a $15 million contribution to the U.N. fund. On June 21, the administration threatened a veto of the fiscal 1991 bill if the two agencies were funded. *(Veto message, 1989 Almanac, p. 41-C)*

The debate ended with the same result for fiscal 1991, as family planning proponents failed to get funds for the agency included in either the House or Senate versions of the bill.

Romanian Example

In 1990, family planning proponents tried to use the plight of Romanian children as an emotional wedge on the issue. The regime of the late dictator Nicolae Ceauşescu banned virtually all abortions and birth control, and news reports offered graphic descriptions of thousands of sickly and destitute children languishing in Romanian orphanages.

During House consideration of the foreign aid spending measure, William Lehman, D-Fla., and John Porter, R-Ill., offered an amendment that would have given $1.5 million for health and child-survival projects in Romania and an additional $1.5 million for population planning programs there administered by the UNFPA and the IPPF.

But other members argued that Romania's children could still get help through other family planning organizations that did not support abortion.

The chairman of the House Appropriations Foreign Operations Subcommittee, David R. Obey, D-Wis., who managed the bill on the House floor, opposed the Lehman-Porter language, saying it would kill the bill and delay helping Romania's children.

A broader amendment that would have allowed funding of the IPPF was dropped after proponents failed to get the votes to approve the Lehman-Porter language.

The House eventually accepted, 224-198, an amendment by Christopher H. Smith, R-N.J., to strike the earmarks for the UNFPA and the IPPF. Instead, the $3 million for Romania would be administered by organizations that met U.S. approval. The underlying Lehman amendment was approved by 406-11. *(Votes 201, 202, p. 68-H)*

White House Opposition

The issue entwined old disputes over the role of foreign aid with the contentious politics of abortion and family planning. Since the mid-1980s, global family planning organizations had received a cold shoulder from Washington. The Reagan administration, arguing that a Third World population boom did not necessarily hamper economic development, curtailed donations to groups that supported abortion.

The White House particularly opposed funding any population agency, such as the U.N. fund, that operated in China.

"The UNFPA continues to support, defend and comanage a program that relies heavily on abortion and forced sterilization to implement its one-child-per-family policy," said Smith.

Supporters of the UNFPA countered that steps could be taken to ensure that U.S. funds were not used in China and insisted that funds for the agency should not be held hostage to the China question.

"We need to fund family planning worldwide because of the effect overpopulation has on the environment, on human suffering and on political instability," said Jim Moody, D-Wis.

The rancor that permeated the domestic abortion debate was just as evident in the UNFPA debate. Some leading UNFPA supporters claimed that opponents of the agency ultimately would like to gut international family planning efforts.

"Some conservatives of the Ghengis Khan variety will never be satisfied with any population planning assistance," asserted Werner H. Fornos, president of the Population Institute.

But Douglas Johnson, legislative director of the National Right to Life Committee, disagreed: "We don't take a position on population assistance."

HR 5114, Atkins argued that the two non-communist groups were collaborating directly with the Khmer Rouge, making a mockery out of the assumption that aid to Sihanouk and the NLAF could be kept from the detested Khmer Rouge. The panel added a provision to bar any aid to Cambodian rebels.

But in House debate over the bill, Solarz warned that the provision would "greatly diminish the prospect for a peaceful solution.... It would greatly diminish the incentive Vietnam has to agree to a peaceful settlement."

House Foreign Affairs Chairman Dante B. Fascell, D-Fla., backed Solarz, insisting that it was essential to keep alive "at least the figment ... of a third force," as an alternative to the existing regime and the Khmer Rouge.

Atkins dismissed the claim that the non-communist forces would carry political weight in a settlement: "The negotiations have failed. There is no possibility at this point of any peaceful negotiation."

. . . Denied Funds in Foreign Aid Bill

The United States helped set up the UNFPA in 1969, said executive director Nafis Sadik. "The U.S. is still a major actor in world politics and development," she said. "Morally, the U.S. has an obligation to fund it."

But Smith, citing China's population policies, retorted that by not funding the agency, "We're expressing the highest form of moral leadership in saying that human rights conditions there have meaning to us."

For a decade the United States was the agency's largest contributor. But in the mid-1980s Washington shifted gears on international family planning policy.

In a 1984 U.N. population conference in Mexico City, the Reagan administration announced that it would not provide funds to private organizations overseas that offered abortion-related services. This policy effectively cut off funds to the IPPF.

Also at the Mexico city conference, the administration reversed longstanding policy and challenged the assumption that population booms deterred economic development in poor countries. Population expansion was inherently a "neutral" phenomenon, the administration argued. While family planning could contribute to population stability, the White House said, free-market economic policies were the "natural mechanism for slowing population growth."

"At Mexico City we backed away from our traditional stance and focused instead on being anti-abortion and promoting capitalism," said J. Joseph Speidel, president of the Population Crisis Committee. The Reagan administration also emphasized bilateral aid programs over multilateral ones, such as the U.N. program, where U.S. influence would be diluted.

The Bush administration showed little interest in reversing the Mexico City policy.

China Policy

The China controversy erupted in January 1985, when media reports revealed that the Beijing government's one-couple, one-child policy included forced sterilizations, abortions and even infanticide. Beijing vehemently denied condoning such actions. The UNFPA denied supporting abortion as a method of family planning. But the Reagan administration withheld $10 million of the $46 million that Congress had appropriated for the agency for fiscal 1985. The $10 million was equal to the U.N. agency's program in China.

Congress subsequently enacted legislation that led to a total funding cutoff.

An amendment by then-Rep. Jack F. Kemp, R-N.Y., and Sen. Bob Kasten, R-Wis., to a fiscal 1985 supplemental appropriations bill (PL 99-88) prohibited funding of any organization that supported programs that included forced abortions or involuntary sterilizations. The provision also stated that the determination was up to the president or the secretary of State. *(1985 Almanac, p. 350)*

"Passage of the Kemp-Kasten language was the high point of the right-to-life movement in Congress. They beat us," said Mark S. Kirk, a former aide to Rep. Porter.

In November 1989, abortion rights and family planning groups thought they had scored a victory when the House and the Senate voted to mandate a $15 million contribution to the U.N. agency in the fiscal 1990 foreign aid spending bill. The amendment, sponsored by Sen. Barbara A. Mikulski, D-Md., stipulated that the money had to be kept in a separate account and could not be used in China.

But anti-abortion groups strongly opposed the provision, and Bush vetoed the bill, asserting that U.S. policy should warn "all family planning organizations that they must refrain from supporting coercive programs."

Congress passed a new version of the bill, minus the population provision, and Bush signed it into law.

Population planning advocates were outraged by the administration's failure to fund the multilateral population program over the narrow China issue. "Suppose there are irregularities that we disapprove of," said Moody. "Should other programs in other countries be held hostage?"

In May 1990, the United Nations estimated that world population, then 5.3 billion, could almost triple in 100 years. Virtually all the growth would be in developing countries.

"I've long believed that we need to address the population problem," said Sen. Mark O. Hatfield, R-Ore. "I was appalled last year that the administration saw fit to veto the foreign aid bill after Congress assured the administration that no money would go to China."

In the Senate, Hatfield, Mikulski, Foreign Operations Appropriations Chairman Patrick J. Leahy, D-Vt., and Foreign Relations Committee member Nancy Landon Kassebaum, R-Kan., asked Bush to reconsider and resume funding the UNFPA.

"Renewed confrontation serves no one's interest," they wrote in a March 5 letter to the White House.

But funding for the U.N. program failed, once again, to make it into the final bill.

Leahy included $15 million for the agency in the committee-approved bill, but the funds were removed during Senate floor consideration.

Supporting Atkins, Robert J. Mrazek, D-N.Y., told the House: "It is a lie to say that our aid does not benefit the Khmer Rouge. . . . Sihanouk supplies the Khmer Rouge . . . because his people don't have the will to fight."

That is "flatly untrue," Solarz retorted. "I stake my reputation for integrity on the proposition that there is no credible evidence whatsoever [that] our aid is going to the Khmer Rouge." He said the amendment would require an immediate aid cutoff to any group the president found "engaged in a pattern of military cooperation" to help the Khmer Rouge.

El Salvador Provision Unchanged

The House left in the bill a challenge to Bush over aid to El Salvador.

The bill halved military aid to the government of President Alfredo Cristiani. In part, this reflected Democrats' anger over human rights violations by the Salvadoran military. It also reflected a desire to press Cristiani's government to negotiate a settlement with leftist guerrillas of that country's long and bloody civil war.

Population-Control Funds

The House dodged a battle with the administration over aid to international population-control groups.

In 1989, Bush had vetoed similar legislation over the family planning issue, saying that the bill would have allowed U.S. aid to international groups that countenanced abortion. *(1989 Almanac, p. 780)*

Family planning proponents tried to use Romania as an emotional wedge. The regime of the late dictator Nicolae Ceauşescu banned virtually all abortions and birth control, and news reports offered graphic descriptions of thousands of sickly and destitute children languishing in Romanian orphanages. A bipartisan amendment by Florida Democrat William Lehman and Illinois Republican Porter called for $1.5 million for health and child survival projects in Romania and an additional $1.5 million for population planning programs there administered by the UNFPA and IPPF. "These organizations have been invited to Romania," said Porter. "They're on the ground and only need resources."

But other members, agreeing that Romania's children needed help, differed over who would handle the program. "The argument that we need family planning assistance in Romania, that we need family planning assistance around the world, is uncontested," countered Alan B. Mollohan, D-W.Va. "But it is not necessary to support these two abortion-promoting organizations to do that."

In a 224-198 vote, the House accepted an amendment by Christopher H. Smith, R-N.J., to strike the earmarks for the UNFPA and IPPF. Instead, the $3 million for Romania would be administered by organizations that met U.S. government approval. Smith later called that vote "a decisive victory for the pro-life forces in Congress."

The underlying Lehman amendment was approved by 406-11. *(Votes 201, 202, p. 68-H)*

Obey, who managed the bill on the House floor, opposed the Lehman-Porter language, saying it would kill his bill and delay helping Romania's children.

"Both these amendments attempt to provide help for these kids. Unfortunately, we're not really talking about these kids. We're talking about politics," Obey said.

The $3 million was to come from the account for population and development aid, a House staff member said.

A broader amendment that effectively would have allowed funding of IPPF was dropped after proponents failed to get the votes needed to approve the Lehman-Porter language.

Accross-the-Board Cut

During wrap-up action, James A. Traficant Jr., D-Ohio, proposed an amendment that would have cut by 10 percent all programs in the bill, with few exemptions. This would have reduced funds in the bill by $1.49 billion.

However, by voice vote, the House substituted for Traficant's language an amendment by Bob Clement, D-Tenn., that would apply a 2 percent reduction from which many programs were exempt. This amendment would reduce the amount appropriated by only about $140 million.

After refusing Traficant's demand for a recorded vote on the Clement substitute, the House adopted the gutted Traficant amendment by voice vote.

The House also adopted by voice vote amendments:

- By Mary Rose Oakar, D-Ohio, to earmark $7.5 million in development assistance for Lebanon.
- By Obey, to increase by $5 million (to $25 million) the amount earmarked for the International Fund for Agricultural Development. This amendment also included a provision that Afghan women receive an equitable share of the $70 million in aid earmarked for the Afghan people.

SENATE COMMITTEE ACTION

By the time the Senate Appropriations Foreign Operations Subcommittee took up HR 5114 on Oct. 2, Germany was unified, centrally planned economies were marching toward capitalism and the United States was on the brink of war with Iraq.

The Senate subcommittee focused much of its attention on U.S. policy in the Persian Gulf when it marked up its $15.3 billion foreign aid bill. The subcommittee approved an administration plan to forgive Egypt's $6.7 billion military debt, a proposal that the House had deferred after intense criticism.

The panel also backed an amendment offered by Frank R. Lautenberg, D-N.J., to cut off assistance to any country that violated the global embargo against Iraq.

However, the Foreign Operations Subcommittee deferred other controversial issues, ensuring that the Senate would revisit some old battles when it took up the foreign aid spending bill.

The subcommittee followed the House's lead and put heavy conditions on the $85 million military-assistance program for El Salvador. The panel also included $15 million in support for the United Nations population fund.

One other aspect of the subcommittee's deliberations remained unchanged over previous years: There was not enough money to fulfill all the foreign aid wishes of senators. In fact, the Foreign Operations panel was given an especially low allocation for outlays — $574 million below the House-passed legislation — when the full Appropriations Committee set spending limits in July.

The tight allocation reflected the view of Appropriations Committee Chairman Byrd, never a staunch proponent of foreign assistance.

As a result, the subcommittee chairman, Patrick J. Leahy, D-Vt., felt compelled to warn members who had amendments to offer, "If it costs money, you will have to identify specifically what you propose to cut to pay for your amendment and ensure that there are sufficient outlays."

Operation Desert Shield

At a news briefing before the markup, Leahy ruminated over how uncomfortable it would be for lawmakers to support debt forgiveness for Egypt during a time of tight budgets in the United States.

Many House members evidently saw that possibility as well. In approving a supplemental appropriation for Operation Desert Shield, the U.S. mobilization in the Middle East, the House voted on Sept. 30 to grant Egypt a temporary debt-payment waiver but deferred the broader question of debt forgiveness.

But the administration succeeded in convincing some senators that Egyptian President Mubarak's fate might depend on debt relief. Leahy, who originally was critical of debt forgiveness, said, "If we were to renege now, I would not want to be a political oddsmaker on Mubarak's future."

The subcommittee also took a different tack than the House on military assistance for Turkey.

The subcommittee earmarked $545 million in military

aid for Turkey, primarily in recognition of that government's contribution to Operation Desert Shield. The House had capped military aid for Turkey at $430 million.

Because military assistance for Greece had been fixed for several years at a 7-10 ratio with Turkey, aid to Athens was increased as well, from a House-passed ceiling of $301 million to $375 million.

The subcommittee approved another amendment intended to bolster U.S. policy in the Middle East, language offered by Lautenberg to punish nations for trading with Iraq. If approved, the measure could require a cutoff of aid to Jordan, which continued to trade with Iraq.

Although Jordan was not always a reliable U.S. ally, it was strategically located and was an important factor in any diplomatic resolution of the gulf crisis.

The administration, which had chosen mostly to overlook Jordan's violations of the Iraq embargo, had not expressed its views on the Lautenberg amendment. But the legislation included a provision for a waiver for national security considerations.

Israel was singled out for favorable recognition by the subcommittee. Leahy cited recent estimates that Israel had spent up to $1 billion on increased air patrols because of the threat from Iraq.

Partly to defray those costs, the panel approved an amendment that gave the Israeli government greater latitude in the expenditure of approximately $200 million from the Economic Support Fund.

El Salvador

Opponents of aid to El Salvador felt that they had their best opportunity yet to place meaningful restrictions on the program, but supporters of the Cristiani government were pulling out all stops to prevent that.

A turning point in the Senate's consideration of the issue came in August, when Christopher J. Dodd, D-Conn., agreed to back a Leahy plan, which was similar in intent to House-passed language, for restrictions on fiscal 1991 military aid to El Salvador. Dodd had opposed previous attempts to restrict aid to the Cristiani government.

The Leahy-Dodd proposal tied military aid to a U.N.-drafted plan for settling the conflict in El Salvador. The $85 million in aid would depend on three major conditions:

- Aid would be cut off completely if the president determined that El Salvador's government had rejected the peace plan but the country's leftist guerrillas (the FMLN) had accepted it.
- It would also be eliminated if the president reported that El Salvador's government "has failed to conduct a thorough and professional" investigation into the murders of six Jesuit priests in November 1989. Leahy described the progress in the case as a "fiasco."
- It would be cut in half if the leftists cooperated in peace talks. The full $85 million would be provided if the president determined that the FMLN has rejected a U.N.-drafted peace settlement that the government accepted, or if the rebels began a major offensive.

The restrictive language was anathema to the White House, which placed its hopes for a resolution of the conflict on continued support for the Cristiani government.

Other Battles

Like the Salvadoran aid issue, other controversial issues, such as funding for the U.N. Population Fund, were expected to be resolved on the Senate floor. Leahy chose to include $15 million in support for the agency.

While the subcommittee-passed bill required that no U.S. funds be used in China, that restriction was unlikely to satisfy the administration.

The subcommittee struck a provision for aid to the non-communist rebels in Cambodia, which was passed by the full House in June.

Democratic senators were particularly divided over aid to the resistance because of its alleged ties to the murderous Khmer Rouge.

The situation in Cambodia had changed considerably since the House vote. The five permanent members of the U.N. Security Council approved a framework for a Cambodian peace agreement in August, and the administration had started direct talks with Vietnam over the Cambodian war. The administration argued that to cut off aid would jeopardize ongoing diplomatic progress toward resolving the conflict.

Full Committee

The Senate Appropriations Committee sent a handful of nettlesome foreign policy questions to the floor when it marked up HR 5114 on Oct. 10.

The top issue awaiting resolution was the administration's proposal to forgive Egypt's $6.7 billion military debt. While the committee backed the plan, Tom Harkin, D-Iowa, said he would offer an amendment to require multilateral efforts to relieve Egypt's debt burden.

The Senate also was asked to resolve proposals to make future military assistance to El Salvador dependent on progress toward a peaceful settlement of the country's decade-long civil war.

Leahy and Dodd were leading efforts to ensure that the El Salvador military undertook reforms before reaping a full allotment of $85 million in military aid.

The Appropriations panel approved an amendment to the legislation, offered by Daniel K. Inouye, D-Hawaii, and Bob Kasten, R-Wis., to expedite the release of defense equipment to Israel and Turkey.

SENATE FLOOR

With adjournment nearing, the Senate passed HR 5114, 76-23, on Oct. 24. But passage came only after a surprise effort by two of the Senate's most powerful leaders to send a message of discontent to Israel and a new clash between the administration and critics of its policy toward El Salvador. *(Vote 306, p. 60-S)*

Debate Over Israel

The strained relations between the United States and Israel came under new pressure Oct. 19 because of the surprise amendment cosponsored by Minority Leader Bob Dole, R-Kan., and Appropriations Chairman Byrd and tabled only after a sharp debate.

The amendment would have required the president to report to Congress on Israel's policy for housing Soviet immigrants. Aides said the amendment was clearly intended to send a message to Israel.

Byrd said he was "deeply disturbed" by events in Israel, including the killing of 21 Palestinian protesters by security forces on Oct. 8. The housing policy also had come under fire because Israeli Foreign Minister David Levy had backed away from a promise not to settle more Soviet immigrants in East Jerusalem. The pledge was made as part of an agreement under which Israel was to receive a $400 million housing loan guarantee.

Sen. Arlen Specter, R-Pa., who opposed the Dole-Byrd proposal, called the measure "highly inflammatory."

Senators voted by a lopsided 90-8 margin to table the amendment. *(Vote 294, p. 58-S)*

In later debate, Byrd also tried to strip the Inouye-Kasten amendment to expedite release of aid to Israel from the bill. The attempt was rejected Oct. 22 by a near-unanimous 1-97. *(Vote 300, p. 59-S)*

Byrd vowed to continue to demand that Israel be viewed in a new light. In a sharply worded floor speech on Oct. 22, Byrd described "a certain psychology" under which "any vote against anything for Israel means that you are against Israel." He called that attitude as "bunk."

Congressional supporters of Israel said they were reassured by the huge numbers of senators who opposed Byrd's amendments.

El Salvador

The Senate on Oct. 19 also voted 74-25 to require an immediate 50 percent cut in military aid to El Salvador, approving the amendment offered by Leahy and Dodd. *(Vote 293, p. 58-S)*

Senators rejected (39-58) a milder, administration-backed amendment by Bob Graham, D-Fla. *(Vote 295, p. 58-S)*

In June, the House had signaled that the congressional mood on El Salvador had changed, approving an amendment to its foreign aid appropriations bill that was similar to the Leahy-Dodd language. The administration undertook negotiations with lawmakers from both bodies in an attempt to moderate the House-passed provision.

The negotiations never gained momentum, in part because the administration was diverted by the crisis in the Persian Gulf. State Department officials never engaged in serious talks with key members such as Joe Moakley, D-Mass., chairman of the House Task Force on El Salvador. When the administration finally focused on the issue, a surprising majority in the Senate had already made up their minds.

In lining up votes for their amendment, Leahy and Dodd said they noticed that many senators had grown tired of dealing with the war in El Salvador, particularly in light of reduced superpower tensions. According to both men, the government's long record of human rights violations, climaxed by the murder of the Jesuit priests, also soured many lawmakers.

Dodd said the wide margin of victory illustrated how "fed up" senators were with the ongoing violence.

As sentiment tilted against military aid to El Salvador, Jesuits and members of other religious orders tried to solidify the opposition. The religious orders, especially Roman Catholics, had long been in the forefront of opposition to military aid, but the killings of the Jesuits lent their message urgency.

While supporters of the Leahy-Dodd amendment believed it would send a signal to the Salvadoran military, they had no illusions that the legislation alone would halt the cycle of violence.

CONFERENCE/FINAL ACTION

The final provisions of the $15.4 billion foreign aid spending bill were crafted in a grueling all-night session of House and Senate conferees Oct. 25-26.

The conferees approved, with minor modificiations, the amendment reducing military aid to El Salvador as well as the administration's plan to forgive Egypt's $6.7 billion military debt.

But agreement on both amendments came only after some verbal brawling. Rep. Obey, who presided over the conference, fought with Sen. Leahy over the debt provision. At one point, Obey ridiculed Leahy's attempt to take the high ground in defending the amendment. "We have foreign policy junkies in here who can give speeches, but that disregards the populism on the House floor," he shouted.

Leahy played the policy card just as hard, pounding his fist on the conference table as he reiterated the administration's argument for the provision. "I don't want a war to start in the Middle East because people question our commitment," the senator thundered.

In the end, it took several closed-door caucuses before the confereees were able to reach a final agreement.

Twin Roadblocks

As the conference ran on into the early morning hours of Oct. 26, Obey said he wanted to delay consideration of controversial issues until the "underbrush [minor topics] had been cleared away." But some of the underbrush proved to be unexpectedly thorny, and the conferees did not begin seriously debating issues involving Egypt and El Salvador until well after 3 a.m.

At that point, reflecting the political linkage between the two measures, members bounced back and forth between topics, depending on which one was less contentious at the moment. Obey initiated the fireworks over Egypt by offering a proposal to reduce, rather than forgive, Egyptian debt. In addition, he said, "the president would be required to get other allies to write it [Egyptian debt] down also."

The purpose of the new provision was to provide political cover for House members who would be reluctant to support debt relief during economic hard times. "The fact is that I can count votes," said Obey. And what he discovered during that count was "every Southern member of the House telling me, 'I can't vote for it.' "

But the administration was successful in persuading the only Southern Democrat present, Rep. Wilson of Texas, to support the plan as drafted by the administration. Said Wilson, "Egypt is the glue that holds the Arabs together" in Operation Desert Shield.

Following a caucus on the issue, Obey returned to the conference room with a scaled-down proposal, which essentially left the forgiveness plan intact.

"The bottom line is the president has made a pledge to forgive [the debt]," Leahy said. "This legislation gives him the tools to carry out that pledge."

Leahy followed Obey onto the hot seat when Republicans, led by Oklahoma's Rep. Edwards, tried to weaken the amendment on El Salvador.

Edwards urged that, in the case of a total aid cutoff, the president be granted the authority to restore military assistance to the government if he determined that it was in full compliance with the complex conditions included in the amendment. Under the amendment offered by Dodd and Leahy, the aid could be restored only with approval by Congress.

Both Leahy and Obey rejected the proposal.

But Edwards pressed on, restating the administration's veto threat. "If it gets to that point," Leahy said testily, "then let him veto the damn thing."

Finally, Edwards and Kasten, Leahy's Republican counterpart on the Senate committee, crafted a compromise under which Leahy promised to request expedited procedures for restoring the aid, if the circumstance arose. The compromise also excluded all military assistance "in the pipeline" — appropriated but not yet delivered — from the Leahy-Dodd restrictions.

Other Provisions

On other issues, the conferees approved an amendment offered by Senate Majority Leader George J. Mitchell, D-Maine, providing for $20 million in overt assistance for the non-communist resistance in Cambodia. But at the behest of Obey, the conference panel required that the funds be subject to congressional oversight.

Obey also strongly objected to language in the Senate bill permitting any country receiving U.S. foreign military aid to be granted unlimited amounts of "excess" Defense Department weaponry. The conferees approved the gist of the Senate provision, although they included excess non-lethal supplies as well.

The conferees also approved an amendment to the Senate bill offered by Don Nickles, R-Okla., that prohibited direct assistance to Yugoslavia because of human rights violations. At the request of House members, again led by Obey, Nickles included language giving the secretary of State authority to waive the restriction.

The committee also compromised on a provision barring development funds for Zaire because of that country's poor human rights record. The conferees said that funds could be provided only through non-governmental organizations, private volunteer organizations or universities.

Changing Times

While the foreign aid bill represented a concession to budget realities in the United States, it also was an acknowledgment of the changes in the geopolitical landscape during the year.

With the passing of the Cold War, Congress had grown increasingly dubious of the need for foreign military grants, aside from those provided to allies in the Middle East. Excluding the $3.1 billion specified for Israel and Egypt, the bill would cut the administration request for grants by nearly 25 percent. The bill would replace some of the grants with low-interest loans.

Perhaps more important, the legislation reduced by $400 million the administration request for Economic Support Fund (ESF) aid. Such aid was widely used, especially by the Reagan and Bush administrations, to bolster the economies of U.S. military allies.

Aside from the slightly more than $2 billion in ESF funds earmarked for Israel and Egypt, the State Department was given only about $1 billion to spread among other countries.

"It's clear that ESF has been hit the hardest," said one administration official. The official said that an existing prohibition on aid to Pakistan could work to the advantage of other ESF recipients, who could otherwise face a reduction. The administration had requested $210 million in ESF aid for Pakistan, along with $228 million in military grants, but assistance to that country had been suspended Oct. 1 because of its emerging nuclear capability. *(Pakistan aid suspension, p. 768)*

Having taken money from security-related accounts such as ESF, Congress redirected the money toward a variety of purposes. The $369.7 million in assistance for Eastern Europe represented a compromise between the House- and Senate-passed figures and a $140 million increase over the administration's original request. The $70 million request for a U.S. contribution for the European Development Bank, which provided loans for Eastern European countries, also was fully funded.

Lawmakers substantially increased the assistance earmarked for sub-Saharan Africa. The bill included $800 million for the Development Fund for Africa, more than $230 million above the administration's request. The Senate Appropriations panel, in its report on the foreign aid bill, expressed "growing alarm at the decline in living standards" throughout the region.

Congress also increased funding for a number of international health and welfare programs over the level requested by the administration. The House and Senate agreed to provide $100 million for the Child Survival Fund, aimed at helping poverty-stricken children in less-developed nations; the administration had asked for $74 million to fund the program.

Lawmakers provided $250 million in funding for international population control programs, an increase of more than 25 percent over the administration request.

They also targeted $52 million to control the spread of AIDS in the developing world, nearly $14 million over the administration figure.

Desert Shield Response

As they had for several years, two countries — Egypt and Israel — dominated foreign aid spending. The legislation specified $2.15 billion in military and security-related assistance for Egypt, and $3 billion for Israel.

Israel also benefited from other provisions, including new authorization for the president to transfer up to $700 million of defense supplies to the country and to pre-position another $300 million worth of U.S. defense stockpiles in Israel.

Congressional sources acknowledged that the amendments also were motivated by a desire to reassure the Israeli government, which was concerned by administration plans to sell $6.7 billion in arms to Saudi Arabia. With adoption of the provisions to aid Israel, critics of the Saudi sale dropped plans to press for a resolution blocking the transfer. *(Saudi arms sale, p. 734)*

The bill passed by the Senate contained a host of new provisions aimed at aiding Israel for the increased military costs it had incurred because of heightened tensions in the Middle East. The conferees agreed to the amendments, altering them only slightly. The most important measure, the Kasten-Inouye amendment, authorized the president to provide the Israelis at least $700 million worth of equipment from Defense Department stocks. The conferees gave the president wider discretion to implement the program than existed in the original Kasten-Inouye language.

In addition, conferees approved Senate-passed language allowing Israel to use up to $200 million in Economic Support Funds for its own defense purposes. They also backed a provision to enable Israel to receive an accelerated disbursement of $1.7 billion in military financing.

Jordan, another nation caught in the vortex of events in the Middle East, was not as fortunate. The House-Senate conference dropped a House-passed provision specifying $50 million in military financing for the kingdom. The conferees retained $35 million in economic aid earmarked for Jordan, however.

The Senate Appropriations Committee, which opposed all earmarked aid for Jordan, said in its report that it was disturbed by Amman's "unwillingness to comply fully" with the U.N.-approved embargo against Iraq.

In another action taken in response to the gulf crisis, lawmakers waived a ban on military sales to Qatar, a small, independent state bordering Saudi Arabia.

Congress also dealt with the painful issue of Americans trapped in Kuwait and Iraq, as well as those held hostage for several years in Lebanon. The legislation set aside $10 million to provide health insurance benefits to the hostages and their families. The detainees also could receive a salary from the government, at an annual rate of up to $32,000, for the period of their captivity.

The bill wrapped several proposed anti-Iraq amendments into an "Iraq Sanctions Act of 1990," which granted the president the authority to cut off trade with nations not complying with the global embargo against Baghdad.

Other Issues

As Obey had noted, the House-Senate conference empowered the president to write down Poland's $2.85 billion official debt. In their explanatory statement, the conferees said they provided authority for the president to recognize the "uncollectibility" of the debt.

The legislation also extended the authority of the Export-Import Bank and the Overseas Private Investment Corporation to operate in Eastern Europe. Conferees retained Obey's provision conditioning U.S. contribution to the new Eastern European development bank on progress in easing Poland's debt.

But Congress stopped short of providing aid to the three Baltic States that had proclaimed their independence from Moscow. Conferees rejected a Senate amendment amendment that would have provided $10 million in medical aid and humanitarian assistance to the three: Latvia, Lithuania and Estonia.

The bill also sought to prod further changes in U.S. policy in Southeast Asia. The administration had revised its policy toward Cambodia in July, authorizing the first direct talks with the Vietnam-backed government in Phnom Penh. Congress approved $20 million in aid for Cambodia and pressed the administration to lift the trade embargo on that country's government.

Reflecting congressional skepticism over the administration's prosecution of the international war on drugs, lawmakers reduced a request for $141 million in military aid for three Andean countries to $118 million. In a direct slap at the State Department's Bureau of International Narcotics, Congress restricted funding for the agency until it provided a report detailing steps being taken to correct its "management deficiencies."

Despite opposition from the administration, and many in the Senate, the legislation included a House-passed amendment providing $20 million for the International Fund for Ireland.

The fund was established in 1986 to promote economic development in Northern Ireland and nearby parts of the Republic of Ireland.

Bush Signing

In signing the bill Nov. 5, Bush said he was "especially pleased" by the Egyptian debt forgiveness provisions, calling congressional approval of his proposal "in accord with the finest traditions of bipartisan cooperation."

The president also said he was "appreciative" of provisions giving him latitude in providing assistance to Eastern Europe.

But Bush called the restrictions on aid to El Salvador "troublesome," warning that they could complicate efforts to reach an accord between the government and the leftist guerrillas. And he also complained of the restrictions on aid to Cambodia, cuts in aid to Turkey and bans on military aid to Malaysia and other countries. ■

Defense Cuts Finance Pork-Filled Bill

Congress cleared a $4.3 billion supplemental spending (HR 4404) bill for fiscal 1990 in the early morning hours of May 25, sending President Bush a pork-filled measure partly financed by $2 billion in defense cuts. The bill included $720 million for Nicaragua and Panama, aid urgently sought by Bush.

The president signed the measure the same day.

BACKGROUND

President Bush got the supplemental bill started on Jan. 25 when he requested $570 million — $500 million of it for the new government of Panama, which had taken office following a U.S. military invasion in December 1989, and $70 million for assistance to cover the larger-than-budgeted cost of arriving refugees, most of them Jews from the Soviet Union.

On March 13, he added $300 million for Nicaragua, bringing his request to $870 million.

Bush asked Congress to act quickly so the money would be available by April 25, when the U.S.-backed Nicaraguan president-elect, Violeta Chamorro, was scheduled to take office.

Bush proposed to pay for the aid with various cuts in the Pentagon budget. *(Nicaragua aid, p. 770; Panama aid, p. 774)*

When the Appropriations committees took up the bill, they added dozens of domestic items, assuming that the engine of aid to Central America would pull them through. When the bill cleared, it provided $4.3 billion in spending:

- $885 million in foreign aid, including $720 million for Panama and Nicaragua, most of the Bush request.
- $2.1 billion for mandatory programs over which appropriators had little control. That figure rose from $1.2 billion in the House version and $1.6 billion in the Senate, primarily because the administration kept increasing its estimate for providing food stamps to all qualified people.
- $1.4 billion for discretionary domestic programs. That rose from about $250 million in the House bill and $1.2 billion in the Senate bill, much but not all of it requested by the administration.

The bill also included $2 billion in defense cuts, offsetting nearly half the new spending.

HOUSE ACTION

The House Appropriations Committee completed its work on the bill March 27, keeping all but $80 million of

Bush's $870 million request and tacking on some $1.5 billion for a raft of domestic programs that were expected to run short of funds, including food stamps and disaster assistance.

The committee bill also contained a more subtle change: a revision of the Pentagon budget cuts that Bush had proposed to offset the new spending.

Defense Offsets

To pay for part of the $2.4 billion measure, the chairman of the Subcommittee on Defense, John P. Murtha, D-Pa., added provisions to rescind a total of $1.79 billion previously appropriated for various Pentagon programs. Included in that amount was more than $600 million that Defense Secretary Dick Cheney had planned to use for another controversial purpose. Cheney had proposed to "reprogram" the funds to restore payroll cuts that had been imposed in 1989. That raised the ire of House Armed Services Committee Chairman Les Aspin, D-Wis., who, with the strong backing of Speaker Thomas S. Foley, D-Wash., blocked the reprogramming. *(Defense reprogramming, p. 676)*

The dispute originated in the budget battles of 1989. In an end-of-session deal, Congress and the administration had agreed to accept partial cuts imposed under the Gramm-Rudman antideficit law as part of a final deficit-reduction package.

The administration could have exempted Pentagon personnel accounts from the across-the-board cuts at the time, but it chose not to. Instead, in early 1990 the Pentagon offered its own proposal to cover the personnel accounts with money from some congressionally popular programs that it cared less about.

Aspin argued that the administration was trying to ease the pain to the Pentagon of Gramm-Rudman cuts, known as sequestration. "If you allow the Pentagon to reprogram without pain, then sequestration doesn't hurt defense," Aspin said. That, he felt, would give the administration the advantage in future budget battles.

With Cheney's proposed funding sources thus preempted, Aspin offered to negotiate a new list of programs from which the funds could be reprogrammed. But he said the Pentagon would have to accept cuts that hurt.

Foreign Aid

The only change the committee made in Bush's foreign aid request was an $80 million reduction in the $500 million requested for Panama. The money was allocated to three areas:

- $30 million to support refugees outside the United States, including $5 million for Soviet Jews who emigrated to Israel.

Though it did not entail a new appropriation, the bill also provided $400 million in housing loan guarantees to help Israel settle Soviet Jews.

- $30 million for aid to Africa, replacing a similar amount drawn from funds earmarked for Somalia and the Sudan to cover the cost of an initial allocation of $42 million in emergency aid to Panama approved in February.

Of the funds for Africa, $10 million was earmarked for the newly independent country of Namibia, $10 million to promote democracy in South Africa, and $2.5 million each for aid to Zambia and Mozambique.

- $20 million for aid to the countries of the eastern Caribbean, including $5 million to deal with the effects of Hurricane Hugo, which ripped through that region in September 1989 before striking the U.S. coast.

The committee also increased by $1.6 billion the amount of "callable capital" available to the World Bank.

Domestic Add-ons

The Appropriations Committee added about $1.5 billion in spending for domestic programs, including:

- $510 million for the food stamp program, the largest single domestic add-on.

Though Congress had appropriated $1.5 billion more than the administration requested for fiscal 1990, the committee cited estimates that the program might run short by an additional $510 million.

- $433 million to help cover the cost of fighting forest fires: $177 million for the Bureau of Land Management and $256 million for the Forest Service.
- $390 million for the Department of Veterans Affairs: $190 million for salaries and pensions, $150 million for the home loan guarantee revolving fund and $50 million for salaries and benefits associated with veterans' medical care.
- $111 million to cover the unusually high cost of disaster-relief efforts after Hurricane Hugo, flooding in Southeastern states and the 1989 San Francisco earthquake.

Floor Action

The House passed the bill by a vote of 362-59 on April 3. *(Vote 65, p. 26-H)*

Though the measure received bipartisan support, the debate was marked by traditional objections to sending money abroad when pressing problems existed at home. Nick J. Rahall II, W.Va., and James A. Traficant Jr., Ohio, both Democrats from economically depressed Rust Belt districts, led the assault with a series of unsuccessful amendments.

The House voted 38-379 to reject a package of amendments by Rahall to delete all foreign aid. By similar margins, it then defeated amendments by Traficant, voting first 64-354 against a 5 percent cut and then 72-346 against a 3 percent cut. Gus Savage, D-Ill., who had been criticized for anti-Semitism in his recently successful primary race, lost 2-418 when he tried to strike the entire $75 million intended for resettling Soviet Jews in the United States and Israel.

Only George W. Crockett Jr., D-Mich., supported him. *(Votes 61, 62, 63, 64, p. 26-H)*

SENATE ACTION

Even before the House vote, Democratic leaders in the Senate served notice that they did not plan to move quickly on the measure.

"I do not believe we should appropriate the full amount requested," Majority Leader George J. Mitchell, D-Maine, said on April 2, "until the administration submits a mean-

> **BOXSCORE**
>
> **Legislation:** Dire Emergency Supplemental Appropriations Act, PL 101-302 (HR 4404).
>
> **Major action:** Signed, May 25. Conference report adopted by Senate, May 25 (session of May 24); House, 308-108, May 24. Passed by Senate, May 1; by House, 362-59, April 3.
>
> **Reports:** Conference Report (H Rept 101-493); Appropriations (S Rept 101-272); Appropriations H Rept 101-434.

ingful long-term foreign aid plan."

The bill was stalled further while Senate leaders and the White House tried to resolve an unrelated conflict over when to bring up a bill to cut capital gains tax rates. That obstacle evaporated with little public explanation April 24.

Hours later, Appropriations Chairman Robert C. Byrd, D-W. Va., convened his committee. With little debate, the committee draft of the bill was approved by a vote of 24-0.

When it left the committee that evening, the bill contained about $1 billion more than the House version, including significant increases for food stamps and veterans' assistance and substantial funding for programs not covered in the House bill, including $110 million for the 1990 census, $165.7 million for Head Start and $185 million for a fingerprinting laboratory for the FBI. Also included was funding for disaster relief, forest firefighting and measles immunizations.

The $3.7 billion price tag on the bill was largely offset by defense transfers and rescissions, which had grown to $2.9 billion.

The bill restored $780 million in outlays for military pay that had been cut in the 1989 budget deal. To achieve this, it trimmed by an estimated 1.6 percent the unobligated balances in all Pentagon accounts, reducing budget authority by $1.347 billion.

Floor Action

The bill arrived on the Senate floor April 25, only to become swamped with amendments and tangled in a fight over abortion.

But a visit to Capitol Hill April 30 by Panama's new president, Guillermo Endara, who was waiting for the $420 million in aid, gave senators a crucial push. Disputes that had been holding up final action — over abortion, the death penalty, and financing for the savings and loan bailout — evaporated, and the bill was approved May 1 by voice vote.

Language in the committee bill that would have allowed the District of Columbia to use local funds to pay for abortions had drawn an immediate White House veto threat. After anti-abortion conservatives failed to strip the provision from the bill, they used arcane Senate rules to attach a pro-death penalty amendment to the abortion rights language.

The new provision would have allowed the death penalty for drug-related murders in the Distict, which prohibited capital punishment. Senators finally punted the whole issue to conferees, approving the two-pronged provision without a roll-call vote.

The committee had also included a little-noticed provision to take spending needed to salvage the thrift industry and pay off depositors in failed institutions out of budget calculations under the Gramm-Rudman-Hollings anti-deficit law. Ernest F. Hollings, D-S.C., raised a point of order, arguing that the act should not be changed in an appropriations bill.

And he threatened to bring up his own proposals to take the Social Security trust funds out of deficit calculations and roll back Social Security payroll taxes. Not wanting to entangle the supplemental in a budget fight, budget leaders backed down and the provision was dropped.

CONFERENCE ACTION

When the two bills reached the conference stage May 9, House Appropriations Chairman Jamie L. Whitten, D-Miss., was clearly annoyed at the $1.3 billion in spending that had been added by the Senate.

As he saw it, the House had been a team player, expediting its version quickly and resisting many members' attempts to pile on pet projects.

"He's looking for an equalization here. He's saying, 'Either you take yours out, or you give us some,' " said a Democratic member of House Appropriations.

In the end, House conferees added at least $100 million worth of constituent-pleasing amendments to the already-loaded bill.

The new add-ons, in the form of flood-relief money for the Southeast and many earmarks for the districts of well-placed members, were approved virtually without opposition from Senate negotiators.

The conferees scrapped the most controversial provision, which would have allowed the District to use its own money to pay for abortions for poor women; the pro-death penalty language also died with it.

Final conference action on what had become a $4.3 billion bill was delayed by a last-minute debate over defense cuts.

Conferees had to nickle-and-dime a slew of defense programs to reach their goal of $2 billion in offsets.

Lawmakers reduced the Pentagon's fuel supplies, saving $200 million.

They shifted $140 million from the discontinued SR-71 spy plane, and killed or cut $253 million worth of military construction projects, most of them overseas.

The repair of the recently exploded turret on the battleship *Iowa* was deferred, saving $11 million.

Another $83 million was cut from payroll accounts, derived from an earlier civilian hiring freeze. NASA lost $30 million of the Air Force's annual contribution to the space shuttle program. Congress shifted $180 million from various missile accounts, including the MX and the Sidewinder.

Almost $95 million was cut from aircraft-buying accounts, much of it from spare parts and the Air Force's F-4G Wild Weasel.

But conferees still were unable to put together a successful plan for covering the payroll accounts. Defense appropriators and the administration came up with a $1.4 billion reprogramming plan. But under informal rules governing such matters, the proposal also required the approval of the chairmen of the two congressional Armed Services committees.

Aspin balked, insisting on cuts from the Pentagon's favorite weapons programs, such as the B-2 stealth bomber, the strategic defense initiative (SDI), and the *Seawolf*-class nuclear submarine.

A compromise was finally put together, but it fell apart when Cheney refused to accept $200 million-plus in big-weapons cuts.

The dispute was not resolved until after the bill had cleared.

On June 7, Cheney announced that he and Foley had broken the deadlock. Cheney agreed to reprogram $58 million from major weapons programs, but none of it came from the B-2 or SDI.

The House approved the conference report, 308-108, on May 24, but only after defeating several attempts by conservative Republicans to kill the pet projects of other members.

The Senate then cleared the bill by voice vote May 25, shortly after midnight. *(Vote 138, p. 48-H)* ■

$188.2 Billion for Labor/HHS/Education

There was plenty of drama during the passage of the $182.2 billion fiscal 1991 spending bill for the Departments of Labor, Health and Human Services (HHS), and Education and related agencies even though the annual argument over abortion funding was resolved relatively early.

The Senate finally cleared the conference report on the bill (HR 5257) by voice vote late Oct. 26, ending four days of bouncing the bill back and forth between the two chambers.

In the end, the key sticking point between the two houses, $2 million for a commission to measure progress toward meeting a set of educational goals developed by the nation's governors and President Bush, stayed in, although in slightly altered form.

The final compromise, pushed by Sen. Jeff Bingaman, D-N.M., provided funding for the commission only if the panel was specifically authorized. Bingaman said he hoped to clear an authorization bill early in 1991, in time to take advantage of the available funding.

BOXSCORE

Legislation: Fiscal 1991 Labor, Health and Human Services, Education and related agencies appropriations, PL 101-517 (HR 5257).

Major action: Signed, Nov. 5. Cleared by Senate, Oct. 26; conference report adopted by Senate, 82-15, Oct. 25; by House, 335-74, Oct. 22. Passed by Senate, 76-15, Oct. 12; by House, 359-58, July 19.

Reports: Conference report (H Rept 101-908). Appropriations (S Rept 101-516); Appropriations (H Rept 101-591).

But while the bill was traveling back and forth, it picked up other riders as well. Besides adding Bingaman's commission funding late Oct. 25, the Senate tacked on an entire bill to overhaul the Job Training Partnership Act (JTPA), and $10 million for grants to states to plan to meet public health goals.

The House stripped off the latter two amendments early Oct. 26, before sending the conference report back to the Senate, which ended the tennis match by clearing the bill.

For the first time in years, the abortion issue, which had held fiscal 1990 bill hostage for weeks in 1989 and gotten one version vetoed by Bush, was not a factor in the bill's delay. The 1989 appropriations bill provided $156.7 billion in fiscal 1990 spending. *(Fiscal 1990 Labor-HHS appropriations, 1989 Almanac, p. 707)*

While the Senate version of the fiscal 1991 measure would have permitted federal funding of abortions in certain cases of rape or incest, a floor amendment to that amendment would have required that abortion providers receiving funds under the bill (including hospitals and other large health facilities) notify the parents of a minor 48 hours before the abortion could be performed.

Because it was procedurally impossible to separate the parental-notification language from the rape and incest language, abortion rights advocates who wanted the rape and incest exceptions decided to drop the issue entirely for the year.

But another issue — allocating funds for cities and states hard-hit by the AIDS virus — provided some of the drama that was usually generated by the abortion debate. Congress on Aug. 4 had cleared legislation (S 2240) authorizing $875 million to help cities and states cope with the huge costs of the AIDS crisis. *(AIDS emergency relief bill, p. 582)*

Neither the House nor the Senate Appropriations Labor-HHS Subcommittee included new funding for the AIDS measure in their versions of the spending bill. After an acrimonious fight between AIDS groups, which wanted to find funds by paring back other health programs, and organizations representing the programs the AIDS groups wanted to cut, conferees eventually agreed to $221 million for the AIDS relief programs.

The overall fiscal 1991 spending level of $182.2 billion was $7.4 billion more than Bush's request and $25.5 billion over the $156.7 billion in the fiscal 1990 Labor-HHS bill.

HOUSE COMMITTEE ACTION

With members literally singing its praises, the House Appropriations Committee on July 12 approved a $170.4 billion fiscal 1991 Labor-HHS spending bill. The Labor-HHS Subcommittee had approved the bill on June 20.

As approved by the full committee, the bill carried the same language that had been law since 1981 — prohibiting funds from being spent on abortions unless the pregnancy endangered the woman's life.

But the abortion question was not raised by either side during the markup, primarily because those in both camps knew that for procedural reasons, whatever happened could easily be undone on the floor.

"The issue will be joined," said committee member Vic Fazio, D-Calif., one of the leaders of House efforts to relax the ban and permit federal funding of abortions in cases of rape or incest. "We are going to deal with it on the floor."

With the abortion battle deferred another day, committee members heaped praise on the second-biggest appropriations bill (only defense was larger) and on its sponsor, Labor-HHS Subcommittee Chairman William H. Natcher, D-Ky.

It was, in fact, while Silvio O. Conte, Mass., ranking Republican on both the Labor-HHS Subcommittee and the full Appropriations panel, was wondering whether HR 5257 or Natcher could more appropriately be called "America's Bill," that the singing began. It started as a low hum from somewhere in the Republican ranks to accompany Conte's accolades but soon spread across the aisle until junior members from both parties burst into "The Battle Hymn of the Republic."

Since the bill funded some of the most popular government programs, members found little to complain about.

Most of the measure's funding — $123.9 billion — was not even within the committee's jurisdiction because it paid for entitlement programs such as Medicaid, the joint federal-state health program for the poor; portions of Medicare, the federal health program for the elderly and disabled; and Aid to Families with Dependent Children, the nation's principal welfare program.

Still, the remaining $43.9 billion in "discretionary"

Fiscal 1991 Appropriations for Labor . . .

Following are the budget authority totals in the fiscal 1991 appropriations bill (HR 5257 — PL 101-517) for the Departments of Labor, Health and Human Services (HHS), and Education and related agencies [including, in some cases, funds appropriated for subsequent fiscal years].

(Figures, in thousands of dollars, may not add due to rounding.)

Agency	Bush Request	House [1] Bill	Senate Bill	Conference/ [2] Final
Department of Labor				
Employment and Training Administration	$ 4,864,621	$ 5,264,817	$ 5,212,868	$ 5,160,552
Labor-Management Service	90,051	90,051	90,051	87,880
Employment Standards Administration	1,433,900	1,438,940	1,438,940	1,433,580
Occupational Safety and Health Administration	287,893	291,243	295,893	286,663
Mine Safety and Health Administration	172,500	177,767	179,823	174,947
Bureau of Labor Statistics	205,084	207,274	206,674	205,206
Departmental Management	175,776	178,501	169,522	167,709
Subtotal	**$ 7,229,825**	**$ 7,648,593**	**$ 7,593,771**	**$ 7,516,537**
Health and Human Services				
Health Resources and Services	1,937,457	1,865,875	2,713,440	2,326,325
Centers for Disease Control	1,171,595	997,701	1,322,698	1,318,197
National Institutes of Health	7,927,989	8,317,654	8,347,085	8,306,648
Alcohol, Drug Abuse and Mental Health Administration	2,836,152	2,837,891	3,012,283	2,907,109
Assistant Secretary for Health	224,107	247,965	276,643	282,484
Health Care Financing Administration	84,881,262	84,175,932	85,807,354	85,904,313
Social Security Administration	46,958	46,958	46,958	46,958
Black Lung Benefits	829,081	829,081	829,081	829,081
Supplemental Security Income	17,575,394	15,551,594	17,504,618	17,552,170
Family Support Administration	14,370,913	14,037,446	16,870,526	17,002,540
Human Development Services	8,551,433	6,855,409	10,112,559	9,577,423
Departmental Management	162,552	162,502	154,752	157,707
Undistributed salary and expense savings	0	0	-50,000	-50,000
Subtotal	**$ 140,514,893**	**$ 135,926,008**	**$ 146,947,997**	**$ 146,160,955**
Department of Education				
Compensatory Education	$ 5,838,939	$ 6,225,250	$ 6,376,674	$ 6,224,516
Impact Aid	660,854	800,000	800,000	780,720
School Improvement Programs	1,704,916	1,529,045	1,685,247	1,582,654
Bilingual, Immigrant and Refugee	205,537	205,000	196,779	198,014
Handicapped Education	2,137,421	2,747,730	2,253,503	2,467,446
Rehabilitation Services	1,839,073	1,851,911	1,903,862	1,896,499
Special Institutions	117,979	117,654	119,042	115,610
Vocational and Adult Education	1,169,389	245,000	1,244,879	1,245,536

funding over which the committee did have control was $5.6 billion more than the comparable total for fiscal 1990 and $3.2 billion more than Bush requested.

That number was expected to go even higher, because, as was his custom, Natcher deferred funding for programs not yet authorized.

The subcommittee set aside $5.5 billion for programs awaiting reauthorization, including the popular Head Start program for disadvantaged preschoolers (which received $1.55 billion in fiscal 1990), the Low Income Home Energy Assistance Program (funded at $1.4 billion in fiscal 1990) and vocational education assistance ($929.7 million). Together, the unauthorized programs had received $5.9 billion in fiscal 1990; Bush requested $5.5 billion for them for fiscal 1991.

The subcommittee also set aside an additional $2.9 bil-

. . . HHS, Education and Related Agencies

Agency	Bush Request	House [1] Bill	Senate Bill	Conference/ [2] Final
Department of Education				
Student Financial Assistance	6,352,415	6,777,000	6,873,950	6,709,584
Guaranteed Student Loans	4,539,780	3,900,000	4,539,780	4,539,780
Higher Education	657,648	763,616	785,592	762,638
Howard University	185,446	200,036	195,536	195,215
College Housing Loans	13,449	38,449	13,449	37,726
Education Research and Statistics	174,726	133,860	139,726	135,070
Libraries	39,062	140,800	146,428	142,898
Departmental Management	406,700	406,700	402,700	392,386
Subtotal	**$ 26,043,334**	**$ 26,082,051**	**$ 27,677,147**	**$ 27,426,292**
Related Agencies				
Action	192,424	191,659	200,136	191,292
Corporation for Public Broadcasting	306,505	306,505	341,940	318,636
Federal Mediation and Conciliation Service	26,312	27,705	27,705	27,037
Federal Mine Safety and Health Review Commission	4,292	4,292	4,292	4,189
Postsecondary Education	0	0	1,000	0
National AIDS Commission	3,000	3,000	3,000	2,928
National Commission on Children	0	0	1,100	1,073
National Commission on Libraries	777	750	750	732
National Commission to Prevent Infant Mortality	0	400	400	390
National Commission on Financing Postsecondary Education	662	0	0	0
National Council on Disability	1,200	1,200	1,750	1,439
National Labor Relations Board	151,103	151,103	140,111	147,461
National Mediation Board	6,675	6,675	6,675	6,514
Occupational Safety and Health Review Commission	6,401	6,401	6,401	6,247
Railroad Retirement Board	303,100	310,100	317,400	309,327
Soldiers' and Airmen's Home	47,999	0	53,083	51,804
Institute of Peace	7,270	8,000	9,200	8,393
White House Conference on Library and Information Services	0	0	1,000	488
Subtotal	**$ 1,057,720**	**$ 1,017,790**	**$ 1,115,943**	**$ 1,077,950**
TOTAL	**$ 174,845,772**	**$ 170,674,442** [1]	**$ 183,334,858**	**$ 182,181,734** [2]

[1] *The House did not appropriate funds for unauthorized programs.*
[2] *Reflects an across-the-board reduction of 2.41 percent for each discretionary spending item.*

lion for new programs expected to be approved before Congress adjourned. Among them were authorizations contained in comprehensive child-care legislation, programs to help hard-hit areas cope with the AIDS epidemic, and a new program to help pay the cost of screening women for breast and cervical cancers. *(Child care, p. 547; AIDS, p. 582; cancer screening, p. 606)*

Of the programs for which the appropriations measure did set specific funding totals, the biggest percentage increase went to the Chapter 1 education program, which provided remedial services for educationally disadvantaged children. The panel approved $6.2 billion, an increase of slightly more than $1 billion from fiscal 1990 and $757 million more than Bush requested.

Another big funding boost went to the National Institutes of Health (NIH). The bill appropriated $8.3 billion

— $1.04 billion more than 1990 funding and $694 million more than the Bush request. The measure did not include about $300 million worth of research training programs not yet reauthorized for fiscal 1991.

Among programs that were net losers was the new Agency for Health Care Policy and Research, created in the fiscal 1990 budget-reconciliation bill (PL 101-239) to coordinate the government's efforts to determine the effectiveness and cost-efficiency of various medical treatments.

The subcommittee bill appropriated $89.7 million for the agency, which was $9.1 million less than the fiscal 1990 appropriation and $20.5 million less than the administration requested.

HOUSE PASSAGE

The House on July 19 approved a $170.7 billion Labor-HHS spending bill after a daylong debate over drugs, deficits and "The Wizard of Oz."

The measure passed by an overwhelming margin — 359-58 — but only after a bitter and sometimes partisan debate that was in marked contrast to the lovefest at the Appropriations Committee markup. *(Vote 252, p. 84-H)*

The biggest winner on July 19 was the Bush administration's drug policy director, William J. Bennett. A day earlier, he had strongly criticized lawmakers because the bill provided $231.4 million less than the administration had asked for drug treatment and education programs.

"The conventional rap on us is that we're too much for law enforcement," Bennett told The Associated Press. "For a year now, we have been flogged for this. Now they cut our damned budget proposal on the demand side. Who are these clowns?"

Members on both sides of the aisle bashed Bennett for his comments but in the end agreed to restore the funding by drawing down a reserve set aside to pay for new programs expected to be enacted later in the year.

"We've been given a very bad rap by the czar," complained Conte, the Appropriations Committee's ranking Republican. The panel did not provide the administration's full request, he said, because the antidrug programs "can't handle all the money we've been throwing at them."

But even though subcommittee Chairman Natcher and Conte defended the funding decisions, they joined to sponsor an amendment to restore the funding — reportedly at the urging of the House Democratic leadership.

Ironically, the administration officially called the bill's funding levels too high. "Increases of this magnitude are unwarranted," an administration policy statement read.

Amendments Fail

The other big winner of the day was Natcher, whose standing in the House was such that no amendment lacking his personal endorsement was added to the bill.

Not that no one tried.

The first to fall was a series of four amendments offered by Robert S. Walker, R-Pa. The man who the day before sought in vain to cut the Agriculture appropriations bill (HR 5268) by $19.90, Walker had no better luck seeking to cut the Labor-HHS bill by amounts from $65,000 to $10 million. *(Agriculture appropriations, p. 867)*

By the time Walker reached his third amendment, to reduce by $65,000 funds for the Physician Payment Review Commission, which advised Congress on Medicare reimbursement for doctors, tempers were fraying.

Snapped David R. Obey, D-Wis., a member of the Labor-HHS Subcommittee, paraphrasing from "The Wizard of Oz": "This is a Munchkin amendment in a town besieged by a Munchkin mentality." The amendment was defeated, 115-293, as was a subsequent amendment to trim $450,000 from the U.S. Institute of Peace. That failed by 194-220. *(Votes 247, 248, p. 84-H)*

More substantial but no more successful was an amendment offered by Bill Frenzel, R-Minn., to cut by 15 percent the $43.9 billion in the bill for discretionary programs over which the committee had direct control.

"This will make substantial cuts in programs many of you love," Frenzel said. "This has nothing to do with the Lollipop Guild or Munchkin land. This has to do with the great and powerful Oz."

But Frenzel's amendment failed, 85-333. *(Vote 249, p. 84-H)*

Democrats who sought to cut the bill fared no better. By 160-253, members first rejected a proposal by Timothy J. Penny, D-Minn., to cut most discretionary programs in the bill by 2 percent. Then, by 204-212 they rejected an amendment offered by George Miller, D-Calif., to reduce by a total of $6.8 million the administrative accounts controlled by the secretaries of Labor, HHS and Education. *(Votes 250, 251, p. 84-H)*

The latter amendment drew some of the most partisan volleys of the day. "These gratuitous potshots are getting out of control," said Conte, who accused Democrats of offering the amendment "just so they can go home and say, 'I voted for a cut.' "

About the only contentious issue that members did not fight over was the one everyone was braced for: abortion.

As passed by the House, the bill would permit federal funding of abortion only when necessary to save a woman's life. For procedural and parliamentary reasons, supporters of language to broaden those exceptions to allow funding in cases of rape or incest did not seek to amend the bill before it left the House. But they warned that they were still spoiling for a fight.

"This is but the first inning," said Les AuCoin, D-Ore., a leading abortion rights supporter. Before the bill went to the president, AuCoin warned, "Every member is going to have a chance to vote on this issue."

SENATE COMMITTEE ACTION

On Sept. 12, the Senate Appropriations Labor-HHS Subcommittee approved a $183 billion fiscal 1991 appropriations bill.

But AIDS activists cried foul over the spending bill because an emergency AIDS relief measure (PL 101-381) enacted in August authorized $875 million for areas hardest hit by the epidemic. But the subcommittee's funding measure provided no increase over existing funding for programs related to AIDS testing and health and social services for those with AIDS or HIV, the AIDS virus.

The appropriations bill, approved by voice vote, did provide $600 million in budget authority for the programs. But it stipulated that $490 million of that would not be available until Oct. 1, 1991, the first day of fiscal 1992. The $110 million that would be available in fiscal 1991 was the same amount appropriated for in fiscal 1990.

That angered those who worked hard to pass the emergency authorization bill before the start of fiscal 1991. Writing the bill so that it provided budget authority that could not be spent until fiscal 1992 "is disingenuous, cold and callous," said Tom Sheridan of the AIDS Action Council, a Washington-based lobbying group. "That year's worth of funding is a literal lifetime for people with AIDS."

The House version of the bill did not cover the AIDS programs. The House measure traditionally did not appropriate for unauthorized programs, and the authorization was not yet law when that chamber passed its version on July 19.

However, the House committee report on the measure specifically mentioned the AIDS bill as among those programs for which it was reserving $2.9 billion of its allocation, to be distributed when authorizations were complete.

Rep. Henry A. Waxman, D-Calif., a chief sponsor of the AIDS measure, said he was disappointed with the Senate appropriations bill. "We need a commitment of real dollars to deal with the real and immediate crisis of the AIDS epidemic," he said.

This was not the first time the Senate had provided phantom funding for a program. In 1989, $1.2 billion in budget authority was provided for a new child-care grant program as envisioned in the child-care bill (S 5) passed by the Senate in June 1989. But that money would not have been available until September 1990, the last month of the fiscal year, resulting in projected outlays of only about $5 million.

But the funding was dropped from the final fiscal 1990 appropriations measure. *(Child-care bill, 1989 Almanac, p. 203; fiscal 1990 funding removal, p. 712)*

Other Programs Get Increases

The problem, explained Senate Labor-HHS Appropriations Subcommittee Chairman Tom Harkin, D-Iowa, was a shortage of available funds for so many popular programs.

Not only did the panel receive funding requests from every member of the Appropriations panel and 99 of the 100 senators, Harkin said at the markup, but at $53.2 billion, the subcommittee's discretionary funding ceiling — the only funding level over which it had direct control — was $800 million less than was available to the House committee.

Programs that received major increases over fiscal 1990 funding levels in the Senate bill included:

- Head Start, which received $2 billion in fiscal 1991. That was $448 million more than the program received in fiscal 1990 and $114 million more that the Bush administration requested. The House deferred Head Start funding because it was awaiting reauthorization.
- Chapter 1, which provided remedial education services to disadvantaged elementary and secondary school students; it received $6.4 billion. That was $1.2 billion more than the fiscal 1990 level, $922 million more than the administration request, and $165 million more than the House bill.
- Pell grants, the largest need-based federal aid program for college students. The Senate bill's $5.34 billion reflected a $100 increase in the existing maximum annual award of $2,300 — an amount, Harkin noted at the markup, that had not been increased in three years. That funding level was $530 million more than in fiscal 1990 and $59 million more than the administration request. But even though the House would retain the existing cap at $2,300, it provided $78 million more.

Abortion Fights Delayed

It was not mentioned at the subcommittee markup, but the abortion issue continued to hang over the bill like an ominous cloud.

As it had every year for more than a decade, the House bill incorporated the so-called Hyde amendment language, which forbade the use of funds appropriated in the bill to pay for abortions unless carrying the fetus to term would endanger the woman's life.

And as the Senate had for many of those years, the version approved by Harkin's subcommittee would permit federal abortion funding in cases of rape and incest as well.

But administration officials continued to warn that Bush would not sign any bill that permitted federal abortion funding in rape and incest cases.

Full Committee Action

Abortion was also not mentioned at the full Appropriations Committee markup of its $183.3 billion legislation Oct. 10. As in the subcommittee markup, the most contentious issue was AIDS — specifically the failure of the measure to fund new AIDS-care programs approved overwhelmingly by Congress earlier in 1990.

Outraged members of AIDS groups who helped pass the AIDS authorization immediately began campaigning to find the funding, ultimately enlisting in their behalf three members of the Appropriations Committee: Brock Adams, D-Wash.; Frank R. Lautenberg, D-N.J.; and Alfonse M. D'Amato, R-N.Y.

But the senators' proposed solution — an across-the-board cut of just under 1 percent for programs in the bill set to receive an increase higher than inflation — touched off a backlash of its own.

A coalition of more than 70 health, education and social service groups launched a counterattack, pleading with the senators to "avoid a self-destructive struggle that pits one vital human need against another."

Harkin did find himself with an additional $326 million in fiscal 1991 outlays as a result of the committee's reallocation to comply with the budget resolution approved Oct. 8, but most of it was consumed within the bill for technical reasons.

And the $27 million that was left for the AIDS bill was not enough to satisfy Adams and company.

"What we have here is a disaster, which the Senate has voted as being a disaster by a vote of 95-4," said Adams, referring to the original Senate passage of the AIDS authorization bill May 16.

Said D'Amato: "We're talking about a total collapse of medical systems in our country. It's not just AIDS patients being affected. It's the quality of care for all."

But theirs was a distinctly minority view. "There isn't a program that's not underfunded in this bill," said subcommittee Republican Ted Stevens of Alaska. "It's not a fair way to do it."

The amendment was defeated by voice vote.

SENATE FLOOR ACTION

The abortion controversy finally surfaced during Senate floor debate of the Labor-HHS spending bill Oct. 12.

After members approved HR 5257 by a 76-15 vote, both sides of the abortion debate had something in the bill to like and something to hate. *(Vote 269, p. 90-H)*

After an unusual parliamentary minuet, members by voice vote agreed to add to the measure an amendment to permit federal funding of abortions in cases of rape or incest. However, the amendment also required that facilities receiving funds in the bill that performed abortions notify at least one parent of "an emancipated female under the age of 18" at least 48 hours before the abortion was to be performed.

But it was proponents of the rape and incest exception who found themselves on the ropes. Once the two amendments were joined, it was virtually impossible procedurally to separate them, leaving abortion rights supporters with an all-or-nothing proposition to take to the House-Senate conference. Dropping both would probably have been acceptable to abortion opponents; existing law barred all federal abortion funding except in cases in which the woman's life was in danger.

The "parental notification" amendment, offered by William L. Armstrong, R-Colo., was similar to one he succeeded in adding to a federal family planning reauthorization (S 110) killed by the Senate on Sept. 26. *(Family planning authorization, p. 604)*

Armstrong's amendment required that at least one parent be notified 48 hours in advance of an abortion involving a minor "except in instances where an attending physician certifies in such minor's medical record that the abortion was performed due to a medical emergency requiring immediate attention."

Armstrong argued that such notification was warranted for a procedure "far more serious than giving blood or having your ears pierced" — both of which routinely required parental consent.

Opponents of the amendment were led by subcommittee Chairman Harkin, whose support of abortion rights had become a major re-election issue. They argued that the amendment would not facilitate teenagers talking to their parents. Instead, Harkin said, "a young woman in that situation would obviously end up in the back alleys."

Both Armstrong and Harkin regaled the Senate with horror stories about young women who suffered from complications associated with abortions either because of — or because of the lack of — state parental notification laws.

Harkin, noting that the Senate had voted on the politically sensitive matter only two weeks earlier, originally offered to accept Armstrong's amendment by voice vote. Armstrong, however, insisted on a roll call.

But when the motion to table (kill) the amendment failed on a tie vote of 48-48, members agreed by voice votes to adopt both the notification and rape-incest amendments. *(Vote 266, p. 88-H)*

Although they lost by having the Armstong amendment added, abortion-rights supporters said they were buoyed by the closeness of the vote, which they expected to lose.

Other Fights

After the abortion question was settled, most of the remaining Senate floor debate centered on the question of AIDS funding.

Several senators were upset that the measure appropriated only $159 million of $875 million authorized by the emergency AIDS treatment measure.

Among the AIDS treatment programs not fully funded by the spending bill was one authorizing $275 million to emergency disaster assistance to the 16 cities hardest hit by the epidemic.

"We have a plague on our hands Mr. President," said New Jersey's Lautenberg, who represented two cities — Jersey City and Newark — slated to receive funds under the bill. "I think it is cruel and inhuman to discuss here whether or not we can afford it."

But because of the funding squeeze that prevented Harkin from being able to fund the programs in the first place, the only AIDS amendment offered would have reduced, not increased, AIDS funding.

The first, by Jesse Helms, R-N.C., would have deleted $441 million for the AIDS treatment programs for fiscal 1992. Harkin provided the 1992 funding for the programs when he was unable, because of his budget outlay ceiling, to fund the programs in fiscal 1991.

Helms found that objectionable. "We should not be appropriating money for fiscal year 1992 before we even get our fiscal house in order for fiscal year 1991," he said.

But the "forward funding" was defended by the subcommittee's ranking Republican, Arlen Specter, Pa., who argued that it "ought to remain in the bill as a commitment for the future because of the extraordinary nature of this problem."

Helms' amendment was tabled, 70-24. Also tabled, on a 69-23 vote, was a subsequent Helms amendment to transfer $120 million in AIDS-related funding to programs to address health problems of children and persons suffering from Alzheimer's disease. *(Votes 267, 268, p. 54-S)*

Other amendments adopted included:

- By Harkin (for Bill Bradley, D-N.J.), to increase by $748,000 funding for education programs for gifted and talented children.
- By Harkin (for Jeff Bingaman, D-N.M.) to appropriate $1 million for the School Year Extension Study Commission and $2 million for the National Council on Educational Goals. To make the amendment budget-neutral, it cut from $14 million to $11 million the amount provided for disaster-assistance payments under the Education Department's Impact Aid program.

FINAL ACTION

House-Senate conferees finished work on HR 5257 on Oct. 19, paving the way for final approval. For the 10th consecutive year, the spending measure barred all funding for abortions except when a pregnancy would endanger a woman's life.

Because of the two abortion-related amendments added by the Senate, which could not be procedurally disentangled, and because abortion rights supporters opposed the parental-notification requirement more than they wanted the rape and incest language, they decided to drop both amendments during an Oct. 18 House-Senate conference meeting.

"We're folding up the tent," said a disappointed Oregon Democrat AuCoin, a leader of the abortion rights forces in the House, on Oct. 16.

On Oct. 19, Senate Labor-HHS Subcommittee Chairman Harkin, said, "It was just something we had to do."

Since the 1989 votes on the issue indicated that a majority of both the House and Senate supported the rape and incest language, anti-abortion activists devised a sort of "poison pill" strategy to maintain existing law.

During Senate debate in April on a fiscal 1990 supplemental appropriation bill (HR 4404 — PL 101-302), abortion opponent Phil Gramm, R-Texas, appended language authorizing the death penalty for drug-related murders in the nation's capital to an amendment permitting the District of Columbia to use local tax money for abortions. *(Supplemental appropriations bill, p. 844)*

In the end, both amendments were dropped.

For the Labor-HHS funding bill, abortion opponents decided to meet the rape-incest provision, the abortion rights issue with the widest political support, with the parental-notification language, their own most popular position. It barely worked: The parental-notification language was added by voice vote after a motion to kill it failed on a 48-48 tie Oct. 12.

Abortion rights advocates, having lost another round, vowed to be back in 1991. "We're not going to be content to sit here ... being stymied by these shabby little procedures," said AuCoin.

LIHEAP Funding

Conferees agreed to provide $1.45 billion for the Low Income Home Energy Assistance Program (LIHEAP), plus a contingency fund of $200 million.

Rep. Conte, ranking Republican on the Appropriations Committee, tried but failed to increase the funding to $1.63 billion.

He warned that as the nation headed into a recession and the price of oil soared, more people would need help in the winter with their heating bills. But conferees rejected his proposal to shift about $36 million from public broadcasting funds to LIHEAP.

Education Commission

As Congress struggled the week of Oct. 22 to complete the $182.2 billion fiscal 1991 HHS spending bill, it got hung up over a $2 million appropriation for an education commission that might never exist.

Although no one seemed to believe that the government's second-largest appropriations bill would actually founder over a $2 million allocation for the National Council on Educational Goals, the provision did stop the bill in its tracks for several days.

Funding for the independent council, whose mission would be to assess progress toward meeting the set of goals adopted by Bush and the nation's governors, was added to the bill on the Senate floor Oct. 12.

But because subcommittee Chairman Harkin forgot to offer it before final passage, the provision was added afterwards. When Republicans complained, it was dropped from the bill before the House-Senate conference.

During the conference, the appropriation was restored on the condition that the money could not be spent unless the commission was authorized. However, it was again deleted when the House took up the conference report on the measure Oct. 22.

The House approved the measure, minus the $2 million, by a vote of 335-74. *(Vote 504, p. 160-H)*

Partisan Jockeying

Although there were technical and procedural reasons why the funding was dropped both from the original Senate bill and on the House floor, the underlying reason was that the White House opposed creation of the commission, which would have made its first report in the presidential election year of 1992.

"I got a call from the White House saying they were going to veto the bill if this was in it," said Conte.

Said Bingaman: "I think it's real clear [Bush administration officials] are nervous about what any such panel is likely to say about how this country is doing on education and how this administration is doing."

The entire fight could have been unnecessary because Bingaman's bill to authorize the commission (S 3095) was dumped from an omnibus education bill (HR 5115) after the White House threatened to veto that measure if the commission was included. *(Education bill, p. 610)*

That did not stop Bingaman, who proceeded to reattach his amendment after the Senate on Oct. 25 approved the conference report on the Labor-HHS bill, 82-15. *(Vote 315, p. 62-S)*

There was opposition, both substantive and procedural.

"Here's another commission with another bucket they want filled up with $2 million to do something that's already being done," complained Sen. Thad Cochran, R-Miss.

Said Specter, ranking Republican on the Senate Labor-HHS Subcommittee: "It's an authorizing matter, and it ought to be taken up by the authorizing committee."

When Cochran's motion to kill Bingaman's amendment failed on a vote of 42-55, Republicans fought back by appending to the bill a big separate bill to revise the Job Training Partnership Act. *(Vote 316, p. 62-S)*

"If the majority wants to use appropriations bills to carry authorizing legislation, then we ought to give it some legislation to carry," said Orrin G. Hatch, R-Utah.

The job training legislation was adopted by 95-1. The lone holdout was Senate Appropriations Committee Chairman Robert C. Byrd, D-W.Va.

"I don't want to see the legislative process perverted here, and that's exactly what we're doing when we put authorizing legislation into appropriations bills," Byrd complained. *(Vote 318, p. 62-S)*

The House stripped off the jobs bill early Oct. 26, along with $10 million added by Harkin the night before for a health program. But with the Senate having officially adopted the Bingaman proposal the day before, the House left the commission funding in the bill. That resolved the last known dispute, and the Senate cleared the bill.

Funding Levels

Although bill sponsors got a significant boost in funding for the bill as a result of the Oct. 8 budget agreement, members still found themselves squeezed to increase funds as much as they wanted for many programs.

Rising fuel prices and a weakening economy meant that conferees were forced at the last minute to find $1.2 billion to pay for unexpected increases in unemployment insurance and the energy emergency contingency fund. They got the money by imposing an across-the-board cut of 2.4 percent for each of the discretionary funding items in the bill.

Even with the cut, however, many key health and education programs got large increases.

For example, Head Start received $1.95 billion even after the 2 percent cut. That was nearly $500 million more than the program got in 1990 and the largest increase in its history.

Chapter 1, which provided remedial education for disadvantaged students, gained $6.2 billion, up $800 million from fiscal 1990.

And the National Institutes of Health gained $8.3 billion, an increase over fiscal 1990 of $700 million.

Among the programs that received less than many members would have liked was a new one to help cities and states cope with the costs of the AIDS epidemic. Conferees agreed to provide only $221 million of the $875 million authorized in the AIDS-care bill, cleared earlier in the year.

After the across-the-board reduction, $220.6 million remained. Of that amount, $87.8 million was appropriated for emergency aid to hard-hit cities, an identical amount for states and $44.9 million for grants to provide early intervention services for those with AIDS and HIV, the AIDS virus. ■

VA/HUD Bill Trims Housing, Boosts NASA

The House on Oct. 26 cleared by voice vote a $78 billion fiscal 1991 appropriations bill (HR 5158) to fund the Departments of Veterans Affairs (VA), Housing and Urban Development (HUD) and related independent agencies, including NASA, the Environmental Protection Agency (EPA) and the National Science Foundation (NSF).

The House had first approved the conference report by 366-32 on Oct. 20. But the Senate amended and approved the measure five days later by voice vote, requiring the House to agree to it one more time. *(Vote 495, p. 156-H)*

As in past years, housing and space programs were pitted against each other in the annual fight over the spending bill.

Despite significant increases in funds for both programs, last-minute jockeying to boost NASA's bottom line ended up taking away from subsidized housing for the poor.

President Bush had requested a 24 percent increase for NASA to proceed with major projects such as the space station and the moon-Mars initiative. Congress, however, provided NASA with $13.9 billion in fiscal 1991 — nowhere near the $15.1 billion that the administration requested. *(NASA authorization, p. 434)*

The space station, which had encountered numerous technical problems, was funded at $1.9 billion, $313 million more than the Senate-passed bill and approximately $350 million less than the House level. The administration had requested $2.45 billion. *(Space station, p. 436)*

The moon-Mars program, to send astronauts to the moon and Mars, was virtually zeroed out.

By increasing the space agency's funds above the Senate recommendation, lawmakers had to take from HUD's assisted housing fund, which helped low-income families pay their rent.

Despite a House recommendation of $11.4 billion and a Senate recommendation of $10.6 billion for assisted housing, only $9.3 billion was approved by conferees.

The legislation also provided $31.3 billion to the VA, an increase over the previous year's $29.7 billion. The EPA's budget was increased to $6.1 billion in fiscal 1991 from $5.5 billion in fiscal 1990. And the NSF received $2.3 billion in fiscal 1991, compared with $2.1 billion in fiscal 1990.

The measure also provided $22 billion to the Federal Deposit Insurance Corporation to cover the costs of buying out promissory notes and assets given to purchasers of 200 failed thrifts in 1988. That money was not counted toward the bill's bottom line.

BOXSCORE

Legislation: Departments of Veterans Affairs, Housing and Urban Development and independent agencies fiscal 1991 appropriations, PL 101-507 (HR 5158).

Major action: Signed, Nov. 5. Conference report adopted by House, Oct. 26; by Senate, Oct. 25; first adopted by House, 366-32, Oct. 20. Passed by Senate, 90-8, Oct. 3; by House, 355-48, June 28.

Reports: Conference report (H Rept 101-900). Appropriations (S Rept 101-474); Appropriations (H Rept 101-556).

HOUSE COMMITTEE ACTION

NASA took a hit from the House Appropriations Subcommittee on Veterans Affairs, Housing and Urban Development and Independent Agencies on June 12 when members decided to slash the president's request for the space agency by $829 million, signaling concern over costs for the proposed lunar-Mars initiative.

The subcommittee approved a total of $80.7 billion for the spending bill. That was a significant increase over fiscal 1990's $66.2 billion. Much of the increase was in mandatory items, such as veterans' pensions.

Bush had requested a 24 percent increase for NASA over fiscal 1990, to $15.2 billion in budget authority. The subcommittee recommended that the space agency receive $14.3 billion.

The smaller increase meant that NASA could not proceed with studies in fiscal 1991 for the project to send people to the moon and Mars. Of the $829 million cut from Bush's request, about $300 million was slated for the lunar-Mars initiative.

The panel also pared $195 million from Bush's $2 billion request for NASA's space station.

Increase for Housing

The subcommittee provided an increase of $4.6 billion for federal housing programs, such as public housing and rental certificates and vouchers.

The large housing increase was in response to legislation in both the House and the Senate (HR 1180, S 556) to reauthorize and expand federal housing programs to benefit the homeless and others who were unable to find affordable housing. *(Housing overhaul, p. 631)*

Bush had recommended a total of $21.4 billion in budget authority for housing programs, while the subcommittee provided $25.9 billion in budget authority.

In housing, the bill provided $11.7 billion in new budget authority for 120,667 additional units of assisted housing. In 1990, the number was only 75,604. Bush's budget proposed adding 82,049 units to the assisted housing rolls in 1991.

Of the 120,667 new units, 45,000 were to come from Section 8 vouchers, 55,000 from Section 8 certificates, 7,000 from public housing major reconstruction, and 8,000 from Section 202 housing construction for the elderly and disabled.

Other budget authority levels for programs in the bill included $31.3 billion for the VA, which was $100 million above Bush's budget; $6.1 billion for the EPA, $431 million above Bush's request; and $2.3 billion for the NSF, $46 million below Bush's request.

The NSF was the only major agency besides NASA to receive less money than the president requested. NSF research and related activities were cut by $100 million; science education activities increased by $34 million.

Full Committee Action

The House Appropriations Committee on June 26 approved HR 5158, adding about $11 million for veterans'

VA-HUD Appropriations

Following are budget authority totals in the fiscal 1991 appropriations bill (HR 5158 — PL 101-507) for the Departments of Veterans Affairs, Housing and Urban Development and related independent agencies.

(Figures, in thousands of dollars, may not add due to rounding.)

Agency	President's Request	House Bill	Senate Bill	Conference Final
Department of Veterans Affairs				
Benefits	$ 16,881,294	$ 16,953,461	$ 16,953,461	$ 16,953,461
Health and Research	12,473,816	12,579,816	12,501,816	12,579,316
Administration	1,689,859	1,748,815	1,636,219	1,740,859
Total, VA	31,044,969	31,282,092	31,091,496	31,273,836
Department of Housing and Urban Development				
Housing Programs [1]	17,392,005	22,079,106	20,821,276	19,632,476
Assisted housing	7,115,942	11,388,711	10,573,625	9,288,625
Expiring Section 8 subsidies	7,734,985	7,734,985	7,734,985	7,734,985
Rental Rehabilitation Grants	70,000	135,000	70,000	70,000
Federal Housing Administration	317,366	317,366	317,366	317,366
Homeless Assistance	425,448	340,000	333,019	339,427
Community Development	2,796,000	3,015,000	3,213,000	3,213,000
Policy Development and Research	23,000	30,000	27,000	28,500
Fair Housing	12,200	12,200	12,410	12,410
Management and Administration	426,124	426,124	432,000	429,500
Inspector General	29,283	29,283	29,283	29,283
Guaranteed Loan Limits	(155,000,000)	(155,140,000)	(155,250,000)	(155,250,000)
Government National Mortgage Association	(80,000,000)	(80,000,000)	(80,000,000)	(80,000,000)
Total, HUD	21,104,060	25,931,713	24,867,988	23,684,596
Independent Agencies				
American Battle Monuments Commission	$ 15,402	$ 15,900	$ 15,402	$ 15,900
Army Cemeterial Expenses	12,236	12,236	12,236	12,236
Commission on National Service	—	—	100,000	57,000
Consumer Information Center	1,540	1,540	1,540	1,540
Consumer Product Safety Commission	35,609	37,109	36,709	37,109
Council on Environmental Quality	2,780	2,780	1,465	1,873
Court of Veterans Appeals	9,560	9,560	4,127	7,481
Environmental Protection Agency	5,580,709	6,012,625	6,017,937	6,094,353
Federal Deposit Insurance Corporation [1]	(22,000,000)	(2,915,744)	(4,398,000)	(22,000,000)
Federal Emergency Management Agency	819,272	656,787	546,793	562,975
Interagency Council on the Homeless	1,214	1,214	1,083	1,083
NASA	15,125,200	14,290,325	13,451,200	13,868,300
National Credit Union Administration [2]	(600,000)	(600,000)	(600,000)	(600,000)
National Institute of Building Sciences	—	250	—	—
National Science Foundation	2,383,000	2,337,000	2,364,192	2,316,028
National Space Council	1,363	1,000	1,363	1,363
Neighborhood Reinvestment Corporation	24,500	24,500	25,554	25,554
Office of Consumer Affairs	1,889	1,889	1,964	1,964
Office of Science and Technology Policy	3,300	3,300	3,560	3,560
Points of Light Initiative Foundation	—	—	5,000	5,000
Resolution Trust Corporation [3]	10,785	10,785	10,785	10,785
Selective Service System	26,635	26,635	26,635	26,635
TOTAL	**$ 76,177,418**	**$ 80,659,240**	**$ 78,587,029**	**$ 78,011,205**

[1] *Total includes accounts in addition to those listed.*
[2] *Limitation on direct loans*
[3] *Appropriation for office of inspector general*

SOURCE: House Appropriations Committee

medical care, construction at VA hospitals, the Neighborhood Reinvestment Corporation, the Consumer Product Safety Commission and two EPA projects.

The committee bill recommended new budget authority of $83.6 billion in fiscal 1991, an increase of $12.3 billion over fiscal 1990.

Most hurt by the reductions from Bush's request for NASA was the Space Exploration Initiative — also known as the moon-Mars initiative.

The committee also cut $195 million out of the president's request for $2.5 billion for the development of Space Station Freedom, as well as imposing a $200 million reduction in appropriations for space flight, control and data communications.

HOUSE ACTION

The House on June 28 passed, 355-48, the $83.6 billion VA-HUD appropriations bill that gave federal programs for veterans, housing and space exploration a $12 billion, 17 percent increase over fiscal 1990. *(Vote 210, p. 72-H)*

Most of the increase, $7.7 billion, was required by HUD's expiring rent contracts. While these needed new budget authority for multi-year contracts, they had little impact on fiscal 1991 outlays, the yardstick by which Gramm-Rudman measurements were taken.

NASA was given a 17 percent increase to $14.3 billion. Bush had requested a 24 percent increase to $15.1 billion. The Office of Management and Budget (OMB) complained about the reduction but did not directly threaten a veto. "The $820 million reduction from the president's request seriously compromises a number of NASA programs that are critical to the nation's space leadership," an OMB statement said.

Bill Frenzel, R-Minn., took the first shot at cutting the bill. He proposed an amendment to cut all programs except medical care for veterans and renewals of expiring rent subsidies by 14.5 percent, in order to reduce the bill's total appropriation to its fiscal 1990 level. Frenzel said he offered the amendment knowing it would not succeed, and he was right. It lost 72-337. *(Vote 207, p. 72-H)*

A more modest cut offered by California Republican William E. Dannemeyer, to trim all discretionary accounts by 5 percent, lost 53-343. *(Vote 208, p. 72-H)*

And members rejected an amendment from Timothy J. Penny, D-Minn., to pare the bill by 2 percent in all discretionary accounts except for veterans' medical care and HUD Section 8 subsidy contracts. That vote was 172-235. *(Vote 209, p. 72-H)*

Extraterrestrial Intelligence

Only one amendment during floor debate succeeded in stripping out any money from the bill. Ronald K. Machtley, R-R.I., took to the podium to complain about $6.1 million in NASA's budget for a "search for extraterrestrial intelligence." He asked, "Does any congressperson think he or she can explain to their constituents how important it is to spend $6.1 million to find out if E. T. really exists? And then that we're going to raise taxes to pay for it?"

If there really was intelligent life out there, he said, "might it be easier to listen and let them call us?"

Bill Green of New York, the subcommittee's ranking Republican, noted that the administration originally had requested $12.1 million for the program, which received $4 million in fiscal 1990. "What the gentleman wants us to do now is take away the last penny that the president has requested for this program?" asked Traxler. Machtley did, and his amendment eliminating the $6.1 million passed by voice vote.

Rental Units Increase

Noticeably absent from the House debate was any attempt to transfer funds from space exploration to domestic programs.

In 1989, Charles E. Schumer, D-N.Y., proposed shifting $714 million from NASA to other programs but was defeated. He had vowed to try again but apparently was dissuaded by the $11.1 billion increase for HUD, $4.5 billion more than the president's request. That amount would have provided 118,035 additional subsidized housing units compared with 73,560 in fiscal 1990. Bush had requested 74,144 incremental units for 1991. *(1989 Almanac, p. 715)*

The administration opposed the increase in rental units to HUD, citing both fiscal and policy reasons. OMB said that while the administration supported the goal of providing more assistance to low-income families, it preferred to use tenant rental assistance and low-income home ownership programs.

The bulk of the increase, however, stemmed from the scheduled expiration over the following five years of about 1 million Section 8 rental assistance contracts. Renewal of existing contracts being provided to low-income households was to cost the federal government $32 billion over that period. Bush requested and was granted $7.7 billion to renew rental certificate and voucher contracts for 294,495 housing units.

One of the losers among the bill's 20 independent agencies and offices was the Federal Emergency Management Agency, which was cut by $1.1 billion. In fiscal 1990, the agency received $1.8 billion. Bush proposed new budget authority of $819 million, while the Appropriations subcommittee chose $657 million. "This amount is clearly too low given the highly unpredictable level of disasters in any year," the OMB statement said. "Underfunding the disaster relief fund is an unacceptable budget gimmick."

SENATE COMMITTEE ACTION

Despite last-minute lobbying by Vice President Dan Quayle, Senate appropriators gave space programs far less money than the president requested, and funds for his moon-Mars initiative were virtually zeroed out.

With a smaller pot to work from, the Senate Appropriations Subcommittee on VA, HUD and Independent Agencies cut $2 billion that the House had appropriated for housing and space programs. The Senate subcommittee agreed by voice vote Sept. 13 to move the bill to full committee.

Altogether, the subcommittee provided $78.6 billion in fiscal 1991 for federal programs funded under the VA-HUD spending bill.

That amount was $2 billion less than the House would provide, almost $3 billion more than the administration had proposed and $12.4 billion more than was spent in fiscal 1990.

Barbara A. Mikulski, D-Md., the subcommittee chairman, complained that there was not enough money to go around. Compounding the problem, she said, were 900 requests from senators for special projects totaling $26 billion. In 1989, the subcommittee received 500 requests.

Shortly before the markup, Quayle telephoned Mikulski to ask for more money to send astronauts to the moon and Mars, one of Bush's top space priorities. Quayle, chairman of the National Space Council, also asked for more money for a space station and for NASA in general.

The administration had proposed spending $15.1 billion in fiscal 1991; $12.2 billion was spent for space programs in fiscal 1990.

While both the House and the Senate subcommittees agreed to increase spending for space programs, neither came close to the president's request. The Senate wanted to spend $13.5 billion in fiscal 1991 — $855 million less than the House level.

The Senate also provided $1.6 billion for a space station, which was $863.6 million less than Bush's budget request and $162 million less than in fiscal 1990.

The House had essentially cut out funds for the moon-Mars project, but the Senate subcommittee left in about $34 million for propulsion work that could be counted toward the initiative.

Slashing Housing Programs

As the spending legislation made its way from the House to the Senate, housing suffered the deepest cuts, losing $1.1 billion from the House appropriations measure. At the same time, housing was also responsible for a major increase in the bottom line of the total bill.

In fiscal 1990, HUD received $14.9 billion. For fiscal 1991, Bush requested $21.4 billion. The House wanted to spend $25.9 billion, while the Senate would have cut that to $24.9 billion.

The recommended 67 percent increase reflected the need to appropriate $9.5 billion to renew expiring rental assistance contracts and to fulfill contracts that had run out of money. If those contracts were not renewed, several hundred thousand families were to lose their homes.

Tenants in about 300,000 apartments around the country were also at risk of eviction by landlords paying off their federally subsidized mortgages. The mortgages required owners to provide affordable rents to low-income tenants. Once they paid off those loans, however, the landlords were free to raise rents or convert their buildings to condominiums — forcing their renters out.

The Senate subcommittee provided $440 million in subsidies to landlords to persuade them not to pay off their mortgages.

Roasting the Archenemy of Pork

Rep. Lawrence Coughlin, R-Pa., offered his amendment to the VA-HUD spending bill during the House Appropriations Committee markup June 26 just like anyone else — with little description and no mention of cost.

When he mentioned that the provision would benefit Lebanon, Pa., however, smirks broke out. One member called out: "Whose district is that?"

But everyone already knew the answer. Robert S. Walker, R-Pa., self-proclaimed crusader against pork-barrel spending, had requested a little favor for his constituents in HR 5158.

VA-HUD Subcommittee Chairman Bob Traxler, D-Mich., solemnly explained that he had meant to include the provision in the committee print, but somehow it was left out because of an oversight. His statement was greeted with laughter.

And Traxler repeatedly let his colleagues know the exact cost of the amendment. "That's $479,000 in outlays," he said. "$479,000 of pork."

To underscore the point one more time, Traxler said the item was not funded based on merit.

Proceeds From Land Sale

The provision exempted the southeastern Pennsylvania city from a HUD requirement that it give the federal government the proceeds from the sale of land that was reclaimed with federal assistance.

Lebanon received $20 million in HUD grants in 1973-79 for an urban renewal project to reclaim a flood plain. The city contended that it should not have to repay the $479,000 it got for the land because it had to pay $5 million to complete the project.

The HUD regional office approved Lebanon's request, but headquarters overruled the decision.

So Walker set out to help his district.

First, he got a provision in a 1987 House bill reauthorizing housing and community development programs. But it was dropped in conference. *(1987 Almanac, p. 682)*

In 1990 he got the provision included during committee consideration of the big housing reauthorization bill (HR 1180). But as of spring, that bill's prospects for final enactment were uncertain. *(Housing reauthorization, p. 631)*

Finally, Walker pulled Traxler aside and asked him to place the item in the VA-HUD bill, just as other members did with similar items. "I assured him that we would give him every consideration," Traxler said in an interview. "We're doing for Mr. Walker what we have done for others."

A few weeks later, Traxler and Walker clashed on the floor during the May 24 debate over the fiscal 1990 supplemental appropriations bill. *(Supplemental appropriations, p. 844)*

Walker, continuing his struggle for pork-free legislation, complained that the supplemental required HUD to fund 37 community development projects that the housing agency did not want. That, he said, was exactly like the politicized process of handing out grants, loans and contracts at HUD in the Reagan administration.

"If we take a look at the list of where all of these meritorious projects went, 28 of the 37 go to either people who were in the conference, people who serve on the subcommittee or serve on the committee," Walker said.

"These were not picked because they are the most meritorious projects in the country. They were picked because people who were sitting in the room had the political clout to get something in that they wanted, and that is all that it is," Walker said.

"Is my good friend suggesting," Traxler responded, "that I ought not to put the language in a bill this year that he has requested to forgive the indebtedness on that urban renewal project?"

Walker protested that the provision "does not cost the government a dime and the gentleman knows that."

But Bill Green, N.Y., ranking Republican on the VA-HUD Appropriations Subcommittee, pointed out that forgiving repayment did indeed cost money.

The administration opposed Walker's request, saying it and similar provisions would set a bad precedent.

'Having Fun at My Expense'

In an interview, Walker said he did not view the provision — which stayed in the bill through enactment (PL 101-507) — as pork. "My definition of pork is when we're actually spending money. We're not spending any money here," he said.

Still, he said, "It's uncomfortable because I do think I carry an important message about keeping this process clean. So they're having fun at my expense."

Altogether, the Senate bill provided funds for 125,000 new units of housing — 40,000 more than were created in fiscal 1990. Housing for the elderly and disabled was to increase by 4,000 units from fiscal 1990 to 12,000 units in fiscal 1991. Of that, 500 units were to be set aside for people with AIDS.

Senators provided $2.8 billion to modernize public housing and remove lead paint, $50 million more than the fiscal 1990 level and $45 million more than the House level. And because of rising oil prices, the subcommittee provided $1.3 million more than the House's $2 billion to operate low-income housing projects.

The bill did not provide money for new programs in the omnibus housing reauthorization bill that was awaiting conference action.

The appropriations bill did include money for public housing home ownership, a pet program of HUD Secretary Jack F. Kemp. The subcommittee set aside $50 million for "special purpose grants," including $18.9 million for Kenilworth-Parkside, a Washington, D.C., public housing home ownership project, and $5.9 million for Carr Square, a St. Louis public housing home ownership project.

For the homeless, the bill gave a major boost to the single-room occupancy program, providing 2,700 new units of permanent housing. Funds would increase 43 percent from fiscal 1990, from $73.2 million to $105 million.

In other programs for the homeless, emergency shelter grants were frozen at the fiscal 1990 level of $73.2 million; money for a transitional and supportive housing demonstration program rose from $126.8 million in fiscal 1990 to $143.6 million; and aid to homeless shelters increased from $10.8 million in fiscal 1990 to $11.3 million in fiscal 1991.

Two other agencies, the VA and EPA, also received increases over fiscal 1990.

The Senate provided $31 billion for the VA, $1.4 billion more than in fiscal 1990 and $632 million more than Bush's requested but $190 million less than the House had recommended.

In particular, medical care for veterans was increased to $12.2 billion from $11.4 billion in fiscal 1990. The House provided $12.3 billion for medical care.

The subcommittee bill also provided $6 billion for the EPA — $5 million more than the House bill contained. That was $500 million more than the agency received in fiscal 1990 and $437 million more than Bush's request.

Mikulski noted that Frank R. Lautenberg, D-N.J., had pushed repeatedly for more money for the agency, particularly for the "superfund" program to clean up toxic waste sites.

Superfund received $1.6 billion under the Senate proposal, $6 million more than the House provided. Still, that was less than the Bush request of $1.7 billion. In fiscal 1990, superfund received $1.5 billion.

Full Committee Action

The Senate Appropriations Committee approved the VA-HUD spending bill on Sept. 25 with Jake Garn, R-Utah, promising to fight for more money for space programs when the bill reached the Senate floor.

HR 5158 was approved by a vote of 20-0. The senators did not alter spending levels within the nearly $78.6 billion plan as set by the VA-HUD Subcommittee.

Despite a 10 percent increase in funding for NASA over fiscal 1990, the committee proposal was still $1.7 billion short of Bush's fiscal 1991 request and $839 million less than the House version, passed June 28.

Altogether, the Senate provided $13.5 billion for NASA — not enough money for a space station or for the moon-Mars project, both favored by Bush.

Garn, a fervent space and science booster who once flew aboard the shuttle *Challenger*, said the committee was being "terribly shortsighted to put space on hold."

He extolled the virtues of space, noting that pharmaceuticals could be processed more efficiently and purely in that medium.

"I think you're going to find cures for diseases out there," Garn said.

But he said he would wait to offer amendments to increase the amount of money for NASA until the bill went to the Senate floor.

For housing, the committee report included strong language on the problems of lead-based paint in public housing and privately owned, federally assisted housing. The report said HUD had "no known policy, priorities, goals or cost estimates for making these government-supported dwellings free of danger to children's health from lead paint poisoning."

Of the 1.8 million public housing units, more than 800,000 were built before 1978 and could contain harmful levels of lead paint, the report said.

In 1990, HUD was only required to address the issue of lead-based paint in public housing, and the report said those efforts had been "unduly cumbersome and incomplete."

HUD issued guidelines for lead-paint testing and removal that took effect April 1, 1990, but the agency still had not sent those guidelines to one-third of the country's 3,300 public and Indian housing authorities.

The committee directed the HUD secretary to submit a report on the agency's plans to achieve lead-safe, HUD-subsidized housing — private, nonprofit, public and HUD-owned — by April 1, 1991.

SENATE ACTION

The Senate on Oct. 3 approved, 90-8, the VA-HUD spending bill providing $78.6 billion for housing, the environment, space and veterans' programs. *(Vote 260, p. 52-S)*

In the latest skirmish of a long-running battle over who controlled policy and purse strings, the Senate tried to force the Bush administration to spend $51 million in housing funds for special projects that did not necessarily have to do with housing.

The fight, pitting HUD Secretary Kemp against his former Capitol Hill colleagues, stemmed from 1989 efforts to clean house at HUD. Kemp tried to stamp out political favoritism used to fund programs.

But his attempt to eliminate such projects ran afoul of Congress' cherished prerogative of earmarking funds in appropriations bills for projects members wanted to bring home.

Determined to have the last word, members of the Senate Appropriations Committee had put $50 million in earmarked projects in HR 5158.

During floor action, senators by voice vote added another $1 million to the special-projects list — to relocate a soup kitchen in Kansas City, Kan.

The Bush administration, however, issued a a strong veto threat, condemning senators for earmarking their projects, for including money to build 10,000 units of public housing that the administration had vehemently opposed as not the best way to provide homes, and for failing to appropriate money for Kemp's new programs that had yet to be authorized.

Funding Projects

Lawmakers and the administration also clashed over the issue of whether the administration had to fund projects that were earmarked in report language rather than directed by statute in spending bills.

Kemp, accusing lawmakers of "disgraceful" pork-barrel behavior on the heels of the 1989 HUD Reform Act (PL 101-235), refused to fund about 40 projects worth almost $30 million that had been earmarked in the conference report to the fiscal 1990 VA-HUD appropriations bill (PL 101-144). *(HUD reform act, 1989 Almanac, p. 631; earmarked projects, p. 720)*

The projects included money for street improvements in Dayton, Wash.; a library on Mackinac Island, Mich.; and a shelter for battered women in Highland, Calif.

By May, lawmakers struck back. Senate appropriators required Kemp to fund the projects by law — inserting the language into the fiscal 1990 supplemental spending bill.

Nudging Kemp

In marking up their fiscal 1991 VA-HUD spending bill, Senate appropriators dealt a largely symbolic slap, eliminating HUD's Office of Public Affairs and its 27 employees, and they axed Kemp's travel budget, forbidding first-class travel.

The panel also moved to prohibit money transfers between accounts in the Senate's version of the spending bill. And another action targeted Kemp's showpiece — home ownership at the Kenilworth-Parkside public housing project in Washington, D.C. With a ceremony scheduled for Sept. 28 to turn over the keys to tenants, Kemp needed about $9 million right away to provide subsidies for tenants in 464 units over the following five years.

But Appropriations subcommittee Chairmen Traxler and Mikulski refused to give the secretary permission to transfer fiscal 1990 funds from one account to another.

"Jack, we are not opposed to expanding home-ownership opportunities for public housing residents," Mikulski and Traxler wrote in a Sept. 27 letter to Kemp. "We do have great reservations about selling the nation's public housing stock."

However, they said they would honor the commitment to the project — in fiscal 1991.

After receiving calls from reporters, Mikulski and Traxler backed down and allowed Kemp to take the money he needed for the Kenilworth-Parkside project. The ceremony went on as planned. Not in attendance were Mikulski and Traxler. Mikulski did not receive an invitation until two days before the event.

Also, in an amendment offered by Mikulski on the floor, the Senate by voice vote restored $35,000 to Kemp's travel allowance and some of HUD's ability to transfer funds.

The Senate subcommittee did provide $18.9 million for Kenilworth-Parkside and $5.9 million for Carr Square Village project in St. Louis, Mo., in the fiscal 1991 bill.

And Mikulski's panel put the money in a place where Kemp could not help but notice it — a new account that revived the Senate's earmarks.

Special Purpose Grants

Although the reform act had effectively killed the account where earmarks were usually attached, Senate appropriators created another one: special purpose grants.

Although no authorizing legislation existed for the grants, appropriators wrote it into their bill — in addition to the report — providing their $50 million for 29 grants.

"Less than one year after the enactment of the HUD Reform Act, Congress has taken one of the most abused HUD programs, given it a new name, put it under a new department and funded it at $50 million," said HUD spokeswoman Mary S. Brunette. "And, of course, we find that objectionable."

One Hill staff member acknowledged that the special-purpose grants violated the spirit of the reform act. The earmarks were of the same ilk as those Kemp had protested in 1989.

The House appropriations measure for fiscal 1991 did not include such earmarks under housing. But lawmakers on both sides of the aisle and in both chambers defended the practice.

In the Senate, staff members pointed out that the projects were relatively small, were scrutinized closely and did not contain odd programs unrelated to the mission of HUD. None went to Mikulski's state of Maryland.

In addition, they noted that the two top money-getters were for Kemp's pet projects — $25 million for the Washington, D.C., and St. Louis home-ownership projects.

However, the money designated for Kenilworth-Parkside was no longer necessary since HUD had been allowed to take it from fiscal 1990 funds.

Mikulski declined to discuss the matter. But one of her aides said the subcommittee's actions were "not personal," but "a matter of priorities to guarantee that what we're funding gets spent."

Traxler also refused to talk about the flap. And Green, the ranking House subcommittee Republican, said he thought it was inappropriate to talk about it before the House-Senate conference.

But Green said he was not altogether happy with the way Kemp and HUD had been functioning.

"I'm sensing a typical bureaucratic overreaction to scandal," he said. "As a result, everything seems to be dead in the water."

Space Contracting

During Senate floor debate, Garn complained that the funding levels in the legislation for NASA and the National Science Foundation were "wholly inadequate."

Under the Senate bill, the space agency was to receive $13.5 billion in fiscal 1991, a 10 percent increase over the previous year, but still far short of the $15.1 billion requested by the Bush administration. The House provided $14.3 billion for NASA.

The NSF received $2.4 billion under the Senate's legislation, about $27 million more than the House version and about $20 million short of the president's recommendation.

Garn said he had intended to offer an amendment to increase the agencies' bottom line. But he decided to hold off because of the Sept. 30 White House-congressional budget agreement, saying he hoped that more money could be allocated during the House-Senate conference.

Mikulski agreed, and said that if the subcommittee received an increase in its allocation, the money would go to NASA.

In particular, the subcommittee wanted to provide more money to the space station program, which was cut by $863.6 million from the president's request and $162 million below fiscal 1990.

The Senate agreed by voice vote to an amendment by Maine's two senators — Democrat George J. Mitchell, the majority leader, and Republican William S. Cohen — to set aside $15 million to award a second contract to develop and produce the "throat" entrance of the Advanced Solid Rocket Motor (ASRM) nozzle. The ASRM program, which was expected to cost $2 billion, was developing a new type of motor and nozzle for the space shuttle after the *Challenger* explosion.

NASA had already awarded a contract to do the work to Textron Inc. in Providence, R.I. But a company called Fiber Materials Inc., based in Biddeford, Maine, did not bid on the contract the first time around, sources said, and wanted a chance to work on the project.

Altogether, the second contract, which was to be awarded on a competitive basis, could cost NASA as much as $145 million to repeat Textron's work.

Second-source contracts were sometimes used to spur competition among companies to produce the best work. Under the amendment, the second contract would not be awarded if the president told Congress that it would delay the project or cost too much.

Also agreed to was an amendment from John McCain, R-Ariz., to provide $23 million from HUD funds for housing vouchers to chronically mentally ill and homeless veterans.

The vouchers, used to help pay for rent, were to be

combined with counseling and social services paid for out of other funds.

FINAL ACTION

Just minutes before conferees for the VA-HUD appropriations bill were to start their meeting Oct. 16, key members met privately to make a few last trims to the $78 billion bottom line.

But by the time the formal conference was over, they had managed to exceed the discretionary outlay limit by $23 million. Staff members began looking for ways to cut that number before the conference report was sent to the House and Senate for floor votes.

NASA Gets an Increase

Funding for NASA grew by 13 percent over fiscal 1990. Still, space program booster Garn renewed his complaint that not enough money was going to the space agency.

The House and Senate split the difference between their two recommendations, providing the space agency $13.9 billion in fiscal 1991 — $420 million more than the Senate level and $400 million less than the House.

Bush had requested a 24 percent increase for NASA to proceed with major projects such as the space station and the moon-Mars initiative.

The space station, troubled by numerous technical problems, was to be funded at $1.9 billion, $313 million more than the Senate-passed bill, about $350 million less than the House level and far less than the $2.5 billion the administration requested.

The moon-Mars program was virtually zeroed out. "We're essentially not doing moon-Mars," Senate Appropriations Subcommittee Chairman Mikulski declared.

House Appropriations Subcommittee Chairman Traxler pointed out that the budgets of NASA, EPA and NSF all increased by about 13.5 percent. "Even though it's a yeoman's leap forward, we do have to recognize the shortfalls," Traxler said.

Housing Funds Cut

By increasing the space agency's funds above the Senate recommendation, the legislation dealt a blow to the HUD subsidized housing account.

Those programs, which helped poor people pay for housing, received $9.5 billion in fiscal 1991. That was down $1.3 billion from the Senate recommendation and $2.1 billion from the House.

Altogether, HUD received $23.7 billion in fiscal 1991, a drop from the House recommendation of $25.9 billion and the Senate suggestion of $24.9 billion.

But the bottom line was still an $8.7 billion jump over the previous year.

The huge increase was needed, however, to renew expiring rental subsidy contracts to maintain the number of people receiving rental vouchers and certificates. Excluding that, the agency received a $2.1 billion overall increase.

Conferees dropped $18.9 million earmarked for HUD Secretary Kemp's plan to turn over ownership of 464 public housing units to residents at a project in Washington. Instead, they allowed the secretary to take that money from another fiscal 1990 account.

Members accepted an amendment by Mikulski to remove a cap on the number of public housing units that could be sold in fiscal 1991.

Appropriators had wanted to send a clear signal to Kemp that they disapproved of his plan to sell public housing. They initially said that HUD could not sell more than 750 units in 1991. With the cap removed, Kemp's home ownership program, which was authorized in the omnibus housing bill (S 566), was free to move forward.

Lawmakers also agreed to reduce the HUD public affairs office from 29 positions to 20. Kemp's travel budget was to be restored, but first-class travel was forbidden unless it was medically necessary or a flight was longer than seven hours.

Members bemoaned the fact that there was not enough money throughout the bill. For example, Traxler noted that in 1981, $25 billion was appropriated for low-income housing. In fiscal 1990, that number had dropped to $7.5 billion. In fiscal 1991, $9.5 billion was appropriated.

"That represents the largest single reduction of any major program in the entire government over the past 10 years," Traxler said.

Despite the pain of cutting programs and paring the deficit, the conferees managed to fund 61 "special purpose grants worth $54 million, requested by members for their districts.

The administration had complained that these projects had not gone through a competitive process and were not authorized by law. Although the 1989 Housing and Urban Development Reform Act effectively killed the account where special projects were stashed, appropriators created a category under assisted housing and funded them out of that.

Among the projects were $995,000 for a performing arts and cultural center in North Miami Beach, Fla., and $795,000 to renovate the Old Post Office Building in Lynn, Mass. Traxler's home state, Michigan, was to get $790,000 for park improvements and shoreline protection in Saginaw and $769,000 for park improvements in Bay City.

On the House floor, Steve Bartlett, R-Texas, complained that the projects were pork, that the funds were given according to whom a member knew in the leadership or the Appropriations Committee, and that it was taking away from those who needed it most.

"We know that there are in excess of 5,000 low-income families that will not have a place to live, that will not have a Section 8 certificate," Bartlett said, "in order to satisfy our own political interests." He urged his colleagues to defeat a Traxler amendment to add the special projects, but the House approved it, 232-167. *(Vote 496, p. 158-H)*

Bush Signing Statement

In signing the bill into law Nov. 5, Bush said the measure "meets the needs of our nation's veterans." He also expressed pleasure with the 13.5 percent increase in NASA's overall budget.

But Bush said that he was "disappointed" by Congress' refusal to provide "the small amount of funding" requested to start work on the moon-Mars mission. He pointedly noted that NASA had the authority to reprogram funds to continue existing in-house mission studies.

The president also said that he was "greatly concerned over the significant reduction" in the space station program, which he said "remains, for me, a high priority."

Bush also voiced disappointment with the cuts for the NSF and with the refusal to fund the administration's HOPE home-ownership initiative. But he concluded in a conciliatory tone by recognizing that Congress had "an especially difficult task balancing the competing priorities funded in this diverse act." ■

$20.2 Billion for Energy, Water Projects

The Senate on Oct. 20 gave voice vote approval to a $20.2 billion spending bill (HR 5019) for energy and water projects, clearing the measure for President Bush.

The House had approved the conference report — a compromise based on the two chambers' original versions of the bill — on Oct. 19. The House debated some provisions of the compromise, but attempts to change it failed on lopsided votes, and the House-Senate conference report was adopted by a vote of 362-51. *(Vote 489, p. 156-H)*

Increases over energy and water appropriations for fiscal 1990 totaled $1.7 billion. Most of the extra money was to pay for cleaning up the Energy Department's nuclear bomb plants and civilian research facilities. *(1989 Almanac, p. 737)*

BOXSCORE

Legislation: Fiscal 1991 energy and water development appropriations, PL 101-514 (HR 5019).

Major action: Signed, Nov. 5. Conference report adopted by Senate, Oct. 20; by House, 362-51, Oct. 19. Passed by Senate, Aug. 2; by House, 355-59, June 19.

Reports: Conference report (H Rept 101-889). Appropriations (S Rept 101-378); Appropriations (H Rept 101-536).

Bush requested $2.8 billion for cleanup efforts, but the bill raised that figure to $3.1 billion. Estimates of the total cost of the cleanup ranged from $60 billion to $200 billion over the following 20 to 50 years.

The bill also:

- Cut Bush's request for the proposed superconducting super collider (SSC) by $75 million to $243 million. Both houses had approved Bush's full $318 million request for the Texas project, but conferees cut that figure as they slashed millions from domestic programs to comply with the 1990 budget agreement. *(Super collider, p. 438)*

"It's not a death blow, but it's a serious blow," said Rep. Jim Chapman, D-Texas, the project's main booster. "The conference is telling us that until the Energy Department can tell us what it's going to cost, it's going to be an attractive target."

The project's estimated cost had continually grown; 1990 estimates ranged up to $11.7 billion, but the administration had yet to settle on a final figure.

Bush's request for other Energy Department general science programs was also cut, leaving only $1.1 billion, roughly what they had gotten in fiscal 1990.

In another science account, Energy Department biology programs received a healthy increase to nearly $400 million, including Bush's $46 million request for a proposed multibillion-dollar gene-mapping project. The project received $87.6 million more through the National Institutes of Health in the Labor-HHS appropriations bill (HR 5257 — PL 101-517), down from Bush's $100 million-plus request for NIH genome work. *(Labor-HHS appropriations bill, p. 847)*

- Denied Bush's requests for two new plutonium facilities that were part of a plan to modernize the Energy Department's bomb program. Both projects — one at Rocky Flats, Colo., the other at Los Alamos, N.M. — would eventually cost hundreds of millions of dollars and had generated local opposition.

Opponents had tried unsuccessfully to kill Bush's $65 million request for the Rocky Flats project when the bill first reached the House floor June 19, but conferees removed the money after it became clear that the fiscal 1991 defense bill (HR 4739) would not authorize the project. *(Defense authorization bill, p. 671)*

Also stripped was $20.6 million requested for the Los Alamos project, which had been granted by the Senate but denied by the House.

- Provided $3.3 billion for Corps of Engineers water projects, including more than 25 new projects. *(Water projects, p. 299)*
- Provided nearly $90 million for research facilities in the states of well-placed members of Congress.

Dropped from that part of the bill was a $4 million earmark for hydrogen research advocated by Rep. Robert S. Walker, R-Pa., the Science Committee's ranking minority member.

During the initial House floor debate, Walker complained that many of the bill's allocations for research programs ignored priorities set by his committee. To appease him, the bill's drafters accepted his $4 million amendment on the House floor — then stripped it from the bill in conference. *(Hydrogen research, p. 318)*

- Increased Bush's $2.1 billion request for energy supply research programs to $2.5 billion, providing a bit more for solar ($131 million) than Bush wanted and much less for nuclear ($306 million) and fusion ($275 million).
- Provided federal support for two projects opposed by environmentalists but supported by influential senators.

For Democrat Daniel K. Inouye of Hawaii, the bill included $5 million to study a geothermal project in his state that some feared would endanger a rain forest.

Sen. James A. McClure, R-Idaho, inserted $1 million for a hydroelectric project opposed by environmentalists and fishing interests worried about its impact on a trout-rich Idaho stream known as the Henry's Fork of the Snake River.

HOUSE COMMITTEE ACTION

The House Appropriations Subcommittee on Energy and Water Development approved HR 5019 on June 7 providing $20.9 billion for fiscal 1991 for the Energy Department, Army Corps of Engineers and related programs.

The total was more than $500 million over what Bush requested.

Pushing aside concerns about rising costs, key House appropriators planned to grant Bush his full $318 million request toward building a massive atom smasher that was expected to cost $8 billion.

"We think it's a great project," subcommittee Chairman Tom Bevill, D-Ala., said of the superconducting super collider, planned for Waxahachie, Texas. "Every member of that panel feels that is something we need to do."

The bill included all sorts of additions and money shifts favored by influential lawmakers that were opposed by the administration. Those protests, however, were tempered by Bush's active support for super collider funding, which included close to $170 million for construction, enough to put the project well on its way toward the scheduled 1998 completion.

Full funding for the atom smasher had the implicit approval of one of the Texas project's biggest critics — Silvio O. Conte, Mass., the Appropriations Committee's ranking Republican. "We've decided not to make a run at it," said Conte, who had been considering such a move.

The Energy panel's report on the bill was expected to say members were "very concerned" about the project's rising costs but to place no restrictions on the use of the money, said Chapman, the state's point man for the project on the Appropriations Committee.

Nor was there an effort to cap federal spending on the project at $5 billion. The House put such a provision in a separate authorization bill (HR 4380), that passed the House May 2, 309-109. *(Vote 94, p. 34-H)*

As approved by the subcommittee, the spending bill also included:

- $3.3 billion toward cleaning up Energy Department nuclear facilities, including its bomb plants, a job that was expected to cost up to $110 billion or more over the following 25 years. The 1991 total was $487 million more than Bush's request, Bevill said.
- Up to $50 million for home-state university science facilities favored by five well-placed Appropriations Committee members, including Bevill, who inserted $10 million for a biomedical research center at the University of Alabama in Birmingham.

The subcommittee had declined to earmark Energy Department money for research centers in the past couple of years, but in 1990 it decided to hand out some favors.

Also in line for up to $10 million each, according to Bevill, were Boston College, which was advocated by Conte; the University of New Orleans, advocated by Lindy (Mrs. Hale) Boggs, D-La.; Case Western University, advocated by Louis Stokes, D-Ohio; and Indiana State, advocated by John T. Myers, the subcommittee's ranking Republican.

- Money for about 25 new Corps of Engineers water projects not requested by the administration but backed by various members. Combined with money for projects begun in previous years, the bill allocated about $1.4 billion for corps construction, more than 10 percent over Bush's request, Bevill said.

Energy and Water Appropriations

Following are the budget authority totals in the fiscal 1991 energy and water appropriations bill (HR 5019 — PL 101-514).

(Figures, in thousands of dollars, may not add due to rounding.)

	President's Request	House Bill	Senate Bill	Final Bill
Army Corps of Engineers				
General Construction	$ 1,226,000	$ 1,362,025	$ 1,308,043	$ 1,143,086
Operation and Maintenance	1,389,500	1,457,488	1,408,791	1,450,669
Other	706,100	742,778	719,528	708,741
Subtotal	**$ 3,321,600**	**$ 3,562,291**	**$ 3,436,362**	**$ 3,302,496**
Bureau of Reclamation (Interior)				
Construction	609,430	649,697	641,027	642,897
Operation and Maintenance	231,516	231,516	231,516	221,516
Other	74,426	75,896	75,491	76,191
Subtotal	**$ 915,372**	**$ 957,109**	**$ 948,034**	**$ 940,604**
Energy Department				
Atomic Energy Defense	8,544,900	10,915,148	10,980,258	10,914,014
Energy Supply R&D	2,105,337	2,703,272	2,745,615	2,527,082
Environmental Restoration and Waste Management	2,818,436	(3,278,492)	(3,194,301)	(3,144,301)
Defense function (Atomic Energy)	(2,361,751)	(2,714,807)	(2,680,616)	(2,704,722)
Non-defense function	(429,685)	(563,685)	(513,685)	(439,579)
Uranium Supply and Enrichment				
Expenditures	1,340,018	1,406,018	1,340,018	1,340,018
Revenues	−1,450,400	−1,530,500	−1,450,400	−1,450,400
General Science	1,273,732	1,273,732	1,273,732	1,148,732
Superconducting Super Collider	(317,866)	(317,866)	(317,866)	(242,866)
Nuclear Waste	292,833	292,833	292,833	242,833
Power Marketing Administrations	326,387	326,387	326,387	326,387
Federal Energy Regulatory Commission				
Expenditures	122,750	122,750	122,750	122,750
Revenues	−122,750	−122,750	−122,750	−122,750
Other	252,928	253,596	253,596	243,596
Subtotal	**$ 15,504,171**	**$ 15,640,486**	**$ 15,762,039**	**$ 15,292,262**
Independent Agencies				
Appalachian Regional Commission	50,000	150,000	180,000	170,000
Nuclear Regulatory Commission				
Expenditures	475,000	475,000	475,000	465,000
Revenues	−156,750	−156,750	−156,750	−153,450
Tennessee Valley Authority	91,302	135,000	125,000	135,000
Other	13,682	12,382	12,720	12,720
Subtotal	**$ 473,234**	**$ 615,632**	**$ 635,970**	**$ 629,270**
GRAND TOTAL	**$ 20,214,377**	**$ 20,775,518**	**$ 20,782,405**	**$ 20,164,632**

SOURCE: House Appropriations Committee

Flood control, dams, levees, beach restoration, dikes, harbors and other water projects were the staple of the bill, but Bush asked the subcommittee to refrain from funding new starts because it had approved so many (32) in 1989.

Full Committee Action

The House Appropriations Committee on June 13 gave speedy voice vote approval to HR 5019, a $20.8 billion measure for energy and water development.

The committee left the bill virtually intact as it came from the Energy and Water Development Subcommittee on June 7. No substantive amendments were approved, and the bill had the enthusiastic backing of Myers, the panel's ranking Republican. "How can you improve upon perfection?" he asked.

Despite that assessment, Myers warned that some provisions could cause trouble with the administration. He noted that the bill reflected several spending priorities that were at odds with the administration's, including continued strong support for the Appalachian Regional Commission and higher funding for nuclear waste cleanup.

However, the bill also included Bush's full funding request of $318 million for the superconducting super collider.

The bill's total was $575 million more than the administration had requested and more than $2.3 billion above what was appropriated for fiscal 1990.

Most of the increase was due to almost $3.3 billion to clean up nuclear weapons plants. The committee recommended $2.7 billion to clean up waste connected with the Energy Department's defense-related work and about $564 million for non-defense cleanup and environmental restoration. The $3.3 billion total was almost $500 million more than the administration had requested.

No similar waste-cleanup funds were provided for fiscal 1990.

As in the past, about half the money ($10.9 billion) was for atomic weapons activities of the Energy Department. The defense-waste cleanup was partly offset by cuts of about 13 percent to 14 percent in several other atomic weapons accounts, including research and development and testing.

The bill provided no money for two weapons programs that the administration said it wanted to cancel, the warhead for the Follow-on-to-Lance missile and modernizing the 155mm Artillery Fired Atomic Projectile.

Also included in the bill:

- About $2 billion to build Army Corps of Engineers and Bureau of Reclamation water projects, including 25 new projects.
- $150 million for the Appalachian Regional Commission, $100 million more than the administration sought.
- $195 million for solar and renewable energy programs, $20 million more than requested.

HOUSE FLOOR ACTION

The House on June 19 approved a $20.8 billion energy and water spending bill by 355-59. *(Vote 181, p. 64-H)*

Confident that President Bush would not veto a bill that included funding for his favorite project — the gigantic atom smasher in Texas — House members approved HR 5019 that also contained start-up money for well over $1 billion worth of their own pet proposals.

The 1990 bill signaled a changed dynamic on the annual spending measure, a perennial whipping boy for Republican administration critics of Democratic spending habits. There appeared to be an implicit quid pro quo between the Bush administration and Congress: constant funding for the $8 billion superconducting super collider in exchange for a plethora of smaller congressional undertakings.

Said Vic Fazio, D-Calif.: "I wouldn't say there's a direct correlation, but if the administration is going to remain as committed as they are [to the super collider], obviously there's going to be some give and take."

Committee Members Benefit

To that end, Fazio was one of many influential Appropriations Committee members and other well-placed members who successfully advocated projects in the bill for their districts.

As approved by the House, the bill included 25 new water projects — flood control, locks and dams, beach erosion and the like — with a total of almost $45 million in fiscal 1991 funds.

The administration did not want to start any new projects. Spread across the country, the projects eventually would cost the federal government an estimated $1.6 billion-plus to complete, according to administration estimates.

More than half benefited the states and districts of Appropriations Committee members. A flood control and harbor project, for instance, would be ordered in committee Chairman Jaime L. Whitten's home state of Mississippi..

Additional flood control projects were also successfully advocated by Appropriations members Fazio; Bill Alexander, D-Ark.; Wes Watkins, D-Okla.; Carl D. Pursell, R-Mich.; Bill Lowery, R-Calif.; and Virginia Smith, R-Neb.

Majority Leader Richard A. Gephardt, D-Mo., and Rules Committee member Alan Wheat, D-Mo., also backed flood control projects in the bill.

HR 5019 also included more than $80 million for university facilities and hospital improvement projects. Among them were research facilities for the home states of five Appropriations Committee members, including subcommittee Chairman Bevill and ranking Republican Myers and Conte, Republican leader of the full committee.

Bevill also inserted a paragraph into the committee's report on the bill urging the Energy Department to expand the super collider program at the University of Alabama. It was one of scores of schools involved in the project but the only one mentioned in Bevill's report.

Bush met with Bevill and Myers before the fiscal 1990 bill was drafted to lobby them on the super collider. The lawmakers then brought up the need for new water projects, said Chapman.

Bevill had denied that there was a quid pro quo, but Chapman said: "That was direct last year. We know that was discussed. Myers and Bevill asked the president to give us some breathing room on some public works projects. They were saying, 'Mr. President, we need some help.' "

Weeks later, though neither Bevill nor Myers had seemed particularly enthusiastic about the super collider and its rising costs, their strong backing helped supporters resoundingly beat back an attempt to cut its funding substantially. It was the pivotal vote in the project's decade-long history.

During the 1990 debate on the bill, no one even took a shot at the project, despite a $2 billion jump in its estimated cost. Most of the biggest critics, including Republican Conte and Democrats David R. Obey, Wis., Howard Wolpe, Mich., and Dennis E. Eckart, Ohio, had agreed not to offer anti-collider amendments. Bill Frenzel, R-Minn., caused a last-minute panic among supporters when he signaled his intention to offer an amendment to strike the SSC's $318 million allocation.

But Chapman and Republican Joe L. Barton, whose Texas district was the proposed home of the project, begged him to reconsider.

Frenzel never offered the amendment, saying he had more important things to do, such as the ongoing budget summit with the White House.

Instead, Frenzel and other Republican critics of pork-barrel politics tried to cut the whole bill back. But they got little support from the White House.

"The administration, in order to keep the superconducting super collider funded at the level they want, is being friendly" to the bill's Democratic drafters, said Walker.

"The superconducting super collider does have a pretty powerful influence over the direction of this bill."

Concern, but No Veto

The official White House position statement on the bill pointedly avoided the use of the word "veto" — a positive signal in the eyes of the bill's drafters.

"We haven't gotten any love letters from the president," Chapman said. "But there's been no explicit veto threat."

The White House statement said: "The administration is deeply concerned about the excessive amount of unjustified spending for new construction starts and other unrequested items in the bill."

The statement also complained about 80 unrequested planning studies related to possible future projects.

The administration called the bill, coming on the heels of all the new starts added by the House and Senate the previous year, "irresponsible" and said it would commit the Army Corps of Engineers to a construction schedule it "cannot possibly meet."

Barton and some of his conservative Texas compatriots also tempered their criticism of the bill; several cast votes against spending-cut proposals because of the super collider — cuts they said they otherwise would have backed.

There were four such votes, but supporters of the bill won each time by lopsided margins, with a majority of Republicans voting against a majority of Democrats. A 2 percent across-the-board cut to the bill — offered by Democrat Timothy J. Penny of Minnesota — came the closest, but it still lost, 175-232. *(Vote 180, p. 64-H)*

"This is another meat-ax approach," Bevill complained.

Frenzel, who had earlier advocated much bigger reductions, replied: "This very blunt meat ax, as it has been described, is actually a cream puff. It is a marshmallow. It is hardly worth voting for." He urged everyone to vote for it nonetheless.

Earlier, the House defeated cuts of 10.5 percent (offered by Frenzel) and 5 percent (offered by William E. Dannemeyer, R-Calif.), on votes of 98-314 and 124-285, respectively. *(Votes 178, 179, p. 62-H)*

The Democrats likewise won, 260-157, on a procedural vote aimed at allowing Republicans to try to pare domestic spending in all of the fiscal 1991 appropriations bills. *(Vote 173, p. 62-H)*

In other significant action on the bill, the House:

- Approved without debate a $487 million increase in Bush's request for the Energy Department's civilian and military nuclear cleanup effort. The bill included $3.3 billion for the effort, which the committee said was expected to cost between $60 billion and $200 billion over the following 20 to 50 years.
- Earmarked $4 million for hydrogen energy research programs, as requested by Walker, by voice vote.
- Approved, 413-7, a provision that would prevent the administration from spending $65 million toward building a new $571 million plutonium recovery facility at the Rocky Flats Nuclear Weapons Plant outside Denver until 30 days after Congress had received a report on the Energy Department's plans for modernizing its weapons complex. The amendment was offered by David E. Skaggs, D-Colo., after a move by Patricia Schroeder, D-Colo., and other arms controllers to strip the money from the bill failed 142-278. *(Votes 176, 175; p. 62-H)*
- Rejected an amendment by Thomas E. Petri, R-Wis., by 140-277, that would have stricken from the bill a provision to require the federal government to pay for the cost of salmon protection efforts near the Shasta Dam in Northern California, instead of passing off the costs to ratepayers who used power from the hydroelectric facility. *(Vote 177, p. 62-H)*

  Members said the costs totaled $11 million.
- Approved, by voice vote, an amendment by James H. Scheuer, D-N.Y., to earmark $1.3 million for an Energy Department program aimed at reducing the export of atom-bomb grade uranium by supporting research into low-grade alternatives.

SENATE COMMITTEE ACTION

Rejecting positions taken by the House, the Senate Appropriations Committee on July 19 voted to kill a dozen water projects, boost energy research funds, cut nuclear cleanup accounts and declare that the world's biggest atom smasher should be built in Texas even if foreign countries failed to chip in.

The actions came as the committee by voice vote approved its $20.8 billion version of HR 5019. The Subcommittee on Energy and Water Development had approved the spending measure on July 18.

As usual, the bill was full of home-state projects advocated by well-placed senators, who stripped out House projects to make room for their own.

Overseeing the bill was Energy and Water Subcommittee Chairman J. Bennett Johnston, D-La., who faced a tough re-election fight in 1990. He inserted lots of money for Louisiana.

The bill included nearly $150 million for Louisiana water projects, much more than Bush or the House had recommended; $12.5 million for Louisiana State University's Biomedical Research Institute; and $750,000 for Louisiana Tech University.

Strong Signal for Collider

A good-sized chunk of money from the proposed $8 billion super collider, for which the committee approved Bush's full fiscal 1991 request of $318 million, was also likely to end up in Louisiana.

Two companies bidding on the project's $1 billion-plus contract to build the massive magnets for the experimental device had promised to set up factories in the oil-depressed state.

Johnston had been regarded as skeptical about the SSC, but he was convinced that it was worthwhile, and his enthusiasm was reflected in the Appropriations Committee's report on the bill. Unlike its House counterpart, the report made no mention of the project's recent $2 billion cost increase.

The report also implicitly rejected a House-approved provision, included in the super collider authorization bill that required at least 20 percent of the project's cost to come from foreign countries.

"It is the continued consensus of the committee that the SSC should proceed whether foreign participation is forthcoming or not," the report said. "The benefits to be gained . . . outweigh the budgetary requirements that appear to require foreign participation."

Johnston, who also chaired the Energy Committee, said he had no plans to do a separate authorization because many of the players who would draft such a bill already oversaw the project's budget on the Appropriations panel.

Other Provisions

Other significant provisions in the Senate committee's energy and water spending bill included:

- **Water projects.** The bill set funding for all Army Corps of Engineers construction projects at $1.3 billion, $54 million less than the House version and $82 million more than Bush wanted.

Aides said the bill stripped out about half of the 25 new flood control, beach erosion and lock and dam projects that were in the House bill. Almost all of the so-called new starts that remained in the Senate bill were taken from the House version.

- **Energy programs.** The bill boosted funding for energy research and development accounts by $42 million over the House bill to $2.75 billion, compared with Bush's $2.1 billion request.

Money for solar programs ($130 million) was slightly below that in the House bill and well above Bush's request. Conversely, nuclear research funds ($330 million) were below Bush's request but above those in the House bill.

At the last minute, subcommittee members had decided to cut in half development funds for a nuclear power pack that would provide energy for civilian and defense space systems. Mark O. Hatfield, R-Ore., called it "Chernobyl in space." The account was reduced to $7.3 million.

- **Science programs.** The bill included exactly what Bush wanted and what the House allowed for all Energy Department science programs (including the super collider): $1.3 billion, compared with $1.1 billion in 1990.

Biological research also fared well, with the committee allowing almost $400 million, more than in both Bush's budget and the House bill.

Included was Bush's request of $46 million for an ongoing effort to map human genes.

The mapping project was a joint effort with the National Institutes of Health (NIH) that had been been the subject of an interagency dispute over who would control the project, a fight the NIH won. Now the Senate committee was pressing the Energy Department to reassert more control over the project.

Also approved in the energy and water bill was Energy Secretary James D. Watkins' last-minute proposal to allow him to spend unspecified funds "to improve mathematics, science and engineering education and skill levels in the United States."

- **Nuclear cleanup.** The bill cut by $84 million the House's $3.28 billion down payment on the Energy Department's multibillion-dollar, long-term effort to restore the environment around its civilian and defense nuclear facilities. That was still substantially more than the administration's $2.8 billion request.

- **University projects.** Senators stripped from the bill money for a handful of university building projects the House approved at the behest of well-placed members, replacing them with their own projects.

Those who landed from $4 million to $12.5 million apiece for their states were Louisiana's Johnston; Oregon's Hatfield; committee Chairman Robert C. Byrd, D-W.Va.; Ernest F. Hollings, D-S.C.; Tom Harkin, D-Iowa; Thad Cochran, R-Miss.; and Minority Leader Bob Dole, R-Kan. Other state-specific earmarks benefited the states of committee members McClure, Inouye, and Harry Reid, D-Nev.

Reid publicly begged Johnston to increase the committee's allocation to help Nevada, its local governments and universities help oversee the Energy Department's plan to put a nuclear-waste dump in Yucca Mountain.

Even though committee members believed the state was trying to "use every possible legal means to frustrate and obstruct" the plan, according to the report, Johnston agreed to more than double the total to $15.4 million.

SENATE FLOOR ACTION

The Senate on Aug. 2 approved by voice vote the $20.8 billion spending bill for energy and water programs after sponsors persuaded a Republican member to drop his attempt to nick less than 3 percent off the bill to bring its total in line with Bush's request.

The Senate's version of HR 5019 exceeded administration requests by more than $580 million, as did the House-passed version.

Following the lead of House Republicans who had consistently tried to trim spending bills, Rudy Boschwitz, R-Minn., wanted to whittle the measure back. But he gave up after voicing fear on the Senate floor that the bill's top Republican advocate would attempt to take the money from projects in Minnesota.

"That's a pretty tough way to do business," Boschwitz told Hatfield, the Appropriations Committee's ranking Republican, on Aug. 1, when the Senate began work on the bill.

Hatfield had cryptically announced that he might offer an amendment to Boschwitz's proposal, but did not specify what he had in mind.

The next day, Boschwitz said he decided not to offer his amendment. He said Hatfield had persuaded him to drop the idea by showing that the bill was within outlines approved by the Budget Committee (H Con Res 310).

In passing the bill, the Senate granted Bush's full fiscal 1991 request for the proposed superconducting super collider but shuffled other presidential priorities.

The measure included $318 million for the huge atom smasher.

There was no mention on the floor of the project's rising costs, now estimated at up to $8.6 billion, up from the previous year's estimate of $5.3 billion.

The bill was approved in much the same form as it left the Senate Appropriations Committee.

Late on Aug. 1, members approved by voice votes and without debate a dozen amendments, most of them setting aside money for home-state projects.

The parochial amendments, ranging in cost from $60,000 to several million dollars, benefited the following states: Idaho, California, Nevada, Tennessee, Rhode Island, Arkansas, Wyoming and Oregon.

Also approved was an amendment by Frank H. Murkowski, R-Alaska, to block foreign companies from bidding on U.S. public works projects if their home countries unfairly restricted U.S. firms bidding on projects there.

The Senate also passed an amendment by Jeff Bingaman, D-N.M., that increased funds for arms control programs by cutting weapons production accounts.

Fights over contested amendments by Tim Wirth, D-Colo., and Ted Stevens, R-Alaska, were avoided Aug. 2 when they agreed to a compromise requiring the administration to study the supercomputer needs of certain research projects in their states. Wirth's involved global warming; Stevens' involved efforts to tap energy from the aurora borealis. Wirth and Stevens had wanted to earmark money to buy computing equipment for the projects.

McClure won the only roll call, 76-23, when the Senate set aside $1 million for a hydroelectric project on the Snake River in his state. The cooperative that undertook the job missed the expiration deadline for energy tax credits because of delays caused by environmental studies, McClure said. *(Vote 205, p. 43-S)*

Opponents, led by Bill Bradley, D-N.J., said it was a bad precedent to appropriate money for those who had lost tax benefits.

"It will have no end," Bradley said of the practice.

In other areas, the bill included initial funding for 15 new water projects, most of them also approved by the House in its version of the bill. But the Senate killed some other projects advocated by the House, construction efforts that could have cost more than $1.5 billion.

Bush did not want to begin any new projects in fiscal 1991, and the administration praised the Senate for showing more restraint. But it still opposed the ones that were included.

The administration, reflecting ongoing differences over what constituted a new start, said that there were actually 16 and that they would cost $300 million over the following five years; the Senate committee staff disputed that figure, saying it was as much as $100 million too high.

The Senate voted for more energy research funds than the House. Within those accounts, the Senate approved more for nuclear programs than the House, but less for solar energy.

Senators cut the House's total for Energy Department programs to clean up nuclear-weapons and civilian research facilities, though the Senate figure was still considerably more than Bush's.

The bill included $3.2 billion for that purpose — an effort that was expected to cost tens or hundreds of billions of dollars over the following few decades. Bush wanted to spend only $2.8 billion in fiscal 1991, while the House advocated $3.3 billion.

At least nine Appropriations Committee members managed to get multimillion-dollar earmarks included in the bill, most of them for university research efforts.

FINAL ACTION

Congressional negotiators put finishing touches on HR 5019 on Oct. 12, agreeing to a $20 billion-plus spending measure that cut funds for the super collider.

House and Senate conference committee members also cut funding for a slew of water projects and Energy Department programs in the bill, while succumbing to a last-minute appeal from Democratic Sen. Inouye to fund a $5 million study for a controversial geothermal energy project in Hawaii that was opposed by environmentalists.

Lawmakers had to trim the bill's domestic programs by about $750 million below what the two chambers already had approved, members said.

That move was, in effect, forced by the tentative budget agreement outline (H Con Res 310) approved by Congress on Oct. 8. Using that outline, the full Appropriations Committees capped domestic spending for the Energy and Water subcommittees at levels far below what they had approved.

The budget deal prevented members from raiding the bill's defense funds, so they had to trim $750 million from domestic accounts, which made up less than half of the bill's total, said House subcommitee Chairman Bevill.

Said his Senate counterpart, Johnston, "It's tough and difficult, and it will inflict a lot of pain."

The first to feel the pinch was the big $8 billion-plus atom smasher, which had been set to get $318 million in both bills. Members cut that figure by $75 million.

Conferees also rejected a request by Rep. Chapman to reimburse the state of Texas if it made up the difference on the super collider cuts and if the project was subsequently canceled. The House in May had overwhelmingly rejected just such a proposal on a separate authorization bill, but Chapman was unfazed. "You don't get anything if you don't ask for it," he said.

Panel members also cut another estimated $375 million from Energy Department programs and $250 million from Army Corps of Engineers construction projects, although none of roughly 30 new projects were killed outright. Chapman said no corps projects in Texas were cut, possibly because the big super collider cut "made them feel a little guilty."

Agreeing to Compromises

After approving the conference report Oct. 19, the House held separate votes on two compromises with the Senate.

The first, which was approved 246-172, authorized the Interior Secretary to pay $1 million to the Fall River Electric Cooperative as reimbursement for environmental protection costs for the Island Park Dam and Reservoir in Idaho. *(Vote 490, p. 156-H)*

The second, approved 308-108, earmarked $45 million in unauthorized biomedical research grants, steering them largely to universities in districts and states represented by many of the conferees. *(Vote 491, p. 156-H)*

Rep. Walker, ranking Republican on the House Science Committee, protested the earmarks.

"Once again, we're expendable people who have no say in the process whatsoever," Walker said of himself and fellow authorizers.

Signed by Bush

Bush signed the bill Nov. 5. In a statement, he criticized Congress for cutting the funds for the super collider while using the money saved to finance "large numbers of economically unjustified water projects" in the Corps of Engineers and the Bureau of Reclamation.

The president also faulted Congress for cutting his overall request for scientific research "while protecting $170 million of funds overall earmarked ... for special interest projects."

"Research projects should be selected after competitive evaluation on the basis of merit and research priorities, not on the basis of parochial interests," Bush wrote. ■

Food Assistance Boosted in Agriculture Bill

The Senate on Oct. 23 cleared a fiscal 1991 appropriations bill (HR 5268) for the Department of Agriculture and related agencies that provided $52.2 billion for farm, nutrition and rural development programs in fiscal 1991.

The House had adopted the conference report by voice vote Oct. 22. The Senate followed suit, also by voice vote, after midnight in the same day's session.

The most notable feature of the fiscal 1991 bill was a compromise worked out by House Appropriations Committee Chairman Jamie L. Whitten, D-Miss., to preserve but overhaul the financially troubled crop insurance program.

For the Commodity Credit Corporation, the federal entity that funded crop subsidy programs, the bill provided $5 billion — $1.1 billion less than President Bush had requested.

There was a $3 billion increase over fiscal 1990 spending — to $27.6 billion — for domestic nutrition programs. That included $19 billion for food stamps, an increase of $2.2 billion over fiscal 1990, and $2.4 billion for the Women, Infants and Children (WIC) program, an increase of $224 million.

Bush had requested a total of $26.4 billion for the programs.

For the PL 480 Food for Peace program, which provided surplus commodities for foreign countries, the bill provided for a program level of $1.6 billion, which was $54 million more than in fiscal 1990.

Of that total, $880 million was earmarked for credit sales, in which recipient governments received low-interest, short- and medium-term loans to purchase U.S. commodities. And the remaining $696 million was provided for commodity donations abroad, an increase of $23.4 million.

For rural development programs, the bill provided loan authority of $11.9 billion, an increase of $2.3 billion. There was a $150 million increase for rural water and sewer facility loans, bringing the program level up to $500 million.

The bill provided $1.2 billion for low-income housing loans, including $50 million for direct loans, $70 million for government guarantees of private loans and another $30 million to subsidize interest rates on private loans.

Conservation programs received $2.3 billion, an increase of $282 million. Most of the increase would be for the Conservation Reserve Program, which paid farmers to remove environmentally fragile land from production.

The bill provided about $100 million less than Bush's overall budget request, but shifted about $1 billion from agriculture programs to domestic food programs.

The increases for food and rural development programs drove the total amount about $7 billion over the $45.2 billion that was provided in fiscal 1990 by the agriculture spending bill Congress passed in 1989 and a fiscal 1990 supplemental appropriations bill cleared by Congress on May 25. *(Supplemental appropriations, p. 844; fiscal 1990 appropriations, 1989 Almanac, p. 741)*

BOXSCORE

Legislation: Fiscal 1991 appropriations for the Department of Agriculture, rural development and related agencies, PL 101-506 (HR 5268).

Major action: Signed, Nov. 5. Conference report adopted by Senate, Oct. 23 (Oct. 22 session); by House, Oct. 22. Passed by Senate, 79-19, Sept. 25; by House, 335-86, July 18.

Reports: Conference report (H Rept 101-907). Appropriations (S Rept 101-468); Appropriations (H Rept 101-598).

HOUSE COMMITTEE ACTION

The House Appropriations Committee on July 13 approved a $50.35 billion spending bill for agriculture that terminated the federal crop insurance program.

The panel, which approved the fiscal 1991 spending measure by voice vote with no amendments, also agreed to give a big boost to the Agriculture Department's food stamp program — approving a $19.04 billion appropriation, $2.1 billion more than in fiscal 1990 and $2.2 billion more than Bush had requested.

Crop Insurance Program

Committee Chairman Whitten, who also chaired the Agriculture subcommittee, said high costs and low farmer participation had made the crop insurance program unworkable. "We tried for 10 years to make crop insurance actuarially sound," Whitten said.

The Bush administration had proposed eliminating crop insurance and replacing it with direct disaster payments to farmers affected by weather.

The bill provided $101.6 million to cover the cost of the federal subsidy on crop insurance policies sold before Oct. 1. But no money was available for new policies.

The decision to cut the crop insurance program was made despite objections from the Agriculture Committee, which was working on restructuring the program. In a letter to Whitten, committee members said "arbitrary action to deny access to insurance" would be unfair.

Other Programs

For the Commodity Credit Corporation, the bill provided $5.3 billion, $1.4 billion less than the administration said it would need.

Rural development loan and grant programs were given $13.1 billion — a $1.4 billion increase, but $1.6 billion less than the administration requested. For emergency disaster loans, the committee approved an authorization level of $600 million; the administration asked for $25 million.

Although the committee appropriated more than requested for food stamps, it made the funds contingent upon receiving a formal request from the administration for the additional $2.1 billion.

Whitten said the administration had consistently underestimated the cost of the program. He wanted it to justify any increase.

HOUSE FLOOR ACTION

The House on July 18 passed, 335-86, a $50.35 billion dollar spending bill (HR 5268) for farm, nutrition and rural development programs after a debate that focused more on the budget deficit than on farm programs. *(Vote 243, p. 82-H)*

Debating the Deficit

The day before, the House had narrowly rejected a proposed constitutional amendment that would have generally banned federal budget deficits. *(Balanced-budget amendment, p. 174)*

Pennsylvania Republican Robert S. Walker decided to use the agriculture spending bill to continue the debate, and he showed that he was willing to go pretty far — all the way down to $19.90 — to embarrass House Democrats on the issue.

Walker tweaked the Democrats for voting overwhelmingly to reject, in succession, amendments proposing across-the-board cuts of 7.7 percent, 5 percent and 2 percent in the agriculture budget. The first two, sponsored by Republicans, failed by nearly identical margins: 115-305 and 115-300. The last, offered by Democrat Timothy J. Penny of Minnesota, came closer, 202-216, with Democrats dividing 58-190 against it. *(Votes 239-241, p. 82-H)*

So Walker came up with an amendment to impose an across-the-board cut of cut 0.0000000004 percent — or $19.90 out of the $50 billion bill.

"If in 1990 we can cut $19.90, then next year we can muster the courage to go to $19.91," Walker said.

Democrats met Walker's challenge by blaming the rising deficits on the two recent Republican administrations.

"When poor old beleaguered Jimmy Carter left office the national debt was $932 billion," David R. Obey, D-Wis., said. "The national debt today is $3.38 trillion. It has been tripled because this Congress gutlessly and spinelessly followed the policies of the Reagan administration and its successor."

With that said, Democrats united to defeat Walker's amendment. The vote was 175-214, with just 19 Democrats taking Walker's bait. Eleven Republicans crossed party lines to vote against the amendment. *(Vote 242, p. 82-H)*

Agriculture Bill Defended

Most lawmakers showed little interest in debating crop subsidies, rural lending, food stamps or any of the many other Agriculture Department programs funded in the bill. But House Appropriations Chairman Whitten defended the bill down to the last dollar.

"I just can't understand the efforts to cut," Whitten said. "I get asked about the balanced budget. I advise that I believe in the balanced budget but not at the expense of sound programs that are absolutely essential to the well-being of the American people."

Whitten did make drastic cuts in federal crop insurance in a move to eliminate the program. The bill made available $101.6 million to cover policies sold before Oct. 1. No money was to be available after that.

"We have a long record of trying to work out an actuarially sound crop insurance program," Whitten said. "I don't know if that can be done or not. . . . The big money goes to those engaged in the insurance business."

Supporters of the program did not try to amend the bill to restore the funds, but they said they would try to save it, either by restructuring crop insurance in the omnibus farm programs authorization bill (HR 3950) or by securing additional funds in the Senate version of the agriculture spending bill. *(Omnibus farm bill, p. 323)*

"I am concerned that the action taken here by the committee might send the wrong signal," said Agriculture Committee Chairman E. "Kika" de la Garza, D-Texas. "Crop insurance has become a tool of the new farming era."

Other Programs

The bill also included $100 million for a new program of rural housing loans, in which the department both guaranteed private-sector loans and subsidized the interest rate. The Bush administration had requested loan authorization for $297 million for both subsidized and unsubsidized loans. Whitten expressed "doubts about the willingness of lending institutions to participate," but he provided enough funding for a pilot program.

As in past years, the bill placed limits on funding for two commodity export subsidy programs. The Targeted Export Assistance Program was to be limited to $200 million in fiscal 1991, the same as in fiscal 1990; the Export Enhancement Program was to be capped at $500 million, $270 million less than could be used in fiscal 1990.

SENATE COMMITTEE ACTION

The Senate Agriculture Appropriations Subcommittee approved a $51.6 billion fiscal 1991 spending bill Sept. 11 that intended to rescue the federal crop insurance program from elimination.

As approved by the subcommittee, the bill provided $663.2 million to cover the federal subsidy on crop insurance policies, as well as to pay for administrative costs of the Federal Crop Insurance Corporation.

Asserting that the crop insurance program was faulty and too expensive, the Bush administration had proposed scrapping it and replacing it with permanent authority for direct disaster assistance to farmers. The House version of the annual agriculture appropriations bill provided no funds for crop insurance policies issued after Sept. 30.

"It's fine to say that crop insurance is too expensive and the program needs to be strengthened, but you can't just drop it like a hot potato," said Quentin N. Burdick, D-N.D., chairman of the Appropriations Subcommittee on Agriculture, Rural Development and Related Agencies.

Controversy also flared over an amendment by Bob Kasten, R-Wis., that would have required the Food and Drug Administration (FDA) to issue federal standards governing a dairy product known as light butter, which was lower in fat and cholesterol than real butter.

Arlen Specter, R-Pa., said Kasten's amendment, which would have required the light product to be composed of at least 50 percent butter, would harm dairy producers in Pennsylvania and other states, whose light butter contained more than half non-dairy ingredients.

Kasten withdrew the amendment until full committee consideration of the bill. He acknowledged that the amendment was an effort to end-run a nutrition labeling bill reported by the Labor and Human Resources Committee in April. *(Nutrition labeling bill, p. 575)*

The spending bill provided $1.6 billion for the PL 480 Food for Peace program in fiscal 1991, a modest increase over fiscal 1990. For the Commodity Credit Corporation the bill included $5 billion, the same as the House and $1.1 billion less than the administration requested.

SENATE FLOOR ACTION

On Sept. 25, the Senate passed, 79-19, the $52.3 billion agriculture appropriations bill for fiscal 1991. *(Vote 251, p. 51-S)*

All action but the vote on passage had been completed during initial floor consideration of the bill the week of Sept. 17.

But lawmakers agreed to put off the final vote because of Rosh Hashana, the Jewish New Year.

The spending bill, which was approved on a voice vote by the Appropriations Committee on Sept. 19 and ratified on the floor the next day, contained $1.9 billion more than the House-passed version and about $483 million less than requested by the Bush administration.

The Senate then closed off any further amendments and scheduled a vote for final passage for the following week.

Committee members had approved three amendments shifting about $70 million.

In each case, the rural housing loan program was reduced to offset increases elsewhere, including an additional $60 million for farm operating loans and $1.5 million for a pilot program to help disabled farmers.

The administration proposed a tripling of the funding for programs to prevent water pollution caused by agriculture.

But the committee cut the request from $15.5 million to $10.4 million, the same as the House.

Lawmakers refused to fund an administration proposal to subsidize interest on guaranteed loans under the low-income rural housing program. The administration had requested $362 million for the program as part of its ongoing effort to shift out of direct lending and into federal guarantees for private lenders.

Food Inspection

For the FDA, the committee had provided the full $14 million requested by the administration to expand federal fish inspections.

The Senate on Sept. 12 passed legislation (S 2924) to establish a new mandatory fish-inspection program in the Agriculture Department.

The House agricultural spending bill provided only $5 million for fish inspection.

The fish inspection bill stalled, however, because of disputes over which agency — the FDA or the Agriculture Department — should be given the new responsibility. *(Fish inspection, p. 396)*

Overall, FDA received $661.7 million — an increase of $95 million over fiscal 1990 — for carrying out its food-

Agriculture Appropriations

Following are the budget authority totals in the fiscal 1991 bill (HR 5268 — PL 101-506) for the Agriculture Department and related agencies.

(Figures, in thousands of dollars, may not add due to rounding.)

	President's Request	House Bill	Senate Bill	Final Bill
Agriculture Programs				
Production, processing and marketing	$ 2,664,454	$ 2,774,654	$ 2,830,815	$ 2,818,807
Federal Crop Insurance Corp.	663,222	264,518	663,222	586,000
Commodity Credit Corp.	6,100,000	5,000,000	5,000,000	5,000,000
Other	506	511	511	511
Subtotal	**$ 9,428,182**	**$ 8,039,683**	**$ 8,494,548**	**$ 8,405,318**
Rural Development Programs				
Farmers Home Administration				
Rural Housing Insurance Fund				
New budget authority	3,287,646	2,475,286	2,975,286	2,975,286
(Loan authorization)	(1,621,350)	(2,014,340)	(1,942,823)	(1,978,581)
Agricultural Credit Insurance Fund				
New budget authority	6,049,583	5,623,659	6,018,356	6,018,106
(Loan authorization)	(3,300,000)	(4,704,600)	(4,604,600)	(4,654,600)
Rural Development Insurance Fund				
New budget authority	1,666,160	1,466,160	1,666,160	1,666,160
(Loan authorization)	(445,700)	(760,000)	(760,000)	(760,000)
Rural housing vouchers	189,928	0	0	0
Other rural development	611,447	839,734	885,704	862,452
(Other rural loans)	(30,000)	(25,000)	(40,000)	(32,500)
Rural Electrification Administration				
New budget authority	34,319	334,632	334,632	334,632
(Loan authorization)	(200,000)	(1,794,375)	(1,932,375)	(1,794,375)
Soil Conservation Service	723,947	777,096	765,419	771,257
Conservation Reserve Program	1,878,038	1,314,926	1,314,926	1,314,926
Other conservation	214,265	246,182	235,648	241,521
Subtotal				
New budget authority	**$ 14,655,333**	**$ 13,077,675**	**$ 14,196,131**	**$ 14,184,872**
(Loan authorization)	**(5,597,050)**	**(9,298,815)**	**(9,280,298)**	**(9,220,556)**
Domestic Food Programs				
Child nutrition programs	880,698	569,038	880,698	880,698
Transfer from Sec. 32	4,696,501	4,696,501	4,696,501	4,696,501
Women, Infants and Children (WIC)	2,215,248	2,325,000	2,350,000	2,350,000
Food stamp program	18,078,168	19,038,806	19,050,901	19,050,901
Other food programs	616,906	663,520	638,520	638,520
Subtotal	**$ 26,487,521**	**$ 27,292,865**	**$ 27,616,620**	**$ 27,616,620**
International Programs				
PL 480 (Food for Peace)	897,853	1,010,853	1,010,853	1,010,853
(Program level)	(1,463,000)	(1,576,000)	(1,576,000)	(1,576,000)
Other	107,634	111,691	113,566	113,487
Subtotal	**$ 1,005,487**	**$ 1,122,544**	**$ 1,124,419**	**$ 1,124,342**
Related Agencies				
Food and Drug Administration	527,997	688,770	698,114	690,481
Farm Credit System assistance	99,330	90,000	90,000	90,000
Commodity Futures Trading Commission	44,960	39,691	44,960	43,960
Subtotal	**$ 672,287**	**$ 818,461**	**$ 833,074**	**$ 824,441**
GRAND TOTALS				
New budget (obligational) authority	**$ 52,248,810**	**$ 50,351,228**	**$ 52,264,792**	**$ 52,155,593**
Direct and insured loan level	2,256,610	5,227,795	5,142,778	5,116,036
Guaranteed loan level	2,863,560	4,297,120	4,363,620	4,330,620

SOURCE: House Appropriations Committee

monitoring inspection and research. The administration requested $164 million less.

FINAL ACTION

The Senate cleared HR 5268 on Oct. 23, providing $52.2 billion for agriculture spending. The bill preserved the financially plagued crop insurance program, but ordered its overhaul.

The House-Senate compromise was worked out in a short conference Oct. 19.

While the House had proposed to eliminate the crop insurance program, the final bill actually put the Agriculture Department back in the business of overseeing the program to offer farmers insurance policies against losses. Thus, it reversed a 1980 law that gave private insurers a subsidy for offering crop insurance.

In addition, the program had to possess reserves sufficient to cover at least 75 percent of its expected losses.

House Appropriations Chairman Whitten demanded the changes in return for abandoning his opposition to providing subsidies for new private insurance policies.

The effect of the changes, according to a House Appropriations Committee aide, was to significantly raise crop insurance premiums in certain regions and for certain crops, particularly in the Wheat Belt. But Whitten, the aide said, hoped that outcome would put crop insurance on a sounder financial footing, obviating further infusions of funds from the Commodity Credit Corporation.

"Since 1980, the [crop insurance] program has lost over $2.6 billion in indemnity payments," Whitten said.

About half the money in the bill, $27.6 billion, went to feeding programs, including $19 billion for food stamps and $2.4 billion for the WIC program. ■

Art, Owls, Oil Drilling Argued in Interior Bill

Final congressional action on an $11.7 billion fiscal 1991 appropriations bill for the Interior Department and related agencies (HR 5769) came only after lawmakers crafted temporizing positions on several contentious issues, including offshore oil drilling, protection of the northern spotted owl, and federal funding for sexually explicit artworks.

Total spending contained in the conference report on the bill, cleared by the Senate Oct. 27 after adoption by the House earlier that day, was $1.9 billion more than President Bush had requested.

Funding for the National Endowment for the Arts (NEA) had generated bruising fights in both chambers because of complaints that grants were being awarded to artists for works that critics labeled obscene or sacrilegious.

The dispute was resolved by a compromise, crafted largely by supporters of the endowment, that left issues of obscenity to the courts rather than the NEA. *(NEA funding, p. 430)*

Artists found guilty of obscenity would be required to return funds to the NEA, and they could be barred from receiving additional grants for three years unless they paid the money back. Existing law required the NEA to ensure in advance that money did not go to obscene, homoerotic or sadomasochistic works.

The House language also instructed the NEA, in judging applications, to take into account "general standards of decency and respect for the diverse beliefs and values of the American public."

During the conference, the Senate agreed to drop an amendment by Sen. Jesse Helms, R-N.C., to ban funding of works that denigrated religion.

Conferees split the difference on funding for the arts agency, agreeing to $175 million for fiscal 1991.

BOXSCORE

Legislation: Fiscal 1991 Interior Department and related agencies appropriations, PL 101-512 (HR 5769).

Major action: Signed, Nov. 5. Conference report adopted by Senate, Oct. 27; by House, 298-43, Oct. 27. Passed by Senate, 92-6, Oct. 24; by House, 327-80, Oct. 15.

Reports: Conference report (H Rept 101-971). Appropriations (S Rept 101-534); Appropriations (H Rept 101-789).

The issue of protecting the endangered northern spotted owl from loss of habitat due to logging in the Pacific Northwest's "old-growth" forests was the latest of a number of battles between environmentalists and the timber industry to be fought out on the Interior Department's annual spending bill. For fiscal 1991, conferees agreed on a provision to require a 20 percent reduction in the amount of timber to be harvested from U.S. Forest Service lands in Oregon and Washington. *(Spotted owl, p. 296)*

Environmentalists wanted an even larger reduction, arguing that the 3.2 billion board feet (bbf) permitted could not be cut without violating Endangered Species Act protections of the threatened owl. The timber industry wanted to maintain at least the 3.85 bbf level approved in 1989.

More comprehensive bills were pushed in House Agriculture and Interior subcommittees, but they stalled because of deep disagreements among members.

Late in the session, the Bush administration weighed in with its own proposal to exempt timber sales in the Pacific Northwest from the Endangered Species Act, but the proposal was widely criticized as unrealistic.

The issue of limiting federal leasing for offshore oil and gas drilling had been fought out on the Interior Department spending bill since fiscal 1982.

Congress had imposed a series of one-year moratoriums on offshore drilling, and the provision added to the fiscal 1991 bill was the most extensive to date — barring drilling off most U.S. shores.

President Bush had hoped to forestall legislative action in 1990 when he announced on June 26 a ban for the rest of the century on drilling in huge areas off the California, Florida and New England coasts. But lawmakers whose regions were left unprotected by the administration's decision lobbied for a more restrictive policy.

The one-year moratorium included in the fiscal 1991 Interior appropriations bill encompassed all the areas included in the administration's drilling ban, as well as Alaska's Bristol Bay, the Florida Panhandle and a portion of the mid-Atlantic region stretching from New Jersey to Maryland.

Senate conferees accepted the House-passed provision in exchange for a House agreement to drop a provision to raise fees for cattle ranchers who grazed herds on public lands.

Other House-passed provisions backed by an alliance of environmentalists and budget-cutters were also dropped. They included provisions aimed at cutting back public lands subsidies for timber, mining and livestock industries.

In addition to the grazing fee, House conferees agreed to drop a one-year moratorium on the issuance of mining patents on federal lands. Under a 118-year-old mining law, federal land could be sold for as little as $2.50 an acre to anyone who staked a mining claim.

Conferees compromised on funding for construction of logging roads, approving $181 million.

In 1989, Congress appropriated $11.18 billion for the Interior Department and related agencies in fiscal 1990. *(1989 Almanac, p. 731)*

HOUSE COMMITTEE ACTION

When the House Appropriations Subcommittee on the Interior took up its fiscal 1991 spending bill July 24, it proposed a legislative package to resolve competing pressures to protect northern spotted owls and the ancient Pacific-Northwest forests where they resided and to preserve the region's timber economy.

Subcommittee members reluctantly took center stage in the effort to save both jobs and owls, approving a spending measure to cut timber sales in the bird's old-growth habitat by about 20 percent in fiscal 1991, to the lowest level in 30 years.

But saving the spotted owl was only one of several controversies in the $12.8 billion spending bill, which the Interior Subcommittee approved in closed session. To the dismay of the oil industry, members also agreed to impose a one-year moratorium on drilling off the coasts of much of the United States, including areas not included in the Bush administration's existing ban.

And although no restrictions were attached to the subcommittee's $180 million allocation for the NEA, members said an effort to stop federal aid for "obscene" or "indecent" projects was likely when the full committee considered the bill.

Subcommittee Chairman Sidney R. Yates, D-Ill., said those issues made the fiscal 1991 spending bill the most difficult he had faced in his 15 years as chairman. "We have some issues that generate tremendous emotion and passion," he said.

Owls vs. Jobs

The Interior Department's Fish and Wildlife Service on June 22 officially listed the spotted owl as a threatened species, requiring the federal government to come up with a long-term plan to preserve the owl and its ancient forest habitat.

But shortly after that announcement, Agriculture Secretary Clayton Yeutter said a plan for protecting the owl on Forest Service lands would not be completed until Sept. 1. The administration was seeking an approach that would minimize job losses. That delay shifted the spotted owl debate to Congress.

In 1989 Congress settled for a quick fix to the spotted owl controversy when it tacked a one-year agreement limiting old-growth timber harvest levels and providing some protection for the owl onto the fiscal 1990 Interior appropriations bill.

The subcommittee's 1990 spending bill would provide funds in fiscal 1991 for about 3 bbf of timber sales on Forest Service lands in Washington and Oregon. Another 200 million board feet would be carried over from fiscal 1990.

If timber sales fell below that level, the leftover funds would go toward timber sale preparation.

Timber lobbyists immediately criticized the funding levels as too low.

"I don't know what the right adjective is — mortified or shocked," David A. Ford of the National Forest Products Association said. "It's a question of how many more people are going to be unemployed because of a ratcheting down on the program."

But Jay Watson, a forest issues specialist with The Wilderness Society, countered that the harvest levels approved in the bill were "unquestionably in excess" of what should be allowed if the owl was to be saved.

Yates had pushed for funding levels that would have allowed less than 2.7 bbf of timber sales in the region. That figure would have matched the cuts in timber sales recommended in an owl-protection plan prepared by a group of government scientists.

Yates also sought language in the committee report to indicate support for the findings of that scientific panel, but he said that provision was stripped from the report at the behest of subcommittee members from the Pacific Northwest. "They are really being squeezed up there," Yates said.

Subcommittee Democrats Les AuCoin of Oregon and Norm Dicks of Washington said they were pleased with the final agreement, while conceding it would be a bitter pill for their states.

AuCoin said the legislation would serve as a "wakeup call, although not a very welcome one," for his timber-dependent state.

The timber industry took blows in other parts of the country as well.

The Interior Subcommittee approved funds for an administration proposal to phase out money-losing timber sales in 12 national forests.

The one-year pilot program would test whether the loss in local timber receipts could be offset by increases in recreational uses of the land. Report language was also included directing the administration to expand the phase-out to all federal lands where timber sales brought in less revenue than the federal government spent on logging roads and other preparation costs.

Environmental groups had long opposed such "below-cost sales" as harmful to the environment and a waste of taxpayers' money.

Approval of that program came despite the strong opposition of Harold L. Volkmer, D-Mo., chairman of the House Agriculture Subcommittee on Forests, Family Farms and Energy, who said it was poorly planned and would hurt local economies.

The subcommittee's spending bill also cut the administration's request for funds to construct timber roads by $30 million, for a total of $151.6 million.

Yates had sought larger reductions.

Timber lobbyists were worried that such a cut would make it impossible for timber sales to reach even the reduced levels funded in the spending bill — 9.26 bbf nationwide, compared with the fiscal 1990 target of 11.13 bbf.

Drilling Limits Expanded

The subcommittee also took action to limit oil drilling off U.S. coasts, acceding to members who wanted the administration's limited ban on offshore oil activities extended to their states.

Bush had announced June 26 that he would end oil drilling for at least 10 years off the coasts of California, southwest Florida, all of Washington and Oregon, and all of New England north of Rhode Island.

The Interior Subcommittee approved a one-year ban on oil drilling in all the areas in the Bush proposal. It also extended a moratorium on drilling in Alaska's Bristol Bay and banned for one year leasing and pre-leasing sales off North Carolina, the Florida Panhandle and New Jersey.

The North Carolina ban would not interfere with an existing lease to the oil giant Mobil Corp., despite strong lobbying by Walter B. Jones, D-N.C., to stop that project. Subcommittee members were concerned that prohibiting Mobil's oil exploration would leave the federal government liable for the company's losses, AuCoin said.

Whitten Attacks NEA

While no restrictions were included in the bill on funding for the NEA, Appropriations Committee Chairman Jamie L. Whitten, D-Miss., offered a surprise handwritten amendment in the subcommittee markup that would have barred NEA funds for what he called "filthy pictures."

The subcommittee agreed to put off Whitten's amendment and another by ranking Republican Ralph Regula of Ohio until later action on the bill. Whitten was expected to pursue the issue in his Appropriations Committee. Regula said he preferred taking his amendment to the floor.

Yates, who was Congress' strongest supporter of the NEA, said he was not put off by efforts to include restrictions in his subcommittee bill. "Lots of my friends feel there ought to be restrictions," he said.

But another subcommittee member said approval of the Whitten language would have been a tremendous blow to Yates. "I've never seen a full-committee chairman come into a subcommittee where the chairman has such clear feelings ... and offer an amendment so completely contrary," he said.

Full Committee Action

Despite Republican efforts to cast offshore oil drilling moratoriums as a recipe for dependence on Iraqi President Saddam Hussein, the House Appropriations Committee on Oct. 1 approved its version of an $11.9 billion fiscal 1991 Interior spending bill to protect large tracts off the U.S. coast from oil and gas development.

The one-year ban on drilling covered California, Washington and Oregon, Alaska's Bristol Bay, New England, parts of the North Atlantic and the Florida Panhandle.

Some of the coastal areas were included in Bush's ban on offshore oil drilling, but appropriators accommodated members from other states as well, who wanted to ensure that their beaches remained free of oil slicks.

Louisiana Republican Bob Livingston criticized the committee for succumbing to "environmental hysteria" in approving the far-reaching legislation. "Congress has a rotten energy policy," he said. "We're not developing domestic resources, and we're becoming more and more dependent on people like Saddam Hussein."

The committee turned back a number of proposals by Livingston and Regula to narrow the scope of the bans, particularly off the coast of Florida. Committee members succeeded in getting the committee to approve, by voice vote, an amendment to remove North Carolina and Virginia from the moratorium.

A one-year ban on drilling off North Carolina already was approved as part of oil spill legislation (HR 1465 — PL 101-380) signed by the president on Aug. 18. *(Oil spill liability bill, p. 283)*

A committee aide said the Virginia delegation had not pushed for a ban off the coast of their state.

NEA Debate Postponed

An equally contentious debate over whether federal funds should be spent on artistic projects some members considered obscene was put off until floor action. As approved by the committee, the legislation attached no strings to the $180 million in NEA funds.

Regula agreed to withdraw his amendment to restrict NEA funds in exchange for a commitment from subcommittee Chairman Yates to allow the proposal to be debated on the floor.

Regula's amendment was to limit NEA grants to projects appropriate for a "general audience." It also required that projects supported by the NEA be "sensitive to the nature of public sponsorship." No NEA money could go for art determined to be obscene or indecent under standards outlined in several court cases.

The committee defeated, by voice vote, a proposal by Tom DeLay, R-Texas, to bar any funding for the NEA in the absence of a reauthorization bill. Opponents characterized the DeLay amendment as an attempt to kill the agency. "The fundamental question is whether you are for or against the NEA," Yates said.

Yates had been delaying work on the Interior bill in hope that Congress would resolve the NEA issue when it reauthorized the agency.

Texas Wetlands

Much of the committee's time was spent debating a more local issue: whether 3,802 acres of Texas wetlands should be released from federal protection so a reservoir project could proceed.

The proposed reservoir was to be in the district of Ralph M. Hall, D-Texas, who had been pushing hard for legislation (HR 188) to relinquish the conservation easement. The wetlands were donated to the U.S. Fish and Wildlife Service by the Little Sandy Hunting and Fishing Club, which still had access to the land.

The bill was approved by the Merchant Marine Committee on Aug. 1, but Hall wanted to boost its chances by attaching it to the spending bill as well.

A long list of environmental organizations opposed the measure, however, arguing that the land was important waterfowl habitat and should be protected. Opponents also said it would set a bad precedent to remove land from the National Wildlife Refuge for the first time.

Texas Democrat Jim Chapman, who offered the amendment on behalf of Hall, said the land had been donated by the club to prevent development and protect the hunting and fishing privileges of its 87 members. "It is ridiculous that wealthy people can give an easement and deny water resources for the whole state," he said. The amendment was defeated, 17-26.

HOUSE ACTION

The House on Oct. 15 approved HR 5769, providing $11.9 billion for Department of the Interior programs for fiscal 1991. The vote was 327-80. *(Vote 464, p. 148-H)*

House members had settled the controversy over the NEA on Oct. 11 when they agreed to compromise language during consideration of the agency's reauthorization measure (HR 4825).

The House compromise had been worked out between Pat Williams, D-Mont., and E. Thomas Coleman, R-Mo. The House overwhelmingly adopted it, by a vote of 349-76, on the reauthorization bill. *(Vote 449, p. 144-H)*

Anticipating the Senate's inability to reauthorize the endowment, the House inserted the same language on arts funding into the Interior spending bill Oct. 15. Again, the House definitively supported the plan, 342-58. *(Vote 462, p. 148-H)*

The compromise stated that the NEA should not fund obscene projects, but it left the determination of what was obscene to the courts. After a hearing, the NEA could order grant recipients to return the federal money if they were found guilty of violating obscenity standards.

"What the House did overwhelmingly was to isolate the far right and accept a moderate approach. That overwhelming vote should embolden each member of the Senate," Williams said.

Cattle Grazing Fees

Oklahoma Democrat Mike Synar had been trying for years to level the field for cattle ranchers. He wanted to cut back on federal subsidies enjoyed almost exclusively in the West and Great Plains, but his proposal had gone nowhere in a House Interior Committee dominated by members from those states.

After three years of pleading with the Rules Committee to allow him to bypass the committee and bring the issue straight to the floor, Synar on Oct. 15 finally got his vote: By a large margin of 251-155, the House agreed to gradually impose a 500 percent increase in fees on ranchers who grazed their cattle on public lands. *(Vote 460, p. 146-H)*

The Senate, which was generally

Interior Appropriations

Following are the budget authority totals in the fiscal 1991 appropriations bill (HR 5769 — PL 101-512) for the Interior Department and related agencies.

(Figures, in thousands of dollars, may not add due to rounding.)

	President's Request	House Bill	Senate Bill	Final Bill
Interior Department				
Bureau of Land Management				
Management of lands	$ 466,384	$ 503,451	$ 496,899	$ 500,112
Firefighting	165,585	246,892	168,765	168,765
Other	219,992	235,073	242,688	236,799
Subtotal	851,961	985,416	908,352	905,676
Fish and Wildlife Service	545,661	650,983	677,374	697,535
National Park Service				
Operations	830,804	874,178	873,791	881,317
Recreation, preservation	10,125	17,968	16,278	18,398
Construction	99,766	227,111	227,710	271,871
Land acquisition, state aid	80,153	152,386	144,478	137,513
Kennedy Center	8,150	21,150	21,150	21,150
Other	3,665	24,915	4,915	5,085
Subtotal	1,032,663	1,317,708	1,288,322	1,355,164
Geological Survey	506,578	571,904	567,412	573,704
Minerals Management Service	194,810	200,128	193,103	197,028
Bureau of Mines	145,712	171,443	185,155	182,182
Office of Surface Mining	260,741	311,433	311,633	311,433
Bureau of Indian Affairs				
Indian programs	1,018,185	1,329,259	1,303,379	1,326,997
Construction	103,099	166,935	162,501	168,536
Payments to Indians	52,407	53,931	56,431	56,431
Navajo Trust Fund	0	2,000	4,000	3,000
Indian loan fund	11,487	11,487	11,987	11,787
(Guaranteed loans)	(45,000)	(45,000)	(0)	(0)
Subtotal	1,185,178	1,563,612	1,538,298	1,566,751
Territorial affairs	121,003	184,719	177,281	179,726
Departmental offices	113,826	109,811	111,452	111,126
Interior Subtotal	**$ 4,958,133**	**$ 6,067,157**	**$ 5,958,382**	**$ 6,080,325**
Related Agencies				
Forest Service				
Forest research	148,672	167,693	165,284	168,512
State and private forestry	231,617	132,806	190,932	183,377
National forest system	1,211,543	1,274,021	1,303,847	1,302,687
Firefighting	297,849	304,507	299,507	299,507
Construction	222,906	243,705	299,208	278,593
(Timber receipts)	(−96,280)	(−96,280)	(−96,280)	(−96,280)
Land acquisition	88,869	92,579	85,519	89,163
Other	15,900	7,316	6,816	7,316
Subtotal	$ 2,217,356	$ 2,222,627	$ 2,351,113	$ 2,329,155
Energy Department				
Clean coal technology	−500,000	−565,000	−500,000	−565,000
Fossil energy research	202,309	443,258	459,322	461,167
Naval Petroleum Reserve	210,610	224,310	210,610	224,310
Energy conservation	212,591	497,684	470,941	497,784
Strategic Petroleum Reserve	195,633	195,633	201,633	201,633
SPR oil account	119,935	119,935	0	0
Other	89,483	92,041	92,786	93,236
Subtotal	$ 530,561	$ 998,261	$ 925,692	903,530
Indian Health	1,292,080	1,586,936	1,580,456	1,585,879
Indian Education	75,762	75,762	75,762	75,762
Smithsonian Institution	307,690	328,358	325,111	327,837
National Endowment for the Arts	175,000	180,000	170,000	175,000
National Endowment for the Humanities	165,000	170,700	168,300	170,900
Other agencies	135,320	154,342	146,121	152,405
Related Agencies Subtotal	**$ 4,898,769**	**$ 5,716,986**	**$ 5,742,555**	**$ 5,720,468**
General reduction of appropriations	0	0	0	−64,968
GRAND TOTAL	**$ 9,856,902**	**$ 11,784,143**	**$ 11,700,937**	**$ 11,735,825**

SOURCE: House Appropriations Committee

more sympathetic to rural interests, subsequently struck the proposal from its version of the bill, leaving the issue to be resolved in conference.

Westerners disputed Synar's contention that the low grazing fees amounted to a subsidy. Cattle ranchers who used public lands, said New Mexico Republican Joe Skeen, were required to build and maintain fences, make water improvements and cover other costs not charged to ranchers leasing private lands.

But in the urban-dominated House, the amendment proved irresistible. It had the support of both the fiscally conservative American Taxpayers Union and major environmental groups, such as the Wilderness Society and the National Wildlife Federation, which argued that public lands were suffering from overgrazing encouraged by low federal fees.

The dual benefit of Synar's proposal — bringing in new federal revenue and offering members a pro-environmental vote — proved tantalizing enough to override emotional appeals by members from the Western and Great Plains states, where most federal lands were located. The Westerners characterized the amendment as an attack by environmentalists whose real aim was to drive livestock operators and other industries that relied on public lands out of business.

"Eliminate the livestock," Bob Smith, R-Ore., sniped. "Eliminate the timber industry with the spotted owl. Eliminate the sheep industry in this country. Let us vote for the Synar amendment and eliminate all of us."

Synar said only a small number of cattle ranchers were benefiting from the subsidies, at a cost to taxpayers of $100 million a year. "Is it fair to subsidize 3 percent of the cattle producers in the country at the expense of the rest?" he asked.

The issue centered on the discrepancies between what cattle ranchers who leased public lands paid to graze their livestock — $1.81 to graze a cow and calf for a month — and the fees paid for use of private lands, which ranged as high as $14. In fiscal 1989, the federal government took in $25 million in grazing revenues, but spent $77 million to run the grazing program.

The public fees were based on a formula established by the Public Rangelands Improvement Act of 1978, which was to be followed for a seven-year trial period. President Ronald Reagan in 1986 issued an executive order to extend use of the formula and set a "floor" fee of $1.35 a month.

Synar's amendment increased grazing fees on public lands to $8.70 by fiscal 1994, the same amount charged for unintentional trespass by cattle ranchers on public lands.

Opponents said that higher fee was arbitrary and did not take into account the hidden costs of leasing public grazing lands. "If we take all things into consideration, it costs more to graze livestock on public lands than it does on leased private lands," said Colorado Democrat Ben Nighthorse Campbell.

'Below Cost' Timber Sales

During House debate, Jim Jontz, D-Ind., declined to offer an amendment to cut "below cost" timber sales on federal lands in exchange for an agreement from Agriculture's Forests Subcommittee Chairman Volkmer to take up the issue in 1991.

Below cost sales occurred in forests when the federal government spent more on timber-preparation costs, such as building logging roads, than it made from selling timber. The Jontz amendment would have ensured that no more than 20 percent of federal timber sales came from national forests that operated below cost.

SENATE COMMITTEE ACTION

Robert C. Byrd, D-W.Va., the powerful chairman of the Senate Appropriations Committee, rejected compromise language on obscenity and federal funding of the arts, pitting himself between the right and left on funding for the NEA.

Byrd placed restrictions on the NEA in the committee's version of an $11.7 billion fiscal 1991 Interior appropriations bill — the same restrictions that were enacted in the spending bill in 1989. The committee approved the bill by voice vote on Oct. 16.

"A lot of people are deathly afraid of Byrd," said Orrin G. Hatch, R-Utah, who preferred to have the courts decide questions of obscenity. But senators who feared angering the man who controlled the purse also were leery of approaching the obscenity issue. "I see a lot of jitteriness, a lot of worry and a lot of pain," Hatch said.

Under the Byrd language, the endowment would continue to be forbidden to fund projects that "may be considered obscene, including but not limited to, depictions of sadomasochism, homoeroticism, the sexual exploitation of children, or individuals engaged in sex acts and which, when taken as a whole, do not have serious literary, artistic, political or scientific value."

The measure also required grant recipients to sign a pledge that they would comply with the restrictions. Artists had been required by the endowment, but not by law, to sign a pledge.

Byrd's move essentially gutted a separate reauthorization measure (S 2724) worked out in the Senate Labor and Human Resources Committee. After months of closed-door meetings, senators had agreed to place the onus on the courts to decide what was and what was not obscene. Artists found guilty of violating obscenity or child pornography laws would be required to return the money they received and would be barred from receiving any other grants for at least three years. This language was similar to the House-approved compromise.

Despite requests from members of the Labor Committee, Byrd refused to include their language in his bill.

Oil Drilling Bans

The NEA language was only one of a number of controversial issues that were part of the spending bill.

During markup by the Interior Subcommittee, which Byrd also chaired, Byrd struck from the Senate version one-year moratoriums on oil drilling in areas in the Atlantic Ocean, the Gulf of Mexico, the Pacific Ocean and in Bristol Bay, Alaska.

Some of those areas were already included in the president's 10-year offshore drilling ban. But the one-year moratoriums in the House spending bill were expanded to other areas under pressure from members from Florida and other states who did not want unsightly oil rigs off their shores.

In 1989, the Senate Appropriations Committee had left somewhat less extensive House-imposed bans on drilling largely intact.

Byrd also declined to accept a House floor amendment to raise fees for grazing cattle and sheep on public lands.

The committee bill made no changes, however, in House provisions that addressed northern spotted owl habitat in the Pacific Northwest. Both versions included funds for 3.2 bbf in timber sales in the region, the same amount called for in the administration's spotted owl proposal. Environmentalists had been pushing for lower timber harvests in the owl's ancient forest habitat, but timber lobbyists wanted no reduction from the 1990 level of 3.85 bbf.

The administration argued that the 3.2 bbf in timber sales could go forward without violating Endangered Species Act requirements and without significant timber job losses in fiscal 1991.

Oregon Republican Bob Packwood planned to offer an amendment to the Senate bill to allow an Endangered Species Committee to weigh the value of protecting the spotted owl in future years against the economic and social costs to timber communities of the Pacific Northwest.

The Senate bill also included a somewhat higher national timber sale level than the House bill — 9.6 bbf, compared with 9.3 bbf — and more money for construction of logging roads.

SENATE FLOOR ACTION

After stripping out Byrd's language restricting funding for the NEA, the Senate on Oct. 24 passed HR 5769, an $11.7 billion Interior spending bill. The vote was 92-6. *(Vote 309, p. 60-S)*

Adopting language similar to that of the House, senators agreed to leave decisions on obscenity to the courts. NEA grant recipients were required, however, to return money used to produce any work of art that the courts declared to be obscene. They could also be barred for three years from recieving additional grants. The amendment, by Orrin G. Hatch, R-Utah, was adopted 73-24. *(Vote 308, p. 60-S)*

Senators also rejected even stiffer obscenity restrictions offered by Helms. But arts supporters left the floor before work on the measure was completed, which alowed Helms to gain voice vote approval of an amendment to ban funding of art works that denigrated religion. That provision was expected to be dropped in conference, however.

'God-Squad' Plan Dies

On Oct. 23, the Senate shot down provisions to convene what was termed a Cabinet-level "God Squad" to determine whether protecting the northern spotted owl could be reconciled with salvaging timber industry jobs in the Pacific Northwest.

Packwood failed by a vote of 34-62 to attach the proposal to the spending bill. *(Vote 303, p. 60-S)*

Packwood said he knew that he was short the votes needed but pursued the issue anyway. "It's worth losing on occasion so it goes into your . . . notes who your friends are," he said.

The proposal, which would have amended the Endangered Species Act, was a cornerstone of the Bush administration's plan to balance spotted owl protections with preserving timber industry jobs.

The idea was to jump-start formation of a committee made up of the secretaries of Agriculture and the Interior, among others, to develop a long-term forest management strategy for the owl and the Pacific Northwest. The committee would have been authorized to weigh economic and social values alongside the biological values of species protection.

The committee was called the God Squad because it would be empowered to abandon efforts to protect the owl from extinction if the social and economic costs were deemed too high.

Under existing law, the committee was convened only if all other alternatives had been exhausted, leaving a conflict between a proposed federal action — such as selling timber or building a dam — and a species' survival. Otherwise, the act required that science be the only factor in developing plans to protect the owl and other endangered or threatened species from extinction.

Stacking the Deck?

Packwood said the estimated loss of 28,000 jobs in the Pacific Northwest justified congressional action to circumvent existing law and convene the committee immediately.

He said the proposal was "value-neutral" and did not preordain whether the committee would develop a strong protection plan for the owl, or decide that such protection was too costly for the region.

Opponents, including Senate Majority Leader George J. Mitchell, D-Maine, argued that the Endangered Species Act was working and should be allowed to run its course without interference from Congress. Since the act was written in 1973, Mitchell said, the U.S. Fish and Wildlife Service had barred only three projects from going forward out of the 10,000 reviewed for compliance with the law's requirements.

Al Gore, D-Tenn., said the Packwood proposal "stacked the deck" against owl protection and "virtually ensures the destruction" of the bird's ancient forest habitat. "Congress is being asked to step in and convene the Endangered Species Committee not as a last resort but as the first resort," he said.

Packwood said after the vote that many senators failed to back him up only because they faced no economic devastation in their own states.

He criticized Gore, in particular, for taking the opposite position on endangered species protection when jobs in his state were at issue. The first time the committee was convened, in the late 1970s, was when the habitat of a three-inch fish known as the snail darter was threatened by completion of the Tellico Dam project in Tennessee.

The committee at that time determined that construction of the dam should be halted to protect the fish, but Congress, with Gore's vote, overruled that decision and ordered the dam completed anyway. "I'm touched, deeply touched, that he has so much concern for the environment in my state," Packwood said. "I wish he had as much concern for the environment in his state."

Gore said the earlier situation was different because his vote came after the consultative process required by the Endangered Species Act had been completed.

Mining Moratorium Killed

Western senators were more successful during work on the spending bill in beating back efforts to cut federal support for mining and logging on public lands.

After a six-hour debate the night of Oct. 22, which Ted Stevens, R-Alaska, threatened to turn into a filibuster, the Senate voted, 48-50, to kill a one-year moratorium on the issuance of new mining patents on federal lands. *(Vote 301, p. 59-S)*

Dale Bumpers, D-Ark., wanted the moratorium in place to prevent a "headlong mad dash" of patent applications, while Congress worked in 1991 to overhaul an 1872 mining law. The Senate Appropriations Committee had added Bumpers' amendment to its version of the spending bill by a vote of 18-10. Under the 118-year-old law, federal land could be sold for as little as $2.50 an acre to anyone who staked a mining claim and invested at least $100 a year in developing it.

"The original rationale for giving away the public domain for $2.50 an acre to go West and settle is hardly a legitimate rationale in this year of Our Lord 1990," Bumpers argued.

A General Accounting Office study had found that under that law the federal government had sold land worth up to $47 million for $4,500. In some cases, the mining company had then resold the land for substantial profits. The federal government collected no royalties on minerals developed on the patented land.

Western senators said that the law was working to promote domestic minerals development and should not be changed. They argued that miners made substantial investments of about $250,000 to establish that minerals existed on the land and to apply for a patent.

Suspending the patent process, Nevada Democrat Richard H. Bryan said, would leave mining companies "in a state of suspended animation," unable to secure financing to develop their claims.

Logging Roads

As debate on the bill continued Oct. 23, the Senate voted, 52-44, to kill a proposal by Wyche Fowler Jr., D-Ga., to cut $100 million from the $196.6 million in the Senate bill for construction of logging roads. The House bill included $151.6 million for road construction. *(Vote 302, p. 60-S)*

Those funds were viewed by critics, including the conservative Heritage Foundation and the environmentalist Wilderness Society, as a subsidy for the timber industry. In many national forests, the federal government spent more to build access roads, particularly in remote, mountainous areas, than it brought in by selling timber, although the program did operate at a surplus nationwide.

"Those roads are built, thousands of miles every year, mainly to accommodate logging companies in a timber subsidy program that loses money in 102 of 120 national forests in this country," Fowler said.

A similar amendment by Fowler was attached to to the appropriations measure in 1989 but was deleted in conference. Republican support eroded in 1990, a Fowler aide said, largely due to opposition by Oregon Republican Mark O. Hatfield, who was in a tight battle for re-election.

Hatfield called the amendment a "job wrecker" that would close down one- or two-mill communities in Oregon and put 25,000 loggers and other timber-related employees out of work. "Mill towns into ghost towns — that is what the Fowler amendment creates in my state," he said.

FINAL ACTION

With late Senate passage of HR 5769, conferees had to move fast to complete work on the bill. The conference report was filed Oct. 27, the last full day of the session, and adopted by both chambers that day.

Floor Action

The House adopted the conference report by a vote of 298-43, with 36 Republicans and seven Democrats voting against it. The Senate cleared the bill by voice vote later that day. *(Vote 532, p. 168-H)*

The NEA issue generated no further floor debate, even though the lawmakers who presented the report in each chamber — Yates in the House, Byrd in the Senate — each said the final compromise was not to his liking.

House Republicans did take the chance, however, to tweak one of the Senate conferees, Democrat Tom Harkin of Iowa, for earmarking Energy Department funds for a metal casting research center at the University of Northern Iowa.

Robert S. Walker, R-Pa., noted that the House's version of the bill provided $1 million for a metal casting center at the University of Alabama and inquired, sarcastically, what qualifications the Iowa school had in the field.

Yates answered that when the Senate conferees discovered the House had one casting laboratory, "the Senate decided that perhaps it ought to be balanced by one that it approved. . . ."

"I understand the gentleman's problem," said Walker, a Science Committee member and frequent critic of pork-barrel projects. "I would suggest," he added, "that this is not exactly science the way I think of science being done."

Harkin was in a tough contest for re-election against GOP Rep. Tom Tauke. Harkin won with 54 percent of the vote.

Signed by Bush

In signing the bill Nov. 5, Bush avoided discussion of the NEA funding dispute. But he did criticize several provisions of the bill, including the offshore drilling moratorium and restrictions on reorganization of the Bureau of Indian Affairs. *(Indian legislation, p. 421)* ■

Pennsylvania Tiff Stalls Transportation Bill

Congress approved a $12.9 billion fiscal 1991 appropriations bill for the Department of Transportation and related agencies in the final hours of the session after resolving a feud among Pennsylvania lawmakers over state highway funds.

The House cleared the measure (HR 5229) for President Bush in the early morning hours of Oct. 28 (session of Oct. 27) by agreeing to a Senate amendment that softened a provision sought by House Democratic Whip William H. Gray III of Philadelphia. Gray wanted to try to force the state of Pennsylvania to increase mass transit aid for the Philadelphia region, but the state's two Republican senators — John Heinz and Arlen Specter — resisted the move.

The House had originally adopted the conference report, 394-17, on Oct. 19 — with Gray's provision calling for cutting about $142 million from Pennsylvania's federal highway funds unless the state legislature adopted a dedicated funding source for mass transit. *(Vote 492, 156-H)*

The Senate agreed to the conference report on Oct. 26 by voice vote, but Heinz and Specter held up final action by a vigorous, three-hour fight that forced Majority Leader George J. Mitchell, D-Maine, to pull the bill.

Heinz and Specter argued that the provision was a federal intrusion into state revenue decisions and "blackmail" aimed at helping urban transit at the expense of state highway funds.

Mitchell called in Senate Appropriations Chairman Robert C. Byrd, D-W.Va., to mediate the dispute. Byrd, the three Pennsylvania lawmakers and the chairmen and ranking members of the Transportation Appropriations subcommittees met in Byrd's office the next day.

They agreed to keep the Gray provision in the bill but to delay its threatened funding cuts until 1992. The state legislature and governor also could avoid the federal cuts by declaring opposition to any direct funding mechanism for mass transit.

With that conflict out of the way, the final version of the conference report sailed through both chambers, clearing the House about 12:30 a.m. on Oct. 28 — less than two hours before Congress' final adjournment.

Senate Transportation Appropriations Chairman Frank R. Lautenberg, D-N.J., praised the final bill for being within budget agreement limits. Still, the measure called for an 11 percent increase in Federal Highway Administration funding, a 14 percent increase in Federal Aviation Administration spending and a 24 percent increase in spending for the Coast Guard.

The fiscal 1990 bill provided $11.97 billion in funding for the Transportation Department and other agencies covered in the bill. Bush had requested $11.88 billion for fiscal 1991. *(1989 Almanac, p. 749)*

Rather than pick and choose which of each chamber's road demonstration projects to accept, conferees simply accepted almost every one — but with a general 15 percent cut in most of the 33 requests.

Total road demonstration projects, apart from highway safety grants, were $763 million less than in fiscal 1990, but $471 million more than the administration requested.

Conferees also agreed to spend $625 million on Amtrak, $5 million more than the Senate proposal and $7 million less than the House bill. The administration had proposed no funding for the passenger railroad corporation.

Among other earmarks was $125 million for the electrification of rail lines from New Haven, Conn., to Boston. The switch from diesel trains was expected to shorten the length of the five-hour trip from New York City to Boston by two hours.

BOXSCORE

Legislation: Fiscal 1991 appropriations for the Department of Transportation and related agencies, PL 101-516 (HR 5229).

Major action: Signed, Nov. 5. Conference report cleared by House, Oct. 28 (session of Oct. 27); adopted by Senate, with amendment, Oct. 26; by House, 394-17, Oct. 19. Passed by Senate, Aug. 4; by House, 385-31, July 12.

Reports: Conference report (H Rept 101-892). Appropriations (S Rept 101-398); Appropriations (H Rept 101-584).

HOUSE COMMITTEE ACTION

The House Appropriations Subcommittee on Transportation approved a $13.08 billion fiscal 1991 spending bill June 19 that boosted federal spending for highways and airport improvement.

Local transit officials and members of the House Public Works Committee had lambasted the Bush administration's 1990 transportation policy for shifting too much responsibility for the nation's infrastructure needs onto the states and users of the transportation system.

Instead, the subcommittee's appropriations bill called for increased spending from the federal highway and airport trust funds.

The legislation, approved in closed session, capped spending from the Highway Trust Fund at $14.5 billion, $2.49 billion more than the administration's proposal and $2.29 billion more than in fiscal 1990, House aides said.

Funds for Airport Improvement Grants were increased to $1.8 billion, compared with the administration's request of $1.5 billion.

The overall amount appropriated for the Federal Aviation Administration (FAA) was $8.17 billion, $1.05 billion more than in fiscal 1990 but below the administration's request of $8.28 billion.

Deep Cuts Prevented

As in past years, the subcommittee fended off administration efforts to make deep cuts in funding for the Amtrak national passenger railroad and for Urban Mass Transit Administration (UMTA) grants.

Members approved $632 million for Amtrak, up from the $615 million in fiscal 1990, and $2 billion for UMTA, an increase from $1.91 billion in the previous year. The president had requested no funds for Amtrak and had proposed cutting mass transit grant funding to $1.16 billion.

The bill appropriated less than the administration requested for the U.S. Coast Guard, FAA facilities and equipment, and salaries and expenses for the Transportation secretary.

A number of unauthorized highway demonstration projects were included in the bill, subcommittee Chairman William Lehman, D-Fla., said, but only after members requesting the projects produced letters of approval from the chairmen of the relevant authorizing committees. However, similar assurances in 1989 did not stave off an unsuccessful effort by Public Works Chairman Glenn M. Anderson, D-Calif., to strike the demonstration projects.

No Glamour

The bill included no controversial legislative proposals. In 1989, the spending bill became the vehicle for legislation to ban smoking on domestic airline flights.

"This is not a glamorous bill," Lehman said. "It's a bill that deals basically with the real needs of this country."

The House was likely to be at odds with the Senate in at least one respect, however: The subcommittee legislation cut funds for the rural essential air service to $23.6 million, $7.04 million less than in fiscal 1990. Many small communities relied on the federal subsidies to maintain airports because it was unprofitable for airlines to offer flights in rural areas where there were few passengers per flight.

The subcommittee had proposed a far more drastic cut of over 60 percent in the fiscal 1990 spending bill. But that proposal did not get past Senate Appropriations Committee Chairman Byrd, a strong supporter of the program.

HOUSE FLOOR ACTION

The House approved a $13.1 billion fiscal 1991 transportation spending bill July 12 by 385-31, with only Republicans voting against the measure. *(Vote 225, p. 78-H)*

The Appropriations Committee had approved the bill July 10 by voice vote.

Aviation Trust Fund Deal

Leaders of the Public Works and Appropriations committees had traditionally clashed over aviation funding priorities and pet highway projects. But in 1990, passage was smoothed in part by a deal between James L. Oberstar, D-Minn., chairman of the Public Works Aviation Subcommittee, and Appropriations subcommittee Chairman Lehman to spend down the $7.6 billion surplus in the Airport and Airway Trust Fund.

Public Works members and the aviation industry had long contended that appropriators, in conjunction with the White House, had hoarded the trust fund surplus to disguise the size of the general budget deficit. The fund was fed by taxes on airline tickets, fuel and cargo.

Members of the Appropriations Committee and Bush administration officials, on the other hand, argued that aviation users had been getting at least as much money in federal aviation programs as they contributed to the trust fund, because general taxpayers were picking up a large share of the cost of operating the FAA.

Appropriators and the Congressional Budget Office attributed the extra burden on general revenues to Public Works-generated legislation that, since 1982, had shifted $5.3 billion of the cost of FAA operations from the trust fund to the general taxpayer. *(1982 Almanac, p. 333)*

This "penalty clause" was designed to spur the Appropriations Committee to keep capital projects fully funded. It automatically cut the amount of money that could be appropriated from the trust fund for FAA operations whenever appropriations for airport improvement projects fell below authorized levels. The trust funds available for FAA operations had to be reduced by twice the amount the capital programs were underfunded.

The penalty clause failed to stop the appropriators from approving less than the authorized amount for airport improvement programs.

To break the logjam, Oberstar agreed to repeal the penalty clause in exchange for a commitment from Lehman to recommend $1.8 billion in fiscal 1991 for airport development and planning grants, an increase of about 21 percent over the previous year. The penalty clause repeal was included in a bill (HR 5170) to authorize aviation programs that passed the House Aug. 2. *(Aviation package, p. 384)*

The result was that about 75 percent of the cost of FAA operations and maintenance would come from the trust fund, compared with 50 percent to 55 percent in previous years.

Both Sides Happy

The spending bill also included a 24 percent increase over fiscal 1990 in spending on FAA facilities and equipment, for a total of $2.14 billion. Spending from the Highway Trust Fund increased to $14.5 billion, $2.29 billion more than in fiscal 1990.

As in past years, the House turned back administration efforts to eliminate subsidies for the Amtrak national passenger railroad and to cut funds for mass transit.

Both sides were pleased with the final result. "We've been wanting to do something about that penalty clause for a long time," Lehman said.

"I think what we've got here is a very productive agreement that depends on mutual trust," Oberstar said. He added that some members of the Public Works Committee remained concerned that appropriators would not continue to "deliver in the future."

The House approved, 331-88, an amendment by Gerald B. H. Solomon, R-N.Y., to require 2 percent annual reductions in federal highway aid to states that did not suspend the driver's licenses of convicted drug offenders for at least six months. *(Vote 223, p. 78-H)*

The bill also appropriated funds for 35 unauthorized highway projects, including:

- $20 million for a reconstruction project on Pennsylvania Route 56 in Cambria, Somerset and Westmoreland counties. Requested by John P. Murtha, D-Pa.
- $7 million for work on U.S. 27 in Palm Beach County, Fla. Requested by Tom Lewis, R-Fla.
- $6.3 million for a Michigan Bristol Road relocation project in Flint and Genesee County. Requested by Dale E. Kildee, D-Mich.
- $6 million for a toll road project on the Monongahela Valley Expressway, a 70-mile highway extending from U.S. 48 near Morgantown, W.Va., to the Penn-Lincoln Highway near Pittsburgh. Requested by Joseph M. Gaydos, D-Pa.
- $5 million for Lake Road Outlet Bridge in Irondequoit, N.Y. Requested by Louise M. Slaughter, D-N.Y., and Frank Horton, R-N.Y.
- $4 million for a bypass of Pennsylvania State Route 711 in Ligonier. Requested by Joe Kolter, D-Pa.
- $4 million for a Florida causeway tunnel project in Fort Lauderdale. Requested by E. Clay Shaw Jr., R-Fla.
- $3 million for an Illinois interchange on I-80 and Houbolt Road near Joliet. Requested by George E. Sangmeister, D-Ill.
- $3 million for a Hubbard Expressway project in Youngstown, Ohio. Requested by James A. Traficant Jr., D-Ohio.
- $3 million for a Washington State Route 509 East-West corridor project in Tacoma. Requested by Norm Dicks, D-Wash.
- $2.5 million for an I-65 and State Road 46 interchange in Columbus, Ind. Requested by Philip R. Sharp, D-Ind., and Lee H. Hamilton, D-Ind.
- $2.5 million for a Michigan M-84 expansion in Saginaw and Bay counties. Requested by Bob Traxler, D-Mich.
- $2 million for Norrell Road and Interstate 20 in Hinds County, Miss. Requested by Mike Espy, D-Miss.

Rural Air Service

The bill allocated $23.6 million in subsidies to rural airports, a cut of $7 million from fiscal 1990. Funds were eliminated for 10 communities.

The 10 least cost-effective airports, the Transportation Department said, were in Lewiston, Mont.; Jonesboro, Ark.; Miles City, Mont.; Hot Springs, Ark.; Gadsden, Ala.; Laconia, N.H.; Worthington, Minn.; Enid, Okla.; Mount Vernon, Ill.; and Brownwood, Texas.

SENATE COMMITTEE ACTION

The Senate Appropriations Committee on July 27 completed work on a $13.19 billion fiscal 1991 transportation spending bill, boosting money for Amtrak and highway and airport improvements.

The bill's total came in just under the allocation set by the Senate's budget resolution.

The committee bill spent more in almost every category than the administration's request, which sought $11.9 billion. It was slightly more than the $13.09 billion House version passed July 12.

Bush's request counted on savings from cuts in mass transit and zero funding for Amtrak to pay for more airport improvements and Coast Guard spending.

"That obviously didn't wash with us," said Lautenberg, chairman of the Appropriations Subcommittee on Transportation.

The bill allocated $620 million to Amtrak, $5 million more than in fiscal 1990. However, that was $12 million less than the House voted to provide.

The Senate bill also provided $114 million less than the House had allotted for the Urban Mass Transit Administration, but it raised a trust fund cap on mass transit spending by $200 million more than the House bill, to $1.4 billion.

Lautenberg also put in a $125 million project to electrify the rail line between New Haven, Conn., and Boston. The switch from diesel to electric trains was expected to shorten travel from New York to Boston by two hours, he said.

The Coast Guard was to receive more money for oil spills and drug interdiction. Defense Subcommittee Chairman Daniel K. Inouye, D-Hawaii, and ranking Republican Ted Stevens of Alaska agreed to shift $300 million from their bill for Coast Guard drug-interdiction activities.

Conferees were going to have to resolve how much to open the spigot of the airport trust fund, which was capped at $1.4 billion in fiscal 1990.

House appropriators, at the urging of the Public Works and Transportation Committee, voted to increase trust fund spending by 21 percent, to $1.8 billion. In exchange, Public Works agreed to drop the penalty clause that would have punished appropriators for spending less than authorized levels for airport improvement projects.

Transportation Appropriations

Following are the budget authority totals in the fiscal 1991 appropriations bill (HR 5229 — PL 101-516) for the Transportation Department and related agencies.

(Figures, in thousands of dollars, may not add due to rounding.)

	President's Request	House Bill	Senate Bill	Final Bill
Transportation Department				
Office of the Secretary	$ 102,745	$ 188,901	$ 195,987	$ 198,871
Rural airline subsidies	(23,600)	(23,600)	(26,600)	(26,600)
Coast Guard	3,393,472	3,180,647	3,081,593	3,043,023
Operating expenses	(2,391,351)	(2,192,000)	(2,051,103)	(2,039,839)
Acquisition, construction	(419,536)	(391,994)	(432,396)	(406,331)
Federal Aviation Administration	6,777,700	6,370,615	6,474,269	6,137,407
Operations	(4,087,700)	(4,037,000)	(4,038,551)	(4,037,000)
Facilities and equipment	(2,500,000)	(2,138,615)	(2,240,018)	(2,095,407)
(limitation on obligations)	*(1,500,000)*	*(1,800,000)*	*(1,650,000)*	*(1,800,000)*
Federal Highway Administration	45,719	289,300	356,230	517,045
New demonstration projects	(0)	(101,450)	(187,730)	(246,330)
(limitation on obligations)	*(12,083,000)*	*(14,571,500)*	*(13,920,000)*	*(14,571,500)*
National Highway Traffic Safety Administration	117,326	109,036	117,058	118,713
(limitation on obligations)	*(125,622)*	*(125,622)*	*(131,655)*	*(129,655)*
Federal Railroad Administration	69,579	736,514	864,198	893,810
Amtrak	(0)	(632,000)	(620,000)	(625,080)
Portion applied to debt reduction	(−3,097)	(−3,097)	(—3,097)	(−3,097)
Urban Mass Transit Administration	1,160,202	2,003,770	1,889,496	1,869,683
(limitations on obligations)	*(1,140,000)*	*(1,200,000)*	*(1,400,000)*	*(1,400,000)*
Other	72,259	68,137	69,108	69,000
Subtotal	**$ 11,739,002**	**$ 12,946,920**	**$ 13,047,939**	**$ 12,847,552**
Related Agencies				
Architectural and Transportation Barriers Compliance Board	2,100	2,700	2,700	2,700
National Transportation Safety Board	30,940	30,940	32,000	31,470
Interstate Commerce Commission	43,777	45,369	43,777	43,777
Panama Canal Commission *(limitation on expenses)*	*(0)*	*(448,497)*	*(459,000)*	*(459,000)*
St. Lawrence Seaway Toll Rebate	10,789	10,500	10,500	10,500
Washington Metro Transit Authority (interest payments)	51,664	51,664	51,664	51,664
Subtotal	**$ 139,270**	**$ 141,173**	**$ 140,641**	**$ 140,111**
GRAND TOTALS				
New budget authority	**$ 11,878,272**	**$ 13,088,093**	**$ 13,188,580**	**$ 12,987,663**
(Limitations on obligations)	*($14,849,097)*	*($17,697,597)*	*($17,102,130)*	*($17,901,630)*

SOURCE: House Appropriations Committee

The Senate made no such deal, and its bill allocated an increase of only 10 percent in trust fund spending.

Subsidies for rural airports also fared better under the Senate bill.

The House cut subsidies by $7 million, to $23.6 million. Lautenberg and Appropriations Chairman Byrd, a big advocate, met the House halfway. The Senate bill included $26.6 million, $4 million less than in fiscal 1990.

SENATE FLOOR ACTION

The Senate on Aug. 4 passed by voice vote HR 5229, a $13.19 billion transportation spending bill for fiscal 1991, rejecting President Bush's proposal to cut mass transit, highway and rail funds. Senate leaders said that the bill's 11 percent increase in budget authority over Bush's $11.9 billion request was needed to begin rebuilding the nation's transit networks.

"We are now paying the price for our lax attention to these infrastructure needs," said subcommittee Chairman Lautenberg.

Authority for mass transit spending would be increased from fiscal 1990 levels by $260 million to $1.4 billion — in part, Lautenberg said, to meet anticipated expenses of clean air and disabled-rights legislation. *(Clean air, p. 229; disabled rights, p. 447)*

A proposed increase of $215 million for Federal Aviation Administration operating expenses included money for an additional 495 air-traffic controllers and 406 safety inspectors. The bill increased spending from the Airport and Airway Trust Fund, but by only $225 million — $150 million less than the House agreed to July 12.

Among the policy initiatives in the bill, a Lautenberg provision barred interstate truckers and bus drivers from using police radar detectors.

A provision by Alfonse M. D'Amato, N.Y., the subcommittee's ranking Republican, penalized states for not suspending the driver's license for at least six months of anyone convicted of drug offenses. It cut off 5 percent of a non-complying state's federal highway money in the first year and 10 percent in later years.

Lautenberg said his subcommittee received 497 requests from 85 senators for transportation project earmarks. One that made it into the bill was a request from Minority Leader Bob Dole, R-Kan., for $11 million for a road construction project in Wichita.

CONFERENCE ACTION

The House on Oct. 19 adopted the conference report to a $12.9 billion fiscal 1991 transportation appropriations bill, after conferees dropped Senate provisions that would have required drug testing for mass transit workers and a ban on radar detectors for trucks.

The conference report, which passed on a vote of 394-17, cut transportation spending by $68.6 million from fiscal 1990. It came in at $100 million under the original House-passed bill, but was still $1 billion over Bush's request.

The Senate gave up its language to prohibit the use of radar detectors by interstate truck and bus drivers. Instead, the Transportation Department agreed to study their use.

The Senate also caved in on an attempt by Sen. D'Amato to require drug and alcohol testing for 179,000 mass transit workers.

The conference meeting on Oct. 16 forced a few issues into the open. In an unusual move, Lautenberg, chairman of the conference, bluntly denied a request by Senate colleague Specter to address the conferees about a state transportation issue. Specter was not a member of the conference and had no right to speak, Lautenberg ruled.

Rep. Gray, a conferee, had added language to cut Pennsylvania's federal highway funds by 25 percent unless the state agreed to dedicate funding for mass transit systems in the state.

Lautenberg, who represented thousands of New Jersey voters who commuted to jobs in Philadelphia, supported Gray's effort, which Specter called blackmail of rural Pennsylvanians.

"I know of no precedent for a senator objecting to a unanimous-consent request to speak before a committee," Specter fumed in the hallway afterward.

Reps. Bob Carr, D-Mich., and Robert J. Mrazek, D-N.Y., both argued for more money for programs of interest to them or their districts. But they employed different methods — and got different results.

Carr was upset that the Senate had earmarked $4 million of its $25 million allotment for research on computerized traffic management to demonstration projects in Minnesota, New Jersey and New York. The House had set aside $12 million, with none of the funds earmarked for specific states.

"At these levels of funding we really shouldn't be doing any earmarking," Carr said. "It's not a good deal for Oakland County, Michigan."

After nearly 10 minutes of Carr's protests, however, it was clear that Lautenberg would not back down. Nor would House Transportation Appropriations Chairman Lehman. "I have to stay with the deal I made because it ties into others," Lehman said. Carr lost badly on a show of hands, and the conferees moved to the next item.

Mrazek's approach was more conciliatory. The House had agreed to spend $12 million for magnetic levitation train research, an idea of personal interest to Mrazek. The Senate had appropriated only $7 million.

Mrazek also objected to earmarks in magnetic levitation research, but told Lautenberg he had no intention of challenging them. Rather, he said, "if the Senate went higher, I wouldn't mind."

Lautenberg and the conferees amicably agreed to fund the program at $10 million.

In other conference-related action, D'Amato, under pressure from a threatened veto, backed away from language to pay higher salaries to air-traffic controllers in the New York-New Jersey metropolitan area. Instead, the conferees ordered a study of the issue.

Conferees agreed to raise the ceiling on obligations to the Airport and Airway Trust Fund from the House level of $1.8 billion.

The House prevailed with its plan to raise the obligation ceiling for the Highway Trust Fund to $14.5 billion, higher than the Senate figure of $13.85 billion.

Senate Delay

The Senate on Oct. 26 appeared set to clear the $12.9 billion transportation appropriations bill but was stymied by the protracted efforts of the Pennsylvania senators to protect their state's highway funds.

The only floor debate on the conference agreement was over a provision put into the House bill by Gray to cut an estimated $144 million, or 25 percent, of Pennsylvania's highway funds unless the state adopted a dedicated, tax-based revenue source for the state's mass transit programs.

The state's GOP senators, Specter and Heinz, both protested the provision. Specter called it "a gun to the head of Pennsylvania . . . to accede to the wishes of the federal government."

Lautenberg and Gray wanted Pennsylvania to dedicate funds for mass transit, particularly for the Philadelphia-based Southeastern Pennsylvania Transit Authority (SEPTA). Lautenberg, who had thousands of New Jersey constituents who commuted to Philadelphia, blasted the city's mass transit safety record.

Lautenberg succeeded in killing Specter's effort to remove the Gray language, prevailing on a tabling motion by a party-line vote of 54-42. A Heinz effort to reconsider the vote also was tabled, 52-44. *(Votes 321, 322, p. 63-S)*

But Heinz and Specter refused to concede defeat and continued debating the issue. Majority Leader Mitchell eventually pulled the bill from the floor.

After the three Pennsylvania lawmakers and the chairmen and ranking members of the Transportation Appropriations Subcommittees met in Senate Appropriations Chairman Byrd's office, they agreed to keep the Gray provision in the bill but to delay its threatened funding cuts until 1992.

They also agreed that the Pennsylvania legislature and governor could avoid the cuts by certifying that they opposed a direct funding mechanism for mass transit. ■

Justice Funds Hiked in $19.3 Billion Bill

Congress on Oct. 24 cleared a $19.3 billion fiscal 1991 appropriations bill for the Departments of Commerce, Justice, State and the federal judiciary, after resolving a dispute over Securities and Exchange Commission (SEC) fees and beating back attempts to restrict grants under the Legal Services Corporation (LSC).

The conference report for the spending bill (HR 5021) was accepted by voice vote in the Senate and by 377-40 in the House on Oct. 23. *(Vote 506, p. 160-H)*

The bill faced little opposition during debate before both floor votes. The fiscal 1990 conference final was $17.2 billion. *(1989 Almanac, p. 725)*

The House and Senate agreed to allow the SEC to increase filing fees by $30 million annually. The rate hike was intended to allow the agency to hire more personnel to investigate and oversee securities transactions.

In House action Oct. 23, members by voice vote removed the new SEC fees from the bill after the Ways and Means Committee protested that the provision was a tax that should not be included on an appropriations bill.

The following day, the Senate, also by voice vote, reinserted the provision, with a change in accounting procedures so that the new funds would directly offset SEC spending. The House then accepted the change.

During earlier House consideration, Charles W. Stenholm, D-Texas, said he wanted to restrict the activities of the LSC. The Texas Democrat and a handful of other members had long tried to curtail legal-aid lawyers' work, contending that the lawyers were more involved in policy issues than day-to-day help for the poor and needy.

Under Stenholm's proposal, similar to one he offered in 1989, lawyer-grantees would have had to keep records on the types of cases they took and on how much time was spent on various disputes. Overall, it was aimed at pushing government-funded lawyers away from class-action lawsuits and more exclusively into aid for individuals with common problems such as landlord-tenant disputes and child-support cases.

In the end, Stenholm said he did not have the votes for his amendment and agreed not to press it. *(Legal Services Corporation, p. 531)*

Others items in dispute during the conference involved funding for government-sponsored television broadcasting to Cuba, known as TV Marti, and a restriction on post-employment lobbying by the U.S. trade representative.

The House and Senate agreed on a compromise to fund TV Marti, and the lobbying restriction was dropped from the bill.

The department that drew the largest share of the appropriation was Justice, where members boosted funds for law enforcement efforts against bank fraud and illegal drug trafficking.

The department's appropriation of $8.5 billion was $1.4 billion over the fiscal 1990 appropriation, not counting 1990 funds for a one-time prison expansion.

The conferees stressed in their report the need for more federal investigations and prosecutions in a number of high-profile areas, such as the savings and loan industry. *(Thrift fraud crackdown, p. 182)*

Additionally, members from the Appropriations committees expressed concern that the Justice Department was not devoting enough attention and resources to telemarketing fraud, which conferees described as a serious national problem. The bill required the department to report within six months on what it was doing to safeguard telephone transactions involving credit cards, facsimile machines and other wire activities.

On a State Department issue, the administration was rebuffed in its request for funds to tear down and rebuild the bug-riddled U.S. Embassy in Moscow. Instead, appropriators limited the administration to a $3.8 million reprogramming to begin a design study. *(Moscow embassy, p. 760)*

BOXSCORE

Legislation: Fiscal 1991 appropriations for the Departments of Commerce, Justice, State and the federal judiciary, PL 101-515 (HR 5021).

Major action: Signed, Nov. 5. Conference report adopted by Senate, Oct. 24; by House, 377-40, Oct. 23. Passed by Senate, 91-7, Oct. 11; by House, 358-55, June 26.

Reports: Conference report (H Rept 101-909). Appropriations (S Rept 101-515), Appropriations (H Rept 101-537).

HOUSE COMMITTEE ACTION

By voice vote, the House Appropriations Subcommittee on Commerce, Justice, State and the Judiciary on June 7 approved a spending bill that provided about $19.4 billion in fiscal 1991.

As was the practice of the subcommittee, panel members approved funds only for programs that were authorized by Congress.

The bill appropriated $10.5 billion for authorized programs and "reserved" for other, unauthorized programs $8.9 billion.

Full Committee Action

The full Appropriations Committee on June 13 also approved its version of HR 5021 by voice vote.

The measure provided $10.5 billion — a highly misleading figure because, for the third year in a row, Commerce, Justice, State Subcommittee Chairman Neal Smith, D-Iowa, refused to fund the dozens of agencies and programs that had not been authorized.

Like the subcommittee, the committee did set aside $8.9 billion for those programs.

The $10.5 billion figure was below both the $11.7 billion fiscal 1990 appropriation for comparable programs and an $11.1 billion administration request. But Smith said he was generally pleased with the total allocated. "It's a little deficient but not too bad," he said.

The measure contained about $1 billion more spending than in fiscal 1990 for antidrug programs. But according to Smith, that figure was also misleading, because the funding was mostly at levels similar to those provided on a part-year basis late in 1989.

Continued on p. 884

Fiscal 1991 Appropriations for Commerce . . .

Following are the budget authority totals in the fiscal 1991 spending bill (HR 5021 — PL 101-515) for the Departments of Commerce, Justice and State and for the federal judiciary.

(Figures, in thousands of dollars, may not add due to rounding.)

Agency	Bush Request	House Bill	Senate Bill	Final Bill
Department of Commerce				
General administration	$ 45,441	$ 44,454	$ 43,545	$ 43,995
Census Bureau total	431,337	423,767	383,428	382,950
Economic and Statistical Analysis	39,948	38,456	39,948	36,200
Economic Development Administration	20,000	41,418	232,035	201,018
International Trade Administration	189,020	24,421	183,620	185,620
Export Administration	44,373	— *	43,599	43,099
Minority Business Development Agency	46,161	— *	42,549	40,549
U.S. Travel and Tourism Administration	14,362	— *	19,596	19,596
National Oceanic and Atmospheric Administration	1,354,784	1,041,664	1,413,450	1,397,376
Patent and Trademark Office	112,027	109,807	— *	91,000
Technology Administration	4,583	— *	4,433	4,200
National Institute of Standards and Technology	198,408	— *	224,328	215,328
National Telecommunications and Information Administration	15,252	— *	14,882	15,252
New budget (obligational) authority	**$ 2,515,696**	**$ 1,744,820**	**$ 2,667,246**	**$ 2,698,016**
Related Agencies				
Federal Communications Commission	117,998	— *	117,794	115,794
Federal Maritime Commission	15,894	15,894	15,894	15,894
Federal Trade Commission	56,990	— *	56,095	54,095
International Trade Commission	42,430	— *	40,671	40,299
Marine Mammal Commission	1,003	1,003	1,153	1,153
Maritime Administration	296,687	— *	294,685	294,000
Martin Luther King Jr. Federal Holiday Commission	300	— *	300	300
Office of the U.S. Trade Representative	18,936	— *	18,936	20,000
Securities and Exchange Commission	192,385	— *	162,385	157,485
Small Business Administration	446,501	437,700	439,819	469,578
Department of Justice				
General administration	129,443	— *	123,108	126,108
U.S. Parole Commission	9,869	— *	9,869	10,051
Legal activities	2,252,397	1,087,063	2,310,634	2,300,731
Organized-crime drug enforcement	330,000	— *	330,000	328,000
Federal Bureau of Investigation	1,640,237	— *	1,690,962	1,687,962
Drug Enforcement Administration	700,000	— *	696,900	694,340
Immigration and Naturalization Service	884,349	— *	896,551	894,550
Federal prison system	1,756,247	— *	1,744,208	1,742,208
Office of Justice Programs	613,590	601,396	685,106	686,254
Subtotal	**$ 8,316,132**	**$ 1,763,459**	**$ 8,487,338**	**$ 8,470,204**
Related Agencies				
Christopher Columbus Quincentenary Jubilee Commission	214	214	214	214
Commission on the Bicentennial of the U.S. Constitution	16,884	14,973	14,973	14,973

* *The House did not appropriate funds for unauthorized programs.*

. . . Justice, State and the Federal Judiciary

Agency	Bush Request	House Bill	Senate Bill	Final Bill
Related Agencies				
Commission on Agricultural Workers	657	1,457	1,457	1,457
Commission on Civil Rights	10,152	6,075	7,825	7,075
Equal Employment Opportunity Commission	195,867	194,500	200,700	198,300
Legal Services Corporation	343,000	— *	329,186	327,186
State Justice Institute	15,000	14,000	12,360	13,000
Department of State				
Administration of foreign affairs	2,658,580	2,261,441	2,248,429	2,249,957
International organizations and conferences	1,414,104	909,905	909,905	909,905
International commissions	35,600	36,340	37,047	37,047
Bilateral Science and Technology Agreements	5,000	5,000	4,000	4,500
Asia Foundation	13,978	13,978	13,978	13,978
Soviet-East European research and training	4,600	4,784	4,600	4,600
Fishermen's guaranty fund	900	— *	900	900
Fishermen's protective fund	500	500	500	500
British American Parliamentary Group	—	—	50	50
Subtotal	**$ 4,133,262**	**$ 3,231,948**	**$ 3,219,409**	**$ 3,221,437**
Related Agencies				
Arms Control and Disarmament Agency	30,000	30,000	36,040	37,040
Board for International Broadcasting	201,258	192,586	201,258	197,750
Commission for the Preservation of America's Heritage Abroad	200	200	200	200
Commission on Security and Cooperation in Europe	991	991	991	991
Commission on the Ukraine Famine	—	— *	—	—
Commission for the Study of International Migration and Cooperative Economic Development	—	— *	—	—
Competitiveness Policy Council	—	— *	750	750
Japan-U.S. Friendship Trust Fund	1,250	1,250	1,250	1,250
U.S. Information Agency	986,708	990,076	1,005,737	1,006,237
The Judiciary				
Supreme Court	22,677	22,260	22,482	22,482
U.S. Court of Appeals for Federal Circuit	9,766	9,590	9,304	9,711
U.S. Court of International Trade	8,838	8,721	8,721	8,721
Court of Appeals, District Courts and other judicial services	1,943,059	1,843,647	1,865,650	1,852,643
Administrative Office of the U.S. Courts	38,487	37,712	37,178	37,400
Federal Judicial Center	15,866	13,918	13,918	13,918
Judicial Retirement Funds	5,000	5,000	5,000	5,000
U.S. Sentencing Commission	9,300	8,422	8,422	8,422
Subtotal, the judiciary	**$ 2,052,993**	**$ 1,949,270**	**$ 1,970,675**	**$ 1,958,297**
Total, Related Agencies	**$ 2,991,305**	**$ 1,901,419**	**$ 2,961,211**	**$ 2,975,521**
GRAND TOTAL	**$ 20,009,388**	**$ 10,590,916**	**$ 19,305,879**	**$ 19,323,475**

** The House did not appropriate funds for unauthorized programs.*

Continued from p. 881

With the work of the 1990 census winding down, funding for the Census Bureau was slashed from $1.5 billion to $423 million.

The committee recommended $788 million for contributions to international organizations, such as the United Nations, enough to pay existing obligations and 20 percent of the arrears the United States owed. *(U.N. funding, p. 802)*

Among the agencies for which the committee provided no money were the Drug Enforcement Administration, FBI, Federal Communications Commission, Federal Trade Commission, LSC, SEC and U.S. Trade Representative. Nor were funds provided for federal prisons or Justice Department salaries or to tear down and rebuild the U.S. Embassy in Moscow.

HOUSE FLOOR ACTION

By a vote of 358-55, the House on June 26 approved HR 5021, providing $10.6 billion for the Departments of Commerce, Justice and State and the federal judiciary. *(Vote 196, p. 68-H)*

The bill was approved after the House easily rejected two amendments that would have cut the appropriations across the board, first by 5 percent, then by 2 percent.

Forty-nine of the members who opposed the bill were Republicans, many of whom said they were against increasing spending levels when congressional leaders had not made significant headway in resolving the budget deficit.

The amendment to cut 5 percent from all discretionary accounts in the bill was offered by William E. Dannemeyer, R-Calif., and was defeated 88-323. *(Vote 195, p. 68-H)*

Dannemeyer said, "I do not think there is a program functioning in the government of the United States that cannot be reduced by 5 percent, including the appropriation for the legislative branch of the House of Representatives and the U.S. Senate."

Subcommittee Chairman Smith responded that the funds were within guidelines for budgetary allocations.

"Most of the programs in the bill are either at no more than the administration's request or less than the administration's request," Smith said. "Also, virtually every program in here is funded at less than the members of the House, in great numbers, wanted for the programs that were their high priorities."

The amendment to cut 2 percent, by Timothy J. Penny, D-Minn., was rejected by voice vote. Penny had estimated that the 2 percent cut would reduce the deficit by $200 million, which was about one-tenth of 1 percent of the estimated federal deficit.

There was little substantive debate on HR 5021, in part because slightly less than half the funds for the departments covered by the bill, a "reserved" $8.9 billion, had not yet been allocated.

The subcommittee had a tradition of not spelling out spending proposals for unauthorized programs in the bill until after the Senate had acted separately on the spending bill and a conference was under way.

Savings and Loan Fraud Funds

In earlier action, House members approved $75 million for Justice Department investigations into savings and loan fraud and rejected an attempt to cut funds for U.S. television broadcasts to Cuba.

Most of the bill's floor time June 20 was consumed by members' railing against criminal activity associated with the financial crisis in the nation's savings and loan associations and warning that wrongdoers were going unprosecuted.

Appropriations subcommittee Chairman Smith offered the amendment to set aside $65 million for investigations and prosecutions and $10 million for related civil actions to recover funds. The $75 million was the full amount that was authorized for fiscal 1991 under savings and loan reform legislation passed in August 1989 (PL 101-73). *(1989 Almanac, p. 117)*

Frank Annunzio, D-Ill., chairman of the House Banking Subcommittee on Financial Institutions, said more than 21,000 criminal referrals had been made to the Justice Department relating to the savings and loan scandal.

The $75 million amendment passed 420-1, with Philip M. Crane, R-Ill., the lone dissenter. *(Vote 187, p. 64-H)*

TV to Cuba

In other action, Bill Alexander, D-Ark., proposed that $8 million be cut from the $16 million allocated for television broadcasts to Cuba.

Some members of Congress said TV Marti was hindering U.S.-Cuban relations or was a waste of money. But its continued operation was one of a number of goals of a Cuban-American lobby.

Alexander said the funds could be better spent because Cuban President Fidel Castro had ordered the broadcasts jammed. Alexander also said that with easing of U.S.-Soviet tensions, the Cold War was virtually over and the United States did not have to broadcast its ideas and way of life to Cuba.

Dante B. Fascell, D-Fla., chairman of the Foreign Affairs Committee, was among the members arguing against the reduction. He likened U.S. broadcasts to Cuba to "providing food to starving people."

The Alexander amendment was rejected 111-306. *(Vote 188, p. 66-H)*

Administration Objections

The Bush administration objected to a number of the bill's spending proposals and said it thought less money should be appropriated. None of the administration's specific concerns were discussed during House debate.

In a statement of administration policy on June 19, the Office of Management and Budget (OMB) said it was particularly opposed to appropriations for programs that the administration had tried to eliminate or shrink.

The OMB pointed first to the bill's $41 million appropriation for the Economic Development Administration, saying that the agency's funds should be reduced and that its mission of regional development should be left to the private sector.

SENATE COMMITTEE ACTION

On Sept 12, the Senate Appropriations Subcommittee on Commerce, Justice, State and the Judiciary approved by voice vote a $19.6 billion fiscal 1991 spending bill for programs under its jurisdiction.

Members also gave voice vote approval to an amendment to increase funding for programs affected by the Senate-passed crime bill (S 1970) and for costs resulting from the Persian Gulf troop deployment. *(Crime bill, p. 486; Persian Gulf crisis, p. 717)*

Subcommittee Chairman Ernest F. Hollings, D-S.C.,

and ranking minority member Warren B. Rudman, R-N.H., offered the amendment, which added about $1 billion to the measure.

The $19.6 billion was $400 million less than the Bush administration request and about $200 million more than the House version.

The amendment included $203 million for U.S. payments to international organizations. The committee bill allocated $615 million to pay U.S. dues for fiscal 1991 — nearly $80 million less than the administration requested.

In recent years, Congress had withheld portions of U.S. dues to force the United Nations to change its practices. Bush requested $464 million to pay the past-due U.S. contributions, called "arrearages," over the following five years.

At first, the panel's bill included no funds for arrearages. But the amendment increased the fiscal 1991 payment to meet Bush's request and included nearly $93 million (or roughly 20 percent of the $464 million requested) for the first-year payment on U.S. arrearages.

The $203 million also included $31 million for arrearages to the U.N. peacekeeping forces. That was in addition to the $91 million already in the bill for U.S. contributions in fiscal 1991.

The subcommittee also included in its amendment a $79 million boost in funds for the Ready Reserve Force. That force consisted of 96 ships that could, on a moment's notice, go on active duty. Forty-one of those ships had already been deployed to the Persian Gulf. The $79 million would fund five more ships.

Targeting Savings and Loan Fraud

The savings and loan scandal had caused members across the political spectrum to feel the heat of public discontent. To deflect some of this criticism, lawmakers had pushed for investigations of fraud and abuse.

The subcommittee approved $117 million in its amendment to pay for fiscal 1991 probes into savings and loan fraud. The investigations were authorized in the Senate's crime bill. That was $17 million more than Bush's request and $42 million more than the House put in its bill.

The amendment also included $577 million to meet Bush's request to bolster crime fighting and antidrug programs. Of that amount, $203 million went for prison construction, bringing the bill's prison total to nearly $311 million.

The subcommittee measure also gave the State Department $10 million to knock down and rebuild the bug-riddled U.S. Embassy in Moscow.

President Bush decided in 1989 to raze the building and start again. He requested $270 million in fiscal 1991. *(1989 Almanac, p. 536)*

Full Committee Action

The spending measure was easily approved by a unanimous Senate Appropriations Committee on Oct. 10. The panel's chairman, Robert C. Byrd, D-W.Va., said the total was $716 million lower than Bush had requested.

The lion's share of the funds, however, went to the Justice Department, where appropriators endorsed higher spending levels than the administration had sought.

The Justice Department appropriation of $8.5 billion was more than $300 million higher than the 1990 appropriation. And that did not tell the whole story because a big chunk of the fiscal 1990 appropriation was for a one-year prison construction program. If the prison expansion was excluded, Justice received $1.4 billion, or 19 percent, more than it received in fiscal 1990.

Hollings and Rudman, chairman and ranking minority member, respectively, of the Commerce, Justice, State Subcommittee, said they agreed that the priority would be to expand U.S. law enforcement.

The committee members by voice vote accepted a provision to deny an export license for the sale of supercomputer technology to any country helping Iraq improve its rocket technology or chemical, biological or nuclear weapons capability. Bob Kasten, R-Wis., who pushed the amendment, said, "If you do business with Iraq, you can't do business with the United States."

SENATE FLOOR ACTION

The Senate on Oct. 11 approved HR 5021, providing $19.3 billion for programs in the Departments of Commerce, Justice, State and the federal judiciary. The vote was 91-7 after little debate. *(Vote 265, p. 53-S)*

The spending measure included $109.5 million in increased funds for savings and loan crime prosecution and funding boosts for other anticrime efforts.

The bill was about $200 million less than the House had appropriated or reserved for unauthorized programs.

The money for savings and loan inquiries and prosecution reflected legislation passed by both chambers to create stiff new penalties for bank fraud and to provide more money for Justice Department enforcement activities.

Hollings said the Justice Department could hire nearly 1,000 new FBI and drug enforcement agents to pursue bank fraud and illegal drug-trafficking.

He added, "We provided the money to activate one new prison and expand the capacity of 13 existing penal institutions." Hollings said the expansion would boost federal prison capacity from 56,400 to 62,450 inmates.

The bill also provided more money for the federal courts to meet higher caseloads: $2 billion, up from the $1.7 billion allocated for fiscal 1990. However, funds for proposed new judgeships were not included. The House on Sept. 27 passed a bill (HR 3134) for 59 new judgeships, and the Senate Judiciary Committee had approved 77 new positions in S 2648. *(New judgeships, p. 520)*

As approved by the Senate, the spending bill also addressed the issue of U.N. contributions. The bill included funds for repayment of those previously withheld dues and increased contributions to international organizations and for peacekeeping activities in the Persian Gulf, for a total of $902.6 million in fiscal 1991.

FINAL ACTION

House-Senate conferees Oct. 18 approved HR 5021.

The bill included $109.5 million for savings and loan fraud investigations and a prohibition on the export of U.S. supercomputer technology to countries helping Iraq improve its weapons capability.

As modified by the conferees, the bill denied an export license for the sale of any supercomputer to a country whose government or nationals were helping Iraq.

In the latter case, the license would be denied "only if the president determines that the government of the country has made inadequate efforts to restrict such involvement by its citizens or corporations and so reports to the Congress."

The committee left two differences between the chambers to be resolved in floor action. Conferees could not reach agreement on how much money to provide for government-sponsored television broadcasting to Cuba, TV Marti, or on a provision to restrict former employees of the Office of the U.S. Trade Representative from handling clients who did business with the government.

The House and Senate finally agreed to a compromise on funding for TV Marti — accepting the House figure of $16 million for TV Marti and the Senate figure of $15 million for Radio Marti — and the lobbying restriction was eventually dropped from the bill.

Bush Statements

In signing the bill Nov. 5, Bush voiced reservations about two appointment-related provisions.

He said that a provision creating a three-member Central European Small Enterprise Development Commission failed to specify who would appoint its members and that he would construe it "to require that the members of the Commission are to be appointed by me or my delegate."

He also said he would interpret a provision regarding powers of the Legal Services Corporation board of directors not to impose special limits on them as recess appointees.

Later in the month, in signing the omnibus crime bill (S 3266 — PL 101-647) on Nov. 29, Bush criticized another provision in the spending bill: an $11 million line item for 17 "death penalty resource centers."

Bush said that without new restrictions he recommended on death row inmates' legal challenges, "these Federal funds will inevitably be used in part to foster repetitive attacks on State court judgments and to delay unjustly the implementation of State sentences." ■

Federal Pay Hike in Treasury Spending Bill

A sweeping reform of the federal pay system was the centerpiece of the $20.9 billion fiscal 1991 appropriations bill for the Treasury Department, U.S. Postal Service, the Executive Office of the President and a number of independent agencies.

The House had approved the conference report, 343-67, Oct. 22; the Senate approved it by voice vote on Oct. 23.

After settling some minor amendments in disagreement, the House cleared and sent the bill to President Bush on Oct. 24.

Bush had threatened to veto the bill over provisions preventing the Office of Management and Budget (OMB) from establishing an accounting-standards process for the federal government, but ended up signing the measure Nov. 5.

Under pay reform provisions agreed to by the administration and House and Senate conferees the week of Oct. 15, federal workers were to receive raises equal to the average annual salary increases in the private sector beginning in 1992. Employees were guaranteed salary increases of up to 5 percent annually, based on the Employment Cost Index, which kept track of changes in the private local labor markets. *(Federal pay system overhaul, p. 405)*

The agreement marked the end of negotiations between Congress and the administration over how much authority the president had to limit or deny pay increases.

The aim was to close the gap between federal and private-sector salaries. According to the president's pay advisers, federal pay had fallen an average of 30 percent behind private-sector wages.

In 1990, all federal workers of the same rank received the same pay, regardless of where they lived.

Beginning in fiscal 1994, federal workers in high-cost cities would qualify for extra locality-based pay increases. For nine years, starting in 1995, the remaining gap was to be closed by 10 percent per year.

Under the bill, the president could opt not to increase salaries only in the event of war or negative growth of the gross national product for two consecutive quarters. After 1995, the president was given broader discretion to alter the agreement.

The measure also gave all federal workers a 4.1 percent pay increase effective Jan. 1. Bush had asked for a 3.5 percent increase.

Total spending in the bill was about $200 million higher than Bush had requested. In 1989, Congress had provided $18.4 billion for the agencies in the fiscal 1990 spending measure. *(1989 Almanac, p. 745)*

BOXSCORE

Legislation: Fiscal 1991 appropriations for Treasury Department, U.S. Postal Service and general government, PL 101-509 (HR 5241).

Major action: Signed, Nov. 5. Conference report cleared by House, Oct. 24; adopted by Senate, with amendment, Oct. 23; by House, 343-67, Oct. 22. Passed by Senate, 93-6, Sept. 11; by House, 300-72, July 13.

Reports: Conference report (H Rept 101-906). Appropriations (S Rept 101-411); Appropriations (H Rept 101-589)

HOUSE ACTION

The House Appropriations Subcommittee on Treasury, Postal Service and General Government approved a $20.4 billion spending package June 13, after members voted to close the markup.

However, sources said members of the subcommittee refused to agree to a request by Government Operations Chairman John Conyers Jr., D-Mich., to withhold funding for the Office of Information and Regulatory Affairs (OIRA), the division of OMB that affected the form and content of agency regulations.

Subcommittee members agreed to leave the matter for the full committee to decide, sources said.

Conyers, who attended the markup, presented subcommittee members with a letter signed by six other House chairmen. In the letter, Conyers said OIRA should not be funded until an agreement could be reached with OMB to limit its control over agency regulations.

During full committee consideration of the bill July 11, an amendment was approved allowing the U.S. Secret Ser-

Treasury, Postal Service Appropriations

Following are the budget authority totals in the fiscal 1991 appropriations bill (HR 5241 — PL 101-509) for the Treasury, Postal Service, Executive Office of the President and independent agencies.

(Figures, in thousands of dollars, may not add due to rounding.)

	President's Request	House Bill	Senate Bill	Final Bill
Treasury Department				
Financial Management Service	$ 218,742	$ 218,742	$ 218,742	$ 218,742
Bureau of Alcohol, Tobacco and Firearms	275,284	296,284	305,704	301,854
U.S. Customs Service	1,280,140	1,264,140	1,273,079	1,263,315
Bureau of the Public Debt	175,139	175,139	175,139	175,139
Internal Revenue Service	6,135,000	6,135,000	5,906,925	6,107,925
Administration and management	(136,072)	(136,072)	(142,279)	(142,279)
Processing tax returns, assistance	(1,444,517)	(1,444,517)	(1,521,595)	(1,521,595)
Examinations and appeals	(0)	(0)	(0)	(0)
Investigations, collection	(0)	(0)	(0)	(0)
Tax law enforcement	(3,560,484)	(3,560,484)	(3,310,119)	(3,501,119)
Information systems	(993,927)	(993,927)	(932,932)	(942,932)
U.S. Secret Service	397,640	397,640	412,740	406,700
Other	219,337	219,337	254,205	244,903
Subtotal	**$ 8,701,282**	**$ 8,706,282**	**$ 8,546,534**	**$ 8,718,578**
Postal Service				
Postal subsidies	484,592	484,592	470,592	472,592
Fund for non-funded liabilities	38,142	38,142	38,142	38,142
Executive Office of President				
President's compensation	250	250	250	250
Administration and residence	68,791	68,791	69,291	69,291
Vice president's residence	626	626	626	626
Council of Economic Advisers	3,064	3,064	3,064	3,064
National Security Council	5,893	5,893	5,893	5,893
Office of Management and Budget	49,305	49,305	48,343	48,343
Office of National Drug Control Policy	194,500	194,500	145,500	145,000
Other activities	7,544	7,544	7,709	7,709
Subtotal	**$ 329,973**	**$ 329,973**	**$ 280,676**	**$ 280,176**
Independent Agencies				
Federal Election Commission	17,150	17,150	17,150	17,150
General Services Administration	1,600,320	1,592,079	1,814,228	1,829,098
Federal Buildings Fund	(1,365,353)	(1,408,870)	(1,578,380)	(1,645,733)
(limitations)	*(5,184,330)*	*(5,279,209)*	*(5,099,809)*	*(5,268,852)*
National Archives	128,879	139,756	131,469	138,219
Office of Personnel Management	9,324,436	9,324,436	9,323,436	9,324,436
Other personnel agencies	47,615	47,615	47,615	47,865
U.S. Tax Court	31,598	31,598	31,598	31,598
Other agencies	8,471	8,471	8,471	8,471
Subtotal	**$11,158,469**	**$11,161,105**	**$11,373,967**	**$11,396,837**
GRAND TOTAL	**$20,712,458**	**$20,720,094**	**$20,709,911**	**$20,906,325**

SOURCE: House Appropriations Committee

vice to investigate crimes committed by savings and loan officials.

Hardly anyone opposed the provision, offered by Treasury Subcommittee Chairman Edward R. Roybal, D-Calif., although there was considerable debate about who should receive the credit.

"I guess the chairman decided it was going to be a Democrat-sponsored bill," said Silvio O. Conte of Massachusetts, the full committee's ranking Republican, who said he had been working on just such an amendment during the July Fourth recess. "It does give the federal government an added tool to put those crooks in jail," he said.

Others noted that Dennis E. Eckart, D-Ohio, had introduced a separate bill (HR 5098) to give Secret Service agents authority to investigate wrongdoing at savings and loans. Although the Bush administration opposed his measure, Eckart said, it was needed "to bring these scoundrels to justice."

Conte chimed in: "I was going to offer this amendment, and something happened on the way to the forum."

Earlier, Appropriations Chairman Jamie L. Whitten, D-Miss., had offered this solution: "When the Appropriations Committee passes the bill, all of us can take credit."

House Passage

The House approved the $20.7 billion fiscal 1991 spending bill for the Treasury Department and Postal Service on July 13. The vote was 300-72. *(Vote 233, p. 80-H)*

As passed by the House, the bill included only $7.8 million more than Bush requested.

A principal target for a spending increase was the Internal Revenue Service (IRS), for which funding for tax law enforcement and collection increased by more than $600 million, from $5.5 billion in fiscal 1990 to a total of $6.1 billion.

A new account of nearly $1 billion funded a new computer information system, which the IRS said would help it track down tax evaders.

The bill also provided $484.6 million requested by the U.S. Postal Service for nonprofit mail subsidies, a $31 million increase over fiscal 1990.

The committee had approved every request by the president for White House functions, including a $626,000 appropriation for operations and renovation of the vice president's mansion — a $52,000 increase over fiscal 1990. Vice President Dan Quayle's wife, Marilyn, had conducted a personal lobbying campaign to improve the structure of the house.

The OMB was also given an increase of $5 million, up to $49.3 million, which included funding for OIRA, the controversial regulatory review office.

Deal on OMB Unit

HR 5241 sailed smoothly through the House partly because of an eleventh-hour deal struck between Government Operations Chairman Conyers and OMB Director Richard G. Darman.

Conyers had threatened to raise a point of order against the bill that would have deleted $4.5 million in funding for OMB's regulatory affairs office, OIRA.

It had been operating without authorization, and Conyers was set to argue that funding could not be approved without authorization.

Conyers had been trying to restrict the office's control of the regulatory review process, arguing that OMB used its power to affect the form and content of agency regulations to further administration policy goals.

Conyers and Frank Horton of New York, the ranking Republican on Government Operations, thought they had struck a gentleman's agreement with Darman: They would draft a straight reauthorization of OIRA without language limiting OIRA's control; Darman, in return, would agree to regulatory review limits in an informal sidebar agreement.

Later, however, the White House said such an agreement was never made.

Conyers said his and Darman's staffs met until 2 a.m. July 13 trying to hammer out a compromise. Conyers, Horton and Sen. John Glenn, D-Ohio, chairman of the Senate Governmental Affairs Committee, then met with Darman later that day to seal the deal.

Under the new agreement, the president would limit OIRA's regulatory control by issuing an executive order — a far more stringent action than Conyers' original agreement with Darman, a sign that the White House feared Congress would go along with Conyers' plans to strike OIRA's funding.

"We had to go all the way to the wire," Conyers said outside the House chamber.

Requested Projects

The bill also shouldered its usual weight of pork-barrel projects in the form of new construction projects for the General Services Administration (GSA), the government's landlord.

More than half of the projects listed as "new construction" were not requested by the GSA but by individual members, including Majority Whip William H. Gray III, D-Pa., and Rules Committee Chairman Joe Moakley, D-Mass. In some cases, the projects had nothing to do with federal buildings.

The Bush administration, in a statement of opposition to the bill, called on the House to "stop this totally inappropriate use" of the GSA account, although it stopped short of issuing a veto threat.

Subcommittee aides said the projects numbered no more than usual. As passed, the bill appropriated the following:

- $200,000 for a California State University grant.
- $39,000 for a Japanese-American National Museum in Los Angeles.
- $5 million for Loyola University, Marymount, Calif.
- $2 million for Children's Hospital in San Diego.
- $2 million for the American Indian Higher Education Consortium in Washington, D.C.
- $2 million for the D.C. Children's National Medical Center.
- $2 million for the Mount Sinai Medical Center in Miami.
- $5 million for the Christopher Columbus Center on Marine Research and Exploration in Baltimore.
- $1.5 million for the University of Maryland in College Park, Md.
- $51.3 million for the Federal Building-Courthouse in Boston.
- $5 million for the National Center for Complex Systems, Brandeis University, Waltham, Mass.
- $6 million for the Marine Biomedical Institute for Advanced Studies in Woods Hole, Mass.
- $2 million for the Michigan Technological University in Houghton, Mich.
- $5 million for the Primate Research Institute in Alamogordo, N.M.
- $2 million for the Rochester Institute of Technology in Rochester, N.Y.
- $778,000 for the Parents Against Drugs in Philadelphia.
- $1 million for Texas A&M University to establish an Institute for National Drug Abatement Research in College Station, Texas.
- $2 million for the University of Texas in El Paso, Texas.

Floor Amendments

An amendment by James A. Traficant Jr., D-Ohio, authorizing the IRS to establish a training program to teach IRS employees to be courteous to taxpayers, was adopted by voice vote.

Traficant argued that taxpayers were harassed and

made to feel like criminals in the face of IRS scrutiny.

Andrew Jacobs Jr., D-Ind., offered an amendment cutting from $2 million to $449,200 the appropriation for pensions and allowances to former presidents.

But Jacobs' amendment was amended by Joe Skeen of New Mexico, the subcommittee's ranking Republican, striking the figure $449,200 and inserting $1.84 million, the same amount that had been appropriated in fiscal 1990. The Skeen amendment was adopted 300-91. *(Vote 229, p. 80-H)*

An amendment by Harris W. Fawell, R-Ill., that would have cut out $43 million in GSA construction grants failed by voice vote.

Bill Frenzel, R-Minn., offered an amendment to reduce discretionary spending to the fiscal 1990 level, except for the IRS budget. The House rejected it, 130-254. *(Vote 231, p. 80-H)*

Another amendment by Timothy J. Penny, D-Minn., to make a 2 percent across-the-board cut in discretionary accounts in the bill failed, 178-201. *(Vote 232, p. 80-H)*

SENATE COMMITTEE ACTION

The Senate Appropriations Committee approved a $20.7 billion spending bill (HR 5241) for the Treasury and Postal Service on Aug. 1. The subcommittee had approved the bill July 31.

During the full committee markup, federal budget constraints collided with parochial pork-barrel interests as members stripped $200 million from the Bush administration request for the IRS, but added millions more for grants and building projects in their home states.

The committee recommended a total of $5.9 billion in fiscal 1991 spending for the IRS. That represented a $405 million increase over the agency's fiscal 1990 appropriation but was still far short of the president's $6.1 billion request, which was approved by the House.

The IRS had planned to use the extra funding primarily for modernization of its operations including new computer systems.

"We could not give the president everything he requested for new initiatives," said New Mexico's Pete V. Domenici, ranking Republican on the Senate Appropriations Subcommittee on the Treasury, Postal Service and General Government. "We weren't able to give them a wholly modern computer system, but we made a start," he said.

Meanwhile, Senate appropriators also stripped from the House version a list of pork-barrel projects in the form of new construction for the GSA.

In their place, the Senate panel inserted its own pork projects, including $80.4 million for a new federal building in Charleston, W.Va., the home state of Democrat Robert C. Byrd, chairman of the full committee.

Struggle Over Government Processes

Another move by the Senate committee highlighted an ongoing power struggle between Congress and the executive branch over control of government processes.

Senate appropriators included language designed to fend off a plan by the OMB to establish a new accounting-standards process for the federal government. According to the report accompanying the bill, OMB was planning to put the new rules into effect "unilaterally" by an executive order of the president. The plan "undermines Congress' ability to oversee federal spending," the report stated.

As approved by the committee, the bill prevented "any department, agency or office of the United States" from using appropriated funds to issue new accounting principles or standards without the agreement of the comptroller general.

Antidrug Efforts

Many federal agencies covered by the bill received slight increases over fiscal 1990 spending, including the U.S. Customs Service and the Secret Service.

But the committee scrapped a Bush request, approved by the House, to establish a National Drug Intelligence Center under the joint supervision of the Justice Department and the Office of National Drug Control Policy.

The committee instead chose to provide $83 million — $33 million more than the president requested — for "high intensity drug trafficking areas" that were also home for many of their constituents. The money provided local aid to enhance antidrug efforts in New York, Los Angeles, Miami, Houston and the Southwest border — hot spots the committee said the Drug Control Policy Office cited in January.

SENATE FLOOR ACTION

On a 93-6 vote, the Senate on Sept. 11 passed its version of HR 5241, providing $20.7 billion in fiscal 1991 spending for the Treasury and Postal Service. *(Vote 231, p. 47-S)*

Senators added provisions to overhaul the federal pay system to make salaries more competitive with the private sector.

In an attempt to stick to its budget allocation, the Senate Appropriations Committee recommended $2.5 million less in new spending authority than President Bush requested and $10 million less than the House bill.

The main difference between the Senate and House versions was the funding level for the IRS. The Senate bill provided the IRS with $5.9 billion in fiscal 1991, $428 million more than fiscal 1990 but $228 million less than requested by the president and approved by the House.

Governmental Affairs Committee Chairman Glenn offered an amendment to provide the IRS an additional $55.5 million to hire 1,000 more employees to collect unpaid debts to the federal government. Glenn said that as of June, "deadbeats" owed the government about $96 billion.

However, Dennis DeConcini, D-Ariz., chairman of the Treasury Appropriations Subcommittee, argued that the amendment was out of order because it would have pushed the bill over its budget limits.

Joseph I. Lieberman, D-Conn., sought to waive the budget restrictions (a motion that required 60 votes), arguing that the IRS needed to show a get-tough policy on unpaid taxes. "How can we seriously contemplate raising taxes that honest, hard-working, taxpaying Americans will have to pay, if we are unwilling to make that extra effort to collect the billions that are already owed to our government?" Lieberman asked.

The Senate rejected the waiver motion, 35-64. *(Vote 228, p. 47-S)*

Private Sector-Size Raises

The federal pay overhaul was offered by Glenn and William V. Roth Jr., R-Del., chairman and ranking Republican, respectively, of the Governmental Affairs Committee, and incorporated the language of a bill (S 2274) approved by their committee on July 25.

The amendment granted pay increases to federal workers equivalent to the average annual salary increases in the private sector and also granted extra locality-based pay increases to government employees in high-cost cities. The amendment, however, incorporated several changes to the language in S 2274.

Most important, it retained the unlimited discretion the president had to limit or deny pay raises in the event of "serious economic conditions affecting the general welfare."

The Senate gave voice vote approval to an amendment by DeConcini to raise the starting salaries of federal officers by $3,000 a year; grant cost of living bonuses to officers assigned to the nation's 13 highest costing cities; and provide relocation, retention and language-skill bonuses. DeConcini's staff estimated the cost of his amendment at $250 million in fiscal 1992, although the administration had placed it at nearly double that figure.

FINAL ACTION

House and Senate conferees approved the final version of HR 5241 on Oct. 19, after days of negotiations with the administration over concerns that the federal pay-overhaul plan might erode the president's authority.

Administration officials took exception to a number of provisions in the bill, including one that could hinder the president's power to limit or deny pay raises.

An agreement was finally negotiated by Rep. Steny H. Hoyer, D-Md., representing the conferees, and OMB officials. The resulting language was a combination of the administration's own proposals and different bills introduced by Rep. Gary L. Ackerman, D-N.Y., and Hoyer, Senate Governmental Affairs Chairman Glenn and ranking Republican Roth.

Beginning in 1992, federal workers were to receive pay raises equal to the average annual salary increases in the private sector.

Starting in fiscal 1994, federal workers in high-cost cities also were to qualify for extra locality-based pay increases. Increases were to be phased in over nine years beginning in 1994, to bring federal pay in line with local levels for the same work.

Barring unusual economic circumstances, the president would have to increase salaries for federal employees in areas with a gap of 5 percent or greater. The gap would have to be closed by at least 20 percent in the first year and an additional 10 percent each year until federal workers were brought to within 95 percent of full comparability.

After 1995, the president would have broad discretion to alter the agreement.

After some debate, conferees also agreed to provide a 4.1 percent pay raise for federal workers for fiscal 1991. President Bush had asked for a 3.5 percent increase.

OMB Under Scrutiny

Meanwhile, conferees left in the spending bill provisions that would prevent OMB from establishing an accounting-standards process for the federal government.

Bush had threatened to veto the bill over the provisions, which prohibited any department or agency from using its funds to issue new accounting principles or standards without the agreement of the comptroller general, an officer of Congress.

Conferees also had a host of other sticking points that slowed down the bill.

House conferees, at the urging of House Appropriations Chairman Whitten, wanted to cut $2 million from the appropriation for OMB.

OMB had requested $49.3 million, and initially the House had agreed to the request. The Senate allocated $48.3 million. House conferees wanted to cut the Senate figure by $2 million because they said OMB had used some 1990 funds to purchase equipment and had therefore come out $2 million ahead for fiscal 1991.

DeConcini and Domenici argued against the move, which some saw as a jab at OMB Director Darman. "Whether we like them or not, I think they do a good job," Domenici said.

"Whether we like Mr. Darman or not, I think he does a good job."

Domenici said Darman had asked him to raise the issue in conference. House Treasury Subcommittee Chairman Roybal agreed to take the matter back to Whitten. Conferees eventually settled on the Senate number.

Splitting Differences

Conferees resolved one longstanding problem in a way that could become a model for future appropriations negotiations — that is, how to divide dollars for competing pork projects.

These annual disputes usually involved relatively small amounts of money but resolving them could mean hours of haggling in conference.

In 1990, DeConcini suggested that the House and Senate delegations merely split the difference between their aggregate figures for construction projects, then let each side decide how to split up its own pot to determine which projects survived.

"One of my concerns is if we do not divide it evenly, 50-50, we are going to have a race on who's going to load up," DeConcini told Roybal, who agreed with the idea.

Because the committees had to cut about $75 million from the bill to meet budget targets, the Senate was forced to shave about $9 million off its list of projects, while the House had to cut about $8 million.

DeConcini said that in 1990 the Senate could agree to take about $2 million less than the House. "I'm willing to give you a couple more than the Senate, just because I want to close the thing," DeConcini said.

But he added: "I want to make it clear that next year I don't want to do that."

Signed by Bush

In a written statement issued when he signed the bill Nov. 5, Bush made no mention of the pay raise for federal workers.

Bush thanked Congress, however, for a little-noticed section of the bill softening a provision of the fiscal 1988 omnibus continuing resolution (PL 100-202) aimed at barring enforcement of non-disclosure agreements required of federal employees with access to classified information.

Section 617 of HR 5241 allowed enforcement of such agreements as long as they contained a written statement that the restrictions did not supersede laws protecting government whistleblowers.

Bush said the previous act "raised profound constitutional concerns and resulted in lengthy litigation." The new provision, he said, "accommodates the concerns of the executive branch, provided that it is not construed in a manner that interferes with my constitutional authority to protect national security information." ■

Abortion-Free D.C. Bill OK'd by Senate

The Senate on Oct. 27 cleared and sent to the president a $4.4 billion fiscal 1991 spending package for the District of Columbia after controversial language to ease restrictions on abortion funding was removed.

A House-Senate conference agreement on the bill (HR 5311) was rejected twice by the House, which had originally included liberalized abortion language without a fight. Given the repeated veto threats that President Bush had held over the bill, Senate and House appropriators decided to give up and leave existing D.C. abortion funding restrictions intact.

After the language was removed, the bill passed both the House and the Senate by voice vote.

HR 5311, as first agreed to by conferees, would have allowed the District to use its federal appropriation to pay for abortions for poor women in cases of rape or incest or to save the woman's life, and to use its locally raised revenues as it chose.

Existing law, enacted in 1988, prohibited the District from paying for abortions other than to save the woman's life. *(1988 Almanac, p. 713)*

The conference report was first rejected by the House on a 185-211 vote and rejected a second time on a 195-211 vote. *(Vote 494, p. 156-H; vote 523, p. 164-H)*

As cleared, the bill provided $549.7 million in federal funds, including a federal payment of $430.5 million to the District in lieu of taxes for the use of District land, the same figure as in fiscal 1990. The total federal contribution for fiscal 1990 was $538 million. *(1989 Almanac, p. 757)*

The federal contribution was 13 percent of the District's total spending of $4.4 billion; the rest of the funds were raised from local taxes.

The fiscal 1991 bill also included language that barred the District from using federal or locally raised revenues to fund a shadow delegation elected by the city to lobby Congress for statehood. The bill did not include any provisions restricting the right of homosexuals to participate in organizations that worked with children.

The Senate had included an amendment by William L. Armstrong, R-Colo., to permit organizations to decide whether to accept homosexuals as counselors. Also included was a compromise amendment by Brock Adams, D-Wash., chairman of the District of Columbia Subcommittee, that would have allowed organizations to exclude anyone to whom a parent objected because of the person's sexual orientation.

Both amendments were removed in conference Oct. 12.

BOXSCORE

Legislation: Fiscal 1991 appropriations for the District of Columbia, PL 101-518 (HR 5311).

Major action: Signed, Nov. 5. Conference report adopted by Senate, Oct. 27 (session of Oct. 26); by House, Oct. 26. Original conference report rejected by House, 195-211, Oct. 25; 185-211, Oct. 20. Passed by Senate, Sept. 18; by House, 241-178, July 26.

Reports: Conference report (H Rept 101-958). Appropriations (S Rept 101-397); Appropriations (H Rept 101-607).

HOUSE COMMITTEE ACTION

The House Appropriations District of Columbia Subcommittee on July 12 set the stage for yet another battle over abortion funding in the nation's capital by approving a fiscal 1991 spending bill that would allow the use of all District government funds — both federal and local — to pay for some abortions.

Thus, the D.C. Subcommittee returned to its original 1989 stance, when it won a landmark battle on the House floor but was forced to concede defeat to Bush after he vetoed two successive D.C. appropriations bills over the issue. Congress finally agreed to prohibit the District from funding any abortions, except those to save a woman's life. *(Veto messages, 1989 Almanac, pp. 39-C, 42-C)*

Subcommittee Chairman Julian C. Dixon, D-Calif., said he would not try to amend the language to suit Bush, as the committee had done grudgingly in 1989. "I'm not interested in sending it up over and over again," Dixon said.

Under the fiscal 1991 bill approved by the subcommittee, District officials could use locally raised taxes as they saw fit. Federal funds would still be restricted, although they could be used to pay for abortions in cases of rape or incest or when the woman's life was in danger.

The $4.3 billion spending bill included $519.3 million in federal funds to the District, the same as requested by the administration and $39 million less than in fiscal 1990. The federal payment to the city, made in lieu of taxes for the use of District land, remained the same as the 1990 appropriation of $430.5 million.

The subcommittee also approved the District's plans for raising $3.8 billion through taxes and other means, including the D.C. lottery.

The full Appropriations Committee approved HR 5311 by voice vote on July 19 and left intact the subcommittee's abortion language.

HOUSE FLOOR ACTION

The House on July 26 approved, by a vote of 241-178, a $4.3 billion spending bill for the District of Columbia. *(Vote 274, p. 90-H)*

House members shied away from a floor battle over language allowing the District to use both federal and locally raised money to pay for abortions.

As passed, HR 5311 included about $540 million in federal appropriations for the District on top of about $3.9 billion to be raised through District taxes.

The bill allowed the District to use its own funds to pay for abortions but limited the use of federal funds for abortions to cases of rape or incest or to save the life of the woman.

The Bush administration, which vetoed two D.C. appropriations bills in 1989, had again threatened to veto the bill over the abortion language. It wanted Congress to craft a bill that allowed the District to fund abortions only to save a woman's life.

Robert K. Dornan, R-Calif., had intended to offer an amendment to delete the broad abortion language in favor of a ban on other District-funded abortions except to save the woman's life. But he did not, an aide said, because the amendment could have been ruled out of order on procedural grounds.

Although the abortion issue was not addressed on the House floor, a number of amendments were aimed at decreasing the District's funding.

Bill Frenzel, R-Minn., proposed to cut the District's budget across the board by 4.4 percent, or about $25 million. The House rejected that proposal, 195-219. *(Vote 273, p. 90-H)*

However, an amendment by Timothy J. Penny, D-Minn., to cut the District's budget by 2 percent was approved by voice vote.

The House also took aim at funding for the University of the District of Columbia (UDC), voting 297-123 to cut $1.6 million the school had planned to use to renovate a building to display a controversial ceramic art piece titled "The Dinner Party." Conservative Republicans called the artwork obscene. *(Vote 272, p. 90-H)*

SENATE COMMITTEE ACTION

The Senate Appropriations District of Columbia Subcommittee approved its version of a D.C. spending bill on July 24, but panel members first signaled their low opinion of statehood for the District of Columbia.

The members gave bipartisan, voice vote approval to an amendment to HR 5311 prohibiting the city from using federal or locally raised revenues to fund its plan to elect "shadow senators" to lobby for statehood. The District also could not use its funding to pay for any other attempts to push for statehood.

In February, the City Council had authorized the election in the fall of 1990 of a shadow delegation — two senators and one House representative. But the council stopped short of appropriating $1.3 million it estimated would be needed to pay the delegation and their staffs.

Because the District had never asked Congress to approve funding for the shadow delegation, the amendment offered by the subcommittee's ranking Republican, Phil Gramm of Texas, was understood by D.C. officials as a political gesture.

"It has little or no effect on the budget as it exists now," said Richard W. Clark, liaison officer for the City Council.

But Clark said members were unfair in "prohibiting the District from using its own funds to communicate with Congress."

Larry Neal, Gramm's press secretary, explained the amendment's purpose this way: "This is in effect saying, 'If this is in your mind, forget it.' "

Congress had strongly opposed D.C. statehood in the past. In 1989, Congress would not allow the city to spend $150,000 for a statehood lobbying office.

Gramm believed that the District should not be allowed to spend taxpayers' dollars on a statehood lobbying effort, Neal said, when other states did not. He pointed to Texas' admittance to the Union in 1845 after the U.S.-Mexican War.

"We did it the old-fashioned way — we earned it," Neal said. "In Texas we had a revolution."

Full Committee

The full Appropriations Committee approved HR 5311 on July 27.

Committee members agreed to reverse the House's 2 percent budget cut and restore the $1.6 million in funding for the University of the District of Columbia that the House had deleted.

The Senate committee also stayed away from the abortion issue, putting off a confrontation until the bill reached the floor.

In restoring the UDC funds, District Subcommittee Chairman Adams argued that the money was part of the school's operating funds, and he suggested that the committee send a letter of disapproval to the university instead.

However, Senate Appropriations Committee Chairman Robert C. Byrd, D-W.Va., said he opposed allowing the school to use the money in connection with the artwork.

"I'm very much opposed to spending the taxpayers' money for this, and people can call it censorship if they want to," Byrd said.

D.C. Appropriations

Following are the budget authority totals for the fiscal 1991 appropriations bill (HR 5311 — PL 101-518) for the District of Columbia.

(Figures, in thousands of dollars, may not add due to rounding.)

	President's Request	House Bill	Senate Bill	Final Bill
Federal Funds				
Federal payment	$ 430,500	$ 430,500	$ 430,500	$ 430,500
Contributions to retirement fund	52,070	52,070	52,070	52,070
St. Elizabeths Hospital	10,000	10,000	10,000	10,000
Drug Emergency	26,708	26,708	26,708	26,708
Other	0	21,340	30,350	30,422
Subtotal	$ 519,278	$ 540,618	$ 549,628	$ 549,700
2% across-the-board reduction	—	−10,812	—	—
Subtotal, federal funds	**$ 519,278**	**$ 529,806**	**$ 549,628**	**$ 549,700**
D.C. Funds	**$ 3,818,652**	**$ 3,852,792**	**$ 3,861,502**	**$ 3,862,574**
TOTAL DISTRICT BUDGET	**$ 4,337,930**	**$ 4,383,598**	**$ 4,411,130**	**$ 4,412,274**

SOURCE: House Appropriations Committee

SENATE FLOOR ACTION

When the D.C. spending bill went to the Senate floor Sept. 12, it bogged down over extraneous issues including homosexual rights and interstate trash disposal.

Senators eventually passed the $4.4 billion spending bill by voice vote on Sept. 18.

William L. Armstrong, R-Colo., offered an amendment on the floor to allow organizations such as the Boy Scouts of America to decide whether to accept homosexuals as counselors. Under the District's antidiscrimination ordinance, such organizations could not refuse to accept homosexuals.

Subcommittee Chairman Adams proposed a compromise to allow the organizations to exclude any person convicted of a sex crime involving a juvenile, anyone posing a threat of sexually abusing a minor, or anyone to whom a parent objected based on the person's sexual orientation.

The Adams amendment was adopted 98-0, but Adams' motion to table (kill) the Armstrong amendment failed on a vote of 45-54. Thus, both provisions remained in the bill as it went to conference. *(Votes 233, 234, p. 47-S)*

Trash Wars

Floor action then stalled after Daniel R. Coats, R-Ind., offered an amendment to allow states to choose whether to accept trash from other states and allow them to charge a fee for storing another state's garbage.

Coats had been trying all year to get the Senate to consider his bill (S 1921) to allow states such as Indiana to bar transportation and disposal of trash and refuse from other states. In May, he tried to attach it as an amendment to a chemical weapons sanctions bill (S 195), but a cloture vote shut off all non-germane amendments. *(Chemical weapons sanctions, p. 198)*

Coats then held up action on a bill to prohibit backhauling of garbage in food trucks, insisting on a vote on his legislation to allow states to refuse disposal of out-of-state garbage. *(Backhauling bill, p. 382)*

Coats finally won Sept. 18 when the Senate, on a 68-31 vote, agreed to attach his garbage-restrictive language to the D.C. spending bill. *(Vote 244, p. 49-S)*

The action came despite arguments from Adams that the amendment was not germane to the bill and despite a floor attack from New Jersey Democrats Frank R. Lautenberg and Bill Bradley.

They accused Coats of pushing the amendment as part of his re-election bid.

"It is ill-timed. It is an insult," Bradley said. "I hope that the senator will understand that what goes around comes around."

This time around, however, the amendment received bipartisan support. States that had developed their own 20-year solid-waste management plans would be allowed to ban imports of solid waste — but not hazardous waste — from other states.

It would also allow states to charge larger dumping fees for imported waste than for garbage generated within the state. States could still enter into regional compacts with other states for garbage disposal.

FINAL ACTION

Despite its surprising success in the Senate, Coats' plan to allow states to bar transportation and disposal of garbage from other states was unceremoniously stripped from HR 5311.

House and Senate conferees on the $4.4 billion bill agreed Oct. 12 to drop Coats' amendment.

House conferees, led by House D.C. Appropriations Subcommittee Chairman Dixon, argued that the amendment was not germane to the appropriations bill. In addition, Dixon said, John D. Dingell, D-Mich., the powerful House Energy and Commerce Committee chairman, had asked that the matter be studied further and fully aired in both houses.

Sen. Gramm contended that the amendment was ruled germane by a vote from the Senate and should be included. "I think the merits are overwhelming," he said.

But Rep. Bill Green, R-N.Y., reminded Gramm that the germaneness rules of the House differed from those of the Senate. Those rules, he said, "would make it almost impossible for us to pass it in the House."

'Shadow' Plans

Conferees also had a lengthy debate over provisions in both bills prohibiting the District from using federal funds and locally raised revenues to fund its plan to send a "shadow" delegation to Congress to lobby for statehood. After haggling over the wording, the House language was retained.

Dixon said he opposed including any such restrictive language but preferred to retain the House provision since it at least allowed District officials, if not shadow representatives, to lobby for statehood.

Gramm said he doubted that the House language would do the job. "Down the road we're creating a lot of problems for the District and ourselves if we don't go on and end this shadow business," Gramm said.

Report Rejected Over Abortion

The conferees also did not change the House abortion language in the bill, causing a highly charged debate when the conference report reached the House floor the week of Oct. 22. Anti-abortion advocates in the House claimed victory after defeating the conference report.

Their efforts, backed by President Bush's repeated veto threats, forced conferees to strike language to allow the District to use locally raised revenues to fund abortions.

The 195-211 defeat of HR 5311 on Oct. 25 followed an earlier 185-211 vote to reject the measure on Oct. 20. But with several members absent for that Saturday session, Democratic leaders decided to bring the bill back to the floor unchanged.

Both votes represented a significant reversal of a House vote in 1989, when an amendment to strip liberalized abortion language from the D.C. spending bill lost, 206-216. That provision was removed, however, following two vetoes by Bush.

Dixon conceded defeat after the second vote. He said the liberalized abortion provision would be dropped and the bill sent back to the House for passage late Oct. 26.

Dixon said, however, that he did not view the vote as a victory for anti-abortion forces. He said some members could have been expressing displeasure at the conduct of D.C. Mayor Marion S. Barry Jr., who was arrested and tried on drug charges in 1990, and at what they viewed as severe mismanagement of the city. *(D.C. politics, p. 428)*

The House adopted the conference report by voice vote Oct. 26 and sent it to the Senate, which cleared the measure, also by voice vote, in the early hours of Oct. 27.

In presenting the conference report to the Senate, subcommittee Chairman Adams noted that it appropriated $350,000 to begin a program for boarder babies and the children of drug abusers and $500,000 for a residential aftercare program for pregnant drug abusers. He also noted that the measure provided an additional $1 million for a Senate-recommended early childhood program.

Adams ended by voicing regret at the abortion funding restrictions. "I hope that in the future the president will permit District citizens the same rights as other citizens have and allow their local elected officials to decide how local tax dollars are spent," he said. ■

With Budget Tight, Congress' Funds Raised

The Senate on Oct. 27 sent President Bush a $2.16 billion fiscal 1991 appropriations bill for the legislative branch.

The Senate's voice vote clearing the conference report on the bill (HR 5399) came after the House had given its final approval to the measure the same day by 259-129. *(Vote 529, p. 166-H)*

Despite efforts to scale back the money Congress spent on itself, the appropriations bill was 11 percent more than the amount provided in the previous year. Final fiscal 1990 appropriations for Congress' own operations totaled $1.94 billion. *(1989 Almanac, p. 728)*

The spending measure also provided funding for several agencies related to Congress, including the Government Printing Office, the General Accounting Office and the Library of Congress.

BOXSCORE

Legislation: Fiscal 1991 appropriations for the legislative branch, PL 101-520 (HR 5399, S 3207).

Major action: Signed, Nov. 5. Conference report adopted by Senate, Oct. 27; by House, 259-129, Oct. 27. Passed by Senate, 72-24, Oct. 25; by House, 292-117, Oct. 21.

Reports: Conference report (H Rept 101-965). Appropriations (S Rept 101-533); Appropriations (H Rept 101-648).

Conferees included without major change proposals to impose new restrictions on the use of congressional mailing privileges in both the House and Senate. The bill still provided $122 million to pay for the franking privilege — including $33.2 million to make up for a shortfall in fiscal 1990 appropriations. *(Legislative mail, p. 75)*

Vic Fazio, Democrat of California and chairman of the House Appropriations Subcommittee on the Legislative Branch, said that if the $33.2 million in back mail payments was not counted in the fiscal 1991 total, the spending increase for fiscal 1991 was less than 8 percent.

The provisions restricting House mail, for the first time, required each House member to disclose the amount spent on franked mailings, gave each member a mailing budget, and required all mass mailings to be approved by the House Franking Commission. The Senate provisions restricted senators' ability to augment or transfer mail funds.

The main issue decided by the House-Senate conference committee was how much to cut from the spending increases recommended by the two chambers' Appropriations committees. During House floor debate, members voted to trim its $1.7 billion version of the bill, which did not yet include Senate funds, by 2 percent, or $34 million. The Senate voted to cut its $2.17 billion version of the bill, which included money for both the House and Senate, by 5 percent, or $109 million.

In conference, negotiators agreed to cut the compromise total of $2.2 billion by $34 million — a cut of less than 2 percent. The cuts were taken from more than a dozen different activities in the bill.

The reductions included $4.5 million from the $648 million provided for the House and $4.7 million from the $38.4 million for Senate office buildings.

Conferees retained House language authorizing a $50,000 increase in the budget each House member had to pay staff salaries, but it was unclear that there was enough money in the bill to finance such an increase. Fazio said that money would have to be shifted from other appropriations accounts to increase pay.

The conferees were at odds over a House provision to bar senators from using personal and political money to supplement their office expense accounts — a source of funds prohibited to House members. Conferees went along with the Senate version, which provided the prohibition would take effect Oct. 1, 1991.

Political Eyesore

Even though the bill included significant limits on the much criticized franking privilege, that accomplishment could not overshadow the political eyesore of Congress squabbling over funds for the House beauty salon, a proposed staff gym and modular office furniture while the rest of the government was nearly paralyzed over ways to reduce the federal deficit.

The appropriations bill for the legislative branch was a perennial target for criticism because it included financing for such perquisites as staff salaries, mailing privileges and office expenses.

But the political nerves exposed by the bill were especially raw in 1990 as hostility toward the government establishment rumbled across the electorate. To make matters worse, the bill came to the House and Senate floors less than three weeks before Election Day.

"It is ironic that after all the blood, sweat and tears, we finally pull up the last appropriations bill to reach the floor: the bill to feather our own nest," said Rep. Silvio O. Conte of Massachusetts, ranking Republican on the Appropriations Committee. "We've saved the best for last!"

But members' attacks on Congress' own budget were derided by Senate Appropriations Committee Chairman Robert C. Byrd, D-W.Va., as acts of "self-flagellation" that only encouraged public hostility to government.

"We should stop fouling our own nest," said Byrd. "He that maketh himself an ass must not take it ill if men ride him."

HOUSE COMMITTEE ACTION

The House Appropriations Subcommittee on the Legislative Branch on July 24 approved a 10 percent increase in spending for House operations in fiscal 1991, including $50,000 for every House member to raise staff salaries. But it put off handling the divisive issue of curbing congressional mailing privileges.

The subcommittee voted to provide $1.75 billion for running the House and other legislative operations in fiscal 1991.

The Senate was expected to add $500 million to the bill for its operations, bringing total appropriations for the legislative branch to $2.2 billion in fiscal 1991 — up from about $2 billion in fiscal 1990.

As the bill moved toward floor consideration, subcommittee Chairman Fazio said he expected the Rules Committee to structure floor debate to allow consideration of one or more plans to change franking. Fazio had been circulating proposals to impose new limits on the frank, which critics claimed was abused for political purposes. But he ran into resistance from incumbents of both parties.

As approved by the subcommittee, the appropriations bill included $59 million for franking in fiscal 1991 and about $33 million to pay for a big cost overrun in the House's fiscal 1990 mail budget.

The subcommittee bill included provisions that could make it easier for the House to cover future overruns without approving supplemental appropriations. The bill gave the subcommittee new authority to shift any unused money in other House operating accounts to pay for mail if appropriations for franking fell short.

The additional money for House staff salaries came just six months after House members received a controversial salary boost from $89,500 to $96,600 in February 1990. *(1989 Almanac, p. 51)*

Fazio said it was the first increase in the ceiling on members' staff salary accounts — about $447,000 per office in 1990 — other than cost of living hikes since 1975.

Subcommittee member David R. Obey, D-Wis., had pushed for bigger staff salary increases, arguing that better pay in the Senate and the private sector was contributing to high employee turnover in the House.

Full Committee

The House Appropriations Committee approved a fiscal 1991 legislative branch spending bill on July 30.

As approved by the committee, HR 5399 provided $1.7 billion for the House and other agencies; Senate spending was expected to bring the total to $2.2 billion.

Fazio had circulated a proposal to give each House member for the first time a mailing budget. Each member would be allotted the cost of three mailings to each household in his district — on average, $160,000 a year, although that figure was a point of contention. Members would also be allowed to use money from office and staff accounts for additional mail.

Some Democrats opposed any curbs on their mail, which was at the time without limit. But Republicans generally backed the proposed limits, and many sought fuller disclosure requirements.

The Senate on July 31 added mail curbs to a campaign finance bill (S 137). *(Campaign financing, p. 59)*

HOUSE FLOOR ACTION

The House passed its version of HR 5399 by 292-117 in an unusual Sunday session Oct. 21. *(Vote 501, p. 158-H)*

Before approving the bill, the House adopted several amendments that cut a total of $77 million from the Appropriations Committee recommendations, including $16 million to boost staff salaries.

The most rancorous debate erupted over a proposal by Harris W. Fawell, R-Ill., to cut $375,000 for renovating the House beauty salon. Female lawmakers said it was sexist because the cut did not apply to the House barbershop. The amendment, rejected by voice vote, also would have cut $25,000 to study the feasibility of a staff gym.

Another amendment, approved on a 35-21 standing vote, dropped a $500,000 allocation to study the use of modular furniture.

Mail Restrictions

The new restrictions on House mail were adopted on the floor by voice vote. They were designed to address criticism that the frank had been misused by incumbents for their political advantage. The Senate already had similar rules limiting members' mail budgets and requiring disclosure of how much each senator spent.

The deal struck by House leaders was an acknowledgment by the Democratic leadership that the cost of fighting the battle to preserve the frank as it existed in 1990 was not worth the gain, if it could be won at all. The franking privilege allowed members to sign their name to mail in lieu of postage. It was a popular device for members to communicate with constituents that had been routinely

Legislative Appropriations

Following are the budget authority totals in the fiscal 1991 appropriations bill (HR 5399 — PL 101-520) for the legislative branch:

(Figures, in thousands of dollars, may not add due to rounding.)

Agency	Fiscal 1990 Appropriations	House Bill	Senate Bill	Final Bill
Congressional Operations				
Senate	$ 392,429	—	$ 437,083	$ 437,083
House of Representatives	571,798	647,550	647,550	647,550
Joint Items	99,824	106,867	107,067	106,867
Office of Technology Assessment	18,376	19,557	19,557	19,557
Biomedical Ethics Board	590	—	—	—
Congressional Budget Office	19,229	19,229	21,183	21,183
Architect of the Capitol	114,847	97,415	137,426	139,806
Congressional Research Service	45,820	51,885	52,743	52,743
Government Printing Office (congressional printing)	74,149	77,365	79,515	79,615
SUBTOTAL	**$ 1,336,971**	**$ 1,019,868**	**$ 1,502,224**	**$ 1,504,404**
Related Agencies				
Botanic Garden	2,590	3,519	3,519	3,519
Library of Congress	207,240	227,579	231,364	232,369
Architect of the Capitol (library buildings)	7,136	14,868	10,268	15,268
Copyright Royalty Tribunal	101	127	127	127
Government Printing Office (non-congressional printing)	24,214	25,745	26,500	26,500
General Accounting Office	363,661	413,215	407,500	413,215
SUBTOTAL	**$ 604,942**	**$ 685,053**	**$ 679,278**	**$ 690,998**
General reduction	—	34,098	109,075	34,035
GRAND TOTAL	**$ 1,941,913**	**$ 1,670,823**	**$ 2,072,426**	**$ 2,161,367**

SOURCE: House Appropriations Committee

Record Number of Stopgap Spending Bills

A record number of stopgap spending measures or "continuing resolutions" (CRs) were approved in 1990 because none of the 13 regular appropriations bills were cleared by Oct. 1, 1990, the start of fiscal 1991. Six short-term bills were approved by Congress, but President Bush vetoed one, objecting that it was not accompanied by a deficit-reduction package.

The five CRs that were enacted — surpassing the previous record four CRs in 1987 — were needed to give budget negotiators time to craft a deal acceptable to both parties and then to give Congress time to wrap up work on the appropriations bills.

In addition to providing stopgap spending, the measures suspended automatic spending cuts that would have been triggered Oct. 1 under the Gramm-Rudman antideficit law; all but the first also extended the limit on federal borrowing.

The first CR provided supplemental funding for the military operations in the Persian Gulf, called Operation Desert Shield. *(Persian Gulf crisis, p. 717)*

Bush vetoed one of the CRs because the bipartisan budget agreement sent to the House on Oct. 5 was decisively rejected. A revolt by House Republicans killed the agreement and forced the White House and congressional budget negotiators back to the summit table. *(Budget summit, p. 129; veto message, p. 137)*

The president's veto of the stopgap measure shut down "non-essential" branches of the government and kept Congress in Washington and at work during the Columbus Day weekend Oct. 6-8.

Congress had passed one or more continuing resolutions every year since 1954 except 1988, when lawmakers completed the final appropriations bill one minute before the start of the new fiscal year. Three CRs were enacted in 1989, Bush's first year in office. *(1988 Almanac, p. 649; 1989 Almanac, p. 705)*

First Stopgap Spending Bill

The first fiscal 1991 CR (H J Res 655 — PL 101-403) was cleared Sept. 30, when Congress came to the end of fiscal 1990 without having finished work on any of the 13 regular appropriations bills. The House passed the short-term funding measure that day on a 382-41 vote; the Senate followed by voice vote. President Bush signed it into law Oct. 1. *(Vote 394, p. 128-H)*

H J Res 655 set defense spending at $263 billion in total obligational authority. For other programs, the resolution specified that spending was allowed to continue through Oct. 5 at the following levels:

- For bills that had passed both chambers, spending was at the lowest of the House-passed, the Senate-passed or the fiscal 1990 appropriations bills.
- For bills that had passed only the House, at the lower of the House-passed or fiscal 1990 bills.
- For bills not yet passed, at fiscal 1990 levels.

H J Res 655 also contained supplemental appropriations for fiscal 1990 of $2 billion for Operation Desert Shield. And it suspended automatic Gramm-Rudman cuts through Oct. 5.

The House Appropriations Committee approved the measure, 32-20, on Sept. 25 (H Rept 101-754). The committee rejected, 31-21, a move by panel Republicans to strip out the Desert Shield funding and offer it as a separate bill.

Republicans maintained that the Desert Shield funds should not be held hostage to the rest of the bill, which Bush had threatened to veto over the provision to suspend the Gramm-Rudman cuts for 20 days.

The committee also approved, by voice vote, an amendment by David R. Obey, D-Wis., to suspend foreign aid restrictions temporarily and permit the United States to continue aid to Egypt, a key U.S. ally in the Persian Gulf crisis, without regard to its ability to make payments on its outstanding debts to the United States.

Bush Vetoes Bill

Congress worked late in the day Oct. 5 to pass a new continuing appropriations bill (H J Res 660) that leaders hoped would prevent a shutdown of the government when existing spending authority expired at midnight.

But Bush ended up vetoing the bill Oct. 6, insisting that Congress first agree on an acceptable budget. The government shutdown was felt sporadically over the weekend and on Columbus Day, Monday Oct. 8.

This second CR would have permitted government agencies to continue spending money for another week at the same levels in effect since the new fiscal year began Oct. 1.

The House had approved the measure, 300-113, a little after 7 p.m. Oct. 5. The Senate cleared it by voice vote later that night. *(Vote 431, p. 140-H)*

In a Saturday session Oct. 6, the House failed on a 260-138 vote to override Bush's veto — only six votes short of the two-thirds majority that Democrats needed to beat the president.

It was a narrow escape, but a heartening win for both

abused by some members as a campaign tool.

In 1989, the House agreed to limit members to using their franking privilege no more than three times a year for newsletters sent to every postal patron. But the House refused to join the Senate in making each member publicly accountable for a mail budget.

As crafted by Fazio and Minnesota Republican Bill Frenzel, the new House rules:

- Gave each member an individual mail budget equal to the amount needed to make three first-class mailings to every non-business address in his district.
- Allowed members to supplement their mail budget by transferring up to $25,000 a year from other accounts for other office expenses.
- Required the amount each member spent to be reported quarterly.
- Required all mailings to more than 500 recipients to be approved by the House Franking Commission.

SENATE ACTION

The Senate Appropriations Committee approved its

Needed During Struggle for Budget Accord

House Republicans and Bush. *(Vote 433, p. 140-H)*

Second Stopgap Bill Enacted

Over the weekend, Congress adopted a new budget resolution, leading Bush to accept a new stopgap measure that it sent to him in the early hours of Tuesday, Oct. 9 (H J Res 666 — PL 101-412). Bush signed it that morning, restoring full federal government operations just in time for the start of the first normal workday after the three-day holiday weekend.

The new stopgap spending measure permitted the government to continue operating through Oct. 19. The formula for continued spending was the same as in the other emergency spending bills: For appropriations bills that had passed both chambers, funding was continued at the lowest of the two versions or the fiscal 1990 level; for bills that had passed only the House, the total was the House level or 1990, whichever was lower; for bills not yet passed, it was the 1990 levels.

The CR also allowed the government to continue borrowing money through Oct. 19 and suspended automatic cuts under the Gramm-Rudman antideficit law during the same period.

Amendments offered by House Minority Leader Robert H. Michel, R-Ill., to change the expiration date of the resolution to Oct. 12 and to put in place limited Gramm-Rudman cuts failed, the first by voice vote and the second by a vote of 186-224. The bill was approved Oct. 8 on a 305-105 vote. *(Votes 437, 438, p. 140-H)*

The Senate passed the bill by voice vote that evening, with amendments. The House cleared it, 362-3, shortly before 2 a.m. the next morning. *(Vote 439, p. 140-H)*

Third CR

With little fanfare — and none of the acrimony that had accompanied similar actions since the end of September — the House passed another stopgap spending bill (H J Res 677 — PL 101-444) on Oct. 18 to keep the government functioning through midnight Oct. 24. The Senate followed suit Oct. 19, the day that the previous CR was set to expire.

The measure also further suspended automatic spending cuts triggered by the Gramm-Rudman law and allowed a temporary increase in the federal government's limit on total borrowing to stay in effect through Oct. 24.

Bush indicated Oct. 18 that he would not object to a further stopgap measure, provided conferees were making progress on the reconciliation bill (HR 5835). That assurance removed a threat that the government would face another temporary shutdown like the one over the Columbus Day weekend. *(Budget reconciliation, p. 138)*

The new bill continued spending for appropriated government accounts at the lowest of the following spending levels for each regular appropriations bill: the level agreed on in conference committee, the House-passed level, the Senate-passed level, or the fiscal 1990 spending level.

The formula, according to Silvio O. Conte of Massachusetts, ranking Republican on the House Appropriations Committee, was the equivalent of an annual $28.5 billion reduction in new budget authority and an $11.5 billion cut in outlays below the spending levels assumed in the final budget resolution for fiscal 1991 (H Con Res 310) that had been adopted Oct. 9. *(Budget resolution, p. 136)*

The House passed the latest measure by a 379-37 vote, and the Senate did so by unanimous consent. Bush signed it Oct. 19. *(Vote 487, p. 154-H)*

Fourth CR

With a final deal on a reconciliation bill in sight — and none of the 13 regular appropriations bills signed into law — Congress on Oct. 24 cleared yet another stopgap spending measure. The latest emergency bill, the fourth since the fiscal year began Oct. 1, kept the government going through midnight Oct. 27. Bush signed the bill Oct. 25.

Like its predecessors, the bill (H J Res 681 — PL 101-461) took the place of unfinished appropriations bills, suspended automatic spending cuts triggered by the Gramm-Rudman act and allowed a temporary increase in the federal government's borrowing limit.

The House passed the bill by a vote of 380-45 the evening of Oct. 24. The Senate cleared it the same evening by voice vote. *(Vote 518, p. 164-H)*

Fifth and Final Stopgap Bill

The fifth and final CR to be enacted was cleared Oct. 27 and signed by Bush on Oct. 28 (H J Res 687 — PL 101-467).

The measure provided government funding through Nov. 5 in order to give the president time to sign the 13 appropriations bills.

The House passed the bill, 283-49, on Oct. 27; the Senate cleared it by voice vote later the same day. *(Vote 533, p. 168-H)*

version (S 3207) of a legislative branch spending bill on Oct. 16.

The $33 million allocated for mail in the Senate bill was expected to fall during floor action.

The Senate spent $17 million on mail in fiscal 1990, less than the $23 million that was appropriated, according to Harry Reid, D-Nev., chairman of the Legislative Branch Subcommittee.

Reid attributed the reduction to the Senate's decision in 1989 to force disclosure of individual spending.

Don Nickles of Oklahoma, the ranking Republican on the subcommittee, attempted to offer amendments to bar senators from transferring mail funds among one another and from carrying forward unspent funds from one year to the next.

He also sought to limit the amount a senator could transfer into the mail account from other office accounts or from his mail account into his office accounts.

At the request of Appropriations Committee Chairman Byrd, Nickles agreed to hold his amendments for floor action. Byrd said he did not want to trespass on matters in the Rules Committee's purview.

The Senate on Oct. 25 approved its version of HR 5399 72-24, after cutting 5 percent from the amount recommended by the Appropriations Committee. The amendment by Nickles was approved by voice vote after a motion to table it failed 32-60. *(Votes 314, 310, p. 61-S)*

The Senate also adopted, by voice vote, another Nickles amendment to reduce the amount included for Senate mail to $30 million.

Nickles initially sought $24 million, the fiscal 1990 amount — but compromised in the face of vigorous objections from Ted Stevens, R-Alaska.

Other amendments adopted during the Senate debate:

- Allowed senators to retain unused mail funds for future use but only until the next fiscal year.
- Allowed senators to transfer money from their mail accounts to other accounts in amounts not exceeding $100,000 or 50 percent of their mass mail budget, whichever was less. The Appropriations Committee proposed allowing that new transfer authority with no limit on the amount.
- Barred the transfer of mail funds from one senator to another, as was allowed in 1990 without restriction.

During the House-Senate conference, negotiators accepted without major change both the House and Senate proposals to impose new restrictions on the use of congressional mailing privileges. ■

Chapter 13

POLITICAL REPORT

1990 Elections Overview 901
  Voter Turnout 901
Personal Characteristics, New Members, 101st Congress .. 902
Incumbents' Performance 903
  Incumbent Re-Election Rates, 1946-90 903
  Incumbents' Falloff 904
  Close Calls in House 905
  Personal Lows 906
  1990 Vote Totals by Party 907
Congressional Election Spending 908
Yeutter Selected To Head RNC 909
Senate Races 911
Senate Membership — 102nd Congress 912
  Senate Membership Changes 913
Seymour Appointed To Succeed Wilson 913
Years of Expiration of Senate Terms 914
House Races 916
  House Members Defeated 917
  House Membership Changes 918
  Party Gains and Losses 919
House Membership — 102nd Congress 920
Independent Bernard Sanders 922
Characteristics of 102nd Congress 923
  Minorities in Congress 924
  Occupations, Religion 925
Gubernatorial Races 926
  1991 Statehouse Occupants 927
Reapportionment and Redistricting 930
  Key Redistricting States 931
Patronage Ruling 933
1990 Special Elections 934
1990 Election Results 935

Voters React More to Local Issues

Most members survived, but many margins narrow

Peace and prosperity were the two issues that had driven the 1988 elections. But while war and recession hovered ominously over the 1990 campaign, neither figured prominently in its outcome. Instead, the election campaigns looked more like a series of hard-fought city council contests, shaped largely by personalities, local issues and a pronounced absence of clear-cut national themes.

While frustrated voters talked tough, on Nov. 6 they returned incumbents to Washington en masse.

The ambiguous results reinforced two of the traits — the lack of party discipline and the erosion of confidence in government — that had made Congress so hard to lead. Incumbents prospered most by blaming the mess on somebody else, in effect running against Washington. And neither party emerged with a mandate — not that either sought one.

By compromising on the budget, President Bush and Congress' Democratic leadership prevented the election from becoming a referendum on economic policy. Divisive issues such as taxes and abortion played out inconsistently across party and state lines. Even the growing prospects for war with Iraq failed to stir a wide-ranging debate over U.S. policy in the Persian Gulf.

The mixed signals were illustrated by the warning shots fired at two high-profile incumbents. New Jersey voters, riled at tax hikes pushed by their Democratic governor, James J. Florio, vented their spleen on Democratic Sen. Bill Bradley, widely regarded as presidential timber. They sent Bradley back for a third term, but just by a 3 percentage point margin.

House GOP Whip Newt Gingrich of Georgia led the charge against taxes in Washington, but he escaped defeat in the Atlanta suburbs by fewer than 1,000 votes. His inattentiveness to striking Eastern Airlines workers almost cost him re-election. The message, Gingrich said, was this: "It's to pay more attention, to listen more, to reach out to people more to make sure you're their incumbent."

The lineup on Capitol Hill would look familiar come 1991. Not one committee chairman who sought re-election lost, although only five subcommittee chairmen fell.

Bush's hand was weakened. Republicans lost one Senate seat and eight House seats. He faced the possibility of

PARTY LINEUP

102nd Congress
(As of Jan. 10, 1991)

Senate		House	
Democrats	56	Democrats	267
Republicans	44	Republicans	167
		Independent	1

101st Congress
(As of Oct. 28, 1990)

Senate		House [1]	
Democrats	55	Democrats	258
Republicans	45	Republicans	175

[1] *Two vacancies at end of session. One seat had been held by a Democrat, one by a Republican.*

1990 Voter Turnout: Onward and Downward

Midterm Election Turnouts Since 1962, Based on House Votes Cast

(Percentage of voting-age population)

The voter turnout rate in midterm elections had been declining since 1962. It fell sharply after the voting age was lowered to 18 in 1971 and continued downward, except for the recession year of 1982.

In 1990, turnout for House contests was 33.0 percent, the lowest point since the wartime election of 1942.

Turnout was below 20 percent in three states: Louisiana, where only one district was decided in November; Mississippi; and Tennessee.

In only four states did a majority of the voting-age population participate in voting for the House: Maine (55.6 percent), Minnesota (54.8 percent), Montana (54.6 percent) and Alaska (52.5 percent).

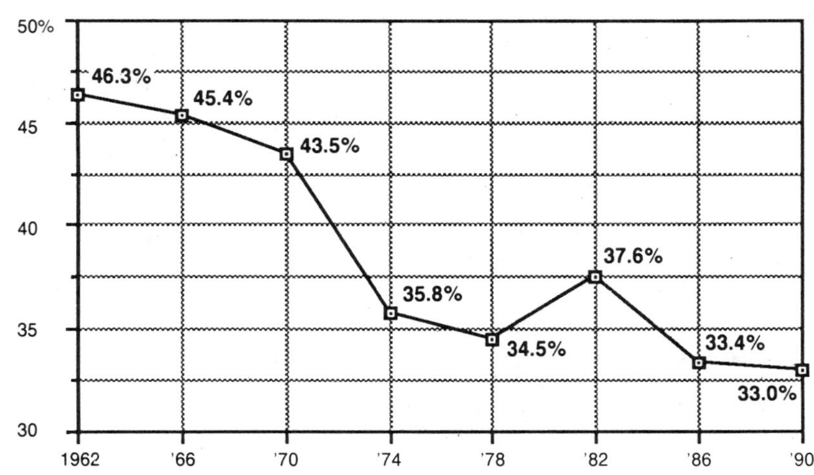

SOURCE: Census Bureau, 1962-86; Congressional Quarterly, 1990, using voting-age population projections from Census Bureau.

finding it tougher to sustain vetoes in the House. The GOP's greatest damage, however, sprang from its failure to meet its own expectations, announced before Bush's shift on taxes and when his soaring popularity held out the hope of defying history and gaining seats or breaking even.

Conversely, the Democratic leadership emerged slightly stronger, although it still lacked the troops to easily override a veto. Nor were the House's Democratic incumbents, many re-elected by their thinnest margins in years, likely to act with abandon; many did not know who they would represent after redistricting.

"A window has opened for Democrats; the question is whether they are going to be able to go through it," said Peter H. Fenn, a Democratic political consultant.

Some Trends Seen

The statehouse proved to be the real workshop of democracy in 1990. The throw-the-bums-out sentiment overtook incumbent Republican governors in Florida, Nebraska, Kansas and Rhode Island, and Democrats in Michigan and Minnesota. Seven other statehouses also changed hands, to Republicans in Vermont, Ohio, Arizona and Massachusetts, and to Democrats in Oklahoma, Texas and New Mexico. Republicans running as independents won in Connecticut and Alaska. *(Gubernatorial races, p. 926)*

Moreover, California and Colorado joined Oklahoma's earlier decision to impose term limits on officeholders. But the broad anti-incumbent sentiment expressed toward Congress in pre-election polls did not materialize in the polling place. *(Term limits, p. 13)*

In the Senate, 31 of 32 incumbents seeking re-election won. The lone victor among Senate challengers, Democrat Paul Wellstone of Minnesota, described a system stacked against a challenger.

"There are so many advantages — the franking privilege, a tremendous mismatch of resources in terms of finances — that, you know, I still think the incumbents have a tremendous advantage even when people are very dissatisfied," Wellstone said. *(Senate races, p. 911)*

In the House, the anti-incumbent sentiment was translated into marginal victories rather than outright defeats. Of the 407 House incumbents who sought re-election in 1990, 392 won — a 96 percent re-election rate. Total turnover, including retirements, amounted to just 10 percent. Still, there was ample cause for concern: About 85 incumbents won with less than 60 percent of the vote, roughly double the number of 1988. Fifty-three House members were re-elected with their lowest winning percentage ever, while 57 won with their lowest vote share since they were first elected. *(Personal lows, p. 906)*

"Obviously, the anti-incumbent sentiment didn't end today," warned Edward J. Rollins, executive director of the National Republican Campaign Committee, the House GOP's campaign arm. Democratic pollster Harrison Hickman added: "If anybody dodged the bullet, my advice would be, don't assume it's the only bullet in the gun."

The depressed margins of victory also accounted for an anomaly: Despite winning more House seats (267) in 1990 than in any election since the recession-year contest of 1982, the Democrats' share of the total, nationwide congressional vote was their lowest for any midterm election since 1966.

In 1990, Democratic candidates drew just 52.9 percent of all House votes cast across the country. By comparison, when Democrats captured 269 seats in 1982 (just two more than in 1990), their share of the total nationwide congressional vote was 55.2 percent, more than 2 percentage points higher than in 1990. *(Vote totals by party, p. 907)*

The election also taught incumbents a lesson certain to complicate the leadership's task. Insiders trying to look like outsiders would be even less likely to blindly hew to party lines. House Republicans in particular had less reason to take their lead from the White House. But Democratic leaders bent on sharpening their differences with Republicans on the tax "fairness" issue could also find it hard to bring their members along. *(House races, p. 916)*

Backlash Backfires

Republicans entered the year confident that a solid front against new taxes would produce a confrontation over the budget and a subsequent backlash against Democrats. They got their confrontation, but the subsequent compromise killed the backlash. Taxes went up, but voters did not know who to blame. The upshot was that the tax issue, like

Personal Characteristics

New Members 101st Congress, 2nd Session

Following is a compilation of information about individual members who joined the 101st Congress during 1990 — their birth dates, occupations, religions and seniority within their parties. Two members joined after the 101st Congress had adjourned: Robert E. Andrews, elected to the House in a special election Nov. 6, and Robert C. Smith, appointed to the Senate on Dec. 7. *(Membership changes, p. 14; 1990 special elections, p. 934; characteristics, other members, 1989 Almanac, p. 3-E)*

SENATE

HAWAII

Daniel K. Akaka (D) -- Sept. 11, 1924. Occupation: elementary school teacher, public official. Religion: Congregationalist. Seniority: 55.

NEW HAMPSHIRE

Robert C. Smith (R) -- March 30, 1941. Occupation: real estate broker. Religion: Roman Catholic. Seniority: 45.

HOUSE

HAWAII

2 Patsy T. Mink (D) -- Dec. 6, 1927. Occupation: lawyer. Religion: Protestant. Seniority: 258.

NEW YORK

14 Susan Molinari (R) -- March 27, 1958. Occupation: public official. Religion: Roman Catholic. Seniority: 175.

18 Jose E. Serrano (D) -- Oct. 24, 1943. Occupation: public official. Religion: Roman Catholic. Seniority: 257.

NEW JERSEY

1 Robert E. Andrews (D) -- Aug. 4, 1957. Occupation: law professor. Religion: Episcopalian. Seniority: 259.

two of 1990's other prominent issues, abortion and the savings and loan debacle, cut unevenly.

Voters defeated two anti-abortion rights initiatives in Oregon, but returned Sen. Mark O. Hatfield, a Republican whose stance against abortion served as a reminder that single issues only rarely decided elections. Likewise, voters in Iowa re-elected anti-abortion GOP Gov. Terry E. Branstad but also sent abortion rights Democrat Tom Harkin back to the Senate.

Ties to S&L operators helped turn out House incumbents Denny Smith, R-Ore.; Douglas H. Bosco, D-Calif.; and Charles "Chip" Pashayan Jr., R-Calif. But similar campaigns mounted against Reps. Bill Lowery, R-Calif.; Doug Barnard Jr., D-Ga.; and David E. Price, D-N.C., failed.

The biggest victim on Election Day was the GOP's four-year plan to wrest Congress from the Democrats. The strategy called for chipping away at Democratic margins in the House and Senate in 1990, while holding key governorships in Florida, Texas and California, states slated together to gain 14 new House seats after reapportionment. The GOP was then to go over the top in at least one chamber in 1992, when Democrats would have to defend 20 Senate seats, compared with 15 for the GOP.

Republicans kept the crown jewel, the California governorship, but the rest of the strategy fell apart. Democrats not only captured statehouses in Florida and Texas, but also increased their ranks in Congress.

The GOP sought to put the defeats in their best light: The party would have a say, either through a legislative chamber or a governor, in how 231 House seats were redrawn for 1992, up from 65 in 1982. *(State legislature races and redistricting, p. 930)*

For his part, Democratic National Committee Chairman Ronald H. Brown called the election a "referendum on the leadership — or lack thereof — of George Bush, and he failed that test." Like many Democrats, Brown saw a wounded president in the election returns, and the White House in the offing.

The alignment on Capitol Hill beckoned confrontation to test the limits of divided government. Voters asked for change Nov. 6, but they did not demand it. The question hanging over the following two years was whether the voters would go so easily on incumbents next time. ■

Incumbents Battle Local Voter Distrust

Although few members of Congress were defeated in 1990, the voting for House incumbents contained more indications of voter dissatisfaction than was apparent in the simple tally of wins and losses.

Only 16 House members were defeated, producing the fourth straight election that House incumbents had a 95-percent-plus re-election rate. *(Incumbents' re-election rates 1946-90, this page)*

While few incumbents were beaten, however, many were chastened. According to computations by Congressional Quarterly, the average vote for House incumbents with major-party opposition fell in 1990 to 63.5 percent. That was nearly 5 percentage points below the incumbent average in 1986 and 1988, and barely 2 points above the incumbent average in the volatile Watergate election of 1974 or the more competitive congressional elections of the 1950s. *(Incumbents' vote percentage, p. 908)*

In addition, 53 House members were re-elected in 1990 with their lowest winning percentage ever, and 57 won with their lowest vote share since they were first elected. Combined, these two categories constituted about one-fourth of the House membership in the 102nd Congress. *(Personal lows, p. 906)*

The group was geographically diverse. Counting both kinds of lows, the group included members from 30 states.

Still, voter reaction was particularly acute in certain states or regions, — such as Georgia, Missouri and Southern California.

The cast of incumbents that hit the skids in 1990 was bipartisan, which in itself was noteworthy.

On the average, Democratic congressional candidates ran several percentage points better in midterm elections than they did in presidential years, when they usually had to buck the tide produced by a strong Republican national ticket.

In 1990, however, about three of five House members

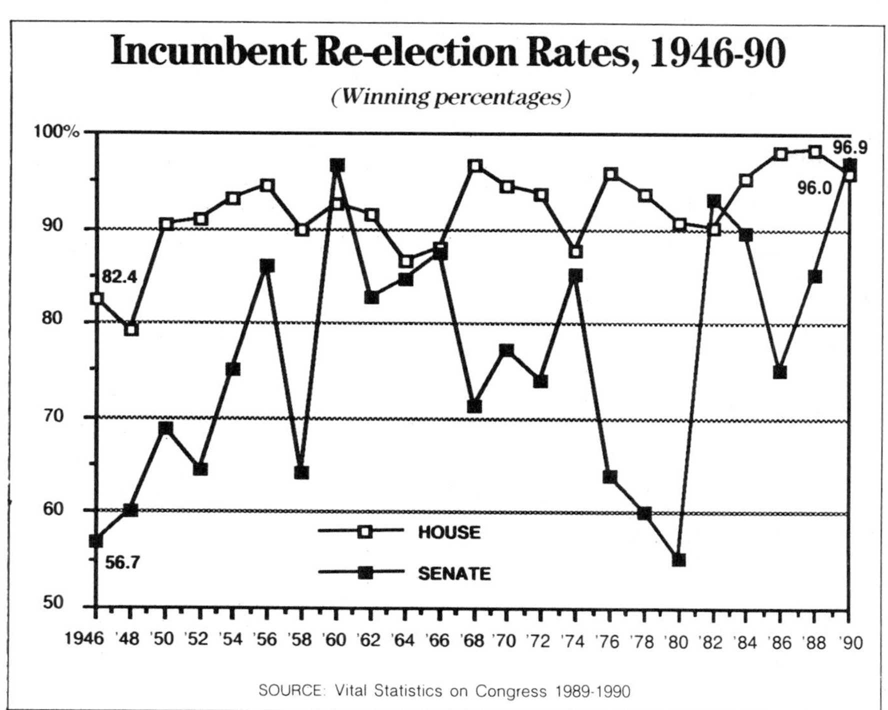

SOURCE: Vital Statistics on Congress 1989-1990

The 1990 Incumbents' Falloff

Although the vast majority of congressional and gubernatorial incumbents won re-election Nov. 6, many saw their vote shares drop off dramatically from their last race.

Below is a list of the incumbents who suffered the greatest falloff in percentage point terms from their last general election: 1988 for members of the House, 1984 for members of the Senate, and 1986 for most incumbent governors. Only incumbents who faced major-party competition in both elections are included.

House	1990 Vote Percent	Change in (% points)	Result	Years in Office
Douglas H. Bosco, D-Calif. (1)	42	−27	Lost	8
Charles "Chip" Pashayan Jr., R-Calif. (17)	45	−26	Lost	12
Herbert H. Bateman, R-Va. (1)	51	−22	Won	8
Ralph Regula, R-Ohio (16)	59	−20	Won	18
Richard T. Schulze, R-Pa. (5)	57	−20	Won	16
Bill Lowery, R-Calif. (41)	49	−19	Won	10
John J. LaFalce, D-N.Y. (32)	54	−18	Won	16
Don Sundquist, R-Tenn. (7)	62	−18	Won	8
Al McCandless, R-Calif. (37)	49	−17	Won	8
Jim Bates, D-Calif. (44)	45	−17	Lost	8
Earl Hutto, D-Fla. (1)	52	−17	Won	12
Jack Buechner, R-Mo. (2)	50	−17	Lost	4
Stan Parris, R-Va. (8)	45	−17	Lost	12
Chalmers P. Wylie, R-Ohio (15)	59	−16	Won	24
Toby Roth, R-Wis. (8)	54	−16	Won	12
Olympia J. Snowe, R-Maine (2)	51	−15	Won	12
Thomas C. Sawyer, D-Ohio (14)	60	−15	Won	4
Rod Chandler, R-Wash. (8)	56	−15	Won	8
Bob Stump, R-Ariz. (3)	57	−14	Won	14
Pete Stark, D-Calif. (9)	59	−14	Won	18
Carlos J. Moorhead, R-Calif. (22)	59	−14	Won	18
Jan Meyers, R-Kan. (3)	60	−14	Won	6
Gerry E. Studds, D-Mass. (10)	53	−14	Won	18
Guy Vander Jagt, R-Mich. (9)	55	−14	Won	24
Joe Kolter, D-Pa. (4)	56	−14	Won	8
Doug Walgren, D-Pa. (18)	49	−14	Lost	14

Senate	1990 Vote Percent	Change in (% points)	Result	Years in Office
Larry Pressler, R-S.D.	52	−22	Won	12
Alan K. Simpson, R-Wyo.	64	−14	Won	12
Bill Bradley, D-N.J.	51	−13	Won	12
William S. Cohen, R-Maine	61	−12	Won	12
Mark O. Hatfield, R-Ore.	54	−12	Won	24
Claiborne Pell, D-R.I.	62	−11	Won	30
Rudy Boschwitz, R-Minn.	48	−10	Lost	12

Governors	1990 Vote Percent	Change in (% points)	Result	Years in Office
Edward D. DiPrete, R-R.I.	26	−25	Lost	6
William Donald Schaefer, D-Md.	60	−22	Won	4
James J. Blanchard, D-Mich.	50	−18	Lost	8
Mario M. Cuomo, D-N.Y.	53	−12	Won	8
Bob Martinez, R-Fla.	43	−12	Lost	4

NOTE: Percentages for 1990 are based on nearly complete, unofficial returns. In most races they reflect only the major-party vote, although in some contests, especially in California and New York, the third-party vote was included. The 1988 House vote percentages that are used as a point of comparison are based on nearly complete, unofficial returns published in the 1988 CQ Almanac. The Senate and gubernatorial vote percentages from earlier years are based on official returns.

who registered either a personal low winning percentage or their lowest since their first election were Democrats.

In other words, Democrats were about as common on the list of low-percentage winners as they were in the House itself.

The depressed margins accounted for an anomaly: Despite winning more House seats (267) in 1990 than in any election since the recession-year contest of 1982, the Democrats' share of the total, nationwide congressional vote was their lowest for any midterm election since 1966.

In 1990, Democratic candidates drew just 52.9 percent of all House votes cast across the country. By comparison, when Democrats captured 269 seats in 1982 (just two more than in 1990), their share of the total nationwide congressional vote was 55.2 percent, more than 2 percentage points higher than in 1990. *(Vote totals by party, p. 907)*

For many incumbents, identification with Washington was no asset. And, to a degree, vulnerability seemed to increase with seniority. The vast majority of members (40 of the 53) who registered their lowest winning percentage in 1990 had served at least three terms; 22 had served six or more terms.

A number of House heavyweights were among those members registering their lowest winning percentage. There was Majority Leader Richard A. Gephardt of Missouri, and the No. 2 and No. 3 members of the House GOP leadership: Whip Newt Gingrich of Georgia, who won a seventh term by less than 1,000 votes; and Republican Conference Chairman Jerry Lewis of California.

The two parties' campaign chiefs — Vic Fazio, Calif., chairman of the Democratic Congressional Campaign Committee (DCCC), and Guy Vander Jagt of Michigan, chairman of the National Republican Congressional Committee (NRCC) — won re-election in 1990 with less than 55 percent of the vote. (Fazio became DCCC chairman after the election.)

Several Democratic committee chairmen also registered personal lows, including Judiciary Committee Chairman Jack Brooks of Texas, Small Business Committee Chairman John J. LaFalce of New York, and Post Office and Civil Service Committee Chairman William L. Clay, who represented the St. Louis district adjacent to Gephardt's.

1990 House Elections: More Close Calls

There was a marked upsurge in competitive House elections in 1990 after a relative paucity of such contests in the late 1980s. Sixty members (35 Democrats, 25 Republicans) won seats in 1990 year with no more than 55 percent of the vote, up from 38 members in 1988. Moreover, 35 of the 1990 crop of "marginal" victors were incumbents, up from 21 in 1988. Of the others who won with 55 percent or less in 1990, 13 were competing for open seats and 12 were challengers.

A sub-55 showing can be an ominous sign for a veteran member. Of the 21 incumbents who won re-election in 1988 with no more than 55 percent, five were then beaten in 1990 (Democrats Roy Dyson of Maryland and James McClure Clarke of North Carolina and Republicans John Hiler of Indiana, Arlan Stangeland of Minnesota and Denny Smith of Oregon). A sixth, Republican Patricia Saiki of Hawaii, ran unsuccessfully for the Senate.

For less-senior members, a low percentage may be less cause for alarm. Of the 17 House freshmen who were elected in 1988 with no more than 55 percent, only one was beaten in 1990 (Republican Peter Smith of Vermont), and just four others were back on the "marginal" list last year.

In the chart below, House incumbents are designated by the letter "I," with the year they were first elected appearing in parentheses. Members who won in 1990 as challengers are designated by "C" and open-seat winners by "OS."

The numbers at right are their percentage shares of the 1990 vote, based on official returns from state election agencies, and are based on total votes cast (not just major-party votes).

Democrats

	Member	Status	%
1)	Frank Pallone Jr. (N.J. 3)	I ('88)	49.1
2)	Joan Kelly Horn (Mo. 2)	C	50.0
3)	Bernard J. Dwyer (N.J. 6)	I ('80)	50.5
	Al Swift (Wash. 2)	I ('78)	50.5
5)	Carl C. Perkins (Ky. 7)	I ('84)	50.8
6)	Tim Roemer (Ind. 3)	C	50.9
7)	Charles Luken (Ohio 1)	OS	51.1
8)	James P. Moran Jr. (Va. 8)	C	51.7
9)	Jim Bacchus (Fla. 11)	OS	51.9
10)	Nick J. Rahall II (W.Va. 4)	I ('76)	52.0
11)	Rosa DeLauro (Conn. 3)	OS	52.1
12)	Chester G. Atkins (Mass. 5)	I ('84)	52.2
	Earl Hutto (Fla. 1)	I ('78)	52.2
14)	Ben Jones (Ga. 4)	I ('88)	52.4
15)	William J. Jefferson (La. 2)	OS	52.5
16)	George E. Brown Jr. (Calif. 36)	I ('62)	52.7
	Dick Swett (N.H. 2)	C	52.7
18)	Larry LaRocco (Idaho 1)	OS	53.0
	Marilyn Lloyd (Tenn. 3)	I ('74)	53.0
20)	Jim Jontz (Ind. 5)	I ('86)	53.1
21)	Robert J. Mrazek (N.Y. 3)	I ('82)	53.3
22)	Gerry E. Studds (Mass. 10)	I ('72)	53.4
23)	Chet Edwards (Texas 11)	OS	53.5
	Collin C. Peterson (Minn. 7)	C	53.5
25)	Frank Annunzio (Ill. 11)	I ('64)	53.6
26)	Jolene Unsoeld (Wash. 3)	I ('88)	53.8
27)	Robert E. Andrews (N.J. 1)	OS	54.3
	Greg Laughlin (Texas 14)	I ('88)	54.3
29)	Calvin Dooley (Calif. 17)	C	54.5
30)	John W. Cox Jr. (Ill. 16)	OS	54.6
31)	Vic Fazio (Calif. 4)	I ('78)	54.7
	Frank McCloskey (Ind. 8)	I ('82)	54.7
33)	John J. LaFalce (N.Y. 32)	I ('74)	55.0
	W. G. "Bill" Hefner (N.C. 8)	I ('74)	55.0
	Mike Kopetski (Ore. 5)	C	55.0

Republicans

	Member	Status	%
1)	Frank Riggs (Calif. 1)	C	43.3
2)	Randy "Duke" Cunningham (Calif. 44)	C	46.3
3)	Bill Lowery (Calif. 41)	I ('80)	49.2
4)	Al McCandless (Calif. 37)	I ('82)	49.7
5)	Jim Nussle (Iowa 2)	OS	49.8
6)	Newt Gingrich (Ga. 6)	I ('78)	50.3
7)	Charles H. Taylor (N.C. 11)	C	50.7
8)	Olympia J. Snowe (Maine 2)	I ('78)	51.0
	Herbert H. Bateman (Va. 1)	I ('82)	51.0
10)	Bill Barrett (Neb. 3)	OS	51.1
11)	Bill Dickinson (Ala. 2)	I ('64)	51.3
12)	Rick Santorum (Pa. 18)	C	51.4
13)	John T. Doolittle (Calif. 14)	OS	51.5
14)	Don Young (Alaska AL)	I ('73)	51.7
	Gary Franks (Conn. 5)	OS	51.7
16)	E. Thomas Coleman (Mo. 6)	I ('76)	51.9
17)	John Miller (Wash. 1)	I ('84)	52.0
18)	Mel Hancock (Mo. 7)	I ('88)	52.1
	James V. Hansen (Utah 1)	I ('80)	52.1
20)	Scott L. Klug (Wis. 2)	C	53.2
21)	Toby Roth (Wis. 8)	I ('78)	53.5
22)	Wayne Allard (Colo. 4)	OS	54.1
23)	Robert J. Lagomarsino (Calif. 19)	I ('74)	54.6
	Raymond J. McGrath (N.Y. 5)	I ('80)	54.6
25)	Guy Vander Jagt (Mich. 9)	I ('66)	54.8

Some incumbents' all-time lows reflected less vulnerability than others'.

For example, in 1990 the all-time low for Democrat Kweisi Mfume, who represented a black-majority district in Baltimore, was 85 percent.

Similarly, Democrat Ted Weiss, who represented a liberal constituency on Manhattan's West Side, had a personal low of 80 percent.

The lowest winning percentage for Republican Joel Hefley, whose district was anchored by the military-oriented Colorado Springs, was 66 percent.

Of the 53 House incumbents who hit a personal low in 1990, 35 drew less than 60 percent of the vote. For them, the results were likely to be a wakeup call for 1992, when lingering or intensified antipolitician sentiment could be expected to interact with new district lines to put them at greater risk.

Political Geography

Whatever message voters were sending members of

Hitting Personal Lows

Members' winning percentages in 1990

Only 15 House incumbents were defeated for re-election in November 1990, but 53 others scored their lowest winning percentage ever. Six were members of the class of 1988 — Democrats Ben Jones of Georgia, Frank Pallone Jr. of New Jersey and Jim McDermott of Washington; and Republicans Dana Rohrabacher of California, Mel Hancock of Missouri and Ronald K. Machtley of Rhode Island.

The other 47 are listed in order of seniority in the chart below. Their official share of the vote in 1990 is compared with their lowest share in any previous general election. All percentages are based on total votes cast.

Not on this list are many House veterans who made their weakest showing in years. Among them: Frank Horton, R-N.Y., who drew his lowest percentage (63) since 1964; Walter B. Jones, D-N.C., his lowest (65) since 1966 and Frank Annunzio, D-Ill., his lowest (54) since 1972. Even Speaker Thomas S. Foley, D-Wash., had his lowest percentage (69) since 1982.

	First Elected	1990 Percentage	Previous Low Percentage	Win
Jack Brooks, D-Texas 9	1952	57.7	58.8	1984
Guy Vander Jagt, R-Mich. 9	1966	54.8	56.6	1974
Chalmers P. Wylie, R-Ohio 15	1966	59.1	59.9	1966
William L. Clay, D-Mo. 1	1968	60.9	64.0	1972
Charles Wilson, D-Texas 2	1972	55.6	59.3	1984
John J. LaFalce, D-N.Y. 32	1974	55.0	59.6	1974
Richard T. Schulze, R-Pa. 5	1974	57.1	59.5	1976
Doug Barnard Jr., D-Ga. 10	1976	58.3	64.0	1988
Tom Coleman, R-Mo. 6	1976	51.9	55.3	1982
Richard A. Gephardt, D-Mo. 3	1976	56.8	62.8	1988
Ed Jenkins, D-Ga. 9	1976	55.8	62.9	1988
Dale E. Kildee, D-Mich. 7	1976	68.4	70.0	1976
Mary Rose Oakar, D-Ohio 20	1976	73.3	81.0	1976
Don J. Pease, D-Ohio 13	1976	56.7	61.2	1982
Ted Weiss, D-N.Y. 17	1976	80.4	81.5	1984
Julian C. Dixon, D-Calif. 28	1978	72.7	75.6	1984
Vic Fazio, D-Calif. 4	1978	54.7	55.4	1978
Newt Gingrich, R-Ga. 6	1978	50.3	54.4	1978
Earl Hutto, D-Fla. 1	1978	52.2	61.2	1980
Jerry Lewis, R-Calif. 35	1978	60.6	61.4	1978
Toby Roth, R-Wis. 8	1978	53.5	57.2	1982
Al Swift, D-Wash. 2	1978	50.5	51.4	1978
Bernard J. Dwyer, D-N.J. 6	1980	50.5	53.4	1980
Bill Lowery, R-Calif. 41	1980	49.2	52.7	1980
Raymond J. McGrath, R-N.Y. 5	1980	54.6	57.7	1980
Gus Savage, D-Ill. 2	1980	78.2	82.7	1988
Herbert H. Bateman, R-Va. 1	1982	51.0	53.9	1982
Dan Burton, R-Ind. 6	1982	63.5	64.9	1982
Rod Chandler, R-Wash. 8	1982	56.2	57.0	1982
Joe Kolter, D-Pa. 4	1982	55.9	56.8	1984
Al McCandless, R-Calif. 37	1982	49.7	59.1	1982
Richard Ray, D-Ga. 3	1982	63.2	71.0	1982
J. Roy Rowland, D-Ga. 8	1982	68.7	86.4	1986
Harley O. Staggers Jr., D-W.Va. 2	1982	55.5	56.0	1984
Chester G. Atkins, D-Mass. 5	1984	52.2	53.4	1984
Albert Bustamante, D-Texas 23	1984	63.5	64.5	1988
Harris G. W. Fawell, R-Ill. 13	1984	65.8	67.0	1984
Carl C. Perkins, D-Ky. 7	1984	50.8	58.7	1988
H. James Saxton, R-N.J. 13	1984	58.1	60.7	1984
Peter J. Visclosky, D-Ind. 1	1984	66.0	70.7	1984
Benjamin L. Cardin, D-Md. 3	1986	69.7	72.9	1988
Elton Gallegly, R-Calif. 21	1986	58.4	68.4	1986
Joel Hefley, R-Colo. 5	1986	66.4	69.8	1986
Jon Kyl, R-Ariz. 4	1986	61.3	64.6	1986
H. Martin Lancaster, D-N.C. 3	1986	59.3	64.5	1986
Kweisi Mfume, D-Md. 7	1986	85.0	86.7	1986
Fred Upton, R-Mich. 4	1986	57.8	61.9	1986

Congress in 1990, it was directed at incumbents of both parties. While 1st District Democrat Earl Hutto was being elected to a seventh term in the Florida Panhandle with his lowest percentage (52 percent), Democrat-turned-Republican Bill Grant in the neighboring 2nd District was being ousted from office.

Across the border in Georgia, the near upset of Gingrich drew national headlines, obscuring the fact that five of his Democratic colleagues in the state's congressional delegation were also being held to their lowest winning percentage. Among them were Ed Jenkins and Doug Barnard Jr., both members of the House class of 1976 who had never fallen below 60 percent before.

Gingrich was "way too confident," said Emory University political scientist Merle Black.

His constituents felt that he had "gotten too big for his district," a mix of small towns and suburbs that sprawled from the outskirts of Atlanta to the Alabama state line, added Black.

Black saw case-by-case considerations pulling down the Democrats — Barnard was a key member of the House Banking Committee and was linked to the savings and loan crisis; Jenkins represented a fast-growing district to the north of Atlanta that was becoming increasingly suburbanized.

But throughout Georgia, there was also a GOP upsurge. Republicans offered their most competitive gubernatorial candidate in nearly a quarter-century, helping the GOP congressional candidates as a group win almost 40 percent of the vote statewide.

Clearly, incumbents were more apt to be given the benefit of the doubt in some states than in others.

In Mississippi, all five Democratic incumbents were re-elected with at least 64.9 percent of the vote. "Historically," said Mississippi's Republican National Committeeman Haley Barbour, "our guys are re-elected until they die or quit or run for another office."

But in states with a heritage of congressional competition or a rapidly changing population, incumbents were more likely to encounter trouble.

Of Missouri's nine incumbents, one was beaten (Republican Jack Buechner by Joan Kelly Horn) and four hit personal lows (Republicans Tom Coleman and Mel Hancock and

Democrats Gephardt and Clay). In addition, Democrat Alan Wheat of Kansas City was held to his lowest winning percentage since he first won his seat in 1982.

Voter volatility was also apparent in a broad band extending from Chicago to Boston, affecting an array of the House's quiet as well as quietly powerful members.

In Ohio alone, Democrats Don J. Pease and Mary Rose Oakar (both from the class of 1976) hit all-time lows, as did Republican Chalmers P. Wylie, who was first elected in 1966.

Several of Wylie's Buckeye State GOP colleagues, including 13-termer Clarence E. Miller and 10-termer Ralph Regula, had their lowest winning percentages since they were first elected.

And in California, a decade with a virtual absence of congressional competition ended with a spurt of action. Three incumbents were defeated, seven sank to their lowest winning percentage ever, and eight others fell to their lowest vote share since they were first elected.

The downdraft pulled down the reelection percentages of veteran Democrats Fazio, Robert T. Matsui and George Miller, as well as a host of Southern California Republicans, including Lewis, Bill Thomas and William E. Dannemeyer (all elected in 1978); Bill Lowery and David Dreier (both elected in 1980); and Al McCandless and Ron Packard (both elected in 1982).

Several forces seemed to be at play in California in 1990.

Voter frustration over the performance of politicians in general was fanned by a ballot initiative limiting the terms of state legislators; it passed. *(Term limits, p. 13)*

Booming population throughout the decade, particularly in the southern counties below Los Angeles, had dramatically altered the political terrain of a number of districts by 1990. And many California voters in 1990 cast their ballots for third-party candidates, so that of the six members of the 102nd Congress elected with less than a majority of the vote, four were from California. *(House elections: close calls, p. 905)*

While Vermont voters elected independent Bernard Sanders to their at-large House seat, third-party candidates as a group tended to run particularly well in districts in the two largest states, California and New York.

In California, the third-party options were offered by the Peace and Freedom and the Libertarian parties; in New York, they were posed mainly by the Conservative and the Right to Life parties.

Yet voters in 1990 opted most often for independent or third-party candidates at the gubernatorial level, delivering them nearly 3 million votes.

Walter J. Hickel in Alaska and Lowell P. Weicker Jr. in Connecticut each won their governorships as independents. The Conservative Party candidate in New York, who billed himself as the "real Republican" in the race, received 20 percent of the vote and barely missed finishing second to Democratic Gov. Mario M. Cuomo.

And an independent right-to-life entry in Oregon drew more than 10 percent, probably costing Republican candidate Dave Frohnmayer the governor's chair. *(Gubernatorial races, p. 926)*

Ten governors were elected with less than 50 percent, and a runoff in Arizona was required because neither Republican Fife Symington nor Democrat Terry Goddard

1990 Vote Totals by Party

Even though the Democrats in 1990 won more House seats (267) than in any election since the recession-year contest of 1982, the Democrats' share of the total nationwide congressional vote was smaller than in any midterm election since 1966.

In midterm contests from 1970 through 1986, the Democratic percentage of the nationwide House vote ranged from a high of 57.1 percent in the post-Watergate election of 1974 to a low of 53 percent in 1970. In 1990, Democratic candidates drew 52.9 percent of all House votes cast across the country.

The fall-off in the Democratic vote in 1990 attested to the strength of antipolitician sentiment, which whittled down the victory margins of many House incumbents in both parties. By comparison, when Democrats captured 269 seats in 1982 (just two more than in 1990), their share of the total nationwide congressional vote was 55.2 percent, 2.3 percentage points higher than the party's share last year.

In the following chart, the House vote from all races includes results from the 423 districts in which votes were tallied.

In seven districts in Louisiana, the House members were elected in the state's open primary in October. In five districts in Florida, candidates ran unopposed in November, and no vote was recorded.

The vote from contested races is limited to the 350 House contests (213 won by the Democrats, 131 by the Republicans and one by an independent) in which both major parties fielded candidates.

	Total Vote	Democrats Vote	%	Republicans Vote	%	Others Vote	%
House							
All Races	61,352,951	32,471,851	52.9	27,602,241	45.0	1,278,859	2.1
Contested	54,000,715	28,417,086	52.6	24,773,563	45.9	810,066	1.5
Senate	34,919,650	17,907,507	51.3	16,495,462	47.2	516,681	1.5
Governor	54,054,094	26,939,727	49.8	24,261,647	44.9	2,852,720	5.3

If just Democratic and Republican votes are counted, the Democrats' share of the vote in all 1990 House races was 54.1 percent, while their share of the major-party vote in contested races was 53.4 percent.

The aggregate vote totals in the chart above were compiled by Congressional Quarterly from official returns supplied by the 50 state election agencies.

The vote for others includes independents, third-party candidates and assorted write-ins. The Republican gubernatorial vote includes 10,941 votes cast for the party's original nominee in Minnesota, Jon Grunseth.

won the majority required by state law. (Symington won the February runoff.)

Voter consideration of third-party alternatives stood out against the continuing decline in voter turnout, which hit a postwar low for House races. *(Voter turnout 1962-90, p. 901)*

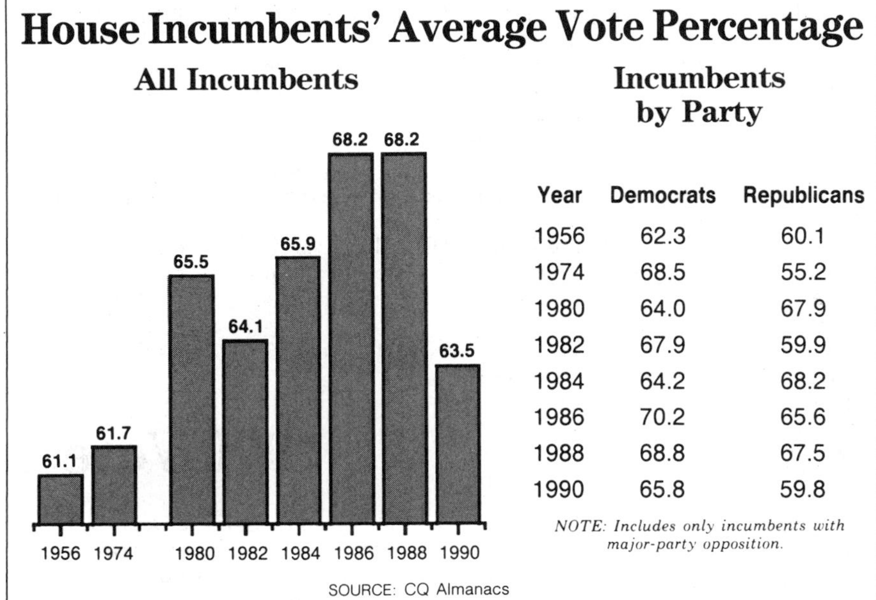

Incumbents by Party

Year	Democrats	Republicans
1956	62.3	60.1
1974	68.5	55.2
1980	64.0	67.9
1982	67.9	59.9
1984	64.2	68.2
1986	70.2	65.6
1988	68.8	67.5
1990	65.8	59.8

NOTE: Includes only incumbents with major-party opposition.

Some Exceptions

Not all House incumbents were caught in a downward spiral.

Nearly 100 members hit personal highs, although two-thirds did so because they had no major-party opposition or because they were winning their first re-election (having first been elected in 1988 or in a more recent special election).

Newer members benefited from what became known as the "sophomore surge."

For some second-termers, the surge was dramatic.

Democrat Jill Long, who in 1989 captured the northeast Indiana seat held previously by Vice President Dan Quayle and GOP Sen. Daniel R. Coats, saw her vote jump from 51 percent in the special election to 61 percent in 1990. Democrat Pete Geren of Texas, who took the Fort Worth district of former House Speaker Jim Wright in 1989 with 51 percent, won a full term in 1990 with 71 percent.

On the other hand, among veteran House members (those at least in their third term in 1990) who had major-party opponents, a relatively small number hit personal highs in 1990.

Democrats who recorded personal highs were Lane Evans of Illinois, Thomas M. Foglietta of Pennsylvania, Wayne Owens of Utah, Timothy J. Penny of Minnesota, Bill Richardson of New Mexico, Martin Olav Sabo of Minnesota, Richard Stallings of Idaho and James A. Traficant Jr. of Ohio.

Republicans who scored personal highs were Dick Armey of Texas, Helen Delich Bentley of Maryland, Howard Coble of North Carolina, Paul B. Henry of Michigan, Nancy L. Johnson of Connecticut, Jim Ross Lightfoot of Iowa, Don Ritter of Pennsylvania and Bob Smith of Oregon.

The new-high group was a diverse mix of Rust Belt and prairie populists, conservative and moderate Republicans, and a few House members who found themselves tenuously positioned in districts whose natural inclination would be to vote for the other party.

For these members, constituents had to be assiduously courted, and virtually all of them were "one-district congressmen" who attempted to become household names only among their own constituents.

None were "old bulls" — only Ritter and Sabo were elected before 1980.

Many were skilled at what DCCC political director Doug Sosnik called the main ingredients for securing a seat: "Do a good job for the district and effectively communicate with the district."

Incumbents who were as likely to be identified with Capitol Hill as with their districts often found their national prestige no protection against trouble back home. ■

1990 Congressional Election Spending Dips

Congressional elections cost less in 1990 than in 1988: $445 million, down from $459 million, according to the summary of 1990 campaign finances the Federal Election Commission (FEC) released Feb. 21, 1991. Less certain was why spending fell — and competing explanations were likely to figure prominently in the renewed debate on campaign finance legislation in the 102nd Congress.

The 3 percent decline from 1988 levels brought campaign spending to its lowest point in six years. It was also the first time that spending fell from one election cycle to the next since FEC recordkeeping began in the 1970s. *(Campaign spending 1978-90, p. 909)*

A slate of Senate contests marked by a lack of competition accounted for all of the decline. The 35 Senate races in 1990 cost $180 million, down 10 percent from 1988's races. Spending in House campaigns increased slightly, rising 3 percent to $265 million.

It was the second straight election cycle to produce signs that the cost of congressional elections had begun to stabilize. The trend emerged in 1988, when the cost advanced 2 percent from 1986, an increase that lagged behind the inflation rate. It marked a significant shift from the double-digit increases posted in previous cycles.

The numbers were likely to be cited in the 1991 debate over campaign financing legislation because a central issue dividing the parties was whether to impose a spending limit on campaigns. *(Campaign financing legislation, p. 59)*

Democrats argued that campaigns operated like nations locked in an arms race, with each candidate trying to outspend the other; they contended that a firm cap was the only way to halt the escalation. Republicans, on the other hand, had opposed spending limits and could argue that the spending slowdown alleviated the need for a cap.

Campaign Spending By Election Year

(In millions of dollars)

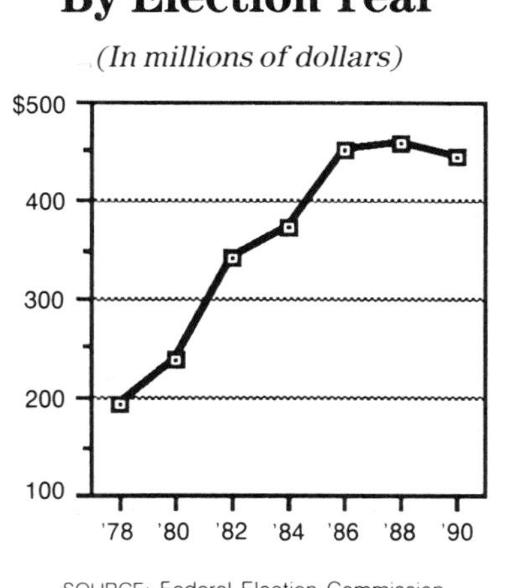

SOURCE: Federal Election Commission

But the FEC report was just as likely to fuel the arguments of those who contended that the campaign system was increasingly tilted against challengers. In state after state, incumbents outgunned challengers with money. According to Common Cause, the public interest lobby pressing Congress for spending limits and public financing of campaigns, 145 of 206 Republican challengers in the House each raised less than $100,000. Only 10 Senate challengers had even half as much money available as the incumbent.

All told, House and Senate incumbents raised $300 million during the two-year election cycle, compared with $102 million for challengers. Incumbents spent $276 million, compared with $101 million for challengers. Incumbents ended the campaign with a $95 million cash surplus — proof that they had plenty of firepower to summon had they felt the need.

Senate: 'The Rich Got Richer'

At first glance, the chief explanation for the spending slowdown appeared to be the unique nature of the 1990 election cycle.

There were no Senate races in four of the most heavily populated states: California, Florida, New York and Pennsylvania. So despite the addition in 1990 of special elections in Hawaii and Indiana, the 1990 election cycle still touched the fewest potential voters of the three Senate classes, 99 million, compared with 135 million in 1988 and 128 million in 1986.

Moreover, in four other states — Arkansas, Georgia, Mississippi and Virginia — incumbents ran without major-party opposition. It had been unusual for even one Senate seat to go uncontested.

Driving overall costs down even further were "a number of lightly opposed races that lacked credible challengers," observed Larry J. Sabato, a political scientist at the University of Virginia. This meant incumbents had to spend less in those races as well. *(Senate races, p. 911)*

The FEC report also made it clear that incumbent senators had more to spend if they had needed it. Texas Republican Phil Gramm coasted to reelection after spending $12.5 million, more than seven times more than his opponent. He had $4.1 million left over. Three other senators, all Democrats, finished with more than $1 million in the bank: Sam Nunn of Georgia, Howell Heflin of Alabama, and David Pryor of Arkansas.

"What you have is the rich growing richer and the poor poorer," Common Cause President Fred Wertheimer said. "Challengers as a group in the House and Senate did not have the resources to be competitive.

"This is the first election where we are beginning to see the House phenomenon in the Senate: of members not just building up large sums in advance but building up huge carry-over surpluses."

House: $77 Million Left Over

House incumbents in 1990 again widened their fund-raising advantage over challengers to nearly 4-to-1. Incumbents raised $181 million, up from $175 million in 1988. Meanwhile, challengers raised $47 million, down from $51 million in 1988.

Roughly 24 of every 25 House incumbents who ran won, but they did not need to spend all their money to do it. The incumbents spent only $163 million, giving them a surplus to apply to the 1992 election. Altogether, incumbents ended the 1990 campaign with $77 million, an increase of more than $13 million over 1988. *(House races, p. 916)*

"Some incumbents are beginning to conclude that they don't need to" spend ever-larger amounts, said Frank J. Sorauf, a University of Minnesota political scientist. Incumbents have learned how to run efficient campaigns, and their challengers often trailed so far behind financially that there was no need to keep spending, Sorauf said.

On the other hand, some incumbents in tight races woke up too late to spend as much as they might have otherwise. Democrat Al Swift of Washington, for one, finished with 50.5 percent of the vote in a three-way race. He spent $465,249 and never ran a TV ad — but not for lack of money. He finished the campaign with $168,462. ■

Bush Selects Clayton Yeutter To Head RNC

President Bush selected Agriculture Secretary Clayton Yeutter to head the Republican National Committee (RNC) after his initial choice, "drug czar" and former Education Secretary William J. Bennett, changed his mind about taking the job.

Yeutter's selection, widely reported on Jan. 4, 1991, ended an embarrassing three-week period following Bennett's announcement on Dec. 13, 1990.

Bennett's explanation that ethics laws would not allow him to serve as RNC chairman while also collecting substantial speaking fees puzzled many people, and subsequent reports on the extensive search for a new party chief became an embarrassment and distraction for Bush and his party.

Bush formally announced his choice of Yeutter on Jan. 7; the RNC unanimously confirmed him for the post on Jan. 25. As committee chairman, Yeutter was to be the party spokesman, chief operating officer and fundraiser for the 1992 election cycle.

He replaced Lee Atwater, Bush's 1988 campaign manager. Atwater had been diagnosed with an inoperable brain tumor in March 1990; he died March 29, 1991. *(Atwater's selection, 1989 Almanac, p. 5-A)*

Bennett Selected, Withdraws

Bush announced his initial selection of former drug czar Bennett to be party chairman on Nov. 30, two weeks after it had been reported that Bennett was White House Chief of Staff John H. Sununu's choice. Bush's selection of Bennett was interpreted both as an overture to the party's right and as an attempt to harness Bennett's personal political energy.

Bennett did not become a Republican until 1986. But as drug czar, secretary of Education (1985-88) and chairman of the National Endowment for the Humanities (1981-85), his tough and strongly articulated views attracted admirers on the political right. He had announced his resignation as director of the Office of Drug Control Policy on Nov. 8. *(Drug czar post, p. 503)*

A former college professor of philosophy, Bennett had been expected to spearhead party efforts and lock horns with Democratic spokesmen; he was an uninhibited debater and a wide-ranging commentator.

President Ronald Reagan had appointed Bennett chairman of the National Endowment for the Humanities, then to the Education seat in the Cabinet — where his often-acerbic style soon found a wider audience. He attracted frequent criticism from teachers' groups and affirmative action advocates. Bush named him to the drug czar's position, and in that post, too, he often tangled with Democrats over strategy and progress in the fight against drugs.

Hours after his RNC selection became known, Bennett told reporters he looked forward to debating affirmative action with the Democrats during the next election cycle. Two weeks later, however, Bennett sent a letter to the president saying he no longer wanted the job. Bennett said that it appeared that ethics laws would not allow him, as a former administration official, to serve as RNC chairman while also collecting substantial speaking fees from private interests.

The stunned White House issued a statement of regret, attributing the situation to 1978 legislation governing former officials' activities in their first year out of office.

Bennett was to be paid $125,000 a year, but he had expected to augment that amount with his writing and with the five-figure speaker fees a figure of his prominence could command. Bennett had expected to expand on this precedent considerably, in part to repay a substantial advance from the publishing house Simon & Schuster. Bennett said he would be too busy as RNC chairman to write two books he owed the publisher.

Whatever considerations entered into Bennett's decision, what came out of it was an undeniable embarrassment for the president. The Democratic National Committee (DNC) immediately issued a mock want ad for the position, and DNC Chairman Ronald H. Brown said the White House's recent theme of a "new paradigm" looked more like a "new paralysis."

Settling on Yeutter

Yeutter himself sparked controversy three days before his formal election to the party post when he suggested that voters would punish the 45 Democrats in the Senate and 179 in the House who had voted against the Persian Gulf use-of-force resolutions on the floor Jan. 12. Yeutter had said he thought 90 percent of the Democrats who voted against that resolution wished they had voted the other way. *(Persian Gulf crisis, p. 717)*

The remarks drew sharp rebukes from House Speaker Thomas S. Foley of Washington, who said Yeutter's "judgment deserted him," and from DNC Chairman Brown, who called the remarks "a disgrace."

In a Jan. 25 speech, Yeutter did not read many of the prepared remarks in which he was to have attacked Democrats on domestic issues.

But he did pledge to press the GOP's case as "vigorously and aggressively as the situation demands" and not to be "intimidated by anyone" in his role as party spokesman for the next two years.

As both an agricultural economist and a practicing farmer, Yeutter had been generally regarded as one of the best qualified Agriculture secretaries ever. *(Yeutter's confirmation, 1989 Almanac, p. 397)*

To members of Congress, however, he frequently came across as arrogant and too clever. And the prize that Yeutter wanted most of all — an agreement liberalizing world trade in agriculture — eluded him.

Democrats, in particular, were frustrated by Yeutter's ability to navigate around many of the partisan traps laid for the Bush administration during the 1990 debate over federal farm subsidies.

Throughout the spring and summer, Yeutter refused to say by how much he wanted to see farm subsidies cut, thus denying Democrats a potent issue.

Yeutter irked even some Republican lawmakers by seeming to ignore Capitol Hill.

He focused his attention on trade negotiations abroad, first as U.S. trade representative in Reagan's second term, then as an assistant to Bush's Trade Representative Carla A. Hills in the effort to eradicate agriculture subsidies worldwide.

Lawmakers frequently charged that Yeutter would have preferred to see the U.S. farm policy "written in Geneva." But the negotiations broke down in December over the European Community's unwillingness to make deep cuts in their farmers' export subsidies.

Yeutter had seemed to have reached the top of his chosen profession by running the Department of Agriculture. But he let it be known that he did not consider that his last stop in public life.

During the 1990 campaign, he was in demand in farm states and communities in which GOP candidates needed the crowds and publicity he could generate.

Yeutter kept an operating ranch in Nebraska even after he moved permanently to Washington, and it had been observed that his home state had two Democratic senators and a Democratic governor at whom he might take aim.

Yeutter raised eyebrows back home by singling out Sen. Bob Kerrey, D-Neb., for criticism after the use-of-force vote on the Hill. Some observers speculated on a potential Yeutter challenge to Kerrey in 1994; Yeutter's RNC term ran to 1993.

"Americans do not share the negative and depressed viewpoints of Sen. Kerrey and others," Yeutter said.

Kerrey took to the Senate floor to respond, saying Yeutter's comments "trivialize the deep misgivings which all Americans have about sending our sons and daughters into combat." ■

GOP Senate Showing Below Expectations

U.S. SENATE

102nd Congress
(As of Jan 10, 1991)

Democrats	56
Freshmen	1
Incumbents re-elected	17
Incumbents defeated	0
Republicans	44
Freshmen	4
Incumbents re-elected	14
Incumbent defeated	1

101st Congress

Democrats	55
Republicans	45

In real numbers, the Republican Party on Nov. 6 held its Senate losses to a minimum. The Republicans suffered a net drop of one Senate seat — well below the average for the White House party in recent off-year elections.

In terms of expectations, however, the 1990 Senate campaign was a major Republican setback. National GOP strategists initially billed the election as one in which they would cut into the 55-45 Democratic Senate majority. The stage would then have been set for a big Republican push in 1992, when Democrats would have to defend 20 seats to the Republicans' 15.

Instead, Republicans slipped further into the minority, with 44 seats to 56 for the Democrats. *(Changes in Senate membership, p. 913)*

The Democratic gain came despite a national party strategy aimed at protecting their existing majority by defending incumbents. Officials of the Democratic Senatorial Campaign Committee made only a token effort to recruit challengers against Republican incumbents. They were pleasantly surprised when some of their self-starters did well, especially Paul Wellstone, a college professor with a colorful personality who upset seemingly invulnerable two-term Republican Sen. Rudy Boschwitz in Minnesota.

The National Republican Senatorial Committee (NRSC), on the other hand, invested its hopes — and millions of dollars — in the campaigns of five House members and one former member running against Democratic incumbents in Hawaii, Illinois, Iowa, Michigan, Nebraska and Rhode Island. All lost, some by landslides.

In fact, the only real GOP threat to unseat a Democrat came in a New Jersey race that Republican officials had written off. Sen. Bill Bradley, heavily favored, was caught in a reaction to a Democratic-backed state tax hike and held to under 51 percent of the vote by Christine Todd Whitman, a former public utilities commissioner.

The Republicans managed to stave off a deeper net loss only because they played better defense than offense. The generic "economic fairness" issue that emerged during the mid-October federal budget debate combined with local factors to put three Republican incumbents — Jesse Helms of North Carolina, Mark O. Hatfield of Oregon and Mitch McConnell of Kentucky — at unexpected risk. However, each had time and money to halt the slides.

The overall Senate results contrasted sharply with pre-election predictions of a national anti-incumbent mood. The 1990 Senate incumbent re-election rate of 96.9 percent (31 of 32) was the highest since direct elections began in 1914. The rate even edged past that of the House, where incumbents had in recent years tended to be statistically less vulnerable to challenge than senators. *(Incumbents' re-election rates 1946-90, p. 903)*

Anatomy of an Upset

Wellstone's victory in Minnesota would have stood out even in a more generally competitive year.

Boschwitz had won a second Senate term in 1984 with 58 percent of the vote and entered the 1990 campaign as the state's most popular politician. Wellstone was a political science professor at Carleton College who was best-known as state co-chairman for Jesse Jackson's 1988 presidential campaign. The contest was a financial mismatch: As of Oct. 17, Boschwitz had raised $7.3 million to Wellstone's $818,000.

However, Wellstone grabbed the voters' attention with an imaginative campaign. To underline his low-budget status, he toured in an old green school bus. Wellstone also reeled off a series of clever TV commercials. In one, a takeoff of the movie "Roger and Me," the elfin Wellstone "searched" for Boschwitz to challenge him to a debate.

This approach leavened Wellstone's otherwise harsh criticism of Boschwitz as a right-wing toady of big business who ignored pressing social needs. Another Wellstone ad showed children scrawling on oversized checks made out to "Rudy." The message, however, was tough. "If kids had money, maybe he wouldn't have one of the worst records in the Senate on children's issues," Wellstone narrated.

Boschwitz was slow to respond and was thus primed for a free fall when the state GOP organization erupted in campaign chaos. In late October, GOP gubernatorial candidate Jon Grunseth was confronted with reports alleging sexual improprieties. His political collapse threatened the entire Republican ticket.

When Grunseth dropped out Oct. 28, Boschwitz supported Republican primary runner-up Arne Carlson. Although Boschwitz opposed abortion, his support for the pro-abortion rights Carlson over Cal Ludeman, the anti-abortion 1986 Republican candidate for governor, alienated many conservatives.

Boschwitz tried to reverse the negative tide by assailing Wellstone as an ultraliberal on national health insurance and other costly social spending. Although he rebounded in the polls, Boschwitz struck many voters as strident and desperate.

Boschwitz's status as the only incumbent to lose was ironic. He had served as NRSC chairman during the 100th Congress, recruiting candidates and helping raise millions of dollars for them.

After his 1984 campaign, Boschwitz wrote a memo to fellow Republicans suggesting that they could ensure re-election by raising lots of money and by tying themselves to the president. But by the time Boschwitz ran again, the public mood had turned against incumbents' constant appeals for money. And the president, who came to campaign for Boschwitz, was not the triumphant Ronald Reagan of 1984 but the struggling George Bush of 1990.

Venting Frustration

Bradley, the only incumbent to suffer near defeat, became a surrogate for voters angry at another Democrat, New Jersey Gov. James J. Florio. Elected in 1989, Florio

Senate Membership — 102nd Congress

Democrats	56	**1990 winners in *italics***	**Seats That Switched:**
Republicans	44	**# Freshmen**	**Democrat to Republican — 0**
Freshmen	5	**† Seat switched parties**	**Republican to Democrat — 1**

Alabama
Howell Heflin (D)
Richard C. Shelby (D)

Alaska
Frank H. Murkowski (R)
Ted Stevens (R)

Arizona
Dennis DeConcini (D)
John McCain (R)

Arkansas
Dale Bumpers (D)
David Pryor (D)

California
Alan Cranston (D)
John Seymour (R)# *

Colorado
Tim Wirth (D)
Hank Brown (R)#

Connecticut
Christopher J. Dodd (D)
Joseph I. Lieberman (D)

Delaware
Joseph R. Biden Jr. (D)
William V. Roth Jr. (R)

Florida
Bob Graham (D)
Connie Mack (R)

Georgia
Wyche Fowler Jr. (D)
Sam Nunn (D)

Hawaii
Daniel K. Akaka (D)
Daniel K. Inouye (D)

Idaho
Larry E. Craig (R)#
Steve Symms (R)

Illinois
Alan J. Dixon (D)
Paul Simon (D)

Indiana
Daniel R. Coats (R)
Richard G. Lugar (R)

Iowa
Tom Harkin (D)
Charles E. Grassley (R)

Kansas
Bob Dole (R)
Nancy Landon Kassebaum (R)

Kentucky
Wendell H. Ford (D)
Mitch McConnell (R)

Louisiana
John B. Breaux (D)
J. Bennett Johnston (D)

Maine
George J. Mitchell (D)
William S. Cohen (R)

Maryland
Barbara A. Mikulski (D)
Paul S. Sarbanes (D)

Massachusetts
Edward M. Kennedy (D)
John Kerry (D)

Michigan
Carl Levin (D)
Donald W. Riegle Jr. (D)

Minnesota †
Paul Wellstone (D)#
Dave Durenberger (R)

Mississippi
Thad Cochran (R)
Trent Lott (R)

Missouri
Christopher S. Bond (R)
John C. Danforth (R)

Montana
Max Baucus (D)
Conrad Burns (R)

Nebraska
Jim Exon (D)
Bob Kerrey (D)

Nevada
Harry Reid (D)
Richard H. Bryan (D)

New Hampshire
Warren B. Rudman (R)
Robert C. Smith (R)#

New Jersey
Bill Bradley (D)
Frank R. Lautenberg (D)

New Mexico
Jeff Bingaman (D)
Pete V. Domenici (R)

New York
Daniel Patrick Moynihan (D)
Alfonse M. D'Amato (R)

North Carolina
Terry Sanford (D)
Jesse Helms (R)

North Dakota
Quentin N. Burdick (D)
Kent Conrad (D)

Ohio
John Glenn (D)
Howard M. Metzenbaum (D)

Oklahoma
David L. Boren (D)
Don Nickles (R)

Oregon
Mark O. Hatfield (R)
Bob Packwood (R)

Pennsylvania
John Heinz (R)
Arlen Specter (R)

Rhode Island
Claiborne Pell (D)
John H. Chafee (R)

South Carolina
Ernest F. Hollings (D)
Strom Thurmond (R)

South Dakota
Tom Daschle (D)
Larry Pressler (R)

Tennessee
Al Gore (D)
Jim Sasser (D)

Texas
Lloyd Bentsen (D)
Phil Gramm (R)

Utah
Jake Garn (R)
Orrin G. Hatch (R)

Vermont
Patrick J. Leahy (D)
James M. Jeffords (R)

Virginia
Charles S. Robb (D)
John W. Warner (R)

Washington
Brock Adams (D)
Slade Gorton (R)

West Virginia
Robert C. Byrd (D)
John D. Rockefeller IV (D)

Wisconsin
Herb Kohl (D)
Bob Kasten (R)

Wyoming
Alan K. Simpson (R)
Malcolm Wallop (R)

* *John Seymour was sworn in Jan. 10, 1991, after being appointed by California Gov. Pete Wilson to the Senate seat vacated by Wilson. He was to serve until Jan. 3, 1993; a special election was to be held in November 1992 for the remaining two years of the term, and a regular election was to be held in November 1994 for a full six-year term.*

addressed a budget shortfall by pushing a $2.8 billion tax increase package through the Democratic-controlled Legislature.

Although Florio argued that it would shift the tax burden to the wealthy, the measure (and Florio) were overwhelmingly unpopular.

Whitman was an unfamiliar figure, but she was the available messenger for the antitax movement. In no other Senate race was the anti-incumbent mood so manifest: Whitman's campaign bumper stickers read, "Get Florio, Dump Bradley."

The nail-biting finish was nonetheless viewed incredulously by most observers.

Bradley, who won a second term in 1984 with 64 percent of the vote, was often mentioned as a possible presidential candidate. He used a huge financial advantage ($12.5 million to $543,000, as of Oct. 17) to highlight positive aspects of his record.

It appeared for a time that Massachusetts Democrat John Kerry might be a victim of state fiscal problems too. Businessman Jim Rappaport spent more than $2.8 million to link Kerry to the unpopular administration of retiring Democratic Gov. Michael S. Dukakis. However, Kerry responded with an effective campaign that mocked the 34-year-old Rappaport as a spoiled rich kid trying to buy a Senate seat.

Changes in Senate Membership

State	Winner	Loser	Incumbent
California	John Seymour (R)	—	Pete Wilson (R) [1]
Colorado	Hank Brown (R)	Josie Heath (D)	William L. Armstrong (R) [2]
Idaho	Larry E. Craig (R)	Ron J. Twilegar (D)	James A. McClure (R) [2]
New Hampshire	Robert C. Smith (R)	John A. Durkin (D)	Gordon J. Humphrey (R) [2]
Minnesota	Paul Wellstone (D)	Rudy Boschwitz (R)	Boschwitz

[1] *Sen. Pete Wilson was elected governor of California. Wilson appointed John Seymour, who was sworn in as senator Jan. 10, 1991.*
[2] *Retired.*

Squandered Capital

Whitman supporters complained that a greater investment by the national party might have brought them victory. But the NRSC was preoccupied with the effort to salvage its first-line challenges that were going bust.

The GOP focused on a handful of Democratic Senate incumbents: Tom Harkin of Iowa, Carl Levin of Michigan, Paul Simon of Illinois, Jim Exon of Nebraska and Claiborne Pell of Rhode Island. When Democratic Sen. Spark M. Matsunaga's death forced a November special election in Hawaii, the GOP targeted his appointed successor, Rep. Daniel K. Akaka.

The NRSC's drafting of Republican House veterans to run for these seats initially looked like a coup. Five challengers — Tom Tauke of Iowa, Lynn Martin of Illinois, Bill Schuette of Michigan, Claudine Schneider of Rhode Island and Patricia Saiki of Hawaii — sacrificed promising House careers to run. A former House member, Hal Daub of Nebraska (1981-89), who lost a 1988 Senate bid, jumped at a second chance.

But the incumbents were well prepared. Each used a financial advantage to promote a "man of the people" image, foiling efforts to apply the liberal label.

The issues also broke to the advantage of each of the Democratic incumbents. Foreign Relations Committee Chairman Pell and Armed Services Committee member Levin, for example, gained positive publicity for visiting U.S. troops deployed against Iraq in the Persian Gulf.

The economic debate bolstered Democrats. Harkin's ads accused Tauke of supporting tax breaks for the rich. Levin linked Schuette's opposition to a toxic chemical regulation to his ownership of a large block of Dow Chemical Co. stock; in doing so, he obliquely reminded voters of Schuette's wealth.

Meanwhile, the Republicans, each of whom took a "no new taxes" pledge, were undercut by Bush's budget maneuverings. Also, the GOP could hardly take advantage of anti-Washington attitudes when its key challengers were Capitol Hill denizens.

Hawaii and Illinois might have been the keenest GOP disappointments. Although the low-key Akaka had served in Congress for 14 years, Republicans were confident that two-termer Saiki's more assertive personality would give her the edge. But they discounted the strength of the

California's Seymour

Republican Gov. Pete Wilson of California appointed GOP state Sen. John Seymour to succeed him in the Senate. Seymour was a longtime personal ally who mirrored Wilson's own image of a consensus-minded mainstream conservative.

Seymour filled the seat Wilson vacated when Wilson was sworn in as governor Jan. 7, 1991. Seymour was sworn in as senator Jan. 10.

The new senator faced the prospect of back-to-back elections. He would have to face the voters in 1992 to secure the right to the final two years of the term Wilson won in 1988; the seat would then be up again in 1994.

In announcing his choice Jan. 2, 1991, Wilson surprised California political observers. Seymour's name had not appeared on most lists of possible appointees.

Getting into politics, Seymour won an Anaheim City Council seat in 1974, then was elected mayor in 1978. He was best known for negotiating the move of the Los Angeles Rams football team to Anaheim Stadium.

Seymour also spent eight years as one of 40 state senators. In his one campaign for statewide office, he lost the June 1990 Republican primary for lieutenant governor to another state senator, Marian Bergeson (who lost to incumbent Democrat Leo McCarthy in November).

Although his state Senate record was mainly conservative, Seymour angered some hard-liners by coming out in 1989 for abortion rights and against offshore oil drilling. His new positions on both issues reflected Wilson's.

Years of Expiration of Senate Terms

— 1992 —

(35 Senators: 20 Democrats, 15 Republicans) †

Adams, Brock, D-Wash.
Bond, Christopher S., R-Mo.
Breaux, John B., D-La.
Bumpers, Dale, D-Ark.
Coats, Daniel R., R-Ind.
Conrad, Kent, D-N.D.
Cranston, Alan, D-Calif.
D'Amato, Alfonse M., R-N.Y.
Daschle, Tom, D-S.D.
Dixon, Alan J., D-Ill.
Dodd, Christopher J., D-Conn.
Dole, Bob, R-Kan.
Ford, Wendell H., D-Ky.
Fowler, Wyche Jr., D-Ga.
Garn, Jake, R-Utah
Glenn, John, D-Ohio
Graham, Bob, D-Fla.
Grassley, Charles E., R-Iowa
Hollings, Ernest F., D-S.C.
Inouye, Daniel K., D-Hawaii
Kasten, Bob, R-Wis.
Leahy, Patrick J., D-Vt.
McCain, John, R-Ariz.
Mikulski, Barbara A., D-Md.
Murkowski, Frank H., R-Alaska
Nickles, Don, R-Okla.
Packwood, Bob, R-Ore.
Reid, Harry, D-Nev.
Rudman, Warren B., R-N.H.
Sanford, Terry, D-N.C.
Seymour, John, R-Calif. †
Shelby, Richard C., D-Ala.
Specter, Arlen, R-Pa.
Symms, Steve, R-Idaho
Wirth, Tim, D-Colo.

— 1994 —

(33 Senators: 19 Democrats, 13 Republicans, 1 Undetermined) †

Akaka, Daniel K., D-Hawaii
Bentsen, Lloyd, D-Texas
Bingaman, Jeff, D-N.M.
Bryan, Richard H., D-Nev.
Burdick, Quentin N., D-N.D.
Burns, Conrad, R-Mont.
Byrd, Robert C., D-W.Va.
Chafee, John H., R-R.I.
Danforth, John C., R-Mo.
DeConcini, Dennis, D-Ariz.
Durenberger, Dave, R-Minn.
Gorton, Slade, R-Wash.
Hatch, Orrin G., R-Utah
Heinz, John, R-Pa.
Jeffords, James M., R-Vt.
Kennedy, Edward M., D-Mass.
Kerrey, Bob, D-Neb.
Kohl, Herbert, D-Wis.
Lautenberg, Frank R., D-N.J.
Lieberman, Joseph I., D-Conn.
Lott, Trent, R-Miss.
Lugar, Richard G., R-Ind.
Mack, Connie, R-Fla.
Metzenbaum, Howard M., D-Ohio
Mitchell, George J., D-Maine
Moynihan, Daniel Patrick, D-N.Y.
Riegle, Donald W. Jr., D-Mich.
Robb, Charles S., D-Va.
Roth, William V. Jr., R-Del.
Sarbanes, Paul S., D-Md.
Sasser, Jim, D-Tenn.
Wallop, Malcolm, R-Wyo.
California Seat †

— 1996 —

(33 Senators: 17 Democrats, 16 Republicans)

Baucus, Max, D-Mont.
Biden, Joseph R. Jr., D-Del.
Boren, David L., D-Okla.
Bradley, Bill, D-N.J.
Brown, Hank, R-Colo.
Cochran, Thad, R-Miss.
Cohen, William S., R-Maine
Craig, Larry E., R-Idaho
Domenici, Pete V., R-N.M.
Exon, Jim, D-Neb.
Gore, Al, D-Tenn.
Gramm, Phil, R-Texas
Harkin, Tom, D-Iowa
Hatfield, Mark O., R-Ore.
Heflin, Howell, D-Ala.
Helms, Jesse, R-N.C.
Johnston, J. Bennett, D-La.
Kassebaum, Nancy Landon, R-Kan.
Kerry, John, D-Mass.
Levin, Carl, D-Mich.
McConnell, Mitch, R-Ky.
Nunn, Sam, D-Ga.
Pell, Claiborne, D-R.I.
Pressler, Larry, R-S.D.
Pryor, David, D-Ark.
Rockefeller, John D. IV, D-W.Va.
Simon, Paul, D-Ill.
Simpson, Alan K., R-Wyo.
Smith, Robert C., R-N.H.
Stevens, Ted, R-Alaska
Thurmond, Strom, R-S.C.
Warner, John W., R-Va.
Wellstone, Paul, D-Minn.

** John Seymour was sworn in as senator Jan. 10, 1991, to the seat vacated by Pete Wilson, who was elected governor of California. Seymour was to face a special election in 1992 to complete Wilson's term, and the winner of that election was to face re-election in 1994.*

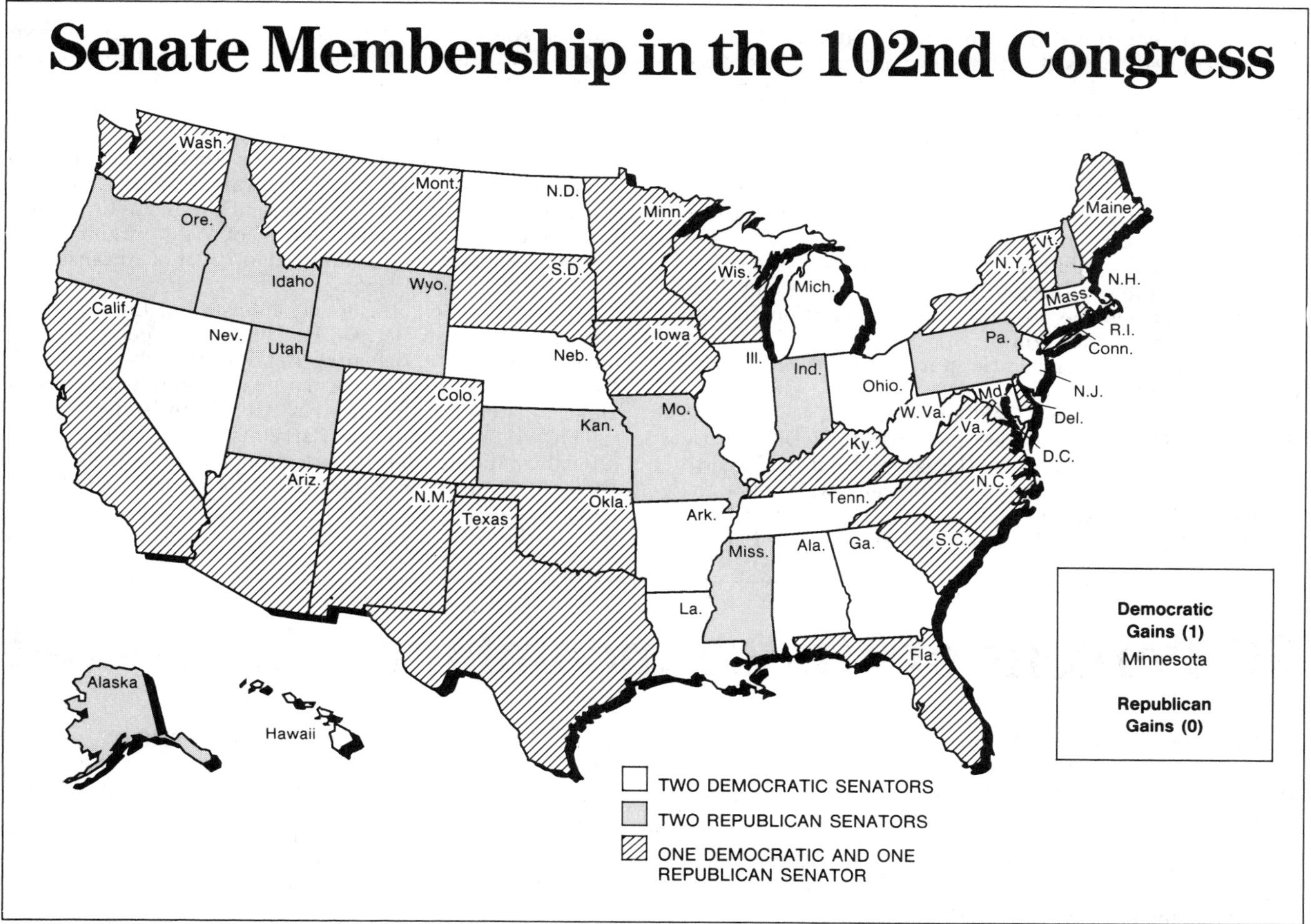

Democratic machine that dominated Hawaii: Akaka won with 54 percent.

Martin's campaign in Illinois was plagued by gaffes and finance problems. Yet Simon's 65 percent share of the vote was an eyebrow-raiser. Martin, a former vice chairman of the House Republican Conference, was once regarded as the Republicans' blue-chip candidate: Simon, a 50 percent winner in 1984 and an unsuccessful 1988 presidential candidate, was viewed as vulnerable.

GOP House members did much better in holding the seats of retiring GOP senators: In New Hampshire, Republican Rep. Robert C. Smith crushed former Democratic Sen. John A. Durkin's comeback bid to succeed Sen. Gordon J. Humphrey. Easy wins were also scored by Idaho Rep. Larry E. Craig, to succeed Sen. James A. McClure, and Colorado Rep. Hank Brown, to replace Sen. William L. Armstrong.

Holding the Line

Except for Boschwitz, Republican Senate veterans were as successful as Democrats at holding seats. The fiercest contest was in North Carolina.

Conservative Republican crusader Helms won a fourth term by fending off Harvey B. Gantt, a Democratic former mayor of Charlotte who was seeking to become the first black sent to the Senate from the South since Reconstruction.

To Democratic activists, Helms' survival skills were nearly as infuriating as his liberal-bashing rhetoric. In 1984, Helms had edged then-Democratic Gov. James B. Hunt Jr. after a heated campaign.

Helms' defeat of the popular Hunt and his awesome fundraising ability led most to discount Gantt's chances. Gantt also had to prove that a black candidate could compete in a state with a history of racial divisiveness.

Gantt's unthreatening manner initially belied Helms' effort to portray him as an extreme liberal. Accusing Helms of neglecting pressing social needs, Gantt surged ahead in some polls.

Helms fought back with TV ads that accused Gantt of supporting unrestricted abortion and, most damagingly, of backing racial quotas. Although Gantt accused Helms of running a racist campaign, the incumbent managed to energize a conservative constituency that had lacked enthusiasm earlier.

In Oregon, a late spate of advertising also saved Hatfield's bid for a fifth term. For much of the campaign, Hatfield had ignored Democratic businessman Harry Lonsdale, a first-time candidate who struck a nerve with voters by portraying Hatfield as losing touch with the state.

However, Hatfield came home and raised questions about Lonsdale's business practices, including his laboratory's toxic-waste disposal practices.

Kentucky's McConnell had to fight off a late effort by his Democratic opponent, former Louisville Mayor Harvey Sloane, who portrayed the incumbent as beholden to big business interests. A Sloane TV ad depicted McConnell as a marionette controlled by a costumed "fat cat." McConnell "inoculated" himself with his own ad on the tax issue, in which he said, "I think everyone should pay their fair share, including the rich."

Two other Republican candidates were never seriously endangered, but won by modest margins.

South Dakota Sen. Larry Pressler won 52 percent to 45 percent, despite Democrat Ted Muenster's efforts to tar him as a junketeer.

In Indiana, Republican Daniel R. Coats — who was appointed in 1988 to the seat that had been held by Vice President Dan Quayle — won a special election for the final two years of the term.

Coats defeated Democratic state Rep. Baron P. Hill with 54 percent.

Maine Republican Sen. William S. Cohen easily won a third term. However, a determined effort by Democratic state Rep. Neil Rolde to raise the issue of national health care helped him hold Cohen to 61 percent, well below the 73 percent he received in 1984.

Other Republicans who won comfortably were Pete V. Domenici of New Mexico, Phil Gramm of Texas, Nancy Landon Kassebaum of Kansas, Alan K. Simpson of Wyoming, Ted Stevens of Alaska and Strom Thurmond of South Carolina.

Thad Cochran of Mississippi and John W. Warner of Virginia had no Democratic opponents.

Democrats who coasted included Max Baucus of Montana, Joseph R. Biden Jr. of Delaware, David L. Boren of Oklahoma, Al Gore of Tennessee, Howell Heflin of Alabama and John D. Rockefeller IV of West Virginia.

Sam Nunn of Georgia and David Pryor of Arkansas had no Republican opponents.

Democratic Sen. J. Bennett Johnston of Louisiana had been re-elected on Oct. 6 when he won 54 percent of the open-primary vote, defeating Republican state Sen. David Duke in a race that drew national attention because of Duke's history as a former Ku Klux Klan leader.

The state's Republican Party disavowed Duke, and its official candidate, Ben Bagert, dropped out Oct. 4 to deny Duke a chance at a runoff with Johnston. Nonetheless, Duke was estimated to have won 60 percent of the white vote in the balloting. ■

96 Percent of House Incumbents Re-Elected

The 1990 elections reaffirmed the aphorism that a House seat is a very difficult thing for an incumbent party to lose. Nonetheless, on Nov. 6, incumbent-party candidates in 21 congressional districts managed to do just that.

Fifteen incumbents — six Democrats and nine Republicans — lost their jobs, and Democrats captured six open seats that had been held by the GOP. *(House members defeated, p. 917)*

Democrats tallied a net gain of nine seats (including a win in the vacant New Jersey 1st); Republicans suffered a net loss of eight seats (counting a GOP win in the vacant Ohio 8th). Vermont's Bernard Sanders, a self-described socialist who ran as an independent, defeated freshman GOP Rep. Peter Smith. *(Changes in House membership, p. 918; Sanders' status in House, p. 922)*

U.S. HOUSE

102nd Congress
(As of Jan. 3, 1991)

Democrats	267
Net gain	9
Freshmen	25
Incumbents re-elected	242
Incumbents defeated	6
Republicans	167
Net loss	8
Freshmen	18
Incumbents re-elected	149
Incumbents defeated	9
Independent	1

101st Congress
(As of Oct. 28, 1990)

Democrats	258
Republicans	175
Vacancies	2

Of the 407 House members who sought re-election in 1990 — including Ohio Republican Donald E. "Buz" Lukens, who lost his primary and later resigned — 391 won. The return rate of 96 percent was down from the 98 percent re-election rate in 1988. *(Incumbents' re-election rates 1946-90, p. 903)*

Among the 44-member freshman class of the 102nd Congress were:

- The first black Republican House member since 1935 — Gary Franks of Connecticut.
- The first Democrat elected from northwestern Illinois since 1850 (four years before the Republican Party was born) — John W. Cox Jr.
- The first black member of Congress from Louisiana since Reconstruction — Democrat William J. Jefferson.
- The first Democrat to win in Idaho's western 1st District in more than a quarter-century — Larry LaRocco.
- The first socialist House member (Sanders) since 1929.
- One son of an incumbent member of Congress — Ohio Democrat Charles Luken, replacing his father, Thomas A. Luken — and two sons-in-law of current members — Indiana Democrat Tim Roemer (related to Sen. J. Bennett Johnston, D-La.) and New Hampshire Democrat Dick Swett (related to Rep. Tom Lantos, D-Calif.).
- Two former members of the House — Democrats Ray Thornton of Arkansas (1973-79) and Neil Abercrombie of Hawaii (1986-87).
- Four women (all Democrats) — Maxine Waters of California, Rosa DeLauro of Connecticut, Barbara-Rose Collins of Michigan and Joan Kelly Horn of Missouri — and four blacks (three Democrats, one Republican) — Waters, Jefferson, Collins and Franks.

The elections — resulting in a partisan makeup of 267 Democrats, 167 Republicans and one independent — demonstrated the Democratic Party's continuing prowess in House contests. Democrats gained House seats for the third straight election. The last time a party gained seats in as many consecutive elections was when Democrats registered pickups in 1954, 1956 and 1958.

Democratic gains in Arkansas, Hawaii, Idaho, Utah and Virginia gave the party a majority of members in those states' House delegations. Republicans took the lead in the

Pennsylvania and Wisconsin delegations. *(House makeup, p. 919)*

Perhaps no state showcased the Democratic domination at the House level better than Indiana. In 1981, Republicans, in control of the state legislature and the governor's office, produced a gerrymandered congressional map designed to produce a GOP majority in the state's House delegation. But over the course of the decade, Democrats gained the upper hand, and in 1990 the defeat of Republican Rep. John Hiler gave Democrats an 8-2 delegation majority.

House Members Defeated

	Terms
Jim Bates, D-Calif.	4
Douglas H. Bosco, D-Calif.	4
Charles "Chip" Pashayan Jr., R-Calif.	6
Bill Grant, R-Fla.	2
John Hiler, R-Ind.	5
Roy Dyson, D-Md.	5
Arlan Stangeland, R-Minn.	6 †
Jack Buechner, R-Mo.	2
Chuck Douglas, R-N.H.	1
James McClure Clarke, D-N.C.	3
Denny Smith, R-Ore.	5
Doug Walgren, D-Pa.	7
Peter Smith, R-Vt.	1
Stan Parris, R-Va.	6
Robert W. Kastenmeier, D-Wis.	16

† Elected in a special election in 1977.
Donald E. "Buz" Lukens, R-Ohio, was defeated in primary, then resigned Oct. 24, 1990.

Faults and Foibles

As in 1988, when six of the seven House incumbents defeated for renomination or re-election were tarred by ethical questions, eight of the 16 losers in 1990 were dogged by some charge of unethical conduct.

Public outrage over the increasingly expensive bailout of failed savings and loan institutions zapped some of the losers. Republicans Hiler, Denny Smith of Oregon, Charles "Chip" Pashayan Jr. of California and Stan Parris of Virginia, and Democrat Douglas H. Bosco of California either confronted charges of personal wrongdoing or were blamed for failing to avert the problems. But two Democrats whose opponents accused them of complicity in the S&L debacle, Frank Annunzio of Illinois and Doug Barnard Jr. of Georgia, managed sizable if not quite comfortable victories.

Personal scandals helped halt the House careers of Democrats Jim Bates of California and Roy Dyson of Maryland and Republicans Lukens and Arlan Stangeland of Minnesota.

In choosing elected officials, voters often gave more weight to personality than policy, and some members' abrasive or blustery temperaments were apparently too much for their constituents to take. Parris, long known for conservative bombast, wearied many with his diatribes against liberals and the District of Columbia's government. (The Democrat who ousted him, though, James P. Moran Jr., matched him blow for rhetorical blow.)

Similarly, the forcefulness of two Republicans, New Hampshire's Chuck Douglas and Missouri's Jack Buechner, contributed to their losses. (New Hampshire Republicans also blamed Douglas' public feuding with White House Chief of Staff John H. Sununu, a former New Hampshire governor, for his loss.)

One incumbent, North Carolina Democrat James McClure Clarke, lost through no particular fault of his own but because of the extremely competitive nature of his 11th District. Every House race in the 11th since 1980 had been decided by fewer than 5,000 votes. In 1988, Clarke became the first to win re-election in the district since 1978, but in 1990 voters turned to Republican Charles H. Taylor, a former state legislator who had lost to Clarke by 1,529 votes in 1988. Taylor prevailed by 2,673 votes.

Dwindling Margins

The late adjournment date of Oct. 28 — Congress had not been in session as close to Election Day since 1942 — coupled with unflattering publicity over Congress' protracted budget negotiations helped to explain significantly lower percentages for many entrenched incumbents and a marked increase in competitive House races. *(Incumbents' falloffs, p. 904; House elections: close calls, p. 905)*

More than anything else, benign neglect — inability to campaign in person and refute opponents' charges that they had lost touch with their constituents — led to the defeat of two Democrats who had been considered safe bets for re-election, Doug Walgren of Pennsylvania and Robert W. Kastenmeier of Wisconsin. Both Rick Santorum (Walgren's GOP challenger) and Scott L. Klug (Kastenmeier's foe) campaigned on anti-incumbent themes.

Unstable state political climates affected some House races. Angry antitax voters in New Jersey and Massachusetts held Democratic incumbents well below their usual re-election marks. On Long Island, antitax voters hurt Democratic and Republican incumbents alike.

Some House leaders were targets of voter antipathy toward incumbents. In one of the country's closest races, House Minority Whip Newt Gingrich of Georgia won a seventh term by fewer than 1,000 votes.

House Majority Leader Richard A. Gephardt of Missouri also had a closer-than-expected race. Ways and Means Committee Chairman Dan Rostenkowski of Illinois saw 21 percent of his district's vote go to a third-party candidate; no Republican was on the ballot.

Michigan GOP Rep. Guy Vander Jagt, who was under siege as chairman of the National Republican Congressional Committee (the NRCC, which worked to elect Republicans to the House), was held to 55 percent. Vander Jagt's challenger for the NRCC chairmanship, Tennessee Rep. Don Sundquist, got just 62 percent against an underfunded political unknown.

Californian Vic Fazio, expected to chair the Democratic Congressional Campaign Committee in the 102nd Congress and one of the most prominent defenders of congressional pay raises and mailing privileges, dropped to 55 percent.

Party switching lost some of its cachet as a tool for increasing GOP strength in the House. In 1989, two members converted to the GOP, but evidently voters in their districts did not. Florida's Bill Grant was soundly rejected for re-election. And Arkansas' Tommy F. Robinson, another 1989 switcher, left to run for governor and his House seat went to a Democrat.

The Gulf and Abortion

While the budget flap, late adjournment and President Bush's reneging on his "no new taxes" pledge damaged some members, Bush's late-campaign strategy of concentrating on U.S. policy in the Persian Gulf and denouncing Iraqi President Saddam Hussein might have rescued some others. *(Persian Gulf crisis, p. 717)*

In Alabama, Bill Dickinson, ranking Republican on the Armed Services Committee, was facing questions over his

Changes in House Membership

State	District	Old	New	Winner	Loser	Incumbent
Alabama	5	D	D	Bud Cramer (D)	Albert McDonald (R)	Ronnie G. Flippo (D) [1]
Arkansas	2	R	D	Ray Thornton (D)	Jim Keet (R)	Tommy F. Robinson (R) [1]
California	1	D	R	Frank Riggs (R)	Douglas H. Bosco (D)	Bosco
	14	R	R	John T. Doolittle (R)	Patricia Malberg (D)	Norman D. Shumway (R) [2]
	17	R	D	Calvin Dooley (D)	Charles "Chip" Pashayan Jr. (R)	Pashayan
	29	D	D	Maxine Waters (D)	Bill DeWitt (R)	Augustus F. Hawkins (D) [2]
	44	D	R	Randy "Duke" Cunningham (R)	Jim Bates (D)	Bates
Colorado	4	R	R	Wayne Allard (R)	Dick Bond (D)	Hank Brown (R) [3]
Connecticut	3	D	D	Rosa DeLauro (D)	Thomas Scott (R)	Bruce A. Morrison (D) [1]
	5	R	R	Gary Franks (R)	Toby Moffett (D)	John G. Rowland (R) [1]
Florida	2	R	D	Pete Peterson (D)	Bill Grant (R)	Grant
	11	D	D	Jim Bacchus (D)	Bill Tolley (R)	Bill Nelson (D) [1]
Hawaii	1	R	D	Neil Abercrombie (D)	Mike Liu (R)	Patricia Saiki (R) [3]
Idaho	1	R	D	Larry LaRocco (D)	C. A. "Skip" Smyser (R)	Larry E. Craig (R) [3]
Illinois	16	R	D	John W. Cox Jr. (D)	John W. Hallock Jr. (R)	Lynn Martin (R) [3]
Indiana	3	R	D	Tim Roemer (D)	John Hiler (R)	Hiler
Iowa	2	R	R	Jim Nussle (R)	Eric Tabor (D)	Tom Tauke (R) [3]
Kansas	5	R	R	Dick Nichols (R)	George Wingert (D)	Bob Whittaker (R) [2]
Louisiana	2	D	D	William J. Jefferson (D)	Marc H. Morial (D)	Lindy (Mrs. Hale) Boggs (D) [2]
Maine	1	D	D	Thomas H. Andrews (D)	David F. Emery (R)	Joseph E. Brennan (D) [1]
Maryland	1	D	R	Wayne T. Gilchrest (R)	Roy Dyson (D)	Dyson
Michigan	10	R	R	David Camp (R)	Joan Louise Dennison (D)	Bill Schuette (R) [3]
	13	D	D	Barbara-Rose Collins (D)	Carl R. Edwards Sr. (R)	George W. Crockett Jr. (D) [2]
Minnesota	3	R	R	Jim Ramstad (R)	Lewis DeMars (D)	Bill Frenzel (R) [2]
	7	R	D	Collin C. Peterson (D)	Arlan Stangeland (R)	Stangeland
Missouri	2	R	D	Joan Kelly Horn (D)	Jack Buechner (R)	Buechner
Nebraska	3	R	R	Bill Barrett (R)	Sandra K. Scofield (D)	Virginia Smith (R) [2]
New Hampshire	1	R	R	Bill Zeliff (R)	Joseph F. Keefe (D)	Robert C. Smith (R) [3]
	2	R	D	Dick Swett (D)	Chuck Douglas (R)	Douglas
New Jersey	1	D	D	Robert E. Andrews (D)	Daniel J. Mangini (R)	James J. Florio (D) [4]
	12	R	R	Dick Zimmer (R)	Marguerite Chandler (D)	Jim Courter (R) [2]
North Carolina	11	D	R	Charles H. Taylor (R)	James McClure Clarke (D)	Clarke
Ohio	1	D	D	Charles Luken (D)	J. Kenneth Blackwell (R)	Thomas A. Luken (D) [2]
	7	R	R	David L. Hobson (R)	Jack Schira (D)	Mike DeWine (R) [5]
	8	R	R	John A. Boehner (R)	Gregory V. Jolivette (D)	Donald E. "Buz" Lukens (R) [6]
Oklahoma	3	D	D	Bill Brewster (D)	Patrick K. Miller (R)	Wes Watkins (D) [1]
Oregon	5	R	D	Mike Kopetski (D)	Denny Smith (R)	Smith
Pennsylvania	18	D	R	Rick Santorum (R)	Doug Walgren (D)	Walgren
Rhode Island	2	R	D	John F. Reed (D)	Trudy Coxe (R)	Claudine Schneider (R) [3]
Texas	11	D	D	Chet Edwards (D)	Hugh D. Shine (R)	Marvin Leath (D) [2]
Utah	3	R	D	Bill Orton (D)	Karl Snow (R)	Howard C. Nielson (R) [2]
Vermont	AL	R	I	Bernard Sanders (I)	Peter Smith (R)	Smith
Virginia	8	R	D	James P. Moran Jr. (D)	Stan Parris (R)	Parris
Wisconsin	2	D	R	Scott L. Klug (R)	Robert W. Kastenmeier (D)	Kastenmeier

[1] *Ran for governor*
[2] *Retired*
[3] *Ran for Senate*
[4] *Resigned Jan. 16, 1990, to become governor of New Jersey*
[5] *Ran for lieutenant governor*
[6] *Defeated in primary, then resigned Oct. 24, 1990*

House Makeup, Party Gains and Losses

	Seats	101st Congress Dem.	101st Congress Rep.	102nd Congress Dem.	102nd Congress Rep.	Gain/ Loss
Ala.	7	5	2	5	2	
Alaska	1	0	1	0	1	
Ariz.	5	1	4	1	4	
Ark.	4	2	2	3	1	+1D/−1R
Calif.	45	27	18	26	19	−1D/+1R
Colo.	6	3	3	3	3	
Conn.	6	3	3	3	3	
Del.	1	1	0	1	0	
Fla.	19	8	11	9	10	+1D/−1R
Ga.	10	9	1	9	1	
Hawaii	2	1	1	2	0	+1D/−1R
Idaho	2	1	1	2	0	+1D/−1R
Ill.	22	14	8	15	7	+1D/−1R
Ind.	10	7	3	8	2	+1D/−1R
Iowa	6	2	4	2	4	
Kan.	5	2	3	2	3	
Ky.	7	4	3	4	3	
La.	8	4	4	4	4	
Maine	2	1	1	1	1	
Md.	8	6	2	5	3	−1D/+1R
Mass.	11	10	1	10	1	
Mich.	18	11	7	11	7	
Minn.	8	5	3	6	2	+1D/−1R
Miss.	5	5	0	5	0	
Mo.	9	5	4	6	3	+1D/−1R
Mont.	2	1	1	1	1	
Neb.	3	1	2	1	2	
Nev.	2	1	1	1	1	
N.H.	2	0	2	1	1	+1D/−1R
N.J.	14	7	6	8	6	+1D [1]
N.M.	3	1	2	1	2	
N.Y.	34	21	13	21	13	
N.C.	11	8	3	7	4	−1D/+1R
N.D.	1	1	0	1	0	
Ohio	21	11	9	11	10	+1R [2]
Okla.	6	4	2	4	2	
Ore.	5	3	2	4	1	+1D/−1R
Pa.	23	12	11	11	12	−1D/+1R
R.I.	2	0	2	1	1	+1D/−1R
S.C.	6	4	2	4	2	
S.D.	1	1	0	1	0	
Tenn.	9	6	3	6	3	
Texas	27	19	8	19	8	
Utah	3	1	2	2	1	+1D/−1R
Vt.	1	0	1	0	0	−1R [3]
Va.	10	5	5	6	4	+1D/−1R
Wash.	8	5	3	5	3	
W.Va.	4	4	0	4	0	
Wis.	9	5	4	4	5	−1D/+1R
Wyo.	1	0	1	0	1	
TOTALS	435 [4]	258	175	267	167	+9D/−8R

[1] *James J. Florio, D-N.J., resigned Jan. 16, 1990, to become governor of New Jersey.*
[2] *Donald E. "Buz" Lukens, R-Ohio, resigned Oct. 24, 1990.*
[3] *Bernard Sanders was elected as an independent in Vermont, replacing Republican Peter Smith.*

[4] *There were two vacancies at the end of the 101st Congress. Bernard Sanders was elected as an independent from Vermont to the 102nd Congress.*

financial dealings. The late shift in focus to the Persian Gulf helped boost him to a 4,400-vote win.

In Virginia's 1st District, another Armed Services Republican, Herbert H. Bateman, was struggling to win a fifth term. But Bateman, a tireless promoter of the 1st's extensive military and shipbuilding facilities, pulled out a win by fewer than 2,900 votes.

After the Supreme Court's 1989 decision in *Webster v. Reproductive Health Services,* many predicted that abortion would be one of the most electric political issues of 1990. In House races where anti-abortion incumbents were targeted for defeat, national abortion rights organizations scored several successes. Denny Smith and Parris fell, and support for abortion rights aided Horn in her campaign to defeat anti-abortion GOP Rep. Buechner. In Idaho's open 1st District, Democrat LaRocco made his abortion rights stance a central feature of his winning campaign.

But another prime target of abortion rights advocates, Florida Republican Craig T. James, won a second term with 56 percent. *(Abortion, p. 528)*

GOP Suffers in Open Seats

Twenty-seven open seats were up for election on Nov. 6. Democrats held all 10 of their open seats, while Republicans lost six of their 17 open seats.

Because of their one-sided political nature, four of the Democrats' open districts were a lock: the urban seats of the California 29th, Louisiana 2nd, Michigan 13th and the rural Oklahoma 3rd. Four GOP seats either began as or quickly became virtual locks for retention: the Kansas 5th, Michigan 10th, Minnesota 3rd and Ohio 7th. All eight districts stayed in the incumbent party's hands.

But of the remaining 19 open seats, 13 had been held by Republicans, and Democrats won six.

The GOP had to defend the seats of six Republicans who retired, and GOP recruiting for governor and the Senate compounded the party's open-seat headaches. Two House Republicans ran for governor: Robinson of Arkansas and John G. Rowland of Connecticut. Robinson lost in the primary and did nothing to help Republicans keep his district; Democrat Thornton easily won. Rowland lost statewide Nov. 6; Franks held the House seat for the GOP.

Five Democrats ran for governor either in primaries or the general election: Wes Watkins of Oklahoma, Joseph E. Brennan of Maine, Ronnie G. Flippo of Alabama, Bruce A. Morrison of Connecticut and Bill Nelson of Florida. All five lost, but all five House seats remained Democratic. *(Gubernatorial races, p. 926)*

Eight House members — all Republican — ran for the Senate in the general election. Three won: Hank Brown of Colorado, Larry E. Craig of Idaho and Robert C. Smith of

Continued on p. 922

House Membership in 102nd Congress

Lineup

Democrats	**267**	**Freshmen**	**25**
Republicans	**167**	**Freshmen**	**18**
Independents	**1**	**Freshmen**	**1**

 # Freshman representative

ALABAMA

1 Sonny Callahan (R)
2 Bill Dickinson (R)
3 Glen Browder (D)
4 Tom Bevill (D)
5 Bud Cramer (D)#
6 Ben Erdreich (D)
7 Claude Harris (D)

ALASKA

AL Don Young (R)

ARIZONA

1 John J. Rhodes III (R)
2 Morris K. Udall (D)
3 Bob Stump (R)
4 Jon Kyl (R)
5 Jim Kolbe (R)

ARKANSAS

1 Bill Alexander (D)
2 Ray Thornton (D)#
3 John Paul Hammerschmidt (R)
4 Beryl Anthony Jr. (D)

CALIFORNIA

1 Frank Riggs (R)#
2 Wally Herger (R)
3 Robert T. Matsui (D)
4 Vic Fazio (D)
5 Nancy Pelosi (D)
6 Barbara Boxer (D)
7 George Miller (D)
8 Ronald V. Dellums (D)
9 Pete Stark (D)
10 Don Edwards (D)
11 Tom Lantos (D)
12 Tom Campbell (R)
13 Norman Y. Mineta (D)
14 John T. Doolittle (R) #
15 Gary Condit (D)
16 Leon E. Panetta (D)
17 Calvin Dooley (D)#
18 Richard H. Lehman (D)
19 Robert J. Lagomarsino (R)
20 Bill Thomas (R)
21 Elton Gallegly (R)
22 Carlos J. Moorhead (R)
23 Anthony C. Beilenson (D)
24 Henry A. Waxman (D)
25 Edward R. Roybal (D)
26 Howard L. Berman (D)
27 Mel Levine (D)
28 Julian C. Dixon (D)
29 Maxine Waters (D)#
30 Matthew G. Martinez (D)
31 Mervyn M. Dymally (D)
32 Glenn M. Anderson (D)
33 David Dreier (R)
34 Esteban E. Torres (D)
35 Jerry Lewis (R)
36 George E. Brown Jr. (D)
37 Al McCandless (R)
38 Robert K. Dornan (R)
39 William E. Dannemeyer (R)
40 C. Christopher Cox (R)
41 Bill Lowery (R)
42 Dana Rohrabacher (R)
43 Ron Packard (R)
44 Randy "Duke" Cunningham (R)#
45 Duncan Hunter (R)

COLORADO

1 Patricia Schroeder (D)
2 David E. Skaggs (D)
3 Ben Nighthorse Campbell (D)
4 Wayne Allard (R)#
5 Joel Hefley (R)
6 Dan Schaefer (R)

CONNECTICUT

1 Barbara B. Kennelly (D)
2 Sam Gejdenson (D)
3 Rosa DeLauro (D)#
4 Christopher Shays (R)
5 Gary Franks (R)#
6 Nancy L. Johnson (R)

DELAWARE

AL Thomas R. Carper (D)

FLORIDA

1 Earl Hutto (D)
2 Pete Peterson (D)#
3 Charles E. Bennett (D)
4 Craig T. James (R)
5 Bill McCollum (R)
6 Cliff Stearns (R)
7 Sam M. Gibbons (D)
8 C.W. Bill Young (R)
9 Michael Bilirakis (R)
10 Andy Ireland (R)
11 Jim Bacchus (D)#
12 Tom Lewis (R)
13 Porter J. Goss (R)
14 Harry A. Johnston (D)
15 E. Clay Shaw Jr. (R)
16 Lawrence J. Smith (D)
17 William Lehman (D)
18 Ileana Ros-Lehtinen (R)
19 Dante B. Fascell (D)

GEORGIA

1 Lindsay Thomas (D)
2 Charles Hatcher (D)
3 Richard Ray (D)
4 Ben Jones (D)
5 John Lewis (D)
6 Newt Gingrich (R)
7 George "Buddy" Darden (D)
8 J. Roy Rowland (D)
9 Ed Jenkins (D)
10 Doug Barnard Jr. (D)

HAWAII

1 Neil Abercrombie (D)#
2 Patsy T. Mink (D)

IDAHO

1 Larry LaRocco (D)#
2 Richard Stallings (D)

ILLINOIS

1 Charles A. Hayes (D)
2 Gus Savage (D)
3 Marty Russo (D)
4 George E. Sangmeister (D)
5 William O. Lipinski (D)
6 Henry J. Hyde (R)
7 Cardiss Collins (D)
8 Dan Rostenkowski (D)
9 Sidney R. Yates (D)
10 John Porter (R)
11 Frank Annunzio (D)
12 Philip M. Crane (R)
13 Harris W. Fawell (R)
14 Dennis Hastert (R)
15 Edward Madigan (R)
16 John W. Cox Jr. (D)#
17 Lane Evans (D)
18 Robert H. Michel (R)
19 Terry L. Bruce (D)
20 Richard J. Durbin (D)
21 Jerry F. Costello (D)
22 Glenn Poshard (D)

INDIANA

1 Peter J. Visclosky (D)
2 Philip R. Sharp (D)
3 Tim Roemer (D)#
4 Jill Long (D)
5 Jim Jontz (D)
6 Dan Burton (R)
7 John T. Myers (R)
8 Frank McCloskey (D)
9 Lee H. Hamilton (D)
10 Andrew Jacobs Jr. (D)

IOWA

1 Jim Leach (R)
2 Jim Nussle (R)#
3 Dave Nagle (D)
4 Neal Smith (D)
5 Jim Ross Lightfoot (R)
6 Fred Grandy (R)

KANSAS

1 Pat Roberts (R)
2 Jim Slattery (D)
3 Jan Meyers (R)
4 Dan Glickman (D)
5 Dick Nichols (R)#

KENTUCKY

1 Carroll Hubbard Jr. (D)
2 William H. Natcher (D)
3 Romano L. Mazzoli (D)
4 Jim Bunning (R)
5 Harold Rogers (R)
6 Larry J. Hopkins (R)
7 Carl C. Perkins (D)

LOUISIANA

1 Bob Livingston (R)
2 William J. Jefferson (D)#
3 W. J. "Billy" Tauzin (D)
4 Jim McCrery (R)
5 Jerry Huckaby (D)
6 Richard H. Baker (R)
7 Jimmy Hayes (D)
8 Clyde C. Holloway (R)

MAINE

1 Thomas H. Andrews (D)#
2 Olympia J. Snowe (R)

MARYLAND

1 Wayne T. Gilchrest (R)#
2 Helen Delich Bentley (R)
3 Benjamin L. Cardin (D)
4 Tom McMillen (D)
5 Steny H. Hoyer (D)
6 Beverly B. Byron (D)
7 Kweisi Mfume (D)
8 Constance A. Morella (R)

MASSACHUSETTS

1 Silvio O. Conte (R)
2 Richard E. Neal (D)
3 Joseph D. Early (D)
4 Barney Frank (D)
5 Chester G. Atkins (D)
6 Nicholas Mavroules (D)
7 Edward J. Markey (D)
8 Joseph P. Kennedy II (D)
9 Joe Moakley (D)
10 Gerry E. Studds (D)
11 Brian Donnelly (D)

MICHIGAN

1 John Conyers Jr. (D)
2 Carl D. Pursell (R)
3 Howard Wolpe (D)
4 Fred Upton (R)
5 Paul B. Henry (R)
6 Bob Carr (D)
7 Dale E. Kildee (D)
8 Bob Traxler (D)
9 Guy Vander Jagt (R)
10 Dave Camp (R)#
11 Robert W. Davis (R)
12 David E. Bonior (D)
13 Barbara-Rose Collins (D)#
14 Dennis M. Hertel (D)
15 William D. Ford (D)
16 John D. Dingell (D)

17 Sander M. Levin (D)
18 William S. Broomfield (R)

MINNESOTA

1 Timothy J. Penny (D)
2 Vin Weber (R)
3 Jim Ramstad (R)#
4 Bruce F. Vento (D)
5 Martin Olav Sabo (D)
6 Gerry Sikorski (D)
7 Collin C. Peterson (D)#
8 James L. Oberstar (D)

MISSISSIPPI

1 Jamie L. Whitten (D)
2 Mike Espy (D)
3 G.V. "Sonny" Montgomery (D)
4 Mike Parker (D)
5 Gene Taylor (D)

MISSOURI

1 William L. Clay (D)
2 Joan Kelly Horn (D)#
3 Richard A. Gephardt (D)
4 Ike Skelton (D)
5 Alan Wheat (D)
6 E. Thomas Coleman (R)
7 Mel Hancock (R)
8 Bill Emerson (R)
9 Harold L. Volkmer (D)

MONTANA

1 Pat Williams (D)
2 Ron Marlenee (R)

NEBRASKA

1 Doug Bereuter (R)
2 Peter Hoagland (D)
3 Bill Barrett (R)#

NEVADA

1 James Bilbray (D)
2 Barbara F. Vucanovich (R)

NEW HAMPSHIRE

1 Bill Zeliff (R)#
2 Dick Swett (D)#

NEW JERSEY

1 Robert E. Andrews (D)#
2 William J. Hughes (D)
3 Frank Pallone Jr. (D)
4 Christopher H. Smith (R)
5 Marge Roukema (R)
6 Bernard J. Dwyer (D)
7 Matthew J. Rinaldo (R)
8 Robert A. Roe (D)
9 Robert G. Torricelli (D)
10 Donald M. Payne (D)
11 Dean A. Gallo (R)
12 Dick Zimmer (R)#
13 H. James Saxton (R)
14 Frank J. Guarini (D)

NEW MEXICO

1 Steven H. Schiff (R)
2 Joe Skeen (R)
3 Bill Richardson (D)

NEW YORK

1 George J. Hochbrueckner (D)
2 Thomas J. Downey (D)
3 Robert J. Mrazek (D)
4 Norman F. Lent (R)
5 Raymond J. McGrath (R)
6 Floyd H. Flake (D)
7 Gary L. Ackerman (D)
8 James H. Scheuer (D)
9 Thomas J. Manton (D)
10 Charles E. Schumer (D)
11 Ed Towns (D)
12 Major R. Owens (D)
13 Stephen J. Solarz (D)
14 Susan Molinari (R)
15 Bill Green (R)
16 Charles B. Rangel (D)
17 Ted Weiss (D)
18 Jose E. Serrano (D)
19 Eliot L. Engel (D)
20 Nita M. Lowey (D)
21 Hamilton Fish Jr. (R)
22 Benjamin A. Gilman (R)
23 Michael R. McNulty (D)
24 Gerald B. H. Solomon (R)
25 Sherwood Boehlert (R)
26 David O'B. Martin (R)
27 James T. Walsh (R)
28 Matthew F. McHugh (D)
29 Frank Horton (R)
30 Louise M. Slaughter (D)
31 Bill Paxon (R)
32 John J. LaFalce (D)
33 Henry J. Nowak (D)
34 Amo Houghton (R)

NORTH CAROLINA

1 Walter B. Jones (D)
2 Tim Valentine (D)
3 H. Martin Lancaster (D)
4 David E. Price (D)
5 Stephen L. Neal (D)
6 Howard Coble (R)
7 Charlie Rose (D)
8 W. G. "Bill" Hefner (D)
9 Alex McMillan (R)
10 Cass Ballenger (R)
11 Charles H. Taylor (R)#

NORTH DAKOTA

AL Byron L. Dorgan (D)

OHIO

1 Charles Luken (D)#
2 Bill Gradison (R)
3 Tony P. Hall (D)
4 Michael G. Oxley (R)
5 Paul E. Gillmor (R)
6 Bob McEwen (R)
7 David L. Hobson (R)#
8 John A. Boehner (R)#
9 Marcy Kaptur (D)
10 Clarence E. Miller (R)
11 Dennis E. Eckart (D)
12 John R. Kasich (R)
13 Don J. Pease (D)
14 Thomas C. Sawyer (D)
15 Chalmers P. Wylie (R)
16 Ralph Regula (R)
17 James A. Traficant Jr. (D)
18 Doug Applegate (D)
19 Edward F. Feighan (D)
20 Mary Rose Oakar (D)
21 Louis Stokes (D)

OKLAHOMA

1 James M. Inhofe (R)
2 Mike Synar (D)
3 Bill Brewster (D)#
4 Dave McCurdy (D)
5 Mickey Edwards (R)
6 Glenn English (D)

OREGON

1 Les AuCoin (D)
2 Bob Smith (R)
3 Ron Wyden (D)
4 Peter A. DeFazio (D)
5 Mike Kopetski (D)#

PENNSYLVANIA

1 Thomas M. Foglietta (D)
2 William H. Gray III (D)
3 Robert A. Borski (D)
4 Joe Kolter (D)
5 Richard T. Schulze (R)
6 Gus Yatron (D)
7 Curt Weldon (R)
8 Peter H. Kostmayer (D)
9 Bud Shuster (R)
10 Joseph M. McDade (R)
11 Paul E. Kanjorski (D)
12 John P. Murtha (D)
13 Lawrence Coughlin (R)
14 William J. Coyne (D)
15 Don Ritter (R)
16 Robert S. Walker (R)
17 George W. Gekas (R)
18 Rick Santorum (R)#
19 Bill Goodling (R)
20 Joseph M. Gaydos (D)
21 Tom Ridge (R)
22 Austin J. Murphy (D)
23 William F. Clinger Jr. (R)

RHODE ISLAND

1 Ronald K. Machtley (R)
2 John F. Reed (D)#

SOUTH CAROLINA

1 Arthur Ravenel Jr. (R)
2 Floyd D. Spence (R)
3 Butler Derrick (D)
4 Liz J. Patterson (D)
5 John M. Spratt Jr. (D)
6 Robin Tallon (D)

SOUTH DAKOTA

AL Tim Johnson (D)

TENNESSEE

1 James H. Quillen (R)
2 John J. "Jimmy" Duncan Jr. (R)
3 Marilyn Lloyd (D)
4 Jim Cooper (D)
5 Bob Clement (D)
6 Bart Gordon (D)
7 Don Sundquist (R)
8 John Tanner (D)
9 Harold E. Ford (D)

TEXAS

1 Jim Chapman (D)
2 Charles Wilson (D)
3 Steve Bartlett (R)
4 Ralph M. Hall (D)
5 John Bryant (D)
6 Joe L. Barton (R)
7 Bill Archer (R)
8 Jack Fields (R)
9 Jack Brooks (D)
10 J. J. "Jake" Pickle (D)
11 Chet Edwards (D)#
12 Pete Geren (D)
13 Bill Sarpalius (D)
14 Greg Laughlin (D)
15 E. "Kika" de la Garza (D)
16 Ronald D. Coleman (D)
17 Charles W. Stenholm (D)
18 Craig Washington (D)
19 Larry Combest (R)
20 Henry B. Gonzalez (D)
21 Lamar Smith (R)
22 Tom DeLay (R)
23 Albert G. Bustamante (D)
24 Martin Frost (D)
25 Michael A. Andrews (D)
26 Dick Armey (R)
27 Solomon P. Ortiz (D)

UTAH

1 James V. Hansen (R)
2 Wayne Owens (D)
3 Bill Orton (D)#

VERMONT

AL Bernard Sanders (I)#

VIRGINIA

1 Herbert H. Bateman (R)
2 Owen B. Pickett (D)
3 Thomas J. Bliley Jr. (R)
4 Norman Sisisky (D)
5 Lewis F. Payne Jr. (D)
6 Jim Olin (D)
7 D. French Slaughter Jr. (R)
8 James P. Moran Jr. (D)#
9 Rick Boucher (D)
10 Frank R. Wolf (R)

WASHINGTON

1 John Miller (R)
2 Al Swift (D)
3 Jolene Unsoeld (D)
4 Sid Morrison (R)
5 Thomas S. Foley (D)
6 Norm Dicks (D)
7 Jim McDermott (D)
8 Rod Chandler (R)

WEST VIRGINIA

1 Alan B. Mollohan (D)
2 Harley O. Staggers Jr. (D)
3 Bob Wise (D)
4 Nick J. Rahall II (D)

WISCONSIN

1 Les Aspin (D)
2 Scott L. Klug (R)#
3 Steve Gunderson (R)
4 Gerald D. Kleczka (D)
5 Jim Moody (D)
6 Thomas E. Petri (R)
7 David R. Obey (D)
8 Toby Roth (R)
9 F. James Sensenbrenner Jr. (R)

WYOMING

AL Craig Thomas (R)

Independent Sanders

Bernard Sanders' election in 1990 to the at-large House seat from Vermont made him the first truly independent member of the House since 1955 and the first avowed socialist to win a seat in Congress in six decades.

Sanders, the former four-term mayor of Burlington, Vermont's largest city, ousted freshman GOP Rep. Peter Smith with 56 percent of the vote. Sanders had narrowly lost to Smith two years earlier.

A self-described socialist, Sanders ran as an independent. He used populist themes in his campaign, accusing Republicans and Democrats alike of pursuing the priorities of big business and ignoring the needs of the middle class, the poor and the elderly.

During his campaign and after the election, Sanders said he planned to join in the Democratic Caucus. In the face of opposition from a broad array of House Democrats, however, Sanders withdrew that request after being assured he would receive committee assignments.

"He will not be allowed in the Democratic Caucus because he is not a Democrat," House Rules Committee Chairman Joe Moakley, D-Mass., explained.

Sanders was the first truly independent House member since Henry Frazier Reams of Ohio (1951-55). Reams served two terms before being defeated by a Democrat, Thomas Ludlow Ashley.

The last House member elected as an independent was Thomas M. Foglietta of Pennsylvania in 1980. Foglietta defeated a Democratic incumbent convicted in the Abscam scandal — Michael "Ozzie" Myers — and joined the Democrats when he assumed his seat in 1981. *(1980 Almanac, p. 515)*

The last Socialist House member was Victor Luitpold Berger of Milwaukee (1911-13, 1923-29). One other representative was elected and served throughout his House career as a Socialist: Meyer London of New York (1915-19, 1921-23).

In addition, New York's Fiorello H. LaGuardia won election as a Socialist in 1924 after having served in the House two terms as a Republican (1917-19, 1923-25). LaGuardia was listed as a Socialist for two years and then served again as a Republican from 1927-33.

Two House members sometimes counted as Socialists — Vito Marcantonio of New York (1935-37, 1939-51) and Leo Isacson (1948-49), both of New York — were actually members of the more militant American Labor Party. Marcantonio served his first term as a Republican.

Continued from p. 919

New Hampshire. Five lost: Bill Schuette of Michigan, Lynn Martin of Illinois, Patricia Saiki of Hawaii, Claudine Schneider of Rhode Island and Tom Tauke of Iowa. *(Senate races, p. 911)*

Of the eight House seats Republicans left behind, Democrats picked off four: those of Craig, Martin, Saiki and Schneider.

Democrats fielded strong candidates in all eight races. In Hawaii, Democrats nominated Abercrombie, a popular former legislator. In 1986, Abercrombie won and lost a seat in the House on the same day: He won a special election to replace Rep. Cecil Heftel but lost the Democratic primary for a full term. In 1990, Abercrombie sailed past GOP state Rep. Mike Liu.

In Idaho, Democrats offered LaRocco, who gave Craig a tough run in 1982 and was well-known for his work as an aide to Sen. Frank Church (1957-81) in the 1970s and on a statewide referendum in 1988. A tough primary boosted his visibility in 1990. LaRocco and his lesser-known GOP foe, state Sen. C. A. "Skip" Smyser, battled bitterly, but LaRocco won with 53 percent.

In Illinois, Democrats scarcely hoped to compete in a seat that had not elected a member of their party in well over a century. But the GOP nominee, state Rep. John W. Hallock Jr., bumbled through the campaign. Democrat John W. Cox Jr., a former prosecutor, won by 9 percentage points.

In Rhode Island, Republicans thought they had picked an ideal successor for Schneider: Trudy Coxe, an environmental activist with Schneider's moderate-to-liberal GOP inclinations. Coxe, however, turned out to be a less than adept candidate. Democratic state Sen. John F. Reed, a West Point graduate who recounted his military experiences eagerly and often, was helped by the focus on the Persian Gulf crisis and his long record of opposition to reviled Republican Gov. Edward D. DiPrete. With Coxe stumbling and DiPrete plummeting to a humiliating defeat, Reed ran up a 59 percent win.

Eleven House members retired, but only one retiree's seat switched parties: that of Utah Republican Howard C. Nielson. In one of the country's most Republican districts, a corrosive GOP primary, a conservative Democratic nominee and ethical questions surrounding the Republican nominee, former state Sen. Karl Snow, combined to elect first-time candidate Bill Orton.

One special election was held Nov. 6. In the vacant New Jersey 1st, complete, official returns gave Democrat Robert E. Andrews 72,324 votes (55 percent); Republican Daniel J. Mangini had 58,671 votes (45 percent). Andrews won a full term in the 102nd Congress by a similar margin. There was no special election in the vacant Ohio 8th, to be represented by Republican John Boehner in the 102nd Congress. *(1990 special elections, p. 934)*

Lose-to-Win Strategy

The best training for a successful House campaign had often been a losing one. The House had many members who first lost at least one race before winning a seat.

Seven of 1990's first-time House winners had previously lost at least one race in their district: Abercrombie, LaRocco, Sanders, Taylor, Maryland Republican Wayne T. Gilchrest, Oregon Democrat Mike Kopetski and Minnesota Democrat Collin C. Peterson.

The most persistent of these was Peterson, who lost to Stangeland in 1984 and 1986 (the latter by only 121 votes) and lost bids for the Democratic nomination in 1982 and 1988.

Some repeat challengers improved in 1990 on previous outings but failed to break through.

Georgia's Worley, who got 41 percent against Gingrich in 1988, nearly won in 1990.

In Massachusetts, Republican Jon L. Bryan rode the state's anti-Democratic fever to a 47 percent tally against Democratic Rep. Gerry E. Studds; in 1988, Bryan got only one-third of the vote against Studds.

But two other second-chancers fared poorly in closely watched races. In Indiana, Republican Mike Pence held Democratic Rep. Philip R. Sharp to 53 percent in 1988, but Sharp won the 1990 rematch easily. In North Carolina, Republican Ted Blanton, who nearly ambushed longtime Democratic Rep. W. G. "Bill" Hefner in 1988, lost Nov. 6 by 10 percentage points.

Poor Return on Investment

For some candidates, 1990 proved that money cannot buy everything — in this case, a seat in the House.

North Carolina Republican John Carrington spent more than $890,000 — much of it his own — against Democratic Rep. David E. Price. Price won with 58 percent.

In New York, Republican William W. Koeppel raised eyebrows when he reported spending more than $430,000 against Democratic Rep. Ted Weiss. Weiss, who spent $112,000, ended up with 80 percent of the vote to Koeppel's 16 percent.

In New Jersey's open 12th, Democrat Marguerite Chandler, a businesswoman and philanthropist, spent more than $1.7 million on her congressional bid. But on Election Day, she took just 31 percent. Early in 1990, Chandler appeared to be a viable challenger to GOP Rep. Jim Courter, who was damaged after losing the 1989 governor's race. But once Courter pulled out and a mainstream Republican, Dick Zimmer, won the nomination, Chandler had no chance. ■

Record Number of Blacks, Women Elected

Election Day 1990 sent record numbers of women and blacks to the House, although both remained underrepresented in comparison with their proportions of the population.

Thirty-one women were elected to serve in the 102nd Congress — 29 in the House, two in the Senate. That was four more women than were elected in November 1988 but equal to the number of women at the end of the 101st Congress.

The newcomers, all House members, were Barbara-Rose Collins, D-Mich.; Rosa DeLauro, D-Conn.; Joan Kelly Horn, D-Mo.; Maxine Waters, D-Calif.; and Eleanor Holmes Norton, D-D.C., a non-voting delegate.

Twenty-five women were elected to the House two years earlier. Four more — Ileana Ros-Lehtinen, R-Fla.; Jill Long, D-Ind.; Susan Molinari, R-N.Y.; and Patsy T. Mink, D-Hawaii — won special elections in 1989 and 1990.

Five women left the House after the 101st Congress. Patricia Saiki, R-Hawaii, Lynn Martin, R-Ill., and Claudine Schneider, R-R.I., left to wage unsuccessful Senate races. Virginia Smith, R-Neb., and Lindy (Mrs. Hale) Boggs, D-La., retired.

AVERAGE AGE

102nd Congress [1]

	All	Senate	House
Both parties	53.6	57.2	52.8
Democrats	53.4	57.5	52.6
Republicans	53.9	56.8	53.2

90th-101st Congresses [2]

	All	Senate	House
101st	52.8	55.6	52.1
100th	52.5	54.4	50.7
99th	50.5	54.2	49.7
98th	47.0	53.4	45.5
97th	49.2	52.5	48.4
96th	50.9	55.5	49.8
95th	50.3	54.7	49.3
94th	50.9	55.5	49.8
93th	52.0	55.3	51.1
92th	52.7	56.4	51.9
91st	53.0	56.6	52.2
90th	52.1	57.7	50.8

[1] *Ages as of Nov. 9, 1990*
[2] *Average age calculated at or near the beginning of each Congress*

Women made no gains in the Senate, although eight ran as major-party candidates. That left Nancy Landon Kassebaum, R-Kan., and Barbara A. Mikulski, D-Md., as the only women in the Senate. Kassebaum won re-election with 74 percent of the vote; Mikulski's term was not up until 1992. *(Women in Congress, p. 924)*

Although 31 was the highest number of women to serve in a Congress, they still made up only 2 percent of the Senate and 6.7 percent of the House. Women constituted more than half of the population and more than half of all voters.

Blacks, Other Minorities

Blacks, too, remained underrepresented as a group, de spite a record 26 members elected to the House (one of whom was a non-voting delegate from the District of Columbia). That gave blacks 6 percent of House seats, while they constituted 12.1 percent of the population, according to the 1990 census.

No black had served in the Senate since Edward W. Brooke, R-Mass. (1967-79), lost his re-election bid in 1978. North Carolina Democrat Harvey B. Gantt ran against GOP Sen. Jesse Helms in 1990 but lost by 53 percent to 47 percent after a campaign that featured last-minute advertising by Helms asserting that Gantt supported racial job quotas.

The elections gave blacks two noteworthy gains. Three of the newly elected women — Collins, Norton and Waters — joined Rep. Cardiss Collins, D-Ill., to make the largest black women's caucus since the period from 1973 to 1979, when four black women served. And Gary Franks, an alderman from Waterbury, Conn., became the first black Republican to serve in the House since Oscar De Priest of Illinois (1929-35). Franks defeated former Democratic Rep. Toby Moffett for a seat vacated by Republican John G. Rowland.

No new Hispanic lawmakers were elected to the House on Nov. 6. Tony Coelho, D-Calif. (1979-89), and Robert Garcia, D-N.Y. (1978-90), resigned during the 101st Congress, but Ros-Lehtinen and Jose E. Serrano, D-N.Y. (who replaced Garcia), kept the net number of Hispanics in the House at 12.

Hawaiian politics reduced the number of Asian and Pacific Island House members by one. Saiki lost her bid to unseat Democratic Sen. Daniel K. Akaka. Saiki's seat was won by Democrat Neil Abercrombie. Mink, who filled Akaka's vacant seat in 1990 and won re-election, brought the total number of Asian and Pacific Island lawmakers to seven.

Like blacks, Hispanics and Asian-Americans remained underrepresented in Congress compared with their shares

Minorities in Congress

Women

House (29)

California: Nancy Pelosi, D; Barbara Boxer, D.; Maxine Waters, D.
Colorado: Patricia Schroeder, D.
Connecticut: Barbara B. Kennelly, D; Rosa DeLauro, D; Nancy L. Johnson, R.
District of Columbia: Eleanor Holmes Norton, D.*
Florida: Ileana Ros-Lehtinen, R.
Hawaii: Patsy T. Mink, D.
Illinois: Cardiss Collins, D.
Indiana: Jill Long, D.
Kansas: Jan Meyers, R.
Maine: Olympia J. Snowe, R.
Maryland: Helen Delich Bentley, R; Beverly B. Byron, D; Constance A. Morella, R.
Michigan: Barbara-Rose Collins, D.
Missouri: Joan Kelly Horn, D.
Nevada: Barbara F. Vucanovich, R.
New Jersey: Marge Roukema, R.
New York: Susan Molinari, R; Nita M. Lowey, D.; Louise M. Slaughter, D.
Ohio: Marcy Kaptur, D; Mary Rose Oakar, D.
South Carolina: Liz J. Patterson, D.
Tennessee: Marilyn Lloyd, D.
Washington: Jolene Unsoeld, D.

Senate (2)

Kansas: Nancy Landon Kassebaum, R.
Maryland: Barbara A. Mikulski, D.

Blacks

House (26)

California: Ronald V. Dellums, D; Julian C. Dixon, D; Maxine Waters, D.; Mervyn M. Dymally, D.
Connecticut: Gary Franks, R.
District of Columbia: Eleanor Holmes Norton, D.*
Georgia: John Lewis, D.
Illinois: Charles A. Hayes, D; Gus Savage, D; Cardiss Collins, D.
Louisiana: William Jefferson, D.
Maryland: Kweisi Mfume, D.
Michigan: John Conyers Jr., D; Barbara-Rose Collins, D.
Mississippi: Mike Espy, D.
Missouri: William L. Clay, D; Alan Wheat, D.
New Jersey: Donald M. Payne, D.
New York: Floyd H. Flake, D; Edolphus Towns, D; Major R. Owens, D; Charles B. Rangel, D.
Ohio: Louis Stokes, D.
Pennsylvania: William H. Gray III, D.
Tennessee: Harold E. Ford, D.
Texas: Craig Washington, D.

Hispanics

House (12)

California: Edward R. Roybal, D; Matthew G. Martinez, D; Esteban E. Torres, D.
Florida: Ileana Ros-Lehtinen, R.
New Mexico: Bill Richardson, D.
New York: Jose E. Serrano, D.
Puerto Rico: Jaime B. Fuster, Popular Dem.*
Texas: E. "Kika" de la Garza, D; Henry B. Gonzalez, D; Albert G. Bustamante, D; Solomon P. Ortiz, D.
Virgin Islands: Ron de Lugo, D.*

Asians and Pacific Islanders

House (5)

American Samoa: Eni F. H. Faleomavaega, D.*
California: Robert T. Matsui, D, Norman Y. Mineta, D.
Guam: Ben Blaz, R.*
Hawaii: Patsy T. Mink, D.

Senate (2)

Hawaii: Daniel K. Inouye, D.; Daniel K. Akaka, D.

* *Non-voting delegate*

of the total population. Hispanics numbered just under 3 percent of the House membership, compared with 9 percent of the overall population; Asian-Americans and Pacific Islanders held under 2 percent of the House seats, compared with 2.9 percent of the overall population. *(Minorities in Congress, this page)*

Blacks lost a bit of power on Capitol Hill in the 102nd Congress as two of their number left House chairmanships. Augustus F. Hawkins, D-Calif., chairman of the Education and Labor Committee, retired. Julian C. Dixon, D-Calif., gave up his chairmanship of the Committee on Standards of Official Conduct, after several extensions beyond the Democrats' traditional two-term limit.

Women made little headway on the Capitol Hill leadership ladder during the 101st Congress, apart from the ascension of Mikulski to chair the Appropriations Subcommittee on VA, HUD and Independent Agencies.

In the House, women chaired no committees at the start of the 102nd Congress, and they had netted no new subcommittee gavels in the previous two years. Patricia Schroeder, D-Colo., and Beverly B. Byron, D-Md., chaired Armed Services subcommittees.

Mary Rose Oakar, D-Ohio, Marilyn Lloyd, D-Tenn., and Cardiss Collins headed subcommittees on the Banking; Science, Space and Technology; and Government Operations committees, respectively.

On Feb. 28, 1991, however, Schroeder was named to chair the Select Committee on Youth, Children and Families. She succeeded George Miller, D-Calif., who became acting chairman of the Interior Committee while Morris K. Udall, D-Ariz., was recuperating from the combined effects of a fall and Parkinson's disease.

Women lost a seat on the House Rules Committee, after the departure of Lynn Martin. Cardiss Collins was the only woman on the Energy and Commerce Committee, which had four vacancies in 1991.

The Graying of Congress

As of Nov. 9, 1990, the average age of members who would be serving in the 102nd Congress was 53.6, the oldest since the 85th Congress, when the average age was 53.8. The average age for senators was 57.2; for House members, 52.8. *(Average age 90th-102nd Congresses, p. 923)*

The oldest senator remained Strom Thurmond, R-S.C., who turned

88 less than a month after Election Day. The retirement of Hawkins, 83, and George W. Crockett Jr., D-Mich., 81, left Sidney R. Yates, D-Ill., as the oldest House member at 81.

The average age had been creeping upward since the 98th Congress, when members were the youngest of the post-World War II era. The trend was partly attributable to the aging trend of the nation's population. But low turnover was a bigger factor.

Only five freshmen joined the Senate in January 1991 (four elected in November and John Seymour appointed to replace Pete Wilson in California), the fewest of the postwar era.

In the House, the 44 freshmen made up only 10 percent of the voting membership. That was up from the 7.6 percent of 1988 but low by historical standards. The youngest freshman — and the youngest member of Congress — was Jim Nussle, R-Iowa, who was 30. The oldest member of the freshman class was Dick Nichols, R-Kan., who was 64.

Occupations

In comparison with the 101st Congress, the 1991 House and Senate had three fewer lawyers, 51 fewer members whose occupations were in public service or politics before joining Congress, five more farmers, 14 more educators, eight fewer journalists and 12 fewer in business or banking. *(Members' occupations, this page)*

The 102nd Congress had 244 lawyers, 45.6 percent of all members. The high was 316 in 1963.

The trend away from lawyers was more evident among Republicans than Democrats and more apparent in the House than the Senate. GOP lawyers in the House dropped from 117 in 1953 to 57 in the 102nd Congress.

There were 61 Senate lawyers in 1991; 63 was the average over the previous 40 years. Of five freshman senators, only Rep. Hank Brown, R-Colo., held a law degree. College professor Paul Wellstone, D-Minn., held a doctorate. Larry E. Craig, R-Idaho, and Robert C. Smith, R-N.H., were former House members who listed occupations in real estate, as did Seymour.

Thirteen former members ran for House seats in the 1990 election cycle. Of those, eight lost in primaries, three lost in the general election, and two won. The winners were Ray Thornton, D-Ark., who served from 1973 to 1979, and Neil Abercrombie, who served a little more than three months at the end of the 99th Congress in 1986-87.

Members' Occupations

	House			Senate			Congress
	D	R	Total	D	R	Total	Total
Actor/Entertainer	1	1	2	0	0	0	2
Aeronautics	0	1	1	1	0	1	2
Agriculture	11	9	20	3	5	8	28
Business or Banking	77	80	157	15	17	32	189
Clergy	2	0	2	0	1	1	3
Education	37	19	57 †	6	4	10	67 †
Engineering	4	3	7	0	0	0	7
Journalism	14	10	25 †	8	2	10	35 †
Labor Officials	3	0	3	0	0	0	3
Law	126	57	183	35	25	60	243
Law Enforcement	4	1	5	0	0	0	5
Medicine	3	2	5	0	0	0	5
Military	0	1	1	0	1	1	2
Professional Sports	2	1	3	1	0	1	4
Public Service/Politics	41	20	61	4	0	4	65

** Because some members have more than one occupation, totals are higher than total membership.*
† Includes Sanders, I-Vt.

Religious Affiliations

	House			Senate			Congress
	D	R	Total	D	R	Total	Total
African Methodist Episcopal	2	0	2	0	0	0	2
Apostolic Christian	0	1	1	0	0	0	1
Baptist	35	12	47	4	8	12	59
Christian Church	1	0	1	0	0	0	1
Christian Reformed Church	0	1	1	0	0	0	1
Christian Science	0	2	2	0	0	0	2
Church of Christ	3	1	4	0	0	0	4
Disciples of Christ	1	0	1	0	0	0	1
Episcopalian	24	17	41	6	12	18	59
French Huguenot	0	1	1	0	0	0	1
Greek Orthodox	2	4	6	1	0	1	7
Jewish	26	6	33 †	6	2	8	41 †
Lutheran	10	9	19	2	1	3	22
Methodist	38	24	62	9	4	13	75
Mormon	6	4	10	1	2	3	13
Presbyterian	15	27	42	7	2	9	51
Roman Catholic	85	37	122	12	8	20	142
Seventh-day Adventist	0	1	1	0	0	0	1
Unitarian	5	2	7	1	2	3	10
United Church of Christ and Congregationalist	3	2	5	5	2	7	12
Unspecified Protestant	10	17	27	1	2	3	30
Unspecified	5	0	5	0	0	0	5

** Statistics based on apparent winners as of Nov. 9, 1990.)*
† Includes Sanders, I-Vt.

The House freshman class included 18 who held law degrees, 14 in business, four who practiced real estate, four whose primary career was as political activists and three former congressional or state legislative aides.

Abercrombie, Wayne Allard, R-Colo., and Tim Roemer, D-Ind., were the only new House members who held non-law doctorates. Twenty-eight had advanced degrees, while Barbara-Rose Collins was the only freshman who did not hold a degree.

Roman Catholics continued to be the largest single religious bloc on Capitol Hill, with 122 members in the House and 20 in the Senate, up from a total of 139 elected in 1988. But the various Protestant denominations outnumbered their ranks. The new Congress included 75 Methodists, 59 Episcopalians, 51 Presbyterians and 59 Baptists. Jews in the 102nd Congress numbered 41, a net gain of one from the 101st Congress. *(Members' religious affiliations, p. 925)* ■

Governors First in Line of Voters' Ire

Electoral turbulence rattled many of the nation's statehouses Nov. 6, swinging control of 14 governorships from one party to another and toppling more incumbent governors than in any year since 1970.

In results that appeared to mirror general voter ambivalence about politics and politicians, neither party emerged as an overall winner. Democrats dropped from 29 governorships to 28, Republicans from 21 to 19. Two new governors were elected under the banners of independent parties, and a third governorship was left temporarily undecided.

The question mark hung over Arizona's open-seat race, when write-in votes prevented either Republican Fife Symington or Democrat Terry Goddard from reaching the majority required by state law. Republicans finished the election cycle with 20 seats when Symington defeated Goddard in the Feb. 26, 1991, runoff, adding about 2 percentage points to the 49.6 percent plurality he had recorded in November.

GOVERNORSHIPS

1991	
Democrats	27
Net loss	2*
Incumbents re-elected	10
Incumbents defeated	2
Republicans	21*
Net change	0
Incumbents re-elected	7
Incumbents defeated	4
Independents	2
1990	
Democrats	29
Republicans	21
Independents	0

** Includes Louisiana's Buddy Roemer, who switched parties March 11, 1991.*

Republicans picked up one more statehouse when Louisiana's Buddy Roemer, elected as a Democrat in 1987, switched parties March 11, 1991. That made the final lineup 27 Democrats, 21 Republicans and two independents.

Talk of voter anger in the fall of 1990 had focused on congressional antics over the federal budget. But when voters vented their anti-incumbent frustrations, they apparently did so more at their governors than their federal officeholders. Only one incumbent senator seeking re-election was defeated, while six of 23 gubernatorial incumbents who ran lost their jobs.

Democratic incumbents James J. Blanchard of Michigan and Rudy Perpich of Minnesota were surprise losers. On the Republican side, four incumbents widely regarded as vulnerable — Bob Martinez of Florida, Mike Hayden of Kansas, Kay A. Orr of Nebraska and Edward D. DiPrete of Rhode Island — were defeated.

In Alabama, freshman GOP incumbent Guy Hunt had to go all out to defeat Democrat Paul Hubbert, top lobbyist for the state teachers' union. The state's Democratic tradition accounted for some of Hunt's troubles, but Hubbert also convinced many voters that Hunt was a flawed leader.

New York's Democratic incumbent Mario M. Cuomo was expected to rack up Olympian totals against nominee Pierre A. Rinfret, who seemed to spend most of his campaign bashing fellow Republicans. Instead, Cuomo won with only 53 percent, while Rinfret and the Conservative Party nominee split most of the remaining vote.

Voters even managed to spank one governor who did not appear on the ballot: New Jersey Democrat James J. Florio. Many New Jersey voters were furious with Florio for raising taxes after indicating that he would not, and they lashed out at Democratic Sen. Bill Bradley, who had a surprisingly close re-election win.

Observers said the incumbents' losses or low victory margins showed that voters were holding governors, more than other elected officials, accountable for unfavorable conditions. "The action in American government is in the states," said University of Virginia political scientist Larry J. Sabato. "And so is the action on election night."

Still, plenty of incumbents cruised to easy victories, and it was difficult to find clear themes.

"It's one of the wackiest years I can remember," said Michele Davis, executive director of the Republican Governors Association. "The pieces just don't fit together yet."

Her counterpart at the Democratic Governors' Association, Mark Gearan, also cautioned against superimposing national trends on the state results.

Instead, both party aides saw the number of incumbent losses as evidence of the front-line role played by governors, particularly in the wake of Reagan-era federalism that shifted many responsibilities to the states.

"They're out there every day either making people happy or making choices that alienate people," said the Democrats' Gearan.

They Did It Their Way

For Democrats, the results were somewhat disappointing. They had hoped for a net gain of several governorships. But independents, not Republicans, were the prime beneficiaries of Democratic weakness.

In Connecticut, former GOP Sen. Lowell P. Weicker Jr. won the seat vacated by Democrat William A. O'Neill. Weicker, a maverick liberal Republican who lost a 1988 Senate re-election bid, chose to run on his own ticket ("A

1991 Occupants of Statehouses

Following are the governors of the 50 states as of March 1991, and the year in which the next election for each office was to be held. The names of governors elected in 1990 are in **boldface.**

Alabama — Guy Hunt (R) 1994 [1]
Alaska — Walter J. Hickel (I) 1994
Arizona — Fife Symington (R) 1994 [2]
Arkansas — Bill Clinton (D) 1994
California — Pete Wilson (R) 1994
Colorado — Roy Romer (D) 1994
Connecticut — Lowell P. Weicker Jr. (I) 1994
Delaware — Michael N. Castle (R) 1992 [1]
Florida — Lawton Chiles (D) 1994
Georgia — Zell Miller (D) 1994
Hawaii — John Waihee III (D) 1994 [1]
Idaho — Cecil D. Andrus (D) 1994
Illinois — Jim Edgar (R) 1994
Indiana — Evan Bayh (D) 1992
Iowa — Terry E. Branstad (R) 1994
Kansas — Joan Finney (D) 1994
Kentucky — Wallace G. Wilkinson (D) 1991 [1]
Louisiana — Buddy Roemer (R) 1991 [3]
Maine — John R. McKernan Jr. (R) 1994 [1]
Maryland — William Donald Schaefer (D) 1994 [1]
Massachusetts — William F. Weld (R) 1994
Michigan — John Engler (R) 1994
Minnesota — Arne Carlson (R) 1994
Mississippi — Ray Mabus (D) 1991
Missouri — John Ashcroft (R) 1992 [1]
Montana — Stan Stephens (R) 1992
Nebraska — Ben Nelson (D) 1994
Nevada — Bob Miller (D) 1994
New Hampshire — Judd Gregg (R) 1992
New Jersey — James J. Florio (D) 1993
New Mexico — Bruce King (D) 1994
New York — Mario M. Cuomo (D) 1994
North Carolina — James G. Martin (R) 1992 [1]
North Dakota — George Sinner (D) 1992
Ohio — George V. Voinovich (R) 1994
Oklahoma — David Walters (D) 1994
Oregon — Barbara Roberts (D) 1994
Pennsylvania — Robert P. Casey (D) 1994 [1]
Rhode Island — Bruce Sundlun (D) 1992
South Carolina — Carroll A. Campbell Jr. (R) 1994 [1]
South Dakota — George S. Mickelson (R) 1994 [1]
Tennessee — Ned McWherter (D) 1994 [1]
Texas — Ann W. Richards (D) 1994
Utah — Norman H. Bangerter (R) 1992
Vermont — Richard A. Snelling (R) 1992
Virginia — L. Douglas Wilder (D) 1993 [1]
Washington — Booth Gardner (D) 1992
West Virginia — Gaston Caperton (D) 1992
Wisconsin — Tommy G. Thompson (R) 1994
Wyoming — Mike Sullivan (D) 1994

[1] *Barred by state law from seeking re-election.* [2] *Fife Symington was elected in a runoff Feb. 26, 1991.*
[3] *Buddy Roemer, elected as a Democrat, switched to the Republican Party on March 11, 1991.*

Connecticut Party") rather than compete for the GOP nomination. Yet he became the immediate favorite against two House members, Republican John G. Rowland and Democrat Bruce A. Morrison.

In a race focused on the states' fiscal woes, voters gravitated toward Weicker, a familiar entity who nonetheless seemed to offer change. They ignored warnings that Weicker's brusque character and independence would make it impossible for him to deal with a partisan legislature.

Alaska voters were similarly unfettered by convention, electing former Republican Gov. Walter J. Hickel. The former governor had thrown the race into disarray by jumping in on the Alaska Independence Party ticket only six weeks before the election. Republicans had nominated State Sen. Arliss Sturgulewski, the 1986 GOP nominee, but some were uncomfortable with her abortion rights stance, and even her running mate abandoned her ticket to run with Hickel.

Hickel had also run against Sturgulewski in 1986 as a write-in candidate, drawing enough votes to help elect Democrat Steve Cowper. Democrats hoped that pattern would repeat itself and elect their man, former Anchorage Mayor Tony Knowles. Instead, Hickel surged to victory on his image of strength and his anti-abortion, pro-business platform.

While Weicker's views probably placed him somewhere in between the major parties, Hickel's win could arguably be viewed as a Republican victory. Hickel had disavowed the platform of the Alaska Independence Party, which sought to make Alaska an independent country.

This was the first time voters elected two independents as governor, but political observers did not expect a stampede toward third-party banners.

"They did it their way, but their way was the hard way," political scientist Sabato said of Weicker and Hickel. Neither received an outright majority, and, as former statewide officeholders, both had unusually strong political contacts and name recognition.

Remapping Looms

Gubernatorial races drew particular attention in 1990 because governors and legislatures were poised to redraw districts for state and federal legislators. Governors typically had veto power over new district maps and could influence the process to aid their party.

No race was more important in this regard than California, which was expected to add seven congressional seats for a total of 52. Republicans tapped Sen. Pete Wilson as their nominee, and his victory was their greatest election-night trophy.

Both Wilson and Democratic nominee Dianne Feinstein, a former mayor of San Francisco, were moderates and favored abortion rights, the death penalty and environmental protection. At times, the two candidates seemed to struggle to find distinguishing issues. Feinstein endorsed "Big Green," a sweeping environmental ballot initiative that was defeated. Wilson aligned himself with another, successful initiative to limit the terms of state legislators.

Ultimately, the contest was one of resources and personalities. Wilson outspent Feinstein $16 million to $13 million in the general election campaign and was backed by more extensive party organizing. He projected a solid if unexciting image of experience, while Feinstein offered a more dramatic personality and political history.

Republicans also won governorships in several states expected to lose House seats, among them Michigan, Ohio and Illinois.

But Democrats countered with former Sen. Lawton Chiles' win in Florida and state Treasurer Ann W. Richards' eleventh-hour triumph in Texas. Between them, Florida and Texas were expected to gain seven congressional seats in 1992.

Texas was the bigger surprise, as many Democrats had given up on Richards by early fall. Polls had consistently shown Richards trailing Republican nominee Clayton Williams, a millionaire oilman and political first-timer, despite his political inexperience and frequent verbal gaffes.

Richards kept jabbing at Williams, however, and her persistence paid off. Richards began to gather momentum by discrediting Williams' image as a successful businessman and tapping voter discontent over soaring health insurance rates.

Williams helped out when he refused to shake Richards' hand at a joint forum, a dangerous violation of the cowboy code that had served him so well politically. And in the final week, Williams plugged two more bullets into his own candidacy. First, he could not recall how he had voted on his absentee ballot on a proposed constitutional amendment on gubernatorial appointments. Then he revealed that he had paid no income tax in 1986, claiming his businesses were struggling that year.

In Florida, Republican incumbent Bob Martinez dug himself out of dismal approval ratings with an unusual "mea culpa" television ad in which he apologized to voters for past mistakes. Martinez had pushed, then abandoned, an unpopular package of tax increases; his standing also suffered when he unsuccessfully sought to push restrictive abortion measures through a special session of the Legislature.

Chiles, who stepped down from his Senate job in 1988 citing "burnout," admitted that he was taking the drug Prozac to treat his depression. But Chiles limited campaign contributions to $100, talked of mending the torn social fabric and spent many campaign days studying the ins and outs of various state programs rather than hunting down voters. His unusual campaign energized Democratic supporters, while Martinez saw many Republican voters stay on the sidelines.

All of the so-called Big Three gubernatorial races were also Big Money contests. Only in California, however, did the better-financed candidate win. Williams spent $20 million, including more than $8 million of his own money, to lose in Texas, about twice as much as Richards. The ratio was similar in Florida.

Economic Anxiety

Many of 1990's gubernatorial races took place against a backdrop of economic difficulty, if not decay. In the Northeast, three Democratic incumbents — Michael S. Dukakis in Massachusetts, O'Neill in Connecticut and Madeleine M. Kunin in Vermont — chose to step down rather than campaign in hard times.

Rhode Island's DiPrete, a Republican, got just 26 percent in losing to Democratic businessman Bruce Sundlun, whom he had defeated twice before. While DiPrete's image was tarnished by corruption charges, he was also held to blame for rising taxes and the state's economic downturn.

In Maine, Republican incumbent John R. McKernan Jr. had been assailed by his Democratic predecessor and 1990 challenger, Rep. Joseph E. Brennan, for mismanaging the state budget. McKernan rallied to win but took less than 50 percent of the overall vote.

Only New Hampshire's GOP Gov. Judd Gregg slipped through the region's fiscal minefield without serious wounds, winning easily despite having agreed to a series of tax increases.

In Michigan, Blanchard had been expected to win a third term against Republican Senate leader John Engler. But Engler hammered away at taxes and other economic issues. Engler backed a 20 percent cut in property taxes and gave away nickels to symbolize how little he claimed Blanchard's tax relief plans would aid the average property owner each week.

In Kansas, Republican Hayden had been pounded for presiding over a property tax overhaul that sent many tax bills soaring. He barely defeated an antitax challenger in the primary and could not hold off Democratic nominee Joan Finney, the 65-year-old state treasurer, who also cut into his GOP base by opposing abortion.

In Nebraska, voters were similarly dismayed at Orr for raising taxes despite a no-taxes pledge. She lost to Democrat Ben Nelson, an Omaha lawyer in his first try for elective office, who warned voters, "Don't be fooled again."

But in Illinois' close race, taxes were not fatal to Republican Secretary of State Jim Edgar. Democratic Attorney General Neil F. Hartigan hammered away at Edgar's call to extend a temporary income tax increase to pay for schools, instead promising to provide the school funding from budget savings. Hartigan did make headway on the issue, but many voters remained skeptical that the Democrat could make good on his no-tax promise.

Edgar tried to turn the issue into a question of trust, promising "no surprises" after Election Day. Hartigan was also hurt by weakened black support in his home city of Chicago, where activists fielded an all-black Harold Washington Party slate.

Oklahoma voters also turned aside a Republican candidate, former U.S. Attorney Bill Price, who sought to repeal a tax package to pay for education that had been backed by retiring Republican Gov. Henry Bellmon. Democratic businessman David Walters, who lost to Bellmon in 1986, backed the school tax and won easily.

As predicted, abortion was a focal issue in many gubernatorial races and might have tipped the balance in some. Abortion rights activists counted Florida and Texas as their clearest wins. In Florida, Martinez outraged abortion rights advocates when he called a special session to pass restrictive anti-abortion laws. State legislators rebuffed him, but that was not enough for some. One anti-Martinez bumper sticker urged, "Abort Martinez before a second term."

Chiles, who had come to an abortion rights stance after taking several anti-abortion positions in the Senate, was initially reluctant to press the issue. But in the closing weeks, Chiles did talk up his abortion rights views, seemingly to his benefit.

Texas also offered a clear choice between an abortion rights supporter — Richards — and Williams, an abortion opponent. Williams tried to frame the issue to his advantage, pressing Richards to join him in backing parental

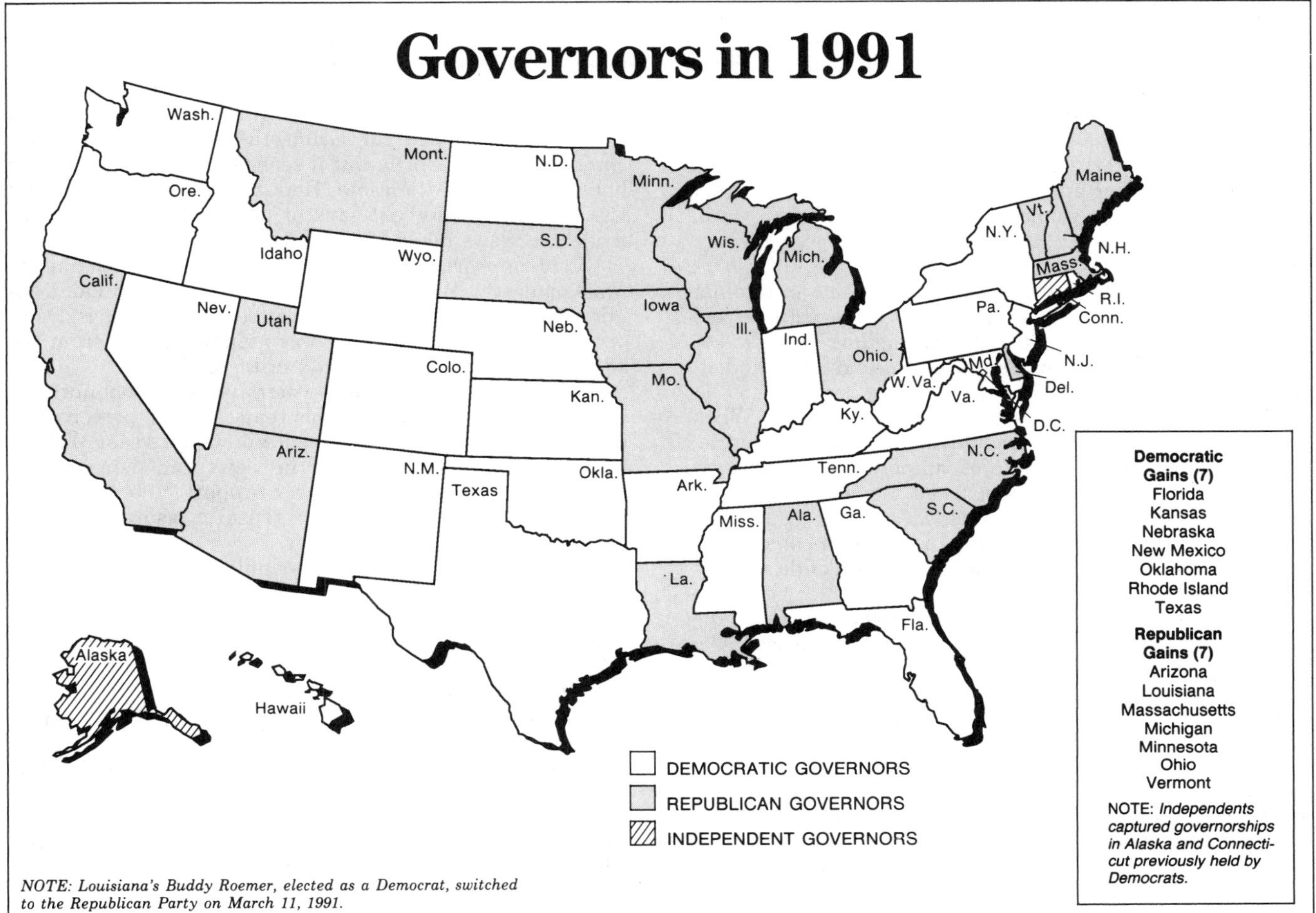

NOTE: Louisiana's Buddy Roemer, elected as a Democrat, switched to the Republican Party on March 11, 1991.

notification laws for minors seeking an abortion. But Richards' abortion rights views probably helped cement critical support among Republican women.

In Idaho, Democrat Cecil D. Andrus had no trouble winning re-election despite anger among anti-abortion groups over his veto of a law restricting abortion.

But anti-abortion governors were elected in Kansas, Ohio and Alaska, three seats previously held by abortion rights supporters. Abortion rights forces had targeted Blanchard's race in Michigan, but were unable to stave off his loss to abortion opponent John Engler.

After a much-publicized flip-flop on the issue, Ohio Attorney General Anthony J. Celebrezze Jr. hoped his new-found abortion rights stand would help him defeat Republican opponent George V. Voinovich, the former mayor of Cleveland. The issue did help keep the race close, but Voinovich prevailed in a race that centered more on shooing away the ethical clouds of the existing Democratic administration.

In Iowa, where many believed state House Speaker Donald D. Avenson's abortion rights views would be a powerful weapon against Republican incumbent Terry E. Branstad, Branstad won handily. Several other anti-abortion incumbents considered potentially vulnerable on the issue — Democrat Robert P. Casey in Pennsylvania and Republicans Tommy G. Thompson in Wisconsin and Gregg in New Hampshire — were not noticeably damaged by the issue.

Abortion may have played a decisive role in the Oregon race: as a spoiler. Both major-party nominees, Democrat Barbara Roberts and Republican Attorney General Dave Frohnmayer, supported abortion rights. But anti-abortion candidate Al Mobley drew 13 percent of the vote, votes Republicans believe came primarily at Frohnmayer's expense. Roberts won with 46 percent of the vote.

New Women Elected

Roberts was one of three women elected governor in 1990, along with Richards in Texas and Finney in Kansas. That held the total number of women governors steady at three.

Rose Mofford in Arizona and Kunin in Vermont did not run for re-election. Nebraska incumbent Orr was defeated, as were three female Republican challengers — rancher Mary Mead in Wyoming, Barbara Hafer in Pennsylvania and Sturgulewski in Alaska — and Democrat Feinstein in California.

There had been speculation that the abortion issue and voters' hankering for change would benefit women candidates. That dynamic was at work in several races.

In California, Feinstein stressed her sex in an attempt to quench voters' thirst for change. Feinstein also suggested that she would be a stronger defender of abortion rights. Some voters did respond, although Feinstein may also have been hurt by stereotypes that male politicians were better equipped to battle crime and balance budgets.

Roberts had better success in Oregon, where her charisma also contrasted well with Frohnmayer's bland personality. Frohnmayer attacked Roberts as weak on crime, but polls suggested that voters saw Roberts as more direct.

But Finney won without the issues, or support, typically associated with female candidates. Instead, her strength was convincing voters that she was the best choice to keep taxes down, and her anti-abortion views actually cost her support among some women and women's groups.

Familiar Faces

In 1990, new political wine sometimes came in familiar bottles. Three of the "new" governors were actually old governors — Republican Richard A. Snelling in Vermont, Democrat Bruce King in New Mexico, and independent Hickel in Alaska.

Snelling was Vermont's governor in 1977-85. When Kunin announced that she would not seek another term, Snelling quickly became the front-runner. But Snelling was not well-loved as governor and faced a spirited challenge from former state Sen. Peter Welch.

King was more popular during his two non-consecutive terms as governor in 1970 and 1978, and his likable manner helped him in his comeback.

But prior service was not always rewarded. Over the summer it looked as though Brennan would unseat McKernan in Maine, largely by reminding voters of the sunnier economic picture when he was governor. But McKernan found negative ammunition in Brennan's record as well and was able to hold on.

In Arizona, Republican primary voters sternly turned away a comeback bid by former Gov. Evan Mecham. But Mecham's memory continued to muddy the waters: A runoff law in response to Mecham's 1986 win forced the gubernatorial candidates into their runoff. The one-paragraph law left much unanswered, however, and it took until late February 1991 before the election was decided. Democrat and former Phoenix Mayor Goddard had been favored to win in November, but finished slightly behind Symington.

In the Feb. 26, 1991, runoff, Symington beat Goddard with 52 percent of the vote. Arizona law required an absolute majority. Write-in votes in November frustrated Symington, a millionaire land developer seeking office for the first time. He bettered Goddard, a former Phoenix mayor, the first time around by about 4,200 votes.

The new faces around the country included seasoned politicians and newcomers, moderates and mavericks. Many of the Republican newcomers were solid, moderate politicians. Two of them, state Auditor Arne Carlson in Minnesota and William F. Weld in Massachusetts, were sharply attacked in the primary as too liberal. Carlson, who supported abortion rights, actually lost his primary to the more conservative Jon Grunseth. But Carlson became the last-minute nominee when Grunseth dropped out amid charges of sexual impropriety.

Democrats hoped the Grunseth affair would save incumbent Rudy Perpich, but it seemed instead to prompt a house-cleaning (Minnesota Republican Rudy Boschwitz was the only incumbent senator defeated). And Carlson's moderate views made him a palatable crossover prospect.

Weld appeared to benefit from a similar dynamic in Massachusetts. While public disgust with the Dukakis administration fanned Republican gubernatorial hopes, Democratic nominee John Silber was arguably as far from the administration, and as harsh a critic, as Weld.

But many Massachusetts voters were not comfortable with Silber's arrogance, and his remarks were perceived as hostile to minorities and women. Voters opted for Weld, a Republican moderate enough in views and demeanor to draw heavy Democratic crossover support. Voters simultaneously rejected a stringent tax repeal measure supported by Weld and opposed by Silber.

Georgia Democrats had a similar candidate in Zell Miller, who defeated GOP state Rep. Johnny Isakson. The liberal-to-moderate Miller was the state's longest-serving lieutenant governor.

Hardy Perennials

Even in a year of change, plenty of incumbents won reelection without difficulty.

Republican Carroll A. Campbell Jr. of South Carolina enjoyed the highest victory margin of any incumbent, winning 71 percent. Campbell won the backing of some black leaders despite running against a black state legislator, Theo Mitchell. Republican incumbent George S. Mickelson also won easily in South Dakota.

Republicans began the year with high hopes that businessman Sheffield Nelson could unseat 10-year Democratic incumbent Bill Clinton in Arkansas. But Clinton successfully defended his performance while keeping Nelson off balance.

Among other Democratic incumbents, Colorado's Roy Romer, Hawaii's John Waihee III, Nevada's Bob Miller, Tennessee's Ned McWherter and Wyoming's Mike Sullivan all won more than 60 percent of the vote in races that were never particularly competitive. Maryland Democrat William Donald Schaefer won with just under 60 percent, but had been expected to do even better than that against the husband and wife GOP ticket of William S. and Lois Shepard. ■

Census Sets Battle Lines for Redistricting

The Dec. 26 release of the official census results and the Nov. 6 nationwide election results set the battle lines for the decennial redrawing of congressional districts. The census results confirmed earlier projections that 19 House seats would cross state lines in the 103rd Congress, with eight states gaining seats and 13 states losing at least one seat each. On Election Day, meanwhile, Democrats increased their hold on state legislative chambers across the country.

The December official results pegged the national population at 249,632,692. The tally added about 4 million people to the preliminary fall numbers. Census Bureau Director Barbara Everitt Bryant said the new number depicted an increase in many cities that had complained about undercounts. The Commerce Department said it would decide by July 15, 1991, whether to use its authority to adjust the census tally to correct for undercounting.

The population flow was to the West, South and South-

Key Redistricting States

Seat Change in 1992	State	Party Control After 1990 Elections State House	State Senate	Gov.	Comments
+7	Calif.	D	D	R	GOP's gubernatorial win was bulwark against repeat of partisan Democratic remap enacted in last redistricting round.
+4	Fla.	D	D	D	Gubernatorial takeover plus Senate hold gave Democrats complete remap control. But influx of Republican voters expected to ensure GOP share of new seats.
+3	Texas	D	D	D	Democrats took governorship, but legislative alliance between Republicans and conservative Democrats plus GOP growth in state likely to help GOP in remapping.
+1	Ariz.	R	D	R	Democrats took over Senate, but lost governorship; demographics favored GOP.
+1	Ga.	D	D	D	Democrats were to draw new district.
+1	N.C.	D	D	R	Democratic gains in House weakened Republican role in deciding how to draw new district; GOP governor had no veto power.
+1	Va.	D	D	D	Democrats held all legs of process after '89 elections.
+1	Wash.	D	R	D	Remapping was to be done by a bipartisan commission with broad powers.
−3	N.Y.	D	R	D	Lackluster showing by Gov. Mario M. Cuomo helped Republicans hold off Democrats challenging GOP Senate control. Seat loss expected to hit both parties.
−2	Ill.	D	D	R	Democrats protected slim Senate lead but did not wrest governorship from GOP, so both parties faced likely hit in remapping.
−2	Mich.	D	R	R	Democrats skittish after GOP picked up governorship and held Senate.
−2	Ohio	D	R	R	Republicans won governorship, held Senate. Seat loss likely to hit both parties.
−2	Pa.	D	R	D	Chambers remained closely divided and split between parties, so both parties were expected to yield a seat in remap.
−1	Iowa	D	D	R	Maps to be drawn by nonpartisan agency, but Democratic legislature, GOP governor held veto.
−1	Kan.	D	R	D	Democrats took over governorship and state House, putting pressure on 5th District GOP newcomer Dick Nichols.
−1	La.	D	D	R	Complete Democratic control of process upset by Gov. Buddy Roemer's March 1991 switch from Democrats to GOP.
−1	Mass.	D	D	R	Low Republican clout in legislature offset by gubernatorial win.
−1	Ky.; N.J.; W.Va.	D	D	D	Democrats controlled governorship and both legislative chambers in each state.

west. California was to gain seven seats (for an unprecedented 52-seat delegation) and Washington was to gain one. In the South, Florida was to gain four; North Carolina, Virginia and Georgia, one each. In the Southwest, Texas was to pick up three seats and Arizona, one.

Northeastern and Midwestern delegations would take the biggest hits. New York was to lose three seats; Illinois, Michigan, Ohio and Pennsylvania were each to lose two.

Slated to lose one representative each were Iowa, Kansas, Kentucky, Louisiana, Massachusetts, Montana, New Jersey and West Virginia. (Montana was to drop from two seats to one, elected on an at-large basis.) *(Key redistricting states, this page)*

For Republicans, the November elections capped a disappointing decade that saw a thwarting of their hopes to institutionalize these favorable demographic trends and overcome their minority status in the U.S. House.

With redistricting battles set to begin, Democrats were to have total control of the process in Texas and Florida, where they controlled governorships and both chambers of the legislatures.

Democrats on Nov. 6 won control of five new state legislative chambers, including the state Senates in Arizona, Montana and Nevada, and state Houses in Indiana and Kansas. Overall, according to the National Conference of State Legislatures, Democrats controlled 72 chambers, with GOP autonomy slipping to 23 chambers; three chambers were tied, and one — Nebraska — was unicameral and nonpartisan. Going into the election, the Democratic advantage was 69-28, with one tie.

But there was some good election news for the GOP, as the party won the biggest redistricting prize — California's governorship — and won three megastate governorships in the Midwest.

The GOP also controlled the governorship or at least one legislative chamber in the five states losing more than one seat.

Democratic National Committee Chairman Ronald H. Brown called the state legislative results the "greatest area of Democratic victory." But Charles Black, chief spokesman for the Republican National Committee, said, "Our party is very well positioned not only for 1992 but for the rest of this decade."

The official 1990 census results — setting the U.S. population at 249,632,692 — showed an increase of more than 23 million people (10.2 percent) over the 1980 total.

While officials in big cities braced themselves for bad news, they were still upset with the extent of their population losses and many challenged the accuracy of the count. Rural areas also experienced deterioration after making a comeback in the 1970s. *(Reaction to census, p. 415)*

Questions of Undercount

The counting controversy at center stage of the census debate involved the historical undercount in predominantly minority communities. The Census Bureau said it had particular trouble tallying in such areas, where there often were fewer English-speaking residents and more distrust between residents and census enumerators than was the case in other communities.

In 1980 the bureau estimated that it counted about 99 percent of the white population, but only about 94 percent of blacks.

The undercounted areas were represented in Congress mostly by Democrats, and they were the most outspoken in calling on the Census Bureau to make a statistical adjustment of the tally to account for people who were missed. But the Commerce Department announced in 1987 that it would not make an adjustment, a ruling that fueled lawsuits and charges of partisanship.

"Unfortunately, I am not sure that this Republican administration wants to count everyone in this very Democratic city," New York Democratic Rep. Charles E. Schumer said in a March conference highlighting census glitches in his hometown.

In response to the lawsuit brought by New York City (along with other cities, states and civil rights organizations), the Commerce Department agreed in 1989 to keep the adjustment question open until 1991. But that Commerce concession did not quiet critics.

Early in 1990, the plaintiffs in the New York City case reopened their lawsuit in an effort to get the Commerce Department to draft new guidelines to require the department to adjust the count in 1991, unless it could demonstrate that a statistical change would not be more accurate than the actual tally.

In something of a split decision, a federal district court in New York ruled June 7 that an adjustment would be constitutional and said that the Commerce Department would "clearly incur a heavier burden" to explain an anti-adjustment decision in 1991. But Judge Joseph M. McLaughlin also ruled that the Commerce Department's guidelines on the matter were not inadequate or biased.

In addition, Commerce critics said the low mail-in response rate — which was not the same as the undercount — had occurred because the administration was not committed to counting hard-to-reach people. "I think [the low response] is the direct result of the cynicism with which this administration and the previous administration approached the whole question of the census," said Rep. Mervyn M. Dymally, D-Calif., an adjustment advocate who headed the Post Office Subcommittee on Census and Population in the 101st Congress.

But some Republicans suggested that critics of the census had a political agenda of their own.

"Instead of using [low response] as an opportunity maybe to push one side or the other of the adjustment question, it would be much better if people became part of the solution and helped to get a better enumeration," said Tom Hofeller, director of redistricting for the National Republican Congressional Committee.

Who Benefits?

It was generally thought that urban areas would benefit from an adjustment. Schumer estimated that 450,000 New York City residents were missed in 1980; others said an adjustment might have spared New York state some of its five-seat loss in the 1981 House reapportionment.

But some questioned the assumptions of adjustment advocates. "A person from New York will get up and say, 'Well, we might find 350 or 400 thousand people. That's a big portion of a congressional district; therefore we will get one more congressional seat,' " said Hofeller. "What they don't remember is that Florida is also finding more people, and so is Texas, and so is California. It is very possible that a city could pick up more people and still lose."

William P. O'Hare of the Population Reference Bureau, a Washington-based private research group, said he thought that an adjusted census would yield about the same reapportionment of House seats as the actual census. "My first bet would be that it wouldn't shift any seats," he said.

O'Hare noted that urban centers were not the only areas where an adjustment could boost population. It was also hard to count people in many rural areas. "Some of the data from previous censuses indicate that those areas, particularly in the rural South, are undercounted at about the same rate as central cities," he said.

For those who worried that an undercount of their area would deprive it of federal funds distributed on the basis of population, skeptics of an adjustment noted that using population formulas to allocate federal funds was merely a statutory decision, not a constitutional mandate.

"The funding issue is in many ways a totally spurious issue," said Hofeller, "because if Congress decided it wanted to change the funding formulas, it could do it."

Because population data were the building blocks of reapportionment and redistricting, problems with the census had the potential to greatly complicate the 1990s line-drawing process. Even before the problems with the 1990 census surfaced, many redistricting experts were predicting that the coming round of remapping would be a litigious one, because of disputes over such issues as minority representation and population equality among districts.

POLITICAL OUTLOOK

While census questions made up a large part of the redistricting debate, the political scenario was just as important. Both national parties devoted serious efforts and resources on legislative campaigns throughout the nation.

Overall, Democrats emerged from the Nov. 6 vote holding redistricting monopolies in 17 states. Republicans held total control only in the small-population states of New Hampshire and Utah (which were not projected to gain or lose House seats) and South Dakota (which had only a single, at-large House member.)

Influencing Winners and Losers

The national parties directed a large chunk of the millions of dollars they spent in 1990 to influence state elections in the 21 states projected either to gain or lose a total of 19 seats because of population shifts measured in the 1990 census.

Legislative control, however, was also important in

states keeping their existing number of districts, because lines could be gerrymandered to help or hurt incumbents.

In those states expecting numerical changes in congressional districts, Democrats wrested control of the governorships in Florida, Texas and Kansas and picked up a net of three legislative chambers.

Republicans, meanwhile, gained crucial governorships in Ohio, Michigan and Massachusetts, and they maintained control of the executive offices in Illinois and Iowa. The GOP gained control of only one legislative chamber — the Oregon state House. Oregon, which had a Democratic state Senate and governor, expected no change in its House strength in reapportionment.

Democrats had expected to hold another governorship — in Arizona — but Republicans retook it when Phoenix real estate developer Fife Symington defeated the favored Democratic nominee, former Phoenix Mayor Terry Goddard, in a February 1991 runoff. Symington's win countered the Democrats' gaining control of the state Senate.

Some Solace for GOP

GOP legislative disappointments were offset to some degree by Sen. Pete Wilson's narrow victory over former San Francisco Mayor Dianne Feinstein in the California governor's race. The state was expected to gain seven congressional seats, and loss of the governorship would have opened the way for Democrats — who controlled the Legislature — to push through a highly partisan plan similar to that drawn a decade earlier.

Democratic Rep. Phillip Burton (1964-83) drew that plan, artfully offsetting population growth in GOP suburban areas. Because Democrats controlled all three prongs of the redistricting process, a 22-21 Democratic edge within the congressional delegation became a lopsided 28-17 advantage after the 1982 elections.

After California, perhaps the brightest spot for the GOP came in Michigan, where they held onto a narrow margin in the state Senate, and Republican John Engler felled Democratic Gov. James J. Blanchard in a razor-close race. Michigan Democrats had reason to be nervous; the state expected to lose two seats in reapportionment, and most of the districts that lost residents were held by Democrats.

In Florida — expected to gain four seats — former Sen. Lawton Chiles' gubernatorial victory over GOP Gov. Bob Martinez gave Democrats a clean sweep of the remap triad.

But while Democrats also managed to stanch their eight-year bleeding in the Florida state Senate, in redistricting they would not be able to ignore the fact that Republicans were a large part of the population in rapidly developing areas.

Similarly in Texas, despite a Democratic trifecta crowned by state Treasurer Ann W. Richards' gubernatorial win, demographic imperatives and a legislative coalition of Republicans and conservative Democrats had the potential of blunting a partisan remap.

New York, which faced the fifth consecutive decade of multiple-seat House losses (it was expected to drop three seats), emerged from the election with no change in its redistricting power configuration.

Democrats, who controlled the House, had hoped to close a 33-26 gap in the state Senate. But Republicans held on to the Senate, thanks to an unexpectedly poor 53 percent showing by Democratic Gov. Mario M. Cuomo that provided no coattails effect.

In the last round of redistricting, a similarly split New York Legislature divided the redistricting damage evenly by merging two Republican and two Democratic districts.

Closely divided chambers in Pennsylvania were targeted by both parties. Democrats maintained control of the governorship and the state House, yet failed to gain control of the GOP-held state Senate.

The state was expected to lose two House seats, and congressional redistricting — unlike state legislative redistricting, which was handled by a bipartisan commission — followed the normal legislative process and would likely be tinged by regional rivalries.

In Illinois, which stood to lose two House seats in reapportionment, Republicans ensured themselves at least some say in remapping with Secretary of State Jim Edgar's gubernatorial win over Democratic state Attorney General Neil F. Hartigan.

In other states of interest, Democrats overcame a two-seat deficit to gain control of the state House in Indiana, where Republicans drew a gerrymandered map in the last redistricting round. Democrats also controlled the Indiana governorship, but the GOP held the state Senate.

In Kansas, which expected to lose a seat in 1992, Democrats gained control of both the governorship and the state House, perhaps putting the state's 5th District and GOP newcomer Dick Nichols in jeopardy. ■

Patronage System Setback

In a rejection of the longstanding tradition of political patronage, the Supreme Court ruled June 21 that it is unconstitutional to hire, promote or transfer most public employees based on party affiliation.

By a 5-4 vote, the court said that the patronage system impermissibly infringed on the First Amendment rights of public employees unless party membership was "an appropriate requirement" for the job.

The case of *Rutan v. Republican Party of Illinois* was brought after Illinois Gov. James R. Thompson, a Republican, began a government hiring and promotions freeze in 1980, affecting 60,000 state positions. His executive order allowed no exceptions but those granted by the governor's personnel office.

The plaintiffs alleged that the personnel office discriminated against them because they did not support the state's Republican Party.

In its ruling, the Supreme Court said the Illinois Republican system penalized workers who did not affiliate with the Republican Party by denying them pay increases, better hours and — in cases of "temporary" layoffs — their jobs.

"These are significant penalties and are imposed for the exercise of rights guaranteed by the First Amendment," wrote Justice William J. Brennan Jr. for the court. He added: "To the victor belong only those spoils that may be constitutionally obtained."

With Brennan in the majority were Justices Byron R. White, Thurgood Marshall, Harry A. Blackmun and John Paul Stevens.

Dissenting were Chief Justice William H. Rehnquist and Justices Sandra Day O'Connor, Antonin Scalia and Anthony M. Kennedy. ■

No Party Shifts in 1990 Special Elections

Continuity was the rule in the four special House elections held in 1990 as none of the seats changed partisan hands. By contrast, three of eight special House elections in 1989 saw the seat shift from one party to the other. *(1989 special elections, 1989 Almanac, p. 8-A)*

Two special House elections were held in New York City on March 20. The 14th District (Staten Island; southwest Brooklyn) stayed Republican, as City Council member Susan Molinari swept past Democratic lawyer Robert Gigante.

In the 18th District (South Bronx), Democratic state Rep. Jose E. Serrano swamped the GOP candidate, lawyer Simeon Golar.

In Hawaii's 2nd District, vacated when Daniel K. Akaka resigned to assume an open Senate seat, a Sept. 22 special election saw former Democratic Rep. Patsy T. Mink (1965-77) sent back to Congress.

In New Jersey's 1st District, Democrat Robert E. Andrews succeeded James J. Florio, who resigned in January to become governor.

Molinari Succeeds Father in New York 14th

Molinari succeeded her father, popular five-term Rep. Guy V. Molinari, who resigned the 14th District seat Jan. 1 after being elected Staten Island borough president in November 1989.

Susan Molinari, serving her second term in the City Council, took conservative stands on such issues as crime and defense. But she also described herself as an environmental activist, touting her efforts to reduce the trash flow into Staten Island's Fresh Kills landfill and blaming several oil spills into waters off Staten Island on "corporate America's sloppiness and greed."

Molinari was also a supporter of abortion rights. While this stance spurred an active campaign by Right-to-Life Party candidate Barbara Bollaert, it gave no leeway to Gigante, who also was pro-abortion rights.

Gigante, a local Democratic Party official who had not run for office since an unsuccessful 1980 House primary bid, seemed to be reaching for issues. He assailed the Molinari "dynasty," said he would be more effective than Molinari in the House because Democrats controlled the chamber and described himself as more typical of the average district voter because he had four children while Molinari had none.

Carl Grillo, the Liberal Party candidate, trailed the field. Official returns:

Molinari (R-C)	29,336	(59.0%)
Gigante (D)	17,302	(34.8%)
Bollaert (RTL)	2,649	(5.3%)
Grillo (L)	427	(0.9%)

Serrano Rolls in New York 18th

Serrano extended the line of Democratic members of Puerto Rican ancestry in New York's 18th District, begun by Herman Badillo (1971-77) and continued by Robert Garcia (1978-90), who resigned Jan. 7 after his conviction in the Wedtech influence-peddling case. *(Garcia resignation, p. 107)*

Serrano, in his eighth term in the state Assembly, was promoted as the heir to the seat. He worked to energize his core support but eschewed the description of the 18th as a "Hispanic seat." Blacks numbered nearly half the district's residents.

Golar, a black lawyer and developer who served in the administration of Mayor John V. Lindsay, had serious liabilities. Once a member of New York's Liberal Party, Golar ran three unsuccessful House primary races as a Democrat in Queens' 6th District during the 1980s. As a resident of Queens running in the 18th, Golar was vulnerable to the carpetbagger charge.

Serrano, who also had the Liberal line, left Golar and Conservative Party candidate Kevin Brawley far behind. Official returns:

Serrano (D-L)	26,928	(92.4%)
Golar (R)	2,079	(7.1%)
Brawley (C)	126	(0.5%)

Mink Succeeds Akaka in Hawaii 2nd

Mink, who served in the House from 1965 to 1977, returned to Congress by winning the Sept. 22 special election for Hawaii's 2nd District seat, vacated by Daniel K. Akaka. He resigned in May when named by Democratic Gov. John Waihee III as the interim replacement to the late Democratic Sen. Spark M. Matsunaga.

Mink staved off a challenge from Mufi F. Hannemann, a businessman who was the 1986 Democratic House nominee in the 1st District. At the same time, she also won the party's nomination for a full term in the Democratic primary that coincided with the special election, again by edging out Hannemann.

Mink established herself as the front-runner early in the race, but Hannemann made it close. An executive with a Hawaii corporation, Hannemann nonetheless received support from several large unions.

Official results:

Mink (D)	51,841	(38.5%)
Hannemann (D)	50,164	(37.3%)
Menor (D)	23,629	(17.6%)
Poepoe (R)	8,872	(6.6%)

Andrews Elected in New Jersey's 1st

New Jersey's 1st District held a special election coinciding with the regular general election on Nov. 6 to fill a vacancy in the 101st Congress caused by Florio's resignation to assume the state's governorship on Jan. 16, 1990. The seat had been vacant since then.

In the special election, Andrews, the Camden County freeholder director, defeated Daniel J. Mangini, a Gloucester County freeholder. Andrews had 72,324 votes (55.3 percent) to 58,671 votes (44.7 percent) for Mangini.

Andrews became a member of the already adjourned 101st Congress upon winning his special election; he won a two-year term at the same time over Mangini and three minor-party candidates, gathering 54 percent of the vote to Mangini's 43 percent.

Official 1990 Election Results

Following are the official 1990 vote returns for the Senate, House and gubernatorial elections compiled by Congressional Quarterly from figures supplied by each state's election agency. The box below provides a key to party designation. Also included are write-in candidates that received at least 0.1 percent of the vote. Because of rounding and because scattered write-in votes are not listed, percentages do not always add to 100.

Other symbols:

• incumbent;

x candidate without major-party opposition; no vote available.

ALABAMA

	Candidate	Vote Total	%
Governor			
	• Guy Hunt (R)	633,520	52.1
	Paul Hubbert (D)	582,106	47.9
Senate			
	• Howell Heflin (D)	717,814	60.6
	Bill Cabaniss (R)	467,190	39.4
House			
1	• Sonny Callahan (R)	82,185	99.6
	(No Democratic candidate)		
2	• Bill Dickinson (R)	87,649	51.3
	Faye Baggiano (D)	83,243	48.7
3	• Glen Browder (D)	101,923	73.7
	Don Sledge (R)	36,317	26.3
4	• Tom Bevill (D)	129,872	99.7
	(No Republican candidate)		
5	Bud Cramer (D)	113,047	67.1
	Albert McDonald (R)	55,326	32.9
6	• Ben Erdreich (D)	134,412	92.8
	David A. Alvarez (I)	8,640	6.0
	Nathaniel Ivory (I)	1,745	1.2
7	• Claude Harris (D)	127,490	70.5
	Michael D. Barker (R)	53,258	29.5

ALASKA

	Candidate	Vote Total	%
Governor			
	Walter J. Hickel (I)	75,721	38.9
	Tony Knowles (D)	60,201	30.9
	Arliss Sturgulewski (R)	50,991	26.2
	Jim Sykes (Green)	6,563	3.4
	Michael O'Callaghan (P)	942	0.5
Senate			
	• Ted Stevens (R)	125,806	66.2
	Michael Beasley (D)	61,152	32.2
House			
AL	• Don Young (R)	99,003	51.7
	John E. Devens (D)	91,677	47.8

ARIZONA

	Candidate	Vote Total	%
Governor *			
	Fife Symington (R)	492,569	52.4
	Terry Goddard (D)	448,168	47.6
House			
1	• John J. Rhodes III (R)	166,223	99.5
	(No Democratic candidate)		
	Tim Rose (write-in)	621	0.4
	Betsy McDonald (write-in)	172	0.1
2	• Morris K. Udall (D)	76,549	65.9
	Joseph D. Sweeney (R)	39,586	34.1
3	• Bob Stump (R)	134,279	56.6
	Roger Hartstone (D)	103,018	43.4
4	• Jon Kyl (R)	141,843	61.3
	Mark Ivey Jr. (D)	89,395	38.7
5	• Jim Kolbe (R)	138,975	64.8
	Chuck Phillips (D)	75,642	35.2

* *Gubernatorial results from Feb. 16, 1991, runoff election.*

ARKANSAS

	Candidate	Vote Total	%
Governor			
	• Bill Clinton (D)	400,386	57.5
	Sheffield Nelson (R)	295,925	42.5
Senate			
	• David Pryor (D)	493,910	99.8
	(No Republican candidate)		
	Betty White (write-in)	825	0.2
House			
1	• Bill Alexander (D)	101,026	64.3
	Terry Hayes (R)	56,071	35.7
2	Ray Thornton (D)	103,471	60.4
	Jim Keet (R)	67,800	39.6
3	• John Paul Hammerschmidt (R)	129,876	70.5
	Dan Ivy (D)	54,332	29.5
4	• Beryl Anthony Jr. (D)	110,365	72.4
	Roy Rood (R)	42,130	27.6

CALIFORNIA

	Candidate	Vote Total	%
Governor			
	Pete Wilson (R)	3,791,904	49.2
	Dianne Feinstein (D)	3,525,197	45.8
	Dennis Thompson (LIBERT)	145,628	1.9
	Jerome "Jerry" McCready (AMI)	139,661	1.8
	Maria Elizabeth Munoz (PF)	96,795	1.3
House			
1	Frank Riggs (R)	99,782	43.3
	• Douglas H. Bosco (D)	96,468	41.9
	Darlene G. Comingore (PF)	34,011	14.8
2	• Wally Herger (R)	133,315	63.7
	Erwin E. "Bill" Rush (D)	65,333	31.2
	Ross Crain (LIBERT)	10,753	5.1
3	• Robert T. Matsui (D)	132,143	60.3
	Lowell P. Landowski (R)	76,148	34.8
	David M. McCann (LIBERT)	10,797	4.9
4	• Vic Fazio (D)	115,090	54.7
	Mark Baughman (R)	82,738	39.3
	Bryce Bigwood (LIBERT)	12,626	6.0
5	• Nancy Pelosi (D)	120,633	77.2
	Alan Nichols (R)	35,671	22.8
6	• Barbara Boxer (D)	137,306	68.1
	Bill Boerum (R)	64,402	31.9
7	• George Miller (D)	121,080	60.5
	Roger A. Payton (R)	79,031	39.5
8	• Ronald V. Dellums (D)	119,645	61.3
	Barbara Galewski (R)	75,544	38.7
9	• Pete Stark (D)	94,739	58.4
	Victor Romero (R)	67,412	41.6
10	• Don Edwards (D)	81,875	62.7
	Mark Patrosso (R)	48,747	37.3
11	• Tom Lantos (D)	105,029	65.9
	G. M. "Bill" Quraishi (R)	45,818	28.8
	June R. Genis (LIBERT)	8,518	5.3
12	• Tom Campbell (R)	125,157	60.8
	Robert Palmer (D)	69,270	33.7
	Chuck Olson (LIBERT)	11,271	5.5
13	• Norman Y. Mineta (D)	97,286	58.0
	David E. Smith (R)	59,773	35.7
	John H. Webster (LIBERT)	10,587	6.3
14	John T. Doolittle (R)	128,309	51.5
	Patricia Malberg (D)	120,742	48.5
15	• Gary Condit (D)	97,147	66.2
	Cliff Burris (R)	49,634	33.8
16	• Leon E. Panetta (D)	134,236	74.2
	Jerry M. Reiss (R)	39,885	22.0
	Brian H. Tucker (LIBERT)	6,881	3.8
17	Calvin Dooley (D)	82,611	54.5
	• Charles "Chip" Pashayan Jr. (R)	68,848	45.5
18	• Richard H. Lehman (D)	98,804	100
	(No Republican candidate)		
19	• Robert J. Lagomarsino (R)	94,599	54.6
	Anita Perez Ferguson (D)	76,991	44.4
	Mindy Lorenz (write-in)	1,655	1.0
20	• Bill Thomas (R)	112,962	59.8
	Michael A. Thomas (D)	65,101	34.4
	William H. Dilbeck (LIBERT)	10,555	5.6
	Lita Martin Reid (write-in)	307	0.2
21	• Elton Gallegly (R)	118,326	58.4
	Richard D. Freiman (D)	68,921	34.0
	Peggy Christensen (LIBERT)	15,364	7.6
22	• Carlos J. Moorhead (R)	108,634	60.0
	David Bayer (D)	61,630	34.1
	William H. Wilson (LIBERT)	6,702	3.7
	Jan B. Tucker (PF)	3,963	2.2
23	• Anthony C. Beilenson (D)	103,141	61.7
	Jim Salomon (R)	57,118	34.2
	John Honigsfeld (PF)	6,834	4.1
24	• Henry A. Waxman (D)	71,562	68.9
	John N. Cowles (R)	26,607	25.6
	Maggie Phair (PF)	5,706	5.5
25	• Edward R. Roybal (D)	48,120	70.0
	Steven J. Renshaw (R)	17,021	24.8
	Robert H. Scott (LIBERT)	3,576	5.2

Abbreviations for Party Designations

AM — American
AMI — American Independent
ACP — A Connecticut Party
AM — American Party
ASI — American Systems Independent
BAG — Better Affordable Government
C — Conservative
CC — Concerned Citizens
COP — Concerns of People
D — Democratic
ER — Earth Rights
GR — Grass Roots
I — Independent
I-C — Independent Conservative
IHT — Independent High-Tech
IS — Illinois Solidarity
L — Liberal
LIBERT — Libertarian
LU — Liberty Union
NA — New Alliance
P — Political
PB — Colorado Prohibition
PF — Peace and Freedom
PH — Pride & Honesty
POP — Populist
R — Republican
RTL — Right to Life
SIS — Staten Island Secession
SW — Socialist Workers
TIC — Tisch Independent Citizens
UC — United Citizens
WW — Workers World
WWW — World Without War

		Candidate	Vote Total	%
26	●	Howard L. Berman (D)	78,031	61.1
		Roy Dahlson (R)	44,492	34.8
		Bernard Zimring (LIBERT)	5,268	4.1
27	●	Mel Levine (D)	90,857	58.2
		David Barrett Cohen (R)	58,140	37.2
		Edward E. Ferrer (PF)	7,101	4.5
28	●	Julian C. Dixon (D)	69,482	72.7
		George Z. Adams (R)	21,245	22.2
		William R. Williams (PF)	2,723	2.8
		Bob Weber (LIBERT)	2,150	2.2
29		Maxine Waters (D)	51,350	79.4
		Bill DeWitt (R)	12,054	18.6
		Waheed R. Boctor (LIBERT)	1,268	2.0
30	●	Matthew G. Martinez (D)	45,456	58.2
		Reuben D. Franco (R)	28,914	37.0
		G. Curtis Feger (LIBERT)	3,713	4.8
31	●	Mervyn M. Dymally (D)	56,394	67.1
		Eunice A. Sato (R)	27,593	32.9
32	●	Glenn M. Anderson (D)	68,268	61.5
		Sanford W. Kahn (R)	42,692	38.5
33	●	David Dreier (R)	101,336	63.7
		Georgia Houston Webb (D)	49,981	31.4
		Gail Lightfoot (LIBERT)	7,840	4.9
34	●	Esteban E. Torres (D)	55,646	60.7
		John Eastman (R)	36,024	39.3
35	●	Jerry Lewis (R)	121,602	60.6
		Barry Norton (D)	66,100	32.9
		Jerry Johnson (LIBERT)	13,020	6.5
36	●	George E. Brown Jr. (D)	72,409	52.7
		Robert Hammock (R)	64,961	47.3
37	●	Al McCandless (R)	115,469	49.7
		Ralph Waite (D)	103,961	44.8
		Gary R. Odom (AMI)	6,474	2.8
		Bonnie Flickinger (LIBERT)	6,178	2.7
38	●	Robert K. Dornan (R)	60,561	58.1
		Barbara Jackson (D)	43,693	41.9
39	●	William E. Dannemeyer (R)	113,849	65.3
		Francis X. Hoffman (D)	53,670	30.8
		Maxine B. Quirk (PF)	6,709	3.9
40	●	C. Christopher Cox (R)	142,299	67.6
		Eugene C. Gratz (D)	68,087	32.4
41	●	Bill Lowery (R)	105,723	49.2
		Dan Kripke (D)	93,586	43.6
		Karen S. R. Works (PF)	15,428	7.2
42	●	Dana Rohrabacher (R)	109,353	59.3
		Guy C. Kimbrough (D)	67,189	36.5
		Richard Gibb Martin (LIBERT)	7,744	4.2
43	●	Ron Packard (R)	151,206	68.1
		(No Democratic candidate)		
		Doug Hansen (PF)	40,212	18.1
		Richard L. Arnold (LIBERT)	30,720	13.8
44		Randy "Duke" Cunningham (R)	50,377	46.3
	●	Jim Bates (D)	48,712	44.8
		Donna White (PF)	5,237	4.8
		John Wallner (LIBERT)	4,385	4.0
45	●	Duncan Hunter (R)	123,591	72.8
		(No Democratic candidate)		
		Joe Shea (LIBERT)	46,068	27.2

COLORADO

		Candidate	Vote Total	%
Governor				
	●	Roy Romer (D)	626,032	61.9
		John Andrews (R)	358,403	35.4
		David Aitken (LIBERT)	18,932	1.9
		Wm. David Livingston (PB)	7,907	0.8
Senate				
		Hank Brown (R)	569,048	55.7
		Josie Heath (D)	425,746	41.7
		John Heckman (COP)	15,432	1.5
		Earl F. Dodge (PB)	11,801	1.1
House				
1	●	Patricia Schroeder (D)	82,176	63.7
		Gloria Gonzales Roemer (R)	46,802	36.3
2	●	David E. Skaggs (D)	105,248	60.7
		Jason Lewis (R)	68,226	39.3
House				
1	●	Patricia Schroeder (D)	82,176	63.7
		Gloria Gonzales Roemer (R)	46,802	36.3
2	●	David E. Skaggs (D)	105,248	60.7
		Jason Lewis (R)	68,226	39.3
3	●	Ben Nighthorse Campbell (D)	124,487	70.2
		Bob Ellis (R)	49,961	28.2
		Howard E. Fields (POP-Colo)	2,859	1.6
4		Wayne Allard (R)	89,285	54.1
		Dick Bond (D)	75,901	45.9
5	●	Joel Hefley (R)	127,740	66.4
		Cal Johnston (D)	57,776	30.0
		Keith L. Hamburger (LIBERT)	6,761	3.5
6	●	Dan Schaefer (R)	105,312	64.5
		Don Jarrett (D)	57,961	35.5

CONNECTICUT

		Candidate	Vote Total	%
Governor				
		Lowell P. Weicker Jr. (ACP)	460,576	40.4
		John G. Rowland (R)	427,840	37.5
		Bruce A. Morrison (D)	236,641	20.7
		Joseph A. Zdonczyk (CC)	16,044	1.4
House				
1	●	Barbara B. Kennelly (D)	126,566	71.4
		James M. Garvey (R)	50,690	28.6
2	●	Sam Gejdenson (D)	105,085	59.7
		John M. Ragsdale (R)	70,922	40.3
3		Rosa DeLauro (D)	90,772	52.1
		Thomas Scott (R)	83,440	47.9
4	●	Christopher Shays (R)	105,682	76.5
		Al Smith (D)	32,352	23.4
5		Gary Franks (R)	93,912	51.7
		Toby Moffett (D)	85,803	47.2
		William G. Hare (Liberty)	1,888	1.0
6	●	Nancy L. Johnson (R)	141,105	74.4
		Paul Kulas (D)	48,628	25.6

DELAWARE

		Candidate	Vote Total	%
Senate				
	●	Joseph R. Biden Jr. (D)	112,918	62.7
		M. Jane Brady (R)	64,554	35.8
		Lee Rosenbaum (LIBERT)	2,680	1.5
House				
AL	●	Thomas R. Carper (D)	116,274	65.5
		Ralph O. Williams (R)	58,037	32.7
		Richard A. Cohen (LIBERT)	3,121	1.8

FLORIDA

		Candidate	Vote Total	%
Governor				
		Lawton Chiles (D)	1,995,206	56.5
	●	Bob Martinez (R)	1,535,068	43.5
House				
1	●	Earl Hutto (D)	88,416	52.2
		Terry Ketchel (R)	80,851	47.8
2		Pete Peterson (D)	103,032	56.9
	●	Bill Grant (R)	77,939	43.1
3	●	Charles E. Bennett (D)	84,280	72.7
		Rod Sullivan (R)	31,727	27.3
4	●	Craig T. James (R)	120,895	55.9
		Reid Hughes (D)	95,320	44.1
5	●	Bill McCollum (R)	94,453	59.9
		Bob Fletcher (D)	63,253	40.1
6	●	Cliff Stearns (R)	138,588	59.2
		Art Johnson (D)	95,421	40.8
7	●	Sam M. Gibbons (D)	99,464	67.6
		Charles D. Prout (R)	47,765	32.4
8	●	C. W. Bill Young (R)	x	x
		(No Democratic candidate)		
9	●	Michael Bilirakis (R)	142,163	58.1
		Cheryl Davis Knapp (D)	102,503	41.9
10	●	Andy Ireland (R)	x	x
		(No Democratic candidate)		
11		Jim Bacchus (D)	120,991	51.9
		Bill Tolley (R)	111,970	48.1
12	●	Tom Lewis (R)	x	x
		(No Democratic candidate)		
13	●	Porter J. Goss (R)	x	x
		(No Democratic candidate)		
14	●	Harry A. Johnston (D)	156,055	66.0
		Scott Shore (R)	80,249	34.0
15	●	E. Clay Shaw Jr. (R)	104,295	97.8
		(No Democratic candidate)		
		Charles Goodmon (write-in)	2,374	2.2
16	●	Lawrence J. Smith (D)	x	x
		(No Republican candidate)		
17	●	William Lehman (D)	79,569	78.3
		Earl Rodney (R)	22,029	21.7
18	●	Ileana Ros-Lehtinen (R)	56,364	60.4
		Bernard Anscher (D)	36,978	39.6
19	●	Dante B. Fascell (D)	87,696	62.0
		Bob Allen (R)	53,796	38.0

GEORGIA

		Candidate	Vote Total	%
Governor				
		Zell Miller (D)	766,662	52.9
		Johnny Isakson (R)	645,625	44.5
		Carole Ann Rand (LIBERT)	37,365	2.6
Senate				
	●	Sam Nunn (D)	1,033,439	100
		(No Republican candidate)		
House				
1	●	Lindsay Thomas (D)	80,515	71.2
		Chris Meredith (R)	32,532	28.8
2	●	Charles Hatcher (D)	77,910	73.0
		Jonathan Perry Waters (R)	28,781	27.0
3	●	Richard Ray (D)	72,961	63.2
		Paul Broun (R)	42,561	36.8
4	●	Ben Jones (D)	96,526	52.4
		John Linder (R)	87,569	47.6
5	●	John Lewis (D)	86,037	75.6
		J. W. Tibbs Jr. (R)	27,781	24.4
6	●	Newt Gingrich (R)	78,768	50.3
		David Worley (D)	77,794	49.7
7	●	George "Buddy" Darden (D)	95,817	60.1
		Al Beverly (R)	63,588	39.9
8	●	J. Roy Rowland (D)	81,344	68.7
		Robert F. Cunningham (R)	36,980	31.3
9	●	Ed Jenkins (D)	96,197	55.8
		Joe Hoffman (R)	76,121	44.2
10	●	Doug Barnard Jr. (D)	89,683	58.3
		Sam Jones (R)	64,184	41.7

HAWAII

		Candidate	Vote Total	%
Governor				
	●	John Waihee III (D)	203,491	59.8
		Fred Hemmings (R)	131,310	38.6
		Triaka-Don Smith (LIBERT)	2,885	0.8
		Peggy Ha'o Ross (Nonpartisan)	2,446	0.7
Senate				
	●	Daniel K. Akaka (D)	188,901	54.0
		Patricia Saiki (R)	155,978	44.6
		Ken Schoolland (LIBERT)	4,787	1.4
House				
1		Neil Abercrombie (D)	97,622	60.0
		Mike Liu (R)	62,982	38.7
		Roger Lee Taylor (LIBERT)	2,107	1.3
2	●	Patsy T. Mink (D)	118,155	66.3
		Andy Poepoe (R)	54,625	30.6
		Lloyd Jeffrey Mallan (LIBERT)	5,508	3.1

IDAHO

		Candidate	Vote Total	%
Governor				
	●	Cecil D. Andrus (D)	218,673	68.2
		Roger Fairchild (R)	101,937	31.8
Senate				
		Larry E. Craig (R)	193,641	61.3
		Ron J. Twilegar (D)	122,295	38.7
House				
1		Larry LaRocco (D)	85,054	53.0
		C. A. "Skip" Smyser (R)	75,406	47.0
2	●	Richard Stallings (D)	98,008	63.6
		Sean McDevitt (R)	56,044	36.4

ILLINOIS

	Candidate	Vote Total	%
Governor			
	Jim Edgar (R)	1,653,126	50.7
	Neil F. Hartigan (D)	1,569,217	48.2
	Jessie Fields (IS)	35,067	1.1
Senate			
	• Paul Simon (D)	2,115,377	65.1
	Lynn Martin (R)	1,135,628	34.9
House			
1	• Charles A. Hayes (D)	100,890	93.8
	Babette Peyton (R)	6,708	6.2
2	• Gus Savage (D)	80,245	78.2
	William T. Hespel (R)	22,350	21.8
3	• Marty Russo (D)	110,512	70.9
	Carl L. Klein (R)	45,299	29.1
4	• George E. Sangmeister (D)	77,290	59.2
	Manny Hoffman (R)	53,258	40.8
5	• William O. Lipinski (D)	73,805	66.3
	David J. Shestokas (R)	34,440	31.0
	Ronald Bartos (IS)	3,001	2.7
6	• Henry J. Hyde (R)	96,410	66.7
	Robert J. Cassidy (D)	48,155	33.3
7	• Cardiss Collins (D)	80,021	79.9
	Michael Dooley (R)	20,099	20.1
8	• Dan Rostenkowski (D)	70,151	79.1
	(No Republican candidate)		
	Robert Marshall (LIBERT)	18,529	20.9
9	• Sidney R. Yates (D)	96,557	71.2
	Herbert Sohn (R)	39,031	28.8
10	• John Porter (R)	104,070	67.7
	Peg McNamara (D)	47,286	30.8
	Herbert L. Gorrell (IS)	2,243	1.5
11	• Frank Annunzio (D)	82,703	53.6
	Walter W. Dudycz (R)	68,850	44.6
	Larry Saska (IS)	2,692	1.7
12	• Philip M. Crane (R)	113,081	82.2
	(No Democratic candidate)		
	Steve Pedersen (IS)	24,450	17.8
13	• Harris W. Fawell (R)	116,048	65.8
	Steven Thomas (D)	60,305	34.2
14	• Dennis Hastert (R)	112,383	66.9
	Donald J. Westphal (D)	55,592	33.1
15	• Edward Madigan (R)	119,812	100
	(No Democratic candidate)		
16	John W. Cox Jr. (D)	83,061	54.6
	John W. Hallock Jr. (R)	69,105	45.4
17	• Lane Evans (D)	102,062	66.5
	Dan Lee (R)	51,380	33.5
18	• Robert H. Michel (R)	105,693	98.4
	(No Democratic candidate)		
	Walter Gillin (write-in)	1,524	1.4
	Alan J. Port (write-in)	153	0.1
19	• Terry L. Bruce (D)	113,958	66.3
	Robert F. Kerans (R)	55,680	32.4
	Brian James O'Neill II (IS)	2,250	1.3
20	• Richard J. Durbin (D)	130,114	66.2
	Paul E. Jurgens (R)	66,433	33.8
21	• Jerry F. Costello (D)	95,208	66.0
	Robert H. Gaffner (R)	48,949	34.0
22	• Glenn Poshard (D)	138,425	83.7
	(No Republican candidate)		
	Jim Wham (Jim Wham Party)	26,896	16.3

INDIANA

	Candidate	Vote Total	%
Senate			
	• Daniel R. Coats (R)	806,048	53.6
	Baron P. Hill (D)	696,639	46.4
House			
1	• Peter J. Visclosky (D)	68,920	66.0
	William B. Costas (R)	35,450	34.0
2	• Philip R. Sharp (D)	93,495	59.4
	Mike Pence (R)	63,980	40.6
3	Tim Roemer (D)	80,740	50.9
	• John Hiler (R)	77,911	49.1
4	• Jill Long (D)	99,347	60.7
	Rick Hawks (R)	64,415	39.3
5	• Jim Jontz (D)	81,373	53.1
	John A. Johnson (R)	71,750	46.9
6	• Dan Burton (R)	116,470	63.5
	James P. Fadely (D)	67,024	36.5
7	• John T. Myers (R)	88,598	57.6
	John W. Riley Sr. (D)	65,248	42.4
8	• Frank McCloskey (D)	97,465	54.7
	Richard E. Mourdock (R)	80,645	45.3
9	• Lee H. Hamilton (D)	107,526	69.0
	Floyd Eugene Coates (R)	48,325	31.0
10	• Andrew Jacobs Jr. (D)	69,362	66.4
	Janos Horvath (R)	35,049	33.6

IOWA

	Candidate	Vote Total	%
Governor			
	• Terry E. Branstad (R)	591,852	60.6
	Donald D. Avenson (D)	379,372	38.9
	Nan Bailey (SW)	4,263	0.4
Senate			
	• Tom Harkin (D)	535,975	54.5
	Tom Tauke (R)	446,869	45.4
House			
1	• Jim Leach (R)	90,042	99.8
	(No Democratic candidate)		
2	Jim Nussle (R)	82,650	49.8
	Eric Tabor (D)	81,008	48.8
	Jan J. Zonneveld (I)	2,325	1.4
3	• Dave Nagle (D)	100,947	99.2
	(No Republican candidate)		
4	• Neal Smith (D)	127,812	97.9
	(No Republican candidate)		
5	• Jim Ross Lightfoot (R)	99,978	68.0
	Rod Powell (D)	47,022	32.0
6	• Fred Grandy (R)	112,333	71.8
	Mike D. Earll (D)	44,063	28.2

KANSAS

	Candidate	Vote Total	%
Governor			
	Joan Finney (D)	380,609	48.6
	• Mike Hayden (R)	333,589	42.6
	Christina Campbell-Cline (I)	69,127	8.8
Senate			
	• Nancy Landon Kassebaum (R)	578,605	73.6
	Dick Williams (D)	207,491	26.4
House			
1	• Pat Roberts (R)	102,974	62.6
	Duane West (D)	61,396	37.4
2	• Jim Slattery (D)	99,093	62.8
	Scott Morgan (R)	58,643	37.2
3	• Jan Meyers (R)	88,725	60.1
	Leroy Jones (D)	58,923	39.9
4	• Dan Glickman (D)	112,015	70.8
	Roger M. Grund (R)	46,283	29.2
5	Dick Nichols (R)	90,555	59.3
	George Wingert (D)	62,244	40.7

KENTUCKY

	Candidate	Vote Total	%
Senate			
	• Mitch McConnell (R)	478,034	52.2
	Harvey Sloane (D)	437,976	47.8
House			
1	• Carroll Hubbard Jr. (D)	85,323	86.9
	(No Republican candidate)		
	Marvin H. Seat (POP)	12,879	13.1
2	• William H. Natcher (D)	77,057	66.0
	Martin A. Tori (R)	39,624	34.0
3	• Romano L. Mazzoli (D)	84,750	60.6
	Al Brown (R)	55,188	39.4
4	• Jim Bunning (R)	101,680	69.3
	Galen Martin (D)	44,979	30.7
5	• Harold Rogers (R)	64,660	100
	(No Democratic candidate)		
6	• Larry J. Hopkins (R)	76,859	100
	(No Democratic candidate)		
7	• Carl C. Perkins (D)	61,330	50.8
	Will T. Scott (R)	59,377	49.2

LOUISIANA

	Candidate	Vote Total	%
Senate			
	• J. Bennett Johnston (D)	x	x
House			
1	• Bob Livingston (R)	x	x
2	William J. Jefferson (D)	55,621	52.5
	Marc H. Morial (D)	50,232	47.5
3	• W. J. "Billy" Tauzin (D)	x	x
4	• Jim McCrery (R)	x	x
5	• Jerry Huckaby (D)	x	x
6	• Richard H. Baker (R)	x	x
7	• Jimmy Hayes (D)	x	x
8	• Clyde C. Holloway (R)	x	x

MAINE

	Candidate	Vote Total	%
Governor			
	• John R. McKernan Jr. (R)	243,766	46.7
	Joseph E. Brennan (D)	230,038	44.0
	Andrew Adam (Unenrolled)	48,377	9.3
Senate			
	• William S. Cohen (R)	319,167	61.3
	Neil Rolde (D)	201,053	38.6
House			
1	Thomas H. Andrews (D)	167,623	60.1
	David F. Emery (R)	110,836	39.7
2	• Olympia J. Snowe (R)	121,704	51.0
	Patrick K. McGowan (D)	116,798	49.0

MARYLAND

	Candidate	Vote Total	%
Governor			
	• William Donald Schaefer (D)	664,015	59.8
	William S. Shepard (R)	446,980	40.2
House			
1	Wayne T. Gilchrest (R)	88,920	56.8
	• Roy Dyson (D)	67,518	43.2
2	• Helen Delich Bentley (R)	115,398	74.4
	Ronald P. Bowers (D)	39,785	25.6
3	• Benjamin L. Cardin (D)	82,545	69.7
	Harwood Nichols (R)	35,841	30.3
4	• Tom McMillen (D)	85,601	58.9
	Robert P. Duckworth (R)	59,846	41.1
5	• Steny H. Hoyer (D)	84,747	80.7
	Lee F. Breuer (R)	20,314	19.3
6	• Beverly B. Byron (D)	106,502	65.3
	Christopher P. Fiotes Jr. (R)	56,479	34.7
7	• Kweisi Mfume (D)	59,628	85.0
	Kenneth Kondner (R)	10,529	15.0
8	• Constance A. Morella (R)	130,059	73.5
	James Walker Jr. (D)	39,343	22.2
	Sidney Altman (I)	7,485	4.2

MASSACHUSETTS

	Candidate	Vote Total	%
Governor			
	William F. Weld (R)	1,175,817	50.2
	John Silber (D)	1,099,878	46.9
	Leonard Umina (IHT)	62,703	2.7
Senate			
	• John Kerry (D)	1,321,712	57.1
	Jim Rappaport (R)	992,917	42.9

			Vote Total	%
House				
1	•	Silvio O. Conte (R)	150,748	77.5
		John R. Arden (D)	43,611	22.4
2	•	Richard E. Neal (D)	134,152	99.8
		(No Republican candidate)		
3	•	Joseph D. Early (D)	150,992	99.4
		(No Republican candidate)		
4	•	Barney Frank (D)	143,473	65.5
		John R. Soto (R)	75,454	34.5
5	•	Chester G. Atkins (D)	110,232	52.2
		John F. MacGovern (R)	101,017	47.8
6	•	Nicholas Mavroules (D)	149,284	65.0
		Edgar L. Kelley (R)	80,177	34.9
7	•	Edward J. Markey (D)	155,380	99.9
		(No Republican candidate)		
8	•	Joseph P. Kennedy II (D)	125,479	72.2
		Glenn W. Fiscus (R)	39,310	22.6
		Susan C. Davies (NA)	8,806	5.1
9	•	Joe Moakley (D)	124,534	70.3
		(No Republican candidate)		
		Robert Horan (I)	52,660	29.7
10	•	Gerry E. Studds (D)	137,805	53.4
		Jon L. Bryan (R)	120,217	46.6
11	•	Brian Donnelly (D)	145,480	99.7
		(No Republican candidate)		

MICHIGAN

			Vote Total	%
Governor				
		John Engler (R)	1,276,134	49.8
	•	James J. Blanchard (D)	1,258,539	49.1
		William Roundtree (WW)	28,091	1.1
Senate				
	•	Carl Levin (D)	1,471,753	57.5
		Bill Schuette (R)	1,055,695	41.2
		Susan Farquhar (WW)	32,796	1.3
House				
1	•	John Conyers Jr. (D)	76,556	89.3
		Ray Shoulders (R)	7,298	8.5
		Robert Mays (No affiliation)	1,134	1.3
		Jonathan Paul Flint (LIBERT)	764	0.9
2	•	Carl D. Pursell (R)	95,962	64.1
		Elmer White (D)	49,678	33.2
		Paul S. Jensen (TIC)	4,119	2.7
3	•	Howard Wolpe (D)	82,376	57.9
		Brad Haskins (R)	60,007	42.1
4	•	Fred Upton (R)	75,850	57.8
		JoAnne McFarland (D)	55,449	42.2
5	•	Paul B. Henry (R)	126,308	75.4
		Thomas Trzybinski (D)	41,170	24.6
6	•	Bob Carr (D)	97,547	99.8
		(No Republican candidate)		
7	•	Dale E. Kildee (D)	90,307	68.4
		David J. Morrill (R)	41,759	31.6
8	•	Bob Traxler (D)	98,903	68.6
		James White (R)	45,259	31.4
9	•	Guy Vander Jagt (R)	89,078	54.8
		Geraldine Greene (D)	73,604	45.2
10		Dave Camp (R)	99,952	65.0
		Joan Louise Dennison (D)	50,923	33.1
		Charles Congdon (LIBERT)	2,496	1.6
11	•	Robert W. Davis (R)	94,555	61.3
		Marcia Gould (D)	59,759	38.7
12	•	David E. Bonior (D)	98,232	64.7
		Jim Dingeman (R)	51,119	33.7
		Robert W. Roddis (LIBERT)	2,472	1.6
13		Barbara-Rose Collins (D)	54,345	80.1
		Carl R. Edwards Sr. (R)	11,203	16.5
		Joyce Ann Griffin (WW)	1,090	1.6
		Jeff J. Hampton (LIBERT)	649	1.0
		Cleve Andrew Pulley (none)	530	0.8
14	•	Dennis M. Hertel (D)	78,506	63.6
		Kenneth C. McNealy (R)	40,499	32.8
		Robert John Gale (TIC)	2,692	2.2
		Kenneth G. Morris (LIBERT)	1,721	1.4
15	•	William D. Ford (D)	68,742	61.2
		Burl C. Adkins (R)	41,092	36.6
		David R. Hunt (LIBERT)	2,497	2.2
16	•	John D. Dingell (D)	88,962	66.6
		Frank Beaumont (R)	42,629	31.9
		Roger Conant Pope (LIBERT)	2,019	1.5
17	•	Sander M. Levin (D)	92,205	69.7
		Blaine L. Lankford (R)	40,100	30.3
18	•	William S. Broomfield (R)	126,629	66.4
		Walter O. Briggs IV (D)	64,185	33.6

MINNESOTA

			Vote Total	%
Governor				
		Arne Carlson (R)	895,988	49.6
	•	Rudy Perpich (D)	836,218	46.3
		Heart Warrior (Judith Ann) Chosa (ER)	21,139	1.2
		Ross S. Culverhouse (GR)	17,176	1.0
		Jon Grunseth (originally GOP nominee)	10,941	0.6
		Wendy Lyons (SW)	6,701	0.4
Senate				
		Paul Wellstone (D)	911,999	50.4
	•	Rudy Boschwitz (R)	864,375	47.8
		Russell B. Bentley (GR)	29,820	1.6
House				
1	•	Timothy J. Penny (D)	156,749	78.1
		Doug Andersen (R)	43,856	21.9
2	•	Vin Weber (R)	126,367	61.8
		Jim Stone (D)	77,935	38.1
3		Jim Ramstad (R)	195,833	66.9
		Lewis DeMars (D)	96,395	32.9
4	•	Bruce F. Vento (D)	143,353	64.7
		Ian Maitland (R)	77,639	35.1
5	•	Martin Olav Sabo (D)	144,682	72.9
		Raymond C. "Buzz" Gilbertson (R)	53,720	27.1
6	•	Gerry Sikorski (D)	164,816	64.6
		Bruce D. Anderson (R)	90,138	35.3
7		Collin C. Peterson (D)	107,126	53.5
	•	Arlan Stangeland (R)	92,876	46.4
8	•	James L. Oberstar (D)	151,145	72.9
		Jerry Shuster (R)	56,068	27.0

MISSISSIPPI

			Vote Total	%
Senate				
	•	Thad Cochran (R)	274,244	100
		(No Democratic candidate)		
House				
1	•	Jamie L. Whitten (D)	43,668	64.9
		Bill Bowlin (R)	23,650	35.1
2	•	Mike Espy (D)	59,393	84.1
		Dorothy Benford (R)	11,224	15.9
3	•	G. V. "Sonny" Montgomery (D)	49,162	100
		(No Republican candidate)		
4	•	Mike Parker (D)	57,137	80.6
		Jerry "Rev" Parks (R)	13,754	19.4
5	•	Gene Taylor (D)	89,926	81.4
		Sheila Smith (R)	20,588	18.6

MISSOURI

			Vote Total	%
House				
1	•	William L. Clay (D)	62,550	60.9
		Wayne G. Piotrowski (R)	40,160	39.1
2		Joan Kelly Horn (D)	94,378	50.0
	•	Jack Buechner (R)	94,324	50.0
3	•	Richard A. Gephardt (D)	88,950	56.8
		Malcolm L. Holekamp (R)	67,659	43.2
4	•	Ike Skelton (D)	105,527	61.8
		David Eyerly (R)	65,095	38.2
5	•	Alan Wheat (D)	71,890	62.1
		Robert H. Gardner (R)	43,897	37.9
6	•	E. Thomas Coleman (R)	78,956	51.9
		Bob McClure (D)	73,093	48.1
7	•	Mel Hancock (R)	83,609	52.1
		Thomas Patrick Deaton (D)	76,725	47.9
8	•	Bill Emerson (R)	81,452	57.3
		Russ Carnahan (D)	60,751	42.7
9	•	Harold L. Volkmer (D)	94,156	57.5
		Don Curtis (R)	69,514	42.5

MONTANA

			Vote Total	%
Senate				
	•	Max Baucus (D)	217,563	68.1
		Allen C. Kolstad (R)	93,836	29.4
		Westley F. Deitchler (LIBERT)	7,937	2.5
House				
1	•	Pat Williams (D)	100,409	61.1
		Brad Johnson (R)	63,837	38.9
2	•	Ron Marlenee (R)	96,449	63.0
		Don Burris (D)	56,739	37.0

NEBRASKA

			Vote Total	%
Governor				
		Ben Nelson (D)	292,771	49.9
	•	Kay A. Orr (R)	288,741	49.2
		Mort Sullivan (write-in)	1,887	0.3
Senate				
	•	Jim Exon (D)	349,779	58.9
		Hal Daub (R)	243,013	40.9
House				
1	•	Doug Bereuter (R)	129,654	64.7
		Larry Hall (D)	70,587	35.2
2	•	Peter Hoagland (D)	111,903	57.9
		Ally Milder (R)	80,845	41.8
3		Bill Barrett (R)	98,607	51.1
		Sandra K. Scofield (D)	94,234	48.8

NEVADA

			Vote Total	%
Governor				
	•	Bob Miller (D)	207,878	64.8
		Jim Gallaway (R)	95,789	29.9
		None of these	9,017	2.8
		James Frye (LIBERT)	8,059	2.5
House				
1	•	James Bilbray (D)	84,650	61.4
		Bob Dickinson (R)	47,377	34.4
		William Moore (LIBERT)	5,825	4.2
2	•	Barbara F. Vucanovich (R)	103,508	59.1
		Jane Wisdom (D)	59,581	34.0
		Dan Becan (LIBERT)	12,120	6.9

NEW HAMPSHIRE

			Vote Total	%
Governor				
	•	Judd Gregg (R)	177,611	60.2
		J. Joseph Grandmaison (D)	101,886	34.6
		Miriam F. Luce (LIBERT)	14,348	4.9
Senate				
		Robert C. Smith (R)	189,630	65.1
		John A. Durkin (D)	91,262	31.3
		John Elsnau (LIBERT)	9,717	3.3
House				
1		Bill Zeliff (R)	81,684	55.1
		Joseph F. Keefe (D)	66,176	44.6
2		Dick Swett (D)	74,829	52.7
	•	Chuck Douglas (R)	67,063	47.2

NEW JERSEY

			Vote Total	%
Senate				
	•	Bill Bradley (D)	977,810	50.4
		Christine Todd Whitman (R)	918,874	47.4
		John L. Kucek (POP)	19,978	1.0
		Louis M. Stefanelli (LIBERT)	13,988	0.7
		Don Mackle (SW)	7,804	0.4
House				
1		Robert E. Andrews (D)	73,522	54.3
		Daniel J. Mangini (R)	57,801	42.7
		Jerry Zeldin (LIBERT)	1,599	1.2
		Walter E. Konstanty (PH)	1,431	1.0
		William Henry Harris (POP)	1,078	0.8

		Vote Total	%
2	• William J. Hughes (D)	98,734	88.2
	(No Republican candidate)		
	William A. Kanengiser (POP)	13,246	11.8
3	• Frank Pallone Jr. (D)	77,709	49.1
	Paul A. Kapalko (R)	73,451	46.4
	Richard D. McKean (I)	4,390	2.8
	William Stewart (LIBERT)	1,875	1.2
	Joseph A. Plonski (POP)	867	0.5
4	• Christopher H. Smith (R)	101,508	62.9
	Mark Setaro (D)	55,454	34.4
	Carl Peters (LIBERT)	2,168	1.3
	Joseph J. Notarangelo (POP)	1,219	0.8
	J. M. Carter (God We Trust)	1,029	0.6
5	• Marge Roukema (R)	118,101	75.7
	Lawrence Wayne Olsen (D)	35,010	22.4
	Mark Richards (POP)	2,998	1.9
6	• Bernard J. Dwyer (D)	63,696	50.5
	Paul Danielczyk (R)	58,209	46.2
	Randolph Waller (POP)	2,364	1.9
	Howard F. Schoen (LIBERT)	1,784	1.4
7	• Matthew J. Rinaldo (R)	100,274	74.6
	Bruce H. Bergen (D)	31,114	23.2
	Thomas V. Sarnowski (POP)	2,929	2.2
8	• Robert A. Roe (D)	55,212	76.9
	(No Republican candidate)		
	Stephen Sibilia (I-C)	13,239	18.4
	Bruce Eden (POP)	3,347	4.7
9	• Robert G. Torricelli (D)	82,736	57.0
	Peter J. Russo (R)	59,759	41.2
	Chester Grabowski (POP)	2,573	1.8
10	• Donald M. Payne (D)	42,616	81.5
	Howard E. Berkeley (R)	9,072	17.3
	George Mehrabian (SW)	617	1.2
11	• Dean A. Gallo (R)	95,198	64.9
	Michael Gordon (D)	47,782	32.6
	Jasper Gould (POP)	3,610	2.5
12	Dick Zimmer (R)	108,173	64.0
	Marguerite Chandler (D)	52,498	31.1
	Joan I. Bottcher (Back to Basics)	4,443	2.6
	C. Max Kortepeter (I-Reform)	2,442	1.4
	Michael A. Notarangelo (POP)	1,408	0.8
13	• H. James Saxton (R)	100,537	58.1
	John H. Adler (D)	68,286	39.5
	Howard Scott Pearlman (WWW)	4,178	2.4
14	• Frank J. Guarini (D)	57,581	66.1
	Fred J. Theemling Jr. (R)	25,473	29.2
	Michael Ziruolo (BAG)	1,897	2.2
	Jane E. Harris (SW)	1,355	1.5
	Donald K. Stoveken Sr. (POP)	519	0.6
	Louis Vernotico (Right to Vote)	324	0.4

NEW MEXICO

		Vote Total	%
Governor			
	Bruce King (D)	224,564	54.6
	Frank M. Bond (R)	185,692	45.2
	Joseph E. Knight (write-in)	788	0.2
Senate			
	• Pete V. Domenici (R)	296,712	72.9
	Tom R. Benavides (D)	110,033	27.1
House			
1	• Steven H. Schiff (R)	97,375	70.2
	Rebecca Vigil-Giron (D)	41,306	29.8
2	• Joe Skeen (R)	80,677	100
	(No Democratic candidate)		
3	• Bill Richardson (D)	104,225	74.5
	Phil T. Archuletta (R)	35,751	25.5

NEW YORK

		Vote Total	%
Governor			
	• Mario M. Cuomo (D, L)	2,157,087	53.2
	Pierre A. Rinfret (R)	865,948	21.3
	Herbert I. London (C)	827,614	20.4
	Louis P. Wein (RTL)	137,804	3.4
	Lenora B. Fulani (NA)	31,089	0.8
	W. Gary Johnson (LIBERT)	24,611	0.6
	Craig Gannon (SW)	12,743	0.3
House			
1	• George J. Hochbrueckner (D, Tax Break)	75,211	56.3
	Francis W. Creighton (R)	46,380	34.7
	Clayton Baldwin Jr. (C)	6,883	5.2
	Peter J. O'Hara (RTL)	5,111	3.8
2	• Thomas J. Downey (D)	56,722	55.8
	John W. Bugler (R, RTL, Tax Cut)	36,859	36.2
	Dominic A. Curcio (C)	8,150	8.0
3	• Robert J. Mrazek (D, L)	73,029	53.3
	Robert Previdi (R, C)	59,089	43.1
	Francis A. Dreger (RTL)	4,915	3.6
4	• Norman F. Lent (R, C)	79,304	61.2
	Francis T. Goban (D)	41,308	31.8
	John J. Dunkle (RTL)	6,706	5.2
	Ben-Zion J. Heyman (L)	2,343	1.8
5	• Raymond J. McGrath (R, C)	71,948	54.6
	Mark S. Epstein (D, L)	53,920	40.9
	Edward K. Kitt (RTL)	6,000	4.5
6	• Floyd H. Flake (D, L)	44,306	73.1
	William Sampol (R)	13,224	21.8
	John Cronin (RTL)	3,111	5.1
7	• Gary L. Ackerman (D, L)	51,091	100
	(No Republican candidate)		
8	• James H. Scheuer (D, L)	56,396	72.3
	Gustave Reifenkugel (R)	21,646	27.7
9	• Thomas J. Manton (D)	35,177	64.4
	Ann Pfoser Darby (R, Anti-corruption)	13,330	24.4
	Thomas V. Ognibene (C)	6,137	11.2
10	• Charles E. Schumer (D, L)	61,468	80.4
	Patrick J. Kinsella (R, C)	14,963	19.6
11	• Ed Towns (D, L)	36,286	92.9
	(No Republican candidate)		
	Ernest Johnson (C)	1,676	4.3
	Lorraine Stevens (NA)	1,094	2.8
12	• Major R. Owens (D, L)	40,570	94.9
	(No Republican candidate)		
	Joseph N. O. Caesar (C)	1,159	2.7
	Mamie Moore (NA)	1,021	2.4
13	• Stephen J. Solarz (D, L)	47,446	80.4
	Edwin Ramos (R, C)	11,557	19.6
14	• Susan Molinari (R, C)	58,616	60.0
	Anthony J. Pocchia (D, L, SIS)	34,625	35.5
	Christine Sacchi (RTL)	4,370	4.5
15	• Bill Green (R)	52,919	58.8
	Frances L. Reiter (D)	33,464	37.2
	Michael T. Berns (C)	3,654	4.0
16	• Charles B. Rangel (D, R, L)	55,882	97.2
	Alvaader Frazier (NA)	1,592	2.8
17	• Ted Weiss (D, L)	79,161	80.4
	William W. Koeppel (R)	15,219	15.5
	Mark Goret (C)	2,928	3.0
	John Patterson (NA)	1,087	1.1
18	• Jose E. Serrano (D, L)	38,024	93.2
	Joseph Chiavaro (R)	1,189	2.9
	Mary Rivera (NA)	866	2.1
	Anna Johnson (C)	717	1.8
19	• Eliot L. Engel (D, L)	45,758	61.2
	William J. Gouldman (R)	17,135	22.9
	Kevin Brawley (C, RTL)	11,868	15.9
20	• Nita M. Lowey (D)	82,203	62.8
	Glenn D. Belitto (R)	35,575	27.2
	John M. Schafer (C, RTL)	13,030	10.0
21	• Hamilton Fish Jr. (R, C)	99,866	71.4
	Richard L. Barbuto (D)	34,128	24.4
	Richard S. Curtin II (RTL)	5,925	4.2
22	• Benjamin A. Gilman (R)	95,495	68.6
	John G. Dow (D)	37,034	26.6
	Margaret M. Beirne (RTL)	6,656	4.8
23	• Michael R. McNulty (D, C)	117,239	64.1
	Margaret B. Buhrmaster (R)	65,760	35.9
24	• Gerald B. H. Solomon (R, C, RTL)	121,206	68.1
	Bob Lawrence (D)	56,671	31.9
25	• Sherwood Boehlert (R)	91,348	83.9
	(No Democratic candidate)		
	William L. Griffen (L)	17,481	16.1
26	• David O'B. Martin (R, C)	97,340	100
	(No Democratic candidate)		
27	• James T. Walsh (R, C)	95,220	63.2
	Peggy L. Murray (D, L)	52,438	34.8
	Stephen K. Hoff (RTL)	3,097	2.0
28	• Matthew F. McHugh (D)	97,815	64.8
	Seymour Krieger (R)	53,077	35.2
29	• Frank Horton (R)	89,105	63.0
	Alton F. Eber (D)	34,835	24.6
	Peter DeMauro (C)	12,599	8.9
	Donald M. Peters (RTL)	4,878	3.4
30	• Louise M. Slaughter (D)	97,280	59.0
	John M. Regan Jr. (R, C, RTL)	67,534	41.0
31	• Bill Paxon (R, C, RTL)	90,237	56.6
	Kevin P. Gaughan (D, L)	69,328	43.4
32	• John J. LaFalce (D, L)	68,367	55.0
	Michael T. Waring (R)	39,053	31.4
	Kenneth J. Kowalski (C, RTL)	16,853	13.6
33	• Henry J. Nowak (D, L)	84,905	77.5
	Thomas K. Kepfer (R)	18,181	16.6
	Louis P. Corrigan Jr. (C)	6,460	5.9
34	• Amo Houghton (R, C)	89,831	69.6
	Joseph P. Leahey (D)	37,421	29.0
	Nevin K. Eklund (L)	1,807	1.4

NORTH CAROLINA

		Vote Total	%
Senate			
	• Jesse Helms (R)	1,088,331	52.6
	Harvey B. Gantt (D)	981,573	47.4
House			
1	• Walter B. Jones (D)	105,832	64.8
	Howard D. Moye (R)	57,526	35.2
2	• Tim Valentine (D)	130,979	74.7
	Hal C. Sharpe (R)	44,263	25.3
3	• H. Martin Lancaster (D)	83,930	59.3
	Don Davis (R)	57,605	40.7
4	• David E. Price (D)	139,396	58.1
	John Carrington (R)	100,661	41.9
5	• Stephen L. Neal (D)	113,814	59.1
	Ken Bell (R)	78,747	40.9
6	• Howard Coble (R)	125,392	66.6
	Helen R. Allegrone (D)	62,913	33.4
7	• Charlie Rose (D)	94,946	65.6
	Robert C. Anderson (R)	49,681	34.4
8	• W. G. "Bill" Hefner (D)	98,700	55.0
	Ted Blanton (R)	80,852	45.0
9	• Alex McMillan (R)	131,936	62.0
	David P. McKnight (D)	80,802	38.0
10	• Cass Ballenger (R)	106,400	61.8
	Daniel R. Green Jr. (D)	65,710	38.2
11	Charles H. Taylor (R)	101,991	50.7
	• James McClure Clarke (D)	99,318	49.3

NORTH DAKOTA

		Vote Total	%
House			
AL	• Byron L. Dorgan (D)	152,530	65.2
	Edward T. Schafer (R)	81,443	34.8

OHIO

		Vote Total	%
Governor			
	George V. Voinovich (R)	1,938,103	55.7
	Anthony J. Celebrezze Jr. (D)	1,539,416	44.3
House			
1	Charles Luken (D)	83,932	51.1
	J. Kenneth Blackwell (R)	80,362	48.9
2	• Bill Gradison (R)	103,817	64.4
	Tyrone K. Yates (D)	57,345	35.6
3	• Tony P. Hall (D)	116,797	100
	(No Republican candidate)		
4	• Michael G. Oxley (R)	103,897	61.7
	Thomas E. Burkhart (D)	64,467	38.3

		Vote Total	%
5	• Paul E. Gillmor (R)	113,615	68.5
	P. Scott Mange (D)	41,693	25.1
	John E. Jackson (I)	10,612	6.4
6	• Bob McEwen (R)	117,220	71.2
	Ray Mitchell (D)	47,415	28.8
7	David L. Hobson (R)	97,123	62.1
	Jack Schira (D)	59,349	37.9
8	John A. Boehner (R)	99,955	61.1
	Gregory V. Jolivette (D)	63,584	38.9
9	• Marcy Kaptur (D)	117,681	77.7
	Jerry D. Lammers (R)	33,791	22.3
10	• Clarence E. Miller (R)	106,009	63.2
	John M. Buchanan (D)	61,656	36.8
11	• Dennis E. Eckart (D)	111,923	65.7
	Margaret Mueller (R)	58,372	34.3
12	• John R. Kasich (R)	130,495	72.0
	Mike Gelpi (D)	50,784	28.0
13	• Don J. Pease (D)	93,431	56.7
	William D. Nielsen (R)	60,925	36.9
	John Michael Ryan (I)	10,506	6.4
14	• Thomas C. Sawyer (D)	97,875	59.6
	Jean E. Bender (R)	66,460	40.4
15	• Chalmers P. Wylie (R)	99,251	59.1
	Thomas V. Erney (D)	68,510	40.8
	William L. Buckel (write-in)	158	0.1
16	• Ralph Regula (R)	101,097	58.9
	Warner D. Mendenhall (D)	70,516	41.1
17	• James A. Traficant Jr. (D)	133,207	77.7
	Robert R. DeJulio Jr. (R)	38,199	22.3
18	• Doug Applegate (D)	120,782	74.3
	John A. Hales (R)	41,823	25.7
19	• Edward F. Feighan (D)	132,951	64.8
	Susan M. Lawko (R)	72,315	35.2
20	• Mary Rose Oakar (D)	109,390	73.3
	Bill Smith (R)	39,749	26.7
21	• Louis Stokes (D)	103,338	80.0
	Franklin H. Roski (R)	25,906	20.0

OKLAHOMA

		Vote Total	%
Governor			
	David Walters (D)	523,196	57.4
	Bill Price (R)	297,584	32.7
	Thomas D. Ledgerwood II (I)	90,534	9.9
Senate			
	• David L. Boren (D)	735,684	83.2
	Stephen Jones (R)	148,814	16.8
House			
1	• James M. Inhofe (R)	75,618	56.0
	Kurt G. Glassco (D)	59,521	44.0
2	• Mike Synar (D)	90,820	61.3
	Terry M. Gorham (R)	57,331	38.7
3	Bill Brewster (D)	107,641	80.4
	Patrick K. Miller (R)	26,261	19.6
4	• Dave McCurdy (D)	100,879	73.6
	Howard Bell (R)	36,232	26.4
5	• Mickey Edwards (R)	114,608	69.6
	Bryce Baggett (D)	50,086	30.4
6	• Glenn English (D)	110,100	80.0
	Robert Burns (R)	27,540	20.0

OREGON

		Vote Total	%
Governor			
	Barbara Roberts (D)	508,749	45.7
	Dave Frohnmayer (R)	444,646	40.0
	Al Mobley (I)	144,062	12.9
	Fred Oerther (LIBERT)	14,583	1.3
Senate			
	• Mark O. Hatfield (R)	590,095	53.7
	Harry Lonsdale (D)	507,743	46.2
House			
1	• Les AuCoin (D)	150,292	63.1
	Earl Molander (R)	72,382	30.4
	Rick Livingston (I)	15,585	6.5
2	• Bob Smith (R)	127,998	68.0
	Jim Smiley (D)	60,131	32.0
3	• Ron Wyden (D)	169,731	80.8
	Philip E. Mooney (R)	40,216	19.1
4	• Peter A. DeFazio (D)	162,494	85.8
	(No Republican candidate)		
	Tonie Nathan (LIBERT)	26,432	14.0
5	Mike Kopetski (D)	124,610	55.0
	• Denny Smith (R)	101,650	44.9

PENNSYLVANIA

		Vote Total	%
Governor			
	• Robert P. Casey (D)	2,065,244	67.7
	Barbara Hafer (R)	987,516	32.3
House			
1	• Thomas M. Foglietta (D)	73,423	79.4
	James Love Jackson (R)	19,018	20.6
2	• William H. Gray III (D)	94,584	92.1
	Donald Bakove (R)	8,118	7.9
3	• Robert A. Borski (D)	89,908	60.0
	Joseph Marc McColgan (R)	59,901	40.0
4	• Joe Kolter (D)	74,114	55.9
	Gordon R. Johnston (R)	58,469	44.1
5	• Richard T. Schulze (R)	75,097	57.1
	Samuel C. Stretton (D)	50,597	38.5
	Lewis Dupont Smith (ASI)	5,795	4.4
6	• Gus Yatron (D)	74,394	57.0
	John F. Hicks (R)	56,093	43.0
7	• Curt Weldon (R)	105,868	65.3
	John Innelli (D)	56,292	34.7
8	• Peter H. Kostmayer (D)	85,015	56.6
	Audrie Zettick Schaller (R)	65,100	43.4
9	• Bud Shuster (R, D)	106,632	100
10	• Joseph M. McDade (R, D)	113,490	100
11	• Paul E. Kanjorski (D)	88,219	100
	(No Republican candidate)		
12	• John P. Murtha (D)	80,686	61.7
	William Choby (R)	50,007	38.3
13	• Lawrence Coughlin (R)	89,577	60.3
	Bernard Tomkin (D)	58,967	39.7
14	• William J. Coyne (D)	77,636	71.8
	Richard Edward Caligiuri (R)	30,497	28.2
15	• Don Ritter (R)	77,178	60.6
	Richard J. Orloski (D)	50,233	39.4
16	• Robert S. Walker (R)	85,596	66.1
	Ernest Eric Guyll (D)	43,849	33.9
17	• George W. Gekas (R, D)	110,317	100
18	Rick Santorum (R)	85,697	51.4
	• Doug Walgren (D)	80,880	48.6
19	• Bill Goodling (R)	96,336	100
	(No Democratic candidate)		
20	• Joseph M. Gaydos (D)	82,080	65.6
	Robert C. Lee (R)	43,054	34.4
21	• Tom Ridge (R)	92,732	100
	(No Democratic candidate)		
22	• Austin J. Murphy (D)	78,375	63.3
	Suzanne Hayden (R)	45,509	36.7
23	• William F. Clinger Jr. (R)	78,189	59.4
	Daniel J. Shannon (D)	53,465	40.6

RHODE ISLAND

		Vote Total	%
Governor			
	Bruce Sundlun (D)	264,411	74.2
	• Edward D. DiPrete (R)	92,177	25.8
Senate			
	• Claiborne Pell (D)	225,105	61.8
	Claudine Schneider (R)	138,947	38.2
1	• Ronald K. Machtley (R)	89,963	55.2
	Scott Wolf (D)	73,131	44.8
House			
2	John F. Reed (D)	108,818	59.2
	Gertrude M. "Trudy" Coxe (R)	74,953	40.8

SOUTH CAROLINA

		Vote Total	%
Governor			
	• Carroll A. Campbell Jr. (R)	528,831	69.5
	Theo Mitchell (D)	212,034	27.9
	John Peeples (AM)	17,302	2.3
Senate			
	• Strom Thurmond (R)	482,032	64.2
	Bob Cunningham (D)	244,112	32.5
	William H. Griffin (LIBERT)	13,805	1.8
	Marion C. Metts (AM)	10,317	1.4
House			
1	• Arthur Ravenel Jr. (R)	80,839	65.5
	Eugene Platt (D)	42,555	34.5
2	• Floyd D. Spence (R)	90,054	88.7
	(No Democratic candidate)		
	Geb Sommer (LIBERT)	11,101	10.9
3	• Butler Derrick (D)	72,561	58.0
	Ray Haskett (R)	52,419	41.9
4	• Liz J. Patterson (D)	81,927	61.4
	Terry E. Haskins (R)	51,338	38.4
5	• John M. Spratt Jr. (D)	91,775	99.9
	(No Republican candidate)		
6	• Robin Tallon (D)	94,121	99.6
	(No Republican candidate)		

SOUTH DAKOTA

		Vote Total	%
Governor			
	• George S. Mickelson (R)	151,198	58.9
	Bob L. Samuelson (D)	105,525	41.1
Senate			
	• Larry Pressler (R)	135,682	52.4
	Ted Muenster (D)	116,727	45.1
	Dean L. Sinclair (I)	6,567	2.5
House			
AL	• Tim Johnson (D)	173,814	67.6
	Don Frankenfeld (R)	83,484	32.4

TENNESSEE

		Vote Total	%
Governor			
	• Ned McWherter (D)	480,885	60.8
	Dwight Henry (R)	289,348	36.6
	W. Curtis Jacox (I)	10,993	1.4
	David Brandon Shepard (I)	9,109	1.2
Senate			
	• Al Gore (D)	530,898	67.7
	William R. Hawkins (R)	233,703	29.8
	Bill Jacox (I)	11,191	1.4
	Charles Gordon Vick (I)	8,021	1.0
House			
1	• James H. Quillen (R)	47,796	99.9
	(No Democratic candidate)		
2	• John J. "Jimmy" Duncan Jr. (R)	62,797	80.6
	(No Democratic candidate)		
	Peter Hebert (I)	15,127	19.4
3	• Marilyn Lloyd (D)	49,662	53.0
	Grady L. Rhoden (R)	36,855	39.3
	Peter T. Melcher (I)	5,598	6.0
	George E. Googe (I)	1,546	1.7
4	• Jim Cooper (D)	52,101	67.4
	Claiborne "Clay" Sanders (R)	22,890	29.6
	Gene M. Bullington (I)	2,281	3.0
5	• Bob Clement (D)	55,607	72.4
	(No Republican candidate)		
	Tom Stone (I)	13,577	17.7
	Al Borgman (I)	5,383	7.0
	Maurice C. Kuttab (I)	2,192	2.9

	Candidate	Vote Total	%
6	● Bart Gordon (D)	60,538	66.7
	Gregory Cochran (R)	26,424	29.1
	Ken Brown (I)	3,793	4.2
7	● Don Sundquist (R)	66,141	62.0
	Ken Bloodworth (D)	40,516	38.0
8	● John Tanner (D)	62,241	100
	(No Republican candidate)		
9	● Harold E. Ford (D)	48,629	58.1
	Aaron C. Davis (R)	25,730	30.8
	Thomas M. Davidson (I)	7,249	8.7
	Isaac Richmond (I)	2,032	2.4

TEXAS

	Candidate	Vote Total	%
Governor			
	Ann W. Richards (D)	1,925,670	49.5
	Clayton Williams (R)	1,826,431	46.9
	Jeff Daiell (LIBERT)	129,157	3.3
	Bubbles Cash (write-in)	3,275	0.1
Senate			
	● Phil Gramm (R)	2,302,357	60.2
	Hugh Parmer (D)	1,429,986	37.4
	Gary Johnson (LIBERT)	89,089	2.3
House			
1	● Jim Chapman (D)	89,241	61.0
	Hamp Hodges (R)	56,954	39.0
2	● Charles Wilson (D)	76,974	55.6
	Donna Peterson (R)	61,555	44.4
3	● Steve Bartlett (R)	153,857	99.6
	(No Democratic candidate)		
	Noel Kopala (write-in)	617	0.4
4	● Ralph M. Hall (D)	108,300	99.6
	(No Republican candidate)		
	Tim J. McCord (write in)	394	0.4
5	● John Bryant (D)	65,228	59.6
	Jerry Rucker (R)	41,307	37.7
	Kenneth Ashby (LIBERT)	2,939	2.7
6	● Joe L. Barton (R)	125,049	66.5
	John E. Welch (D)	62,344	33.1
	Michael Worsham (write in)	737	0.4
7	● Bill Archer (R)	114,254	100
	(No Democratic candidate)		
8	● Jack Fields (R)	60,603	100
	(No Democratic candidate)		
9	● Jack Brooks (D)	79,786	57.7
	Maury Meyers (R)	58,399	42.3
10	● J. J. "Jake" Pickle (D)	152,784	64.9
	David Beilharz (R)	73,766	31.3
	Jeff Davis (LIBERT)	8,905	3.8
11	Chet Edwards (D)	73,810	53.5
	Hugh D. Shine (R)	64,269	46.5
12	● Pete Geren (D)	98,026	71.3
	Mike McGinn (R)	39,438	28.7
13	● Bill Sarpalius (D)	81,815	56.5
	Dick Waterfield (R)	63,045	43.5
14	● Greg Laughlin (D)	89,251	54.3
	Joe Dial (R)	75,098	45.7
15	● E. "Kika" de la Garza (D)	72,461	100
	(No Republican candidate)		
16	● Ronald D. Coleman (D)	62,455	95.6
	(No Republican candidate)		
	William Burgett (write-in)	2,854	4.4
17	● Charles W. Stenholm (D)	104,100	100
	(No Republican candidate)		
18	● Craig Washington (D)	54,477	99.6
	(No Republican candidate)		
	Timothy John Hattenbach (write-in)	166	0.3
	Shirley Fobbs (write-in)	38	0.1
19	● Larry Combest (R)	83,795	100
	(No Democratic candidate)		
20	● Henry B. Gonzalez (D)	56,318	100
	(No Republican candidate)		
21	● Lamar Smith (R)	144,570	74.8
	Kirby J. Roberts (D)	48,585	25.2
22	● Tom DeLay (R)	93,425	71.2
	Bruce Director (D)	37,721	28.8
23	● Albert G. Bustamante (D)	71,052	63.5
	Jerome L. "Jerry" Gonzales (R)	40,856	36.5
24	● Martin Frost (D)	86,297	100
	(No Republican candidate)		
25	● Michael A. Andrews (D)	67,427	100
	(No Republican candidate)		
26	● Dick Armey (R)	147,856	70.4
	John Wayne Caton (D)	62,158	29.6
27	● Solomon P. Ortiz (D)	62,822	100
	(No Republican candidate)		

UTAH

	Candidate	Vote Total	%
House			
1	● James V. Hansen (R)	82,746	52.1
	Kenley Brunsdale (D)	69,491	43.8
	Reva Marx Wadsworth (AM)	6,429	4.1
2	● Wayne Owens (D)	85,167	57.6
	Genevieve Atwood (R)	58,869	39.8
	Lawrence Rey Topham (I-Utah)	3,424	2.3
	Eleanor Garcia (SW)	411	0.3
3	Bill Orton (D)	79,163	58.3
	Karl Snow (R)	49,452	36.4
	Robert J. Smith (AM)	6,542	4.8
	Anthony Melvin Dutrow (SW)	519	0.4

VERMONT

	Candidate	Vote Total	%
Governor			
	Richard A. Snelling (R)	109,540	51.8
	Peter Welch (D)	97,321	46.0
	David Atkinson (LIBERT)	2,777	1.3
	Richard F. Gottlieb (LU)	1,389	0.7
House			
AL	Bernard Sanders (I)	117,522	56.0
	● Peter Smith (R)	82,938	39.5
	Dolores Sandoval (D)	6,315	3.0
	Peter Diamondstone (LU)	1,965	0.9

VIRGINIA

	Candidate	Vote Total	%
Senate			
	● John W. Warner (R)	876,782	80.9
	(No Democratic candidate)		
	Nancy B. Spannaus (I)	196,755	18.2
House			
1	● Herbert H. Bateman (R)	72,000	51.0
	Andrew H. Fox (D)	69,194	49.0
2	● Owen B. Pickett (D)	55,179	75.0
	(No Republican candidate)		
	Harry G. Broskie (I)	15,915	21.6
3	● Thomas J. Bliley Jr. (R)	77,125	65.3
	Jay Starke (D)	36,253	30.7
	Rose L. Simpson (I)	4,317	3.7
4	● Norman Sisisky (D)	71,051	78.3
	(No Republican candidate)		
	Don L. Reynolds (I)	12,295	13.6
	Loretta F. Chandler (I)	7,102	7.8
5	● Lewis F. Payne Jr. (D)	66,532	99.4
	(No Republican candidate)		
6	● Jim Olin (D)	92,968	82.7
	(No Republican candidate)		
	Gerald E. "Laser" Berg (I)	18,148	16.1
7	● D. French Slaughter Jr. (R)	81,688	58.1
	David M. Smith (D)	58,684	41.7
8	James P. Moran Jr. (D)	88,475	51.7
	● Stan Parris (R)	76,367	44.6
	Robert T. Murphy (I)	5,958	3.5
9	● Rick Boucher (D)	67,215	97.1
	(No Republican candidate)		
10	● Frank R. Wolf (R)	103,761	61.5
	N. MacKenzie Canter III (D)	57,249	33.9
	Barbara S. Minnich (I)	5,273	3.1
	Lyndon H. LaRouche Jr. (I)	2,293	1.4

WASHINGTON

	Candidate	Vote Total	%
House			
1	● John Miller (R)	100,339	52.0
	Cynthia Sullivan (D)	92,447	48.0
2	● Al Swift (D)	92,837	50.5
	Doug Smith (R)	75,669	41.2
	William L. McCord (LIBERT)	15,165	8.3
3	● Jolene Unsoeld (D)	95,645	53.8
	Bob Williams (R)	82,269	46.2
4	● Sid Morrison (R)	106,545	70.7
	Ole Hougen (D)	44,241	29.3
5	● Thomas S. Foley (D)	110,234	68.8
	Marlyn A. Derby (R)	49,965	31.2
6	● Norm Dicks (D)	79,079	61.4
	Norbert Mueller (R)	49,786	38.6
7	● Jim McDermott (D)	106,761	72.3
	Larry Penberthy (R)	35,511	24.1
	Robbie Scherr (SW)	5,370	3.6
8	● Rod Chandler (R)	96,323	56.2
	David E. Giles (D)	75,031	43.8

WEST VIRGINIA

	Candidate	Vote Total	%
Senate			
	● John D. Rockefeller IV (D)	276,234	68.3
	John Yoder (R)	128,071	31.7
House			
1	● Alan B. Mollohan (D)	72,849	67.1
	Howard K. Tuck (R)	35,657	32.9
2	● Harley O. Staggers Jr. (D)	63,174	55.5
	Oliver Luck (R)	50,708	44.5
3	● Bob Wise (D)	75,327	100
	(No Republican candidate)		
4	● Nick J. Rahall II (D)	39,948	52.0
	Marianne R. Brewster (R)	36,946	48.0

WISCONSIN

	Candidate	Vote Total	%
Governor			
	● Tommy G. Thompson (R)	802,321	58.2
	Thomas Loftus (D)	576,280	41.8
House			
1	● Les Aspin (D)	93,961	99.4
	(No Republican candidate)		
2	Scott L. Klug (R)	96,938	53.2
	● Robert W. Kastenmeier (D)	85,156	46.8
3	● Steve Gunderson (R)	94,509	61.0
	James L. Ziegeweid (D)	60,409	39.0
4	● Gerald D. Kleczka (D)	96,981	69.2
	Joseph L. Cook (R)	43,001	30.7
5	● Jim Moody (D)	77,557	68.0
	Donalda Arnell Hammersmith (R)	31,255	27.4
	Nathaniel J. Stampley (I)	4,968	4.4
6	● Thomas E. Petri (R)	111,036	99.5
	(No Democratic candidate)		
7	● David R. Obey (D)	100,069	62.1
	John L. McEwen (R)	60,961	37.9
8	● Toby Roth (R)	95,902	53.5
	Jerome Van Sistine (D)	83,199	46.4
9	● F. James Sensenbrenner Jr. (R)	117,967	99.7
	(No Democratic candidate)		

WYOMING

	Candidate	Vote Total	%
Governor			
	● Mike Sullivan (D)	104,638	65.4
	Mary Mead (R)	55,471	34.6
Senate			
	● Alan K. Simpson (R)	100,784	63.9
	Kathy Helling (D)	56,848	36.1
House			
AL	● Craig Thomas (R)	87,078	55.1
	Pete Maxfield (D)	70,977	44.9

CQ

Appendix A

PUBLIC LAWS

Public Laws, 101st Congress, 2nd Session

PL 101-241 (H J Res 82) Designate Feb. 8, 1989, as "National Women and Girls in Sports Day." Introduced by SNOWE, R-Maine, Jan. 19, 1989. House Post Office and Civil Service discharged. House passed, amended, Jan. 31, 1990. Senate passed Feb. 5. President signed Feb. 12, 1990.

PL 101-242 (S J Res 217) Designate the week of Feb. 4, 1990, as "National Burn Awareness Week." Introduced by WILSON, R-Calif., Oct. 20, 1989. Senate Judiciary reported Oct. 26. Senate passed, amended, Oct. 27. House Post Office and Civil Service discharged. House passed Feb. 6, 1990. President signed Feb. 12, 1990.

PL 101-243 (HR 3952) Authorize assistance and trade benefits for Panama. Introduced by FASCELL, D-Fla., Feb. 6, 1990. Foreign Affairs reported Feb. 7 (H Rept 101-401, Part I). Ways and Means reported Feb. 7 (H Rept 101-401, Part II). House passed, under suspension of the rules, Feb. 7. Senate passed Feb. 7. President signed Feb. 14, 1990.

PL 101-244 (S J Res 103) Designate the week of Feb. 18, 1990, as "National Visiting Nurse Associations Week." Introduced by BRADLEY, D-N.J., April 18, 1989. Senate Judiciary discharged. Senate passed Jan. 30, 1990. House Post Office and Civil Service discharged. House passed Feb. 6. President signed Feb. 14, 1990.

PL 101-245 (S J Res 130) Designate the week of Feb. 11, 1990, as "Vocational-Technical Education Week." Introduced by SARBANES, D-Md., May 12, 1989. Senate Judiciary reported June 8. Senate passed June 9. House Post Office and Civil Service discharged. House passed Jan. 31, 1990. President signed Feb. 14, 1990.

PL 101-246 (HR 3792) Authorize fiscal 1990-91 State Department appropriations. Introduced by FASCELL, D-Fla., Nov. 21, 1989. House passed, under suspension of the rules, Nov. 21. Senate passed Jan. 30, 1990. President signed Feb. 16, 1990.

PL 101-247 (H J Res 149) Designate Feb. 16, 1990, as "Lithuanian Independence Day." Introduced by RUSSO, D-Ill., Feb. 22, 1989. House Post Office and Civil Service discharged. House passed June 29. Senate Judiciary discharged. Senate passed Jan. 30. President signed Feb. 16, 1990.

PL 101-248 (S J Res 186) Designate the week of March 1, 1990, as "National Quarter Horse Week." Introduced by McCLURE, R-Idaho, Aug. 3, 1989. Senate Judiciary reported Oct. 18. Senate passed Oct. 20. House Post Office and Civil Service discharged. House passed Feb. 21, 1990. President signed Feb. 27, 1990.

PL 101-249 (HR 150) Amend the Immigration and Nationality Act to allow an alien who dies while on active duty with the U.S. armed forces during certain hostilities to be considered a U.S. citizen at the time of death. Introduced by DONNELLY, D-Mass., Jan. 3, 1989. House Judiciary reported, amended, Nov. 13 (H Rept 101-350). House passed, amended, under suspension of the rules, Nov. 13. Senate Judiciary reported Feb. 1, 1990. Senate passed Feb. 20. President signed March 6, 1990.

PL 101-250 (HR 2281) Amend the Elementary and Secondary Education Act of 1965 to extend the authorization for certain school-dropout demonstration programs. Introduced by HAYES, D-Ill., May 9, 1989. House Education and Labor reported, amended, June 13 (H Rept 101-82). House passed, amended, under suspension of the rules, June 13. Senate passed Feb. 20, 1990. President signed March 6, 1990.

PL 101-251 (S J Res 227) Designate the week of March 11, 1990, as "Deaf Awareness Week." Introduced by KASTEN, R-Wis., Nov. 16, 1989. Senate Judiciary reported Feb. 22, 1990. Senate passed Feb. 26. House Post Office and Civil Service discharged. House passed March 7. President signed March 13, 1990.

PL 101-252 (S J Res 257) Designate March 10, 1990, as "Harriet Tubman Day." Introduced by BIDEN, D-Del., Feb. 20, 1990. Senate Judiciary discharged. Senate passed March 6. House Post Office and Civil Service discharged. House passed March 7. President signed March 13, 1990.

PL 101-253 (S 1016) Change the name of Marion Lake, northwest of Marion, Kan., to Marion Reservoir. Introduced by DOLE, R-Kan., May 17, 1989. Senate Environment and Public Works reported, amended, Aug. 1. Senate passed, amended, Aug. 2. House Interior and Insular Affairs discharged. House passed, under suspension of the rules, Feb. 27, 1990. President signed March 14, 1990.

PL 101-254 (HR 2742) Extend and amend the Library Services and Construction Act. Introduced by WILLIAMS, D-Mont., June 22, 1989. House Education and Labor reported, amended, Sept. 12 (H Rept 101-237). House passed, amended, under suspension of the rules, Sept. 12. Senate passed, amended, Oct. 12. House agreed to conference report, under suspension of the rules, Feb. 27, 1990 (H Rept 101-407). Senate agreed to conference report March 1. President signed March 15, 1990.

PL 101-255 (HR 4010) Give the Agriculture secretary authority regarding the sale of sterile screwworms. Introduced by de la GARZA, D-Texas, Feb. 20, 1990. House Agriculture reported Feb. 27 (H Rept 101-408). House passed, under suspension of the rules, Feb. 27. Senate Agriculture, Nutrition and Forestry discharged. Senate passed March 5. President signed March 15, 1990.

PL 101-256 (S J Res 243) Designate March 25, 1990, as "Greek Independence Day: A Day of Celebration of Greek and American Democracy." Introduced by LAUTENBERG, D-N.J., Jan. 30, 1990. Senate Judiciary reported Feb. 22. Senate passed Feb. 26. House Post Office and Civil Service discharged. House passed March 14. President signed March 20, 1990.

PL 101-257 (HR 2749) Authorize the conveyance of a parcel of land in Whitney Lake, Texas. Introduced by BARTON, R-Texas, June 27, 1989. House Public Works and Transportation discharged. House passed, amended, June 28. Senate Armed Services discharged. Senate Environment and Public Works reported Nov. 17. Senate passed March 5, 1990. President signed March 20, 1990.

PL 101-258 (S J Res 237) Provide for the commemoration of the 100th anniversary of the birth of Dwight D. Eisenhower. Introduced by DOLE, R-Kan., Jan. 23, 1990. Senate Judiciary discharged. Senate passed March 1. House passed March 21. President signed March 27, 1990.

PL 101-259 (HR 3311) Redesignate the U.S. post office/courthouse in Salt Lake City as the Frank E. Moss Federal Building. Introduced by OWENS, D-Utah, Sept. 20, 1989. House Public Works and Transportation reported, amended, Nov. 17 (H Rept 101-375). House passed, amended, Nov. 17. Senate Environment and Public Works reported March 9, 1990. Senate passed March 20. President signed March 30, 1990.

PL 101-260 (S 1091) Provide for the striking of medals commemorating the Coast Guard's bicentennial. Introduced by GRAHAM, D-Fla., June 1, 1989. Senate Banking, Housing and Urban Affairs reported Sept. 29. Senate passed Oct. 3. House passed, under suspension of the rules, March 20, 1990. President signed March 30, 1990.

PL 101-261 (S J Res 229) Designate April 1990 as "National Prevent-A-Litter Month." Introduced by CRANSTON, D-Calif., Nov. 20, 1989. Senate Judiciary reported Feb. 22, 1990. Senate passed Feb. 26. House Post Office and Civil Service discharged. House passed March 14. President signed March 30, 1990.

PL 101-262 (S 2231) Amend the Energy Policy and Conservation Act to extend the authority for Titles I and II. Introduced by JOHNSTON, D-La., March 5, 1990. Senate Energy and Natural Resources reported March 5 (S Rept 101-247). Senate passed March 9. House passed March 20. President signed March 31, 1990.

PL 101-263 (S 1521) Amend PL 91-34 relating to the police force of the National Zoological Park of the Smithsonian Institution. Introduced by MOYNIHAN, D-N.Y., Aug. 3, 1989. Senate Rules and Administration reported Sept. 28 (S Rept 101-145). Senate passed Oct. 2. House passed, amended, under suspension of the rules, Jan. 30, 1990. Senate agreed to House amendments March 20. President signed April 4, 1990.

PL 101-264 (S J Res 250) Designate April 1990 as "National Recycling Month." Introduced by CHAFEE, R-R.I., Feb. 5, 1990. Senate Judiciary reported Feb. 22. Senate passed Feb. 26. House Post Office and Civil Service discharged. House passed March 28. President signed April 4, 1990.

PL 101-265 (S J Res 266) Designate March 1990 as "United

States Naval Reserve Month." Introduced by JEFFORDS, R-Vt., March 5, 1990. Senate Judiciary discharged. Senate passed March 20. House Post Office and Civil Service discharged. House passed March 28. President signed April 4, 1990.

PL 101-266 (S J Res 190) Designate April 9, 1990, as "National Former Prisoners of War Recognition Day." Introduced by HEINZ, R-Pa., Aug. 4, 1989. Senate Judiciary reported Feb. 22, 1990. Senate passed Feb. 26. House Post Office and Civil Service discharged. House passed March 20. President signed April 5, 1990.

PL 101-267 (H J Res 500) Designate April 6, 1990, as "Education Day, U.S.A." Introduced by MICHEL, R-Ill., March 5, 1990. House Post Office and Civil Service discharged. House passed March 28. Senate passed March 29. President signed April 6, 1990.

PL 101-268 (HR 2692) Amend the Woodrow Wilson Memorial Act of 1968 to provide that the Education secretary and two other private individuals shall be trustees of the Woodrow Wilson International Center for Scholars. Introduced by OAKAR, D-Ohio, June 20, 1989. House passed, under suspension of the rules, March 20, 1990. Senate Rules and Administration discharged. Senate passed March 26. President signed April 9, 1990.

PL 101-269 (S 2151) Allow the transfer of the obsolete submarine USS *Requin* to the Carnegie Institute in Pittsburgh, Pa., before the expiration of the 60-day waiting period that would otherwise be applicable to the transfer. Introduced by HEINZ, R-Pa., Feb. 21, 1990. Senate Armed Services reported Feb. 27. Senate passed March 5. House Armed Services discharged. House passed March 28. President signed April 9, 1990.

PL 101-270 (HR 4099) Suspend Section 332 of the Agriculture Adjustment Act of 1938 for the 1991 crop of wheat. Introduced by de la GARZA, D-Texas, Feb. 26, 1990. House Agriculture reported March 6 (H Rept 101-414). House passed, under suspension of the rules, March 6. Senate Agriculture, Nutrition and Forestry discharged. Senate passed March 28. President signed April 10, 1990.

PL 101-271 (S 388) Provide for five-year staggered terms for members of the Federal Energy Regulatory Commission. Introduced by BINGAMAN, D-N.M., Feb. 8, 1989. Senate Energy and Natural Resources reported, amended, July 12 (S Rept 101-76). Senate passed, amended, Nov. 15. House passed, amended, March 27, 1990. Senate agreed to House amendment March 29. President signed April 11, 1990.

PL 101-272 (S 1813) Ensure that funds provided under Section 4213 of the Indian Alcohol and Substances Abuse Prevention and Treatment Act of 1986 may be used to acquire land for emergency shelters. Introduced by GORTON, R-Wash., Oct. 31, 1989. Senate Indian Affairs reported, amended, Nov. 15 (S Rept 101-207). Senate passed, amended, Nov. 16. House Interior and Insular Affairs reported March 27, 1990 (H Rept 101-432, Part I). House passed, under suspension of the rules, April 3. President signed April 18, 1990.

PL 101-273 (S 1949) Amend the Labor Management Relations Act of 1947 to permit parties engaged in collective bargaining to bargain over the establishment and administration of trust funds to provide financial assistance for employee housing. Introduced by KENNEDY, D-Mass., Nov. 20, 1989. Senate Labor and Human Resources discharged. Senate passed, amended, Nov. 22. House Education and Labor discharged. House passed April 3, 1990. President signed April 18, 1990.

PL 101-274 (HR 3968) Amend the Organ Transplant Amendments Act of 1988 to change an effective date. Introduced by WALGREN, D-Pa., Feb. 6, 1990. House Energy and Commerce reported, amended, April 3 (H Rept 101-447). House passed, amended, April 4. Senate passed April 4. President signed April 23, 1990.

PL 101-275 (HR 1048) Provide for the acquisition and publication of data about crimes that manifest prejudice based on race, religion, homosexuality or heterosexuality, or ethnicity. Introduced by CONYERS, D-Mich., Feb. 22, 1989. House Judiciary reported, amended, June 23 (H Rept 101-109). House passed, amended, under suspension of the rules, June 27. Senate Judiciary discharged. Senate passed, amended, Feb. 8, 1990. House agreed to Senate amendments, under suspension of the rules, April 4. President signed April 23, 1990.

PL 101-276 (S J Res 242) Designate the week of April 22, 1990, as "National Crime Victims' Rights Week." Introduced by THURMOND, R-S.C., Jan. 25, 1990. Senate Judiciary discharged. Senate passed April 4. House Post Office and Civil Service discharged. House passed April 18. President signed April 25, 1990.

PL 101-277 (S 1096) Provide for the use and distribution of funds awarded the Seminole Indians in Dockets 73, 151 and 73A of the Indians Claims Commission. Introduced by NICKLES, R-Okla., June 1, 1989. Senate Indian Affairs reported, amended, Nov. 19 (S Rept 101-212). Senate passed, amended, Nov. 22. House Interior and Insular Affairs reported, amended, Feb. 6, 1990 (H Rept 101-399). House passed, amended, under suspension of the rules, Feb. 6. House agreed to conference report, under suspension of the rules, April 3 (H Rept 101-439). Senate agreed to conference report April 5. President signed April 30, 1990.

PL 101-278 (HR 2334) Redesignate the Post Office at 300 E. Ninth Street in Austin, Texas, as the Homer Thornberry Judicial Building. Introduced by PICKLE, D-Texas, May 11, 1989. House Public Works and Transportation discharged. House passed Aug. 5. Senate Governmental Affairs discharged. Senate passed April 5, 1990. President signed May 1, 1990.

PL 101-279 (S J Res 258) Authorize the president to proclaim the last Friday of April 1990 as "National Arbor Day." Introduced by BRADLEY, D-N.J., Feb. 20, 1990. Senate Judiciary reported Feb. 22. Senate passed Feb. 26. House Post Office and Civil Service discharged. House passed April 24. President signed May 1, 1990.

PL 101-280 (H J Res 553) Make technical changes in the Ethics Reform Act of 1989. Introduced by FAZIO, D-Calif., April 23, 1990. House passed, under suspension of the rules, April 24. Senate passed April 26. President signed May 4, 1990.

PL 101-281 (S 2533) Amend the Federal Aviation Act of 1958 to extend the civil penalty assessment demonstration program. Introduced by FORD, D-Ky., April 26, 1990. Senate passed April 26. House passed, under suspension of the rules, May 1. President signed May 4, 1990.

PL 101-282 (S J Res 236) Designate the week of May 6, 1990, as "Be Kind to Animals and National Pet Week." Introduced by WILSON, R-Calif., Jan. 23, 1990. Senate Judiciary reported Feb. 22. Senate passed Feb. 26. House Post Office and Civil Service discharged. House passed May 1. President signed May 8, 1990.

PL 101-283 (HR 3802) Designate the month of May as "Asian/Pacific American Heritage Month." Introduced by HORTON, R-N.Y., Nov. 21, 1989. House Post Office and Civil Service discharged. House passed, amended, May 3, 1990. Senate passed May 3. President signed May 9, 1990.

PL 101-284 (S J Res 153) Designate the third week in May 1990 as "National Tourism Week." Introduced by ROCKEFELLER, D-W.Va., June 7, 1989. Senate Judiciary discharged. Senate passed Feb. 28, 1990. House Post Office and Civil Service discharged. House passed, amended, April 18. Senate agreed to House amendments April 24. President signed May 9, 1990.

PL 101-285 (S J Res 230) Designate the week of May 6, 1990, as "National Drinking Water Week." Introduced by DeCONCINI, D-Ariz., Nov. 20, 1989. Senate Judiciary reported Feb. 22, 1990. Senate passed Feb. 26. House Post Office and Civil Service discharged. House passed May 1. President signed May 9, 1990.

PL 101-286 (HR 1011) Provide for the establishment of the National Commission on Natural Resources Disasters and to provide for increased planning and cooperation with local firefighting forces in the event of forest fires. Introduced by HERGER, R-Calif., Feb. 9, 1989. House Agriculture reported, amended, Nov. 7 (H Rept 101-333, Part I). House passed, amended, under suspension of the rules, Nov. 13. Senate Agriculture, Nutrition, and Forestry discharged. Senate passed April 26, 1990. President signed May 9, 1990.

PL 101-287 (H J Res 546) Designate May 13, 1990, as "Infant Mortality Awareness Day." Introduced by HARRIS, D-Ala., April 4, 1990. Post Office and Civil Service discharged. House Energy and Commerce discharged. House passed April 24. Senate passed April 26. President signed May 10, 1990.

PL 101-288 (S 1485) Grant the consent of Congress to the Quad Cities Interstate Metropolitan Authority Compact entered into between the states of Illinois and Iowa. Introduced by GRASSLEY, R-Iowa, Aug. 3, 1989. Senate Judiciary reported Nov. 6. Senate passed Nov. 15. House Judiciary reported April 25, 1990 (H Rept 101-462). House passed, under suspension of the rules,

May 1. President signed May 10, 1990.

PL 101-289 (S J Res 224) Designate the month of May 1990 as "National Trauma Awareness Month." Introduced by BYRD, D-W.Va., Nov. 7, 1989. Senate Judiciary discharged. Senate passed April 24, 1990. House Post Office and Civil Service discharged. House passed May 1. President signed May 10, 1990.

PL 101-290 (S J Res 241) Designate the week of April 29, 1990, as "Jewish Heritage Week." Introduced by D'AMATO, R-N.Y., Jan. 25, 1990. Senate Judiciary reported, amended, Feb. 22. Senate passed, amended, Feb. 26. House Post Office and Civil Service discharged. House passed May 1. President signed May 10, 1990.

PL 101-291 (HR 922) Designate the building located at 1515 Sam Houston Street in Liberty, Texas, as the M. P. Daniel and Thomas F. Calhoun Sr., Post Office Building. Introduced by WILSON, D-Texas, Feb. 7, 1989. House passed, under suspension of the rules, Oct. 30. Senate Environment and Public Works reported May 7, 1990. Senate passed May 9. President signed May 17, 1990.

PL 101-292 (HR 1472) Establish the Grand Island National Recreation area in Michigan. Introduced by KILDEE, D-Mich., March 16, 1989. House Interior and Insular Affairs reported, amended, June 8 (H Rept 101-78, Part I). House Agriculture reported, amended, July 21 (H Rept 101-78, Part II). House passed, amended, under suspension of the rules, July 31. Senate Energy and Natural Resources reported, amended, March 5, 1990. Senate passed, amended, March 20. House agreed to Senate amendments May 1. President signed May 17, 1990.

PL 101-293 (HR 4637) Amend P L 101-86 to eliminate the six-month limitation on the period for which civilian and military retirees may serve as temporary employees, in connection with the 1990 decennial census of population, without being subject to certain offsets from pay or other benefits. Introduced by SAWYER, D-Ohio, April 26, 1990. House passed, under suspension of the rules, May 1. Senate passed May 7. President signed May 17, 1990.

PL 101-294 (H J Res 453) Designate May 1990 as "National Digestive Disease Awareness Month." Introduced by ROYBAL, D-Calif, Nov. 21, 1989. House Post Office and Civil Service discharged. House passed May 8, 1990. Senate passed May 9. President signed May 17, 1990.

PL 101-295 (H J Res 490) Commemorate May 18, 1990, as the 25th anniversary of Head Start. Introduced by KILDEE, D-Mich., Feb. 27, 1990. House Post Office and Civil Service discharged. House passed May 1. Senate passed May 4. President signed May 17, 1990.

PL 101-296 (S 1853) Award a Congressional Gold Medal to Laurence Spelman Rockefeller. Introduced by CHAFEE, R-R.I., Nov. 8, 1989. Senate Banking, Housing and Urban Affairs reported March 21, 1990. Senate passed, amended, March 26. House passed, under suspension of the rules, May 1. President signed May 17, 1990.

PL 101-297 (HR 2890) Redesignate the federal buildings and courthouse located in East St. Louis, Ill., as the Melvin Price Federal Courthouse. Introduced by COSTELLO, D-Ill., July 13, 1989. House Public Works and Transportation reported, amended, Nov. 1 (H Rept 101-326). House passed, amended, under suspension of the rules, Nov. 7. Senate Environment and Public Works reported May 7, 1990. Senate passed May 9. President signed May 22, 1990.

PL 101-298 (S 993) Implement the Convention on the Prohibition of the Development, Production, and Stockpiling of Bacteriological (Biological) and Toxin Weapons and Their Destruction, by prohibiting certain conduct relating to biological weapons. Introduced by KOHL, D-Wis., May 16, 1989. Senate Judiciary reported, amended, Nov. 16 (S Rept 101-210). Senate passed, amended, Nov. 21. House passed May 8, 1990. President signed May 22, 1990.

PL 101-299 (S J Res 275) Designate May 13, 1990, as the "National Day in Support of Freedom and Human Rights in China and Tibet." Introduced by PELL, D-R.I., March 20, 1990. Senate Judiciary discharged. Senate passed April 5. House Post Office and Civil Service discharged. House passed May 10. President signed May 23, 1990.

PL 101-300 (S 2300) Provide financial assistance to the Simon Wiesenthal Center in Los Angeles for the education programs of the Museum of Tolerance. Introduced by KENNEDY, D-Mass., March 20, 1990. Senate Labor and Human Resources reported April 24. Senate passed, amended, May 1. House passed May 10. President signed May 24, 1990.

PL 101-301 (S 1846) Make miscellaneous amendments to Indian laws. Introduced by INOUYE, D-Hawaii, Nov. 7, 1989. Senate Select Indian Affairs reported, amended, Nov. 21 (S Rept 101- 226). Senate passed, amended, May 2, 1990. House passed May 10. President signed May 24, 1990.

PL 101-302 (HR 4404) Make dire emergency supplemental appropriations for disaster assistance, food stamps, unemployment compensation administration, and other urgent needs, and transfers, and reduce funds budgeted for military spending for the fiscal year ending Sept. 30, 1990. Introduced by WHITTEN, D-Miss., March 27, 1990. House Appropriations reported March 27 (H Rept 101-434). House passed, amended, April 3. Senate Appropriations reported, amended, April 24 (S Rept 101-272). Senate passed, amended, May 1. House agreed to conference report May 24 (H Rept 101-493). Senate agreed to conference report May 24. President signed May 25, 1990.

PL 101-303 (HR 1805) Amend Title 5, of the U.S. Code, to allow federal annuitants to make contributions for health benefits through direct payments rather than through annuity withholdings if the annuity is insufficient to cover the required withholdings; to eliminate the reinsurance requirement under the federal employees' life insurance program; and to make a technical correction relating to the life insurance program. Introduced by ACKERMAN, D-N.Y., April 12, 1989. House Post Office and Civil Service reported, amended, Nov. 1 (H Rept 101-327). House passed, amended, under suspension of the rules, Nov. 6. Senate passed, amended, April 26, 1990. House agreed to Senate amendments, disagreed to Senate amendment, and agreed with amendment to the Senate amendment to the title May 8. Senate receded from its amendment and agreed to House amendment to Senate amendment to the title May 14. President signed May 29, 1990.

PL 101-304 (HR 3961) Redesignate the federal building located at 1800 5th Ave. North, in Birmingham, Ala., as the Robert S. Vance Federal Building. Introduced by ERDREICH, D-Ala., Feb. 6, 1990. House Public Works and Transportation reported, amended, April 19 (H Rept 101-453). House passed, amended, under suspension of the rules, April 24. Senate Environment and Public Works discharged. Senate passed May 10. President signed May 29, 1990.

PL 101-305 (HR 3910) Require the secretary of Education to conduct a comprehensive national assessment of programs carried out with assistance under Chapter 1 of Title 1 of the Elementary and Secondary Education Act of 1965. Introduced by HAWKINS, D-Calif., Jan. 30, 1990. House Education and Labor reported, amended, Feb. 20 (H Rept 101-404). House passed, amended, under suspension of the rules, Feb. 27. Senate passed, amended, May 7. House agreed to Senate amendment with amendment May 10. Senate agreed to House amendment to Senate amendment May 14. President signed May 30, 1990.

PL 101-306 (HR 644) Amend the Wild and Scenic Rivers Act by designating segments of the East Fork of the Jemez and Pecos rivers in New Mexico as components of the National Wild and Scenic Rivers System. Introduced by RICHARDSON, D-N.M., Jan. 24, 1989. House Interior and Insular Affairs reported, amended, Sept. 7 (H Rept 101-232). House passed, amended, April 19, 1990. Senate passed May 22. President signed June 6, 1990.

PL 101-307 (S J Res 231) Designate the week of June 10, 1990, as "State-Supported Homes for Veterans Week." Introduced by GRASSLEY, R-Iowa, Nov. 20, 1989. Senate Judiciary reported Feb. 22, 1990. Senate passed Feb. 26. House Post Office and Civil Service discharged. House passed May 22. President signed June 6, 1990.

PL 101-308 (S J Res 267) Authorize and request the president to designate May 1990 as "National Physical Fitness and Sports Month." Introduced by THURMOND, R-S.C., March 6, 1990. Senate Judiciary discharged. Senate passed May 8. House Post Office and Civil Service discharged. House passed May 24. President signed June 6, 1990.

PL 101-309 (S J Res 251) Designate "Baltic Freedom Day." Introduced by RIEGLE, D-Mich., Feb. 7, 1990. Senate Judiciary reported Feb. 22. Senate passed Feb. 26. House Foreign Affairs and House Post Office and Civil Service discharged. House passed June 12. President signed June 18, 1990.

PL 101-310 (H J Res 516) Designate the week of June 10, 1990, as "National Scleroderma Awareness Week." Introduced by

HUGHES, D-N.J., March 14, 1990. House Post Office and Civil Service discharged. House passed June 7. Senate Judiciary discharged. Senate passed June 11. President signed June 18, 1990.

PL 101-311 (HR 4612) Amend Title 11 of the U.S. Code regarding swap agreements and forward contracts. Introduced by BROOKS, D-Texas, April 25, 1990. House Judiciary reported May 14 (H Rept 101-484). House passed, amended, under suspension of the rules, May 15. Senate passed June 6. President signed June 25, 1990.

PL 101-312 (S 2700) Authorize the secretary of Veterans Affairs to proceed with a proposed administrative reorganization of the regional field offices of the Veterans Health Services and Research Administration of the Department of Veterans Affairs, notwithstanding the notice-and-wait provisions in Section 210(b) of Title 38, of the U.S. Code. Introduced by CRANSTON, D-Calif., May 24, 1990. Senate passed June 6. House passed June 12. President signed June 25, 1990.

PL 101-313 (S 286) Establish the Petroglyph National Monument in New Mexico. Introduced by DOMENICI, R-N.M., Jan. 31, 1989. Senate Energy and Natural Resources reported, amended, Dec. 20 (S Rept 101-230). Senate passed, amended, Jan. 24, 1990. House Interior and Insular Affairs reported, amended, May 21 (H Rept 101-491). House passed, amended, under suspension of the rules, May 22. Senate agreed to House amendments with amendments June 12. House agreed to Senate amendments June 14. President signed June 27, 1990.

PL 101-314 (S J Res 245) Designate July 3, 1990, as "Idaho Centennial Day." Introduced by McCLURE, R-Idaho, Jan. 30, 1990. Senate Judiciary reported Feb. 22. Senate passed Feb. 26. House Post Office and Civil Service discharged. House passed June 12. President signed June 28, 1990.

PL 101-315 (H J Res 575) Designate June 25, 1990, as "Korean War Remembrance Day." Introduced by SANGMEISTER, D-Ill., May 22, 1990. House Post Office and Civil Service discharged. House passed June 19. Senate passed June 22. President signed June 28, 1990.

PL 101-316 (S J Res 264) Commemorate the 50th anniversary of the National Sheriffs' Association. Introduced by BIDEN, D-Del., March 1, 1990. Senate Judiciary discharged. Senate passed May 15. House Post Office and Civil Service discharged. House passed June 19. President signed June 28, 1990.

PL 101-317 (S J Res 246) Call on the United Nations to repeal General Assembly Resolution 3379. Introduced by BOSCHWITZ, R-Minn., Jan. 31, 1990. Senate Foreign Relations reported March 6. Senate passed May 3. House passed, under suspension of the rules, June 18. President signed June 29, 1990.

PL 101-318 (HR 1622) Amend Title 17, of the U.S. Code, to change the fee schedule of the Copyright Office and to make technical amendments. Introduced by KASTENMEIER, D-Wis., March 23, 1990. House Judiciary reported Oct. 13 (H Rept 101-279). House passed, amended, under suspension of the rules, Oct. 16. Senate Judiciary reported April 19 (S Rept 101-267). Senate passed June 13. President signed July 3, 1990.

PL 101-319 (HR 3046) Reduce the number of commissioners on the Copyright Royalty Tribunal to change the salary classification rates for members of the Copyright Royalty Tribunal and the U.S. Parole Commission and for the deputy and assistant commissioners of the Patent and Trademark Office. Introduced by KASTENMEIER, D-Wis., July 28, 1989. House Judiciary reported, amended, Nov. 3 (H Rept 101-329). House passed, amended, under suspension of the rules, Nov. 13. Senate Judiciary reported April 19, 1990, (S Rept 101-268). Senate passed June 13. President signed July 3, 1990.

PL 101-320 (HR 3545) Amend the Chesapeake and Ohio Canal Development Act to make changes relating to the Chesapeake and Ohio Canal National Historical Park Commission. Introduced by BYRON, D-Md., Oct. 30, 1989. House Interior and Insular Affairs reported April 24, 1990, (H Rept 101-456). House passed, under suspension of the rules, April 24. Senate Energy and Natural Resources reported June 7 (S Rept 101-312). Senate passed June 14. President signed July 3, 1990.

PL 101-321 (HR 3834) Amend the National Trails System Act to designate the route from Selma, Ala., to Montgomery, Ala., for study for potential addition to the national trails system. Introduced by LEWIS, D-Ga., Nov. 21, 1989. House Interior and Insular Affairs reported, amended, March 20, 1990, (H Rept 101-425). House passed, amended, under suspension of the rules, March 20. Senate Energy and Natural Resources reported June 7 (S Rept 101-313). Senate passed June 14. President signed July 3, 1990.

PL 101-322 (HR 5075) Amend the Rail Passenger Service Act to authorize appropriations for the National Railroad Passenger Corporation. Introduced by LUKEN, D-Ohio, June 19, 1990. House passed, under suspension of the rules, June 25. Senate passed June 25. President signed July 6, 1990.

PL 101-323 (H J Res 555) Commemorate the bicentennial of the enactment of the law that provided civil government for the territory from which Tennessee was formed. Introduced by QUILLEN, R-Tenn., April 24, 1990. House Post Office and Civil Service discharged. House passed May 24. Senate Judiciary reported June 14. Senate passed June 18. President signed July 6, 1990.

PL 101-324 (S 1999) Amend the Higher Education Act of 1965 to clarify the administrative procedures of the National Commission on Responsibilities for Financing Postsecondary Education. Introduced by HEINZ, R-Pa., Nov. 21, 1989. Senate passed Nov. 22. House Education and Labor reported, amended, June 5 (H Rept 101-517). House passed, under suspension of the rules, June 5. Senate agreed to House amendments June 22. President signed July 6, 1990.

PL 101-325 (S J Res 271) Designate July 10, 1990, as "Wyoming Centennial Day." Introduced by WALLOP, R-Wyo., March 8, 1990. Senate Judiciary reported June 14. Senate passed June 18. House Post Office and Civil Service discharged. House passed June 28. President signed July 6, 1990.

PL 101-326 (S J Res 315) Designate July 22, 1990, as "Rose Fitzgerald Kennedy Family Appreciation Day." Introduced by LEAHY, D-Vt., May 15, 1990. Senate passed May 15. House Post Office and Civil Service discharged. House passed June 21. President signed July 6, 1990.

PL 101-327 (S J Res 320) Designate July 2, 1990, as "National Literacy Day." Introduced by LAUTENBERG, D-N.J., May 18, 1990. Senate Judiciary reported June 14. Senate passed June 18. House Post Office and Civil Service discharged. House passed June 21. President signed July 6, 1990.

PL 101-328 (S 2124) Authorize appropriations for the National Space Council. Introduced by HOLLINGS, D-S.C., Feb. 8, 1990. Senate passed Feb. 20. House passed, under suspension of the rules, June 26. President signed July 8, 1990.

PL 101-329 (S J Res 278) Designate July 19, 1990, as "Flight Attendant Safety Professionals' Day." Introduced by ROCKEFELLER, D-W.Va., March 28, 1990. Senate Judiciary reported June 14. Senate passed June 18. House Post Office and Civil Service discharged. House passed June 26. President signed July 8, 1990.

PL 101-330 (HR 5149) Amend the Child Nutrition Act of 1966 to provide that the secretary of Agriculture may not consider, in allocating amounts to a state agency under the special supplemental food program for women, infants and children for fiscal year 1991, any amounts returned by such agency for reallocation during fiscal 1990 and to allow amounts allocated to a state for such program for fiscal 1991 to be expended for expenses incurred in fiscal 1990. Introduced by HALL, D-Ohio, June 25, 1990. House Education and Labor discharged. House passed, amended, June 28. Senate passed June 29. President signed on July 12, 1990.

PL 101-331 (H J Res 599) Designate July 1, 1990, as "National Ducks and Wetlands Day." Introduced by STANGELAND, R-Minn., June 12, 1990. House Post Office and Civil Service discharged. House passed June 28. Senate passed June 29. President signed July 13, 1990.

PL 101-332 (HR 1028) Require the secretary of the Treasury to mint coins in commemoration of the Golden Anniversary of the Mount Rushmore National Memorial. Introduced by JOHNSON, D-S.D., Feb. 21, 1989. House passed, amended, under suspension of the rules, May 15, 1990. Senate Banking, Housing and Urban Affairs discharged. Senate passed June 29. President signed July 16, 1990.

PL 101-333 (HR 4252) Authorize the secretary of the Air Force to purchase certain property at Pease Air Force Base, N.H. Introduced by MARTIN, R-N.Y., March 13, 1990. House Armed Services discharged. House passed, amended, May 21. Senate Armed Services reported June 28. Senate passed June 29. President signed July 16, 1990.

PL 101-334 (HR 4525) Amend the Ethics in Government

Act of 1978 to increase the authorization of appropriations for the Office of Government Ethics. Introduced by FRANK, D-Mass., April 18, 1990. House Judiciary reported May 31 (H Rept 101-502, Part I). House Post Office and Civil Service reported June 21 (H Rept 101-502, Part II). House passed, under suspension of the rules, June 25. Senate passed June 29. President signed July 16, 1990.

PL 101-335 (HR 2514) Amend Subchapter III of Chapter 84 of Title 5, of the U.S. Code. Introduced by ACKERMAN, D-N.Y., May 31, 1989. House Post Office and Civil Service reported, amended, April 19, 1990, (H Rept 101-452). House passed, under suspension of the rules, April 24. Senate Banking, Housing and Urban Affairs discharged. Senate Governmental Affairs reported June 7. Senate passed June 27. President signed July 17, 1990.

PL 101-336 (S 933) Establish a clear and comprehensive prohibition against discrimination on the basis of disability. Introduced by HARKIN, D-Iowa, May 9, 1990. Senate Labor and Human Resources reported, amended, Aug. 30 (S Rept 101-116). Senate passed, amended, Sept. 7. House passed, amended, May 22. Conference report filed in the House on June 26 (H Rept 101-558). Senate recommitted conference report July 11. House agreed to conference report July 12 (H Rept 101-596). Senate agreed to conference report July 13. President signed July 26, 1990.

PL 101-337 (HR 2844) Improve the ability of the secretary of the Interior to properly manage certain resources of the National Park System. Introduced by VENTO, D-Minn., June 29, 1989. House Interior and Insular Affairs discharged. House passed July 19, 1989. Senate Energy and Natural Resources reported, amended, June 8 (S Rept 101-328). Senate passed, amended, June 19. House agreed to Senate amendment July 10. President signed July 27, 1990.

PL 101-338 (S J Res 276) Designate the week of July 22, 1990, as "Lyme Disease Awareness Week." Introduced by LIEBERMAN, D-Conn., March 22, 1990. Senate Judiciary reported June 14. Senate passed June 18. House Post Office and Civil Service discharged. House passed July 17. President signed July 27, 1990.

PL 101-339 (S J Res 75) Relating to NASA and the International Space Year. Introduced by MATSUNAGA, D-Hawaii, March 9, 1989. Senate Foreign Relations reported, amended, March 6, 1990. Senate passed, amended, March 7. House Science, Space and Technology reported, amended, June 7 (H Rept 101-532, Part I). House passed, amended, under suspension of the rules, June 12. Senate agreed to House amendments July 19. President signed July 31, 1990.

PL 101-340 (S J Res 281) Designate Sept. 13, 1990, as "National DARE (Drug Abuse Resistance Education) Day." Introduced by DeCONCINI, D-Ariz., March 29, 1990. Senate Judiciary reported June 14. Senate passed June 18. House Post Office and Civil Service discharged. House passed July 17. President signed July 31, 1990.

PL 101-341 (S J Res 339) Designate Aug. 1, 1990, as "Helsinki Human Rights Day." Introduced by DeCONCINI, D-Ariz., June 22, 1990. Senate Judiciary reported June 27. Senate passed June 29. House Post Office and Civil Service and House Foreign Affairs discharged. House passed July 26. President signed July 31, 1990.

PL 101-342 (H J Res 591) Designate the third Sunday of August 1990 as "National Senior Citizens Day." Introduced by SMITH, D-Fla., June 7, 1990. House Post Office and Civil Service discharged. House passed July 17. Senate Judiciary discharged. Senate passed July 19. President signed Aug. 2, 1990.

PL 101-343 (H J Res 577) Authorize and request the president to proclaim November 1990 and every November thereafter "National American Indian Heritage Month." Introduced by FALEOMAVAEGA, D-Am. Samoa, May 24, 1990. House Post Office and Civil Service discharged. House passed, amended, June 26. Senate Judiciary discharged. Senate passed July 19. President signed Aug. 3, 1990.

PL 101-344 (HR 2843) Establish the Kino Missions National Monument in Arizona. Introduced by UDALL, D-Ariz., June 29, 1989. House Interior and Insular Affairs reported, amended, March 13, 1990 (H Rept 101-418). House passed, amended, under suspension of the rules, March 13. Senate Energy and Natural Resources reported July 11 (S Rept 101-362). Senate passed July 23. President signed Aug. 6, 1990.

PL 101-345 (H J Res 625) Designate Aug. 6, 1990, as "Voting Rights Celebration Day." Introduced by GEPHARDT, D-Mo., July 19, 1990. House Post Office and Civil Service discharged. House passed July 31. Senate passed Aug. 1. President signed Aug. 7, 1990.

PL 101-346 (H J Res 548) Designate the week of Aug. 19, 1990, as "National Agricultural Research Week." Introduced by WEBER, R-Minn., April 4, 1990. House Post Office and Civil Service discharged. House passed July 17. Senate passed July 27. President signed Aug. 9, 1990.

PL 101-347 (S J Res 77) Recognize the National Fallen Firefighters' Memorial at the National Fire Academy in Emmitsburg, Md., as the official national memorial to volunteer and career firefighters who die in the line of duty. Introduced by SARBANES, D-Md., March 9, 1989. Senate Rules and Administration reported May 18 (S Rept 101-31). Senate passed Nov. 1. House Administration discharged. House passed July 30, 1990. President signed Aug. 9, 1990.

PL 101-348 (S J Res 256) Designate the week of Oct. 7, 1990, as "Mental Illness Awareness Week." Introduced by SIMON, D-Ill., Feb. 8, 1990. Senate Judiciary reported June 14. Senate passed June 18. House Post Office and Civil Service discharged. House passed July 31. President signed Aug. 9, 1990.

PL 101-349 (S J Res 316) Designate the second Sunday in October of 1990 as "National Children's Day." Introduced by HATFIELD, R-Ore., May 16, 1990. Senate Judiciary reported June 14. Senate passed June 18. House Post Office and Civil Service discharged. House passed July 31. President signed Aug. 9, 1990.

PL 101-350 (HR 5350) Provide for a temporary increase in the public debt limit. Introduced by ROSTENKOWSKI, D-Ill., July 24, 1990. House Ways and Means reported July 26 (H Rept 101-631). House passed, amended, Aug. 3. Senate passed Aug. 4. President signed Aug. 9, 1990.

PL 101-351 (HR 5432) Extend the expiration date of the Defense Production Act of 1950. Introduced by GONZALEZ, D-Texas, Aug. 2, 1990. House Banking, Finance and Urban Affairs discharged. House passed Aug. 2. Senate passed Aug. 4. President signed Aug. 9, 1990.

PL 101-352 (HR 293) Direct the secretary of Health and Human Services to promulgate fire safety standards for cigarettes. Introduced by MOAKLEY, D-Mass., Jan. 3, 1989. House passed, amended, under suspension of the rules, July 30, 1990. Senate passed July 30. President signed Aug. 10, 1990.

PL 101-353 (HR 3048) Designate the Agricultural Research Service, U.S. Department of Agriculture animal health research building in Clay Center, Neb., as the "Virginia D. Smith Animal Health Research Laboratory." Introduced by ROBERTS, R-Kan., July 28, 1989. House passed, under suspension of the rules, May 1, 1990. Senate Environment and Public Works discharged. Senate passed Aug. 4. President signed Aug. 10, 1990.

PL 101-354 (HR 4790) Amend the Public Health Service Act to establish a program of grants for the prevention and control of breast and cervical cancer. Introduced by WAXMAN, D-Calif., May 10, 1990. House Energy and Commerce reported June 18 (H Rept 101-543). House passed, amended, under suspension of the rules, June 18. Senate Labor and Human Resources discharged. Senate passed, amended, Aug. 4. House agreed to Senate amendment Aug. 4. President signed Aug. 10, 1990.

PL 101-355 (H J Res 467) Designate Sept. 21, 1990, as "National POW/MIA Recognition Day," and recognize the National League of Families POW/MIA flag. Introduced by SOLARZ, D-N.Y., Feb. 5, 1990. House Post Office and Civil Service discharged. House passed May 24. Senate Judiciary discharged. Senate passed Aug. 2. President signed Aug. 10, 1990.

PL 101-356 (S 1046) Designate the Merrimack River in New Hampshire as a river to be studied for inclusion in the National Wild and Scenic Rivers System. Introduced by RUDMAN, R-N.H., May 18, 1989. Senate Energy and Natural Resources reported, amended Dec. 20 (S Rept 101-233). Senate passed, amended, Jan. 24, 1990. House Interior and Insular Affairs reported July 30 (H Rept 101-640). House passed, under suspension of the rules, July 30. President signed Aug. 10, 1990.

PL 101-357 (S 1524) Amend the Wild and Scenic Rivers Act of 1968 by designating segments of the Pemigewasset River in New Hampshire for study as a National Wild and Scenic River. Introduced by HUMPHREY, R-N.H., Aug. 3, 1989. Senate Energy and Natural Resources discharged. Senate passed, amended, Nov. 21.

House Interior and Insular Affairs reported July 30, 1990 (H Rept 101-639). House passed, under suspension of the rules, July 30. President signed Aug. 10, 1990.

PL 101-358 (S 1543) Authorize the Colonial Dames at Gunston Hall to establish a memorial to George Mason in the District of Columbia. Introduced by ROBB, D-Va., Aug. 4, 1989. Senate Rules and Administration reported, amended, Feb. 28, 1990 (S Rept 101-245). Senate passed, amended, March 7. House Administration discharged. House passed July 31. President signed Aug. 10, 1990.

PL 101-359 (S 1875) Redesignate the Calamus Dam and Reservoir authorized under the Reclamation Project Authorization Act of 1972 as the "Virginia Smith Dam and Calamus Lake Recreation Area." Introduced by EXON, D-Neb., Nov. 14, 1989. Senate Environment and Public Works reported, amended May 22, 1990. Senate passed, amended, June 12. House Public Works and Transportation discharged. House Interior and Insular Affairs discharged. House passed July 31. President signed Aug. 10, 1990.

PL 101-360 (S 2952) Amend the Energy Policy and Conservation Act to extend the authority for Titles I and II. Introduced by JOHNSTON, D-La., Aug. 2, 1990. Senate passed Aug. 2. House passed Aug. 4. President signed Aug. 10, 1990.

PL 101-361 (S J Res 296) Designate Aug. 7, 1990, as "National Neighborhood Crime Watch Day." Introduced by SPECTER, R-Pa., April 20, 1990. Senate Judiciary reported June 14. Senate passed June 18. House Post Office and Civil Service discharged. House passed Aug. 4. President signed Aug. 10, 1990.

PL 101-362 (S J Res 343) Designate the week of Aug. 13, 1990, as "Home Health Aide Week." Introduced by DOMENICI, R-N.M., June 28, 1990. Senate Judiciary discharged. Senate passed July 12. House Post Office and Civil Service discharged. House passed Aug. 4. President signed Aug. 10, 1990.

PL 101-363 (HR 4872) Establish the National Advisory Council on the Public Service Act. Introduced by FORD, D-Mich., May 21, 1990. House Post Office and Civil Service reported June 21 (H Rept 101-551). House passed, under suspension of the rules, June 25. Senate passed July 27. President signed Aug. 14, 1990.

PL 101-364 (HR 76) Amend the Wild and Scenic Rivers Act to study the eligibility of the St. Marys River in Florida and Georgia for potential addition to the National Wild and Scenic Rivers System. Introduced by BENNETT, D-Fla., Jan. 3, 1989. House Interior and Insular Affairs reported, amended, Oct. 16 (H Rept 101-284). House passed, amended, under suspension of the rules, Oct. 16. Senate Energy and Natural Resources reported, amended June 7, 1990 (S Rept 101-311). Senate passed, amended, June 14. House agreed to Senate amendment Aug. 1. President signed Aug. 15, 1990.

PL 101-365 (HR 1159) Amend the National Trails System Act by designating the Juan Bautista de Anza National Historic Trail. Introduced by MILLER, D-Calif., Feb. 28, 1989. House Interior and Insular Affairs reported, amended, March 5, 1990 (H Rept 101-412). House passed, amended, under suspension of the rules, March 6. Senate Energy and Natural Resources reported, amended, May 15 (S Rept 101-290). Senate passed, amended, May 22. House agreed to Senate amendment Aug. 1. President signed Aug. 15, 1990.

PL 101-366 (HR 1199) Amend Title 38, of the U.S. Code, to improve recruitment and retention of nurses in the Department of Veterans Affairs by providing greater flexibility in the pay system for those nurses. Introduced by KENNEDY, D-Mass., March 1, 1989. House Veterans' Affairs reported, amended, June 22 (H Rept 101-106). House passed, amended, under suspension of the rules, June 27. Senate Veterans' Affairs discharged. Senate passed, amended, Aug. 2. House agreed to Senate amendments Aug. 3. President signed Aug. 15, 1990.

PL 101-367 (HR 4035) Designate the federal building located at 777 Sonoma Ave. in Santa Rosa, Calif., as the "John F. Shea Federal Building." Introduced by BOSCO, D-Calif., Feb. 21, 1990. House Public Works and Transportation reported, amended, April 19 (H Rept 101-454). House passed, amended, under suspension of the rules, April 24. Senate Environment and Public Works discharged. Senate passed Aug. 2. President signed Aug. 15, 1990.

PL 101-368 (HR 4273) Amend the Public Health Service Act to extend the program of grants for preventive health services with respect to tuberculosis. Introduced by WAXMAN, D-Calif., March 14, 1990. House Energy and Commerce reported, amended, June 18 (H Rept 101-542). House passed, amended, under suspension of the rules, June 18. Senate Labor and Human Resources discharged. Senate passed Aug. 4. President signed Aug. 15, 1990.

PL 101-369 (HR 4314) Implement the Inter-American Convention on International Commercial Arbitration. Introduced by BROOKS, D-Texas, March 20, 1990. House Judiciary reported, amended, May 31 (H Rept 101-501). House passed, amended, under suspension of the rules, June 5. Senate Foreign Relations discharged. Senate passed Aug. 4. President signed Aug. 15, 1990.

PL 101-370 (HR 5131) Amend the Federal Aviation Act of 1958 to extend the civil penalty assessment demonstration program. Introduced by OBERSTAR, D-Minn., June 21, 1990. House Public Works and Transportation reported, amended, July 13 (H Rept 101-602). House passed, amended, under suspension of the rules, July 16. Senate Commerce, Science, and Transportation reported Aug. 3 (S Rept 101-425). Senate passed Aug. 4. President signed Aug. 15, 1990.

PL 101-371 (H J Res 515) Designate the week of Sept. 16, 1990, as "National Give Kids a Fighting Chance Week." Introduced by FROST, D-Texas, March 14, 1990. House Post Office and Civil Service discharged. House passed July 31. Senate Judiciary discharged. Senate passed Aug. 4. President signed Aug. 15, 1990.

PL 101-372 (H J Res 554) Designate the week of Jan. 6, 1991, as "National Law Enforcement Training Week." Introduced by ASPIN, D-Wis., April 24, 1990. House Post Office and Civil Service discharged. House passed July 17. Senate Judiciary discharged. Senate passed Aug. 2. President signed Aug. 15, 1990.

PL 101-373 (H J Res 627) Designate Labor Day weekend, Sept. 1 through Sept. 3, 1990, as "National Drive for Life Weekend." Introduced by MINETA, D-Calif., July 19, 1990. House Post Office and Civil Service discharged. House passed Aug. 4. President signed Aug. 15, 1990.

PL 101-374 (S 2461) Reauthorize appropriations to provide for and improve the drug treatment waiting period reduction grant program under the Public Health Service Act. Introduced by KENNEDY, D-Mass., April 19, 1990. Senate Labor and Human Resources reported, amended, June 25 (S Rept 101-336). Senate passed, amended, June 29. House passed, amended, under suspension of the rules, July 30. Senate agreed to House amendments Aug. 4. President signed Aug. 15, 1990.

PL 101-375 (S J Res 248) Designate September 1990 as "International Visitor's Month." Introduced by BOSCHWITZ, R-Minn., Feb. 1, 1990. Senate Judiciary reported June 14. Senate passed June 18. House Post Office and Civil Service discharged. House passed Aug. 4. President signed Aug. 15, 1990.

PL 101-376 (HR 3086) Amend Title 5, of the U.S. Code, to grant appeal rights to members of the excepted service affected by adverse personnel actions. Introduced by SIKORSKI, D-Minn., Aug. 2, 1989. House Post Office and Civil Service reported, amended, Nov. 3 (H Rept 101-328). House passed, amended, under suspension of the rules, Nov. 6. Senate Governmental Affairs reported, amended, May 15, 1990. Senate passed, amended, July 30. House agreed to Senate amendments Aug. 4. President signed Aug. 17, 1990.

PL 101-377 (HR 3248) Revise the boundary of Gettysburg National Military Park in Pennsylvania. Introduced by GOODLING, R-Pa., Sept. 12, 1989. House Interior and Insular Affairs reported, amended, May 1, 1990 (H Rept 101-467). House passed, amended, under suspension of the rules, May 1. Senate passed Aug. 4. President signed Aug. 17, 1990.

PL 101-378 (S 666) Enroll 20 individuals under the Alaska Native Claims Settlement Act. Introduced by MURKOWSKI, R-Alaska, March 17, 1989. Senate Energy and Natural Resources reported, amended, May 18, 1990 (S Rept 101-297). Senate passed, amended, June 6. House Interior and Insular Affairs reported, amended, July 10 (H Rept 101-575). House passed, amended, under suspension of the rules, July 10. Senate agreed to House amendments with amendments July 23. House agreed to Senate amendments to the House amendments Aug. 1. President signed Aug. 17, 1990.

PL 101-379 (HR 498) Clarify and strengthen the authority for certain Department of the Interior law enforcement services, activities and officers on Indian reservations. Introduced by RHODES, R-Ariz., Jan. 4, 1989. House Interior and Insular Affairs reported, amended, May 23, 1989 (H Rept 101-60). House passed, amended, under suspension of the rules, May 23. Senate Indian Affairs reported, amended, Oct. 18 (S Rept 101-167). Senate passed, amended, Nov. 18. House agreed to Senate amendment with amendments Aug. 1, 1990. Senate agreed to House amendments to Senate amendment Aug. 4. President signed Aug. 18, 1990.

PL 101-380 (HR 1465) Establish limitations on liability for damages resulting from oil pollution and to establish a fund for the payment of compensation for such damages. Introduced by JONES, D-N.C., March 16, 1989. House Public Works and Transportation reported, amended, Sept. 18 (H Rept 101-242, Part I). House Merchant Marine and Fisheries reported, amended, Sept. 18 (H Rept 101-242, Part II). House Foreign Affairs and House Interior and Insular Affairs discharged. House Science, Space and Technology reported, amended, Sept. 20 (H Rept 101-242, Part III). House Public Works and Transportation filed supplemental report Oct. 3 (H Rept 101-242, Part IV). House Merchant Marine and Fisheries filed supplemental report Oct. 4 (H Rept 101-242, Part V). House passed, amended, Nov. 9. Senate passed, amended, Nov. 19. Conference report filed in the House Aug. 1, 1990 (H Rept 101-653). Senate agreed to conference report Aug. 2. House agreed to conference report Aug. 4. President signed Aug. 18, 1990.

PL 101-381 (S 2240) Amend the Public Health Service Act to provide grants to improve the quality and availability of care for individuals and families who test HIV-positive. Introduced by KENNEDY, D-Mass., March 6, 1990. Senate Labor and Human Resources reported, amended April 24 (S Rept 101-273). Senate passed, amended, May 16. House passed, amended, June 13. Conference report filed in the House July 31 (H Rept 101-652). House agreed to conference report Aug. 4. Senate agreed to conference report Aug. 4. President signed Aug. 18, 1990.

PL 101-382 (HR 1594) Extend non-discriminatory treatment to the products of the Peoples' Republic of Hungary for five years. Introduced by GIBBONS, D-Fla., March 23, 1989. House Ways and Means reported, amended, June 21 (H Rept 101-99). House failed to pass under suspension of the rules June 27. House passed, amended, Sept. 7. Senate Finance reported, amended March 22, 1990 (S Rept 101-252). Senate passed, amended April 24. House agreed to Senate amendment to the text with amendment and agreed to Senate amendment to the title May 9. Conference report filed in the House on July 30 (H Rept 101-650). Senate agreed to conference report July 31. House agreed to conference report Aug. 4. President signed Aug. 20, 1990.

PL 101-383 (S 2088) Amend the Energy Policy and Conservation Act to extend the authority for Titles I and II. Introduced by JOHNSTON, D-La., Feb. 7, 1990. Senate Energy and Natural Resources reported, amended, May 15 (S Rept 101-289). Senate passed, amended, May 22. House passed, amended, July 16. House agreed to conference report Sept. 13 (H Rept 101-698). Senate agreed to conference report Sept. 13. President signed Sept. 15, 1990.

PL 101-384 (S 3033) Amend Title 39, of the U.S. Code, to allow free mailing privileges to be extended to members of the armed forces while engaged in temporary military operations under arduous circumstances. Introduced by PRYOR, D-Ark., Sept. 12, 1990. Senate Governmental Affairs discharged. Senate passed Sept. 14. House passed, under suspension of the rules, Sept. 17. President signed Sept. 18, 1990.

PL 101-385 (H J Res 568) Designate the week beginning Sept. 16, 1990, as "Emergency Medical Services Week." Introduced by MANTON, D-N.Y., May 15, 1990. House Post Office and Civil Service discharged. House passed Sept. 13. Senate passed Sept. 17. President signed Sept. 20, 1990.

PL 101-386 (S 2597) Amend the Act of June 20, 1910, to clarify in New Mexico authority to exchange lands granted by the United States in trust and to validate prior land exchanges. Introduced by DOMENICI, R-N.M., May 9, 1990. Senate Energy and Natural Resources discharged. Senate passed Aug. 2. House passed, under suspension of the rules, Sept. 10. President signed Sept. 20, 1990.

PL 101-387 (S J Res 285) Designate the period commencing Sept. 9, 1990, and ending Sept. 15, 1990, as "National Historically Black Colleges Week." Introduced by THURMOND, R-S.C., April 4, 1990. Senate Judiciary reported June 14. Senate passed June 18. House Post Office and Civil Service discharged. House passed Sept. 10. President signed Sept. 20, 1990.

PL 101-388 (S J Res 289) Designate October 1990 as "Polish American Heritage Month." Introduced by SIMON, D-Ill., April 19, 1990. Senate Judiciary reported June 14. Senate passed June 18. House Post Office and Civil Service discharged. House passed Sept. 10. President signed Sept. 20, 1990.

PL 101-389 (S J Res 309) Designate October 1990 as "Crime Prevention Month." Introduced by BIDEN, D-Del., May 8, 1990. Senate Judiciary discharged. Senate passed July 31. House Post Office and Civil Service discharged. House passed Sept. 10. President signed Sept. 20, 1990.

PL 101-390 (S J Res 279) Designate the week of Sept. 16, 1990, as "National Rehabilitation Week." Introduced by SPECTER, R-Pa., March 29, 1990. Senate Judiciary reported June 27. Senate passed June 29. House Post Office and Civil Service discharged. House passed Sept. 10. President signed Sept. 21, 1990.

PL 101-391 (HR 94) Amend the Federal Fire Prevention and Control Act of 1974 to allow for the development and issuance of guidelines concerning the use and installation of automatic sprinkler systems and smoke detectors in places of public accommodation affecting commerce. Introduced by BOEHLERT, R-N.Y., Jan. 3, 1989. House Science, Space and Technology reported, amended, Nov. 14 (H Rept 101-357). House passed, under suspension of the rules, amended, Nov. 17. Senate Commerce, Science, and Transportation reported, amended, Aug. 1, 1990 (S Rept 101-408). Senate passed, amended, Aug. 4. House agreed to Senate amendments under suspension of the rules Sept. 10. President signed Sept. 25, 1990.

PL 101-392 (HR 7) Amend the Carl D. Perkins Vocational Education Act to extend the authorities contained in the act through fiscal 1995. Introduced by HAWKINS, D-Calif., Jan. 3, 1989. House Education and Labor reported, amended, April 28 (H Rept 101-41). House passed, amended, May 9. Senate Labor and Human Resources reported April 3, 1990. Senate passed, amended, April 5. Senate agreed to conference report Aug. 2 (H Rept 101-660). House agreed to conference report Sept. 13. President signed Sept. 25, 1990.

PL 101-393 (S J Res 313) Designate Oct. 3, 1990, as "National Teacher Appreciation Day." Introduced by HEFLIN, D-Ala., May 14, 1990. Senate Judiciary reported June 27. Senate passed June 29. House Post Office and Civil Service discharged. House passed Sept. 17. President signed Sept. 25, 1990.

PL 101-394 (S J Res 331) Designate the week of Sept. 23, 1990, as "Religious Freedom Week." Introduced by PELL, D-R.I., May 24, 1990. Senate Judiciary reported June 14. Senate passed June 18. House Post Office and Civil Service discharged. House passed Sept. 17. President signed Sept. 25, 1990.

PL 101-395 (S J Res 333) Designate the week of Sept. 30, 1990, as "National Job Skills Week." Introduced by GORE, D-Tenn., June 5, 1990. Senate Judiciary reported June 14. Senate passed June 18. House Post Office and Civil Service discharged. House passed Sept. 17. President signed Sept. 25, 1990.

PL 101-396 (HR 3265) Amend the Communications Act of 1934 to provide authorization of appropriations for the Federal Communications Commission. Introduced by MARKEY, D-Mass., Sept. 13, 1989. House Energy and Commerce reported, amended, Oct. 27 (H Rept 101-316). House passed, under suspension of the rules, amended, Oct. 30. Senate Commerce, Science and Transportation discharged. Senate passed, amended, July 19, 1990. House agreed to Senate amendment Sept. 13. President signed Sept. 28, 1990.

PL 101-397 (HR 1101) Extend the authorization of the Water Resources Research Act of 1984 through fiscal 1993. Introduced by MILLER, D-Calif., Feb. 23, 1989. House Interior and Insular Affairs reported, amended, June 6 (H Rept 101-76). House passed, under suspension of the rules, amended, June 6. Senate Environment and Public Works discharged. Senate passed, amended, Aug. 2. House agreed to Senate amendment Sept. 11. President signed Sept. 28, 1990.

101-398 (HR 2174) Establish a commission to prepare a report on the feasibility of creating a Mississippi River National Heritage Corridor. Introduced by ESPY, D-Miss., May 2, 1989. House Interior and Insular Affairs reported, amended, June 5, 1990 (H Rept 101-525). House passed, under suspension of the rules, amended, June 12. Senate Energy and Natural Resources reported Aug. 3 (S Rept 101-423). Senate passed Sept. 11. President signed Sept. 28, 1990.

PL 101-399 (HR 4501) Provide for the acquisition of the William Johnson House and its addition to the Natchez National Historical Park. Introduced by PARKER, D-Miss., April 4, 1990. House Interior and Insular Affairs reported, amended, June 21

(H Rept 101-550). House passed, under suspension of the rules, amended, June 25. Senate Energy and Natural Resources reported Aug. 3 (S Rept 101-424). Senate passed Sept. 11. President signed Sept. 28, 1990.

PL 101-400 (S 963) Authorize a study on methods to commemorate Route 66. Introduced by DOMENICI, R-N.M., May 10, 1989. Senate Energy and Natural Resources reported, amended, July 27 (S Rept 101-89). Senate passed, amended, Aug. 2. House Interior and Insular Affairs discharged. House passed, amended, July 31, 1990. Senate agreed to House amendment Sept. 13. President signed Sept. 28, 1990.

PL 101-401 (S 2205) Designate certain lands in Maine as wilderness. Introduced by MITCHELL, D-Maine, Feb. 28, 1990. Senate Agriculture, Nutrition and Forestry reported, amended, May 21 (S Rept 101-299). Senate passed, amended, June 6. House Agriculture reported Sept. 17 (H Rept 101-714, Part I). House passed, under suspension of the rules, Sept. 17. President signed Sept. 28, 1990.

PL 101-402 (HR 5747) Provide for the temporary extension of certain programs relating to housing and community development. Introduced by GONZALEZ, D-Texas, Sept. 28, 1990. House passed, under suspension of the rules, Sept. 28. Senate passed Sept. 28. President signed Oct. 1, 1990.

PL 101-403 (H J Res 655) Make continuing appropriations for fiscal 1991 and supplemental appropriations for "Operation Desert Shield" for fiscal 1990. Introduced by WHITTEN, D-Miss., Sept. 25, 1990. House Appropriations reported Sept. 25 (H Rept 101-754). House passed, amended, Sept. 30. Senate passed Sept. 30. President signed Oct. 1, 1990.

PL 101-404 (HR 2761) Require the secretary of the Treasury to mint coins in commemoration of the 50th anniversary of the United Services Organization. Introduced by RIDGE, R-Pa., June 27, 1989. House passed, under suspension of the rules, amended, May 15, 1990. Senate Banking, Housing and Urban Affairs discharged. Senate passed Sept. 20. President signed Oct. 2, 1990.

PL 101-405 (HR 5755) Extend the temporary increase in the public debt limit. Introduced by ROSTENKOWSKI, D-Ill., Sept. 30, 1990. Ways and Means discharged. House passed Sept. 30. Senate passed Sept. 30. President signed Oct. 2, 1990.

PL 101-406 (HR 4962) Authorize the minting of commemorative coins to support the training of American athletes participating in the 1992 Olympic Games. Introduced by LEHMAN, D-Calif., June 5, 1990. House passed, under suspension of the rules, amended, Sept. 17. Senate passed Sept. 20. President signed Oct. 3, 1990.

PL 101-407 (HR 5725) Extend the expiration date of the Defense Production Act of 1950. Introduced by OAKAR, D-Ohio, Sept. 26, 1990. House Banking, Finance, and Urban Affairs discharged. House passed Sept. 27. Senate passed, amended, Sept. 30. House agreed to Senate amendment Oct. 1. President signed Oct. 4, 1990.

PL 101-408 (S 2075) Authorize grants to improve the capability of Indian tribal governments to regulate environmental quality. Introduced by McCAIN, R-Ariz., Feb. 6, 1990. Senate Indian Affairs reported, amended, May 16 (S Rept 101-295). Senate passed, amended, May 23. House Interior and Insular Affairs reported Sept. 24 (H Rept 101-743). House passed, under suspension of the rules, Sept. 24. President signed Oct. 4, 1990.

PL 101-409 (HR 4773) Authorize the president to call and conduct a National White House Conference on Small Business. Introduced by LaFALCE, D-N.Y., May 9, 1990. House Small Business reported, amended Aug. 4 (H Rept 101-669). House passed, under suspension of the rules, amended, Sept. 10. Senate passed Sept. 18. President signed Oct. 5, 1990.

PL 101-410 (S 535) Increase civil monetary penalties based on the effect of inflation. Introduced by LAUTENBERG, D-N.J., March 8, 1989. Senate Governmental Affairs reported Jan. 31, 1990 (S Rept 101-240). Senate passed, amended, Feb. 22. House Government Operations reported Sept. 13 (H Rept 101-697). House passed, under suspension of the rules, Sept. 24. President signed Oct. 5, 1990.

PL 101-411 (S 3155) Extend the expiration date of the Defense Production Act of 1950 to Oct. 20, 1990. Introduced by RIEGLE, D-Mich., Oct. 3, 1990. Senate passed Oct. 3. House passed Oct. 5. President signed Oct. 6, 1990.

PL 101-412 (H J Res 666) Make further continuing appropriations for fiscal 1991. Introduced by WHITTEN, D-Miss., Oct. 7, 1990. House Ways and Means and House Appropriations discharged. House passed Oct. 8. Senate passed, amended, Oct. 8. House agreed to Senate amendments Oct. 9. President signed Oct. 9, 1990.

PL 101-413 (H J Res 469) Designate Oct. 6, 1990, as "German-American Day." Introduced by LUKEN, D-Ohio, Feb. 6, 1990. House Post Office and Civil Service discharged. House passed July 31. Senate Judiciary reported Sept. 27. Senate passed Sept. 28. President signed Oct. 11, 1990.

PL 101-414 (H J Res 603) Designate October 1990 as "Country Music Month." Introduced by CLEMENT, D-Tenn., June 14, 1990. House Post Office and Civil Service discharged. House passed Sept. 17. Senate Judiciary reported Sept. 27. Senate passed Sept. 28. President signed Oct. 11, 1990.

PL 101-415 (S J Res 301) Designate October 1990 as "National Breast Cancer Awareness Month." Introduced by PELL, D-R.I., April 26, 1990. Senate Judiciary reported June 14. Senate passed June 18. House Post Office and Civil Service discharged. House passed Oct. 1. President signed Oct. 11, 1990.

PL 101-416 (HR 5643) Grant a temporary extension on the authority under which the government may accept the voluntary services of private-sector executives, and clarify the status of federal employees assigned to private-sector positions while participating in an executive exchange program. Introduced by SIKORSKI, D-Minn., Sept. 18, 1990. House passed, under suspension of the rules, amended, Sept. 28. Senate passed Oct. 2. President signed Oct. 12, 1990.

PL 101-417 (H J Res 398) Commemorate the centennial of the designation by Congress of Yosemite National Park. Introduced by LEHMAN, D-Calif., Sept. 6, 1989. House Post Office and Civil Service discharged. House passed March 7, 1990. Senate Judiciary discharged. Senate passed Oct. 1. President signed Oct. 12, 1990.

PL 101-418 (H J Res 482) Designate March 1990 as "Irish-American Heritage Month." Introduced by MANTON, D-N.Y., Feb. 20, 1990. House Post Office and Civil Service discharged. House passed, amended, Aug. 4. Senate Judiciary discharged. Senate passed Oct. 1. President signed Oct. 12, 1990.

PL 101-419 (S 1738) Convey certain Oregon and California Railroad Grant Lands in Josephine County, Ore., to the Rogue Community College District. Introduced by HATFIELD, R-Ore., Oct. 6, 1989. Senate Energy and Natural Resources reported, amended, May 8, 1990 (S Rept 101-282). Senate passed, amended, May 17. House Interior and Insular Affairs reported Sept. 24 (H Rept 101-741). House passed, under suspension of the rules, Sept. 27. President signed Oct. 12, 1990.

PL 101-420 (S 2588) Amend Section 5948 of Title 5 of the U.S. Code to reauthorize physicians' comparability allowances. Introduced by STEVENS, R-Alaska, May 8, 1990. Senate Governmental Affairs discharged. Senate passed Sept. 26. House passed, under suspension of the rules, Oct. 1. President signed Oct. 12, 1990.

PL 101-421 (HR 3007) Amend the Contract Services for Drug Dependent Federal Offenders Act of 1978 to provide additional authorization for appropriations. Introduced by HUGHES, D-N.J., July 25, 1989. House Judiciary reported Oct. 6 (H Rept 101-272). House passed, under suspension of the rules, Oct. 10. Senate Judiciary reported Sept. 27, 1990. Senate passed Sept. 28. President signed Oct. 12, 1990.

PL 101-422 (HR 3897) Authorize appropriations for the Administrative Conference of the United States for fiscal 1991, 1992, 1993 and 1994. Introduced by BROOKS, D-Texas, Jan. 24, 1990. House Judiciary reported, amended, May 31 (H Rept 101-500). House passed, under suspension of the rules, amended, June 5. Senate Judiciary reported Sept. 14. Senate passed, amended, Sept. 17. House agreed to Senate amendment, under suspension of the rules, Oct. 1. President signed Oct. 12, 1990.

PL 101-423 (S J Res 57) Establish a national policy on permanent papers. Introduced by PELL, D-R.I., Feb. 8, 1989. Senate Governmental Affairs discharged. Senate passed July 31. House Government Operations and House Administration discharged. House passed, amended, Sept. 17, 1990. Senate agreed to House amendments Sept. 26. President signed Oct. 12, 1990.

PL 101-424 (S J Res 181) Establish calendar year 1992 the "Year of Clean Water." Introduced by MITCHELL, D-Maine, July 19, 1989. Senate Judiciary reported Oct. 18. Senate passed

Oct. 20. House Post Office and Civil Service discharged. House passed Oct. 1, 1990. President signed Oct. 12, 1990.

PL 101-425 (HR 1243) Require the secretary of Energy to establish three Centers for Metal Casting Competitiveness Research. Introduced by ERDREICH, D-Ala., March 2, 1989. House Science, Space and Technology reported, amended, March 1, 1990 (H Rept 101-410). House passed, under suspension of the rules, amended, March 6. Senate Commerce, Science and Transportation discharged. Senate Energy and Natural Resources reported, amended, March 28 (S Rept 101-258). Senate passed, amended, April 3. House agreed to Senate amendment with amendments Sept. 24. Senate agreed to House amendments to Senate amendment Sept. 28. President signed Oct. 15, 1990.

PL 101-426 (HR 2372) Provide jurisdiction and procedures for claims for compassionate payments for injuries due to exposure to radiation from nuclear testing. Introduced by OWENS, D-Utah, May 16, 1989. House Judiciary reported, amended, April 25 (H Rept 101-463). House passed, under suspension of the rules, amended, June 5. Senate passed, amended, Aug. 2. House agreed to Senate amendment, under suspension of the rules, Sept. 27. President signed Oct. 15, 1990.

PL 101-427 (S 2806) Redesignate the Interstate Highway System as the Dwight D. Eisenhower Interstate Highway System. Introduced by HEINZ, R-Pa., June 28, 1990. Senate Environment and Public Works reported Sept. 26. Senate passed, amended, Oct. 4. House passed Oct. 10. President signed Oct. 15, 1990.

PL 101-428 (HR 5641) Amend Title 5 of the U.S. Code, with respect to retirement of members of the Capitol Police. Introduced by OAKAR, D-Ohio, Sept. 18, 1990. House passed, under suspension of the rules, Sept. 27. Senate passed Oct. 2. President signed Oct. 15, 1990.

PL 101-429 (S 647) Amend the federal securities laws in order to provide additional enforcement remedies for violations of those laws. Introduced by DODD, D-Conn., March 17, 1989. Senate Banking, Housing and Urban Affairs reported, amended, June 26, 1990 (S Rept 101-337). Senate passed, amended, July 18. House passed, amended, July 23. Senate agreed to House amendments with amendment Sept. 27. House agreed to Senate amendment to House amendments under suspension of the rules Oct. 1. President signed Oct. 15, 1990.

PL 101-430 (S 1230) Authorize the acquisition of additional lands containing Indian burial grounds for inclusion in the Knife River Indian Villages National Historic Site, North Dakota, and to provide additional development funding for the historic site visitor center. Introduced by BURDICK, D-N.D., June 22, 1989. Senate Environment and Public Works discharged. Senate Energy and Natural Resources reported, amended, March 22, 1990 (S Rept 101-256). Senate passed, amended, March 28. House Interior and Insular Affairs reported, amended, July 30 (H Rept 101-638). House passed, under suspension of the rules, amended, July 30. Senate agreed to House amendment Oct. 2. President signed Oct. 15, 1990.

PL 101-431 (S 1974) Require new televisions to have built-in decoder circuitry. Introduced by HARKIN, D-Iowa, Nov. 21, 1989. Senate Commerce, Science and Transportation reported, amended, July 25, 1990 (S Rept 101-393). Senate passed, amended, Aug. 2. House Energy and Commerce discharged. House passed Oct. 1. President signed Oct. 15, 1990.

PL 101-432 (HR 3657) Amend the Securities Exchange Act of 1934 to provide additional authorities to the Securities and Exchange Commission to prevent disruptions to the nation's securities markets. Introduced by MARKEY, D-Mass., Nov. 14, 1989. House Energy and Commerce reported, amended, June 5, 1990 (H Rept 101-524). House passed, under suspension of the rules, amended, June 5. Senate passed, amended, Sept. 25. House agreed to Senate amendments, under suspension of the rules, Sept. 28. President signed Oct. 16, 1990.

PL 101-433 (S 1511) Amend the Age Discrimination in Employment Act of 1967 to clarify the protections given to older individuals in regard to employee benefit plans. Introduced by PRYOR, D-Ark., Aug. 3, 1989. Senate Labor and Human Resources reported, amended, April 5, 1990 (S Rept 101-263). Senate considered Sept. 17, 18. Senate passed, amended, Sept. 24. House considered Oct. 2. House passed, under suspension of the rules, Oct. 3. President signed Oct. 16, 1990.

PL 101-434 (HR 435) Amend the Appalachian Regional Development Act of 1965 to include Columbiana County, Ohio, as part of the Appalachian region. Introduced by APPLEGATE, D-Ohio, Jan. 4, 1989. House Public Works and Transportation reported Nov. 17 (H Rept 101-374). House passed Nov. 17. Senate Environment and Public Works reported Sept. 26. Senate passed Oct. 4. President signed Oct. 17, 1990.

PL 101-435 (HR 971) Require the Federal Communications Commission to prescribe rules to protect consumers from unfair practices in the provision of operator services. Introduced by COOPER, D-Tenn., Feb. 9, 1989. House Energy and Commerce reported, amended, Aug. 3 (H Rept 101-213). House passed, under suspension of the rules, amended, Sept. 25. Senate Commerce, Science and Transportation discharged. Senate passed, amended, Oct. 1, 1990. House agreed to Senate amendment Oct. 3. President signed Oct. 17, 1990.

PL 101-436 (HR 2809) Provide for the conveyance of certain lands to California. Introduced by LEHMAN, D-Calif., June 29, 1989. House Interior and Insular Affairs reported, amended, Nov. 9 (H Rept 101-337). House passed, under suspension of the rules, amended, Nov. 13. Senate Energy and Natural Resources reported, amended, Aug. 30, 1990 (S Rept 101-430). Senate passed, amended, Sept. 11. House agreed to Senate amendments Oct. 3. President signed Oct. 17, 1990.

PL 101-437 (HR 1677) Require the Federal Communications Commission to reinstate restrictions on advertising during children's television and to enforce the obligation of broadcasters to meet the educational and informational needs of the child audience. Introduced by BRYANT, D-Texas, April 5, 1990. House Energy and Commerce reported Nov. 21 (H Rept 101-385). House passed, under suspension of the rules, amended, July 23, 1990. Senate passed, amended, Sept. 24. House agreed to Senate amendment, under suspension of the rules, Oct. 1. Became law without the president's signature Oct. 17, 1990.

PL 101-438 (HR 4758) Provide for the construction, operation and maintenance of an extension of the American Canal at El Paso, Texas. Introduced by COLEMAN, D-Texas, May 9, 1990. House passed, under suspension of the rules, June 12. Senate Environment and Public Works reported Sept. 26. Senate passed Oct. 4. President signed Oct. 18, 1990.

PL 101-439 (H J Res 602) Designate October 1990 as "National Domestic Violence Awareness Month." Introduced by SLAUGHTER, D-N.Y., June 13, 1990. House Post Office and Civil Service discharged. House passed Oct. 1. Senate Judiciary discharged. Senate passed Oct. 10. President signed Oct. 18, 1990.

PL 101-440 (S 247) Amend the Energy Policy and Conservation Act to increase the efficiency and effectiveness of state energy conservation programs carried out pursuant to such act. Introduced by METZENBAUM, D-Ohio, Jan. 25, 1989. Senate Energy and Natural Resources reported, amended, Jan. 10, 1990 (S Rept 101-235). Senate passed, amended, Jan. 25. House Energy and Commerce discharged. House passed, amended, Oct. 1. Senate agreed to House amendment Oct. 4. President signed Oct. 18, 1990.

PL 101-441 (S 830) Amend PL 99-647, establishing the Blackstone River Valley Heritage Corridor Commission, to authorize the commission to take immediate action in furtherance of its purposes and to increase the authorization of appropriations for it. Introduced by PELL, D-R.I., April 18, 1989. Senate Energy and Natural Resources reported, amended, July 6 (S Rept 101-63). Senate passed, amended, July 14. House Interior and Insular Affairs reported, amended, Sept. 17, 1990 (H Rept 101-712). House passed, under suspension of the rules, amended, Sept. 17. Senate agreed to House amendment Oct. 3. President signed Oct. 18, 1990.

PL 101-442 (S 2437) Authorize the acquisition of certain lands in Louisiana for inclusion in the Vicksburg National Military Park. Introduced by JOHNSTON, D-La., April 5, 1990. Senate Energy and Natural Resources reported, amended, June 7 (S Rept 101-309). Senate passed, amended, June 14. House Interior and Insular Affairs reported, amended, Sept. 24, 1990 (H Rept 101-744). House passed, under suspension of the rules, amended, Sept. 27. Senate agreed to House amendment Oct. 3. President signed Oct. 18, 1990.

PL 101-443 (HR 3468) Amend the act titled "An Act to Extend the Wetlands Loan Act," to provide for the expansion of the Stewart B. McKinney National Wildlife Refuge. Introduced by MORRISON, D-Conn., Oct. 13, 1989. House Merchant Marine and Fisheries reported, amended, June 5 1990 (H Rept 101-522). House passed, amended, July 19. Senate Environment and Public Works reported Oct. 1 (S Rept 101-484). Senate passed Oct. 9.

President signed Oct. 19, 1990.

PL 101-444 (H J Res 677) Make further continuing appropriations for fiscal 1991. Introduced by WHITTEN, D-Miss., Oct. 18, 1990. House Appropriations and House Ways and Means discharged. House passed Oct. 18. Senate passed Oct. 19. President signed Oct. 19, 1990.

PL 101-445 (HR 1608) Strengthen national nutrition monitoring by requiring the secretary of Agriculture and the secretary of Health and Human Services to prepare and implement a 10-year plan to assess the dietary and nutritional status of the United States population; to support research on, and development of, nutrition monitoring; to foster national nutrition education; and to establish dietary guidelines. Introduced by de la GARZA, D-Texas, March 23, 1989. House Agriculture reported, amended, Oct. 2, 1990 (H Rept 101-788). House passed, under suspension of the rules, amended, Oct. 2. Senate passed Oct. 5. President signed Oct. 22, 1990.

PL 101-446 (HR 4522) Improve the information available to emergency response personnel in the field. Introduced by MEYERS, R-Kan., April 18, 1990. House Science, Space and Technology reported May 3 (H Rept 101-473). House passed, under suspension of the rules, May 8. Senate Commerce, Science and Transportation reported Aug. 30 (S Rept 101-452). Senate passed Oct. 5. President signed Oct. 22, 1990.

PL 101-447 (HR 4593) Transfer to the secretary of the Interior the administration of the surface rights in approximately 10,650 acres of land presently within the boundaries of the San Carlos Indian Reservation, Ariz., and managed by the Forest Service as part of the Coronado National Forest. Introduced by KYL, R-Ariz., April 24, 1990. House Interior and Insular Affairs reported, amended, Aug. 3 (H Rept 101-666). House passed, amended, Oct. 1. Senate passed Oct. 5. President signed Oct. 22, 1990.

PL 101-448 (HR 4985) Designate the federal building located at 51 Southwest First Ave. in Miami as the "Claude Pepper Federal Building." Introduced by ROS-LEHTINEN, R-Fla., June 7, 1990. House Public Works and Transportation reported Sept. 10 (H Rept 101-689). House passed, under suspension of the rules, Sept. 10. Senate Environment and Public Works discharged. Senate passed Oct. 5. President signed Oct. 22, 1990.

PL 101-449 (HR 5070) Amend the John F. Kennedy Center Act to authorize appropriations for maintenance, repair, alteration and other services necessary for the John F. Kennedy Center for the Performing Arts. Introduced by BOSCO, D-Calif., June 19, 1990. House Public Works and Transportation reported, amended, Aug. 3 (H Rept 101-662). House passed, under suspension of the rules, amended, Sept. 10. Senate Environment and Public Works discharged. Senate passed Oct. 5. President signed Oct. 22, 1990.

PL 101-450 (S J Res 304) Designate Oct. 17, 1990, as "National Drug-Free Schools and Communities Education and Awareness Day." Introduced by SHELBY, D-Ala., May 3, 1990. Senate Judiciary reported June 14. Senate passed June 18. House Post Office and Civil Service discharged. House passed Oct. 16. President signed Oct. 22, 1990.

PL 101-451 (S J Res 317) Designate the week of Oct. 14, 1990, as "National Radon Action Week." Introduced by LAUTENBERG, D-N.J., May 16, 1990. Senate Judiciary reported June 14. Senate passed June 18. House Post Office and Civil Service discharged. House passed Oct. 16. President signed Oct. 22, 1990.

PL 101-452 (HR 3787) Authorize a joint federal, state and tribal study for the restoration of the fishery resources of the Chehalis River Basin, Washington. Introduced by UNSOELD, D-Wash., Nov. 20, 1989. House Merchant Marine and Fisheries reported, amended, July 12, 1990 (H Rept 101-594). House passed, under suspension of the rules, amended, July 16. Senate Environment and Public Works reported Oct. 1 (S Rept 101-485). Senate passed Oct. 9. President signed Oct. 24, 1990.

PL 101-453 (HR 4279) Amend Title 31 of the U.S. Code, to improve cash management of funds transferred between the federal government and the states. Introduced by CONYERS, D-Mich., March 15, 1990. House Government Operations reported, amended, Sept. 13 (H Rept 101-696). House passed, under suspension of the rules, amended, Sept. 24. Senate passed Oct. 10. President signed Oct. 24, 1990.

PL 101-454 (S 2017) Provide a permanent endowment for the Eisenhower Exchange Fellowship Program. Introduced by DOLE, R-Kan., Jan. 23, 1990. Senate Foreign Relations reported, amended, June 28. Senate passed, amended, Sept. 27. House passed, amended, Oct. 3. Senate agreed to House amendment Oct. 9. President signed Oct. 24, 1990.

PL 101-455 (S 2540) Authorize the board of regents of the Smithsonian Institution to plan, design, construct and equip space in the East Court of the National Museum of Natural History building. Introduced by GARN, R-Utah, April 27, 1990. Senate Rules and Administration reported June 27 (S Rept 101-342). Senate passed July 10. House Administration and House Public Works discharged. House passed Oct. 10. President signed Oct. 24, 1990.

PL 101-456 (S 3046) Redesignate the federal building located at 1 Bowling Green in New York, N.Y., as the "Alexander Hamilton United States Custom House." Introduced by MOYNIHAN, D-N.Y., Sept. 13, 1990. Senate Environment and Public Works reported Sept. 26. Senate passed Oct. 4. House passed Oct. 10. President signed Oct. 24, 1990.

PL 101-457 (S 3127) Designate the Department of Veterans Affairs Medical Center in Albany, N.Y., as the "Samuel S. Stratton Department of Veterans Affairs Medical Center." Introduced by MOYNIHAN, D-N.Y., Sept. 27, 1990. Senate passed Sept. 27. House Veterans' Affairs discharged. House passed Oct. 15. President signed Oct. 24, 1990.

PL 101-458 (S J Res 342) Designate October 1990 as "Ending Hunger Month." Introduced by SIMON, D-Ill., June 28, 1990. Senate Judiciary reported Sept. 27. Senate passed Sept. 28. House Post Office and Civil Service discharged. House passed Oct. 16. President signed Oct. 24, 1990.

PL 101-459 (S J Res 346) Designate the week of Oct. 20, 1990, as "National Red Ribbon Week for a Drug-Free America." Introduced by BOSCHWITZ, R-Minn., July 11, 1990. Senate Judiciary discharged. Senate passed Sept. 17. House Post Office and Civil Service discharged. House passed Oct. 16. President signed Oct. 24, 1990.

PL 101-460 (S J Res 349) Designate October 1990 as "Italian-American Heritage and Culture Month." Introduced by DeCONCINI, D-Ariz., July 13, 1990. Senate Judiciary reported Sept. 27. Senate passed Sept. 28. House Post Office and Civil Service discharged. House passed Oct. 16. President signed Oct. 24, 1990.

PL 101-461 (H J Res 681) Make further continuing appropriations for fiscal 1991. Introduced by WHITTEN, D-Miss., Oct. 24, 1990. House Appropriations and House Ways and Means discharged. House passed Oct. 24. Senate passed Oct. 24. President signed Oct. 25, 1990.

PL 101-462 (HR 4757) Provide for the extension of certain authority for the marshal of the U.S. Supreme Court and the U.S. Supreme Court Police. Introduced by BROOKS, D-Texas, May 9, 1990. House Judiciary reported, amended, May 31 (H Rept 101-503). House passed, under suspension of the rules, amended, June 5. Senate passed, amended, Oct. 5. House agreed to Senate amendments under suspension of the rules Oct. 16. President signed Oct. 25, 1990.

PL 101-463 (H J Res 214) Designate the week of Oct. 23, 1990, as "Eating Disorders Awareness Week." Introduced by FISH, R-N.Y., March 22, 1989. House Post Office and Civil Service discharged. House passed, amended, Oct. 16, 1990. Senate passed Oct. 18. President signed Oct. 25, 1990.

PL 101-464 (H J Res 518) Designate the week of Oct. 13, 1990, as "American Textile Industry Bicentennial Week." Introduced by LLOYD, D-Tenn., March 14, 1990. House Post Office and Civil Service discharged. House passed Oct. 16. Senate passed Oct. 18. President signed Oct. 25, 1990.

PL 101-465 (S J Res 158) Designate the week of Oct. 21, 1990, as "World Population Awareness Week." Introduced by KERRY, D-Mass., June 16, 1989. Senate Judiciary discharged. Senate passed Oct. 6. House Post Office and Civil Service discharged. House passed, amended, Oct. 16, 1990. Senate agreed to House amendments Oct. 18. President signed Oct. 25, 1990.

PL 101-466 (H J Res 682) Waive certain enrollment requirements with respect to any reconciliation bill, appropriation bill or continuing resolution for the remainder of the 101st Congress. Introduced by GRAY, D-Pa., Oct. 24, 1990. House passed Oct. 24. Senate passed Oct. 26. President signed Oct. 27, 1990.

PL 101-467 (H J Res 687) Make further continuing appropriations for fiscal 1991. Introduced by WHITTEN, D-Miss., Oct. 27, 1990. House Appropriations and House Ways and Means discharged. House passed Oct. 27. Senate passed Oct. 27. President signed Oct. 28, 1990.

PL 101-468 (S J Res 270) Designate the week of Feb. 17, 1991, as "National Visiting Nurse Associations Week." Introduced by BRADLEY, D-N.J., March 8, 1990. Senate Judiciary reported Sept. 27. Senate passed Sept. 28. House Post Office and Civil Service discharged. House passed Oct. 16. President signed Oct. 30, 1990.

PL 101-469 (S J Res 323) Designate the week of Nov. 11, 1990, as "Geography Awareness Week." Introduced by BRADLEY, D-N.J., May 22, 1990. Senate Judiciary reported Sept. 27. Senate passed Sept. 28. House Post Office and Civil Service discharged. House passed Oct. 16. President signed Oct. 30, 1990.

PL 101-470 (S J Res 347) Designate the week of April 7, 1991, as "National County Government Week." Introduced by BURNS, R-Mont., July 12, 1990. Senate Judiciary reported Sept. 27. Senate passed Sept. 28. House Post Office and Civil Service discharged. House passed Oct. 16. President signed Oct. 30, 1990.

PL 101-471 (S J Res 351) Designate May 1991 as "National Trauma Awareness Month." Introduced by BYRD, D-W.Va., July 13, 1990. Senate Judiciary discharged. Senate passed Oct. 1. House Post Office and Civil Service discharged. House passed Oct. 16. President signed Oct. 30, 1990.

PL 101-472 (S J Res 362) Designate the week of Nov. 18, 1990, as "National Adoption Week." Introduced by HATCH, R-Utah, Sept. 12, 1990. Senate Judiciary reported Sept. 27. Senate passed Sept. 28. House Post Office and Civil Service discharged. House passed Oct. 16. President signed Oct. 30, 1990.

PL 101-473 (S J Res 366) Designate March 30, 1991, as "National Doctors Day." Introduced by COCHRAN, R-Miss., Sept. 17, 1990. Senate Judiciary reported Sept. 27. Senate passed Sept. 28. House Post Office and Civil Service discharged. House passed Oct. 16. President signed Oct. 30, 1990.

PL 101-474 (HR 4174) Establish a comprehensive personnel system for employees of the Administrative Office of the U.S. Courts. Introduced by FORD, D-Mich., March 5, 1990. House Post Office and Civil Service reported, amended, Sept. 28 (H Rept 101-770, Part I). House passed, under suspension of the rules, amended, Oct. 1. Senate passed Oct. 11. President signed Oct. 30, 1990.

PL 101-475 (HR 5579) Amend Section 28(w) of the Mineral Leasing Act. Introduced by RAHALL, D-W.Va., Nov. 11, 1990. House Interior and Insular Affairs reported Oct. 10 (H Rept 101-833). House passed, under suspension of the rules, Oct. 10. Senate passed Oct. 15. President signed Oct. 30, 1990.

PL 101-476 (S 1824) Reauthorize the Education of the Handicapped Act. Introduced by HARKIN, D-Iowa, Oct. 31, 1989. Senate Labor and Human Resources reported, amended, Nov. 15 (S Rept 101-204). Senate passed, amended, Nov. 16. House Education and Labor discharged. House passed, amended, June 18, 1990. Senate agreed to conference report Oct. 2 (H Rept 101-787). House agreed to conference report, under suspension of the rules, Oct. 15. President signed Oct. 30, 1990.

PL 101-477 (S 2167) Reauthorize the Tribally Controlled Community College Assistance Act of 1978 and the Navajo Community College Act. Introduced by McCAIN, R-Ariz., Feb. 22, 1990. Senate Indian Affairs reported, amended, July 16 (S Rept 101-371). Senate passed, amended, Oct. 11. House passed Oct. 12. President signed Oct. 30, 1990.

PL 101-478 (S 3091) Amend the act incorporating the American Legion so as to redefine eligibility for membership therein. Introduced by THURMOND, R-S.C., Sept. 24, 1990. Senate Judiciary reported Sept. 27. Senate passed Sept. 28. House Judiciary discharged. House passed Oct. 16. President signed Oct. 30, 1990.

PL 101-479 (HR 3888) Allow a certain parcel of land in Rockingham County, Va., to be used for a child-care center. Introduced by OLIN, D-Va., Jan. 24, 1990. House Interior and Insular Affairs reported, amended, July 10 (H Rept 101-578). House passed, under suspension of the rules, amended, July 10. Senate Energy and Natural Resources reported Oct. 11 (S Rept 101-525). Senate passed Oct. 18. President signed Oct. 31, 1990.

PL 101-480 (HR 5749) Amend the act titled "An Act to Incorporate The American University," approved Feb. 24, 1893, to clarify the relationship between the board of trustees of The American University and the general board of Higher Education and Ministry of the United Methodist Church. Introduced by DELLUMS, D-Calif., Sept. 28, 1990. House District of Columbia reported Oct. 5 (H Rept 101-805). House passed, under suspension of the rules, Oct. 15. Senate passed Oct. 18. President signed Oct. 31, 1990.

PL 101-481 (H J Res 519) Designate April 16, 1990, as "National Sarcoidosis Awareness Day." Introduced by SLATTERY, D-Kan., March 14, 1990. House Post Office and Civil Service discharged. House passed, amended, Aug. 4. Senate Judiciary discharged. Senate passed Oct. 16. President signed Oct. 31, 1990.

PL 101-482 (H J Res 566) Acknowledge the sacrifices that military families have made in behalf of the nation and designate Nov. 19, 1990, as "National Military Families Recognition Day." Introduced by ESPY, D-Miss., May 9, 1990. House Post Office and Civil Service discharged. House passed Oct. 16. Senate passed Oct. 18. President signed Oct. 31, 1990.

PL 101-483 (H J Res 587) Commit to the private sector the responsibility for support of the Civic Achievement Award Program in Honor of the Office of Speaker of the House of Representatives. Introduced by CLAY, D-Mo., June 6, 1990. House passed, under suspension of the rules, Oct. 15. Senate passed Oct. 19. President signed Oct. 31, 1990.

PL 101-484 (S 1747) Provide for the restoration of federal recognition to the Ponca Tribe of Nebraska. Introduced by EXON, D-Neb., Oct. 11, 1989. Senate Indian Affairs reported, amended, June 12, 1990 (S Rept 101-330). Senate passed, amended, July 18. House Interior and Insular Affairs reported, amended, Oct. 1 (H Rept 101-776). House passed, under suspension of the rules, amended, Oct. 10. Senate agreed to House amendments Oct. 16. President signed Oct. 31, 1990.

PL 101-485 (S 2059) Establish the Weir Farm National Historic Site in Connecticut. Introduced by LIEBERMAN, D-Conn., Feb. 5, 1990. Senate Energy and Natural Resources reported, amended, June 8 (S Rept 101-318). Senate passed, amended, June 14. House Interior and Insular Affairs reported, amended, Oct. 1 (H Rept 101-782). House passed, under suspension of the rules, amended, Oct. 10. Senate agreed to House amendments Oct. 18. President signed Oct. 31, 1990.

PL 101-486 (S 2203) Settle certain claims of the Zuni Indian Tribe. Introduced by DOMENICI, R-N.M., Feb. 28, 1990. Senate Indian Affairs reported, amended, June 6 (S Rept 101-306). Senate passed, amended, June 21. House Interior and Insular Affairs discharged. House passed, amended, Oct. 10. Senate agreed to House amendments Oct. 15. President signed Oct. 31, 1990.

PL 101-487 (S 3032) Designate the planned Department of Veterans Affairs Medical Center in Honolulu as the "Spark M. Matsunaga Department of Veterans Affairs Medical Center." Introduced by AKAKA, D-Hawaii, Sept. 12, 1990. Senate Veterans' Affairs discharged. Senate passed Oct. 18. House passed Oct. 20. President signed Oct. 31, 1990.

PL 101-488 (S 3216) Designate the Department of Veterans Affairs Medical Center in Charleston, S.C., as the "Ralph H. Johnson Department of Veterans Affairs Medical Center." Introduced by SYMMS, R-Idaho, Oct. 17, 1990. Senate passed Oct. 18. House passed Oct. 20. President signed Oct. 31, 1990.

PL 101-489 (S J Res 293) Designate Nov. 6, 1990, as "National Philanthropy Day." Introduced by RIEGLE, D-Mich., April 19, 1990. Senate Judiciary reported Sept. 27. Senate passed Sept. 28. House Post Office and Civil Service discharged. House passed Oct. 16. President signed Oct. 31, 1990.

PL 101-490 (S J Res 307) Designate the week of Nov. 11, 1990, as "National Women Veterans Recognition Week." Introduced by CRANSTON, D-Calif., May 4, 1990. Senate Judiciary reported Sept. 27. Senate passed Sept. 28. House Post Office and Civil Service discharged. House passed Oct. 16. President signed Oct. 31, 1990.

PL 101-491 (S J Res 324) Designate the week of June 3, 1990, as "Week of the National Observance of the 50th Anniversary of World War II." Introduced by DOLE, R-Kan., May 22, 1990. Senate Judiciary reported June 27. Senate passed June 29. House Post Office and Civil Service discharged. House passed, amended, Oct. 16. Senate agreed to House amendments Oct. 19. President signed Oct. 31, 1990.

PL 101-492 (S J Res 353) Designate September 1991 as "National Rice Month." Introduced by JOHNSTON, D-La., July 24, 1990. Senate Judiciary reported Sept. 27. Senate passed Sept. 28. House Post Office and Civil Service discharged. House passed

Oct. 16. President signed Oct. 31, 1990.

PL 101-493 (HR 5209) Amend Title 39 of the U.S. Code to make non-mailable any unsolicited sample of a drug or other hazardous household substance that does not meet child-resistant packaging requirements. Introduced by McCLOSKEY, D-Ind., June 28, 1990. House Post Office and Civil Service reported, amended, Sept. 26 (H Rept 101-758). House passed, under suspension of the rules, amended, Oct. 1. Senate passed Oct. 16. President signed Oct. 31, 1990.

PL 101-494 (HR 5933) Provide for the temporary extension of certain laws relating to housing and community development. Introduced by GONZALEZ, D-Texas, Oct. 26, 1990. House passed, under suspension of the rules, amended, Oct. 27. Senate passed, amended, Oct. 27. House agreed to Senate amendments, under suspension of the rules, Oct. 27. President signed Oct. 31, 1990.

PL 101-495 (S 2737) Require the secretary of the Treasury to mint a silver dollar coin in commemoration of the 38th anniversary of the ending of the Korean War and in honor of those who served. Introduced by ARMSTRONG, R-Colo., June 14, 1990. Senate Banking, Housing, and Urban Affairs discharged. Senate passed July 27. House passed, under suspension of the rules, amended, Oct. 10. Senate agreed to House amendment Oct. 18. President signed Oct. 31, 1990.

PL 101-496 (S 2753) Reauthorize the Developmental Disabilities Assistance and Bill of Rights Act. Introduced by HARKIN, D-Iowa, June 19, 1990. Senate Labor and Human Resources reported, amended, July 18 (S Rept 101-376). Senate passed, amended, Aug. 2. House Energy and Commerce discharged. House passed, amended, Oct. 10. Senate agreed to House amendments Oct. 12. President signed Oct. 31, 1990.

PL 101-497 (S J Res 388) Waive certain enrollment requirements with respect to S 2830, The Food, Agriculture, Conservation and Trade Act of 1990. Introduced by LEAHY, D-Vt., Oct. 27, 1990. Senate passed Oct. 27. House passed Oct. 28. President signed Oct. 31, 1990.

PL 101-498 (HR 4111) Amend the Mining and Mineral Resources Research Institute Act of 1984. Introduced by CRAIG, R-Idaho, Feb. 27, 1990. House Interior and Insular Affairs reported, amended, April 26 (H Rept 101-465). House passed, under suspension of the rules, amended, July 10. Senate Energy and Natural Resources reported Oct. 3 (S Rept 101-496). Senate passed Oct. 16. President signed Nov. 2, 1990.

PL 101-499 (S 2846) Authorize and direct the secretary of the Interior to conduct a study of the feasibility of establishing a unit of the national park system to interpret and commemorate the origins, development, and progression of jazz in the United States. Introduced by JOHNSTON, D-La., July 12, 1990. Senate Energy and Natural Resources reported, amended, Sept. 20 (S Rept 101-469). Senate passed, amended, Sept. 26. House Interior and Insular Affairs reported, amended, Oct. 15 (H Rept 101-879). House passed, under suspension of the rules, amended, Oct. 16. Senate agreed to House amendment Oct. 19. President signed Nov. 2, 1990.

PL 101-500 (HR 3386) Prohibit the use of refrigerated motor vehicles for the transportation of solid waste and to prohibit the use of cargo tanks in providing motor vehicle transportation of food and hazardous materials. Introduced by CLINGER, R-Pa., Oct. 2, 1989. House Public Works and Transportation reported, amended, Dec. 1 (H Rept 101-390, Part I). House Energy and Commerce reported, amended, March 15, 1990 (H Rept 101-390, Part II). House passed, under suspension of the rules, amended, March 27. Senate Commerce, Science and Transportation discharged. Senate passed, amended, Sept. 20. House agreed to Senate amendment with amendments Oct. 16. Senate agreed to House amendments to Senate amendments Oct. 19. President signed Nov. 3, 1990.

PL 101-501 (HR 4151) Authorize appropriations for fiscal 1991 through 1994 to carry out the Head Start Act, the Follow Through Act, the Community Services Block Grant Act, and the Low-Income Home Energy Assistance Act of 1981. Introduced by KILDEE, D-Mich., March 1, 1990. House Education and Labor reported, amended, May 9 (H Rept 101-480). House passed, amended, May 16. Senate Labor and Human Resources reported, amended, Aug. 3 (S Rept 101-421). Senate passed, amended, Sept. 18. House agreed to conference report, under suspension of the rules, Oct. 10 (H Rept 101-816). Senate agreed to conference report Oct. 19. President signed Nov. 3, 1990.

PL 101-502 (HR 4238) Amend the Public Health Service Act to extend various programs with respect to vaccine-preventable diseases. Introduced by WAXMAN, D-Calif., March 8, 1990. House Energy and Commerce reported July 23 (H Rept 101-611). House passed, under suspension of the rules, amended, July 23. Senate passed, amended, Oct. 12. House agreed to Senate amendment, under suspension of the rules Oct. 16. President signed Nov. 3, 1990.

PL 101-503 (HR 5367) Provide for the renegotiation of certain leases of the Seneca Nation. Introduced by HOUGHTON, R-N.Y., July 25, 1990. House Interior and Insular Affairs, reported, amended, Oct. 10 (H Rept 101-832). House passed, under suspension of the rules, amended, Oct. 10. Senate passed Oct. 16. President signed Nov. 3, 1990.

PL 101-504 (HR 5794) Amend the Age Discrimination Claims Assistance Act of 1988 to extend the statute of limitations applicable to certain additional claims under the Age Discrimination in Employment Act of 1967. Introduced by ROYBAL, D-Calif., Oct. 4, 1990. House Education and Labor discharged. House passed, amended, Oct. 11. Senate Labor and Human Resources discharged. Senate passed Oct. 19. President signed Nov. 3, 1990.

PL 101-505 (H J Res 520) Grant the consent of Congress to amendments to the Washington Metropolitan Area Transit Regulation Compact. Introduced by HOYER, D-Md., March 15, 1990. House Judiciary reported, amended, May 31 (H Rept 101-504). House passed, under suspension of the rules, amended, June 5. Senate Judiciary reported Aug. 30. Senate passed, amended, Sept. 27. House agreed to Senate amendments, under suspension of the rules, Oct. 16. President signed Nov. 3, 1990.

PL 101-506 (HR 5268) Make appropriations for Rural Development, Agriculture and Related Agencies programs for fiscal 1991. Introduced by WHITTEN, D-Miss., July 13, 1990. House Appropriations reported July 13 (H Rept 101-598). House passed July 18. Senate Appropriations reported, amended, Sept. 19 (S Rept 101-468). Senate passed, amended, Sept. 25. House agreed to conference report Oct. 22 (H Rept 101-907). House receded and concurred in Senate amendments Oct. 22. House receded and concurred with amendments in Senate amendments Oct. 22. Senate agreed to conference report Oct. 23. Senate agreed to House amendments to Senate amendments Oct. 23. President signed Nov. 5, 1990.

PL 101-507 (HR 5158) Make appropriations for the Departments of Veterans Affairs and Housing and Urban Development, and for sundry independent agencies, commissions, corporations and offices for fiscal 1991. Introduced by TRAXLER, D-Mich., June 26, 1990. House Appropriations reported June 26 (H Rept 101-556). House passed, amended, June 28. Senate Appropriations reported, amended, Sept. 26 (S Rept 101-474). Senate passed, amended, Oct. 3. House agreed to conference report Oct. 20 (H Rept 101-900). House receded and concurred in Senate amendments Oct. 20. House receded and concurred with amendments in Senate amendments Oct. 20. House insisted on its disagreement to Senate amendment Oct. 20. Senate agreed to conference report Oct. 25. Senate agreed to House amendments to Senate amendments Oct. 25. Senate agreed to House amendments to Senate amendments with amendments Oct. 25. Senate receded from its amendment Oct. 25. House agreed to Senate amendments to House amendments to Senate amendments Oct. 26. President signed Nov. 5, 1990.

PL 101-508 (HR 5835) Provide for reconciliation pursuant to Section 4 of the concurrent resolution on the budget for fiscal 1991. Introduced by PANETTA, D-Calif., Oct. 15, 1990. House Budget reported Oct. 16 (H Rept 101-881). House passed, amended, Oct. 16. Senate passed, amended, Oct. 19. House agreed to conference report Oct. 27 (H Rept 101-964). Senate agreed to conference report Oct. 27. President signed Nov. 5, 1990.

PL 101-509 (HR 5241) Make appropriations for the Treasury Department, the U.S. Postal Service, the Executive Office of the President and certain independent agencies for fiscal 1991. Introduced by ROYBAL, D-Calif., July 11, 1990. House Appropriations reported July 11 (H Rept 101-589). House passed, amended, July 13. Senate Appropriations reported, amended, Aug. 1 (S Rept 101-411). Senate passed, amended, Sept. 11. House agreed to conference report Oct. 22 (H Rept 101-906). House receded and concurred in Senate amendments Oct. 22. Senate agreed to conference report Oct. 23. Senate agreed to House amendment to Senate amendment with amendment Oct. 23. House agreed to Senate amendment to House amendment to Senate amendment Oct. 24. President signed Nov. 5, 1990.

PL 101-510 (HR 4739) Authorize appropriations for fiscal 1991 for military functions of the Department of Defense and to prescribe military personnel levels for fiscal 1991. Introduced by ASPIN, D-Wis., May 8, 1990. House Armed Services reported, amended, Aug. 3 (H Rept 101-665). House passed, amended, Sept. 19. Senate passed, amended, Sept. 25. House agreed to conference report Oct. 24 (H Rept 101-923). Senate agreed to conference report Oct. 26. President signed Nov. 5, 1990.

PL 101-511 (HR 5803) Make appropriations for the Department of Defense for fiscal 1991. Introduced by MURTHA, D-Pa., Oct. 9, 1990. House Appropriations reported Oct. 9 (H Rept 101-822). House passed, amended, Oct. 12. Senate passed, amended, Oct. 15. House agreed to conference report Oct. 25 (H Rept 101-938). Senate agreed to conference report Oct. 26. President signed Nov. 5, 1990.

PL 101-512 (HR 5769) Make appropriations for the Department of the Interior and related agencies for fiscal 1991. Introduced by YATES, D-Ill., Oct. 2, 1990. House Appropriations reported Oct. 2 (H Rept 101-789). House considered Oct. 12. House passed, amended, Oct. 15. Senate Appropriations reported, amended, Oct. 16 (S Rept 101-534). Senate passed, amended, Oct. 24. House agreed to conference report Oct. 27 (H Rept 101-971). Senate agreed to conference report Oct. 27. President signed Nov. 5, 1990.

PL 101-513 (HR 5114) Make appropriations for foreign operations, export financing and related programs for fiscal 1991. Introduced by OBEY, D-Wis., June 21, 1990. House Appropriations reported June 21 (H Rept 101-553). House passed, amended, June 27. Senate Appropriations reported, amended, Oct. 10 (S Rept 101-519). Senate considered Oct. 12, 19, 20, 22. Recommitted to Senate Appropriations Oct. 23. Senate Appropriations reported, amended, Oct. 23. Senate passed, amended, Oct. 24. House agreed to conference report Oct. 27 (H Rept 101-968). Senate agreed to conference report Oct. 27. President signed Nov. 5, 1990.

PL 101-514 (HR 5019) Make appropriations for energy and water development for fiscal 1991. Introduced by BEVILL, D-Ala., June 13, 1990. House Appropriations reported June 13 (H Rept 101-536). House passed, amended, June 19. Senate Appropriations reported, amended, July 19 (S Rept 101-378). Senate considered Aug. 1. Senate passed, amended, Aug. 2. House agreed to conference report Oct. 19 (H Rept 101-889). House receded and concurred with amendments in Senate amendments Oct. 19. Senate agreed to conference report Oct. 20. Senate agreed to House amendments to Senate amendments Oct. 20. President signed Nov. 5, 1990.

PL 101-515 (HR 5021) Make appropriations for the Departments of Commerce, Justice, State, the judiciary and related agencies for fiscal 1991. Introduced by SMITH, D-Iowa, June 13, 1990. House Appropriations reported June 13 (H Rept 101-537). House considered June 20. House passed, amended, June 26. Senate Appropriations reported, amended, Oct. 10 (S Rept 101-515). Senate passed, amended, Oct. 11. House agreed to conference report Oct. 23 (H Rept 101-909). House receded and concurred with amendments in Senate amendments Oct. 23. House insisted on its disagreement to Senate amendment Oct. 23. Senate agreed to conference report Oct. 24. Senate agreed to House amendments to Senate amendments Oct. 24. Senate receded from its amendment Oct. 24. House agreed to Senate amendment to House amendment to Senate amendment Oct. 24. President signed Nov. 5, 1990.

PL 101-516 (HR 5229) Make appropriations for the Department of Transportation and related agencies for fiscal 1991. LEHMAN, D-Fla., July 10, 1990. House Appropriations reported July 10 (H Rept 101-584). House passed, amended, July 12. Senate Appropriations reported, amended, July 27 (S Rept 101-398). Senate passed, amended, Aug. 4. House agreed to conference report Oct. 19 (H Rept 101-892). House receded and concurred in Senate amendments Oct. 19. House receded and concurred with amendments in Senate amendments Oct. 19. Senate agreed to conference report Oct. 26. Senate agreed to House amendments to Senate amendments Oct. 26. Senate agreed to House amendment to Senate amendment with amendment Oct. 27. Senate agreed to House amendment to Senate amendment Oct. 27. House agreed to Senate amendment to House amendment to Senate amendment Oct. 28. President signed Nov. 5, 1990.

PL 101-517 (HR 5257) Make appropriations for the Departments of Labor, Health and Human Services, and Education, and related agencies for fiscal 1991. Introduced by NATCHER, D-Ky., July 12, 1990. House Appropriations reported July 12 (H Rept 101-591). House passed, amended, July 19. Senate Appropriations reported, amended, Oct. 10 (S Rept 101-516). Senate passed, amended, Oct. 12. House agreed to conference report Oct. 22 (H Rept 101-908). House receded and concurred with amendments in Senate amendments Oct. 22. Senate agreed to conference report Oct. 25. Senate agreed to House amendments with amendments Oct. 25. House agreed to Senate amendment to House amendment to Senate amendment Oct. 26. House disagreed to Senate amendments to House amendments to Senate amendments Oct. 26. Senate receded from its amendments to House amendments to Senate amendments Oct. 26. President signed Nov. 5, 1990.

PL 101-518 (HR 5311) Make appropriations for the government of the District of Columbia and other activities chargeable in whole or in part against the District's revenues for fiscal 1991. Introduced by DIXON, D-Calif., July 19, 1990. House Appropriations reported July 19 (H Rept 101-607). House passed, amended, July 26. Senate Appropriations reported, amended, July 27 (S Rept 101-397). Senate considered Sept. 11, 12 and 14. Senate passed, amended, Sept 18. House rejected conference report Oct. 20 (H Rept 101-897). House rejected conference report Oct. 25 (H Rept 101-935). House agreed to conference report Oct. 26 (H Rept 101-958). Senate agreed to conference report Oct. 27. President signed Nov. 5, 1990.

PL 101-519 (HR 5313) Make appropriations for military construction for the Department of Defense for fiscal 1991. Introduced by HEFNER, D-N.C., July 19, 1990. House Appropriations reported July 19 (H Rept 101-608). House passed, amended, July 30. Senate Appropriations reported, amended, Aug. 1 (S Rept 101-410). Senate passed, amended, Oct. 1. House agreed to conference report Oct. 19 (H Rept 101-888). House receded and concurred in Senate amendment Oct. 19. House receded and concurred with amendments in Senate amendments Oct. 19. House insisted on its disagreement to Senate amendments Oct. 19. Senate agreed to conference report Oct. 27. Senate agreed to House amendments to Senate amendments Oct. 27. Senate receded from its amendments Oct. 28. President signed Nov. 5, 1990.

PL 101-520 (HR 5399) Make appropriations for the legislative branch for fiscal 1991. Introduced by FAZIO, D-Calif., July 30, 1990. House Appropriations reported July 30 (H Rept 101-648). House passed, amended, Oct. 21. Senate considered Oct. 24. Recommitted to Senate Appropriations on Oct. 24. Senate Appropriations reported, amended, Oct. 24. Senate passed, amended, Oct. 25. House agreed to conference report Oct. 27 (H Rept 101-965). Senate agreed to conference report Oct. 27. President signed Nov. 5, 1990.

PL 101-521 (HR 5759) Amend the Age Discrimination in Employment Act of 1967 to clarify the application of such act to employee group health plans. Introduced by GOODLING, R-Pa., Oct. 1, 1990. House passed, under suspension of the rules, Oct. 2. Senate Labor and Human Resources discharged. Senate passed with amendment Oct. 16. House agreed to Senate amendment Oct. 17. President signed Nov. 5, 1990.

PL 101-522 (HR 3840) Establish the Newberry Volcanoes National Monument in Oregon. Introduced by BOB SMITH, R-Ore., Nov. 21, 1989. House Interior and Insular Affairs reported, amended, Oct. 10, 1990 (H Rept 101-827). House passed, under suspension of the rules, amended, Oct. 10. Senate Energy and Natural Resources discharged. Senate passed Oct. 23. President signed Nov. 5, 1990.

PL 101-523 (HR 5144) Establish the Vancouver National Historical Reserve in Washington state. Introduced by UNSOELD, D-Wash., June 21, 1990. House Interior and Insular Affairs reported, amended, Sept. 24 (H Rept 101-740). House passed, under suspension of the rules, amended, Sept. 27. Senate Energy and Natural Resources discharged. Senate passed Oct. 15. President signed Nov. 5, 1990.

PL 101-524 (HR 2331) Amend Title 39 of the U.S. Code to designate as non-mailable solicitations of donations that could reasonably be misconstrued as a bill, invoice or statement of account due, solicitations for the purchase of products or services that the federal government provides either free or at a lower price, and solicitations offered in terms implying any federal government connection or endorsement, unless such matter contains an appropriate conspicuous disclaimer. Introduced by McCLOSKEY, D-Ind., May 11, 1989. House Post Office and Civil Service reported, amended, July 26 (H Rept 101-178). House passed, under suspension of the rules, amended, July 31. Senate Governmental Affairs discharged. Senate passed, amended, Oct. 4, 1990. House agreed to Senate amendments Oct. 19. President signed Nov. 6, 1990.

PL 101-525 (HR 5275) Amend the Congressional Award Act to temporarily extend the Congressional Awards Board and to otherwise revise such act. Introduced by OWENS, D-N.Y., July 13, 1990. House Education and Labor reported, amended, July 23 (H Rept 101-618). House passed, under suspension of the rules, amended, July 23. Governmental Affairs discharged. Senate passed, amended, Oct. 20. House agreed to Senate amendment Oct. 22. President signed Nov. 6, 1990.

PL 101-526 (HR 5482) Waive the period of congressional review of certain District of Columbia acts authorizing the issuance of certain District of Columbia revenue bonds. Introduced by FAUNTROY, D-D.C., Aug. 3, 1990. House passed, under suspension of the rules, Sept. 24. Governmental Affairs discharged. Senate passed, amended, Oct. 16. House agreed to Senate amendment, under suspension of the rules, Oct. 22. President signed Nov. 6, 1990.

PL 101-527 (HR 5702) Amend the Public Health Service Act to provide for an improvement in the health of members of minority groups. Introduced by WAXMAN, D-Calif., Sept. 24, 1990. House Education and Labor reported, amended, Oct. 5 (H Rept 101-804). House passed, under suspension of the rules, amended, Oct. 10. Senate passed Oct. 16. President signed Nov. 6, 1990.

PL 101-528 (H J Res 525) Designate the weeks of Nov. 18, 1990, and Nov. 17, 1991, as "National Family Caregivers Week." Introduced by SNOWE, R-Maine, March 20, 1990. House Post Office and Civil Service discharged. House passed, amended, Oct. 16. Senate passed Oct. 18. President signed Nov. 6, 1990.

PL 101-529 (H J Res 667) Designate Nov. 16, 1990, as "National Federation of the Blind Day." Introduced by KANJORSKI, D-Pa., Oct. 10, 1990. House Post Office and Civil Service discharged. House passed Oct. 18. Senate passed Oct. 23. President signed Nov. 6, 1990.

PL 101-530 (S 1890) Amend Title 5 of the U.S. Code to provide relief from certain inequities remaining in the crediting of National Guard technician service in connection with civil service retirement. Introduced by THURMOND, R-S.C., Nov. 16, 1989. Senate Governmental Affairs discharged. Senate passed, amended, Oct. 10, 1990. House passed, under suspension of the rules, Oct. 22. President signed Nov. 6, 1990.

PL 101-531 (S 3062) Transfer the responsibility for operation and maintenance of Highway 82 Bridge at Greenville, Miss., to the states of Mississippi and Arkansas. Introduced by LOTT, R-Miss., Sept. 17, 1990. Senate Environment and Public Works reported Sept. 26. Senate passed Oct. 4. House passed, under suspension of the rules, Oct. 22. President signed Nov. 6, 1990.

PL 101-532 (H J Res 669) Salute and congratulate the people of Poland as they commemorate the 200th anniversary of the adoption of the Polish Constitution on May 3, 1991. Introduced by CONTE, R-Mass., Oct. 16, 1990. House Post Office and Civil Service discharged. House passed Oct. 16. Senate passed Oct. 18. President signed on Nov. 7, 1990.

PL 101-533 (S 2516) Augment and improve the quality of international data compiled by the Bureau of Economic Analysis under the International Investment and Trade in Services Survey Act by allowing that agency to share statistical establishment list information compiled by the Bureau of the Census. Introduced by EXON, D-Neb., April 25, 1990. Senate Commerce, Science and Transportation reported, amended, Aug. 30 (S Rept 101-443). Senate passed, amended, Oct. 19. House passed, under suspension of the rules, Oct. 23. President signed Nov. 7, 1990.

PL 101-534 (HR 3911) Amend Title 5 of the U.S. Code to increase the allowance for services of attendants. KENNEDY, D-Mass., Jan. 30, 1990. House passed, under suspension of the rules, Oct. 15. Senate passed, amended, Oct. 25. House agreed to Senate amendment Oct. 25. President signed Nov. 7, 1990.

PL 101-535 (HR 3562) Amend the federal Food, Drug and Cosmetic Act to prescribe nutrition labeling for foods. Introduced by WAXMAN, D-Calif., Oct. 31, 1989. House Energy and Commerce reported, amended, June 13, 1990 (H Rept 101-538). House passed, under suspension of the rules, amended, July 30. Senate passed, amended, Oct. 24. House agreed to Senate amendments, under suspension of the rules, Oct. 26. President signed Nov. 8, 1990.

PL 101-536 (HR 4090) Authorize the establishment of the Glorieta National Battlefield in New Mexico. Introduced by RICHARDSON, D-N.M., Feb. 22, 1990. House Interior and Insular Affairs reported, amended, Oct. 10 (H Rept 101-828). House passed, under suspension of the rules, amended, Oct. 10. Senate Energy and Natural Resources discharged. Senate passed Oct. 25. President signed Nov. 8, 1990.

PL 101-537 (HR 4299) Authorize a study of the fishery resources of the Great Lakes. Introduced by NOWAK, D-N.Y., March 19, 1990. House Merchant Marine and Fisheries reported, amended, Sept. 24 (H Rept 101-748). House passed, under suspension of the rules, amended, Oct. 1. Senate passed Oct. 24. President signed Nov. 8, 1990.

PL 101-538 (HR 5004) Amend the Wild and Scenic Rivers Act to designate certain segments of the Mills River in North Carolina for potential addition to the Wild and Scenic Rivers System. Introduced by CLARKE, D-N.C., June 12, 1990. House Interior and Insular Affairs reported, amended, Oct. 1 (H Rept 101-780). House passed, under suspension of the rules, amended, Oct. 10. Senate Energy and Natural Resources discharged. Senate passed Oct. 25. President signed Nov. 8, 1990.

PL 101-539 (HR 5433) Direct the secretary of Agriculture to release on behalf of the United States a condition in a deed conveying certain lands to the Conservation Commission of West Virginia. Introduced by STAGGERS, D-W.Va., Aug. 2, 1990. House passed, under suspension of the rules, amended, Oct. 10. Senate passed, Oct. 25. President signed Nov. 8, 1990.

PL 101-540 (HR 5872) Amend Title I of the Employee Retirement Income Security Act of 1974 to require qualifying employer securities to include interest in publicly traded partnerships. Introduced by CLAY, D-Mo., Oct. 19, 1990. House Education and Labor discharged. House passed Oct. 22. Senate passed Oct. 25. President signed Nov. 8, 1990.

PL 101-541 (H J Res 649) Approve the extension of nondiscriminatory treatment (most-favored-nation treatment) to the products of Czechoslovakia. Introduced by GEPHARDT, D-Mo., Sept. 10, 1990. House Ways and Means reported Oct. 1 (H Rept 101-773). House passed Oct. 17. Senate passed Oct. 24. President signed Nov. 8, 1990.

PL 101-542 (S 580) Require institutions of higher education receiving federal financial assistance to provide certain information with respect to the graduation rates of student-athletes at such institutions. Introduced by BRADLEY, D-N.J., March 15, 1989. Senate Labor and Human Resources reported, amended, Nov. 16 (S Rept 101-209). Senate passed, amended, Feb. 22, 1990. House Education and Labor discharged. House passed, amended, June 5. Senate agreed to House amendment with amendment Sept. 13. House agreed to conference report, under suspension of the rules, Oct. 22 (H Rept 101-883). Senate agreed to conference report Oct. 24. President signed Nov. 8, 1990.

PL 101-543 (S 1756) Provide for the preservation and interpretation of sites associated with Acadian culture in Maine. Introduced by MITCHELL, D-Maine, Oct. 16, 1989. Senate Energy and Natural Resources reported, amended, June 7, 1990 (S Rept 101-308). Senate passed, amended, June 14. House Interior and Insular Affairs reported, amended, Sept. 24 (H Rept 101-742). House passed, under suspension of the rules, amended, Sept. 27. Senate agreed to House amendment with amendments Oct. 16. House agreed to Senate amendments and disagreed to other Senate amendments Oct. 18. Senate receded from its amendments Oct. 23. President signed Nov. 8, 1990.

PL 101-544 (S J Res 375) Designate Oct. 30, 1990, as "Refugee Day." Introduced by BOSCHWITZ, R-Minn., Oct. 4, 1990. Senate Judiciary discharged. Senate passed Oct. 25. House Post Office and Civil Service discharged. House passed Oct. 27. President signed Nov. 8, 1990.

PL 101-545 (HR 5007) Designate the facility of the U.S. Postal Service located at 100 South John F. Kennedy Drive, Carpentersville, Ill., as the "Robert McClory Post Office." Introduced by HASTERT, R-Ill., June 12, 1990. House Post Office and Civil Service reported, amended, Sept. 26 (H Rept 101-756). House passed, under suspension of the rules, amended, Oct. 1. Senate passed Oct. 27. President signed Nov. 14, 1990.

PL 101-546 (HR 5409) Designate the post office building at 222 W. Center Street, in Orem, Utah, as the "Arthur V. Watkins Post Office." Introduced by NIELSON, R-Utah, July 30, 1990. House Post Office and Civil Service reported, amended, Sept. 26 (H Rept 101-757). House passed, under suspension of the rules, amended, Oct. 1. Senate Governmental Affairs discharged. Senate passed Oct. 25. President signed Nov. 14, 1990.

PL 101-547 (H J Res 673) Designate Nov. 2, 1990, as a national day of prayer for members of American forces and American citizens stationed or held in the Middle East, and for their families. Introduced by DUNCAN, R-Tenn., Oct. 17, 1990. House Post Office and Civil Service discharged. House passed Oct. 24. Senate Judiciary discharged. Senate passed Oct. 28. President signed Nov. 14, 1990.

PL 101-548 (S 3156) Correct a clerical error in PL 101-383, Energy Policy and Conservation Act amendments. Introduced by CRANSTON, D-Calif., Oct. 3, 1990. Senate passed Oct. 3. House passed Oct. 27. President signed Nov. 14, 1990.

PL 101-549 (S 1630) Amend the Clean Air Act to provide for the attainment and maintenance of health protective national ambient air quality standards. Introduced by BAUCUS, D-Mont., Sept. 14, 1989. Senate Environment and Public Works reported, amended, Dec. 20 (S Rept 101-228). Senate passed, amended, April 3, 1990. House passed, amended, May 23. House agreed to conference report Oct. 26 (H Rept 101-952). Senate agreed to conference report Oct. 27. President signed Nov. 15, 1990.

PL 101-550 (HR 1396) Amend the federal securities laws in order to facilitate cooperation between the United States and foreign countries in securities law enforcement. Introduced by MARKEY, D-Mass., March 14, 1989. House Energy and Commerce reported, amended, Sept. 12 (H Rept 101-240). House passed, under suspension of the rules, amended, Sept. 25. Senate passed, amended, Nov. 16. House agreed to Senate amendment with amendment Oct. 1, 1990. Senate agreed to conference report Oct. 25 (H Rept 101-924). House agreed to conference report, under suspension of the rules, Oct. 26. President signed Nov. 15, 1990.

PL 101-551 (HR 1463) Amend the National Capital Transportation Act of 1969 relating to the Washington Metrorail System. Introduced by DELLUMS, D-Calif., March 16, 1989. House District of Columbia reported, amended, March 23, 1990 (H Rept 101-430). House passed, amended, March 28. Senate Governmental Affairs discharged. Senate passed, amended, Oct. 25. House agreed to Senate amendment Oct. 26. President signed Nov. 15, 1990.

PL 101-552 (HR 2497) Authorize and encourage federal agencies to use mediation, conciliation, arbitration, and other techniques for the prompt and informal resolution of disputes. Introduced by GLICKMAN, D-Kan., May 25, 1989. House Judiciary reported, amended, June 1, 1990 (H Rept 101-513). House passed, under suspension of the rules, amended, June 5. Senate Governmental Affairs discharged. Senate passed, amended, Oct. 25. Senate vitiated its passage Oct. 25. Senate passed, amended, Oct. 25. House agreed to Senate amendment, under suspension of the rules, Oct. 26. President signed Nov. 15, 1990.

PL 101-553 (HR 3045) Amend Chapters 5 and 9 of Title 17 of the U.S. Code to clarify that states, instrumentalities of states, and officers and employees of states acting in their official capacity, are subject to suit in federal court by any person for infringement of copyright and infringement of exclusive rights in mask works, and that all the remedies can be obtained in such suit that can be obtained in a suit against a private person or against other public entities. Introduced by KASTENMEIER, D-Wis., July 28, 1989. House Judiciary reported Oct. 13 (H Rept 101-282). House passed, under suspension of the rules, Oct. 16. Senate Judiciary reported June 5, 1990 (S Rept 101-305). Senate passed, amended, June 26. Senate agreed to conference report Oct. 20 (H Rept 101-887). House agreed to conference report Oct. 26. President signed Nov. 15, 1990.

PL 101-554 (HR 3069) Amend the Job Training Partnership Act to establish an employment training program for displaced homemakers. Introduced by MARTINEZ, D-Calif., Aug. 1, 1989. House passed, under suspension of the rules, amended, Oct. 15, 1990. Senate passed, amended, Oct. 20. House agreed to Senate amendments Oct. 24. President signed Nov. 15, 1990.

PL 101-555 (HR 3310) Authorize appropriations for activities of the National Telecommunications and Information Administration for fiscal 1990 and 1991. Introduced by MARKEY, D-Mass., Sept. 20, 1989. House Energy and Commerce reported Oct. 27 (H Rept 101-317). House passed, under suspension of the rules, Oct. 30. Senate Commerce, Science and Transportation discharged. Senate passed, amended, Oct. 25, 1990. House agreed to Senate amendment, under suspension of the rules, Oct. 26. President signed Nov. 15, 1990.

PL 101-556 (HR 4630) Exchange certain lands in New Mexico. Introduced by RICHARDSON, D-N.M., April 25, 1990. House Interior and Insular Affairs reported, amended, Oct. 1 (H Rept 101-783, Part I). House passed, under suspension of the rules, amended, Oct. 10. Senate Energy and Natural Resources discharged. Senate passed, amended, Oct. 25. House agreed to Senate amendments Oct. 27. President signed Nov. 15, 1990.

PL 101-557 (HR 5112) Amend the Public Health Service Act to extend certain programs for health-care services in the home. Introduced by BRUCE, D-Ill., June 21, 1990. House Energy and Commerce reported, amended, July 23 (H Rept 101-612). House passed, under suspension of the rules, amended, July 23. Senate passed, amended, Oct. 23. House considered Senate amendments, under suspension of the rules, Oct. 23. House agreed to Senate amendments, under suspension of the rules, Oct. 25. President signed Nov. 15, 1990.

PL 101-558 (HR 5113) Amend the Public Health Service Act to revise and extend the program for the prevention and control of injuries. Introduced by BRUCE, D-Ill., June 21, 1990. House Energy and Commerce reported, amended, July 23 (H Rept 101-613). House passed, under suspension of the rules, July 23. Senate passed, amended, Oct. 24. House agreed to Senate amendments, under suspension of the rules, Oct. 26. President signed Nov. 15, 1990.

PL 101-559 (HR 5419) Designate the federal building at 88 W. 200 North in Provo, Utah, as the "J. Will Robinson Federal Building." Introduced by NIELSON, R-Utah, July 31, 1990. House Public Works and Transportation reported, amended, Oct. 5 (H Rept 101-811). House passed, under suspension of the rules, amended, Oct. 10. Senate passed Oct. 28. President signed Nov. 15, 1990.

PL 101-560 (HR 5507) Regarding the Early Winters Resort. Introduced by MORRISON, R-Wash., Aug. 3, 1990. House Interior and Insular Affairs reported, amended, Oct. 10 (H Rept 101-843, Part I). House passed, under suspension of the rules, amended, Oct. 10. Senate Energy and Natural Resources discharged. Senate passed Oct. 26. President signed Nov. 15, 1990.

PL 101-561 (HR 5667) Amend the Water Resources Development Act of 1974 to establish a deadline for the transfer of jurisdiction of the Big South Fork National River and Recreation Area from the secretary of the Army to the secretary of the Interior. Introduced by COOPER, D-Tenn., Sept. 19, 1990. House Interior and Insular Affairs reported, amended, Oct. 10 (H Rept 101-841, Part I). House passed, under suspension of the rules, amended, Oct. 10. Senate Environment and Public Works discharged. Senate passed Oct. 26. President signed Nov. 15, 1990.

PL 101-562 (HR 5708) Authorize acquisition of certain real property for the Library of Congress. Introduced by ANDERSON, D-Calif., Sept. 25, 1990. House Public Works and Transportation reported Oct. 5 (H Rept 101-809). House passed, under suspension of the rules, Oct. 10. Senate passed Oct. 27. President signed Nov. 15, 1990.

PL 101-563 (H J Res 562) Designate the week of Oct. 21, 1990, as "National Humanities Week." Introduced by OAKAR, D-Ohio, May 3, 1990. House Post Office and Civil Service discharged. House passed Oct. 24. Senate Judiciary discharged. Senate passed Oct. 28. President signed Nov. 15, 1990.

PL 101-564 (H J Res 652) Designate March 25, 1991, as "National Medal of Honor Day." Introduced by CHANDLER, R-Wash., Sept. 24, 1990. House Post Office and Civil Service discharged. House passed Oct. 27. Senate Judiciary discharged. Senate passed Oct. 28. President signed Nov. 15, 1990.

PL 101-565 (H J Res 657) Grant the consent of the Congress to amendments to the Delaware-New Jersey Compact. Introduced by HUGHES, D-N.J., Sept. 26, 1990. House Judiciary reported, amended, Oct. 19 (H Rept 101-905). House passed, under suspension of the rules, amended, Oct. 22. Senate passed Oct. 23. President signed Nov. 15, 1990.

PL 101-566 (S 639) Establish a hydrogen research and development program. Introduced by MATSUNAGA, D-Hawaii,

March 16, 1989. Senate Energy and Natural Resources reported, amended, July 23, 1990 (S Rept 101-385). Senate passed, amended, Oct. 16. House passed, under suspension of the rules, Oct. 23. President signed Nov. 15, 1990.

PL 101-567 (S 1805) Authorize the secretary of the Interior to reinstate oil and gas lease LA 033164. Introduced by INOUYE, D-Hawaii, Oct. 27, 1989. Senate Energy and Natural Resources reported, amended, July 26, 1990 (S Rept 101-395). Senate passed, amended, Sept. 11. House Interior and Insular Affairs reported, amended, Oct. 10 (H Rept 101-837). House passed, under suspension of the rules, Oct. 10. Senate disagreed to House amendments Oct. 23. House receded from its amendments Oct. 27. President signed Nov. 15, 1990.

PL 101-568 (S 3215) Authorize the transfer by lease of a specified naval landing ship dock to the government of Brazil. Introduced by NUNN, D-Ga., Oct. 17, 1990. Senate passed, amended, Oct. 18. House passed, under suspension of the rules, Oct. 23. President signed Nov. 15, 1990.

PL 101-569 (S J Res 318) Provide for the appointment of Ira Michael Heyman of California as a citizen regent of the Board of Regents of the Smithsonian Institution. Introduced by MOYNIHAN, D-N.Y., May 17, 1990. Senate Rules and Administration reported June 27 (S Rept 101-346). Senate passed July 10. House passed, under suspension of the rules, amended, Oct. 23. Senate agreed to House amendments Oct. 25. President signed Nov. 15, 1990.

PL 101-570 (S J Res 369) Designate 1991 as "The Year of Thanksgiving for the Blessing of Liberty." Introduced by DOLE, R-Kan., Sept. 24, 1990. Senate Judiciary discharged. Senate passed Oct. 1. House Post Office and Civil Service discharged. House passed Oct. 24. President signed Nov. 15, 1990.

PL 101-571 (HR 2419) Authorize the secretary of Agriculture to exchange certain property in the Chattahoochee National Forest for the construction of facilities in the national forest. Introduced by JENKINS, D-Ga., May 18, 1989. House Agriculture reported, amended, Sept. 17, 1990 (H Rept 101-713). House passed, amended, under suspension of the rules, Sept. 17. Senate Agriculture, Nutrition and Forestry discharged. Senate passed Oct. 27. President signed Nov. 15, 1990.

PL 101-572 (HR 3656) Clarify the application of the functional relationship test to gas utility holding companies registered under the Public Utility Holding Company Act of 1935. Introduced by MARKEY, D-Mass., Nov. 14, 1989. House Energy and Commerce reported, amended, May 8, 1990 (H Rept 101-477). House passed, amended, under suspension of the rules, May 8. Senate Banking, Housing and Urban Affairs discharged and returned to House on June 11 pursuant to H Res 405. Senate passed, amended, Oct. 27. House agreed to Senate amendments, under suspension of the rules, Oct. 27. President signed Nov. 15, 1990.

PL 101-573 (HR 4107) Direct the secretary of the Interior to permit certain uses of lands within Richmond National Battlefield Park and Colonial National Historical Park in Virginia. Introduced by BLILEY, R-Va., Feb. 27, 1990. House Interior and Insular Affairs reported, amended, Sept. 17 (H Rept 101-706). House passed, amended, under suspension of the rules, Sept. 17. Senate Energy and Natural Resources discharged. Senate passed Oct. 27. President signed Nov. 15, 1990.

PL 101-574 (HR 4793) Amend the Small Business Act and the Small Business Investment Act of 1958. Introduced by LaFALCE, D-N.Y., May 10, 1990. House Small Business reported, amended, Aug. 3 (H Rept 101-667). House passed, amended, Sept. 25. Senate passed, amended, Oct. 27. House agreed to Senate amendment Oct. 28. President signed Nov. 15, 1990.

PL 101-575 (HR 4808) Encourage solar, wind and geothermal power production by removing the size limitation contained in the Public Utility Regulatory Policies Act of 1978. Introduced by SHARP, D-Ind., May 14, 1990. House Energy and Commerce reported, Oct. 16 (H Rept 101-885). House passed, amended, under suspension of the rules, Oct. 23. Senate passed, amended, Oct. 27. House agreed to Senate amendment, under suspension of the rules, Oct. 28. President signed Nov. 15, 1990.

PL 101-576 (HR 5687) Amend Title 31 of the U.S. Code to improve the financial management of the federal government by establishing a chief financial officer of the United States within the Office of Management and Budget; by establishing a chief financial officer within each executive department and within each major executive agency; and by requiring the development of systems that provide complete, accurate and timely reporting of financial information. Introduced by CONYERS, D-Mich., Sept. 21, 1990. House Government Operations reported, amended, Oct. 6 (H Rept 101-818, Part I). House Post Office and Civil Service discharged. House passed, amended, under suspension of the rules, Oct. 15. Senate passed, amended, Oct. 27. House agreed to Senate amendments, under suspension of the rules, Oct. 28. President signed Nov. 15, 1990.

PL 101-577 (HR 5871) Amend the farm poundage quota provisions of Section 319(g), (h) and (i) of the Agricultural Adjustment Act of 1938. Introduced by HOPKINS, R-Ky., Oct. 19, 1990. House Agriculture discharged. House passed Oct. 20. Senate Agriculture, Nutrition and Forestry discharged. Senate passed Oct. 26. President signed Nov. 15, 1990.

PL 101-578 (HR 5796) Conduct certain studies in New Mexico. Introduced by RICHARDSON, D-N.M., Oct. 5, 1990. House Interior and Insular Affairs reported, amended, Oct. 15 (H Rept 101-878). House passed, amended, under suspension of the rules, Oct. 16. Senate Energy and Natural Resources discharged. Senate passed Oct. 26. President signed Nov. 15, 1990.

PL 101-579 (H J Res 606) Designate Feb. 16, 1991, as "Lithuanian Independence Day." Introduced by RUSSO, D-Ill., June 19, 1990. House Post Office and Civil Service discharged. House passed Oct. 24. Senate Judiciary discharged. Senate passed Oct. 28. President signed Nov. 15, 1990.

PL 101-580 (S 459) Amend Title 35 of the U.S. Code and the National Aeronautics and Space Act of 1958, with respect to the use of inventions in outer space. Introduced by GORE, D-Tenn., Feb. 28, 1989. Senate Judiciary reported, amended, April 19, 1990 (S Rept 101-266). Senate passed, amended, May 1. House Judiciary discharged. House passed Oct. 26. President signed Nov. 15, 1990.

PL 101-581 (S 1931) Prevent the discharge in a Chapter 13 bankruptcy proceeding of certain debts arising out of the debtor's operation of a motor vehicle while legally intoxicated. Introduced by DANFORTH, R-Mo., Nov. 20, 1989. Senate Judiciary reported, amended, Aug. 30, 1990 (S Rept 101-434). Senate passed, amended, Sept. 18. House passed, amended, under suspension of the rules, Oct. 26. Senate agreed to House amendments Oct. 27. President signed Nov. 15, 1990.

PL 101-582 (S 2056) Amend Title XIX of the Public Health Service Act to provide grants to states and implement state health objectives plans. Introduced by HARKIN, D-Iowa, Feb. 1, 1990. Senate Labor and Human Resources reported, amended, Aug. 3 (S Rept 101-417). Senate passed, amended, Oct. 20. House passed, amended, under suspension of the rules, Oct. 26. Senate agreed to House amendments Oct. 27. President signed Nov. 15, 1990.

PL 101-583 (S 2930) Eliminate substantial documentary evidence requirement for minimum wage determination for American Samoa. Introduced by McCLURE, R-Idaho, July 27, 1990. Senate Labor and Human Resources discharged. Senate passed Aug. 4. House passed, amended, Oct. 18. Senate agreed to House amendments Oct. 27. President signed Nov. 15, 1990.

PL 101-584 (S 3187) Address immediate problems affecting environmental cleanup activities. Introduced by BURDICK, D-N.D., Oct. 11, 1990. Senate Environment and Public Works reported Oct. 11 (S Rept 101-520). Senate passed, amended, Oct. 19. House passed, under suspension of the rules, Oct. 26. President signed Nov. 15, 1990.

PL 101-585 (S 3237) Authorize the secretary of the Treasury to sell certain silver proof coin sets. Introduced by BRYAN, D-Nev., Oct. 23, 1990. Senate passed Oct. 23. House Banking, Finance and Urban Affairs discharged. House passed Oct. 27. President signed Nov. 15, 1990.

PL 101-586 (S J Res 302) Provide for the reappointment of Anne L. Armstrong as a citizen regent of the Board of Regents of the Smithsonian Institution. Introduced by GARN, R-Utah, April 27, 1990. Senate Rules and Administration reported June 27 (S Rept 101-345). Senate passed July 10. House passed, amended, under suspension of the rules, Oct. 23. Senate agreed to House amendments Oct. 25. President signed Nov. 15, 1990.

PL 101-587 (S J Res 357) Designate Sept. 15, 1990, to Oct. 15, 1990, as "Community Center Month." Introduced by PACKWOOD, R-Ore., Aug. 2, 1990. Senate Judiciary discharged. Senate passed Aug. 4. House Post Office and Civil Service discharged. House passed, amended, Oct. 24. Senate agreed to House amendments Oct. 28. President signed Nov. 15, 1990.

PL 101-588 (HR 29) Amend the Clayton Act regarding interlocking directorates and officers. Introduced by FISH, R-N.Y., Jan. 3, 1989. House Judiciary reported, amended, May 14, 1990 (H Rept 101-483). House passed, amended, under suspension of the rules, May 15. Senate passed, amended, Oct. 27. House agreed to Senate amendments, under suspension of the rules, Oct. 28. President signed Nov. 16, 1990.

PL 101-589 (HR 996) Establish the Congressional Scholarships for Science, Mathematics and Engineering. Introduced by WALGREN, D-Pa., Feb. 9, 1989. House Science, Space and Technology reported, amended, Aug. 4 (H Rept 101-220). House passed, amended, under suspension of the rules, Sept. 12. Senate Labor and Human Resources reported Aug. 2, 1990. Senate passed, amended, Aug. 4. House agreed to conference report Oct. 25 (H Rept 101-937). Senate agreed to conference report Oct. 26. President signed Nov. 16, 1990.

PL 101-590 (HR 1602) Amend the Public Health Service Act to improve emergency medical services and trauma care. Introduced by BATES, D-Calif., March 23, 1989. House Energy and Commerce reported, amended, Nov. 13 (H Rept 101-346). House passed, amended, under suspension of the rules, Nov. 14. Senate Labor and Human Resources discharged. Senate passed, amended, Oct. 19, 1990. House agreed to conference report, under suspension of the rules, Oct. 26 (H Rept 101-956). Senate agreed to conference report Oct. 27. President signed Nov. 16, 1990.

PL 101-591 (HR 2840) Reauthorize the Coastal Barrier Resources Act. Introduced by STUDDS, D-Mass., June 29, 1989. House Merchant Marine and Fisheries reported, amended, Aug. 2, 1990 (H Rept 101-657, Part I). House Public Works and Transportation discharged. House Banking, Finance and Urban Affairs reported, amended, Sept. 19 (H Rept 101-657, Part II). House passed, amended, under suspension of the rules, Sept. 28. Senate passed, amended, Oct. 26. House agreed to Senate amendments, under suspension of the rules, Oct. 27. President signed Nov. 16, 1990.

PL 101-592 (HR 3000) Require that certain fasteners sold in commerce conform to the specifications to which they are represented to be manufactured, to provide for accreditation of laboratories engaged in fastener testing, and to require inspection, testing and certification, in accordance with standardized methods, of fasteners used in critical applications to increase fastener quality and reduce the danger of fastener failure. Introduced by DINGELL, D-Mich., July 25, 1989. House Science, Space and Technology reported Aug. 2 (H Rept 101-211, Part I). House Energy and Commerce reported Sept. 12 (H Rept 101-211, Part II). House passed, amended, under suspension of the rules, Sept. 19. Senate Commerce, Science and Transportation reported, amended, July 23, 1990 (S Rept 101-388). Senate passed, amended, Oct. 26. House agreed to Senate amendment, under suspension of the rules, Oct. 26. President signed Nov. 16, 1990.

PL 101-593 (HR 3338) Direct the secretary of the Interior to convey all interest of the United States in a fish hatchery to South Carolina. Introduced by SPRATT, D-S.C., Sept. 25, 1989. House Merchant Marine and Fisheries reported, amended, July 11, 1990 (H Rept 101-586). House passed, amended, under suspension of the rules, July 16. Senate Environment and Public Works reported, amended, Oct. 11 (S Rept 101-522). Senate passed, amended, Oct. 26. House agreed to Senate amendments, under suspension of the rules, Oct. 27. President signed Nov. 16, 1990.

PL 101-594 (HR 3977) Protect and conserve the continent of Antarctica. Introduced by CONTE, R-Mass., Feb. 7, 1990. House Merchant Marine and Fisheries reported, amended, Sept. 10 (H Rept 101-692, Part I). House Interior and Insular Affairs discharged. House passed, amended, under suspension of the rules, Oct. 15. Senate passed, amended, Oct. 25. House agreed to Senate amendment Oct. 26. President signed Nov. 16, 1990.

PL 101-595 (HR 4009) Authorize appropriations for fiscal 1991 for the Federal Maritime Commission. Introduced by JONES, D-N.C., Feb. 20, 1990. House Merchant Marine and Fisheries reported, amended, April 2 (H Rept 101-440). House passed, amended, under suspension of the rules, April 3. Senate Commerce, Science and Transportation discharged. Senate passed, amended, Aug. 4. House agreed to Senate amendment with amendment, under suspension of the rules, Oct. 15. Senate agreed to House amendment to Senate amendment with amendment Oct. 27. House agreed to Senate amendment to House amendment to Senate amendment Oct. 28. President signed Nov. 16, 1990.

PL 101-596 (HR 4323) Amend the federal Water Pollution Control Act relating to water quality in the Great Lakes. Introduced by NOWAK, D-N.Y., March 20, 1990. House Public Works and Transportation reported, amended, Sept. 14 (H Rept 101-704). House passed, amended, under suspension of the rules, Sept. 24. Senate Environment and Public Works discharged. Senate passed, amended, Oct. 18. House agreed to Senate amendment, under suspension of the rules, Oct. 27. President signed Nov. 16, 1990.

PL 101-597 (HR 4487) Amend the Public Health Service Act to revise and extend the program for the National Health Service Corps and to establish a program of grants to the states with respect to offices of rural health. Introduced by RICHARDSON, D-N.M., April 4, 1990. House Energy and Commerce reported, amended, July 30 (H Rept 101-642). House passed, amended, under suspension of the rules, July 30. Senate passed, amended, Aug. 4. House agreed to conference report, under suspension of the rules, Oct. 26 (H Rept 101-945). Senate agreed to conference report Oct. 27. President signed Nov. 16, 1990.

PL 101-598 (HR 4721) Designate the federal building located at 340 North Pleasant Valley Road in Winchester, Va., as the "J. Kenneth Robinson Postal Building." Introduced by SLAUGHTER, R-Va., May 2, 1990. House passed, under suspension of the rules, June 25. Senate Governmental Affairs discharged. Senate passed Oct. 25. President signed Nov. 16, 1990.

PL 101-599 (HR 4888) Improve navigational safety and reduce the hazards to navigation resulting from vessel collisions with pipelines in the marine environment. Introduced by TAUZIN, D-La., May 23, 1990. House Public Works and Transportation reported, amended, Oct. 5 (H Rept 101-814, Part I). House Energy and Commerce reported, amended, Oct. 10 (H Rept 101-814, Part II). House Merchant Marine and Fisheries reported, amended, Oct. 10 (H Rept 101-814, Part III). House passed, amended, under suspension of the rules, Oct. 15. Senate passed Oct. 27. President signed Nov. 16, 1990.

PL 101-600 (HR 5140) Amend the Elementary and Secondary Education Act of 1965 to improve secondary school programs for basic skills improvement and dropout reduction. Introduced by SERRANO, D-N.Y., June 21, 1990. House Education and Labor reported, amended, July 6 (H Rept 101-574). House passed, amended, under suspension of the rules, July 10. Senate Labor and Human Resources discharged. Senate passed, amended, Oct. 25. House agreed to Senate amendment Oct. 27. President signed Nov. 16, 1990.

PL 101-601 (HR 5237) Provide for the protection of American Indian graves. Introduced by UDALL, D-Ariz., July 10, 1990. House Interior and Insular Affairs reported, amended, Oct. 15 (H Rept 101-877). House passed, amended, under suspension of the rules, Oct. 22. Senate passed, amended, Oct. 25. Senate vitiated its passage Oct. 25. Senate passed, amended, Oct. 26. House agreed to Senate amendments Oct. 27. President signed Nov. 16, 1990.

PL 101-602 (HR 5308) Approve the Fort Hall Indian Water Rights Settlement. Introduced by STALLINGS, D-Idaho, July 18, 1990. House Interior and Insular Affairs reported, amended, Oct. 10 (H Rept 101-831). House passed, amended, under suspension of the rules, Oct. 10. Senate Indian Affairs discharged. Senate passed Oct. 28. President signed Nov. 16, 1990.

PL 101-603 (HR 5497) Authorize the secretary of the Interior to acquire certain lands to be added to the Fort Raleigh National Historic Site and the Alligator River National Wildlife Refuge in North Carolina. Introduced by JONES, D-N.C., Aug. 3, 1990. House Interior and Insular Affairs reported, amended, Oct. 10 (H Rept 101-840, Part I). House passed, amended, under suspension of the rules, Oct. 10. Senate Energy and Natural Resources discharged. Senate passed Oct. 27. President signed Nov. 16, 1990.

PL 101-604 (HR 5732) Promote and strengthen aviation security. Introduced by OBERSTAR, D-Minn., Sept. 27, 1990. House passed, amended, under suspension of the rules, Oct. 1. Senate passed, amended, Oct. 23. House agreed to Senate amendment Oct. 24. President signed Nov. 16, 1990.

PL 101-605 (HR 5909) Establish the Florida Keys National Marine Sanctuary. Introduced by FASCELL, D-Fla., Oct. 24, 1990. House passed, under suspension of the rules, Oct. 26. Senate passed Oct. 27. President signed Nov. 16, 1990.

PL 101-606 (S 169) Amend the National Science and Technology Policy, Organization and Priorities Act of 1976 to provide for improved coordination of national scientific research efforts and to provide for a national plan to improve scientific understanding of the Earth system and the effect of changes in that system on climate and human well-being. Introduced by HOLLINGS, D-S.C., Jan. 25, 1989. Senate Commerce, Science and Transportation reported, amended, May 31 (S Rept 101-40). Senate passed, amended, Feb. 6, 1990. House passed, amended, under suspension of the rules, Oct. 26. Senate agreed to House amendments Oct. 28. President signed Nov. 16, 1990.

PL 101-607 (S 555) Establish in the Department of the Interior the De Soto Expedition Trail Commission. Introduced by GRAHAM, D-Fla., March 9, 1989. Senate Energy and Natural Resources reported, amended, Dec. 20 (S Rept 101-232). Senate passed, amended, Jan. 24, 1990. House passed, amended, under suspension of the rules, Oct. 22. Senate agreed to House amendment Oct. 27. President signed Nov. 16, 1990.

PL 101-608 (S 605) Authorize appropriations for the Consumer Product Safety Commission. Introduced by BRYAN, D-Nev., March 16, 1989. Senate Commerce, Science and Transportation reported, amended, May 25 (S Rept 101-37). Senate passed, amended, Aug. 3. House Energy and Commerce discharged. House passed, amended, July 16, 1990. Senate agreed to conference report Oct. 23 (H Rept 101-914). House considered conference report, under suspension of the rules, Oct. 23. House agreed to conference report, under suspension of the rules, Oct. 25. President signed Nov. 16, 1990.

PL 101-609 (S 677) Amend the Arctic Research and Policy Act of 1984 to improve and clarify its provisions. Introduced by MURKOWSKI, R-Alaska, March 17, 1989. Senate Governmental Affairs reported, amended, July 31, 1990 (S Rept 101-405). Senate passed, amended, Sept. 24. House Science, Space and Technology discharged. House passed Oct. 26. President signed Nov. 16, 1990.

PL 101-610 (S 1430) Enhance national and community service. Introduced by KENNEDY, D-Mass., July 27, 1989. Senate Labor and Human Resources reported, amended, Oct. 27 (S Rept 101-176). Senate considered Feb. 26, 27, and 28, 1990. Senate passed, amended, March 1. House Education and Labor discharged. House passed, amended, Sept. 13. Senate agreed to conference report Oct. 16 (H Rept 101-893). House agreed to conference report Oct. 24. President signed Nov. 16, 1990.

PL 101-611 (S 2287) Authorize appropriations to the National Aeronautics and Space Administration for research and development, space flight, control and data communications, construction of facilities, and research and program management. Introduced by GORE, D-Tenn., March 9, 1990. Senate Commerce, Science and Transportation reported, amended, Sept. 11 (S Rept 101-455). Senate passed, amended, Oct. 25. House passed Oct. 25. President signed Nov. 16, 1990.

PL 101-612 (S 2566) Establish the Smith River National Recreation Area, to redesignate the Sunset Crater National Monument. Introduced by McCAIN, R-Ariz., May 2, 1990. Senate Energy and Natural Resources reported June 7 (S Rept 101-310). Senate passed June 14. House Interior and Insular Affairs discharged. House passed, amended, Oct. 27. Senate agreed to House amendment Oct. 28. President signed Nov. 16, 1990.

PL 101-613 (S 2857) Amend the Public Health Service Act to reauthorize certain institutes of the National Institutes of Health. Introduced by KENNEDY, D-Mass., July 16, 1990. Senate Labor and Human Resources reported, amended, Sept. 12 (S Rept 101-459). Senate passed, amended, Oct. 19. House passed, amended, under suspension of the rules, Oct. 27. Senate agreed to House amendments Oct. 27. President signed Nov. 16, 1990.

PL 101-614 (S 2789) Authorize appropriations for the Earthquake Hazards Reduction Act of 1977. Introduced by GORE, D-Tenn., June 26, 1990. Senate Commerce, Science and Transportation reported, amended, Aug. 30 (S Rept 101-446). Senate passed, amended, Oct. 19. House passed Oct. 20. President signed Nov. 16, 1990.

PL 101-615 (S 2936) Amend the Hazardous Materials Transportation Act to authorize appropriations for fiscal 1990, 1991 and 1992. Introduced by EXON, D-Neb., July 30, 1990. Senate Commerce, Science and Transportation reported, amended, Aug. 30 (S Rept 101-449). Senate passed, amended, Oct. 23. House passed, amended, Oct. 25. Senate agreed to House amendment Oct. 26. President signed Nov. 16, 1990.

PL 101-616 (S 2946) Amend the Public Health Service Act to revise and extend the program establishing the National Bone Marrow Donor Registry. Introduced by KENNEDY, D-Mass., July 31, 1990. Senate Labor and Human Resources reported, amended, Oct. 12 (S Rept 101-530). Senate passed, amended, Oct. 25. House passed, under suspension of the rules, Oct. 26. President signed Nov. 16, 1990.

PL 101-617 (S 3069) Provide a method of locating private and government research on environmental issues by geographic location. Introduced by JEFFORDS, R-Vt., Sept. 18, 1990. Senate Environment and Public Works reported Oct. 19 (S Rept 101-541). Senate passed Oct. 26. House Science, Space and Technology discharged. House passed Oct. 28. President signed Nov. 16, 1990.

PL 101-618 (S 3084) Provide for the settlement of water rights claims of the Fallon Paiute-Shoshone Indian Tribe. Introduced by REID, D-Nev., Sept. 20, 1990. Senate Indian Affairs reported, amended, Oct. 25 (S Rept 101-555). Senate passed, amended, Oct. 26. House Interior and Insular Affairs discharged. House passed Oct. 28. President signed Nov. 16, 1990.

PL 101-619 (S 3176) Promote environmental education. Introduced by BURDICK, D-N.D., Oct. 10, 1990. Senate Environment and Public Works discharged. Senate passed, amended, Oct. 26. House passed Oct. 27. President signed Nov. 16, 1990.

PL 101-620 (S J Res 206) Call for the United States to encourage immediate negotiations toward a new agreement among Antarctic Treaty consultative parties for the full protection of Antarctica as a global ecological commons. Introduced by GORE, D-Tenn., Sept. 26, 1989. Senate Foreign Relations reported, amended, Sept. 17, 1990. Senate passed, amended, Oct. 4. House passed, amended, under suspension of the rules, Oct. 23. Senate agreed to House amendment Oct. 25. President signed Nov. 16, 1990.

PL 101-621 (HR 4559) Establish the Red Rock Canyon National Conservation Area. Introduced by BILBRAY, D-Nev., April 19, 1990. House Interior and Insular Affairs reported, amended, Sept. 24 (H Rept 101-739). House passed, amended, under suspension of the rules, Sept. 25. Senate Energy and Natural Resources reported, amended, Oct. 12 (S Rept 101-527). Senate passed, amended, Oct. 19. House agreed to Senate amendment with amendment, under suspension of the rules, Oct. 26. Senate agreed to House amendment to Senate amendment Oct. 27. President signed Nov. 16, 1990.

PL 101-622 (HR 5264) Authorize modification of the boundaries of the Alaska Maritime National Wildlife Refuge. Introduced by YOUNG, R-Alaska, July 12, 1990. House Merchant Marine and Fisheries reported, amended, Sept. 14 (H Rept 101-703, Part I). House Interior and Insular Affairs discharged. House passed, amended, under suspension of the rules, Sept. 28. Senate Energy and Natural Resources discharged. Senate passed Oct. 27. President signed Nov. 21, 1990.

PL 101-623 (HR 5567) Authorize international narcotics control activities for fiscal 1991. Introduced by FASCELL, D-Fla., Sept. 11, 1990. House passed, amended, under suspension of the rules, Oct. 22. Senate passed, amended, Oct. 26. House agreed to Senate amendments, under suspension of the rules, Oct. 27. President signed Nov. 21, 1990.

PL 101-624 (S 2830) Extend and revise agricultural price-support and related programs, to provide for agricultural export, resource conservation, farm credit, and agricultural research and related programs, and to ensure consumers an abundance of food and fiber at reasonable prices. Introduced by LEAHY, D-Vt., July 6, 1990. Senate Agriculture, Nutrition and Forestry reported July 6 (S Rept 101-357). Senate considered July 19, 20, 23, 24, 25, 26. Senate passed, amended, July 27. House passed, amended, Aug. 4. House agreed to conference report Oct. 23 (H Rept 101-916). Senate agreed to conference report Oct. 25. President signed Nov. 28, 1990.

PL 101-625 (S 566) Authorize a new corporation to support state and local strategies for achieving more affordable housing and to increase home ownership. Introduced by CRANSTON, D-Calif., March 15, 1989. Senate Banking, Housing and Urban Affairs reported, amended, June 8, 1990 (S Rept 101-316). Senate considered June 18, 19, 20, 21, 22. Senate passed, amended, June 27. House passed, amended, Aug. 1. House recommitted the conference report Oct. 24 (H Rept 101-922). House agreed to conference report Oct. 25 (H Rept 101-943). Senate agreed to conference report Oct. 27. President signed Nov. 28, 1990.

PL 101-626 (HR 987) Amend the Alaska National Interest Lands Conservation Act and designate certain lands in the

Tongass National Forest as wilderness. Introduced by MRAZEK, D-N.Y., Feb. 9, 1989. House Interior and Insular Affairs reported, amended, June 13 (H Rept 101-84, Part I). House Agriculture reported, amended, June 29 (H Rept 101-84, Part II). House passed, amended, July 13. Senate Energy and Natural Resources reported, amended, March 30, 1990 (S Rept 101-261). Senate considered June 12. Senate passed, amended, June 13. Senate agreed to conference report Oct. 24 (H Rept 101-931). House agreed to conference report, under suspension of the rules, Oct. 26. President signed Nov. 28, 1990.

PL 101-627 (HR 2061) Authorize appropriations to carry out the Magnuson Fishery Conservation and Management Act through fiscal 1992. Introduced by STUDDS, D-Mass., April 18, 1989. House Merchant Marine and Fisheries reported, amended, Dec. 15 (H Rept 101-393). House passed, amended, under suspension of the rules, Feb. 6, 1990. Senate Commerce, Science and Transportation discharged. Senate passed, amended, Oct. 11. House agreed to Senate amendment with amendment, under suspension of the rules, Oct. 23. Senate agreed to House amendment to Senate amendment with amendment Oct. 27. House agreed to Senate amendment to House amendment to Senate amendment, under suspension of the rules, Oct. 27. President signed Nov. 28, 1990.

PL 101-628 (HR 2570) Provide for the designation of certain public lands as wilderness in Arizona. Introduced by UDALL, D-Ariz., June 7, 1989. House Interior and Insular Affairs reported, amended, Feb. 21, 1990 (H Rept 101-405). House passed, amended, Feb. 28. Senate Energy and Natural Resources reported, amended, July 10 (S Rept 101-359). Senate passed, amended, Oct. 27. House agreed to Senate amendment with amendment, under suspension of the rules, Oct. 28. Senate agreed to House amendment to Senate amendment Oct. 28. President signed Nov. 28, 1990.

PL 101-629 (HR 3095) Amend the federal Food, Drug and Cosmetic Act to make improvements in the regulation of medical devices. Introduced by WAXMAN, D-Calif., Aug. 2, 1989. House Energy and Commerce reported, amended, Oct. 5, 1990 (H Rept 101-808). House passed, amended, under suspension of the rules, Oct. 10. Senate passed, amended, Oct. 12. House agreed to conference report, under suspension of the rules, Oct. 27 (H Rept 101-959). Senate agreed to conference report Oct. 27. President signed Nov. 28, 1990.

PL 101-630 (HR 3703) Authorize the Rumsey Indian Rancheria to convey a certain parcel of land. Introduced by FAZIO, D-Calif., Nov. 17, 1989. House Interior and Insular Affairs reported Sept. 10, 1990 (H Rept 101-687). House passed Oct. 1. Senate Indian Affairs discharged. Senate passed, amended, Oct. 25. House agreed to Senate amendment Oct. 26. President signed Nov. 28, 1990.

PL 101-631 (HR 4567) Authorize an exchange of lands in South Dakota and Colorado. Introduced by JOHNSON, D-S.D., April 19, 1990. House Interior and Insular Affairs reported, amended, Sept. 21 (H Rept 101-728, Part I). House Agriculture reported, amended, Sept. 24 (H Rept 101-728, Part II). House passed, amended, under suspension of the rules, Sept. 27. Senate Energy and Natural Resources reported Oct. 17 (S Rept 101-536). Senate passed Oct. 26. President signed Nov. 28, 1990.

PL 101-632 (HR 4834) Provide for a visitor center at Salem Maritime National Historic Site in Massachusetts. Introduced by MAVROULES, D-Mass., May 16, 1990. House Interior and Insular Affairs reported, amended, July 10 (H Rept 101-576). House passed, amended, under suspension of the rules, July 10. Senate Energy and Natural Resources reported Oct. 5 (H Rept 101-506). Senate passed Oct. 28. President signed Nov. 28, 1990.

PL 101-633 (HR 5428) Designate certain public lands in Illinois as wilderness. Introduced by POSHARD, D-Ill., Aug. 1, 1990. House Interior and Insular Affairs reported, amended, Oct. 1 (H Rept 101-784, Part I). House passed, under suspension of the rules, Oct. 10. Senate Agriculture, Nutrition and Forestry discharged. Senate passed Oct. 27. President signed Nov. 28, 1990.

PL 101-634 (S 319) Effect an exchange of lands between the U.S. Forest Service and the Salt Lake City Corp. within Utah. Introduced by GARN, R-Utah, Jan. 31, 1989. Senate Energy and Natural Resources reported, amended, Dec. 20 (S Rept 101-231). Senate passed, amended, Jan. 24, 1990. House Interior and Insular Affairs reported, amended, June 20 (H Rept 101-547, Part I). House Agriculture reported, amended, Oct. 2 (H Rept 101-547,Part II). House passed, amended, under suspension of the rules, Oct. 10. Senate agreed to House amendment Oct. 26. President signed Nov. 28, 1990.

PL 101-635 (S 845) Amend the Food, Drug and Cosmetic Act to revitalize the Food and Drug Administration. Introduced by HATCH, R-Utah, April 19, 1989. Senate Labor and Human Resources reported, amended, Feb. 1, 1990 (S Rept 101-242). Senate passed, amended, Oct. 25. House considered, under suspension of the rules, Oct. 24. House passed, under suspension of the rules, Oct. 27. President signed Nov. 28, 1990.

PL 101-636 (S 1859) Restructure repayment terms and conditions for loans by the secretary of the Interior to the Wolf Trap Foundation for the Performing Arts for the reconstruction of the Filene Center in Wolf Trap Farm Park in Fairfax County, Va. Introduced by WARNER, R-Va., Nov. 8, 1989. Senate Energy and Natural Resources reported March 22, 1990 (S Rept 101-257). Senate passed March 29. House Interior and Insular Affairs reported, amended, Oct. 10 (H Rept 101-838). House passed, amended, under suspension of the rules, Oct. 10. Senate agreed to House amendment Oct. 28. President signed Nov. 28, 1990.

PL 101-637 (S 1893) Reauthorize the Asbestos School Hazard Abatement Act of 1984. Introduced by LAUTENBERG, D-N.J., Nov. 16, 1989. Senate Environment and Public Works reported, amended, June 28, 1990 (S Rept 101-353). Senate passed, amended, Oct. 15. House passed, under suspension of the rules, Oct. 26. President signed Nov. 28, 1990.

PL 101-638 (S 1939) Extend the authorization of appropriations for the Taft Institute. Introduced by MOYNIHAN, D-N.Y., Nov. 20, 1989. Senate passed Nov. 20. House passed, amended, June 7, 1990. House agreed to conference report, under suspension of the rules, Oct. 22 (H Rept 101-884). Senate agreed to conference report Oct. 27. President signed Nov. 28, 1990.

PL 101-639 (S 2628) Amend the Public Health Service Act to reauthorize certain National Institute of Mental Health grants and to improve provisions concerning the state comprehensive mental health services plan. Introduced by KENNEDY, D-Mass., May 15, 1990. Senate Labor and Human Resources reported, amended, July 24 (H Rept 101-389). Senate passed, amended, Aug. 4. House passed, amended, under suspension of the rules, Oct. 23. Senate agreed to House amendment Oct. 25. President signed Nov. 28, 1990.

PL 101-640 (S 2740) Provide for the conservation and development of water and related resources and authorize the Army Corps of Engineers civil works program to construct various projects for improvements to the nation's infrastructure. Introduced by BURDICK, D-N.D., June 14, 1990. Senate Environment and Public Works reported June 14 (S Rept 101-333). Senate passed, amended, Aug. 2. House passed, amended, Sept. 26. House agreed to conference report, under suspension of the rules, Oct. 27 (H Rept 101-966). Senate agreed to conference report Oct. 27. President signed Nov. 28, 1990.

PL 101-641 (S 3012) Amend the Independent Safety Board Act of 1974 to authorize appropriations for fiscal 1991, 1992 and 1993. Introduced by HOLLINGS, D-S.C., Aug. 30, 1990. Senate Commerce, Science and Transportation reported Aug. 30 (S Rept 101-450). Senate passed Oct. 27. House passed, under suspension of the rules, Oct. 28. President signed Nov. 28, 1990.

PL 101-642 (S J Res 329) Designate the week of Nov. 3, 1990, as "National Week to Commemorate the Victims of the Famine in the Ukraine, 1932-1933," and to commemorate the Ukrainian famine of 1932-1933 and the policies of Russification to suppress Ukrainian identity. Introduced by KASTEN, R-Wis., May 24, 1990. Senate Foreign Relations discharged. Senate passed, amended, Oct. 20. House Post Office and Civil Service and House Foreign Affairs discharged. House passed Oct. 27. President signed Nov. 28, 1990.

PL 101-643 (S J Res 364) Designate the third week of February 1991 as "National Parents and Teachers Association Week." Introduced by REID, D-Nev., Sept. 14, 1990. Senate Judiciary discharged. Senate passed Oct. 10. House Post Office and Civil Service discharged. House passed Oct. 27. President signed Nov. 28, 1990.

PL 101-644 (HR 2006) Expand the powers of the Indian Arts and Crafts Board. Introduced by KYL, R-Ariz., April 17, 1989. House Interior and Insular Affairs reported, amended, Feb. 6, 1990 (H Rept 101-400, Part I). House Judiciary reported, amended, Sept. 21 (H Rept 101-400, Part II). House passed, amended, under suspension of the rules, Sept. 27. Senate Indian Affairs discharged. Senate passed, amended, Oct. 25. House agreed to Senate amendment with amendments Oct. 27. Senate agreed to House amendments to Senate amendment Oct. 28. President signed Nov. 29, 1990.

PL 101-645 (HR 3789) Amend the Stewart B. McKinney Homeless Assistance Act to extend programs providing urgently needed assistance for the homeless. Introduced by VENTO, D-Minn., Nov. 20, 1989. House Banking, Finance and Urban Affairs reported, amended, July 10, 1990 (H Rept 101-583, Part I). House Energy and Commerce reported, amended, July 30 (H Rept 101-583, Part II). House passed, amended, under suspension of the rules, Oct. 10. Senate passed, amended, Oct. 12. House agreed to conference report Oct. 26 (H Rept 101-951). Senate agreed to conference report Oct. 26. President signed Nov. 29, 1990.

PL 101-646 (HR 5390) Prevent and control infestations of the coastal inland waters of the United States by the zebra mussel and non-indigenous aquatic nuisance species. Introduced by HERTEL, D-Mich., July 27, 1990. House passed, amended, Oct. 1. Senate passed, amended, Oct. 26. House agreed to Senate amendment, under suspension of the rules, Oct. 27. President signed Nov. 29, 1990.

PL 101-647 (S 3266) Control crime. Introduced by MITCHELL, D-Maine, Oct. 27, 1990. Senate passed Oct. 27. House passed, under suspension of the rules, Oct. 27. President signed Nov. 29, 1990.

PL 101-648 (S 303) Establish a framework for the conduct of negotiated rulemaking by federal agencies. Introduced by LEVIN, D-Mich., Jan. 31, 1989. Senate Governmental Affairs reported, amended, July 31 (S Rept 101-97). Senate passed, amended, Aug. 3. House Judiciary discharged. House passed, amended, May 1, 1990. Senate agreed to House amendment with amendments Oct. 4. House agreed to Senate amendments to House amendment, under suspension of the rules, Oct. 22. President signed Nov. 29, 1990.

PL 101-649 (S 358) Amend the Immigration and Nationality Act to change the level of and preference system for admission of immigrants to the United States and to provide for administrative naturalization. Introduced by KENNEDY, D-Mass., Feb. 7, 1989. Senate Judiciary reported, amended, June 19 (S Rept 101-55). Senate considered July 11 and 12. Senate passed, amended, July 13. House Judiciary discharged. House passed, amended, Oct. 3, 1990. Senate agreed to conference report Oct. 26 (H Rept 101-955). House agreed to conference report Oct. 27. President signed Nov. 29, 1990.

PL 101-650 (HR 5316) Provide for the appointment of additional federal circuit and district judges. Introduced by BROOKS, D-Texas, July 19, 1990. House Judiciary reported, amended, Sept. 21 (H Rept 101-733). House passed, amended, under suspension of the rules, Sept. 27. Senate passed, amended, Oct. 27. House agreed to Senate amendment, under suspension of the rules, Oct. 28. President signed Dec. 1, 1990. ■

CQ

Appendix B

VOTING STUDIES

CQ Key Votes 3-B
Interest Group Ratings................................ 22-B

Key Votes Made More Heat, Less Policy

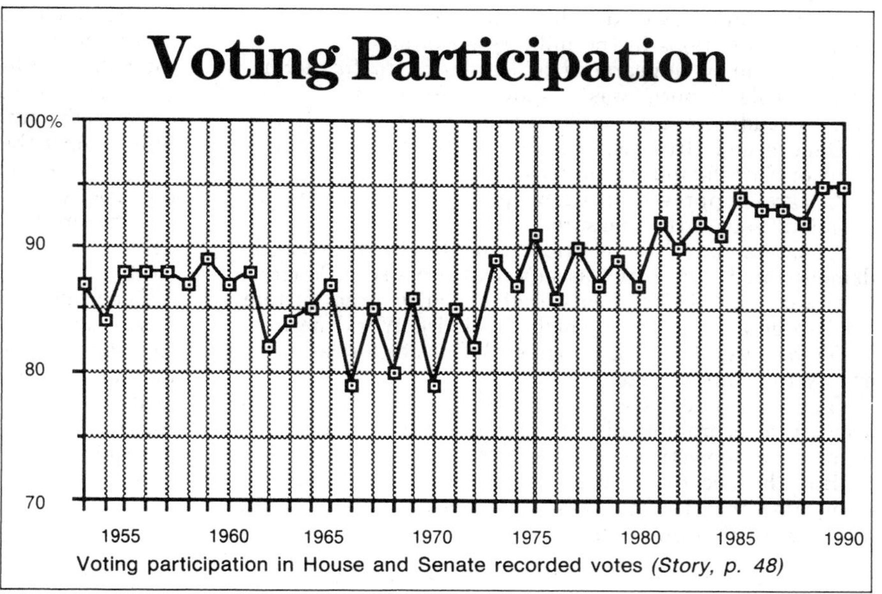

Voting participation in House and Senate recorded votes *(Story, p. 48)*

In his first term as Speaker, Thomas S. Foley went to the well of the House just three times to debate legislation. The 1990 budget battle drew the Washington Democrat out twice. His other appearance came on a proposed constitutional amendment aimed at prohibiting flag burning — a clash between two revered American symbols, Old Glory and the Bill of Rights.

Foley's decision to speak out in the flap over flag burning illustrated how issues could shoot to the top of Congress' agenda and fizzle just as quickly. Leading up to the House vote that rejected the amendment, lawmakers and political observers were warning that opponents might have to pay a political price in November. By the time the elections came around, however, voters were focusing on other issues — including the budget and the Persian Gulf crisis. As an electoral issue, flag burning proved to be strictly flash-in-the-pan.

It was not an unusual story in 1990 for Congress. Many of the issues that produced key votes — flag burning, Rep. Barney Frank's ethics case, abortions in military hospitals, the immigration status of Chinese students and the National Endowment for the Arts (NEA) — gained prominence as metaphors for broader principles or from judgments about their potential for campaign advertisements, not from their long-term impact on the commonweal. There were plenty of reminders that writing laws is only one facet of politics on Capitol Hill.

The year's first showdown between congressional Democrats and President Bush, ostensibly over the immigration status of Chinese students, set the tone. The president had vetoed legislation to defer the students' deportation and instead had taken administrative steps to protect them. This cast the Jan. 25 override vote as a debate over policy toward China in the wake of the Tiananmen Square massacre, as an opportunity for Democrats to prove they could override a veto, and as a test of the president's determination to keep a free hand on foreign policy.

Bush's victory preserved his unbroken string of wins on veto overrides and prevented Congress from dictating his China policy.

Conservative disdain for the federal government's role in education found an outlet in what appeared to be a sideshow to an $800 million package of education initiatives negotiated by the White House and Democrats. Sen. Jesse Helms, R-N.C., sought to strip a $25 million grant sought by Democrats for the privately run National Board for Professional Teaching Standards, arguing that eventually the federal government would try to impose the certification standards on the states.

Helms lost this battle, but he won the war; he led conservative objectors who killed the measure by keeping it off the Senate floor late in the session.

The moral overtones emanating from the ethics case against Frank left many House members nervous over whether they should reprimand him or apply the stronger punishment of censure. The liberal Massachusetts Democrat's relationship with a male prostitute and Republican threats to make a campaign issue of the vote to punish Frank worried members who feared that the case could haunt their elections.

But voters did not hold the scandal against any House member, much less Frank, who took 66 percent of the vote on Election Day.

Symbol and Substance

The Frank case was not the year's only morality play. Congress backed away from setting standards on the sexual content of government-funded art only a year after it prohibited the NEA from funding works considered obscene, sadomasochistic or homoerotic. The House dropped these restrictions in favor of letting the courts decide what is obscene.

Congress made its perennial run at the abortion issue but never hit it head-on. Instead, the two major floor

How Congressional Quarterly Picks Key Votes

Since 1945, Congressional Quarterly has selected a series of key votes on major issues of the year.

An issue is judged by the extent that it represents a matter of major controversy; a matter of presidential or political power; or a decision of potentially great impact on the nation and lives of Americans. For each group of related votes on an issue, one key vote usually is chosen — one that, in the opinion of CQ editors, was important in determining the outcome.

Charts showing how each member of Congress voted on these issues follow the narrative summaries.

battles on abortion came on peripheral aspects of the issue: whether the parents of young women should be notified before their daughters have abortions and whether abortions should be performed in overseas military hospitals. The status quo prevailed in both cases: no parental notification, no abortions in the military hospitals.

The biennial appearance of legislation to further restrict textile imports was a show of force aimed at an overseas audience: international trade negotiators meeting in Geneva and Brussels, Belgium, on the General Agreement on Tariffs and Trade (GATT).

Congress approved stiff new quotas and, as usual, the president vetoed the measure.

Congress failed to override, but the 10-vote margin demonstrated that there was sufficient support in Congress to thwart any GATT treaty that curtailed even current textile quotas, a position sought by Third World nations.

To be sure, the 101st Congress did not devote all of its energy to symbolic acts.

The budget deal, clean air legislation, the farm bill and a measure to prohibit discrimination against the disabled topped the domestic agenda.

But the accord between the White House and Hill Democrats that led to a costly new clean air law and a deficit-reduction bill with higher taxes was noticeably absent on the civil rights legislation that Bush vetoed.

It was likely to be among the first issues the Democrats would take up in 1991.

The year's biggest foreign policy issue, Operation Desert Shield, did not produce a major vote; the money to cover the initial troop deployment was wrapped into a catchall spending measure. But while Congress avoided going on record about Bush's Persian Gulf policy in a direct, substantive manner, many members argued forcefully against the president's desire to forgo the $6.7 billion the Egyptian government owed the United States for military goods.

The president sought and won the authority to grant debt relief so he could make a gesture of gratitude to a key Arab ally.

The fight over Egyptian debt relief was only one demonstration that the fall of the Berlin Wall did not dull all of the edges to the debate over national security policy. Some familiar hot spots, among them Angola and El Salvador, continued to bring the left and right into conflict on Capitol Hill.

And as the "peace dividend" slowly disappeared in the sands of Saudi Arabia, the post-Cold War order looked dangerous enough that Congress failed to kill a single major weapons system. ■

Key Senate Votes

1. Chinese Students Veto

The first vote of the year was set up as a test of the strength of President Bush's veto. Bush had prevailed on all nine previous vetoes, but Democratic leaders thought they would have a breakthrough with a bill to allow Chinese students to remain in the United States rather than return home to face possible reprisals by the repressive Chinese government. The bill (HR 2712) had cleared near the end of the first session without a dissenting vote in either chamber. When the House took up the veto override, only 25 Republicans stuck by the president.

In the Senate, Bush marshaled a strong display of GOP solidarity. Only eight Republicans went with the Democrats, and the 62-37 vote fell four short of the two-thirds majority needed to override the veto: R 8-37; D 54-0 (ND 38-0, SD 16-0). The Republican senators who provided the margin of victory expressed their positions in partisan terms as support for the chief executive, rather than support for Bush's China policy.

It was a theme that played out for the rest of the year. Bush ended the Congress without having any of his 19 vetoes of public bills overridden, and a credible veto threat was one of the few bargaining chips that the Republican minority had on numerous pieces of legislation.

The bill would have permitted Chinese students who were in the United States at the time of the Tiananmen Square massacre in June 1989 to remain for an indeterminate period and to seek permanent resident status without returning to China. It also would have waived for four years a requirement that Chinese exchange students on "J" visas return home for at least two years before applying for permanent U.S. residency.

Bush vetoed the legislation Nov. 30, 1989, while Congress was in recess. The action was part of the administration's effort to restore cordial relations with China despite that country's repression of pro-democracy forces.

The Chinese government had threatened to permanently pull out of the Fulbright scholarship program and other education exchanges if HR 2712 became law. Bush originally said he considered his veto to be a pocket veto not subject to override by Congress, but did not press the issue when congressional leaders moved ahead with override votes; they argued that a pocket veto could occur only after the adjournment of a full Congress.

Administration officials said they were trying privately to persuade the government in Beijing to ease oppression. Bush had taken other steps to lessen U.S.-Chinese tensions, including sending U.S. officials to Beijing — a secret delegation in July 1989 and a public visit in December 1989 by national security adviser Brent Scowcroft.

Administration officials pointed to Beijing's lifting of martial law as a sign of human rights progress. But members of Congress were skeptical. Rep. Nancy Pelosi, D-Calif., sponsor of HR 2712, said: "Beijing can lift martial law because it does not need martial law to crush dissent.... I am confident the Congress will see through these feeble attempts by Chinese leaders to mislead Western governments."

Members who voted to uphold the veto denounced Chinese oppression, but said they believed Bush's behind-the-scenes efforts would do more to help democracy than would congressional action. The House vote to override, 390-25, came a day before the Senate vote.

2. Education

Two weeks after the Senate reconvened in 1990, Jesse Helms, R-N.C., tied up President Bush's education initiative for two days with complaints about a $25 million grant tacked on to the legislation (S 695) by Democrats. Though his amendment to delete the provision was defeated on Feb. 6, 35-64 (R 35-10; D 0-54; ND 0-37, SD 0-17), the same issue came back to kill the package on the last day of the 101st Congress.

The grant was to go to the National Board for Professional Teaching Standards, headed by former North Carolina Gov. James B. Hunt Jr., who had challenged Helms in 1984 for his Senate seat in a rancorous campaign.

The board, which was created in 1987 with funding from the Carnegie Corporation of New York and a number of other foundations, was drawing up guidelines for voluntary certification of teachers nationwide.

Helms charged that the board was dominated by teachers' unions, and he predicted that its voluntary certification guidelines would soon turn into mandatory licensing standards for teachers.

"The labor unions want to control education in America. No one else need apply," he said.

Proponents of the plan stressed that certification was not designed to take the place of state and local standards for teachers. "All we are trying to do is to retain the good teachers, attract new ones and provide some recognition for their accomplishments in what they are doing," said Christopher J. Dodd, D-Conn. Despite administration opposition to the grant, 10 Republicans joined Democrats to defeat the Helms amendment.

But at the end of the session, Helms had another chance. S 695 came back to the Senate in the form of HR 5932. The new bill included the president's education proposals plus literacy and teacher training provisions, and had been worked out with the House in an informal conference.

When Majority Leader George J. Mitchell, D-Maine, tried to call the bill up for a vote on Oct. 27, the last full day of the session, Helms and a number of other conservative Republicans objected. The group kept a rolling hold on the bill, with some objecting to a smaller, $10 million grant to the National Board, and with others objecting to different provisions.

In the end, Helms won his battle to kill the grant as well as the entire bill. In a campaign appearance in North Carolina, Helms boasted that he had saved taxpayers $800 million — the cost of the entire education package.

3. Clean Air

The environment lobby had been waiting years for a vote like this one — yes or no on a get-tough amendment to the most important antipollution bill (S 1630) in a decade. It seemed that such a vote would separate the black hats from the white hats, prove the movement's true strength in the Senate and provide campaign fodder for years to come.

For all the frantic lobbying beforehand, however, the outcome the week of March 19 was far from a definitive indication of the new environmental politics. Instead, it proved to be a pivotal show of strength for an unusual alliance: the Republican White House, which had introduced and backed clean air legislation for the first time in a decade, and Senate leaders of both parties, who had fashioned a compromise off the floor in the hope of winning passage for the first time since the Clean Air Act was last amended in 1977.

At stake was an amendment by Sens. Tim Wirth, D-Colo., and Pete Wilson, R-Calif. They wanted to make the bill's auto-emissions controls and clean-fuel provisions substantially tougher than the White House-leadership compromise.

Wirth and Wilson wanted to require an automatic, second round of tailpipe emissions reductions in 2002 — not a conditional review based on how much progress had been made, as called for in the White House compromise. They also wanted to require the use of cleaner burning gasoline mixes by 1993 in all smog-heavy areas — 60 to 70 in all — not just in the nine worst cities, as the compromise stipulated.

The Senate killed Wirth-Wilson, 52-46, on a motion to table: R 25-19; D 27-27 (ND 14-23; SD 13-4), March 20.

The result, however, appeared to be less a measure of environmentalist vs. industry muscle than of the unusual political alliances that formed around the Senate bill.

Farm-state members liked the Wirth-Wilson amendment because they believed it favored grain-based ethanol as an alternative clean fuel. Others went for it thinking it would help small businesses by shifting more of the pain of cleaning the air to big oil companies and car manufacturers.

Meanwhile, usually pro-environment senators voted against the amendment, fearing that it would scuttle the still-tenuous compromise with the Bush administration. Majority Leader George J. Mitchell, D-Maine, and his Republican counterpart, Bob Dole of Kansas, made the vote a test of the compromise's survival.

Much of the debate over Wirth-Wilson focused on whether it would indeed doom the bill's chances for yet another year. The environment lobby, dominated by purists, had made it clear that it did not think much of the Mitchell-Dole-White House compromise.

The Wirth-Wilson amendment was the group's main shot at shoring up the bill, so the lobby fought hard to counter the argument that it would harm its chances.

But many of their traditional allies remained swayed by Mitchell and voted with him to table the amendment. Voting to table were senators who usually voted the environmentalist position, including Democrats Christopher J. Dodd of Connecticut, Paul S. Sarbanes of Maryland and Howard M. Metzenbaum of Ohio, and Republican Gordon J. Humphrey of New Hampshire.

Then again, some usually pro-industry senators voted for the Wirth-Wilson amendment — at least one hoping that it would indeed become a "dealbuster."

Voting for Wirth-Wilson were Republicans who rarely toed the environment lobby's line, including Jesse Helms of North Carolina, James A. McClure and Steve Symms of Idaho, Jake Garn and Orrin G. Hatch of Utah, and Malcolm Wallop of Wyoming.

The defeat of Wirth-Wilson was followed the next day by another close vote on an amendment by Bob Kerrey, D-Neb., to toughen the urban smog provisions of the deal. It, too, was killed on a 53-46 tabling vote.

After those votes, the Senate compromise was able to survive all onslaughts — including another test in the attempt by Robert C. Byrd, D-W.Va., to ensure job-loss benefits for coal miners.

4. Job-Loss Benefits

Ostensibly, the two-week fight over Robert C. Byrd's amendment to the Senate clean air bill (S 1630) was over job-loss benefits for coal miners. The narrow defeat of the West Virginia Democrat's proposal, however, said little about the Senate's sympathy for miners thrown out of work by the bill: The chamber later approved a less ambitious House-crafted package as part of the final bill.

What the episode did show was the complex nature of power within the Senate. When the roll call was taken March 29, traditional liberal-conservative divisions broke down, and members were driven more by loyalty, fear and trickery.

The debate pitted Byrd's formidable force as chairman of the Appropriations Committee against Majority Leader George J. Mitchell of Maine, who had become inextricably linked in an alliance of convenience with the White House. The fight was the climax to Byrd's long struggle against a new clean air law. As the Democrats' leader before Mitchell, Byrd for years helped block such bills, knowing well that reducing acid rain would involve weaning the nation from West Virginia's high-sulfur coal.

Once Byrd stepped down from that post, he lost much of his power over the issue. President Bush was committed to signing a clear air bill so that he could become the "environmental president," and Mitchell had long advocated such legislation.

So Byrd made the best of the situation: He tried to extract a price from the bill's supporters in the form of hundreds of millions of dollars for his constituents.

A master of debate, Byrd spent hours on the floor pleading for support. "Have we looked into the eyes of a hungry coal miner's child?" he asked at one point. For days, few would publicly oppose him; he joked that he had been forced into negotiations with himself.

But the White House remained adamantly opposed, pointedly hinting that President Bush would veto the entire bill over Byrd's amendment. Mitchell fought it hard, but only to preserve a broad clean air deal with the White House; his sympathies clearly rested with Byrd on the need for unemployment benefits.

Byrd took advantage of Mitchell's dilemma. During a photo session the day before the vote, Byrd put his arm around a coal miner's son and said: "Sen. Mitchell is fighting for what he believes in, and I'm fighting for what I believe in."

Byrd had more than symbolic strength, however. His pockets were full of IOUs from 32 years in the Senate, and as the new chairman of the Appropriations Committee, he had plenty of future chits to hand out.

His office-to-office campaign served as a not-so-subtle reminder to his colleagues of what each had at stake in the fight. A large majority of his Democratic colleagues were too loyal or too afraid to vote against him, as were many Republicans. "Had I offered an amendment like this, I would not get five votes," said Republican leader Bob Dole of Kansas.

Minutes before the vote, it looked like Byrd might just win. Said Mitchell: "None of us like the choice we now face."

The White House, however, stole two of Byrd's votes, and thus victory, with a last-minute bit of apparent double-dealing.

During the roll call, Bush's chief of staff, John H. Sununu, assured Joseph R. Biden Jr., D-Del., that the president would veto the bill if Byrd won. Not wanting to scuttle the bill, Biden voted no. Earlier Sununu had told Steve Symms, R-Idaho, just the opposite — that Bush would not veto the whole bill just because he opposed the Byrd amendment.

Symms, convinced that the clean air bill was too expensive already, had been looking for a way to derail it. Assured that the Byrd amendment would not do the trick, he voted against making what he thought was a bad bill worse.

Byrd's amendment fell short by one vote, 49-50: R 11-34; D 38-16 (ND 29-9, SD 9-7).

5. Assault Weapons

Senate Democrats surprised themselves May 23 by gathering enough votes to preserve in an anticrime bill (S 1970) a ban on semiautomatic assault-style weapons. The vote temporarily snagged the bill in the Senate, and ultimately, Congress backed away from the controversial topics of gun control and the death penalty as it settled for a much less sweeping anticrime bill than it had planned.

The provision would have outlawed the manufacture, sale or possession of nine semiautomatic weapons, including the AK-47, used in a January 1989 schoolyard massacre in Stockton, Calif., that sparked an outcry over criminal use of semiautomatics. The gun control provision squeaked by the Senate Judiciary Committee in July 1989 on a 7-6 vote, largely because two usual opponents of gun control did not contest it.

The crime bill made it to the floor 10 months later, with President Bush on numerous occasions criticizing Congress for inaction. Gun control opponents tried to delete the assault-weapons ban, but their motion failed 48-52: R 36-9; D 12-43 (ND 5-33, SD 7-10). Two hours later, gun control advocates prevailed again as a motion to reconsider fell short, 49-50. Dennis DeConcini, D-Ariz., whose sponsorship of the gun ban had touched off a brief recall effort in Arizona, brought off the one-vote victory.

The Senate gun vote marked that chamber's biggest defeat for the National Rifle Association (NRA), which was known for its lobbying muscle and hefty campaign contributions. The NRA had been able to dissuade both chambers from voting for restrictions on handguns. But assault weapons were a different story, since they had come to be a symbol of the drug trade.

DeConcini was supported by a handful of Southern Democrats who had generally opposed gun control, including Lloyd Bentsen of Texas, David L. Boren of Oklahoma, Sam Nunn of Georgia and Al Gore of Tennessee. He also won the vote of Majority Leader George J. Mitchell of Maine, who came from a big sporting state and who had been quoted in the past as saying he did not believe in gun control.

The Senate did, however, reject an amendment by Howard M. Metzenbaum, D-Ohio, that would have permanently banned 12 more types of semiautomatic rifles and pistols and limited ammunition magazines to 15 rounds.

Gun control, opposed by most Republicans and the Bush administration, was one of the disputed items that hung up passage of a comprehensive anticrime bill. House conferees would not give up on racial protections for death penalty defendants, which the Senate had rejected. Senate conferees would not relinquish gun control. Both subjects were stripped from the final bill, paving the way for passage.

6. Flag Burning

Closing out a chapter that began a year earlier, the Senate on June 26 defeated a resolution (S J Res 332) for a constitutional amendment to protect the flag. The 58-42 vote was nine short of the two-thirds needed to pass the amendment: R 38-7; D 20-35 (ND 10-28, SD 10-7).

The resolution stated: "The Congress and the states shall have the power to prohibit the physical desecration of the flag of the United States."

It was a loss for President Bush, who had been pushing for an amendment to the Constitution since the Supreme Court first ruled on June 21, 1989, that a Texas law against flag burning infringed on First Amendment guarantees of free expression. A second Supreme Court ruling, on June 11, 1990, striking down a federal flag law, touched off the second round of political rhetoric on whether the flag needed special protection. But the second ruling sparked much less public outcry than the first, and that gave opponents of a constitutional amendment an edge.

Members against the amendment asserted that it was politically inspired and too radical a solution to the few flag-burning incidents that occurred. Some members thought defeat of the amendment would be used in the fall elections, since it had been mostly Republicans championing the constitutional amendment. But hardly a peep on the flag was heard.

The Senate had rejected a constitutional amendment to protect the flag a year earlier, after the first court ruling. As an alternative, Congress on Oct. 12, 1989, cleared the statute (HR 2978 — PL 101-131) to safeguard the flag from physical desecration; that was the law struck down by the high court in June.

The Senate's June 26 vote was superfluous because a week earlier the House had failed by 34 votes to gain the necessary two-thirds to pass the amendment. Approval by both chambers was needed to send an amendment to the states for ratification.

7. Americans with Disabilities Act

In contrast to the high-profile debates in 1990 over flag burning, pornographic art and the budget, Congress passed the Americans with Disabilities Act (ADA) with comparatively little fanfare. But while it was barely noticed by most of the general public, the sweeping civil rights measure would affect the lives of far more Americans than the 43 million with physical or mental disabilities.

The ADA (S 933) guaranteed to those with disabilities protections against discrimination in employment, public transit, public accommodations and telecommunications. It required employers to make "reasonable accommodations" needed by workers with disabilities, and business owners to make "readily achievable" changes to make facilities accessible to and usable by those with disabilities. It also required telecommunications companies to operate relay systems that allowed those with speech or hearing impairments to use the telephone.

Backed by candidate George Bush on the campaign trail in 1988 and by a bipartisan corps in Congress that included leaders of both parties from both chambers, there was never much doubt that the ADA would become law during the 101st Congress. But there were some tense moments for backers of the bill when progress was stalled temporarily over two relatively minor issues: how to include Congress as a covered entity and whether people with AIDS could be transferred out of food handling jobs.

Both issues were ultimately resolved by mid-July, with the House approving a second conference report on the measure by a vote of 377-28 on July 12. A day later, after a brief but emotional debate during which Orrin G. Hatch, R-Utah, broke down as he spoke of the courage with which his late brother-in-law battled polio, the Senate overwhelmingly cleared the measure by a vote of 91-6: R 37-6; D 54-0 (ND 37-0, SD 17-0). President Bush signed the bill (PL 101-336) on July 26 at a huge outdoor ceremony on the White House grounds.

8. Farm Price Supports

In the weeks leading up to Senate floor action on the 1990 farm bill in July, there was plenty of fierce politicking on the issue of farm price supports. Much of the action centered on supports for one crop, sugar. Sugar seemed to be emerging as a sacrificial lamb, the one crop subsidy program among the multitude that Congress might dare to cut — not so much to save money as to save face: Politically, the sugar program had become almost indefensible.

The opportunity came on an amendment by Bill Bradley, D-N.J., to the farm bill (S 2830) to cut the 18-cent sugar support price by 2 cents. Candy makers and soda companies had directed a steady barrage of invective at the program that guaranteed prices for sugar that were far above world market levels. They charged that it was protectionist and gouged consumers at home and some of our best and poorest allies abroad. Though by law it cost taxpayers nothing, it hurt consumers by artificially bolstering the price of sugar and hurt the nation's sugar-producing allies by preventing them from selling their main product in the United States.

The sugar industry countered that cutting the support price would be devastating, from the cane fields of Hawaii, Louisiana and Florida to the sugar beet and corn fields of the Midwest, all the way to the processing plants in New York, California and elsewhere.

For several months, the Bush administration had been flip-flopping, caught between its support for lifting "trade-distorting" subsidies around the world and the need to bolster the fortunes of Republican Senate candidates in states where the need for a high sugar price verged on gospel.

But before the vote on the Bradley amendment, all the signs suggested that it had a good chance of passing. Agriculture Secretary Clayton Yeutter had unequivocally endorsed it. So had Cargill, the giant Midwestern agribusiness company. That raised the possibility that farm-state lawmakers, who usually banded together to defeat assaults on individual programs, might split their votes.

In fact, the vote proved that the farm coalition remained powerful and mostly unified. The 2-cent cut was tabled, or killed, on July 24 by a vote of 54-44: R, 17-26; D, 37-18 (ND 22-16, SD 15-2).

Later that day, during debate on its version of the farm bill, the House also rebuffed a similar amendment, 150-271.

The Senate sugar vote foreshadowed what would occur throughout floor action on the farm bill. Amendments cutting or eliminating specific crop programs were repeatedly rejected, often by wide margins.

Many lawmakers said they realized that the budget would require deep cuts in farm programs, but they preferred to leave that responsibility in the hands of the budget summit negotiators.

9. Campaign Finance

Perhaps the most surprising thing about the Senate's July 30 vote on taxpayer financing of congressional campaigns was that it took place at all.

It was one of 17 roll call votes on amendments that, taken together, showed how far campaign finance legislation had come since the 100th Congress, when the action never advanced beyond a Republican filibuster.

But the results also showed how far there was to go before there was substantive change in the law.

The bill put before the Senate by the Democrats (S 137) sought to impose state-by-state spending limits on Senate races and eliminate political action committees (an idea borrowed from the GOP). But because spending limits had to be voluntary, the bill called for wide-ranging use of public monies to lure participation.

The incentives offered to participants included discounts on campaign mail; a voucher worth 20 percent of the spending limit for the state, to be used to purchase television time in blocks of one minute or more; and contingent public financing if an opposing candidate exceeded the spending limits. The cost to the Treasury was estimated at more than $56 million a year.

While proponents argued that this was a small price to pay for their vision of reform, opponents ridiculed the idea of asking taxpayers to pay for congressional elections in an era of $300 billion federal deficits.

Republicans opposed both spending limits and public financing. Kentucky Sen. Mitch McConnell, the Republican floor manager, argued that because the U.S. election system equated spending with free speech — an opinion expressed by the Supreme Court in its 1976 *Buckley v. Valeo* decision — the government would in effect punish candidates who chose to exercise their First Amendment rights, by giving money to their opponents. Republicans, moreover, were convinced that rigid spending limits would deter their efforts to retake the Senate.

McConnell moved to strip all forms of taxpayer financing from the bill. It was rejected 46-49: R 44-0; D 2-49 (ND 1-34, SD 1-15). The narrow, basically party-line defeat signaled that the Democrats would be in firm control of the debate.

But that partisan cast brought a firm veto threat from President Bush, and while the House also passed a bill, the two chambers never attempted to resolve the considerable differences between Democrats at different ends of the Capitol.

10. Abortion/Parental Notification

For several years, the conventional wisdom about the abortion debate held that while it was difficult to tell from opinion surveys how available most Americans thought the procedure should be, two issues regularly claimed large majorities. One was the question of abortion in cases of rape and incest, which both sides conceded was supported by a substantial majority of the public. The other was whether minors should have to notify or obtain consent from their parents before an abortion could be performed. On that question, too, supporters of abortion rights as well as abortion opponents agreed that the public favored some sort of parental notification. Thus, while rape and incest came to be viewed as the weakest issue for abortion opponents, parental notification was considered the Achilles' heel for abortion rights supporters.

Congress had voted often on providing federal funding in cases of rape and incest, and the House's shift in 1989 to support such funding signaled abortion rights gains in the backlash from the Supreme Court's decision in *Webster v. Reproductive Health Services*. That July 1989 decision gave states broader authority to restrict abortion than at any time since the court struck down state abortion bans in the 1973 *Roe v. Wade* decision.

By contrast, Congress had almost no track record on parental notification, an issue generally debated at the state level. Sen. William L. Armstrong, R-Colo., a leader of anti-abortion forces, made a first attempt to force votes on the issue Sept. 26 when he offered an amendment to a family planning reauthorization bill (S 110) that would require federally supported family planning agencies to notify a parent of a minor 48 hours before an abortion could be performed. But a roll call was muddied by the fact that it was tied to an unrelated amendment urging President Bush to tap the Strategic Petroleum Reserve. The amendment was eventually added to the bill by voice vote, but S 110 died the next day when it failed to achieve cloture to limit debate.

But the question was more clear-cut on Oct. 12, when Armstrong sought to append a similar amendment to the fiscal 1991 appropriations bill for the Departments of Labor, Health and Human Services (HHS), and Education (HR 5257). In contrast to the earlier vote, this time abortion rights supporters worked to defeat the amendment, and, to their surprise, they almost succeeded. It was added to the bill only after a motion by Labor-HHS Subcommittee Chairman Tom Harkin, D-Iowa, to table it failed on a 48-48 tie: R 8-34; D 40-14 (ND 31-6, SD 9-8).

In the end, the parental notification language and an amendment permitting abortion funding in cases of rape or incest, to which the notification amendment had been added, were both dropped to clear the bill.

Still, abortion rights supporters were buoyed by the strength of the vote on their weakest issue. And Congress might in the future be influenced further by the defeat Nov. 6 of a parental notification ballot proposal in Oregon. Even abortion rights supporters, who vehemently opposed the proposal, had expected it to pass.

11. U.S. Troops in Europe

The budget crunch and the dramatic improvement in U.S.-Soviet relations added high-octane fuel to the long-simmering congressional unhappiness over the cost of stationing U.S. forces overseas.

Since the mid-1970s, a growing coalition in Congress had argued that high Pentagon budgets were, in effect, subsidies for the United States' strongest commercial competitors, particularly Japan and Germany. The critics argued that countries protected by the U.S. shield could spend a smaller share of their national wealth on defense programs, making available more money for productive investments. Presidents of both parties had countered that overseas deployments directly serve U.S. security interests. But they also had pressed the major allies to begin picking up a larger share of the cost of alliance defense efforts.

In 1990, with the Soviet-led Warsaw Pact disintegrating and a treaty slashing the size of conventional forces in Europe (CFE) nearing completion, demands to bring home some of the 311,000 Army and Air Force personnel in Europe rose to a crescendo. The House and Senate each approved a provision in the fiscal 1991 defense authorization bill (HR 4739) to cut the overseas deployment by 50,000.

By the time the Senate took up the companion defense appropriations bill (HR 5803) on Oct. 15, critics had another grievance: the allies' paltry commitments to the U.S.-led deployments to the Persian Gulf to confront Iraq.

An amendment to the appropriations measure by Kent Conrad, D-N.D., would have sliced U.S. manpower in Europe by 80,000 — a reduction of 30,000 more than each chamber had approved.

It was only narrowly rejected, 46-50: R 8-34; D 38-16 (ND 31-6; SD 7-10).

Days later, in negotiations over the authorization measure, the 80,000-troop-cut was accepted by the administration for fear that even deeper cuts would win out. The final version of the appropriations bill settled on a cut of 78,600 personnel.

12. Stealth Bomber

The B-2 stealth bomber, designed to penetrate Soviet air defenses but controversial because of its cost, ran into more congressional flak during the year because of the declining Pentagon budget and the receding Soviet threat.

The plane's exotic materials and complex shape were intended to prevent an enemy from locating it with sufficient precision to shoot it down. But those factors also produced a price tag that was all too visible on the political battlefield — between $450 million and $850 million per copy, according to competing estimates.

For decades, liberals had challenged the need for bombers with sophisticated equipment designed to slip through Soviet defenses. The same missions could be performed more cheaply by small, long-range cruise missiles launched from planes flying beyond the reach of Soviet defenses, the critics argued.

Air Force leaders and congressional backers of the program contended that the B-2's hard-to-detect design would give U.S. forces a revolutionary advantage in conventional conflicts, as well as in a nuclear war. To get control of the program's soaring cost, the Pentagon in April cut the planned B-2 fleet from 132 planes to 75. But the argument that the plane simply cost too much, particularly in light of eased U.S.-Soviet relations, made significant headway, even among Senate and House Republicans.

In 1990, a bipartisan coalition persuaded the House to oppose building any more B-2s beyond the 15 planes funded in previous budgets. The Senate approved funds for two additional planes in fiscal 1991, and the two bodies wrestled the issue to an intentionally ambiguous draw: authorizing and appropriating more B-2 procurement money, but not specifying whether it could be used for anything more than unanticipated cost increases on the previously funded bombers.

Even in the Senate, where support for the B-2 had been stronger, opponents made a creditable showing, reaching their high-water mark on an amendment to the fiscal 1991 defense appropriations bill that would have halted B-2 production. The amendment, by Patrick J. Leahy, D-Vt., was rejected 44-50: R 9-32; D 35-18 (ND 30-7; SD 5-11).

13. Tax and Spending-Cut Package

The House vote to defeat the budget summit deal Oct. 5 deprived the Senate of a chance to weigh in on the most controversial aspect of the budget debate — not that many senators complained. Only two weeks later — after both chambers had given their committees the responsibility for ironing out the specifics of how to raise taxes and cut spending — did the Senate face a tough vote. *(House Key Vote 11, p. 18-B)*

The action came on a budget-reconciliation bill rolled together by the Senate Budget Committee after other committees had filled in the details of a bare-bones budget resolution. Again, the House had acted first.

Armed with their 83-vote majority, House Democrats ignored GOP complaints and passed a highly partisan Democratic alternative reconciliation bill that skewed tax increases heavily toward the wealthiest taxpayers. *(House Key Vote 14, p. 20-B)*

The narrower 10-vote Democratic margin in the Senate forced party leaders to temper their reconciliation bill from the start. After lengthy negotiations with GOP leaders and White House officials over the measure's tax and entitlement program components, Democratic leaders agreed to back a much more moderate reconciliation measure.

That put Senate Majority Leader George J. Mitchell, D-Maine, and other top Democrats on the defensive during floor debate — primarily against attacks from liberals in their own party.

Democratic senators made repeated attempts to amend the reconciliation bill to make it more like the one the House had passed, but Mitchell and Senate Budget Committee Chairman Jim Sasser, D-Tenn., had to fight each amendment on the grounds that it would violate their deal with Republican leaders and the White House, and thereby kill the bill.

They succeeded in killing proposals that appealed to Democrats, such as a proposal by Al Gore, D-Tenn., and Barbara A. Mikulski, D-Md., to raise taxes on the wealthy in order to cut back a proposed increase in the gasoline tax and eliminate proposed increases in payments by Medicare beneficiaries.

The debate stretched over three days, Oct. 17-19. When it came time for a vote on final passage shortly after 1 a.m. on Oct. 19, liberal Democrats had been unable to change it, and conservative Republicans, who were bitterly opposed to the package's broad new taxes, had been unable to kill it.

Leaders had agreed that both parties would provide a majority of their members in support of the package, and that took some doing. Some senators with tough re-election races wanted desperately to vote against the measure.

The measure went over the top only when GOP leaders persuaded two Republican senators to switch their no votes to yeses; others then followed.

In the end, the Senate approved the bill 54-46: R 23-22; D 31-24 (ND 20-18; SD 11-6).

The final package that President Bush signed looked more like the Senate bill than the House version.

14. El Salvador Aid

Few foreign policy issues had been more contentious during the past decade than military aid for El Salvador. Conservatives had argued that the support was essential to prevent left-wing guerrillas from taking over; liberals objected to the assistance because of the poor human rights record of the government in San Salvador.

Although the issue caused fierce ideological divisions, the Reagan and Bush administrations managed to win continued military assistance during the 1980s, thanks to backing in the Senate from Republicans and centrist Democrats. But that loose coalition fell apart in 1990, primarily because of the military's alleged role in yet another atrocity.

Senators from both parties agreed that the character of the issue changed substantially on Nov. 16, 1989, when six Jesuit priests and their two housekeepers were murdered. Eight soldiers were arrested after the execution-style slayings, and there were suspicions that high-ranking officers — including the head of military forces — had prior knowledge of the murders. A House task force concluded that the government botched its investigation of the case, and the House voted in May to cut U.S. aid by half. *(House Key Vote 1, p. 14-B)*

The murders and charges of a coverup resulted in a backlash against the Salvadoran military. That sentiment was bolstered by Congress' waning interest in Third World conflicts that had served as proxies for superpower rivalry during the Cold War.

The Senate followed the House in slashing aid Oct. 19, approving an immediate 50 percent cut in the $85 million military aid package for El Salvador by a vote of 74-25: R 19-25; D 55-0 (ND 38-0, SD 17-0).

The measure, an amendment to the foreign aid appropriations bill (HR 5114), was sponsored by Democratic Sens. Christopher J. Dodd, Conn., and Patrick J. Leahy, Vt. Support for the amendment crossed partisan and ideological lines.

Dodd said senators were "fed up" with El Salvador's continuing human rights abuses.

An administration-backed amendment aimed at weakening the Dodd-Leahy provision, offered by Bob Graham, D-Fla., was subsequently defeated, also by a wide margin (39-58).

President Bush initially had vowed to veto the foreign aid bill if it included restrictions on military aid, but the threat was eventually withdrawn, and he signed the bill.

15. Egyptian Debt

After Iraq's invasion of Kuwait on Aug. 2, the White House assiduously cultivated Arab backing for the U.N. embargo against the regime of Saddam Hussein and for the U.S. military buildup in the Persian Gulf.

Egypt was considered particularly crucial to the alliance. As a reward for its help and to relieve its economic burden, the White House decided to forgive $6.7 billion in military debts the Egyptian government owed.

The action triggered far more congressional criticism than the initial dispatch of 200,000 troops to the region. Lawmakers from both parties, while recognizing the unique contributions of President Hosni Mubarak's government to the multilateral coalition against Iraq, were concerned that it could set a precedent for debt forgiveness that would lead to new problems. Sen. Patrick J. Leahy, D-Vt., said, "If we grant relief to all of the nations that request it, the total cost could be $60 billion, $61 billion."

But Leahy, chairman of the Senate Appropriations Subcommittee on Foreign Operations, eventually supported the debt relief offer. He led successful opposition to an amendment by Sen. Tom Harkin, D-Iowa, that would have stricken the debt-relief provision from the foreign aid appropriations bill (HR 5114). On Oct. 19, the Harkin amendment was defeated 42-55: R 10-34; D 32-21 (ND 20-16, SD 12-5).

There was no up-or-down vote on the provision in the House because work on the foreign aid appropriations bill had been completed well before the Iraqi invasion. But intense opposition to the provision contributed to the narrow margin (188-162) by which the conference report on the final aid bill was passed by the House on Oct. 27.

16. Civil Rights

By a single vote, the Senate on Oct. 24 failed to override President Bush's veto of a sweeping civil rights bill (S 2104 — H Rept 101-856). The result was the first defeat of a major civil rights bill in the last quarter century.

The vote was 66-34: R 11-34; D 55-0 (ND 38-0, SD 17-0). Democratic sponsors complained that the administration was not honest in its months-long negotiations on the legislation and that Bush likely never intended to sign the measure, which would have made it easier to prove job discrimination.

The administration rejoined that the Hill sponsors wanted too much too fast and were unwilling to compromise. On the day of the override vote, black House members ringed the Senate floor, and in the gallery sat Jesse Jackson and, separately, David Duke, a failed Louisiana senatorial candidate and former Ku Klux Klan leader who had run against affirmative action.

The bill would have countered six 1989 Supreme Court rulings that narrowed the rights and remedies of victims of job discrimination. It also would have responded to four other court decisions from the 1980s by making it easier for lawyers for prevailing plaintiffs to recover costs and fees.

Unrelated to high court action, the bill would have amended Title VII of the 1964 Civil Rights Act to allow victims of intentional discrimination to recover compensatory damages and, in egregious cases, punitive damages. Title VII forbade racial, sex, religious and ethnic bias in the workplace. Title VII remedies were limited to back pay and benefits, attorneys' fees and court orders to correct discriminatory practices. The bill also would have allowed jury trials.

The arguments against the bill could be stated in one word: quotas.

Bush and business groups contended that the bill would cause companies to adopt hiring quotas for women and minorities so that they would not be subject to frivolous lawsuits based on the presence of a higher percentage of male or white workers.

That argument arose primarily from the centerpiece of the legislation, intended to reverse the court's June 1989 ruling in *Wards Cove Packing Co. v. Atonio.* The bill would have made it more difficult for an employer to justify in court job practices that were fair in form but that had an adverse impact on minorities or women. Examples of such practices were skill tests or physical requirements.

Key House Votes

1. El Salvador Aid

For Rep. Joe Moakley, D-Mass., chairman of the powerful Rules Committee and head of a House task force on El Salvador, tolerance for rights abuses perpetrated by the Salvadoran military reached a breaking point in 1990. "Enough is enough," said Moakley during the House debate on the fiscal 1990 foreign aid supplemental authorization bill (HR 4636).

His colleagues agreed and on May 22 approved a 50 percent cut in military aid to the government in San Salvador by adopting a Moakley amendment 250-163: R 31-135; D 219-28 (ND 166-4, SD 53-24). It was the first of several defeats for the administration on the issue, culminating in Senate passage Oct. 19 of an amendment to the fiscal 1991 foreign aid appropriations bill that also required a 50 percent aid cut. *(Senate Key Vote 14, p. 15-B)*

In a pattern later repeated in the Senate, liberal House opponents of the aid to El Salvador were able to enlist more moderate members — such as John P. Murtha, D-Pa., chairman of the Defense Appropriations Subcommittee — who in the past had been strong backers of the Salvadoran military. Murtha, a member of the Moakley task force, which traveled to El Salvador to investigate the 1989 murders of six Jesuit priests, cosponsored the measure to reduce the aid.

Still, it took some time for a consistent House position on the issue to jell. On May 24, with the El Salvador aid as only one of the issues in dispute, the House voted down the foreign aid bill to which the language sponsored by Moakley and Murtha was attached. But by June, when the House considered the fiscal 1991 foreign aid appropriations bill (HR 5114), support for a 50 percent aid cut had solidified. The bill including the aid cut passed the House, and eventually the Senate, by a wide margin.

As it turned out, David R. Obey, D-Wis., chairman of the Appropriations Subcommittee on Foreign Operations, was prescient in characterizing the May 22 action. "That's the position of the House," said Obey; it was essentially the position that later became law.

2. Job-Loss Benefits

Most of the battles on the clean air package in 1990 were fought along regional rather than partisan lines. But one debate sent the parties scrambling back to their corners: Whether to provide job-loss relief for workers displaced by the new law.

House Democrats, spurning White House veto threats, approved such a measure by a wide margin May 23. In doing so, West Virginia Democrat Bob Wise achieved what his powerful Senate counterpart, Robert C. Byrd, could not.

Wise, along with cosponsors Tom Ridge, R-Pa., and Thomas J. Downey, D-N.Y., patterned his amendment after similar relief available to U.S. workers under the Trade Adjustment Assistance Act. The amendment offered 26 additional weeks of unemployment and retraining benefits to workers who could show that the clean air law was "an important contributing factor" to their job loss. It authorized $250 million in funding over five years.

The Senate barely rejected a similar but more expensive program on a 49-50 vote March 29, marking a rare defeat for Appropriations Chairman Byrd, who — like Wise — was trying to help coal miners in his state. *(Senate Key Vote 4, p. 14-B)*

But part of the appeal of the Wise amendment was its application to workers in all fields and geographic regions, while Byrd's $500 million plan offered aid only to coal miners.

House Democrats pushed the amendment through on a vote of

274-146: R 43-126; D 231-20 (ND 169-2, SD 62-18).

Still, administration threats to veto the entire bill over the provision remained. President Bush argued that it would become an open-ended entitlement that would cost far more than $250 million. And though it was unclear whether Senate conferees would abandon their previous pact with the White House and go along with a compromise job-loss provision, Wise never took the veto threat seriously: "I can't believe the president's going to veto the environmental bill of the decade over $50 million a year."

Wise was right. The amendment was modified in conference — with help from the administration — to address Bush's concerns. Instead of continuing mandatory benefits, conferees agreed to a $250 million needs-based program that would be administered through the Job Training Partnership Act. Qualified displaced workers would be guaranteed cash supplemental payments after their unemployment assistance ran out as long as they remained in a job-retraining program.

3. Clean Air

For a decade, clean air bills were stalled in Congress. But when a package (HR 3030) finally made it to the House floor May 23, members approved the sweeping rewrite of the antipollution law by an overwhelming 401-21 vote: R 154-16; D 247-5 (ND 169-4; SD 78-1). The vote, which followed only two days of largely nonpartisan debate, demonstrated what environmentalists had long maintained: They had the support they needed on the floor, if only a bill could be navigated through key committee obstructionists — in particular, auto industry ally John D. Dingell, D-Mich. As chairman of the House Energy and Commerce Committee, Dingell for years had blocked a series of earlier bills that would have placed new controls on automobiles and smokestacks.

This time, however, the Energy Committee had produced so many agreements on so many divisive issues that the rest of the House was given only a handful of choices to make before final passage. The long-awaited floor showdown that some lobbyists had promoted as the environmental vote of the decade looked at times like a bipartisan love-in, with members clamoring to take credit for a series of compromise amendments, most of which passed on overwhelming votes.

In the end, the vote on final passage locked in the legislation's major components as the bill entered the next stage — grueling conference negotiations with the Senate — which ended barely in time for a bill to be sent to President Bush's desk before Congress adjourned. Dingell, Henry A. Waxman, D-Calif., the main House advocate of clean air legislation, and Norman F. Lent, N.Y., the ranking Republican on Energy and Commerce, were committed to standing by many parts of the House bill through conference with the Senate, unless all three could agree on a compromise.

House conferees did spend much of their time renegotiating parts of their bill to make it less burdensome on businesses; although pro-environment conferees had the leverage of a strong floor vote, pro-industry conferees had the clock on their side.

Oddly, the soundness of House floor support may have done more to bolster the position of Senate conferees, most of whom supported a stronger clean air rewrite than the bill (S 1630) that passed their chamber. Senate conferees, led by Majority Leader George J. Mitchell, D-Maine, had been forced to strike a deal with the White House, watering down the legislation to get it past strident Senate opposition.

Once in conference, however, Senate negotiators felt free to abandon the White House deal and give in to House-passed language in important areas, opting, for example, to recede entirely to the House's tougher antismog provisions.

4. Flag Burning

An early-strike strategy by House opponents of a constitutional amedment to protect the U.S. flag led to a June 21 defeat of the proposed amendment (H J Res 350). The opponents had contended in this politically charged debate that the First Amendment and the Bill of Rights needed more protection than the flag.

The 254-177 vote fell 34 short of the two-thirds necessary for passage: R 159-17; D 95-160 (ND 43-130, SD 52-30).

The resolution stated: "The Congress and the states shall have the power to prohibit the physical desecration of the flag of the United States."

The amendment was proposed after the Supreme Court on June 11 struck down a federal statute that made it illegal to burn, mutilate or otherwise desecrate the flag. As the court had ruled in 1989 on a Texas flag-burning statute, the majority said protesters who burned the U.S. flag were protected by the First Amendment right to free speech.

Supporters of an amendment to reverse the court believed that public sentiment was on their side. But they failed to organize outside interest groups, such as veterans, to write and call members of Congress. At the same time, foes of a flag amendment had spent months putting in place an opposition strategy, anticipating the court's decision to strike down the statute.

Democrats suggested that Republicans were trying to stir up pre-election defensiveness, just as George Bush had challenged Democratic nominee Michael S. Dukakis' patriotism during the 1988 presidential campaign. They used the Bill of Rights as both a legal argument and a symbol, trying to defuse those who argued that support for the flag was a test of patriotism. House Speaker Thomas S. Foley of Washington, who had led opposition to the constitutional amendment, made a rare floor appearance to close debate. In the end, the House vote on the amendment wasn't even close to the two-thirds necessary, and the issue was not a major factor in the fall elections.

5. Family and Medical Leave

"We shall override, someday," vowed Patricia Schroeder, D-Colo., of legislation vetoed by President Bush that would have required employers to grant unpaid leave to workers caring for newborn children or sick relatives.

That day was not July 25, when the House by a wide, 54-vote margin failed to revive the family and medical leave bill (HR 770). Indeed, Schroeder's wistful pledge seemed aimed not only at family leave — it also spoke of Democrats' frustration at being unable to override any of the Bush presidency's vetoes.

The legislation would have protected jobs for workers who took up to 12 weeks of unpaid leave to care for a newborn, adopted or ill child at no cost to the employee. It also would have covered time off for personal medical emergencies, including caring for family members. The bill would have applied only to businesses with 50 or more employees.

Sponsors argued that federal minimum requirements were needed to bring U.S. businesses in line with the changing workplace, with about 60 percent of mothers working outside the home. They also said the United States was virtually alone among industrialized nations in lacking a national family and medical leave policy, though opponents said employees were forced to pay into mandatory leave benefit plans in many other countries.

Bush, in vetoing the bill June 29, said he supported the concept of parental and medical leave but believed such arrangements should be decided in labor-management negotiations.

Despite heavy lobbying, Democrats found the goal of getting a two-thirds vote in the House insurmountable. In fact, sponsors lost eight votes from when the bill was passed by the chamber May 10. The override attempt was rejected 232-195: R 38-138; D 194-57 (ND 156-14, SD 38-43).

Democrats howled that Bush was falling short on a campaign promise to support families. But with 57 Democrats sustaining the veto, Bush could not be held solely accountable. Election-year pressure by business groups opposing the bill swayed more than a few votes.

But Bush's seeming invincibility and popularity over the summer also helped him trounce Democrats resoundingly in their own back yard.

6. Farm Programs

If there was an underlying theme to the 1990 farm bill, it was class warfare. Rich, successful farmers found themselves scorned as "fat cats" who were milking the taxpayer for millions of dollars. Pitted against them were the poorer farmers who produced less of the nation's food and received less of its subsidy bounty. Conflict was inevitable because the budget crisis meant that for the first time in years, farmers would be getting less, not more, government aid. The matter came to a head July 26, when the House debated an amendment to the farm bill (HR 3950) that would have denied crop subsidies to farmers with gross adjusted incomes of more than $100,000 a year. The four-hour debate on the amendment cut to the philosophical underpinnings of farm programs.

The amendment was the handiwork of Charles E. Schumer, D-N.Y., and Dick Armey, R-Texas, the leaders of a coalition of urban liberals who disliked farm subsidies going to a few farmers while programs for the poor had been under pressure, and of Republican conservatives, who clung to a hope of a free market farm sector.

Farm-state lawmakers saw the amendment as a strike at the heart of the program. Having wealthy farmers with large operations in the program was desirable, they argued, because it gave the government more control over those who produced most of the nation's food, and thus over prices and supply. Kick out those affluent farmers, they argued, and the government would have a tougher time keeping food prices stable.

Critics had long contended that the farm program was inequitable, but they had little success in changing it. With the budget crisis, however, 1990 seemed different. Armey and Schumer argued that, in addition to correcting the inequities of the farm program, their amendment would save the government money. In effect, their proposal would convert farm subsidies into a more explicit welfare program for needy farmers.

However, farm-state lawmakers had an alternative: Instead of soaking the rich, they proposed reducing every farmer's subsidy check. In the end, the alternative proved more acceptable. The amendment was defeated 159-263: R 66-109; D 93-154 (ND 85-82, SD 8-72).

7. Ethics Reprimand

Buffeted by a yearlong string of scandals, the House navigated unusually partisan, emotional waters when it debated how harshly to punish Barney Frank, D-Mass., for improperly using his office to help a male prostitute.

The debate came at a time when many politicians were evincing election-year jitters about Congress' scandal-scarred image. The drama of floor debate centered on whether nervous incumbents would go along with the recommendation of the House ethics committee to reprimand Frank or impose the stiffer sanction of censuring him.

The key vote came when the House on July 26 rejected a Republican motion to censure Frank 141-287: R 129-46; D 12-241 (ND 1-171, SD 11-70); clearing the way for overwhelming approval of a reprimand.

Frank's case was the most publicized of several congressional sex scandals of 1990. After investigating of allegations that first surfaced in The Washington Times in August 1989, the ethics committee concluded that Frank "reflected discredit upon the House" by writing a misleading memorandum in behalf of Steve Gobie, a male prostitute with whom Frank associated in 1985-87, and by improperly using his status as a congressman to fix 33 parking tickets. However, the committee found no conclusive evidence to back up allegations that Frank knew Gobie was running a prostitution service out of the congressman's apartment.

Frank did not contest the committee's recommendation that he be reprimanded. The motion to increase the punishment to censure was offered by House GOP Whip Newt Gingrich of Georgia, who had instigated the 1989 ethics inquiry that led to the resignation of House Speaker Jim Wright of Texas.

The voting breakdown on the censure motion showed how partisan the ethics issue had become, especially in Frank's case. Disciplinary votes usually did not break down along party lines. But the ethics committee itself, before deciding to recommend a reprimand, had been riven by unusually deep partisan divisions over how far to go. Although the committee's recommendation had been approved unanimously, three Republican committee members voted for censure on the floor.

Solid Democratic opposition to the censure motion was, in part, a measure of Democrats' deep hostility toward Gingrich. Many resented his role in the Wright affair and were irritated that he was criticizing the same ethics committee that he had praised earlier in the year for clearing his own name.

In the end, ethics committee Chairman Julian C. Dixon, D-Calif., depicted the censure vote as a referendum on the ethics panel itself. He portrayed it as a choice between a unanimous, bipartisan committee that had studied the case for almost a year and GOP demagogues who would throw their colleagues to the wolves. Said Dixon, "This case boils down to, really, who do you trust?"

8. Strategic Defense Initiative

Congress continued its persistent effort to reorient and reduce long-term funding for the strategic defense initiative (SDI), the antimissile defense program launched in 1983 by President Ronald Reagan.

The sweeping rhetoric Reagan used in promoting the program — offering the potential to make nuclear missiles "impotent and obsolete" — had long since been supplanted by the more modest goal of deploying by the end of the 1990s a network of space-based missiles that could protect the U.S. nuclear deterrent against a Soviet first strike.

But in 1990, both the revised goal and President Bush's $4.7 billion SDI funding request for fiscal 1991 were wanting in congressional support.

Following the Senate's lead, the final defense authorization bill included provisions intended to reduce funding for the planned network of space-based missiles while increasing funding for two other kinds of missile defenses: ground-based antimissile interceptors that could head off a small attack or a few accidentally launched missiles; and lasers and other futuristic weapons that might in the next century begin to realize Reagan's grander vision.

Congress also slashed the SDI funding request to $2.89 billion — a compromise between the $3.57 billion authorized by the Senate and the $2.3 billion authorized by the House. The House accepted that figure in an amendment sponsored by Charles E. Bennett, D-Fla., and Tom Ridge, R-Pa., which was adopted by 225-189: R 20-150; D 205-39 (ND 157-7; SD 48-32).

9. Abortion at Military Facilities

The Supreme Court's 1989 decision in *Webster v. Reproductive Health Services*, which gave states new latitude to restrict access to abortion, galvanized abortion rights forces in the country and on Capitol Hill. But abortion rights supporters, while enjoying considerable success in Congress that year on abortion-related issues, were unable to alter policy because they could not muster majorities large enough to override four Bush vetoes.

By 1990, abortion rights backers were looking for new issues on which they might be able to roll back some of the myriad federal restrictions that had cropped up in the years since abortion was legalized nationwide by the Supreme Court's 1973 *Roe v. Wade* decision.

The one they ultimately set out to overturn was a 1988 Defense Department directive forbidding abortions in overseas military facilities, even if the woman paid for the procedure herself.

The first test came in the Senate on Aug. 3, where Tim Wirth, D-Colo., tried to add the amendment overturning the ban to the defense authorization bill (S 2884). Sponsors mustered a majority but fell two votes short of the 60 needed to stop a filibuster.

By the time the issue got to the House, debate had sharpened.

Supporters painted the issue as a vote on simply ensuring access to abortion services for members of the military and their dependents. But opponents portrayed it as a vote for "abortion on demand," which they said would lead to abortions of fetuses potentially able to live outside the womb or for sex selection.

That argument carried the day; an amendment similar to the Senate proposal, offered by Vic Fazio, D-Calif., could not even muster a majority, failing Sept. 18 by 200-216: R 35-139; D 165-77 (ND 113-50, SD 52-27).

10. Immigration

The House on Oct. 3 voted to increase immigration by more than 60 percent and offer amnesty, under certain conditions, to thousands of people living in the United States illegally.

The generous House bill (HR 4300) set the stage for negotiations with the Senate, which had passed a less-sweeping bill (S 358) in July 1989. The compromise that was cleared for the president did not open the door as wide as the House bill would have. But the House's position forced the Senate to broaden its approach toward the numbers and types of immigrants allowed in.

The House legislation passed 231-192: R 45-127; D 186-65 (ND 159-13, SD 27-52). The administration had opposed the measure largely because of its country-specific amnesty and huge increases in visa levels.

The broad purpose of the legislation — and that of the bill that cleared — was to bring in more specially trained workers and increase immigration from countries adversely affected under the existing visa allotment system that favored Latin Americans and Asians. The House bill differed from the Senate legislation beyond sheer numbers. It would have allowed a stay of deportation for illegal immigrants from El Salvador, Lebanon, Liberia and Kuwait. It would have granted more visas to spouses and unmarried minor children of lawful permanent residents under the terms similar to those for immediate relatives of U.S. citizens.

It also would have been more generous in barring deportation of children and spouses of foreigners who were legalized under the 1986 Immigration Reform and Control Act. The children and spouses did not have visas.

During House floor debate, members beat back several attempts to decrease the number of new visas in the bill. The issue divided members who argued that a generous immigration policy was a good thing for reuniting families, adding diversity to the population and building the talent pool, and those who said the government should discourage foreigners and concentrate its money on essential services for U.S.-born.

John Bryant, D-Texas, protested, "We have a shortage of jobs and training, not a shortage of people."

His point of view did not prevail on the House floor or in conference. Under the measure cleared Oct. 27, legal immigration was raised from about 500,000 annually to about 700,000 during each of the first three years of the act. After that, a permanent level of 675,000 would be set. The only country-specific amnesty that remained in the bill was an 18-month stay of deportation for people from El Salvador living in the United States illegally.

11. Budget Summit Agreement

In one of 1990's most dramatic congressional votes, House leaders unsure of their vote counts rolled the dice at 1 a.m. Oct. 5 in a last-ditch attempt to save a budget deal produced by nearly five months of increasingly desperate negotiations between Congress and the Bush administration. When White House and congressional leaders announced the package Sept. 30, they hoped that the pressure of automatic budget cuts threatened by the Gramm-Rudman deficit-reduction law would bring members into line. But five days later, with the House in open rebellion and support for the budget package fading by the minute, leaders felt they had little choice but to gamble. They lost. In a stunning rebuke of President Bush and House leaders of both parties, the House refused to adopt the conference report on the budget resolution 179-254: R 71-105; D 108-149 (ND 63-111, SD 45-38).

The defeat of the budget deal meant that Congress was held hostage in Washington for another three weeks of negotiations — the longest election-year session since World War II — before Congress adopted a final budget-reconciliation package Oct. 27.

By the time of the Oct. 5 vote, many House members felt they had already been prisoners of the budget wars since the talks began in mid-May. Some blamed the defeat on the package's most politically odious components: new taxes and cuts in safety net programs such as Medicare. But others said it was at least in part an angry backlash by members frustrated at having been left out as an elite corps of congressional and White House officials negotiated behind closed doors, only to hand the rank and file a tough, take-it-or-leave-it package just weeks before the fall elections.

The process began in early May when President Bush, driven by fear that the economy would collapse on his watch, agreed to convene a no-preconditions budget summit with congressional leaders. When the talks threatened to stall in June, he abandoned his no-new-taxes pledge to get the negotiations started again.

That shifted the terms of the debate from whether to tax to whom to tax, and how much. Democrats who had been on the defensive over taxes for the decade since Ronald Reagan became president suddenly found themselves making political headway with the "fairness" issue. When Republicans demanded a cut in the capital gains tax to stimulate a dangerously weakening economy, Democrats countered that the cut would be a sop to rich taxpayers that would have little or no effect on the nation's economic health. Instead, they insisted on a hike in the top tax rate for the wealthiest taxpayers.

When it became clear that the budget summit deal would include substantial new taxes, negotiator and House Minority Whip Newt Gingrich of Georgia jumped ship and declared war on the process. When the deal itself was announced Sept. 30, Gingrich refused to attend the Rose Garden ceremony where Bush and congressional leaders said they would support it despite disliking it. Gingrich's defection was an omen.

Backers of the budget deal spent the week furiously lobbying Congress. Early indications were that the Senate would go along but that the package was in trouble in the House. Bush himself went on television to ask for national support, but that only appeared to generate more phone calls to congressional offices against the package. With a stopgap spending bill set to run out at midnight Oct. 5, the House had to vote on the deal less than a week after it was unveiled.

There had long been an understanding that both parties would have to produce a majority of their members to support the package on the floor, but a significant bloc of conservative Republicans had solidified around Gingrich in opposition, and when it became clear that the GOP would not produce its votes, Democrats deserted in droves as well. Ultimately, the deal was done in by a rare alliance between conservative Republicans and liberal Democrats. The Republicans hated the taxes, and the Democrats hated the cuts in Medicare and other programs.

After three more weeks of negotiations, the final budget deal still had both taxes and safety-net cuts, but each in either smaller quantities or more politically palatable forms.

12. Textile Quotas

It had become routine for Congress to send bills to the president mandating stiff new quotas on textile, apparel and shoe imports in an effort to shore up domestic producers. It was just as routine for him to veto those bills and for the House to fail to override the veto by a narrow margin.

It happened in 1986, in 1988 and again in 1990. The show of support for the nation's textile industry had barely wavered on Capitol Hill. But that fact, quota supporters said, was important for the long-term survival of the domestic industry.

Textile-quota bills also had been altered somewhat over time in an effort to pick up votes; the 1990 version would have allowed textile and apparel imports to grow by 1 percent annually, and shoe imports would have been frozen permanently at 1989 levels. It also would have given incentives to countries that purchased U.S. farm goods.

Critics said stiff quotas were needed to preserve a shrinking domestic manufacturing base, while opponents argued that a constricted supply would drive up prices for consumers. Besides, they said, the domestic textile industry had never been healthier. Apparel makers, but not their unions, opposed the quota measure.

Although the House had come up a few votes short of overriding the president's veto each time, 1990 was the first time either chamber summoned more than a two-thirds majority for a textile-quota bill. In July, the Senate had passed the measure (HR 4328) by 68-32, and opponents feared for the first time that there might be enough congressional support for the measure to ram it through.

But Oct. 10, when the vetoed bill was returned to the House floor for an override attempt, history repeated itself. Supporters could not quite muster the required two-thirds majority — falling 10 votes short — and the override effort failed 275-152: R 70-103; D 205-49 (ND 131-41; SD 74-8).

Quota supporter Ed Jenkins, D-Ga., said he was not surprised at the outcome. But neither was he completely disheartened. He and others said it was important that congressional support for quotas remained strong because international trade negotiators meeting in Geneva and Brussels, Belgium, were hoping to make major changes in the General Agreement on Tariffs and Trade before the end of 1990. A central element of those talks was the proposal to phase out an existing scheme of negotiated bilateral textile and apparel quotas. Third World suppliers of textiles in particular wanted an end to restrictions on textile trade.

Any such trade agreement would have to be submitted to Congress for approval before it could take effect. And Jenkins said after the override attempt failed that if a new trade agreement was reached that would put an end to the existing quota regime, it was clear that Congress would refuse to support it.

13. Obscenity Debate

A year after Congress restricted the National Endowment for the Arts (NEA) from funding works that could be considered obscene, sadomasochistic or homoerotic, lawmakers pulled back. The House on Oct. 11 chose to drop the restrictions in favor of a substitute by Pat Williams, D-Mont., and E. Thomas Coleman, R-Mo., by a vote of 382-42: R 142-31; D 240-11 (ND 160-11, SD 80-0).

The House's lopsided vote marked a turning of the tide in favor of artistic freedom over the concerns of the religious right.

Approval of the Williams-Coleman language, as an amendment to a bill to reauthorize the NEA (HR 4825), followed months of stalemate among arts advocates who wanted to preserve the endowment without any restrictions, moderate Republicans who wanted to include language opposing obscenity and conservatives who wanted to abolish the agency.

The impetus for the compromise between Williams and Coleman was a 15-1 vote in the Senate Labor and Human Resources Committee to reauthorize the arts endowment while leaving the courts to decide what was obscene. Similar to the Senate language, the Williams-Coleman substitute dropped the existing restrictions and placed the onus on courts to determine questions of obscenity.

If an artist was convicted of violating obscenity standards, the NEA could order him or her to return the federal money. In a nod to the right, the substitute included language drafted by Paul B. Henry, R-Mich., stating that although artistic excellence was the standard by which grant applications were judged, "general standards of decency and respect for the diverse beliefs and values of the American public" should be taken into account.

The only serious opposition to the amendment came from Dana Rohrabacher, R-Calif., and a few other conservatives. Rohrabacher offered an amendment containing a series of restrictions aimed at curbing obscenity, blasphemy, flag desecration and racism in NEA-funded projects.

But Amo Houghton, R-N.Y., called Rohrabacher's effort to further restrict the NEA "a ruse" designed to gut federal arts spending. The House agreed, rejecting Rohrabacher's amendment, 175-249, before approving the Williams-Coleman language.

Ultimately, the House plan was adopted in conference on the fiscal 1991 Interior appropriations bill (HR 5769 — PL 101-512), which funded the NEA.

14. Tax and Spending-Cut Package

For much of the year, Democratic congressional leaders worked with their Republican counterparts and White House officials to craft a budget deal that could win majority support from both sides of the aisle. But after the House on Oct. 5 overwhelmingly rejected the best compromise leaders could strike, Democrats decided it was time to take a more partisan tack.

Bowing to pressure from rank-and-file members — most of whom had been shut out of the high-level budget deliberations — House leaders agreed to allow a largely political Democratic alternative to be offered as a floor amendment to the fiscal 1991 reconciliation bill (HR 5835). The alternative did what many Democrats had clamored for throughout the year but which leaders had discouraged because of the ongoing negotiations with the White House.

The package, drafted by Ways and Means Committee Democrats, shifted a much larger share of the tax burden onto the wealthy and made smaller spending cuts in Medicare and other social programs. In short, it did everything President Bush opposed in the budget talks. It raised the top rate for the wealthiest taxpayers from 28 percent to 33 percent and imposed a 10 percent surtax on millionaires. It called for a capital gains tax break but only for the middle class, and it reduced proposed Medicare savings from $60 billion to $43 billion.

As expected, support for the Democratic alternative split along party lines. The amendment was adopted Oct. 16 by a vote of 238-192: R 10-164; D 228-28 (ND 157-16, SD 71-12). The package helped refocus the tax debate from one concerning how much revenue should be raised to one concerning who should pay, and its passage in the House forced conferees to shape a final reconciliation bill much more to Democrats' liking. *(Senate Key Vote 13, p. 15-B)*

15. Civil Rights

The House voted Oct. 16 to pass a comprehensive civil rights measure, but the vote was 12 short of what would have been needed to override a veto. And, ultimately, it was a veto by President Bush that killed the bill aimed at making it easier for workers to sue and win awards for discrimination.

The House passed the legislation (S 2104 — H Rept 101-755) by a vote of 273-154: R 34-139; D 239-15 (ND 169-3, SD 70-12). The veto override attempt failed in the Senate by a single vote, so it never came back to the House. *(Senate Key Vote 16, p. 15-B)*

The bill would have countered six 1989 Supreme Court rulings that narrowed the rights and remedies of victims of job discrimination. In response to four other court decisions from the 1980s, it would have given lawyers a greater chance to obtain costs and fees.

The legislation also would have amended Title VII of the 1964 Civil Rights Act to allow victims of intentional discrimination to recover compensatory damages and, in egregious cases, punitive damages. Under current law, Title VII remedies were limited to back pay and benefits, attorneys' fees and court orders to stop discriminatory practices. The bill also would have allowed jury trials for discrimination victims.

Civil rights advocates and labor groups said the legislation was needed to protect workers from bias. The administration and business argued, however, that its pro-employee slant would have opened the door for frivolous lawsuits and led to quota hiring by employers trying to protect themselves.

16. Aid to Angolan Rebels

President Ronald Reagan had terrific problems persuading Congress to view the Nicaraguan contras as "freedom fighters," but he had a far easier time obtaining support for covert assistance to antigovernment rebels in Angola.

For years, a broad coalition of lawmakers, including a substantial number of Democrats, backed secret military assistance for the rebels, who were led by the public-relations savvy Jonas Savimbi.

But the argument in favor of such programs was far more convincing for many lawmakers when the Soviet Union was aggressively funding communist regimes in the Third World. With the Cold War ending and the Soviets less interested in fueling regional conflicts, support for anticommunist movements such as Savimbi's waned.

In October, the House approved tough new restrictions on aid for the National Union for the Total Independence of Angola (UNITA) rebels as part of its fiscal 1991 intelligence authorization bill (HR 5422). While the complicated conditions ultimately were eased somewhat by a House-Senate conference committee, the House vote demonstrated growing congressional skepticism toward large-scale secret programs.

The Angola restrictions, sponsored by Stephen J. Solarz, D-N.Y., a member of the Intelligence Committee, passed Oct. 17 by one vote: Speaker Thomas S. Foley, D-Wash., was called on to cast the deciding vote to approve the Solarz amendment 207-206: R 12-156; D 195-50 (ND 158-10, SD 37-40).

Given the razor-thin margin of passage, the administration was confident that the provision would be dropped in conference.

The Senate, in its consideration of the intelligence bill, attached only minor conditions on aid for UNITA. But the conference committee approved language by Solarz withholding half of the military aid for UNITA until congressional intelligence committees approved its release. Solarz termed that a "remarkable victory." The rebels reportedly received about $60 million a year from the United States, about half in military aid.

	1	2	3	4	5	6	7	8
ALABAMA								
Heflin	Y	N	Y	Y	Y	Y	Y	Y
Shelby	Y	N	Y	Y	Y	Y	Y	Y
ALASKA								
Murkowski	N	Y	Y	N	Y	Y	Y	N
Stevens	N	Y	?	Y	Y	Y	Y	Y
ARIZONA								
DeConcini	Y	N	N	Y	N	Y	Y	Y
McCain	N	Y	N	N	Y	Y	Y	N
ARKANSAS								
Bumpers	Y	N	Y	Y	N	N	Y	Y
Pryor	Y	N	Y	N	N	N	Y	Y
CALIFORNIA								
Cranston	Y	N	N	Y	N	N	Y	Y
Wilson	Y	Y	N	N	N	Y	Y	Y
COLORADO								
Wirth	Y	N	N	Y	N	N	Y	Y
Armstrong	Y	Y	N	N	Y	Y	Y	N
CONNECTICUT								
Dodd	Y	N	Y	N	N	N	Y	Y
Lieberman	Y	N	N	Y	N	N	Y	N
DELAWARE								
Biden	Y	N	Y	N	N	N	Y	N
Roth	N	N	N	N	Y	Y	Y	N
FLORIDA								
Graham	Y	N	N	N	N	Y	Y	Y
Mack	N	Y	Y	N	Y	Y	Y	Y
GEORGIA								
Fowler	Y	N	N	N	N	Y	Y	Y
Nunn	Y	N	N	N	N	Y	Y	N
HAWAII								
Inouye	Y	N	Y	Y	N	N	Y	Y
Akaka †					N	N	Y	Y
IDAHO								
McClure	N	Y	N	Y	Y	Y	?	Y
Symms	N	Y	N	N	Y	Y	N	Y
ILLINOIS								
Dixon	Y	N	Y	Y	N	Y	Y	Y
Simon	Y	N	N	Y	N	N	Y	Y
INDIANA								
Coats	N	Y	Y	Y	Y	Y	Y	N
Lugar	N	Y	Y	N	Y	Y	Y	N
IOWA								
Harkin	Y	N	N	Y	N	N	Y	Y
Grassley	N	Y	Y	Y	Y	Y	Y	N
KANSAS								
Dole	N	Y	Y	N	N	Y	Y	N
Kassebaum	N	Y	N	N	N	Y	Y	N
KENTUCKY								
Ford	Y	N	Y	Y	Y	Y	Y	Y
McConnell	N	Y	Y	Y	Y	Y	Y	N
LOUISIANA								
Breaux	?	N	Y	N	Y	Y	Y	Y
Johnston	Y	N	Y	+	Y	Y	Y	Y
MAINE								
Mitchell	Y	N	Y	N	N	N	Y	N
Cohen	Y	N	N	N	Y	Y	Y	N
MARYLAND								
Mikulski	Y	N	N	Y	N	N	Y	Y
Sarbanes	Y	N	Y	N	N	N	Y	N
MASSACHUSETTS								
Kennedy	Y	N	N	Y	N	N	Y	N
Kerry	Y	N	N	Y	N	N	Y	N
MICHIGAN								
Levin	Y	N	Y	N	N	N	Y	Y
Riegle	Y	N	Y	N	N	N	Y	Y
MINNESOTA								
Boschwitz	Y	Y	N	N	Y	Y	Y	Y
Durenberger	N	N	Y	N	Y	N	Y	Y
MISSISSIPPI								
Cochran	N	N	Y	Y	Y	Y	Y	Y
Lott	N	Y	Y	N	Y	Y	Y	Y
MISSOURI								
Bond	N	Y	Y	Y	Y	Y	N	N
Danforth	N	Y	Y	Y	Y	N	Y	N
MONTANA								
Baucus	Y	N	Y	N	Y	Y	Y	Y
Burns	N	Y	N	N	Y	Y	Y	Y
NEBRASKA								
Exon	Y	N	Y	Y	Y	Y	Y	Y
Kerrey	Y	N	Y	Y	N	N	Y	Y
NEVADA								
Bryan	Y	N	N	Y	Y	Y	Y	N
Reid	Y	-	N	Y	Y	Y	Y	N
NEW HAMPSHIRE								
Humphrey	N	Y	Y	N	Y	N	N	N
Rudman	N	Y	Y	N	Y	N	Y	N
NEW JERSEY								
Bradley	Y	N	N	Y	N	N	Y	N
Lautenberg	Y	N	N	Y	N	N	Y	N
NEW MEXICO								
Bingaman	Y	N	N	Y	Y	N	Y	N
Domenici	N	Y	Y	N	Y	Y	Y	N
NEW YORK								
Moynihan	Y	N	N	Y	N	N	Y	N
D'Amato	N	Y	N	N	N	Y	Y	Y
NORTH CAROLINA								
Sanford	Y	N	Y	Y	Y	N	Y	Y
Helms	Y	Y	N	N	Y	Y	N	Y
NORTH DAKOTA								
Burdick	Y	N	Y	Y	N	Y	Y	Y
Conrad	Y	N	N	Y	N	Y	Y	Y
OHIO								
Glenn	Y	N	Y	Y	N	N	Y	N
Metzenbaum	Y	N	Y	Y	N	N	Y	N
OKLAHOMA								
Boren	Y	N	Y	N	N	N	Y	Y
Nickles	N	Y	Y	N	Y	Y	Y	N
OREGON								
Hatfield	N	N	N	Y	N	Y	Y	N
Packwood	N	Y	N	N	N	N	Y	N
PENNSYLVANIA								
Heinz	N	N	Y	Y	Y	Y	Y	N
Specter	N	N	Y	Y	Y	Y	Y	N
RHODE ISLAND								
Pell	Y	N	N	Y	N	N	Y	N
Chafee	N	N	Y	N	N	N	Y	N
SOUTH CAROLINA								
Hollings	Y	N	Y	Y	Y	Y	Y	Y
Thurmond	N	Y	Y	N	Y	Y	Y	Y
SOUTH DAKOTA								
Daschle	Y	N	N	N	N	N	Y	Y
Pressler	Y	Y	N	N	Y	Y	Y	?
TENNESSEE								
Gore	Y	N	N	Y	N	N	Y	Y
Sasser	Y	N	Y	Y	N	N	Y	Y
TEXAS								
Bentsen	Y	N	Y	Y	N	Y	Y	Y
Gramm	N	Y	Y	N	Y	Y	Y	Y
UTAH								
Garn	N	Y	N	N	Y	Y	N	?
Hatch	N	N	N	N	Y	Y	Y	Y
VERMONT								
Leahy	Y	N	N	N	N	N	Y	Y
Jeffords	N	N	Y	N	N	N	Y	N
VIRGINIA								
Robb	Y	N	Y	N	N	N	Y	N
Warner	N	Y	Y	N	N	Y	Y	N
WASHINGTON								
Adams	Y	N	N	Y	N	N	Y	Y
Gorton	Y	Y	N	N	Y	Y	Y	N
WEST VIRGINIA								
Byrd	Y	N	N	Y	N	Y	Y	Y
Rockefeller	Y	N	N	Y	N	Y	?	Y
WISCONSIN								
Kohl	Y	N	N	Y	N	N	Y	N
Kasten	Y	Y	Y	N	Y	Y	Y	N
WYOMING								
Simpson	N	Y	Y	N	Y	Y	+	Y
Wallop	N	Y	N	N	Y	Y	N	Y

KEY

Y Voted for (yea).
Paired for.
\+ Announced for.
N Voted against (nay).
X Paired against.
\- Announced against.
P Voted "present."
C Voted "present" to avoid possible conflict of interest.
? Did not vote or otherwise make a position known.

Democrats ***Republicans***

ND Northern Democrats SD Southern Democrats

Southern states - Ala., Ark., Fla., Ga., Ky., La., Miss., N.C., Okla., S.C., Tenn., Texas, Va.

1. HR 2712. Chinese Students/Veto Override. Passage, over President Bush's Nov. 30 veto, of the bill to defer indefinitely the deportation of Chinese students whose visas expire and to waive for students on "J" visas a requirement that they return to their home country for two years before applying for permanent residence in the United States. Rejected 62-37: R 8-37; D 54-0 (ND 38-0, SD 16-0), Jan. 25, 1990. A two-thirds majority of those present and voting (66 in this case) of both houses is required to override a veto. A "nay" was a vote supporting the president's position.

2. S 695. Education Programs/National Standards. Helms, R-N.C., amendment to delete $25 million in federal matching funds for the National Board for Professional Teaching Standards, which is developing guidelines for voluntary certification of teachers. Rejected 35-64: R 35-10; D 0-54 (ND 0-37, SD 0-17), Feb. 6, 1990. A "yea" was a vote supporting the president's position.

3. S 1630. Clean Air Act Reauthorization/Motor Vehicles. Mitchell, D-Maine, motion to table (kill) the Wirth, D-Colo., amendment to provide for a second round of tailpipe emissions reductions in the year 2003; to require cleaner-burning reformulated gasoline in all ozone non-attainment areas; to require light-duty vehicles to meet new-car emission standards for 100,000 miles; and to provide for use of clean fuels and clean-fuel vehicles in the nation's smoggiest cities. Motion agreed to 52-46: R 25-19; D 27-27 (ND 14-23, SD 13-4), March 20, 1990. A "yea" was a vote supporting the president's position.

4. S 1630. Clean Air Act Reauthorization/Coal Miner Benefits. Byrd, D-W.Va., amendment to provide severance pay and retraining benefits to coal miners who lose their jobs as a result of provisions to control acid rain. Rejected 49-50: R 11-34; D 38-16 (ND 29-9, SD 9-7), March 29, 1990. A "nay" was a vote supporting the president's position.

5. S 1970. Omnibus Crime Package/Assault-Style Weapons. Hatch, R-Utah, amendment to strike provisions that would prohibit for three years making, selling and possessing nine types of semiautomatic assault-style weapons. Rejected 48-52: R 36-9; D 12-43 (ND 5-33, SD 7-10), May 23, 1990. A "yea" was a vote supporting the president's position.

6. S J Res 332. Constitutional Amendment on the Flag/Passage. Passage of the joint resolution to propose an amendment to the Constitution to prohibit the physical desecration of the U.S. flag. Rejected 58-42: R 38-7; D 20-35 (ND 10-28, SD 10-7), June 26, 1990. A two-thirds majority of those present and voting (67 in this case) of both houses is required for passage of a joint resolution proposing an amendment to the Constitution. A "yea" was a vote supporting the president's position.

7. S 933. Americans with Disabilities Act/Conference Report. Adoption of the conference report (thus clearing the measure for the president) on the bill to prohibit discrimination against the disabled in public facilities and employment and to guarantee them access to mass transit and telecommunications services. Adopted 91-6: R 37-6; D 54-0 (ND 37-0, SD 17-0), July 13, 1990. A "yea" was a vote supporting the president's position.

8. S 2830. Farm Programs Reauthorization/Sugar Price Supports. Akaka, D-Hawaii, motion to table (kill) the Bradley, D-N.J., amendment to extend the current sugar program for five years and lower the sugar price-support program loan rate from 18 cents per pound to 16 cents per pound. Motion agreed to 54-44: R 17-26; D 37-18 (ND 22-16, SD 15-2), July 24, 1990.

† Daniel K. Akaka was appointed April 28, 1990.

	9	10	11	12	13	14	15	16
ALABAMA								
Heflin	?	N	N	N	N	Y	Y	Y
Shelby	N	N	Y	N	N	Y	Y	Y
ALASKA								
Murkowski	Y	N	N	N	Y	Y	N	N
Stevens	Y	Y	N	N	Y	Y	N	N
ARIZONA								
DeConcini	-	N	Y	Y	N	Y	N	Y
McCain	Y	N	N	Y	N	N	N	N
ARKANSAS								
Bumpers	N	Y	Y	Y	Y	Y	Y	Y
Pryor	N	Y	Y	Y	Y	Y	Y	Y
CALIFORNIA								
Cranston	N	Y	Y	Y	Y	Y	N	Y
Wilson	Y	?	?	?	N	N	N	N
COLORADO								
Wirth	N	Y	Y	Y	Y	Y	N	Y
Armstrong	?	N	N	N	N	N	N	N
CONNECTICUT								
Dodd	N	Y	Y	N	Y	Y	Y	Y
Lieberman	N	Y	N	Y	N	Y	N	Y
DELAWARE								
Biden	N	Y	Y	Y	N	Y	Y	Y
Roth	Y	N	N	Y	N	Y	N	N
FLORIDA								
Graham	N	Y	N	Y	N	Y	Y	Y
Mack	Y	N	N	N	N	N	N	N
GEORGIA								
Fowler	N	Y	Y	N	Y	Y	N	Y
Nunn	N	N	N	N	Y	Y	Y	Y
HAWAII								
Inouye	N	Y	N	N	Y	Y	N	Y
Akaka	N	Y	N	Y	N	Y	Y	Y
IDAHO								
McClure	Y	N	N	Y	Y	N	N	N
Symms	Y	N	N	N	N	N	N	N
ILLINOIS								
Dixon	N	N	Y	N	Y	Y	Y	Y
Simon	N	Y	Y	Y	N	Y	Y	Y
INDIANA								
Coats	Y	N	N	N	N	N	Y	N
Lugar	Y	N	N	N	Y	N	N	N
IOWA								
Harkin	N	Y	Y	Y	N	Y	Y	Y
Grassley	Y	N	N	Y	N	Y	Y	N
KANSAS								
Dole	Y	N	N	N	Y	N	N	N
Kassebaum	Y	N	?	?	Y	Y	Y	N
KENTUCKY								
Ford	N	N	N	N	Y	Y	Y	Y
McConnell	Y	N	N	N	N	N	N	N
LOUISIANA								
Breaux	N	N	N	N	Y	Y	Y	Y
Johnston	N	N	N	N	N	Y	Y	Y
MAINE								
Mitchell	N	Y	Y	Y	Y	Y	N	Y
Cohen	Y	Y	Y	Y	N	Y	Y	Y
MARYLAND								
Mikulski	?	Y	Y	Y	Y	Y	Y	Y
Sarbanes	N	Y	Y	Y	Y	Y	N	Y
MASSACHUSETTS								
Kennedy	N	Y	Y	Y	Y	Y	N	Y
Kerry	N	Y	+	#	N	Y	Y	Y
MICHIGAN								
Levin	N	Y	Y	N	N	Y	Y	Y
Riegle	N	Y	Y	Y	N	Y	?	Y
MINNESOTA								
Boschwitz	Y	N	N	N	Y	Y	Y	Y
Durenberger	Y	N	N	N	Y	Y	N	Y
MISSISSIPPI								
Cochran	Y	N	N	N	Y	N	N	N
Lott	Y	N	N	N	N	N	Y	N
MISSOURI								
Bond	Y	N	N	N	Y	N	N	N
Danforth	Y	N	N	N	Y	Y	N	Y
MONTANA								
Baucus	N	Y	Y	Y	N	Y	Y	Y
Burns	Y	N	N	N	N	N	N	N
NEBRASKA								
Exon	Y	N	Y	N	N	Y	Y	Y
Kerrey	N	Y	Y	Y	N	Y	Y	Y
NEVADA								
Bryan	N	Y	Y	N	Y	Y	Y	Y
Reid	N	N	Y	Y	Y	Y	Y	Y
NEW HAMPSHIRE								
Humphrey	Y	N	Y	Y	N	N	Y	N
Rudman	Y	Y	N	N	Y	N	N	N
NEW JERSEY								
Bradley	N	Y	Y	Y	N	Y	N	Y
Lautenberg	N	Y	Y	Y	N	Y	N	Y
NEW MEXICO								
Bingaman	N	Y	Y	N	Y	Y	N	Y
Domenici	Y	?	N	N	Y	Y	N	Y
NEW YORK								
Moynihan	N	Y	Y	Y	Y	Y	N	Y
D'Amato	Y	N	Y	N	N	Y	N	N
NORTH CAROLINA								
Sanford	N	Y	Y	X	N	Y	Y	Y
Helms	Y	N	Y	N	N	N	Y	N
NORTH DAKOTA								
Burdick	N	Y	Y	Y	Y	Y	Y	Y
Conrad	N	N	Y	Y	N	Y	Y	Y
OHIO								
Glenn	N	Y	N	Y	Y	Y	N	Y
Metzenbaum	N	?	Y	Y	N	Y	N	Y
OKLAHOMA								
Boren	N	N	Y	N	Y	Y	N	Y
Nickles	Y	N	Y	N	N	N	N	N
OREGON								
Hatfield	Y	?	+	#	N	Y	Y	Y
Packwood	Y	Y	Y	Y	Y	Y	N	Y
PENNSYLVANIA								
Heinz	Y	Y	N	Y	Y	Y	N	Y
Specter	Y	Y	N	N	Y	Y	N	Y
RHODE ISLAND								
Pell	-	Y	Y	Y	N	Y	Y	Y
Chafee	Y	Y	N	N	Y	Y	N	Y
SOUTH CAROLINA								
Hollings	Y	Y	N	Y	N	Y	Y	Y
Thurmond	Y	N	N	N	Y	N	N	N
SOUTH DAKOTA								
Daschle	N	Y	Y	Y	Y	Y	+	Y
Pressler	Y	N	Y	Y	N	Y	Y	N
TENNESSEE								
Gore	N	Y	N	N	Y	Y	N	Y
Sasser	N	Y	Y	Y	Y	Y	Y	Y
TEXAS								
Bentsen	N	N	N	N	Y	Y	N	Y
Gramm	Y	N	N	N	N	?	?	N
UTAH								
Garn	Y	N	N	N	Y	N	N	N
Hatch	Y	N	N	N	Y	N	N	N
VERMONT								
Leahy	N	Y	N	Y	Y	Y	N	Y
Jeffords	Y	Y	N	X	Y	Y	N	Y
VIRGINIA								
Robb	N	Y	N	N	Y	Y	N	Y
Warner	Y	N	N	N	Y	Y	N	N
WASHINGTON								
Adams	N	Y	Y	Y	N	Y	N	Y
Gorton	Y	N	N	N	N	N	N	N
WEST VIRGINIA								
Byrd	N	N	N	Y	Y	Y	Y	Y
Rockefeller	N	Y	Y	Y	Y	Y	Y	Y
WISCONSIN								
Kohl	N	Y	Y	Y	Y	Y	Y	Y
Kasten	Y	N	Y	N	N	N	N	N
WYOMING								
Simpson	Y	N	N	N	Y	N	N	N
Wallop	Y	N	N	N	N	N	N	N

KEY

Y Voted for (yea).
Paired for.
+ Announced for.
N Voted against (nay).
X Paired against.
- Announced against.
P Voted "present."
C Voted "present" to avoid possible conflict of interest.
? Did not vote or otherwise make a position known.

Democrats *Republicans*

ND Northern Democrats SD Southern Democrats

Southern states - Ala., Ark., Fla., Ga., Ky., La., Miss., N.C., Okla., S.C., Tenn., Texas, Va.

9. S 137. Campaign Finance Overhaul/Taxpayer Funding. McConnell, R-Ky., amendment to the Boren, D-Okla., substitute amendment to eliminate all taxpayer funding of Senate campaigns. Rejected 46-49: R 44-0; D 2-49 (ND 1-34, SD 1-15), July 30, 1990.

10. HR 5257. Fiscal 1991 Labor, HHS and Education Appropriations/Abortion. Harkin, D-Iowa, motion to table (kill) the Armstrong, R-Colo., amendment to the committee amendment to permit federal funding of abortion in cases of rape or incest. The Armstrong amendment would require organizations receiving funds to notify a parent or legal guardian 48 hours before performing an abortion for a minor, unless there is a medical emergency. Motion rejected 48-48: R 8-34; D 40-14 (ND 31-6, SD 9-8), Oct. 12, 1990. (Subsequently, the Armstrong amendment was adopted by voice vote.)

11. S 3189. Fiscal 1991 Defense Appropriations/Troop Cuts. Conrad, D-N.D., amendment to reduce U.S. forces in NATO by 30,000 troops below the Senate-passed authorization level and reduce the Department of Defense military personnel level by a corresponding 30,000 below the authorized level. Rejected 46-50: R 8-34; D 38-16 (ND 31-6, SD 7-10), Oct. 15, 1990. A "nay" was a vote supporting the president's position.

12. S 3189. Fiscal 1991 Defense Appropriations/B-2 Bomber. Leahy, D-Vt., amendment to cut funds for the two additional B-2 bombers in the bill thereby terminating the expansion of the program with the 15 bombers being produced and tested. Rejected 44-50: R 9-32; D 35-18 (ND 30-7, SD 5-11), Oct. 15, 1990. A "nay" was a vote supporting the president's position.

13. S 3209. Fiscal 1991 Budget Reconciliation Act/Passage. Passage of the bill to cut spending and raise revenues as required by the reconciliation instructions in the budget resolution and make changes in the budget process. Passed 54-46: R 23-22; D 31-24 (ND 20-18, SD 11-6), in the session that began, and the Congressional Record dated, Oct. 18, 1990. (The Senate subsequently passed HR 5835 by voice vote after striking everything after the enacting clause and inserting in lieu thereof the text of S 3209.)

14. HR 5114. Fiscal 1991 Foreign Operations Appropriations/El Salvador. Leahy, D-Vt., amendment to the committee amendment, to reduce military aid to the government of El Salvador by 50 percent and link future military aid to improvements in human rights and progress toward a negotiated peace settlement. Adopted 74-25: R 19-25; D 55-0 (ND 38-0, SD 17-0), Oct. 19, 1990. A "nay" was a vote supporting the president's position.

15. HR 5114. Fiscal 1991 Foreign Operations Appropriations/Egyptian Debt. Harkin, D-Iowa, amendment to the committee amendment, to strike provisions canceling Egypt's debt to the United States and to require the president to develop in cooperation with Congress a proposal to restructure that debt and convene an international conference to develop a comprehensive and multilateral solution to Egypt's international debt problem. Rejected 42-55: R 10-34; D 32-21 (ND 20-16, SD 12-5), Oct. 19, 1990. A "nay" was a vote supporting the president's position.

16. S 2104. Civil Rights Act of 1990/Veto Override. Passage, over President Bush's Oct. 22 veto, of the bill to reverse or modify six recent Supreme Court decisions that narrowed the reach and remedies of job discrimination law and to authorize monetary damages under Title VII of the 1964 Civil Rights Act. Rejected 66-34: R 11-34; D 55-0 (ND 38-0, SD 17-0), Oct. 24, 1990. A two-thirds majority of those present and voting (67 in this case) of both houses is required to override a veto. A "nay" was a vote supporting the president's position.

KEY HOUSE VOTES 1, 2, 3, 4, 5, 6, 7, 8

1. HR 4636. Fiscal 1990 Foreign Aid Supplemental Authorizations/Military Aid. Moakley, D-Mass., amendment to suspend 50 percent of El Salvador's military aid planned for fiscal years 1990 and 1991, depending on actions by the Salvadoran government or by the leftist guerrillas. Adopted 250-163: R 31-135; D 219-28 (ND 166-4, SD 53-24), May 22, 1990. A "nay" was a vote supporting the president's position.

2. HR 3030. Clean Air Act Reauthorization/Transition Aid. Wise, D-W.Va., amendment to authorize $250 million over a five-year period for a Clean Air Employment Transition Assistance program to provide workers who lose their jobs or have their wages reduced as a result of the bill with retraining assistance and up to six months of additional unemployment benefits. Adopted 274-146: R 43-126; D 231-20 (ND 169-2, SD 62-18), May 23, 1990. A "nay" was a vote supporting the president's position.

3. HR 3030. Clean Air Act Reauthorization/Passage. Passage of the bill (thus clearing for the president) to amend the Clean Air Act to attain and maintain national ambient air quality standards, require reductions of emissions in motor vehicles, control toxic air pollutants, reduce acid rain, establish a system of federal permits and enforcement, and otherwise improve the quality of the nation's air. Passed 401-21: R 154-16; D 247-5 (ND 169-4, SD 78-1), May 23, 1990.

4. H J Res 350. Constitutional Amendment on the Flag/-Passage. Brooks, D-Texas, motion to suspend the rules and pass the joint resolution to propose an amendment to the Constitution to prohibit the physical desecration of the U.S. flag. Rejected 254-177: R 159-17; D 95-160 (ND 43-130, SD 52-30), June 21, 1990. A two-thirds majority of those present and voting (288 in this case) of both houses is required for passage of a joint resolution proposing an amendment to the Constitution. A "yea" was a vote supporting the president's position.

5. HR 770. Family and Medical Leave Act/Veto Override. Passage, over President Bush's June 29 veto, of the bill to require public and private employers to give unpaid leave to care for a newborn child or a seriously ill child, parent or spouse, or to use as medical leave due to a serious health condition. Rejected 232-195: R 38-138; D 194-57 (ND 156-14, SD 38-43), July 25, 1990. A two-thirds majority or those present and voting (285 in this case) of both houses is required to override a veto. A "nay" was a vote supporting the president's position.

6. HR 3950. Farm Programs Reauthorization/High-Income Farmers. Schumer, D-N.Y., amendment to prohibit all payments, purchases and loans under the wheat, feed grains, cotton, honey, rice, oil seeds, and wool and mohair programs for any person with an adjusted gross income of $100,000 or more. Rejected 159-263: R 66-109; D 93-154 (ND 85-82, SD 8-72), July 25, 1990.

7. H Res 440. Frank Reprimand/Censure. Gingrich, R-Ga., motion to recommit the resolution reprimanding Frank to the Committee on Standards of Official Conduct with instructions to report back a recommendation of censure instead of reprimand. Motion rejected 141-287: R 129-46; D 12-241 (ND 1-171, SD 11-70), July 26, 1990.

8. HR 4739. Fiscal 1991 Defense Authorization/SDI Funding. Bennett, D-Fla., amendment to reduce spending for the strategic defense initiative by $600 million to a new level of $2.3 billion. Adopted 225-189: R 20-150; D 205-39 (ND 157-7, SD 48-32), Sept. 18, 1990. A "nay" was a vote supporting the president's position.

† Patsy T. Mink, D-Hawaii, was sworn in Sept. 27, 1990.

KEY

- Y Voted for (yea).
- \# Paired for.
- \+ Announced for.
- N Voted against (nay).
- X Paired against.
- \- Announced against.
- P Voted "present."
- C Voted "present" to avoid possible conflict of interest.
- ? Did not vote or otherwise make a position known.

Democrats ***Republicans***

	1	2	3	4	5	6	7	8
ALABAMA								
1 ***Callahan***	Y	N	Y	Y	N	N	N	N
2 ***Dickinson***	N	N	Y	Y	N	Y	Y	N
3 Browder	Y	Y	Y	Y	N	N	N	N
4 Bevill	Y	Y	Y	Y	N	N	N	N
5 Flippo	?	?	?	Y	Y	N	N	N
6 Erdreich	Y	Y	Y	Y	Y	N	N	N
7 Harris	Y	Y	Y	Y	N	N	N	N
ALASKA								
AL ***Young***	N	N	Y	Y	Y	N	N	N
ARIZONA								
1 ***Rhodes***	N	N	Y	Y	N	N	Y	N
2 Udall	Y	Y	Y	N	Y	N	N	Y
3 ***Stump***	N	N	N	Y	N	C	Y	N
4 ***Kyl***	N	N	Y	Y	N	N	Y	N
5 ***Kolbe***	X	N	Y	N	N	N	Y	N
ARKANSAS								
1 Alexander	?	?	?	Y	Y	N	N	Y
2 ***Robinson***	?	?	?	Y	N	N	Y	N
3 ***Hammerschmidt***	?	N	Y	Y	N	N	Y	N
4 Anthony	Y	Y	Y	N	Y	N	N	Y
CALIFORNIA								
1 Bosco	Y	Y	Y	N	Y	N	N	Y
2 ***Herger***	N	Y	Y	Y	N	N	Y	?
3 Matsui	Y	Y	Y	N	Y	N	N	Y
4 Fazio	Y	Y	Y	N	Y	N	N	Y
5 Pelosi	Y	Y	Y	N	Y	Y	N	Y
6 Boxer	Y	Y	Y	N	Y	N	N	Y
7 Miller	Y	Y	Y	N	Y	Y	N	Y
8 Dellums	Y	Y	Y	N	Y	Y	N	Y
9 Stark	Y	Y	Y	N	Y	Y	N	Y
10 Edwards	Y	Y	Y	N	Y	N	N	Y
11 Lantos	Y	Y	Y	N	Y	Y	N	Y
12 ***Campbell***	Y	N	Y	Y	Y	Y	N	Y
13 Mineta	Y	Y	Y	N	Y	N	N	Y
14 ***Shumway***	N	N	Y	Y	N	N	Y	N
15 Condit	Y	Y	Y	Y	Y	N	N	Y
16 Panetta	Y	Y	Y	N	Y	Y	N	Y
17 ***Pashayan***	Y	Y	Y	Y	N	N	N	N
18 Lehman	Y	Y	Y	N	Y	N	N	Y
19 ***Lagomarsino***	N	N	Y	Y	N	Y	Y	N
20 ***Thomas***	X	X	?	Y	N	N	Y	N
21 ***Gallegly***	N	N	Y	Y	N	N	Y	N
22 ***Moorhead***	N	N	Y	Y	N	N	Y	N
23 Beilenson	Y	N	Y	N	Y	Y	N	Y
24 Waxman	Y	Y	Y	N	Y	Y	N	Y
25 Roybal	Y	Y	Y	N	Y	N	N	Y
26 Berman	Y	Y	Y	N	Y	Y	N	Y
27 Levine	Y	Y	Y	N	Y	Y	N	Y
28 Dixon	Y	Y	Y	N	Y	N	N	Y
29 Hawkins	#	Y	Y	N	Y	N	N	?
30 Martinez	Y	Y	Y	Y	Y	?	N	Y
31 Dymally	Y	Y	Y	N	Y	N	N	Y
32 Anderson	Y	Y	Y	N	Y	N	N	Y
33 ***Dreier***	N	N	Y	Y	N	Y	Y	N
34 Torres	Y	Y	Y	N	Y	N	N	Y
35 ***Lewis***	N	N	Y	Y	N	N	N	N
36 Brown	?	Y	Y	N	Y	N	N	Y
37 ***McCandless***	N	N	Y	Y	N	N	Y	N
38 ***Dornan***	N	N	Y	Y	N	N	Y	N
39 ***Dannemeyer***	N	N	N	Y	N	Y	Y	N
40 ***Cox***	N	N	Y	Y	N	Y	Y	N
41 ***Lowery***	N	N	Y	Y	N	N	N	N
42 ***Rohrabacher***	N	N	Y	Y	N	Y	Y	N
43 ***Packard***	N	N	Y	Y	N	N	Y	N
44 Bates	Y	Y	Y	N	Y	Y	N	Y
45 ***Hunter***	N	N	Y	Y	N	N	Y	N
COLORADO								
1 Schroeder	Y	Y	Y	N	Y	Y	N	Y
2 Skaggs	Y	Y	Y	N	Y	N	N	Y
3 Campbell	Y	Y	Y	Y	N	N	N	Y
4 ***Brown***	N	N	Y	Y	N	Y	Y	N
5 ***Hefley***	N	N	Y	Y	N	N	Y	N
6 ***Schaefer***	N	Y	Y	Y	N	N	Y	N
CONNECTICUT								
1 Kennelly	Y	Y	Y	N	Y	Y	N	Y
2 Gejdenson	Y	Y	Y	N	Y	Y	N	Y
3 Morrison	Y	Y	Y	N	Y	Y	N	Y
4 ***Shays***	Y	N	Y	N	Y	Y	Y	Y
5 ***Rowland***	N	N	Y	Y	Y	Y	Y	N
6 ***Johnson***	N	Y	Y	N	Y	Y	Y	N
DELAWARE								
AL Carper	Y	Y	Y	N	Y	Y	N	Y
FLORIDA								
1 Hutto	N	N	Y	Y	N	N	Y	N
2 ***Grant***	N	N	Y	Y	N	N	Y	Y
3 Bennett	Y	Y	Y	Y	Y	Y	N	Y
4 ***James***	N	N	Y	Y	N	N	Y	N
5 ***McCollum***	N	N	Y	Y	N	Y	Y	N
6 ***Stearns***	N	N	Y	Y	N	Y	Y	N
7 Gibbons	Y	Y	Y	N	Y	Y	N	Y
8 ***Young***	N	N	Y	Y	N	Y	Y	N
9 ***Bilirakis***	N	N	Y	Y	N	N	Y	?
10 ***Ireland***	N	N	Y	Y	N	N	Y	N
11 Nelson	#	#	+	Y	+	-	-	N
12 ***Lewis***	N	N	Y	Y	N	N	Y	N
13 ***Goss***	N	N	Y	Y	N	Y	Y	N
14 Johnston	Y	Y	Y	N	Y	Y	N	Y
15 ***Shaw***	N	N	Y	Y	N	Y	Y	N
16 Smith	Y	Y	Y	N	Y	N	N	Y
17 Lehman	Y	Y	Y	N	Y	Y	N	Y
18 ***Ros-Lehtinen***	N	N	Y	Y	Y	Y	Y	N
19 Fascell	Y	Y	Y	N	Y	N	N	Y
GEORGIA								
1 Thomas	N	Y	Y	Y	N	N	Y	Y
2 Hatcher	N	Y	Y	Y	N	N	N	Y
3 Ray	N	N	Y	Y	N	N	Y	Y
4 Jones	Y	Y	Y	N	N	N	N	Y
5 Lewis	Y	Y	Y	N	Y	N	N	Y
6 ***Gingrich***	N	N	Y	Y	N	N	Y	N
7 Darden	N	Y	Y	Y	N	N	N	N
8 Rowland	Y	Y	Y	Y	N	N	Y	Y
9 Jenkins	N	N	Y	Y	Y	N	N	Y
10 Barnard	#	Y	Y	Y	N	N	Y	?
HAWAII								
1 ***Saiki***	N	N	Y	Y	Y	N	Y	N
2 Mink †								
IDAHO								
1 ***Craig***	X	X	Y	Y	N	N	Y	N
2 Stallings	Y	?	Y	Y	N	N	N	Y
ILLINOIS								
1 Hayes	Y	Y	Y	N	Y	N	N	Y
2 Savage	Y	Y	Y	N	Y	Y	P	Y
3 Russo	Y	Y	Y	N	Y	Y	N	Y
4 Sangmeister	Y	Y	Y	Y	Y	N	N	Y
5 Lipinski	N	Y	Y	Y	Y	Y	N	N
6 ***Hyde***	N	N	Y	Y	Y	N	Y	N
7 Collins	Y	Y	Y	N	Y	N	N	Y
8 Rostenkowski	Y	Y	Y	N	Y	Y	N	Y
9 Yates	Y	Y	Y	N	Y	Y	N	Y
10 ***Porter***	N	N	Y	N	N	Y	Y	N
11 Annunzio	Y	Y	Y	Y	Y	Y	N	Y
12 ***Crane***	N	N	N	Y	N	Y	Y	N
13 ***Fawell***	N	N	Y	Y	N	Y	Y	N
14 ***Hastert***	N	N	Y	Y	N	N	Y	N
15 ***Madigan***	N	N	Y	Y	N	N	Y	N
16 ***Martin***	N	Y	Y	Y	Y	N	N	N
17 Evans	Y	Y	Y	N	Y	N	N	Y
18 ***Michel***	N	N	Y	Y	N	N	Y	N
19 Bruce	Y	Y	Y	N	Y	N	N	Y
20 Durbin	Y	Y	Y	N	Y	N	N	Y
21 Costello	Y	Y	N	Y	Y	N	N	Y
22 Poshard	Y	Y	N	N	Y	N	Y	Y
INDIANA								
1 Visclosky	Y	Y	Y	N	Y	Y	N	Y
2 Sharp	Y	Y	Y	Y	Y	N	N	?
3 ***Hiler***	N	N	Y	Y	N	N	Y	N

ND Northern Democrats SD Southern Democrats

	1	2	3	4	5	6	7	8
4 Long	Y	Y	Y	Y	Y	N	N	Y
5 Jontz	Y	Y	Y	N	Y	N	N	Y
6 ***Burton***	N	N	N	Y	N	N	Y	N
7 ***Myers***	N	N	N	Y	N	N	N	N
8 McCloskey	Y	Y	Y	N	Y	N	N	Y
9 Hamilton	Y	Y	Y	N	N	N	N	Y
10 Jacobs	Y	Y	Y	Y	Y	Y	N	Y
IOWA								
1 ***Leach***	Y	N	Y	N	N	N	N	Y
2 ***Tauke***	Y	N	Y	Y	N	N	N	N
3 Nagle	Y	Y	Y	N	N	N	N	Y
4 Smith	Y	Y	Y	N	Y	N	N	N
5 ***Lightfoot***	N	N	N	Y	N	N	Y	N
6 ***Grandy***	Y	N	Y	N	N	N	N	Y
KANSAS								
1 ***Roberts***	N	N	Y	Y	N	N	Y	N
2 Slattery	Y	Y	Y	N	N	N	N	Y
3 ***Meyers***	N	N	Y	Y	N	N	Y	N
4 Glickman	Y	Y	Y	N	N	N	N	Y
5 ***Whittaker***	N	N	Y	Y	N	N	N	N
KENTUCKY								
1 Hubbard	Y	Y	N	Y	N	N	N	Y
2 Natcher	Y	Y	Y	Y	Y	N	N	Y
3 Mazzoli	Y	Y	Y	Y	Y	Y	N	Y
4 ***Bunning***	N	Y	Y	Y	N	N	Y	N
5 ***Rogers***	N	Y	Y	Y	N	N	Y	N
6 ***Hopkins***	N	Y	Y	Y	N	N	Y	N
7 Perkins	Y	Y	Y	Y	Y	N	N	Y
LOUISIANA								
1 ***Livingston***	N	N	Y	Y	N	Y	Y	N
2 Boggs	Y	Y	Y	N	Y	N	N	N
3 Tauzin	N	N	Y	Y	N	N	N	N
4 ***McCrery***	N	N	Y	Y	N	N	Y	N
5 Huckaby	N	N	Y	Y	N	N	N	N
6 ***Baker***	N	N	Y	Y	N	N	Y	N
7 Hayes	Y	Y	Y	Y	N	N	N	N
8 ***Holloway***	N	?	?	Y	N	N	Y	N
MAINE								
1 Brennan	Y	Y	Y	N	Y	Y	N	Y
2 ***Snowe***	N	N	Y	Y	Y	Y	N	Y
MARYLAND								
1 Dyson	Y	Y	Y	Y	Y	N	N	N
2 ***Bentley***	N	Y	Y	Y	N	N	Y	N
3 Cardin	Y	Y	Y	N	Y	Y	N	Y
4 McMillen	Y	Y	Y	Y	Y	Y	N	Y
5 Hoyer	Y	Y	Y	N	Y	N	N	Y
6 Byron	N	Y	Y	Y	N	N	N	N
7 Mfume	Y	Y	Y	N	Y	Y	N	Y
8 ***Morella***	Y	N	Y	N	Y	Y	N	Y
MASSACHUSETTS								
1 ***Conte***	Y	N	Y	N	Y	Y	N	Y
2 Neal	Y	Y	Y	Y	Y	Y	N	+
3 Early	Y	N	Y	N	Y	?	N	Y
4 Frank	Y	Y	Y	N	Y	Y	C	Y
5 Atkins	Y	Y	Y	N	Y	Y	N	Y
6 Mavroules	Y	Y	Y	N	Y	Y	N	Y
7 Markey	Y	Y	Y	N	Y	Y	N	Y
8 Kennedy	Y	Y	Y	N	Y	Y	N	Y
9 Moakley	Y	Y	Y	Y	Y	N	N	Y
10 Studds	Y	Y	Y	N	Y	Y	N	Y
11 Donnelly	Y	Y	Y	Y	N	Y	N	Y
MICHIGAN								
1 Conyers	Y	Y	Y	N	Y	N	N	Y
2 ***Pursell***	Y	Y	Y	Y	N	N	Y	Y
3 Wolpe	Y	Y	Y	N	Y	N	N	Y
4 ***Upton***	Y	Y	Y	Y	N	N	Y	N
5 ***Henry***	Y	Y	Y	N	N	N	Y	N
6 Carr	Y	Y	Y	N	N	N	N	Y
7 Kildee	Y	Y	Y	N	Y	N	N	Y
8 Traxler	Y	Y	Y	Y	Y	N	N	Y
9 ***Vander Jagt***	N	N	Y	Y	N	N	Y	N
10 ***Schuette***	N	Y	Y	Y	N	N	Y	N
11 ***Davis***	N	Y	Y	Y	Y	N	N	?
12 Bonior	Y	Y	Y	N	Y	Y	N	Y
13 Crockett	Y	Y	Y	N	Y	?	N	?
14 Hertel	Y	Y	Y	N	Y	Y	N	Y
15 Ford	Y	Y	Y	N	Y	N	N	Y
16 Dingell	Y	Y	Y	N	Y	N	N	Y
17 Levin	Y	Y	Y	N	Y	Y	N	Y
18 ***Broomfield***	N	Y	Y	Y	N	Y	Y	N
MINNESOTA								
1 Penny	Y	Y	Y	N	N	N	N	Y
2 ***Weber***	N	N	Y	Y	N	N	Y	N
3 ***Frenzel***	N	N	?	Y	N	Y	N	N
4 Vento	Y	Y	Y	N	Y	Y	N	Y

	1	2	3	4	5	6	7	8
5 Sabo	Y	Y	Y	N	Y	Y	N	Y
6 Sikorski	Y	Y	Y	N	Y	N	N	Y
7 ***Stangeland***	N	Y	Y	Y	N	N	N	N
8 Oberstar	Y	Y	Y	N	Y	N	N	Y
MISSISSIPPI								
1 Whitten	Y	Y	Y	Y	Y	N	N	N
2 Espy	Y	Y	Y	N	Y	N	N	Y
3 Montgomery	N	N	Y	Y	N	N	N	N
4 Parker	N	N	Y	Y	N	N	N	N
5 Taylor	Y	Y	Y	Y	N	N	Y	N
MISSOURI								
1 Clay	Y	Y	Y	N	Y	N	N	Y
2 ***Buechner***	N	N	Y	Y	N	Y	Y	N
3 Gephardt	Y	Y	Y	N	Y	N	N	Y
4 Skelton	N	Y	Y	Y	N	N	N	N
5 Wheat	Y	Y	Y	N	Y	N	N	Y
6 ***Coleman***	N	N	Y	Y	N	N	N	N
7 ***Hancock***	N	N	N	Y	N	Y	Y	N
8 ***Emerson***	N	Y	Y	Y	N	N	Y	N
9 Volkmer	Y	Y	Y	Y	Y	N	N	Y
MONTANA								
1 Williams	Y	#	Y	N	Y	N	N	Y
2 ***Marlenee***	X	N	N	Y	N	N	N	N
NEBRASKA								
1 ***Bereuter***	Y	N	Y	Y	N	N	N	N
2 Hoagland	N	Y	Y	N	N	N	N	Y
3 ***Smith***	N	N	Y	Y	N	N	Y	N
NEVADA								
1 Bilbray	Y	Y	Y	Y	Y	Y	N	Y
2 ***Vucanovich***	N	N	Y	Y	N	N	Y	N
NEW HAMPSHIRE								
1 ***Smith***	N	N	Y	Y	N	Y	Y	N
2 ***Douglas***	N	N	Y	Y	N	Y	Y	N
NEW JERSEY								
1 Vacancy								
2 Hughes	Y	Y	Y	N	?	Y	N	Y
3 Pallone	Y	Y	Y	Y	Y	Y	N	Y
4 ***Smith***	N	Y	Y	Y	Y	Y	Y	N
5 ***Roukema***	Y	N	Y	Y	Y	Y	Y	Y
6 Dwyer	Y	Y	Y	N	Y	Y	N	Y
7 ***Rinaldo***	Y	Y	Y	Y	Y	Y	Y	N
8 Roe	Y	Y	Y	Y	Y	?	N	Y
9 Torricelli	Y	Y	Y	N	Y	Y	N	?
10 Payne	Y	Y	Y	N	Y	Y	N	Y
11 ***Gallo***	N	N	Y	Y	N	Y	Y	N
12 ***Courter***	N	N	Y	Y	N	Y	Y	N
13 ***Saxton***	N	N	Y	Y	N	Y	Y	Y
14 Guarini	Y	Y	Y	Y	Y	Y	N	Y
NEW MEXICO								
1 ***Schiff***	N	Y	Y	Y	N	N	N	N
2 ***Skeen***	N	N	Y	Y	N	N	Y	N
3 Richardson	Y	Y	Y	Y	Y	N	N	N
NEW YORK								
1 Hochbrueckner	Y	Y	Y	Y	Y	Y	N	Y
2 Downey	Y	Y	Y	N	Y	Y	N	Y
3 Mrazek	Y	Y	Y	N	Y	Y	N	Y
4 ***Lent***	N	N	Y	Y	N	Y	N	N
5 ***McGrath***	Y	Y	Y	Y	Y	Y	N	N
6 Flake	Y	Y	Y	N	?	?	N	Y
7 Ackerman	Y	Y	Y	N	Y	N	N	Y
8 Scheuer	Y	Y	Y	N	Y	Y	N	Y
9 Manton	Y	Y	Y	Y	Y	Y	N	Y
10 Schumer	Y	Y	Y	N	Y	Y	N	Y
11 Towns	Y	Y	Y	N	Y	N	N	Y
12 Owens	Y	Y	Y	N	Y	Y	N	Y
13 Solarz	Y	Y	Y	N	Y	Y	N	Y
14 ***Molinari***	N	N	Y	Y	Y	Y	N	N
15 ***Green***	Y	N	Y	N	Y	Y	N	Y
16 Rangel	Y	Y	Y	?	Y	Y	N	Y
17 Weiss	Y	Y	Y	N	Y	Y	N	Y
18 Serrano	Y	Y	Y	N	Y	Y	N	Y
19 Engel	Y	Y	Y	N	Y	Y	N	Y
20 Lowey	Y	Y	Y	N	Y	Y	N	Y
21 ***Fish***	?	Y	Y	Y	Y	N	N	N
22 ***Gilman***	Y	Y	Y	Y	Y	N	N	N
23 McNulty	Y	Y	Y	Y	Y	Y	N	N
24 ***Solomon***	N	Y	Y	Y	Y	N	Y	N
25 ***Boehlert***	Y	N	Y	Y	Y	N	N	N
26 ***Martin***	N	Y	Y	Y	Y	N	N	N
27 ***Walsh***	Y	Y	Y	Y	N	N	Y	N
28 McHugh	Y	Y	Y	N	Y	N	N	Y
29 ***Horton***	Y	Y	Y	Y	Y	N	N	Y
30 Slaughter	Y	Y	Y	N	Y	N	N	Y
31 ***Paxon***	N	N	Y	Y	N	N	Y	N

	1	2	3	4	5	6	7	8
32 LaFalce	Y	Y	Y	N	N	Y	N	Y
33 Nowak	Y	Y	Y	N	Y	Y	N	Y
34 ***Houghton***	N	Y	Y	N	N	N	N	N
NORTH CAROLINA								
1 Jones	Y	Y	Y	Y	N	N	N	Y
2 Valentine	Y	N	Y	N	N	N	N	Y
3 Lancaster	N	Y	Y	Y	N	N	N	N
4 Price	Y	Y	Y	N	Y	Y	N	Y
5 Neal	Y	N	Y	N	N	N	N	Y
6 ***Coble***	N	N	Y	Y	N	Y	Y	Y
7 Rose	Y	Y	Y	N	Y	N	N	Y
8 Hefner	Y	Y	Y	Y	N	N	N	Y
9 ***McMillan***	N	N	Y	Y	N	Y	Y	N
10 ***Ballenger***	N	N	Y	Y	N	Y	Y	N
11 Clarke	Y	N	Y	Y	N	Y	N	Y
NORTH DAKOTA								
AL Dorgan	Y	Y	Y	N	Y	N	N	Y
OHIO								
1 Luken	Y	Y	Y	Y	Y	N	N	Y
2 ***Gradison***	N	N	Y	Y	N	Y	Y	N
3 Hall	Y	Y	Y	N	Y	N	N	Y
4 ***Oxley***	N	Y	Y	Y	N	N	Y	N
5 ***Gillmor***	N	N	Y	Y	Y	N	Y	N
6 ***McEwen***	N	Y	N	Y	N	N	Y	N
7 ***DeWine***	N	Y	N	Y	Y	N	Y	N
8 ***Lukens***	?	?	?	Y	N	N	P	N
9 Kaptur	Y	Y	Y	N	?	N	N	Y
10 ***Miller***	N	Y	N	Y	N	Y	Y	?
11 Eckart	Y	Y	Y	Y	Y	Y	N	Y
12 ***Kasich***	N	Y	N	Y	N	N	Y	N
13 Pease	Y	Y	Y	N	Y	Y	N	Y
14 Sawyer	Y	Y	Y	N	Y	N	N	Y
15 ***Wylie***	N	N	Y	Y	N	Y	Y	N
16 ***Regula***	Y	Y	Y	Y	Y	Y	Y	N
17 Traficant	Y	Y	Y	Y	Y	N	N	Y
18 Applegate	Y	Y	N	Y	Y	N	N	Y
19 Feighan	Y	Y	Y	N	Y	Y	N	?
20 Oakar	Y	Y	Y	N	Y	Y	N	Y
21 Stokes	#	Y	Y	N	Y	N	N	Y
OKLAHOMA								
1 ***Inhofe***	N	N	Y	Y	N	N	Y	N
2 Synar	Y	Y	Y	N	Y	N	N	Y
3 Watkins	?	Y	Y	Y	N	N	Y	?
4 McCurdy	N	N	Y	N	Y	N	N	Y
5 ***Edwards***	N	N	Y	Y	N	N	Y	N
6 English	N	Y	Y	Y	Y	N	N	N
OREGON								
1 AuCoin	Y	Y	Y	N	Y	N	N	?
2 ***Smith, B.***	N	Y	Y	Y	N	N	Y	N
3 Wyden	Y	Y	Y	N	Y	Y	N	Y
4 DeFazio	Y	Y	Y	N	Y	N	N	Y
5 ***Smith, D.***	-	N	Y	Y	N	N	Y	N
PENNSYLVANIA								
1 Foglietta	Y	Y	Y	N	Y	Y	N	Y
2 Gray	Y	Y	Y	N	Y	Y	N	Y
3 Borski	Y	Y	Y	N	Y	Y	N	Y
4 Kolter	Y	Y	Y	Y	Y	?	N	Y
5 ***Schulze***	N	Y	Y	Y	N	Y	Y	N
6 Yatron	Y	Y	Y	Y	Y	Y	N	Y
7 ***Weldon***	Y	Y	Y	Y	Y	Y	N	N
8 Kostmayer	Y	Y	Y	N	Y	Y	N	Y
9 ***Shuster***	N	N	N	Y	N	Y	Y	N
10 ***McDade***	N	Y	Y	Y	Y	N	N	?
11 Kanjorski	Y	Y	Y	Y	Y	Y	N	Y
12 Murtha	Y	Y	Y	Y	Y	N	N	?
13 ***Coughlin***	Y	N	Y	Y	Y	Y	N	Y
14 Coyne	Y	Y	Y	N	Y	Y	N	Y
15 ***Ritter***	N	Y	Y	Y	N	N	N	N
16 ***Walker***	N	N	Y	Y	N	Y	Y	N
17 ***Gekas***	N	N	Y	Y	N	N	Y	?
18 Walgren	Y	Y	Y	N	Y	Y	N	Y
19 ***Goodling***	N	Y	Y	Y	N	Y	Y	N
20 Gaydos	Y	Y	Y	Y	Y	Y	N	Y
21 ***Ridge***	Y	Y	Y	Y	N	N	N	Y
22 Murphy	Y	Y	Y	Y	Y	Y	N	Y
23 ***Clinger***	N	+	+	N	N	N	N	N
RHODE ISLAND								
1 ***Machtley***	Y	N	Y	Y	Y	Y	N	Y
2 ***Schneider***	Y	N	Y	N	Y	Y	N	Y
SOUTH CAROLINA								
1 ***Ravenel***	N	N	Y	Y	Y	N	N	N
2 ***Spence***	N	N	Y	Y	N	N	N	N
3 Derrick	Y	Y	Y	Y	N	N	N	Y
4 Patterson	Y	Y	Y	Y	N	N	Y	N
5 Spratt	Y	Y	Y	N	N	N	N	N
6 Tallon	N	Y	Y	N	N	N	N	N

	1	2	3	4	5	6	7	8
SOUTH DAKOTA								
AL Johnson	Y	Y	Y	Y	Y	N	N	Y
TENNESSEE								
1 ***Quillen***	N	Y	Y	Y	N	N	Y	N
2 ***Duncan***	N	Y	Y	Y	N	Y	Y	N
3 Lloyd	N	Y	Y	Y	N	N	N	N
4 Cooper	N	N	Y	N	N	C	N	Y
5 Clement	Y	Y	Y	Y	Y	N	N	Y
6 Gordon	Y	Y	Y	N	Y	N	N	Y
7 ***Sundquist***	N	N	Y	Y	N	N	Y	N
8 Tanner	Y	Y	Y	N	N	N	N	Y
9 Ford	Y	Y	Y	N	Y	?	N	Y
TEXAS								
1 Chapman	Y	Y	Y	Y	Y	N	?	Y
2 Wilson	N	Y	Y	Y	Y	N	N	N
3 ***Bartlett***	N	N	Y	Y	N	N	Y	N
4 Hall	N	N	Y	?	N	N	Y	N
5 Bryant	Y	Y	Y	N	Y	N	N	Y
6 ***Barton***	?	?	Y	Y	N	N	Y	N
7 ***Archer***	N	N	Y	Y	N	Y	Y	N
8 ***Fields***	N	N	Y	Y	N	N	Y	N
9 Brooks	Y	Y	Y	Y	Y	N	N	Y
10 Pickle	Y	N	Y	N	N	N	N	N
11 Leath	?	Y	?	Y	N	N	N	?
12 Geren	N	Y	Y	Y	N	N	N	N
13 Sarpalius	N	Y	Y	Y	N	N	Y	N
14 Laughlin	N	Y	Y	Y	N	N	Y	Y
15 de la Garza	Y	Y	Y	Y	Y	N	N	Y
16 Coleman	Y	Y	Y	N	Y	N	N	N
17 Stenholm	N	N	Y	N	N	N	N	N
18 Washington	Y	Y	Y	N	?	N	N	Y
19 ***Combest***	N	N	N	Y	N	N	Y	N
20 Gonzalez	Y	Y	Y	N	Y	N	N	Y
21 ***Smith***	N	N	Y	Y	Y	N	Y	N
22 ***DeLay***	N	N	N	Y	N	N	Y	N
23 Bustamante	Y	Y	Y	Y	Y	N	N	Y
24 Frost	Y	Y	Y	N	Y	N	N	Y
25 Andrews	Y	N	Y	Y	Y	N	N	Y
26 ***Armey***	N	N	N	Y	N	Y	Y	N
27 Ortiz	Y	Y	Y	Y	Y	N	N	Y
UTAH								
1 ***Hansen***	N	N	Y	Y	N	Y	Y	N
2 Owens	Y	Y	Y	N	Y	Y	N	Y
3 ***Nielson***	N	N	Y	Y	N	Y	Y	N
VERMONT								
AL ***Smith***	Y	N	Y	N	Y	N	Y	Y
VIRGINIA								
1 ***Bateman***	N	N	Y	Y	N	N	Y	N
2 Pickett	N	N	Y	Y	N	N	N	N
3 ***Bliley***	N	N	Y	Y	N	Y	Y	N
4 Sisisky	N	N	Y	Y	N	N	N	N
5 Payne	Y	Y	Y	Y	N	N	N	N
6 Olin	Y	Y	Y	Y	N	N	N	Y
7 ***Slaughter***	N	N	Y	Y	N	N	Y	N
8 ***Parris***	N	N	Y	Y	N	N	Y	N
9 Boucher	Y	Y	Y	N	Y	Y	N	Y
10 ***Wolf***	N	N	Y	Y	N	Y	Y	N
WASHINGTON								
1 ***Miller***	Y	N	Y	Y	Y	Y	N	N
2 Swift	Y	Y	Y	N	Y	N	N	Y
3 Unsoeld	Y	Y	Y	N	Y	N	N	+
4 ***Morrison***	Y	N	Y	Y	Y	N	N	N
5 Foley				N			N	
6 Dicks	Y	Y	Y	N	Y	N	N	Y
7 McDermott	Y	Y	Y	N	Y	N	N	Y
8 ***Chandler***	Y	N	Y	N	N	N	N	Y
WEST VIRGINIA								
1 Mollohan	Y	Y	N	Y	Y	N	N	Y
2 Staggers	Y	Y	Y	Y	Y	N	N	Y
3 Wise	Y	Y	Y	Y	Y	Y	N	Y
4 Rahall	Y	Y	Y	Y	Y	N	N	Y
WISCONSIN								
1 Aspin	Y	Y	Y	N	N	Y	N	Y
2 Kastenmeier	Y	Y	Y	N	Y	N	N	Y
3 ***Gunderson***	N	N	Y	Y	N	N	N	N
4 Kleczka	Y	Y	Y	N	Y	Y	N	Y
5 Moody	Y	Y	Y	N	Y	Y	N	Y
6 ***Petri***	N	N	Y	N	N	Y	Y	N
7 Obey	Y	Y	Y	N	Y	Y	N	Y
8 ***Roth***	N	N	Y	Y	N	Y	Y	N
9 ***Sensenbrenner***	N	N	Y	Y	N	Y	Y	N
WYOMING								
AL ***Thomas***	N	N	Y	Y	N	N	Y	N

Southern states - Ala., Ark., Fla., Ga., Ky., La., Miss., N.C., Okla., S.C., Tenn., Texas, Va.
Omitted votes are quorum calls, which CQ does not include in its vote charts.

HOUSE VOTES 9, 10, 11, 12

9. HR 4739. Fiscal 1991 Defense Authorization/Abortion Services. Fazio, D-Calif., amendment to provide military personnel and their dependents stationed overseas with reproductive health services, including privately paid abortions, at military hospitals. Rejected 200-216: R 35-139; D 165-77 (ND 113-50, SD 52-27), Sept. 18, 1990. A "nay" was a vote supporting the president's position.

10. HR 4300. Legal Immigration Revision/Passage. Passage of the bill to increase the number of visas for relatives and people coming to the United States to work; suspend deportation for the spouses and children of newly legalized aliens; establish diversity visas for immigrants from countries that currently account for a low number of immigrants to the United States; and reform and revise other immigration procedures. Passed 231-192: R 45-127; D 186-65 (ND 159-13, SD 27-52), Oct. 3, 1990. A "nay" was a vote supporting the president's position.

11. H Con Res 310. Fiscal 1991 Budget Resolution/Conference Report. Adoption of the conference report to set binding budget levels for fiscal 1991: budget authority, $1.49 trillion; outlays, $1.24 trillion; revenues, $1.173 trillion; deficit, $64 billion, by incorporating the spending and revenue targets announced Sept. 30 at the budget summit. The agreement contains reconciliation instructions providing cost-saving changes in entitlement programs, increases in various user fees and taxes, and caps on annual appropriations for defense, international affairs and domestic programs to reduce the deficit by $40.1 billion in fiscal 1991 and $500 billion in fiscal 1991 through 1995. Rejected 179-254: R 71-105; D 108-149 (ND 63-111, SD 45-38), Oct. 5, 1990 (in the session that began, and the Congressional Record dated, Oct. 4, 1990). A "yea" was a vote supporting the president's position.

12. HR 4328. Textile Trade Act/Veto Override. Passage, over President Bush's Oct. 5 veto, of the bill to limit the growth of imports of textiles and apparel to 1 percent annually, establish permanent quotas for most non-rubber footwear imports at 1989 levels, authorize the special allocation of textile quotas for countries increasing their purchases of U.S. agricultural goods, and for other purposes. Rejected 275-152: R 70-103; D 205-49 (ND 131-41, SD 74-8), Oct. 10, 1990. A two-thirds majority of those present and voting (285 in this case) of both chambers is required to override a veto. A "nay" was a vote supporting the president's position.

† Patsy T. Mink, D-Hawaii, was sworn in Sept. 27, 1990.

KEY

- Y Voted for (yea).
- # Paired for.
- \+ Announced for.
- N Voted against (nay).
- X Paired against.
- \- Announced against.
- P Voted "present."
- C Voted "present" to avoid possible conflict of interest.
- ? Did not vote or otherwise make a position known.

Democrats *Republicans*

	9	10	11	12
ALABAMA				
1 ***Callahan***	N	N	N	Y
2 ***Dickinson***	N	N	Y	Y
3 Browder	N	N	N	Y
4 Bevill	N	N	Y	Y
5 Flippo	N	?	Y	Y
6 Erdreich	Y	N	Y	Y
7 Harris	N	N	N	Y
ALASKA				
AL ***Young***	N	Y	Y	Y
ARIZONA				
1 ***Rhodes***	N	N	Y	N
2 Udall	Y	Y	Y	N
3 ***Stump***	N	N	N	N
4 ***Kyl***	N	N	N	N
5 ***Kolbe***	Y	N	Y	N
ARKANSAS				
1 Alexander	Y	Y	N	Y
2 ***Robinson***	N	N	Y	N
3 ***Hammerschmidt***	N	N	Y	Y
4 Anthony	Y	Y	N	Y
CALIFORNIA				
1 Bosco	Y	Y	Y	Y
2 ***Herger***	N	N	N	N
3 Matsui	Y	Y	Y	N
4 Fazio	Y	Y	Y	Y
5 Pelosi	Y	Y	N	N
6 Boxer	Y	Y	N	N
7 Miller	Y	Y	N	N
8 Dellums	Y	Y	N	Y
9 Stark	Y	Y	N	N
10 Edwards	Y	Y	N	Y
11 Lantos	Y	Y	Y	Y
12 ***Campbell***	Y	?	N	N
13 Mineta	Y	Y	Y	Y
14 ***Shumway***	N	N	Y	N
15 Condit	Y	Y	N	Y
16 Panetta	Y	Y	Y	N
17 ***Pashayan***	N	Y	N	Y
18 Lehman	Y	Y	N	Y
19 ***Lagomarsino***	N	N	N	N
20 ***Thomas***	Y	Y	N	Y
21 ***Gallegly***	N	N	N	N
22 ***Moorhead***	N	N	N	N
23 Beilenson	Y	N	Y	N
24 Waxman	Y	Y	N	N
25 Roybal	Y	Y	N	Y
26 Berman	Y	Y	N	N
27 Levine	Y	Y	N	N
28 Dixon	Y	Y	N	Y
29 Hawkins	?	Y	N	Y
30 Martinez	Y	Y	N	Y
31 Dymally	Y	Y	N	Y
32 Anderson	Y	Y	Y	N
33 ***Dreier***	N	N	N	N
34 Torres	Y	Y	Y	Y
35 ***Lewis***	N	N	Y	N
36 Brown	Y	Y	N	Y
37 ***McCandless***	Y	N	N	N
38 ***Dornan***	N	Y	N	Y
39 ***Dannemeyer***	N	N	N	N
40 ***Cox***	N	N	N	N
41 ***Lowery***	N	N	Y	N
42 ***Rohrabacher***	N	Y	N	N
43 ***Packard***	N	N	N	N
44 Bates	Y	Y	N	Y
45 ***Hunter***	N	Y	N	Y
COLORADO				
1 Schroeder	Y	Y	N	N
2 Skaggs	Y	Y	Y	N
3 Campbell	Y	Y	N	Y
4 ***Brown***	Y	N	N	N
5 ***Hefley***	N	N	N	N
6 ***Schaefer***	N	N	N	Y
CONNECTICUT				
1 Kennelly	Y	Y	Y	N
2 Gejdenson	Y	Y	Y	Y
3 Morrison	Y	Y	N	Y
4 ***Shays***	Y	Y	Y	Y
5 ***Rowland***	Y	?	N	X
6 ***Johnson***	Y	Y	Y	N
DELAWARE				
AL Carper	Y	Y	Y	Y
FLORIDA				
1 Hutto	N	N	N	Y
2 ***Grant***	N	N	N	Y
3 Bennett	Y	N	Y	Y
4 ***James***	N	N	N	N
5 ***McCollum***	N	N	N	N
6 ***Stearns***	N	N	N	N
7 Gibbons	Y	Y	Y	N
8 ***Young***	N	N	Y	N
9 ***Bilirakis***	?	N	N	N
10 ***Ireland***	N	N	Y	N
11 Nelson	Y	N	Y	N
12 ***Lewis***	N	N	N	N
13 ***Goss***	N	N	N	N
14 Johnston	Y	N	N	Y
15 ***Shaw***	N	N	Y	N
16 Smith	Y	Y	N	Y
17 Lehman	Y	Y	Y	Y
18 ***Ros-Lehtinen***	N	Y	N	N
19 Fascell	Y	Y	Y	Y
GEORGIA				
1 Thomas	Y	N	Y	Y
2 Hatcher	Y	N	Y	Y
3 Ray	N	N	Y	Y
4 Jones	Y	?	N	Y
5 Lewis	Y	Y	N	Y
6 ***Gingrich***	N	Y	N	Y
7 Darden	Y	Y	Y	Y
8 Rowland	Y	N	Y	Y
9 Jenkins	N	N	N	Y
10 Barnard	N	N	N	Y
HAWAII				
1 ***Saiki***	Y	Y	N	N
2 Mink †		Y	N	Y
IDAHO				
1 ***Craig***	N	N	N	N
2 Stallings	N	N	N	N
ILLINOIS				
1 Hayes	Y	Y	N	Y
2 Savage	Y	N	N	Y
3 Russo	N	Y	N	Y
4 Sangmeister	N	Y	N	N
5 Lipinski	N	Y	N	Y
6 ***Hyde***	N	Y	N	N
7 Collins	Y	Y	N	Y
8 Rostenkowski	N	Y	Y	N
9 Yates	Y	Y	N	Y
10 ***Porter***	Y	Y	Y	N
11 Annunzio	N	Y	N	Y
12 ***Crane***	N	N	N	N
13 ***Fawell***	Y	N	N	N
14 ***Hastert***	N	N	Y	N
15 ***Madigan***	N	Y	Y	N
16 ***Martin***	Y	Y	N	N
17 Evans	Y	Y	N	Y
18 ***Michel***	N	N	Y	N
19 Bruce	N	Y	N	Y
20 Durbin	N	Y	N	Y
21 Costello	N	Y	N	Y
22 Poshard	N	Y	N	Y
INDIANA				
1 Visclosky	Y	Y	Y	Y
2 Sharp	Y	Y	N	Y
3 ***Hiler***	N	N	N	N

ND Northern Democrats SD Southern Democrats

	9	10	11	12
4 Long	Y	N	N	Y
5 Jontz	Y	Y	N	Y
6 ***Burton***	N	N	N	Y
7 ***Myers***	N	N	N	N
8 McCloskey	Y	Y	N	Y
9 Hamilton	Y	Y	Y	N
10 Jacobs	Y	Y	N	Y
IOWA				
1 ***Leach***	Y	Y	Y	N
2 ***Tauke***	N	Y	N	N
3 Nagle	Y	Y	Y	Y
4 Smith	Y	Y	Y	N
5 ***Lightfoot***	N	N	N	N
6 ***Grandy***	N	N	Y	N
KANSAS				
1 ***Roberts***	N	N	Y	N
2 Slattery	Y	Y	Y	N
3 ***Meyers***	Y	N	Y	N
4 Glickman	Y	Y	Y	N
5 ***Whittaker***	N	N	Y	N
KENTUCKY				
1 Hubbard	Y	N	N	Y
2 Natcher	N	N	N	Y
3 Mazzoli	N	N	N	N
4 ***Bunning***	N	N	N	N
5 ***Rogers***	N	N	N	Y
6 ***Hopkins***	N	N	N	Y
7 Perkins	N	N	N	Y
LOUISIANA				
1 ***Livingston***	N	N	Y	N
2 Boggs	?	?	Y	?
3 Tauzin	N	N	N	Y
4 ***McCrery***	N	N	N	Y
5 Huckaby	N	N	N	Y
6 ***Baker***	N	N	Y	Y
7 Hayes	N	N	N	Y
8 ***Holloway***	N	N	N	Y
MAINE				
1 Brennan	Y	Y	N	Y
2 ***Snowe***	Y	Y	N	Y
MARYLAND				
1 Dyson	N	N	N	Y
2 ***Bentley***	N	N	N	Y
3 Cardin	Y	Y	Y	Y
4 McMillen	Y	Y	Y	Y
5 Hoyer	Y	Y	Y	Y
6 Byron	N	N	Y	Y
7 Mfume	Y	Y	N	Y
8 ***Morella***	Y	Y	Y	N
MASSACHUSETTS				
1 ***Conte***	N	Y	Y	Y
2 Neal	+	Y	N	#
3 Early	N	N	N	Y
4 Frank	Y	Y	N	Y
5 Atkins	Y	Y	N	Y
6 Mavroules	N	Y	N	Y
7 Markey	Y	Y	N	Y
8 Kennedy	Y	Y	N	Y
9 Moakley	N	Y	Y	Y
10 Studds	Y	Y	N	Y
11 Donnelly	N	Y	N	Y
MICHIGAN				
1 Conyers	Y	Y	Y	Y
2 ***Pursell***	N	N	N	N
3 Wolpe	Y	Y	N	Y
4 ***Upton***	N	N	N	N
5 ***Henry***	N	N	N	?
6 Carr	Y	Y	N	Y
7 Kildee	N	Y	N	Y
8 Traxler	N	Y	Y	Y
9 ***Vander Jagt***	N	N	Y	N
10 ***Schuette***	N	N	N	?
11 ***Davis***	N	N	N	Y
12 Bonior	N	Y	N	Y
13 Crockett	?	?	?	N
14 Hertel	N	Y	N	Y
15 Ford	?	Y	N	Y
16 Dingell	Y	Y	Y	Y
17 Levin	Y	Y	Y	Y
18 ***Broomfield***	N	N	N	N
MINNESOTA				
1 Penny	N	Y	Y	N
2 ***Weber***	N	Y	N	N
3 ***Frenzel***	Y	N	Y	N
4 Vento	Y	Y	N	Y

	9	10	11	12
5 Sabo	Y	Y	Y	Y
6 Sikorski	N	Y	Y	Y
7 ***Stangeland***	N	Y	N	N
8 Oberstar	N	Y	Y	Y
MISSISSIPPI				
1 Whitten	N	?	N	Y
2 Espy	Y	Y	N	Y
3 Montgomery	N	N	Y	Y
4 Parker	N	N	Y	Y
5 Taylor	N	N	N	Y
MISSOURI				
1 Clay	Y	Y	N	Y
2 ***Buechner***	N	N	Y	N
3 Gephardt	?	Y	Y	Y
4 Skelton	N	N	Y	Y
5 Wheat	Y	Y	N	Y
6 ***Coleman***	N	N	Y	Y
7 ***Hancock***	N	N	N	N
8 ***Emerson***	N	N	N	Y
9 Volkmer	N	N	N	Y
MONTANA				
1 Williams	Y	Y	N	Y
2 ***Marlenee***	N	N	N	N
NEBRASKA				
1 ***Bereuter***	N	N	N	N
2 Hoagland	Y	N	N	Y
3 ***Smith***	N	N	Y	N
NEVADA				
1 Bilbray	N	Y	Y	Y
2 ***Vucanovich***	N	?	Y	Y
NEW HAMPSHIRE				
1 ***Smith***	N	N	N	Y
2 ***Douglas***	N	N	N	Y
NEW JERSEY				
1 Vacancy				
2 Hughes	Y	N	N	Y
3 Pallone	Y	Y	N	Y
4 ***Smith***	N	Y	N	Y
5 ***Roukema***	Y	N	N	Y
6 Dwyer	Y	Y	N	Y
7 ***Rinaldo***	N	Y	N	Y
8 Roe	N	Y	N	Y
9 Torricelli	?	Y	N	Y
10 Payne	Y	Y	N	Y
11 ***Gallo***	Y	N	Y	N
12 ***Courter***	Y	Y	Y	N
13 ***Saxton***	N	N	N	N
14 Guarini	Y	Y	N	Y
NEW MEXICO				
1 ***Schiff***	Y	Y	Y	Y
2 ***Skeen***	N	Y	Y	Y
3 Richardson	?	Y	Y	Y
NEW YORK				
1 Hochbrueckner	N	Y	N	Y
2 Downey	Y	Y	N	N
3 Mrazek	Y	Y	N	Y
4 ***Lent***	N	Y	Y	N
5 ***McGrath***	N	Y	N	Y
6 Flake	Y	Y	N	Y
7 Ackerman	Y	Y	Y	Y
8 Scheuer	Y	Y	Y	Y
9 Manton	N	Y	Y	Y
10 Schumer	Y	Y	N	N
11 Towns	Y	Y	N	Y
12 Owens	Y	Y	N	#
13 Solarz	Y	Y	Y	N
14 ***Molinari***	Y	Y	Y	N
15 ***Green***	Y	Y	Y	N
16 Rangel	Y	Y	N	Y
17 Weiss	Y	Y	N	Y
18 Serrano	Y	Y	Y	Y
19 Engel	Y	?	N	Y
20 Lowey	Y	Y	N	Y
21 ***Fish***	N	Y	Y	Y
22 ***Gilman***	Y	Y	N	Y
23 McNulty	N	Y	Y	Y
24 ***Solomon***	N	N	N	Y
25 ***Boehlert***	Y	Y	Y	Y
26 ***Martin***	N	N	Y	Y
27 ***Walsh***	N	Y	N	N
28 McHugh	Y	Y	Y	N
29 ***Horton***	Y	Y	Y	Y
30 Slaughter	Y	Y	N	Y
31 ***Paxon***	N	N	N	N

		10	11	12
32 LaFalce	N	Y	Y	N
33 Nowak	N	Y	N	Y
34 ***Houghton***	Y	N	Y	Y
NORTH CAROLINA				
1 Jones	Y	Y	N	Y
2 Valentine	Y	N	Y	Y
3 Lancaster	Y	N	Y	Y
4 Price	Y	Y	Y	Y
5 Neal	Y	N	N	Y
6 ***Coble***	N	N	N	Y
7 Rose	Y	Y	Y	Y
8 Hefner	Y	N	N	Y
9 ***McMillan***	N	N	Y	Y
10 ***Ballenger***	N	N	N	Y
11 Clarke	Y	Y	N	Y
NORTH DAKOTA				
AL Dorgan	N	Y	N	N
OHIO				
1 Luken	N	Y	Y	Y
2 ***Gradison***	N	Y	Y	N
3 Hall	N	Y	Y	Y
4 ***Oxley***	N	N	Y	N
5 ***Gillmor***	N	N	Y	N
6 ***McEwen***	N	N	N	N
7 ***DeWine***	N	Y	Y	N
8 ***Lukens***	N	N	Y	Y
9 Kaptur	N	Y	Y	Y
10 ***Miller***	N	N	Y	Y
11 Eckart	Y	Y	N	Y
12 ***Kasich***	N	N	N	N
13 Pease	Y	Y	Y	N
14 Sawyer	Y	Y	Y	N
15 ***Wylie***	N	N	Y	N
16 ***Regula***	N	N	N	Y
17 Traficant	Y	N	N	Y
18 Applegate	N	N	N	Y
19 Feighan	?	Y	N	Y
20 Oakar	N	Y	N	Y
21 Stokes	Y	Y	N	Y
OKLAHOMA				
1 ***Inhofe***	N	N	N	N
2 Synar	Y	Y	N	N
3 Watkins	?	N	Y	Y
4 McCurdy	Y	N	Y	N
5 ***Edwards***	N	N	N	N
6 English	N	N	N	N
OREGON				
1 AuCoin	?	Y	Y	N
2 ***Smith, B.***	N	N	N	N
3 Wyden	Y	Y	N	N
4 DeFazio	Y	Y	N	N
5 ***Smith, D.***	N	N	N	Y
PENNSYLVANIA				
1 Foglietta	N	Y	Y	Y
2 Gray	Y	Y	Y	Y
3 Borski	N	Y	N	Y
4 Kolter	N	Y	N	Y
5 ***Schulze***	N	N	N	Y
6 Yatron	N	Y	N	Y
7 ***Weldon***	N	+	N	Y
8 Kostmayer	Y	Y	Y	Y
9 ***Shuster***	N	N	N	Y
10 ***McDade***	?	Y	Y	Y
11 Kanjorski	N	Y	N	Y
12 Murtha	N	Y	Y	Y
13 ***Coughlin***	Y	N	Y	N
14 Coyne	Y	Y	N	Y
15 ***Ritter***	N	N	N	Y
16 ***Walker***	N	N	N	N
17 ***Gekas***	N	N	Y	Y
18 Walgren	Y	Y	N	Y
19 ***Goodling***	N	N	Y	Y
20 Gaydos	N	Y	N	Y
21 ***Ridge***	Y	N	Y	Y
22 Murphy	N	Y	N	Y
23 ***Clinger***	N	N	Y	Y
RHODE ISLAND				
1 ***Machtley***	Y	Y	N	Y
2 ***Schneider***	Y	Y	N	Y
SOUTH CAROLINA				
1 ***Ravenel***	N	N	N	Y
2 ***Spence***	N	N	N	Y
3 Derrick	Y	N	Y	Y
4 Patterson	Y	N	N	Y
5 Spratt	Y	N	Y	Y
6 Tallon	N	N	Y	Y

	9	10	11	12
SOUTH DAKOTA				
AL Johnson	Y	Y	N	Y
TENNESSEE				
1 ***Quillen***	N	N	Y	Y
2 ***Duncan***	N	N	N	Y
3 Lloyd	N	N	Y	Y
4 Cooper	Y	N	Y	Y
5 Clement	Y	N	Y	Y
6 Gordon	Y	N	Y	Y
7 ***Sundquist***	N	N	Y	N
8 Tanner	Y	N	Y	Y
9 Ford	Y	Y	N	Y
TEXAS				
1 Chapman	Y	N	Y	Y
2 Wilson	Y	Y	Y	Y
3 ***Bartlett***	N	N	Y	N
4 Hall	N	N	Y	Y
5 Bryant	Y	N	N	Y
6 ***Barton***	N	N	N	N
7 ***Archer***	N	N	Y	N
8 ***Fields***	N	N	N	N
9 Brooks	Y	Y	N	Y
10 Pickle	Y	Y	Y	N
11 Leath	?	N	Y	Y
12 Geren	Y	N	N	N
13 Sarpalius	N	N	N	Y
14 Laughlin	N	N	N	Y
15 de la Garza	N	Y	Y	Y
16 Coleman	Y	Y	Y	Y
17 Stenholm	N	N	Y	Y
18 Washington	Y	Y	N	Y
19 ***Combest***	N	N	Y	Y
20 Gonzalez	Y	Y	N	Y
21 ***Smith***	N	N	N	Y
22 ***DeLay***	N	N	N	N
23 Bustamante	?	Y	Y	Y
24 Frost	Y	Y	Y	Y
25 Andrews	Y	N	Y	Y
26 ***Armey***	N	N	N	N
27 Ortiz	N	Y	Y	Y
UTAH				
1 ***Hansen***	N	N	Y	N
2 Owens	Y	Y	Y	N
3 ***Nielson***	N	N	N	N
VERMONT				
AL ***Smith***	Y	Y	Y	Y
VIRGINIA				
1 ***Bateman***	N	N	Y	N
2 Pickett	Y	Y	N	Y
3 ***Bliley***	N	N	N	Y
4 Sisisky	Y	N	Y	Y
5 Payne	Y	N	Y	Y
6 Olin	Y	N	Y	Y
7 ***Slaughter***	N	N	N	Y
8 ***Parris***	N	N	N	Y
9 Boucher	Y	Y	N	Y
10 ***Wolf***	N	N	Y	N
WASHINGTON				
1 ***Miller***	Y	Y	Y	N
2 Swift	Y	Y	Y	N
3 Unsoeld	+	Y	N	N
4 ***Morrison***	Y	Y	Y	N
5 Foley			Y	
6 Dicks	Y	Y	Y	N
7 McDermott	Y	Y	Y	N
8 ***Chandler***	Y	N	Y	N
WEST VIRGINIA				
1 Mollohan	N	Y	Y	Y
2 Staggers	N	Y	N	Y
3 Wise	Y	Y	N	Y
4 Rahall	N	Y	N	Y
WISCONSIN				
1 Aspin	Y	Y	Y	Y
2 Kastenmeier	Y	Y	N	Y
3 ***Gunderson***	N	Y	N	Y
4 Kleczka	N	Y	N	N
5 Moody	Y	Y	N	Y
6 ***Petri***	N	N	N	N
7 Obey	Y	Y	N	Y
8 ***Roth***	N	N	N	Y
9 ***Sensenbrenner***	N	N	N	N
WYOMING				
AL ***Thomas***	N	N	N	N

Southern states - Ala., Ark., Fla., Ga., Ky., La., Miss., N.C., Okla., S.C., Tenn., Texas, Va.
Omitted votes are quorum calls, which CQ does not include in its vote charts.

13. HR 4825. Fiscal 1991-95 NEA Authorization/NEA Funding Standards. Williams, D-Mont., substitute amendment to require the chairman of the National Endowment for the Arts (NEA) in funding projects to take into account not only artistic excellence and merit but general standards of decency and respect for the diverse beliefs and values of Americans. The amendment also gives states a larger share of NEA funds and leaves the courts to decide what constitutes obscenity; requires artists convicted of obscenity to repay their grants; and makes changes in the grant application process. Adopted 382-42: R 142-31; D 240-11 (ND 160-11, SD 80-0), Oct. 11, 1990.

14. HR 5835. Fiscal 1991 Omnibus Reconciliation Act/-Democratic Alternative. Rostenkowski, D-Ill., en bloc amendment to provide smaller increases in the Medicare premium and deductible; delete revenue provisions, including the gas tax, the petroleum fuels tax, the extension of the Medicare tax to additional state and local employees, and the limit on itemized deductions; eliminate the "bubble" and lift the top marginal tax rate to 33 percent; create a 10 percent surtax on income above $1 million; increase the minimum tax rate; delay indexing for one year; provide a limited tax break for capital gains; and for other purposes. Adopted 238-192: R 10-164; D 228-28 (ND 157-16, SD 71-12), Oct. 16, 1990. A "nay" was a vote supporting the president's position.

15. S 2104. Civil Rights Act of 1990/Conference Report. Adoption of the conference report on the bill to reverse or modify six recent Supreme Court decisions that narrowed the reach and remedies of job discrimination laws and to authorize monetary damages under Title VII of the 1964 Civil Rights Act. Adopted 273-154: R 34-139; D 239-15 (ND 169-3, SD 70-12), Oct. 17, 1990. A "nay" was a vote supporting the president's position.

16. HR 5422. Fiscal 1991 Intelligence Appropriations/Aid to UNITA. Separate vote at the request of Hyde, R-Ill., on the Solarz, D-N.Y., amendment to suspend military aid to the National Union for the Total Independence of Angola (UNITA) — a rebel group fighting the Angolan government — if the government of Angola agrees to accept a cease-fire and a political settlement for the conflict in Angola; receives no military aid from the Soviet Union; and offers free and fair multiparty elections in which UNITA is free to participate. Adopted 207-206: R 12-156; D 195-50 (ND 158-10, SD 37-40), Oct. 17, 1990. A "nay" was a vote supporting the president's

KEY

Y Voted for (yea).
\# Paired for.
\+ Announced for.
N Voted against (nay).
X Paired against.
\- Announced against.
P Voted "present."
C Voted "present" to avoid possible conflict of interest.
? Did not vote or otherwise make a position known.

Democrats ***Republicans***

	13	14	15	16
ALABAMA				
1 ***Callahan***	Y	N	N	N
2 ***Dickinson***	Y	N	N	N
3 Browder	Y	Y	Y	N
4 Bevill	Y	Y	Y	N
5 Flippo	Y	Y	Y	Y
6 Erdreich	Y	Y	Y	N
7 Harris	Y	Y	Y	N
ALASKA				
AL ***Young***	Y	N	N	N
ARIZONA				
1 ***Rhodes***	Y	N	N	N
2 Udall	Y	Y	Y	Y
3 ***Stump***	N	N	N	N
4 ***Kyl***	N	N	N	N
5 ***Kolbe***	Y	N	N	N
ARKANSAS				
1 Alexander	Y	Y	Y	Y
2 ***Robinson***	N	N	N	N
3 ***Hammerschmidt***	Y	N	N	N
4 Anthony	Y	Y	Y	Y
CALIFORNIA				
1 Bosco	Y	N	Y	Y
2 ***Herger***	N	N	N	N
3 Matsui	Y	Y	Y	Y
4 Fazio	Y	Y	Y	Y
5 Pelosi	Y	Y	Y	Y
6 Boxer	N	Y	Y	Y
7 Miller	Y	Y	Y	Y
8 Dellums	N	Y	Y	Y
9 Stark	Y	Y	Y	Y
10 Edwards	Y	Y	Y	Y
11 Lantos	Y	Y	Y	N
12 ***Campbell***	N	N	Y	N
13 Mineta	Y	Y	Y	Y
14 ***Shumway***	N	N	N	N
15 Condit	Y	N	Y	Y
16 Panetta	Y	Y	Y	Y
17 ***Pashayan***	Y	N	N	N
18 Lehman	Y	Y	Y	Y
19 ***Lagomarsino***	Y	N	N	N
20 ***Thomas***	Y	?	N	N
21 ***Gallegly***	Y	N	N	N
22 ***Moorhead***	Y	N	N	N
23 Beilenson	Y	Y	Y	Y
24 Waxman	N	Y	Y	Y
25 Roybal	Y	Y	Y	Y
26 Berman	N	Y	Y	Y
27 Levine	N	Y	Y	Y
28 Dixon	Y	Y	Y	Y
29 Hawkins	Y	Y	Y	?
30 Martinez	Y	Y	Y	Y
31 Dymally	Y	Y	Y	Y
32 Anderson	Y	Y	Y	Y
33 ***Dreier***	N	N	N	N
34 Torres	Y	Y	Y	Y
35 ***Lewis***	Y	N	N	N
36 Brown	Y	Y	Y	Y
37 ***McCandless***	Y	N	N	N
38 ***Dornan***	N	N	N	N
39 ***Dannemeyer***	Y	N	N	N
40 ***Cox***	N	N	N	N
41 ***Lowery***	Y	N	N	N
42 ***Rohrabacher***	N	N	N	N
43 ***Packard***	Y	N	N	N
44 Bates	Y	Y	Y	Y
45 ***Hunter***	N	N	N	N
COLORADO				
1 Schroeder	Y	Y	Y	Y
2 Skaggs	Y	Y	Y	Y
3 Campbell	Y	N	Y	N
4 ***Brown***	Y	N	N	N
5 ***Hefley***	Y	N	N	N
6 ***Schaefer***	Y	N	N	N
CONNECTICUT				
1 Kennelly	Y	Y	Y	Y
2 Gejdenson	Y	Y	Y	Y
3 Morrison	+	Y	+	+
4 ***Shays***	Y	N	Y	Y
5 ***Rowland***	?	?	?	?
6 ***Johnson***	Y	N	Y	N
DELAWARE				
AL Carper	Y	Y	Y	Y
FLORIDA				
1 Hutto	Y	Y	N	N
2 ***Grant***	Y	N	Y	N
3 Bennett	Y	Y	Y	Y
4 ***James***	Y	N	Y	N
5 ***McCollum***	Y	N	N	N
6 ***Stearns***	Y	N	N	N
7 Gibbons	Y	Y	Y	Y
8 ***Young***	Y	N	N	N
9 ***Bilirakis***	Y	N	N	N
10 ***Ireland***	Y	N	N	N
11 Nelson	Y	Y	Y	N
12 ***Lewis***	Y	N	N	N
13 ***Goss***	Y	N	N	N
14 Johnston	Y	Y	Y	Y
15 ***Shaw***	Y	N	N	N
16 Smith	Y	Y	Y	N
17 Lehman	Y	Y	Y	Y
18 ***Ros-Lehtinen***	Y	N	Y	N
19 Fascell	Y	Y	Y	N
GEORGIA				
1 Thomas	Y	Y	Y	N
2 Hatcher	Y	Y	Y	N
3 Ray	Y	Y	Y	N
4 Jones	Y	N	Y	N
5 Lewis	Y	Y	Y	Y
6 ***Gingrich***	Y	N	N	N
7 Darden	Y	Y	N	N
8 Rowland	Y	Y	Y	N
9 Jenkins	Y	Y	N	N
10 Barnard	Y	N	N	N
HAWAII				
1 ***Saiki***	Y	N	Y	N
2 Mink	Y	Y	Y	Y
IDAHO				
1 ***Craig***	N	N	N	N
2 Stallings	Y	N	Y	N
ILLINOIS				
1 Hayes	?	Y	Y	Y
2 Savage	Y	N	Y	Y
3 Russo	Y	Y	N	Y
4 Sangmeister	Y	N	Y	Y
5 Lipinski	Y	Y	N	Y
6 ***Hyde***	Y	N	N	N
7 Collins	Y	Y	Y	Y
8 Rostenkowski	Y	Y	Y	Y
9 Yates	Y	Y	Y	Y
10 ***Porter***	Y	N	N	N
11 Annunzio	Y	N	N	Y
12 ***Crane***	N	N	N	N
13 ***Fawell***	Y	N	N	N
14 ***Hastert***	Y	N	N	N
15 ***Madigan***	Y	N	N	N
16 ***Martin***	Y	N	?	?
17 Evans	Y	Y	Y	Y
18 ***Michel***	Y	N	N	N
19 Bruce	Y	Y	Y	Y
20 Durbin	Y	Y	Y	Y
21 Costello	Y	Y	Y	Y
22 Poshard	Y	Y	Y	Y
INDIANA				
1 Visclosky	Y	Y	Y	Y
2 Sharp	Y	Y	Y	Y
3 ***Hiler***	Y	N	N	N

ND Northern Democrats SD Southern Democrats

	13	14	15	16
4 Long	Y	N	Y	Y
5 Jontz	Y	Y	Y	Y
6 ***Burton***	Y	N	N	N
7 ***Myers***	Y	N	N	N
8 McCloskey	Y	Y	Y	Y
9 Hamilton	Y	Y	Y	Y
10 Jacobs	Y	Y	Y	Y
IOWA				
1 ***Leach***	Y	Y	Y	Y
2 ***Tauke***	Y	N	N	Y
3 Nagle	Y	Y	Y	Y
4 Smith	Y	Y	Y	Y
5 ***Lightfoot***	N	N	N	N
6 ***Grandy***	Y	N	N	Y
KANSAS				
1 ***Roberts***	Y	N	N	N
2 Slattery	Y	Y	Y	Y
3 ***Meyers***	Y	N	Y	N
4 Glickman	Y	Y	Y	Y
5 ***Whittaker***	Y	N	N	N
KENTUCKY				
1 Hubbard	Y	N	Y	N
2 Natcher	Y	Y	Y	Y
3 Mazzoli	Y	Y	Y	Y
4 ***Bunning***	Y	N	N	N
5 ***Rogers***	Y	N	N	N
6 ***Hopkins***	Y	N	N	N
7 Perkins	Y	Y	Y	Y
LOUISIANA				
1 ***Livingston***	N	N	N	N
2 Boggs	?	Y	Y	Y
3 Tauzin	Y	N	Y	N
4 ***McCrery***	Y	N	N	N
5 Huckaby	Y	Y	N	N
6 ***Baker***	Y	N	N	N
7 Hayes	Y	N	Y	?
8 ***Holloway***	N	N	N	N
MAINE				
1 Brennan	Y	?	?	?
2 ***Snowe***	Y	N	Y	N
MARYLAND				
1 Dyson	Y	N	Y	Y
2 ***Bentley***	Y	N	N	N
3 Cardin	Y	Y	Y	Y
4 McMillen	Y	Y	Y	Y
5 Hoyer	Y	Y	Y	Y
6 Byron	Y	Y	Y	N
7 Mfume	Y	Y	Y	Y
8 ***Morella***	Y	Y	Y	Y
MASSACHUSETTS				
1 ***Conte***	Y	Y	Y	N
2 Neal	Y	Y	Y	Y
3 Early	Y	Y	Y	Y
4 Frank	Y	Y	Y	Y
5 Atkins	Y	Y	Y	Y
6 Mavroules	Y	Y	Y	Y
7 Markey	Y	Y	Y	Y
8 Kennedy	Y	Y	Y	Y
9 Moakley	Y	Y	Y	Y
10 Studds	N	Y	Y	Y
11 Donnelly	Y	Y	Y	N
MICHIGAN				
1 Conyers	Y	Y	Y	Y
2 ***Pursell***	Y	N	Y	N
3 Wolpe	Y	Y	Y	Y
4 ***Upton***	Y	N	N	N
5 ***Henry***	Y	N	Y	N
6 Carr	Y	Y	Y	Y
7 Kildee	Y	Y	Y	Y
8 Traxler	Y	Y	Y	Y
9 ***Vander Jagt***	N	N	N	N
10 ***Schuette***	?	N	?	?
11 ***Davis***	Y	Y	Y	N
12 Bonior	Y	Y	Y	Y
13 Crockett	Y	Y	Y	?
14 Hertel	Y	Y	Y	Y
15 Ford	Y	Y	Y	?
16 Dingell	Y	Y	Y	Y
17 Levin	Y	Y	Y	Y
18 ***Broomfield***	Y	N	N	N
MINNESOTA				
1 Penny	Y	Y	Y	Y
2 ***Weber***	N	N	N	N
3 ***Frenzel***	Y	N	N	?
4 Vento	Y	Y	Y	Y

	13	14	15	16
5 Sabo	Y	Y	Y	Y
6 Sikorski	Y	Y	Y	Y
7 ***Stangeland***	Y	N	N	N
8 Oberstar	Y	Y	Y	Y
MISSISSIPPI				
1 Whitten	Y	Y	Y	N
2 Espy	Y	Y	Y	Y
3 Montgomery	Y	Y	N	N
4 Parker	Y	Y	N	N
5 Taylor	Y	N	N	N
MISSOURI				
1 Clay	Y	Y	Y	Y
2 ***Buechner***	Y	N	N	N
3 Gephardt	Y	Y	Y	Y
4 Skelton	Y	Y	Y	N
5 Wheat	Y	Y	Y	Y
6 ***Coleman***	Y	N	N	?
7 ***Hancock***	N	N	N	N
8 ***Emerson***	Y	N	N	N
9 Volkmer	Y	Y	Y	Y
MONTANA				
1 Williams	Y	Y	Y	?
2 ***Marlenee***	Y	N	N	N
NEBRASKA				
1 ***Bereuter***	Y	N	N	N
2 Hoagland	Y	Y	Y	Y
3 ***Smith***	Y	N	N	N
NEVADA				
1 Bilbray	Y	N	Y	Y
2 ***Vucanovich***	N	N	N	N
NEW HAMPSHIRE				
1 ***Smith***	N	N	N	N
2 ***Douglas***	Y	N	N	N
NEW JERSEY				
1 Vacancy				
2 Hughes	Y	Y	Y	N
3 Pallone	Y	N	Y	Y
4 ***Smith***	Y	N	N	N
5 ***Roukema***	Y	N	Y	N
6 Dwyer	Y	Y	Y	Y
7 ***Rinaldo***	Y	N	Y	N
8 Roe	Y	Y	Y	N
9 Torricelli	Y	Y	Y	Y
10 Payne	Y	Y	Y	Y
11 ***Gallo***	Y	N	N	N
12 ***Courter***	Y	N	N	?
13 ***Saxton***	Y	N	N	N
14 Guarini	Y	Y	Y	Y
NEW MEXICO				
1 ***Schiff***	Y	N	Y	N
2 ***Skeen***	Y	N	N	N
3 Richardson	Y	Y	Y	Y
NEW YORK				
1 Hochbrueckner	Y	Y	Y	Y
2 Downey	Y	Y	Y	Y
3 Mrazek	N	Y	Y	Y
4 ***Lent***	Y	N	N	N
5 ***McGrath***	Y	Y	N	N
6 Flake	Y	Y	Y	Y
7 Ackerman	N	Y	Y	?
8 Scheuer	Y	Y	Y	Y
9 Manton	Y	Y	Y	Y
10 Schumer	Y	Y	Y	Y
11 Towns	Y	Y	Y	Y
12 Owens	Y	Y	Y	Y
13 Solarz	Y	Y	Y	Y
14 ***Molinari***	Y	Y	N	N
15 ***Green***	Y	N	Y	Y
16 Rangel	Y	Y	Y	Y
17 Weiss	N	Y	Y	Y
18 Serrano	Y	Y	Y	Y
19 Engel	Y	Y	Y	Y
20 Lowey	Y	Y	Y	Y
21 ***Fish***	Y	Y	Y	?
22 ***Gilman***	Y	N	Y	Y
23 McNulty	Y	Y	Y	Y
24 ***Solomon***	Y	N	N	N
25 ***Boehlert***	Y	Y	Y	N
26 ***Martin***	Y	N	N	N
27 ***Walsh***	Y	N	Y	N
28 McHugh	Y	Y	Y	Y
29 ***Horton***	Y	Y	Y	N
30 Slaughter	Y	Y	Y	Y
31 ***Paxon***	Y	N	N	N

	13	14	15	16
32 LaFalce	Y	Y	Y	Y
33 Nowak	Y	Y	Y	Y
34 ***Houghton***	Y	N	Y	Y
NORTH CAROLINA				
1 Jones	Y	Y	Y	N
2 Valentine	Y	Y	Y	N
3 Lancaster	Y	Y	Y	N
4 Price	Y	Y	Y	Y
5 Neal	Y	Y	Y	?
6 ***Coble***	Y	N	N	N
7 Rose	?	Y	?	Y
8 Hefner	Y	Y	Y	Y
9 ***McMillan***	Y	N	N	N
10 ***Ballenger***	Y	N	N	N
11 Clarke	Y	Y	Y	Y
NORTH DAKOTA				
AL Dorgan	Y	Y	Y	Y
OHIO				
1 Luken	Y	Y	Y	Y
2 ***Gradison***	Y	N	N	N
3 Hall	?	Y	Y	Y
4 ***Oxley***	Y	N	N	N
5 ***Gillmor***	Y	N	N	N
6 ***McEwen***	Y	N	N	N
7 ***DeWine***	Y	N	Y	N
8 ***Lukens***	Y	N	N	N
9 Kaptur	Y	Y	Y	Y
10 ***Miller***	Y	N	N	N
11 Eckart	Y	Y	Y	Y
12 ***Kasich***	Y	N	N	N
13 Pease	Y	Y	Y	Y
14 Sawyer	Y	Y	Y	Y
15 ***Wylie***	?	N	N	N
16 ***Regula***	Y	N	Y	N
17 Traficant	Y	N	Y	Y
18 Applegate	Y	N	Y	Y
19 Feighan	Y	Y	Y	Y
20 Oakar	Y	Y	Y	Y
21 Stokes	Y	Y	Y	Y
OKLAHOMA				
1 ***Inhofe***	Y	N	N	N
2 Synar	Y	Y	Y	Y
3 Watkins	Y	Y	Y	N
4 McCurdy	Y	Y	Y	N
5 ***Edwards***	Y	N	N	N
6 English	Y	Y	Y	N
OREGON				
1 AuCoin	Y	Y	Y	Y
2 ***Smith, B.***	N	N	N	N
3 Wyden	Y	Y	Y	Y
4 DeFazio	Y	Y	Y	Y
5 ***Smith, D.***	Y	N	N	N
PENNSYLVANIA				
1 Foglietta	Y	Y	Y	Y
2 Gray	Y	Y	Y	Y
3 Borski	Y	Y	Y	Y
4 Kolter	Y	N	Y	Y
5 ***Schulze***	Y	N	Y	N
6 Yatron	Y	N	Y	Y
7 ***Weldon***	Y	N	N	N
8 Kostmayer	N	Y	Y	Y
9 ***Shuster***	Y	N	N	N
10 ***McDade***	Y	N	N	N
11 Kanjorski	Y	Y	Y	Y
12 Murtha	Y	Y	Y	N
13 ***Coughlin***	Y	N	Y	N
14 Coyne	Y	Y	Y	Y
15 ***Ritter***	Y	N	N	N
16 ***Walker***	N	N	N	N
17 ***Gekas***	Y	N	N	N
18 Walgren	Y	Y	Y	Y
19 ***Goodling***	Y	N	N	N
20 Gaydos	Y	N	Y	Y
21 ***Ridge***	Y	N	N	N
22 Murphy	Y	Y	Y	Y
23 ***Clinger***	Y	N	N	N
RHODE ISLAND				
1 ***Machtley***	Y	N	Y	Y
2 ***Schneider***	Y	N	Y	Y
SOUTH CAROLINA				
1 ***Ravenel***	Y	N	N	N
2 ***Spence***	Y	N	N	N
3 Derrick	Y	Y	Y	Y
4 Patterson	Y	N	Y	Y
5 Spratt	Y	Y	Y	Y
6 Tallon	Y	Y	Y	N

	13	14	15	16
SOUTH DAKOTA				
AL Johnson	Y	Y	Y	Y
TENNESSEE				
1 ***Quillen***	Y	N	N	N
2 ***Duncan***	Y	N	N	N
3 Lloyd	Y	Y	Y	N
4 Cooper	Y	Y	Y	N
5 Clement	Y	Y	Y	Y
6 Gordon	Y	Y	Y	Y
7 ***Sundquist***	Y	N	N	N
8 Tanner	Y	Y	Y	N
9 Ford	Y	Y	Y	?
TEXAS				
1 Chapman	Y	Y	Y	Y
2 Wilson	?	Y	Y	?
3 ***Bartlett***	N	N	N	N
4 Hall	Y	N	N	Y
5 Bryant	Y	Y	Y	Y
6 ***Barton***	N	N	Y	N
7 ***Archer***	Y	N	N	N
8 ***Fields***	Y	N	N	N
9 Brooks	Y	Y	Y	?
10 Pickle	Y	Y	Y	N
11 Leath	Y	N	N	Y
12 Geren	Y	N	Y	N
13 Sarpalius	Y	N	N	N
14 Laughlin	Y	N	Y	N
15 de la Garza	Y	Y	Y	?
16 Coleman	Y	Y	Y	Y
17 Stenholm	Y	Y	N	N
18 Washington	Y	Y	Y	Y
19 ***Combest***	N	N	N	N
20 Gonzalez	Y	Y	Y	Y
21 ***Smith***	Y	N	N	N
22 ***DeLay***	N	N	N	N
23 Bustamante	Y	Y	Y	Y
24 Frost	Y	Y	Y	Y
25 Andrews	Y	Y	Y	Y
26 ***Armey***	N	N	N	N
27 Ortiz	Y	Y	Y	Y
UTAH				
1 ***Hansen***	N	N	N	N
2 Owens	Y	Y	Y	Y
3 ***Nielson***	Y	N	N	N
VERMONT				
AL ***Smith***	Y	Y	Y	?
VIRGINIA				
1 ***Bateman***	Y	N	N	N
2 Pickett	Y	Y	Y	Y
3 ***Bliley***	Y	N	Y	N
4 Sisisky	Y	Y	Y	N
5 Payne	Y	Y	Y	Y
6 Olin	Y	Y	Y	N
7 ***Slaughter***	Y	N	N	N
8 ***Parris***	Y	N	N	N
9 Boucher	Y	Y	Y	Y
10 ***Wolf***	Y	N	N	N
WASHINGTON				
1 ***Miller***	Y	N	N	Y
2 Swift	Y	Y	Y	Y
3 Unsoeld	Y	Y	Y	Y
4 ***Morrison***	Y	N	N	Y
5 Foley				Y
6 Dicks	Y	Y	Y	Y
7 McDermott	N	Y	Y	Y
8 ***Chandler***	Y	N	N	N
WEST VIRGINIA				
1 Mollohan	Y	Y	Y	N
2 Staggers	Y	Y	Y	Y
3 Wise	Y	Y	Y	Y
4 Rahall	Y	Y	Y	Y
WISCONSIN				
1 Aspin	Y	Y	Y	Y
2 Kastenmeier	Y	Y	Y	Y
3 ***Gunderson***	Y	N	N	N
4 Kleczka	Y	Y	Y	Y
5 Moody	Y	Y	Y	Y
6 ***Petri***	N	N	N	N
7 Obey	Y	Y	Y	Y
8 ***Roth***	Y	N	N	N
9 ***Sensenbrenner***	N	N	N	N
WYOMING				
AL ***Thomas***	Y	N	N	N

Southern states - Ala., Ark., Fla., Ga., Ky., La., Miss., N.C., Okla., S.C., Tenn., Texas, Va.
Omitted votes are quorum calls, which CQ does not include in its vote charts.

Ratings Find Ideological Edges Softened

With Congress tackling bedrock economic issues such as taxes, job protections and worker benefits in 1990, national business and labor organizations found plenty of litmus-test votes on which to judge members. But, despite election-year politicking, ideological interest groups had trouble finding floor tests of their pet issues.

Selecting congressional votes to use in rating members of Congress is an annual exercise for groups representing conservatives, liberals, business, labor and other interests.

The AFL-CIO and the U.S. Chamber of Commerce were, as usual, often at loggerheads in the 1990 session, but both organizations agreed that Congress addressed their interests on a long list of meaningful votes. Floor confrontations took place on child care, employee safety, worker discrimination and the role of federal workers in the political process. Congress also dealt with important commerce concerns when it took roll call votes on imposing new air pollution controls, setting trade quotas, altering the treatment of vertical price fixing, and revising the Davis-Bacon Act.

On the other hand, two ideologically oriented groups, the American Conservative Union (ACU) and the liberal Americans for Democratic Action (ADA), found fewer direct tests on their biggest issues.

Members "spent the better part of the last year bickering, and they avoided some of the more important issues which affect the lives of all Americans," said Wendy Isaacs, the national director of ADA.

The two groups found fewer votes to use in rating members than in 1989, partly because election years tend to blunt ideological tendencies and partly because attention at the end of the year was focused on the Persian Gulf and foreign policy. The ADA and ACU often relied on votes that re-fought old battles on the death penalty, the strategic defense initiative, abortion and constitutional amendments to protect the flag and to require a balanced budget. *(1989 group ratings, 1989 Almanac, p. 63-B)*

Perhaps reflecting election-year pressures to compromise, all the groups found clear-cut victories hard to come by. The Chamber of Commerce and the ACU posted their worst success rates of the past three years. The ACU was battered in the House, where it won only three of 22 contests, and the Chamber saw its success rate plummet. However, several of those groups' defeats, such as the initial passage of the Family and Medical Leave Act, were salvaged by President Bush's successful use of the veto. *(How intererst groups fared, p. 24-B)*

While the groups' positions did not often prevail, there was not a large decline in members' support scores. This apparent anomaly is largely explained by the prevalence of votes in the studies that required a "supermajority" (two-thirds or, in some cases, 60 Senate votes). Thus, a group could see its position defeated even when it won a majority.

Party Scores

Average scores for members of each party in each chamber, as computed by four interest groups:

	House	Senate
AFL-CIO		
Democrats	82%	71%
Republicans	17	31
U.S. Chamber of Commerce		
Democrats	34	26
Republicans	75	74
Americans for Democratic Action		
Democrats	71	72
Republicans	19	20
American Conservative Union		
Democrats	20	20
Republicans	73	75

The AFL-CIO, for instance, fell short of its goals in the Senate while winning a majority of votes on three veto overrides and one motion to shut off debate.

Representatives of all interest groups agreed that the ideological balance in Congress did not shift significantly during 1990.

Robert D. Billings, legislative director of the ACU, said, "The House and the Senate moved a little more towards the middle," continuing "a lessening of the polarization that we saw during the Reagan years."

If the second session of the 101st Congress showed any trend, it was slightly to the left. The ADA's overall "liberal quotient," the average number of times members of Congress voted in support of the ADA's stated position on selected votes, improved slightly in the Senate, where its 49 percent score was the second highest in the previous 15 years. (It was four points higher in 1987.) At 41 percent, the ACU lost two points from its 1989 House support score and three points from 1988, while the Chamber's average support scores fell by more than 10 percentage points in both chambers.

'Use Them Gingerly'

Interest groups compile ratings of members of Congress to help inform their memberships of who is watching out for their interests on Capitol Hill and, in some cases, to decide who gets campaign help from the groups. The compilations by the ACU, ADA, AFL-CIO and the U.S. Chamber of Commerce are four of the most often cited ratings.

While the ratings are widely read, their value as an analytical tool is debated. The studies use a small number of votes selected by groups with a vested interest in what Congress does, making them a limited and potentially misleading barometer of what is happening on Capitol Hill.

"Use them gingerly to understand the Congress," Roger Davidson, a political science professor at the University of Maryland, commented. "They are of some utility, but the positions may be more subtle than might be reflected in these simple indices."

For instance, on what was probably the biggest vote of 1990 — the Oct. 5 House vote that rejected the budget-summit agreement — members who voted against it helped their cause with both the ADA and its ideological opponent, the ACU. Both groups opposed the agreement, although for different reasons: conservatives because it depended on new taxes, liberals because the tax burden did not fall heavily enough on the rich and because cuts were proposed in social services.

The scores can change drastically with one or two votes. If a senator opposed the AFL-CIO on only one vote in 1990, his score was lowered by 11 percentage points. The AFL-CIO and the Chamber both said their studies were significantly altered by one or two unusual votes in 1990.

When the House voted 312-86 to loosen controls on exports of high technology to Eastern Europe — in agreement with the Chamber's position — the core of opposition came from conservatives who distrusted the Soviet Union, with 82 Republicans voting no. They apparently saw it more as a test of ideology than of business.

Largely because of such votes, only six House members got perfect scores from the Chamber in 1990, compared with 98 members who tallied 100 percent in 1989. In the Senate, Republicans Connie Mack, Fla., Trent Lott, Miss., and Don Nickles, Okla., all received perfect scores from the Chamber; four senators notched perfect scores in 1989.

For the AFL-CIO, votes on such issues as fuel-efficiency standards and workers' safety proved a nemesis; they prevented any senator from receiving a perfect score in support. Twenty-six senators had perfect labor support scores in 1989. In the House, 77 representatives — the same number as in 1989 — supported the AFL-CIO's position on every vote it selected.

Year of the Veto

The large number of votes that required a supermajority underscored the importance of Bush's active use of the veto — 11 bills in 1990 — in analyzing legislative action in the 101st Congress. All four groups used at least one veto override attempt in their ratings.

Nowhere was the influence of the presidential veto, threatened or real, more evident than on labor issues. The AFL-CIO included three veto-override attempts — one-third of the total votes it used — in its study of the Senate, and it also used a cloture vote on motor vehicle fuel-efficiency standards, which required 60 votes to pass.

The AFL-CIO used override attempts instead of final-passage votes because its leaders felt the overrides mattered more. "Some members think they can vote one way to please their constituency and then turn around and vote another way to please the president," said Peggy Taylor, assistant director of the AFL-CIO's legislative department.

If the veto-override attempts were removed from the study, the AFL-CIO would have won about 75 percent of its House votes and 50 percent of its Senate votes in 1990, said Taylor.

Despite its lower overall scores, the labor leaders were optimistic about the 1990 legislative session, mainly because average support scores did not fall significantly.

"It's a pretty heavy duty to override the president," said Taylor. "We don't fault the Congress."

The Chamber took the opposite tack, basing its optimism — in the face of a losing record and declining average support scores — on the veto. Christine Russell, House legislative liaison for the Chamber, said the Chamber prevailed in the end on the issues that mattered most, such as blocking the civil rights and parental leave bills.

"We won on more of the major issues than we lost; therefore, we are not pessimistic about 1990 at all," Russell said.

Looking for the Votes

Both the ACU and ADA reported difficulty finding solid votes on which to base their ratings.

ADA leaders perceived a lot of political posturing on Capitol Hill in 1990, Isaacs said. Usually, the ADA selected 20 votes from each chamber, but for 1990 the group found only 18 votes per chamber that met its standards.

Twenty-nine House members voted with the ADA on every vote in their study, up from 25 in 1989, and an increase of 13 members from 1988. Sens. Daniel K. Akaka, D-Hawaii, Alan Cranston, D-Calif., Edward M. Kennedy, D-Mass., and Frank R. Lautenberg, D-N.J., led their chamber with perfect ADA scores. Two senators had perfect ADA scores in 1989.

The ACU saw its average member support score in the House drop from 43 percent in 1989 to 41 percent in 1990. In the Senate, the average ACU rating fell from 46 percent in 1989 to 45 percent in 1990.

Jesse Helms, R-N.C., and Steve Symms, R-Idaho, were the ACU's big supporters in the Senate, both scoring 100 percent. Helms had scored 100 percent since his second year in office in 1974. In the House, five members drew perfect scores from the ACU, down from nine in 1989.

The ACU's Billings said the election played a role in lowering its average scores, as a lot of members did not want to risk opposing legislation that they believed to be popular among their voters, such as the civil rights bill.

Billings said there was a "general feeling among some Republicans that it's all right to compromise a little bit in the spirit of bipartisanship. After eight years of conservatism, it is time to sit back and digest a little bit." ■

Votes Used in Interest Groups' Ratings

Following are the positions advocated by four major interest groups on congressional votes they used to rate members in 1990. A "Y" or "N" indicates whether the group favored a yea or nay vote; "won" or "lost" indicates whether the group's position prevailed. *(Individual scores, House, p. 28-B; Senate, p. 30-B)*

AMERICANS FOR DEMOCRATIC ACTION

Since 1947, ADA ratings have been a standard, if sometimes disputed, measure of liberalism. The ADA based its ratings on 18 Senate votes and 18 House votes.

House Votes

The ADA supported:

Automatically registering eligible citizens to vote when they applied for, renewed or changed a driver's license, and making voter-registration forms available at certain public offices. *(Vote 11; Y — won)*

Passing, over Bush's veto, the bill to establish a commission to investigate and report on the management dispute between Eastern Airlines and its unions. *(Vote 22; Y — lost)*

Barring the use of federal funds for religious worship or instruction at child-care centers and prohibiting religious discrimination in the hiring of child-care workers by sectarian institutions receiving federal funds *(Vote 56; Y — lost)*

Requiring eight-year/80,000 mile warranties for catalytic converters and electronic control units. *(Vote 133; Y — won)*

Passing, over Bush's veto, the bill to allow greater political activity by federal employees and to protect them from political pressure. *(Vote 184; Y — won)*

Passing, over Bush's veto, the bill requiring employers to give unpaid leave to workers caring for a new child or sick relative. *(Vote 262; Y — lost)*

Terminating the strategic defense initiative (SDI) program by limiting basic research on it in fiscal 1991 to $1.5 billion. *(Vote 337; Y — lost)*

Rejecting the death penalty as a maximum sentence in favor of mandatory life imprisonment without the possibility of parole. *(Vote 143; Y — lost)*

Barring the execution of prisoners who demonstrated that their death sentence was imposed because of racial discrimination. *(Vote 423; N to strike — won)*

Amending the budget agreement to provide smaller increases in the Medicare premium and deductible; delete revenue provisions; eliminate the tax "bubble" and lift the top marginal tax rate to 33 percent; create a 10 percent surtax on income above $1 million; increase the minimum tax rate; delay indexing for one year; and provide a limited tax break for capital gains. *(Vote 474; Y — won)*

The ADA opposed:

Allowing an employer to transfer a worker with a communicable disease out of a food-handling position, provided the employer offered the worker a similar position. *(Vote 118; N — lost)*

Proposing a constitutional amendment to prohibit the physical desecration of the flag. *(Vote 192; N — won)*

Proposing a constitutional amendment to require a balanced budget *(Vote 238; N — won)*

Defining "business necessity" in the civil rights bill as a practice that had a clear relationship to the employment in question or that served a legitimate employment goal; striking the bill's damages provisions; and reducing or deleting a number of the bill's other provisions. *(Vote 309; N — won)*

Lowering the limit on political action committees' donations; requiring that at least half of a House candidate's campaign funds come from his constituents; banning leadership PACs; prohibiting the transfer between PACs and candidate committees; banning the use of "soft money" by state and federal parties; and prohibiting the use of union or corporate funds for voter registration or participation campaigns directed at members or employees. *(Vote 316; N — won)*

Allowing semiautomatic weapons that have been banned from importation to be assembled from domestic parts. *(Vote 416; N — lost)*

Adopting the Sept. 30 budget agreement between congressional leaders and the Bush administration setting binding budget levels for fiscal 1991 by incorporating cost-saving measures in entitlement programs and increasing various user fees and taxes. *(Vote 421; N — won)*

Prohibiting the National Endowment for the Arts from funding obscene material, material deemed indecent by the Federal Communications Commission, or works denigrating a religion or an individual on the basis of race, sex, handicap or national origin. *(Vote 447; N — won)*

Senate Votes

The ADA supported:

Requiring a second round of tailpipe emissions reductions by 2003; the use of reformulated gasoline in ozone non-attainment areas; and the use of clean fuel in vehicles in the nation's smoggiest cities. *(Vote 35; N to table — lost)*

Prohibiting the death penalty if a defendant could prove that race played a role in his sentencing. *(Vote 108; N to strike provisions — lost)*

Passing, over President Bush's veto, the bill to allow greater political activity by federal employees and to protect them from political pressure. *(Vote 121; Y — lost)*

Banning for three years the production, sale and possession of nine types of semiautomatic assault-style weapons. *(Vote 133; Y — won)*

Rejecting the death penalty as a maximum sentence in favor of mandatory life imprisonment without the possibility of parole. *(Vote 143; Y — lost)*

Reversing or modifying six recent Supreme Court decisions that narrowed the reach and remedies of job discrimination laws. *(Vote 161; Y — won)*

Halting the construction of the B-2 bomber at six test aircraft. *(Vote 208; Y — lost)*

Reducing by $594 million the amount authorized for the strategic defense initiative (SDI) in 1991. *(Vote 225; N to table — lost)*

Requiring federally funded facilities assisting pregnant women to advise them, on request, of all their legal and medical options, including abortion. *(Vote 252; Y — won)*

How Interest Groups Fared

(On 1990 votes they selected)

	Won-Lost		Average Scores	
	1990	1989	1990	1989
AFL-CIO				
House	7-5	9-3	55.8%	56.0%
Senate	3-6	8-2	53.4	59.0
U.S. Chamber of Commerce				
House	4-10	7-3	50.7	64.0
Senate	4-8	4-4	47.2	60.0
Americans for Democratic Action				
House	11-7	11-9	49.0	50.0
Senate	7-11	8-12	49.0	45.0
American Conservative Union				
House	3-19	8-17	41.0	43.0
Senate	7-14	7-17	45.0	46.0

Invoking cloture (thus limiting debate) on a proposal to allow eligible citizens to register to vote when they applied for or renewed driver's licenses. *(Vote 257; Y — lost)*

Eliminating the income tax rate bubble; increasing the alternative minimum tax; providing a surtax of 10 percent on taxable income above $1 million; deleting all new burdens placed on Medicare recipients; reducing the increase in the gas tax; and removing all provisions that would disallow 5 percent of itemized deductions on the portion of income above $100,000. *(Vote 280; Y — lost)*

Reducing military aid to El Salvador by 50 percent and linking future military aid to improvements in human rights and progress toward a negotiated peace settlement. *(Vote 293; Y — won)*

The ADA opposed:

Allowing an employer to transfer a worker with a communicable disease out of a food-handling position, provided the employer offered the worker a similar position. *(Vote 110; Y to table — lost)*

Proposing a constitutional amendment to prohibit the physical desecration of the flag. *(Vote 128; N — won)*

Allowing all workers covered by union contracts, including union members, to opt out of paying dues or other fees that went for any activity other than bargaining contracts. *(Vote 189; N-won)*

Confirming David H. Souter to be an associate justice of the U.S. Supreme Court. *(Vote 259; N — lost)*

Requiring federally funded health facilities to notify at least one parent of a minor seeking an abortion. *(Vote 266; Y to table — lost)*

Prohibiting the National Endowment for the Arts from using federal funds to promote, distribute, disseminate or produce materials that depicted or described, in a patently offensive way, sexual or excretory activities or organs. *(Vote 307; N — won)*

ADA Scores

House Highs and Lows

High scorers. Twenty-seven Northern and two Southern Democrats scored 100 percent. Twenty-seven Northern Democrats scored 94 percent.

Among Southern Democrats, Gonzalez, Texas, and Lewis, Ga., each scored 100 percent. Smith, Fla.; Synar, Okla.; and Washington, Texas, scored 94 percent.

Conte, Mass., and Schneider, R.I., scored highest among Republicans with 78 percent. Shays, Conn., followed with 72 percent.

Low scorers. Thirteen Republicans scored 0 percent. Forty-six scored 6 percent.

Hall of Texas scored lowest among Southern Democrats with

6 percent, followed by Leath of Texas with 11 percent.

Lowest scoring among Northern Democrats were Byron, Md., and Skelton, Mo., with 33 percent. Stallings, Idaho, and Volkmer, Mo., followed with 39 percent.

Senate Highs and Lows

High scorers. Four Northern Democrats scored 100 percent: Akaka, Hawaii; Cranston, Calif.; Kennedy, Mass.; and Lautenberg, N.J. Ten Northern Democrats scored 94 percent.

Highest among Southern Democrats was Gore, Tenn., with 78 percent. Bumpers, Ark.; Fowler, Ga.; and Sasser, Tenn., followed with 72 percent.

The highest scoring Republican was Hatfield, Ore., with 78 percent. Jeffords, Vt., and Packwood, Ore., each scored 72 percent.

Low scorers. Eight Republicans scored 0 percent: Coats, Ind.; Cochran, Miss.; Dole, Kan.; Gramm, Texas; Lott, Miss.; Mack, Fla.; McConnell, Ky.; Nickles, Okla. Ten scored 6 percent.

Among Southern Democrats, Heflin, Ala., scored lowest with 28 percent. Breaux, La., and Shelby, Ala., each scored 33 percent.

Exon of Nebraska scored lowest among Northern Democrats with 33 percent. Dixon, Ill., had the next-lowest score with 44 percent.

AFL-CIO

The umbrella group for organized labor, which has rated members of Congress since 1955, says its ratings represent "votes for or against the interest of workers." The AFL-CIO based its ratings on nine Senate votes and 12 House votes.

House Votes

The AFL-CIO supported:

Automatically registering eligible citizens to vote when they applied for, renewed or changed an address on a driver's license, and making voter-registration forms available at certain public offices. *(Vote 10; N to recommit — won)*

Passing, over Bush's veto, the bill to establish a commission to investigate and report on the management dispute between Eastern Airlines and its unions. *(Vote 22; Y — lost)*

Authorizing $250 million over five years for retraining and additional unemployment benefits for workers who lost their jobs or had their pay cut as a result of the Clean Air Act. *(Vote 132; Y — won)*

Passing, over Bush's veto, a bill requiring employers to give unpaid leave to workers caring for a new child or sick relative. *(Vote 262; Y — lost)*

Continuing the regulation of modular homes by state and local construction and safety codes. *(Vote 291; Y — lost)*

Requiring employers who hired foreign workers to certify that they had agreed to provide education and training for U.S. workers or students. *(Vote 400; Y — lost)*

Passing, over Bush's veto, the bill imposing stiff quotas on imported textiles, apparel and shoes. *(Vote 440; Y — lost)*

Amending the budget agreement to provide smaller increases in the Medicare premium and deductible; delete revenue provisions; eliminate the tax "bubble" and lift the top marginal tax rate to 33 percent; create a 10 percent surtax on income above $1 million; increase the minimum tax rate; delay indexing for one year; and provide a limited tax break for capital gains. *(Vote 474; Y — won)*

Establishing a national shellfish inspection program to be administered by the FDA, requiring the president to submit to Congress a proposal for a comprehensive mandatory fish inspection program, and providing whistleblower protections. *(Vote 514; Y — won)*

The AFL-CIO opposed:

Adopting a substitute to the child-care bill that would generally provide smaller funding increases than were included in the Democratic leadership bill and would not require states to impose child-care standards in certain areas or authorize a new school-based program for before- and after-school care. *(Vote 57; N — won)*

Proposing a constitutional amendment to require a balanced budget. *(Vote 238; N — won)*

Defining "business necessity" in the civil rights bill as a practice that had a clear relationship to the employment in question or that served a legitimate employment goal; striking the bill's damages provisions; and reducing or deleting a number of the bill's other provisions. *(Vote 309; N — won)*

Senate Votes

The AFL-CIO supported:

Providing severance pay and retraining benefits to coal miners who lost their jobs as a result of the Clean Air Act. *(Vote 47; Y — lost)*

Passing, over President Bush's veto, the bill to reauthorize Amtrak for fiscal 1989-92. *(Vote 115; Y — lost)*

Passing, over Bush's veto, the bill to allow greater political activity by federal employees and to protect them from political pressure. *(Vote 121; Y — lost)*

Limiting growth in imports of textiles, textile products and non-rubber footwear to 1 percent annually. *(Vote 157; Y — won)*

Directing the secretaries of Health and Human Services and Commerce, instead of the Department of Agriculture, to establish a safety and quality program for fish and fish products with protections for whistleblowers. *(Vote 232; Y — lost)*

Setting minimum civil penalties for violations of worker safety and health standards set by the Occupational Safety and Health Administration. *(Vote 282; Y — lost)*

Passing, over Bush's veto, the bill reversing or modifying six recent Supreme Court decisions that narrowed the reach and remedies of job discrimination laws. *(Vote 304; Y — lost)*

The AFL-CIO opposed:

Exempting federal low-income housing construction and rehabilitation projects of less than $1 million from the Davis-Bacon Act. *(Vote 122; Y to table — won)*

Invoking cloture (thus limiting debate) on a proposal requiring automakers to increase 1988 corporate average Fuel economy (CAFE) levels 20 percent by 1995 and 40 percent by 2001. *(Vote 248; N — won)*

AFL-CIO Scores

House Highs and Lows

High scorers. Seventy-seven Democrats received perfect scores of 100 percent. The breakdown was 10 Southern Democrats and 67 Northern Democrats.

Conte, Mass., led Republicans with 92 percent. Davis, Mich., and Horton, N.Y., followed with 83 percent.

Low scorers. Thirty-six Republicans received 0 percent. Forty-nine scored 8 percent.

Hall, Texas, scored lowest among Democrats with 20 percent. Six Southern Democrats scored 25 percent.

Among Northern Democrats, Stallings, Idaho, scored lowest with 27 percent. Byron, Md.; Penny, Minn.; and Skelton, Mo., each scored 50 percent.

Senate Highs and Lows

High scorers. Five Northern Democrats scored 89 percent: Byrd, W.Va.; Inouye, Hawaii; Kennedy, Mass.; Kerry, Mass.; and Metzenbaum, Ohio.

Gore, Tenn., and Ford, Ky., led Southern Democrats with 89 percent. Johnston, La., followed with 86 percent.

Specter, Pa., scored highest among Republicans with 89 percent. Heinz, Pa., received 78 percent.

Low scorers. Three Republicans — Gorton, Wash.; Pressler, S.D. and Wilson, Calif.— received 0 percent. Ten Republicans scored 11 percent.

Fowler, Ga., and Gramm, Fla., scored lowest among Southern Democrats with 44 percent each. Four Southern Democrats scored 56 percent.

Lowest scorer among Northern Democrats was Baucus, Mont., with 44 percent. Seven Northern Democrats scored 56 percent.

U.S. CHAMBER OF COMMERCE

The Chamber selected votes that it said provided "a fair representation of floor votes on issues important to business — including large and small firms." Twelve Senate votes and 14

House votes were chosen for the study.

House Votes

The Chamber supported:

Adopting a substitute to the child-care bill that would generally provide smaller funding increases than were included in the Democratic leadership bill and would not require states to impose child-care standards in certain areas or authorize a new school-based program for before- and after-school care. *(Vote 57; Y — lost)*

Limiting the remedies in the Americans with Disabilities Act to those available under Title VII of the 1964 Civil Rights Act: injunctive relief, back pay and attorneys' fees. *(Vote 121; Y — lost)*

Easing restrictions on certain U.S. exports to U.S. allies and Eastern European countries and, to a lesser extent, the Soviet Union. *(Vote 160; Y — won)*

Limiting federal tax-revenue growth to the growth rate of national income, unless a specific tax increase is enacted by a three-fifths vote of each chamber. *(Vote 236; Y — lost)*

Proposing a constitutional amendment to require a balanced budget. *(Vote 238; Y — lost)*

Defining "business necessity" in the civil rights bill as a practice that had a clear relationship to the employment in question or that served a legitimate employment goal; striking the bill's damages provisions; and reducing or deleting a number of the bill's other provisions. *(Vote 309; Y — lost)*

Raising the number of visas granted annually, drawing immigrants from Europe and other areas shut out under current law and allowing entry of more skilled workers. *(Vote 530; Y — won)*

The Chamber opposed:

Clarifying the evidence necessary to establish resale (vertical) price fixing. *(Vote 74; N — lost)*

Requiring employers to give unpaid leave to workers caring for a new child or sick relative. *(Vote 107; N — lost)*

Requiring eight-year/80,000 mile warranties for catalytic converters and electronic control units. *(Vote 133; N — lost)*

Passing, over Bush's veto, the bill requiring employers to give unpaid leave to workers caring for a new child or sick relative. *(Vote 262; N — won)*

Adopting the Sept. 30 budget agreement between congressional leaders and the Bush administration setting binding budget levels for fiscal 1991 by incorporating cost-saving measures in entitlement programs and increasing various user fees and taxes. *(Vote 421; N — won)*

Denying most-favored-nation trade status to China. *(Vote 483; N — lost)*

Passing the fiscal 1991 Budget Reconciliation Act containing provisions to reduce spending and raise revenues. *(Vote 326; N — lost)*

Senate Votes

The Chamber supported:

Allowing states to issue operating permits without full review by the Environmental Protection Agency to facilitate enforcement of the Clean Air Act. *(Vote 53; Y — lost)*

Granting the president the legislative line-item veto. *(Vote 111; Y — lost)*

Exempting federal low-income housing construction and rehabilitation projects of less than $1 million from the Davis-Bacon Act. *(Vote 122; N to table — lost)*

Eliminating taxpayer funding of Senate campaigns. *(Vote 188; Y — lost)*

Reducing the Social Security payroll tax gradually over six years and returning Social Security to a pay-as-you-go basis. *(Vote 262; Y — lost)*

Lessening the burden of proof in civil rights lawsuits for employers defending practices that were fair in form but had the effect of discriminating against women and minorities. *(Vote 275; Y — lost)*

The Chamber opposed:

Establishing blending limits for alternative fuels and requiring that reformulated gasoline replace conventional gasoline in the nation's nine smoggiest cities. *(Vote 48; Y to table — lost)*

Passing, over President Bush's veto, the bill to reauthorize Amtrak for fiscal years 1989-92. *(Vote 115; N — won)*

Setting minimum civil penalties for violations of worker safety and health standards set by the Occupational Safety and Health Administration. *(Vote 282; N — won)*

Reinstating the windfall profit tax on domestic crude oil. *(Vote 288; N — won)*

Passing, over Bush's veto, the bill reversing or modifying six recent Supreme Court decisions that narrowed the reach and remedies of job discrimination laws. *(Vote 304; N — won)*

Passing the fiscal 1991 Budget Reconciliation Act containing provisions to reduce spending and raise revenues. *(Vote 326; N — lost)*

Chamber Scores

House Highs and Lows

High scorers. Six Republicans scored 100 percent. Sarpalius, Texas, led Southern Democrats with 92 percent. Stallings, Idaho, led Northern Democrats with 79 percent.

Low scorers. Nelson, Fla., who missed 10 of 14 Chamber votes in 1990, scored 0 percent. Five Northern Democrats scored 8 percent.

Next to Nelson, the lowest-scoring Southern Democrats were Fascell, Fla., and Frost, Texas, each with 14 percent.

Lowest among Republicans were Conte, Mass., and Gilman, N.Y., with 14 percent each.

Senate Highs and Lows

High scorers. Three Republicans scored 100 percent: Lott, Miss.; Mack, Fla.; and Nickles, Okla.

Heflin, Ala., led Southern Democrats with 64 percent.

Exon, Neb., scored highest among Northern Democrats with 55 percent.

Low scorers. Kennedy, Mass., scored lowest among Northern Democrats with 0 percent. Six other Northern Democrats received scores of 8 percent.

The lowest-scoring Southern Democrats were Tennessee's Gore and Sasser, each with 17 percent.

Hatfield, Ore., scored lowest among Republicans with 22 percent.

AMERICAN CONSERVATIVE UNION

The ACU seeks "to mobilize resources of responsible conservative thought across the country and further the general cause of conservatism." It based its ratings on 21 Senate and 22 House votes.

House Votes

The ACU supported:

Adopting a substitute to the child-care bill that would generally provide smaller funding increases than were included in the Democratic leadership bill and would not require states to impose child-care standards in certain areas or authorize a new school-based program for before- and after-school care. *(Vote 57; Y — lost)*

Allowing an employer to transfer a worker with a communicable disease out of a food-handling position, provided the employer offered the worker a similar position. *(Vote 118; Y — won)*

Prohibiting the export of machine tools to the Soviet Union. *(Vote 158; Y — lost)*

Proposing a constitutional amendment to prohibit the physical desecration of the flag. *(Vote 192; Y — lost)*

Proposing a constitutional amendment to require a balanced budget. The ACU double-weighted this vote in calculating its scores. *(Vote 238; Y — lost)*

Censuring Rep. Barney Frank, D-Mass., rather than imposing the lighter reprimand he received. *(Vote 270; Y — lost)*

Increasing funding by $1.3 billion to $4.2 billion for the SDI. *(Vote 336; Y-lost)*

Prohibiting the National Endowment for the Arts from funding obscene material, material deemed indecent by the Federal Communications Commission, or works denigrating a religion or an individual on the basis of race, sex, handicap or national origin. *(Vote 447; Y — lost)*

The ACU opposed:

Automatically registering eligible citizens to vote when they applied for, renewed or changed a driver's license, and making voter-registration forms available at certain public offices. *(Vote 11; N — lost)*

Elevating the Environmental Protection Agency to Cabinet status. *(Vote 50; N — lost)*

Reducing the budget deficit to $63.8 billion through greater defense cuts and larger revenue increases than called for in the House budget plan. *(Vote 88; N — won)*

Requiring employers to give unpaid leave to workers caring for a newborn child or sick relative. *(Vote 107; N — lost)*

Suspending 50 percent of El Salvador's military aid for fiscal years 1990 and 1991, depending on the actions by the Salvadoran government or by the leftist guerrillas. *(Vote 127; N — lost)*

Amending the Clean Air Act to attain and maintain national air quality standards and otherwise improving the quality of the nation's air. *(Vote 137; N — lost)*

Providing $6 million for a fish and wildlife refuge in central Iowa. *(Vote 139; N — lost)*

Allowing greater political activity by federal employees and protecting them from political pressure. *(Vote 163; N — lost)*

Reversing or modifying six recent Supreme Court decisions that narrowed the reach and remedies of job discrimination laws. The ACU double-weighted this vote in calculating its scores. *(Vote 310; N — lost)*

Reducing spending for SDI by $600 million to a new level of $2.3 billion. *(Vote 339; N — lost)*

Adopting the Sept. 30 budget agreement between congressional leaders and the White House setting binding budget levels for fiscal 1991 by incorporating cost-saving measures in entitlement programs and increasing various user fees and taxes. *(Vote 421; N — won)*

Barring the execution of prisoners who demonstrated that their death sentence was imposed because of racial discrimination. *(Vote 423; Y to strike — lost)*

Passing the fiscal 1991 Budget Reconciliation Act containing provisions to reduce spending and raise revenues. *(Vote 326; N — lost)*

Suspending military aid to the National Union for the Total Independence of Angola (UNITA) — a rebel group fighting the Angolan government — if the government of Angola agreed to certain conditions. *(Vote 482; N — lost)*

Senate Votes

The ACU supported:

Using any savings from the "peace dividend" to balance the budget and to return any funds beyond that to the taxpayers. *(Vote 22; Y — lost)*

Allowing an employer to transfer a worker with a communicable disease out of a food-handling position, provided the employer offered the worker a similar position. *(Vote 110; N to table — won)*

Exempting federal low-income housing construction and rehabilitation projects of less than $1 million from the Davis-Bacon Act. *(Vote 122; N to table — lost)*

Proposing a constitutional amendment to prohibit the physical desecration of the flag. *(Vote 128; Y — lost)*

Prohibiting U.S. financial institutions from extending credit to the Soviet Union at interest rates below those offered to American farmers. *(Vote 178; Y — won)*

Eliminating taxpayer funding of Senate campaigns. *(Vote 188; Y — lost)*

Excluding private nonprofit organizations such as Planned Parenthood from receiving direct federal funding under Title X of the Public Health Service Act of 1970. *(Vote 253; Y — lost)*

Confirming David H. Souter to be an associate justice of the U.S. Supreme Court. *(Vote 259; Y — won)*

Prohibiting the National Endowment for the Arts from using federal funds to promote, distribute, disseminate or produce materials that depicted or described, in a patently offensive way, sexual or excretory activities or organs. *(Vote 307; Y — lost)*

The ACU opposed:

Limiting the right of organizations in the District of Columbia to exclude homosexuals and bisexuals from coaching, teaching or serving as mentors to minors. *(Vote 23; Y to table — lost)*

Allowing greater political activity by federal employees. *(Vote 90; N — lost)*

Banning for three years the production, sale and possession of nine types of semiautomatic assault-style weapons. *(Vote 103; Y to strike provisions — lost)*

Prohibiting the death penalty if a defendant could prove that race played a role in his sentencing. *(Vote 108; Y to strike provisions — won)*

Halting the construction of the B-2 bomber at six test aircraft. *(Vote 208; N — won)*

Barring the closure of any domestic military base in fiscal 1991 and requiring any future closures to be part of a long-term plan for the future shape of the military. *(Vote 221; N — won)*

Changing priorities within the strategic defense initiative (SDI); providing more money for research on ground-based antimissile systems; and reducing funding for the so-called brilliant pebbles program of space-based interceptor missiles. The ACU double-weighted this vote in calculating its scores. *(Vote 223; N — lost)*

Appropriating $183.3 billion — nearly $11.6 billion more than the president requested — for the Departments of Labor, Health and Human Services, and Education and related agencies in fiscal 1991. *(Vote 269; N — lost)*

Passing the bill to reduce spending and raise revenues as required by the reconciliation instructions in the budget resolution. *(Vote 292; N — lost)*

Reducing military aid to El Salvador by 50 percent and linking future military aid to improvements in human rights and progress toward a negotiated peace settlement. *(Vote 293; N — lost)*

Passing, over President Bush's veto, the bill reversing or modifying six recent Supreme Court decisions that narrowed the reach and remedies of job discrimination laws. The ACU double-weighted this vote in calculating its scores. *(Vote 304; N — won)*

Amending the Clean Air Act to attain and maintain national air quality standards, and otherwise improving the quality of the nation's air. *(Vote 324; N — lost)*

ACU Scores

House Highs and Lows

High scorers. Five Republicans received perfect scores of 100 percent. Nine Republicans scored 96 percent.

Barnard, Ga., led Southern Democrats with 81 percent. Hutto, Fla., received the next highest score among Southern Democrats with 78 percent.

Among Northern Democrats, Lipinski, Ill., scored highest with 54 percent, followed by Skelton, Mo., with 50 percent.

Low scorers. Twenty Northern Democrats scored 0 percent. Fifty-three Northern Democrats scored 4 percent.

Lehman, Fla., was the only Southern Democrat to receive a 0 percent score. Boggs, La., Gonzalez, Texas, and Lewis, Ga., all scored 4 percent.

Conte, Mass., was the lowest-scoring Republican with 8 percent. Green, N.Y., scored next lowest among Republicans with 13 percent.

Senate Highs and Lows

High scorers. Two Republicans received perfect 100 percent scores: Helms, N.C., and Symms, Idaho. Coats, Ind.; Mack, Fla.; and Nickles, Okla., each scored 96 percent.

Exon, Neb., led all Democrats with 61 percent. The next highest Northern Democratic scorer was Baucus, Mont., with 41 percent.

Heflin, Ala., scored highest among Southern Democrats with 55 percent. Hollings, S.C., and Shelby, Ala., followed, each with 48 percent.

Low scorers. Cranston, Calif., and Kennedy, Mass., scored lowest among Northern Democrats with 0 percent. Four Northern Democrats scored 4 percent.

The lowest-scoring Southern Democrats were Tennessee's Gore and Sasser, each with 9 percent. Sanford, N.C., scored 17 percent.

Among Republicans, Jeffords, Vt., scored lowest with 26 percent. Oregon's Hatfield and Packwood each received 35 percent.

ADA (Americans for Democratic Action) — The percentage of time each representative voted in accordance with the ADA position on 18 selected votes in 1990. The percentages were compiled by the ADA. Failure to vote lowers scores.

AFL-CIO (American Federation of Labor-Congress of Industrial Organizations) — The percentage of time each representative voted for or was paired in favor of the AFL-CIO position on 12 selected votes in 1990. The percentages were computed by Congressional Quarterly based on the selected votes. Failure to vote does not lower scores.

CCUS (Chamber of Commerce of the United States) — The percentage of time each representative voted with the Chamber's position on 14 selected votes in 1990. The percentages were compiled by the Chamber. Failure to vote does not lower scores.

ACU (American Conservative Union) — The percentage of time each representative voted with the ACU position on 22 selected votes in 1990. The percentages were compiled by the ACU. Failure to vote does not lower scores.

[1] *Rep. Patsy T. Mink was sworn in Sept. 27, 1990, to succeed Daniel K. Akaka, D, who was appointed to replace the late Democratic Sen. Spark M. Matsunaga. Mink was not rated by the ADA.*

[2] *Rep. Thomas S. Foley as Speaker of the House, voted at his discretion. He was rated only by the ACU on the basis of three votes.*

KEY

ADA — Americans for Democratic Action

AFL-CIO — American Federation of Labor-Congress of Industrial Organizations

CCUS — Chamber of Commerce of the United States

ACU — American Conservative Union

Democrats ***Republicans***

	ADA	AFL-CIO	CCUS	ACU
Alabama				
1 ***Callahan***	6	17	92	87
2 ***Dickinson***	0	17	79	88
3 Browder	33	50	71	58
4 Bevill	22	50	57	58
5 Flippo	33	78	29	56
6 Erdreich	39	75	36	54
7 Harris	33	50	57	58
Alaska				
AL ***Young***	33	33	64	67
Arizona				
1 ***Rhodes***	17	17	71	63
2 Udall	89	92	8	4
3 ***Stump***	6	9	80	100
4 ***Kyl***	6	0	86	92
5 ***Kolbe***	22	8	86	61
Arkansas				
1 Alexander	50	73	50	17
2 ***Robinson***	22	27	78	76
3 ***Hammerschmidt***	6	8	77	82
4 Anthony	67	58	50	17
California				
1 Bosco	50	75	43	21
2 ***Herger***	6	8	79	96
3 Matsui	94	92	21	0
4 Fazio	89	100	21	4
5 Pelosi	100	92	15	4
6 Boxer	94	83	8	4
7 Miller	100	83	21	4
8 Dellums	100	100	29	4
9 Stark	100	83	23	4
10 Edwards	100	100	21	4
11 Lantos	78	92	21	17
12 ***Campbell***	44	27	71	46
13 Mineta	94	92	15	0
14 ***Shumway***	0	0	86	92
15 Condit	56	67	36	29
16 Panetta	83	83	21	8
17 ***Pashayan***	11	18	79	64
18 Lehman	94	83	15	4
19 ***Lagomarsino***	11	0	79	92
20 ***Thomas***	17	9	91	74
21 ***Gallegly***	11	0	86	92
22 ***Moorhead***	6	8	86	96
23 Beilenson	83	75	8	8
24 Waxman	100	92	21	4
25 Roybal	100	100	36	4
26 Berman	100	92	23	4
27 Levine	100	92	21	4
28 Dixon	100	100	23	4
29 Hawkins	89	100	10	11
30 Martinez	78	92	38	9
31 Dymally	100	100	36	4
32 Anderson	94	92	21	4
33 ***Dreier***	17	8	79	83
34 Torres	89	100	21	0
35 ***Lewis***	6	0	58	76
36 Brown	89	83	31	4
37 ***McCandless***	6	8	79	92
38 ***Dornan***	6	18	79	91
39 ***Dannemeyer***	6	8	71	100
40 ***Cox***	11	0	85	88
41 ***Lowery***	11	8	77	70
42 ***Rohrabacher***	6	8	86	96
43 ***Packard***	11	8	93	88
44 Bates	94	92	31	18
45 ***Hunter***	6	17	86	96
Colorado				
1 Schroeder	100	92	21	13
2 Skaggs	89	83	21	8
3 Campbell	56	67	77	33
4 ***Brown***	11	0	79	83
5 ***Hefley***	6	0	79	92
6 ***Schaefer***	11	25	79	79
Connecticut				
1 Kennelly	83	92	14	8
2 Gejdenson	94	100	14	4
3 Morrison	94	100	23	9
4 ***Shays***	72	50	36	25
5 ***Rowland***	44	40	58	52
6 ***Johnson***	44	33	57	50
Delaware				
AL Carper	78	92	21	17
Florida				
1 Hutto	28	50	77	78
2 ***Grant***	22	8	77	67
3 Bennett	39	83	21	42
4 ***James***	17	8	79	71
5 ***McCollum***	17	8	71	88
6 ***Stearns***	17	8	71	83
7 Gibbons	61	55	31	27
8 ***Young***	17	8	57	79
9 ***Bilirakis***	17	9	85	80
10 ***Ireland***	11	8	64	82
11 Nelson	50	89	0	27
12 ***Lewis***	6	0	79	90
13 ***Goss***	33	8	86	79
14 Johnston	83	83	38	25
15 ***Shaw***	6	8	57	83
16 Smith	94	100	21	9
17 Lehman	89	92	21	0
18 ***Ros-Lehtinen***	33	8	54	65
19 Fascell	83	92	14	8
Georgia				
1 Thomas	28	42	69	50
2 Hatcher	28	42	57	50
3 Ray	22	25	71	50
4 Jones	61	67	57	33
5 Lewis	100	100	21	4
6 ***Gingrich***	17	25	92	86
7 Darden	28	50	57	58
8 Rowland	33	42	57	42
9 Jenkins	39	42	67	54
10 Barnard	22	50	86	81
Hawaii				
1 ***Saiki***	44	36	67	54
2 Mink [1]		100	50	20
Idaho				
1 ***Craig***	11	0	82	86
2 Stallings	39	27	79	46
Illinois				
1 Hayes	100	100	29	4
2 Savage	89	92	14	9
3 Russo	78	83	23	17
4 Sangmeister	56	75	38	33
5 Lipinski	44	75	54	54
6 ***Hyde***	11	17	64	88
7 Collins	94	100	31	5
8 Rostenkowski	67	83	17	14
9 Yates	100	92	17	5
10 ***Porter***	22	17	79	67
11 Annunzio	56	75	43	38
12 ***Crane***	11	0	79	100
13 ***Fawell***	11	8	93	88
14 ***Hastert***	6	0	86	79
15 ***Madigan***	0	0	79	86
16 ***Martin***	11	27	83	61
17 Evans	100	100	21	4
18 ***Michel***	11	0	71	76
19 Bruce	83	100	36	8
20 Durbin	83	92	31	4
21 Costello	67	92	36	29
22 Poshard	78	92	29	29
Indiana				
1 Visclosky	72	92	14	13
2 Sharp	67	83	46	22
3 ***Hiler***	11	0	86	88

	ADA	AFL-CIO	CCUS	ACU
4 Long	50	67	43	38
5 Jontz	89	83	36	17
6 ***Burton***	11	17	85	96
7 ***Myers***	11	0	86	83
8 McCloskey	83	92	21	8
9 Hamilton	67	58	43	13
10 Jacobs	78	83	43	25
Iowa				
1 ***Leach***	61	42	57	21
2 ***Tauke***	28	0	85	57
3 Nagle	83	75	36	8
4 Smith	83	83	29	8
5 ***Lightfoot***	6	0	93	92
6 ***Grandy***	28	0	86	42
Kansas				
1 ***Roberts***	6	0	79	75
2 Slattery	61	67	43	22
3 ***Meyers***	22	0	57	67
4 Glickman	72	67	31	17
5 ***Whittaker***	11	17	86	71
Kentucky				
1 Hubbard	39	42	79	52
2 Natcher	61	75	36	25
3 Mazzoli	78	83	29	13
4 ***Bunning***	6	8	79	87
5 ***Rogers***	6	17	86	83
6 ***Hopkins***	11	17	79	83
7 Perkins	78	100	21	13
Louisiana				
1 ***Livingston***	6	8	79	83
2 Boggs	67	100	21	4
3 Tauzin	22	25	85	58
4 ***McCrery***	17	8	86	88
5 Huckaby	22	25	79	71
6 ***Baker***	0	18	83	86
7 Hayes	22	45	75	55
8 ***Holloway***	11	18	92	91
Maine				
1 Brennan	89	82	33	17
2 ***Snowe***	28	33	43	54
Maryland				
1 Dyson	44	75	36	38
2 ***Bentley***	11	25	77	83
3 Cardin	83	92	14	4
4 McMillen	56	83	29	17
5 Hoyer	89	100	14	0
6 Byron	33	50	57	48
7 Mfume	94	92	29	13
8 ***Morella***	67	58	29	17
Massachusetts				
1 ***Conte***	78	92	14	8
2 Neal	83	92	29	18
3 Early	72	82	36	19
4 Frank	94	100	23	4
5 Atkins	89	100	21	4
6 Mavroules	94	100	21	8
7 Markey	94	100	21	4
8 Kennedy	89	92	21	4
9 Moakley	78	100	14	4
10 Studds	100	100	21	4
11 Donnelly	61	83	36	29
Michigan				
1 Conyers	78	100	15	0
2 ***Pursell***	28	18	92	57
3 Wolpe	100	100	21	13
4 ***Upton***	17	17	93	71
5 ***Henry***	33	9	86	63
6 Carr	72	67	57	25
7 Kildee	94	100	21	4
8 Traxler	56	100	17	9
9 ***Vander Jagt***	6	8	85	83
10 ***Schuette***	17	22	100	76
11 ***Davis***	56	83	29	43
12 Bonior	94	100	31	8
13 Crockett	61	92	10	0
14 Hertel	94	100	21	17
15 Ford	78	100	33	5
16 Dingell	67	100	15	4
17 Levin	89	100	21	4
18 ***Broomfield***	17	17	100	83
Minnesota				
1 Penny	67	50	43	25
2 ***Weber***	22	0	92	83
3 ***Frenzel***	17	0	82	61
4 Vento	100	100	21	4
5 Sabo	94	100	14	0
6 Sikorski	89	100	8	0
7 ***Stangeland***	17	8	100	79
8 Oberstar	78	100	15	0
Mississippi				
1 Whitten	44	75	38	43
2 Espy	67	83	31	17
3 Montgomery	22	25	71	63
4 Parker	22	25	79	63
5 Taylor	28	50	64	63
Missouri				
1 Clay	94	100	31	4
2 ***Buechner***	22	17	71	67
3 Gephardt	83	100	14	4
4 Skelton	33	50	62	50
5 Wheat	100	100	21	4
6 ***Coleman***	28	17	57	65
7 ***Hancock***	11	0	79	100
8 ***Emerson***	11	17	85	78
9 Volkmer	39	75	36	38
Montana				
1 Williams	89	82	33	9
2 ***Marlenee***	6	0	93	87
Nebraska				
1 ***Bereuter***	17	0	100	67
2 Hoagland	72	83	50	29
3 ***Smith***	0	0	71	70
Nevada				
1 Bilbray	50	75	29	25
2 ***Vucanovich***	6	8	79	88
New Hampshire				
1 ***Smith***	6	17	71	91
2 ***Douglas***	17	17	79	88
New Jersey				
1 Vacancy				
2 Hughes	78	91	38	13
3 Pallone	61	83	43	29
4 ***Smith***	56	50	64	63
5 ***Roukema***	28	42	58	59
6 Dwyer	83	100	31	9
7 ***Rinaldo***	50	67	54	46
8 Roe	67	92	36	18
9 Torricelli	83	100	31	10
10 Payne	89	100	29	4
11 ***Gallo***	17	8	77	65
12 ***Courter***	17	8	64	73
13 ***Saxton***	33	17	92	63
14 Guarini	78	92	31	13
New Mexico				
1 ***Schiff***	22	17	71	58
2 ***Skeen***	6	8	79	71
3 Richardson	61	92	21	26
New York				
1 Hochbrueckner	89	100	21	13
2 Downey	100	92	21	8
3 Mrazek	100	100	29	9
4 ***Lent***	17	9	77	63
5 ***McGrath***	50	75	36	52
6 Flake	89	91	38	4
7 Ackerman	94	100	15	0
8 Scheuer	89	100	14	0
9 Manton	67	100	21	9
10 Schumer	94	92	21	4
11 Towns	94	100	31	4
12 Owens	94	100	29	4
13 Solarz	89	92	21	0
14 ***Molinari***	31	40	57	57
15 ***Green***	61	42	36	13
16 Rangel	89	100	29	4
17 Weiss	100	100	29	4
18 Serrano	88	100	14	0
19 Engel	100	100	21	9
20 Lowey	100	100	21	4
21 ***Fish***	56	50	43	32
22 ***Gilman***	61	83	14	29
23 McNulty	78	92	21	21
24 ***Solomon***	22	36	64	83
25 ***Boehlert***	61	50	50	33
26 ***Martin***	28	33	64	63
27 ***Walsh***	44	33	62	58
28 McHugh	89	92	14	4
29 ***Horton***	61	83	36	25
30 Slaughter	94	92	29	17
31 ***Paxon***	6	8	86	88
32 LaFalce	72	67	46	21
33 Nowak	89	100	31	4
34 ***Houghton***	33	25	54	43
North Carolina				
1 Jones	50	82	54	39
2 Valentine	33	42	43	42
3 Lancaster	39	50	43	50
4 Price	61	75	29	21
5 Neal	50	55	43	32
6 ***Coble***	6	8	93	83
7 Rose	61	75	23	21
8 Hefner	44	58	50	38
9 ***McMillan***	11	17	79	67
10 ***Ballenger***	6	8	86	83
11 Clarke	56	50	57	29
North Dakota				
AL Dorgan	72	73	43	21
Ohio				
1 Luken	50	92	31	17
2 ***Gradison***	11	0	86	75
3 Hall	72	100	8	8
4 ***Oxley***	0	17	93	79
5 ***Gillmor***	11	17	57	74
6 ***McEwen***	6	8	93	100
7 ***DeWine***	17	17	54	83
8 ***Lukens***	0	10	88	89
9 Kaptur	72	100	15	8
10 ***Miller***	0	25	71	91
11 Eckart	56	92	29	29
12 ***Kasich***	11	17	86	92
13 Pease	89	92	21	4
14 Sawyer	89	92	14	0
15 ***Wylie***	11	8	71	74
16 ***Regula***	17	42	71	63
17 Traficant	72	92	29	13
18 Applegate	50	92	36	33
19 Feighan	94	100	29	9
20 Oakar	83	92	23	4
21 Stokes	100	100	29	4
Oklahoma				
1 ***Inhofe***	11	0	77	88
2 Synar	94	91	21	8
3 Watkins	28	58	70	58
4 McCurdy	56	58	14	33
5 ***Edwards***	6	0	79	92
6 English	50	58	64	54
Oregon				
1 AuCoin	78	82	21	0
2 ***Smith***	6	8	93	88
3 Wyden	89	92	29	4
4 DeFazio	83	83	36	14
5 ***Smith***	6	8	100	85
Pennsylvania				
1 Foglietta	78	100	14	4
2 Gray	94	92	14	0
3 Borski	83	100	21	8
4 Kolter	44	92	36	30
5 ***Schulze***	17	27	86	71
6 Yatron	44	92	36	33
7 ***Weldon***	33	42	69	54
8 Kostmayer	89	100	14	0
9 ***Shuster***	11	9	92	96
10 ***McDade***	33	58	46	57
11 Kanjorski	67	92	21	21
12 Murtha	56	100	21	22
13 ***Coughlin***	33	17	64	35
14 Coyne	100	100	29	4
15 ***Ritter***	6	25	79	83
16 ***Walker***	11	8	71	96
17 ***Gekas***	0	17	86	91
18 Walgren	78	92	23	17
19 ***Goodling***	22	27	64	68
20 Gaydos	50	83	50	33
21 ***Ridge***	22	33	57	58
22 Murphy	50	83	69	33
23 ***Clinger***	28	18	77	55
Rhode Island				
1 ***Machtley***	61	50	64	25
2 ***Schneider***	78	58	54	25
South Carolina				
1 ***Ravenel***	28	25	57	63
2 ***Spence***	17	17	71	79
3 Derrick	44	58	62	33
4 Patterson	44	50	64	54
5 Spratt	56	67	36	33
6 Tallon	50	58	43	42
South Dakota				
AL Johnson	67	83	36	25
Tennessee				
1 ***Quillen***	6	25	92	83
2 ***Duncan***	11	25	79	88
3 Lloyd	44	58	50	46
4 Cooper	56	67	64	29
5 Clement	44	83	29	29
6 Gordon	67	92	21	13
7 ***Sundquist***	6	8	86	79
8 Tanner	44	58	54	29
9 Ford	89	100	27	5
Texas				
1 Chapman	33	83	43	27
2 Wilson	44	83	17	40
3 ***Bartlett***	0	8	86	83
4 Hall	6	20	77	71
5 Bryant	83	92	29	17
6 ***Barton***	6	0	77	87
7 ***Archer***	0	8	86	88
8 ***Fields***	6	8	93	88
9 Brooks	61	100	23	17
10 Pickle	61	33	50	25
11 Leath	11	30	67	56
12 Geren	39	50	79	46
13 Sarpalius	28	45	92	74
14 Laughlin	28	36	83	59
15 de la Garza	61	83	15	23
16 Coleman	67	83	23	17
17 Stenholm	22	25	71	67
18 Washington	94	100	31	5
19 ***Combest***	0	8	79	96
20 Gonzalez	100	100	21	4
21 ***Smith***	11	25	86	83
22 ***DeLay***	6	8	93	92
23 Bustamante	50	92	36	17
24 Frost	67	100	14	8
25 Andrews	56	75	29	25
26 ***Armey***	6	8	93	96
27 Ortiz	56	83	43	21
Utah				
1 ***Hansen***	0	0	79	92
2 Owens	72	75	23	13
3 ***Nielson***	11	8	93	83
Vermont				
AL ***Smith***	50	50	42	26
Virginia				
1 ***Bateman***	6	0	79	83
2 Pickett	50	75	64	42
3 ***Bliley***	17	17	93	83
4 Sisisky	39	50	50	42
5 Payne	33	50	64	33
6 Olin	50	58	43	38
7 ***Slaughter***	6	17	86	92
8 ***Parris***	17	17	93	83
9 Boucher	72	100	23	13
10 ***Wolf***	6	0	71	83
Washington				
1 ***Miller***	39	17	54	46
2 Swift	89	92	21	4
3 Unsoeld	83	92	36	9
4 ***Morrison***	22	17	64	50
5 Foley [2]				0
6 Dicks	83	92	21	4
7 McDermott	94	92	21	0
8 ***Chandler***	28	8	85	50
West Virginia				
1 Mollohan	61	100	21	21
2 Staggers	72	83	29	13
3 Wise	72	100	21	13
4 Rahall	78	100	36	13
Wisconsin				
1 Aspin	61	92	38	8
2 Kastenmeier	100	92	29	4
3 ***Gunderson***	33	8	77	63
4 Kleczka	89	83	23	17
5 Moody	94	83	42	14
6 ***Petri***	22	8	86	75
7 Obey	83	91	21	9
8 ***Roth***	6	8	93	83
9 ***Sensenbrenner***	6	0	86	83
Wyoming				
AL ***Thomas***	11	0	100	79

	ADA	AFL-CIO	CCUS	ACU
Alabama				
Heflin	28	78	64	55
Shelby	33	78	50	48
Alaska				
Murkowski	11	44	83	76
Stevens	33	67	64	65
Arizona				
DeConcini	61	56	50	20
McCain	11	22	83	87
Arkansas				
Bumpers	72	56	33	23
Pryor	67	56	25	18
California				
Cranston	100	67	8	0
Wilson	17	0	80	69
Colorado				
Wirth	83	56	17	10
Armstrong	6	22	91	95
Connecticut				
Dodd	61	78	9	9
Lieberman	83	78	17	22
Delaware				
Biden	83	67	36	17
Roth	22	33	67	87
Florida				
Graham	67	44	36	30
Mack	0	11	100	96
Georgia				
Fowler	72	44	33	35
Nunn	50	56	42	32
Hawaii				
Akaka	100	88	10	11
Inouye	72	89	17	13
Idaho				
McClure	6	33	83	91
Symms	6	11	83	100
Illinois				
Dixon	44	78	50	39
Simon	94	78	25	13
Indiana				
Coats	0	22	83	96
Lugar	6	11	75	83

	ADA	AFL-CIO	CCUS	ACU
Iowa				
Harkin	94	78	17	22
Grassley	17	33	83	87
Kansas				
Dole	0	33	75	83
Kassebaum	44	22	67	64
Kentucky				
Ford	39	89	33	35
McConnell	0	33	92	87
Louisiana				
Breaux	33	78	33	39
Johnston	39	86	33	38
Maine				
Mitchell	83	56	17	9
Cohen	61	33	42	48
Maryland				
Mikulski	94	75	10	5
Sarbanes	83	67	8	4
Massachusetts				
Kennedy	100	89	0	0
Kerry	94	89	18	5
Michigan				
Levin	78	78	33	22
Riegle	83	78	25	9
Minnesota				
Boschwitz	22	11	67	68
Durenberger	44	56	25	45
Mississippi				
Cochran	0	33	83	87
Lott	0	22	100	91
Missouri				
Bond	11	44	67	77
Danforth	39	44	67	43
Montana				
Baucus	56	44	45	41
Burns	6	11	83	91
Nebraska				
Exon	33	67	55	61
Kerrey	83	67	25	13
Nevada				
Bryan	56	78	25	30
Reid	61	67	17	30

	ADA	AFL-CIO	CCUS	ACU
New Hampshire				
Humphrey	11	22	92	87
Rudman	17	11	75	77
New Jersey				
Bradley	94	67	8	13
Lautenberg	100	78	17	4
New Mexico				
Bingaman	67	56	17	19
Domenici	22	56	67	50
New York				
Moynihan	94	78	17	4
D'Amato	28	44	67	70
North Carolina				
Sanford	67	67	25	17
Helms	6	22	92	100
North Dakota				
Burdick	89	78	17	9
Conrad	67	56	42	30
Ohio				
Glenn	89	67	25	9
Metzenbaum	78	89	8	10
Oklahoma				
Boren	56	63	55	23
Nickles	0	11	100	96
Oregon				
Hatfield	78	67	22	35
Packwood	72	44	42	35
Pennsylvania				
Heinz	33	78	42	48
Specter	39	89	50	48
Rhode Island				
Pell	94	78	18	19
Chafee	50	11	55	43
South Carolina				
Hollings	50	67	42	48
Thurmond	6	33	75	83
South Dakota				
Daschle	83	56	33	9
Pressler	22	0	83	83
Tennessee				
Gore	78	89	17	9
Sasser	72	78	17	9

KEY

ADA — Americans for Democratic Action

AFL-CIO — American Federation of Labor-Congress of Industrial Organizations

CCUS — Chamber of Commerce of the United States

ACU — American Conservative Union

Democrats ***Republicans***

	ADA	AFL-CIO	CCUS	ACU
Texas				
Bentsen	44	78	25	32
Gramm	0	22	92	91
Utah				
Garn	6	33	92	95
Hatch	11	33	92	87
Vermont				
Leahy	94	56	17	4
Jeffords	72	44	25	26
Virginia				
Robb	61	56	33	22
Warner	28	56	75	70
Washington				
Adams	94	78	8	9
Gorton	17	0	92	78
West Virginia				
Byrd	56	89	25	26
Rockefeller	83	78	25	13
Wisconsin				
Kohl	94	67	8	9
Kasten	6	44	83	91
Wyoming				
Simpson	11	11	75	73
Wallop	6	11	92	95

ADA (Americans for Democratic Action) — The percentage of time each senator voted in accordance with the ADA position on 18 selected votes in 1990. The percentages were compiled by the ADA. Failure to vote lowers scores.

AFL-CIO (American Federation of Labor-Congress of Industrial Organizations) — The percentage of time each senator voted for or was paired in favor of the AFL-CIO position on nine selected votes in 1990. The percentages were computed by Congressional Quarterly based on the selected votes. Failure to vote does not lower scores.

CCUS (Chamber of Commerce of the United States) — The percentage of time each senator voted with the Chamber's position on 12 selected votes in 1990. The percentages were compiled by the Chamber. Failure to vote does not lower scores.

ACU (American Conservative Union) — The percentage of time each senator voted with the ACU position on 21 selected votes in 1990. The percentages were compiled by the ACU. Failure to vote does not lower scores.

Appendix C

CONGRESS AND ITS MEMBERS

Legislative Process in Brief 3-C
How a Bill Becomes Law 4-C
Glossary 7-C

The Legislative Process in Brief

(Parliamentary terms used below are defined in the glossary, p. 7-C.)

Introduction of Bills

A House member (including the resident commissioner of Puerto Rico and non-voting delegates of the District of Columbia, Guam, the Virgin Islands and American Samoa) may introduce any one of several types of bills and resolutions by handing it to the clerk of the House or placing it in a box called the hopper.

A senator first gains recognition of the presiding officer to announce the introduction of a bill. If objection is offered by any senator, the introduction of the bill is postponed until the following day.

As the next step in either the House or Senate, the bill is numbered, referred to committee, labeled with the sponsor's name and sent to the Government Printing Office so that copies can be made for subsequent study and action. Senate bills may be jointly sponsored and carry several senators' names.

Until 1978, the House limited the number of members who could cosponsor any one bill; the ceiling was eliminated at the beginning of the 96th Congress.

A bill written in the executive branch and proposed as an administration measure usually is introduced by the chairman of the congressional committee that has jurisdiction over the subject.

Bills—Prefixed with HR in the House, S in the Senate, followed by a number. Used as the form for most legislation, whether general or special, public or private.

Joint Resolutions—Designated H J Res or S J Res. Subject to the same procedure as bills, with the exception of a joint resolution proposing an amendment to the Constitution. The latter must be approved by two-thirds of both houses and is thereupon sent directly to the administrator of general services for submission to the states for ratification instead of being presented to the president for his approval.

Concurrent Resolutions—Designated H Con Res or S Con Res. Used for matters affecting the operations of both houses. These resolutions do not become law.

Resolutions—Designated H Res or S Res. Used for a matter concerning the operation of either house alone and adopted only by the chamber in which it originates.

Committee Action

With few exceptions, bills are referred to the appropriate standing committees. The job of referral formally is the responsibility of the Speaker of the House and the presiding officer of the Senate, but this task usually is carried out on their behalf by the parliamentarians of the House and Senate.

Precedent, statute and the jurisdictional mandates of the committees as set forth in the rules of the House and Senate determine which committees receive what kinds of bills. An exception is the referral of private bills, which are sent to whatever committee is designated by their sponsors. Bills are technically considered "read for the first time" when referred to House committees.

When a bill reaches a committee, it is placed on the committee's calendar. At that time the bill comes under the sharpest congressional focus. Its chances for passage are quickly determined; the great majority of bills falls by the legislative roadside.

Failure of a committee to act on a bill is equivalent to killing it; the measure can be withdrawn from the committee's purview only by a discharge petition signed by a majority of the House membership on House bills or by adoption of a special resolution in the Senate. Discharge attempts rarely succeed.

The first committee action taken on a bill usually is a request for comment on it by interested government agencies. The committee chairman may assign the bill to a subcommittee for study and hearings, or it may be considered by the full committee. Hearings may be public, closed (executive session) or both. After considering a bill, a subcommittee reports to the full committee its recommendations for action and any proposed amendments.

The full committee then votes on its recommendation to the House or Senate. This procedure is called "ordering a bill reported."

Occasionally a committee may order a bill reported unfavorably; most of the time a report, submitted by the committee chairman to the House or Senate, calls for favorable action on the measure since the committee can effectively "kill" a bill by simply not taking any action.

After the bill is reported, the committee chairman instructs the staff to prepare a written report. The report describes the bill's purposes and scope, explains the committee revisions, notes proposed changes in existing law and, usually, includes the views of the executive branch agencies consulted. Often committee members opposing a bill include dissenting views in the report.

Usually, the committee "marks up" or proposes amendments to the bill. If they are substantial and the measure is complicated, the committee may order a "clean bill" introduced, which will embody the proposed amendments. The original bill then is put aside and the clean bill, with a new number, is reported to the floor.

The chamber must approve, alter or reject the committee amendments before the bill itself can be put to a vote.

Floor Action

After a bill is reported back to the house where it originated, it is placed on the calendar.

There are five legislative calendars in the House, issued in one cumulative calendar titled *Calendars of the United States House of Representatives and History of Legislation.* The House calendars are:

The Union Calendar to which are referred bills raising revenues, general appropriations bills and any measures directly or indirectly appropriating money or property. It is the Calendar of the Committee of the Whole House on the State of the Union.

The House Calendar to which are referred bills of pub-

How a Bill Becomes Law

This graphic shows the most typical way in which proposed legislation is enacted into law. There are more complicated, as well as simpler, routes, and most bills never become law. The process is illustrated with two hypothetical bills, House bill No. 1 (HR 1) and Senate bill No. 2 (S 2). Bills must be passed by both houses in identical form before they can be sent to the president. The path of HR 1 is traced by a solid line, that of S 2 by a broken line. In practice, most bills begin as similar proposals in both houses.

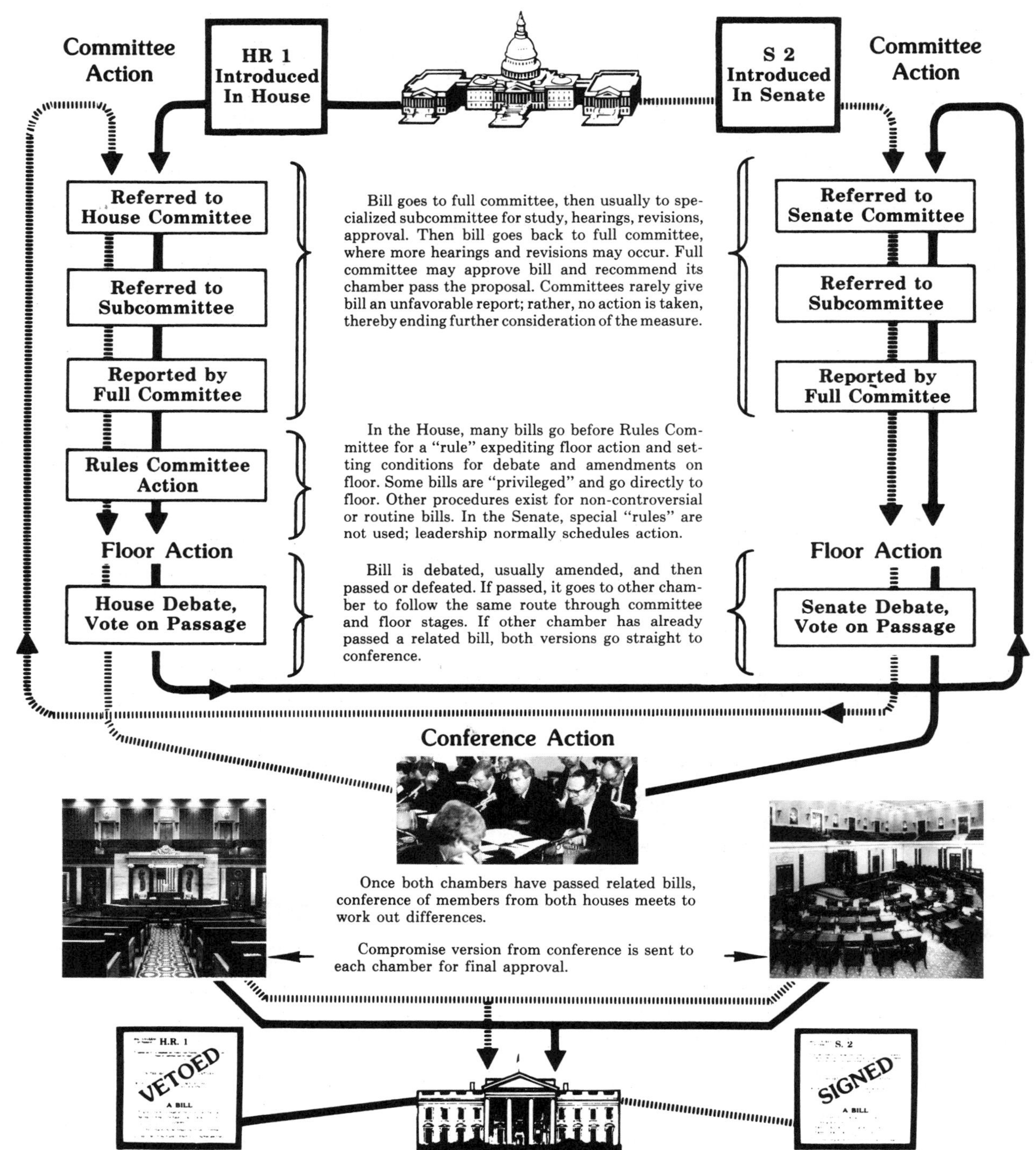

Compromise bill approved by both houses is sent to the president, who may sign it into law, allow it to become law without his signature, or veto it and return it to Congress. Congress may override veto by two-thirds majority vote in both houses; bill then becomes law without president's signature.

lic character not raising revenue or appropriating money or property.

The Consent Calendar to which are referred bills of a non-controversial nature that are passed without debate when the Consent Calendar is called on the first and third Mondays of each month.

The Private Calendar to which are referred bills for relief in the nature of claims against the United States or private immigration bills that are passed without debate when the Private Calendar is called the first and third Tuesdays of each month.

The Discharge Calendar to which are referred motions to discharge committees when the necessary signatures are signed to a discharge petition.

There is only one legislative calendar in the Senate and one "executive calendar" for treaties and nominations submitted to the Senate. When the Senate Calendar is called, each senator is limited to five minutes' debate on each bill.

Debate. A bill is brought to debate by varying procedures. If it is a routine measure, it may await the call of the calendar. If it is urgent or important, it can be taken up in the Senate either by unanimous consent or by a majority vote. The majority leader, in consultation with the minority leader and others, schedules the bills that will be taken up for debate.

In the House, precedence is granted if a special rule is obtained from the Rules Committee. A request for a special rule usually is made by the chairman of the committee that favorably reported the bill, supported by the bill's sponsor and other committee members. The request, considered by the Rules Committee in the same way that other committees consider legislative measures, is in the form of a resolution providing for immediate consideration of the bill.

The Rules Committee reports the resolution to the House, where it is debated and voted upon in the same fashion as regular bills. If the Rules Committee should fail to report a rule requested by a committee, there are several ways to bring the bill to the House floor — under suspension of the rules, on Calendar Wednesday or by a discharge motion.

The resolutions providing special rules are important because they specify how long the bill may be debated and whether it may be amended from the floor. If floor amendments are banned, the bill is considered under a "closed rule," which permits only members of the committee that first reported the measure to the House to alter its language, subject to chamber acceptance.

When a bill is debated under an "open rule," amendments may be offered from the floor. Committee amendments always are taken up first but may be changed, like all amendments up to the second degree; that is, an amendment to an amendment to an amendment is not in order.

Duration of debate in the House depends on whether the bill is under discussion by the House proper or before the House when it is sitting as the Committee of the Whole House on the State of the Union.

In the House, the amount of time for debate either is determined by special rule or is allocated with an hour for each member if the measure is under consideration without a rule.

In the Committee of the Whole, the amount of time agreed on for general debate is equally divided between proponents and opponents. At the end of general discussion, the bill is read section by section for amendment. Debate on an amendment is limited to five minutes for each side; this is called the "five-minute rule." In practice, amendments regularly are debated more than 10 minutes, with members gaining the floor by offering pro forma amendments or obtaining unanimous consent to speak longer than five minutes.

Senate debate usually is unlimited. It can be halted only by unanimous consent or by "cloture," which requires a three-fifths majority of the entire Senate or, in the case of a proposed change in the Senate rules, a two-thirds vote.

The House considers almost all important bills within a parliamentary framework known as the Committee of the Whole. It is not a committee as the word usually is understood; it is the full House meeting under another name for the purpose of speeding action on legislation.

Technically, the House sits as the Committee of the Whole when it considers any tax measure or bill dealing with public appropriations. It also can resolve itself into the Committee of the Whole if a member moves to do so and the motion is carried. The Speaker appoints a member to serve as the chairman.

The rules of the House permit the Committee of the Whole to meet when a quorum of 100 members is present on the floor and to amend and act on bills, within certain time limitations. When the Committee of the Whole has acted, it "rises," the Speaker returns as the presiding officer of the House and the member appointed chairman of the Committee of the Whole reports the action of the committee and its recommendations.

The Committee of the Whole cannot pass a bill; it reports the measure to the full House with whatever changes it has approved. The full House then may pass or reject the bill — or, on occasion, recommit the bill to committee. Amendments adopted in the Committee of the Whole may be put to a second vote in the full House.

Votes. Voting on bills may occur repeatedly before they are finally approved or rejected. The House votes on the rule for the bill and on various amendments to the bill. Voting on amendments often is a more illuminating test of a bill's support than is the final tally. Sometimes members approve final passage of bills after vigorously supporting amendments that, if adopted, would scuttle the legislation.

The Senate has three different methods of voting: an untabulated voice vote, a standing vote (called a division) and a recorded roll call to which members answer "yea" or "nay" when their names are called.

The House also employs voice and standing votes, but since January 1973 yeas and nays have been recorded by an electronic voting device, eliminating the need for time-consuming roll calls.

Another method of voting, used in the House only, is the teller vote. Traditionally, members filed up the center aisle past counters; only vote totals were announced. Since 1971, one-fifth of a quorum can demand that the votes of individual members be recorded, thereby forcing them to take a public position on amendments to key bills.

After amendments to a bill have been voted upon, a vote may be taken on a motion to recommit the bill to committee. If carried, this vote removes the bill from the chamber's calendar and is usually a death blow to the bill. If the motion is unsuccessful, the bill then is "read for the third time." An actual reading usually is dispensed with. Until 1965, an opponent of a bill could delay this move by objecting and asking for a full reading of an engrossed (certified in final form) copy of the bill. After the "third reading," the vote on final passage is taken.

The final vote may be followed by a motion to reconsider, and this motion may be followed by a move to lay the motion on the table. Usually, those voting for the bill's passage vote for the tabling motion, thus safeguarding the final passage action. With that, the bill has been formally passed by the chamber. While a motion to reconsider a Senate vote is pending on a bill, the measure cannot be sent to the House.

Action in Second House

After a bill is passed, it is sent to the other chamber. This body may then take one of several steps. It may pass the bill as is — accepting the other chamber's language. It may send the bill to committee for scrutiny or alteration, or reject the entire bill, advising the other house of its actions. Or it simply may ignore the bill submitted while it continues work on its own version of the proposed legislation. Frequently, one chamber may approve a version of a bill that is greatly at variance with the version passed by the other house, and then substitute its contents for the language of the other, retaining only the latter's bill number.

A provision of the Legislative Reorganization Act of 1970 permits a separate House vote on any non-germane amendment added by the Senate to a House-passed bill and requires a majority vote to retain the amendment. Previously, the House was forced to act on the bill as a whole; the only way to defeat the non-germane amendment was to reject the entire bill.

Often, the second chamber makes only minor changes. If these are readily agreed to by the other house, the bill then is sent to the president.

If the opposite chamber significantly alters the bill submitted to it, however, the measure usually is "sent to conference." The chamber that has possession of the "papers" (engrossed bill, engrossed amendments, messages of transmittal) requests a conference and the other chamber must agree to it. If the second house does not agree, the bill dies.

Conference, Final Action

Conference. A conference reconciles the differences between House and Senate versions of a legislative bill. The conferees usually are senior members appointed by the presiding officers of the two houses, from the committees that managed the bills. Under this arrangement the conferees of one house have the duty of trying to maintain their chamber's position in the face of amending actions by the conferees (also referred to as "managers") of the other house.

The number of conferees from each chamber varies, depending upon the length or complexity of the bill involved. A majority vote controls the action of each group; a large representation does not give one chamber a voting advantage over the other.

Theoretically, conferees are not allowed to write new legislation in reconciling the two versions before them, but this curb sometimes is bypassed. Many bills have been put into acceptable compromise form only after new language was provided by the conferees.

The 1970 Reorganization Act attempted to tighten restrictions on conferees by forbidding them to introduce any language on a topic that neither chamber sent to conference or to modify any topic beyond the scope of the differing versions of the bill.

Frequently, the ironing out of difficulties takes days or even weeks. As a conference proceeds, conferees reconcile differences between the versions. Generally, they grant concessions only insofar as they are sure that the chamber they represent will accept the compromises.

Occasionally, uncertainty over how either house will react, or the refusal of a chamber to back down on a disputed amendment, results in an impasse, and the bills die in conference even though each was approved by its sponsoring chamber.

Conferees may go back to their respective chambers for further instructions, when they report certain portions in disagreement. Then the chamber concerned can either "recede and concur" in the amendment of the other house or "insist on its amendment."

When the conferees have reached agreement, they prepare a conference report embodying their recommendations. The report, in document form, must be submitted to each house.

The conference report must be adopted by each house; adoption of the report is approval of the compromise bill. The chamber which asked for a conference yields to the other chamber the opportunity to vote first.

Final Steps. After a bill has been passed by both the House and Senate in identical form, all of the original papers are sent to the enrolling clerk of the chamber in which the bill originated. He then prepares an enrolled bill, which is printed on parchment paper.

When this bill has been certified as correct by the secretary of the Senate or the clerk of the House, depending on which chamber originated the bill, it is signed first (no matter whether it originated in the Senate or House) by the Speaker of the House and then by the president of the Senate. It is next sent to the White House to await action.

If the president approves the bill, he signs it, dates it and usually writes the word "approved" on the document. If he does not sign it within 10 days (Sundays excepted) and Congress is in session, the bill becomes law without his signature. Should Congress adjourn before the 10 days expire, and the president fails to sign the measure, it does not become law. This procedure is called the pocket veto.

A president vetoes a bill by refusing to sign it and, before the 10-day period expires, returning it to Congress with a message stating his reasons. The message is sent to the chamber that originated the bill. If no action is taken on the message, the bill dies.

Congress, however, can attempt to override the veto and enact the bill, "the objections of the president to the contrary notwithstanding." Overriding a veto requires a two-thirds vote of those present, who must number a quorum and vote by roll call.

Debate can precede this vote, with motions permitted to lay the message on the table, postpone action on it or refer it to committee. If the president's veto is overridden in both houses, the bill becomes law. Otherwise, it is dead.

When bills are passed finally and signed, or passed over a veto, they are given law numbers in numerical order as they become law. There are two series of numbers, one for public and one for private laws, starting at the number "1" for each two-year term of Congress. They are then identified by law number and by Congress — for example, Private Law 21, 97th Congress; Public Law 250, 97th Congress (or PL 97-250).

Glossary of Congressional Terms

Act—The term for legislation once it has passed both houses of Congress and has been signed by the president or passed over his veto, thus becoming law. *(See also Veto, Pocket Veto.)*

Also used in parliamentary terminology for a bill that has been passed by one house and engrossed. *(See Engrossed Bill.)*

Adjournment Sine Die—Adjournment without definitely fixing a day for reconvening; literally, "adjournment without a day." Usually used to connote the final adjournment of a session of Congress. A session can continue until noon, Jan. 3, of the following year, when, under the 20th Amendment to the Constitution, it automatically terminates. Both houses must agree to a concurrent resolution for either house to adjourn for more than three days.

Adjournment to a Day Certain—Adjournment under a motion or resolution that fixes the next time of meeting. Under the Constitution, neither house can adjourn for more than three days without the concurrence of the other. A session of Congress is not ended by adjournment to a day certain.

Amendment—A proposal of a member of Congress to alter the language, provisions or stipulations in a bill or in another amendment. An amendment usually is printed, debated and voted upon in the same manner as a bill.

Amendment in the Nature of a Substitute—Usually an amendment that seeks to replace the entire text of a bill. Passage of this type of amendment strikes out everything after the enacting clause and inserts a new version of the bill. An amendment in the nature of a substitute also can refer to an amendment that replaces a large portion of the text of a bill.

Appeal—A member's challenge of a ruling or decision made by the presiding officer of the chamber. In the Senate, the senator appeals to members of the chamber to override the decision. If carried by a majority vote, the appeal nullifies the chair's ruling. In the House, the decision of the Speaker traditionally has been final; seldom are there appeals to the members to reverse the Speaker's stand. To appeal a ruling is considered an attack on the Speaker.

Appropriations Bill—A bill that gives legal authority to spend or obligate money from the Treasury. The Constitution disallows money to be drawn from the Treasury "but in Consequence of Appropriations made by Law."

By congressional custom, an appropriations bill originates in the House, and it is not supposed to be considered by the full House or Senate until a related measure authorizing the funding is enacted. An appropriations bill grants the actual money approved by authorization bills, but not necessarily the full amount permissible under the authorization. The 1985 Gramm-Rudman anti-deficit law stipulated that the House is to pass by June 30 the last regular appropriations bill for the fiscal year starting the following Oct. 1. (There is no such deadline for the Senate.) However, for decades appropriations often have not been final until well after the fiscal year begins, requiring a succession of stopgap bills to continue the government's functions. In addition, much federal spending — about half of all budget authority, notably that for Social Security and interest on the federal debt — does not require annual appropriations; those programs exist under permanent appropriations. *(See also Authorization, Budget Process, Backdoor Spending Authority, Entitlement Program.)*

In addition to general appropriations bills, there are two specialized types. *(See Continuing Resolution, Supplemental Appropriations Bill.)*

Authorization—Basic, substantive legislation that establishes or continues the legal operation of a federal program or agency, either indefinitely or for a specific period of time, or which sanctions a particular type of obligation or expenditure. An authorization normally is a prerequisite for an appropriation or other kind of budget authority. Under the rules of both chambers, the appropriation for a program or agency may not be considered until its authorization has been considered (although this requirement is often waived). An authorization sets the maximum amount of funds that can be given to a program or agency, but sometimes it merely authorizes "such sums as may be necessary." *(See also Backdoor Spending Authority.)*

Backdoor Spending Authority—Budget authority provided in legislation outside the normal appropriations process. The most common forms of backdoor spending are borrowing authority, contract authority, entitlements and loan guarantees that commit the government to payments of principal and interest on loans — such as Guaranteed Student Loans — made by banks or other private lenders. Loan guarantees result in actual outlays only when there is a default by the borrower.

In some cases, such as interest on the public debt, a permanent appropriation is provided that becomes available without further action by Congress.

Bills—Most legislative proposals before Congress are in the form of bills and are designated by HR in the House of Representatives or S in the Senate, according to the house in which they originate, and by a number assigned in the order in which they are introduced during the two-year period of a congressional term. "Public bills" deal with general questions and become public laws if approved by Congress and signed by the president. "Private bills" deal with individual matters such as claims against the government, immigration and naturalization cases or land titles, and become private laws if approved and signed. *(See also Concurrent Resolution, Joint Resolution, Resolution.)*

Bills Introduced—In both the House and Senate, any number of members may join in introducing a single bill or resolution. The first member listed is the sponsor of the bill, and all subsequent members listed are the bill's cosponsors.

Many bills are committee bills and are introduced under the name of the chairman of the committee or subcommittee. All appropriations bills fall into this category. A committee frequently holds hearings on a number of related bills and may agree to one of them or to an entirely new bill. *(See also Report, Clean Bill, By Request.)*

Bills Referred—When introduced, a bill is referred to the committee or committees that have jurisdiction over the subject with which the bill is concerned. Under the standing rules of the House and Senate, bills are referred by the Speaker in the House and by the presiding officer in the Senate. In practice, the House and Senate parliamentarians act for these officials and refer the vast majority of bills.

Borrowing Authority—Statutory authority that permits a federal agency to incur obligations and make payments for specified purposes with borrowed money.

Budget—The document sent to Congress by the president early each year estimating government revenue and expenditures for the ensuing fiscal year.

Budget Act—The common name for the Congressional Budget and Impoundment Control Act of 1974, which established the current budget process and created the Congressional Budget Office. The act also put limits on presidential authority to spend appropriated money. *(See Impoundments, Budget Process.)*

Budget Authority—Authority to enter into obligations that will result in immediate or future outlays involving federal funds. The basic forms of budget authority are appropriations, contract authority and borrowing authority. Budget authority may be classified by (1) the period of availability (one-year, multiple-year or without a time limitation), (2) the timing of congressional action (current or permanent) or (3) the manner of determining the amount available (definite or indefinite).

Budget process — Congress in 1990 overhauled its budget procedures for the third time since it created the congressional budget process in 1974. The 1990 Budget Enforcement Act departed from its predecessor budget laws by holding Congress harmless until fiscal 1994 for budget-deficit increases that it did not explicitly cause.

If the deficit increased because of recession, war or specifically exempted programs, that would no longer trigger the automatic spending cuts ("sequester") threatened by the Gramm-Rudman antideficit law, enacted in 1985 and amended in 1987.

The new budget rules did require, however, that spending programs be hit with a sequester if Congress exceeded pre-agreed caps on discretionary spending (appropriations bills) or violated new "pay-as-you-go" rules for mandatory spending (entitlement programs such as Medicare or food stamps) or tax cuts. *(See also Sequester Order.)*

Discretionary spending was divided into three categories — domestic, defense and international — for fiscal years 1991-93. Each category had a spending cap, and money could not be taken from one category to increase another. For fiscal years 1994-95, the three categories were to be collapsed into a single pot of money with a single cap.

For taxes and entitlements, the pay-as-you-go plan required that new entitlement spending or tax cuts be deficit-neutral. If Congress cut taxes, created a new entitlement program or expanded eligibility or benefits for an existing program, it had to offset the cost or subject entitlement spending programs to a sequester.

The 1990 law made minor changes in the timetable for presidential submission of budgets and for congressional approval of budget resolutions and reconciliation bills, two mechanisms created by the Congressional Budget and Impoundment Control Act of 1974. The president was given until the first Monday in February to submit his proposed budget. Congressional budget resolutions, due by April 15 annually, set guidelines for congressional action on spending and tax measures; they were to be adopted by the House and Senate but not signed by the president and did not have the force of law. Reconciliation bills, due by June 15, made the actual changes in existing law to meet budget resolution goals.

Budget Resolution—A concurrent resolution passed by both houses of Congress, but not requiring the president's signature, setting forth or revising the congressional budget for each of three fiscal years. The budget resolution sets forth various budget totals and functional allocations and may include reconciliation instructions. *(See Functions, Reconciliation.)*

By Request—A phrase used when a senator or representative introduces a bill at the request of an executive agency or private organization but does not necessarily endorse the legislation.

Calendar—An agenda or list of business awaiting possible action by each chamber. The House uses five legislative calendars. *(See Consent, Discharge, House, Private and Union Calendar.)*

In the Senate, all legislative matters reported from committee go on one calendar. They are listed there in the order in which committees report them or the Senate places them on the calendar, but they may be called up out of order by the majority leader, either by obtaining unanimous consent of the Senate or by a motion to call up a bill. The Senate also uses one non-legislative calendar; this is used for treaties and nominations. *(See Executive Calendar.)*

Calendar Wednesday—A procedure in the House, now rarely used, whereby committees, on Wednesdays, may be called in the order in which they appear in Rule X of the House, for the purpose of bringing up any of their bills from either the House or the Union Calendar, except bills that are privileged. General debate is limited to two hours. Bills called up from the Union Calendar are considered in Committee of the Whole. Calendar Wednesday is not observed during the last two weeks of a session and may be dispensed with at other times by a two-thirds vote. This procedure is now routinely is dispensed with by unanimous consent.

Call of the Calendar—Senate bills that are not brought up for debate by a motion, unanimous consent or a unanimous consent agreement are brought before the Senate for action when the calendar listing them is "called." Bills must be called in the order listed. Measures considered by this method usually are noncontroversial, and debate on the bill and any proposed amendments is limited to a total of five minutes for each senator.

Chamber—The meeting place for the membership of either the House or the Senate; also the membership of the House or Senate meeting as such.

Clean Bill—Frequently after a committee has finished a major revision of a bill, one of the committee members, usually the chairman, will assemble the changes and what is left of the original bill into a new measure and introduce it as a "clean bill." The revised measure, which is given a new number, then is referred back to the committee, which reports it to the floor for consideration. This often is a timesaver, as committee-recommended changes in a clean bill do not have to be considered and voted on by the chamber. Reporting a clean bill also protects committee amendments that could be subject to points of order concerning germaneness.

Clerk of the House—Chief administrative officer of the House of Representatives, with duties corresponding to those of the secretary of the Senate. *(See also Secretary of the Senate.)*

Cloture—The process by which a filibuster can be ended in the Senate other than by unanimous consent. A motion for cloture can apply to any measure before the Senate, including a proposal to change the chamber's rules. A cloture motion requires the signatures of 16 senators to be introduced. To end a filibuster, the cloture motion must obtain the votes of three-fifths of the entire Senate membership (60 if there are no vacancies), except when the filibuster is against a proposal to amend the standing rules of the Senate and a two-thirds vote of senators present and voting is required. The cloture request is put to a roll call vote one hour after the Senate meets on the second day following introduction of the motion. If approved, cloture limits each senator to one hour of debate. The bill or amendment in question comes to a final vote after 30 hours of consideration (including debate time and the time it takes to conduct roll calls, quorum calls and other procedural motions). *(See Filibuster.)*

Committee—A division of the House or Senate that prepares legislation for action by the parent chamber or makes investigations as directed by the parent chamber.

There are several types of committees. *(See Standing and Select or Special Committees.)* Most standing committees are divided into subcommittees, which study legislation, hold hearings and report bills, with or without amendments, to the full committee. Only the full committee can report legislation for action by the House or Senate.

Committee of the Whole—The working title of what is formally "The Committee of the Whole House [of Representatives] on the State of the Union." The membership is composed of all House members sitting as a committee. Any 100 members who are present on the floor of the chamber to consider legislation comprise a quorum of the committee. Any legislation, however, must first have passed through the regular legislative or Appropriations committee and have been placed on the calendar.

Technically, the Committee of the Whole considers only bills directly or indirectly appropriating money, authorizing appropriations or involving taxes or charges on the public. Because the Committee of the Whole need number only 100 representatives, a quorum is more readily attained, and legislative business is expedited. Before 1971, members' positions were not individually recorded on votes taken in the Committee of the Whole. *(See Teller Vote.)*

When the full House resolves itself into the Committee of the Whole, it replaces the Speaker with a "chairman." A measure is debated and amendments may be proposed, with votes on amendments as needed. *(See Five-Minute Rule.)*

When the committee completes its work on the measure, it dissolves itself by "rising." The Speaker returns, and the chairman of the Committee of the Whole reports to the House that the committee's work has been completed. At this time members may demand a roll call vote on any amendment adopted in the Committee of the Whole. The final vote is on passage of the legislation.

Committee Veto—A requirement added to a few statutes directing that certain policy directives by an executive department or agency be reviewed by certain congressional committees before they are implemented. Under common practice, the government department or agency and the committees involved are expected to reach a consensus before the directives are carried out. *(See also Legislative Veto.)*

Concurrent Resolution—A concurrent resolution, designated H Con Res or S Con Res, must be adopted by both houses, but it is not sent to the president for approval and therefore does not have the force of law. A concurrent resolution, for example, is used to fix the time for adjournment of a Congress. It also is used as the vehicle for expressing the sense of Congress on a foreign policy or domestic issue, and it serves as the vehicle for coordinated decisions on the federal budget under the 1974 Congressional Budget and Impoundment Control Act. *(See also Bills, Joint Resolution, Resolution.)*

Conference—A meeting between the representatives of the House and the Senate to reconcile differences between the two houses on provisions of a bill passed by both chambers. Members of the conference committee are appointed by the Speaker and the presiding officer of the Senate and are called "managers" for their respective chambers. A majority of the managers for each house must reach agreement on the provisions of the bill (often a compromise between the versions of the two chambers) before it can be considered by either chamber in the form of a "conference report." When the conference report goes to the floor, it cannot be amended, and, if it is not approved by both chambers, the bill may go back to conference under certain situations, or a new conference must be convened. Many rules and informal practices govern the conduct of conference committees.

Bills that are passed by both houses with only minor differences need not be sent to conference. Either chamber may "concur" in the other's amendments, completing action on the legislation. Sometimes leaders of the committees of jurisdiction work out an informal compromise instead of having a formal conference. *(See Custody of the Papers.)*

Confirmations—*(See Nominations.)*

Congressional Record—The daily, printed account of proceedings in both the House and Senate chambers, showing substantially verbatim debate, statements and a record of floor action. Highlights of legislative and committee action are embodied in a Daily Digest section of the Record, and members are entitled to have their extraneous remarks printed in an appendix known as "Extension of Remarks." Members may edit and revise remarks made on the floor during debate, and quotations from debate reported by the press are not always found in the Record.

The Congressional Record provides a way to distinguish remarks spoken on the floor of the House and Senate from undelivered speeches. In the Senate, all speeches, articles and other matter that members insert in the Record without actually reading them on the floor are set off by large black dots, or bullets. However, a loophole allows a member to avoid the bulleting if he delivers any portion of the speech in person. In the House, undelivered speeches and other material are printed in a distinctive typeface. *(See also Journal)*

Congressional Terms of Office—Normally begin on Jan. 3 of the year following a general election and are two years for representatives and six years for senators. Representatives elected in special elections are sworn in for the remainder of a term. A person may be appointed to fill a Senate vacancy and serves until a successor is elected; the successor serves until the end of the term applying to the vacant seat.

Consent Calendar—Members of the House may place on this calendar most bills on the Union or House Calendar that are considered to be non-controversial. Bills on the Consent Calendar normally are called on the first and third Mondays of each month. On the first occasion that a bill is called in this manner, consideration may be blocked by the objection of any member. The second time, if there are three objections, the bill is stricken from the Consent Calendar. If fewer than three members object, the bill is given immediate consideration.

A bill on the Consent Calendar may be postponed in another way. A member may ask that the measure be passed over "without prejudice." In that case, no objection is recorded against the bill, and its status on the Consent Calendar remains unchanged. A bill stricken from the Consent Calendar remains on the Union or House Calendar.

Continuing Resolution—A joint resolution, cleared by Congress and signed by the president (when the new fiscal year is about to begin or has begun), to provide new budget authority for federal agencies and programs to continue in operation until the regular appropriations acts are enacted. The continuing resolution usually specifies a maximum rate at which an agency may incur obligations, based on the rate of the prior year, the president's budget request or an appropriations bill passed by either or both houses of Congress but not yet enacted. Continuing resolutions also are called "CRs" or continuing appropriations.

Contract Authority—Budget authority contained in an authorization bill that permits the federal government to enter into contracts or other obligations for future payments from funds not yet appropriated by Congress. The assumption is that funds will be available for payment in a subsequent appropriation act.

Controllable Budget Items—In federal budgeting, this term refers to programs for which the budget authority or outlays during a fiscal year can be controlled without changing existing, substantive law. The concept "relatively uncontrollable under current law" includes outlays for open-ended programs and fixed costs such as interest on the public debt, Social Security benefits, veterans' benefits and outlays to liquidate prior-year obligations. More and more spending for federal programs has become uncontrollable or relatively uncontrollable.

Correcting Recorded Votes—Rules prohibit members from changing their votes after the result has been announced. But, occasionally, hours, days or months after a vote has been taken, a member may announce he was "incorrectly recorded." In the Senate, a request to change one's vote almost always receives unanimous consent. In the House, members are prohibited from changing their votes if tallied by the electronic voting system. If the vote was taken by roll call, a change is permissible if consent is granted.

Cosponsor—*(See Bills Introduced.)*

Current Services Estimates—Estimated budget authority and outlays for federal programs and operations for the forthcoming fiscal year based on continuation of existing levels of service without policy changes. These estimates of budget authority and outlays, accompanied by the underlying economic and policy assumptions upon which they are based, are transmitted by the president to Congress when the budget is submitted.

Custody of the Papers—To reconcile differences between the House and Senate versions of a bill, a conference may be arranged. The chamber with "custody of the papers" — the engrossed bill, engrossed amendments, messages of transmittal — is the only body empowered to request the conference. By custom, the chamber that asks for a conference is the last to act on the conference report once agreement has been reached on the bill by the conferees.

Custody of the papers sometimes is manipulated to ensure that a particular chamber acts either first or last on the conference report.

Deferral—Executive branch action to defer, or delay, the spending of appropriated money. The 1974 Congressional Budget and Impoundment Control Act requires a special message from the president to Congress reporting a proposed deferral of spending. Deferrals may not extend beyond the end of the fiscal year in which the message is transmitted. A federal district court in 1986 struck down the president's authority to defer spending for policy reasons; the ruling was upheld by a federal appeals court in 1987. Congress can prohibit proposed deferrals by enacting a law doing so; most often, cancellations of proposed deferrals are included in appropriations bills. *(See also Rescission.)*

Dilatory Motion—A motion made for the purpose of killing time and preventing action on a bill or amendment. House rules outlaw dilatory motions, but enforcement is largely within the discretion of the Speaker or chairman of the Committee of the Whole. The Senate does not have a rule banning dilatory motions, except under cloture.

Discharge a Committee—Occasionally, attempts are made to relieve a committee from jurisdiction over a measure before it. This is attempted more often in the House than in the Senate, and the procedure rarely is successful.

In the House, if a committee does not report a bill within 30 days after the measure is referred to it, any member may file a discharge motion. Once offered, the motion is treated as a petition needing the signatures of a majority of members (218 if there are no vacancies). After the required signatures have been obtained, there is a delay of seven days. Thereafter, on the second and fourth Mondays of each month, except during the last six days of a session, any member who has signed the petition must be recognized, if he so desires, to move that the committee be discharged. Debate on the motion to discharge is limited to 20 minutes, and, if the motion is carried, consideration of the bill becomes a matter of high privilege.

If a resolution to consider a bill is held up in the Rules Committee for more than seven legislative days, any member may enter a motion to discharge the committee. The motion is handled like any other discharge petition in the House. Occasionally, to expedite non-controversial legislative business, a committee is discharged by unanimous consent of the House, and a petition is not required. *(Senate procedure, see Discharge Resolution.)*

Discharge Calendar—The House calendar to which motions to discharge committees are referred when they have the required number of signatures (218) and are awaiting floor action.

Discharge Petition—*(See Discharge a Committee.)*

Discharge Resolution—In the Senate, a special motion that any senator may introduce to relieve a committee from consideration of a bill before it. The resolution can be called up for Senate approval or disapproval in the same manner as any other Senate business. *(House procedure, see Discharge a Committee.)*

Division of a Question for Voting—A practice that is more common in the Senate but also used in the House whereby a member may demand a division of an amendment or a motion for purposes of voting. Where an amendment or motion can be divided, the individual parts are voted on separately when a member demands a division. This procedure occurs most often during the consideration of conference reports.

Division Vote—*(See Standing Vote.)*

Enacting Clause—Key phrase in bills beginning, "Be it enacted by the Senate and House of Representatives . . ." A successful motion to strike it from legislation kills the measure.

Engrossed Bill—The final copy of a bill as passed by one chamber, with the text as amended by floor action and certified by the clerk of the House or the secretary of the Senate.

Enrolled Bill—The final copy of a bill that has been passed in identical form by both chambers. It is certified by an officer of the house of origin (clerk of the House or secretary of the Senate) and then sent on for the signatures of the House Speaker, the Senate president pro tempore and the president of the United States. An enrolled bill is printed on parchment.

Entitlement Program—A federal program that guarantees a certain level of benefits to persons or other entities who meet requirements set by law, such as Social Security, farm price supports or unemployment benefits. It thus leaves no discretion with Congress on how much money to appropriate, and some entitlements carry permanent appropriations.

Executive Calendar—This is a non-legislative calendar in the Senate on which presidential documents such as treaties and nominations are listed.

Executive Document—A document, usually a treaty, sent to the Senate by the president for consideration or approval. Executive documents are identified for each session of Congress according to the following pattern: Executive A, 97th Congress, 1st Session; Executive B, and so on. They are referred to committee in the same manner as other measures. Unlike legislative documents, however, treaties do not die at the end of a Congress but remain "live" proposals until acted on by the Senate or withdrawn by the president.

Executive Session—A meeting of a Senate or House committee (or occasionally of either chamber) that only its members may attend. Witnesses regularly appear at committee meetings in executive session — for example, Defense Department officials during presentations of classified defense information. Other members of Congress may be invited, but the public and press are not allowed to attend.

Expenditures—The actual spending of money as distinguished from the appropriation of funds. Expenditures are made by the disbursing officers of the administration; appropriations are made only by Congress. The two are rarely identical in any fiscal year. In addition to some current budget authority, expenditures may represent budget authority made available one, two or more years earlier.

Filibuster—A time-delaying tactic associated with the Senate and used by a minority in an effort to prevent a vote on a bill or amendment that probably would pass if voted upon directly. The most common method is to take advantage of the Senate's rules permitting unlimited debate, but other forms of parliamentary maneuvering may be used. The stricter rules of the House make filibusters more difficult, but delaying tactics are employed occasionally through various procedural devices allowed by House rules. *(Senate filibusters, see Cloture.)*

Fiscal Year—Financial operations of the government are carried out in a 12-month fiscal year, beginning on Oct. 1 and ending on Sept. 30. The fiscal year carries the date of the calendar year in which it ends. (From fiscal year 1844 to fiscal year 1976, the fiscal year began July 1 and ended the following June 30.)

Five-Minute Rule—A debate-limiting rule of the House that is invoked when the House sits as the Committee of the Whole. Under the rule, a member offering an amendment is allowed to speak five minutes in its favor, and an opponent of the amendment is allowed to speak five minutes in opposition. Debate is then closed. In practice, amendments regularly are debated more than 10 minutes, with members gaining the floor by offering pro forma amendments or obtaining unanimous consent to speak longer than five minutes. *(See Strike Out the Last Word.)*

Floor Manager—A member who has the task of steering legislation through floor debate and the amendment process to a final vote in the House or the Senate. Floor managers usually are chairmen or ranking members of the committee that reported the bill. Managers are responsible for apportioning the debate time granted supporters of the bill. The ranking minority member of the committee normally apportions time for the minority party's participation in the debate.

Frank—A member's facsimile signature, which is used on envelopes in lieu of stamps, for the member's official outgoing mail. The "franking privilege" is the right to send mail postage-free.

Germane—Pertaining to the subject matter of the measure at hand. All House amendments must be germane to the bill being considered. The Senate requires that amendments be germane when they are proposed to general appropriations bills or to bills being considered once cloture has been adopted or, frequently, when the Senate is proceeding under a unanimous consent agreement placing a time limit on consideration of a bill. The 1974 budget act also requires that amendments to concurrent budget resolutions be germane. In the House, floor debate must be germane, and the first three hours of debate each day in the Senate must be germane to the pending business.

Gramm-Rudman-Hollings Deficit Reduction Act—*(See Budget Process, Sequestration.)*

Grandfather Clause—A provision that exempts persons or other entities already engaged in an activity from rules or legislation affecting that activity. Grandfather clauses sometimes are added to legislation in order to avoid antagonizing groups with established interests in the activities affected.

Hearings—Committee sessions for taking testimony from witnesses. At hearings on legislation, witnesses usually include specialists, government officials and spokespersons for individuals or entities affected by the bill or bills under study. Hearings related to special investigations bring forth a variety of witnesses. Committees sometimes use their subpoena power to summon reluctant witnesses. The public and press may attend open hearings but are barred from closed, or "executive," hearings. The vast majority of hearings are open to the public. *(See Executive Session.)*

Hold-Harmless Clause—A provision added to legislation to ensure that recipients of federal funds do not receive less in a future year than they did in the current year if a new formula for allocating funds authorized in the legislation would result in a reduction to the recipients. This clause has been used most often to soften the impact of sudden reductions in federal grants.

Hopper—Box on House clerk's desk where members deposit bills and resolutions to introduce them. *(See also Bills Introduced.)*

Hour Rule—A provision in the rules of the House that permits one hour of debate time for each member on amendments debated in the House of Representatives sitting as the House. Therefore, the House normally amends bills while sitting as the Committee of the Whole, where the five-minute rule on amendments operates. *(See Committee of the Whole, Five-Minute Rule.)*

House—The House of Representatives, as distinct from the Senate, although each body is a "house" of Congress.

House as in Committee of the Whole—A procedure that can be used to expedite consideration of certain measures such as continuing resolutions and, when there is debate, private bills. The procedure only can be invoked with the unanimous consent of the House or a rule from the Rules Committee and has procedural elements of both the House sitting as the House of Representatives, such as the Speaker presiding and the previous question motion being in order, and the House sitting as the Committee of the Whole, such as the five-minute rule pertaining.

House Calendar—A listing for action by the House of public bills that do not directly or indirectly appropriate money or raise revenue.

Immunity—The constitutional privilege of members of Congress to make verbal statements on the floor and in committee for which they cannot be sued or arrested for slander or libel. Also, freedom from arrest while traveling to or from sessions of Congress or on official business. Members in this status may be arrested only for treason, felonies or a breach of the peace, as defined by congressional manuals.

Joint Committee—A committee composed of a specified number of members of both the House and Senate. A joint committee may be investigative or research-oriented, an example of the latter being the Joint Economic Committee. Others have housekeeping duties such as the joint committees on Printing and on the Library of Congress.

Joint Resolution—A joint resolution, designated H J Res or S J Res, requires the approval of both houses and the signature of the president, just as a bill does, and has the force of law if approved. There is no practical difference between a bill and a joint resolution. A joint resolution generally is used to deal with a limited matter such as a single appropriation.

Joint resolutions also are used to propose amendments to the Constitution. They do not require a presidential signature but become a part of the Constitution when three-fourths of the states have ratified them.

Journal—The official record of the proceedings of the House and Senate. The Journal records the actions taken in each chamber, but, unlike the Congressional Record, it does not include the substantially verbatim report of speeches, debates, statements and the like.

Law—An act of Congress that has been signed by the president or passed over his veto by Congress. Public bills, when signed, become public laws, and are cited by the letters PL and a hyphenated number. The number before the hyphen corresponds to the Congress, and the one or more digits after the hyphen refer to the numerical sequence in which the president signed the bills during that Congress. Private bills, when signed, become private laws. *(See also Pocket Veto, Slip Laws, Statutes at Large, U.S. Code.)*

Legislative Day—The "day" extending from the time either house meets after an adjournment until the time it next adjourns. Because the House normally adjourns from day to day, legislative days and calendar days usually coincide. But in the Senate, a legislative day may, and frequently does, extend over several calendar days. *(See Recess.)*

Legislative Veto—A procedure, held unconstitutional by the Supreme Court, permitting either the House or Senate, or both chambers, to review proposed executive branch regulations or actions and to block or modify those with which they disagreed.

The specifics of the procedure varied, but Congress generally provided for a legislative veto by including in a bill a provision that administrative rules or action taken to implement the law were to go into effect at the end of a designated period of time unless blocked by either or both houses of Congress. Another version of the veto provided for congressional reconsideration and rejection of regulations already in effect.

The Supreme Court in 1983 struck down the legislative veto as an unconstitutional violation of the lawmaking procedure provided in the Constitution.

Loan Guarantees—Loans to third parties for which the federal government in the event of default guarantees, in whole or in part, the repayment of principal or interest to a lender or holder of a security.

Lobby—A group seeking to influence the passage or defeat of legislation. Originally the term referred to persons frequenting the lobbies or corridors of legislative chambers to speak to lawmakers.

The definition of a lobby and the activity of lobbying is a matter of differing interpretation. By some definitions, lobbying is limited to direct attempts to influence lawmakers through personal interviews and persuasion. Under other definitions, lobbying includes attempts at indirect, or "grass-roots," influence, such as persuading members of a group to write or visit their district's representative and state's senators or attempting to create a climate of opinion favorable to a desired legislative goal.

The right to attempt to influence legislation is based on the First Amendment to the Constitution, which says Congress shall make no law abridging the right of the people "to petition the government for a redress of grievances."

Majority Leader—Floor leader for the majority party in each chamber. In the Senate, in consultation with the minority leader and his colleagues, the majority leader directs the legislative schedule for the chamber. He also is his party's spokesperson and chief strategist. In the House, the majority leader is second to the Speaker in the majority party's leadership and serves as his party's legislative strategist.

Majority Whip—In effect, the assistant majority leader, in either the House or Senate. His job is to help marshal majority forces in support of party strategy and legislation.

Manual—The official handbook in each house prescribing in detail its organization, procedures and operations.

Marking Up a Bill—Going through the contents of a piece of legislation in committee or subcommittee to, for example, consider its provisions in large and small portions, act on amendments to provisions and proposed revisions to the language, and insert new sections and phraseology. If the bill is extensively amended, the committee's version may be introduced as a separate bill, with a new number, before being considered by the full House or Senate. *(See Clean Bill.)*

Minority Leader—Floor leader for the minority party in each chamber. *(See also Majority Leader.)*

Minority Whip—Performs duties of whip for the minority party. *(See also Majority Whip.)*

Morning Hour—The time set aside at the beginning of each legislative day for the consideration of regular, routine business. The "hour" is of indefinite duration in the House, where it is rarely used.

In the Senate, it is the first two hours of a session following an adjournment, as distinguished from a recess. The morning hour can be terminated earlier if the morning business has been completed. Business includes such matters as messages from the president, communications from the heads of departments, messages from the House, the presentation of petitions, reports of standing and select committees and the introduction of bills and resolutions. During the first hour of the morning hour in the Senate, no motion to proceed to the consideration of any bill on the calendar is in order except by unanimous consent. During the second hour, motions can be made but must be decided without debate. Senate committees may meet while the Senate conducts morning hour.

Motion—In the House or Senate chamber, a request by a member to institute any one of a wide array of parliamentary actions. He "moves" for a certain procedure, such as the consideration of a measure. The precedence of motions, and whether they are debatable, is set forth in the House and Senate manuals.

Nominations—Presidential appointments to office subject to Senate confirmation. Although most nominations win quick Senate approval, some are controversial and become the topic of hearings and debate. Sometimes senators object to appointees for patronage reasons — for example, when a nomination to a local federal job is made without consulting the senators of the state concerned. In some situations a senator may object that the nominee is "personally obnoxious" to him. Usually other senators join in blocking such appointments out of courtesy to their colleagues. *(See Senatorial Courtesy.)*

One-Minute Speeches—Addresses by House members at the beginning of a legislative day. The speeches may cover any subject but are limited to one minute's duration.

Outlays—Payments made (generally through the issuance of checks or disbursement of cash) to liquidate obligations. Outlays during a fiscal year may be for the payment of obligations incurred in prior years or in the same year.

Override a Veto—If the president disapproves a bill and sends it back to Congress with his objections, Congress may try to override his veto and enact the bill into law. Neither house is required to attempt to override a veto. The override of a veto requires a recorded vote with a two-thirds majority of those present and voting in each chamber. The question put to each house is: "Shall the bill pass, the objections of the president to the contrary notwithstanding?" *(See also Pocket Veto, Veto.)*

Oversight Committee—A congressional committee, or designated subcommittee of a committee, that is charged with general oversight of one or more federal agencies' programs and activities. Usually, the oversight panel for a particular agency also is the authorizing committee for that agency's programs and operations.

Pair—A voluntary, informal arrangement that two lawmakers, usually on opposite sides of an issue, make on recorded votes. In many cases the result is to subtract a vote from each side, with no effect on the outcome. Pairs are not authorized in the rules of either house, are not counted in tabulating the final result and have no official standing. However, members pairing are identified in the Congressional Record, along with their positions on such votes, if known. A member who expects to be absent for a vote can pair with a member who plans to vote, with the latter agreeing to withhold his vote.

There are three types of pairs: 1) A live pair involves a member who is present for a vote and another who is absent. The member in attendance votes and then withdraws the vote, announcing that he has a live pair with colleague "X" and stating how the two members would have voted, one in favor, the other opposed. A live pair may affect the outcome of a closely contested vote, since it subtracts one "yea" or one "nay" from the final tally. A live pair may cover one or several specific issues. 2) A general pair, widely used in the House, does not entail any arrangement between two members and does not affect the vote. Members who expect to be absent notify the clerk that they wish to make a general pair. Each member then is paired with another desiring a pair, and their names are listed in the Congressional Record. The member may or may not be paired with another taking the opposite position, and no indication of how the members would have voted is given. 3) A specific pair is similar to a general pair, except that the opposing stands of the two members are identified and printed in the Record.

Petition—A request or plea sent to one or both chambers from an organization or private citizens' group asking support of particular legislation or favorable consideration of a matter not yet receiving congressional attention. Petitions are referred to appropriate committees.

Pocket Veto—The act of the president in withholding his approval of a bill after Congress has adjourned. When Congress is in session, a bill becomes law without the president's signature if he does not act upon it within 10 days, excluding Sundays, from the time he gets it. But if Congress adjourns sine die within that 10-day period, the bill will die even if the president does not formally veto it.

The Supreme Court in 1986 agreed to decide whether the president can pocket veto a bill during recesses and between sessions of the same Congress or only between Congresses. The justices in 1987 declared the case moot, however, because the bill in question was invalid once the case reached the court. *(See also Veto.)*

Point of Order—An objection raised by a member that the chamber is departing from rules governing its conduct of business. The objector cites the rule violated, the chair sustaining his objection if correctly made. Order is restored by the chair's suspending proceedings of the chamber until it conforms to the prescribed "order of business."

President of the Senate—Under the Constitution, the vice president of the United States presides over the Senate. In his absence, the president pro tempore, or a senator designated by the president pro tempore, presides over the chamber.

President Pro Tempore—The chief officer of the Senate in the absence of the vice president; literally, but loosely, the president for a time. The president pro tempore is elected by his fellow senators, and the recent practice has been to elect the senator of the majority party with the longest period of continuous service.

Previous Question—A motion for the previous question, when carried, has the effect of cutting off all debate, preventing the offering of further amendments and forcing a vote on the pending matter. In the House, the previous question is not permitted in the Committee of the Whole. The motion for the previous question is a debate-limiting device and is not in order in the Senate.

Printed Amendment—A House rule guarantees five minutes of floor debate in support and five minutes in opposition, and no other debate time, on amendments printed in the Congressional Record at least one day prior to the amendment's consideration in the Committee of the Whole. In the Senate, while amendments may be submitted for printing, they have no parliamentary standing or status. An amendment submitted for printing in the Senate, however, may be called up by any senator.

Private Calendar—In the House, private bills dealing with individual matters such as claims against the government, immigration or land titles are put on this calendar. The private calendar must be called on the first Tuesday of each month, and the Speaker may call it on the third Tuesday of each month as well.

When a private bill is before the chamber, two members may block its consideration, which recommits the bill to committee. Backers of a recommitted private bill have recourse. The measure can be put into an "omnibus claims bill" — several private bills rolled into one. As with any bill, no part of an omnibus claims bill may be deleted without a vote. When the private bill goes back to the House floor in this form, it can be deleted from the omnibus bill only by majority vote.

Privileged Questions—The order in which bills, motions and other legislative measures are considered on the floor of the Senate and House is governed by strict priorities. A motion to table, for instance, is more privileged than a motion to recommit. Thus, if a member moves to recommit a bill to committee for further consideration, another member could supersede the first action by moving to table it, and a vote would occur first on the motion to table (or kill) the motion to recommit. A motion to adjourn is considered "of the highest privilege" and would have to be considered before virtually any other motion. *(See also Questions of Privilege.)*

Pro Forma Amendment—*(See Strike Out the Last Word.)*

Public Laws—*(See Law.)*

Questions of Privilege—These are matters affecting members of Congress individually or collectively. Matters affecting the rights, safety, dignity and integrity of proceedings of the House or Senate as a whole are questions of privilege in both chambers.

Questions involving individual members are called questions of "personal privilege." A member rising to ask a question of personal privilege is given precedence over almost all other proceedings. For instance, if a member feels that he has been improperly impugned in comments by another member, he can immediately demand to be heard on the floor on a question of personal privilege. An annotation in the House rules points out that the privilege rests primarily on the Constitution, which gives him a conditional immunity from arrest and an unconditional freedom to speak in the House. *(See also Privileged Questions.)*

Quorum—The number of members whose presence is necessary for the transaction of business. In the Senate and House, it is a majority of the membership. A quorum is 100 in the Committee of the Whole House. If a point of order is made that a quorum is not present, the only business that is in order is either a motion to adjourn or a motion to direct the sergeant-at-arms to request the attendance of absentees.

Readings of Bills—Traditional parliamentary procedure required bills to be read three times before they were passed. This custom is of little modern significance. Normally a bill is considered to have its first reading when it is introduced and printed, by title, in the Congressional Record. In the House, its second reading comes when floor consideration begins. (This is the most likely point at which there is an actual reading of the bill, if there is any.) The second reading in the Senate is supposed to occur on the legislative day after the measure is introduced, but before it is referred to committee. The third reading (again, usually by title) takes place when floor action has been completed on amendments.

Recess—Distinguished from adjournment in that a recess does not end a legislative day and therefore does not interrupt unfinished business. The rules in each house set forth certain matters to be taken up and disposed of at the beginning of each legislative day. The House usually adjourns from day to day. The Senate often recesses, thus meeting on the same legislative day for several calendar days or even weeks at a time.

Recognition—The power of recognition of a member is lodged in the Speaker of the House and the presiding officer of the Senate. The presiding officer names the member to speak first when two or more members simultaneously request recognition.

Recommit to Committee—A motion, made on the floor after a bill has been debated, to return it to the committee that reported it. If approved, recommittal usually is considered a death blow to the bill. In the House, a motion to recommit can be made only by a member opposed to the bill, and, in recognizing a member to make the motion, the Speaker gives preference to members of the minority party over majority-party members.

A motion to recommit may include instructions to the committee to report the bill again with specific amendments or by a certain date. Or the instructions may direct that a particular study be made, with no definite deadline for further action. If the recommittal motion includes instructions to "report the bill back forthwith" and the motion is adopted, floor action on the bill continues; the committee does not actually reconsider the legislation.

Reconciliation—The 1974 budget act provides for a "reconciliation" procedure for bringing existing tax and spending laws into conformity with ceilings enacted in the congressional budget resolution. Under the procedure, Congress instructs designated legislative committees to approve measures adjusting revenues and expenditures by a certain amount. The committees have a deadline by which they must report the legislation, but they have the discretion of deciding what changes are to be made. The recommendations of the various committees are consolidated without change by the Budget committees into an omnibus reconciliation bill, which then must be considered and approved by both houses of Congress. The orders to congressional committees to report recommendations for reconciliation bills are called reconciliation instructions, and they are contained in the budget resolution. Reconciliation instructions are not binding, but Congress must meet annual Gramm-Rudman deficit targets to avoid the automatic spending cuts of sequestration, which means it must also meet the goal of reconciliation. *(See also Budget Resolution, Sequestration.)*

Reconsider a Vote—A motion to reconsider the vote by which an action was taken has, until it is disposed of, the effect of putting the action in abeyance. In the Senate, the motion can be made only by a member who voted on the prevailing side of the original question or by a member who did not vote at all. In the House, it can be made only by a member on the prevailing side.

A common practice in the Senate after close votes on an issue is a motion to reconsider, followed by a motion to table the motion to reconsider. On this motion to table, senators vote as they voted on the original question, which allows the motion to table to prevail, assuming there are no switches. The matter then is finally closed and further motions to reconsider are not entertained. In the House, as a routine precaution, a motion to reconsider usually is made every time a measure is passed. Such a motion almost always is tabled immediately, thus shutting off the possibility of future reconsideration, except by unanimous consent.

Motions to reconsider must be entered in the Senate within the next two days of actual session after the original vote has been taken. In the House, they must be entered either on the same day or on the next succeeding day the House is in session.

Recorded Vote—A vote upon which each member's stand is individually made known. In the Senate, this is accomplished through a roll call of the entire membership, to which each senator on the floor must answer "yea," "nay" or "present." Since January 1973, the House has used an electronic voting system for recorded votes, including yea-and-nay votes formerly taken by roll calls.

When not required by the Constitution, a recorded vote can be obtained on questions in the House on the demand of one-fifth (44 members) of a quorum or one-fourth (25) of a quorum in the Committee of the Whole. *(See Yeas and Nays.)*

Report—Both a verb and a noun as a congressional term. A committee that has been examining a bill referred to it by the parent chamber "reports" its findings and recommendations to the chamber when it completes consideration and returns the measure. The process is called "reporting" a bill.

A "report" is the document setting forth the committee's explanation of its action. Senate and House reports are numbered separately and are designated S Rept or H Rept. When a committee report is not unanimous, the dissenting committee members may file a statement of their views, called minority or dissenting views and referred to as a minority report. Members in disagreement with some provisions of a bill may file additional or supplementary views. Sometimes a bill is reported without a committee recommendation.

Adverse reports occasionally are submitted by legislative committees. However, when a committee is opposed to a bill, it usually fails to report the bill at all. Some laws require that committee reports — favorable or adverse — be made.

Rescission—An item in an appropriations bill rescinding or canceling budget authority previously appropriated but not spent. Also, the repeal of a previous appropriation by Congress at the request of the president to cut spending or because the budget authority no longer is needed. Under the 1974 budget act, however, unless Congress approves a rescission within 45 days of continuous session after receipt of the proposal, the funds must be made available for obligation. *(See also Deferral.)*

Resolution—A "simple" resolution, designated H Res or S Res, deals with matters entirely within the prerogatives of one house or the other. It requires neither passage by the other chamber nor approval by the president, and it does not have the force of law. Most resolutions deal with the rules or procedures of one house. They also are used to express the sentiments of a single house such as condolences to the family of a deceased member or to comment on foreign policy or executive business. A simple resolution is the vehicle for a "rule" from the House Rules Committee. *(See also Concurrent and Joint Resolutions, Rules.)*

Rider—An amendment, usually not germane, that its sponsor hopes to get through more easily by including it in other legislation. Riders become law if the bills embodying them are enacted. Amendments providing legislative directives in appropriations bills are outstanding examples of riders, though technically legislation is banned from appropriations bills.

The House, unlike the Senate, has a strict germaneness rule; thus, riders usually are Senate devices to get legislation enacted quickly or to bypass lengthy House consideration and, possibly, opposition.

Rules—A rule is a standing order governing the conduct of House or Senate business and listed among the permanent rules of either chamber. The rules deal with issues such as duties of officers, the order of business, admission to the floor, parliamentary procedures on handling amendments and voting and jurisdictions of committees.

In the House, a rule also may be a resolution reported by its Rules Committee to govern the handling of a particular bill on the floor. The committee may report a "rule," also called a "special order," in the form of a simple resolution. If the resolution is adopted by the House, the temporary rule becomes as valid as any standing rule and lapses only after action has been completed on the measure to which it pertains. A rule sets the time limit on general debate. It also may waive points of order against provisions of the bill in question such as non-germane language or against certain amendments intended to be proposed to the bill from the floor. It may even forbid all amendments or all amendments except those proposed by the legislative committee that handled the bill. In this instance, it is known as a "closed" rule as opposed to an "open" rule, which puts no limitation on floor amendments, thus leaving the bill completely open to alteration by the adoption of germane amendments.

Secretary of the Senate—Chief administrative officer of the Senate, responsible for overseeing the duties of Senate employees, educating Senate pages, administering oaths, overseeing the registration of lobbyists and handling other tasks necessary for the continuing operation of the Senate. *(See also Clerk of the House.)*

Select or Special Committee—A committee set up for a special purpose and, usually, for a limited time by resolution of either the House or Senate. Most special committees are investigative and lack legislative authority: legislation is not referred to them, and they cannot report bills to their parent chamber. *(See also Standing Committees.)*

Senatorial Courtesy—Sometimes referred to as "the courtesy of the Senate," it is a general practice — with no written rule — applied to consideration of executive nominations. Generally, it means that nominations from a state are not to be confirmed unless they have been approved by the senators of the president's party of that state, with other senators following their colleagues' lead in the attitude they take toward consideration of such nominations. *(See Nominations.)*

Sequester order — Under procedures put in place by the 1985 Gramm-Rudman antideficit law, Congress was threatened with year-end, across-the-board spending cuts known as a sequester if the deficit exceeded a pre-set maximum. The Budget Enforcement Act of 1990 effectively did away with that form of sequester for fiscal years 1991-93, replacing it with a series of targeted "mini-sequesters." *(See also Budget Process.)*

For fiscal 1991-93, discretionary spending in any of the 13 regular appropriations bills that exceeded the cap for its particular category (domestic, defense or international) would trigger a sequester in that category only. For fiscal 1994-95, however, the three categories were collapsed into a single pot of money, which meant that a sequester would affect all discretionary spending. The sequester would take place 15 days after adjournment.

New "pay-as-you-go" rules required that mandatory spending (entitlement programs such as Medicare and food stamps) and tax cuts be deficit-neutral. If Congress cut taxes, expanded existing entitlement programs or created new entitlements, the cost had to be offset. If there was no offset, a sequester of all non-exempt entitlement programs would take place 15 days after Congress adjourns.

Two other types of sequesters affected supplemental appropriations bills. A supplemental that exceeded discretionary spending limits and was enacted before July 1 would trigger a "within-session" sequester within 15 days of enactment. That sequester would require a cutback in spending for the offending category during the current fiscal year.

A supplemental that exceeded the caps and was enacted after June 30 would trigger a "look-back" sequester, which would reduce the cap for the offending category for the next fiscal year by the amount of the excess spending.

Sine Die—*(See Adjournment Sine Die.)*

Slip Laws—The first official publication of a bill that has been enacted and signed into law. Each is published separately in unbound single-sheet or pamphlet form. *(See also Law, Statutes at Large, U.S. Code.)*

Speaker—The presiding officer of the House of Representatives, selected by the caucus of the party to which he belongs and formally elected by the whole House.

Special Session—A session of Congress after it has adjourned sine die, completing its regular session. Special sessions are convened by the president.

Spending Authority—The 1974 budget act defines spending authority as borrowing authority, contract authority and entitlement authority for which budget authority is not provided in advance by appropriation acts.

Sponsor—*(See Bills Introduced.)*

Standing Committees—Committees that are permanently established by House and Senate rules. The standing committees of the House were last reorganized by the committee reorganization of 1974. The last major realignment of Senate committees was in the committee system reorganization of 1977. The standing committees are legislative committees — legislation may be referred to them and they may report bills and resolutions to their parent chambers. *(See also Select or Special Committees.)*

Standing Vote—A non-recorded vote used in both the House and Senate. (A standing vote also is called a division vote.) Members in favor of a proposal stand and are counted by the presiding officer. Then members opposed stand and are counted. There is no record of how individual members voted.

Statutes at Large—A chronological arrangement of the laws enacted in each session of Congress. Though indexed, the laws are not arranged by subject matter, and there is not an indication of how they changed previously enacted laws. *(See also Law, Slip Laws, U.S. Code.)*

Strike From the Record—Remarks made on the House floor may offend some member, who moves that the offending words be "taken down" for the Speaker's cognizance, and then expunged from the debate as published in the Congressional Record.

Strike Out the Last Word—A motion whereby a House member is entitled to speak for five minutes on an amendment then being debated by the chamber. A member gains recognition from the chair by moving to "strike out the last word" of the amendment or section of the bill under consideration. The motion is pro forma, requires no vote and does not change the amendment being debated.

Substitute—A motion, amendment or entire bill introduced in place of the pending legislative business. Passage of a substitute measure kills the original measure by supplanting it. The substitute also may be amended. *(See also Amendment in the Nature of a Substitute.)*

Supplemental Appropriations Bill—Legislation appropriating funds after the regular annual appropriations bill for a federal department or agency has been enacted. A supplemental appropriation provides additional budget authority beyond original estimates for programs or activities, including new programs authorized after the enactment of the regular appropriation act, for which the need for funds is too urgent to be postponed until enactment of the next year's regular appropriation bill.

Suspend the Rules—Often a time-saving procedure for passing bills in the House. The wording of the motion, which may be made by any member recognized by the Speaker, is: "I move to suspend the rules and pass the bill . . ." A favorable vote by two-thirds of those present is required for passage. Debate is limited to 40 minutes and no amendments from the floor are permitted. If a two-thirds favorable vote is not attained, the bill may be considered later under regular procedures. The suspension procedure is in order every Monday and Tuesday and is intended to be reserved for non-controversial bills.

Table a Bill—Motions to table, or to "lay on the table," are used to block or kill amendments or other parliamentary questions. When approved, a tabling motion is considered the final disposition of that issue. One of the most widely used parliamentary procedures, the motion to table is not debatable, and adoption requires a simple majority vote.

In the Senate, however, different language sometimes is used. The motion may be worded to let a bill "lie on the table," perhaps for subsequent "picking up." This motion is more flexible, keeping the bill pending for later action, if desired. Tabling motions on amendments are effective debate-ending devices in the Senate.

Teller Vote—This is a largely moribund House procedure in the Committee of the Whole. Members file past tellers and are counted as for or against a measure, but they are not recorded individually. In the House, tellers are ordered upon demand of one-fifth of a quorum. This is 44 in the House, 20 in the Committee of the Whole.

The House also has a recorded teller vote, now largely supplanted by the electronic voting procedure, under which the votes of each member are made public just as they would be on a recorded vote.

Treaties—Executive proposals — in the form of resolutions of ratification — which must be submitted to the Senate for approval by two-thirds of the senators present. Treaties are normally sent to the Foreign Relations Committee for scrutiny before the Senate takes action. Foreign Relations has jurisdiction over all treaties, regardless of the subject matter. Treaties are read three times and debated on the floor in much the same manner as legislative proposals. After approval by the Senate, treaties are formally ratified by the president.

Trust Funds—Funds collected and used by the federal government for carrying out specific purposes and programs according to terms of a trust agreement or statute such as the Social Security and unemployment compensation trust funds. Such funds are administered by the government in a fiduciary capacity and are not available for the general purposes of the government.

Unanimous Consent—Proceedings of the House or Senate and action on legislation often take place upon the unanimous consent of the chamber, whether or not a rule of the chamber is being violated. Unanimous consent is used to expedite floor action and frequently is used in a routine fashion such as by a senator requesting the unanimous consent of the Senate to have specified members of his staff present on the floor during debate on a specific amendment.

Unanimous Consent Agreement—A device used in the Senate to expedite legislation. Much of the Senate's legislative business, dealing with both minor and controversial issues, is conducted through unanimous consent or unanimous consent agreements. On major legislation, such agreements usually are printed and transmitted to all senators in advance of floor debate. Once agreed to, they are binding on all members unless the Senate, by unanimous consent, agrees to modify them. An agreement may list the order in which various bills are to be considered, specify the length of time bills and contested amendments are to be debated and when they are to be voted upon and, frequently, require that all amendments introduced be germane to the bill under consideration.

In this regard, unanimous consent agreements are similar to the "rules" issued by the House Rules Committee for bills pending in the House.

Union Calendar—Bills that directly or indirectly appropriate money or raise revenue are placed on this House calendar according to the date they are reported from committee.

U.S. Code—A consolidation and codification of the general and permanent laws of the United States arranged by subject under 50 titles, the first six dealing with general or political subjects, and the other 44 alphabetically arranged from agriculture to war. The U.S. Code is updated annually, and a new set of bound volumes is published every six years. *(See also Law, Slip Laws, Statutes at Large.)*

Veto—Disapproval by the president of a bill or joint resolution (other than one proposing an amendment to the Constitution). When Congress is in session, the president must veto a bill within 10 days, excluding Sundays, after he has received it; otherwise, it becomes law without his signature. When the president vetoes a bill, he returns it to the house of origin along with a message stating his objections. *(See also Pocket Veto, Override a Veto.)*

Voice Vote—In either the House or Senate, members answer "aye" or "no" in chorus, and the presiding officer decides the result. The term also is used loosely to indicate action by unanimous consent or without objection.

Whip—*(See Majority and Minority Whip.)*

Without Objection—Used in lieu of a vote on non-controversial motions, amendments or bills that may be passed in either the House or Senate if no member voices an objection.

Yeas and Nays—The Constitution requires that yea-and-nay votes be taken and recorded when requested by one-fifth of the members present. In the House, the Speaker determines whether one-fifth of the members present requested a vote. In the Senate, practice requires only 11 members. The Constitution requires the yeas and nays on a veto override attempt. *(See Recorded Vote.)*

Yielding—When a member has been recognized to speak, no other member may speak unless he obtains permission from the member recognized. This permission is called yielding and usually is requested in the form, "Will the gentleman (or gentlelady) yield to me?" While this activity occasionally is seen in the Senate, the Senate has no rule or practice to parcel out time.

CQ

Appendix H

HOUSE ROLL-CALL VOTES

2. Procedural Motion. Boehlert, R-N.Y., motion to approve the House Journal of Tuesday, Jan. 23. Motion agreed to 312-89: R 78-87; D 234-2 (ND 156-2, SD 78-0), Jan. 24, 1990.

3. HR 2712. Chinese Students/Veto Override. Michel, R-Ill., motion to refer the bill and President Bush's Nov. 30, 1989, memorandum of disapproval to the Foreign Affairs and Judiciary committees for review in light of events in China since passage of the bill to stay the deportation of Chinese students in the United States whose visas have expired, provide work permits for the students and waive a requirement that Chinese nationals on "J" exchange visas return home for two years before applying for permanent residency in the United States. Motion rejected 137-276: R 137-32; D 0-244 (ND 0-164, SD 0-80), Jan. 24, 1990.

4. HR 2712. Chinese Students/Veto Override. Passage, over President Bush's Nov. 30, 1989, veto, of the bill to stay the deportation of Chinese students in the United States whose visas have expired, provide work permits for the students and waive a requirement that Chinese nationals on "J" exchange visas return home for two years before applying for permanent residency in the United States. Passed (thus cleared for Senate action) 390-25: R 145-25; D 245-0 (ND 165-0, SD 80-0), Jan. 24, 1990. A two-thirds majority of those present and voting (277 in this case) of both houses is required to override a veto. A "nay" was a vote supporting the president's position.

KEY

- Y Voted for (yea).
- # Paired for.
- + Announced for.
- N Voted against (nay).
- X Paired against.
- - Announced against.
- P Voted "present."
- C Voted "present" to avoid possible conflict of interest.
- ? Did not vote or otherwise make a position known.

Democrats ***Republicans***

	2	3	4
ALABAMA			
1 ***Callahan***	Y	Y	Y
2 ***Dickinson***	N	Y	Y
3 Browder	Y	N	Y
4 Bevill	Y	N	Y
5 Flippo	?	?	?
6 Erdreich	Y	N	Y
7 Harris	Y	N	Y
ALASKA			
AL ***Young***	?	?	?
ARIZONA			
1 ***Rhodes***	N	Y	Y
2 Udall	Y	N	Y
3 ***Stump***	N	Y	N
4 ***Kyl***	N	Y	Y
5 ***Kolbe***	?	?	#
ARKANSAS			
1 Alexander	Y	N	Y
2 ***Robinson***	Y	Y	N
3 ***Hammerschmidt***	Y	Y	N
4 Anthony	Y	N	Y
CALIFORNIA			
1 Bosco	Y	N	Y
2 ***Herger***	N	Y	Y
3 Matsui	Y	N	Y
4 Fazio	Y	N	Y
5 Pelosi	Y	N	Y
6 Boxer	Y	N	Y
7 Miller	Y	N	Y
8 Dellums	Y	N	Y
9 Stark	Y	N	Y
10 Edwards	Y	N	Y
11 Lantos	Y	N	Y
12 ***Campbell***	Y	N	Y
13 Mineta	Y	N	Y
14 ***Shumway***	Y	Y	Y
15 Condit	Y	N	Y
16 Panetta	Y	N	Y
17 ***Pashayan***	N	Y	Y
18 Lehman	Y	N	Y
19 ***Lagomarsino***	N	N	Y
20 ***Thomas***	N	Y	Y
21 ***Gallegly***	N	Y	Y
22 ***Moorhead***	N	Y	Y
23 Beilenson	?	N	Y
24 Waxman	?	N	Y
25 Roybal	Y	N	Y
26 Berman	Y	N	Y
27 Levine	Y	N	Y
28 Dixon	Y	N	Y
29 Hawkins	Y	N	Y
30 Martinez	Y	N	Y
31 Dymally	Y	N	Y
32 Anderson	Y	N	Y
33 ***Dreier***	N	Y	Y
34 Torres	Y	N	Y
35 ***Lewis***	N	Y	Y
36 Brown	Y	N	Y
37 ***McCandless***	N	Y	Y
38 ***Dornan***	N	Y	Y
39 ***Dannemeyer***	N	Y	Y
40 ***Cox***	N	N	Y
41 ***Lowery***	N	Y	Y
42 ***Rohrabacher***	Y	N	Y
43 ***Packard***	Y	Y	Y
44 Bates	Y	N	Y
45 ***Hunter***	N	Y	Y
COLORADO			
1 Schroeder	N	N	Y
2 Skaggs	Y	N	Y
3 Campbell	Y	N	Y
4 ***Brown***	Y	N	Y
5 ***Hefley***	N	Y	Y
6 ***Schaefer***	Y	Y	Y
CONNECTICUT			
1 Kennelly	Y	N	Y
2 Gejdenson	Y	N	Y
3 Morrison	Y	N	Y
4 ***Shays***	N	Y	Y
5 ***Rowland***	Y	N	Y
6 ***Johnson***	Y	Y	Y
DELAWARE			
AL Carper	Y	N	Y
FLORIDA			
1 Hutto	Y	N	Y
2 ***Grant***	Y	Y	Y
3 Bennett	Y	N	Y
4 ***James***	Y	Y	Y
5 ***McCollum***	N	Y	Y
6 ***Stearns***	Y	Y	Y
7 Gibbons	Y	N	Y
8 ***Young***	Y	Y	N
9 ***Bilirakis***	?	#	#
10 ***Ireland***	N	Y	N
11 Nelson	+	-	+
12 ***Lewis***	N	Y	Y
13 ***Goss***	N	Y	N
14 Johnston	Y	N	Y
15 ***Shaw***	Y	Y	Y
16 Smith	Y	N	Y
17 Lehman	Y	N	Y
18 ***Ros-Lehtinen***	N	Y	Y
19 Fascell	Y	N	Y
GEORGIA			
1 Thomas	Y	N	Y
2 Hatcher	Y	N	Y
3 Ray	Y	N	Y
4 Jones	Y	N	Y
5 Lewis	Y	N	Y
6 ***Gingrich***	N	Y	Y
7 Darden	Y	N	Y
8 Rowland	Y	N	Y
9 Jenkins	Y	N	Y
10 Barnard	Y	N	Y
HAWAII			
1 ***Saiki***	Y	N	Y
2 Akaka	Y	N	Y
IDAHO			
1 ***Craig***	N	Y	Y
2 Stallings	Y	N	Y
ILLINOIS			
1 Hayes	Y	N	Y
2 Savage	Y	N	Y
3 Russo	Y	N	Y
4 Sangmeister	Y	N	Y
5 Lipinski	Y	N	Y
6 ***Hyde***	Y	Y	Y
7 Collins	Y	N	Y
8 Rostenkowski	Y	N	Y
9 Yates	Y	N	Y
10 ***Porter***	Y	N	Y
11 Annunzio	Y	N	Y
12 ***Crane***	N	Y	Y
13 ***Fawell***	N	Y	Y
14 ***Hastert***	N	Y	N
15 ***Madigan***	N	Y	N
16 ***Martin***	N	Y	Y
17 Evans	Y	N	Y
18 ***Michel***	Y	Y	N
19 Bruce	Y	N	Y
20 Durbin	Y	N	Y
21 Costello	Y	N	Y
22 Poshard	Y	N	Y
INDIANA			
1 Visclosky	Y	N	Y
2 Sharp	Y	N	Y
3 ***Hiler***	Y	Y	Y

ND Northern Democrats SD Southern Democrats

	2	3	4
4 Long	Y	N	Y
5 Jontz	Y	N	Y
6 ***Burton***	N	Y	Y
7 ***Myers***	Y	Y	Y
8 McCloskey	Y	N	Y
9 Hamilton	Y	N	Y
10 Jacobs	N	N	Y
IOWA			
1 ***Leach***	N	Y	Y
2 ***Tauke***	N	Y	Y
3 Nagle	Y	N	Y
4 Smith	Y	N	Y
5 ***Lightfoot***	N	Y	Y
6 ***Grandy***	Y	Y	Y
KANSAS			
1 ***Roberts***	Y	Y	Y
2 Slattery	Y	N	Y
3 ***Meyers***	Y	Y	Y
4 Glickman	Y	N	Y
5 ***Whittaker***	N	Y	Y
KENTUCKY			
1 Hubbard	Y	N	Y
2 Natcher	Y	N	Y
3 Mazzoli	+	N	Y
4 ***Bunning***	N	Y	Y
5 ***Rogers***	N	Y	Y
6 ***Hopkins***	N	Y	Y
7 Perkins	Y	N	Y
LOUISIANA			
1 ***Livingston***	Y	Y	Y
2 Boggs	Y	N	Y
3 Tauzin	Y	N	Y
4 ***McCrery***	Y	Y	N
5 Huckaby	Y	N	Y
6 ***Baker***	N	Y	N
7 Hayes	Y	N	Y
8 ***Holloway***	Y	Y	N
MAINE			
1 Brennan	Y	N	Y
2 ***Snowe***	Y	N	Y
MARYLAND			
1 Dyson	Y	N	Y
2 ***Bentley***	N	Y	Y
3 Cardin	Y	N	Y
4 McMillen	Y	N	Y
5 Hoyer	Y	N	Y
6 Byron	Y	N	Y
7 Mfume	Y	N	Y
8 ***Morella***	Y	N	Y
MASSACHUSETTS			
1 ***Conte***	Y	N	Y
2 Neal	Y	N	Y
3 Early	Y	N	Y
4 Frank	Y	N	Y
5 Atkins	Y	N	Y
6 Mavroules	Y	N	Y
7 Markey	Y	N	Y
8 Kennedy	Y	N	Y
9 Moakley	Y	N	Y
10 Studds	Y	N	Y
11 Donnelly	?	?	?
MICHIGAN			
1 Conyers	?	N	Y
2 ***Pursell***	Y	N	Y
3 Wolpe	Y	N	Y
4 ***Upton***	N	Y	Y
5 ***Henry***	Y	N	Y
6 Carr	?	?	?
7 Kildee	Y	N	Y
8 Traxler	Y	N	Y
9 ***Vander Jagt***	?	?	?
10 ***Schuette***	N	N	Y
11 ***Davis***	Y	Y	Y
12 Bonior	Y	N	Y
13 Crockett	Y	N	Y
14 Hertel	Y	N	Y
15 Ford	Y	N	Y
16 Dingell	Y	N	Y
17 Levin	Y	N	Y
18 ***Broomfield***	Y	Y	Y
MINNESOTA			
1 Penny	Y	N	Y
2 ***Weber***	?	Y	Y
3 ***Frenzel***	P	Y	Y
4 Vento	Y	N	Y
5 Sabo	Y	N	Y
6 Sikorski	?	X	?
7 ***Stangeland***	N	Y	Y
8 Oberstar	Y	N	Y
MISSISSIPPI			
1 Whitten	Y	N	Y
2 Espy	?	N	Y
3 Montgomery	Y	N	Y
4 Parker	Y	N	Y
5 Taylor	Y	N	Y
MISSOURI			
1 Clay	P	N	Y
2 ***Buechner***	Y	Y	Y
3 Gephardt	Y	N	Y
4 Skelton	Y	N	Y
5 Wheat	Y	N	Y
6 ***Coleman***	N	Y	Y
7 ***Hancock***	N	Y	Y
8 ***Emerson***	Y	Y	Y
9 Volkmer	Y	N	Y
MONTANA			
1 Williams	Y	N	Y
2 ***Marlenee***	N	Y	Y
NEBRASKA			
1 ***Bereuter***	Y	N	Y
2 Hoagland	Y	N	Y
3 ***Smith***	Y	Y	Y
NEVADA			
1 Bilbray	Y	N	Y
2 ***Vucanovich***	?	?	Y
NEW HAMPSHIRE			
1 ***Smith***	N	N	Y
2 ***Douglas***	N	N	Y
NEW JERSEY			
1 Vacancy			
2 Hughes	?	N	Y
3 Pallone	Y	N	Y
4 ***Smith***	Y	N	Y
5 ***Roukema***	N	N	Y
6 Dwyer	Y	N	Y
7 ***Rinaldo***	Y	N	Y
8 Roe	Y	N	Y
9 Torricelli	Y	N	Y
10 Payne	Y	N	Y
11 ***Gallo***	Y	Y	Y
12 ***Courter***	N	Y	Y
13 ***Saxton***	N	Y	Y
14 Guarini	Y	N	Y
NEW MEXICO			
1 ***Schiff***	Y	Y	Y
2 ***Skeen***	Y	Y	Y
3 Richardson	Y	N	Y
NEW YORK			
1 Hochbrueckner	Y	N	Y
2 Downey	Y	N	Y
3 Mrazek	Y	N	Y
4 ***Lent***	Y	Y	N
5 ***McGrath***	N	Y	Y
6 Flake	Y	?	?
7 Ackerman	Y	N	Y
8 Scheuer	Y	N	Y
9 Manton	Y	N	Y
10 Schumer	Y	N	Y
11 Towns	Y	N	Y
12 Owens	Y	N	Y
13 Solarz	Y	N	Y
14 Vacancy			
15 ***Green***	P	N	Y
16 Rangel	?	N	Y
17 Weiss	Y	N	Y
18 Vacancy			
19 Engel	Y	N	Y
20 Lowey	Y	N	Y
21 ***Fish***	Y	Y	Y
22 ***Gilman***	N	N	Y
23 McNulty	Y	N	Y
24 ***Solomon***	N	Y	Y
25 ***Boehlert***	N	N	Y
26 ***Martin***	Y	Y	Y
27 ***Walsh***	Y	N	Y
28 McHugh	Y	N	Y
29 ***Horton***	?	Y	Y
30 Slaughter	Y	N	Y
31 ***Paxon***	N	Y	Y
32 LaFalce	Y	N	Y
33 Nowak	?	N	Y
34 ***Houghton***	Y	Y	Y
NORTH CAROLINA			
1 Jones	Y	N	Y
2 Valentine	Y	N	Y
3 Lancaster	Y	N	Y
4 Price	Y	N	Y
5 Neal	Y	N	Y
6 ***Coble***	N	Y	Y
7 Rose	Y	N	Y
8 Hefner	Y	N	Y
9 ***McMillan***	Y	Y	Y
10 ***Ballenger***	N	Y	Y
11 Clarke	Y	N	Y
NORTH DAKOTA			
AL Dorgan	Y	N	Y
OHIO			
1 Luken	Y	?	Y
2 ***Gradison***	Y	Y	Y
3 Hall	Y	N	Y
4 ***Oxley***	Y	Y	Y
5 ***Gillmor***	Y	Y	N
6 ***McEwen***	Y	Y	Y
7 ***DeWine***	N	Y	Y
8 ***Lukens***	N	N	Y
9 Kaptur	Y	N	Y
10 ***Miller***	N	Y	Y
11 Eckart	Y	N	Y
12 ***Kasich***	Y	N	Y
13 Pease	Y	N	Y
14 Sawyer	Y	N	Y
15 ***Wylie***	Y	Y	Y
16 ***Regula***	N	Y	Y
17 Traficant	Y	N	Y
18 Applegate	Y	N	Y
19 Feighan	Y	N	Y
20 Oakar	?	?	?
21 Stokes	Y	N	Y
OKLAHOMA			
1 ***Inhofe***	N	Y	Y
2 Synar	Y	N	Y
3 Watkins	Y	N	Y
4 McCurdy	?	N	Y
5 ***Edwards***	N	Y	Y
6 English	Y	N	Y
OREGON			
1 AuCoin	?	X	?
2 ***Smith, B.***	N	Y	Y
3 Wyden	Y	N	Y
4 DeFazio	Y	N	Y
5 ***Smith, D.***	N	N	Y
PENNSYLVANIA			
1 Foglietta	Y	N	Y
2 Gray	Y	N	Y
3 Borski	Y	N	Y
4 Kolter	?	?	?
5 ***Schulze***	Y	Y	Y
6 Yatron	Y	N	Y
7 ***Weldon***	Y	Y	Y
8 Kostmayer	Y	N	Y
9 ***Shuster***	Y	Y	Y
10 ***McDade***	?	#	X
11 Kanjorski	Y	N	Y
12 Murtha	Y	N	Y
13 ***Coughlin***	N	Y	N
14 Coyne	Y	N	Y
15 ***Ritter***	Y	Y	Y
16 ***Walker***	N	Y	Y
17 ***Gekas***	N	Y	N
18 Walgren	Y	N	Y
19 ***Goodling***	N	Y	Y
20 Gaydos	Y	N	Y
21 ***Ridge***	N	Y	Y
22 Murphy	?	?	?
23 ***Clinger***	Y	Y	Y
RHODE ISLAND			
1 ***Machtley***	N	N	Y
2 ***Schneider***	Y	N	Y
SOUTH CAROLINA			
1 ***Ravenel***	Y	Y	Y
2 ***Spence***	Y	Y	Y
3 Derrick	Y	N	Y
4 Patterson	Y	N	Y
5 Spratt	Y	N	Y
6 Tallon	Y	N	Y
SOUTH DAKOTA			
AL Johnson	Y	N	Y
TENNESSEE			
1 ***Quillen***	Y	Y	N
2 ***Duncan***	Y	Y	Y
3 Lloyd	Y	N	Y
4 Cooper	Y	N	Y
5 Clement	Y	N	Y
6 Gordon	Y	N	Y
7 ***Sundquist***	N	Y	N
8 Tanner	Y	N	Y
9 Ford	Y	?	Y
TEXAS			
1 Chapman	Y	N	Y
2 Wilson	Y	N	?
3 ***Bartlett***	Y	Y	Y
4 Hall	Y	N	Y
5 Bryant	Y	N	Y
6 ***Barton***	N	Y	Y
7 ***Archer***	Y	Y	Y
8 ***Fields***	N	Y	Y
9 Brooks	Y	N	Y
10 Pickle	Y	N	Y
11 Leath	Y	N	Y
12 Geren	Y	N	Y
13 Sarpalius	Y	N	Y
14 Laughlin	Y	N	Y
15 de la Garza	Y	N	Y
16 Coleman	Y	N	Y
17 Stenholm	Y	N	Y
18 Washington	Y	N	Y
19 ***Combest***	Y	Y	N
20 Gonzalez	Y	N	Y
21 ***Smith***	N	Y	N
22 ***DeLay***	N	Y	N
23 Bustamante	Y	N	Y
24 Frost	Y	N	Y
25 Andrews	Y	N	Y
26 ***Armey***	N	Y	Y
27 Ortiz	Y	N	Y
UTAH			
1 ***Hansen***	Y	Y	N
2 Owens	Y	N	Y
3 ***Nielson***	Y	Y	Y
VERMONT			
AL ***Smith***	Y	N	Y
VIRGINIA			
1 ***Bateman***	Y	Y	N
2 Pickett	Y	N	Y
3 ***Bliley***	N	Y	Y
4 Sisisky	Y	N	Y
5 Payne	Y	N	Y
6 Olin	Y	N	Y
7 ***Slaughter***	N	Y	Y
8 ***Parris***	N	N	Y
9 Boucher	Y	N	Y
10 ***Wolf***	N	Y	Y
WASHINGTON			
1 ***Miller***	N	N	Y
2 Swift	Y	N	Y
3 Unsoeld	Y	N	Y
4 ***Morrison***	Y	Y	Y
5 Foley			
6 Dicks	Y	N	Y
7 McDermott	Y	N	Y
8 ***Chandler***	N	Y	Y
WEST VIRGINIA			
1 Mollohan	Y	N	Y
2 Staggers	Y	N	Y
3 Wise	Y	N	Y
4 Rahall	Y	N	Y
WISCONSIN			
1 Aspin	Y	N	Y
2 Kastenmeier	Y	N	Y
3 ***Gunderson***	Y	Y	Y
4 Kleczka	Y	N	Y
5 Moody	?	N	Y
6 ***Petri***	Y	Y	N
7 Obey	Y	N	Y
8 ***Roth***	Y	Y	Y
9 ***Sensenbrenner***	N	Y	N
WYOMING			
AL ***Thomas***	Y	Y	Y

Southern states - Ala., Ark., Fla., Ga., Ky., La., Miss., N.C., Okla., S.C., Tenn., Texas, Va.
Omitted votes are quorum calls, which CQ does not include in its vote charts.

HOUSE VOTES 5, 6

5. Procedural Motion. Douglas, R-N.H., motion to approve the House Journal of Tuesday, Jan. 30. Motion agreed to 301-100: R 75-94; D 226-6 (ND 152-6, SD 74-0), Jan. 31, 1990.

6. HR 2190. Voter Registration/Rule. Adoption of the rule (H Res 309) to provide for House floor consideration of the bill to establish national voter registration procedures for elections to federal office. Adopted 254-166: R 6-166; D 248-0 (ND 167-0, SD 81-0), Jan. 31, 1990.

KEY

Y Voted for (yea).
\# Paired for.
\+ Announced for.
N Voted against (nay).
X Paired against.
\- Announced against.
P Voted "present."
C Voted "present" to avoid possible conflict of interest.
? Did not vote or otherwise make a position known.

Democrats ***Republicans***

	5	6
ALABAMA		
1 ***Callahan***	Y	N
2 ***Dickinson***	N	?
3 Browder	Y	Y
4 Bevill	Y	Y
5 Flippo	Y	Y
6 Erdreich	Y	Y
7 Harris	Y	Y
ALASKA		
AL ***Young***	N	N
ARIZONA		
1 ***Rhodes***	N	N
2 Udall	Y	Y
3 ***Stump***	N	N
4 ***Kyl***	N	N
5 ***Kolbe***	N	N
ARKANSAS		
1 Alexander	Y	Y
2 ***Robinson***	Y	N
3 ***Hammerschmidt***	Y	N
4 Anthony	Y	Y
CALIFORNIA		
1 Bosco	?	?
2 ***Herger***	N	N
3 Matsui	Y	Y
4 Fazio	Y	Y
5 Pelosi	Y	Y
6 Boxer	Y	Y
7 Miller	Y	Y
8 Dellums	Y	Y
9 Stark	Y	Y
10 Edwards	Y	Y
11 Lantos	?	?
12 ***Campbell***	Y	N
13 Mineta	Y	Y
14 ***Shumway***	Y	N
15 Condit	Y	Y
16 Panetta	Y	Y
17 ***Pashayan***	N	N
18 Lehman	Y	Y
19 ***Lagomarsino***	N	N
20 ***Thomas***	N	Y
21 ***Gallegly***	N	N
22 ***Moorhead***	N	N
23 Beilenson	Y	Y
24 Waxman	Y	Y
25 Roybal	?	Y
26 Berman	Y	Y
27 Levine	Y	Y
28 Dixon	Y	Y
29 Hawkins	N	Y
30 Martinez	?	Y
31 Dymally	Y	Y
32 Anderson	Y	Y
33 ***Dreier***	N	N
34 Torres	Y	Y
35 ***Lewis***	N	N
36 Brown	Y	Y
37 ***McCandless***	N	N
38 ***Dornan***	N	N
39 ***Dannemeyer***	N	N
40 ***Cox***	Y	N
41 ***Lowery***	?	N
42 ***Rohrabacher***	Y	N
43 ***Packard***	Y	N
44 Bates	Y	Y
45 ***Hunter***	N	N
COLORADO		
1 Schroeder	N	Y
2 Skaggs	Y	Y
3 Campbell	Y	Y
4 ***Brown***	N	N
5 ***Hefley***	N	N
6 ***Schaefer***	N	N
CONNECTICUT		
1 Kennelly	Y	Y
2 Gejdenson	Y	Y
3 Morrison	Y	Y
4 ***Shays***	N	N
5 ***Rowland***	Y	N
6 ***Johnson***	Y	N
DELAWARE		
AL Carper	Y	Y
FLORIDA		
1 Hutto	?	?
2 ***Grant***	Y	N
3 Bennett	Y	Y
4 ***James***	?	N
5 ***McCollum***	Y	N
6 ***Stearns***	N	N
7 Gibbons	Y	Y
8 ***Young***	N	N
9 ***Bilirakis***	N	N
10 ***Ireland***	N	N
11 Nelson	Y	Y
12 ***Lewis***	N	N
13 ***Goss***	N	N
14 Johnston	Y	Y
15 ***Shaw***	Y	N
16 Smith	Y	Y
17 Lehman	Y	Y
18 ***Ros-Lehtinen***	N	N
19 Fascell	?	Y
GEORGIA		
1 Thomas	Y	Y
2 Hatcher	Y	Y
3 Ray	Y	Y
4 Jones	Y	Y
5 Lewis	Y	Y
6 ***Gingrich***	N	N
7 Darden	Y	Y
8 Rowland	Y	Y
9 Jenkins	Y	Y
10 Barnard	?	Y
HAWAII		
1 ***Saiki***	Y	N
2 Akaka	Y	Y
IDAHO		
1 ***Craig***	N	N
2 Stallings	Y	Y
ILLINOIS		
1 Hayes	Y	Y
2 Savage	Y	Y
3 Russo	Y	Y
4 Sangmeister	Y	Y
5 Lipinski	Y	Y
6 ***Hyde***	Y	N
7 Collins	Y	Y
8 Rostenkowski	Y	Y
9 Yates	Y	Y
10 ***Porter***	Y	N
11 Annunzio	Y	Y
12 ***Crane***	N	N
13 ***Fawell***	Y	N
14 ***Hastert***	N	N
15 ***Madigan***	N	?
16 ***Martin***	N	N
17 Evans	Y	Y
18 ***Michel***	Y	N
19 Bruce	Y	Y
20 Durbin	Y	Y
21 Costello	Y	Y
22 Poshard	Y	Y
INDIANA		
1 Visclosky	Y	Y
2 Sharp	Y	Y
3 ***Hiler***	N	Y

ND Northern Democrats SD Southern Democrats

	5	6
4 Long	Y	Y
5 Jontz	Y	Y
6 ***Burton***	N	N
7 ***Myers***	Y	N
8 McCloskey	Y	Y
9 Hamilton	Y	Y
10 Jacobs	N	Y
IOWA		
1 ***Leach***	N	N
2 ***Tauke***	N	N
3 Nagle	Y	Y
4 Smith	?	?
5 ***Lightfoot***	N	N
6 ***Grandy***	N	N
KANSAS		
1 ***Roberts***	?	N
2 Slattery	Y	Y
3 ***Meyers***	Y	N
4 Glickman	Y	Y
5 ***Whittaker***	N	N
KENTUCKY		
1 Hubbard	Y	Y
2 Natcher	Y	Y
3 Mazzoli	Y	Y
4 ***Bunning***	N	N
5 ***Rogers***	N	N
6 ***Hopkins***	N	N
7 Perkins	Y	Y
LOUISIANA		
1 ***Livingston***	Y	N
2 Boggs	Y	Y
3 Tauzin	Y	Y
4 ***McCrery***	Y	Y
5 Huckaby	Y	Y
6 ***Baker***	N	N
7 Hayes	Y	Y
8 ***Holloway***	N	N
MAINE		
1 Brennan	Y	Y
2 ***Snowe***	Y	N
MARYLAND		
1 Dyson	?	Y
2 ***Bentley***	N	N
3 Cardin	Y	Y
4 McMillen	Y	Y
5 Hoyer	Y	Y
6 Byron	Y	Y
7 Mfume	Y	Y
8 ***Morella***	Y	N
MASSACHUSETTS		
1 ***Conte***	Y	N
2 Neal	Y	Y
3 Early	Y	Y
4 Frank	Y	Y
5 Atkins	Y	Y
6 Mavroules	?	Y
7 Markey	Y	Y
8 Kennedy	Y	Y
9 Moakley	Y	Y
10 Studds	Y	Y
11 Donnelly	Y	Y
MICHIGAN		
1 Conyers	Y	Y
2 ***Pursell***	Y	N
3 Wolpe	Y	Y
4 ***Upton***	N	Y
5 ***Henry***	N	N
6 Carr	P	Y
7 Kildee	Y	Y
8 Traxler	Y	Y
9 ***Vander Jagt***	Y	N
10 ***Schuette***	N	Y
11 ***Davis***	Y	N
12 Bonior	Y	Y
13 Crockett	Y	Y
14 Hertel	Y	Y
15 Ford	Y	Y
16 Dingell	?	?
17 Levin	Y	Y
18 ***Broomfield***	Y	N
MINNESOTA		
1 Penny	Y	Y
2 ***Weber***	N	N
3 ***Frenzel***	Y	N
4 Vento	Y	Y

	5	6
5 Sabo	Y	Y
6 Sikorski	N	Y
7 ***Stangeland***	N	N
8 Oberstar	Y	Y
MISSISSIPPI		
1 Whitten	Y	Y
2 Espy	Y	Y
3 Montgomery	Y	Y
4 Parker	Y	Y
5 Taylor	Y	Y
MISSOURI		
1 Clay	N	Y
2 ***Buechner***	N	N
3 Gephardt	Y	Y
4 Skelton	Y	Y
5 Wheat	Y	Y
6 ***Coleman***	N	N
7 ***Hancock***	N	N
8 ***Emerson***	Y	N
9 Volkmer	Y	Y
MONTANA		
1 Williams	Y	Y
2 ***Marlenee***	N	N
NEBRASKA		
1 ***Bereuter***	Y	N
2 Hoagland	Y	Y
3 ***Smith***	Y	N
NEVADA		
1 Bilbray	Y	Y
2 ***Vucanovich***	N	N
NEW HAMPSHIRE		
1 ***Smith***	N	N
2 ***Douglas***	N	N
NEW JERSEY		
1 Vacancy		
2 Hughes	Y	Y
3 Pallone	Y	Y
4 ***Smith***	Y	N
5 ***Roukema***	N	N
6 Dwyer	Y	Y
7 ***Rinaldo***	Y	N
8 Roe	Y	Y
9 Torricelli	Y	Y
10 Payne	Y	Y
11 ***Gallo***	Y	N
12 ***Courter***	N	N
13 ***Saxton***	Y	N
14 Guarini	Y	Y
NEW MEXICO		
1 ***Schiff***	Y	N
2 ***Skeen***	Y	N
3 Richardson	?	Y
NEW YORK		
1 Hochbrueckner	Y	Y
2 Downey	Y	Y
3 Mrazek	Y	Y
4 ***Lent***	Y	N
5 ***McGrath***	N	N
6 Flake	Y	Y
7 Ackerman	Y	Y
8 Scheuer	Y	Y
9 Manton	Y	Y
10 Schumer	Y	Y
11 Towns	Y	Y
12 Owens	Y	Y
13 Solarz	Y	Y
14 Vacancy		
15 ***Green***	Y	N
16 Rangel	Y	Y
17 Weiss	Y	Y
18 Vacancy		
19 Engel	?	Y
20 Lowey	Y	Y
21 ***Fish***	Y	N
22 ***Gilman***	Y	N
23 McNulty	?	Y
24 ***Solomon***	N	N
25 ***Boehlert***	N	N
26 ***Martin***	Y	N
27 ***Walsh***	Y	N
28 McHugh	Y	Y
29 ***Horton***	Y	N
30 Slaughter	Y	Y
31 ***Paxon***	N	N

	5	6
32 LaFalce	Y	Y
33 Nowak	Y	Y
34 ***Houghton***	Y	N
NORTH CAROLINA		
1 Jones	Y	Y
2 Valentine	Y	Y
3 Lancaster	Y	Y
4 Price	Y	Y
5 Neal	?	Y
6 ***Coble***	N	N
7 Rose	Y	Y
8 Hefner	?	?
9 ***McMillan***	Y	N
10 ***Ballenger***	Y	N
11 Clarke	Y	Y
NORTH DAKOTA		
AL Dorgan	Y	Y
OHIO		
1 Luken	Y	Y
2 ***Gradison***	Y	N
3 Hall	?	Y
4 ***Oxley***	Y	N
5 ***Gillmor***	Y	N
6 ***McEwen***	Y	N
7 ***DeWine***	N	N
8 ***Lukens***	N	N
9 Kaptur	Y	Y
10 ***Miller***	N	N
11 Eckart	Y	Y
12 ***Kasich***	Y	N
13 Pease	Y	Y
14 Sawyer	Y	Y
15 ***Wylie***	Y	N
16 ***Regula***	N	N
17 Traficant	Y	Y
18 Applegate	Y	Y
19 Feighan	Y	Y
20 Oakar	Y	Y
21 Stokes	Y	Y
OKLAHOMA		
1 ***Inhofe***	N	N
2 Synar	Y	Y
3 Watkins	?	Y
4 McCurdy	Y	Y
5 ***Edwards***	N	N
6 English	Y	Y
OREGON		
1 AuCoin	Y	?
2 ***Smith, B.***	N	N
3 Wyden	Y	Y
4 DeFazio	Y	Y
5 ***Smith, D.***	N	N
PENNSYLVANIA		
1 Foglietta	Y	Y
2 Gray	Y	Y
3 Borski	Y	Y
4 Kolter	Y	Y
5 ***Schulze***	Y	N
6 Yatron	Y	Y
7 ***Weldon***	Y	N
8 Kostmayer	?	?
9 ***Shuster***	Y	N
10 ***McDade***	Y	N
11 Kanjorski	Y	Y
12 Murtha	Y	Y
13 ***Coughlin***	N	N
14 Coyne	?	Y
15 ***Ritter***	Y	N
16 ***Walker***	?	N
17 ***Gekas***	N	N
18 Walgren	Y	Y
19 ***Goodling***	N	N
20 Gaydos	Y	Y
21 ***Ridge***	N	N
22 Murphy	N	Y
23 ***Clinger***	Y	N
RHODE ISLAND		
1 ***Machtley***	N	N
2 ***Schneider***	Y	N
SOUTH CAROLINA		
1 ***Ravenel***	Y	N
2 ***Spence***	Y	N
3 Derrick	Y	Y
4 Patterson	Y	Y
5 Spratt	Y	Y
6 Tallon	Y	Y

	5	6
SOUTH DAKOTA		
AL Johnson	Y	Y
TENNESSEE		
1 ***Quillen***	Y	N
2 ***Duncan***	N	N
3 Lloyd	Y	Y
4 Cooper	Y	Y
5 Clement	Y	Y
6 Gordon	Y	Y
7 ***Sundquist***	N	N
8 Tanner	Y	Y
9 Ford	?	Y
TEXAS		
1 Chapman	Y	Y
2 Wilson	Y	Y
3 ***Bartlett***	Y	N
4 Hall	Y	Y
5 Bryant	Y	Y
6 ***Barton***	N	N
7 ***Archer***	Y	N
8 ***Fields***	N	N
9 Brooks	?	Y
10 Pickle	Y	Y
11 Leath	Y	Y
12 Geren	Y	Y
13 Sarpalius	Y	Y
14 Laughlin	Y	Y
15 de la Garza	?	Y
16 Coleman	Y	Y
17 Stenholm	Y	Y
18 Washington	Y	Y
19 ***Combest***	Y	N
20 Gonzalez	Y	Y
21 ***Smith***	N	N
22 ***DeLay***	N	N
23 Bustamante	Y	Y
24 Frost	Y	Y
25 Andrews	Y	Y
26 ***Armey***	N	N
27 Ortiz	Y	Y
UTAH		
1 ***Hansen***	N	N
2 Owens	Y	Y
3 ***Nielson***	Y	N
VERMONT		
AL ***Smith***	Y	N
VIRGINIA		
1 ***Bateman***	?	N
2 Pickett	Y	Y
3 ***Bliley***	N	N
4 Sisisky	Y	Y
5 Payne	Y	Y
6 Olin	Y	Y
7 ***Slaughter***	N	N
8 ***Parris***	N	N
9 Boucher	Y	Y
10 ***Wolf***	N	N
WASHINGTON		
1 ***Miller***	N	N
2 Swift	Y	Y
3 Unsoeld	Y	Y
4 ***Morrison***	Y	Y
5 Foley		
6 Dicks	Y	Y
7 McDermott	Y	Y
8 ***Chandler***	?	?
WEST VIRGINIA		
1 Mollohan	Y	Y
2 Staggers	Y	Y
3 Wise	Y	Y
4 Rahall	Y	Y
WISCONSIN		
1 Aspin	Y	Y
2 Kastenmeier	Y	Y
3 ***Gunderson***	Y	N
4 Kleczka	Y	Y
5 Moody	Y	Y
6 ***Petri***	Y	N
7 Obey	Y	Y
8 ***Roth***	Y	N
9 ***Sensenbrenner***	N	N
WYOMING		
AL ***Thomas***	Y	N

Southern states - Ala., Ark., Fla., Ga., Ky., La., Miss., N.C., Okla., S.C., Tenn., Texas, Va.
Omitted votes are quorum calls, which CQ does not include in its vote charts.

HOUSE VOTES 7, 8, 9, 10, 11, 12, 13, 14

7. HR 2061. Magnuson Fisheries Act/Passage. Studds, D-Mass., motion to suspend the rules and pass the bill to authorize appropriations for the Magnuson Fishery Conservation and Management Act through fiscal 1992. Passed 396-21: R 151-17; D 245-4 (ND 163-4, SD 82-0), Feb. 6, 1990. A two-thirds majority of those present and voting (278 in this case) is required for passage under suspension of the rules. A "nay" was a vote supporting the president's position.

8. H Con Res 254. U.N. Participation in Cambodia/Passage. Solarz, D-N.Y., motion to suspend the rules and adopt the concurrent resolution expressing the sense of Congress urging negotiations for a political settlement in Cambodia. Motion agreed to 413-0: R 168-0; D 245-0 (ND 163-0, SD 82-0), Feb. 6, 1990. A two-thirds majority of those present and voting (276 in this case) is required for passage under suspension of the rules.

9. HR 2190. Voter Registration/State Discretion. Roberts, R-Kan., en bloc amendments to make voluntary and leave to the discretion of the states the provisions of the bill to automatically register to vote anyone applying for, renewing or changing an address on a driver's license, and to provide $120 million for block grants to fund state programs to increase voter registration and protect voters from fraudulent voter rolls and ineligible voters. Motion rejected 129-291: R 128-41; D 1-250 (ND 1-168, SD 0-82), Feb. 6, 1990.

10. HR 2190. Voter Registration/Recommittal Motion. Gillmor, R-Ohio, motion to recommit to the House Administration Committee the bill to automatically register to vote anyone applying for, renewing or changing an address on a driver's license and to make voter-registration forms available at certain public offices, with instructions to report it back to the House after adding provisions for formal authentication of mail-in registrations and penalties for offers of payment for voting, filing false information regarding a campaign and using the postal system to perpetrate such fraud; and deleting provisions to require designated locations to accept and transmit completed registration forms to state election officials. Motion rejected 156-265: R 155-14; D 1-251 (ND 1-169, SD 0-82), Feb. 6, 1990.

11. HR 2190. Voter Registration/Passage. Passage of the bill to automatically register to vote anyone applying for, renewing or changing an address on a driver's license and to make voter-registration forms available at certain public offices. Passed 289-132: R 61-108; D 228-24 (ND 162-8, SD 66-16), Feb. 6, 1990. A "nay" was a vote supporting the president's position.

12. H Con Res 262. Operation Just Cause/Passage. Fascell, D-Fla., motion to suspend the rules and adopt the concurrent resolution to express the sense of Congress praising the Dec. 20, 1989, U.S. invasion of Panama, expressing sadness over the deaths of U.S. soldiers and Panamanian residents, commending the president's efforts to recall the remaining troops involved in the action and urging the president to continue trying to foster democracy in Panama. Motion agreed to 389-26: R 174-0; D 215-26 (ND 139-24, SD 76-2), Feb. 7, 1990. A two-thirds majority of those present and voting (277 in this case) is required for passage under suspension of the rules.

13. H Res 330. Privileges of the House/Adoption. Adoption of the resolution to instruct the House Administration Committee to report on the propriety of allowing House members to delete and revise their floor remarks in the Congressional Record. The resolution was prompted by the removal from the Record of remarks made by Rep. Gus Savage, D-Ill., criticizing Reps. Patricia Schroeder, D-Colo., Barney Frank, D-Mass., and Matthew F. McHugh, D-N.Y., for instigating an ethics committee investigation of him. Adopted 373-30: R 170-0; D 203-30 (ND 130-27, SD 73-3), Feb. 7, 1990.

14. HR 1465. Oil-Spill Liability/Instruction of Conferees. Gallo, R-N.J., motion to instruct the House conferees to insist upon including in the conference report a requirement to equip new and existing tank vessels with double bottoms or double hulls as part of the bill to set national oil-spill liability limits, provide for the payment of cleanup and damage-compensation costs beyond those limits, and establish a series of requirements to help prevent spills and improve response to spills that do occur. Motion agreed to 376-37: R 150-21; D 226-16 (ND 161-2, SD 65-14), Feb. 7, 1990.

KEY

- Y Voted for (yea).
- # Paired for.
- + Announced for.
- N Voted against (nay).
- X Paired against.
- - Announced against.
- P Voted "present."
- C Voted "present" to avoid possible conflict of interest.
- ? Did not vote or otherwise make a position known.

Democrats ***Republicans***

	7	8	9	10	11	12	13	14
ALABAMA								
1 ***Callahan***	Y	Y	Y	Y	N	Y	Y	N
2 ***Dickinson***	Y	Y	Y	Y	N	Y	Y	?
3 Browder	Y	Y	N	N	N	Y	Y	Y
4 Bevill	Y	Y	N	N	N	Y	Y	Y
5 Flippo	Y	Y	N	N	N	?	Y	Y
6 Erdreich	Y	Y	N	N	N	Y	Y	Y
7 Harris	Y	Y	N	N	N	?	?	Y
ALASKA								
AL ***Young***	Y	Y	Y	Y	Y	Y	Y	Y
ARIZONA								
1 ***Rhodes***	Y	Y	Y	Y	N	Y	Y	Y
2 Udall	Y	Y	N	N	Y	Y	Y	Y
3 ***Stump***	N	Y	Y	Y	N	Y	Y	N
4 ***Kyl***	Y	Y	Y	Y	N	Y	Y	Y
5 ***Kolbe***	Y	Y	Y	Y	Y	Y	Y	Y
ARKANSAS								
1 Alexander	Y	Y	N	N	Y	Y	Y	N
2 ***Robinson***	Y	Y	N	N	Y	Y	Y	?
3 ***Hammerschmidt***	Y	Y	Y	Y	N	Y	Y	Y
4 Anthony	Y	Y	N	N	Y	Y	Y	Y
CALIFORNIA								
1 Bosco	Y	Y	N	N	Y	Y	Y	Y
2 ***Herger***	Y	Y	Y	Y	N	Y	Y	Y
3 Matsui	Y	Y	N	N	Y	Y	Y	Y
4 Fazio	Y	Y	N	N	Y	Y	P	Y
5 Pelosi	Y	Y	N	N	Y	Y	Y	Y
6 Boxer	Y	Y	N	N	Y	Y	Y	Y
7 Miller	Y	Y	N	N	Y	N	Y	Y
8 Dellums	Y	Y	N	N	Y	N	N	Y
9 Stark	N	Y	N	N	Y	Y	Y	Y
10 Edwards	Y	Y	N	N	Y	N	Y	Y
11 Lantos	Y	Y	N	N	Y	Y	Y	Y
12 ***Campbell***	Y	Y	Y	Y	N	Y	Y	Y
13 Mineta	Y	Y	N	N	Y	Y	Y	Y
14 ***Shumway***	Y	Y	Y	Y	N	Y	Y	Y
15 Condit	Y	Y	N	N	Y	Y	Y	Y
16 Panetta	Y	Y	N	N	Y	Y	Y	Y
17 ***Pashayan***	?	?	?	?	?	Y	P	Y
18 Lehman	Y	Y	N	N	Y	Y	N	Y
19 ***Lagomarsino***	Y	Y	Y	Y	N	Y	Y	Y
20 ***Thomas***	N	Y	N	Y	Y	Y	Y	Y
21 ***Gallegly***	Y	Y	Y	Y	N	Y	Y	Y
22 ***Moorhead***	Y	Y	Y	Y	N	Y	Y	Y
23 Beilenson	Y	Y	N	N	Y	N	Y	Y
24 Waxman	?	?	N	N	Y	Y	Y	Y
25 Roybal	Y	Y	N	N	Y	N	N	Y
26 Berman	Y	Y	N	N	Y	Y	Y	Y
27 Levine	Y	Y	N	N	Y	Y	Y	Y
28 Dixon	N	Y	N	N	Y	Y	P	Y
29 Hawkins	N	Y	N	N	Y	?	P	Y
30 Martinez	Y	Y	N	N	Y	Y	Y	Y
31 Dymally	?	?	N	N	Y	N	N	Y
32 Anderson	N	Y	N	N	Y	Y	Y	Y
33 ***Dreier***	N	Y	Y	Y	N	Y	Y	Y
34 Torres	Y	Y	N	N	Y	Y	Y	Y
35 ***Lewis***	?	?	?	?	?	?	?	?
36 Brown	Y	Y	N	N	Y	Y	Y	?
37 ***McCandless***	N	Y	Y	Y	N	Y	Y	N
38 ***Dornan***	?	?	#	?	X	Y	Y	Y
39 ***Dannemeyer***	N	Y	N	Y	N	Y	Y	Y
40 ***Cox***	Y	Y	Y	Y	N	Y	Y	Y
41 ***Lowery***	N	Y	Y	Y	N	Y	Y	Y
42 ***Rohrabacher***	N	Y	Y	Y	N	Y	Y	Y
43 ***Packard***	Y	Y	Y	Y	N	Y	Y	Y
44 Bates	Y	Y	N	N	Y	N	Y	Y
45 ***Hunter***	N	Y	Y	Y	N	Y	Y	Y
COLORADO								
1 Schroeder	Y	Y	N	N	Y	Y	P	Y
2 Skaggs	Y	Y	N	N	N	Y	Y	Y
3 Campbell	Y	Y	N	N	Y	Y	Y	Y
4 ***Brown***	Y	Y	Y	Y	N	Y	Y	Y
5 ***Hefley***	Y	Y	Y	Y	N	Y	Y	Y
6 ***Schaefer***	Y	Y	Y	Y	N	Y	Y	Y
CONNECTICUT								
1 Kennelly	Y	Y	N	N	Y	Y	Y	Y
2 Gejdenson	Y	Y	N	N	Y	Y	Y	Y
3 Morrison	Y	Y	N	N	Y	Y	Y	Y
4 ***Shays***	Y	Y	N	Y	Y	Y	Y	Y
5 ***Rowland***	Y	Y	Y	Y	Y	Y	Y	Y
6 ***Johnson***	Y	Y	Y	Y	Y	Y	Y	Y
DELAWARE								
AL Carper	Y	Y	N	N	Y	Y	Y	Y
FLORIDA								
1 Hutto	Y	Y	N	N	N	Y	Y	Y
2 ***Grant***	Y	Y	Y	Y	Y	Y	Y	Y
3 Bennett	Y	Y	N	N	Y	Y	Y	Y
4 ***James***	Y	Y	Y	Y	Y	Y	Y	Y
5 ***McCollum***	Y	Y	Y	Y	Y	Y	Y	Y
6 ***Stearns***	Y	Y	Y	Y	Y	Y	Y	Y
7 Gibbons	Y	Y	N	N	N	Y	Y	Y
8 ***Young***	Y	Y	Y	Y	Y	Y	Y	Y
9 ***Bilirakis***	?	?	Y	Y	Y	Y	Y	Y
10 ***Ireland***	Y	Y	N	N	Y	Y	Y	Y
11 Nelson	Y	Y	N	N	Y	Y	Y	Y
12 ***Lewis***	Y	Y	Y	Y	N	Y	Y	Y
13 ***Goss***	Y	Y	Y	Y	Y	Y	Y	Y
14 Johnston	Y	Y	N	N	Y	Y	Y	Y
15 ***Shaw***	Y	Y	Y	Y	N	Y	Y	Y
16 Smith	Y	Y	N	N	Y	Y	Y	Y
17 Lehman	Y	Y	N	N	Y	Y	Y	Y
18 ***Ros-Lehtinen***	Y	Y	N	Y	Y	Y	Y	Y
19 Fascell	Y	Y	N	N	Y	Y	Y	Y
GEORGIA								
1 Thomas	Y	Y	N	N	Y	Y	Y	Y
2 Hatcher	Y	Y	N	N	N	Y	Y	Y
3 Ray	Y	Y	N	N	Y	Y	Y	N
4 Jones	Y	Y	N	N	Y	Y	N	Y
5 Lewis	Y	Y	N	N	Y	N	N	Y
6 ***Gingrich***	Y	Y	N	Y	Y	Y	Y	Y
7 Darden	Y	Y	N	N	Y	Y	Y	Y
8 Rowland	Y	Y	N	N	Y	Y	Y	Y
9 Jenkins	Y	Y	N	N	Y	Y	Y	Y
10 Barnard	Y	Y	N	N	N	Y	Y	Y
HAWAII								
1 ***Saiki***	Y	Y	N	N	Y	Y	Y	Y
2 Akaka	Y	Y	N	N	Y	Y	Y	Y
IDAHO								
1 ***Craig***	Y	Y	Y	Y	N	Y	Y	Y
2 Stallings	Y	Y	N	N	N	Y	Y	Y
ILLINOIS								
1 Hayes	Y	Y	N	N	Y	N	N	Y
2 Savage	Y	Y	N	N	Y	N	P	Y
3 Russo	Y	Y	N	N	N	Y	Y	Y
4 Sangmeister	Y	Y	N	N	Y	Y	Y	Y
5 Lipinski	Y	Y	N	N	N	Y	Y	Y
6 ***Hyde***	Y	Y	Y	Y	N	Y	Y	Y
7 Collins	Y	Y	N	N	Y	N	N	Y
8 Rostenkowski	Y	Y	N	N	N	Y	Y	Y
9 Yates	Y	Y	N	N	Y	N	Y	Y
10 ***Porter***	Y	Y	Y	Y	N	Y	Y	Y
11 Annunzio	Y	Y	N	N	Y	Y	Y	Y
12 ***Crane***	N	Y	Y	Y	N	Y	Y	N
13 ***Fawell***	Y	Y	Y	Y	N	Y	Y	Y
14 ***Hastert***	Y	Y	Y	Y	N	Y	Y	Y
15 ***Madigan***	Y	Y	Y	Y	N	Y	Y	Y
16 ***Martin***	Y	Y	Y	Y	N	Y	Y	Y
17 Evans	Y	Y	N	N	Y	Y	Y	Y
18 ***Michel***	Y	Y	Y	Y	N	Y	Y	Y
19 Bruce	Y	Y	N	N	Y	Y	Y	Y
20 Durbin	Y	?	N	N	Y	Y	N	Y
21 Costello	Y	Y	N	N	Y	Y	Y	Y
22 Poshard	Y	Y	N	N	Y	Y	Y	Y
INDIANA								
1 Visclosky	Y	Y	N	N	N	Y	Y	N
2 Sharp	?	?	N	N	Y	Y	Y	Y
3 ***Hiler***	Y	Y	N	Y	Y	Y	Y	Y

ND Northern Democrats SD Southern Democrats

Member	7	8	9	10	11	12	13	14
4 Long	Y	Y	N	N	Y	Y	Y	Y
5 Jontz	Y	Y	N	N	Y	Y	Y	Y
6 ***Burton***	Y	Y	Y	Y	N	Y	Y	Y
7 ***Myers***	Y	Y	Y	Y	N	Y	Y	Y
8 McCloskey	Y	Y	N	N	Y	Y	Y	?
9 Hamilton	Y	Y	N	N	Y	Y	Y	Y
10 Jacobs	Y	Y	N	N	Y	Y	Y	Y
IOWA								
1 ***Leach***	Y	Y	N	Y	Y	Y	Y	Y
2 ***Tauke***	?	?	?	?	?	Y	Y	Y
3 Nagle	Y	Y	N	N	Y	Y	Y	Y
4 Smith	Y	Y	N	N	Y	Y	Y	Y
5 ***Lightfoot***	Y	Y	Y	Y	N	Y	Y	Y
6 ***Grandy***	Y	Y	Y	Y	Y	Y	P	Y
KANSAS								
1 ***Roberts***	Y	Y	Y	Y	N	Y	Y	Y
2 Slattery	Y	Y	N	N	Y	Y	Y	Y
3 ***Meyers***	Y	Y	Y	Y	Y	Y	Y	Y
4 Glickman	Y	Y	N	N	Y	Y	Y	Y
5 ***Whittaker***	Y	Y	Y	Y	N	Y	Y	Y
KENTUCKY								
1 Hubbard	Y	Y	N	N	Y	Y	Y	Y
2 Natcher	Y	Y	N	N	Y	Y	Y	Y
3 Mazzoli	Y	Y	N	N	Y	Y	Y	Y
4 ***Bunning***	Y	Y	Y	Y	N	Y	Y	N
5 ***Rogers***	Y	Y	Y	Y	N	Y	Y	Y
6 ***Hopkins***	Y	Y	Y	Y	Y	Y	Y	Y
7 Perkins	Y	Y	N	N	Y	Y	Y	Y
LOUISIANA								
1 ***Livingston***	Y	Y	Y	Y	N	Y	Y	N
2 Boggs	Y	Y	N	N	Y	Y	?	N
3 Tauzin	Y	Y	N	N	Y	Y	Y	N
4 ***McCrery***	Y	Y	N	Y	Y	Y	Y	N
5 Huckaby	Y	Y	N	N	N	Y	Y	Y
6 ***Baker***	Y	Y	Y	Y	N	Y	Y	N
7 Hayes	Y	Y	N	N	Y	Y	Y	N
8 ***Holloway***	Y	Y	Y	Y	N	Y	Y	N
MAINE								
1 Brennan	Y	Y	N	N	Y	Y	Y	Y
2 ***Snowe***	Y	Y	N	Y	N	Y	Y	Y
MARYLAND								
1 Dyson	Y	Y	N	N	Y	Y	Y	Y
2 ***Bentley***	Y	Y	Y	Y	N	Y	Y	Y
3 Cardin	Y	?	N	N	Y	Y	Y	Y
4 McMillen	Y	Y	N	N	Y	Y	Y	Y
5 Hoyer	Y	Y	N	N	Y	+	Y	Y
6 Byron	Y	Y	N	N	Y	Y	Y	Y
7 Mfume	Y	Y	N	N	Y	N	N	Y
8 ***Morella***	Y	Y	N	N	Y	Y	Y	Y
MASSACHUSETTS								
1 ***Conte***	Y	Y	N	N	Y	Y	Y	Y
2 Neal	Y	Y	N	N	Y	Y	Y	Y
3 Early	?	?	?	?	?	?	?	?
4 Frank	Y	Y	N	N	Y	Y	P	Y
5 Atkins	Y	Y	N	N	Y	Y	P	Y
6 Mavroules	Y	Y	N	N	Y	Y	Y	Y
7 Markey	Y	Y	N	N	Y	Y	N	Y
8 Kennedy	Y	Y	N	N	Y	Y	Y	Y
9 Moakley	Y	Y	N	N	Y	Y	Y	Y
10 Studds	Y	Y	N	N	Y	P	Y	Y
11 Donnelly	Y	Y	Y	Y	N	Y	Y	Y
MICHIGAN								
1 Conyers	Y	Y	N	N	Y	N	N	Y
2 ***Pursell***	Y	Y	N	Y	Y	Y	Y	Y
3 Wolpe	Y	Y	N	N	Y	Y	Y	Y
4 ***Upton***	Y	Y	N	Y	Y	Y	Y	Y
5 ***Henry***	Y	Y	Y	Y	Y	Y	Y	Y
6 Carr	Y	Y	N	N	Y	Y	Y	Y
7 Kildee	Y	Y	N	N	Y	Y	Y	Y
8 Traxler	Y	Y	N	N	Y	Y	Y	Y
9 ***Vander Jagt***	Y	Y	Y	Y	N	Y	Y	?
10 ***Schuette***	Y	Y	N	N	Y	Y	Y	Y
11 ***Davis***	Y	Y	N	N	Y	Y	Y	Y
12 Bonior	Y	Y	N	N	Y	Y	Y	Y
13 Crockett	Y	Y	N	N	Y	N	N	?
14 Hertel	Y	Y	N	N	Y	Y	Y	Y
15 Ford	Y	Y	N	N	Y	?	Y	Y
16 Dingell	Y	Y	N	N	Y	Y	Y	Y
17 Levin	Y	Y	N	N	Y	Y	Y	Y
18 ***Broomfield***	Y	Y	Y	Y	N	Y	Y	Y
MINNESOTA								
1 Penny	Y	Y	N	N	Y	Y	Y	Y
2 ***Weber***	Y	Y	N	Y	Y	Y	Y	Y
3 ***Frenzel***	N	Y	X	?	#	Y	Y	Y
4 Vento	Y	Y	N	N	Y	Y	?	Y

Member	7	8	9	10	11	12	13	14
5 Sabo	Y	Y	N	N	Y	Y	Y	Y
6 Sikorski	Y	Y	N	N	Y	Y	Y	Y
7 ***Stangeland***	Y	Y	Y	Y	Y	Y	Y	N
8 Oberstar	Y	Y	N	N	Y	Y	Y	Y
MISSISSIPPI								
1 Whitten	Y	Y	N	N	Y	Y	?	Y
2 Espy	Y	Y	N	N	Y	Y	Y	N
3 Montgomery	Y	Y	N	N	Y	Y	Y	X
4 Parker	Y	Y	N	N	Y	Y	Y	N
5 Taylor	Y	Y	N	N	Y	Y	Y	Y
MISSOURI								
1 Clay	Y	Y	N	N	Y	N	N	Y
2 ***Buechner***	Y	Y	Y	Y	Y	Y	Y	Y
3 Gephardt	Y	Y	N	N	Y	Y	N	Y
4 Skelton	Y	Y	N	N	Y	Y	Y	Y
5 Wheat	Y	Y	N	N	Y	Y	Y	Y
6 ***Coleman***	Y	Y	Y	Y	N	Y	Y	Y
7 ***Hancock***	Y	Y	Y	Y	N	Y	Y	N
8 ***Emerson***	Y	Y	Y	Y	N	Y	Y	N
9 Volkmer	Y	Y	N	N	N	Y	Y	Y
MONTANA								
1 Williams	Y	Y	N	N	Y	P	?	Y
2 ***Marlenee***	?	?	Y	Y	N	Y	Y	Y
NEBRASKA								
1 ***Bereuter***	Y	Y	Y	Y	N	Y	Y	Y
2 Hoagland	Y	Y	N	N	Y	Y	Y	Y
3 ***Smith***	Y	Y	Y	Y	N	Y	Y	Y
NEVADA								
1 Bilbray	Y	Y	N	N	Y	Y	Y	?
2 ***Vucanovich***	Y	Y	Y	Y	N	Y	Y	Y
NEW HAMPSHIRE								
1 ***Smith***	Y	Y	Y	Y	N	Y	Y	Y
2 ***Douglas***	Y	Y	Y	Y	N	Y	Y	Y
NEW JERSEY								
1 Vacancy								
2 Hughes	Y	Y	N	N	Y	Y	Y	Y
3 Pallone	Y	Y	N	N	Y	Y	Y	Y
4 ***Smith***	Y	Y	N	N	Y	Y	Y	Y
5 ***Roukema***	Y	Y	N	Y	N	Y	Y	Y
6 Dwyer	Y	Y	N	N	Y	Y	P	Y
7 ***Rinaldo***	Y	Y	N	Y	Y	Y	Y	Y
8 Roe	Y	Y	N	N	Y	Y	Y	Y
9 Torricelli	Y	Y	N	N	Y	Y	Y	Y
10 Payne	Y	Y	N	N	Y	N	N	Y
11 ***Gallo***	Y	Y	Y	Y	N	Y	Y	Y
12 ***Courter***	Y	Y	Y	Y	Y	Y	Y	Y
13 ***Saxton***	Y	Y	Y	Y	N	Y	?	Y
14 Guarini	Y	?	N	N	Y	Y	Y	Y
NEW MEXICO								
1 ***Schiff***	Y	Y	Y	Y	Y	Y	Y	Y
2 ***Skeen***	Y	Y	Y	Y	N	Y	Y	Y
3 Richardson	Y	Y	N	N	Y	Y	Y	Y
NEW YORK								
1 Hochbrueckner	Y	Y	N	N	Y	Y	Y	Y
2 Downey	Y	Y	N	N	Y	Y	Y	Y
3 Mrazek	Y	?	?	N	Y	Y	Y	Y
4 ***Lent***	Y	Y	Y	Y	Y	Y	Y	Y
5 ***McGrath***	Y	Y	Y	Y	Y	Y	Y	Y
6 Flake	Y	Y	N	N	Y	N	N	Y
7 Ackerman	Y	Y	N	N	Y	Y	N	Y
8 Scheuer	Y	Y	N	N	Y	Y	Y	Y
9 Manton	Y	Y	N	N	Y	Y	N	N
10 Schumer	Y	Y	N	N	Y	Y	Y	Y
11 Towns	Y	Y	N	N	Y	N	N	Y
12 Owens	Y	Y	N	N	Y	N	N	Y
13 Solarz	Y	Y	N	N	Y	?	Y	Y
14 Vacancy								
15 ***Green***	Y	Y	N	N	Y	Y	Y	Y
16 Rangel	Y	Y	N	N	Y	?	N	Y
17 Weiss	Y	Y	N	N	Y	N	N	Y
18 Vacancy								
19 Engel	Y	Y	N	N	Y	Y	Y	Y
20 Lowey	Y	Y	N	N	Y	Y	Y	Y
21 ***Fish***	Y	Y	N	Y	Y	Y	Y	Y
22 ***Gilman***	Y	Y	N	Y	Y	Y	Y	Y
23 McNulty	Y	Y	N	N	Y	Y	Y	Y
24 ***Solomon***	Y	Y	Y	Y	N	Y	Y	Y
25 ***Boehlert***	Y	Y	N	Y	Y	Y	Y	Y
26 ***Martin***	Y	Y	Y	Y	N	Y	Y	Y
27 ***Walsh***	Y	Y	N	N	Y	Y	Y	Y
28 McHugh	Y	Y	N	N	Y	Y	P	Y
29 ***Horton***	Y	Y	N	N	Y	Y	Y	Y
30 Slaughter	Y	Y	N	N	Y	Y	Y	Y
31 ***Paxon***	Y	Y	Y	Y	N	Y	Y	Y

Member	7	8	9	10	11	12	13	14
32 LaFalce	Y	Y	N	N	Y	Y	Y	Y
33 Nowak	Y	Y	N	N	Y	Y	Y	Y
34 ***Houghton***	Y	Y	Y	Y	Y	Y	Y	Y
NORTH CAROLINA								
1 Jones	Y	Y	N	N	Y	Y	Y	Y
2 Valentine	Y	Y	N	N	N	Y	Y	Y
3 Lancaster	Y	Y	N	N	N	Y	Y	Y
4 Price	Y	Y	N	N	Y	Y	Y	Y
5 Neal	Y	Y	N	N	Y	Y	Y	Y
6 ***Coble***	Y	Y	Y	Y	N	Y	Y	Y
7 Rose	Y	Y	N	N	Y	Y	Y	Y
8 Hefner	Y	Y	N	N	Y	Y	Y	Y
9 ***McMillan***	Y	Y	Y	Y	Y	Y	Y	Y
10 ***Ballenger***	Y	Y	Y	Y	N	Y	Y	Y
11 Clarke	Y	Y	N	N	Y	Y	Y	Y
NORTH DAKOTA								
AL Dorgan	Y	Y	N	N	Y	Y	Y	Y
OHIO								
1 Luken	Y	Y	N	N	Y	Y	Y	Y
2 ***Gradison***	Y	Y	N	Y	N	Y	Y	Y
3 Hall	Y	Y	N	N	Y	Y	Y	Y
4 ***Oxley***	Y	Y	Y	Y	N	Y	Y	Y
5 ***Gillmor***	Y	Y	Y	Y	N	Y	Y	Y
6 ***McEwen***	Y	Y	Y	Y	N	Y	Y	Y
7 ***DeWine***	Y	Y	Y	Y	N	Y	Y	Y
8 ***Lukens***	Y	Y	Y	Y	N	Y	Y	Y
9 Kaptur	Y	Y	N	N	Y	Y	Y	Y
10 ***Miller***	N	Y	Y	Y	N	Y	Y	Y
11 Eckart	Y	Y	N	N	Y	Y	Y	Y
12 ***Kasich***	Y	Y	Y	Y	N	Y	Y	Y
13 Pease	Y	Y	N	N	Y	Y	Y	Y
14 Sawyer	Y	Y	N	N	Y	Y	Y	Y
15 ***Wylie***	Y	Y	Y	Y	N	Y	Y	Y
16 ***Regula***	Y	Y	Y	Y	N	Y	Y	Y
17 Traficant	Y	Y	N	N	Y	Y	N	Y
18 Applegate	Y	Y	N	N	Y	Y	Y	Y
19 Feighan	Y	Y	N	N	Y	Y	Y	Y
20 Oakar	Y	Y	N	N	Y	Y	Y	Y
21 Stokes	Y	Y	N	N	Y	N	N	Y
OKLAHOMA								
1 ***Inhofe***	Y	Y	Y	Y	Y	Y	Y	N
2 Synar	Y	Y	N	N	Y	Y	P	N
3 Watkins	Y	Y	N	N	N	?	?	?
4 McCurdy	Y	Y	N	N	Y	Y	Y	Y
5 ***Edwards***	Y	Y	Y	Y	N	Y	Y	Y
6 English	Y	Y	N	N	Y	Y	Y	Y
OREGON								
1 AuCoin	?	?	?	?	?	?	?	#
2 ***Smith, B.***	Y	Y	Y	Y	N	Y	Y	Y
3 Wyden	Y	Y	N	N	Y	Y	Y	Y
4 DeFazio	Y	Y	N	N	Y	N	Y	Y
5 ***Smith, D.***	Y	Y	Y	Y	N	Y	Y	Y
PENNSYLVANIA								
1 Foglietta	Y	Y	N	N	Y	Y	N	Y
2 Gray	Y	Y	N	N	Y	Y	N	?
3 Borski	Y	Y	N	N	Y	Y	Y	Y
4 Kolter	Y	Y	N	N	Y	Y	Y	Y
5 ***Schulze***	?	?	?	?	?	Y	Y	Y
6 Yatron	Y	Y	N	N	Y	Y	Y	Y
7 ***Weldon***	Y	Y	N	Y	Y	Y	Y	Y
8 Kostmayer	Y	Y	N	N	Y	Y	Y	Y
9 ***Shuster***	Y	Y	Y	Y	N	Y	Y	Y
10 ***McDade***	Y	Y	N	N	Y	Y	Y	Y
11 Kanjorski	Y	Y	N	N	Y	Y	Y	Y
12 Murtha	Y	Y	N	N	Y	Y	Y	Y
13 ***Coughlin***	Y	Y	N	Y	Y	Y	Y	Y
14 Coyne	Y	Y	N	N	Y	Y	N	Y
15 ***Ritter***	Y	Y	Y	Y	N	Y	Y	Y
16 ***Walker***	N	Y	Y	Y	N	Y	Y	Y
17 ***Gekas***	N	Y	Y	Y	N	Y	Y	Y
18 Walgren	Y	Y	N	N	Y	Y	Y	Y
19 ***Goodling***	Y	Y	Y	Y	N	Y	Y	Y
20 Gaydos	Y	Y	N	N	Y	Y	P	Y
21 ***Ridge***	Y	Y	N	Y	N	Y	Y	Y
22 Murphy	Y	Y	N	N	Y	Y	Y	Y
23 ***Clinger***	Y	Y	N	Y	Y	Y	Y	Y
RHODE ISLAND								
1 ***Machtley***	Y	Y	N	N	Y	Y	Y	Y
2 ***Schneider***	Y	Y	N	N	Y	Y	Y	Y
SOUTH CAROLINA								
1 ***Ravenel***	Y	Y	Y	Y	N	Y	Y	Y
2 ***Spence***	Y	Y	Y	Y	N	Y	Y	Y
3 Derrick	Y	Y	N	N	Y	Y	Y	?
4 Patterson	Y	Y	N	N	Y	Y	Y	Y
5 Spratt	Y	Y	N	N	Y	Y	Y	Y
6 Tallon	Y	Y	N	N	Y	Y	Y	Y

Member	7	8	9	10	11	12	13	14
SOUTH DAKOTA								
AL Johnson	Y	Y	N	N	Y	Y	Y	Y
TENNESSEE								
1 ***Quillen***	Y	Y	Y	Y	N	Y	Y	N
2 ***Duncan***	N	Y	Y	Y	N	Y	Y	Y
3 Lloyd	Y	Y	N	N	Y	Y	Y	Y
4 Cooper	Y	Y	N	N	Y	Y	Y	Y
5 Clement	Y	Y	N	N	Y	Y	Y	Y
6 Gordon	Y	Y	N	N	Y	Y	Y	Y
7 ***Sundquist***	Y	Y	Y	Y	N	Y	Y	Y
8 Tanner	Y	Y	N	N	Y	Y	Y	Y
9 Ford	?	?	?	?	?	?	?	?
TEXAS								
1 Chapman	Y	Y	N	N	Y	Y	Y	Y
2 Wilson	Y	Y	N	N	Y	Y	Y	Y
3 ***Bartlett***	Y	Y	Y	Y	N	Y	Y	Y
4 Hall	Y	Y	N	N	Y	Y	Y	N
5 Bryant	Y	Y	N	N	Y	Y	Y	Y
6 ***Barton***	N	Y	Y	Y	N	Y	Y	N
7 ***Archer***	Y	Y	Y	Y	N	Y	Y	N
8 ***Fields***	Y	Y	Y	Y	N	Y	Y	N
9 Brooks	Y	Y	N	N	Y	Y	Y	Y
10 Pickle	Y	Y	N	N	Y	Y	Y	Y
11 Leath	Y	Y	N	N	Y	?	Y	Y
12 Geren	Y	Y	N	N	Y	Y	Y	N
13 Sarpalius	Y	Y	N	N	Y	Y	Y	N
14 Laughlin	Y	Y	N	N	Y	Y	Y	N
15 de la Garza	Y	Y	N	N	Y	Y	Y	Y
16 Coleman	Y	Y	N	N	Y	Y	N	Y
17 Stenholm	Y	Y	N	N	N	Y	Y	N
18 Washington	Y	Y	N	N	Y	Y	Y	Y
19 ***Combest***	Y	Y	Y	Y	N	Y	Y	N
20 Gonzalez	Y	Y	N	N	Y	N	P	Y
21 ***Smith***	Y	Y	Y	Y	N	Y	Y	N
22 ***DeLay***	N	Y	Y	Y	N	Y	Y	N
23 Bustamante	Y	Y	N	N	Y	Y	Y	Y
24 Frost	Y	Y	N	N	Y	Y	Y	Y
25 Andrews	Y	Y	N	N	Y	Y	Y	N
26 ***Armey***	Y	Y	Y	Y	N	Y	Y	N
27 Ortiz	Y	Y	N	N	Y	Y	Y	Y
UTAH								
1 ***Hansen***	Y	Y	Y	Y	N	Y	Y	Y
2 Owens	Y	Y	N	N	Y	Y	Y	Y
3 ***Nielson***	Y	Y	Y	Y	N	Y	Y	Y
VERMONT								
AL ***Smith***	Y	Y	Y	Y	Y	Y	Y	Y
VIRGINIA								
1 ***Bateman***	Y	Y	Y	Y	N	Y	Y	Y
2 Pickett	Y	Y	N	N	N	Y	Y	Y
3 ***Bliley***	Y	Y	N	Y	Y	Y	Y	Y
4 Sisisky	Y	Y	N	N	Y	Y	Y	Y
5 Payne	Y	Y	N	N	Y	Y	Y	Y
6 Olin	Y	Y	N	N	N	Y	Y	Y
7 ***Slaughter***	Y	Y	Y	Y	N	Y	Y	Y
8 ***Parris***	Y	Y	Y	Y	N	Y	Y	Y
9 Boucher	Y	Y	N	N	Y	Y	Y	Y
10 ***Wolf***	Y	Y	Y	Y	N	Y	Y	Y
WASHINGTON								
1 ***Miller***	Y	Y	N	Y	Y	Y	Y	Y
2 Swift	Y	Y	N	N	Y	Y	N	?
3 Unsoeld	Y	Y	N	N	Y	Y	Y	Y
4 ***Morrison***	Y	Y	N	Y	Y	Y	Y	Y
5 Foley								
6 Dicks	Y	Y	N	N	Y	Y	Y	Y
7 McDermott	Y	Y	N	N	Y	Y	Y	Y
8 ***Chandler***	Y	Y	N	Y	Y	Y	Y	Y
WEST VIRGINIA								
1 Mollohan	Y	Y	N	N	Y	Y	P	Y
2 Staggers	Y	Y	N	N	Y	Y	Y	Y
3 Wise	Y	Y	N	N	Y	Y	Y	Y
4 Rahall	Y	Y	N	N	Y	Y	Y	Y
WISCONSIN								
1 Aspin	Y	Y	N	N	Y	Y	Y	?
2 Kastenmeier	Y	Y	N	N	Y	N	Y	Y
3 ***Gunderson***	Y	Y	N	Y	Y	Y	Y	Y
4 Kleczka	Y	Y	N	N	Y	N	Y	Y
5 Moody	Y	Y	N	N	Y	Y	Y	Y
6 ***Petri***	Y	Y	Y	Y	N	Y	P	Y
7 Obey	?	?	?	?	?	?	?	?
8 ***Roth***	Y	Y	Y	Y	N	Y	Y	Y
9 ***Sensenbrenner***	N	Y	Y	Y	N	Y	Y	Y
WYOMING								
AL ***Thomas***	Y	Y	Y	Y	N	Y	Y	Y

Southern states - Ala., Ark., Fla., Ga., Ky., La., Miss., N.C., Okla., S.C., Tenn., Texas, Va.
Omitted votes are quorum calls, which CQ does not include in its vote charts.

15. HR 2570. Arizona Desert Wilderness Act/Adoption. Adoption of the rule (H Res 338) to provide for House floor consideration of the bill to provide for the designation of certain public lands as wilderness areas in Arizona. Adopted 386-0: R 156-0; D 230-0 (ND 159-0, SD 71-0), Feb. 21, 1990.

KEY

- Y Voted for (yea).
- # Paired for.
- + Announced for.
- N Voted against (nay).
- X Paired against.
- - Announced against.
- P Voted "present."
- C Voted "present" to avoid possible conflict of interest.
- ? Did not vote or otherwise make a position known.

Democrats *Republicans*

	15
ALABAMA	
1 ***Callahan***	Y
2 ***Dickinson***	Y
3 Browder	Y
4 Bevill	Y
5 Flippo	Y
6 Erdreich	Y
7 Harris	Y
ALASKA	
AL ***Young***	Y
ARIZONA	
1 ***Rhodes***	Y
2 Udall	Y
3 ***Stump***	Y
4 ***Kyl***	Y
5 ***Kolbe***	Y
ARKANSAS	
1 Alexander	Y
2 ***Robinson***	Y
3 ***Hammerschmidt***	Y
4 Anthony	Y
CALIFORNIA	
1 Bosco	Y
2 ***Herger***	Y
3 Matsui	Y
4 Fazio	Y
5 Pelosi	Y
6 Boxer	?
7 Miller	Y
8 Dellums	?
9 Stark	Y
10 Edwards	Y
11 Lantos	Y
12 ***Campbell***	Y
13 Mineta	Y
14 ***Shumway***	Y
15 Condit	Y
16 Panetta	Y
17 ***Pashayan***	Y
18 Lehman	Y
19 ***Lagomarsino***	Y
20 ***Thomas***	Y
21 ***Gallegly***	?
22 ***Moorhead***	Y
23 Beilenson	Y
24 Waxman	Y
25 Roybal	Y
26 Berman	Y
27 Levine	Y
28 Dixon	Y
29 Hawkins	Y
30 Martinez	Y
31 Dymally	Y
32 Anderson	Y
33 ***Dreier***	Y
34 Torres	Y
35 ***Lewis***	Y
36 Brown	?
37 ***McCandless***	Y
38 ***Dornan***	Y
39 ***Dannemeyer***	Y
40 ***Cox***	?
41 ***Lowery***	Y
42 ***Rohrabacher***	Y
43 ***Packard***	Y
44 Bates	Y
45 ***Hunter***	Y
COLORADO	
1 Schroeder	Y
2 Skaggs	Y
3 Campbell	Y
4 ***Brown***	Y
5 ***Hefley***	Y
6 ***Schaefer***	Y
CONNECTICUT	
1 Kennelly	Y
2 Gejdenson	Y
3 Morrison	Y
4 ***Shays***	Y
5 ***Rowland***	Y
6 ***Johnson***	Y
DELAWARE	
AL Carper	Y
FLORIDA	
1 Hutto	Y
2 ***Grant***	Y
3 Bennett	Y
4 ***James***	Y
5 ***McCollum***	Y
6 ***Stearns***	Y
7 Gibbons	?
8 ***Young***	Y
9 ***Bilirakis***	?
10 ***Ireland***	Y
11 Nelson	Y
12 ***Lewis***	Y
13 ***Goss***	?
14 Johnston	?
15 ***Shaw***	?
16 Smith	Y
17 Lehman	Y
18 ***Ros-Lehtinen***	Y
19 Fascell	Y
GEORGIA	
1 Thomas	Y
2 Hatcher	Y
3 Ray	Y
4 Jones	Y
5 Lewis	Y
6 ***Gingrich***	Y
7 Darden	Y
8 Rowland	Y
9 Jenkins	Y
10 Barnard	Y
HAWAII	
1 ***Saiki***	Y
2 Akaka	Y
IDAHO	
1 ***Craig***	Y
2 Stallings	Y
ILLINOIS	
1 Hayes	Y
2 Savage	?
3 Russo	Y
4 Sangmeister	Y
5 Lipinski	Y
6 ***Hyde***	Y
7 Collins	Y
8 Rostenkowski	?
9 Yates	Y
10 ***Porter***	Y
11 Annunzio	Y
12 ***Crane***	Y
13 ***Fawell***	Y
14 ***Hastert***	Y
15 ***Madigan***	Y
16 ***Martin***	Y
17 Evans	Y
18 ***Michel***	Y
19 Bruce	Y
20 Durbin	?
21 Costello	Y
22 Poshard	Y
INDIANA	
1 Visclosky	Y
2 Sharp	Y
3 ***Hiler***	Y

ND Northern Democrats SD Southern Democrats

	15
4 Long	Y
5 Jontz	?
6 ***Burton***	Y
7 ***Myers***	Y
8 McCloskey	Y
9 Hamilton	Y
10 Jacobs	Y
IOWA	
1 ***Leach***	Y
2 ***Tauke***	Y
3 Nagle	Y
4 Smith	Y
5 ***Lightfoot***	Y
6 ***Grandy***	Y
KANSAS	
1 ***Roberts***	Y
2 Slattery	Y
3 ***Meyers***	Y
4 Glickman	Y
5 ***Whittaker***	Y
KENTUCKY	
1 Hubbard	Y
2 Natcher	Y
3 Mazzoli	Y
4 ***Bunning***	Y
5 ***Rogers***	Y
6 ***Hopkins***	Y
7 Perkins	Y
LOUISIANA	
1 ***Livingston***	Y
2 Boggs	Y
3 Tauzin	?
4 ***McCrery***	Y
5 Huckaby	Y
6 ***Baker***	?
7 Hayes	Y
8 ***Holloway***	Y
MAINE	
1 Brennan	Y
2 ***Snowe***	Y
MARYLAND	
1 Dyson	Y
2 ***Bentley***	Y
3 Cardin	Y
4 McMillen	Y
5 Hoyer	Y
6 Byron	Y
7 Mfume	Y
8 ***Morella***	Y
MASSACHUSETTS	
1 ***Conte***	Y
2 Neal	Y
3 Early	Y
4 Frank	Y
5 Atkins	Y
6 Mavroules	Y
7 Markey	Y
8 Kennedy	Y
9 Moakley	?
10 Studds	Y
11 Donnelly	?
MICHIGAN	
1 Conyers	Y
2 ***Pursell***	?
3 Wolpe	Y
4 ***Upton***	Y
5 ***Henry***	Y
6 Carr	Y
7 Kildee	Y
8 Traxler	?
9 ***Vander Jagt***	Y
10 ***Schuette***	Y
11 ***Davis***	Y
12 Bonior	Y
13 Crockett	Y
14 Hertel	Y
15 Ford	Y
16 Dingell	Y
17 Levin	Y
18 ***Broomfield***	Y
MINNESOTA	
1 Penny	Y
2 ***Weber***	Y
3 ***Frenzel***	?
4 Vento	?

	15
5 Sabo	Y
6 Sikorski	Y
7 ***Stangeland***	Y
8 Oberstar	Y
MISSISSIPPI	
1 Whitten	Y
2 Espy	?
3 Montgomery	Y
4 Parker	Y
5 Taylor	Y
MISSOURI	
1 Clay	Y
2 ***Buechner***	Y
3 Gephardt	Y
4 Skelton	?
5 Wheat	Y
6 ***Coleman***	Y
7 ***Hancock***	Y
8 ***Emerson***	Y
9 Volkmer	Y
MONTANA	
1 Williams	Y
2 ***Marlenee***	Y
NEBRASKA	
1 ***Bereuter***	Y
2 Hoagland	Y
3 ***Smith***	Y
NEVADA	
1 Bilbray	Y
2 ***Vucanovich***	Y
NEW HAMPSHIRE	
1 ***Smith***	Y
2 ***Douglas***	Y
NEW JERSEY	
1 Vacancy	
2 Hughes	Y
3 Pallone	Y
4 ***Smith***	Y
5 ***Roukema***	Y
6 Dwyer	Y
7 ***Rinaldo***	Y
8 Roe	Y
9 Torricelli	Y
10 Payne	Y
11 ***Gallo***	Y
12 ***Courter***	Y
13 ***Saxton***	Y
14 Guarini	Y
NEW MEXICO	
1 ***Schiff***	?
2 ***Skeen***	Y
3 Richardson	Y
NEW YORK	
1 Hochbrueckner	Y
2 Downey	Y
3 Mrazek	Y
4 ***Lent***	?
5 ***McGrath***	Y
6 Flake	Y
7 Ackerman	Y
8 Scheuer	Y
9 Manton	Y
10 Schumer	Y
11 Towns	Y
12 Owens	Y
13 Solarz	Y
14 Vacancy	
15 ***Green***	Y
16 Rangel	Y
17 Weiss	Y
18 Vacancy	
19 Engel	Y
20 Lowey	?
21 ***Fish***	Y
22 ***Gilman***	Y
23 McNulty	Y
24 ***Solomon***	Y
25 ***Boehlert***	Y
26 ***Martin***	Y
27 ***Walsh***	Y
28 McHugh	Y
29 ***Horton***	Y
30 Slaughter	Y
31 ***Paxon***	Y

	15
32 LaFalce	Y
33 Nowak	Y
34 ***Houghton***	Y
NORTH CAROLINA	
1 Jones	Y
2 Valentine	Y
3 Lancaster	Y
4 Price	Y
5 Neal	Y
6 ***Coble***	Y
7 Rose	Y
8 Hefner	Y
9 ***McMillan***	Y
10 ***Ballenger***	Y
11 Clarke	Y
NORTH DAKOTA	
AL Dorgan	Y
OHIO	
1 Luken	Y
2 ***Gradison***	?
3 Hall	Y
4 ***Oxley***	Y
5 ***Gillmor***	Y
6 ***McEwen***	Y
7 ***DeWine***	Y
8 ***Lukens***	Y
9 Kaptur	Y
10 ***Miller***	Y
11 Eckart	Y
12 ***Kasich***	Y
13 Pease	Y
14 Sawyer	Y
15 ***Wylie***	?
16 ***Regula***	Y
17 Traficant	Y
18 Applegate	Y
19 Feighan	Y
20 Oakar	Y
21 Stokes	Y
OKLAHOMA	
1 ***Inhofe***	?
2 Synar	Y
3 Watkins	Y
4 McCurdy	Y
5 ***Edwards***	Y
6 English	Y
OREGON	
1 AuCoin	Y
2 ***Smith, B.***	Y
3 Wyden	Y
4 DeFazio	Y
5 ***Smith, D.***	Y
PENNSYLVANIA	
1 Foglietta	Y
2 Gray	?
3 Borski	Y
4 Kolter	Y
5 ***Schulze***	?
6 Yatron	Y
7 ***Weldon***	Y
8 Kostmayer	Y
9 ***Shuster***	Y
10 ***McDade***	Y
11 Kanjorski	Y
12 Murtha	Y
13 ***Coughlin***	Y
14 Coyne	Y
15 ***Ritter***	?
16 ***Walker***	Y
17 ***Gekas***	Y
18 Walgren	Y
19 ***Goodling***	Y
20 Gaydos	Y
21 ***Ridge***	Y
22 Murphy	Y
23 ***Clinger***	Y
RHODE ISLAND	
1 ***Machtley***	Y
2 ***Schneider***	Y
SOUTH CAROLINA	
1 ***Ravenel***	Y
2 ***Spence***	Y
3 Derrick	?
4 Patterson	Y
5 Spratt	Y
6 Tallon	Y

	15
SOUTH DAKOTA	
AL Johnson	Y
TENNESSEE	
1 ***Quillen***	?
2 ***Duncan***	Y
3 Lloyd	?
4 Cooper	Y
5 Clement	Y
6 Gordon	Y
7 ***Sundquist***	Y
8 Tanner	Y
9 Ford	?
TEXAS	
1 Chapman	Y
2 Wilson	?
3 ***Bartlett***	Y
4 Hall	Y
5 Bryant	Y
6 ***Barton***	Y
7 ***Archer***	Y
8 ***Fields***	Y
9 Brooks	?
10 Pickle	Y
11 Leath	Y
12 Geren	Y
13 Sarpalius	?
14 Laughlin	Y
15 de la Garza	Y
16 Coleman	Y
17 Stenholm	Y
18 Washington	Y
19 ***Combest***	Y
20 Gonzalez	?
21 ***Smith***	Y
22 ***DeLay***	Y
23 Bustamante	Y
24 Frost	Y
25 Andrews	Y
26 ***Armey***	Y
27 Ortiz	?
UTAH	
1 ***Hansen***	Y
2 Owens	Y
3 ***Nielson***	Y
VERMONT	
AL ***Smith***	Y
VIRGINIA	
1 ***Bateman***	Y
2 Pickett	Y
3 ***Bliley***	Y
4 Sisisky	Y
5 Payne	Y
6 Olin	Y
7 ***Slaughter***	Y
8 ***Parris***	Y
9 Boucher	Y
10 ***Wolf***	Y
WASHINGTON	
1 ***Miller***	?
2 Swift	Y
3 Unsoeld	Y
4 ***Morrison***	Y
5 Foley	
6 Dicks	Y
7 McDermott	Y
8 ***Chandler***	?
WEST VIRGINIA	
1 Mollohan	Y
2 Staggers	Y
3 Wise	Y
4 Rahall	Y
WISCONSIN	
1 Aspin	Y
2 Kastenmeier	Y
3 ***Gunderson***	Y
4 Kleczka	Y
5 Moody	Y
6 ***Petri***	Y
7 Obey	Y
8 ***Roth***	Y
9 ***Sensenbrenner***	Y
WYOMING	
AL ***Thomas***	?

Southern states - Ala., Ark., Fla., Ga., Ky., La., Miss., N.C., Okla., S.C., Tenn., Texas, Va.
Omitted votes are quorum calls, which CQ does not include in its vote charts.

16. HR 2742. Library Grants/Conference Report. Williams, D-Mont., motion to suspend the rules and adopt the conference report on the bill to amend and reauthorize through fiscal 1994 the Library Services and Construction Act. The bill would authorize $207.5 million in fiscal 1990 and "such sums as necessary" in succeeding years. Motion agreed to 401-4: R 158-4; D 243-0 (ND 164-0, SD 79-0), Feb. 27, 1990. A two-thirds majority of those present and voting (270 in this case) is required for passage under suspension of the rules.

17. H Con Res 87. Persecution of Iranian Baha'is/Adoption. Dymally, D-Calif., motion to suspend the rules and adopt the concurrent resolution stating concern over Iranian persecution of the Baha'is and calling on the Iranian government to grant the Baha'is internationally recognized human rights. Motion agreed to 404-0: R 162-0; D 242-0 (ND 163-0, SD 79-0), Feb. 27, 1990. A two-thirds majority of those present and voting (270 in this case) is required for passage under suspension of the rules.

18. HR 2570. Arizona Desert Wilderness Act/Passage. Passage of the bill to designate certain public lands as wilderness areas in Arizona. Passed 356-45: R 127-38; D 229-7 (ND 157-3, SD 72-4), Feb. 28, 1990.

KEY

Y Voted for (yea).
\# Paired for.
\+ Announced for.
N Voted against (nay).
X Paired against.
\- Announced against.
P Voted "present."
C Voted "present" to avoid possible conflict of interest.
? Did not vote or otherwise make a position known.

Democrats ***Republicans***

	16	17	18
ALABAMA			
1 ***Callahan***	Y	Y	Y
2 ***Dickinson***	Y	Y	Y
3 Browder	Y	Y	Y
4 Bevill	Y	Y	Y
5 Flippo	Y	Y	Y
6 Erdreich	Y	Y	Y
7 Harris	Y	Y	Y
ALASKA			
AL ***Young***	Y	Y	Y
ARIZONA			
1 ***Rhodes***	Y	Y	Y
2 Udall	Y	Y	Y
3 ***Stump***	N	Y	N
4 ***Kyl***	Y	Y	Y
5 ***Kolbe***	Y	Y	Y
ARKANSAS			
1 Alexander	Y	Y	Y
2 ***Robinson***	Y	Y	N
3 ***Hammerschmidt***	Y	Y	N
4 Anthony	Y	Y	?
CALIFORNIA			
1 Bosco	Y	Y	Y
2 ***Herger***	Y	Y	N
3 Matsui	Y	Y	Y
4 Fazio	Y	Y	?
5 Pelosi	Y	Y	Y
6 Boxer	Y	Y	Y
7 Miller	Y	Y	Y
8 Dellums	Y	Y	?
9 Stark	Y	Y	Y
10 Edwards	Y	Y	Y
11 Lantos	Y	Y	Y
12 ***Campbell***	Y	Y	Y
13 Mineta	Y	Y	Y
14 ***Shumway***	Y	Y	N
15 Condit	Y	Y	Y
16 Panetta	Y	Y	Y
17 ***Pashayan***	Y	Y	Y
18 Lehman	?	?	Y
19 ***Lagomarsino***	+	+	Y
20 ***Thomas***	Y	Y	N
21 ***Gallegly***	Y	Y	Y
22 ***Moorhead***	Y	Y	Y
23 Beilenson	Y	Y	Y
24 Waxman	Y	Y	Y
25 Roybal	Y	Y	Y
26 Berman	Y	Y	Y
27 Levine	?	?	?
28 Dixon	Y	Y	Y
29 Hawkins	Y	Y	Y
30 Martinez	Y	Y	Y
31 Dymally	Y	Y	Y
32 Anderson	Y	Y	Y
33 ***Dreier***	Y	Y	Y
34 Torres	Y	Y	Y
35 ***Lewis***	Y	Y	N
36 Brown	Y	Y	Y
37 ***McCandless***	Y	Y	N
38 ***Dornan***	Y	Y	N
39 ***Dannemeyer***	Y	Y	N
40 ***Cox***	?	?	Y
41 ***Lowery***	?	?	?

	16	17	18
42 ***Rohrabacher***	Y	Y	Y
43 ***Packard***	Y	Y	Y
44 Bates	Y	Y	Y
45 ***Hunter***	Y	Y	N
COLORADO			
1 Schroeder	Y	Y	Y
2 Skaggs	Y	Y	Y
3 Campbell	Y	Y	N
4 ***Brown***	Y	Y	N
5 ***Hefley***	Y	Y	Y
6 ***Schaefer***	?	?	N
CONNECTICUT			
1 Kennelly	Y	Y	Y
2 Gejdenson	Y	Y	Y
3 Morrison	+	+	Y
4 ***Shays***	Y	Y	Y
5 ***Rowland***	Y	Y	Y
6 ***Johnson***	Y	Y	Y
DELAWARE			
AL Carper	Y	Y	Y
FLORIDA			
1 Hutto	Y	Y	Y
2 ***Grant***	Y	Y	Y
3 Bennett	Y	Y	Y
4 ***James***	Y	Y	Y
5 ***McCollum***	Y	Y	Y
6 ***Stearns***	Y	Y	Y
7 Gibbons	Y	Y	Y
8 ***Young***	Y	Y	Y
9 ***Bilirakis***	Y	Y	Y
10 ***Ireland***	Y	Y	Y
11 Nelson	Y	Y	+
12 ***Lewis***	+	+	+
13 ***Goss***	Y	Y	Y
14 Johnston	Y	Y	Y
15 ***Shaw***	Y	Y	Y
16 Smith	Y	Y	?
17 Lehman	Y	Y	Y
18 ***Ros-Lehtinen***	Y	Y	Y
19 Fascell	Y	Y	Y
GEORGIA			
1 Thomas	Y	Y	Y
2 Hatcher	Y	Y	Y
3 Ray	Y	Y	Y
4 Jones	Y	Y	Y
5 Lewis	Y	Y	Y
6 ***Gingrich***	Y	Y	Y
7 Darden	Y	Y	Y
8 Rowland	Y	Y	Y
9 Jenkins	Y	Y	Y
10 Barnard	Y	Y	Y
HAWAII			
1 ***Saiki***	Y	Y	Y
2 Akaka	Y	Y	Y
IDAHO			
1 ***Craig***	Y	Y	N
2 Stallings	Y	Y	N
ILLINOIS			
1 Hayes	Y	Y	Y
2 Savage	Y	Y	Y
3 Russo	Y	Y	Y
4 Sangmeister	Y	Y	Y
5 Lipinski	Y	Y	Y
6 ***Hyde***	?	?	?
7 Collins	?	?	Y
8 Rostenkowski	Y	Y	Y
9 Yates	?	?	?
10 ***Porter***	Y	Y	Y
11 Annunzio	Y	Y	Y
12 ***Crane***	N	Y	N
13 ***Fawell***	Y	Y	Y
14 ***Hastert***	?	?	Y
15 ***Madigan***	Y	Y	Y
16 ***Martin***	Y	Y	?
17 Evans	Y	Y	Y
18 ***Michel***	Y	Y	?
19 Bruce	Y	Y	Y
20 Durbin	?	?	Y
21 Costello	+	+	Y
22 Poshard	Y	Y	Y
INDIANA			
1 Visclosky	Y	Y	Y
2 Sharp	Y	Y	Y
3 ***Hiler***	Y	Y	Y

ND Northern Democrats SD Southern Democrats

	16	17	18
4 Long	Y	Y	Y
5 Jontz	Y	Y	Y
6 ***Burton***	Y	Y	N
7 ***Myers***	Y	Y	Y
8 McCloskey	Y	Y	Y
9 Hamilton	Y	Y	Y
10 Jacobs	Y	Y	Y
IOWA			
1 ***Leach***	Y	Y	Y
2 ***Tauke***	+	+	Y
3 Nagle	Y	Y	Y
4 Smith	Y	Y	Y
5 ***Lightfoot***	Y	Y	Y
6 ***Grandy***	Y	Y	Y
KANSAS			
1 ***Roberts***	Y	Y	N
2 Slattery	Y	Y	Y
3 ***Meyers***	Y	Y	Y
4 Glickman	Y	Y	Y
5 ***Whittaker***	Y	Y	N
KENTUCKY			
1 Hubbard	Y	Y	Y
2 Natcher	Y	Y	Y
3 Mazzoli	Y	Y	Y
4 ***Bunning***	Y	Y	Y
5 ***Rogers***	Y	Y	N
6 ***Hopkins***	Y	Y	Y
7 Perkins	Y	Y	Y
LOUISIANA			
1 ***Livingston***	Y	Y	Y
2 Boggs	Y	Y	Y
3 Tauzin	Y	Y	Y
4 ***McCrery***	Y	Y	?
5 Huckaby	Y	Y	Y
6 ***Baker***	Y	Y	Y
7 Hayes	Y	Y	Y
8 ***Holloway***	Y	Y	Y
MAINE			
1 Brennan	Y	Y	Y
2 ***Snowe***	Y	Y	Y
MARYLAND			
1 Dyson	Y	Y	Y
2 ***Bentley***	Y	Y	Y
3 Cardin	Y	Y	Y
4 McMillen	Y	Y	Y
5 Hoyer	Y	Y	Y
6 Byron	Y	Y	?
7 Mfume	Y	Y	Y
8 ***Morella***	Y	Y	Y
MASSACHUSETTS			
1 ***Conte***	Y	Y	Y
2 Neal	Y	Y	Y
3 Early	Y	Y	Y
4 Frank	Y	Y	Y
5 Atkins	Y	Y	Y
6 Mavroules	Y	Y	Y
7 Markey	Y	Y	Y
8 Kennedy	Y	Y	Y
9 Moakley	Y	Y	Y
10 Studds	?	?	Y
11 Donnelly	Y	Y	Y
MICHIGAN			
1 Conyers	Y	Y	Y
2 ***Pursell***	Y	Y	Y
3 Wolpe	Y	Y	?
4 ***Upton***	Y	Y	Y
5 ***Henry***	Y	Y	Y
6 Carr	Y	Y	Y
7 Kildee	Y	Y	Y
8 Traxler	Y	Y	Y
9 ***Vander Jagt***	Y	Y	Y
10 ***Schuette***	Y	Y	Y
11 ***Davis***	Y	Y	Y
12 Bonior	Y	Y	Y
13 Crockett	Y	Y	Y
14 Hertel	Y	Y	Y
15 Ford	Y	Y	?
16 Dingell	Y	Y	Y
17 Levin	Y	Y	Y
18 ***Broomfield***	Y	Y	Y
MINNESOTA			
1 Penny	Y	Y	Y
2 ***Weber***	Y	Y	Y
3 ***Frenzel***	Y	Y	Y
4 Vento	Y	Y	Y

	16	17	18
5 Sabo	Y	Y	Y
6 Sikorski	Y	Y	Y
7 ***Stangeland***	Y	Y	Y
8 Oberstar	Y	Y	Y
MISSISSIPPI			
1 Whitten	Y	Y	Y
2 Espy	Y	Y	Y
3 Montgomery	Y	Y	N
4 Parker	Y	Y	Y
5 Taylor	Y	Y	Y
MISSOURI			
1 Clay	Y	Y	Y
2 ***Buechner***	Y	Y	Y
3 Gephardt	Y	Y	Y
4 Skelton	Y	Y	N
5 Wheat	Y	Y	?
6 ***Coleman***	Y	Y	Y
7 ***Hancock***	Y	Y	N
8 ***Emerson***	Y	Y	N
9 Volkmer	Y	Y	Y
MONTANA			
1 Williams	Y	Y	Y
2 ***Marlenee***	Y	Y	N
NEBRASKA			
1 ***Bereuter***	Y	Y	Y
2 Hoagland	Y	Y	Y
3 ***Smith***	Y	Y	Y
NEVADA			
1 Bilbray	Y	Y	Y
2 ***Vucanovich***	Y	Y	N
NEW HAMPSHIRE			
1 ***Smith***	Y	Y	Y
2 ***Douglas***	Y	Y	Y
NEW JERSEY			
1 Vacancy			
2 Hughes	Y	Y	Y
3 Pallone	Y	Y	Y
4 ***Smith***	Y	Y	Y
5 ***Roukema***	Y	Y	Y
6 Dwyer	Y	Y	Y
7 ***Rinaldo***	Y	Y	Y
8 Roe	Y	Y	Y
9 Torricelli	Y	Y	Y
10 Payne	Y	Y	Y
11 ***Gallo***	Y	Y	?
12 ***Courter***	Y	Y	Y
13 ***Saxton***	Y	Y	Y
14 Guarini	Y	Y	Y
NEW MEXICO			
1 ***Schiff***	Y	Y	Y
2 ***Skeen***	Y	Y	N
3 Richardson	Y	Y	Y
NEW YORK			
1 Hochbrueckner	Y	Y	Y
2 Downey	Y	Y	Y
3 Mrazek	Y	?	Y
4 ***Lent***	Y	Y	Y
5 ***McGrath***	Y	Y	Y
6 Flake	Y	Y	Y
7 Ackerman	Y	Y	Y
8 Scheuer	Y	Y	Y
9 Manton	?	?	?
10 Schumer	Y	Y	Y
11 Towns	Y	Y	Y
12 Owens	Y	Y	Y
13 Solarz	Y	Y	?
14 Vacancy			
15 ***Green***	Y	Y	Y
16 Rangel	Y	Y	Y
17 Weiss	Y	Y	Y
18 Vacancy			
19 Engel	Y	Y	Y
20 Lowey	Y	Y	Y
21 ***Fish***	Y	Y	Y
22 ***Gilman***	Y	Y	Y
23 McNulty	Y	Y	Y
24 ***Solomon***	Y	Y	Y
25 ***Boehlert***	Y	Y	Y
26 ***Martin***	Y	Y	Y
27 ***Walsh***	Y	Y	Y
28 McHugh	Y	Y	Y
29 ***Horton***	Y	Y	Y
30 Slaughter	Y	Y	Y
31 ***Paxon***	Y	Y	Y

	16	17	18
32 LaFalce	Y	Y	Y
33 Nowak	Y	Y	Y
34 ***Houghton***	?	?	?
NORTH CAROLINA			
1 Jones	Y	Y	Y
2 Valentine	Y	Y	Y
3 Lancaster	Y	Y	Y
4 Price	Y	Y	Y
5 Neal	Y	Y	Y
6 ***Coble***	Y	Y	N
7 Rose	Y	Y	Y
8 Hefner	Y	Y	Y
9 ***McMillan***	Y	Y	Y
10 ***Ballenger***	Y	Y	Y
11 Clarke	Y	Y	Y
NORTH DAKOTA			
AL Dorgan	Y	Y	Y
OHIO			
1 Luken	Y	Y	Y
2 ***Gradison***	Y	Y	Y
3 Hall	Y	Y	Y
4 ***Oxley***	Y	Y	Y
5 ***Gillmor***	Y	Y	Y
6 ***McEwen***	Y	Y	Y
7 ***DeWine***	Y	Y	Y
8 ***Lukens***	Y	Y	Y
9 Kaptur	Y	Y	Y
10 ***Miller***	Y	Y	Y
11 Eckart	Y	Y	Y
12 ***Kasich***	Y	Y	Y
13 Pease	Y	Y	Y
14 Sawyer	Y	Y	Y
15 ***Wylie***	Y	Y	Y
16 ***Regula***	Y	Y	Y
17 Traficant	Y	Y	Y
18 Applegate	Y	Y	Y
19 Feighan	Y	Y	Y
20 Oakar	Y	Y	Y
21 Stokes	Y	Y	Y
OKLAHOMA			
1 ***Inhofe***	Y	Y	Y
2 Synar	Y	Y	Y
3 Watkins	Y	Y	Y
4 McCurdy	Y	Y	Y
5 ***Edwards***	Y	Y	?
6 English	Y	Y	Y
OREGON			
1 AuCoin	Y	Y	?
2 ***Smith, B.***	?	?	N
3 Wyden	Y	Y	Y
4 DeFazio	Y	Y	Y
5 ***Smith, D.***	Y	Y	N
PENNSYLVANIA			
1 Foglietta	Y	Y	Y
2 Gray	Y	Y	?
3 Borski	Y	Y	Y
4 Kolter	Y	Y	?
5 ***Schulze***	?	?	Y
6 Yatron	Y	Y	Y
7 ***Weldon***	Y	Y	Y
8 Kostmayer	Y	Y	Y
9 ***Shuster***	Y	Y	N
10 ***McDade***	Y	Y	Y
11 Kanjorski	Y	Y	Y
12 Murtha	Y	Y	Y
13 ***Coughlin***	Y	Y	Y
14 Coyne	Y	Y	Y
15 ***Ritter***	Y	Y	Y
16 ***Walker***	Y	Y	Y
17 ***Gekas***	Y	Y	N
18 Walgren	Y	Y	Y
19 ***Goodling***	Y	Y	Y
20 Gaydos	Y	Y	Y
21 ***Ridge***	Y	Y	Y
22 Murphy	Y	Y	Y
23 ***Clinger***	Y	Y	Y
RHODE ISLAND			
1 ***Machtley***	Y	Y	Y
2 ***Schneider***	Y	Y	Y
SOUTH CAROLINA			
1 ***Ravenel***	Y	Y	Y
2 ***Spence***	Y	Y	Y
3 Derrick	Y	Y	?
4 Patterson	Y	Y	Y
5 Spratt	Y	Y	Y
6 Tallon	Y	Y	Y

	16	17	18
SOUTH DAKOTA			
AL Johnson	Y	Y	Y
TENNESSEE			
1 ***Quillen***	Y	Y	Y
2 ***Duncan***	Y	Y	Y
3 Lloyd	Y	Y	Y
4 Cooper	Y	Y	Y
5 Clement	Y	Y	Y
6 Gordon	Y	Y	Y
7 ***Sundquist***	Y	Y	N
8 Tanner	Y	Y	Y
9 Ford	?	?	?
TEXAS			
1 Chapman	Y	Y	Y
2 Wilson	Y	Y	Y
3 ***Bartlett***	N	Y	Y
4 Hall	Y	Y	N
5 Bryant	Y	Y	Y
6 ***Barton***	Y	Y	N
7 ***Archer***	Y	Y	Y
8 ***Fields***	Y	Y	N
9 Brooks	Y	Y	Y
10 Pickle	Y	Y	Y
11 Leath	Y	Y	N
12 Geren	Y	Y	Y
13 Sarpalius	?	?	Y
14 Laughlin	Y	Y	Y
15 de la Garza	Y	Y	Y
16 Coleman	Y	Y	Y
17 Stenholm	Y	Y	N
18 Washington	?	?	?
19 ***Combest***	Y	Y	N
20 Gonzalez	Y	Y	Y
21 ***Smith***	Y	Y	Y
22 ***DeLay***	Y	Y	N
23 Bustamante	Y	Y	Y
24 Frost	?	?	Y
25 Andrews	Y	Y	?
26 ***Armey***	N	Y	N
27 Ortiz	Y	Y	Y
UTAH			
1 ***Hansen***	Y	Y	N
2 Owens	Y	Y	Y
3 ***Nielson***	Y	Y	N
VERMONT			
AL ***Smith***	Y	Y	Y
VIRGINIA			
1 ***Bateman***	Y	Y	Y
2 Pickett	Y	Y	Y
3 ***Bliley***	Y	Y	Y
4 Sisisky	Y	Y	Y
5 Payne	Y	Y	Y
6 Olin	Y	Y	Y
7 ***Slaughter***	Y	Y	Y
8 ***Parris***	Y	Y	?
9 Boucher	Y	Y	Y
10 ***Wolf***	Y	Y	Y
WASHINGTON			
1 ***Miller***	?	?	Y
2 Swift	Y	Y	Y
3 Unsoeld	Y	Y	Y
4 ***Morrison***	Y	Y	Y
5 Foley			
6 Dicks	Y	Y	Y
7 McDermott	Y	Y	Y
8 ***Chandler***	Y	Y	Y
WEST VIRGINIA			
1 Mollohan	Y	Y	Y
2 Staggers	Y	Y	Y
3 Wise	Y	Y	Y
4 Rahall	Y	Y	Y
WISCONSIN			
1 Aspin	Y	Y	Y
2 Kastenmeier	Y	Y	Y
3 ***Gunderson***	Y	Y	Y
4 Kleczka	Y	Y	Y
5 Moody	Y	Y	Y
6 ***Petri***	Y	Y	Y
7 Obey	Y	Y	Y
8 ***Roth***	?	?	Y
9 ***Sensenbrenner***	Y	Y	Y
WYOMING			
AL ***Thomas***	Y	Y	N

Southern states - Ala., Ark., Fla., Ga., Ky., La., Miss., N.C., Okla., S.C., Tenn., Texas, Va.
Omitted votes are quorum calls, which CQ does not include in its vote charts.

19. Procedural Motion. Upton, R-Mich., motion to approve the House Journal of Monday, March 5. Motion agreed to 284-101: R 66-95; D 218-6 (ND 143-6, SD 75-0), March 6, 1990.

20. HR 1109. National Trails System/Passage. Vento, D-Minn., motion to suspend the rules and pass the bill to amend the National Trails System Act to designate the California National Historic Trail and Pony Express National Historic Trail as components of the National Trails System. Motion agreed to 416-0: R 171-0; D 245-0 (ND 166-0, SD 79-0), March 6, 1990. A two-thirds majority of those present and voting (278 in this case) is required for passage under suspension of the rules.

21. HR 1243. Metal Casting Competitiveness/Passage. Lloyd, D-Tenn., motion to suspend the rules and pass the bill to require the Energy secretary to establish three centers for metal casting competitiveness. Motion agreed to 382-27: R 144-26; D 238-1 (ND 160-1, SD 78-0), March 6, 1990. A two-thirds majority of those present and voting (273 in this case) is required for passage under suspension of the rules.

22. HR 1231. Eastern Airlines Strike Emergency Board/Veto Override. Passage, over President Bush's Nov. 21, 1989, veto, of the bill to establish a commission to investigate and report on the dispute between Eastern Airlines and its unions. Rejected 261-160: R 25-147; D 236-13 (ND 169-1, SD 67-12), March 7, 1990. A two-thirds majority of those present and voting (282 in this case) of both houses is required to override a veto. A "nay" was a vote supporting the president's position.

KEY

- Y Voted for (yea).
- # Paired for.
- + Announced for.
- N Voted against (nay).
- X Paired against.
- \- Announced against.
- P Voted "present."
- C Voted "present" to avoid possible conflict of interest.
- ? Did not vote or otherwise make a position known.

Democrats ***Republicans***

	19	20	21	22
ALABAMA				
1 ***Callahan***	Y	Y	Y	N
2 ***Dickinson***	N	Y	Y	N
3 Browder	Y	Y	Y	Y
4 Bevill	Y	Y	Y	Y
5 Flippo	Y	Y	Y	Y
6 Erdreich	Y	Y	Y	Y
7 Harris	Y	Y	Y	Y
ALASKA				
AL ***Young***	N	Y	Y	Y
ARIZONA				
1 ***Rhodes***	N	Y	Y	N
2 Udall	?	Y	Y	Y
3 ***Stump***	N	Y	N	N
4 ***Kyl***	N	Y	N	N
5 ***Kolbe***	N	Y	Y	N
ARKANSAS				
1 Alexander	Y	Y	Y	Y
2 ***Robinson***	?	?	?	Y
3 ***Hammerschmidt***	Y	Y	Y	N
4 Anthony	Y	Y	Y	Y
CALIFORNIA				
1 Bosco	Y	Y	Y	Y
2 ***Herger***	N	Y	Y	N
3 Matsui	Y	Y	Y	Y
4 Fazio	Y	Y	Y	Y
5 Pelosi	Y	Y	Y	Y
6 Boxer	?	Y	Y	Y
7 Miller	?	Y	Y	Y
8 Dellums	Y	Y	Y	Y
9 Stark	Y	Y	Y	Y
10 Edwards	Y	Y	Y	Y
11 Lantos	Y	Y	Y	Y
12 ***Campbell***	Y	Y	Y	C
13 Mineta	Y	Y	Y	Y
14 ***Shumway***	?	Y	Y	N
15 Condit	Y	Y	Y	Y
16 Panetta	?	Y	Y	Y
17 ***Pashayan***	N	Y	Y	N
18 Lehman	Y	Y	Y	Y
19 ***Lagomarsino***	N	Y	Y	N
20 ***Thomas***	N	Y	Y	N
21 ***Gallegly***	N	Y	Y	N
22 ***Moorhead***	N	Y	Y	N
23 Beilenson	Y	Y	Y	Y
24 Waxman	Y	Y	Y	Y
25 Roybal	Y	Y	Y	Y
26 Berman	?	Y	Y	Y
27 Levine	?	?	?	Y
28 Dixon	?	Y	Y	Y
29 Hawkins	N	Y	Y	Y
30 Martinez	Y	Y	Y	Y
31 Dymally	Y	Y	Y	Y
32 Anderson	Y	Y	Y	Y
33 ***Dreier***	N	Y	Y	N
34 Torres	Y	Y	Y	Y
35 ***Lewis***	N	Y	Y	N
36 Brown	Y	Y	Y	Y
37 ***McCandless***	N	Y	N	N
38 ***Dornan***	Y	Y	Y	N
39 ***Dannemeyer***	N	Y	N	N
40 ***Cox***	N	Y	N	N
41 ***Lowery***	N	Y	Y	N
42 ***Rohrabacher***	Y	Y	Y	N
43 ***Packard***	?	Y	Y	N
44 Bates	Y	Y	?	Y
45 ***Hunter***	N	Y	Y	N
COLORADO				
1 Schroeder	N	Y	Y	Y
2 Skaggs	Y	Y	Y	Y
3 Campbell	?	Y	Y	Y
4 ***Brown***	N	Y	Y	N
5 ***Hefley***	N	Y	N	N
6 ***Schaefer***	N	Y	Y	N
CONNECTICUT				
1 Kennelly	Y	Y	Y	Y
2 Gejdenson	Y	Y	Y	Y
3 Morrison	Y	Y	Y	Y
4 ***Shays***	N	Y	Y	N
5 ***Rowland***	Y	Y	Y	Y
6 ***Johnson***	Y	Y	Y	Y
DELAWARE				
AL Carper	Y	Y	N	Y
FLORIDA				
1 Hutto	Y	Y	Y	Y
2 ***Grant***	Y	Y	Y	N
3 Bennett	Y	Y	Y	Y
4 ***James***	N	Y	Y	N
5 ***McCollum***	Y	Y	N	N
6 ***Stearns***	N	Y	N	N
7 Gibbons	Y	Y	Y	Y
8 ***Young***	N	Y	N	N
9 ***Bilirakis***	?	Y	Y	N
10 ***Ireland***	N	Y	Y	N
11 Nelson	+	+	+	Y
12 ***Lewis***	N	Y	Y	N
13 ***Goss***	N	Y	N	N
14 Johnston	Y	Y	Y	Y
15 ***Shaw***	?	Y	Y	N
16 Smith	Y	Y	Y	Y
17 Lehman	Y	Y	Y	N
18 ***Ros-Lehtinen***	Y	Y	Y	N
19 Fascell	Y	Y	Y	Y
GEORGIA				
1 Thomas	Y	Y	Y	Y
2 Hatcher	Y	Y	Y	Y
3 Ray	Y	Y	Y	N
4 Jones	Y	Y	Y	Y
5 Lewis	Y	Y	Y	Y
6 ***Gingrich***	Y	Y	Y	Y
7 Darden	Y	Y	Y	Y
8 Rowland	Y	Y	Y	Y
9 Jenkins	Y	Y	Y	Y
10 Barnard	Y	Y	Y	Y
HAWAII				
1 ***Saiki***	Y	Y	Y	N
2 Akaka	Y	Y	Y	Y
IDAHO				
1 ***Craig***	N	Y	N	X
2 Stallings	Y	Y	Y	Y
ILLINOIS				
1 Hayes	Y	Y	Y	Y
2 Savage	Y	Y	Y	Y
3 Russo	Y	Y	Y	Y
4 Sangmeister	Y	Y	Y	Y
5 Lipinski	Y	Y	Y	Y
6 ***Hyde***	Y	Y	Y	N
7 Collins	?	?	?	Y
8 Rostenkowski	Y	Y	Y	Y
9 Yates	?	?	?	#
10 ***Porter***	Y	Y	Y	Y
11 Annunzio	Y	Y	Y	Y
12 ***Crane***	N	Y	N	N
13 ***Fawell***	Y	Y	Y	N
14 ***Hastert***	N	Y	Y	N
15 ***Madigan***	N	Y	Y	N
16 ***Martin***	N	Y	Y	N
17 Evans	Y	Y	Y	Y
18 ***Michel***	N	Y	Y	N
19 Bruce	Y	Y	Y	Y
20 Durbin	Y	Y	Y	Y
21 Costello	Y	Y	Y	Y
22 Poshard	Y	Y	Y	Y
INDIANA				
1 Visclosky	?	Y	Y	Y
2 Sharp	Y	Y	?	Y
3 ***Hiler***	N	Y	Y	N

ND Northern Democrats SD Southern Democrats

	19	20	21	22
4 Long	Y	Y	Y	Y
5 Jontz	Y	Y	Y	Y
6 ***Burton***	N	Y	N	N
7 ***Myers***	?	Y	Y	N
8 McCloskey	Y	Y	Y	Y
9 Hamilton	Y	Y	Y	Y
10 Jacobs	N	Y	Y	Y
IOWA				
1 ***Leach***	N	Y	Y	N
2 ***Tauke***	N	Y	Y	N
3 Nagle	Y	Y	Y	Y
4 Smith	Y	Y	Y	Y
5 ***Lightfoot***	?	Y	Y	N
6 ***Grandy***	N	Y	Y	N
KANSAS				
1 ***Roberts***	N	Y	Y	N
2 Slattery	Y	Y	Y	Y
3 ***Meyers***	Y	Y	Y	N
4 Glickman	Y	Y	Y	Y
5 ***Whittaker***	N	Y	Y	Y
KENTUCKY				
1 Hubbard	Y	Y	Y	Y
2 Natcher	Y	Y	Y	Y
3 Mazzoli	Y	Y	Y	Y
4 ***Bunning***	N	Y	N	N
5 ***Rogers***	N	Y	Y	N
6 ***Hopkins***	N	Y	Y	N
7 Perkins	Y	Y	Y	Y
LOUISIANA				
1 ***Livingston***	Y	Y	N	N
2 Boggs	Y	Y	Y	Y
3 Tauzin	Y	Y	Y	N
4 ***McCrery***	Y	Y	Y	N
5 Huckaby	Y	Y	Y	N
6 ***Baker***	N	Y	Y	N
7 Hayes	Y	Y	Y	?
8 ***Holloway***	N	Y	Y	N
MAINE				
1 Brennan	Y	Y	Y	Y
2 ***Snowe***	Y	Y	Y	N
MARYLAND				
1 Dyson	Y	Y	Y	Y
2 ***Bentley***	N	Y	Y	N
3 Cardin	Y	Y	Y	Y
4 McMillen	Y	Y	Y	Y
5 Hoyer	Y	Y	Y	Y
6 Byron	Y	Y	Y	N
7 Mfume	Y	Y	Y	Y
8 ***Morella***	Y	Y	Y	N
MASSACHUSETTS				
1 ***Conte***	Y	Y	Y	Y
2 Neal	Y	Y	Y	Y
3 Early	Y	Y	Y	Y
4 Frank	Y	Y	Y	Y
5 Atkins	Y	Y	Y	Y
6 Mavroules	Y	Y	Y	Y
7 Markey	Y	Y	Y	Y
8 Kennedy	Y	Y	Y	Y
9 Moakley	Y	Y	Y	Y
10 Studds	Y	Y	Y	Y
11 Donnelly	?	Y	Y	Y
MICHIGAN				
1 Conyers	Y	Y	Y	+
2 ***Pursell***	?	Y	Y	N
3 Wolpe	Y	Y	Y	Y
4 ***Upton***	N	Y	Y	N
5 ***Henry***	N	Y	Y	N
6 Carr	Y	Y	Y	Y
7 Kildee	Y	Y	Y	Y
8 Traxler	Y	Y	Y	Y
9 ***Vander Jagt***	Y	Y	Y	N
10 ***Schuette***	N	Y	Y	N
11 ***Davis***	Y	Y	Y	Y
12 Bonior	Y	Y	Y	Y
13 Crockett	Y	Y	Y	Y
14 Hertel	Y	Y	Y	Y
15 Ford	Y	Y	Y	Y
16 Dingell	Y	Y	Y	Y
17 Levin	Y	Y	Y	Y
18 ***Broomfield***	Y	Y	Y	N
MINNESOTA				
1 Penny	Y	Y	Y	Y
2 ***Weber***	N	Y	Y	N
3 ***Frenzel***	N	Y	N	N
4 Vento	Y	Y	Y	Y

	19	20	21	22
5 Sabo	Y	Y	Y	Y
6 Sikorski	N	Y	Y	Y
7 ***Stangeland***	N	Y	Y	N
8 Oberstar	Y	Y	Y	Y
MISSISSIPPI				
1 Whitten	?	Y	Y	Y
2 Espy	Y	Y	Y	Y
3 Montgomery	Y	Y	Y	N
4 Parker	Y	Y	Y	N
5 Taylor	Y	Y	Y	Y
MISSOURI				
1 Clay	?	?	?	?
2 ***Buechner***	N	Y	Y	N
3 Gephardt	Y	Y	Y	Y
4 Skelton	Y	Y	Y	Y
5 Wheat	Y	Y	Y	Y
6 ***Coleman***	N	Y	Y	Y
7 ***Hancock***	N	Y	N	N
8 ***Emerson***	Y	Y	Y	N
9 Volkmer	Y	Y	Y	Y
MONTANA				
1 Williams	?	Y	Y	Y
2 ***Marlenee***	N	Y	?	N
NEBRASKA				
1 ***Bereuter***	Y	Y	Y	N
2 Hoagland	Y	Y	Y	Y
3 ***Smith***	Y	Y	Y	N
NEVADA				
1 Bilbray	Y	Y	Y	Y
2 ***Vucanovich***	N	Y	N	N
NEW HAMPSHIRE				
1 ***Smith***	N	Y	Y	N
2 ***Douglas***	?	Y	Y	N
NEW JERSEY				
1 Vacancy				
2 Hughes	Y	Y	Y	Y
3 Pallone	Y	Y	Y	Y
4 ***Smith***	Y	Y	Y	Y
5 ***Roukema***	N	Y	Y	Y
6 Dwyer	Y	Y	Y	Y
7 ***Rinaldo***	?	Y	Y	Y
8 Roe	Y	Y	Y	Y
9 Torricelli	Y	Y	Y	Y
10 Payne	Y	Y	Y	Y
11 ***Gallo***	N	Y	Y	N
12 ***Courter***	N	Y	Y	N
13 ***Saxton***	N	Y	Y	Y
14 Guarini	Y	Y	Y	Y
NEW MEXICO				
1 ***Schiff***	Y	Y	Y	N
2 ***Skeen***	Y	Y	N	N
3 Richardson	Y	Y	Y	Y
NEW YORK				
1 Hochbrueckner	Y	Y	Y	Y
2 Downey	?	Y	Y	Y
3 Mrazek	Y	Y	Y	Y
4 ***Lent***	?	?	?	N
5 ***McGrath***	?	?	?	Y
6 Flake	Y	Y	Y	Y
7 Ackerman	Y	Y	Y	Y
8 Scheuer	Y	Y	Y	Y
9 Manton	Y	Y	Y	Y
10 Schumer	Y	Y	Y	Y
11 Towns	Y	Y	Y	Y
12 Owens	Y	Y	Y	Y
13 Solarz	?	Y	Y	Y
14 Vacancy				
15 ***Green***	Y	Y	Y	N
16 Rangel	?	Y	Y	Y
17 Weiss	?	Y	Y	Y
18 Vacancy				
19 Engel	?	?	?	Y
20 Lowey	Y	Y	Y	Y
21 ***Fish***	Y	Y	Y	N
22 ***Gilman***	Y	Y	Y	Y
23 McNulty	Y	Y	Y	Y
24 ***Solomon***	N	Y	Y	?
25 ***Boehlert***	N	Y	Y	Y
26 ***Martin***	Y	Y	Y	N
27 ***Walsh***	Y	Y	Y	Y
28 McHugh	Y	Y	Y	Y
29 ***Horton***	Y	Y	Y	Y
30 Slaughter	Y	Y	Y	Y
31 ***Paxon***	N	Y	Y	N

	19	20	21	22
32 LaFalce	Y	Y	Y	Y
33 Nowak	Y	Y	Y	Y
34 ***Houghton***	Y	Y	Y	N
NORTH CAROLINA				
1 Jones	Y	Y	Y	Y
2 Valentine	?	Y	Y	N
3 Lancaster	Y	Y	Y	Y
4 Price	Y	Y	Y	Y
5 Neal	Y	Y	Y	?
6 ***Coble***	N	Y	Y	N
7 Rose	Y	Y	Y	Y
8 Hefner	Y	Y	Y	Y
9 ***McMillan***	Y	Y	Y	N
10 ***Ballenger***	N	Y	Y	N
11 Clarke	Y	Y	Y	Y
NORTH DAKOTA				
AL Dorgan	Y	Y	Y	Y
OHIO				
1 Luken	Y	Y	Y	Y
2 ***Gradison***	Y	Y	Y	N
3 Hall	Y	Y	Y	Y
4 ***Oxley***	Y	Y	Y	N
5 ***Gillmor***	Y	Y	Y	N
6 ***McEwen***	Y	Y	Y	N
7 ***DeWine***	N	Y	Y	N
8 ***Lukens***	N	Y	Y	N
9 Kaptur	Y	Y	Y	Y
10 ***Miller***	N	Y	Y	N
11 Eckart	Y	Y	Y	Y
12 ***Kasich***	?	Y	Y	N
13 Pease	?	Y	Y	Y
14 Sawyer	Y	Y	Y	Y
15 ***Wylie***	Y	Y	Y	N
16 ***Regula***	N	Y	Y	N
17 Traficant	Y	Y	Y	Y
18 Applegate	Y	Y	Y	Y
19 Feighan	N	Y	Y	Y
20 Oakar	Y	Y	Y	Y
21 Stokes	Y	Y	Y	Y
OKLAHOMA				
1 ***Inhofe***	N	Y	Y	N
2 Synar	?	Y	Y	Y
3 Watkins	?	Y	Y	Y
4 McCurdy	Y	Y	Y	Y
5 ***Edwards***	Y	Y	Y	N
6 English	Y	Y	Y	Y
OREGON				
1 AuCoin	Y	Y	?	Y
2 ***Smith, B.***	N	Y	Y	N
3 Wyden	Y	Y	Y	Y
4 DeFazio	Y	Y	Y	Y
5 ***Smith, D.***	?	?	?	N
PENNSYLVANIA				
1 Foglietta	?	?	?	Y
2 Gray	?	Y	Y	Y
3 Borski	Y	Y	?	Y
4 Kolter	Y	Y	Y	Y
5 ***Schulze***	Y	Y	Y	N
6 Yatron	Y	Y	Y	Y
7 ***Weldon***	Y	Y	Y	Y
8 Kostmayer	Y	Y	Y	Y
9 ***Shuster***	Y	Y	Y	N
10 ***McDade***	Y	Y	Y	Y
11 Kanjorski	Y	Y	Y	Y
12 Murtha	Y	Y	Y	Y
13 ***Coughlin***	N	Y	Y	N
14 Coyne	?	Y	Y	Y
15 ***Ritter***	Y	Y	Y	N
16 ***Walker***	N	Y	Y	N
17 ***Gekas***	N	Y	N	N
18 Walgren	Y	Y	Y	Y
19 ***Goodling***	N	Y	Y	N
20 Gaydos	Y	Y	Y	Y
21 ***Ridge***	N	Y	Y	Y
22 Murphy	N	Y	Y	Y
23 ***Clinger***	Y	Y	Y	N
RHODE ISLAND				
1 ***Machtley***	N	Y	Y	Y
2 ***Schneider***	Y	Y	Y	Y
SOUTH CAROLINA				
1 ***Ravenel***	Y	Y	Y	N
2 ***Spence***	Y	Y	Y	N
3 Derrick	Y	Y	Y	Y
4 Patterson	Y	Y	Y	Y
5 Spratt	Y	Y	Y	Y
6 Tallon	Y	Y	Y	Y

	19	20	21	22
SOUTH DAKOTA				
AL Johnson	Y	Y	?	Y
TENNESSEE				
1 ***Quillen***	Y	Y	Y	N
2 ***Duncan***	Y	Y	N	N
3 Lloyd	Y	Y	Y	Y
4 Cooper	Y	Y	Y	Y
5 Clement	Y	Y	Y	Y
6 Gordon	Y	Y	?	Y
7 ***Sundquist***	N	Y	Y	N
8 Tanner	Y	Y	Y	Y
9 Ford	?	?	?	#
TEXAS				
1 Chapman	Y	Y	Y	Y
2 Wilson	Y	Y	Y	N
3 ***Bartlett***	Y	Y	Y	N
4 Hall	Y	Y	Y	N
5 Bryant	Y	Y	Y	Y
6 ***Barton***	N	Y	Y	N
7 ***Archer***	Y	Y	N	N
8 ***Fields***	N	Y	Y	N
9 Brooks	?	?	?	?
10 Pickle	Y	Y	Y	N
11 Leath	Y	Y	Y	N
12 Geren	Y	Y	Y	Y
13 Sarpalius	Y	Y	Y	Y
14 Laughlin	?	?	?	Y
15 de la Garza	Y	Y	Y	Y
16 Coleman	Y	Y	Y	Y
17 Stenholm	Y	Y	Y	N
18 Washington	Y	Y	Y	Y
19 ***Combest***	Y	Y	Y	N
20 Gonzalez	Y	Y	Y	Y
21 ***Smith***	N	Y	Y	N
22 ***DeLay***	N	Y	N	N
23 Bustamante	Y	Y	Y	Y
24 Frost	Y	Y	Y	Y
25 Andrews	Y	Y	Y	Y
26 ***Armey***	N	Y	N	N
27 Ortiz	Y	Y	Y	Y
UTAH				
1 ***Hansen***	N	Y	Y	N
2 Owens	Y	Y	Y	Y
3 ***Nielson***	Y	Y	N	N
VERMONT				
AL ***Smith***	Y	Y	Y	N
VIRGINIA				
1 ***Bateman***	Y	Y	Y	N
2 Pickett	Y	Y	Y	Y
3 ***Bliley***	N	Y	Y	N
4 Sisisky	Y	Y	Y	Y
5 Payne	Y	Y	Y	Y
6 Olin	Y	Y	Y	Y
7 ***Slaughter***	N	Y	Y	N
8 ***Parris***	N	Y	Y	Y
9 Boucher	Y	Y	Y	Y
10 ***Wolf***	N	Y	Y	N
WASHINGTON				
1 ***Miller***	N	Y	Y	N
2 Swift	?	Y	Y	Y
3 Unsoeld	Y	?	?	Y
4 ***Morrison***	Y	Y	Y	N
5 Foley				
6 Dicks	Y	Y	Y	Y
7 McDermott	Y	Y	Y	Y
8 ***Chandler***	N	Y	Y	N
WEST VIRGINIA				
1 Mollohan	Y	Y	Y	Y
2 Staggers	Y	Y	Y	Y
3 Wise	Y	Y	Y	Y
4 Rahall	Y	Y	Y	Y
WISCONSIN				
1 Aspin	?	Y	Y	Y
2 Kastenmeier	Y	Y	Y	Y
3 ***Gunderson***	Y	Y	Y	N
4 Kleczka	Y	Y	Y	Y
5 Moody	Y	Y	Y	Y
6 ***Petri***	Y	Y	Y	N
7 Obey	Y	Y	Y	Y
8 ***Roth***	Y	Y	Y	N
9 ***Sensenbrenner***	N	Y	Y	N
WYOMING				
AL ***Thomas***	Y	Y	N	N

Southern states - Ala., Ark., Fla., Ga., Ky., La., Miss., N.C., Okla., S.C., Tenn., Texas, Va.
Omitted votes are quorum calls, which CQ does not include in its vote charts.

24. HR 3581. Rural Economic Development Act/Rule. Adoption of the rule (H Res 355) to provide for House floor consideration of the bill to enhance rural economic development by allowing the Agriculture secretary to transfer funds among various rural development accounts at the request of states. Adopted 315-99: R 74-96; D 241-3 (ND 165-2, SD 76-1), March 14, 1990.

25. Procedural Motion. Brown, R-Colo., motion to approve the House Journal of Wednesday, March 14. Motion agreed to 292-98: R 67-93; D 225-5 (ND 147-5, SD 78-0), March 15, 1990.

27. HR 3581. Rural Economic Development Act/Funds Transfers. Rose, D-N.C., amendment to strike provisions that would allow the Agriculture secretary to transfer funds among various rural development accounts at the request of states. Adopted 204-193: R 68-96; D 136-97 (ND 98-60, SD 38-37), March 15, 1990.

KEY

- Y Voted for (yea).
- # Paired for.
- + Announced for.
- N Voted against (nay).
- X Paired against.
- \- Announced against.
- P Voted "present."
- C Voted "present" to avoid possible conflict of interest.
- ? Did not vote or otherwise make a position known.

Democrats ***Republicans***

	24	25	27
ALABAMA			
1 ***Callahan***	Y	Y	N
2 ***Dickinson***	N	N	N
3 Browder	Y	Y	N
4 Bevill	Y	Y	?
5 Flippo	?	?	?
6 Erdreich	Y	Y	N
7 Harris	Y	Y	N
ALASKA			
AL ***Young***	Y	?	?
ARIZONA			
1 ***Rhodes***	N	N	N
2 Udall	Y	Y	Y
3 ***Stump***	?	?	?
4 ***Kyl***	N	N	Y
5 ***Kolbe***	N	N	N
ARKANSAS			
1 Alexander	Y	Y	Y
2 ***Robinson***	Y	Y	Y
3 ***Hammerschmidt***	?	?	Y
4 Anthony	Y	Y	Y
CALIFORNIA			
1 Bosco	Y	Y	N
2 ***Herger***	N	N	N
3 Matsui	Y	Y	Y
4 Fazio	Y	Y	Y
5 Pelosi	Y	Y	Y
6 Boxer	Y	Y	Y
7 Miller	Y	Y	Y
8 Dellums	Y	?	Y
9 Stark	Y	Y	Y
10 Edwards	Y	Y	Y
11 Lantos	Y	Y	Y
12 ***Campbell***	N	Y	N
13 Mineta	Y	Y	Y
14 ***Shumway***	N	Y	N
15 Condit	Y	Y	Y
16 Panetta	Y	Y	Y
17 ***Pashayan***	Y	N	N
18 Lehman	Y	Y	Y
19 ***Lagomarsino***	N	N	N
20 ***Thomas***	N	N	Y
21 ***Gallegly***	N	N	N
22 ***Moorhead***	N	N	N
23 Beilenson	Y	Y	Y
24 Waxman	Y	Y	Y
25 Roybal	Y	Y	Y
26 Berman	Y	Y	Y
27 Levine	Y	Y	?
28 Dixon	Y	?	Y
29 Hawkins	Y	Y	Y
30 Martinez	Y	?	Y
31 Dymally	Y	Y	Y
32 Anderson	Y	Y	N
33 ***Dreier***	N	N	N
34 Torres	Y	Y	Y
35 ***Lewis***	N	N	Y
36 Brown	Y	Y	N
37 ***McCandless***	N	N	Y
38 ***Dornan***	N	?	N
39 ***Dannemeyer***	N	N	N
40 ***Cox***	N	Y	N
41 ***Lowery***	N	N	Y

	24	25	27
42 ***Rohrabacher***	N	N	N
43 ***Packard***	N	Y	Y
44 Bates	Y	Y	Y
45 ***Hunter***	N	N	Y
COLORADO			
1 Schroeder	Y	N	Y
2 Skaggs	Y	Y	N
3 Campbell	Y	Y	N
4 ***Brown***	N	N	N
5 ***Hefley***	N	N	N
6 ***Schaefer***	N	N	N
CONNECTICUT			
1 Kennelly	?	Y	Y
2 Gejdenson	Y	Y	Y
3 Morrison	Y	Y	?
4 ***Shays***	N	N	N
5 ***Rowland***	Y	Y	Y
6 ***Johnson***	Y	Y	N
DELAWARE			
AL Carper	Y	Y	N
FLORIDA			
1 Hutto	Y	Y	Y
2 ***Grant***	Y	Y	Y
3 Bennett	Y	Y	Y
4 ***James***	N	N	Y
5 ***McCollum***	N	N	Y
6 ***Stearns***	N	N	Y
7 Gibbons	Y	Y	Y
8 ***Young***	N	Y	Y
9 ***Bilirakis***	N	N	Y
10 ***Ireland***	N	N	Y
11 Nelson	+	+	+
12 ***Lewis***	N	N	Y
13 ***Goss***	N	N	Y
14 Johnston	Y	Y	Y
15 ***Shaw***	N	Y	Y
16 Smith	Y	Y	Y
17 Lehman	Y	Y	Y
18 ***Ros-Lehtinen***	N	N	Y
19 Fascell	Y	Y	Y
GEORGIA			
1 Thomas	Y	Y	N
2 Hatcher	Y	Y	N
3 Ray	Y	Y	N
4 Jones	Y	Y	N
5 Lewis	Y	Y	N
6 ***Gingrich***	N	N	N
7 Darden	Y	Y	N
8 Rowland	Y	Y	N
9 Jenkins	Y	Y	N
10 Barnard	Y	Y	N
HAWAII			
1 ***Saiki***	Y	Y	N
2 Akaka	Y	Y	Y
IDAHO			
1 ***Craig***	N	N	N
2 Stallings	Y	Y	N
ILLINOIS			
1 Hayes	Y	Y	Y
2 Savage	?	Y	Y
3 Russo	Y	Y	Y
4 Sangmeister	Y	Y	Y
5 Lipinski	Y	Y	Y
6 ***Hyde***	N	N	Y
7 Collins	?	?	?
8 Rostenkowski	Y	Y	Y
9 Yates	?	?	?
10 ***Porter***	N	Y	N
11 Annunzio	Y	Y	N
12 ***Crane***	N	N	N
13 ***Fawell***	N	Y	N
14 ***Hastert***	N	N	N
15 ***Madigan***	Y	N	N
16 ***Martin***	Y	N	N
17 Evans	Y	Y	Y
18 ***Michel***	Y	N	N
19 Bruce	Y	Y	Y
20 Durbin	Y	Y	Y
21 Costello	Y	Y	Y
22 Poshard	Y	Y	Y
INDIANA			
1 Visclosky	Y	Y	N
2 Sharp	Y	Y	N
3 ***Hiler***	Y	N	N

ND Northern Democrats SD Southern Democrats

	24	25	27
4 Long	Y	Y	N
5 Jontz	Y	Y	N
6 ***Burton***	N	N	N
7 ***Myers***	Y	Y	Y
8 McCloskey	Y	Y	N
9 Hamilton	Y	P	N
10 Jacobs	Y	N	N
IOWA			
1 ***Leach***	Y	N	N
2 ***Tauke***	Y	N	N
3 Nagle	Y	Y	Y
4 Smith	Y	Y	Y
5 ***Lightfoot***	Y	N	N
6 ***Grandy***	Y	N	N
KANSAS			
1 ***Roberts***	Y	N	N
2 Slattery	Y	Y	N
3 ***Meyers***	N	Y	N
4 Glickman	Y	Y	N
5 ***Whittaker***	Y	?	N
KENTUCKY			
1 Hubbard	Y	Y	Y
2 Natcher	Y	Y	Y
3 Mazzoli	Y	Y	Y
4 ***Bunning***	N	N	Y
5 ***Rogers***	N	N	Y
6 ***Hopkins***	N	N	Y
7 Perkins	Y	Y	Y
LOUISIANA			
1 ***Livingston***	N	Y	Y
2 Boggs	Y	Y	Y
3 Tauzin	Y	Y	N
4 ***McCrery***	Y	?	N
5 Huckaby	Y	Y	N
6 ***Baker***	N	N	N
7 Hayes	Y	?	?
8 ***Holloway***	Y	N	N
MAINE			
1 Brennan	Y	Y	Y
2 ***Snowe***	Y	Y	Y
MARYLAND			
1 Dyson	Y	Y	N
2 ***Bentley***	N	N	N
3 Cardin	Y	Y	Y
4 McMillen	Y	Y	Y
5 Hoyer	Y	Y	Y
6 Byron	Y	?	N
7 Mfume	Y	Y	?
8 ***Morella***	Y	N	N
MASSACHUSETTS			
1 ***Conte***	N	Y	Y
2 Neal	Y	Y	Y
3 Early	Y	Y	N
4 Frank	Y	Y	Y
5 Atkins	Y	Y	Y
6 Mavroules	?	Y	N
7 Markey	Y	Y	?
8 Kennedy	Y	Y	Y
9 Moakley	Y	Y	Y
10 Studds	Y	Y	Y
11 Donnelly	Y	Y	Y
MICHIGAN			
1 Conyers	Y	Y	?
2 ***Pursell***	N	Y	Y
3 Wolpe	Y	?	N
4 ***Upton***	N	N	N
5 ***Henry***	N	N	N
6 Carr	Y	Y	Y
7 Kildee	Y	Y	N
8 Traxler	Y	Y	Y
9 ***Vander Jagt***	Y	Y	N
10 ***Schuette***	Y	N	N
11 ***Davis***	Y	Y	Y
12 Bonior	Y	Y	Y
13 Crockett	Y	?	?
14 Hertel	Y	Y	Y
15 Ford	Y	Y	N
16 Dingell	Y	Y	N
17 Levin	Y	Y	N
18 ***Broomfield***	N	Y	N
MINNESOTA			
1 Penny	Y	Y	N
2 ***Weber***	Y	N	Y
3 ***Frenzel***	N	N	N
4 Vento	Y	Y	Y
5 Sabo	Y	Y	Y
6 Sikorski	Y	N	Y
7 ***Stangeland***	Y	N	Y
8 Oberstar	Y	Y	Y
MISSISSIPPI			
1 Whitten	Y	Y	Y
2 Espy	Y	Y	N
3 Montgomery	Y	Y	Y
4 Parker	Y	Y	Y
5 Taylor	Y	Y	Y
MISSOURI			
1 Clay	?	N	Y
2 ***Buechner***	N	Y	N
3 Gephardt	Y	Y	N
4 Skelton	Y	Y	Y
5 Wheat	Y	Y	N
6 ***Coleman***	Y	Y	N
7 ***Hancock***	N	N	N
8 ***Emerson***	Y	Y	N
9 Volkmer	Y	Y	Y
MONTANA			
1 Williams	N	?	?
2 ***Marlenee***	N	N	Y
NEBRASKA			
1 ***Bereuter***	Y	Y	N
2 Hoagland	Y	Y	N
3 ***Smith***	Y	Y	?
NEVADA			
1 Bilbray	Y	Y	N
2 ***Vucanovich***	N	?	N
NEW HAMPSHIRE			
1 ***Smith***	N	N	Y
2 ***Douglas***	N	N	Y
NEW JERSEY			
1 Vacancy			
2 Hughes	Y	Y	Y
3 Pallone	Y	Y	Y
4 ***Smith***	Y	Y	Y
5 ***Roukema***	N	N	Y
6 Dwyer	Y	Y	Y
7 ***Rinaldo***	N	Y	Y
8 Roe	Y	Y	Y
9 Torricelli	Y	Y	?
10 Payne	Y	Y	?
11 ***Gallo***	N	?	Y
12 ***Courter***	N	N	Y
13 ***Saxton***	N	?	Y
14 Guarini	Y	?	?
NEW MEXICO			
1 ***Schiff***	N	Y	Y
2 ***Skeen***	Y	Y	Y
3 Richardson	Y	Y	N
NEW YORK			
1 Hochbrueckner	Y	Y	Y
2 Downey	Y	?	Y
3 Mrazek	Y	Y	Y
4 ***Lent***	Y	Y	?
5 ***McGrath***	Y	N	Y
6 Flake	Y	Y	Y
7 Ackerman	Y	Y	Y
8 Scheuer	Y	Y	Y
9 Manton	Y	Y	Y
10 Schumer	Y	?	Y
11 Towns	Y	Y	Y
12 Owens	Y	Y	Y
13 Solarz	Y	?	Y
14 Vacancy			
15 ***Green***	Y	Y	Y
16 Rangel	Y	?	Y
17 Weiss	Y	Y	Y
18 Vacancy			
19 Engel	Y	Y	Y
20 Lowey	Y	Y	Y
21 ***Fish***	Y	Y	?
22 ***Gilman***	Y	Y	N
23 McNulty	Y	Y	N
24 ***Solomon***	Y	N	Y
25 ***Boehlert***	Y	Y	Y
26 ***Martin***	Y	N	N
27 ***Walsh***	Y	Y	N
28 McHugh	Y	Y	Y
29 ***Horton***	Y	Y	N
30 Slaughter	Y	Y	Y
31 ***Paxon***	N	N	N
32 LaFalce	Y	Y	N
33 Nowak	Y	Y	Y
34 ***Houghton***	N	Y	N
NORTH CAROLINA			
1 Jones	Y	Y	Y
2 Valentine	Y	Y	Y
3 Lancaster	Y	Y	Y
4 Price	Y	Y	Y
5 Neal	Y	Y	Y
6 ***Coble***	N	N	Y
7 Rose	Y	Y	Y
8 Hefner	Y	Y	Y
9 ***McMillan***	N	N	Y
10 ***Ballenger***	N	N	Y
11 Clarke	Y	Y	Y
NORTH DAKOTA			
AL Dorgan	N	Y	N
OHIO			
1 Luken	Y	Y	N
2 ***Gradison***	Y	Y	N
3 Hall	Y	Y	N
4 ***Oxley***	Y	Y	N
5 ***Gillmor***	Y	?	?
6 ***McEwen***	Y	Y	N
7 ***DeWine***	Y	N	N
8 ***Lukens***	N	?	?
9 Kaptur	Y	Y	N
10 ***Miller***	Y	N	N
11 Eckart	Y	Y	N
12 ***Kasich***	N	Y	N
13 Pease	Y	Y	N
14 Sawyer	Y	Y	N
15 ***Wylie***	Y	Y	N
16 ***Regula***	N	Y	N
17 Traficant	Y	Y	N
18 Applegate	Y	?	N
19 Feighan	Y	Y	N
20 Oakar	Y	?	?
21 Stokes	Y	Y	Y
OKLAHOMA			
1 ***Inhofe***	Y	N	N
2 Synar	Y	Y	N
3 Watkins	Y	Y	?
4 McCurdy	Y	Y	N
5 ***Edwards***	Y	Y	N
6 English	Y	Y	N
OREGON			
1 AuCoin	Y	Y	N
2 ***Smith, B.***	Y	N	Y
3 Wyden	Y	Y	N
4 DeFazio	Y	Y	Y
5 ***Smith, D.***	N	N	N
PENNSYLVANIA			
1 Foglietta	Y	Y	Y
2 Gray	Y	?	N
3 Borski	Y	?	?
4 Kolter	Y	Y	?
5 ***Schulze***	N	Y	Y
6 Yatron	Y	Y	N
7 ***Weldon***	N	Y	N
8 Kostmayer	Y	Y	Y
9 ***Shuster***	Y	Y	Y
10 ***McDade***	Y	N	Y
11 Kanjorski	Y	Y	Y
12 Murtha	Y	Y	Y
13 ***Coughlin***	N	N	Y
14 Coyne	Y	Y	Y
15 ***Ritter***	N	?	N
16 ***Walker***	N	N	N
17 ***Gekas***	N	N	N
18 Walgren	Y	Y	N
19 ***Goodling***	Y	N	N
20 Gaydos	Y	Y	N
21 ***Ridge***	Y	N	N
22 Murphy	Y	Y	N
23 ***Clinger***	-	Y	Y
RHODE ISLAND			
1 ***Machtley***	Y	N	Y
2 ***Schneider***	Y	Y	Y
SOUTH CAROLINA			
1 ***Ravenel***	?	Y	Y
2 ***Spence***	N	Y	Y
3 Derrick	Y	Y	Y
4 Patterson	Y	Y	Y
5 Spratt	Y	Y	Y
6 Tallon	N	Y	Y
SOUTH DAKOTA			
AL Johnson	Y	Y	Y
TENNESSEE			
1 ***Quillen***	Y	Y	Y
2 ***Duncan***	Y	Y	N
3 Lloyd	Y	Y	Y
4 Cooper	Y	Y	N
5 Clement	Y	Y	Y
6 Gordon	Y	Y	Y
7 ***Sundquist***	Y	N	N
8 Tanner	Y	Y	?
9 Ford	?	?	?
TEXAS			
1 Chapman	Y	Y	N
2 Wilson	?	Y	?
3 ***Bartlett***	N	Y	N
4 Hall	Y	Y	N
5 Bryant	Y	Y	N
6 ***Barton***	Y	?	?
7 ***Archer***	N	Y	N
8 ***Fields***	N	?	?
9 Brooks	?	Y	N
10 Pickle	Y	Y	N
11 Leath	?	Y	N
12 Geren	Y	Y	N
13 Sarpalius	Y	Y	N
14 Laughlin	Y	Y	N
15 de la Garza	Y	Y	N
16 Coleman	Y	Y	N
17 Stenholm	Y	Y	N
18 Washington	Y	Y	N
19 ***Combest***	N	Y	N
20 Gonzalez	Y	Y	N
21 ***Smith***	N	N	N
22 ***DeLay***	N	?	?
23 Bustamante	Y	Y	N
24 Frost	Y	Y	N
25 Andrews	Y	?	N
26 ***Armey***	N	N	N
27 Ortiz	Y	Y	N
UTAH			
1 ***Hansen***	N	N	N
2 Owens	Y	?	N
3 ***Nielson***	Y	Y	N
VERMONT			
AL ***Smith***	Y	Y	N
VIRGINIA			
1 ***Bateman***	?	Y	Y
2 Pickett	Y	Y	Y
3 ***Bliley***	N	N	Y
4 Sisisky	Y	Y	Y
5 Payne	Y	Y	Y
6 Olin	Y	Y	Y
7 ***Slaughter***	Y	Y	Y
8 ***Parris***	Y	N	Y
9 Boucher	Y	Y	Y
10 ***Wolf***	Y	N	Y
WASHINGTON			
1 ***Miller***	Y	N	N
2 Swift	Y	N	N
3 Unsoeld	Y	Y	N
4 ***Morrison***	Y	Y	N
5 Foley			
6 Dicks	Y	Y	Y
7 McDermott	Y	Y	N
8 ***Chandler***	Y	N	N
WEST VIRGINIA			
1 Mollohan	Y	Y	Y
2 Staggers	Y	Y	N
3 Wise	Y	Y	N
4 Rahall	Y	Y	Y
WISCONSIN			
1 Aspin	Y	Y	Y
2 Kastenmeier	Y	Y	N
3 ***Gunderson***	Y	Y	N
4 Kleczka	Y	Y	N
5 Moody	Y	?	N
6 ***Petri***	N	Y	N
7 Obey	Y	Y	Y
8 ***Roth***	N	Y	Y
9 ***Sensenbrenner***	N	N	?
WYOMING			
AL ***Thomas***	Y	N	N

Southern states - Ala., Ark., Fla., Ga., Ky., La., Miss., N.C., Okla., S.C., Tenn., Texas, Va.
Omitted votes are quorum calls, which CQ does not include in its vote charts.

28. Procedural Motion. Stearns, R-Fla., motion to approve the House Journal of Monday, March 19. Motion agreed to 258-121: R 47-115; D 211-6 (ND 137-6, SD 74-0), March 20, 1990.

29. HR 4167. Strategic Petroleum Reserve/Passage. Sharp, D-Ind., motion to suspend the rules and pass the bill to extend from April 1, 1990, to Aug. 15, 1990, the Energy Department's authority to draw down the strategic petroleum reserve. Motion agreed to 397-0: R 165-0; D 232-0 (ND 155-0, SD 77-0), March 20, 1990. A two-thirds majority of those present and voting (265 in this case) is required for passage under suspension of the rules. (Passage was subsequently vacated and S 2231, a similar Senate-passed bill, was passed by voice vote, clearing the measure for the president.)

30. HR 2692. Woodrow Wilson Memorial Act/Passage. Clay, D-Mo., motion to suspend the rules and pass the bill to amend the act to provide that the Education secretary and two additional private citizens shall be members of the board of trustees of the Woodrow Wilson International Center for Scholars in Washington. Motion agreed to 399-0: R 165-0; D 234-0 (ND 157-0, SD 77-0), March 20, 1990. A two-thirds majority of those present and voting (266 in this case) is required for passage under suspension of the rules.

31. S 1091. Coast Guard Bicentennial Medals/Passage. Lehman, D-Calif., motion to suspend the rules and pass the bill to provide for the striking of medals to commemorate the bicentennial of the Coast Guard. Motion agreed to 402-0: R 167-0; D 235-0 (ND 158-0, SD 77-0), March 20, 1990. A two-thirds majority of those present and voting (268 in this case) is required for passage under suspension of the rules.

32. HR 3182. Yosemite National Park Centennial Medals/Passage. Lehman, D-Calif., motion to suspend the rules and pass the bill to provide for the striking of medals to commemorate the centennial of Yosemite National Park. Motion agreed to 401-0: R 168-0; D 233-0 (ND 156-0, SD 77-0), March 20, 1990. A two-thirds majority of those present and voting (268 in this case) is required for passage under suspension of the rules.

33. HR 3834. National Trails System/Passage. Vento, D-Minn., motion to suspend the rules and pass the bill to amend the National Trails System Act to designate the route from Selma to Montgomery, Ala., for study for addition to the national trails system. Motion agreed to 400-0: R 166-0; D 234-0 (ND 156-0, SD 78-0), March 20, 1990. A two-thirds majority of those present and voting (267 in this case) is required for passage under suspension of the rules.

34. HR 2566. Property Rights on San Juan Island, Wash./Passage. Vento, D-Minn., motion to suspend the rules and pass the bill to direct the Interior secretary to transfer all federal rights, title and interest in certain property on San Juan Island, Wash., to people who were sold the property because of an erroneous survey. Motion agreed to 401-0: R 167-0; D 234-0 (ND 157-0, SD 77-0), March 20, 1990. A two-thirds majority of those present and voting (268 in this case) is required for passage under suspension of the rules.

KEY

- Y Voted for (yea).
- # Paired for.
- + Announced for.
- N Voted against (nay).
- X Paired against.
- - Announced against.
- P Voted "present."
- C Voted "present" to avoid possible conflict of interest.
- ? Did not vote or otherwise make a position known.

Democrats *Republicans*

	28	29	30	31	32	33	34
ALABAMA							
1 *Callahan*	Y	Y	Y	Y	Y	Y	Y
2 *Dickinson*	N	Y	Y	Y	Y	Y	Y
3 Browder	Y	Y	Y	Y	Y	Y	Y
4 Bevill	Y	Y	Y	Y	Y	Y	Y
5 Flippo	?	?	?	?	?	?	?
6 Erdreich	Y	Y	Y	Y	Y	Y	Y
7 Harris	Y	Y	Y	Y	Y	Y	Y
ALASKA							
AL *Young*	N	Y	Y	Y	Y	Y	Y
ARIZONA							
1 *Rhodes*	N	Y	Y	Y	Y	Y	Y
2 Udall	?	Y	Y	Y	Y	Y	Y
3 *Stump*	?	?	?	?	?	?	?
4 *Kyl*	N	Y	Y	Y	Y	Y	Y
5 *Kolbe*	N	Y	Y	Y	Y	Y	Y
ARKANSAS							
1 Alexander	Y	Y	Y	?	Y	Y	Y
2 *Robinson*	Y	Y	Y	Y	Y	Y	Y
3 *Hammerschmidt*	N	Y	Y	Y	Y	Y	Y
4 Anthony	Y	Y	Y	Y	Y	Y	Y
CALIFORNIA							
1 Bosco	Y	Y	Y	Y	Y	Y	Y
2 *Herger*	N	Y	Y	Y	Y	Y	Y
3 Matsui	Y	Y	Y	Y	Y	Y	Y
4 Fazio	Y	Y	Y	Y	Y	Y	Y
5 Pelosi	Y	Y	Y	Y	Y	Y	Y
6 Boxer	Y	Y	Y	Y	Y	Y	Y
7 Miller	Y	Y	Y	Y	Y	Y	Y
8 Dellums	Y	Y	Y	Y	Y	Y	Y
9 Stark	?	Y	Y	Y	Y	Y	Y
10 Edwards	Y	Y	Y	Y	Y	Y	Y
11 Lantos	Y	Y	Y	Y	Y	Y	Y
12 *Campbell*	Y	Y	Y	Y	Y	Y	Y
13 Mineta	Y	Y	Y	Y	Y	Y	Y
14 *Shumway*	?	Y	Y	Y	Y	Y	Y
15 Condit	?	Y	Y	Y	Y	Y	Y
16 Panetta	?	Y	Y	Y	Y	Y	Y
17 *Pashayan*	N	Y	Y	Y	Y	Y	Y
18 Lehman	Y	Y	Y	Y	Y	Y	Y
19 *Lagomarsino*	N	Y	Y	Y	Y	Y	Y
20 *Thomas*	N	Y	Y	Y	Y	Y	Y
21 *Gallegly*	N	Y	Y	Y	Y	Y	Y
22 *Moorhead*	N	Y	Y	Y	Y	Y	Y
23 Beilenson	Y	Y	Y	Y	Y	Y	Y
24 Waxman	Y	Y	Y	Y	Y	Y	Y
25 Roybal	P	Y	Y	Y	Y	Y	Y
26 Berman	Y	Y	Y	Y	Y	Y	Y
27 Levine	Y	Y	Y	Y	Y	Y	Y
28 Dixon	Y	Y	Y	Y	Y	Y	Y
29 Hawkins	Y	Y	Y	Y	?	?	?
30 Martinez	Y	Y	Y	Y	Y	Y	Y
31 Dymally	Y	Y	Y	Y	Y	Y	Y
32 Anderson	Y	Y	Y	Y	Y	Y	Y
33 *Dreier*	N	Y	Y	Y	Y	Y	Y
34 Torres	Y	Y	Y	Y	Y	Y	Y
35 *Lewis*	N	Y	Y	Y	Y	Y	Y
36 Brown	?	?	?	?	?	?	?
37 *McCandless*	N	Y	Y	Y	Y	Y	Y
38 *Dornan*	N	Y	Y	Y	Y	Y	Y
39 *Dannemeyer*	N	Y	Y	Y	Y	Y	Y
40 *Cox*	Y	Y	Y	Y	Y	Y	Y
41 *Lowery*	N	Y	Y	Y	Y	Y	Y
42 *Rohrabacher*	N	Y	Y	Y	Y	Y	Y
43 *Packard*	N	Y	Y	Y	Y	Y	Y
44 Bates	Y	Y	Y	Y	Y	Y	Y
45 *Hunter*	N	Y	Y	Y	Y	Y	Y
COLORADO							
1 Schroeder	N	Y	Y	Y	Y	Y	Y
2 Skaggs	Y	Y	Y	Y	Y	Y	Y
3 Campbell	Y	Y	Y	Y	Y	Y	Y
4 *Brown*	N	Y	Y	Y	Y	Y	Y
5 *Hefley*	N	Y	Y	Y	Y	Y	Y
6 *Schaefer*	N	Y	Y	Y	Y	Y	Y
CONNECTICUT							
1 Kennelly	Y	Y	Y	Y	Y	Y	Y
2 Gejdenson	Y	Y	Y	Y	Y	Y	Y
3 Morrison	?	+	+	+	+	+	+
4 *Shays*	N	Y	Y	Y	Y	Y	Y
5 *Rowland*	Y	Y	Y	Y	Y	Y	Y
6 *Johnson*	Y	Y	Y	Y	Y	Y	Y
DELAWARE							
AL Carper	Y	Y	Y	Y	Y	Y	Y
FLORIDA							
1 Hutto	Y	Y	Y	Y	Y	Y	Y
2 *Grant*	Y	Y	Y	Y	Y	Y	Y
3 Bennett	Y	Y	Y	Y	Y	Y	Y
4 *James*	N	Y	Y	Y	Y	Y	Y
5 *McCollum*	Y	Y	Y	Y	Y	Y	Y
6 *Stearns*	N	Y	Y	Y	Y	Y	Y
7 Gibbons	?	?	?	?	?	?	?
8 *Young*	?	?	?	?	Y	Y	Y
9 *Bilirakis*	N	Y	Y	Y	Y	Y	Y
10 *Ireland*	N	Y	Y	Y	Y	Y	Y
11 Nelson	+	+	+	+	+	+	+
12 *Lewis*	?	Y	Y	Y	Y	Y	Y
13 *Goss*	N	Y	Y	Y	Y	Y	Y
14 Johnston	Y	Y	Y	Y	Y	Y	Y
15 *Shaw*	Y	Y	Y	Y	Y	Y	Y
16 Smith	Y	Y	Y	Y	Y	Y	Y
17 Lehman	Y	Y	Y	Y	Y	Y	Y
18 *Ros-Lehtinen*	N	Y	Y	Y	Y	Y	Y
19 Fascell	Y	Y	Y	Y	Y	Y	Y
GEORGIA							
1 Thomas	Y	Y	Y	Y	Y	Y	Y
2 Hatcher	Y	Y	Y	Y	Y	Y	Y
3 Ray	Y	Y	Y	Y	Y	Y	Y
4 Jones	Y	Y	Y	Y	Y	Y	Y
5 Lewis	Y	Y	Y	Y	Y	Y	Y
6 *Gingrich*	N	Y	Y	Y	Y	Y	Y
7 Darden	Y	Y	Y	Y	Y	Y	Y
8 Rowland	Y	Y	Y	Y	Y	Y	Y
9 Jenkins	Y	Y	Y	Y	Y	Y	Y
10 Barnard	Y	Y	Y	Y	Y	Y	Y
HAWAII							
1 *Saiki*	Y	Y	Y	Y	Y	Y	Y
2 Akaka	Y	Y	Y	Y	Y	Y	Y
IDAHO							
1 *Craig*	?	?	?	?	?	?	?
2 Stallings	Y	Y	Y	Y	Y	Y	Y
ILLINOIS							
1 Hayes	?	?	?	?	?	?	?
2 Savage	?	?	?	?	?	?	?
3 Russo	Y	Y	Y	Y	Y	Y	Y
4 Sangmeister	?	?	?	?	?	?	?
5 Lipinski	?	?	?	?	?	?	?
6 *Hyde*	N	Y	Y	Y	Y	Y	Y
7 Collins	?	?	?	?	?	?	?
8 Rostenkowski	Y	Y	Y	Y	Y	Y	Y
9 Yates	?	?	?	?	?	?	?
10 *Porter*	N	Y	Y	Y	Y	Y	Y
11 Annunzio	?	?	?	?	?	?	?
12 *Crane*	-	-	-	+	+	-	+
13 *Fawell*	N	Y	Y	Y	Y	Y	Y
14 *Hastert*	N	Y	Y	Y	Y	Y	Y
15 *Madigan*	N	Y	Y	Y	Y	Y	Y
16 *Martin*	?	?	?	?	?	?	?
17 Evans	Y	Y	Y	Y	Y	Y	Y
18 *Michel*	N	Y	Y	Y	Y	Y	Y
19 Bruce	Y	Y	Y	Y	Y	Y	Y
20 Durbin	Y	Y	Y	Y	Y	Y	Y
21 Costello	Y	Y	Y	Y	Y	Y	Y
22 Poshard	Y	Y	Y	Y	Y	Y	Y
INDIANA							
1 Visclosky	Y	Y	Y	Y	Y	Y	Y
2 Sharp	Y	Y	Y	Y	Y	Y	Y
3 *Hiler*	N	Y	Y	Y	Y	Y	Y

ND Northern Democrats SD Southern Democrats

	28	29	30	31	32	33	34
4 Long	Y	Y	Y	Y	Y	Y	Y
5 Jontz	Y	Y	Y	Y	Y	Y	Y
6 ***Burton***	N	Y	Y	Y	Y	Y	Y
7 ***Myers***	Y	Y	Y	Y	Y	Y	Y
8 McCloskey	Y	Y	Y	Y	Y	Y	Y
9 Hamilton	Y	Y	Y	Y	Y	Y	Y
10 Jacobs	N	Y	Y	Y	Y	Y	Y
IOWA							
1 ***Leach***	N	Y	Y	Y	Y	Y	Y
2 ***Tauke***	Y	Y	Y	Y	Y	Y	Y
3 Nagle	Y	Y	Y	Y	Y	Y	Y
4 Smith	Y	Y	Y	Y	Y	Y	Y
5 ***Lightfoot***	N	Y	Y	Y	Y	Y	Y
6 ***Grandy***	N	Y	Y	Y	Y	Y	Y
KANSAS							
1 ***Roberts***	N	Y	Y	Y	Y	Y	Y
2 Slattery	Y	Y	Y	Y	Y	Y	Y
3 ***Meyers***	Y	Y	Y	Y	Y	Y	Y
4 Glickman	Y	Y	Y	Y	Y	Y	Y
5 ***Whittaker***	N	Y	Y	Y	Y	Y	Y
KENTUCKY							
1 Hubbard	Y	Y	Y	Y	Y	Y	Y
2 Natcher	Y	Y	Y	Y	Y	Y	Y
3 Mazzoli	Y	Y	Y	Y	Y	Y	Y
4 ***Bunning***	N	Y	Y	Y	Y	Y	Y
5 ***Rogers***	N	Y	Y	Y	Y	Y	Y
6 ***Hopkins***	N	Y	Y	Y	Y	Y	Y
7 Perkins	Y	Y	Y	Y	Y	Y	Y
LOUISIANA							
1 ***Livingston***	Y	Y	Y	Y	Y	Y	Y
2 Boggs	Y	Y	Y	Y	Y	Y	Y
3 Tauzin	Y	Y	Y	Y	Y	Y	Y
4 ***McCrery***	Y	Y	Y	Y	Y	Y	Y
5 Huckaby	Y	Y	Y	Y	Y	Y	Y
6 ***Baker***	N	Y	Y	Y	Y	Y	Y
7 Hayes	Y	Y	Y	Y	Y	Y	Y
8 ***Holloway***	N	Y	Y	Y	Y	Y	Y
MAINE							
1 Brennan	Y	Y	Y	Y	Y	Y	Y
2 ***Snowe***	Y	Y	Y	Y	Y	Y	Y
MARYLAND							
1 Dyson	Y	Y	Y	Y	Y	Y	Y
2 ***Bentley***	N	Y	Y	Y	Y	Y	Y
3 Cardin	Y	Y	Y	Y	Y	Y	Y
4 McMillen	Y	Y	Y	Y	Y	Y	Y
5 Hoyer	Y	Y	?	Y	Y	Y	Y
6 Byron	Y	Y	Y	Y	Y	Y	Y
7 Mfume	Y	Y	Y	Y	Y	Y	Y
8 ***Morella***	N	Y	Y	Y	Y	Y	Y
MASSACHUSETTS							
1 ***Conte***	Y	Y	Y	Y	Y	Y	Y
2 Neal	?	Y	Y	Y	Y	Y	Y
3 Early	Y	Y	Y	Y	Y	Y	Y
4 Frank	Y	Y	Y	Y	Y	Y	Y
5 Atkins	Y	Y	Y	Y	Y	Y	Y
6 Mavroules	Y	Y	Y	Y	Y	Y	Y
7 Markey	Y	Y	Y	Y	Y	Y	Y
8 Kennedy	Y	Y	Y	Y	Y	Y	Y
9 Moakley	Y	Y	Y	Y	Y	Y	Y
10 Studds	Y	Y	Y	Y	Y	Y	Y
11 Donnelly	?	Y	Y	Y	Y	Y	Y
MICHIGAN							
1 Conyers	?	?	?	?	?	?	?
2 ***Pursell***	N	Y	Y	Y	Y	Y	Y
3 Wolpe	Y	?	Y	Y	Y	Y	Y
4 ***Upton***	N	Y	Y	Y	Y	Y	Y
5 ***Henry***	N	Y	Y	Y	Y	Y	Y
6 Carr	Y	Y	Y	Y	Y	?	?
7 Kildee	Y	Y	Y	Y	Y	Y	Y
8 Traxler	Y	Y	Y	Y	Y	Y	Y
9 ***Vander Jagt***	?	Y	Y	Y	Y	Y	Y
10 ***Schuette***	?	?	?	?	?	?	?
11 ***Davis***	Y	Y	Y	Y	Y	Y	Y
12 Bonior	Y	Y	Y	Y	Y	Y	Y
13 Crockett	?	?	?	?	?	?	Y
14 Hertel	Y	Y	Y	Y	Y	Y	Y
15 Ford	?	Y	Y	Y	Y	Y	Y
16 Dingell	Y	Y	Y	Y	Y	Y	Y
17 Levin	Y	Y	Y	Y	Y	Y	Y
18 ***Broomfield***	Y	Y	Y	Y	Y	Y	Y
MINNESOTA							
1 Penny	Y	Y	Y	Y	Y	Y	Y
2 ***Weber***	N	Y	Y	Y	Y	Y	Y
3 ***Frenzel***	N	Y	Y	Y	Y	Y	Y
4 Vento	Y	Y	Y	Y	Y	Y	Y
5 Sabo	Y	Y	Y	Y	Y	Y	Y
6 Sikorski	N	Y	Y	Y	Y	Y	Y
7 ***Stangeland***	N	Y	Y	Y	Y	Y	Y
8 Oberstar	Y	Y	Y	Y	Y	Y	Y
MISSISSIPPI							
1 Whitten	Y	Y	Y	Y	?	Y	Y
2 Espy	Y	Y	Y	Y	Y	Y	Y
3 Montgomery	Y	Y	Y	Y	Y	Y	Y
4 Parker	Y	Y	Y	Y	Y	Y	Y
5 Taylor	Y	Y	Y	Y	Y	Y	Y
MISSOURI							
1 Clay	N	Y	Y	Y	Y	Y	Y
2 ***Buechner***	N	Y	Y	Y	Y	Y	Y
3 Gephardt	Y	Y	Y	Y	Y	Y	Y
4 Skelton	Y	Y	Y	Y	Y	Y	Y
5 Wheat	Y	Y	Y	Y	Y	Y	Y
6 ***Coleman***	N	Y	Y	Y	Y	Y	Y
7 ***Hancock***	N	Y	Y	Y	Y	Y	Y
8 ***Emerson***	N	Y	Y	Y	Y	?	Y
9 Volkmer	Y	Y	Y	Y	Y	Y	Y
MONTANA							
1 Williams	Y	Y	Y	Y	Y	Y	Y
2 ***Marlenee***	N	Y	Y	Y	Y	Y	Y
NEBRASKA							
1 ***Bereuter***	N	Y	Y	Y	Y	Y	Y
2 Hoagland	Y	Y	Y	Y	Y	Y	Y
3 ***Smith***	N	Y	Y	Y	Y	Y	Y
NEVADA							
1 Bilbray	Y	?	Y	Y	Y	Y	Y
2 ***Vucanovich***	N	Y	Y	Y	Y	Y	Y
NEW HAMPSHIRE							
1 ***Smith***	N	Y	Y	Y	Y	Y	Y
2 ***Douglas***	N	?	?	Y	Y	Y	Y
NEW JERSEY							
1 Vacancy							
2 Hughes	?	?	?	?	?	?	?
3 Pallone	Y	Y	Y	Y	Y	Y	Y
4 ***Smith***	Y	?	Y	Y	Y	Y	Y
5 ***Roukema***	N	Y	Y	Y	Y	Y	Y
6 Dwyer	Y	Y	Y	Y	Y	Y	Y
7 ***Rinaldo***	Y	Y	Y	Y	Y	Y	Y
8 Roe	Y	Y	Y	Y	Y	Y	Y
9 Torricelli	Y	Y	Y	Y	Y	Y	Y
10 Payne	Y	Y	Y	Y	Y	Y	Y
11 ***Gallo***	N	Y	Y	Y	Y	Y	Y
12 ***Courter***	N	Y	Y	Y	Y	Y	Y
13 ***Saxton***	N	Y	Y	Y	Y	Y	Y
14 Guarini	Y	Y	Y	Y	?	Y	Y
NEW MEXICO							
1 ***Schiff***	Y	Y	Y	Y	Y	Y	Y
2 ***Skeen***	Y	Y	Y	Y	Y	Y	Y
3 Richardson	Y	Y	Y	Y	Y	Y	Y
NEW YORK							
1 Hochbrueckner	Y	Y	Y	Y	Y	Y	Y
2 Downey	Y	?	Y	Y	Y	Y	Y
3 Mrazek	Y	Y	Y	Y	Y	Y	Y
4 ***Lent***	Y	Y	Y	Y	Y	Y	Y
5 ***McGrath***	N	Y	Y	Y	Y	Y	Y
6 Flake	?	?	?	?	?	?	?
7 Ackerman	Y	Y	Y	Y	Y	Y	Y
8 Scheuer	Y	Y	Y	Y	Y	Y	Y
9 Manton	Y	Y	Y	Y	Y	Y	Y
10 Schumer	Y	Y	Y	Y	Y	Y	Y
11 Towns	?	Y	Y	Y	Y	Y	Y
12 Owens	?	Y	Y	Y	Y	Y	Y
13 Solarz	Y	Y	Y	Y	Y	Y	Y
14 Vacancy							
15 ***Green***	Y	Y	Y	Y	Y	Y	Y
16 Rangel	?	Y	Y	Y	Y	Y	Y
17 Weiss	?	Y	Y	Y	Y	Y	Y
18 Vacancy							
19 Engel	?	Y	Y	Y	Y	Y	Y
20 Lowey	Y	Y	Y	Y	Y	Y	Y
21 ***Fish***	Y	Y	Y	Y	Y	Y	Y
22 ***Gilman***	Y	Y	Y	Y	Y	Y	Y
23 McNulty	Y	Y	Y	Y	Y	Y	Y
24 ***Solomon***	N	Y	Y	Y	Y	Y	Y
25 ***Boehlert***	N	Y	Y	Y	Y	Y	Y
26 ***Martin***	N	Y	Y	Y	Y	Y	Y
27 ***Walsh***	N	Y	Y	Y	Y	Y	Y
28 McHugh	Y	Y	Y	Y	Y	Y	Y
29 ***Horton***	Y	Y	Y	Y	Y	Y	Y
30 Slaughter	Y	Y	Y	Y	Y	Y	Y
31 ***Paxon***	N	Y	Y	Y	Y	Y	Y
32 LaFalce	Y	Y	Y	Y	Y	Y	Y
33 Nowak	Y	Y	Y	Y	Y	Y	Y
34 ***Houghton***	Y	Y	Y	Y	Y	Y	Y
NORTH CAROLINA							
1 Jones	Y	Y	Y	Y	Y	Y	Y
2 Valentine	Y	Y	Y	Y	Y	Y	Y
3 Lancaster	Y	Y	Y	Y	Y	Y	Y
4 Price	Y	Y	Y	Y	Y	Y	Y
5 Neal	Y	Y	Y	Y	Y	Y	Y
6 ***Coble***	N	Y	Y	Y	Y	Y	Y
7 Rose	Y	Y	Y	Y	Y	Y	Y
8 Hefner	Y	Y	Y	Y	Y	Y	Y
9 ***McMillan***	N	Y	Y	Y	Y	Y	Y
10 ***Ballenger***	N	Y	Y	Y	Y	Y	Y
11 Clarke	Y	Y	Y	Y	Y	Y	Y
NORTH DAKOTA							
AL Dorgan	Y	Y	Y	Y	Y	Y	Y
OHIO							
1 Luken	Y	Y	Y	Y	Y	Y	Y
2 ***Gradison***	N	Y	Y	Y	Y	Y	Y
3 Hall	Y	Y	Y	Y	Y	Y	Y
4 ***Oxley***	N	Y	Y	Y	Y	Y	Y
5 ***Gillmor***	Y	Y	Y	Y	Y	Y	Y
6 ***McEwen***	Y	Y	Y	Y	Y	Y	Y
7 ***DeWine***	N	Y	Y	Y	Y	Y	Y
8 ***Lukens***	N	Y	Y	Y	Y	Y	Y
9 Kaptur	Y	Y	Y	Y	Y	Y	Y
10 ***Miller***	N	Y	Y	Y	Y	Y	Y
11 Eckart	Y	Y	Y	Y	Y	Y	Y
12 ***Kasich***	Y	Y	Y	Y	Y	Y	Y
13 Pease	Y	Y	Y	Y	Y	Y	Y
14 Sawyer	Y	Y	Y	Y	Y	Y	Y
15 ***Wylie***	Y	Y	Y	Y	Y	Y	Y
16 ***Regula***	N	Y	Y	Y	Y	Y	Y
17 Traficant	Y	Y	Y	Y	Y	Y	Y
18 Applegate	Y	Y	Y	Y	Y	Y	Y
19 Feighan	?	?	?	?	?	?	?
20 Oakar	?	?	?	?	?	?	?
21 Stokes	N	Y	Y	Y	Y	Y	Y
OKLAHOMA							
1 ***Inhofe***	N	Y	Y	Y	Y	Y	Y
2 Synar	Y	Y	Y	Y	Y	Y	Y
3 Watkins	?	Y	Y	Y	Y	Y	Y
4 McCurdy	Y	Y	Y	Y	Y	Y	Y
5 ***Edwards***	?	?	?	?	?	?	?
6 English	Y	Y	Y	Y	Y	Y	Y
OREGON							
1 AuCoin	Y	Y	Y	Y	Y	Y	Y
2 ***Smith, B.***	N	Y	Y	Y	Y	Y	Y
3 Wyden	Y	Y	Y	Y	Y	Y	Y
4 DeFazio	Y	Y	Y	Y	Y	Y	Y
5 ***Smith, D.***	N	Y	Y	Y	Y	Y	Y
PENNSYLVANIA							
1 Foglietta	?	Y	Y	Y	Y	Y	Y
2 Gray	?	Y	Y	Y	Y	Y	Y
3 Borski	Y	Y	Y	Y	Y	Y	Y
4 Kolter	Y	Y	Y	Y	Y	Y	Y
5 ***Schulze***	Y	Y	Y	Y	Y	Y	Y
6 Yatron	Y	Y	Y	Y	Y	Y	Y
7 ***Weldon***	N	Y	Y	Y	Y	Y	Y
8 Kostmayer	Y	Y	Y	Y	Y	Y	Y
9 ***Shuster***	N	Y	Y	Y	Y	Y	Y
10 ***McDade***	N	Y	Y	Y	Y	Y	?
11 Kanjorski	Y	Y	Y	Y	Y	Y	Y
12 Murtha	Y	Y	Y	Y	Y	Y	Y
13 ***Coughlin***	N	Y	Y	Y	Y	Y	Y
14 Coyne	Y	Y	Y	Y	Y	Y	Y
15 ***Ritter***	Y	Y	Y	Y	Y	Y	Y
16 ***Walker***	N	Y	Y	Y	Y	Y	Y
17 ***Gekas***	N	Y	+	Y	Y	Y	Y
18 Walgren	Y	Y	Y	Y	Y	Y	Y
19 ***Goodling***	N	Y	Y	Y	Y	Y	Y
20 Gaydos	Y	Y	Y	Y	Y	Y	Y
21 ***Ridge***	N	Y	Y	Y	Y	Y	Y
22 Murphy	N	Y	Y	Y	Y	Y	Y
23 ***Clinger***	N	Y	Y	Y	Y	Y	Y
RHODE ISLAND							
1 ***Machtley***	N	Y	Y	Y	Y	Y	Y
2 ***Schneider***	Y	Y	Y	Y	Y	Y	Y
SOUTH CAROLINA							
1 ***Ravenel***	Y	Y	Y	Y	Y	Y	Y
2 ***Spence***	N	Y	Y	Y	Y	Y	Y
3 Derrick	Y	Y	Y	Y	Y	Y	Y
4 Patterson	Y	Y	Y	Y	Y	Y	Y
5 Spratt	Y	Y	Y	Y	Y	Y	Y
6 Tallon	Y	Y	Y	Y	Y	Y	Y
SOUTH DAKOTA							
AL Johnson	Y	Y	Y	Y	Y	Y	Y
TENNESSEE							
1 ***Quillen***	Y	Y	Y	Y	Y	Y	Y
2 ***Duncan***	Y	Y	Y	Y	Y	Y	Y
3 Lloyd	?	Y	Y	Y	Y	Y	Y
4 Cooper	Y	Y	Y	Y	Y	Y	Y
5 Clement	Y	Y	Y	Y	Y	Y	Y
6 Gordon	Y	Y	Y	Y	Y	Y	Y
7 ***Sundquist***	N	Y	Y	Y	Y	Y	Y
8 Tanner	?	?	?	?	?	?	?
9 Ford	?	?	?	Y	Y	Y	Y
TEXAS							
1 Chapman	Y	Y	Y	Y	Y	Y	Y
2 Wilson	?	Y	Y	Y	Y	Y	Y
3 ***Bartlett***	Y	Y	Y	Y	Y	Y	Y
4 Hall	Y	Y	Y	Y	Y	Y	Y
5 Bryant	Y	Y	Y	Y	Y	Y	Y
6 ***Barton***	?	Y	Y	Y	Y	Y	Y
7 ***Archer***	Y	Y	Y	Y	Y	Y	Y
8 ***Fields***	?	?	?	?	?	?	?
9 Brooks	Y	Y	Y	Y	Y	Y	Y
10 Pickle	Y	Y	Y	Y	Y	Y	Y
11 Leath	Y	Y	Y	Y	Y	Y	Y
12 Geren	Y	Y	Y	Y	Y	Y	?
13 Sarpalius	Y	Y	Y	Y	Y	Y	Y
14 Laughlin	Y	Y	Y	Y	Y	Y	Y
15 de la Garza	Y	Y	Y	Y	Y	Y	Y
16 Coleman	Y	Y	Y	Y	Y	Y	Y
17 Stenholm	Y	Y	Y	Y	Y	Y	Y
18 Washington	Y	?	?	?	?	?	?
19 ***Combest***	Y	Y	Y	Y	Y	Y	Y
20 Gonzalez	Y	Y	Y	Y	Y	Y	Y
21 ***Smith***	?	Y	Y	Y	Y	Y	Y
22 ***DeLay***	N	Y	Y	Y	Y	Y	Y
23 Bustamante	Y	Y	Y	Y	Y	Y	Y
24 Frost	Y	Y	Y	Y	Y	Y	Y
25 Andrews	Y	Y	Y	Y	Y	Y	Y
26 ***Armey***	N	Y	Y	Y	Y	Y	Y
27 Ortiz	Y	Y	Y	Y	Y	Y	Y
UTAH							
1 ***Hansen***	N	Y	Y	Y	Y	Y	Y
2 Owens	Y	Y	Y	Y	Y	Y	Y
3 ***Nielson***	Y	Y	Y	Y	Y	Y	Y
VERMONT							
AL ***Smith***	Y	Y	Y	Y	Y	Y	Y
VIRGINIA							
1 ***Bateman***	Y	Y	Y	Y	Y	Y	Y
2 Pickett	Y	Y	Y	Y	Y	Y	Y
3 ***Bliley***	N	Y	Y	Y	Y	Y	Y
4 Sisisky	Y	Y	Y	Y	Y	Y	Y
5 Payne	Y	Y	Y	Y	Y	Y	Y
6 Olin	Y	Y	Y	Y	Y	Y	Y
7 ***Slaughter***	N	Y	Y	Y	Y	Y	Y
8 ***Parris***	N	Y	Y	Y	Y	?	Y
9 Boucher	?	Y	Y	Y	Y	Y	Y
10 ***Wolf***	N	Y	Y	Y	Y	Y	Y
WASHINGTON							
1 ***Miller***	N	Y	Y	Y	Y	Y	Y
2 Swift	Y	Y	Y	Y	Y	Y	Y
3 Unsoeld	Y	Y	Y	Y	Y	Y	Y
4 ***Morrison***	Y	Y	Y	Y	Y	Y	Y
5 Foley							
6 Dicks	Y	Y	Y	Y	Y	Y	Y
7 McDermott	Y	Y	Y	Y	Y	Y	Y
8 ***Chandler***	N	Y	Y	Y	Y	Y	Y
WEST VIRGINIA							
1 Mollohan	Y	Y	Y	Y	Y	Y	Y
2 Staggers	Y	Y	Y	Y	Y	Y	Y
3 Wise	Y	Y	Y	Y	Y	Y	Y
4 Rahall	Y	Y	Y	Y	Y	Y	Y
WISCONSIN							
1 Aspin	Y	Y	Y	Y	Y	Y	Y
2 Kastenmeier	Y	Y	Y	Y	Y	Y	Y
3 ***Gunderson***	Y	Y	Y	Y	Y	Y	Y
4 Kleczka	Y	Y	Y	Y	Y	Y	Y
5 Moody	Y	Y	Y	Y	Y	Y	Y
6 ***Petri***	N	Y	Y	Y	Y	Y	Y
7 Obey	Y	Y	Y	Y	Y	Y	Y
8 ***Roth***	N	Y	Y	Y	Y	Y	Y
9 ***Sensenbrenner***	N	Y	Y	Y	Y	Y	Y
WYOMING							
AL ***Thomas***	N	Y	Y	Y	Y	Y	Y

Southern states - Ala., Ark., Fla., Ga., Ky., La., Miss., N.C., Okla., S.C., Tenn., Texas, Va.
Omitted votes are quorum calls, which CQ does not include in its vote charts.

HOUSE VOTES 35, 36, 37, 38, 39, 40

35. Procedural Motion. Morella, R-Md., motion to approve the House Journal of Tuesday, March 20. Motion agreed to 282-124: R 50-118; D 232-6 (ND 156-6, SD 76-0), March 21, 1990.

36. H Res 346. Committee Funding/Passage. Adoption of the resolution to provide $56.8 million in 1990 for expenses for investigations and studies by House committees. Adopted 349-71: R 102-70; D 247-1 (ND 170-1, SD 77-0), March 21, 1990.

37. H Res 362. Flag Protection/Previous Question. Michel, R-Ill., motion to order the previous question (thus ending debate and the possibility of amendment) on the resolution to withdraw the House counsel's brief regarding Supreme Court review of the Anti-Flag Desecration Act. The brief urged that the court wait until its October 1990 term to consider the constitutionality of the statute. Motion rejected 203-204: R 166-0; D 37-204 (ND 12-152, SD 25-52), March 22, 1990.

38. H Res 362. Flag Protection/Refferral Motion. Gephardt, D-Mo., motion to refer to the House Judiciary Committee the resolution to withdraw the House counsel's brief for the Supreme Court's review of the Anti-Flag Desecration Act. The brief urged the court to wait until its October 1990 term to consider the constitutionality of the statute. Motion rejected 176-233: R 0-167; D 176-66 (ND 146-21, SD 30-45), March 22, 1990.

39. H Res 362. Flag Protection/Adoption. Adoption of the resolution to withdraw the House counsel's brief urging the Supreme Court to wait until its October 1990 term to review the constitutionality of the Anti-Flag Desecration Act. Adopted 309-101: R 167-0; D 142-101 (ND 76-90, SD 66-11), March 22, 1990.

40. HR 3581. Rural Economic Development Act/Passage. Passage of the bill to expand existing rural development programs, establish within the Agriculture Department a new Rural Development Administration to coordinate federal rural development programs and to create a new delivery system for rural development grants and loans, permitting the Agriculture secretary to transfer funds among existing accounts in response to economic development plans by states. Passed 360-45: R 123-42; D 237-3 (ND 161-1, SD 76-2), March 22, 1990. A "nay" was a vote supporting the president's position.

KEY

Y Voted for (yea).
Paired for.
\+ Announced for.
N Voted against (nay).
X Paired against.
\- Announced against.
P Voted "present."
C Voted "present" to avoid possible conflict of interest.
? Did not vote or otherwise make a position known.

Democrats ***Republicans***

	35	36	37	38	39	40
ALABAMA						
1 ***Callahan***	N	N	Y	N	Y	Y
2 ***Dickinson***	N	Y	Y	N	Y	Y
3 Browder	Y	Y	?	N	Y	Y
4 Bevill	Y	Y	Y	N	Y	Y
5 Flippo	?	?	?	?	?	?
6 Erdreich	Y	Y	Y	N	Y	Y
7 Harris	Y	Y	Y	N	Y	Y
ALASKA						
AL ***Young***	N	N	Y	N	Y	Y
ARIZONA						
1 ***Rhodes***	N	Y	Y	N	Y	Y
2 Udall	?	Y	N	Y	Y	Y
3 ***Stump***	?	#	#	X	#	X
4 ***Kyl***	N	N	Y	N	Y	N
5 ***Kolbe***	N	Y	Y	N	Y	Y
ARKANSAS						
1 Alexander	Y	Y	N	Y	Y	N
2 ***Robinson***	Y	N	Y	N	Y	Y
3 ***Hammerschmidt***	Y	Y	Y	N	Y	Y
4 Anthony	Y	Y	N	Y	Y	Y
CALIFORNIA						
1 Bosco	Y	Y	N	Y	Y	Y
2 ***Herger***	N	Y	Y	N	Y	Y
3 Matsui	Y	Y	N	Y	Y	Y
4 Fazio	Y	Y	N	Y	N	Y
5 Pelosi	Y	Y	N	Y	N	Y
6 Boxer	Y	Y	N	Y	N	Y
7 Miller	Y	Y	N	Y	N	Y
8 Dellums	Y	Y	N	Y	N	Y
9 Stark	Y	Y	N	Y	N	Y
10 Edwards	Y	Y	N	Y	N	Y
11 Lantos	Y	Y	N	Y	Y	Y
12 ***Campbell***	N	N	Y	N	Y	N
13 Mineta	Y	Y	N	Y	N	Y
14 ***Shumway***	?	N	Y	N	Y	N
15 Condit	Y	Y	N	Y	Y	Y
16 Panetta	Y	Y	N	Y	N	Y
17 ***Pashayan***	N	Y	Y	N	Y	Y
18 Lehman	Y	Y	N	Y	Y	Y
19 ***Lagomarsino***	N	Y	Y	N	Y	N
20 ***Thomas***	N	Y	Y	N	Y	Y
21 ***Gallegly***	N	Y	Y	N	Y	Y
22 ***Moorhead***	N	N	Y	N	Y	N
23 Beilenson	Y	Y	N	Y	N	Y
24 Waxman	Y	Y	N	?	N	Y
25 Roybal	Y	Y	N	Y	N	Y
26 Berman	Y	Y	N	Y	N	Y
27 Levine	Y	Y	N	Y	N	Y
28 Dixon	Y	Y	N	Y	N	Y
29 Hawkins	?	Y	N	Y	N	Y
30 Martinez	?	Y	N	Y	N	Y
31 Dymally	Y	Y	N	Y	N	Y
32 Anderson	Y	Y	N	Y	Y	Y
33 ***Dreier***	N	N	Y	N	Y	N
34 Torres	Y	Y	N	Y	Y	Y
35 ***Lewis***	N	Y	Y	N	Y	?
36 Brown	?	Y	X	#	?	?
37 ***McCandless***	N	N	Y	N	Y	N
38 ***Dornan***	N	N	?	N	Y	N
39 ***Dannemeyer***	N	N	Y	N	Y	N
40 ***Cox***	N	N	Y	N	Y	N
41 ***Lowery***	N	Y	Y	N	Y	Y
42 ***Rohrabacher***	N	N	Y	N	Y	N
43 ***Packard***	N	Y	Y	N	Y	Y
44 Bates	Y	Y	N	Y	N	N
45 ***Hunter***	N	N	Y	N	Y	Y
COLORADO						
1 Schroeder	N	Y	N	Y	N	Y
2 Skaggs	Y	Y	N	Y	N	Y
3 Campbell	Y	Y	Y	Y	Y	Y
4 ***Brown***	N	N	Y	N	Y	Y
5 ***Hefley***	N	N	Y	N	Y	N
6 ***Schaefer***	N	N	Y	N	Y	N
CONNECTICUT						
1 Kennelly	Y	Y	N	Y	Y	Y
2 Gejdenson	Y	Y	N	Y	N	Y
3 Morrison	Y	Y	?	?	?	?
4 ***Shays***	N	N	Y	N	Y	N
5 ***Rowland***	Y	Y	Y	N	Y	Y
6 ***Johnson***	Y	N	Y	N	Y	Y
DELAWARE						
AL Carper	Y	Y	N	Y	Y	Y
FLORIDA						
1 Hutto	Y	Y	Y	N	Y	Y
2 ***Grant***	Y	N	Y	N	Y	Y
3 Bennett	Y	Y	Y	N	Y	Y
4 ***James***	N	Y	Y	N	Y	Y
5 ***McCollum***	N	Y	Y	N	Y	N
6 ***Stearns***	N	N	Y	N	Y	N
7 Gibbons	?	?	N	Y	Y	Y
8 ***Young***	N	Y	Y	N	Y	Y
9 ***Bilirakis***	N	Y	Y	N	Y	Y
10 ***Ireland***	N	Y	?	?	?	?
11 Nelson	+	+	X	#	X	+
12 ***Lewis***	N	N	Y	N	Y	Y
13 ***Goss***	N	Y	Y	N	Y	N
14 Johnston	Y	Y	N	Y	Y	Y
15 ***Shaw***	Y	Y	Y	N	Y	Y
16 Smith	Y	Y	N	Y	N	Y
17 Lehman	Y	Y	N	Y	N	Y
18 ***Ros-Lehtinen***	N	Y	Y	N	Y	Y
19 Fascell	Y	Y	N	?	?	Y
GEORGIA						
1 Thomas	Y	Y	Y	N	Y	Y
2 Hatcher	Y	Y	N	N	Y	Y
3 Ray	Y	Y	N	N	Y	Y
4 Jones	Y	Y	N	N	Y	Y
5 Lewis	Y	Y	N	Y	N	Y
6 ***Gingrich***	N	Y	Y	N	Y	Y
7 Darden	Y	Y	Y	N	Y	Y
8 Rowland	Y	Y	Y	N	Y	Y
9 Jenkins	Y	Y	Y	N	Y	Y
10 Barnard	?	Y	Y	N	Y	Y
HAWAII						
1 ***Saiki***	Y	Y	Y	N	Y	Y
2 Akaka	Y	Y	N	Y	Y	Y
IDAHO						
1 ***Craig***	?	X	#	X	?	#
2 Stallings	Y	Y	N	N	Y	Y
ILLINOIS						
1 Hayes	Y	Y	N	Y	N	Y
2 Savage	?	?	?	?	?	?
3 Russo	Y	Y	N	N	Y	Y
4 Sangmeister	Y	Y	Y	N	Y	Y
5 Lipinski	Y	Y	N	N	Y	Y
6 ***Hyde***	N	Y	Y	N	Y	N
7 Collins	?	?	?	?	X	?
8 Rostenkowski	Y	Y	N	Y	Y	Y
9 Yates	?	Y	N	Y	N	Y
10 ***Porter***	N	N	Y	N	Y	N
11 Annunzio	Y	Y	Y	N	Y	Y
12 ***Crane***	N	N	Y	N	Y	N
13 ***Fawell***	Y	N	Y	N	Y	N
14 ***Hastert***	N	Y	Y	N	Y	Y
15 ***Madigan***	N	Y	Y	N	Y	Y
16 ***Martin***	N	N	Y	N	Y	Y
17 Evans	Y	Y	N	Y	N	Y
18 ***Michel***	N	Y	Y	N	Y	Y
19 Bruce	Y	Y	N	Y	Y	Y
20 Durbin	Y	Y	N	Y	N	Y
21 Costello	Y	Y	N	N	Y	Y
22 Poshard	Y	Y	N	N	Y	Y
INDIANA						
1 Visclosky	Y	Y	?	Y	N	Y
2 Sharp	Y	Y	N	N	#	Y
3 ***Hiler***	N	Y	Y	N	Y	Y

ND Northern Democrats SD Southern Democrats

	35	36	37	38	39	40
4 Long	Y	Y	N	N	Y	Y
5 Jontz	Y	Y	N	Y	N	Y
6 ***Burton***	N	N	Y	N	Y	N
7 ***Myers***	Y	Y	Y	N	Y	Y
8 McCloskey	Y	Y	N	Y	N	Y
9 Hamilton	Y	Y	N	Y	Y	Y
10 Jacobs	N	N	N	Y	Y	Y
IOWA						
1 ***Leach***	N	N	Y	N	Y	Y
2 ***Tauke***	N	N	Y	N	Y	Y
3 Nagle	Y	Y	N	Y	N	Y
4 Smith	Y	Y	N	Y	N	Y
5 ***Lightfoot***	N	Y	Y	N	Y	Y
6 ***Grandy***	N	Y	Y	N	Y	Y
KANSAS						
1 ***Roberts***	N	Y	Y	N	Y	Y
2 Slattery	Y	Y	N	Y	N	Y
3 ***Meyers***	Y	Y	Y	N	Y	Y
4 Glickman	Y	Y	N	Y	N	Y
5 ***Whittaker***	N	N	Y	N	Y	Y
KENTUCKY						
1 Hubbard	Y	Y	Y	N	Y	Y
2 Natcher	Y	Y	Y	Y	Y	Y
3 Mazzoli	Y	Y	N	Y	N	Y
4 ***Bunning***	N	N	Y	N	Y	N
5 ***Rogers***	N	Y	Y	N	Y	N
6 ***Hopkins***	N	N	Y	N	Y	N
7 Perkins	Y	Y	Y	N	Y	N
LOUISIANA						
1 ***Livingston***	Y	Y	Y	N	Y	N
2 Boggs	Y	Y	N	N	Y	Y
3 Tauzin	Y	Y	Y	N	Y	Y
4 ***McCrery***	N	Y	Y	N	Y	Y
5 Huckaby	Y	Y	Y	N	Y	Y
6 ***Baker***	N	Y	Y	N	Y	Y
7 Hayes	Y	Y	Y	N	Y	Y
8 ***Holloway***	N	N	Y	N	Y	Y
MAINE						
1 Brennan	Y	Y	N	Y	Y	Y
2 ***Snowe***	Y	Y	Y	N	Y	?
MARYLAND						
1 Dyson	Y	Y	Y	N	Y	Y
2 ***Bentley***	N	Y	Y	N	Y	Y
3 Cardin	Y	Y	N	Y	N	Y
4 McMillen	Y	Y	N	Y	N	Y
5 Hoyer	Y	Y	N	Y	N	Y
6 Byron	Y	Y	N	N	Y	Y
7 Mfume	Y	Y	N	Y	N	Y
8 ***Morella***	Y	Y	Y	N	Y	Y
MASSACHUSETTS						
1 ***Conte***	Y	N	Y	N	Y	Y
2 Neal	Y	Y	N	Y	Y	Y
3 Early	Y	Y	N	Y	N	Y
4 Frank	Y	Y	N	Y	Y	Y
5 Atkins	Y	Y	N	Y	N	Y
6 Mavroules	Y	Y	N	Y	Y	Y
7 Markey	Y	Y	N	Y	N	Y
8 Kennedy	Y	Y	N	Y	N	Y
9 Moakley	Y	Y	N	Y	Y	Y
10 Studds	Y	Y	N	Y	N	Y
11 Donnelly	Y	Y	N	Y	Y	Y
MICHIGAN						
1 Conyers	Y	Y	N	Y	Y	Y
2 ***Pursell***	?	N	Y	N	Y	N
3 Wolpe	Y	Y	N	Y	N	Y
4 ***Upton***	N	N	Y	N	Y	Y
5 ***Henry***	N	Y	Y	N	Y	N
6 Carr	Y	Y	N	Y	Y	Y
7 Kildee	Y	Y	N	Y	N	Y
8 Traxler	Y	Y	N	Y	N	?
9 ***Vander Jagt***	Y	Y	Y	N	Y	Y
10 ***Schuette***	N	N	Y	N	Y	#
11 ***Davis***	Y	Y	Y	N	Y	Y
12 Bonior	Y	Y	N	Y	N	Y
13 Crockett	Y	Y	N	Y	N	Y
14 Hertel	Y	Y	N	Y	Y	Y
15 Ford	?	Y	N	Y	N	Y
16 Dingell	?	Y	N	Y	N	Y
17 Levin	Y	Y	N	Y	Y	Y
18 ***Broomfield***	Y	Y	Y	N	Y	Y
MINNESOTA						
1 Penny	Y	Y	?	Y	Y	Y
2 ***Weber***	N	Y	Y	N	Y	Y
3 ***Frenzel***	N	Y	Y	N	Y	N
4 Vento	Y	Y	N	Y	N	Y

	35	36	37	38	39	40
5 Sabo	Y	Y	N	Y	N	Y
6 Sikorski	N	Y	N	Y	N	Y
7 ***Stangeland***	N	Y	Y	N	Y	Y
8 Oberstar	Y	Y	N	Y	N	Y
MISSISSIPPI						
1 Whitten	Y	Y	Y	Y	Y	Y
2 Espy	Y	Y	N	Y	Y	Y
3 Montgomery	Y	Y	Y	N	Y	Y
4 Parker	Y	Y	Y	N	Y	Y
5 Taylor	Y	Y	Y	N	Y	Y
MISSOURI						
1 Clay	N	Y	N	Y	N	Y
2 ***Buechner***	N	Y	Y	N	Y	Y
3 Gephardt	Y	Y	N	Y	N	Y
4 Skelton	Y	Y	Y	N	Y	Y
5 Wheat	Y	Y	N	Y	N	Y
6 ***Coleman***	N	Y	Y	N	Y	Y
7 ***Hancock***	N	N	Y	N	Y	N
8 ***Emerson***	Y	Y	Y	N	Y	Y
9 Volkmer	Y	Y	N	N	Y	Y
MONTANA						
1 Williams	?	Y	N	Y	N	Y
2 ***Marlenee***	N	Y	#	?	?	X
NEBRASKA						
1 ***Bereuter***	N	Y	Y	N	Y	Y
2 Hoagland	Y	Y	N	Y	Y	Y
3 ***Smith***	Y	Y	Y	N	Y	Y
NEVADA						
1 Bilbray	Y	Y	N	N	Y	Y
2 ***Vucanovich***	N	Y	Y	N	Y	Y
NEW HAMPSHIRE						
1 ***Smith***	N	N	Y	N	Y	N
2 ***Douglas***	N	N	Y	N	Y	N
NEW JERSEY						
1 Vacancy						
2 Hughes	Y	Y	Y	Y	Y	Y
3 Pallone	Y	Y	N	Y	Y	Y
4 ***Smith***	Y	Y	Y	N	Y	Y
5 ***Roukema***	N	Y	Y	N	Y	Y
6 Dwyer	Y	Y	N	Y	Y	?
7 ***Rinaldo***	Y	Y	Y	N	Y	Y
8 Roe	Y	Y	N	Y	Y	?
9 Torricelli	Y	Y	N	Y	N	Y
10 Payne	Y	Y	N	Y	N	Y
11 ***Gallo***	?	Y	Y	N	Y	Y
12 ***Courter***	N	N	Y	N	Y	Y
13 ***Saxton***	N	Y	Y	N	Y	Y
14 Guarini	Y	Y	N	Y	N	Y
NEW MEXICO						
1 ***Schiff***	N	Y	Y	N	Y	Y
2 ***Skeen***	Y	Y	?	N	Y	Y
3 Richardson	Y	Y	N	Y	Y	Y
NEW YORK						
1 Hochbrueckner	Y	Y	Y	N	Y	Y
2 Downey	Y	Y	N	Y	Y	Y
3 Mrazek	Y	Y	?	?	?	?
4 ***Lent***	Y	N	Y	N	Y	Y
5 ***McGrath***	N	Y	Y	N	Y	Y
6 Flake	Y	Y	N	Y	N	Y
7 Ackerman	Y	Y	N	Y	N	Y
8 Scheuer	Y	Y	N	Y	N	Y
9 Manton	Y	Y	N	Y	Y	Y
10 Schumer	Y	Y	N	Y	N	Y
11 Towns	Y	Y	N	Y	N	Y
12 Owens	Y	Y	N	Y	?	Y
13 Solarz	Y	Y	N	Y	N	Y
14 Vacancy						
15 ***Green***	Y	Y	Y	N	Y	Y
16 Rangel	Y	Y	N	Y	N	Y
17 Weiss	Y	Y	N	Y	N	Y
18 Vacancy						
19 Engel	Y	Y	N	Y	Y	Y
20 Lowey	Y	Y	N	Y	Y	Y
21 ***Fish***	Y	N	Y	N	Y	Y
22 ***Gilman***	Y	Y	Y	N	Y	Y
23 McNulty	Y	Y	N	Y	Y	Y
24 ***Solomon***	N	N	Y	N	Y	Y
25 ***Boehlert***	N	Y	Y	N	Y	Y
26 ***Martin***	N	Y	Y	N	Y	Y
27 ***Walsh***	Y	Y	Y	N	Y	Y
28 McHugh	Y	Y	N	Y	N	Y
29 ***Horton***	?	Y	Y	N	Y	Y
30 Slaughter	Y	Y	N	Y	Y	Y
31 ***Paxon***	N	N	Y	N	Y	Y

	35	36	37	38	39	40
32 LaFalce	Y	Y	N	Y	N	Y
33 Nowak	?	Y	N	Y	Y	Y
34 ***Houghton***	Y	N	Y	N	Y	Y
NORTH CAROLINA						
1 Jones	Y	Y	N	Y	Y	Y
2 Valentine	Y	Y	N	N	Y	Y
3 Lancaster	Y	Y	N	N	Y	Y
4 Price	Y	Y	N	Y	Y	Y
5 Neal	Y	Y	N	Y	Y	Y
6 ***Coble***	N	N	Y	N	Y	Y
7 Rose	Y	Y	N	Y	Y	Y
8 Hefner	Y	Y	N	N	Y	Y
9 ***McMillan***	N	N	Y	N	Y	Y
10 ***Ballenger***	N	N	Y	N	Y	N
11 Clarke	Y	Y	N	N	Y	Y
NORTH DAKOTA						
AL Dorgan	Y	Y	—	Y	N	Y
OHIO						
1 Luken	Y	Y	N	Y	Y	?
2 ***Gradison***	Y	Y	Y	N	Y	N
3 Hall	Y	Y	N	Y	Y	Y
4 ***Oxley***	Y	Y	Y	N	Y	Y
5 ***Gillmor***	Y	Y	Y	N	Y	Y
6 ***McEwen***	Y	Y	Y	N	Y	Y
7 ***DeWine***	N	N	Y	N	Y	Y
8 ***Lukens***	N	Y	Y	N	Y	Y
9 Kaptur	Y	Y	N	Y	Y	Y
10 ***Miller***	N	N	Y	N	Y	Y
11 Eckart	Y	Y	N	Y	Y	Y
12 ***Kasich***	Y	Y	Y	N	Y	N
13 Pease	Y	Y	N	Y	Y	Y
14 Sawyer	Y	Y	N	Y	Y	Y
15 ***Wylie***	Y	Y	Y	N	Y	Y
16 ***Regula***	N	Y	Y	N	Y	Y
17 Traficant	Y	Y	N	Y	Y	Y
18 Applegate	Y	Y	Y	N	Y	Y
19 Feighan	Y	Y	N	Y	Y	Y
20 Oakar	Y	Y	Y	Y	Y	Y
21 Stokes	N	Y	N	Y	N	Y
OKLAHOMA						
1 ***Inhofe***	N	N	Y	N	Y	Y
2 Synar	Y	Y	N	Y	N	Y
3 Watkins	Y	Y	Y	N	Y	Y
4 McCurdy	Y	Y	N	Y	N	Y
5 ***Edwards***	N	Y	Y	N	Y	Y
6 English	Y	Y	N	N	Y	Y
OREGON						
1 AuCoin	Y	Y	N	Y	N	Y
2 ***Smith, B.***	N	N	Y	N	Y	Y
3 Wyden	Y	Y	N	Y	N	Y
4 DeFazio	Y	Y	N	Y	N	Y
5 ***Smith, D.***	N	N	Y	N	Y	Y
PENNSYLVANIA						
1 Foglietta	Y	Y	N	Y	N	Y
2 Gray	Y	Y	N	Y	N	Y
3 Borski	Y	Y	N	Y	Y	Y
4 Kolter	Y	Y	N	Y	Y	?
5 ***Schulze***	?	?	?	?	?	Y
6 Yatron	Y	Y	N	N	Y	Y
7 ***Weldon***	N	Y	Y	N	Y	Y
8 Kostmayer	Y	Y	N	Y	N	Y
9 ***Shuster***	N	Y	Y	N	Y	Y
10 ***McDade***	N	Y	Y	N	Y	Y
11 Kanjorski	Y	Y	N	Y	Y	Y
12 Murtha	Y	Y	N	Y	Y	Y
13 ***Coughlin***	N	Y	Y	N	Y	Y
14 Coyne	Y	Y	N	Y	N	Y
15 ***Ritter***	Y	N	Y	N	Y	Y
16 ***Walker***	N	Y	Y	N	Y	N
17 ***Gekas***	N	Y	Y	N	Y	Y
18 Walgren	Y	Y	N	Y	Y	Y
19 ***Goodling***	N	Y	Y	N	Y	Y
20 Gaydos	Y	Y	N	N	Y	?
21 ***Ridge***	N	Y	Y	N	Y	Y
22 Murphy	N	Y	Y	N	Y	Y
23 ***Clinger***	Y	Y	Y	N	Y	Y
RHODE ISLAND						
1 ***Machtley***	N	N	Y	N	Y	Y
2 ***Schneider***	Y	Y	Y	N	Y	Y
SOUTH CAROLINA						
1 ***Ravenel***	Y	Y	Y	N	Y	Y
2 ***Spence***	N	Y	Y	N	Y	Y
3 Derrick	Y	Y	N	N	Y	Y
4 Patterson	Y	Y	N	N	Y	Y
5 Spratt	Y	Y	N	N	Y	Y
6 Tallon	Y	Y	N	N	Y	Y

	35	36	37	38	39	40
SOUTH DAKOTA						
AL Johnson	Y	Y	N	Y	Y	Y
TENNESSEE						
1 ***Quillen***	Y	Y	Y	N	?	?
2 ***Duncan***	Y	N	Y	N	Y	Y
3 Lloyd	Y	Y	Y	N	Y	Y
4 Cooper	Y	Y	N	?	Y	Y
5 Clement	Y	Y	N	Y	Y	Y
6 Gordon	Y	Y	N	Y	Y	Y
7 ***Sundquist***	N	Y	?	?	?	?
8 Tanner	?	?	?	?	?	?
9 Ford	Y	Y	N	?	?	?
TEXAS						
1 Chapman	Y	Y	N	N	Y	Y
2 Wilson	?	Y	N	N	Y	Y
3 ***Bartlett***	Y	Y	Y	N	Y	N
4 Hall	Y	Y	Y	N	Y	Y
5 Bryant	Y	Y	N	Y	N	Y
6 ***Barton***	N	N	Y	N	Y	Y
7 ***Archer***	Y	Y	Y	N	Y	N
8 ***Fields***	N	N	Y	N	Y	N
9 Brooks	?	?	X	Y	N	Y
10 Pickle	Y	Y	N	Y	Y	Y
11 Leath	Y	Y	N	?	Y	Y
12 Geren	Y	Y	Y	N	Y	Y
13 Sarpalius	Y	Y	Y	N	Y	Y
14 Laughlin	Y	Y	N	N	Y	Y
15 de la Garza	Y	Y	N	Y	Y	Y
16 Coleman	Y	Y	N	Y	N	Y
17 Stenholm	Y	Y	N	N	Y	Y
18 Washington	Y	Y	N	Y	N	Y
19 ***Combest***	Y	Y	Y	N	Y	Y
20 Gonzalez	Y	Y	N	Y	N	Y
21 ***Smith***	N	Y	Y	N	Y	Y
22 ***DeLay***	N	N	Y	N	Y	N
23 Bustamante	Y	?	?	?	?	?
24 Frost	Y	Y	N	Y	Y	Y
25 Andrews	Y	Y	N	Y	Y	Y
26 ***Armey***	N	N	Y	N	Y	N
27 Ortiz	Y	Y	N	Y	Y	Y
UTAH						
1 ***Hansen***	Y	N	Y	?	Y	Y
2 Owens	Y	Y	N	Y	N	Y
3 ***Nielson***	Y	N	Y	N	Y	Y
VERMONT						
AL ***Smith***	Y	Y	Y	N	Y	Y
VIRGINIA						
1 ***Bateman***	Y	Y	Y	N	Y	Y
2 Pickett	Y	Y	N	N	Y	Y
3 ***Bliley***	N	N	Y	N	Y	Y
4 Sisisky	Y	Y	N	N	Y	Y
5 Payne	Y	Y	N	N	Y	Y
6 Olin	Y	Y	N	N	Y	Y
7 ***Slaughter***	N	N	Y	N	Y	Y
8 ***Parris***	N	Y	Y	N	Y	Y
9 Boucher	Y	Y	N	Y	Y	Y
10 ***Wolf***	N	Y	Y	N	Y	Y
WASHINGTON						
1 ***Miller***	N	N	Y	N	Y	Y
2 Swift	Y	Y	N	Y	N	Y
3 Unsoeld	Y	Y	N	Y	N	Y
4 ***Morrison***	Y	Y	Y	N	Y	Y
5 Foley						
6 Dicks	Y	Y	N	Y	N	Y
7 McDermott	Y	Y	N	Y	N	Y
8 ***Chandler***	N	Y	Y	N	Y	Y
WEST VIRGINIA						
1 Mollohan	Y	Y	?	Y	N	Y
2 Staggers	Y	Y	N	Y	N	Y
3 Wise	Y	Y	N	Y	N	Y
4 Rahall	Y	Y	Y	N	Y	Y
WISCONSIN						
1 Aspin	Y	Y	N	Y	Y	Y
2 Kastenmeier	Y	Y	N	Y	N	Y
3 ***Gunderson***	Y	Y	Y	N	Y	Y
4 Kleczka	Y	Y	N	Y	Y	Y
5 Moody	Y	Y	N	Y	N	Y
6 ***Petri***	Y	N	Y	N	Y	Y
7 Obey	Y	Y	N	Y	N	Y
8 ***Roth***	N	N	?	?	?	?
9 ***Sensenbrenner***	N	N	Y	N	Y	N
WYOMING						
AL ***Thomas***	N	N	Y	N	Y	Y

Southern states - Ala., Ark., Fla., Ga., Ky., La., Miss., N.C., Okla., S.C., Tenn., Texas, Va.
Omitted votes are quorum calls, which CQ does not include in its vote charts.

HOUSE VOTES 42, 43, 44, 45, 46, 47

42. HR 4328. Fiscal 1991-92 Customs and Trade Authorization/Passage. Rostenkowski, D-Ill., motion to suspend the rules and pass the bill to authorize appropriations for fiscal 1991-92 for the customs and trade agencies. Motion agreed to 424-0: R 172-0; D 252-0 (ND 171-0, SD 81-0), March 27, 1990. A two-thirds majority of those present and voting (283 in this case) is required for passage under suspension of the rules.

43. HR 2209. Soybean Promotion Act/Passage. De la Garza, D-Texas, motion to suspend the rules and pass the bill to enable the producers of soybeans to develop, finance and carry out a nationally coordinated program for soybean promotion, research and consumer information. Motion agreed to 416-9: R 165-8; D 251-1 (ND 170-1, SD 81-0), March 27, 1990. A two-thirds majority of those present and voting (284 in this case) is required for passage under suspension of the rules.

44. HR 908. FERC Member Terms/Passage. Sharp, D-Ind., motion to suspend the rules and pass the bill to provide for five-year, staggered terms for members of the Federal Energy Regulatory Commission. Motion agreed to 426-0: R 173-0; D 253-0 (ND 172-0, SD 81-0), March 27, 1990. A two-thirds majority of those present and voting (284 in this case) is required for passage under suspension of the rules. Passage was subsequently vacated and S 388 was passed in lieu after being amended to contain the language of the House bill.

45. HR 3386. Garbage Backhauling/Passage. Anderson, D-Calif., motion to suspend the rules and pass the bill to require the Transportation Department to issue regulations governing the "backhauling" of food, solid waste and hazardous materials and to prohibit using cargo tanks in transporting food and hazardous materials by motor vehicles. Motion agreed to 410-15: R 157-15; D 253-0 (ND 172-0, SD 81-0), March 27, 1990. A two-thirds majority of those present and voting (284 in this case) is required for passage under suspension of the rules. A "nay" was a vote supporting the president's position.

46. H J Res 471. Corrections to Fiscal 1990 Commerce, Justice and State Appropriations/Adoption. Smith, D-Iowa, motion to suspend the rules and adopt the resolution to make technical changes and correct enrollment errors in the fiscal 1990 Commerce, Justice, State, the judiciary and related agencies appropriations and to make technical changes in the fiscal 1990-91 foreign relations authorization. The effect would have been to authorize more spending for the State Department and the U.S. Information Agency and to lift the overall cap on spending by the federal government. Motion rejected 276-149: R 87-85; D 189-64 (ND 139-33, SD 50-31), March 27, 1990. A two-thirds majority of those present and voting (284 in this case) is required for passage under suspension of the rules. A "yea" was a vote supporting the president's position.

47. Procedural Motion. McNulty, D-N.Y., motion to approve the House Journal of Tuesday, March 27. Motion agreed to 299-108: R 61-103; D 238-5 (ND 158-5, SD 80-0), March 28, 1990.

† Susan Molinari was sworn in March 27, 1990. The first vote for which she was eligible was 42.

† † Jose E. Serrano was sworn in March 28, 1990. The first vote for which he was eligible was 47.

KEY

- Y Voted for (yea).
- # Paired for.
- \+ Announced for.
- N Voted against (nay).
- X Paired against.
- \- Announced against.
- P Voted "present."
- C Voted "present" to avoid possible conflict of interest.
- ? Did not vote or otherwise make a position known.

Democrats ***Republicans***

	42	43	44	45	46	47
ALABAMA						
1 ***Callahan***	Y	Y	Y	Y	N	Y
2 ***Dickinson***	Y	Y	Y	Y	Y	N
3 Browder	Y	Y	Y	Y	N	Y
4 Bevill	Y	Y	Y	Y	N	Y
5 Flippo	Y	Y	Y	Y	N	Y
6 Erdreich	Y	Y	Y	Y	N	Y
7 Harris	Y	Y	Y	Y	N	Y
ALASKA						
AL ***Young***	Y	Y	Y	Y	N	?
ARIZONA						
1 ***Rhodes***	Y	Y	Y	Y	Y	N
2 Udall	Y	Y	Y	Y	Y	?
3 ***Stump***	?	?	?	X	?	?
4 ***Kyl***	Y	Y	Y	Y	N	N
5 ***Kolbe***	Y	Y	Y	Y	Y	N
ARKANSAS						
1 Alexander	Y	Y	Y	Y	Y	Y
2 ***Robinson***	Y	Y	Y	Y	Y	Y
3 ***Hammerschmidt***	Y	Y	Y	Y	N	Y
4 Anthony	Y	Y	Y	Y	Y	Y
CALIFORNIA						
1 Bosco	Y	Y	Y	Y	Y	Y
2 ***Herger***	Y	Y	Y	Y	N	N
3 Matsui	Y	Y	Y	Y	Y	Y
4 Fazio	Y	Y	Y	Y	Y	Y
5 Pelosi	Y	Y	Y	Y	Y	Y
6 Boxer	Y	Y	Y	Y	N	Y
7 Miller	Y	Y	Y	Y	N	Y
8 Dellums	Y	Y	Y	Y	N	Y
9 Stark	Y	Y	Y	Y	N	Y
10 Edwards	Y	Y	Y	Y	Y	Y
11 Lantos	Y	Y	Y	Y	Y	Y
12 ***Campbell***	Y	Y	Y	Y	N	N
13 Mineta	Y	Y	Y	Y	Y	Y
14 ***Shumway***	Y	Y	Y	N	N	Y
15 Condit	Y	Y	Y	Y	Y	Y
16 Panetta	Y	Y	Y	Y	N	Y
17 ***Pashayan***	Y	Y	Y	Y	N	P
18 Lehman	Y	Y	Y	Y	Y	Y
19 ***Lagomarsino***	Y	Y	Y	Y	Y	N
20 ***Thomas***	Y	Y	Y	Y	N	N
21 ***Gallegly***	Y	Y	Y	Y	Y	N
22 ***Moorhead***	Y	Y	Y	Y	N	N
23 Beilenson	Y	Y	Y	Y	Y	Y
24 Waxman	Y	Y	Y	Y	Y	Y
25 Roybal	Y	Y	Y	Y	Y	?
26 Berman	Y	Y	Y	Y	Y	Y
27 Levine	Y	Y	Y	Y	Y	Y
28 Dixon	Y	Y	Y	Y	Y	Y
29 Hawkins	Y	Y	Y	Y	Y	Y
30 Martinez	Y	Y	Y	Y	Y	Y
31 Dymally	Y	Y	Y	Y	Y	Y
32 Anderson	Y	Y	Y	Y	Y	Y
33 ***Dreier***	Y	Y	Y	Y	N	N
34 Torres	Y	Y	Y	Y	Y	Y
35 ***Lewis***	Y	Y	Y	Y	Y	N
36 Brown	Y	Y	Y	Y	Y	Y
37 ***McCandless***	Y	Y	Y	Y	N	N
38 ***Dornan***	Y	Y	Y	N	N	N
39 ***Dannemeyer***	Y	N	Y	N	N	N
40 ***Cox***	Y	N	Y	Y	N	N
41 ***Lowery***	Y	Y	Y	Y	Y	N
42 ***Rohrabacher***	Y	N	Y	Y	N	N
43 ***Packard***	Y	Y	Y	Y	N	Y
44 Bates	?	?	?	?	?	Y
45 ***Hunter***	Y	Y	Y	Y	N	N
COLORADO						
1 Schroeder	Y	Y	Y	Y	N	N
2 Skaggs	Y	Y	Y	Y	Y	Y
3 Campbell	Y	Y	Y	Y	Y	Y
4 ***Brown***	Y	Y	Y	Y	N	N
5 ***Hefley***	Y	N	Y	Y	N	N
6 ***Schaefer***	Y	Y	Y	Y	N	N
CONNECTICUT						
1 Kennelly	Y	Y	Y	Y	Y	Y
2 Gejdenson	Y	Y	Y	Y	Y	Y
3 Morrison	Y	Y	Y	Y	Y	Y
4 ***Shays***	Y	Y	Y	Y	N	N
5 ***Rowland***	Y	Y	Y	Y	N	Y
6 ***Johnson***	Y	Y	Y	Y	Y	Y
DELAWARE						
AL Carper	Y	Y	Y	Y	N	Y
FLORIDA						
1 Hutto	Y	Y	Y	Y	Y	Y
2 ***Grant***	Y	Y	Y	Y	Y	Y
3 Bennett	Y	Y	Y	Y	N	Y
4 ***James***	Y	Y	Y	Y	N	N
5 ***McCollum***	?	Y	Y	Y	Y	Y
6 ***Stearns***	Y	Y	Y	Y	N	N
7 Gibbons	Y	Y	Y	Y	Y	Y
8 ***Young***	Y	Y	Y	Y	Y	Y
9 ***Bilirakis***	?	?	?	#	?	N
10 ***Ireland***	Y	Y	Y	Y	Y	N
11 Nelson	Y	Y	Y	Y	Y	Y
12 ***Lewis***	Y	Y	Y	Y	N	N
13 ***Goss***	Y	Y	Y	Y	N	N
14 Johnston	Y	Y	Y	Y	Y	Y
15 ***Shaw***	Y	Y	Y	Y	Y	Y
16 Smith	Y	Y	Y	Y	Y	P
17 Lehman	Y	Y	Y	Y	Y	Y
18 ***Ros-Lehtinen***	Y	Y	Y	Y	Y	?
19 Fascell	Y	Y	Y	Y	Y	?
GEORGIA						
1 Thomas	Y	Y	Y	Y	N	Y
2 Hatcher	Y	Y	Y	Y	Y	Y
3 Ray	Y	Y	Y	Y	N	Y
4 Jones	Y	Y	Y	Y	Y	Y
5 Lewis	Y	Y	Y	Y	Y	Y
6 ***Gingrich***	Y	Y	Y	Y	Y	N
7 Darden	Y	Y	Y	Y	Y	Y
8 Rowland	Y	Y	Y	Y	Y	Y
9 Jenkins	Y	Y	Y	Y	N	Y
10 Barnard	?	?	?	#	?	Y
HAWAII						
1 ***Saiki***	Y	Y	Y	Y	Y	Y
2 Akaka	Y	Y	Y	Y	Y	Y
IDAHO						
1 ***Craig***	Y	Y	Y	Y	N	?
2 Stallings	Y	Y	Y	Y	N	Y
ILLINOIS						
1 Hayes	Y	Y	Y	Y	N	Y
2 Savage	Y	Y	Y	Y	N	Y
3 Russo	Y	Y	Y	Y	N	Y
4 Sangmeister	Y	Y	Y	Y	Y	Y
5 Lipinski	Y	Y	Y	Y	Y	Y
6 ***Hyde***	Y	Y	Y	Y	Y	N
7 Collins	Y	Y	Y	Y	N	Y
8 Rostenkowski	Y	Y	Y	Y	Y	Y
9 Yates	Y	Y	Y	Y	N	Y
10 ***Porter***	Y	Y	Y	Y	Y	N
11 Annunzio	Y	Y	Y	Y	Y	Y
12 ***Crane***	Y	N	Y	N	N	N
13 ***Fawell***	Y	Y	Y	Y	N	Y
14 ***Hastert***	Y	Y	Y	Y	N	N
15 ***Madigan***	Y	Y	Y	N	Y	N
16 ***Martin***	Y	Y	Y	Y	N	N
17 Evans	Y	Y	Y	Y	Y	Y
18 ***Michel***	Y	Y	Y	Y	Y	N
19 Bruce	Y	Y	Y	Y	Y	Y
20 Durbin	Y	Y	Y	Y	Y	?
21 Costello	Y	Y	Y	Y	N	Y
22 Poshard	Y	Y	Y	Y	N	Y
INDIANA						
1 Visclosky	Y	Y	Y	Y	Y	Y
2 Sharp	Y	Y	Y	Y	N	Y
3 ***Hiler***	Y	Y	Y	Y	?	N

ND Northern Democrats SD Southern Democrats

	42	43	44	45	46	47
4 Long	Y	Y	Y	Y	Y	Y
5 Jontz	Y	N	Y	Y	Y	Y
6 ***Burton***	Y	Y	Y	N	N	N
7 ***Myers***	Y	Y	Y	Y	Y	Y
8 McCloskey	Y	Y	Y	Y	Y	Y
9 Hamilton	Y	Y	Y	Y	Y	Y
10 Jacobs	Y	Y	Y	Y	N	N
IOWA						
1 ***Leach***	Y	Y	Y	?	Y	N
2 ***Tauke***	Y	Y	Y	Y	Y	N
3 Nagle	Y	Y	Y	Y	Y	Y
4 Smith	Y	Y	Y	Y	Y	Y
5 ***Lightfoot***	Y	Y	Y	Y	Y	N
6 ***Grandy***	Y	Y	Y	Y	N	Y
KANSAS						
1 ***Roberts***	Y	Y	Y	Y	N	N
2 Slattery	Y	Y	Y	Y	Y	Y
3 ***Meyers***	Y	Y	Y	Y	Y	Y
4 Glickman	Y	Y	Y	Y	N	Y
5 ***Whittaker***	Y	Y	Y	Y	Y	N
KENTUCKY						
1 Hubbard	Y	Y	Y	Y	N	Y
2 Natcher	Y	Y	Y	Y	Y	Y
3 Mazzoli	Y	Y	Y	Y	Y	Y
4 ***Bunning***	Y	Y	Y	Y	N	N
5 ***Rogers***	Y	Y	Y	Y	Y	N
6 ***Hopkins***	Y	Y	Y	Y	N	N
7 Perkins	Y	Y	Y	Y	Y	Y
LOUISIANA						
1 ***Livingston***	Y	Y	Y	Y	Y	Y
2 Boggs	Y	Y	Y	Y	Y	Y
3 Tauzin	Y	Y	Y	Y	N	Y
4 ***McCrery***	Y	Y	Y	Y	Y	Y
5 Huckaby	Y	Y	Y	Y	N	Y
6 ***Baker***	Y	Y	Y	Y	N	N
7 Hayes	Y	Y	Y	Y	N	Y
8 ***Holloway***	Y	N	Y	Y	N	N
MAINE						
1 Brennan	Y	Y	Y	Y	Y	Y
2 ***Snowe***	Y	Y	Y	Y	Y	N
MARYLAND						
1 Dyson	Y	Y	Y	Y	Y	Y
2 ***Bentley***	Y	Y	Y	Y	N	N
3 Cardin	Y	Y	Y	Y	Y	Y
4 McMillen	Y	Y	Y	Y	Y	Y
5 Hoyer	Y	Y	Y	Y	Y	Y
6 Byron	Y	Y	Y	Y	N	Y
7 Mfume	Y	Y	Y	Y	Y	Y
8 ***Morella***	Y	Y	Y	Y	Y	Y
MASSACHUSETTS						
1 ***Conte***	Y	Y	Y	Y	Y	Y
2 Neal	Y	Y	Y	Y	Y	Y
3 Early	Y	Y	Y	Y	Y	Y
4 Frank	Y	Y	Y	Y	Y	Y
5 Atkins	Y	Y	Y	Y	Y	?
6 Mavroules	Y	Y	Y	Y	Y	?
7 Markey	Y	Y	Y	Y	Y	Y
8 Kennedy	Y	Y	Y	Y	Y	Y
9 Moakley	Y	Y	Y	Y	Y	Y
10 Studds	Y	Y	Y	Y	Y	Y
11 Donnelly	Y	Y	Y	Y	N	Y
MICHIGAN						
1 Conyers	Y	Y	Y	Y	Y	Y
2 ***Pursell***	Y	Y	Y	Y	Y	Y
3 Wolpe	Y	Y	Y	Y	Y	Y
4 ***Upton***	Y	Y	Y	Y	N	N
5 ***Henry***	Y	Y	Y	Y	N	N
6 Carr	Y	Y	Y	Y	Y	Y
7 Kildee	Y	Y	Y	Y	Y	Y
8 Traxler	Y	Y	Y	Y	Y	Y
9 ***Vander Jagt***	Y	Y	Y	Y	Y	Y
10 ***Schuette***	Y	Y	Y	Y	N	N
11 ***Davis***	Y	Y	Y	Y	Y	Y
12 Bonior	Y	Y	Y	Y	Y	Y
13 Crockett	Y	Y	Y	Y	Y	Y
14 Hertel	Y	Y	Y	Y	Y	Y
15 Ford	Y	Y	Y	Y	Y	Y
16 Dingell	Y	Y	Y	Y	Y	?
17 Levin	Y	Y	Y	Y	Y	Y
18 ***Broomfield***	Y	Y	Y	Y	Y	Y
MINNESOTA						
1 Penny	Y	Y	Y	Y	N	Y
2 ***Weber***	Y	Y	Y	Y	N	N
3 ***Frenzel***	Y	Y	Y	N	N	N
4 Vento	Y	Y	Y	Y	Y	Y

	42	43	44	45	46	47
5 Sabo	Y	Y	Y	Y	Y	Y
6 Sikorski	Y	Y	Y	Y	Y	N
7 ***Stangeland***	Y	Y	Y	Y	Y	N
8 Oberstar	Y	Y	Y	Y	Y	Y
MISSISSIPPI						
1 Whitten	Y	Y	Y	Y	Y	Y
2 Espy	Y	Y	Y	Y	Y	Y
3 Montgomery	Y	Y	Y	Y	Y	Y
4 Parker	Y	Y	Y	Y	Y	Y
5 Taylor	Y	Y	Y	Y	N	Y
MISSOURI						
1 Clay	Y	Y	Y	Y	Y	N
2 ***Buechner***	Y	Y	Y	Y	N	N
3 Gephardt	Y	Y	Y	Y	Y	Y
4 Skelton	Y	Y	Y	Y	N	Y
5 Wheat	Y	Y	Y	Y	Y	Y
6 ***Coleman***	Y	Y	Y	Y	Y	N
7 ***Hancock***	Y	Y	Y	Y	N	N
8 ***Emerson***	Y	Y	Y	Y	N	?
9 Volkmer	Y	Y	Y	Y	Y	Y
MONTANA						
1 Williams	Y	Y	Y	Y	Y	?
2 ***Marlenee***	Y	Y	Y	N	N	?
NEBRASKA						
1 ***Bereuter***	Y	Y	Y	Y	Y	N
2 Hoagland	+	+	Y	Y	N	Y
3 ***Smith***	Y	Y	Y	Y	Y	?
NEVADA						
1 Bilbray	Y	Y	Y	Y	Y	Y
2 ***Vucanovich***	Y	Y	Y	Y	Y	?
NEW HAMPSHIRE						
1 ***Smith***	Y	N	Y	Y	N	N
2 ***Douglas***	Y	Y	Y	Y	N	N
NEW JERSEY						
1 Vacancy						
2 Hughes	Y	Y	Y	Y	Y	Y
3 Pallone	Y	Y	Y	Y	Y	Y
4 ***Smith***	Y	Y	Y	Y	Y	Y
5 ***Roukema***	Y	Y	Y	Y	Y	N
6 Dwyer	Y	Y	Y	Y	Y	Y
7 ***Rinaldo***	Y	Y	Y	Y	Y	Y
8 Roe	Y	Y	Y	Y	Y	Y
9 Torricelli	Y	Y	Y	Y	Y	Y
10 Payne	Y	Y	Y	Y	Y	Y
11 ***Gallo***	Y	Y	Y	Y	Y	N
12 ***Courter***	Y	Y	Y	Y	Y	N
13 ***Saxton***	Y	Y	Y	Y	Y	N
14 Guarini	Y	Y	Y	Y	Y	Y
NEW MEXICO						
1 ***Schiff***	Y	Y	Y	Y	Y	Y
2 ***Skeen***	Y	Y	Y	Y	Y	Y
3 Richardson	Y	Y	Y	Y	Y	Y
NEW YORK						
1 Hochbrueckner	Y	Y	Y	Y	Y	Y
2 Downey	Y	Y	Y	Y	N	Y
3 Mrazek	Y	Y	Y	Y	Y	Y
4 ***Lent***	Y	Y	Y	Y	Y	Y
5 ***McGrath***	Y	Y	Y	Y	Y	N
6 Flake	Y	Y	Y	Y	Y	Y
7 Ackerman	Y	Y	Y	Y	Y	Y
8 Scheuer	Y	Y	Y	Y	Y	Y
9 Manton	Y	Y	Y	Y	Y	Y
10 Schumer	Y	Y	Y	Y	Y	Y
11 Towns	Y	Y	Y	Y	Y	Y
12 Owens	Y	Y	Y	Y	Y	Y
13 Solarz	Y	Y	Y	Y	Y	Y
14 ***Molinari*** †	Y	Y	Y	Y	Y	Y
15 ***Green***	Y	Y	Y	Y	Y	Y
16 Rangel	Y	Y	Y	Y	Y	Y
17 Weiss	Y	Y	Y	Y	Y	Y
18 Serrano ††						
19 Engel	Y	Y	Y	Y	Y	Y
20 Lowey	Y	Y	Y	Y	Y	Y
21 ***Fish***	Y	Y	Y	Y	Y	Y
22 ***Gilman***	Y	Y	Y	Y	Y	Y
23 McNulty	Y	Y	Y	Y	Y	Y
24 ***Solomon***	Y	Y	Y	Y	N	N
25 ***Boehlert***	Y	Y	Y	Y	Y	N
26 ***Martin***	Y	Y	Y	Y	Y	N
27 ***Walsh***	Y	Y	Y	Y	Y	Y
28 McHugh	Y	Y	Y	Y	Y	Y
29 ***Horton***	Y	Y	Y	Y	Y	Y
30 Slaughter	Y	Y	Y	Y	Y	Y
31 ***Paxon***	Y	Y	Y	Y	N	N

	42	43	44	45	46	47
32 LaFalce	Y	Y	Y	Y	Y	Y
33 Nowak	Y	Y	Y	Y	Y	Y
34 ***Houghton***	Y	Y	Y	Y	Y	Y
NORTH CAROLINA						
1 Jones	Y	Y	Y	Y	Y	Y
2 Valentine	Y	Y	Y	Y	Y	Y
3 Lancaster	Y	Y	Y	Y	Y	Y
4 Price	Y	Y	Y	Y	Y	Y
5 Neal	Y	Y	Y	Y	N	Y
6 ***Coble***	Y	Y	Y	Y	N	N
7 Rose	Y	Y	Y	Y	Y	Y
8 Hefner	Y	Y	Y	Y	Y	Y
9 ***McMillan***	Y	Y	Y	Y	N	N
10 ***Ballenger***	Y	Y	Y	Y	Y	N
11 Clarke	Y	Y	Y	Y	Y	Y
NORTH DAKOTA						
AL Dorgan	Y	Y	Y	Y	N	Y
OHIO						
1 Luken	Y	Y	Y	Y	Y	Y
2 ***Gradison***	Y	Y	Y	Y	Y	Y
3 Hall	Y	Y	Y	Y	Y	Y
4 ***Oxley***	Y	Y	Y	Y	Y	Y
5 ***Gillmor***	Y	Y	Y	Y	Y	Y
6 ***McEwen***	Y	Y	Y	Y	N	Y
7 ***DeWine***	Y	Y	Y	Y	Y	N
8 ***Lukens***	Y	Y	Y	Y	Y	N
9 Kaptur	Y	Y	Y	Y	Y	Y
10 ***Miller***	Y	Y	Y	Y	N	N
11 Eckart	Y	Y	Y	Y	Y	Y
12 ***Kasich***	Y	Y	Y	Y	N	Y
13 Pease	Y	Y	Y	Y	Y	Y
14 Sawyer	Y	Y	Y	Y	Y	Y
15 ***Wylie***	Y	Y	Y	Y	Y	Y
16 ***Regula***	Y	Y	Y	Y	Y	N
17 Traficant	Y	Y	Y	Y	Y	Y
18 Applegate	Y	Y	Y	Y	Y	Y
19 Feighan	Y	Y	Y	Y	Y	Y
20 Oakar	Y	Y	Y	Y	Y	Y
21 Stokes	Y	Y	Y	Y	Y	?
OKLAHOMA						
1 ***Inhofe***	Y	Y	Y	Y	N	N
2 Synar	Y	Y	Y	Y	Y	Y
3 Watkins	Y	Y	Y	Y	N	Y
4 McCurdy	Y	Y	Y	Y	N	Y
5 ***Edwards***	Y	Y	Y	Y	Y	N
6 English	Y	Y	Y	Y	N	Y
OREGON						
1 AuCoin	Y	Y	Y	Y	Y	Y
2 ***Smith, B.***	Y	Y	Y	Y	N	N
3 Wyden	Y	Y	Y	Y	Y	Y
4 DeFazio	Y	Y	Y	Y	Y	Y
5 ***Smith, D.***	?	?	?	?	?	?
PENNSYLVANIA						
1 Foglietta	Y	Y	Y	Y	Y	Y
2 Gray	Y	Y	Y	Y	Y	Y
3 Borski	Y	Y	Y	Y	Y	Y
4 Kolter	Y	Y	Y	Y	N	Y
5 ***Schulze***	Y	Y	Y	Y	N	Y
6 Yatron	Y	Y	Y	Y	Y	Y
7 ***Weldon***	Y	Y	Y	Y	N	Y
8 Kostmayer	Y	Y	Y	Y	Y	Y
9 ***Shuster***	Y	Y	Y	Y	N	Y
10 ***McDade***	Y	Y	Y	Y	Y	N
11 Kanjorski	Y	Y	Y	Y	N	Y
12 Murtha	Y	Y	Y	Y	Y	Y
13 ***Coughlin***	Y	Y	Y	Y	Y	N
14 Coyne	Y	Y	Y	Y	Y	Y
15 ***Ritter***	Y	Y	Y	Y	N	Y
16 ***Walker***	Y	Y	Y	Y	N	N
17 ***Gekas***	Y	Y	Y	Y	N	N
18 Walgren	Y	Y	Y	Y	Y	Y
19 ***Goodling***	Y	Y	Y	Y	N	N
20 Gaydos	Y	Y	Y	Y	N	Y
21 ***Ridge***	Y	Y	Y	Y	N	N
22 Murphy	Y	Y	Y	Y	N	N
23 ***Clinger***	Y	Y	Y	Y	Y	N
RHODE ISLAND						
1 ***Machtley***	Y	Y	Y	Y	Y	N
2 ***Schneider***	Y	Y	Y	Y	Y	Y
SOUTH CAROLINA						
1 ***Ravenel***	Y	Y	Y	Y	N	Y
2 ***Spence***	Y	Y	Y	Y	N	Y
3 Derrick	Y	Y	Y	Y	Y	Y
4 Patterson	Y	Y	Y	Y	N	Y
5 Spratt	Y	Y	Y	Y	Y	Y
6 Tallon	Y	Y	Y	Y	N	Y

	42	43	44	45	46	47
SOUTH DAKOTA						
AL Johnson	Y	Y	Y	Y	N	Y
TENNESSEE						
1 ***Quillen***	Y	Y	Y	Y	Y	Y
2 ***Duncan***	Y	Y	Y	Y	N	Y
3 Lloyd	Y	Y	Y	Y	N	Y
4 Cooper	Y	Y	Y	Y	Y	Y
5 Clement	Y	Y	Y	Y	N	Y
6 Gordon	Y	Y	Y	Y	Y	Y
7 ***Sundquist***	Y	Y	Y	Y	N	N
8 Tanner	Y	Y	Y	Y	N	Y
9 Ford	?	?	?	?	?	?
TEXAS						
1 Chapman	Y	Y	Y	Y	Y	Y
2 Wilson	Y	Y	Y	Y	Y	Y
3 ***Bartlett***	Y	Y	Y	Y	N	Y
4 Hall	Y	Y	Y	Y	N	Y
5 Bryant	Y	Y	Y	Y	N	Y
6 ***Barton***	Y	Y	Y	Y	N	N
7 ***Archer***	Y	Y	Y	N	Y	Y
8 ***Fields***	Y	Y	Y	N	N	N
9 Brooks	Y	Y	Y	Y	Y	Y
10 Pickle	Y	Y	Y	Y	Y	Y
11 Leath	Y	Y	Y	Y	N	Y
12 Geren	Y	Y	Y	Y	Y	Y
13 Sarpalius	Y	Y	Y	Y	N	Y
14 Laughlin	Y	Y	Y	Y	Y	Y
15 de la Garza	Y	Y	Y	Y	Y	Y
16 Coleman	Y	Y	Y	Y	Y	Y
17 Stenholm	Y	Y	Y	Y	N	Y
18 Washington	Y	Y	Y	Y	Y	Y
19 ***Combest***	Y	Y	Y	N	N	Y
20 Gonzalez	Y	Y	Y	Y	Y	Y
21 ***Smith***	Y	Y	Y	Y	Y	N
22 ***DeLay***	Y	Y	Y	N	N	N
23 Bustamante	Y	Y	Y	Y	Y	Y
24 Frost	Y	Y	Y	Y	Y	Y
25 Andrews	Y	Y	Y	Y	Y	Y
26 ***Armey***	Y	N	Y	N	N	N
27 Ortiz	Y	Y	Y	Y	Y	Y
UTAH						
1 ***Hansen***	Y	Y	Y	N	N	?
2 Owens	Y	Y	Y	Y	Y	?
3 ***Nielson***	Y	Y	Y	N	N	Y
VERMONT						
AL ***Smith***	Y	Y	Y	Y	Y	Y
VIRGINIA						
1 ***Bateman***	Y	Y	Y	Y	Y	Y
2 Pickett	Y	Y	Y	Y	N	Y
3 ***Bliley***	Y	Y	Y	Y	N	N
4 Sisisky	Y	Y	Y	Y	N	Y
5 Payne	Y	Y	Y	Y	N	Y
6 Olin	Y	Y	Y	Y	Y	Y
7 ***Slaughter***	Y	Y	Y	Y	N	N
8 ***Parris***	Y	Y	Y	Y	Y	N
9 Boucher	Y	Y	Y	Y	Y	Y
10 ***Wolf***	Y	Y	Y	Y	Y	N
WASHINGTON						
1 ***Miller***	Y	Y	Y	Y	Y	N
2 Swift	Y	Y	Y	Y	Y	Y
3 Unsoeld	Y	Y	Y	Y	Y	Y
4 ***Morrison***	Y	Y	Y	Y	Y	Y
5 Foley						
6 Dicks	Y	Y	Y	Y	Y	Y
7 McDermott	Y	Y	Y	Y	Y	?
8 ***Chandler***	Y	Y	Y	Y	Y	N
WEST VIRGINIA						
1 Mollohan	Y	Y	Y	Y	Y	Y
2 Staggers	Y	Y	Y	Y	N	Y
3 Wise	Y	Y	Y	Y	Y	Y
4 Rahall	Y	Y	Y	Y	N	Y
WISCONSIN						
1 Aspin	Y	Y	Y	Y	Y	Y
2 Kastenmeier	Y	Y	Y	Y	N	Y
3 ***Gunderson***	Y	Y	Y	Y	N	Y
4 Kleczka	Y	Y	Y	Y	Y	Y
5 Moody	Y	Y	Y	Y	Y	Y
6 ***Petri***	Y	Y	Y	Y	Y	Y
7 Obey	Y	Y	Y	Y	Y	Y
8 ***Roth***	Y	Y	Y	Y	Y	Y
9 ***Sensenbrenner***	Y	Y	Y	Y	N	N
WYOMING						
AL ***Thomas***	Y	Y	Y	Y	N	?

Southern states - Ala., Ark., Fla., Ga., Ky., La., Miss., N.C., Okla., S.C., Tenn., Texas, Va.
Omitted votes are quorum calls, which CQ does not include in its vote charts.

HOUSE VOTES 49, 50, 51, 52, 53, 54

49. HR 3847. Department of Environmental Protection/Substitute. Hastert, R-Ill., substitute amendment to elevate the EPA to Cabinet level by eliminating virtually all other provisions of the bill, including those that would restrict the contracting out of "inherently governmental" functions; authorize a National Academy of Sciences study; and establish specific departmental offices, a Bureau of Environmental Statistics and a Commission on Improving Environmental Protection. Rejected 161-266: R 136-38; D 25-228 (ND 5-166, SD 20-62), March 28, 1990. A "yea" was a vote supporting the president's position.

50. HR 3847. Department of Environmental Protection/Passage. Passage of the bill to establish a Department of Environmental Protection; restrict the contracting out of "inherently governmental" functions; authorize a National Academy of Sciences study; and establish specific departmental offices, including an independent Bureau of Environmental Statistics and a Commission on Improving Environmental Protection. Passed 371-55: R 132-42; D 239-13 (ND 166-5, SD 73-8), March 28, 1990. A "nay" was a vote supporting the president's position.

51. HR 1463. National Capital Transportation Amendments/Drug Testing. Solomon, R-N.Y., amendment to establish a program that would require the Washington, D.C.-area Metropolitan Transit Authority to conduct random testing of its employees responsible for safety-sensitive mass transportation functions for the illegal use of controlled substances. Adopted 405-3: R 169-0; D 236-3 (ND 164-1, SD 72-2), March 28, 1990.

52. HR 1463. National Capital Transportation Amendments/Passage. Passage of the bill to amend the act to authorize an additional $2.2 billion over 11 years to finish the 103-mile Washington, D.C.-area Metrorail system. Local jurisdictions would have to continue to provide some of the funds, with the federal government paying 80 percent of the cost. Passed 260-150: R 46-123; D 214-27 (ND 150-16, SD 64-11), March 28, 1990. A "nay" was a vote supporting the president's position.

53. HR 3. Child Care/Previous Question. Frost, D-Texas, motion to order the previous question (thus ending debate and the possibility of amendment) on the rule (H Res 368) to provide for House floor consideration of the bill to expand programs providing federal aid for child care and increase the earned income tax credit for poor working families with children. Motion agreed to 251-171: R 0-170; D 251-1 (ND 172-1, SD 79-0), March 29, 1990.

54. HR 3. Child Care/Rule. Adoption of the rule (H Res 368) to provide for House floor consideration of the bill to expand programs providing federal aid for child care and increase the earned income tax credit for poor working families with children. Adopted 246-176: R 0-171; D 246-5 (ND 167-5, SD 79-0), March 29, 1990.

KEY

Y Voted for (yea).
Paired for.
+ Announced for.
N Voted against (nay).
X Paired against.
- Announced against.
P Voted "present."
C Voted "present" to avoid possible conflict of interest.
? Did not vote or otherwise make a position known.

Democrats ***Republicans***

	49	50	51	52	53	54
ALABAMA						
1 ***Callahan***	Y	N	?	?	N	N
2 ***Dickinson***	Y	Y	Y	N	N	N
3 Browder	N	Y	Y	Y	Y	Y
4 Bevill	Y	Y	Y	Y	Y	Y
5 Flippo	N	?	?	?	?	?
6 Erdreich	N	Y	Y	Y	Y	Y
7 Harris	N	Y	?	?	Y	Y
ALASKA						
AL ***Young***	Y	N	Y	N	N	N
ARIZONA						
1 ***Rhodes***	Y	Y	Y	N	N	N
2 Udall	N	N	Y	Y	Y	Y
3 ***Stump***	#	X	?	X	?	X
4 ***Kyl***	Y	Y	Y	N	N	N
5 ***Kolbe***	Y	Y	Y	Y	N	N
ARKANSAS						
1 Alexander	N	Y	Y	Y	Y	Y
2 ***Robinson***	Y	Y	Y	N	N	N
3 ***Hammerschmidt***	Y	Y	Y	N	N	N
4 Anthony	N	Y	Y	Y	Y	Y
CALIFORNIA						
1 Bosco	N	Y	Y	Y	Y	Y
2 ***Herger***	Y	N	Y	N	N	N
3 Matsui	N	Y	Y	Y	Y	Y
4 Fazio	N	Y	Y	Y	Y	Y
5 Pelosi	N	Y	Y	Y	Y	Y
6 Boxer	N	Y	Y	Y	Y	Y
7 Miller	N	Y	Y	Y	Y	Y
8 Dellums	N	Y	Y	Y	Y	Y
9 Stark	N	Y	Y	Y	Y	Y
10 Edwards	N	Y	Y	Y	Y	Y
11 Lantos	N	Y	Y	Y	Y	Y
12 ***Campbell***	N	Y	Y	N	N	N
13 Mineta	N	Y	Y	Y	Y	Y
14 ***Shumway***	Y	N	Y	N	N	N
15 Condit	N	Y	Y	Y	Y	Y
16 Panetta	N	Y	Y	Y	Y	Y
17 ***Pashayan***	Y	Y	Y	N	N	N
18 Lehman	N	Y	Y	Y	Y	Y
19 ***Lagomarsino***	Y	Y	Y	N	N	N
20 ***Thomas***	Y	Y	Y	N	N	N
21 ***Gallegly***	Y	Y	Y	N	N	N
22 ***Moorhead***	Y	N	Y	N	N	N
23 Beilenson	N	Y	Y	Y	Y	Y
24 Waxman	N	Y	?	?	Y	Y
25 Roybal	?	Y	Y	Y	Y	Y
26 Berman	N	Y	Y	Y	Y	Y
27 Levine	N	Y	Y	Y	Y	Y
28 Dixon	N	Y	Y	Y	Y	Y
29 Hawkins	?	?	Y	Y	Y	Y
30 Martinez	N	Y	Y	Y	Y	Y
31 Dymally	N	Y	?	Y	Y	Y
32 Anderson	N	Y	Y	Y	Y	Y
33 ***Dreier***	N	Y	Y	N	N	N
34 Torres	N	Y	Y	Y	Y	Y
35 ***Lewis***	Y	N	Y	N	N	N
36 Brown	N	Y	Y	Y	Y	Y
37 ***McCandless***	Y	N	Y	N	N	N
38 ***Dornan***	Y	Y	Y	N	N	N
39 ***Dannemeyer***	Y	N	Y	N	N	N
40 ***Cox***	Y	Y	Y	N	N	N
41 ***Lowery***	Y	Y	Y	N	N	N
42 ***Rohrabacher***	Y	N	Y	N	N	N
43 ***Packard***	Y	N	Y	N	N	N
44 Bates	N	?	Y	Y	Y	Y
45 ***Hunter***	Y	N	Y	N	N	N
COLORADO						
1 Schroeder	N	N	Y	Y	Y	Y
2 Skaggs	N	Y	Y	Y	Y	Y
3 Campbell	Y	Y	Y	Y	Y	Y
4 ***Brown***	N	Y	Y	N	N	N
5 ***Hefley***	Y	Y	Y	N	N	N
6 ***Schaefer***	N	Y	Y	Y	N	N
CONNECTICUT						
1 Kennelly	N	Y	Y	Y	Y	Y
2 Gejdenson	N	Y	Y	Y	Y	Y
3 Morrison	N	Y	Y	Y	Y	Y
4 ***Shays***	N	Y	Y	Y	N	N
5 ***Rowland***	N	Y	Y	Y	N	N
6 ***Johnson***	Y	Y	Y	Y	N	N
DELAWARE						
AL Carper	N	Y	Y	Y	Y	Y
FLORIDA						
1 Hutto	Y	Y	Y	Y	Y	Y
2 ***Grant***	Y	Y	Y	N	N	N
3 Bennett	N	Y	Y	N	Y	Y
4 ***James***	N	Y	Y	N	N	N
5 ***McCollum***	Y	Y	Y	N	N	N
6 ***Stearns***	Y	Y	Y	N	N	N
7 Gibbons	N	Y	Y	Y	Y	Y
8 ***Young***	Y	Y	Y	Y	N	N
9 ***Bilirakis***	N	Y	Y	N	N	N
10 ***Ireland***	Y	Y	Y	Y	N	N
11 Nelson	N	Y	Y	Y	Y	Y
12 ***Lewis***	Y	Y	Y	N	N	N
13 ***Goss***	Y	Y	Y	N	N	N
14 Johnston	N	Y	Y	Y	Y	Y
15 ***Shaw***	Y	Y	Y	N	N	N
16 Smith	N	Y	Y	Y	Y	Y
17 Lehman	N	Y	Y	Y	Y	Y
18 ***Ros-Lehtinen***	N	Y	Y	Y	N	N
19 Fascell	N	Y	?	?	Y	Y
GEORGIA						
1 Thomas	N	Y	Y	Y	Y	Y
2 Hatcher	N	Y	Y	Y	Y	Y
3 Ray	Y	N	Y	Y	Y	Y
4 Jones	Y	Y	Y	Y	Y	Y
5 Lewis	N	Y	Y	Y	Y	Y
6 ***Gingrich***	Y	Y	Y	N	N	N
7 Darden	N	Y	Y	Y	Y	Y
8 Rowland	N	Y	Y	Y	Y	Y
9 Jenkins	N	Y	?	?	?	?
10 Barnard	Y	Y	Y	N	Y	Y
HAWAII						
1 ***Saiki***	Y	Y	Y	Y	N	N
2 Akaka	N	Y	Y	Y	Y	Y
IDAHO						
1 ***Craig***	Y	N	Y	Y	N	N
2 Stallings	Y	Y	Y	Y	Y	#
ILLINOIS						
1 Hayes	N	Y	Y	Y	Y	Y
2 Savage	N	Y	Y	Y	?	Y
3 Russo	N	Y	Y	N	Y	N
4 Sangmeister	N	Y	Y	Y	Y	Y
5 Lipinski	N	Y	Y	N	Y	Y
6 ***Hyde***	Y	Y	Y	N	N	N
7 Collins	N	Y	Y	Y	Y	Y
8 Rostenkowski	N	Y	Y	N	Y	N
9 Yates	N	Y	Y	Y	Y	Y
10 ***Porter***	N	Y	Y	N	N	N
11 Annunzio	N	Y	Y	N	Y	Y
12 ***Crane***	Y	N	Y	N	?	?
13 ***Fawell***	Y	Y	Y	N	N	N
14 ***Hastert***	Y	Y	Y	N	N	N
15 ***Madigan***	Y	N	Y	Y	N	N
16 ***Martin***	N	Y	Y	N	N	N
17 Evans	N	Y	Y	Y	Y	Y
18 ***Michel***	Y	N	Y	Y	N	N
19 Bruce	N	Y	Y	Y	Y	Y
20 Durbin	N	Y	Y	Y	Y	Y
21 Costello	N	Y	Y	N	Y	Y
22 Poshard	N	Y	Y	N	Y	Y
INDIANA						
1 Visclosky	N	Y	Y	Y	Y	Y
2 Sharp	N	Y	Y	N	Y	N
3 ***Hiler***	Y	Y	Y	N	N	N

ND Northern Democrats SD Southern Democrats

	49	50	51	52	53	54
4 Long	N	Y	Y	Y	Y	Y
5 Jontz	N	Y	Y	Y	Y	Y
6 ***Burton***	Y	N	Y	N	N	N
7 ***Myers***	Y	N	Y	N	N	N
8 McCloskey	N	Y	Y	Y	Y	Y
9 Hamilton	N	Y	Y	N	Y	Y
10 Jacobs	N	N	Y	N	N	N
IOWA						
1 ***Leach***	N	Y	Y	N	N	N
2 ***Tauke***	N	Y	Y	N	N	N
3 Nagle	N	Y	Y	Y	Y	Y
4 Smith	N	Y	Y	Y	Y	Y
5 ***Lightfoot***	Y	N	Y	N	N	N
6 ***Grandy***	Y	N	Y	N	N	N
KANSAS						
1 ***Roberts***	Y	Y	Y	Y	N	N
2 Slattery	N	Y	Y	Y	Y	Y
3 ***Meyers***	Y	Y	Y	N	N	N
4 Glickman	N	Y	Y	Y	Y	Y
5 ***Whittaker***	Y	Y	Y	N	N	N
KENTUCKY						
1 Hubbard	N	Y	Y	N	Y	Y
2 Natcher	N	Y	Y	Y	Y	Y
3 Mazzoli	N	Y	Y	Y	Y	Y
4 ***Bunning***	Y	Y	Y	N	N	N
5 ***Rogers***	Y	Y	Y	N	N	N
6 ***Hopkins***	Y	Y	Y	N	N	N
7 Perkins	N	Y	N	Y	Y	Y
LOUISIANA						
1 ***Livingston***	Y	N	Y	N	N	N
2 Boggs	N	Y	Y	Y	Y	Y
3 Tauzin	N	Y	Y	Y	Y	Y
4 ***McCrery***	Y	N	Y	Y	?	N
5 Huckaby	N	Y	Y	N	Y	Y
6 ***Baker***	Y	N	Y	Y	N	N
7 Hayes	Y	N	Y	Y	Y	Y
8 ***Holloway***	Y	N	Y	N	N	N
MAINE						
1 Brennan	N	Y	Y	Y	Y	Y
2 ***Snowe***	N	Y	Y	N	N	N
MARYLAND						
1 Dyson	N	Y	Y	Y	Y	Y
2 ***Bentley***	Y	Y	Y	Y	N	N
3 Cardin	N	Y	Y	Y	Y	Y
4 McMillen	N	Y	Y	Y	Y	Y
5 Hoyer	N	Y	Y	Y	Y	Y
6 Byron	Y	Y	Y	Y	Y	Y
7 Mfume	N	Y	Y	Y	Y	Y
8 ***Morella***	N	Y	Y	Y	N	N
MASSACHUSETTS						
1 ***Conte***	N	Y	Y	Y	N	N
2 Neal	N	Y	Y	Y	Y	Y
3 Early	N	N	Y	N	Y	Y
4 Frank	N	Y	Y	Y	Y	Y
5 Atkins	N	Y	Y	Y	Y	Y
6 Mavroules	N	Y	Y	Y	Y	Y
7 Markey	N	Y	Y	Y	Y	Y
8 Kennedy	N	Y	Y	Y	Y	Y
9 Moakley	N	Y	Y	Y	Y	Y
10 Studds	N	Y	Y	Y	Y	Y
11 Donnelly	N	Y	Y	Y	Y	?
MICHIGAN						
1 Conyers	N	Y	Y	Y	Y	Y
2 ***Pursell***	Y	Y	Y	N	N	N
3 Wolpe	N	Y	Y	Y	Y	Y
4 ***Upton***	Y	Y	Y	N	N	N
5 ***Henry***	N	Y	Y	N	N	N
6 Carr	N	Y	Y	N	Y	Y
7 Kildee	N	Y	Y	Y	Y	Y
8 Traxler	N	Y	Y	Y	Y	Y
9 ***Vander Jagt***	Y	Y	Y	N	N	N
10 ***Schuette***	N	Y	Y	N	N	N
11 ***Davis***	Y	Y	Y	Y	N	N
12 Bonior	N	Y	Y	Y	Y	Y
13 Crockett	N	Y	?	?	Y	Y
14 Hertel	N	Y	Y	Y	Y	Y
15 Ford	N	Y	Y	Y	Y	Y
16 Dingell	N	Y	N	Y	Y	Y
17 Levin	N	Y	Y	Y	Y	Y
18 ***Broomfield***	Y	Y	Y	N	N	N
MINNESOTA						
1 Penny	N	Y	Y	N	Y	Y
2 ***Weber***	N	Y	Y	Y	N	N
3 ***Frenzel***	Y	Y	Y	N	N	N
4 Vento	N	Y	Y	Y	Y	Y

	49	50	51	52	53	54
5 Sabo	N	Y	Y	Y	Y	Y
6 Sikorski	N	Y	Y	Y	Y	Y
7 ***Stangeland***	Y	Y	Y	Y	N	N
8 Oberstar	N	Y	Y	Y	Y	Y
MISSISSIPPI						
1 Whitten	N	Y	?	?	Y	Y
2 Espy	N	Y	Y	Y	Y	Y
3 Montgomery	Y	N	Y	Y	Y	Y
4 Parker	Y	N	Y	Y	Y	Y
5 Taylor	N	Y	Y	Y	Y	Y
MISSOURI						
1 Clay	N	Y	Y	Y	Y	Y
2 ***Buechner***	N	Y	Y	N	N	N
3 Gephardt	N	Y	Y	Y	Y	Y
4 Skelton	N	Y	Y	Y	Y	Y
5 Wheat	N	Y	Y	Y	Y	Y
6 ***Coleman***	Y	Y	Y	Y	N	N
7 ***Hancock***	Y	N	Y	N	N	N
8 ***Emerson***	Y	Y	Y	N	N	N
9 Volkmer	Y	Y	Y	N	Y	Y
MONTANA						
1 Williams	N	Y	Y	N	Y	N
2 ***Marlenee***	Y	N	Y	N	N	N
NEBRASKA						
1 ***Bereuter***	Y	Y	Y	N	N	N
2 Hoagland	N	Y	Y	Y	Y	Y
3 ***Smith***	Y	Y	Y	N	N	N
NEVADA						
1 Bilbray	N	Y	Y	Y	Y	Y
2 ***Vucanovich***	Y	N	Y	N	N	N
NEW HAMPSHIRE						
1 ***Smith***	N	Y	Y	N	N	N
2 ***Douglas***	N	Y	Y	N	N	N
NEW JERSEY						
1 Vacancy						
2 Hughes	N	Y	Y	Y	Y	Y
3 Pallone	N	Y	Y	Y	Y	Y
4 ***Smith***	N	Y	?	?	N	N
5 ***Roukema***	N	Y	Y	Y	N	N
6 Dwyer	N	Y	?	?	Y	Y
7 ***Rinaldo***	N	Y	Y	Y	?	?
8 Roe	N	Y	Y	Y	Y	Y
9 Torricelli	N	Y	Y	Y	Y	Y
10 Payne	N	Y	Y	Y	Y	Y
11 ***Gallo***	N	Y	Y	Y	N	N
12 ***Courter***	Y	Y	Y	Y	N	N
13 ***Saxton***	N	Y	Y	Y	N	N
14 Guarini	N	Y	Y	N	Y	Y
NEW MEXICO						
1 ***Schiff***	Y	Y	Y	N	N	N
2 ***Skeen***	Y	Y	Y	N	N	N
3 Richardson	N	Y	Y	Y	Y	Y
NEW YORK						
1 Hochbrueckner	N	Y	Y	Y	Y	Y
2 Downey	N	Y	Y	Y	Y	Y
3 Mrazek	N	Y	Y	Y	Y	Y
4 ***Lent***	Y	Y	?	?	?	?
5 ***McGrath***	Y	Y	Y	Y	N	N
6 Flake	N	Y	Y	Y	Y	Y
7 Ackerman	N	Y	Y	Y	Y	Y
8 Scheuer	N	Y	Y	Y	Y	Y
9 Manton	N	Y	Y	Y	Y	Y
10 Schumer	N	Y	Y	Y	Y	Y
11 Towns	N	Y	Y	Y	Y	Y
12 Owens	N	Y	Y	Y	Y	Y
13 Solarz	N	Y	Y	Y	Y	Y
14 ***Molinari***	N	Y	Y	Y	N	N
15 ***Green***	N	Y	Y	Y	N	N
16 Rangel	N	Y	Y	Y	Y	Y
17 Weiss	N	Y	Y	Y	Y	Y
18 Serrano	N	Y	Y	Y	Y	Y
19 Engel	N	Y	Y	Y	Y	Y
20 Lowey	N	Y	Y	Y	Y	Y
21 ***Fish***	Y	Y	Y	N	N	N
22 ***Gilman***	N	Y	Y	N	N	N
23 McNulty	N	Y	Y	Y	Y	Y
24 ***Solomon***	Y	Y	Y	N	N	N
25 ***Boehlert***	N	Y	Y	Y	N	N
26 ***Martin***	Y	Y	Y	Y	N	N
27 ***Walsh***	N	Y	Y	Y	N	N
28 McHugh	N	Y	Y	Y	Y	Y
29 ***Horton***	Y	Y	Y	Y	N	N
30 Slaughter	N	Y	Y	Y	Y	Y
31 ***Paxon***	Y	Y	Y	N	N	N

	49	50	51	52	53	54
32 LaFalce	N	Y	Y	Y	Y	Y
33 Nowak	N	Y	Y	Y	Y	Y
34 ***Houghton***	Y	Y	Y	N	N	N
NORTH CAROLINA						
1 Jones	N	Y	Y	Y	Y	Y
2 Valentine	N	Y	Y	N	Y	Y
3 Lancaster	N	Y	Y	Y	Y	Y
4 Price	N	Y	Y	Y	Y	Y
5 Neal	N	Y	Y	N	Y	Y
6 ***Coble***	Y	Y	Y	N	N	N
7 Rose	N	Y	?	?	Y	Y
8 Hefner	N	Y	Y	N	Y	Y
9 ***McMillan***	Y	Y	Y	N	N	N
10 ***Ballenger***	Y	Y	Y	N	N	N
11 Clarke	N	Y	Y	Y	Y	Y
NORTH DAKOTA						
AL Dorgan	N	Y	Y	Y	Y	Y
OHIO						
1 Luken	N	Y	Y	Y	Y	Y
2 ***Gradison***	Y	Y	Y	N	N	N
3 Hall	N	Y	?	?	Y	Y
4 ***Oxley***	Y	Y	Y	Y	N	N
5 ***Gillmor***	N	Y	Y	N	N	N
6 ***McEwen***	Y	N	Y	N	N	N
7 ***DeWine***	Y	Y	Y	N	N	N
8 ***Lukens***	Y	Y	Y	N	N	N
9 Kaptur	N	Y	Y	Y	Y	Y
10 ***Miller***	Y	N	Y	N	N	N
11 Eckart	N	Y	Y	Y	Y	Y
12 ***Kasich***	Y	Y	Y	N	N	N
13 Pease	N	Y	Y	Y	Y	Y
14 Sawyer	N	Y	Y	Y	Y	Y
15 ***Wylie***	Y	Y	Y	N	N	N
16 ***Regula***	Y	Y	Y	N	N	N
17 Traficant	N	Y	Y	Y	Y	Y
18 Applegate	N	N	Y	Y	Y	Y
19 Feighan	N	Y	Y	Y	Y	Y
20 Oakar	N	Y	Y	Y	Y	Y
21 Stokes	N	Y	Y	Y	Y	Y
OKLAHOMA						
1 ***Inhofe***	Y	Y	Y	N	N	N
2 Synar	N	Y	Y	Y	Y	Y
3 Watkins	N	Y	Y	N	Y	Y
4 McCurdy	N	Y	Y	Y	Y	Y
5 ***Edwards***	Y	N	Y	N	N	N
6 English	N	Y	Y	N	Y	Y
OREGON						
1 AuCoin	N	Y	Y	Y	Y	Y
2 ***Smith, B.***	Y	N	Y	N	N	N
3 Wyden	N	Y	Y	Y	Y	Y
4 DeFazio	N	Y	Y	Y	Y	Y
5 ***Smith, D.***	?	?	?	?	?	?
PENNSYLVANIA						
1 Foglietta	N	Y	Y	Y	Y	Y
2 Gray	N	Y	Y	Y	Y	Y
3 Borski	N	Y	Y	Y	Y	Y
4 Kolter	N	Y	Y	Y	Y	Y
5 ***Schulze***	Y	Y	Y	N	N	N
6 Yatron	N	Y	Y	Y	Y	Y
7 ***Weldon***	N	Y	?	?	N	N
8 Kostmayer	N	Y	Y	Y	Y	Y
9 ***Shuster***	Y	N	Y	N	N	N
10 ***McDade***	Y	Y	Y	Y	N	N
11 Kanjorski	N	Y	Y	Y	Y	Y
12 Murtha	N	Y	Y	Y	Y	Y
13 ***Coughlin***	Y	Y	Y	N	N	N
14 Coyne	N	Y	?	?	Y	Y
15 ***Ritter***	Y	Y	Y	N	N	N
16 ***Walker***	Y	N	Y	N	N	N
17 ***Gekas***	Y	N	Y	N	N	N
18 Walgren	N	Y	Y	Y	Y	Y
19 ***Goodling***	Y	Y	Y	N	N	N
20 Gaydos	N	Y	Y	Y	Y	Y
21 ***Ridge***	Y	Y	Y	Y	N	N
22 Murphy	N	Y	Y	Y	Y	Y
23 ***Clinger***	Y	Y	Y	N	N	N
RHODE ISLAND						
1 ***Machtley***	N	Y	Y	N	N	N
2 ***Schneider***	N	Y	Y	Y	N	N
SOUTH CAROLINA						
1 ***Ravenel***	Y	Y	Y	Y	N	N
2 ***Spence***	Y	Y	Y	N	N	N
3 Derrick	N	Y	Y	Y	Y	Y
4 Patterson	Y	Y	Y	N	Y	Y
5 Spratt	N	Y	Y	Y	Y	Y
6 Tallon	Y	Y	Y	N	Y	Y

	49	50	51	52	53	54
SOUTH DAKOTA						
AL Johnson	N	Y	Y	Y	Y	Y
TENNESSEE						
1 ***Quillen***	Y	N	Y	N	N	N
2 ***Duncan***	Y	N	Y	N	N	N
3 Lloyd	N	Y	Y	Y	Y	Y
4 Cooper	N	Y	Y	Y	Y	Y
5 Clement	N	Y	Y	Y	Y	Y
6 Gordon	N	Y	Y	Y	Y	Y
7 ***Sundquist***	Y	N	Y	N	N	N
8 Tanner	N	Y	Y	Y	Y	Y
9 Ford	X	#	?	?	?	?
TEXAS						
1 Chapman	Y	Y	Y	Y	Y	Y
2 Wilson	N	Y	?	Y	Y	Y
3 ***Bartlett***	Y	Y	Y	N	N	N
4 Hall	Y	N	Y	Y	Y	Y
5 Bryant	N	Y	Y	Y	Y	Y
6 ***Barton***	Y	N	Y	N	N	N
7 ***Archer***	Y	Y	Y	N	N	N
8 ***Fields***	Y	Y	Y	N	N	N
9 Brooks	N	Y	Y	Y	Y	Y
10 Pickle	N	Y	Y	Y	Y	Y
11 Leath	Y	Y	Y	Y	Y	Y
12 Geren	Y	Y	Y	Y	Y	Y
13 Sarpalius	Y	Y	Y	Y	Y	Y
14 Laughlin	Y	N	Y	Y	?	?
15 de la Garza	N	Y	Y	Y	Y	Y
16 Coleman	N	Y	?	?	Y	Y
17 Stenholm	Y	N	Y	Y	Y	Y
18 Washington	N	Y	N	Y	Y	Y
19 ***Combest***	Y	N	Y	N	N	N
20 Gonzalez	N	Y	Y	Y	Y	Y
21 ***Smith***	Y	Y	Y	N	N	N
22 ***DeLay***	Y	N	Y	N	N	N
23 Bustamante	N	Y	Y	Y	Y	Y
24 Frost	N	Y	Y	Y	Y	Y
25 Andrews	N	Y	Y	Y	Y	Y
26 ***Armey***	Y	N	Y	N	N	N
27 Ortiz	N	Y	Y	Y	Y	Y
UTAH						
1 ***Hansen***	Y	N	Y	N	N	N
2 Owens	N	Y	Y	Y	Y	Y
3 ***Nielson***	Y	N	Y	N	N	N
VERMONT						
AL ***Smith***	N	Y	Y	Y	N	N
VIRGINIA						
1 ***Bateman***	Y	Y	Y	Y	N	N
2 Pickett	Y	Y	Y	Y	Y	Y
3 ***Bliley***	Y	Y	Y	Y	N	N
4 Sisisky	Y	Y	Y	Y	Y	Y
5 Payne	N	Y	Y	Y	Y	Y
6 Olin	Y	N	Y	Y	Y	Y
7 ***Slaughter***	Y	Y	Y	Y	N	N
8 ***Parris***	Y	Y	Y	Y	N	N
9 Boucher	N	Y	Y	Y	Y	Y
10 ***Wolf***	Y	Y	Y	Y	N	N
WASHINGTON						
1 ***Miller***	N	Y	+	−	N	N
2 Swift	N	Y	Y	Y	Y	Y
3 Unsoeld	N	Y	Y	Y	Y	Y
4 ***Morrison***	Y	Y	Y	Y	N	N
5 Foley						
6 Dicks	N	Y	Y	Y	Y	Y
7 McDermott	N	Y	Y	Y	Y	Y
8 ***Chandler***	Y	Y	Y	N	N	N
WEST VIRGINIA						
1 Mollohan	Y	Y	Y	Y	Y	Y
2 Staggers	?	?	?	?	Y	Y
3 Wise	N	Y	Y	Y	Y	Y
4 Rahall	N	Y	Y	N	Y	Y
WISCONSIN						
1 Aspin	N	Y	?	?	Y	Y
2 Kastenmeier	N	Y	Y	Y	Y	Y
3 ***Gunderson***	Y	Y	Y	N	N	N
4 Kleczka	N	Y	Y	Y	Y	Y
5 Moody	N	Y	?	#	Y	Y
6 ***Petri***	Y	Y	Y	N	N	N
7 Obey	N	Y	Y	Y	Y	Y
8 ***Roth***	Y	Y	Y	N	N	N
9 ***Sensenbrenner***	Y	Y	Y	N	N	N
WYOMING						
AL ***Thomas***	Y	Y	Y	N	N	N

Southern states - Ala., Ark., Fla., Ga., Ky., La., Miss., N.C., Okla., S.C., Tenn., Texas, Va.
Omitted votes are quorum calls, which CQ does not include in its vote charts.

55. HR 3. Child Care/Mandates. Price, D-N.C., amendment to permit rather than require states to have a child-care voucher program. Rejected 182-243: R 10-163; D 172-80 (ND 131-42, SD 41-38), March 29, 1990.

56. HR 3. Child Care/Religious Programs. Edwards, D-Calif., amendment to prohibit the use of federal funds provided under the Social Services Block Grant program for sectarian purposes. Rejected 125-297: R 11-160; D 114-137 (ND 98-75, SD 16-62), March 29, 1990.

57. HR 3. Child Care/Substitute. Stenholm, D-Texas, substitute amendment to provide expanded funding for Head Start and for the Social Services Block Grant program and to increase the existing earned income tax credit for poor working families with children. (The Stenholm substitute would generally provide smaller increases than were included in the Democratic leadership bill to require states to impose child-care standards in certain areas and to authorize a new school-based program for before- and after-school care.) Rejected 195-225: R 157-14; D 38-211 (ND 6-165, SD 32-46), March 29, 1990. A "yea" was a vote supporting the president's position.

58. HR 3. Child Care/Leadership Substitute. Democratic leadership substitute amendment (text of HR 4381) to expand programs providing federal aid for child care and increase the earned income tax credit for poor working families with children. Adopted 263-158: R 39-132; D 224-26 (ND 163-8, SD 61-18), March 29, 1990. A "nay" was a vote supporting the president's position.

59. HR 3. Child Care/Recommittal Motion. Gingrich, R-Ga., motion to recommit jointly to the Ways and Means and Budget committees the bill to expand programs providing federal aid for child care and increase the earned income tax credit for poor working families with children, with instructions to hold hearings on the bill and its net deficit effects. Motion rejected 152-259: R 151-16; D 1-243 (ND 0-166, SD 1-77), March 29, 1990.

60. HR 3. Child Care/Passage. Passage of the bill to expand programs providing federal aid for child care and increase the earned income tax credit for poor working families with children. Passed 265-145: R 47-119; D 218-26 (ND 154-13, SD 64-13), March 29, 1990. A "nay" was a vote supporting the president's position.

KEY

- Y Voted for (yea).
- # Paired for.
- \+ Announced for.
- N Voted against (nay).
- X Paired against.
- \- Announced against.
- P Voted "present."
- C Voted "present" to avoid possible conflict of interest.
- ? Did not vote or otherwise make a position known.

Democrats *Republicans*

	55	56	57	58	59	60
ALABAMA						
1 ***Callahan***	N	N	Y	N	Y	N
2 ***Dickinson***	N	N	Y	N	?	X
3 Browder	Y	N	Y	N	N	Y
4 Bevill	N	N	Y	N	N	Y
5 Flippo	?	?	?	?	?	?
6 Erdreich	N	N	Y	N	N	Y
7 Harris	N	N	Y	N	N	Y
ALASKA						
AL ***Young***	N	Y	Y	N	Y	N
ARIZONA						
1 ***Rhodes***	N	N	Y	N	Y	N
2 Udall	Y	Y	N	Y	N	Y
3 ***Stump***	?	?	X	?	?	?
4 ***Kyl***	N	N	Y	N	Y	N
5 ***Kolbe***	N	N	Y	N	Y	N
ARKANSAS						
1 Alexander	Y	N	N	Y	N	Y
2 ***Robinson***	N	N	Y	N	?	?
3 ***Hammerschmidt***	N	N	Y	N	Y	N
4 Anthony	N	N	N	Y	N	Y
CALIFORNIA						
1 Bosco	Y	N	N	Y	N	Y
2 ***Herger***	N	N	Y	N	Y	N
3 Matsui	Y	Y	N	Y	N	Y
4 Fazio	Y	Y	N	Y	N	Y
5 Pelosi	Y	Y	N	Y	N	Y
6 Boxer	Y	Y	N	Y	N	Y
7 Miller	Y	Y	N	Y	N	Y
8 Dellums	Y	Y	N	N	N	N
9 Stark	Y	Y	N	Y	N	Y
10 Edwards	Y	Y	N	N	?	?
11 Lantos	Y	Y	N	Y	N	Y
12 ***Campbell***	N	N	Y	Y	Y	Y
13 Mineta	Y	Y	N	Y	N	Y
14 ***Shumway***	N	N	Y	N	Y	N
15 Condit	N	N	N	Y	N	Y
16 Panetta	Y	N	N	Y	N	Y
17 ***Pashayan***	N	N	Y	N	Y	Y
18 Lehman	Y	Y	N	Y	N	Y
19 ***Lagomarsino***	N	N	Y	N	Y	Y
20 ***Thomas***	N	N	Y	N	Y	N
21 ***Gallegly***	N	N	Y	N	Y	Y
22 ***Moorhead***	N	N	Y	N	Y	N
23 Beilenson	Y	Y	N	Y	N	N
24 Waxman	Y	Y	N	Y	N	Y
25 Roybal	Y	Y	N	Y	N	Y
26 Berman	Y	Y	N	Y	N	Y
27 Levine	Y	Y	N	Y	N	Y
28 Dixon	Y	Y	N	Y	N	Y
29 Hawkins	Y	Y	N	Y	N	Y
30 Martinez	Y	Y	N	Y	N	Y
31 Dymally	Y	Y	N	Y	N	Y
32 Anderson	Y	Y	N	Y	N	Y
33 ***Dreier***	N	N	Y	N	Y	N
34 Torres	Y	Y	N	Y	N	Y
35 ***Lewis***	N	N	Y	N	Y	N
36 Brown	Y	N	N	Y	N	Y
37 ***McCandless***	N	N	Y	N	Y	N
38 ***Dornan***	N	N	Y	N	Y	N
39 ***Dannemeyer***	N	N	Y	N	Y	N
40 ***Cox***	N	N	Y	N	Y	N
41 ***Lowery***	N	N	Y	N	Y	N
42 ***Rohrabacher***	N	N	Y	N	Y	N
43 ***Packard***	N	N	Y	N	Y	N
44 Bates	Y	Y	N	Y	N	Y
45 ***Hunter***	N	N	Y	N	Y	N
COLORADO						
1 Schroeder	Y	Y	N	Y	N	Y
2 Skaggs	Y	Y	N	Y	N	Y
3 Campbell	Y	Y	N	Y	N	Y
4 ***Brown***	N	N	Y	N	Y	N
5 ***Hefley***	N	N	Y	N	Y	N
6 ***Schaefer***	N	N	Y	N	Y	N
CONNECTICUT						
1 Kennelly	Y	N	N	Y	N	Y
2 Gejdenson	Y	Y	N	Y	N	Y
3 Morrison	Y	Y	N	Y	N	Y
4 ***Shays***	N	Y	N	Y	N	Y
5 ***Rowland***	N	N	Y	Y	N	Y
6 ***Johnson***	N	N	Y	Y	Y	Y
DELAWARE						
AL Carper	Y	N	N	Y	N	Y
FLORIDA						
1 Hutto	N	N	Y	N	N	N
2 ***Grant***	N	N	Y	Y	Y	Y
3 Bennett	Y	N	Y	Y	N	Y
4 ***James***	N	N	Y	Y	Y	Y
5 ***McCollum***	N	N	Y	N	Y	N
6 ***Stearns***	N	N	Y	N	Y	N
7 Gibbons	Y	N	?	Y	N	Y
8 ***Young***	Y	N	Y	N	Y	Y
9 ***Bilirakis***	Y	N	Y	Y	Y	Y
10 ***Ireland***	N	N	Y	N	Y	N
11 Nelson	Y	Y	N	Y	N	Y
12 ***Lewis***	N	N	Y	N	Y	N
13 ***Goss***	N	N	Y	N	Y	N
14 Johnston	Y	Y	N	Y	N	Y
15 ***Shaw***	N	N	Y	N	Y	X
16 Smith	Y	Y	N	Y	N	Y
17 Lehman	Y	Y	N	Y	N	Y
18 ***Ros-Lehtinen***	N	N	Y	Y	Y	Y
19 Fascell	Y	Y	N	Y	N	Y
GEORGIA						
1 Thomas	N	N	Y	Y	N	Y
2 Hatcher	N	N	Y	Y	?	?
3 Ray	N	N	Y	N	Y	N
4 Jones	Y	N	Y	Y	N	Y
5 Lewis	Y	Y	N	Y	N	Y
6 ***Gingrich***	N	N	Y	N	Y	N
7 Darden	N	N	Y	Y	N	Y
8 Rowland	N	N	Y	Y	N	Y
9 Jenkins	N	N	Y	Y	N	Y
10 Barnard	N	N	Y	N	N	N
HAWAII						
1 ***Saiki***	N	N	Y	Y	Y	Y
2 Akaka	Y	Y	N	Y	N	Y
IDAHO						
1 ***Craig***	N	N	Y	N	Y	N
2 Stallings	N	N	Y	Y	N	N
ILLINOIS						
1 Hayes	Y	Y	N	Y	N	Y
2 Savage	Y	Y	N	Y	N	Y
3 Russo	Y	Y	N	Y	N	Y
4 Sangmeister	Y	N	N	Y	N	Y
5 Lipinski	N	N	Y	Y	?	?
6 ***Hyde***	N	N	Y	N	Y	N
7 Collins	Y	Y	N	Y	N	Y
8 Rostenkowski	Y	N	N	Y	N	Y
9 Yates	Y	Y	N	Y	N	Y
10 ***Porter***	N	N	Y	N	Y	N
11 Annunzio	N	N	N	Y	N	Y
12 ***Crane***	N	N	Y	N	Y	N
13 ***Fawell***	N	N	Y	N	Y	N
14 ***Hastert***	N	N	Y	N	Y	N
15 ***Madigan***	N	N	Y	N	Y	N
16 ***Martin***	N	N	Y	Y	Y	Y
17 Evans	Y	Y	N	Y	N	Y
18 ***Michel***	N	N	Y	N	Y	N
19 Bruce	Y	Y	N	Y	N	Y
20 Durbin	N	N	N	Y	N	Y
21 Costello	N	Y	N	Y	N	Y
22 Poshard	N	Y	N	Y	N	Y
INDIANA						
1 Visclosky	Y	N	N	Y	N	Y
2 Sharp	N	N	N	Y	N	Y
3 ***Hiler***	N	N	Y	N	Y	N

ND Northern Democrats SD Southern Democrats

	55	56	57	58	59	60
4 Long	Y	N	N	N	N	N
5 Jontz	Y	Y	N	Y	N	Y
6 ***Burton***	N	N	Y	N	Y	N
7 ***Myers***	N	N	Y	N	Y	N
8 McCloskey	Y	N	N	Y	N	Y
9 Hamilton	Y	N	N	Y	N	Y
10 Jacobs	N	N	N	Y	N	Y
IOWA						
1 ***Leach***	Y	Y	N	Y	Y	Y
2 ***Tauke***	N	N	Y	N	Y	Y
3 Nagle	Y	N	N	Y	N	Y
4 Smith	N	Y	N	Y	N	Y
5 ***Lightfoot***	N	N	Y	N	Y	N
6 ***Grandy***	N	N	Y	N	Y	N
KANSAS						
1 ***Roberts***	N	N	Y	N	Y	N
2 Slattery	Y	N	Y	N	N	N
3 ***Meyers***	Y	N	Y	N	Y	N
4 Glickman	Y	N	N	Y	N	Y
5 ***Whittaker***	N	N	Y	N	Y	N
KENTUCKY						
1 Hubbard	N	N	Y	N	N	Y
2 Natcher	N	N	N	Y	N	Y
3 Mazzoli	N	N	N	Y	N	Y
4 ***Bunning***	N	N	Y	N	Y	N
5 ***Rogers***	N	N	Y	N	Y	N
6 ***Hopkins***	N	N	Y	N	Y	N
7 Perkins	Y	N	N	Y	N	Y
LOUISIANA						
1 ***Livingston***	N	N	Y	N	Y	N
2 Boggs	N	N	N	Y	N	Y
3 Tauzin	N	N	Y	Y	N	Y
4 ***McCrery***	N	N	Y	N	Y	N
5 Huckaby	N	N	Y	N	N	N
6 ***Baker***	N	N	Y	N	?	?
7 Hayes	N	N	Y	Y	N	Y
8 ***Holloway***	N	N	Y	N	Y	N
MAINE						
1 Brennan	Y	Y	N	Y	N	Y
2 ***Snowe***	N	N	N	Y	N	Y
MARYLAND						
1 Dyson	N	N	N	Y	N	Y
2 ***Bentley***	N	N	Y	N	Y	N
3 Cardin	Y	Y	N	Y	N	Y
4 McMillen	Y	N	N	Y	N	Y
5 Hoyer	Y	Y	N	Y	N	Y
6 Byron	N	N	Y	N	Y	Y
7 Mfume	Y	Y	N	Y	N	Y
8 ***Morella***	Y	Y	N	Y	N	Y
MASSACHUSETTS						
1 ***Conte***	N	N	N	Y	Y	Y
2 Neal	Y	Y	N	Y	N	Y
3 Early	N	N	N	Y	N	Y
4 Frank	Y	N	N	Y	N	Y
5 Atkins	N	N	N	Y	N	Y
6 Mavroules	Y	Y	N	Y	N	Y
7 Markey	Y	N	N	Y	N	Y
8 Kennedy	Y	Y	N	Y	N	Y
9 Moakley	N	N	N	Y	N	Y
10 Studds	Y	Y	N	Y	N	Y
11 Donnelly	N	N	N	Y	N	Y
MICHIGAN						
1 Conyers	Y	Y	N	Y	N	Y
2 ***Pursell***	N	N	Y	N	Y	N
3 Wolpe	Y	Y	N	Y	?	Y
4 ***Upton***	N	N	Y	N	Y	N
5 ***Henry***	N	N	Y	N	Y	N
6 Carr	Y	Y	N	Y	N	Y
7 Kildee	N	N	N	Y	N	Y
8 Traxler	N	N	?	?	X	#
9 ***Vander Jagt***	N	N	Y	N	Y	N
10 ***Schuette***	N	N	Y	N	Y	N
11 ***Davis***	Y	Y	N	Y	N	Y
12 Bonior	Y	Y	N	Y	N	Y
13 Crockett	Y	Y	N	Y	N	Y
14 Hertel	Y	Y	N	Y	N	Y
15 Ford	Y	Y	N	Y	N	Y
16 Dingell	Y	N	N	Y	N	Y
17 Levin	Y	Y	N	Y	N	Y
18 ***Broomfield***	N	N	Y	N	Y	N
MINNESOTA						
1 Penny	Y	N	N	Y	N	Y
2 ***Weber***	N	N	Y	N	Y	N
3 ***Frenzel***	N	?	#	?	?	X
4 Vento	Y	Y	N	Y	N	Y

	55	56	57	58	59	60
5 Sabo	Y	Y	N	Y	N	Y
6 Sikorski	Y	N	N	Y	N	Y
7 ***Stangeland***	N	N	Y	N	Y	N
8 Oberstar	Y	N	N	Y	N	Y
MISSISSIPPI						
1 Whitten	Y	N	N	Y	N	Y
2 Espy	N	N	N	Y	N	Y
3 Montgomery	N	N	Y	N	N	N
4 Parker	N	N	Y	N	N	N
5 Taylor	N	N	Y	N	N	N
MISSOURI						
1 Clay	Y	Y	N	N	N	N
2 ***Buechner***	N	N	Y	N	Y	N
3 Gephardt	Y	N	N	Y	N	Y
4 Skelton	N	N	Y	N	N	N
5 Wheat	Y	Y	N	Y	N	Y
6 ***Coleman***	N	N	Y	N	Y	N
7 ***Hancock***	N	N	Y	N	Y	N
8 ***Emerson***	N	N	Y	N	Y	N
9 Volkmer	N	N	N	Y	N	Y
MONTANA						
1 Williams	Y	Y	N	N	N	N
2 ***Marlenee***	N	N	Y	N	Y	N
NEBRASKA						
1 ***Bereuter***	N	N	Y	N	Y	Y
2 Hoagland	Y	Y	N	Y	N	Y
3 ***Smith***	N	N	Y	N	Y	N
NEVADA						
1 Bilbray	N	N	N	Y	N	Y
2 ***Vucanovich***	N	N	Y	N	Y	N
NEW HAMPSHIRE						
1 ***Smith***	N	N	Y	N	Y	N
2 ***Douglas***	N	N	Y	N	Y	N
NEW JERSEY						
1 Vacancy						
2 Hughes	N	N	N	Y	N	Y
3 Pallone	N	N	N	Y	N	Y
4 ***Smith***	N	N	Y	Y	N	Y
5 ***Roukema***	?	?	X	?	#	?
6 Dwyer	X	?	X	?	X	#
7 ***Rinaldo***	N	N	N	Y	N	Y
8 Roe	N	N	N	Y	N	Y
9 Torricelli	N	N	?	?	?	#
10 Payne	Y	Y	N	Y	N	Y
11 ***Gallo***	N	?	#	?	?	?
12 ***Courter***	N	N	Y	N	Y	N
13 ***Saxton***	Y	N	Y	Y	N	Y
14 Guarini	N	N	N	Y	N	Y
NEW MEXICO						
1 ***Schiff***	N	Y	Y	Y	Y	Y
2 ***Skeen***	N	N	Y	N	Y	N
3 Richardson	N	N	N	Y	N	Y
NEW YORK						
1 Hochbrueckner	Y	Y	N	Y	N	Y
2 Downey	Y	Y	N	Y	N	Y
3 Mrazek	Y	Y	N	Y	N	Y
4 ***Lent***	N	N	Y	N	Y	N
5 ***McGrath***	N	N	N	Y	N	Y
6 Flake	Y	Y	N	Y	N	Y
7 Ackerman	Y	Y	N	Y	N	N
8 Scheuer	Y	Y	N	Y	N	Y
9 Manton	N	N	N	Y	N	Y
10 Schumer	Y	Y	N	Y	N	Y
11 Towns	Y	Y	N	Y	N	Y
12 Owens	Y	Y	N	Y	N	Y
13 Solarz	Y	N	N	Y	N	Y
14 ***Molinari***	N	N	N	Y	N	Y
15 ***Green***	N	N	Y	Y	Y	Y
16 Rangel	Y	Y	N	Y	N	Y
17 Weiss	Y	Y	N	Y	N	N
18 Serrano	Y	Y	N	Y	N	Y
19 Engel	Y	Y	N	Y	N	Y
20 Lowey	Y	Y	N	Y	N	Y
21 ***Fish***	N	Y	Y	Y	Y	Y
22 ***Gilman***	N	N	N	Y	N	Y
23 McNulty	N	Y	N	Y	N	Y
24 ***Solomon***	N	N	Y	N	Y	N
25 ***Boehlert***	N	Y	Y	Y	N	Y
26 ***Martin***	N	N	Y	Y	N	N
27 ***Walsh***	N	N	Y	Y	N	Y
28 McHugh	N	N	N	Y	N	Y
29 ***Horton***	N	Y	Y	Y	Y	Y
30 Slaughter	N	Y	N	Y	N	Y
31 ***Paxon***	N	N	Y	N	Y	N

	55	56	57	58	59	60
32 LaFalce	N	N	Y	Y	N	Y
33 Nowak	N	N	N	Y	N	Y
34 ***Houghton***	N	N	Y	N	Y	N
NORTH CAROLINA						
1 Jones	#	?	?	?	?	#
2 Valentine	Y	N	N	Y	N	Y
3 Lancaster	Y	N	Y	Y	N	Y
4 Price	Y	N	N	Y	N	Y
5 Neal	Y	N	N	Y	N	Y
6 ***Coble***	N	N	Y	N	Y	N
7 Rose	Y	N	N	Y	N	Y
8 Hefner	Y	N	N	Y	N	Y
9 ***McMillan***	N	N	Y	N	Y	N
10 ***Ballenger***	N	N	Y	N	Y	N
11 Clarke	Y	N	N	Y	N	Y
NORTH DAKOTA						
AL Dorgan	N	N	N	Y	N	Y
OHIO						
1 Luken	N	N	N	Y	N	Y
2 ***Gradison***	N	N	Y	N	Y	N
3 Hall	N	N	N	Y	N	Y
4 ***Oxley***	N	N	Y	N	Y	N
5 ***Gillmor***	N	N	Y	Y	Y	Y
6 ***McEwen***	N	N	Y	N	Y	N
7 ***DeWine***	N	N	Y	N	Y	N
8 ***Lukens***	N	N	Y	N	Y	N
9 Kaptur	N	Y	N	Y	N	Y
10 ***Miller***	N	N	Y	N	Y	N
11 Eckart	Y	N	N	Y	N	Y
12 ***Kasich***	N	N	Y	N	Y	N
13 Pease	Y	Y	N	Y	N	Y
14 Sawyer	Y	Y	N	Y	N	Y
15 ***Wylie***	N	N	Y	N	Y	Y
16 ***Regula***	N	N	Y	N	Y	N
17 Traficant	Y	N	N	Y	N	Y
18 Applegate	Y	N	N	Y	N	Y
19 Feighan	Y	Y	N	Y	N	Y
20 Oakar	N	N	N	Y	N	Y
21 Stokes	Y	Y	N	N	N	N
OKLAHOMA						
1 ***Inhofe***	N	N	Y	N	Y	N
2 Synar	Y	Y	N	Y	N	Y
3 Watkins	N	N	Y	Y	N	Y
4 McCurdy	N	N	N	Y	N	Y
5 ***Edwards***	N	N	Y	N	Y	N
6 English	N	N	Y	Y	N	Y
OREGON						
1 AuCoin	Y	Y	N	Y	N	Y
2 ***Smith, B.***	N	N	Y	N	Y	N
3 Wyden	Y	Y	N	Y	N	Y
4 DeFazio	Y	Y	N	Y	N	Y
5 ***Smith, D.***	?	?	#	?	#	X
PENNSYLVANIA						
1 Foglietta	Y	N	N	Y	N	Y
2 Gray	Y	Y	N	Y	N	Y
3 Borski	Y	N	N	Y	N	Y
4 Kolter	N	N	N	Y	N	Y
5 ***Schulze***	N	N	Y	N	Y	N
6 Yatron	Y	N	N	Y	N	Y
7 ***Weldon***	N	N	Y	Y	Y	Y
8 Kostmayer	Y	Y	N	Y	N	Y
9 ***Shuster***	N	N	Y	N	Y	N
10 ***McDade***	N	N	Y	Y	Y	Y
11 Kanjorski	N	N	N	Y	N	Y
12 Murtha	N	N	N	Y	N	Y
13 ***Coughlin***	Y	N	Y	Y	Y	Y
14 Coyne	Y	Y	N	Y	N	Y
15 ***Ritter***	N	N	Y	N	Y	N
16 ***Walker***	N	N	Y	N	Y	N
17 ***Gekas***	N	N	Y	N	Y	N
18 Walgren	Y	N	N	Y	N	Y
19 ***Goodling***	N	N	Y	N	Y	N
20 Gaydos	N	N	N	Y	N	Y
21 ***Ridge***	N	N	Y	Y	Y	Y
22 Murphy	Y	N	N	Y	?	?
23 ***Clinger***	N	N	Y	N	Y	N
RHODE ISLAND						
1 ***Machtley***	Y	Y	N	Y	N	Y
2 ***Schneider***	Y	Y	N	Y	N	Y
SOUTH CAROLINA						
1 ***Ravenel***	N	N	Y	Y	Y	Y
2 ***Spence***	N	N	Y	N	?	?
3 Derrick	Y	N	Y	Y	N	Y
4 Patterson	Y	N	Y	Y	N	Y
5 Spratt*	N	N	N	Y	N	Y
6 Tallon	N	N	N	Y	N	Y

	55	56	57	58	59	60
SOUTH DAKOTA						
AL Johnson	Y	N	N	Y	N	Y
TENNESSEE						
1 ***Quillen***	N	N	Y	N	Y	N
2 ***Duncan***	N	N	Y	N	Y	N
3 Lloyd	N	N	Y	N	N	N
4 Cooper	Y	N	Y	N	N	N
5 Clement	Y	Y	N	Y	N	Y
6 Gordon	Y	N	N	Y	N	Y
7 ***Sundquist***	N	N	Y	N	Y	N
8 Tanner	N	N	N	Y	N	Y
9 Ford	Y	Y	N	Y	N	Y
TEXAS						
1 Chapman	N	N	N	Y	N	Y
2 Wilson	Y	Y	N	Y	N	Y
3 ***Bartlett***	N	N	Y	N	Y	N
4 Hall	N	N	Y	Y	N	Y
5 Bryant	Y	N	N	Y	N	?
6 ***Barton***	N	N	Y	N	Y	N
7 ***Archer***	N	N	Y	N	Y	N
8 ***Fields***	N	N	Y	N	Y	N
9 Brooks	Y	N	N	Y	N	Y
10 Pickle	Y	Y	N	Y	N	Y
11 Leath	N	?	Y	N	N	N
12 Geren	N	N	N	Y	N	Y
13 Sarpalius	?	?	?	?	?	?
14 Laughlin	?	?	?	?	?	?
15 de la Garza	Y	N	N	Y	N	Y
16 Coleman	Y	Y	N	Y	N	Y
17 Stenholm	N	N	Y	N	N	N
18 Washington	Y	Y	N	Y	N	Y
19 ***Combest***	N	N	Y	N	Y	N
20 Gonzalez	Y	Y	N	Y	N	Y
21 ***Smith***	N	N	Y	N	Y	N
22 ***DeLay***	N	N	Y	N	Y	N
23 Bustamante	Y	N	N	Y	N	Y
24 Frost	Y	N	N	Y	N	Y
25 Andrews	N	N	N	Y	N	Y
26 ***Armey***	N	N	Y	N	Y	N
27 Ortiz	N	N	Y	Y	N	Y
UTAH						
1 ***Hansen***	N	N	Y	N	Y	N
2 Owens	Y	N	N	Y	?	?
3 ***Nielson***	N	N	Y	N	Y	N
VERMONT						
AL ***Smith***	N	N	N	Y	N	Y
VIRGINIA						
1 ***Bateman***	N	N	Y	N	Y	N
2 Pickett	N	Y	N	N	N	N
3 ***Bliley***	N	N	Y	N	Y	N
4 Sisisky	Y	N	N	Y	N	Y
5 Payne	Y	N	N	Y	N	Y
6 Olin	Y	Y	N	N	N	N
7 ***Slaughter***	N	N	Y	N	Y	N
8 ***Parris***	N	N	Y	N	Y	Y
9 Boucher	Y	N	N	Y	N	Y
10 ***Wolf***	N	N	Y	N	Y	N
WASHINGTON						
1 ***Miller***	N	N	Y	Y	Y	Y
2 Swift	Y	Y	N	Y	N	N
3 Unsoeld	Y	Y	N	Y	N	Y
4 ***Morrison***	N	N	Y	Y	Y	Y
5 Foley						
6 Dicks	Y	Y	N	Y	N	Y
7 McDermott	Y	Y	N	Y	N	N
8 ***Chandler***	N	N	Y	N	Y	N
WEST VIRGINIA						
1 Mollohan	Y	N	N	Y	N	Y
2 Staggers	Y	N	N	Y	N	Y
3 Wise	Y	N	N	Y	N	Y
4 Rahall	Y	N	N	Y	N	Y
WISCONSIN						
1 Aspin	Y	N	N	Y	N	Y
2 Kastenmeier	Y	Y	N	Y	N	Y
3 ***Gunderson***	N	N	Y	N	Y	N
4 Kleczka	Y	Y	N	Y	N	Y
5 Moody	Y	Y	N	Y	N	Y
6 ***Petri***	N	N	Y	Y	Y	Y
7 Obey	Y	N	N	Y	N	Y
8 ***Roth***	N	N	Y	N	Y	N
9 ***Sensenbrenner***	N	N	Y	N	Y	N
WYOMING						
AL ***Thomas***	N	N	Y	N	Y	N

Southern states - Ala., Ark., Fla., Ga., Ky., La., Miss., N.C., Okla., S.C., Tenn., Texas, Va.
Omitted votes are quorum calls, which CQ does not include in its vote charts.

61. HR 4404. Fiscal 1990 Supplemental Appropriations/ Foreign Aid. Rahall, D-W.Va., en bloc amendments to strike the foreign aid parts of the bill. Rejected 38-379: R 10-163; D 28-216 (ND 17-150, SD 11-66), April 3, 1990.

62. HR 4404. Fiscal 1990 Supplemental Appropriations/ Foreign Aid. Traficant, D-Ohio, en bloc amendments to cut 5 percent of the foreign aid funds in the bill except for hurricane assistance to the Eastern Caribbean. Rejected 64-354: R 20-152; D 44-202 (ND 28-141, SD 16-61), April 3, 1990.

63. HR 4404. Fiscal 1990 Supplemental Appropriations/ Foreign Aid. Traficant, D-Ohio, en bloc amendments to cut 3 percent of the foreign aid funds in the bill except for hurricane assistance to the Eastern Caribbean. Rejected 72-346: R 25-148; D 47-198 (ND 31-136, SD 16-62), April 3, 1990.

64. HR 4404. Fiscal 1990 Supplemental Appropriations/ Refugee Assistance. Savage, D-Ill., amendment to strike provisions of the bill that would provide $75 million in migration and refugee assistance, with not less than $5 million of the funds available to Soviet, Eastern European and other refugees resettling in Israel. Rejected 2-418: R 0-172; D 2-246 (ND 2-168, SD 0-78), April 3, 1990.

65. HR 4404. Fiscal 1990 Supplemental Appropriations/ Passage. Passage of the bill to appropriate $2.4 billion in supplemental funds, including $870 million for assistance to Panama, Nicaragua and other foreign nations and $1.5 billion for domestic programs, including food stamps, low-income heating assistance, unemployment compensation and disaster assistance. The bill would rescind $1.8 billion in fiscal 1990 defense appropriations to offset most of the new spending. Passed 362-59: R 139-34; D 223-25 (ND 152-19, SD 71-6), April 3, 1990.

66. HR 1048. Hate Crimes Statistics Act/Passage. Schumer, D-N.Y., motion to suspend the rules and pass the bill (thus clearing the measure for the president) to require the Justice Department to collect and publish data on certain crimes that manifest prejudice based on race, religion, sexual orientation or ethnicity. Motion agreed to 402-18: R 156-18; D 246-0 (ND 167-0, SD 79-0), April 4, 1990. A two-thirds majority of those present and voting (280 in this case) is required for passage under suspension of the rules. A "yea" was a vote supporting the president's position.

67. H Con Res 289. Lithuanian Independence/Adoption. Hamilton, D-Ind., motion to suspend the rules and adopt the concurrent resolution to express U.S. support for the independence of Lithuania and call on the president to "plan for and take those steps, at the earliest possible time, that would normalize diplomatic relations" between the United States and the new government of Lithuania. Motion agreed to 416-3: R 173-0; D 243-3 (ND 164-3, SD 79-0), April 4, 1990. A two-thirds majority of those present and voting (280 in this case) is required for passage under suspension of the rules.

68. HR 2015. Public Works and Economic Development Act/Passage. Passage of the bill to aid economically distressed areas of the nation by authorizing in each of fiscal years 1991-93 $276 million for the Economic Development Administration of the Commerce Department and $185 million for the Appalachian Regional Commission. Passed 340-82: R 97-78; D 243-4 (ND 165-3, SD 78-1), April 4, 1990. A "nay" was a vote supporting the president's position.

KEY

- Y Voted for (yea).
- # Paired for.
- + Announced for.
- N Voted against (nay).
- X Paired against.
- - Announced against.
- P Voted "present."
- C Voted "present" to avoid possible conflict of interest.
- ? Did not vote or otherwise make a position known.

Democrats *Republicans*

	61	62	63	64	65	66	67	68
ALABAMA								
1 ***Callahan***	N	N	N	N	Y	Y	Y	Y
2 ***Dickinson***	N	N	N	N	N	Y	Y	Y
3 Browder	N	N	N	N	Y	Y	Y	Y
4 Bevill	N	N	N	N	Y	Y	Y	Y
5 Flippo	?	?	?	?	?	?	?	?
6 Erdreich	N	N	N	N	Y	Y	Y	Y
7 Harris	N	N	N	N	Y	Y	Y	Y
ALASKA								
AL ***Young***	N	N	Y	N	Y	Y	Y	Y
ARIZONA								
1 ***Rhodes***	N	N	N	N	Y	Y	Y	N
2 Udall	?	N	N	-	Y	Y	Y	Y
3 ***Stump***	#	#	#	?	X	X	?	X
4 ***Kyl***	N	N	N	N	Y	N	Y	N
5 ***Kolbe***	N	N	N	N	Y	Y	Y	N
ARKANSAS								
1 Alexander	Y	?	N	N	Y	Y	Y	Y
2 ***Robinson***	N	N	N	N	Y	Y	Y	Y
3 ***Hammerschmidt***	N	N	N	N	Y	N	Y	Y
4 Anthony	N	N	N	N	Y	Y	Y	Y
CALIFORNIA								
1 Bosco	N	N	N	N	Y	Y	Y	Y
2 ***Herger***	N	N	Y	N	Y	Y	Y	Y
3 Matsui	N	N	N	N	Y	Y	Y	Y
4 Fazio	N	N	N	N	Y	Y	Y	Y
5 Pelosi	N	N	N	N	Y	Y	Y	Y
6 Boxer	N	N	N	N	Y	Y	Y	Y
7 Miller	Y	N	N	N	N	Y	Y	Y
8 Dellums	N	N	N	N	Y	Y	Y	Y
9 Stark	Y	Y	Y	N	N	Y	Y	Y
10 Edwards	N	N	N	N	Y	Y	Y	Y
11 Lantos	N	N	N	N	Y	Y	Y	Y
12 ***Campbell***	N	N	N	N	Y	Y	Y	N
13 Mineta	N	N	N	N	Y	Y	Y	Y
14 ***Shumway***	N	N	N	N	N	N	Y	N
15 Condit	N	N	N	N	Y	Y	Y	Y
16 Panetta	N	N	N	N	Y	Y	Y	Y
17 ***Pashayan***	N	N	N	N	Y	Y	Y	Y
18 Lehman	N	N	N	N	Y	Y	Y	Y
19 ***Lagomarsino***	N	N	N	N	Y	Y	Y	N
20 ***Thomas***	N	N	N	N	Y	Y	Y	N
21 ***Gallegly***	N	N	N	N	Y	Y	Y	N
22 ***Moorhead***	N	Y	Y	N	N	Y	Y	N
23 Beilenson	N	N	N	N	Y	Y	Y	Y
24 Waxman	N	N	N	N	Y	Y	Y	Y
25 Roybal	N	N	N	N	Y	Y	Y	Y
26 Berman	N	N	N	N	Y	Y	Y	Y
27 Levine	N	N	N	N	Y	Y	Y	Y
28 Dixon	N	N	N	N	Y	Y	Y	Y
29 Hawkins	?	?	?	N	Y	Y	Y	?
30 Martinez	N	N	N	N	Y	Y	Y	Y
31 Dymally	N	Y	Y	N	Y	Y	Y	Y
32 Anderson	N	N	N	N	Y	Y	Y	Y
33 ***Dreier***	N	N	N	N	Y	Y	Y	N
34 Torres	N	N	N	N	Y	Y	Y	Y
35 ***Lewis***	N	N	N	N	Y	Y	Y	Y
36 Brown	N	N	N	N	Y	Y	Y	?
37 ***McCandless***	Y	Y	Y	N	N	Y	Y	N
38 ***Dornan***	N	N	N	N	N	N	Y	N
39 ***Dannemeyer***	N	Y	Y	N	N	N	Y	N
40 ***Cox***	N	N	N	N	Y	Y	Y	N
41 ***Lowery***	N	N	N	N	Y	Y	Y	Y
42 ***Rohrabacher***	N	N	N	N	Y	Y	Y	N
43 ***Packard***	N	N	N	N	N	Y	Y	Y
44 Bates	N	N	N	N	Y	Y	Y	Y
45 ***Hunter***	N	N	N	N	Y	N	Y	Y
COLORADO								
1 Schroeder	Y	Y	Y	N	Y	Y	Y	Y
2 Skaggs	N	N	N	N	Y	Y	Y	Y
3 Campbell	?	?	?	?	?	Y	Y	Y
4 ***Brown***	N	N	N	N	Y	Y	Y	N
5 ***Hefley***	N	N	N	N	Y	Y	Y	N
6 ***Schaefer***	N	Y	Y	N	Y	Y	Y	N
CONNECTICUT								
1 Kennelly	N	N	N	N	Y	Y	Y	Y
2 Gejdenson	N	N	N	N	Y	Y	Y	Y
3 Morrison	N	N	N	N	Y	Y	Y	Y
4 ***Shays***	N	N	N	N	Y	Y	Y	N
5 ***Rowland***	N	N	N	N	Y	Y	Y	Y
6 ***Johnson***	N	N	N	N	Y	Y	Y	Y
DELAWARE								
AL Carper	N	N	N	N	Y	Y	Y	N
FLORIDA								
1 Hutto	N	N	N	N	Y	Y	Y	Y
2 ***Grant***	N	N	N	N	Y	Y	Y	Y
3 Bennett	N	N	N	N	Y	Y	Y	Y
4 ***James***	N	N	N	N	Y	Y	Y	Y
5 ***McCollum***	N	N	N	N	Y	Y	Y	N
6 ***Stearns***	N	N	N	N	Y	Y	Y	N
7 Gibbons	N	N	N	N	Y	Y	Y	Y
8 ***Young***	N	N	N	N	Y	Y	Y	Y
9 ***Bilirakis***	N	N	N	N	Y	Y	Y	N
10 ***Ireland***	N	N	N	N	Y	Y	Y	N
11 Nelson	X	X	X	-	#	#	+	#
12 ***Lewis***	N	N	N	N	N	Y	Y	N
13 ***Goss***	N	N	N	N	Y	Y	Y	N
14 Johnston	N	N	N	N	Y	Y	Y	Y
15 ***Shaw***	N	N	N	N	Y	Y	Y	N
16 Smith	N	N	N	N	Y	Y	Y	Y
17 Lehman	N	N	N	N	Y	Y	Y	Y
18 ***Ros-Lehtinen***	N	N	N	N	Y	Y	Y	Y
19 Fascell	N	N	N	N	Y	Y	Y	Y
GEORGIA								
1 Thomas	N	N	N	N	Y	Y	Y	Y
2 Hatcher	N	N	N	N	Y	?	Y	Y
3 Ray	N	N	N	N	N	Y	Y	Y
4 Jones	N	N	N	N	Y	Y	Y	Y
5 Lewis	N	N	N	N	Y	Y	Y	Y
6 ***Gingrich***	N	N	N	N	Y	?	?	Y
7 Darden	N	N	N	N	Y	Y	Y	Y
8 Rowland	N	N	N	N	Y	Y	Y	Y
9 Jenkins	N	Y	Y	N	Y	Y	Y	Y
10 Barnard	N	N	N	N	N	Y	Y	Y
HAWAII								
1 ***Saiki***	N	N	N	N	Y	Y	Y	N
2 Akaka	N	N	N	N	Y	+	Y	Y
IDAHO								
1 ***Craig***	N	N	N	N	N	Y	Y	Y
2 Stallings	N	N	N	N	Y	Y	Y	Y
ILLINOIS								
1 Hayes	N	Y	N	N	Y	Y	Y	Y
2 Savage	N	N	N	Y	Y	Y	Y	Y
3 Russo	Y	Y	Y	N	N	Y	Y	Y
4 Sangmeister	N	Y	Y	N	Y	Y	Y	Y
5 Lipinski	N	N	N	N	Y	Y	Y	Y
6 ***Hyde***	N	N	N	N	Y	Y	Y	N
7 Collins	N	N	N	N	Y	Y	Y	Y
8 Rostenkowski	N	N	N	N	Y	Y	Y	Y
9 Yates	N	?	?	?	?	?	?	?
10 ***Porter***	N	N	N	N	Y	Y	Y	N
11 Annunzio	N	N	N	N	Y	Y	Y	Y
12 ***Crane***	N	Y	Y	N	N	N	Y	N
13 ***Fawell***	N	N	N	N	N	Y	Y	N
14 ***Hastert***	N	N	N	N	Y	Y	Y	N
15 ***Madigan***	N	N	N	N	Y	Y	Y	Y
16 ***Martin***	N	N	N	N	Y	Y	Y	Y
17 Evans	N	N	N	N	Y	Y	Y	Y
18 ***Michel***	N	N	N	N	Y	Y	Y	Y
19 Bruce	N	N	N	N	Y	Y	Y	Y
20 Durbin	N	N	N	N	Y	Y	Y	Y
21 Costello	N	Y	Y	N	Y	Y	Y	Y
22 Poshard	Y	Y	Y	N	Y	Y	Y	Y
INDIANA								
1 Visclosky	N	N	N	N	Y	Y	Y	Y
2 Sharp	N	N	Y	N	Y	Y	Y	Y
3 ***Hiler***	N	N	N	N	Y	Y	Y	N

ND Northern Democrats SD Southern Democrats

	61	62	63	64	65	66	67	68
4 Long	N	Y	Y	N	N	Y	Y	Y
5 Jontz	Y	Y	Y	N	N	Y	Y	Y
6 ***Burton***	N	N	N	N	Y	N	Y	N
7 ***Myers***	N	N	N	N	Y	Y	Y	Y
8 McCloskey	N	N	N	N	Y	Y	Y	Y
9 Hamilton	N	N	N	N	Y	Y	Y	Y
10 Jacobs	N	Y	Y	N	Y	Y	?	Y
IOWA								
1 ***Leach***	N	N	N	N	Y	Y	Y	N
2 ***Tauke***	N	N	N	N	Y	Y	Y	N
3 Nagle	N	?	?	N	Y	Y	N	Y
4 Smith	N	N	N	N	Y	Y	Y	Y
5 ***Lightfoot***	N	N	N	N	Y	Y	Y	Y
6 ***Grandy***	N	N	N	N	Y	Y	Y	Y
KANSAS								
1 ***Roberts***	N	N	N	N	Y	Y	Y	N
2 Slattery	N	N	N	N	Y	Y	Y	Y
3 ***Meyers***	N	N	N	N	Y	Y	Y	N
4 Glickman	N	N	N	N	Y	Y	Y	Y
5 ***Whittaker***	?	?	?	?	?	Y	Y	N
KENTUCKY								
1 Hubbard	N	Y	Y	N	N	Y	Y	Y
2 Natcher	N	N	N	N	Y	Y	Y	Y
3 Mazzoli	N	N	N	N	Y	Y	Y	Y
4 ***Bunning***	N	N	N	N	Y	Y	Y	Y
5 ***Rogers***	N	N	N	N	Y	Y	Y	Y
6 ***Hopkins***	Y	Y	Y	N	Y	N	Y	N
7 Perkins	Y	Y	Y	N	Y	Y	Y	Y
LOUISIANA								
1 ***Livingston***	N	?	N	?	Y	Y	Y	N
2 Boggs	N	N	N	N	Y	Y	Y	Y
3 Tauzin	N	Y	N	N	Y	Y	Y	Y
4 ***McCrery***	N	N	N	N	N	Y	Y	Y
5 Huckaby	N	N	N	N	Y	Y	Y	Y
6 ***Baker***	N	N	N	N	Y	Y	Y	Y
7 Hayes	?	?	?	?	X	Y	Y	Y
8 ***Holloway***	N	Y	Y	N	N	N	Y	Y
MAINE								
1 Brennan	N	N	N	N	Y	Y	Y	Y
2 ***Snowe***	N	N	N	N	Y	Y	Y	Y
MARYLAND								
1 Dyson	Y	N	N	N	Y	Y	Y	Y
2 ***Bentley***	N	N	N	N	Y	Y	Y	Y
3 Cardin	N	N	N	N	Y	Y	Y	Y
4 McMillen	N	N	N	N	Y	Y	Y	Y
5 Hoyer	N	N	N	N	Y	Y	Y	Y
6 Byron	N	N	N	N	Y	Y	Y	Y
7 Mfume	N	N	N	N	Y	Y	Y	Y
8 ***Morella***	N	N	N	N	Y	Y	Y	N
MASSACHUSETTS								
1 ***Conte***	N	N	N	N	Y	Y	Y	Y
2 Neal	N	N	N	N	Y	Y	Y	Y
3 Early	N	N	N	N	Y	Y	Y	Y
4 Frank	N	N	N	N	Y	Y	Y	Y
5 Atkins	N	N	N	N	Y	Y	Y	Y
6 Mavroules	N	N	N	N	Y	Y	Y	Y
7 Markey	N	N	N	N	Y	Y	Y	Y
8 Kennedy	N	N	N	N	Y	Y	Y	Y
9 Moakley	N	N	N	N	Y	Y	Y	Y
10 Studds	N	N	N	N	Y	Y	Y	Y
11 Donnelly	N	N	N	N	Y	Y	Y	Y
MICHIGAN								
1 Conyers	Y	Y	Y	N	N	Y	Y	Y
2 ***Pursell***	N	N	N	N	Y	Y	Y	N
3 Wolpe	N	N	N	N	Y	Y	Y	Y
4 ***Upton***	N	N	N	N	N	Y	Y	Y
5 ***Henry***	Y	Y	Y	N	N	Y	Y	Y
6 Carr	N	N	N	N	Y	Y	Y	N
7 Kildee	N	N	N	N	Y	Y	Y	Y
8 Traxler	N	N	N	N	Y	Y	Y	Y
9 ***Vander Jagt***	N	N	N	N	Y	Y	Y	Y
10 ***Schuette***	?	?	?	?	?	Y	Y	Y
11 ***Davis***	N	N	N	N	Y	Y	Y	Y
12 Bonior	N	N	N	N	Y	Y	Y	Y
13 Crockett	N	Y	Y	Y	N	Y	N	?
14 Hertel	N	N	N	N	Y	Y	Y	Y
15 Ford	N	N	N	N	Y	?	?	Y
16 Dingell	N	N	N	N	Y	Y	Y	Y
17 Levin	N	N	N	N	Y	Y	Y	Y
18 ***Broomfield***	N	N	N	N	Y	Y	Y	Y
MINNESOTA								
1 Penny	N	Y	Y	N	N	Y	Y	N
2 ***Weber***	N	N	N	N	Y	Y	?	Y
3 ***Frenzel***	N	N	N	N	N	Y	Y	N
4 Vento	N	N	Y	N	Y	?	?	Y
5 Sabo	N	N	N	N	Y	Y	Y	Y
6 Sikorski	N	N	N	N	N	Y	Y	Y
7 ***Stangeland***	N	N	Y	N	Y	Y	Y	Y
8 Oberstar	N	N	N	N	Y	Y	Y	Y
MISSISSIPPI								
1 Whitten	N	N	N	N	Y	Y	Y	Y
2 Espy	N	N	N	N	Y	Y	Y	Y
3 Montgomery	N	N	N	N	Y	Y	Y	Y
4 Parker	N	N	N	N	Y	Y	Y	Y
5 Taylor	Y	Y	Y	N	Y	Y	Y	Y
MISSOURI								
1 Clay	N	N	N	N	Y	#	?	Y
2 ***Buechner***	N	N	N	N	Y	Y	Y	N
3 Gephardt	N	N	N	N	Y	Y	Y	Y
4 Skelton	N	N	N	N	Y	Y	Y	Y
5 Wheat	N	N	N	N	Y	Y	Y	Y
6 ***Coleman***	N	N	N	N	Y	Y	Y	Y
7 ***Hancock***	N	Y	Y	N	N	N	Y	N
8 ***Emerson***	N	Y	Y	N	Y	Y	Y	Y
9 Volkmer	N	N	?	N	Y	Y	Y	Y
MONTANA								
1 Williams	N	N	N	N	N	Y	Y	Y
2 ***Marlenee***	N	Y	Y	N	Y	N	Y	N
NEBRASKA								
1 ***Bereuter***	N	N	Y	N	Y	Y	Y	N
2 Hoagland	N	N	N	N	Y	Y	Y	Y
3 ***Smith***	N	N	N	N	Y	Y	Y	N
NEVADA								
1 Bilbray	N	N	N	N	Y	Y	Y	Y
2 ***Vucanovich***	N	N	N	N	Y	Y	Y	Y
NEW HAMPSHIRE								
1 ***Smith***	N	N	N	N	N	N	Y	N
2 ***Douglas***	N	N	N	N	Y	Y	Y	N
NEW JERSEY								
1 Vacancy								
2 Hughes	N	N	Y	N	N	Y	Y	Y
3 Pallone	N	N	N	N	Y	Y	Y	Y
4 ***Smith***	N	N	N	N	Y	Y	Y	Y
5 ***Roukema***	N	N	N	N	Y	Y	Y	Y
6 Dwyer	N	N	N	N	Y	Y	Y	Y
7 ***Rinaldo***	N	N	N	N	Y	Y	Y	Y
8 Roe	N	N	N	N	Y	Y	Y	Y
9 Torricelli	?	N	N	N	Y	Y	Y	Y
10 Payne	N	N	N	N	Y	Y	Y	Y
11 ***Gallo***	N	N	N	N	Y	Y	Y	Y
12 ***Courter***	N	N	N	N	Y	Y	Y	Y
13 ***Saxton***	N	N	N	N	Y	Y	Y	Y
14 Guarini	N	N	N	N	Y	Y	Y	Y
NEW MEXICO								
1 ***Schiff***	N	N	N	N	Y	Y	Y	Y
2 ***Skeen***	N	N	N	N	Y	Y	Y	N
3 Richardson	N	N	N	N	Y	Y	Y	Y
NEW YORK								
1 Hochbrueckner	N	N	N	N	Y	Y	Y	Y
2 Downey	N	N	N	N	Y	Y	Y	Y
3 Mrazek	N	N	N	N	Y	Y	Y	Y
4 ***Lent***	N	N	N	N	Y	Y	Y	Y
5 ***McGrath***	N	N	N	N	Y	Y	Y	Y
6 Flake	N	N	N	N	Y	Y	Y	Y
7 Ackerman	N	N	N	N	Y	Y	Y	Y
8 Scheuer	N	N	N	N	Y	Y	Y	Y
9 Manton	N	N	N	N	Y	Y	Y	Y
10 Schumer	N	N	N	N	Y	Y	Y	Y
11 Towns	N	N	N	N	Y	Y	Y	Y
12 Owens	N	N	N	N	Y	Y	Y	Y
13 Solarz	N	N	N	N	Y	Y	Y	Y
14 ***Molinari***	N	N	N	N	Y	Y	Y	Y
15 ***Green***	N	N	N	N	Y	Y	Y	Y
16 Rangel	N	N	N	N	Y	Y	Y	Y
17 Weiss	N	N	N	N	Y	Y	Y	Y
18 Serrano	N	N	N	N	Y	Y	Y	Y
19 Engel	?	N	N	N	Y	Y	Y	Y
20 Lowey	N	N	N	N	Y	?	?	Y
21 ***Fish***	N	N	N	N	Y	Y	Y	Y
22 ***Gilman***	N	N	N	N	Y	Y	Y	Y
23 McNulty	N	N	N	N	Y	Y	Y	Y
24 ***Solomon***	N	N	N	N	Y	Y	Y	N
25 ***Boehlert***	N	N	N	N	Y	Y	Y	Y
26 ***Martin***	N	N	N	N	Y	Y	Y	Y
27 ***Walsh***	N	N	N	N	Y	Y	Y	Y
28 McHugh	N	N	N	N	Y	Y	Y	Y
29 ***Horton***	N	N	N	N	Y	Y	Y	Y
30 Slaughter	N	N	?	N	Y	Y	Y	Y
31 ***Paxon***	N	N	N	N	Y	Y	Y	Y
32 LaFalce	N	N	N	N	Y	Y	Y	Y
33 Nowak	N	N	N	N	Y	Y	Y	Y
34 ***Houghton***	N	N	N	N	Y	Y	Y	Y
NORTH CAROLINA								
1 Jones	Y	Y	Y	N	Y	Y	Y	Y
2 Valentine	Y	Y	Y	N	Y	Y	Y	Y
3 Lancaster	N	N	N	N	Y	Y	Y	Y
4 Price	N	N	N	N	Y	Y	Y	Y
5 Neal	?	N	N	N	Y	Y	Y	Y
6 ***Coble***	N	N	N	N	Y	Y	Y	N
7 Rose	N	N	N	N	Y	Y	Y	Y
8 Hefner	N	Y	Y	N	Y	Y	Y	Y
9 ***McMillan***	N	N	N	N	Y	Y	Y	N
10 ***Ballenger***	N	N	N	N	Y	Y	Y	Y
11 Clarke	N	N	N	N	Y	Y	Y	Y
NORTH DAKOTA								
AL Dorgan	N	Y	Y	N	N	Y	Y	Y
OHIO								
1 Luken	?	N	N	N	Y	Y	Y	Y
2 ***Gradison***	N	N	N	N	Y	Y	Y	Y
3 Hall	N	N	N	N	Y	Y	Y	?
4 ***Oxley***	N	N	N	N	Y	Y	Y	N
5 ***Gillmor***	N	N	N	N	Y	Y	Y	Y
6 ***McEwen***	N	N	N	N	Y	N	Y	Y
7 ***DeWine***	N	N	N	N	Y	Y	Y	Y
8 ***Lukens***	N	N	N	N	Y	Y	Y	Y
9 Kaptur	N	N	N	N	Y	Y	Y	Y
10 ***Miller***	Y	Y	Y	N	N	Y	Y	Y
11 Eckart	Y	Y	Y	N	Y	Y	Y	Y
12 ***Kasich***	N	N	N	N	N	Y	Y	N
13 Pease	Y	Y	Y	N	N	Y	Y	Y
14 Sawyer	N	N	N	N	Y	Y	Y	Y
15 ***Wylie***	N	N	N	N	Y	Y	Y	N
16 ***Regula***	N	N	Y	N	Y	Y	Y	Y
17 Traficant	Y	Y	Y	N	Y	Y	Y	Y
18 Applegate	Y	Y	Y	N	N	Y	Y	Y
19 Feighan	?	?	?	?	?	?	?	?
20 Oakar	N	Y	Y	N	Y	Y	Y	Y
21 Stokes	N	N	N	N	Y	Y	Y	Y
OKLAHOMA								
1 ***Inhofe***	N	N	N	N	Y	Y	Y	Y
2 Synar	N	N	N	N	Y	Y	Y	Y
3 Watkins	N	Y	Y	N	Y	Y	Y	Y
4 McCurdy	N	N	N	N	Y	Y	Y	Y
5 ***Edwards***	N	N	N	N	Y	Y	Y	N
6 English	N	Y	Y	N	Y	Y	Y	Y
OREGON								
1 AuCoin	N	N	N	N	Y	Y	Y	Y
2 ***Smith, B.***	N	N	N	N	Y	Y	Y	Y
3 Wyden	N	N	N	N	Y	Y	Y	Y
4 DeFazio	N	N	N	N	Y	Y	Y	Y
5 ***Smith, D.***	N	N	N	N	N	Y	Y	N
PENNSYLVANIA								
1 Foglietta	N	N	N	N	Y	Y	Y	Y
2 Gray	N	N	N	N	Y	Y	Y	Y
3 Borski	N	N	N	N	Y	Y	Y	Y
4 Kolter	N	N	Y	N	Y	Y	Y	Y
5 ***Schulze***	N	N	N	N	Y	Y	Y	Y
6 Yatron	N	N	N	N	Y	Y	Y	Y
7 ***Weldon***	N	N	N	N	Y	Y	Y	Y
8 Kostmayer	N	N	N	N	Y	Y	Y	Y
9 ***Shuster***	N	N	N	N	Y	Y	Y	Y
10 ***McDade***	N	N	N	N	Y	Y	Y	Y
11 Kanjorski	Y	Y	Y	N	N	Y	Y	Y
12 Murtha	N	N	N	N	Y	Y	Y	Y
13 ***Coughlin***	N	N	N	N	Y	Y	Y	N
14 Coyne	N	N	N	N	Y	Y	Y	Y
15 ***Ritter***	N	N	N	N	Y	Y	Y	Y
16 ***Walker***	N	N	N	N	N	Y	Y	N
17 ***Gekas***	N	N	N	N	Y	Y	Y	Y
18 Walgren	N	Y	Y	N	Y	Y	Y	Y
19 ***Goodling***	N	N	N	N	Y	Y	Y	Y
20 Gaydos	N	Y	Y	N	N	Y	Y	Y
21 ***Ridge***	N	N	N	N	Y	Y	Y	Y
22 Murphy	Y	Y	Y	N	N	Y	Y	Y
23 ***Clinger***	N	N	N	N	Y	Y	Y	Y
RHODE ISLAND								
1 ***Machtley***	N	N	N	N	Y	Y	Y	Y
2 ***Schneider***	N	N	N	N	Y	Y	Y	Y
SOUTH CAROLINA								
1 ***Ravenel***	N	N	N	N	Y	Y	Y	Y
2 ***Spence***	N	N	N	N	Y	Y	Y	Y
3 Derrick	N	N	N	N	Y	Y	Y	Y
4 Patterson	N	Y	Y	N	N	Y	Y	Y
5 Spratt	N	N	N	N	Y	Y	Y	Y
6 Tallon	Y	Y	Y	N	Y	Y	Y	Y
SOUTH DAKOTA								
AL Johnson	N	N	N	N	Y	Y	Y	Y
TENNESSEE								
1 ***Quillen***	N	N	N	N	Y	Y	Y	Y
2 ***Duncan***	Y	Y	Y	N	N	Y	Y	Y
3 Lloyd	N	N	N	N	Y	Y	Y	Y
4 Cooper	N	N	N	N	Y	Y	Y	Y
5 Clement	N	N	N	N	Y	Y	Y	Y
6 Gordon	N	N	N	N	Y	Y	Y	Y
7 ***Sundquist***	N	N	N	N	Y	Y	Y	Y
8 Tanner	Y	Y	Y	N	Y	Y	Y	Y
9 Ford	?	?	?	?	?	?	?	?
TEXAS								
1 Chapman	N	N	N	N	Y	Y	Y	Y
2 Wilson	N	N	N	N	Y	Y	Y	Y
3 ***Bartlett***	N	N	N	N	Y	Y	Y	N
4 Hall	Y	Y	Y	N	Y	Y	Y	Y
5 Bryant	Y	Y	Y	N	Y	Y	Y	Y
6 ***Barton***	N	Y	Y	N	N	Y	Y	N
7 ***Archer***	N	N	N	N	N	Y	Y	N
8 ***Fields***	Y	Y	Y	N	N	Y	Y	N
9 Brooks	N	N	N	N	Y	Y	Y	Y
10 Pickle	N	N	N	N	Y	Y	Y	Y
11 Leath	N	N	N	N	?	Y	Y	Y
12 Geren	N	N	N	N	Y	Y	Y	Y
13 Sarpalius	N	N	N	N	Y	Y	Y	Y
14 Laughlin	N	N	N	N	Y	Y	Y	Y
15 de la Garza	N	N	N	N	Y	Y	Y	Y
16 Coleman	N	N	N	N	Y	Y	Y	Y
17 Stenholm	N	N	N	N	Y	Y	Y	N
18 Washington	Y	Y	Y	N	Y	Y	Y	?
19 ***Combest***	N	Y	Y	N	N	N	Y	N
20 Gonzalez	Y	N	N	N	N	Y	Y	Y
21 ***Smith***	N	N	N	N	Y	Y	Y	N
22 ***DeLay***	N	N	N	N	N	N	Y	N
23 Bustamante	?	?	?	?	#	Y	Y	Y
24 Frost	N	N	N	N	Y	Y	Y	Y
25 Andrews	N	N	N	N	Y	Y	Y	Y
26 ***Armey***	N	N	N	N	N	N	Y	N
27 Ortiz	N	N	Y	N	Y	Y	Y	Y
UTAH								
1 ***Hansen***	N	N	N	N	N	Y	Y	N
2 Owens	N	N	N	N	Y	Y	Y	Y
3 ***Nielson***	Y	Y	Y	N	N	N	Y	N
VERMONT								
AL ***Smith***	N	N	N	N	Y	Y	Y	Y
VIRGINIA								
1 ***Bateman***	N	N	N	N	Y	Y	Y	Y
2 Pickett	N	N	N	N	N	Y	?	Y
3 ***Bliley***	N	N	N	N	Y	Y	Y	N
4 Sisisky	N	N	N	N	Y	Y	Y	Y
5 Payne	N	N	N	N	Y	Y	Y	Y
6 Olin	N	N	N	N	Y	Y	Y	Y
7 ***Slaughter***	N	N	N	N	Y	Y	Y	N
8 ***Parris***	N	N	N	N	Y	Y	Y	Y
9 Boucher	N	N	N	N	Y	Y	Y	Y
10 ***Wolf***	N	N	N	N	Y	Y	Y	Y
WASHINGTON								
1 ***Miller***	N	N	N	N	Y	Y	Y	N
2 Swift	N	N	N	N	Y	Y	Y	Y
3 Unsoeld	N	N	N	N	Y	Y	Y	Y
4 ***Morrison***	N	N	N	N	Y	Y	Y	Y
5 Foley								
6 Dicks	N	N	N	N	Y	Y	Y	Y
7 McDermott	N	N	N	N	Y	Y	Y	Y
8 ***Chandler***	N	N	N	N	Y	Y	Y	Y
WEST VIRGINIA								
1 Mollohan	Y	Y	Y	N	Y	Y	Y	Y
2 Staggers	N	N	N	N	Y	Y	Y	Y
3 Wise	N	N	N	N	Y	Y	Y	Y
4 Rahall	Y	Y	Y	N	N	Y	Y	Y
WISCONSIN								
1 Aspin	N	N	N	N	Y	Y	Y	Y
2 Kastenmeier	Y	Y	Y	N	N	Y	Y	Y
3 ***Gunderson***	N	N	N	N	Y	Y	Y	Y
4 Kleczka	N	Y	Y	N	Y	Y	Y	Y
5 Moody	N	N	N	N	Y	Y	Y	Y
6 ***Petri***	Y	Y	Y	N	N	Y	Y	N
7 Obey	N	N	N	N	Y	Y	N	Y
8 ***Roth***	Y	Y	Y	N	N	Y	Y	Y
9 ***Sensenbrenner***	Y	Y	Y	N	N	Y	Y	N
WYOMING								
AL ***Thomas***	N	N	N	N	Y	Y	Y	N

Southern states - Ala., Ark., Fla., Ga., Ky., La., Miss., N.C., Okla., S.C., Tenn., Texas, Va.
Omitted votes are quorum calls, which CQ does not include in its vote charts.

HOUSE VOTES 69, 71, 72, 73, 74, 75

69. HR 1236. Vertical Price Fixing/Previous Question. Moakley, D-Mass., motion to order the previous question (thus ending debate and the possibility of amendment) on the rule (H Res 373) to provide for House consideration of the bill to clarify the evidence necessary to establish resale (vertical) price fixing. Republicans sought to defeat the motion to make in order an amendment that contained the text of President Bush's anticrime package. Motion agreed to 235-157: R 0-156; D 235-1 (ND 160-1, SD 75-0), April 18, 1990.

71. HR 1236. Vertical Price Fixing/Evidentiary Standards. Douglas, R-N.H., substitute amendment to codify a 1911 Supreme Court ruling that resale price fixing is per se illegal under antitrust laws and to delete all evidentiary standards contained in the bill. Rejected 155-242: R 136-25; D 19-217 (ND 2-158, SD 17-59), April 18, 1990.

72. HR 1236. Vertical Price Fixing/Evidentiary Standards. Fish, R-N.Y., amendment to require that before an antitrust case of this type may go to trial, the plaintiff make a preliminary showing that a manufacturer and retailer conspired to fix a minimum price for a product and that a complaining retailer's decision to sell the product at a lower price was the major cause of the manufacturer's decision to terminate that retailer's contract. Rejected 192-204: R 156-4; D 36-200 (ND 12-148, SD 24-52), April 18, 1990.

73. HR 1236. Vertical Price Fixing/Allowable Defense. Campbell, R-Calif., amendment to make it a defense to price-fixing actions brought under the bill that the defendant had such a small share of the relevant market as to lack market power. Rejected 190-199: R 153-3; D 37-196 (ND 15-144, SD 22-52), April 18, 1990.

74. HR 1236. Vertical Price Fixing/Passage. Passage of the bill to clarify the evidence necessary to establish resale (vertical) price fixing. Passed 235-157: R 23-134; D 212-23 (ND 157-4, SD 55-19), April 18, 1990. A "nay" was a vote supporting the president's position.

75. HR 644. Wild and Scenic Rivers/Passage. Passage of the bill to include segments of the Jemez and Pecos rivers in New Mexico as part of the National Wild and Scenic Rivers System. Passed 391-1: R 156-1; D 235-0 (ND 161-0, SD 74-0), April 19, 1990.

KEY

Y Voted for (yea).
\# Paired for.
\+ Announced for.
N Voted against (nay).
X Paired against.
\- Announced against.
P Voted "present."
C Voted "present" to avoid possible conflict of interest.
? Did not vote or otherwise make a position known.

Democrats ***Republicans***

	69	71	72	73	74	75
ALABAMA						
1 ***Callahan***	N	Y	Y	Y	N	?
2 ***Dickinson***	N	Y	Y	Y	N	Y
3 Browder	Y	N	N	N	N	Y
4 Bevill	Y	N	N	N	Y	Y
5 Flippo	?	?	?	?	?	?
6 Erdreich	Y	N	Y	N	Y	Y
7 Harris	Y	N	Y	N	Y	Y
ALASKA						
AL ***Young***	N	Y	Y	Y	N	Y
ARIZONA						
1 ***Rhodes***	N	Y	Y	Y	N	Y
2 Udall	Y	N	N	Y	Y	Y
3 ***Stump***	X	#	#	#	X	X
4 ***Kyl***	N	Y	Y	Y	N	Y
5 ***Kolbe***	N	Y	Y	Y	N	Y
ARKANSAS						
1 Alexander	Y	N	N	N	Y	Y
2 ***Robinson***	?	?	?	?	?	Y
3 ***Hammerschmidt***	N	Y	Y	Y	N	Y
4 Anthony	Y	N	N	N	Y	Y
CALIFORNIA						
1 Bosco	Y	N	N	N	Y	Y
2 ***Herger***	N	Y	Y	Y	N	Y
3 Matsui	Y	N	N	N	Y	?
4 Fazio	Y	N	N	N	Y	Y
5 Pelosi	Y	N	N	N	Y	Y
6 Boxer	Y	N	N	N	Y	?
7 Miller	Y	N	N	N	Y	Y
8 Dellums	Y	N	N	N	Y	Y
9 Stark	Y	N	N	N	Y	Y
10 Edwards	Y	N	N	N	Y	Y
11 Lantos	Y	N	N	N	Y	Y
12 ***Campbell***	N	N	Y	Y	N	Y
13 Mineta	?	?	?	?	?	Y
14 ***Shumway***	N	Y	Y	Y	N	Y
15 Condit	Y	N	N	Y	Y	Y
16 Panetta	Y	N	N	N	Y	Y
17 ***Pashayan***	N	Y	Y	Y	N	Y
18 Lehman	Y	N	N	N	Y	?
19 ***Lagomarsino***	N	Y	Y	Y	N	Y
20 ***Thomas***	X	#	#	#	X	?
21 ***Gallegly***	N	Y	Y	Y	N	Y
22 ***Moorhead***	N	Y	Y	Y	N	Y
23 Beilenson	Y	?	?	?	?	?
24 Waxman	Y	N	N	N	Y	Y
25 Roybal	Y	N	N	N	Y	Y
26 Berman	Y	N	N	N	?	Y
27 Levine	Y	N	N	N	Y	Y
28 Dixon	Y	N	N	N	Y	Y
29 Hawkins	Y	N	?	?	#	Y
30 Martinez	Y	N	N	?	N	Y
31 Dymally	Y	N	N	N	Y	Y
32 Anderson	Y	N	N	N	Y	Y
33 ***Dreier***	N	Y	Y	Y	N	Y
34 Torres	Y	N	N	Y	Y	Y
35 ***Lewis***	X	#	#	#	X	?
36 Brown	?	?	?	?	?	?
37 ***McCandless***	N	Y	Y	Y	N	Y
38 ***Dornan***	?	?	Y	Y	N	Y
39 ***Dannemeyer***	N	Y	Y	Y	Y	Y
40 ***Cox***	N	Y	Y	Y	N	Y
41 ***Lowery***	N	Y	Y	Y	N	Y
42 ***Rohrabacher***	N	Y	Y	Y	N	Y
43 ***Packard***	N	Y	Y	Y	N	Y
44 Bates	Y	N	N	N	Y	?
45 ***Hunter***	N	Y	Y	Y	N	Y
COLORADO						
1 Schroeder	Y	N	N	N	Y	Y
2 Skaggs	Y	N	Y	Y	Y	Y
3 Campbell	Y	N	Y	N	N	Y
4 ***Brown***	N	N	Y	Y	N	Y
5 ***Hefley***	N	Y	Y	Y	N	Y
6 ***Schaefer***	N	Y	Y	Y	N	Y
CONNECTICUT						
1 Kennelly	Y	N	N	N	Y	Y
2 Gejdenson	Y	N	N	N	Y	Y
3 Morrison	Y	N	N	?	Y	Y
4 ***Shays***	N	N	Y	Y	Y	Y
5 ***Rowland***	N	N	Y	Y	Y	Y
6 ***Johnson***	N	N	Y	Y	Y	Y
DELAWARE						
AL Carper	Y	N	N	Y	Y	Y
FLORIDA						
1 Hutto	Y	Y	Y	Y	N	Y
2 ***Grant***	?	?	?	?	?	?
3 Bennett	Y	N	N	N	Y	Y
4 ***James***	N	Y	Y	Y	N	Y
5 ***McCollum***	N	N	Y	Y	Y	?
6 ***Stearns***	N	Y	Y	Y	N	Y
7 Gibbons	Y	N	N	N	Y	Y
8 ***Young***	N	N	Y	Y	Y	Y
9 ***Bilirakis***	N	Y	Y	Y	N	Y
10 ***Ireland***	N	Y	Y	Y	N	Y
11 Nelson	+	X	X	X	#	+
12 ***Lewis***	N	Y	Y	Y	N	Y
13 ***Goss***	N	Y	Y	Y	N	Y
14 Johnston	Y	N	N	Y	Y	Y
15 ***Shaw***	N	Y	Y	Y	N	Y
16 Smith	Y	N	N	N	Y	Y
17 Lehman	Y	N	N	N	Y	Y
18 ***Ros-Lehtinen***	N	Y	Y	Y	Y	Y
19 Fascell	Y	N	N	N	Y	Y
GEORGIA						
1 Thomas	Y	N	N	N	Y	Y
2 Hatcher	Y	N	N	N	Y	Y
3 Ray	Y	Y	Y	Y	N	?
4 Jones	Y	N	Y	N	Y	Y
5 Lewis	Y	N	N	N	Y	Y
6 ***Gingrich***	N	Y	?	?	?	Y
7 Darden	Y	N	N	N	Y	Y
8 Rowland	Y	N	N	N	Y	Y
9 Jenkins	?	#	#	?	X	?
10 Barnard	Y	Y	Y	Y	N	?
HAWAII						
1 ***Saiki***	–	–	–	–	+	+
2 Akaka	#	X	X	X	#	Y
IDAHO						
1 ***Craig***	X	#	#	#	?	?
2 Stallings	Y	Y	Y	Y	N	Y
ILLINOIS						
1 Hayes	Y	N	N	N	Y	Y
2 Savage	?	N	N	N	Y	Y
3 Russo	Y	N	N	N	Y	Y
4 Sangmeister	Y	N	N	N	Y	Y
5 Lipinski	Y	N	N	N	Y	Y
6 ***Hyde***	N	N	N	N	Y	Y
7 Collins	#	X	?	X	#	?
8 Rostenkowski	Y	N	N	N	Y	Y
9 Yates	Y	N	N	N	Y	Y
10 ***Porter***	N	N	N	N	Y	Y
11 Annunzio	Y	N	N	N	Y	Y
12 ***Crane***	N	Y	Y	Y	N	N
13 ***Fawell***	N	Y	Y	Y	N	Y
14 ***Hastert***	N	Y	Y	Y	N	Y
15 ***Madigan***	N	Y	Y	Y	N	Y
16 ***Martin***	N	Y	Y	Y	N	Y
17 Evans	Y	N	N	N	Y	Y
18 ***Michel***	?	Y	Y	Y	N	Y
19 Bruce	Y	N	N	N	Y	Y
20 Durbin	+	–	–	–	+	Y
21 Costello	Y	N	N	N	Y	Y
22 Poshard	Y	N	N	N	Y	Y
INDIANA						
1 Visclosky	Y	N	N	Y	Y	Y
2 Sharp	Y	N	N	Y	Y	Y
3 ***Hiler***	N	Y	Y	Y	N	Y

ND Northern Democrats SD Southern Democrats

	69	71	72	73	74	75
4 Long	Y	N	N	Y	Y	Y
5 Jontz	Y	N	N	N	Y	Y
6 ***Burton***	N	Y	Y	Y	N	Y
7 ***Myers***	N	Y	Y	Y	N	Y
8 McCloskey	Y	N	N	N	Y	Y
9 Hamilton	Y	N	N	Y	Y	Y
10 Jacobs	N	N	N	N	Y	Y
IOWA						
1 ***Leach***	N	Y	Y	Y	N	Y
2 ***Tauke***	?	?	?	?	?	Y
3 Nagle	Y	N	?	N	Y	Y
4 Smith	Y	N	N	N	Y	Y
5 ***Lightfoot***	N	Y	Y	Y	N	Y
6 ***Grandy***	N	Y	Y	Y	N	Y
KANSAS						
1 ***Roberts***	N	Y	Y	Y	N	Y
2 Slattery	Y	N	N	N	Y	Y
3 ***Meyers***	N	Y	Y	Y	Y	Y
4 Glickman	Y	N	N	N	Y	Y
5 ***Whittaker***	N	Y	Y	Y	N	Y
KENTUCKY						
1 Hubbard	Y	Y	Y	Y	N	Y
2 Natcher	Y	N	N	N	Y	Y
3 Mazzoli	Y	N	N	N	Y	Y
4 ***Bunning***	N	Y	Y	Y	N	Y
5 ***Rogers***	N	Y	Y	Y	N	Y
6 ***Hopkins***	N	N	Y	Y	N	Y
7 Perkins	Y	N	N	N	Y	Y
LOUISIANA						
1 ***Livingston***	N	Y	Y	Y	N	Y
2 Boggs	Y	N	N	N	Y	Y
3 Tauzin	Y	Y	Y	?	X	Y
4 ***McCrery***	N	Y	Y	Y	N	Y
5 Huckaby	Y	N	Y	N	Y	Y
6 ***Baker***	N	Y	Y	Y	N	Y
7 Hayes	Y	N	N	?	X	Y
8 ***Holloway***	N	Y	Y	Y	N	?
MAINE						
1 Brennan	Y	N	N	N	Y	Y
2 ***Snowe***	N	Y	Y	Y	Y	Y
MARYLAND						
1 Dyson	Y	N	N	N	Y	Y
2 ***Bentley***	N	Y	Y	Y	N	Y
3 Cardin	Y	N	N	N	Y	Y
4 McMillen	Y	N	N	N	Y	Y
5 Hoyer	Y	N	N	N	Y	Y
6 Byron	Y	Y	Y	Y	N	Y
7 Mfume	Y	N	N	N	Y	Y
8 ***Morella***	N	Y	Y	Y	N	Y
MASSACHUSETTS						
1 ***Conte***	N	N	Y	Y	Y	Y
2 Neal	Y	N	N	N	Y	Y
3 Early	Y	N	N	N	Y	?
4 Frank	Y	N	N	N	Y	Y
5 Atkins	Y	N	N	N	Y	Y
6 Mavroules	Y	N	N	N	Y	Y
7 Markey	Y	N	N	N	Y	Y
8 Kennedy	Y	N	N	N	Y	Y
9 Moakley	Y	N	N	N	Y	Y
10 Studds	Y	N	N	N	Y	Y
11 Donnelly	Y	N	N	N	Y	Y
MICHIGAN						
1 Conyers	Y	N	N	N	Y	Y
2 ***Pursell***	N	N	Y	Y	N	Y
3 Wolpe	Y	N	N	N	Y	Y
4 ***Upton***	N	Y	Y	Y	N	Y
5 ***Henry***	N	N	Y	Y	Y	Y
6 Carr	Y	N	N	N	Y	Y
7 Kildee	Y	N	N	N	Y	Y
8 Traxler	Y	N	N	N	Y	Y
9 ***Vander Jagt***	N	Y	Y	Y	N	Y
10 ***Schuette***	N	Y	Y	Y	N	Y
11 ***Davis***	N	Y	Y	Y	N	Y
12 Bonior	Y	N	N	N	?	#
13 Crockett	?	?	?	?	?	?
14 Hertel	Y	N	N	N	Y	Y
15 Ford	Y	N	N	N	Y	Y
16 Dingell	?	X	X	N	Y	Y
17 Levin	Y	N	N	N	Y	Y
18 ***Broomfield***	N	Y	Y	Y	N	Y
MINNESOTA						
1 Penny	Y	N	N	N	Y	Y
2 ***Weber***	N	Y	Y	Y	N	Y
3 ***Frenzel***	N	Y	?	?	?	Y
4 Vento	Y	N	N	N	Y	Y

	69	71	72	73	74	75
5 Sabo	Y	N	N	N	Y	Y
6 Sikorski	Y	N	N	N	Y	Y
7 ***Stangeland***	N	Y	Y	Y	N	Y
8 Oberstar	Y	N	N	N	Y	Y
MISSISSIPPI						
1 Whitten	Y	N	N	N	Y	Y
2 Espy	Y	N	N	Y	Y	Y
3 Montgomery	Y	Y	Y	Y	N	Y
4 Parker	Y	Y	Y	Y	N	Y
5 Taylor	Y	Y	Y	Y	N	Y
MISSOURI						
1 Clay	?	?	?	?	?	?
2 ***Buechner***	N	Y	Y	Y	N	Y
3 Gephardt	Y	N	N	N	Y	Y
4 Skelton	Y	N	Y	Y	Y	Y
5 Wheat	Y	N	N	N	Y	Y
6 ***Coleman***	N	Y	Y	Y	N	Y
7 ***Hancock***	N	Y	Y	Y	N	Y
8 ***Emerson***	N	Y	Y	Y	N	Y
9 Volkmer	Y	N	N	Y	Y	Y
MONTANA						
1 Williams	Y	N	N	N	Y	Y
2 ***Marlenee***	N	Y	Y	Y	N	Y
NEBRASKA						
1 ***Bereuter***	N	Y	Y	Y	N	Y
2 Hoagland	Y	N	N	N	Y	Y
3 ***Smith***	?	Y	Y	Y	N	Y
NEVADA						
1 Bilbray	Y	N	Y	N	Y	Y
2 ***Vucanovich***	N	Y	Y	Y	N	?
NEW HAMPSHIRE						
1 ***Smith***	N	N	Y	Y	Y	Y
2 ***Douglas***	N	Y	Y	Y	N	Y
NEW JERSEY						
1 Vacancy						
2 Hughes	Y	N	N	N	Y	Y
3 Pallone	Y	N	N	N	Y	Y
4 ***Smith***	N	N	Y	Y	Y	Y
5 ***Roukema***	N	N	Y	Y	Y	Y
6 Dwyer	Y	N	N	N	Y	Y
7 ***Rinaldo***	N	N	N	?	#	Y
8 Roe	Y	N	N	N	Y	Y
9 Torricelli	Y	N	N	N	Y	?
10 Payne	Y	N	N	N	Y	Y
11 ***Gallo***	N	N	Y	Y	Y	Y
12 ***Courter***	N	Y	Y	Y	N	Y
13 ***Saxton***	N	N	Y	Y	Y	Y
14 Guarini	Y	N	N	N	Y	Y
NEW MEXICO						
1 ***Schiff***	N	Y	Y	Y	N	Y
2 ***Skeen***	N	Y	Y	Y	N	Y
3 Richardson	Y	?	N	N	Y	Y
NEW YORK						
1 Hochbrueckner	Y	N	N	N	Y	Y
2 Downey	Y	N	N	N	Y	Y
3 Mrazek	Y	N	N	N	Y	Y
4 ***Lent***	?	?	?	?	?	Y
5 ***McGrath***	?	?	?	?	?	?
6 Flake	Y	N	N	N	Y	Y
7 Ackerman	Y	N	N	N	Y	Y
8 Scheuer	Y	N	N	N	Y	Y
9 Manton	Y	?	N	N	Y	Y
10 Schumer	Y	N	N	N	Y	Y
11 Towns	Y	N	N	N	Y	Y
12 Owens	#	N	N	N	Y	Y
13 Solarz	Y	N	N	N	Y	Y
14 ***Molinari***	N	Y	Y	Y	N	Y
15 ***Green***	N	Y	Y	Y	N	Y
16 Rangel	Y	N	N	N	Y	Y
17 Weiss	Y	N	N	N	Y	Y
18 Serrano	Y	N	N	N	Y	Y
19 Engel	Y	N	N	N	Y	Y
20 Lowey	Y	N	N	N	Y	Y
21 ***Fish***	N	Y	Y	Y	N	Y
22 ***Gilman***	N	N	Y	Y	Y	Y
23 McNulty	Y	N	N	N	Y	Y
24 ***Solomon***	N	Y	Y	Y	N	Y
25 ***Boehlert***	N	Y	Y	Y	N	Y
26 ***Martin***	N	Y	Y	Y	N	Y
27 ***Walsh***	N	Y	Y	Y	N	Y
28 McHugh	Y	N	N	N	Y	Y
29 ***Horton***	?	Y	Y	Y	N	?
30 Slaughter	Y	N	N	N	Y	Y
31 ***Paxon***	N	Y	Y	Y	N	Y

	69	71	72	73	74	75
32 LaFalce	Y	N	N	N	Y	Y
33 Nowak	Y	N	N	N	Y	Y
34 ***Houghton***	N	Y	Y	#	?	?
NORTH CAROLINA						
1 Jones	Y	N	N	N	Y	Y
2 Valentine	Y	Y	Y	Y	N	Y
3 Lancaster	Y	N	N	N	Y	Y
4 Price	Y	N	N	N	Y	Y
5 Neal	Y	Y	Y	Y	N	Y
6 ***Coble***	N	Y	Y	Y	N	Y
7 Rose	Y	N	N	N	Y	Y
8 Hefner	?	N	N	N	Y	Y
9 ***McMillan***	N	Y	Y	Y	N	Y
10 ***Ballenger***	N	Y	Y	Y	N	Y
11 Clarke	Y	N	N	N	Y	Y
NORTH DAKOTA						
AL Dorgan	Y	N	N	?	Y	Y
OHIO						
1 Luken	Y	N	N	N	Y	Y
2 ***Gradison***	N	Y	Y	Y	N	Y
3 Hall	Y	N	N	N	Y	Y
4 ***Oxley***	N	Y	Y	Y	N	Y
5 ***Gillmor***	N	Y	Y	Y	N	Y
6 ***McEwen***	N	Y	Y	Y	N	Y
7 ***DeWine***	N	Y	Y	Y	N	Y
8 ***Lukens***	?	?	?	?	?	Y
9 Kaptur	Y	N	N	N	Y	Y
10 ***Miller***	N	Y	Y	Y	N	Y
11 Eckart	Y	N	N	N	Y	Y
12 ***Kasich***	N	Y	Y	Y	N	Y
13 Pease	Y	N	N	N	Y	Y
14 Sawyer	Y	N	N	N	Y	Y
15 ***Wylie***	N	Y	Y	Y	Y	Y
16 ***Regula***	N	Y	Y	Y	N	Y
17 Traficant	Y	N	N	N	Y	Y
18 Applegate	Y	N	Y	N	Y	Y
19 Feighan	Y	N	N	N	Y	Y
20 Oakar	Y	N	N	N	Y	Y
21 Stokes	Y	N	N	N	Y	Y
OKLAHOMA						
1 ***Inhofe***	?	?	?	?	?	?
2 Synar	Y	N	N	N	Y	Y
3 Watkins	?	?	?	?	?	?
4 McCurdy	Y	N	N	N	Y	Y
5 ***Edwards***	N	Y	Y	Y	N	?
6 English	Y	Y	Y	Y	N	Y
OREGON						
1 AuCoin	Y	N	Y	Y	Y	Y
2 ***Smith, B.***	N	Y	Y	Y	N	Y
3 Wyden	Y	N	N	N	Y	Y
4 DeFazio	Y	N	Y	N	Y	Y
5 ***Smith, D.***	N	Y	Y	Y	N	Y
PENNSYLVANIA						
1 Foglietta	Y	N	N	N	Y	Y
2 Gray	Y	N	N	N	Y	Y
3 Borski	Y	N	N	N	Y	Y
4 Kolter	Y	N	N	N	Y	Y
5 ***Schulze***	N	Y	Y	Y	N	Y
6 Yatron	Y	N	Y	N	Y	Y
7 ***Weldon***	N	Y	Y	?	?	Y
8 Kostmayer	Y	N	N	N	Y	Y
9 ***Shuster***	N	Y	Y	Y	N	Y
10 ***McDade***	N	N	N	N	Y	Y
11 Kanjorski	Y	N	N	N	Y	Y
12 Murtha	Y	N	N	N	Y	Y
13 ***Coughlin***	N	Y	Y	Y	N	Y
14 Coyne	Y	N	N	N	Y	Y
15 ***Ritter***	N	Y	Y	Y	N	Y
16 ***Walker***	N	Y	Y	Y	N	Y
17 ***Gekas***	N	Y	Y	Y	N	Y
18 Walgren	Y	N	N	N	Y	Y
19 ***Goodling***	N	N	Y	Y	Y	Y
20 Gaydos	Y	N	N	N	Y	Y
21 ***Ridge***	N	N	Y	Y	N	?
22 Murphy	Y	N	Y	N	Y	Y
23 ***Clinger***	N	N	Y	Y	N	Y
RHODE ISLAND						
1 ***Machtley***	?	Y	Y	Y	N	Y
2 ***Schneider***	N	Y	Y	Y	N	Y
SOUTH CAROLINA						
1 ***Ravenel***	N	Y	Y	Y	Y	Y
2 ***Spence***	N	Y	Y	Y	N	Y
3 Derrick	Y	Y	Y	N	N	Y
4 Patterson	Y	Y	Y	Y	N	Y
5 Spratt	Y	N	N	N	Y	Y
6 Tallon	Y	N	Y	Y	Y	Y

	69	71	72	73	74	75
SOUTH DAKOTA						
AL Johnson	Y	N	N	Y	Y	Y
TENNESSEE						
1 ***Quillen***	N	Y	Y	Y	N	Y
2 ***Duncan***	N	Y	Y	Y	N	Y
3 Lloyd	Y	Y	N	Y	N	Y
4 Cooper	Y	N	N	N	Y	Y
5 Clement	Y	N	N	N	Y	Y
6 Gordon	Y	N	N	N	Y	Y
7 ***Sundquist***	N	Y	Y	Y	N	Y
8 Tanner	?	?	?	?	?	?
9 Ford	?	?	X	X	?	?
TEXAS						
1 Chapman	Y	N	N	N	Y	Y
2 Wilson	Y	N	N	N	Y	Y
3 ***Bartlett***	N	Y	Y	Y	N	Y
4 Hall	Y	Y	Y	Y	N	Y
5 Bryant	Y	N	N	N	Y	Y
6 ***Barton***	N	Y	Y	Y	N	Y
7 ***Archer***	N	Y	Y	Y	N	Y
8 ***Fields***	N	Y	Y	Y	N	Y
9 Brooks	Y	N	N	N	Y	Y
10 Pickle	Y	N	N	Y	Y	Y
11 Leath	?	?	?	?	?	Y
12 Geren	Y	N	N	N	Y	Y
13 Sarpalius	Y	N	Y	Y	N	Y
14 Laughlin	Y	N	N	N	Y	?
15 de la Garza	Y	N	N	N	Y	Y
16 Coleman	Y	N	N	N	Y	Y
17 Stenholm	Y	Y	Y	Y	N	Y
18 Washington	Y	N	N	N	Y	Y
19 ***Combest***	N	Y	Y	Y	N	Y
20 Gonzalez	Y	N	N	N	Y	Y
21 ***Smith***	N	N	Y	Y	N	?
22 ***DeLay***	N	Y	Y	Y	N	?
23 Bustamante	Y	N	N	N	Y	Y
24 Frost	Y	N	N	N	Y	Y
25 Andrews	Y	N	N	N	Y	Y
26 ***Armey***	N	Y	Y	Y	N	Y
27 Ortiz	Y	N	N	N	Y	Y
UTAH						
1 ***Hansen***	N	Y	Y	Y	N	Y
2 Owens	?	?	?	?	?	Y
3 ***Nielson***	N	Y	Y	Y	N	Y
VERMONT						
AL ***Smith***	N	Y	Y	Y	N	Y
VIRGINIA						
1 ***Bateman***	N	Y	Y	Y	N	Y
2 Pickett	Y	Y	Y	Y	N	Y
3 ***Bliley***	N	Y	Y	Y	N	Y
4 Sisisky	Y	N	Y	Y	Y	Y
5 Payne	Y	N	Y	Y	N	Y
6 Olin	Y	N	N	N	Y	Y
7 ***Slaughter***	N	Y	Y	Y	N	Y
8 ***Parris***	?	Y	Y	Y	N	Y
9 Boucher	Y	N	N	N	Y	Y
10 ***Wolf***	N	Y	Y	Y	N	Y
WASHINGTON						
1 ***Miller***	–	+	+	+	+	Y
2 Swift	Y	N	N	N	Y	Y
3 Unsoeld	Y	N	N	N	Y	Y
4 ***Morrison***	N	Y	Y	Y	N	Y
5 Foley						
6 Dicks	Y	N	N	N	Y	Y
7 McDermott	Y	N	N	N	Y	Y
8 ***Chandler***	?	?	?	?	?	?
WEST VIRGINIA						
1 Mollohan	Y	N	N	N	Y	Y
2 Staggers	Y	N	N	N	Y	Y
3 Wise	Y	N	N	N	Y	Y
4 Rahall	?	?	?	?	Y	Y
WISCONSIN						
1 Aspin	Y	N	Y	N	Y	?
2 Kastenmeier	Y	N	N	N	Y	Y
3 ***Gunderson***	N	Y	Y	?	N	Y
4 Kleczka	Y	N	N	N	Y	Y
5 Moody	X	X	X	X	#	Y
6 ***Petri***	N	Y	Y	Y	N	Y
7 Obey	Y	N	N	N	Y	Y
8 ***Roth***	N	Y	Y	Y	N	Y
9 ***Sensenbrenner***	N	Y	Y	Y	N	Y
WYOMING						
AL ***Thomas***	N	Y	Y	Y	N	Y

Southern states - Ala., Ark., Fla., Ga., Ky., La., Miss., N.C., Okla., S.C., Tenn., Texas, Va.
Omitted votes are quorum calls, which CQ does not include in its vote charts.

76. H Res 354. Human Rights in Liberia/Adoption. Yatron, D-Pa., motion to suspend the rules and adopt the resolution to express the sense of the House condemning recent human rights abuses in Nimba County, Liberia, and urging the president not to permit military assistance to the Republic of Liberia. Motion agreed to 417-0: R 170-0; D 247-0 (ND 168-0, SD 79-0), April 24, 1990. A two-thirds majority of those present and voting (278 in this case) is required for passage under suspension of the rules.

77. H Con Res 290. Status of Jerusalem/Adoption. Fascell, D-Fla., motion to suspend the rules and adopt the resolution to express the sense of Congress that Jerusalem is and should remain the undivided capital of Israel, with free and open access to all people and all religions. Motion agreed to 378-34: R 157-10; D 221-24 (ND 146-21, SD 75-3), April 24, 1990. A two-thirds majority of those present and voting (275 in this case) is required for passage under suspension of the rules.

78. HR 3961. Vance Federal Building/Passage. Anderson, D-Calif., motion to suspend the rules and pass the bill to redesignate the federal building in Birmingham, Ala., as the Robert S. Vance Federal Building and United States Courthouse. Motion agreed to 417-0: R 169-0; D 248-0 (ND 168-0, SD 80-0), April 24, 1990. A two-thirds majority of those present and voting (278 in this case) is required for passage under suspension of the rules.

80. HR 3848. Money Laundering/Check-Cashing Fees. Foglietta, D-Pa., amendment to suggest uniform state guidelines under which check-cashing businesses could charge no more than 1.5 percent of the value of the check or $8, whichever is less. Adopted 207-200: R 30-132; D 177-68 (ND 144-23, SD 33-45), April 25, 1990.

81. HR 3848. Money Laundering/Record-Keeping. Torres, D-Calif., amendment to require the Treasury Department to establish a pilot program to record international electronic transfers of funds by having customers supply to banks the names, addresses and account numbers of parties involved. Rejected 127-283: R 6-158; D 121-125 (ND 101-67, SD 20-58), April 25, 1990.

82. HR 3848. Money Laundering/Passage. Passage of the bill to establish and extend programs to discourage financial institutions from participating in money-laundering schemes. Passed 406-0: R 163-0; D 243-0 (ND 166-0, SD 77-0), April 25, 1990. A "yea" was a vote supporting the president's position.

84. H Con Res 310. Fiscal 1991 Budget Resolution/Substitute Amendment. Kasich, R-Ohio, substitute amendment to freeze budget authority for defense and all discretionary domestic programs at fiscal 1990 levels, to cut $3.2 billion in Medicare spending, to increase revenues by $13.2 billion, to create $5.6 billion in new user fees and increased collections of debts owed the government, and to project a deficit of $63.6 billion. Rejected 106-305: R 79-89; D 27-216 (ND 7-160, SD 20-56), April 26, 1990.

85. H Con Res 310. Fiscal 1991 Budget Resolution/Substitute Amendment. Dannemeyer, R-Calif., substitute amendment to freeze budget authority and outlays for all defense spending and for all domestic discretionary programs except for science, space, and administration of justice programs, which would receive inflationary adjustments. The substitute also would save $39 billion in interest costs by refinancing the national debt with long-term, gold-backed bonds, increase revenues by $26.5 billion by collecting taxes owed the government, call for a cut in capital gains tax and project a deficit of $61.9 billion, and it would not cut entitlement programs. Rejected 48-354: R 42-119; D 6-235 (ND 2-164, SD 4-71), April 26, 1990.

KEY

Y Voted for (yea).
\# Paired for.
\+ Announced for.
N Voted against (nay).
X Paired against.
\- Announced against.
P Voted "present."
C Voted "present" to avoid possible conflict of interest.
? Did not vote or otherwise make a position known.

Democrats ***Republicans***

	76	77	78	80	81	82	84	85
ALABAMA								
1 ***Callahan***	Y	Y	Y	N	N	Y	Y	Y
2 ***Dickinson***	Y	P	Y	N	N	Y	Y	N
3 Browder	Y	Y	Y	N	N	Y	N	N
4 Bevill	Y	Y	Y	N	N	Y	N	N
5 Flippo	?	?	?	?	?	?	?	N
6 Erdreich	Y	Y	Y	N	N	Y	N	N
7 Harris	Y	Y	Y	N	N	Y	N	N
ALASKA								
AL ***Young***	Y	Y	Y	N	N	Y	N	Y
ARIZONA								
1 ***Rhodes***	Y	Y	Y	N	N	Y	N	N
2 Udall	Y	Y	Y	Y	Y	Y	N	N
3 ***Stump***	?	?	?	?	?	?	?	#
4 ***Kyl***	Y	Y	Y	N	N	Y	N	N
5 ***Kolbe***	Y	Y	Y	N	N	Y	Y	N
ARKANSAS								
1 Alexander	Y	Y	Y	Y	Y	Y	N	?
2 ***Robinson***	Y	Y	Y	N	N	Y	N	N
3 ***Hammerschmidt***	Y	Y	Y	N	N	Y	N	Y
4 Anthony	Y	Y	Y	Y	N	Y	N	N
CALIFORNIA								
1 Bosco	Y	Y	Y	Y	N	Y	?	?
2 ***Herger***	Y	Y	Y	N	N	Y	Y	Y
3 Matsui	Y	Y	Y	Y	N	Y	N	N
4 Fazio	Y	Y	Y	Y	Y	Y	N	N
5 Pelosi	Y	Y	Y	Y	Y	Y	N	N
6 Boxer	Y	Y	Y	Y	Y	Y	N	N
7 Miller	Y	Y	Y	Y	Y	Y	N	N
8 Dellums	Y	N	Y	Y	Y	Y	N	N
9 Stark	Y	Y	?	Y	Y	Y	N	?
10 Edwards	Y	Y	Y	Y	Y	Y	N	N
11 Lantos	Y	Y	Y	Y	Y	Y	N	N
12 ***Campbell***	Y	N	Y	N	N	Y	N	N
13 Mineta	Y	Y	Y	Y	Y	Y	N	N
14 ***Shumway***	Y	Y	Y	N	N	Y	N	Y
15 Condit	Y	Y	Y	N	Y	Y	Y	N
16 Panetta	Y	Y	Y	Y	Y	Y	N	N
17 ***Pashayan***	Y	Y	Y	?	N	Y	N	N
18 Lehman	Y	Y	Y	Y	Y	Y	N	N
19 ***Lagomarsino***	Y	Y	Y	N	N	Y	N	N
20 ***Thomas***	Y	Y	Y	N	N	Y	Y	N
21 ***Gallegly***	Y	Y	Y	N	N	Y	N	N
22 ***Moorhead***	Y	Y	Y	N	N	Y	Y	Y
23 Beilenson	Y	Y	Y	?	?	?	N	N
24 Waxman	Y	Y	Y	Y	Y	Y	N	N
25 Roybal	Y	N	Y	Y	Y	Y	N	N
26 Berman	Y	Y	Y	Y	Y	Y	N	N
27 Levine	Y	Y	Y	Y	Y	Y	N	N
28 Dixon	Y	Y	Y	Y	Y	Y	N	N
29 Hawkins	?	?	?	?	?	?	N	N
30 Martinez	Y	Y	Y	Y	N	Y	N	N
31 Dymally	Y	N	Y	Y	Y	Y	N	N
32 Anderson	Y	Y	Y	N	Y	Y	N	N
33 ***Dreier***	Y	Y	Y	N	N	Y	N	N
34 Torres	Y	Y	Y	Y	Y	Y	N	N
35 ***Lewis***	Y	Y	Y	N	N	Y	N	N
36 Brown	Y	Y	Y	Y	Y	Y	N	N
37 ***McCandless***	Y	Y	Y	N	N	Y	N	N
38 ***Dornan***	Y	Y	Y	?	?	?	Y	Y
39 ***Dannemeyer***	Y	Y	Y	N	N	Y	Y	Y
40 ***Cox***	Y	Y	Y	N	N	Y	N	Y
41 ***Lowery***	?	?	?	N	N	Y	Y	N
42 ***Rohrabacher***	Y	Y	Y	N	N	Y	Y	Y
43 ***Packard***	Y	Y	Y	N	N	Y	N	Y
44 Bates	Y	Y	Y	Y	Y	Y	N	N
45 ***Hunter***	Y	Y	Y	Y	N	Y	N	N
COLORADO								
1 Schroeder	Y	Y	Y	+	–	+	N	N
2 Skaggs	Y	N	Y	N	N	Y	Y	N
3 Campbell	Y	Y	Y	Y	N	Y	N	N
4 ***Brown***	Y	Y	Y	N	N	Y	N	N
5 ***Hefley***	Y	Y	Y	N	N	Y	N	N
6 ***Schaefer***	Y	Y	Y	N	N	Y	N	Y
CONNECTICUT								
1 Kennelly	Y	Y	Y	Y	Y	Y	N	N
2 Gejdenson	Y	Y	Y	Y	Y	Y	N	N
3 Morrison	Y	Y	Y	Y	Y	Y	N	N
4 ***Shays***	Y	Y	Y	Y	Y	Y	Y	N
5 ***Rowland***	Y	Y	Y	N	N	Y	Y	N
6 ***Johnson***	Y	Y	Y	N	N	Y	Y	N
DELAWARE								
AL Carper	Y	Y	Y	Y	Y	Y	Y	N
FLORIDA								
1 Hutto	Y	Y	Y	N	N	Y	N	N
2 ***Grant***	Y	Y	Y	N	N	Y	N	N
3 Bennett	Y	N	Y	Y	Y	Y	Y	N
4 ***James***	Y	Y	Y	N	N	Y	N	N
5 ***McCollum***	Y	Y	Y	N	N	Y	Y	N
6 ***Stearns***	Y	Y	Y	N	N	Y	N	N
7 Gibbons	Y	Y	Y	Y	Y	Y	N	N
8 ***Young***	?	?	?	N	N	Y	N	N
9 ***Bilirakis***	Y	Y	Y	N	N	Y	N	N
10 ***Ireland***	Y	Y	Y	N	N	Y	Y	N
11 Nelson	+	+	+	-	-	+	N	N
12 ***Lewis***	Y	Y	Y	N	N	Y	Y	N
13 ***Goss***	Y	Y	Y	N	N	Y	Y	N
14 Johnston	Y	Y	Y	N	N	Y	?	?
15 ***Shaw***	Y	Y	Y	Y	Y	Y	N	N
16 Smith	Y	Y	Y	Y	Y	Y	N	N
17 Lehman	Y	Y	Y	Y	Y	Y	N	N
18 ***Ros-Lehtinen***	Y	Y	Y	?	?	+	N	N
19 Fascell	Y	Y	Y	?	?	?	N	N
GEORGIA								
1 Thomas	Y	Y	Y	N	N	Y	Y	N
2 Hatcher	Y	Y	Y	N	N	Y	N	N
3 Ray	Y	Y	Y	N	N	Y	Y	N
4 Jones	Y	Y	Y	Y	Y	Y	N	N
5 Lewis	Y	Y	Y	Y	Y	Y	N	N
6 ***Gingrich***	Y	Y	Y	N	N	Y	Y	Y
7 Darden	Y	Y	Y	N	N	Y	Y	?
8 Rowland	Y	Y	Y	N	N	Y	Y	N
9 Jenkins	Y	Y	Y	N	N	Y	N	N
10 Barnard	Y	Y	Y	N	N	Y	Y	N
HAWAII								
1 ***Saiki***	Y	Y	Y	N	N	Y	N	N
2 Akaka	Y	Y	Y	Y	Y	Y	N	N
IDAHO								
1 ***Craig***	Y	Y	Y	N	N	Y	N	Y
2 Stallings	Y	Y	Y	N	N	Y	N	N
ILLINOIS								
1 Hayes	Y	N	Y	Y	Y	Y	N	N
2 Savage	Y	N	Y	Y	Y	Y	N	N
3 Russo	Y	Y	Y	Y	Y	Y	?	?
4 Sangmeister	Y	Y	Y	Y	N	Y	N	N
5 Lipinski	Y	Y	Y	Y	Y	Y	N	N
6 ***Hyde***	Y	N	Y	?	?	?	N	N
7 Collins	?	?	?	?	?	?	?	?
8 Rostenkowski	Y	Y	Y	N	N	Y	N	N
9 Yates	Y	Y	Y	Y	Y	Y	N	N
10 ***Porter***	Y	Y	Y	N	N	Y	Y	Y
11 Annunzio	Y	Y	Y	Y	Y	Y	N	N
12 ***Crane***	Y	Y	Y	N	N	Y	Y	Y
13 ***Fawell***	Y	Y	Y	N	N	Y	Y	N
14 ***Hastert***	Y	Y	Y	N	N	Y	Y	?
15 ***Madigan***	Y	Y	Y	N	N	Y	N	N
16 ***Martin***	Y	Y	Y	N	N	Y	N	N
17 Evans	Y	Y	Y	Y	Y	Y	N	N
18 ***Michel***	Y	Y	Y	N	N	Y	?	?
19 Bruce	Y	Y	Y	Y	N	Y	N	N
20 Durbin	Y	Y	Y	Y	N	Y	N	N
21 Costello	Y	Y	Y	Y	N	Y	N	N
22 Poshard	Y	Y	Y	Y	Y	Y	N	N
INDIANA								
1 Visclosky	Y	Y	Y	N	N	Y	N	N
2 Sharp	Y	Y	Y	Y	N	Y	N	N
3 ***Hiler***	Y	Y	Y	N	N	Y	Y	N

ND Northern Democrats SD Southern Democrats

	76	77	78	80	81	82	84	85
4 Long	Y	Y	Y	N	N	Y	N	N
5 Jontz	Y	Y	Y	Y	Y	Y	N	N
6 ***Burton***	Y	Y	Y	N	N	Y	Y	Y
7 ***Myers***	Y	Y	Y	N	N	Y	N	N
8 McCloskey	Y	Y	Y	Y	N	Y	N	N
9 Hamilton	Y	N	Y	N	N	Y	N	N
10 Jacobs	Y	N	Y	Y	N	Y	N	N
IOWA								
1 ***Leach***	Y	Y	Y	N	N	Y	Y	N
2 ***Tauke***	Y	Y	Y	N	N	Y	Y	N
3 Nagle	Y	Y	Y	N	N	Y	N	N
4 Smith	Y	Y	Y	N	N	Y	N	N
5 ***Lightfoot***	Y	Y	Y	N	N	Y	N	N
6 ***Grandy***	Y	Y	Y	N	N	Y	Y	N
KANSAS								
1 ***Roberts***	Y	N	Y	?	?	?	Y	N
2 Slattery	Y	Y	Y	—	—	+	N	N
3 ***Meyers***	Y	Y	Y	Y	N	Y	N	N
4 Glickman	Y	Y	Y	N	N	Y	N	N
5 ***Whittaker***	Y	N	Y	Y	N	Y	Y	N
KENTUCKY								
1 Hubbard	Y	Y	Y	N	N	Y	N	N
2 Natcher	Y	Y	Y	N	N	Y	N	N
3 Mazzoli	Y	—	Y	N	N	Y	N	N
4 ***Bunning***	Y	Y	Y	N	N	Y	N	N
5 ***Rogers***	Y	Y	Y	N	N	Y	Y	N
6 ***Hopkins***	?	?	?	X	?	?	?	X
7 Perkins	Y	Y	Y	Y	Y	Y	N	N
LOUISIANA								
1 ***Livingston***	Y	Y	Y	N	N	Y	N	Y
2 Boggs	Y	Y	Y	N	N	Y	N	N
3 Tauzin	Y	Y	Y	N	N	Y	Y	Y
4 ***McCrery***	Y	Y	Y	N	N	Y	N	N
5 Huckaby	Y	Y	Y	N	N	Y	Y	N
6 ***Baker***	Y	Y	Y	N	N	Y	N	N
7 Hayes	Y	Y	Y	N	N	Y	Y	N
8 ***Holloway***	Y	Y	Y	N	Y	Y	N	Y
MAINE								
1 Brennan	Y	Y	Y	Y	Y	Y	N	N
2 ***Snowe***	Y	Y	Y	Y	N	Y	N	N
MARYLAND								
1 Dyson	Y	Y	Y	Y	N	Y	N	N
2 ***Bentley***	?	Y	Y	Y	N	Y	N	Y
3 Cardin	Y	Y	Y	Y	N	Y	N	N
4 McMillen	Y	Y	Y	Y	N	Y	N	N
5 Hoyer	Y	Y	Y	Y	N	Y	N	N
6 Byron	Y	Y	Y	N	N	Y	N	N
7 Mfume	Y	Y	Y	Y	Y	Y	?	N
8 ***Morella***	Y	Y	Y	?	?	+	N	N
MASSACHUSETTS								
1 ***Conte***	Y	Y	Y	Y	Y	Y	N	N
2 Neal	Y	Y	Y	Y	N	Y	N	N
3 Early	Y	Y	Y	Y	Y	Y	N	Y
4 Frank	Y	Y	Y	Y	N	Y	N	N
5 Atkins	Y	Y	Y	Y	Y	Y	N	N
6 Mavroules	Y	Y	Y	Y	Y	Y	N	N
7 Markey	Y	Y	Y	Y	N	Y	N	N
8 Kennedy	Y	Y	Y	Y	Y	Y	N	N
9 Moakley	Y	Y	Y	Y	N	Y	N	N
10 Studds	Y	N	Y	Y	Y	Y	N	N
11 Donnelly	Y	Y	Y	Y	Y	Y	N	N
MICHIGAN								
1 Conyers	Y	N	Y	Y	Y	Y	N	N
2 ***Pursell***	Y	Y	Y	N	N	Y	?	?
3 Wolpe	Y	Y	Y	Y	Y	Y	N	N
4 ***Upton***	Y	Y	Y	N	N	Y	Y	N
5 ***Henry***	Y	Y	Y	N	N	Y	N	N
6 Carr	Y	Y	Y	Y	N	Y	N	N
7 Kildee	Y	Y	Y	Y	Y	Y	N	N
8 Traxler	?	?	?	Y	Y	Y	N	N
9 ***Vander Jagt***	Y	Y	Y	N	N	Y	Y	N
10 ***Schuette***	Y	Y	Y	N	N	Y	?	?
11 ***Davis***	Y	Y	Y	N	N	Y	N	N
12 Bonior	Y	N	Y	Y	Y	Y	N	N
13 Crockett	Y	N	Y	Y	Y	Y	N	?
14 Hertel	Y	Y	Y	Y	Y	Y	N	N
15 Ford	Y	N	Y	Y	Y	Y	N	N
16 Dingell	Y	N	Y	Y	N	Y	N	N
17 Levin	Y	Y	Y	Y	N	Y	N	N
18 ***Broomfield***	Y	Y	Y	N	N	Y	N	N
MINNESOTA								
1 Penny	Y	Y	Y	N	N	Y	N	N
2 ***Weber***	Y	Y	Y	N	N	Y	Y	Y
3 ***Frenzel***	Y	Y	Y	N	N	Y	Y	N
4 Vento	Y	Y	Y	Y	Y	Y	N	N
5 Sabo	Y	Y	Y	Y	Y	Y	Y	N
6 Sikorski	Y	Y	Y	Y	Y	Y	N	N
7 ***Stangeland***	Y	Y	Y	N	N	Y	Y	Y
8 Oberstar	Y	Y	Y	Y	Y	Y	N	N
MISSISSIPPI								
1 Whitten	Y	Y	Y	N	N	Y	N	N
2 Espy	Y	Y	Y	Y	N	Y	?	?
3 Montgomery	Y	Y	Y	N	N	Y	N	N
4 Parker	Y	Y	Y	N	N	Y	N	N
5 Taylor	Y	Y	Y	N	Y	Y	Y	Y
MISSOURI								
1 Clay	Y	N	Y	Y	Y	Y	N	N
2 ***Buechner***	Y	Y	Y	N	N	Y	Y	N
3 Gephardt	Y	Y	Y	Y	Y	Y	N	N
4 Skelton	Y	Y	Y	N	N	Y	N	N
5 Wheat	Y	Y	Y	Y	Y	Y	N	N
6 ***Coleman***	Y	P	Y	N	N	Y	N	N
7 ***Hancock***	Y	Y	?	N	N	Y	N	Y
8 ***Emerson***	Y	Y	Y	N	N	Y	N	N
9 Volkmer	Y	Y	Y	N	N	Y	N	N
MONTANA								
1 Williams	Y	Y	Y	Y	N	Y	N	N
2 ***Marlenee***	Y	Y	Y	Y	N	?	N	N
NEBRASKA								
1 ***Bereuter***	Y	Y	Y	Y	N	Y	Y	N
2 Hoagland	Y	Y	Y	Y	N	Y	Y	N
3 ***Smith***	Y	Y	Y	N	N	Y	Y	N
NEVADA								
1 Bilbray	Y	Y	Y	N	N	Y	N	N
2 ***Vucanovich***	Y	Y	Y	?	?	?	N	Y
NEW HAMPSHIRE								
1 ***Smith***	Y	Y	Y	N	N	Y	N	Y
2 ***Douglas***	Y	Y	Y	N	N	Y	N	Y
NEW JERSEY								
1 Vacancy								
2 Hughes	Y	Y	Y	Y	N	Y	N	N
3 Pallone	Y	Y	Y	Y	N	Y	N	N
4 ***Smith***	?	?	Y	Y	N	Y	N	N
5 ***Roukema***	Y	Y	Y	Y	N	Y	N	N
6 Dwyer	Y	Y	Y	Y	N	Y	N	N
7 ***Rinaldo***	Y	Y	Y	Y	N	Y	N	N
8 Roe	Y	Y	Y	Y	Y	Y	N	N
9 Torricelli	Y	Y	Y	Y	N	Y	N	N
10 Payne	Y	Y	Y	Y	Y	Y	N	N
11 ***Gallo***	Y	Y	Y	Y	N	Y	Y	N
12 ***Courter***	Y	Y	Y	Y	N	Y	N	N
13 ***Saxton***	Y	Y	Y	Y	N	Y	Y	N
14 Guarini	Y	Y	Y	Y	Y	Y	N	N
NEW MEXICO								
1 ***Schiff***	Y	Y	Y	N	N	Y	N	N
2 ***Skeen***	Y	Y	Y	N	N	Y	Y	N
3 Richardson	Y	Y	Y	Y	Y	Y	N	N
NEW YORK								
1 Hochbrueckner	Y	Y	Y	Y	Y	Y	N	N
2 Downey	Y	Y	Y	Y	Y	Y	Y	N
3 Mrazek	Y	Y	Y	Y	Y	Y	?	N
4 ***Lent***	Y	Y	Y	N	N	Y	Y	N
5 ***McGrath***	Y	Y	Y	Y	N	Y	N	N
6 Flake	Y	Y	Y	Y	Y	Y	N	N
7 Ackerman	Y	Y	Y	Y	Y	Y	X	?
8 Scheuer	Y	Y	Y	Y	Y	Y	N	N
9 Manton	Y	Y	Y	Y	N	Y	N	N
10 Schumer	Y	Y	Y	Y	Y	Y	N	N
11 Towns	Y	Y	Y	Y	Y	Y	N	N
12 Owens	?	?	?	#	Y	Y	N	N
13 Solarz	Y	Y	Y	?	?	?	N	N
14 ***Molinari***	Y	Y	Y	N	N	Y	N	N
15 ***Green***	Y	Y	Y	Y	N	Y	N	N
16 Rangel	Y	Y	Y	Y	Y	Y	N	N
17 Weiss	Y	Y	Y	Y	Y	Y	N	N
18 Serrano	Y	Y	Y	Y	Y	Y	N	N
19 Engel	Y	Y	Y	Y	Y	Y	N	N
20 Lowey	Y	Y	Y	Y	Y	Y	N	N
21 ***Fish***	Y	Y	Y	Y	N	Y	Y	N
22 ***Gilman***	Y	Y	?	Y	Y	Y	N	N
23 McNulty	Y	Y	Y	Y	N	Y	N	N
24 ***Solomon***	Y	Y	Y	N	N	Y	?	?
25 ***Boehlert***	Y	Y	Y	Y	N	Y	N	N
26 ***Martin***	Y	Y	Y	?	N	Y	Y	N
27 ***Walsh***	Y	Y	Y	N	N	Y	N	N
28 McHugh	Y	Y	Y	N	N	Y	N	N
29 ***Horton***	Y	Y	Y	Y	N	Y	N	N
30 Slaughter	Y	Y	Y	Y	Y	Y	N	N
31 ***Paxon***	Y	Y	Y	N	N	Y	N	N
32 LaFalce	Y	Y	Y	N	N	Y	N	N
33 Nowak	Y	Y	Y	Y	N	Y	N	N
34 ***Houghton***	Y	Y	Y	N	N	Y	Y	N
NORTH CAROLINA								
1 Jones	Y	Y	Y	Y	Y	Y	N	N
2 Valentine	Y	Y	Y	Y	N	Y	N	N
3 Lancaster	Y	Y	Y	Y	N	Y	Y	N
4 Price	Y	Y	Y	Y	N	Y	N	N
5 Neal	Y	Y	Y	Y	N	Y	N	N
6 ***Coble***	Y	Y	Y	N	N	Y	Y	N
7 Rose	Y	Y	Y	N	Y	Y	N	N
8 Hefner	?	Y	Y	N	N	Y	N	N
9 ***McMillan***	Y	Y	Y	N	N	Y	Y	N
10 ***Ballenger***	Y	Y	Y	—	—	+	Y	N
11 Clarke	Y	Y	Y	Y	N	Y	N	N
NORTH DAKOTA								
AL Dorgan	Y	Y	Y	N	N	Y	N	N
OHIO								
1 Luken	Y	Y	Y	Y	N	Y	N	N
2 ***Gradison***	Y	Y	Y	N	N	Y	N	N
3 Hall	Y	Y	Y	Y	N	Y	N	N
4 ***Oxley***	Y	Y	Y	N	N	Y	Y	N
5 ***Gillmor***	Y	Y	Y	N	N	Y	Y	N
6 ***McEwen***	Y	Y	Y	N	N	Y	Y	Y
7 ***DeWine***	Y	Y	Y	N	N	Y	Y	N
8 ***Lukens***	Y	Y	Y	N	N	Y	Y	N
9 Kaptur	Y	Y	Y	Y	Y	Y	N	N
10 ***Miller***	Y	N	Y	N	Y	Y	Y	N
11 Eckart	Y	Y	Y	Y	N	Y	N	N
12 ***Kasich***	Y	Y	Y	N	N	Y	Y	Y
13 Pease	Y	N	Y	Y	Y	Y	N	N
14 Sawyer	Y	Y	Y	Y	N	Y	N	N
15 ***Wylie***	Y	Y	Y	N	N	Y	Y	N
16 ***Regula***	Y	Y	Y	Y	N	Y	N	N
17 Traficant	Y	N	Y	Y	Y	Y	N	N
18 Applegate	Y	Y	Y	Y	N	Y	N	N
19 Feighan	Y	Y	Y	Y	N	Y	N	N
20 Oakar	Y	N	Y	Y	Y	Y	N	N
21 Stokes	Y	Y	Y	Y	Y	Y	N	N
OKLAHOMA								
1 ***Inhofe***	Y	Y	Y	N	N	Y	N	N
2 Synar	Y	Y	Y	Y	Y	Y	N	N
3 Watkins	Y	Y	Y	?	?	?	?	?
4 McCurdy	Y	Y	Y	N	N	Y	N	N
5 ***Edwards***	Y	Y	Y	?	?	?	Y	N
6 English	Y	Y	Y	N	Y	Y	Y	N
OREGON								
1 AuCoin	Y	Y	Y	Y	Y	Y	N	N
2 ***Smith, B.***	Y	Y	Y	N	N	Y	N	N
3 Wyden	Y	Y	Y	Y	Y	Y	N	N
4 DeFazio	Y	Y	Y	Y	Y	?	N	N
5 ***Smith, D.***	Y	Y	Y	N	N	Y	N	Y
PENNSYLVANIA								
1 Foglietta	Y	Y	Y	Y	Y	Y	N	N
2 Gray	Y	Y	Y	Y	Y	Y	N	N
3 Borski	Y	Y	Y	Y	N	Y	N	N
4 Kolter	Y	P	Y	Y	N	Y	N	N
5 ***Schulze***	Y	Y	Y	N	N	Y	Y	Y
6 Yatron	Y	Y	Y	Y	N	Y	N	N
7 ***Weldon***	Y	Y	Y	N	N	Y	N	N
8 Kostmayer	Y	Y	Y	Y	Y	Y	N	N
9 ***Shuster***	Y	Y	Y	N	N	Y	N	N
10 ***McDade***	Y	Y	Y	Y	N	Y	N	N
11 Kanjorski	Y	Y	Y	Y	N	Y	N	N
12 Murtha	Y	Y	Y	Y	N	Y	N	N
13 ***Coughlin***	Y	Y	Y	N	N	Y	Y	N
14 Coyne	Y	Y	Y	Y	Y	Y	N	N
15 ***Ritter***	Y	Y	Y	Y	N	Y	Y	Y
16 ***Walker***	Y	Y	Y	Y	N	Y	N	Y
17 ***Gekas***	Y	Y	Y	Y	N	Y	Y	Y
18 Walgren	Y	Y	Y	Y	Y	Y	N	Y
19 ***Goodling***	Y	Y	Y	Y	N	Y	N	N
20 Gaydos	Y	Y	Y	Y	N	Y	N	X
21 ***Ridge***	Y	N	?	N	N	Y	Y	?
22 Murphy	Y	P	Y	Y	Y	Y	N	N
23 ***Clinger***	Y	N	Y	N	N	Y	Y	?
RHODE ISLAND								
1 ***Machtley***	Y	Y	Y	N	N	Y	N	?
2 ***Schneider***	Y	Y	Y	Y	N	Y	N	N
SOUTH CAROLINA								
1 ***Ravenel***	Y	Y	Y	N	N	Y	Y	Y
2 ***Spence***	Y	Y	Y	N	N	Y	Y	Y
3 Derrick	Y	Y	Y	N	N	Y	N	N
4 Patterson	Y	Y	Y	N	N	Y	Y	N
5 Spratt	Y	Y	Y	N	N	Y	N	N
6 Tallon	Y	Y	Y	N	N	Y	Y	N
SOUTH DAKOTA								
AL Johnson	Y	Y	Y	N	Y	Y	N	N
TENNESSEE								
1 ***Quillen***	Y	Y	Y	N	N	Y	N	?
2 ***Duncan***	Y	Y	Y	N	N	Y	Y	N
3 Lloyd	Y	Y	Y	N	N	Y	N	N
4 Cooper	Y	N	Y	Y	Y	C	Y	N
5 Clement	Y	Y	Y	Y	N	Y	N	N
6 Gordon	Y	Y	Y	Y	N	Y	Y	N
7 ***Sundquist***	Y	Y	Y	N	N	Y	Y	Y
8 Tanner	Y	Y	Y	N	N	Y	N	N
9 Ford	?	?	?	?	?	?	?	?
TEXAS								
1 Chapman	Y	Y	Y	Y	N	Y	Y	N
2 Wilson	Y	Y	Y	Y	N	Y	N	N
3 ***Bartlett***	Y	Y	Y	N	N	Y	Y	Y
4 Hall	Y	Y	Y	N	N	Y	Y	Y
5 Bryant	Y	P	Y	Y	Y	Y	N	N
6 ***Barton***	Y	Y	Y	N	N	Y	N	N
7 ***Archer***	Y	Y	Y	N	N	Y	N	N
8 ***Fields***	Y	Y	Y	N	N	Y	N	Y
9 Brooks	Y	Y	Y	Y	N	Y	N	N
10 Pickle	Y	Y	Y	Y	N	Y	Y	N
11 Leath	Y	Y	Y	N	N	Y	?	N
12 Geren	Y	Y	Y	N	N	Y	N	N
13 Sarpalius	Y	Y	Y	N	N	Y	N	N
14 Laughlin	Y	Y	Y	N	N	Y	N	N
15 de la Garza	Y	Y	Y	Y	N	Y	N	?
16 Coleman	Y	Y	Y	Y	Y	Y	N	N
17 Stenholm	Y	Y	Y	N	N	Y	Y	Y
18 Washington	Y	N	Y	Y	Y	Y	N	N
19 ***Combest***	Y	Y	Y	N	N	Y	Y	N
20 Gonzalez	Y	Y	Y	N	N	Y	N	N
21 ***Smith***	Y	Y	Y	N	N	Y	N	N
22 ***DeLay***	Y	Y	Y	N	N	Y	Y	Y
23 Bustamante	Y	Y	Y	Y	Y	Y	?	?
24 Frost	Y	Y	Y	Y	Y	Y	N	N
25 Andrews	Y	Y	Y	Y	N	Y	N	N
26 ***Armey***	Y	Y	Y	N	N	Y	#	#
27 Ortiz	Y	Y	Y	Y	Y	Y	N	N
UTAH								
1 ***Hansen***	Y	Y	Y	N	N	Y	N	Y
2 Owens	Y	Y	Y	Y	N	Y	Y	N
3 ***Nielson***	Y	N	Y	N	N	Y	Y	#
VERMONT								
AL ***Smith***	Y	Y	Y	Y	N	Y	N	?
VIRGINIA								
1 ***Bateman***	Y	P	Y	N	N	Y	Y	N
2 Pickett	Y	Y	Y	Y	N	Y	N	N
3 ***Bliley***	Y	Y	Y	N	N	Y	Y	N
4 Sisisky	Y	Y	Y	N	N	Y	N	N
5 Payne	Y	Y	Y	N	N	Y	N	N
6 Olin	Y	Y	Y	N	N	Y	N	N
7 ***Slaughter***	Y	Y	Y	N	N	Y	Y	N
8 ***Parris***	Y	Y	Y	N	N	Y	N	N
9 Boucher	Y	Y	Y	N	N	Y	N	N
10 ***Wolf***	Y	Y	Y	N	N	Y	N	N
WASHINGTON								
1 ***Miller***	Y	Y	Y	—	—	+	Y	N
2 Swift	Y	Y	Y	Y	N	Y	N	N
3 Unsoeld	Y	Y	Y	Y	Y	?	N	N
4 ***Morrison***	Y	Y	Y	N	N	Y	N	N
5 Foley								
6 Dicks	Y	Y	Y	Y	N	Y	N	N
7 McDermott	Y	Y	Y	Y	N	Y	N	N
8 ***Chandler***	Y	Y	Y	?	?	?	Y	N
WEST VIRGINIA								
1 Mollohan	?	?	?	N	N	Y	N	N
2 Staggers	Y	Y	Y	Y	Y	Y	N	N
3 Wise	Y	Y	Y	Y	Y	Y	N	N
4 Rahall	Y	N	Y	Y	N	Y	?	?
WISCONSIN								
1 Aspin	Y	Y	Y	N	N	Y	N	N
2 Kastenmeier	?	N	Y	Y	Y	Y	N	N
3 ***Gunderson***	Y	Y	Y	N	N	Y	N	N
4 Kleczka	Y	Y	Y	Y	Y	Y	N	N
5 Moody	Y	Y	Y	N	Y	Y	N	N
6 ***Petri***	Y	N	Y	N	N	Y	Y	N
7 Obey	Y	N	Y	Y	Y	Y	N	N
8 ***Roth***	Y	N	Y	N	N	Y	Y	Y
9 ***Sensenbrenner***	Y	Y	Y	N	N	Y	Y	Y
WYOMING								
AL ***Thomas***	Y	?	Y	N	N	Y	?	X

Southern states - Ala., Ark., Fla., Ga., Ky., La., Miss., N.C., Okla., S.C., Tenn., Texas, Va.
Omitted votes are quorum calls, which CQ does not include in its vote charts.

86. HR 743. Negotiated Rulemaking/Passage. Frank, D-Mass., motion to suspend the rules and pass the bill to establish a statutory framework for federal agencies to use in negotiated rulemaking procedures, under which affected parties can work with agency officials to seek a consensus before a rule is published in the Federal Register. Motion agreed to 411-0: R 165-0; D 246-0 (ND 167-0, SD 79-0), May 1, 1990. A two-thirds majority of those present and voting (275 in this case) is required for passage under suspension of the rules. (Passage was subsequently vacated and the House passed a similar Senate bill, S 303, after substituting the language of HR 743.)

87. S 1485. Quad Cities Interstate Compact/Passage. Frank, D-Mass., motion to suspend the rules and pass the bill (thus clearing the measure for the president) to grant the consent of Congress to the compact between Illinois and Iowa to provide facilities and foster cooperative efforts for the economic development and public benefit of Scott County, Iowa, and Rock Island County, Ill. Motion agreed to 413-0: R 165-0; D 248-0 (ND 168-0, SD 80-0), May 1, 1990. A two-thirds majority of those present and voting (276 in this case) is required for passage under suspension of the rules.

88. H Con Res 310. Fiscal 1991 Budget Resolution/Defense Cuts. Dellums, D-Calif., substitute amendment to cut defense funding by $56.4 billion in authority and $27.4 billion in outlays from the current inflation-adjusted level (compared with the resolution's cuts of $32.8 billion and $11.5 billion, respectively), reallocating the funds to education, job training, health, housing, food and nutrition, environmental, veterans, anti-drug abuse and other domestic programs. The Dellums amendment assumes $19.8 billion in increased revenues (compared with the $13.9 billion in the resolution). Rejected 90-334: R 0-174; D 90-160 (ND 82-88, SD 8-72), May 1, 1990.

89. H Con Res 310. Fiscal 1991 Budget Resolution/Adoption. Adoption of the resolution to set binding budget levels for the fiscal year ending Sept. 30, 1991: budget authority, $1.388 trillion; outlays, $1.239 trillion; revenues, $1.175 trillion; deficit, $63.75 billion. Adopted 218-208: R 0-174; D 218-34 (ND 159-12, SD 59-22), May 1, 1990. A "nay" was a vote supporting the president's position.

KEY

- Y Voted for (yea).
- # Paired for.
- + Announced for.
- N Voted against (nay).
- X Paired against.
- \- Announced against.
- P Voted "present."
- C Voted "present" to avoid possible conflict of interest.
- ? Did not vote or otherwise make a position known.

Democrats *Republicans*

	86	87	88	89
ALABAMA				
1 ***Callahan***	Y	Y	N	N
2 ***Dickinson***	Y	Y	N	N
3 Browder	Y	Y	N	N
4 Bevill	Y	Y	N	Y
5 Flippo	Y	Y	N	Y
6 Erdreich	Y	Y	N	Y
7 Harris	Y	Y	N	Y
ALASKA				
AL ***Young***	Y	Y	N	N
ARIZONA				
1 ***Rhodes***	Y	Y	N	N
2 Udall	Y	Y	Y	Y
3 ***Stump***	Y	Y	N	N
4 ***Kyl***	Y	?	N	N
5 ***Kolbe***	Y	Y	N	N
ARKANSAS				
1 Alexander	Y	Y	N	N
2 ***Robinson***	Y	Y	N	N
3 ***Hammerschmidt***	Y	Y	N	N
4 Anthony	Y	Y	N	Y
CALIFORNIA				
1 Bosco	Y	Y	N	Y
2 ***Herger***	Y	Y	N	N
3 Matsui	Y	Y	Y	N
4 Fazio	Y	Y	N	Y
5 Pelosi	Y	Y	Y	Y
6 Boxer	Y	Y	Y	Y
7 Miller	Y	Y	Y	Y
8 Dellums	Y	Y	Y	Y
9 Stark	Y	Y	Y	Y
10 Edwards	Y	Y	Y	Y
11 Lantos	Y	Y	N	Y
12 ***Campbell***	Y	Y	N	N
13 Mineta	Y	Y	Y	Y
14 ***Shumway***	Y	Y	N	N
15 Condit	Y	Y	N	Y
16 Panetta	Y	Y	N	Y
17 ***Pashayan***	Y	Y	N	N
18 Lehman	Y	Y	Y	Y
19 ***Lagomarsino***	Y	Y	N	N
20 ***Thomas***	Y	Y	N	N
21 ***Gallegly***	Y	Y	N	N
22 ***Moorhead***	Y	Y	N	N
23 Beilenson	Y	Y	N	Y
24 Waxman	Y	Y	Y	Y
25 Roybal	Y	Y	Y	Y
26 Berman	Y	Y	Y	Y
27 Levine	Y	Y	Y	Y
28 Dixon	Y	Y	Y	Y
29 Hawkins	?	?	Y	Y
30 Martinez	?	Y	Y	Y
31 Dymally	Y	Y	Y	Y
32 Anderson	Y	Y	N	Y
33 ***Dreier***	Y	Y	N	N
34 Torres	Y	Y	Y	Y
35 ***Lewis***	Y	Y	N	N
36 Brown	Y	Y	Y	Y
37 ***McCandless***	Y	Y	N	N
38 ***Dornan***	?	?	N	N
39 ***Dannemeyer***	Y	Y	N	N
40 ***Cox***	Y	Y	N	N
41 ***Lowery***	Y	Y	N	N
42 ***Rohrabacher***	Y	Y	N	N
43 ***Packard***	Y	Y	N	N
44 Bates	?	Y	Y	Y
45 ***Hunter***	Y	Y	N	N
COLORADO				
1 Schroeder	Y	Y	Y	Y
2 Skaggs	Y	Y	N	Y
3 Campbell	Y	Y	N	Y
4 ***Brown***	Y	Y	N	N
5 ***Hefley***	Y	Y	N	N
6 ***Schaefer***	Y	Y	N	N
CONNECTICUT				
1 Kennelly	Y	Y	N	Y
2 Gejdenson	Y	Y	N	Y
3 Morrison	Y	Y	N	Y
4 ***Shays***	Y	Y	N	N
5 ***Rowland***	Y	Y	N	N
6 ***Johnson***	Y	Y	N	N
DELAWARE				
AL Carper	Y	Y	N	Y
FLORIDA				
1 Hutto	Y	Y	N	N
2 ***Grant***	?	Y	N	N
3 Bennett	Y	Y	N	N
4 ***James***	Y	Y	N	N
5 ***McCollum***	Y	Y	N	N
6 ***Stearns***	Y	Y	N	N
7 Gibbons	Y	Y	N	Y
8 ***Young***	Y	Y	N	N
9 ***Bilirakis***	Y	Y	N	N
10 ***Ireland***	P	Y	N	N
11 Nelson	+	+	-	Y
12 ***Lewis***	+	+	-	X
13 ***Goss***	Y	Y	N	N
14 Johnston	Y	Y	N	Y
15 ***Shaw***	Y	Y	N	N
16 Smith	?	?	?	?
17 Lehman	Y	Y	Y	Y
18 ***Ros-Lehtinen***	+	+	N	N
19 Fascell	Y	Y	N	Y
GEORGIA				
1 Thomas	Y	Y	N	Y
2 Hatcher	Y	Y	N	Y
3 Ray	Y	Y	N	N
4 Jones	Y	Y	N	Y
5 Lewis	Y	Y	Y	Y
6 ***Gingrich***	Y	Y	N	N
7 Darden	Y	Y	N	Y
8 Rowland	Y	Y	N	Y
9 Jenkins	Y	Y	N	Y
10 Barnard	Y	Y	N	N
HAWAII				
1 ***Saiki***	Y	Y	N	N
2 Akaka	Y	Y	Y	Y
IDAHO				
1 ***Craig***	Y	Y	N	N
2 Stallings	Y	Y	N	Y
ILLINOIS				
1 Hayes	Y	Y	Y	Y
2 Savage	Y	Y	Y	Y
3 Russo	Y	Y	N	Y
4 Sangmeister	Y	Y	N	Y
5 Lipinski	Y	Y	N	Y
6 ***Hyde***	Y	Y	N	N
7 Collins	?	?	?	#
8 Rostenkowski	Y	Y	N	Y
9 Yates	Y	Y	Y	Y
10 ***Porter***	Y	?	N	N
11 Annunzio	Y	Y	N	Y
12 ***Crane***	Y	Y	N	N
13 ***Fawell***	Y	Y	N	N
14 ***Hastert***	Y	Y	N	N
15 ***Madigan***	Y	Y	N	N
16 ***Martin***	Y	Y	N	N
17 Evans	Y	Y	Y	Y
18 ***Michel***	?	?	N	X
19 Bruce	Y	Y	N	Y
20 Durbin	Y	Y	Y	Y
21 Costello	Y	Y	N	Y
22 Poshard	Y	Y	N	Y
INDIANA				
1 Visclosky	Y	Y	N	Y
2 Sharp	Y	Y	N	N
3 ***Hiler***	Y	Y	N	N

ND Northern Democrats SD Southern Democrats

	86	87	88	89
4 Long	Y	Y	N	N
5 Jontz	Y	Y	Y	Y
6 ***Burton***	Y	Y	N	N
7 ***Myers***	Y	Y	N	N
8 McCloskey	Y	Y	N	Y
9 Hamilton	Y	Y	N	N
10 Jacobs	Y	Y	Y	N
IOWA				
1 ***Leach***	Y	Y	N	N
2 ***Tauke***	Y	Y	N	N
3 Nagle	Y	Y	Y	Y
4 Smith	Y	Y	N	Y
5 ***Lightfoot***	Y	Y	N	N
6 ***Grandy***	Y	Y	N	N
KANSAS				
1 ***Roberts***	Y	Y	N	N
2 Slattery	Y	Y	N	Y
3 ***Meyers***	Y	Y	N	N
4 Glickman	Y	Y	N	Y
5 ***Whittaker***	Y	Y	N	N
KENTUCKY				
1 Hubbard	Y	Y	N	Y
2 Natcher	Y	Y	N	Y
3 Mazzoli	Y	Y	N	Y
4 ***Bunning***	Y	Y	N	N
5 ***Rogers***	Y	Y	N	N
6 ***Hopkins***	Y	Y	N	N
7 Perkins	Y	Y	Y	Y
LOUISIANA				
1 ***Livingston***	Y	Y	N	N
2 Boggs	?	?	Y	Y
3 Tauzin	Y	Y	N	N
4 ***McCrery***	Y	Y	N	N
5 Huckaby	Y	Y	N	Y
6 ***Baker***	Y	Y	N	N
7 Hayes	Y	Y	N	Y
8 ***Holloway***	Y	Y	N	N
MAINE				
1 Brennan	Y	Y	N	Y
2 ***Snowe***	Y	Y	N	N
MARYLAND				
1 Dyson	Y	Y	N	Y
2 ***Bentley***	Y	Y	N	N
3 Cardin	Y	Y	N	Y
4 McMillen	Y	Y	N	Y
5 Hoyer	Y	Y	Y	Y
6 Byron	Y	Y	N	N
7 Mfume	Y	Y	Y	Y
8 ***Morella***	Y	Y	N	N
MASSACHUSETTS				
1 ***Conte***	Y	Y	N	N
2 Neal	Y	Y	Y	Y
3 Early	Y	?	Y	Y
4 Frank	Y	Y	Y	Y
5 Atkins	Y	Y	Y	Y
6 Mavroules	Y	Y	N	Y
7 Markey	Y	Y	Y	Y
8 Kennedy	Y	Y	Y	Y
9 Moakley	Y	Y	Y	Y
10 Studds	Y	Y	Y	Y
11 Donnelly	Y	Y	N	Y
MICHIGAN				
1 Conyers	Y	Y	Y	Y
2 ***Pursell***	Y	Y	N	N
3 Wolpe	Y	Y	N	Y
4 ***Upton***	Y	Y	N	N
5 ***Henry***	Y	Y	N	N
6 Carr	Y	Y	N	N
7 Kildee	Y	Y	Y	Y
8 Traxler	Y	Y	Y	Y
9 ***Vander Jagt***	Y	Y	N	N
10 ***Schuette***	Y	Y	N	N
11 ***Davis***	Y	Y	N	N
12 Bonior	Y	Y	N	Y
13 Crockett	Y	Y	Y	Y
14 Hertel	Y	Y	N	Y
15 Ford	Y	Y	Y	Y
16 Dingell	Y	Y	?	Y
17 Levin	Y	Y	N	Y
18 ***Broomfield***	Y	Y	N	N
MINNESOTA				
1 Penny	Y	Y	N	Y
2 ***Weber***	Y	Y	N	N
3 ***Frenzel***	Y	Y	N	N
4 Vento	Y	Y	Y	Y

	86	87	88	89
5 Sabo	Y	Y	Y	Y
6 Sikorski	Y	Y	Y	Y
7 ***Stangeland***	Y	Y	N	N
8 Oberstar	Y	Y	Y	Y
MISSISSIPPI				
1 Whitten	?	Y	N	Y
2 Espy	Y	Y	Y	Y
3 Montgomery	Y	Y	N	Y
4 Parker	Y	Y	N	Y
5 Taylor	Y	Y	N	N
MISSOURI				
1 Clay	Y	Y	Y	Y
2 ***Buechner***	Y	Y	N	N
3 Gephardt	Y	Y	N	Y
4 Skelton	Y	Y	N	N
5 Wheat	Y	Y	Y	Y
6 ***Coleman***	Y	Y	N	N
7 ***Hancock***	Y	Y	N	N
8 ***Emerson***	Y	Y	N	N
9 Volkmer	Y	Y	N	Y
MONTANA				
1 Williams	Y	Y	Y	Y
2 ***Marlenee***	Y	Y	N	N
NEBRASKA				
1 ***Bereuter***	Y	Y	N	N
2 Hoagland	Y	Y	N	Y
3 ***Smith***	Y	Y	N	N
NEVADA				
1 Bilbray	Y	Y	N	Y
2 ***Vucanovich***	Y	Y	N	N
NEW HAMPSHIRE				
1 ***Smith***	?	Y	N	N
2 ***Douglas***	Y	Y	N	N
NEW JERSEY				
1 Vacancy				
2 Hughes	Y	Y	N	Y
3 Pallone	Y	Y	N	Y
4 ***Smith***	?	?	N	N
5 ***Roukema***	Y	Y	N	N
6 Dwyer	Y	Y	N	Y
7 ***Rinaldo***	Y	Y	N	N
8 Roe	Y	Y	N	Y
9 Torricelli	Y	Y	N	Y
10 Payne	Y	Y	Y	Y
11 ***Gallo***	Y	Y	N	N
12 ***Courter***	Y	Y	N	N
13 ***Saxton***	Y	Y	N	N
14 Guarini	Y	Y	N	Y
NEW MEXICO				
1 ***Schiff***	Y	Y	N	N
2 ***Skeen***	Y	Y	N	N
3 Richardson	Y	Y	N	Y
NEW YORK				
1 Hochbrueckner	Y	Y	N	Y
2 Downey	Y	Y	N	Y
3 Mrazek	Y	Y	N	Y
4 ***Lent***	Y	Y	N	N
5 ***McGrath***	Y	Y	N	N
6 Flake	Y	Y	Y	Y
7 Ackerman	?	?	?	#
8 Scheuer	Y	Y	Y	Y
9 Manton	Y	Y	N	Y
10 Schumer	Y	Y	Y	Y
11 Towns	Y	Y	Y	Y
12 Owens	Y	Y	Y	Y
13 Solarz	Y	Y	Y	Y
14 ***Molinari***	Y	Y	N	N
15 ***Green***	Y	Y	N	N
16 Rangel	Y	Y	Y	Y
17 Weiss	Y	Y	Y	Y
18 Serrano	Y	Y	Y	Y
19 Engel	?	?	N	Y
20 Lowey	Y	Y	Y	Y
21 ***Fish***	?	?	N	N
22 ***Gilman***	Y	Y	N	N
23 McNulty	Y	Y	N	Y
24 ***Solomon***	Y	Y	N	N
25 ***Boehlert***	Y	Y	N	N
26 ***Martin***	Y	Y	N	N
27 ***Walsh***	Y	Y	N	N
28 McHugh	Y	Y	N	N
29 ***Horton***	Y	Y	N	N
30 Slaughter	Y	Y	Y	Y
31 ***Paxon***	Y	Y	N	N

	86	87	88	89
32 LaFalce	Y	Y	N	N
33 Nowak	Y	Y	Y	Y
34 ***Houghton***	Y	Y	N	N
NORTH CAROLINA				
1 Jones	Y	Y	N	Y
2 Valentine	Y	Y	N	Y
3 Lancaster	Y	Y	N	Y
4 Price	Y	Y	N	Y
5 Neal	Y	Y	N	Y
6 ***Coble***	Y	Y	N	N
7 Rose	Y	Y	N	Y
8 Hefner	Y	Y	N	Y
9 ***McMillan***	Y	Y	N	N
10 ***Ballenger***	Y	Y	N	N
11 Clarke	Y	Y	N	Y
NORTH DAKOTA				
AL Dorgan	Y	Y	N	Y
OHIO				
1 Luken	Y	Y	N	Y
2 ***Gradison***	Y	Y	N	N
3 Hall	Y	Y	N	Y
4 ***Oxley***	Y	Y	N	N
5 ***Gillmor***	Y	Y	N	N
6 ***McEwen***	Y	Y	N	N
7 ***DeWine***	Y	Y	N	N
8 ***Lukens***	Y	Y	N	N
9 Kaptur	Y	Y	N	Y
10 ***Miller***	Y	Y	N	N
11 Eckart	Y	Y	N	Y
12 ***Kasich***	Y	?	N	N
13 Pease	Y	Y	N	Y
14 Sawyer	Y	Y	Y	Y
15 ***Wylie***	Y	Y	N	N
16 ***Regula***	Y	Y	N	N
17 Traficant	Y	Y	Y	Y
18 Applegate	Y	Y	N	N
19 Feighan	Y	Y	N	Y
20 Oakar	Y	Y	Y	Y
21 Stokes	Y	Y	Y	Y
OKLAHOMA				
1 ***Inhofe***	Y	Y	N	N
2 Synar	Y	Y	N	Y
3 Watkins	Y	Y	N	N
4 McCurdy	Y	Y	N	N
5 ***Edwards***	Y	Y	N	N
6 English	Y	Y	N	N
OREGON				
1 AuCoin	Y	Y	Y	Y
2 ***Smith, B.***	Y	Y	N	N
3 Wyden	Y	Y	Y	Y
4 DeFazio	Y	Y	Y	Y
5 ***Smith, D.***	Y	Y	N	N
PENNSYLVANIA				
1 Foglietta	Y	Y	Y	Y
2 Gray	Y	Y	Y	Y
3 Borski	Y	Y	N	Y
4 Kolter	Y	Y	N	Y
5 ***Schulze***	Y	Y	N	N
6 Yatron	Y	Y	N	Y
7 ***Weldon***	Y	Y	N	N
8 Kostmayer	Y	Y	Y	Y
9 ***Shuster***	Y	Y	N	N
10 ***McDade***	Y	Y	N	N
11 Kanjorski	Y	Y	N	Y
12 Murtha	Y	Y	N	Y
13 ***Coughlin***	Y	Y	N	N
14 Coyne	Y	Y	Y	Y
15 ***Ritter***	?	?	?	N
16 ***Walker***	Y	Y	N	N
17 ***Gekas***	Y	Y	N	N
18 Walgren	Y	Y	Y	Y
19 ***Goodling***	Y	Y	N	N
20 Gaydos	Y	Y	N	Y
21 ***Ridge***	Y	Y	N	N
22 Murphy	Y	Y	N	Y
23 ***Clinger***	Y	Y	N	N
RHODE ISLAND				
1 ***Machtley***	Y	Y	N	N
2 ***Schneider***	Y	Y	N	N
SOUTH CAROLINA				
1 ***Ravenel***	Y	Y	N	N
2 ***Spence***	Y	Y	N	N
3 Derrick	Y	Y	N	Y
4 Patterson	Y	Y	N	N
5 Spratt	Y	Y	N	Y
6 Tallon	Y	Y	N	N

	86	87	88	89
SOUTH DAKOTA				
AL Johnson	Y	Y	Y	Y
TENNESSEE				
1 ***Quillen***	Y	Y	N	N
2 ***Duncan***	Y	Y	N	N
3 Lloyd	Y	Y	N	Y
4 Cooper	Y	Y	N	Y
5 Clement	Y	Y	N	Y
6 Gordon	Y	Y	N	Y
7 ***Sundquist***	Y	Y	N	N
8 Tanner	Y	Y	N	Y
9 Ford	Y	Y	Y	?
TEXAS				
1 Chapman	Y	Y	N	N
2 Wilson	Y	Y	N	N
3 ***Bartlett***	Y	Y	N	N
4 Hall	Y	Y	N	N
5 Bryant	Y	Y	N	Y
6 ***Barton***	Y	Y	N	N
7 ***Archer***	?	?	N	N
8 ***Fields***	Y	Y	N	N
9 Brooks	Y	Y	N	Y
10 Pickle	Y	Y	N	Y
11 Leath	Y	Y	?	N
12 Geren	Y	Y	N	Y
13 Sarpalius	Y	Y	N	N
14 Laughlin	Y	Y	N	N
15 de la Garza	Y	Y	N	Y
16 Coleman	Y	Y	N	Y
17 Stenholm	Y	Y	N	Y
18 Washington	Y	Y	Y	Y
19 ***Combest***	Y	Y	N	N
20 Gonzalez	Y	Y	Y	Y
21 ***Smith***	Y	Y	N	N
22 ***DeLay***	Y	Y	N	N
23 Bustamante	Y	Y	N	Y
24 Frost	Y	Y	N	Y
25 Andrews	Y	Y	N	Y
26 ***Armey***	Y	Y	N	N
27 Ortiz	Y	Y	N	N
UTAH				
1 ***Hansen***	Y	Y	N	N
2 Owens	Y	Y	N	N
3 ***Nielson***	Y	Y	N	N
VERMONT				
AL ***Smith***	Y	Y	N	N
VIRGINIA				
1 ***Bateman***	Y	Y	N	N
2 Pickett	Y	Y	N	N
3 ***Bliley***	Y	Y	N	N
4 Sisisky	Y	Y	N	N
5 Payne	Y	Y	N	Y
6 Olin	Y	Y	N	Y
7 ***Slaughter***	Y	Y	N	N
8 ***Parris***	Y	Y	N	N
9 Boucher	Y	Y	N	Y
10 ***Wolf***	Y	Y	N	N
WASHINGTON				
1 ***Miller***	Y	Y	N	N
2 Swift	Y	Y	N	Y
3 Unsoeld	Y	Y	N	Y
4 ***Morrison***	Y	Y	N	N
5 Foley				
6 Dicks	Y	Y	N	Y
7 McDermott	Y	Y	Y	Y
8 ***Chandler***	Y	Y	N	N
WEST VIRGINIA				
1 Mollohan	Y	Y	N	Y
2 Staggers	Y	Y	N	Y
3 Wise	Y	Y	N	Y
4 Rahall	?	?	?	?
WISCONSIN				
1 Aspin	Y	Y	N	Y
2 Kastenmeier	Y	Y	Y	Y
3 ***Gunderson***	Y	Y	N	N
4 Kleczka	Y	Y	N	Y
5 Moody	Y	Y	Y	Y
6 ***Petri***	Y	Y	N	N
7 Obey	Y	Y	N	Y
8 ***Roth***	Y	Y	N	N
9 ***Sensenbrenner***	Y	Y	N	N
WYOMING				
AL ***Thomas***	Y	Y	N	N

Southern states - Ala., Ark., Fla., Ga., Ky., La., Miss., N.C., Okla., S.C., Tenn., Texas, Va.
Omitted votes are quorum calls, which CQ does not include in its vote charts.

HOUSE VOTES 90, 92, 93, 94, 95, 96

90. HR 4380. Super Collider Authorization/Rule. Adoption of the rule (H Res 379) to provide for House floor consideration of the bill to authorize funds for the superconducting super collider. Adopted 406-0: R 169-0; D 237-0 (ND 160-0, SD 77-0), May 2, 1990.

92. HR 4380. Super Collider Authorization/Plan Evaluation. Wolpe, D-Mich., amendment to require a General Accounting Office evaluation of the summary project plan before $1.17 billion could be obligated. The amendment also would require various reports and audits certifying success throughout the project before additional funds could be obligated. Adopted 420-0: R 171-0; D 249-0 (ND 171-0, SD 78-0), May 2, 1990.

93. HR 4380. Super Collider Authorization/Texas. Sensenbrenner, R-Wis., amendment to delete provisions of the bill that would refund Texas its contribution if the project is terminated before Oct. 1, 1995. Adopted 256-163: R 139-32; D 117-131 (ND 95-74, SD 22-57), May 2, 1990.

94. HR 4380. Super Collider Authorization/Passage. Passage of the bill to authorize $5 billion in federal funds and $7.4 billion overall, with additional funds coming from Texas and international sources, for the development and construction of the superconducting super collider to break subatomic particles into their basic elements. Passed 309-109: R 115-57; D 194-52 (ND 124-43, SD 70-9), May 2, 1990. A "yea" was a vote supporting the president's position.

95. Procedural Motion. Machtley, R-R.I., motion to approve the House Journal of Wednesday, May 2. Motion agreed to 283-106: R 59-101; D 224-5 (ND 154-5, SD 70-0), May 3, 1990.

96. HR 4404. Fiscal 1990 Supplemental Appropriations/Instruction of Conferees. Conte, R-Mass., motion to instruct the House conferees on the fiscal 1990 supplemental appropriations bill to agree to Senate amendments on food stamps, veterans programs and the census, but to disagree on amendments that are not "dire emergencies." Motion agreed to 388-8: R 163-1; D 225-7 (ND 156-6, SD 69-1), May 3, 1990.

KEY

Y Voted for (yea).
\# Paired for.
\+ Announced for.
N Voted against (nay).
X Paired against.
\- Announced against.
P Voted "present."
C Voted "present" to avoid possible conflict of interest.
? Did not vote or otherwise make a position known.

Democrats *Republicans*

	90	92	93	94	95	96
ALABAMA						
1 *Callahan*	Y	Y	N	Y	N	Y
2 *Dickinson*	Y	Y	N	Y	N	Y
3 Browder	Y	Y	N	Y	?	Y
4 Bevill	Y	Y	N	Y	Y	Y
5 Flippo	?	?	?	?	?	?
6 Erdreich	Y	Y	N	Y	Y	Y
7 Harris	Y	Y	N	Y	Y	Y
ALASKA						
AL *Young*	Y	Y	N	Y	N	Y
ARIZONA						
1 *Rhodes*	Y	Y	Y	Y	N	Y
2 Udall	Y	Y	Y	Y	Y	Y
3 *Stump*	Y	Y	N	Y	?	?
4 *Kyl*	Y	Y	?	?	?	?
5 *Kolbe*	Y	Y	Y	Y	N	Y
ARKANSAS						
1 Alexander	?	?	N	Y	?	?
2 *Robinson*	Y	Y	Y	Y	Y	Y
3 *Hammerschmidt*	Y	Y	Y	Y	Y	Y
4 Anthony	?	Y	N	Y	Y	Y
CALIFORNIA						
1 Bosco	?	Y	N	Y	Y	Y
2 *Herger*	Y	Y	Y	N	N	Y
3 Matsui	?	Y	N	Y	Y	Y
4 Fazio	Y	Y	N	Y	Y	Y
5 Pelosi	Y	Y	N	Y	Y	Y
6 Boxer	Y	Y	Y	Y	Y	Y
7 Miller	Y	Y	Y	N	Y	Y
8 Dellums	Y	Y	N	Y	?	Y
9 Stark	Y	Y	Y	N	Y	Y
10 Edwards	Y	Y	N	Y	Y	Y
11 Lantos	Y	Y	Y	Y	Y	Y
12 *Campbell*	Y	Y	Y	N	N	Y
13 Mineta	Y	Y	N	Y	Y	Y
14 *Shumway*	Y	Y	Y	Y	Y	Y
15 Condit	Y	Y	N	Y	Y	Y
16 Panetta	Y	Y	Y	Y	Y	Y
17 *Pashayan*	Y	Y	N	Y	N	Y
18 Lehman	?	Y	N	Y	Y	?
19 *Lagomarsino*	Y	Y	Y	Y	N	Y
20 *Thomas*	Y	Y	Y	Y	N	Y
21 *Gallegly*	Y	Y	Y	Y	N	Y
22 *Moorhead*	Y	Y	Y	Y	N	Y
23 Beilenson	Y	Y	Y	N	Y	Y
24 Waxman	Y	Y	Y	Y	Y	Y
25 Roybal	Y	Y	N	Y	Y	Y
26 Berman	Y	Y	N	Y	Y	Y
27 Levine	Y	Y	?	?	Y	Y
28 Dixon	Y	Y	N	Y	Y	Y
29 Hawkins	Y	Y	N	Y	N	Y
30 Martinez	Y	Y	N	Y	Y	Y
31 Dymally	Y	Y	N	Y	?	Y
32 Anderson	Y	Y	Y	Y	Y	Y
33 *Dreier*	Y	Y	Y	Y	N	Y
34 Torres	Y	Y	N	Y	Y	Y
35 *Lewis*	Y	Y	N	Y	N	Y
36 Brown	Y	Y	N	Y	Y	Y
37 *McCandless*	Y	Y	Y	Y	N	Y
38 *Dornan*	Y	Y	Y	Y	N	Y
39 *Dannemeyer*	Y	Y	Y	Y	N	Y
40 *Cox*	Y	Y	Y	Y	N	Y
41 *Lowery*	Y	Y	Y	Y	?	Y
42 *Rohrabacher*	Y	Y	Y	N	N	Y
43 *Packard*	Y	Y	Y	Y	Y	Y
44 Bates	Y	Y	Y	N	Y	Y
45 *Hunter*	Y	Y	Y	Y	N	Y
COLORADO						
1 Schroeder	Y	Y	Y	N	N	Y
2 Skaggs	Y	Y	N	Y	Y	Y
3 Campbell	Y	Y	Y	Y	?	Y
4 *Brown*	Y	Y	Y	Y	N	Y
5 *Hefley*	Y	Y	Y	N	N	Y
6 *Schaefer*	Y	Y	Y	Y	N	Y
CONNECTICUT						
1 Kennelly	Y	Y	Y	Y	Y	Y
2 Gejdenson	Y	Y	Y	Y	Y	Y
3 Morrison	Y	Y	Y	N	Y	Y
4 *Shays*	Y	Y	Y	N	N	Y
5 *Rowland*	Y	Y	Y	N	Y	Y
6 *Johnson*	Y	Y	?	N	Y	Y
DELAWARE						
AL Carper	Y	Y	Y	N	Y	Y
FLORIDA						
1 Hutto	Y	Y	N	Y	Y	Y
2 *Grant*	Y	Y	N	Y	Y	Y
3 Bennett	Y	Y	Y	Y	Y	Y
4 *James*	Y	Y	Y	N	N	Y
5 *McCollum*	Y	Y	Y	Y	?	Y
6 *Stearns*	Y	Y	Y	Y	N	Y
7 Gibbons	Y	Y	N	Y	Y	Y
8 *Young*	Y	Y	Y	Y	Y	Y
9 *Bilirakis*	Y	Y	Y	Y	N	Y
10 *Ireland*	Y	Y	Y	Y	N	Y
11 Nelson	Y	+	-	+	+	+
12 *Lewis*	Y	Y	Y	Y	N	Y
13 *Goss*	Y	Y	Y	Y	N	Y
14 Johnston	Y	Y	Y	Y	Y	Y
15 *Shaw*	Y	Y	Y	Y	Y	Y
16 Smith	?	?	?	?	?	?
17 Lehman	Y	Y	N	Y	Y	Y
18 *Ros-Lehtinen*	Y	Y	Y	N	N	Y
19 Fascell	Y	Y	N	Y	Y	Y
GEORGIA						
1 Thomas	Y	Y	Y	Y	Y	Y
2 Hatcher	Y	Y	N	Y	Y	Y
3 Ray	Y	Y	Y	Y	Y	Y
4 Jones	Y	Y	N	Y	Y	Y
5 Lewis	Y	Y	Y	Y	Y	Y
6 *Gingrich*	Y	Y	Y	Y	N	Y
7 Darden	Y	Y	Y	Y	?	Y
8 Rowland	Y	Y	Y	Y	Y	Y
9 Jenkins	Y	Y	Y	Y	Y	?
10 Barnard	Y	Y	Y	Y	Y	?
HAWAII						
1 *Saiki*	?	Y	Y	Y	Y	Y
2 Akaka	?	Y	N	Y	?	?
IDAHO						
1 *Craig*	?	?	#	X	?	?
2 Stallings	Y	Y	N	Y	Y	Y
ILLINOIS						
1 Hayes	Y	Y	N	Y	Y	Y
2 Savage	?	Y	N	Y	?	?
3 Russo	Y	Y	Y	Y	Y	Y
4 Sangmeister	Y	Y	Y	Y	Y	Y
5 Lipinski	Y	Y	Y	Y	Y	Y
6 *Hyde*	Y	Y	Y	N	N	Y
7 Collins	?	?	?	?	?	?
8 Rostenkowski	Y	Y	Y	N	Y	Y
9 Yates	Y	Y	Y	Y	Y	Y
10 *Porter*	Y	Y	Y	N	N	Y
11 Annunzio	Y	Y	Y	Y	Y	Y
12 *Crane*	Y	Y	Y	N	N	Y
13 *Fawell*	Y	Y	Y	Y	Y	Y
14 *Hastert*	Y	Y	Y	N	N	Y
15 *Madigan*	Y	Y	N	Y	N	Y
16 *Martin*	Y	Y	Y	Y	N	Y
17 Evans	Y	Y	Y	N	Y	Y
18 *Michel*	Y	Y	Y	Y	N	Y
19 Bruce	Y	Y	Y	Y	Y	Y
20 Durbin	Y	Y	Y	N	Y	Y
21 Costello	Y	Y	Y	Y	Y	Y
22 Poshard	Y	Y	Y	Y	Y	Y
INDIANA						
1 Visclosky	Y	Y	N	Y	Y	Y
2 Sharp	Y	Y	Y	N	?	Y
3 *Hiler*	Y	Y	Y	N	Y	Y

ND Northern Democrats SD Southern Democrats

	90	92	93	94	95	96
4 Long	Y	Y	Y	N	Y	Y
5 Jontz	Y	Y	Y	N	Y	Y
6 ***Burton***	Y	Y	Y	N	N	Y
7 ***Myers***	Y	Y	Y	Y	?	?
8 McCloskey	Y	Y	Y	Y	Y	Y
9 Hamilton	Y	Y	Y	N	Y	Y
10 Jacobs	Y	Y	Y	N	N	Y
IOWA						
1 ***Leach***	Y	Y	Y	Y	N	Y
2 ***Tauke***	Y	Y	Y	N	N	Y
3 Nagle	Y	Y	N	Y	Y	Y
4 Smith	Y	Y	N	Y	Y	Y
5 ***Lightfoot***	?	?	?	?	?	?
6 ***Grandy***	Y	Y	Y	N	N	Y
KANSAS						
1 ***Roberts***	Y	Y	Y	Y	N	Y
2 Slattery	Y	Y	Y	N	Y	Y
3 ***Meyers***	Y	Y	Y	Y	Y	Y
4 Glickman	Y	Y	Y	N	Y	Y
5 ***Whittaker***	Y	Y	Y	Y	N	Y
KENTUCKY						
1 Hubbard	Y	Y	N	Y	Y	Y
2 Natcher	Y	Y	N	Y	Y	Y
3 Mazzoli	Y	Y	Y	Y	Y	Y
4 ***Bunning***	Y	Y	Y	N	N	Y
5 ***Rogers***	Y	Y	Y	Y	N	Y
6 ***Hopkins***	Y	Y	Y	Y	N	Y
7 Perkins	Y	Y	N	Y	Y	Y
LOUISIANA						
1 ***Livingston***	Y	Y	N	Y	Y	Y
2 Boggs	Y	Y	N	Y	Y	N
3 Tauzin	Y	Y	N	Y	Y	Y
4 ***McCrery***	Y	Y	N	Y	Y	Y
5 Huckaby	Y	?	?	?	?	?
6 ***Baker***	Y	Y	N	Y	N	Y
7 Hayes	Y	Y	N	Y	Y	Y
8 ***Holloway***	Y	Y	N	Y	N	N
MAINE						
1 Brennan	Y	Y	Y	Y	Y	Y
2 ***Snowe***	Y	Y	Y	N	N	Y
MARYLAND						
1 Dyson	Y	Y	Y	N	Y	Y
2 ***Bentley***	Y	Y	Y	Y	N	Y
3 Cardin	Y	Y	N	Y	Y	Y
4 McMillen	Y	Y	N	Y	Y	Y
5 Hoyer	Y	Y	N	Y	?	Y
6 Byron	Y	Y	N	Y	Y	Y
7 Mfume	Y	Y	Y	Y	?	Y
8 ***Morella***	Y	Y	Y	Y	N	Y
MASSACHUSETTS						
1 ***Conte***	Y	Y	Y	Y	Y	Y
2 Neal	Y	Y	Y	Y	Y	Y
3 Early	Y	Y	Y	N	Y	Y
4 Frank	Y	Y	Y	Y	Y	Y
5 Atkins	Y	Y	N	Y	Y	Y
6 Mavroules	?	Y	N	Y	Y	Y
7 Markey	Y	Y	N	Y	?	Y
8 Kennedy	Y	Y	Y	Y	Y	Y
9 Moakley	Y	Y	Y	Y	Y	Y
10 Studds	Y	Y	Y	N	Y	Y
11 Donnelly	Y	Y	N	Y	Y	Y
MICHIGAN						
1 Conyers	Y	Y	N	Y	Y	Y
2 ***Pursell***	Y	Y	N	Y	?	?
3 Wolpe	Y	Y	Y	N	Y	Y
4 ***Upton***	Y	Y	Y	N	N	Y
5 ***Henry***	Y	Y	Y	N	N	Y
6 Carr	Y	Y	N	N	Y	Y
7 Kildee	Y	Y	Y	N	Y	Y
8 Traxler	Y	Y	Y	Y	?	?
9 ***Vander Jagt***	?	Y	Y	N	Y	Y
10 ***Schuette***	Y	Y	Y	N	N	Y
11 ***Davis***	Y	Y	Y	N	Y	Y
12 Bonior	Y	Y	Y	N	Y	Y
13 Crockett	?	Y	Y	N	?	?
14 Hertel	Y	Y	Y	N	Y	Y
15 Ford	Y	Y	N	Y	Y	Y
16 Dingell	Y	Y	N	Y	Y	N
17 Levin	Y	Y	Y	Y	Y	Y
18 ***Broomfield***	Y	Y	Y	N	Y	Y
MINNESOTA						
1 Penny	Y	Y	Y	N	Y	N
2 ***Weber***	Y	Y	Y	Y	N	Y
3 ***Frenzel***	?	Y	Y	N	N	Y
4 Vento	Y	Y	Y	N	Y	N

	90	92	93	94	95	96
5 Sabo	Y	Y	Y	Y	Y	Y
6 Sikorski	Y	Y	Y	N	N	N
7 ***Stangeland***	Y	Y	Y	N	N	Y
8 Oberstar	Y	Y	Y	N	Y	Y
MISSISSIPPI						
1 Whitten	Y	Y	N	Y	Y	Y
2 Espy	Y	Y	N	Y	Y	Y
3 Montgomery	Y	Y	N	Y	Y	Y
4 Parker	Y	Y	N	Y	Y	Y
5 Taylor	Y	Y	N	Y	Y	Y
MISSOURI						
1 Clay	Y	Y	Y	Y	?	Y
2 ***Buechner***	Y	Y	Y	N	N	Y
3 Gephardt	Y	Y	N	Y	Y	Y
4 Skelton	Y	Y	Y	Y	Y	Y
5 Wheat	?	Y	Y	Y	Y	Y
6 ***Coleman***	Y	Y	Y	Y	N	Y
7 ***Hancock***	Y	Y	Y	N	N	Y
8 ***Emerson***	Y	Y	Y	Y	Y	Y
9 Volkmer	Y	Y	N	Y	Y	Y
MONTANA						
1 Williams	Y	Y	Y	N	Y	Y
2 ***Marlenee***	Y	Y	Y	N	N	Y
NEBRASKA						
1 ***Bereuter***	Y	Y	Y	N	N	Y
2 Hoagland	Y	Y	Y	N	Y	Y
3 ***Smith***	Y	Y	Y	Y	Y	Y
NEVADA						
1 Bilbray	Y	Y	N	Y	Y	Y
2 ***Vucanovich***	Y	Y	Y	Y	N	Y
NEW HAMPSHIRE						
1 ***Smith***	Y	Y	Y	N	N	Y
2 ***Douglas***	Y	Y	Y	N	N	Y
NEW JERSEY						
1 Vacancy						
2 Hughes	Y	Y	Y	Y	Y	Y
3 Pallone	Y	Y	N	Y	Y	Y
4 ***Smith***	Y	Y	N	Y	Y	Y
5 ***Roukema***	Y	Y	Y	N	N	Y
6 Dwyer	Y	Y	N	Y	Y	?
7 ***Rinaldo***	Y	Y	N	Y	Y	Y
8 Roe	Y	Y	N	Y	Y	Y
9 Torricelli	?	Y	N	Y	Y	Y
10 Payne	Y	Y	N	Y	Y	Y
11 ***Gallo***	Y	Y	N	Y	Y	Y
12 ***Courter***	Y	Y	Y	Y	N	Y
13 ***Saxton***	Y	Y	N	Y	Y	Y
14 Guarini	Y	Y	Y	Y	Y	Y
NEW MEXICO						
1 ***Schiff***	Y	Y	N	Y	?	Y
2 ***Skeen***	Y	Y	N	Y	Y	Y
3 Richardson	Y	Y	N	Y	Y	Y
NEW YORK						
1 Hochbrueckner	Y	Y	N	Y	Y	Y
2 Downey	Y	Y	Y	Y	Y	Y
3 Mrazek	Y	Y	Y	Y	Y	Y
4 ***Lent***	Y	Y	Y	Y	Y	Y
5 ***McGrath***	Y	Y	Y	Y	N	Y
6 Flake	Y	Y	Y	Y	Y	Y
7 Ackerman	?	?	?	?	?	?
8 Scheuer	Y	Y	N	Y	Y	Y
9 Manton	Y	Y	N	Y	Y	Y
10 Schumer	Y	Y	Y	Y	Y	Y
11 Towns	Y	Y	N	Y	Y	Y
12 Owens	Y	Y	N	Y	Y	Y
13 Solarz	Y	Y	Y	Y	Y	Y
14 ***Molinari***	Y	Y	Y	Y	N	Y
15 ***Green***	Y	Y	Y	Y	Y	Y
16 Rangel	Y	Y	X	#	Y	Y
17 Weiss	Y	Y	Y	N	Y	Y
18 Serrano	?	Y	N	Y	Y	Y
19 Engel	Y	Y	N	Y	Y	Y
20 Lowey	Y	Y	Y	Y	Y	?
21 ***Fish***	Y	Y	Y	Y	Y	Y
22 ***Gilman***	Y	Y	Y	Y	Y	Y
23 McNulty	Y	Y	N	Y	Y	Y
24 ***Solomon***	Y	Y	Y	N	N	Y
25 ***Boehlert***	Y	Y	Y	Y	N	Y
26 ***Martin***	Y	Y	Y	N	N	Y
27 ***Walsh***	Y	Y	Y	Y	Y	Y
28 McHugh	Y	Y	Y	Y	Y	Y
29 ***Horton***	Y	Y	Y	Y	Y	Y
30 Slaughter	Y	Y	Y	Y	Y	Y
31 ***Paxon***	Y	Y	Y	N	N	Y

	90	92	93	94	95	96
32 LaFalce	Y	Y	Y	N	Y	Y
33 Nowak	Y	Y	N	Y	Y	Y
34 ***Houghton***	Y	Y	Y	Y	Y	Y
NORTH CAROLINA						
1 Jones	Y	Y	N	Y	?	Y
2 Valentine	Y	Y	N	Y	Y	Y
3 Lancaster	Y	Y	N	Y	Y	Y
4 Price	Y	Y	N	Y	Y	Y
5 Neal	Y	Y	Y	N	Y	Y
6 ***Coble***	Y	Y	Y	N	N	Y
7 Rose	Y	Y	N	Y	Y	Y
8 Hefner	Y	Y	N	Y	Y	Y
9 ***McMillan***	Y	Y	Y	Y	N	Y
10 ***Ballenger***	Y	Y	N	Y	?	Y
11 Clarke	Y	Y	Y	Y	Y	Y
NORTH DAKOTA						
AL Dorgan	Y	Y	N	Y	Y	Y
OHIO						
1 Luken	Y	Y	N	Y	Y	?
2 ***Gradison***	Y	Y	Y	N	Y	Y
3 Hall	?	Y	Y	Y	Y	Y
4 ***Oxley***	Y	Y	Y	N	N	Y
5 ***Gillmor***	Y	Y	N	Y	Y	Y
6 ***McEwen***	Y	Y	Y	N	Y	Y
7 ***DeWine***	Y	Y	Y	Y	N	Y
8 ***Lukens***	?	?	?	?	?	?
9 Kaptur	Y	Y	N	Y	Y	?
10 ***Miller***	Y	Y	Y	Y	N	Y
11 Eckart	Y	Y	Y	N	Y	Y
12 ***Kasich***	Y	Y	Y	Y	Y	Y
13 Pease	Y	Y	Y	N	Y	Y
14 Sawyer	Y	Y	Y	N	Y	Y
15 ***Wylie***	Y	Y	Y	Y	Y	Y
16 ***Regula***	Y	Y	Y	N	N	Y
17 Traficant	Y	Y	N	Y	Y	Y
18 Applegate	Y	Y	N	Y	Y	Y
19 Feighan	Y	Y	Y	Y	Y	Y
20 Oakar	Y	Y	N	Y	Y	Y
21 Stokes	Y	Y	N	Y	Y	Y
OKLAHOMA						
1 ***Inhofe***	Y	Y	Y	Y	N	Y
2 Synar	Y	Y	Y	N	Y	Y
3 Watkins	Y	Y	N	Y	Y	Y
4 McCurdy	Y	Y	N	Y	Y	Y
5 ***Edwards***	Y	Y	Y	Y	Y	?
6 English	Y	Y	N	Y	Y	Y
OREGON						
1 AuCoin	Y	Y	Y	Y	Y	Y
2 ***Smith, B.***	Y	Y	Y	N	N	Y
3 Wyden	Y	Y	Y	Y	Y	Y
4 DeFazio	Y	Y	Y	N	Y	Y
5 ***Smith, D.***	Y	Y	Y	Y	N	Y
PENNSYLVANIA						
1 Foglietta	Y	Y	Y	Y	Y	Y
2 Gray	Y	Y	N	Y	Y	Y
3 Borski	Y	Y	Y	Y	Y	Y
4 Kolter	Y	Y	N	Y	Y	Y
5 ***Schulze***	Y	Y	Y	N	Y	Y
6 Yatron	Y	Y	Y	Y	Y	Y
7 ***Weldon***	Y	Y	Y	N	Y	Y
8 Kostmayer	Y	Y	Y	N	Y	Y
9 ***Shuster***	Y	Y	Y	N	Y	Y
10 ***McDade***	Y	Y	Y	Y	Y	Y
11 Kanjorski	Y	Y	N	N	Y	Y
12 Murtha	Y	Y	N	Y	Y	Y
13 ***Coughlin***	Y	Y	Y	N	N	Y
14 Coyne	Y	Y	N	Y	Y	Y
15 ***Ritter***	Y	Y	Y	N	?	?
16 ***Walker***	Y	Y	Y	Y	N	Y
17 ***Gekas***	Y	Y	Y	Y	N	Y
18 Walgren	Y	Y	Y	Y	Y	Y
19 ***Goodling***	Y	?	N	Y	N	Y
20 Gaydos	Y	Y	N	Y	Y	Y
21 ***Ridge***	Y	Y	Y	N	N	Y
22 Murphy	Y	Y	Y	N	N	Y
23 ***Clinger***	Y	Y	Y	Y	Y	Y
RHODE ISLAND						
1 ***Machtley***	Y	Y	Y	N	N	Y
2 ***Schneider***	Y	Y	Y	N	Y	Y
SOUTH CAROLINA						
1 ***Ravenel***	Y	Y	Y	Y	Y	Y
2 ***Spence***	Y	Y	Y	Y	Y	Y
3 Derrick	Y	Y	Y	N	Y	Y
4 Patterson	Y	Y	Y	Y	Y	Y
5 Spratt	Y	Y	Y	N	Y	Y
6 Tallon	Y	Y	N	N	Y	Y

	90	92	93	94	95	96
SOUTH DAKOTA						
AL Johnson	Y	Y	Y	Y	Y	Y
TENNESSEE						
1 ***Quillen***	Y	Y	Y	Y	Y	Y
2 ***Duncan***	Y	Y	Y	N	N	Y
3 Lloyd	Y	Y	N	Y	Y	Y
4 Cooper	Y	Y	Y	Y	Y	?
5 Clement	Y	Y	Y	N	Y	Y
6 Gordon	?	Y	Y	Y	Y	Y
7 ***Sundquist***	Y	Y	Y	N	N	Y
8 Tanner	Y	Y	N	Y	Y	Y
9 Ford	Y	Y	N	Y	?	?
TEXAS						
1 Chapman	Y	Y	N	Y	Y	Y
2 Wilson	?	Y	N	Y	Y	?
3 ***Bartlett***	Y	Y	N	Y	Y	Y
4 Hall	Y	Y	N	Y	Y	Y
5 Bryant	Y	Y	N	Y	Y	Y
6 ***Barton***	Y	Y	N	Y	?	?
7 ***Archer***	Y	Y	N	Y	Y	Y
8 ***Fields***	Y	Y	N	Y	N	Y
9 Brooks	Y	Y	N	Y	?	Y
10 Pickle	Y	Y	N	Y	?	?
11 Leath	Y	Y	N	Y	?	?
12 Geren	Y	Y	N	Y	Y	Y
13 Sarpalius	Y	Y	N	Y	Y	Y
14 Laughlin	Y	Y	N	Y	Y	Y
15 de la Garza	Y	Y	N	Y	Y	Y
16 Coleman	Y	Y	N	Y	Y	Y
17 Stenholm	Y	Y	N	Y	Y	Y
18 Washington	Y	Y	N	Y	Y	Y
19 ***Combest***	Y	Y	N	Y	Y	Y
20 Gonzalez	Y	Y	N	Y	Y	Y
21 ***Smith***	Y	Y	N	Y	N	Y
22 ***DeLay***	Y	Y	N	Y	Y	Y
23 Bustamante	Y	Y	N	Y	Y	Y
24 Frost	Y	Y	N	Y	?	?
25 Andrews	Y	Y	N	Y	Y	Y
26 ***Armey***	Y	Y	N	Y	?	?
27 Ortiz	Y	Y	N	Y	Y	Y
UTAH						
1 ***Hansen***	?	Y	Y	Y	Y	Y
2 Owens	Y	Y	N	?	Y	Y
3 ***Nielson***	Y	Y	Y	Y	Y	Y
VERMONT						
AL ***Smith***	Y	?	Y	Y	Y	Y
VIRGINIA						
1 ***Bateman***	Y	Y	N	Y	Y	Y
2 Pickett	Y	Y	N	Y	Y	Y
3 ***Bliley***	Y	Y	Y	Y	?	Y
4 Sisisky	Y	Y	Y	N	Y	Y
5 Payne	Y	Y	Y	N	Y	Y
6 Olin	Y	Y	Y	N	Y	Y
7 ***Slaughter***	Y	Y	Y	Y	N	Y
8 ***Parris***	Y	Y	Y	Y	N	?
9 Boucher	Y	Y	N	Y	Y	Y
10 ***Wolf***	Y	Y	Y	Y	?	Y
WASHINGTON						
1 ***Miller***	Y	Y	Y	Y	N	Y
2 Swift	Y	Y	Y	Y	Y	Y
3 Unsoeld	Y	Y	N	Y	Y	Y
4 ***Morrison***	Y	Y	N	Y	Y	Y
5 Foley						
6 Dicks	Y	Y	Y	Y	Y	Y
7 McDermott	Y	Y	Y	Y	Y	Y
8 ***Chandler***	Y	Y	Y	Y	N	Y
WEST VIRGINIA						
1 Mollohan	Y	Y	N	Y	Y	N
2 Staggers	Y	Y	N	Y	Y	N
3 Wise	Y	Y	N	Y	Y	Y
4 Rahall	?	?	?	?	?	?
WISCONSIN						
1 Aspin	Y	Y	N	Y	Y	Y
2 Kastenmeier	Y	Y	Y	N	Y	Y
3 ***Gunderson***	Y	Y	Y	N	Y	Y
4 Kleczka	Y	Y	Y	N	Y	Y
5 Moody	Y	Y	Y	?	Y	Y
6 ***Petri***	Y	Y	Y	N	Y	Y
7 Obey	Y	Y	Y	N	Y	Y
8 ***Roth***	Y	Y	Y	Y	N	Y
9 ***Sensenbrenner***	Y	Y	Y	N	N	Y
WYOMING						
AL ***Thomas***	Y	Y	Y	N	N	Y

Southern states - Ala., Ark., Fla., Ga., Ky., La., Miss., N.C., Okla., S.C., Tenn., Texas, Va.
Omitted votes are quorum calls, which CQ does not include in its vote charts.

HOUSE VOTES 97, 98, 99, 100, 101, 102, 103, 104

97. Procedural Motion. Bunning, R-Ky., motion to approve the House Journal of Monday, May 7. Motion agreed to 263-106: R 56-100; D 207-6 (ND 140-6, SD 67-0), May 8, 1990.

98. HR 4522. Emergency Response Information/Passage. Valentine, D-N.C., motion to suspend the rules and pass the bill to require the U.S. Fire Administration to review and make recommendations to improve information used by firefighters and other state and local emergency personnel in responding to medical emergencies, fires, the release of hazardous materials and natural emergencies. Motion agreed to 410-0: R 169-0; D 241-0 (ND 165-0, SD 76-0), May 8, 1990. A two-thirds majority of those present and voting (274 in this case) is required for passage under suspension of the rules.

99. HR 237. Biological Weapons/Passage. Kastenmeier, D-Wis., motion to suspend the rules and pass the bill to prohibit development or possession of biological weapons and to prohibit assisting a foreign state or organization that is trying to develop or possess biological weapons. The bill would implement an international convention ratified by the Senate in 1974 and signed by 111 nations. Motion agreed to 408-0: R 169-0; D 239-0 (ND 164-0, SD 75-0), May 8, 1990. A two-thirds majority of those present and voting (272 in this case) is required for passage under suspension of the rules.

100. Procedural Motion. Paxon, R-N.Y., motion to approve the House Journal of Tuesday, May 8. Motion agreed to 298-108: R 64-102; D 234-6 (ND 156-6, SD 78-0), May 9, 1990.

101. Procedural Motion. Yates, D-Ill., motion to allow Torricelli, D-N.J., to proceed in order after the chair ruled that he had transgressed proper debate by saying the president was "intellectually dishonest" with regard to his pledge not to raise taxes. Motion agreed to 246-167: R 0-167; D 246-0 (ND 167-0, SD 79-0), May 9, 1990.

102. HR 3. Child-Care Programs/Instruction of Conferees. Archer, R-Texas, motion to instruct the House conferees on the bill to reject the Senate amendments to establish a new child-care grant program (the Act for Better Child Care). Motion agreed to 411-0: R 166-0; D 245-0 (ND 169-0, SD 76-0), May 9, 1990.

103. HR 2364. Amtrak Reauthorization/Conference Report. Adoption of the conference report on the bill to reauthorize Amtrak for fiscal 1989-92 and to require the Interstate Commerce Commission to review proposed acquisitions of major railroads by non-railroad companies. Adopted 322-93: R 84-83; D 238-10 (ND 167-2, SD 71-8), May 9, 1990. A "nay" was a vote supporting the president's position.

104. HR 770. Parental and Medical Leave Act/Rule. Adoption of the rule (H Res 388) to provide for House floor consideration of the bill to require employers to provide benefits for employees with a new child, a seriously ill child or parent, or a serious health condition. Adopted 251-151: R 18-146; D 233-5 (ND 159-1, SD 74-4), May 9, 1990.

KEY

- Y Voted for (yea).
- # Paired for.
- \+ Announced for.
- N Voted against (nay).
- X Paired against.
- \- Announced against.
- P Voted "present."
- C Voted "present" to avoid possible conflict of interest.
- ? Did not vote or otherwise make a position known.

Democrats ***Republicans***

	97	98	99	100	101	102	103	104
ALABAMA								
1 ***Callahan***	Y	Y	Y	Y	N	Y	Y	N
2 ***Dickinson***	N	Y	Y	?	?	?	X	X
3 Browder	?	Y	Y	Y	Y	Y	Y	Y
4 Bevill	Y	Y	Y	Y	Y	Y	Y	Y
5 Flippo	?	?	?	?	?	?	?	?
6 Erdreich	Y	Y	Y	Y	Y	Y	Y	Y
7 Harris	Y	Y	?	Y	Y	Y	Y	Y
ALASKA								
AL ***Young***	N	Y	Y	N	N	Y	N	N
ARIZONA								
1 ***Rhodes***	N	Y	Y	N	N	Y	N	N
2 Udall	?	?	?	?	?	?	?	?
3 ***Stump***	N	Y	Y	N	N	Y	N	N
4 ***Kyl***	N	Y	Y	N	N	Y	N	N
5 ***Kolbe***	?	?	?	N	N	Y	N	N
ARKANSAS								
1 Alexander	?	Y	Y	?	?	?	Y	Y
2 ***Robinson***	?	?	?	?	?	?	?	?
3 ***Hammerschmidt***	Y	Y	Y	Y	N	Y	Y	N
4 Anthony	Y	Y	Y	Y	Y	Y	Y	Y
CALIFORNIA								
1 Bosco	Y	Y	Y	Y	Y	Y	Y	Y
2 ***Herger***	N	Y	Y	N	N	Y	N	N
3 Matsui	Y	Y	Y	Y	Y	Y	Y	Y
4 Fazio	Y	Y	Y	Y	Y	Y	Y	Y
5 Pelosi	Y	Y	Y	Y	Y	Y	Y	Y
6 Boxer	Y	Y	Y	Y	Y	Y	Y	Y
7 Miller	Y	Y	Y	Y	Y	Y	Y	Y
8 Dellums	Y	Y	Y	Y	Y	Y	Y	Y
9 Stark	Y	Y	Y	Y	Y	Y	Y	Y
10 Edwards	Y	Y	Y	Y	Y	Y	Y	Y
11 Lantos	Y	Y	Y	Y	Y	Y	Y	Y
12 ***Campbell***	–	+	+	N	N	Y	N	N
13 Mineta	Y	Y	Y	Y	Y	Y	Y	Y
14 ***Shumway***	Y	Y	Y	Y	N	Y	N	N
15 Condit	Y	Y	Y	Y	?	Y	Y	Y
16 Panetta	Y	Y	Y	Y	Y	Y	Y	Y
17 ***Pashayan***	N	Y	Y	N	N	Y	Y	N
18 Lehman	?	Y	Y	Y	Y	Y	Y	Y
19 ***Lagomarsino***	N	Y	Y	N	N	Y	Y	N
20 ***Thomas***	N	Y	Y	N	N	Y	Y	N
21 ***Gallegly***	N	Y	Y	N	N	Y	Y	N
22 ***Moorhead***	N	Y	Y	N	N	Y	N	N
23 Beilenson	Y	Y	Y	Y	Y	Y	Y	Y
24 Waxman	Y	Y	Y	Y	Y	Y	Y	?
25 Roybal	Y	Y	Y	Y	Y	Y	Y	Y
26 Berman	Y	Y	Y	Y	Y	Y	Y	Y
27 Levine	Y	Y	Y	Y	Y	Y	?	?
28 Dixon	Y	Y	Y	Y	Y	Y	Y	Y
29 Hawkins	N	?	?	N	Y	Y	?	?
30 Martinez	Y	Y	Y	Y	Y	Y	Y	Y
31 Dymally	Y	Y	Y	Y	Y	Y	Y	Y
32 Anderson	Y	Y	Y	Y	Y	Y	Y	Y
33 ***Dreier***	N	Y	Y	N	N	Y	N	N
34 Torres	Y	Y	Y	Y	Y	Y	Y	Y
35 ***Lewis***	N	Y	Y	N	N	?	X	X
36 Brown	Y	Y	Y	Y	Y	Y	Y	Y
37 ***McCandless***	N	Y	Y	N	N	Y	N	N
38 ***Dornan***	?	Y	Y	Y	N	Y	N	N
39 ***Dannemeyer***	N	Y	Y	N	N	Y	N	N
40 ***Cox***	N	Y	Y	N	N	Y	N	N
41 ***Lowery***	N	Y	Y	?	N	Y	N	N
42 ***Rohrabacher***	N	Y	Y	N	N	Y	N	N
43 ***Packard***	Y	Y	Y	Y	N	Y	N	N
44 Bates	Y	Y	Y	?	Y	Y	Y	Y
45 ***Hunter***	N	Y	Y	?	N	Y	?	N
COLORADO								
1 Schroeder	N	Y	Y	N	Y	Y	Y	Y
2 Skaggs	Y	Y	Y	Y	Y	Y	Y	Y
3 Campbell	Y	Y	Y	Y	Y	Y	N	Y
4 ***Brown***	N	Y	Y	N	N	Y	N	N
5 ***Hefley***	N	Y	Y	N	N	Y	N	N
6 ***Schaefer***	N	Y	Y	N	N	Y	N	N
CONNECTICUT								
1 Kennelly	Y	Y	Y	Y	Y	Y	Y	Y
2 Gejdenson	Y	Y	Y	Y	Y	Y	Y	Y
3 Morrison	?	Y	Y	?	Y	Y	Y	Y
4 ***Shays***	N	Y	Y	N	N	Y	Y	Y
5 ***Rowland***	?	Y	Y	Y	N	Y	Y	Y
6 ***Johnson***	Y	Y	Y	Y	N	Y	Y	N
DELAWARE								
AL Carper	Y	Y	Y	Y	Y	Y	Y	Y
FLORIDA								
1 Hutto	Y	Y	Y	Y	Y	Y	Y	Y
2 ***Grant***	Y	Y	Y	Y	N	Y	Y	N
3 Bennett	Y	Y	Y	Y	Y	Y	Y	Y
4 ***James***	N	Y	Y	N	N	Y	N	N
5 ***McCollum***	Y	Y	Y	Y	N	Y	N	N
6 ***Stearns***	Y	Y	Y	N	N	Y	N	N
7 Gibbons	Y	Y	Y	Y	Y	Y	Y	Y
8 ***Young***	?	Y	Y	?	?	?	?	?
9 ***Bilirakis***	N	Y	Y	N	N	Y	N	N
10 ***Ireland***	?	Y	Y	N	N	Y	N	N
11 Nelson	+	+	+	+	+	+	#	#
12 ***Lewis***	N	Y	Y	N	N	Y	N	N
13 ***Goss***	N	Y	Y	N	N	Y	N	N
14 Johnston	?	Y	Y	Y	Y	Y	Y	Y
15 ***Shaw***	?	Y	Y	Y	N	Y	N	N
16 Smith	Y	Y	Y	Y	Y	Y	Y	Y
17 Lehman	?	Y	Y	Y	Y	Y	Y	Y
18 ***Ros-Lehtinen***	N	Y	Y	N	N	Y	N	N
19 Fascell	Y	Y	Y	Y	Y	Y	Y	Y
GEORGIA								
1 Thomas	Y	Y	Y	Y	Y	Y	Y	Y
2 Hatcher	Y	Y	Y	Y	Y	Y	Y	Y
3 Ray	Y	Y	Y	Y	Y	Y	Y	Y
4 Jones	Y	Y	Y	Y	Y	Y	Y	Y
5 Lewis	Y	Y	Y	Y	Y	Y	Y	Y
6 ***Gingrich***	N	Y	Y	Y	N	Y	N	N
7 Darden	Y	Y	Y	Y	Y	Y	Y	Y
8 Rowland	Y	Y	Y	Y	Y	Y	Y	Y
9 Jenkins	Y	Y	Y	Y	Y	Y	Y	Y
10 Barnard	Y	Y	Y	Y	Y	Y	Y	Y
HAWAII								
1 ***Saiki***	Y	Y	Y	Y	N	Y	Y	Y
2 Akaka	Y	Y	Y	Y	Y	Y	Y	Y
IDAHO								
1 ***Craig***	?	?	?	?	?	?	X	X
2 Stallings	Y	Y	Y	Y	Y	Y	Y	Y
ILLINOIS								
1 Hayes	Y	Y	Y	Y	Y	Y	Y	Y
2 Savage	?	Y	Y	?	Y	Y	Y	?
3 Russo	Y	Y	Y	Y	Y	Y	Y	Y
4 Sangmeister	Y	Y	Y	Y	Y	Y	Y	Y
5 Lipinski	Y	Y	Y	Y	Y	Y	Y	Y
6 ***Hyde***	?	Y	Y	N	N	Y	N	N
7 Collins	?	?	?	?	?	?	#	?
8 Rostenkowski	Y	Y	Y	Y	Y	Y	Y	Y
9 Yates	Y	Y	Y	Y	Y	Y	Y	Y
10 ***Porter***	Y	Y	Y	Y	N	Y	N	N
11 Annunzio	Y	Y	Y	Y	Y	Y	Y	Y
12 ***Crane***	N	Y	Y	N	N	Y	N	N
13 ***Fawell***	?	Y	Y	Y	N	Y	N	N
14 ***Hastert***	N	Y	Y	N	N	Y	Y	N
15 ***Madigan***	N	Y	Y	N	N	Y	Y	N
16 ***Martin***	N	Y	Y	N	N	Y	N	N
17 Evans	Y	Y	Y	Y	Y	Y	Y	Y
18 ***Michel***	N	Y	Y	N	N	Y	N	N
19 Bruce	Y	Y	Y	Y	Y	Y	Y	Y
20 Durbin	Y	Y	Y	Y	Y	Y	Y	Y
21 Costello	Y	Y	Y	Y	Y	Y	Y	Y
22 Poshard	Y	Y	Y	Y	Y	Y	Y	Y
INDIANA								
1 Visclosky	?	?	?	Y	Y	Y	Y	Y
2 Sharp	Y	Y	Y	Y	Y	Y	Y	Y
3 ***Hiler***	N	Y	Y	N	N	Y	N	N

ND Northern Democrats SD Southern Democrats

	97	98	99	100	101	102	103	104
4 Long	Y	Y	Y	Y	Y	Y	Y	Y
5 Jontz	Y	Y	Y	Y	Y	Y	Y	Y
6 ***Burton***	N	Y	Y	N	N	Y	N	N
7 ***Myers***	Y	Y	Y	Y	N	Y	Y	N
8 McCloskey	Y	Y	Y	Y	Y	Y	Y	Y
9 Hamilton	Y	Y	Y	Y	Y	Y	Y	Y
10 Jacobs	N	Y	Y	N	Y	Y	Y	Y
IOWA								
1 ***Leach***	N	Y	Y	N	N	Y	Y	N
2 ***Tauke***	N	Y	Y	N	N	Y	Y	N
3 Nagle	Y	Y	Y	Y	Y	Y	Y	Y
4 Smith	Y	Y	Y	Y	Y	Y	Y	Y
5 ***Lightfoot***	N	Y	Y	N	N	Y	Y	N
6 ***Grandy***	N	Y	Y	N	N	Y	Y	N
KANSAS								
1 ***Roberts***	N	Y	Y	N	N	Y	Y	N
2 Slattery	Y	Y	Y	Y	Y	Y	Y	Y
3 ***Meyers***	Y	Y	Y	Y	N	Y	Y	N
4 Glickman	Y	Y	Y	Y	Y	Y	Y	Y
5 ***Whittaker***	N	Y	Y	N	N	Y	Y	N
KENTUCKY								
1 Hubbard	?	?	?	Y	Y	Y	N	N
2 Natcher	Y	Y	Y	Y	Y	Y	Y	Y
3 Mazzoli	Y	Y	Y	Y	Y	Y	Y	Y
4 ***Bunning***	N	Y	Y	N	N	Y	N	N
5 ***Rogers***	N	Y	Y	N	N	Y	N	N
6 ***Hopkins***	N	Y	Y	N	N	Y	N	N
7 Perkins	Y	Y	Y	Y	Y	Y	Y	Y
LOUISIANA								
1 ***Livingston***	Y	Y	Y	Y	N	Y	N	?
2 Boggs	?	Y	Y	Y	Y	Y	Y	Y
3 Tauzin	Y	Y	Y	?	Y	Y	Y	Y
4 ***McCrery***	Y	Y	Y	Y	N	Y	N	N
5 Huckaby	Y	Y	Y	Y	Y	Y	N	?
6 ***Baker***	N	Y	Y	N	N	Y	N	N
7 Hayes	Y	Y	Y	Y	Y	Y	Y	Y
8 ***Holloway***	N	Y	Y	N	N	Y	N	N
MAINE								
1 Brennan	Y	Y	Y	Y	Y	Y	Y	Y
2 ***Snowe***	N	Y	Y	Y	N	Y	N	Y
MARYLAND								
1 Dyson	Y	Y	Y	Y	Y	Y	Y	Y
2 ***Bentley***	?	Y	Y	?	?	?	?	?
3 Cardin	Y	Y	Y	Y	Y	Y	Y	Y
4 McMillen	Y	Y	Y	Y	Y	Y	Y	Y
5 Hoyer	Y	Y	Y	Y	Y	Y	Y	Y
6 Byron	Y	Y	Y	Y	P	Y	Y	Y
7 Mfume	N	Y	Y	Y	Y	Y	Y	Y
8 ***Morella***	N	Y	Y	Y	N	Y	Y	Y
MASSACHUSETTS								
1 ***Conte***	Y	Y	Y	Y	N	Y	Y	N
2 Neal	?	?	?	Y	Y	?	Y	Y
3 Early	Y	Y	Y	Y	Y	Y	N	Y
4 Frank	Y	Y	Y	Y	Y	Y	#	#
5 Atkins	Y	Y	Y	Y	Y	Y	Y	Y
6 Mavroules	Y	Y	Y	?	Y	Y	Y	Y
7 Markey	Y	Y	Y	Y	Y	Y	Y	Y
8 Kennedy	Y	Y	Y	?	Y	Y	Y	Y
9 Moakley	Y	Y	Y	Y	Y	Y	Y	Y
10 Studds	Y	Y	Y	Y	Y	Y	Y	Y
11 Donnelly	Y	Y	Y	Y	Y	Y	Y	Y
MICHIGAN								
1 Conyers	Y	Y	Y	Y	Y	Y	Y	?
2 ***Pursell***	?	Y	Y	N	N	Y	Y	?
3 Wolpe	Y	Y	Y	Y	Y	Y	Y	Y
4 ***Upton***	N	Y	Y	N	N	Y	N	N
5 ***Henry***	N	Y	Y	N	N	Y	Y	N
6 Carr	Y	Y	Y	Y	Y	Y	Y	N
7 Kildee	Y	Y	Y	Y	Y	Y	Y	Y
8 Traxler	?	Y	Y	Y	Y	Y	Y	Y
9 ***Vander Jagt***	Y	Y	Y	Y	N	Y	Y	N
10 ***Schuette***	?	?	?	N	N	Y	N	N
11 ***Davis***	Y	Y	Y	Y	N	Y	Y	Y
12 Bonior	Y	Y	Y	Y	Y	Y	Y	Y
13 Crockett	?	Y	Y	?	?	Y	Y	?
14 Hertel	Y	Y	Y	Y	Y	Y	Y	Y
15 Ford	Y	Y	Y	Y	Y	Y	Y	Y
16 Dingell	?	Y	Y	Y	Y	Y	Y	?
17 Levin	Y	Y	Y	Y	Y	Y	Y	Y
18 ***Broomfield***	Y	Y	Y	Y	N	Y	N	N
MINNESOTA								
1 Penny	Y	Y	Y	Y	Y	Y	Y	Y
2 ***Weber***	N	Y	Y	N	N	Y	N	N
3 ***Frenzel***	?	Y	Y	N	N	Y	N	N
4 Vento	?	Y	Y	Y	Y	Y	Y	Y

	97	98	99	100	101	102	103	104
5 Sabo	Y	Y	Y	Y	Y	Y	Y	Y
6 Sikorski	?	Y	Y	N	Y	Y	Y	Y
7 ***Stangeland***	N	Y	Y	N	N	Y	Y	N
8 Oberstar	Y	Y	Y	Y	Y	Y	Y	Y
MISSISSIPPI								
1 Whitten	Y	Y	Y	Y	Y	Y	Y	Y
2 Espy	Y	Y	Y	Y	Y	Y	Y	Y
3 Montgomery	Y	Y	Y	Y	Y	Y	Y	Y
4 Parker	?	Y	Y	Y	Y	Y	Y	Y
5 Taylor	Y	Y	Y	Y	Y	Y	Y	Y
MISSOURI								
1 Clay	N	Y	Y	N	Y	Y	Y	Y
2 ***Buechner***	N	Y	Y	N	N	Y	N	N
3 Gephardt	Y	Y	Y	Y	Y	Y	Y	Y
4 Skelton	Y	Y	Y	Y	Y	Y	Y	Y
5 Wheat	Y	Y	Y	Y	Y	Y	Y	Y
6 ***Coleman***	N	Y	Y	N	N	Y	Y	N
7 ***Hancock***	N	Y	Y	N	N	Y	N	N
8 ***Emerson***	?	Y	Y	?	?	?	?	?
9 Volkmer	?	Y	Y	Y	Y	Y	Y	Y
MONTANA								
1 Williams	Y	Y	Y	?	?	Y	Y	Y
2 ***Marlenee***	N	Y	Y	N	N	Y	Y	N
NEBRASKA								
1 ***Bereuter***	N	Y	Y	N	N	Y	Y	N
2 Hoagland	Y	Y	Y	Y	Y	Y	Y	Y
3 ***Smith***	Y	Y	Y	Y	N	Y	Y	N
NEVADA								
1 Bilbray	Y	Y	Y	Y	Y	Y	Y	Y
2 ***Vucanovich***	N	Y	Y	N	N	Y	N	N
NEW HAMPSHIRE								
1 ***Smith***	N	Y	Y	N	N	Y	N	N
2 ***Douglas***	N	Y	Y	N	N	Y	N	N
NEW JERSEY								
1 Vacancy								
2 Hughes	Y	Y	Y	Y	Y	Y	Y	Y
3 Pallone	?	Y	Y	Y	Y	Y	Y	Y
4 ***Smith***	Y	Y	Y	Y	N	Y	Y	Y
5 ***Roukema***	N	Y	Y	Y	N	P	Y	Y
6 Dwyer	Y	Y	Y	Y	Y	Y	Y	?
7 ***Rinaldo***	Y	Y	Y	Y	N	Y	Y	Y
8 Roe	?	Y	Y	Y	Y	Y	Y	Y
9 Torricelli	Y	Y	Y	Y	Y	Y	Y	Y
10 Payne	Y	Y	Y	Y	Y	Y	Y	Y
11 ***Gallo***	Y	Y	Y	Y	N	Y	Y	N
12 ***Courter***	?	Y	Y	N	N	Y	Y	N
13 ***Saxton***	Y	Y	Y	Y	N	Y	Y	N
14 Guarini	Y	Y	Y	Y	Y	Y	Y	Y
NEW MEXICO								
1 ***Schiff***	Y	Y	Y	Y	N	Y	Y	N
2 ***Skeen***	Y	Y	Y	Y	N	Y	Y	N
3 Richardson	Y	Y	Y	Y	Y	Y	Y	Y
NEW YORK								
1 Hochbrueckner	Y	Y	Y	Y	Y	Y	Y	Y
2 Downey	Y	Y	Y	Y	Y	Y	Y	Y
3 Mrazek	?	Y	Y	Y	Y	Y	Y	Y
4 ***Lent***	Y	Y	Y	Y	N	Y	Y	N
5 ***McGrath***	N	Y	Y	N	N	Y	Y	Y
6 Flake	Y	Y	Y	Y	Y	Y	Y	Y
7 Ackerman	Y	Y	Y	Y	Y	Y	Y	Y
8 Scheuer	Y	Y	?	Y	Y	Y	Y	Y
9 Manton	Y	Y	Y	Y	Y	Y	?	#
10 Schumer	?	Y	Y	Y	Y	Y	Y	Y
11 Towns	Y	Y	Y	Y	Y	Y	Y	?
12 Owens	?	?	?	Y	Y	Y	Y	Y
13 Solarz	Y	Y	Y	Y	Y	Y	Y	Y
14 ***Molinari***	N	Y	Y	N	N	Y	N	N
15 ***Green***	Y	Y	Y	Y	N	Y	Y	Y
16 Rangel	?	Y	Y	?	Y	Y	Y	Y
17 Weiss	Y	Y	Y	Y	Y	Y	Y	Y
18 Serrano	Y	Y	Y	Y	Y	Y	Y	Y
19 Engel	?	Y	Y	Y	Y	Y	Y	Y
20 Lowey	Y	Y	Y	Y	Y	Y	Y	Y
21 ***Fish***	Y	Y	Y	Y	N	Y	Y	N
22 ***Gilman***	Y	Y	Y	Y	N	Y	Y	Y
23 McNulty	Y	Y	Y	Y	Y	Y	Y	Y
24 ***Solomon***	N	Y	Y	N	N	Y	Y	N
25 ***Boehlert***	N	Y	Y	N	N	Y	Y	N
26 ***Martin***	N	Y	Y	N	N	Y	Y	N
27 ***Walsh***	Y	Y	Y	Y	N	Y	Y	N
28 McHugh	Y	Y	Y	?	Y	Y	Y	Y
29 ***Horton***	Y	Y	Y	Y	N	Y	Y	N
30 Slaughter	Y	Y	Y	Y	Y	?	Y	Y
31 ***Paxon***	N	Y	Y	N	N	Y	Y	N

	97	98	99	100	101	102	103	104
32 LaFalce	Y	Y	Y	Y	Y	Y	Y	Y
33 Nowak	Y	Y	Y	Y	Y	Y	Y	Y
34 ***Houghton***	N	Y	Y	Y	N	Y	Y	N
NORTH CAROLINA								
1 Jones	Y	Y	Y	Y	Y	Y	Y	Y
2 Valentine	Y	Y	Y	Y	Y	Y	Y	Y
3 Lancaster	?	Y	Y	Y	Y	Y	Y	Y
4 Price	Y	Y	Y	Y	Y	Y	Y	Y
5 Neal	Y	Y	Y	Y	Y	Y	N	?
6 ***Coble***	N	Y	Y	N	N	Y	N	N
7 Rose	Y	Y	Y	Y	Y	Y	Y	Y
8 Hefner	Y	Y	Y	Y	Y	Y	Y	Y
9 ***McMillan***	N	Y	Y	Y	N	Y	Y	N
10 ***Ballenger***	N	Y	Y	Y	N	Y	N	N
11 Clarke	Y	Y	Y	Y	Y	Y	Y	N
NORTH DAKOTA								
AL Dorgan	Y	Y	Y	Y	Y	Y	Y	Y
OHIO								
1 Luken	?	Y	Y	Y	Y	Y	Y	Y
2 ***Gradison***	Y	Y	Y	Y	N	Y	N	N
3 Hall	Y	Y	Y	Y	?	Y	Y	?
4 ***Oxley***	N	Y	Y	N	N	Y	Y	N
5 ***Gillmor***	Y	Y	Y	Y	N	Y	N	N
6 ***McEwen***	Y	Y	Y	?	?	?	?	?
7 ***DeWine***	N	Y	Y	N	N	Y	Y	N
8 ***Lukens***	?	?	?	N	N	Y	N	?
9 Kaptur	?	Y	Y	Y	Y	Y	Y	Y
10 ***Miller***	N	Y	Y	N	N	Y	N	Y
11 Eckart	Y	Y	Y	Y	Y	Y	Y	Y
12 ***Kasich***	Y	Y	Y	Y	N	Y	N	Y
13 Pease	Y	Y	Y	Y	Y	Y	Y	Y
14 Sawyer	Y	Y	Y	Y	Y	Y	Y	Y
15 ***Wylie***	?	?	?	Y	N	Y	Y	N
16 ***Regula***	N	Y	Y	N	N	Y	Y	N
17 Traficant	Y	Y	Y	Y	Y	Y	Y	Y
18 Applegate	Y	Y	Y	Y	Y	Y	Y	Y
19 Feighan	Y	Y	Y	Y	Y	Y	Y	Y
20 Oakar	?	?	?	Y	Y	Y	Y	Y
21 Stokes	?	?	?	Y	Y	Y	Y	Y
OKLAHOMA								
1 ***Inhofe***	N	Y	Y	N	N	Y	N	N
2 Synar	Y	Y	Y	Y	Y	Y	Y	Y
3 Watkins	?	Y	Y	Y	Y	Y	N	Y
4 McCurdy	Y	Y	Y	Y	Y	Y	N	Y
5 ***Edwards***	N	Y	Y	?	?	Y	N	N
6 English	Y	Y	Y	Y	Y	Y	N	Y
OREGON								
1 AuCoin	Y	Y	Y	Y	Y	Y	Y	Y
2 ***Smith, B.***	N	Y	Y	N	N	Y	Y	N
3 Wyden	Y	Y	Y	Y	Y	Y	Y	Y
4 DeFazio	P	Y	Y	Y	Y	Y	Y	Y
5 ***Smith, D.***	N	Y	Y	N	N	Y	N	N
PENNSYLVANIA								
1 Foglietta	?	Y	Y	Y	Y	Y	Y	Y
2 Gray	Y	Y	Y	Y	Y	Y	Y	Y
3 Borski	Y	Y	Y	Y	Y	Y	Y	Y
4 Kolter	Y	Y	Y	Y	Y	Y	Y	Y
5 ***Schulze***	Y	Y	Y	Y	N	Y	Y	N
6 Yatron	Y	Y	Y	Y	Y	Y	Y	Y
7 ***Weldon***	Y	Y	Y	Y	N	Y	Y	Y
8 Kostmayer	Y	Y	Y	Y	Y	Y	Y	Y
9 ***Shuster***	Y	Y	Y	Y	N	Y	Y	N
10 ***McDade***	Y	Y	Y	Y	N	Y	Y	?
11 Kanjorski	Y	Y	Y	Y	Y	Y	Y	Y
12 Murtha	Y	Y	Y	Y	Y	Y	Y	Y
13 ***Coughlin***	N	Y	Y	N	N	Y	Y	N
14 Coyne	Y	Y	Y	?	Y	Y	Y	Y
15 ***Ritter***	Y	Y	Y	Y	N	Y	Y	N
16 ***Walker***	N	Y	Y	N	N	Y	N	N
17 ***Gekas***	N	Y	Y	N	N	Y	Y	N
18 Walgren	Y	Y	Y	Y	Y	Y	Y	Y
19 ***Goodling***	N	Y	Y	N	N	Y	Y	N
20 Gaydos	Y	Y	Y	Y	Y	Y	Y	Y
21 ***Ridge***	N	Y	Y	N	N	Y	Y	Y
22 Murphy	N	Y	Y	N	Y	Y	Y	Y
23 ***Clinger***	Y	Y	Y	Y	N	Y	Y	N
RHODE ISLAND								
1 ***Machtley***	N	Y	Y	N	?	?	Y	N
2 ***Schneider***	Y	Y	Y	Y	N	Y	Y	N
SOUTH CAROLINA								
1 ***Ravenel***	Y	Y	Y	Y	N	Y	Y	N
2 ***Spence***	Y	Y	Y	Y	N	Y	Y	N
3 Derrick	Y	Y	Y	Y	Y	Y	Y	Y
4 Patterson	Y	Y	Y	Y	Y	Y	Y	Y
5 Spratt	?	Y	Y	Y	Y	Y	Y	Y
6 Tallon	Y	Y	Y	Y	Y	Y	Y	Y

	97	98	99	100	101	102	103	104
SOUTH DAKOTA								
AL Johnson	Y	Y	Y	Y	Y	Y	Y	Y
TENNESSEE								
1 ***Quillen***	Y	Y	Y	Y	N	Y	N	N
2 ***Duncan***	Y	Y	Y	N	N	Y	N	N
3 Lloyd	Y	Y	Y	Y	Y	Y	Y	Y
4 Cooper	Y	Y	Y	Y	Y	Y	Y	Y
5 Clement	Y	Y	Y	Y	Y	Y	Y	Y
6 Gordon	Y	Y	Y	Y	Y	Y	Y	Y
7 ***Sundquist***	N	Y	Y	N	N	Y	N	N
8 Tanner	Y	Y	Y	Y	Y	Y	Y	Y
9 Ford	?	?	?	Y	Y	Y	Y	Y
TEXAS								
1 Chapman	Y	Y	Y	Y	Y	Y	Y	Y
2 Wilson	?	?	?	Y	Y	Y	Y	Y
3 ***Bartlett***	Y	Y	Y	Y	N	Y	N	N
4 Hall	Y	Y	Y	Y	Y	Y	N	N
5 Bryant	Y	Y	?	Y	Y	Y	Y	Y
6 ***Barton***	N	Y	Y	N	N	Y	N	N
7 ***Archer***	Y	Y	Y	Y	N	Y	N	N
8 ***Fields***	N	Y	Y	N	N	Y	N	N
9 Brooks	?	?	Y	Y	Y	?	Y	Y
10 Pickle	Y	Y	Y	Y	Y	?	Y	Y
11 Leath	Y	Y	Y	Y	Y	?	?	?
12 Geren	Y	Y	Y	Y	Y	Y	Y	Y
13 Sarpalius	Y	Y	Y	Y	Y	Y	Y	Y
14 Laughlin	Y	Y	Y	?	Y	Y	Y	Y
15 de la Garza	Y	Y	Y	Y	Y	Y	Y	Y
16 Coleman	Y	Y	Y	Y	Y	Y	Y	Y
17 Stenholm	Y	Y	Y	Y	Y	Y	N	Y
18 Washington	Y	?	?	Y	?	Y	Y	Y
19 ***Combest***	Y	Y	Y	Y	N	Y	N	N
20 Gonzalez	Y	Y	Y	Y	Y	Y	Y	Y
21 ***Smith***	N	Y	Y	N	N	Y	Y	N
22 ***DeLay***	N	Y	Y	N	N	Y	N	N
23 Bustamante	Y	Y	Y	Y	Y	?	Y	Y
24 Frost	?	Y	Y	Y	Y	Y	?	Y
25 Andrews	Y	Y	Y	Y	Y	Y	Y	Y
26 ***Armey***	N	Y	Y	N	N	Y	N	N
27 Ortiz	Y	Y	Y	Y	Y	Y	Y	Y
UTAH								
1 ***Hansen***	N	Y	Y	N	N	Y	N	N
2 Owens	Y	Y	Y	Y	Y	Y	Y	Y
3 ***Nielson***	Y	Y	Y	Y	N	Y	N	N
VERMONT								
AL ***Smith***	Y	Y	Y	N	N	Y	Y	Y
VIRGINIA								
1 ***Bateman***	Y	Y	Y	Y	N	Y	Y	N
2 Pickett	Y	Y	Y	Y	Y	Y	Y	Y
3 ***Bliley***	N	Y	Y	N	N	Y	Y	N
4 Sisisky	Y	Y	Y	Y	Y	Y	Y	Y
5 Payne	Y	Y	Y	Y	Y	Y	Y	Y
6 Olin	Y	Y	Y	Y	Y	Y	Y	N
7 ***Slaughter***	N	Y	Y	N	N	Y	Y	N
8 ***Parris***	N	Y	Y	N	N	Y	Y	N
9 Boucher	Y	Y	Y	Y	Y	Y	Y	Y
10 ***Wolf***	N	Y	Y	N	N	Y	Y	N
WASHINGTON								
1 ***Miller***	N	Y	Y	N	N	Y	Y	N
2 Swift	Y	Y	Y	Y	Y	Y	Y	Y
3 Unsoeld	Y	Y	Y	Y	Y	Y	Y	Y
4 ***Morrison***	?	Y	Y	Y	N	Y	Y	N
5 Foley								
6 Dicks	Y	Y	Y	Y	Y	Y	Y	Y
7 McDermott	Y	Y	Y	Y	Y	Y	Y	Y
8 ***Chandler***	N	Y	Y	N	N	Y	Y	N
WEST VIRGINIA								
1 Mollohan	?	Y	Y	Y	Y	Y	Y	Y
2 Staggers	Y	Y	Y	Y	Y	Y	Y	Y
3 Wise	Y	Y	Y	Y	Y	Y	Y	Y
4 Rahall	?	?	?	Y	Y	Y	Y	Y
WISCONSIN								
1 Aspin	Y	Y	Y	Y	Y	Y	Y	Y
2 Kastenmeier	Y	Y	Y	Y	Y	Y	Y	Y
3 ***Gunderson***	Y	Y	Y	Y	N	Y	Y	N
4 Kleczka	Y	Y	Y	Y	Y	Y	Y	Y
5 Moody	Y	Y	Y	Y	Y	Y	Y	Y
6 ***Petri***	Y	Y	Y	Y	N	Y	Y	N
7 Obey	Y	Y	Y	Y	Y	?	Y	Y
8 ***Roth***	Y	Y	Y	Y	N	Y	N	N
9 ***Sensenbrenner***	N	Y	Y	N	N	Y	N	N
WYOMING								
AL ***Thomas***	Y	Y	Y	N	N	Y	N	N

Southern states - Ala., Ark., Fla., Ga., Ky., La., Miss., N.C., Okla., S.C., Tenn., Texas, Va.
Omitted votes are quorum calls, which CQ does not include in its vote charts.

HOUSE VOTES 105, 106, 107

105. HR 770. Parental and Medical Leave Act/Substitute Amendment. Gordon, D-Tenn., substitute amendment to require the federal government and private companies with 50 or more employees to provide employees with up to 12 weeks per year of unpaid leave to care for a new child, or a seriously ill child, parent or spouse, or to use as medical leave due to a serious health condition. Only one parent at a time may take leave to care for a newborn, and leave to care for a seriously ill person could be used only for a spouse, a biological parent or a person raised by the employee. Illness must be certified by a doctor. Adopted 259-157: R 47-123; D 212-34 (ND 161-8, SD 51-26), May 10, 1990.

106. HR 770. Parental and Medical Leave Act/Recommittal Motion. Grandy, R-Iowa, motion to recommit the bill to the House Education and Labor Committee with instructions to report it back to the House with provisions to establish a commission to study and make recommendations on existing and proposed policies regarding family and medical leave. Motion rejected 155-264: R 129-39; D 26-225 (ND 4-168, SD 22-57), May 10, 1990.

107. HR 770. Parental and Medical Leave Act/Passage. Passage of the bill to require public and private employers to give unpaid leave to care for a new child, or a seriously ill child, parent or spouse, or to use as medical leave due to a serious health condition. Passed 237-187: R 39-133; D 198-54 (ND 159-14, SD 39-40), May 10, 1990. A "nay" was a vote supporting the president's position.

KEY

Y Voted for (yea).
Paired for.
+ Announced for.
N Voted against (nay).
X Paired against.
- Announced against.
P Voted "present."
C Voted "present" to avoid possible conflict of interest.
? Did not vote or otherwise make a position known.

Democrats ***Republicans***

	105	106	107
ALABAMA			
1 ***Callahan***	N	Y	N
2 ***Dickinson***	N	Y	N
3 Browder	Y	N	N
4 Bevill	Y	Y	N
5 Flippo	?	?	?
6 Erdreich	Y	N	Y
7 Harris	Y	Y	N
ALASKA			
AL ***Young***	Y	Y	Y
ARIZONA			
1 ***Rhodes***	N	Y	N
2 Udall	?	N	Y
3 ***Stump***	N	Y	N
4 ***Kyl***	N	Y	N
5 ***Kolbe***	N	Y	N
ARKANSAS			
1 Alexander	Y	N	Y
2 ***Robinson***	?	?	?
3 ***Hammerschmidt***	N	Y	N
4 Anthony	Y	N	Y
CALIFORNIA			
1 Bosco	Y	N	Y
2 ***Herger***	N	Y	N
3 Matsui	Y	N	Y
4 Fazio	Y	N	Y
5 Pelosi	Y	N	Y
6 Boxer	Y	N	Y
7 Miller	Y	N	Y
8 Dellums	Y	N	Y
9 Stark	Y	N	Y
10 Edwards	Y	N	Y
11 Lantos	Y	N	Y
12 ***Campbell***	N	N	Y
13 Mineta	Y	N	Y
14 ***Shumway***	N	Y	N
15 Condit	Y	N	Y
16 Panetta	Y	N	Y
17 ***Pashayan***	Y	Y	N
18 Lehman	Y	N	Y
19 ***Lagomarsino***	N	Y	N
20 ***Thomas***	N	Y	N
21 ***Gallegly***	N	+	N
22 ***Moorhead***	N	Y	N
23 Beilenson	Y	N	Y
24 Waxman	Y	N	Y
25 Roybal	Y	N	Y
26 Berman	Y	N	Y
27 Levine	Y	N	Y
28 Dixon	Y	N	Y
29 Hawkins	Y	N	Y
30 Martinez	Y	N	Y
31 Dymally	Y	N	Y
32 Anderson	Y	N	Y
33 ***Dreier***	N	Y	N
34 Torres	Y	N	Y
35 ***Lewis***	X	#	X
36 Brown	Y	?	Y
37 ***McCandless***	N	Y	N
38 ***Dornan***	N	Y	N
39 ***Dannemeyer***	N	Y	N
40 ***Cox***	N	Y	N
41 ***Lowery***	N	Y	N
42 ***Rohrabacher***	N	Y	N
43 ***Packard***	N	Y	N
44 Bates	Y	N	Y
45 ***Hunter***	N	?	N
COLORADO			
1 Schroeder	Y	N	Y
2 Skaggs	Y	N	Y
3 Campbell	N	N	N
4 ***Brown***	N	Y	N
5 ***Hefley***	N	Y	N
6 ***Schaefer***	N	Y	N
CONNECTICUT			
1 Kennelly	Y	N	Y
2 Gejdenson	Y	N	Y
3 Morrison	Y	N	Y
4 ***Shays***	Y	N	Y
5 ***Rowland***	Y	N	Y
6 ***Johnson***	Y	N	Y
DELAWARE			
AL Carper	Y	N	Y
FLORIDA			
1 Hutto	N	N	N
2 ***Grant***	N	Y	N
3 Bennett	Y	N	Y
4 ***James***	N	Y	N
5 ***McCollum***	N	Y	N
6 ***Stearns***	N	Y	N
7 Gibbons	Y	N	Y
8 ***Young***	Y	Y	N
9 ***Bilirakis***	Y	Y	N
10 ***Ireland***	N	Y	N
11 Nelson	#	X	#
12 ***Lewis***	N	Y	N
13 ***Goss***	N	Y	N
14 Johnston	Y	N	Y
15 ***Shaw***	N	Y	N
16 Smith	Y	N	Y
17 Lehman	Y	N	Y
18 ***Ros-Lehtinen***	Y	N	Y
19 Fascell	Y	N	Y
GEORGIA			
1 Thomas	N	N	N
2 Hatcher	Y	N	N
3 Ray	N	N	N
4 Jones	Y	N	N
5 Lewis	Y	N	Y
6 ***Gingrich***	N	Y	N
7 Darden	N	N	N
8 Rowland	N	N	N
9 Jenkins	Y	N	Y
10 Barnard	N	Y	N
HAWAII			
1 ***Saiki***	Y	N	Y
2 Akaka	Y	N	Y
IDAHO			
1 ***Craig***	N	Y	N
2 Stallings	N	Y	N
ILLINOIS			
1 Hayes	Y	N	Y
2 Savage	Y	N	Y
3 Russo	Y	N	Y
4 Sangmeister	Y	N	Y
5 Lipinski	Y	N	Y
6 ***Hyde***	Y	N	Y
7 Collins	Y	N	Y
8 Rostenkowski	?	?	?
9 Yates	Y	N	Y
10 ***Porter***	N	Y	N
11 Annunzio	Y	N	Y
12 ***Crane***	N	Y	N
13 ***Fawell***	N	Y	N
14 ***Hastert***	N	Y	N
15 ***Madigan***	Y	Y	N
16 ***Martin***	Y	N	Y
17 Evans	Y	N	Y
18 ***Michel***	N	Y	N
19 Bruce	Y	N	Y
20 Durbin	Y	N	Y
21 Costello	Y	N	Y
22 Poshard	Y	N	Y
INDIANA			
1 Visclosky	Y	N	Y
2 Sharp	Y	N	Y
3 ***Hiler***	N	Y	N

ND Northern Democrats SD Southern Democrats

	105	106	107
4 Long	Y	N	Y
5 Jontz	Y	N	Y
6 ***Burton***	N	?	N
7 ***Myers***	N	Y	N
8 McCloskey	Y	N	Y
9 Hamilton	Y	N	N
10 Jacobs	Y	N	Y
IOWA			
1 ***Leach***	N	Y	N
2 ***Tauke***	N	Y	N
3 Nagle	Y	Y	N
4 Smith	Y	N	Y
5 ***Lightfoot***	N	Y	N
6 ***Grandy***	N	Y	N
KANSAS			
1 ***Roberts***	N	Y	N
2 Slattery	N	N	N
3 ***Meyers***	N	Y	N
4 Glickman	N	N	N
5 ***Whittaker***	N	Y	N
KENTUCKY			
1 Hubbard	N	Y	N
2 Natcher	Y	N	Y
3 Mazzoli	Y	N	Y
4 ***Bunning***	N	Y	N
5 ***Rogers***	N	Y	N
6 ***Hopkins***	N	Y	N
7 Perkins	Y	N	Y
LOUISIANA			
1 ***Livingston***	N	Y	N
2 Boggs	Y	N	Y
3 Tauzin	Y	Y	N
4 ***McCrery***	N	Y	N
5 Huckaby	N	Y	N
6 ***Baker***	N	Y	N
7 Hayes	Y	Y	N
8 ***Holloway***	N	Y	N
MAINE			
1 Brennan	Y	N	Y
2 ***Snowe***	Y	N	Y
MARYLAND			
1 Dyson	Y	N	Y
2 ***Bentley***	?	?	—
3 Cardin	Y	N	Y
4 McMillen	Y	N	Y
5 Hoyer	Y	N	Y
6 Byron	N	N	N
7 Mfume	Y	N	Y
8 ***Morella***	Y	N	Y
MASSACHUSETTS			
1 ***Conte***	Y	N	Y
2 Neal	Y	N	Y
3 Early	Y	N	Y
4 Frank	Y	N	Y
5 Atkins	Y	N	Y
6 Mavroules	Y	N	Y
7 Markey	Y	N	Y
8 Kennedy	Y	N	Y
9 Moakley	Y	N	Y
10 Studds	Y	N	Y
11 Donnelly	N	N	N
MICHIGAN			
1 Conyers	Y	N	Y
2 ***Pursell***	N	Y	N
3 Wolpe	Y	N	Y
4 ***Upton***	N	Y	N
5 ***Henry***	N	Y	N
6 Carr	Y	Y	N
7 Kildee	Y	N	Y
8 Traxler	Y	N	Y
9 ***Vander Jagt***	N	Y	N
10 ***Schuette***	N	Y	N
11 ***Davis***	Y	N	Y
12 Bonior	Y	N	Y
13 Crockett	Y	N	Y
14 Hertel	Y	N	Y
15 Ford	Y	N	Y
16 Dingell	Y	N	Y
17 Levin	Y	N	Y
18 ***Broomfield***	N	Y	N
MINNESOTA			
1 Penny	N	Y	N
2 ***Weber***	N	Y	N
3 ***Frenzel***	N	Y	N
4 Vento	Y	N	Y

	105	106	107
5 Sabo	Y	N	Y
6 Sikorski	Y	N	Y
7 ***Stangeland***	N	Y	N
8 Oberstar	Y	N	Y
MISSISSIPPI			
1 Whitten	Y	N	Y
2 Espy	Y	N	Y
3 Montgomery	N	N	N
4 Parker	N	Y	N
5 Taylor	Y	Y	N
MISSOURI			
1 Clay	Y	N	Y
2 ***Buechner***	N	Y	N
3 Gephardt	Y	N	Y
4 Skelton	N	N	N
5 Wheat	Y	N	Y
6 ***Coleman***	N	Y	N
7 ***Hancock***	N	Y	N
8 ***Emerson***	?	?	?
9 Volkmer	Y	N	Y
MONTANA			
1 Williams	Y	N	Y
2 ***Marlenee***	N	Y	N
NEBRASKA			
1 ***Bereuter***	Y	Y	N
2 Hoagland	Y	N	N
3 ***Smith***	Y	N	Y
NEVADA			
1 Bilbray	Y	N	Y
2 ***Vucanovich***	N	Y	N
NEW HAMPSHIRE			
1 ***Smith***	N	Y	N
2 ***Douglas***	N	Y	N
NEW JERSEY			
1 Vacancy			
2 Hughes	Y	N	Y
3 Pallone	Y	N	Y
4 ***Smith***	Y	N	Y
5 ***Roukema***	Y	N	Y
6 Dwyer	Y	N	Y
7 ***Rinaldo***	Y	N	Y
8 Roe	Y	N	Y
9 Torricelli	Y	N	Y
10 Payne	Y	N	Y
11 ***Gallo***	N	Y	N
12 ***Courter***	N	Y	N
13 ***Saxton***	N	Y	N
14 Guarini	Y	N	Y
NEW MEXICO			
1 ***Schiff***	Y	Y	N
2 ***Skeen***	N	Y	N
3 Richardson	Y	N	Y
NEW YORK			
1 Hochbrueckner	Y	N	Y
2 Downey	Y	N	Y
3 Mrazek	Y	N	Y
4 ***Lent***	N	Y	N
5 ***McGrath***	Y	N	Y
6 Flake	Y	N	Y
7 Ackerman	Y	N	Y
8 Scheuer	Y	N	Y
9 Manton	Y	N	Y
10 Schumer	Y	N	Y
11 Towns	Y	N	Y
12 Owens	Y	N	Y
13 Solarz	Y	N	Y
14 ***Molinari***	Y	N	Y
15 ***Green***	Y	N	Y
16 Rangel	Y	N	Y
17 Weiss	Y	N	Y
18 Serrano	Y	N	Y
19 Engel	?	N	Y
20 Lowey	Y	N	Y
21 ***Fish***	Y	N	Y
22 ***Gilman***	Y	N	Y
23 McNulty	Y	N	Y
24 ***Solomon***	Y	?	Y
25 ***Boehlert***	Y	N	Y
26 ***Martin***	Y	N	Y
27 ***Walsh***	N	N	N
28 McHugh	Y	N	Y
29 ***Horton***	Y	N	Y
30 Slaughter	Y	N	Y
31 ***Paxon***	N	Y	N

	105	106	107
32 LaFalce	Y	N	N
33 Nowak	Y	N	Y
34 ***Houghton***	N	Y	N
NORTH CAROLINA			
1 Jones	Y	Y	Y
2 Valentine	N	Y	N
3 Lancaster	Y	Y	N
4 Price	Y	N	Y
5 Neal	N	Y	N
6 ***Coble***	?	Y	N
7 Rose	Y	N	Y
8 Hefner	Y	N	N
9 ***McMillan***	N	Y	N
10 ***Ballenger***	N	Y	N
11 Clarke	N	Y	N
NORTH DAKOTA			
AL Dorgan	Y	N	Y
OHIO			
1 Luken	Y	N	Y
2 ***Gradison***	N	Y	N
3 Hall	Y	N	Y
4 ***Oxley***	N	Y	N
5 ***Gillmor***	Y	Y	Y
6 ***McEwen***	N	Y	N
7 ***DeWine***	Y	N	Y
8 ***Lukens***	N	Y	N
9 Kaptur	Y	N	Y
10 ***Miller***	N	Y	N
11 Eckart	Y	N	Y
12 ***Kasich***	N	Y	N
13 Pease	Y	N	Y
14 Sawyer	Y	N	Y
15 ***Wylie***	N	Y	N
16 ***Regula***	Y	N	Y
17 Traficant	Y	N	Y
18 Applegate	Y	N	Y
19 Feighan	Y	N	Y
20 Oakar	Y	N	Y
21 Stokes	Y	N	Y
OKLAHOMA			
1 ***Inhofe***	N	Y	N
2 Synar	Y	N	Y
3 Watkins	?	?	?
4 McCurdy	Y	N	Y
5 ***Edwards***	?	Y	N
6 English	Y	N	Y
OREGON			
1 AuCoin	Y	N	Y
2 ***Smith, B.***	N	Y	N
3 Wyden	Y	N	Y
4 DeFazio	Y	N	Y
5 ***Smith, D.***	N	Y	N
PENNSYLVANIA			
1 Foglietta	Y	N	Y
2 Gray	Y	N	Y
3 Borski	Y	N	Y
4 Kolter	Y	N	Y
5 ***Schulze***	N	Y	N
6 Yatron	Y	N	Y
7 ***Weldon***	Y	N	Y
8 Kostmayer	Y	N	Y
9 ***Shuster***	N	Y	N
10 ***McDade***	Y	N	Y
11 Kanjorski	Y	N	Y
12 Murtha	Y	N	Y
13 ***Coughlin***	Y	N	Y
14 Coyne	Y	N	Y
15 ***Ritter***	Y	Y	N
16 ***Walker***	N	Y	N
17 ***Gekas***	N	Y	N
18 Walgren	Y	N	Y
19 ***Goodling***	N	Y	N
20 Gaydos	Y	N	Y
21 ***Ridge***	N	Y	N
22 Murphy	Y	N	Y
23 ***Clinger***	N	N	N
RHODE ISLAND			
1 ***Machtley***	Y	N	Y
2 ***Schneider***	Y	N	Y
SOUTH CAROLINA			
1 ***Ravenel***	Y	N	Y
2 ***Spence***	Y	Y	N
3 Derrick	N	Y	N
4 Patterson	N	N	N
5 Spratt	Y	N	N
6 Tallon	N	Y	N

	105	106	107
SOUTH DAKOTA			
AL Johnson	Y	N	Y
TENNESSEE			
1 ***Quillen***	N	Y	N
2 ***Duncan***	N	Y	N
3 Lloyd	?	Y	N
4 Cooper	N	Y	N
5 Clement	Y	N	Y
6 Gordon	Y	N	Y
7 ***Sundquist***	N	Y	N
8 Tanner	N	Y	N
9 Ford	Y	N	Y
TEXAS			
1 Chapman	Y	N	Y
2 Wilson	?	N	Y
3 ***Bartlett***	N	Y	N
4 Hall	N	Y	N
5 Bryant	Y	N	Y
6 ***Barton***	N	Y	N
7 ***Archer***	N	Y	N
8 ***Fields***	N	Y	N
9 Brooks	Y	N	Y
10 Pickle	N	N	N
11 Leath	N	N	N
12 Geren	N	N	N
13 Sarpalius	N	Y	N
14 Laughlin	?	?	?
15 de la Garza	Y	N	Y
16 Coleman	Y	N	Y
17 Stenholm	N	N	N
18 Washington	Y	N	Y
19 ***Combest***	N	Y	N
20 Gonzalez	Y	N	Y
21 ***Smith***	Y	N	Y
22 ***DeLay***	N	Y	N
23 Bustamante	Y	N	Y
24 Frost	Y	N	Y
25 Andrews	Y	N	Y
26 ***Armey***	N	Y	N
27 Ortiz	Y	N	Y
UTAH			
1 ***Hansen***	N	Y	N
2 Owens	+	N	Y
3 ***Nielson***	Y	N	N
VERMONT			
AL ***Smith***	Y	N	Y
VIRGINIA			
1 ***Bateman***	N	Y	N
2 Pickett	N	N	N
3 ***Bliley***	N	Y	N
4 Sisisky	Y	N	N
5 Payne	N	N	N
6 Olin	Y	Y	N
7 ***Slaughter***	N	Y	N
8 ***Parris***	N	Y	N
9 Boucher	Y	N	Y
10 ***Wolf***	N	Y	N
WASHINGTON			
1 ***Miller***	Y	N	Y
2 Swift	?	N	Y
3 Unsoeld	Y	N	Y
4 ***Morrison***	Y	N	Y
5 Foley			
6 Dicks	Y	N	Y
7 McDermott	Y	N	Y
8 ***Chandler***	N	Y	N
WEST VIRGINIA			
1 Mollohan	Y	N	Y
2 Staggers	Y	N	Y
3 Wise	Y	N	Y
4 Rahall	Y	N	Y
WISCONSIN			
1 Aspin	Y	N	N
2 Kastenmeier	Y	N	Y
3 ***Gunderson***	N	Y	N
4 Kleczka	Y	N	Y
5 Moody	Y	N	Y
6 ***Petri***	N	Y	N
7 Obey	Y	N	Y
8 ***Roth***	N	Y	N
9 ***Sensenbrenner***	N	Y	N
WYOMING			
AL ***Thomas***	N	Y	N

Southern states - Ala., Ark., Fla., Ga., Ky., La., Miss., N.C., Okla., S.C., Tenn., Texas, Va.
Omitted votes are quorum calls, which CQ does not include in its vote charts.

108. H Res 381. Cuban Human Rights Abuses/Adoption. Yatron, D-Pa., motion to suspend the rules and adopt the resolution to condemn the Cuban government for human rights abuses and to call upon Cuba to release human rights activists and other political prisoners, particularly those who testified before the Cuba Working Group of the U.N. Human Rights Commission under the promise that they would not be punished. Motion agreed to 391-2: R 162-0; D 229-2 (ND 153-1, SD 76-1), May 15, 1990. A two-thirds majority of those present and voting (262 in this case) is required for passage under suspension of the rules.

109. Procedural Motion. Slaughter, R-Va., motion to approve the House Journal of Tuesday, May 15. Motion agreed to 267-113: R 56-108; D 211-5 (ND 136-5, SD 75-0), May 16, 1990.

110. HR 4151. Head Start Reauthorization/Rule. Adoption of the rule (H Res 392) to provide for House floor consideration of the bill to authorize appropriations for fiscal years 1991-94 to carry out the Head Start Act, the Follow Through Act, the Community Services Block Grant Act and other programs to help low-income individuals and families. Adopted 408-0: R 171-0; D 237-0 (ND 163-0, SD 74-0), May 16, 1990.

111. HR 4151. Head Start Reauthorization/Passage. Passage of the bill to authorize $2.9 billion for fiscal year 1991 and $19.6 billion for fiscal years 1992-94 to carry out the Head Start Act, the Follow Through Act, the Community Services Block Grant Act and other programs to help low-income individuals and families. Passed 404-14: R 156-14; D 248-0 (ND 170-0, SD 78-0), May 16, 1990. A "nay" was a vote supporting the president's position.

** Rep. Daniel K. Akaka, D-Hawaii, resigned May 16, 1990, to fill the vacancy created by the April 15 death of Sen. Spark M. Matsunaga. The last House vote for which he was eligible was vote 108.*

KEY

Y Voted for (yea).
\# Paired for.
\+ Announced for.
N Voted against (nay).
X Paired against.
\- Announced against.
P Voted "present."
C Voted "present" to avoid possible conflict of interest.
? Did not vote or otherwise make a position known.

Democrats ***Republicans***

	108	109	110	111
ALABAMA				
1 ***Callahan***	Y	N	Y	Y
2 ***Dickinson***	Y	N	?	Y
3 Browder	Y	Y	Y	Y
4 Bevill	Y	Y	Y	Y
5 Flippo	?	?	?	?
6 Erdreich	Y	Y	Y	Y
7 Harris	Y	Y	Y	Y
ALASKA				
AL ***Young***	Y	N	Y	Y
ARIZONA				
1 ***Rhodes***	Y	?	Y	Y
2 Udall	Y	Y	Y	Y
3 ***Stump***	Y	N	Y	N
4 ***Kyl***	Y	N	Y	Y
5 ***Kolbe***	Y	N	Y	Y
ARKANSAS				
1 Alexander	?	?	?	?
2 ***Robinson***	Y	Y	Y	Y
3 ***Hammerschmidt***	?	Y	Y	Y
4 Anthony	Y	?	Y	Y
CALIFORNIA				
1 Bosco	Y	Y	Y	Y
2 ***Herger***	Y	N	Y	Y
3 Matsui	Y	Y	Y	Y
4 Fazio	Y	Y	Y	Y
5 Pelosi	Y	Y	Y	Y
6 Boxer	?	Y	Y	Y
7 Miller	Y	Y	Y	Y
8 Dellums	?	?	Y	Y
9 Stark	Y	?	Y	Y
10 Edwards	Y	Y	Y	Y
11 Lantos	Y	Y	?	Y
12 ***Campbell***	Y	N	Y	Y
13 Mineta	Y	?	Y	Y
14 ***Shumway***	Y	Y	Y	Y
15 Condit	Y	?	Y	Y
16 Panetta	?	Y	Y	Y
17 ***Pashayan***	Y	N	Y	Y
18 Lehman	Y	Y	Y	Y
19 ***Lagomarsino***	Y	N	Y	Y
20 ***Thomas***	Y	N	Y	Y
21 ***Gallegly***	Y	N	Y	Y
22 ***Moorhead***	Y	N	Y	Y
23 Beilenson	Y	Y	Y	Y
24 Waxman	Y	Y	Y	Y
25 Roybal	Y	Y	Y	?
26 Berman	Y	Y	Y	Y
27 Levine	?	?	Y	Y
28 Dixon	Y	?	Y	Y
29 Hawkins	Y	N	Y	Y
30 Martinez	Y	Y	Y	Y
31 Dymally	Y	?	Y	Y
32 Anderson	Y	Y	Y	Y
33 ***Dreier***	Y	N	Y	Y
34 Torres	Y	Y	Y	Y
35 ***Lewis***	Y	N	Y	Y
36 Brown	Y	?	Y	Y
37 ***McCandless***	Y	N	Y	Y
38 ***Dornan***	Y	Y	Y	Y
39 ***Dannemeyer***	Y	N	Y	N
40 ***Cox***	Y	N	Y	Y
41 ***Lowery***	Y	N	Y	Y
42 ***Rohrabacher***	Y	N	Y	Y
43 ***Packard***	Y	Y	Y	Y
44 Bates	Y	?	Y	Y
45 ***Hunter***	Y	?	Y	Y
COLORADO				
1 Schroeder	Y	N	Y	Y
2 Skaggs	Y	Y	Y	Y
3 Campbell	Y	Y	Y	Y
4 ***Brown***	Y	N	Y	Y
5 ***Hefley***	Y	N	Y	Y
6 ***Schaefer***	Y	N	Y	Y
CONNECTICUT				
1 Kennelly	Y	Y	Y	Y
2 Gejdenson	Y	Y	Y	Y
3 Morrison	+	?	?	Y
4 ***Shays***	Y	N	Y	Y
5 ***Rowland***	Y	Y	Y	Y
6 ***Johnson***	Y	Y	Y	Y
DELAWARE				
AL Carper	Y	Y	Y	Y
FLORIDA				
1 Hutto	Y	Y	Y	Y
2 ***Grant***	?	Y	Y	Y
3 Bennett	Y	Y	Y	Y
4 ***James***	Y	N	Y	Y
5 ***McCollum***	Y	N	Y	Y
6 ***Stearns***	Y	N	Y	Y
7 Gibbons	Y	Y	Y	Y
8 ***Young***	?	?	?	?
9 ***Bilirakis***	Y	N	Y	Y
10 ***Ireland***	Y	N	Y	Y
11 Nelson	+	+	+	+
12 ***Lewis***	Y	N	Y	Y
13 ***Goss***	Y	N	Y	Y
14 Johnston	Y	Y	Y	Y
15 ***Shaw***	Y	Y	Y	Y
16 Smith	Y	Y	Y	Y
17 Lehman	Y	Y	?	Y
18 ***Ros-Lehtinen***	Y	N	Y	Y
19 Fascell	Y	Y	Y	?
GEORGIA				
1 Thomas	Y	Y	Y	Y
2 Hatcher	Y	Y	Y	Y
3 Ray	Y	Y	Y	Y
4 Jones	Y	Y	Y	Y
5 Lewis	Y	Y	Y	Y
6 ***Gingrich***	?	N	Y	Y
7 Darden	Y	Y	Y	Y
8 Rowland	Y	Y	Y	Y
9 Jenkins	Y	Y	Y	Y
10 Barnard	Y	Y	Y	Y
HAWAII				
1 ***Saiki***	Y	Y	Y	Y
2 Vacancy *	Y			
IDAHO				
1 ***Craig***	?	?	?	?
2 Stallings	Y	Y	Y	Y
ILLINOIS				
1 Hayes	Y	?	Y	Y
2 Savage	?	Y	Y	Y
3 Russo	Y	Y	Y	Y
4 Sangmeister	Y	Y	Y	Y
5 Lipinski	Y	Y	Y	Y
6 ***Hyde***	Y	N	Y	Y
7 Collins	?	?	Y	Y
8 Rostenkowski	?	?	Y	Y
9 Yates	Y	Y	Y	Y
10 ***Porter***	Y	?	Y	Y
11 Annunzio	Y	Y	Y	Y
12 ***Crane***	Y	N	Y	N
13 ***Fawell***	Y	N	Y	Y
14 ***Hastert***	Y	?	Y	Y
15 ***Madigan***	Y	N	Y	Y
16 ***Martin***	Y	N	Y	Y
17 Evans	Y	Y	Y	Y
18 ***Michel***	?	N	Y	Y
19 Bruce	Y	Y	Y	Y
20 Durbin	Y	Y	Y	Y
21 Costello	Y	Y	Y	Y
22 Poshard	Y	?	Y	Y
INDIANA				
1 Visclosky	Y	Y	Y	Y
2 Sharp	Y	?	?	?
3 ***Hiler***	Y	N	Y	Y

ND Northern Democrats SD Southern Democrats

	108	109	110	111
4 Long	Y	Y	Y	Y
5 Jontz	Y	Y	Y	Y
6 ***Burton***	Y	N	Y	Y
7 ***Myers***	Y	Y	Y	Y
8 McCloskey	Y	Y	Y	Y
9 Hamilton	Y	Y	Y	Y
10 Jacobs	Y	N	Y	Y
IOWA				
1 ***Leach***	Y	N	Y	Y
2 ***Tauke***	Y	N	Y	Y
3 Nagle	Y	?	Y	Y
4 Smith	Y	Y	Y	Y
5 ***Lightfoot***	Y	N	Y	Y
6 ***Grandy***	Y	N	Y	Y
KANSAS				
1 ***Roberts***	Y	N	Y	Y
2 Slattery	Y	Y	Y	Y
3 ***Meyers***	Y	N	Y	Y
4 Glickman	Y	Y	Y	Y
5 ***Whittaker***	Y	N	Y	Y
KENTUCKY				
1 Hubbard	Y	Y	Y	Y
2 Natcher	Y	Y	Y	Y
3 Mazzoli	Y	Y	Y	Y
4 ***Bunning***	Y	N	Y	Y
5 ***Rogers***	Y	N	Y	Y
6 ***Hopkins***	Y	N	Y	Y
7 Perkins	Y	Y	Y	Y
LOUISIANA				
1 ***Livingston***	Y	Y	Y	Y
2 Boggs	Y	Y	Y	Y
3 Tauzin	Y	Y	Y	Y
4 ***McCrery***	?	?	Y	Y
5 Huckaby	Y	Y	Y	Y
6 ***Baker***	Y	N	Y	Y
7 Hayes	Y	Y	Y	Y
8 ***Holloway***	Y	N	Y	?
MAINE				
1 Brennan	Y	Y	Y	Y
2 ***Snowe***	Y	N	Y	Y
MARYLAND				
1 Dyson	Y	?	Y	Y
2 ***Bentley***	Y	N	Y	Y
3 Cardin	Y	Y	Y	Y
4 McMillen	Y	Y	Y	Y
5 Hoyer	Y	Y	Y	Y
6 Byron	Y	Y	Y	Y
7 Mfume	Y	?	Y	Y
8 ***Morella***	Y	Y	Y	Y
MASSACHUSETTS				
1 ***Conte***	+	Y	Y	Y
2 Neal	Y	Y	Y	Y
3 Early	Y	Y	Y	Y
4 Frank	Y	Y	Y	Y
5 Atkins	Y	Y	Y	Y
6 Mavroules	Y	Y	?	Y
7 Markey	Y	?	Y	Y
8 Kennedy	Y	Y	Y	Y
9 Moakley	Y	Y	Y	Y
10 Studds	Y	Y	Y	Y
11 Donnelly	Y	Y	Y	Y
MICHIGAN				
1 Conyers	?	?	Y	Y
2 ***Pursell***	Y	Y	Y	Y
3 Wolpe	Y	Y	Y	Y
4 ***Upton***	Y	N	Y	Y
5 ***Henry***	Y	N	Y	Y
6 Carr	Y	Y	Y	Y
7 Kildee	Y	Y	Y	Y
8 Traxler	Y	?	Y	Y
9 ***Vander Jagt***	Y	Y	Y	Y
10 ***Schuette***	Y	N	Y	Y
11 ***Davis***	?	Y	Y	Y
12 Bonior	Y	Y	?	Y
13 Crockett	N	Y	Y	Y
14 Hertel	Y	Y	Y	Y
15 Ford	Y	Y	Y	Y
16 Dingell	Y	Y	Y	Y
17 Levin	Y	Y	Y	Y
18 ***Broomfield***	Y	Y	Y	Y
MINNESOTA				
1 Penny	Y	Y	Y	Y
2 ***Weber***	Y	N	Y	Y
3 ***Frenzel***	?	N	Y	N
4 Vento	Y	Y	Y	Y

	108	109	110	111
5 Sabo	Y	Y	Y	Y
6 Sikorski	Y	N	Y	Y
7 ***Stangeland***	Y	N	Y	Y
8 Oberstar	+	Y	Y	Y
MISSISSIPPI				
1 Whitten	?	Y	Y	Y
2 Espy	Y	Y	Y	Y
3 Montgomery	Y	Y	Y	Y
4 Parker	Y	Y	Y	Y
5 Taylor	Y	Y	Y	Y
MISSOURI				
1 Clay	Y	N	Y	Y
2 ***Buechner***	Y	N	Y	Y
3 Gephardt	?	Y	Y	Y
4 Skelton	Y	Y	Y	Y
5 Wheat	Y	Y	Y	Y
6 ***Coleman***	Y	N	Y	Y
7 ***Hancock***	Y	N	Y	N
8 ***Emerson***	Y	Y	Y	Y
9 Volkmer	Y	Y	Y	Y
MONTANA				
1 Williams	Y	?	Y	Y
2 ***Marlenee***	Y	N	Y	N
NEBRASKA				
1 ***Bereuter***	Y	N	Y	Y
2 Hoagland	Y	Y	Y	Y
3 ***Smith***	Y	Y	Y	Y
NEVADA				
1 Bilbray	Y	Y	Y	Y
2 ***Vucanovich***	Y	N	Y	?
NEW HAMPSHIRE				
1 ***Smith***	Y	N	Y	Y
2 ***Douglas***	Y	N	Y	Y
NEW JERSEY				
1 Vacancy				
2 Hughes	Y	Y	Y	Y
3 Pallone	Y	Y	Y	Y
4 ***Smith***	Y	Y	Y	Y
5 ***Roukema***	Y	N	Y	Y
6 Dwyer	Y	Y	Y	Y
7 ***Rinaldo***	Y	Y	Y	Y
8 Roe	Y	Y	Y	Y
9 Torricelli	Y	Y	Y	Y
10 Payne	Y	?	Y	Y
11 ***Gallo***	Y	Y	Y	Y
12 ***Courter***	Y	N	Y	?
13 ***Saxton***	Y	Y	Y	Y
14 Guarini	Y	Y	Y	Y
NEW MEXICO				
1 ***Schiff***	Y	Y	Y	Y
2 ***Skeen***	Y	Y	Y	Y
3 Richardson	Y	Y	Y	Y
NEW YORK				
1 Hochbrueckner	Y	Y	Y	Y
2 Downey	Y	Y	Y	Y
3 Mrazek	Y	Y	Y	Y
4 ***Lent***	Y	Y	Y	Y
5 ***McGrath***	Y	N	Y	Y
6 Flake	Y	Y	Y	Y
7 Ackerman	Y	+	Y	Y
8 Scheuer	Y	Y	Y	Y
9 Manton	Y	?	?	Y
10 Schumer	Y	Y	Y	Y
11 Towns	Y	Y	Y	Y
12 Owens	Y	Y	Y	Y
13 Solarz	Y	Y	Y	Y
14 ***Molinari***	Y	N	Y	Y
15 ***Green***	Y	Y	Y	Y
16 Rangel	Y	?	Y	Y
17 Weiss	+	Y	Y	Y
18 Serrano	Y	Y	Y	Y
19 Engel	?	?	?	?
20 Lowey	Y	?	?	Y
21 ***Fish***	Y	Y	Y	Y
22 ***Gilman***	Y	+	Y	Y
23 McNulty	Y	Y	Y	Y
24 ***Solomon***	Y	N	Y	Y
25 ***Boehlert***	Y	N	Y	Y
26 ***Martin***	Y	N	Y	Y
27 ***Walsh***	Y	?	Y	Y
28 McHugh	Y	Y	Y	Y
29 ***Horton***	Y	Y	Y	Y
30 Slaughter	Y	Y	Y	Y
31 ***Paxon***	Y	N	Y	Y

	108	109	110	111
32 LaFalce	Y	Y	Y	Y
33 Nowak	Y	Y	Y	Y
34 ***Houghton***	Y	Y	Y	Y
NORTH CAROLINA				
1 Jones	Y	Y	Y	Y
2 Valentine	Y	Y	Y	Y
3 Lancaster	Y	Y	Y	Y
4 Price	Y	Y	Y	Y
5 Neal	Y	?	Y	Y
6 ***Coble***	Y	N	Y	Y
7 Rose	Y	Y	Y	Y
8 Hefner	Y	Y	Y	Y
9 ***McMillan***	Y	Y	Y	Y
10 ***Ballenger***	+	?	Y	Y
11 Clarke	Y	Y	Y	Y
NORTH DAKOTA				
AL Dorgan	Y	Y	Y	Y
OHIO				
1 Luken	Y	Y	Y	Y
2 ***Gradison***	Y	Y	Y	Y
3 Hall	Y	Y	Y	Y
4 ***Oxley***	Y	N	Y	Y
5 ***Gillmor***	Y	Y	Y	Y
6 ***McEwen***	Y	Y	Y	N
7 ***DeWine***	Y	N	Y	Y
8 ***Lukens***	Y	Y	Y	Y
9 Kaptur	Y	Y	Y	Y
10 ***Miller***	Y	N	Y	Y
11 Eckart	Y	Y	Y	Y
12 ***Kasich***	Y	Y	Y	Y
13 Pease	Y	Y	Y	Y
14 Sawyer	Y	Y	Y	Y
15 ***Wylie***	Y	Y	Y	Y
16 ***Regula***	Y	N	Y	Y
17 Traficant	Y	Y	Y	Y
18 Applegate	Y	Y	Y	Y
19 Feighan	Y	Y	Y	Y
20 Oakar	?	Y	?	Y
21 Stokes	Y	Y	Y	Y
OKLAHOMA				
1 ***Inhofe***	Y	N	Y	Y
2 Synar	Y	Y	Y	Y
3 Watkins	Y	Y	Y	Y
4 McCurdy	Y	Y	Y	Y
5 ***Edwards***	Y	N	Y	Y
6 English	Y	Y	Y	Y
OREGON				
1 AuCoin	Y	?	Y	Y
2 ***Smith, B.***	Y	N	Y	Y
3 Wyden	Y	Y	Y	Y
4 DeFazio	Y	Y	Y	Y
5 ***Smith, D.***	Y	N	Y	Y
PENNSYLVANIA				
1 Foglietta	?	Y	Y	Y
2 Gray	?	Y	Y	Y
3 Borski	Y	Y	Y	Y
4 Kolter	?	?	?	Y
5 ***Schulze***	Y	Y	Y	Y
6 Yatron	Y	Y	Y	Y
7 ***Weldon***	Y	N	Y	Y
8 Kostmayer	Y	Y	Y	Y
9 ***Shuster***	Y	Y	Y	Y
10 ***McDade***	Y	Y	Y	Y
11 Kanjorski	Y	Y	Y	Y
12 Murtha	Y	Y	Y	Y
13 ***Coughlin***	Y	N	Y	Y
14 Coyne	Y	Y	Y	Y
15 ***Ritter***	Y	?	Y	Y
16 ***Walker***	Y	N	Y	N
17 ***Gekas***	Y	N	Y	N
18 Walgren	Y	Y	Y	Y
19 ***Goodling***	Y	N	Y	Y
20 Gaydos	Y	Y	Y	Y
21 ***Ridge***	Y	N	Y	Y
22 Murphy	?	?	Y	Y
23 ***Clinger***	Y	Y	Y	Y
RHODE ISLAND				
1 ***Machtley***	Y	N	Y	Y
2 ***Schneider***	Y	Y	Y	Y
SOUTH CAROLINA				
1 ***Ravenel***	Y	Y	Y	Y
2 ***Spence***	Y	Y	Y	Y
3 Derrick	Y	Y	Y	Y
4 Patterson	Y	Y	Y	Y
5 Spratt	Y	Y	Y	Y
6 Tallon	Y	Y	Y	Y

	108	109	110	111
SOUTH DAKOTA				
AL Johnson	Y	Y	Y	Y
TENNESSEE				
1 ***Quillen***	Y	Y	Y	Y
2 ***Duncan***	Y	N	Y	N
3 Lloyd	Y	Y	Y	Y
4 Cooper	Y	Y	Y	Y
5 Clement	Y	Y	+	+
6 Gordon	Y	Y	Y	Y
7 ***Sundquist***	Y	N	Y	Y
8 Tanner	Y	Y	Y	Y
9 Ford	?	?	?	Y
TEXAS				
1 Chapman	Y	Y	Y	Y
2 Wilson	Y	Y	Y	Y
3 ***Bartlett***	Y	Y	Y	Y
4 Hall	Y	Y	Y	Y
5 Bryant	Y	Y	Y	Y
6 ***Barton***	Y	N	?	Y
7 ***Archer***	?	Y	Y	N
8 ***Fields***	Y	N	Y	N
9 Brooks	Y	Y	Y	Y
10 Pickle	Y	Y	?	Y
11 Leath	Y	?	?	Y
12 Geren	Y	Y	Y	Y
13 Sarpalius	Y	Y	Y	Y
14 Laughlin	Y	Y	Y	Y
15 de la Garza	Y	Y	Y	Y
16 Coleman	Y	Y	Y	Y
17 Stenholm	Y	Y	Y	Y
18 Washington	?	?	?	Y
19 ***Combest***	Y	Y	Y	Y
20 Gonzalez	N	Y	Y	Y
21 ***Smith***	Y	N	Y	Y
22 ***DeLay***	Y	N	Y	N
23 Bustamante	Y	Y	Y	Y
24 Frost	Y	Y	Y	Y
25 Andrews	Y	Y	Y	Y
26 ***Armey***	Y	N	Y	N
27 Ortiz	Y	Y	Y	Y
UTAH				
1 ***Hansen***	Y	N	Y	Y
2 Owens	Y	Y	Y	Y
3 ***Nielson***	?	Y	Y	Y
VERMONT				
AL ***Smith***	Y	Y	Y	Y
VIRGINIA				
1 ***Bateman***	Y	Y	Y	Y
2 Pickett	Y	Y	Y	Y
3 ***Bliley***	Y	N	Y	Y
4 Sisisky	Y	Y	Y	Y
5 Payne	Y	Y	Y	Y
6 Olin	Y	Y	Y	Y
7 ***Slaughter***	Y	N	Y	Y
8 ***Parris***	?	?	?	?
9 Boucher	Y	Y	Y	Y
10 ***Wolf***	Y	N	Y	Y
WASHINGTON				
1 ***Miller***	Y	N	Y	Y
2 Swift	Y	Y	Y	Y
3 Unsoeld	Y	?	Y	Y
4 ***Morrison***	Y	Y	Y	Y
5 Foley				
6 Dicks	Y	Y	Y	Y
7 McDermott	Y	Y	Y	Y
8 ***Chandler***	Y	N	Y	Y
WEST VIRGINIA				
1 Mollohan	?	Y	Y	Y
2 Staggers	Y	Y	Y	Y
3 Wise	Y	Y	Y	Y
4 Rahall	Y	Y	Y	Y
WISCONSIN				
1 Aspin	Y	Y	Y	Y
2 Kastenmeier	Y	Y	Y	Y
3 ***Gunderson***	Y	Y	Y	Y
4 Kleczka	?	Y	Y	Y
5 Moody	Y	Y	Y	Y
6 ***Petri***	Y	Y	Y	Y
7 Obey	Y	Y	Y	Y
8 ***Roth***	Y	Y	Y	Y
9 ***Sensenbrenner***	Y	N	Y	Y
WYOMING				
AL ***Thomas***	Y	N	Y	Y

Southern states - Ala., Ark., Fla., Ga., Ky., La., Miss., N.C., Okla., S.C., Tenn., Texas, Va.
Omitted votes are quorum calls, which CQ does not include in its vote charts.

HOUSE VOTES 112, 113, 114, 116, 117, 118

112. Procedural Motion. Hastert, R-Ill., motion to approve the House Journal of Wednesday, May 16. Motion agreed to 285-103: R 60-99; D 225-4 (ND 151-4, SD 74-0), May 17, 1990.

113. HR 2273. Americans With Disabilities Act/Previous Question. Gordon, D-Tenn., motion to order the previous question (thus ending debate and the possibility of amendment) on the rule (H Res 394) to provide for House floor consideration of the bill to guarantee disabled Americans equal access to public facilities, mass transit and jobs. Motion agreed to 251-162: R 7-160; D 244-2 (ND 167-1, SD 77-1), May 17, 1990.

114. HR 2273. Americans With Disabilities Act/Rule. Adoption of the rule (H Res 394) to provide for House floor consideration of the bill to guarantee disabled Americans equal access to public facilities, mass transit and jobs. Adopted 237-172: R 14-154; D 223-18 (ND 163-1, SD 60-17), May 17, 1990.

116. HR 2273. Americans With Disabilities Act/Phase-In. LaFalce, D-N.Y., amendment to allow small businesses an extended phase-in period for the public accommodations part of the bill. Businesses with 25 or fewer employees and annual gross receipts less than $1 million would be exempt from enforcement actions for the first six months after the section takes effect (18 months after enactment), and businesses with 10 or fewer employees and annual gross receipts less than $500,000 would be exempt from enforcement actions for an additional year. Adopted 401-0: R 153-0; D 248-0 (ND 173-0, SD 75-0), May 17, 1990.

117. HR 2273. Americans With Disabilities Act/Undue Hardship Limit. Olin, D-Va., amendment to provide that it would be an "undue hardship" for an employer to incur costs to facilitate the employment of a disabled worker if the costs exceeded 10 percent of the employee's salary. Rejected 187-213: R 119-39; D 68-174 (ND 21-145, SD 47-29), May 17, 1990.

118. HR 2273. Americans With Disabilities Act/Communicable Diseases. Chapman, D-Texas, amendment to allow employers to move an employee with a communicable disease out of a food-handling position, provided that the employer offers an alternative position in which the employee would sustain no economic damage. Adopted 199-187: R 120-31; D 79-156 (ND 26-133, SD 53-23), May 17, 1990.

KEY

Y Voted for (yea).
Paired for.
+ Announced for.
N Voted against (nay).
X Paired against.
- Announced against.
P Voted "present."
C Voted "present" to avoid possible conflict of interest.
? Did not vote or otherwise make a position known.

Democrats ***Republicans***

	112	113	114	116	117	118
ALABAMA						
1 ***Callahan***	Y	N	N	Y	Y	Y
2 ***Dickinson***	N	N	N	Y	Y	Y
3 Browder	Y	Y	Y	Y	N	Y
4 Bevill	Y	Y	Y	Y	N	Y
5 Flippo	?	?	?	?	?	?
6 Erdreich	Y	Y	Y	Y	N	Y
7 Harris	Y	Y	Y	Y	N	Y
ALASKA						
AL ***Young***	N	N	Y	Y	Y	Y
ARIZONA						
1 ***Rhodes***	N	N	N	Y	N	Y
2 Udall	Y	Y	?	Y	N	N
3 ***Stump***	N	N	N	Y	Y	Y
4 ***Kyl***	N	N	N	Y	Y	Y
5 ***Kolbe***	N	N	N	Y	N	Y
ARKANSAS						
1 Alexander	?	?	?	?	?	?
2 ***Robinson***	?	?	?	?	?	?
3 ***Hammerschmidt***	?	?	?	?	?	?
4 Anthony	Y	Y	Y	Y	Y	N
CALIFORNIA						
1 Bosco	Y	Y	Y	Y	Y	N
2 ***Herger***	N	N	N	Y	Y	Y
3 Matsui	Y	Y	Y	Y	X	X
4 Fazio	Y	Y	Y	Y	N	N
5 Pelosi	Y	Y	Y	Y	N	N
6 Boxer	Y	Y	Y	Y	N	N
7 Miller	?	Y	Y	Y	N	N
8 Dellums	Y	Y	Y	Y	N	N
9 Stark	Y	Y	Y	Y	N	N
10 Edwards	Y	Y	Y	Y	N	N
11 Lantos	Y	Y	Y	Y	N	N
12 ***Campbell***	N	N	N	Y	N	N
13 Mineta	Y	Y	Y	Y	N	N
14 ***Shumway***	Y	N	N	Y	Y	Y
15 Condit	Y	Y	Y	Y	N	N
16 Panetta	Y	Y	Y	Y	N	N
17 ***Pashayan***	N	N	N	Y	?	#
18 Lehman	Y	Y	Y	Y	N	N
19 ***Lagomarsino***	N	N	N	Y	Y	Y
20 ***Thomas***	N	N	N	Y	?	#
21 ***Gallegly***	N	N	N	Y	Y	Y
22 ***Moorhead***	N	N	N	Y	Y	Y
23 Beilenson	Y	Y	Y	Y	N	N
24 Waxman	Y	Y	Y	Y	N	N
25 Roybal	Y	Y	Y	Y	N	N
26 Berman	Y	Y	Y	Y	N	N
27 Levine	Y	Y	Y	Y	N	N
28 Dixon	?	Y	Y	Y	N	N
29 Hawkins	?	Y	Y	Y	N	?
30 Martinez	Y	Y	Y	Y	N	N
31 Dymally	Y	Y	Y	Y	N	N
32 Anderson	Y	Y	Y	Y	N	N
33 ***Dreier***	N	N	N	Y	Y	Y
34 Torres	Y	Y	Y	Y	N	N
35 ***Lewis***	N	N	N	Y	Y	Y
36 Brown	Y	?	?	Y	N	N
37 ***McCandless***	N	N	N	Y	Y	Y
38 ***Dornan***	N	N	N	Y	Y	Y
39 ***Dannemeyer***	N	N	N	Y	Y	Y
40 ***Cox***	N	N	N	Y	Y	Y
41 ***Lowery***	?	N	N	Y	?	?
42 ***Rohrabacher***	Y	N	N	Y	Y	Y
43 ***Packard***	Y	N	N	Y	Y	N
44 Bates	Y	Y	Y	Y	N	N
45 ***Hunter***	?	N	N	Y	N	Y
COLORADO						
1 Schroeder	N	Y	Y	Y	N	N
2 Skaggs	Y	Y	Y	Y	N	N
3 Campbell	Y	Y	Y	Y	Y	N
4 ***Brown***	N	N	N	Y	Y	Y
5 ***Hefley***	N	N	N	Y	Y	Y
6 ***Schaefer***	N	N	N	Y	Y	Y
CONNECTICUT						
1 Kennelly	Y	Y	Y	Y	N	N
2 Gejdenson	Y	Y	Y	Y	N	N
3 Morrison	Y	Y	Y	Y	N	N
4 ***Shays***	N	N	N	Y	N	N
5 ***Rowland***	Y	Y	Y	Y	N	N
6 ***Johnson***	Y	N	X	Y	N	N
DELAWARE						
AL Carper	Y	Y	Y	Y	N	N
FLORIDA						
1 Hutto	Y	Y	N	?	Y	Y
2 ***Grant***	Y	N	N	?	Y	Y
3 Bennett	Y	Y	Y	Y	N	Y
4 ***James***	N	N	N	?	Y	Y
5 ***McCollum***	Y	N	N	Y	Y	Y
6 ***Stearns***	N	N	N	+	Y	Y
7 Gibbons	Y	Y	Y	Y	N	Y
8 ***Young***	?	N	N	?	Y	Y
9 ***Bilirakis***	N	N	Y	?	Y	Y
10 ***Ireland***	N	N	N	?	Y	?
11 Nelson	+	#	#	+	-	+
12 ***Lewis***	N	N	N	+	#	+
13 ***Goss***	N	N	N	+	Y	Y
14 Johnston	Y	Y	Y	Y	N	Y
15 ***Shaw***	Y	N	N	Y	Y	Y
16 Smith	Y	Y	Y	Y	N	N
17 Lehman	Y	Y	Y	Y	N	N
18 ***Ros-Lehtinen***	N	N	N	+	Y	Y
19 Fascell	Y	Y	Y	?	N	N
GEORGIA						
1 Thomas	Y	Y	Y	Y	Y	Y
2 Hatcher	Y	Y	Y	Y	Y	Y
3 Ray	Y	Y	Y	Y	Y	N
4 Jones	Y	Y	Y	Y	Y	N
5 Lewis	Y	Y	Y	Y	N	N
6 ***Gingrich***	N	N	N	?	Y	Y
7 Darden	Y	Y	Y	Y	Y	Y
8 Rowland	Y	Y	Y	Y	Y	N
9 Jenkins	Y	Y	Y	Y	Y	Y
10 Barnard	Y	Y	Y	Y	Y	Y
HAWAII						
1 ***Saiki***	?	N	N	Y	N	Y
2 Vacancy						
IDAHO						
1 ***Craig***	?	X	X	?	#	#
2 Stallings	Y	Y	Y	Y	N	Y
ILLINOIS						
1 Hayes	Y	Y	Y	Y	N	N
2 Savage	Y	Y	Y	Y	N	N
3 Russo	Y	Y	Y	Y	N	N
4 Sangmeister	Y	Y	Y	Y	N	Y
5 Lipinski	Y	Y	Y	Y	Y	Y
6 ***Hyde***	N	N	N	Y	N	Y
7 Collins	?	Y	Y	Y	N	?
8 Rostenkowski	Y	Y	Y	Y	?	?
9 Yates	Y	Y	Y	Y	?	X
10 ***Porter***	N	N	N	Y	Y	Y
11 Annunzio	Y	Y	Y	Y	N	N
12 ***Crane***	?	N	N	?	?	?
13 ***Fawell***	N	N	N	Y	Y	Y
14 ***Hastert***	N	N	N	Y	Y	Y
15 ***Madigan***	N	N	N	Y	Y	Y
16 ***Martin***	N	N	N	Y	Y	Y
17 Evans	Y	Y	Y	Y	N	N
18 ***Michel***	N	N	N	+	Y	?
19 Bruce	Y	Y	Y	Y	N	N
20 Durbin	Y	Y	Y	Y	N	N
21 Costello	Y	Y	Y	Y	N	N
22 Poshard	Y	Y	Y	Y	N	N
INDIANA						
1 Visclosky	Y	Y	Y	Y	Y	N
2 Sharp	Y	Y	Y	Y	N	N
3 ***Hiler***	N	N	N	Y	Y	Y

ND Northern Democrats SD Southern Democrats

	112	113	114	116	117	118
4 Long	Y	Y	Y	Y	Y	Y
5 Jontz	Y	Y	Y	Y	N	N
6 ***Burton***	N	N	N	Y	Y	Y
7 ***Myers***	Y	N	N	Y	Y	Y
8 McCloskey	Y	Y	Y	Y	N	N
9 Hamilton	Y	Y	Y	Y	Y	N
10 Jacobs	N	?	Y	Y	N	N
IOWA						
1 ***Leach***	N	N	N	Y	N	N
2 ***Tauke***	N	N	N	Y	N	Y
3 Nagle	Y	Y	Y	Y	N	N
4 Smith	Y	Y	Y	Y	N	N
5 ***Lightfoot***	N	N	N	Y	Y	Y
6 ***Grandy***	N	N	N	Y	?	N
KANSAS						
1 ***Roberts***	N	N	N	Y	Y	Y
2 Slattery	Y	Y	Y	Y	N	Y
3 ***Meyers***	Y	N	N	Y	N	Y
4 Glickman	Y	Y	Y	Y	N	Y
5 ***Whittaker***	N	N	N	Y	Y	Y
KENTUCKY						
1 Hubbard	Y	Y	Y	Y	?	?
2 Natcher	Y	Y	Y	Y	N	N
3 Mazzoli	Y	Y	Y	+	X	X
4 ***Bunning***	N	N	N	Y	Y	Y
5 ***Rogers***	N	N	N	?	?	?
6 ***Hopkins***	N	N	N	Y	Y	Y
7 Perkins	Y	Y	Y	Y	N	N
LOUISIANA						
1 ***Livingston***	Y	N	N	Y	Y	Y
2 Boggs	Y	Y	Y	Y	N	N
3 Tauzin	Y	Y	N	Y	Y	Y
4 ***McCrery***	Y	Y	N	Y	Y	N
5 Huckaby	Y	Y	Y	Y	Y	Y
6 ***Baker***	N	N	N	Y	Y	?
7 Hayes	Y	Y	Y	Y	Y	Y
8 ***Holloway***	N	N	N	Y	Y	Y
MAINE						
1 Brennan	Y	Y	Y	Y	N	N
2 ***Snowe***	Y	N	N	Y	N	Y
MARYLAND						
1 Dyson	Y	Y	Y	Y	Y	Y
2 ***Bentley***	N	N	N	Y	Y	Y
3 Cardin	Y	Y	Y	Y	N	N
4 McMillen	Y	Y	Y	Y	Y	N
5 Hoyer	Y	Y	Y	Y	N	N
6 Byron	Y	Y	Y	Y	Y	N
7 Mfume	Y	Y	Y	Y	N	N
8 ***Morella***	Y	Y	Y	Y	N	N
MASSACHUSETTS						
1 ***Conte***	Y	Y	Y	Y	N	N
2 Neal	Y	Y	Y	Y	N	N
3 Early	Y	Y	Y	Y	N	?
4 Frank	Y	Y	Y	Y	N	N
5 Atkins	Y	Y	Y	Y	N	N
6 Mavroules	Y	Y	Y	Y	N	N
7 Markey	Y	Y	Y	Y	N	N
8 Kennedy	Y	Y	Y	Y	N	N
9 Moakley	Y	Y	Y	Y	N	N
10 Studds	Y	Y	Y	Y	N	N
11 Donnelly	Y	Y	Y	Y	N	Y
MICHIGAN						
1 Conyers	?	Y	Y	Y	N	?
2 ***Pursell***	Y	N	N	?	?	?
3 Wolpe	Y	N	N	Y	N	N
4 ***Upton***	N	N	N	Y	N	Y
5 ***Henry***	N	N	N	Y	N	N
6 Carr	?	?	?	Y	N	N
7 Kildee	Y	Y	Y	Y	N	N
8 Traxler	Y	Y	Y	Y	N	N
9 ***Vander Jagt***	Y	N	N	Y	Y	Y
10 ***Schuette***	?	?	?	?	#	?
11 ***Davis***	Y	?	N	?	?	?
12 Bonior	Y	Y	Y	Y	N	N
13 Crockett	Y	?	?	Y	?	?
14 Hertel	Y	Y	Y	Y	N	Y
15 Ford	?	Y	Y	Y	N	N
16 Dingell	Y	Y	Y	Y	N	N
17 Levin	Y	Y	Y	Y	N	N
18 ***Broomfield***	Y	N	N	Y	Y	Y
MINNESOTA						
1 Penny	Y	Y	Y	Y	Y	N
2 ***Weber***	N	N	N	Y	N	Y
3 ***Frenzel***	N	N	N	Y	Y	N
4 Vento	Y	Y	Y	Y	N	N
5 Sabo	Y	Y	Y	Y	N	N
6 Sikorski	N	Y	Y	Y	N	N
7 ***Stangeland***	N	N	N	Y	Y	Y
8 Oberstar	?	Y	Y	Y	—	—
MISSISSIPPI						
1 Whitten	?	Y	Y	Y	N	Y
2 Espy	Y	Y	Y	Y	Y	Y
3 Montgomery	Y	Y	Y	Y	Y	Y
4 Parker	Y	Y	N	Y	Y	Y
5 Taylor	Y	Y	N	Y	Y	Y
MISSOURI						
1 Clay	?	Y	Y	Y	N	N
2 ***Buechner***	N	N	N	Y	N	Y
3 Gephardt	Y	Y	Y	Y	N	N
4 Skelton	?	Y	Y	Y	Y	Y
5 Wheat	Y	Y	Y	Y	N	N
6 ***Coleman***	N	N	N	Y	Y	Y
7 ***Hancock***	N	N	N	Y	Y	Y
8 ***Emerson***	Y	N	N	Y	Y	Y
9 Volkmer	Y	Y	Y	Y	Y	Y
MONTANA						
1 Williams	?	Y	Y	Y	N	N
2 ***Marlenee***	N	N	N	Y	Y	Y
NEBRASKA						
1 ***Bereuter***	N	N	N	Y	Y	Y
2 Hoagland	Y	Y	Y	Y	N	Y
3 ***Smith***	Y	N	N	Y	Y	Y
NEVADA						
1 Bilbray	Y	Y	Y	Y	Y	N
2 ***Vucanovich***	N	N	N	Y	Y	Y
NEW HAMPSHIRE						
1 ***Smith***	N	N	N	Y	Y	Y
2 ***Douglas***	N	N	N	Y	Y	Y
NEW JERSEY						
1 Vacancy						
2 Hughes	Y	Y	Y	Y	N	N
3 Pallone	Y	Y	Y	Y	N	N
4 ***Smith***	Y	N	Y	Y	N	N
5 ***Roukema***	?	N	N	Y	Y	?
6 Dwyer	Y	Y	Y	Y	N	?
7 ***Rinaldo***	Y	Y	Y	Y	N	N
8 Roe	Y	Y	Y	Y	N	?
9 Torricelli	Y	Y	Y	Y	N	N
10 Payne	Y	Y	Y	Y	N	N
11 ***Gallo***	Y	N	N	Y	Y	Y
12 ***Courter***	?	?	?	?	?	?
13 ***Saxton***	Y	N	N	Y	Y	Y
14 Guarini	Y	Y	Y	Y	N	N
NEW MEXICO						
1 ***Schiff***	Y	N	N	Y	N	N
2 ***Skeen***	Y	N	N	Y	Y	Y
3 Richardson	Y	Y	Y	Y	Y	N
NEW YORK						
1 Hochbrueckner	Y	Y	Y	Y	N	N
2 Downey	Y	Y	Y	Y	N	N
3 Mrazek	Y	Y	Y	Y	N	N
4 ***Lent***	Y	N	N	Y	Y	Y
5 ***McGrath***	N	N	N	Y	N	?
6 Flake	Y	Y	?	Y	N	N
7 Ackerman	Y	+	Y	Y	N	N
8 Scheuer	Y	Y	?	Y	N	N
9 Manton	Y	Y	Y	Y	N	N
10 Schumer	Y	Y	Y	Y	N	N
11 Towns	Y	Y	Y	Y	N	N
12 Owens	Y	Y	Y	Y	N	N
13 Solarz	Y	Y	Y	Y	X	X
14 ***Molinari***	N	N	N	Y	Y	Y
15 ***Green***	Y	N	N	Y	N	N
16 Rangel	?	Y	Y	Y	N	N
17 Weiss	Y	Y	Y	Y	N	N
18 Serrano	Y	Y	Y	Y	N	N
19 Engel	Y	Y	Y	Y	N	N
20 Lowey	Y	Y	Y	Y	N	N
21 ***Fish***	?	N	N	Y	N	N
22 ***Gilman***	Y	Y	Y	Y	N	N
23 McNulty	Y	Y	Y	Y	N	N
24 ***Solomon***	?	N	N	Y	Y	Y
25 ***Boehlert***	N	N	N	Y	N	N
26 ***Martin***	Y	N	N	Y	N	N
27 ***Walsh***	Y	N	Y	Y	N	N
28 McHugh	Y	Y	Y	Y	N	N
29 ***Horton***	Y	N	Y	Y	N	N
30 Slaughter	Y	Y	+	Y	N	N
31 ***Paxon***	N	N	N	Y	Y	Y
32 LaFalce	Y	Y	Y	Y	N	Y
33 Nowak	Y	Y	Y	Y	N	N
34 ***Houghton***	Y	N	N	Y	X	?
NORTH CAROLINA						
1 Jones	Y	Y	Y	Y	Y	N
2 Valentine	Y	Y	N	Y	Y	Y
3 Lancaster	Y	N	N	Y	Y	Y
4 Price	Y	Y	N	Y	Y	Y
5 Neal	?	Y	N	Y	Y	Y
6 ***Coble***	N	N	N	Y	Y	Y
7 Rose	Y	Y	Y	Y	Y	Y
8 Hefner	Y	Y	N	Y	Y	Y
9 ***McMillan***	Y	N	N	Y	Y	Y
10 ***Ballenger***	N	N	N	Y	Y	Y
11 Clarke	Y	Y	N	Y	Y	N
NORTH DAKOTA						
AL Dorgan	?	Y	Y	Y	Y	Y
OHIO						
1 Luken	Y	Y	Y	Y	?	?
2 ***Gradison***	Y	N	N	Y	Y	N
3 Hall	Y	Y	Y	Y	N	Y
4 ***Oxley***	Y	N	N	Y	Y	Y
5 ***Gillmor***	Y	N	N	Y	Y	Y
6 ***McEwen***	Y	N	N	Y	Y	Y
7 ***DeWine***	N	N	N	Y	?	?
8 ***Lukens***	N	N	N	Y	Y	?
9 Kaptur	Y	Y	Y	Y	N	Y
10 ***Miller***	N	N	N	?	Y	Y
11 Eckart	Y	Y	Y	Y	Y	Y
12 ***Kasich***	Y	N	N	Y	N	Y
13 Pease	Y	Y	Y	Y	N	N
14 Sawyer	Y	Y	Y	Y	Y	N
15 ***Wylie***	Y	N	N	Y	Y	Y
16 ***Regula***	N	N	N	Y	Y	Y
17 Traficant	Y	Y	Y	Y	N	N
18 Applegate	Y	Y	Y	Y	Y	Y
19 Feighan	Y	Y	Y	Y	N	N
20 Oakar	?	Y	Y	Y	N	N
21 Stokes	Y	Y	Y	Y	N	N
OKLAHOMA						
1 ***Inhofe***	N	N	N	Y	Y	Y
2 Synar	Y	Y	Y	Y	N	N
3 Watkins	Y	Y	Y	Y	Y	Y
4 McCurdy	Y	Y	Y	Y	Y	Y
5 ***Edwards***	N	N	N	Y	Y	Y
6 English	Y	Y	N	Y	Y	Y
OREGON						
1 AuCoin	Y	Y	#	Y	N	—
2 ***Smith, B.***	N	N	N	Y	Y	Y
3 Wyden	Y	Y	Y	Y	N	N
4 DeFazio	Y	Y	Y	Y	N	N
5 ***Smith, D.***	N	N	N	?	?	?
PENNSYLVANIA						
1 Foglietta	Y	Y	Y	Y	N	N
2 Gray	?	Y	Y	Y	N	N
3 Borski	Y	Y	Y	Y	N	N
4 Kolter	Y	Y	Y	Y	N	Y
5 ***Schulze***	?	X	X	?	#	?
6 Yatron	Y	Y	Y	Y	N	Y
7 ***Weldon***	Y	N	N	Y	Y	Y
8 Kostmayer	Y	Y	Y	Y	N	N
9 ***Shuster***	Y	N	N	Y	Y	Y
10 ***McDade***	N	N	N	Y	Y	Y
11 Kanjorski	Y	Y	Y	Y	Y	Y
12 Murtha	Y	Y	?	Y	N	Y
13 ***Coughlin***	N	N	N	Y	Y	N
14 Coyne	?	Y	Y	Y	N	N
15 ***Ritter***	N	N	N	Y	Y	Y
16 ***Walker***	N	N	N	Y	Y	Y
17 ***Gekas***	?	N	N	Y	Y	Y
18 Walgren	Y	Y	Y	Y	N	Y
19 ***Goodling***	N	?	Y	Y	Y	N
20 Gaydos	?	Y	Y	Y	N	Y
21 ***Ridge***	N	N	N	Y	N	Y
22 Murphy	N	Y	Y	Y	Y	N
23 ***Clinger***	Y	?	?	Y	Y	N
RHODE ISLAND						
1 ***Machtley***	N	N	N	Y	N	N
2 ***Schneider***	Y	N	N	Y	N	N
SOUTH CAROLINA						
1 ***Ravenel***	Y	Y	Y	Y	N	N
2 ***Spence***	Y	N	Y	Y	Y	Y
3 Derrick	Y	Y	Y	Y	N	Y
4 Patterson	Y	Y	Y	Y	N	Y
5 Spratt	Y	Y	Y	Y	Y	Y
6 Tallon	Y	Y	Y	Y	Y	Y
SOUTH DAKOTA						
AL Johnson	Y	Y	Y	Y	Y	Y
TENNESSEE						
1 ***Quillen***	N	N	N	Y	Y	Y
2 ***Duncan***	Y	N	N	Y	Y	Y
3 Lloyd	Y	Y	Y	Y	Y	Y
4 Cooper	Y	Y	N	Y	Y	N
5 Clement	Y	Y	Y	Y	Y	Y
6 Gordon	Y	Y	Y	Y	Y	N
7 ***Sundquist***	N	N	N	Y	Y	Y
8 Tanner	Y	Y	N	Y	Y	Y
9 Ford	?	Y	Y	Y	N	N
TEXAS						
1 Chapman	Y	Y	Y	Y	Y	Y
2 Wilson	?	Y	Y	Y	N	Y
3 ***Bartlett***	Y	N	N	Y	N	Y
4 Hall	Y	Y	N	Y	Y	Y
5 Bryant	Y	Y	Y	Y	N	N
6 ***Barton***	N	N	N	Y	Y	Y
7 ***Archer***	Y	N	N	Y	Y	Y
8 ***Fields***	N	N	N	Y	Y	Y
9 Brooks	Y	Y	Y	Y	N	Y
10 Pickle	Y	Y	Y	Y	N	N
11 Leath	Y	Y	?	Y	Y	Y
12 Geren	Y	Y	N	Y	Y	Y
13 Sarpalius	Y	Y	Y	Y	Y	Y
14 Laughlin	Y	Y	Y	Y	N	Y
15 de la Garza	?	Y	Y	Y	Y	N
16 Coleman	Y	?	?	?	?	?
17 Stenholm	Y	Y	Y	Y	Y	Y
18 Washington	Y	Y	Y	Y	N	N
19 ***Combest***	Y	N	N	Y	Y	Y
2 [B0 Gonzalez	Y	Y	Y	Y	N	N
21 ***Smith***	N	N	N	Y	Y	#
22 ***DeLay***	N	N	N	Y	Y	Y
23 Bustamante	?	#	#	?	?	?
24 Frost	Y	Y	Y	Y	N	Y
25 Andrews	Y	Y	Y	Y	Y	Y
26 ***Armey***	N	N	N	Y	Y	Y
27 Ortiz	Y	Y	Y	Y	N	N
UTAH						
1 ***Hansen***	Y	N	Y	Y	Y	Y
2 Owens	Y	Y	Y	Y	N	N
3 ***Nielson***	Y	N	N	Y	Y	Y
VERMONT						
AL ***Smith***	Y	N	N	Y	N	Y
VIRGINIA						
1 ***Bateman***	Y	N	N	Y	Y	Y
2 Pickett	Y	Y	Y	Y	Y	Y
3 ***Bliley***	N	N	N	Y	Y	?
4 Sisisky	Y	Y	N	Y	Y	Y
5 Payne	Y	Y	N	Y	Y	Y
6 Olin	Y	Y	Y	Y	Y	Y
7 ***Slaughter***	?	N	N	Y	Y	Y
8 ***Parris***	N	N	N	Y	Y	Y
9 Boucher	Y	Y	Y	Y	N	Y
10 ***Wolf***	N	N	N	Y	N	Y
WASHINGTON						
1 ***Miller***	N	N	N	Y	Y	N
2 Swift	Y	Y	Y	Y	N	N
3 Unsoeld	Y	Y	Y	Y	N	N
4 ***Morrison***	Y	N	N	Y	Y	Y
5 Foley						
6 Dicks	Y	Y	Y	Y	N	N
7 McDermott	Y	Y	Y	Y	N	N
8 ***Chandler***	N	N	N	Y	Y	Y
WEST VIRGINIA						
1 Mollohan	Y	Y	Y	Y	N	Y
2 Staggers	Y	Y	Y	Y	N	N
3 Wise	Y	Y	Y	Y	N	N
4 Rahall	Y	Y	Y	Y	N	N
WISCONSIN						
1 Aspin	Y	Y	Y	Y	N	N
2 Kastenmeier	Y	Y	Y	Y	N	N
3 ***Gunderson***	?	N	N	Y	N	N
4 Kleczka	?	Y	Y	Y	N	N
5 Moody	Y	Y	Y	Y	N	N
6 ***Petri***	Y	N	N	Y	Y	Y
7 Obey	Y	Y	Y	Y	N	N
8 ***Roth***	Y	N	N	Y	Y	Y
9 ***Sensenbrenner***	N	N	N	Y	Y	Y
WYOMING						
AL ***Thomas***	Y	N	N	Y	Y	Y

Southern states - Ala., Ark., Fla., Ga., Ky., La., Miss., N.C., Okla., S.C., Tenn., Texas, Va.
Omitted votes are quorum calls, which CQ does not include in its vote charts.

119. HR 2273. Americans with Disabilities Act/Commuter Rail Service. Lipinski, D-Ill., amendment to exempt commuter rail services from the bill's requirement that new rail cars purchased or leased be readily accessible to the disabled if, within five years, at least one car per train is accessible. Rejected 110-290: R 87-78; D 23-212 (ND 10-152, SD 13-60), May 22, 1990.

120. HR 2273. Americans with Disabilities Act/Urban Fixed-Route Systems. Shuster, R-Pa., amendment to allow the Transportation secretary to exempt fixed-route systems in non-urban areas or in urbanized areas with populations of 200,000 or less from requirements that new vehicles be accessible to the disabled, provided that the local transit authority, in consultation with an advisory committee representing disabled people, develops an alternative plan that meets no substantial opposition from those it serves. Rejected 148-266: R 116-54; D 32-212 (ND 12-155, SD 20-57), May 22, 1990.

121. HR 2273. Americans with Disabilities Act/Remedies. Sensenbrenner, R-Wis., amendment to give victims of job discrimination based on disability only the remedies available under the Civil Rights Act of 1964 — injunctive relief, back pay and attorneys' fees — not compensatory or punitive damages. Rejected 192-227: R 146-24; D 46-203 (ND 10-161, SD 36-42), May 22, 1990. A "yea" was a vote supporting the president's position.

122. HR 2273. Americans with Disabilities Act/Recommittal Motion. DeLay, R-Texas, motion to recommit the bill to committee with instructions to report it back with provisions to allow an employer to take into account an employee's history of drug or alcohol abuse before assigning him to a safety-sensitive job and to expand the bill to apply to the executive and judicial branches of the federal government. Motion rejected 143-280: R 135-37; D 8-243 (ND 3-170, SD 5-73), May 22, 1990.

123. S 933. Americans with Disabilities Act/Passage. Passage of the bill to prohibit discrimination against the disabled in public facilities and employment and to guarantee them access to mass transit and telecommunications services. Passed 403-20: R 155-17; D 248-3 (ND 173-0, SD 75-3), May 22, 1990. A "yea" was a vote supporting the president's position. Prior to passage, the text of HR 2273 was substituted for the text of S 933, a similar Senate bill.

124. S 286. Petroglyph National Monument/Passage. Vento, D-Minn., motion to suspend the rules and pass the bill to designate the site of prehistoric and historic petroglyphs (rock art) on cliffs or rocks near Albuquerque, N.M., as the Petroglyph National Monument, a unit of the National Park System. Motion agreed to 415-0: R 169-0; D 246-0 (ND 172-0, SD 74-0), May 22, 1990. A two-thirds majority of those present and voting (277 in this case) is required for passage under suspension of the rules.

125. HR 4636. Fiscal 1990 Foreign Aid Supplemental Authorizations/Rule. Adoption of the rule (H Res 395) to provide for House floor consideration of the bill to make supplemental authorizations for foreign aid programs in fiscal 1990, including $470 million to Panama and $340 million to Nicaragua. Adopted 305-108: R 66-103; D 239-5 (ND 164-4, SD 75-1), May 22, 1990.

126. HR 4636. Fiscal 1990 Foreign Aid Supplemental Authorizations/El Savador. Broomfield, R-Mich., substitute amendment to allow the president to withhold up to 25 percent of El Salvador's military aid in fiscal year 1991, depending on actions by the government of El Salvador or by the leftist guerrillas. Rejected 175-243: R 152-18; D 23-225 (ND 2-169, SD 21-56), May 22, 1990. A "yea" was a vote supporting the president's position.

KEY

- Y Voted for (yea).
- # Paired for.
- + Announced for.
- N Voted against (nay).
- X Paired against.
- \- Announced against.
- P Voted "present."
- C Voted "present" to avoid possible conflict of interest.
- ? Did not vote or otherwise make a position known.

Democrats *Republicans*

	119	120	121	122	123	124	125	126
ALABAMA								
1 *Callahan*	?	Y	Y	Y	Y	Y	Y	Y
2 *Dickinson*	Y	Y	Y	Y	Y	Y	N	Y
3 Browder	N	N	N	N	Y	Y	Y	N
4 Bevill	N	N	N	N	Y	Y	Y	N
5 Flippo	?	?	?	?	?	?	?	?
6 Erdreich	N	N	N	N	Y	Y	Y	N
7 Harris	N	N	N	N	Y	Y	Y	N
ALASKA								
AL *Young*	?	?	Y	Y	Y	Y	N	Y
ARIZONA								
1 *Rhodes*	Y	Y	Y	Y	Y	Y	Y	Y
2 Udall	N	N	N	N	Y	Y	?	N
3 *Stump*	Y	Y	Y	Y	N	Y	N	Y
4 *Kyl*	Y	Y	Y	Y	Y	Y	N	Y
5 *Kolbe*	N	Y	Y	Y	Y	?	?	#
ARKANSAS								
1 Alexander	?	?	?	?	?	?	?	?
2 *Robinson*	N	Y	Y	Y	Y	Y	N	#
3 *Hammerschmidt*	?	?	?	?	?	?	?	?
4 Anthony	X	N	Y	N	Y	Y	Y	N
CALIFORNIA								
1 Bosco	N	N	N	N	Y	Y	Y	N
2 *Herger*	Y	Y	Y	Y	N	Y	N	Y
3 Matsui	N	N	N	N	Y	Y	Y	N
4 Fazio	N	N	N	N	Y	Y	Y	N
5 Pelosi	N	N	N	N	Y	Y	Y	N
6 Boxer	N	N	N	N	Y	Y	Y	N
7 Miller	?	N	N	N	Y	Y	Y	N
8 Dellums	N	N	N	N	Y	Y	Y	N
9 Stark	N	N	N	N	Y	Y	Y	N
10 Edwards	N	N	N	N	Y	Y	Y	N
11 Lantos	?	N	N	N	Y	Y	Y	N
12 *Campbell*	N	Y	Y	Y	Y	Y	N	N
13 Mineta	N	N	N	N	Y	Y	Y	N
14 *Shumway*	Y	Y	Y	Y	N	Y	N	Y
15 Condit	Y	Y	N	N	Y	Y	Y	N
16 Panetta	N	N	N	N	Y	Y	Y	N
17 *Pashayan*	N	N	N	Y	Y	Y	Y	Y
18 Lehman	N	N	N	N	Y	Y	Y	N
19 *Lagomarsino*	Y	N	Y	Y	Y	Y	Y	Y
20 *Thomas*	#	?	#	#	?	?	?	#
21 *Gallegly*	Y	Y	Y	Y	Y	Y	Y	Y
22 *Moorhead*	Y	Y	Y	Y	Y	Y	N	Y
23 Beilenson	N	N	N	N	Y	Y	Y	N
24 Waxman	N	N	N	N	Y	Y	Y	N
25 Roybal	N	N	N	N	Y	Y	Y	N
26 Berman	N	N	N	N	Y	Y	Y	N
27 Levine	N	N	N	N	Y	Y	Y	N
28 Dixon	N	N	N	N	Y	Y	Y	N
29 Hawkins	N	N	N	N	Y	?	Y	X
30 Martinez	N	N	N	N	Y	Y	Y	N
31 Dymally	N	N	N	N	Y	Y	Y	N
32 Anderson	N	N	N	N	Y	Y	Y	N
33 *Dreier*	N	Y	Y	Y	Y	Y	N	Y
34 Torres	N	N	N	N	Y	Y	Y	N
35 *Lewis*	Y	Y	Y	Y	Y	Y	N	Y
36 Brown	N	N	N	N	Y	Y	Y	N
37 *McCandless*	Y	Y	Y	Y	Y	Y	N	Y
38 *Dornan*	?	?	Y	Y	Y	Y	N	Y
39 *Dannemeyer*	Y	Y	Y	Y	N	Y	N	Y
40 *Cox*	Y	Y	Y	Y	Y	Y	N	Y
41 *Lowery*	Y	Y	Y	Y	Y	Y	N	Y
42 *Rohrabacher*	N	Y	Y	Y	Y	Y	N	Y
43 *Packard*	Y	Y	Y	Y	N	Y	N	Y
44 Bates	N	N	N	N	Y	Y	Y	N
45 *Hunter*	Y	Y	Y	Y	Y	Y	N	Y
COLORADO								
1 Schroeder	N	N	N	N	Y	Y	Y	N
2 Skaggs	N	N	N	N	Y	Y	Y	N
3 Campbell	N	N	N	N	Y	Y	Y	N
4 *Brown*	Y	Y	Y	Y	Y	Y	N	Y
5 *Hefley*	Y	Y	Y	Y	Y	Y	N	Y
6 *Schaefer*	Y	Y	Y	Y	Y	Y	N	N
CONNECTICUT								
1 Kennelly	N	N	N	N	Y	Y	Y	N
2 Gejdenson	N	N	N	N	Y	Y	Y	N
3 Morrison	N	N	N	N	Y	Y	Y	N
4 *Shays*	N	N	N	N	Y	Y	Y	N
5 *Rowland*	N	N	N	N	Y	Y	N	Y
6 *Johnson*	N	Y	Y	Y	Y	Y	Y	Y
DELAWARE								
AL Carper	N	N	N	N	Y	Y	Y	N
FLORIDA								
1 Hutto	+	+	Y	N	Y	Y	Y	Y
2 *Grant*	Y	Y	Y	Y	Y	Y	Y	Y
3 Bennett	N	N	N	N	Y	Y	Y	N
4 *James*	N	N	Y	Y	Y	Y	N	Y
5 *McCollum*	Y	Y	Y	Y	Y	Y	N	Y
6 *Stearns*	N	Y	Y	Y	Y	Y	Y	Y
7 Gibbons	N	N	N	Y	Y	Y	Y	N
8 *Young*	Y	Y	Y	Y	Y	Y	N	Y
9 *Bilirakis*	N	N	Y	Y	Y	Y	N	Y
10 *Ireland*	Y	Y	Y	Y	Y	Y	N	Y
11 Nelson	X	X	X	X	#	?	?	X
12 *Lewis*	Y	Y	Y	Y	Y	Y	N	Y
13 *Goss*	Y	Y	Y	Y	Y	Y	Y	Y
14 Johnston	N	N	Y	N	Y	Y	Y	N
15 *Shaw*	Y	Y	Y	Y	Y	Y	N	Y
16 Smith	N	N	N	N	Y	Y	Y	N
17 Lehman	N	N	N	N	Y	Y	Y	N
18 *Ros-Lehtinen*	N	N	?	Y	Y	Y	Y	Y
19 Fascell	N	N	N	N	Y	Y	Y	N
GEORGIA								
1 Thomas	N	Y	Y	N	Y	Y	Y	Y
2 Hatcher	Y	N	N	N	Y	Y	Y	Y
3 Ray	N	N	Y	N	Y	Y	Y	Y
4 Jones	N	N	N	N	Y	Y	Y	N
5 Lewis	N	N	N	N	Y	Y	Y	N
6 *Gingrich*	N	N	Y	Y	Y	Y	N	Y
7 Darden	N	Y	N	N	Y	Y	Y	Y
8 Rowland	N	Y	Y	N	Y	Y	Y	Y
9 Jenkins	N	Y	Y	N	Y	Y	Y	Y
10 Barnard	N	Y	Y	N	Y	Y	Y	Y
HAWAII								
1 *Saiki*	N	N	N	N	Y	Y	Y	N
2 Vacancy								
IDAHO								
1 *Craig*	#	#	#	#	X	?	?	#
2 Stallings	N	N	Y	N	Y	Y	Y	N
ILLINOIS								
1 Hayes	N	N	N	N	Y	Y	Y	N
2 Savage	N	N	N	N	Y	Y	Y	N
3 Russo	Y	N	N	N	Y	Y	Y	N
4 Sangmeister	Y	N	N	N	Y	Y	Y	N
5 Lipinski	Y	Y	Y	Y	Y	Y	Y	N
6 *Hyde*	Y	Y	Y	Y	Y	Y	N	Y
7 Collins	N	N	N	N	Y	Y	Y	N
8 Rostenkowski	Y	N	N	N	Y	Y	Y	N
9 Yates	N	N	N	N	Y	Y	Y	N
10 *Porter*	N	Y	Y	Y	Y	Y	N	Y
11 Annunzio	N	N	N	N	Y	Y	Y	N
12 *Crane*	Y	Y	Y	Y	N	Y	N	Y
13 *Fawell*	Y	Y	Y	Y	Y	Y	N	Y
14 *Hastert*	Y	Y	Y	Y	Y	Y	Y	Y
15 *Madigan*	N	Y	Y	Y	Y	Y	Y	Y
16 *Martin*	Y	Y	Y	Y	Y	+	N	Y
17 Evans	N	N	N	N	Y	Y	Y	N
18 *Michel*	?	Y	Y	Y	Y	Y	Y	Y
19 Bruce	Y	Y	N	N	Y	Y	Y	N
20 Durbin	?	N	N	N	Y	Y	Y	N
21 Costello	N	N	N	N	Y	Y	Y	N
22 Poshard	Y	N	N	N	Y	Y	Y	N
INDIANA								
1 Visclosky	N	N	N	N	Y	Y	Y	N
2 Sharp	N	N	N	N	Y	Y	Y	N
3 *Hiler*	Y	Y	Y	Y	Y	Y	N	Y

ND Northern Democrats SD Southern Democrats

	119	120	121	122	123	124	125	126
4 Long	N	N	Y	N	Y	Y	Y	N
5 Jontz	N	N	N	N	Y	Y	Y	N
6 ***Burton***	Y	Y	Y	Y	N	Y	N	Y
7 ***Myers***	Y	Y	Y	Y	Y	Y	Y	Y
8 McCloskey	N	N	N	N	Y	Y	Y	N
9 Hamilton	N	N	N	N	Y	Y	Y	N
10 Jacobs	N	N	N	N	Y	Y	Y	N
IOWA								
1 ***Leach***	N	N	N	Y	Y	Y	N	N
2 ***Tauke***	N	Y	Y	Y	Y	Y	N	N
3 Nagle	N	N	N	N	Y	Y	?	N
4 Smith	N	N	Y	N	Y	Y	Y	N
5 ***Lightfoot***	Y	Y	Y	Y	N	Y	N	Y
6 ***Grandy***	Y	Y	Y	Y	Y	Y	N	Y
KANSAS								
1 ***Roberts***	Y	Y	Y	Y	Y	Y	N	Y
2 Slattery	N	N	N	N	Y	Y	Y	N
3 ***Meyers***	Y	N	Y	Y	Y	Y	Y	Y
4 Glickman	N	N	N	N	Y	Y	Y	N
5 ***Whittaker***	N	Y	Y	Y	Y	Y	N	Y
KENTUCKY								
1 Hubbard	Y	Y	Y	Y	Y	Y	Y	N
2 Natcher	N	N	N	N	Y	Y	Y	N
3 Mazzoli	N	N	N	N	Y	Y	Y	N
4 ***Bunning***	Y	Y	Y	Y	Y	Y	N	Y
5 ***Rogers***	Y	Y	Y	Y	Y	Y	Y	Y
6 ***Hopkins***	Y	N	Y	Y	Y	Y	N	Y
7 Perkins	N	N	N	N	Y	Y	Y	N
LOUISIANA								
1 ***Livingston***	Y	Y	Y	Y	Y	Y	N	Y
2 Boggs	N	N	N	N	Y	Y	Y	N
3 Tauzin	N	N	Y	N	Y	Y	Y	Y
4 ***McCrery***	Y	Y	Y	Y	Y	Y	N	Y
5 Huckaby	Y	Y	Y	N	Y	Y	Y	Y
6 ***Baker***	?	Y	Y	Y	Y	Y	Y	Y
7 Hayes	N	N	Y	N	Y	Y	Y	N
8 ***Holloway***	?	Y	Y	Y	Y	Y	N	Y
MAINE								
1 Brennan	N	N	N	N	Y	Y	Y	N
2 ***Snowe***	N	N	N	N	Y	Y	Y	Y
MARYLAND								
1 Dyson	N	Y	N	N	Y	Y	Y	N
2 ***Bentley***	Y	N	Y	Y	Y	Y	N	Y
3 Cardin	N	N	N	N	Y	Y	Y	N
4 McMillen	N	N	N	N	Y	Y	Y	N
5 Hoyer	N	N	N	N	Y	Y	Y	N
6 Byron	?	?	N	N	Y	Y	Y	Y
7 Mfume	N	N	N	N	Y	Y	Y	N
8 ***Morella***	N	N	N	N	Y	Y	Y	N
MASSACHUSETTS								
1 ***Conte***	N	N	N	N	Y	Y	Y	N
2 Neal	N	N	N	N	Y	Y	Y	N
3 Early	N	N	N	N	Y	Y	Y	N
4 Frank	?	?	?	N	Y	Y	Y	N
5 Atkins	N	N	N	N	Y	Y	Y	N
6 Mavroules	N	N	N	N	Y	Y	Y	N
7 Markey	N	N	N	N	Y	Y	Y	N
8 Kennedy	N	N	N	N	Y	Y	Y	N
9 Moakley	N	N	N	N	Y	Y	Y	N
10 Studds	N	N	N	N	Y	Y	Y	N
11 Donnelly	N	N	N	N	Y	Y	Y	N
MICHIGAN								
1 Conyers	N	N	N	N	Y	Y	Y	N
2 ***Pursell***	Y	N	Y	N	Y	Y	?	Y
3 Wolpe	N	N	N	N	Y	Y	Y	N
4 ***Upton***	Y	Y	Y	Y	Y	Y	N	Y
5 ***Henry***	N	N	Y	N	Y	Y	N	Y
6 Carr	N	N	N	N	Y	Y	Y	N
7 Kildee	N	N	N	N	Y	Y	Y	N
8 Traxler	N	N	N	N	Y	Y	Y	N
9 ***Vander Jagt***	N	Y	Y	Y	Y	Y	N	Y
10 ***Schuette***	N	Y	Y	Y	Y	Y	N	Y
11 ***Davis***	Y	N	Y	N	Y	Y	Y	Y
12 Bonior	N	N	N	N	Y	Y	Y	N
13 Crockett	N	N	N	N	Y	Y	Y	N
14 Hertel	N	N	N	N	Y	Y	Y	N
15 Ford	N	N	N	N	Y	Y	Y	N
16 Dingell	N	N	N	N	Y	Y	Y	N
17 Levin	N	N	N	N	Y	Y	Y	N
18 ***Broomfield***	N	Y	Y	Y	Y	Y	Y	Y
MINNESOTA								
1 Penny	N	Y	N	N	Y	Y	Y	N
2 ***Weber***	N	Y	Y	Y	Y	Y	N	Y
3 ***Frenzel***	Y	Y	?	Y	Y	Y	N	Y
4 Vento	N	N	N	N	Y	Y	Y	N

	119	120	121	122	123	124	125	126
5 Sabo	N	N	N	N	Y	Y	Y	N
6 Sikorski	N	N	N	N	Y	Y	Y	N
7 ***Stangeland***	Y	Y	Y	Y	Y	Y	Y	Y
8 Oberstar	—	—	X	N	Y	Y	Y	N
MISSISSIPPI								
1 Whitten	N	N	N	N	Y	?	Y	N
2 Espy	?	N	N	N	Y	Y	Y	N
3 Montgomery	Y	Y	Y	N	Y	Y	Y	Y
4 Parker	Y	Y	Y	N	Y	Y	Y	Y
5 Taylor	N	N	N	N	Y	Y	Y	Y
MISSOURI								
1 Clay	N	N	N	N	Y	Y	?	N
2 ***Buechner***	N	N	N	N	Y	Y	Y	Y
3 Gephardt	N	N	N	N	Y	Y	Y	N
4 Skelton	Y	?	Y	N	Y	Y	Y	Y
5 Wheat	?	?	N	N	Y	Y	Y	N
6 ***Coleman***	N	Y	Y	Y	Y	Y	Y	Y
7 ***Hancock***	Y	Y	Y	Y	N	Y	N	Y
8 ***Emerson***	N	Y	Y	Y	Y	Y	Y	Y
9 Volkmer	N	Y	Y	N	Y	Y	Y	N
MONTANA								
1 Williams	N	N	N	N	Y	Y	?	N
2 ***Marlenee***	Y	Y	Y	Y	N	Y	N	Y
NEBRASKA								
1 ***Bereuter***	N	Y	Y	Y	Y	Y	N	Y
2 Hoagland	N	Y	N	N	Y	Y	Y	N
3 ***Smith***	Y	Y	Y	Y	Y	Y	Y	Y
NEVADA								
1 Bilbray	N	N	N	N	Y	Y	Y	N
2 ***Vucanovich***	Y	Y	Y	Y	Y	Y	N	Y
NEW HAMPSHIRE								
1 ***Smith***	N	Y	Y	Y	Y	Y	N	Y
2 ***Douglas***	Y	Y	Y	Y	Y	Y	N	Y
NEW JERSEY								
1 Vacancy								
2 Hughes	N	N	N	N	Y	Y	N	N
3 Pallone	N	N	N	N	Y	Y	Y	N
4 ***Smith***	N	N	Y	N	Y	Y	Y	Y
5 ***Roukema***	N	N	Y	Y	Y	Y	N	N
6 Dwyer	N	N	N	N	Y	Y	Y	N
7 ***Rinaldo***	N	N	N	N	Y	Y	Y	N
8 Roe	N	N	N	N	Y	Y	Y	N
9 Torricelli	N	N	N	N	Y	Y	Y	N
10 Payne	N	N	N	N	Y	Y	Y	N
11 ***Gallo***	Y	N	Y	N	Y	Y	Y	Y
12 ***Courter***	Y	N	N	N	Y	Y	N	Y
13 ***Saxton***	N	N	Y	N	Y	Y	N	Y
14 Guarini	N	N	N	N	Y	Y	Y	N
NEW MEXICO								
1 ***Schiff***	N	N	Y	Y	Y	Y	N	Y
2 ***Skeen***	Y	Y	Y	Y	Y	Y	Y	Y
3 Richardson	N	N	N	N	Y	Y	Y	N
NEW YORK								
1 Hochbrueckner	N	N	N	N	Y	Y	Y	N
2 Downey	N	N	N	N	Y	Y	Y	N
3 Mrazek	?	N	N	N	Y	Y	Y	N
4 ***Lent***	N	N	Y	N	Y	Y	N	Y
5 ***McGrath***	N	N	N	N	Y	Y	Y	Y
6 Flake	N	N	N	N	Y	Y	Y	N
7 Ackerman	N	N	N	N	Y	Y	Y	N
8 Scheuer	N	N	N	N	Y	Y	Y	N
9 Manton	?	N	N	N	Y	Y	Y	N
10 Schumer	N	N	N	N	Y	Y	Y	N
11 Towns	N	N	N	N	Y	Y	Y	N
12 Owens	N	N	N	N	Y	Y	Y	N
13 Solarz	N	N	N	N	Y	Y	?	N
14 ***Molinari***	N	Y	Y	Y	Y	Y	Y	Y
15 ***Green***	N	N	N	N	Y	Y	Y	N
16 Rangel	N	N	N	N	Y	Y	Y	N
17 Weiss	N	N	N	N	Y	Y	Y	N
18 Serrano	N	N	N	N	Y	Y	Y	N
19 Engel	N	N	N	N	Y	Y	Y	N
20 Lowey	N	N	N	N	Y	Y	Y	N
21 ***Fish***	N	N	N	N	Y	Y	Y	Y
22 ***Gilman***	N	N	N	N	Y	Y	Y	Y
23 McNulty	N	N	N	N	Y	Y	Y	N
24 ***Solomon***	N	N	Y	Y	Y	Y	Y	Y
25 ***Boehlert***	N	N	Y	N	Y	Y	Y	Y
26 ***Martin***	N	N	Y	Y	Y	Y	Y	Y
27 ***Walsh***	N	N	N	N	Y	Y	Y	N
28 McHugh	N	N	N	N	Y	Y	Y	N
29 ***Horton***	N	N	N	N	Y	Y	Y	N
30 Slaughter	N	N	N	N	Y	Y	Y	N
31 ***Paxon***	Y	Y	Y	Y	Y	Y	N	Y

	119	120	121	122	123	124	125	126
32 LaFalce	N	N	Y	N	Y	Y	Y	N
33 Nowak	N	N	N	N	Y	Y	Y	N
34 ***Houghton***	N	N	N	Y	Y	Y	N	Y
NORTH CAROLINA								
1 Jones	Y	N	N	N	Y	Y	Y	X
2 Valentine	N	N	Y	N	Y	Y	Y	N
3 Lancaster	Y	Y	Y	N	Y	Y	Y	N
4 Price	N	N	Y	N	Y	Y	Y	N
5 Neal	N	N	N	N	Y	Y	Y	N
6 ***Coble***	Y	Y	Y	Y	Y	Y	N	Y
7 Rose	N	Y	Y	N	Y	Y	Y	N
8 Hefner	N	Y	Y	N	Y	Y	Y	N
9 ***McMillan***	Y	Y	Y	Y	Y	Y	Y	Y
10 ***Ballenger***	Y	Y	Y	Y	Y	Y	N	Y
11 Clarke	?	N	Y	N	Y	Y	Y	N
NORTH DAKOTA								
AL Dorgan	N	N	N	N	Y	Y	Y	N
OHIO								
1 Luken	N	N	N	N	Y	Y	Y	N
2 ***Gradison***	Y	Y	Y	Y	Y	Y	Y	Y
3 Hall	N	N	N	N	Y	Y	Y	N
4 ***Oxley***	N	Y	Y	Y	Y	Y	N	Y
5 ***Gillmor***	N	N	Y	N	Y	Y	N	Y
6 ***McEwen***	Y	Y	Y	Y	Y	Y	N	Y
7 ***DeWine***	N	Y	Y	Y	Y	Y	N	Y
8 ***Lukens***	?	?	?	?	?	?	?	?
9 Kaptur	N	N	N	N	Y	Y	Y	N
10 ***Miller***	N	Y	Y	Y	Y	Y	Y	Y
11 Eckart	N	N	N	N	Y	Y	Y	N
12 ***Kasich***	N	N	Y	N	Y	Y	N	Y
13 Pease	N	Y	N	N	Y	Y	Y	N
14 Sawyer	N	N	N	N	Y	Y	Y	N
15 ***Wylie***	N	N	Y	Y	Y	Y	Y	Y
16 ***Regula***	N	Y	Y	Y	Y	Y	Y	Y
17 Traficant	N	N	N	N	Y	Y	N	N
18 Applegate	N	N	Y	N	Y	Y	Y	N
19 Feighan	N	N	N	N	Y	Y	Y	N
20 Oakar	N	N	N	N	Y	Y	Y	N
21 Stokes	N	N	N	N	Y	Y	Y	X
OKLAHOMA								
1 ***Inhofe***	Y	Y	Y	Y	Y	Y	N	Y
2 Synar	N	N	N	N	Y	Y	Y	N
3 Watkins	?	?	?	?	?	?	?	?
4 McCurdy	N	N	N	N	Y	Y	Y	N
5 ***Edwards***	Y	Y	Y	Y	Y	Y	Y	Y
6 English	N	N	Y	N	Y	Y	Y	N
OREGON								
1 AuCoin	N	N	N	N	Y	Y	Y	N
2 ***Smith, B.***	N	Y	Y	Y	Y	Y	N	Y
3 Wyden	N	N	N	N	Y	Y	Y	N
4 DeFazio	N	N	N	N	Y	Y	Y	N
5 ***Smith, D.***	Y	Y	Y	Y	Y	Y	N	Y
PENNSYLVANIA								
1 Foglietta	N	N	N	N	Y	Y	Y	N
2 Gray	N	N	N	N	Y	Y	Y	N
3 Borski	Y	N	N	N	Y	Y	Y	N
4 Kolter	N	N	N	N	Y	Y	Y	N
5 ***Schulze***	Y	Y	Y	Y	Y	Y	Y	Y
6 Yatron	N	N	Y	N	Y	Y	Y	N
7 ***Weldon***	?	Y	Y	N	Y	Y	Y	Y
8 Kostmayer	N	N	N	N	Y	Y	Y	N
9 ***Shuster***	Y	Y	Y	Y	N	Y	N	Y
10 ***McDade***	N	Y	N	N	Y	Y	Y	Y
11 Kanjorski	N	N	N	N	Y	Y	Y	N
12 Murtha	N	N	N	N	Y	Y	Y	N
13 ***Coughlin***	N	Y	Y	Y	Y	Y	N	Y
14 Coyne	N	N	N	N	Y	Y	Y	N
15 ***Ritter***	Y	Y	Y	Y	Y	Y	Y	Y
16 ***Walker***	N	Y	Y	Y	Y	Y	N	Y
17 ***Gekas***	N	Y	Y	Y	Y	Y	N	Y
18 Walgren	N	Y	N	N	Y	Y	Y	N
19 ***Goodling***	N	Y	Y	N	Y	Y	?	Y
20 Gaydos	N	N	N	N	Y	Y	Y	N
21 ***Ridge***	N	Y	Y	N	Y	Y	N	N
22 Murphy	N	N	Y	Y	Y	Y	N	N
23 ***Clinger***	Y	Y	Y	N	Y	Y	N	Y
RHODE ISLAND								
1 ***Machtley***	N	N	Y	N	Y	Y	Y	N
2 ***Schneider***	N	N	N	N	Y	Y	Y	N
SOUTH CAROLINA								
1 ***Ravenel***	N	N	N	N	Y	Y	Y	Y
2 ***Spence***	N	N	Y	Y	Y	?	N	Y
3 Derrick	N	N	Y	N	Y	Y	Y	N
4 Patterson	N	N	N	N	Y	Y	Y	N
5 Spratt	N	N	N	N	Y	Y	Y	N
6 Tallon	Y	N	N	N	Y	Y	Y	Y

	119	120	121	122	123	124	125	126
SOUTH DAKOTA								
AL Johnson	N	N	N	Y	Y	Y	Y	N
TENNESSEE								
1 ***Quillen***	Y	N	Y	Y	Y	Y	Y	Y
2 ***Duncan***	Y	Y	Y	Y	Y	Y	N	Y
3 Lloyd	N	N	N	N	Y	Y	Y	N
4 Cooper	N	N	Y	N	N	Y	Y	N
5 Clement	N	N	N	N	Y	Y	Y	N
6 Gordon	N	N	N	N	Y	Y	Y	N
7 ***Sundquist***	N	Y	Y	Y	Y	Y	N	Y
8 Tanner	N	N	Y	N	Y	Y	Y	N
9 Ford	?	?	?	X	?	?	?	N
TEXAS								
1 Chapman	N	Y	Y	N	Y	Y	Y	N
2 Wilson	?	N	N	N	Y	?	N	Y
3 ***Bartlett***	Y	Y	Y	Y	Y	Y	N	Y
4 Hall	Y	N	N	Y	Y	Y	Y	Y
5 Bryant	N	N	N	N	Y	Y	Y	N
6 ***Barton***	Y	Y	N	Y	N	Y	N	Y
7 ***Archer***	Y	Y	Y	Y	N	Y	N	Y
8 ***Fields***	Y	Y	Y	Y	Y	Y	N	Y
9 Brooks	N	N	N	N	Y	Y	Y	N
10 Pickle	N	N	N	N	Y	Y	Y	N
11 Leath	Y	Y	Y	N	Y	?	?	?
12 Geren	N	Y	Y	N	Y	Y	Y	N
13 Sarpalius	Y	Y	Y	N	Y	Y	Y	Y
14 Laughlin	N	N	Y	N	Y	Y	Y	N
15 de la Garza	N	N	N	N	Y	Y	Y	N
16 Coleman	N	N	N	N	Y	Y	Y	N
17 Stenholm	Y	Y	Y	Y	N	Y	Y	Y
18 Washington	N	N	N	N	Y	?	?	N
19 ***Combest***	Y	Y	Y	Y	Y	Y	N	Y
20 Gonzalez	N	N	N	N	Y	Y	Y	N
21 ***Smith***	Y	Y	Y	Y	Y	Y	Y	Y
22 ***DeLay***	Y	Y	Y	Y	N	Y	N	Y
23 Bustamante	N	N	N	N	Y	Y	Y	Y
24 Frost	N	N	N	N	Y	Y	Y	N
25 Andrews	N	Y	Y	N	Y	Y	Y	N
26 ***Armey***	Y	Y	Y	Y	N	Y	Y	Y
27 Ortiz	N	N	Y	N	Y	Y	Y	N
UTAH								
1 ***Hansen***	Y	Y	Y	Y	Y	Y	Y	Y
2 Owens	N	N	N	N	Y	Y	Y	N
3 ***Nielson***	Y	Y	Y	Y	N	Y	N	Y
VERMONT								
AL ***Smith***	N	N	N	N	Y	Y	Y	N
VIRGINIA								
1 ***Bateman***	Y	Y	Y	Y	N	Y	N	Y
2 Pickett	N	N	Y	N	Y	Y	Y	Y
3 ***Bliley***	N	N	Y	N	Y	Y	N	Y
4 Sisisky	N	Y	Y	N	Y	Y	Y	Y
5 Payne	N	N	Y	N	Y	Y	Y	N
6 Olin	Y	Y	Y	Y	N	Y	Y	N
7 ***Slaughter***	Y	N	Y	Y	Y	Y	N	Y
8 ***Parris***	N	N	Y	N	Y	Y	N	Y
9 Boucher	N	N	N	N	Y	Y	Y	N
10 ***Wolf***	N	N	Y	N	Y	Y	N	Y
WASHINGTON								
1 ***Miller***	Y	Y	Y	Y	Y	Y	Y	Y
2 Swift	N	N	N	N	Y	Y	Y	N
3 Unsoeld	N	N	N	N	Y	Y	Y	N
4 ***Morrison***	Y	Y	Y	Y	Y	Y	Y	N
5 Foley								
6 Dicks	N	N	N	N	Y	Y	Y	N
7 McDermott	N	N	N	N	Y	Y	Y	N
8 ***Chandler***	N	N	Y	Y	Y	Y	Y	Y
WEST VIRGINIA								
1 Mollohan	N	N	N	N	Y	Y	Y	N
2 Staggers	N	N	N	N	Y	Y	Y	N
3 Wise	N	N	N	N	Y	Y	Y	N
4 Rahall	?	?	N	N	Y	Y	N	N
WISCONSIN								
1 Aspin	Y	Y	N	N	Y	Y	Y	N
2 Kastenmeier	N	N	N	N	Y	Y	Y	N
3 ***Gunderson***	N	N	N	Y	Y	Y	Y	Y
4 Kleczka	N	N	N	N	Y	Y	Y	N
5 Moody	?	Y	N	N	Y	Y	Y	N
6 ***Petri***	N	Y	Y	Y	Y	Y	N	Y
7 Obey	N	Y	N	N	Y	Y	Y	N
8 ***Roth***	N	Y	Y	Y	Y	Y	N	Y
9 ***Sensenbrenner***	N	Y	Y	Y	Y	Y	N	Y
WYOMING								
AL ***Thomas***	Y	N	Y	Y	Y	Y	Y	Y

Southern states - Ala., Ark., Fla., Ga., Ky., La., Miss., N.C., Okla., S.C., Tenn., Texas, Va.
Omitted votes are quorum calls, which CQ does not include in its vote charts.

HOUSE VOTES 127,128,129,130,131,132,133,134

127. HR 4636. Fiscal 1990 Foreign Aid Supplemental Authorizations/Military Aid. Moakley, D-Mass., amendment to suspend 50 percent of El Salvador's military aid planned for fiscal years 1990 and 1991, depending on actions by the Salvadoran government or by the leftist guerrillas. Adopted 250-163: R 31-135; D 219-28 (ND 166-4, SD 53-24), May 22, 1990. A "nay" was a vote supporting the president's position.

128. HR 4636. Fiscal 1990 Foreign Aid Supplemental Authorizations/Passage. Passage of the bill to make supplemental authorizations for foreign aid programs in fiscal 1990, including $470 million to Panama and $340 million to Nicaragua. Rejected 171-244: R 16-150; D 155-94 (ND 124-47, SD 31-47), May 22, 1990. A "nay" was a vote supporting the president's position.

129. HR 3030. Clean Air Act Reauthorization/Previous Question. Gordon, D-Tenn., motion to order the previous question (thus ending debate and the possibility of amendment) on the rule (H Res 399) to provide for House floor consideration of the bill to amend the Clean Air Act to provide for attainment and maintenance of national ambient air quality standards, require emissions reductions in motor vehicles, control toxic air pollutants, reduce acid rain, establish a system of federal permits and enforcement, and make other improvements in the quality of the nation's air. Motion agreed to 312-106: R 94-75; D 218-31 (ND 148-23, SD 70-8), May 23, 1990.

130. HR 3030. Clean Air Act Reauthorization/Rule. Adoption of the rule (H Res 399) to provide for House floor consideration of the joint resolution to amend the Clean Air Act to provide for attainment and maintenance of national ambient air quality standards, require emissions reductions in motor vehicles, control toxic air pollutants, reduce acid rain, establish a system of federal permits and enforcement, and make other improvements in the quality of the nation's air. Adopted 317-105: R 98-72; D 219-33 (ND 149-23, SD 70-10), May 23, 1990.

131. HR 3030. Clean Air Act Reauthorization/Fees. Rostenkowski, D-Ill., en bloc amendments to strike provisions from the bill authorizing or mandating the imposition of various fees and charges. Rejected 170-253: R 75-95; D 95-158 (ND 68-105, SD 27-53), May 23, 1990.

132. HR 3030. Clean Air Act Reauthorization /Transition Aid. Wise, D-W.Va., amendment to authorize $250 million over a five-year period for a Clean Air Employment Transition Assistance program to provide workers who lose their jobs or have their wages reduced as a result of the bill with retraining assistance and up to six months of additional unemployment benefits. Adopted 274-146: R 43-126; D 231-20 (ND 169-2, SD 62-18), May 23, 1990. A "nay" was a vote supporting the president's position.

133. HR 3030. Clean Air Act Reauthorization/Catalytic Converters. Sikorski, D-Minn., amendment to require automobile manufacturers to provide an eight-year/80,000-mile warranty for catalytic converters and electronic control units. Adopted 239-180: R 61-106: D 178-74 (ND 137-35, SD 41-39), May 23, 1990.

134. HR 3030. Clean Air Act Reauthorization/CFCs. Dingell, D-Mich., amendment to phase out production and use of chlorofluorocarbons (CFCs) and other substances that deplete the ozone layer. Adopted 416-0: R 170-0; D 246-0 (ND 169-0, SD 77-0), May 23, 1990.

KEY

Y Voted for (yea).
\# Paired for.
\+ Announced for.
N Voted against (nay).
X Paired against.
\- Announced against.
P Voted "present."
C Voted "present" to avoid possible conflict of interest.
? Did not vote or otherwise make a position known.

Democrats *Republicans*

	127	128	129	130	131	132	133	134
ALABAMA								
1 *Callahan*	Y	N	Y	Y	N	N	N	Y
2 *Dickinson*	N	N	Y	Y	Y	N	N	Y
3 Browder	Y	N	Y	Y	N	Y	N	Y
4 Bevill	Y	Y	Y	Y	N	Y	N	Y
5 Flippo	?	?	?	?	?	?	?	?
6 Erdreich	Y	N	Y	Y	Y	Y	Y	Y
7 Harris	Y	N	Y	Y	N	Y	N	Y
ALASKA								
AL *Young*	N	N	N	N	Y	N	N	Y
ARIZONA								
1 *Rhodes*	N	N	Y	Y	Y	N	N	Y
2 Udall	Y	Y	Y	Y	Y	Y	Y	Y
3 *Stump*	N	N	N	N	Y	N	N	Y
4 *Kyl*	N	N	N	N	Y	N	N	Y
5 *Kolbe*	X	X	Y	Y	N	N	N	Y
ARKANSAS								
1 Alexander	?	?	N	N	?	?	?	?
2 *Robinson*	?	X	?	#	?	?	#	?
3 *Hammerschmidt*	?	?	N	N	Y	N	N	Y
4 Anthony	Y	N	N	N	Y	Y	Y	Y
CALIFORNIA								
1 Bosco	Y	Y	Y	Y	N	Y	N	Y
2 *Herger*	N	N	N	N	Y	Y	N	Y
3 Matsui	Y	Y	N	N	Y	Y	Y	Y
4 Fazio	Y	Y	Y	Y	N	Y	Y	Y
5 Pelosi	Y	Y	Y	Y	Y	Y	Y	Y
6 Boxer	Y	Y	N	Y	Y	Y	Y	Y
7 Miller	Y	Y	Y	Y	Y	Y	Y	Y
8 Dellums	Y	Y	Y	Y	N	Y	Y	Y
9 Stark	Y	N	N	N	Y	Y	Y	Y
10 Edwards	Y	Y	Y	Y	Y	Y	Y	Y
11 Lantos	Y	Y	Y	Y	N	Y	Y	Y
12 *Campbell*	Y	Y	Y	Y	N	N	Y	Y
13 Mineta	Y	Y	Y	Y	Y	Y	Y	Y
14 *Shumway*	N	N	N	N	Y	N	N	Y
15 Condit	Y	Y	Y	Y	N	Y	Y	Y
16 Panetta	Y	Y	Y	Y	Y	Y	Y	Y
17 *Pashayan*	Y	N	Y	Y	Y	Y	N	Y
18 Lehman	Y	Y	Y	Y	N	Y	Y	Y
19 *Lagomarsino*	N	N	Y	Y	N	N	Y	Y
20 *Thomas*	X	?	?	X	#	X	X	?
21 *Gallegly*	N	N	Y	Y	N	N	Y	Y
22 *Moorhead*	N	N	Y	Y	N	N	N	Y
23 Beilenson	Y	Y	Y	Y	Y	N	Y	Y
24 Waxman	Y	Y	Y	Y	N	Y	Y	Y
25 Roybal	Y	N	Y	Y	Y	Y	Y	Y
26 Berman	Y	Y	Y	Y	N	Y	Y	Y
27 Levine	Y	Y	Y	Y	N	Y	Y	Y
28 Dixon	Y	Y	Y	Y	N	Y	Y	Y
29 Hawkins	#	#	Y	Y	N	Y	Y	Y
30 Martinez	Y	Y	Y	Y	N	Y	Y	Y
31 Dymally	Y	Y	Y	Y	N	Y	Y	Y
32 Anderson	Y	Y	Y	Y	N	Y	Y	Y
33 *Dreier*	N	N	Y	Y	Y	N	Y	Y
34 Torres	Y	Y	Y	Y	Y	Y	Y	Y
35 *Lewis*	N	N	Y	Y	N	N	N	Y
36 Brown	?	Y	Y	Y	N	Y	Y	?
37 *McCandless*	N	N	Y	Y	N	N	N	Y
38 *Dornan*	N	N	N	Y	Y	N	N	Y
39 *Dannemeyer*	N	N	N	N	Y	N	N	Y
40 *Cox*	N	N	N	Y	Y	N	+	Y
41 *Lowery*	N	N	Y	Y	N	N	N	Y
42 *Rohrabacher*	N	N	N	N	Y	N	N	Y
43 *Packard*	N	N	N	N	N	N	N	Y
44 Bates	Y	Y	Y	Y	N	Y	Y	Y
45 *Hunter*	N	N	N	N	Y	N	N	Y
COLORADO								
1 Schroeder	Y	N	Y	Y	N	Y	Y	Y
2 Skaggs	Y	Y	Y	Y	N	Y	Y	Y
3 Campbell	Y	N	Y	Y	N	Y	N	Y
4 *Brown*	N	N	N	N	Y	N	Y	Y
5 *Hefley*	N	N	N	N	Y	N	N	Y
6 *Schaefer*	N	N	Y	Y	N	Y	N	Y
CONNECTICUT								
1 Kennelly	Y	Y	N	N	Y	Y	Y	Y
2 Gejdenson	Y	Y	Y	Y	N	Y	Y	Y
3 Morrison	Y	Y	Y	Y	N	Y	Y	Y
4 *Shays*	Y	Y	Y	Y	N	N	Y	Y
5 *Rowland*	N	N	Y	Y	N	N	Y	Y
6 *Johnson*	N	N	N	N	Y	Y	Y	Y
DELAWARE								
AL Carper	Y	Y	Y	Y	N	Y	Y	Y
FLORIDA								
1 Hutto	N	N	N	N	N	N	N	+
2 *Grant*	N	N	Y	Y	N	N	Y	Y
3 Bennett	Y	Y	Y	Y	N	Y	Y	Y
4 *James*	N	N	N	N	N	N	Y	Y
5 *McCollum*	N	N	N	N	N	N	Y	Y
6 *Stearns*	N	N	Y	Y	N	N	Y	Y
7 Gibbons	Y	Y	N	N	N	Y	Y	Y
8 *Young*	N	N	N	N	N	N	Y	Y
9 *Bilirakis*	N	N	Y	Y	N	N	N	Y
10 *Ireland*	N	N	N	N	Y	N	Y	Y
11 Nelson	#	#	#	#	X	#	#	+
12 *Lewis*	N	N	N	N	Y	N	N	Y
13 *Goss*	N	N	Y	Y	Y	N	Y	Y
14 Johnston	Y	Y	Y	Y	N	Y	Y	Y
15 *Shaw*	N	N	N	N	Y	N	Y	Y
16 Smith	Y	Y	Y	Y	N	Y	Y	Y
17 Lehman	Y	Y	Y	Y	N	Y	Y	Y
18 *Ros-Lehtinen*	N	N	Y	Y	N	N	Y	Y
19 Fascell	Y	Y	Y	Y	N	Y	Y	Y
GEORGIA								
1 Thomas	N	N	Y	Y	N	Y	N	Y
2 Hatcher	N	N	Y	Y	Y	Y	N	Y
3 Ray	N	N	Y	Y	N	N	N	Y
4 Jones	Y	N	Y	Y	Y	Y	N	Y
5 Lewis	Y	Y	Y	Y	N	Y	Y	Y
6 *Gingrich*	N	N	N	Y	N	N	N	Y
7 Darden	N	N	Y	Y	N	Y	N	Y
8 Rowland	Y	N	Y	Y	N	Y	N	Y
9 Jenkins	N	N	N	N	Y	N	N	Y
10 Barnard	#	N	Y	Y	N	Y	N	Y
HAWAII								
1 *Saiki*	N	N	Y	Y	N	N	N	Y
2 Vacancy								
IDAHO								
1 *Craig*	X	?	X	X	?	X	X	Y
2 Stallings	Y	N	Y	Y	N	?	Y	Y
ILLINOIS								
1 Hayes	Y	N	Y	Y	Y	Y	Y	Y
2 Savage	Y	N	?	Y	Y	Y	Y	Y
3 Russo	Y	N	N	N	Y	Y	Y	Y
4 Sangmeister	Y	N	Y	Y	Y	Y	Y	Y
5 Lipinski	N	N	Y	Y	Y	Y	N	Y
6 *Hyde*	N	N	Y	Y	Y	N	N	Y
7 Collins	Y	Y	Y	Y	N	Y	Y	Y
8 Rostenkowski	Y	N	N	N	Y	Y	Y	Y
9 Yates	Y	Y	Y	Y	Y	Y	Y	Y
10 *Porter*	N	N	N	N	Y	N	N	Y
11 Annunzio	Y	N	Y	Y	Y	Y	Y	Y
12 *Crane*	N	N	N	N	Y	N	Y	Y
13 *Fawell*	N	N	N	Y	N	N	N	Y
14 *Hastert*	N	N	N	N	Y	N	N	Y
15 *Madigan*	N	N	Y	Y	N	N	N	Y
16 *Martin*	N	N	Y	Y	N	Y	N	Y
17 Evans	Y	Y	Y	Y	N	Y	Y	Y
18 *Michel*	N	N	Y	Y	Y	N	N	Y
19 Bruce	Y	Y	Y	Y	N	Y	N	Y
20 Durbin	Y	Y	Y	Y	Y	Y	N	Y
21 Costello	Y	N	N	N	Y	Y	Y	Y
22 Poshard	Y	N	N	N	Y	Y	Y	Y
INDIANA								
1 Visclosky	Y	Y	Y	Y	Y	Y	Y	Y
2 Sharp	Y	N	Y	Y	N	Y	N	Y
3 *Hiler*	N	N	Y	Y	Y	N	N	Y

ND Northern Democrats SD Southern Democrats

	127	128	129	130	131	132	133	134
4 Long	Y	N	Y	Y	Y	Y	Y	Y
5 Jontz	Y	N	Y	Y	N	Y	Y	Y
6 ***Burton***	N	N	N	N	Y	N	N	Y
7 ***Myers***	N	N	Y	Y	Y	N	N	Y
8 McCloskey	Y	Y	?	?	Y	Y	Y	Y
9 Hamilton	Y	Y	N	Y	Y	Y	N	Y
10 Jacobs	Y	Y	Y	Y	Y	Y	Y	Y
IOWA								
1 ***Leach***	Y	Y	Y	Y	N	N	Y	Y
2 ***Tauke***	Y	N	Y	Y	N	N	Y	Y
3 Nagle	Y	Y	Y	Y	N	Y	Y	Y
4 Smith	Y	Y	Y	Y	Y	Y	Y	Y
5 ***Lightfoot***	N	N	N	N	N	N	N	Y
6 ***Grandy***	Y	N	Y	N	Y	N	N	Y
KANSAS								
1 ***Roberts***	N	N	N	N	N	N	N	Y
2 Slattery	Y	Y	Y	Y	N	Y	Y	Y
3 ***Meyers***	N	N	Y	Y	N	N	Y	Y
4 Glickman	Y	Y	Y	Y	N	Y	Y	Y
5 ***Whittaker***	N	N	Y	Y	N	N	N	Y
KENTUCKY								
1 Hubbard	Y	N	Y	Y	N	Y	N	Y
2 Natcher	Y	Y	Y	Y	N	Y	Y	Y
3 Mazzoli	Y	N	Y	Y	N	Y	Y	Y
4 ***Bunning***	N	N	N	N	Y	Y	N	Y
5 ***Rogers***	N	N	N	N	Y	Y	N	Y
6 ***Hopkins***	N	N	N	N	Y	Y	N	Y
7 Perkins	Y	N	Y	Y	N	Y	Y	Y
LOUISIANA								
1 ***Livingston***	N	N	Y	Y	Y	N	N	Y
2 Boggs	Y	Y	Y	Y	Y	Y	Y	Y
3 Tauzin	N	N	Y	Y	Y	N	N	Y
4 ***McCrery***	N	N	Y	Y	N	N	N	Y
5 Huckaby	N	N	Y	Y	N	N	N	Y
6 ***Baker***	N	N	N	N	N	N	N	Y
7 Hayes	Y	N	Y	Y	N	Y	N	Y
8 ***Holloway***	N	N	N	N	Y	?	?	?
MAINE								
1 Brennan	Y	Y	Y	Y	N	Y	Y	Y
2 ***Snowe***	N	N	Y	Y	N	N	Y	Y
MARYLAND								
1 Dyson	Y	N	Y	Y	Y	Y	N	Y
2 ***Bentley***	N	N	N	N	Y	Y	N	Y
3 Cardin	Y	Y	N	N	Y	Y	Y	Y
4 McMillen	Y	N	Y	Y	N	Y	N	Y
5 Hoyer	Y	Y	Y	Y	N	Y	Y	Y
6 Byron	N	N	N	Y	Y	Y	N	Y
7 Mfume	Y	Y	Y	Y	N	Y	Y	Y
8 ***Morella***	Y	Y	Y	Y	N	N	Y	Y
MASSACHUSETTS								
1 ***Conte***	Y	Y	Y	Y	N	N	Y	Y
2 Neal	Y	Y	Y	Y	N	Y	Y	Y
3 Early	Y	Y	Y	Y	N	N	Y	Y
4 Frank	Y	Y	Y	Y	N	Y	Y	Y
5 Atkins	Y	Y	Y	Y	N	Y	Y	Y
6 Mavroules	Y	Y	Y	Y	N	Y	Y	Y
7 Markey	Y	Y	Y	Y	N	Y	Y	Y
8 Kennedy	Y	Y	Y	Y	N	Y	Y	Y
9 Moakley	Y	Y	Y	Y	N	Y	Y	Y
10 Studds	Y	Y	Y	Y	N	Y	Y	Y
11 Donnelly	Y	Y	N	N	Y	Y	Y	Y
MICHIGAN								
1 Conyers	Y	Y	Y	Y	N	Y	N	Y
2 ***Pursell***	Y	N	Y	Y	N	Y	N	Y
3 Wolpe	Y	Y	Y	Y	N	Y	Y	Y
4 ***Upton***	Y	N	N	N	N	Y	N	Y
5 ***Henry***	Y	N	Y	Y	N	Y	N	Y
6 Carr	Y	N	Y	Y	N	Y	N	Y
7 Kildee	Y	Y	Y	Y	N	Y	Y	Y
8 Traxler	Y	N	Y	Y	N	Y	N	Y
9 ***Vander Jagt***	N	N	Y	Y	Y	N	N	Y
10 ***Schuette***	N	N	Y	Y	N	Y	N	Y
11 ***Davis***	N	N	Y	Y	N	Y	Y	Y
12 Bonior	Y	Y	Y	Y	N	Y	N	Y
13 Crockett	Y	Y	Y	Y	Y	Y	Y	Y
14 Hertel	Y	Y	Y	Y	N	Y	Y	Y
15 Ford	Y	Y	Y	Y	N	Y	N	Y
16 Dingell	Y	Y	Y	Y	N	Y	N	Y
17 Levin	Y	Y	N	N	Y	Y	N	Y
18 ***Broomfield***	N	N	Y	Y	N	Y	N	Y
MINNESOTA								
1 Penny	Y	Y	Y	Y	Y	Y	Y	Y
2 ***Weber***	N	N	Y	Y	N	N	Y	Y
3 ***Frenzel***	N	N	?	?	Y	N	N	?
4 Vento	Y	Y	Y	Y	N	Y	Y	Y

	127	128	129	130	131	132	133	134
5 Sabo	Y	Y	Y	Y	Y	Y	Y	Y
6 Sikorski	Y	N	Y	Y	N	Y	Y	Y
7 ***Stangeland***	N	N	Y	Y	Y	Y	N	Y
8 Oberstar	Y	Y	Y	Y	N	Y	Y	Y
MISSISSIPPI								
1 Whitten	Y	Y	Y	Y	N	Y	N	Y
2 Espy	Y	Y	Y	Y	N	Y	N	Y
3 Montgomery	N	N	Y	Y	N	N	N	Y
4 Parker	N	N	Y	Y	N	N	N	Y
5 Taylor	Y	N	Y	N	N	Y	Y	Y
MISSOURI								
1 Clay	Y	Y	Y	Y	N	Y	Y	Y
2 ***Buechner***	N	N	N	N	N	N	Y	Y
3 Gephardt	Y	Y	Y	Y	N	Y	Y	Y
4 Skelton	N	N	Y	Y	Y	Y	N	Y
5 Wheat	Y	Y	Y	Y	N	Y	Y	Y
6 ***Coleman***	N	N	Y	Y	N	N	Y	Y
7 ***Hancock***	N	N	N	N	Y	N	N	Y
8 ***Emerson***	N	N	N	N	N	Y	N	Y
9 Volkmer	Y	N	Y	Y	N	Y	N	Y
MONTANA								
1 Williams	Y	N	Y	Y	N	#	#	?
2 ***Marlenee***	X	?	N	N	N	N	N	Y
NEBRASKA								
1 ***Bereuter***	Y	N	Y	Y	N	N	N	Y
2 Hoagland	N	N	Y	Y	N	Y	Y	Y
3 ***Smith***	N	N	Y	Y	N	N	N	Y
NEVADA								
1 Bilbray	Y	Y	Y	Y	N	Y	Y	Y
2 ***Vucanovich***	N	N	N	N	Y	N	N	Y
NEW HAMPSHIRE								
1 ***Smith***	N	N	Y	Y	N	N	N	Y
2 ***Douglas***	N	N	Y	Y	N	N	Y	Y
NEW JERSEY								
1 Vacancy								
2 Hughes	Y	N	Y	Y	Y	Y	Y	Y
3 Pallone	Y	Y	Y	Y	N	Y	Y	Y
4 ***Smith***	N	N	Y	Y	N	Y	Y	Y
5 ***Roukema***	Y	N	Y	Y	N	N	Y	Y
6 Dwyer	Y	Y	Y	Y	N	Y	Y	Y
7 ***Rinaldo***	Y	N	Y	Y	N	Y	Y	Y
8 Roe	Y	Y	Y	Y	N	Y	Y	Y
9 Torricelli	Y	Y	Y	Y	Y	Y	Y	Y
10 Payne	Y	Y	Y	Y	N	Y	Y	Y
11 ***Gallo***	N	N	Y	Y	N	N	Y	Y
12 ***Courter***	N	N	Y	Y	N	N	Y	Y
13 ***Saxton***	N	N	Y	Y	N	N	?	Y
14 Guarini	Y	N	N	N	Y	Y	Y	Y
NEW MEXICO								
1 ***Schiff***	N	N	Y	Y	N	Y	N	Y
2 ***Skeen***	N	N	Y	Y	N	N	N	Y
3 Richardson	Y	Y	Y	Y	N	Y	Y	Y
NEW YORK								
1 Hochbrueckner	Y	N	Y	Y	N	Y	Y	Y
2 Downey	Y	Y	N	N	Y	Y	Y	Y
3 Mrazek	Y	Y	Y	Y	Y	Y	Y	Y
4 ***Lent***	N	N	Y	Y	N	N	N	Y
5 ***McGrath***	Y	N	N	N	Y	Y	Y	Y
6 Flake	Y	Y	Y	Y	N	Y	N	Y
7 Ackerman	Y	Y	Y	Y	N	Y	Y	Y
8 Scheuer	Y	Y	Y	Y	N	Y	Y	Y
9 Manton	Y	Y	Y	Y	N	Y	N	Y
10 Schumer	Y	Y	Y	Y	Y	Y	Y	Y
11 Towns	Y	Y	Y	Y	N	Y	N	Y
12 Owens	Y	Y	Y	Y	N	Y	Y	Y
13 Solarz	Y	Y	Y	Y	N	Y	Y	Y
14 ***Molinari***	N	N	Y	Y	N	N	Y	Y
15 ***Green***	Y	Y	Y	Y	N	N	Y	Y
16 Rangel	Y	Y	N	N	Y	Y	Y	Y
17 Weiss	Y	Y	Y	Y	N	Y	Y	Y
18 Serrano	Y	Y	Y	Y	N	Y	Y	Y
19 Engel	Y	Y	Y	Y	N	Y	Y	Y
20 Lowey	Y	Y	Y	Y	Y	Y	Y	Y
21 ***Fish***	?	?	Y	Y	N	Y	Y	Y
22 ***Gilman***	Y	Y	Y	Y	N	Y	Y	Y
23 McNulty	Y	Y	Y	Y	N	Y	Y	Y
24 ***Solomon***	N	N	Y	Y	N	Y	Y	Y
25 ***Boehlert***	Y	Y	Y	Y	N	N	Y	Y
26 ***Martin***	N	N	Y	Y	N	Y	Y	Y
27 ***Walsh***	Y	N	Y	Y	N	Y	Y	Y
28 McHugh	Y	Y	Y	Y	N	Y	Y	Y
29 ***Horton***	Y	Y	Y	Y	N	Y	Y	Y
30 Slaughter	Y	Y	Y	Y	N	Y	Y	Y
31 ***Paxon***	N	N	Y	Y	N	N	N	Y

	127	128	129	130	131	132	133	134
32 LaFalce	Y	Y	Y	Y	N	Y	Y	Y
33 Nowak	Y	Y	Y	Y	N	Y	Y	Y
34 ***Houghton***	N	N	Y	Y	Y	Y	Y	Y
NORTH CAROLINA								
1 Jones	Y	N	Y	Y	Y	Y	N	Y
2 Valentine	Y	N	Y	Y	N	N	Y	Y
3 Lancaster	N	N	Y	Y	Y	Y	Y	Y
4 Price	Y	Y	Y	Y	N	Y	Y	Y
5 Neal	Y	N	Y	Y	N	N	Y	Y
6 ***Coble***	N	N	N	N	Y	N	N	Y
7 Rose	Y	Y	Y	Y	Y	Y	Y	Y
8 Hefner	Y	N	Y	Y	Y	Y	Y	Y
9 ***McMillan***	N	N	Y	Y	N	N	N	Y
10 ***Ballenger***	N	N	N	N	Y	N	N	Y
11 Clarke	Y	Y	Y	Y	N	N	Y	Y
NORTH DAKOTA								
AL Dorgan	Y	Y	N	N	Y	Y	N	Y
OHIO								
1 Luken	Y	Y	Y	Y	N	Y	N	Y
2 ***Gradison***	N	N	Y	Y	N	N	N	Y
3 Hall	Y	Y	Y	Y	N	Y	Y	Y
4 ***Oxley***	N	N	Y	Y	N	Y	N	Y
5 ***Gillmor***	N	N	Y	Y	N	N	Y	Y
6 ***McEwen***	N	N	N	N	Y	Y	N	Y
7 ***DeWine***	N	N	N	N	N	Y	N	Y
8 ***Lukens***	?	?	?	?	?	?	?	?
9 Kaptur	Y	N	Y	Y	N	Y	Y	Y
10 ***Miller***	N	N	N	N	Y	Y	N	Y
11 Eckart	Y	N	Y	Y	N	Y	N	Y
12 ***Kasich***	N	N	N	N	Y	Y	N	Y
13 Pease	Y	N	N	N	Y	Y	Y	Y
14 Sawyer	Y	N	Y	N	N	Y	Y	Y
15 ***Wylie***	N	N	Y	Y	N	N	Y	Y
16 ***Regula***	Y	N	N	N	Y	Y	N	Y
17 Traficant	Y	N	N	Y	Y	Y	N	Y
18 Applegate	Y	N	N	N	Y	Y	N	Y
19 Feighan	Y	Y	Y	Y	N	Y	Y	Y
20 Oakar	Y	N	N	N	N	Y	N	Y
21 Stokes	#	#	Y	N	N	Y	Y	Y
OKLAHOMA								
1 ***Inhofe***	N	N	N	N	Y	N	N	Y
2 Synar	Y	Y	Y	Y	N	Y	Y	Y
3 Watkins	?	?	?	?	N	Y	N	Y
4 McCurdy	N	N	Y	Y	N	N	Y	Y
5 ***Edwards***	N	N	N	N	Y	N	N	Y
6 English	N	N	Y	Y	N	Y	N	Y
OREGON								
1 AuCoin	Y	Y	Y	Y	Y	Y	Y	Y
2 ***Smith, B.***	N	N	N	N	N	Y	N	Y
3 Wyden	Y	Y	Y	Y	N	Y	Y	Y
4 DeFazio	Y	Y	Y	Y	N	Y	Y	Y
5 ***Smith, D.***	-	X	N	Y	Y	N	N	Y
PENNSYLVANIA								
1 Foglietta	Y	Y	Y	Y	Y	Y	Y	Y
2 Gray	Y	Y	Y	Y	N	Y	Y	?
3 Borski	Y	Y	Y	Y	Y	Y	Y	Y
4 Kolter	Y	N	Y	Y	Y	Y	N	Y
5 ***Schulze***	N	N	N	N	Y	Y	Y	Y
6 Yatron	Y	Y	Y	Y	Y	Y	N	Y
7 ***Weldon***	Y	N	Y	Y	N	Y	Y	Y
8 Kostmayer	Y	Y	Y	Y	Y	Y	Y	Y
9 ***Shuster***	N	N	N	N	Y	N	N	Y
10 ***McDade***	N	N	Y	Y	N	Y	Y	Y
11 Kanjorski	Y	N	Y	Y	Y	Y	Y	Y
12 Murtha	Y	Y	Y	Y	Y	Y	Y	Y
13 ***Coughlin***	Y	N	Y	Y	N	N	Y	Y
14 Coyne	Y	Y	N	N	Y	Y	Y	Y
15 ***Ritter***	N	N	N	N	Y	Y	N	Y
16 ***Walker***	N	N	N	N	Y	N	Y	Y
17 ***Gekas***	N	N	N	N	Y	N	N	Y
18 Walgren	Y	N	Y	Y	N	Y	Y	Y
19 ***Goodling***	N	Y	N	N	N	Y	N	Y
20 Gaydos	Y	N	Y	Y	Y	Y	Y	Y
21 ***Ridge***	Y	Y	?	Y	?	Y	Y	Y
22 Murphy	Y	N	Y	Y	Y	Y	N	Y
23 ***Clinger***	N	N	N	N	Y	+	+	+
RHODE ISLAND								
1 ***Machtley***	Y	Y	Y	Y	N	N	Y	Y
2 ***Schneider***	Y	Y	Y	Y	N	N	Y	Y
SOUTH CAROLINA								
1 ***Ravenel***	N	N	Y	Y	N	N	Y	Y
2 ***Spence***	N	N	Y	Y	N	N	Y	Y
3 Derrick	Y	N	Y	Y	Y	Y	Y	Y
4 Patterson	Y	N	Y	Y	N	Y	Y	Y
5 Spratt	Y	Y	Y	Y	N	Y	Y	Y
6 Tallon	N	N	Y	Y	Y	Y	Y	Y

	127	128	129	130	131	132	133	134
SOUTH DAKOTA								
AL Johnson	Y	N	Y	Y	N	Y	Y	Y
TENNESSEE								
1 ***Quillen***	N	N	N	Y	Y	Y	N	Y
2 ***Duncan***	N	N	N	N	Y	Y	N	Y
3 Lloyd	N	N	Y	Y	Y	Y	Y	Y
4 Cooper	N	N	Y	Y	N	N	N	Y
5 Clement	Y	Y	Y	Y	Y	Y	N	Y
6 Gordon	Y	Y	Y	Y	N	Y	Y	Y
7 ***Sundquist***	N	N	N	N	Y	N	N	Y
8 Tanner	Y	N	Y	Y	N	Y	N	Y
9 Ford	Y	Y	Y	N	Y	Y	Y	Y
TEXAS								
1 Chapman	Y	N	Y	Y	N	Y	N	Y
2 Wilson	N	N	Y	Y	N	Y	Y	Y
3 ***Bartlett***	N	N	N	N	Y	N	N	Y
4 Hall	N	N	Y	Y	N	N	N	Y
5 Bryant	Y	N	Y	Y	N	Y	Y	Y
6 ***Barton***	?	?	?	?	?	?	X	Y
7 ***Archer***	N	N	N	N	Y	N	N	Y
8 ***Fields***	N	N	Y	Y	N	N	N	Y
9 Brooks	Y	Y	Y	Y	Y	Y	Y	Y
10 Pickle	Y	Y	N	N	Y	N	Y	Y
11 Leath	?	?	?	Y	Y	Y	N	?
12 Geren	N	N	Y	Y	Y	Y	N	Y
13 Sarpalius	N	N	Y	Y	N	Y	N	Y
14 Laughlin	N	N	Y	Y	Y	Y	N	Y
15 de la Garza	Y	Y	Y	Y	Y	Y	Y	Y
16 Coleman	Y	Y	Y	Y	N	Y	Y	Y
17 Stenholm	N	N	Y	Y	Y	N	N	Y
18 Washington	Y	Y	?	Y	N	Y	Y	?
19 ***Combest***	N	N	N	N	Y	N	N	Y
20 Gonzalez	Y	Y	Y	Y	N	Y	Y	Y
21 ***Smith***	N	N	N	N	Y	N	N	Y
22 ***DeLay***	N	N	N	N	Y	N	N	Y
23 Bustamante	Y	Y	Y	Y	N	Y	N	Y
24 Frost	Y	Y	Y	Y	Y	Y	Y	Y
25 Andrews	Y	N	N	N	Y	N	Y	Y
26 ***Armey***	N	N	N	N	Y	N	N	Y
27 Ortiz	Y	Y	Y	Y	Y	Y	N	Y
UTAH								
1 ***Hansen***	N	N	N	N	Y	N	N	Y
2 Owens	Y	Y	Y	Y	N	Y	Y	Y
3 ***Nielson***	N	N	Y	Y	N	N	N	Y
VERMONT								
AL ***Smith***	Y	Y	Y	Y	N	N	Y	Y
VIRGINIA								
1 ***Bateman***	N	N	Y	Y	Y	N	N	Y
2 Pickett	N	N	Y	Y	Y	N	N	Y
3 ***Bliley***	N	N	Y	Y	N	N	N	Y
4 Sisisky	N	N	N	N	Y	N	N	Y
5 Payne	Y	N	Y	Y	N	Y	N	Y
6 Olin	Y	Y	Y	Y	N	Y	Y	Y
7 ***Slaughter***	N	N	N	N	Y	N	N	Y
8 ***Parris***	N	N	Y	Y	N	N	N	Y
9 Boucher	Y	Y	Y	Y	N	Y	N	Y
10 ***Wolf***	N	N	Y	Y	N	N	N	Y
WASHINGTON								
1 ***Miller***	Y	Y	Y	Y	N	N	Y	Y
2 Swift	Y	Y	Y	Y	N	Y	Y	Y
3 Unsoeld	Y	Y	Y	Y	N	Y	Y	Y
4 ***Morrison***	Y	Y	Y	N	Y	N	N	Y
5 Foley								
6 Dicks	Y	Y	Y	Y	N	Y	Y	?
7 McDermott	Y	N	Y	N	Y	Y	Y	Y
8 ***Chandler***	Y	N	N	N	Y	N	N	Y
WEST VIRGINIA								
1 Mollohan	Y	N	Y	N	Y	Y	N	Y
2 Staggers	Y	Y	Y	Y	Y	Y	N	Y
3 Wise	Y	Y	Y	Y	N	Y	N	Y
4 Rahall	Y	N	Y	Y	Y	Y	Y	Y
WISCONSIN								
1 Aspin	Y	N	Y	Y	N	Y	N	Y
2 Kastenmeier	Y	Y	Y	Y	N	Y	Y	Y
3 ***Gunderson***	N	N	Y	Y	N	N	Y	Y
4 Kleczka	Y	Y	Y	Y	Y	Y	Y	Y
5 Moody	Y	Y	N	N	Y	Y	Y	Y
6 ***Petri***	N	N	N	Y	N	N	Y	Y
7 Obey	Y	Y	Y	Y	N	Y	Y	Y
8 ***Roth***	N	N	N	N	N	N	N	Y
9 ***Sensenbrenner***	N	N	N	N	N	N	N	Y
WYOMING								
AL ***Thomas***	N	N	Y	N	Y	N	N	Y

Southern states - Ala., Ark., Fla., Ga., Ky., La., Miss., N.C., Okla., S.C., Tenn., Texas, Va.
Omitted votes are quorum calls, which CQ does not include in its vote charts.

HOUSE VOTES 135, 136, 137, 138, 139, 140, 141, 142

135. HR 3030. Clean Air Act Reauthorization/Offshore Emissions. Dingell, D-Mich., amendment to regulate emissions from offshore oil and gas platforms. Adopted 411-5: R 166-4; D 245-1 (ND 168-0, SD 77-1), May 23, 1990.

136. HR 3030. Clean Air Act Reauthorization/Demonstration Program. Dingell, D-Mich., amendment to require the use of clean-fuel vehicles in commercial motor vehicle fleets and urban bus fleets in the nation's largest or most polluted cities, and to establish a clean-fuel vehicle demonstration program in California. Adopted 405-15: R 154-15; D 251-0 (ND 173-0, SD 78-0), May 23, 1990.

137. HR 3030. Clean Air Act Reauthorization/Passage. Passage of the bill to amend the Clean Air Act to attain and maintain national ambient air quality standards, require reductions of emissions in motor vehicles, control toxic air pollutants, reduce acid rain, establish a system of federal permits and enforcement, and otherwise improve the quality of the nation's air. Passed 401-21: R 154-16; D 247-5 (ND 169-4, SD 78-1), May 23, 1990.

138. HR 4404. Fiscal 1990 Supplemental Appropriations/Conference Report. Adoption of the conference report on the bill to provide $4.3 billion in new budget authority, including $3.5 billion for domestic programs and $885 million for foreign aid, of which $420 million is for Panama and $300 million is for Nicaragua. The bill would also rescind $2 billion in previously appropriated defense funds to offset new spending. Adopted 308-108: R 105-64; D 203-44 (ND 137-33, SD 66-11), May 24, 1990.

139. HR 4404. Fiscal 1990 Supplemental Appropriations/Fish Farms. Whitten, D-Miss., motion that the House recede from its disagreement with a Senate amendment to procure a fish farming laboratory in Arkansas. Approval was necessary to allow the House to consider an amendment to provide $6 million to procure a fish and wildlife refugee in central Iowa. Motion agreed to 246-160: R 32-130; D 214-30 (ND 152-17, SD 62-13), May 24, 1990. (The amendment was subsequently approved by voice vote.)

140. HR 4404. Fiscal 1990 Supplemental Appropriations/Samoan Ferry. Whitten, D-Miss., motion that the House recede from its disagreement to a Senate amendment to provide funds to transfer a ferryboat to the government of American Samoa. Motion agreed to 284-123: R 50-116; D 234-7 (ND 160-5, SD 74-2), May 24, 1990.

141. HR 4404. Fiscal 1990 Supplemental Appropriations/Explosives Production. Whitten, D-Miss., motion that the House recede from its disagreement with a Senate amendment to provide $238 million to build an explosives production facility at the Louisiana Army Ammunition Plant. Rejected 33-376: R 6-162; D 27-214 (ND 10-156, SD 17-58), May 24, 1990.

142. HR 4404. Fiscal 1990 Supplemental Appropriations/Prior Authorization. Whitten, D-Miss., motion that the House recede from its disagreement and concur in the Senate amendment to waive requirements that prohibit foreign aid appropriations without prior authorization. Motion agreed to 277-126: R 156-8; D 121-118 (ND 61-101, SD 60-17), May 24, 1990.

KEY

Y Voted for (yea).
\# Paired for.
\+ Announced for.
N Voted against (nay).
X Paired against.
\- Announced against.
P Voted "present."
C Voted "present" to avoid possible conflict of interest.
? Did not vote or otherwise make a position known.

Democrats ***Republicans***

	135	136	137	138	139	140	141	142
ALABAMA								
1 ***Callahan***	Y	Y	Y	N	?	?	?	?
2 ***Dickinson***	Y	Y	Y	Y	N	N	N	Y
3 Browder	Y	Y	Y	Y	Y	Y	N	Y
4 Bevill	Y	Y	Y	Y	Y	Y	Y	Y
5 Flippo	?	?	?	?	?	?	?	?
6 Erdreich	Y	Y	Y	Y	Y	Y	N	Y
7 Harris	Y	Y	Y	Y	Y	Y	N	Y
ALASKA								
AL ***Young***	N	N	Y	Y	Y	Y	Y	?
ARIZONA								
1 ***Rhodes***	Y	Y	Y	Y	N	Y	N	Y
2 Udall	Y	Y	Y	Y	?	?	?	?
3 ***Stump***	N	N	N	N	N	N	N	Y
4 ***Kyl***	Y	Y	Y	Y	N	N	N	Y
5 ***Kolbe***	Y	Y	Y	Y	N	N	N	Y
ARKANSAS								
1 Alexander	?	?	?	?	?	?	?	?
2 ***Robinson***	?	#	?	?	?	?	?	?
3 ***Hammerschmidt***	Y	N	Y	Y	N	N	N	Y
4 Anthony	Y	Y	Y	Y	Y	Y	N	N
CALIFORNIA								
1 Bosco	Y	Y	Y	Y	Y	Y	N	Y
2 ***Herger***	Y	Y	Y	N	N	N	N	Y
3 Matsui	Y	Y	Y	Y	Y	Y	N	N
4 Fazio	Y	Y	Y	Y	Y	Y	Y	Y
5 Pelosi	Y	Y	Y	Y	Y	Y	N	N
6 Boxer	Y	Y	Y	Y	Y	Y	N	N
7 Miller	?	Y	Y	N	Y	Y	N	N
8 Dellums	Y	Y	Y	Y	Y	Y	N	N
9 Stark	Y	Y	Y	N	Y	Y	N	N
10 Edwards	Y	Y	Y	Y	Y	Y	N	?
11 Lantos	Y	Y	Y	Y	Y	Y	N	N
12 ***Campbell***	Y	Y	Y	N	N	N	N	Y
13 Mineta	Y	Y	Y	Y	Y	Y	N	Y
14 ***Shumway***	Y	N	Y	N	N	N	N	Y
15 Condit	Y	Y	Y	Y	Y	?	N	N
16 Panetta	Y	Y	Y	N	N	Y	N	N
17 ***Pashayan***	Y	Y	Y	N	Y	Y	N	Y
18 Lehman	Y	Y	Y	Y	Y	Y	N	N
19 ***Lagomarsino***	Y	Y	Y	Y	N	Y	N	Y
20 ***Thomas***	?	X	?	?	?	?	?	?
21 ***Gallegly***	Y	Y	Y	Y	N	N	N	Y
22 ***Moorhead***	Y	Y	Y	N	N	N	N	Y
23 Beilenson	Y	Y	Y	Y	Y	Y	N	Y
24 Waxman	Y	Y	Y	Y	Y	Y	?	N
25 Roybal	Y	Y	Y	Y	Y	Y	Y	N
26 Berman	Y	Y	Y	Y	Y	Y	N	N
27 Levine	Y	Y	Y	Y	Y	Y	N	N
28 Dixon	Y	Y	Y	Y	Y	Y	N	N
29 Hawkins	?	Y	Y	N	Y	Y	N	?
30 Martinez	Y	Y	Y	Y	Y	Y	Y	N
31 Dymally	Y	Y	Y	?	?	?	?	X
32 Anderson	Y	Y	Y	Y	Y	Y	N	Y
33 ***Dreier***	Y	Y	Y	Y	N	N	N	Y
34 Torres	Y	Y	Y	Y	Y	Y	N	Y
35 ***Lewis***	Y	Y	Y	Y	Y	Y	N	Y
36 Brown	Y	Y	Y	Y	Y	Y	N	Y
37 ***McCandless***	Y	Y	Y	N	N	N	N	Y
38 ***Dornan***	Y	Y	Y	N	N	Y	N	Y
39 ***Dannemeyer***	Y	Y	N	N	N	N	N	Y
40 ***Cox***	Y	Y	Y	N	N	N	N	Y
41 ***Lowery***	Y	Y	Y	Y	?	Y	N	Y
42 ***Rohrabacher***	Y	Y	Y	N	N	N	N	Y
43 ***Packard***	Y	Y	Y	N	N	Y	N	Y
44 Bates	Y	Y	Y	N	N	N	N	N
45 ***Hunter***	Y	Y	Y	Y	N	Y	N	Y
COLORADO								
1 Schroeder	Y	Y	Y	N	N	Y	N	N
2 Skaggs	Y	Y	Y	Y	Y	Y	N	N
3 Campbell	Y	Y	Y	Y	Y	Y	N	N
4 ***Brown***	Y	Y	Y	Y	N	N	N	N
5 ***Hefley***	Y	N	Y	N	N	N	N	Y
6 ***Schaefer***	Y	Y	Y	N	N	N	N	Y
CONNECTICUT								
1 Kennelly	Y	Y	Y	N	Y	Y	N	N
2 Gejdenson	Y	Y	Y	Y	Y	Y	N	N
3 Morrison	Y	Y	Y	N	Y	Y	N	—
4 ***Shays***	Y	Y	Y	Y	N	N	N	Y
5 ***Rowland***	Y	Y	Y	N	N	N	N	Y
6 ***Johnson***	Y	Y	Y	Y	N	N	N	Y
DELAWARE								
AL Carper	Y	Y	Y	Y	N	Y	N	N
FLORIDA								
1 Hutto	Y	Y	Y	Y	N	Y	N	Y
2 ***Grant***	Y	Y	Y	Y	N	N	N	Y
3 Bennett	Y	Y	Y	Y	Y	Y	N	Y
4 ***James***	Y	Y	Y	Y	N	N	N	Y
5 ***McCollum***	Y	Y	Y	Y	N	N	N	Y
6 ***Stearns***	Y	Y	Y	Y	N	N	N	Y
7 Gibbons	Y	Y	Y	?	?	Y	N	Y
8 ***Young***	Y	Y	Y	Y	N	Y	N	Y
9 ***Bilirakis***	Y	Y	Y	Y	N	N	N	Y
10 ***Ireland***	Y	Y	Y	?	?	?	?	?
11 Nelson	+	+	+	#	+	+	—	+
12 ***Lewis***	Y	Y	Y	N	—	—	—	—
13 ***Goss***	Y	Y	Y	Y	N	Y	N	Y
14 Johnston	Y	Y	Y	Y	N	Y	N	N
15 ***Shaw***	Y	Y	Y	Y	N	Y	N	Y
16 Smith	Y	Y	Y	Y	Y	Y	Y	Y
17 Lehman	Y	Y	Y	Y	Y	Y	Y	Y
18 ***Ros-Lehtinen***	Y	Y	Y	Y	N	N	N	Y
19 Fascell	Y	Y	Y	Y	Y	Y	Y	N
GEORGIA								
1 Thomas	Y	?	Y	Y	Y	Y	N	Y
2 Hatcher	Y	Y	Y	Y	?	Y	N	Y
3 Ray	Y	Y	Y	N	Y	Y	N	N
4 Jones	Y	Y	Y	Y	Y	Y	N	Y
5 Lewis	Y	Y	Y	Y	Y	Y	N	N
6 ***Gingrich***	Y	Y	Y	Y	?	N	N	Y
7 Darden	Y	Y	Y	Y	Y	Y	N	Y
8 Rowland	Y	Y	Y	N	Y	Y	N	Y
9 Jenkins	?	Y	Y	N	Y	Y	N	Y
10 Barnard	Y	Y	Y	X	?	?	?	?
HAWAII								
1 ***Saiki***	Y	Y	Y	Y	N	Y	N	Y
2 Vacancy								
IDAHO								
1 ***Craig***	Y	Y	Y	N	N	N	N	Y
2 Stallings	Y	Y	Y	Y	Y	Y	N	Y
ILLINOIS								
1 Hayes	Y	Y	Y	Y	Y	Y	Y	N
2 Savage	Y	Y	Y	Y	Y	Y	N	N
3 Russo	?	Y	Y	N	Y	Y	N	N
4 Sangmeister	Y	Y	Y	N	Y	Y	N	N
5 Lipinski	Y	Y	Y	Y	Y	Y	N	Y
6 ***Hyde***	Y	Y	Y	Y	N	Y	N	Y
7 Collins	Y	Y	Y	Y	Y	Y	N	Y
8 Rostenkowski	?	Y	Y	N	N	Y	N	N
9 Yates	Y	Y	Y	Y	Y	Y	N	Y
10 ***Porter***	Y	Y	Y	Y	Y	Y	N	Y
11 Annunzio	Y	Y	Y	Y	Y	Y	N	Y
12 ***Crane***	Y	N	N	N	N	Y	N	N
13 ***Fawell***	Y	Y	Y	N	N	N	N	Y
14 ***Hastert***	Y	Y	Y	N	N	N	N	Y
15 ***Madigan***	Y	Y	Y	Y	N	Y	N	Y
16 ***Martin***	Y	Y	Y	Y	N	N	N	Y
17 Evans	Y	Y	Y	Y	Y	Y	N	N
18 ***Michel***	Y	Y	Y	Y	?	N	N	Y
19 Bruce	Y	Y	Y	Y	Y	Y	N	N
20 Durbin	Y	Y	Y	Y	Y	Y	N	Y
21 Costello	Y	Y	N	Y	Y	Y	N	N
22 Poshard	Y	Y	N	Y	Y	Y	N	N
INDIANA								
1 Visclosky	Y	Y	Y	Y	Y	Y	N	N
2 Sharp	Y	Y	Y	N	Y	Y	N	Y
3 ***Hiler***	Y	Y	Y	Y	N	N	N	Y

ND Northern Democrats SD Southern Democrats

	135	136	137	138	139	140	141	142
4 Long	Y	Y	Y	N	N	Y	N	Y
5 Jontz	Y	Y	Y	N	Y	Y	N	N
6 ***Burton***	Y	N	N	Y	N	Y	N	Y
7 ***Myers***	Y	Y	N	N	Y	N	N	Y
8 McCloskey	Y	Y	Y	Y	Y	Y	N	N
9 Hamilton	Y	Y	Y	Y	N	N	N	N
10 Jacobs	Y	Y	Y	Y	N	Y	N	N
IOWA								
1 ***Leach***	Y	Y	Y	Y	Y	N	N	Y
2 ***Tauke***	Y	Y	Y	N	Y	N	N	Y
3 Nagle	Y	Y	Y	Y	Y	?	N	?
4 Smith	Y	Y	Y	Y	Y	Y	Y	Y
5 ***Lightfoot***	Y	Y	N	Y	Y	Y	N	Y
6 ***Grandy***	Y	Y	Y	Y	Y	Y	N	Y
KANSAS								
1 ***Roberts***	Y	Y	Y	N	N	Y	N	Y
2 Slattery	Y	Y	Y	N	N	Y	N	N
3 ***Meyers***	Y	Y	Y	Y	N	N	N	Y
4 Glickman	Y	Y	Y	N	N	Y	N	Y
5 ***Whittaker***	Y	Y	Y	Y	N	N	N	Y
KENTUCKY								
1 Hubbard	Y	Y	N	N	Y	Y	N	N
2 Natcher	Y	Y	Y	Y	Y	Y	Y	Y
3 Mazzoli	Y	Y	Y	Y	Y	Y	N	Y
4 ***Bunning***	Y	Y	Y	?	?	?	?	#
5 ***Rogers***	Y	Y	Y	Y	Y	N	N	Y
6 ***Hopkins***	Y	Y	Y	N	N	N	N	N
7 Perkins	Y	Y	Y	Y	Y	Y	N	Y
LOUISIANA								
1 ***Livingston***	Y	Y	Y	Y	Y	N	Y	Y
2 Boggs	Y	Y	Y	Y	Y	Y	Y	Y
3 Tauzin	Y	Y	Y	Y	Y	Y	Y	Y
4 ***McCrery***	Y	Y	Y	Y	N	Y	Y	Y
5 Huckaby	Y	Y	Y	Y	N	Y	Y	Y
6 ***Baker***	Y	Y	Y	N	N	N	Y	Y
7 Hayes	Y	Y	Y	N	Y	Y	Y	Y
8 ***Holloway***	?	?	?	Y	N	N	Y	Y
MAINE								
1 Brennan	Y	Y	Y	Y	Y	Y	N	Y
2 ***Snowe***	Y	Y	Y	N	N	N	N	N
MARYLAND								
1 Dyson	Y	Y	Y	Y	Y	Y	N	Y
2 ***Bentley***	Y	N	Y	Y	N	N	N	Y
3 Cardin	Y	Y	Y	Y	Y	Y	N	N
4 McMillen	Y	Y	Y	Y	Y	Y	N	Y
5 Hoyer	Y	Y	Y	Y	Y	Y	N	Y
6 Byron	Y	Y	Y	Y	Y	Y	N	Y
7 Mfume	Y	Y	Y	Y	Y	Y	N	N
8 ***Morella***	Y	Y	Y	Y	N	N	N	Y
MASSACHUSETTS								
1 ***Conte***	Y	Y	Y	Y	Y	N	N	Y
2 Neal	Y	Y	Y	Y	Y	Y	N	N
3 Early	Y	Y	Y	Y	Y	Y	N	Y
4 Frank	Y	Y	Y	Y	Y	Y	N	N
5 Atkins	Y	Y	Y	Y	Y	Y	N	N
6 Mavroules	Y	Y	Y	Y	Y	Y	N	N
7 Markey	Y	Y	Y	Y	Y	Y	N	N
8 Kennedy	Y	Y	Y	Y	Y	Y	N	N
9 Moakley	Y	Y	Y	Y	Y	Y	N	?
10 Studds	Y	Y	Y	Y	Y	Y	N	N
11 Donnelly	Y	Y	Y	N	Y	Y	N	N
MICHIGAN								
1 Conyers	Y	Y	Y	Y	Y	Y	N	N
2 ***Pursell***	Y	Y	Y	Y	Y	Y	N	Y
3 Wolpe	Y	Y	Y	N	N	Y	N	N
4 ***Upton***	Y	Y	Y	N	N	N	N	Y
5 ***Henry***	Y	Y	Y	N	N	?	N	Y
6 Carr	Y	Y	Y	Y	Y	Y	N	Y
7 Kildee	Y	Y	Y	Y	Y	Y	N	Y
8 Traxler	Y	Y	Y	Y	Y	Y	N	Y
9 ***Vander Jagt***	Y	Y	Y	N	N	N	N	Y
10 ***Schuette***	Y	Y	Y	Y	N	N	N	Y
11 ***Davis***	Y	Y	Y	Y	Y	Y	N	Y
12 Bonior	Y	Y	Y	Y	Y	Y	N	Y
13 Crockett	Y	Y	Y	N	Y	?	N	N
14 Hertel	Y	Y	Y	Y	Y	Y	N	N
15 Ford	Y	Y	Y	Y	Y	?	N	N
16 Dingell	Y	Y	Y	Y	Y	Y	N	Y
17 Levin	Y	Y	Y	Y	Y	Y	N	Y
18 ***Broomfield***	Y	Y	Y	Y	N	Y	N	Y
MINNESOTA								
1 Penny	Y	Y	Y	N	N	N	N	N
2 ***Weber***	Y	Y	Y	Y	?	?	N	Y
3 ***Frenzel***	?	?	?	N	?	N	N	Y
4 Vento	Y	Y	Y	Y	Y	Y	N	N

	135	136	137	138	139	140	141	142
5 Sabo	Y	Y	Y	Y	Y	Y	Y	Y
6 Sikorski	Y	Y	Y	Y	Y	Y	N	N
7 ***Stangeland***	Y	Y	Y	Y	N	N	N	Y
8 Oberstar	Y	Y	Y	Y	Y	Y	N	Y
MISSISSIPPI								
1 Whitten	Y	Y	Y	Y	Y	Y	Y	Y
2 Espy	Y	Y	Y	Y	Y	Y	N	Y
3 Montgomery	Y	Y	Y	Y	Y	Y	N	Y
4 Parker	Y	Y	Y	Y	Y	Y	N	Y
5 Taylor	Y	Y	Y	Y	Y	Y	N	N
MISSOURI								
1 Clay	Y	Y	Y	Y	Y	Y	N	N
2 ***Buechner***	Y	Y	Y	Y	N	N	N	?
3 Gephardt	Y	Y	Y	Y	Y	Y	N	Y
4 Skelton	Y	Y	Y	Y	Y	Y	N	Y
5 Wheat	Y	Y	Y	Y	Y	Y	N	N
6 ***Coleman***	Y	Y	Y	?	N	Y	N	Y
7 ***Hancock***	Y	N	N	N	N	N	N	Y
8 ***Emerson***	Y	Y	Y	Y	Y	N	N	Y
9 Volkmer	Y	Y	Y	Y	Y	Y	N	Y
MONTANA								
1 Williams	?	Y	Y	Y	Y	Y	N	N
2 ***Marlenee***	Y	Y	N	Y	Y	Y	N	Y
NEBRASKA								
1 ***Bereuter***	Y	Y	Y	Y	N	Y	N	Y
2 Hoagland	Y	Y	Y	Y	Y	Y	N	Y
3 ***Smith***	Y	Y	Y	Y	Y	Y	N	Y
NEVADA								
1 Bilbray	Y	Y	Y	Y	Y	Y	N	N
2 ***Vucanovich***	Y	N	Y	Y	N	Y	N	Y
NEW HAMPSHIRE								
1 ***Smith***	Y	Y	Y	N	N	N	N	Y
2 ***Douglas***	Y	Y	Y	N	N	N	N	Y
NEW JERSEY								
1 Vacancy								
2 Hughes	Y	Y	Y	N	Y	N	N	N
3 Pallone	Y	Y	Y	Y	Y	Y	N	Y
4 ***Smith***	Y	Y	Y	Y	N	Y	N	Y
5 ***Roukema***	Y	Y	Y	N	N	N	N	N
6 Dwyer	Y	Y	Y	Y	Y	Y	N	Y
7 ***Rinaldo***	Y	Y	Y	Y	Y	N	N	Y
8 Roe	Y	Y	Y	Y	Y	Y	?	?
9 Torricelli	Y	Y	Y	Y	Y	Y	N	Y
10 Payne	Y	Y	Y	Y	Y	Y	N	N
11 ***Gallo***	Y	Y	Y	Y	Y	Y	N	Y
12 ***Courter***	Y	Y	Y	Y	Y	Y	N	Y
13 ***Saxton***	Y	Y	Y	Y	Y	N	N	Y
14 Guarini	Y	Y	Y	Y	Y	Y	N	N
NEW MEXICO								
1 ***Schiff***	Y	Y	Y	Y	N	N	N	Y
2 ***Skeen***	Y	Y	Y	Y	Y	Y	N	Y
3 Richardson	Y	Y	Y	Y	Y	Y	N	Y
NEW YORK								
1 Hochbrueckner	Y	Y	Y	Y	Y	Y	N	N
2 Downey	Y	Y	Y	Y	Y	Y	N	N
3 Mrazek	Y	Y	Y	Y	?	?	?	N
4 ***Lent***	Y	Y	Y	Y	N	Y	N	Y
5 ***McGrath***	Y	Y	Y	Y	N	N	N	Y
6 Flake	Y	Y	Y	Y	Y	Y	N	N
7 Ackerman	Y	Y	Y	Y	Y	Y	N	Y
8 Scheuer	Y	Y	Y	Y	Y	Y	N	?
9 Manton	Y	Y	Y	Y	Y	Y	?	?
10 Schumer	Y	Y	Y	Y	Y	Y	N	Y
11 Towns	Y	Y	Y	?	Y	Y	N	N
12 Owens	Y	Y	Y	Y	Y	Y	Y	N
13 Solarz	Y	Y	Y	Y	Y	Y	N	N
14 ***Molinari***	Y	Y	Y	Y	N	N	N	Y
15 ***Green***	Y	Y	Y	Y	Y	Y	N	Y
16 Rangel	Y	Y	Y	Y	Y	Y	N	N
17 Weiss	Y	Y	Y	Y	Y	Y	N	N
18 Serrano	Y	Y	Y	Y	Y	Y	N	Y
19 Engel	Y	Y	Y	+	+	+	+	Y
20 Lowey	Y	Y	Y	Y	Y	Y	N	Y
21 ***Fish***	Y	Y	Y	Y	N	N	N	Y
22 ***Gilman***	Y	Y	Y	Y	N	N	N	Y
23 McNulty	Y	Y	Y	Y	Y	Y	N	Y
24 ***Solomon***	Y	Y	Y	N	N	N	N	Y
25 ***Boehlert***	Y	Y	Y	Y	N	N	N	Y
26 ***Martin***	Y	Y	Y	Y	N	N	N	Y
27 ***Walsh***	Y	Y	Y	Y	N	N	N	Y
28 McHugh	Y	Y	Y	Y	Y	Y	N	Y
29 ***Horton***	Y	Y	Y	Y	N	Y	N	Y
30 Slaughter	Y	Y	Y	Y	N	Y	N	N
31 ***Paxon***	Y	Y	Y	Y	N	N	N	Y

	135	136	137	138	139	140	141	142
32 LaFalce	Y	Y	Y	Y	Y	Y	N	N
33 Nowak	Y	Y	Y	Y	Y	Y	N	Y
34 ***Houghton***	Y	Y	Y	Y	N	Y	N	Y
NORTH CAROLINA								
1 Jones	Y	Y	Y	Y	Y	Y	?	Y
2 Valentine	Y	Y	Y	Y	N	Y	N	Y
3 Lancaster	Y	Y	Y	Y	Y	Y	N	Y
4 Price	Y	Y	Y	Y	Y	Y	N	Y
5 Neal	Y	Y	Y	Y	Y	Y	N	N
6 ***Coble***	Y	Y	Y	Y	N	N	N	Y
7 Rose	Y	Y	Y	Y	Y	Y	N	Y
8 Hefner	Y	Y	Y	Y	Y	Y	N	Y
9 ***McMillan***	Y	Y	Y	Y	N	N	N	Y
10 ***Ballenger***	Y	+	Y	Y	?	N	N	Y
11 Clarke	Y	Y	Y	Y	Y	Y	N	Y
NORTH DAKOTA								
AL Dorgan	Y	Y	Y	N	Y	Y	N	?
OHIO								
1 Luken	Y	Y	Y	Y	Y	Y	N	N
2 ***Gradison***	Y	Y	Y	N	N	N	N	Y
3 Hall	Y	Y	Y	Y	Y	Y	N	Y
4 ***Oxley***	Y	Y	Y	Y	N	Y	N	?
5 ***Gillmor***	Y	Y	Y	Y	Y	N	N	Y
6 ***McEwen***	Y	N	N	N	N	N	N	Y
7 ***DeWine***	Y	Y	N	Y	N	N	N	Y
8 ***Lukens***	?	?	?	?	?	?	?	?
9 Kaptur	Y	Y	Y	Y	Y	Y	N	Y
10 ***Miller***	Y	Y	N	N	N	N	Y	Y
11 Eckart	Y	Y	Y	N	N	Y	N	Y
12 ***Kasich***	Y	Y	N	N	N	N	N	Y
13 Pease	Y	Y	Y	N	Y	Y	N	N
14 Sawyer	Y	Y	Y	Y	Y	Y	N	N
15 ***Wylie***	Y	Y	Y	Y	N	N	N	Y
16 ***Regula***	Y	Y	Y	Y	Y	Y	N	Y
17 Traficant	Y	Y	Y	N	Y	Y	N	N
18 Applegate	Y	Y	N	N	Y	Y	N	N
19 Feighan	Y	Y	Y	Y	Y	Y	N	N
20 Oakar	Y	Y	Y	N	Y	Y	N	N
21 Stokes	Y	Y	Y	Y	Y	Y	N	N
OKLAHOMA								
1 ***Inhofe***	Y	Y	Y	N	N	N	N	Y
2 Synar	Y	Y	Y	Y	Y	Y	N	Y
3 Watkins	Y	Y	Y	Y	Y	?	?	?
4 McCurdy	Y	Y	Y	Y	N	Y	N	Y
5 ***Edwards***	Y	Y	Y	N	N	N	N	Y
6 English	Y	Y	Y	Y	N	Y	N	Y
OREGON								
1 AuCoin	Y	Y	Y	Y	Y	Y	N	N
2 ***Smith, B.***	Y	Y	Y	N	N	N	N	Y
3 Wyden	Y	Y	Y	Y	Y	Y	N	N
4 DeFazio	Y	Y	Y	Y	Y	Y	N	N
5 ***Smith, D.***	Y	Y	Y	N	N	N	N	Y
PENNSYLVANIA								
1 Foglietta	Y	Y	Y	Y	Y	Y	N	Y
2 Gray	Y	Y	Y	Y	Y	Y	N	Y
3 Borski	Y	Y	Y	Y	Y	Y	N	N
4 Kolter	Y	Y	Y	N	Y	Y	N	Y
5 ***Schulze***	Y	Y	Y	N	N	N	N	Y
6 Yatron	Y	Y	Y	Y	N	Y	N	N
7 ***Weldon***	Y	Y	Y	Y	Y	N	N	Y
8 Kostmayer	Y	Y	Y	Y	Y	Y	N	N
9 ***Shuster***	Y	Y	N	N	N	N	N	Y
10 ***McDade***	Y	Y	Y	Y	Y	Y	N	Y
11 Kanjorski	Y	Y	Y	Y	Y	Y	N	Y
12 Murtha	Y	Y	Y	Y	Y	Y	Y	Y
13 ***Coughlin***	Y	Y	Y	Y	Y	Y	N	Y
14 Coyne	Y	Y	Y	Y	Y	Y	N	N
15 ***Ritter***	Y	Y	Y	Y	N	N	N	Y
16 ***Walker***	Y	N	Y	N	N	N	N	N
17 ***Gekas***	Y	Y	Y	N	N	N	N	Y
18 Walgren	Y	Y	Y	Y	Y	Y	N	N
19 ***Goodling***	Y	Y	Y	Y	N	N	N	Y
20 Gaydos	Y	Y	Y	N	Y	Y	N	Y
21 ***Ridge***	Y	Y	Y	Y	N	N	N	N
22 Murphy	Y	Y	Y	N	N	Y	N	N
23 ***Clinger***	+	+	+	+	−	−	−	+
RHODE ISLAND								
1 ***Machtley***	Y	Y	Y	Y	Y	Y	N	Y
2 ***Schneider***	Y	Y	Y	Y	N	N	N	Y
SOUTH CAROLINA								
1 ***Ravenel***	Y	Y	Y	Y	Y	Y	N	Y
2 ***Spence***	Y	Y	Y	N	N	Y	N	Y
3 Derrick	Y	Y	Y	Y	Y	Y	N	Y
4 Patterson	Y	Y	Y	Y	N	Y	N	N
5 Spratt	Y	Y	Y	Y	N	Y	N	Y
6 Tallon	Y	Y	Y	N	N	Y	N	N

	135	136	137	138	139	140	141	142
SOUTH DAKOTA								
AL Johnson	Y	Y	Y	N	N	Y	N	N
TENNESSEE								
1 ***Quillen***	Y	Y	Y	N	N	N	N	Y
2 ***Duncan***	Y	Y	Y	N	N	N	N	N
3 Lloyd	Y	Y	Y	Y	Y	Y	N	Y
4 Cooper	Y	Y	Y	N	Y	Y	N	Y
5 Clement	Y	Y	Y	Y	Y	Y	N	N
6 Gordon	Y	Y	Y	Y	Y	Y	N	Y
7 ***Sundquist***	Y	Y	Y	Y	N	N	N	Y
8 Tanner	Y	Y	Y	Y	Y	Y	N	Y
9 Ford	Y	Y	Y	Y	?	Y	N	N
TEXAS								
1 Chapman	Y	Y	Y	Y	Y	Y	Y	Y
2 Wilson	Y	Y	Y	Y	Y	Y	Y	Y
3 ***Bartlett***	Y	Y	Y	N	N	N	N	Y
4 Hall	Y	Y	Y	Y	N	N	N	N
5 Bryant	Y	Y	Y	Y	Y	Y	N	N
6 ***Barton***	Y	Y	Y	N	N	N	N	Y
7 ***Archer***	Y	Y	Y	N	N	N	N	Y
8 ***Fields***	Y	Y	Y	N	N	N	N	Y
9 Brooks	Y	Y	Y	Y	Y	Y	Y	Y
10 Pickle	Y	Y	Y	Y	Y	Y	N	N
11 Leath	?	?	?	Y	Y	Y	Y	Y
12 Geren	Y	Y	Y	Y	Y	Y	Y	Y
13 Sarpalius	Y	Y	Y	N	N	Y	N	N
14 Laughlin	Y	Y	Y	N	Y	Y	N	Y
15 de la Garza	Y	Y	Y	?	Y	?	?	Y
16 Coleman	Y	Y	Y	Y	Y	Y	Y	Y
17 Stenholm	Y	Y	Y	N	N	Y	N	N
18 Washington	N	Y	Y	Y	?	?	?	?
19 ***Combest***	N	Y	N	N	N	N	N	Y
20 Gonzalez	Y	Y	Y	Y	Y	Y	N	Y
21 ***Smith***	Y	Y	Y	Y	N	N	N	Y
22 ***DeLay***	N	N	N	Y	Y	N	N	Y
23 Bustamante	Y	Y	Y	Y	Y	Y	Y	Y
24 Frost	Y	Y	Y	Y	Y	Y	N	Y
25 Andrews	Y	Y	Y	Y	N	Y	N	Y
26 ***Armey***	Y	N	N	N	N	N	N	Y
27 Ortiz	Y	Y	Y	Y	Y	Y	N	Y
UTAH								
1 ***Hansen***	Y	N	Y	N	N	Y	N	?
2 Owens	Y	Y	Y	Y	Y	Y	N	N
3 ***Nielson***	Y	Y	Y	N	N	Y	N	Y
VERMONT								
AL ***Smith***	Y	Y	Y	Y	N	N	N	Y
VIRGINIA								
1 ***Bateman***	Y	Y	Y	Y	N	Y	N	Y
2 Pickett	Y	Y	Y	N	Y	Y	N	Y
3 ***Bliley***	Y	Y	Y	N	N	N	N	Y
4 Sisisky	Y	Y	Y	Y	Y	Y	N	Y
5 Payne	Y	Y	Y	Y	Y	Y	N	Y
6 Olin	Y	Y	Y	Y	Y	Y	N	Y
7 ***Slaughter***	Y	Y	Y	N	N	N	N	Y
8 ***Parris***	Y	Y	Y	Y	N	N	N	Y
9 Boucher	Y	Y	Y	Y	Y	Y	N	Y
10 ***Wolf***	Y	Y	Y	Y	N	N	N	Y
WASHINGTON								
1 ***Miller***	Y	Y	Y	Y	N	N	N	Y
2 Swift	Y	Y	Y	Y	Y	Y	N	N
3 Unsoeld	Y	Y	Y	Y	Y	Y	N	N
4 ***Morrison***	Y	Y	Y	Y	N	Y	N	Y
5 Foley								
6 Dicks	Y	Y	Y	Y	Y	Y	N	N
7 McDermott	Y	Y	Y	Y	Y	Y	N	N
8 ***Chandler***	Y	Y	Y	Y	N	N	N	Y
WEST VIRGINIA								
1 Mollohan	Y	Y	N	Y	Y	Y	Y	Y
2 Staggers	Y	Y	Y	Y	Y	Y	N	N
3 Wise	Y	Y	Y	Y	Y	Y	N	Y
4 Rahall	Y	Y	Y	Y	Y	Y	Y	N
WISCONSIN								
1 Aspin	Y	Y	Y	Y	Y	Y	N	Y
2 Kastenmeier	Y	Y	Y	N	Y	Y	N	N
3 ***Gunderson***	Y	Y	Y	Y	N	N	N	Y
4 Kleczka	Y	Y	Y	Y	Y	Y	N	Y
5 Moody	Y	Y	Y	N	Y	N	N	N
6 ***Petri***	Y	Y	Y	N	N	N	N	Y
7 Obey	Y	Y	Y	Y	Y	Y	N	Y
8 ***Roth***	Y	Y	Y	N	N	N	N	Y
9 ***Sensenbrenner***	Y	Y	Y	N	N	N	N	Y
WYOMING								
AL ***Thomas***	Y	Y	Y	Y	N	N	N	Y

Southern states - Ala., Ark., Fla., Ga., Ky., La., Miss., N.C., Okla., S.C., Tenn., Texas, Va.
Omitted votes are quorum calls, which CQ does not include in its vote charts.

143. HR 4404. Fiscal 1990 Supplemental Appropriations/ Rural Technology. Whitten, D-Miss., motion that the House recede from its disagreement with a Senate amendment to provide $1 million for the Appropriate Technology for Rural Areas program. Approval was necessary to allow a House amendment to change the funding level to $827,000, which was subsequently agreed to by voice vote. Motion agreed to 231-165: R 28-134; D 203-31 (ND 138-19, SD 65-12), May 24, 1990.

144. HR 4404. Fiscal 1990 Supplemental Appropriations/ Community Development Block Grants. Whitten, D-Miss., motion that the House recede from its disagreement with a Senate amendment and concur in an amendment to force the administration to fund projects under the Community Development Block Grant program. Motion agreed 230-166: R 43-119; D 187-47 (ND 127-31, SD 60-16), May 24, 1990.

145. HR 4404. Fiscal 1990 Supplemental Appropriations/ Capitol Preservation. Whitten, D-Miss., motion that the House recede from its disagreement with a Senate amendment to clarify the authority of the U.S. Capitol Preservation Commission. Motion agreed 208-163: R 0-152; D 208-11 (ND 143-9, SD 65-2), May 24, 1990.

146. HR 4404. Fiscal 1990 Supplemental Appropriations/ Franking. Whitten, D-Miss., motion that the House recede from its disagreement with a Senate amendment and concur in an amendment to allow unused legislative appropriations from past years to be used for other purposes, a general authority intended to allow $25 million from past years to be used to pay fiscal 1990 congressional mailing expenses. Rejected 161-208: R 1-148; D 160-60 (ND 121-30, SD 39-30), May 24, 1990.

KEY

- Y Voted for (yea).
- # Paired for.
- + Announced for.
- N Voted against (nay).
- X Paired against.
- \- Announced against.
- P Voted "present."
- C Voted "present" to avoid possible conflict of interest.
- ? Did not vote or otherwise make a position known.

Democrats ***Republicans***

	143	144	145	146
ALABAMA				
1 ***Callahan***	?	?	?	?
2 ***Dickinson***	N	N	?	?
3 Browder	Y	Y	Y	N
4 Bevill	Y	Y	Y	Y
5 Flippo	?	?	?	?
6 Erdreich	Y	N	Y	N
7 Harris	Y	Y	Y	N
ALASKA				
AL ***Young***	?	?	?	?
ARIZONA				
1 ***Rhodes***	N	N	N	N
2 Udall	?	Y	Y	Y
3 ***Stump***	N	N	N	N
4 ***Kyl***	N	N	N	N
5 ***Kolbe***	N	N	N	N
ARKANSAS				
1 Alexander	?	?	?	?
2 ***Robinson***	?	?	?	?
3 ***Hammerschmidt***	N	N	N	N
4 Anthony	Y	Y	Y	Y
CALIFORNIA				
1 Bosco	Y	Y	Y	Y
2 ***Herger***	N	N	N	N
3 Matsui	Y	Y	Y	Y
4 Fazio	Y	Y	Y	Y
5 Pelosi	Y	Y	Y	Y
6 Boxer	Y	Y	Y	Y
7 Miller	Y	Y	Y	Y
8 Dellums	Y	?	Y	Y
9 Stark	Y	Y	N	Y
10 Edwards	?	?	?	?
11 Lantos	Y	N	Y	Y
12 ***Campbell***	N	N	N	N
13 Mineta	Y	Y	Y	Y
14 ***Shumway***	N	N	N	N
15 Condit	Y	Y	Y	Y
16 Panetta	N	N	N	N
17 ***Pashayan***	Y	Y	N	N
18 Lehman	Y	Y	Y	Y
19 ***Lagomarsino***	Y	N	N	N
20 ***Thomas***	?	?	?	?
21 ***Gallegly***	N	N	N	N
22 ***Moorhead***	N	N	N	N
23 Beilenson	Y	Y	Y	Y
24 Waxman	Y	Y	?	?
25 Roybal	Y	Y	Y	Y
26 Berman	Y	Y	Y	Y
27 Levine	Y	Y	Y	Y
28 Dixon	Y	Y	Y	Y
29 Hawkins	?	?	?	?
30 Martinez	?	?	?	?
31 Dymally	?	?	?	?
32 Anderson	Y	Y	Y	N
33 ***Dreier***	Y	N	N	N
34 Torres	Y	N	Y	Y
35 ***Lewis***	Y	Y	N	N
36 Brown	?	?	?	?
37 ***McCandless***	N	N	N	N
38 ***Dornan***	N	N	N	N
39 ***Dannemeyer***	N	N	N	N
40 ***Cox***	N	N	N	N
41 ***Lowery***	Y	Y	N	N
42 ***Rohrabacher***	N	N	N	N
43 ***Packard***	N	N	N	N
44 Bates	Y	N	Y	N
45 ***Hunter***	N	N	N	N
COLORADO				
1 Schroeder	N	Y	N	N
2 Skaggs	Y	Y	Y	Y
3 Campbell	Y	N	Y	Y
4 ***Brown***	N	N	?	?
5 ***Hefley***	?	?	?	?
6 ***Schaefer***	N	N	N	N
CONNECTICUT				
1 Kennelly	N	Y	Y	N
2 Gejdenson	Y	Y	Y	Y
3 Morrison	+	–	+	–
4 ***Shays***	N	N	N	N
5 ***Rowland***	N	N	?	?
6 ***Johnson***	N	N	N	N
DELAWARE				
AL Carper	N	N	Y	N
FLORIDA				
1 Hutto	N	N	Y	N
2 ***Grant***	N	N	N	N
3 Bennett	Y	N	N	N
4 ***James***	N	N	N	N
5 ***McCollum***	N	N	N	N
6 ***Stearns***	N	N	N	N
7 Gibbons	Y	N	Y	Y
8 ***Young***	N	Y	N	N
9 ***Bilirakis***	N	Y	N	?
10 ***Ireland***	?	?	?	?
11 Nelson	+	+	+	–
12 ***Lewis***	–	–	–	–
13 ***Goss***	N	N	N	N
14 Johnston	Y	Y	?	#
15 ***Shaw***	N	N	N	N
16 Smith	Y	Y	?	?
17 Lehman	Y	Y	Y	Y
18 ***Ros-Lehtinen***	N	N	N	N
19 Fascell	Y	Y	Y	Y
GEORGIA				
1 Thomas	Y	Y	Y	N
2 Hatcher	Y	Y	Y	Y
3 Ray	Y	N	Y	N
4 Jones	Y	Y	Y	Y
5 Lewis	Y	Y	Y	Y
6 ***Gingrich***	N	N	N	N
7 Darden	Y	Y	Y	N
8 Rowland	Y	Y	?	?
9 Jenkins	N	Y	Y	N
10 Barnard	?	?	?	?
HAWAII				
1 ***Saiki***	Y	Y	N	N
2 Vacancy				
IDAHO				
1 ***Craig***	N	N	?	?
2 Stallings	?	?	?	?
ILLINOIS				
1 Hayes	Y	Y	Y	Y
2 Savage	Y	Y	Y	Y
3 Russo	N	Y	Y	Y
4 Sangmeister	Y	Y	Y	N
5 Lipinski	Y	Y	?	?
6 ***Hyde***	N	N	N	N
7 Collins	Y	Y	Y	Y
8 Rostenkowski	N	N	N	?
9 Yates	Y	Y	Y	Y
10 ***Porter***	N	N	N	N
11 Annunzio	Y	Y	Y	Y
12 ***Crane***	N	N	N	N
13 ***Fawell***	N	N	N	N
14 ***Hastert***	N	N	N	N
15 ***Madigan***	?	N	?	?
16 ***Martin***	N	N	N	N
17 Evans	Y	N	Y	Y
18 ***Michel***	N	Y	N	N
19 Bruce	Y	Y	Y	Y
20 Durbin	Y	Y	Y	Y
21 Costello	Y	Y	Y	N
22 Poshard	Y	Y	Y	N
INDIANA				
1 Visclosky	Y	Y	Y	Y
2 Sharp	Y	Y	Y	N
3 ***Hiler***	N	N	N	N

ND Northern Democrats SD Southern Democrats

	143	144	145	146
4 Long	Y	N	Y	N
5 Jontz	Y	Y	Y	Y
6 ***Burton***	N	N	N	N
7 ***Myers***	N	Y	N	N
8 McCloskey	Y	Y	Y	Y
9 Hamilton	N	N	N	N
10 Jacobs	N	N	N	N
IOWA				
1 ***Leach***	Y	Y	N	N
2 ***Tauke***	N	Y	N	N
3 Nagle	?	?	?	?
4 Smith	Y	Y	Y	Y
5 ***Lightfoot***	Y	N	N	N
6 ***Grandy***	N	N	N	N
KANSAS				
1 ***Roberts***	N	N	N	N
2 Slattery	N	N	?	?
3 ***Meyers***	N	N	N	N
4 Glickman	Y	N	Y	N
5 ***Whittaker***	N	N	N	N
KENTUCKY				
1 Hubbard	Y	N	Y	Y
2 Natcher	Y	Y	Y	Y
3 Mazzoli	Y	Y	Y	Y
4 ***Bunning***	?	?	?	?
5 ***Rogers***	N	Y	N	N
6 ***Hopkins***	N	N	N	N
7 Perkins	Y	Y	Y	Y
LOUISIANA				
1 ***Livingston***	Y	Y	N	N
2 Boggs	Y	Y	Y	Y
3 Tauzin	Y	N	?	N
4 ***McCrery***	N	Y	N	N
5 Huckaby	Y	N	Y	N
6 ***Baker***	N	N	N	N
7 Hayes	Y	Y	Y	N
8 ***Holloway***	N	N	?	N
MAINE				
1 Brennan	Y	Y	Y	N
2 ***Snowe***	N	N	N	N
MARYLAND				
1 Dyson	Y	Y	Y	N
2 ***Bentley***	Y	N	N	N
3 Cardin	Y	Y	Y	Y
4 McMillen	Y	N	Y	Y
5 Hoyer	Y	Y	Y	Y
6 Byron	N	N	Y	N
7 Mfume	N	N	Y	Y
8 ***Morella***	N	N	N	N
MASSACHUSETTS				
1 ***Conte***	Y	Y	N	N
2 Neal	Y	Y	Y	Y
3 Early	Y	Y	N	?
4 Frank	Y	N	Y	Y
5 Atkins	Y	Y	Y	Y
6 Mavroules	Y	Y	Y	Y
7 Markey	Y	Y	Y	Y
8 Kennedy	Y	Y	Y	Y
9 Moakley	Y	Y	Y	Y
10 Studds	Y	?	Y	Y
11 Donnelly	N	Y	Y	Y
MICHIGAN				
1 Conyers	Y	Y	?	?
2 ***Pursell***	N	Y	N	N
3 Wolpe	Y	Y	Y	Y
4 ***Upton***	N	N	N	N
5 ***Henry***	N	N	N	N
6 Carr	Y	Y	Y	Y
7 Kildee	Y	Y	Y	Y
8 Traxler	Y	Y	Y	Y
9 ***Vander Jagt***	N	Y	N	N
10 ***Schuette***	N	Y	N	N
11 ***Davis***	Y	Y	N	N
12 Bonior	Y	Y	Y	Y
13 Crockett	Y	?	?	?
14 Hertel	Y	Y	Y	Y
15 Ford	Y	Y	?	Y
16 Dingell	?	Y	Y	Y
17 Levin	Y	Y	Y	Y
18 ***Broomfield***	N	N	N	N
MINNESOTA				
1 Penny	N	N	N	N
2 ***Weber***	N	N	N	N
3 ***Frenzel***	N	N	N	N
4 Vento	Y	Y	Y	Y

	143	144	145	146
5 Sabo	Y	Y	Y	Y
6 Sikorski	Y	N	?	#
7 ***Stangeland***	Y	N	N	N
8 Oberstar	Y	Y	Y	Y
MISSISSIPPI				
1 Whitten	Y	Y	Y	Y
2 Espy	Y	?	?	?
3 Montgomery	Y	Y	?	Y
4 Parker	Y	Y	Y	N
5 Taylor	N	Y	Y	N
MISSOURI				
1 Clay	?	Y	Y	Y
2 ***Buechner***	?	?	?	?
3 Gephardt	Y	Y	Y	Y
4 Skelton	Y	Y	Y	Y
5 Wheat	Y	Y	Y	Y
6 ***Coleman***	N	N	?	N
7 ***Hancock***	N	N	N	N
8 ***Emerson***	N	N	N	N
9 Volkmer	Y	N	Y	Y
MONTANA				
1 Williams	Y	Y	Y	N
2 ***Marlenee***	Y	N	N	N
NEBRASKA				
1 ***Bereuter***	Y	N	N	N
2 Hoagland	Y	Y	Y	N
3 ***Smith***	N	Y	N	N
NEVADA				
1 Bilbray	Y	Y	Y	Y
2 ***Vucanovich***	Y	?	?	N
NEW HAMPSHIRE				
1 ***Smith***	N	N	N	N
2 ***Douglas***	N	N	N	N
NEW JERSEY				
1 Vacancy				
2 Hughes	N	N	Y	Y
3 Pallone	N	Y	Y	N
4 ***Smith***	N	N	N	Y
5 ***Roukema***	N	N	N	N
6 Dwyer	Y	Y	Y	Y
7 ***Rinaldo***	N	N	N	N
8 Roe	?	?	?	?
9 Torricelli	Y	Y	Y	Y
10 Payne	Y	Y	Y	Y
11 ***Gallo***	Y	Y	N	N
12 ***Courter***	N	N	N	N
13 ***Saxton***	N	N	N	N
14 Guarini	Y	Y	Y	N
NEW MEXICO				
1 ***Schiff***	N	N	N	N
2 ***Skeen***	N	Y	N	N
3 Richardson	Y	Y	Y	Y
NEW YORK				
1 Hochbrueckner	Y	Y	Y	N
2 Downey	Y	Y	Y	Y
3 Mrazek	Y	Y	Y	Y
4 ***Lent***	N	Y	N	?
5 ***McGrath***	N	Y	N	N
6 Flake	Y	Y	Y	Y
7 Ackerman	Y	?	?	?
8 Scheuer	?	?	?	?
9 Manton	?	?	?	?
10 Schumer	Y	N	Y	Y
11 Towns	Y	Y	Y	Y
12 Owens	Y	Y	Y	Y
13 Solarz	Y	Y	Y	Y
14 ***Molinari***	N	Y	N	N
15 ***Green***	Y	Y	N	N
16 Rangel	?	Y	Y	Y
17 Weiss	Y	Y	Y	Y
18 Serrano	Y	Y	Y	Y
19 Engel	Y	Y	Y	Y
20 Lowey	Y	Y	Y	Y
21 ***Fish***	N	N	N	N
22 ***Gilman***	N	N	N	N
23 McNulty	Y	Y	Y	Y
24 ***Solomon***	N	N	N	N
25 ***Boehlert***	N	Y	N	?
26 ***Martin***	N	N	?	?
27 ***Walsh***	N	Y	N	N
28 McHugh	Y	Y	Y	Y
29 ***Horton***	Y	Y	?	?
30 Slaughter	Y	N	Y	N
31 ***Paxon***	N	N	N	N

	143	144	145	146
32 LaFalce	Y	Y	Y	Y
33 Nowak	Y	Y	Y	?
34 ***Houghton***	N	Y	N	N
NORTH CAROLINA				
1 Jones	Y	Y	Y	Y
2 Valentine	N	Y	Y	N
3 Lancaster	Y	Y	?	#
4 Price	Y	Y	Y	Y
5 Neal	Y	Y	Y	Y
6 ***Coble***	N	N	N	N
7 Rose	Y	Y	Y	Y
8 Hefner	Y	Y	Y	N
9 ***McMillan***	N	N	N	N
10 ***Ballenger***	N	?	N	N
11 Clarke	Y	Y	Y	N
NORTH DAKOTA				
AL Dorgan	?	N	Y	Y
OHIO				
1 Luken	Y	Y	Y	Y
2 ***Gradison***	N	N	N	N
3 Hall	Y	Y	Y	Y
4 ***Oxley***	Y	Y	N	N
5 ***Gillmor***	N	N	N	N
6 ***McEwen***	N	N	N	N
7 ***DeWine***	N	Y	N	N
8 ***Lukens***	?	?	?	?
9 Kaptur	Y	Y	Y	Y
10 ***Miller***	Y	N	N	N
11 Eckart	Y	Y	N	Y
12 ***Kasich***	N	N	N	N
13 Pease	N	N	?	X
14 Sawyer	Y	Y	Y	Y
15 ***Wylie***	N	N	N	N
16 ***Regula***	Y	N	N	N
17 Traficant	Y	Y	Y	Y
18 Applegate	Y	Y	Y	N
19 Feighan	Y	Y	Y	Y
20 Oakar	Y	Y	Y	Y
21 Stokes	Y	Y	Y	Y
OKLAHOMA				
1 ***Inhofe***	N	N	N	N
2 Synar	Y	Y	Y	Y
3 Watkins	?	?	?	?
4 McCurdy	N	N	Y	Y
5 ***Edwards***	N	N	N	?
6 English	Y	Y	Y	N
OREGON				
1 AuCoin	Y	Y	Y	Y
2 ***Smith, B.***	N	N	N	N
3 Wyden	Y	Y	Y	Y
4 DeFazio	Y	Y	?	Y
5 ***Smith, D.***	?	N	N	?
PENNSYLVANIA				
1 Foglietta	Y	Y	Y	Y
2 Gray	Y	Y	Y	Y
3 Borski	Y	Y	Y	Y
4 Kolter	Y	Y	Y	Y
5 ***Schulze***	N	N	N	N
6 Yatron	N	N	Y	N
7 ***Weldon***	Y	N	N	N
8 Kostmayer	Y	N	Y	Y
9 ***Shuster***	N	N	N	N
10 ***McDade***	Y	Y	?	?
11 Kanjorski	Y	Y	Y	Y
12 Murtha	Y	Y	Y	Y
13 ***Coughlin***	N	Y	N	N
14 Coyne	Y	Y	Y	Y
15 ***Ritter***	N	N	N	N
16 ***Walker***	N	N	N	N
17 ***Gekas***	N	N	N	N
18 Walgren	N	Y	Y	N
19 ***Goodling***	N	N	N	N
20 Gaydos	Y	N	Y	N
21 ***Ridge***	N	N	N	N
22 Murphy	N	N	Y	Y
23 ***Clinger***	—	—	—	—
RHODE ISLAND				
1 ***Machtley***	N	N	N	N
2 ***Schneider***	N	N	N	N
SOUTH CAROLINA				
1 ***Ravenel***	Y	Y	N	N
2 ***Spence***	Y	Y	N	N
3 Derrick	Y	Y	Y	Y
4 Patterson	N	N	Y	N
5 Spratt	Y	Y	Y	Y
6 Tallon	N	N	Y	N

	143	144	145	146
SOUTH DAKOTA				
AL Johnson	Y	N	Y	N
TENNESSEE				
1 ***Quillen***	N	Y	N	?
2 ***Duncan***	N	Y	N	N
3 Lloyd	Y	Y	Y	N
4 Cooper	Y	Y	Y	Y
5 Clement	Y	Y	N	Y
6 Gordon	Y	Y	Y	Y
7 ***Sundquist***	N	Y	N	N
8 Tanner	Y	Y	Y	Y
9 Ford	Y	Y	Y	Y
TEXAS				
1 Chapman	Y	Y	Y	Y
2 Wilson	Y	Y	?	?
3 ***Bartlett***	N	N	N	N
4 Hall	N	N	Y	N
5 Bryant	Y	Y	Y	N
6 ***Barton***	N	N	N	N
7 ***Archer***	N	N	N	N
8 ***Fields***	N	N	N	N
9 Brooks	Y	Y	Y	Y
10 Pickle	Y	Y	Y	N
11 Leath	Y	Y	?	Y
12 Geren	Y	Y	Y	Y
13 Sarpalius	N	N	Y	N
14 Laughlin	N	Y	Y	N
15 de la Garza	Y	Y	Y	Y
16 Coleman	Y	Y	Y	Y
17 Stenholm	N	N	Y	N
18 Washington	?	?	?	?
19 ***Combest***	N	N	N	N
20 Gonzalez	Y	N	Y	Y
21 ***Smith***	N	N	N	N
22 ***DeLay***	N	Y	N	N
23 Bustamante	Y	Y	Y	Y
24 Frost	Y	Y	Y	Y
25 Andrews	N	N	Y	N
26 ***Armey***	N	N	N	N
27 Ortiz	Y	Y	?	?
UTAH				
1 ***Hansen***	?	?	?	?
2 Owens	Y	Y	Y	Y
3 ***Nielson***	N	Y	N	N
VERMONT				
AL ***Smith***	N	Y	N	N
VIRGINIA				
1 ***Bateman***	N	Y	N	?
2 Pickett	Y	Y	Y	N
3 ***Bliley***	N	N	N	N
4 Sisisky	Y	Y	Y	X
5 Payne	Y	Y	Y	Y
6 Olin	Y	Y	Y	N
7 ***Slaughter***	N	N	N	N
8 ***Parris***	N	N	N	N
9 Boucher	Y	Y	Y	Y
10 ***Wolf***	N	Y	N	N
WASHINGTON				
1 ***Miller***	N	N	N	N
2 Swift	Y	Y	Y	Y
3 Unsoeld	Y	Y	Y	Y
4 ***Morrison***	Y	N	N	N
5 Foley				
6 Dicks	Y	Y	Y	Y
7 McDermott	Y	Y	Y	Y
8 ***Chandler***	N	N	N	N
WEST VIRGINIA				
1 Mollohan	Y	Y	Y	Y
2 Staggers	Y	Y	Y	Y
3 Wise	Y	Y	Y	Y
4 Rahall	Y	Y	Y	N
WISCONSIN				
1 Aspin	Y	Y	Y	Y
2 Kastenmeier	Y	Y	Y	Y
3 ***Gunderson***	N	N	N	N
4 Kleczka	Y	Y	Y	Y
5 Moody	Y	N	Y	Y
6 ***Petri***	N	N	N	N
7 Obey	Y	Y	Y	Y
8 ***Roth***	N	N	?	N
9 ***Sensenbrenner***	N	N	N	N
WYOMING				
AL ***Thomas***	Y	N	N	N

Southern states - Ala., Ark., Fla., Ga., Ky., La., Miss., N.C., Okla., S.C., Tenn., Texas, Va.
Omitted votes are quorum calls, which CQ does not include in its vote charts.

HOUSE VOTES 147, 148, 149, 150, 151, 152

147. Procedural Motion. Burton, R-Ind., motion to approve the House Journal of Tuesday, June 5. Motion agreed to 272-104: R 64-98; D 208-6 (ND 138-6, SD 70-0), June 6, 1990.

148. HR 4653. Export Administration Act Reauthorization/Funding. Roth, R-Wis., amendment to reduce the amount authorized from $47 million to $29 million for the Bureau of Export Administration to carry out the bill's provisions in fiscal 1991. Rejected 117-291: R 107-63; D 10-228 (ND 6-156, SD 4-72), June 6, 1990.

149. HR 4653. Export Administration Act Reauthorization/Exports to Soviet Union. Durbin, D-Ill., amendment to prohibit easing restrictions on exports to the Soviet Union until the president certifies that the Soviet Union has begun serious negotiations with the elected government of Lithuania on allowing self-determination, is conducting such negotiations without economic coercion and is not restricting the emigration of Soviet Jews. Adopted 390-24: R 165-5; D 225-19 (ND 152-13, SD 73-6), June 6, 1990.

150. HR 4653. Export Administration Act Reauthorization/Exports to China. Solomon, R-N.Y., amendment to eliminate the authority in current law for the administration to issue distribution licenses for exports to China. Adopted 352-62: R 147-25; D 205-37 (ND 139-25, SD 66-12), June 6, 1990.

151. HR 4653. Export Administration Act Reauthorization/Satellite Exports to China. Solomon, R-N.Y., amendment, as amended by Gejdenson, D-Conn., on a voice vote, to remove waivers in current law that allow the administration to permit the export of satellites to China. Adopted 393-15: R 164-7; D 229-8 (ND 155-6, SD 74-2), June 6, 1990.

152. HR 4653. Export Administration Act Reauthorization/Exports to Eastern Europe. AuCoin, D-Ore., amendment to clarify that Poland, Hungary and Czechoslovakia are eligible for the bill's reduced restrictions on exports, provided that they meet the bill's criteria for the use of these exports and for adequate safeguards against diversion to other countries. Adopted 409-0: R 170-0; D 239-0 (ND 162-0, SD 77-0), June 6, 1990.

KEY

- Y Voted for (yea).
- # Paired for.
- + Announced for.
- N Voted against (nay).
- X Paired against.
- - Announced against.
- P Voted "present."
- C Voted "present" to avoid possible conflict of interest.
- ? Did not vote or otherwise make a position known.

Democrats ***Republicans***

	147	148	149	150	151	152
ALABAMA						
1 ***Callahan***	N	Y	Y	Y	Y	Y
2 ***Dickinson***	N	Y	Y	Y	Y	Y
3 Browder	Y	N	Y	Y	Y	Y
4 Bevill	Y	N	Y	Y	Y	Y
5 Flippo	?	?	?	?	?	?
6 Erdreich	Y	N	Y	Y	Y	Y
7 Harris	Y	N	Y	Y	Y	Y
ALASKA						
AL ***Young***	?	Y	Y	Y	Y	Y
ARIZONA						
1 ***Rhodes***	Y	Y	Y	Y	Y	Y
2 Udall	Y	N	Y	?	Y	Y
3 ***Stump***	N	Y	Y	Y	Y	Y
4 ***Kyl***	N	Y	Y	Y	Y	Y
5 ***Kolbe***	N	Y	Y	Y	Y	Y
ARKANSAS						
1 Alexander	Y	N	Y	N	Y	Y
2 ***Robinson***	Y	Y	Y	Y	N	Y
3 ***Hammerschmidt***	Y	Y	N	N	N	Y
4 Anthony	?	?	Y	Y	Y	Y
CALIFORNIA						
1 Bosco	Y	N	Y	Y	Y	Y
2 ***Herger***	N	Y	Y	Y	Y	Y
3 Matsui	Y	N	Y	Y	Y	Y
4 Fazio	?	?	?	?	?	?
5 Pelosi	Y	N	Y	Y	Y	Y
6 Boxer	?	?	?	?	?	?
7 Miller	?	?	?	?	?	?
8 Dellums	?	?	?	?	?	?
9 Stark	Y	N	Y	Y	Y	Y
10 Edwards	Y	?	N	Y	Y	Y
11 Lantos	Y	N	Y	Y	Y	Y
12 ***Campbell***	N	N	N	N	N	Y
13 Mineta	Y	N	Y	Y	Y	Y
14 ***Shumway***	Y	Y	Y	Y	Y	Y
15 Condit	Y	Y	Y	Y	Y	Y
16 Panetta	Y	N	Y	Y	Y	Y
17 ***Pashayan***	?	N	Y	Y	Y	Y
18 Lehman	?	?	?	?	?	?
19 ***Lagomarsino***	N	Y	Y	Y	Y	Y
20 ***Thomas***	N	N	Y	N	Y	Y
21 ***Gallegly***	-	+	+	+	+	Y
22 ***Moorhead***	N	Y	Y	Y	Y	Y
23 Beilenson	Y	N	Y	N	Y	Y
24 Waxman	Y	N	Y	Y	Y	Y
25 Roybal	Y	N	Y	Y	Y	?
26 Berman	?	N	Y	Y	Y	Y
27 Levine	Y	N	Y	Y	Y	Y
28 Dixon	?	N	Y	Y	Y	Y
29 Hawkins	N	N	Y	N	Y	Y
30 Martinez	Y	?	Y	N	Y	Y
31 Dymally	Y	N	N	N	N	Y
32 Anderson	Y	N	Y	Y	Y	Y
33 ***Dreier***	N	Y	Y	Y	Y	Y
34 Torres	Y	N	Y	Y	Y	Y
35 ***Lewis***	?	?	?	?	?	?
36 Brown	?	N	Y	Y	Y	Y
37 ***McCandless***	N	Y	Y	Y	Y	Y
38 ***Dornan***	N	Y	Y	Y	Y	Y
39 ***Dannemeyer***	N	Y	Y	Y	Y	Y
40 ***Cox***	?	Y	Y	Y	Y	Y
41 ***Lowery***	?	#	?	?	?	?
42 ***Rohrabacher***	Y	Y	Y	Y	Y	Y
43 ***Packard***	Y	Y	Y	Y	Y	Y
44 Bates	?	?	?	?	?	?
45 ***Hunter***	N	Y	Y	Y	Y	Y
COLORADO						
1 Schroeder	N	N	Y	Y	Y	Y
2 Skaggs	Y	N	Y	Y	Y	Y
3 Campbell	Y	N	Y	Y	Y	Y
4 ***Brown***	N	Y	Y	Y	Y	Y
5 ***Hefley***	N	Y	Y	Y	Y	Y
6 ***Schaefer***	N	Y	Y	Y	Y	Y
CONNECTICUT						
1 Kennelly	Y	N	Y	N	Y	Y
2 Gejdenson	Y	N	Y	Y	Y	Y
3 Morrison	Y	N	Y	Y	Y	Y
4 ***Shays***	N	N	Y	N	Y	Y
5 ***Rowland***	Y	N	Y	Y	Y	Y
6 ***Johnson***	Y	N	Y	N	Y	Y
DELAWARE						
AL Carper	Y	N	Y	Y	Y	Y
FLORIDA						
1 Hutto	Y	N	Y	Y	Y	Y
2 ***Grant***	Y	Y	Y	Y	Y	Y
3 Bennett	Y	Y	Y	Y	Y	Y
4 ***James***	N	Y	Y	Y	Y	Y
5 ***McCollum***	Y	Y	Y	Y	Y	Y
6 ***Stearns***	N	Y	Y	Y	Y	Y
7 Gibbons	Y	N	Y	Y	Y	Y
8 ***Young***	Y	N	Y	Y	Y	Y
9 ***Bilirakis***	N	Y	Y	Y	Y	Y
10 ***Ireland***	N	Y	Y	Y	Y	Y
11 Nelson	+	X	+	-	+	+
12 ***Lewis***	N	Y	Y	Y	Y	Y
13 ***Goss***	N	Y	Y	Y	Y	Y
14 Johnston	?	N	Y	Y	Y	Y
15 ***Shaw***	Y	Y	Y	Y	Y	Y
16 Smith	?	N	Y	Y	Y	Y
17 Lehman	Y	N	Y	N	Y	Y
18 ***Ros-Lehtinen***	N	N	Y	Y	Y	Y
19 Fascell	Y	N	Y	Y	Y	Y
GEORGIA						
1 Thomas	Y	N	Y	Y	Y	Y
2 Hatcher	Y	N	Y	Y	Y	Y
3 Ray	Y	N	Y	Y	Y	Y
4 Jones	Y	N	Y	Y	Y	Y
5 Lewis	Y	N	Y	Y	Y	Y
6 ***Gingrich***	N	Y	Y	Y	Y	Y
7 Darden	?	N	Y	Y	Y	Y
8 Rowland	Y	N	Y	Y	Y	Y
9 Jenkins	Y	N	Y	Y	Y	Y
10 Barnard	Y	N	Y	Y	Y	Y
HAWAII						
1 ***Saiki***	Y	N	Y	Y	Y	Y
2 Vacancy						
IDAHO						
1 ***Craig***	N	Y	Y	Y	Y	Y
2 Stallings	Y	N	Y	Y	Y	Y
ILLINOIS						
1 Hayes	Y	N	Y	Y	Y	Y
2 Savage	?	N	N	N	N	Y
3 Russo	Y	N	Y	Y	Y	Y
4 Sangmeister	Y	N	Y	Y	Y	Y
5 Lipinski	?	N	Y	Y	Y	Y
6 ***Hyde***	N	N	Y	Y	Y	Y
7 Collins	Y	N	Y	Y	Y	Y
8 Rostenkowski	Y	N	Y	N	Y	Y
9 Yates	Y	N	Y	Y	Y	Y
10 ***Porter***	Y	N	Y	Y	Y	Y
11 Annunzio	Y	N	Y	Y	Y	Y
12 ***Crane***	N	Y	Y	Y	Y	Y
13 ***Fawell***	N	Y	Y	Y	Y	Y
14 ***Hastert***	N	N	Y	Y	Y	Y
15 ***Madigan***	N	Y	Y	Y	Y	Y
16 ***Martin***	N	N	Y	Y	Y	Y
17 Evans	Y	N	Y	Y	Y	Y
18 ***Michel***	N	N	Y	Y	Y	Y
19 Bruce	Y	N	Y	Y	Y	Y
20 Durbin	Y	N	Y	Y	Y	Y
21 Costello	Y	N	Y	Y	Y	Y
22 Poshard	Y	N	Y	Y	Y	Y
INDIANA						
1 Visclosky	Y	N	Y	Y	Y	Y
2 Sharp	Y	N	Y	N	Y	Y
3 ***Hiler***	N	Y	Y	Y	Y	Y

ND Northern Democrats SD Southern Democrats

	147	148	149	150	151	152
4 Long	Y	N	Y	Y	Y	Y
5 Jontz	Y	N	Y	Y	Y	Y
6 ***Burton***	N	Y	Y	Y	Y	Y
7 ***Myers***	Y	Y	Y	N	Y	Y
8 McCloskey	Y	N	Y	Y	?	Y
9 Hamilton	Y	N	N	N	Y	Y
10 Jacobs	N	Y	Y	Y	Y	Y
IOWA						
1 ***Leach***	N	Y	Y	Y	Y	Y
2 ***Tauke***	N	N	Y	Y	Y	Y
3 Nagle	Y	N	Y	Y	Y	Y
4 Smith	Y	N	N	N	N	Y
5 ***Lightfoot***	N	Y	Y	Y	Y	Y
6 ***Grandy***	N	Y	Y	Y	Y	Y
KANSAS						
1 ***Roberts***	N	N	Y	N	Y	Y
2 Slattery	?	?	?	?	?	?
3 ***Meyers***	N	Y	Y	Y	Y	Y
4 Glickman	Y	N	Y	N	Y	Y
5 ***Whittaker***	N	Y	Y	Y	Y	Y
KENTUCKY						
1 Hubbard	Y	N	Y	Y	Y	Y
2 Natcher	Y	N	Y	Y	Y	Y
3 Mazzoli	Y	N	N	Y	Y	Y
4 ***Bunning***	N	Y	Y	Y	Y	Y
5 ***Rogers***	N	N	Y	N	Y	Y
6 ***Hopkins***	N	N	Y	Y	Y	Y
7 Perkins	Y	N	Y	Y	Y	Y
LOUISIANA						
1 ***Livingston***	Y	N	Y	Y	Y	Y
2 Boggs	Y	N	Y	Y	Y	Y
3 Tauzin	Y	Y	Y	N	Y	Y
4 ***McCrery***	Y	Y	Y	N	Y	Y
5 Huckaby	Y	N	Y	N	Y	Y
6 ***Baker***	N	Y	Y	N	Y	Y
7 Hayes	Y	Y	Y	Y	Y	Y
8 ***Holloway***	N	Y	Y	Y	Y	Y
MAINE						
1 Brennan	Y	N	Y	Y	Y	Y
2 ***Snowe***	Y	N	Y	Y	Y	Y
MARYLAND						
1 Dyson	Y	Y	Y	Y	Y	Y
2 ***Bentley***	N	N	Y	Y	Y	Y
3 Cardin	Y	N	Y	Y	Y	Y
4 McMillen	Y	N	Y	Y	Y	Y
5 Hoyer	Y	N	Y	Y	Y	Y
6 Byron	Y	N	Y	Y	Y	Y
7 Mfume	?	N	Y	Y	Y	Y
8 ***Morella***	Y	N	Y	Y	Y	?
MASSACHUSETTS						
1 ***Conte***	Y	N	Y	Y	Y	Y
2 Neal	Y	N	Y	Y	Y	Y
3 Early	Y	N	Y	Y	Y	Y
4 Frank	Y	N	Y	N	Y	Y
5 Atkins	Y	N	Y	Y	Y	Y
6 Mavroules	Y	N	Y	Y	?	Y
7 Markey	Y	N	Y	Y	Y	Y
8 Kennedy	Y	N	Y	Y	Y	Y
9 Moakley	Y	N	Y	Y	Y	Y
10 Studds	Y	N	Y	Y	Y	Y
11 Donnelly	?	?	Y	Y	Y	Y
MICHIGAN						
1 Conyers	Y	N	Y	Y	Y	Y
2 ***Pursell***	Y	Y	Y	Y	Y	Y
3 Wolpe	Y	N	Y	Y	Y	Y
4 ***Upton***	N	Y	Y	Y	Y	Y
5 ***Henry***	N	N	Y	Y	Y	Y
6 Carr	Y	N	Y	Y	Y	Y
7 Kildee	Y	N	Y	Y	Y	Y
8 Traxler	?	N	Y	Y	Y	Y
9 ***Vander Jagt***	Y	Y	Y	Y	?	Y
10 ***Schuette***	?	Y	Y	Y	Y	Y
11 ***Davis***	?	Y	Y	Y	Y	Y
12 Bonior	Y	N	Y	Y	Y	Y
13 Crockett	?	N	N	N	N	?
14 Hertel	Y	N	Y	Y	Y	Y
15 Ford	?	N	Y	Y	Y	Y
16 Dingell	?	N	Y	Y	N	Y
17 Levin	Y	N	Y	Y	Y	Y
18 ***Broomfield***	Y	Y	Y	Y	Y	Y
MINNESOTA						
1 Penny	Y	N	Y	N	Y	Y
2 ***Weber***	N	N	Y	N	Y	Y
3 ***Frenzel***	N	N	N	N	N	Y
4 Vento	Y	N	Y	Y	Y	Y
5 Sabo	Y	N	Y	Y	Y	Y
6 Sikorski	N	N	Y	Y	Y	Y
7 ***Stangeland***	N	N	Y	Y	Y	Y
8 Oberstar	Y	N	Y	Y	Y	Y
MISSISSIPPI						
1 Whitten	Y	N	Y	Y	Y	Y
2 Espy	?	?	?	?	?	?
3 Montgomery	Y	N	N	N	Y	Y
4 Parker	Y	N	Y	Y	Y	Y
5 Taylor	Y	N	Y	Y	Y	Y
MISSOURI						
1 Clay	N	N	Y	Y	Y	Y
2 ***Buechner***	N	Y	Y	Y	Y	Y
3 Gephardt	Y	N	Y	Y	Y	Y
4 Skelton	Y	N	Y	Y	Y	Y
5 Wheat	Y	N	Y	Y	Y	Y
6 ***Coleman***	N	N	Y	Y	Y	Y
7 ***Hancock***	N	Y	Y	Y	Y	Y
8 ***Emerson***	Y	N	Y	Y	Y	Y
9 Volkmer	Y	N	Y	Y	Y	Y
MONTANA						
1 Williams	Y	Y	Y	Y	Y	?
2 ***Marlenee***	N	Y	N	N	Y	?
NEBRASKA						
1 ***Bereuter***	N	Y	Y	N	Y	Y
2 Hoagland	Y	N	Y	Y	Y	Y
3 ***Smith***	Y	Y	Y	Y	Y	Y
NEVADA						
1 Bilbray	Y	N	Y	Y	Y	Y
2 ***Vucanovich***	N	Y	Y	Y	Y	Y
NEW HAMPSHIRE						
1 ***Smith***	N	Y	Y	Y	Y	Y
2 ***Douglas***	N	Y	Y	Y	Y	Y
NEW JERSEY						
1 Vacancy						
2 Hughes	Y	N	Y	Y	Y	Y
3 Pallone	Y	N	Y	Y	Y	Y
4 ***Smith***	Y	N	Y	Y	Y	Y
5 ***Roukema***	N	N	Y	Y	Y	Y
6 Dwyer	Y	N	Y	Y	Y	Y
7 ***Rinaldo***	Y	N	Y	Y	Y	Y
8 Roe	?	N	Y	N	Y	Y
9 Torricelli	Y	N	Y	N	Y	Y
10 Payne	Y	N	Y	Y	Y	Y
11 ***Gallo***	Y	N	Y	Y	Y	Y
12 ***Courter***	N	Y	Y	Y	Y	Y
13 ***Saxton***	Y	N	Y	Y	Y	Y
14 Guarini	?	N	Y	Y	Y	Y
NEW MEXICO						
1 ***Schiff***	?	?	?	Y	Y	Y
2 ***Skeen***	Y	Y	Y	Y	Y	Y
3 Richardson	?	N	Y	Y	Y	Y
NEW YORK						
1 Hochbrueckner	Y	N	Y	Y	Y	Y
2 Downey	Y	N	N	Y	Y	Y
3 Mrazek	Y	N	Y	Y	Y	Y
4 ***Lent***	Y	N	Y	Y	Y	Y
5 ***McGrath***	N	N	Y	Y	Y	Y
6 Flake	Y	N	Y	Y	Y	Y
7 Ackerman	Y	N	Y	Y	Y	Y
8 Scheuer	Y	N	Y	Y	Y	Y
9 Manton	Y	N	Y	Y	Y	Y
10 Schumer	Y	N	Y	Y	Y	Y
11 Towns	Y	N	Y	Y	Y	Y
12 Owens	Y	N	Y	Y	Y	Y
13 Solarz	?	N	Y	Y	Y	Y
14 ***Molinari***	N	Y	Y	Y	Y	Y
15 ***Green***	Y	N	Y	Y	N	Y
16 Rangel	Y	N	Y	Y	Y	Y
17 Weiss	?	N	N	Y	Y	Y
18 Serrano	Y	N	Y	Y	Y	Y
19 Engel	Y	N	Y	Y	Y	Y
20 Lowey	?	N	Y	Y	Y	Y
21 ***Fish***	Y	N	Y	Y	Y	Y
22 ***Gilman***	Y	N	Y	Y	Y	Y
23 McNulty	Y	N	Y	Y	Y	Y
24 ***Solomon***	N	Y	Y	Y	Y	Y
25 ***Boehlert***	N	N	Y	Y	Y	Y
26 ***Martin***	N	Y	Y	Y	Y	?
27 ***Walsh***	Y	N	Y	Y	Y	Y
28 McHugh	Y	N	N	Y	Y	Y
29 ***Horton***	Y	N	Y	Y	Y	Y
30 Slaughter	Y	N	Y	N	Y	Y
31 ***Paxon***	N	Y	Y	Y	Y	Y
32 LaFalce	Y	N	Y	Y	Y	Y
33 Nowak	Y	N	Y	Y	Y	Y
34 ***Houghton***	Y	N	Y	N	N	Y
NORTH CAROLINA						
1 Jones	Y	N	Y	Y	Y	Y
2 Valentine	Y	N	Y	N	Y	?
3 Lancaster	Y	N	Y	Y	Y	Y
4 Price	Y	N	Y	Y	Y	Y
5 Neal	Y	N	Y	Y	Y	Y
6 ***Coble***	N	Y	Y	Y	Y	Y
7 Rose	Y	N	Y	Y	Y	Y
8 Hefner	Y	N	Y	Y	Y	Y
9 ***McMillan***	Y	N	Y	Y	Y	Y
10 ***Ballenger***	N	Y	Y	Y	Y	Y
11 Clarke	Y	N	Y	Y	Y	Y
NORTH DAKOTA						
AL Dorgan	Y	N	Y	Y	Y	Y
OHIO						
1 Luken	Y	N	Y	Y	Y	Y
2 ***Gradison***	Y	Y	Y	Y	Y	Y
3 Hall	Y	N	Y	Y	Y	Y
4 ***Oxley***	P	Y	Y	Y	Y	Y
5 ***Gillmor***	Y	Y	Y	Y	Y	Y
6 ***McEwen***	Y	Y	Y	Y	Y	Y
7 ***DeWine***	N	Y	Y	Y	Y	Y
8 ***Lukens***	N	N	Y	Y	Y	Y
9 Kaptur	?	N	Y	Y	Y	Y
10 ***Miller***	N	N	Y	Y	Y	Y
11 Eckart	Y	N	Y	Y	Y	Y
12 ***Kasich***	Y	Y	Y	Y	Y	Y
13 Pease	Y	N	Y	N	N	Y
14 Sawyer	Y	N	Y	Y	Y	Y
15 ***Wylie***	Y	Y	Y	Y	Y	Y
16 ***Regula***	Y	N	Y	N	Y	Y
17 Traficant	Y	N	Y	Y	Y	Y
18 Applegate	Y	N	Y	Y	Y	Y
19 Feighan	Y	N	Y	Y	Y	Y
20 Oakar	Y	N	Y	Y	Y	Y
21 Stokes	Y	N	Y	Y	Y	Y
OKLAHOMA						
1 ***Inhofe***	N	Y	Y	Y	Y	Y
2 Synar	Y	-	Y	Y	Y	Y
3 Watkins	Y	N	Y	Y	Y	Y
4 McCurdy	Y	N	Y	Y	Y	Y
5 ***Edwards***	Y	?	?	Y	Y	Y
6 English	Y	N	Y	Y	Y	Y
OREGON						
1 AuCoin	Y	N	Y	N	Y	Y
2 ***Smith, B.***	N	Y	Y	Y	Y	Y
3 Wyden	Y	N	Y	N	Y	Y
4 DeFazio	Y	N	Y	Y	Y	Y
5 ***Smith, D.***	N	Y	Y	Y	Y	Y
PENNSYLVANIA						
1 Foglietta	Y	N	Y	Y	Y	Y
2 Gray	Y	N	Y	Y	?	Y
3 Borski	Y	N	Y	Y	Y	Y
4 Kolter	Y	N	Y	Y	Y	Y
5 ***Schulze***	Y	Y	Y	Y	Y	Y
6 Yatron	Y	N	Y	Y	Y	Y
7 ***Weldon***	Y	N	Y	Y	Y	Y
8 Kostmayer	Y	N	Y	Y	Y	Y
9 ***Shuster***	Y	Y	Y	Y	Y	Y
10 ***McDade***	?	?	?	?	?	?
11 Kanjorski	Y	Y	Y	Y	Y	Y
12 Murtha	Y	N	Y	Y	Y	Y
13 ***Coughlin***	N	Y	Y	Y	Y	Y
14 Coyne	Y	N	Y	N	Y	Y
15 ***Ritter***	Y	Y	Y	Y	Y	Y
16 ***Walker***	N	Y	Y	Y	Y	Y
17 ***Gekas***	?	Y	Y	Y	Y	Y
18 Walgren	?	N	Y	Y	Y	Y
19 ***Goodling***	N	Y	Y	Y	Y	Y
20 Gaydos	Y	N	Y	Y	Y	Y
21 ***Ridge***	N	N	Y	Y	Y	Y
22 Murphy	N	Y	Y	Y	Y	Y
23 ***Clinger***	Y	Y	Y	Y	Y	Y
RHODE ISLAND						
1 ***Machtley***	N	N	Y	Y	Y	Y
2 ***Schneider***	Y	N	Y	Y	Y	Y
SOUTH CAROLINA						
1 ***Ravenel***	Y	N	Y	Y	Y	Y
2 ***Spence***	Y	N	Y	Y	Y	Y
3 Derrick	Y	N	Y	Y	Y	Y
4 Patterson	Y	N	Y	Y	Y	Y
5 Spratt	Y	N	Y	Y	Y	Y
6 Tallon	Y	N	N	N	N	Y
SOUTH DAKOTA						
AL Johnson	Y	N	Y	Y	?	Y
TENNESSEE						
1 ***Quillen***	Y	N	Y	Y	Y	Y
2 ***Duncan***	N	Y	Y	Y	Y	Y
3 Lloyd	Y	N	Y	Y	Y	Y
4 Cooper	Y	Y	Y	Y	Y	Y
5 Clement	Y	N	Y	Y	Y	Y
6 Gordon	Y	N	Y	Y	Y	Y
7 ***Sundquist***	N	N	Y	Y	Y	Y
8 Tanner	Y	N	Y	Y	Y	Y
9 Ford	?	?	Y	Y	Y	Y
TEXAS						
1 Chapman	Y	N	Y	Y	Y	Y
2 Wilson	?	N	Y	Y	Y	Y
3 ***Bartlett***	Y	N	Y	N	Y	Y
4 Hall	Y	N	Y	N	Y	Y
5 Bryant	Y	N	N	Y	Y	Y
6 ***Barton***	N	Y	Y	Y	Y	Y
7 ***Archer***	Y	Y	Y	N	Y	Y
8 ***Fields***	?	Y	Y	N	Y	Y
9 Brooks	Y	N	Y	Y	Y	Y
10 Pickle	Y	N	Y	N	Y	Y
11 Leath	?	N	Y	?	?	Y
12 Geren	Y	N	Y	Y	Y	Y
13 Sarpalius	Y	N	Y	N	Y	Y
14 Laughlin	Y	N	Y	Y	Y	Y
15 de la Garza	?	?	?	?	?	?
16 Coleman	Y	N	Y	Y	Y	Y
17 Stenholm	Y	N	N	N	Y	Y
18 Washington	?	N	Y	Y	?	?
19 ***Combest***	Y	N	Y	Y	Y	Y
20 Gonzalez	Y	N	N	Y	P	Y
21 ***Smith***	N	Y	Y	Y	Y	Y
22 ***DeLay***	N	Y	Y	N	Y	Y
23 Bustamante	?	N	Y	Y	Y	Y
24 Frost	Y	N	Y	Y	Y	Y
25 Andrews	Y	N	Y	Y	Y	Y
26 ***Armey***	N	Y	Y	N	Y	Y
27 Ortiz	Y	N	Y	Y	Y	Y
UTAH						
1 ***Hansen***	Y	Y	Y	N	Y	Y
2 Owens	Y	N	Y	Y	Y	Y
3 ***Nielson***	Y	Y	Y	Y	Y	Y
VERMONT						
AL ***Smith***	Y	N	Y	Y	Y	Y
VIRGINIA						
1 ***Bateman***	Y	N	Y	Y	Y	Y
2 Pickett	Y	N	Y	N	N	Y
3 ***Bliley***	N	Y	Y	Y	Y	Y
4 Sisisky	Y	N	Y	Y	Y	Y
5 Payne	Y	N	Y	Y	Y	Y
6 Olin	Y	N	Y	Y	Y	Y
7 ***Slaughter***	N	Y	Y	Y	Y	Y
8 ***Parris***	N	Y	Y	Y	Y	Y
9 Boucher	Y	N	Y	Y	Y	Y
10 ***Wolf***	N	N	Y	Y	Y	Y
WASHINGTON						
1 ***Miller***	N	N	Y	Y	Y	Y
2 Swift	Y	N	Y	Y	Y	Y
3 Unsoeld	Y	N	Y	Y	Y	Y
4 ***Morrison***	Y	N	Y	N	Y	Y
5 Foley						
6 Dicks	?	N	Y	Y	Y	Y
7 McDermott	Y	N	Y	N	Y	Y
8 ***Chandler***	N	N	Y	N	Y	Y
WEST VIRGINIA						
1 Mollohan	Y	N	Y	Y	Y	Y
2 Staggers	Y	N	Y	Y	Y	Y
3 Wise	?	N	Y	Y	Y	Y
4 Rahall	Y	N	N	Y	Y	Y
WISCONSIN						
1 Aspin	Y	N	N	N	Y	Y
2 Kastenmeier	Y	N	N	N	Y	Y
3 ***Gunderson***	Y	Y	Y	Y	Y	Y
4 Kleczka	Y	N	Y	Y	Y	Y
5 Moody	?	?	?	?	?	?
6 ***Petri***	Y	Y	N	N	N	Y
7 Obey	Y	N	N	N	Y	Y
8 ***Roth***	?	Y	Y	Y	Y	Y
9 ***Sensenbrenner***	N	Y	Y	Y	Y	Y
WYOMING						
AL ***Thomas***	N	Y	Y	Y	Y	Y

Southern states - Ala., Ark., Fla., Ga., Ky., La., Miss., N.C., Okla., S.C., Tenn., Texas, Va.
Omitted votes are quorum calls, which CQ does not include in its vote charts.

HOUSE VOTES 153, 154, 155, 156, 157, 158, 159, 160

153. HR 4653. Export Administration Act Reauthorization/Munitions. Hyde, R-Ill., amendment to remove the bill's requirement that the U.S. munition list be the same as that of the 17-nation Coordinating Committee for Multilateral Export Controls, retain the bill's definition of munition and give the president authority to determine whether a commodity is to be controlled. Rejected 136-281: R 115-58; D 21-223 (ND 7-158, SD 14-65), June 6, 1990.

154. HR 4653. Export Administration Act Reauthorization/Telecommunications. Hunter, R-Calif., amendment to strike provisions easing U.S. export restrictions on telecommunications equipment and technology. Rejected 47-365: R 44-127; D 3-238 (ND 1-163, SD 2-75), June 6, 1990.

155. HR 4653. Export Administration Act Reauthorization/Telecommunications. Wyden, D-Ore., amendment to ensure that certain items are included in the definition of telecommunications for the purposes of reduced export controls. Adopted 348-45: R 125-41; D 223-4 (ND 155-0, SD 68-4), June 6, 1990.

156. HR 4653. Export Administration Act Reauthorization/Telecommunications Exports to Soviet Union. Hunter, R-Calif., amendment to prohibit the export of telecommunications equipment to the Soviet Union. Rejected 78-315: R 73-93; D 5-222 (ND 2-154, SD 3-68), June 6, 1990.

157. HR 4653. Export Administration Act Reauthorization/Commodity Control List. Engel, D-N.Y., amendment to change the bill's procedure for indexing certain classes of items on the Commodity Control List, the Commerce Department's main list of sensitive products subject to export controls. Adopted 388-2: R 165-0; D 223-2 (ND 150-2, SD 73-0), June 6, 1990.

158. HR 4653. Export Administration Act Reauthorization/Exports to Soviet Union. Hunter, R-Calif., amendment to prohibit the export of machine tools to the Soviet Union. Rejected 90-304: R 85-82; D 5-222 (ND 2-152, SD 3-70), June 6, 1990.

159. HR 4653. Export Administration Act Reauthorization/Recommittal Motion. Burton, R-Ind., motion to recommit the bill to committee with instructions to report it back to the House with provisions to prohibit the easing of restrictions on exports to the Soviet Union until the president certifies that the Soviets have halted military assistance to Cuba and Afghanistan. Motion rejected 143-252: R 133-36; D 10-216 (ND 2-151, SD 8-65), June 6, 1990.

160. HR 4653. Export Administration Act Reauthorization/Passage. Passage of the bill to ease restrictions on certain U.S. exports to U.S. allies and Eastern European countries and, to a lesser extent, the Soviet Union. Passed 312-86: R 87-82; D 225-4 (ND 153-1, SD 72-3), June 6, 1990.

KEY

Y Voted for (yea).
\# Paired for.
\+ Announced for.
N Voted against (nay).
X Paired against.
\- Announced against.
P Voted "present."
C Voted "present" to avoid possible conflict of interest.
? Did not vote or otherwise make a position known.

Democrats ***Republicans***

	153	154	155	156	157	158	159	160
ALABAMA								
1 ***Callahan***	Y	Y	Y	Y	Y	Y	Y	Y
2 ***Dickinson***	Y	Y	Y	Y	Y	Y	Y	N
3 Browder	N	N	Y	N	Y	N	N	Y
4 Bevill	N	N	Y	N	Y	N	N	Y
5 Flippo	?	?	?	?	?	?	?	?
6 Erdreich	N	N	Y	N	Y	N	N	Y
7 Harris	N	N	Y	N	Y	N	N	Y
ALASKA								
AL ***Young***	Y	N	Y	N	Y	Y	Y	N
ARIZONA								
1 ***Rhodes***	Y	N	Y	N	Y	N	Y	N
2 Udall	N	N	Y	?	Y	N	?	?
3 ***Stump***	Y	Y	N	Y	Y	Y	Y	N
4 ***Kyl***	Y	Y	N	Y	Y	Y	Y	N
5 ***Kolbe***	N	N	Y	N	Y	N	Y	Y
ARKANSAS								
1 Alexander	N	N	Y	N	Y	N	N	Y
2 ***Robinson***	N	N	Y	Y	Y	Y	Y	N
3 ***Hammerschmidt***	Y	N	Y	Y	Y	Y	Y	N
4 Anthony	N	N	Y	N	Y	N	N	Y
CALIFORNIA								
1 Bosco	N	N	Y	N	Y	N	N	Y
2 ***Herger***	Y	Y	N	Y	Y	Y	Y	N
3 Matsui	N	N	Y	N	Y	N	N	Y
4 Fazio	?	X	#	N	Y	N	N	Y
5 Pelosi	N	N	Y	N	Y	N	?	?
6 Boxer	?	?	?	?	?	?	?	?
7 Miller	N	N	Y	N	Y	N	N	Y
8 Dellums	?	N	Y	N	Y	N	N	Y
9 Stark	N	N	Y	N	N	N	?	?
10 Edwards	N	N	Y	N	Y	N	N	Y
11 Lantos	N	N	Y	N	Y	N	N	Y
12 ***Campbell***	N	N	Y	N	Y	N	N	Y
13 Mineta	N	N	Y	N	Y	N	N	Y
14 ***Shumway***	Y	Y	N	Y	Y	Y	Y	N
15 Condit	Y	N	Y	Y	Y	N	N	Y
16 Panetta	N	N	Y	N	Y	N	N	Y
17 ***Pashayan***	Y	N	Y	N	Y	N	Y	N
18 Lehman	?	?	?	?	?	?	?	?
19 ***Lagomarsino***	Y	N	Y	Y	Y	Y	Y	Y
20 ***Thomas***	N	N	Y	N	Y	N	Y	Y
21 ***Gallegly***	Y	N	Y	Y	Y	Y	Y	Y
22 ***Moorhead***	Y	N	Y	Y	Y	Y	Y	N
23 Beilenson	N	N	Y	N	Y	N	N	Y
24 Waxman	N	N	Y	N	Y	?	N	Y
25 Roybal	N	N	Y	N	Y	N	N	Y
26 Berman	N	N	Y	N	Y	N	N	Y
27 Levine	N	N	Y	N	Y	N	N	Y
28 Dixon	N	N	Y	N	Y	?	?	?
29 Hawkins	N	?	Y	?	?	?	?	?
30 Martinez	Y	Y	Y	?	?	?	?	?
31 Dymally	N	N	Y	N	Y	N	N	Y
32 Anderson	N	N	Y	N	Y	N	N	Y
33 ***Dreier***	Y	N	Y	Y	Y	Y	Y	N
34 Torres	N	N	Y	N	Y	N	N	Y
35 ***Lewis***	?	?	?	?	?	?	Y	N
36 Brown	N	N	Y	N	Y	N	N	Y
37 ***McCandless***	Y	Y	N	Y	Y	Y	Y	N
38 ***Dornan***	Y	N	N	Y	Y	Y	Y	N
39 ***Dannemeyer***	Y	Y	N	Y	Y	Y	Y	N
40 ***Cox***	Y	Y	N	Y	Y	Y	Y	N
41 ***Lowery***	?	?	?	?	?	?	?	?
42 ***Rohrabacher***	Y	Y	N	Y	Y	Y	Y	N
43 ***Packard***	N	N	Y	N	Y	N	Y	Y
44 Bates	?	?	?	?	?	?	N	Y
45 ***Hunter***	Y	Y	N	Y	Y	Y	Y	N
COLORADO								
1 Schroeder	N	N	Y	N	Y	N	N	Y
2 Skaggs	N	N	Y	N	Y	N	N	Y
3 Campbell	N	N	Y	N	Y	N	?	?
4 ***Brown***	N	N	Y	N	Y	N	Y	Y
5 ***Hefley***	Y	Y	N	Y	Y	Y	Y	N
6 ***Schaefer***	Y	N	Y	N	Y	N	Y	N
CONNECTICUT								
1 Kennelly	N	N	Y	N	Y	Y	N	Y
2 Gejdenson	N	N	Y	N	Y	N	N	Y
3 Morrison	N	N	Y	N	Y	N	N	Y
4 ***Shays***	N	N	Y	N	Y	N	N	Y
5 ***Rowland***	Y	N	Y	Y	Y	Y	Y	Y
6 ***Johnson***	N	N	Y	N	Y	N	N	Y
DELAWARE								
AL Carper	N	N	Y	N	Y	N	N	Y
FLORIDA								
1 Hutto	Y	?	?	?	?	?	?	?
2 ***Grant***	Y	Y	N	Y	Y	Y	Y	N
3 Bennett	Y	Y	N	Y	Y	Y	Y	N
4 ***James***	Y	N	Y	N	Y	N	Y	N
5 ***McCollum***	Y	Y	Y	Y	Y	Y	Y	N
6 ***Stearns***	Y	Y	N	Y	Y	Y	Y	N
7 Gibbons	N	N	Y	N	Y	N	Y	Y
8 ***Young***	Y	N	Y	Y	Y	Y	Y	N
9 ***Bilirakis***	Y	Y	N	Y	Y	Y	Y	N
10 ***Ireland***	Y	N	Y	Y	Y	Y	Y	N
11 Nelson	-	-	+	-	-	-	-	+
12 ***Lewis***	Y	Y	N	Y	Y	Y	Y	N
13 ***Goss***	Y	Y	N	Y	Y	Y	Y	Y
14 Johnston	N	N	Y	N	Y	N	N	Y
15 ***Shaw***	N	N	N	Y	Y	Y	Y	N
16 Smith	N	N	?	N	Y	N	N	Y
17 Lehman	N	N	?	N	Y	N	N	Y
18 ***Ros-Lehtinen***	N	Y	N	Y	Y	Y	Y	N
19 Fascell	N	N	Y	N	Y	N	N	Y
GEORGIA								
1 Thomas	N	N	Y	N	Y	N	N	Y
2 Hatcher	N	N	?	?	?	?	N	Y
3 Ray	Y	N	Y	N	Y	N	N	Y
4 Jones	N	N	Y	N	Y	N	N	Y
5 Lewis	N	N	Y	N	Y	N	N	Y
6 ***Gingrich***	Y	N	?	Y	?	?	Y	N
7 Darden	N	N	Y	N	Y	N	N	Y
8 Rowland	N	N	Y	N	Y	N	N	Y
9 Jenkins	N	N	Y	N	Y	N	N	Y
10 Barnard	N	N	Y	N	Y	N	N	Y
HAWAII								
1 ***Saiki***	N	N	Y	N	Y	N	Y	Y
2 Vacancy								
IDAHO								
1 ***Craig***	Y	#	X	#	?	Y	Y	N
2 Stallings	N	N	Y	N	Y	N	N	Y
ILLINOIS								
1 Hayes	N	N	Y	N	Y	N	N	Y
2 Savage	N	N	Y	N	Y	N	N	N
3 Russo	N	N	Y	N	Y	N	N	Y
4 Sangmeister	N	N	Y	N	Y	N	N	Y
5 Lipinski	Y	N	Y	N	Y	N	N	Y
6 ***Hyde***	Y	Y	N	Y	Y	Y	Y	N
7 Collins	N	N	Y	N	Y	N	N	Y
8 Rostenkowski	N	N	Y	N	Y	N	N	Y
9 Yates	N	N	Y	?	?	?	?	?
10 ***Porter***	Y	N	Y	N	Y	N	Y	Y
11 Annunzio	N	N	Y	N	Y	N	N	Y
12 ***Crane***	Y	Y	N	Y	Y	Y	Y	N
13 ***Fawell***	Y	Y	N	Y	Y	Y	Y	N
14 ***Hastert***	Y	N	Y	N	Y	Y	Y	Y
15 ***Madigan***	Y	N	Y	N	Y	N	N	N
16 ***Martin***	N	N	Y	N	Y	N	Y	Y
17 Evans	N	N	Y	N	Y	N	N	Y
18 ***Michel***	Y	N	N	N	Y	N	Y	N
19 Bruce	N	N	Y	N	Y	N	N	Y
20 Durbin	N	N	Y	N	Y	N	N	Y
21 Costello	N	N	Y	N	Y	N	N	Y
22 Poshard	N	N	Y	N	Y	N	N	Y
INDIANA								
1 Visclosky	N	N	Y	N	Y	N	N	Y
2 Sharp	N	N	Y	N	Y	N	N	Y
3 ***Hiler***	Y	N	Y	N	Y	Y	Y	N

ND Northern Democrats SD Southern Democrats

	153	154	155	156	157	158	159	160
4 Long	N	N	Y	N	Y	N	N	Y
5 Jontz	N	N	Y	N	Y	N	N	Y
6 ***Burton***	Y	Y	N	Y	Y	Y	Y	N
7 ***Myers***	N	N	Y	N	Y	N	Y	N
8 McCloskey	N	N	Y	N	Y	N	N	Y
9 Hamilton	N	N	Y	N	Y	N	N	Y
10 Jacobs	N	N	Y	N	Y	N	N	Y
IOWA								
1 ***Leach***	N	N	Y	N	Y	N	N	Y
2 ***Tauke***	N	N	Y	N	Y	N	N	Y
3 Nagle	N	N	Y	N	Y	N	N	Y
4 Smith	N	N	Y	N	Y	N	N	Y
5 ***Lightfoot***	Y	N	Y	Y	Y	Y	Y	Y
6 ***Grandy***	N	N	Y	N	Y	N	N	Y
KANSAS								
1 ***Roberts***	Y	N	Y	N	Y	N	Y	Y
2 Slattery	?	?	?	?	?	?	N	Y
3 ***Meyers***	Y	N	Y	Y	Y	Y	Y	Y
4 Glickman	N	N	Y	N	Y	N	N	Y
5 ***Whittaker***	Y	N	Y	N	Y	N	Y	Y
KENTUCKY								
1 Hubbard	Y	N	Y	N	Y	N	Y	Y
2 Natcher	N	N	Y	N	Y	N	N	Y
3 Mazzoli	N	N	Y	N	Y	N	N	Y
4 ***Bunning***	Y	Y	N	Y	Y	Y	Y	N
5 ***Rogers***	Y	N	Y	N	Y	Y	Y	Y
6 ***Hopkins***	Y	N	Y	N	Y	Y	Y	N
7 Perkins	N	N	Y	N	Y	N	N	Y
LOUISIANA								
1 ***Livingston***	Y	Y	N	Y	Y	Y	Y	N
2 Boggs	N	N	Y	N	Y	N	N	Y
3 Tauzin	N	N	Y	N	Y	N	Y	Y
4 ***McCrery***	Y	N	Y	?	Y	Y	Y	N
5 Huckaby	N	N	Y	?	Y	N	N	Y
6 ***Baker***	Y	N	Y	?	Y	Y	Y	N
7 Hayes	N	N	Y	N	Y	N	N	Y
8 ***Holloway***	Y	N	Y	N	Y	N	Y	N
MAINE								
1 Brennan	N	N	Y	N	Y	N	N	Y
2 ***Snowe***	N	N	Y	N	Y	N	Y	Y
MARYLAND								
1 Dyson	N	N	Y	N	Y	N	N	Y
2 ***Bentley***	Y	Y	N	Y	Y	Y	Y	N
3 Cardin	N	N	Y	N	Y	N	N	Y
4 McMillen	N	N	Y	N	Y	N	N	Y
5 Hoyer	N	N	Y	N	Y	N	N	Y
6 Byron	Y	N	?	?	?	?	N	Y
7 Mfume	N	N	Y	N	Y	N	N	Y
8 ***Morella***	N	N	Y	N	Y	N	N	Y
MASSACHUSETTS								
1 ***Conte***	N	N	Y	N	Y	N	N	Y
2 Neal	N	N	Y	N	Y	N	N	Y
3 Early	N	N	?	?	?	?	N	Y
4 Frank	N	N	Y	N	Y	N	N	Y
5 Atkins	N	N	Y	N	Y	N	N	Y
6 Mavroules	N	N	Y	N	Y	N	N	Y
7 Markey	N	N	?	N	Y	N	N	Y
8 Kennedy	N	N	Y	N	Y	N	N	Y
9 Moakley	N	N	Y	N	Y	N	N	Y
10 Studds	N	N	Y	N	Y	N	N	Y
11 Donnelly	Y	N	Y	N	Y	N	N	Y
MICHIGAN								
1 Conyers	N	N	?	?	?	N	?	?
2 ***Pursell***	Y	N	Y	N	Y	N	?	?
3 Wolpe	N	N	Y	N	Y	N	N	Y
4 ***Upton***	Y	N	Y	N	Y	N	Y	Y
5 ***Henry***	N	N	Y	N	Y	N	N	Y
6 Carr	N	N	Y	N	Y	N	N	Y
7 Kildee	N	N	Y	N	Y	N	N	Y
8 Traxler	N	N	Y	N	Y	N	N	Y
9 ***Vander Jagt***	N	N	Y	N	Y	N	Y	Y
10 ***Schuette***	Y	N	Y	Y	Y	Y	Y	Y
11 ***Davis***	Y	Y	Y	Y	?	?	Y	N
12 Bonior	N	N	Y	N	Y	N	N	Y
13 Crockett	?	?	?	?	Y	?	?	?
14 Hertel	N	N	Y	N	Y	N	N	Y
15 Ford	N	N	?	?	?	?	?	?
16 Dingell	N	N	Y	N	Y	N	N	Y
17 Levin	N	N	Y	N	Y	N	N	Y
18 ***Broomfield***	Y	N	Y	N	Y	Y	+	+
MINNESOTA								
1 Penny	N	N	Y	N	Y	N	N	Y
2 ***Weber***	N	N	Y	N	Y	N	N	Y
3 ***Frenzel***	N	N	Y	N	Y	N	N	Y
4 Vento	N	N	Y	N	Y	N	N	Y
5 Sabo	N	N	Y	N	Y	N	N	Y
6 Sikorski	N	N	Y	N	Y	N	N	Y
7 ***Stangeland***	Y	N	Y	N	Y	N	N	Y
8 Oberstar	N	N	Y	N	Y	N	N	Y
MISSISSIPPI								
1 Whitten	Y	N	Y	?	?	?	?	?
2 Espy	?	?	?	?	?	?	?	?
3 Montgomery	Y	N	Y	N	Y	N	N	Y
4 Parker	Y	N	Y	N	Y	N	N	Y
5 Taylor	Y	Y	N	Y	Y	N	Y	N
MISSOURI								
1 Clay	N	N	Y	N	?	N	N	Y
2 ***Buechner***	N	N	Y	N	Y	N	N	Y
3 Gephardt	N	N	Y	N	Y	N	N	Y
4 Skelton	N	N	Y	N	Y	N	N	Y
5 Wheat	N	N	Y	N	Y	N	N	Y
6 ***Coleman***	Y	N	Y	N	Y	N	Y	N
7 ***Hancock***	Y	Y	N	Y	Y	Y	Y	N
8 ***Emerson***	Y	N	Y	N	Y	Y	N	Y
9 Volkmer	N	N	Y	N	Y	N	N	Y
MONTANA								
1 Williams	N	N	?	N	Y	N	?	?
2 ***Marlenee***	Y	N	Y	N	Y	Y	Y	Y
NEBRASKA								
1 ***Bereuter***	N	N	Y	N	Y	N	N	Y
2 Hoagland	N	N	Y	N	Y	N	N	Y
3 ***Smith***	Y	N	Y	N	Y	N	N	Y
NEVADA								
1 Bilbray	N	N	Y	N	Y	N	N	Y
2 ***Vucanovich***	Y	Y	Y	Y	Y	Y	Y	N
NEW HAMPSHIRE								
1 ***Smith***	Y	Y	N	Y	Y	Y	Y	N
2 ***Douglas***	Y	N	Y	Y	Y	Y	Y	N
NEW JERSEY								
1 Vacancy								
2 Hughes	N	N	Y	N	Y	N	N	Y
3 Pallone	N	N	Y	N	Y	N	N	Y
4 ***Smith***	Y	N	Y	N	Y	N	Y	Y
5 ***Roukema***	N	N	Y	N	Y	N	N	Y
6 Dwyer	N	N	Y	N	Y	N	N	Y
7 ***Rinaldo***	Y	N	Y	N	Y	N	Y	Y
8 Roe	N	N	Y	N	Y	N	N	Y
9 Torricelli	N	N	?	N	Y	N	N	Y
10 Payne	N	N	Y	N	Y	N	N	Y
11 ***Gallo***	N	N	Y	N	Y	N	N	Y
12 ***Courter***	Y	N	Y	N	Y	N	Y	Y
13 ***Saxton***	Y	N	Y	N	Y	N	N	Y
14 Guarini	N	N	Y	N	Y	N	-	+
NEW MEXICO								
1 ***Schiff***	N	N	Y	N	Y	N	Y	Y
2 ***Skeen***	Y	N	Y	N	Y	N	Y	Y
3 Richardson	N	N	Y	N	Y	?	N	Y
NEW YORK								
1 Hochbrueckner	N	N	Y	N	Y	N	N	Y
2 Downey	N	N	?	N	Y	N	N	Y
3 Mrazek	N	N	Y	N	Y	N	?	Y
4 ***Lent***	N	N	Y	?	?	N	Y	Y
5 ***McGrath***	N	N	Y	N	Y	Y	Y	Y
6 Flake	N	N	Y	N	Y	N	N	Y
7 Ackerman	N	N	?	?	?	N	N	Y
8 Scheuer	Y	N	Y	N	Y	N	N	Y
9 Manton	N	N	Y	N	?	?	N	Y
10 Schumer	N	N	Y	N	Y	N	N	Y
11 Towns	N	N	Y	N	Y	?	?	?
12 Owens	N	N	Y	N	Y	N	N	Y
13 Solarz	N	N	Y	N	Y	N	N	Y
14 ***Molinari***	Y	Y	N	Y	Y	Y	Y	Y
15 ***Green***	N	N	Y	N	Y	N	N	Y
16 Rangel	N	N	Y	N	?	N	N	Y
17 Weiss	N	N	Y	N	Y	N	N	Y
18 Serrano	N	N	?	N	Y	N	N	Y
19 Engel	N	N	Y	N	Y	N	N	Y
20 Lowey	N	N	Y	N	Y	N	N	Y
21 ***Fish***	N	N	Y	N	Y	N	N	Y
22 ***Gilman***	Y	Y	N	Y	Y	Y	Y	N
23 McNulty	N	N	Y	N	Y	N	N	Y
24 ***Solomon***	Y	Y	N	Y	Y	Y	Y	N
25 ***Boehlert***	N	N	Y	N	Y	N	N	Y
26 ***Martin***	Y	N	Y	N	Y	N	Y	N
27 ***Walsh***	N	N	Y	N	Y	N	Y	Y
28 McHugh	N	N	Y	N	Y	N	N	Y
29 ***Horton***	N	N	Y	N	Y	N	N	Y
30 Slaughter	N	N	Y	N	Y	N	N	Y
31 ***Paxon***	Y	N	Y	N	Y	Y	Y	N
32 LaFalce	N	N	Y	N	Y	Y	N	Y
33 Nowak	N	N	Y	N	Y	N	N	Y
34 ***Houghton***	N	N	Y	N	Y	N	N	Y
NORTH CAROLINA								
1 Jones	N	N	Y	N	Y	N	N	Y
2 Valentine	N	N	?	N	Y	N	N	Y
3 Lancaster	N	N	Y	N	Y	N	Y	Y
4 Price	N	N	Y	N	Y	N	N	Y
5 Neal	N	N	N	N	Y	Y	N	Y
6 ***Coble***	N	N	Y	Y	Y	Y	Y	Y
7 Rose	N	N	Y	N	Y	N	N	Y
8 Hefner	N	N	Y	N	Y	N	N	Y
9 ***McMillan***	N	N	Y	N	Y	N	Y	Y
10 ***Ballenger***	Y	N	Y	N	Y	N	Y	N
11 Clarke	N	N	Y	N	Y	N	N	Y
NORTH DAKOTA								
AL Dorgan	N	N	Y	N	N	N	N	Y
OHIO								
1 Luken	N	N	Y	N	Y	N	N	Y
2 ***Gradison***	N	N	Y	N	Y	N	N	Y
3 Hall	Y	N	Y	N	Y	N	?	?
4 ***Oxley***	Y	N	Y	N	Y	N	Y	Y
5 ***Gillmor***	Y	N	Y	Y	?	?	Y	N
6 ***McEwen***	Y	Y	Y	Y	Y	Y	Y	N
7 ***DeWine***	Y	Y	N	Y	Y	Y	Y	N
8 ***Lukens***	Y	?	?	Y	Y	Y	?	?
9 Kaptur	N	N	Y	N	Y	N	N	Y
10 ***Miller***	Y	Y	N	Y	Y	Y	Y	N
11 Eckart	N	N	Y	N	Y	N	N	Y
12 ***Kasich***	Y	N	Y	Y	Y	Y	Y	N
13 Pease	N	N	Y	N	Y	N	N	Y
14 Sawyer	N	N	Y	N	Y	N	N	Y
15 ***Wylie***	N	N	Y	N	Y	N	Y	Y
16 ***Regula***	N	N	Y	N	Y	Y	Y	Y
17 Traficant	N	N	Y	N	Y	N	Y	Y
18 Applegate	N	N	Y	Y	Y	N	Y	Y
19 Feighan	N	N	Y	N	Y	N	N	Y
20 Oakar	N	?	?	?	?	?	?	?
21 Stokes	N	N	Y	N	?	N	N	Y
OKLAHOMA								
1 ***Inhofe***	Y	Y	Y	Y	Y	Y	Y	N
2 Synar	N	N	Y	N	Y	N	N	Y
3 Watkins	N	N	Y	Y	Y	Y	?	Y
4 McCurdy	N	N	Y	N	Y	N	N	Y
5 ***Edwards***	Y	N	Y	Y	Y	Y	Y	N
6 English	N	N	Y	N	Y	N	N	Y
OREGON								
1 AuCoin	N	N	Y	N	Y	N	N	Y
2 ***Smith, B.***	N	N	Y	N	Y	Y	Y	Y
3 Wyden	N	N	Y	N	Y	N	N	Y
4 DeFazio	N	N	Y	N	Y	?	N	Y
5 ***Smith, D.***	N	N	Y	?	Y	N	Y	Y
PENNSYLVANIA								
1 Foglietta	N	N	Y	N	Y	N	N	Y
2 Gray	N	N	Y	N	?	N	N	Y
3 Borski	N	N	Y	N	Y	N	N	Y
4 Kolter	N	N	Y	N	?	N	N	Y
5 ***Schulze***	Y	N	Y	?	?	?	Y	Y
6 Yatron	N	N	Y	N	Y	N	N	Y
7 ***Weldon***	Y	N	Y	Y	Y	Y	Y	Y
8 Kostmayer	N	N	Y	N	Y	N	N	Y
9 ***Shuster***	Y	N	N	Y	Y	Y	?	?
10 ***McDade***	?	?	?	?	?	?	?	?
11 Kanjorski	N	N	Y	N	Y	N	N	Y
12 Murtha	N	N	Y	N	Y	N	N	Y
13 ***Coughlin***	Y	N	Y	N	Y	N	Y	Y
14 Coyne	N	N	Y	N	Y	N	N	Y
15 ***Ritter***	Y	Y	N	Y	Y	Y	Y	N
16 ***Walker***	Y	Y	?	?	?	?	Y	N
17 ***Gekas***	N	N	N	Y	Y	Y	Y	N
18 Walgren	N	N	Y	N	Y	N	N	Y
19 ***Goodling***	Y	Y	?	Y	Y	?	Y	Y
20 Gaydos	N	N	Y	X	Y	N	N	Y
21 ***Ridge***	N	N	Y	N	Y	N	N	Y
22 Murphy	N	N	Y	N	?	N	N	Y
23 ***Clinger***	Y	N	Y	N	Y	N	N	N
RHODE ISLAND								
1 ***Machtley***	N	N	Y	N	Y	N	N	Y
2 ***Schneider***	N	N	Y	N	Y	N	N	Y
SOUTH CAROLINA								
1 ***Ravenel***	Y	N	Y	N	Y	N	Y	Y
2 ***Spence***	Y	Y	Y	Y	Y	Y	Y	N
3 Derrick	N	N	Y	N	Y	N	N	Y
4 Patterson	N	N	Y	N	Y	N	N	Y
5 Spratt	N	N	Y	N	Y	N	N	Y
6 Tallon	Y	N	Y	N	Y	N	N	Y
SOUTH DAKOTA								
AL Johnson	N	N	Y	N	Y	N	N	Y
TENNESSEE								
1 ***Quillen***	N	N	N	N	Y	N	Y	Y
2 ***Duncan***	Y	Y	N	Y	Y	Y	Y	N
3 Lloyd	N	N	Y	N	Y	N	N	Y
4 Cooper	N	N	Y	N	Y	N	N	Y
5 Clement	N	N	Y	N	Y	N	N	Y
6 Gordon	N	N	Y	N	Y	N	N	Y
7 ***Sundquist***	N	N	Y	N	Y	N	Y	Y
8 Tanner	N	N	Y	N	Y	N	N	Y
9 Ford	N	N	Y	N	Y	N	N	Y
TEXAS								
1 Chapman	N	N	Y	N	Y	N	N	Y
2 Wilson	Y	N	?	?	?	?	?	?
3 ***Bartlett***	N	N	Y	N	Y	N	N	Y
4 Hall	Y	N	Y	N	Y	N	Y	Y
5 Bryant	N	N	Y	N	Y	N	N	Y
6 ***Barton***	Y	N	Y	Y	Y	Y	Y	N
7 ***Archer***	Y	N	Y	N	Y	Y	Y	Y
8 ***Fields***	Y	N	?	N	Y	N	Y	Y
9 Brooks	N	N	N	N	Y	N	N	Y
10 Pickle	N	N	Y	N	Y	N	N	Y
11 Leath	N	?	?	?	?	?	?	?
12 Geren	N	N	Y	N	Y	N	N	Y
13 Sarpalius	N	N	Y	N	Y	N	N	Y
14 Laughlin	N	N	Y	N	Y	N	N	Y
15 de la Garza	?	?	?	?	?	?	?	?
16 Coleman	N	N	Y	N	Y	N	N	Y
17 Stenholm	N	N	Y	N	Y	N	N	Y
18 Washington	N	N	Y	?	?	?	?	Y
19 ***Combest***	Y	Y	N	Y	Y	Y	Y	N
20 Gonzalez	N	N	Y	N	Y	N	N	Y
21 ***Smith***	Y	N	Y	N	Y	N	Y	Y
22 ***DeLay***	Y	N	Y	N	Y	N	Y	N
23 Bustamante	N	N	Y	N	Y	N	N	Y
24 Frost	N	N	Y	N	Y	N	N	Y
25 Andrews	N	N	Y	N	Y	N	N	Y
26 ***Armey***	Y	N	Y	N	Y	N	Y	N
27 Ortiz	Y	N	Y	N	Y	N	N	Y
UTAH								
1 ***Hansen***	Y	N	N	Y	Y	Y	Y	N
2 Owens	N	N	Y	N	Y	N	N	Y
3 ***Nielson***	N	N	Y	N	Y	N	Y	N
VERMONT								
AL ***Smith***	N	N	Y	N	Y	N	N	Y
VIRGINIA								
1 ***Bateman***	Y	Y	N	Y	Y	Y	Y	N
2 Pickett	Y	N	Y	N	Y	N	N	Y
3 ***Bliley***	Y	N	Y	Y	Y	Y	Y	N
4 Sisisky	Y	N	Y	N	Y	N	Y	Y
5 Payne	N	N	Y	?	Y	N	N	Y
6 Olin	N	N	Y	N	Y	N	N	Y
7 ***Slaughter***	Y	N	Y	Y	Y	Y	Y	N
8 ***Parris***	Y	N	Y	Y	Y	Y	Y	Y
9 Boucher	N	N	Y	N	Y	N	N	Y
10 ***Wolf***	Y	N	?	Y	Y	Y	Y	N
WASHINGTON								
1 ***Miller***	N	N	Y	N	Y	N	N	Y
2 Swift	N	N	Y	N	Y	N	N	Y
3 Unsoeld	N	N	Y	N	Y	N	N	Y
4 ***Morrison***	N	N	Y	N	?	N	N	Y
5 Foley								
6 Dicks	N	N	Y	N	Y	N	N	Y
7 McDermott	N	N	Y	N	Y	N	N	Y
8 ***Chandler***	N	N	Y	N	Y	N	N	Y
WEST VIRGINIA								
1 Mollohan	N	N	Y	N	Y	N	N	Y
2 Staggers	N	N	Y	N	Y	N	N	Y
3 Wise	N	N	Y	N	Y	N	N	Y
4 Rahall	N	N	Y	N	Y	N	N	Y
WISCONSIN								
1 Aspin	N	N	Y	N	Y	N	N	Y
2 Kastenmeier	N	N	Y	N	Y	N	N	Y
3 ***Gunderson***	Y	N	Y	N	Y	N	?	?
4 Kleczka	N	N	Y	N	Y	N	N	Y
5 Moody	?	?	?	?	?	?	?	?
6 ***Petri***	N	N	Y	N	Y	N	N	Y
7 Obey	N	N	Y	N	Y	N	N	Y
8 ***Roth***	N	N	Y	N	Y	N	Y	Y
9 ***Sensenbrenner***	Y	N	Y	N	Y	N	Y	Y
WYOMING								
AL ***Thomas***	N	N	Y	N	Y	N	Y	Y

Southern states - Ala., Ark., Fla., Ga., Ky., La., Miss., N.C., Okla., S.C., Tenn., Texas, Va.
Omitted votes are quorum calls, which CQ does not include in its vote charts.

161. Procedural Motion. Fields, R-Texas, motion to approve the House Journal of Wednesday, June 6. Motion agreed to 283-106: R 61-101; D 222-5 (ND 147-5, SD 75-0), June 7, 1990.

162. HR 2364. Amtrak Reauthorization/Veto Override. Passage, over President Bush's May 24 veto, of the bill to reauthorize the National Railroad Passenger Corporation (Amtrak) for fiscal years 1989-92. Passed (thus clearing the measure for Senate action) 294-123: R 58-116; D 236-7 (ND 166-0, SD 70-7), June 7, 1990. A two-thirds majority of those present and voting (278 in this case) of both houses is required to override a veto. A "nay" was a vote supporting the president's position.

KEY

- Y Voted for (yea).
- # Paired for.
- \+ Announced for.
- N Voted against (nay).
- X Paired against.
- \- Announced against.
- P Voted "present."
- C Voted "present" to avoid possible conflict of interest.
- ? Did not vote or otherwise make a position known.

Democrats ***Republicans***

	161	162
ALABAMA		
1 ***Callahan***	Y	Y
2 ***Dickinson***	N	N
3 Browder	Y	Y
4 Bevill	Y	Y
5 Flippo	?	?
6 Erdreich	Y	Y
7 Harris	Y	Y
ALASKA		
AL ***Young***	?	N
ARIZONA		
1 ***Rhodes***	N	N
2 Udall	?	Y
3 ***Stump***	N	N
4 ***Kyl***	N	N
5 ***Kolbe***	N	N
ARKANSAS		
1 Alexander	Y	Y
2 ***Robinson***	Y	N
3 ***Hammerschmidt***	Y	N
4 Anthony	Y	Y
CALIFORNIA		
1 Bosco	Y	Y
2 ***Herger***	N	N
3 Matsui	Y	Y
4 Fazio	Y	Y
5 Pelosi	Y	Y
6 Boxer	?	?
7 Miller	Y	Y
8 Dellums	Y	Y
9 Stark	Y	Y
10 Edwards	Y	Y
11 Lantos	Y	Y
12 ***Campbell***	N	N
13 Mineta	Y	Y
14 ***Shumway***	Y	N
15 Condit	?	Y
16 Panetta	Y	Y
17 ***Pashayan***	N	Y
18 Lehman	?	?
19 ***Lagomarsino***	N	Y
20 ***Thomas***	N	Y
21 ***Gallegly***	N	N
22 ***Moorhead***	N	N
23 Beilenson	Y	Y
24 Waxman	Y	Y
25 Roybal	?	Y
26 Berman	Y	Y
27 Levine	?	Y
28 Dixon	Y	Y
29 Hawkins	?	?
30 Martinez	?	Y
31 Dymally	Y	Y
32 Anderson	Y	Y
33 ***Dreier***	N	N
34 Torres	?	Y
35 ***Lewis***	N	N
36 Brown	Y	Y
37 ***McCandless***	N	N
38 ***Dornan***	N	N
39 ***Dannemeyer***	N	N
40 ***Cox***	?	N
41 ***Lowery***	?	N
42 ***Rohrabacher***	N	N
43 ***Packard***	Y	N
44 Bates	Y	Y
45 ***Hunter***	?	N
COLORADO		
1 Schroeder	N	Y
2 Skaggs	Y	Y
3 Campbell	Y	Y
4 ***Brown***	Y	N
5 ***Hefley***	N	N
6 ***Schaefer***	N	Y
CONNECTICUT		
1 Kennelly	Y	Y
2 Gejdenson	Y	Y
3 Morrison	Y	Y
4 ***Shays***	N	Y
5 ***Rowland***	Y	Y
6 ***Johnson***	Y	Y
DELAWARE		
AL Carper	Y	Y
FLORIDA		
1 Hutto	?	?
2 ***Grant***	Y	N
3 Bennett	Y	Y
4 ***James***	N	N
5 ***McCollum***	N	N
6 ***Stearns***	N	N
7 Gibbons	?	Y
8 ***Young***	N	N
9 ***Bilirakis***	N	N
10 ***Ireland***	N	N
11 Nelson	+	+
12 ***Lewis***	N	N
13 ***Goss***	N	N
14 Johnston	Y	?
15 ***Shaw***	Y	N
16 Smith	?	Y
17 Lehman	Y	Y
18 ***Ros-Lehtinen***	N	N
19 Fascell	Y	Y
GEORGIA		
1 Thomas	Y	Y
2 Hatcher	Y	Y
3 Ray	Y	Y
4 Jones	Y	Y
5 Lewis	Y	Y
6 ***Gingrich***	N	N
7 Darden	Y	Y
8 Rowland	Y	Y
9 Jenkins	Y	Y
10 Barnard	Y	Y
HAWAII		
1 ***Saiki***	Y	N
2 Vacancy		
IDAHO		
1 ***Craig***	?	N
2 Stallings	Y	Y
ILLINOIS		
1 Hayes	Y	Y
2 Savage	Y	Y
3 Russo	Y	Y
4 Sangmeister	Y	Y
5 Lipinski	Y	Y
6 ***Hyde***	N	N
7 Collins	Y	Y
8 Rostenkowski	Y	Y
9 Yates	Y	Y
10 ***Porter***	N	N
11 Annunzio	Y	Y
12 ***Crane***	?	N
13 ***Fawell***	N	N
14 ***Hastert***	N	N
15 ***Madigan***	N	Y
16 ***Martin***	?	N
17 Evans	Y	Y
18 ***Michel***	Y	N
19 Bruce	Y	Y
20 Durbin	Y	Y
21 Costello	Y	Y
22 Poshard	Y	Y
INDIANA		
1 Visclosky	Y	Y
2 Sharp	Y	Y
3 ***Hiler***	N	N

ND Northern Democrats SD Southern Democrats

	161	162
4 Long	Y	Y
5 Jontz	Y	Y
6 ***Burton***	N	N
7 ***Myers***	Y	Y
8 McCloskey	?	Y
9 Hamilton	Y	Y
10 Jacobs	N	Y
IOWA		
1 ***Leach***	N	Y
2 ***Tauke***	N	Y
3 Nagle	Y	Y
4 Smith	Y	Y
5 ***Lightfoot***	N	Y
6 ***Grandy***	N	Y
KANSAS		
1 ***Roberts***	N	Y
2 Slattery	Y	Y
3 ***Meyers***	Y	Y
4 Glickman	Y	Y
5 ***Whittaker***	N	Y
KENTUCKY		
1 Hubbard	Y	N
2 Natcher	Y	Y
3 Mazzoli	Y	Y
4 ***Bunning***	N	N
5 ***Rogers***	N	N
6 ***Hopkins***	N	N
7 Perkins	Y	Y
LOUISIANA		
1 ***Livingston***	Y	N
2 Boggs	Y	Y
3 Tauzin	Y	Y
4 ***McCrery***	?	N
5 Huckaby	Y	Y
6 ***Baker***	N	N
7 Hayes	Y	Y
8 ***Holloway***	N	N
MAINE		
1 Brennan	Y	Y
2 ***Snowe***	Y	Y
MARYLAND		
1 Dyson	Y	Y
2 ***Bentley***	N	Y
3 Cardin	Y	Y
4 McMillen	Y	Y
5 Hoyer	Y	Y
6 Byron	Y	Y
7 Mfume	?	?
8 ***Morella***	Y	Y
MASSACHUSETTS		
1 ***Conte***	Y	Y
2 Neal	Y	Y
3 Early	Y	Y
4 Frank	Y	Y
5 Atkins	Y	Y
6 Mavroules	Y	Y
7 Markey	Y	Y
8 Kennedy	Y	Y
9 Moakley	Y	Y
10 Studds	Y	Y
11 Donnelly	Y	Y
MICHIGAN		
1 Conyers	?	Y
2 ***Pursell***	Y	?
3 Wolpe	Y	Y
4 ***Upton***	N	N
5 ***Henry***	N	N
6 Carr	Y	Y
7 Kildee	Y	Y
8 Traxler	Y	Y
9 ***Vander Jagt***	Y	Y
10 ***Schuette***	N	N
11 ***Davis***	Y	Y
12 Bonior	Y	Y
13 Crockett	?	Y
14 Hertel	Y	Y
15 Ford	Y	Y
16 Dingell	Y	Y
17 Levin	Y	Y
18 ***Broomfield***	Y	N
MINNESOTA		
1 Penny	Y	Y
2 ***Weber***	?	N
3 ***Frenzel***	Y	N
4 Vento	Y	Y

	161	162
5 Sabo	Y	Y
6 Sikorski	N	Y
7 ***Stangeland***	N	Y
8 Oberstar	Y	Y
MISSISSIPPI		
1 Whitten	Y	Y
2 Espy	?	Y
3 Montgomery	Y	Y
4 Parker	Y	Y
5 Taylor	Y	Y
MISSOURI		
1 Clay	N	Y
2 ***Buechner***	N	N
3 Gephardt	Y	Y
4 Skelton	Y	Y
5 Wheat	Y	Y
6 ***Coleman***	N	N
7 ***Hancock***	N	N
8 ***Emerson***	?	Y
9 Volkmer	Y	Y
MONTANA		
1 Williams	?	Y
2 ***Marlenee***	?	Y
NEBRASKA		
1 ***Bereuter***	N	N
2 Hoagland	Y	Y
3 ***Smith***	Y	N
NEVADA		
1 Bilbray	Y	Y
2 ***Vucanovich***	N	N
NEW HAMPSHIRE		
1 ***Smith***	N	N
2 ***Douglas***	N	N
NEW JERSEY		
1 Vacancy		
2 Hughes	Y	Y
3 Pallone	Y	Y
4 ***Smith***	Y	Y
5 ***Roukema***	N	Y
6 Dwyer	Y	Y
7 ***Rinaldo***	Y	Y
8 Roe	Y	Y
9 Torricelli	Y	Y
10 Payne	Y	Y
11 ***Gallo***	Y	Y
12 ***Courter***	Y	N
13 ***Saxton***	?	?
14 Guarini	Y	Y
NEW MEXICO		
1 ***Schiff***	Y	N
2 ***Skeen***	Y	N
3 Richardson	Y	Y
NEW YORK		
1 Hochbrueckner	Y	Y
2 Downey	Y	Y
3 Mrazek	Y	Y
4 ***Lent***	Y	Y
5 ***McGrath***	N	Y
6 Flake	Y	Y
7 Ackerman	Y	Y
8 Scheuer	Y	Y
9 Manton	Y	Y
10 Schumer	Y	Y
11 Towns	Y	Y
12 Owens	Y	Y
13 Solarz	Y	Y
14 ***Molinari***	N	N
15 ***Green***	Y	Y
16 Rangel	?	Y
17 Weiss	Y	Y
18 Serrano	Y	Y
19 Engel	Y	Y
20 Lowey	Y	Y
21 ***Fish***	Y	N
22 ***Gilman***	Y	Y
23 McNulty	Y	Y
24 ***Solomon***	N	Y
25 ***Boehlert***	?	Y
26 ***Martin***	Y	Y
27 ***Walsh***	Y	Y
28 McHugh	Y	Y
29 ***Horton***	Y	Y
30 Slaughter	Y	Y
31 ***Paxon***	N	N

	161	162
32 LaFalce	Y	Y
33 Nowak	Y	Y
34 ***Houghton***	Y	N
NORTH CAROLINA		
1 Jones	Y	Y
2 Valentine	Y	Y
3 Lancaster	Y	Y
4 Price	Y	Y
5 Neal	Y	N
6 ***Coble***	N	N
7 Rose	Y	Y
8 Hefner	Y	Y
9 ***McMillan***	N	Y
10 ***Ballenger***	N	N
11 Clarke	Y	Y
NORTH DAKOTA		
AL Dorgan	Y	Y
OHIO		
1 Luken	Y	Y
2 ***Gradison***	Y	N
3 Hall	?	Y
4 ***Oxley***	N	N
5 ***Gillmor***	Y	N
6 ***McEwen***	Y	N
7 ***DeWine***	N	Y
8 ***Lukens***	N	N
9 Kaptur	Y	Y
10 ***Miller***	N	N
11 Eckart	Y	Y
12 ***Kasich***	Y	N
13 Pease	Y	Y
14 Sawyer	Y	Y
15 ***Wylie***	Y	N
16 ***Regula***	N	Y
17 Traficant	Y	Y
18 Applegate	Y	Y
19 Feighan	Y	Y
20 Oakar	?	?
21 Stokes	?	Y
OKLAHOMA		
1 ***Inhofe***	N	N
2 Synar	Y	Y
3 Watkins	Y	N
4 McCurdy	Y	N
5 ***Edwards***	N	N
6 English	Y	N
OREGON		
1 AuCoin	Y	Y
2 ***Smith, B.***	N	Y
3 Wyden	Y	Y
4 DeFazio	Y	Y
5 ***Smith, D.***	Y	N
PENNSYLVANIA		
1 Foglietta	Y	Y
2 Gray	Y	Y
3 Borski	Y	Y
4 Kolter	?	Y
5 ***Schulze***	Y	N
6 Yatron	Y	Y
7 ***Weldon***	Y	Y
8 Kostmayer	Y	Y
9 ***Shuster***	Y	Y
10 ***McDade***	N	N
11 Kanjorski	Y	Y
12 Murtha	Y	Y
13 ***Coughlin***	N	N
14 Coyne	Y	Y
15 ***Ritter***	Y	N
16 ***Walker***	N	N
17 ***Gekas***	N	N
18 Walgren	Y	Y
19 ***Goodling***	?	N
20 Gaydos	Y	Y
21 ***Ridge***	N	Y
22 Murphy	N	Y
23 ***Clinger***	Y	N
RHODE ISLAND		
1 ***Machtley***	N	Y
2 ***Schneider***	Y	Y
SOUTH CAROLINA		
1 ***Ravenel***	Y	Y
2 ***Spence***	Y	N
3 Derrick	Y	Y
4 Patterson	Y	Y
5 Spratt	Y	Y
6 Tallon	Y	Y

	161	162
SOUTH DAKOTA		
AL Johnson	Y	Y
TENNESSEE		
1 ***Quillen***	N	N
2 ***Duncan***	N	N
3 Lloyd	Y	Y
4 Cooper	Y	Y
5 Clement	Y	Y
6 Gordon	Y	Y
7 ***Sundquist***	N	N
8 Tanner	Y	Y
9 Ford	Y	Y
TEXAS		
1 Chapman	Y	Y
2 Wilson	Y	Y
3 ***Bartlett***	Y	N
4 Hall	Y	N
5 Bryant	Y	Y
6 ***Barton***	N	N
7 ***Archer***	Y	N
8 ***Fields***	N	N
9 Brooks	Y	Y
10 Pickle	Y	Y
11 Leath	?	?
12 Geren	Y	N
13 Sarpalius	Y	Y
14 Laughlin	Y	Y
15 de la Garza	Y	Y
16 Coleman	Y	?
17 Stenholm	Y	Y
18 Washington	?	Y
19 ***Combest***	Y	N
20 Gonzalez	Y	Y
21 ***Smith***	N	Y
22 ***DeLay***	N	N
23 Bustamante	Y	Y
24 Frost	Y	Y
25 Andrews	Y	Y
26 ***Armey***	N	N
27 Ortiz	Y	Y
UTAH		
1 ***Hansen***	N	N
2 Owens	?	?
3 ***Nielson***	N	N
VERMONT		
AL ***Smith***	Y	Y
VIRGINIA		
1 ***Bateman***	Y	Y
2 Pickett	Y	Y
3 ***Bliley***	N	Y
4 Sisisky	Y	Y
5 Payne	Y	Y
6 Olin	Y	Y
7 ***Slaughter***	N	Y
8 ***Parris***	N	Y
9 Boucher	Y	Y
10 ***Wolf***	N	Y
WASHINGTON		
1 ***Miller***	N	Y
2 Swift	Y	Y
3 Unsoeld	Y	Y
4 ***Morrison***	Y	N
5 Foley		
6 Dicks	Y	Y
7 McDermott	Y	Y
8 ***Chandler***	N	N
WEST VIRGINIA		
1 Mollohan	Y	Y
2 Staggers	Y	Y
3 Wise	Y	Y
4 Rahall	Y	Y
WISCONSIN		
1 Aspin	Y	Y
2 Kastenmeier	Y	Y
3 ***Gunderson***	Y	N
4 Kleczka	Y	Y
5 Moody	?	?
6 ***Petri***	Y	Y
7 Obey	Y	Y
8 ***Roth***	Y	N
9 ***Sensenbrenner***	N	N
WYOMING		
AL ***Thomas***	N	N

Southern states - Ala., Ark., Fla., Ga., Ky., La., Miss., N.C., Okla., S.C., Tenn., Texas, Va.
Omitted votes are quorum calls, which CQ does not include in its vote charts.

HOUSE VOTES 163, 164, 165, 166, 167, 168

163. HR 20. Hatch Act Revisions/Passage. Ford, D-Mich., motion to suspend the rules and concur in the Senate amendments to the bill (thus clearing the measure for the president) to allow greater political activity by federal employees and to protect them from political pressure. Motion agreed to 334-87: R 90-84; D 244-3 (ND 165-2, SD 79-1), June 12, 1990. A two-thirds majority of those present and voting (281 in this case) is required for passage under suspension of the rules. A "nay" was a vote supporting the president's position.

164. HR 4785. AIDS Prevention Act/Rule. Adoption of the rule (H Res 408) to provide for House floor consideration of the bill to authorize emergency relief to cities with the largest numbers of AIDS cases, provide grants for health-care facilities to provide AIDS testing and counseling to help prevent the spread of AIDS, create a system to notify emergency workers of possible exposure to infectious diseases, authorize various other grant and demonstration projects, and require certain studies. Adopted 308-109: R 61-109; D 247-0 (ND 168-0, SD 79-0), June 13, 1990.

165. HR 2567. Reclamation Project Authorization/Rule. Adoption of the rule (H Res 409) to provide for House floor consideration of the bill to authorize the Bureau of Reclamation to study, design, construct or modify a number of water and power projects. Adopted 250-167: R 30-140; D 220-27 (ND 157-11, SD 63-16), June 13, 1990.

166. HR 4785. AIDS Prevention Act/Name Reporting. Rowland, D-Ga., substitute amendment to the Dannemeyer, R-Calif., amendment, to state that nothing shall be construed to require or prohibit a state from reporting to public health authorities identifying information about people testing positive for HIV, the virus that causes AIDS. Adopted 312-113: R 70-103; D 242-10 (ND 170-1, SD 72-9), June 13, 1990.

167. HR 4785. AIDS Prevention Act/Name Reporting. Dannemeyer, R-Calif., amendment to allow states to decide whether to establish a reporting system for entities performing HIV testing to confidentially report to public health officials identifying information about people testing positive for HIV. Before being amended by Rowland, D-Ga., the Dannemeyer amendment would have required states to set up a reporting system before they could receive federal grants. Adopted 422-1: R 171-1; D 251-0 (ND 169-0, SD 82-0), June 13, 1990.

168. HR 4785. AIDS Prevention Act/Passage. Passage of the bill to authorize $2.76 billion over five years for emergency relief to cities with the largest numbers of AIDS cases and grants for health-care facilities to provide AIDS testing and counseling to help prevent the spread of AIDS and to help implement a system to notify emergency workers of possible exposure to infectious diseases, authorize various other grant and demonstration projects, and require certain studies. Passed 408-14: R 159-14; D 249-0 (ND 168-0, SD 81-0), June 13, 1990. A "nay" was a vote supporting the president's position. (The House subsequently passed S 2240 by voice vote after substituting the text of HR 4785 for the Senate-passed text of S 2240.)

KEY

Y Voted for (yea).
Paired for.
+ Announced for.
N Voted against (nay).
X Paired against.
- Announced against.
P Voted "present."
C Voted "present" to avoid possible conflict of interest.
? Did not vote or otherwise make a position known.

Democrats ***Republicans***

	163	164	165	166	167	168
ALABAMA						
1 ***Callahan***	N	Y	N	N	Y	Y
2 ***Dickinson***	N	N	N	Y	Y	Y
3 Browder	Y	Y	Y	Y	Y	Y
4 Bevill	Y	Y	Y	Y	Y	Y
5 Flippo	Y	Y	Y	Y	Y	Y
6 Erdreich	Y	Y	Y	Y	Y	Y
7 Harris	Y	Y	Y	Y	Y	Y
ALASKA						
AL ***Young***	Y	Y	N	Y	Y	Y
ARIZONA						
1 ***Rhodes***	Y	N	N	Y	Y	Y
2 Udall	Y	Y	Y	Y	Y	Y
3 ***Stump***	N	N	N	N	Y	N
4 ***Kyl***	N	N	N	N	Y	N
5 ***Kolbe***	Y	N	N	Y	Y	Y
ARKANSAS						
1 Alexander	?	Y	Y	Y	Y	Y
2 ***Robinson***	Y	N	N	Y	Y	Y
3 ***Hammerschmidt***	Y	N	N	N	Y	Y
4 Anthony	Y	Y	Y	Y	Y	Y
CALIFORNIA						
1 Bosco	Y	Y	Y	Y	Y	Y
2 ***Herger***	N	N	N	N	Y	Y
3 Matsui	Y	Y	N	Y	Y	Y
4 Fazio	Y	Y	N	Y	Y	Y
5 Pelosi	Y	Y	Y	Y	Y	Y
6 Boxer	Y	Y	Y	Y	Y	Y
7 Miller	Y	Y	Y	Y	Y	Y
8 Dellums	Y	?	Y	Y	Y	Y
9 Stark	Y	Y	Y	Y	Y	Y
10 Edwards	Y	Y	Y	Y	Y	Y
11 Lantos	Y	Y	Y	Y	Y	Y
12 ***Campbell***	Y	N	Y	Y	Y	Y
13 Mineta	Y	Y	Y	Y	Y	Y
14 ***Shumway***	N	N	N	N	Y	Y
15 Condit	Y	Y	N	Y	Y	Y
16 Panetta	Y	Y	N	Y	Y	Y
17 ***Pashayan***	Y	Y	P	Y	Y	Y
18 Lehman	Y	Y	N	Y	Y	Y
19 ***Lagomarsino***	N	N	N	N	Y	Y
20 ***Thomas***	Y	?	N	N	Y	Y
21 ***Gallegly***	N	N	N	N	Y	Y
22 ***Moorhead***	N	Y	N	N	Y	Y
23 Beilenson	N	Y	Y	Y	Y	Y
24 Waxman	Y	Y	Y	Y	Y	Y
25 Roybal	Y	Y	Y	Y	Y	Y
26 Berman	Y	Y	Y	Y	Y	Y
27 Levine	Y	Y	Y	Y	Y	Y
28 Dixon	Y	Y	Y	Y	Y	Y
29 Hawkins	Y	?	Y	?	?	?
30 Martinez	Y	Y	Y	Y	Y	Y
31 Dymally	Y	Y	Y	Y	Y	Y
32 Anderson	Y	Y	Y	Y	Y	Y
33 ***Dreier***	Y	N	N	N	Y	Y
34 Torres	Y	Y	Y	Y	Y	Y
35 ***Lewis***	N	N	N	Y	Y	Y
36 Brown	Y	Y	Y	Y	Y	Y
37 ***McCandless***	N	N	N	Y	Y	Y
38 ***Dornan***	N	N	N	N	Y	Y
39 ***Dannemeyer***	N	N	N	N	Y	Y
40 ***Cox***	N	N	N	N	Y	Y
41 ***Lowery***	Y	N	N	N	Y	Y
42 ***Rohrabacher***	N	N	N	N	Y	Y
43 ***Packard***	N	N	N	N	Y	Y
44 Bates	Y	Y	Y	Y	Y	Y
45 ***Hunter***	N	N	N	N	Y	N
COLORADO						
1 Schroeder	Y	Y	Y	Y	Y	Y
2 Skaggs	Y	Y	Y	Y	Y	Y
3 Campbell	Y	Y	N	Y	Y	Y
4 ***Brown***	N	N	N	N	Y	Y
5 ***Hefley***	N	N	Y	N	Y	Y
6 ***Schaefer***	Y	N	N	N	Y	N
CONNECTICUT						
1 Kennelly	Y	Y	Y	Y	Y	Y
2 Gejdenson	Y	Y	Y	Y	Y	Y
3 Morrison	Y	Y	Y	Y	Y	Y
4 ***Shays***	Y	Y	Y	Y	Y	Y
5 ***Rowland***	Y	Y	N	Y	Y	Y
6 ***Johnson***	N	N	N	Y	Y	Y
DELAWARE						
AL Carper	Y	Y	Y	Y	Y	Y
FLORIDA						
1 Hutto	Y	Y	N	N	Y	Y
2 ***Grant***	Y	Y	N	Y	Y	Y
3 Bennett	N	Y	Y	Y	Y	Y
4 ***James***	N	N	N	N	Y	Y
5 ***McCollum***	N	N	N	N	Y	Y
6 ***Stearns***	N	N	N	N	Y	Y
7 Gibbons	Y	Y	Y	Y	Y	Y
8 ***Young***	Y	N	N	N	Y	Y
9 ***Bilirakis***	Y	N	N	N	Y	Y
10 ***Ireland***	N	N	N	N	Y	Y
11 Nelson	+	+	+	+	+	+
12 ***Lewis***	N	N	N	N	Y	Y
13 ***Goss***	Y	N	N	Y	Y	Y
14 Johnston	Y	Y	Y	Y	Y	Y
15 ***Shaw***	N	N	N	N	Y	Y
16 Smith	Y	Y	Y	Y	Y	Y
17 Lehman	Y	Y	Y	Y	Y	Y
18 ***Ros-Lehtinen***	Y	Y	Y	Y	Y	Y
19 Fascell	Y	Y	Y	Y	Y	Y
GEORGIA						
1 Thomas	Y	Y	Y	Y	Y	Y
2 Hatcher	Y	Y	N	Y	Y	Y
3 Ray	Y	Y	?	Y	Y	Y
4 Jones	Y	Y	Y	Y	Y	Y
5 Lewis	Y	Y	Y	Y	Y	Y
6 ***Gingrich***	N	N	N	N	Y	Y
7 Darden	Y	Y	Y	Y	Y	Y
8 Rowland	Y	Y	Y	Y	Y	Y
9 Jenkins	Y	Y	Y	Y	Y	Y
10 Barnard	Y	Y	Y	Y	Y	Y
HAWAII						
1 ***Saiki***	Y	Y	Y	Y	Y	Y
2 Vacancy						
IDAHO						
1 ***Craig***	Y	N	N	N	Y	Y
2 Stallings	Y	Y	N	Y	Y	Y
ILLINOIS						
1 Hayes	Y	Y	Y	Y	Y	Y
2 Savage	Y	Y	Y	Y	Y	Y
3 Russo	Y	Y	Y	Y	Y	Y
4 Sangmeister	Y	Y	Y	Y	Y	Y
5 Lipinski	Y	Y	Y	Y	Y	Y
6 ***Hyde***	N	N	N	N	Y	Y
7 Collins	Y	Y	Y	Y	Y	Y
8 Rostenkowski	?	?	?	?	?	?
9 Yates	Y	Y	Y	Y	Y	Y
10 ***Porter***	N	N	Y	Y	Y	Y
11 Annunzio	Y	Y	?	Y	Y	Y
12 ***Crane***	N	N	N	N	Y	N
13 ***Fawell***	N	N	N	N	Y	Y
14 ***Hastert***	Y	N	N	N	Y	Y
15 ***Madigan***	N	Y	N	N	Y	Y
16 ***Martin***	Y	N	N	N	Y	Y
17 Evans	Y	Y	Y	Y	Y	Y
18 ***Michel***	Y	Y	N	N	Y	Y
19 Bruce	Y	Y	Y	Y	Y	Y
20 Durbin	Y	Y	Y	Y	Y	Y
21 Costello	Y	Y	Y	Y	Y	Y
22 Poshard	Y	Y	Y	Y	Y	Y
INDIANA						
1 Visclosky	Y	Y	Y	Y	Y	Y
2 Sharp	Y	Y	Y	Y	Y	Y
3 ***Hiler***	N	N	Y	N	Y	Y

ND Northern Democrats SD Southern Democrats

	163	164	165	166	167	168
4 Long	Y	Y	Y	Y	Y	Y
5 Jontz	Y	Y	Y	Y	Y	Y
6 ***Burton***	Y	N	N	N	Y	Y
7 ***Myers***	Y	Y	N	N	Y	Y
8 McCloskey	Y	Y	Y	Y	Y	Y
9 Hamilton	Y	Y	Y	Y	Y	Y
10 Jacobs	Y	Y	Y	Y	Y	Y
IOWA						
1 ***Leach***	N	Y	N	Y	Y	Y
2 ***Tauke***	Y	N	N	Y	Y	Y
3 Nagle	Y	Y	Y	Y	Y	Y
4 Smith	Y	Y	Y	Y	Y	Y
5 ***Lightfoot***	N	?	?	?	?	?
6 ***Grandy***	Y	N	N	Y	Y	Y
KANSAS						
1 ***Roberts***	N	N	N	N	Y	Y
2 Slattery	Y	Y	Y	Y	Y	Y
3 ***Meyers***	N	Y	Y	Y	Y	Y
4 Glickman	Y	Y	Y	Y	Y	Y
5 ***Whittaker***	Y	N	N	Y	Y	Y
KENTUCKY						
1 Hubbard	Y	Y	N	N	Y	Y
2 Natcher	Y	Y	Y	Y	Y	Y
3 Mazzoli	Y	Y	Y	Y	Y	+
4 ***Bunning***	N	N	N	N	Y	Y
5 ***Rogers***	N	N	N	N	Y	Y
6 ***Hopkins***	N	Y	N	Y	Y	Y
7 Perkins	Y	Y	N	Y	Y	Y
LOUISIANA						
1 ***Livingston***	Y	N	N	N	Y	Y
2 Boggs	Y	Y	Y	Y	Y	Y
3 Tauzin	Y	Y	N	N	Y	Y
4 ***McCrery***	N	Y	Y	Y	Y	Y
5 Huckaby	Y	Y	Y	Y	Y	Y
6 ***Baker***	N	N	N	N	Y	Y
7 Hayes	Y	Y	Y	Y	Y	Y
8 ***Holloway***	Y	N	N	N	N	N
MAINE						
1 Brennan	Y	Y	Y	Y	Y	Y
2 ***Snowe***	N	Y	Y	Y	Y	Y
MARYLAND						
1 Dyson	Y	Y	Y	Y	Y	Y
2 ***Bentley***	Y	N	N	N	Y	Y
3 Cardin	Y	Y	Y	Y	Y	Y
4 McMillen	Y	Y	Y	Y	Y	Y
5 Hoyer	Y	Y	Y	Y	Y	Y
6 Byron	Y	Y	N	Y	Y	Y
7 Mfume	Y	Y	Y	Y	Y	Y
8 ***Morella***	Y	Y	Y	Y	Y	Y
MASSACHUSETTS						
1 ***Conte***	Y	Y	Y	Y	Y	Y
2 Neal	Y	Y	Y	Y	Y	Y
3 Early	Y	Y	Y	Y	Y	Y
4 Frank	Y	Y	Y	Y	Y	Y
5 Atkins	Y	Y	Y	Y	Y	Y
6 Mavroules	Y	Y	Y	Y	Y	Y
7 Markey	Y	Y	Y	Y	Y	Y
8 Kennedy	Y	Y	Y	Y	Y	?
9 Moakley	Y	Y	Y	Y	Y	Y
10 Studds	Y	Y	Y	Y	Y	Y
11 Donnelly	Y	Y	Y	Y	Y	Y
MICHIGAN						
1 Conyers	Y	Y	Y	Y	Y	Y
2 ***Pursell***	Y	?	N	N	Y	N
3 Wolpe	Y	Y	Y	Y	Y	Y
4 ***Upton***	Y	N	N	N	Y	Y
5 ***Henry***	N	N	N	Y	Y	Y
6 Carr	Y	Y	Y	Y	Y	Y
7 Kildee	Y	Y	Y	Y	Y	Y
8 Traxler	Y	Y	Y	Y	Y	Y
9 ***Vander Jagt***	?	N	N	N	Y	Y
10 ***Schuette***	Y	N	N	N	Y	Y
11 ***Davis***	Y	N	N	N	Y	Y
12 Bonior	Y	Y	Y	Y	Y	Y
13 Crockett	Y	?	?	Y	?	Y
14 Hertel	Y	Y	Y	Y	Y	Y
15 Ford	Y	Y	Y	Y	Y	Y
16 Dingell	Y	Y	?	Y	Y	Y
17 Levin	Y	Y	Y	Y	Y	Y
18 ***Broomfield***	N	N	N	N	Y	Y
MINNESOTA						
1 Penny	Y	Y	Y	Y	Y	Y
2 ***Weber***	N	N	N	N	Y	Y
3 ***Frenzel***	?	?	?	?	?	?
4 Vento	Y	Y	Y	Y	Y	Y

	163	164	165	166	167	168
5 Sabo	Y	Y	Y	Y	Y	Y
6 Sikorski	Y	Y	Y	Y	Y	Y
7 ***Stangeland***	N	N	N	N	Y	Y
8 Oberstar	Y	Y	Y	Y	Y	Y
MISSISSIPPI						
1 Whitten	Y	Y	Y	Y	Y	Y
2 Espy	Y	Y	N	Y	Y	Y
3 Montgomery	Y	Y	N	Y	Y	Y
4 Parker	Y	Y	N	N	Y	Y
5 Taylor	Y	Y	N	N	Y	Y
MISSOURI						
1 Clay	Y	Y	Y	Y	Y	Y
2 ***Buechner***	Y	N	N	Y	Y	Y
3 Gephardt	Y	Y	Y	Y	Y	Y
4 Skelton	Y	Y	Y	Y	Y	Y
5 Wheat	Y	Y	Y	Y	Y	Y
6 ***Coleman***	N	Y	N	Y	Y	Y
7 ***Hancock***	N	N	N	N	Y	N
8 ***Emerson***	Y	Y	N	N	Y	Y
9 Volkmer	Y	Y	Y	N	Y	Y
MONTANA						
1 Williams	Y	Y	Y	Y	Y	Y
2 ***Marlenee***	N	N	N	N	Y	N
NEBRASKA						
1 ***Bereuter***	Y	N	Y	Y	Y	Y
2 Hoagland	Y	Y	Y	Y	Y	Y
3 ***Smith***	N	N	N	Y	Y	Y
NEVADA						
1 Bilbray	Y	Y	N	Y	Y	Y
2 ***Vucanovich***	Y	N	N	N	Y	Y
NEW HAMPSHIRE						
1 ***Smith***	N	N	Y	N	Y	Y
2 ***Douglas***	Y	N	N	N	Y	Y
NEW JERSEY						
1 Vacancy						
2 Hughes	Y	Y	Y	Y	Y	Y
3 Pallone	Y	Y	Y	Y	Y	Y
4 ***Smith***	Y	Y	Y	N	Y	Y
5 ***Roukema***	N	Y	N	N	Y	Y
6 Dwyer	Y	Y	Y	Y	Y	Y
7 ***Rinaldo***	Y	Y	Y	Y	Y	Y
8 Roe	Y	Y	Y	Y	Y	Y
9 Torricelli	Y	Y	Y	Y	Y	Y
10 Payne	Y	Y	Y	Y	Y	Y
11 ***Gallo***	Y	Y	Y	Y	Y	Y
12 ***Courter***	N	Y	N	Y	Y	Y
13 ***Saxton***	Y	Y	Y	N	Y	Y
14 Guarini	Y	Y	Y	Y	Y	Y
NEW MEXICO						
1 ***Schiff***	N	N	N	Y	Y	Y
2 ***Skeen***	Y	N	N	Y	Y	Y
3 Richardson	Y	Y	Y	Y	Y	Y
NEW YORK						
1 Hochbrueckner	Y	Y	Y	Y	Y	Y
2 Downey	Y	Y	Y	Y	Y	Y
3 Mrazek	Y	Y	Y	Y	Y	Y
4 ***Lent***	Y	Y	Y	N	Y	Y
5 ***McGrath***	Y	Y	Y	Y	Y	Y
6 Flake	Y	?	Y	Y	Y	Y
7 Ackerman	Y	Y	Y	Y	Y	Y
8 Scheuer	Y	Y	Y	Y	Y	Y
9 Manton	Y	Y	Y	Y	Y	Y
10 Schumer	Y	Y	Y	Y	Y	Y
11 Towns	Y	Y	Y	Y	Y	Y
12 Owens	Y	Y	Y	Y	Y	Y
13 Solarz	Y	Y	Y	Y	Y	Y
14 ***Molinari***	Y	N	?	Y	Y	Y
15 ***Green***	Y	Y	Y	Y	Y	Y
16 Rangel	Y	Y	Y	Y	?	?
17 Weiss	Y	Y	Y	Y	Y	Y
18 Serrano	Y	Y	?	Y	Y	Y
19 Engel	Y	Y	Y	Y	Y	Y
20 Lowey	Y	Y	Y	Y	Y	Y
21 ***Fish***	Y	Y	N	Y	Y	Y
22 ***Gilman***	Y	Y	Y	Y	Y	Y
23 McNulty	Y	Y	Y	Y	Y	Y
24 ***Solomon***	Y	Y	N	N	Y	N
25 ***Boehlert***	Y	Y	N	Y	Y	Y
26 ***Martin***	Y	?	N	Y	Y	Y
27 ***Walsh***	Y	Y	N	N	Y	Y
28 McHugh	Y	Y	Y	Y	Y	Y
29 ***Horton***	Y	Y	Y	Y	Y	Y
30 Slaughter	Y	Y	Y	Y	Y	Y
31 ***Paxon***	N	N	N	N	Y	Y

	163	164	165	166	167	168
32 LaFalce	Y	Y	Y	Y	Y	?
33 Nowak	Y	Y	Y	Y	Y	Y
34 ***Houghton***	Y	Y	N	Y	Y	Y
NORTH CAROLINA						
1 Jones	Y	Y	Y	Y	Y	Y
2 Valentine	Y	Y	N	Y	Y	Y
3 Lancaster	Y	Y	Y	Y	Y	Y
4 Price	Y	Y	Y	Y	Y	Y
5 Neal	Y	Y	Y	Y	Y	Y
6 ***Coble***	N	N	N	N	Y	Y
7 Rose	Y	Y	Y	Y	Y	Y
8 Hefner	Y	Y	Y	Y	Y	Y
9 ***McMillan***	Y	Y	N	N	Y	Y
10 ***Ballenger***	N	N	N	Y	Y	Y
11 Clarke	Y	Y	Y	Y	Y	Y
NORTH DAKOTA						
AL Dorgan	Y	Y	Y	Y	Y	Y
OHIO						
1 Luken	Y	Y	Y	Y	Y	Y
2 ***Gradison***	N	Y	N	Y	Y	Y
3 Hall	Y	Y	Y	Y	Y	Y
4 ***Oxley***	N	N	N	Y	Y	Y
5 ***Gillmor***	N	N	Y	Y	Y	Y
6 ***McEwen***	N	?	N	N	Y	Y
7 ***DeWine***	Y	N	N	Y	Y	Y
8 ***Lukens***	N	N	N	Y	Y	Y
9 Kaptur	Y	Y	Y	Y	Y	Y
10 ***Miller***	Y	Y	N	N	Y	Y
11 Eckart	Y	Y	Y	Y	Y	Y
12 ***Kasich***	Y	Y	N	Y	Y	Y
13 Pease	Y	Y	Y	Y	Y	Y
14 Sawyer	Y	Y	Y	Y	Y	Y
15 ***Wylie***	Y	N	N	N	Y	Y
16 ***Regula***	Y	Y	Y	N	Y	Y
17 Traficant	Y	Y	Y	Y	Y	Y
18 Applegate	Y	Y	Y	Y	Y	Y
19 Feighan	Y	Y	Y	Y	Y	Y
20 Oakar	Y	Y	Y	Y	Y	Y
21 Stokes	Y	Y	Y	Y	Y	Y
OKLAHOMA						
1 ***Inhofe***	N	N	N	N	Y	Y
2 Synar	Y	Y	Y	Y	Y	Y
3 Watkins	?	Y	N	Y	Y	Y
4 McCurdy	Y	Y	?	Y	Y	Y
5 ***Edwards***	N	N	N	N	Y	N
6 English	Y	Y	N	Y	Y	Y
OREGON						
1 AuCoin	Y	Y	Y	Y	Y	Y
2 ***Smith, B.***	Y	N	N	Y	Y	Y
3 Wyden	Y	Y	Y	Y	Y	Y
4 DeFazio	?	Y	Y	Y	Y	Y
5 ***Smith, D.***	N	N	N	-	+	+
PENNSYLVANIA						
1 Foglietta	N	Y	Y	Y	Y	Y
2 Gray	?	Y	Y	Y	Y	Y
3 Borski	Y	Y	Y	Y	Y	Y
4 Kolter	?	Y	Y	Y	Y	Y
5 ***Schulze***	N	N	Y	N	Y	Y
6 Yatron	Y	Y	Y	Y	Y	Y
7 ***Weldon***	Y	Y	N	Y	Y	Y
8 Kostmayer	Y	Y	Y	Y	Y	Y
9 ***Shuster***	Y	N	N	N	Y	Y
10 ***McDade***	Y	Y	N	Y	Y	Y
11 Kanjorski	Y	Y	Y	Y	Y	Y
12 Murtha	Y	Y	Y	Y	Y	Y
13 ***Coughlin***	Y	Y	N	Y	Y	Y
14 Coyne	Y	Y	Y	Y	Y	Y
15 ***Ritter***	N	N	N	N	Y	Y
16 ***Walker***	N	N	N	N	Y	N
17 ***Gekas***	N	N	N	N	Y	N
18 Walgren	Y	Y	Y	Y	Y	Y
19 ***Goodling***	Y	Y	?	N	Y	Y
20 Gaydos	Y	Y	Y	Y	Y	Y
21 ***Ridge***	Y	N	N	Y	Y	Y
22 Murphy	Y	Y	Y	Y	Y	Y
23 ***Clinger***	Y	N	N	Y	Y	Y
RHODE ISLAND						
1 ***Machtley***	Y	Y	N	Y	Y	Y
2 ***Schneider***	Y	N	N	Y	Y	Y
SOUTH CAROLINA						
1 ***Ravenel***	Y	Y	N	Y	Y	Y
2 ***Spence***	Y	Y	N	N	Y	Y
3 Derrick	Y	Y	Y	Y	Y	Y
4 Patterson	Y	Y	Y	Y	Y	Y
5 Spratt	Y	Y	Y	Y	Y	Y
6 Tallon	Y	Y	Y	N	Y	Y

	163	164	165	166	167	168
SOUTH DAKOTA						
AL Johnson	Y	Y	Y	Y	Y	Y
TENNESSEE						
1 ***Quillen***	Y	Y	N	Y	Y	Y
2 ***Duncan***	Y	N	N	N	Y	N
3 Lloyd	Y	Y	Y	Y	Y	Y
4 Cooper	Y	Y	Y	Y	Y	Y
5 Clement	Y	Y	Y	Y	Y	Y
6 Gordon	Y	Y	Y	Y	Y	Y
7 ***Sundquist***	Y	N	N	N	Y	Y
8 Tanner	Y	Y	Y	Y	Y	Y
9 Ford	Y	Y	Y	Y	Y	Y
TEXAS						
1 Chapman	Y	Y	Y	Y	Y	Y
2 Wilson	Y	?	Y	Y	Y	Y
3 ***Bartlett***	N	N	N	N	Y	Y
4 Hall	Y	Y	?	N	Y	Y
5 Bryant	Y	Y	Y	Y	Y	Y
6 ***Barton***	N	N	N	N	Y	Y
7 ***Archer***	N	N	N	N	Y	Y
8 ***Fields***	N	N	N	N	Y	Y
9 Brooks	Y	Y	Y	Y	Y	Y
10 Pickle	Y	Y	Y	Y	Y	Y
11 Leath	Y	?	Y	?	Y	Y
12 Geren	Y	Y	N	Y	Y	Y
13 Sarpalius	Y	Y	Y	Y	Y	Y
14 Laughlin	Y	Y	Y	N	Y	Y
15 de la Garza	Y	Y	N	Y	Y	Y
16 Coleman	Y	Y	N	Y	Y	Y
17 Stenholm	Y	Y	Y	N	Y	Y
18 Washington	Y	?	Y	Y	Y	Y
19 ***Combest***	N	N	Y	N	Y	Y
20 Gonzalez	Y	Y	Y	Y	Y	Y
21 ***Smith***	N	N	N	N	Y	Y
22 ***DeLay***	N	N	N	N	Y	Y
23 Bustamante	Y	Y	Y	Y	Y	Y
24 Frost	Y	Y	Y	Y	Y	Y
25 Andrews	Y	Y	Y	Y	Y	Y
26 ***Armey***	N	N	Y	N	Y	Y
27 Ortiz	Y	Y	N	Y	Y	Y
UTAH						
1 ***Hansen***	N	N	?	N	Y	Y
2 Owens	?	Y	Y	Y	Y	Y
3 ***Nielson***	Y	Y	N	N	Y	Y
VERMONT						
AL ***Smith***	Y	N	N	Y	Y	Y
VIRGINIA						
1 ***Bateman***	N	Y	N	Y	Y	Y
2 Pickett	Y	Y	Y	Y	Y	Y
3 ***Bliley***	Y	Y	N	N	Y	Y
4 Sisisky	Y	Y	Y	Y	Y	Y
5 Payne	Y	Y	Y	Y	Y	Y
6 Olin	Y	Y	Y	Y	Y	Y
7 ***Slaughter***	N	Y	N	N	Y	Y
8 ***Parris***	Y	Y	N	N	?	Y
9 Boucher	Y	Y	Y	Y	Y	Y
10 ***Wolf***	N	Y	N	N	Y	Y
WASHINGTON						
1 ***Miller***	Y	Y	N	Y	Y	Y
2 Swift	Y	Y	N	Y	Y	Y
3 Unsoeld	Y	Y	Y	Y	Y	Y
4 ***Morrison***	Y	Y	Y	Y	Y	Y
5 Foley						
6 Dicks	Y	Y	Y	Y	Y	Y
7 McDermott	Y	Y	Y	Y	Y	Y
8 ***Chandler***	Y	Y	N	Y	Y	Y
WEST VIRGINIA						
1 Mollohan	Y	Y	Y	Y	Y	Y
2 Staggers	Y	Y	Y	Y	Y	Y
3 Wise	Y	Y	Y	Y	Y	Y
4 Rahall	Y	Y	Y	Y	Y	Y
WISCONSIN						
1 Aspin	Y	Y	Y	Y	Y	Y
2 Kastenmeier	Y	Y	Y	Y	Y	Y
3 ***Gunderson***	Y	Y	N	Y	Y	Y
4 Kleczka	Y	Y	Y	Y	Y	Y
5 Moody	?	Y	N	Y	Y	Y
6 ***Petri***	Y	N	Y	N	Y	Y
7 Obey	Y	Y	Y	Y	Y	Y
8 ***Roth***	N	N	N	N	Y	Y
9 ***Sensenbrenner***	N	N	N	N	Y	Y
WYOMING						
AL ***Thomas***	Y	Y	N	Y	Y	Y

Southern states - Ala., Ark., Fla., Ga., Ky., La., Miss., N.C., Okla., S.C., Tenn., Texas, Va.
Omitted votes are quorum calls, which CQ does not include in its vote charts.

169. HR 2567. Reclamation Project Authorization/Family Trusts. Lehman, D-Calif., amendment to the Miller, D-Calif., amendment to specify that provisions regarding trusts would not apply to "family trusts," which are trusts for which all beneficiaries are from no more than three generations of the same family, are related by blood and are at least 18 years old. Rejected 118-297: R 75-93; D 43-204 (ND 19-149, SD 24-55), June 14, 1990.

170. HR 2567. Reclamation Project Authorization/Water Subsidies. Miller, D-Calif., amendment to revise provisions of the 1982 Reclamation Reform Act to ensure that no farm larger than 960 acres (or no farm operation composed of separate parcels totaling more than 960 acres) may receive federally subsidized irrigation water and to require that all entities receiving subsidized irrigation water must be composed of U.S. citizens or resident aliens. Adopted 316-97: R 107-64; D 209-33 (ND 152-13, SD 57-20), June 14, 1990.

171. HR 2567. Reclamation Project Authorization/Water Subsidies. Gejdenson, D-Conn., amendment to phase out federal subsidies for irrigation water used to grow surplus crops if the secretary of Agriculture determines that there are enough surplus crops stored in reserve that can be reasonably expected to meet a shortage of crops caused by a disruption in the supply. Adopted 338-55: R 124-38; D 214-17 (ND 147-12, SD 67-5), June 14, 1990.

KEY

- Y Voted for (yea).
- # Paired for.
- + Announced for.
- N Voted against (nay).
- X Paired against.
- \- Announced against.
- P Voted "present."
- C Voted "present" to avoid possible conflict of interest.
- ? Did not vote or otherwise make a position known.

Democrats ***Republicans***

	169	170	171
ALABAMA			
1 ***Callahan***	N	Y	Y
2 ***Dickinson***	Y	Y	Y
3 Browder	N	Y	Y
4 Bevill	Y	Y	?
5 Flippo	N	Y	Y
6 Erdreich	N	Y	Y
7 Harris	N	Y	Y
ALASKA			
AL ***Young***	Y	N	N
ARIZONA			
1 ***Rhodes***	Y	N	Y
2 Udall	Y	Y	Y
3 ***Stump***	Y	N	N
4 ***Kyl***	Y	N	Y
5 ***Kolbe***	Y	N	Y
ARKANSAS			
1 Alexander	Y	N	?
2 ***Robinson***	?	?	?
3 ***Hammerschmidt***	Y	N	Y
4 Anthony	N	Y	Y
CALIFORNIA			
1 Bosco	N	Y	Y
2 ***Herger***	Y	N	N
3 Matsui	Y	N	N
4 Fazio	Y	N	N
5 Pelosi	N	Y	Y
6 Boxer	N	Y	Y
7 Miller	N	Y	Y
8 Dellums	N	Y	Y
9 Stark	N	Y	Y
10 Edwards	N	Y	Y
11 Lantos	N	Y	Y
12 ***Campbell***	N	Y	Y
13 Mineta	N	Y	Y
14 ***Shumway***	Y	N	N
15 Condit	Y	N	N
16 Panetta	Y	N	N
17 ***Pashayan***	Y	N	N
18 Lehman	Y	N	N
19 ***Lagomarsino***	Y	N	Y
20 ***Thomas***	Y	N	N
21 ***Gallegly***	Y	N	Y
22 ***Moorhead***	Y	N	N
23 Beilenson	N	Y	Y
24 Waxman	N	Y	Y
25 Roybal	N	Y	Y
26 Berman	?	#	?
27 Levine	N	Y	Y
28 Dixon	N	Y	Y
29 Hawkins	N	Y	Y
30 Martinez	Y	N	Y
31 Dymally	N	Y	Y
32 Anderson	Y	Y	Y
33 ***Dreier***	N	N	N
34 Torres	N	Y	Y
35 ***Lewis***	Y	N	N
36 Brown	Y	Y	Y
37 ***McCandless***	Y	N	N
38 ***Dornan***	Y	Y	N
39 ***Dannemeyer***	Y	N	Y
40 ***Cox***	N	N	Y
41 ***Lowery***	Y	N	X
42 ***Rohrabacher***	N	Y	Y
43 ***Packard***	Y	N	N
44 Bates	N	Y	Y
45 ***Hunter***	Y	N	N
COLORADO			
1 Schroeder	N	Y	Y
2 Skaggs	N	Y	Y
3 Campbell	Y	N	N
4 ***Brown***	N	Y	Y
5 ***Hefley***	Y	Y	Y
6 ***Schaefer***	Y	N	N
CONNECTICUT			
1 Kennelly	N	Y	Y
2 Gejdenson	N	Y	Y
3 Morrison	N	Y	+
4 ***Shays***	N	Y	Y
5 ***Rowland***	N	Y	?
6 ***Johnson***	N	Y	Y
DELAWARE			
AL Carper	N	Y	Y
FLORIDA			
1 Hutto	Y	Y	Y
2 ***Grant***	Y	N	Y
3 Bennett	N	Y	Y
4 ***James***	N	Y	Y
5 ***McCollum***	Y	Y	Y
6 ***Stearns***	N	Y	Y
7 Gibbons	N	Y	Y
8 ***Young***	Y	Y	Y
9 ***Bilirakis***	N	Y	Y
10 ***Ireland***	Y	N	Y
11 Nelson	-	+	+
12 ***Lewis***	Y	Y	Y
13 ***Goss***	N	Y	Y
14 Johnston	N	Y	Y
15 ***Shaw***	N	Y	?
16 Smith	N	Y	Y
17 Lehman	N	Y	Y
18 ***Ros-Lehtinen***	N	Y	Y
19 Fascell	N	Y	Y
GEORGIA			
1 Thomas	N	Y	Y
2 Hatcher	Y	N	?
3 Ray	N	Y	Y
4 Jones	N	Y	Y
5 Lewis	N	Y	Y
6 ***Gingrich***	Y	Y	Y
7 Darden	N	Y	Y
8 Rowland	N	Y	Y
9 Jenkins	N	Y	Y
10 Barnard	N	Y	Y
HAWAII			
1 ***Saiki***	N	Y	Y
2 Vacancy			
IDAHO			
1 ***Craig***	Y	N	N
2 Stallings	Y	N	N
ILLINOIS			
1 Hayes	N	Y	Y
2 Savage	N	Y	Y
3 Russo	N	Y	Y
4 Sangmeister	N	Y	Y
5 Lipinski	N	Y	Y
6 ***Hyde***	?	Y	Y
7 Collins	N	?	Y
8 Rostenkowski	?	?	?
9 Yates	N	Y	Y
10 ***Porter***	N	Y	Y
11 Annunzio	N	Y	Y
12 ***Crane***	N	Y	Y
13 ***Fawell***	N	Y	Y
14 ***Hastert***	N	Y	Y
15 ***Madigan***	Y	N	N
16 ***Martin***	N	Y	Y
17 Evans	N	Y	Y
18 ***Michel***	?	N	Y
19 Bruce	N	Y	Y
20 Durbin	Y	Y	Y
21 Costello	N	Y	Y
22 Poshard	N	Y	Y
INDIANA			
1 Visclosky	N	Y	Y
2 Sharp	N	Y	Y
3 ***Hiler***	N	Y	Y

ND Northern Democrats SD Southern Democrats

	169	170	171
4 Long	N	Y	Y
5 Jontz	N	Y	Y
6 ***Burton***	N	Y	Y
7 ***Myers***	Y	N	Y
8 McCloskey	N	Y	Y
9 Hamilton	N	Y	Y
10 Jacobs	N	Y	Y
IOWA			
1 ***Leach***	N	Y	Y
2 ***Tauke***	N	Y	Y
3 Nagle	Y	N	Y
4 Smith	Y	N	?
5 ***Lightfoot***	Y	N	N
6 ***Grandy***	Y	N	Y
KANSAS			
1 ***Roberts***	Y	N	N
2 Slattery	N	Y	Y
3 ***Meyers***	N	Y	Y
4 Glickman	N	Y	Y
5 ***Whittaker***	Y	N	N
KENTUCKY			
1 Hubbard	Y	N	Y
2 Natcher	N	Y	Y
3 Mazzoli	N	Y	Y
4 ***Bunning***	Y	N	Y
5 ***Rogers***	Y	Y	Y
6 ***Hopkins***	Y	Y	Y
7 Perkins	Y	N	N
LOUISIANA			
1 ***Livingston***	N	N	Y
2 Boggs	N	Y	Y
3 Tauzin	N	N	Y
4 ***McCrery***	N	Y	Y
5 Huckaby	N	N	Y
6 ***Baker***	N	N	N
7 Hayes	N	Y	Y
8 ***Holloway***	Y	N	N
MAINE			
1 Brennan	N	Y	Y
2 ***Snowe***	N	Y	Y
MARYLAND			
1 Dyson	N	Y	Y
2 ***Bentley***	N	Y	Y
3 Cardin	N	Y	Y
4 McMillen	N	Y	Y
5 Hoyer	N	Y	Y
6 Byron	Y	N	Y
7 Mfume	N	Y	Y
8 ***Morella***	+	-	Y
MASSACHUSETTS			
1 ***Conte***	N	Y	Y
2 Neal	N	Y	Y
3 Early	N	Y	Y
4 Frank	N	?	?
5 Atkins	N	Y	Y
6 Mavroules	?	?	?
7 Markey	N	Y	Y
8 Kennedy	N	Y	Y
9 Moakley	N	Y	Y
10 Studds	N	Y	Y
11 Donnelly	N	Y	Y
MICHIGAN			
1 Conyers	N	Y	Y
2 ***Pursell***	N	Y	Y
3 Wolpe	N	Y	Y
4 ***Upton***	N	Y	Y
5 ***Henry***	N	Y	Y
6 Carr	N	Y	Y
7 Kildee	N	Y	Y
8 Traxler	N	?	?
9 ***Vander Jagt***	N	N	Y
10 ***Schuette***	?	?	?
11 ***Davis***	N	Y	Y
12 Bonior	N	Y	Y
13 Crockett	?	?	?
14 Hertel	N	Y	Y
15 Ford	N	Y	Y
16 Dingell	N	Y	Y
17 Levin	N	Y	Y
18 ***Broomfield***	N	Y	Y
MINNESOTA			
1 Penny	N	Y	Y
2 ***Weber***	?	?	?
3 ***Frenzel***	N	Y	Y
4 Vento	N	Y	Y

	169	170	171
5 Sabo	N	Y	Y
6 Sikorski	N	Y	Y
7 ***Stangeland***	Y	N	N
8 Oberstar	N	Y	Y
MISSISSIPPI			
1 Whitten	N	Y	Y
2 Espy	Y	N	N
3 Montgomery	Y	N	Y
4 Parker	Y	N	#
5 Taylor	Y	Y	Y
MISSOURI			
1 Clay	N	Y	?
2 ***Buechner***	N	Y	Y
3 Gephardt	N	Y	N
4 Skelton	N	Y	Y
5 Wheat	N	Y	Y
6 ***Coleman***	Y	N	Y
7 ***Hancock***	Y	N	Y
8 ***Emerson***	Y	N	N
9 Volkmer	N	Y	Y
MONTANA			
1 Williams	Y	N	N
2 ***Marlenee***	Y	N	N
NEBRASKA			
1 ***Bereuter***	Y	Y	N
2 Hoagland	N	Y	Y
3 ***Smith***	Y	N	N
NEVADA			
1 Bilbray	Y	Y	Y
2 ***Vucanovich***	Y	N	N
NEW HAMPSHIRE			
1 ***Smith***	N	Y	Y
2 ***Douglas***	N	Y	Y
NEW JERSEY			
1 Vacancy			
2 Hughes	N	Y	Y
3 Pallone	N	Y	Y
4 ***Smith***	N	Y	Y
5 ***Roukema***	N	Y	Y
6 Dwyer	N	Y	Y
7 ***Rinaldo***	N	Y	Y
8 Roe	N	Y	Y
9 Torricelli	N	Y	Y
10 Payne	N	Y	Y
11 ***Gallo***	N	Y	Y
12 ***Courter***	N	Y	?
13 ***Saxton***	N	Y	Y
14 Guarini	N	Y	Y
NEW MEXICO			
1 ***Schiff***	Y	N	Y
2 ***Skeen***	Y	N	N
3 Richardson	N	Y	Y
NEW YORK			
1 Hochbrueckner	N	Y	Y
2 Downey	N	Y	Y
3 Mrazek	N	Y	Y
4 ***Lent***	N	Y	Y
5 ***McGrath***	N	Y	Y
6 Flake	N	Y	Y
7 Ackerman	N	Y	Y
8 Scheuer	N	Y	Y
9 Manton	N	Y	Y
10 Schumer	N	Y	Y
11 Towns	N	Y	Y
12 Owens	N	Y	?
13 Solarz	N	Y	Y
14 ***Molinari***	N	Y	Y
15 ***Green***	N	Y	Y
16 Rangel	?	?	?
17 Weiss	N	Y	Y
18 Serrano	N	Y	Y
19 Engel	N	Y	Y
20 Lowey	N	Y	Y
21 ***Fish***	N	Y	Y
22 ***Gilman***	N	Y	Y
23 McNulty	N	Y	Y
24 ***Solomon***	N	Y	Y
25 ***Boehlert***	N	Y	Y
26 ***Martin***	N	Y	Y
27 ***Walsh***	N	Y	Y
28 McHugh	N	Y	Y
29 ***Horton***	N	Y	Y
30 Slaughter	N	Y	Y
31 ***Paxon***	N	Y	?

	169	170	171
32 LaFalce	N	Y	Y
33 Nowak	N	Y	Y
34 ***Houghton***	N	Y	Y
NORTH CAROLINA			
1 Jones	N	Y	Y
2 Valentine	N	N	Y
3 Lancaster	N	Y	Y
4 Price	N	Y	Y
5 Neal	N	Y	Y
6 ***Coble***	N	Y	Y
7 Rose	N	Y	Y
8 Hefner	N	Y	Y
9 ***McMillan***	Y	Y	Y
10 ***Ballenger***	N	Y	Y
11 Clarke	N	Y	Y
NORTH DAKOTA			
AL Dorgan	N	Y	?
OHIO			
1 Luken	N	Y	Y
2 ***Gradison***	?	Y	Y
3 Hall	N	Y	Y
4 ***Oxley***	N	Y	Y
5 ***Gillmor***	Y	Y	Y
6 ***McEwen***	Y	Y	Y
7 ***DeWine***	N	Y	Y
8 ***Lukens***	Y	N	N
9 Kaptur	N	Y	?
10 ***Miller***	Y	Y	Y
11 Eckart	N	Y	Y
12 ***Kasich***	N	Y	Y
13 Pease	N	Y	Y
14 Sawyer	N	Y	Y
15 ***Wylie***	N	Y	Y
16 ***Regula***	N	Y	Y
17 Traficant	N	Y	Y
18 Applegate	N	Y	Y
19 Feighan	N	Y	Y
20 Oakar	N	Y	Y
21 Stokes	N	Y	Y
OKLAHOMA			
1 ***Inhofe***	Y	N	N
2 Synar	N	Y	?
3 Watkins	?	?	?
4 McCurdy	N	Y	N
5 ***Edwards***	Y	Y	N
6 English	Y	Y	Y
OREGON			
1 AuCoin	N	Y	N
2 ***Smith, B.***	Y	N	N
3 Wyden	N	Y	Y
4 DeFazio	N	Y	Y
5 ***Smith, D.***	Y	N	N
PENNSYLVANIA			
1 Foglietta	N	Y	Y
2 Gray	N	Y	Y
3 Borski	N	Y	Y
4 Kolter	N	Y	Y
5 ***Schulze***	N	Y	Y
6 Yatron	N	Y	Y
7 ***Weldon***	N	Y	Y
8 Kostmayer	N	Y	Y
9 ***Shuster***	Y	Y	?
10 ***McDade***	N	Y	Y
11 Kanjorski	N	Y	Y
12 Murtha	N	Y	Y
13 ***Coughlin***	N	Y	Y
14 Coyne	N	Y	Y
15 ***Ritter***	N	Y	?
16 ***Walker***	N	Y	Y
17 ***Gekas***	N	Y	Y
18 Walgren	N	Y	Y
19 ***Goodling***	N	Y	+
20 Gaydos	N	Y	Y
21 ***Ridge***	N	Y	Y
22 Murphy	N	Y	Y
23 ***Clinger***	Y	N	Y
RHODE ISLAND			
1 ***Machtley***	N	Y	Y
2 ***Schneider***	N	Y	Y
SOUTH CAROLINA			
1 ***Ravenel***	N	Y	Y
2 ***Spence***	N	Y	Y
3 Derrick	Y	N	Y
4 Patterson	Y	Y	Y
5 Spratt	N	Y	Y
6 Tallon	N	N	Y

	169	170	171
SOUTH DAKOTA			
AL Johnson	N	Y	N
TENNESSEE			
1 ***Quillen***	Y	N	X
2 ***Duncan***	N	Y	Y
3 Lloyd	N	Y	Y
4 Cooper	N	Y	Y
5 Clement	N	Y	Y
6 Gordon	N	Y	Y
7 ***Sundquist***	N	N	?
8 Tanner	N	Y	Y
9 Ford	N	Y	Y
TEXAS			
1 Chapman	N	Y	Y
2 Wilson	N	Y	Y
3 ***Bartlett***	N	Y	Y
4 Hall	?	?	?
5 Bryant	N	Y	Y
6 ***Barton***	Y	N	Y
7 ***Archer***	N	Y	Y
8 ***Fields***	Y	Y	Y
9 Brooks	N	Y	Y
10 Pickle	N	Y	Y
11 Leath	Y	?	Y
12 Geren	Y	N	N
13 Sarpalius	Y	N	Y
14 Laughlin	Y	Y	Y
15 de la Garza	Y	N	?
16 Coleman	?	?	?
17 Stenholm	Y	N	Y
18 Washington	N	Y	Y
19 ***Combest***	Y	N	N
20 Gonzalez	N	Y	Y
21 ***Smith***	Y	Y	Y
22 ***DeLay***	N	Y	Y
23 Bustamante	Y	N	Y
24 Frost	N	?	?
25 Andrews	N	Y	Y
26 ***Armey***	N	Y	Y
27 Ortiz	Y	N	N
UTAH			
1 ***Hansen***	Y	N	N
2 Owens	N	Y	Y
3 ***Nielson***	?	X	?
VERMONT			
AL ***Smith***	N	Y	Y
VIRGINIA			
1 ***Bateman***	Y	N	Y
2 Pickett	N	Y	Y
3 ***Bliley***	Y	N	Y
4 Sisisky	N	Y	Y
5 Payne	Y	N	Y
6 Olin	Y	N	Y
7 ***Slaughter***	Y	N	Y
8 ***Parris***	Y	N	Y
9 Boucher	Y	Y	Y
10 ***Wolf***	N	Y	Y
WASHINGTON			
1 ***Miller***	N	Y	Y
2 Swift	Y	N	N
3 Unsoeld	N	Y	Y
4 ***Morrison***	Y	N	N
5 Foley			
6 Dicks	N	Y	Y
7 McDermott	N	Y	Y
8 ***Chandler***	Y	N	N
WEST VIRGINIA			
1 Mollohan	N	Y	Y
2 Staggers	N	Y	Y
3 Wise	N	Y	Y
4 Rahall	N	Y	Y
WISCONSIN			
1 Aspin	N	Y	Y
2 Kastenmeier	N	Y	Y
3 ***Gunderson***	Y	N	Y
4 Kleczka	Y	Y	#
5 Moody	N	Y	Y
6 ***Petri***	N	Y	Y
7 Obey	N	Y	Y
8 ***Roth***	N	Y	Y
9 ***Sensenbrenner***	N	Y	Y
WYOMING			
AL ***Thomas***	Y	N	N

Southern states - Ala., Ark., Fla., Ga., Ky., La., Miss., N.C., Okla., S.C., Tenn., Texas, Va.
Omitted votes are quorum calls, which CQ does not include in its vote charts.

HOUSE VOTES 172, 173, 174, 175, 176, 177, 178, 179

172. Procedural Motion. Duncan, R-Tenn., motion to approve the House Journal of Monday, June 18. Motion agreed to 280-115: R 54-110; D 226-5 (ND 150-4, SD 76-1), June 19, 1990.

173. HR 5019. Fiscal 1991 Energy and Water Appropriations/Previous Question. Derrick, D-S.C., motion to order the previous question (thus ending debate and the possibility of amendment) on the rule (H Res 413) to provide for House floor consideration and to waive points of order against certain provisions of the bill to appropriate $20.8 billion in fiscal 1991 for the energy, water and nuclear weapons programs. Motion agreed to 260-157: R 14-155; D 246-2 (ND 167-2, SD 79-0), June 19, 1990. (Opponents of the rule were trying to defeat the previous question in order to offer an alternative rule. The alternative would have used fiscal 1990 spending levels plus inflation, rather than spending levels provided in the House-passed budget resolution, H Con Res 310, to set limits on fiscal 1991 appropriations.)

174. HR 5019. Fiscal 1991 Energy and Water Appropriations/Rule. Adoption of the rule (H Res 413) to provide for House floor consideration and to waive points of order against certain provisions of the bill to appropriate $20.8 billion in fiscal 1991 for the energy, water and nuclear weapons programs. The rule also establishes budget guidelines for House consideration of all fiscal 1991 general appropriation bills. Adopted 276-136: R 32-134; D 244-2 (ND 167-1, SD 77-1), June 19, 1990.

175. HR 5019. Fiscal 1991 Energy and Water Appropriations/Rocky Flats Plant. Schroeder, D-Colo., amendment to cut the $65 million for the Plutonium Recovery Modification Project at the Rocky Flats Plant in Colorado. Rejected 142-278: R 32-139; D 110-139 (ND 95-75, SD 15-64), June 19, 1990.

176. HR 5019. Fiscal 1991 Energy and Water Appropriations/Rocky Flats Plant. Skaggs, D-Colo., amendment to prohibit the use of $65 million for the Plutonium Recovery Modification Project at the Rocky Flats Plant in Colorado until 30 days after the Energy Department has submitted its "Facilities Modernization Report" to Congress. Adopted 413-7: R 166-6; D 247-1 (ND 169-1, SD 78-0), June 19, 1990.

177. HR 5019. Fiscal 1991 Energy and Water Appropriations/Shasta Dam. Petri, R-Wis., amendment to cut the power purchase rebate for the Shasta Dam in California. Rejected 140-277: R 98-70; D 42-207 (ND 34-136, SD 8-71), June 19, 1990.

178. HR 5019. Fiscal 1991 Energy and Water Appropriations/Across-the-Board Cuts. Frenzel, R-Minn., amendment to provide a 10.53 percent across-the-board cut in all discretionary accounts in the bill. Rejected 98-314: R 86-85; D 12-229 (ND 7-157, SD 5-72), June 19, 1990.

179. HR 5019. Fiscal 1991 Energy and Water Appropriations/Across-the-Board Cuts. Dannemeyer, R-Calif., amendment to provide a 5 percent across-the-board cut in all discretionary accounts in the bill. Rejected 124-285: R 99-72; D 25-213 (ND 14-148, SD 11-65), June 19, 1990.

KEY

Y Voted for (yea).
\# Paired for.
\+ Announced for.
N Voted against (nay).
X Paired against.
\- Announced against.
P Voted "present."
C Voted "present" to avoid possible conflict of interest.
? Did not vote or otherwise make a position known.

Democrats ***Republicans***

	172	173	174	175	176	177	178	179
ALABAMA								
1 ***Callahan***	N	Y	Y	N	Y	N	N	N
2 ***Dickinson***	N	N	N	?	Y	N	N	N
3 Browder	Y	Y	Y	Y	Y	N	N	N
4 Bevill	Y	Y	Y	N	Y	N	N	N
5 Flippo	Y	Y	Y	N	Y	N	N	?
6 Erdreich	Y	Y	Y	N	Y	N	N	N
7 Harris	Y	Y	Y	N	Y	N	N	N
ALASKA								
AL ***Young***	N	Y	Y	N	N	N	N	N
ARIZONA								
1 ***Rhodes***	N	N	N	N	Y	N	N	N
2 Udall	Y	Y	Y	N	Y	N	N	N
3 ***Stump***	N	N	N	N	N	Y	Y	Y
4 ***Kyl***	N	N	N	N	N	Y	N	N
5 ***Kolbe***	N	N	Y	N	Y	N	N	N
ARKANSAS								
1 Alexander	Y	Y	Y	N	Y	N	N	N
2 ***Robinson***	Y	N	N	N	Y	Y	Y	Y
3 ***Hammerschmidt***	Y	N	N	N	Y	Y	Y	Y
4 Anthony	Y	Y	Y	N	Y	N	N	N
CALIFORNIA								
1 Bosco	Y	Y	Y	Y	Y	N	N	N
2 ***Herger***	N	N	N	N	?	N	N	N
3 Matsui	Y	Y	Y	Y	Y	N	N	N
4 Fazio	Y	Y	Y	N	Y	N	N	N
5 Pelosi	Y	Y	Y	Y	Y	N	N	N
6 Boxer	Y	Y	Y	Y	Y	N	N	N
7 Miller	Y	Y	Y	Y	Y	N	N	N
8 Dellums	?	Y	Y	Y	Y	N	N	N
9 Stark	Y	Y	Y	Y	Y	N	N	N
10 Edwards	Y	Y	Y	Y	Y	N	?	?
11 Lantos	Y	Y	Y	N	Y	N	N	N
12 ***Campbell***	N	N	N	Y	Y	Y	Y	Y
13 Mineta	Y	Y	Y	N	Y	N	N	N
14 ***Shumway***	Y	N	N	N	Y	N	Y	Y
15 Condit	Y	Y	Y	Y	Y	N	N	N
16 Panetta	Y	Y	Y	Y	Y	N	N	N
17 ***Pashayan***	N	N	N	N	Y	N	N	N
18 Lehman	Y	Y	Y	Y	Y	N	N	N
19 ***Lagomarsino***	N	N	N	N	Y	N	N	N
20 ***Thomas***	N	N	N	N	Y	N	Y	Y
21 ***Gallegly***	N	N	N	N	Y	N	N	N
22 ***Moorhead***	N	N	N	N	Y	N	Y	Y
23 Beilenson	Y	Y	Y	Y	Y	N	N	N
24 Waxman	Y	Y	Y	Y	Y	N	N	N
25 Roybal	Y	Y	Y	N	Y	N	N	N
26 Berman	Y	Y	Y	Y	Y	N	N	N
27 Levine	Y	Y	Y	Y	Y	N	N	N
28 Dixon	Y	Y	Y	N	Y	N	N	N
29 Hawkins	?	Y	?	?	Y	N	?	?
30 Martinez	Y	Y	Y	N	Y	N	N	?
31 Dymally	Y	Y	Y	Y	Y	N	N	N
32 Anderson	Y	Y	Y	N	Y	N	N	N
33 ***Dreier***	N	N	N	N	Y	N	Y	Y
34 Torres	Y	Y	Y	Y	Y	N	N	N
35 ***Lewis***	N	N	Y	N	Y	N	N	N
36 Brown	Y	Y	Y	N	Y	N	N	N
37 ***McCandless***	N	N	N	N	Y	N	Y	Y
38 ***Dornan***	N	N	N	N	Y	N	N	Y
39 ***Dannemeyer***	N	N	N	N	Y	Y	Y	Y
40 ***Cox***	N	N	?	N	Y	Y	Y	Y
41 ***Lowery***	?	N	Y	N	Y	N	N	N
42 ***Rohrabacher***	Y	N	N	N	Y	N	Y	Y
43 ***Packard***	Y	N	N	N	Y	N	Y	Y
44 Bates	Y	Y	Y	Y	Y	Y	N	Y
45 ***Hunter***	N	?	N	N	Y	N	Y	Y
COLORADO								
1 Schroeder	N	Y	Y	Y	Y	N	Y	Y
2 Skaggs	Y	Y	Y	Y	Y	N	N	N
3 Campbell	Y	Y	Y	Y	Y	N	N	N
4 ***Brown***	N	N	N	Y	Y	N	Y	Y
5 ***Hefley***	N	N	N	Y	Y	N	Y	Y
6 ***Schaefer***	N	N	N	Y	Y	N	N	Y
CONNECTICUT								
1 Kennelly	Y	Y	Y	N	Y	Y	N	N
2 Gejdenson	Y	Y	Y	Y	Y	Y	N	N
3 Morrison	Y	Y	Y	Y	+	+	Y	Y
4 ***Shays***	N	N	N	Y	Y	Y	Y	Y
5 ***Rowland***	Y	N	N	N	Y	Y	Y	Y
6 ***Johnson***	Y	N	N	N	Y	Y	Y	Y
DELAWARE								
AL Carper	Y	Y	Y	N	Y	N	N	N
FLORIDA								
1 Hutto	Y	Y	Y	N	Y	N	N	N
2 ***Grant***	Y	N	N	N	Y	N	N	Y
3 Bennett	Y	Y	Y	Y	Y	N	Y	Y
4 ***James***	N	N	—	N	Y	Y	N	N
5 ***McCollum***	Y	N	N	N	Y	N	N	Y
6 ***Stearns***	Y	N	N	N	Y	Y	Y	Y
7 Gibbons	Y	Y	Y	Y	Y	N	N	N
8 ***Young***	N	N	N	N	Y	N	N	N
9 ***Bilirakis***	N	N	N	N	Y	Y	Y	Y
10 ***Ireland***	N	?	?	N	Y	N	Y	Y
11 Nelson	+	+	+	-	+	-	-	-
12 ***Lewis***	N	N	N	N	Y	N	Y	N
13 ***Goss***	N	N	N	N	Y	Y	N	N
14 Johnston	Y	Y	Y	Y	Y	Y	Y	Y
15 ***Shaw***	Y	N	Y	N	Y	Y	N	N
16 Smith	Y	Y	Y	?	Y	N	N	N
17 Lehman	Y	Y	Y	N	Y	N	N	N
18 ***Ros-Lehtinen***	N	N	N	Y	Y	N	N	N
19 Fascell	Y	Y	Y	Y	Y	N	N	N
GEORGIA								
1 Thomas	Y	Y	Y	N	Y	N	N	N
2 Hatcher	Y	Y	Y	N	Y	N	N	N
3 Ray	Y	?	?	N	Y	Y	N	N
4 Jones	Y	Y	Y	N	Y	N	N	N
5 Lewis	Y	Y	Y	Y	Y	N	N	N
6 ***Gingrich***	N	N	N	N	Y	?	Y	Y
7 Darden	Y	Y	Y	N	Y	N	N	Y
8 Rowland	Y	Y	Y	N	Y	N	N	N
9 Jenkins	Y	Y	Y	N	Y	N	N	Y
10 Barnard	Y	Y	Y	N	Y	N	N	Y
HAWAII								
1 ***Saiki***	Y	N	N	Y	Y	N	N	N
2 Vacancy								
IDAHO								
1 ***Craig***	N	?	N	N	Y	N	N	Y
2 Stallings	Y	Y	Y	N	Y	N	N	N
ILLINOIS								
1 Hayes	Y	Y	Y	Y	Y	N	N	N
2 Savage	?	Y	Y	N	Y	N	N	N
3 Russo	Y	Y	Y	Y	Y	Y	N	N
4 Sangmeister	Y	Y	Y	Y	Y	N	N	N
5 Lipinski	Y	Y	Y	N	Y	N	N	N
6 ***Hyde***	N	N	Y	N	Y	Y	N	N
7 Collins	Y	Y	Y	Y	Y	N	N	N
8 Rostenkowski	Y	Y	Y	Y	Y	N	N	N
9 Yates	Y	Y	Y	Y	Y	N	N	N
10 ***Porter***	N	N	N	N	Y	Y	N	N
11 Annunzio	Y	Y	Y	N	Y	N	N	N
12 ***Crane***	N	N	N	N	Y	Y	Y	Y
13 ***Fawell***	N	N	N	Y	Y	Y	Y	Y
14 ***Hastert***	N	N	N	N	Y	Y	Y	N
15 ***Madigan***	N	N	N	N	Y	Y	N	N
16 ***Martin***	N	N	N	Y	Y	Y	Y	Y
17 Evans	Y	Y	Y	Y	Y	Y	N	N
18 ***Michel***	Y	N	N	N	Y	Y	Y	Y
19 Bruce	Y	Y	Y	Y	Y	Y	N	N
20 Durbin	Y	Y	Y	Y	Y	N	N	N
21 Costello	Y	Y	Y	Y	Y	Y	N	N
22 Poshard	Y	Y	Y	Y	Y	Y	N	N
INDIANA								
1 Visclosky	Y	Y	Y	N	Y	N	N	N
2 Sharp	Y	Y	Y	Y	Y	Y	Y	Y
3 ***Hiler***	N	N	N	N	Y	Y	Y	Y

ND Northern Democrats SD Southern Democrats

	172	173	174	175	176	177	178	179
4 Long	Y	Y	Y	Y	Y	Y	N	Y
5 Jontz	Y	Y	Y	Y	Y	Y	Y	Y
6 ***Burton***	N	N	N	N	Y	Y	Y	Y
7 ***Myers***	Y	Y	Y	N	Y	N	N	N
8 McCloskey	Y	Y	Y	N	Y	Y	N	N
9 Hamilton	Y	Y	Y	Y	Y	Y	Y	Y
10 Jacobs	?	N	N	Y	Y	Y	Y	Y
IOWA								
1 ***Leach***	N	N	N	Y	Y	Y	Y	Y
2 ***Tauke***	N	N	N	Y	Y	Y	Y	Y
3 Nagle	?	Y	Y	Y	Y	N	N	N
4 Smith	?	Y	Y	N	Y	N	N	N
5 ***Lightfoot***	N	N	N	N	Y	Y	Y	Y
6 ***Grandy***	N	N	P	N	Y	Y	N	N
KANSAS								
1 ***Roberts***	N	N	N	Y	Y	Y	N	N
2 Slattery	Y	Y	Y	Y	Y	Y	N	N
3 ***Meyers***	Y	N	N	Y	Y	Y	N	N
4 Glickman	Y	Y	Y	Y	Y	Y	N	N
5 ***Whittaker***	N	N	N	Y	Y	N	Y	Y
KENTUCKY								
1 Hubbard	Y	Y	Y	N	Y	N	N	N
2 Natcher	Y	Y	Y	N	Y	N	N	N
3 Mazzoli	Y	Y	Y	N	Y	N	N	N
4 ***Bunning***	N	N	N	N	N	Y	Y	Y
5 ***Rogers***	N	N	Y	N	Y	N	N	N
6 ***Hopkins***	N	N	N	N	Y	Y	Y	Y
7 Perkins	Y	Y	Y	N	Y	N	N	N
LOUISIANA								
1 ***Livingston***	Y	N	Y	N	Y	N	N	N
2 Boggs	Y	Y	Y	N	Y	N	N	N
3 Tauzin	Y	Y	Y	N	Y	N	N	N
4 ***McCrery***	Y	Y	?	N	Y	N	N	N
5 Huckaby	Y	Y	Y	N	Y	N	N	N
6 ***Baker***	N	Y	?	N	Y	N	N	Y
7 Hayes	Y	Y	Y	N	Y	N	N	?
8 ***Holloway***	N	Y	Y	N	Y	Y	N	N
MAINE								
1 Brennan	Y	Y	Y	Y	Y	N	N	N
2 ***Snowe***	Y	N	N	Y	Y	Y	Y	Y
MARYLAND								
1 Dyson	?	Y	Y	N	Y	N	N	N
2 ***Bentley***	N	N	N	N	Y	Y	Y	Y
3 Cardin	Y	Y	Y	Y	Y	N	N	N
4 McMillen	Y	Y	Y	N	Y	N	N	N
5 Hoyer	Y	Y	Y	N	Y	N	N	N
6 Byron	?	?	?	N	Y	Y	N	Y
7 Mfume	Y	Y	Y	Y	Y	N	N	N
8 ***Morella***	N	N	N	Y	Y	Y	N	N
MASSACHUSETTS								
1 ***Conte***	Y	N	Y	N	Y	N	N	N
2 Neal	Y	Y	Y	Y	Y	N	N	N
3 Early	Y	Y	Y	N	Y	N	N	N
4 Frank	Y	Y	Y	Y	Y	N	N	N
5 Atkins	Y	Y	Y	Y	Y	N	N	N
6 Mavroules	Y	Y	Y	Y	Y	N	N	N
7 Markey	Y	?	Y	Y	Y	N	N	N
8 Kennedy	Y	Y	Y	Y	Y	N	N	N
9 Moakley	Y	Y	Y	N	Y	N	N	N
10 Studds	Y	Y	Y	Y	Y	Y	N	N
11 Donnelly	Y	Y	Y	Y	Y	N	N	N
MICHIGAN								
1 Conyers	Y	Y	Y	Y	Y	N	N	N
2 ***Pursell***	Y	Y	Y	N	Y	?	N	N
3 Wolpe	Y	Y	Y	Y	Y	Y	N	N
4 ***Upton***	N	N	N	N	Y	Y	Y	Y
5 ***Henry***	N	N	N	Y	Y	Y	Y	Y
6 Carr	Y	Y	Y	N	Y	N	N	N
7 Kildee	Y	Y	Y	Y	Y	Y	N	N
8 Traxler	Y	Y	Y	N	Y	N	N	N
9 ***Vander Jagt***	?	N	N	N	Y	Y	Y	Y
10 ***Schuette***	?	?	?	?	?	?	?	?
11 ***Davis***	Y	N	N	N	Y	Y	N	N
12 Bonior	Y	Y	Y	Y	Y	N	N	N
13 Crockett	?	Y	?	Y	Y	N	?	?
14 Hertel	Y	Y	Y	Y	N	Y	N	N
15 Ford	?	Y	Y	N	Y	N	N	?
16 Dingell	Y	Y	Y	N	Y	Y	N	N
17 Levin	Y	Y	Y	N	Y	N	N	N
18 ***Broomfield***	Y	N	N	N	Y	Y	Y	Y
MINNESOTA								
1 Penny	Y	N	Y	N	Y	Y	N	Y
2 ***Weber***	N	N	N	Y	Y	Y	N	N
3 ***Frenzel***	N	N	N	Y	Y	Y	Y	Y
4 Vento	Y	Y	Y	N	Y	N	?	N

	172	173	174	175	176	177	178	179
5 Sabo	Y	Y	Y	N	Y	N	N	N
6 Sikorski	N	Y	Y	Y	Y	Y	Y	N
7 ***Stangeland***	N	N	Y	N	Y	?	N	N
8 Oberstar	Y	Y	Y	N	Y	N	N	N
MISSISSIPPI								
1 Whitten	Y	Y	Y	N	Y	N	N	N
2 Espy	Y	Y	Y	N	Y	N	N	N
3 Montgomery	Y	Y	Y	N	Y	N	N	N
4 Parker	?	Y	Y	N	Y	N	N	N
5 Taylor	Y	Y	Y	N	Y	N	N	N
MISSOURI								
1 Clay	N	Y	Y	N	Y	N	N	?
2 ***Buechner***	N	N	N	N	Y	N	N	N
3 Gephardt	Y	Y	Y	Y	Y	N	N	N
4 Skelton	Y	Y	Y	N	Y	N	N	N
5 Wheat	Y	Y	Y	Y	Y	N	N	N
6 ***Coleman***	N	N	N	N	Y	N	Y	Y
7 ***Hancock***	N	N	N	N	Y	Y	Y	Y
8 ***Emerson***	Y	N	Y	N	Y	N	N	N
9 Volkmer	Y	Y	Y	N	Y	N	N	N
MONTANA								
1 Williams	Y	Y	Y	Y	Y	N	N	N
2 ***Marlenee***	N	N	N	N	Y	N	N	N
NEBRASKA								
1 ***Bereuter***	N	N	N	N	Y	N	N	N
2 Hoagland	Y	Y	Y	Y	Y	Y	N	N
3 ***Smith***	Y	N	Y	N	Y	N	N	N
NEVADA								
1 Bilbray	Y	Y	Y	Y	Y	N	N	N
2 ***Vucanovich***	?	?	?	?	?	?	?	?
NEW HAMPSHIRE								
1 ***Smith***	N	N	N	N	Y	Y	Y	Y
2 ***Douglas***	N	N	N	N	Y	Y	Y	Y
NEW JERSEY								
1 Vacancy								
2 Hughes	Y	Y	Y	N	Y	N	N	N
3 Pallone	?	Y	Y	N	Y	Y	N	N
4 ***Smith***	Y	N	Y	N	Y	Y	N	N
5 ***Roukema***	N	N	N	Y	Y	N	N	Y
6 Dwyer	Y	Y	Y	N	Y	N	N	N
7 ***Rinaldo***	Y	Y	Y	N	Y	Y	N	N
8 Roe	Y	Y	Y	N	Y	N	N	N
9 Torricelli	?	?	?	Y	Y	N	N	N
10 Payne	Y	Y	Y	N	Y	N	N	N
11 ***Gallo***	N	N	N	N	Y	Y	N	N
12 ***Courter***	N	N	N	N	Y	N	N	Y
13 ***Saxton***	N	N	N	N	Y	Y	N	N
14 Guarini	Y	Y	Y	Y	Y	N	N	Y
NEW MEXICO								
1 ***Schiff***	Y	N	N	N	Y	N	N	N
2 ***Skeen***	Y	N	Y	N	Y	N	N	N
3 Richardson	Y	Y	Y	N	Y	N	N	N
NEW YORK								
1 Hochbrueckner	Y	Y	Y	N	Y	N	N	N
2 Downey	Y	Y	Y	Y	Y	N	N	N
3 Mrazek	Y	Y	Y	Y	Y	N	N	N
4 ***Lent***	Y	Y	N	N	Y	Y	Y	?
5 ***McGrath***	N	N	N	N	Y	Y	Y	Y
6 Flake	Y	Y	Y	N	Y	N	N	N
7 Ackerman	Y	Y	Y	Y	Y	N	N	N
8 Scheuer	Y	Y	Y	Y	Y	N	N	N
9 Manton	?	Y	Y	N	Y	N	N	N
10 Schumer	Y	Y	Y	Y	Y	N	N	N
11 Towns	?	Y	Y	Y	Y	N	N	N
12 Owens	Y	Y	Y	Y	Y	N	N	N
13 Solarz	Y	Y	Y	Y	Y	N	N	N
14 ***Molinari***	N	N	N	N	Y	Y	Y	Y
15 ***Green***	Y	N	Y	Y	Y	Y	N	N
16 Rangel	Y	Y	Y	?	?	?	?	?
17 Weiss	Y	Y	Y	Y	Y	Y	N	N
18 Serrano	Y	Y	Y	N	Y	N	N	N
19 Engel	?	?	?	?	?	?	?	?
20 Lowey	Y	Y	Y	N	Y	Y	N	N
21 ***Fish***	Y	N	N	Y	Y	?	?	?
22 ***Gilman***	Y	N	Y	Y	Y	Y	N	N
23 McNulty	Y	Y	Y	N	Y	N	N	N
24 ***Solomon***	N	N	N	N	Y	Y	Y	Y
25 ***Boehlert***	N	N	N	Y	Y	Y	N	N
26 ***Martin***	N	N	N	N	Y	N	N	Y
27 ***Walsh***	Y	N	N	Y	Y	N	N	Y
28 McHugh	Y	Y	Y	N	Y	N	N	N
29 ***Horton***	Y	Y	Y	N	Y	N	N	N
30 Slaughter	Y	Y	Y	Y	Y	N	N	N
31 ***Paxon***	Y	N	N	N	Y	Y	N	N

	172	173	174	175	176	177	178	179
32 LaFalce	Y	Y	Y	N	Y	Y	N	?
33 Nowak	Y	Y	Y	N	Y	N	N	N
34 ***Houghton***	Y	N	N	N	Y	Y	Y	Y
NORTH CAROLINA								
1 Jones	Y	Y	Y	Y	Y	N	N	N
2 Valentine	Y	Y	Y	Y	Y	Y	N	Y
3 Lancaster	Y	Y	N	N	Y	N	N	N
4 Price	Y	Y	Y	Y	Y	N	N	N
5 Neal	Y	Y	Y	N	?	Y	N	Y
6 ***Coble***	N	N	N	Y	Y	Y	Y	Y
7 Rose	Y	Y	Y	N	?	N	N	N
8 Hefner	?	Y	Y	N	Y	N	N	N
9 ***McMillan***	?	N	N	N	Y	Y	Y	Y
10 ***Ballenger***	N	N	N	N	Y	Y	Y	Y
11 Clarke	N	Y	Y	Y	Y	N	N	N
NORTH DAKOTA								
AL Dorgan	Y	Y	Y	N	Y	N	N	N
OHIO								
1 Luken	Y	Y	Y	N	Y	N	N	N
2 ***Gradison***	Y	N	N	N	Y	Y	Y	Y
3 Hall	?	Y	Y	Y	Y	N	N	Y
4 ***Oxley***	N	N	N	N	Y	Y	Y	Y
5 ***Gillmor***	Y	N	N	N	Y	Y	N	N
6 ***McEwen***	Y	N	Y	N	Y	Y	Y	Y
7 ***DeWine***	N	N	N	N	Y	Y	Y	Y
8 ***Lukens***	N	N	N	N	N	N	Y	Y
9 Kaptur	Y	Y	Y	N	Y	N	N	N
10 ***Miller***	N	N	Y	N	Y	N	Y	Y
11 Eckart	Y	Y	Y	Y	Y	Y	N	N
12 ***Kasich***	?	N	N	N	Y	Y	Y	Y
13 Pease	Y	Y	Y	N	Y	N	N	N
14 Sawyer	Y	Y	Y	N	Y	Y	N	N
15 ***Wylie***	?	?	?	?	?	?	?	?
16 ***Regula***	N	N	N	N	Y	Y	N	N
17 Traficant	Y	Y	Y	Y	Y	N	N	N
18 Applegate	Y	Y	Y	N	Y	Y	N	N
19 Feighan	Y	Y	Y	Y	Y	N	N	N
20 Oakar	Y	Y	Y	Y	Y	N	N	N
21 Stokes	?	Y	Y	N	Y	N	N	N
OKLAHOMA								
1 ***Inhofe***	N	N	N	N	Y	Y	N	N
2 Synar	Y	Y	?	Y	Y	N	N	N
3 Watkins	?	?	Y	N	Y	N	N	N
4 McCurdy	Y	Y	Y	N	Y	N	N	N
5 ***Edwards***	N	N	N	N	Y	Y	N	N
6 English	Y	Y	Y	N	Y	N	N	N
OREGON								
1 AuCoin	Y	Y	Y	N	Y	N	N	N
2 ***Smith, B.***	N	N	N	N	Y	N	Y	Y
3 Wyden	Y	Y	Y	Y	Y	N	N	N
4 DeFazio	Y	Y	Y	Y	Y	N	N	N
5 ***Smith, D.***	N	N	N	N	Y	N	Y	Y
PENNSYLVANIA								
1 Foglietta	?	Y	Y	Y	Y	N	N	N
2 Gray	Y	Y	Y	N	Y	N	N	N
3 Borski	Y	Y	Y	Y	Y	N	N	N
4 Kolter	Y	Y	Y	N	Y	N	?	?
5 ***Schulze***	Y	N	Y	N	Y	N	Y	Y
6 Yatron	Y	Y	Y	N	Y	N	N	N
7 ***Weldon***	?	N	N	N	Y	Y	Y	Y
8 Kostmayer	Y	Y	Y	Y	Y	Y	N	N
9 ***Shuster***	Y	N	N	N	Y	Y	Y	Y
10 ***McDade***	N	N	N	N	Y	N	N	N
11 Kanjorski	Y	Y	Y	Y	Y	N	N	N
12 Murtha	Y	Y	Y	N	Y	N	N	N
13 ***Coughlin***	N	N	Y	N	Y	N	N	N
14 Coyne	Y	Y	Y	N	Y	N	?	N
15 ***Ritter***	?	?	?	?	Y	Y	Y	Y
16 ***Walker***	N	N	N	N	Y	Y	Y	Y
17 ***Gekas***	N	N	N	N	Y	N	Y	Y
18 Walgren	Y	Y	Y	Y	Y	N	N	Y
19 ***Goodling***	N	N	N	N	Y	Y	Y	Y
20 Gaydos	Y	Y	Y	N	Y	N	N	N
21 ***Ridge***	?	N	N	Y	Y	Y	Y	Y
22 Murphy	N	Y	Y	Y	Y	N	N	N
23 ***Clinger***	Y	N	N	N	Y	Y	Y	Y
RHODE ISLAND								
1 ***Machtley***	N	N	N	Y	Y	N	Y	Y
2 ***Schneider***	Y	N	N	Y	Y	Y	Y	Y
SOUTH CAROLINA								
1 ***Ravenel***	Y	N	N	N	Y	N	N	Y
2 ***Spence***	N	N	N	N	Y	N	N	Y
3 Derrick	Y	Y	Y	N	Y	N	N	N
4 Patterson	Y	Y	Y	N	Y	Y	Y	Y
5 Spratt	Y	Y	Y	N	Y	N	N	N
6 Tallon	Y	Y	Y	N	Y	Y	Y	Y

	172	173	174	175	176	177	178	179
SOUTH DAKOTA								
AL Johnson	Y	Y	Y	Y	Y	N	N	N
TENNESSEE								
1 ***Quillen***	Y	N	N	N	Y	Y	N	N
2 ***Duncan***	N	N	N	N	Y	Y	Y	Y
3 Lloyd	?	Y	Y	N	Y	N	N	N
4 Cooper	Y	Y	Y	Y	Y	N	N	N
5 Clement	Y	Y	Y	Y	Y	N	N	N
6 Gordon	Y	Y	Y	N	Y	N	N	N
7 ***Sundquist***	N	N	N	N	Y	Y	N	N
8 Tanner	Y	Y	Y	N	Y	N	N	N
9 Ford	Y	Y	Y	Y	Y	N	?	N
TEXAS								
1 Chapman	Y	Y	Y	N	Y	N	N	N
2 Wilson	Y	Y	Y	N	Y	N	N	N
3 ***Bartlett***	Y	Y	Y	N	Y	Y	N	N
4 Hall	?	?	?	?	?	?	?	?
5 Bryant	Y	Y	Y	N	Y	N	N	N
6 ***Barton***	N	Y	Y	N	Y	Y	N	N
7 ***Archer***	Y	N	N	N	Y	Y	Y	Y
8 ***Fields***	N	Y	Y	N	Y	Y	N	N
9 Brooks	Y	Y	Y	N	Y	N	N	N
10 Pickle	Y	Y	Y	N	Y	N	?	?
11 Leath	Y	Y	Y	N	?	?	?	?
12 Geren	Y	Y	Y	N	Y	N	N	N
13 Sarpalius	Y	Y	Y	N	Y	Y	N	N
14 Laughlin	Y	Y	Y	N	Y	N	N	N
15 de la Garza	Y	Y	Y	N	Y	N	N	N
16 Coleman	Y	Y	Y	N	Y	N	N	N
17 Stenholm	Y	Y	Y	N	Y	Y	Y	Y
18 Washington	Y	Y	Y	?	Y	?	?	?
19 ***Combest***	?	N	N	N	Y	Y	Y	Y
20 Gonzalez	Y	Y	?	N	Y	N	N	N
21 ***Smith***	?	N	Y	N	Y	Y	N	N
22 ***DeLay***	N	N	Y	N	Y	Y	N	N
23 Bustamante	Y	Y	Y	N	Y	N	N	N
24 Frost	Y	Y	Y	N	Y	N	N	N
25 Andrews	Y	Y	Y	N	Y	N	N	N
26 ***Armey***	N	N	N	N	Y	Y	N	Y
27 Ortiz	Y	Y	Y	N	Y	N	N	N
UTAH								
1 ***Hansen***	Y	N	N	N	N	N	N	Y
2 Owens	Y	Y	Y	Y	Y	N	N	N
3 ***Nielson***	Y	N	N	N	Y	N	N	N
VERMONT								
AL ***Smith***	Y	N	N	Y	Y	Y	Y	Y
VIRGINIA								
1 ***Bateman***	Y	N	N	N	Y	N	N	N
2 Pickett	Y	Y	Y	N	Y	N	N	N
3 ***Bliley***	N	N	N	N	Y	N	Y	Y
4 Sisisky	Y	Y	Y	Y	Y	Y	N	N
5 Payne	Y	Y	Y	N	Y	N	N	Y
6 Olin	Y	Y	Y	N	Y	N	N	N
7 ***Slaughter***	N	N	N	N	Y	N	Y	Y
8 ***Parris***	N	N	N	N	Y	?	?	Y
9 Boucher	Y	Y	Y	N	Y	N	N	N
10 ***Wolf***	N	N	N	N	Y	Y	N	N
WASHINGTON								
1 ***Miller***	N	N	N	N	Y	Y	N	Y
2 Swift	Y	Y	Y	N	Y	N	N	N
3 Unsoeld	Y	Y	Y	N	Y	N	N	N
4 ***Morrison***	Y	Y	Y	N	Y	N	N	N
5 Foley								
6 Dicks	Y	Y	Y	N	Y	N	N	N
7 McDermott	Y	Y	Y	Y	Y	N	?	N
8 ***Chandler***	N	N	N	N	Y	N	N	N
WEST VIRGINIA								
1 Mollohan	Y	Y	Y	N	Y	N	N	N
2 Staggers	Y	Y	Y	N	Y	N	N	N
3 Wise	Y	Y	Y	N	Y	N	N	N
4 Rahall	Y	Y	Y	N	Y	N	N	N
WISCONSIN								
1 Aspin	?	Y	Y	N	Y	N	N	?
2 Kastenmeier	Y	Y	Y	Y	Y	N	N	N
3 ***Gunderson***	N	N	N	N	Y	Y	N	N
4 Kleczka	Y	Y	Y	N	Y	Y	N	N
5 Moody	Y	Y	Y	Y	Y	N	N	Y
6 ***Petri***	Y	N	N	N	Y	Y	Y	Y
7 Obey	Y	Y	Y	N	Y	N	N	N
8 ***Roth***	N	N	N	N	Y	Y	Y	Y
9 ***Sensenbrenner***	N	N	N	Y	Y	Y	Y	Y
WYOMING								
AL ***Thomas***	Y	N	N	Y	Y	N	Y	Y

Southern states - Ala., Ark., Fla., Ga., Ky., La., Miss., N.C., Okla., S.C., Tenn., Texas, Va.
Omitted votes are quorum calls, which CQ does not include in its vote charts.

HOUSE VOTES 180, 181, 182, 183, 184, 185, 186, 187

180. HR 5019. Fiscal 1991 Energy and Water Appropriations/Across-the-Board Cuts. Penny, D-Minn., amendment to provide a 2 percent across-the-board cut in all discretionary accounts in the bill. Rejected 175-232: R 126-42; D 49-190 (ND 28-135, SD 21-55), June 19, 1990.

181. HR 5019. Fiscal 1991 Energy and Water Appropriations/Passage. Passage of the bill to appropriate $20.8 billion in fiscal 1991 for energy, water and nuclear weapons programs. Passed 355-59: R 121-48; D 234-11 (ND 159-8, SD 75-3), June 19, 1990.

182. HR 3859. Washington Center Financial Assistance/Passage. Williams, D-Mont., motion to suspend the rules and pass the bill to authorize $12 million in financial assistance to the Washington Center for Internships and Academic Seminars to help construct a student residence and classroom building. Rejected 91-313: R 10-157; D 81-156 (ND 64-100, SD 17-56), June 19, 1990. A two-thirds majority of those present and voting (270 in this case) is required for passage under suspension of the rules. A "nay" was a vote supporting the president's position.

183. Procedural Motion. McEwen, R-Ohio, motion to approve the House Journal of Tuesday, June 19. Motion agreed to 281-121: R 55-116; D 226-5 (ND 153-5, SD 73-0), June 20, 1990.

184. HR 20. Hatch Act Revisions/Veto Override. Passage, over President Bush's June 15 veto, of the bill to allow greater political activity by federal employees and to protect them from political pressure. Passed (thus cleared for Senate action) 327-93: R 84-90; D 243-3 (ND 164-2, SD 79-1), June 20, 1990. A two-thirds majority of those present and voting of both houses (280 in this case) is required to override a veto. A "nay" was a vote supporting the president's position.

185. HR 3. Child-Care Programs/Instruction of Conferees. Brown, R-Colo., motion to instruct the House conferees to accept, with an amendment, Senate language to relax the Social Security earnings test. The Brown amendment would delay implementing a part of the Senate change until 1996 in order to keep the provision revenue neutral. Motion agreed to 384-36: R 174-1; D 210-35 (ND 136-30, SD 74-5), June 20, 1990.

186. HR 3. Child-Care Programs/Instruction of Conferees. Goodling, R-Pa., motion to instruct the House conferees to reject the Senate amendments to establish a new child-care grant program (the Act for Better Child Care). Motion agreed to 416-0: R 173-0; D 243-0 (ND 164-0, SD 79-0), June 20, 1990. (The Goodling motion to instruct was identical to an Archer, R-Texas, motion to instruct. The Archer motion was agreed to May 9, but most members felt that conferees had not adhered to it. Motions to instruct are non-binding.)

187. HR 5021. Fiscal 1991 Commerce, Justice, State and the Judiciary Appropriations/Savings and Loan Investigations. Smith, D-Iowa, amendment to appropriate $75 million to the Justice Department to investigate and prosecute fraud and other crimes at savings and loan institutions. Adopted 420-1: R 173-1; D 247-0 (ND 167-0, SD 80-0), June 20, 1990.

KEY

Y Voted for (yea).
\# Paired for.
\+ Announced for.
N Voted against (nay).
X Paired against.
\- Announced against.
P Voted "present."
C Voted "present" to avoid possible conflict of interest.
? Did not vote or otherwise make a position known.

Democrats *Republicans*

	180	181	182	183	184	185	186	187
ALABAMA								
1 ***Callahan***	N	Y	N	Y	N	Y	Y	Y
2 ***Dickinson***	N	Y	N	N	N	Y	Y	Y
3 Browder	N	Y	N	Y	Y	Y	Y	Y
4 Bevill	N	Y	N	Y	Y	Y	Y	Y
5 Flippo	?	Y	N	Y	Y	Y	Y	Y
6 Erdreich	N	Y	N	Y	Y	Y	Y	Y
7 Harris	N	Y	N	Y	Y	Y	Y	Y
ALASKA								
AL ***Young***	N	Y	N	N	Y	Y	Y	Y
ARIZONA								
1 ***Rhodes***	Y	Y	N	N	Y	Y	Y	Y
2 Udall	N	Y	N	Y	Y	N	Y	Y
3 ***Stump***	Y	N	N	N	N	Y	Y	Y
4 ***Kyl***	Y	Y	N	N	N	Y	Y	Y
5 ***Kolbe***	Y	Y	N	N	Y	Y	Y	Y
ARKANSAS								
1 Alexander	N	Y	Y	?	Y	Y	Y	Y
2 ***Robinson***	Y	N	N	Y	Y	Y	Y	Y
3 ***Hammerschmidt***	Y	Y	N	Y	Y	Y	Y	Y
4 Anthony	N	Y	Y	Y	Y	Y	Y	Y
CALIFORNIA								
1 Bosco	N	Y	N	Y	Y	Y	Y	Y
2 ***Herger***	Y	Y	N	N	N	Y	Y	Y
3 Matsui	N	Y	Y	Y	Y	N	Y	Y
4 Fazio	N	Y	Y	Y	Y	Y	Y	Y
5 Pelosi	N	Y	Y	Y	Y	Y	Y	Y
6 Boxer	N	Y	N	Y	Y	Y	Y	Y
7 Miller	N	Y	N	Y	Y	Y	Y	Y
8 Dellums	N	Y	Y	Y	Y	N	Y	Y
9 Stark	N	Y	N	Y	Y	Y	Y	Y
10 Edwards	?	Y	Y	Y	Y	N	Y	Y
11 Lantos	N	Y	N	Y	Y	Y	Y	Y
12 ***Campbell***	Y	N	N	N	Y	Y	Y	Y
13 Mineta	N	Y	Y	Y	Y	Y	Y	Y
14 ***Shumway***	Y	Y	N	Y	N	Y	Y	Y
15 Condit	Y	Y	N	Y	Y	Y	Y	Y
16 Panetta	N	Y	N	Y	Y	N	Y	Y
17 ***Pashayan***	N	Y	N	N	Y	Y	Y	+
18 Lehman	N	Y	N	Y	Y	Y	Y	Y
19 ***Lagomarsino***	Y	Y	N	N	N	Y	Y	Y
20 ***Thomas***	Y	Y	N	N	Y	Y	Y	Y
21 ***Gallegly***	Y	Y	N	N	N	Y	Y	Y
22 ***Moorhead***	Y	Y	N	N	N	Y	Y	Y
23 Beilenson	N	Y	N	Y	N	N	Y	Y
24 Waxman	N	Y	Y	Y	Y	Y	Y	Y
25 Roybal	N	Y	Y	Y	Y	Y	Y	Y
26 Berman	N	Y	Y	Y	Y	Y	Y	Y
27 Levine	N	Y	Y	Y	Y	Y	Y	Y
28 Dixon	N	Y	N	?	Y	Y	Y	Y
29 Hawkins	?	?	?	?	Y	Y	Y	Y
30 Martinez	?	Y	N	Y	Y	Y	Y	Y
31 Dymally	N	Y	Y	Y	Y	N	Y	Y
32 Anderson	N	Y	Y	Y	Y	Y	Y	Y
33 ***Dreier***	Y	Y	N	N	N	Y	Y	Y
34 Torres	N	Y	Y	Y	Y	Y	Y	Y
35 ***Lewis***	N	Y	N	N	N	Y	Y	Y
36 Brown	N	Y	Y	Y	Y	Y	Y	Y
37 ***McCandless***	Y	Y	N	N	N	Y	Y	Y
38 ***Dornan***	?	Y	N	N	N	Y	Y	Y
39 ***Dannemeyer***	Y	Y	N	N	N	Y	Y	Y
40 ***Cox***	Y	Y	N	N	N	Y	Y	Y
41 ***Lowery***	N	Y	N	N	Y	Y	Y	Y
42 ***Rohrabacher***	Y	Y	N	N	N	Y	Y	Y
43 ***Packard***	Y	Y	N	Y	N	Y	Y	Y
44 Bates	Y	N	Y	Y	Y	Y	Y	Y
45 ***Hunter***	Y	Y	N	N	N	Y	Y	Y
COLORADO								
1 Schroeder	Y	N	N	N	Y	Y	Y	Y
2 Skaggs	N	Y	N	Y	Y	Y	Y	+
3 Campbell	N	Y	N	Y	Y	?	?	?
4 ***Brown***	Y	N	N	N	N	Y	Y	Y
5 ***Hefley***	Y	Y	N	N	N	Y	Y	Y
6 ***Schaefer***	Y	Y	N	N	Y	Y	Y	Y
CONNECTICUT								
1 Kennelly	N	Y	Y	Y	Y	N	Y	Y
2 Gejdenson	N	Y	Y	Y	Y	Y	Y	Y
3 Morrison	Y	N	N	+	Y	Y	Y	Y
4 ***Shays***	Y	N	N	N	Y	Y	Y	Y
5 ***Rowland***	Y	N	N	Y	Y	Y	Y	Y
6 ***Johnson***	Y	N	N	Y	N	Y	Y	Y
DELAWARE								
AL Carper	N	Y	Y	Y	Y	Y	Y	Y
FLORIDA								
1 Hutto	Y	Y	N	Y	Y	Y	Y	Y
2 ***Grant***	Y	Y	N	Y	Y	Y	Y	Y
3 Bennett	Y	Y	N	Y	N	Y	Y	Y
4 ***James***	N	Y	N	N	N	Y	Y	Y
5 ***McCollum***	Y	Y	N	N	N	Y	Y	Y
6 ***Stearns***	Y	Y	N	N	N	Y	Y	Y
7 Gibbons	?	?	?	Y	Y	Y	Y	Y
8 ***Young***	N	Y	N	N	Y	Y	Y	Y
9 ***Bilirakis***	Y	Y	N	N	Y	Y	Y	Y
10 ***Ireland***	Y	Y	N	N	N	Y	Y	Y
11 Nelson	-	+	-	+	+	+	+	+
12 ***Lewis***	N	Y	N	N	N	Y	Y	Y
13 ***Goss***	N	Y	N	N	Y	Y	Y	Y
14 Johnston	Y	N	Y	Y	Y	Y	Y	Y
15 ***Shaw***	Y	Y	N	Y	N	Y	Y	Y
16 Smith	N	Y	Y	Y	Y	Y	Y	Y
17 Lehman	N	Y	Y	Y	Y	Y	Y	Y
18 ***Ros-Lehtinen***	N	Y	N	N	Y	Y	Y	Y
19 Fascell	N	Y	Y	Y	Y	Y	Y	Y
GEORGIA								
1 Thomas	N	Y	N	Y	Y	Y	Y	Y
2 Hatcher	N	Y	Y	Y	Y	Y	Y	Y
3 Ray	N	Y	N	Y	?	Y	Y	Y
4 Jones	N	Y	N	Y	Y	Y	Y	Y
5 Lewis	N	Y	N	Y	Y	Y	Y	Y
6 ***Gingrich***	Y	N	N	N	N	Y	?	Y
7 Darden	Y	Y	N	Y	Y	Y	Y	Y
8 Rowland	N	Y	N	Y	Y	Y	Y	Y
9 Jenkins	Y	Y	N	Y	Y	Y	Y	Y
10 Barnard	Y	Y	?	?	Y	Y	?	Y
HAWAII								
1 ***Saiki***	N	Y	N	Y	Y	Y	Y	Y
2 Vacancy								
IDAHO								
1 ***Craig***	Y	Y	?	N	Y	Y	Y	Y
2 Stallings	N	Y	N	Y	Y	Y	Y	Y
ILLINOIS								
1 Hayes	N	Y	Y	Y	Y	Y	Y	Y
2 Savage	N	Y	N	Y	Y	Y	Y	Y
3 Russo	Y	N	N	Y	Y	Y	Y	Y
4 Sangmeister	Y	Y	N	Y	Y	Y	Y	Y
5 Lipinski	Y	Y	N	Y	Y	Y	Y	Y
6 ***Hyde***	N	Y	N	N	N	Y	Y	Y
7 Collins	N	Y	N	Y	Y	Y	Y	Y
8 Rostenkowski	N	Y	Y	Y	Y	N	Y	Y
9 Yates	N	Y	N	Y	Y	Y	Y	Y
10 ***Porter***	Y	Y	Y	Y	N	Y	Y	Y
11 Annunzio	N	Y	N	Y	Y	Y	Y	Y
12 ***Crane***	Y	N	N	N	N	Y	Y	N
13 ***Fawell***	Y	Y	N	N	N	Y	Y	Y
14 ***Hastert***	Y	Y	N	N	Y	Y	Y	Y
15 ***Madigan***	?	?	?	N	N	Y	Y	Y
16 ***Martin***	Y	N	N	N	+	Y	Y	Y
17 Evans	N	Y	N	Y	Y	Y	Y	Y
18 ***Michel***	Y	N	N	N	Y	Y	?	Y
19 Bruce	N	Y	N	Y	Y	Y	Y	Y
20 Durbin	N	Y	N	Y	Y	Y	Y	Y
21 Costello	N	Y	N	Y	Y	Y	Y	Y
22 Poshard	N	Y	Y	Y	Y	Y	Y	Y
INDIANA								
1 Visclosky	N	Y	N	Y	Y	N	Y	Y
2 Sharp	Y	N	N	Y	Y	Y	Y	Y
3 ***Hiler***	Y	N	N	N	N	Y	Y	Y

ND Northern Democrats SD Southern Democrats

	180	181	182	183	184	185	186	187
4 Long	Y	Y	N	Y	Y	Y	Y	Y
5 Jontz	Y	N	Y	Y	Y	Y	Y	Y
6 ***Burton***	Y	N	N	N	Y	Y	Y	Y
7 ***Myers***	N	Y	N	Y	Y	Y	Y	Y
8 McCloskey	N	Y	N	Y	Y	Y	Y	Y
9 Hamilton	Y	Y	Y	Y	Y	Y	Y	Y
10 Jacobs	Y	N	N	N	Y	N	Y	Y
IOWA								
1 ***Leach***	?	?	?	N	N	Y	Y	Y
2 ***Tauke***	Y	N	Y	N	Y	Y	Y	Y
3 Nagle	N	Y	Y	Y	Y	Y	Y	Y
4 Smith	N	Y	Y	Y	Y	Y	Y	Y
5 ***Lightfoot***	Y	Y	Y	N	N	Y	Y	Y
6 ***Grandy***	Y	Y	N	N	Y	Y	Y	Y
KANSAS								
1 ***Roberts***	Y	Y	N	N	N	Y	Y	Y
2 Slattery	Y	Y	N	Y	Y	N	Y	Y
3 ***Meyers***	Y	Y	N	N	N	Y	Y	Y
4 Glickman	Y	Y	N	Y	Y	Y	Y	Y
5 ***Whittaker***	Y	Y	N	N	N	Y	Y	Y
KENTUCKY								
1 Hubbard	Y	Y	N	Y	Y	Y	Y	Y
2 Natcher	N	Y	N	Y	Y	Y	Y	Y
3 Mazzoli	N	Y	N	Y	Y	Y	Y	Y
4 ***Bunning***	Y	N	N	N	N	Y	Y	Y
5 ***Rogers***	Y	N	N	N	N	Y	Y	Y
6 ***Hopkins***	Y	Y	N	N	N	Y	Y	Y
7 Perkins	N	Y	Y	Y	Y	Y	Y	Y
LOUISIANA								
1 ***Livingston***	N	Y	N	Y	Y	Y	Y	Y
2 Boggs	N	Y	Y	?	Y	Y	Y	Y
3 Tauzin	N	Y	?	Y	Y	Y	Y	Y
4 ***McCrery***	N	Y	N	Y	N	Y	Y	Y
5 Huckaby	N	Y	N	Y	Y	Y	Y	Y
6 ***Baker***	Y	Y	N	N	N	Y	Y	Y
7 Hayes	?	?	?	Y	Y	Y	Y	Y
8 ***Holloway***	N	Y	N	N	Y	Y	Y	Y
MAINE								
1 Brennan	Y	Y	N	Y	Y	Y	Y	Y
2 ***Snowe***	Y	N	N	N	N	N	Y	Y
MARYLAND								
1 Dyson	N	Y	N	?	Y	Y	Y	Y
2 ***Bentley***	Y	Y	N	N	Y	Y	Y	Y
3 Cardin	N	Y	N	?	Y	N	Y	Y
4 McMillen	N	Y	N	Y	Y	Y	Y	Y
5 Hoyer	N	Y	Y	Y	Y	N	Y	Y
6 Byron	Y	Y	N	Y	Y	Y	Y	Y
7 Mfume	N	Y	N	Y	Y	N	Y	Y
8 ***Morella***	Y	Y	N	N	Y	Y	Y	Y
MASSACHUSETTS								
1 ***Conte***	N	Y	N	Y	Y	Y	Y	Y
2 Neal	N	Y	Y	Y	Y	Y	Y	Y
3 Early	N	Y	Y	Y	Y	N	Y	Y
4 Frank	N	Y	N	Y	Y	Y	Y	Y
5 Atkins	N	Y	N	Y	Y	Y	Y	Y
6 Mavroules	N	Y	Y	Y	Y	Y	Y	Y
7 Markey	N	Y	?	Y	Y	Y	Y	Y
8 Kennedy	N	Y	N	Y	+	Y	Y	Y
9 Moakley	N	Y	N	Y	Y	Y	Y	Y
10 Studds	N	Y	N	Y	Y	Y	Y	Y
11 Donnelly	N	Y	Y	Y	Y	Y	Y	Y
MICHIGAN								
1 Conyers	N	Y	Y	?	Y	Y	Y	Y
2 ***Pursell***	N	Y	Y	Y	Y	Y	Y	Y
3 Wolpe	N	Y	N	Y	Y	Y	Y	Y
4 ***Upton***	Y	N	N	N	Y	Y	Y	Y
5 ***Henry***	Y	N	N	N	N	Y	Y	Y
6 Carr	N	Y	N	Y	Y	Y	Y	Y
7 Kildee	N	Y	Y	Y	Y	Y	Y	Y
8 Traxler	N	Y	N	Y	Y	Y	Y	Y
9 ***Vander Jagt***	Y	Y	N	Y	Y	Y	Y	Y
10 ***Schuette***	?	?	?	N	Y	Y	Y	Y
11 ***Davis***	N	Y	Y	Y	Y	Y	Y	Y
12 Bonior	N	Y	Y	Y	Y	Y	Y	Y
13 Crockett	?	?	?	?	Y	Y	Y	Y
14 Hertel	N	Y	Y	Y	Y	Y	Y	Y
15 Ford	?	Y	Y	Y	Y	Y	Y	Y
16 Dingell	N	Y	N	Y	Y	N	Y	Y
17 Levin	N	Y	N	Y	Y	N	Y	Y
18 ***Broomfield***	Y	Y	N	Y	N	Y	Y	Y
MINNESOTA								
1 Penny	Y	Y	N	Y	Y	Y	Y	Y
2 ***Weber***	Y	Y	N	N	N	Y	Y	Y
3 ***Frenzel***	Y	N	N	?	N	Y	Y	Y
4 Vento	N	Y	Y	Y	Y	N	Y	Y

	180	181	182	183	184	185	186	187
5 Sabo	N	Y	Y	Y	Y	N	Y	Y
6 Sikorski	Y	N	N	N	Y	Y	Y	Y
7 ***Stangeland***	N	Y	N	N	N	Y	Y	Y
8 Oberstar	N	Y	Y	Y	Y	Y	Y	Y
MISSISSIPPI								
1 Whitten	N	Y	N	Y	Y	N	Y	Y
2 Espy	N	Y	N	Y	Y	Y	Y	Y
3 Montgomery	N	Y	N	Y	Y	Y	Y	Y
4 Parker	Y	Y	N	Y	Y	Y	Y	Y
5 Taylor	N	Y	N	Y	Y	Y	Y	Y
MISSOURI								
1 Clay	?	Y	Y	N	Y	?	Y	Y
2 ***Buechner***	Y	Y	N	N	Y	Y	Y	Y
3 Gephardt	N	Y	Y	Y	Y	N	Y	Y
4 Skelton	Y	Y	N	Y	Y	Y	Y	Y
5 Wheat	N	Y	Y	Y	Y	Y	Y	Y
6 ***Coleman***	Y	Y	N	N	N	Y	Y	Y
7 ***Hancock***	Y	N	N	N	Y	Y	Y	Y
8 ***Emerson***	N	Y	Y	Y	Y	Y	Y	Y
9 Volkmer	N	Y	N	Y	Y	Y	Y	Y
MONTANA								
1 Williams	N	Y	Y	?	Y	Y	Y	Y
2 ***Marlenee***	N	Y	N	N	N	Y	Y	Y
NEBRASKA								
1 ***Bereuter***	Y	Y	N	N	Y	Y	Y	Y
2 Hoagland	N	Y	Y	Y	Y	Y	Y	Y
3 ***Smith***	N	Y	N	Y	N	Y	Y	Y
NEVADA								
1 Bilbray	Y	Y	N	Y	Y	Y	Y	Y
2 ***Vucanovich***	?	?	?	?	Y	Y	Y	Y
NEW HAMPSHIRE								
1 ***Smith***	Y	N	N	N	N	Y	Y	Y
2 ***Douglas***	Y	N	N	N	Y	Y	Y	Y
NEW JERSEY								
1 Vacancy								
2 Hughes	N	Y	Y	Y	Y	Y	Y	Y
3 Pallone	N	Y	N	Y	Y	Y	Y	Y
4 ***Smith***	N	Y	?	Y	Y	Y	Y	Y
5 ***Roukema***	Y	Y	Y	N	N	Y	Y	Y
6 Dwyer	N	Y	Y	Y	Y	Y	Y	Y
7 ***Rinaldo***	N	Y	N	Y	Y	Y	Y	Y
8 Roe	N	Y	Y	Y	Y	Y	Y	Y
9 Torricelli	N	Y	N	Y	Y	N	Y	Y
10 Payne	N	Y	Y	?	?	?	?	?
11 ***Gallo***	N	Y	N	N	Y	Y	Y	Y
12 ***Courter***	Y	Y	N	N	N	Y	Y	Y
13 ***Saxton***	N	Y	N	N	Y	Y	Y	Y
14 Guarini	Y	Y	N	Y	Y	Y	Y	Y
NEW MEXICO								
1 ***Schiff***	N	Y	N	Y	N	Y	Y	Y
2 ***Skeen***	N	Y	N	Y	N	Y	Y	Y
3 Richardson	N	Y	N	Y	Y	Y	Y	Y
NEW YORK								
1 Hochbrueckner	N	Y	N	Y	Y	Y	Y	Y
2 Downey	N	Y	N	Y	Y	N	Y	Y
3 Mrazek	N	Y	N	Y	Y	Y	Y	Y
4 ***Lent***	?	?	?	Y	Y	Y	Y	Y
5 ***McGrath***	Y	N	N	N	Y	Y	Y	Y
6 Flake	N	Y	N	Y	Y	Y	Y	Y
7 Ackerman	N	Y	Y	Y	Y	Y	Y	Y
8 Scheuer	N	Y	N	Y	Y	N	Y	Y
9 Manton	N	Y	N	Y	Y	Y	Y	Y
10 Schumer	Y	Y	N	Y	Y	Y	Y	Y
11 Towns	N	Y	Y	Y	Y	Y	Y	Y
12 Owens	?	?	?	?	?	?	?	Y
13 Solarz	N	Y	N	Y	Y	Y	Y	Y
14 ***Molinari***	Y	N	N	N	Y	Y	Y	Y
15 ***Green***	N	Y	N	Y	Y	Y	Y	Y
16 Rangel	?	?	?	?	?	?	?	?
17 Weiss	N	Y	Y	Y	Y	Y	Y	Y
18 Serrano	N	Y	Y	+	+	+	+	+
19 Engel	?	?	?	?	Y	Y	Y	Y
20 Lowey	N	Y	Y	Y	Y	Y	Y	Y
21 ***Fish***	?	?	?	Y	Y	Y	Y	Y
22 ***Gilman***	Y	Y	N	Y	Y	Y	Y	Y
23 McNulty	N	Y	N	Y	Y	Y	Y	Y
24 ***Solomon***	Y	N	N	N	Y	Y	Y	Y
25 ***Boehlert***	Y	Y	N	N	Y	Y	Y	Y
26 ***Martin***	Y	N	N	N	Y	Y	Y	Y
27 ***Walsh***	Y	Y	N	Y	Y	Y	Y	Y
28 McHugh	N	Y	N	?	Y	Y	Y	Y
29 ***Horton***	N	Y	Y	Y	Y	Y	Y	Y
30 Slaughter	N	Y	N	Y	Y	Y	Y	Y
31 ***Paxon***	Y	Y	N	N	N	Y	Y	Y

	180	181	182	183	184	185	186	187
32 LaFalce	N	Y	N	Y	Y	Y	?	Y
33 Nowak	N	Y	Y	Y	Y	Y	Y	Y
34 ***Houghton***	Y	Y	N	Y	Y	Y	Y	Y
NORTH CAROLINA								
1 Jones	N	Y	Y	Y	Y	Y	Y	Y
2 Valentine	Y	Y	N	Y	Y	Y	Y	Y
3 Lancaster	N	Y	?	Y	Y	Y	Y	Y
4 Price	N	Y	N	Y	Y	Y	Y	Y
5 Neal	Y	N	N	?	Y	Y	Y	Y
6 ***Coble***	Y	N	N	N	N	Y	Y	Y
7 Rose	N	Y	Y	Y	Y	Y	Y	Y
8 Hefner	N	Y	N	Y	Y	Y	Y	Y
9 ***McMillan***	Y	N	N	?	?	?	?	?
10 ***Ballenger***	Y	N	N	N	N	Y	Y	Y
11 Clarke	Y	Y	N	Y	Y	Y	Y	Y
NORTH DAKOTA								
AL Dorgan	N	Y	N	Y	Y	Y	Y	Y
OHIO								
1 Luken	N	Y	N	Y	Y	Y	Y	Y
2 ***Gradison***	Y	N	N	Y	N	Y	Y	Y
3 Hall	Y	Y	N	Y	Y	Y	Y	Y
4 ***Oxley***	Y	N	N	N	N	Y	Y	Y
5 ***Gillmor***	Y	Y	N	Y	N	Y	Y	Y
6 ***McEwen***	Y	N	N	Y	N	Y	Y	Y
7 ***DeWine***	Y	Y	N	N	Y	Y	Y	Y
8 ***Lukens***	Y	N	N	N	N	Y	Y	Y
9 Kaptur	N	Y	N	Y	Y	Y	Y	Y
10 ***Miller***	Y	Y	Y	N	N	Y	Y	Y
11 Eckart	N	Y	N	Y	?	?	?	?
12 ***Kasich***	Y	N	N	Y	Y	Y	Y	Y
13 Pease	N	Y	N	Y	Y	N	Y	Y
14 Sawyer	Y	Y	N	Y	Y	Y	Y	Y
15 ***Wylie***	?	?	?	Y	N	Y	Y	Y
16 ***Regula***	Y	Y	N	N	Y	Y	Y	Y
17 Traficant	N	Y	N	Y	Y	Y	Y	Y
18 Applegate	Y	Y	N	Y	Y	Y	Y	Y
19 Feighan	N	Y	N	Y	Y	Y	Y	Y
20 Oakar	N	Y	Y	Y	Y	Y	Y	Y
21 Stokes	N	Y	Y	Y	Y	Y	Y	Y
OKLAHOMA								
1 ***Inhofe***	Y	Y	N	N	N	Y	Y	Y
2 Synar	N	Y	Y	Y	Y	Y	Y	Y
3 Watkins	N	Y	N	Y	Y	Y	Y	Y
4 McCurdy	Y	Y	N	Y	Y	Y	Y	Y
5 ***Edwards***	N	Y	N	?	N	Y	Y	Y
6 English	Y	Y	N	Y	Y	Y	Y	Y
OREGON								
1 AuCoin	N	Y	N	?	Y	Y	Y	Y
2 ***Smith, B.***	Y	Y	N	N	N	Y	Y	Y
3 Wyden	N	Y	N	Y	Y	Y	Y	Y
4 DeFazio	N	Y	N	Y	Y	Y	Y	Y
5 ***Smith, D.***	Y	Y	N	N	N	Y	Y	Y
PENNSYLVANIA								
1 Foglietta	N	Y	Y	Y	N	Y	Y	Y
2 Gray	N	Y	?	Y	Y	N	?	Y
3 Borski	N	Y	N	Y	Y	Y	Y	Y
4 Kolter	N	Y	?	Y	Y	Y	Y	Y
5 ***Schulze***	N	Y	N	Y	N	Y	Y	Y
6 Yatron	N	Y	N	Y	Y	Y	Y	Y
7 ***Weldon***	Y	Y	N	Y	Y	Y	Y	Y
8 Kostmayer	N	Y	N	Y	Y	Y	Y	Y
9 ***Shuster***	Y	Y	N	Y	Y	Y	Y	Y
10 ***McDade***	N	Y	N	Y	Y	Y	Y	Y
11 Kanjorski	N	Y	N	Y	Y	Y	Y	Y
12 Murtha	N	Y	N	Y	Y	Y	Y	Y
13 ***Coughlin***	N	Y	N	N	Y	Y	Y	Y
14 Coyne	N	Y	Y	Y	Y	N	Y	Y
15 ***Ritter***	Y	N	N	Y	N	Y	Y	Y
16 ***Walker***	Y	N	N	N	N	Y	Y	Y
17 ***Gekas***	Y	N	N	N	N	Y	Y	Y
18 Walgren	Y	Y	N	Y	Y	Y	Y	Y
19 ***Goodling***	Y	Y	N	N	Y	Y	Y	Y
20 Gaydos	N	Y	N	Y	Y	Y	Y	Y
21 ***Ridge***	Y	Y	Y	N	Y	Y	Y	Y
22 Murphy	N	Y	N	N	Y	Y	Y	Y
23 ***Clinger***	Y	Y	N	N	Y	Y	Y	Y
RHODE ISLAND								
1 ***Machtley***	Y	Y	N	N	Y	Y	Y	Y
2 ***Schneider***	Y	N	N	Y	Y	Y	Y	Y
SOUTH CAROLINA								
1 ***Ravenel***	Y	Y	N	Y	Y	Y	Y	Y
2 ***Spence***	Y	Y	N	Y	Y	Y	Y	Y
3 Derrick	N	Y	N	Y	Y	Y	Y	Y
4 Patterson	Y	Y	N	Y	Y	Y	Y	Y
5 Spratt	N	Y	N	Y	Y	Y	Y	Y
6 Tallon	Y	Y	N	Y	Y	Y	Y	Y

	180	181	182	183	184	185	186	187
SOUTH DAKOTA								
AL Johnson	N	Y	Y	Y	Y	Y	Y	Y
TENNESSEE								
1 ***Quillen***	Y	Y	N	Y	Y	Y	Y	Y
2 ***Duncan***	Y	N	N	N	Y	Y	Y	Y
3 Lloyd	N	Y	N	Y	Y	Y	Y	Y
4 Cooper	Y	Y	N	Y	Y	Y	Y	Y
5 Clement	N	Y	Y	Y	Y	Y	Y	Y
6 Gordon	N	Y	N	Y	Y	Y	Y	Y
7 ***Sundquist***	Y	Y	N	N	Y	Y	Y	Y
8 Tanner	Y	Y	N	Y	Y	Y	Y	Y
9 Ford	N	Y	N	Y	Y	N	Y	Y
TEXAS								
1 Chapman	N	Y	N	Y	Y	Y	Y	Y
2 Wilson	N	Y	N	?	Y	Y	Y	Y
3 ***Bartlett***	N	Y	N	Y	N	Y	Y	Y
4 Hall	?	?	?	?	?	?	?	?
5 Bryant	N	Y	N	?	Y	Y	Y	Y
6 ***Barton***	N	Y	N	N	N	Y	Y	Y
7 ***Archer***	Y	N	N	Y	N	Y	Y	Y
8 ***Fields***	N	Y	N	N	N	Y	Y	Y
9 Brooks	N	Y	Y	Y	Y	Y	Y	Y
10 Pickle	N	Y	N	Y	Y	N	Y	Y
11 Leath	?	?	?	Y	Y	?	Y	Y
12 Geren	Y	Y	N	Y	Y	Y	Y	Y
13 Sarpalius	N	Y	N	Y	Y	Y	Y	Y
14 Laughlin	N	Y	N	Y	Y	Y	Y	Y
15 de la Garza	N	Y	N	Y	Y	Y	Y	Y
16 Coleman	N	Y	?	Y	Y	Y	Y	Y
17 Stenholm	Y	Y	N	Y	Y	Y	Y	Y
18 Washington	?	Y	Y	?	Y	?	?	?
19 ***Combest***	Y	N	N	Y	N	Y	Y	Y
20 Gonzalez	N	Y	Y	Y	Y	Y	Y	Y
21 ***Smith***	Y	Y	N	N	N	Y	Y	Y
22 ***DeLay***	Y	Y	N	N	N	Y	Y	Y
23 Bustamante	N	Y	N	?	Y	Y	Y	Y
24 Frost	N	Y	Y	Y	Y	Y	Y	Y
25 Andrews	Y	Y	N	Y	Y	N	Y	Y
26 ***Armey***	Y	N	N	N	N	Y	Y	Y
27 Ortiz	N	Y	N	Y	Y	Y	Y	Y
UTAH								
1 ***Hansen***	Y	Y	N	N	N	Y	Y	Y
2 Owens	N	Y	Y	Y	Y	Y	Y	Y
3 ***Nielson***	N	Y	N	?	Y	Y	Y	Y
VERMONT								
AL ***Smith***	Y	Y	N	Y	Y	Y	Y	Y
VIRGINIA								
1 ***Bateman***	Y	Y	N	Y	N	N	Y	Y
2 Pickett	N	N	N	Y	Y	Y	Y	Y
3 ***Bliley***	Y	N	N	N	Y	Y	Y	Y
4 Sisisky	N	Y	N	Y	Y	Y	Y	Y
5 Payne	Y	Y	N	Y	Y	Y	Y	Y
6 Olin	N	Y	?	Y	Y	N	Y	Y
7 ***Slaughter***	Y	N	N	N	N	Y	Y	Y
8 ***Parris***	Y	N	N	N	Y	Y	Y	Y
9 Boucher	N	Y	N	Y	Y	Y	Y	Y
10 ***Wolf***	Y	Y	N	N	N	Y	Y	Y
WASHINGTON								
1 ***Miller***	Y	Y	N	N	Y	Y	Y	Y
2 Swift	N	Y	Y	Y	Y	Y	Y	Y
3 Unsoeld	N	Y	N	Y	Y	N	Y	Y
4 ***Morrison***	N	Y	N	Y	Y	Y	Y	Y
5 Foley								
6 Dicks	N	Y	Y	Y	Y	Y	Y	Y
7 McDermott	N	Y	Y	Y	Y	Y	Y	Y
8 ***Chandler***	Y	Y	N	N	Y	Y	Y	Y
WEST VIRGINIA								
1 Mollohan	N	Y	N	Y	Y	Y	Y	Y
2 Staggers	N	Y	N	Y	?	Y	?	Y
3 Wise	N	Y	N	Y	Y	Y	Y	Y
4 Rahall	N	Y	Y	Y	Y	Y	Y	Y
WISCONSIN								
1 Aspin	?	?	?	Y	Y	N	Y	Y
2 Kastenmeier	Y	Y	Y	Y	Y	Y	Y	Y
3 ***Gunderson***	Y	Y	N	Y	Y	Y	Y	Y
4 Kleczka	N	Y	N	Y	Y	Y	Y	Y
5 Moody	Y	Y	N	Y	Y	N	Y	Y
6 ***Petri***	Y	N	N	Y	Y	Y	Y	Y
7 Obey	N	Y	N	Y	Y	Y	Y	Y
8 ***Roth***	Y	N	N	Y	N	Y	Y	Y
9 ***Sensenbrenner***	Y	N	N	N	N	Y	Y	Y
WYOMING								
AL ***Thomas***	Y	Y	N	N	Y	Y	Y	Y

Southern states - Ala., Ark., Fla., Ga., Ky., La., Miss., N.C., Okla., S.C., Tenn., Texas, Va.
Omitted votes are quorum calls, which CQ does not include in its vote charts.

188. HR 5021. Fiscal 1991 Commerce, Justice, State and the Judiciary Appropriations/TV Marti. Alexander, D-Ark., amendment to reduce from $16 million to $8 million the appropriation for TV Marti, the U.S. Information Agency's television broadcast to Cuba. Rejected 111-306: R 8-166; D 103-140 (ND 91-73, SD 12-67), June 20, 1990.

189. Procedural Motion. McCrery, R-La., motion to approve the House Journal of Wednesday, June 20. Motion agreed to 286-114: R 59-108; D 227-6 (ND 150-6, SD 77-0), June 21, 1990.

190. H J Res 350. Constitutional Amendment on the Flag/Previous Question. Bonior, D-Mich., motion to order the previous question (thus ending debate and the possibility of amendment) on the rule (H Res 417) to provide for House floor consideration of the joint resolution to propose an amendment to the Constitution to prohibit the physical desecration of the U.S. flag. Motion agreed to 232-191: R 0-176; D 232-15 (ND 162-3, SD 70-12), June 21, 1990.

191. H J Res 350. Constitutional Amendment on the Flag/Rule. Adoption of the rule (H Res 417) to provide for House floor consideration of the joint resolution to propose an amendment to the Constitution to prohibit the physical desecration of the U.S. flag. Adopted 231-192: R 1-174; D 230-18 (ND 160-6, SD 70-12), June 21, 1990.

192. H J Res 350. Constitutional Amendment on the Flag/Passage. Brooks, D-Texas, motion to suspend the rules and pass the joint resolution to propose an amendment to the Constitution to prohibit the physical desecration of the U.S. flag. Rejected 254-177: R 159-17; D 95-160 (ND 43-130, SD 52-30), June 21, 1990. A two-thirds majority of those present and voting (288 in this case) of both houses is required for passage of a joint resolution proposing an amendment to the Constitution. A "yea" was a vote supporting the president's position.

193. HR 5091. Flag Protection Act/Passage. Cooper, D-Tenn., motion to suspend the rules and pass the bill to make it a federal crime to destroy or damage a U.S. flag with intent to provoke imminent violence and in circumstances reasonably likely to produce imminent violence, or to destroy or damage a federally owned U.S. flag or a flag on federal property. Rejected 179-236: R 17-154; D 162-82 (ND 103-61, SD 59-21), June 21, 1990. A two-thirds majority of those present and voting (277 in this case) is required for passage under suspension of the rules.

KEY

- Y Voted for (yea).
- # Paired for.
- \+ Announced for.
- N Voted against (nay).
- X Paired against.
- \- Announced against.
- P Voted "present."
- C Voted "present" to avoid possible conflict of interest.
- ? Did not vote or otherwise make a position known.

Democrats *Republicans*

	188	189	190	191	192	193
ALABAMA						
1 ***Callahan***	N	Y	N	N	Y	Y
2 ***Dickinson***	N	N	N	N	Y	N
3 Browder	N	Y	Y	Y	Y	Y
4 Bevill	N	Y	Y	Y	Y	Y
5 Flippo	N	Y	Y	Y	Y	Y
6 Erdreich	N	Y	Y	Y	Y	Y
7 Harris	N	Y	Y	Y	Y	Y
ALASKA						
AL ***Young***	N	N	N	N	Y	N
ARIZONA						
1 ***Rhodes***	N	Y	N	N	Y	N
2 Udall	N	?	Y	Y	N	Y
3 ***Stump***	N	N	N	N	Y	N
4 ***Kyl***	N	N	N	N	Y	N
5 ***Kolbe***	N	N	N	N	N	N
ARKANSAS						
1 Alexander	Y	Y	Y	Y	Y	Y
2 ***Robinson***	X	Y	N	N	Y	?
3 ***Hammerschmidt***	N	Y	N	N	Y	N
4 Anthony	#	Y	Y	Y	N	Y
CALIFORNIA						
1 Bosco	Y	Y	Y	Y	N	N
2 ***Herger***	N	?	N	N	Y	N
3 Matsui	N	Y	Y	Y	N	N
4 Fazio	Y	Y	Y	Y	N	Y
5 Pelosi	N	Y	Y	Y	N	N
6 Boxer	N	Y	Y	Y	N	Y
7 Miller	Y	Y	Y	Y	N	?
8 Dellums	Y	Y	Y	Y	N	N
9 Stark	Y	Y	Y	Y	N	Y
10 Edwards	Y	Y	Y	Y	N	N
11 Lantos	N	Y	Y	Y	N	Y
12 ***Campbell***	N	N	N	N	Y	N
13 Mineta	Y	Y	Y	Y	N	Y
14 ***Shumway***	N	Y	N	N	Y	N
15 Condit	Y	Y	Y	Y	Y	Y
16 Panetta	Y	Y	Y	Y	N	N
17 ***Pashayan***	N	N	N	N	Y	Y
18 Lehman	N	Y	Y	Y	N	Y
19 ***Lagomarsino***	N	N	N	N	Y	N
20 ***Thomas***	N	N	N	N	Y	N
21 ***Gallegly***	N	N	N	N	Y	N
22 ***Moorhead***	N	N	N	N	Y	N
23 Beilenson	Y	Y	Y	Y	N	Y
24 Waxman	Y	Y	Y	Y	N	?
25 Roybal	Y	Y	Y	Y	N	N
26 Berman	N	Y	Y	Y	N	?
27 Levine	N	Y	Y	Y	N	N
28 Dixon	N	?	Y	Y	N	Y
29 Hawkins	Y	Y	Y	Y	N	Y
30 Martinez	N	Y	Y	Y	Y	N
31 Dymally	Y	Y	Y	Y	N	N
32 Anderson	Y	Y	Y	Y	N	Y
33 ***Dreier***	N	N	N	N	Y	N
34 Torres	Y	Y	Y	Y	N	Y
35 ***Lewis***	N	N	N	N	Y	?
36 Brown	Y	Y	Y	Y	N	Y
37 ***McCandless***	N	N	N	N	Y	N
38 ***Dornan***	N	N	N	N	Y	N
39 ***Dannemeyer***	N	N	N	N	Y	N
40 ***Cox***	N	N	N	N	Y	N
41 ***Lowery***	N	?	N	N	Y	N
42 ***Rohrabacher***	N	N	N	N	Y	N
43 ***Packard***	N	Y	N	N	Y	N
44 Bates	N	Y	Y	Y	N	Y
45 ***Hunter***	N	N	N	N	Y	N
COLORADO						
1 Schroeder	Y	N	Y	Y	N	N
2 Skaggs	Y	Y	Y	Y	N	N
3 Campbell	?	?	?	?	Y	Y
4 ***Brown***	N	Y	N	N	Y	Y
5 ***Hefley***	N	N	N	N	Y	N
6 ***Schaefer***	N	N	N	N	Y	N
CONNECTICUT						
1 Kennelly	Y	Y	Y	Y	N	N
2 Gejdenson	N	Y	Y	Y	N	Y
3 Morrison	Y	Y	Y	Y	N	Y
4 ***Shays***	N	N	N	N	N	N
5 ***Rowland***	N	Y	N	N	Y	N
6 ***Johnson***	N	Y	N	N	N	Y
DELAWARE						
AL Carper	N	Y	Y	N	N	Y
FLORIDA						
1 Hutto	N	Y	N	N	Y	Y
2 ***Grant***	N	Y	N	N	Y	N
3 Bennett	N	Y	Y	Y	Y	Y
4 ***James***	N	N	N	N	Y	N
5 ***McCollum***	N	Y	N	N	Y	N
6 ***Stearns***	N	N	N	N	Y	N
7 Gibbons	N	Y	Y	Y	N	Y
8 ***Young***	N	N	N	N	Y	N
9 ***Bilirakis***	N	N	N	N	Y	N
10 ***Ireland***	N	N	N	N	Y	N
11 Nelson	-	+	N	N	Y	Y
12 ***Lewis***	N	N	N	N	Y	N
13 ***Goss***	N	Y	N	N	Y	N
14 Johnston	N	Y	Y	Y	N	Y
15 ***Shaw***	N	Y	N	N	Y	N
16 Smith	N	Y	Y	Y	N	?
17 Lehman	N	Y	Y	Y	N	Y
18 ***Ros-Lehtinen***	N	N	N	N	Y	Y
19 Fascell	N	Y	Y	Y	N	Y
GEORGIA						
1 Thomas	N	Y	Y	Y	Y	Y
2 Hatcher	N	Y	Y	Y	Y	N
3 Ray	N	Y	N	N	Y	N
4 Jones	N	Y	Y	Y	N	Y
5 Lewis	Y	Y	Y	Y	N	N
6 ***Gingrich***	N	?	N	N	Y	N
7 Darden	N	Y	Y	Y	Y	Y
8 Rowland	N	Y	Y	Y	Y	Y
9 Jenkins	N	Y	Y	Y	Y	Y
10 Barnard	N	Y	Y	Y	Y	Y
HAWAII						
1 ***Saiki***	N	Y	N	N	Y	N
2 Vacancy						
IDAHO						
1 ***Craig***	N	N	N	N	Y	N
2 Stallings	N	Y	Y	Y	Y	N
ILLINOIS						
1 Hayes	Y	Y	Y	Y	N	Y
2 Savage	Y	Y	Y	Y	N	N
3 Russo	Y	Y	Y	Y	N	N
4 Sangmeister	N	Y	Y	Y	Y	Y
5 Lipinski	N	Y	Y	Y	Y	Y
6 ***Hyde***	N	N	N	N	Y	N
7 Collins	Y	Y	Y	Y	N	Y
8 Rostenkowski	N	Y	Y	Y	N	Y
9 Yates	Y	Y	Y	Y	N	N
10 ***Porter***	N	Y	N	N	N	N
11 Annunzio	N	Y	Y	Y	Y	N
12 ***Crane***	N	N	N	N	Y	N
13 ***Fawell***	N	N	N	N	Y	N
14 ***Hastert***	N	N	N	N	Y	N
15 ***Madigan***	N	N	N	N	Y	N
16 ***Martin***	N	N	N	N	Y	N
17 Evans	Y	Y	Y	Y	N	Y
18 ***Michel***	N	N	N	N	Y	N
19 Bruce	Y	Y	Y	Y	N	Y
20 Durbin	Y	Y	Y	Y	N	Y
21 Costello	Y	Y	Y	Y	Y	?
22 Poshard	Y	Y	Y	Y	N	N
INDIANA						
1 Visclosky	N	Y	Y	Y	N	Y
2 Sharp	Y	Y	Y	Y	Y	Y
3 ***Hiler***	N	N	N	N	Y	N

ND Northern Democrats SD Southern Democrats

	188	189	190	191	192	193
4 Long	Y	Y	Y	Y	Y	Y
5 Jontz	Y	Y	Y	Y	N	Y
6 ***Burton***	N	N	N	N	Y	N
7 ***Myers***	N	Y	N	N	Y	N
8 McCloskey	Y	Y	Y	Y	N	N
9 Hamilton	N	Y	Y	Y	N	Y
10 Jacobs	Y	N	N	N	Y	Y
IOWA						
1 ***Leach***	N	N	N	N	N	Y
2 ***Tauke***	Y	N	N	N	Y	Y
3 Nagle	Y	Y	Y	Y	N	N
4 Smith	N	Y	Y	Y	N	N
5 ***Lightfoot***	N	N	N	N	Y	N
6 ***Grandy***	N	N	N	N	N	N
KANSAS						
1 ***Roberts***	N	N	N	N	Y	N
2 Slattery	N	Y	Y	Y	N	Y
3 ***Meyers***	N	N	N	N	Y	Y
4 Glickman	Y	Y	Y	Y	N	Y
5 ***Whittaker***	N	N	N	N	Y	N
KENTUCKY						
1 Hubbard	N	Y	Y	Y	Y	N
2 Natcher	Y	Y	Y	Y	Y	Y
3 Mazzoli	N	Y	Y	Y	Y	Y
4 ***Bunning***	N	N	N	N	Y	N
5 ***Rogers***	N	N	N	N	Y	N
6 ***Hopkins***	N	N	N	N	Y	N
7 Perkins	Y	Y	Y	Y	Y	Y
LOUISIANA						
1 ***Livingston***	N	?	N	N	Y	N
2 Boggs	N	Y	Y	Y	N	N
3 Tauzin	N	Y	Y	Y	Y	N
4 ***McCrery***	N	Y	N	N	Y	N
5 Huckaby	?	Y	N	N	Y	N
6 ***Baker***	N	N	N	N	Y	N
7 Hayes	N	Y	Y	Y	Y	N
8 ***Holloway***	N	N	N	N	Y	N
MAINE						
1 Brennan	Y	Y	Y	Y	N	Y
2 ***Snowe***	N	Y	N	N	Y	N
MARYLAND						
1 Dyson	N	Y	Y	Y	Y	N
2 ***Bentley***	N	N	N	N	Y	N
3 Cardin	N	Y	Y	Y	N	Y
4 McMillen	N	Y	Y	Y	Y	Y
5 Hoyer	N	Y	Y	Y	N	Y
6 Byron	Y	Y	Y	Y	Y	N
7 Mfume	Y	?	Y	Y	N	N
8 ***Morella***	Y	?	N	N	N	Y
MASSACHUSETTS						
1 ***Conte***	N	Y	N	N	N	N
2 Neal	N	Y	Y	Y	Y	Y
3 Early	Y	Y	Y	Y	N	Y
4 Frank	Y	Y	Y	Y	N	N
5 Atkins	Y	Y	Y	Y	N	Y
6 Mavroules	N	Y	Y	Y	N	Y
7 Markey	Y	Y	Y	Y	N	N
8 Kennedy	Y	Y	Y	Y	N	Y
9 Moakley	N	Y	Y	Y	Y	Y
10 Studds	Y	Y	Y	Y	N	Y
11 Donnelly	N	Y	Y	Y	Y	Y
MICHIGAN						
1 Conyers	Y	?	Y	Y	N	N
2 ***Pursell***	N	N	N	N	Y	N
3 Wolpe	Y	Y	Y	Y	N	Y
4 ***Upton***	N	N	N	N	Y	N
5 ***Henry***	N	N	N	N	N	Y
6 Carr	Y	Y	Y	Y	N	Y
7 Kildee	Y	Y	Y	Y	N	Y
8 Traxler	N	Y	Y	Y	Y	Y
9 ***Vander Jagt***	N	Y	N	N	Y	N
10 ***Schuette***	N	N	N	N	Y	N
11 ***Davis***	N	Y	N	N	Y	N
12 Bonior	Y	Y	Y	Y	N	Y
13 Crockett	Y	Y	?	?	N	N
14 Hertel	Y	Y	Y	Y	N	Y
15 Ford	?	Y	?	Y	N	Y
16 Dingell	N	?	Y	Y	N	Y
17 Levin	N	Y	Y	Y	N	Y
18 ***Broomfield***	N	Y	N	N	Y	N
MINNESOTA						
1 Penny	Y	Y	Y	Y	N	Y
2 ***Weber***	N	N	N	N	Y	N
3 ***Frenzel***	Y	?	N	N	Y	N
4 Vento	Y	Y	Y	Y	N	N

	188	189	190	191	192	193
5 Sabo	Y	Y	Y	Y	N	N
6 Sikorski	Y	N	Y	Y	N	Y
7 ***Stangeland***	N	N	N	N	Y	N
8 Oberstar	Y	Y	Y	Y	N	Y
MISSISSIPPI						
1 Whitten	N	Y	Y	Y	Y	Y
2 Espy	N	Y	Y	Y	N	Y
3 Montgomery	N	Y	N	N	Y	N
4 Parker	N	Y	N	N	Y	N
5 Taylor	N	Y	N	N	Y	Y
MISSOURI						
1 Clay	Y	N	Y	Y	N	N
2 ***Buechner***	N	N	N	N	Y	N
3 Gephardt	N	Y	Y	Y	N	Y
4 Skelton	N	Y	Y	Y	Y	N
5 Wheat	N	Y	Y	Y	N	N
6 ***Coleman***	N	N	N	N	N	N
7 ***Hancock***	N	N	N	N	Y	N
8 ***Emerson***	N	Y	N	N	Y	N
9 Volkmer	N	Y	Y	Y	Y	N
MONTANA						
1 Williams	Y	Y	Y	Y	N	N
2 ***Marlenee***	N	N	N	N	Y	?
NEBRASKA						
1 ***Bereuter***	N	N	N	N	Y	N
2 Hoagland	N	Y	Y	Y	N	Y
3 ***Smith***	N	Y	N	N	Y	N
NEVADA						
1 Bilbray	N	Y	Y	Y	Y	Y
2 ***Vucanovich***	N	N	N	N	Y	N
NEW HAMPSHIRE						
1 ***Smith***	N	N	N	N	Y	N
2 ***Douglas***	N	N	N	N	Y	N
NEW JERSEY						
1 Vacancy						
2 Hughes	Y	Y	Y	N	N	N
3 Pallone	N	Y	Y	Y	Y	Y
4 ***Smith***	N	Y	N	N	Y	N
5 ***Roukema***	N	N	N	N	Y	Y
6 Dwyer	N	Y	Y	Y	N	Y
7 ***Rinaldo***	N	Y	N	N	Y	N
8 Roe	N	Y	Y	Y	Y	N
9 Torricelli	N	Y	Y	Y	N	Y
10 Payne	?	Y	Y	Y	N	N
11 ***Gallo***	N	N	N	N	Y	N
12 ***Courter***	N	N	N	N	Y	N
13 ***Saxton***	N	N	N	N	Y	N
14 Guarini	N	Y	Y	Y	Y	N
NEW MEXICO						
1 ***Schiff***	N	Y	N	N	Y	N
2 ***Skeen***	N	Y	N	N	Y	N
3 Richardson	N	Y	Y	Y	Y	?
NEW YORK						
1 Hochbrueckner	Y	Y	Y	Y	Y	Y
2 Downey	Y	?	Y	Y	N	N
3 Mrazek	Y	Y	Y	Y	N	N
4 ***Lent***	N	Y	N	N	Y	N
5 ***McGrath***	N	N	N	N	Y	N
6 Flake	Y	?	?	?	N	N
7 Ackerman	N	Y	Y	Y	N	?
8 Scheuer	Y	Y	Y	Y	N	N
9 Manton	N	Y	Y	Y	Y	Y
10 Schumer	?	?	?	?	N	Y
11 Towns	Y	Y	Y	Y	N	Y
12 Owens	Y	Y	Y	Y	N	N
13 Solarz	N	Y	Y	Y	N	Y
14 ***Molinari***	N	N	N	N	Y	N
15 ***Green***	N	Y	N	N	N	N
16 Rangel	?	?	?	?	?	?
17 Weiss	Y	Y	Y	Y	N	N
18 Serrano	—	?	?	?	N	Y
19 Engel	N	Y	Y	Y	N	Y
20 Lowey	N	Y	Y	Y	N	Y
21 ***Fish***	N	Y	N	N	Y	?
22 ***Gilman***	N	Y	N	N	Y	Y
23 McNulty	N	Y	Y	Y	Y	Y
24 ***Solomon***	N	N	N	N	Y	N
25 ***Boehlert***	N	N	N	N	Y	N
26 ***Martin***	N	N	N	N	Y	N
27 ***Walsh***	N	?	N	N	Y	N
28 McHugh	Y	Y	Y	Y	N	N
29 ***Horton***	N	Y	N	N	Y	N
30 Slaughter	Y	Y	Y	Y	N	Y
31 ***Paxon***	N	N	N	N	Y	N

	188	189	190	191	192	193
32 LaFalce	N	Y	Y	Y	N	Y
33 Nowak	N	Y	Y	Y	N	Y
34 ***Houghton***	N	Y	N	N	N	Y
NORTH CAROLINA						
1 Jones	Y	Y	Y	Y	Y	Y
2 Valentine	N	Y	Y	Y	N	Y
3 Lancaster	N	Y	Y	Y	Y	Y
4 Price	N	Y	Y	Y	N	Y
5 Neal	Y	?	Y	Y	N	Y
6 ***Coble***	N	N	N	N	Y	N
7 Rose	N	Y	Y	Y	N	Y
8 Hefner	N	?	Y	Y	Y	Y
9 ***McMillan***	?	Y	N	N	Y	N
10 ***Ballenger***	N	N	N	N	Y	N
11 Clarke	N	Y	Y	Y	Y	Y
NORTH DAKOTA						
AL Dorgan	Y	Y	Y	Y	N	Y
OHIO						
1 Luken	N	Y	Y	Y	Y	Y
2 ***Gradison***	N	Y	N	N	Y	N
3 Hall	?	?	Y	Y	N	Y
4 ***Oxley***	N	N	N	N	Y	N
5 ***Gillmor***	N	Y	N	N	Y	Y
6 ***McEwen***	N	Y	N	?	Y	N
7 ***DeWine***	N	N	N	N	Y	N
8 ***Lukens***	N	Y	N	N	Y	N
9 Kaptur	N	Y	Y	Y	N	Y
10 ***Miller***	Y	N	N	N	Y	N
11 Eckart	?	?	?	?	Y	Y
12 ***Kasich***	Y	Y	N	N	Y	N
13 Pease	Y	Y	Y	Y	N	N
14 Sawyer	Y	Y	Y	Y	N	N
15 ***Wylie***	N	Y	N	N	Y	N
16 ***Regula***	Y	N	N	N	Y	N
17 Traficant	N	Y	Y	Y	Y	Y
18 Applegate	N	Y	N	N	Y	Y
19 Feighan	N	Y	Y	Y	N	N
20 Oakar	N	Y	Y	Y	N	Y
21 Stokes	Y	Y	Y	Y	N	N
OKLAHOMA						
1 ***Inhofe***	N	N	N	N	Y	N
2 Synar	Y	Y	Y	Y	N	Y
3 Watkins	N	Y	N	N	Y	Y
4 McCurdy	N	Y	Y	Y	N	Y
5 ***Edwards***	N	?	N	N	Y	N
6 English	N	Y	N	N	Y	N
OREGON						
1 AuCoin	Y	?	Y	Y	N	N
2 ***Smith, B.***	N	N	N	N	Y	N
3 Wyden	Y	Y	Y	Y	N	Y
4 DeFazio	Y	Y	Y	Y	N	N
5 ***Smith, D.***	N	N	N	N	Y	?
PENNSYLVANIA						
1 Foglietta	N	N	Y	Y	N	Y
2 Gray	Y	Y	Y	Y	N	Y
3 Borski	N	?	Y	Y	N	Y
4 Kolter	N	Y	Y	Y	Y	Y
5 ***Schulze***	N	Y	N	N	Y	N
6 Yatron	N	Y	Y	Y	Y	Y
7 ***Weldon***	N	Y	N	N	Y	N
8 Kostmayer	N	Y	Y	Y	N	N
9 ***Shuster***	Y	Y	N	N	Y	N
10 ***McDade***	N	Y	N	N	Y	N
11 Kanjorski	Y	Y	Y	Y	Y	Y
12 Murtha	N	Y	Y	Y	Y	N
13 ***Coughlin***	N	N	N	N	Y	N
14 Coyne	N	Y	Y	Y	N	Y
15 ***Ritter***	N	?	N	N	Y	N
16 ***Walker***	N	N	N	N	Y	N
17 ***Gekas***	N	N	N	N	Y	N
18 Walgren	N	?	Y	Y	N	Y
19 ***Goodling***	N	N	N	N	Y	N
20 Gaydos	Y	?	Y	Y	Y	Y
21 ***Ridge***	N	N	N	N	Y	N
22 Murphy	Y	N	Y	Y	Y	Y
23 ***Clinger***	N	Y	N	N	N	Y
RHODE ISLAND						
1 ***Machtley***	N	N	N	N	Y	N
2 ***Schneider***	N	Y	N	N	N	Y
SOUTH CAROLINA						
1 ***Ravenel***	N	Y	N	N	Y	N
2 ***Spence***	N	Y	N	N	Y	N
3 Derrick	N	Y	Y	Y	Y	Y
4 Patterson	N	Y	Y	Y	Y	Y
5 Spratt	N	Y	Y	N	N	Y
6 Tallon	N	Y	Y	Y	N	Y

	188	189	190	191	192	193
SOUTH DAKOTA						
AL Johnson	N	Y	Y	Y	Y	Y
TENNESSEE						
1 ***Quillen***	Y	Y	N	N	Y	N
2 ***Duncan***	N	N	N	N	Y	N
3 Lloyd	N	Y	Y	Y	Y	Y
4 Cooper	N	Y	Y	Y	N	Y
5 Clement	Y	Y	Y	Y	Y	?
6 Gordon	N	Y	Y	Y	N	Y
7 ***Sundquist***	N	N	N	N	Y	N
8 Tanner	N	Y	Y	Y	N	Y
9 Ford	Y	Y	Y	Y	N	Y
TEXAS						
1 Chapman	N	Y	Y	Y	Y	Y
2 Wilson	N	Y	N	N	Y	N
3 ***Bartlett***	N	Y	N	N	Y	N
4 Hall	?	?	?	?	?	?
5 Bryant	N	Y	Y	Y	N	Y
6 ***Barton***	N	N	N	N	Y	N
7 ***Archer***	N	Y	N	N	Y	N
8 ***Fields***	N	N	N	N	Y	N
9 Brooks	N	Y	Y	Y	Y	Y
10 Pickle	N	Y	Y	Y	N	Y
11 Leath	N	?	Y	Y	Y	N
12 Geren	N	Y	Y	Y	Y	Y
13 Sarpalius	N	Y	Y	Y	Y	N
14 Laughlin	N	Y	N	Y	Y	Y
15 de la Garza	N	Y	Y	Y	Y	Y
16 Coleman	N	Y	Y	Y	N	Y
17 Stenholm	N	Y	Y	Y	N	N
18 Washington	N	?	Y	Y	N	N
19 ***Combest***	N	Y	N	N	Y	N
20 Gonzalez	Y	Y	Y	Y	N	N
21 ***Smith***	N	N	N	N	Y	N
22 ***DeLay***	N	N	N	N	Y	N
23 Bustamante	Y	Y	Y	Y	Y	Y
24 Frost	N	Y	Y	Y	N	Y
25 Andrews	N	Y	Y	Y	Y	Y
26 ***Armey***	N	N	N	N	Y	N
27 Ortiz	N	Y	Y	Y	Y	Y
UTAH						
1 ***Hansen***	N	N	N	N	Y	N
2 Owens	N	Y	Y	Y	N	N
3 ***Nielson***	N	N	N	N	Y	N
VERMONT						
AL ***Smith***	N	Y	N	N	N	N
VIRGINIA						
1 ***Bateman***	N	Y	N	N	Y	N
2 Pickett	N	Y	N	N	Y	N
3 ***Bliley***	N	N	N	N	Y	N
4 Sisisky	N	Y	Y	Y	Y	N
5 Payne	N	Y	Y	Y	Y	N
6 Olin	Y	Y	Y	Y	Y	N
7 ***Slaughter***	N	N	N	N	Y	N
8 ***Parris***	N	N	N	N	Y	N
9 Boucher	N	Y	Y	Y	N	Y
10 ***Wolf***	N	N	N	N	Y	N
WASHINGTON						
1 ***Miller***	N	N	N	N	Y	N
2 Swift	Y	Y	Y	Y	N	N
3 Unsoeld	Y	Y	Y	Y	N	N
4 ***Morrison***	N	Y	N	N	Y	N
5 Foley					N	
6 Dicks	N	Y	Y	Y	N	Y
7 McDermott	Y	Y	Y	Y	N	—
8 ***Chandler***	N	N	N	N	N	N
WEST VIRGINIA						
1 Mollohan	Y	Y	Y	Y	Y	Y
2 Staggers	Y	Y	Y	Y	Y	N
3 Wise	N	Y	Y	Y	Y	Y
4 Rahall	Y	Y	N	N	Y	N
WISCONSIN						
1 Aspin	N	Y	Y	Y	N	?
2 Kastenmeier	Y	Y	Y	Y	N	N
3 ***Gunderson***	N	Y	N	N	Y	N
4 Kleczka	?	Y	Y	Y	N	Y
5 Moody	N	Y	Y	Y	N	Y
6 ***Petri***	N	Y	N	N	Y	Y
7 Obey	Y	Y	Y	N	N	Y
8 ***Roth***	N	Y	N	N	Y	N
9 ***Sensenbrenner***	N	N	N	N	Y	N
WYOMING						
AL ***Thomas***	N	N	N	N	Y	N

Southern states - Ala., Ark., Fla., Ga., Ky., La., Miss., N.C., Okla., S.C., Tenn., Texas, Va.
Omitted votes are quorum calls, which CQ does not include in its vote charts.

HOUSE VOTES 195, 196, 197, 198, 199, 200, 201, 202

195. HR 5021. Fiscal 1991 Commerce, Justice, State and the Judiciary Appropriations/Across-the-Board Cuts. Dannemeyer, R-Calif., amendment to provide a 5 percent across-the-board cut in all discretionary accounts in the bill. Rejected 88-323: R 75-94; D 13-229 (ND 5-161, SD 8-68), June 26, 1990.

196. HR 5021. Fiscal 1991 Commerce, Justice, State and the Judiciary Appropriations/Passage. Passage of the bill to appropriate $10.5 billion for the Departments of Commerce, Justice and State, the federal judiciary and related agencies in fiscal 1991 for programs that are currently authorized. The bill does not appropriate any funds for unauthorized programs, deferring $8.9 billion within its Section 302 (b) budget allocation to cover programs not yet authorized. Passed 358-55: R 121-49; D 237-6 (ND 163-4, SD 74-2), June 26, 1990.

197. S 280. Niobrara River Scenic River Designation Act/Substitute. Smith, R-Neb., substitute amendment to provide for further study of the Niobrara River in Nebraska to determine whether any segments of the river should be designated under the Wild and Scenic Rivers Act. Rejected 115-302: R 98-73; D 17-229 (ND 10-157, SD 7-72), June 26, 1990.

198. S 280. Niobrara River Scenic River Designation Act/Condemnation. Young, R-Alaska, amendment to prohibit the Interior Department from acquiring any land, scenic easements or other interests in land within the designated river corridors through condemnation. Rejected 93-323: R 83-89; D 10-234 (ND 7-159, SD 3-75), June 26, 1990.

199. S 280. Niobrara River Scenic River Designation Act/Passage. Passage of the bill to designate segments of the Niobrara River in Nebraska as a scenic river under the National Wild and Scenic Rivers Act and designate segments of the Niobrara and Missouri rivers as recreational rivers. The bill would also require studies and establish an advisory commission. Passed 358-59: R 114-58; D 244-1 (ND 166-0, SD 78-1), June 26, 1990.

200. HR 5114. Fiscal 1991 Foreign Operations Appropriations/Rule. Adoption of the rule (H Res 425) to provide for House floor consideration of the bill to appropriate $15.8 billion for foreign military and economic assistance and export financing in fiscal 1991. Adopted 262-157: R 19-150; D 243-7 (ND 165-6, SD 78-1), June 27, 1990.

201. HR 5114. Fiscal 1991 Foreign Operations Appropriations/Romania. Smith, R-N.J., amendment to the Lehman, D-Fla., amendment to allow the Agency for International Development (AID) to provide funds to organizations AID has identified as putting together a new international family planning program to deliver family planning assistance to Romania. The Lehman amendment would have designated the International Planned Parenthood Federation and the United Nations Fund for Population Activities as the agencies to deliver family planning assistance to Romania. Adopted 224-198: R 138-36; D 86-162 (ND 51-118, SD 35-44), June 27, 1990.

202. HR 5114. Fiscal 1991 Foreign Operations Appropriations/Romania. Lehman, D-Fla., amendment to earmark $1.5 million for voluntary family planning in Romania and $1.5 million for other health and child survival projects. The family planning funds would be used for contraceptives, birth control counseling and education, but no funds could be used for abortions. Adopted 406-11: R 166-7; D 240-4 (ND 164-2, SD 76-2), June 27, 1990.

KEY

- Y Voted for (yea).
- # Paired for.
- + Announced for.
- N Voted against (nay).
- X Paired against.
- \- Announced against.
- P Voted "present."
- C Voted "present" to avoid possible conflict of interest.
- ? Did not vote or otherwise make a position known.

Democrats *Republicans*

	195	196	197	198	199	200	201	202
ALABAMA								
1 *Callahan*	Y	N	Y	Y	Y	N	Y	Y
2 *Dickinson*	N	Y	Y	Y	Y	N	N	?
3 Browder	N	Y	N	N	Y	Y	Y	Y
4 Bevill	?	?	Y	N	Y	Y	Y	Y
5 Flippo	?	?	N	N	Y	Y	Y	Y
6 Erdreich	Y	Y	N	N	Y	Y	N	Y
7 Harris	N	Y	N	N	Y	Y	Y	Y
ALASKA								
AL *Young*	N	Y	Y	Y	N	Y	Y	Y
ARIZONA								
1 *Rhodes*	N	Y	Y	Y	N	N	Y	Y
2 Udall	?	Y	N	N	Y	Y	N	Y
3 *Stump*	Y	N	Y	Y	N	N	Y	N
4 *Kyl*	N	Y	Y	Y	N	N	Y	Y
5 *Kolbe*	N	Y	Y	Y	Y	N	N	Y
ARKANSAS								
1 Alexander	N	Y	N	N	Y	Y	N	Y
2 *Robinson*	Y	Y	Y	Y	Y	N	Y	Y
3 *Hammerschmidt*	Y	Y	Y	Y	N	N	Y	Y
4 Anthony	N	Y	N	N	Y	Y	N	Y
CALIFORNIA								
1 Bosco	N	Y	N	N	Y	Y	N	Y
2 *Herger*	Y	N	Y	Y	N	N	Y	Y
3 Matsui	N	Y	N	N	Y	Y	N	Y
4 Fazio	N	Y	N	N	Y	Y	N	Y
5 Pelosi	N	Y	N	N	Y	Y	N	Y
6 Boxer	N	Y	N	N	Y	Y	N	Y
7 Miller	N	Y	N	N	Y	Y	N	?
8 Dellums	N	Y	N	N	Y	Y	N	Y
9 Stark	N	Y	N	N	Y	Y	N	Y
10 Edwards	N	Y	N	N	Y	Y	N	Y
11 Lantos	N	Y	N	N	Y	Y	N	Y
12 *Campbell*	Y	N	N	N	Y	N	N	Y
13 Mineta	N	Y	N	N	Y	Y	N	Y
14 *Shumway*	Y	N	Y	Y	N	N	Y	Y
15 Condit	N	Y	Y	N	Y	Y	N	Y
16 Panetta	N	Y	N	N	Y	Y	?	Y
17 *Pashayan*	Y	N	Y	Y	N	N	Y	Y
18 Lehman	N	Y	N	N	Y	Y	N	Y
19 *Lagomarsino*	Y	Y	Y	Y	N	N	Y	Y
20 *Thomas*	#	X	N	N	Y	N	Y	Y
21 *Gallegly*	Y	Y	Y	Y	N	N	Y	Y
22 *Moorhead*	Y	N	N	N	Y	N	Y	Y
23 Beilenson	N	Y	N	N	Y	Y	N	Y
24 Waxman	N	Y	N	N	Y	Y	N	Y
25 Roybal	N	Y	N	N	Y	Y	N	Y
26 Berman	N	Y	N	N	Y	Y	N	?
27 Levine	N	Y	N	N	Y	Y	N	Y
28 Dixon	N	Y	Y	N	Y	Y	N	Y
29 Hawkins	N	Y	N	N	Y	Y	N	Y
30 Martinez	N	Y	N	Y	Y	Y	N	Y
31 Dymally	N	Y	N	N	Y	Y	N	Y
32 Anderson	N	Y	Y	N	Y	Y	N	Y
33 *Dreier*	Y	Y	N	N	Y	N	Y	Y
34 Torres	N	Y	N	N	Y	Y	N	Y
35 *Lewis*	N	Y	Y	Y	N	N	N	Y
36 Brown	N	Y	Y	N	Y	Y	N	Y
37 *McCandless*	Y	N	N	Y	N	N	Y	Y
38 *Dornan*	Y	Y	Y	Y	Y	N	Y	Y
39 *Dannemeyer*	Y	N	Y	Y	N	N	Y	Y
40 *Cox*	Y	N	N	N	Y	N	Y	Y
41 *Lowery*	N	Y	N	Y	Y	Y	Y	Y
42 *Rohrabacher*	Y	N	Y	Y	N	N	Y	Y
43 *Packard*	Y	N	Y	Y	N	N	Y	Y
44 Bates	N	Y	N	N	Y	Y	N	Y
45 *Hunter*	Y	Y	Y	Y	N	N	Y	Y
COLORADO								
1 Schroeder	N	Y	N	N	Y	Y	N	Y
2 Skaggs	N	Y	N	N	Y	Y	N	Y
3 Campbell	N	Y	Y	Y	Y	Y	N	Y
4 *Brown*	N	Y	Y	Y	Y	Y	N	Y
5 *Hefley*	Y	Y	N	Y	Y	N	Y	Y
6 *Schaefer*	Y	Y	Y	Y	Y	N	Y	Y
CONNECTICUT								
1 Kennelly	N	Y	N	N	Y	Y	N	Y
2 Gejdenson	N	Y	N	N	Y	Y	N	Y
3 Morrison	-	+	-	-	+	+	–	+
4 *Shays*	Y	N	N	N	Y	N	N	Y
5 *Rowland*	N	Y	N	N	Y	Y	N	Y
6 *Johnson*	Y	N	Y	Y	Y	Y	N	Y
DELAWARE								
AL Carper	N	Y	N	N	Y	Y	N	Y
FLORIDA								
1 Hutto	N	Y	N	N	Y	Y	Y	Y
2 *Grant*	N	Y	N	Y	Y	N	Y	Y
3 Bennett	Y	Y	N	N	Y	Y	Y	Y
4 *James*	N	Y	N	N	Y	N	Y	Y
5 *McCollum*	N	Y	N	Y	Y	N	Y	Y
6 *Stearns*	N	Y	N	Y	Y	N	Y	Y
7 Gibbons	N	Y	N	N	Y	Y	Y	Y
8 *Young*	?	Y	N	Y	Y	N	Y	Y
9 *Bilirakis*	Y	Y	N	N	Y	N	Y	Y
10 *Ireland*	Y	Y	N	N	Y	N	Y	Y
11 Nelson	-	+	-	-	+	+	-	+
12 *Lewis*	Y	Y	Y	N	Y	N	Y	Y
13 *Goss*	Y	N	N	N	Y	N	Y	Y
14 Johnston	N	Y	N	N	Y	Y	N	Y
15 *Shaw*	N	Y	N	Y	Y	N	Y	Y
16 Smith	N	Y	N	N	Y	Y	N	Y
17 Lehman	N	Y	N	N	Y	Y	N	Y
18 *Ros-Lehtinen*	N	Y	N	N	Y	N	Y	Y
19 Fascell	N	Y	N	N	Y	Y	N	Y
GEORGIA								
1 Thomas	N	Y	N	N	Y	Y	N	Y
2 Hatcher	N	Y	N	N	Y	Y	N	Y
3 Ray	?	?	N	N	Y	Y	Y	Y
4 Jones	N	Y	N	N	Y	Y	N	Y
5 Lewis	N	Y	N	N	Y	Y	N	Y
6 *Gingrich*	Y	N	Y	N	Y	Y	Y	Y
7 Darden	N	Y	N	N	Y	Y	N	Y
8 Rowland	N	Y	N	N	Y	Y	N	Y
9 Jenkins	N	Y	N	N	Y	Y	Y	Y
10 Barnard	N	#	N	N	Y	Y	Y	Y
HAWAII								
1 *Saiki*	N	Y	N	N	Y	N	N	Y
2 Vacancy								
IDAHO								
1 *Craig*	N	Y	Y	Y	Y	Y	Y	Y
2 Stallings	N	Y	N	Y	Y	Y	Y	Y
ILLINOIS								
1 Hayes	N	Y	N	N	Y	Y	N	Y
2 Savage	N	Y	N	N	Y	N	Y	N
3 Russo	N	Y	N	N	Y	Y	Y	Y
4 Sangmeister	N	Y	N	N	Y	Y	Y	Y
5 Lipinski	N	Y	N	N	Y	Y	Y	Y
6 *Hyde*	N	Y	Y	N	Y	?	Y	Y
7 Collins	N	Y	N	N	Y	Y	N	Y
8 Rostenkowski	N	Y	N	N	Y	Y	Y	Y
9 Yates	N	Y	N	N	Y	Y	N	Y
10 *Porter*	N	Y	N	N	Y	Y	N	Y
11 Annunzio	N	Y	Y	N	Y	Y	Y	Y
12 *Crane*	Y	N	Y	Y	N	N	Y	N
13 *Fawell*	Y	N	Y	N	Y	N	N	Y
14 *Hastert*	N	Y	Y	Y	Y	N	Y	Y
15 *Madigan*	Y	Y	Y	Y	N	N	Y	Y
16 *Martin*	N	Y	N	N	Y	N	N	Y
17 Evans	N	Y	N	N	Y	Y	N	Y
18 *Michel*	Y	N	Y	Y	N	N	Y	Y
19 Bruce	N	Y	N	N	Y	Y	Y	Y
20 Durbin	N	Y	N	N	Y	Y	N	Y
21 Costello	N	Y	N	N	Y	Y	Y	Y
22 Poshard	N	Y	N	N	Y	Y	Y	Y
INDIANA								
1 Visclosky	N	Y	N	N	Y	Y	N	Y
2 Sharp	Y	Y	N	N	Y	N	N	Y
3 *Hiler*	Y	Y	N	N	Y	N	Y	Y

ND Northern Democrats SD Southern Democrats

	195	196	197	198	199	200	201	202
4 Long	N	Y	N	N	Y	Y	N	Y
5 Jontz	N	Y	N	N	Y	Y	N	Y
6 ***Burton***	Y	N	Y	Y	N	N	Y	Y
7 ***Myers***	N	Y	Y	Y	N	N	Y	Y
8 McCloskey	N	Y	N	N	Y	Y	Y	Y
9 Hamilton	Y	Y	N	N	Y	Y	N	Y
10 Jacobs	Y	N	N	N	Y	N	N	Y
IOWA								
1 ***Leach***	N	Y	N	N	Y	N	N	Y
2 ***Tauke***	N	Y	Y	N	Y	N	Y	Y
3 Nagle	?	Y	N	N	Y	Y	N	Y
4 Smith	N	Y	N	N	Y	Y	N	Y
5 ***Lightfoot***	N	Y	Y	Y	N	N	Y	Y
6 ***Grandy***	N	Y	Y	N	N	N	Y	Y
KANSAS								
1 ***Roberts***	Y	N	Y	Y	N	N	Y	Y
2 Slattery	N	Y	N	N	Y	Y	Y	Y
3 ***Meyers***	N	Y	Y	N	Y	N	N	Y
4 Glickman	N	Y	N	N	Y	Y	N	Y
5 ***Whittaker***	?	?	?	?	?	?	Y	Y
KENTUCKY								
1 Hubbard	N	Y	N	N	Y	Y	Y	Y
2 Natcher	N	Y	N	N	Y	Y	Y	Y
3 Mazzoli	N	Y	N	N	Y	Y	Y	Y
4 ***Bunning***	Y	N	Y	Y	N	N	Y	Y
5 ***Rogers***	N	Y	Y	Y	N	N	Y	Y
6 ***Hopkins***	Y	Y	Y	Y	N	N	Y	Y
7 Perkins	N	Y	N	N	Y	Y	Y	Y
LOUISIANA								
1 ***Livingston***	N	Y	Y	Y	N	N	Y	Y
2 Boggs	N	Y	N	N	Y	Y	Y	Y
3 Tauzin	Y	Y	N	Y	Y	N	Y	N
4 ***McCrery***	N	Y	Y	Y	Y	?	Y	Y
5 Huckaby	Y	Y	N	N	Y	Y	Y	Y
6 ***Baker***	Y	Y	Y	Y	N	N	Y	Y
7 Hayes	N	Y	N	N	Y	?	?	?
8 ***Holloway***	?	Y	Y	Y	N	?	Y	Y
MAINE								
1 Brennan	N	Y	N	N	Y	Y	N	Y
2 ***Snowe***	N	Y	Y	N	Y	Y	N	Y
MARYLAND								
1 Dyson	N	Y	N	N	Y	Y	Y	Y
2 ***Bentley***	Y	N	Y	Y	N	N	Y	Y
3 Cardin	N	Y	N	N	Y	Y	N	Y
4 McMillen	N	Y	N	N	Y	Y	N	Y
5 Hoyer	N	Y	N	N	Y	Y	N	Y
6 Byron	N	Y	N	N	Y	Y	Y	Y
7 Mfume	N	Y	N	N	Y	Y	N	Y
8 ***Morella***	N	Y	N	N	Y	Y	N	Y
MASSACHUSETTS								
1 ***Conte***	N	Y	N	N	Y	Y	N	Y
2 Neal	N	Y	N	N	Y	Y	Y	Y
3 Early	N	Y	N	Y	Y	Y	Y	Y
4 Frank	N	Y	N	?	?	Y	N	Y
5 Atkins	N	Y	N	N	Y	Y	N	Y
6 Mavroules	N	Y	N	N	Y	Y	Y	Y
7 Markey	N	Y	N	N	Y	Y	N	Y
8 Kennedy	N	Y	N	N	Y	Y	N	Y
9 Moakley	N	Y	N	N	Y	Y	Y	Y
10 Studds	N	Y	N	N	Y	Y	N	Y
11 Donnelly	N	Y	N	N	Y	Y	Y	Y
MICHIGAN								
1 Conyers	Y	N	N	N	Y	Y	N	Y
2 ***Pursell***	N	N	N	N	Y	N	N	Y
3 Wolpe	N	Y	N	N	Y	Y	N	Y
4 ***Upton***	Y	Y	Y	N	Y	N	N	Y
5 ***Henry***	Y	N	N	N	Y	N	Y	Y
6 Carr	N	Y	N	N	Y	Y	N	Y
7 Kildee	N	Y	N	N	Y	Y	Y	Y
8 Traxler	N	Y	N	N	Y	Y	Y	Y
9 ***Vander Jagt***	Y	Y	Y	N	Y	N	Y	Y
10 ***Schuette***	N	Y	N	N	Y	?	Y	Y
11 ***Davis***	N	Y	Y	Y	N	N	Y	Y
12 Bonior	N	Y	N	N	Y	Y	Y	Y
13 Crockett	N	Y	?	?	?	?	?	?
14 Hertel	N	Y	N	N	Y	Y	Y	Y
15 Ford	N	?	N	N	Y	Y	N	?
16 Dingell	N	Y	N	N	Y	Y	N	Y
17 Levin	N	Y	N	N	Y	Y	N	Y
18 ***Broomfield***	N	Y	Y	N	Y	N	Y	Y
MINNESOTA								
1 Penny	N	Y	N	Y	Y	Y	Y	Y
2 ***Weber***	N	Y	Y	N	Y	N	Y	Y
3 ***Frenzel***	Y	N	N	N	Y	N	X	Y
4 Vento	N	Y	N	N	Y	Y	N	Y
5 Sabo	N	Y	N	N	Y	Y	N	Y
6 Sikorski	N	Y	N	N	Y	N	N	Y
7 ***Stangeland***	N	Y	Y	Y	N	N	Y	Y
8 Oberstar	N	Y	N	N	Y	Y	Y	Y
MISSISSIPPI								
1 Whitten	N	Y	Y	N	Y	Y	Y	Y
2 Espy	N	Y	?	?	Y	Y	N	Y
3 Montgomery	N	Y	N	N	Y	Y	Y	Y
4 Parker	Y	Y	N	N	Y	Y	Y	Y
5 Taylor	N	Y	N	N	Y	Y	Y	N
MISSOURI								
1 Clay	N	Y	N	N	Y	Y	N	Y
2 ***Buechner***	N	Y	N	N	Y	N	Y	Y
3 Gephardt	N	Y	N	N	Y	Y	N	Y
4 Skelton	N	Y	N	N	Y	Y	Y	Y
5 Wheat	N	Y	N	N	Y	Y	N	Y
6 ***Coleman***	N	Y	Y	N	Y	N	Y	Y
7 ***Hancock***	Y	N	Y	Y	N	N	Y	N
8 ***Emerson***	N	Y	Y	Y	N	N	Y	Y
9 Volkmer	N	Y	N	N	Y	Y	Y	Y
MONTANA								
1 Williams	N	Y	N	N	Y	Y	N	Y
2 ***Marlenee***	?	?	#	#	X	N	Y	N
NEBRASKA								
1 ***Bereuter***	N	Y	N	N	Y	N	Y	Y
2 Hoagland	N	Y	N	N	Y	Y	N	Y
3 ***Smith***	N	Y	Y	Y	N	N	Y	Y
NEVADA								
1 Bilbray	N	Y	N	N	Y	Y	Y	Y
2 ***Vucanovich***	Y	Y	Y	Y	N	N	Y	Y
NEW HAMPSHIRE								
1 ***Smith***	Y	N	N	N	Y	N	Y	Y
2 ***Douglas***	Y	N	N	N	Y	N	Y	Y
NEW JERSEY								
1 Vacancy								
2 Hughes	N	Y	N	N	Y	Y	N	Y
3 Pallone	N	Y	N	N	Y	Y	N	Y
4 ***Smith***	N	Y	N	N	Y	Y	Y	Y
5 ***Roukema***	N	Y	Y	N	Y	N	N	N
6 Dwyer	N	Y	N	N	Y	Y	N	Y
7 ***Rinaldo***	N	Y	N	N	Y	N	Y	Y
8 Roe	N	Y	N	N	Y	Y	Y	Y
9 Torricelli	N	Y	N	N	Y	Y	N	Y
10 Payne	N	Y	N	N	Y	Y	N	Y
11 ***Gallo***	N	Y	Y	N	Y	N	N	Y
12 ***Courter***	N	Y	N	N	Y	N	N	Y
13 ***Saxton***	N	Y	N	N	Y	Y	Y	Y
14 Guarini	N	Y	N	N	Y	Y	N	Y
NEW MEXICO								
1 ***Schiff***	N	Y	Y	N	Y	N	Y	Y
2 ***Skeen***	N	Y	Y	Y	N	N	Y	Y
3 Richardson	N	Y	N	N	Y	Y	N	Y
NEW YORK								
1 Hochbrueckner	N	Y	N	N	Y	Y	N	Y
2 Downey	N	Y	N	N	Y	Y	N	Y
3 Mrazek	N	Y	N	N	Y	Y	N	Y
4 ***Lent***	N	N	Y	N	Y	N	Y	Y
5 ***McGrath***	N	Y	N	N	Y	N	Y	Y
6 Flake	N	Y	N	N	Y	Y	N	Y
7 Ackerman	N	Y	N	N	Y	Y	N	Y
8 Scheuer	?	?	?	?	?	Y	N	Y
9 Manton	?	Y	N	N	Y	Y	Y	Y
10 Schumer	N	Y	?	?	?	Y	N	Y
11 Towns	N	Y	N	N	Y	Y	N	Y
12 Owens	N	Y	N	N	Y	Y	N	Y
13 Solarz	N	Y	N	N	Y	Y	N	Y
14 ***Molinari***	N	Y	Y	N	Y	N	N	Y
15 ***Green***	N	Y	N	N	Y	Y	N	Y
16 Rangel	N	Y	N	N	Y	Y	N	Y
17 Weiss	N	Y	N	N	Y	Y	N	Y
18 Serrano	N	?	N	N	Y	Y	N	Y
19 Engel	N	Y	N	N	Y	Y	N	Y
20 Lowey	N	Y	N	N	Y	Y	N	Y
21 ***Fish***	N	Y	N	N	Y	N	Y	Y
22 ***Gilman***	N	Y	N	N	Y	Y	N	Y
23 McNulty	N	Y	N	N	Y	Y	N	Y
24 ***Solomon***	Y	N	N	N	Y	N	Y	Y
25 ***Boehlert***	N	Y	N	N	Y	N	N	Y
26 ***Martin***	N	Y	N	N	Y	N	Y	Y
27 ***Walsh***	N	Y	N	N	Y	N	N	Y
28 McHugh	N	Y	Y	N	Y	Y	N	Y
29 ***Horton***	N	Y	N	N	Y	Y	N	Y
30 Slaughter	N	Y	N	N	Y	Y	N	Y
31 ***Paxon***	N	Y	N	Y	Y	N	Y	Y
32 LaFalce	N	Y	N	N	Y	Y	Y	Y
33 Nowak	N	Y	N	N	Y	Y	Y	Y
34 ***Houghton***	N	Y	Y	Y	Y	N	N	Y
NORTH CAROLINA								
1 Jones	N	Y	N	N	Y	Y	N	Y
2 Valentine	N	Y	N	N	Y	Y	N	Y
3 Lancaster	N	Y	N	N	Y	Y	N	Y
4 Price	N	Y	N	N	Y	Y	N	Y
5 Neal	N	Y	N	N	Y	Y	N	Y
6 ***Coble***	Y	N	N	N	Y	N	Y	Y
7 Rose	N	Y	N	N	?	Y	N	Y
8 Hefner	N	Y	N	N	Y	Y	Y	Y
9 ***McMillan***	Y	N	N	N	Y	N	Y	Y
10 ***Ballenger***	Y	Y	?	N	Y	N	Y	Y
11 Clarke	N	Y	N	N	Y	Y	Y	Y
NORTH DAKOTA								
AL Dorgan	N	Y	Y	Y	Y	Y	Y	Y
OHIO								
1 Luken	N	N	N	N	Y	Y	Y	Y
2 ***Gradison***	Y	N	Y	N	Y	N	Y	Y
3 Hall	N	Y	N	N	Y	Y	Y	Y
4 ***Oxley***	N	Y	Y	Y	N	N	Y	Y
5 ***Gillmor***	N	Y	Y	N	Y	N	Y	?
6 ***McEwen***	Y	N	N	N	Y	Y	Y	Y
7 ***DeWine***	N	Y	N	N	Y	N	Y	Y
8 ***Lukens***	N	N	Y	Y	Y	N	Y	Y
9 Kaptur	N	Y	N	N	Y	Y	Y	Y
10 ***Miller***	Y	Y	Y	Y	N	N	Y	Y
11 Eckart	N	Y	N	N	Y	Y	N	Y
12 ***Kasich***	Y	Y	N	N	Y	N	Y	Y
13 Pease	N	Y	N	N	Y	Y	N	?
14 Sawyer	N	Y	N	N	Y	Y	N	Y
15 ***Wylie***	Y	Y	Y	N	N	N	Y	Y
16 ***Regula***	N	Y	Y	N	Y	N	Y	Y
17 Traficant	N	Y	N	N	Y	Y	N	Y
18 Applegate	N	Y	N	N	Y	Y	Y	Y
19 Feighan	N	Y	N	N	Y	Y	N	Y
20 Oakar	N	Y	Y	N	Y	Y	Y	Y
21 Stokes	N	Y	N	N	Y	Y	N	Y
OKLAHOMA								
1 ***Inhofe***	N	Y	Y	N	Y	N	Y	Y
2 Synar	N	Y	N	N	Y	Y	N	Y
3 Watkins	N	Y	N	N	Y	Y	N	Y
4 McCurdy	N	Y	N	N	Y	Y	N	Y
5 ***Edwards***	N	Y	?	?	?	N	Y	Y
6 English	N	Y	Y	N	Y	Y	Y	Y
OREGON								
1 AuCoin	?	?	?	?	#	Y	N	Y
2 ***Smith, B.***	N	Y	Y	Y	N	N	Y	Y
3 Wyden	N	Y	N	N	Y	Y	N	Y
4 DeFazio	N	Y	N	N	Y	Y	N	Y
5 ***Smith, D.***	N	Y	Y	Y	N	N	Y	Y
PENNSYLVANIA								
1 Foglietta	N	Y	N	N	Y	Y	N	Y
2 Gray	N	Y	N	N	Y	Y	?	Y
3 Borski	N	Y	N	N	Y	Y	Y	Y
4 Kolter	N	Y	N	N	Y	Y	Y	Y
5 ***Schulze***	?	?	?	?	?	?	#	?
6 Yatron	N	Y	N	N	Y	Y	Y	Y
7 ***Weldon***	N	Y	N	N	Y	N	Y	Y
8 Kostmayer	N	Y	N	N	Y	Y	N	Y
9 ***Shuster***	Y	N	Y	Y	N	N	Y	Y
10 ***McDade***	N	Y	Y	N	Y	?	Y	Y
11 Kanjorski	N	Y	N	N	Y	Y	Y	Y
12 Murtha	N	Y	N	N	Y	Y	Y	Y
13 ***Coughlin***	N	Y	N	N	Y	N	N	Y
14 Coyne	N	Y	N	N	Y	Y	N	Y
15 ***Ritter***	N	Y	N	N	Y	N	Y	Y
16 ***Walker***	Y	N	Y	Y	N	N	Y	Y
17 ***Gekas***	Y	N	Y	Y	N	N	N	Y
18 Walgren	Y	Y	N	N	Y	Y	N	Y
19 ***Goodling***	N	Y	Y	N	Y	N	Y	Y
20 Gaydos	N	Y	N	N	Y	Y	Y	Y
21 ***Ridge***	Y	?	N	N	Y	N	Y	Y
22 Murphy	N	N	N	N	Y	N	Y	Y
23 ***Clinger***	N	Y	Y	N	Y	N	Y	Y
RHODE ISLAND								
1 ***Machtley***	N	Y	N	N	Y	Y	N	Y
2 ***Schneider***	N	Y	N	N	Y	N	N	Y
SOUTH CAROLINA								
1 ***Ravenel***	Y	Y	N	N	Y	N	Y	Y
2 ***Spence***	N	Y	N	Y	Y	N	Y	Y
3 Derrick	N	Y	N	N	Y	Y	N	Y
4 Patterson	N	Y	N	N	Y	Y	N	Y
5 Spratt	N	Y	N	N	Y	Y	N	Y
6 Tallon	N	Y	N	N	Y	Y	N	Y
SOUTH DAKOTA								
AL Johnson	N	Y	N	Y	Y	Y	Y	Y
TENNESSEE								
1 ***Quillen***	N	Y	Y	Y	N	Y	Y	Y
2 ***Duncan***	Y	N	Y	Y	N	N	Y	Y
3 Lloyd	N	Y	N	?	Y	Y	Y	Y
4 Cooper	N	Y	N	N	Y	Y	Y	Y
5 Clement	N	Y	N	N	Y	Y	Y	Y
6 Gordon	N	Y	N	N	Y	Y	N	Y
7 ***Sundquist***	?	?	N	Y	Y	N	Y	Y
8 Tanner	N	Y	N	N	Y	Y	N	Y
9 Ford	?	N	N	N	Y	Y	N	Y
TEXAS								
1 Chapman	?	Y	N	N	Y	Y	Y	Y
2 Wilson	N	Y	N	N	Y	Y	N	Y
3 ***Bartlett***	Y	N	Y	N	N	N	Y	Y
4 Hall	?	?	?	?	?	?	?	?
5 Bryant	N	Y	N	N	Y	Y	N	Y
6 ***Barton***	Y	N	Y	Y	N	N	Y	Y
7 ***Archer***	N	Y	N	Y	Y	N	Y	Y
8 ***Fields***	Y	N	Y	Y	N	N	Y	Y
9 Brooks	N	Y	N	N	Y	Y	N	Y
10 Pickle	N	Y	N	Y	N	Y	N	Y
11 Leath	N	Y	N	N	Y	?	Y	Y
12 Geren	N	Y	N	N	Y	Y	Y	Y
13 Sarpalius	Y	Y	N	N	Y	Y	Y	Y
14 Laughlin	Y	Y	N	N	Y	Y	Y	Y
15 de la Garza	N	Y	N	N	Y	Y	N	?
16 Coleman	N	Y	N	N	Y	Y	N	Y
17 Stenholm	Y	Y	Y	N	Y	Y	Y	Y
18 Washington	N	?	?	?	?	Y	?	?
19 ***Combest***	Y	N	Y	Y	N	N	Y	Y
20 Gonzalez	N	Y	N	N	Y	Y	N	Y
21 ***Smith***	N	Y	N	N	Y	N	Y	Y
22 ***DeLay***	N	Y	Y	Y	N	N	Y	Y
23 Bustamante	N	Y	N	N	Y	Y	N	Y
24 Frost	N	Y	N	N	Y	Y	N	Y
25 Andrews	N	Y	N	N	Y	Y	N	Y
26 ***Armey***	Y	N	Y	Y	N	N	Y	Y
27 Ortiz	N	Y	N	N	Y	Y	Y	Y
UTAH								
1 ***Hansen***	Y	N	Y	Y	N	N	Y	Y
2 Owens	N	Y	N	N	Y	Y	N	Y
3 ***Nielson***	Y	N	Y	Y	N	N	Y	Y
VERMONT								
AL ***Smith***	N	Y	N	N	Y	N	N	Y
VIRGINIA								
1 ***Bateman***	N	Y	Y	Y	Y	N	Y	Y
2 Pickett	N	N	N	Y	Y	Y	N	Y
3 ***Bliley***	Y	Y	N	N	Y	N	Y	Y
4 Sisisky	N	Y	N	N	Y	Y	N	Y
5 Payne	N	Y	N	N	Y	Y	Y	Y
6 Olin	N	Y	Y	N	Y	Y	N	Y
7 ***Slaughter***	Y	N	Y	Y	Y	N	Y	Y
8 ***Parris***	Y	Y	Y	Y	N	N	Y	Y
9 Boucher	N	Y	N	N	Y	Y	N	Y
10 ***Wolf***	N	Y	Y	N	Y	N	Y	Y
WASHINGTON								
1 ***Miller***	N	Y	N	N	Y	N	N	Y
2 Swift	N	Y	N	N	Y	Y	N	?
3 Unsoeld	N	Y	N	N	Y	Y	N	Y
4 ***Morrison***	N	Y	Y	Y	Y	N	N	Y
5 Foley								
6 Dicks	N	Y	N	N	Y	Y	N	Y
7 McDermott	N	Y	N	N	Y	Y	N	Y
8 ***Chandler***	N	Y	N	N	Y	N	N	Y
WEST VIRGINIA								
1 Mollohan	N	Y	N	N	Y	Y	Y	Y
2 Staggers	N	Y	N	N	Y	Y	Y	Y
3 Wise	X	+	X	X	+	Y	N	Y
4 Rahall	N	Y	N	N	Y	N	Y	N
WISCONSIN								
1 Aspin	N	Y	N	N	Y	Y	Y	Y
2 Kastenmeier	N	Y	N	N	Y	Y	N	Y
3 ***Gunderson***	N	Y	N	N	Y	N	Y	Y
4 Kleczka	N	Y	N	N	Y	Y	N	Y
5 Moody	N	Y	N	N	Y	Y	N	Y
6 ***Petri***	Y	Y	N	N	Y	N	Y	N
7 Obey	N	Y	N	N	Y	Y	Y	Y
8 ***Roth***	N	Y	N	Y	Y	N	Y	Y
9 ***Sensenbrenner***	Y	N	N	N	Y	N	Y	N
WYOMING								
AL ***Thomas***	Y	Y	Y	Y	N	N	Y	Y

Southern states - Ala., Ark., Fla., Ga., Ky., La., Miss., N.C., Okla., S.C., Tenn., Texas, Va.
Omitted votes are quorum calls, which CQ does not include in its vote charts.

203. HR 5114. Fiscal 1991 Foreign Operations Appropriations/Cambodia. Solarz, D-N.Y., amendment to earmark $7 million for non-lethal aid to the non-communist resistance in Cambodia. Any assistance to the Khmer Rouge would be prohibited. Adopted 260-163: R 153-22; D 107-141 (ND 54-115, SD 53-26), June 27, 1990.

204. HR 5114. Fiscal 1991 Foreign Operations Appropriations/Passage. Passage of the bill to appropriate $15.66 billion for foreign military and economic assistance and export financing in fiscal 1991. Passed 308-117: R 108-67; D 200-50 (ND 145-25, SD 55-25), June 27, 1990.

205. HR 5158. Fiscal 1991 VA and HUD Appropriations/Rule. Adoption of the rule (H Res 426) to provide for House floor consideration for and waive certain points of order against the bill to appropriate $83.6 billion for the Department of Housing and Urban Development (HUD), the Department of Veterans Affairs (VA) and independent agencies in fiscal 1991. Adopted 351-59: R 108-59; D 243-0 (ND 165-0, SD 78-0), June 28, 1990.

KEY

- Y Voted for (yea).
- # Paired for.
- \+ Announced for.
- N Voted against (nay).
- X Paired against.
- \- Announced against.
- P Voted "present."
- C Voted "present" to avoid possible conflict of interest.
- ? Did not vote or otherwise make a position known.

Democrats ***Republicans***

	203	204	205
ALABAMA			
1 ***Callahan***	Y	N	?
2 ***Dickinson***	Y	N	Y
3 Browder	Y	Y	Y
4 Bevill	Y	Y	Y
5 Flippo	Y	Y	Y
6 Erdreich	Y	Y	Y
7 Harris	Y	Y	Y
ALASKA			
AL ***Young***	Y	Y	N
ARIZONA			
1 ***Rhodes***	Y	Y	Y
2 Udall	Y	Y	Y
3 ***Stump***	Y	N	N
4 ***Kyl***	Y	Y	N
5 ***Kolbe***	Y	Y	N
ARKANSAS			
1 Alexander	Y	N	Y
2 ***Robinson***	Y	N	Y
3 ***Hammerschmidt***	Y	N	Y
4 Anthony	Y	Y	Y
CALIFORNIA			
1 Bosco	Y	Y	Y
2 ***Herger***	Y	N	N
3 Matsui	N	Y	Y
4 Fazio	N	Y	Y
5 Pelosi	N	Y	Y
6 Boxer	N	Y	Y
7 Miller	N	N	Y
8 Dellums	N	Y	Y
9 Stark	N	N	Y
10 Edwards	N	Y	Y
11 Lantos	N	Y	Y
12 ***Campbell***	N	Y	Y
13 Mineta	N	Y	Y
14 ***Shumway***	Y	N	N
15 Condit	Y	Y	Y
16 Panetta	N	Y	Y
17 ***Pashayan***	N	N	Y
18 Lehman	N	Y	Y
19 ***Lagomarsino***	Y	Y	N
20 ***Thomas***	Y	Y	N
21 ***Gallegly***	Y	Y	N
22 ***Moorhead***	Y	N	N
23 Beilenson	Y	Y	?
24 Waxman	N	Y	Y
25 Roybal	N	N	Y
26 Berman	N	Y	Y
27 Levine	N	Y	Y
28 Dixon	N	Y	Y
29 Hawkins	N	Y	Y
30 Martinez	Y	Y	?
31 Dymally	Y	Y	Y
32 Anderson	Y	Y	Y
33 ***Dreier***	Y	Y	N
34 Torres	N	Y	Y
35 ***Lewis***	Y	N	Y
36 Brown	N	Y	Y
37 ***McCandless***	Y	N	N
38 ***Dornan***	Y	Y	N
39 ***Dannemeyer***	Y	N	N
40 ***Cox***	Y	Y	Y
41 ***Lowery***	Y	Y	Y
42 ***Rohrabacher***	Y	Y	Y
43 ***Packard***	Y	N	N
44 Bates	N	Y	Y
45 ***Hunter***	Y	Y	N
COLORADO			
1 Schroeder	N	N	Y
2 Skaggs	N	Y	Y
3 Campbell	Y	Y	Y
4 ***Brown***	Y	Y	N
5 ***Hefley***	Y	Y	N
6 ***Schaefer***	Y	Y	N
CONNECTICUT			
1 Kennelly	Y	Y	Y
2 Gejdenson	N	Y	Y
3 Morrison	X	+	+
4 ***Shays***	Y	Y	N
5 ***Rowland***	Y	Y	Y
6 ***Johnson***	Y	Y	Y
DELAWARE			
AL Carper	N	Y	Y
FLORIDA			
1 Hutto	Y	Y	Y
2 ***Grant***	Y	Y	Y
3 Bennett	Y	N	Y
4 ***James***	Y	N	Y
5 ***McCollum***	Y	N	Y
6 ***Stearns***	Y	N	Y
7 Gibbons	Y	N	Y
8 ***Young***	Y	N	Y
9 ***Bilirakis***	Y	N	Y
10 ***Ireland***	Y	Y	Y
11 Nelson	+	+	+
12 ***Lewis***	Y	N	Y
13 ***Goss***	Y	Y	Y
14 Johnston	N	Y	Y
15 ***Shaw***	Y	Y	Y
16 Smith	Y	Y	Y
17 Lehman	N	Y	Y
18 ***Ros-Lehtinen***	Y	Y	Y
19 Fascell	Y	Y	Y
GEORGIA			
1 Thomas	Y	Y	Y
2 Hatcher	Y	Y	Y
3 Ray	Y	N	Y
4 Jones	N	Y	Y
5 Lewis	N	Y	Y
6 ***Gingrich***	Y	Y	Y
7 Darden	Y	Y	Y
8 Rowland	Y	Y	Y
9 Jenkins	Y	N	Y
10 Barnard	Y	N	Y
HAWAII			
1 ***Saiki***	Y	Y	Y
2 Vacancy			
IDAHO			
1 ***Craig***	Y	N	Y
2 Stallings	N	Y	Y
ILLINOIS			
1 Hayes	N	Y	Y
2 Savage	N	N	Y
3 Russo	N	N	?
4 Sangmeister	N	Y	Y
5 Lipinski	Y	Y	Y
6 ***Hyde***	Y	Y	?
7 Collins	N	Y	Y
8 Rostenkowski	N	Y	Y
9 Yates	N	Y	Y
10 ***Porter***	N	Y	N
11 Annunzio	Y	Y	Y
12 ***Crane***	Y	N	N
13 ***Fawell***	Y	Y	N
14 ***Hastert***	Y	Y	N
15 ***Madigan***	Y	Y	Y
16 ***Martin***	N	N	N
17 Evans	N	Y	Y
18 ***Michel***	Y	Y	Y
19 Bruce	N	Y	Y
20 Durbin	N	Y	Y
21 Costello	N	Y	Y
22 Poshard	N	N	Y
INDIANA			
1 Visclosky	N	Y	Y
2 Sharp	N	Y	Y
3 ***Hiler***	Y	Y	Y

ND Northern Democrats SD Southern Democrats

	203	204	205
4 Long	Y	Y	Y
5 Jontz	N	Y	Y
6 ***Burton***	Y	Y	N
7 ***Myers***	Y	Y	Y
8 McCloskey	N	Y	Y
9 Hamilton	N	Y	Y
10 Jacobs	N	N	Y
IOWA			
1 ***Leach***	N	Y	Y
2 ***Tauke***	N	N	Y
3 Nagle	N	Y	Y
4 Smith	N	Y	Y
5 ***Lightfoot***	Y	Y	N
6 ***Grandy***	N	Y	Y
KANSAS			
1 ***Roberts***	Y	N	Y
2 Slattery	Y	N	Y
3 ***Meyers***	Y	N	Y
4 Glickman	Y	Y	Y
5 ***Whittaker***	Y	N	Y
KENTUCKY			
1 Hubbard	Y	N	Y
2 Natcher	N	Y	Y
3 Mazzoli	N	N	Y
4 ***Bunning***	Y	N	N
5 ***Rogers***	Y	N	N
6 ***Hopkins***	Y	N	N
7 Perkins	N	N	Y
LOUISIANA			
1 ***Livingston***	Y	N	Y
2 Boggs	Y	Y	Y
3 Tauzin	Y	N	Y
4 ***McCrery***	Y	Y	Y
5 Huckaby	Y	N	Y
6 ***Baker***	Y	N	Y
7 Hayes	?	?	?
8 ***Holloway***	Y	Y	Y
MAINE			
1 Brennan	N	Y	Y
2 ***Snowe***	N	N	Y
MARYLAND			
1 Dyson	Y	Y	Y
2 ***Bentley***	Y	Y	Y
3 Cardin	N	Y	Y
4 McMillen	Y	Y	Y
5 Hoyer	Y	Y	Y
6 Byron	Y	Y	Y
7 Mfume	Y	Y	Y
8 ***Morella***	N	Y	Y
MASSACHUSETTS			
1 ***Conte***	N	Y	Y
2 Neal	N	Y	Y
3 Early	N	N	Y
4 Frank	N	Y	Y
5 Atkins	N	Y	Y
6 Mavroules	N	Y	Y
7 Markey	N	Y	Y
8 Kennedy	N	Y	Y
9 Moakley	N	Y	Y
10 Studds	N	Y	Y
11 Donnelly	?	?	?
MICHIGAN			
1 Conyers	N	Y	?
2 ***Pursell***	Y	Y	Y
3 Wolpe	N	Y	Y
4 ***Upton***	Y	Y	N
5 ***Henry***	Y	N	N
6 Carr	N	Y	Y
7 Kildee	N	Y	Y
8 Traxler	N	Y	Y
9 ***Vander Jagt***	Y	Y	?
10 ***Schuette***	Y	Y	Y
11 ***Davis***	N	Y	Y
12 Bonior	N	Y	?
13 Crockett	?	?	Y
14 Hertel	N	Y	Y
15 Ford	N	Y	Y
16 Dingell	N	Y	Y
17 Levin	N	Y	Y
18 ***Broomfield***	Y	Y	Y
MINNESOTA			
1 Penny	Y	Y	Y
2 ***Weber***	Y	Y	Y
3 ***Frenzel***	Y	Y	N
4 Vento	N	Y	Y

	203	204	205
5 Sabo	N	Y	Y
6 Sikorski	N	Y	Y
7 ***Stangeland***	Y	N	Y
8 Oberstar	N	Y	Y
MISSISSIPPI			
1 Whitten	N	Y	Y
2 Espy	Y	Y	Y
3 Montgomery	Y	N	Y
4 Parker	Y	Y	Y
5 Taylor	Y	N	Y
MISSOURI			
1 Clay	N	Y	Y
2 ***Buechner***	N	Y	N
3 Gephardt	N	Y	Y
4 Skelton	Y	Y	Y
5 Wheat	N	Y	Y
6 ***Coleman***	Y	Y	N
7 ***Hancock***	Y	N	N
8 ***Emerson***	Y	Y	Y
9 Volkmer	Y	N	Y
MONTANA			
1 Williams	N	N	Y
2 ***Marlenee***	Y	N	N
NEBRASKA			
1 ***Bereuter***	Y	Y	Y
2 Hoagland	Y	Y	Y
3 ***Smith***	Y	N	Y
NEVADA			
1 Bilbray	Y	Y	Y
2 ***Vucanovich***	Y	Y	N
NEW HAMPSHIRE			
1 ***Smith***	Y	N	N
2 ***Douglas***	N	Y	Y
NEW JERSEY			
1 Vacancy			
2 Hughes	Y	N	Y
3 Pallone	Y	Y	Y
4 ***Smith***	Y	Y	Y
5 ***Roukema***	Y	N	Y
6 Dwyer	N	Y	Y
7 ***Rinaldo***	Y	Y	Y
8 Roe	Y	Y	Y
9 Torricelli	Y	Y	Y
10 Payne	N	Y	Y
11 ***Gallo***	Y	Y	Y
12 ***Courter***	Y	Y	Y
13 ***Saxton***	Y	Y	Y
14 Guarini	N	N	Y
NEW MEXICO			
1 ***Schiff***	N	Y	Y
2 ***Skeen***	Y	Y	Y
3 Richardson	?	Y	Y
NEW YORK			
1 Hochbrueckner	Y	Y	Y
2 Downey	N	Y	Y
3 Mrazek	N	Y	Y
4 ***Lent***	Y	Y	?
5 ***McGrath***	N	Y	Y
6 Flake	Y	Y	Y
7 Ackerman	Y	Y	Y
8 Scheuer	Y	Y	Y
9 Manton	Y	Y	Y
10 Schumer	N	Y	Y
11 Towns	N	Y	Y
12 Owens	N	Y	Y
13 Solarz	Y	Y	Y
14 ***Molinari***	Y	Y	Y
15 ***Green***	Y	Y	Y
16 Rangel	N	Y	Y
17 Weiss	N	Y	Y
18 Serrano	N	Y	Y
19 Engel	Y	Y	Y
20 Lowey	Y	Y	Y
21 ***Fish***	Y	Y	Y
22 ***Gilman***	Y	Y	Y
23 McNulty	Y	Y	Y
24 ***Solomon***	Y	N	Y
25 ***Boehlert***	Y	Y	Y
26 ***Martin***	Y	Y	Y
27 ***Walsh***	Y	Y	Y
28 McHugh	Y	Y	Y
29 ***Horton***	N	Y	Y
30 Slaughter	N	Y	Y
31 ***Paxon***	Y	Y	Y

	203	204	205
32 LaFalce	Y	Y	Y
33 Nowak	Y	Y	Y
34 ***Houghton***	Y	Y	N
NORTH CAROLINA			
1 Jones	N	N	Y
2 Valentine	N	N	Y
3 Lancaster	Y	Y	Y
4 Price	Y	Y	Y
5 Neal	Y	N	Y
6 ***Coble***	Y	Y	N
7 Rose	Y	Y	Y
8 Hefner	N	N	Y
9 ***McMillan***	Y	Y	Y
10 ***Ballenger***	Y	N	N
11 Clarke	Y	Y	Y
NORTH DAKOTA			
AL Dorgan	N	Y	Y
OHIO			
1 Luken	N	Y	Y
2 ***Gradison***	Y	N	Y
3 Hall	N	Y	?
4 ***Oxley***	Y	N	Y
5 ***Gillmor***	Y	Y	Y
6 ***McEwen***	Y	Y	N
7 ***DeWine***	Y	Y	Y
8 ***Lukens***	N	Y	N
9 Kaptur	N	Y	Y
10 ***Miller***	Y	N	Y
11 Eckart	Y	Y	Y
12 ***Kasich***	Y	Y	N
13 Pease	N	N	Y
14 Sawyer	N	Y	Y
15 ***Wylie***	Y	N	Y
16 ***Regula***	Y	Y	Y
17 Traficant	N	N	Y
18 Applegate	N	N	Y
19 Feighan	Y	Y	Y
20 Oakar	N	Y	Y
21 Stokes	N	Y	Y
OKLAHOMA			
1 ***Inhofe***	Y	Y	Y
2 Synar	N	Y	Y
3 Watkins	Y	N	Y
4 McCurdy	Y	Y	Y
5 ***Edwards***	Y	Y	N
6 English	Y	N	Y
OREGON			
1 AuCoin	N	Y	Y
2 ***Smith, B.***	N	N	N
3 Wyden	N	Y	Y
4 DeFazio	N	Y	Y
5 ***Smith, D.***	Y	Y	N
PENNSYLVANIA			
1 Foglietta	N	Y	Y
2 Gray	N	Y	Y
3 Borski	Y	Y	Y
4 Kolter	Y	N	Y
5 ***Schulze***	#	?	?
6 Yatron	Y	Y	Y
7 ***Weldon***	Y	N	Y
8 Kostmayer	Y	Y	Y
9 ***Shuster***	Y	N	N
10 ***McDade***	Y	Y	Y
11 Kanjorski	Y	Y	Y
12 Murtha	Y	Y	Y
13 ***Coughlin***	Y	Y	Y
14 Coyne	N	Y	Y
15 ***Ritter***	Y	Y	Y
16 ***Walker***	Y	N	?
17 ***Gekas***	Y	N	N
18 Walgren	Y	N	Y
19 ***Goodling***	Y	N	N
20 Gaydos	N	N	Y
21 ***Ridge***	Y	Y	?
22 Murphy	N	N	Y
23 ***Clinger***	Y	Y	Y
RHODE ISLAND			
1 ***Machtley***	N	Y	Y
2 ***Schneider***	N	Y	Y
SOUTH CAROLINA			
1 ***Ravenel***	Y	Y	Y
2 ***Spence***	Y	N	Y
3 Derrick	N	Y	Y
4 Patterson	N	N	Y
5 Spratt	N	Y	Y
6 Tallon	Y	Y	Y

	203	204	205
SOUTH DAKOTA			
AL Johnson	N	Y	Y
TENNESSEE			
1 ***Quillen***	Y	Y	Y
2 ***Duncan***	Y	N	N
3 Lloyd	Y	N	Y
4 Cooper	Y	Y	Y
5 Clement	Y	Y	Y
6 Gordon	N	Y	Y
7 ***Sundquist***	Y	Y	Y
8 Tanner	N	N	Y
9 Ford	N	Y	Y
TEXAS			
1 Chapman	Y	Y	Y
2 Wilson	Y	N	?
3 ***Bartlett***	Y	Y	N
4 Hall	?	?	?
5 Bryant	Y	N	Y
6 ***Barton***	Y	N	?
7 ***Archer***	Y	N	N
8 ***Fields***	Y	N	Y
9 Brooks	N	Y	Y
10 Pickle	Y	Y	Y
11 Leath	?	Y	Y
12 Geren	Y	Y	Y
13 Sarpalius	Y	Y	Y
14 Laughlin	N	Y	Y
15 de la Garza	Y	Y	Y
16 Coleman	N	Y	Y
17 Stenholm	Y	Y	Y
18 Washington	N	Y	Y
19 ***Combest***	Y	N	N
20 Gonzalez	N	N	Y
21 ***Smith***	Y	Y	Y
22 ***DeLay***	Y	N	Y
23 Bustamante	Y	Y	?
24 Frost	Y	Y	Y
25 Andrews	N	Y	Y
26 ***Armey***	Y	N	Y
27 Ortiz	Y	Y	Y
UTAH			
1 ***Hansen***	Y	N	Y
2 Owens	Y	Y	Y
3 ***Nielson***	Y	N	?
VERMONT			
AL ***Smith***	N	Y	Y
VIRGINIA			
1 ***Bateman***	Y	Y	N
2 Pickett	Y	Y	Y
3 ***Bliley***	Y	Y	Y
4 Sisisky	N	Y	Y
5 Payne	Y	Y	Y
6 Olin	N	Y	Y
7 ***Slaughter***	Y	N	Y
8 ***Parris***	Y	N	Y
9 Boucher	Y	Y	Y
10 ***Wolf***	Y	Y	Y
WASHINGTON			
1 ***Miller***	Y	Y	Y
2 Swift	N	Y	Y
3 Unsoeld	N	Y	Y
4 ***Morrison***	Y	Y	Y
5 Foley			
6 Dicks	Y	Y	Y
7 McDermott	N	Y	Y
8 ***Chandler***	Y	Y	N
WEST VIRGINIA			
1 Mollohan	Y	N	Y
2 Staggers	N	N	Y
3 Wise	N	Y	Y
4 Rahall	Y	N	Y
WISCONSIN			
1 Aspin	Y	Y	Y
2 Kastenmeier	N	N	Y
3 ***Gunderson***	Y	Y	Y
4 Kleczka	N	Y	Y
5 Moody	N	Y	Y
6 ***Petri***	Y	N	N
7 Obey	N	Y	Y
8 ***Roth***	Y	N	Y
9 ***Sensenbrenner***	N	N	N
WYOMING			
AL ***Thomas***	Y	N	Y

Southern states - Ala., Ark., Fla., Ga., Ky., La., Miss., N.C., Okla., S.C., Tenn., Texas, Va.
Omitted votes are quorum calls, which CQ does not include in its vote charts.

207. HR 5158. Fiscal 1991 VA and HUD Appropriations/Across-the-Board Cuts. Frenzel, R-Minn., amendment to provide for an across-the-board 14.5 percent cut in all discretionary accounts except for medical care and veterans health service and research administration accounts. Rejected 72-337: R 65-105; D 7-232 (ND 2-162, SD 5-70), June 28, 1990.

208. HR 5158. Fiscal 1991 VA and HUD Appropriations/Across-the-Board Cuts. Dannemeyer, R-Calif., amendment to provide for an across-the-board 5 percent cut in all discretionary accounts in the bill. Rejected 53-343: R 48-108; D 5-235 (ND 3-161, SD 2-74), June 28, 1990.

209. HR 5158. Fiscal 1991 VA and HUD Appropriations/Across-the-Board Cuts. Penny, D-Minn., amendment to provide for an across-the-board 2 percent cut in all discretionary accounts except for the Department of Veterans Affairs medical care and Department of Housing and Urban Development Section 8 subsidy contracts. Rejected 172-235: R 124-46; D 48-189 (ND 27-135, SD 21-54), June 28, 1990.

210. HR 5158. Fiscal 1991 VA and HUD Appropriations/Passage. Passage of the bill to appropriate $83.6 billion in fiscal 1991 for the Department of Housing and Urban Development (HUD), the Department of Veterans Affairs (VA), the Environmental Protection Agency, NASA, the National Science Foundation and various other agencies. Passed 355-48: R 128-39; D 227-9 (ND 155-7, SD 72-2), June 28, 1990.

KEY

- Y Voted for (yea).
- # Paired for.
- + Announced for.
- N Voted against (nay).
- X Paired against.
- - Announced against.
- P Voted "present."
- C Voted "present" to avoid possible conflict of interest.
- ? Did not vote or otherwise make a position known.

Democrats ***Republicans***

	207	208	209	210
ALABAMA				
1 ***Callahan***	N	N	Y	Y
2 ***Dickinson***	N	Y	Y	Y
3 Browder	N	N	N	Y
4 Bevill	N	N	N	Y
5 Flippo	N	N	N	Y
6 Erdreich	N	N	N	Y
7 Harris	N	N	N	Y
ALASKA				
AL ***Young***	N	N	N	Y
ARIZONA				
1 ***Rhodes***	N	N	Y	Y
2 Udall	N	N	Y	Y
3 ***Stump***	N	N	Y	N
4 ***Kyl***	N	N	Y	N
5 ***Kolbe***	N	N	Y	Y
ARKANSAS				
1 Alexander	N	N	N	Y
2 ***Robinson***	Y	Y	Y	?
3 ***Hammerschmidt***	N	N	Y	Y
4 Anthony	N	N	N	Y
CALIFORNIA				
1 Bosco	N	N	N	Y
2 ***Herger***	Y	?	Y	N
3 Matsui	N	N	N	Y
4 Fazio	N	N	N	Y
5 Pelosi	N	N	N	Y
6 Boxer	N	N	N	Y
7 Miller	N	N	N	Y
8 Dellums	N	N	N	Y
9 Stark	?	?	?	?
10 Edwards	N	N	N	Y
11 Lantos	N	N	N	Y
12 ***Campbell***	Y	Y	Y	N
13 Mineta	N	N	N	Y
14 ***Shumway***	Y	Y	Y	N
15 Condit	N	N	Y	P
16 Panetta	N	N	N	Y
17 ***Pashayan***	Y	N	Y	Y
18 Lehman	N	N	Y	Y
19 ***Lagomarsino***	N	Y	Y	Y
20 ***Thomas***	Y	Y	Y	Y
21 ***Gallegly***	N	Y	Y	Y
22 ***Moorhead***	Y	Y	Y	N
23 Beilenson	N	Y	Y	N
24 Waxman	N	N	N	Y
25 Roybal	N	N	N	Y
26 Berman	N	N	N	Y
27 Levine	N	N	N	Y
28 Dixon	N	N	N	Y
29 Hawkins	N	N	N	Y
30 Martinez	N	N	?	?
31 Dymally	N	N	N	Y
32 Anderson	N	N	N	Y
33 ***Dreier***	Y	Y	Y	Y
34 Torres	N	N	N	Y
35 ***Lewis***	N	N	N	#
36 Brown	N	N	N	Y
37 ***McCandless***	Y	?	Y	Y
38 ***Dornan***	Y	N	Y	Y
39 ***Dannemeyer***	Y	Y	Y	N
40 ***Cox***	Y	Y	Y	N
41 ***Lowery***	?	N	N	Y
42 ***Rohrabacher***	N	Y	Y	N
43 ***Packard***	Y	Y	Y	N
44 Bates	N	N	N	Y
45 ***Hunter***	N	Y	Y	Y
COLORADO				
1 Schroeder	N	N	Y	Y
2 Skaggs	N	N	N	Y
3 Campbell	N	N	Y	Y
4 ***Brown***	N	Y	Y	Y
5 ***Hefley***	Y	Y	Y	Y
6 ***Schaefer***	Y	N	Y	Y
CONNECTICUT				
1 Kennelly	N	N	N	Y
2 Gejdenson	N	N	N	Y
3 Morrison	–	–	–	+
4 ***Shays***	N	N	Y	Y
5 ***Rowland***	N	N	Y	Y
6 ***Johnson***	Y	Y	Y	N
DELAWARE				
AL Carper	N	N	N	Y
FLORIDA				
1 Hutto	N	N	N	Y
2 ***Grant***	N	N	N	Y
3 Bennett	Y	Y	Y	Y
4 ***James***	N	N	N	Y
5 ***McCollum***	N	N	Y	Y
6 ***Stearns***	N	N	Y	Y
7 Gibbons	N	N	Y	Y
8 ***Young***	N	N	N	Y
9 ***Bilirakis***	N	N	N	Y
10 ***Ireland***	Y	Y	Y	Y
11 Nelson	-	-	-	#
12 ***Lewis***	N	N	N	Y
13 ***Goss***	N	N	Y	Y
14 Johnston	N	N	N	Y
15 ***Shaw***	N	N	Y	Y
16 Smith	N	N	?	?
17 Lehman	N	N	N	Y
18 ***Ros-Lehtinen***	N	N	N	Y
19 Fascell	N	N	N	Y
GEORGIA				
1 Thomas	N	N	N	Y
2 Hatcher	N	N	N	Y
3 Ray	N	N	Y	Y
4 Jones	N	N	N	Y
5 Lewis	N	N	N	Y
6 ***Gingrich***	Y	N	Y	Y
7 Darden	N	N	Y	Y
8 Rowland	N	N	N	Y
9 Jenkins	?	?	?	?
10 Barnard	N	N	Y	Y
HAWAII				
1 ***Saiki***	N	N	N	Y
2 Vacancy				
IDAHO				
1 ***Craig***	N	Y	Y	Y
2 Stallings	N	N	Y	Y
ILLINOIS				
1 Hayes	N	N	N	Y
2 Savage	N	N	N	Y
3 Russo	N	Y	Y	N
4 Sangmeister	N	N	N	Y
5 Lipinski	N	N	N	Y
6 ***Hyde***	N	Y	Y	Y
7 Collins	N	N	N	Y
8 Rostenkowski	N	N	N	Y
9 Yates	N	N	N	Y
10 ***Porter***	Y	Y	Y	Y
11 Annunzio	N	N	N	Y
12 ***Crane***	Y	Y	Y	N
13 ***Fawell***	Y	?	Y	N
14 ***Hastert***	Y	Y	Y	Y
15 ***Madigan***	N	N	N	Y
16 ***Martin***	?	?	#	X
17 Evans	N	N	N	Y
18 ***Michel***	Y	N	Y	N
19 Bruce	N	N	N	Y
20 Durbin	N	N	N	Y
21 Costello	N	N	N	Y
22 Poshard	N	N	N	Y
INDIANA				
1 Visclosky	N	N	N	Y
2 Sharp	Y	N	N	Y
3 ***Hiler***	N	?	Y	Y

ND Northern Democrats SD Southern Democrats

	207	208	209	210
4 Long	N	N	Y	Y
5 Jontz	N	N	Y	Y
6 ***Burton***	N	N	Y	Y
7 ***Myers***	N	N	N	Y
8 McCloskey	N	N	N	Y
9 Hamilton	Y	Y	Y	Y
10 Jacobs	N	N	Y	N
IOWA				
1 ***Leach***	N	N	Y	Y
2 ***Tauke***	N	N	Y	N
3 Nagle	N	N	N	Y
4 Smith	N	N	N	Y
5 ***Lightfoot***	Y	Y	Y	Y
6 ***Grandy***	N	N	Y	Y
KANSAS				
1 ***Roberts***	Y	N	Y	N
2 Slattery	N	N	Y	Y
3 ***Meyers***	N	Y	Y	Y
4 Glickman	N	N	Y	Y
5 ***Whittaker***	Y	N	Y	Y
KENTUCKY				
1 Hubbard	N	N	N	Y
2 Natcher	N	N	N	Y
3 Mazzoli	N	N	N	Y
4 ***Bunning***	Y	Y	Y	N
5 ***Rogers***	N	N	Y	Y
6 ***Hopkins***	N	Y	Y	N
7 Perkins	N	N	N	Y
LOUISIANA				
1 ***Livingston***	N	N	Y	Y
2 Boggs	N	N	N	Y
3 Tauzin	Y	N	Y	Y
4 ***McCrery***	N	?	Y	Y
5 Huckaby	N	N	Y	Y
6 ***Baker***	N	N	Y	Y
7 Hayes	N	N	N	Y
8 ***Holloway***	N	N	N	Y
MAINE				
1 Brennan	N	N	N	Y
2 ***Snowe***	N	N	Y	Y
MARYLAND				
1 Dyson	N	N	Y	P
2 ***Bentley***	N	N	N	Y
3 Cardin	N	N	N	Y
4 McMillen	N	N	N	Y
5 Hoyer	N	N	N	Y
6 Byron	N	N	Y	N
7 Mfume	N	N	N	Y
8 ***Morella***	N	N	N	Y
MASSACHUSETTS				
1 ***Conte***	N	N	N	Y
2 Neal	N	N	N	Y
3 Early	N	N	N	Y
4 Frank	N	N	N	Y
5 Atkins	N	N	N	Y
6 Mavroules	N	N	N	Y
7 Markey	N	N	N	Y
8 Kennedy	N	?	N	Y
9 Moakley	?	?	X	Y
10 Studds	N	N	N	Y
11 Donnelly	?	?	?	?
MICHIGAN				
1 Conyers	?	?	?	?
2 ***Pursell***	N	N	N	Y
3 Wolpe	N	N	N	Y
4 ***Upton***	Y	N	Y	N
5 ***Henry***	Y	N	Y	N
6 Carr	N	N	N	Y
7 Kildee	N	N	N	Y
8 Traxler	N	N	N	Y
9 ***Vander Jagt***	Y	?	Y	Y
10 ***Schuette***	N	N	N	?
11 ***Davis***	N	N	N	Y
12 Bonior	N	N	N	Y
13 Crockett	N	N	?	?
14 Hertel	N	N	N	Y
15 Ford	N	N	N	Y
16 Dingell	N	N	N	Y
17 Levin	N	N	N	Y
18 ***Broomfield***	N	N	Y	Y
MINNESOTA				
1 Penny	N	N	Y	N
2 ***Weber***	N	N	Y	Y
3 ***Frenzel***	Y	Y	Y	N
4 Vento	N	N	N	Y
5 Sabo	N	N	N	Y
6 Sikorski	N	N	N	Y
7 ***Stangeland***	Y	N	Y	Y
8 Oberstar	N	N	N	Y
MISSISSIPPI				
1 Whitten	N	N	N	Y
2 Espy	N	N	N	Y
3 Montgomery	N	N	N	Y
4 Parker	N	N	N	Y
5 Taylor	N	N	N	Y
MISSOURI				
1 Clay	N	N	N	Y
2 ***Buechner***	N	N	N	Y
3 Gephardt	N	N	N	Y
4 Skelton	N	N	N	Y
5 Wheat	N	N	N	Y
6 ***Coleman***	N	N	Y	Y
7 ***Hancock***	Y	Y	Y	N
8 ***Emerson***	N	N	N	Y
9 Volkmer	N	N	N	Y
MONTANA				
1 Williams	N	N	?	N
2 ***Marlenee***	Y	N	N	Y
NEBRASKA				
1 ***Bereuter***	N	N	Y	Y
2 Hoagland	N	N	Y	Y
3 ***Smith***	N	N	Y	Y
NEVADA				
1 Bilbray	N	N	N	Y
2 ***Vucanovich***	N	?	Y	Y
NEW HAMPSHIRE				
1 ***Smith***	Y	Y	Y	N
2 ***Douglas***	Y	Y	Y	N
NEW JERSEY				
1 Vacancy				
2 Hughes	N	N	Y	Y
3 Pallone	N	N	N	Y
4 ***Smith***	N	N	N	Y
5 ***Roukema***	N	N	Y	Y
6 Dwyer	N	N	N	Y
7 ***Rinaldo***	N	N	N	Y
8 Roe	N	N	N	Y
9 Torricelli	N	N	N	Y
10 Payne	N	N	N	Y
11 ***Gallo***	N	N	Y	Y
12 ***Courter***	Y	Y	Y	Y
13 ***Saxton***	N	N	Y	Y
14 Guarini	?	N	Y	Y
NEW MEXICO				
1 ***Schiff***	N	N	N	Y
2 ***Skeen***	N	N	N	Y
3 Richardson	N	N	N	Y
NEW YORK				
1 Hochbrueckner	N	N	N	Y
2 Downey	N	N	N	Y
3 Mrazek	N	N	N	Y
4 ***Lent***	N	N	N	Y
5 ***McGrath***	N	N	N	Y
6 Flake	N	N	N	Y
7 Ackerman	N	N	N	Y
8 Scheuer	N	N	N	Y
9 Manton	?	?	?	?
10 Schumer	N	N	N	Y
11 Towns	N	N	N	Y
12 Owens	N	N	N	Y
13 Solarz	N	N	N	Y
14 ***Molinari***	N	N	N	Y
15 ***Green***	N	N	N	Y
16 Rangel	N	N	N	Y
17 Weiss	N	N	N	Y
18 Serrano	N	N	N	Y
19 Engel	N	N	N	Y
20 Lowey	N	N	N	Y
21 ***Fish***	N	N	Y	Y
22 ***Gilman***	N	N	N	Y
23 McNulty	N	N	N	Y
24 ***Solomon***	N	N	N	Y
25 ***Boehlert***	N	N	N	Y
26 ***Martin***	N	N	?	Y
27 ***Walsh***	N	N	Y	Y
28 McHugh	N	N	N	Y
29 ***Horton***	N	N	N	Y
30 Slaughter	N	N	Y	Y
31 ***Paxon***	N	N	N	Y
32 LaFalce	N	N	N	Y
33 Nowak	N	N	N	Y
34 ***Houghton***	Y	Y	Y	Y
NORTH CAROLINA				
1 Jones	N	N	Y	Y
2 Valentine	N	N	N	Y
3 Lancaster	N	N	Y	Y
4 Price	N	N	N	Y
5 Neal	N	N	Y	Y
6 ***Coble***	Y	N	Y	Y
7 Rose	?	N	N	Y
8 Hefner	N	N	N	Y
9 ***McMillan***	Y	N	Y	N
10 ***Ballenger***	Y	—	Y	Y
11 Clarke	N	N	N	Y
NORTH DAKOTA				
AL Dorgan	N	N	Y	Y
OHIO				
1 Luken	?	?	?	?
2 ***Gradison***	Y	Y	Y	N
3 Hall	N	N	Y	Y
4 ***Oxley***	Y	?	Y	Y
5 ***Gillmor***	N	?	Y	Y
6 ***McEwen***	Y	?	Y	N
7 ***DeWine***	N	N	Y	Y
8 ***Lukens***	N	N	Y	?
9 Kaptur	N	N	Y	P
10 ***Miller***	Y	N	Y	Y
11 Eckart	N	N	N	Y
12 ***Kasich***	Y	N	Y	Y
13 Pease	N	N	N	N
14 Sawyer	N	N	N	Y
15 ***Wylie***	N	N	Y	Y
16 ***Regula***	N	N	N	Y
17 Traficant	N	N	N	Y
18 Applegate	N	N	N	Y
19 Feighan	N	?	?	Y
20 Oakar	N	N	N	Y
21 Stokes	N	N	N	Y
OKLAHOMA				
1 ***Inhofe***	N	N	Y	Y
2 Synar	N	N	N	Y
3 Watkins	N	N	N	Y
4 McCurdy	N	N	Y	Y
5 ***Edwards***	N	N	Y	Y
6 English	N	N	Y	Y
OREGON				
1 AuCoin	N	N	N	Y
2 ***Smith, B.***	Y	N	Y	Y
3 Wyden	N	N	N	Y
4 DeFazio	N	N	N	Y
5 ***Smith, D.***	Y	?	Y	Y
PENNSYLVANIA				
1 Foglietta	N	N	N	Y
2 Gray	N	N	N	Y
3 Borski	N	N	N	Y
4 Kolter	N	N	N	Y
5 ***Schulze***	?	?	#	?
6 Yatron	N	N	N	Y
7 ***Weldon***	N	N	Y	Y
8 Kostmayer	N	N	N	Y
9 ***Shuster***	Y	Y	Y	N
10 ***McDade***	N	N	N	Y
11 Kanjorski	N	N	N	Y
12 Murtha	N	N	N	Y
13 ***Coughlin***	N	N	N	Y
14 Coyne	N	N	N	Y
15 ***Ritter***	?	N	N	Y
16 ***Walker***	Y	Y	Y	N
17 ***Gekas***	N	Y	Y	N
18 Walgren	?	N	Y	Y
19 ***Goodling***	N	N	Y	Y
20 Gaydos	N	N	N	Y
21 ***Ridge***	N	N	Y	Y
22 Murphy	N	N	Y	Y
23 ***Clinger***	Y	Y	Y	Y
RHODE ISLAND				
1 ***Machtley***	N	N	N	Y
2 ***Schneider***	N	N	N	Y
SOUTH CAROLINA				
1 ***Ravenel***	N	N	N	Y
2 ***Spence***	N	N	N	Y
3 Derrick	N	N	N	Y
4 Patterson	N	N	Y	Y
5 Spratt	N	N	N	Y
6 Tallon	N	N	N	Y
SOUTH DAKOTA				
AL Johnson	N	N	N	Y
TENNESSEE				
1 ***Quillen***	N	N	N	Y
2 ***Duncan***	Y	Y	Y	N
3 Lloyd	N	N	N	Y
4 Cooper	Y	N	Y	Y
5 Clement	N	N	Y	Y
6 Gordon	N	N	N	Y
7 ***Sundquist***	N	N	Y	Y
8 Tanner	N	N	N	Y
9 Ford	N	N	N	Y
TEXAS				
1 Chapman	N	N	N	Y
2 Wilson	?	?	?	?
3 ***Bartlett***	Y	Y	Y	N
4 Hall	?	?	?	?
5 Bryant	?	?	N	Y
6 ***Barton***	?	?	?	?
7 ***Archer***	Y	Y	Y	N
8 ***Fields***	Y	Y	Y	N
9 Brooks	N	N	N	Y
10 Pickle	N	N	Y	?
11 Leath	N	N	N	Y
12 Geren	N	N	Y	Y
13 Sarpalius	N	N	N	Y
14 Laughlin	N	N	N	Y
15 de la Garza	?	?	?	?
16 Coleman	N	N	N	Y
17 Stenholm	Y	Y	Y	Y
18 Washington	N	N	N	Y
19 ***Combest***	Y	?	?	?
20 Gonzalez	N	N	N	Y
21 ***Smith***	N	N	N	Y
22 ***DeLay***	N	Y	Y	N
23 Bustamante	?	?	X	?
24 Frost	N	N	?	?
25 Andrews	N	N	Y	Y
26 ***Armey***	Y	Y	Y	N
27 Ortiz	N	N	N	Y
UTAH				
1 ***Hansen***	Y	?	Y	Y
2 Owens	N	N	N	Y
3 ***Nielson***	?	?	?	X
VERMONT				
AL ***Smith***	N	N	N	Y
VIRGINIA				
1 ***Bateman***	N	N	Y	Y
2 Pickett	N	N	N	N
3 ***Bliley***	Y	?	Y	Y
4 Sisisky	N	N	N	Y
5 Payne	N	N	Y	Y
6 Olin	Y	N	Y	N
7 ***Slaughter***	Y	N	Y	Y
8 ***Parris***	N	?	Y	Y
9 Boucher	N	N	N	Y
10 ***Wolf***	N	N	Y	Y
WASHINGTON				
1 ***Miller***	N	N	Y	Y
2 Swift	N	N	N	Y
3 Unsoeld	N	N	N	Y
4 ***Morrison***	N	N	Y	Y
5 Foley				
6 Dicks	N	N	N	Y
7 McDermott	N	N	N	Y
8 ***Chandler***	N	N	Y	Y
WEST VIRGINIA				
1 Mollohan	N	N	N	Y
2 Staggers	N	N	N	Y
3 Wise	N	N	N	Y
4 Rahall	N	N	N	Y
WISCONSIN				
1 Aspin	N	N	N	Y
2 Kastenmeier	N	N	N	Y
3 ***Gunderson***	Y	N	Y	Y
4 Kleczka	N	N	N	Y
5 Moody	N	N	Y	Y
6 ***Petri***	Y	Y	Y	N
7 Obey	N	N	N	Y
8 ***Roth***	Y	Y	Y	Y
9 ***Sensenbrenner***	Y	Y	Y	N
WYOMING				
AL ***Thomas***	Y	Y	Y	N

Southern states - Ala., Ark., Fla., Ga., Ky., La., Miss., N.C., Okla., S.C., Tenn., Texas, Va.
Omitted votes are quorum calls, which CQ does not include in its vote charts.

211. HR 4834. Salem Maritime Visitor Center/Passage. Vento, D-Minn., motion to suspend the rules and pass the bill to authorize the Interior Department to lease or acquire part of the Salem, Mass., Armory to establish a maritime visitors center to help preserve the history of maritime shipping and commerce. Motion agreed to 393-8: R 156-8; D 237-0 (ND 161-0, SD 76-0), July 10, 1990. A two-thirds majority of those present and voting (268 in this case) is required for passage under suspension of the rules.

212. S 666. Alaska Native Claims Amendments/Passage. Vento, D-Minn., motion to suspend the rules and pass the bill to make 20 people eligible for benefits under the Alaska Native Claims Settlement Act of 1971 (PL 92-203). The bill would also modify procedures to transfer stocks issued by native corporations under the act and improve management of federal lands on Alaska's Admiralty Island. Motion agreed to 361-43: R 130-35; D 231-8 (ND 159-4, SD 72-4), July 10, 1990. A two-thirds majority of those present and voting (270 in this case) is required for passage under suspension of the rules.

213. HR 988. Utah Land Exchange/Passage. Vento, D-Minn., motion to suspend the rules and pass the bill to authorize an equal-value exchange of Bureau of Land Management lands for private lands in and around Camp W. G. Williams, an active military installation, in Salt Lake and Utah counties, Utah, in order to restrict public access to lands littered by unexploded munitions that pose a safety hazard. Motion agreed to 401-1: R 163-1; D 238-0 (ND 162-0, SD 76-0), July 10, 1990. A two-thirds majority of those present and voting (268 in this case) is required for passage under suspension of the rules.

214. HR 5064. Drug Abuse Resistance Education Act/Passage. Unsoeld, D-Wash., motion to suspend the rules and pass the bill to require the Education Department to reserve $15 million of funds appropriated under the Drug-Free Schools and Community Act to establish a grant program to develop an antidrug education strategy to teach elementary school children to resist the pressures that lead to drug use. Motion agreed to 388-13: R 148-13; D 240-0 (ND 164-0, SD 76-0), July 10, 1990. A two-thirds majority of those present and voting (268 in this case) is required for passage under suspension of the rules. A "nay" was a vote supporting the president's position.

KEY

Y Voted for (yea).
Paired for.
+ Announced for.
N Voted against (nay).
X Paired against.
- Announced against.
P Voted "present."
C Voted "present" to avoid possible conflict of interest.
? Did not vote or otherwise make a position known.

Democrats *Republicans*

	211	212	213	214
ALABAMA				
1 *Callahan*	Y	Y	Y	Y
2 *Dickinson*	Y	Y	Y	Y
3 Browder	Y	Y	Y	Y
4 Bevill	Y	Y	Y	Y
5 Flippo	Y	Y	Y	Y
6 Erdreich	Y	Y	Y	Y
7 Harris	Y	Y	Y	Y
ALASKA				
AL *Young*	Y	Y	Y	Y
ARIZONA				
1 *Rhodes*	Y	Y	Y	Y
2 Udall	Y	Y	Y	Y
3 *Stump*	N	N	Y	N
4 *Kyl*	?	?	?	?
5 *Kolbe*	Y	Y	Y	Y
ARKANSAS				
1 Alexander	Y	Y	Y	Y
2 *Robinson*	Y	Y	Y	Y
3 *Hammerschmidt*	Y	Y	Y	Y
4 Anthony	Y	Y	Y	Y
CALIFORNIA				
1 Bosco	Y	Y	Y	Y
2 *Herger*	Y	N	Y	Y
3 Matsui	Y	Y	Y	Y
4 Fazio	Y	Y	Y	Y
5 Pelosi	Y	Y	Y	Y
6 Boxer	Y	Y	Y	Y
7 Miller	?	?	?	?
8 Dellums	Y	Y	Y	Y
9 Stark	Y	Y	Y	Y
10 Edwards	Y	N	Y	Y
11 Lantos	Y	Y	Y	Y
12 *Campbell*	Y	Y	Y	Y
13 Mineta	Y	Y	Y	Y
14 *Shumway*	Y	N	Y	N
15 Condit	?	Y	Y	Y
16 Panetta	Y	Y	Y	Y
17 *Pashayan*	Y	Y	Y	Y
18 Lehman	Y	Y	Y	Y
19 *Lagomarsino*	Y	Y	Y	Y
20 *Thomas*	Y	Y	Y	Y
21 *Gallegly*	Y	Y	Y	Y
22 *Moorhead*	Y	N	Y	Y
23 Beilenson	Y	N	Y	Y
24 Waxman	Y	Y	Y	Y
25 Roybal	Y	Y	Y	Y
26 Berman	Y	Y	Y	Y
27 Levine	Y	Y	Y	Y
28 Dixon	Y	Y	Y	Y
29 Hawkins	Y	Y	Y	Y
30 Martinez	Y	Y	Y	Y
31 Dymally	Y	Y	Y	Y
32 Anderson	Y	Y	Y	Y
33 *Dreier*	Y	Y	Y	Y
34 Torres	Y	Y	Y	Y
35 *Lewis*	Y	Y	Y	Y
36 Brown	Y	Y	Y	Y
37 *McCandless*	Y	Y	Y	Y
38 *Dornan*	Y	Y	Y	Y
39 *Dannemeyer*	Y	N	Y	Y
40 *Cox*	Y	N	Y	Y
41 *Lowery*	Y	Y	Y	Y
42 *Rohrabacher*	?	?	?	?
43 *Packard*	Y	N	Y	N
44 Bates	Y	Y	Y	Y
45 *Hunter*	?	?	?	?
COLORADO				
1 Schroeder	Y	Y	Y	Y
2 Skaggs	Y	Y	Y	Y
3 Campbell	Y	Y	Y	Y
4 *Brown*	Y	Y	Y	Y
5 *Hefley*	Y	Y	Y	Y
6 *Schaefer*	Y	Y	Y	Y
CONNECTICUT				
1 Kennelly	Y	Y	Y	Y
2 Gejdenson	Y	Y	Y	Y
3 Morrison	Y	Y	Y	Y
4 *Shays*	Y	Y	Y	Y
5 *Rowland*	Y	Y	Y	Y
6 *Johnson*	Y	Y	Y	?
DELAWARE				
AL Carper	Y	Y	Y	Y
FLORIDA				
1 Hutto	Y	Y	Y	Y
2 *Grant*	Y	Y	Y	Y
3 Bennett	Y	Y	Y	Y
4 *James*	?	Y	Y	Y
5 *McCollum*	Y	Y	Y	Y
6 *Stearns*	N	N	Y	Y
7 Gibbons	Y	Y	Y	Y
8 *Young*	Y	Y	Y	Y
9 *Bilirakis*	Y	Y	Y	?
10 *Ireland*	?	?	?	?
11 Nelson	+	+	+	+
12 *Lewis*	Y	Y	Y	Y
13 *Goss*	Y	Y	Y	Y
14 Johnston	Y	Y	Y	Y
15 *Shaw*	Y	Y	Y	Y
16 Smith	?	?	?	?
17 Lehman	Y	Y	Y	Y
18 *Ros-Lehtinen*	Y	Y	Y	Y
19 Fascell	Y	Y	Y	Y
GEORGIA				
1 Thomas	Y	Y	Y	Y
2 Hatcher	Y	Y	Y	Y
3 Ray	Y	Y	Y	Y
4 Jones	Y	Y	Y	Y
5 Lewis	Y	Y	Y	Y
6 *Gingrich*	Y	N	Y	Y
7 Darden	Y	Y	Y	Y
8 Rowland	Y	Y	Y	Y
9 Jenkins	Y	N	Y	Y
10 Barnard	Y	N	Y	Y
HAWAII				
1 *Saiki*	Y	Y	Y	Y
2 Vacancy				
IDAHO				
1 *Craig*	?	?	?	?
2 Stallings	Y	Y	Y	Y
ILLINOIS				
1 Hayes	Y	Y	Y	Y
2 Savage	?	Y	Y	Y
3 Russo	Y	Y	Y	Y
4 Sangmeister	Y	Y	Y	Y
5 Lipinski	Y	Y	Y	Y
6 *Hyde*	Y	Y	Y	Y
7 Collins	Y	Y	Y	Y
8 Rostenkowski	Y	Y	Y	Y
9 Yates	Y	Y	Y	Y
10 *Porter*	Y	N	Y	+
11 Annunzio	Y	Y	Y	Y
12 *Crane*	N	Y	N	N
13 *Fawell*	Y	Y	Y	Y
14 *Hastert*	Y	Y	Y	Y
15 *Madigan*	Y	Y	Y	Y
16 *Martin*	Y	Y	Y	Y
17 Evans	Y	Y	Y	Y
18 *Michel*	Y	Y	Y	N
19 Bruce	Y	Y	Y	Y
20 Durbin	Y	Y	Y	Y
21 Costello	Y	Y	Y	Y
22 Poshard	Y	Y	Y	Y
INDIANA				
1 Visclosky	Y	Y	Y	Y
2 Sharp	Y	Y	Y	Y
3 *Hiler*	Y	Y	Y	Y

ND Northern Democrats SD Southern Democrats

	211	212	213	214
4 Long	Y	Y	Y	Y
5 Jontz	Y	Y	Y	Y
6 ***Burton***	N	Y	Y	N
7 ***Myers***	Y	Y	Y	Y
8 McCloskey	Y	Y	Y	?
9 Hamilton	Y	Y	Y	Y
10 Jacobs	Y	Y	Y	Y
IOWA				
1 ***Leach***	Y	Y	Y	Y
2 ***Tauke***	Y	Y	Y	Y
3 Nagle	Y	Y	Y	Y
4 Smith	Y	Y	Y	Y
5 ***Lightfoot***	Y	Y	Y	Y
6 ***Grandy***	Y	Y	Y	Y
KANSAS				
1 ***Roberts***	Y	Y	Y	Y
2 Slattery	Y	Y	Y	Y
3 ***Meyers***	Y	Y	Y	Y
4 Glickman	Y	Y	Y	Y
5 ***Whittaker***	Y	Y	Y	Y
KENTUCKY				
1 Hubbard	Y	Y	Y	Y
2 Natcher	Y	Y	Y	Y
3 Mazzoli	Y	Y	Y	Y
4 ***Bunning***	Y	Y	Y	Y
5 ***Rogers***	Y	Y	Y	Y
6 ***Hopkins***	Y	N	Y	Y
7 Perkins	Y	Y	Y	Y
LOUISIANA				
1 ***Livingston***	Y	Y	Y	Y
2 Boggs	Y	Y	Y	Y
3 Tauzin	Y	Y	Y	Y
4 ***McCrery***	Y	Y	Y	Y
5 Huckaby	Y	Y	Y	Y
6 ***Baker***	Y	Y	Y	Y
7 Hayes	Y	Y	Y	Y
8 ***Holloway***	Y	N	Y	Y
MAINE				
1 Brennan	Y	Y	Y	Y
2 ***Snowe***	Y	Y	Y	Y
MARYLAND				
1 Dyson	Y	Y	Y	Y
2 ***Bentley***	Y	Y	Y	Y
3 Cardin	Y	Y	Y	Y
4 McMillen	Y	Y	Y	Y
5 Hoyer	Y	Y	Y	Y
6 Byron	Y	Y	Y	Y
7 Mfume	Y	Y	Y	Y
8 ***Morella***	Y	Y	Y	Y
MASSACHUSETTS				
1 ***Conte***	Y	Y	Y	Y
2 Neal	Y	Y	Y	Y
3 Early	Y	Y	Y	?
4 Frank	Y	Y	Y	Y
5 Atkins	?	?	?	Y
6 Mavroules	Y	Y	Y	Y
7 Markey	Y	Y	Y	Y
8 Kennedy	Y	Y	Y	Y
9 Moakley	Y	Y	Y	Y
10 Studds	Y	Y	Y	Y
11 Donnelly	Y	Y	Y	Y
MICHIGAN				
1 Conyers	Y	Y	Y	Y
2 ***Pursell***	Y	Y	Y	Y
3 Wolpe	Y	Y	Y	Y
4 ***Upton***	Y	Y	Y	Y
5 ***Henry***	Y	N	Y	Y
6 Carr	Y	Y	Y	Y
7 Kildee	Y	Y	Y	Y
8 Traxler	Y	Y	Y	Y
9 ***Vander Jagt***	Y	Y	Y	Y
10 ***Schuette***	Y	Y	Y	Y
11 ***Davis***	Y	Y	Y	Y
12 Bonior	Y	Y	Y	Y
13 Crockett	?	?	?	?
14 Hertel	Y	Y	Y	Y
15 Ford	Y	Y	?	Y
16 Dingell	Y	Y	Y	Y
17 Levin	Y	Y	Y	Y
18 ***Broomfield***	Y	Y	Y	Y
MINNESOTA				
1 Penny	Y	Y	Y	Y
2 ***Weber***	Y	Y	Y	Y
3 ***Frenzel***	Y	N	Y	N
4 Vento	Y	Y	Y	Y

	211	212	213	214
5 Sabo	Y	Y	Y	Y
6 Sikorski	Y	Y	Y	Y
7 ***Stangeland***	Y	Y	Y	Y
8 Oberstar	Y	Y	Y	Y
MISSISSIPPI				
1 Whitten	Y	Y	Y	Y
2 Espy	Y	Y	Y	Y
3 Montgomery	Y	Y	Y	Y
4 Parker	Y	Y	Y	Y
5 Taylor	Y	Y	Y	Y
MISSOURI				
1 Clay	?	?	?	?
2 ***Buechner***	Y	Y	Y	Y
3 Gephardt	Y	Y	Y	Y
4 Skelton	Y	Y	Y	Y
5 Wheat	Y	Y	Y	Y
6 ***Coleman***	Y	Y	Y	Y
7 ***Hancock***	N	N	Y	N
8 ***Emerson***	Y	Y	Y	Y
9 Volkmer	Y	Y	Y	Y
MONTANA				
1 Williams	Y	Y	Y	Y
2 ***Marlenee***	?	?	?	?
NEBRASKA				
1 ***Bereuter***	Y	Y	Y	Y
2 Hoagland	Y	Y	Y	Y
3 ***Smith***	Y	Y	Y	Y
NEVADA				
1 Bilbray	Y	Y	Y	Y
2 ***Vucanovich***	Y	Y	Y	Y
NEW HAMPSHIRE				
1 ***Smith***	N	N	Y	Y
2 ***Douglas***	Y	N	Y	Y
NEW JERSEY				
1 Vacancy				
2 Hughes	Y	Y	Y	Y
3 Pallone	Y	Y	Y	Y
4 ***Smith***	Y	Y	Y	Y
5 ***Roukema***	Y	Y	Y	Y
6 Dwyer	Y	Y	Y	Y
7 ***Rinaldo***	Y	Y	Y	Y
8 Roe	Y	Y	Y	Y
9 Torricelli	Y	Y	Y	Y
10 Payne	Y	Y	Y	Y
11 ***Gallo***	Y	Y	Y	Y
12 ***Courter***	Y	Y	Y	Y
13 ***Saxton***	Y	Y	Y	Y
14 Guarini	?	?	?	?
NEW MEXICO				
1 ***Schiff***	Y	Y	Y	Y
2 ***Skeen***	Y	Y	Y	Y
3 Richardson	Y	Y	Y	Y
NEW YORK				
1 Hochbrueckner	Y	Y	Y	Y
2 Downey	Y	Y	Y	Y
3 Mrazek	Y	Y	Y	Y
4 ***Lent***	?	?	?	?
5 ***McGrath***	Y	Y	Y	Y
6 Flake	Y	Y	Y	Y
7 Ackerman	Y	Y	Y	Y
8 Scheuer	Y	Y	Y	Y
9 Manton	Y	Y	Y	Y
10 Schumer	Y	Y	Y	Y
11 Towns	?	?	?	?
12 Owens	Y	Y	Y	Y
13 Solarz	Y	Y	Y	Y
14 ***Molinari***	Y	Y	Y	Y
15 ***Green***	Y	Y	Y	Y
16 Rangel	Y	Y	Y	Y
17 Weiss	Y	Y	Y	Y
18 Serrano	Y	Y	Y	Y
19 Engel	Y	Y	Y	Y
20 Lowey	Y	Y	Y	Y
21 ***Fish***	Y	Y	Y	Y
22 ***Gilman***	Y	Y	Y	Y
23 McNulty	Y	Y	Y	Y
24 ***Solomon***	Y	N	Y	Y
25 ***Boehlert***	Y	Y	Y	Y
26 ***Martin***	Y	Y	Y	Y
27 ***Walsh***	Y	Y	Y	Y
28 McHugh	Y	Y	Y	Y
29 ***Horton***	Y	Y	Y	Y
30 Slaughter	Y	Y	Y	Y
31 ***Paxon***	Y	Y	Y	?

	211	212	213	214
32 LaFalce	Y	Y	Y	Y
33 Nowak	Y	Y	Y	Y
34 ***Houghton***	Y	Y	Y	Y
NORTH CAROLINA				
1 Jones	Y	Y	Y	Y
2 Valentine	Y	Y	Y	Y
3 Lancaster	Y	Y	Y	Y
4 Price	Y	Y	Y	Y
5 Neal	Y	N	Y	Y
6 ***Coble***	Y	Y	Y	Y
7 Rose	Y	Y	Y	Y
8 Hefner	Y	Y	Y	Y
9 ***McMillan***	Y	Y	Y	Y
10 ***Ballenger***	Y	Y	Y	Y
11 Clarke	Y	Y	Y	Y
NORTH DAKOTA				
AL Dorgan	Y	Y	Y	Y
OHIO				
1 Luken	Y	Y	Y	Y
2 ***Gradison***	Y	Y	Y	Y
3 Hall	Y	Y	Y	Y
4 ***Oxley***	Y	Y	Y	Y
5 ***Gillmor***	Y	Y	Y	Y
6 ***McEwen***	Y	Y	Y	Y
7 ***DeWine***	Y	Y	Y	Y
8 ***Lukens***	?	?	?	?
9 Kaptur	Y	Y	Y	Y
10 ***Miller***	Y	Y	Y	Y
11 Eckart	Y	Y	Y	Y
12 ***Kasich***	Y	Y	Y	Y
13 Pease	Y	Y	Y	Y
14 Sawyer	Y	Y	Y	Y
15 ***Wylie***	Y	Y	Y	Y
16 ***Regula***	Y	Y	Y	Y
17 Traficant	Y	Y	Y	Y
18 Applegate	Y	Y	Y	Y
19 Feighan	?	?	?	Y
20 Oakar	Y	Y	Y	Y
21 Stokes	Y	Y	Y	Y
OKLAHOMA				
1 ***Inhofe***	Y	N	Y	Y
2 Synar	Y	Y	Y	Y
3 Watkins	Y	Y	Y	Y
4 McCurdy	Y	Y	Y	Y
5 ***Edwards***	Y	Y	Y	Y
6 English	Y	Y	Y	Y
OREGON				
1 AuCoin	Y	Y	Y	Y
2 ***Smith, B.***	Y	Y	Y	Y
3 Wyden	Y	Y	Y	Y
4 DeFazio	Y	Y	Y	Y
5 ***Smith, D.***	Y	N	Y	Y
PENNSYLVANIA				
1 Foglietta	?	?	?	Y
2 Gray	Y	Y	Y	Y
3 Borski	Y	Y	Y	Y
4 Kolter	Y	Y	Y	Y
5 ***Schulze***	Y	Y	Y	Y
6 Yatron	Y	Y	Y	Y
7 ***Weldon***	Y	Y	Y	Y
8 Kostmayer	Y	Y	Y	Y
9 ***Shuster***	Y	Y	Y	Y
10 ***McDade***	Y	Y	Y	Y
11 Kanjorski	Y	N	Y	Y
12 Murtha	Y	Y	Y	Y
13 ***Coughlin***	Y	Y	Y	Y
14 Coyne	Y	Y	Y	Y
15 ***Ritter***	Y	Y	Y	Y
16 ***Walker***	N	N	Y	Y
17 ***Gekas***	Y	Y	Y	Y
18 Walgren	Y	Y	Y	Y
19 ***Goodling***	Y	Y	Y	Y
20 Gaydos	Y	Y	Y	Y
21 ***Ridge***	Y	Y	Y	Y
22 Murphy	Y	Y	Y	Y
23 ***Clinger***	Y	Y	Y	Y
RHODE ISLAND				
1 ***Machtley***	Y	Y	Y	Y
2 ***Schneider***	Y	Y	Y	Y
SOUTH CAROLINA				
1 ***Ravenel***	Y	Y	Y	Y
2 ***Spence***	Y	Y	Y	Y
3 Derrick	Y	Y	Y	Y
4 Patterson	Y	Y	Y	Y
5 Spratt	?	?	?	?
6 Tallon	Y	Y	Y	Y

	211	212	213	214
SOUTH DAKOTA				
AL Johnson	Y	Y	Y	Y
TENNESSEE				
1 ***Quillen***	Y	Y	Y	Y
2 ***Duncan***	Y	Y	Y	Y
3 Lloyd	Y	Y	Y	Y
4 Cooper	Y	N	Y	Y
5 Clement	Y	Y	Y	Y
6 Gordon	Y	Y	Y	Y
7 ***Sundquist***	Y	N	Y	N
8 Tanner	Y	Y	Y	Y
9 Ford	?	?	?	?
TEXAS				
1 Chapman	Y	Y	Y	Y
2 Wilson	?	?	?	?
3 ***Bartlett***	Y	N	Y	Y
4 Hall	?	?	?	?
5 Bryant	Y	Y	Y	Y
6 ***Barton***	Y	N	Y	Y
7 ***Archer***	Y	N	Y	N
8 ***Fields***	?	?	?	?
9 Brooks	Y	Y	Y	Y
10 Pickle	Y	Y	Y	Y
11 Leath	Y	Y	Y	Y
12 Geren	Y	Y	Y	Y
13 Sarpalius	Y	Y	Y	Y
14 Laughlin	?	?	?	?
15 de la Garza	Y	Y	Y	Y
16 Coleman	Y	Y	Y	Y
17 Stenholm	Y	Y	Y	Y
18 Washington	Y	Y	Y	Y
19 ***Combest***	Y	Y	Y	Y
20 Gonzalez	Y	Y	Y	Y
21 ***Smith***	Y	N	Y	Y
22 ***DeLay***	Y	N	Y	N
23 Bustamante	Y	Y	Y	Y
24 Frost	Y	Y	Y	Y
25 Andrews	Y	Y	Y	Y
26 ***Armey***	Y	N	Y	Y
27 Ortiz	Y	Y	Y	Y
UTAH				
1 ***Hansen***	Y	N	Y	N
2 Owens	Y	Y	Y	Y
3 ***Nielson***	Y	N	Y	N
VERMONT				
AL ***Smith***	Y	N	?	Y
VIRGINIA				
1 ***Bateman***	Y	Y	Y	Y
2 Pickett	Y	Y	Y	Y
3 ***Bliley***	Y	Y	Y	Y
4 Sisisky	Y	Y	Y	Y
5 Payne	Y	Y	Y	Y
6 Olin	Y	Y	Y	Y
7 ***Slaughter***	Y	Y	Y	Y
8 ***Parris***	Y	Y	Y	Y
9 Boucher	Y	Y	Y	Y
10 ***Wolf***	Y	Y	Y	Y
WASHINGTON				
1 ***Miller***	Y	N	Y	Y
2 Swift	Y	Y	Y	Y
3 Unsoeld	Y	Y	Y	Y
4 ***Morrison***	Y	Y	Y	Y
5 Foley				
6 Dicks	Y	Y	Y	Y
7 McDermott	Y	Y	Y	Y
8 ***Chandler***	?	?	?	?
WEST VIRGINIA				
1 Mollohan	?	?	?	?
2 Staggers	Y	Y	Y	Y
3 Wise	Y	Y	Y	Y
4 Rahall	Y	Y	Y	Y
WISCONSIN				
1 Aspin	?	?	?	?
2 Kastenmeier	Y	Y	Y	Y
3 ***Gunderson***	Y	Y	Y	Y
4 Kleczka	Y	Y	Y	Y
5 Moody	Y	N	Y	Y
6 ***Petri***	Y	N	Y	Y
7 Obey	Y	Y	Y	Y
8 ***Roth***	Y	N	Y	Y
9 ***Sensenbrenner***	N	N	Y	Y
WYOMING				
AL ***Thomas***	?	?	?	?

Southern states - Ala., Ark., Fla., Ga., Ky., La., Miss., N.C., Okla., S.C., Tenn., Texas, Va.
Omitted votes are quorum calls, which CQ does not include in its vote charts.

216. HR 4329. Commerce Department Technical Programs Reauthorization/Tax Credit. Roe, D-N.J., en bloc amendment to delete provisions of the bill under the jurisdiction of the Ways and Means Committee, including a sense of the Congress resolution supporting a permanent extension of the research and experimentation tax credit. Adopted 264-160: R 22-153; D 242-7 (ND 166-5, SD 76-2), July 11, 1990.

217. HR 4329. Commerce Department Technical Programs Reauthorization/Commission on Capital Costs. Roe, D-N.J., amendment to rename the "Presidential Commission on Reducing Capital Costs for Emerging Technology" the "National Commission on Reducing Capital Costs for Emerging Technology" and to have both the president and Congress appoint members to the commission instead of just the president. Adopted 249-174: R 1-174; D 248-0 (ND 170-0, SD 78-0), July 11, 1990.

218. HR 4329. Commerce Department Technical Programs Reauthorization/Funding Level. Walker, R-Pa., amendment to change the bill's fiscal 1992 authorization for the Advanced Technology Program from $250 million to "such sums as may be necessary." Rejected 150-272: R 145-29; D 5-243 (ND 2-167, SD 3-76), July 11, 1990.

219. HR 4329. Commerce Department Technical Programs Reauthorization/Salary. Horton, R-N.Y., amendment to delete provisions to elevate the salary level of the White House Office of Science and Technology's director to Level I (currently $107,300) from Level II ($96,600). Adopted 227-195: R 172-2; D 55-193 (ND 35-135, SD 20-58), July 11, 1990.

220. HR 4329. Commerce Department Technical Programs Reauthorization/Recommittal Motion. Walker, R-Pa., motion to recommit the bill to the House Science, Space and Technology Committee, with instructions to report it back to the House with the bill's fiscal 1992 authorization for the Advanced Technology Program changed from $250 million to $150 million. Motion rejected 165-257: R 158-15; D 7-242 (ND 2-168, SD 5-74), July 11, 1990.

221. HR 4329. Commerce Department Technical Programs Reauthorization/Passage. Passage of the bill to improve U.S. technological competitiveness, fund the National Institute of Standards and Technology through fiscal 1992 and provide funds for the U.S. research consortia to speed the commercial development of high-definition television and other new technologies. Passed 327-93: R 83-90; D 244-3 (ND 169-1, SD 75-2), July 11, 1990. A "nay" was a vote supporting the president's position.

KEY

- Y Voted for (yea).
- # Paired for.
- + Announced for.
- N Voted against (nay).
- X Paired against.
- \- Announced against.
- P Voted "present."
- C Voted "present" to avoid possible conflict of interest.
- ? Did not vote or otherwise make a position known.

Democrats ***Republicans***

	216	217	218	219	220	221
ALABAMA						
1 ***Callahan***	N	N	Y	Y	Y	Y
2 ***Dickinson***	N	N	N	Y	Y	Y
3 Browder	Y	Y	N	N	N	Y
4 Bevill	Y	Y	N	N	N	Y
5 Flippo	Y	Y	N	N	N	Y
6 Erdreich	Y	Y	N	N	N	Y
7 Harris	Y	Y	N	N	N	Y
ALASKA						
AL ***Young***	N	Y	?	Y	Y	Y
ARIZONA						
1 ***Rhodes***	N	N	Y	Y	Y	N
2 Udall	Y	Y	N	N	N	Y
3 ***Stump***	N	N	Y	Y	Y	N
4 ***Kyl***	N	N	Y	Y	Y	N
5 ***Kolbe***	N	N	Y	Y	Y	N
ARKANSAS						
1 Alexander	Y	Y	N	N	N	Y
2 ***Robinson***	N	N	Y	Y	Y	Y
3 ***Hammerschmidt***	Y	N	N	Y	Y	Y
4 Anthony	Y	Y	N	N	N	Y
CALIFORNIA						
1 Bosco	Y	Y	N	N	N	Y
2 ***Herger***	N	N	Y	Y	Y	N
3 Matsui	Y	Y	N	N	N	Y
4 Fazio	Y	Y	N	N	N	Y
5 Pelosi	Y	Y	N	Y	N	Y
6 Boxer	Y	Y	N	N	N	Y
7 Miller	Y	Y	N	N	N	Y
8 Dellums	Y	Y	N	N	N	Y
9 Stark	Y	Y	N	N	N	Y
10 Edwards	Y	Y	N	N	N	Y
11 Lantos	Y	Y	N	N	N	Y
12 ***Campbell***	N	N	Y	Y	Y	Y
13 Mineta	Y	Y	N	N	N	Y
14 ***Shumway***	N	N	Y	Y	Y	N
15 Condit	Y	Y	Y	Y	N	Y
16 Panetta	Y	Y	N	N	N	Y
17 ***Pashayan***	N	N	N	Y	Y	Y
18 Lehman	Y	Y	N	N	N	Y
19 ***Lagomarsino***	N	N	Y	Y	Y	N
20 ***Thomas***	Y	N	N	Y	Y	N
21 ***Gallegly***	N	N	Y	Y	Y	N
22 ***Moorhead***	N	N	Y	Y	Y	N
23 Beilenson	Y	Y	N	N	N	Y
24 Waxman	Y	Y	N	N	N	Y
25 Roybal	Y	Y	N	N	N	Y
26 Berman	Y	Y	N	N	N	Y
27 Levine	Y	Y	N	N	N	Y
28 Dixon	Y	Y	N	Y	N	Y
29 Hawkins	Y	?	N	N	N	Y
30 Martinez	Y	Y	N	Y	N	Y
31 Dymally	Y	Y	N	N	N	Y
32 Anderson	Y	Y	N	N	N	Y
33 ***Dreier***	N	N	Y	Y	Y	N
34 Torres	Y	Y	N	N	N	Y
35 ***Lewis***	N	N	N	Y	Y	Y
36 Brown	Y	Y	N	N	N	Y
37 ***McCandless***	N	N	Y	Y	Y	N
38 ***Dornan***	N	N	Y	Y	Y	N
39 ***Dannemeyer***	N	N	N	Y	Y	N
40 ***Cox***	N	N	Y	Y	Y	N
41 ***Lowery***	N	N	Y	Y	Y	Y
42 ***Rohrabacher***	N	N	Y	Y	Y	N
43 ***Packard***	N	N	Y	Y	Y	N
44 Bates	Y	Y	N	N	N	Y
45 ***Hunter***	N	N	Y	Y	Y	N
COLORADO						
1 Schroeder	N	Y	N	N	N	Y
2 Skaggs	Y	Y	N	N	N	Y
3 Campbell	Y	Y	N	N	N	Y
4 ***Brown***	N	N	Y	Y	Y	N
5 ***Hefley***	N	N	Y	Y	Y	N
6 ***Schaefer***	N	N	Y	Y	Y	N
CONNECTICUT						
1 Kennelly	Y	Y	N	Y	N	Y
2 Gejdenson	N	Y	N	N	N	Y
3 Morrison	N	Y	N	?	X	?
4 ***Shays***	N	N	Y	Y	Y	Y
5 ***Rowland***	N	N	Y	Y	Y	Y
6 ***Johnson***	Y	N	Y	Y	Y	Y
DELAWARE						
AL Carper	Y	Y	N	N	N	Y
FLORIDA						
1 Hutto	Y	Y	N	N	Y	Y
2 ***Grant***	N	N	N	Y	Y	Y
3 Bennett	Y	Y	N	Y	Y	Y
4 ***James***	N	N	N	Y	Y	N
5 ***McCollum***	N	N	N	Y	Y	Y
6 ***Stearns***	N	N	N	Y	Y	N
7 Gibbons	Y	Y	N	N	N	Y
8 ***Young***	N	N	N	Y	Y	Y
9 ***Bilirakis***	N	N	Y	Y	Y	Y
10 ***Ireland***	N	N	Y	Y	Y	N
11 Nelson	+	#	-	-	-	+
12 ***Lewis***	N	N	N	Y	Y	Y
13 ***Goss***	N	N	Y	Y	Y	N
14 Johnston	Y	Y	N	N	N	Y
15 ***Shaw***	Y	N	Y	Y	Y	N
16 Smith	Y	Y	N	N	N	Y
17 Lehman	Y	Y	N	N	N	Y
18 ***Ros-Lehtinen***	N	N	Y	Y	Y	Y
19 Fascell	Y	Y	N	N	N	Y
GEORGIA						
1 Thomas	Y	Y	N	N	N	Y
2 Hatcher	Y	Y	N	N	N	Y
3 Ray	Y	Y	N	Y	N	Y
4 Jones	Y	Y	N	N	N	Y
5 Lewis	Y	Y	N	N	N	Y
6 ***Gingrich***	N	N	Y	Y	Y	N
7 Darden	Y	Y	N	N	N	Y
8 Rowland	Y	Y	N	N	N	Y
9 Jenkins	Y	Y	N	?	?	?
10 Barnard	Y	Y	N	N	N	Y
HAWAII						
1 ***Saiki***	N	N	Y	Y	Y	Y
2 Vacancy						
IDAHO						
1 ***Craig***	N	N	Y	Y	Y	N
2 Stallings	Y	Y	N	N	N	Y
ILLINOIS						
1 Hayes	Y	Y	N	N	N	Y
2 Savage	Y	Y	N	Y	N	Y
3 Russo	Y	Y	N	N	N	Y
4 Sangmeister	Y	Y	N	Y	N	Y
5 Lipinski	Y	Y	N	N	N	Y
6 ***Hyde***	N	N	Y	Y	Y	Y
7 Collins	Y	Y	N	N	N	Y
8 Rostenkowski	Y	Y	N	N	N	Y
9 Yates	Y	Y	N	N	N	Y
10 ***Porter***	N	N	Y	Y	Y	N
11 Annunzio	Y	Y	N	N	N	Y
12 ***Crane***	Y	N	Y	Y	Y	N
13 ***Fawell***	N	N	Y	Y	Y	Y
14 ***Hastert***	N	N	Y	Y	Y	N
15 ***Madigan***	N	N	Y	Y	Y	N
16 ***Martin***	N	N	Y	Y	Y	Y
17 Evans	Y	Y	N	N	N	Y
18 ***Michel***	N	N	Y	Y	Y	N
19 Bruce	Y	Y	N	N	N	Y
20 Durbin	Y	Y	N	N	N	Y
21 Costello	Y	Y	N	N	N	Y
22 Poshard	Y	Y	N	N	N	Y
INDIANA						
1 Visclosky	Y	Y	N	N	N	Y
2 Sharp	Y	Y	N	N	N	Y
3 ***Hiler***	N	N	Y	Y	Y	N

ND Northern Democrats SD Southern Democrats

	216	217	218	219	220	221
4 Long	Y	Y	N	Y	N	Y
5 Jontz	Y	Y	N	Y	N	Y
6 ***Burton***	N	N	Y	Y	Y	N
7 ***Myers***	N	N	Y	Y	Y	Y
8 McCloskey	Y	Y	N	N	N	Y
9 Hamilton	Y	Y	N	N	N	Y
10 Jacobs	Y	Y	N	Y	Y	N
IOWA						
1 ***Leach***	Y	N	Y	Y	Y	Y
2 ***Tauke***	N	N	Y	Y	Y	Y
3 Nagle	Y	Y	N	N	N	Y
4 Smith	Y	Y	N	N	N	Y
5 ***Lightfoot***	N	N	Y	Y	Y	N
6 ***Grandy***	N	N	Y	Y	Y	N
KANSAS						
1 ***Roberts***	N	N	Y	Y	Y	N
2 Slattery	Y	Y	N	Y	N	Y
3 ***Meyers***	N	N	Y	Y	Y	Y
4 Glickman	Y	Y	N	N	N	Y
5 ***Whittaker***	N	N	N	Y	Y	Y
KENTUCKY						
1 Hubbard	Y	Y	N	Y	N	Y
2 Natcher	Y	Y	N	N	N	Y
3 Mazzoli	Y	Y	N	N	N	Y
4 ***Bunning***	N	N	Y	Y	Y	N
5 ***Rogers***	N	N	Y	Y	Y	Y
6 ***Hopkins***	N	N	Y	Y	Y	Y
7 Perkins	Y	Y	N	N	N	Y
LOUISIANA						
1 ***Livingston***	N	N	Y	Y	Y	Y
2 Boggs	Y	Y	N	N	N	Y
3 Tauzin	Y	Y	N	Y	N	Y
4 ***McCrery***	N	N	Y	Y	Y	N
5 Huckaby	Y	Y	N	Y	N	Y
6 ***Baker***	N	N	Y	Y	Y	Y
7 Hayes	Y	Y	N	N	N	Y
8 ***Holloway***	N	N	Y	Y	Y	N
MAINE						
1 Brennan	Y	Y	N	N	N	Y
2 ***Snowe***	N	N	Y	Y	Y	Y
MARYLAND						
1 Dyson	Y	Y	N	N	N	Y
2 ***Bentley***	N	N	N	N	N	Y
3 Cardin	Y	Y	N	Y	N	Y
4 McMillen	Y	Y	N	N	N	Y
5 Hoyer	Y	Y	N	N	N	Y
6 Byron	Y	Y	N	Y	N	Y
7 Mfume	Y	Y	N	Y	N	Y
8 ***Morella***	N	N	Y	Y	N	Y
MASSACHUSETTS						
1 ***Conte***	Y	N	N	Y	Y	Y
2 Neal	Y	Y	N	N	N	Y
3 Early	Y	Y	N	Y	N	Y
4 Frank	Y	Y	N	N	N	Y
5 Atkins	Y	Y	?	N	N	Y
6 Mavroules	Y	?	N	N	N	Y
7 Markey	Y	Y	N	N	N	Y
8 Kennedy	Y	Y	N	N	N	Y
9 Moakley	Y	Y	N	N	N	Y
10 Studds	Y	Y	N	N	N	Y
11 Donnelly	Y	Y	N	N	N	Y
MICHIGAN						
1 Conyers	Y	Y	N	Y	N	Y
2 ***Pursell***	N	N	N	Y	Y	Y
3 Wolpe	Y	Y	N	N	N	Y
4 ***Upton***	N	N	Y	Y	Y	N
5 ***Henry***	N	N	N	Y	N	Y
6 Carr	Y	Y	N	Y	N	Y
7 Kildee	Y	Y	N	N	N	Y
8 Traxler	Y	Y	?	Y	N	Y
9 ***Vander Jagt***	Y	N	Y	Y	Y	Y
10 ***Schuette***	N	N	Y	Y	Y	Y
11 ***Davis***	Y	N	Y	Y	Y	Y
12 Bonior	Y	Y	N	N	N	Y
13 Crockett	?	?	?	?	?	?
14 Hertel	Y	Y	N	N	N	Y
15 Ford	Y	Y	N	N	N	Y
16 Dingell	Y	Y	N	N	N	Y
17 Levin	Y	Y	N	Y	N	Y
18 ***Broomfield***	N	N	Y	Y	Y	Y
MINNESOTA						
1 Penny	Y	Y	Y	N	N	Y
2 ***Weber***	N	N	Y	Y	Y	N
3 ***Frenzel***	Y	N	Y	Y	Y	N
4 Vento	Y	Y	N	N	N	Y

	216	217	218	219	220	221
5 Sabo	Y	Y	N	N	N	Y
6 Sikorski	Y	Y	N	N	N	Y
7 ***Stangeland***	N	N	N	Y	N	Y
8 Oberstar	Y	Y	N	N	N	Y
MISSISSIPPI						
1 Whitten	Y	Y	N	N	N	Y
2 Espy	Y	Y	N	Y	N	Y
3 Montgomery	Y	Y	N	Y	N	Y
4 Parker	Y	Y	Y	Y	Y	Y
5 Taylor	Y	Y	N	N	N	Y
MISSOURI						
1 Clay	Y	Y	N	Y	N	Y
2 ***Buechner***	N	N	Y	Y	Y	Y
3 Gephardt	Y	Y	N	N	N	Y
4 Skelton	Y	Y	N	N	N	Y
5 Wheat	Y	Y	N	N	N	Y
6 ***Coleman***	N	N	Y	Y	Y	Y
7 ***Hancock***	N	N	Y	Y	Y	N
8 ***Emerson***	N	N	N	Y	Y	Y
9 Volkmer	Y	Y	N	N	N	Y
MONTANA						
1 Williams	Y	Y	N	N	N	Y
2 ***Marlenee***	N	N	Y	Y	Y	N
NEBRASKA						
1 ***Bereuter***	N	N	Y	Y	N	Y
2 Hoagland	Y	Y	N	N	N	Y
3 ***Smith***	N	N	Y	Y	Y	Y
NEVADA						
1 Bilbray	Y	Y	N	N	N	Y
2 ***Vucanovich***	N	N	Y	Y	Y	N
NEW HAMPSHIRE						
1 ***Smith***	N	N	Y	Y	Y	N
2 ***Douglas***	N	N	Y	Y	#	N
NEW JERSEY						
1 Vacancy						
2 Hughes	Y	Y	N	N	N	Y
3 Pallone	Y	Y	N	N	N	Y
4 ***Smith***	Y	N	N	Y	N	Y
5 ***Roukema***	Y	N	Y	Y	Y	Y
6 Dwyer	Y	Y	N	N	N	Y
7 ***Rinaldo***	Y	N	N	Y	N	Y
8 Roe	Y	Y	N	N	N	Y
9 Torricelli	Y	Y	N	N	N	Y
10 Payne	Y	Y	N	N	N	Y
11 ***Gallo***	N	N	Y	Y	Y	Y
12 ***Courter***	Y	N	Y	Y	Y	Y
13 ***Saxton***	N	N	Y	Y	Y	Y
14 Guarini	Y	Y	N	N	N	Y
NEW MEXICO						
1 ***Schiff***	N	N	Y	Y	N	Y
2 ***Skeen***	N	N	Y	Y	Y	N
3 Richardson	Y	Y	N	Y	N	Y
NEW YORK						
1 Hochbrueckner	Y	Y	N	N	N	Y
2 Downey	Y	Y	N	N	N	Y
3 Mrazek	Y	Y	N	N	N	Y
4 ***Lent***	N	N	Y	Y	Y	N
5 ***McGrath***	Y	N	Y	Y	Y	N
6 Flake	Y	Y	N	Y	N	Y
7 Ackerman	Y	Y	N	?	?	?
8 Scheuer	Y	Y	N	N	N	Y
9 Manton	Y	Y	N	N	N	Y
10 Schumer	Y	Y	N	N	N	Y
11 Towns	Y	Y	N	Y	N	Y
12 Owens	Y	Y	N	N	N	Y
13 Solarz	Y	Y	N	N	N	Y
14 ***Molinari***	N	N	Y	Y	Y	Y
15 ***Green***	N	N	Y	Y	Y	Y
16 Rangel	Y	Y	N	Y	N	Y
17 Weiss	Y	Y	N	Y	N	Y
18 Serrano	Y	Y	N	N	N	Y
19 Engel	Y	Y	N	N	N	Y
20 Lowey	Y	Y	N	N	N	Y
21 ***Fish***	N	N	Y	Y	Y	?
22 ***Gilman***	N	N	Y	Y	N	Y
23 McNulty	Y	Y	N	N	N	Y
24 ***Solomon***	N	N	Y	Y	Y	N
25 ***Boehlert***	N	N	Y	Y	Y	Y
26 ***Martin***	N	N	Y	Y	Y	Y
27 ***Walsh***	N	N	Y	Y	Y	Y
28 McHugh	N	Y	N	N	N	Y
29 ***Horton***	N	N	N	N	N	Y
30 Slaughter	Y	Y	N	Y	N	Y
31 ***Paxon***	N	N	Y	Y	Y	N

	216	217	218	219	220	221
32 LaFalce	Y	Y	N	N	N	Y
33 Nowak	Y	Y	N	N	N	Y
34 ***Houghton***	N	N	Y	Y	Y	N
NORTH CAROLINA						
1 Jones	Y	Y	N	N	N	Y
2 Valentine	Y	Y	N	N	N	Y
3 Lancaster	Y	Y	N	N	N	Y
4 Price	Y	Y	N	N	N	Y
5 Neal	Y	?	N	N	Y	N
6 ***Coble***	N	N	Y	Y	Y	N
7 Rose	Y	Y	N	Y	N	Y
8 Hefner	Y	Y	N	N	N	Y
9 ***McMillan***	N	N	N	Y	Y	N
10 ***Ballenger***	N	N	Y	Y	Y	N
11 Clarke	Y	Y	N	N	N	Y
NORTH DAKOTA						
AL Dorgan	Y	Y	N	Y	N	Y
OHIO						
1 Luken	Y	Y	N	N	N	Y
2 ***Gradison***	Y	N	Y	Y	Y	N
3 Hall	Y	Y	N	N	N	Y
4 ***Oxley***	N	N	Y	Y	Y	N
5 ***Gillmor***	N	N	N	Y	Y	N
6 ***McEwen***	Y	N	Y	Y	Y	N
7 ***DeWine***	N	N	Y	Y	Y	Y
8 ***Lukens***	?	X	?	?	?	?
9 Kaptur	Y	Y	N	N	N	Y
10 ***Miller***	N	N	Y	Y	Y	N
11 Eckart	Y	Y	N	N	N	Y
12 ***Kasich***	N	N	Y	Y	Y	N
13 Pease	Y	Y	N	Y	N	Y
14 Sawyer	Y	Y	N	N	N	Y
15 ***Wylie***	N	N	Y	Y	Y	N
16 ***Regula***	N	N	Y	Y	Y	N
17 Traficant	Y	Y	N	N	N	Y
18 Applegate	Y	Y	N	N	N	Y
19 Feighan	Y	Y	N	N	N	Y
20 Oakar	Y	Y	N	Y	N	Y
21 Stokes	Y	Y	N	N	N	Y
OKLAHOMA						
1 ***Inhofe***	N	N	Y	Y	Y	N
2 Synar	Y	Y	N	N	N	Y
3 Watkins	Y	Y	N	Y	N	Y
4 McCurdy	Y	Y	N	N	N	Y
5 ***Edwards***	N	N	N	?	?	?
6 English	N	Y	N	Y	N	Y
OREGON						
1 AuCoin	Y	Y	N	N	N	Y
2 ***Smith, B.***	N	N	Y	Y	Y	Y
3 Wyden	Y	Y	N	N	N	Y
4 DeFazio	Y	Y	N	N	N	Y
5 ***Smith, D.***	N	N	Y	Y	Y	N
PENNSYLVANIA						
1 Foglietta	Y	Y	N	N	N	Y
2 Gray	?	Y	N	N	N	Y
3 Borski	Y	Y	N	N	N	Y
4 Kolter	Y	Y	N	N	N	Y
5 ***Schulze***	Y	N	Y	Y	Y	Y
6 Yatron	Y	Y	N	Y	N	Y
7 ***Weldon***	N	N	Y	Y	Y	Y
8 Kostmayer	Y	Y	N	Y	N	Y
9 ***Shuster***	N	N	Y	Y	Y	N
10 ***McDade***	N	N	Y	Y	Y	Y
11 Kanjorski	Y	Y	N	Y	N	Y
12 Murtha	Y	Y	N	N	N	Y
13 ***Coughlin***	N	N	Y	Y	Y	Y
14 Coyne	Y	Y	N	N	N	Y
15 ***Ritter***	N	N	N	N	N	Y
16 ***Walker***	N	N	Y	Y	Y	N
17 ***Gekas***	N	N	Y	Y	Y	N
18 Walgren	Y	Y	N	N	N	Y
19 ***Goodling***	N	N	Y	Y	Y	Y
20 Gaydos	Y	Y	N	N	N	Y
21 ***Ridge***	N	N	Y	Y	N	Y
22 Murphy	Y	Y	N	Y	N	Y
23 ***Clinger***	N	N	N	Y	Y	Y
RHODE ISLAND						
1 ***Machtley***	N	N	Y	Y	Y	Y
2 ***Schneider***	N	N	Y	Y	Y	Y
SOUTH CAROLINA						
1 ***Ravenel***	N	N	N	Y	N	Y
2 ***Spence***	N	N	Y	Y	Y	Y
3 Derrick	Y	Y	N	N	N	?
4 Patterson	Y	Y	N	Y	N	Y
5 Spratt	Y	Y	N	N	N	?
6 Tallon	Y	Y	N	N	N	Y

	216	217	218	219	220	221
SOUTH DAKOTA						
AL Johnson	Y	Y	N	N	Y	Y
TENNESSEE						
1 ***Quillen***	N	N	Y	Y	Y	N
2 ***Duncan***	N	N	Y	Y	Y	N
3 Lloyd	Y	Y	N	N	N	Y
4 Cooper	Y	Y	N	N	N	Y
5 Clement	Y	Y	N	N	N	Y
6 Gordon	Y	Y	N	N	N	Y
7 ***Sundquist***	Y	N	Y	Y	Y	N
8 Tanner	Y	Y	N	N	N	Y
9 Ford	?	?	?	?	?	?
TEXAS						
1 Chapman	?	Y	N	N	N	Y
2 Wilson	Y	Y	N	N	N	Y
3 ***Bartlett***	N	N	Y	Y	Y	N
4 Hall	?	?	?	?	?	?
5 Bryant	Y	Y	N	Y	N	Y
6 ***Barton***	N	N	Y	Y	Y	N
7 ***Archer***	Y	N	Y	Y	Y	N
8 ***Fields***	N	N	Y	Y	Y	N
9 Brooks	Y	Y	N	N	N	Y
10 Pickle	Y	Y	N	N	N	Y
11 Leath	?	?	N	N	N	Y
12 Geren	Y	Y	Y	Y	N	Y
13 Sarpalius	Y	Y	N	Y	N	Y
14 Laughlin	Y	Y	N	N	N	Y
15 de la Garza	Y	Y	N	N	N	Y
16 Coleman	N	Y	N	N	N	Y
17 Stenholm	Y	Y	Y	Y	N	Y
18 Washington	Y	Y	?	?	N	Y
19 ***Combest***	N	N	Y	Y	Y	N
20 Gonzalez	Y	Y	N	N	N	Y
21 ***Smith***	N	N	Y	Y	Y	Y
22 ***DeLay***	N	N	Y	Y	Y	N
23 Bustamante	Y	Y	N	Y	N	Y
24 Frost	Y	Y	N	N	N	Y
25 Andrews	Y	Y	N	N	N	Y
26 ***Armey***	N	N	Y	Y	Y	N
27 Ortiz	Y	Y	N	N	N	Y
UTAH						
1 ***Hansen***	N	N	Y	Y	Y	N
2 Owens	Y	Y	N	Y	N	Y
3 ***Nielson***	N	N	Y	Y	Y	N
VERMONT						
AL ***Smith***	N	N	Y	Y	Y	Y
VIRGINIA						
1 ***Bateman***	N	N	Y	Y	Y	Y
2 Pickett	Y	Y	N	N	N	Y
3 ***Bliley***	N	N	Y	Y	Y	N
4 Sisisky	Y	Y	N	Y	N	Y
5 Payne	Y	Y	N	Y	N	Y
6 Olin	Y	Y	N	Y	Y	N
7 ***Slaughter***	N	N	Y	Y	Y	N
8 ***Parris***	Y	N	Y	Y	Y	Y
9 Boucher	Y	Y	N	N	N	Y
10 ***Wolf***	N	N	N	Y	N	Y
WASHINGTON						
1 ***Miller***	N	N	Y	Y	Y	Y
2 Swift	Y	Y	N	N	N	Y
3 Unsoeld	Y	Y	N	N	N	Y
4 ***Morrison***	N	N	Y	Y	Y	Y
5 Foley						
6 Dicks	Y	Y	N	N	N	Y
7 McDermott	Y	Y	N	N	N	Y
8 ***Chandler***	Y	N	Y	Y	Y	Y
WEST VIRGINIA						
1 Mollohan	Y	Y	N	N	N	Y
2 Staggers	Y	Y	N	N	N	Y
3 Wise	Y	Y	N	N	N	Y
4 Rahall	Y	Y	N	N	N	Y
WISCONSIN						
1 Aspin	Y	Y	N	N	N	Y
2 Kastenmeier	Y	Y	N	N	N	Y
3 ***Gunderson***	N	N	Y	Y	Y	N
4 Kleczka	Y	Y	N	N	N	Y
5 Moody	Y	Y	N	N	N	Y
6 ***Petri***	N	N	Y	Y	Y	N
7 Obey	N	Y	?	Y	N	Y
8 ***Roth***	N	N	Y	Y	Y	N
9 ***Sensenbrenner***	N	N	Y	Y	Y	N
WYOMING						
AL ***Thomas***	N	N	Y	Y	Y	N

Southern states - Ala., Ark., Fla., Ga., Ky., La., Miss., N.C., Okla., S.C., Tenn., Texas, Va.
Omitted votes are quorum calls, which CQ does not include in its vote charts.

HOUSE VOTES 222, 223, 224, 225, 226, 227, 228

222. HR 5115. Equity and Excellence in Education/Rule. Adoption of the rule (H Res 430) to provide for House floor consideration of the bill to authorize $5.3 billion in fiscal 1991-95 for a series of new educational initiatives. Adopted 267-151: R 25-150; D 242-1 (ND 166-1, SD 76-0), July 12, 1990.

223. HR 5229. Fiscal 1991 Transportation Appropriations/License Suspension. Solomon, R-N.Y., amendment to require that federal highway grants to individual states be reduced by 2 percent annually unless the state suspends the driver's licenses of people convicted of selling or using drugs. Adopted 331-88: R 160-13; D 171-75 (ND 112-57, SD 59-18), July 12, 1990.

224. HR 5229. Fiscal 1991 Transportation Appropriations/Discretionary Accounts. Penny, D-Minn., amendment to provide an across-the-board 2 percent cut in all discretionary accounts in the bill. Rejected 133-283: R 112-62; D 21-221 (ND 11-154, SD 10-67), July 12, 1990.

225. HR 5229. Fiscal 1991 Transportation Appropriations/Passage. Passage of the bill to appropriate $13.1 billion in fiscal 1991 for the Department of Transportation and related agencies, $1.2 billion more than requested by the administration. Passed 385-31: R 142-31; D 243-0 (ND 167-0, SD 76-0), July 12, 1990.

226. S 933. Americans with Disabilities Act/Rule. Adoption of the rule (H Res 427) to provide for House floor consideration of and waive certain points of order against the conference report on the bill to prohibit discrimination against the disabled in public facilities and employment and to guarantee them access to mass transit and telecommunications services. Adopted 355-58: R 115-56; D 240-2 (ND 166-1, SD 74-1), July 12, 1990.

227. S 933. Americans with Disabilities Act/Recommittal Motion. Dannemeyer, R-Calif., motion to recommit to the conference committee the conference report on the bill to prohibit discrimination against the disabled in public facilities and employment and to guarantee them access to mass transit and telecommunications services, with instructions to report it back with the Chapman, D-Texas, amendment to allow employers to move an employee with a communicable disease out of a food-handling position, provided the employer offers an alternative position in which the employee would sustain no economic damage. Motion rejected 180-224: R 124-42; D 56-182 (ND 16-146, SD 40-36), July 12, 1990.

228. S 933. Americans with Disabilities Act/Conference Report. Adoption of the conference report on the bill to prohibit discrimination against the disabled in public facilities and employment and to guarantee them access to mass transit and telecommunications services. Adopted 377-28: R 145-23; D 232-5 (ND 161-0, SD 71-5), July 12, 1990. A "yea" was a vote supporting the president's position.

KEY

Y Voted for (yea).
Paired for.
\+ Announced for.
N Voted against (nay).
X Paired against.
\- Announced against.
P Voted "present."
C Voted "present" to avoid possible conflict of interest.
? Did not vote or otherwise make a position known.

Democrats ***Republicans***

	222	223	224	225	226	227	228
ALABAMA							
1 ***Callahan***	N	Y	N	Y	Y	Y	Y
2 ***Dickinson***	N	Y	N	Y	Y	Y	Y
3 Browder	Y	Y	N	Y	Y	Y	Y
4 Bevill	Y	N	N	Y	Y	Y	Y
5 Flippo	Y	Y	N	Y	Y	Y	Y
6 Erdreich	Y	Y	N	Y	Y	Y	Y
7 Harris	Y	Y	N	Y	Y	Y	Y
ALASKA							
AL ***Young***	Y	Y	N	Y	Y	Y	Y
ARIZONA							
1 ***Rhodes***	N	Y	Y	N	Y	Y	Y
2 Udall	Y	N	N	Y	Y	N	Y
3 ***Stump***	N	Y	Y	N	N	Y	N
4 ***Kyl***	N	Y	Y	N	N	Y	Y
5 ***Kolbe***	N	N	Y	N	Y	Y	Y
ARKANSAS							
1 Alexander	Y	N	N	Y	N	Y	Y
2 ***Robinson***	N	Y	Y	Y	Y	?	?
3 ***Hammerschmidt***	N	Y	Y	Y	N	Y	Y
4 Anthony	Y	Y	N	Y	Y	N	Y
CALIFORNIA							
1 Bosco	Y	N	N	Y	Y	N	Y
2 ***Herger***	N	Y	Y	N	N	Y	N
3 Matsui	Y	N	N	Y	Y	N	Y
4 Fazio	Y	Y	N	Y	Y	N	Y
5 Pelosi	Y	Y	N	Y	Y	N	Y
6 Boxer	Y	Y	N	Y	Y	N	Y
7 Miller	Y	Y	N	Y	Y	N	Y
8 Dellums	Y	N	N	Y	Y	N	Y
9 Stark	Y	N	N	Y	Y	N	Y
10 Edwards	Y	N	N	Y	Y	N	Y
11 Lantos	Y	Y	N	Y	Y	N	Y
12 ***Campbell***	N	N	Y	Y	Y	N	Y
13 Mineta	Y	N	N	Y	Y	N	Y
14 ***Shumway***	N	Y	Y	N	N	Y	N
15 Condit	Y	Y	Y	Y	Y	N	Y
16 Panetta	Y	Y	?	Y	Y	N	Y
17 ***Pashayan***	N	Y	Y	Y	Y	Y	Y
18 Lehman	Y	Y	N	Y	Y	N	Y
19 ***Lagomarsino***	N	Y	Y	Y	Y	Y	Y
20 ***Thomas***	N	Y	Y	Y	N	Y	Y
21 ***Gallegly***	N	Y	Y	Y	Y	Y	Y
22 ***Moorhead***	N	Y	Y	Y	Y	Y	Y
23 Beilenson	Y	N	N	Y	Y	N	Y
24 Waxman	Y	N	N	Y	Y	N	Y
25 Roybal	Y	N	N	Y	Y	N	Y
26 Berman	Y	N	N	Y	Y	N	Y
27 Levine	Y	Y	N	Y	Y	N	Y
28 Dixon	Y	Y	N	Y	Y	N	Y
29 Hawkins	Y	N	N	Y	Y	N	Y
30 Martinez	?	?	?	?	?	?	?
31 Dymally	Y	N	N	Y	Y	N	Y
32 Anderson	Y	N	N	Y	Y	N	Y
33 ***Dreier***	N	Y	Y	Y	Y	Y	Y
34 Torres	Y	Y	N	+	Y	N	Y
35 ***Lewis***	N	Y	N	Y	N	Y	N
36 Brown	Y	Y	N	Y	Y	N	Y
37 ***McCandless***	N	Y	N	Y	Y	Y	Y
38 ***Dornan***	N	Y	Y	Y	N	Y	Y
39 ***Dannemeyer***	N	Y	Y	N	N	Y	N
40 ***Cox***	N	Y	Y	Y	N	Y	Y
41 ***Lowery***	N	Y	N	Y	Y	?	Y
42 ***Rohrabacher***	N	Y	Y	Y	N	Y	Y
43 ***Packard***	N	Y	Y	Y	N	Y	N
44 Bates	Y	N	Y	Y	Y	N	Y
45 ***Hunter***	N	Y	Y	Y	N	Y	Y
COLORADO							
1 Schroeder	Y	Y	Y	Y	Y	N	Y
2 Skaggs	Y	N	N	Y	Y	N	Y
3 Campbell	Y	Y	Y	Y	N	N	Y
4 ***Brown***	N	Y	Y	Y	N	Y	Y
5 ***Hefley***	N	N	Y	Y	N	Y	Y
6 ***Schaefer***	N	Y	Y	Y	Y	Y	Y
CONNECTICUT							
1 Kennelly	Y	Y	N	Y	Y	N	Y
2 Gejdenson	Y	Y	N	Y	Y	N	Y
3 Morrison	+	+	−	+	+	−	+
4 ***Shays***	Y	Y	Y	Y	Y	N	Y
5 ***Rowland***	Y	Y	N	Y	Y	N	Y
6 ***Johnson***	N	Y	Y	N	Y	N	Y
DELAWARE							
AL Carper	Y	Y	N	Y	Y	N	Y
FLORIDA							
1 Hutto	Y	Y	Y	Y	Y	Y	Y
2 ***Grant***	N	Y	N	Y	Y	Y	Y
3 Bennett	Y	Y	N	Y	Y	N	Y
4 ***James***	N	Y	N	Y	N	Y	Y
5 ***McCollum***	N	Y	N	Y	N	Y	Y
6 ***Stearns***	N	Y	Y	Y	N	Y	Y
7 Gibbons	Y	Y	N	Y	Y	N	Y
8 ***Young***	N	Y	N	Y	N	Y	Y
9 ***Bilirakis***	Y	Y	N	Y	Y	Y	Y
10 ***Ireland***	N	Y	N	Y	N	Y	Y
11 Nelson	+	+	-	+	+	+	+
12 ***Lewis***	N	Y	N	Y	N	Y	Y
13 ***Goss***	N	Y	N	Y	N	N	Y
14 Johnston	Y	Y	N	Y	Y	N	Y
15 ***Shaw***	N	Y	N	Y	N	Y	Y
16 Smith	Y	Y	N	Y	Y	N	Y
17 Lehman	Y	N	N	Y	Y	N	Y
18 ***Ros-Lehtinen***	N	Y	N	Y	Y	Y	Y
19 Fascell	Y	Y	N	Y	Y	N	Y
GEORGIA							
1 Thomas	Y	Y	N	Y	Y	Y	Y
2 Hatcher	?	?	?	?	?	?	?
3 Ray	Y	Y	N	Y	Y	N	Y
4 Jones	Y	+	X	+	+	−	+
5 Lewis	Y	N	N	Y	Y	N	Y
6 ***Gingrich***	N	Y	Y	N	N	Y	Y
7 Darden	Y	Y	N	Y	Y	Y	Y
8 Rowland	Y	Y	N	Y	Y	N	Y
9 Jenkins	?	?	?	?	?	?	?
10 Barnard	?	Y	N	Y	Y	Y	Y
HAWAII							
1 ***Saiki***	Y	Y	N	Y	Y	N	Y
2 Vacancy							
IDAHO							
1 ***Craig***	N	Y	Y	Y	Y	Y	Y
2 Stallings	Y	Y	N	Y	Y	Y	Y
ILLINOIS							
1 Hayes	Y	N	N	Y	Y	N	Y
2 Savage	?	N	N	Y	Y	N	Y
3 Russo	Y	Y	N	Y	Y	N	Y
4 Sangmeister	Y	Y	N	Y	Y	N	Y
5 Lipinski	Y	N	N	Y	Y	Y	Y
6 ***Hyde***	N	Y	Y	Y	N	Y	Y
7 Collins	Y	N	N	Y	Y	N	Y
8 Rostenkowski	Y	Y	?	Y	Y	N	Y
9 Yates	Y	N	N	Y	Y	N	Y
10 ***Porter***	N	Y	Y	Y	N	Y	Y
11 Annunzio	Y	Y	N	Y	Y	N	Y
12 ***Crane***	N	Y	Y	N	N	Y	N
13 ***Fawell***	N	Y	Y	N	N	N	Y
14 ***Hastert***	N	Y	Y	Y	N	Y	N
15 ***Madigan***	N	Y	N	Y	Y	N	Y
16 ***Martin***	N	Y	Y	Y	Y	Y	Y
17 Evans	Y	Y	N	Y	Y	N	Y
18 ***Michel***	N	Y	Y	N	Y	Y	Y
19 Bruce	Y	Y	N	Y	Y	N	Y
20 Durbin	Y	Y	N	Y	Y	N	Y
21 Costello	Y	Y	N	Y	Y	N	Y
22 Poshard	Y	Y	N	Y	Y	N	Y
INDIANA							
1 Visclosky	Y	N	N	Y	Y	N	Y
2 Sharp	Y	Y	N	Y	Y	N	Y
3 ***Hiler***	N	Y	Y	Y	Y	Y	Y

ND Northern Democrats SD Southern Democrats

	222	223	224	225	226	227	228
4 Long	Y	Y	N	Y	Y	N	Y
5 Jontz	Y	N	N	Y	Y	N	Y
6 **Burton**	N	Y	Y	N	N	Y	N
7 **Myers**	Y	Y	N	Y	Y	Y	Y
8 McCloskey	Y	Y	N	Y	Y	N	Y
9 Hamilton	Y	Y	Y	Y	Y	N	Y
10 Jacobs	N	Y	Y	Y	Y	N	Y
IOWA							
1 **Leach**	N	Y	Y	Y	Y	N	Y
2 **Tauke**	N	Y	Y	Y	Y	Y	Y
3 Nagle	Y	N	N	Y	Y	N	Y
4 Smith	Y	N	N	Y	Y	N	Y
5 **Lightfoot**	N	Y	N	Y	Y	Y	N
6 **Grandy**	N	Y	Y	Y	Y	N	Y
KANSAS							
1 **Roberts**	N	Y	Y	N	N	N	Y
2 Slattery	Y	Y	Y	Y	Y	N	Y
3 **Meyers**	N	Y	Y	Y	N	Y	Y
4 Glickman	Y	Y	N	Y	Y	N	Y
5 **Whittaker**	Y	Y	N	Y	Y	N	Y
KENTUCKY							
1 Hubbard	Y	Y	Y	Y	Y	Y	Y
2 Natcher	Y	N	N	Y	Y	N	Y
3 Mazzoli	Y	Y	N	Y	Y	N	Y
4 **Bunning**	N	Y	Y	Y	N	Y	Y
5 **Rogers**	N	Y	N	Y	Y	Y	Y
6 **Hopkins**	N	Y	Y	?	Y	Y	Y
7 Perkins	Y	N	N	Y	Y	N	Y
LOUISIANA							
1 **Livingston**	N	Y	N	Y	N	Y	Y
2 Boggs	Y	Y	N	Y	Y	N	Y
3 Tauzin	Y	Y	N	Y	Y	Y	Y
4 **McCrery**	N	Y	Y	Y	Y	N	Y
5 Huckaby	Y	Y	Y	Y	?	?	?
6 **Baker**	N	Y	Y	Y	Y	Y	Y
7 Hayes	Y	Y	N	Y	Y	Y	Y
8 **Holloway**	N	Y	Y	Y	N	Y	N
MAINE							
1 Brennan	Y	Y	N	Y	Y	N	Y
2 **Snowe**	Y	Y	Y	Y	Y	N	Y
MARYLAND							
1 Dyson	Y	Y	N	Y	Y	N	Y
2 **Bentley**	N	Y	N	Y	N	Y	Y
3 Cardin	Y	N	N	Y	Y	N	Y
4 McMillen	Y	Y	N	Y	Y	N	Y
5 Hoyer	Y	N	N	Y	Y	N	Y
6 Byron	Y	Y	N	Y	Y	N	Y
7 Mfume	Y	N	N	Y	Y	N	Y
8 **Morella**	Y	Y	N	Y	Y	N	Y
MASSACHUSETTS							
1 **Conte**	Y	Y	N	Y	Y	N	Y
2 Neal	Y	Y	N	Y	Y	N	Y
3 Early	Y	Y	N	Y	Y	Y	Y
4 Frank	Y	N	N	Y	Y	N	Y
5 Atkins	Y	Y	N	Y	Y	N	Y
6 Mavroules	?	Y	N	Y	Y	N	Y
7 Markey	Y	N	N	Y	Y	N	Y
8 Kennedy	Y	Y	N	Y	Y	N	Y
9 Moakley	Y	Y	N	Y	Y	N	Y
10 Studds	Y	Y	N	Y	Y	N	Y
11 Donnelly	Y	Y	N	Y	Y	Y	Y
MICHIGAN							
1 Conyers	Y	Y	N	Y	Y	N	Y
2 **Pursell**	N	Y	N	Y	Y	?	?
3 Wolpe	Y	Y	N	Y	Y	N	Y
4 **Upton**	N	Y	N	Y	N	Y	Y
5 **Henry**	N	Y	Y	N	Y	N	Y
6 Carr	Y	Y	N	Y	Y	N	Y
7 Kildee	Y	N	N	Y	Y	N	Y
8 Traxler	Y	Y	N	Y	Y	?	?
9 **Vander Jagt**	N	Y	Y	Y	Y	Y	Y
10 **Schuette**	N	?	?	?	?	?	?
11 **Davis**	Y	Y	N	Y	Y	Y	Y
12 Bonior	Y	Y	N	Y	Y	N	Y
13 Crockett	?	?	?	?	?	?	?
14 Hertel	Y	Y	N	Y	Y	N	Y
15 Ford	Y	N	N	Y	?	?	?
16 Dingell	Y	Y	N	Y	Y	N	Y
17 Levin	Y	N	N	Y	Y	N	Y
18 **Broomfield**	Y	Y	N	Y	Y	Y	Y
MINNESOTA							
1 Penny	Y	Y	Y	Y	Y	N	Y
2 **Weber**	N	Y	Y	Y	Y	Y	Y
3 **Frenzel**	N	Y	Y	N	Y	?	Y
4 Vento	Y	Y	N	Y	Y	N	Y
5 Sabo	Y	N	N	Y	Y	N	Y
6 Sikorski	Y	Y	N	Y	Y	?	?
7 **Stangeland**	Y	Y	N	Y	Y	Y	Y
8 Oberstar	Y	N	N	Y	Y	N	Y
MISSISSIPPI							
1 Whitten	Y	N	N	Y	Y	N	Y
2 Espy	Y	Y	N	Y	Y	N	Y
3 Montgomery	Y	Y	N	Y	Y	Y	Y
4 Parker	Y	Y	Y	Y	Y	Y	N
5 Taylor	Y	Y	N	Y	Y	Y	Y
MISSOURI							
1 Clay	Y	N	N	Y	Y	N	Y
2 **Buechner**	N	Y	Y	Y	Y	N	Y
3 Gephardt	Y	N	?	Y	Y	N	Y
4 Skelton	Y	Y	N	Y	Y	Y	Y
5 Wheat	Y	N	N	Y	Y	N	Y
6 **Coleman**	N	Y	N	Y	Y	Y	Y
7 **Hancock**	N	Y	Y	N	N	Y	N
8 **Emerson**	N	Y	N	Y	N	Y	Y
9 Volkmer	Y	Y	N	Y	Y	Y	Y
MONTANA							
1 Williams	Y	N	N	?	Y	N	Y
2 **Marlenee**	N	Y	N	Y	N	Y	N
NEBRASKA							
1 **Bereuter**	Y	Y	N	Y	Y	Y	Y
2 Hoagland	Y	Y	N	Y	Y	Y	Y
3 **Smith**	N	Y	N	Y	Y	Y	Y
NEVADA							
1 Bilbray	Y	Y	N	Y	Y	N	Y
2 **Vucanovich**	N	Y	Y	Y	Y	Y	Y
NEW HAMPSHIRE							
1 **Smith**	N	Y	Y	N	N	Y	Y
2 **Douglas**	N	Y	Y	Y	N	Y	Y
NEW JERSEY							
1 Vacancy							
2 Hughes	Y	Y	N	Y	Y	N	Y
3 Pallone	Y	Y	N	Y	Y	N	Y
4 **Smith**	N	Y	Y	Y	Y	N	Y
5 **Roukema**	Y	Y	N	Y	Y	Y	Y
6 Dwyer	Y	Y	N	Y	Y	N	Y
7 **Rinaldo**	Y	Y	N	Y	Y	N	Y
8 Roe	Y	Y	N	Y	Y	N	Y
9 Torricelli	Y	?	?	?	?	?	?
10 Payne	Y	N	N	Y	Y	N	Y
11 **Gallo**	N	Y	N	Y	Y	N	Y
12 **Courter**	N	Y	N	Y	Y	Y	Y
13 **Saxton**	N	Y	Y	Y	Y	N	Y
14 Guarini	Y	Y	N	Y	Y	N	+
NEW MEXICO							
1 **Schiff**	N	Y	N	Y	Y	N	Y
2 **Skeen**	N	Y	N	Y	Y	Y	Y
3 Richardson	Y	Y	N	Y	Y	N	Y
NEW YORK							
1 Hochbrueckner	Y	Y	N	Y	Y	N	Y
2 Downey	Y	Y	N	Y	Y	N	Y
3 Mrazek	Y	Y	N	Y	Y	N	Y
4 **Lent**	N	Y	Y	Y	Y	Y	Y
5 **McGrath**	N	Y	Y	Y	Y	N	Y
6 Flake	Y	Y	?	Y	Y	?	?
7 Ackerman	Y	N	N	Y	Y	N	Y
8 Scheuer	Y	N	N	Y	Y	?	?
9 Manton	Y	Y	N	Y	Y	N	Y
10 Schumer	Y	Y	N	Y	Y	?	?
11 Towns	Y	N	N	Y	Y	N	Y
12 Owens	Y	N	N	Y	Y	N	Y
13 Solarz	Y	Y	N	Y	Y	N	Y
14 **Molinari**	N	Y	Y	Y	Y	N	Y
15 **Green**	N	Y	N	Y	Y	N	Y
16 Rangel	Y	Y	N	Y	?	N	Y
17 Weiss	Y	N	N	Y	Y	N	Y
18 Serrano	Y	Y	N	Y	Y	N	Y
19 Engel	Y	Y	N	Y	Y	N	Y
20 Lowey	Y	Y	N	Y	Y	N	Y
21 **Fish**	N	Y	N	Y	Y	N	Y
22 **Gilman**	Y	Y	N	Y	Y	N	Y
23 McNulty	Y	Y	N	Y	Y	N	Y
24 **Solomon**	N	Y	Y	Y	Y	Y	Y
25 **Boehlert**	Y	Y	Y	Y	Y	N	Y
26 **Martin**	N	Y	N	Y	Y	N	Y
27 **Walsh**	N	Y	Y	Y	Y	N	Y
28 McHugh	Y	Y	N	Y	Y	N	Y
29 **Horton**	Y	N	N	Y	Y	N	Y
30 Slaughter	Y	Y	N	Y	Y	N	Y
31 **Paxon**	N	Y	Y	Y	Y	Y	Y
32 LaFalce	Y	Y	N	Y	Y	N	Y
33 Nowak	Y	Y	N	Y	Y	N	Y
34 **Houghton**	N	Y	Y	Y	Y	N	Y
NORTH CAROLINA							
1 Jones	Y	Y	N	Y	Y	N	Y
2 Valentine	Y	Y	N	Y	Y	Y	Y
3 Lancaster	Y	N	N	Y	Y	Y	Y
4 Price	Y	Y	N	Y	Y	N	Y
5 Neal	Y	Y	Y	Y	Y	Y	Y
6 **Coble**	N	Y	Y	Y	Y	Y	Y
7 Rose	Y	Y	N	Y	Y	Y	Y
8 Hefner	Y	Y	N	Y	Y	Y	Y
9 **McMillan**	N	Y	Y	Y	Y	Y	Y
10 **Ballenger**	N	Y	Y	Y	N	Y	Y
11 Clarke	Y	Y	Y	Y	Y	N	Y
NORTH DAKOTA							
AL Dorgan	Y	Y	N	Y	Y	Y	Y
OHIO							
1 Luken	Y	Y	N	Y	Y	N	Y
2 **Gradison**	N	Y	Y	N	Y	N	Y
3 Hall	Y	Y	Y	Y	Y	Y	Y
4 **Oxley**	N	Y	Y	Y	Y	Y	Y
5 **Gillmor**	Y	N	Y	Y	Y	Y	Y
6 **McEwen**	N	Y	Y	Y	Y	Y	N
7 **DeWine**	N	Y	Y	Y	Y	Y	Y
8 **Lukens**	?	?	#	?	?	?	?
9 Kaptur	Y	Y	N	Y	Y	N	Y
10 **Miller**	N	Y	Y	Y	Y	Y	N
11 Eckart	Y	Y	N	Y	Y	N	Y
12 **Kasich**	N	Y	Y	Y	N	Y	Y
13 Pease	Y	Y	N	Y	Y	N	Y
14 Sawyer	Y	Y	N	Y	Y	N	Y
15 **Wylie**	N	Y	Y	Y	Y	Y	Y
16 **Regula**	N	Y	Y	Y	Y	Y	Y
17 Traficant	Y	Y	N	Y	Y	N	Y
18 Applegate	Y	Y	N	Y	Y	Y	Y
19 Feighan	Y	Y	N	Y	Y	N	Y
20 Oakar	Y	Y	N	Y	Y	N	Y
21 Stokes	Y	N	N	Y	Y	N	Y
OKLAHOMA							
1 **Inhofe**	N	Y	Y	Y	Y	Y	Y
2 Synar	Y	N	N	Y	Y	N	Y
3 Watkins	Y	Y	N	Y	Y	Y	Y
4 McCurdy	Y	Y	N	Y	Y	Y	Y
5 **Edwards**	N	?	Y	N	Y	Y	N
6 English	Y	Y	N	Y	Y	Y	Y
OREGON							
1 AuCoin	Y	Y	N	Y	Y	N	Y
2 **Smith, B.**	N	Y	Y	Y	Y	Y	Y
3 Wyden	Y	Y	N	Y	Y	N	Y
4 DeFazio	Y	Y	N	Y	Y	N	Y
5 **Smith, D.**	N	Y	Y	Y	N	Y	Y
PENNSYLVANIA							
1 Foglietta	Y	Y	N	Y	Y	N	Y
2 Gray	Y	Y	N	Y	Y	?	?
3 Borski	Y	N	N	Y	Y	N	Y
4 Kolter	Y	N	N	Y	Y	N	Y
5 **Schulze**	N	Y	Y	Y	N	Y	Y
6 Yatron	Y	Y	N	Y	Y	Y	Y
7 **Weldon**	N	Y	Y	Y	Y	Y	Y
8 Kostmayer	Y	Y	N	Y	Y	N	Y
9 **Shuster**	N	N	N	Y	N	Y	N
10 **McDade**	N	Y	N	Y	?	?	?
11 Kanjorski	Y	Y	N	Y	Y	N	Y
12 Murtha	Y	N	N	Y	Y	Y	Y
13 **Coughlin**	N	Y	N	Y	Y	N	Y
14 Coyne	Y	Y	N	Y	Y	N	Y
15 **Ritter**	N	Y	Y	Y	N	Y	Y
16 **Walker**	N	Y	Y	N	N	Y	Y
17 **Gekas**	N	Y	Y	N	N	Y	Y
18 Walgren	Y	Y	Y	Y	Y	Y	Y
19 **Goodling**	N	Y	Y	Y	Y	?	?
20 Gaydos	Y	Y	N	Y	Y	Y	Y
21 **Ridge**	N	Y	Y	Y	Y	Y	Y
22 Murphy	Y	N	N	Y	Y	Y	Y
23 **Clinger**	Y	Y	N	Y	Y	N	Y
RHODE ISLAND							
1 **Machtley**	Y	Y	N	Y	Y	N	Y
2 **Schneider**	Y	Y	N	Y	Y	N	Y
SOUTH CAROLINA							
1 **Ravenel**	Y	Y	N	Y	Y	N	Y
2 **Spence**	N	Y	Y	Y	Y	Y	Y
3 Derrick	Y	Y	N	Y	Y	N	Y
4 Patterson	Y	Y	Y	Y	Y	N	Y
5 Spratt	Y	Y	N	Y	Y	N	Y
6 Tallon	Y	Y	N	Y	Y	Y	Y
SOUTH DAKOTA							
AL Johnson	Y	Y	N	Y	Y	Y	Y
TENNESSEE							
1 **Quillen**	Y	N	N	Y	Y	Y	Y
2 **Duncan**	N	Y	Y	N	Y	Y	Y
3 Lloyd	Y	Y	N	Y	Y	Y	Y
4 Cooper	Y	Y	Y	Y	Y	Y	N
5 Clement	Y	Y	N	?	Y	Y	Y
6 Gordon	Y	Y	N	Y	Y	N	Y
7 **Sundquist**	N	Y	Y	Y	?	Y	Y
8 Tanner	Y	Y	N	Y	Y	Y	Y
9 Ford	?	?	?	?	?	?	?
TEXAS							
1 Chapman	Y	Y	N	Y	Y	Y	N
2 Wilson	Y	Y	N	Y	Y	Y	Y
3 **Bartlett**	N	Y	Y	Y	Y	Y	Y
4 Hall	?	?	?	?	?	?	?
5 Bryant	Y	Y	N	Y	Y	N	Y
6 **Barton**	N	Y	Y	N	N	Y	N
7 **Archer**	N	Y	Y	N	N	Y	N
8 **Fields**	N	Y	Y	Y	N	Y	Y
9 Brooks	Y	Y	N	Y	Y	N	Y
10 Pickle	Y	Y	N	Y	Y	N	Y
11 Leath	Y	N	N	Y	Y	Y	Y
12 Geren	Y	N	Y	Y	Y	Y	Y
13 Sarpalius	Y	Y	N	Y	Y	Y	Y
14 Laughlin	Y	N	N	Y	Y	Y	Y
15 de la Garza	Y	Y	N	Y	?	N	Y
16 Coleman	Y	Y	N	Y	Y	N	Y
17 Stenholm	Y	Y	Y	Y	Y	Y	N
18 Washington	?	N	N	Y	Y	N	Y
19 **Combest**	N	Y	Y	Y	Y	Y	Y
20 Gonzalez	Y	N	N	Y	Y	N	Y
21 **Smith**	N	Y	Y	Y	?	?	?
22 **DeLay**	N	N	N	Y	N	Y	N
23 Bustamante	Y	Y	N	Y	Y	N	Y
24 Frost	Y	N	N	Y	Y	N	Y
25 Andrews	Y	Y	N	Y	Y	N	Y
26 **Armey**	N	Y	Y	N	N	Y	N
27 Ortiz	Y	Y	N	Y	Y	N	Y
UTAH							
1 **Hansen**	N	Y	Y	N	Y	Y	Y
2 Owens	Y	Y	N	Y	Y	N	Y
3 **Nielson**	N	Y	Y	N	Y	Y	N
VERMONT							
AL **Smith**	N	N	Y	N	Y	Y	Y
VIRGINIA							
1 **Bateman**	N	Y	Y	Y	N	Y	N
2 Pickett	Y	N	N	Y	Y	Y	Y
3 **Bliley**	N	Y	Y	Y	Y	Y	Y
4 Sisisky	Y	Y	N	Y	Y	Y	Y
5 Payne	Y	N	N	Y	Y	Y	Y
6 Olin	Y	N	N	Y	Y	Y	N
7 **Slaughter**	N	Y	Y	Y	Y	Y	Y
8 **Parris**	N	Y	N	Y	Y	Y	Y
9 Boucher	Y	Y	N	Y	Y	N	Y
10 **Wolf**	N	Y	N	Y	Y	Y	Y
WASHINGTON							
1 **Miller**	N	Y	N	Y	Y	N	Y
2 Swift	Y	N	N	Y	Y	N	Y
3 Unsoeld	Y	N	N	Y	Y	N	Y
4 **Morrison**	N	N	N	Y	Y	N	Y
5 Foley							
6 Dicks	Y	Y	N	Y	Y	N	Y
7 McDermott	Y	N	N	Y	Y	N	Y
8 **Chandler**	N	Y	Y	Y	Y	?	?
WEST VIRGINIA							
1 Mollohan	Y	N	N	Y	Y	N	Y
2 Staggers	Y	Y	N	Y	Y	N	Y
3 Wise	Y	Y	N	Y	Y	N	Y
4 Rahall	Y	Y	N	Y	Y	N	Y
WISCONSIN							
1 Aspin	Y	Y	N	Y	Y	N	Y
2 Kastenmeier	Y	N	N	Y	Y	N	Y
3 **Gunderson**	N	N	Y	Y	Y	N	Y
4 Kleczka	Y	N	N	Y	Y	N	Y
5 Moody	?	Y	Y	Y	Y	N	Y
6 **Petri**	N	N	Y	Y	Y	Y	Y
7 Obey	Y	N	N	Y	Y	N	Y
8 **Roth**	N	Y	N	Y	Y	Y	Y
9 **Sensenbrenner**	N	Y	Y	N	Y	Y	Y
WYOMING							
AL **Thomas**	N	N	Y	N	Y	Y	Y

Southern states - Ala., Ark., Fla., Ga., Ky., La., Miss., N.C., Okla., S.C., Tenn., Texas, Va.
Omitted votes are quorum calls, which CQ does not include in its vote charts.

HOUSE VOTES 229, 230, 231, 232, 233, 234, 235, 236

229. HR 5241. Fiscal 1991 Treasury-Postal Appropriations/Presidential Pensions. Skeen, R-N.M., amendment to the Jacobs, D-Ind., amendment, to reduce appropriations for pensions and allowances for former presidents from $2 million to $1.8 million. The Jacobs amendment would have reduced the appropriations from $2 million to $449,200. Adopted 300-91: R 139-25; D 161-66 (ND 98-58, SD 63-8), July 13, 1990.

230. HR 5241. Fiscal 1991 Treasury-Postal Appropriations/Presidential Pensions. Jacobs, D-Ind., amendment to reduce the bill's appropriation for pensions and allowances for former presidents from $2 million to $1.8 million. The amendment would leave each of the four living former presidents with a pension of $107,300 and Mrs. Lyndon B. Johnson with a pension of $20,000. Adopted 379-7: R 156-3; D 223-4 (ND 152-4, SD 71-0), July 13, 1990.

231. HR 5241. Fiscal 1991 Treasury-Postal Appropriations/Across-the-Board Cuts. Frenzel, R-Minn., amendment to provide for an across-the-board 6.9 percent cut in all discretionary accounts except for the Internal Revenue Service which would reduce the amountsto fiscla 1990 levels. Rejected 130-254: R 103-58; D 27-196 (ND 14-140, SD 13-56), July 13, 1990.

232. HR 5241. Fiscal 1991 Treasury-Postal Appropriations/Across-the-Board Cuts. Penny, D-Minn., amendment to provide for an across-the-board 2 percent cut in all discretionary accounts except for the Internal Revenue Service. Rejected 178-201: R 128-29; D 50-172 (ND 24-130, SD 26-42), July 13, 1990.

233. HR 5241. Fiscal 1991 Treasury-Postal Appropriations/Passage. Passage of the bill to appropriate $20.7 billion for the Treasury Department, the Postal Service and other government agencies in 1991, $2.3 billion more than in fiscal 1990 and $8 million more than requested by the administration. Passed 300-72: R 86-66; D 214-6 (ND 149-5, SD 65-1), July 13, 1990.

234. HR 4982. Math and Science Education Amendments/Passage. Sawyer, D-Ohio, motion to suspend the rules and pass the bill to provide incentives to make it easier to recruit math and science teachers, promote the study of math and science in elementary and secondary schools, and increase the authorization level for the Eisenhower Mathematics and Science Education Act to $250 million in fiscal 1991, $300 million in fiscal 1992 and $400 million in fiscal 1993. Motion agreed to 347-19: R 131-19; D 216-0 (ND 147-0, SD 69-0), July 17, 1990. A two-thirds majority of those present and voting (244 in this case) is required for passage under suspension of the rules.

235. H J Res 268. Balanced Budget Constitutional Amendment/Rule. Adoption of the rule (H Res 434) to provide for House floor consideration of the joint resolution to propose an amendment to the Constitution to require a balanced budget, mandating that federal outlays not exceed estimated receipts in any fiscal year unless Congress approves a specific excess expenditure by a three-fifths vote. Adopted 348-59: R 108-56; D 240-3 (ND 163-2, SD 77-1), July 17, 1990.

236. H J Res 268. Balanced Budget Constitutional Amendment/Substitute. Barton, R-Texas, substitute amendment to add the requirement that estimated receipts not be allowed to increase faster than the previous year's rate of increase in national income, unless a specific tax increase is enacted by a three-fifths vote of each house. Rejected 184-244: R 149-25; D 35-219 (ND 8-165, SD 27-54), July 17, 1990.

KEY

Y Voted for (yea).
\# Paired for.
\+ Announced for.
N Voted against (nay).
X Paired against.
\- Announced against.
P Voted "present."
C Voted "present" to avoid possible conflict of interest.
? Did not vote or otherwise make a position known.

Democrats ***Republicans***

	229	230	231	232	233	234	235	236
ALABAMA								
1 ***Callahan***	Y	Y	Y	Y	Y	Y	N	Y
2 ***Dickinson***	Y	Y	N	N	Y	Y	Y	Y
3 Browder	Y	Y	N	Y	Y	Y	Y	Y
4 Bevill	Y	Y	N	N	Y	Y	Y	Y
5 Flippo	Y	Y	?	?	?	Y	Y	Y
6 Erdreich	Y	Y	N	Y	Y	Y	Y	Y
7 Harris	Y	Y	N	Y	Y	Y	Y	Y
ALASKA								
AL ***Young***	Y	Y	Y	N	Y	?	Y	Y
ARIZONA								
1 ***Rhodes***	Y	Y	Y	Y	N	Y	Y	Y
2 Udall	Y	Y	N	N	Y	Y	?	N
3 ***Stump***	N	Y	Y	Y	N	N	N	#
4 ***Kyl***	Y	Y	Y	Y	N	Y	N	Y
5 ***Kolbe***	Y	Y	N	Y	Y	Y	N	Y
ARKANSAS								
1 Alexander	Y	Y	N	N	Y	Y	Y	N
2 ***Robinson***	?	?	?	?	?	Y	Y	Y
3 ***Hammerschmidt***	Y	Y	Y	Y	N	Y	Y	Y
4 Anthony	Y	Y	N	N	Y	?	?	N
CALIFORNIA								
1 Bosco	N	Y	N	N	Y	Y	Y	Y
2 ***Herger***	Y	Y	Y	Y	N	N	Y	Y
3 Matsui	Y	Y	?	?	Y	?	Y	N
4 Fazio	Y	Y	N	N	Y	Y	Y	N
5 Pelosi	Y	N	N	N	Y	?	?	N
6 Boxer	?	?	?	?	?	Y	Y	N
7 Miller	N	Y	N	N	Y	Y	Y	N
8 Dellums	Y	Y	N	N	Y	Y	Y	N
9 Stark	?	?	?	?	?	Y	Y	N
10 Edwards	N	Y	N	N	Y	Y	Y	N
11 Lantos	N	Y	N	Y	Y	Y	Y	N
12 ***Campbell***	N	Y	Y	Y	N	Y	N	Y
13 Mineta	N	Y	X	?	Y	Y	Y	N
14 ***Shumway***	Y	Y	Y	Y	N	N	Y	Y
15 Condit	Y	Y	N	Y	Y	?	Y	N
16 Panetta	Y	Y	N	N	Y	Y	Y	N
17 ***Pashayan***	Y	Y	N	N	Y	Y	Y	N
18 Lehman	Y	Y	N	N	Y	Y	Y	N
19 ***Lagomarsino***	Y	Y	Y	Y	Y	Y	N	Y
20 ***Thomas***	Y	Y	Y	Y	N	Y	N	Y
21 ***Gallegly***	Y	Y	Y	Y	Y	Y	N	Y
22 ***Moorhead***	Y	Y	Y	Y	N	Y	N	Y
23 Beilenson	Y	Y	N	N	Y	Y	Y	N
24 Waxman	Y	Y	N	N	Y	Y	Y	N
25 Roybal	Y	Y	N	N	Y	Y	Y	N
26 Berman	Y	Y	N	N	Y	?	Y	N
27 Levine	Y	Y	N	N	Y	Y	Y	N
28 Dixon	Y	Y	N	N	Y	?	Y	N
29 Hawkins	N	?	N	?	Y	?	?	N
30 Martinez	?	?	?	?	?	?	Y	N
31 Dymally	N	N	N	N	Y	Y	Y	N
32 Anderson	Y	Y	N	N	Y	Y	N	N
33 ***Dreier***	Y	Y	Y	Y	N	Y	N	Y
34 Torres	Y	Y	N	N	Y	Y	Y	N
35 ***Lewis***	Y	Y	N	X	?	?	N	Y
36 Brown	?	?	?	?	?	Y	Y	N
37 ***McCandless***	Y	Y	Y	Y	Y	Y	Y	Y
38 ***Dornan***	Y	Y	Y	Y	N	Y	?	Y
39 ***Dannemeyer***	N	Y	Y	Y	N	N	N	Y
40 ***Cox***	Y	Y	Y	Y	?	Y	N	Y
41 ***Lowery***	Y	Y	N	N	Y	Y	N	Y
42 ***Rohrabacher***	N	Y	Y	Y	N	N	N	Y
43 ***Packard***	Y	Y	Y	Y	N	Y	N	Y
44 Bates	Y	Y	Y	Y	Y	Y	Y	N
45 ***Hunter***	Y	Y	Y	Y	N	?	N	Y
COLORADO								
1 Schroeder	N	Y	Y	Y	Y	Y	Y	N
2 Skaggs	Y	Y	N	N	Y	Y	Y	Y
3 Campbell	Y	Y	N	Y	Y	Y	Y	Y
4 ***Brown***	N	Y	Y	Y	N	Y	N	Y
5 ***Hefley***	Y	Y	Y	Y	N	Y	Y	Y
6 ***Schaefer***	Y	Y	Y	Y	N	Y	Y	Y
CONNECTICUT								
1 Kennelly	Y	Y	N	Y	Y	Y	Y	N
2 Gejdenson	Y	Y	N	N	Y	Y	Y	N
3 Morrison	+	+	-	-	+	?	?	N
4 ***Shays***	N	Y	Y	Y	N	Y	Y	Y
5 ***Rowland***	Y	Y	N	?	Y	?	?	Y
6 ***Johnson***	Y	Y	Y	Y	N	Y	Y	Y
DELAWARE								
AL Carper	N	Y	N	N	Y	Y	Y	N
FLORIDA								
1 Hutto	Y	Y	Y	Y	Y	Y	Y	Y
2 ***Grant***	N	Y	N	Y	Y	Y	Y	Y
3 Bennett	N	Y	Y	Y	Y	Y	Y	Y
4 ***James***	Y	Y	N	Y	Y	Y	N	Y
5 ***McCollum***	Y	Y	Y	Y	Y	?	Y	Y
6 ***Stearns***	N	Y	Y	Y	Y	N	N	Y
7 Gibbons	Y	Y	N	N	Y	Y	Y	N
8 ***Young***	N	Y	Y	Y	Y	Y	N	N
9 ***Bilirakis***	Y	Y	N	Y	Y	Y	Y	Y
10 ***Ireland***	Y	Y	Y	Y	N	Y	Y	N
11 Nelson	+	+	-	-	+	+	+	X
12 ***Lewis***	Y	Y	Y	Y	N	Y	N	Y
13 ***Goss***	Y	Y	Y	Y	N	Y	N	Y
14 Johnston	?	?	?	?	#	Y	Y	N
15 ***Shaw***	Y	Y	Y	Y	Y	Y	Y	N
16 Smith	Y	Y	N	N	Y	Y	Y	N
17 Lehman	Y	Y	N	N	Y	Y	Y	N
18 ***Ros-Lehtinen***	Y	Y	N	N	Y	Y	Y	Y
19 Fascell	Y	Y	?	?	?	Y	Y	N
GEORGIA								
1 Thomas	Y	Y	N	N	Y	Y	Y	N
2 Hatcher	?	?	?	?	?	Y	Y	N
3 Ray	Y	Y	Y	Y	Y	Y	Y	N
4 Jones	Y	Y	N	Y	Y	+	Y	N
5 Lewis	N	Y	N	N	Y	Y	Y	N
6 ***Gingrich***	Y	Y	Y	Y	N	?	N	Y
7 Darden	Y	Y	N	Y	Y	Y	Y	N
8 Rowland	Y	Y	N	N	Y	Y	Y	N
9 Jenkins	?	?	?	?	?	Y	Y	Y
10 Barnard	Y	Y	Y	Y	Y	Y	Y	Y
HAWAII								
1 ***Saiki***	Y	Y	N	N	Y	Y	Y	Y
2 Vacancy								
IDAHO								
1 ***Craig***	N	Y	Y	Y	N	Y	Y	Y
2 Stallings	Y	Y	N	N	Y	Y	Y	N
ILLINOIS								
1 Hayes	N	Y	N	N	Y	Y	Y	N
2 Savage	Y	Y	N	N	Y	Y	Y	N
3 Russo	N	Y	N	Y	N	Y	Y	N
4 Sangmeister	Y	Y	N	N	Y	Y	Y	Y
5 Lipinski	Y	Y	N	N	Y	Y	Y	N
6 ***Hyde***	Y	Y	N	?	?	Y	N	Y
7 Collins	Y	Y	N	N	Y	Y	Y	N
8 Rostenkowski	Y	Y	N	N	Y	Y	Y	N
9 Yates	Y	Y	N	N	Y	Y	Y	N
10 ***Porter***	Y	Y	Y	Y	Y	Y	N	Y
11 Annunzio	Y	Y	N	N	Y	Y	Y	N
12 ***Crane***	N	Y	Y	Y	N	N	N	Y
13 ***Fawell***	Y	Y	Y	Y	N	Y	N	Y
14 ***Hastert***	Y	Y	?	?	?	Y	N	Y
15 ***Madigan***	Y	Y	Y	N	Y	Y	Y	Y
16 ***Martin***	Y	Y	N	Y	N	Y	Y	Y
17 Evans	N	Y	N	N	Y	Y	Y	N
18 ***Michel***	Y	Y	Y	Y	N	?	Y	N
19 Bruce	Y	Y	N	N	Y	Y	Y	N
20 Durbin	N	Y	N	N	Y	Y	Y	N
21 Costello	N	Y	N	N	Y	Y	Y	N
22 Poshard	Y	Y	N	N	Y	Y	Y	N
INDIANA								
1 Visclosky	N	Y	Y	N	Y	Y	Y	N
2 Sharp	N	Y	Y	Y	Y	?	Y	N
3 ***Hiler***	Y	Y	Y	Y	Y	Y	Y	Y

ND Northern Democrats SD Southern Democrats

	229	230	231	232	233	234	235	236
4 Long	N	Y	Y	Y	Y	Y	Y	N
5 Jontz	N	Y	N	Y	Y	?	Y	N
6 ***Burton***	N	Y	Y	Y	N	N	N	Y
7 ***Myers***	Y	Y	N	N	Y	Y	Y	Y
8 McCloskey	N	Y	N	N	Y	?	Y	N
9 Hamilton	N	Y	Y	Y	Y	Y	Y	N
10 Jacobs	N	Y	Y	Y	Y	?	Y	N
IOWA								
1 ***Leach***	Y	?	N	Y	Y	?	Y	Y
2 ***Tauke***	Y	Y	N	Y	N	Y	?	Y
3 Nagle	Y	Y	N	N	Y	?	Y	N
4 Smith	Y	Y	N	N	Y	Y	N	N
5 ***Lightfoot***	Y	Y	Y	Y	N	Y	N	Y
6 ***Grandy***	Y	Y	N	Y	Y	Y	N	Y
KANSAS								
1 ***Roberts***	Y	Y	Y	Y	N	?	?	Y
2 Slattery	Y	Y	Y	Y	Y	Y	Y	N
3 ***Meyers***	Y	Y	N	N	Y	Y	Y	N
4 Glickman	?	?	?	?	?	Y	Y	N
5 ***Whittaker***	Y	Y	Y	Y	Y	Y	Y	Y
KENTUCKY								
1 Hubbard	Y	Y	N	Y	Y	Y	Y	Y
2 Natcher	Y	Y	N	N	Y	Y	Y	N
3 Mazzoli	Y	Y	N	N	Y	Y	Y	N
4 ***Bunning***	Y	Y	Y	Y	N	?	?	Y
5 ***Rogers***	Y	Y	N	N	Y	Y	Y	Y
6 ***Hopkins***	Y	Y	Y	Y	N	Y	N	Y
7 Perkins	Y	Y	N	N	Y	Y	Y	N
LOUISIANA								
1 ***Livingston***	Y	Y	N	N	Y	Y	Y	Y
2 Boggs	Y	Y	N	N	Y	Y	Y	N
3 Tauzin	Y	Y	N	N	?	Y	Y	Y
4 ***McCrery***	Y	Y	Y	Y	Y	Y	Y	Y
5 Huckaby	Y	Y	Y	Y	Y	Y	Y	Y
6 ***Baker***	Y	Y	?	?	?	?	?	?
7 Hayes	?	?	?	?	?	Y	Y	N
8 ***Holloway***	Y	Y	Y	Y	N	Y	Y	Y
MAINE								
1 Brennan	Y	Y	N	N	Y	Y	Y	N
2 ***Snowe***	Y	Y	Y	Y	Y	Y	Y	Y
MARYLAND								
1 Dyson	Y	Y	N	N	Y	Y	Y	N
2 ***Bentley***	Y	Y	Y	N	Y	Y	N	Y
3 Cardin	Y	Y	N	N	Y	Y	Y	N
4 McMillen	Y	Y	N	N	Y	Y	Y	N
5 Hoyer	Y	Y	N	N	Y	?	Y	N
6 Byron	Y	Y	N	N	Y	Y	Y	N
7 Mfume	Y	Y	N	N	Y	?	Y	N
8 ***Morella***	?	?	?	?	?	?	Y	N
MASSACHUSETTS								
1 ***Conte***	Y	N	N	N	Y	Y	Y	N
2 Neal	Y	Y	N	N	?	Y	Y	N
3 Early	Y	?	?	?	?	Y	Y	N
4 Frank	N	Y	N	N	Y	Y	Y	N
5 Atkins	N	Y	N	N	Y	Y	Y	N
6 Mavroules	N	Y	N	N	Y	Y	Y	N
7 Markey	N	Y	?	?	?	?	?	N
8 Kennedy	?	?	?	?	?	Y	Y	N
9 Moakley	Y	Y	N	N	Y	Y	Y	N
10 Studds	N	Y	N	N	Y	Y	Y	N
11 Donnelly	N	Y	N	N	Y	?	Y	N
MICHIGAN								
1 Conyers	N	Y	N	N	Y	?	Y	N
2 ***Pursell***	Y	?	N	N	Y	Y	Y	Y
3 Wolpe	N	Y	N	N	Y	Y	Y	N
4 ***Upton***	N	Y	Y	Y	N	Y	N	Y
5 ***Henry***	Y	Y	Y	Y	N	Y	Y	Y
6 Carr	N	Y	N	N	Y	Y	Y	N
7 Kildee	N	Y	N	N	Y	Y	Y	N
8 Traxler	N	Y	N	N	?	Y	Y	N
9 ***Vander Jagt***	N	N	Y	Y	Y	?	Y	Y
10 ***Schuette***	Y	Y	N	N	Y	Y	Y	Y
11 ***Davis***	Y	Y	N	N	Y	Y	?	N
12 Bonior	Y	Y	N	N	Y	Y	Y	N
13 Crockett	?	?	?	?	?	?	?	N
14 Hertel	N	Y	N	N	Y	Y	Y	N
15 Ford	?	?	?	X	?	?	Y	N
16 Dingell	N	Y	N	N	Y	Y	Y	N
17 Levin	N	Y	N	N	Y	Y	Y	N
18 ***Broomfield***	Y	Y	Y	Y	Y	Y	Y	Y
MINNESOTA								
1 Penny	N	Y	Y	Y	N	Y	Y	N
2 ***Weber***	Y	Y	N	Y	Y	?	?	Y
3 ***Frenzel***	Y	Y	Y	Y	N	?	?	Y
4 Vento	N	Y	N	N	Y	Y	Y	N

	229	230	231	232	233	234	235	236
5 Sabo	Y	Y	N	N	Y	Y	Y	N
6 Sikorski	N	Y	N	N	Y	Y	Y	N
7 ***Stangeland***	Y	Y	Y	Y	N	Y	Y	Y
8 Oberstar	Y	Y	N	N	Y	Y	Y	N
MISSISSIPPI								
1 Whitten	Y	Y	N	N	Y	Y	Y	N
2 Espy	Y	Y	N	N	Y	?	Y	N
3 Montgomery	Y	Y	N	Y	Y	Y	Y	N
4 Parker	Y	Y	Y	Y	Y	?	Y	Y
5 Taylor	Y	Y	Y	N	Y	Y	Y	Y
MISSOURI								
1 Clay	?	Y	N	N	Y	Y	Y	N
2 ***Buechner***	Y	Y	Y	Y	?	Y	N	Y
3 Gephardt	Y	Y	N	N	Y	?	Y	N
4 Skelton	?	Y	N	Y	Y	?	?	N
5 Wheat	Y	Y	N	N	Y	Y	Y	N
6 ***Coleman***	Y	Y	N	Y	Y	Y	Y	N
7 ***Hancock***	N	Y	Y	Y	N	N	N	Y
8 ***Emerson***	N	Y	N	Y	Y	Y	Y	Y
9 Volkmer	N	Y	N	N	Y	Y	Y	N
MONTANA								
1 Williams	N	Y	N	Y	Y	?	?	N
2 ***Marlenee***	Y	Y	N	Y	N	Y	N	Y
NEBRASKA								
1 ***Bereuter***	N	Y	-	Y	N	Y	Y	Y
2 Hoagland	Y	Y	N	N	Y	Y	Y	N
3 ***Smith***	Y	Y	N	Y	Y	Y	Y	Y
NEVADA								
1 Bilbray	Y	Y	N	N	Y	Y	Y	N
2 ***Vucanovich***	Y	Y	Y	Y	Y	Y	N	Y
NEW HAMPSHIRE								
1 ***Smith***	?	?	?	?	?	N	N	Y
2 ***Douglas***	Y	Y	Y	#	X	N	N	Y
NEW JERSEY								
1 Vacancy								
2 Hughes	Y	Y	N	N	Y	Y	Y	N
3 Pallone	Y	Y	N	Y	N	Y	Y	Y
4 ***Smith***	Y	Y	N	N	Y	Y	Y	Y
5 ***Roukema***	N	Y	N	Y	N	Y	Y	N
6 Dwyer	Y	Y	N	N	Y	Y	Y	N
7 ***Rinaldo***	Y	Y	N	N	Y	?	Y	Y
8 Roe	Y	Y	N	N	Y	Y	Y	N
9 Torricelli	?	?	?	?	?	Y	Y	N
10 Payne	Y	Y	N	N	Y	Y	Y	N
11 ***Gallo***	Y	Y	N	Y	Y	Y	Y	Y
12 ***Courter***	Y	Y	N	Y	Y	?	Y	Y
13 ***Saxton***	Y	Y	N	Y	?	Y	Y	Y
14 Guarini	N	Y	N	N	Y	Y	Y	N
NEW MEXICO								
1 ***Schiff***	Y	Y	N	N	Y	Y	Y	N
2 ***Skeen***	Y	Y	N	N	Y	Y	Y	Y
3 Richardson	Y	Y	N	N	Y	Y	Y	N
NEW YORK								
1 Hochbrueckner	Y	Y	N	N	Y	Y	Y	N
2 Downey	Y	Y	N	N	?	Y	Y	N
3 Mrazek	Y	Y	N	N	Y	Y	Y	N
4 ***Lent***	Y	?	N	Y	Y	?	?	Y
5 ***McGrath***	Y	Y	N	Y	Y	Y	N	N
6 Flake	?	?	?	?	?	Y	Y	N
7 Ackerman	Y	Y	N	N	Y	Y	Y	N
8 Scheuer	N	Y	N	N	Y	?	Y	N
9 Manton	Y	Y	N	N	Y	Y	Y	N
10 Schumer	Y	Y	N	N	Y	Y	Y	N
11 Towns	Y	Y	N	N	Y	Y	Y	N
12 Owens	Y	Y	N	N	Y	Y	Y	N
13 Solarz	Y	Y	N	N	Y	Y	Y	N
14 ***Molinari***	Y	Y	N	Y	Y	Y	Y	Y
15 ***Green***	Y	Y	N	N	Y	?	Y	N
16 Rangel	Y	Y	N	N	Y	Y	Y	N
17 Weiss	Y	N	N	N	Y	+	Y	N
18 Serrano	Y	Y	N	N	Y	Y	Y	N
19 Engel	Y	Y	N	N	Y	Y	Y	N
20 Lowey	Y	Y	N	N	Y	Y	Y	N
21 ***Fish***	Y	Y	N	Y	Y	Y	Y	Y
22 ***Gilman***	Y	Y	N	N	Y	Y	Y	N
23 McNulty	Y	Y	N	N	Y	Y	Y	N
24 ***Solomon***	Y	Y	N	N	Y	Y	Y	Y
25 ***Boehlert***	Y	Y	N	N	Y	Y	Y	N
26 ***Martin***	?	?	?	?	?	Y	Y	Y
27 ***Walsh***	Y	Y	N	Y	?	Y	N	N
28 McHugh	Y	Y	N	N	Y	Y	Y	N
29 ***Horton***	Y	Y	N	N	Y	Y	Y	N
30 Slaughter	Y	Y	N	N	Y	Y	Y	N
31 ***Paxon***	?	?	?	?	?	?	?	Y

	229	230	231	232	233	234	235	236
32 LaFalce	?	Y	N	N	Y	Y	Y	N
33 Nowak	Y	Y	N	N	Y	Y	Y	N
34 ***Houghton***	?	?	#	#	?	Y	Y	N
NORTH CAROLINA								
1 Jones	Y	Y	N	N	Y	?	?	N
2 Valentine	N	Y	N	N	Y	Y	Y	N
3 Lancaster	Y	Y	N	Y	Y	Y	Y	N
4 Price	Y	Y	N	N	Y	?	Y	N
5 Neal	N	Y	Y	Y	Y	?	Y	N
6 ***Coble***	Y	Y	Y	Y	Y	Y	N	Y
7 Rose	Y	Y	N	N	Y	Y	Y	N
8 Hefner	Y	Y	N	N	Y	Y	Y	N
9 ***McMillan***	Y	Y	Y	Y	N	Y	Y	Y
10 ***Ballenger***	Y	Y	Y	Y	Y	Y	Y	Y
11 Clarke	N	Y	N	N	Y	+	Y	N
NORTH DAKOTA								
AL Dorgan	N	Y	N	Y	Y	Y	Y	N
OHIO								
1 Luken	Y	Y	N	N	Y	Y	Y	N
2 ***Gradison***	Y	Y	Y	Y	N	Y	Y	N
3 Hall	Y	Y	N	Y	Y	Y	Y	N
4 ***Oxley***	Y	Y	Y	#	?	Y	Y	Y
5 ***Gillmor***	Y	Y	N	Y	Y	Y	Y	N
6 ***McEwen***	N	N	Y	Y	N	Y	Y	Y
7 ***DeWine***	Y	Y	Y	Y	N	Y	Y	N
8 ***Lukens***	Y	Y	Y	Y	N	Y	Y	Y
9 Kaptur	Y	Y	N	N	Y	Y	Y	N
10 ***Miller***	Y	Y	Y	Y	Y	N	Y	Y
11 Eckart	N	Y	N	N	Y	Y	Y	N
12 ***Kasich***	Y	Y	Y	Y	?	?	Y	Y
13 Pease	N	Y	N	N	N	Y	Y	N
14 Sawyer	Y	Y	N	N	Y	Y	Y	N
15 ***Wylie***	Y	Y	Y	Y	Y	Y	Y	Y
16 ***Regula***	?	?	?	?	?	Y	Y	Y
17 Traficant	Y	Y	N	N	Y	Y	Y	N
18 Applegate	Y	Y	N	Y	Y	Y	Y	N
19 Feighan	Y	Y	N	N	Y	Y	Y	N
20 Oakar	Y	Y	N	N	Y	Y	Y	N
21 Stokes	N	Y	N	N	Y	Y	Y	N
OKLAHOMA								
1 ***Inhofe***	Y	Y	Y	Y	Y	Y	Y	Y
2 Synar	N	Y	N	N	Y	Y	N	N
3 Watkins	?	?	?	?	?	?	?	Y
4 McCurdy	N	Y	N	N	Y	Y	Y	N
5 ***Edwards***	N	Y	Y	Y	Y	?	Y	Y
6 English	Y	Y	N	N	Y	Y	Y	N
OREGON								
1 AuCoin	N	Y	?	N	Y	Y	Y	N
2 ***Smith, B.***	Y	Y	Y	Y	Y	Y	Y	Y
3 Wyden	Y	Y	N	N	Y	Y	Y	N
4 DeFazio	N	Y	N	N	Y	Y	Y	N
5 ***Smith, D.***	?	?	?	?	?	Y	N	Y
PENNSYLVANIA								
1 Foglietta	Y	N	N	N	Y	Y	Y	N
2 Gray	Y	?	N	N	Y	Y	Y	N
3 Borski	N	Y	N	N	Y	Y	Y	N
4 Kolter	Y	Y	Y	N	Y	Y	Y	N
5 ***Schulze***	Y	Y	Y	Y	Y	Y	Y	Y
6 Yatron	N	Y	Y	Y	Y	Y	Y	N
7 ***Weldon***	Y	?	N	Y	Y	?	Y	Y
8 Kostmayer	+	+	-	X	?	Y	Y	N
9 ***Shuster***	Y	Y	Y	Y	N	Y	Y	Y
10 ***McDade***	?	?	?	?	?	Y	Y	Y
11 Kanjorski	N	Y	N	N	Y	Y	Y	N
12 Murtha	?	?	?	?	?	Y	Y	N
13 ***Coughlin***	Y	Y	N	Y	Y	Y	Y	Y
14 Coyne	?	?	?	?	?	Y	Y	N
15 ***Ritter***	Y	Y	Y	Y	Y	?	Y	Y
16 ***Walker***	Y	Y	Y	Y	N	N	N	N
17 ***Gekas***	Y	Y	Y	Y	N	N	N	Y
18 Walgren	Y	Y	N	Y	Y	Y	Y	N
19 ***Goodling***	+	+	Y	Y	Y	Y	Y	Y
20 Gaydos	Y	Y	Y	Y	Y	Y	Y	Y
21 ***Ridge***	Y	Y	Y	Y	Y	Y	Y	N
22 Murphy	N	Y	Y	Y	Y	Y	Y	Y
23 ***Clinger***	?	?	?	?	?	Y	Y	Y
RHODE ISLAND								
1 ***Machtley***	Y	Y	N	N	?	Y	Y	Y
2 ***Schneider***	Y	Y	N	Y	Y	Y	Y	Y
SOUTH CAROLINA								
1 ***Ravenel***	Y	Y	Y	Y	Y	Y	Y	Y
2 ***Spence***	Y	Y	Y	Y	Y	Y	N	Y
3 Derrick	Y	Y	N	Y	?	Y	Y	Y
4 Patterson	Y	Y	Y	Y	Y	Y	Y	Y
5 Spratt	Y	Y	N	N	Y	Y	Y	N
6 Tallon	Y	Y	Y	Y	Y	Y	Y	Y

	229	230	231	232	233	234	235	236
SOUTH DAKOTA								
AL Johnson	Y	Y	N	N	Y	Y	Y	N
TENNESSEE								
1 ***Quillen***	Y	Y	N	Y	Y	Y	Y	Y
2 ***Duncan***	Y	Y	N	Y	Y	N	Y	Y
3 Lloyd	Y	Y	N	N	Y	Y	Y	Y
4 Cooper	Y	Y	Y	Y	Y	Y	Y	Y
5 Clement	?	?	?	?	?	Y	Y	N
6 Gordon	Y	Y	N	N	Y	Y	Y	Y
7 ***Sundquist***	Y	Y	Y	Y	N	Y	Y	Y
8 Tanner	Y	Y	Y	Y	Y	Y	Y	N
9 Ford	?	?	?	?	?	?	?	?
TEXAS								
1 Chapman	Y	Y	N	N	Y	?	Y	N
2 Wilson	N	Y	N	N	Y	Y	Y	N
3 ***Bartlett***	Y	Y	Y	Y	N	N	Y	Y
4 Hall	?	?	?	?	?	Y	Y	Y
5 Bryant	Y	Y	N	N	Y	Y	Y	N
6 ***Barton***	Y	Y	Y	Y	N	Y	Y	Y
7 ***Archer***	Y	Y	Y	Y	N	?	?	Y
8 ***Fields***	Y	Y	Y	Y	N	?	Y	Y
9 Brooks	Y	Y	N	N	Y	Y	Y	N
10 Pickle	Y	Y	N	N	Y	Y	Y	Y
11 Leath	Y	Y	N	N	Y	?	Y	N
12 Geren	Y	Y	N	Y	Y	Y	Y	Y
13 Sarpalius	Y	Y	N	N	N	Y	Y	Y
14 Laughlin	Y	Y	N	N	Y	Y	Y	Y
15 de la Garza	Y	Y	N	N	Y	?	Y	N
16 Coleman	Y	Y	N	N	Y	Y	Y	N
17 Stenholm	Y	Y	Y	Y	Y	Y	Y	N
18 Washington	?	?	?	?	?	Y	Y	N
19 ***Combest***	Y	Y	Y	Y	Y	Y	N	Y
20 Gonzalez	Y	Y	N	N	Y	Y	Y	N
21 ***Smith***	?	?	?	?	?	Y	Y	Y
22 ***DeLay***	Y	Y	Y	N	Y	N	N	Y
23 Bustamante	Y	Y	N	?	Y	Y	Y	Y
24 Frost	?	?	?	?	?	Y	Y	N
25 Andrews	Y	Y	N	N	Y	Y	Y	N
26 ***Armey***	N	Y	Y	Y	N	Y	N	Y
27 Ortiz	Y	Y	N	N	Y	Y	Y	N
UTAH								
1 ***Hansen***	Y	Y	Y	Y	N	N	Y	Y
2 Owens	Y	Y	Y	N	Y	Y	Y	N
3 ***Nielson***	Y	Y	Y	Y	N	N	Y	Y
VERMONT								
AL ***Smith***	N	Y	Y	Y	Y	Y	N	Y
VIRGINIA								
1 ***Bateman***	Y	Y	N	Y	Y	Y	Y	Y
2 Pickett	Y	Y	N	Y	Y	Y	Y	N
3 ***Bliley***	Y	Y	Y	Y	N	Y	N	Y
4 Sisisky	Y	Y	N	Y	Y	Y	Y	N
5 Payne	Y	Y	N	Y	Y	Y	Y	N
6 Olin	Y	Y	N	Y	Y	Y	Y	N
7 ***Slaughter***	Y	Y	Y	Y	N	Y	N	Y
8 ***Parris***	Y	Y	N	N	Y	Y	Y	Y
9 Boucher	?	?	?	?	?	Y	Y	N
10 ***Wolf***	Y	Y	N	N	Y	Y	Y	Y
WASHINGTON								
1 ***Miller***	Y	Y	Y	Y	Y	Y	Y	Y
2 Swift	Y	Y	N	N	Y	Y	Y	N
3 Unsoeld	N	Y	N	N	Y	?	Y	N
4 ***Morrison***	Y	?	Y	Y	Y	Y	Y	N
5 Foley								
6 Dicks	Y	Y	N	N	Y	Y	Y	N
7 McDermott	N	Y	N	N	Y	Y	Y	N
8 ***Chandler***	Y	Y	?	?	?	Y	Y	Y
WEST VIRGINIA								
1 Mollohan	Y	Y	N	N	Y	Y	Y	N
2 Staggers	N	Y	N	N	Y	Y	Y	N
3 Wise	N	Y	N	N	Y	Y	Y	N
4 Rahall	N	Y	N	N	Y	Y	Y	Y
WISCONSIN								
1 Aspin	Y	Y	N	N	Y	Y	Y	N
2 Kastenmeier	Y	Y	N	N	Y	Y	Y	N
3 ***Gunderson***	Y	Y	N	Y	Y	Y	Y	Y
4 Kleczka	Y	Y	N	N	Y	Y	Y	N
5 Moody	Y	Y	N	N	Y	Y	Y	N
6 ***Petri***	N	Y	Y	Y	N	Y	N	Y
7 Obey	N	Y	N	N	Y	Y	Y	N
8 ***Roth***	N	Y	Y	Y	N	Y	Y	Y
9 ***Sensenbrenner***	N	Y	Y	Y	N	Y	N	Y
WYOMING								
AL ***Thomas***	Y	Y	Y	Y	N	Y	Y	Y

Southern states - Ala., Ark., Fla., Ga., Ky., La., Miss., N.C., Okla., S.C., Tenn., Texas, Va.
Omitted votes are quorum calls, which CQ does not include in its vote charts.

237. H J Res 268. Balanced Budget Constitutional Amendment/Effective Date. Stenholm, D-Texas, substitute amendment to change the effective date to fiscal 1995 or the second year after ratification, whichever is later. Adopted 276-152: R 169-4; D 107-148 (ND 43-130, SD 64-18), July 17, 1990.

238. H J Res 268. Balanced Budget Constitutional Amendment/Passage. Passage of the joint resolution to propose an amendment to the Constitution to require a balanced budget, mandating that federal outlays not exceed estimated receipts in any fiscal year unless Congress approved a specific excess expenditure by a three-fifths vote. Rejected 279-150: R 169-5; D 110-145 (ND 44-129, SD 66-16), July 17, 1990. A two-thirds majority of those present and voting (286 in this case) of both houses is required for passage of a joint resolution proposing an amendment to the Constitution. A "yea" was a vote supporting the president's position.

239. HR 5268. Fiscal 1991 Agriculture Appropriations/Across-the-Board Cuts. Frenzel, R-Minn., amendment to provide an across-the-board 7.7 percent cut in all discretionary accounts, which would reduce the accounts to fiscal 1990 levels. Rejected 115-305: R 104-67; D 11-238 (ND 8-159, SD 3-79), July 18, 1990.

240. HR 5268. Fiscal 1991 Agriculture Appropriations/Across-the-Board Cuts. Dannemeyer, R-Calif., amendment to provide an across-the-board 5 percent cut in all discretionary accounts in the bill. Rejected 115-300: R 102-67; D 13-233 (ND 9-158, SD 4-75), July 18, 1990.

241. HR 5268. Fiscal 1991 Agriculture Appropriations/Across-the-Board Cuts. Penny, D-Minn., amendment to provide an across-the-board 2 percent cut in all discretionary accounts in the bill except the special supplemental Food Program for Women, Infants and Children. Rejected 202-216: R 144-26; D 58-190 (ND 35-133, SD 23-57), July 18, 1990.

242. HR 5268. Fiscal 1991 Agriculture Appropriations/Across-the-Board Cuts. Walker, R-Pa., amendment to provide an across-the-board 0.0000000002 percent cut in all discretionary accounts, resulting in $19.90 in savings. Rejected 175-214: R 156-11; D 19-203 (ND 12-138, SD 7-65), July 18, 1990.

243. HR 5268. Fiscal 1991 Agriculture Appropriations/Passage. Passage of the bill to appropriate $50.35 billion in fiscal 1991 for the Agriculture Department's agriculture, rural development, domestic food assistance and international programs, and several other related agencies. The total is $5.2 billion more than in fiscal 1990 and $86.5 million less than requested by the administration. Passed 335-86: R 96-75; D 239-11 (ND 160-8, SD 79-3), July 18, 1990.

244. HR 5258. Balanced Budget Statute/Rule. Adoption of the rule (H Res 433) to provide for House floor consideration of the bill to require that the president submit a balanced budget, that the Budget committees report balanced budgets and that both chambers consider a balanced budget each year. Adopted 251-173: R 0-172; D 251-1 (ND 171-0, SD 80-1), July 18, 1990.

KEY

- Y Voted for (yea).
- # Paired for.
- + Announced for.
- N Voted against (nay).
- X Paired against.
- - Announced against.
- P Voted "present."
- C Voted "present" to avoid possible conflict of interest.
- ? Did not vote or otherwise make a position known.

Democrats ***Republicans***

	237	238	239	240	241	242	243	244
ALABAMA								
1 ***Callahan***	Y	Y	N	Y	Y	Y	Y	N
2 ***Dickinson***	Y	Y	N	?	?	?	?	N
3 Browder	Y	Y	N	N	N	P	Y	Y
4 Bevill	Y	Y	N	N	N	N	Y	Y
5 Flippo	Y	Y	N	N	N	N	Y	Y
6 Erdreich	Y	Y	N	N	Y	Y	Y	Y
7 Harris	Y	Y	N	N	N	N	Y	Y
ALASKA								
AL ***Young***	Y	Y	N	N	N	Y	Y	N
ARIZONA								
1 ***Rhodes***	Y	N	Y	Y	Y	Y	N	N
2 Udall	N	N	N	N	N	N	Y	Y
3 ***Stump***	+	+	#	#	#	+	X	-
4 ***Kyl***	Y	Y	Y	Y	Y	Y	N	N
5 ***Kolbe***	Y	Y	Y	Y	Y	Y	Y	N
ARKANSAS								
1 Alexander	N	N	N	N	N	N	Y	Y
2 ***Robinson***	Y	Y	Y	Y	Y	Y	Y	N
3 ***Hammerschmidt***	Y	Y	N	N	Y	Y	Y	N
4 Anthony	Y	Y	N	N	N	N	Y	Y
CALIFORNIA								
1 Bosco	Y	Y	N	Y	Y	P	Y	Y
2 ***Herger***	Y	Y	Y	Y	Y	Y	?	N
3 Matsui	N	N	N	N	N	P	Y	Y
4 Fazio	N	N	N	N	N	N	Y	Y
5 Pelosi	N	N	N	N	N	N	Y	Y
6 Boxer	N	N	N	N	N	N	Y	Y
7 Miller	N	N	N	N	N	N	Y	Y
8 Dellums	N	N	N	N	N	N	Y	Y
9 Stark	N	N	N	N	N	N	Y	Y
10 Edwards	N	N	N	N	N	N	Y	Y
11 Lantos	N	Y	N	N	N	N	Y	Y
12 ***Campbell***	Y	Y	Y	Y	Y	Y	N	N
13 Mineta	N	N	X	X	X	—	#	+
14 ***Shumway***	Y	Y	Y	Y	Y	Y	N	N
15 Condit	Y	Y	N	N	Y	P	Y	Y
16 Panetta	N	N	N	N	N	N	Y	Y
17 ***Pashayan***	Y	Y	N	N	N	N	Y	N
18 Lehman	N	N	N	N	N	N	Y	Y
19 ***Lagomarsino***	Y	Y	Y	Y	Y	Y	N	N
20 ***Thomas***	Y	Y	Y	Y	Y	Y	Y	N
21 ***Gallegly***	Y	Y	Y	Y	Y	Y	N	N
22 ***Moorhead***	Y	Y	Y	Y	Y	Y	N	N
23 Beilenson	N	N	N	N	N	N	Y	Y
24 Waxman	N	N	N	N	N	N	Y	Y
25 Roybal	N	N	N	N	N	N	Y	Y
26 Berman	N	N	N	N	N	N	Y	Y
27 Levine	N	N	N	N	N	N	Y	Y
28 Dixon	N	N	N	N	N	N	Y	Y
29 Hawkins	N	N	N	N	N	N	Y	Y
30 Martinez	N	N	N	N	N	N	Y	Y
31 Dymally	N	N	N	N	N	N	Y	Y
32 Anderson	N	N	N	N	Y	Y	Y	Y
33 ***Dreier***	Y	Y	Y	Y	Y	Y	N	N
34 Torres	N	N	—	—	—	—	Y	Y
35 ***Lewis***	Y	Y	Y	N	N	Y	Y	N
36 Brown	N	N	N	N	N	N	Y	Y
37 ***McCandless***	Y	Y	Y	Y	Y	Y	N	N
38 ***Dornan***	Y	Y	#	#	Y	Y	N	N
39 ***Dannemeyer***	Y	Y	Y	Y	Y	Y	N	N
40 ***Cox***	Y	Y	Y	Y	Y	Y	N	N
41 ***Lowery***	Y	Y	N	N	N	Y	Y	N
42 ***Rohrabacher***	Y	Y	Y	Y	Y	Y	N	N
43 ***Packard***	Y	Y	Y	Y	Y	Y	N	N
44 Bates	Y	Y	Y	Y	Y	P	N	Y
45 ***Hunter***	Y	Y	Y	Y	Y	Y	N	N
COLORADO								
1 Schroeder	N	N	Y	Y	Y	N	Y	Y
2 Skaggs	N	N	N	N	N	P	Y	Y
3 Campbell	Y	Y	N	N	Y	N	Y	Y
4 ***Brown***	Y	Y	Y	Y	Y	Y	N	N
5 ***Hefley***	Y	Y	Y	Y	Y	Y	N	N
6 ***Schaefer***	Y	Y	Y	Y	Y	Y	N	N
CONNECTICUT								
1 Kennelly	N	N	N	N	N	N	Y	Y
2 Gejdenson	N	N	N	N	N	N	Y	Y
3 Morrison	N	N	#	#	#	—	X	#
4 ***Shays***	Y	Y	Y	Y	Y	Y	N	N
5 ***Rowland***	Y	Y	?	?	?	Y	Y	?
6 ***Johnson***	Y	Y	Y	Y	Y	Y	N	N
DELAWARE								
AL Carper	Y	Y	N	N	N	Y	Y	Y
FLORIDA								
1 Hutto	Y	Y	N	N	Y	N	Y	Y
2 ***Grant***	Y	Y	N	N	N	Y	Y	N
3 Bennett	Y	Y	N	Y	Y	Y	Y	Y
4 ***James***	Y	Y	N	N	Y	Y	Y	N
5 ***McCollum***	Y	Y	Y	Y	Y	Y	N	N
6 ***Stearns***	Y	Y	N	Y	Y	Y	Y	N
7 Gibbons	Y	Y	N	N	Y	N	Y	Y
8 ***Young***	Y	Y	Y	?	?	Y	Y	N
9 ***Bilirakis***	Y	Y	N	N	Y	Y	Y	N
10 ***Ireland***	Y	Y	Y	Y	Y	Y	Y	N
11 Nelson	+	+	X	X	X	-	#	+
12 ***Lewis***	Y	Y	N	N	N	Y	Y	N
13 ***Goss***	Y	Y	Y	Y	Y	Y	Y	N
14 Johnston	Y	Y	N	N	N	N	Y	Y
15 ***Shaw***	Y	Y	Y	Y	Y	Y	N	N
16 Smith	N	N	N	N	Y	N	Y	Y
17 Lehman	N	N	N	N	N	N	Y	Y
18 ***Ros-Lehtinen***	Y	Y	N	N	Y	Y	Y	N
19 Fascell	N	N	N	Y	Y	N	N	Y
GEORGIA								
1 Thomas	Y	Y	N	N	N	N	Y	Y
2 Hatcher	Y	Y	N	N	N	N	Y	Y
3 Ray	Y	Y	N	N	N	N	Y	Y
4 Jones	Y	Y	N	N	Y	N	Y	Y
5 Lewis	N	N	N	N	N	N	Y	Y
6 ***Gingrich***	Y	Y	Y	Y	Y	Y	N	N
7 Darden	Y	Y	N	N	Y	P	Y	Y
8 Rowland	Y	Y	N	N	N	N	Y	Y
9 Jenkins	Y	Y	N	N	Y	P	Y	Y
10 Barnard	Y	Y	N	N	Y	N	Y	Y
HAWAII								
1 ***Saiki***	Y	Y	N	N	Y	Y	Y	N
2 Vacancy								
IDAHO								
1 ***Craig***	Y	Y	Y	Y	Y	Y	Y	X
2 Stallings	Y	Y	N	N	Y	N	Y	Y
ILLINOIS								
1 Hayes	N	N	N	N	N	N	Y	Y
2 Savage	N	N	?	?	N	N	Y	Y
3 Russo	N	N	N	N	Y	N	N	Y
4 Sangmeister	Y	Y	N	N	Y	Y	Y	Y
5 Lipinski	Y	Y	N	N	Y	P	Y	Y
6 ***Hyde***	Y	Y	Y	Y	Y	Y	N	N
7 Collins	N	N	N	N	N	N	Y	Y
8 Rostenkowski	N	N	N	N	N	N	Y	Y
9 Yates	N	N	N	N	N	N	Y	Y
10 ***Porter***	Y	Y	Y	Y	Y	?	N	N
11 Annunzio	Y	Y	N	N	N	P	Y	Y
12 ***Crane***	Y	Y	Y	Y	Y	Y	N	N
13 ***Fawell***	N	Y	Y	Y	Y	Y	N	N
14 ***Hastert***	Y	Y	Y	Y	Y	Y	Y	N
15 ***Madigan***	Y	Y	N	N	N	Y	Y	N
16 ***Martin***	Y	Y	N	N	Y	Y	N	N
17 Evans	N	N	N	N	N	N	Y	Y
18 ***Michel***	Y	Y	Y	Y	?	?	?	N
19 Bruce	N	N	N	N	N	Y	Y	Y
20 Durbin	N	N	N	N	N	N	Y	Y
21 Costello	Y	Y	N	N	N	N	Y	Y
22 Poshard	Y	Y	N	N	N	N	Y	Y
INDIANA								
1 Visclosky	N	N	N	N	N	Y	Y	Y
2 Sharp	Y	Y	N	N	Y	P	Y	Y
3 ***Hiler***	Y	Y	Y	Y	Y	Y	Y	N

ND Northern Democrats SD Southern Democrats

	237	238	239	240	241	242	243	244
4 Long	N	Y	N	N	Y	P	Y	Y
5 Jontz	Y	Y	N	N	N	P	Y	Y
6 ***Burton***	Y	Y	Y	Y	Y	Y	N	N
7 ***Myers***	Y	Y	N	N	N	N	Y	N
8 McCloskey	N	N	N	N	N	N	Y	Y
9 Hamilton	N	N	Y	Y	Y	Y	Y	Y
10 Jacobs	N	Y	Y	Y	Y	Y	N	Y
IOWA								
1 ***Leach***	Y	Y	N	N	Y	Y	N	N
2 ***Tauke***	Y	Y	N	N	Y	Y	N	N
3 Nagle	N	N	N	N	N	N	Y	Y
4 Smith	N	N	N	N	N	N	Y	Y
5 ***Lightfoot***	Y	Y	N	N	Y	Y	N	N
6 ***Grandy***	Y	Y	N	N	Y	?	N	N
KANSAS								
1 ***Roberts***	Y	Y	Y	Y	Y	Y	N	N
2 Slattery	N	N	Y	N	Y	Y	N	Y
3 ***Meyers***	Y	Y	N	N	Y	Y	N	N
4 Glickman	N	N	N	N	Y	N	Y	Y
5 ***Whittaker***	Y	Y	Y	Y	Y	Y	N	N
KENTUCKY								
1 Hubbard	Y	Y	N	N	N	Y	Y	Y
2 Natcher	N	Y	N	N	N	N	Y	Y
3 Mazzoli	N	N	N	N	N	N	Y	Y
4 ***Bunning***	Y	Y	Y	Y	Y	Y	N	N
5 ***Rogers***	Y	Y	N	N	N	Y	Y	N
6 ***Hopkins***	Y	Y	Y	Y	Y	Y	Y	N
7 Perkins	N	N	N	N	N	N	Y	Y
LOUISIANA								
1 ***Livingston***	Y	Y	Y	N	Y	Y	Y	N
2 Boggs	N	N	N	N	N	N	Y	Y
3 Tauzin	Y	Y	Y	?	Y	N	Y	Y
4 ***McCrery***	Y	Y	N	N	Y	Y	Y	N
5 Huckaby	Y	Y	N	N	N	N	Y	Y
6 ***Baker***	?	?	?	?	?	?	?	?
7 Hayes	Y	Y	N	N	N	P	Y	Y
8 ***Holloway***	Y	Y	N	N	Y	Y	Y	N
MAINE								
1 Brennan	Y	Y	N	N	Y	N	Y	Y
2 ***Snowe***	Y	Y	Y	Y	Y	Y	Y	N
MARYLAND								
1 Dyson	Y	Y	N	N	N	N	Y	Y
2 ***Bentley***	Y	Y	Y	Y	Y	Y	N	N
3 Cardin	N	N	N	N	N	N	Y	Y
4 McMillen	Y	Y	N	N	N	N	Y	Y
5 Hoyer	N	N	N	N	N	N	Y	Y
6 Byron	Y	Y	N	N	Y	N	Y	Y
7 Mfume	Y	Y	N	N	N	N	Y	Y
8 ***Morella***	Y	Y	N	N	Y	Y	Y	N
MASSACHUSETTS								
1 ***Conte***	N	N	N	N	Y	N	Y	N
2 Neal	Y	Y	N	N	N	N	Y	Y
3 Early	Y	Y	N	N	N	N	Y	Y
4 Frank	N	N	N	N	N	N	Y	Y
5 Atkins	N	N	N	N	N	N	Y	Y
6 Mavroules	N	N	N	N	N	N	Y	Y
7 Markey	N	N	N	N	N	N	Y	Y
8 Kennedy	N	N	N	N	N	N	Y	Y
9 Moakley	N	N	N	N	N	N	Y	Y
10 Studds	N	N	N	N	N	N	Y	Y
11 Donnelly	N	N	N	N	N	N	Y	Y
MICHIGAN								
1 Conyers	N	N	N	N	N	N	Y	Y
2 ***Pursell***	Y	Y	N	Y	Y	Y	Y	N
3 Wolpe	N	N	N	N	N	N	Y	Y
4 ***Upton***	Y	Y	Y	Y	Y	Y	N	N
5 ***Henry***	Y	Y	Y	Y	Y	Y	N	N
6 Carr	Y	Y	N	N	N	Y	Y	Y
7 Kildee	N	N	N	N	N	N	Y	Y
8 Traxler	N	N	N	N	N	N	Y	Y
9 ***Vander Jagt***	Y	Y	Y	Y	Y	Y	Y	N
10 ***Schuette***	Y	Y	N	N	Y	Y	Y	N
11 ***Davis***	Y	Y	N	N	N	N	Y	N
12 Bonior	N	N	N	N	N	N	Y	Y
13 Crockett	N	N	?	?	?	?	Y	Y
14 Hertel	N	N	N	N	N	N	N	Y
15 Ford	N	N	N	N	N	N	Y	Y
16 Dingell	N	N	N	N	N	N	Y	Y
17 Levin	N	N	N	N	N	N	Y	Y
18 ***Broomfield***	Y	Y	Y	Y	Y	Y	N	N
MINNESOTA								
1 Penny	Y	Y	Y	Y	Y	N	N	Y
2 ***Weber***	Y	Y	N	N	N	Y	Y	N
3 ***Frenzel***	Y	Y	Y	Y	Y	Y	N	N
4 Vento	N	N	N	N	N	N	Y	Y

	237	238	239	240	241	242	243	244
5 Sabo	N	N	N	N	N	N	Y	Y
6 Sikorski	N	N	N	N	N	N	Y	Y
7 ***Stangeland***	Y	Y	N	N	Y	Y	Y	N
8 Oberstar	N	N	N	N	N	N	Y	Y
MISSISSIPPI								
1 Whitten	N	Y	N	N	N	N	Y	Y
2 Espy	Y	Y	N	N	N	N	Y	Y
3 Montgomery	Y	Y	N	N	N	N	Y	Y
4 Parker	Y	Y	N	N	N	N	Y	Y
5 Taylor	Y	Y	N	N	N	N	Y	Y
MISSOURI								
1 Clay	N	N	N	N	N	N	Y	Y
2 ***Buechner***	Y	Y	Y	Y	Y	Y	Y	N
3 Gephardt	N	N	N	N	?	?	?	Y
4 Skelton	Y	Y	N	N	N	N	Y	Y
5 Wheat	N	N	N	N	N	N	Y	Y
6 ***Coleman***	Y	Y	N	N	N	Y	Y	N
7 ***Hancock***	Y	Y	Y	Y	Y	Y	N	N
8 ***Emerson***	Y	Y	N	N	N	Y	Y	N
9 Volkmer	Y	Y	N	N	N	N	Y	Y
MONTANA								
1 Williams	N	N	N	N	N	?	Y	Y
2 ***Marlenee***	Y	Y	N	N	N	Y	Y	N
NEBRASKA								
1 ***Bereuter***	Y	Y	N	N	Y	Y	Y	N
2 Hoagland	Y	Y	N	N	Y	Y	Y	Y
3 ***Smith***	Y	Y	N	N	N	Y	Y	N
NEVADA								
1 Bilbray	Y	Y	N	N	N	N	Y	Y
2 ***Vucanovich***	Y	Y	Y	Y	Y	Y	Y	N
NEW HAMPSHIRE								
1 ***Smith***	Y	Y	Y	Y	Y	Y	N	N
2 ***Douglas***	Y	Y	Y	Y	Y	Y	N	N
NEW JERSEY								
1 Vacancy								
2 Hughes	N	N	N	N	Y	N	Y	Y
3 Pallone	Y	Y	Y	Y	Y	Y	N	Y
4 ***Smith***	Y	Y	N	N	Y	Y	Y	N
5 ***Roukema***	Y	Y	N	N	Y	Y	N	N
6 Dwyer	N	N	N	N	N	N	Y	Y
7 ***Rinaldo***	Y	Y	N	N	Y	Y	Y	N
8 Roe	N	N	N	N	N	N	Y	Y
9 Torricelli	N	N	N	N	N	N	Y	Y
10 Payne	N	N	N	N	N	N	Y	Y
11 ***Gallo***	Y	Y	N	N	Y	Y	Y	N
12 ***Courter***	Y	Y	N	N	Y	Y	Y	N
13 ***Saxton***	Y	Y	Y	Y	Y	Y	Y	N
14 Guarini	N	N	N	N	Y	P	Y	Y
NEW MEXICO								
1 ***Schiff***	Y	Y	N	N	N	P	Y	N
2 ***Skeen***	Y	Y	N	N	N	N	Y	N
3 Richardson	Y	Y	N	?	N	N	Y	Y
NEW YORK								
1 Hochbrueckner	N	N	N	N	N	N	Y	Y
2 Downey	N	N	N	N	N	N	Y	Y
3 Mrazek	N	N	N	N	N	N	Y	Y
4 ***Lent***	Y	Y	N	Y	Y	Y	Y	N
5 ***McGrath***	Y	Y	Y	Y	Y	Y	N	N
6 Flake	N	N	N	N	N	N	Y	Y
7 Ackerman	N	N	N	N	N	N	Y	Y
8 Scheuer	N	N	N	N	N	N	Y	Y
9 Manton	N	N	N	N	N	N	Y	Y
10 Schumer	N	N	N	Y	Y	N	Y	Y
11 Towns	N	N	N	N	N	N	Y	Y
12 Owens	N	N	N	N	N	N	Y	Y
13 Solarz	N	N	N	N	N	N	Y	Y
14 ***Molinari***	Y	Y	Y	Y	Y	Y	N	N
15 ***Green***	N	N	N	N	N	N	Y	N
16 Rangel	N	N	N	N	N	N	Y	Y
17 Weiss	N	N	N	N	N	N	Y	Y
18 Serrano	N	N	N	N	N	N	Y	Y
19 Engel	N	N	N	N	N	N	Y	Y
20 Lowey	N	N	N	N	N	N	Y	Y
21 ***Fish***	Y	Y	Y	Y	Y	Y	Y	N
22 ***Gilman***	Y	N	N	N	N	N	Y	N
23 McNulty	N	Y	N	N	N	N	Y	Y
24 ***Solomon***	Y	Y	Y	?	Y	Y	N	N
25 ***Boehlert***	Y	Y	N	N	Y	N	Y	N
26 ***Martin***	Y	Y	N	N	Y	Y	Y	N
27 ***Walsh***	Y	Y	N	N	Y	Y	Y	N
28 McHugh	N	N	N	N	N	N	Y	Y
29 ***Horton***	Y	Y	N	N	N	N	Y	N
30 Slaughter	N	Y	N	N	N	N	Y	Y
31 ***Paxon***	Y	Y	Y	Y	Y	Y	Y	N

	237	238	239	240	241	242	243	244
32 LaFalce	Y	N	N	N	Y	N	Y	Y
33 Nowak	Y	N	N	N	N	N	Y	Y
34 ***Houghton***	N	N	Y	Y	Y	Y	Y	N
NORTH CAROLINA								
1 Jones	Y	Y	N	N	N	N	Y	Y
2 Valentine	Y	Y	N	N	N	N	Y	Y
3 Lancaster	Y	Y	N	X	N	N	Y	Y
4 Price	Y	Y	N	N	N	N	Y	Y
5 Neal	Y	Y	N	N	?	N	Y	Y
6 ***Coble***	Y	Y	Y	Y	Y	Y	Y	N
7 Rose	Y	Y	N	N	N	N	Y	Y
8 Hefner	Y	Y	N	N	N	N	Y	Y
9 ***McMillan***	Y	Y	Y	Y	Y	Y	N	N
10 ***Ballenger***	Y	Y	Y	Y	Y	Y	N	N
11 Clarke	Y	Y	N	N	Y	Y	Y	Y
NORTH DAKOTA								
AL Dorgan	Y	Y	N	N	N	N	+	Y
OHIO								
1 Luken	Y	Y	N	N	N	N	Y	Y
2 ***Gradison***	Y	Y	Y	Y	Y	Y	N	N
3 Hall	N	N	N	N	Y	Y	Y	Y
4 ***Oxley***	Y	Y	Y	Y	Y	Y	Y	N
5 ***Gillmor***	Y	Y	N	N	N	Y	Y	N
6 ***McEwen***	Y	Y	Y	Y	Y	Y	N	N
7 ***DeWine***	Y	Y	N	Y	Y	Y	Y	N
8 ***Lukens***	Y	Y	?	Y	Y	Y	N	N
9 Kaptur	N	N	N	N	N	N	Y	Y
10 ***Miller***	Y	Y	Y	Y	Y	Y	Y	N
11 Eckart	Y	Y	N	N	N	N	Y	Y
12 ***Kasich***	Y	Y	Y	Y	Y	Y	N	N
13 Pease	N	N	N	N	N	N	N	Y
14 Sawyer	Y	N	N	N	N	N	Y	Y
15 ***Wylie***	Y	Y	Y	Y	Y	Y	Y	N
16 ***Regula***	Y	Y	N	N	N	Y	Y	N
17 Traficant	N	N	N	N	N	N	Y	Y
18 Applegate	N	N	N	N	Y	N	Y	Y
19 Feighan	N	N	N	N	N	N	Y	Y
20 Oakar	N	N	N	N	N	N	Y	Y
21 Stokes	N	N	N	N	N	N	Y	Y
OKLAHOMA								
1 ***Inhofe***	Y	Y	Y	Y	Y	Y	N	N
2 Synar	N	N	N	N	N	N	Y	Y
3 Watkins	Y	Y	N	N	N	N	Y	Y
4 McCurdy	Y	Y	N	N	Y	N	N	Y
5 ***Edwards***	Y	Y	Y	Y	Y	Y	N	N
6 English	Y	Y	N	N	N	Y	N	N
OREGON								
1 AuCoin	N	N	N	N	N	N	Y	Y
2 ***Smith, B.***	Y	Y	N	N	Y	Y	Y	N
3 Wyden	N	N	N	N	N	N	Y	Y
4 DeFazio	Y	Y	X	N	N	N	Y	Y
5 ***Smith, D.***	Y	Y	Y	Y	Y	Y	Y	N
PENNSYLVANIA								
1 Foglietta	N	N	N	N	N	N	Y	Y
2 Gray	N	N	N	N	N	N	Y	Y
3 Borski	N	N	N	N	N	N	Y	Y
4 Kolter	N	N	N	N	N	N	Y	Y
5 ***Schulze***	Y	Y	Y	Y	Y	Y	Y	N
6 Yatron	N	N	N	N	Y	N	Y	Y
7 ***Weldon***	Y	Y	Y	Y	Y	Y	Y	N
8 Kostmayer	N	N	N	N	Y	P	Y	Y
9 ***Shuster***	Y	Y	Y	Y	Y	Y	N	N
10 ***McDade***	Y	Y	N	N	N	Y	Y	N
11 Kanjorski	N	N	N	N	Y	N	Y	Y
12 Murtha	N	N	N	N	N	N	Y	Y
13 ***Coughlin***	Y	Y	N	N	N	Y	Y	N
14 Coyne	N	N	N	N	N	N	Y	Y
15 ***Ritter***	Y	Y	Y	Y	Y	Y	Y	N
16 ***Walker***	Y	Y	Y	Y	Y	Y	N	N
17 ***Gekas***	Y	Y	Y	Y	Y	Y	N	N
18 Walgren	Y	Y	Y	Y	Y	N	Y	Y
19 ***Goodling***	Y	Y	Y	N	Y	N	Y	N
20 Gaydos	Y	Y	N	N	Y	?	Y	Y
21 ***Ridge***	Y	Y	N	N	Y	?	Y	N
22 Murphy	Y	Y	N	N	Y	P	Y	Y
23 ***Clinger***	Y	Y	N	N	Y	Y	Y	N
RHODE ISLAND								
1 ***Machtley***	Y	Y	N	N	Y	Y	Y	N
2 ***Schneider***	Y	Y	N	N	Y	Y	Y	N
SOUTH CAROLINA								
1 ***Ravenel***	Y	Y	Y	Y	Y	Y	Y	N
2 ***Spence***	Y	Y	Y	N	Y	Y	Y	N
3 Derrick	Y	Y	N	N	Y	N	Y	Y
4 Patterson	Y	Y	N	N	Y	Y	Y	Y
5 Spratt	Y	Y	N	N	Y	N	Y	Y
6 Tallon	Y	Y	N	N	N	N	Y	Y

	237	238	239	240	241	242	243	244
SOUTH DAKOTA								
AL Johnson	Y	Y	N	N	N	N	Y	Y
TENNESSEE								
1 ***Quillen***	Y	Y	N	N	N	Y	Y	N
2 ***Duncan***	Y	Y	Y	Y	Y	Y	N	N
3 Lloyd	Y	Y	N	N	N	?	Y	Y
4 Cooper	Y	Y	Y	Y	Y	Y	Y	Y
5 Clement	Y	Y	N	N	Y	N	Y	Y
6 Gordon	Y	Y	N	N	N	N	Y	Y
7 ***Sundquist***	Y	Y	Y	Y	Y	Y	N	N
8 Tanner	Y	Y	N	N	N	P	Y	Y
9 Ford	N	N	N	N	N	N	Y	Y
TEXAS								
1 Chapman	Y	Y	N	N	N	N	Y	Y
2 Wilson	Y	Y	N	N	N	N	Y	Y
3 ***Bartlett***	Y	Y	Y	Y	Y	Y	N	N
4 Hall	Y	Y	N	N	N	N	Y	Y
5 Bryant	N	Y	N	N	N	N	Y	Y
6 ***Barton***	Y	Y	Y	Y	Y	Y	N	N
7 ***Archer***	Y	Y	Y	Y	Y	Y	N	N
8 ***Fields***	Y	Y	Y	Y	Y	Y	N	N
9 Brooks	N	N	N	N	N	N	Y	Y
10 Pickle	Y	Y	N	N	Y	N	Y	Y
11 Leath	Y	Y	N	N	N	?	Y	?
12 Geren	Y	Y	N	N	N	P	Y	Y
13 Sarpalius	Y	Y	N	N	N	N	Y	Y
14 Laughlin	Y	Y	N	N	N	N	Y	Y
15 de la Garza	Y	Y	N	N	N	N	Y	Y
16 Coleman	Y	Y	N	N	N	N	Y	Y
17 Stenholm	Y	Y	Y	Y	Y	N	Y	Y
18 Washington	N	N	N	?	?	?	Y	Y
19 ***Combest***	Y	Y	Y	Y	Y	Y	N	N
20 Gonzalez	N	N	N	N	N	N	Y	Y
21 ***Smith***	Y	Y	Y	N	Y	Y	Y	N
22 ***DeLay***	Y	Y	Y	Y	Y	Y	N	N
23 Bustamante	Y	Y	N	N	N	N	Y	Y
24 Frost	N	N	N	N	N	N	Y	Y
25 Andrews	Y	Y	N	N	Y	N	Y	Y
26 ***Armey***	Y	Y	Y	Y	Y	Y	N	N
27 Ortiz	Y	Y	N	N	N	P	Y	Y
UTAH								
1 ***Hansen***	Y	Y	Y	Y	Y	Y	N	N
2 Owens	Y	Y	N	N	Y	N	Y	Y
3 ***Nielson***	Y	Y	Y	Y	Y	Y	N	N
VERMONT								
AL ***Smith***	Y	Y	N	N	Y	Y	Y	N
VIRGINIA								
1 ***Bateman***	Y	Y	N	N	Y	P	Y	N
2 Pickett	N	N	N	N	Y	N	Y	Y
3 ***Bliley***	Y	Y	Y	Y	Y	Y	Y	N
4 Sisisky	Y	Y	N	N	N	N	Y	Y
5 Payne	Y	Y	N	N	Y	N	Y	Y
6 Olin	Y	Y	N	N	N	N	Y	Y
7 ***Slaughter***	Y	Y	Y	Y	Y	Y	Y	N
8 ***Parris***	Y	Y	Y	Y	Y	Y	Y	N
9 Boucher	Y	N	N	N	N	N	Y	Y
10 ***Wolf***	Y	Y	Y	Y	Y	Y	Y	N
WASHINGTON								
1 ***Miller***	Y	Y	N	N	Y	Y	Y	N
2 Swift	N	N	N	N	N	N	Y	Y
3 Unsoeld	N	N	N	N	N	N	Y	Y
4 ***Morrison***	Y	Y	N	N	N	N	Y	N
5 Foley								
6 Dicks	N	N	N	N	N	N	Y	Y
7 McDermott	N	N	N	N	N	N	Y	Y
8 ***Chandler***	Y	Y	N	N	Y	Y	N	N
WEST VIRGINIA								
1 Mollohan	N	N	N	N	N	N	Y	Y
2 Staggers	N	N	N	N	N	N	Y	Y
3 Wise	N	N	N	N	N	N	Y	Y
4 Rahall	Y	N	N	N	N	N	Y	Y
WISCONSIN								
1 Aspin	N	N	N	N	N	?	?	Y
2 Kastenmeier	N	N	N	N	N	N	Y	Y
3 ***Gunderson***	Y	Y	N	N	Y	Y	Y	N
4 Kleczka	Y	Y	N	N	N	N	Y	Y
5 Moody	Y	Y	N	N	Y	P	Y	Y
6 ***Petri***	Y	Y	Y	Y	Y	Y	N	N
7 Obey	N	N	N	N	N	?	Y	Y
8 ***Roth***	Y	Y	Y	N	Y	Y	Y	N
9 ***Sensenbrenner***	Y	Y	Y	Y	Y	Y	N	N
WYOMING								
AL ***Thomas***	?	Y	Y	Y	Y	Y	N	N

Southern states - Ala., Ark., Fla., Ga., Ky., La., Miss., N.C., Okla., S.C., Tenn., Texas, Va.
Omitted votes are quorum calls, which CQ does not include in its vote charts.

HOUSE VOTES 245, 246, 247, 248, 249, 250, 251, 252

245. HR 5258. Balanced Budget Statute/Recommittal Motion. Horton, R-N.Y., motion to recommit to committee the bill to require that the president submit a balanced budget, that the Budget committees report balanced budgets and that both chambers consider a balanced budget each year, with instructions to hold hearings on the bill. Motion rejected 181-244: R 173-0; D 8-244 (ND 2-168, SD 6-76), July 18, 1990.

246. HR 5258. Balanced Budget Statute/Passage. Passage of the bill to require that the president submit a balanced budget, that the Budget committees report balanced budgets and that both chambers consider a balanced budget each year. Passed 282-144: R 42-131; D 240-13 (ND 161-10, SD 79-3), July 18, 1990.

247. HR 5257. Fiscal 1991 Labor, HHS and Education Appropriations/Payment Review Commission. Walker, R-Pa., amendment to cut $65,000 from the Physician Payment Review Commission account, reducing the account to its fiscal 1990 level of $3.8 million. The Physician Payment Review Commission advises Congress and the secretary of Health and Human Services on Medicare physician reimbursement. Rejected 115-293: R 112-50; D 3-243 (ND 0-168, SD 3-75), July 19, 1990.

248. HR 5257. Fiscal 1991 Labor, HHS and Education Appropriations/Institute for Peace. Walker, R-Pa., amendment to cut $450,000 from the U.S. Institute of Peace account, reducing the account to its fiscal 1990 level of $7.55 million. The Institute provides education and training, basic and applied research, and information services to promote international peace and the resolution of conflicts. Rejected 194-220: R 144-26; D 50-194 (ND 20-146, SD 30-48), July 19, 1990.

249. HR 5257. Fiscal 1991 Labor, HHS and Education Appropriations/Across-the-Board Cuts. Frenzel, R-Minn., amendment to provide an across-the-board 15.2 percent cut in all discretionary accounts to reduce spending in the bill to fiscal 1990 levels. Rejected 85-333: R 83-86; D 2-247 (ND 0-169, SD 2-78), July 19, 1990.

250. HR 5257. Fiscal 1991 Labor, HHS and Education Appropriations/Across-the-Board Cuts. Penny, D-Minn., amendment to provide an across-the-board 2 percent cut in all discretionary accounts to reduce discretionary spending in the bill, except for spending on Chapter 1 compensatory education, education for the disabled, higher education, student financial assistance and library assistance programs. Rejected 160-253: R 122-43; D 38-210 (ND 17-151, SD 21-59), July 19, 1990.

251. HR 5257. Fiscal 1991 Labor, HHS and Education Appropriations/Administrative Funding. Miller, D-Calif., amendment to reduce funding for the offices of the secretary of Labor by $2 million, the secretary of Health and Human Services by $2.8 million and the secretary of Education by $2 million. Rejected 204-212: R 92-74; D 112-138 (ND 73-97, SD 39-41), July 19, 1990.

252. HR 5257. Fiscal 1991 Labor, HHS and Education Appropriations/Passage. Passage of the bill to appropriate $170.4 billion for the Departments of Labor, Health and Human Services, and Education and related agencies, $150.7 billion in fiscal 1991, $19.4 billion in fiscal 1992, and $306.5 million in fiscal 1993. The bill appropriates $17.3 billion more than in fiscal 1990 and $4.2 billion more than requested for the three-year period by the administration. Passed 359-58: R 108-58; D 251-0 (ND 170-0, SD 81-0), July 19, 1990.

KEY

Y Voted for (yea).
\# Paired for.
\+ Announced for.
N Voted against (nay).
X Paired against.
\- Announced against.
P Voted "present."
C Voted "present" to avoid possible conflict of interest.
? Did not vote or otherwise make a position known.

Democrats ***Republicans***

	245	246	247	248	249	250	251	252
ALABAMA								
1 ***Callahan***	Y	N	Y	Y	Y	Y	Y	Y
2 ***Dickinson***	Y	N	Y	Y	N	Y	N	Y
3 Browder	N	Y	N	N	N	N	N	Y
4 Bevill	N	Y	N	N	N	N	N	Y
5 Flippo	N	Y	N	Y	N	Y	Y	Y
6 Erdreich	N	Y	N	Y	N	N	Y	Y
7 Harris	N	Y	N	Y	N	N	Y	Y
ALASKA								
AL ***Young***	Y	N	Y	N	N	N	N	Y
ARIZONA								
1 ***Rhodes***	Y	N	Y	Y	Y	Y	N	Y
2 Udall	N	Y	N	N	N	N	Y	Y
3 ***Stump***	#	X	+	#	#	#	?	X
4 ***Kyl***	Y	N	Y	Y	Y	Y	Y	N
5 ***Kolbe***	Y	N	Y	Y	Y	Y	N	Y
ARKANSAS								
1 Alexander	N	Y	N	N	N	N	N	Y
2 ***Robinson***	Y	N	Y	Y	N	Y	N	Y
3 ***Hammerschmidt***	Y	N	Y	Y	N	N	N	Y
4 Anthony	N	Y	X	X	N	N	Y	Y
CALIFORNIA								
1 Bosco	N	Y	N	N	N	N	N	Y
2 ***Herger***	Y	N	Y	Y	Y	Y	Y	N
3 Matsui	N	Y	N	N	N	N	N	Y
4 Fazio	N	Y	N	N	N	N	N	Y
5 Pelosi	N	Y	N	N	N	N	Y	Y
6 Boxer	N	Y	N	N	N	N	Y	Y
7 Miller	N	Y	N	N	N	N	Y	Y
8 Dellums	N	N	N	N	N	N	N	Y
9 Stark	N	Y	N	N	N	N	Y	Y
10 Edwards	N	Y	N	N	?	N	N	Y
11 Lantos	N	Y	N	N	N	N	Y	Y
12 ***Campbell***	Y	N	Y	Y	Y	Y	Y	Y
13 Mineta	-	+	N	N	N	N	N	Y
14 ***Shumway***	Y	N	Y	Y	Y	Y	Y	N
15 Condit	N	Y	N	N	N	Y	Y	Y
16 Panetta	N	Y	N	N	N	?	Y	Y
17 ***Pashayan***	Y	N	Y	Y	N	Y	N	Y
18 Lehman	N	Y	N	N	N	N	Y	Y
19 ***Lagomarsino***	Y	N	Y	Y	N	Y	Y	Y
20 ***Thomas***	Y	N	Y	Y	Y	Y	Y	#
21 ***Gallegly***	Y	N	Y	Y	N	Y	Y	Y
22 ***Moorhead***	Y	N	Y	Y	Y	Y	Y	N
23 Beilenson	N	Y	N	N	N	N	Y	Y
24 Waxman	N	N	N	N	N	N	N	#
25 Roybal	N	Y	N	N	N	N	N	Y
26 Berman	N	Y	N	N	N	N	N	Y
27 Levine	N	Y	N	N	N	N	Y	Y
28 Dixon	N	Y	N	N	N	N	N	Y
29 Hawkins	N	Y	N	N	X	N	N	Y
30 Martinez	N	Y	N	?	N	N	N	Y
31 Dymally	N	Y	N	N	X	X	N	Y
32 Anderson	N	Y	N	N	N	N	N	Y
33 ***Dreier***	Y	N	Y	Y	Y	Y	Y	N
34 Torres	N	Y	N	N	N	N	N	Y
35 ***Lewis***	Y	N	N	N	N	N	N	Y
36 Brown	N	Y	N	N	N	N	N	Y
37 ***McCandless***	Y	N	N	Y	Y	Y	Y	Y
38 ***Dornan***	Y	N	#	Y	Y	Y	N	N
39 ***Dannemeyer***	Y	N	?	?	#	?	?	X
40 ***Cox***	Y	N	Y	Y	Y	Y	Y	N
41 ***Lowery***	Y	N	N	Y	N	N	N	Y
42 ***Rohrabacher***	Y	N	Y	Y	Y	Y	Y	N
43 ***Packard***	Y	N	Y	Y	Y	Y	Y	N
44 Bates	N	Y	N	N	N	N	Y	Y
45 ***Hunter***	Y	N	Y	Y	Y	Y	N	N
COLORADO								
1 Schroeder	N	Y	N	N	N	N	Y	Y
2 Skaggs	N	Y	N	N	N	N	N	Y
3 Campbell	N	Y	N	Y	N	Y	N	Y
4 ***Brown***	Y	Y	Y	Y	Y	Y	Y	Y
5 ***Hefley***	Y	Y	Y	Y	Y	Y	Y	N
6 ***Schaefer***	Y	Y	Y	Y	Y	Y	Y	N
CONNECTICUT								
1 Kennelly	N	Y	N	N	N	N	Y	Y
2 Gejdenson	N	Y	N	N	N	N	Y	Y
3 Morrison	X	#	N	N	N	N	Y	Y
4 ***Shays***	Y	Y	Y	Y	N	Y	Y	Y
5 ***Rowland***	Y	Y	N	Y	N	Y	Y	Y
6 ***Johnson***	Y	Y	N	Y	Y	Y	N	N
DELAWARE								
AL Carper	N	N	N	Y	N	N	N	Y
FLORIDA								
1 Hutto	N	Y	N	Y	N	Y	Y	Y
2 ***Grant***	Y	N	Y	Y	N	N	N	Y
3 Bennett	N	Y	Y	Y	Y	Y	Y	Y
4 ***James***	Y	N	Y	Y	N	N	N	Y
5 ***McCollum***	Y	N	Y	Y	Y	Y	N	Y
6 ***Stearns***	Y	Y	Y	Y	Y	Y	Y	Y
7 Gibbons	N	Y	N	N	N	N	Y	Y
8 ***Young***	Y	N	N	N	N	N	N	Y
9 ***Bilirakis***	Y	N	N	Y	N	Y	Y	Y
10 ***Ireland***	Y	N	Y	Y	Y	Y	N	Y
11 Nelson	X	#	-	-	-	-	-	#
12 ***Lewis***	Y	N	Y	Y	N	Y	N	Y
13 ***Goss***	Y	N	Y	Y	N	Y	N	Y
14 Johnston	N	Y	N	N	N	N	Y	Y
15 ***Shaw***	Y	N	Y	Y	N	Y	N	Y
16 Smith	N	Y	N	N	N	N	Y	Y
17 Lehman	N	Y	N	N	N	N	N	Y
18 ***Ros-Lehtinen***	Y	Y	Y	Y	N	Y	Y	Y
19 Fascell	N	Y	N	N	N	N	N	Y
GEORGIA								
1 Thomas	N	Y	N	N	N	N	N	Y
2 Hatcher	N	Y	N	N	N	N	N	Y
3 Ray	Y	Y	N	Y	N	N	N	Y
4 Jones	N	Y	N	N	N	N	N	Y
5 Lewis	N	Y	N	N	N	N	Y	Y
6 ***Gingrich***	Y	N	Y	Y	Y	?	?	N
7 Darden	N	Y	N	Y	N	Y	N	Y
8 Rowland	N	Y	N	Y	N	N	N	Y
9 Jenkins	N	Y	N	Y	N	Y	Y	Y
10 Barnard	N	Y	N	Y	N	Y	Y	Y
HAWAII								
1 ***Saiki***	Y	Y	N	N	N	Y	N	Y
2 Vacancy								
IDAHO								
1 ***Craig***	#	X	#	#	?	#	?	X
2 Stallings	N	Y	N	N	N	N	Y	Y
ILLINOIS								
1 Hayes	N	Y	N	N	N	N	N	Y
2 Savage	N	N	N	N	N	N	N	Y
3 Russo	N	Y	N	N	N	Y	Y	Y
4 Sangmeister	N	Y	N	Y	N	N	Y	Y
5 Lipinski	N	Y	N	N	N	N	Y	Y
6 ***Hyde***	Y	N	N	N	N	Y	N	Y
7 Collins	N	Y	N	N	N	N	Y	Y
8 Rostenkowski	N	Y	N	N	N	N	Y	Y
9 Yates	N	Y	N	N	N	N	N	Y
10 ***Porter***	Y	N	N	N	N	N	N	Y
11 Annunzio	N	Y	N	N	N	N	N	Y
12 ***Crane***	Y	N	Y	Y	Y	Y	Y	N
13 ***Fawell***	Y	N	N	Y	Y	Y	Y	N
14 ***Hastert***	Y	Y	Y	Y	Y	Y	N	Y
15 ***Madigan***	Y	N	Y	Y	Y	Y	N	Y
16 ***Martin***	Y	N	Y	Y	N	Y	Y	N
17 Evans	N	Y	N	N	N	N	N	Y
18 ***Michel***	Y	N	Y	Y	Y	?	?	N
19 Bruce	N	Y	N	N	N	N	N	Y
20 Durbin	N	Y	N	N	N	N	Y	Y
21 Costello	N	Y	N	N	N	N	Y	Y
22 Poshard	N	Y	N	N	N	N	Y	Y
INDIANA								
1 Visclosky	N	Y	N	N	N	N	Y	Y
2 Sharp	N	Y	N	N	N	N	Y	Y
3 ***Hiler***	Y	N	Y	Y	N	Y	Y	Y

ND Northern Democrats SD Southern Democrats

	245	246	247	248	249	250	251	252
4 Long	N	Y	N	N	N	Y	Y	Y
5 Jontz	N	Y	N	N	N	N	Y	Y
6 ***Burton***	Y	N	Y	Y	Y	Y	Y	N
7 ***Myers***	Y	N	N	N	N	N	N	Y
8 McCloskey	N	Y	N	N	N	N	Y	Y
9 Hamilton	N	Y	N	N	N	N	Y	Y
10 Jacobs	N	Y	N	N	N	Y	Y	Y
IOWA								
1 ***Leach***	Y	Y	Y	N	N	Y	Y	N
2 ***Tauke***	Y	Y	Y	Y	N	Y	Y	N
3 Nagle	Y	N	N	N	N	N	N	Y
4 Smith	N	Y	N	N	N	N	N	Y
5 ***Lightfoot***	Y	N	Y	Y	N	Y	Y	N
6 ***Grandy***	Y	N	Y	Y	N	Y	Y	Y
KANSAS								
1 ***Roberts***	Y	N	Y	Y	Y	Y	Y	N
2 Slattery	N	Y	N	N	N	Y	Y	Y
3 ***Meyers***	Y	Y	Y	Y	N	Y	Y	Y
4 Glickman	N	Y	N	N	N	Y	Y	Y
5 ***Whittaker***	Y	Y	Y	N	Y	Y	Y	Y
KENTUCKY								
1 Hubbard	N	Y	N	Y	N	Y	Y	Y
2 Natcher	N	Y	N	N	N	N	N	Y
3 Mazzoli	N	Y	N	N	N	N	N	Y
4 ***Bunning***	Y	N	Y	Y	Y	Y	Y	N
5 ***Rogers***	Y	N	N	Y	N	N	N	Y
6 ***Hopkins***	Y	N	?	Y	Y	Y	Y	N
7 Perkins	N	Y	N	N	N	N	N	Y
LOUISIANA								
1 ***Livingston***	Y	N	N	Y	N	N	N	Y
2 Boggs	N	Y	N	N	N	N	N	Y
3 Tauzin	N	Y	N	Y	N	N	Y	Y
4 ***McCrery***	Y	Y	Y	Y	N	N	N	Y
5 Huckaby	N	Y	N	N	N	Y	Y	Y
6 ***Baker***	?	?	?	?	?	?	?	?
7 Hayes	N	Y	N	N	N	N	N	Y
8 ***Holloway***	Y	Y	Y	Y	N	Y	Y	Y
MAINE								
1 Brennan	N	Y	N	N	N	N	N	Y
2 ***Snowe***	Y	Y	Y	Y	N	Y	Y	Y
MARYLAND								
1 Dyson	N	Y	N	Y	N	N	Y	Y
2 ***Bentley***	Y	N	?	Y	Y	?	?	?
3 Cardin	N	N	N	N	N	N	N	Y
4 McMillen	N	Y	N	N	N	N	N	Y
5 Hoyer	N	Y	N	?	N	N	N	Y
6 Byron	N	Y	N	Y	N	Y	N	Y
7 Mfume	N	Y	N	N	N	N	N	Y
8 ***Morella***	Y	N	N	N	N	N	N	Y
MASSACHUSETTS								
1 ***Conte***	Y	Y	N	N	N	N	N	Y
2 Neal	N	Y	N	Y	N	N	N	Y
3 Early	N	Y	N	N	N	N	N	Y
4 Frank	N	Y	N	N	N	N	N	Y
5 Atkins	N	Y	N	N	N	N	N	Y
6 Mavroules	N	Y	N	Y	N	N	N	Y
7 Markey	N	Y	?	N	N	N	N	Y
8 Kennedy	N	Y	N	N	N	N	N	Y
9 Moakley	N	Y	N	N	N	N	N	Y
10 Studds	N	Y	N	N	N	N	Y	Y
11 Donnelly	N	Y	N	Y	N	N	N	Y
MICHIGAN								
1 Conyers	N	Y	N	N	N	N	N	Y
2 ***Pursell***	Y	Y	N	N	N	N	N	Y
3 Wolpe	N	Y	N	N	N	N	Y	Y
4 ***Upton***	Y	Y	Y	Y	Y	Y	Y	N
5 ***Henry***	Y	Y	N	Y	Y	Y	Y	N
6 Carr	N	Y	N	N	N	N	Y	Y
7 Kildee	N	Y	N	N	N	N	N	Y
8 Traxler	N	Y	N	N	N	N	Y	Y
9 ***Vander Jagt***	Y	Y	Y	Y	Y	Y	N	Y
10 ***Schuette***	Y	N	Y	Y	N	N	Y	Y
11 ***Davis***	Y	N	N	N	N	N	N	Y
12 Bonior	N	Y	N	N	N	N	N	Y
13 Crockett	N	Y	N	N	N	N	?	Y
14 Hertel	N	Y	N	N	N	N	N	Y
15 Ford	N	Y	N	N	N	N	N	Y
16 Dingell	N	Y	N	N	N	N	N	Y
17 Levin	N	Y	N	N	N	N	Y	Y
18 ***Broomfield***	Y	Y	Y	Y	Y	Y	Y	Y
MINNESOTA								
1 Penny	N	Y	N	Y	N	Y	Y	Y
2 ***Weber***	Y	N	N	N	N	N	N	Y
3 ***Frenzel***	Y	N	Y	Y	Y	?	?	N
4 Vento	N	Y	N	N	N	Y	Y	Y

	245	246	247	248	249	250	251	252
5 Sabo	N	N	?	N	N	N	N	Y
6 Sikorski	N	Y	N	N	N	N	Y	Y
7 ***Stangeland***	Y	N	N	Y	N	N	N	Y
8 Oberstar	N	Y	N	N	N	N	Y	Y
MISSISSIPPI								
1 Whitten	N	Y	N	N	N	N	N	Y
2 Espy	N	Y	N	N	N	N	N	Y
3 Montgomery	Y	Y	N	Y	N	N	Y	Y
4 Parker	Y	Y	N	Y	N	Y	Y	Y
5 Taylor	N	Y	N	Y	N	Y	Y	Y
MISSOURI								
1 Clay	N	Y	N	N	N	N	N	Y
2 ***Buechner***	Y	N	Y	Y	N	Y	Y	Y
3 Gephardt	N	Y	N	N	N	?	N	Y
4 Skelton	N	Y	N	Y	N	N	N	Y
5 Wheat	N	N	N	N	N	N	N	Y
6 ***Coleman***	Y	N	Y	Y	N	Y	N	Y
7 ***Hancock***	Y	N	Y	Y	Y	Y	Y	N
8 ***Emerson***	Y	Y	N	Y	N	N	N	Y
9 Volkmer	N	Y	N	Y	N	N	Y	Y
MONTANA								
1 Williams	N	Y	N	N	N	N	N	Y
2 ***Marlenee***	Y	Y	N	Y	Y	Y	N	N
NEBRASKA								
1 ***Bereuter***	Y	Y	N	Y	N	N	Y	Y
2 Hoagland	N	Y	N	N	N	Y	Y	Y
3 ***Smith***	Y	Y	N	Y	N	N	N	Y
NEVADA								
1 Bilbray	N	Y	N	N	N	N	N	Y
2 ***Vucanovich***	Y	N	Y	Y	N	N	N	Y
NEW HAMPSHIRE								
1 ***Smith***	Y	N	Y	Y	Y	Y	Y	N
2 ***Douglas***	Y	N	Y	Y	Y	Y	Y	N
NEW JERSEY								
1 Vacancy								
2 Hughes	N	Y	N	Y	N	Y	Y	Y
3 Pallone	N	Y	N	N	N	Y	Y	Y
4 ***Smith***	Y	Y	N	Y	N	N	N	Y
5 ***Roukema***	Y	Y	N	Y	N	Y	Y	Y
6 Dwyer	N	Y	N	N	N	N	N	Y
7 ***Rinaldo***	Y	Y	N	N	N	N	N	Y
8 Roe	N	Y	N	N	N	N	N	Y
9 Torricelli	N	Y	N	N	N	N	Y	Y
10 Payne	N	N	N	N	N	N	N	Y
11 ***Gallo***	Y	N	N	N	N	Y	N	Y
12 ***Courter***	Y	N	N	Y	N	N	N	Y
13 ***Saxton***	Y	N	Y	Y	N	N	N	Y
14 Guarini	N	Y	N	N	N	N	Y	Y
NEW MEXICO								
1 ***Schiff***	Y	N	Y	Y	N	N	N	Y
2 ***Skeen***	Y	N	N	Y	N	N	N	Y
3 Richardson	N	Y	N	N	N	N	N	Y
NEW YORK								
1 Hochbrueckner	N	Y	N	N	N	N	Y	Y
2 Downey	N	Y	N	N	N	N	Y	Y
3 Mrazek	N	Y	N	N	N	N	N	Y
4 ***Lent***	Y	N	Y	Y	Y	Y	N	Y
5 ***McGrath***	Y	N	Y	Y	N	Y	Y	Y
6 Flake	N	Y	N	X	N	N	N	Y
7 Ackerman	N	Y	N	N	N	N	N	Y
8 Scheuer	N	Y	N	N	N	N	N	Y
9 Manton	N	Y	N	N	N	N	N	Y
10 Schumer	N	Y	N	?	N	N	Y	Y
11 Towns	N	Y	N	N	N	N	N	Y
12 Owens	N	Y	N	N	N	X	?	#
13 Solarz	N	Y	N	N	N	N	N	Y
14 ***Molinari***	Y	N	Y	Y	N	Y	Y	Y
15 ***Green***	Y	N	N	N	N	N	N	Y
16 Rangel	N	Y	N	N	N	N	N	Y
17 Weiss	N	Y	N	N	N	N	N	Y
18 Serrano	N	Y	N	N	N	N	N	Y
19 Engel	N	Y	N	N	N	N	Y	Y
20 Lowey	N	Y	N	N	N	N	N	Y
21 ***Fish***	Y	N	?	Y	N	Y	N	Y
22 ***Gilman***	Y	N	N	N	N	N	N	Y
23 McNulty	N	Y	N	N	N	N	N	Y
24 ***Solomon***	Y	N	Y	Y	?	Y	Y	N
25 ***Boehlert***	Y	N	N	N	N	N	N	Y
26 ***Martin***	Y	N	N	Y	N	N	N	Y
27 ***Walsh***	Y	N	N	Y	N	Y	N	Y
28 McHugh	N	Y	N	N	N	N	N	Y
29 ***Horton***	Y	N	N	N	N	N	N	Y
30 Slaughter	N	Y	N	N	N	N	Y	Y
31 ***Paxon***	Y	N	Y	Y	Y	Y	Y	N

	245	246	247	248	249	250	251	252
32 LaFalce	N	Y	N	?	N	N	Y	Y
33 Nowak	N	Y	N	Y	N	N	N	Y
34 ***Houghton***	Y	N	N	Y	Y	Y	N	Y
NORTH CAROLINA								
1 Jones	N	Y	N	N	N	N	N	Y
2 Valentine	N	Y	N	Y	N	N	N	Y
3 Lancaster	N	Y	N	N	N	N	Y	Y
4 Price	N	Y	N	N	N	N	N	Y
5 Neal	N	Y	N	N	N	Y	Y	Y
6 ***Coble***	Y	N	Y	Y	Y	Y	Y	Y
7 Rose	N	Y	N	N	N	N	N	Y
8 Hefner	N	Y	N	Y	N	N	Y	Y
9 ***McMillan***	Y	N	Y	Y	Y	Y	Y	N
10 ***Ballenger***	Y	N	Y	Y	Y	Y	Y	N
11 Clarke	N	Y	N	N	N	N	Y	Y
NORTH DAKOTA								
AL Dorgan	N	Y	N	N	N	Y	Y	Y
OHIO								
1 Luken	N	Y	?	?	?	?	?	?
2 ***Gradison***	Y	N	Y	Y	Y	Y	Y	N
3 Hall	N	Y	N	?	N	Y	Y	Y
4 ***Oxley***	Y	N	N	Y	Y	Y	N	N
5 ***Gillmor***	Y	N	Y	Y	N	N	N	Y
6 ***McEwen***	Y	N	Y	Y	Y	Y	Y	N
7 ***DeWine***	Y	N	Y	Y	N	Y	Y	Y
8 ***Lukens***	Y	N	?	Y	Y	Y	Y	N
9 Kaptur	N	Y	N	N	N	N	N	Y
10 ***Miller***	Y	Y	Y	Y	Y	Y	Y	Y
11 Eckart	N	Y	N	N	N	N	N	Y
12 ***Kasich***	Y	N	Y	Y	Y	Y	Y	N
13 Pease	N	Y	N	N	N	N	N	Y
14 Sawyer	N	Y	N	N	N	N	N	Y
15 ***Wylie***	Y	N	Y	Y	Y	Y	Y	Y
16 ***Regula***	Y	Y	Y	Y	N	Y	N	Y
17 Traficant	N	Y	N	N	N	N	N	Y
18 Applegate	N	Y	N	Y	N	N	N	Y
19 Feighan	N	Y	N	N	N	N	Y	Y
20 Oakar	?	Y	N	N	N	N	N	Y
21 Stokes	N	Y	N	N	N	N	N	Y
OKLAHOMA								
1 ***Inhofe***	Y	N	Y	Y	Y	Y	Y	Y
2 Synar	N	Y	N	Y	N	N	Y	Y
3 Watkins	N	Y	?	?	?	?	?	?
4 McCurdy	N	Y	N	N	N	Y	Y	Y
5 ***Edwards***	Y	N	Y	Y	Y	Y	Y	N
6 English	N	Y	N	Y	N	Y	Y	Y
OREGON								
1 AuCoin	N	Y	N	N	N	N	N	Y
2 ***Smith, B.***	Y	N	Y	Y	N	Y	Y	Y
3 Wyden	N	Y	N	N	N	N	N	Y
4 DeFazio	N	Y	N	N	N	N	Y	Y
5 ***Smith, D.***	Y	N	Y	Y	Y	Y	Y	X
PENNSYLVANIA								
1 Foglietta	N	Y	?	N	N	N	Y	Y
2 Gray	N	Y	X	N	N	N	N	Y
3 Borski	N	Y	N	N	N	N	Y	Y
4 Kolter	N	Y	N	N	N	N	N	Y
5 ***Schulze***	Y	N	Y	Y	Y	Y	N	Y
6 Yatron	N	Y	N	Y	N	Y	Y	Y
7 ***Weldon***	Y	N	N	Y	N	N	N	Y
8 Kostmayer	N	Y	N	N	N	N	Y	Y
9 ***Shuster***	Y	N	Y	Y	Y	Y	Y	N
10 ***McDade***	Y	N	?	?	?	?	?	+
11 Kanjorski	N	Y	N	Y	N	N	N	Y
12 Murtha	N	N	N	N	N	N	N	Y
13 ***Coughlin***	Y	N	Y	Y	N	N	N	Y
14 Coyne	N	Y	N	N	N	N	N	Y
15 ***Ritter***	Y	N	?	N	Y	Y	Y	Y
16 ***Walker***	Y	N	Y	Y	Y	Y	Y	N
17 ***Gekas***	Y	N	Y	Y	Y	Y	Y	N
18 Walgren	N	Y	N	N	N	N	Y	Y
19 ***Goodling***	Y	N	?	N	N	N	N	Y
20 Gaydos	N	Y	N	Y	N	N	N	Y
21 ***Ridge***	Y	N	Y	Y	N	Y	Y	?
22 Murphy	N	Y	N	Y	N	N	N	Y
23 ***Clinger***	Y	N	Y	Y	N	Y	Y	Y
RHODE ISLAND								
1 ***Machtley***	Y	Y	N	Y	N	N	N	Y
2 ***Schneider***	Y	Y	N	N	N	Y	N	Y
SOUTH CAROLINA								
1 ***Ravenel***	Y	N	N	Y	N	Y	Y	Y
2 ***Spence***	Y	Y	N	Y	Y	Y	N	Y
3 Derrick	N	Y	N	N	N	Y	Y	Y
4 Patterson	N	Y	N	Y	N	Y	Y	Y
5 Spratt	N	Y	N	N	N	N	Y	Y
6 Tallon	N	Y	N	Y	N	N	Y	Y

	245	246	247	248	249	250	251	252
SOUTH DAKOTA								
AL Johnson	N	Y	N	N	N	N	Y	Y
TENNESSEE								
1 ***Quillen***	Y	N	Y	Y	Y	Y	N	Y
2 ***Duncan***	Y	Y	Y	Y	N	Y	Y	Y
3 Lloyd	N	Y	N	N	N	N	N	Y
4 Cooper	N	Y	N	Y	N	Y	Y	Y
5 Clement	N	Y	N	N	N	N	N	Y
6 Gordon	N	Y	N	N	N	N	Y	Y
7 ***Sundquist***	Y	N	Y	Y	Y	Y	Y	N
8 Tanner	N	Y	Y	Y	N	N	Y	Y
9 Ford	N	Y	N	N	N	N	Y	Y
TEXAS								
1 Chapman	N	Y	?	Y	N	N	N	Y
2 Wilson	N	Y	N	N	N	N	N	Y
3 ***Bartlett***	Y	N	Y	Y	Y	Y	N	N
4 Hall	Y	Y	N	N	N	N	N	Y
5 Bryant	N	Y	N	N	N	N	N	Y
6 ***Barton***	Y	N	Y	Y	Y	Y	Y	N
7 ***Archer***	Y	N	Y	Y	N	?	Y	N
8 ***Fields***	Y	N	Y	Y	Y	Y	Y	N
9 Brooks	N	Y	N	N	N	N	N	Y
10 Pickle	N	Y	N	Y	N	N	N	Y
11 Leath	N	N	?	?	?	N	N	Y
12 Geren	N	Y	N	N	N	N	Y	Y
13 Sarpalius	N	Y	N	N	N	N	N	Y
14 Laughlin	N	Y	N	Y	N	Y	Y	Y
15 de la Garza	N	Y	N	N	N	N	N	Y
16 Coleman	N	Y	N	N	N	N	N	Y
17 Stenholm	Y	Y	Y	Y	Y	Y	Y	Y
18 Washington	N	Y	N	N	N	?	?	Y
19 ***Combest***	Y	N	Y	Y	Y	Y	Y	N
20 Gonzalez	N	N	N	N	N	N	N	Y
21 ***Smith***	Y	N	Y	Y	N	Y	Y	Y
22 ***DeLay***	Y	N	Y	Y	Y	Y	Y	N
23 Bustamante	N	Y	N	?	N	N	N	Y
24 Frost	N	Y	N	N	N	N	N	Y
25 Andrews	N	Y	N	Y	N	Y	Y	Y
26 ***Armey***	Y	N	Y	Y	Y	Y	Y	N
27 Ortiz	N	Y	N	N	N	N	N	Y
UTAH								
1 ***Hansen***	Y	N	Y	Y	Y	Y	Y	N
2 Owens	N	Y	N	N	N	Y	Y	Y
3 ***Nielson***	Y	N	?	Y	Y	Y	Y	N
VERMONT								
AL ***Smith***	Y	Y	N	N	N	N	N	Y
VIRGINIA								
1 ***Bateman***	Y	N	N	Y	N	Y	N	Y
2 Pickett	Y	N	N	N	N	N	N	Y
3 ***Bliley***	Y	N	Y	Y	Y	Y	Y	Y
4 Sisisky	N	Y	N	N	N	N	N	Y
5 Payne	N	Y	N	Y	N	Y	N	Y
6 Olin	N	Y	N	Y	N	Y	Y	Y
7 ***Slaughter***	Y	N	Y	Y	Y	Y	Y	Y
8 ***Parris***	Y	Y	N	Y	N	N	N	Y
9 Boucher	N	Y	N	N	N	N	N	Y
10 ***Wolf***	Y	N	N	Y	N	Y	N	Y
WASHINGTON								
1 ***Miller***	Y	N	−	−	−	+	+	+
2 Swift	N	Y	N	N	N	N	N	Y
3 Unsoeld	N	Y	N	N	N	N	Y	Y
4 ***Morrison***	Y	Y	N	N	N	N	N	Y
5 Foley								
6 Dicks	Y	Y	N	N	N	N	N	Y
7 McDermott	N	Y	N	N	N	N	Y	Y
8 ***Chandler***	Y	N	N	N	Y	Y	Y	Y
WEST VIRGINIA								
1 Mollohan	N	Y	N	N	N	N	N	Y
2 Staggers	N	Y	N	N	N	N	Y	Y
3 Wise	N	Y	N	N	N	N	Y	Y
4 Rahall	N	Y	N	N	N	N	N	Y
WISCONSIN								
1 Aspin	N	Y	N	N	N	N	Y	Y
2 Kastenmeier	N	Y	N	N	N	Y	Y	Y
3 ***Gunderson***	Y	N	Y	Y	N	N	Y	Y
4 Kleczka	N	Y	N	Y	N	N	N	Y
5 Moody	N	Y	N	N	N	N	Y	Y
6 ***Petri***	Y	Y	Y	Y	Y	Y	Y	N
7 Obey	N	Y	N	N	N	N	N	Y
8 ***Roth***	Y	Y	Y	Y	Y	Y	Y	Y
9 ***Sensenbrenner***	Y	N	Y	Y	Y	Y	Y	N
WYOMING								
AL ***Thomas***	Y	Y	Y	Y	Y	Y	Y	N

Southern states - Ala., Ark., Fla., Ga., Ky., La., Miss., N.C., Okla., S.C., Tenn., Texas, Va.
Omitted votes are quorum calls, which CQ does not include in its vote charts.

HOUSE VOTES 253,254,255,256,257,258,259,260

253. HR 5115. Omnibus Education Authorizations/Open Enrollment Study. Hawkins, D-Calif., en bloc amendment to provide $40 million in grants to study open enrollment "choice" programs in schools, parental as well as business and community involvement in public schools, and improved public education finance. It would also permit school districts to enter into educational performance agreements with the federal government to cut red tape involving federal dollars to local schools, amend the Adult Education Act, amend the Bilingual Education Act, clarify the auditing process within the Education Department's Office of Administrative Law Judges, and for other purposes. Adopted 387-0: R 153-0; D 234-0 (ND 163-0, SD 71-0), July 20, 1990.

254. HR 5115. Omnibus Education Authorizations/Student Aid Eligibility. Roukema, R-N.J., amendment to change the formula for student aid eligibility and address the student loan default rate. Rejected 122-264: R 101-53; D 21-211 (ND 14-150, SD 7-61), July 20, 1990.

255. HR 5115. Omnibus Education Authorizations/Student Aid Suspensions. Solomon, R-N.Y., amendment to suspend student financial assistance to students convicted of offenses involving the possession or sale of illegal drugs. Adopted 315-59: R 148-0; D 167-59 (ND 106-52, SD 61-7), July 20, 1990.

256. HR 5115. Omnibus Education Authorizations/Passage. Passage of the bill to authorize $1.1 billion in fiscal 1991-95 for a series of new educational initiatives to increase the high school graduation rate to at least 90 percent, promote math and science education, combat adult illiteracy and boost the recruitment of quality teachers. Passed 350-25: R 123-25; D 227-0 (ND 159-0, SD 68-0), July 20, 1990.

257. HR 3950. Farm Programs Reauthorization/Rule. Adoption of the rule (H Res 439) to provide for House floor consideration of the bill to revise and extend federal farm price- and income-support programs for major commodities as well as Agriculture Department nutrition programs. Adopted 283-80: R 89-58; D 194-22 (ND 142-1, SD 52-21), July 23, 1990.

258. HR 3950. Farm Programs Reauthorization/Sugar Price Supports. Downey, D-N.Y., amendment to change the sugar price-support program loan rate from 18 cents per pound to 16 cents per pound through fiscal 1995. Rejected 150-271: R 70-102; D 80-169 (ND 67-103, SD 13-66), July 24, 1990.

259. HR 3950. Farm Programs Reauthorization/Dairy Price Supports. Volkmer, D-Mo., amendment to change the dairy price-support program from $10.10 per hundredweight to $10.60 per hundredweight in fiscal 1991 and to be adjusted annually thereafter by the Agriculture Department. The amendment would also establish a "two tier" price-support system, to take effect if dairy surpluses were estimated to exceed 5 billion pounds a year. Rejected 70-353: R 10-165; D 60-188 (ND 45-125, SD 15-63), July 24, 1990.

260. HR 3950. Farm Programs Reauthorization/Dairy Allowances. Obey, D-Wis., amendment to provide that no state may establish a dairy "make allowance" greater than that used by the Agriculture Department. The make allowance was a surcharge dairy farmers pay to have dairy products processed; California used a make allowance greater than that used by the Agriculture Department. Adopted 307-114: R 150-22; D 157-92 (ND 121-49, SD 36-43), July 24, 1990.

KEY

Y Voted for (yea).
\# Paired for.
\+ Announced for.
N Voted against (nay).
X Paired against.
\- Announced against.
P Voted "present."
C Voted "present" to avoid possible conflict of interest.
? Did not vote or otherwise make a position known.

Democrats ***Republicans***

	253	254	255	256	257	258	259	260
ALABAMA								
1 ***Callahan***	Y	Y	?	?	N	N	N	Y
2 ***Dickinson***	Y	Y	Y	Y	N	N	N	Y
3 Browder	Y	N	Y	Y	N	N	N	Y
4 Bevill	Y	?	Y	Y	N	N	N	Y
5 Flippo	Y	N	Y	Y	N	N	N	Y
6 Erdreich	Y	N	Y	Y	N	N	N	Y
7 Harris	Y	N	Y	Y	N	N	N	N
ALASKA								
AL ***Young***	Y	N	Y	Y	N	N	N	N
ARIZONA								
1 ***Rhodes***	Y	N	Y	N	N	Y	N	N
2 Udall	?	N	?	Y	Y	Y	Y	Y
3 ***Stump***	?	#	+	-	N	N	N	Y
4 ***Kyl***	Y	Y	Y	N	N	Y	N	Y
5 ***Kolbe***	Y	Y	Y	Y	Y	Y	N	Y
ARKANSAS								
1 Alexander	Y	N	Y	Y	N	N	Y	Y
2 ***Robinson***	?	?	?	?	Y	N	N	Y
3 ***Hammerschmidt***	Y	N	Y	Y	Y	Y	Y	Y
4 Anthony	Y	N	Y	Y	N	N	Y	Y
CALIFORNIA								
1 Bosco	Y	N	Y	Y	Y	N	N	N
2 ***Herger***	Y	Y	Y	N	Y	N	N	N
3 Matsui	Y	N	Y	Y	Y	N	N	N
4 Fazio	Y	N	?	Y	Y	N	N	N
5 Pelosi	Y	N	N	Y	Y	N	N	N
6 Boxer	Y	N	?	?	?	N	N	N
7 Miller	?	?	?	?	Y	N	N	N
8 Dellums	Y	N	N	Y	Y	N	N	N
9 Stark	Y	N	N	Y	Y	N	N	N
10 Edwards	Y	N	N	Y	Y	Y	N	N
11 Lantos	Y	Y	Y	Y	Y	N	N	N
12 ***Campbell***	Y	Y	Y	Y	Y	Y	N	N
13 Mineta	Y	N	N	Y	Y	N	N	N
14 ***Shumway***	Y	Y	Y	N	N	N	N	N
15 Condit	Y	N	Y	Y	Y	N	Y	N
16 Panetta	Y	N	Y	Y	Y	N	N	N
17 ***Pashayan***	Y	N	Y	Y	#	N	N	N
18 Lehman	Y	N	Y	Y	?	N	N	N
19 ***Lagomarsino***	Y	N	Y	Y	N	N	N	N
20 ***Thomas***	?	X	?	?	Y	N	N	N
21 ***Gallegly***	Y	Y	Y	Y	N	N	N	N
22 ***Moorhead***	Y	N	Y	Y	N	N	N	N
23 Beilenson	Y	N	Y	Y	Y	Y	N	N
24 Waxman	Y	N	?	?	Y	Y	N	N
25 Roybal	Y	N	N	Y	Y	N	N	N
26 Berman	Y	N	N	Y	Y	Y	N	N
27 Levine	Y	N	N	Y	?	Y	N	N
28 Dixon	Y	N	N	Y	+	Y	N	N
29 Hawkins	Y	N	N	Y	Y	Y	N	N
30 Martinez	Y	N	Y	Y	Y	N	N	N
31 Dymally	Y	N	N	Y	?	N	N	N
32 Anderson	Y	N	N	Y	?	N	N	N
33 ***Dreier***	Y	Y	Y	Y	N	N	N	N
34 Torres	Y	N	Y	Y	+	N	N	N
35 ***Lewis***	?	?	?	?	?	N	N	Y
36 Brown	Y	N	Y	Y	Y	N	N	N
37 ***McCandless***	Y	Y	Y	Y	?	N	N	N
38 ***Dornan***	Y	#	?	?	N	N	N	N
39 ***Dannemeyer***	?	?	?	?	?	N	N	N
40 ***Cox***	?	?	?	?	?	Y	N	N
41 ***Lowery***	Y	N	Y	Y	Y	N	N	N
42 ***Rohrabacher***	Y	Y	Y	N	N	Y	N	N
43 ***Packard***	Y	Y	?	?	X	Y	N	N
44 Bates	Y	N	Y	Y	Y	Y	N	Y
45 ***Hunter***	Y	Y	Y	N	N	N	N	N
COLORADO								
1 Schroeder	Y	N	Y	Y	Y	Y	N	Y
2 Skaggs	Y	N	Y	Y	Y	N	N	Y
3 Campbell	Y	N	Y	Y	Y	N	N	Y
4 ***Brown***	Y	Y	Y	Y	N	N	N	Y
5 ***Hefley***	Y	Y	Y	Y	N	N	N	Y
6 ***Schaefer***	Y	Y	Y	Y	?	N	N	Y
CONNECTICUT								
1 Kennelly	Y	N	Y	Y	Y	Y	N	Y
2 Gejdenson	Y	N	Y	Y	Y	Y	N	Y
3 Morrison	+	-	+	+	+	+	-	+
4 ***Shays***	Y	Y	Y	Y	Y	Y	N	Y
5 ***Rowland***	?	?	?	?	?	Y	N	Y
6 ***Johnson***	Y	Y	Y	Y	Y	Y	N	Y
DELAWARE								
AL Carper	Y	N	Y	Y	Y	Y	N	Y
FLORIDA								
1 Hutto	Y	N	Y	Y	N	N	N	Y
2 ***Grant***	Y	Y	Y	Y	Y	N	N	Y
3 Bennett	Y	Y	Y	Y	Y	Y	N	Y
4 ***James***	Y	N	Y	Y	N	N	N	Y
5 ***McCollum***	?	?	?	?	N	N	N	Y
6 ***Stearns***	Y	Y	Y	Y	N	N	N	Y
7 Gibbons	Y	N	Y	Y	Y	Y	N	N
8 ***Young***	Y	N	Y	Y	N	Y	N	Y
9 ***Bilirakis***	Y	N	Y	Y	N	?	N	Y
10 ***Ireland***	Y	Y	Y	Y	N	N	N	?
11 Nelson	+	-	+	+	+	#	-	-
12 ***Lewis***	Y	Y	Y	Y	Y	N	N	Y
13 ***Goss***	Y	Y	Y	Y	Y	N	N	Y
14 Johnston	Y	N	Y	Y	Y	N	N	Y
15 ***Shaw***	Y	Y	Y	Y	N	Y	N	Y
16 Smith	Y	N	Y	Y	Y	N	N	Y
17 Lehman	Y	Y	N	Y	Y	Y	N	Y
18 ***Ros-Lehtinen***	Y	N	Y	Y	N	N	N	Y
19 Fascell	Y	N	Y	Y	Y	N	N	Y
GEORGIA								
1 Thomas	Y	N	Y	Y	N	N	N	N
2 Hatcher	Y	N	Y	Y	Y	N	N	N
3 Ray	Y	N	Y	Y	Y	N	N	N
4 Jones	Y	N	Y	Y	Y	N	N	N
5 Lewis	Y	N	N	Y	Y	Y	N	N
6 ***Gingrich***	Y	Y	?	Y	?	N	N	Y
7 Darden	Y	N	Y	Y	Y	N	N	Y
8 Rowland	Y	N	Y	Y	?	N	N	N
9 Jenkins	Y	N	Y	Y	Y	N	N	Y
10 Barnard	?	?	?	?	Y	Y	N	N
HAWAII								
1 ***Saiki***	Y	Y	Y	Y	Y	N	N	Y
2 Vacancy								
IDAHO								
1 ***Craig***	?	?	?	?	X	N	N	Y
2 Stallings	?	?	?	?	Y	N	N	N
ILLINOIS								
1 Hayes	Y	N	N	Y	Y	N	N	Y
2 Savage	Y	N	N	Y	Y	Y	N	Y
3 Russo	Y	N	Y	Y	Y	N	N	N
4 Sangmeister	Y	N	Y	Y	Y	N	N	Y
5 Lipinski	Y	N	Y	Y	?	N	N	Y
6 ***Hyde***	Y	Y	Y	Y	N	Y	N	Y
7 Collins	Y	N	Y	Y	Y	N	N	Y
8 Rostenkowski	Y	N	Y	Y	Y	Y	N	Y
9 Yates	Y	N	N	Y	Y	Y	N	Y
10 ***Porter***	+	-	+	+	Y	Y	N	Y
11 Annunzio	Y	N	Y	Y	Y	Y	N	Y
12 ***Crane***	Y	Y	Y	N	N	Y	N	Y
13 ***Fawell***	Y	Y	Y	Y	N	Y	N	Y
14 ***Hastert***	Y	Y	Y	Y	Y	N	N	Y
15 ***Madigan***	Y	Y	Y	Y	Y	N	N	Y
16 ***Martin***	Y	Y	Y	Y	?	Y	N	Y
17 Evans	Y	N	N	Y	Y	N	Y	Y
18 ***Michel***	Y	Y	Y	Y	Y	N	N	Y
19 Bruce	Y	N	Y	Y	Y	N	Y	Y
20 Durbin	Y	N	Y	Y	Y	N	N	Y
21 Costello	Y	N	Y	Y	Y	N	N	Y
22 Poshard	Y	N	Y	Y	Y	N	N	Y
INDIANA								
1 Visclosky	?	?	?	?	Y	Y	Y	Y
2 Sharp	Y	N	Y	Y	?	Y	N	Y
3 ***Hiler***	Y	Y	Y	Y	Y	Y	N	Y

ND Northern Democrats SD Southern Democrats

	253	254	255	256	257	258	259	260
4 Long	Y	N	Y	Y	Y	N	N	N
5 Jontz	Y	N	N	Y	Y	N	Y	N
6 ***Burton***	Y	Y	Y	N	Y	Y	Y	Y
7 ***Myers***	?	?	?	?	Y	N	N	Y
8 McCloskey	Y	N	N	Y	Y	N	N	Y
9 Hamilton	Y	N	Y	Y	Y	Y	N	Y
10 Jacobs	Y	N	Y	Y	N	Y	N	N
IOWA								
1 ***Leach***	Y	Y	Y	Y	Y	Y	N	Y
2 ***Tauke***	Y	N	Y	Y	Y	N	N	Y
3 Nagle	Y	N	Y	Y	Y	N	Y	N
4 Smith	?	?	?	?	Y	N	N	Y
5 ***Lightfoot***	Y	Y	Y	N	N	N	N	Y
6 ***Grandy***	Y	N	Y	Y	Y	N	N	Y
KANSAS								
1 ***Roberts***	Y	Y	Y	Y	Y	N	N	Y
2 Slattery	Y	N	Y	Y	Y	Y	N	Y
3 ***Meyers***	Y	Y	Y	Y	Y	Y	N	Y
4 Glickman	Y	Y	Y	Y	Y	N	N	N
5 ***Whittaker***	Y	Y	Y	Y	Y	N	N	Y
KENTUCKY								
1 Hubbard	Y	N	Y	Y	Y	N	N	Y
2 Natcher	Y	N	Y	Y	Y	N	N	N
3 Mazzoli	Y	N	Y	Y	Y	Y	N	Y
4 ***Bunning***	Y	Y	Y	Y	N	N	N	Y
5 ***Rogers***	Y	Y	Y	Y	N	N	N	Y
6 ***Hopkins***	Y	Y	Y	Y	Y	N	N	Y
7 Perkins	Y	N	N	Y	Y	N	Y	N
LOUISIANA								
1 ***Livingston***	Y	N	Y	Y	N	N	N	Y
2 Boggs	?	?	?	?	N	N	N	N
3 Tauzin	?	X	?	?	Y	N	N	N
4 ***McCrery***	Y	N	Y	Y	N	N	N	Y
5 Huckaby	Y	Y	Y	Y	N	N	N	N
6 ***Baker***	?	?	?	?	?	N	N	N
7 Hayes	?	?	?	?	N	N	N	N
8 ***Holloway***	Y	Y	Y	Y	N	N	N	Y
MAINE								
1 Brennan	Y	N	Y	Y	Y	Y	N	Y
2 ***Snowe***	Y	Y	Y	Y	Y	Y	N	Y
MARYLAND								
1 Dyson	?	?	?	?	Y	N	N	N
2 ***Bentley***	?	?	?	?	Y	N	N	Y
3 Cardin	Y	N	Y	Y	Y	N	N	Y
4 McMillen	Y	N	Y	Y	Y	N	N	Y
5 Hoyer	Y	N	Y	Y	Y	N	N	N
6 Byron	Y	Y	Y	Y	Y	N	N	Y
7 Mfume	Y	N	Y	Y	Y	N	N	Y
8 ***Morella***	Y	N	Y	Y	Y	?	N	Y
MASSACHUSETTS								
1 ***Conte***	Y	N	Y	Y	Y	Y	N	Y
2 Neal	Y	N	Y	Y	?	Y	N	Y
3 Early	?	?	?	?	Y	Y	N	Y
4 Frank	Y	N	N	Y	Y	Y	N	Y
5 Atkins	Y	N	N	Y	Y	Y	N	Y
6 Mavroules	Y	N	Y	Y	?	N	N	N
7 Markey	Y	N	N	Y	Y	Y	N	Y
8 Kennedy	Y	N	Y	Y	Y	Y	N	Y
9 Moakley	Y	N	Y	Y	Y	Y	N	Y
10 Studds	Y	N	Y	Y	Y	Y	N	Y
11 Donnelly	Y	N	Y	Y	?	Y	N	Y
MICHIGAN								
1 Conyers	Y	N	Y	Y	Y	Y	Y	N
2 ***Pursell***	Y	N	Y	Y	Y	N	N	Y
3 Wolpe	Y	N	Y	Y	Y	N	Y	Y
4 ***Upton***	Y	Y	Y	Y	Y	Y	N	Y
5 ***Henry***	Y	Y	Y	Y	Y	Y	N	Y
6 Carr	Y	N	Y	Y	?	N	N	Y
7 Kildee	Y	N	N	Y	Y	N	Y	Y
8 Traxler	Y	N	Y	Y	Y	N	Y	Y
9 ***Vander Jagt***	Y	Y	Y	Y	Y	N	N	Y
10 ***Schuette***	?	?	?	?	?	N	N	Y
11 ***Davis***	?	?	?	?	?	N	N	Y
12 Bonior	Y	N	Y	Y	Y	N	Y	Y
13 Crockett	Y	?	?	Y	?	?	?	?
14 Hertel	Y	N	Y	Y	Y	N	N	Y
15 Ford	Y	N	N	Y	Y	N	N	Y
16 Dingell	Y	N	N	Y	Y	N	N	Y
17 Levin	Y	N	Y	Y	Y	N	N	Y
18 ***Broomfield***	Y	X	?	?	?	Y	N	Y
MINNESOTA								
1 Penny	Y	N	Y	Y	Y	N	N	Y
2 ***Weber***	Y	N	Y	Y	Y	N	N	Y
3 ***Frenzel***	Y	N	Y	Y	N	Y	N	?
4 Vento	Y	N	N	Y	Y	N	Y	Y

	253	254	255	256	257	258	259	260
5 Sabo	Y	N	N	Y	Y	N	Y	Y
6 Sikorski	Y	N	Y	Y	Y	N	Y	Y
7 ***Stangeland***	Y	N	Y	Y	Y	N	Y	Y
8 Oberstar	Y	N	N	Y	Y	N	Y	Y
MISSISSIPPI								
1 Whitten	Y	N	Y	Y	Y	N	N	N
2 Espy	?	?	?	?	N	N	Y	N
3 Montgomery	Y	N	Y	Y	Y	N	N	Y
4 Parker	Y	N	Y	Y	Y	N	N	N
5 Taylor	Y	Y	Y	Y	N	N	N	N
MISSOURI								
1 Clay	Y	N	Y	Y	Y	Y	N	N
2 ***Buechner***	Y	Y	Y	Y	N	N	N	Y
3 Gephardt	Y	N	Y	?	Y	N	Y	N
4 Skelton	Y	N	Y	Y	Y	N	Y	Y
5 Wheat	Y	N	N	Y	Y	N	Y	N
6 ***Coleman***	Y	N	Y	Y	Y	N	N	Y
7 ***Hancock***	Y	Y	Y	N	?	Y	N	Y
8 ***Emerson***	Y	N	Y	Y	Y	N	Y	Y
9 Volkmer	Y	N	Y	Y	Y	N	Y	N
MONTANA								
1 Williams	Y	N	N	Y	Y	N	Y	Y
2 ***Marlenee***	Y	Y	Y	Y	?	N	N	N
NEBRASKA								
1 ***Bereuter***	Y	Y	Y	Y	Y	N	N	Y
2 Hoagland	Y	N	Y	Y	Y	N	Y	N
3 ***Smith***	?	?	?	?	Y	N	N	Y
NEVADA								
1 Bilbray	Y	N	Y	Y	Y	N	N	N
2 ***Vucanovich***	Y	N	Y	+	N	N	N	Y
NEW HAMPSHIRE								
1 ***Smith***	Y	Y	Y	N	N	Y	N	Y
2 ***Douglas***	Y	Y	Y	N	N	Y	N	Y
NEW JERSEY								
1 Vacancy								
2 Hughes	Y	N	Y	Y	Y	Y	N	Y
3 Pallone	Y	Y	Y	Y	Y	Y	N	Y
4 ***Smith***	Y	N	Y	Y	Y	Y	N	Y
5 ***Roukema***	Y	Y	Y	N	?	Y	N	Y
6 Dwyer	Y	Y	?	?	Y	Y	N	Y
7 ***Rinaldo***	Y	Y	Y	Y	Y	Y	N	Y
8 Roe	Y	N	Y	Y	Y	N	N	Y
9 Torricelli	?	Y	Y	Y	?	N	N	Y
10 Payne	Y	N	N	Y	?	Y	Y	Y
11 ***Gallo***	Y	Y	Y	Y	Y	Y	N	Y
12 ***Courter***	?	?	?	?	Y	Y	N	Y
13 ***Saxton***	Y	N	Y	Y	Y	Y	N	Y
14 Guarini	Y	Y	Y	Y	Y	Y	N	Y
NEW MEXICO								
1 ***Schiff***	Y	N	Y	Y	Y	N	N	Y
2 ***Skeen***	Y	Y	Y	Y	N	N	N	Y
3 Richardson	Y	N	Y	Y	Y	N	N	Y
NEW YORK								
1 Hochbrueckner	Y	N	Y	Y	Y	Y	N	Y
2 Downey	Y	N	N	Y	Y	Y	N	Y
3 Mrazek	Y	N	N	?	Y	Y	N	Y
4 ***Lent***	Y	Y	Y	Y	N	Y	N	Y
5 ***McGrath***	Y	N	Y	Y	?	Y	N	Y
6 Flake	Y	N	N	Y	?	N	N	?
7 Ackerman	Y	N	N	Y	?	N	N	Y
8 Scheuer	Y	N	N	Y	Y	Y	N	N
9 Manton	Y	N	Y	Y	?	N	Y	Y
10 Schumer	Y	Y	Y	Y	Y	Y	N	Y
11 Towns	Y	N	N	Y	?	N	Y	Y
12 Owens	Y	N	N	Y	Y	Y	N	Y
13 Solarz	Y	N	N	Y	Y	Y	N	Y
14 ***Molinari***	Y	Y	Y	Y	?	N	N	Y
15 ***Green***	Y	Y	Y	Y	Y	Y	N	Y
16 Rangel	Y	N	N	Y	Y	Y	N	Y
17 Weiss	Y	N	N	Y	+	Y	N	Y
18 Serrano	Y	N	N	Y	Y	Y	N	Y
19 Engel	Y	N	Y	Y	?	N	N	Y
20 Lowey	Y	N	Y	Y	?	?	N	Y
21 ***Fish***	Y	N	Y	Y	Y	N	N	Y
22 ***Gilman***	Y	Y	Y	Y	Y	N	Y	Y
23 McNulty	Y	N	Y	Y	#	Y	N	Y
24 ***Solomon***	?	Y	Y	Y	?	N	N	Y
25 ***Boehlert***	Y	N	Y	Y	Y	N	Y	Y
26 ***Martin***	Y	?	?	?	Y	N	N	Y
27 ***Walsh***	Y	N	Y	Y	?	N	N	Y
28 McHugh	Y	N	Y	Y	Y	Y	N	Y
29 ***Horton***	Y	N	Y	Y	Y	N	N	Y
30 Slaughter	Y	N	Y	Y	Y	N	N	Y
31 ***Paxon***	Y	Y	Y	Y	Y	N	N	Y

	253	254	255	256	257	258	259	260
32 LaFalce	Y	N	Y	Y	?	Y	N	Y
33 Nowak	Y	N	Y	Y	Y	Y	N	Y
34 ***Houghton***	Y	N	Y	Y	?	Y	N	+
NORTH CAROLINA								
1 Jones	Y	N	N	Y	Y	N	N	N
2 Valentine	Y	Y	Y	Y	Y	N	N	Y
3 Lancaster	Y	N	Y	Y	Y	N	N	N
4 Price	Y	N	Y	Y	Y	N	N	N
5 Neal	Y	N	Y	Y	Y	N	N	Y
6 ***Coble***	Y	Y	Y	Y	Y	N	N	Y
7 Rose	Y	N	Y	Y	Y	N	Y	N
8 Hefner	Y	N	Y	Y	?	N	N	Y
9 ***McMillan***	Y	Y	Y	Y	N	N	N	Y
10 ***Ballenger***	Y	Y	Y	N	N	N	N	Y
11 Clarke	Y	N	Y	Y	Y	N	N	Y
NORTH DAKOTA								
AL Dorgan	Y	Y	Y	Y	Y	N	Y	Y
OHIO								
1 Luken	Y	N	Y	Y	Y	N	Y	Y
2 ***Gradison***	Y	Y	Y	Y	Y	Y	N	Y
3 Hall	Y	N	Y	Y	Y	Y	?	Y
4 ***Oxley***	Y	Y	Y	N	Y	N	N	Y
5 ***Gillmor***	Y	Y	?	?	Y	N	N	Y
6 ***McEwen***	Y	Y	?	?	Y	N	N	Y
7 ***DeWine***	Y	N	Y	Y	Y	Y	N	Y
8 ***Lukens***	Y	N	Y	N	N	Y	N	Y
9 Kaptur	Y	Y	Y	Y	?	N	Y	Y
10 ***Miller***	Y	Y	Y	N	Y	Y	N	Y
11 Eckart	Y	Y	Y	Y	Y	Y	Y	Y
12 ***Kasich***	Y	Y	Y	Y	Y	N	N	Y
13 Pease	Y	N	N	Y	Y	Y	N	Y
14 Sawyer	Y	N	N	Y	Y	Y	N	Y
15 ***Wylie***	Y	Y	Y	Y	Y	Y	N	Y
16 ***Regula***	Y	Y	Y	Y	Y	Y	N	Y
17 Traficant	Y	N	Y	Y	Y	N	Y	Y
18 Applegate	Y	N	Y	Y	Y	N	Y	Y
19 Feighan	Y	N	Y	Y	Y	Y	N	Y
20 Oakar	Y	N	Y	Y	?	Y	Y	Y
21 Stokes	Y	N	N	Y	Y	N	N	N
OKLAHOMA								
1 ***Inhofe***	Y	N	Y	Y	N	N	N	Y
2 Synar	Y	?	?	?	Y	N	N	N
3 Watkins	?	?	?	?	?	?	?	?
4 McCurdy	?	?	?	?	?	Y	N	N
5 ***Edwards***	?	Y	Y	Y	?	N	N	Y
6 English	Y	Y	Y	Y	?	N	Y	N
OREGON								
1 AuCoin	Y	N	Y	Y	Y	N	N	N
2 ***Smith, B.***	Y	Y	Y	Y	Y	N	N	Y
3 Wyden	Y	N	Y	Y	Y	N	N	Y
4 DeFazio	Y	N	N	Y	Y	N	N	[illegible]
5 ***Smith, D.***	?	?	?	?	?	N	N	Y
PENNSYLVANIA								
1 Foglietta	Y	N	N	Y	Y	N	N	Y
2 Gray	Y	N	Y	Y	Y	N	N	Y
3 Borski	Y	N	Y	Y	Y	Y	N	Y
4 Kolter	Y	N	Y	Y	Y	N	Y	Y
5 ***Schulze***	Y	Y	Y	Y	Y	Y	N	Y
6 Yatron	Y	Y	Y	Y	?	Y	Y	Y
7 ***Weldon***	Y	Y	Y	Y	?	Y	N	Y
8 Kostmayer	Y	Y	N	Y	Y	Y	N	Y
9 ***Shuster***	Y	Y	Y	Y	Y	N	N	Y
10 ***McDade***	Y	N	?	?	Y	Y	Y	Y
11 Kanjorski	Y	N	Y	Y	Y	Y	Y	Y
12 Murtha	Y	N	Y	Y	Y	N	Y	Y
13 ***Coughlin***	Y	Y	Y	Y	?	?	N	Y
14 Coyne	Y	N	N	Y	Y	Y	Y	Y
15 ***Ritter***	Y	Y	Y	Y	Y	Y	N	Y
16 ***Walker***	Y	Y	Y	N	N	Y	N	Y
17 ***Gekas***	Y	N	Y	N	N	Y	N	Y
18 Walgren	Y	N	Y	Y	Y	Y	N	Y
19 ***Goodling***	Y	N	Y	Y	Y	Y	N	Y
20 Gaydos	Y	N	Y	Y	Y	N	Y	Y
21 ***Ridge***	Y	Y	Y	Y	Y	Y	N	Y
22 Murphy	Y	N	Y	Y	Y	N	Y	Y
23 ***Clinger***	Y	N	Y	Y	Y	Y	N	Y
RHODE ISLAND								
1 ***Machtley***	Y	N	Y	Y	N	Y	N	Y
2 ***Schneider***	Y	N	Y	Y	Y	Y	N	Y
SOUTH CAROLINA								
1 ***Ravenel***	Y	Y	Y	Y	Y	N	N	N
2 ***Spence***	Y	N	Y	Y	Y	N	N	Y
3 Derrick	Y	N	Y	Y	Y	N	N	Y
4 Patterson	Y	N	Y	Y	Y	N	N	Y
5 Spratt	Y	N	Y	Y	Y	Y	N	Y
6 Tallon	Y	N	Y	Y	Y	N	N	N

	253	254	255	256	257	258	259	260
SOUTH DAKOTA								
AL Johnson	Y	Y	Y	Y	Y	N	Y	Y
TENNESSEE								
1 ***Quillen***	Y	N	Y	Y	Y	N	N	Y
2 ***Duncan***	Y	Y	Y	Y	Y	N	N	Y
3 Lloyd	Y	N	Y	Y	Y	Y	N	N
4 Cooper	Y	N	Y	Y	Y	Y	N	N
5 Clement	Y	N	Y	Y	Y	N	N	Y
6 Gordon	Y	N	Y	Y	Y	Y	N	Y
7 ***Sundquist***	Y	N	Y	Y	N	Y	N	Y
8 Tanner	Y	N	Y	Y	N	N	Y	Y
9 Ford	?	?	?	?	?	?	?	?
TEXAS								
1 Chapman	Y	N	?	Y	N	N	Y	Y
2 Wilson	Y	N	Y	Y	?	N	Y	Y
3 ***Bartlett***	Y	Y	Y	Y	N	Y	N	Y
4 Hall	?	?	?	?	N	N	N	N
5 Bryant	Y	N	Y	Y	N	N	Y	Y
6 ***Barton***	Y	Y	Y	Y	N	N	N	Y
7 ***Archer***	Y	Y	Y	Y	N	Y	N	Y
8 ***Fields***	Y	Y	Y	Y	N	Y	N	Y
9 Brooks	?	?	?	?	Y	N	N	Y
10 Pickle	Y	N	Y	?	Y	N	N	Y
11 Leath	Y	N	Y	Y	?	N	?	N
12 Geren	Y	N	Y	Y	Y	N	Y	N
13 Sarpalius	?	?	?	?	Y	N	N	N
14 Laughlin	Y	N	Y	Y	Y	N	N	N
15 de la Garza	Y	N	N	Y	Y	N	N	N
16 Coleman	Y	N	Y	Y	N	N	Y	N
17 Stenholm	Y	Y	Y	Y	Y	N	N	N
18 Washington	Y	N	N	Y	Y	Y	?	Y
19 ***Combest***	Y	Y	Y	N	N	N	N	Y
20 Gonzalez	Y	N	N	Y	Y	N	Y	N
21 ***Smith***	Y	N	Y	Y	N	N	N	Y
22 ***DeLay***	Y	Y	Y	N	N	Y	N	Y
23 Bustamante	Y	N	Y	Y	Y	N	Y	N
24 Frost	Y	N	Y	Y	Y	N	Y	N
25 Andrews	Y	N	Y	Y	N	N	N	Y
26 ***Armey***	Y	Y	Y	N	N	Y	N	Y
27 Ortiz	Y	?	?	?	N	N	N	N
UTAH								
1 ***Hansen***	Y	N	Y	N	?	X	?	?
2 Owens	Y	N	Y	Y	?	Y	N	Y
3 ***Nielson***	Y	Y	Y	N	N	Y	N	Y
VERMONT								
AL ***Smith***	+	N	Y	Y	?	N	Y	Y
VIRGINIA								
1 ***Bateman***	Y	N	Y	Y	Y	N	N	Y
2 Pickett	Y	N	Y	Y	Y	N	N	?
3 ***Bliley***	Y	Y	Y	Y	Y	N	N	Y
4 Sisisky	Y	N	Y	Y	?	C	N	Y
5 Payne	Y	N	Y	Y	Y	N	N	N
6 Olin	Y	N	Y	Y	Y	N	N	N
7 ***Slaughter***	Y	Y	Y	Y	Y	N	N	Y
8 ***Parris***	Y	N	Y	Y	Y	N	N	Y
9 Boucher	Y	N	Y	Y	Y	Y	N	Y
10 ***Wolf***	Y	Y	Y	Y	Y	Y	N	Y
WASHINGTON								
1 ***Miller***	?	N	Y	Y	N	Y	N	Y
2 Swift	Y	N	Y	Y	Y	N	N	Y
3 Unsoeld	Y	N	Y	Y	Y	N	N	Y
4 ***Morrison***	Y	N	Y	Y	Y	N	N	Y
5 Foley								
6 Dicks	?	?	?	?	Y	N	N	Y
7 McDermott	Y	N	N	?	Y	Y	N	Y
8 ***Chandler***	Y	Y	Y	Y	Y	Y	N	Y
WEST VIRGINIA								
1 Mollohan	Y	N	Y	Y	Y	N	N	N
2 Staggers	Y	N	Y	Y	Y	N	N	N
3 Wise	Y	N	Y	Y	Y	N	N	N
4 Rahall	Y	N	Y	Y	Y	N	N	Y
WISCONSIN								
1 Aspin	Y	N	?	Y	Y	N	Y	Y
2 Kastenmeier	Y	N	N	Y	Y	N	Y	Y
3 ***Gunderson***	Y	N	Y	Y	Y	N	N	Y
4 Kleczka	Y	N	Y	Y	Y	N	Y	Y
5 Moody	Y	N	N	Y	Y	Y	Y	Y
6 ***Petri***	Y	Y	Y	Y	Y	Y	N	Y
7 Obey	Y	N	N	Y	Y	N	Y	Y
8 ***Roth***	Y	Y	Y	Y	Y	N	N	Y
9 ***Sensenbrenner***	Y	Y	Y	N	Y	Y	Y	Y
WYOMING								
AL ***Thomas***	?	#	?	?	Y	N	N	Y

Southern states - Ala., Ark., Fla., Ga., Ky., La., Miss., N.C., Okla., S.C., Tenn., Texas, Va.
Omitted votes are quorum calls, which CQ does not include in its vote charts.

HOUSE VOTES 261, 262, 263, 264, 265, 266

261. Procedural Motion. Pursell, R-Mich., motion to approve the House Journal of Tuesday, July 24. Motion agreed to 288-111: R 58-104; D 230-7 (ND 155-7, SD 75-0), July 25, 1990.

262. HR 770. Family and Medical Leave Act/Veto Override Attempt. Passage, over President Bush's June 29 veto, of the bill to require public and private employers to give unpaid leave to care for a newborn child or a seriously ill child, parent or spouse, or to use as medical leave due to a serious health condition. Rejected 232-195: R 38-138; D 194-57 (ND 156-14, SD 38-43), July 25, 1990. A two-thirds majority or those present and voting (285 in this case) of both houses is required to override a veto. A "nay" was a vote supporting the president's position.

263. HR 3950. Farm Programs Reauthorization/Dairy Surpluses. Walsh, R-N.Y., amendment to reduce from 7 billion pounds to 6 billion pounds the level of dairy surpluses that would trigger implementation of an Agriculture Department inventory management program. Adopted 256-164: R 87-85; D 169-79 (ND 123-44, SD 46-35), July 25, 1990.

264. HR 3950. Farm Programs Reauthorization/Wheat and Feed Grains. Madigan, R-Ill., en bloc amendment to allow the Agriculture Department to reduce wheat and feed grain loan rates by 10 percent below the previous year's level in any of the next five years, if the Agriculture Department finds it necessary to keep U.S. wheat and feed grains competitive on world markets and to require the Agriculture Department to increase target prices for wheat and feed grains if the acreage reduction required of producers that year is more than 22.5 percent. Adopted 219-210: R 152-24; D 67-186 (ND 56-115, SD 11-71), July 25, 1990.

265. HR 3950. Farm Programs Reauthorization/High-Income Farmers. Glickman, D-Kan., substitute amendment to the Schumer, D-N.Y., amendment to prohibit deficiency payments to any producer whose total income from the sale of wheat, feed grains, cotton or rice exceeds $1 million annually. Rejected 174-251: R 70-106; D 104-145 (ND 74-93, SD 30-52), July 25, 1990.

266. HR 3950. Farm Programs Reauthorization/High-Income Farmers. Schumer, D-N.Y., amendment to prohibit all payments, purchases and loans under the wheat, feed grains, cotton, honey, rice, oilseeds, and wool and mohair programs for any person with an adjusted gross income of $100,000 or more. Rejected 159-263: R 66-109; D 93-154 (ND 85-82, SD 8-72), July 25, 1990.

KEY

Y Voted for (yea).
\# Paired for.
\+ Announced for.
N Voted against (nay).
X Paired against.
\- Announced against.
P Voted "present."
C Voted "present" to avoid possible conflict of interest.
? Did not vote or otherwise make a position known.

Democrats ***Republicans***

	261	262	263	264	265	266
ALABAMA						
1 ***Callahan***	N	N	Y	Y	N	N
2 ***Dickinson***	?	N	Y	Y	N	Y
3 Browder	Y	N	Y	N	Y	N
4 Bevill	Y	N	Y	N	Y	N
5 Flippo	Y	Y	Y	N	N	N
6 Erdreich	Y	Y	Y	N	N	N
7 Harris	Y	N	Y	N	Y	N
ALASKA						
AL ***Young***	N	Y	N	N	N	N
ARIZONA						
1 ***Rhodes***	N	N	N	Y	N	N
2 Udall	Y	Y	Y	Y	N	N
3 ***Stump***	N	N	N	Y	N	C
4 ***Kyl***	N	N	?	Y	N	N
5 ***Kolbe***	N	N	N	Y	N	N
ARKANSAS						
1 Alexander	?	Y	Y	N	N	N
2 ***Robinson***	Y	N	Y	N	N	N
3 ***Hammerschmidt***	Y	N	Y	N	N	N
4 Anthony	Y	Y	Y	N	Y	N
CALIFORNIA						
1 Bosco	Y	Y	Y	N	Y	N
2 ***Herger***	?	N	N	Y	N	N
3 Matsui	Y	Y	N	N	N	N
4 Fazio	Y	Y	N	N	Y	N
5 Pelosi	Y	Y	?	N	N	Y
6 Boxer	Y	Y	N	N	Y	N
7 Miller	Y	Y	N	Y	Y	Y
8 Dellums	Y	Y	N	N	Y	Y
9 Stark	Y	Y	N	Y	Y	Y
10 Edwards	Y	Y	N	N	Y	N
11 Lantos	Y	Y	N	N	N	Y
12 ***Campbell***	N	Y	N	Y	N	Y
13 Mineta	Y	Y	N	N	Y	N
14 ***Shumway***	Y	N	N	Y	N	N
15 Condit	N	Y	N	N	N	N
16 Panetta	Y	Y	N	N	Y	Y
17 ***Pashayan***	N	N	N	N	N	N
18 Lehman	Y	Y	N	N	N	N
19 ***Lagomarsino***	N	N	N	Y	Y	Y
20 ***Thomas***	N	N	N	Y	Y	N
21 ***Gallegly***	N	N	N	Y	Y	N
22 ***Moorhead***	N	N	N	Y	Y	N
23 Beilenson	Y	Y	N	N	N	Y
24 Waxman	Y	Y	N	N	Y	Y
25 Roybal	Y	Y	N	N	Y	N
26 Berman	Y	Y	N	N	N	Y
27 Levine	Y	Y	N	N	Y	Y
28 Dixon	Y	Y	N	N	Y	N
29 Hawkins	Y	Y	N	N	N	N
30 Martinez	Y	Y	Y	N	?	?
31 Dymally	Y	Y	Y	N	Y	N
32 Anderson	Y	Y	N	N	Y	N
33 ***Dreier***	N	N	N	Y	N	Y
34 Torres	Y	Y	N	N	Y	N
35 ***Lewis***	N	N	N	Y	Y	N
36 Brown	Y	Y	Y	N	Y	N
37 ***McCandless***	N	N	N	Y	Y	N
38 ***Dornan***	N	N	N	Y	Y	N
39 ***Dannemeyer***	N	N	N	Y	Y	Y
40 ***Cox***	Y	N	N	Y	N	Y
41 ***Lowery***	N	N	N	Y	Y	N
42 ***Rohrabacher***	N	N	N	Y	N	Y
43 ***Packard***	Y	N	N	Y	N	N
44 Bates	Y	Y	N	Y	N	Y
45 ***Hunter***	N	N	N	Y	Y	N
COLORADO						
1 Schroeder	N	Y	Y	N	N	Y
2 Skaggs	Y	Y	Y	N	Y	N
3 Campbell	Y	N	Y	N	N	N
4 ***Brown***	N	N	N	Y	N	Y
5 ***Hefley***	N	N	N	Y	Y	N
6 ***Schaefer***	N	N	N	Y	Y	N
CONNECTICUT						
1 Kennelly	Y	Y	N	Y	Y	Y
2 Gejdenson	Y	Y	Y	N	N	Y
3 Morrison	Y	Y	Y	Y	N	Y
4 ***Shays***	N	Y	Y	Y	N	Y
5 ***Rowland***	Y	Y	Y	Y	N	Y
6 ***Johnson***	Y	Y	Y	Y	N	Y
DELAWARE						
AL Carper	Y	Y	N	Y	N	Y
FLORIDA						
1 Hutto	Y	N	N	Y	Y	N
2 ***Grant***	Y	N	N	Y	Y	N
3 Bennett	Y	Y	Y	Y	N	Y
4 ***James***	N	N	N	Y	Y	N
5 ***McCollum***	N	N	N	Y	N	Y
6 ***Stearns***	N	N	N	Y	Y	Y
7 Gibbons	Y	Y	Y	Y	N	Y
8 ***Young***	N	N	N	Y	N	Y
9 ***Bilirakis***	N	N	?	Y	Y	N
10 ***Ireland***	N	N	N	Y	Y	N
11 Nelson	+	+	-	+	-	-
12 ***Lewis***	N	N	N	Y	Y	N
13 ***Goss***	N	N	N	Y	N	Y
14 Johnston	Y	Y	Y	N	N	Y
15 ***Shaw***	Y	N	N	Y	Y	Y
16 Smith	Y	Y	N	N	N	N
17 Lehman	Y	Y	N	Y	N	Y
18 ***Ros-Lehtinen***	N	Y	N	Y	Y	Y
19 Fascell	?	Y	N	N	Y	N
GEORGIA						
1 Thomas	Y	N	N	N	N	N
2 Hatcher	Y	N	N	N	N	N
3 Ray	Y	N	N	N	N	N
4 Jones	Y	N	N	N	Y	N
5 Lewis	Y	Y	N	N	N	N
6 ***Gingrich***	?	N	N	Y	Y	N
7 Darden	Y	N	N	N	Y	N
8 Rowland	Y	N	N	N	Y	N
9 Jenkins	Y	Y	N	Y	Y	N
10 Barnard	Y	N	N	N	N	N
HAWAII						
1 ***Saiki***	Y	Y	Y	Y	N	N
2 Vacancy						
IDAHO						
1 ***Craig***	N	N	N	N	N	N
2 Stallings	Y	N	Y	N	N	N
ILLINOIS						
1 Hayes	Y	Y	N	N	Y	N
2 Savage	Y	Y	N	N	Y	Y
3 Russo	Y	Y	Y	Y	N	Y
4 Sangmeister	?	Y	Y	Y	Y	N
5 Lipinski	Y	Y	Y	Y	N	Y
6 ***Hyde***	Y	Y	N	Y	Y	N
7 Collins	Y	Y	N	N	N	N
8 Rostenkowski	Y	Y	Y	Y	N	Y
9 Yates	Y	Y	N	Y	N	Y
10 ***Porter***	Y	N	?	Y	N	Y
11 Annunzio	Y	Y	Y	Y	N	Y
12 ***Crane***	N	N	N	Y	N	Y
13 ***Fawell***	N	N	Y	Y	N	Y
14 ***Hastert***	?	N	N	Y	Y	N
15 ***Madigan***	N	N	Y	Y	Y	N
16 ***Martin***	N	Y	Y	Y	Y	N
17 Evans	Y	Y	Y	N	Y	N
18 ***Michel***	?	N	N	Y	N	N
19 Bruce	Y	Y	Y	Y	Y	N
20 Durbin	Y	Y	Y	Y	Y	N
21 Costello	Y	Y	Y	Y	Y	N
22 Poshard	Y	Y	Y	Y	Y	N
INDIANA						
1 Visclosky	Y	Y	Y	Y	N	Y
2 Sharp	Y	Y	Y	N	Y	N
3 ***Hiler***	N	N	Y	Y	N	N

ND Northern Democrats SD Southern Democrats

	261	262	263	264	265	266
4 Long	Y	Y	Y	N	N	N
5 Jontz	Y	Y	Y	N	N	N
6 ***Burton***	N	N	Y	Y	N	N
7 ***Myers***	Y	N	Y	N	N	N
8 McCloskey	Y	Y	Y	N	Y	N
9 Hamilton	Y	N	Y	Y	Y	N
10 Jacobs	N	Y	N	Y	Y	Y
IOWA						
1 ***Leach***	N	N	Y	N	Y	N
2 ***Tauke***	N	N	Y	N	Y	N
3 Nagle	Y	N	Y	N	Y	N
4 Smith	Y	Y	Y	N	N	N
5 ***Lightfoot***	N	N	Y	N	Y	N
6 ***Grandy***	N	N	Y	Y	Y	N
KANSAS						
1 ***Roberts***	N	N	N	N	N	N
2 Slattery	Y	N	Y	N	Y	N
3 ***Meyers***	?	N	Y	Y	Y	N
4 Glickman	Y	N	Y	N	Y	N
5 ***Whittaker***	N	N	N	Y	N	N
KENTUCKY						
1 Hubbard	Y	N	Y	Y	N	N
2 Natcher	Y	Y	Y	N	N	N
3 Mazzoli	Y	Y	N	Y	N	Y
4 ***Bunning***	N	N	N	Y	N	N
5 ***Rogers***	N	N	Y	Y	N	N
6 ***Hopkins***	N	N	Y	Y	N	N
7 Perkins	Y	Y	Y	N	N	N
LOUISIANA						
1 ***Livingston***	Y	N	N	Y	Y	Y
2 Boggs	Y	Y	N	N	N	N
3 Tauzin	Y	N	Y	N	N	N
4 ***McCrery***	?	N	Y	Y	N	N
5 Huckaby	Y	N	Y	N	N	N
6 ***Baker***	N	N	N	Y	Y	N
7 Hayes	Y	N	Y	N	N	N
8 ***Holloway***	N	N	Y	Y	Y	N
MAINE						
1 Brennan	Y	Y	Y	Y	N	Y
2 ***Snowe***	Y	Y	Y	Y	N	Y
MARYLAND						
1 Dyson	Y	Y	Y	N	N	N
2 ***Bentley***	?	N	N	Y	Y	N
3 Cardin	Y	Y	?	N	Y	Y
4 McMillen	Y	Y	Y	Y	N	Y
5 Hoyer	Y	Y	Y	N	Y	N
6 Byron	Y	N	Y	N	Y	N
7 Mfume	Y	Y	Y	N	N	Y
8 ***Morella***	N	Y	Y	Y	N	Y
MASSACHUSETTS						
1 ***Conte***	Y	Y	N	Y	N	Y
2 Neal	Y	Y	N	N	N	Y
3 Early	Y	Y	N	?	?	?
4 Frank	Y	Y	N	Y	N	Y
5 Atkins	Y	Y	N	Y	N	Y
6 Mavroules	Y	Y	Y	Y	N	Y
7 Markey	Y	Y	Y	N	N	Y
8 Kennedy	Y	Y	N	N	N	Y
9 Moakley	Y	Y	Y	N	N	N
10 Studds	Y	Y	N	Y	N	Y
11 Donnelly	Y	N	Y	Y	N	Y
MICHIGAN						
1 Conyers	Y	Y	Y	N	N	N
2 ***Pursell***	Y	N	Y	Y	Y	N
3 Wolpe	Y	Y	Y	N	Y	N
4 ***Upton***	N	N	Y	Y	N	N
5 ***Henry***	N	N	Y	Y	Y	N
6 Carr	Y	N	Y	Y	?	N
7 Kildee	Y	Y	Y	N	N	N
8 Traxler	Y	Y	Y	N	N	N
9 ***Vander Jagt***	Y	N	Y	Y	Y	N
10 ***Schuette***	N	N	Y	Y	Y	N
11 ***Davis***	Y	Y	Y	Y	N	N
12 Bonior	Y	Y	Y	N	Y	Y
13 Crockett	?	Y	Y	N	?	?
14 Hertel	Y	Y	Y	N	Y	Y
15 Ford	Y	Y	Y	N	Y	N
16 Dingell	?	Y	Y	N	N	N
17 Levin	Y	Y	Y	N	N	Y
18 ***Broomfield***	Y	N	N	Y	N	Y
MINNESOTA						
1 Penny	Y	N	Y	N	Y	N
2 ***Weber***	N	N	Y	N	N	N
3 ***Frenzel***	?	N	N	Y	N	Y
4 Vento	Y	Y	?	N	N	Y

	261	262	263	264	265	266
5 Sabo	Y	Y	Y	N	N	Y
6 Sikorski	N	Y	Y	N	Y	N
7 ***Stangeland***	N	N	Y	N	N	N
8 Oberstar	Y	Y	Y	N	Y	N
MISSISSIPPI						
1 Whitten	Y	Y	N	N	N	N
2 Espy	Y	Y	N	N	N	N
3 Montgomery	Y	N	Y	N	N	N
4 Parker	Y	N	N	N	N	N
5 Taylor	Y	N	N	N	N	N
MISSOURI						
1 Clay	N	Y	Y	N	N	N
2 ***Buechner***	N	N	N	Y	Y	Y
3 Gephardt	?	Y	Y	N	Y	N
4 Skelton	Y	N	Y	N	N	N
5 Wheat	Y	Y	Y	N	Y	N
6 ***Coleman***	N	N	N	N	N	N
7 ***Hancock***	N	N	Y	Y	N	Y
8 ***Emerson***	Y	N	Y	N	N	N
9 Volkmer	N	Y	Y	N	Y	N
MONTANA						
1 Williams	Y	Y	Y	N	N	N
2 ***Marlenee***	N	N	Y	N	N	N
NEBRASKA						
1 ***Bereuter***	N	N	Y	N	Y	N
2 Hoagland	Y	N	Y	N	Y	N
3 ***Smith***	Y	N	N	N	N	N
NEVADA						
1 Bilbray	Y	Y	Y	N	N	Y
2 ***Vucanovich***	?	N	N	Y	Y	N
NEW HAMPSHIRE						
1 ***Smith***	N	N	Y	Y	N	Y
2 ***Douglas***	N	N	Y	Y	N	Y
NEW JERSEY						
1 Vacancy						
2 Hughes	Y	?	N	Y	N	Y
3 Pallone	Y	Y	Y	N	N	Y
4 ***Smith***	Y	Y	Y	Y	N	Y
5 ***Roukema***	N	Y	N	Y	N	Y
6 Dwyer	Y	Y	Y	Y	N	Y
7 ***Rinaldo***	Y	Y	Y	Y	N	Y
8 Roe	Y	Y	Y	Y	Y	?
9 Torricelli	Y	Y	Y	Y	N	Y
10 Payne	Y	Y	Y	N	N	Y
11 ***Gallo***	N	N	Y	Y	N	Y
12 ***Courter***	N	N	N	Y	Y	Y
13 ***Saxton***	Y	N	Y	Y	N	Y
14 Guarini	Y	Y	Y	Y	N	Y
NEW MEXICO						
1 ***Schiff***	Y	N	Y	Y	N	N
2 ***Skeen***	Y	N	N	Y	N	N
3 Richardson	Y	Y	Y	N	N	N
NEW YORK						
1 Hochbrueckner	Y	Y	Y	Y	N	Y
2 Downey	Y	Y	Y	Y	N	Y
3 Mrazek	Y	Y	Y	Y	?	Y
4 ***Lent***	Y	N	N	Y	N	Y
5 ***McGrath***	N	Y	Y	Y	N	Y
6 Flake	?	?	?	?	?	?
7 Ackerman	Y	Y	Y	N	Y	N
8 Scheuer	Y	Y	Y	N	N	Y
9 Manton	Y	Y	Y	N	N	Y
10 Schumer	Y	Y	Y	Y	N	Y
11 Towns	Y	Y	Y	N	N	N
12 Owens	Y	Y	Y	N	N	Y
13 Solarz	Y	Y	Y	N	N	Y
14 ***Molinari***	N	Y	Y	Y	N	Y
15 ***Green***	Y	Y	?	Y	N	Y
16 Rangel	Y	Y	N	N	N	Y
17 Weiss	Y	Y	N	Y	N	Y
18 Serrano	Y	Y	Y	N	N	Y
19 Engel	Y	Y	Y	N	N	Y
20 Lowey	Y	Y	Y	N	N	Y
21 ***Fish***	Y	Y	Y	Y	Y	N
22 ***Gilman***	Y	Y	Y	Y	Y	N
23 McNulty	Y	Y	Y	Y	N	Y
24 ***Solomon***	N	Y	Y	Y	N	N
25 ***Boehlert***	N	Y	Y	Y	N	N
26 ***Martin***	N	Y	Y	Y	N	N
27 ***Walsh***	Y	N	Y	Y	N	N
28 McHugh	Y	Y	Y	N	Y	N
29 ***Horton***	?	Y	Y	Y	N	N
30 Slaughter	Y	Y	Y	Y	Y	N
31 ***Paxon***	N	N	Y	Y	Y	N

	261	262	263	264	265	266
32 LaFalce	Y	N	Y	Y	N	Y
33 Nowak	Y	Y	Y	Y	N	Y
34 ***Houghton***	Y	N	Y	Y	Y	N
NORTH CAROLINA						
1 Jones	Y	N	Y	N	N	N
2 Valentine	?	N	N	N	Y	N
3 Lancaster	Y	N	Y	N	Y	N
4 Price	Y	Y	N	N	N	Y
5 Neal	Y	N	N	N	Y	N
6 ***Coble***	N	N	N	Y	Y	Y
7 Rose	Y	Y	N	N	Y	N
8 Hefner	Y	N	Y	N	N	N
9 ***McMillan***	N	N	N	Y	N	Y
10 ***Ballenger***	N	N	N	Y	Y	Y
11 Clarke	Y	N	N	Y	N	Y
NORTH DAKOTA						
AL Dorgan	Y	Y	Y	N	Y	N
OHIO						
1 Luken	Y	Y	Y	N	N	N
2 ***Gradison***	Y	N	Y	Y	N	Y
3 Hall	Y	Y	Y	Y	N	N
4 ***Oxley***	Y	N	Y	Y	Y	N
5 ***Gillmor***	Y	Y	Y	Y	Y	N
6 ***McEwen***	Y	N	Y	Y	N	N
7 ***DeWine***	N	Y	Y	Y	Y	N
8 ***Lukens***	N	N	Y	Y	N	N
9 Kaptur	?	?	?	N	Y	N
10 ***Miller***	N	N	Y	Y	Y	Y
11 Eckart	Y	Y	Y	N	N	Y
12 ***Kasich***	Y	N	Y	Y	Y	N
13 Pease	Y	Y	Y	N	Y	Y
14 Sawyer	Y	Y	Y	N	Y	N
15 ***Wylie***	Y	N	Y	Y	N	Y
16 ***Regula***	N	Y	Y	Y	Y	Y
17 Traficant	Y	Y	Y	N	Y	N
18 Applegate	?	Y	Y	Y	Y	N
19 Feighan	?	Y	Y	N	N	Y
20 Oakar	Y	Y	Y	N	N	Y
21 Stokes	Y	Y	Y	N	N	N
OKLAHOMA						
1 ***Inhofe***	N	N	N	Y	Y	N
2 Synar	Y	Y	Y	N	N	N
3 Watkins	?	N	Y	N	N	N
4 McCurdy	Y	Y	Y	N	N	N
5 ***Edwards***	N	N	N	N	N	N
6 English	Y	Y	Y	N	N	N
OREGON						
1 AuCoin	?	Y	Y	N	N	N
2 ***Smith, B.***	N	N	N	N	N	N
3 Wyden	Y	Y	N	N	N	Y
4 DeFazio	Y	Y	Y	N	N	N
5 ***Smith, D.***	N	N	N	N	N	N
PENNSYLVANIA						
1 Foglietta	Y	Y	Y	Y	N	Y
2 Gray	?	Y	Y	N	Y	Y
3 Borski	Y	Y	Y	N	N	Y
4 Kolter	Y	Y	Y	Y	N	?
5 ***Schulze***	Y	N	N	Y	N	Y
6 Yatron	Y	Y	Y	Y	N	Y
7 ***Weldon***	Y	Y	Y	Y	N	Y
8 Kostmayer	Y	Y	N	Y	N	Y
9 ***Shuster***	Y	N	Y	Y	N	Y
10 ***McDade***	?	Y	Y	Y	N	N
11 Kanjorski	Y	Y	Y	Y	N	Y
12 Murtha	Y	Y	Y	Y	Y	N
13 ***Coughlin***	?	Y	Y	N	N	Y
14 Coyne	Y	Y	Y	Y	Y	Y
15 ***Ritter***	Y	N	N	Y	N	N
16 ***Walker***	N	N	N	Y	N	Y
17 ***Gekas***	N	N	Y	Y	N	N
18 Walgren	Y	Y	Y	Y	Y	Y
19 ***Goodling***	N	N	Y	Y	Y	Y
20 Gaydos	Y	Y	N	Y	N	Y
21 ***Ridge***	N	N	Y	Y	Y	N
22 Murphy	N	Y	Y	Y	N	Y
23 ***Clinger***	Y	N	Y	Y	Y	N
RHODE ISLAND						
1 ***Machtley***	N	Y	Y	Y	N	Y
2 ***Schneider***	Y	Y	Y	Y	N	Y
SOUTH CAROLINA						
1 ***Ravenel***	Y	Y	Y	Y	Y	N
2 ***Spence***	N	N	N	Y	N	N
3 Derrick	Y	N	N	N	N	N
4 Patterson	Y	N	N	N	N	N
5 Spratt	Y	N	N	N	N	N
6 Tallon	Y	N	N	N	N	N

	261	262	263	264	265	266
SOUTH DAKOTA						
AL Johnson	Y	Y	Y	N	Y	N
TENNESSEE						
1 ***Quillen***	Y	N	N	Y	Y	N
2 ***Duncan***	Y	N	N	Y	N	Y
3 Lloyd	Y	N	Y	Y	Y	N
4 Cooper	Y	N	N	N	Y	C
5 Clement	Y	Y	N	N	Y	N
6 Gordon	Y	Y	Y	N	Y	N
7 ***Sundquist***	N	N	Y	Y	Y	N
8 Tanner	Y	N	Y	N	Y	N
9 Ford	?	Y	Y	Y	Y	?
TEXAS						
1 Chapman	?	Y	Y	N	Y	N
2 Wilson	Y	Y	Y	N	Y	N
3 ***Bartlett***	?	N	N	Y	Y	N
4 Hall	Y	N	Y	N	N	N
5 Bryant	Y	Y	Y	N	Y	N
6 ***Barton***	N	N	Y	Y	N	N
7 ***Archer***	Y	N	N	Y	N	Y
8 ***Fields***	N	N	N	Y	N	N
9 Brooks	Y	Y	Y	N	Y	N
10 Pickle	Y	N	Y	N	Y	N
11 Leath	Y	N	Y	N	N	N
12 Geren	Y	N	Y	N	Y	N
13 Sarpalius	Y	N	Y	N	N	N
14 Laughlin	Y	N	Y	N	N	N
15 de la Garza	Y	Y	Y	N	N	N
16 Coleman	Y	Y	Y	N	Y	N
17 Stenholm	Y	N	Y	N	N	N
18 Washington	?	?	?	N	N	N
19 ***Combest***	Y	N	N	N	N	N
20 Gonzalez	Y	Y	Y	N	N	N
21 ***Smith***	N	Y	Y	N	N	N
22 ***DeLay***	N	N	N	Y	N	N
23 Bustamante	Y	Y	Y	N	N	N
24 Frost	Y	Y	Y	N	Y	N
25 Andrews	Y	Y	Y	N	Y	N
26 ***Armey***	N	N	N	Y	N	Y
27 Ortiz	Y	Y	Y	N	N	N
UTAH						
1 ***Hansen***	Y	N	N	Y	Y	Y
2 Owens	Y	Y	N	Y	Y	Y
3 ***Nielson***	N	N	N	Y	N	Y
VERMONT						
AL ***Smith***	Y	Y	Y	Y	N	N
VIRGINIA						
1 ***Bateman***	Y	N	N	Y	Y	N
2 Pickett	Y	N	N	N	Y	N
3 ***Bliley***	N	N	N	Y	Y	Y
4 Sisisky	Y	N	N	N	N	N
5 Payne	Y	N	N	N	N	N
6 Olin	Y	N	N	N	N	N
7 ***Slaughter***	N	N	N	N	Y	N
8 ***Parris***	Y	N	N	Y	N	N
9 Boucher	Y	Y	N	N	N	Y
10 ***Wolf***	N	N	N	Y	N	Y
WASHINGTON						
1 ***Miller***	N	Y	N	Y	N	Y
2 Swift	Y	Y	Y	N	Y	N
3 Unsoeld	Y	Y	Y	N	Y	N
4 ***Morrison***	Y	Y	Y	Y	N	N
5 Foley						
6 Dicks	Y	Y	Y	N	Y	N
7 McDermott	Y	Y	Y	N	Y	N
8 ***Chandler***	N	N	Y	Y	Y	N
WEST VIRGINIA						
1 Mollohan	Y	Y	Y	N	Y	N
2 Staggers	Y	Y	N	N	Y	N
3 Wise	Y	Y	Y	N	Y	Y
4 Rahall	Y	Y	N	Y	Y	N
WISCONSIN						
1 Aspin	?	N	Y	N	N	Y
2 Kastenmeier	Y	Y	Y	N	Y	N
3 ***Gunderson***	Y	N	Y	Y	Y	N
4 Kleczka	Y	Y	?	Y	N	Y
5 Moody	Y	Y	Y	N	Y	Y
6 ***Petri***	Y	N	Y	Y	Y	Y
7 Obey	Y	Y	Y	N	N	Y
8 ***Roth***	Y	N	Y	Y	N	Y
9 ***Sensenbrenner***	N	N	Y	Y	N	Y
WYOMING						
AL ***Thomas***	N	N	N	Y	Y	N

Southern states - Ala., Ark., Fla., Ga., Ky., La., Miss., N.C., Okla., S.C., Tenn., Texas, Va.
Omitted votes are quorum calls, which CQ does not include in its vote charts.

HOUSE VOTES 268, 270, 271, 272, 273, 274

268. H Res 442. Frank Expulsion/Adoption. Adoption of the resolution to expel Barney Frank, D-Mass., from the House of Representatives. Rejected 38-390: R 36-138; D 2-252 (ND 0-172, SD 2-80), July 26, 1990. A two-thirds majority of those present and voting (286 in this case) is required to expel a member of the House.

270. H Res 440. Frank Reprimand/Censure. Gingrich, R-Ga., motion to recommit the resolution to the Committee on Standards of Official Conduct with instructions to report back a recommendation of censure instead of reprimand. Motion rejected 141-287: R 129-46; D 12-241 (ND 1-171, SD 11-70), July 26, 1990.

271. H Res 440. Frank Reprimand/Adoption. Adoption of the resolution to reprimand Rep. Barney Frank, D-Mass., for improperly using his political influence by putting misleading statements favorable to his personal assistant, Stephen L. Gobie, in a memorandum concerning Gobie's probation, and for abusing his congressional authority by having 33 District of Columbia parking tickets dismissed that were not incurred on official House business. Adopted 408-18: R 164-11; D 244-7 (ND 165-6, SD 79-1), July 26, 1990.

272. HR 5311. Fiscal 1991 D.C. Appropriations/UDC Funds. Parris, R-Va., amendment to eliminate $1.6 million for the University of the District of Columbia (UDC) capital account, which is the amount UDC plans to spend to renovate a building to house the sculpture "Dinner Party" by Judy Chicago. Proponents of the amendment say the sculpture is obscene. Adopted 297-123: R 162-12; D 135-111 (ND 71-97, SD 64-14), July 26, 1990.

273. HR 5311. Fiscal 1991 D.C. Appropriations/Across-the-Board Cuts. Frenzel, R-Minn., amendment to make an across-the-board cut of 4.4 percent ($25 million) in federal funds in the bill in fiscal 1991. Rejected 195-219: R 142-26; D 53-193 (ND 24-142, SD 29-51), July 26, 1990.

274. HR 5311. Fiscal 1991 D.C. Appropriations/Passage. Passage of the bill to appropriate $543 million in federal funds in fiscal 1991 and to approve spending $3.9 billion in funds raised from local taxes for the District of Columbia, $24 million more than President Bush requested in federal funds and $38 million more than he wanted approved from local taxes. The bill would not limit the District in using local tax revenues for abortions. Passed 241-178: R 37-134; D 204-44 (ND 145-23, SD 59-21), July 26, 1990.

KEY

- Y Voted for (yea).
- # Paired for.
- + Announced for.
- N Voted against (nay).
- X Paired against.
- \- Announced against.
- P Voted "present."
- C Voted "present" to avoid possible conflict of interest.
- ? Did not vote or otherwise make a position known.

Democrats ***Republicans***

	268	270	271	272	273	274
ALABAMA						
1 ***Callahan***	N	N	Y	Y	Y	N
2 ***Dickinson***	N	Y	Y	Y	Y	N
3 Browder	N	N	Y	Y	N	Y
4 Bevill	N	N	Y	Y	N	Y
5 Flippo	N	N	Y	Y	N	Y
6 Erdreich	N	N	Y	Y	N	Y
7 Harris	N	N	Y	Y	N	Y
ALASKA						
AL ***Young***	N	N	Y	Y	?	N
ARIZONA						
1 ***Rhodes***	N	Y	Y	Y	Y	N
2 Udall	N	N	Y	Y	Y	Y
3 ***Stump***	Y	Y	N	Y	Y	N
4 ***Kyl***	N	Y	Y	Y	Y	N
5 ***Kolbe***	N	Y	Y	Y	Y	Y
ARKANSAS						
1 Alexander	N	N	Y	Y	N	Y
2 ***Robinson***	Y	Y	Y	Y	#	X
3 ***Hammerschmidt***	N	Y	Y	Y	Y	N
4 Anthony	N	N	Y	N	N	Y
CALIFORNIA						
1 Bosco	N	N	Y	N	N	Y
2 ***Herger***	Y	Y	N	Y	Y	N
3 Matsui	N	N	Y	N	N	Y
4 Fazio	N	N	Y	N	N	Y
5 Pelosi	N	N	N	N	N	Y
6 Boxer	N	N	Y	N	N	Y
7 Miller	N	N	Y	N	N	Y
8 Dellums	N	N	P	N	N	Y
9 Stark	N	N	Y	N	N	Y
10 Edwards	N	N	Y	N	N	Y
11 Lantos	N	N	Y	N	N	Y
12 ***Campbell***	N	N	Y	N	Y	N
13 Mineta	N	N	Y	N	N	Y
14 ***Shumway***	Y	Y	Y	Y	Y	N
15 Condit	N	N	Y	?	?	?
16 Panetta	N	N	Y	Y	N	Y
17 ***Pashayan***	N	N	Y	Y	Y	N
18 Lehman	N	N	Y	Y	N	Y
19 ***Lagomarsino***	N	Y	Y	Y	Y	N
20 ***Thomas***	N	Y	Y	Y	Y	N
21 ***Gallegly***	N	Y	Y	Y	Y	N
22 ***Moorhead***	Y	Y	Y	Y	Y	N
23 Beilenson	N	N	Y	N	N	Y
24 Waxman	N	N	N	N	N	Y
25 Roybal	N	N	Y	N	N	Y
26 Berman	N	N	Y	N	N	Y
27 Levine	N	N	Y	N	N	Y
28 Dixon	N	N	Y	N	N	Y
29 Hawkins	N	N	Y	N	X	?
30 Martinez	N	N	Y	N	N	Y
31 Dymally	N	N	N	N	N	Y
32 Anderson	N	N	Y	N	N	Y
33 ***Dreier***	N	Y	Y	Y	Y	N
34 Torres	N	N	Y	Y	N	Y
35 ***Lewis***	N	N	Y	N	N	Y
36 Brown	N	N	Y	N	N	Y
37 ***McCandless***	N	Y	Y	Y	Y	N
38 ***Dornan***	Y	Y	N	Y	Y	N
39 ***Dannemeyer***	Y	Y	N	Y	Y	N
40 ***Cox***	N	Y	Y	Y	Y	N
41 ***Lowery***	N	N	Y	Y	Y	N
42 ***Rohrabacher***	N	Y	Y	Y	Y	N
43 ***Packard***	Y	Y	Y	Y	Y	N
44 Bates	N	N	Y	N	N	Y
45 ***Hunter***	Y	Y	N	Y	?	N
COLORADO						
1 Schroeder	N	N	Y	N	Y	Y
2 Skaggs	N	N	Y	N	N	Y
3 Campbell	N	N	Y	Y	N	Y
4 ***Brown***	N	Y	Y	Y	Y	N
5 ***Hefley***	N	Y	Y	Y	Y	N
6 ***Schaefer***	N	Y	Y	Y	Y	N
CONNECTICUT						
1 Kennelly	N	N	Y	N	?	Y
2 Gejdenson	N	N	Y	N	N	Y
3 Morrison	N	N	Y	Y	N	Y
4 ***Shays***	N	Y	Y	Y	Y	Y
5 ***Rowland***	N	Y	Y	Y	Y	Y
6 ***Johnson***	N	Y	Y	Y	N	Y
DELAWARE						
AL Carper	N	N	Y	Y	N	Y
FLORIDA						
1 Hutto	N	Y	Y	Y	Y	N
2 ***Grant***	N	Y	Y	Y	Y	N
3 Bennett	N	N	Y	Y	Y	Y
4 ***James***	N	Y	Y	Y	Y	N
5 ***McCollum***	N	Y	Y	Y	Y	N
6 ***Stearns***	Y	Y	Y	Y	Y	N
7 Gibbons	N	N	Y	Y	N	Y
8 ***Young***	N	Y	Y	Y	N	Y
9 ***Bilirakis***	?	Y	Y	Y	Y	N
10 ***Ireland***	N	Y	Y	Y	Y	N
11 Nelson	-	-	+	-	X	+
12 ***Lewis***	N	Y	Y	Y	Y	N
13 ***Goss***	N	Y	Y	Y	Y	N
14 Johnston	N	N	Y	N	N	Y
15 ***Shaw***	N	Y	Y	Y	Y	N
16 Smith	N	N	Y	?	?	Y
17 Lehman	N	N	Y	N	N	Y
18 ***Ros-Lehtinen***	N	Y	Y	Y	N	N
19 Fascell	N	N	Y	N	N	Y
GEORGIA						
1 Thomas	N	Y	Y	Y	N	Y
2 Hatcher	N	N	Y	Y	N	Y
3 Ray	N	Y	Y	Y	Y	N
4 Jones	N	N	Y	Y	N	Y
5 Lewis	N	N	Y	N	N	Y
6 ***Gingrich***	N	Y	N	Y	Y	N
7 Darden	N	N	Y	Y	N	Y
8 Rowland	N	Y	Y	Y	N	Y
9 Jenkins	N	N	Y	Y	Y	N
10 Barnard	N	Y	Y	Y	Y	N
HAWAII						
1 ***Saiki***	N	Y	Y	Y	Y	Y
2 Vacancy						
IDAHO						
1 ***Craig***	N	Y	Y	Y	Y	N
2 Stallings	N	N	Y	Y	N	N
ILLINOIS						
1 Hayes	N	N	Y	N	N	Y
2 Savage	P	P	P	N	N	Y
3 Russo	N	N	Y	Y	Y	N
4 Sangmeister	N	N	Y	Y	Y	N
5 Lipinski	N	N	Y	Y	Y	N
6 ***Hyde***	N	Y	Y	Y	Y	N
7 Collins	N	N	Y	N	N	Y
8 Rostenkowski	N	N	Y	?	?	?
9 Yates	N	N	N	N	N	Y
10 ***Porter***	Y	Y	Y	Y	Y	Y
11 Annunzio	N	N	Y	Y	N	Y
12 ***Crane***	Y	Y	Y	Y	Y	N
13 ***Fawell***	Y	Y	Y	Y	Y	Y
14 ***Hastert***	Y	Y	Y	Y	Y	N
15 ***Madigan***	N	Y	Y	Y	Y	N
16 ***Martin***	N	N	Y	Y	Y	N
17 Evans	N	N	Y	N	N	Y
18 ***Michel***	N	Y	Y	Y	Y	N
19 Bruce	N	N	Y	Y	N	Y
20 Durbin	N	N	Y	Y	N	Y
21 Costello	N	N	Y	Y	N	Y
22 Poshard	N	Y	Y	Y	N	Y
INDIANA						
1 Visclosky	N	N	Y	Y	N	Y
2 Sharp	N	N	Y	Y	Y	Y
3 ***Hiler***	N	Y	Y	Y	Y	N

ND Northern Democrats SD Southern Democrats

	268	270	271	272	273	274
4 Long	N	N	Y	Y	Y	Y
5 Jontz	N	N	Y	N	N	Y
6 ***Burton***	Y	Y	N	Y	Y	N
7 ***Myers***	N	N	Y	Y	N	Y
8 McCloskey	N	N	Y	N	N	Y
9 Hamilton	N	N	Y	Y	Y	Y
10 Jacobs	N	N	Y	N	Y	Y
IOWA						
1 ***Leach***	N	N	Y	Y	Y	N
2 ***Tauke***	N	N	Y	Y	Y	N
3 Nagle	N	N	Y	Y	N	Y
4 Smith	N	N	Y	N	N	Y
5 ***Lightfoot***	Y	Y	Y	Y	Y	N
6 ***Grandy***	N	N	Y	Y	Y	N
KANSAS						
1 ***Roberts***	N	Y	Y	Y	Y	N
2 Slattery	N	N	Y	Y	Y	N
3 ***Meyers***	N	Y	Y	Y	Y	N
4 Glickman	N	N	Y	Y	Y	N
5 ***Whittaker***	N	N	Y	Y	Y	N
KENTUCKY						
1 Hubbard	N	N	Y	Y	Y	N
2 Natcher	N	N	Y	Y	N	Y
3 Mazzoli	N	N	Y	N	N	Y
4 ***Bunning***	Y	Y	Y	Y	Y	N
5 ***Rogers***	Y	Y	Y	Y	Y	N
6 ***Hopkins***	Y	Y	Y	Y	Y	N
7 Perkins	N	N	Y	Y	N	Y
LOUISIANA						
1 ***Livingston***	Y	Y	Y	?	?	?
2 Boggs	N	N	Y	N	N	Y
3 Tauzin	N	N	Y	Y	Y	N
4 ***McCrery***	N	Y	Y	?	?	?
5 Huckaby	N	N	Y	Y	Y	N
6 ***Baker***	N	Y	Y	Y	Y	N
7 Hayes	N	N	Y	Y	Y	N
8 ***Holloway***	Y	Y	N	Y	Y	N
MAINE						
1 Brennan	N	N	Y	Y	N	Y
2 ***Snowe***	N	N	Y	Y	Y	N
MARYLAND						
1 Dyson	N	N	Y	Y	N	Y
2 ***Bentley***	N	Y	Y	Y	Y	N
3 Cardin	N	N	Y	N	N	Y
4 McMillen	N	N	Y	Y	N	Y
5 Hoyer	N	N	Y	N	N	Y
6 Byron	N	N	Y	Y	Y	N
7 Mfume	N	N	Y	N	N	Y
8 ***Morella***	N	N	Y	N	N	#
MASSACHUSETTS						
1 ***Conte***	N	N	Y	N	N	Y
2 Neal	N	N	Y	Y	N	Y
3 Early	N	N	Y	?	?	?
4 Frank	C	C	C	N	N	Y
5 Atkins	N	N	Y	N	N	Y
6 Mavroules	N	N	Y	N	N	Y
7 Markey	N	N	Y	N	N	Y
8 Kennedy	N	N	Y	N	N	Y
9 Moakley	N	N	Y	Y	N	Y
10 Studds	N	N	Y	N	N	Y
11 Donnelly	N	N	Y	Y	N	Y
MICHIGAN						
1 Conyers	N	N	Y	N	N	Y
2 ***Pursell***	N	Y	Y	Y	Y	N
3 Wolpe	N	N	Y	N	N	Y
4 ***Upton***	N	Y	Y	Y	Y	N
5 ***Henry***	N	Y	Y	Y	Y	N
6 Carr	N	N	Y	N	N	Y
7 Kildee	N	N	Y	N	N	N
8 Traxler	N	N	Y	Y	N	Y
9 ***Vander Jagt***	N	Y	Y	Y	Y	N
10 ***Schuette***	Y	Y	Y	Y	Y	N
11 ***Davis***	N	N	Y	Y	?	?
12 Bonior	N	N	Y	N	N	Y
13 Crockett	N	N	Y	N	N	Y
14 Hertel	N	N	Y	N	N	Y
15 Ford	N	N	Y	N	N	Y
16 Dingell	N	N	Y	N	N	Y
17 Levin	N	N	Y	N	N	Y
18 ***Broomfield***	N	Y	Y	Y	Y	N
MINNESOTA						
1 Penny	N	N	Y	Y	Y	N
2 ***Weber***	N	Y	Y	Y	Y	N
3 ***Frenzel***	N	N	Y	Y	Y	N
4 Vento	N	N	Y	N	N	Y
5 Sabo	N	N	Y	N	N	Y
6 Sikorski	N	N	Y	N	N	Y
7 ***Stangeland***	N	N	Y	Y	Y	Y
8 Oberstar	N	N	Y	N	N	Y
MISSISSIPPI						
1 Whitten	N	N	Y	Y	N	?
2 Espy	N	N	Y	N	N	Y
3 Montgomery	N	N	Y	Y	Y	N
4 Parker	N	N	Y	Y	Y	N
5 Taylor	N	Y	Y	Y	Y	N
MISSOURI						
1 Clay	N	N	N	N	N	Y
2 ***Buechner***	N	Y	Y	Y	Y	N
3 Gephardt	N	N	Y	N	N	Y
4 Skelton	N	N	Y	Y	Y	N
5 Wheat	N	N	Y	N	N	Y
6 ***Coleman***	N	N	Y	Y	Y	N
7 ***Hancock***	Y	Y	N	Y	Y	N
8 ***Emerson***	N	Y	Y	Y	Y	N
9 Volkmer	N	N	Y	Y	Y	N
MONTANA						
1 Williams	N	N	Y	N	N	N
2 ***Marlenee***	N	N	Y	Y	Y	N
NEBRASKA						
1 ***Bereuter***	N	N	Y	Y	Y	N
2 Hoagland	N	N	Y	Y	Y	N
3 ***Smith***	N	Y	Y	Y	Y	N
NEVADA						
1 Bilbray	N	N	Y	Y	N	Y
2 ***Vucanovich***	Y	Y	Y	Y	Y	N
NEW HAMPSHIRE						
1 ***Smith***	Y	Y	Y	Y	Y	N
2 ***Douglas***	N	Y	Y	Y	Y	N
NEW JERSEY						
1 Vacancy						
2 Hughes	N	N	Y	Y	Y	N
3 Pallone	N	N	Y	Y	Y	N
4 ***Smith***	N	Y	Y	Y	Y	N
5 ***Roukema***	N	Y	Y	Y	Y	Y
6 Dwyer	N	N	Y	N	N	Y
7 ***Rinaldo***	N	Y	Y	Y	Y	N
8 Roe	N	N	Y	Y	N	Y
9 Torricelli	N	N	Y	Y	N	Y
10 Payne	N	N	Y	N	N	Y
11 ***Gallo***	N	Y	Y	N	N	Y
12 ***Courter***	N	Y	Y	Y	Y	N
13 ***Saxton***	N	Y	Y	Y	Y	N
14 Guarini	N	N	Y	Y	Y	Y
NEW MEXICO						
1 ***Schiff***	N	N	Y	Y	N	Y
2 ***Skeen***	N	Y	Y	Y	?	Y
3 Richardson	N	N	Y	Y	N	Y
NEW YORK						
1 Hochbrueckner	N	N	Y	Y	Y	Y
2 Downey	N	N	Y	N	N	Y
3 Mrazek	N	N	N	N	N	Y
4 ***Lent***	N	N	Y	Y	Y	N
5 ***McGrath***	N	N	Y	Y	Y	N
6 Flake	N	N	Y	N	N	Y
7 Ackerman	N	N	Y	N	N	Y
8 Scheuer	N	N	Y	N	N	Y
9 Manton	N	N	Y	N	N	Y
10 Schumer	N	N	Y	N	N	Y
11 Towns	N	N	Y	N	N	Y
12 Owens	N	N	Y	N	?	Y
13 Solarz	N	N	Y	N	N	Y
14 ***Molinari***	N	N	Y	Y	Y	Y
15 ***Green***	N	N	Y	N	N	Y
16 Rangel	N	N	Y	N	N	Y
17 Weiss	N	N	Y	N	N	Y
18 Serrano	N	N	Y	N	N	Y
19 Engel	N	N	Y	N	N	Y
20 Lowey	N	N	Y	?	?	?
21 ***Fish***	N	N	Y	N	N	Y
22 ***Gilman***	N	N	Y	N	N	Y
23 McNulty	N	N	Y	Y	N	Y
24 ***Solomon***	N	Y	Y	Y	Y	N
25 ***Boehlert***	N	N	Y	Y	N	Y
26 ***Martin***	N	N	Y	Y	N	Y
27 ***Walsh***	N	Y	Y	Y	N	N
28 McHugh	N	N	Y	N	N	Y
29 ***Horton***	N	N	Y	Y	N	Y
30 Slaughter	N	N	Y	N	N	Y
31 ***Paxon***	N	Y	Y	Y	Y	N
32 LaFalce	N	N	Y	N	N	N
33 Nowak	N	N	Y	Y	N	Y
34 ***Houghton***	N	N	Y	Y	Y	Y
NORTH CAROLINA						
1 Jones	N	N	Y	N	N	Y
2 Valentine	N	N	Y	Y	Y	Y
3 Lancaster	N	N	Y	Y	Y	Y
4 Price	N	N	Y	Y	N	Y
5 Neal	N	N	Y	Y	Y	N
6 ***Coble***	Y	Y	Y	Y	Y	N
7 Rose	N	N	Y	Y	N	Y
8 Hefner	N	N	Y	Y	N	Y
9 ***McMillan***	N	Y	Y	Y	Y	Y
10 ***Ballenger***	N	Y	Y	Y	Y	N
11 Clarke	N	N	Y	Y	N	Y
NORTH DAKOTA						
AL Dorgan	N	N	Y	Y	Y	Y
OHIO						
1 Luken	N	N	Y	Y	N	N
2 ***Gradison***	N	Y	Y	Y	Y	N
3 Hall	N	N	Y	Y	N	Y
4 ***Oxley***	N	Y	Y	Y	Y	N
5 ***Gillmor***	N	Y	Y	Y	N	Y
6 ***McEwen***	Y	Y	Y	Y	Y	N
7 ***DeWine***	N	Y	Y	Y	Y	N
8 ***Lukens***	P	P	P	Y	Y	N
9 Kaptur	N	N	Y	Y	N	Y
10 ***Miller***	N	Y	Y	Y	Y	N
11 Eckart	N	N	Y	Y	Y	Y
12 ***Kasich***	N	Y	Y	Y	Y	N
13 Pease	N	N	Y	N	N	Y
14 Sawyer	N	N	Y	N	N	Y
15 ***Wylie***	Y	Y	Y	Y	Y	N
16 ***Regula***	N	Y	Y	Y	N	Y
17 Traficant	N	N	Y	Y	N	Y
18 Applegate	N	N	Y	Y	N	N
19 Feighan	N	N	Y	Y	N	Y
20 Oakar	N	N	Y	N	N	Y
21 Stokes	N	N	Y	N	N	Y
OKLAHOMA						
1 ***Inhofe***	N	Y	Y	Y	Y	N
2 Synar	N	N	Y	N	N	Y
3 Watkins	N	Y	Y	Y	Y	N
4 McCurdy	N	N	Y	Y	Y	N
5 ***Edwards***	N	Y	Y	Y	?	N
6 English	N	N	Y	Y	Y	N
OREGON						
1 AuCoin	N	N	Y	N	N	Y
2 ***Smith, B.***	Y	Y	Y	Y	Y	N
3 Wyden	N	N	Y	N	N	Y
4 DeFazio	N	N	Y	Y	Y	N
5 ***Smith, D.***	Y	Y	Y	Y	Y	N
PENNSYLVANIA						
1 Foglietta	N	N	Y	N	N	Y
2 Gray	N	N	Y	N	N	Y
3 Borski	N	N	Y	Y	N	Y
4 Kolter	N	N	Y	Y	N	Y
5 ***Schulze***	Y	Y	Y	Y	Y	N
6 Yatron	N	N	Y	Y	N	N
7 ***Weldon***	N	N	Y	Y	Y	N
8 Kostmayer	N	N	Y	N	N	Y
9 ***Shuster***	N	Y	Y	Y	Y	N
10 ***McDade***	N	N	Y	Y	N	Y
11 Kanjorski	N	N	Y	Y	N	Y
12 Murtha	N	N	Y	N	N	Y
13 ***Coughlin***	N	N	Y	Y	N	N
14 Coyne	N	N	Y	N	N	Y
15 ***Ritter***	N	N	Y	Y	Y	N
16 ***Walker***	N	Y	N	Y	Y	N
17 ***Gekas***	N	Y	Y	Y	Y	N
18 Walgren	N	N	Y	Y	N	Y
19 ***Goodling***	N	Y	Y	Y	Y	Y
20 Gaydos	N	N	Y	Y	N	Y
21 ***Ridge***	N	N	Y	N	Y	Y
22 Murphy	N	N	Y	Y	Y	N
23 ***Clinger***	N	N	Y	Y	Y	N
RHODE ISLAND						
1 ***Machtley***	N	N	Y	N	N	Y
2 ***Schneider***	N	N	Y	N	N	Y
SOUTH CAROLINA						
1 ***Ravenel***	N	N	Y	Y	Y	Y
2 ***Spence***	N	N	Y	Y	Y	N
3 Derrick	N	N	Y	Y	Y	Y
4 Patterson	N	Y	Y	Y	Y	Y
5 Spratt	N	N	Y	Y	N	Y
6 Tallon	N	N	Y	Y	Y	N
SOUTH DAKOTA						
AL Johnson	N	N	Y	Y	N	N
TENNESSEE						
1 ***Quillen***	Y	Y	Y	Y	Y	N
2 ***Duncan***	Y	Y	Y	Y	Y	N
3 Lloyd	N	N	Y	Y	Y	N
4 Cooper	N	N	Y	Y	Y	Y
5 Clement	N	N	Y	Y	N	Y
6 Gordon	N	N	?	Y	N	Y
7 ***Sundquist***	Y	Y	N	Y	Y	N
8 Tanner	N	N	Y	Y	N	Y
9 Ford	N	N	Y	N	N	Y
TEXAS						
1 Chapman	N	?	?	?	#	?
2 Wilson	N	N	Y	Y	N	Y
3 ***Bartlett***	N	Y	Y	Y	Y	N
4 Hall	Y	Y	Y	Y	Y	N
5 Bryant	N	N	Y	Y	N	Y
6 ***Barton***	Y	Y	Y	Y	Y	N
7 ***Archer***	N	Y	Y	Y	Y	N
8 ***Fields***	N	Y	Y	Y	Y	N
9 Brooks	N	N	Y	Y	Y	Y
10 Pickle	N	N	Y	Y	N	Y
11 Leath	N	N	Y	Y	Y	Y
12 Geren	N	N	Y	Y	N	Y
13 Sarpalius	Y	Y	Y	Y	Y	N
14 Laughlin	N	Y	Y	Y	Y	N
15 de la Garza	N	N	Y	Y	N	Y
16 Coleman	N	N	Y	Y	N	Y
17 Stenholm	N	N	Y	Y	Y	N
18 Washington	N	N	N	?	N	Y
19 ***Combest***	N	Y	Y	Y	Y	N
20 Gonzalez	N	N	Y	N	N	Y
21 ***Smith***	N	Y	Y	Y	Y	N
22 ***DeLay***	N	Y	Y	Y	Y	N
23 Bustamante	N	N	Y	Y	N	Y
24 Frost	N	N	Y	Y	N	Y
25 Andrews	N	N	Y	Y	N	Y
26 ***Armey***	N	Y	Y	Y	Y	N
27 Ortiz	N	N	Y	N	N	Y
UTAH						
1 ***Hansen***	N	Y	Y	Y	Y	N
2 Owens	N	N	Y	Y	N	Y
3 ***Nielson***	N	Y	Y	Y	Y	N
VERMONT						
AL ***Smith***	N	Y	Y	Y	Y	Y
VIRGINIA						
1 ***Bateman***	N	Y	Y	Y	N	Y
2 Pickett	N	N	Y	Y	N	Y
3 ***Bliley***	N	Y	Y	Y	N	Y
4 Sisisky	N	N	Y	Y	N	Y
5 Payne	N	N	Y	Y	N	Y
6 Olin	N	N	Y	N	N	Y
7 ***Slaughter***	N	Y	Y	Y	Y	N
8 ***Parris***	N	Y	Y	Y	N	Y
9 Boucher	N	N	Y	?	N	Y
10 ***Wolf***	N	Y	Y	Y	N	N
WASHINGTON						
1 ***Miller***	N	N	Y	Y	Y	N
2 Swift	N	N	Y	N	N	Y
3 Unsoeld	N	N	Y	Y	N	Y
4 ***Morrison***	N	N	Y	Y	Y	N
5 Foley	N	N	Y			
6 Dicks	N	N	Y	N	N	Y
7 McDermott	N	N	Y	N	N	Y
8 ***Chandler***	N	N	Y	Y	Y	N
WEST VIRGINIA						
1 Mollohan	N	N	Y	Y	N	N
2 Staggers	N	N	Y	Y	N	Y
3 Wise	N	N	Y	Y	N	Y
4 Rahall	N	N	Y	Y	N	Y
WISCONSIN						
1 Aspin	N	N	Y	Y	N	Y
2 Kastenmeier	N	N	Y	N	N	Y
3 ***Gunderson***	N	N	Y	Y	Y	N
4 Kleczka	N	N	Y	Y	N	Y
5 Moody	N	N	Y	N	N	Y
6 ***Petri***	N	Y	Y	Y	Y	N
7 Obey	N	N	Y	P	N	Y
8 ***Roth***	Y	Y	Y	Y	Y	N
9 ***Sensenbrenner***	N	Y	Y	Y	Y	N
WYOMING						
AL ***Thomas***	N	Y	Y	Y	Y	N

Southern states - Ala., Ark., Fla., Ga., Ky., La., Miss., N.C., Okla., S.C., Tenn., Texas, Va.
Omitted votes are quorum calls, which CQ does not include in its vote charts.

HOUSE VOTES 275, 276, 277, 278, 279, 280, 281, 282

275. HR 1180. Housing Programs Reauthorization/Rule. Adoption of the rule (H Res 435) to provide for House floor consideration of the bill to reauthorize and expand existing federal housing programs. Adopted 303-98: R 67-98; D 236-0 (ND 157-0, SD 79-0), July 27, 1990.

276. HR 3950. Farm Programs Reauthorization/Sanctions. Glickman, D-Kan., amendment to the Gejdenson, D-Conn., amendment, to deny credit guarantees to countries that violate human rights or support international terrorism and reallocate such guarantees to other countries, including emerging democracies. Adopted 234-175: R 84-84; D 150-91 (ND 115-47, SD 35-44), July 27, 1990.

277. HR 3950. Farm Programs Reauthorization/Sanctions. Bereuter, R-Neb., amendment to the Gejdenson, D-Conn., amendment, to allow the secretary of Agriculture to suspend credit restrictions, if the secretary finds the impact of the restrictions would harm American farmers more than it would harm the country violating human rights or supporting international terrorism. Adopted 208-191: R 109-56; D 99-135 (ND 53-106, SD 46-29), July 27, 1990.

278. HR 3950. Farm Programs Reauthorization/Honey Price Supports. Conte, R-Mass., substitute amendment to the Armey, R-Texas, amendment, to phase out the honey price support program over four years. Rejected 178-215: R 95-68; D 83-147 (ND 71-84, SD 12-63), July 27, 1990.

279. HR 5313. Fiscal 1991 Military Construction Appropriations/Previous Question. Hall, D-Ohio, motion to order the previous question (thus ending debate and the possibility of amendment) on the rule (H Res 441) to provide for House floor consideration of the bill to appropriate funds for the construction of military facilities at home and overseas in fiscal 1991. Motion agreed to 289-93: R 67-92; D 222-1 (ND 148-1, SD 74-0), July 30, 1990.

280. HR 5313. Fiscal 1991 Military Construction Appropriations/Rule. Adoption of the rule (H Res 441) to provide for House floor consideration of the bill to appropriate funds for the construction of military facilities at home and overseas in fiscal 1991. Adopted 299-93: R 72-93; D 227-0 (ND 152-0, SD 75-0), July 30, 1990.

281. HR 5313. Fiscal 1991 Military Construction Appropriations/Across-the-Board Cuts. Penny, D-Minn., amendment to make an across-the-board cut of 2 percent in all discretionary accounts in the bill, cutting a total of about $166 million. Rejected 164-239: R 112-56; D 52-183 (ND 42-116, SD 10-67), July 30, 1990.

282. HR 5313. Fiscal 1991 Military Construction Appropriations/Across-the-Board Cuts. Frenzel, R-Minn., amendment to make an across-the-board cut of 0.8 percent in all discretionary accounts in the bill, cutting a total of about $70 million. Rejected 180-214: R 120-40; D 60-174 (ND 48-111, SD 12-63), July 30, 1990.

KEY

- Y Voted for (yea).
- # Paired for.
- + Announced for.
- N Voted against (nay).
- X Paired against.
- \- Announced against.
- P Voted "present."
- C Voted "present" to avoid possible conflict of interest.
- ? Did not vote or otherwise make a position known.

Democrats *Republicans*

	275	276	277	278	279	280	281	282
ALABAMA								
1 *Callahan*	N	Y	Y	N	N	N	N	Y
2 *Dickinson*	N	N	Y	N	N	Y	Y	N
3 Browder	Y	Y	Y	N	Y	Y	N	N
4 Bevill	Y	Y	N	N	Y	Y	N	?
5 Flippo	Y	N	?	?	Y	Y	N	N
6 Erdreich	Y	Y	N	Y	Y	Y	Y	Y
7 Harris	Y	Y	N	N	Y	Y	N	N
ALASKA								
AL *Young*	Y	Y	N	N	Y	Y	N	N
ARIZONA								
1 *Rhodes*	N	Y	Y	Y	N	N	Y	Y
2 Udall	?	N	N	N	Y	Y	N	Y
3 *Stump*	N	N	Y	N	N	N	N	?
4 *Kyl*	N	Y	N	Y	N	N	Y	Y
5 *Kolbe*	N	Y	Y	N	N	Y	N	Y
ARKANSAS								
1 Alexander	Y	N	+	N	Y	Y	N	N
2 *Robinson*	?	?	?	X	Y	Y	Y	Y
3 *Hammerschmidt*	N	N	Y	N	Y	Y	Y	?
4 Anthony	Y	N	Y	N	Y	Y	N	N
CALIFORNIA								
1 Bosco	Y	N	Y	N	Y	Y	Y	Y
2 *Herger*	N	N	Y	N	N	N	Y	Y
3 Matsui	Y	N	Y	N	Y	Y	N	N
4 Fazio	Y	N	Y	N	Y	Y	N	N
5 Pelosi	Y	Y	N	N	Y	Y	N	N
6 Boxer	Y	Y	?	?	Y	Y	Y	Y
7 Miller	Y	Y	N	Y	Y	Y	N	N
8 Dellums	Y	N	N	N	?	?	Y	Y
9 Stark	Y	Y	?	?	Y	Y	Y	N
10 Edwards	Y	Y	N	N	Y	Y	N	N
11 Lantos	Y	Y	N	Y	?	?	?	?
12 *Campbell*	Y	Y	N	Y	-	-	Y	Y
13 Mineta	Y	Y	N	N	Y	Y	N	N
14 *Shumway*	N	N	Y	N	Y	N	Y	Y
15 Condit	Y	N	Y	N	Y	Y	Y	Y
16 Panetta	Y	N	Y	N	Y	Y	N	N
17 *Pashayan*	Y	N	Y	N	Y	Y	Y	Y
18 Lehman	Y	N	Y	N	Y	Y	N	N
19 *Lagomarsino*	N	Y	N	Y	N	N	Y	Y
20 *Thomas*	N	N	#	N	Y	Y	N	N
21 *Gallegly*	N	Y	N	Y	N	N	Y	Y
22 *Moorhead*	N	Y	Y	N	N	N	Y	Y
23 Beilenson	Y	Y	N	Y	Y	Y	N	N
24 Waxman	Y	Y	N	Y	Y	Y	N	N
25 Roybal	Y	Y	?	N	Y	Y	N	N
26 Berman	?	Y	N	Y	Y	Y	N	N
27 Levine	Y	Y	N	Y	Y	Y	N	N
28 Dixon	?	?	N	N	Y	Y	N	N
29 Hawkins	Y	Y	N	?	?	?	?	?
30 Martinez	?	Y	N	N	Y	Y	N	N
31 Dymally	Y	N	Y	N	Y	Y	#	#
32 Anderson	Y	Y	N	N	Y	Y	N	N
33 *Dreier*	N	Y	Y	Y	N	N	Y	Y
34 Torres	Y	?	N	N	Y	Y	N	N
35 *Lewis*	N	N	Y	N	N	N	N	N
36 Brown	Y	Y	N	N	Y	Y	N	N
37 *McCandless*	Y	Y	Y	N	N	N	Y	Y
38 *Dornan*	N	Y	N	N	N	N	Y	Y
39 *Dannemeyer*	N	Y	Y	Y	N	N	Y	Y
40 *Cox*	N	Y	N	Y	N	N	?	?
41 *Lowery*	?	N	Y	N	Y	Y	N	N
42 *Rohrabacher*	N	Y	N	Y	N	N	Y	Y
43 *Packard*	N	Y	Y	Y	?	?	Y	Y
44 Bates	Y	N	Y	Y	Y	Y	Y	Y
45 *Hunter*	N	Y	Y	Y	N	N	N	N
COLORADO								
1 Schroeder	Y	Y	N	Y	Y	Y	N	Y
2 Skaggs	Y	Y	N	N	Y	Y	N	N
3 Campbell	Y	Y	N	N	Y	Y	Y	Y
4 *Brown*	N	Y	N	Y	N	N	Y	Y
5 *Hefley*	N	Y	Y	Y	?	N	Y	Y
6 *Schaefer*	N	Y	Y	Y	N	N	Y	Y
CONNECTICUT								
1 Kennelly	Y	Y	N	N	Y	Y	N	N
2 Gejdenson	Y	Y	N	Y	Y	Y	N	N
3 Morrison	+	#	X	#	+	+	#	#
4 *Shays*	Y	N	Y	Y	Y	Y	Y	Y
5 *Rowland*	?	?	?	?	Y	Y	N	N
6 *Johnson*	?	N	Y	Y	N	N	Y	Y
DELAWARE								
AL Carper	Y	Y	Y	Y	Y	Y	N	?
FLORIDA								
1 Hutto	Y	Y	Y	N	?	?	N	N
2 *Grant*	Y	N	Y	N	Y	Y	N	N
3 Bennett	Y	Y	N	Y	Y	Y	N	N
4 *James*	N	Y	N	N	N	N	Y	Y
5 *McCollum*	Y	Y	N	N	Y	Y	Y	Y
6 *Stearns*	Y	Y	#	?	N	N	Y	Y
7 Gibbons	Y	N	Y	Y	Y	Y	?	?
8 *Young*	N	N	N	Y	Y	Y	N	N
9 *Bilirakis*	?	?	?	?	?	?	?	#
10 *Ireland*	N	Y	N	Y	N	Y	Y	Y
11 Nelson	+	+	-	-	+	+	-	X
12 *Lewis*	N	N	Y	N	N	N	Y	+
13 *Goss*	N	Y	N	Y	N	N	Y	Y
14 Johnston	Y	Y	N	N	Y	Y	Y	Y
15 *Shaw*	Y	Y	Y	Y	Y	Y	Y	Y
16 Smith	?	?	?	?	Y	Y	N	Y
17 Lehman	Y	Y	N	Y	Y	Y	N	N
18 *Ros-Lehtinen*	N	Y	N	Y	N	N	Y	Y
19 Fascell	Y	Y	N	N	?	?	N	N
GEORGIA								
1 Thomas	Y	N	Y	N	Y	Y	N	N
2 Hatcher	Y	N	Y	N	Y	Y	N	N
3 Ray	Y	N	Y	N	Y	Y	N	N
4 Jones	Y	Y	N	N	Y	Y	N	N
5 Lewis	Y	Y	N	N	Y	Y	Y	Y
6 *Gingrich*	N	N	Y	Y	?	N	Y	Y
7 Darden	Y	N	Y	N	Y	Y	N	N
8 Rowland	Y	N	Y	N	Y	Y	N	N
9 Jenkins	Y	N	Y	N	Y	Y	N	N
10 Barnard	Y	N	Y	N	Y	Y	X	X
HAWAII								
1 *Saiki*	?	N	Y	N	+	+	—	—
2 Vacancy								
IDAHO								
1 *Craig*	N	Y	Y	N	N	N	N	Y
2 Stallings	Y	N	Y	N	Y	Y	N	N
ILLINOIS								
1 Hayes	Y	Y	Y	N	Y	Y	Y	Y
2 Savage	Y	N	Y	N	Y	Y	Y	Y
3 Russo	Y	Y	N	Y	Y	Y	N	Y
4 Sangmeister	Y	Y	Y	N	?	?	#	?
5 Lipinski	Y	Y	N	N	Y	Y	N	N
6 *Hyde*	Y	N	Y	Y	N	N	Y	Y
7 Collins	Y	Y	N	N	Y	Y	Y	Y
8 Rostenkowski	?	?	?	?	Y	Y	N	N
9 Yates	Y	Y	N	Y	Y	Y	N	N
10 *Porter*	N	Y	N	Y	N	N	Y	Y
11 Annunzio	Y	Y	N	Y	Y	Y	N	N
12 *Crane*	N	Y	N	Y	N	N	Y	Y
13 *Fawell*	N	N	Y	Y	N	N	Y	Y
14 *Hastert*	N	N	Y	Y	N	N	Y	Y
15 *Madigan*	Y	N	Y	N	Y	Y	?	?
16 *Martin*	Y	N	Y	Y	N	N	Y	Y
17 Evans	Y	Y	N	N	Y	Y	N	N
18 *Michel*	Y	N	Y	Y	Y	Y	Y	?
19 Bruce	Y	N	Y	N	+	+	N	N
20 Durbin	Y	Y	N	Y	Y	Y	N	N
21 Costello	Y	N	Y	N	Y	Y	N	N
22 Poshard	Y	Y	N	N	Y	Y	N	N
INDIANA								
1 Visclosky	Y	N	Y	N	Y	Y	N	N
2 Sharp	Y	N	Y	Y	Y	Y	Y	Y
3 *Hiler*	Y	N	Y	Y	Y	Y	N	N

ND Northern Democrats SD Southern Democrats

	275	276	277	278	279	280	281	282
4 Long	Y	N	Y	N	Y	Y	Y	Y
5 Jontz	Y	N	Y	N	Y	Y	N	N
6 ***Burton***	N	?	?	?	N	N	Y	Y
7 ***Myers***	Y	N	Y	N	N	Y	N	N
8 McCloskey	Y	N	Y	Y	Y	Y	N	N
9 Hamilton	Y	N	Y	Y	Y	Y	Y	Y
10 Jacobs	?	?	?	#	N	Y	Y	Y
IOWA								
1 ***Leach***	Y	Y	Y	N	N	N	Y	Y
2 ***Tauke***	N	N	Y	N	Y	N	Y	Y
3 Nagle	Y	N	Y	N	Y	Y	N	Y
4 Smith	Y	N	Y	N	Y	Y	N	N
5 ***Lightfoot***	N	N	Y	N	N	N	N	Y
6 ***Grandy***	Y	N	Y	N	N	N	Y	Y
KANSAS								
1 ***Roberts***	N	N	Y	N	N	N	Y	Y
2 Slattery	Y	Y	N	N	Y	Y	Y	Y
3 ***Meyers***	Y	N	Y	Y	N	N	Y	Y
4 Glickman	Y	Y	N	N	Y	Y	N	N
5 ***Whittaker***	N	N	Y	Y	N	N	Y	Y
KENTUCKY								
1 Hubbard	Y	N	Y	N	Y	Y	Y	Y
2 Natcher	Y	N	Y	N	Y	Y	N	N
3 Mazzoli	Y	N	Y	Y	Y	Y	N	N
4 ***Bunning***	N	Y	Y	N	N	N	Y	Y
5 ***Rogers***	N	N	Y	N	N	Y	N	Y
6 ***Hopkins***	N	N	Y	N	N	N	Y	Y
7 Perkins	Y	N	Y	N	Y	Y	N	N
LOUISIANA								
1 ***Livingston***	?	?	?	?	N	N	N	N
2 Boggs	?	?	?	?	Y	Y	N	N
3 Tauzin	Y	N	Y	N	Y	Y	N	N
4 ***McCrery***	?	?	?	?	?	?	N	N
5 Huckaby	Y	N	Y	N	Y	Y	Y	Y
6 ***Baker***	Y	N	Y	Y	N	N	Y	Y
7 Hayes	Y	N	Y	N	Y	Y	N	N
8 ***Holloway***	N	N	?	?	N	N	N	Y
MAINE								
1 Brennan	Y	Y	N	Y	Y	Y	N	N
2 ***Snowe***	Y	Y	N	Y	Y	Y	N	N
MARYLAND								
1 Dyson	Y	Y	N	N	Y	Y	N	N
2 ***Bentley***	N	Y	Y	Y	N	N	N	N
3 Cardin	Y	Y	N	Y	Y	Y	N	N
4 McMillen	Y	Y	N	Y	Y	Y	N	N
5 Hoyer	?	?	N	N	Y	Y	N	N
6 Byron	Y	Y	Y	N	?	?	N	N
7 Mfume	Y	Y	N	Y	Y	Y	N	Y
8 ***Morella***	Y	Y	N	Y	Y	N	Y	Y
MASSACHUSETTS								
1 ***Conte***	Y	Y	N	Y	Y	Y	N	?
2 Neal	Y	Y	N	Y	?	?	?	?
3 Early	?	?	?	?	Y	Y	N	N
4 Frank	Y	Y	N	Y	Y	Y	N	N
5 Atkins	Y	Y	N	Y	?	?	?	?
6 Mavroules	Y	Y	N	?	Y	Y	N	N
7 Markey	Y	Y	N	N	Y	Y	N	N
8 Kennedy	Y	Y	N	Y	Y	Y	N	N
9 Moakley	Y	Y	N	?	Y	Y	N	N
10 Studds	Y	Y	N	Y	Y	Y	N	N
11 Donnelly	Y	Y	N	?	Y	Y	N	N
MICHIGAN								
1 Conyers	Y	N	?	?	Y	Y	Y	N
2 ***Pursell***	N	Y	N	Y	?	N	Y	Y
3 Wolpe	Y	Y	N	Y	Y	Y	N	N
4 ***Upton***	N	Y	N	Y	N	N	Y	Y
5 ***Henry***	N	Y	N	Y	N	N	Y	Y
6 Carr	Y	N	N	Y	?	?	N	N
7 Kildee	Y	Y	N	N	Y	Y	N	N
8 Traxler	Y	N	Y	N	Y	Y	N	N
9 ***Vander Jagt***	Y	Y	Y	Y	Y	Y	Y	Y
10 ***Schuette***	Y	Y	N	N	?	?	?	?
11 ***Davis***	?	N	Y	N	Y	Y	N	N
12 Bonior	Y	Y	N	Y	Y	Y	N	N
13 Crockett	?	?	?	?	?	?	?	?
14 Hertel	?	?	?	?	Y	Y	N	N
15 Ford	Y	N	N	Y	?	Y	N	N
16 Dingell	Y	N	Y	N	Y	Y	N	N
17 Levin	Y	Y	N	Y	Y	Y	N	N
18 ***Broomfield***	N	Y	N	Y	N	Y	Y	?
MINNESOTA								
1 Penny	Y	N	Y	N	Y	Y	Y	Y
2 ***Weber***	Y	N	Y	N	N	N	Y	Y
3 ***Frenzel***	N	N	Y	Y	N	N	Y	Y
4 Vento	Y	Y	N	Y	Y	Y	N	N
5 Sabo	Y	Y	Y	N	Y	Y	N	N
6 Sikorski	Y	Y	N	N	Y	Y	N	N
7 ***Stangeland***	N	N	Y	N	?	N	Y	Y
8 Oberstar	Y	Y	N	N	Y	Y	N	N
MISSISSIPPI								
1 Whitten	Y	N	Y	N	Y	Y	N	N
2 Espy	Y	N	Y	N	Y	Y	N	N
3 Montgomery	Y	Y	Y	N	Y	Y	N	?
4 Parker	Y	N	Y	X	Y	Y	Y	Y
5 Taylor	Y	N	Y	N	Y	Y	N	N
MISSOURI								
1 Clay	Y	Y	?	Y	?	?	?	?
2 ***Buechner***	N	Y	Y	Y	Y	Y	Y	Y
3 Gephardt	Y	Y	Y	N	Y	Y	?	?
4 Skelton	Y	N	Y	N	Y	Y	N	N
5 Wheat	Y	N	Y	Y	Y	Y	N	N
6 ***Coleman***	N	N	Y	N	N	Y	N	Y
7 ***Hancock***	N	N	Y	Y	N	N	Y	Y
8 ***Emerson***	Y	N	Y	N	N	Y	Y	Y
9 Volkmer	Y	N	Y	N	?	?	Y	Y
MONTANA								
1 Williams	Y	N	Y	N	Y	Y	N	N
2 ***Marlenee***	N	N	Y	N	N	N	Y	Y
NEBRASKA								
1 ***Bereuter***	Y	N	Y	N	Y	N	Y	Y
2 Hoagland	Y	N	Y	N	Y	Y	N	Y
3 ***Smith***	Y	N	Y	N	N	N	Y	Y
NEVADA								
1 Bilbray	Y	Y	N	Y	?	?	N	N
2 ***Vucanovich***	N	N	Y	Y	?	?	N	N
NEW HAMPSHIRE								
1 ***Smith***	N	Y	N	Y	N	N	Y	Y
2 ***Douglas***	N	Y	N	Y	N	N	Y	Y
NEW JERSEY								
1 Vacancy								
2 Hughes	Y	Y	N	Y	Y	Y	Y	Y
3 Pallone	Y	Y	N	Y	Y	Y	N	N
4 ***Smith***	Y	Y	N	Y	Y	Y	N	Y
5 ***Roukema***	?	?	?	#	Y	Y	Y	Y
6 Dwyer	?	?	?	?	Y	Y	N	N
7 ***Rinaldo***	Y	Y	N	Y	Y	Y	Y	Y
8 Roe	Y	Y	Y	N	Y	Y	N	N
9 Torricelli	Y	Y	N	Y	Y	Y	N	Y
10 Payne	Y	Y	N	Y	Y	Y	Y	Y
11 ***Gallo***	Y	Y	N	Y	N	N	N	N
12 ***Courter***	Y	Y	N	Y	N	N	Y	N
13 ***Saxton***	Y	Y	N	N	N	N	N	N
14 Guarini	Y	Y	N	N	Y	Y	Y	Y
NEW MEXICO								
1 ***Schiff***	N	N	Y	N	N	Y	N	N
2 ***Skeen***	N	N	Y	N	Y	Y	N	N
3 Richardson	Y	Y	Y	N	Y	Y	N	N
NEW YORK								
1 Hochbrueckner	Y	Y	N	Y	Y	Y	N	N
2 Downey	Y	Y	N	Y	Y	Y	N	N
3 Mrazek	?	Y	N	Y	Y	Y	?	?
4 ***Lent***	Y	Y	N	Y	Y	Y	N	Y
5 ***McGrath***	Y	Y	N	Y	Y	Y	N	N
6 Flake	Y	Y	N	N	Y	Y	Y	N
7 Ackerman	Y	Y	N	Y	Y	Y	N	N
8 Scheuer	Y	Y	N	Y	Y	Y	N	N
9 Manton	Y	Y	N	N	Y	Y	N	N
10 Schumer	Y	Y	N	Y	Y	Y	Y	Y
11 Towns	Y	N	N	N	Y	Y	Y	N
12 Owens	Y	Y	N	Y	Y	Y	Y	Y
13 Solarz	Y	Y	N	Y	Y	Y	N	N
14 ***Molinari***	N	Y	N	Y	Y	N	N	N
15 ***Green***	Y	Y	N	Y	Y	Y	N	N
16 Rangel	Y	N	N	N	?	Y	X	N
17 Weiss	Y	Y	N	Y	Y	Y	N	N
18 Serrano	Y	Y	N	?	?	?	N	N
19 Engel	Y	Y	N	N	Y	Y	N	N
20 Lowey	Y	Y	N	N	Y	Y	Y	Y
21 ***Fish***	Y	Y	N	N	Y	Y	Y	Y
22 ***Gilman***	Y	Y	N	N	Y	Y	N	N
23 McNulty	Y	Y	N	Y	Y	Y	N	N
24 ***Solomon***	Y	Y	N	Y	?	?	Y	Y
25 ***Boehlert***	Y	Y	N	N	Y	Y	N	N
26 ***Martin***	Y	N	Y	?	N	N	N	N
27 ***Walsh***	Y	N	Y	N	Y	Y	Y	Y
28 McHugh	Y	Y	N	N	Y	Y	N	N
29 ***Horton***	Y	Y	N	?	Y	Y	?	?
30 Slaughter	Y	Y	N	N	Y	Y	Y	Y
31 ***Paxon***	N	Y	N	N	N	N	Y	Y
32 LaFalce	Y	Y	Y	?	Y	Y	Y	Y
33 Nowak	Y	Y	N	Y	Y	Y	Y	Y
34 ***Houghton***	N	N	Y	N	Y	N	Y	Y
NORTH CAROLINA								
1 Jones	Y	Y	N	N	Y	Y	N	N
2 Valentine	Y	Y	Y	N	Y	Y	N	N
3 Lancaster	Y	Y	Y	N	Y	Y	N	N
4 Price	Y	Y	N	N	Y	Y	N	N
5 Neal	Y	Y	N	N	Y	Y	N	N
6 ***Coble***	N	N	Y	N	?	N	Y	Y
7 Rose	Y	Y	N	N	Y	Y	N	N
8 Hefner	Y	N	Y	N	Y	Y	N	N
9 ***McMillan***	Y	N	Y	Y	Y	Y	Y	Y
10 ***Ballenger***	N	N	Y	Y	N	N	Y	Y
11 Clarke	Y	Y	N	Y	Y	Y	N	Y
NORTH DAKOTA								
AL Dorgan	Y	N	Y	N	Y	Y	Y	Y
OHIO								
1 Luken	Y	N	Y	N	Y	Y	N	N
2 ***Gradison***	N	N	Y	Y	Y	Y	Y	Y
3 Hall	?	N	Y	Y	Y	Y	N	N
4 ***Oxley***	N	N	Y	?	N	N	Y	Y
5 ***Gillmor***	N	N	Y	Y	Y	Y	N	Y
6 ***McEwen***	N	N	Y	N	?	?	?	?
7 ***DeWine***	N	Y	Y	Y	Y	Y	Y	Y
8 ***Lukens***	N	Y	N	Y	N	N	Y	Y
9 Kaptur	Y	Y	Y	N	?	?	X	X
10 ***Miller***	Y	N	Y	Y	Y	Y	Y	Y
11 Eckart	Y	Y	Y	Y	Y	Y	Y	Y
12 ***Kasich***	N	Y	Y	N	Y	Y	?	?
13 Pease	Y	Y	N	N	Y	Y	Y	Y
14 Sawyer	Y	N	Y	Y	Y	Y	Y	Y
15 ***Wylie***	Y	N	Y	Y	N	N	Y	?
16 ***Regula***	Y	Y	Y	Y	Y	Y	Y	Y
17 Traficant	Y	Y	N	Y	Y	Y	Y	Y
18 Applegate	Y	Y	N	Y	?	?	Y	Y
19 Feighan	?	N	Y	Y	?	?	?	?
20 Oakar	Y	N	Y	Y	Y	Y	N	Y
21 Stokes	Y	Y	?	Y	?	?	N	N
OKLAHOMA								
1 ***Inhofe***	N	Y	Y	Y	Y	N	Y	Y
2 Synar	Y	Y	N	N	Y	Y	N	N
3 Watkins	Y	N	Y	N	Y	Y	N	N
4 McCurdy	Y	N	Y	N	Y	Y	N	N
5 ***Edwards***	N	N	Y	Y	Y	Y	N	N
6 English	Y	N	Y	N	?	?	N	N
OREGON								
1 AuCoin	Y	Y	N	N	Y	Y	N	N
2 ***Smith, B.***	N	N	Y	N	N	N	Y	Y
3 Wyden	Y	Y	N	Y	Y	Y	N	N
4 DeFazio	Y	Y	N	N	?	?	?	Y
5 ***Smith, D.***	N	N	Y	N	N	N	Y	Y
PENNSYLVANIA								
1 Foglietta	Y	Y	N	N	Y	Y	N	N
2 Gray	?	?	?	?	Y	Y	N	N
3 Borski	Y	Y	N	Y	Y	Y	N	N
4 Kolter	Y	Y	N	N	?	Y	N	N
5 ***Schulze***	Y	Y	Y	Y	Y	Y	Y	Y
6 Yatron	Y	Y	N	Y	Y	Y	Y	Y
7 ***Weldon***	Y	Y	Y	Y	Y	Y	Y	Y
8 Kostmayer	Y	Y	N	Y	Y	Y	N	N
9 ***Shuster***	N	N	Y	Y	N	Y	Y	Y
10 ***McDade***	Y	Y	N	Y	Y	Y	N	N
11 Kanjorski	Y	Y	N	Y	Y	Y	N	N
12 Murtha	Y	Y	N	N	Y	Y	N	N
13 ***Coughlin***	N	Y	N	Y	N	Y	N	N
14 Coyne	Y	Y	N	N	Y	Y	N	N
15 ***Ritter***	Y	Y	N	Y	Y	Y	Y	Y
16 ***Walker***	N	N	Y	Y	N	N	Y	Y
17 ***Gekas***	N	N	N	N	N	N	Y	Y
18 Walgren	Y	Y	N	Y	Y	Y	Y	Y
19 ***Goodling***	Y	N	Y	N	Y	Y	N	Y
20 Gaydos	Y	Y	N	Y	Y	Y	N	N
21 ***Ridge***	?	Y	N	Y	Y	Y	Y	Y
22 Murphy	Y	Y	Y	Y	Y	Y	Y	Y
23 ***Clinger***	Y	Y	Y	N	Y	Y	Y	Y
RHODE ISLAND								
1 ***Machtley***	Y	Y	N	Y	Y	Y	N	N
2 ***Schneider***	Y	Y	N	Y	Y	Y	Y	Y
SOUTH CAROLINA								
1 ***Ravenel***	N	Y	Y	Y	Y	N	Y	Y
2 ***Spence***	Y	X	?	?	N	Y	N	N
3 Derrick	Y	Y	N	N	Y	Y	N	N
4 Patterson	Y	Y	N	Y	Y	Y	N	N
5 Spratt	Y	Y	N	Y	Y	Y	N	N
6 Tallon	Y	Y	X	X	Y	Y	N	N
SOUTH DAKOTA								
AL Johnson	Y	N	Y	N	Y	Y	N	N
TENNESSEE								
1 ***Quillen***	Y	N	Y	N	Y	Y	N	N
2 ***Duncan***	N	N	Y	Y	Y	Y	N	Y
3 Lloyd	Y	Y	N	N	Y	Y	N	N
4 Cooper	Y	Y	N	Y	Y	Y	N	N
5 Clement	Y	N	Y	N	Y	Y	Y	Y
6 Gordon	Y	Y	N	Y	Y	Y	N	N
7 ***Sundquist***	Y	Y	Y	Y	N	N	Y	Y
8 Tanner	Y	Y	N	N	?	?	N	N
9 Ford	Y	Y	?	?	?	?	?	?
TEXAS								
1 Chapman	?	?	Y	N	Y	Y	N	N
2 Wilson	Y	N	Y	N	Y	Y	N	N
3 ***Bartlett***	Y	Y	Y	Y	Y	N	Y	Y
4 Hall	Y	N	Y	N	Y	Y	N	N
5 Bryant	Y	Y	N	N	Y	Y	Y	Y
6 ***Barton***	N	Y	Y	Y	Y	N	Y	Y
7 ***Archer***	N	N	Y	Y	N	N	Y	Y
8 ***Fields***	N	N	Y	Y	N	N	Y	Y
9 Brooks	Y	N	Y	N	Y	Y	N	N
10 Pickle	Y	Y	Y	N	Y	Y	N	N
11 Leath	Y	N	Y	N	Y	Y	N	N
12 Geren	Y	N	Y	N	Y	Y	N	N
13 Sarpalius	Y	N	Y	N	Y	Y	N	N
14 Laughlin	Y	N	?	?	?	?	?	?
15 de la Garza	Y	N	N	N	Y	Y	N	N
16 Coleman	Y	N	Y	N	Y	Y	N	N
17 Stenholm	Y	N	Y	N	?	Y	Y	Y
18 Washington	Y	N	Y	Y	?	?	?	?
19 ***Combest***	N	N	Y	N	N	Y	N	N
20 Gonzalez	Y	N	N	N	Y	Y	N	N
21 ***Smith***	Y	N	Y	N	Y	Y	N	Y
22 ***DeLay***	N	N	Y	Y	?	?	N	N
23 Bustamante	Y	N	N	N	Y	Y	N	N
24 Frost	Y	Y	N	N	Y	Y	N	N
25 Andrews	Y	N	Y	Y	Y	Y	Y	Y
26 ***Armey***	N	Y	N	Y	N	N	Y	Y
27 Ortiz	Y	N	Y	N	Y	Y	N	N
UTAH								
1 ***Hansen***	N	N	Y	Y	Y	Y	N	N
2 Owens	Y	Y	N	Y	Y	Y	Y	Y
3 ***Nielson***	N	N	Y	Y	N	N	Y	Y
VERMONT								
AL ***Smith***	N	Y	N	N	N	N	Y	Y
VIRGINIA								
1 ***Bateman***	Y	N	Y	N	?	?	N	N
2 Pickett	Y	N	Y	N	Y	Y	N	N
3 ***Bliley***	Y	N	Y	Y	?	N	N	N
4 Sisisky	Y	Y	N	N	Y	Y	N	N
5 Payne	Y	Y	N	N	Y	Y	N	N
6 Olin	Y	N	Y	N	Y	Y	N	N
7 ***Slaughter***	N	N	Y	N	Y	Y	N	N
8 ***Parris***	N	N	Y	Y	Y	Y	Y	?
9 Boucher	Y	Y	Y	N	Y	Y	N	N
10 ***Wolf***	Y	Y	N	Y	Y	Y	N	Y
WASHINGTON								
1 ***Miller***	N	Y	N	Y	N	N	Y	Y
2 Swift	Y	Y	N	N	Y	Y	N	N
3 Unsoeld	Y	Y	N	N	Y	Y	N	N
4 ***Morrison***	Y	N	Y	N	N	Y	Y	Y
5 Foley								
6 Dicks	Y	Y	N	N	Y	Y	N	N
7 McDermott	Y	Y	Y	?	Y	Y	Y	Y
8 ***Chandler***	Y	Y	N	N	Y	N	Y	Y
WEST VIRGINIA								
1 Mollohan	Y	N	N	N	Y	Y	N	N
2 Staggers	Y	Y	N	N	Y	Y	N	N
3 Wise	Y	Y	N	Y	Y	Y	N	N
4 Rahall	Y	N	Y	Y	Y	Y	N	N
WISCONSIN								
1 Aspin	Y	N	Y	Y	Y	Y	N	N
2 Kastenmeier	Y	N	Y	N	Y	Y	Y	Y
3 ***Gunderson***	Y	N	Y	N	N	Y	N	N
4 Kleczka	Y	Y	N	Y	?	?	N	N
5 Moody	Y	Y	Y	Y	Y	Y	Y	Y
6 ***Petri***	N	N	Y	Y	N	N	Y	Y
7 Obey	Y	N	Y	N	Y	Y	N	N
8 ***Roth***	Y	N	Y	N	N	N	Y	Y
9 ***Sensenbrenner***	N	Y	N	Y	N	N	Y	Y
WYOMING								
AL ***Thomas***	N	N	Y	N	N	N	Y	Y

Southern states - Ala., Ark., Fla., Ga., Ky., La., Miss., N.C., Okla., S.C., Tenn., Texas, Va.
Omitted votes are quorum calls, which CQ does not include in its vote charts.

HOUSE VOTES 283, 284, 286, 287, 288, 290, 291

283. HR 5313. Fiscal 1991 Military Construction Appropriations/Passage. Passage of the bill to appropriate $8.3 billion in fiscal 1991 for the construction of military facilities in the United States and overseas. The bill's funding is $815 million less than requested by the president and $183 million less than the fiscal 1990 level. Passed 312-82: R 107-54; D 205-28 (ND 134-26, SD 71-2), July 30, 1990.

284. HR 5355. Debt-Limit Increase/Rule. Adoption of the rule (H Res 443) to provide for House floor consideration of the bill to increase the statutory limit on the public debt to $3.444 trillion. Adopted 274-148: R 30-143; D 244-5 (ND 169-2, SD 75-3), July 31, 1990.

286. HR 5355. Debt-Limit Increase/Social Security. Dorgan, D-N.D., amendment to remove the Social Security trust funds from the Gramm-Rudman deficit calculations, starting in fiscal 1992, and to create a point of order against legislation that would create a net increase in Social Security benefits or a net reduction in Social Security payroll tax receipts, beyond a certain threshold level. Adopted 413-15: R 164-10; D 249-5 (ND 168-5, SD 81-0), July 31, 1990. A "nay" was a vote supporting the president's position.

287. HR 5355. Debt-Limit Increase/Passage. Passage of the bill to increase the statutory limit on the public debt to $3.444 trillion and remove the Social Security trust funds from the Gramm-Rudman deficit calculations in fiscal 1992. Passed 221-205: R 46-129; D 175-76 (ND 130-42, SD 45-34), July 31, 1990.

288. HR 5401. Savings and Loan Crime Bill/Passage. Schumer, D-N.Y., motion to suspend the rules and pass the bill to strengthen criminal penalties for crimes involving savings and loan institutions and banks, to authorize additional funds for investigations, prosecutions and civil actions, to establish a special counsel in the Justice Department to investigate savings and loan crimes, and to establish a commission to study the causes of the savings and loan crisis and make recommendations. Motion agreed to 424-4: R 174-1; D 250-3 (ND 171-1, SD 79-2), July 31, 1990. A two-thirds majority of those present and voting (286 in this case) is required for passage under suspension of the rules.

290. HR 1180. Housing Programs Reauthorization/FHA Mortgages. Vento, D-Minn., amendment to phase out over five years the upfront Federal Housing Administration (FHA) mortgage insurance premium of 3.8 percent of the loan amount, requiring instead that 1.35 percent be paid at settlement and 0.6 percent be paid annually over the life of the loan; to prohibit the issuance of FHA mortgages that exceed the market value of a property; to eliminate the rebate of unearned insurance premiums when mortgages are prepaid; and to improve financial security of the FHA fund by raising capital standards to 1.25 percent of loans. Adopted 418-2: R 171-1; D 247-1 (ND 169-0, SD 78-1), July 31, 1990.

291. HR 1180. Housing Programs Reauthorization/Modular Home Regulation. Oakar, D-Ohio, amendment to ensure that modular homes continue to be regulated by state and local construction and safety codes. Rejected 200-211: R 22-147; D 178-64 (ND 145-20, SD 33-44), July 31, 1990.

KEY

- Y Voted for (yea).
- # Paired for.
- + Announced for.
- N Voted against (nay).
- X Paired against.
- - Announced against.
- P Voted "present."
- C Voted "present" to avoid possible conflict of interest.
- ? Did not vote or otherwise make a position known.

Democrats ***Republicans***

	283	284	286	287	288	290	291
ALABAMA							
1 ***Callahan***	Y	N	Y	N	Y	Y	N
2 ***Dickinson***	Y	N	Y	N	Y	Y	N
3 Browder	Y	Y	Y	N	Y	Y	N
4 Bevill	?	Y	Y	Y	Y	Y	N
5 Flippo	?	Y	Y	N	Y	Y	N
6 Erdreich	Y	Y	Y	N	Y	Y	N
7 Harris	Y	Y	Y	N	Y	Y	N
ALASKA							
AL ***Young***	Y	Y	Y	N	Y	Y	N
ARIZONA							
1 ***Rhodes***	Y	N	Y	N	Y	Y	N
2 Udall	Y	Y	Y	Y	Y	Y	Y
3 ***Stump***	?	N	Y	N	Y	Y	N
4 ***Kyl***	N	N	Y	N	Y	Y	N
5 ***Kolbe***	Y	N	Y	N	Y	Y	N
ARKANSAS							
1 Alexander	Y	Y	Y	N	Y	Y	Y
2 ***Robinson***	Y	N	Y	N	Y	Y	Y
3 ***Hammerschmidt***	?	N	Y	N	Y	Y	N
4 Anthony	Y	Y	Y	N	Y	Y	N
CALIFORNIA							
1 Bosco	Y	Y	Y	N	Y	Y	Y
2 ***Herger***	Y	N	Y	N	Y	Y	N
3 Matsui	Y	Y	N	N	Y	Y	Y
4 Fazio	Y	Y	Y	Y	Y	Y	?
5 Pelosi	Y	Y	Y	Y	Y	Y	Y
6 Boxer	N	Y	Y	Y	Y	Y	Y
7 Miller	Y	Y	Y	Y	Y	Y	Y
8 Dellums	N	?	Y	Y	Y	Y	Y
9 Stark	N	Y	Y	Y	Y	Y	Y
10 Edwards	Y	Y	Y	Y	Y	Y	Y
11 Lantos	?	Y	Y	Y	Y	Y	Y
12 ***Campbell***	N	N	Y	N	Y	Y	Y
13 Mineta	Y	Y	N	Y	Y	Y	Y
14 ***Shumway***	N	N	Y	N	Y	Y	N
15 Condit	Y	Y	Y	N	Y	Y	Y
16 Panetta	Y	Y	Y	Y	Y	Y	Y
17 ***Pashayan***	Y	Y	Y	N	Y	Y	N
18 Lehman	Y	Y	Y	Y	Y	Y	N
19 ***Lagomarsino***	Y	N	Y	N	Y	Y	N
20 ***Thomas***	Y	N	Y	N	Y	Y	N
21 ***Gallegly***	Y	N	Y	N	Y	Y	N
22 ***Moorhead***	Y	N	Y	N	Y	Y	N
23 Beilenson	Y	Y	Y	Y	Y	Y	N
24 Waxman	Y	Y	Y	Y	Y	Y	Y
25 Roybal	Y	Y	Y	Y	Y	Y	Y
26 Berman	Y	Y	Y	Y	Y	Y	Y
27 Levine	Y	Y	Y	Y	Y	Y	Y
28 Dixon	Y	Y	Y	Y	Y	Y	Y
29 Hawkins	?	Y	Y	Y	Y	?	?
30 Martinez	Y	Y	Y	Y	Y	Y	Y
31 Dymally	X	Y	Y	Y	Y	Y	Y
32 Anderson	Y	Y	Y	Y	Y	Y	Y
33 ***Dreier***	Y	N	Y	N	Y	Y	N
34 Torres	Y	Y	Y	Y	Y	Y	Y
35 ***Lewis***	Y	N	Y	Y	Y	Y	N
36 Brown	Y	Y	Y	Y	Y	Y	N
37 ***McCandless***	Y	N	Y	N	Y	Y	N
38 ***Dornan***	N	N	Y	N	Y	Y	N
39 ***Dannemeyer***	N	N	Y	N	Y	Y	N
40 ***Cox***	?	N	Y	N	Y	Y	?
41 ***Lowery***	Y	?	Y	Y	Y	Y	N
42 ***Rohrabacher***	Y	N	Y	N	Y	Y	N
43 ***Packard***	N	N	Y	N	Y	Y	N
44 Bates	N	Y	Y	N	Y	Y	Y
45 ***Hunter***	N	N	Y	Y	Y	Y	N
COLORADO							
1 Schroeder	?	Y	Y	N	Y	Y	Y
2 Skaggs	Y	Y	Y	Y	Y	Y	N
3 Campbell	N	Y	Y	N	Y	Y	Y
4 ***Brown***	N	Y	Y	N	Y	Y	N
5 ***Hefley***	Y	N	Y	N	Y	Y	N
6 ***Schaefer***	Y	N	Y	N	Y	Y	N
CONNECTICUT							
1 Kennelly	Y	Y	Y	Y	Y	Y	Y
2 Gejdenson	Y	Y	Y	Y	Y	Y	Y
3 Morrison	N	Y	Y	Y	Y	Y	Y
4 ***Shays***	Y	N	Y	N	Y	Y	Y
5 ***Rowland***	Y	N	Y	N	Y	Y	Y
6 ***Johnson***	N	N	Y	Y	Y	Y	N
DELAWARE							
AL Carper	?	Y	Y	N	Y	Y	Y
FLORIDA							
1 Hutto	Y	Y	Y	N	Y	Y	N
2 ***Grant***	Y	N	Y	N	Y	Y	N
3 Bennett	Y	Y	Y	Y	Y	Y	Y
4 ***James***	Y	N	Y	N	Y	Y	N
5 ***McCollum***	Y	N	Y	N	Y	Y	N
6 ***Stearns***	Y	N	Y	N	Y	Y	N
7 Gibbons	?	Y	Y	N	Y	Y	N
8 ***Young***	Y	N	Y	N	Y	Y	N
9 ***Bilirakis***	?	?	?	X	?	?	X
10 ***Ireland***	N	N	Y	N	Y	Y	N
11 Nelson	+	+	+	#	+	+	#
12 ***Lewis***	X	N	Y	N	Y	Y	N
13 ***Goss***	N	N	Y	N	Y	Y	N
14 Johnston	Y	Y	Y	Y	Y	Y	N
15 ***Shaw***	Y	Y	Y	N	Y	Y	N
16 Smith	Y	Y	Y	Y	Y	Y	Y
17 Lehman	Y	Y	Y	Y	Y	Y	Y
18 ***Ros-Lehtinen***	Y	N	Y	N	Y	Y	N
19 Fascell	Y	Y	Y	Y	Y	Y	N
GEORGIA							
1 Thomas	Y	Y	Y	N	Y	Y	N
2 Hatcher	Y	Y	Y	Y	Y	Y	N
3 Ray	Y	Y	Y	N	Y	Y	N
4 Jones	Y	Y	Y	Y	Y	Y	Y
5 Lewis	N	Y	Y	Y	Y	Y	Y
6 ***Gingrich***	N	N	Y	Y	Y	Y	N
7 Darden	Y	Y	Y	N	Y	Y	N
8 Rowland	Y	Y	Y	Y	Y	Y	N
9 Jenkins	Y	Y	Y	Y	Y	Y	N
10 Barnard	#	Y	Y	N	Y	Y	Y
HAWAII							
1 ***Saiki***	+	Y	Y	Y	Y	Y	N
2 Vacancy							
IDAHO							
1 ***Craig***	Y	N	Y	N	Y	Y	N
2 Stallings	Y	Y	Y	N	Y	Y	Y
ILLINOIS							
1 Hayes	N	Y	Y	Y	Y	Y	Y
2 Savage	N	Y	Y	Y	Y	Y	Y
3 Russo	Y	Y	Y	N	Y	Y	Y
4 Sangmeister	?	Y	Y	N	Y	Y	Y
5 Lipinski	Y	Y	Y	Y	Y	Y	Y
6 ***Hyde***	Y	N	Y	Y	Y	Y	N
7 Collins	N	Y	Y	Y	Y	Y	Y
8 Rostenkowski	Y	Y	Y	Y	Y	Y	Y
9 Yates	Y	Y	Y	Y	Y	Y	Y
10 ***Porter***	Y	Y	Y	Y	Y	Y	Y
11 Annunzio	Y	Y	Y	Y	Y	Y	Y
12 ***Crane***	N	N	N	N	N	Y	N
13 ***Fawell***	N	N	Y	N	Y	Y	N
14 ***Hastert***	N	N	Y	N	Y	Y	N
15 ***Madigan***	?	Y	Y	Y	Y	Y	N
16 ***Martin***	N	N	Y	N	Y	Y	N
17 Evans	Y	Y	Y	Y	Y	Y	Y
18 ***Michel***	?	Y	N	Y	Y	Y	N
19 Bruce	Y	Y	Y	Y	Y	Y	Y
20 Durbin	Y	Y	Y	Y	Y	Y	Y
21 Costello	Y	Y	Y	N	Y	Y	Y
22 Poshard	Y	Y	Y	N	Y	Y	Y
INDIANA							
1 Visclosky	Y	Y	Y	N	Y	Y	N
2 Sharp	Y	Y	Y	Y	Y	Y	N
3 ***Hiler***	Y	N	Y	N	Y	Y	N

ND Northern Democrats SD Southern Democrats

	283	284	286	287	288	290	291
4 Long	Y	Y	Y	Y	Y	Y	N
5 Jontz	Y	Y	Y	Y	Y	Y	Y
6 ***Burton***	N	N	Y	N	Y	Y	N
7 ***Myers***	Y	Y	N	N	Y	Y	N
8 McCloskey	Y	Y	Y	Y	Y	Y	Y
9 Hamilton	Y	Y	Y	Y	Y	Y	N
10 Jacobs	Y	N	Y	N	Y	Y	N
IOWA							
1 ***Leach***	N	N	Y	N	Y	Y	Y
2 ***Tauke***	N	N	Y	N	Y	Y	N
3 Nagle	N	Y	Y	N	Y	Y	Y
4 Smith	Y	Y	Y	Y	Y	Y	Y
5 ***Lightfoot***	Y	N	Y	N	Y	Y	N
6 ***Grandy***	N	N	Y	N	Y	Y	N
KANSAS							
1 ***Roberts***	N	N	Y	N	Y	Y	N
2 Slattery	Y	N	Y	N	Y	Y	Y
3 ***Meyers***	N	N	Y	N	Y	Y	N
4 Glickman	Y	Y	Y	N	Y	Y	N
5 ***Whittaker***	N	N	Y	N	Y	Y	N
KENTUCKY							
1 Hubbard	N	Y	Y	N	Y	Y	N
2 Natcher	Y	Y	Y	Y	Y	Y	N
3 Mazzoli	Y	Y	Y	Y	Y	Y	Y
4 ***Bunning***	N	N	Y	N	Y	Y	N
5 ***Rogers***	Y	N	Y	N	Y	Y	N
6 ***Hopkins***	Y	N	Y	N	Y	Y	N
7 Perkins	Y	Y	Y	Y	Y	Y	Y
LOUISIANA							
1 ***Livingston***	Y	N	Y	N	Y	Y	N
2 Boggs	Y	Y	Y	Y	Y	Y	Y
3 Tauzin	Y	Y	Y	N	Y	Y	N
4 ***McCrery***	Y	N	Y	Y	Y	Y	N
5 Huckaby	Y	Y	Y	N	Y	Y	N
6 ***Baker***	Y	N	Y	N	Y	Y	N
7 Hayes	Y	Y	Y	N	Y	Y	Y
8 ***Holloway***	Y	N	Y	N	Y	Y	N
MAINE							
1 Brennan	Y	Y	Y	Y	Y	Y	Y
2 ***Snowe***	Y	N	Y	N	Y	Y	N
MARYLAND							
1 Dyson	Y	Y	Y	N	Y	Y	Y
2 ***Bentley***	Y	N	Y	N	Y	Y	Y
3 Cardin	Y	Y	Y	Y	Y	Y	Y
4 McMillen	Y	Y	Y	Y	Y	Y	Y
5 Hoyer	Y	Y	Y	Y	Y	Y	#
6 Byron	Y	Y	Y	N	Y	Y	N
7 Mfume	Y	Y	Y	Y	Y	Y	Y
8 ***Morella***	Y	Y	Y	Y	Y	Y	Y
MASSACHUSETTS							
1 ***Conte***	?	Y	Y	Y	Y	Y	Y
2 Neal	Y	Y	Y	N	Y	Y	Y
3 Early•	Y	Y	Y	N	Y	Y	Y
4 Frank	Y	Y	Y	Y	Y	Y	Y
5 Atkins	?	Y	Y	Y	Y	Y	Y
6 Mavroules	Y	Y	Y	Y	Y	Y	Y
7 Markey	Y	Y	Y	Y	Y	Y	Y
8 Kennedy	Y	Y	Y	Y	Y	Y	N
9 Moakley	Y	Y	Y	Y	Y	Y	Y
10 Studds	Y	Y	Y	Y	Y	Y	Y
11 Donnelly	Y	Y	Y	Y	Y	Y	Y
MICHIGAN							
1 Conyers	N	Y	Y	Y	Y	Y	?
2 ***Pursell***	N	N	Y	N	Y	Y	N
3 Wolpe	Y	Y	Y	Y	Y	Y	Y
4 ***Upton***	N	N	Y	N	Y	Y	N
5 ***Henry***	N	N	Y	N	Y	Y	N
6 Carr	Y	Y	Y	N	Y	Y	N
7 Kildee	Y	Y	Y	Y	Y	Y	Y
8 Traxler	Y	Y	Y	Y	Y	Y	Y
9 ***Vander Jagt***	Y	Y	Y	Y	Y	Y	N
10 ***Schuette***	?	N	Y	N	Y	?	?
11 ***Davis***	Y	Y	Y	Y	Y	Y	Y
12 Bonior	Y	Y	Y	Y	Y	Y	Y
13 Crockett	?	Y	Y	Y	Y	Y	Y
14 Hertel	Y	Y	Y	N	Y	Y	Y
15 Ford	Y	Y	Y	N	Y	Y	?
16 Dingell	Y	Y	Y	Y	Y	Y	Y
17 Levin	Y	Y	Y	Y	Y	Y	Y
18 ***Broomfield***	?	N	Y	N	Y	Y	N
MINNESOTA							
1 Penny	N	Y	Y	Y	Y	Y	N
2 ***Weber***	Y	N	Y	Y	Y	Y	N
3 ***Frenzel***	N	N	N	N	Y	Y	N
4 Vento	Y	Y	Y	Y	Y	Y	Y

	283	284	286	287	288	290	291
5 Sabo	Y	Y	Y	Y	Y	Y	Y
6 Sikorski	Y	Y	Y	Y	Y	Y	Y
7 ***Stangeland***	N	N	Y	N	Y	Y	N
8 Oberstar	Y	Y	Y	Y	Y	Y	Y
MISSISSIPPI							
1 Whitten	?	Y	Y	Y	Y	Y	N
2 Espy	Y	Y	Y	Y	Y	Y	Y
3 Montgomery	?	Y	Y	Y	Y	Y	N
4 Parker	Y	Y	Y	Y	Y	Y	N
5 Taylor	Y	N	Y	N	Y	Y	N
MISSOURI							
1 Clay	?	Y	Y	Y	Y	Y	Y
2 ***Buechner***	N	—	Y	N	Y	Y	Y
3 Gephardt	?	Y	Y	Y	Y	Y	Y
4 Skelton	Y	Y	Y	Y	Y	Y	N
5 Wheat	Y	Y	Y	Y	Y	Y	Y
6 ***Coleman***	Y	N	Y	Y	Y	Y	N
7 ***Hancock***	N	N	Y	N	Y	Y	N
8 ***Emerson***	Y	N	Y	N	Y	Y	N
9 Volkmer	Y	Y	Y	Y	Y	Y	Y
MONTANA							
1 Williams	Y	Y	Y	N	?	Y	?
2 ***Marlenee***	Y	N	Y	N	Y	Y	N
NEBRASKA							
1 ***Bereuter***	Y	N	Y	N	Y	Y	N
2 Hoagland	Y	Y	Y	N	Y	Y	Y
3 ***Smith***	Y	N	Y	N	Y	Y	N
NEVADA							
1 Bilbray	Y	Y	Y	Y	Y	Y	N
2 ***Vucanovich***	Y	N	Y	N	Y	Y	N
NEW HAMPSHIRE							
1 ***Smith***	Y	N	Y	N	Y	Y	N
2 ***Douglas***	N	N	Y	N	Y	Y	N
NEW JERSEY							
1 Vacancy							
2 Hughes	N	Y	Y	N	Y	Y	Y
3 Pallone	N	Y	Y	N	Y	Y	Y
4 ***Smith***	Y	Y	Y	Y	Y	Y	N
5 ***Roukema***	N	N	Y	Y	Y	?	X
6 Dwyer	Y	Y	Y	Y	Y	Y	Y
7 ***Rinaldo***	Y	N	Y	N	Y	Y	Y
8 Roe	Y	Y	Y	Y	Y	Y	Y
9 Torricelli	Y	Y	Y	Y	Y	Y	Y
10 Payne	Y	Y	Y	Y	Y	Y	Y
11 ***Gallo***	Y	N	Y	Y	Y	Y	N
12 ***Courter***	Y	N	Y	N	Y	Y	N
13 ***Saxton***	Y	N	Y	N	Y	Y	N
14 Guarini	N	Y	Y	N	Y	Y	Y
NEW MEXICO							
1 ***Schiff***	Y	N	Y	Y	Y	Y	N
2 ***Skeen***	Y	N	Y	N	Y	Y	N
3 Richardson	Y	Y	Y	Y	Y	Y	Y
NEW YORK							
1 Hochbrueckner	Y	Y	Y	Y	Y	Y	Y
2 Downey	Y	Y	Y	Y	Y	Y	Y
3 Mrazek	?	Y	Y	Y	Y	Y	Y
4 ***Lent***	Y	N	Y	Y	Y	Y	?
5 ***McGrath***	Y	Y	Y	Y	Y	Y	N
6 Flake	Y	Y	Y	Y	Y	Y	N
7 Ackerman	Y	Y	Y	Y	Y	Y	Y
8 Scheuer	Y	Y	Y	Y	Y	Y	Y
9 Manton	Y	Y	Y	Y	Y	Y	Y
10 Schumer	Y	Y	Y	Y	Y	Y	Y
11 Towns	N	Y	Y	Y	Y	Y	Y
12 Owens	N	Y	Y	Y	Y	Y	Y
13 Solarz	Y	?	Y	Y	Y	Y	Y
14 ***Molinari***	Y	N	Y	Y	Y	Y	N
15 ***Green***	Y	Y	N	Y	Y	Y	N
16 Rangel	Y	Y	Y	Y	Y	Y	Y
17 Weiss	Y	Y	N	N	Y	Y	Y
18 Serrano	Y	Y	Y	Y	Y	Y	Y
19 Engel	Y	Y	N	Y	Y	Y	Y
20 Lowey	Y	Y	Y	Y	Y	Y	Y
21 ***Fish***	Y	Y	Y	Y	Y	Y	N
22 ***Gilman***	Y	N	Y	N	Y	Y	Y
23 McNulty	Y	Y	Y	Y	Y	Y	Y
24 ***Solomon***	Y	N	Y	N	Y	Y	N
25 ***Boehlert***	Y	Y	Y	Y	Y	Y	Y
26 ***Martin***	Y	Y	Y	Y	Y	Y	N
27 ***Walsh***	Y	Y	Y	Y	Y	Y	N
28 McHugh	Y	Y	Y	Y	Y	Y	Y
29 ***Horton***	?	Y	Y	Y	Y	Y	Y
30 Slaughter	Y	Y	Y	Y	Y	Y	Y
31 ***Paxon***	Y	N	Y	N	Y	Y	N

	283	284	286	287	288	290	291
32 LaFalce	Y	Y	Y	Y	Y	Y	Y
33 Nowak	Y	Y	Y	Y	Y	Y	Y
34 ***Houghton***	N	N	N	N	Y	Y	N
NORTH CAROLINA							
1 Jones	Y	Y	Y	Y	Y	Y	Y
2 Valentine	Y	?	Y	N	Y	Y	N
3 Lancaster	Y	Y	Y	Y	Y	Y	N
4 Price	Y	Y	Y	Y	Y	Y	N
5 Neal	Y	N	Y	N	Y	Y	N
6 ***Coble***	Y	N	Y	N	Y	Y	N
7 Rose	Y	Y	Y	Y	Y	Y	Y
8 Hefner	Y	Y	Y	N	Y	Y	N
9 ***McMillan***	Y	N	Y	N	Y	Y	N
10 ***Ballenger***	N	Y	Y	N	Y	Y	N
11 Clarke	Y	Y	Y	Y	Y	Y	N
NORTH DAKOTA							
AL Dorgan	Y	Y	Y	Y	Y	Y	?
OHIO							
1 Luken	Y	Y	Y	Y	Y	Y	Y
2 ***Gradison***	N	N	Y	Y	Y	Y	N
3 Hall	Y	Y	N	Y	Y	Y	Y
4 ***Oxley***	N	Y	Y	Y	Y	Y	N
5 ***Gillmor***	Y	N	Y	Y	Y	Y	N
6 ***McEwen***	?	N	Y	N	Y	Y	N
7 ***DeWine***	Y	N	Y	N	Y	Y	N
8 ***Lukens***	N	N	Y	N	Y	Y	N
9 Kaptur	#	Y	Y	Y	Y	Y	Y
10 ***Miller***	Y	Y	Y	N	Y	Y	Y
11 Eckart	N	Y	Y	N	Y	Y	Y
12 ***Kasich***	?	N	Y	N	Y	Y	N
13 Pease	N	Y	Y	Y	Y	Y	Y
14 Sawyer	Y	Y	Y	Y	Y	Y	Y
15 ***Wylie***	?	Y	Y	Y	Y	Y	N
16 ***Regula***	Y	Y	Y	N	Y	Y	Y
17 Traficant	N	Y	Y	N	Y	Y	Y
18 Applegate	N	Y	Y	N	Y	Y	Y
19 Feighan	?	Y	Y	Y	Y	Y	Y
20 Oakar	Y	Y	Y	Y	Y	Y	Y
21 Stokes	Y	Y	Y	Y	Y	?	Y
OKLAHOMA							
1 ***Inhofe***	Y	N	Y	N	Y	Y	N
2 Synar	Y	Y	Y	Y	Y	Y	?
3 Watkins	Y	Y	Y	N	Y	Y	Y
4 McCurdy	Y	Y	Y	N	Y	Y	N
5 ***Edwards***	Y	N	Y	N	Y	Y	N
6 English	Y	Y	Y	N	Y	Y	Y
OREGON							
1 AuCoin	Y	Y	Y	Y	Y	Y	N
2 ***Smith, B.***	Y	N	Y	N	Y	Y	N
3 Wyden	N	Y	Y	N	Y	Y	Y
4 DeFazio	N	Y	Y	N	Y	?	Y
5 ***Smith, D.***	N	N	Y	N	Y	Y	N
PENNSYLVANIA							
1 Foglietta	Y	Y	Y	Y	Y	Y	Y
2 Gray	Y	Y	Y	Y	Y	?	Y
3 Borski	Y	Y	Y	Y	Y	Y	Y
4 Kolter	Y	Y	Y	N	Y	Y	Y
5 ***Schulze***	N	N	Y	N	Y	Y	N
6 Yatron	Y	Y	Y	N	Y	Y	Y
7 ***Weldon***	Y	N	Y	N	Y	?	X
8 Kostmayer	Y	Y	Y	Y	Y	Y	Y
9 ***Shuster***	Y	N	Y	N	Y	Y	?
10 ***McDade***	Y	N	Y	Y	Y	Y	N
11 Kanjorski	Y	Y	Y	N	N	Y	N
12 Murtha	Y	Y	Y	Y	Y	Y	Y
13 ***Coughlin***	Y	N	Y	N	Y	Y	N
14 Coyne	Y	Y	Y	Y	Y	Y	Y
15 ***Ritter***	N	N	Y	N	Y	Y	N
16 ***Walker***	N	N	Y	N	Y	Y	N
17 ***Gekas***	N	N	Y	Y	Y	Y	N
18 Walgren	Y	Y	Y	Y	Y	Y	Y
19 ***Goodling***	Y	N	Y	Y	Y	Y	N
20 Gaydos	Y	Y	Y	N	Y	Y	Y
21 ***Ridge***	N	N	Y	N	Y	Y	N
22 Murphy	N	Y	Y	N	Y	Y	Y
23 ***Clinger***	Y	N	Y	N	Y	Y	N
RHODE ISLAND							
1 ***Machtley***	Y	N	Y	Y	Y	Y	Y
2 ***Schneider***	N	N	Y	N	Y	Y	Y
SOUTH CAROLINA							
1 ***Ravenel***	Y	N	Y	N	Y	Y	N
2 ***Spence***	Y	N	+	N	Y	Y	N
3 Derrick	Y	Y	Y	Y	Y	Y	N
4 Patterson	Y	Y	Y	N	Y	Y	N
5 Spratt	Y	Y	Y	Y	Y	Y	N
6 Tallon	Y	Y	Y	N	Y	Y	N

	283	284	286	287	288	290	291
SOUTH DAKOTA							
AL Johnson	Y	Y	Y	Y	Y	Y	Y
TENNESSEE							
1 ***Quillen***	Y	Y	Y	Y	Y	Y	N
2 ***Duncan***	Y	N	Y	N	Y	Y	N
3 Lloyd	Y	Y	Y	N	Y	Y	N
4 Cooper	Y	Y	Y	N	Y	N	Y
5 Clement	Y	Y	Y	Y	Y	Y	N
6 Gordon	Y	Y	Y	Y	Y	Y	Y
7 ***Sundquist***	Y	N	Y	N	Y	Y	N
8 Tanner	Y	Y	Y	N	Y	Y	N
9 Ford	?	?	?	X	?	?	?
TEXAS							
1 Chapman	Y	Y	Y	Y	Y	Y	Y
2 Wilson	Y	Y	Y	Y	Y	Y	Y
3 ***Bartlett***	N	N	Y	N	Y	Y	N
4 Hall	Y	Y	Y	N	Y	Y	?
5 Bryant	Y	Y	Y	N	Y	Y	Y
6 ***Barton***	N	N	N	N	Y	Y	N
7 ***Archer***	N	N	N	N	Y	Y	N
8 ***Fields***	N	N	N	N	Y	Y	N
9 Brooks	Y	Y	Y	Y	Y	Y	Y
10 Pickle	Y	Y	Y	Y	Y	Y	N
11 Leath	Y	Y	Y	Y	Y	?	?
12 Geren	Y	Y	Y	+	Y	Y	Y
13 Sarpalius	Y	Y	Y	N	Y	Y	Y
14 Laughlin	?	?	Y	?	Y	Y	N
15 de la Garza	Y	Y	Y	Y	Y	Y	Y
16 Coleman	Y	Y	Y	Y	Y	Y	Y
17 Stenholm	Y	Y	Y	Y	Y	Y	N
18 Washington	?	?	Y	Y	N	?	?
19 ***Combest***	Y	N	Y	N	Y	Y	N
20 Gonzalez	Y	N	Y	N	N	Y	Y
21 ***Smith***	Y	N	Y	N	Y	Y	N
22 ***DeLay***	Y	N	Y	N	Y	Y	N
23 Bustamante	Y	Y	Y	Y	Y	Y	Y
24 Frost	Y	Y	Y	Y	Y	Y	Y
25 Andrews	Y	Y	Y	Y	Y	Y	Y
26 ***Armey***	N	N	N	N	Y	Y	N
27 Ortiz	Y	Y	Y	Y	Y	Y	Y
UTAH							
1 ***Hansen***	Y	N	Y	N	Y	Y	N
2 Owens	N	Y	Y	Y	Y	Y	Y
3 ***Nielson***	N	N	Y	N	Y	Y	N
VERMONT							
AL ***Smith***	Y	N	Y	Y	Y	Y	Y
VIRGINIA							
1 ***Bateman***	Y	Y	N	Y	Y	Y	N
2 Pickett	Y	Y	Y	N	Y	Y	Y
3 ***Bliley***	Y	N	Y	Y	Y	Y	N
4 Sisisky	Y	Y	Y	Y	Y	Y	N
5 Payne	Y	Y	Y	N	Y	Y	N
6 Olin	Y	Y	Y	Y	Y	Y	N
7 ***Slaughter***	Y	N	Y	N	Y	Y	N
8 ***Parris***	Y	N	Y	N	Y	Y	N
9 Boucher	Y	Y	Y	Y	Y	Y	Y
10 ***Wolf***	Y	Y	Y	Y	Y	Y	N
WASHINGTON							
1 ***Miller***	Y	N	Y	Y	Y	Y	N
2 Swift	Y	Y	Y	Y	Y	Y	Y
3 Unsoeld	Y	Y	Y	Y	Y	Y	#
4 ***Morrison***	Y	N	Y	Y	Y	Y	Y
5 Foley							
6 Dicks	Y	Y	Y	Y	Y	Y	Y
7 McDermott	Y	Y	Y	#	Y	Y	Y
8 ***Chandler***	Y	Y	Y	Y	Y	Y	N
WEST VIRGINIA							
1 Mollohan	Y	Y	Y	Y	Y	Y	Y
2 Staggers	Y	Y	Y	Y	Y	Y	N
3 Wise	Y	Y	Y	Y	Y	Y	Y
4 Rahall	Y	Y	Y	N	Y	Y	Y
WISCONSIN							
1 Aspin	Y	Y	Y	Y	Y	Y	Y
2 Kastenmeier	N	Y	Y	Y	Y	Y	Y
3 ***Gunderson***	Y	N	Y	N	Y	Y	N
4 Kleczka	Y	Y	Y	Y	Y	Y	Y
5 Moody	Y	Y	Y	N	Y	Y	Y
6 ***Petri***	N	N	Y	N	Y	N	N
7 Obey	Y	Y	Y	Y	Y	Y	Y
8 ***Roth***	N	N	Y	N	Y	Y	N
9 ***Sensenbrenner***	N	N	Y	N	Y	Y	N
WYOMING							
AL ***Thomas***	Y	N	Y	N	Y	Y	N

Southern states - Ala., Ark., Fla., Ga., Ky., La., Miss., N.C., Okla., S.C., Tenn., Texas, Va.
Omitted votes are quorum calls, which CQ does not include in its vote charts.

HOUSE VOTES 292, 293, 294, 295, 296, 297, 298, 299

292. HR 1180. Housing Programs Reauthorization/Subsidized Mortgages. Carper, D-Del., amendment to modify provisions concerning the prepayment of federally subsidized mortgages. Adopted 400-12: R 168-0; D 232-12 (ND 156-11, SD 76-1) July 31, 1990.

293. HR 1180. Housing Programs Reauthorization/Authorization Levels. Dannemeyer, R-Calif., amendment to provide that the amount of budget authority authorized for each program for fiscal 1991 be reduced on a pro rata basis by the amount necessary to provide that the total fiscal 1991 authorization level is equal to the fiscal 1990 level plus a 4.8 percent increase. Rejected 62-354: R 62-107; D 0-247 (ND 0-170, SD 0-77), Aug. 1, 1990.

294. HR 1180. Housing Programs Reauthorization/Passage. Passage of the bill to authorize $27.9 billion in fiscal 1991 to reauthorize existing housing programs, establish programs to help first-time home buyers purchase homes, permit and assist people receiving public housing assistance to buy their own homes, and encourage the construction of new rental housing. The bill authorizes about $11 billion more than in fiscal 1990. Passed 378-43: R 132-42; D 246-1 (ND 168-1, SD 78-0), Aug. 1, 1990. A "nay" was a vote supporting the president's position. (The House subsequently passed S 566 by voice vote, after substituting the text of HR 1180.)

295. HR 3950. Farm Programs Reauthorization/Payment Limits. Conte, R-Mass., amendment to the Huckaby, D-La., substitute to the Conte amendment, to require the Department of Agriculture to attribute to individuals, in proportion to their ownership shares, any payments made to corporations, partnerships and similar entities. Rejected 171-250: R 81-91; D 90-159 (ND 81-90, SD 9-69), Aug. 1, 1990.

296. HR 3950. Farm Programs Reauthorization/Payment Limits. Huckaby, D-La., substitute amendment to the Conte, R-Mass., amendment, to establish a $50,000 limit on deficiency and land diversion payments; allow a producer to collect deficiency payments as a participant in three different entities with a limit of $100,000 on total payments; establish a $100,000 limit on marketing loan gains, Findley payments and inventory reduction payments; and establish a $200,000 aggregate limit on all payments, which could not be exceeded through participation in more than one farming entity. Adopted 375-45: R 150-21; D 225-24 (ND 148-22, SD 77-2), Aug. 1, 1990.

297. HR 3950. Farm Programs Reauthorization/Organic Foods. DeFazio, D-Ore., substitute amendment to the Stenholm, D-Texas, amendment, to establish specific national standards for foods labeled as "organic" and establish a National Organic Standards Board. Adopted 234-187: R 42-131; D 192-56 (ND 155-16, SD 37-40), Aug. 1, 1990.

298. HR 3950. Farm Programs Reauthorization/Food Stamps. Frenzel, R-Minn., en bloc amendment to strike all provisions regarding Food Stamps and other nutrition programs that result in increases in direct spending above the baseline level. Rejected 83-336: R 83-89; D 0-247 (ND 0-168, SD 0-79), Aug. 1, 1990.

299. HR 3950. Farm Programs Reauthorization/Passage. Passage of the bill to revise and extend federal farm price and income support programs for major commodities as well as Agriculture Department nutrition programs. Passed 327-91: R 117-54; D 210-37 (ND 133-35, SD 77-2), Aug. 1, 1990. A "nay" was a vote supporting the president's position.

KEY

- Y Voted for (yea).
- # Paired for.
- + Announced for.
- N Voted against (nay).
- X Paired against.
- - Announced against.
- P Voted "present."
- C Voted "present" to avoid possible conflict of interest.
- ? Did not vote or otherwise make a position known.

Democrats ***Republicans***

	292	293	294	295	296	297	298	299
ALABAMA								
1 ***Callahan***	Y	Y	Y	N	Y	N	N	Y
2 ***Dickinson***	Y	Y	Y	N	Y	N	Y	Y
3 Browder	Y	N	Y	N	Y	N	N	Y
4 Bevill	Y	N	Y	N	Y	N	N	Y
5 Flippo	Y	?	?	N	Y	N	N	Y
6 Erdreich	Y	N	Y	N	Y	Y	N	Y
7 Harris	Y	N	Y	N	Y	N	N	Y
ALASKA								
AL ***Young***	Y	Y	Y	N	Y	N	N	Y
ARIZONA								
1 ***Rhodes***	Y	N	Y	Y	Y	N	Y	Y
2 Udall	Y	N	Y	N	Y	Y	N	Y
3 ***Stump***	Y	Y	N	C	C	N	Y	N
4 ***Kyl***	Y	Y	N	Y	Y	N	Y	N
5 ***Kolbe***	Y	Y	Y	N	Y	N	Y	Y
ARKANSAS								
1 Alexander	Y	N	Y	N	Y	?	N	Y
2 ***Robinson***	Y	N	Y	N	Y	N	N	Y
3 ***Hammerschmidt***	Y	N	Y	N	Y	N	N	Y
4 Anthony	Y	N	Y	N	Y	Y	N	Y
CALIFORNIA								
1 Bosco	Y	N	Y	N	?	Y	N	Y
2 ***Herger***	Y	Y	N	N	N	N	Y	Y
3 Matsui	Y	N	Y	N	Y	Y	N	Y
4 Fazio	Y	N	Y	N	Y	Y	N	Y
5 Pelosi	Y	N	Y	N	Y	Y	N	Y
6 Boxer	Y	N	Y	N	Y	Y	N	Y
7 Miller	Y	N	Y	Y	N	Y	N	N
8 Dellums	Y	N	Y	N	Y	Y	N	N
9 Stark	Y	N	Y	Y	N	Y	N	N
10 Edwards	Y	N	Y	N	Y	Y	N	N
11 Lantos	Y	N	Y	N	Y	Y	N	Y
12 ***Campbell***	Y	N	Y	Y	N	Y	N	N
13 Mineta	Y	N	Y	N	Y	Y	N	Y
14 ***Shumway***	Y	N	N	N	Y	N	Y	N
15 Condit	Y	N	Y	N	Y	N	N	Y
16 Panetta	Y	N	Y	N	Y	Y	N	Y
17 ***Pashayan***	Y	N	Y	N	Y	N	N	Y
18 Lehman	Y	N	Y	N	Y	Y	N	Y
19 ***Lagomarsino***	Y	N	Y	N	Y	Y	N	N
20 ***Thomas***	Y	N	Y	N	Y	N	Y	Y
21 ***Gallegly***	Y	N	Y	N	Y	Y	N	N
22 ***Moorhead***	Y	Y	N	N	Y	N	N	N
23 Beilenson	Y	N	Y	Y	N	Y	N	N
24 Waxman	Y	N	Y	Y	Y	Y	?	Y
25 Roybal	Y	N	Y	N	Y	N	N	N
26 Berman	Y	N	Y	Y	Y	Y	N	N
27 Levine	Y	N	Y	Y	Y	Y	N	Y
28 Dixon	Y	N	Y	N	Y	Y	N	Y
29 Hawkins	?	N	Y	X	Y	Y	?	?
30 Martinez	Y	N	Y	N	Y	Y	N	Y
31 Dymally	Y	N	Y	N	Y	Y	N	Y
32 Anderson	N	N	Y	N	Y	Y	N	Y
33 ***Dreier***	Y	Y	Y	Y	Y	N	Y	N
34 Torres	N	N	Y	N	Y	Y	N	Y
35 ***Lewis***	Y	N	Y	N	Y	N	N	Y
36 Brown	Y	N	Y	N	Y	Y	N	Y
37 ***McCandless***	Y	N	Y	N	Y	N	Y	Y
38 ***Dornan***	Y	Y	N	Y	N	N	Y	N
39 ***Dannemeyer***	Y	Y	N	Y	N	N	Y	N
40 ***Cox***	Y	Y	N	Y	Y	N	Y	N
41 ***Lowery***	Y	N	Y	N	Y	N	Y	Y
42 ***Rohrabacher***	Y	Y	N	Y	N	N	Y	N
43 ***Packard***	Y	N	Y	N	Y	N	Y	N
44 Bates	Y	N	Y	Y	Y	Y	N	N
45 ***Hunter***	Y	Y	Y	Y	N	N	Y	Y
COLORADO								
1 Schroeder	Y	N	Y	Y	Y	Y	N	N
2 Skaggs	Y	N	Y	Y	Y	Y	N	Y
3 Campbell	Y	N	Y	N	Y	N	N	Y
4 ***Brown***	Y	Y	N	Y	Y	N	Y	N
5 ***Hefley***	Y	Y	N	N	Y	N	Y	Y
6 ***Schaefer***	Y	Y	N	Y	Y	N	Y	Y
CONNECTICUT								
1 Kennelly	Y	N	Y	Y	Y	Y	N	Y
2 Gejdenson	Y	N	Y	Y	Y	Y	N	Y
3 Morrison	Y	N	Y	Y	Y	Y	N	X
4 ***Shays***	Y	N	Y	Y	Y	Y	N	N
5 ***Rowland***	Y	N	Y	Y	Y	Y	N	Y
6 ***Johnson***	Y	N	Y	Y	Y	N	N	Y
DELAWARE								
AL Carper	Y	N	Y	Y	Y	Y	N	Y
FLORIDA								
1 Hutto	Y	N	Y	N	Y	N	N	Y
2 ***Grant***	Y	?	Y	N	Y	N	N	Y
3 Bennett	Y	N	Y	Y	N	Y	N	N
4 ***James***	Y	N	Y	N	Y	N	N	Y
5 ***McCollum***	Y	Y	N	Y	N	N	Y	N
6 ***Stearns***	Y	Y	Y	Y	Y	N	Y	N
7 Gibbons	Y	N	Y	Y	N	Y	N	N
8 ***Young***	Y	N	Y	Y	N	N	Y	N
9 ***Bilirakis***	?	?	?	?	?	?	?	?
10 ***Ireland***	Y	?	N	Y	N	N	Y	N
11 Nelson	+	−	+	+	−	+	−	#
12 ***Lewis***	Y	?	Y	N	Y	N	N	Y
13 ***Goss***	Y	N	Y	Y	Y	N	Y	N
14 Johnston	Y	N	Y	Y	Y	Y	N	Y
15 ***Shaw***	?	N	Y	Y	N	N	Y	Y
16 Smith	Y	N	Y	Y	Y	Y	N	Y
17 Lehman	Y	N	Y	Y	Y	Y	N	Y
18 ***Ros-Lehtinen***	Y	N	Y	Y	Y	Y	N	Y
19 Fascell	Y	N	Y	N	Y	Y	N	Y
GEORGIA								
1 Thomas	Y	N	Y	N	Y	N	N	Y
2 Hatcher	Y	N	Y	N	Y	N	N	Y
3 Ray	Y	N	Y	N	Y	N	N	Y
4 Jones	Y	N	Y	N	Y	Y	N	Y
5 Lewis	Y	N	Y	N	Y	Y	N	Y
6 ***Gingrich***	Y	N	Y	N	Y	N	Y	Y
7 Darden	Y	N	Y	N	Y	N	N	Y
8 Rowland	Y	N	Y	N	Y	N	N	Y
9 Jenkins	Y	N	Y	N	Y	N	N	Y
10 Barnard	Y	N	Y	N	Y	N	N	Y
HAWAII								
1 ***Saiki***	Y	N	Y	N	Y	Y	N	Y
2 Vacancy								
IDAHO								
1 ***Craig***	Y	Y	N	N	Y	N	Y	Y
2 Stallings	Y	N	Y	N	Y	N	N	Y
ILLINOIS								
1 Hayes	Y	N	Y	N	Y	Y	N	Y
2 Savage	Y	N	Y	N	Y	Y	N	Y
3 Russo	Y	N	Y	Y	N	Y	N	N
4 Sangmeister	Y	N	Y	Y	Y	Y	N	N
5 Lipinski	Y	N	Y	N	Y	Y	N	N
6 ***Hyde***	Y	Y	Y	Y	Y	N	N	Y
7 Collins	Y	N	Y	N	Y	Y	N	Y
8 Rostenkowski	Y	N	Y	Y	Y	Y	N	Y
9 Yates	Y	N	Y	Y	N	Y	N	N
10 ***Porter***	Y	Y	Y	Y	Y	Y	Y	N
11 Annunzio	Y	N	Y	N	Y	Y	N	Y
12 ***Crane***	Y	Y	N	Y	N	N	Y	N
13 ***Fawell***	Y	?	N	Y	Y	Y	Y	N
14 ***Hastert***	Y	N	Y	N	Y	N	Y	Y
15 ***Madigan***	Y	Y	Y	N	Y	N	Y	N
16 ***Martin***	Y	N	Y	Y	Y	N	N	Y
17 Evans	Y	N	Y	N	Y	Y	N	Y
18 ***Michel***	Y	N	Y	Y	Y	N	Y	Y
19 Bruce	Y	N	Y	N	Y	Y	N	Y
20 Durbin	Y	N	Y	Y	Y	Y	N	Y
21 Costello	Y	N	Y	N	Y	Y	N	Y
22 Poshard	Y	N	Y	N	Y	Y	N	Y
INDIANA								
1 Visclosky	Y	N	Y	Y	Y	Y	N	Y
2 Sharp	Y	N	Y	N	Y	Y	N	Y
3 ***Hiler***	Y	N	Y	N	Y	N	N	Y

ND Northern Democrats SD Southern Democrats

	292	293	294	295	296	297	298	299
4 Long	Y	N	Y	N	Y	N	N	Y
5 Jontz	Y	N	Y	N	Y	Y	N	Y
6 ***Burton***	Y	Y	N	N	Y	N	Y	Y
7 ***Myers***	Y	N	Y	N	Y	N	N	Y
8 McCloskey	Y	N	Y	N	Y	Y	N	Y
9 Hamilton	Y	N	Y	Y	Y	Y	N	Y
10 Jacobs	Y	N	Y	Y	N	Y	N	N
IOWA								
1 ***Leach***	Y	N	Y	Y	Y	Y	N	Y
2 ***Tauke***	Y	N	Y	N	Y	N	N	Y
3 Nagle	Y	N	Y	N	Y	Y	N	N
4 Smith	Y	N	Y	N	Y	N	N	Y
5 ***Lightfoot***	Y	Y	Y	N	Y	N	Y	Y
6 ***Grandy***	Y	N	Y	N	Y	N	N	Y
KANSAS								
1 ***Roberts***	Y	Y	N	N	Y	N	Y	Y
2 Slattery	Y	N	Y	Y	Y	Y	N	Y
3 ***Meyers***	Y	N	Y	Y	Y	Y	Y	Y
4 Glickman	Y	N	Y	N	Y	Y	N	Y
5 ***Whittaker***	Y	N	Y	N	Y	N	Y	Y
KENTUCKY								
1 Hubbard	Y	N	Y	N	Y	N	N	Y
2 Natcher	Y	N	Y	N	Y	N	N	Y
3 Mazzoli	Y	N	Y	Y	Y	Y	N	Y
4 ***Bunning***	Y	N	Y	N	Y	N	N	Y
5 ***Rogers***	Y	N	Y	N	Y	N	N	Y
6 ***Hopkins***	Y	Y	N	N	Y	N	Y	Y
7 Perkins	Y	N	Y	N	Y	Y	N	Y
LOUISIANA								
1 ***Livingston***	Y	Y	Y	N	Y	N	Y	Y
2 Boggs	Y	N	Y	N	Y	N	N	Y
3 Tauzin	Y	N	Y	N	Y	N	N	Y
4 ***McCrery***	Y	N	Y	N	Y	N	N	Y
5 Huckaby	Y	N	Y	N	Y	N	N	Y
6 ***Baker***	Y	N	Y	N	Y	N	Y	Y
7 Hayes	Y	N	Y	N	Y	N	N	Y
8 ***Holloway***	Y	Y	Y	N	Y	N	N	Y
MAINE								
1 Brennan	Y	N	Y	Y	Y	Y	N	N
2 ***Snowe***	Y	N	Y	Y	Y	Y	N	Y
MARYLAND								
1 Dyson	Y	N	Y	N	Y	N	N	Y
2 ***Bentley***	Y	N	Y	Y	Y	N	Y	Y
3 Cardin	Y	N	Y	Y	Y	Y	N	N
4 McMillen	Y	N	Y	Y	N	Y	N	Y
5 Hoyer	Y	N	?	N	Y	Y	N	Y
6 Byron	Y	N	Y	N	Y	Y	N	Y
7 Mfume	Y	N	Y	Y	N	Y	N	Y
8 ***Morella***	Y	N	Y	Y	N	Y	N	Y
MASSACHUSETTS								
1 ***Conte***	Y	N	Y	Y	N	Y	N	N
2 Neal	Y	N	Y	Y	N	Y	N	N
3 Early	N	N	Y	Y	N	Y	N	N
4 Frank	Y	N	Y	Y	N	#	N	N
5 Atkins	Y	N	Y	Y	N	Y	N	N
6 Mavroules	Y	N	Y	Y	Y	Y	N	Y
7 Markey	N	N	Y	Y	Y	Y	N	Y
8 Kennedy	N	N	Y	Y	Y	Y	N	Y
9 Moakley	Y	N	Y	Y	Y	Y	N	Y
10 Studds	Y	N	Y	Y	N	Y	N	N
11 Donnelly	N	N	Y	Y	N	Y	N	N
MICHIGAN								
1 Conyers	Y	N	Y	N	Y	Y	N	N
2 ***Pursell***	Y	Y	Y	Y	N	Y	Y	Y
3 Wolpe	Y	N	Y	Y	Y	Y	N	Y
4 ***Upton***	Y	N	Y	Y	Y	Y	N	Y
5 ***Henry***	Y	N	Y	Y	Y	N	N	Y
6 Carr	Y	N	Y	N	Y	Y	N	Y
7 Kildee	Y	N	Y	N	Y	Y	N	Y
8 Traxler	N	N	Y	N	Y	N	N	Y
9 ***Vander Jagt***	Y	N	Y	Y	Y	N	Y	Y
10 ***Schuette***	?	N	Y	N	Y	N	N	Y
11 ***Davis***	Y	N	Y	N	Y	Y	N	Y
12 Bonior	Y	N	Y	N	Y	Y	N	Y
13 Crockett	?	?	Y	?	?	?	N	?
14 Hertel	Y	N	Y	Y	N	Y	N	N
15 Ford	?	N	Y	Y	?	Y	N	N
16 Dingell	Y	N	Y	N	N	N	N	Y
17 Levin	Y	N	Y	N	Y	Y	N	Y
18 ***Broomfield***	Y	Y	Y	Y	N	Y	Y	N
MINNESOTA								
1 Penny	Y	N	N	Y	Y	N	N	Y
2 ***Weber***	Y	N	Y	N	Y	N	N	Y
3 ***Frenzel***	Y	N	Y	Y	N	N	Y	N
4 Vento	Y	N	Y	Y	Y	Y	N	Y
5 Sabo	Y	N	Y	Y	Y	Y	N	Y
6 Sikorski	Y	N	Y	Y	Y	Y	N	Y
7 ***Stangeland***	Y	N	Y	N	Y	N	N	Y
8 Oberstar	Y	N	Y	Y	Y	Y	N	Y
MISSISSIPPI								
1 Whitten	Y	N	Y	N	Y	N	N	Y
2 Espy	Y	N	Y	N	Y	N	N	Y
3 Montgomery	Y	N	Y	N	Y	N	N	Y
4 Parker	Y	N	Y	N	Y	N	N	Y
5 Taylor	Y	N	Y	N	Y	N	N	Y
MISSOURI								
1 Clay	Y	N	Y	N	Y	Y	N	Y
2 ***Buechner***	Y	N	Y	Y	Y	N	N	Y
3 Gephardt	Y	N	Y	N	Y	Y	N	Y
4 Skelton	Y	N	Y	N	Y	N	N	Y
5 Wheat	Y	N	Y	N	Y	Y	N	Y
6 ***Coleman***	Y	?	Y	N	Y	N	N	Y
7 ***Hancock***	Y	Y	N	Y	Y	N	Y	N
8 ***Emerson***	Y	N	Y	N	Y	N	N	Y
9 Volkmer	Y	N	Y	N	Y	Y	N	Y
MONTANA								
1 Williams	Y	N	Y	N	Y	Y	N	N
2 ***Marlenee***	Y	N	N	N	Y	N	Y	Y
NEBRASKA								
1 ***Bereuter***	Y	N	Y	N	Y	N	N	Y
2 Hoagland	Y	N	Y	N	Y	Y	N	Y
3 ***Smith***	Y	Y	N	N	Y	N	Y	Y
NEVADA								
1 Bilbray	Y	N	Y	Y	Y	Y	N	Y
2 ***Vucanovich***	Y	N	Y	N	Y	N	Y	N
NEW HAMPSHIRE								
1 ***Smith***	Y	Y	N	Y	N	Y	Y	N
2 ***Douglas***	Y	Y	N	Y	Y	Y	N	N
NEW JERSEY								
1 Vacancy								
2 Hughes	Y	N	Y	Y	Y	Y	N	Y
3 Pallone	Y	N	Y	Y	Y	Y	N	N
4 ***Smith***	Y	N	Y	Y	Y	Y	N	Y
5 ***Roukema***	?	?	?	#	X	X	?	X
6 Dwyer	Y	N	Y	N	Y	Y	N	?
7 ***Rinaldo***	Y	N	Y	Y	Y	Y	N	N
8 Roe	Y	N	Y	N	Y	Y	N	Y
9 Torricelli	Y	N	Y	Y	Y	Y	N	Y
10 Payne	Y	N	Y	Y	Y	Y	N	Y
11 ***Gallo***	Y	N	Y	Y	Y	N	N	N
12 ***Courter***	Y	N	Y	?	?	?	?	?
13 ***Saxton***	Y	N	Y	Y	Y	Y	N	N
14 Guarini	Y	N	Y	Y	Y	Y	N	N
NEW MEXICO								
1 ***Schiff***	Y	N	Y	N	Y	N	N	Y
2 ***Skeen***	Y	N	Y	N	Y	N	Y	Y
3 Richardson	Y	N	Y	Y	Y	Y	N	Y
NEW YORK								
1 Hochbrueckner	Y	N	Y	Y	Y	Y	N	Y
2 Downey	Y	N	Y	Y	Y	Y	N	N
3 Mrazek	?	?	?	Y	Y	Y	N	Y
4 ***Lent***	?	N	Y	Y	Y	Y	N	N
5 ***McGrath***	Y	N	Y	Y	Y	Y	N	N
6 Flake	Y	N	Y	N	Y	Y	?	#
7 Ackerman	Y	N	Y	N	Y	Y	N	Y
8 Scheuer	Y	N	Y	Y	N	Y	N	N
9 Manton	Y	N	Y	N	Y	Y	N	Y
10 Schumer	Y	N	Y	Y	N	Y	N	Y
11 Towns	Y	N	Y	N	Y	N	N	Y
12 Owens	Y	N	Y	Y	Y	Y	N	Y
13 Solarz	Y	?	?	Y	Y	Y	N	Y
14 ***Molinari***	Y	N	Y	Y	Y	N	N	Y
15 ***Green***	Y	N	Y	Y	N	Y	N	N
16 Rangel	Y	N	Y	N	Y	Y	N	Y
17 Weiss	Y	N	Y	Y	N	Y	N	Y
18 Serrano	Y	N	Y	N	Y	Y	N	Y
19 Engel	Y	N	Y	N	Y	Y	N	Y
20 Lowey	Y	N	Y	N	Y	Y	N	Y
21 ***Fish***	?	N	Y	Y	Y	Y	N	?
22 ***Gilman***	Y	N	Y	N	Y	Y	N	Y
23 McNulty	Y	N	Y	N	Y	N	N	Y
24 ***Solomon***	Y	N	Y	N	Y	Y	Y	Y
25 ***Boehlert***	Y	N	Y	N	Y	Y	N	Y
26 ***Martin***	Y	N	Y	N	Y	N	N	Y
27 ***Walsh***	Y	N	Y	N	Y	N	N	Y
28 McHugh	Y	N	Y	N	Y	Y	N	Y
29 ***Horton***	Y	N	Y	N	Y	Y	N	Y
30 Slaughter	Y	N	Y	N	Y	Y	N	Y
31 ***Paxon***	Y	N	Y	Y	Y	N	N	Y
32 LaFalce	Y	N	Y	Y	Y	Y	N	Y
33 Nowak	Y	N	Y	Y	Y	Y	N	Y
34 ***Houghton***	Y	N	Y	Y	Y	Y	N	Y
NORTH CAROLINA								
1 Jones	Y	N	Y	N	Y	Y	N	Y
2 Valentine	Y	N	Y	N	Y	N	N	Y
3 Lancaster	Y	N	Y	N	Y	N	N	Y
4 Price	Y	N	Y	Y	Y	Y	N	Y
5 Neal	Y	N	Y	N	Y	Y	N	Y
6 ***Coble***	Y	Y	Y	N	Y	N	N	Y
7 Rose	Y	N	Y	N	Y	Y	N	Y
8 Hefner	Y	N	Y	N	Y	Y	N	Y
9 ***McMillan***	Y	N	Y	N	Y	N	N	Y
10 ***Ballenger***	Y	Y	N	N	Y	N	N	N
11 Clarke	Y	?	Y	Y	Y	Y	N	Y
NORTH DAKOTA								
AL Dorgan	?	N	Y	Y	Y	Y	N	N
OHIO								
1 Luken	Y	N	Y	N	Y	Y	N	Y
2 ***Gradison***	Y	Y	N	Y	Y	N	Y	N
3 Hall	Y	N	Y	N	Y	Y	N	Y
4 ***Oxley***	Y	Y	Y	N	Y	N	Y	Y
5 ***Gillmor***	Y	N	Y	N	Y	N	N	Y
6 ***McEwen***	Y	N	Y	N	Y	N	Y	Y
7 ***DeWine***	Y	N	Y	N	Y	N	N	Y
8 ***Lukens***	Y	N	N	N	Y	N	N	N
9 Kaptur	Y	N	Y	N	Y	Y	N	Y
10 ***Miller***	Y	Y	Y	Y	Y	N	Y	Y
11 Eckart	Y	N	Y	Y	Y	Y	N	Y
12 ***Kasich***	Y	N	Y	Y	Y	N	N	Y
13 Pease	Y	N	Y	Y	Y	Y	N	Y
14 Sawyer	Y	N	Y	Y	Y	Y	N	Y
15 ***Wylie***	Y	N	Y	Y	Y	N	?	?
16 ***Regula***	Y	N	Y	Y	Y	N	N	Y
17 Traficant	N	N	Y	N	Y	Y	N	Y
18 Applegate	Y	N	Y	Y	Y	Y	N	Y
19 Feighan	Y	N	Y	Y	Y	Y	?	Y
20 Oakar	Y	N	Y	Y	Y	Y	N	Y
21 Stokes	Y	N	Y	N	Y	Y	N	Y
OKLAHOMA								
1 ***Inhofe***	Y	Y	Y	N	Y	N	Y	Y
2 Synar	Y	N	Y	N	Y	Y	N	Y
3 Watkins	Y	N	Y	N	Y	N	N	Y
4 McCurdy	Y	N	Y	N	Y	Y	N	Y
5 ***Edwards***	Y	N	Y	N	Y	N	N	Y
6 English	Y	N	Y	N	Y	N	N	Y
OREGON								
1 AuCoin	Y	N	Y	N	Y	Y	N	Y
2 ***Smith, B.***	Y	N	Y	N	Y	N	N	Y
3 Wyden	Y	N	Y	Y	Y	Y	N	Y
4 DeFazio	Y	N	Y	N	Y	Y	?	Y
5 ***Smith, D.***	Y	Y	Y	N	Y	N	Y	Y
PENNSYLVANIA								
1 Foglietta	Y	N	Y	Y	N	Y	N	Y
2 Gray	Y	N	Y	N	Y	Y	N	Y
3 Borski	Y	N	Y	Y	Y	Y	N	Y
4 Kolter	N	N	Y	N	Y	N	N	Y
5 ***Schulze***	Y	Y	Y	Y	N	N	Y	Y
6 Yatron	Y	N	Y	Y	Y	Y	N	Y
7 ***Weldon***	?	N	Y	Y	Y	Y	N	N
8 Kostmayer	N	N	Y	Y	N	Y	N	Y
9 ***Shuster***	?	Y	N	Y	Y	N	Y	Y
10 ***McDade***	Y	N	Y	N	Y	Y	N	Y
11 Kanjorski	Y	N	Y	Y	Y	Y	N	Y
12 Murtha	Y	N	Y	N	Y	Y	N	Y
13 ***Coughlin***	Y	N	Y	Y	Y	Y	Y	N
14 Coyne	N	N	Y	N	Y	Y	N	Y
15 ***Ritter***	Y	N	Y	Y	Y	Y	Y	Y
16 ***Walker***	Y	Y	N	Y	N	N	Y	N
17 ***Gekas***	Y	N	N	Y	Y	N	Y	Y
18 Walgren	Y	N	Y	N	Y	Y	N	Y
19 ***Goodling***	Y	N	Y	Y	Y	N	N	Y
20 Gaydos	Y	N	Y	N	Y	Y	N	Y
21 ***Ridge***	Y	N	Y	Y	Y	N	N	Y
22 Murphy	Y	N	Y	Y	Y	Y	N	Y
23 ***Clinger***	Y	N	Y	N	Y	N	Y	Y
RHODE ISLAND								
1 ***Machtley***	Y	N	Y	Y	Y	Y	N	Y
2 ***Schneider***	Y	N	Y	Y	Y	Y	N	N
SOUTH CAROLINA								
1 ***Ravenel***	Y	Y	Y	N	Y	Y	N	Y
2 ***Spence***	Y	N	Y	N	Y	N	Y	Y
3 Derrick	Y	N	Y	?	Y	Y	N	Y
4 Patterson	Y	N	Y	N	Y	N	N	Y
5 Spratt	Y	N	Y	N	Y	Y	N	Y
6 Tallon	Y	N	Y	N	Y	N	N	Y
SOUTH DAKOTA								
AL Johnson	Y	N	Y	N	Y	Y	N	N
TENNESSEE								
1 ***Quillen***	Y	Y	Y	N	Y	N	Y	Y
2 ***Duncan***	Y	Y	N	N	Y	N	Y	N
3 Lloyd	Y	N	Y	N	Y	N	N	Y
4 Cooper	Y	N	Y	N	Y	Y	N	Y
5 Clement	Y	N	Y	N	Y	Y	N	Y
6 Gordon	Y	N	Y	N	Y	Y	N	Y
7 ***Sundquist***	Y	N	Y	N	Y	N	Y	Y
8 Tanner	Y	N	Y	N	Y	N	N	Y
9 Ford	?	?	?	?	#	?	?	?
TEXAS								
1 Chapman	Y	N	Y	N	Y	N	N	Y
2 Wilson	Y	N	Y	N	Y	N	N	Y
3 ***Bartlett***	Y	N	Y	Y	Y	N	Y	N
4 Hall	?	?	?	?	?	?	?	?
5 Bryant	Y	N	Y	N	Y	Y	N	Y
6 ***Barton***	Y	Y	Y	N	Y	N	Y	Y
7 ***Archer***	Y	Y	N	Y	Y	N	Y	N
8 ***Fields***	Y	Y	N	Y	Y	N	N	N
9 Brooks	Y	N	Y	N	Y	Y	N	Y
10 Pickle	Y	N	Y	N	Y	Y	N	Y
11 Leath	?	?	?	?	?	?	?	?
12 Geren	Y	N	Y	N	Y	N	N	Y
13 Sarpalius	Y	N	Y	N	Y	N	N	Y
14 Laughlin	Y	N	Y	N	Y	N	N	Y
15 de la Garza	Y	N	Y	N	Y	N	N	Y
16 Coleman	Y	N	Y	N	Y	Y	N	Y
17 Stenholm	Y	N	Y	N	Y	N	N	Y
18 Washington	?	N	Y	N	Y	Y	N	Y
19 ***Combest***	Y	Y	N	N	Y	N	Y	Y
20 Gonzalez	N	N	Y	N	Y	Y	N	Y
21 ***Smith***	Y	N	Y	N	Y	N	N	Y
22 ***DeLay***	Y	Y	N	Y	Y	N	Y	N
23 Bustamante	Y	N	Y	N	Y	Y	N	Y
24 Frost	Y	N	Y	N	Y	Y	N	Y
25 Andrews	?	N	Y	N	Y	Y	N	Y
26 ***Armey***	Y	Y	N	Y	N	N	Y	N
27 Ortiz	Y	N	Y	N	Y	?	N	Y
UTAH								
1 ***Hansen***	Y	N	N	N	Y	N	Y	Y
2 Owens	Y	N	Y	Y	Y	Y	N	N
3 ***Nielson***	Y	Y	N	Y	Y	N	Y	N
VERMONT								
AL ***Smith***	Y	N	Y	Y	Y	Y	N	N
VIRGINIA								
1 ***Bateman***	Y	N	Y	N	Y	N	N	Y
2 Pickett	Y	N	Y	N	Y	N	N	Y
3 ***Bliley***	Y	Y	Y	N	Y	N	N	Y
4 Sisisky	Y	N	Y	N	Y	N	N	Y
5 Payne	Y	N	Y	N	Y	Y	N	Y
6 Olin	Y	N	Y	N	Y	N	N	Y
7 ***Slaughter***	Y	Y	Y	N	Y	N	Y	Y
8 ***Parris***	Y	N	N	N	Y	N	N	Y
9 Boucher	Y	N	Y	Y	Y	Y	N	Y
10 ***Wolf***	Y	N	Y	Y	Y	N	N	Y
WASHINGTON								
1 ***Miller***	Y	N	Y	Y	Y	Y	N	N
2 Swift	?	N	Y	N	Y	Y	N	Y
3 Unsoeld	Y	N	Y	Y	Y	Y	N	Y
4 ***Morrison***	Y	N	Y	N	Y	N	N	Y
5 Foley								
6 Dicks	Y	N	?	Y	Y	Y	N	Y
7 McDermott	Y	N	Y	N	Y	Y	N	Y
8 ***Chandler***	Y	N	Y	N	Y	Y	N	Y
WEST VIRGINIA								
1 Mollohan	Y	N	Y	N	Y	N	N	Y
2 Staggers	Y	N	Y	N	Y	N	N	Y
3 Wise	Y	N	Y	N	Y	Y	N	Y
4 Rahall	Y	N	Y	N	Y	Y	N	Y
WISCONSIN								
1 Aspin	Y	N	Y	N	Y	Y	N	Y
2 Kastenmeier	Y	N	Y	N	Y	Y	N	N
3 ***Gunderson***	Y	N	Y	N	Y	N	N	Y
4 Kleczka	Y	N	Y	Y	Y	Y	N	Y
5 Moody	Y	N	Y	Y	N	Y	N	N
6 ***Petri***	Y	Y	N	Y	?	Y	Y	Y
7 Obey	Y	N	Y	Y	Y	Y	N	Y
8 ***Roth***	Y	Y	Y	N	Y	N	Y	Y
9 ***Sensenbrenner***	Y	Y	N	Y	Y	N	Y	N
WYOMING								
AL ***Thomas***	Y	Y	Y	N	Y	N	Y	Y

Southern states - Ala., Ark., Fla., Ga., Ky., La., Miss., N.C., Okla., S.C., Tenn., Texas, Va.
Omitted votes are quorum calls, which CQ does not include in its vote charts.

HOUSE VOTES 300, 301, 302, 303, 304, 305

300. Procedural Motion. Clinger, R-Pa., motion to approve the House Journal of Wednesday, Aug. 1. Motion agreed to 289-108: R 59-103; D 230-5 (ND 156-5, SD 74-0), Aug. 2, 1990.

301. HR 5170. Aviation Safety and Capacity Expansion/Passenger Facility Charges. Bosco, D-Calif., amendment to eliminate provisions that permit airports to impose passenger facility charges intended to finance airport improvements. Rejected 171-252: R 40-134; D 131-118 (ND 100-70, SD 31-48), Aug. 2, 1990.

302. HR 5170. Aviation Safety and Capacity Expansion/Passage. Passage of the bill to authorize $17.7 billion in fiscal 1991-92 for Federal Aviation Administration programs to operate and develop the national airway system. Passed 405-15: R 169-5; D 236-10 (ND 158-10, SD 78-0), Aug. 2, 1990.

303. HR 5431. Iraq Sanctions/Passage. Passage of the bill to impose sanctions on Iraq in response to its invasion of Kuwait. Passed 416-0: R 173-0; D 243-0 (ND 164-0, SD 79-0), Aug. 2, 1990.

304. HR 4000. Civil Rights Act of 1990/Previous Question. Wheat, D-Mo., motion to order the previous question (thus ending debate and the possibility of amendment) on the rule (H Res 449) to provide for House floor consideration of the bill to reverse or modify six recent Supreme Court decisions that narrowed the reach and remedies of job discrimination laws and to authorize monetary damages under Title VII of the 1964 Civil Rights Act. Motion agreed 247-171: R 2-171; D 245-0 (ND 167-0, SD 78-0), Aug. 2, 1990.

305. HR 4000. Civil Rights Act of 1990/Rule. Adoption of the rule (H Res 449) to provide for House floor consideration of the bill to reverse or modify six recent Supreme Court decisions that narrowed the reach and remedies of job discrimination laws and to authorize monetary damages under Title VII of the 1964 Civil Rights Act. Adopted 246-175: R 3-170; D 243-5 (ND 166-3, SD 77-2), Aug. 2, 1990.

KEY

Y Voted for (yea).
Paired for.
+ Announced for.
N Voted against (nay).
X Paired against.
- Announced against.
P Voted "present."
C Voted "present" to avoid possible conflict of interest.
? Did not vote or otherwise make a position known.

Democrats *Republicans*

	300	301	302	303	304	305
ALABAMA						
1 *Callahan*	?	N	Y	Y	N	N
2 *Dickinson*	N	N	Y	Y	N	N
3 Browder	Y	Y	Y	Y	Y	Y
4 Bevill	Y	Y	Y	Y	Y	Y
5 Flippo	Y	Y	Y	Y	Y	Y
6 Erdreich	Y	Y	Y	Y	Y	Y
7 Harris	Y	Y	Y	Y	Y	Y
ALASKA						
AL *Young*	?	N	Y	Y	N	N
ARIZONA						
1 *Rhodes*	N	N	Y	Y	N	N
2 Udall	?	N	Y	Y	Y	Y
3 *Stump*	N	N	Y	Y	N	N
4 *Kyl*	N	N	Y	Y	N	N
5 *Kolbe*	N	N	Y	Y	N	N
ARKANSAS						
1 Alexander	?	N	Y	Y	Y	Y
2 *Robinson*	Y	N	Y	Y	?	?
3 *Hammerschmidt*	Y	N	Y	Y	N	N
4 Anthony	Y	N	Y	Y	Y	Y
CALIFORNIA						
1 Bosco	Y	Y	N	Y	Y	Y
2 *Herger*	?	Y	Y	Y	N	N
3 Matsui	Y	Y	Y	Y	Y	Y
4 Fazio	Y	N	Y	Y	Y	Y
5 Pelosi	Y	Y	Y	Y	Y	Y
6 Boxer	Y	Y	Y	Y	Y	Y
7 Miller	Y	Y	Y	Y	Y	Y
8 Dellums	Y	Y	Y	Y	Y	Y
9 Stark	Y	N	Y	Y	Y	Y
10 Edwards	Y	Y	Y	Y	Y	Y
11 Lantos	Y	Y	Y	Y	Y	Y
12 *Campbell*	N	N	Y	Y	N	N
13 Mineta	Y	Y	N	Y	Y	Y
14 *Shumway*	Y	N	Y	Y	N	N
15 Condit	Y	Y	N	Y	Y	Y
16 Panetta	Y	N	Y	Y	Y	Y
17 *Pashayan*	N	N	Y	Y	N	N
18 Lehman	Y	N	Y	Y	Y	Y
19 *Lagomarsino*	N	N	Y	Y	N	N
20 *Thomas*	N	N	Y	Y	N	N
21 *Gallegly*	N	N	Y	Y	N	N
22 *Moorhead*	N	N	Y	Y	N	N
23 Beilenson	Y	Y	Y	Y	Y	Y
24 Waxman	Y	N	Y	Y	Y	Y
25 Roybal	Y	Y	Y	Y	Y	Y
26 Berman	Y	Y	Y	Y	Y	Y
27 Levine	Y	Y	Y	Y	Y	Y
28 Dixon	?	N	Y	Y	Y	Y
29 Hawkins	Y	N	Y	Y	Y	Y
30 Martinez	Y	Y	?	Y	Y	Y
31 Dymally	Y	N	Y	Y	Y	Y
32 Anderson	Y	N	Y	?	Y	Y
33 *Dreier*	N	N	Y	Y	N	N
34 Torres	Y	Y	Y	Y	Y	Y
35 *Lewis*	N	N	Y	Y	N	N
36 Brown	?	N	Y	Y	Y	Y
37 *McCandless*	N	N	Y	Y	N	N
38 *Dornan*	N	N	Y	Y	N	N
39 *Dannemeyer*	N	Y	N	Y	N	N
40 *Cox*	?	Y	Y	Y	N	N
41 *Lowery*	?	N	Y	Y	N	N
42 *Rohrabacher*	N	Y	Y	Y	N	N
43 *Packard*	Y	N	Y	Y	N	N
44 Bates	Y	Y	N	Y	Y	Y
45 *Hunter*	N	N	Y	Y	?	N
COLORADO						
1 Schroeder	N	Y	Y	Y	Y	Y
2 Skaggs	Y	Y	Y	Y	Y	Y
3 Campbell	Y	Y	Y	Y	Y	Y
4 *Brown*	N	N	Y	Y	N	N
5 *Hefley*	N	Y	Y	Y	N	N
6 *Schaefer*	N	N	Y	Y	N	N
CONNECTICUT						
1 Kennelly	Y	Y	Y	Y	Y	Y
2 Gejdenson	Y	Y	Y	Y	Y	Y
3 Morrison	?	X	?	Y	Y	Y
4 *Shays*	N	N	Y	Y	N	Y
5 *Rowland*	Y	N	Y	Y	N	N
6 *Johnson*	Y	N	Y	Y	N	Y
DELAWARE						
AL Carper	Y	Y	Y	Y	Y	N
FLORIDA						
1 Hutto	Y	N	Y	Y	Y	Y
2 *Grant*	Y	Y	Y	Y	N	N
3 Bennett	?	N	Y	Y	Y	Y
4 *James*	N	N	Y	Y	N	N
5 *McCollum*	N	N	Y	Y	N	N
6 *Stearns*	N	N	Y	Y	N	N
7 Gibbons	Y	Y	Y	Y	Y	Y
8 *Young*	N	N	Y	Y	N	N
9 *Bilirakis*	?	?	?	?	?	?
10 *Ireland*	?	N	Y	Y	N	N
11 Nelson	+	-	+	+	+	+
12 *Lewis*	N	N	Y	Y	N	N
13 *Goss*	N	N	Y	Y	N	N
14 Johnston	Y	Y	Y	Y	Y	Y
15 *Shaw*	Y	N	Y	Y	N	N
16 Smith	Y	Y	Y	Y	Y	Y
17 Lehman	Y	N	Y	Y	Y	Y
18 *Ros-Lehtinen*	N	Y	Y	Y	N	N
19 Fascell	Y	N	Y	Y	Y	Y
GEORGIA						
1 Thomas	Y	N	Y	Y	Y	Y
2 Hatcher	Y	Y	Y	Y	Y	Y
3 Ray	Y	N	Y	Y	Y	N
4 Jones	Y	Y	Y	Y	Y	Y
5 Lewis	Y	Y	Y	Y	Y	Y
6 *Gingrich*	Y	N	Y	Y	N	N
7 Darden	Y	Y	Y	Y	Y	Y
8 Rowland	Y	N	Y	Y	Y	Y
9 Jenkins	Y	Y	Y	Y	Y	Y
10 Barnard	Y	N	Y	Y	Y	Y
HAWAII						
1 *Saiki*	Y	Y	Y	Y	N	N
2 Vacancy						
IDAHO						
1 *Craig*	N	N	Y	Y	N	N
2 Stallings	Y	Y	Y	Y	Y	N
ILLINOIS						
1 Hayes	Y	N	Y	Y	Y	Y
2 Savage	Y	N	Y	Y	Y	Y
3 Russo	Y	N	Y	Y	Y	Y
4 Sangmeister	Y	Y	N	Y	Y	Y
5 Lipinski	Y	N	Y	?	Y	Y
6 *Hyde*	Y	N	Y	Y	N	N
7 Collins	Y	N	Y	Y	Y	Y
8 Rostenkowski	Y	N	Y	Y	Y	Y
9 Yates	Y	N	Y	Y	Y	Y
10 *Porter*	Y	N	Y	Y	N	N
11 Annunzio	Y	N	Y	Y	Y	Y
12 *Crane*	N	Y	N	Y	N	N
13 *Fawell*	N	N	Y	Y	N	N
14 *Hastert*	N	N	Y	Y	N	N
15 *Madigan*	?	N	Y	Y	N	N
16 *Martin*	N	Y	N	Y	N	N
17 Evans	Y	N	Y	Y	Y	Y
18 *Michel*	Y	N	Y	Y	N	N
19 Bruce	Y	N	Y	Y	Y	Y
20 Durbin	Y	N	Y	Y	Y	Y
21 Costello	Y	N	Y	Y	Y	Y
22 Poshard	Y	N	Y	Y	Y	Y
INDIANA						
1 Visclosky	Y	Y	Y	Y	Y	Y
2 Sharp	Y	Y	Y	Y	Y	Y
3 *Hiler*	N	N	Y	Y	N	N

ND Northern Democrats SD Southern Democrats

	300	301	302	303	304	305
4 Long	Y	N	Y	Y	Y	Y
5 Jontz	Y	Y	Y	Y	Y	Y
6 ***Burton***	N	Y	Y	Y	N	N
7 ***Myers***	Y	N	Y	Y	N	N
8 McCloskey	Y	Y	Y	Y	Y	Y
9 Hamilton	Y	N	Y	Y	Y	Y
10 Jacobs	N	Y	N	Y	Y	Y
IOWA						
1 ***Leach***	N	N	Y	Y	Y	?
2 ***Tauke***	N	N	Y	Y	N	N
3 Nagle	Y	Y	Y	Y	Y	Y
4 Smith	?	N	Y	Y	Y	Y
5 ***Lightfoot***	N	N	Y	Y	N	N
6 ***Grandy***	Y	N	Y	Y	N	N
KANSAS						
1 ***Roberts***	N	N	Y	Y	N	N
2 Slattery	Y	Y	Y	Y	Y	Y
3 ***Meyers***	Y	N	Y	Y	N	N
4 Glickman	Y	Y	Y	Y	Y	Y
5 ***Whittaker***	N	N	Y	Y	N	N
KENTUCKY						
1 Hubbard	Y	N	Y	Y	Y	Y
2 Natcher	Y	N	Y	Y	Y	Y
3 Mazzoli	Y	N	Y	Y	Y	Y
4 ***Bunning***	N	Y	Y	Y	N	N
5 ***Rogers***	N	N	Y	Y	N	N
6 ***Hopkins***	N	N	Y	Y	N	N
7 Perkins	Y	N	Y	Y	Y	Y
LOUISIANA						
1 ***Livingston***	Y	N	Y	Y	N	N
2 Boggs	Y	N	Y	Y	Y	Y
3 Tauzin	Y	N	Y	Y	Y	Y
4 ***McCrery***	?	N	Y	Y	N	N
5 Huckaby	Y	N	Y	Y	Y	Y
6 ***Baker***	N	N	Y	Y	N	N
7 Hayes	Y	N	Y	Y	Y	Y
8 ***Holloway***	?	N	Y	Y	N	N
MAINE						
1 Brennan	Y	Y	Y	Y	Y	Y
2 ***Snowe***	Y	N	Y	Y	N	N
MARYLAND						
1 Dyson	Y	Y	Y	Y	Y	Y
2 ***Bentley***	N	N	Y	Y	N	N
3 Cardin	Y	Y	Y	Y	Y	Y
4 McMillen	Y	Y	Y	Y	Y	Y
5 Hoyer	Y	Y	Y	Y	Y	Y
6 Byron	Y	Y	Y	Y	Y	Y
7 Mfume	Y	Y	Y	Y	Y	Y
8 ***Morella***	Y	Y	Y	Y	Y	Y
MASSACHUSETTS						
1 ***Conte***	Y	N	Y	Y	N	N
2 Neal	Y	Y	Y	Y	Y	Y
3 Early	Y	Y	Y	Y	Y	Y
4 Frank	Y	N	Y	Y	Y	Y
5 Atkins	Y	N	Y	Y	Y	Y
6 Mavroules	Y	Y	Y	Y	Y	Y
7 Markey	Y	N	Y	Y	Y	Y
8 Kennedy	Y	N	Y	Y	Y	Y
9 Moakley	Y	N	Y	Y	Y	Y
10 Studds	Y	N	Y	Y	Y	Y
11 Donnelly	Y	N	Y	Y	Y	Y
MICHIGAN						
1 Conyers	Y	Y	Y	Y	Y	Y
2 ***Pursell***	Y	Y	Y	Y	N	N
3 Wolpe	Y	Y	Y	Y	Y	Y
4 ***Upton***	N	N	Y	Y	N	N
5 ***Henry***	N	N	Y	Y	N	N
6 Carr	Y	Y	N	Y	Y	Y
7 Kildee	Y	Y	Y	Y	Y	Y
8 Traxler	Y	Y	Y	Y	Y	Y
9 ***Vander Jagt***	Y	N	Y	Y	N	N
10 ***Schuette***	N	Y	Y	Y	N	N
11 ***Davis***	Y	N	Y	Y	N	N
12 Bonior	Y	Y	N	Y	Y	Y
13 Crockett	Y	Y	N	?	Y	Y
14 Hertel	Y	Y	N	Y	Y	Y
15 Ford	?	#	?	?	?	?
16 Dingell	?	N	Y	Y	Y	Y
17 Levin	Y	Y	Y	Y	Y	Y
18 ***Broomfield***	?	N	Y	Y	N	N
MINNESOTA						
1 Penny	Y	N	Y	Y	Y	N
2 ***Weber***	N	N	Y	Y	N	N
3 ***Frenzel***	N	N	Y	Y	N	N
4 Vento	Y	N	Y	Y	Y	Y

	300	301	302	303	304	305
5 Sabo	Y	N	Y	Y	Y	Y
6 Sikorski	N	N	Y	Y	Y	Y
7 ***Stangeland***	N	N	Y	Y	N	N
8 Oberstar	Y	N	Y	Y	Y	Y
MISSISSIPPI						
1 Whitten	Y	Y	Y	Y	Y	Y
2 Espy	Y	N	Y	Y	Y	Y
3 Montgomery	Y	N	Y	Y	Y	Y
4 Parker	Y	N	Y	Y	Y	Y
5 Taylor	Y	N	Y	Y	Y	Y
MISSOURI						
1 Clay	N	Y	Y	Y	Y	Y
2 ***Buechner***	N	N	Y	Y	N	N
3 Gephardt	Y	N	Y	Y	?	Y
4 Skelton	Y	N	Y	Y	Y	Y
5 Wheat	Y	N	Y	Y	Y	Y
6 ***Coleman***	Y	N	Y	Y	N	N
7 ***Hancock***	N	N	Y	Y	N	N
8 ***Emerson***	Y	N	Y	Y	N	N
9 Volkmer	Y	Y	Y	Y	Y	Y
MONTANA						
1 Williams	Y	Y	Y	P	Y	Y
2 ***Marlenee***	N	N	Y	Y	N	N
NEBRASKA						
1 ***Bereuter***	N	Y	Y	Y	N	N
2 Hoagland	Y	Y	Y	Y	Y	Y
3 ***Smith***	Y	N	Y	?	N	N
NEVADA						
1 Bilbray	Y	N	Y	Y	Y	Y
2 ***Vucanovich***	N	N	Y	Y	N	N
NEW HAMPSHIRE						
1 ***Smith***	N	Y	Y	Y	N	N
2 ***Douglas***	N	Y	Y	Y	N	N
NEW JERSEY						
1 Vacancy						
2 Hughes	Y	N	Y	Y	Y	Y
3 Pallone	Y	Y	Y	Y	Y	Y
4 ***Smith***	Y	Y	Y	Y	N	N
5 ***Roukema***	?	N	Y	Y	N	N
6 Dwyer	Y	Y	Y	Y	Y	Y
7 ***Rinaldo***	N	Y	Y	Y	N	N
8 Roe	Y	N	Y	Y	Y	Y
9 Torricelli	Y	N	Y	Y	Y	Y
10 Payne	Y	Y	Y	Y	Y	Y
11 ***Gallo***	N	N	Y	Y	N	N
12 ***Courter***	N	N	Y	Y	N	N
13 ***Saxton***	N	Y	Y	Y	N	N
14 Guarini	Y	Y	Y	Y	Y	Y
NEW MEXICO						
1 ***Schiff***	Y	N	Y	Y	N	N
2 ***Skeen***	Y	N	Y	Y	N	N
3 Richardson	Y	Y	Y	Y	Y	Y
NEW YORK						
1 Hochbrueckner	?	Y	Y	Y	Y	Y
2 Downey	Y	Y	Y	Y	Y	Y
3 Mrazek	Y	Y	Y	Y	Y	Y
4 ***Lent***	Y	N	Y	Y	N	N
5 ***McGrath***	N	Y	Y	Y	N	N
6 Flake	?	?	?	?	Y	Y
7 Ackerman	Y	Y	Y	Y	Y	Y
8 Scheuer	?	Y	Y	Y	Y	Y
9 Manton	Y	Y	Y	Y	Y	Y
10 Schumer	Y	Y	Y	Y	Y	Y
11 Towns	?	Y	Y	Y	Y	Y
12 Owens	Y	Y	Y	Y	Y	Y
13 Solarz	Y	N	Y	Y	Y	Y
14 ***Molinari***	N	N	Y	Y	N	N
15 ***Green***	Y	N	Y	Y	N	N
16 Rangel	Y	Y	Y	Y	Y	Y
17 Weiss	Y	Y	Y	Y	Y	Y
18 Serrano	Y	Y	Y	Y	?	Y
19 Engel	Y	Y	Y	Y	Y	Y
20 Lowey	Y	Y	Y	Y	Y	Y
21 ***Fish***	Y	N	Y	Y	N	N
22 ***Gilman***	Y	Y	Y	Y	N	N
23 McNulty	Y	Y	Y	Y	Y	Y
24 ***Solomon***	N	Y	Y	Y	N	N
25 ***Boehlert***	N	N	Y	Y	N	N
26 ***Martin***	N	N	Y	Y	N	N
27 ***Walsh***	Y	N	Y	Y	N	N
28 McHugh	Y	N	Y	Y	Y	Y
29 ***Horton***	Y	N	Y	Y	N	N
30 Slaughter	Y	N	Y	Y	Y	Y
31 ***Paxon***	N	N	Y	Y	N	N

	300	301	302	303	304	305
32 LaFalce	Y	N	Y	?	P	P
33 Nowak	Y	N	Y	Y	Y	Y
34 ***Houghton***	Y	N	Y	Y	N	N
NORTH CAROLINA						
1 Jones	P	N	Y	Y	Y	Y
2 Valentine	Y	N	Y	Y	Y	Y
3 Lancaster	Y	Y	Y	Y	Y	Y
4 Price	Y	Y	Y	Y	Y	Y
5 Neal	?	N	Y	Y	Y	Y
6 ***Coble***	N	N	Y	Y	N	N
7 Rose	Y	N	Y	Y	Y	Y
8 Hefner	Y	N	Y	Y	Y	Y
9 ***McMillan***	N	N	Y	Y	N	N
10 ***Ballenger***	N	N	Y	Y	N	N
11 Clarke	Y	Y	Y	Y	Y	Y
NORTH DAKOTA						
AL Dorgan	Y	N	Y	Y	Y	Y
OHIO						
1 Luken	Y	N	?	?	?	?
2 ***Gradison***	Y	N	Y	Y	N	N
3 Hall	Y	Y	Y	Y	?	?
4 ***Oxley***	N	N	Y	Y	N	N
5 ***Gillmor***	Y	N	Y	Y	N	N
6 ***McEwen***	Y	N	Y	Y	N	N
7 ***DeWine***	N	N	Y	Y	N	N
8 ***Lukens***	N	N	Y	Y	N	N
9 Kaptur	Y	Y	Y	Y	Y	Y
10 ***Miller***	N	N	Y	Y	N	N
11 Eckart	Y	N	Y	Y	Y	Y
12 ***Kasich***	Y	N	Y	Y	N	N
13 Pease	Y	Y	Y	Y	Y	Y
14 Sawyer	Y	N	Y	Y	Y	Y
15 ***Wylie***	?	?	?	?	N	N
16 ***Regula***	N	N	Y	Y	N	N
17 Traficant	Y	Y	Y	Y	Y	Y
18 Applegate	Y	Y	Y	Y	Y	Y
19 Feighan	Y	Y	Y	Y	Y	Y
20 Oakar	Y	Y	Y	Y	Y	Y
21 Stokes	Y	Y	Y	Y	Y	Y
OKLAHOMA						
1 ***Inhofe***	N	N	Y	Y	N	N
2 Synar	Y	Y	Y	Y	Y	Y
3 Watkins	Y	Y	Y	Y	Y	Y
4 McCurdy	Y	Y	Y	Y	Y	Y
5 ***Edwards***	?	N	Y	Y	N	N
6 English	Y	N	Y	Y	Y	Y
OREGON						
1 AuCoin	?	Y	Y	Y	Y	Y
2 ***Smith, B.***	N	Y	Y	Y	N	N
3 Wyden	Y	Y	Y	Y	Y	Y
4 DeFazio	Y	N	Y	Y	Y	Y
5 ***Smith, D.***	Y	N	Y	Y	N	N
PENNSYLVANIA						
1 Foglietta	Y	N	Y	Y	Y	Y
2 Gray	Y	N	Y	Y	Y	Y
3 Borski	Y	N	Y	Y	Y	Y
4 Kolter	Y	Y	Y	Y	Y	Y
5 ***Schulze***	Y	Y	Y	Y	N	N
6 Yatron	Y	Y	Y	Y	Y	Y
7 ***Weldon***	Y	N	Y	Y	N	N
8 Kostmayer	Y	N	Y	Y	Y	Y
9 ***Shuster***	Y	Y	Y	Y	N	N
10 ***McDade***	Y	Y	Y	Y	N	N
11 Kanjorski	Y	Y	Y	Y	Y	Y
12 Murtha	Y	N	Y	Y	Y	Y
13 ***Coughlin***	N	N	Y	Y	N	N
14 Coyne	Y	N	Y	Y	Y	Y
15 ***Ritter***	Y	Y	Y	Y	N	N
16 ***Walker***	N	Y	N	Y	N	N
17 ***Gekas***	N	N	Y	Y	N	N
18 Walgren	Y	N	Y	Y	Y	Y
19 ***Goodling***	N	N	Y	Y	N	N
20 Gaydos	Y	Y	Y	?	Y	Y
21 ***Ridge***	N	Y	Y	Y	N	N
22 Murphy	N	Y	Y	Y	Y	Y
23 ***Clinger***	Y	N	Y	Y	N	N
RHODE ISLAND						
1 ***Machtley***	N	Y	Y	Y	N	N
2 ***Schneider***	Y	N	Y	Y	N	N
SOUTH CAROLINA						
1 ***Ravenel***	Y	Y	Y	Y	N	N
2 ***Spence***	N	Y	Y	Y	N	N
3 Derrick	Y	N	Y	Y	Y	Y
4 Patterson	Y	N	Y	Y	Y	Y
5 Spratt	Y	N	Y	Y	Y	Y
6 Tallon	Y	Y	Y	Y	Y	Y

	300	301	302	303	304	305
SOUTH DAKOTA						
AL Johnson	Y	Y	Y	Y	Y	Y
TENNESSEE						
1 ***Quillen***	Y	Y	Y	Y	N	N
2 ***Duncan***	N	N	Y	Y	N	N
3 Lloyd	Y	N	Y	Y	Y	Y
4 Cooper	Y	N	Y	Y	Y	Y
5 Clement	Y	N	Y	Y	Y	Y
6 Gordon	Y	Y	Y	Y	Y	Y
7 ***Sundquist***	N	N	Y	Y	N	N
8 Tanner	Y	N	Y	Y	Y	Y
9 Ford	?	?	?	?	?	?
TEXAS						
1 Chapman	Y	Y	Y	Y	Y	Y
2 Wilson	Y	Y	Y	Y	Y	Y
3 ***Bartlett***	Y	N	Y	Y	N	N
4 Hall	?	?	?	?	?	?
5 Bryant	Y	N	Y	Y	Y	Y
6 ***Barton***	N	N	Y	Y	N	N
7 ***Archer***	Y	N	Y	Y	N	N
8 ***Fields***	N	N	Y	Y	N	N
9 Brooks	Y	N	Y	Y	Y	Y
10 Pickle	Y	N	Y	Y	Y	Y
11 Leath	?	?	?	?	?	?
12 Geren	Y	N	Y	Y	Y	Y
13 Sarpalius	Y	N	Y	Y	Y	Y
14 Laughlin	Y	N	Y	Y	Y	Y
15 de la Garza	Y	Y	Y	Y	Y	Y
16 Coleman	Y	N	Y	Y	Y	Y
17 Stenholm	Y	N	Y	Y	P	N
18 Washington	Y	Y	Y	Y	Y	Y
19 ***Combest***	Y	N	Y	Y	N	N
20 Gonzalez	Y	N	Y	Y	Y	Y
21 ***Smith***	N	N	Y	Y	N	N
22 ***DeLay***	N	N	Y	Y	N	N
23 Bustamante	Y	Y	Y	Y	Y	Y
24 Frost	?	N	Y	Y	Y	Y
25 Andrews	Y	N	Y	Y	Y	Y
26 ***Armey***	N	N	Y	Y	N	N
27 Ortiz	Y	Y	?	Y	Y	Y
UTAH						
1 ***Hansen***	Y	N	Y	Y	N	N
2 Owens	Y	N	Y	Y	Y	Y
3 ***Nielson***	N	Y	Y	Y	N	N
VERMONT						
AL ***Smith***	N	Y	Y	Y	N	N
VIRGINIA						
1 ***Bateman***	Y	N	Y	Y	N	N
2 Pickett	Y	N	Y	Y	Y	Y
3 ***Bliley***	N	N	Y	Y	N	N
4 Sisisky	Y	N	Y	Y	Y	Y
5 Payne	Y	Y	Y	Y	Y	Y
6 Olin	Y	Y	Y	Y	Y	Y
7 ***Slaughter***	N	Y	Y	Y	N	N
8 ***Parris***	N	N	Y	Y	N	N
9 Boucher	Y	Y	Y	Y	Y	Y
10 ***Wolf***	N	N	Y	Y	N	N
WASHINGTON						
1 ***Miller***	N	N	Y	Y	N	N
2 Swift	Y	Y	Y	Y	Y	Y
3 Unsoeld	Y	Y	Y	Y	Y	Y
4 ***Morrison***	Y	N	Y	Y	N	N
5 Foley						
6 Dicks	Y	N	Y	Y	Y	Y
7 McDermott	Y	Y	Y	Y	Y	Y
8 ***Chandler***	N	N	Y	Y	N	N
WEST VIRGINIA						
1 Mollohan	Y	N	Y	Y	Y	Y
2 Staggers	Y	Y	Y	Y	Y	Y
3 Wise	Y	N	Y	Y	Y	Y
4 Rahall	Y	Y	Y	Y	Y	Y
WISCONSIN						
1 Aspin	Y	N	Y	Y	Y	Y
2 Kastenmeier	Y	Y	Y	Y	Y	Y
3 ***Gunderson***	Y	N	Y	Y	N	N
4 Kleczka	Y	Y	Y	Y	Y	Y
5 Moody	Y	Y	Y	Y	Y	Y
6 ***Petri***	Y	Y	Y	Y	N	N
7 Obey	Y	N	Y	Y	Y	Y
8 ***Roth***	Y	N	Y	Y	N	N
9 ***Sensenbrenner***	N	Y	N	Y	N	N
WYOMING						
AL ***Thomas***	N	N	Y	Y	N	N

Southern states - Ala., Ark., Fla., Ga., Ky., La., Miss., N.C., Okla., S.C., Tenn., Texas, Va.
Omitted votes are quorum calls, which CQ does not include in its vote charts.

HOUSE VOTES 306, 307, 308, 309, 310

306. HR 4000. Civil Rights Act of 1990/Quotas. Andrews, D-Texas, en bloc amendment to state that nothing in the act shall be construed to require an employer to adopt hiring or promotion quotas and that the existence of a statistical imbalance in an employer's work force is not alone sufficient to establish a prima facie case of a disparate impact violation. Adopted 397-24: R 148-23; D 249-1 (ND 170-1, SD 79-0), Aug. 2, 1990.

307. HR 4000. Civil Rights Act of 1990/Punitive Damages. Brooks, D-Texas, amendment to place a cap on punitive damages for employers with fewer than 100 employees of $150,000 or the amount of compensatory damages and equitable monetary relief, whichever is greater. Adopted 289-134: R 80-93; D 209-41 (ND 135-36, SD 74-5), Aug. 2, 1990.

308. Procedural Motion. Kyl, R-Ariz., motion to approve the House Journal of Thursday, Aug. 2. Motion agreed to 270-126: R 45-119; D 225-7 (ND 155-7, SD 70-0), Aug. 3, 1990.

309. HR 4000. Civil Rights Act of 1990/Republican Substitute. Michel, R-Ill., substitute amendment to define "business necessity" as a practice that has a manifest relationship to the employment in question or that serves a legitimate employment goal; to strike the bill's damages provisions; to cut back on the bill's provisions limiting the ability of non-parties to challenge a court decision resolving an employment discrimination claim; to limit the bill's provisions regarding statute of limitations and intentional discrimination; and to not include a number of the bill's other provisions. Rejected 188-238: R 160-14; D 28-224 (ND 6-166, SD 22-58), Aug. 3, 1990.

310. HR 4000. Civil Rights Act of 1990/Passage. Passage of the bill to reverse or modify six recent Supreme Court decisions that narrowed the reach and remedies of job discrimination laws and to authorize monetary damages under Title VII of the 1964 Civil Rights Act. Passed 272-154: R 32-142; D 240-12 (ND 170-2, SD 70-10), Aug. 3, 1990. A "nay" was a vote supporting the president's position.

KEY

Y Voted for (yea).
Paired for.
+ Announced for.
N Voted against (nay).
X Paired against.
- Announced against.
P Voted "present."
C Voted "present" to avoid possible conflict of interest.
? Did not vote or otherwise make a position known.

Democrats ***Republicans***

	306	307	308	309	310
ALABAMA					
1 ***Callahan***	N	N	Y	Y	N
2 ***Dickinson***	Y	N	N	Y	N
3 Browder	Y	Y	Y	N	Y
4 Bevill	Y	Y	Y	N	Y
5 Flippo	Y	Y	Y	N	Y
6 Erdreich	Y	Y	Y	N	Y
7 Harris	Y	Y	Y	N	Y
ALASKA					
AL ***Young***	Y	N	?	Y	N
ARIZONA					
1 ***Rhodes***	Y	N	N	Y	N
2 Udall	Y	Y	?	N	Y
3 ***Stump***	Y	N	N	Y	N
4 ***Kyl***	Y	N	N	Y	N
5 ***Kolbe***	Y	N	N	Y	N
ARKANSAS					
1 Alexander	Y	Y	?	Y	Y
2 ***Robinson***	?	X	?	#	X
3 ***Hammerschmidt***	N	N	Y	Y	N
4 Anthony	Y	Y	Y	Y	Y
CALIFORNIA					
1 Bosco	Y	Y	Y	N	Y
2 ***Herger***	Y	Y	N	Y	N
3 Matsui	Y	Y	?	N	Y
4 Fazio	Y	Y	Y	N	Y
5 Pelosi	Y	N	Y	N	Y
6 Boxer	Y	N	Y	N	Y
7 Miller	Y	N	Y	N	Y
8 Dellums	Y	N	Y	N	Y
9 Stark	Y	N	Y	N	Y
10 Edwards	Y	N	Y	N	Y
11 Lantos	Y	Y	Y	N	Y
12 ***Campbell***	Y	N	N	Y	Y
13 Mineta	Y	N	Y	N	Y
14 ***Shumway***	Y	N	Y	Y	N
15 Condit	Y	Y	Y	N	Y
16 Panetta	Y	Y	Y	N	Y
17 ***Pashayan***	+	Y	N	Y	N
18 Lehman	Y	Y	Y	N	Y
19 ***Lagomarsino***	Y	Y	N	Y	N
20 ***Thomas***	Y	N	N	Y	N
21 ***Gallegly***	Y	N	N	Y	N
22 ***Moorhead***	Y	Y	N	Y	N
23 Beilenson	Y	Y	Y	N	Y
24 Waxman	Y	N	Y	N	Y
25 Roybal	Y	Y	Y	N	Y
26 Berman	Y	Y	Y	N	Y
27 Levine	Y	N	Y	N	Y
28 Dixon	Y	Y	?	N	Y
29 Hawkins	Y	Y	Y	N	Y
30 Martinez	Y	Y	Y	N	Y
31 Dymally	Y	Y	Y	N	Y
32 Anderson	Y	Y	Y	N	Y
33 ***Dreier***	Y	N	N	Y	N
34 Torres	Y	Y	Y	N	Y
35 ***Lewis***	Y	Y	N	Y	N
36 Brown	Y	Y	Y	N	Y
37 ***McCandless***	Y	Y	N	Y	N
38 ***Dornan***	Y	N	N	Y	N
39 ***Dannemeyer***	Y	N	N	Y	N
40 ***Cox***	Y	N	?	Y	N
41 ***Lowery***	N	N	?	Y	N
42 ***Rohrabacher***	Y	N	N	Y	N
43 ***Packard***	Y	Y	N	Y	N
44 Bates	Y	Y	?	N	Y
45 ***Hunter***	Y	Y	N	Y	N
COLORADO					
1 Schroeder	Y	N	N	N	Y
2 Skaggs	Y	Y	Y	N	Y
3 Campbell	Y	Y	Y	N	Y
4 ***Brown***	Y	Y	N	Y	N
5 ***Hefley***	Y	N	N	Y	N
6 ***Schaefer***	Y	Y	N	Y	N
CONNECTICUT					
1 Kennelly	Y	N	Y	N	Y
2 Gejdenson	Y	N	Y	N	Y
3 Morrison	Y	N	Y	N	Y
4 ***Shays***	Y	Y	N	N	Y
5 ***Rowland***	Y	Y	Y	Y	Y
6 ***Johnson***	Y	Y	Y	Y	Y
DELAWARE					
AL Carper	Y	Y	Y	N	Y
FLORIDA					
1 Hutto	Y	Y	Y	Y	N
2 ***Grant***	Y	Y	Y	Y	Y
3 Bennett	Y	Y	Y	N	Y
4 ***James***	Y	Y	N	Y	Y
5 ***McCollum***	Y	N	N	Y	N
6 ***Stearns***	Y	Y	N	Y	N
7 Gibbons	Y	Y	Y	N	Y
8 ***Young***	Y	N	N	Y	N
9 ***Bilirakis***	?	?	?	?	?
10 ***Ireland***	Y	N	N	Y	N
11 Nelson	+	+	+	-	+
12 ***Lewis***	Y	N	N	Y	N
13 ***Goss***	Y	N	N	Y	N
14 Johnston	Y	Y	?	N	Y
15 ***Shaw***	Y	N	Y	Y	N
16 Smith	Y	Y	Y	N	Y
17 Lehman	Y	Y	Y	N	Y
18 ***Ros-Lehtinen***	Y	Y	N	Y	Y
19 Fascell	Y	Y	Y	N	Y
GEORGIA					
1 Thomas	Y	Y	Y	Y	Y
2 Hatcher	Y	Y	Y	Y	Y
3 Ray	Y	Y	Y	Y	Y
4 Jones	Y	Y	Y	N	Y
5 Lewis	Y	N	Y	N	Y
6 ***Gingrich***	N	N	N	Y	N
7 Darden	Y	Y	Y	Y	N
8 Rowland	Y	Y	Y	Y	Y
9 Jenkins	Y	Y	Y	Y	N
10 Barnard	Y	Y	Y	Y	N
HAWAII					
1 ***Saiki***	Y	Y	Y	N	Y
2 Vacancy					
IDAHO					
1 ***Craig***	Y	N	N	Y	N
2 Stallings	Y	Y	Y	Y	Y
ILLINOIS					
1 Hayes	Y	N	Y	N	Y
2 Savage	N	N	Y	N	Y
3 Russo	Y	Y	Y	Y	Y
4 Sangmeister	Y	Y	Y	N	Y
5 Lipinski	Y	Y	Y	Y	N
6 ***Hyde***	Y	N	Y	Y	N
7 Collins	Y	Y	Y	N	Y
8 Rostenkowski	Y	Y	Y	N	Y
9 Yates	Y	Y	Y	N	Y
10 ***Porter***	Y	N	Y	Y	N
11 Annunzio	Y	Y	Y	Y	N
12 ***Crane***	N	N	?	Y	N
13 ***Fawell***	Y	N	N	Y	N
14 ***Hastert***	Y	N	N	Y	N
15 ***Madigan***	N	N	N	Y	N
16 ***Martin***	Y	Y	N	Y	Y
17 Evans	Y	Y	Y	N	Y
18 ***Michel***	N	N	Y	Y	N
19 Bruce	Y	Y	Y	N	Y
20 Durbin	Y	N	Y	N	Y
21 Costello	Y	N	Y	N	Y
22 Poshard	Y	Y	Y	N	Y
INDIANA					
1 Visclosky	Y	Y	Y	N	Y
2 Sharp	Y	Y	Y	N	Y
3 ***Hiler***	Y	N	N	Y	N

ND Northern Democrats SD Southern Democrats

	306	307	308	309	310
4 Long	Y	Y	Y	N	Y
5 Jontz	Y	Y	Y	N	Y
6 ***Burton***	N	N	N	Y	N
7 ***Myers***	N	N	Y	Y	N
8 McCloskey	Y	Y	Y	N	Y
9 Hamilton	Y	Y	Y	N	Y
10 Jacobs	Y	Y	N	N	Y
IOWA					
1 ***Leach***	Y	Y	N	N	Y
2 ***Tauke***	Y	Y	N	Y	N
3 Nagle	Y	N	Y	N	Y
4 Smith	Y	Y	Y	N	Y
5 ***Lightfoot***	Y	Y	N	Y	N
6 ***Grandy***	Y	N	N	Y	N
KANSAS					
1 ***Roberts***	Y	Y	N	Y	N
2 Slattery	Y	Y	Y	N	Y
3 ***Meyers***	Y	Y	Y	Y	Y
4 Glickman	Y	Y	Y	N	Y
5 ***Whittaker***	Y	Y	N	Y	N
KENTUCKY					
1 Hubbard	Y	Y	Y	N	Y
2 Natcher	Y	Y	Y	N	Y
3 Mazzoli	Y	Y	Y	N	Y
4 ***Bunning***	Y	N	N	Y	N
5 ***Rogers***	Y	N	N	Y	N
6 ***Hopkins***	Y	Y	N	Y	N
7 Perkins	Y	N	Y	N	Y
LOUISIANA					
1 ***Livingston***	Y	N	?	Y	N
2 Boggs	Y	Y	Y	N	Y
3 Tauzin	Y	Y	Y	Y	Y
4 ***McCrery***	Y	N	?	Y	N
5 Huckaby	Y	Y	Y	Y	N
6 ***Baker***	N	N	N	Y	N
7 Hayes	Y	Y	Y	Y	Y
8 ***Holloway***	N	N	N	Y	N
MAINE					
1 Brennan	Y	Y	Y	N	Y
2 ***Snowe***	Y	Y	Y	N	Y
MARYLAND					
1 Dyson	Y	Y	?	N	Y
2 ***Bentley***	Y	Y	N	Y	N
3 Cardin	Y	Y	Y	N	Y
4 McMillen	Y	Y	Y	N	Y
5 Hoyer	Y	Y	Y	N	Y
6 Byron	Y	Y	Y	N	Y
7 Mfume	Y	N	Y	N	Y
8 ***Morella***	Y	N	N	N	Y
MASSACHUSETTS					
1 ***Conte***	Y	Y	Y	N	Y
2 Neal	Y	Y	Y	N	Y
3 Early	Y	Y	N	N	Y
4 Frank	Y	N	?	N	Y
5 Atkins	Y	Y	Y	N	Y
6 Mavroules	Y	Y	?	N	Y
7 Markey	Y	Y	Y	N	Y
8 Kennedy	Y	N	Y	N	Y
9 Moakley	Y	Y	Y	N	Y
10 Studds	Y	Y	Y	N	Y
11 Donnelly	Y	Y	Y	N	Y
MICHIGAN					
1 Conyers	Y	Y	Y	N	Y
2 ***Pursell***	Y	Y	Y	Y	N
3 Wolpe	Y	N	Y	N	Y
4 ***Upton***	Y	N	N	Y	N
5 ***Henry***	Y	Y	N	Y	N
6 Carr	Y	Y	Y	N	Y
7 Kildee	Y	Y	Y	N	Y
8 Traxler	Y	Y	Y	N	Y
9 ***Vander Jagt***	?	Y	Y	Y	N
10 ***Schuette***	Y	Y	N	Y	N
11 ***Davis***	Y	Y	N	N	Y
12 Bonior	Y	N	Y	N	Y
13 Crockett	Y	Y	Y	N	Y
14 Hertel	Y	Y	Y	N	Y
15 Ford	?	#	?	X	#
16 Dingell	Y	Y	Y	N	Y
17 Levin	Y	Y	Y	N	Y
18 ***Broomfield***	Y	N	Y	Y	N
MINNESOTA					
1 Penny	Y	Y	Y	N	Y
2 ***Weber***	N	N	N	Y	N
3 ***Frenzel***	Y	N	N	Y	N
4 Vento	Y	Y	Y	N	Y
5 Sabo	Y	Y	Y	N	Y
6 Sikorski	Y	N	N	N	Y
7 ***Stangeland***	N	N	N	Y	N
8 Oberstar	Y	Y	Y	N	Y
MISSISSIPPI					
1 Whitten	Y	Y	Y	N	Y
2 Espy	Y	Y	Y	N	Y
3 Montgomery	Y	Y	Y	Y	N
4 Parker	Y	Y	Y	Y	N
5 Taylor	Y	Y	Y	Y	N
MISSOURI					
1 Clay	Y	Y	N	N	Y
2 ***Buechner***	Y	N	N	Y	N
3 Gephardt	Y	Y	Y	N	Y
4 Skelton	Y	Y	Y	N	Y
5 Wheat	Y	Y	Y	N	Y
6 ***Coleman***	Y	Y	N	Y	N
7 ***Hancock***	Y	N	N	Y	N
8 ***Emerson***	Y	N	N	Y	N
9 Volkmer	Y	Y	Y	N	Y
MONTANA					
1 Williams	Y	N	Y	N	Y
2 ***Marlenee***	Y	N	N	Y	N
NEBRASKA					
1 ***Bereuter***	Y	Y	N	Y	N
2 Hoagland	Y	Y	Y	N	Y
3 ***Smith***	Y	Y	Y	Y	N
NEVADA					
1 Bilbray	Y	Y	?	N	Y
2 ***Vucanovich***	Y	Y	N	Y	N
NEW HAMPSHIRE					
1 ***Smith***	Y	N	N	Y	N
2 ***Douglas***	Y	N	N	Y	N
NEW JERSEY					
1 Vacancy					
2 Hughes	Y	Y	?	N	Y
3 Pallone	Y	N	Y	N	Y
4 ***Smith***	Y	Y	Y	Y	N
5 ***Roukema***	Y	Y	N	Y	Y
6 Dwyer	Y	Y	Y	N	Y
7 ***Rinaldo***	Y	Y	?	N	Y
8 Roe	Y	Y	Y	N	Y
9 Torricelli	Y	Y	Y	N	Y
10 Payne	Y	N	Y	N	Y
11 ***Gallo***	Y	Y	N	Y	N
12 ***Courter***	Y	Y	N	Y	N
13 ***Saxton***	Y	Y	N	Y	N
14 Guarini	Y	Y	Y	N	Y
NEW MEXICO					
1 ***Schiff***	Y	Y	N	Y	Y
2 ***Skeen***	Y	Y	N	Y	N
3 Richardson	Y	Y	Y	N	Y
NEW YORK					
1 Hochbrueckner	Y	Y	Y	N	Y
2 Downey	Y	Y	Y	N	Y
3 Mrazek	Y	Y	Y	N	Y
4 ***Lent***	Y	Y	Y	Y	N
5 ***McGrath***	Y	Y	N	Y	N
6 Flake	Y	Y	Y	N	Y
7 Ackerman	Y	Y	Y	N	Y
8 Scheuer	Y	N	Y	N	Y
9 Manton	Y	Y	Y	N	Y
10 Schumer	Y	Y	Y	N	Y
11 Towns	Y	Y	Y	N	Y
12 Owens	Y	Y	Y	N	Y
13 Solarz	Y	N	Y	N	Y
14 ***Molinari***	Y	N	N	Y	N
15 ***Green***	Y	Y	Y	N	Y
16 Rangel	Y	Y	?	N	Y
17 Weiss	Y	N	Y	N	Y
18 Serrano	Y	Y	Y	N	Y
19 Engel	Y	Y	Y	N	Y
20 Lowey	Y	N	Y	N	Y
21 ***Fish***	Y	Y	Y	N	Y
22 ***Gilman***	Y	Y	Y	N	Y
23 McNulty	Y	Y	Y	N	Y
24 ***Solomon***	Y	Y	N	Y	N
25 ***Boehlert***	Y	Y	N	Y	Y
26 ***Martin***	Y	Y	?	Y	N
27 ***Walsh***	Y	Y	N	N	Y
28 McHugh	Y	Y	Y	N	Y
29 ***Horton***	Y	Y	Y	N	Y
30 Slaughter	Y	Y	Y	N	Y
31 ***Paxon***	Y	N	N	Y	N
32 LaFalce	Y	Y	N	Y	Y
33 Nowak	Y	Y	Y	N	Y
34 ***Houghton***	Y	Y	Y	Y	N
NORTH CAROLINA					
1 Jones	Y	Y	Y	N	Y
2 Valentine	Y	Y	?	N	Y
3 Lancaster	Y	Y	Y	N	Y
4 Price	Y	Y	Y	N	Y
5 Neal	Y	Y	?	N	Y
6 ***Coble***	Y	Y	N	Y	N
7 Rose	Y	Y	?	N	Y
8 Hefner	Y	Y	Y	N	Y
9 ***McMillan***	Y	Y	N	Y	N
10 ***Ballenger***	Y	N	N	Y	N
11 Clarke	Y	Y	Y	N	Y
NORTH DAKOTA					
AL Dorgan	Y	Y	Y	N	Y
OHIO					
1 Luken	?	?	Y	N	Y
2 ***Gradison***	N	N	N	Y	N
3 Hall	Y	Y	Y	N	Y
4 ***Oxley***	Y	N	Y	Y	N
5 ***Gillmor***	Y	Y	Y	Y	N
6 ***McEwen***	Y	Y	Y	Y	N
7 ***DeWine***	Y	N	N	Y	N
8 ***Lukens***	Y	N	N	Y	N
9 Kaptur	Y	Y	Y	N	Y
10 ***Miller***	Y	Y	N	Y	N
11 Eckart	Y	Y	Y	N	Y
12 ***Kasich***	Y	N	Y	Y	N
13 Pease	Y	Y	Y	N	Y
14 Sawyer	Y	Y	Y	N	Y
15 ***Wylie***	Y	N	Y	Y	N
16 ***Regula***	Y	Y	N	Y	Y
17 Traficant	Y	Y	Y	N	Y
18 Applegate	Y	Y	Y	N	Y
19 Feighan	Y	Y	Y	N	Y
20 Oakar	Y	N	Y	N	Y
21 Stokes	Y	Y	Y	N	Y
OKLAHOMA					
1 ***Inhofe***	Y	N	N	Y	N
2 Synar	Y	Y	Y	N	Y
3 Watkins	Y	Y	Y	N	Y
4 McCurdy	Y	Y	Y	N	Y
5 ***Edwards***	Y	N	N	Y	N
6 English	Y	Y	Y	N	Y
OREGON					
1 AuCoin	Y	N	Y	N	Y
2 ***Smith, B.***	Y	N	N	Y	N
3 Wyden	Y	Y	Y	N	Y
4 DeFazio	Y	Y	Y	N	Y
5 ***Smith, D.***	Y	N	N	Y	N
PENNSYLVANIA					
1 Foglietta	Y	N	Y	N	Y
2 Gray	Y	Y	Y	N	Y
3 Borski	Y	Y	Y	N	Y
4 Kolter	Y	Y	Y	N	Y
5 ***Schulze***	N	Y	Y	Y	Y
6 Yatron	Y	Y	Y	N	Y
7 ***Weldon***	Y	Y	N	Y	Y
8 Kostmayer	Y	N	Y	N	Y
9 ***Shuster***	Y	N	Y	Y	N
10 ***McDade***	?	?	Y	Y	N
11 Kanjorski	Y	Y	Y	N	Y
12 Murtha	Y	Y	Y	N	Y
13 ***Coughlin***	Y	N	N	Y	Y
14 Coyne	Y	Y	Y	N	Y
15 ***Ritter***	Y	Y	Y	Y	N
16 ***Walker***	N	N	N	Y	N
17 ***Gekas***	Y	N	N	Y	N
18 Walgren	Y	Y	Y	N	Y
19 ***Goodling***	N	N	N	Y	N
20 Gaydos	Y	Y	Y	N	Y
21 ***Ridge***	Y	Y	N	Y	N
22 Murphy	Y	Y	N	Y	Y
23 ***Clinger***	N	N	Y	Y	N
RHODE ISLAND					
1 ***Machtley***	Y	Y	N	Y	Y
2 ***Schneider***	Y	Y	Y	N	Y
SOUTH CAROLINA					
1 ***Ravenel***	Y	Y	Y	Y	N
2 ***Spence***	Y	Y	N	Y	N
3 Derrick	Y	Y	Y	N	Y
4 Patterson	Y	Y	Y	N	Y
5 Spratt	Y	Y	Y	N	Y
6 Tallon	Y	Y	Y	N	Y
SOUTH DAKOTA					
AL Johnson	Y	Y	Y	N	Y
TENNESSEE					
1 ***Quillen***	Y	Y	Y	Y	N
2 ***Duncan***	Y	Y	N	Y	N
3 Lloyd	Y	Y	?	N	Y
4 Cooper	Y	Y	Y	N	Y
5 Clement	Y	Y	Y	N	Y
6 Gordon	Y	Y	Y	N	Y
7 ***Sundquist***	Y	N	N	Y	N
8 Tanner	Y	Y	Y	N	Y
9 Ford	?	?	?	N	Y
TEXAS					
1 Chapman	Y	Y	Y	Y	Y
2 Wilson	Y	Y	Y	N	Y
3 ***Bartlett***	Y	N	Y	Y	N
4 Hall	?	?	?	?	?
5 Bryant	Y	N	?	N	Y
6 ***Barton***	Y	Y	N	Y	Y
7 ***Archer***	N	N	Y	Y	N
8 ***Fields***	Y	Y	?	Y	N
9 Brooks	Y	Y	Y	N	Y
10 Pickle	Y	Y	?	N	Y
11 Leath	?	?	?	?	?
12 Geren	Y	Y	Y	Y	Y
13 Sarpalius	Y	Y	Y	Y	N
14 Laughlin	Y	Y	Y	Y	Y
15 de la Garza	Y	Y	Y	N	Y
16 Coleman	Y	N	Y	N	Y
17 Stenholm	Y	Y	Y	Y	N
18 Washington	Y	N	Y	N	Y
19 ***Combest***	Y	N	Y	Y	N
20 Gonzalez	Y	Y	Y	N	Y
21 ***Smith***	Y	Y	N	Y	N
22 ***DeLay***	N	N	N	Y	N
23 Bustamante	Y	Y	Y	N	Y
24 Frost	Y	Y	?	N	Y
25 Andrews	Y	Y	Y	N	Y
26 ***Armey***	N	N	N	Y	N
27 Ortiz	Y	Y	Y	N	Y
UTAH					
1 ***Hansen***	Y	N	N	Y	N
2 Owens	Y	Y	Y	N	Y
3 ***Nielson***	Y	N	?	Y	N
VERMONT					
AL ***Smith***	Y	Y	N	Y	Y
VIRGINIA					
1 ***Bateman***	Y	N	Y	Y	N
2 Pickett	Y	Y	Y	N	Y
3 ***Bliley***	Y	Y	N	Y	N
4 Sisisky	Y	Y	Y	N	Y
5 Payne	Y	Y	Y	Y	Y
6 Olin	Y	Y	Y	N	Y
7 ***Slaughter***	Y	N	N	Y	N
8 ***Parris***	Y	N	N	Y	N
9 Boucher	Y	Y	Y	N	Y
10 ***Wolf***	Y	N	N	Y	N
WASHINGTON					
1 ***Miller***	Y	Y	N	Y	N
2 Swift	Y	Y	Y	N	Y
3 Unsoeld	Y	Y	Y	N	Y
4 ***Morrison***	Y	N	N	Y	N
5 Foley					
6 Dicks	Y	Y	Y	N	Y
7 McDermott	Y	Y	Y	N	Y
8 ***Chandler***	Y	N	N	Y	N
WEST VIRGINIA					
1 Mollohan	Y	Y	Y	N	Y
2 Staggers	Y	Y	Y	N	Y
3 Wise	Y	Y	Y	N	Y
4 Rahall	Y	Y	Y	N	Y
WISCONSIN					
1 Aspin	Y	Y	Y	N	Y
2 Kastenmeier	Y	N	Y	N	Y
3 ***Gunderson***	N	N	Y	Y	N
4 Kleczka	Y	Y	Y	N	Y
5 Moody	Y	Y	Y	N	Y
6 ***Petri***	Y	Y	N	Y	N
7 Obey	Y	Y	Y	N	Y
8 ***Roth***	Y	N	Y	Y	N
9 ***Sensenbrenner***	N	N	N	Y	N
WYOMING					
AL ***Thomas***	Y	N	N	Y	N

Southern states - Ala., Ark., Fla., Ga., Ky., La., Miss., N.C., Okla., S.C., Tenn., Texas, Va.
Omitted votes are quorum calls, which CQ does not include in its vote charts.

311. HR 5350. Short-Term Debt Limit Increase/Previous Question. Cooper, D-Tenn., motion to order the previous question (thus ending debate and the possibility of amendment) on the rule (H Res 448) to provide for House floor consideration of the bill to provide for a temporary increase in the statutory public debt limit of $72 billion from $3.123 trillion to $3.195 trillion through Oct. 2, at which time the debt ceiling would drop back to $3.123 trillion. Motion agreed to 284-131: R 41-128; D 243-3 (ND 167-3, SD 76-0), Aug. 3, 1990.

312. HR 5350. Short-Term Debt Limit Increase/Rule. Adoption of the rule (H Res 448) to provide for House floor consideration of the bill to provide for a temporary increase in the statutory public debt limit of $72 billion from $3.123 trillion to $3.195 trillion through Oct. 2, at which time the debt ceiling would drop back to $3.123 trillion. Adopted 285-126: R 46-123; D 239-3 (ND 163-2, SD 76-1), Aug. 3, 1990.

313. HR 5350. Short-Term Debt Limit Increase/Passage. Passage of the bill to provide for a temporary increase in the statutory public debt limit of $72 billion from $3.123 trillion to $3.195 trillion through Oct. 2, at which time the debt ceiling would drop back to $3.123 trillion. Passed 247-172: R 46-126; D 201-46 (ND 143-27, SD 58-19), Aug. 3, 1990.

314. HR 5400. Campaign Finance Overhaul/Rule. Adoption of the rule (H Res 453) to provide for House floor consideration of the bill to revise federal laws governing the financing of federal campaigns. Adopted 232-185: R 0-171; D 232-14 (ND 159-10, SD 73-4), Aug. 3, 1990.

315. Procedural Motion/Adjournment. Walker, R-Pa., motion to adjourn. Rejected 129-275: R 126-38; D 3-237 (ND 1-164, SD 2-73), Aug. 3, 1990.

KEY

- Y Voted for (yea).
- # Paired for.
- + Announced for.
- N Voted against (nay).
- X Paired against.
- \- Announced against.
- P Voted "present."
- C Voted "present" to avoid possible conflict of interest.
- ? Did not vote or otherwise make a position known.

Democrats ***Republicans***

	311	312	313	314	315
ALABAMA					
1 ***Callahan***	N	N	N	N	Y
2 ***Dickinson***	N	N	N	N	Y
3 Browder	Y	Y	Y	Y	N
4 Bevill	?	?	?	?	?
5 Flippo	Y	Y	Y	Y	N
6 Erdreich	Y	Y	N	Y	N
7 Harris	Y	Y	Y	Y	N
ALASKA					
AL ***Young***	N	N	N	N	Y
ARIZONA					
1 ***Rhodes***	N	N	N	N	Y
2 Udall	Y	Y	Y	Y	N
3 ***Stump***	Y	N	N	N	Y
4 ***Kyl***	N	N	N	N	Y
5 ***Kolbe***	N	N	N	N	Y
ARKANSAS					
1 Alexander	Y	Y	Y	N	Y
2 ***Robinson***	?	?	?	?	?
3 ***Hammerschmidt***	N	N	N	N	N
4 Anthony	Y	Y	Y	Y	N
CALIFORNIA					
1 Bosco	Y	Y	Y	Y	N
2 ***Herger***	N	N	N	N	Y
3 Matsui	Y	Y	Y	Y	N
4 Fazio	Y	Y	Y	Y	N
5 Pelosi	Y	Y	Y	Y	N
6 Boxer	Y	Y	Y	Y	N
7 Miller	Y	Y	Y	Y	N
8 Dellums	Y	Y	Y	Y	?
9 Stark	Y	Y	Y	Y	N
10 Edwards	Y	Y	Y	Y	N
11 Lantos	Y	Y	Y	Y	N
12 ***Campbell***	N	N	N	N	N
13 Mineta	Y	Y	Y	Y	N
14 ***Shumway***	N	N	N	N	Y
15 Condit	Y	Y	?	Y	N
16 Panetta	Y	Y	Y	Y	N
17 ***Pashayan***	Y	Y	N	N	N
18 Lehman	Y	Y	Y	Y	N
19 ***Lagomarsino***	N	N	N	N	Y
20 ***Thomas***	N	N	N	N	Y
21 ***Gallegly***	N	N	N	N	Y
22 ***Moorhead***	N	N	N	N	Y
23 Beilenson	Y	Y	Y	Y	N
24 Waxman	Y	Y	Y	Y	N
25 Roybal	Y	Y	Y	Y	N
26 Berman	Y	Y	Y	Y	N
27 Levine	Y	Y	Y	Y	N
28 Dixon	Y	Y	Y	Y	N
29 Hawkins	Y	Y	Y	Y	N
30 Martinez	?	?	Y	Y	N
31 Dymally	Y	Y	Y	Y	N
32 Anderson	Y	Y	Y	Y	N
33 ***Dreier***	N	N	N	N	Y
34 Torres	Y	Y	Y	?	N
35 ***Lewis***	N	N	N	N	Y
36 Brown	Y	Y	Y	Y	N
37 ***McCandless***	N	N	N	N	Y
38 ***Dornan***	N	?	N	N	Y
39 ***Dannemeyer***	N	N	N	N	Y
40 ***Cox***	?	?	N	N	Y
41 ***Lowery***	N	Y	Y	N	Y
42 ***Rohrabacher***	N	N	N	N	Y
43 ***Packard***	N	N	N	N	N
44 Bates	Y	Y	N	Y	N
45 ***Hunter***	Y	Y	Y	N	Y
COLORADO					
1 Schroeder	Y	Y	N	Y	N
2 Skaggs	Y	Y	Y	Y	N
3 Campbell	Y	Y	N	N	N
4 ***Brown***	N	N	N	N	N
5 ***Hefley***	N	N	N	N	Y
6 ***Schaefer***	N	N	N	N	Y
CONNECTICUT					
1 Kennelly	Y	Y	Y	Y	N
2 Gejdenson	Y	Y	Y	Y	N
3 Morrison	Y	Y	Y	Y	N
4 ***Shays***	N	N	N	N	N
5 ***Rowland***	N	N	N	N	Y
6 ***Johnson***	N	Y	Y	N	Y
DELAWARE					
AL Carper	Y	Y	Y	N	N
FLORIDA					
1 Hutto	Y	Y	N	Y	N
2 ***Grant***	Y	N	N	N	Y
3 Bennett	Y	Y	Y	N	N
4 ***James***	N	N	N	N	Y
5 ***McCollum***	N	N	N	N	Y
6 ***Stearns***	N	N	N	N	Y
7 Gibbons	Y	Y	Y	Y	N
8 ***Young***	N	N	N	N	N
9 ***Bilirakis***	?	?	?	?	?
10 ***Ireland***	N	N	N	N	Y
11 Nelson	+	+	#	#	-
12 ***Lewis***	N	N	N	N	Y
13 ***Goss***	N	N	N	N	Y
14 Johnston	Y	Y	Y	Y	N
15 ***Shaw***	Y	N	N	N	Y
16 Smith	Y	Y	Y	Y	N
17 Lehman	Y	Y	+	Y	N
18 ***Ros-Lehtinen***	N	N	N	N	Y
19 Fascell	Y	Y	Y	Y	N
GEORGIA					
1 Thomas	Y	Y	Y	Y	N
2 Hatcher	Y	Y	Y	Y	N
3 Ray	Y	Y	N	Y	N
4 Jones	Y	Y	Y	Y	N
5 Lewis	Y	Y	Y	Y	N
6 ***Gingrich***	N	Y	Y	N	Y
7 Darden	Y	Y	N	Y	N
8 Rowland	Y	Y	Y	Y	N
9 Jenkins	Y	Y	Y	Y	N
10 Barnard	Y	Y	Y	Y	N
HAWAII					
1 ***Saiki***	Y	Y	Y	N	N
2 Vacancy					
IDAHO					
1 ***Craig***	N	N	N	N	Y
2 Stallings	Y	Y	N	Y	N
ILLINOIS					
1 Hayes	Y	Y	Y	Y	N
2 Savage	Y	?	Y	Y	N
3 Russo	Y	Y	N	Y	N
4 Sangmeister	Y	Y	N	Y	N
5 Lipinski	Y	Y	Y	Y	N
6 ***Hyde***	N	N	Y	N	Y
7 Collins	Y	Y	Y	Y	N
8 Rostenkowski	Y	Y	Y	Y	N
9 Yates	Y	Y	Y	Y	N
10 ***Porter***	N	Y	Y	N	N
11 Annunzio	Y	Y	Y	Y	N
12 ***Crane***	N	N	N	N	Y
13 ***Fawell***	N	Y	N	N	Y
14 ***Hastert***	N	N	N	N	Y
15 ***Madigan***	Y	Y	Y	N	N
16 ***Martin***	N	N	N	N	?
17 Evans	Y	Y	Y	Y	N
18 ***Michel***	Y	Y	Y	N	N
19 Bruce	Y	Y	Y	Y	N
20 Durbin	Y	Y	Y	Y	N
21 Costello	Y	Y	N	Y	N
22 Poshard	Y	Y	N	Y	N
INDIANA					
1 Visclosky	Y	Y	N	Y	N
2 Sharp	Y	Y	Y	Y	N
3 ***Hiler***	N	N	N	N	Y

ND Northern Democrats SD Southern Democrats

	311	312	313	314	315
4 Long	Y	Y	Y	Y	N
5 Jontz	Y	Y	Y	Y	N
6 ***Burton***	N	N	N	N	Y
7 ***Myers***	N	N	N	N	Y
8 McCloskey	Y	Y	Y	Y	N
9 Hamilton	Y	Y	Y	Y	N
10 Jacobs	N	Y	N	N	N
IOWA					
1 ***Leach***	N	N	N	N	N
2 ***Tauke***	Y	N	N	N	Y
3 Nagle	Y	?	Y	Y	N
4 Smith	Y	Y	Y	Y	N
5 ***Lightfoot***	N	N	N	N	Y
6 ***Grandy***	N	N	N	N	Y
KANSAS					
1 ***Roberts***	N	Y	N	N	Y
2 Slattery	Y	Y	N	Y	N
3 ***Meyers***	N	Y	N	N	N
4 Glickman	Y	Y	Y	Y	N
5 ***Whittaker***	N	Y	N	N	Y
KENTUCKY					
1 Hubbard	Y	Y	N	Y	N
2 Natcher	Y	Y	Y	Y	N
3 Mazzoli	Y	Y	Y	Y	N
4 ***Bunning***	Y	N	N	N	Y
5 ***Rogers***	Y	N	N	N	Y
6 ***Hopkins***	Y	N	N	N	Y
7 Perkins	Y	Y	Y	Y	Y
LOUISIANA					
1 ***Livingston***	N	N	N	N	Y
2 Boggs	Y	Y	Y	Y	N
3 Tauzin	Y	Y	N	Y	N
4 ***McCrery***	N	Y	N	Y	Y
5 Huckaby	Y	Y	N	Y	N
6 ***Baker***	N	N	N	N	Y
7 Hayes	?	Y	Y	Y	N
8 ***Holloway***	N	N	N	N	Y
MAINE					
1 Brennan	Y	Y	Y	Y	N
2 ***Snowe***	N	N	N	N	N
MARYLAND					
1 Dyson	Y	Y	N	Y	N
2 ***Bentley***	N	N	N	N	N
3 Cardin	Y	Y	Y	Y	N
4 McMillen	Y	Y	Y	Y	N
5 Hoyer	Y	Y	Y	Y	N
6 Byron	Y	Y	N	Y	N
7 Mfume	Y	Y	Y	Y	N
8 ***Morella***	Y	Y	Y	N	N
MASSACHUSETTS					
1 ***Conte***	Y	Y	Y	N	Y
2 Neal	N	N	N	Y	N
3 Early	N	N	N	N	Y
4 Frank	Y	Y	Y	Y	?
5 Atkins	Y	Y	Y	Y	N
6 Mavroules	?	?	Y	Y	N
7 Markey	Y	Y	Y	Y	N
8 Kennedy	Y	Y	Y	Y	N
9 Moakley	Y	Y	Y	Y	N
10 Studds	Y	Y	Y	Y	N
11 Donnelly	Y	Y	Y	N	N
MICHIGAN					
1 Conyers	Y	Y	Y	Y	N
2 ***Pursell***	?	?	X	X	?
3 Wolpe	Y	Y	Y	Y	N
4 ***Upton***	N	N	N	N	Y
5 ***Henry***	N	N	N	N	Y
6 Carr	Y	Y	Y	N	N
7 Kildee	Y	Y	Y	Y	N
8 Traxler	Y	Y	Y	Y	N
9 ***Vander Jagt***	Y	Y	Y	N	Y
10 ***Schuette***	?	?	?	?	?
11 ***Davis***	Y	Y	Y	N	N
12 Bonior	Y	Y	Y	Y	N
13 Crockett	Y	?	?	?	?
14 Hertel	Y	Y	Y	Y	N
15 Ford	?	?	?	#	?
16 Dingell	Y	Y	Y	Y	N
17 Levin	Y	Y	Y	Y	N
18 ***Broomfield***	N	N	N	N	Y
MINNESOTA					
1 Penny	Y	Y	N	Y	N
2 ***Weber***	N	N	N	N	Y
3 ***Frenzel***	Y	Y	Y	N	Y
4 Vento	Y	Y	Y	Y	N

	311	312	313	314	315
5 Sabo	Y	Y	Y	Y	N
6 Sikorski	Y	Y	Y	Y	N
7 ***Stangeland***	N	N	N	N	?
8 Oberstar	Y	Y	Y	Y	N
MISSISSIPPI					
1 Whitten	Y	Y	Y	Y	N
2 Espy	Y	Y	Y	Y	N
3 Montgomery	Y	Y	Y	Y	N
4 Parker	Y	Y	Y	Y	?
5 Taylor	Y	N	N	Y	N
MISSOURI					
1 Clay	Y	Y	Y	N	N
2 ***Buechner***	N	Y	N	N	N
3 Gephardt	Y	Y	Y	Y	N
4 Skelton	Y	Y	Y	Y	N
5 Wheat	Y	Y	Y	Y	N
6 ***Coleman***	N	N	Y	N	Y
7 ***Hancock***	N	N	N	N	Y
8 ***Emerson***	N	N	Y	N	N
9 Volkmer	Y	Y	Y	Y	N
MONTANA					
1 Williams	Y	Y	Y	Y	N
2 ***Marlenee***	N	N	N	N	Y
NEBRASKA					
1 ***Bereuter***	N	N	N	N	N
2 Hoagland	Y	Y	N	Y	N
3 ***Smith***	N	N	N	N	?
NEVADA					
1 Bilbray	Y	Y	Y	Y	N
2 ***Vucanovich***	N	N	N	N	Y
NEW HAMPSHIRE					
1 ***Smith***	N	N	N	N	Y
2 ***Douglas***	N	N	N	N	Y
NEW JERSEY					
1 Vacancy					
2 Hughes	Y	Y	Y	Y	N
3 Pallone	Y	Y	N	Y	N
4 ***Smith***	N	Y	Y	N	N
5 ***Roukema***	Y	Y	Y	X	?
6 Dwyer	Y	Y	Y	Y	N
7 ***Rinaldo***	N	N	N	N	N
8 Roe	Y	Y	Y	N	N
9 Torricelli	Y	Y	Y	N	N
10 Payne	Y	Y	Y	Y	N
11 ***Gallo***	Y	Y	Y	N	N
12 ***Courter***	N	N	N	N	Y
13 ***Saxton***	N	N	N	N	N
14 Guarini	Y	Y	Y	Y	N
NEW MEXICO					
1 ***Schiff***	N	N	Y	N	Y
2 ***Skeen***	N	Y	Y	N	Y
3 Richardson	Y	Y	Y	Y	N
NEW YORK					
1 Hochbrueckner	Y	Y	Y	Y	N
2 Downey	Y	Y	Y	Y	N
3 Mrazek	Y	Y	Y	Y	N
4 ***Lent***	Y	Y	Y	N	Y
5 ***McGrath***	Y	Y	Y	N	?
6 Flake	Y	Y	Y	Y	N
7 Ackerman	Y	Y	Y	Y	N
8 Scheuer	Y	Y	Y	Y	N
9 Manton	Y	Y	Y	Y	N
10 Schumer	Y	Y	Y	Y	N
11 Towns	Y	Y	Y	Y	N
12 Owens	Y	Y	Y	Y	N
13 Solarz	Y	Y	Y	Y	?
14 ***Molinari***	Y	N	Y	N	Y
15 ***Green***	Y	Y	Y	N	N
16 Rangel	Y	Y	Y	Y	N
17 Weiss	Y	Y	Y	Y	N
18 Serrano	Y	Y	Y	Y	N
19 Engel	Y	Y	Y	Y	N
20 Lowey	Y	Y	Y	Y	N
21 ***Fish***	Y	Y	Y	N	Y
22 ***Gilman***	N	N	N	N	N
23 McNulty	Y	Y	Y	Y	N
24 ***Solomon***	Y	N	N	N	Y
25 ***Boehlert***	Y	Y	Y	N	N
26 ***Martin***	Y	N	N	N	Y
27 ***Walsh***	N	N	Y	N	Y
28 McHugh	Y	Y	Y	Y	N
29 ***Horton***	Y	Y	Y	N	N
30 Slaughter	Y	Y	Y	Y	N
31 ***Paxon***	N	N	N	N	Y

	311	312	313	314	315
32 LaFalce	Y	Y	Y	Y	N
33 Nowak	Y	Y	Y	Y	N
34 ***Houghton***	N	N	N	N	N
NORTH CAROLINA					
1 Jones	Y	Y	Y	Y	N
2 Valentine	Y	Y	N	Y	?
3 Lancaster	Y	Y	Y	Y	N
4 Price	Y	Y	Y	Y	N
5 Neal	Y	Y	N	Y	N
6 ***Coble***	N	N	N	N	Y
7 Rose	Y	Y	Y	Y	N
8 Hefner	Y	Y	Y	Y	N
9 ***McMillan***	N	N	N	N	Y
10 ***Ballenger***	N	N	N	N	Y
11 Clarke	Y	Y	Y	Y	N
NORTH DAKOTA					
AL Dorgan	Y	Y	N	Y	N
OHIO					
1 Luken	Y	Y	Y	?	?
2 ***Gradison***	Y	Y	Y	N	Y
3 Hall	Y	Y	Y	Y	?
4 ***Oxley***	Y	Y	Y	N	Y
5 ***Gillmor***	N	Y	Y	N	N
6 ***McEwen***	N	N	N	N	Y
7 ***DeWine***	N	N	N	N	N
8 ***Lukens***	N	N	N	N	Y
9 Kaptur	Y	Y	Y	Y	N
10 ***Miller***	Y	Y	N	N	Y
11 Eckart	Y	Y	N	Y	N
12 ***Kasich***	N	N	N	N	Y
13 Pease	Y	Y	Y	Y	N
14 Sawyer	Y	Y	Y	Y	N
15 ***Wylie***	Y	Y	Y	N	Y
16 ***Regula***	N	Y	N	N	N
17 Traficant	Y	Y	N	N	N
18 Applegate	Y	Y	N	Y	N
19 Feighan	Y	Y	Y	Y	N
20 Oakar	Y	Y	Y	Y	N
21 Stokes	Y	?	Y	Y	N
OKLAHOMA					
1 ***Inhofe***	N	N	N	N	Y
2 Synar	Y	Y	Y	Y	N
3 Watkins	?	?	?	?	?
4 McCurdy	Y	Y	N	Y	N
5 ***Edwards***	N	N	N	N	Y
6 English	Y	Y	N	N	N
OREGON					
1 AuCoin	Y	Y	Y	Y	N
2 ***Smith, B.***	N	N	N	N	Y
3 Wyden	Y	Y	N	Y	N
4 DeFazio	Y	Y	Y	Y	N
5 ***Smith, D.***	N	N	N	N	Y
PENNSYLVANIA					
1 Foglietta	Y	Y	Y	Y	N
2 Gray	Y	Y	Y	Y	?
3 Borski	Y	Y	Y	Y	N
4 Kolter	Y	Y	N	Y	N
5 ***Schulze***	N	N	N	N	Y
6 Yatron	Y	Y	N	Y	N
7 ***Weldon***	Y	N	N	N	Y
8 Kostmayer	Y	Y	Y	Y	N
9 ***Shuster***	N	N	N	N	Y
10 ***McDade***	N	Y	Y	N	N
11 Kanjorski	Y	Y	Y	Y	N
12 Murtha	Y	Y	Y	Y	N
13 ***Coughlin***	?	?	N	N	Y
14 Coyne	Y	Y	Y	Y	N
15 ***Ritter***	N	N	N	N	Y
16 ***Walker***	N	N	N	N	Y
17 ***Gekas***	N	N	N	N	Y
18 Walgren	Y	Y	Y	Y	N
19 ***Goodling***	Y	Y	Y	N	Y
20 Gaydos	Y	Y	N	Y	N
21 ***Ridge***	?	N	N	N	Y
22 Murphy	Y	Y	N	Y	N
23 ***Clinger***	Y	Y	N	N	Y
RHODE ISLAND					
1 ***Machtley***	N	N	N	N	N
2 ***Schneider***	N	N	N	N	N
SOUTH CAROLINA					
1 ***Ravenel***	N	N	N	N	Y
2 ***Spence***	N	N	N	N	Y
3 Derrick	Y	Y	Y	Y	N
4 Patterson	Y	Y	Y	Y	N
5 Spratt	Y	Y	Y	Y	N
6 Tallon	Y	Y	N	Y	N

	311	312	313	314	315
SOUTH DAKOTA					
AL Johnson	Y	?	Y	Y	N
TENNESSEE					
1 ***Quillen***	Y	N	N	N	Y
2 ***Duncan***	N	N	N	N	Y
3 Lloyd	Y	Y	Y	Y	N
4 Cooper	Y	Y	N	Y	N
5 Clement	Y	Y	Y	Y	N
6 Gordon	Y	Y	Y	Y	N
7 ***Sundquist***	N	N	N	N	Y
8 Tanner	Y	Y	N	N	N
9 Ford	Y	Y	Y	Y	N
TEXAS					
1 Chapman	Y	Y	Y	Y	N
2 Wilson	?	?	Y	Y	N
3 ***Bartlett***	N	N	N	N	Y
4 Hall	?	?	?	?	?
5 Bryant	Y	Y	N	Y	N
6 ***Barton***	N	N	N	N	Y
7 ***Archer***	N	N	Y	N	Y
8 ***Fields***	N	N	N	N	?
9 Brooks	Y	Y	Y	Y	N
10 Pickle	Y	Y	Y	Y	N
11 Leath	?	?	?	?	?
12 Geren	Y	Y	Y	Y	N
13 Sarpalius	Y	Y	Y	Y	N
14 Laughlin	Y	Y	N	Y	N
15 de la Garza	Y	Y	Y	Y	?
16 Coleman	Y	Y	Y	Y	N
17 Stenholm	Y	Y	Y	Y	N
18 Washington	Y	Y	Y	?	N
19 ***Combest***	N	N	N	N	Y
20 Gonzalez	Y	Y	N	Y	N
21 ***Smith***	N	N	N	N	N
22 ***DeLay***	N	N	N	N	Y
23 Bustamante	Y	Y	Y	Y	N
24 Frost	Y	Y	Y	Y	N
25 Andrews	Y	Y	Y	Y	N
26 ***Armey***	N	N	N	N	Y
27 Ortiz	Y	Y	Y	Y	N
UTAH					
1 ***Hansen***	N	N	N	N	Y
2 Owens	Y	Y	Y	Y	N
3 ***Nielson***	Y	Y	N	N	?
VERMONT					
AL ***Smith***	N	Y	Y	N	Y
VIRGINIA					
1 ***Bateman***	N	Y	Y	N	Y
2 Pickett	Y	Y	N	Y	N
3 ***Bliley***	N	Y	Y	N	Y
4 Sisisky	Y	Y	Y	Y	N
5 Payne	Y	Y	Y	Y	N
6 Olin	Y	Y	Y	Y	N
7 ***Slaughter***	N	N	N	N	Y
8 ***Parris***	Y	N	N	N	Y
9 Boucher	Y	Y	Y	Y	N
10 ***Wolf***	Y	Y	Y	N	Y
WASHINGTON					
1 ***Miller***	N	N	Y	N	Y
2 Swift	Y	Y	Y	Y	N
3 Unsoeld	Y	Y	Y	Y	N
4 ***Morrison***	Y	Y	Y	N	N
5 Foley					
6 Dicks	Y	Y	Y	Y	N
7 McDermott	Y	Y	Y	Y	N
8 ***Chandler***	N	Y	Y	N	Y
WEST VIRGINIA					
1 Mollohan	Y	Y	Y	Y	N
2 Staggers	Y	Y	Y	Y	N
3 Wise	Y	Y	Y	Y	N
4 Rahall	Y	Y	Y	Y	N
WISCONSIN					
1 Aspin	Y	Y	Y	Y	N
2 Kastenmeier	Y	Y	Y	Y	N
3 ***Gunderson***	N	N	N	N	Y
4 Kleczka	Y	Y	Y	Y	N
5 Moody	Y	Y	Y	Y	N
6 ***Petri***	N	N	N	N	?
7 Obey	Y	Y	Y	Y	N
8 ***Roth***	N	N	N	N	N
9 ***Sensenbrenner***	N	N	N	N	Y
WYOMING					
AL ***Thomas***	Y	N	Y	N	Y

Southern states - Ala., Ark., Fla., Ga., Ky., La., Miss., N.C., Okla., S.C., Tenn., Texas, Va.
Omitted votes are quorum calls, which CQ does not include in its vote charts.

316. HR 5400. Campaign Finance Overhaul/GOP Substitute. Michel, R-Ill., substitute amendment to lower the limit on political action committee (PAC) contributions from $5,000 to $1,000 per candidate; require that at least half of a House candidate's campaign funds come from his constituents; ban leadership PACs; prohibit the transfer between PACs and candidate committees; ban the use of "soft money" by state and federal parties; and prohibit the use of union or corporate funds for nonpartisan registration and get-out-the-vote efforts directed at people connected with the union or the corporation. Rejected 169-241: R 166-1; D 3-240 (ND 1-165, SD 2-75), Aug. 3, 1990.

317. HR 5400. Campaign Finance Overhaul/PAC Limits. Synar, D-Okla., en bloc amendments to limit the total political action committee (PAC) contributions to $220,000 per House candidate; limit to $55,000 the amount a candidate can receive from a PAC that accepts contributions over $240 per member; provide up to $100,000 per candidate in federal funds to match small, individual in-state contributions of less than $50 for House candidates; and to reduce the amount an individual may contribute to federal candidates from $1,000 to $500 per election. Rejected 122-128: R 11-9; D 111-119 (ND 99-55, SD 12-64), Aug. 3, 1990.

318. HR 5400. Campaign Finance Overhaul/Passage. Passage of the bill to set voluntary spending limits of $550,000 per House candidate in return for lower broadcast and mail costs; cap total political action committee (PAC) contributions at $275,000 per House candidate; limit the amount a candidate can receive from a PAC to $1,000 per election unless the PAC only takes contributions of $240 or less per person (then the limit would remain at $5,000); and close loopholes dealing with independent expenditures, bundling and "soft money." Passed 255-155: R 15-152; D 240-3 (ND 165-1, SD 75-2), Aug. 3, 1990. A "nay" was a vote supporting the president's position.

319. HR 1465. Oil-Spill Liability and Compensation/Previous Question. Bonior, D-Mich., motion to order the previous question (thus ending debate and the possibility of amendment) on the rule (H Res 452) to provide for House floor consideration and waive all points of order against the conference report on the bill to provide comprehensive oil-spill liability and compensation, cleanup and prevention measures. The bill would leave states free to maintain their own oil-spill cleanup funds and enforce their own liability laws. Adopted 281-82: R 76-79; D 205-3 (ND 143-1, SD 62-2), Aug. 4, 1990 (in the session that began, and the Congressional Record dated, Aug. 3, 1990). A "nay" was a vote supporting the president's position.

320. HR 1465. Oil-Spill Liability and Compensation/Conference Report. Adoption of the conference report on the bill to provide comprehensive oil-spill liability and compensation, cleanup and prevention measures. The bill would leave states free to maintain their own oil-spill cleanup funds and enforce their own liability laws. Adopted 360-0: R 155-0; D 205-0 (ND 143-0, SD 62-0), Aug. 4, 1990 (in the session that began, and the Congressinal Record dated, Aug. 3, 1990).

KEY

- Y Voted for (yea).
- # Paired for.
- + Announced for.
- N Voted against (nay).
- X Paired against.
- - Announced against.
- P Voted "present."
- C Voted "present" to avoid possible conflict of interest.
- ? Did not vote or otherwise make a position known.

Democrats ***Republicans***

	316	317	318	319	320
ALABAMA					
1 ***Callahan***	Y	P	N	N	Y
2 ***Dickinson***	Y	P	N	Y	Y
3 Browder	N	N	Y	Y	Y
4 Bevill	?	?	?	?	?
5 Flippo	N	N	Y	?	?
6 Erdreich	N	N	Y	Y	Y
7 Harris	N	N	Y	Y	Y
ALASKA					
AL ***Young***	Y	P	N	Y	Y
ARIZONA					
1 ***Rhodes***	Y	P	N	N	Y
2 Udall	N	Y	Y	?	?
3 ***Stump***	Y	P	N	N	Y
4 ***Kyl***	Y	P	N	N	Y
5 ***Kolbe***	Y	P	N	N	Y
ARKANSAS					
1 Alexander	N	N	Y	?	?
2 ***Robinson***	#	?	X	?	?
3 ***Hammerschmidt***	Y	P	N	N	Y
4 Anthony	N	N	Y	Y	Y
CALIFORNIA					
1 Bosco	?	?	?	Y	Y
2 ***Herger***	Y	N	N	N	Y
3 Matsui	N	Y	Y	Y	Y
4 Fazio	N	Y	Y	Y	Y
5 Pelosi	N	Y	Y	Y	Y
6 Boxer	N	Y	Y	Y	Y
7 Miller	N	Y	Y	Y	Y
8 Dellums	N	Y	Y	Y	Y
9 Stark	N	Y	Y	?	?
10 Edwards	N	Y	Y	?	?
11 Lantos	N	N	Y	?	?
12 ***Campbell***	Y	Y	N	Y	Y
13 Mineta	N	P	Y	Y	Y
14 ***Shumway***	P	N	N	N	Y
15 Condit	N	Y	Y	Y	Y
16 Panetta	N	Y	Y	Y	Y
17 ***Pashayan***	Y	P	N	Y	Y
18 Lehman	N	Y	Y	?	?
19 ***Lagomarsino***	Y	P	N	Y	Y
20 ***Thomas***	Y	P	N	N	Y
21 ***Gallegly***	Y	P	N	Y	Y
22 ***Moorhead***	Y	P	N	N	Y
23 Beilenson	N	Y	Y	Y	Y
24 Waxman	N	Y	Y	Y	Y
25 Roybal	N	Y	Y	Y	Y
26 Berman	N	Y	Y	Y	Y
27 Levine	N	Y	Y	Y	Y
28 Dixon	N	Y	Y	Y	Y
29 Hawkins	?	?	#	?	?
30 Martinez	N	N	Y	?	?
31 Dymally	N	Y	Y	Y	Y
32 Anderson	N	Y	Y	Y	Y
33 ***Dreier***	Y	P	N	Y	Y
34 Torres	N	N	Y	Y	Y
35 ***Lewis***	Y	P	N	N	Y
36 Brown	N	Y	Y	?	?
37 ***McCandless***	Y	P	N	N	Y
38 ***Dornan***	Y	P	N	N	Y
39 ***Dannemeyer***	Y	P	N	N	Y
40 ***Cox***	Y	P	N	Y	Y
41 ***Lowery***	Y	P	N	Y	Y
42 ***Rohrabacher***	Y	P	N	N	Y
43 ***Packard***	Y	P	N	N	Y
44 Bates	N	N	Y	Y	Y
45 ***Hunter***	Y	P	N	N	Y
COLORADO					
1 Schroeder	N	Y	Y	Y	Y
2 Skaggs	N	Y	Y	Y	Y
3 Campbell	N	Y	Y	Y	Y
4 ***Brown***	Y	N	N	N	Y
5 ***Hefley***	Y	P	N	N	Y
6 ***Schaefer***	Y	P	N	N	Y
CONNECTICUT					
1 Kennelly	N	Y	Y	Y	Y
2 Gejdenson	N	Y	Y	Y	Y
3 Morrison	N	Y	Y	Y	?
4 ***Shays***	Y	Y	Y	Y	Y
5 ***Rowland***	Y	P	N	Y	Y
6 ***Johnson***	Y	P	N	Y	Y
DELAWARE					
AL Carper	N	Y	Y	Y	Y
FLORIDA					
1 Hutto	N	N	Y	Y	Y
2 ***Grant***	Y	P	N	Y	Y
3 Bennett	Y	N	Y	Y	Y
4 ***James***	Y	P	N	Y	Y
5 ***McCollum***	Y	P	N	Y	Y
6 ***Stearns***	Y	P	N	Y	Y
7 Gibbons	N	N	Y	Y	Y
8 ***Young***	Y	P	N	Y	Y
9 ***Bilirakis***	?	?	?	?	?
10 ***Ireland***	Y	P	N	Y	Y
11 Nelson	X	+	#	+	+
12 ***Lewis***	Y	P	Y	Y	Y
13 ***Goss***	Y	P	N	Y	Y
14 Johnston	N	Y	Y	Y	Y
15 ***Shaw***	Y	P	N	Y	Y
16 Smith	N	Y	Y	?	?
17 Lehman	N	Y	Y	?	?
18 ***Ros-Lehtinen***	Y	P	N	Y	Y
19 Fascell	N	Y	Y	Y	Y
GEORGIA					
1 Thomas	N	N	Y	Y	Y
2 Hatcher	N	N	Y	?	?
3 Ray	X	?	#	?	?
4 Jones	N	N	Y	Y	Y
5 Lewis	N	Y	Y	Y	Y
6 ***Gingrich***	Y	P	N	N	Y
7 Darden	N	N	Y	Y	Y
8 Rowland	N	N	Y	Y	Y
9 Jenkins	N	N	Y	Y	Y
10 Barnard	N	N	Y	Y	Y
HAWAII					
1 ***Saiki***	Y	P	Y	Y	Y
2 Vacancy					
IDAHO					
1 ***Craig***	Y	P	N	N	Y
2 Stallings	N	N	Y	Y	Y
ILLINOIS					
1 Hayes	N	N	Y	Y	Y
2 Savage	Y	Y	Y	?	?
3 Russo	N	N	Y	Y	Y
4 Sangmeister	N	N	Y	Y	Y
5 Lipinski	N	N	Y	Y	Y
6 ***Hyde***	Y	Y	N	N	Y
7 Collins	N	N	Y	Y	Y
8 Rostenkowski	N	N	Y	Y	Y
9 Yates	N	Y	Y	?	?
10 ***Porter***	Y	P	N	N	Y
11 Annunzio	N	N	Y	Y	Y
12 ***Crane***	?	?	?	?	?
13 ***Fawell***	Y	P	N	N	Y
14 ***Hastert***	Y	P	N	N	Y
15 ***Madigan***	Y	P	N	?	?
16 ***Martin***	Y	P	N	Y	Y
17 Evans	N	Y	Y	Y	Y
18 ***Michel***	Y	P	N	N	Y
19 Bruce	N	N	Y	Y	Y
20 Durbin	N	N	Y	Y	Y
21 Costello	N	N	Y	Y	Y
22 Poshard	N	N	Y	Y	Y
INDIANA					
1 Visclosky	N	N	Y	Y	Y
2 Sharp	N	Y	Y	Y	Y
3 ***Hiler***	Y	P	N	Y	Y

ND Northern Democrats SD Southern Democrats

	316	317	318	319	320
4 Long	N	N	Y	Y	Y
5 Jontz	N	N	Y	Y	Y
6 ***Burton***	Y	P	N	N	Y
7 ***Myers***	Y	?	N	N	Y
8 McCloskey	N	Y	Y	Y	Y
9 Hamilton	N	Y	Y	Y	Y
10 Jacobs	N	Y	Y	N	Y
IOWA					
1 ***Leach***	Y	Y	Y	N	Y
2 ***Tauke***	Y	P	N	Y	Y
3 Nagle	N	N	Y	?	Y
4 Smith	N	N	Y	Y	Y
5 ***Lightfoot***	Y	P	N	N	Y
6 ***Grandy***	Y	P	N	N	Y
KANSAS					
1 ***Roberts***	Y	P	N	N	Y
2 Slattery	N	N	Y	Y	Y
3 ***Meyers***	Y	P	N	Y	Y
4 Glickman	N	Y	Y	Y	Y
5 ***Whittaker***	Y	P	N	N	Y
KENTUCKY					
1 Hubbard	N	N	Y	Y	Y
2 Natcher	N	N	Y	Y	Y
3 Mazzoli	N	Y	Y	Y	Y
4 ***Bunning***	Y	P	N	N	Y
5 ***Rogers***	Y	P	N	N	Y
6 ***Hopkins***	Y	P	N	N	Y
7 Perkins	N	N	N	Y	Y
LOUISIANA					
1 ***Livingston***	Y	P	N	N	Y
2 Boggs	N	N	Y	N	Y
3 Tauzin	N	N	Y	Y	Y
4 ***McCrery***	?	?	?	?	?
5 Huckaby	N	N	Y	Y	Y
6 ***Baker***	Y	P	N	N	Y
7 Hayes	N	N	Y	Y	Y
8 ***Holloway***	Y	P	N	N	?
MAINE					
1 Brennan	N	Y	Y	Y	Y
2 ***Snowe***	Y	P	N	Y	Y
MARYLAND					
1 Dyson	N	N	Y	Y	Y
2 ***Bentley***	Y	P	N	Y	Y
3 Cardin	N	Y	Y	Y	Y
4 McMillen	N	Y	Y	Y	Y
5 Hoyer	N	P	Y	Y	Y
6 Byron	N	N	Y	Y	Y
7 Mfume	N	Y	Y	Y	Y
8 ***Morella***	Y	Y	Y	Y	Y
MASSACHUSETTS					
1 ***Conte***	Y	Y	Y	Y	Y
2 Neal	N	Y	Y	Y	Y
3 Early	N	N	Y	Y	Y
4 Frank	N	N	Y	Y	Y
5 Atkins	N	N	Y	Y	Y
6 Mavroules	N	Y	Y	Y	?
7 Markey	N	N	Y	Y	Y
8 Kennedy	N	Y	Y	Y	Y
9 Moakley	N	N	Y	Y	Y
10 Studds	N	Y	Y	Y	Y
11 Donnelly	N	Y	Y	?	?
MICHIGAN					
1 Conyers	N	Y	Y	?	Y
2 ***Pursell***	#	?	X	?	?
3 Wolpe	N	Y	Y	Y	Y
4 ***Upton***	Y	P	N	Y	Y
5 ***Henry***	Y	P	N	Y	Y
6 Carr	N	N	N	Y	Y
7 Kildee	N	Y	Y	Y	Y
8 Traxler	?	?	?	?	?
9 ***Vander Jagt***	Y	P	N	?	?
10 ***Schuette***	?	?	?	?	?
11 ***Davis***	Y	N	N	Y	Y
12 Bonior	N	Y	Y	Y	Y
13 Crockett	?	?	?	?	?
14 Hertel	N	Y	Y	Y	Y
15 Ford	?	?	?	?	?
16 Dingell	N	N	Y	Y	Y
17 Levin	N	P	Y	Y	Y
18 ***Broomfield***	Y	P	N	?	?
MINNESOTA					
1 Penny	N	P	Y	Y	Y
2 ***Weber***	Y	P	N	?	?
3 ***Frenzel***	Y	P	N	N	Y
4 Vento	N	Y	Y	Y	Y
5 Sabo	N	P	Y	Y	Y
6 Sikorski	N	P	Y	Y	Y
7 ***Stangeland***	Y	P	N	Y	Y
8 Oberstar	N	Y	Y	Y	Y
MISSISSIPPI					
1 Whitten	N	N	Y	Y	Y
2 Espy	N	N	Y	Y	Y
3 Montgomery	N	N	Y	?	?
4 Parker	N	N	Y	Y	Y
5 Taylor	Y	N	Y	Y	Y
MISSOURI					
1 Clay	N	Y	Y	Y	?
2 ***Buechner***	Y	P	N	Y	Y
3 Gephardt	N	Y	Y	Y	Y
4 Skelton	N	N	Y	?	?
5 Wheat	N	N	Y	Y	Y
6 ***Coleman***	Y	P	N	Y	Y
7 ***Hancock***	Y	P	N	N	Y
8 ***Emerson***	Y	P	N	N	Y
9 Volkmer	N	N	Y	Y	Y
MONTANA					
1 Williams	N	Y	Y	Y	Y
2 ***Marlenee***	Y	P	N	N	Y
NEBRASKA					
1 ***Bereuter***	Y	P	Y	N	Y
2 Hoagland	N	Y	Y	Y	Y
3 ***Smith***	Y	P	N	?	?
NEVADA					
1 Bilbray	N	N	Y	Y	Y
2 ***Vucanovich***	Y	P	N	N	Y
NEW HAMPSHIRE					
1 ***Smith***	Y	P	N	Y	Y
2 ***Douglas***	Y	P	N	Y	Y
NEW JERSEY					
1 Vacancy					
2 Hughes	N	N	Y	Y	Y
3 Pallone	N	Y	Y	Y	Y
4 ***Smith***	Y	P	Y	Y	Y
5 ***Roukema***	#	?	X	?	?
6 Dwyer	N	Y	Y	?	?
7 ***Rinaldo***	Y	Y	Y	Y	Y
8 Roe	N	N	Y	Y	Y
9 Torricelli	N	N	Y	Y	Y
10 Payne	N	Y	Y	Y	Y
11 ***Gallo***	Y	P	N	Y	Y
12 ***Courter***	Y	P	N	Y	Y
13 ***Saxton***	Y	P	N	Y	Y
14 Guarini	N	Y	Y	Y	Y
NEW MEXICO					
1 ***Schiff***	Y	P	N	Y	Y
2 ***Skeen***	Y	P	N	N	Y
3 Richardson	N	Y	Y	Y	Y
NEW YORK					
1 Hochbrueckner	N	P	Y	Y	Y
2 Downey	N	P	Y	Y	Y
3 Mrazek	N	N	Y	Y	Y
4 ***Lent***	Y	P	N	Y	Y
5 ***McGrath***	Y	N	N	Y	Y
6 Flake	X	?	#	?	?
7 Ackerman	N	Y	Y	Y	Y
8 Scheuer	N	Y	Y	Y	Y
9 Manton	N	N	Y	Y	Y
10 Schumer	N	Y	Y	Y	Y
11 Towns	N	Y	Y	Y	Y
12 Owens	N	Y	Y	Y	Y
13 Solarz	N	Y	Y	Y	Y
14 ***Molinari***	Y	P	N	Y	Y
15 ***Green***	Y	P	N	N	Y
16 Rangel	N	Y	Y	Y	Y
17 Weiss	N	Y	Y	Y	Y
18 Serrano	N	Y	Y	Y	Y
19 Engel	N	Y	Y	Y	Y
20 Lowey	N	Y	Y	Y	Y
21 ***Fish***	Y	P	N	?	?
22 ***Gilman***	Y	Y	Y	Y	Y
23 McNulty	N	Y	Y	Y	Y
24 ***Solomon***	Y	P	N	N	Y
25 ***Boehlert***	N	Y	Y	Y	Y
26 ***Martin***	Y	P	N	Y	Y
27 ***Walsh***	Y	P	N	Y	Y
28 McHugh	N	Y	Y	Y	Y
29 ***Horton***	Y	P	N	Y	Y
30 Slaughter	N	P	Y	Y	Y
31 ***Paxon***	Y	P	N	Y	Y
32 LaFalce	N	Y	Y	?	?
33 Nowak	N	Y	Y	Y	Y
34 ***Houghton***	Y	P	N	N	Y
NORTH CAROLINA					
1 Jones	N	N	Y	Y	Y
2 Valentine	N	N	Y	Y	Y
3 Lancaster	N	N	Y	Y	Y
4 Price	N	P	Y	Y	Y
5 Neal	N	N	Y	Y	Y
6 ***Coble***	Y	P	N	Y	Y
7 Rose	N	N	Y	Y	?
8 Hefner	N	N	Y	Y	Y
9 ***McMillan***	Y	P	N	Y	Y
10 ***Ballenger***	Y	P	N	Y	Y
11 Clarke	N	N	Y	?	?
NORTH DAKOTA					
AL Dorgan	N	Y	Y	Y	Y
OHIO					
1 Luken	?	?	?	?	?
2 ***Gradison***	Y	P	N	?	?
3 Hall	N	Y	Y	Y	Y
4 ***Oxley***	Y	P	N	N	Y
5 ***Gillmor***	Y	P	N	N	Y
6 ***McEwen***	Y	P	N	N	Y
7 ***DeWine***	Y	P	N	N	Y
8 ***Lukens***	Y	P	N	N	Y
9 Kaptur	N	Y	Y	Y	Y
10 ***Miller***	Y	?	N	N	Y
11 Eckart	N	Y	Y	Y	Y
12 ***Kasich***	Y	P	N	N	Y
13 Pease	N	N	Y	Y	Y
14 Sawyer	N	P	Y	Y	Y
15 ***Wylie***	?	?	?	?	?
16 ***Regula***	Y	N	N	N	Y
17 Traficant	N	N	Y	Y	Y
18 Applegate	N	N	Y	Y	Y
19 Feighan	N	N	Y	Y	Y
20 Oakar	N	Y	Y	?	?
21 Stokes	N	Y	Y	Y	Y
OKLAHOMA					
1 ***Inhofe***	Y	P	N	Y	Y
2 Synar	N	Y	Y	?	?
3 Watkins	?	?	?	?	?
4 McCurdy	N	N	Y	Y	Y
5 ***Edwards***	Y	P	N	N	Y
6 English	N	N	Y	Y	Y
OREGON					
1 AuCoin	N	Y	Y	Y	Y
2 ***Smith, B.***	Y	P	N	Y	Y
3 Wyden	N	N	Y	Y	Y
4 DeFazio	N	Y	Y	Y	Y
5 ***Smith, D.***	Y	P	N	Y	Y
PENNSYLVANIA					
1 Foglietta	N	P	Y	Y	Y
2 Gray	N	Y	Y	Y	Y
3 Borski	N	P	Y	Y	Y
4 Kolter	N	N	Y	?	?
5 ***Schulze***	Y	P	N	N	Y
6 Yatron	N	N	Y	?	?
7 ***Weldon***	Y	P	N	Y	Y
8 Kostmayer	N	Y	Y	Y	Y
9 ***Shuster***	Y	N	N	?	?
10 ***McDade***	Y	P	Y	?	?
11 Kanjorski	N	Y	Y	Y	Y
12 Murtha	N	N	Y	Y	Y
13 ***Coughlin***	Y	P	N	Y	Y
14 Coyne	N	Y	Y	?	?
15 ***Ritter***	Y	P	N	Y	Y
16 ***Walker***	Y	P	N	N	Y
17 ***Gekas***	Y	P	N	N	Y
18 Walgren	N	Y	Y	Y	Y
19 ***Goodling***	Y	P	N	?	Y
20 Gaydos	N	N	Y	?	?
21 ***Ridge***	Y	P	N	Y	Y
22 Murphy	N	N	Y	?	?
23 ***Clinger***	Y	P	N	N	Y
RHODE ISLAND					
1 ***Machtley***	Y	P	Y	Y	Y
2 ***Schneider***	Y	P	N	Y	Y
SOUTH CAROLINA					
1 ***Ravenel***	Y	P	N	Y	Y
2 ***Spence***	Y	P	N	Y	Y
3 Derrick	N	N	Y	Y	Y
4 Patterson	N	N	Y	Y	Y
5 Spratt	N	N	Y	Y	Y
6 Tallon	N	N	Y	?	?
SOUTH DAKOTA					
AL Johnson	N	Y	Y	Y	Y
TENNESSEE					
1 ***Quillen***	Y	?	X	?	?
2 ***Duncan***	Y	N	N	N	Y
3 Lloyd	N	N	Y	?	?
4 Cooper	N	N	Y	Y	Y
5 Clement	N	N	Y	Y	Y
6 Gordon	N	N	Y	Y	Y
7 ***Sundquist***	Y	P	N	N	Y
8 Tanner	N	N	Y	Y	Y
9 Ford	N	Y	Y	Y	Y
TEXAS					
1 Chapman	N	N	Y	Y	Y
2 Wilson	N	Y	Y	Y	Y
3 ***Bartlett***	Y	P	N	N	Y
4 Hall	?	?	?	?	?
5 Bryant	N	Y	Y	Y	Y
6 ***Barton***	Y	P	N	N	Y
7 ***Archer***	Y	P	N	N	Y
8 ***Fields***	Y	P	N	N	Y
9 Brooks	N	N	Y	Y	Y
10 Pickle	N	N	Y	Y	?
11 Leath	?	?	?	?	?
12 Geren	N	N	Y	Y	Y
13 Sarpalius	N	N	Y	Y	Y
14 Laughlin	N	N	Y	Y	Y
15 de la Garza	N	N	Y	Y	Y
16 Coleman	N	N	Y	Y	Y
17 Stenholm	N	N	Y	N	Y
18 Washington	N	Y	Y	Y	Y
19 ***Combest***	Y	P	N	N	Y
20 Gonzalez	N	Y	Y	Y	Y
21 ***Smith***	Y	P	N	N	Y
22 ***DeLay***	Y	P	N	N	Y
23 Bustamante	N	N	Y	?	?
24 Frost	N	N	Y	Y	Y
25 Andrews	N	N	Y	Y	Y
26 ***Armey***	Y	P	N	N	Y
27 Ortiz	N	N	Y	Y	Y
UTAH					
1 ***Hansen***	Y	P	N	?	?
2 Owens	N	Y	Y	Y	Y
3 ***Nielson***	Y	P	N	Y	Y
VERMONT					
AL ***Smith***	Y	Y	Y	Y	Y
VIRGINIA					
1 ***Bateman***	Y	P	N	N	Y
2 Pickett	N	N	N	Y	Y
3 ***Bliley***	Y	P	N	N	Y
4 Sisisky	N	N	Y	Y	Y
5 Payne	N	N	Y	Y	Y
6 Olin	N	N	Y	?	?
7 ***Slaughter***	Y	P	N	N	Y
8 ***Parris***	Y	P	N	N	Y
9 Boucher	N	N	Y	?	?
10 ***Wolf***	Y	P	N	N	Y
WASHINGTON					
1 ***Miller***	Y	Y	N	Y	Y
2 Swift	N	N	Y	Y	Y
3 Unsoeld	N	N	Y	Y	Y
4 ***Morrison***	Y	P	Y	Y	Y
5 Foley					
6 Dicks	N	N	Y	?	?
7 McDermott	N	Y	Y	Y	Y
8 ***Chandler***	Y	N	N	Y	Y
WEST VIRGINIA					
1 Mollohan	N	N	Y	Y	Y
2 Staggers	N	Y	Y	Y	Y
3 Wise	N	Y	Y	Y	Y
4 Rahall	N	Y	Y	Y	Y
WISCONSIN					
1 Aspin	N	N	Y	?	?
2 Kastenmeier	N	Y	Y	Y	Y
3 ***Gunderson***	Y	P	N	Y	Y
4 Kleczka	N	Y	Y	Y	Y
5 Moody	N	Y	Y	Y	Y
6 ***Petri***	Y	P	N	?	?
7 Obey	N	Y	Y	Y	Y
8 ***Roth***	Y	P	N	N	Y
9 ***Sensenbrenner***	Y	P	N	Y	Y
WYOMING					
AL ***Thomas***	Y	P	N	Y	Y

Southern states - Ala., Ark., Fla., Ga., Ky., La., Miss., N.C., Okla., S.C., Tenn., Texas, Va.
Omitted votes are quorum calls, which CQ does not include in its vote charts.

HOUSE VOTES 321, 322, 323, 324, 325, 326, 327

321. HR 4739. Fiscal 1991 Defense Authorization/Acquisition Personnel. Mavroules, D-Mass., amendment to create a distinct professional work force in the Defense Department for purchasing and managing the acquisition of defense systems. Before being adopted, the Mavroules amendment was amended by a Gilman, R-N.Y., amendment to help recruit and retain employees with critical skills by permitting federal agencies to pay or reimburse such employees for the cost of their training or student loans. Adopted 413-1: R 169-1; D 244-0 (ND 164-0, SD 80-0), Sept. 11, 1990.

322. HR 4739. Fiscal 1991 Defense Authorization/Staten Island Homeport. Molinari, R-N.Y., substitute amendment to the Bennett, D-Fla., amendment, to prohibit the use of Defense Department funds to close the strategic homeport at Staten Island, N.Y., until 30 days after the Defense Department sends Congress an overall plan to close and realign Navy installations within the United States. Adopted 230-188: R 163-8; D 67-180 (ND 36-130, SD 31-50), Sept. 11, 1990.

323. HR 4739. Fiscal 1991 Defense Authorization/Rule. Adoption of the rule (H Res 461) to provide for further House floor consideration of the bill to establish defense funding levels for fiscal 1991. Adopted 327-65: R 105-59; D 222-6 (ND 147-5, SD 75-1), Sept. 12, 1990.

324. HR 4739. Fiscal 1991 Defense Authorization/Dual Basing. Martin, R-N.Y., en bloc amendment to strike provisions prohibiting the use of any funds to relocate the U.S. Air Force 401st Tactical Fighter Wing of F-16s in Torrejon, Spain, to Crotone, Italy, or any other location outside the United States. The amendment would also strike provisions to require by fiscal 1994 the "dual basing" of U.S. troops. Rejected 174-249: R 159-15; D 15-234 (ND 11-157, SD 4-77), Sept. 12, 1990.

325. HR 4739. Fiscal 1991 Defense Authorization/U.S. Troops in Japan. Bonior, D-Mich., amendment to withdraw 5,000 U.S. troops a year from Japan, unless Japan pays all costs of stationing U.S. forces there. Adopted 370-53: R 141-33; D 229-20 (ND 160-9, SD 69-11), Sept. 12, 1990.

326. HR 4739. Fiscal 1991 Defense Authorization/U.S. Troops in Korea. Mrazek, D-N.Y., amendment to place a permanent ceiling of 30,000 on U.S. troops in Korea to be achieved by fiscal 1993. Rejected 157-265: R 13-160; D 144-105 (ND 119-49, SD 25-56), Sept. 12, 1990.

327. HR 4739. Fiscal 1991 Defense Authorization/Base Closings. Browder, D-Ala., amendment to require the Defense Department to submit a legislative proposal for a new base closure process and to prohibit future domestic base closings until Congress has approved a new closure process or until January 1992, whichever is first. Adopted 287-134: R 45-127; D 242-7 (ND 163-5, SD 79-2), Sept. 12, 1990.

KEY

Y Voted for (yea).
\# Paired for.
\+ Announced for.
N Voted against (nay).
X Paired against.
\- Announced against.
P Voted "present."
C Voted "present" to avoid possible conflict of interest.
? Did not vote or otherwise make a position known.

Democrats ***Republicans***

	321	322	323	324	325	326	327
ALABAMA							
1 ***Callahan***	Y	Y	Y	Y	Y	N	Y
2 ***Dickinson***	Y	Y	Y	Y	N	N	N
3 Browder	Y	Y	Y	N	Y	N	Y
4 Bevill	Y	Y	Y	N	Y	N	Y
5 Flippo	?	Y	Y	N	Y	N	Y
6 Erdreich	Y	Y	Y	N	Y	N	Y
7 Harris	Y	Y	Y	N	Y	N	Y
ALASKA							
AL ***Young***	Y	Y	Y	Y	Y	N	N
ARIZONA							
1 ***Rhodes***	Y	Y	Y	Y	Y	N	N
2 Udall	Y	N	Y	N	Y	?	Y
3 ***Stump***	Y	Y	N	Y	N	N	N
4 ***Kyl***	Y	Y	N	Y	N	N	N
5 ***Kolbe***	Y	Y	Y	Y	Y	N	N
ARKANSAS							
1 Alexander	Y	N	Y	N	Y	Y	Y
2 ***Robinson***	Y	Y	Y	Y	Y	N	Y
3 ***Hammerschmidt***	Y	Y	N	Y	Y	N	N
4 Anthony	Y	N	Y	N	Y	N	Y
CALIFORNIA							
1 Bosco	Y	N	Y	N	Y	Y	Y
2 ***Herger***	Y	Y	Y	Y	Y	N	N
3 Matsui	Y	Y	Y	N	Y	Y	Y
4 Fazio	Y	N	Y	N	Y	N	Y
5 Pelosi	Y	N	Y	N	Y	Y	Y
6 Boxer	Y	N	Y	N	Y	Y	Y
7 Miller	Y	N	Y	N	Y	Y	Y
8 Dellums	Y	N	N	N	Y	Y	Y
9 Stark	Y	N	Y	N	Y	Y	Y
10 Edwards	Y	N	Y	N	Y	Y	Y
11 Lantos	Y	Y	Y	N	Y	N	Y
12 ***Campbell***	Y	Y	?	Y	Y	N	N
13 Mineta	Y	N	Y	N	Y	N	Y
14 ***Shumway***	Y	Y	Y	Y	N	N	N
15 Condit	Y	Y	Y	N	Y	Y	Y
16 Panetta	Y	Y	+	N	Y	Y	Y
17 ***Pashayan***	Y	Y	Y	Y	Y	N	N
18 Lehman	Y	N	Y	N	Y	Y	Y
19 ***Lagomarsino***	Y	Y	Y	Y	N	N	N
20 ***Thomas***	Y	Y	Y	Y	Y	N	N
21 ***Gallegly***	Y	Y	Y	Y	Y	N	N
22 ***Moorhead***	Y	Y	Y	Y	Y	N	N
23 Beilenson	Y	N	Y	N	Y	Y	N
24 Waxman	Y	N	Y	?	Y	N	Y
25 Roybal	Y	N	Y	N	Y	Y	Y
26 Berman	Y	N	Y	Y	Y	N	Y
27 Levine	Y	Y	Y	Y	Y	Y	Y
28 Dixon	Y	N	Y	N	Y	N	Y
29 Hawkins	Y	N	Y	?	?	Y	Y
30 Martinez	Y	N	Y	Y	Y	N	Y
31 Dymally	Y	N	?	N	Y	Y	Y
32 Anderson	Y	N	Y	N	Y	N	Y
33 ***Dreier***	Y	Y	N	Y	Y	N	N
34 Torres	Y	N	Y	N	N	N	Y
35 ***Lewis***	Y	Y	Y	Y	Y	N	N
36 Brown	Y	N	Y	N	Y	Y	Y
37 ***McCandless***	Y	Y	N	Y	Y	N	N
38 ***Dornan***	Y	Y	N	Y	Y	N	N
39 ***Dannemeyer***	Y	Y	N	Y	Y	N	N
40 ***Cox***	Y	Y	Y	Y	N	N	N
41 ***Lowery***	Y	Y	N	Y	Y	N	N
42 ***Rohrabacher***	Y	Y	N	Y	Y	Y	Y
43 ***Packard***	Y	Y	N	Y	N	N	N
44 Bates	Y	N	Y	N	Y	Y	Y
45 ***Hunter***	Y	Y	N	Y	Y	N	N
COLORADO							
1 Schroeder	Y	N	Y	N	Y	Y	Y
2 Skaggs	Y	N	Y	N	N	Y	Y
3 Campbell	Y	N	Y	N	Y	N	Y
4 ***Brown***	Y	N	N	N	Y	Y	N
5 ***Hefley***	Y	Y	N	N	Y	Y	N
6 ***Schaefer***	Y	Y	Y	Y	Y	N	N
CONNECTICUT							
1 Kennelly	Y	N	Y	N	Y	N	Y
2 Gejdenson	Y	N	Y	N	Y	N	Y
3 Morrison	+	-	+	N	+	+	+
4 ***Shays***	Y	Y	N	Y	Y	N	N
5 ***Rowland***	Y	Y	Y	Y	Y	N	Y
6 ***Johnson***	Y	Y	Y	Y	Y	N	N
DELAWARE							
AL Carper	Y	N	Y	N	Y	N	Y
FLORIDA							
1 Hutto	Y	Y	Y	N	N	N	Y
2 ***Grant***	Y	Y	Y	Y	Y	N	Y
3 Bennett	Y	N	Y	N	Y	N	Y
4 ***James***	Y	Y	Y	Y	Y	N	N
5 ***McCollum***	Y	Y	Y	Y	Y	N	N
6 ***Stearns***	Y	Y	Y	Y	Y	N	N
7 Gibbons	Y	N	Y	Y	Y	N	N
8 ***Young***	Y	Y	Y	Y	Y	N	Y
9 ***Bilirakis***	Y	Y	N	Y	Y	N	Y
10 ***Ireland***	Y	Y	?	Y	Y	N	N
11 Nelson	Y	N	Y	N	Y	N	Y
12 ***Lewis***	Y	Y	N	Y	Y	N	Y
13 ***Goss***	Y	Y	N	Y	Y	N	N
14 Johnston	Y	N	Y	N	Y	Y	Y
15 ***Shaw***	Y	Y	N	Y	Y	N	N
16 Smith	Y	N	?	N	Y	N	Y
17 Lehman	Y	N	Y	N	Y	Y	Y
18 ***Ros-Lehtinen***	Y	Y	N	Y	Y	N	N
19 Fascell	Y	N	Y	Y	N	N	Y
GEORGIA							
1 Thomas	Y	N	Y	N	Y	N	Y
2 Hatcher	Y	N	Y	N	Y	N	Y
3 Ray	Y	N	Y	N	N	N	Y
4 Jones	Y	N	Y	N	Y	N	Y
5 Lewis	Y	N	Y	N	Y	Y	Y
6 ***Gingrich***	Y	Y	?	Y	N	N	N
7 Darden	Y	N	Y	N	Y	Y	Y
8 Rowland	Y	Y	Y	N	Y	N	Y
9 Jenkins	Y	N	Y	N	Y	Y	Y
10 Barnard	Y	N	Y	N	Y	N	Y
HAWAII							
1 ***Saiki***	Y	Y	Y	N	Y	N	N
2 Vacancy							
IDAHO							
1 ***Craig***	Y	Y	N	Y	Y	N	N
2 Stallings	Y	N	Y	N	Y	N	Y
ILLINOIS							
1 Hayes	Y	N	Y	N	Y	Y	Y
2 Savage	?	?	?	N	Y	Y	Y
3 Russo	Y	N	?	N	Y	Y	Y
4 Sangmeister	Y	N	Y	N	Y	Y	Y
5 Lipinski	Y	N	Y	N	Y	N	Y
6 ***Hyde***	Y	Y	N	Y	N	N	N
7 Collins	Y	N	Y	N	Y	Y	Y
8 Rostenkowski	Y	N	?	Y	Y	Y	Y
9 Yates	Y	N	Y	N	Y	Y	Y
10 ***Porter***	Y	N	Y	Y	Y	N	N
11 Annunzio	Y	N	?	N	Y	Y	Y
12 ***Crane***	Y	Y	N	Y	N	N	N
13 ***Fawell***	Y	Y	Y	Y	Y	N	N
14 ***Hastert***	Y	Y	N	Y	Y	N	N
15 ***Madigan***	Y	Y	Y	Y	N	N	Y
16 ***Martin***	?	?	Y	N	Y	N	N
17 Evans	Y	N	Y	N	Y	Y	Y
18 ***Michel***	Y	Y	?	Y	N	N	N
19 Bruce	Y	N	Y	N	Y	Y	Y
20 Durbin	Y	N	Y	N	Y	Y	Y
21 Costello	Y	N	Y	N	Y	Y	Y
22 Poshard	Y	N	Y	N	Y	Y	Y
INDIANA							
1 Visclosky	Y	N	Y	N	Y	Y	Y
2 Sharp	Y	N	Y	N	Y	Y	Y
3 ***Hiler***	Y	Y	N	Y	Y	N	N

ND Northern Democrats SD Southern Democrats

	321	322	323	324	325	326	327
4 Long	Y	N	Y	N	Y	Y	Y
5 Jontz	Y	N	Y	N	Y	Y	Y
6 ***Burton***	Y	Y	N	Y	N	N	N
7 ***Myers***	Y	Y	Y	Y	N	N	N
8 McCloskey	Y	N	Y	N	Y	Y	Y
9 Hamilton	Y	N	Y	N	N	N	Y
10 Jacobs	Y	N	N	N	Y	Y	Y
IOWA							
1 ***Leach***	Y	Y	Y	N	Y	N	N
2 ***Tauke***	Y	Y	Y	N	Y	Y	N
3 Nagle	Y	N	Y	N	Y	Y	Y
4 Smith	Y	Y	Y	N	Y	N	Y
5 ***Lightfoot***	Y	Y	N	N	Y	N	N
6 ***Grandy***	Y	Y	Y	N	Y	N	N
KANSAS							
1 ***Roberts***	Y	Y	N	Y	Y	N	N
2 Slattery	?	N	Y	N	Y	N	N
3 ***Meyers***	Y	Y	Y	Y	Y	N	N
4 Glickman	Y	N	Y	N	Y	N	Y
5 ***Whittaker***	Y	Y	Y	Y	Y	N	N
KENTUCKY							
1 Hubbard	Y	Y	Y	Y	Y	Y	Y
2 Natcher	Y	Y	Y	N	Y	N	Y
3 Mazzoli	Y	Y	Y	N	Y	N	Y
4 ***Bunning***	Y	Y	N	Y	N	N	N
5 ***Rogers***	Y	Y	Y	Y	Y	N	N
6 ***Hopkins***	Y	Y	Y	Y	Y	N	N
7 Perkins	Y	Y	Y	N	Y	Y	Y
LOUISIANA							
1 ***Livingston***	Y	Y	Y	Y	N	N	N
2 Boggs	Y	Y	Y	N	Y	N	Y
3 Tauzin	Y	Y	Y	N	Y	N	Y
4 ***McCrery***	Y	Y	Y	Y	Y	N	N
5 Huckaby	Y	N	Y	N	Y	N	Y
6 ***Baker***	Y	Y	Y	Y	Y	N	N
7 Hayes	Y	N	Y	N	Y	N	Y
8 ***Holloway***	Y	Y	N	Y	Y	Y	Y
MAINE							
1 Brennan	Y	N	Y	N	Y	Y	Y
2 ***Snowe***	Y	Y	Y	Y	Y	N	Y
MARYLAND							
1 Dyson	Y	N	?	N	Y	N	Y
2 ***Bentley***	Y	N	Y	Y	Y	N	Y
3 Cardin	?	N	Y	N	Y	Y	Y
4 McMillen	Y	N	Y	N	Y	Y	Y
5 Hoyer	Y	N	Y	N	Y	N	Y
6 Byron	Y	N	Y	N	Y	N	Y
7 Mfume	?	?	Y	N	Y	Y	Y
8 ***Morella***	Y	Y	Y	N	Y	Y	N
MASSACHUSETTS							
1 ***Conte***	Y	Y	?	Y	Y	Y	N
2 Neal	Y	Y	Y	N	Y	Y	Y
3 Early	Y	N	Y	N	Y	Y	Y
4 Frank	Y	Y	Y	N	Y	Y	Y
5 Atkins	Y	Y	Y	N	Y	Y	Y
6 Mavroules	Y	Y	?	N	Y	N	Y
7 Markey	Y	Y	Y	N	Y	Y	Y
8 Kennedy	Y	N	Y	N	Y	Y	N
9 Moakley	Y	N	Y	N	Y	Y	Y
10 Studds	Y	N	Y	N	Y	Y	Y
11 Donnelly	Y	Y	Y	N	Y	Y	Y
MICHIGAN							
1 Conyers	Y	N	N	N	Y	Y	Y
2 ***Pursell***	Y	Y	Y	Y	Y	N	N
3 Wolpe	Y	N	Y	N	Y	Y	Y
4 ***Upton***	Y	Y	N	Y	Y	N	N
5 ***Henry***	Y	N	Y	Y	Y	Y	Y
6 Carr	Y	N	Y	N	Y	N	N
7 Kildee	Y	N	Y	N	Y	Y	Y
8 Traxler	Y	N	Y	N	Y	Y	Y
9 ***Vander Jagt***	Y	Y	Y	Y	Y	N	N
10 ***Schuette***	?	?	Y	Y	Y	N	Y
11 ***Davis***	Y	Y	Y	Y	Y	N	Y
12 Bonior	Y	N	Y	N	Y	Y	Y
13 Crockett	Y	N	Y	N	Y	Y	Y
14 Hertel	Y	N	Y	N	Y	Y	Y
15 Ford	Y	N	?	N	Y	Y	Y
16 Dingell	Y	N	Y	N	Y	Y	Y
17 Levin	Y	N	Y	N	Y	N	Y
18 ***Broomfield***	Y	Y	Y	Y	Y	N	Y
MINNESOTA							
1 Penny	Y	Y	Y	N	N	N	Y
2 ***Weber***	Y	Y	N	Y	N	N	N
3 ***Frenzel***	Y	N	?	Y	N	N	N
4 Vento	Y	N	Y	N	Y	Y	Y
5 Sabo	Y	N	Y	N	Y	Y	Y
6 Sikorski	Y	N	Y	N	Y	Y	Y
7 ***Stangeland***	Y	Y	Y	Y	Y	N	?
8 Oberstar	Y	N	Y	N	Y	Y	Y
MISSISSIPPI							
1 Whitten	Y	Y	?	N	Y	N	Y
2 Espy	Y	N	Y	N	Y	Y	Y
3 Montgomery	Y	Y	Y	N	N	N	Y
4 Parker	Y	Y	Y	N	Y	N	Y
5 Taylor	Y	Y	Y	N	Y	N	Y
MISSOURI							
1 Clay	Y	N	Y	N	Y	Y	Y
2 ***Buechner***	Y	Y	Y	Y	Y	N	N
3 Gephardt	Y	N	?	?	Y	?	?
4 Skelton	Y	N	Y	N	Y	N	Y
5 Wheat	Y	N	Y	N	Y	Y	Y
6 ***Coleman***	Y	Y	Y	Y	Y	N	Y
7 ***Hancock***	Y	Y	N	Y	N	N	N
8 ***Emerson***	Y	Y	Y	N	Y	N	Y
9 Volkmer	Y	?	Y	N	Y	N	Y
MONTANA							
1 Williams	Y	N	Y	N	Y	Y	Y
2 ***Marlenee***	?	Y	N	Y	Y	N	N
NEBRASKA							
1 ***Bereuter***	Y	Y	Y	Y	Y	Y	N
2 Hoagland	Y	N	?	N	Y	N	Y
3 ***Smith***	Y	Y	N	Y	Y	N	N
NEVADA							
1 Bilbray	Y	N	Y	N	Y	N	Y
2 ***Vucanovich***	Y	Y	N	Y	N	N	N
NEW HAMPSHIRE							
1 ***Smith***	?	?	N	Y	Y	N	N
2 ***Douglas***	?	?	N	Y	Y	N	N
NEW JERSEY							
1 Vacancy							
2 Hughes	Y	N	Y	N	Y	N	Y
3 Pallone	Y	Y	Y	N	Y	N	Y
4 ***Smith***	Y	Y	N	Y	Y	N	Y
5 ***Roukema***	Y	Y	Y	Y	Y	N	Y
6 Dwyer	Y	Y	Y	N	Y	N	Y
7 ***Rinaldo***	Y	Y	Y	Y	Y	N	Y
8 Roe	Y	Y	Y	N	Y	Y	Y
9 Torricelli	Y	Y	Y	Y	Y	N	Y
10 Payne	Y	N	Y	N	Y	Y	Y
11 ***Gallo***	Y	Y	N	Y	Y	N	Y
12 ***Courter***	Y	Y	Y	Y	N	N	N
13 ***Saxton***	Y	N	N	Y	Y	N	Y
14 Guarini	Y	Y	Y	N	Y	Y	Y
NEW MEXICO							
1 ***Schiff***	Y	Y	Y	Y	Y	N	Y
2 ***Skeen***	Y	Y	N	Y	Y	N	N
3 Richardson	Y	N	Y	Y	Y	N	Y
NEW YORK							
1 Hochbrueckner	Y	Y	Y	N	Y	Y	Y
2 Downey	Y	Y	Y	N	Y	Y	Y
3 Mrazek	Y	Y	Y	N	Y	Y	Y
4 ***Lent***	Y	Y	Y	Y	Y	N	N
5 ***McGrath***	Y	Y	Y	Y	Y	N	N
6 Flake	Y	N	Y	N	Y	Y	Y
7 Ackerman	Y	N	Y	N	Y	Y	Y
8 Scheuer	Y	N	Y	N	Y	Y	Y
9 Manton	Y	Y	Y	N	Y	Y	Y
10 Schumer	Y	N	Y	N	Y	Y	Y
11 Towns	Y	N	?	N	Y	Y	Y
12 Owens	Y	N	N	N	Y	Y	Y
13 Solarz	Y	N	Y	Y	N	N	Y
14 ***Molinari***	Y	Y	Y	Y	Y	N	N
15 ***Green***	Y	Y	Y	Y	N	N	N
16 Rangel	Y	N	N	N	Y	Y	Y
17 Weiss	Y	N	N	N	N	Y	Y
18 Serrano	?	?	?	?	?	?	?
19 Engel	?	?	?	Y	Y	Y	Y
20 Lowey	Y	N	Y	N	Y	Y	Y
21 ***Fish***	Y	Y	Y	Y	Y	N	Y
22 ***Gilman***	Y	Y	Y	Y	Y	N	Y
23 McNulty	Y	Y	?	N	Y	Y	Y
24 ***Solomon***	Y	Y	Y	Y	Y	N	N
25 ***Boehlert***	Y	Y	Y	Y	Y	N	Y
26 ***Martin***	Y	Y	Y	Y	N	N	N
27 ***Walsh***	Y	Y	Y	Y	Y	N	Y
28 McHugh	Y	Y	Y	N	Y	N	Y
29 ***Horton***	Y	Y	Y	Y	Y	N	Y
30 Slaughter	Y	N	Y	N	Y	Y	Y
31 ***Paxon***	Y	Y	Y	Y	Y	N	N
32 LaFalce	Y	Y	Y	N	N	N	Y
33 Nowak	Y	Y	?	N	Y	Y	Y
34 ***Houghton***	Y	Y	Y	Y	N	N	N
NORTH CAROLINA							
1 Jones	Y	N	Y	N	Y	N	Y
2 Valentine	Y	Y	Y	N	Y	N	Y
3 Lancaster	Y	Y	Y	N	Y	N	Y
4 Price	Y	N	Y	N	Y	N	Y
5 Neal	Y	N	Y	N	Y	N	Y
6 ***Coble***	Y	Y	?	Y	Y	N	Y
7 Rose	Y	N	Y	N	Y	N	Y
8 Hefner	Y	N	Y	N	Y	N	Y
9 ***McMillan***	Y	Y	Y	Y	Y	N	Y
10 ***Ballenger***	Y	Y	N	Y	Y	N	Y
11 Clarke	Y	N	Y	N	Y	N	Y
NORTH DAKOTA							
AL Dorgan	Y	N	Y	N	Y	Y	Y
OHIO							
1 Luken	Y	Y	Y	N	Y	N	Y
2 ***Gradison***	Y	Y	Y	Y	N	N	N
3 Hall	?	N	Y	N	Y	Y	Y
4 ***Oxley***	Y	Y	Y	Y	N	N	N
5 ***Gillmor***	Y	Y	Y	Y	Y	N	N
6 ***McEwen***	Y	Y	N	Y	N	N	N
7 ***DeWine***	Y	Y	N	Y	Y	N	N
8 ***Lukens***	Y	Y	Y	Y	Y	N	N
9 Kaptur	Y	N	Y	N	Y	Y	Y
10 ***Miller***	Y	Y	?	?	?	?	?
11 Eckart	Y	N	Y	N	Y	Y	Y
12 ***Kasich***	Y	Y	Y	Y	Y	N	N
13 Pease	Y	N	?	N	Y	Y	N
14 Sawyer	Y	N	Y	N	Y	N	Y
15 ***Wylie***	Y	Y	Y	Y	Y	N	N
16 ***Regula***	Y	Y	?	Y	Y	Y	N
17 Traficant	Y	Y	Y	N	Y	Y	Y
18 Applegate	Y	N	Y	N	Y	Y	Y
19 Feighan	Y	N	Y	N	Y	N	Y
20 Oakar	Y	Y	Y	N	Y	Y	Y
21 Stokes	Y	N	Y	N	Y	Y	Y
OKLAHOMA							
1 ***Inhofe***	Y	Y	N	Y	Y	N	N
2 Synar	Y	N	Y	N	Y	Y	Y
3 Watkins	?	?	?	?	?	?	?
4 McCurdy	Y	N	Y	N	Y	N	Y
5 ***Edwards***	Y	Y	Y	Y	Y	N	N
6 English	Y	N	Y	N	Y	N	Y
OREGON							
1 AuCoin	?	?	?	?	?	?	?
2 ***Smith, B.***	Y	Y	Y	Y	N	N	Y
3 Wyden	Y	N	Y	N	Y	Y	Y
4 DeFazio	Y	N	Y	N	Y	Y	Y
5 ***Smith, D.***	?	?	?	?	?	?	?
PENNSYLVANIA							
1 Foglietta	Y	N	Y	Y	Y	Y	Y
2 Gray	Y	N	?	N	Y	Y	Y
3 Borski	Y	N	Y	N	Y	Y	Y
4 Kolter	Y	N	Y	N	Y	Y	Y
5 ***Schulze***	Y	Y	Y	N	Y	N	Y
6 Yatron	Y	Y	Y	N	Y	Y	Y
7 ***Weldon***	Y	N	Y	Y	Y	N	Y
8 Kostmayer	Y	N	Y	N	Y	Y	Y
9 ***Shuster***	Y	Y	Y	Y	Y	N	Y
10 ***McDade***	Y	Y	Y	Y	Y	?	N
11 Kanjorski	Y	Y	Y	N	Y	Y	Y
12 Murtha	Y	Y	Y	Y	Y	N	Y
13 ***Coughlin***	Y	Y	N	Y	Y	N	Y
14 Coyne	Y	N	Y	N	Y	N	Y
15 ***Ritter***	Y	Y	Y	Y	Y	N	N
16 ***Walker***	N	Y	N	Y	N	N	N
17 ***Gekas***	Y	Y	N	Y	N	N	Y
18 Walgren	Y	N	Y	N	Y	Y	Y
19 ***Goodling***	Y	Y	Y	Y	Y	N	?
20 Gaydos	Y	N	?	N	Y	Y	?
21 ***Ridge***	Y	Y	Y	Y	Y	N	N
22 Murphy	Y	Y	Y	N	Y	Y	Y
23 ***Clinger***	Y	Y	Y	Y	Y	N	N
RHODE ISLAND							
1 ***Machtley***	Y	Y	Y	Y	Y	N	Y
2 ***Schneider***	Y	Y	Y	N	Y	Y	N
SOUTH CAROLINA							
1 ***Ravenel***	Y	Y	Y	N	Y	N	Y
2 ***Spence***	Y	Y	Y	Y	Y	N	Y
3 Derrick	Y	N	Y	N	Y	N	Y
4 Patterson	Y	N	Y	N	Y	N	Y
5 Spratt	Y	N	Y	N	Y	N	Y
6 Tallon	Y	Y	Y	N	Y	Y	Y
SOUTH DAKOTA							
AL Johnson	Y	N	Y	N	Y	Y	Y
TENNESSEE							
1 ***Quillen***	Y	Y	N	Y	Y	N	Y
2 ***Duncan***	Y	Y	N	Y	Y	Y	N
3 Lloyd	Y	N	Y	N	Y	N	Y
4 Cooper	Y	N	Y	N	N	N	Y
5 Clement	Y	N	Y	N	Y	N	Y
6 Gordon	Y	N	Y	N	Y	Y	Y
7 ***Sundquist***	Y	Y	N	Y	Y	N	Y
8 Tanner	Y	N	Y	N	Y	N	Y
9 Ford	Y	N	?	?	?	?	?
TEXAS							
1 Chapman	Y	Y	Y	N	Y	Y	Y
2 Wilson	?	?	?	Y	Y	Y	N
3 ***Bartlett***	Y	Y	Y	Y	Y	N	N
4 Hall	Y	Y	Y	N	Y	Y	Y
5 Bryant	Y	N	P	N	Y	Y	Y
6 ***Barton***	Y	Y	N	Y	Y	N	N
7 ***Archer***	Y	Y	?	Y	Y	N	N
8 ***Fields***	Y	Y	N	Y	Y	N	N
9 Brooks	Y	N	Y	N	Y	Y	Y
10 Pickle	Y	Y	Y	N	N	Y	Y
11 Leath	Y	Y	Y	N	N	N	Y
12 Geren	Y	Y	Y	N	Y	N	Y
13 Sarpalius	Y	Y	Y	N	Y	N	Y
14 Laughlin	Y	N	Y	N	Y	N	Y
15 de la Garza	Y	Y	Y	N	Y	N	Y
16 Coleman	Y	N	Y	N	Y	N	Y
17 Stenholm	Y	Y	Y	N	N	N	Y
18 Washington	Y	N	Y	N	Y	Y	Y
19 ***Combest***	Y	Y	N	Y	N	N	N
20 Gonzalez	Y	Y	N	N	P	Y	Y
21 ***Smith***	Y	Y	Y	Y	Y	N	N
22 ***DeLay***	Y	Y	N	Y	Y	N	N
23 Bustamante	Y	N	Y	N	Y	Y	Y
24 Frost	Y	N	Y	N	Y	Y	Y
25 Andrews	Y	N	Y	N	Y	Y	Y
26 ***Armey***	Y	Y	N	Y	N	N	N
27 Ortiz	Y	Y	Y	N	Y	N	Y
UTAH							
1 ***Hansen***	Y	Y	Y	Y	Y	N	N
2 Owens	Y	N	Y	N	Y	Y	Y
3 ***Nielson***	Y	Y	Y	Y	Y	N	N
VERMONT							
AL ***Smith***	Y	Y	Y	Y	Y	N	N
VIRGINIA							
1 ***Bateman***	Y	Y	Y	Y	N	N	N
2 Pickett	Y	N	Y	N	N	N	Y
3 ***Bliley***	Y	Y	N	Y	Y	N	N
4 Sisisky	Y	N	Y	N	N	N	Y
5 Payne	Y	Y	?	N	Y	N	Y
6 Olin	Y	N	Y	N	N	N	Y
7 ***Slaughter***	Y	Y	N	Y	Y	N	N
8 ***Parris***	Y	Y	?	Y	Y	N	N
9 Boucher	Y	N	Y	N	Y	Y	Y
10 ***Wolf***	Y	Y	Y	Y	Y	N	N
WASHINGTON							
1 ***Miller***	Y	Y	Y	Y	Y	N	N
2 Swift	Y	Y	Y	N	Y	N	Y
3 Unsoeld	Y	N	Y	N	Y	Y	Y
4 ***Morrison***	Y	Y	Y	Y	Y	N	Y
5 Foley							
6 Dicks	Y	Y	Y	Y	N	N	Y
7 McDermott	Y	N	Y	N	Y	Y	Y
8 ***Chandler***	Y	Y	Y	Y	Y	N	Y
WEST VIRGINIA							
1 Mollohan	Y	N	Y	N	Y	N	Y
2 Staggers	Y	N	Y	N	Y	N	Y
3 Wise	Y	Y	Y	N	Y	N	Y
4 Rahall	Y	N	Y	N	Y	Y	Y
WISCONSIN							
1 Aspin	Y	N	Y	N	N	N	Y
2 Kastenmeier	Y	N	Y	N	Y	Y	Y
3 ***Gunderson***	Y	Y	Y	Y	Y	N	N
4 Kleczka	Y	N	Y	N	Y	Y	Y
5 Moody	Y	N	Y	N	Y	Y	Y
6 ***Petri***	Y	Y	Y	Y	Y	Y	N
7 Obey	Y	N	Y	N	Y	Y	Y
8 ***Roth***	Y	Y	N	N	Y	N	N
9 ***Sensenbrenner***	Y	N	Y	N	Y	N	N
WYOMING							
AL ***Thomas***	Y	Y	Y	Y	Y	N	N

Southern states - Ala., Ark., Fla., Ga., Ky., La., Miss., N.C., Okla., S.C., Tenn., Texas, Va.
Omitted votes are quorum calls, which CQ does not include in its vote charts.

HOUSE VOTES 328, 330, 331

328. Procedural Motion. Schulze, R-Pa., motion to approve the House Journal of Wednesday, Sept. 12. Motion agreed to 281-103: R 60-98; D 221-5 (ND 150-5, SD 71-0), Sept. 13, 1990.

330. HR 4330. National Service Act/Loan Cancellations. Goodling, R-Pa., amendment to strike provisions of the bill that would expand the Perkins loan cancellation program by allowing borrowers to have a portion of their loan principal and all accrued interest canceled for each year that they are full-time volunteers in a tax-exempt organization providing drug counseling and treatment or health care to American Indians. Rejected 200-212: R 166-3; D 34-209 (ND 10-155, SD 24-54), Sept. 13, 1990.

331. S 2088. Strategic Petroleum Reserve/Conference Report. Adoption of the conference report on the bill to reauthorize the Strategic Petroleum Reserve through fiscal 1994, expand its target goal from 750 million barrels to 1 billion barrels and create a reserve for refined petroleum products, such as heating oil, under a three-year test program. Adopted 391-0: R 162-0; D 229-0 (ND 157-0, SD 72-0), Sept. 13, 1990. A "nay" was a vote supporting the president's position.

KEY

Y Voted for (yea).
Paired for.
\+ Announced for.
N Voted against (nay).
X Paired against.
\- Announced against.
P Voted "present."
C Voted "present" to avoid possible conflict of interest.
? Did not vote or otherwise make a position known.

Democrats ***Republicans***

	328	330	331
ALABAMA			
1 ***Callahan***	Y	Y	Y
2 ***Dickinson***	N	Y	Y
3 Browder	Y	N	Y
4 Bevill	Y	N	Y
5 Flippo	Y	N	Y
6 Erdreich	Y	N	Y
7 Harris	Y	N	Y
ALASKA			
AL ***Young***	N	Y	Y
ARIZONA			
1 ***Rhodes***	N	Y	Y
2 Udall	?	N	?
3 ***Stump***	N	Y	Y
4 ***Kyl***	N	Y	Y
5 ***Kolbe***	N	Y	Y
ARKANSAS			
1 Alexander	?	N	Y
2 ***Robinson***	Y	Y	?
3 ***Hammerschmidt***	Y	Y	Y
4 Anthony	Y	N	Y
CALIFORNIA			
1 Bosco	Y	N	+
2 ***Herger***	N	Y	Y
3 Matsui	Y	N	Y
4 Fazio	Y	N	Y
5 Pelosi	Y	N	Y
6 Boxer	Y	?	?
7 Miller	Y	N	Y
8 Dellums	Y	N	Y
9 Stark	Y	N	Y
10 Edwards	Y	N	Y
11 Lantos	Y	N	Y
12 ***Campbell***	N	Y	Y
13 Mineta	Y	N	Y
14 ***Shumway***	Y	Y	Y
15 Condit	?	Y	Y
16 Panetta	?	—	Y
17 ***Pashayan***	N	Y	?
18 Lehman	Y	N	Y
19 ***Lagomarsino***	N	Y	Y
20 ***Thomas***	N	Y	Y
21 ***Gallegly***	N	Y	Y
22 ***Moorhead***	Y	Y	Y
23 Beilenson	Y	N	Y
24 Waxman	Y	N	Y
25 Roybal	Y	?	Y
26 Berman	Y	N	Y
27 Levine	Y	N	Y
28 Dixon	?	N	Y
29 Hawkins	N	N	Y
30 Martinez	Y	N	Y
31 Dymally	Y	N	Y
32 Anderson	Y	N	Y
33 ***Dreier***	N	Y	Y
34 Torres	Y	N	Y
35 ***Lewis***	N	Y	?
36 Brown	Y	N	Y
37 ***McCandless***	N	Y	Y
38 ***Dornan***	?	Y	Y
39 ***Dannemeyer***	N	Y	Y
40 ***Cox***	N	Y	Y
41 ***Lowery***	N	Y	Y
42 ***Rohrabacher***	N	Y	Y
43 ***Packard***	Y	Y	Y
44 Bates	Y	N	Y
45 ***Hunter***	?	Y	Y
COLORADO			
1 Schroeder	N	N	Y
2 Skaggs	Y	N	Y
3 Campbell	Y	N	Y
4 ***Brown***	N	Y	Y
5 ***Hefley***	N	Y	Y
6 ***Schaefer***	N	Y	Y
CONNECTICUT			
1 Kennelly	Y	N	Y
2 Gejdenson	Y	N	Y
3 Morrison	+	-	+
4 ***Shays***	N	Y	Y
5 ***Rowland***	Y	Y	Y
6 ***Johnson***	Y	Y	Y
DELAWARE			
AL Carper	Y	N	Y
FLORIDA			
1 Hutto	Y	Y	Y
2 ***Grant***	Y	Y	Y
3 Bennett	Y	Y	Y
4 ***James***	N	Y	Y
5 ***McCollum***	Y	Y	Y
6 ***Stearns***	N	Y	Y
7 Gibbons	Y	N	Y
8 ***Young***	?	Y	Y
9 ***Bilirakis***	N	Y	Y
10 ***Ireland***	N	Y	Y
11 Nelson	Y	Y	Y
12 ***Lewis***	?	Y	Y
13 ***Goss***	N	Y	Y
14 Johnston	Y	Y	Y
15 ***Shaw***	?	Y	Y
16 Smith	Y	N	Y
17 Lehman	Y	N	Y
18 ***Ros-Lehtinen***	N	Y	Y
19 Fascell	Y	N	Y
GEORGIA			
1 Thomas	Y	N	Y
2 Hatcher	Y	N	Y
3 Ray	Y	N	Y
4 Jones	Y	N	Y
5 Lewis	Y	N	Y
6 ***Gingrich***	?	?	?
7 Darden	Y	N	Y
8 Rowland	Y	N	Y
9 Jenkins	Y	N	Y
10 Barnard	Y	N	?
HAWAII			
1 ***Saiki***	Y	Y	Y
2 Vacancy			
IDAHO			
1 ***Craig***	N	Y	Y
2 Stallings	Y	Y	Y
ILLINOIS			
1 Hayes	Y	N	Y
2 Savage	?	N	Y
3 Russo	Y	N	Y
4 Sangmeister	Y	N	Y
5 Lipinski	Y	N	Y
6 ***Hyde***	Y	Y	Y
7 Collins	Y	N	Y
8 Rostenkowski	?	?	?
9 Yates	Y	N	Y
10 ***Porter***	Y	Y	Y
11 Annunzio	Y	N	Y
12 ***Crane***	?	Y	Y
13 ***Fawell***	N	Y	Y
14 ***Hastert***	N	Y	Y
15 ***Madigan***	N	Y	Y
16 ***Martin***	N	?	?
17 Evans	Y	N	Y
18 ***Michel***	?	?	?
19 Bruce	Y	N	Y
20 Durbin	Y	N	Y
21 Costello	Y	N	Y
22 Poshard	Y	N	Y
INDIANA			
1 Visclosky	Y	N	Y
2 Sharp	Y	N	Y
3 ***Hiler***	N	Y	Y

ND Northern Democrats SD Southern Democrats

	328	330	331
4 Long	Y	N	Y
5 Jontz	Y	N	Y
6 ***Burton***	N	Y	Y
7 ***Myers***	Y	Y	Y
8 McCloskey	Y	N	Y
9 Hamilton	Y	N	Y
10 Jacobs	N	N	Y
IOWA			
1 ***Leach***	N	Y	Y
2 ***Tauke***	N	Y	Y
3 Nagle	Y	N	Y
4 Smith	Y	N	?
5 ***Lightfoot***	N	Y	Y
6 ***Grandy***	N	Y	Y
KANSAS			
1 ***Roberts***	N	Y	Y
2 Slattery	Y	N	Y
3 ***Meyers***	N	Y	Y
4 Glickman	Y	Y	Y
5 ***Whittaker***	N	Y	Y
KENTUCKY			
1 Hubbard	Y	Y	Y
2 Natcher	Y	N	Y
3 Mazzoli	Y	N	Y
4 ***Bunning***	N	Y	Y
5 ***Rogers***	N	Y	Y
6 ***Hopkins***	N	Y	Y
7 Perkins	Y	N	Y
LOUISIANA			
1 ***Livingston***	Y	Y	Y
2 Boggs	?	N	Y
3 Tauzin	Y	Y	Y
4 ***McCrery***	Y	Y	?
5 Huckaby	Y	?	?
6 ***Baker***	N	Y	Y
7 Hayes	Y	Y	Y
8 ***Holloway***	N	Y	Y
MAINE			
1 Brennan	Y	N	Y
2 ***Snowe***	Y	Y	Y
MARYLAND			
1 Dyson	Y	N	Y
2 ***Bentley***	N	Y	Y
3 Cardin	Y	N	Y
4 McMillen	Y	N	Y
5 Hoyer	Y	N	Y
6 Byron	Y	Y	Y
7 Mfume	Y	N	Y
8 ***Morella***	?	N	Y
MASSACHUSETTS			
1 ***Conte***	Y	N	Y
2 Neal	Y	N	Y
3 Early	Y	N	Y
4 Frank	Y	N	Y
5 Atkins	Y	N	Y
6 Mavroules	Y	N	Y
7 Markey	?	N	Y
8 Kennedy	Y	N	Y
9 Moakley	Y	N	Y
10 Studds	Y	N	Y
11 Donnelly	Y	N	?
MICHIGAN			
1 Conyers	Y	N	?
2 ***Pursell***	Y	Y	Y
3 Wolpe	Y	N	Y
4 ***Upton***	N	Y	Y
5 ***Henry***	N	Y	Y
6 Carr	Y	N	Y
7 Kildee	Y	N	Y
8 Traxler	Y	N	Y
9 ***Vander Jagt***	?	Y	Y
10 ***Schuette***	N	Y	Y
11 ***Davis***	Y	Y	Y
12 Bonior	?	N	Y
13 Crockett	?	N	?
14 Hertel	Y	N	Y
15 Ford	?	N	?
16 Dingell	Y	N	Y
17 Levin	Y	N	Y
18 ***Broomfield***	Y	Y	Y
MINNESOTA			
1 Penny	Y	N	Y
2 ***Weber***	N	Y	Y
3 ***Frenzel***	?	?	?
4 Vento	Y	N	Y

	328	330	331
5 Sabo	Y	N	Y
6 Sikorski	N	N	Y
7 ***Stangeland***	N	Y	Y
8 Oberstar	?	N	Y
MISSISSIPPI			
1 Whitten	?	?	?
2 Espy	Y	N	Y
3 Montgomery	Y	N	Y
4 Parker	Y	Y	Y
5 Taylor	Y	Y	Y
MISSOURI			
1 Clay	N	N	Y
2 ***Buechner***	N	Y	+
3 Gephardt	?	?	?
4 Skelton	Y	Y	Y
5 Wheat	Y	N	Y
6 ***Coleman***	Y	Y	Y
7 ***Hancock***	N	Y	Y
8 ***Emerson***	Y	Y	Y
9 Volkmer	Y	N	Y
MONTANA			
1 Williams	?	N	?
2 ***Marlenee***	N	Y	?
NEBRASKA			
1 ***Bereuter***	N	Y	Y
2 Hoagland	Y	Y	Y
3 ***Smith***	Y	Y	Y
NEVADA			
1 Bilbray	Y	N	Y
2 ***Vucanovich***	N	Y	Y
NEW HAMPSHIRE			
1 ***Smith***	N	Y	Y
2 ***Douglas***	N	Y	Y
NEW JERSEY			
1 Vacancy			
2 Hughes	Y	Y	Y
3 Pallone	Y	Y	Y
4 ***Smith***	Y	Y	Y
5 ***Roukema***	N	Y	Y
6 Dwyer	Y	N	Y
7 ***Rinaldo***	Y	Y	Y
8 Roe	Y	N	Y
9 Torricelli	Y	N	?
10 Payne	Y	N	Y
11 ***Gallo***	N	Y	Y
12 ***Courter***	N	Y	Y
13 ***Saxton***	N	Y	Y
14 Guarini	Y	Y	Y
NEW MEXICO			
1 ***Schiff***	Y	Y	Y
2 ***Skeen***	Y	Y	Y
3 Richardson	Y	N	Y
NEW YORK			
1 Hochbrueckner	Y	N	Y
2 Downey	Y	N	Y
3 Mrazek	Y	N	Y
4 ***Lent***	Y	Y	Y
5 ***McGrath***	N	Y	Y
6 Flake	Y	N	Y
7 Ackerman	Y	N	Y
8 Scheuer	Y	N	Y
9 Manton	?	N	Y
10 Schumer	Y	N	Y
11 Towns	Y	N	Y
12 Owens	Y	N	Y
13 Solarz	Y	N	Y
14 ***Molinari***	Y	Y	Y
15 ***Green***	Y	Y	Y
16 Rangel	?	N	Y
17 Weiss	Y	N	Y
18 Serrano	Y	N	Y
19 Engel	Y	N	Y
20 Lowey	Y	N	Y
21 ***Fish***	Y	Y	Y
22 ***Gilman***	Y	?	Y
23 McNulty	Y	N	Y
24 ***Solomon***	N	Y	Y
25 ***Boehlert***	N	Y	Y
26 ***Martin***	N	Y	Y
27 ***Walsh***	Y	Y	Y
28 McHugh	Y	N	Y
29 ***Horton***	Y	Y	Y
30 Slaughter	Y	N	Y
31 ***Paxon***	N	Y	Y

	328	330	331
32 LaFalce	Y	N	Y
33 Nowak	Y	N	Y
34 ***Houghton***	Y	Y	Y
NORTH CAROLINA			
1 Jones	Y	N	Y
2 Valentine	Y	Y	?
3 Lancaster	Y	N	Y
4 Price	Y	N	Y
5 Neal	Y	Y	Y
6 ***Coble***	N	Y	Y
7 Rose	?	N	Y
8 Hefner	Y	N	Y
9 ***McMillan***	Y	Y	Y
10 ***Ballenger***	N	Y	Y
11 Clarke	Y	N	Y
NORTH DAKOTA			
AL Dorgan	Y	N	Y
OHIO			
1 Luken	Y	N	Y
2 ***Gradison***	Y	Y	Y
3 Hall	Y	N	?
4 ***Oxley***	Y	Y	Y
5 ***Gillmor***	Y	Y	Y
6 ***McEwen***	Y	Y	Y
7 ***DeWine***	N	Y	Y
8 ***Lukens***	P	Y	Y
9 Kaptur	Y	N	Y
10 ***Miller***	?	?	?
11 Eckart	Y	N	Y
12 ***Kasich***	Y	Y	Y
13 Pease	Y	N	Y
14 Sawyer	Y	N	Y
15 ***Wylie***	Y	Y	Y
16 ***Regula***	N	Y	Y
17 Traficant	Y	N	Y
18 Applegate	Y	N	Y
19 Feighan	Y	N	Y
20 Oakar	Y	N	Y
21 Stokes	Y	N	Y
OKLAHOMA			
1 ***Inhofe***	N	Y	Y
2 Synar	Y	Y	Y
3 Watkins	?	?	?
4 McCurdy	Y	N	Y
5 ***Edwards***	?	Y	Y
6 English	?	N	Y
OREGON			
1 AuCoin	?	?	?
2 ***Smith, B.***	N	Y	Y
3 Wyden	Y	N	Y
4 DeFazio	Y	?	Y
5 ***Smith, D.***	?	?	?
PENNSYLVANIA			
1 Foglietta	Y	N	Y
2 Gray	Y	N	Y
3 Borski	Y	Y	Y
4 Kolter	Y	N	Y
5 ***Schulze***	Y	Y	?
6 Yatron	Y	N	Y
7 ***Weldon***	Y	Y	Y
8 Kostmayer	Y	N	?
9 ***Shuster***	Y	Y	Y
10 ***McDade***	?	Y	Y
11 Kanjorski	Y	N	Y
12 Murtha	Y	N	Y
13 ***Coughlin***	?	Y	Y
14 Coyne	Y	N	Y
15 ***Ritter***	Y	Y	Y
16 ***Walker***	N	Y	Y
17 ***Gekas***	N	Y	Y
18 Walgren	Y	N	Y
19 ***Goodling***	N	Y	Y
20 Gaydos	Y	N	Y
21 ***Ridge***	N	Y	Y
22 Murphy	?	N	Y
23 ***Clinger***	Y	Y	Y
RHODE ISLAND			
1 ***Machtley***	N	Y	Y
2 ***Schneider***	Y	Y	Y
SOUTH CAROLINA			
1 ***Ravenel***	Y	Y	Y
2 ***Spence***	Y	Y	Y
3 Derrick	Y	N	Y
4 Patterson	+	+	+
5 Spratt	Y	N	Y
6 Tallon	Y	Y	Y

	328	330	331
SOUTH DAKOTA			
AL Johnson	Y	N	Y
TENNESSEE			
1 ***Quillen***	N	N	?
2 ***Duncan***	Y	Y	Y
3 Lloyd	Y	N	Y
4 Cooper	Y	Y	Y
5 Clement	Y	N	Y
6 Gordon	Y	N	Y
7 ***Sundquist***	N	Y	Y
8 Tanner	Y	N	Y
9 Ford	Y	Y	?
TEXAS			
1 Chapman	?	N	Y
2 Wilson	?	Y	Y
3 ***Bartlett***	Y	Y	Y
4 Hall	Y	Y	Y
5 Bryant	Y	N	Y
6 ***Barton***	N	Y	Y
7 ***Archer***	?	Y	Y
8 ***Fields***	N	Y	Y
9 Brooks	Y	N	Y
10 Pickle	Y	N	Y
11 Leath	?	N	Y
12 Geren	Y	Y	Y
13 Sarpalius	?	Y	Y
14 Laughlin	Y	Y	Y
15 de la Garza	Y	N	?
16 Coleman	Y	N	?
17 Stenholm	Y	Y	Y
18 Washington	Y	?	?
19 ***Combest***	Y	Y	Y
20 Gonzalez	Y	N	Y
21 ***Smith***	N	Y	Y
22 ***DeLay***	N	Y	Y
23 Bustamante	Y	N	?
24 Frost	?	N	Y
25 Andrews	Y	N	Y
26 ***Armey***	N	Y	Y
27 Ortiz	Y	N	Y
UTAH			
1 ***Hansen***	N	Y	Y
2 Owens	Y	N	Y
3 ***Nielson***	N	Y	Y
VERMONT			
AL ***Smith***	Y	Y	Y
VIRGINIA			
1 ***Bateman***	Y	Y	Y
2 Pickett	Y	Y	Y
3 ***Bliley***	N	Y	Y
4 Sisisky	Y	Y	Y
5 Payne	Y	N	Y
6 Olin	Y	Y	Y
7 ***Slaughter***	N	Y	Y
8 ***Parris***	N	Y	Y
9 Boucher	Y	N	Y
10 ***Wolf***	N	Y	Y
WASHINGTON			
1 ***Miller***	N	Y	Y
2 Swift	Y	N	Y
3 Unsoeld	Y	N	Y
4 ***Morrison***	Y	Y	Y
5 Foley			
6 Dicks	Y	N	Y
7 McDermott	Y	N	Y
8 ***Chandler***	N	Y	Y
WEST VIRGINIA			
1 Mollohan	Y	N	Y
2 Staggers	Y	N	Y
3 Wise	Y	N	Y
4 Rahall	Y	N	Y
WISCONSIN			
1 Aspin	Y	N	Y
2 Kastenmeier	Y	N	Y
3 ***Gunderson***	Y	Y	Y
4 Kleczka	Y	N	Y
5 Moody	Y	N	Y
6 ***Petri***	Y	Y	Y
7 Obey	Y	N	Y
8 ***Roth***	Y	Y	Y
9 ***Sensenbrenner***	N	Y	Y
WYOMING			
AL ***Thomas***	N	Y	Y

Southern states - Ala., Ark., Fla., Ga., Ky., La., Miss., N.C., Okla., S.C., Tenn., Texas, Va.
Omitted votes are quorum calls, which CQ does not include in its vote charts.

332. S 3033. Free Mailing for Troops in the Persian Gulf/Passage. Hayes, D-Ill., motion to suspend the rules and pass the bill to extend free mailing privileges to members of the armed services engaged in temporary military operations under arduous circumstances. Motion agreed to (thus clearing the measure for the president) 368-0: R 157-0; D 211-0 (ND 140-0, SD 71-0), Sept. 17, 1990. A two-thirds majority of those present and voting (246 in this case) is required for passage under suspension of the rules.

333. HR 5611. Free Mailing for Troops in the Persian Gulf/Recommittal Motion. Ridge, R-Pa., motion to recommit to the Post Office Committee the bill to extend free mailing services to members of the armed services in temporary military operations under arduous circumstances, with instructions to report it back to the House with a provision to fund such mailings through the account for congressional franked mail. Motion agreed to 227-142: R 152-5; D 75-137 (ND 34-107, SD 41-30), Sept. 17, 1990. (The Post Office Committee subsequently reported the bill back with the added provision, and it was passed by voice vote.)

334. HR 4328. Textile Trade Act/Rule. Adoption of the rule (H Res 464) to provide for House floor consideration of the motion to concur in Senate amendments to the bill to limit the growth of imports of textiles and apparel to 1 percent annually; establish permanent quotas for most non-rubber footwear imports at 1989 levels; authorize the special allocation of textile quotas for countries increasing their purchases of U.S. agricultural goods; and for other purposes. Adopted 293-121: R 54-116; D 239-5 (ND 161-5, SD 78-0), Sept. 18, 1990. A "nay" was a vote supporting the president's position.

335. HR 4328. Textile Trade Act/Concur in Senate Amendments. Rostenkowski, D-Ill., motion to concur in Senate amendments to the bill to limit the growth of imports of textiles and apparel to 1 percent annually; establish permanent quotas for most non-rubber footwear imports at 1989 levels; authorize the special allocation of textile quotas for countries increasing their purchases of U.S. agricultural goods; and for other purposes. Motion agreed to 271-149: R 71-101; D 200-48 (ND 129-39, SD 71-9), Sept. 18, 1990. A "nay" was a vote supporting the president's position.

336. HR 4739. Fiscal 1991 Defense Authorization/SDI Funding. Dornan, R-Calif., amendment to increase funding for the strategic defense initiative (SDI) by $1.3 billion to $4.2 billion by proportionally reducing all other defense accounts in the bill and adding the reductions to the SDI account. Rejected 83-338: R 74-99; D 9-239 (ND 1-166, SD 8-73), Sept. 18, 1990.

337. HR 4739. Fiscal 1991 Defense Authorization/SDI Funding. Dellums, D-Calif., amendment to terminate the strategic defense initiative (SDI) program by limiting basic research on SDI in fiscal 1991 to $1.5 billion. Rejected 135-286: R 5-168; D 130-118 (ND 114-53, SD 16-65), Sept. 18, 1990. A "nay" was a vote supporting the president's position.

338. HR 4739. Fiscal 1991 Defense Authorization/SDI Funding. Kyl, R-Ariz., amendment to increase spending for the strategic defense initiative by $670 million to $3.6 billion by reducing spending for the F-16 program by $520 million and for the multi-launch rocket system by $150 million. Rejected 141-273: R 127-45; D 14-228 (ND 1-161, SD 13-67), Sept. 18, 1990.

339. HR 4739. Fiscal 1991 Defense Authorization/SDI Funding. Bennett, D-Fla., amendment to reduce spending for the strategic defense initiative (SDI) by $600 million to a new level of $2.3 billion. Adopted 225-189: R 20-150; D 205-39 (ND 157-7, SD 48-32), Sept. 18, 1990. A "nay" was a vote supporting the president's position.

KEY

- Y Voted for (yea).
- # Paired for.
- + Announced for.
- N Voted against (nay).
- X Paired against.
- - Announced against.
- P Voted "present."
- C Voted "present" to avoid possible conflict of interest.
- ? Did not vote or otherwise make a position known.

Democrats ***Republicans***

	332	333	334	335	336	337	338	339
ALABAMA								
1 ***Callahan***	Y	Y	Y	Y	Y	N	Y	N
2 ***Dickinson***	Y	Y	Y	Y	Y	N	Y	N
3 Browder	Y	Y	Y	Y	Y	N	Y	N
4 Bevill	Y	Y	Y	Y	Y	N	Y	N
5 Flippo	Y	Y	Y	Y	Y	N	Y	N
6 Erdreich	Y	Y	Y	Y	Y	N	Y	N
7 Harris	Y	Y	Y	Y	Y	N	Y	N
ALASKA								
AL ***Young***	?	?	Y	Y	Y	N	Y	N
ARIZONA								
1 ***Rhodes***	Y	Y	N	N	N	N	Y	N
2 Udall	Y	N	Y	N	N	Y	N	Y
3 ***Stump***	Y	Y	N	N	Y	N	Y	N
4 ***Kyl***	Y	Y	N	N	Y	N	Y	N
5 ***Kolbe***	Y	Y	N	N	N	N	Y	N
ARKANSAS								
1 Alexander	Y	N	Y	Y	N	N	N	Y
2 ***Robinson***	Y	Y	N	Y	Y	N	Y	N
3 ***Hammerschmidt***	Y	Y	Y	Y	Y	N	Y	N
4 Anthony	Y	N	Y	Y	N	N	N	Y
CALIFORNIA								
1 Bosco	Y	N	Y	Y	N	N	N	Y
2 ***Herger***	Y	Y	N	N	Y	N	Y	?
3 Matsui	?	?	Y	N	N	Y	N	Y
4 Fazio	Y	N	Y	Y	N	N	N	Y
5 Pelosi	+	N	Y	N	N	Y	N	Y
6 Boxer	?	?	Y	N	N	Y	N	Y
7 Miller	?	?	Y	N	N	Y	N	Y
8 Dellums	Y	N	Y	Y	N	Y	N	Y
9 Stark	Y	N	Y	-	N	Y	N	Y
10 Edwards	Y	N	Y	Y	N	Y	N	Y
11 Lantos	Y	N	Y	Y	N	N	N	Y
12 ***Campbell***	+	+	N	N	N	Y	N	Y
13 Mineta	Y	N	Y	Y	N	Y	N	Y
14 ***Shumway***	Y	Y	N	N	Y	N	Y	N
15 Condit	Y	Y	Y	Y	N	N	N	Y
16 Panetta	+	+	Y	N	N	Y	N	Y
17 ***Pashayan***	Y	Y	Y	Y	N	N	Y	N
18 Lehman	?	?	Y	Y	N	Y	N	Y
19 ***Lagomarsino***	Y	Y	N	N	Y	N	Y	N
20 ***Thomas***	Y	Y	Y	Y	N	N	Y	N
21 ***Gallegly***	Y	Y	N	N	Y	N	Y	N
22 ***Moorhead***	Y	Y	N	N	Y	N	Y	N
23 Beilenson	Y	N	Y	N	N	Y	N	Y
24 Waxman	Y	N	Y	N	N	Y	?	Y
25 Roybal	?	?	Y	Y	N	Y	N	Y
26 Berman	Y	N	Y	N	N	Y	N	Y
27 Levine	Y	N	Y	N	N	Y	N	Y
28 Dixon	Y	N	Y	Y	N	Y	N	Y
29 Hawkins	Y	N	Y	Y	N	Y	N	?
30 Martinez	Y	N	Y	Y	N	N	N	Y
31 Dymally	Y	N	Y	Y	N	Y	?	Y
32 Anderson	?	?	Y	N	N	Y	N	Y
33 ***Dreier***	Y	Y	N	N	Y	N	Y	N
34 Torres	Y	N	Y	Y	N	Y	N	Y
35 ***Lewis***	?	?	N	N	Y	N	Y	N
36 Brown	?	?	Y	Y	N	N	N	Y
37 ***McCandless***	Y	Y	N	N	N	N	Y	N
38 ***Dornan***	Y	Y	?	?	Y	N	Y	N
39 ***Dannemeyer***	Y	Y	N	N	Y	N	Y	N
40 ***Cox***	?	?	N	N	Y	N	Y	N
41 ***Lowery***	Y	Y	?	N	Y	N	Y	N
42 ***Rohrabacher***	Y	Y	N	N	Y	N	Y	N
43 ***Packard***	Y	Y	N	N	Y	N	Y	N
44 Bates	?	?	Y	Y	N	Y	N	Y
45 ***Hunter***	Y	Y	Y	Y	Y	N	Y	N
COLORADO								
1 Schroeder	Y	Y	N	N	N	Y	N	Y
2 Skaggs	Y	N	Y	N	N	Y	N	Y
3 Campbell	Y	Y	Y	Y	N	N	N	Y
4 ***Brown***	Y	Y	N	N	N	N	Y	N
5 ***Hefley***	Y	Y	N	N	Y	N	Y	N
6 ***Schaefer***	Y	Y	Y	Y	N	N	Y	N
CONNECTICUT								
1 Kennelly	Y	N	Y	N	N	Y	N	Y
2 Gejdenson	Y	N	Y	Y	N	Y	N	Y
3 Morrison	+	+	+	Y	N	Y	N	Y
4 ***Shays***	Y	Y	Y	Y	N	Y	N	Y
5 ***Rowland***	?	?	N	N	N	N	Y	N
6 ***Johnson***	+	+	N	N	N	N	?	N
DELAWARE								
AL Carper	Y	N	Y	Y	N	Y	N	Y
FLORIDA								
1 Hutto	?	?	Y	Y	N	N	Y	N
2 ***Grant***	Y	Y	Y	Y	N	N	N	Y
3 Bennett	Y	N	Y	N	N	N	N	Y
4 ***James***	Y	Y	N	N	N	N	Y	N
5 ***McCollum***	Y	Y	N	N	Y	N	Y	N
6 ***Stearns***	Y	Y	N	N	N	N	Y	N
7 Gibbons	Y	N	Y	N	N	Y	N	Y
8 ***Young***	?	?	N	N	Y	N	N	N
9 ***Bilirakis***	?	?	?	?	?	?	?	?
10 ***Ireland***	Y	Y	N	N	Y	N	Y	N
11 Nelson	Y	Y	Y	N	N	N	N	N
12 ***Lewis***	Y	Y	N	N	Y	N	N	N
13 ***Goss***	Y	Y	N	N	Y	N	Y	N
14 Johnston	Y	N	Y	Y	N	Y	N	Y
15 ***Shaw***	Y	Y	N	N	N	N	Y	N
16 Smith	Y	N	Y	Y	N	Y	N	Y
17 Lehman	Y	N	Y	Y	N	Y	N	Y
18 ***Ros-Lehtinen***	Y	Y	N	N	N	N	Y	N
19 Fascell	?	?	Y	Y	N	N	N	Y
GEORGIA								
1 Thomas	Y	Y	Y	Y	N	N	N	Y
2 Hatcher	Y	N	Y	Y	N	N	N	Y
3 Ray	Y	Y	Y	Y	N	N	N	Y
4 Jones	Y	Y	Y	Y	N	N	N	Y
5 Lewis	Y	N	Y	Y	N	Y	N	Y
6 ***Gingrich***	Y	Y	Y	Y	Y	N	Y	N
7 Darden	Y	Y	Y	Y	N	N	N	N
8 Rowland	Y	Y	Y	Y	N	N	N	Y
9 Jenkins	Y	Y	Y	Y	N	N	N	Y
10 Barnard	Y	Y	Y	Y	Y	N	Y	?
HAWAII								
1 ***Saiki***	Y	Y	N	N	N	N	N	N
2 Vacancy								
IDAHO								
1 ***Craig***	Y	Y	N	N	N	N	Y	N
2 Stallings	Y	Y	Y	N	N	N	N	Y
ILLINOIS								
1 Hayes	Y	N	Y	Y	N	Y	N	Y
2 Savage	Y	N	Y	Y	N	Y	N	Y
3 Russo	Y	N	Y	Y	N	Y	N	Y
4 Sangmeister	?	?	Y	N	N	N	N	Y
5 Lipinski	Y	N	Y	Y	N	N	N	N
6 ***Hyde***	Y	Y	N	N	Y	N	Y	N
7 Collins	Y	N	Y	Y	N	Y	N	Y
8 Rostenkowski	Y	N	Y	N	N	N	N	Y
9 Yates	Y	N	Y	Y	N	Y	N	Y
10 ***Porter***	Y	Y	N	N	N	N	N	N
11 Annunzio	Y	N	Y	Y	N	N	N	Y
12 ***Crane***	Y	Y	N	N	Y	N	Y	N
13 ***Fawell***	Y	Y	N	N	N	N	Y	N
14 ***Hastert***	Y	Y	N	-	N	N	Y	N
15 ***Madigan***	Y	Y	N	N	?	N	Y	N
16 ***Martin***	?	?	N	N	N	N	N	N
17 Evans	Y	N	Y	Y	N	Y	N	Y
18 ***Michel***	Y	Y	N	N	Y	N	Y	N
19 Bruce	Y	N	Y	Y	N	Y	N	Y
20 Durbin	Y	N	Y	Y	N	Y	N	Y
21 Costello	Y	Y	Y	Y	N	N	N	Y
22 Poshard	Y	Y	Y	Y	N	Y	N	Y
INDIANA								
1 Visclosky	+	-	Y	Y	N	N	N	Y
2 Sharp	Y	Y	Y	Y	N	N	?	?
3 ***Hiler***	Y	Y	N	N	Y	N	Y	N

ND Northern Democrats SD Southern Democrats

	332	333	334	335	336	337	338	339
4 Long	Y	Y	Y	Y	N	N	N	Y
5 Jontz	Y	Y	Y	Y	N	Y	N	Y
6 ***Burton***	Y	Y	N	Y	Y	N	Y	N
7 ***Myers***	Y	N	N	N	Y	N	Y	N
8 McCloskey	Y	N	Y	Y	N	N	N	Y
9 Hamilton	Y	N	Y	N	N	N	N	Y
10 Jacobs	?	?	N	Y	N	Y	N	Y
IOWA								
1 ***Leach***	Y	Y	N	N	N	Y	N	Y
2 ***Tauke***	?	?	N	N	N	N	N	N
3 Nagle	Y	Y	Y	Y	N	Y	N	Y
4 Smith	Y	N	Y	N	N	N	N	N
5 ***Lightfoot***	Y	Y	N	N	N	N	Y	N
6 ***Grandy***	Y	Y	N	N	N	N	N	Y
KANSAS								
1 ***Roberts***	Y	Y	N	N	N	N	Y	N
2 Slattery	Y	Y	Y	N	N	N	N	Y
3 ***Meyers***	Y	Y	N	N	N	N	N	N
4 Glickman	Y	Y	Y	N	N	Y	N	Y
5 ***Whittaker***	?	?	N	N	Y	N	Y	N
KENTUCKY								
1 Hubbard	Y	Y	Y	Y	N	N	Y	Y
2 Natcher	Y	Y	Y	Y	N	N	N	Y
3 Mazzoli	Y	N	Y	N	N	N	N	Y
4 ***Bunning***	Y	Y	N	N	N	N	Y	N
5 ***Rogers***	Y	Y	Y	Y	N	N	Y	N
6 ***Hopkins***	Y	Y	Y	Y	N	N	N	N
7 Perkins	Y	N	Y	Y	N	Y	N	Y
LOUISIANA								
1 ***Livingston***	Y	N	Y	Y	Y	N	Y	N
2 Boggs	Y	N	Y	Y	N	N	N	N
3 Tauzin	Y	Y	Y	Y	N	N	Y	N
4 ***McCrery***	Y	Y	N	Y	Y	N	Y	N
5 Huckaby	Y	Y	?	Y	N	N	Y	N
6 ***Baker***	Y	N	N	Y	N	N	Y	N
7 Hayes	Y	Y	Y	Y	N	N	N	N
8 ***Holloway***	Y	Y	N	Y	Y	N	Y	N
MAINE								
1 Brennan	Y	Y	Y	Y	N	Y	N	Y
2 ***Snowe***	Y	Y	Y	Y	N	N	N	Y
MARYLAND								
1 Dyson	Y	N	Y	Y	N	N	N	N
2 ***Bentley***	Y	Y	Y	Y	N	N	N	N
3 Cardin	Y	N	Y	Y	N	N	N	Y
4 McMillen	Y	N	Y	Y	N	N	N	Y
5 Hoyer	Y	N	Y	Y	N	N	N	Y
6 Byron	Y	N	Y	Y	N	N	N	N
7 Mfume	Y	N	Y	Y	N	N	Y	Y
8 ***Morella***	Y	Y	N	N	N	N	N	Y
MASSACHUSETTS								
1 ***Conte***	Y	Y	Y	Y	N	Y	N	Y
2 Neal	+	+	+	+	-	+	-	+
3 Early	Y	Y	Y	Y	N	Y	N	Y
4 Frank	Y	N	Y	Y	N	Y	N	Y
5 Atkins	Y	N	Y	Y	N	Y	N	Y
6 Mavroules	Y	N	Y	Y	N	Y	N	Y
7 Markey	Y	N	?	Y	N	Y	N	Y
8 Kennedy	?	?	?	?	?	Y	N	Y
9 Moakley	Y	N	Y	Y	N	Y	N	Y
10 Studds	Y	N	Y	Y	N	Y	N	Y
11 Donnelly	?	?	Y	Y	N	N	N	Y
MICHIGAN								
1 Conyers	Y	N	Y	Y	N	Y	N	Y
2 ***Pursell***	Y	Y	N	N	N	N	N	Y
3 Wolpe	Y	Y	Y	Y	N	Y	N	Y
4 ***Upton***	Y	Y	N	N	N	N	Y	N
5 ***Henry***	Y	Y	Y	Y	N	N	Y	N
6 Carr	Y	N	Y	Y	N	Y	N	Y
7 Kildee	Y	Y	Y	Y	N	Y	N	Y
8 Traxler	Y	N	Y	Y	N	Y	N	Y
9 ***Vander Jagt***	Y	Y	N	N	Y	N	Y	N
10 ***Schuette***	?	?	N	N	N	N	Y	N
11 ***Davis***	Y	Y	Y	Y	Y	N	N	?
12 Bonior	Y	N	Y	Y	N	Y	N	Y
13 Crockett	?	?	Y	N	N	?	?	?
14 Hertel	Y	N	Y	Y	N	Y	N	Y
15 Ford	Y	N	Y	Y	N	Y	N	Y
16 Dingell	Y	N	?	Y	N	Y	N	Y
17 Levin	Y	N	Y	Y	N	Y	N	Y
18 ***Broomfield***	Y	Y	N	N	N	N	Y	N
MINNESOTA								
1 Penny	Y	Y	N	N	N	Y	N	Y
2 ***Weber***	?	?	N	N	Y	N	Y	N
3 ***Frenzel***	?	?	N	N	N	N	N	N
4 Vento	Y	N	Y	Y	N	Y	N	Y
5 Sabo	?	?	Y	Y	N	Y	N	Y
6 Sikorski	Y	N	Y	Y	N	Y	N	Y
7 ***Stangeland***	Y	Y	N	N	Y	N	Y	N
8 Oberstar	Y	N	Y	Y	N	Y	N	Y
MISSISSIPPI								
1 Whitten	Y	N	Y	Y	N	N	N	N
2 Espy	?	?	Y	Y	N	Y	N	Y
3 Montgomery	Y	N	Y	Y	N	N	N	N
4 Parker	Y	Y	Y	Y	N	N	N	N
5 Taylor	Y	N	Y	Y	N	N	N	N
MISSOURI								
1 Clay	Y	N	Y	Y	N	Y	N	Y
2 ***Buechner***	Y	Y	N	N	N	N	Y	N
3 Gephardt	?	?	Y	Y	N	Y	N	Y
4 Skelton	Y	Y	Y	Y	N	N	N	N
5 Wheat	Y	N	Y	Y	N	Y	N	Y
6 ***Coleman***	Y	Y	N	Y	N	N	Y	N
7 ***Hancock***	Y	Y	N	N	Y	N	Y	N
8 ***Emerson***	Y	Y	Y	Y	N	N	Y	N
9 Volkmer	Y	Y	Y	Y	N	N	N	Y
MONTANA								
1 Williams	?	?	Y	Y	N	Y	N	Y
2 ***Marlenee***	Y	Y	N	N	N	N	N	N
NEBRASKA								
1 ***Bereuter***	Y	Y	N	N	N	N	N	N
2 Hoagland	Y	N	Y	Y	N	N	N	Y
3 ***Smith***	Y	Y	N	N	N	N	Y	N
NEVADA								
1 Bilbray	Y	Y	Y	Y	N	N	N	Y
2 ***Vucanovich***	Y	Y	N	Y	Y	N	Y	N
NEW HAMPSHIRE								
1 ***Smith***	Y	Y	N	Y	Y	N	Y	N
2 ***Douglas***	Y	Y	N	Y	Y	N	Y	N
NEW JERSEY								
1 Vacancy								
2 Hughes	Y	N	Y	Y	N	N	N	Y
3 Pallone	Y	Y	Y	Y	N	N	N	Y
4 ***Smith***	Y	Y	Y	Y	N	N	Y	N
5 ***Roukema***	Y	Y	Y	Y	N	N	N	Y
6 Dwyer	Y	Y	Y	Y	N	N	N	Y
7 ***Rinaldo***	Y	Y	Y	Y	N	N	Y	N
8 Roe	Y	Y	Y	Y	N	N	N	Y
9 Torricelli	Y	N	Y	Y	?	?	?	?
10 Payne	Y	N	Y	Y	N	Y	N	Y
11 ***Gallo***	Y	Y	N	N	N	N	Y	N
12 ***Courter***	Y	Y	N	N	Y	N	Y	N
13 ***Saxton***	Y	Y	?	N	N	N	N	Y
14 Guarini	Y	N	Y	Y	N	N	N	Y
NEW MEXICO								
1 ***Schiff***	Y	Y	N	Y	Y	N	Y	N
2 ***Skeen***	Y	Y	Y	Y	Y	N	Y	N
3 Richardson	Y	N	Y	Y	Y	N	Y	N
NEW YORK								
1 Hochbrueckner	Y	N	Y	Y	N	N	N	Y
2 Downey	Y	N	Y	N	N	Y	N	Y
3 Mrazek	Y	N	Y	Y	N	Y	N	Y
4 ***Lent***	Y	Y	?	N	N	N	Y	N
5 ***McGrath***	Y	Y	Y	Y	N	N	N	N
6 Flake	?	?	Y	Y	N	Y	N	Y
7 Ackerman	Y	N	Y	Y	N	Y	N	Y
8 Scheuer	Y	N	Y	Y	N	Y	N	Y
9 Manton	?	?	Y	Y	N	N	N	Y
10 Schumer	Y	N	Y	N	N	Y	N	Y
11 Towns	Y	N	Y	Y	N	Y	N	Y
12 Owens	Y	N	Y	Y	N	Y	N	Y
13 Solarz	Y	N	Y	N	N	Y	N	Y
14 ***Molinari***	Y	Y	N	N	N	N	Y	N
15 ***Green***	Y	Y	N	N	N	N	N	Y
16 Rangel	Y	N	Y	Y	N	Y	N	Y
17 Weiss	Y	N	Y	Y	N	Y	N	Y
18 Serrano	Y	N	Y	Y	N	Y	N	Y
19 Engel	Y	N	Y	Y	N	Y	N	Y
20 Lowey	?	?	Y	Y	N	Y	N	Y
21 ***Fish***	Y	N	Y	Y	N	N	N	N
22 ***Gilman***	Y	N	Y	Y	N	N	Y	N
23 McNulty	Y	N	Y	Y	N	N	N	N
24 ***Solomon***	Y	Y	N	Y	Y	N	Y	N
25 ***Boehlert***	Y	Y	Y	Y	N	N	Y	N
26 ***Martin***	Y	Y	N	Y	Y	N	Y	N
27 ***Walsh***	Y	Y	N	N	Y	N	Y	N
28 McHugh	Y	N	Y	N	N	Y	N	Y
29 ***Horton***	Y	Y	Y	Y	N	N	N	Y
30 Slaughter	Y	N	Y	Y	N	Y	N	Y
31 ***Paxon***	Y	Y	N	N	N	N	Y	N
32 LaFalce	Y	N	Y	N	N	Y	N	Y
33 Nowak	Y	N	Y	Y	N	Y	N	Y
34 ***Houghton***	?	?	Y	Y	N	N	Y	N
NORTH CAROLINA								
1 Jones	Y	N	Y	Y	N	Y	N	Y
2 Valentine	Y	Y	Y	Y	N	N	N	Y
3 Lancaster	Y	Y	Y	Y	N	N	N	N
4 Price	Y	Y	Y	Y	N	N	N	Y
5 Neal	Y	Y	Y	Y	N	N	N	Y
6 ***Coble***	Y	Y	Y	Y	N	N	N	N
7 Rose	?	?	Y	Y	N	Y	N	Y
8 Hefner	Y	Y	Y	Y	N	N	N	Y
9 ***McMillan***	Y	Y	Y	Y	N	N	Y	N
10 ***Ballenger***	Y	Y	Y	Y	N	N	Y	N
11 Clarke	Y	Y	Y	Y	N	N	N	Y
NORTH DAKOTA								
AL Dorgan	Y	N	Y	N	N	Y	N	Y
OHIO								
1 Luken	Y	N	Y	Y	N	N	N	Y
2 ***Gradison***	?	?	N	N	N	N	Y	N
3 Hall	Y	N	Y	Y	N	Y	N	Y
4 ***Oxley***	Y	Y	N	N	N	N	Y	N
5 ***Gillmor***	Y	Y	N	N	N	N	Y	N
6 ***McEwen***	Y	Y	N	N	Y	N	Y	N
7 ***DeWine***	Y	Y	N	N	Y	N	Y	N
8 ***Lukens***	Y	Y	Y	Y	Y	N	Y	N
9 Kaptur	Y	N	Y	Y	N	N	N	Y
10 ***Miller***	Y	Y	N	Y	Y	N	Y	?
11 Eckart	Y	Y	Y	Y	N	N	Y	Y
12 ***Kasich***	Y	Y	N	N	Y	N	Y	N
13 Pease	Y	N	N	N	N	Y	N	Y
14 Sawyer	Y	N	Y	Y	N	Y	N	Y
15 ***Wylie***	Y	Y	N	N	N	N	Y	N
16 ***Regula***	Y	Y	Y	Y	N	N	N	N
17 Traficant	Y	Y	Y	Y	N	N	N	Y
18 Applegate	?	?	Y	Y	N	N	N	Y
19 Feighan	Y	N	?	?	?	?	?	?
20 Oakar	Y	N	Y	Y	N	Y	N	Y
21 Stokes	Y	N	Y	Y	N	Y	N	Y
OKLAHOMA								
1 ***Inhofe***	Y	Y	N	N	Y	N	Y	N
2 Synar	Y	N	Y	N	N	Y	N	Y
3 Watkins	?	?	?	?	?	?	?	?
4 McCurdy	Y	N	Y	N	N	N	N	Y
5 ***Edwards***	Y	Y	N	N	N	N	Y	N
6 English	Y	Y	Y	N	N	N	N	N
OREGON								
1 AuCoin	?	?	?	X	?	?	?	?
2 ***Smith, B.***	Y	Y	N	N	N	N	Y	N
3 Wyden	Y	Y	Y	N	N	Y	N	Y
4 DeFazio	Y	N	Y	N	N	Y	N	Y
5 ***Smith, D.***	Y	Y	Y	Y	N	N	Y	N
PENNSYLVANIA								
1 Foglietta	?	?	Y	Y	N	Y	N	Y
2 Gray	?	?	Y	Y	N	Y	N	Y
3 Borski	Y	N	Y	Y	N	N	N	Y
4 Kolter	?	?	Y	Y	N	N	N	Y
5 ***Schulze***	?	?	Y	Y	N	N	N	N
6 Yatron	Y	Y	Y	Y	N	N	N	Y
7 ***Weldon***	Y	Y	Y	Y	N	N	Y	N
8 Kostmayer	+	+	Y	Y	N	Y	N	Y
9 ***Shuster***	Y	Y	Y	Y	Y	?	?	N
10 ***McDade***	?	?	?	?	?	?	?	?
11 Kanjorski	Y	Y	Y	Y	N	Y	N	Y
12 Murtha	Y	N	Y	Y	N	N	?	?
13 ***Coughlin***	Y	Y	N	N	N	N	N	Y
14 Coyne	?	?	Y	Y	N	Y	N	Y
15 ***Ritter***	Y	Y	Y	Y	N	N	Y	N
16 ***Walker***	Y	Y	N	N	Y	N	Y	N
17 ***Gekas***	Y	Y	N	Y	Y	N	Y	?
18 Walgren	Y	Y	Y	Y	N	Y	N	Y
19 ***Goodling***	Y	Y	Y	Y	N	N	N	N
20 Gaydos	Y	Y	Y	Y	N	N	N	Y
21 ***Ridge***	Y	Y	Y	Y	N	N	N	Y
22 Murphy	Y	N	Y	Y	N	N	N	Y
23 ***Clinger***	Y	Y	Y	Y	N	N	Y	N
RHODE ISLAND								
1 ***Machtley***	Y	Y	Y	Y	N	N	N	Y
2 ***Schneider***	Y	Y	N	Y	N	Y	N	Y
SOUTH CAROLINA								
1 ***Ravenel***	Y	Y	Y	Y	N	N	Y	N
2 ***Spence***	Y	Y	Y	Y	Y	N	Y	N
3 Derrick	Y	Y	Y	Y	N	N	N	Y
4 Patterson	Y	Y	Y	Y	N	N	N	N
5 Spratt	Y	N	Y	Y	N	N	N	N
6 Tallon	Y	Y	Y	Y	N	N	N	N
SOUTH DAKOTA								
AL Johnson	Y	Y	Y	Y	N	Y	N	Y
TENNESSEE								
1 ***Quillen***	Y	Y	Y	Y	Y	N	Y	N
2 ***Duncan***	Y	Y	N	N	N	N	Y	N
3 Lloyd	Y	Y	Y	Y	N	N	N	N
4 Cooper	?	?	Y	Y	N	N	N	Y
5 Clement	Y	N	Y	Y	N	N	N	Y
6 Gordon	Y	N	Y	Y	N	N	N	Y
7 ***Sundquist***	Y	Y	N	N	N	N	Y	N
8 Tanner	?	?	Y	Y	N	N	N	Y
9 Ford	Y	N	Y	#	N	Y	N	Y
TEXAS								
1 Chapman	Y	Y	Y	Y	N	N	N	Y
2 Wilson	?	?	?	Y	Y	N	Y	N
3 ***Bartlett***	Y	Y	N	N	Y	N	N	N
4 Hall	Y	Y	Y	Y	Y	N	Y	N
5 Bryant	Y	N	Y	Y	N	Y	N	Y
6 ***Barton***	Y	Y	N	N	Y	N	N	N
7 ***Archer***	Y	Y	N	N	Y	N	Y	N
8 ***Fields***	Y	Y	N	N	Y	N	N	N
9 Brooks	Y	N	Y	Y	N	N	N	Y
10 Pickle	Y	Y	Y	N	N	N	Y	N
11 Leath	?	?	?	?	?	?	?	?
12 Geren	Y	Y	Y	N	N	N	N	N
13 Sarpalius	Y	Y	Y	Y	N	N	N	N
14 Laughlin	Y	Y	Y	Y	N	N	N	Y
15 de la Garza	Y	Y	Y	Y	N	Y	N	Y
16 Coleman	Y	N	Y	Y	N	N	N	N
17 Stenholm	Y	Y	Y	Y	N	N	N	N
18 Washington	?	?	Y	Y	N	Y	?	Y
19 ***Combest***	Y	Y	N	Y	Y	N	Y	N
20 Gonzalez	Y	N	Y	Y	N	Y	N	Y
21 ***Smith***	Y	Y	N	Y	Y	N	Y	N
22 ***DeLay***	Y	Y	N	N	Y	N	Y	N
23 Bustamante	?	?	?	Y	N	N	N	Y
24 Frost	Y	N	Y	Y	N	N	N	Y
25 Andrews	Y	N	Y	Y	N	N	N	Y
26 ***Armey***	Y	Y	N	N	Y	N	N	N
27 Ortiz	Y	N	Y	Y	N	N	N	Y
UTAH								
1 ***Hansen***	Y	Y	N	N	Y	N	Y	N
2 Owens	?	?	Y	N	N	Y	N	Y
3 ***Nielson***	Y	Y	N	N	N	N	Y	N
VERMONT								
AL ***Smith***	Y	Y	Y	Y	N	N	N	Y
VIRGINIA								
1 ***Bateman***	Y	Y	Y	Y	N	N	Y	N
2 Pickett	Y	Y	Y	Y	N	N	N	N
3 ***Bliley***	Y	Y	Y	Y	Y	N	Y	N
4 Sisisky	Y	Y	Y	Y	N	N	N	N
5 Payne	Y	Y	Y	Y	N	N	N	N
6 Olin	Y	N	Y	Y	N	N	N	Y
7 ***Slaughter***	Y	Y	N	Y	Y	N	Y	N
8 ***Parris***	Y	Y	Y	Y	N	N	Y	N
9 Boucher	?	?	Y	Y	N	Y	N	Y
10 ***Wolf***	Y	Y	Y	N	N	N	Y	N
WASHINGTON								
1 ***Miller***	Y	Y	N	N	N	N	Y	N
2 Swift	Y	N	Y	N	N	Y	N	Y
3 Unsoeld	Y	N	Y	N	-	+	-	+
4 ***Morrison***	Y	Y	N	N	N	N	Y	N
5 Foley								
6 Dicks	Y	N	N	N	N	N	N	Y
7 McDermott	Y	N	Y	N	N	Y	N	Y
8 ***Chandler***	Y	Y	N	N	N	N	N	Y
WEST VIRGINIA								
1 Mollohan	Y	N	Y	Y	N	N	?	Y
2 Staggers	Y	Y	Y	Y	N	Y	N	Y
3 Wise	Y	N	Y	Y	N	N	N	Y
4 Rahall	Y	Y	Y	Y	N	Y	N	Y
WISCONSIN								
1 Aspin	Y	N	Y	Y	N	N	N	Y
2 Kastenmeier	Y	N	Y	Y	N	Y	N	Y
3 ***Gunderson***	Y	Y	Y	Y	N	N	N	N
4 Kleczka	?	?	Y	Y	N	N	N	Y
5 Moody	Y	Y	Y	N	N	Y	N	Y
6 ***Petri***	?	?	N	N	N	N	N	N
7 Obey	Y	N	Y	Y	N	Y	N	Y
8 ***Roth***	Y	Y	Y	Y	N	N	N	N
9 ***Sensenbrenner***	Y	Y	N	N	N	N	N	N
WYOMING								
AL ***Thomas***	Y	Y	N	N	N	N	Y	N

Southern states - Ala., Ark., Fla., Ga., Ky., La., Miss., N.C., Okla., S.C., Tenn., Texas, Va.
Omitted votes are quorum calls, which CQ does not include in its vote charts.

HOUSE VOTES 340, 341, 342, 343, 344, 345, 346, 347

340. HR 4739. Fiscal 1991 Defense Authorization/Economic Adjustment. Hopkins, R-Ky., substitute amendment to the Mavroules, D-Mass., amendment, to increase economic adjustment planning assistance programs funding to $6 million. Rejected 161-253: R 149-23; D 12-230 (ND 2-161, SD 10-69), Sept. 18, 1990.

341. HR 4739. Fiscal 1991 Defense Authorization/Economic Adjustment. Mavroules, D-Mass., amendment to authorize $200 million to create a Defense Economic Adjustment program. Adopted 288-128: R 56-117; D 232-11 (ND 160-3, SD 72-8), Sept. 18, 1990.

342. HR 4739. Fiscal 1991 Defense Authorization/Abortion Services. Fazio, D-Calif., amendment to provide servicemen and their dependents stationed overseas with reproductive health services, including privately paid abortions, at military hospitals. Rejected 200-216: R 35-139; D 165-77 (ND 113-50, SD 52-27), Sept. 18, 1990. A "nay" was a vote supporting the president's position.

343. HR 4739. Fiscal 1991 Defense Authorization/Nuclear Testing. Bosco, D-Calif., amendment to express the sense of the Congress urging the president to negotiate international agreements to achieve early prohibition of nuclear weapons testing. Adopted 234-182: R 36-138; D 198-44 (ND 155-8, SD 43-36), Sept. 18, 1990. A "nay" was a vote supporting the president's position.

344. HR 4739. Fiscal 1991 Defense Authorization/Whistleblowers. Boxer, D-Calif., amendment to prohibit psychiatric examination or hospitalization to be improperly used to harass military whistleblowers. Adopted 334-83: R 113-61; D 221-22 (ND 158-6, SD 63-16), Sept. 18, 1990.

345. HR 4739. Fiscal 1991 Defense Authorization/ICBMs. Frank, D-Mass., amendment to cut $200 million from the $610 million for research and development of mobile intercontinental ballistic missiles (ICBMs). Rejected 153-264: R 27-147; D 126-117 (ND 112-52, SD 14-65), Sept. 18, 1990. A "nay" was a vote supporting the president's position.

346. HR 4739. Fiscal 1991 Defense Authorization/North American Van Lines. Hopkins, R-Ky., amendment to strike provisions that allow the Army to reimburse North American Van Lines for property losses incurred during the invasion of Panama. Rejected 189-228: R 164-9; D 25-219 (ND 15-149, SD 10-70), Sept. 18, 1990.

347. HR 4739. Fiscal 1991 Defense Authorization/Across-the-Board Cut. Traficant, D-Ohio, amendment to reduce all authorizations by 2 percent. Rejected 133-284: R 43-131; D 90-153 (ND 84-79, SD 6-74), Sept. 18, 1990. A "nay" was a vote supporting the president's position.

KEY

Y Voted for (yea).
Paired for.
+ Announced for.
N Voted against (nay).
X Paired against.
- Announced against.
P Voted "present."
C Voted "present" to avoid possible conflict of interest.
? Did not vote or otherwise make a position known.

Democrats ***Republicans***

	340	341	342	343	344	345	346	347
ALABAMA								
1 ***Callahan***	Y	N	N	N	N	N	C	N
2 ***Dickinson***	Y	N	N	N	N	N	Y	N
3 Browder	N	Y	N	N	N	N	N	N
4 Bevill	N	Y	N	N	Y	N	N	N
5 Flippo	N	Y	N	N	Y	N	N	N
6 Erdreich	N	Y	Y	N	Y	N	N	N
7 Harris	N	Y	N	N	Y	N	N	N
ALASKA								
AL ***Young***	Y	N	N	N	N	N	Y	N
ARIZONA								
1 ***Rhodes***	Y	N	N	N	N	N	Y	N
2 Udall	N	Y	Y	Y	Y	Y	Y	N
3 ***Stump***	Y	N	N	N	N	N	Y	N
4 ***Kyl***	Y	N	N	N	N	N	Y	N
5 ***Kolbe***	Y	N	Y	N	N	N	Y	N
ARKANSAS								
1 Alexander	?	Y	Y	Y	Y	N	N	N
2 ***Robinson***	Y	N	N	N	N	N	Y	N
3 ***Hammerschmidt***	Y	Y	N	N	N	N	Y	N
4 Anthony	N	Y	Y	Y	Y	N	N	N
CALIFORNIA								
1 Bosco	N	Y	Y	Y	Y	Y	N	Y
2 ***Herger***	Y	N	N	N	Y	N	Y	Y
3 Matsui	N	Y	Y	Y	Y	Y	N	Y
4 Fazio	N	Y	Y	Y	Y	N	N	N
5 Pelosi	N	Y	Y	Y	Y	Y	N	Y
6 Boxer	N	Y	Y	Y	Y	Y	N	Y
7 Miller	N	Y	Y	Y	Y	Y	N	Y
8 Dellums	N	Y	Y	Y	Y	Y	N	Y
9 Stark	N	Y	Y	Y	Y	Y	N	Y
10 Edwards	N	Y	Y	Y	Y	Y	N	Y
11 Lantos	N	Y	Y	Y	Y	N	N	N
12 ***Campbell***	N	Y	Y	Y	Y	Y	Y	Y
13 Mineta	N	Y	Y	Y	Y	Y	N	Y
14 ***Shumway***	Y	N	N	N	N	N	Y	N
15 Condit	N	Y	Y	Y	Y	N	N	Y
16 Panetta	N	Y	Y	Y	Y	Y	N	N
17 ***Pashayan***	Y	Y	N	N	Y	N	Y	N
18 Lehman	N	Y	Y	Y	Y	Y	N	Y
19 ***Lagomarsino***	Y	N	N	N	Y	N	Y	N
20 ***Thomas***	Y	N	Y	N	Y	N	Y	Y
21 ***Gallegly***	Y	N	N	N	Y	N	Y	N
22 ***Moorhead***	Y	N	N	N	Y	N	Y	N
23 Beilenson	N	Y	Y	Y	Y	Y	N	N
24 Waxman	N	Y	Y	Y	Y	Y	N	N
25 Roybal	N	Y	Y	Y	Y	Y	N	Y
26 Berman	N	Y	Y	Y	Y	Y	N	N
27 Levine	N	Y	Y	Y	Y	Y	N	N
28 Dixon	N	Y	Y	Y	Y	Y	N	N
29 Hawkins	?	?	?	?	?	?	?	?
30 Martinez	N	Y	Y	Y	Y	Y	N	Y
31 Dymally	N	Y	Y	Y	Y	Y	N	Y
32 Anderson	N	Y	Y	Y	Y	Y	N	Y
33 ***Dreier***	Y	N	N	N	Y	N	Y	N
34 Torres	N	Y	Y	Y	Y	Y	N	Y
35 ***Lewis***	Y	Y	N	N	N	N	Y	N
36 Brown	N	Y	Y	Y	Y	N	N	N
37 ***McCandless***	Y	N	Y	N	N	N	Y	N
38 ***Dornan***	Y	N	N	N	Y	N	Y	N
39 ***Dannemeyer***	Y	N	N	N	N	N	Y	Y
40 ***Cox***	Y	N	N	N	Y	N	Y	N
41 ***Lowery***	Y	N	N	N	Y	N	Y	N
42 ***Rohrabacher***	Y	N	N	N	Y	Y	Y	Y
43 ***Packard***	Y	N	N	N	N	N	Y	N
44 Bates	N	Y	Y	Y	Y	Y	N	N
45 ***Hunter***	Y	N	N	N	Y	N	Y	N
COLORADO								
1 Schroeder	N	Y	Y	Y	Y	Y	N	Y
2 Skaggs	N	Y	Y	Y	Y	N	N	N
3 Campbell	N	Y	Y	Y	Y	N	Y	N
4 ***Brown***	Y	N	Y	Y	Y	N	Y	N
5 ***Hefley***	Y	N	N	Y	Y	N	Y	N
6 ***Schaefer***	Y	N	N	Y	Y	N	Y	Y
CONNECTICUT								
1 Kennelly	N	Y	Y	Y	Y	Y	N	N
2 Gejdenson	N	Y	Y	Y	Y	Y	N	N
3 Morrison	N	Y	Y	Y	Y	Y	N	N
4 ***Shays***	N	Y	Y	Y	Y	Y	Y	Y
5 ***Rowland***	Y	Y	Y	Y	Y	Y	Y	N
6 ***Johnson***	Y	Y	Y	Y	Y	Y	Y	N
DELAWARE								
AL Carper	N	Y	Y	Y	Y	N	N	N
FLORIDA								
1 Hutto	N	Y	N	N	N	N	Y	N
2 ***Grant***	Y	?	N	N	Y	N	Y	N
3 Bennett	N	Y	Y	Y	Y	N	Y	N
4 ***James***	Y	N	N	N	Y	N	Y	N
5 ***McCollum***	Y	N	N	N	Y	N	Y	N
6 ***Stearns***	Y	N	N	Y	Y	N	Y	N
7 Gibbons	N	Y	Y	Y	Y	Y	N	N
8 ***Young***	Y	N	N	N	Y	N	Y	N
9 ***Bilirakis***	?	?	?	?	?	?	?	?
10 ***Ireland***	Y	N	N	N	N	N	Y	N
11 Nelson	N	Y	Y	Y	Y	N	N	N
12 ***Lewis***	Y	N	N	N	Y	N	Y	N
13 ***Goss***	Y	N	N	N	N	N	Y	N
14 Johnston	N	Y	Y	Y	Y	N	Y	N
15 ***Shaw***	N	N	N	N	Y	N	Y	N
16 Smith	N	Y	Y	Y	Y	Y	N	N
17 Lehman	N	Y	Y	Y	Y	Y	N	Y
18 ***Ros-Lehtinen***	Y	N	N	N	Y	N	Y	N
19 Fascell	N	Y	Y	Y	Y	N	N	N
GEORGIA								
1 Thomas	N	Y	Y	N	Y	N	N	N
2 Hatcher	N	Y	Y	N	Y	N	N	N
3 Ray	N	Y	N	N	N	N	Y	N
4 Jones	N	Y	Y	Y	Y	N	N	N
5 Lewis	N	Y	Y	Y	Y	Y	N	Y
6 ***Gingrich***	Y	N	N	N	N	N	Y	N
7 Darden	N	Y	Y	N	Y	N	N	N
8 Rowland	N	Y	Y	N	Y	N	N	N
9 Jenkins	N	Y	N	N	Y	N	N	N
10 Barnard	N	Y	N	N	Y	N	N	N
HAWAII								
1 ***Saiki***	N	Y	Y	Y	Y	Y	Y	N
2 Vacancy								
IDAHO								
1 ***Craig***	Y	Y	N	N	Y	N	Y	N
2 Stallings	N	Y	N	Y	Y	Y	N	N
ILLINOIS								
1 Hayes	N	Y	Y	Y	Y	Y	N	Y
2 Savage	N	Y	Y	Y	Y	Y	N	Y
3 Russo	N	Y	N	Y	Y	Y	N	Y
4 Sangmeister	N	Y	N	Y	Y	N	N	N
5 Lipinski	N	N	N	N	Y	N	N	N
6 ***Hyde***	Y	N	N	N	Y	N	Y	N
7 Collins	N	Y	Y	Y	Y	Y	N	Y
8 Rostenkowski	N	Y	N	Y	Y	N	N	N
9 Yates	N	Y	Y	Y	Y	Y	N	N
10 ***Porter***	Y	N	Y	Y	Y	N	Y	Y
11 Annunzio	N	Y	N	Y	Y	Y	N	N
12 ***Crane***	Y	N	N	N	N	N	Y	N
13 ***Fawell***	Y	N	Y	Y	Y	N	Y	Y
14 ***Hastert***	Y	N	N	N	N	Y	Y	Y
15 ***Madigan***	Y	Y	N	N	N	N	N	N
16 ***Martin***	Y	N	Y	Y	Y	N	Y	N
17 Evans	N	Y	Y	Y	Y	Y	N	N
18 ***Michel***	Y	N	N	N	Y	N	Y	N
19 Bruce	N	Y	N	Y	Y	Y	N	N
20 Durbin	N	Y	N	Y	Y	Y	N	Y
21 Costello	N	Y	N	N	Y	N	N	N
22 Poshard	N	Y	N	Y	Y	N	N	N
INDIANA								
1 Visclosky	N	Y	Y	Y	Y	Y	N	N
2 Sharp	N	Y	Y	Y	Y	Y	N	Y
3 ***Hiler***	Y	N	N	N	Y	N	Y	N

ND Northern Democrats SD Southern Democrats

	340	341	342	343	344	345	346	347
4 Long	N	Y	Y	Y	Y	N	N	N
5 Jontz	N	Y	Y	Y	Y	Y	N	Y
6 ***Burton***	Y	N	N	N	N	N	Y	N
7 ***Myers***	Y	N	N	N	N	N	N	N
8 McCloskey	N	Y	Y	Y	Y	N	N	N
9 Hamilton	N	Y	Y	Y	Y	N	N	Y
10 Jacobs	N	Y	Y	Y	Y	Y	N	Y
IOWA								
1 ***Leach***	N	Y	Y	Y	Y	Y	Y	Y
2 ***Tauke***	Y	N	N	Y	Y	Y	Y	Y
3 Nagle	N	Y	Y	Y	Y	N	N	Y
4 Smith	Y	N	Y	Y	Y	N	N	N
5 ***Lightfoot***	Y	N	N	N	Y	N	Y	N
6 ***Grandy***	Y	N	N	N	Y	N	Y	Y
KANSAS								
1 ***Roberts***	Y	N	N	N	Y	N	Y	Y
2 Slattery	N	Y	Y	Y	Y	N	Y	N
3 ***Meyers***	N	Y	Y	Y	Y	Y	Y	Y
4 Glickman	N	Y	Y	Y	Y	N	Y	Y
5 ***Whittaker***	Y	N	N	N	N	N	Y	Y
KENTUCKY								
1 Hubbard	Y	N	Y	N	Y	Y	N	N
2 Natcher	N	Y	N	Y	Y	N	Y	N
3 Mazzoli	N	Y	N	Y	Y	N	Y	N
4 ***Bunning***	Y	N	N	N	N	N	Y	N
5 ***Rogers***	Y	N	N	N	N	N	Y	N
6 ***Hopkins***	Y	N	N	N	N	N	Y	N
7 Perkins	N	Y	N	Y	Y	Y	Y	N
LOUISIANA								
1 ***Livingston***	Y	N	N	N	N	N	Y	N
2 Boggs	?	?	?	?	?	?	?	?
3 Tauzin	Y	Y	N	N	N	N	N	N
4 ***McCrery***	Y	Y	N	N	Y	N	N	N
5 Huckaby	Y	Y	N	N	Y	N	N	N
6 ***Baker***	Y	N	N	N	Y	N	Y	Y
7 Hayes	N	Y	N	N	Y	N	N	N
8 ***Holloway***	Y	N	N	N	N	N	Y	N
MAINE								
1 Brennan	N	Y	Y	Y	Y	Y	N	N
2 ***Snowe***	N	Y	Y	Y	Y	N	Y	Y
MARYLAND								
1 Dyson	N	Y	N	Y	Y	N	N	N
2 ***Bentley***	Y	Y	N	N	Y	N	Y	N
3 Cardin	N	Y	Y	Y	Y	Y	Y	N
4 McMillen	N	Y	Y	Y	Y	N	N	N
5 Hoyer	N	Y	Y	Y	Y	N	N	N
6 Byron	N	Y	N	N	N	N	Y	N
7 Mfume	N	Y	Y	Y	Y	Y	Y	Y
8 ***Morella***	N	Y	Y	Y	Y	Y	Y	Y
MASSACHUSETTS								
1 ***Conte***	N	Y	N	Y	Y	Y	Y	N
2 Neal	-	+	+	+	+	+	-	-
3 Early	N	Y	N	Y	Y	Y	N	N
4 Frank	N	Y	Y	Y	Y	Y	N	Y
5 Atkins	N	Y	Y	Y	Y	Y	N	Y
6 Mavroules	N	Y	N	Y	N	Y	N	N
7 Markey	N	Y	Y	Y	Y	Y	N	Y
8 Kennedy	N	Y	Y	Y	Y	Y	N	N
9 Moakley	N	Y	N	Y	Y	Y	N	?
10 Studds	N	Y	Y	Y	Y	Y	N	N
11 Donnelly	N	Y	N	Y	Y	Y	N	Y
MICHIGAN								
1 Conyers	N	Y	Y	Y	Y	Y	N	Y
2 ***Pursell***	Y	N	N	Y	Y	Y	Y	N
3 Wolpe	N	Y	Y	Y	Y	Y	N	N
4 ***Upton***	Y	N	N	Y	Y	Y	Y	N
5 ***Henry***	Y	N	N	Y	Y	Y	Y	N
6 Carr	N	Y	Y	Y	Y	Y	N	N
7 Kildee	N	Y	N	Y	Y	Y	N	Y
8 Traxler	N	Y	N	Y	Y	Y	N	Y
9 ***Vander Jagt***	Y	N	N	N	Y	N	Y	N
10 ***Schuette***	Y	N	N	N	Y	N	Y	N
11 ***Davis***	Y	Y	N	N	Y	N	Y	N
12 Bonior	N	Y	N	Y	Y	Y	N	Y
13 Crockett	?	?	?	?	?	?	?	?
14 Hertel	N	Y	N	Y	Y	Y	N	N
15 Ford	?	?	?	?	?	?	?	?
16 Dingell	N	Y	Y	Y	Y	Y	N	N
17 Levin	N	Y	Y	Y	Y	Y	N	N
18 ***Broomfield***	Y	N	N	N	Y	N	Y	Y
MINNESOTA								
1 Penny	N	Y	N	Y	Y	N	N	Y
2 ***Weber***	Y	N	N	N	N	N	Y	N
3 ***Frenzel***	Y	N	Y	N	N	Y	Y	Y
4 Vento	N	Y	Y	Y	Y	Y	N	Y

	340	341	342	343	344	345	346	347
5 Sabo	N	Y	Y	Y	Y	Y	N	N
6 Sikorski	N	Y	N	Y	Y	Y	N	Y
7 ***Stangeland***	Y	N	N	N	N	N	Y	N
8 Oberstar	N	Y	N	Y	Y	Y	N	Y
MISSISSIPPI								
1 Whitten	N	Y	N	Y	Y	N	N	N
2 Espy	N	Y	Y	Y	Y	N	N	N
3 Montgomery	N	Y	N	N	N	N	N	N
4 Parker	Y	N	N	N	N	N	N	N
5 Taylor	N	Y	N	N	N	N	N	N
MISSOURI								
1 Clay	N	Y	Y	Y	Y	Y	N	Y
2 ***Buechner***	Y	Y	N	N	Y	N	N	N
3 Gephardt	?	?	?	?	?	?	?	?
4 Skelton	N	Y	N	N	N	N	N	N
5 Wheat	N	Y	Y	Y	Y	Y	N	Y
6 ***Coleman***	Y	N	N	N	Y	N	Y	N
7 ***Hancock***	Y	N	N	N	N	N	Y	Y
8 ***Emerson***	N	Y	N	N	Y	N	N	N
9 Volkmer	N	Y	N	Y	Y	N	N	N
MONTANA								
1 Williams	N	Y	Y	Y	Y	N	N	Y
2 ***Marlenee***	Y	N	N	N	N	N	Y	N
NEBRASKA								
1 ***Bereuter***	Y	N	N	N	Y	N	Y	Y
2 Hoagland	N	Y	Y	Y	N	N	N	N
3 ***Smith***	Y	N	N	Y	Y	Y	Y	Y
NEVADA								
1 Bilbray	N	Y	N	N	Y	N	Y	N
2 ***Vucanovich***	Y	N	N	N	Y	N	Y	N
NEW HAMPSHIRE								
1 ***Smith***	Y	Y	N	N	Y	N	Y	N
2 ***Douglas***	N	Y	N	N	Y	N	Y	Y
NEW JERSEY								
1 Vacancy								
2 Hughes	N	Y	Y	Y	Y	N	N	Y
3 Pallone	N	Y	Y	Y	Y	N	N	N
4 ***Smith***	Y	Y	N	Y	Y	Y	Y	N
5 ***Roukema***	Y	Y	Y	Y	Y	Y	Y	Y
6 Dwyer	N	?	Y	Y	Y	N	N	N
7 ***Rinaldo***	Y	Y	N	Y	Y	N	Y	N
8 Roe	N	Y	N	Y	Y	Y	N	N
9 Torricelli	?	?	?	?	?	?	?	?
10 Payne	N	Y	Y	Y	Y	Y	N	Y
11 ***Gallo***	Y	Y	Y	N	N	N	Y	N
12 ***Courter***	Y	N	Y	N	N	N	Y	N
13 ***Saxton***	Y	Y	N	N	Y	N	Y	N
14 Guarini	N	Y	Y	Y	Y	N	N	N
NEW MEXICO								
1 ***Schiff***	Y	Y	Y	N	Y	N	Y	N
2 ***Skeen***	Y	N	N	N	N	N	Y	N
3 Richardson	N	Y	?	?	Y	N	N	N
NEW YORK								
1 Hochbrueckner	N	Y	N	Y	Y	N	N	N
2 Downey	N	Y	Y	Y	Y	Y	N	Y
3 Mrazek	N	Y	Y	Y	Y	Y	N	Y
4 ***Lent***	Y	Y	N	N	Y	N	Y	N
5 ***McGrath***	Y	Y	N	Y	N	N	Y	N
6 Flake	N	Y	Y	Y	Y	Y	N	Y
7 Ackerman	N	Y	Y	Y	Y	Y	N	Y
8 Scheuer	N	Y	Y	Y	Y	Y	N	Y
9 Manton	N	Y	N	Y	Y	Y	N	N
10 Schumer	N	Y	Y	Y	Y	Y	N	Y
11 Towns	N	Y	Y	Y	Y	Y	N	Y
12 Owens	N	Y	Y	Y	Y	Y	N	Y
13 Solarz	N	Y	Y	Y	Y	Y	N	N
14 ***Molinari***	Y	Y	Y	N	Y	N	Y	N
15 ***Green***	Y	N	Y	Y	Y	Y	Y	N
16 Rangel	N	Y	Y	Y	Y	Y	N	Y
17 Weiss	N	Y	Y	Y	Y	Y	N	Y
18 Serrano	N	Y	Y	Y	Y	Y	N	Y
19 Engel	N	Y	Y	Y	Y	Y	N	N
20 Lowey	N	Y	Y	Y	Y	Y	N	Y
21 ***Fish***	Y	N	N	Y	Y	N	N	N
22 ***Gilman***	N	Y	Y	Y	Y	N	Y	N
23 McNulty	N	Y	N	Y	Y	N	N	N
24 ***Solomon***	N	Y	N	N	Y	N	Y	N
25 ***Boehlert***	N	Y	Y	Y	Y	N	Y	N
26 ***Martin***	?	N	N	N	N	N	Y	N
27 ***Walsh***	Y	Y	N	Y	Y	Y	Y	Y
28 McHugh	N	Y	Y	Y	Y	Y	N	N
29 ***Horton***	N	Y	Y	Y	Y	Y	Y	N
30 Slaughter	N	Y	Y	Y	Y	Y	N	Y
31 ***Paxon***	Y	N	N	N	N	N	Y	N

	340	341	342	343	344	345	346	347
32 LaFalce	N	Y	N	Y	N	Y	Y	N
33 Nowak	N	Y	N	Y	Y	Y	N	Y
34 ***Houghton***	Y	N	Y	N	Y	N	Y	N
NORTH CAROLINA								
1 Jones	N	Y	Y	Y	Y	N	Y	Y
2 Valentine	N	N	Y	N	Y	N	N	N
3 Lancaster	N	Y	Y	N	Y	N	N	N
4 Price	N	Y	Y	Y	Y	N	N	N
5 Neal	N	Y	Y	Y	Y	N	N	N
6 ***Coble***	Y	N	N	N	Y	N	Y	Y
7 Rose	N	Y	Y	Y	N	Y	N	N
8 Hefner	N	Y	Y	Y	Y	N	N	N
9 ***McMillan***	Y	N	N	N	Y	N	Y	Y
10 ***Ballenger***	Y	N	N	N	Y	N	Y	N
11 Clarke	N	Y	Y	Y	Y	N	Y	N
NORTH DAKOTA								
AL Dorgan	N	Y	N	Y	Y	Y	N	Y
OHIO								
1 Luken	N	Y	N	Y	Y	N	N	N
2 ***Gradison***	Y	N	N	N	Y	N	Y	N
3 Hall	Y	N	N	Y	Y	Y	N	N
4 ***Oxley***	Y	N	N	N	N	N	Y	N
5 ***Gillmor***	N	Y	N	N	Y	N	Y	N
6 ***McEwen***	Y	N	N	N	N	N	Y	N
7 ***DeWine***	Y	Y	N	N	Y	N	Y	N
8 ***Lukens***	N	N	N	N	Y	N	Y	N
9 Kaptur	N	Y	N	Y	Y	N	N	N
10 ***Miller***	Y	Y	N	N	Y	N	Y	N
11 Eckart	N	Y	Y	Y	Y	Y	Y	Y
12 ***Kasich***	Y	N	N	N	Y	N	Y	N
13 Pease	N	Y	Y	Y	Y	Y	N	N
14 Sawyer	N	Y	Y	Y	Y	N	N	N
15 ***Wylie***	Y	N	N	N	Y	N	Y	Y
16 ***Regula***	Y	N	N	N	Y	N	Y	Y
17 Traficant	N	Y	Y	Y	Y	Y	N	Y
18 Applegate	N	Y	N	N	Y	Y	Y	Y
19 Feighan	?	?	?	?	?	?	?	?
20 Oakar	N	Y	N	Y	Y	Y	N	Y
21 Stokes	N	Y	Y	Y	Y	Y	N	Y
OKLAHOMA								
1 ***Inhofe***	Y	Y	N	N	N	N	Y	N
2 Synar	N	Y	Y	Y	Y	Y	N	N
3 Watkins	?	?	?	?	?	?	?	?
4 McCurdy	N	Y	Y	N	Y	N	N	N
5 ***Edwards***	Y	Y	N	N	Y	N	Y	N
6 English	N	Y	N	N	Y	N	N	N
OREGON								
1 AuCoin	?	?	?	?	?	?	?	?
2 ***Smith, B.***	Y	N	N	N	N	N	Y	N
3 Wyden	N	Y	Y	Y	Y	Y	N	N
4 DeFazio	N	Y	Y	Y	Y	Y	N	Y
5 ***Smith, D.***	Y	N	N	N	N	N	Y	N
PENNSYLVANIA								
1 Foglietta	N	Y	N	Y	Y	N	N	N
2 Gray	N	Y	Y	Y	Y	Y	N	N
3 Borski	N	Y	N	Y	Y	Y	N	Y
4 Kolter	N	Y	N	Y	Y	N	N	Y
5 ***Schulze***	Y	N	N	N	Y	N	Y	Y
6 Yatron	N	Y	N	Y	Y	N	Y	N
7 ***Weldon***	Y	N	N	N	Y	N	Y	N
8 Kostmayer	N	Y	Y	Y	Y	Y	N	N
9 ***Shuster***	Y	N	N	N	Y	N	Y	N
10 ***McDade***	?	?	?	?	?	?	?	?
11 Kanjorski	N	Y	N	Y	Y	Y	N	Y
12 Murtha	N	Y	N	N	Y	N	N	N
13 ***Coughlin***	Y	Y	Y	N	Y	N	Y	N
14 Coyne	N	Y	Y	Y	Y	Y	N	Y
15 ***Ritter***	N	Y	N	N	Y	Y	Y	Y
16 ***Walker***	Y	N	N	N	N	N	Y	Y
17 ***Gekas***	Y	N	N	N	N	N	Y	N
18 Walgren	N	Y	Y	Y	Y	Y	N	Y
19 ***Goodling***	Y	N	N	N	Y	Y	Y	N
20 Gaydos	N	Y	N	Y	Y	N	N	N
21 ***Ridge***	N	Y	Y	N	Y	N	Y	Y
22 Murphy	N	Y	N	Y	Y	N	N	Y
23 ***Clinger***	Y	N	N	N	Y	N	Y	N
RHODE ISLAND								
1 ***Machtley***	N	Y	Y	Y	Y	Y	Y	N
2 ***Schneider***	N	Y	Y	Y	Y	Y	Y	Y
SOUTH CAROLINA								
1 ***Ravenel***	Y	Y	N	N	Y	N	Y	N
2 ***Spence***	Y	N	N	N	Y	N	Y	N
3 Derrick	N	N	Y	Y	Y	N	N	N
4 Patterson	N	N	N	Y	Y	N	N	N
5 Spratt	N	Y	Y	Y	Y	N	N	N
6 Tallon	N	Y	N	N	Y	N	N	N

	340	341	342	343	344	345	346	347
SOUTH DAKOTA								
AL Johnson	N	Y	Y	Y	Y	Y	N	Y
TENNESSEE								
1 ***Quillen***	Y	Y	N	N	N	N	Y	N
2 ***Duncan***	Y	N	N	N	N	N	Y	Y
3 Lloyd	Y	Y	N	N	N	N	N	N
4 Cooper	Y	N	Y	Y	Y	N	N	N
5 Clement	N	Y	Y	Y	Y	Y	N	N
6 Gordon	N	Y	Y	Y	Y	N	N	N
7 ***Sundquist***	Y	Y	N	N	N	N	Y	N
8 Tanner	N	Y	Y	Y	Y	N	N	N
9 Ford	N	Y	Y	Y	Y	Y	N	Y
TEXAS								
1 Chapman	N	Y	Y	Y	Y	N	N	N
2 Wilson	Y	N	Y	N	N	N	N	N
3 ***Bartlett***	Y	N	N	N	N	N	Y	N
4 Hall	Y	N	N	N	N	N	N	N
5 Bryant	N	Y	Y	Y	Y	Y	N	Y
6 ***Barton***	Y	N	N	N	N	N	Y	N
7 ***Archer***	Y	N	N	N	N	N	Y	N
8 ***Fields***	Y	N	N	N	N	N	Y	N
9 Brooks	N	Y	Y	Y	Y	N	N	N
10 Pickle	N	Y	Y	Y	Y	N	N	N
11 Leath	?	?	?	?	?	?	?	?
12 Geren	N	Y	Y	N	N	N	N	N
13 Sarpalius	Y	Y	N	N	N	N	N	N
14 Laughlin	N	Y	N	N	N	N	Y	N
15 de la Garza	N	Y	N	Y	Y	N	N	N
16 Coleman	N	Y	Y	Y	Y	N	N	N
17 Stenholm	Y	Y	N	N	N	N	N	N
18 Washington	N	Y	Y	Y	Y	Y	N	Y
19 ***Combest***	Y	N	N	N	N	N	Y	N
20 Gonzalez	N	Y	Y	Y	Y	Y	N	N
21 ***Smith***	N	Y	N	N	N	N	Y	N
22 ***DeLay***	Y	N	N	N	N	N	Y	N
23 Bustamante	N	Y	?	?	?	?	N	N
24 Frost	N	Y	Y	Y	Y	N	N	N
25 Andrews	N	Y	Y	Y	Y	N	N	N
26 ***Armey***	Y	N	N	N	N	N	Y	N
27 Ortiz	N	Y	N	Y	Y	N	N	N
UTAH								
1 ***Hansen***	Y	N	N	N	N	N	Y	N
2 Owens	N	Y	Y	Y	Y	Y	N	Y
3 ***Nielson***	Y	N	N	N	N	N	N	Y
VERMONT								
AL ***Smith***	Y	Y	Y	Y	Y	N	Y	N
VIRGINIA								
1 ***Bateman***	Y	N	N	N	N	N	Y	N
2 Pickett	N	Y	Y	N	Y	N	N	N
3 ***Bliley***	Y	N	N	N	Y	N	Y	N
4 Sisisky	N	Y	Y	N	N	N	N	N
5 Payne	N	Y	Y	N	Y	N	N	N
6 Olin	N	Y	Y	Y	Y	N	N	N
7 ***Slaughter***	Y	N	N	N	N	N	Y	N
8 ***Parris***	Y	Y	N	N	Y	N	N	N
9 Boucher	N	Y	Y	Y	Y	Y	N	N
10 ***Wolf***	Y	Y	N	N	Y	N	Y	N
WASHINGTON								
1 ***Miller***	N	Y	Y	N	Y	N	Y	N
2 Swift	N	Y	Y	Y	Y	Y	N	Y
3 Unsoeld	-	+	+	+	+	+	-	+
4 ***Morrison***	?	Y	Y	N	Y	N	Y	N
5 Foley								
6 Dicks	N	Y	Y	Y	Y	N	N	N
7 McDermott	N	Y	Y	Y	Y	Y	N	Y
8 ***Chandler***	Y	N	Y	N	Y	N	Y	Y
WEST VIRGINIA								
1 Mollohan	N	Y	N	N	Y	N	N	N
2 Staggers	N	Y	N	Y	Y	Y	N	Y
3 Wise	N	Y	Y	Y	Y	N	N	Y
4 Rahall	N	Y	N	Y	Y	Y	Y	Y
WISCONSIN								
1 Aspin	N	Y	Y	Y	N	N	N	N
2 Kastenmeier	N	Y	Y	Y	Y	Y	Y	Y
3 ***Gunderson***	Y	N	N	Y	Y	N	Y	N
4 Kleczka	N	Y	N	Y	Y	N	N	Y
5 Moody	?	Y	Y	Y	Y	Y	N	Y
6 ***Petri***	Y	N	N	N	N	N	Y	Y
7 Obey	N	Y	Y	Y	Y	Y	N	Y
8 ***Roth***	Y	N	N	N	Y	N	N	Y
9 ***Sensenbrenner***	Y	N	N	N	N	Y	Y	Y
WYOMING								
AL ***Thomas***	Y	N	N	N	Y	N	Y	Y

Southern states - Ala., Ark., Fla., Ga., Ky., La., Miss., N.C., Okla., S.C., Tenn., Texas, Va.
Omitted votes are quorum calls, which CQ does not include in its vote charts.

HOUSE VOTES 348, 349, 350, 351, 352

348. Procedural Motion. Hefley, R-Colo., motion to approve the House Journal of Tuesday, Sept. 18. Motion agreed to 278-115: R 54-112; D 224-3 (ND 149-3, SD 75-0), Sept. 19, 1990.

349. HR 4739. Fiscal 1991 Defense Authorization/Non-Controversial Amendments. Aspin, D-Wis., en bloc amendment to incorporate various non-controversial amendments into the bill. Adopted 373-45: R 126-45; D 247-0 (ND 168-0, SD 79-0), Sept. 19, 1990.

350. HR 4739. Fiscal 1991 Defense Authorization/Operation Desert Shield. Aspin, D-Wis., en bloc amendment to authorize a net of $948 million for Operation Desert Shield, including $187 million for antichemical and biological weapons defense equipment and training, $540 million for ships and $174 million for personnel compensation. Adopted 413-10: R 165-8; D 248-2 (ND 168-1, SD 80-1), Sept. 19, 1990.

351. HR 4739. Fiscal 1991 Defense Authorization/Recommittal Motion. Dickinson, R-Ala., motion to recommit to the House Armed Services Committee the bill to authorize appropriations for defense programs in fiscal 1991, with instructions to report it back to the House with amendments to reduce funding for F/A-18 aircrafts by $427.5 million, and use that amount to increase by 28,500 the size of the army. Motion rejected 156-254: R 156-12; D 0-242 (ND 0-163, SD 0-79), Sept. 19, 1990.

352. HR 4739. Fiscal 1991 Defense Authorization/Passage. Passage of the bill to authorize appropriations of $283 billion for the Defense Department and defense-related programs, $24 billion less than the administration's request. The Senate's version would authorize $289 billion. Passed 256-155: R 33-135; D 223-20 (ND 145-18, SD 78-2), Sept. 19, 1990. A "nay" was a vote supporting the president's position.

KEY

Y Voted for (yea).
\# Paired for.
\+ Announced for.
N Voted against (nay).
X Paired against.
\- Announced against.
P Voted "present."
C Voted "present" to avoid possible conflict of interest.
? Did not vote or otherwise make a position known.

Democrats *Republicans*

	348	349	350	351	352
ALABAMA					
1 ***Callahan***	Y	N	Y	Y	N
2 ***Dickinson***	N	N	Y	Y	N
3 Browder	Y	Y	Y	N	Y
4 Bevill	Y	Y	Y	N	Y
5 Flippo	Y	Y	Y	N	Y
6 Erdreich	Y	Y	Y	N	Y
7 Harris	Y	Y	Y	N	Y
ALASKA					
AL ***Young***	N	Y	Y	Y	N
ARIZONA					
1 ***Rhodes***	N	Y	Y	Y	N
2 Udall	?	Y	Y	N	Y
3 ***Stump***	N	N	N	Y	N
4 ***Kyl***	N	Y	N	Y	N
5 ***Kolbe***	N	Y	Y	Y	N
ARKANSAS					
1 Alexander	Y	Y	Y	N	Y
2 ***Robinson***	Y	Y	Y	#	X
3 ***Hammerschmidt***	Y	Y	Y	Y	N
4 Anthony	Y	Y	Y	N	Y
CALIFORNIA					
1 Bosco	Y	Y	Y	N	Y
2 ***Herger***	N	Y	Y	Y	N
3 Matsui	Y	Y	Y	?	?
4 Fazio	Y	Y	Y	N	Y
5 Pelosi	Y	Y	Y	N	Y
6 Boxer	Y	Y	Y	?	?
7 Miller	Y	Y	Y	N	Y
8 Dellums	Y	Y	Y	N	N
9 Stark	Y	Y	Y	N	Y
10 Edwards	Y	Y	Y	N	N
11 Lantos	Y	Y	Y	N	Y
12 ***Campbell***	N	Y	Y	Y	N
13 Mineta	Y	Y	Y	N	Y
14 ***Shumway***	?	Y	Y	Y	N
15 Condit	Y	Y	Y	N	Y
16 Panetta	Y	Y	Y	N	Y
17 ***Pashayan***	N	Y	Y	Y	N
18 Lehman	Y	?	Y	N	Y
19 ***Lagomarsino***	N	Y	Y	Y	N
20 ***Thomas***	N	Y	Y	Y	N
21 ***Gallegly***	N	Y	Y	Y	N
22 ***Moorhead***	N	Y	Y	Y	N
23 Beilenson	Y	Y	Y	N	Y
24 Waxman	Y	Y	Y	N	Y
25 Roybal	Y	Y	Y	N	N
26 Berman	Y	Y	Y	N	Y
27 Levine	?	Y	Y	N	Y
28 Dixon	?	Y	Y	N	Y
29 Hawkins	Y	Y	Y	N	Y
30 Martinez	Y	Y	Y	N	Y
31 Dymally	Y	Y	Y	N	Y
32 Anderson	Y	Y	Y	N	Y
33 ***Dreier***	N	Y	Y	Y	N
34 Torres	Y	Y	Y	N	Y
35 ***Lewis***	N	Y	Y	?	N
36 Brown	Y	Y	Y	N	Y
37 ***McCandless***	?	Y	Y	Y	N
38 ***Dornan***	N	N	N	Y	N
39 ***Dannemeyer***	N	N	Y	Y	N
40 ***Cox***	N	Y	Y	Y	N
41 ***Lowery***	?	Y	Y	Y	N
42 ***Rohrabacher***	N	N	Y	Y	N
43 ***Packard***	Y	Y	Y	Y	N
44 Bates	Y	Y	Y	N	Y
45 ***Hunter***	N	Y	Y	Y	N
COLORADO					
1 Schroeder	N	Y	Y	N	Y
2 Skaggs	Y	Y	Y	N	Y
3 Campbell	Y	Y	Y	N	Y
4 ***Brown***	N	Y	Y	Y	N
5 ***Hefley***	N	N	Y	Y	N
6 ***Schaefer***	N	N	Y	Y	N
CONNECTICUT					
1 Kennelly	Y	Y	Y	N	Y
2 Gejdenson	Y	Y	Y	N	Y
3 Morrison	Y	Y	Y	N	Y
4 ***Shays***	N	Y	Y	Y	Y
5 ***Rowland***	Y	Y	Y	Y	Y
6 ***Johnson***	Y	Y	Y	Y	N
DELAWARE					
AL Carper	Y	Y	Y	N	Y
FLORIDA					
1 Hutto	Y	Y	Y	N	Y
2 ***Grant***	Y	Y	Y	Y	N
3 Bennett	Y	Y	Y	N	Y
4 ***James***	N	Y	Y	Y	Y
5 ***McCollum***	Y	Y	Y	Y	N
6 ***Stearns***	N	N	Y	Y	N
7 Gibbons	Y	Y	Y	N	Y
8 ***Young***	N	N	Y	Y	N
9 ***Bilirakis***	?	?	?	?	?
10 ***Ireland***	N	Y	Y	#	#
11 Nelson	Y	Y	Y	N	Y
12 ***Lewis***	N	Y	Y	Y	N
13 ***Goss***	N	N	Y	Y	N
14 Johnston	Y	Y	Y	N	Y
15 ***Shaw***	Y	Y	Y	Y	N
16 Smith	?	Y	Y	?	?
17 Lehman	Y	Y	Y	N	Y
18 ***Ros-Lehtinen***	N	Y	Y	Y	N
19 Fascell	Y	Y	Y	N	Y
GEORGIA					
1 Thomas	Y	Y	Y	N	Y
2 Hatcher	Y	Y	Y	N	Y
3 Ray	Y	Y	Y	N	Y
4 Jones	Y	Y	Y	N	Y
5 Lewis	Y	Y	Y	N	N
6 ***Gingrich***	Y	Y	Y	Y	N
7 Darden	Y	Y	Y	N	Y
8 Rowland	Y	Y	Y	N	Y
9 Jenkins	Y	Y	Y	N	Y
10 Barnard	Y	Y	Y	N	Y
HAWAII					
1 ***Saiki***	Y	Y	Y	Y	Y
2 Vacancy					
IDAHO					
1 ***Craig***	N	Y	Y	Y	N
2 Stallings	Y	Y	Y	N	Y
ILLINOIS					
1 Hayes	Y	Y	Y	N	N
2 Savage	?	Y	N	N	N
3 Russo	Y	Y	Y	N	Y
4 Sangmeister	Y	Y	Y	N	Y
5 Lipinski	Y	Y	Y	N	Y
6 ***Hyde***	N	Y	Y	Y	N
7 Collins	Y	Y	Y	N	N
8 Rostenkowski	Y	Y	Y	N	Y
9 Yates	Y	Y	Y	N	?
10 ***Porter***	Y	Y	Y	Y	Y
11 Annunzio	Y	Y	Y	N	Y
12 ***Crane***	?	N	Y	Y	N
13 ***Fawell***	N	Y	Y	Y	N
14 ***Hastert***	N	Y	Y	Y	N
15 ***Madigan***	N	Y	Y	Y	N
16 ***Martin***	N	Y	Y	Y	N
17 Evans	Y	Y	Y	N	Y
18 ***Michel***	Y	?	Y	Y	N
19 Bruce	Y	Y	Y	N	Y
20 Durbin	Y	Y	Y	N	Y
21 Costello	Y	Y	Y	N	Y
22 Poshard	Y	Y	Y	N	Y
INDIANA					
1 Visclosky	Y	Y	Y	N	Y
2 Sharp	Y	Y	Y	N	Y
3 ***Hiler***	N	Y	Y	Y	N

ND Northern Democrats SD Southern Democrats

	348	349	350	351	352
4 Long	Y	Y	Y	N	Y
5 Jontz	Y	Y	Y	N	Y
6 ***Burton***	N	N	Y	Y	N
7 ***Myers***	Y	Y	Y	Y	N
8 McCloskey	Y	Y	Y	N	Y
9 Hamilton	Y	Y	Y	N	Y
10 Jacobs	N	Y	Y	N	Y
IOWA					
1 ***Leach***	N	Y	Y	N	Y
2 ***Tauke***	N	Y	Y	N	N
3 Nagle	?	Y	Y	N	Y
4 Smith	Y	Y	Y	N	Y
5 ***Lightfoot***	N	Y	Y	Y	N
6 ***Grandy***	N	N	Y	N	N
KANSAS					
1 ***Roberts***	N	N	Y	Y	N
2 Slattery	Y	Y	Y	N	Y
3 ***Meyers***	N	N	Y	Y	N
4 Glickman	Y	Y	Y	N	Y
5 ***Whittaker***	N	N	Y	Y	N
KENTUCKY					
1 Hubbard	Y	Y	Y	N	Y
2 Natcher	Y	Y	Y	N	Y
3 Mazzoli	Y	Y	Y	N	Y
4 ***Bunning***	N	Y	Y	Y	N
5 ***Rogers***	N	Y	Y	Y	N
6 ***Hopkins***	N	Y	Y	Y	Y
7 Perkins	Y	Y	Y	N	Y
LOUISIANA					
1 ***Livingston***	N	N	N	Y	N
2 Boggs	Y	?	Y	N	Y
3 Tauzin	Y	Y	Y	N	Y
4 ***McCrery***	N	N	Y	Y	N
5 Huckaby	Y	Y	Y	N	Y
6 ***Baker***	N	Y	Y	Y	N
7 Hayes	Y	Y	Y	N	Y
8 ***Holloway***	N	Y	Y	Y	N
MAINE					
1 Brennan	Y	Y	Y	N	Y
2 ***Snowe***	Y	Y	Y	Y	Y
MARYLAND					
1 Dyson	?	Y	Y	N	Y
2 ***Bentley***	N	N	Y	Y	N
3 Cardin	Y	Y	Y	N	Y
4 McMillen	Y	Y	Y	N	Y
5 Hoyer	Y	Y	Y	N	Y
6 Byron	Y	Y	Y	N	Y
7 Mfume	Y	Y	Y	N	Y
8 ***Morella***	Y	Y	Y	N	Y
MASSACHUSETTS					
1 ***Conte***	Y	Y	Y	Y	Y
2 Neal	Y	Y	Y	N	Y
3 Early	Y	Y	Y	N	Y
4 Frank	Y	Y	Y	X	?
5 Atkins	Y	Y	Y	N	Y
6 Mavroules	?	Y	Y	N	Y
7 Markey	Y	Y	Y	N	Y
8 Kennedy	Y	Y	Y	N	Y
9 Moakley	Y	Y	Y	N	Y
10 Studds	Y	Y	Y	N	Y
11 Donnelly	Y	Y	Y	N	Y
MICHIGAN					
1 Conyers	?	Y	Y	N	N
2 ***Pursell***	Y	Y	Y	#	X
3 Wolpe	Y	Y	Y	N	Y
4 ***Upton***	N	Y	Y	Y	N
5 ***Henry***	N	Y	Y	Y	N
6 Carr	Y	Y	Y	N	Y
7 Kildee	Y	Y	Y	N	Y
8 Traxler	Y	Y	?	?	?
9 ***Vander Jagt***	Y	Y	Y	Y	N
10 ***Schuette***	N	Y	Y	Y	N
11 ***Davis***	N	Y	Y	Y	N
12 Bonior	Y	Y	Y	N	Y
13 Crockett	?	Y	Y	N	N
14 Hertel	Y	Y	Y	N	Y
15 Ford	?	?	Y	N	Y
16 Dingell	Y	Y	Y	N	Y
17 Levin	Y	Y	Y	N	Y
18 ***Broomfield***	?	Y	Y	Y	N
MINNESOTA					
1 Penny	Y	Y	Y	N	Y
2 ***Weber***	N	N	Y	Y	N
3 ***Frenzel***	N	Y	Y	Y	N
4 Vento	Y	Y	Y	N	Y

	348	349	350	351	352
5 Sabo	Y	Y	Y	N	Y
6 Sikorski	N	Y	Y	N	Y
7 ***Stangeland***	?	Y	Y	Y	N
8 Oberstar	Y	Y	Y	N	Y
MISSISSIPPI					
1 Whitten	Y	Y	Y	N	Y
2 Espy	Y	Y	Y	N	Y
3 Montgomery	Y	Y	Y	N	Y
4 Parker	Y	Y	Y	N	Y
5 Taylor	Y	Y	Y	N	Y
MISSOURI					
1 Clay	?	Y	Y	N	N
2 ***Buechner***	N	Y	Y	N	Y
3 Gephardt	Y	Y	Y	N	Y
4 Skelton	Y	Y	Y	N	Y
5 Wheat	Y	Y	Y	N	Y
6 ***Coleman***	Y	Y	Y	Y	N
7 ***Hancock***	N	N	Y	Y	N
8 ***Emerson***	Y	Y	Y	N	Y
9 Volkmer	Y	Y	Y	N	Y
MONTANA					
1 Williams	?	Y	Y	N	N
2 ***Marlenee***	N	N	N	Y	N
NEBRASKA					
1 ***Bereuter***	N	N	Y	Y	N
2 Hoagland	Y	Y	Y	N	Y
3 ***Smith***	Y	Y	Y	Y	N
NEVADA					
1 Bilbray	Y	Y	Y	N	Y
2 ***Vucanovich***	N	N	Y	Y	N
NEW HAMPSHIRE					
1 ***Smith***	N	N	Y	Y	N
2 ***Douglas***	N	Y	Y	Y	N
NEW JERSEY					
1 Vacancy					
2 Hughes	Y	Y	Y	N	Y
3 Pallone	Y	Y	Y	N	Y
4 ***Smith***	Y	Y	Y	Y	Y
5 ***Roukema***	N	Y	Y	Y	Y
6 Dwyer	Y	Y	Y	N	Y
7 ***Rinaldo***	Y	Y	Y	Y	N
8 Roe	Y	Y	Y	N	Y
9 Torricelli	Y	Y	Y	N	Y
10 Payne	Y	Y	Y	N	N
11 ***Gallo***	N	Y	Y	Y	N
12 ***Courter***	N	Y	Y	Y	N
13 ***Saxton***	Y	Y	Y	Y	N
14 Guarini	Y	Y	Y	N	Y
NEW MEXICO					
1 ***Schiff***	Y	Y	Y	Y	N
2 ***Skeen***	Y	Y	Y	Y	N
3 Richardson	Y	Y	Y	N	Y
NEW YORK					
1 Hochbrueckner	Y	Y	Y	N	Y
2 Downey	Y	Y	Y	N	Y
3 Mrazek	Y	Y	Y	N	Y
4 ***Lent***	Y	Y	Y	Y	N
5 ***McGrath***	N	N	Y	Y	Y
6 Flake	?	Y	Y	N	N
7 Ackerman	Y	Y	Y	N	Y
8 Scheuer	Y	Y	Y	N	Y
9 Manton	Y	Y	Y	N	Y
10 Schumer	Y	Y	Y	?	+
11 Towns	?	?	?	?	?
12 Owens	Y	Y	Y	N	N
13 Solarz	Y	Y	Y	N	Y
14 ***Molinari***	N	Y	Y	Y	N
15 ***Green***	Y	Y	Y	N	Y
16 Rangel	Y	Y	Y	N	N
17 Weiss	Y	Y	Y	N	Y
18 Serrano	Y	Y	Y	N	N
19 Engel	Y	Y	Y	N	Y
20 Lowey	Y	Y	Y	N	Y
21 ***Fish***	Y	Y	Y	Y	N
22 ***Gilman***	Y	Y	Y	Y	Y
23 McNulty	Y	Y	Y	N	Y
24 ***Solomon***	N	N	Y	Y	Y
25 ***Boehlert***	N	Y	Y	Y	Y
26 ***Martin***	N	Y	Y	Y	N
27 ***Walsh***	Y	Y	Y	Y	N
28 McHugh	Y	Y	Y	N	Y
29 ***Horton***	Y	Y	Y	X	#
30 Slaughter	Y	Y	Y	N	Y
31 ***Paxon***	?	?	?	Y	N

	348	349	350	351	352
32 LaFalce	Y	Y	Y	N	Y
33 Nowak	Y	Y	Y	N	Y
34 ***Houghton***	Y	Y	Y	Y	Y
NORTH CAROLINA					
1 Jones	Y	Y	Y	N	Y
2 Valentine	Y	Y	Y	N	Y
3 Lancaster	Y	Y	Y	N	Y
4 Price	Y	Y	Y	N	Y
5 Neal	?	?	Y	N	Y
6 ***Coble***	N	Y	Y	Y	N
7 Rose	Y	Y	Y	N	Y
8 Hefner	Y	Y	Y	N	Y
9 ***McMillan***	N	Y	Y	Y	N
10 ***Ballenger***	N	Y	Y	Y	N
11 Clarke	Y	Y	Y	N	Y
NORTH DAKOTA					
AL Dorgan	Y	Y	Y	N	Y
OHIO					
1 Luken	Y	Y	Y	N	Y
2 ***Gradison***	Y	Y	Y	Y	N
3 Hall	Y	Y	Y	N	Y
4 ***Oxley***	N	Y	Y	Y	N
5 ***Gillmor***	Y	Y	Y	Y	N
6 ***McEwen***	Y	N	N	Y	N
7 ***DeWine***	N	Y	Y	Y	N
8 ***Lukens***	N	Y	Y	Y	N
9 Kaptur	Y	Y	Y	N	Y
10 ***Miller***	N	Y	Y	Y	N
11 Eckart	Y	Y	Y	N	Y
12 ***Kasich***	Y	Y	Y	Y	Y
13 Pease	Y	Y	Y	N	Y
14 Sawyer	Y	Y	Y	N	Y
15 ***Wylie***	Y	Y	Y	Y	N
16 ***Regula***	N	Y	Y	Y	Y
17 Traficant	Y	Y	Y	N	N
18 Applegate	Y	Y	Y	N	Y
19 Feighan	Y	Y	Y	?	Y
20 Oakar	Y	Y	Y	N	Y
21 Stokes	?	Y	Y	N	N
OKLAHOMA					
1 ***Inhofe***	N	Y	Y	Y	N
2 Synar	Y	Y	Y	N	Y
3 Watkins	?	?	?	?	?
4 McCurdy	Y	Y	Y	N	Y
5 ***Edwards***	N	Y	Y	Y	N
6 English	Y	Y	Y	N	Y
OREGON					
1 AuCoin	?	?	?	X	#
2 ***Smith, B.***	N	Y	Y	Y	N
3 Wyden	Y	Y	Y	N	Y
4 DeFazio	?	Y	Y	?	?
5 ***Smith, D.***	N	N	Y	Y	N
PENNSYLVANIA					
1 Foglietta	Y	Y	Y	N	Y
2 Gray	Y	Y	Y	N	Y
3 Borski	Y	Y	Y	N	Y
4 Kolter	Y	Y	Y	N	Y
5 ***Schulze***	Y	N	N	Y	N
6 Yatron	Y	Y	Y	N	Y
7 ***Weldon***	N	Y	Y	Y	Y
8 Kostmayer	Y	Y	Y	N	Y
9 ***Shuster***	Y	Y	Y	Y	N
10 ***McDade***	?	?	?	?	X
11 Kanjorski	Y	Y	Y	N	Y
12 Murtha	Y	Y	Y	N	Y
13 ***Coughlin***	N	Y	Y	Y	Y
14 Coyne	Y	Y	Y	N	Y
15 ***Ritter***	Y	Y	Y	Y	?
16 ***Walker***	N	N	N	Y	N
17 ***Gekas***	N	Y	Y	Y	Y
18 Walgren	Y	Y	Y	N	Y
19 ***Goodling***	?	Y	Y	Y	N
20 Gaydos	Y	Y	Y	N	Y
21 ***Ridge***	N	N	Y	Y	Y
22 Murphy	?	Y	Y	N	Y
23 ***Clinger***	N	Y	Y	Y	N
RHODE ISLAND					
1 ***Machtley***	N	Y	Y	Y	Y
2 ***Schneider***	Y	Y	Y	Y	Y
SOUTH CAROLINA					
1 ***Ravenel***	Y	Y	Y	Y	Y
2 ***Spence***	Y	Y	Y	Y	N
3 Derrick	Y	Y	Y	N	Y
4 Patterson	Y	Y	Y	N	Y
5 Spratt	Y	Y	Y	N	Y
6 Tallon	Y	Y	Y	N	Y

	348	349	350	351	352
SOUTH DAKOTA					
AL Johnson	Y	Y	Y	N	Y
TENNESSEE					
1 ***Quillen***	Y	Y	Y	#	X
2 ***Duncan***	N	N	Y	Y	N
3 Lloyd	?	Y	Y	N	Y
4 Cooper	Y	Y	Y	N	Y
5 Clement	Y	Y	Y	N	Y
6 Gordon	Y	Y	Y	?	Y
7 ***Sundquist***	N	N	Y	Y	N
8 Tanner	Y	Y	Y	N	Y
9 Ford	?	Y	Y	N	Y
TEXAS					
1 Chapman	Y	Y	Y	N	Y
2 Wilson	Y	Y	Y	N	Y
3 ***Bartlett***	Y	Y	Y	Y	N
4 Hall	Y	Y	Y	N	Y
5 Bryant	Y	Y	Y	N	Y
6 ***Barton***	N	N	Y	Y	N
7 ***Archer***	Y	Y	Y	Y	N
8 ***Fields***	N	N	Y	Y	N
9 Brooks	Y	Y	Y	N	Y
10 Pickle	Y	Y	Y	N	Y
11 Leath	?	?	?	?	?
12 Geren	Y	Y	Y	N	Y
13 Sarpalius	?	Y	Y	N	Y
14 Laughlin	Y	Y	Y	N	Y
15 de la Garza	Y	Y	Y	N	Y
16 Coleman	Y	Y	Y	N	Y
17 Stenholm	Y	Y	Y	N	Y
18 Washington	?	Y	Y	N	N
19 ***Combest***	Y	N	Y	Y	N
20 Gonzalez	Y	Y	N	N	Y
21 ***Smith***	N	Y	Y	Y	N
22 ***DeLay***	N	?	Y	Y	N
23 Bustamante	Y	Y	Y	N	Y
24 Frost	Y	Y	Y	N	Y
25 Andrews	Y	Y	Y	N	Y
26 ***Armey***	N	N	Y	Y	N
27 Ortiz	Y	Y	Y	N	Y
UTAH					
1 ***Hansen***	N	N	Y	Y	N
2 Owens	Y	Y	Y	N	Y
3 ***Nielson***	N	N	Y	Y	N
VERMONT					
AL ***Smith***	N	Y	Y	N	Y
VIRGINIA					
1 ***Bateman***	Y	N	Y	Y	Y
2 Pickett	Y	Y	Y	N	Y
3 ***Bliley***	N	Y	Y	Y	N
4 Sisisky	Y	Y	Y	N	Y
5 Payne	Y	Y	Y	N	Y
6 Olin	Y	Y	Y	N	Y
7 ***Slaughter***	N	Y	Y	Y	N
8 ***Parris***	N	Y	Y	Y	N
9 Boucher	Y	Y	Y	N	Y
10 ***Wolf***	N	Y	Y	Y	N
WASHINGTON					
1 ***Miller***	N	Y	Y	Y	N
2 Swift	Y	Y	Y	N	Y
3 Unsoeld	?	+	+	X	#
4 ***Morrison***	Y	Y	Y	Y	N
5 Foley					
6 Dicks	Y	Y	Y	N	Y
7 McDermott	Y	Y	Y	N	Y
8 ***Chandler***	N	Y	Y	N	N
WEST VIRGINIA					
1 Mollohan	Y	Y	Y	N	Y
2 Staggers	Y	Y	Y	N	Y
3 Wise	?	Y	Y	N	Y
4 Rahall	?	Y	Y	N	Y
WISCONSIN					
1 Aspin	Y	Y	Y	N	Y
2 Kastenmeier	Y	Y	Y	N	N
3 ***Gunderson***	Y	Y	Y	Y	N
4 Kleczka	Y	Y	Y	N	Y
5 Moody	Y	Y	Y	N	Y
6 ***Petri***	Y	N	Y	N	N
7 Obey	Y	Y	Y	N	Y
8 ***Roth***	Y	N	Y	N	Y
9 ***Sensenbrenner***	N	N	Y	N	N
WYOMING					
AL ***Thomas***	N	Y	Y	Y	Y

Southern states - Ala., Ark., Fla., Ga., Ky., La., Miss., N.C., Okla., S.C., Tenn., Texas, Va.
Omitted votes are quorum calls, which CQ does not include in its vote charts.

HOUSE VOTES 353, 354, 355, 356, 357, 358, 359, 360

353. HR 3533. Earthquake Hazards Reduction Act Amendments/Second Ordered. Walker, R-Pa., demand for a second on the Roe, D-N.J., motion to suspend the rules and pass the bill to authorize $544.8 million for fiscal 1991 through 1994 for the National Earthquake Hazards Reduction Program. Second ordered 238-151: R 13-149; D 225-2 (ND 148-2, SD 77-0), Sept. 24, 1990. (The bill later was passed on roll call vote 369.)

354. HR 1243. Metal Casting Competitiveness Research/Second Ordered. Walker, R-Pa., demand for a second on the Roe, D-N.J., motion to suspend the rules and adopt the resolution (H Res 470) to agree to the Senate amendment, with amendments to the bill to authorize $15 million in fiscal years 1991 through 1993 for grants by the Energy Department to designate four institutes for metal casting competitiveness research. Second ordered 249-160: R 12-159; D 237-1 (ND 159-1, SD 78-0), Sept. 24, 1990. (The resolution later was adopted on roll call vote 370).

355. HR 486. Defense Production Act Amendments/Second Ordered. Wylie, R-Ohio, demand for a second on the Oakar, D-Ohio, motion to suspend the rules and pass the bill to extend, through fiscal 1992, the authority under the Defense Production Act of 1950 to require companies to fill federal government defense contract orders first and extend the other authorities under the Defense Production Act through fiscal 1995, authorizing $130 million in each fiscal year. Second ordered 243-159: R 8-159; D 235-0 (ND 159-0, SD 76-0), Sept. 24, 1990. (The bill later was passed on roll call vote 371.)

356. HR 4793. Small Business Reauthorization/Previous Question. Slaughter, D-N.Y., motion to order the previous question (thus ending debate and the possibility of amendment) on the rule (H Res 466) to provide for House floor consideration of the bill to authorize the program levels for Small Business Administration loan programs for fiscal 1991 through 1994 and for other purposes. Motion agreed to 400-9: R 162-9; D 238-0 (ND 161-0, SD 77-0), Sept. 24, 1990.

357. HR 4793. Small Business Reauthorization/Rule. Adoption of the rule (H Res 466) to provide for House floor consideration of the bill to authorize the program levels for Small Business Administration loan programs for fiscal 1991 through 1994 and for other purposes. Adopted 406-7: R 164-7; D 242-0 (ND 164-0, SD 78-0), Sept. 24, 1990.

358. HR 5314. Water Resources Development Act/Previous Question. Slaughter, D-N.Y., motion to order the previous question (thus ending debate and the possibility of amendment) on the rule (H Res 469) to provide for House floor consideration of the bill to authorize construction of water resources development projects by the U.S. Army Corps of Engineers for flood control, navigation, port development and related purposes. Motion agreed to 378-33: R 138-33; D 240-0 (ND 163-0, SD 77-0), Sept. 24, 1990.

359. HR 5314. Water Resources Development Act/Rule. Adoption of the rule (H Res 469) to provide for House floor consideration of the bill to authorize construction of water resources development projects by the U.S. Army Corps of Engineers for flood control, navigation, port development and related purposes. Adopted 376-35: R 134-35; D 242-0 (ND 164-0, SD 78-0), Sept. 24, 1990.

360. HR 4450. Coastal Zone Management Reauthorization/Previous Question. Derrick, D-S.C., motion to order the previous question (thus ending debate and the possibility of amendment) on the rule (H Res 468) to provide for House floor consideration of the bill to improve management of the coastal zone and enhance environmental protection of coastal zone resources, by reauthorizing and amending the Coastal Zone Management Act of 1972. Motion agreed to 371-42: R 130-41; D 241-1 (ND 164-1, SD 77-0), Sept. 24, 1990.

KEY

Y Voted for (yea).
Paired for.
+ Announced for.
N Voted against (nay).
X Paired against.
- Announced against.
P Voted "present."
C Voted "present" to avoid possible conflict of interest.
? Did not vote or otherwise make a position known.

Democrats *Republicans*

	353	354	355	356	357	358	359	360
ALABAMA								
1 *Callahan*	N	Y	N	Y	Y	Y	Y	Y
2 *Dickinson*	N	N	N	Y	Y	Y	Y	Y
3 Browder	Y	Y	Y	Y	Y	Y	Y	Y
4 Bevill	Y	Y	Y	Y	Y	Y	Y	Y
5 Flippo	Y	Y	?	?	?	?	?	?
6 Erdreich	Y	Y	Y	Y	Y	Y	Y	Y
7 Harris	Y	Y	Y	Y	Y	Y	Y	Y
ALASKA								
AL *Young*	N	N	N	Y	Y	Y	Y	Y
ARIZONA								
1 *Rhodes*	N	N	N	Y	Y	N	N	N
2 Udall	?	?	?	Y	Y	Y	Y	Y
3 *Stump*	N	N	N	N	N	N	N	N
4 *Kyl*	N	N	N	Y	Y	N	N	N
5 *Kolbe*	N	N	N	Y	Y	Y	Y	N
ARKANSAS								
1 Alexander	Y	Y	Y	Y	Y	Y	Y	Y
2 *Robinson*	Y	N	N	Y	Y	N	N	N
3 *Hammerschmidt*	Y	N	N	Y	Y	Y	Y	N
4 Anthony	Y	Y	Y	Y	Y	Y	Y	Y
CALIFORNIA								
1 Bosco	Y	Y	Y	Y	Y	Y	Y	Y
2 *Herger*	N	N	N	Y	Y	N	Y	N
3 Matsui	Y	Y	Y	Y	Y	Y	Y	Y
4 Fazio	Y	Y	Y	Y	Y	Y	Y	Y
5 Pelosi	Y	Y	Y	Y	Y	Y	Y	Y
6 Boxer	Y	Y	Y	Y	Y	Y	Y	Y
7 Miller	Y	Y	Y	Y	Y	Y	Y	Y
8 Dellums	Y	Y	Y	Y	Y	Y	Y	Y
9 Stark	Y	Y	Y	Y	Y	Y	Y	Y
10 Edwards	Y	Y	Y	Y	Y	?	Y	Y
11 Lantos	Y	Y	Y	Y	Y	Y	Y	Y
12 *Campbell*	Y	N	N	Y	Y	Y	N	Y
13 Mineta	Y	Y	Y	Y	Y	Y	Y	Y
14 *Shumway*	N	N	N	N	N	N	N	N
15 Condit	Y	Y	Y	Y	Y	Y	Y	Y
16 Panetta	Y	Y	Y	Y	Y	Y	Y	Y
17 *Pashayan*	?	N	N	Y	Y	Y	Y	Y
18 Lehman	?	Y	Y	Y	Y	Y	Y	Y
19 *Lagomarsino*	N	N	N	Y	Y	Y	Y	Y
20 *Thomas*	N	N	N	Y	Y	Y	Y	Y
21 *Gallegly*	N	N	N	Y	Y	Y	Y	Y
22 *Moorhead*	N	N	N	Y	Y	Y	Y	Y
23 Beilenson	Y	Y	Y	Y	Y	Y	Y	Y
24 Waxman	Y	Y	Y	Y	Y	Y	Y	Y
25 Roybal	Y	Y	Y	Y	Y	Y	Y	Y
26 Berman	Y	Y	Y	Y	Y	Y	Y	Y
27 Levine	Y	Y	?	Y	Y	Y	Y	Y
28 Dixon	Y	Y	Y	Y	Y	Y	Y	Y
29 Hawkins	Y	?	Y	?	?	?	?	?
30 Martinez	?	Y	Y	Y	Y	Y	Y	Y
31 Dymally	?	Y	Y	Y	Y	Y	Y	Y
32 Anderson	Y	Y	Y	Y	Y	Y	Y	Y
33 *Dreier*	N	N	N	Y	Y	Y	Y	Y
34 Torres	?	Y	Y	Y	Y	Y	Y	Y
35 *Lewis*	N	N	N	N	Y	Y	Y	Y
36 Brown	Y	Y	?	Y	Y	Y	Y	Y
37 *McCandless*	N	N	N	Y	Y	Y	Y	Y
38 *Dornan*	N	N	N	Y	Y	Y	Y	N
39 *Dannemeyer*	?	N	N	N	Y	Y	Y	N
40 *Cox*	?	N	N	Y	Y	Y	N	Y
41 *Lowery*	N	N	N	Y	Y	Y	Y	Y
42 *Rohrabacher*	N	N	N	Y	Y	Y	N	Y
43 *Packard*	N	N	N	Y	Y	Y	Y	N
44 Bates	Y	Y	Y	Y	Y	Y	Y	Y
45 *Hunter*	N	N	N	Y	Y	Y	?	Y
COLORADO								
1 Schroeder	Y	Y	Y	Y	Y	Y	Y	Y
2 Skaggs	Y	Y	Y	Y	Y	Y	Y	Y
3 Campbell	Y	N	Y	Y	Y	Y	Y	Y
4 *Brown*	N	N	N	Y	Y	Y	Y	Y
5 *Hefley*	N	N	N	Y	Y	Y	Y	Y
6 *Schaefer*	N	N	N	Y	Y	Y	Y	N
CONNECTICUT								
1 Kennelly	Y	Y	Y	Y	Y	Y	Y	Y
2 Gejdenson	Y	Y	Y	Y	Y	Y	Y	Y
3 Morrison	+	+	+	+	+	+	+	+
4 *Shays*	N	N	N	Y	Y	Y	Y	Y
5 *Rowland*	?	?	?	?	?	?	?	?
6 *Johnson*	N	N	N	Y	Y	Y	Y	Y
DELAWARE								
AL Carper	Y	Y	Y	Y	Y	Y	Y	Y
FLORIDA								
1 Hutto	Y	Y	Y	Y	Y	Y	Y	Y
2 *Grant*	N	N	N	Y	Y	Y	Y	Y
3 Bennett	Y	Y	Y	Y	Y	Y	Y	Y
4 *James*	?	N	N	Y	Y	Y	Y	Y
5 *McCollum*	N	N	N	Y	Y	Y	Y	Y
6 *Stearns*	N	N	N	Y	Y	N	N	Y
7 Gibbons	Y	Y	Y	Y	Y	Y	Y	Y
8 *Young*	N	N	N	Y	Y	Y	Y	Y
9 *Bilirakis*	N	N	N	Y	Y	Y	Y	Y
10 *Ireland*	N	N	N	Y	Y	Y	Y	Y
11 Nelson	Y	Y	Y	Y	Y	Y	Y	Y
12 *Lewis*	N	N	N	Y	Y	Y	Y	Y
13 *Goss*	N	N	N	Y	Y	Y	Y	Y
14 Johnston	?	?	?	?	?	?	?	?
15 *Shaw*	N	N	N	Y	Y	Y	Y	Y
16 Smith	?	?	?	?	?	?	?	?
17 Lehman	Y	Y	Y	Y	Y	Y	Y	Y
18 *Ros-Lehtinen*	N	N	N	Y	Y	Y	Y	Y
19 Fascell	Y	Y	Y	Y	Y	Y	Y	Y
GEORGIA								
1 Thomas	Y	Y	Y	Y	Y	Y	Y	Y
2 Hatcher	Y	Y	Y	Y	Y	Y	Y	Y
3 Ray	Y	Y	Y	Y	Y	Y	Y	Y
4 Jones	Y	Y	Y	Y	Y	Y	Y	Y
5 Lewis	Y	Y	Y	Y	Y	Y	Y	Y
6 *Gingrich*	N	N	?	Y	Y	Y	Y	Y
7 Darden	Y	Y	Y	Y	Y	Y	Y	Y
8 Rowland	Y	Y	Y	Y	Y	Y	Y	Y
9 Jenkins	Y	Y	Y	Y	Y	Y	Y	Y
10 Barnard	?	?	?	?	?	?	?	?
HAWAII								
1 *Saiki*	Y	N	Y	Y	Y	Y	Y	Y
2 Vacancy								
IDAHO								
1 *Craig*	N	N	N	Y	Y	Y	Y	N
2 Stallings	?	?	?	Y	Y	Y	Y	Y
ILLINOIS								
1 Hayes	Y	Y	Y	Y	Y	Y	Y	Y
2 Savage	Y	Y	Y	Y	Y	Y	Y	Y
3 Russo	Y	Y	Y	Y	Y	Y	Y	Y
4 Sangmeister	Y	Y	Y	Y	Y	Y	Y	Y
5 Lipinski	Y	Y	Y	Y	Y	Y	Y	Y
6 *Hyde*	N	N	N	Y	Y	Y	Y	Y
7 Collins	Y	Y	Y	Y	Y	Y	Y	Y
8 Rostenkowski	Y	Y	Y	Y	Y	Y	Y	Y
9 Yates	Y	Y	Y	Y	Y	Y	Y	Y
10 *Porter*	N	N	N	Y	Y	Y	Y	N
11 Annunzio	Y	Y	Y	Y	Y	Y	Y	Y
12 *Crane*	N	N	N	Y	Y	N	N	N
13 *Fawell*	Y	N	N	Y	Y	Y	Y	Y
14 *Hastert*	N	Y	N	Y	Y	Y	Y	Y
15 *Madigan*	N	N	N	Y	Y	N	?	Y
16 *Martin*	?	?	?	?	?	?	?	?
17 Evans	Y	Y	Y	Y	Y	Y	Y	Y
18 *Michel*	N	Y	Y	Y	Y	N	N	Y
19 Bruce	Y	Y	Y	Y	Y	Y	Y	Y
20 Durbin	Y	Y	Y	Y	Y	Y	Y	Y
21 Costello	Y	Y	Y	Y	Y	Y	Y	Y
22 Poshard	Y	Y	Y	Y	Y	Y	Y	Y
INDIANA								
1 Visclosky	Y	Y	Y	Y	Y	Y	Y	Y
2 Sharp	Y	Y	Y	Y	Y	Y	Y	Y
3 *Hiler*	N	Y	N	Y	Y	N	N	Y

ND Northern Democrats SD Southern Democrats

	353	354	355	356	357	358	359	360
4 Long	Y	Y	Y	Y	Y	Y	Y	Y
5 Jontz	Y	Y	Y	Y	Y	Y	Y	Y
6 ***Burton***	N	N	N	Y	Y	N	N	N
7 ***Myers***	N	N	N	Y	Y	Y	Y	Y
8 McCloskey	Y	Y	Y	Y	Y	Y	Y	Y
9 Hamilton	Y	Y	Y	Y	Y	Y	Y	Y
10 Jacobs	?	Y	Y	Y	Y	Y	Y	N
IOWA								
1 ***Leach***	N	N	N	Y	Y	Y	Y	Y
2 ***Tauke***	N	N	N	Y	Y	Y	Y	Y
3 Nagle	Y	Y	Y	Y	Y	Y	Y	Y
4 Smith	Y	Y	Y	Y	Y	Y	Y	Y
5 ***Lightfoot***	N	N	N	Y	Y	Y	Y	N
6 ***Grandy***	N	N	N	Y	N	N	N	N
KANSAS								
1 ***Roberts***	N	N	N	Y	Y	Y	Y	Y
2 Slattery	Y	Y	Y	Y	Y	Y	Y	Y
3 ***Meyers***	N	N	N	Y	Y	Y	Y	Y
4 Glickman	Y	Y	Y	Y	Y	Y	Y	Y
5 ***Whittaker***	N	N	N	Y	Y	Y	Y	Y
KENTUCKY								
1 Hubbard	Y	Y	Y	Y	Y	Y	Y	Y
2 Natcher	Y	Y	Y	Y	Y	Y	Y	Y
3 Mazzoli	Y	Y	Y	Y	Y	Y	Y	Y
4 ***Bunning***	N	N	N	Y	Y	N	Y	Y
5 ***Rogers***	N	N	N	Y	Y	Y	Y	Y
6 ***Hopkins***	N	N	N	Y	Y	Y	Y	N
7 Perkins	Y	Y	Y	Y	Y	Y	Y	Y
LOUISIANA								
1 ***Livingston***	N	N	N	Y	Y	Y	Y	Y
2 Boggs	Y	Y	Y	Y	Y	Y	Y	Y
3 Tauzin	Y	Y	Y	Y	Y	Y	Y	Y
4 ***McCrery***	?	?	?	?	?	?	?	?
5 Huckaby	Y	Y	Y	Y	Y	Y	Y	Y
6 ***Baker***	N	N	N	Y	Y	Y	N	Y
7 Hayes	Y	Y	Y	Y	Y	Y	Y	Y
8 ***Holloway***	N	N	N	Y	Y	Y	Y	Y
MAINE								
1 Brennan	Y	Y	Y	Y	Y	Y	Y	Y
2 ***Snowe***	N	N	N	Y	Y	Y	Y	Y
MARYLAND								
1 Dyson	Y	Y	Y	Y	Y	Y	Y	Y
2 ***Bentley***	Y	N	Y	Y	Y	Y	Y	N
3 Cardin	Y	Y	Y	Y	Y	Y	Y	Y
4 McMillen	Y	Y	Y	Y	Y	Y	Y	Y
5 Hoyer	Y	Y	Y	Y	Y	Y	Y	Y
6 Byron	?	?	?	?	?	?	?	?
7 Mfume	Y	Y	Y	Y	Y	Y	Y	Y
8 ***Morella***	N	Y	Y	Y	Y	Y	Y	Y
MASSACHUSETTS								
1 ***Conte***	N	N	N	Y	Y	Y	Y	Y
2 Neal	Y	Y	Y	Y	Y	Y	Y	Y
3 Early	Y	Y	Y	Y	Y	Y	Y	Y
4 Frank	Y	Y	Y	Y	Y	Y	Y	Y
5 Atkins	Y	Y	Y	Y	Y	Y	Y	Y
6 Mavroules	Y	Y	Y	Y	Y	Y	Y	Y
7 Markey	Y	Y	Y	Y	Y	Y	Y	Y
8 Kennedy	Y	Y	Y	Y	Y	Y	Y	Y
9 Moakley	Y	Y	Y	Y	Y	Y	Y	Y
10 Studds	Y	Y	Y	Y	Y	Y	Y	Y
11 Donnelly	Y	Y	Y	Y	Y	Y	Y	Y
MICHIGAN								
1 Conyers	Y	Y	Y	Y	Y	Y	Y	Y
2 ***Pursell***	N	N	N	Y	Y	Y	Y	Y
3 Wolpe	?	?	?	?	?	?	?	?
4 ***Upton***	N	N	N	Y	Y	Y	Y	Y
5 ***Henry***	N	Y	N	Y	Y	N	N	N
6 Carr	Y	Y	Y	Y	Y	Y	Y	Y
7 Kildee	Y	Y	Y	Y	Y	Y	Y	Y
8 Traxler	N	Y	Y	Y	Y	Y	Y	Y
9 ***Vander Jagt***	N	N	N	Y	Y	Y	Y	Y
10 ***Schuette***	N	N	N	Y	Y	Y	Y	Y
11 ***Davis***	N	N	N	Y	Y	Y	Y	Y
12 Bonior	Y	Y	Y	Y	Y	Y	Y	Y
13 Crockett	?	?	?	?	?	?	?	?
14 Hertel	Y	Y	Y	Y	Y	Y	Y	Y
15 Ford	?	?	?	Y	Y	Y	Y	Y
16 Dingell	Y	Y	Y	Y	Y	Y	Y	Y
17 Levin	Y	Y	Y	Y	Y	Y	Y	Y
18 ***Broomfield***	N	N	N	Y	Y	Y	Y	Y
MINNESOTA								
1 Penny	Y	Y	Y	Y	Y	Y	Y	Y
2 ***Weber***	N	N	N	Y	Y	Y	Y	Y
3 ***Frenzel***	N	N	?	N	N	N	N	N
4 Vento	Y	Y	Y	Y	Y	Y	Y	Y
5 Sabo	Y	Y	Y	Y	Y	Y	Y	Y
6 Sikorski	Y	Y	Y	Y	Y	Y	Y	Y
7 ***Stangeland***	N	N	N	Y	Y	Y	Y	Y
8 Oberstar	Y	Y	Y	Y	Y	Y	Y	Y
MISSISSIPPI								
1 Whitten	Y	Y	Y	Y	Y	Y	Y	Y
2 Espy	?	?	?	?	?	?	?	?
3 Montgomery	Y	Y	Y	Y	Y	Y	Y	Y
4 Parker	Y	Y	Y	Y	Y	Y	Y	Y
5 Taylor	Y	Y	Y	Y	Y	Y	Y	Y
MISSOURI								
1 Clay	Y	Y	Y	Y	Y	Y	Y	Y
2 ***Buechner***	Y	N	N	Y	Y	Y	Y	Y
3 Gephardt	Y	Y	?	Y	Y	Y	Y	Y
4 Skelton	Y	Y	Y	Y	Y	Y	Y	Y
5 Wheat	Y	Y	Y	Y	Y	Y	Y	Y
6 ***Coleman***	Y	N	N	Y	Y	Y	Y	Y
7 ***Hancock***	Y	N	N	Y	Y	N	N	N
8 ***Emerson***	Y	N	Y	Y	Y	Y	Y	Y
9 Volkmer	Y	Y	Y	Y	Y	Y	Y	Y
MONTANA								
1 Williams	Y	Y	Y	?	?	?	?	Y
2 ***Marlenee***	N	N	N	N	N	N	N	N
NEBRASKA								
1 ***Bereuter***	Y	Y	N	Y	Y	Y	Y	Y
2 Hoagland	Y	Y	Y	Y	Y	Y	Y	Y
3 ***Smith***	N	N	N	Y	Y	Y	Y	N
NEVADA								
1 Bilbray	Y	Y	Y	Y	Y	Y	Y	Y
2 ***Vucanovich***	N	N	N	Y	Y	Y	Y	N
NEW HAMPSHIRE								
1 ***Smith***	N	N	N	Y	Y	N	N	Y
2 ***Douglas***	N	N	?	Y	Y	N	N	Y
NEW JERSEY								
1 Vacancy								
2 Hughes	Y	Y	Y	Y	Y	Y	Y	Y
3 Pallone	Y	Y	Y	Y	Y	Y	Y	Y
4 ***Smith***	N	N	N	Y	Y	Y	Y	Y
5 ***Roukema***	?	N	N	Y	Y	Y	Y	Y
6 Dwyer	Y	Y	Y	Y	Y	Y	Y	Y
7 ***Rinaldo***	N	N	N	Y	Y	Y	Y	Y
8 Roe	Y	Y	Y	Y	Y	Y	Y	Y
9 Torricelli	?	Y	Y	Y	Y	Y	Y	Y
10 Payne	?	?	?	?	?	?	?	?
11 ***Gallo***	N	N	N	Y	Y	Y	Y	Y
12 ***Courter***	N	N	N	Y	Y	Y	Y	Y
13 ***Saxton***	N	N	N	Y	Y	Y	Y	Y
14 Guarini	Y	Y	Y	Y	Y	Y	Y	Y
NEW MEXICO								
1 ***Schiff***	N	N	N	Y	Y	Y	Y	Y
2 ***Skeen***	N	N	N	Y	Y	Y	Y	N
3 Richardson	Y	Y	Y	Y	Y	Y	Y	Y
NEW YORK								
1 Hochbrueckner	Y	Y	Y	Y	Y	Y	Y	Y
2 Downey	Y	Y	Y	Y	Y	Y	Y	Y
3 Mrazek	Y	Y	Y	Y	Y	Y	Y	Y
4 ***Lent***	N	N	N	Y	Y	Y	Y	Y
5 ***McGrath***	Y	N	N	Y	Y	Y	Y	Y
6 Flake	Y	Y	Y	Y	Y	Y	Y	Y
7 Ackerman	Y	Y	Y	Y	Y	Y	Y	Y
8 Scheuer	Y	Y	Y	Y	Y	Y	Y	Y
9 Manton	Y	Y	Y	Y	Y	Y	Y	Y
10 Schumer	Y	Y	Y	Y	Y	Y	Y	Y
11 Towns	Y	Y	Y	Y	Y	Y	Y	Y
12 Owens	?	?	?	?	?	?	?	?
13 Solarz	Y	Y	Y	Y	Y	Y	Y	Y
14 ***Molinari***	N	N	N	Y	Y	Y	Y	Y
15 ***Green***	N	N	N	Y	Y	N	N	Y
16 Rangel	Y	Y	Y	Y	Y	Y	Y	Y
17 Weiss	Y	Y	Y	Y	Y	Y	Y	Y
18 Serrano	Y	Y	Y	Y	Y	Y	Y	Y
19 Engel	Y	Y	Y	Y	Y	Y	Y	Y
20 Lowey	?	Y	Y	Y	Y	Y	Y	Y
21 ***Fish***	N	N	N	Y	Y	Y	Y	Y
22 ***Gilman***	N	Y	N	Y	Y	Y	Y	Y
23 McNulty	Y	Y	Y	Y	Y	Y	Y	Y
24 ***Solomon***	N	N	N	Y	Y	N	N	Y
25 ***Boehlert***	N	N	Y	Y	Y	Y	Y	Y
26 ***Martin***	N	N	N	Y	Y	Y	Y	Y
27 ***Walsh***	N	N	N	Y	Y	Y	Y	Y
28 McHugh	Y	Y	Y	Y	Y	Y	Y	Y
29 ***Horton***	N	Y	Y	Y	Y	Y	Y	Y
30 Slaughter	Y	Y	Y	Y	Y	Y	Y	Y
31 ***Paxon***	N	N	N	Y	Y	Y	Y	Y
32 LaFalce	Y	Y	Y	Y	Y	Y	Y	Y
33 Nowak	Y	Y	Y	Y	Y	Y	Y	Y
34 ***Houghton***	N	N	?	Y	Y	Y	Y	Y
NORTH CAROLINA								
1 Jones	Y	Y	Y	Y	Y	Y	Y	Y
2 Valentine	Y	Y	Y	Y	Y	Y	Y	Y
3 Lancaster	Y	Y	Y	Y	Y	Y	Y	Y
4 Price	Y	Y	Y	Y	Y	Y	Y	Y
5 Neal	Y	Y	Y	Y	Y	Y	Y	Y
6 ***Coble***	N	N	N	Y	Y	Y	Y	Y
7 Rose	Y	Y	Y	Y	Y	Y	Y	Y
8 Hefner	Y	Y	Y	Y	Y	Y	Y	Y
9 ***McMillan***	N	Y	N	Y	Y	Y	Y	Y
10 ***Ballenger***	N	N	N	Y	Y	Y	Y	Y
11 Clarke	Y	Y	Y	Y	Y	Y	Y	Y
NORTH DAKOTA								
AL Dorgan	Y	Y	Y	Y	Y	Y	Y	Y
OHIO								
1 Luken	Y	Y	Y	Y	Y	Y	Y	Y
2 ***Gradison***	N	N	N	Y	Y	N	N	Y
3 Hall	Y	Y	Y	Y	Y	Y	Y	Y
4 ***Oxley***	N	N	N	Y	Y	Y	Y	Y
5 ***Gillmor***	N	N	Y	Y	Y	Y	Y	Y
6 ***McEwen***	N	N	N	Y	Y	Y	Y	Y
7 ***DeWine***	N	N	N	Y	Y	Y	Y	Y
8 ***Lukens***	N	N	N	N	Y	Y	Y	Y
9 Kaptur	?	?	?	Y	Y	Y	Y	Y
10 ***Miller***	N	N	N	Y	Y	Y	Y	Y
11 Eckart	Y	Y	Y	Y	Y	Y	Y	Y
12 ***Kasich***	N	N	N	Y	Y	Y	Y	Y
13 Pease	Y	Y	Y	Y	Y	Y	Y	Y
14 Sawyer	Y	Y	Y	Y	Y	Y	Y	Y
15 ***Wylie***	N	N	N	Y	Y	Y	Y	Y
16 ***Regula***	N	N	N	Y	Y	Y	Y	Y
17 Traficant	Y	Y	Y	Y	Y	Y	Y	Y
18 Applegate	Y	Y	Y	Y	Y	Y	Y	Y
19 Feighan	Y	Y	Y	Y	Y	Y	Y	Y
20 Oakar	Y	Y	Y	Y	Y	Y	Y	Y
21 Stokes	Y	Y	Y	Y	Y	Y	Y	Y
OKLAHOMA								
1 ***Inhofe***	N	N	N	Y	Y	Y	Y	N
2 Synar	Y	Y	Y	Y	Y	Y	Y	Y
3 Watkins	Y	Y	Y	Y	Y	Y	Y	Y
4 McCurdy	Y	Y	Y	Y	Y	Y	Y	Y
5 ***Edwards***	N	N	N	Y	Y	Y	Y	N
6 English	Y	Y	Y	Y	Y	Y	Y	Y
OREGON								
1 AuCoin	Y	Y	Y	Y	Y	Y	Y	Y
2 ***Smith, B.***	N	N	N	Y	Y	Y	N	N
3 Wyden	Y	Y	Y	Y	Y	Y	Y	Y
4 DeFazio	?	Y	Y	Y	Y	Y	Y	Y
5 ***Smith, D.***	?	?	?	?	?	?	?	?
PENNSYLVANIA								
1 Foglietta	Y	Y	Y	Y	Y	Y	Y	Y
2 Gray	?	Y	Y	Y	Y	Y	Y	Y
3 Borski	Y	Y	Y	Y	Y	Y	Y	Y
4 Kolter	Y	Y	Y	Y	Y	Y	Y	Y
5 ***Schulze***	N	N	N	Y	Y	Y	Y	Y
6 Yatron	Y	Y	Y	Y	Y	Y	Y	Y
7 ***Weldon***	N	N	N	Y	Y	Y	Y	Y
8 Kostmayer	Y	Y	Y	Y	Y	Y	Y	Y
9 ***Shuster***	N	N	N	Y	Y	Y	Y	Y
10 ***McDade***	N	N	N	Y	Y	Y	Y	Y
11 Kanjorski	Y	Y	Y	Y	Y	Y	Y	Y
12 Murtha	Y	Y	Y	Y	Y	Y	Y	Y
13 ***Coughlin***	N	N	N	Y	Y	Y	N	Y
14 Coyne	Y	Y	Y	Y	Y	Y	Y	Y
15 ***Ritter***	N	N	N	Y	Y	Y	Y	Y
16 ***Walker***	N	N	N	Y	Y	Y	N	N
17 ***Gekas***	N	N	N	N	Y	Y	N	N
18 Walgren	Y	Y	Y	Y	Y	Y	Y	Y
19 ***Goodling***	N	N	N	Y	Y	Y	Y	Y
20 Gaydos	Y	Y	Y	Y	Y	Y	Y	Y
21 ***Ridge***	?	N	N	Y	Y	Y	Y	Y
22 Murphy	?	Y	Y	Y	Y	Y	Y	Y
23 ***Clinger***	N	N	N	Y	Y	Y	Y	Y
RHODE ISLAND								
1 ***Machtley***	N	N	N	Y	Y	Y	Y	Y
2 ***Schneider***	N	N	N	Y	Y	Y	Y	Y
SOUTH CAROLINA								
1 ***Ravenel***	N	Y	N	Y	Y	Y	Y	Y
2 ***Spence***	N	N	N	Y	Y	Y	Y	Y
3 Derrick	Y	Y	Y	Y	Y	?	Y	?
4 Patterson	Y	Y	Y	Y	Y	Y	Y	Y
5 Spratt	Y	Y	Y	Y	Y	Y	Y	Y
6 Tallon	Y	Y	Y	Y	Y	Y	Y	Y
SOUTH DAKOTA								
AL Johnson	Y	Y	Y	Y	Y	Y	Y	Y
TENNESSEE								
1 ***Quillen***	N	N	N	Y	Y	Y	Y	Y
2 ***Duncan***	N	N	N	Y	Y	Y	Y	N
3 Lloyd	Y	Y	Y	Y	Y	Y	Y	Y
4 Cooper	Y	Y	Y	Y	Y	Y	Y	Y
5 Clement	Y	Y	Y	Y	Y	Y	Y	Y
6 Gordon	Y	Y	Y	Y	Y	Y	Y	Y
7 ***Sundquist***	Y	N	N	Y	Y	Y	Y	Y
8 Tanner	Y	Y	Y	Y	Y	Y	Y	Y
9 Ford	Y	Y	?	Y	Y	Y	Y	Y
TEXAS								
1 Chapman	Y	?	?	Y	Y	Y	Y	Y
2 Wilson	Y	Y	Y	Y	Y	Y	Y	Y
3 ***Bartlett***	N	N	N	Y	Y	N	N	N
4 Hall	Y	Y	Y	Y	Y	Y	Y	Y
5 Bryant	Y	Y	Y	Y	Y	Y	Y	Y
6 ***Barton***	N	N	N	Y	Y	N	N	N
7 ***Archer***	N	N	N	Y	Y	Y	Y	Y
8 ***Fields***	N	N	N	Y	Y	Y	Y	Y
9 Brooks	Y	Y	Y	Y	Y	Y	Y	Y
10 Pickle	Y	Y	Y	Y	Y	Y	Y	Y
11 Leath	Y	Y	Y	Y	Y	Y	Y	Y
12 Geren	Y	Y	Y	Y	Y	Y	Y	Y
13 Sarpalius	Y	Y	Y	Y	Y	Y	Y	Y
14 Laughlin	Y	Y	Y	Y	Y	Y	Y	Y
15 de la Garza	Y	Y	Y	Y	Y	Y	Y	Y
16 Coleman	Y	Y	Y	Y	Y	Y	Y	Y
17 Stenholm	Y	Y	Y	Y	Y	Y	Y	Y
18 Washington	?	Y	Y	Y	Y	Y	Y	Y
19 ***Combest***	N	N	N	Y	Y	Y	Y	N
20 Gonzalez	Y	Y	Y	Y	Y	Y	Y	Y
21 ***Smith***	?	N	N	Y	Y	N	N	N
22 ***DeLay***	N	N	N	Y	Y	N	N	N
23 Bustamante	Y	Y	Y	Y	Y	Y	Y	Y
24 Frost	Y	Y	Y	Y	Y	Y	Y	Y
25 Andrews	Y	Y	Y	Y	Y	Y	Y	Y
26 ***Armey***	N	N	N	Y	N	N	N	Y
27 Ortiz	Y	Y	Y	Y	Y	Y	Y	Y
UTAH								
1 ***Hansen***	N	N	N	Y	Y	Y	Y	N
2 Owens	?	Y	Y	Y	Y	Y	Y	Y
3 ***Nielson***	N	N	N	Y	Y	Y	Y	Y
VERMONT								
AL ***Smith***	N	N	N	Y	Y	N	N	Y
VIRGINIA								
1 ***Bateman***	N	N	N	Y	Y	Y	Y	Y
2 Pickett	Y	Y	Y	Y	Y	Y	Y	Y
3 ***Bliley***	N	N	N	Y	Y	N	Y	Y
4 Sisisky	Y	Y	Y	Y	Y	Y	Y	Y
5 Payne	Y	Y	Y	?	Y	Y	Y	Y
6 Olin	Y	Y	Y	Y	Y	Y	Y	Y
7 ***Slaughter***	N	N	N	Y	Y	N	Y	Y
8 ***Parris***	N	N	N	Y	Y	Y	Y	Y
9 Boucher	?	Y	Y	Y	Y	Y	Y	Y
10 ***Wolf***	N	N	N	Y	Y	Y	Y	Y
WASHINGTON								
1 ***Miller***	?	N	N	Y	Y	Y	Y	Y
2 Swift	Y	Y	Y	?	Y	Y	Y	Y
3 Unsoeld	Y	Y	Y	Y	Y	Y	Y	Y
4 ***Morrison***	—	—	—	—	+	—	+	—
5 Foley								
6 Dicks	Y	Y	Y	Y	Y	Y	Y	Y
7 McDermott	Y	Y	Y	Y	Y	Y	Y	Y
8 ***Chandler***	?	N	N	Y	Y	Y	Y	Y
WEST VIRGINIA								
1 Mollohan	?	?	?	?	?	?	?	?
2 Staggers	Y	Y	Y	Y	Y	Y	Y	Y
3 Wise	?	?	Y	?	Y	Y	Y	Y
4 Rahall	Y	Y	Y	Y	Y	Y	Y	Y
WISCONSIN								
1 Aspin	Y	Y	Y	Y	Y	Y	Y	Y
2 Kastenmeier	Y	Y	Y	Y	Y	Y	Y	Y
3 ***Gunderson***	N	N	N	Y	Y	Y	Y	Y
4 Kleczka	Y	Y	Y	?	Y	Y	Y	Y
5 Moody	Y	Y	Y	Y	Y	Y	Y	Y
6 ***Petri***	N	N	N	Y	Y	Y	Y	N
7 Obey	N	Y	Y	Y	Y	Y	Y	Y
8 ***Roth***	N	N	N	Y	Y	Y	Y	Y
9 ***Sensenbrenner***	N	N	N	N	N	N	N	N
WYOMING								
AL ***Thomas***	N	N	N	Y	Y	Y	Y	Y

Southern states - Ala., Ark., Fla., Ga., Ky., La., Miss., N.C., Okla., S.C., Tenn., Texas, Va.
Omitted votes are quorum calls, which CQ does not include in its vote charts.

HOUSE VOTES 361, 362, 363, 364, 365, 366, 367, 368

361. HR 4450. Coastal Zone Management Reauthorization/Rule. Adoption of the rule (H Res 468) to provide for House floor consideration of the bill to improve management of the coastal zone and enhance environmental protection of coastal zone resources, by reauthorizing and amending the Coastal Zone Management Act of 1972. Adopted 370-44: R 127-44; D 243-0 (ND 165-0, SD 78-0), Sept. 24, 1990.

362. HR 4279. Federal-State Cash Management Improvement Act/Passage. Conyers, D-Mich., motion to suspend the rules and pass the bill to authorize the Treasury Department to regulate disbursement of federal funds to ensure that such funds are transferred to state recipients in a timely manner. Motion agreed to 410-4: R 170-0; D 240-4 (ND 163-2, SD 77-2), Sept. 24, 1990. A two-thirds majority of those present and voting (276 in this case) is required for passage under suspension of the rules.

363. S 535. Federal Civil Penalties Adjustment Act/Passage. Conyers, D-Mich., motion to suspend the rules and pass the bill (thus clearing the measure for the president) to increase civil monetary penalties based on the effect of inflation. Motion agreed to 407-5: R 165-5; D 242-0 (ND 163-0, SD 79-0), Sept. 24, 1990. A two-thirds majority of those present and voting (275 in this case) is required for passage under suspension of the rules.

364. S 2075. Indian Environmental Regulatory Enhancement Act/Passage. Faleomavaega, D-Am. Samoa, motion to suspend the rules and pass the bill to authorize $8 million for each of fiscal years 1991-96 for grants to improve the capability of tribal governments to regulate environmental quality on Indian reservations. Motion agreed to 316-99: R 83-88; D 233-11 (ND 160-5, SD 73-6), Sept. 24, 1990. A two-thirds majority of those present and voting (277 in this case) is required for passage under suspension of the rules. A "nay" was a vote supporting the president's position.

365. HR 4323. Great Lakes Water Quality Improvement Act/Passage. Anderson, D-Calif., motion to suspend the rules and pass the bill to authorize $11 million in fiscal 1991, and $30 million in each of fiscal years 1992-97, for programs to implement the Great Lakes Water Quality Agreement between the United States and Canada. Motion agreed to 376-37: R 133-37; D 243-0 (ND 164-0, SD 79-0), Sept. 24, 1990. A two-thirds majority of those present and voting (276 in this case) is required for passage under suspension of the rules. A "nay" was a vote supporting the president's position.

366. HR 5482. D.C. Revenue Bond Act/Passage. McDermott, D-Wash., motion to suspend the rules and pass the bill to waive the period of congressional review of certain District of Columbia acts authorizing the issuance of eight revenue bonds. Motion agreed to 371-44: R 135-36; D 236-8 (ND 159-6, SD 77-2), Sept. 24, 1990. A two-thirds majority of those present and voting (277 in this case) is required for passage under suspension of the rules.

367. HR 5254. Fish and Wildlife Conservation Authorization/Passage. Studds, D-Mass., motion to suspend the rules and pass the bill to authorize $5 million in both fiscal 1991 and 1992 to reauthorize the Fish and Wildlife Conservation Act. Motion agreed to 408-7: R 165-6; D 243-1 (ND 164-1, SD 79-0), Sept. 24, 1990. A two-thirds majority of those present and voting (277 in this case) is required for passage under suspension of the rules.

368. HR 5255. Fish and Wildlife Foundation Authorization/Passage. Studds, D-Mass., motion to suspend the rules and pass the bill to increase the authorization for federal matching funds for the National Fish and Wildlife Foundation in fiscal 1991-93. Motion agreed to 369-46: R 130-41; D 239-5 (ND 163-2, SD 76-3), Sept. 24, 1990. A two-thirds majority of those present and voting (277 in this case) is required for passage under suspension of the rules.

KEY

- Y Voted for (yea).
- # Paired for.
- \+ Announced for.
- N Voted against (nay).
- X Paired against.
- \- Announced against.
- P Voted "present."
- C Voted "present" to avoid possible conflict of interest.
- ? Did not vote or otherwise make a position known.

Democrats ***Republicans***

	361	362	363	364	365	366	367	368
ALABAMA								
1 ***Callahan***	Y	Y	Y	Y	Y	N	Y	Y
2 ***Dickinson***	Y	Y	Y	Y	Y	Y	Y	N
3 Browder	Y	Y	Y	Y	Y	Y	Y	Y
4 Bevill	Y	Y	Y	Y	Y	Y	Y	Y
5 Flippo	?	?	?	?	?	?	?	?
6 Erdreich	Y	Y	Y	Y	Y	Y	Y	Y
7 Harris	Y	Y	Y	Y	Y	Y	Y	Y
ALASKA								
AL ***Young***	Y	Y	Y	Y	Y	Y	Y	Y
ARIZONA								
1 ***Rhodes***	N	Y	Y	Y	N	Y	Y	Y
2 Udall	Y	Y	Y	Y	Y	Y	Y	Y
3 ***Stump***	N	Y	Y	N	N	N	N	N
4 ***Kyl***	N	Y	Y	Y	N	Y	Y	N
5 ***Kolbe***	N	Y	Y	Y	N	Y	Y	Y
ARKANSAS								
1 Alexander	Y	Y	Y	Y	Y	Y	Y	Y
2 ***Robinson***	N	Y	Y	N	Y	N	Y	Y
3 ***Hammerschmidt***	N	Y	Y	N	Y	Y	Y	N
4 Anthony	Y	Y	Y	Y	Y	Y	Y	Y
CALIFORNIA								
1 Bosco	Y	Y	Y	Y	Y	Y	Y	Y
2 ***Herger***	N	Y	Y	N	N	Y	Y	N
3 Matsui	Y	Y	Y	Y	Y	Y	Y	Y
4 Fazio	Y	Y	Y	Y	Y	Y	Y	Y
5 Pelosi	Y	Y	Y	Y	Y	Y	Y	Y
6 Boxer	Y	Y	Y	Y	Y	Y	Y	Y
7 Miller	Y	Y	Y	Y	Y	Y	Y	Y
8 Dellums	Y	Y	Y	Y	Y	Y	Y	Y
9 Stark	Y	Y	Y	Y	Y	Y	Y	Y
10 Edwards	Y	Y	Y	Y	Y	Y	Y	Y
11 Lantos	Y	Y	Y	Y	Y	Y	Y	Y
12 ***Campbell***	Y	Y	Y	Y	Y	Y	Y	Y
13 Mineta	Y	Y	Y	Y	Y	Y	Y	Y
14 ***Shumway***	N	Y	Y	N	N	Y	Y	N
15 Condit	Y	Y	Y	Y	Y	Y	Y	Y
16 Panetta	Y	Y	Y	Y	Y	Y	Y	Y
17 ***Pashayan***	Y	Y	Y	Y	Y	Y	Y	Y
18 Lehman	Y	Y	Y	Y	Y	Y	Y	Y
19 ***Lagomarsino***	Y	Y	Y	N	Y	N	Y	Y
20 ***Thomas***	Y	Y	Y	Y	Y	Y	Y	Y
21 ***Gallegly***	Y	Y	Y	N	Y	N	Y	Y
22 ***Moorhead***	Y	Y	Y	Y	Y	N	Y	N
23 Beilenson	Y	Y	Y	Y	Y	Y	Y	Y
24 Waxman	Y	Y	Y	Y	Y	Y	Y	Y
25 Roybal	Y	Y	Y	Y	Y	Y	Y	Y
26 Berman	Y	Y	Y	Y	Y	Y	Y	Y
27 Levine	Y	Y	Y	Y	Y	Y	Y	Y
28 Dixon	Y	Y	Y	Y	Y	Y	Y	Y
29 Hawkins	?	Y	Y	Y	?	Y	Y	Y
30 Martinez	Y	Y	Y	Y	Y	Y	Y	Y
31 Dymally	Y	Y	Y	Y	Y	Y	Y	Y
32 Anderson	Y	Y	Y	Y	Y	Y	Y	Y
33 ***Dreier***	Y	Y	Y	Y	Y	Y	Y	Y
34 Torres	Y	Y	Y	Y	Y	Y	Y	Y
35 ***Lewis***	Y	Y	Y	Y	Y	Y	Y	Y
36 Brown	Y	Y	Y	Y	Y	Y	Y	Y
37 ***McCandless***	Y	Y	Y	N	Y	N	Y	N
38 ***Dornan***	N	Y	Y	N	N	N	Y	N
39 ***Dannemeyer***	N	Y	N	N	N	Y	Y	N
40 ***Cox***	Y	Y	Y	Y	Y	Y	Y	Y
41 ***Lowery***	Y	Y	Y	Y	Y	Y	Y	Y
42 ***Rohrabacher***	N	Y	Y	N	Y	Y	Y	Y
43 ***Packard***	Y	Y	Y	N	Y	Y	Y	N
44 Bates	Y	Y	Y	Y	Y	Y	Y	Y
45 ***Hunter***	Y	Y	Y	Y	Y	Y	Y	Y
COLORADO								
1 Schroeder	Y	Y	Y	Y	Y	Y	Y	Y
2 Skaggs	Y	Y	Y	Y	Y	Y	Y	Y
3 Campbell	Y	Y	Y	Y	Y	Y	Y	Y
4 ***Brown***	Y	Y	Y	N	Y	N	Y	Y
5 ***Hefley***	Y	Y	N	N	Y	N	Y	Y
6 ***Schaefer***	N	Y	Y	Y	Y	Y	Y	N
CONNECTICUT								
1 Kennelly	Y	Y	Y	Y	Y	Y	Y	Y
2 Gejdenson	Y	Y	Y	Y	Y	Y	Y	Y
3 Morrison	+	+	+	+	+	+	+	+
4 ***Shays***	Y	Y	Y	Y	Y	Y	Y	Y
5 ***Rowland***	?	?	?	?	?	?	?	?
6 ***Johnson***	Y	Y	Y	Y	Y	Y	Y	Y
DELAWARE								
AL Carper	Y	Y	Y	Y	Y	Y	Y	Y
FLORIDA								
1 Hutto	Y	Y	Y	Y	Y	Y	Y	Y
2 ***Grant***	Y	Y	Y	N	Y	Y	Y	N
3 Bennett	Y	Y	Y	Y	Y	Y	Y	Y
4 ***James***	Y	Y	Y	Y	Y	Y	Y	Y
5 ***McCollum***	Y	Y	Y	N	Y	Y	Y	Y
6 ***Stearns***	Y	Y	Y	N	Y	Y	Y	Y
7 Gibbons	Y	Y	Y	Y	Y	N	Y	Y
8 ***Young***	Y	Y	Y	N	Y	Y	Y	Y
9 ***Bilirakis***	Y	Y	Y	N	Y	Y	Y	Y
10 ***Ireland***	Y	?	Y	N	Y	Y	Y	Y
11 Nelson	Y	Y	Y	Y	Y	Y	Y	Y
12 ***Lewis***	Y	Y	Y	N	Y	Y	Y	Y
13 ***Goss***	Y	Y	Y	Y	Y	Y	Y	Y
14 Johnston	?	?	?	?	?	?	?	?
15 ***Shaw***	Y	Y	Y	N	Y	Y	Y	Y
16 Smith	?	Y	Y	Y	Y	Y	Y	Y
17 Lehman	Y	Y	Y	Y	Y	Y	Y	Y
18 ***Ros-Lehtinen***	Y	Y	Y	Y	Y	Y	Y	Y
19 Fascell	Y	Y	Y	Y	Y	Y	Y	Y
GEORGIA								
1 Thomas	Y	Y	Y	Y	Y	Y	Y	Y
2 Hatcher	Y	Y	Y	Y	Y	Y	Y	Y
3 Ray	Y	Y	Y	Y	Y	Y	Y	Y
4 Jones	Y	Y	Y	N	Y	Y	Y	Y
5 Lewis	Y	Y	Y	Y	Y	Y	Y	Y
6 ***Gingrich***	Y	Y	Y	N	N	N	Y	N
7 Darden	Y	Y	Y	Y	Y	Y	Y	Y
8 Rowland	Y	Y	Y	Y	Y	Y	Y	Y
9 Jenkins	Y	Y	Y	N	Y	Y	Y	N
10 Barnard	?	?	?	?	?	?	?	?
HAWAII								
1 ***Saiki***	Y	Y	Y	Y	Y	Y	Y	Y
2 Vacancy								
IDAHO								
1 ***Craig***	N	Y	Y	Y	N	Y	Y	N
2 Stallings	Y	N	Y	Y	Y	Y	Y	Y
ILLINOIS								
1 Hayes	Y	Y	Y	Y	Y	Y	Y	Y
2 Savage	Y	Y	Y	Y	Y	Y	Y	Y
3 Russo	Y	Y	Y	Y	Y	Y	Y	Y
4 Sangmeister	Y	Y	Y	Y	Y	Y	Y	Y
5 Lipinski	Y	Y	Y	Y	Y	Y	Y	Y
6 ***Hyde***	Y	Y	Y	N	Y	Y	Y	Y
7 Collins	Y	Y	Y	Y	Y	Y	Y	Y
8 Rostenkowski	Y	Y	Y	Y	Y	Y	Y	Y
9 Yates	Y	Y	Y	Y	Y	Y	Y	Y
10 ***Porter***	Y	Y	Y	Y	Y	N	Y	Y
11 Annunzio	Y	Y	Y	Y	Y	Y	Y	Y
12 ***Crane***	Y	Y	Y	N	N	Y	N	N
13 ***Fawell***	Y	Y	Y	Y	Y	Y	Y	Y
14 ***Hastert***	N	Y	Y	N	Y	N	Y	Y
15 ***Madigan***	Y	Y	Y	Y	N	Y	Y	Y
16 ***Martin***	?	?	?	?	?	?	?	?
17 Evans	Y	Y	Y	Y	Y	Y	Y	Y
18 ***Michel***	Y	Y	Y	N	N	Y	Y	Y
19 Bruce	Y	Y	Y	Y	Y	Y	Y	Y
20 Durbin	Y	Y	Y	Y	Y	Y	Y	Y
21 Costello	Y	Y	Y	Y	Y	Y	Y	Y
22 Poshard	Y	Y	Y	Y	Y	Y	Y	Y
INDIANA								
1 Visclosky	Y	Y	Y	Y	Y	Y	Y	Y
2 Sharp	Y	Y	Y	Y	Y	Y	Y	Y
3 ***Hiler***	Y	Y	Y	N	Y	Y	Y	Y

ND Northern Democrats SD Southern Democrats

	361	362	363	364	365	366	367	368
4 Long	Y	Y	Y	Y	Y	Y	Y	Y
5 Jontz	Y	Y	Y	Y	Y	Y	Y	Y
6 ***Burton***	N	Y	Y	N	N	Y	Y	N
7 ***Myers***	Y	Y	Y	N	Y	Y	Y	Y
8 McCloskey	Y	Y	Y	Y	Y	Y	Y	Y
9 Hamilton	Y	Y	Y	Y	Y	Y	Y	Y
10 Jacobs	Y	Y	Y	Y	Y	Y	Y	Y
IOWA								
1 ***Leach***	Y	Y	Y	Y	Y	N	Y	Y
2 ***Tauke***	Y	Y	Y	N	Y	Y	Y	Y
3 Nagle	Y	Y	Y	Y	Y	Y	Y	Y
4 Smith	Y	Y	Y	Y	Y	Y	Y	Y
5 ***Lightfoot***	N	Y	Y	N	Y	Y	Y	N
6 ***Grandy***	N	Y	Y	N	Y	Y	Y	Y
KANSAS								
1 ***Roberts***	Y	Y	Y	Y	Y	Y	Y	N
2 Slattery	Y	Y	Y	Y	Y	Y	Y	N
3 ***Meyers***	Y	Y	Y	N	Y	Y	Y	N
4 Glickman	Y	Y	Y	N	Y	Y	Y	N
5 ***Whittaker***	Y	Y	Y	N	Y	Y	Y	N
KENTUCKY								
1 Hubbard	Y	Y	Y	Y	Y	Y	Y	Y
2 Natcher	Y	Y	Y	Y	Y	Y	Y	Y
3 Mazzoli	Y	Y	Y	Y	Y	Y	Y	Y
4 ***Bunning***	Y	Y	Y	N	Y	Y	Y	N
5 ***Rogers***	N	Y	Y	N	Y	Y	Y	Y
6 ***Hopkins***	N	Y	Y	N	Y	N	Y	Y
7 Perkins	Y	Y	Y	Y	Y	Y	Y	Y
LOUISIANA								
1 ***Livingston***	Y	Y	Y	N	Y	Y	Y	Y
2 Boggs	Y	Y	Y	Y	Y	Y	Y	Y
3 Tauzin	Y	Y	Y	Y	Y	Y	Y	Y
4 ***McCrery***	?	?	?	?	?	?	?	?
5 Huckaby	Y	Y	Y	Y	Y	Y	Y	Y
6 ***Baker***	Y	Y	Y	N	Y	N	Y	Y
7 Hayes	Y	Y	Y	Y	Y	Y	Y	Y
8 ***Holloway***	Y	Y	Y	N	Y	Y	Y	Y
MAINE								
1 Brennan	Y	Y	Y	Y	Y	Y	Y	Y
2 ***Snowe***	Y	Y	Y	Y	Y	Y	Y	Y
MARYLAND								
1 Dyson	Y	Y	Y	Y	Y	Y	Y	Y
2 ***Bentley***	Y	Y	Y	N	Y	Y	Y	Y
3 Cardin	Y	Y	Y	Y	Y	Y	Y	Y
4 McMillen	Y	Y	Y	Y	Y	Y	Y	Y
5 Hoyer	Y	Y	Y	Y	Y	Y	Y	Y
6 Byron	?	?	?	?	?	?	?	?
7 Mfume	Y	Y	Y	Y	Y	Y	Y	Y
8 ***Morella***	Y	Y	Y	Y	Y	Y	Y	Y
MASSACHUSETTS								
1 ***Conte***	Y	Y	Y	Y	Y	Y	Y	Y
2 Neal	Y	Y	Y	Y	Y	Y	Y	Y
3 Early	Y	Y	Y	Y	Y	Y	Y	Y
4 Frank	Y	Y	Y	Y	Y	Y	Y	Y
5 Atkins	Y	Y	Y	Y	Y	Y	Y	Y
6 Mavroules	Y	Y	Y	Y	Y	Y	Y	Y
7 Markey	Y	Y	Y	Y	Y	Y	Y	Y
8 Kennedy	Y	Y	Y	Y	Y	Y	Y	Y
9 Moakley	Y	Y	Y	Y	Y	Y	Y	Y
10 Studds	Y	Y	Y	Y	Y	Y	Y	Y
11 Donnelly	Y	Y	Y	Y	Y	Y	Y	Y
MICHIGAN								
1 Conyers	Y	Y	Y	Y	Y	Y	Y	Y
2 ***Pursell***	Y	Y	Y	Y	Y	Y	Y	Y
3 Wolpe	?	?	?	?	?	?	?	?
4 ***Upton***	Y	Y	Y	Y	Y	Y	Y	Y
5 ***Henry***	N	Y	Y	N	Y	N	Y	Y
6 Carr	Y	Y	Y	N	Y	Y	Y	Y
7 Kildee	Y	Y	Y	Y	Y	Y	Y	Y
8 Traxler	Y	Y	Y	Y	Y	Y	Y	Y
9 ***Vander Jagt***	Y	Y	Y	Y	Y	Y	Y	Y
10 ***Schuette***	Y	Y	Y	Y	Y	Y	Y	Y
11 ***Davis***	Y	Y	Y	Y	Y	Y	Y	Y
12 Bonior	Y	Y	Y	Y	Y	Y	Y	Y
13 Crockett	?	?	?	?	?	?	?	?
14 Hertel	Y	Y	Y	Y	Y	Y	Y	Y
15 Ford	Y	Y	Y	Y	Y	Y	Y	Y
16 Dingell	Y	Y	Y	Y	Y	Y	Y	Y
17 Levin	Y	Y	Y	Y	Y	Y	Y	Y
18 ***Broomfield***	Y	Y	Y	Y	Y	N	Y	Y
MINNESOTA								
1 Penny	Y	N	Y	N	Y	N	N	Y
2 ***Weber***	Y	Y	Y	Y	Y	Y	Y	Y
3 ***Frenzel***	N	Y	Y	N	N	N	N	N
4 Vento	Y	Y	Y	Y	Y	Y	Y	Y
5 Sabo	Y	Y	Y	Y	Y	Y	Y	Y
6 Sikorski	Y	Y	Y	Y	Y	Y	Y	Y
7 ***Stangeland***	Y	Y	Y	Y	Y	Y	Y	Y
8 Oberstar	Y	Y	Y	Y	Y	Y	Y	Y
MISSISSIPPI								
1 Whitten	Y	Y	Y	Y	Y	Y	Y	Y
2 Espy	?	?	?	?	?	?	?	?
3 Montgomery	Y	Y	Y	Y	Y	Y	Y	Y
4 Parker	Y	Y	Y	Y	Y	Y	Y	Y
5 Taylor	Y	Y	Y	Y	Y	Y	Y	Y
MISSOURI								
1 Clay	Y	Y	Y	Y	Y	Y	Y	Y
2 ***Buechner***	Y	Y	Y	Y	Y	Y	Y	Y
3 Gephardt	Y	Y	Y	Y	Y	Y	Y	Y
4 Skelton	Y	Y	Y	N	Y	N	Y	Y
5 Wheat	Y	Y	Y	Y	Y	Y	Y	Y
6 ***Coleman***	Y	Y	Y	N	Y	Y	Y	Y
7 ***Hancock***	N	Y	N	N	N	N	N	N
8 ***Emerson***	Y	Y	Y	N	Y	Y	Y	Y
9 Volkmer	Y	Y	Y	Y	Y	Y	Y	Y
MONTANA								
1 Williams	Y	Y	?	Y	Y	Y	Y	Y
2 ***Marlenee***	N	Y	Y	N	N	N	Y	N
NEBRASKA								
1 ***Bereuter***	Y	Y	Y	Y	Y	Y	Y	Y
2 Hoagland	Y	Y	Y	Y	Y	Y	Y	Y
3 ***Smith***	N	Y	Y	N	N	Y	Y	Y
NEVADA								
1 Bilbray	Y	Y	Y	Y	Y	Y	Y	Y
2 ***Vucanovich***	N	Y	Y	N	N	Y	Y	Y
NEW HAMPSHIRE								
1 ***Smith***	Y	Y	Y	N	Y	N	Y	Y
2 ***Douglas***	Y	Y	Y	Y	Y	N	Y	Y
NEW JERSEY								
1 Vacancy								
2 Hughes	Y	Y	Y	Y	Y	Y	Y	Y
3 Pallone	Y	Y	Y	Y	Y	Y	Y	Y
4 ***Smith***	Y	Y	Y	Y	Y	Y	Y	Y
5 ***Roukema***	Y	Y	Y	N	Y	N	Y	Y
6 Dwyer	Y	Y	Y	Y	Y	Y	Y	Y
7 ***Rinaldo***	Y	Y	Y	Y	Y	Y	Y	Y
8 Roe	Y	Y	Y	Y	Y	Y	Y	Y
9 Torricelli	Y	Y	Y	Y	Y	Y	Y	Y
10 Payne	?	?	?	?	?	?	?	?
11 ***Gallo***	Y	Y	Y	Y	Y	Y	Y	Y
12 ***Courter***	Y	Y	Y	Y	Y	Y	Y	Y
13 ***Saxton***	Y	Y	Y	Y	Y	Y	Y	Y
14 Guarini	Y	Y	Y	N	Y	Y	Y	Y
NEW MEXICO								
1 ***Schiff***	Y	Y	Y	Y	Y	Y	Y	Y
2 ***Skeen***	N	Y	Y	Y	Y	Y	Y	N
3 Richardson	Y	Y	Y	Y	Y	Y	Y	Y
NEW YORK								
1 Hochbrueckner	Y	Y	Y	Y	Y	Y	Y	Y
2 Downey	Y	Y	Y	Y	Y	Y	Y	Y
3 Mrazek	Y	Y	Y	Y	Y	Y	Y	Y
4 ***Lent***	Y	Y	Y	Y	Y	Y	Y	Y
5 ***McGrath***	Y	Y	Y	N	Y	Y	Y	Y
6 Flake	Y	Y	Y	Y	Y	Y	Y	Y
7 Ackerman	Y	Y	Y	Y	Y	Y	Y	Y
8 Scheuer	Y	Y	Y	Y	Y	Y	Y	Y
9 Manton	Y	Y	Y	Y	Y	Y	Y	Y
10 Schumer	Y	Y	Y	Y	Y	Y	Y	Y
11 Towns	Y	Y	Y	Y	Y	Y	Y	Y
12 Owens	?	?	?	?	?	?	?	?
13 Solarz	Y	Y	Y	Y	Y	Y	Y	Y
14 ***Molinari***	Y	Y	Y	N	Y	N	Y	Y
15 ***Green***	Y	Y	Y	N	Y	Y	Y	Y
16 Rangel	Y	Y	Y	Y	Y	Y	Y	Y
17 Weiss	Y	Y	Y	Y	Y	Y	Y	Y
18 Serrano	Y	Y	Y	Y	Y	Y	Y	Y
19 Engel	Y	Y	Y	Y	Y	Y	Y	Y
20 Lowey	Y	Y	Y	Y	Y	Y	Y	Y
21 ***Fish***	Y	Y	Y	Y	Y	Y	Y	Y
22 ***Gilman***	Y	Y	Y	Y	Y	Y	Y	Y
23 McNulty	Y	Y	Y	Y	Y	Y	Y	Y
24 ***Solomon***	N	Y	Y	N	N	Y	Y	Y
25 ***Boehlert***	Y	Y	Y	Y	Y	Y	Y	Y
26 ***Martin***	Y	Y	Y	Y	Y	Y	Y	Y
27 ***Walsh***	Y	Y	Y	Y	Y	Y	Y	Y
28 McHugh	Y	Y	Y	Y	Y	Y	Y	Y
29 ***Horton***	Y	Y	Y	Y	Y	Y	Y	Y
30 Slaughter	Y	Y	Y	Y	Y	Y	Y	Y
31 ***Paxon***	Y	Y	Y	Y	Y	Y	Y	Y
32 LaFalce	Y	Y	Y	Y	Y	Y	Y	Y
33 Nowak	Y	Y	Y	Y	Y	Y	Y	Y
34 ***Houghton***	Y	Y	Y	Y	Y	Y	Y	Y
NORTH CAROLINA								
1 Jones	Y	Y	Y	Y	Y	Y	Y	Y
2 Valentine	Y	Y	Y	Y	Y	Y	Y	Y
3 Lancaster	Y	Y	Y	Y	Y	Y	Y	Y
4 Price	Y	Y	Y	Y	Y	Y	Y	Y
5 Neal	Y	Y	Y	Y	Y	Y	Y	Y
6 ***Coble***	Y	Y	Y	Y	Y	Y	Y	Y
7 Rose	Y	Y	Y	Y	Y	Y	Y	Y
8 Hefner	Y	Y	Y	Y	Y	Y	Y	Y
9 ***McMillan***	Y	Y	Y	N	N	Y	Y	Y
10 ***Ballenger***	Y	Y	Y	N	N	Y	Y	Y
11 Clarke	Y	Y	Y	Y	Y	Y	Y	Y
NORTH DAKOTA								
AL Dorgan	Y	Y	Y	Y	Y	Y	Y	Y
OHIO								
1 Luken	Y	Y	Y	Y	Y	Y	Y	Y
2 ***Gradison***	Y	Y	Y	N	N	Y	Y	Y
3 Hall	Y	Y	Y	Y	Y	Y	Y	Y
4 ***Oxley***	Y	Y	Y	Y	Y	Y	Y	Y
5 ***Gillmor***	Y	Y	Y	Y	Y	N	Y	Y
6 ***McEwen***	Y	Y	Y	N	Y	N	Y	Y
7 ***DeWine***	Y	Y	Y	Y	Y	Y	Y	Y
8 ***Lukens***	Y	Y	Y	Y	Y	Y	Y	N
9 Kaptur	Y	Y	?	Y	Y	Y	Y	Y
10 ***Miller***	Y	Y	Y	N	Y	N	Y	Y
11 Eckart	Y	Y	Y	Y	Y	Y	Y	Y
12 ***Kasich***	Y	Y	?	Y	Y	Y	Y	Y
13 Pease	Y	Y	Y	Y	Y	Y	Y	Y
14 Sawyer	Y	Y	Y	Y	Y	Y	Y	Y
15 ***Wylie***	Y	Y	Y	Y	Y	Y	Y	Y
16 ***Regula***	Y	Y	Y	Y	Y	Y	Y	Y
17 Traficant	Y	Y	Y	Y	Y	Y	Y	Y
18 Applegate	Y	Y	Y	Y	Y	N	Y	Y
19 Feighan	Y	Y	Y	Y	Y	Y	Y	Y
20 Oakar	Y	Y	Y	Y	Y	Y	Y	Y
21 Stokes	Y	Y	Y	Y	Y	Y	Y	Y
OKLAHOMA								
1 ***Inhofe***	N	Y	Y	Y	Y	Y	Y	Y
2 Synar	Y	Y	Y	Y	Y	Y	Y	Y
3 Watkins	Y	Y	Y	Y	Y	Y	Y	Y
4 McCurdy	Y	Y	Y	Y	Y	Y	Y	Y
5 ***Edwards***	N	Y	Y	Y	Y	N	Y	Y
6 English	Y	Y	Y	Y	Y	Y	Y	Y
OREGON								
1 AuCoin	Y	Y	Y	Y	Y	Y	Y	Y
2 ***Smith, B.***	Y	Y	Y	Y	Y	Y	Y	Y
3 Wyden	Y	Y	Y	Y	Y	Y	Y	Y
4 DeFazio	Y	Y	Y	Y	Y	Y	Y	Y
5 ***Smith, D.***	?	?	?	?	?	?	?	?
PENNSYLVANIA								
1 Foglietta	Y	Y	Y	Y	Y	Y	Y	Y
2 Gray	Y	?	?	?	?	?	?	?
3 Borski	Y	Y	Y	Y	Y	Y	Y	Y
4 Kolter	Y	Y	Y	Y	Y	Y	Y	Y
5 ***Schulze***	Y	Y	Y	N	Y	N	Y	Y
6 Yatron	Y	Y	Y	Y	Y	Y	Y	Y
7 ***Weldon***	Y	Y	Y	Y	Y	Y	Y	Y
8 Kostmayer	Y	Y	Y	Y	Y	Y	Y	Y
9 ***Shuster***	N	Y	Y	N	Y	N	Y	N
10 ***McDade***	Y	Y	Y	Y	Y	Y	Y	Y
11 Kanjorski	Y	Y	Y	Y	Y	N	Y	Y
12 Murtha	Y	Y	Y	Y	Y	N	Y	Y
13 ***Coughlin***	Y	Y	Y	N	Y	Y	Y	Y
14 Coyne	Y	Y	Y	Y	Y	Y	Y	Y
15 ***Ritter***	Y	Y	Y	Y	Y	Y	Y	Y
16 ***Walker***	N	Y	Y	N	N	Y	Y	N
17 ***Gekas***	N	Y	Y	N	N	Y	Y	N
18 Walgren	Y	Y	Y	Y	Y	Y	Y	Y
19 ***Goodling***	Y	Y	Y	Y	Y	Y	Y	Y
20 Gaydos	Y	Y	Y	Y	Y	Y	Y	Y
21 ***Ridge***	Y	Y	Y	Y	Y	Y	Y	Y
22 Murphy	Y	Y	Y	Y	Y	N	Y	Y
23 ***Clinger***	Y	Y	Y	N	Y	Y	Y	Y
RHODE ISLAND								
1 ***Machtley***	Y	Y	Y	Y	Y	Y	Y	Y
2 ***Schneider***	Y	Y	Y	Y	Y	Y	Y	Y
SOUTH CAROLINA								
1 ***Ravenel***	Y	Y	Y	Y	Y	Y	Y	Y
2 ***Spence***	Y	Y	Y	N	Y	Y	Y	Y
3 Derrick	Y	Y	Y	Y	Y	Y	Y	Y
4 Patterson	Y	N	Y	Y	Y	Y	Y	Y
5 Spratt	Y	N	Y	Y	Y	Y	Y	Y
6 Tallon	Y	Y	Y	Y	Y	Y	Y	Y
SOUTH DAKOTA								
AL Johnson	Y	Y	Y	Y	Y	Y	Y	Y
TENNESSEE								
1 ***Quillen***	Y	Y	Y	Y	Y	Y	Y	Y
2 ***Duncan***	N	Y	Y	N	Y	N	Y	N
3 Lloyd	Y	Y	Y	Y	Y	Y	Y	Y
4 Cooper	Y	Y	Y	Y	Y	Y	Y	Y
5 Clement	Y	Y	Y	Y	Y	Y	Y	Y
6 Gordon	Y	Y	Y	Y	Y	Y	Y	Y
7 ***Sundquist***	Y	Y	Y	N	N	Y	Y	Y
8 Tanner	Y	Y	Y	Y	Y	Y	Y	Y
9 Ford	Y	Y	Y	Y	Y	Y	Y	Y
TEXAS								
1 Chapman	Y	Y	Y	N	Y	Y	Y	Y
2 Wilson	Y	Y	Y	Y	Y	Y	Y	Y
3 ***Bartlett***	N	Y	Y	N	N	Y	Y	N
4 Hall	Y	Y	Y	Y	Y	N	Y	N
5 Bryant	Y	Y	Y	Y	Y	Y	Y	Y
6 ***Barton***	N	Y	Y	N	N	Y	Y	Y
7 ***Archer***	Y	Y	Y	N	N	N	Y	N
8 ***Fields***	N	Y	Y	N	N	Y	Y	N
9 Brooks	Y	Y	Y	Y	Y	Y	Y	Y
10 Pickle	Y	Y	Y	Y	Y	Y	Y	Y
11 Leath	Y	Y	Y	Y	Y	Y	Y	Y
12 Geren	Y	Y	Y	Y	Y	Y	Y	Y
13 Sarpalius	Y	Y	Y	Y	Y	Y	Y	Y
14 Laughlin	Y	Y	Y	Y	Y	Y	Y	Y
15 de la Garza	Y	Y	Y	Y	Y	Y	Y	Y
16 Coleman	Y	Y	Y	Y	Y	Y	Y	Y
17 Stenholm	Y	Y	Y	Y	Y	Y	Y	Y
18 Washington	Y	Y	Y	Y	Y	Y	Y	Y
19 ***Combest***	N	Y	Y	N	N	Y	Y	Y
20 Gonzalez	Y	Y	Y	Y	Y	Y	Y	Y
21 ***Smith***	N	Y	Y	N	N	Y	Y	N
22 ***DeLay***	N	Y	N	N	N	N	Y	N
23 Bustamante	Y	Y	Y	Y	Y	Y	Y	Y
24 Frost	Y	Y	Y	Y	Y	Y	Y	Y
25 Andrews	Y	Y	Y	Y	Y	Y	Y	Y
26 ***Armey***	N	Y	N	N	N	Y	Y	N
27 Ortiz	Y	Y	Y	Y	Y	Y	Y	Y
UTAH								
1 ***Hansen***	N	Y	Y	N	N	Y	Y	N
2 Owens	Y	Y	Y	Y	Y	Y	Y	Y
3 ***Nielson***	N	Y	Y	N	N	Y	Y	N
VERMONT								
AL ***Smith***	Y	Y	Y	Y	Y	Y	Y	Y
VIRGINIA								
1 ***Bateman***	Y	Y	Y	N	Y	Y	Y	Y
2 Pickett	Y	Y	Y	N	Y	Y	Y	Y
3 ***Bliley***	Y	Y	Y	N	Y	Y	Y	Y
4 Sisisky	Y	Y	Y	N	Y	Y	Y	N
5 Payne	Y	Y	Y	N	Y	Y	Y	Y
6 Olin	Y	Y	Y	Y	Y	Y	Y	Y
7 ***Slaughter***	Y	Y	Y	N	?	Y	Y	Y
8 ***Parris***	Y	Y	Y	N	Y	Y	Y	Y
9 Boucher	Y	Y	Y	Y	Y	Y	Y	Y
10 ***Wolf***	Y	Y	Y	N	Y	Y	Y	Y
WASHINGTON								
1 ***Miller***	Y	Y	Y	Y	Y	Y	Y	Y
2 Swift	Y	Y	Y	Y	Y	Y	Y	Y
3 Unsoeld	Y	Y	Y	Y	Y	Y	Y	Y
4 ***Morrison***	+	+	+	−	+	+	+	+
5 Foley								
6 Dicks	Y	Y	Y	Y	Y	Y	Y	Y
7 McDermott	Y	Y	Y	Y	Y	Y	Y	Y
8 ***Chandler***	Y	Y	Y	Y	Y	Y	Y	Y
WEST VIRGINIA								
1 Mollohan	?	?	?	?	?	?	?	?
2 Staggers	Y	Y	Y	Y	Y	Y	Y	Y
3 Wise	Y	Y	Y	Y	Y	Y	Y	Y
4 Rahall	Y	Y	Y	Y	Y	Y	Y	Y
WISCONSIN								
1 Aspin	Y	Y	Y	Y	Y	Y	Y	Y
2 Kastenmeier	Y	Y	Y	Y	Y	Y	Y	Y
3 ***Gunderson***	Y	Y	Y	N	Y	Y	Y	Y
4 Kleczka	Y	Y	Y	Y	Y	Y	Y	Y
5 Moody	Y	Y	Y	Y	Y	Y	Y	Y
6 ***Petri***	N	Y	Y	N	Y	N	N	N
7 Obey	Y	Y	Y	Y	Y	Y	Y	Y
8 ***Roth***	Y	Y	Y	Y	Y	Y	Y	Y
9 ***Sensenbrenner***	N	Y	Y	N	Y	N	N	N
WYOMING								
AL ***Thomas***	Y	Y	Y	Y	N	Y	Y	Y

Southern states - Ala., Ark., Fla., Ga., Ky., La., Miss., N.C., Okla., S.C., Tenn., Texas, Va.
Omitted votes are quorum calls, which CQ does not include in its vote charts.

HOUSE VOTES 369, 370, 371, 372, 373, 374, 375, 376

369. HR 3533. Earthquake Hazards Reduction Act Amendments/Passage. Roe, D-N.J., motion to suspend the rules and pass the bill to authorize $544.8 million for fiscal 1991-94 for the National Earthquake Reduction Program. Motion agreed to 283-132: R 57-114; D 226-18 (ND 161-4, SD 65-14), Sept. 24, 1990. A two-thirds majority of those present and voting (277 in this case) is required for passage under suspension of the rules. A "nay" was a vote supporting the president's position.

370. HR 1243. Metal Casting Competitiveness Research/Adoption. Roe, D-N.J., motion to suspend the rules and adopt the resolution (H Res 470) to agree to the Senate amendment, with amendments to the bill to authorize $15 million in fiscal years 1991-93 for grants by the Energy Department to designate three institutes for metal casting competitiveness research. Motion agreed to 331-84: R 92-79; D 239-5 (ND 161-4, SD 78-1), Sept. 24, 1990. A two-thirds majority of those present and voting (277 in this case) is required for passage under suspension of the rules.

371. HR 486. Defense Production Act Amendments/Passage. Oakar, D-Ohio, motion to suspend the rules and pass the bill to extend through fiscal 1992 the authority under the Defense Production Act of 1950 to require companies to fill federal government defense contract orders first and to extend the other authorities under the act through fiscal 1995, authorizing $130 million in each fiscal year. Motion agreed to 295-119: R 58-113; D 237-6 (ND 163-1, SD 74-5), Sept. 24, 1990. A two-thirds majority of those present and voting (276 in this case) is required for passage under suspension of the rules.

372. Procedural Motion. Gunderson, R-Wis., motion to approve the House Journal of Monday, Sept. 24. Motion agreed to 266-125: R 48-118; D 218-7 (ND 146-7, SD 72-0), Sept. 25, 1990.

373. HR 5269. Crime Bill/Previous Question. Slaughter, D-N.Y., motion to order the previous question (thus ending debate and the possibility of amendment) on the rule (H Res 473) to provide for House floor consideration of the bill to expand the number of federal crimes subject to the death penalty, restrict federal habeas corpus appeals by state prisoners sentenced to death, increase funds for law enforcement at the state and local levels, and enact into law certain judicially created exceptions to the exclusionary rule. Motion agreed to 214-209: R 1-173; D 213-36 (ND 161-9, SD 52-27), Sept. 25, 1990.

374. HR 5269. Crime Bill/Procedural Motion. Gray, D-Pa., motion to table (kill) the Walker, R-Pa., motion to reconsider the vote on ordering the previous question on the rule (H Res 473), which was previously agreed to. Motion agreed to 244-180: R 0-175; D 244-5 (ND 168-2, SD 76-3), Sept. 25, 1990.

375. HR 5269. Crime Bill/Domestic Firearms. Slaughter, D-N.Y., amendment to the rule (H Res 473) to remove the Unsoeld, D-Wash., amendment banning domestic assembly of non-importable firearms. Adopted 222-202: R 29-146; D 193-56 (ND 139-30, SD 54-26), Sept. 25, 1990.

376. HR 5269. Crime Bill/Rule. Adoption of the rule (H Res 473) to provide for House floor consideration of the bill to expand the number of federal crimes subject to the death penalty, restrict federal habeas corpus appeals by state prisoners sentenced to death, increase funds for law enforcement at the state and local levels, and enact into law certain judicially created exceptions to the exclusionary rule. Rejected 166-258: R 0-174; D 166-84 (ND 129-41, SD 37-43), Sept. 25, 1990.

KEY

Y Voted for (yea).
Paired for.
+ Announced for.
N Voted against (nay).
X Paired against.
- Announced against.
P Voted "present."
C Voted "present" to avoid possible conflict of interest.
? Did not vote or otherwise make a position known.

Democrats ***Republicans***

	369	370	371	372	373	374	375	376
ALABAMA								
1 ***Callahan***	N	Y	N	N	N	N	N	N
2 ***Dickinson***	Y	Y	N	N	N	N	N	N
3 Browder	Y	Y	Y	Y	N	Y	Y	N
4 Bevill	Y	Y	Y	Y	Y	Y	Y	N
5 Flippo	?	?	?	?	?	?	?	?
6 Erdreich	Y	Y	Y	Y	N	N	N	N
7 Harris	Y	Y	Y	Y	N	Y	N	N
ALASKA								
AL ***Young***	Y	Y	Y	?	N	N	N	N
ARIZONA								
1 ***Rhodes***	N	N	N	N	N	N	N	N
2 Udall	Y	Y	Y	?	?	Y	Y	Y
3 ***Stump***	N	N	N	N	N	N	N	N
4 ***Kyl***	N	N	N	N	N	N	N	N
5 ***Kolbe***	N	N	N	N	N	N	N	N
ARKANSAS								
1 Alexander	Y	Y	Y	Y	Y	Y	Y	Y
2 ***Robinson***	Y	Y	Y	Y	N	N	N	N
3 ***Hammerschmidt***	Y	Y	N	Y	N	N	N	N
4 Anthony	Y	Y	Y	?	Y	Y	Y	Y
CALIFORNIA								
1 Bosco	Y	Y	Y	Y	Y	Y	Y	N
2 ***Herger***	N	N	N	N	N	N	N	N
3 Matsui	Y	Y	Y	Y	Y	Y	Y	Y
4 Fazio	Y	Y	Y	Y	Y	Y	Y	Y
5 Pelosi	Y	Y	Y	?	Y	Y	Y	Y
6 Boxer	Y	Y	Y	Y	Y	Y	Y	Y
7 Miller	Y	Y	Y	?	Y	Y	N	Y
8 Dellums	Y	Y	Y	Y	Y	Y	Y	Y
9 Stark	Y	Y	Y	Y	Y	Y	Y	Y
10 Edwards	Y	Y	Y	Y	Y	Y	Y	Y
11 Lantos	Y	Y	Y	Y	Y	Y	Y	N
12 ***Campbell***	Y	N	N	N	N	N	Y	N
13 Mineta	Y	Y	Y	Y	Y	Y	Y	Y
14 ***Shumway***	N	N	N	Y	N	N	N	N
15 Condit	Y	Y	Y	Y	N	Y	N	N
16 Panetta	Y	Y	Y	Y	Y	Y	Y	Y
17 ***Pashayan***	Y	Y	N	N	N	N	N	N
18 Lehman	Y	Y	Y	Y	Y	Y	Y	N
19 ***Lagomarsino***	Y	N	N	N	N	N	N	N
20 ***Thomas***	N	N	N	N	N	N	N	N
21 ***Gallegly***	Y	N	N	N	N	N	N	N
22 ***Moorhead***	Y	N	N	Y	N	N	N	N
23 Beilenson	Y	Y	Y	Y	Y	Y	Y	Y
24 Waxman	Y	Y	Y	?	Y	Y	Y	Y
25 Roybal	Y	Y	Y	Y	Y	Y	Y	Y
26 Berman	Y	Y	Y	Y	Y	Y	Y	Y
27 Levine	Y	Y	Y	Y	Y	Y	Y	Y
28 Dixon	Y	Y	Y	?	Y	Y	Y	Y
29 Hawkins	Y	Y	Y	?	Y	Y	Y	?
30 Martinez	Y	Y	Y	Y	Y	Y	Y	Y
31 Dymally	Y	Y	Y	Y	Y	Y	?	Y
32 Anderson	Y	Y	Y	Y	Y	Y	Y	Y
33 ***Dreier***	Y	N	N	N	N	N	N	N
34 Torres	Y	Y	Y	Y	Y	Y	Y	Y
35 ***Lewis***	Y	Y	Y	N	N	N	N	N
36 Brown	Y	Y	Y	Y	Y	Y	Y	Y
37 ***McCandless***	Y	N	N	N	N	N	N	N
38 ***Dornan***	Y	N	N	N	?	N	N	N
39 ***Dannemeyer***	N	N	N	N	N	N	N	N
40 ***Cox***	Y	N	N	?	N	N	N	N
41 ***Lowery***	Y	Y	N	N	N	N	N	N
42 ***Rohrabacher***	Y	N	N	N	N	N	N	N
43 ***Packard***	Y	N	N	Y	N	N	N	N
44 Bates	Y	Y	Y	?	Y	Y	Y	N
45 ***Hunter***	N	Y	Y	N	N	N	N	N
COLORADO								
1 Schroeder	Y	Y	Y	N	Y	Y	Y	Y
2 Skaggs	Y	Y	Y	Y	Y	Y	Y	Y
3 Campbell	Y	Y	Y	Y	Y	Y	Y	N
4 ***Brown***	N	N	N	N	N	N	N	N
5 ***Hefley***	N	N	N	N	N	N	N	N
6 ***Schaefer***	N	N	Y	N	N	N	N	N
CONNECTICUT								
1 Kennelly	Y	Y	Y	Y	Y	Y	Y	Y
2 Gejdenson	Y	Y	Y	Y	Y	Y	Y	Y
3 Morrison	+	+	+	?	Y	Y	Y	Y
4 ***Shays***	N	N	N	N	N	N	Y	N
5 ***Rowland***	?	?	?	?	?	?	?	?
6 ***Johnson***	N	Y	Y	?	N	N	Y	N
DELAWARE								
AL Carper	Y	N	Y	Y	Y	Y	Y	Y
FLORIDA								
1 Hutto	N	Y	Y	Y	N	Y	N	N
2 ***Grant***	N	Y	N	Y	N	N	N	N
3 Bennett	Y	Y	Y	Y	N	N	Y	N
4 ***James***	Y	Y	Y	N	N	N	N	N
5 ***McCollum***	N	N	N	N	N	N	N	N
6 ***Stearns***	Y	N	N	N	N	N	N	N
7 Gibbons	N	N	N	Y	Y	Y	Y	Y
8 ***Young***	N	N	N	N	N	N	N	N
9 ***Bilirakis***	N	N	N	N	N	N	N	N
10 ***Ireland***	N	N	N	?	N	N	N	N
11 Nelson	Y	Y	Y	Y	Y	Y	Y	Y
12 ***Lewis***	N	N	N	N	N	N	N	N
13 ***Goss***	N	N	N	N	N	N	N	N
14 Johnston	?	?	?	?	Y	Y	Y	Y
15 ***Shaw***	N	Y	N	Y	N	N	N	N
16 Smith	Y	Y	Y	Y	Y	Y	Y	Y
17 Lehman	Y	Y	Y	Y	Y	Y	Y	Y
18 ***Ros-Lehtinen***	Y	Y	N	N	N	N	Y	N
19 Fascell	Y	Y	Y	Y	Y	Y	Y	Y
GEORGIA								
1 Thomas	Y	Y	Y	Y	N	Y	Y	N
2 Hatcher	Y	Y	Y	Y	Y	Y	Y	N
3 Ray	N	Y	N	Y	N	Y	N	N
4 Jones	Y	Y	Y	Y	N	Y	Y	N
5 Lewis	Y	Y	Y	Y	Y	Y	Y	Y
6 ***Gingrich***	N	N	N	?	N	N	N	N
7 Darden	Y	Y	Y	Y	N	Y	Y	N
8 Rowland	Y	Y	Y	Y	N	Y	Y	N
9 Jenkins	N	Y	Y	Y	N	Y	N	N
10 Barnard	?	?	?	Y	N	Y	N	N
HAWAII								
1 ***Saiki***	Y	N	Y	Y	N	N	Y	N
2 Vacancy								
IDAHO								
1 ***Craig***	N	N	N	N	N	N	N	N
2 Stallings	Y	Y	Y	Y	Y	Y	Y	N
ILLINOIS								
1 Hayes	Y	Y	Y	Y	Y	Y	Y	Y
2 Savage	Y	Y	Y	Y	Y	Y	Y	Y
3 Russo	Y	Y	Y	Y	Y	Y	Y	Y
4 Sangmeister	Y	Y	Y	Y	Y	Y	Y	N
5 Lipinski	Y	Y	Y	Y	Y	Y	Y	Y
6 ***Hyde***	N	Y	N	Y	N	N	N	N
7 Collins	Y	Y	Y	Y	Y	Y	Y	Y
8 Rostenkowski	Y	Y	Y	Y	Y	Y	N	Y
9 Yates	N	Y	Y	Y	Y	Y	Y	Y
10 ***Porter***	N	Y	N	N	N	N	Y	N
11 Annunzio	Y	Y	Y	Y	Y	Y	Y	N
12 ***Crane***	N	N	N	?	N	N	N	N
13 ***Fawell***	Y	Y	N	Y	N	N	N	N
14 ***Hastert***	N	Y	N	N	N	N	N	N
15 ***Madigan***	Y	Y	Y	N	N	N	N	N
16 ***Martin***	?	?	?	N	N	N	N	N
17 Evans	Y	Y	Y	Y	Y	Y	Y	Y
18 ***Michel***	N	Y	N	N	N	N	N	N
19 Bruce	Y	Y	Y	Y	Y	Y	Y	N
20 Durbin	Y	Y	Y	Y	Y	Y	Y	N
21 Costello	Y	Y	Y	Y	Y	Y	Y	N
22 Poshard	Y	Y	Y	Y	Y	Y	Y	N
INDIANA								
1 Visclosky	Y	Y	Y	Y	Y	Y	Y	Y
2 Sharp	Y	Y	Y	Y	Y	Y	N	N
3 ***Hiler***	N	Y	N	N	N	N	N	N

ND Northern Democrats SD Southern Democrats

	369	370	371	372	373	374	375	376
4 Long	Y	Y	Y	Y	Y	Y	Y	Y
5 Jontz	Y	Y	Y	Y	Y	Y	Y	Y
6 ***Burton***	N	N	N	N	N	N	N	N
7 ***Myers***	Y	Y	Y	Y	N	N	N	N
8 McCloskey	Y	Y	Y	Y	Y	Y	Y	Y
9 Hamilton	Y	Y	Y	Y	Y	Y	Y	N
10 Jacobs	Y	Y	Y	N	N	Y	Y	N
IOWA								
1 ***Leach***	Y	Y	N	N	N	N	N	N
2 ***Tauke***	N	N	N	N	N	N	N	N
3 Nagle	Y	Y	Y	Y	Y	Y	Y	Y
4 Smith	Y	Y	Y	Y	Y	Y	N	N
5 ***Lightfoot***	N	Y	N	N	N	N	N	N
6 ***Grandy***	N	N	N	N	N	N	N	N
KANSAS								
1 ***Roberts***	N	N	N	N	N	N	N	N
2 Slattery	N	Y	Y	Y	Y	Y	N	Y
3 ***Meyers***	N	Y	Y	N	N	N	Y	N
4 Glickman	Y	Y	Y	Y	Y	Y	N	Y
5 ***Whittaker***	N	N	Y	N	N	N	N	N
KENTUCKY								
1 Hubbard	Y	Y	Y	Y	N	Y	Y	Y
2 Natcher	Y	Y	Y	Y	Y	Y	N	N
3 Mazzoli	Y	Y	Y	Y	Y	Y	Y	Y
4 ***Bunning***	N	N	N	N	N	N	N	N
5 ***Rogers***	N	N	N	N	N	N	N	N
6 ***Hopkins***	Y	N	N	N	N	N	N	N
7 Perkins	Y	Y	Y	Y	Y	Y	N	Y
LOUISIANA								
1 ***Livingston***	N	N	N	N	N	N	N	N
2 Boggs	Y	Y	Y	Y	Y	?	Y	Y
3 Tauzin	Y	Y	Y	Y	Y	Y	N	N
4 ***McCrery***	?	?	?	?	N	N	N	N
5 Huckaby	Y	Y	Y	Y	N	Y	N	N
6 ***Baker***	N	Y	N	N	N	N	N	N
7 Hayes	Y	Y	Y	Y	Y	Y	N	N
8 ***Holloway***	N	Y	N	N	N	N	N	N
MAINE								
1 Brennan	Y	Y	Y	Y	Y	Y	Y	Y
2 ***Snowe***	N	N	Y	N	N	N	N	N
MARYLAND								
1 Dyson	Y	Y	Y	?	Y	Y	N	N
2 ***Bentley***	N	Y	Y	N	N	N	N	N
3 Cardin	Y	Y	Y	Y	Y	Y	Y	Y
4 McMillen	Y	Y	Y	Y	Y	Y	N	Y
5 Hoyer	Y	Y	Y	Y	Y	Y	Y	Y
6 Byron	?	?	?	N	Y	Y	N	N
7 Mfume	Y	Y	Y	?	Y	Y	Y	Y
8 ***Morella***	Y	Y	Y	?	N	N	Y	N
MASSACHUSETTS								
1 ***Conte***	N	Y	Y	Y	N	N	Y	N
2 Neal	Y	Y	Y	Y	Y	Y	Y	Y
3 Early	Y	Y	Y	Y	N	Y	Y	N
4 Frank	Y	Y	Y	?	Y	Y	Y	Y
5 Atkins	Y	Y	Y	Y	Y	Y	Y	Y
6 Mavroules	Y	Y	Y	Y	Y	Y	Y	Y
7 Markey	Y	Y	Y	Y	Y	Y	Y	Y
8 Kennedy	Y	Y	Y	?	Y	Y	Y	Y
9 Moakley	Y	Y	Y	Y	Y	Y	Y	Y
10 Studds	Y	Y	Y	Y	Y	Y	Y	Y
11 Donnelly	Y	Y	Y	Y	Y	?	?	?
MICHIGAN								
1 Conyers	Y	Y	Y	Y	Y	Y	Y	Y
2 ***Pursell***	N	N	N	N	N	N	Y	N
3 Wolpe	?	?	?	Y	Y	Y	Y	Y
4 ***Upton***	N	Y	N	N	N	N	Y	N
5 ***Henry***	N	Y	Y	N	N	N	Y	N
6 Carr	N	Y	Y	Y	Y	Y	N	N
7 Kildee	Y	Y	Y	Y	Y	Y	Y	Y
8 Traxler	Y	Y	Y	Y	Y	Y	N	N
9 ***Vander Jagt***	N	N	N	Y	N	N	N	N
10 ***Schuette***	N	Y	Y	N	N	N	N	N
11 ***Davis***	Y	Y	Y	N	N	N	N	N
12 Bonior	Y	Y	Y	Y	Y	Y	Y	Y
13 Crockett	?	?	?	?	Y	Y	Y	Y
14 Hertel	Y	Y	Y	Y	Y	Y	Y	Y
15 Ford	Y	Y	Y	?	Y	Y	Y	Y
16 Dingell	Y	Y	Y	?	Y	Y	Y	Y
17 Levin	Y	Y	Y	Y	Y	Y	Y	Y
18 ***Broomfield***	N	Y	N	Y	N	N	Y	N
MINNESOTA								
1 Penny	N	N	N	Y	Y	Y	Y	N
2 ***Weber***	N	Y	N	N	N	N	N	N
3 ***Frenzel***	N	N	N	N	N	N	N	N
4 Vento	Y	Y	Y	Y	Y	Y	Y	Y
5 Sabo	Y	Y	Y	Y	Y	Y	Y	Y
6 Sikorski	Y	Y	Y	N	Y	Y	Y	Y
7 ***Stangeland***	Y	Y	N	N	N	N	N	N
8 Oberstar	Y	Y	Y	Y	Y	Y	Y	Y
MISSISSIPPI								
1 Whitten	N	Y	Y	Y	Y	Y	N	N
2 Espy	?	?	?	?	Y	Y	Y	Y
3 Montgomery	Y	Y	Y	Y	N	Y	N	N
4 Parker	Y	Y	Y	Y	N	Y	N	N
5 Taylor	N	Y	Y	Y	N	Y	N	N
MISSOURI								
1 Clay	Y	Y	Y	N	Y	Y	Y	Y
2 ***Buechner***	Y	Y	Y	N	N	N	N	N
3 Gephardt	Y	Y	Y	Y	Y	Y	Y	Y
4 Skelton	Y	Y	Y	Y	Y	Y	N	N
5 Wheat	Y	Y	Y	Y	Y	Y	Y	Y
6 ***Coleman***	Y	Y	Y	N	N	N	Y	N
7 ***Hancock***	Y	N	N	N	N	N	N	N
8 ***Emerson***	Y	Y	Y	Y	N	N	N	N
9 Volkmer	Y	Y	Y	Y	Y	Y	N	N
MONTANA								
1 Williams	Y	Y	?	Y	Y	Y	N	Y
2 ***Marlenee***	N	N	N	N	N	N	N	N
NEBRASKA								
1 ***Bereuter***	N	Y	N	N	N	N	N	N
2 Hoagland	Y	Y	Y	Y	Y	Y	Y	Y
3 ***Smith***	N	N	Y	Y	N	N	N	N
NEVADA								
1 Bilbray	Y	Y	Y	Y	Y	Y	Y	N
2 ***Vucanovich***	N	Y	Y	N	N	N	N	N
NEW HAMPSHIRE								
1 ***Smith***	N	N	N	N	N	N	N	N
2 ***Douglas***	N	N	N	N	N	N	N	N
NEW JERSEY								
1 Vacancy								
2 Hughes	Y	Y	Y	Y	Y	Y	Y	Y
3 Pallone	Y	Y	Y	Y	Y	Y	Y	N
4 ***Smith***	N	Y	Y	Y	N	N	N	N
5 ***Roukema***	N	Y	Y	N	N	N	Y	N
6 Dwyer	Y	Y	Y	Y	Y	Y	Y	Y
7 ***Rinaldo***	N	Y	Y	Y	N	N	N	N
8 Roe	Y	Y	Y	Y	Y	Y	Y	Y
9 Torricelli	Y	Y	Y	Y	Y	Y	Y	Y
10 Payne	?	?	?	Y	Y	Y	Y	Y
11 ***Gallo***	N	Y	N	N	N	N	N	N
12 ***Courter***	Y	Y	N	N	N	N	N	N
13 ***Saxton***	N	Y	N	N	N	N	Y	N
14 Guarini	Y	Y	Y	?	?	?	?	?
NEW MEXICO								
1 ***Schiff***	N	Y	Y	Y	N	N	N	N
2 ***Skeen***	N	Y	Y	Y	N	N	N	N
3 Richardson	Y	Y	Y	Y	Y	Y	N	N
NEW YORK								
1 Hochbrueckner	Y	Y	Y	Y	Y	Y	Y	Y
2 Downey	Y	Y	Y	Y	Y	Y	Y	Y
3 Mrazek	Y	Y	Y	Y	Y	Y	Y	Y
4 ***Lent***	N	Y	Y	Y	N	N	Y	N
5 ***McGrath***	N	Y	N	N	N	N	Y	N
6 Flake	Y	Y	Y	Y	Y	Y	Y	Y
7 Ackerman	Y	Y	Y	Y	Y	Y	Y	Y
8 Scheuer	Y	Y	Y	N	Y	Y	Y	Y
9 Manton	Y	Y	Y	Y	Y	Y	Y	N
10 Schumer	Y	Y	Y	Y	Y	Y	Y	Y
11 Towns	Y	Y	Y	Y	Y	Y	Y	Y
12 Owens	?	?	?	?	Y	Y	Y	Y
13 Solarz	Y	Y	Y	Y	Y	Y	?	Y
14 ***Molinari***	Y	N	N	N	N	N	Y	N
15 ***Green***	N	N	N	Y	N	N	Y	N
16 Rangel	Y	Y	Y	Y	Y	Y	Y	Y
17 Weiss	Y	Y	Y	Y	Y	Y	Y	Y
18 Serrano	Y	Y	Y	Y	Y	Y	Y	Y
19 Engel	Y	Y	Y	Y	Y	Y	Y	Y
20 Lowey	Y	Y	Y	Y	Y	Y	Y	Y
21 ***Fish***	Y	N	N	Y	N	N	N	N
22 ***Gilman***	Y	Y	Y	Y	N	N	N	N
23 McNulty	Y	Y	Y	Y	Y	Y	Y	Y
24 ***Solomon***	N	N	N	N	N	N	N	N
25 ***Boehlert***	Y	Y	Y	N	N	N	Y	N
26 ***Martin***	Y	Y	N	N	N	N	N	N
27 ***Walsh***	Y	Y	Y	N	N	N	Y	N
28 McHugh	Y	Y	Y	Y	Y	Y	Y	Y
29 ***Horton***	Y	Y	Y	Y	N	N	N	N
30 Slaughter	Y	Y	Y	Y	Y	Y	Y	Y
31 ***Paxon***	Y	N	N	N	N	N	N	N
32 LaFalce	Y	Y	Y	Y	Y	Y	Y	Y
33 Nowak	Y	Y	Y	Y	Y	Y	Y	Y
34 ***Houghton***	Y	Y	Y	Y	N	N	N	N
NORTH CAROLINA								
1 Jones	Y	Y	Y	Y	Y	Y	Y	Y
2 Valentine	Y	Y	Y	?	N	Y	Y	N
3 Lancaster	Y	Y	Y	Y	N	Y	N	N
4 Price	Y	Y	Y	Y	Y	Y	Y	Y
5 Neal	N	Y	Y	?	Y	Y	Y	N
6 ***Coble***	Y	Y	Y	N	N	N	N	N
7 Rose	Y	Y	Y	Y	Y	Y	Y	Y
8 Hefner	Y	Y	Y	Y	Y	Y	Y	N
9 ***McMillan***	Y	Y	Y	N	N	N	N	N
10 ***Ballenger***	Y	Y	Y	N	N	N	N	N
11 Clarke	N	Y	Y	Y	Y	Y	N	Y
NORTH DAKOTA								
AL Dorgan	Y	N	Y	Y	Y	Y	N	Y
OHIO								
1 Luken	Y	Y	Y	Y	Y	Y	Y	Y
2 ***Gradison***	N	N	N	Y	N	N	N	N
3 Hall	Y	Y	Y	?	Y	Y	Y	Y
4 ***Oxley***	N	N	Y	N	N	N	N	N
5 ***Gillmor***	N	Y	Y	Y	N	N	N	N
6 ***McEwen***	N	Y	Y	Y	N	N	N	N
7 ***DeWine***	N	Y	N	N	N	N	N	N
8 ***Lukens***	N	N	Y	N	N	N	N	N
9 Kaptur	Y	Y	Y	Y	Y	?	Y	N
10 ***Miller***	N	Y	Y	N	N	N	N	N
11 Eckart	Y	Y	Y	Y	Y	Y	N	Y
12 ***Kasich***	N	N	Y	Y	N	N	N	N
13 Pease	Y	Y	Y	Y	Y	Y	Y	Y
14 Sawyer	Y	Y	Y	Y	Y	Y	Y	Y
15 ***Wylie***	N	Y	Y	Y	N	N	N	N
16 ***Regula***	N	Y	Y	Y	N	N	N	N
17 Traficant	Y	Y	Y	Y	N	Y	Y	Y
18 Applegate	Y	Y	Y	Y	N	N	N	N
19 Feighan	Y	Y	Y	Y	Y	Y	Y	N
20 Oakar	Y	Y	Y	Y	Y	Y	Y	Y
21 Stokes	Y	Y	Y	Y	Y	Y	Y	Y
OKLAHOMA								
1 ***Inhofe***	N	Y	N	N	N	N	N	N
2 Synar	Y	Y	Y	Y	Y	Y	Y	Y
3 Watkins	Y	Y	N	Y	N	Y	Y	N
4 McCurdy	Y	Y	N	Y	N	Y	N	N
5 ***Edwards***	Y	Y	N	N	N	N	N	N
6 English	Y	Y	N	Y	N	Y	N	N
OREGON								
1 AuCoin	Y	Y	Y	Y	Y	Y	Y	Y
2 ***Smith, B.***	N	Y	N	N	N	N	N	N
3 Wyden	Y	Y	Y	Y	Y	Y	Y	Y
4 DeFazio	Y	Y	Y	Y	Y	Y	Y	Y
5 ***Smith, D.***	?	?	?	N	N	N	N	N
PENNSYLVANIA								
1 Foglietta	Y	Y	Y	Y	Y	Y	Y	Y
2 Gray	?	?	?	Y	Y	Y	Y	Y
3 Borski	Y	Y	Y	Y	Y	Y	Y	N
4 Kolter	Y	Y	Y	Y	Y	Y	N	N
5 ***Schulze***	N	Y	Y	Y	N	N	N	N
6 Yatron	Y	N	Y	Y	N	N	N	N
7 ***Weldon***	N	N	Y	N	N	N	N	N
8 Kostmayer	Y	Y	Y	Y	Y	Y	Y	Y
9 ***Shuster***	Y	Y	N	Y	N	N	N	N
10 ***McDade***	N	Y	Y	Y	N	N	N	N
11 Kanjorski	Y	Y	Y	Y	N	Y	N	N
12 Murtha	Y	Y	Y	Y	Y	Y	Y	N
13 ***Coughlin***	N	Y	N	N	N	N	Y	N
14 Coyne	Y	Y	Y	Y	Y	Y	Y	Y
15 ***Ritter***	N	Y	Y	Y	N	N	N	?
16 ***Walker***	N	N	N	N	Y	N	N	N
17 ***Gekas***	N	N	N	N	N	N	N	N
18 Walgren	Y	Y	Y	Y	Y	Y	Y	Y
19 ***Goodling***	Y	Y	N	?	N	N	N	N
20 Gaydos	Y	Y	Y	Y	Y	Y	N	N
21 ***Ridge***	N	Y	Y	N	N	N	N	N
22 Murphy	Y	Y	Y	N	N	Y	N	N
23 ***Clinger***	Y	Y	N	Y	N	N	N	N
RHODE ISLAND								
1 ***Machtley***	Y	Y	N	N	N	N	Y	N
2 ***Schneider***	Y	Y	Y	Y	N	N	Y	N
SOUTH CAROLINA								
1 ***Ravenel***	N	Y	Y	Y	N	N	N	N
2 ***Spence***	Y	Y	Y	N	N	N	N	N
3 Derrick	Y	Y	Y	Y	Y	Y	Y	Y
4 Patterson	Y	Y	Y	Y	N	Y	N	N
5 Spratt	Y	Y	Y	Y	Y	Y	Y	N
6 Tallon	Y	Y	Y	Y	N	Y	N	N
SOUTH DAKOTA								
AL Johnson	Y	Y	Y	Y	N	Y	N	N
TENNESSEE								
1 ***Quillen***	Y	Y	N	N	N	N	N	N
2 ***Duncan***	N	N	N	N	N	N	N	N
3 Lloyd	Y	Y	Y	Y	Y	Y	N	N
4 Cooper	Y	Y	Y	Y	Y	Y	Y	Y
5 Clement	Y	Y	Y	Y	Y	Y	Y	Y
6 Gordon	Y	Y	Y	Y	Y	Y	Y	Y
7 ***Sundquist***	Y	Y	N	N	N	N	N	N
8 Tanner	Y	Y	Y	Y	Y	Y	Y	N
9 Ford	Y	Y	Y	?	Y	Y	Y	Y
TEXAS								
1 Chapman	Y	Y	Y	Y	Y	Y	N	N
2 Wilson	N	Y	Y	?	Y	Y	Y	Y
3 ***Bartlett***	N	N	N	Y	N	N	N	N
4 Hall	Y	Y	Y	Y	N	N	Y	N
5 Bryant	Y	Y	Y	Y	Y	Y	Y	Y
6 ***Barton***	N	N	N	N	N	N	N	N
7 ***Archer***	N	N	N	Y	N	N	N	N
8 ***Fields***	N	N	N	N	N	N	N	N
9 Brooks	Y	Y	Y	Y	Y	Y	Y	Y
10 Pickle	Y	Y	Y	Y	Y	Y	Y	N
11 Leath	Y	Y	Y	?	?	?	?	?
12 Geren	Y	Y	Y	Y	Y	Y	N	Y
13 Sarpalius	Y	Y	Y	?	Y	Y	Y	N
14 Laughlin	Y	Y	Y	Y	N	Y	N	N
15 de la Garza	Y	Y	Y	Y	?	Y	Y	Y
16 Coleman	Y	Y	Y	Y	Y	Y	Y	Y
17 Stenholm	N	Y	Y	Y	Y	Y	N	Y
18 Washington	Y	Y	Y	?	?	?	?	?
19 ***Combest***	N	N	N	Y	N	N	N	N
20 Gonzalez	Y	Y	Y	Y	Y	Y	Y	Y
21 ***Smith***	N	N	N	N	N	N	N	N
22 ***DeLay***	N	N	N	N	N	N	N	N
23 Bustamante	Y	Y	Y	Y	Y	Y	Y	Y
24 Frost	Y	Y	Y	Y	Y	Y	Y	Y
25 Andrews	N	Y	Y	Y	Y	Y	Y	Y
26 ***Armey***	N	N	N	N	N	N	N	N
27 Ortiz	Y	Y	Y	Y	Y	Y	Y	Y
UTAH								
1 ***Hansen***	N	N	N	N	N	N	N	N
2 Owens	Y	Y	Y	Y	Y	Y	Y	N
3 ***Nielson***	N	N	N	Y	N	N	N	N
VERMONT								
AL ***Smith***	N	Y	Y	Y	N	N	Y	N
VIRGINIA								
1 ***Bateman***	N	Y	N	Y	N	N	Y	N
2 Pickett	N	Y	Y	Y	Y	Y	Y	N
3 ***Bliley***	N	N	N	N	N	N	N	N
4 Sisisky	N	Y	Y	Y	Y	Y	Y	N
5 Payne	Y	Y	Y	Y	Y	Y	Y	N
6 Olin	N	Y	Y	Y	N	Y	Y	N
7 ***Slaughter***	N	N	N	N	N	N	N	N
8 ***Parris***	N	Y	Y	N	N	N	N	N
9 Boucher	Y	Y	Y	Y	Y	Y	Y	Y
10 ***Wolf***	N	Y	Y	N	N	N	Y	N
WASHINGTON								
1 ***Miller***	Y	N	N	N	N	N	Y	N
2 Swift	Y	Y	Y	Y	Y	Y	Y	Y
3 Unsoeld	Y	Y	Y	Y	Y	Y	N	Y
4 ***Morrison***	+	+	−	Y	N	N	N	N
5 Foley								
6 Dicks	Y	Y	Y	Y	Y	Y	Y	Y
7 McDermott	Y	Y	Y	Y	Y	Y	Y	Y
8 ***Chandler***	Y	Y	N	N	N	N	N	N
WEST VIRGINIA								
1 Mollohan	?	?	?	?	?	Y	N	Y
2 Staggers	Y	Y	Y	Y	Y	Y	N	Y
3 Wise	Y	Y	Y	Y	Y	Y	Y	Y
4 Rahall	Y	Y	Y	Y	Y	Y	N	Y
WISCONSIN								
1 Aspin	Y	Y	Y	?	Y	Y	Y	Y
2 Kastenmeier	Y	Y	Y	Y	Y	Y	Y	Y
3 ***Gunderson***	N	N	N	Y	N	N	N	N
4 Kleczka	Y	Y	Y	Y	Y	Y	Y	Y
5 Moody	Y	Y	Y	Y	Y	Y	Y	Y
6 ***Petri***	N	Y	N	Y	N	N	N	N
7 Obey	Y	Y	Y	Y	Y	Y	N	Y
8 ***Roth***	N	Y	Y	Y	N	N	N	N
9 ***Sensenbrenner***	N	N	N	N	N	N	N	N
WYOMING								
AL ***Thomas***	N	N	N	N	N	N	N	N

Southern states - Ala., Ark., Fla., Ga., Ky., La., Miss., N.C., Okla., S.C., Tenn., Texas, Va.
Omitted votes are quorum calls, which CQ does not include in its vote charts.

HOUSE VOTES 378, 379, 380, 381, 382, 383, 384, 385

378. HR 4793. Small Business Reauthorization/Tree Planting. Ireland, R-Fla., amendment to strike the Natural Resource Development section of the bill relating to tree planting. Rejected 150-269: R 120-52; D 30-217 (ND 15-151, SD 15-66), Sept. 25, 1990.

379. HR 4793. Small Business Reauthorization/Debenture Prepayments. Ireland, R-Fla., amendment to strike Title II of bill relating to the Small Business Administration's prepayment of debentures at reduced premiums. Rejected 21-399: R 20-155; D 1-244 (ND 0-166, SD 1-78), Sept. 25, 1990.

380. HR 4793. Small Business Reauthorization/Passage. Passage of the bill to authorize the program levels for Small Business Administration loan programs for fiscal 1991 through 1994 and for other purposes. Passed 398-26: R 149-26; D 249-0 (ND 168-0, SD 81-0), Sept. 25, 1990. A "nay" was a vote supporting the president's position.

381. HR 4559. Red Rock Canyon Conservation Area/Second Ordered. Vucanovich, R-Nev., demand for a second on the Vento, D-Minn., motion to suspend the rules and pass the bill to establish the Red Rock Canyon National Conservation Area. Second ordered 407-1: R 171-1; D 236-0 (ND 158-0, SD 78-0), Sept. 25, 1990. (The bill later was passed on roll call vote 383.)

382. HR 4019. Michigan Wild and Scenic Rivers/Second Ordered. Lagomarsino, R-Calif., demand for a second on the Vento, D-Minn., motion to suspend the rules and pass the bill to designate segments of 15 rivers in Michigan as components of the National Wild and Scenic Rivers System. Second ordered 342-53: R 118-53; D 224-0 (ND 147-0, SD 77-0), Sept. 25, 1990.

383. HR 4559. Red Rock Canyon Conservation Area/Passage. Vento, D-Minn., motion to suspend the rules and pass the bill to establish the Red Rock Canyon National Conservation Area. Motion agreed to 382-38: R 139-36; D 243-2 (ND 164-1, SD 79-1), Sept. 25, 1990. A two-thirds majority of those present and voting (280 in this case) is required for passage under suspension of the rules.

384. Procedural Motion. Gunderson, R-Wis., motion to approve the House Journal of Tuesday, Sept. 25. Motion agreed to 275-126: R 41-122; D 234-4 (ND 157-4, SD 77-0), Sept. 26, 1990.

385. HR 5400. Campaign Finance Overhaul/Instruction of Conferees. Thomas, R-Calif., motion to instruct the House conferees on the campaign finance bill to accept Senate amendments requiring reports on franked mail, banning franked mail when the appropriation has been exhausted, and limiting contributions from political action committees. Motion rejected 194-225: R 169-1; D 25-224 (ND 12-154, SD 13-70), Sept. 26, 1990.

KEY

- Y Voted for (yea).
- # Paired for.
- + Announced for.
- N Voted against (nay).
- X Paired against.
- \- Announced against.
- P Voted "present."
- C Voted "present" to avoid possible conflict of interest.
- ? Did not vote or otherwise make a position known.

Democrats ***Republicans***

	378	379	380	381	382	383	384	385
ALABAMA								
1 ***Callahan***	Y	N	Y	Y	Y	Y	N	Y
2 ***Dickinson***	Y	N	Y	Y	Y	Y	N	Y
3 Browder	N	N	Y	Y	Y	Y	Y	N
4 Bevill	N	N	Y	Y	Y	Y	Y	N
5 Flippo	?	?	?	?	?	?	Y	N
6 Erdreich	N	N	Y	Y	Y	Y	Y	N
7 Harris	N	N	Y	Y	Y	Y	Y	N
ALASKA								
AL ***Young***	?	N	Y	Y	Y	N	?	Y
ARIZONA								
1 ***Rhodes***	Y	Y	Y	Y	Y	N	N	Y
2 Udall	N	?	?	?	Y	Y	Y	N
3 ***Stump***	Y	Y	N	Y	N	N	N	Y
4 ***Kyl***	Y	Y	N	Y	Y	Y	N	Y
5 ***Kolbe***	Y	N	Y	Y	Y	N	N	Y
ARKANSAS								
1 Alexander	N	N	Y	Y	Y	Y	Y	N
2 ***Robinson***	N	N	Y	Y	N	N	Y	Y
3 ***Hammerschmidt***	N	N	Y	Y	Y	N	Y	Y
4 Anthony	N	N	Y	Y	Y	Y	Y	N
CALIFORNIA								
1 Bosco	N	N	Y	Y	Y	Y	Y	N
2 ***Herger***	Y	N	Y	Y	N	N	N	Y
3 Matsui	N	N	Y	Y	Y	Y	Y	?
4 Fazio	N	N	Y	Y	Y	Y	Y	N
5 Pelosi	N	N	Y	Y	Y	Y	Y	N
6 Boxer	N	N	Y	Y	Y	Y	Y	N
7 Miller	N	N	Y	Y	Y	Y	Y	N
8 Dellums	N	N	Y	Y	Y	Y	Y	N
9 Stark	N	N	Y	Y	Y	Y	Y	N
10 Edwards	N	N	Y	Y	Y	Y	Y	N
11 Lantos	N	N	Y	Y	Y	Y	Y	N
12 ***Campbell***	N	N	Y	Y	Y	Y	N	Y
13 Mineta	N	N	Y	Y	?	Y	Y	N
14 ***Shumway***	Y	Y	N	Y	N	N	Y	N
15 Condit	N	N	Y	Y	Y	Y	Y	N
16 Panetta	N	N	Y	Y	Y	Y	Y	N
17 ***Pashayan***	N	N	Y	Y	Y	Y	N	Y
18 Lehman	N	N	Y	Y	Y	Y	Y	N
19 ***Lagomarsino***	N	N	Y	Y	Y	Y	N	Y
20 ***Thomas***	Y	N	Y	Y	Y	N	N	Y
21 ***Gallegly***	Y	N	Y	Y	Y	Y	N	Y
22 ***Moorhead***	Y	N	Y	Y	Y	Y	N	Y
23 Beilenson	N	N	Y	Y	Y	Y	Y	N
24 Waxman	N	N	Y	Y	?	Y	Y	N
25 Roybal	N	N	Y	Y	Y	Y	Y	N
26 Berman	N	N	Y	Y	?	Y	?	N
27 Levine	N	N	Y	Y	Y	Y	Y	N
28 Dixon	N	N	Y	Y	Y	Y	?	N
29 Hawkins	?	N	Y	Y	?	Y	Y	N
30 Martinez	N	N	Y	Y	Y	Y	Y	N
31 Dymally	N	N	Y	Y	Y	Y	Y	X
32 Anderson	N	N	Y	Y	Y	Y	Y	N
33 ***Dreier***	N	N	Y	Y	Y	Y	N	Y
34 Torres	N	N	Y	Y	Y	Y	Y	N
35 ***Lewis***	Y	N	Y	Y	N	N	N	Y
36 Brown	N	N	Y	?	Y	Y	Y	?
37 ***McCandless***	Y	N	Y	Y	N	N	N	Y
38 ***Dornan***	Y	N	N	Y	N	Y	N	Y
39 ***Dannemeyer***	?	N	N	Y	Y	N	?	?
40 ***Cox***	N	N	N	Y	Y	Y	N	Y
41 ***Lowery***	Y	N	Y	Y	N	Y	?	Y
42 ***Rohrabacher***	Y	N	N	Y	N	Y	N	Y
43 ***Packard***	Y	N	N	Y	N	N	Y	Y
44 Bates	N	N	Y	Y	?	Y	Y	N
45 ***Hunter***	Y	Y	N	Y	N	N	?	Y
COLORADO								
1 Schroeder	N	N	Y	Y	Y	Y	N	Y
2 Skaggs	Y	N	Y	Y	Y	Y	Y	N
3 Campbell	N	N	Y	Y	Y	Y	Y	N
4 ***Brown***	N	N	Y	Y	N	Y	N	Y
5 ***Hefley***	N	N	Y	Y	Y	Y	N	Y
6 ***Schaefer***	Y	N	Y	Y	N	Y	N	Y
CONNECTICUT								
1 Kennelly	N	N	Y	Y	Y	Y	Y	N
2 Gejdenson	N	N	Y	Y	Y	Y	Y	N
3 Morrison	N	N	Y	?	?	Y	Y	N
4 ***Shays***	N	N	Y	Y	Y	Y	N	Y
5 ***Rowland***	?	?	?	?	?	?	?	?
6 ***Johnson***	Y	N	Y	Y	Y	Y	Y	Y
DELAWARE								
AL Carper	N	N	Y	Y	Y	Y	Y	N
FLORIDA								
1 Hutto	N	N	Y	Y	Y	Y	Y	Y
2 ***Grant***	Y	N	Y	Y	Y	Y	Y	Y
3 Bennett	Y	N	Y	Y	Y	Y	Y	Y
4 ***James***	N	Y	Y	Y	Y	Y	N	Y
5 ***McCollum***	Y	Y	N	Y	?	Y	Y	Y
6 ***Stearns***	Y	N	Y	Y	Y	Y	N	Y
7 Gibbons	Y	N	Y	Y	Y	Y	Y	N
8 ***Young***	Y	N	Y	N	N	Y	N	Y
9 ***Bilirakis***	Y	N	Y	Y	Y	Y	N	Y
10 ***Ireland***	Y	Y	Y	Y	N	Y	N	Y
11 Nelson	Y	N	Y	Y	Y	Y	Y	Y
12 ***Lewis***	Y	N	Y	Y	N	Y	N	Y
13 ***Goss***	Y	N	Y	Y	N	Y	N	Y
14 Johnston	N	N	Y	Y	Y	Y	Y	N
15 ***Shaw***	Y	N	Y	Y	Y	Y	Y	Y
16 Smith	N	Y	Y	Y	?	Y	Y	N
17 Lehman	N	N	Y	Y	Y	Y	Y	N
18 ***Ros-Lehtinen***	Y	N	Y	Y	Y	Y	N	Y
19 Fascell	N	N	Y	Y	Y	Y	Y	N
GEORGIA								
1 Thomas	N	N	Y	Y	Y	Y	Y	N
2 Hatcher	N	N	Y	Y	Y	Y	Y	N
3 Ray	Y	N	Y	Y	Y	Y	Y	N
4 Jones	N	N	Y	Y	Y	Y	Y	N
5 Lewis	N	N	Y	Y	Y	Y	Y	N
6 ***Gingrich***	Y	N	Y	Y	Y	Y	N	Y
7 Darden	N	N	Y	Y	Y	Y	Y	N
8 Rowland	N	N	Y	Y	Y	Y	Y	N
9 Jenkins	N	N	Y	Y	Y	Y	Y	N
10 Barnard	N	N	Y	Y	Y	Y	Y	N
HAWAII								
1 ***Saiki***	N	N	Y	Y	Y	Y	N	Y
2 Vacancy								
IDAHO								
1 ***Craig***	Y	N	Y	Y	N	N	N	Y
2 Stallings	N	N	Y	Y	Y	Y	Y	N
ILLINOIS								
1 Hayes	N	N	Y	Y	Y	Y	Y	N
2 Savage	N	N	Y	Y	Y	Y	Y	N
3 Russo	N	N	Y	Y	?	Y	Y	N
4 Sangmeister	N	N	Y	Y	Y	Y	Y	Y
5 Lipinski	N	N	Y	Y	Y	Y	Y	N
6 ***Hyde***	Y	N	Y	Y	Y	Y	N	Y
7 Collins	N	N	Y	Y	Y	Y	Y	N
8 Rostenkowski	N	N	Y	Y	Y	?	Y	?
9 Yates	N	N	Y	?	Y	Y	Y	N
10 ***Porter***	N	N	Y	Y	Y	Y	N	Y
11 Annunzio	N	N	Y	Y	Y	Y	Y	N
12 ***Crane***	Y	N	N	Y	N	N	?	Y
13 ***Fawell***	N	N	N	Y	Y	Y	N	Y
14 ***Hastert***	Y	N	Y	Y	N	Y	N	Y
15 ***Madigan***	Y	N	Y	Y	Y	Y	N	Y
16 ***Martin***	N	N	Y	Y	Y	Y	?	#
17 Evans	N	N	Y	Y	Y	Y	Y	N
18 ***Michel***	Y	N	Y	Y	Y	Y	N	Y
19 Bruce	N	N	Y	Y	Y	Y	Y	N
20 Durbin	N	N	Y	Y	Y	Y	Y	N
21 Costello	N	N	Y	Y	?	Y	Y	N
22 Poshard	N	N	Y	Y	Y	Y	Y	Y
INDIANA								
1 Visclosky	N	N	Y	Y	Y	Y	Y	N
2 Sharp	?	?	Y	Y	Y	Y	Y	Y
3 ***Hiler***	N	N	Y	Y	N	Y	N	Y

ND Northern Democrats SD Southern Democrats

	378	379	380	381	382	383	384	385
4 Long	N	N	Y	Y	Y	Y	Y	N
5 Jontz	N	N	Y	Y	Y	Y	Y	N
6 **Burton**	Y	N	N	Y	N	N	N	Y
7 **Myers**	Y	N	Y	Y	Y	Y	Y	Y
8 McCloskey	N	N	Y	Y	Y	Y	Y	N
9 Hamilton	N	N	Y	Y	Y	Y	Y	N
10 Jacobs	Y	N	Y	Y	Y	Y	N	Y
IOWA								
1 **Leach**	N	N	Y	Y	Y	Y	N	Y
2 **Tauke**	Y	N	Y	Y	Y	Y	N	Y
3 Nagle	N	N	Y	Y	Y	Y	Y	N
4 Smith	N	N	Y	Y	Y	Y	Y	N
5 **Lightfoot**	Y	N	Y	Y	Y	Y	N	Y
6 **Grandy**	Y	N	Y	Y	N	N	N	Y
KANSAS								
1 **Roberts**	Y	N	Y	Y	Y	Y	N	Y
2 Slattery	Y	N	Y	Y	Y	Y	Y	Y
3 **Meyers**	Y	N	Y	Y	Y	Y	N	Y
4 Glickman	Y	N	Y	Y	Y	Y	Y	Y
5 **Whittaker**	N	N	Y	Y	Y	Y	N	Y
KENTUCKY								
1 Hubbard	N	N	Y	Y	Y	Y	Y	Y
2 Natcher	N	N	Y	Y	Y	Y	Y	N
3 Mazzoli	N	N	Y	Y	Y	Y	Y	N
4 **Bunning**	Y	N	Y	Y	Y	Y	N	Y
5 **Rogers**	Y	N	Y	Y	Y	Y	N	Y
6 **Hopkins**	Y	N	Y	Y	Y	Y	N	Y
7 Perkins	N	N	Y	Y	Y	Y	Y	N
LOUISIANA								
1 **Livingston**	Y	Y	Y	Y	N	Y	N	Y
2 Boggs	N	N	Y	Y	Y	Y	Y	N
3 Tauzin	Y	N	Y	Y	Y	Y	Y	Y
4 **McCrery**	N	N	Y	Y	Y	Y	N	Y
5 Huckaby	Y	N	Y	Y	?	Y	Y	Y
6 **Baker**	Y	N	Y	Y	Y	Y	N	Y
7 Hayes	N	N	Y	Y	Y	Y	Y	Y
8 **Holloway**	Y	Y	Y	Y	N	Y	N	Y
MAINE								
1 Brennan	N	N	Y	Y	Y	Y	Y	N
2 **Snowe**	N	N	Y	Y	Y	Y	N	Y
MARYLAND								
1 Dyson	?	?	?	Y	Y	Y	Y	Y
2 **Bentley**	Y	N	Y	Y	Y	Y	?	Y
3 Cardin	Y	N	Y	?	Y	Y	Y	N
4 McMillen	N	N	Y	Y	Y	Y	Y	N
5 Hoyer	N	N	Y	Y	Y	Y	Y	N
6 Byron	N	N	Y	Y	Y	Y	Y	Y
7 Mfume	Y	N	Y	Y	Y	Y	?	N
8 **Morella**	N	N	Y	Y	Y	Y	N	Y
MASSACHUSETTS								
1 **Conte**	Y	N	Y	Y	Y	Y	Y	Y
2 Neal	N	N	Y	Y	Y	Y	Y	N
3 Early	Y	N	Y	Y	Y	Y	Y	N
4 Frank	N	N	Y	Y	Y	Y	Y	N
5 Atkins	N	N	Y	Y	Y	Y	Y	N
6 Mavroules	N	N	Y	?	Y	Y	Y	N
7 Markey	N	N	Y	?	?	Y	Y	N
8 Kennedy	N	N	Y	Y	Y	Y	Y	N
9 Moakley	N	N	Y	Y	Y	Y	Y	N
10 Studds	N	N	Y	Y	Y	Y	Y	N
11 Donnelly	N	N	Y	Y	Y	Y	Y	N
MICHIGAN								
1 Conyers	N	N	Y	Y	Y	Y	Y	N
2 **Pursell**	N	N	Y	?	Y	Y	N	Y
3 Wolpe	N	N	Y	Y	Y	Y	Y	N
4 **Upton**	Y	N	Y	Y	Y	Y	N	Y
5 **Henry**	Y	N	Y	Y	Y	Y	N	Y
6 Carr	Y	N	Y	Y	Y	Y	Y	N
7 Kildee	N	N	Y	Y	Y	Y	Y	N
8 Traxler	N	N	Y	Y	Y	Y	Y	N
9 **Vander Jagt**	Y	N	Y	Y	Y	Y	Y	Y
10 **Schuette**	N	N	Y	Y	Y	Y	N	Y
11 **Davis**	N	N	Y	Y	Y	Y	N	Y
12 Bonior	N	N	Y	Y	Y	Y	Y	N
13 Crockett	?	N	Y	Y	?	?	?	?
14 Hertel	N	N	Y	Y	Y	Y	Y	N
15 Ford	?	?	?	?	?	?	?	N
16 Dingell	N	N	Y	Y	Y	Y	Y	N
17 Levin	N	N	Y	Y	Y	Y	Y	N
18 **Broomfield**	Y	N	Y	Y	Y	Y	Y	Y
MINNESOTA								
1 Penny	Y	N	Y	Y	Y	Y	Y	N
2 **Weber**	N	N	Y	Y	N	Y	N	Y
3 **Frenzel**	Y	Y	N	Y	Y	Y	N	Y
4 Vento	N	N	Y	Y	Y	Y	Y	N

	378	379	380	381	382	383	384	385
5 Sabo	N	N	Y	Y	Y	Y	Y	N
6 Sikorski	N	N	Y	Y	Y	Y	N	N
7 **Stangeland**	Y	N	Y	Y	Y	N	N	Y
8 Oberstar	N	N	Y	Y	Y	Y	Y	N
MISSISSIPPI								
1 Whitten	N	N	Y	Y	Y	Y	Y	N
2 Espy	N	N	Y	Y	Y	Y	Y	N
3 Montgomery	N	N	Y	Y	Y	Y	Y	N
4 Parker	N	N	Y	Y	Y	Y	Y	Y
5 Taylor	N	N	Y	Y	Y	Y	Y	Y
MISSOURI								
1 Clay	N	N	Y	Y	Y	Y	?	N
2 **Buechner**	N	N	Y	Y	N	Y	N	Y
3 Gephardt	N	N	Y	Y	?	Y	Y	N
4 Skelton	N	N	Y	Y	Y	Y	Y	N
5 Wheat	N	N	Y	Y	Y	Y	Y	N
6 **Coleman**	Y	N	Y	Y	Y	Y	N	Y
7 **Hancock**	Y	Y	N	Y	N	N	N	Y
8 **Emerson**	Y	N	Y	Y	Y	N	N	Y
9 Volkmer	N	N	Y	Y	Y	Y	Y	N
MONTANA								
1 Williams	N	N	Y	Y	Y	Y	?	N
2 **Marlenee**	Y	N	Y	Y	N	N	N	Y
NEBRASKA								
1 **Bereuter**	Y	N	Y	Y	Y	Y	N	Y
2 Hoagland	N	N	Y	Y	Y	Y	Y	N
3 **Smith**	Y	N	Y	Y	N	N	Y	Y
NEVADA								
1 Bilbray	N	N	Y	Y	Y	Y	Y	N
2 **Vucanovich**	Y	N	Y	Y	Y	N	N	Y
NEW HAMPSHIRE								
1 **Smith**	Y	N	Y	Y	Y	Y	N	Y
2 **Douglas**	Y	N	Y	Y	N	Y	N	Y
NEW JERSEY								
1 Vacancy								
2 Hughes	N	N	Y	Y	Y	Y	Y	N
3 Pallone	N	N	Y	Y	Y	Y	Y	Y
4 **Smith**	N	N	Y	Y	Y	Y	Y	Y
5 **Roukema**	N	N	Y	Y	Y	Y	N	Y
6 Dwyer	N	N	Y	Y	Y	Y	Y	N
7 **Rinaldo**	N	N	Y	Y	Y	Y	Y	Y
8 Roe	N	N	Y	Y	Y	Y	Y	N
9 Torricelli	N	N	Y	Y	?	Y	Y	N
10 Payne	N	N	Y	Y	Y	Y	Y	N
11 **Gallo**	Y	N	Y	Y	Y	Y	N	Y
12 **Courter**	Y	N	Y	Y	Y	Y	N	Y
13 **Saxton**	N	N	Y	Y	Y	Y	N	Y
14 Guarini	?	?	?	?	?	?	Y	N
NEW MEXICO								
1 **Schiff**	N	N	Y	Y	Y	Y	Y	Y
2 **Skeen**	Y	N	Y	Y	Y	N	Y	Y
3 Richardson	N	N	Y	Y	?	Y	?	N
NEW YORK								
1 Hochbrueckner	N	N	Y	Y	Y	Y	Y	N
2 Downey	N	N	Y	Y	?	Y	Y	N
3 Mrazek	N	N	Y	?	?	Y	Y	N
4 **Lent**	N	N	Y	Y	N	Y	Y	?
5 **McGrath**	N	N	Y	Y	Y	Y	N	Y
6 Flake	N	N	Y	Y	Y	Y	Y	N
7 Ackerman	N	N	Y	Y	Y	Y	Y	N
8 Scheuer	N	N	Y	Y	Y	Y	Y	N
9 Manton	N	N	Y	Y	Y	Y	Y	N
10 Schumer	N	N	Y	Y	Y	Y	Y	N
11 Towns	N	N	Y	Y	?	Y	Y	N
12 Owens	N	N	Y	Y	Y	Y	Y	N
13 Solarz	N	N	Y	Y	Y	Y	?	N
14 **Molinari**	N	N	Y	Y	N	Y	?	Y
15 **Green**	N	N	Y	Y	Y	Y	Y	Y
16 Rangel	N	N	Y	?	?	Y	?	N
17 Weiss	N	N	Y	Y	Y	Y	Y	N
18 Serrano	N	N	Y	Y	Y	Y	Y	N
19 Engel	N	N	Y	Y	Y	Y	Y	N
20 Lowey	N	N	Y	Y	Y	Y	Y	N
21 **Fish**	N	N	Y	Y	Y	Y	?	+
22 **Gilman**	N	N	Y	Y	Y	Y	Y	Y
23 McNulty	N	N	Y	Y	Y	Y	Y	N
24 **Solomon**	Y	N	Y	Y	N	Y	N	Y
25 **Boehlert**	N	N	Y	Y	Y	Y	N	Y
26 **Martin**	Y	N	Y	Y	N	Y	N	Y
27 **Walsh**	N	N	Y	Y	Y	Y	N	Y
28 McHugh	N	N	Y	Y	?	Y	Y	N
29 **Horton**	N	N	Y	Y	Y	Y	Y	Y
30 Slaughter	N	N	Y	Y	Y	N	Y	N
31 **Paxon**	Y	N	Y	Y	Y	Y	N	Y

	378	379	380	381	382	383	384	385
32 LaFalce	N	N	Y	Y	Y	Y	Y	N
33 Nowak	N	N	Y	Y	Y	Y	Y	N
34 **Houghton**	Y	N	Y	Y	Y	Y	Y	Y
NORTH CAROLINA								
1 Jones	N	N	Y	Y	Y	Y	Y	N
2 Valentine	N	N	Y	?	Y	Y	Y	N
3 Lancaster	N	N	Y	Y	Y	Y	Y	N
4 Price	N	N	Y	Y	Y	Y	Y	N
5 Neal	N	N	Y	?	Y	Y	?	N
6 **Coble**	Y	N	Y	Y	Y	Y	N	Y
7 Rose	N	N	Y	Y	Y	Y	Y	N
8 Hefner	N	N	Y	Y	Y	Y	Y	N
9 **McMillan**	Y	N	Y	Y	Y	Y	N	Y
10 **Ballenger**	Y	N	Y	Y	N	N	N	Y
11 Clarke	Y	N	Y	Y	Y	Y	Y	N
NORTH DAKOTA								
AL Dorgan	N	N	Y	Y	Y	Y	Y	N
OHIO								
1 Luken	N	N	Y	Y	Y	Y	Y	N
2 **Gradison**	Y	Y	Y	Y	Y	Y	Y	Y
3 Hall	Y	N	Y	Y	Y	?	?	N
4 **Oxley**	Y	N	Y	?	Y	Y	N	Y
5 **Gillmor**	N	N	Y	Y	Y	Y	Y	Y
6 **McEwen**	Y	N	Y	Y	Y	N	N	Y
7 **DeWine**	Y	N	Y	Y	Y	Y	?	?
8 **Lukens**	Y	N	N	?	?	Y	N	Y
9 Kaptur	N	N	Y	Y	Y	Y	Y	N
10 **Miller**	Y	N	Y	Y	Y	Y	N	Y
11 Eckart	N	N	Y	Y	Y	Y	Y	Y
12 **Kasich**	Y	N	Y	Y	Y	Y	Y	Y
13 Pease	?	N	Y	Y	Y	Y	Y	N
14 Sawyer	N	N	Y	Y	Y	Y	Y	N
15 **Wylie**	Y	N	Y	Y	Y	Y	Y	Y
16 **Regula**	Y	N	Y	Y	Y	Y	N	Y
17 Traficant	N	N	Y	Y	Y	Y	Y	N
18 Applegate	Y	N	Y	Y	Y	Y	Y	N
19 Feighan	N	N	Y	Y	Y	Y	Y	N
20 Oakar	N	N	Y	Y	Y	Y	Y	?
21 Stokes	N	N	Y	Y	?	Y	Y	N
OKLAHOMA								
1 **Inhofe**	N	N	Y	Y	N	Y	N	Y
2 Synar	N	N	Y	Y	Y	Y	Y	N
3 Watkins	N	N	Y	Y	Y	Y	Y	Y
4 McCurdy	N	N	Y	Y	Y	Y	Y	N
5 **Edwards**	Y	N	Y	Y	N	N	N	Y
6 English	N	N	Y	Y	Y	Y	Y	N
OREGON								
1 AuCoin	N	N	Y	Y	Y	Y	Y	N
2 **Smith, B.**	Y	N	Y	Y	N	N	N	Y
3 Wyden	N	N	Y	Y	Y	Y	Y	N
4 DeFazio	N	N	Y	Y	?	Y	Y	N
5 **Smith, D.**	Y	N	Y	Y	N	N	N	Y
PENNSYLVANIA								
1 Foglietta	N	N	Y	Y	Y	Y	Y	N
2 Gray	N	?	Y	Y	Y	Y	Y	N
3 Borski	N	N	Y	Y	Y	Y	Y	N
4 Kolter	Y	N	Y	?	Y	?	Y	N
5 **Schulze**	Y	N	Y	Y	Y	Y	Y	Y
6 Yatron	Y	N	Y	Y	Y	Y	Y	N
7 **Weldon**	Y	N	Y	Y	Y	Y	N	Y
8 Kostmayer	N	N	Y	Y	Y	?	Y	N
9 **Shuster**	Y	N	Y	Y	Y	Y	Y	Y
10 **McDade**	N	N	Y	Y	N	N	Y	Y
11 Kanjorski	N	N	Y	Y	Y	Y	Y	N
12 Murtha	N	N	Y	Y	Y	Y	Y	N
13 **Coughlin**	Y	N	Y	Y	Y	Y	N	Y
14 Coyne	N	N	Y	Y	Y	Y	Y	N
15 **Ritter**	N	N	Y	Y	N	Y	?	Y
16 **Walker**	Y	Y	N	Y	N	Y	N	Y
17 **Gekas**	Y	N	N	Y	N	Y	N	Y
18 Walgren	N	N	Y	Y	Y	Y	Y	N
19 **Goodling**	Y	N	Y	Y	?	Y	N	Y
20 Gaydos	N	N	Y	Y	Y	Y	Y	N
21 **Ridge**	Y	N	Y	Y	Y	Y	N	Y
22 Murphy	Y	N	Y	?	?	Y	N	N
23 **Clinger**	N	N	Y	Y	Y	Y	Y	Y
RHODE ISLAND								
1 **Machtley**	N	N	Y	Y	?	Y	N	Y
2 **Schneider**	N	N	Y	Y	Y	Y	Y	Y
SOUTH CAROLINA								
1 **Ravenel**	N	N	Y	Y	N	Y	Y	Y
2 **Spence**	Y	N	Y	Y	Y	Y	N	Y
3 Derrick	Y	N	Y	Y	Y	Y	Y	N
4 Patterson	Y	N	Y	Y	Y	Y	Y	N
5 Spratt	N	?	?	?	Y	Y	Y	N
6 Tallon	N	N	Y	Y	Y	Y	Y	N

	378	379	380	381	382	383	384	385
SOUTH DAKOTA								
AL Johnson	N	N	Y	Y	Y	Y	Y	Y
TENNESSEE								
1 **Quillen**	Y	N	Y	Y	Y	Y	N	Y
2 **Duncan**	Y	N	Y	Y	Y	Y	Y	Y
3 Lloyd	N	N	Y	Y	?	Y	Y	N
4 Cooper	Y	N	Y	Y	Y	Y	Y	Y
5 Clement	N	N	Y	Y	Y	Y	Y	N
6 Gordon	N	N	Y	Y	Y	Y	Y	N
7 **Sundquist**	Y	N	Y	Y	Y	Y	N	Y
8 Tanner	Y	N	Y	Y	Y	Y	Y	N
9 Ford	N	?	Y	?	?	Y	?	N
TEXAS								
1 Chapman	Y	N	Y	Y	?	Y	?	N
2 Wilson	N	N	Y	Y	Y	Y	?	N
3 **Bartlett**	Y	Y	N	Y	Y	Y	Y	Y
4 Hall	Y	N	Y	Y	Y	N	Y	Y
5 Bryant	N	N	Y	Y	Y	Y	Y	N
6 **Barton**	Y	Y	Y	Y	N	N	N	Y
7 **Archer**	Y	Y	N	Y	Y	Y	Y	Y
8 **Fields**	Y	N	Y	Y	N	N	N	Y
9 Brooks	N	N	Y	Y	Y	Y	Y	N
10 Pickle	N	N	Y	Y	Y	Y	Y	Y
11 Leath	N	N	Y	Y	Y	Y	?	N
12 Geren	Y	N	Y	Y	Y	Y	Y	N
13 Sarpalius	N	N	Y	Y	Y	Y	Y	N
14 Laughlin	N	N	Y	Y	Y	Y	Y	N
15 de la Garza	N	N	Y	Y	Y	Y	Y	N
16 Coleman	N	N	Y	Y	Y	Y	Y	N
17 Stenholm	Y	N	Y	Y	Y	Y	Y	N
18 Washington	N	?	Y	Y	Y	?	Y	N
19 **Combest**	Y	N	Y	Y	Y	Y	Y	Y
20 Gonzalez	N	N	Y	Y	Y	Y	Y	N
21 **Smith**	Y	N	Y	Y	Y	Y	N	Y
22 **DeLay**	Y	Y	N	Y	N	N	N	Y
23 Bustamante	N	N	Y	Y	Y	Y	Y	N
24 Frost	?	N	Y	Y	Y	Y	Y	N
25 Andrews	N	N	Y	Y	Y	Y	Y	N
26 **Armey**	Y	Y	N	Y	N	Y	N	Y
27 Ortiz	N	N	Y	Y	Y	?	Y	N
UTAH								
1 **Hansen**	Y	Y	N	Y	N	N	N	Y
2 Owens	N	N	Y	Y	Y	Y	Y	N
3 **Nielson**	Y	N	N	Y	Y	N	N	Y
VERMONT								
AL **Smith**	Y	N	Y	Y	Y	Y	Y	Y
VIRGINIA								
1 **Bateman**	?	N	Y	Y	Y	Y	Y	Y
2 Pickett	N	N	Y	Y	Y	Y	Y	N
3 **Bliley**	Y	N	Y	Y	Y	Y	N	Y
4 Sisisky	N	N	Y	Y	Y	Y	Y	N
5 Payne	N	N	Y	Y	Y	Y	Y	N
6 Olin	N	N	Y	Y	Y	Y	Y	N
7 **Slaughter**	Y	N	Y	Y	Y	Y	N	Y
8 **Parris**	Y	N	Y	Y	N	Y	N	Y
9 Boucher	N	N	Y	Y	Y	Y	?	N
10 **Wolf**	Y	N	Y	Y	Y	Y	N	Y
WASHINGTON								
1 **Miller**	N	N	Y	Y	Y	Y	N	Y
2 Swift	N	−	+	+	+	+	+	N
3 Unsoeld	N	N	Y	Y	Y	Y	Y	N
4 **Morrison**	N	N	Y	Y	Y	Y	?	Y
5 Foley								
6 Dicks	N	N	Y	Y	Y	Y	Y	N
7 McDermott	N	N	Y	Y	Y	Y	Y	N
8 **Chandler**	N	N	Y	Y	Y	Y	N	Y
WEST VIRGINIA								
1 Mollohan	N	N	Y	Y	Y	Y	Y	N
2 Staggers	N	N	Y	Y	?	Y	Y	N
3 Wise	N	N	Y	Y	Y	Y	Y	N
4 Rahall	N	N	Y	Y	Y	Y	Y	N
WISCONSIN								
1 Aspin	Y	N	Y	Y	Y	Y	Y	N
2 Kastenmeier	N	N	Y	Y	Y	Y	Y	N
3 **Gunderson**	Y	N	Y	Y	Y	Y	Y	Y
4 Kleczka	N	N	Y	Y	Y	Y	Y	N
5 Moody	N	N	Y	?	?	Y	Y	?
6 **Petri**	Y	N	N	Y	Y	Y	Y	Y
7 Obey	N	N	Y	Y	Y	Y	Y	N
8 **Roth**	N	N	Y	Y	N	Y	Y	Y
9 **Sensenbrenner**	Y	N	N	Y	N	Y	N	Y
WYOMING								
AL **Thomas**	Y	N	Y	Y	Y	Y	N	Y

Southern states - Ala., Ark., Fla., Ga., Ky., La., Miss., N.C., Okla., S.C., Tenn., Texas, Va.
Omitted votes are quorum calls, which CQ does not include in its vote charts.

386. HR 4450. Coastal Zone Reauthorization/Passage. Passage of the bill to reauthorize and recodify the Coastal Zone Management Act, eliminating several existing programs and establishing programs to address pollution of coastal water, to encourage states to improve their management of certain national interests and for other purposes. The bill authorizes $429 million for fiscal 1991-95. Passed 391-32: R 141-31; D 250-1 (ND 170-0, SD 80-1), Sept. 26, 1990. A "nay" was a vote supporting the president's position.

387. HR 5314. Water Resources Development Act/Passage. Passage of the bill to authorize construction of water resources development projects by the U.S. Army Corps of Engineers for flood control, navigation, port development, and related purposes. Passed 350-55: R 116-51; D 234-4 (ND 156-3, SD 78-1), Sept. 26, 1990. A "nay" was a vote supporting the president's position.

KEY

- Y Voted for (yea).
- # Paired for.
- + Announced for.
- N Voted against (nay).
- X Paired against.
- - Announced against.
- P Voted "present."
- C Voted "present" to avoid possible conflict of interest.
- ? Did not vote or otherwise make a position known.

Democrats *Republicans*

	386	387
ALABAMA		
1 *Callahan*	Y	Y
2 *Dickinson*	Y	N
3 Browder	Y	Y
4 Bevill	Y	Y
5 Flippo	Y	Y
6 Erdreich	Y	Y
7 Harris	Y	Y
ALASKA		
AL *Young*	Y	Y
ARIZONA		
1 *Rhodes*	N	N
2 Udall	Y	Y
3 *Stump*	N	N
4 *Kyl*	N	N
5 *Kolbe*	N	Y
ARKANSAS		
1 Alexander	Y	Y
2 *Robinson*	Y	?
3 *Hammerschmidt*	Y	Y
4 Anthony	Y	Y
CALIFORNIA		
1 Bosco	Y	Y
2 *Herger*	N	Y
3 Matsui	Y	Y
4 Fazio	Y	Y
5 Pelosi	Y	Y
6 Boxer	Y	Y
7 Miller	Y	Y
8 Dellums	Y	Y
9 Stark	Y	Y
10 Edwards	Y	Y
11 Lantos	Y	Y
12 *Campbell*	Y	N
13 Mineta	Y	Y
14 *Shumway*	N	N
15 Condit	Y	Y
16 Panetta	Y	Y
17 *Pashayan*	Y	Y
18 Lehman	Y	Y
19 *Lagomarsino*	Y	Y
20 *Thomas*	Y	Y
21 *Gallegly*	Y	Y
22 *Moorhead*	Y	Y
23 Beilenson	Y	Y
24 Waxman	Y	Y
25 Roybal	Y	Y
26 Berman	Y	Y
27 Levine	Y	Y
28 Dixon	Y	Y
29 Hawkins	?	#
30 Martinez	Y	Y
31 Dymally	Y	Y
32 Anderson	Y	Y
33 *Dreier*	Y	Y
34 Torres	Y	Y
35 *Lewis*	Y	Y
36 Brown	Y	Y
37 *McCandless*	Y	Y
38 *Dornan*	Y	Y
39 *Dannemeyer*	?	?
40 *Cox*	Y	Y
41 *Lowery*	Y	Y
42 *Rohrabacher*	Y	Y
43 *Packard*	Y	Y
44 Bates	Y	Y
45 *Hunter*	Y	Y
COLORADO		
1 Schroeder	Y	Y
2 Skaggs	Y	N
3 Campbell	Y	Y
4 *Brown*	Y	N
5 *Hefley*	Y	N
6 *Schaefer*	Y	N
CONNECTICUT		
1 Kennelly	Y	Y
2 Gejdenson	Y	Y
3 Morrison	Y	+
4 *Shays*	Y	N
5 *Rowland*	?	?
6 *Johnson*	Y	N
DELAWARE		
AL Carper	Y	Y
FLORIDA		
1 Hutto	Y	Y
2 *Grant*	Y	Y
3 Bennett	Y	Y
4 *James*	Y	Y
5 *McCollum*	Y	Y
6 *Stearns*	Y	Y
7 Gibbons	Y	Y
8 *Young*	Y	?
9 *Bilirakis*	Y	Y
10 *Ireland*	Y	Y
11 Nelson	Y	Y
12 *Lewis*	Y	Y
13 *Goss*	Y	Y
14 Johnston	Y	Y
15 *Shaw*	Y	Y
16 Smith	Y	Y
17 Lehman	Y	Y
18 *Ros-Lehtinen*	Y	Y
19 Fascell	Y	Y
GEORGIA		
1 Thomas	Y	Y
2 Hatcher	Y	Y
3 Ray	?	Y
4 Jones	Y	Y
5 Lewis	Y	Y
6 *Gingrich*	Y	N
7 Darden	Y	Y
8 Rowland	Y	Y
9 Jenkins	Y	Y
10 Barnard	Y	Y
HAWAII		
1 *Saiki*	Y	Y
2 Vacancy		
IDAHO		
1 *Craig*	N	N
2 Stallings	Y	Y
ILLINOIS		
1 Hayes	Y	Y
2 Savage	Y	Y
3 Russo	Y	Y
4 Sangmeister	Y	Y
5 Lipinski	Y	Y
6 *Hyde*	Y	Y
7 Collins	Y	Y
8 Rostenkowski	Y	?
9 Yates	Y	Y
10 *Porter*	Y	N
11 Annunzio	Y	Y
12 *Crane*	N	N
13 *Fawell*	Y	N
14 *Hastert*	Y	Y
15 *Madigan*	Y	Y
16 *Martin*	?	?
17 Evans	Y	Y
18 *Michel*	Y	N
19 Bruce	Y	Y
20 Durbin	Y	Y
21 Costello	Y	Y
22 Poshard	Y	Y
INDIANA		
1 Visclosky	Y	Y
2 Sharp	Y	?
3 *Hiler*	Y	Y

ND Northern Democrats SD Southern Democrats

	386	387
4 Long	Y	Y
5 Jontz	Y	Y
6 ***Burton***	N	N
7 ***Myers***	Y	Y
8 McCloskey	Y	Y
9 Hamilton	Y	Y
10 Jacobs	Y	N

IOWA

	386	387
1 ***Leach***	Y	N
2 ***Tauke***	Y	Y
3 Nagle	Y	Y
4 Smith	Y	Y
5 ***Lightfoot***	N	Y
6 ***Grandy***	N	Y

KANSAS

	386	387
1 ***Roberts***	N	N
2 Slattery	Y	Y
3 ***Meyers***	Y	Y
4 Glickman	Y	Y
5 ***Whittaker***	Y	N

KENTUCKY

	386	387
1 Hubbard	Y	Y
2 Natcher	Y	Y
3 Mazzoli	Y	Y
4 ***Bunning***	Y	Y
5 ***Rogers***	Y	Y
6 ***Hopkins***	Y	Y
7 Perkins	Y	Y

LOUISIANA

	386	387
1 ***Livingston***	Y	Y
2 Boggs	Y	Y
3 Tauzin	Y	Y
4 ***McCrery***	Y	Y
5 Huckaby	Y	Y
6 ***Baker***	Y	Y
7 Hayes	Y	Y
8 ***Holloway***	Y	Y

MAINE

	386	387
1 Brennan	Y	Y
2 ***Snowe***	Y	N

MARYLAND

	386	387
1 Dyson	Y	Y
2 ***Bentley***	Y	Y
3 Cardin	Y	Y
4 McMillen	Y	Y
5 Hoyer	Y	Y
6 Byron	Y	Y
7 Mfume	Y	Y
8 ***Morella***	Y	Y

MASSACHUSETTS

	386	387
1 ***Conte***	Y	Y
2 Neal	Y	Y
3 Early	Y	Y
4 Frank	Y	Y
5 Atkins	Y	Y
6 Mavroules	Y	Y
7 Markey	Y	Y
8 Kennedy	Y	Y
9 Moakley	Y	Y
10 Studds	Y	Y
11 Donnelly	Y	Y

MICHIGAN

	386	387
1 Conyers	Y	?
2 ***Pursell***	Y	Y
3 Wolpe	Y	Y
4 ***Upton***	Y	Y
5 ***Henry***	Y	N
6 Carr	Y	Y
7 Kildee	Y	Y
8 Traxler	Y	?
9 ***Vander Jagt***	Y	Y
10 ***Schuette***	Y	?
11 ***Davis***	Y	Y
12 Bonior	Y	Y
13 Crockett	?	?
14 Hertel	Y	Y
15 Ford	Y	?
16 Dingell	Y	Y
17 Levin	Y	Y
18 ***Broomfield***	Y	N

MINNESOTA

	386	387
1 Penny	Y	Y
2 ***Weber***	Y	Y
3 ***Frenzel***	N	N
4 Vento	Y	Y
5 Sabo	Y	Y
6 Sikorski	Y	Y
7 ***Stangeland***	Y	Y
8 Oberstar	Y	Y

MISSISSIPPI

	386	387
1 Whitten	Y	Y
2 Espy	Y	Y
3 Montgomery	Y	Y
4 Parker	Y	Y
5 Taylor	Y	Y

MISSOURI

	386	387
1 Clay	Y	?
2 ***Buechner***	Y	Y
3 Gephardt	Y	Y
4 Skelton	Y	Y
5 Wheat	Y	Y
6 ***Coleman***	Y	Y
7 ***Hancock***	N	N
8 ***Emerson***	Y	Y
9 Volkmer	Y	Y

MONTANA

	386	387
1 Williams	Y	Y
2 ***Marlenee***	N	Y

NEBRASKA

	386	387
1 ***Bereuter***	Y	Y
2 Hoagland	Y	Y
3 ***Smith***	N	Y

NEVADA

	386	387
1 Bilbray	Y	Y
2 ***Vucanovich***	N	N

NEW HAMPSHIRE

	386	387
1 ***Smith***	Y	N
2 ***Douglas***	Y	N

NEW JERSEY

	386	387
1 Vacancy		
2 Hughes	Y	Y
3 Pallone	Y	Y
4 ***Smith***	Y	Y
5 ***Roukema***	Y	Y
6 Dwyer	Y	Y
7 ***Rinaldo***	Y	Y
8 Roe	Y	Y
9 Torricelli	Y	Y
10 Payne	Y	Y
11 ***Gallo***	Y	Y
12 ***Courter***	Y	Y
13 ***Saxton***	Y	Y
14 Guarini	Y	Y

NEW MEXICO

	386	387
1 ***Schiff***	Y	Y
2 ***Skeen***	Y	N
3 Richardson	Y	Y

NEW YORK

	386	387
1 Hochbrueckner	Y	Y
2 Downey	Y	Y
3 Mrazek	Y	Y
4 ***Lent***	Y	Y
5 ***McGrath***	Y	Y
6 Flake	Y	Y
7 Ackerman	Y	Y
8 Scheuer	Y	Y
9 Manton	Y	Y
10 Schumer	Y	Y
11 Towns	Y	Y
12 Owens	Y	Y
13 Solarz	Y	Y
14 ***Molinari***	Y	Y
15 ***Green***	Y	Y
16 Rangel	Y	Y
17 Weiss	Y	Y
18 Serrano	Y	Y
19 Engel	Y	Y
20 Lowey	Y	Y
21 ***Fish***	Y	?
22 ***Gilman***	Y	Y
23 McNulty	Y	+
24 ***Solomon***	N	N
25 ***Boehlert***	Y	Y
26 ***Martin***	Y	Y
27 ***Walsh***	Y	Y
28 McHugh	Y	Y
29 ***Horton***	Y	?
30 Slaughter	Y	Y
31 ***Paxon***	Y	Y
32 LaFalce	Y	Y
33 Nowak	Y	Y
34 ***Houghton***	Y	Y

NORTH CAROLINA

	386	387
1 Jones	Y	Y
2 Valentine	Y	Y
3 Lancaster	Y	Y
4 Price	Y	Y
5 Neal	Y	Y
6 ***Coble***	Y	Y
7 Rose	Y	Y
8 Hefner	Y	Y
9 ***McMillan***	Y	Y
10 ***Ballenger***	Y	Y
11 Clarke	Y	Y

NORTH DAKOTA

	386	387
AL Dorgan	Y	+

OHIO

	386	387
1 Luken	Y	Y
2 ***Gradison***	Y	Y
3 Hall	Y	Y
4 ***Oxley***	Y	N
5 ***Gillmor***	Y	Y
6 ***McEwen***	Y	Y
7 ***DeWine***	?	Y
8 ***Lukens***	Y	N
9 Kaptur	Y	Y
10 ***Miller***	Y	Y
11 Eckart	Y	Y
12 ***Kasich***	Y	Y
13 Pease	Y	N
14 Sawyer	Y	Y
15 ***Wylie***	Y	Y
16 ***Regula***	Y	Y
17 Traficant	Y	Y
18 Applegate	Y	Y
19 Feighan	Y	Y
20 Oakar	Y	Y
21 Stokes	Y	Y

OKLAHOMA

	386	387
1 ***Inhofe***	Y	Y
2 Synar	Y	Y
3 Watkins	Y	Y
4 McCurdy	Y	Y
5 ***Edwards***	Y	Y
6 English	Y	Y

OREGON

	386	387
1 AuCoin	Y	Y
2 ***Smith, B.***	Y	Y
3 Wyden	Y	Y
4 DeFazio	Y	Y
5 ***Smith, D.***	Y	N

PENNSYLVANIA

	386	387
1 Foglietta	Y	Y
2 Gray	Y	?
3 Borski	Y	?
4 Kolter	Y	Y
5 ***Schulze***	Y	Y
6 Yatron	Y	Y
7 ***Weldon***	Y	X
8 Kostmayer	Y	Y
9 ***Shuster***	Y	Y
10 ***McDade***	Y	Y
11 Kanjorski	Y	Y
12 Murtha	Y	Y
13 ***Coughlin***	Y	N
14 Coyne	Y	Y
15 ***Ritter***	Y	N
16 ***Walker***	N	N
17 ***Gekas***	N	N
18 Walgren	Y	?
19 ***Goodling***	Y	N
20 Gaydos	Y	Y
21 ***Ridge***	Y	Y
22 Murphy	Y	Y
23 ***Clinger***	Y	Y

RHODE ISLAND

	386	387
1 ***Machtley***	Y	Y
2 ***Schneider***	Y	Y

SOUTH CAROLINA

	386	387
1 ***Ravenel***	Y	Y
2 ***Spence***	Y	Y
3 Derrick	Y	Y
4 Patterson	Y	Y
5 Spratt	Y	Y
6 Tallon	Y	Y

SOUTH DAKOTA

	386	387
AL Johnson	Y	Y

TENNESSEE

	386	387
1 ***Quillen***	Y	N
2 ***Duncan***	N	Y
3 Lloyd	Y	Y
4 Cooper	Y	Y
5 Clement	Y	Y
6 Gordon	Y	Y
7 ***Sundquist***	N	N
8 Tanner	Y	Y
9 Ford	?	?

TEXAS

	386	387
1 Chapman	Y	Y
2 Wilson	Y	?
3 ***Bartlett***	N	N
4 Hall	Y	Y
5 Bryant	Y	Y
6 ***Barton***	N	N
7 ***Archer***	N	Y
8 ***Fields***	N	Y
9 Brooks	Y	Y
10 Pickle	Y	Y
11 Leath	Y	?
12 Geren	Y	Y
13 Sarpalius	Y	Y
14 Laughlin	Y	Y
15 de la Garza	Y	Y
16 Coleman	Y	Y
17 Stenholm	Y	Y
18 Washington	Y	?
19 ***Combest***	Y	N
20 Gonzalez	Y	Y
21 ***Smith***	Y	Y
22 ***DeLay***	N	N
23 Bustamante	Y	Y
24 Frost	Y	Y
25 Andrews	Y	Y
26 ***Armey***	N	N
27 Ortiz	Y	Y

UTAH

	386	387
1 ***Hansen***	N	N
2 Owens	Y	Y
3 ***Nielson***	N	N

VERMONT

	386	387
AL ***Smith***	Y	N

VIRGINIA

	386	387
1 ***Bateman***	Y	Y
2 Pickett	N	N
3 ***Bliley***	Y	Y
4 Sisisky	Y	Y
5 Payne	Y	Y
6 Olin	Y	Y
7 ***Slaughter***	Y	Y
8 ***Parris***	Y	Y
9 Boucher	Y	Y
10 ***Wolf***	Y	Y

WASHINGTON

	386	387
1 ***Miller***	Y	N
2 Swift	+	Y
3 Unsoeld	Y	Y
4 ***Morrison***	Y	Y
5 Foley		
6 Dicks	Y	Y
7 McDermott	Y	Y
8 ***Chandler***	Y	Y

WEST VIRGINIA

	386	387
1 Mollohan	Y	Y
2 Staggers	Y	Y
3 Wise	Y	Y
4 Rahall	Y	Y

WISCONSIN

	386	387
1 Aspin	Y	Y
2 Kastenmeier	Y	Y
3 ***Gunderson***	Y	Y
4 Kleczka	Y	Y
5 Moody	Y	Y
6 ***Petri***	Y	Y
7 Obey	Y	Y
8 ***Roth***	Y	Y
9 ***Sensenbrenner***	Y	N

WYOMING

	386	387
AL ***Thomas***	N	Y

Southern states - Ala., Ark., Fla., Ga., Ky., La., Miss., N.C., Okla., S.C., Tenn., Texas, Va.
Omitted votes are quorum calls, which CQ does not include in its vote charts.

388. Procedural Motion. Holloway, R-La., motion to approve the House Journal of Wednesday, Sept. 26. Motion agreed to 269-115: R 46-111; D 223-4 (ND 150-4, SD 73-0), Sept. 27, 1990.

389. HR 2039. Job Training Partnership Amendments/Passage. Passage of the bill to make changes in the Job Training Partnership Act of 1982 to target job-training programs to individuals who are the hardest to serve and the least prepared to get a job, to provide these individuals with training to become self-sufficient and more productive, and to establish separate programs for adults and at-risk youth. The bill would authorize an estimated $2.16 billion for fiscal 1991 through 1995. Passed 416-1: R 169-1; D 247-0 (ND 167-0, SD 80-0), Sept. 27, 1990.

391. HR 5316. Federal Judgeship Act/Passage. Brooks, D-Texas, motion to suspend the rules and pass the bill to authorize the creation of nine additional federal circuit court judgeships, and an additional 39 permanent and 13 temporary federal district court judgeships. The bill also would require a study of the process used by the U.S. Judicial Conference in recommending to Congress the creation of federal judgeships. Motion agreed to 387-18: R 155-10; D 232-8 (ND 154-8, SD 78-0), Sept. 27, 1990. A two-thirds majority of those present and voting (271 in this case) is required for passage under suspension of the rules.

† Patsy T. Mink, D-Hawaii, was sworn in Sept. 27, 1990. The first vote for which she was eligible was vote 391.

KEY

Y Voted for (yea).
\# Paired for.
\+ Announced for.
N Voted against (nay).
X Paired against.
\- Announced against.
P Voted "present."
C Voted "present" to avoid possible conflict of interest.
? Did not vote or otherwise make a position known.

Democrats ***Republicans***

	388	389	391
ALABAMA			
1 ***Callahan***	Y	Y	Y
2 ***Dickinson***	N	Y	Y
3 Browder	Y	Y	Y
4 Bevill	Y	Y	Y
5 Flippo	Y	Y	Y
6 Erdreich	Y	Y	Y
7 Harris	Y	Y	Y
ALASKA			
AL ***Young***	?	Y	Y
ARIZONA			
1 ***Rhodes***	N	Y	Y
2 Udall	?	Y	P
3 ***Stump***	N	Y	Y
4 ***Kyl***	N	Y	Y
5 ***Kolbe***	N	Y	Y
ARKANSAS			
1 Alexander	Y	Y	?
2 ***Robinson***	?	?	?
3 ***Hammerschmidt***	Y	Y	?
4 Anthony	Y	Y	Y
CALIFORNIA			
1 Bosco	Y	Y	Y
2 ***Herger***	N	Y	Y
3 Matsui	Y	Y	Y
4 Fazio	Y	Y	Y
5 Pelosi	Y	Y	Y
6 Boxer	Y	Y	Y
7 Miller	Y	Y	Y
8 Dellums	Y	Y	Y
9 Stark	Y	Y	Y
10 Edwards	Y	Y	Y
11 Lantos	Y	?	Y
12 ***Campbell***	N	Y	Y
13 Mineta	Y	Y	Y
14 ***Shumway***	Y	Y	Y
15 Condit	Y	Y	Y
16 Panetta	Y	Y	Y
17 ***Pashayan***	N	Y	Y
18 Lehman	Y	Y	Y
19 ***Lagomarsino***	N	Y	Y
20 ***Thomas***	N	Y	Y
21 ***Gallegly***	N	Y	Y
22 ***Moorhead***	N	Y	Y
23 Beilenson	Y	Y	?
24 Waxman	Y	Y	Y
25 Roybal	Y	Y	Y
26 Berman	Y	Y	Y
27 Levine	Y	Y	Y
28 Dixon	?	Y	Y
29 Hawkins	Y	Y	Y
30 Martinez	Y	Y	?
31 Dymally	Y	Y	Y
32 Anderson	Y	Y	Y
33 ***Dreier***	N	Y	Y
34 Torres	Y	Y	Y
35 ***Lewis***	N	Y	?
36 Brown	Y	Y	Y
37 ***McCandless***	N	Y	?
38 ***Dornan***	N	Y	Y
39 ***Dannemeyer***	N	Y	Y
40 ***Cox***	N	Y	Y
41 ***Lowery***	?	Y	Y
42 ***Rohrabacher***	N	Y	Y
43 ***Packard***	Y	Y	Y
44 Bates	Y	Y	Y
45 ***Hunter***	N	Y	Y
COLORADO			
1 Schroeder	N	Y	Y
2 Skaggs	Y	Y	Y
3 Campbell	Y	Y	Y
4 ***Brown***	N	Y	Y
5 ***Hefley***	N	Y	Y
6 ***Schaefer***	N	Y	?
CONNECTICUT			
1 Kennelly	Y	Y	Y
2 Gejdenson	Y	Y	Y
3 Morrison	Y	Y	?
4 ***Shays***	N	Y	Y
5 ***Rowland***	?	?	?
6 ***Johnson***	Y	Y	Y
DELAWARE			
AL Carper	Y	Y	Y
FLORIDA			
1 Hutto	Y	Y	Y
2 ***Grant***	Y	Y	Y
3 Bennett	Y	Y	Y
4 ***James***	N	Y	Y
5 ***McCollum***	N	Y	Y
6 ***Stearns***	N	Y	Y
7 Gibbons	Y	Y	Y
8 ***Young***	N	Y	Y
9 ***Bilirakis***	N	Y	Y
10 ***Ireland***	?	Y	Y
11 Nelson	Y	Y	+
12 ***Lewis***	N	Y	Y
13 ***Goss***	N	Y	Y
14 Johnston	Y	Y	Y
15 ***Shaw***	Y	Y	Y
16 Smith	Y	Y	?
17 Lehman	Y	Y	Y
18 ***Ros-Lehtinen***	N	Y	Y
19 Fascell	Y	Y	Y
GEORGIA			
1 Thomas	Y	Y	Y
2 Hatcher	Y	Y	Y
3 Ray	?	?	Y
4 Jones	Y	Y	Y
5 Lewis	Y	Y	Y
6 ***Gingrich***	?	Y	?
7 Darden	Y	Y	Y
8 Rowland	Y	Y	Y
9 Jenkins	Y	Y	Y
10 Barnard	?	Y	Y
HAWAII			
1 ***Saiki***	N	Y	Y
2 Mink †			Y
IDAHO			
1 ***Craig***	N	Y	Y
2 Stallings	Y	Y	Y
ILLINOIS			
1 Hayes	Y	Y	Y
2 Savage	?	Y	Y
3 Russo	Y	Y	Y
4 Sangmeister	Y	Y	Y
5 Lipinski	Y	Y	Y
6 ***Hyde***	N	Y	Y
7 Collins	?	Y	Y
8 Rostenkowski	?	?	?
9 Yates	Y	Y	Y
10 ***Porter***	N	Y	Y
11 Annunzio	Y	Y	Y
12 ***Crane***	N	N	Y
13 ***Fawell***	N	Y	Y
14 ***Hastert***	N	Y	Y
15 ***Madigan***	N	Y	Y
16 ***Martin***	N	Y	Y
17 Evans	Y	Y	Y
18 ***Michel***	N	Y	Y
19 Bruce	Y	Y	Y
20 Durbin	Y	Y	Y
21 Costello	Y	Y	Y
22 Poshard	Y	Y	Y
INDIANA			
1 Visclosky	Y	Y	N
2 Sharp	Y	Y	Y
3 ***Hiler***	N	Y	Y

ND Northern Democrats SD Southern Democrats

	388	389	391
4 Long	Y	Y	Y
5 Jontz	Y	Y	N
6 ***Burton***	N	Y	Y
7 ***Myers***	Y	Y	Y
8 McCloskey	Y	Y	Y
9 Hamilton	Y	Y	Y
10 Jacobs	N	Y	N
IOWA			
1 ***Leach***	N	Y	Y
2 ***Tauke***	N	Y	Y
3 Nagle	Y	Y	Y
4 Smith	Y	Y	Y
5 ***Lightfoot***	N	Y	Y
6 ***Grandy***	N	Y	Y
KANSAS			
1 ***Roberts***	N	Y	Y
2 Slattery	Y	Y	Y
3 ***Meyers***	N	Y	Y
4 Glickman	Y	Y	N
5 ***Whittaker***	N	Y	Y
KENTUCKY			
1 Hubbard	?	Y	Y
2 Natcher	Y	Y	Y
3 Mazzoli	Y	Y	Y
4 ***Bunning***	N	Y	Y
5 ***Rogers***	N	Y	Y
6 ***Hopkins***	N	Y	Y
7 Perkins	Y	Y	Y
LOUISIANA			
1 ***Livingston***	Y	Y	N
2 Boggs	Y	Y	Y
3 Tauzin	Y	Y	Y
4 ***McCrery***	?	Y	?
5 Huckaby	Y	Y	Y
6 ***Baker***	?	Y	Y
7 Hayes	Y	Y	Y
8 ***Holloway***	N	Y	Y
MAINE			
1 Brennan	Y	Y	Y
2 ***Snowe***	N	Y	Y
MARYLAND			
1 Dyson	Y	Y	Y
2 ***Bentley***	?	Y	Y
3 Cardin	Y	Y	Y
4 McMillen	Y	Y	Y
5 Hoyer	Y	Y	Y
6 Byron	Y	Y	Y
7 Mfume	?	Y	Y
8 ***Morella***	?	Y	Y
MASSACHUSETTS			
1 ***Conte***	Y	Y	Y
2 Neal	Y	Y	Y
3 Early	Y	Y	Y
4 Frank	Y	Y	Y
5 Atkins	Y	Y	Y
6 Mavroules	?	Y	Y
7 Markey	Y	Y	Y
8 Kennedy	Y	Y	Y
9 Moakley	Y	Y	Y
10 Studds	Y	Y	Y
11 Donnelly	Y	Y	Y
MICHIGAN			
1 Conyers	?	?	?
2 ***Pursell***	N	Y	Y
3 Wolpe	Y	Y	Y
4 ***Upton***	N	Y	Y
5 ***Henry***	N	Y	Y
6 Carr	Y	Y	Y
7 Kildee	Y	Y	Y
8 Traxler	Y	Y	Y
9 ***Vander Jagt***	?	Y	Y
10 ***Schuette***	?	?	?
11 ***Davis***	Y	Y	Y
12 Bonior	Y	Y	Y
13 Crockett	?	Y	?
14 Hertel	Y	Y	Y
15 Ford	?	Y	Y
16 Dingell	Y	Y	Y
17 Levin	Y	Y	Y
18 ***Broomfield***	Y	Y	Y
MINNESOTA			
1 Penny	Y	Y	N
2 ***Weber***	N	Y	Y
3 ***Frenzel***	?	Y	Y
4 Vento	Y	Y	Y

	388	389	391
5 Sabo	Y	Y	Y
6 Sikorski	N	Y	Y
7 ***Stangeland***	N	Y	Y
8 Oberstar	Y	Y	Y
MISSISSIPPI			
1 Whitten	Y	Y	Y
2 Espy	Y	Y	Y
3 Montgomery	Y	?	Y
4 Parker	Y	Y	?
5 Taylor	Y	Y	Y
MISSOURI			
1 Clay	?	Y	?
2 ***Buechner***	N	Y	Y
3 Gephardt	Y	Y	Y
4 Skelton	Y	Y	Y
5 Wheat	Y	Y	Y
6 ***Coleman***	N	Y	Y
7 ***Hancock***	N	Y	N
8 ***Emerson***	Y	Y	Y
9 Volkmer	Y	Y	Y
MONTANA			
1 Williams	?	Y	Y
2 ***Marlenee***	N	Y	Y
NEBRASKA			
1 ***Bereuter***	N	Y	Y
2 Hoagland	Y	Y	Y
3 ***Smith***	Y	Y	Y
NEVADA			
1 Bilbray	Y	Y	Y
2 ***Vucanovich***	N	Y	Y
NEW HAMPSHIRE			
1 ***Smith***	N	Y	Y
2 ***Douglas***	N	Y	Y
NEW JERSEY			
1 Vacancy			
2 Hughes	Y	Y	Y
3 Pallone	Y	Y	Y
4 ***Smith***	Y	Y	Y
5 ***Roukema***	N	Y	Y
6 Dwyer	Y	Y	Y
7 ***Rinaldo***	?	Y	Y
8 Roe	Y	Y	Y
9 Torricelli	Y	Y	Y
10 Payne	Y	Y	Y
11 ***Gallo***	Y	Y	Y
12 ***Courter***	N	Y	Y
13 ***Saxton***	N	Y	Y
14 Guarini	Y	Y	Y
NEW MEXICO			
1 ***Schiff***	Y	Y	Y
2 ***Skeen***	Y	Y	Y
3 Richardson	Y	Y	Y
NEW YORK			
1 Hochbrueckner	Y	Y	?
2 Downey	Y	Y	Y
3 Mrazek	?	Y	Y
4 ***Lent***	Y	Y	Y
5 ***McGrath***	?	?	?
6 Flake	?	Y	Y
7 Ackerman	Y	Y	Y
8 Scheuer	Y	Y	Y
9 Manton	Y	?	Y
10 Schumer	Y	Y	Y
11 Towns	?	Y	?
12 Owens	Y	Y	Y
13 Solarz	Y	Y	Y
14 ***Molinari***	N	Y	Y
15 ***Green***	Y	Y	Y
16 Rangel	Y	Y	Y
17 Weiss	Y	Y	Y
18 Serrano	Y	Y	Y
19 Engel	?	Y	Y
20 Lowey	Y	Y	Y
21 ***Fish***	Y	Y	Y
22 ***Gilman***	Y	Y	Y
23 McNulty	Y	Y	Y
24 ***Solomon***	N	Y	Y
25 ***Boehlert***	N	Y	Y
26 ***Martin***	N	?	Y
27 ***Walsh***	N	Y	Y
28 McHugh	Y	Y	Y
29 ***Horton***	Y	Y	Y
30 Slaughter	Y	Y	Y
31 ***Paxon***	N	Y	Y

	388	389	391
32 LaFalce	?	Y	Y
33 Nowak	Y	Y	Y
34 ***Houghton***	Y	Y	Y
NORTH CAROLINA			
1 Jones	Y	Y	Y
2 Valentine	Y	Y	Y
3 Lancaster	Y	Y	Y
4 Price	Y	Y	Y
5 Neal	?	Y	Y
6 ***Coble***	N	Y	N
7 Rose	?	Y	Y
8 Hefner	Y	Y	Y
9 ***McMillan***	N	Y	Y
10 ***Ballenger***	N	Y	N
11 Clarke	Y	Y	Y
NORTH DAKOTA			
AL Dorgan	Y	Y	N
OHIO			
1 Luken	Y	Y	?
2 ***Gradison***	Y	Y	Y
3 Hall	Y	Y	?
4 ***Oxley***	N	Y	Y
5 ***Gillmor***	Y	Y	Y
6 ***McEwen***	Y	Y	Y
7 ***DeWine***	Y	Y	Y
8 ***Lukens***	N	Y	Y
9 Kaptur	Y	Y	Y
10 ***Miller***	N	Y	Y
11 Eckart	Y	Y	Y
12 ***Kasich***	Y	Y	Y
13 Pease	Y	Y	Y
14 Sawyer	Y	Y	Y
15 ***Wylie***	Y	Y	Y
16 ***Regula***	N	Y	Y
17 Traficant	Y	Y	Y
18 Applegate	Y	Y	Y
19 Feighan	Y	Y	Y
20 Oakar	Y	Y	Y
21 Stokes	Y	Y	Y
OKLAHOMA			
1 ***Inhofe***	N	Y	Y
2 Synar	Y	Y	Y
3 Watkins	Y	Y	Y
4 McCurdy	Y	Y	Y
5 ***Edwards***	?	Y	Y
6 English	Y	Y	Y
OREGON			
1 AuCoin	Y	Y	Y
2 ***Smith, B.***	N	Y	Y
3 Wyden	Y	Y	Y
4 DeFazio	Y	Y	Y
5 ***Smith, D.***	N	Y	Y
PENNSYLVANIA			
1 Foglietta	Y	Y	Y
2 Gray	Y	Y	Y
3 Borski	?	Y	Y
4 Kolter	Y	Y	Y
5 ***Schulze***	Y	Y	Y
6 Yatron	Y	Y	Y
7 ***Weldon***	N	Y	Y
8 Kostmayer	Y	Y	Y
9 ***Shuster***	Y	Y	Y
10 ***McDade***	Y	Y	Y
11 Kanjorski	Y	Y	Y
12 Murtha	Y	Y	Y
13 ***Coughlin***	N	Y	Y
14 Coyne	Y	Y	Y
15 ***Ritter***	Y	Y	Y
16 ***Walker***	N	Y	Y
17 ***Gekas***	N	Y	N
18 Walgren	Y	Y	Y
19 ***Goodling***	?	Y	Y
20 Gaydos	?	Y	Y
21 ***Ridge***	N	Y	Y
22 Murphy	N	Y	N
23 ***Clinger***	Y	Y	Y
RHODE ISLAND			
1 ***Machtley***	N	Y	?
2 ***Schneider***	Y	Y	Y
SOUTH CAROLINA			
1 ***Ravenel***	Y	Y	Y
2 ***Spence***	N	Y	Y
3 Derrick	Y	Y	Y
4 Patterson	Y	Y	Y
5 Spratt	Y	Y	Y
6 Tallon	Y	Y	Y

	388	389	391
SOUTH DAKOTA			
AL Johnson	Y	Y	Y
TENNESSEE			
1 ***Quillen***	N	Y	Y
2 ***Duncan***	N	Y	N
3 Lloyd	Y	Y	Y
4 Cooper	Y	Y	Y
5 Clement	Y	Y	Y
6 Gordon	Y	Y	Y
7 ***Sundquist***	N	Y	N
8 Tanner	Y	Y	Y
9 Ford	?	?	?
TEXAS			
1 Chapman	?	Y	Y
2 Wilson	Y	Y	Y
3 ***Bartlett***	Y	Y	Y
4 Hall	Y	Y	Y
5 Bryant	Y	Y	Y
6 ***Barton***	?	Y	Y
7 ***Archer***	Y	Y	Y
8 ***Fields***	N	Y	Y
9 Brooks	Y	Y	Y
10 Pickle	Y	Y	Y
11 Leath	?	Y	Y
12 Geren	Y	Y	Y
13 Sarpalius	?	Y	Y
14 Laughlin	Y	Y	Y
15 de la Garza	Y	Y	Y
16 Coleman	Y	Y	Y
17 Stenholm	Y	Y	Y
18 Washington	?	Y	Y
19 ***Combest***	Y	Y	Y
20 Gonzalez	Y	Y	Y
21 ***Smith***	N	Y	Y
22 ***DeLay***	?	Y	Y
23 Bustamante	Y	Y	Y
24 Frost	Y	Y	Y
25 Andrews	Y	Y	Y
26 ***Armey***	N	Y	N
27 Ortiz	Y	Y	Y
UTAH			
1 ***Hansen***	N	Y	Y
2 Owens	Y	Y	Y
3 ***Nielson***	Y	Y	Y
VERMONT			
AL ***Smith***	N	Y	Y
VIRGINIA			
1 ***Bateman***	Y	Y	Y
2 Pickett	Y	Y	Y
3 ***Bliley***	N	Y	Y
4 Sisisky	Y	Y	Y
5 Payne	Y	Y	Y
6 Olin	Y	Y	Y
7 ***Slaughter***	Y	Y	Y
8 ***Parris***	N	?	Y
9 Boucher	Y	Y	Y
10 ***Wolf***	N	Y	Y
WASHINGTON			
1 ***Miller***	N	Y	Y
2 Swift	Y	+	Y
3 Unsoeld	Y	Y	Y
4 ***Morrison***	Y	Y	Y
5 Foley			
6 Dicks	Y	Y	Y
7 McDermott	Y	Y	Y
8 ***Chandler***	N	Y	Y
WEST VIRGINIA			
1 Mollohan	Y	Y	Y
2 Staggers	Y	?	Y
3 Wise	Y	Y	Y
4 Rahall	Y	Y	Y
WISCONSIN			
1 Aspin	Y	Y	Y
2 Kastenmeier	Y	Y	Y
3 ***Gunderson***	Y	Y	Y
4 Kleczka	Y	Y	Y
5 Moody	Y	Y	Y
6 ***Petri***	Y	Y	N
7 Obey	Y	Y	N
8 ***Roth***	N	Y	Y
9 ***Sensenbrenner***	N	Y	N
WYOMING			
AL ***Thomas***	N	Y	Y

Southern states - Ala., Ark., Fla., Ga., Ky., La., Miss., N.C., Okla., S.C., Tenn., Texas, Va.
Omitted votes are quorum calls, which CQ does not include in its vote charts.

392. Procedural Motion. Sensenbrenner, R-Wis., motion to approve the House Journal of Thursday, Sept. 27. Motion agreed to 239-83: R 43-78; D 196-5 (ND 133-5, SD 63-0), Sept. 28, 1990.

393. H J Res 655. Fiscal 1991 Continuing Appropriations/Passage. Passage of the joint resolution to provide continuing appropriations for fiscal 1991 from Oct. 1 to Oct. 5 for the departments, agencies and programs covered by the 13 regular appropriations bills at funding levels based on each bill's legislative status as of Oct. 1, 1990. The resolution also suspends until Oct. 5 sequestration (automatic budget cuts) required by the Gramm-Rudman antideficit law and provides $2 billion for Operation Desert Shield in the Persian Gulf. Passed 382-41: R 136-37; D 246-4 (ND 165-3, SD 81-1), Sept. 30, 1990.

394. H J Res 658. Persian Gulf Resolution/Passage. Fascell, D-Fla., motion to suspend the rules and pass the joint resolution to express support for the president's deployment of U.S. troops to the Persian Gulf in response to the Iraqi invasion of Kuwait. The resolution emphasizes the continued use of diplomatic and other non-military means to achieve U.S. objectives. The measure does not authorize the deployment of U.S. troops into combat. Motion agreed to 380-29: R 164-0; D 216-29 (ND 138-26, SD 78-3), Oct. 1, 1990. A two-thirds majority of those present and voting (273 in this case) is required for passage under suspension of the rules.

395. H J Res 418. Treaty to Protect Antarctica Resolution/Passage. Yatron, D-Pa., motion to suspend the rules and pass the joint resolution to express support for a comprehensive agreement, treaty or protocol establishing Antarctica as a region closed to commercial mineral development and related activities. Motion agreed to 398-11: R 154-10; D 244-1 (ND 164-0, SD 80-1), Oct. 1, 1990. A two-thirds majority of those present and voting (273 in this case) is required for passage under suspension of the rules. A "yea" was a vote supporting the president's position.

396. H Con Res 329. Sanctions Against Commercial Whaling Resolution/Adoption. Yatron, D-Pa., motion to suspend the rules and adopt the concurrent resolution to express the sense of Congress that the president should use current authority to order an embargo on fishery products entering the United States from nations that violate the International Whaling Commission moratorium on commercial whaling. Motion agreed to 412-0: R 166-0; D 246-0 (ND 164-0, SD 82-0), Oct. 1, 1990. A two-thirds majority of those present and voting (275 in this case) is required for passage under suspension of the rules.

397. HR 3954. Peace Corps Memorial/Passage. Fascell, D-Fla., motion to suspend the rules and pass the bill to authorize the establishment of a seven-member commission to solicit private contributions and conduct other activities to provide for the construction of a Peace Corps Volunteers memorial on federal land in the District of Columbia to honor service in the Peace Corps. Motion agreed to 409-0: R 165-0; D 244-0 (ND 164-0, SD 80-0), Oct. 1, 1990. A two-thirds majority of those present and voting (273 in this case) is required for passage under suspension of the rules.

398. HR 4300. Legal Immigration Revision/Rule. Adoption of the rule (H Res 484) to provide for House floor consideration of the bill to increase the number of visas for those coming to the United States to join families or to work; suspend deportation for the spouses and children of newly legalized aliens; establish "diversity" visas for immigrants from countries that currently account for a low number of immigrants to the United States. Adopted 245-165: R 16-152; D 229-13 (ND 159-5, SD 70-8), Oct. 2, 1990.

399. HR 4300. Legal Immigration Revision/Limits. Smith, R-Texas, amendment to limit legal immigrants to 630,000 per year, including all family and worker immigrants. Rejected 143-266: R 104-56; D 39-210 (ND 8-160, SD 31-50), Oct. 2, 1990.

KEY

Y Voted for (yea).
\# Paired for.
\+ Announced for.
N Voted against (nay).
X Paired against.
\- Announced against.
P Voted "present."
C Voted "present" to avoid possible conflict of interest.
? Did not vote or otherwise make a position known.

Democrats *Republicans*

	392	393	394	395	396	397	398	399
ALABAMA								
1 *Callahan*	?	Y	Y	Y	Y	Y	Y	#
2 *Dickinson*	N	Y	Y	Y	Y	Y	N	Y
3 Browder	Y	Y	Y	Y	Y	Y	Y	Y
4 Bevill	Y	Y	Y	Y	Y	Y	Y	Y
5 Flippo	Y	Y	Y	Y	Y	Y	Y	Y
6 Erdreich	Y	Y	Y	Y	Y	Y	Y	Y
7 Harris	Y	Y	Y	Y	Y	Y	Y	Y
ALASKA								
AL *Young*	N	Y	Y	Y	Y	Y	Y	Y
ARIZONA								
1 *Rhodes*	N	Y	Y	Y	Y	Y	N	?
2 Udall	?	Y	Y	Y	Y	Y	Y	N
3 *Stump*	N	N	Y	N	Y	Y	N	Y
4 *Kyl*	?	Y	Y	Y	Y	Y	N	Y
5 *Kolbe*	N	Y	Y	Y	Y	Y	N	N
ARKANSAS								
1 Alexander	?	Y	?	?	Y	Y	Y	Y
2 *Robinson*	?	Y	Y	Y	Y	Y	N	Y
3 *Hammerschmidt*	Y	Y	Y	N	Y	Y	N	N
4 Anthony	?	Y	Y	Y	Y	Y	Y	N
CALIFORNIA								
1 Bosco	Y	Y	Y	Y	Y	Y	Y	N
2 *Herger*	N	N	Y	Y	Y	Y	N	Y
3 Matsui	Y	Y	Y	Y	Y	Y	Y	N
4 Fazio	Y	Y	Y	Y	Y	Y	Y	N
5 Pelosi	?	Y	N	Y	Y	Y	Y	N
6 Boxer	Y	Y	Y	Y	Y	Y	Y	N
7 Miller	Y	Y	N	Y	Y	Y	Y	?
8 Dellums	Y	Y	N	Y	Y	Y	?	N
9 Stark	Y	Y	N	Y	Y	Y	Y	N
10 Edwards	Y	Y	N	Y	Y	Y	Y	N
11 Lantos	Y	Y	Y	Y	Y	Y	Y	N
12 *Campbell*	N	Y	Y	Y	Y	Y	N	N
13 Mineta	Y	Y	Y	Y	Y	Y	Y	N
14 *Shumway*	?	N	Y	Y	Y	Y	N	N
15 Condit	Y	Y	Y	Y	Y	Y	Y	N
16 Panetta	Y	Y	Y	Y	Y	Y	Y	N
17 *Pashayan*	?	Y	Y	Y	Y	Y	N	N
18 Lehman	Y	Y	Y	Y	Y	Y	Y	N
19 *Lagomarsino*	N	Y	Y	Y	Y	Y	N	Y
20 *Thomas*	?	N	Y	Y	Y	Y	N	?
21 *Gallegly*	?	Y	Y	Y	Y	Y	N	Y
22 *Moorhead*	N	Y	Y	Y	Y	Y	N	Y
23 Beilenson	Y	Y	Y	Y	Y	Y	Y	Y
24 Waxman	Y	Y	Y	Y	Y	Y	Y	N
25 Roybal	?	Y	N	Y	Y	Y	Y	N
26 Berman	Y	Y	Y	Y	Y	Y	Y	N
27 Levine	Y	Y	Y	Y	Y	Y	Y	N
28 Dixon	Y	Y	Y	Y	Y	Y	Y	N
29 Hawkins	?	Y	?	?	?	?	Y	?
30 Martinez	?	?	Y	Y	Y	Y	Y	N
31 Dymally	Y	Y	Y	Y	Y	Y	Y	N
32 Anderson	Y	Y	Y	Y	Y	Y	Y	N
33 *Dreier*	N	N	Y	Y	Y	Y	N	N
34 Torres	Y	Y	N	Y	Y	Y	Y	N
35 *Lewis*	N	Y	Y	Y	Y	Y	N	Y
36 Brown	Y	Y	Y	Y	Y	Y	Y	N
37 *McCandless*	?	Y	Y	Y	Y	Y	N	Y
38 *Dornan*	?	N	Y	Y	Y	Y	N	N
39 *Dannemeyer*	N	N	Y	N	Y	Y	N	Y
40 *Cox*	N	N	Y	Y	Y	Y	?	N
41 *Lowery*	N	Y	Y	Y	Y	Y	N	Y
42 *Rohrabacher*	N	N	Y	Y	Y	Y	N	N
43 *Packard*	Y	N	Y	Y	Y	Y	N	Y
44 Bates	Y	Y	N	Y	Y	Y	Y	N
45 *Hunter*	N	Y	Y	Y	Y	Y	N	Y
COLORADO								
1 Schroeder	N	Y	N	Y	Y	Y	Y	N
2 Skaggs	Y	Y	Y	Y	Y	Y	Y	N
3 Campbell	Y	Y	Y	Y	Y	Y	Y	N
4 *Brown*	?	N	?	?	?	?	N	Y
5 *Hefley*	N	Y	Y	Y	Y	Y	N	Y
6 *Schaefer*	N	Y	Y	Y	Y	Y	N	Y
CONNECTICUT								
1 Kennelly	Y	Y	Y	Y	Y	Y	Y	N
2 Gejdenson	Y	Y	Y	Y	Y	Y	Y	N
3 Morrison	?	+	+	+	+	+	Y	N
4 *Shays*	N	Y	Y	Y	Y	Y	N	N
5 *Rowland*	?	?	?	?	?	?	?	?
6 *Johnson*	Y	Y	Y	Y	Y	Y	Y	N
DELAWARE								
AL Carper	Y	Y	Y	Y	Y	Y	Y	N
FLORIDA								
1 Hutto	Y	Y	Y	Y	Y	Y	N	N
2 *Grant*	Y	Y	Y	Y	Y	Y	N	N
3 Bennett	Y	Y	Y	Y	Y	Y	N	N
4 *James*	N	Y	Y	Y	Y	Y	N	Y
5 *McCollum*	?	Y	Y	Y	Y	Y	N	Y
6 *Stearns*	N	Y	Y	Y	Y	Y	N	Y
7 Gibbons	Y	Y	Y	Y	Y	Y	Y	N
8 *Young*	N	Y	Y	Y	Y	Y	N	Y
9 *Bilirakis*	N	Y	Y	Y	Y	Y	N	N
10 *Ireland*	N	Y	?	?	?	?	N	N
11 Nelson	+	Y	Y	Y	Y	Y	Y	N
12 *Lewis*	N	Y	Y	Y	Y	Y	X	Y
13 *Goss*	N	Y	Y	Y	Y	Y	N	Y
14 Johnston	?	Y	Y	Y	Y	Y	?	N
15 *Shaw*	Y	Y	Y	Y	Y	Y	N	Y
16 Smith	?	Y	Y	Y	Y	Y	Y	N
17 Lehman	?	Y	N	Y	Y	Y	Y	N
18 *Ros-Lehtinen*	?	Y	Y	Y	Y	Y	Y	N
19 Fascell	Y	Y	Y	Y	Y	Y	Y	N
GEORGIA								
1 Thomas	Y	Y	Y	Y	Y	Y	Y	Y
2 Hatcher	Y	Y	?	?	?	?	Y	N
3 Ray	Y	Y	Y	Y	Y	?	Y	Y
4 Jones	?	Y	Y	Y	Y	Y	Y	N
5 Lewis	Y	Y	Y	Y	Y	Y	Y	N
6 *Gingrich*	N	Y	?	?	?	?	N	N
7 Darden	Y	Y	Y	Y	Y	Y	Y	N
8 Rowland	Y	Y	Y	Y	Y	Y	Y	Y
9 Jenkins	Y	Y	Y	Y	Y	Y	Y	Y
10 Barnard	?	Y	Y	Y	Y	Y	N	Y
HAWAII								
1 *Saiki*	?	Y	?	?	?	?	?	X
2 Mink	Y	Y	Y	Y	Y	Y	Y	N
IDAHO								
1 *Craig*	N	Y	Y	Y	Y	Y	N	N
2 Stallings	Y	Y	Y	Y	Y	Y	N	N
ILLINOIS								
1 Hayes	Y	Y	N	Y	Y	Y	Y	N
2 Savage	Y	Y	N	Y	Y	Y	Y	N
3 Russo	Y	Y	Y	Y	Y	Y	Y	N
4 Sangmeister	Y	N	Y	Y	Y	Y	Y	N
5 Lipinski	?	Y	Y	Y	Y	Y	Y	N
6 *Hyde*	?	Y	Y	Y	Y	Y	N	N
7 Collins	Y	Y	N	Y	Y	Y	Y	N
8 Rostenkowski	?	Y	Y	Y	Y	Y	Y	N
9 Yates	Y	Y	N	Y	Y	Y	Y	N
10 *Porter*	Y	N	Y	Y	Y	Y	N	N
11 Annunzio	Y	Y	Y	Y	Y	Y	Y	N
12 *Crane*	?	N	?	?	?	?	N	Y
13 *Fawell*	N	N	Y	Y	Y	Y	N	Y
14 *Hastert*	N	Y	Y	Y	Y	Y	N	?
15 *Madigan*	N	Y	Y	Y	Y	Y	N	N
16 *Martin*	?	?	Y	Y	Y	Y	Y	?
17 Evans	Y	Y	Y	Y	Y	Y	Y	N
18 *Michel*	Y	Y	?	?	Y	Y	N	?
19 Bruce	Y	Y	Y	Y	Y	Y	Y	N
20 Durbin	Y	Y	Y	Y	Y	Y	Y	N
21 Costello	Y	Y	Y	Y	Y	Y	Y	N
22 Poshard	Y	Y	Y	Y	Y	Y	Y	N
INDIANA								
1 Visclosky	Y	Y	Y	Y	Y	Y	Y	N
2 Sharp	Y	Y	Y	Y	Y	Y	Y	N
3 *Hiler*	?	Y	?	?	?	?	N	Y

ND Northern Democrats SD Southern Democrats

	392	393	394	395	396	397	398	399
4 Long	Y	Y	Y	Y	Y	Y	Y	N
5 Jontz	Y	Y	Y	Y	Y	Y	Y	N
6 ***Burton***	N	N	Y	Y	Y	Y	N	Y
7 ***Myers***	Y	Y	Y	Y	Y	Y	?	?
8 McCloskey	Y	Y	Y	Y	Y	Y	Y	N
9 Hamilton	Y	Y	Y	Y	Y	Y	Y	N
10 Jacobs	N	Y	N	Y	Y	Y	N	N
IOWA								
1 ***Leach***	N	Y	Y	Y	Y	Y	N	N
2 ***Tauke***	?	Y	Y	Y	Y	Y	N	N
3 Nagle	Y	Y	Y	Y	Y	Y	Y	N
4 Smith	Y	Y	Y	Y	Y	Y	Y	N
5 ***Lightfoot***	?	N	Y	N	Y	Y	N	Y
6 ***Grandy***	N	Y	Y	Y	Y	Y	N	Y
KANSAS								
1 ***Roberts***	?	Y	Y	Y	Y	Y	N	Y
2 Slattery	Y	Y	Y	Y	Y	Y	N	N
3 ***Meyers***	N	Y	Y	Y	Y	Y	N	Y
4 Glickman	Y	Y	Y	Y	Y	Y	Y	N
5 ***Whittaker***	?	Y	Y	Y	Y	Y	N	Y
KENTUCKY								
1 Hubbard	Y	Y	Y	Y	Y	Y	N	Y
2 Natcher	Y	Y	Y	Y	Y	Y	Y	N
3 Mazzoli	Y	Y	Y	Y	Y	Y	Y	N
4 ***Bunning***	N	Y	Y	Y	Y	Y	N	Y
5 ***Rogers***	N	Y	Y	Y	Y	Y	N	Y
6 ***Hopkins***	N	Y	Y	Y	Y	Y	N	Y
7 Perkins	Y	Y	Y	Y	Y	Y	Y	Y
LOUISIANA								
1 ***Livingston***	Y	Y	Y	Y	Y	Y	N	Y
2 Boggs	Y	Y	Y	Y	Y	Y	?	?
3 Tauzin	?	Y	Y	Y	Y	Y	N	N
4 ***McCrery***	?	Y	Y	Y	Y	Y	N	?
5 Huckaby	Y	Y	Y	Y	Y	Y	Y	Y
6 ***Baker***	?	N	Y	Y	Y	Y	N	Y
7 Hayes	Y	Y	Y	Y	Y	Y	Y	Y
8 ***Holloway***	?	N	Y	Y	Y	Y	N	Y
MAINE								
1 Brennan	Y	Y	Y	Y	Y	Y	Y	N
2 ***Snowe***	Y	Y	Y	Y	Y	Y	N	N
MARYLAND								
1 Dyson	Y	Y	Y	Y	Y	Y	Y	Y
2 ***Bentley***	?	Y	Y	Y	Y	Y	N	Y
3 Cardin	Y	Y	Y	Y	Y	Y	Y	N
4 McMillen	Y	Y	Y	Y	Y	Y	Y	N
5 Hoyer	Y	Y	Y	Y	Y	Y	Y	N
6 Byron	Y	Y	Y	Y	Y	Y	Y	N
7 Mfume	?	Y	N	Y	Y	Y	Y	N
8 ***Morella***	Y	Y	Y	Y	Y	Y	N	N
MASSACHUSETTS								
1 ***Conte***	Y	Y	Y	Y	Y	Y	Y	N
2 Neal	Y	Y	Y	Y	Y	Y	?	N
3 Early	?	Y	Y	Y	Y	Y	Y	N
4 Frank	Y	Y	Y	Y	Y	Y	Y	N
5 Atkins	Y	Y	Y	Y	Y	Y	Y	N
6 Mavroules	?	Y	Y	Y	Y	Y	Y	?
7 Markey	?	Y	Y	Y	Y	Y	Y	N
8 Kennedy	?	Y	Y	Y	Y	Y	?	N
9 Moakley	Y	Y	Y	Y	Y	Y	Y	N
10 Studds	Y	Y	Y	Y	Y	Y	Y	N
11 Donnelly	Y	Y	Y	Y	Y	Y	Y	N
MICHIGAN								
1 Conyers	?	Y	N	Y	Y	Y	Y	N
2 ***Pursell***	Y	N	Y	Y	Y	Y	N	?
3 Wolpe	Y	Y	Y	Y	Y	Y	Y	N
4 ***Upton***	N	N	Y	Y	Y	Y	N	N
5 ***Henry***	?	N	Y	Y	Y	Y	N	Y
6 Carr	Y	Y	Y	Y	Y	Y	Y	N
7 Kildee	Y	Y	Y	Y	Y	Y	Y	N
8 Traxler	Y	Y	N	Y	Y	Y	Y	Y
9 ***Vander Jagt***	?	Y	Y	Y	Y	Y	N	Y
10 ***Schuette***	?	Y	?	?	?	?	N	?
11 ***Davis***	Y	Y	Y	Y	Y	Y	Y	N
12 Bonior	Y	Y	Y	Y	Y	Y	Y	N
13 Crockett	?	?	?	?	?	?	?	N
14 Hertel	Y	Y	Y	Y	Y	Y	Y	N
15 Ford	Y	Y	Y	Y	Y	Y	Y	N
16 Dingell	Y	Y	Y	Y	Y	Y	Y	N
17 Levin	Y	Y	Y	Y	Y	Y	Y	N
18 ***Broomfield***	?	Y	Y	Y	Y	Y	N	Y
MINNESOTA								
1 Penny	Y	N	Y	Y	Y	Y	N	N
2 ***Weber***	N	Y	Y	Y	Y	Y	Y	N
3 ***Frenzel***	?	N	?	?	?	?	N	Y
4 Vento	Y	Y	Y	Y	Y	Y	Y	N

	392	393	394	395	396	397	398	399
5 Sabo	Y	Y	Y	Y	Y	Y	Y	N
6 Sikorski	N	Y	Y	Y	Y	Y	Y	N
7 ***Stangeland***	?	Y	Y	Y	Y	Y	N	N
8 Oberstar	Y	Y	Y	Y	Y	Y	Y	N
MISSISSIPPI								
1 Whitten	Y	Y	Y	Y	Y	Y	?	N
2 Espy	Y	Y	Y	Y	Y	Y	Y	N
3 Montgomery	?	Y	Y	Y	Y	Y	Y	Y
4 Parker	?	N	Y	Y	Y	Y	Y	N
5 Taylor	Y	Y	Y	Y	Y	Y	N	Y
MISSOURI								
1 Clay	?	Y	N	Y	Y	Y	Y	N
2 ***Buechner***	N	Y	Y	Y	Y	Y	N	Y
3 Gephardt	Y	Y	Y	?	?	?	Y	N
4 Skelton	Y	Y	Y	Y	Y	Y	Y	N
5 Wheat	?	Y	Y	Y	Y	Y	Y	N
6 ***Coleman***	Y	Y	Y	Y	Y	Y	N	Y
7 ***Hancock***	N	N	Y	N	Y	Y	N	Y
8 ***Emerson***	Y	Y	Y	Y	Y	Y	N	Y
9 Volkmer	N	Y	Y	Y	Y	Y	Y	Y
MONTANA								
1 Williams	?	Y	P	Y	Y	Y	Y	N
2 ***Marlenee***	?	N	Y	N	Y	Y	N	Y
NEBRASKA								
1 ***Bereuter***	N	Y	Y	Y	Y	Y	N	Y
2 Hoagland	Y	Y	Y	Y	Y	Y	Y	Y
3 ***Smith***	Y	Y	Y	Y	Y	Y	N	Y
NEVADA								
1 Bilbray	Y	Y	Y	Y	Y	Y	Y	N
2 ***Vucanovich***	N	Y	Y	N	Y	Y	N	Y
NEW HAMPSHIRE								
1 ***Smith***	N	N	Y	Y	Y	Y	N	Y
2 ***Douglas***	?	N	?	?	Y	Y	N	Y
NEW JERSEY								
1 Vacancy								
2 Hughes	Y	Y	Y	Y	Y	Y	N	N
3 Pallone	Y	Y	Y	Y	Y	Y	Y	N
4 ***Smith***	?	Y	Y	Y	Y	Y	N	N
5 ***Roukema***	N	Y	Y	Y	Y	Y	N	Y
6 Dwyer	?	Y	Y	Y	Y	Y	Y	N
7 ***Rinaldo***	Y	Y	Y	Y	Y	Y	N	Y
8 Roe	Y	Y	Y	Y	Y	Y	Y	N
9 Torricelli	Y	Y	?	?	?	?	Y	N
10 Payne	Y	Y	N	Y	Y	Y	Y	N
11 ***Gallo***	N	Y	Y	Y	Y	Y	N	Y
12 ***Courter***	?	Y	Y	Y	Y	Y	N	N
13 ***Saxton***	N	Y	Y	Y	Y	Y	N	Y
14 Guarini	Y	Y	Y	Y	Y	Y	Y	N
NEW MEXICO								
1 ***Schiff***	?	Y	Y	Y	Y	Y	N	?
2 ***Skeen***	Y	Y	Y	Y	Y	Y	Y	Y
3 Richardson	?	Y	Y	Y	Y	Y	Y	N
NEW YORK								
1 Hochbrueckner	Y	Y	Y	Y	Y	Y	Y	N
2 Downey	Y	Y	Y	Y	Y	Y	?	N
3 Mrazek	Y	Y	Y	Y	Y	Y	Y	N
4 ***Lent***	Y	Y	Y	Y	Y	Y	N	N
5 ***McGrath***	?	?	Y	Y	Y	Y	Y	N
6 Flake	Y	Y	Y	Y	Y	Y	Y	N
7 Ackerman	?	Y	Y	Y	Y	Y	Y	N
8 Scheuer	Y	Y	Y	Y	Y	Y	Y	N
9 Manton	Y	Y	Y	Y	Y	Y	Y	N
10 Schumer	Y	Y	Y	Y	Y	Y	Y	N
11 Towns	Y	Y	?	?	?	?	?	?
12 Owens	Y	Y	?	?	?	?	?	?
13 Solarz	Y	Y	?	?	?	?	Y	N
14 ***Molinari***	?	Y	Y	Y	Y	Y	Y	N
15 ***Green***	?	Y	Y	Y	Y	Y	N	N
16 Rangel	?	Y	N	Y	Y	Y	?	N
17 Weiss	Y	Y	Y	Y	Y	Y	Y	N
18 Serrano	Y	Y	N	Y	Y	Y	Y	N
19 Engel	?	+	+	+	+	+	#	—
20 Lowey	?	Y	Y	Y	Y	Y	Y	N
21 ***Fish***	Y	Y	Y	Y	Y	Y	?	N
22 ***Gilman***	Y	Y	Y	Y	Y	Y	Y	N
23 McNulty	Y	Y	Y	Y	Y	Y	+	N
24 ***Solomon***	N	Y	Y	Y	Y	Y	N	Y
25 ***Boehlert***	N	Y	Y	Y	Y	Y	N	N
26 ***Martin***	?	Y	Y	Y	Y	Y	N	Y
27 ***Walsh***	?	N	Y	Y	Y	Y	N	N
28 McHugh	Y	Y	Y	Y	Y	Y	Y	N
29 ***Horton***	Y	Y	Y	Y	Y	Y	N	N
30 Slaughter	Y	Y	Y	Y	Y	Y	Y	N
31 ***Paxon***	N	Y	Y	Y	Y	Y	N	N

	392	393	394	395	396	397	398	399
32 LaFalce	?	?	Y	Y	Y	Y	Y	N
33 Nowak	?	Y	Y	Y	Y	Y	Y	N
34 ***Houghton***	Y	Y	+	+	+	+	N	Y
NORTH CAROLINA								
1 Jones	Y	?	Y	Y	Y	Y	Y	N
2 Valentine	Y	Y	Y	Y	Y	Y	Y	N
3 Lancaster	Y	Y	Y	Y	Y	Y	Y	Y
4 Price	?	Y	Y	Y	Y	Y	Y	N
5 Neal	Y	Y	Y	Y	Y	Y	?	N
6 ***Coble***	N	Y	Y	Y	Y	Y	N	Y
7 Rose	?	Y	Y	Y	Y	Y	Y	N
8 Hefner	Y	Y	Y	Y	Y	Y	Y	N
9 ***McMillan***	Y	Y	Y	Y	Y	Y	N	Y
10 ***Ballenger***	N	Y	Y	Y	Y	Y	N	Y
11 Clarke	Y	Y	Y	Y	Y	Y	Y	N
NORTH DAKOTA								
AL Dorgan	Y	Y	Y	Y	Y	Y	Y	Y
OHIO								
1 Luken	?	Y	Y	Y	Y	Y	Y	N
2 ***Gradison***	Y	Y	Y	Y	Y	Y	Y	N
3 Hall	?	Y	Y	Y	Y	Y	Y	N
4 ***Oxley***	Y	Y	Y	Y	Y	Y	N	N
5 ***Gillmor***	Y	Y	Y	Y	Y	Y	N	?
6 ***McEwen***	?	Y	Y	Y	Y	Y	N	N
7 ***DeWine***	N	Y	Y	Y	Y	Y	?	N
8 ***Lukens***	N	Y	Y	Y	Y	Y	N	Y
9 Kaptur	Y	Y	Y	Y	Y	Y	Y	N
10 ***Miller***	N	Y	Y	Y	Y	Y	N	Y
11 Eckart	?	Y	Y	Y	Y	Y	Y	N
12 ***Kasich***	Y	Y	Y	Y	Y	Y	N	Y
13 Pease	Y	N	Y	Y	Y	Y	Y	N
14 Sawyer	Y	Y	Y	Y	Y	Y	Y	N
15 ***Wylie***	Y	Y	Y	Y	Y	Y	N	Y
16 ***Regula***	N	Y	Y	Y	Y	Y	?	Y
17 Traficant	Y	Y	Y	Y	Y	Y	Y	N
18 Applegate	Y	Y	Y	Y	Y	Y	Y	Y
19 Feighan	Y	Y	Y	Y	Y	Y	Y	N
20 Oakar	?	Y	Y	Y	Y	Y	Y	N
21 Stokes	?	Y	N	Y	Y	Y	Y	N
OKLAHOMA								
1 ***Inhofe***	N	Y	Y	Y	Y	Y	N	Y
2 Synar	Y	Y	Y	Y	Y	Y	Y	N
3 Watkins	?	Y	Y	Y	Y	Y	Y	Y
4 McCurdy	Y	Y	Y	Y	Y	Y	Y	Y
5 ***Edwards***	?	Y	Y	Y	Y	Y	?	Y
6 English	Y	Y	Y	Y	Y	Y	Y	Y
OREGON								
1 AuCoin	Y	Y	N	Y	Y	Y	Y	N
2 ***Smith, B.***	N	N	Y	Y	Y	Y	N	Y
3 Wyden	Y	Y	Y	Y	Y	Y	Y	N
4 DeFazio	Y	Y	N	Y	Y	Y	Y	N
5 ***Smith, D.***	N	N	Y	Y	Y	Y	N	Y
PENNSYLVANIA								
1 Foglietta	Y	Y	Y	Y	Y	Y	Y	N
2 Gray	?	Y	Y	Y	Y	Y	Y	N
3 Borski	Y	Y	?	?	?	?	Y	N
4 Kolter	Y	Y	Y	Y	Y	Y	Y	N
5 ***Schulze***	?	N	Y	Y	Y	Y	N	Y
6 Yatron	Y	Y	Y	Y	Y	Y	Y	N
7 ***Weldon***	N	Y	Y	Y	Y	Y	N	Y
8 Kostmayer	Y	Y	Y	Y	Y	Y	Y	N
9 ***Shuster***	Y	Y	Y	Y	Y	Y	N	Y
10 ***McDade***	Y	Y	Y	Y	Y	Y	Y	?
11 Kanjorski	Y	Y	Y	Y	Y	Y	Y	N
12 Murtha	Y	Y	Y	Y	Y	Y	Y	N
13 ***Coughlin***	N	Y	Y	Y	Y	Y	N	Y
14 Coyne	?	Y	Y	Y	Y	Y	Y	N
15 ***Ritter***	?	Y	Y	Y	Y	Y	N	Y
16 ***Walker***	N	Y	Y	Y	Y	Y	N	Y
17 ***Gekas***	N	Y	Y	Y	Y	Y	N	Y
18 Walgren	Y	Y	Y	Y	Y	Y	Y	N
19 ***Goodling***	N	Y	Y	Y	Y	Y	N	Y
20 Gaydos	?	Y	Y	Y	Y	Y	Y	N
21 ***Ridge***	?	Y	Y	Y	Y	Y	N	Y
22 Murphy	N	Y	Y	Y	Y	Y	Y	N
23 ***Clinger***	Y	Y	Y	Y	Y	Y	N	Y
RHODE ISLAND								
1 ***Machtley***	N	Y	Y	Y	Y	Y	N	N
2 ***Schneider***	?	Y	Y	Y	Y	Y	N	N
SOUTH CAROLINA								
1 ***Ravenel***	Y	Y	Y	Y	Y	Y	N	Y
2 ***Spence***	N	Y	Y	Y	Y	Y	N	Y
3 Derrick	Y	Y	Y	Y	Y	Y	Y	N
4 Patterson	Y	Y	Y	Y	Y	Y	Y	N
5 Spratt	Y	Y	Y	Y	Y	Y	Y	N
6 Tallon	Y	Y	Y	Y	Y	Y	Y	Y

	392	393	394	395	396	397	398	399
SOUTH DAKOTA								
AL Johnson	Y	Y	Y	Y	Y	Y	Y	Y
TENNESSEE								
1 ***Quillen***	?	Y	Y	Y	Y	Y	N	Y
2 ***Duncan***	N	Y	Y	Y	Y	Y	N	Y
3 Lloyd	Y	Y	Y	Y	Y	Y	Y	N
4 Cooper	Y	Y	Y	Y	Y	Y	Y	N
5 Clement	Y	Y	Y	Y	Y	Y	Y	N
6 Gordon	Y	Y	Y	Y	Y	Y	Y	N
7 ***Sundquist***	N	Y	Y	Y	Y	Y	N	Y
8 Tanner	Y	Y	Y	Y	Y	Y	Y	N
9 Ford	?	Y	Y	Y	Y	?	Y	?
TEXAS								
1 Chapman	Y	Y	Y	Y	Y	Y	Y	Y
2 Wilson	?	Y	Y	Y	Y	Y	N	Y
3 ***Bartlett***	?	N	Y	Y	Y	Y	N	N
4 Hall	?	Y	Y	N	Y	Y	N	Y
5 Bryant	?	Y	Y	Y	Y	Y	Y	Y
6 ***Barton***	?	N	Y	Y	Y	Y	N	N
7 ***Archer***	Y	Y	Y	Y	Y	Y	N	Y
8 ***Fields***	?	Y	Y	N	Y	Y	N	Y
9 Brooks	Y	Y	Y	Y	Y	Y	Y	N
10 Pickle	Y	Y	Y	Y	Y	Y	Y	N
11 Leath	Y	Y	Y	Y	Y	Y	Y	Y
12 Geren	Y	Y	Y	Y	Y	Y	Y	N
13 Sarpalius	Y	Y	Y	Y	Y	Y	Y	Y
14 Laughlin	Y	Y	Y	Y	Y	Y	Y	N
15 de la Garza	Y	Y	Y	Y	Y	Y	Y	N
16 Coleman	Y	Y	Y	Y	Y	Y	Y	N
17 Stenholm	Y	Y	Y	Y	Y	Y	Y	Y
18 Washington	Y	Y	N	Y	Y	Y	?	N
19 ***Combest***	Y	Y	Y	Y	Y	Y	N	Y
20 Gonzalez	Y	Y	N	Y	Y	Y	Y	N
21 ***Smith***	?	Y	Y	Y	Y	Y	N	Y
22 ***DeLay***	?	N	Y	N	Y	Y	N	Y
23 Bustamante	?	Y	Y	Y	Y	Y	Y	N
24 Frost	Y	Y	Y	Y	Y	Y	Y	N
25 Andrews	Y	Y	Y	Y	Y	Y	Y	Y
26 ***Armey***	N	N	Y	Y	Y	Y	N	N
27 Ortiz	Y	Y	Y	Y	Y	Y	Y	N
UTAH								
1 ***Hansen***	Y	Y	Y	N	Y	Y	N	Y
2 Owens	Y	Y	Y	Y	Y	Y	Y	N
3 ***Nielson***	Y	N	Y	Y	Y	Y	N	Y
VERMONT								
AL ***Smith***	Y	Y	Y	Y	Y	Y	N	N
VIRGINIA								
1 ***Bateman***	Y	Y	Y	Y	Y	Y	Y	N
2 Pickett	Y	Y	Y	Y	Y	Y	Y	N
3 ***Bliley***	N	Y	Y	Y	Y	Y	N	Y
4 Sisisky	Y	Y	Y	Y	Y	Y	Y	N
5 Payne	Y	Y	Y	Y	Y	Y	Y	Y
6 Olin	Y	Y	Y	Y	Y	Y	Y	N
7 ***Slaughter***	Y	Y	Y	Y	Y	Y	N	+
8 ***Parris***	N	Y	Y	Y	Y	Y	N	Y
9 Boucher	?	Y	Y	Y	Y	Y	Y	N
10 ***Wolf***	N	Y	Y	Y	Y	Y	N	Y
WASHINGTON								
1 ***Miller***	N	Y	Y	Y	Y	Y	N	N
2 Swift	+	Y	Y	Y	Y	Y	Y	N
3 Unsoeld	Y	Y	Y	Y	Y	Y	Y	N
4 ***Morrison***	Y	Y	Y	Y	Y	Y	N	N
5 Foley								
6 Dicks	Y	Y	Y	Y	Y	Y	Y	N
7 McDermott	?	Y	N	Y	Y	Y	Y	N
8 ***Chandler***	N	Y	Y	Y	Y	Y	N	Y
WEST VIRGINIA								
1 Mollohan	Y	Y	Y	Y	Y	Y	Y	N
2 Staggers	Y	Y	Y	Y	Y	Y	Y	N
3 Wise	Y	Y	Y	Y	Y	Y	Y	N
4 Rahall	Y	Y	Y	Y	Y	Y	Y	N
WISCONSIN								
1 Aspin	Y	?	Y	Y	Y	Y	Y	N
2 Kastenmeier	Y	Y	N	Y	Y	Y	Y	N
3 ***Gunderson***	Y	Y	Y	Y	Y	Y	N	N
4 Kleczka	Y	Y	Y	Y	Y	Y	Y	N
5 Moody	Y	Y	Y	Y	Y	Y	Y	N
6 ***Petri***	N	N	Y	Y	Y	Y	N	Y
7 Obey	Y	Y	Y	Y	Y	Y	Y	N
8 ***Roth***	?	Y	Y	Y	Y	Y	N	N
9 ***Sensenbrenner***	N	N	Y	Y	Y	Y	N	Y
WYOMING								
AL ***Thomas***	N	Y	Y	Y	Y	Y	N	Y

Southern states - Ala., Ark., Fla., Ga., Ky., La., Miss., N.C., Okla., S.C., Tenn., Texas, Va.
Omitted votes are quorum calls, which CQ does not include in its vote charts.

400. HR 4300. Legal Immigration Revision/Education and Training Fund. Morrison, D-Conn., amendment to replace the education and training fund in the bill with requirements that employers who want to bring in foreign workers certify that they have agreed to provide education and training for U.S. workers or students. Rejected 194-229: R 6-164; D 188-65 (ND 151-20, SD 37-45), Oct. 2, 1990.

401. HR 4300. Legal Immigration Revision/State Government Reimbursements. Smith, R-Texas, amendment to extend from fiscal 1994 to fiscal 1998 the appropriations to reimburse state governments for education and health costs for newly legalized aliens under the State Legalization Impact Assistance Grant program. Rejected 53-368: R 40-130; D 13-238 (ND 1-170, SD 12-68), Oct. 2, 1990.

402. HR 4300. Legal Immigration Revision/Deportations. McCollum, R-Fla., amendment to strike the Moakley, D-Mass., amendment that would suspend detention and deportation of illegal immigrants from El Salvador, Lebanon, Liberia and Kuwait for three years. Rejected 131-285: R 118-49; D 13-236 (ND 1-167, SD 12-69), Oct. 2, 1990.

403. HR 4300. Legal Immigration Revision/State Reimbursements. Lewis, R-Fla., amendment to authorize $500 million a year in fiscal 1991 through 1996 to reimburse states and localities for cash assistance, medical assistance and education for newly arrived foreigners. Rejected 99-319: R 73-97; D 26-222 (ND 8-160, SD 18-62), Oct. 3, 1990. A "nay" was a vote supporting the president's position.

404. HR 4300. Legal Immigration Revision/Family Reunification. Bryant, D-Texas, substitute amendment to delete all provisions of the bill except ones concerning "family reunification." The amendment would prohibit the deportation of spouses and children of legalized aliens; specify that for five years spouses and children of permanent residents would be limited to an overall total of 115,000 and not subject to immigration limits for individual countries; and provide 10,000 additional visas a year for the next five years for unmarried adult children of permanent residents. Rejected 165-257: R 113-58; D 52-199 (ND 11-160, SD 41-39), Oct. 3, 1990. A "yea" was a vote supporting the president's position.

405. HR 4300. Legal Immigration Revision/Recommittal Motion. Smith, R-Texas, motion to recommit to the House Judiciary Committee (thus killing) the bill to increase the number of visas for family relatives and people coming here to work; suspend deportation for the spouses and children of newly legalized aliens; establish "diversity" visas for immigrants from countries that currently account for a low number of immigrants to the United States; and revise other immigration procedures. Motion rejected 176-248: R 137-35; D 39-213 (ND 8-164, SD 31-49), Oct. 3, 1990. A "yea" was a vote supporting the president's position.

406. HR 4300. Legal Immigration Revision/Passage. Passage of the bill to increase the number of visas for family relatives and people coming here to work; suspend deportation for the spouses and children of newly legalized aliens; establish diversity visas for immigrants from countries that currently account for a low number of immigrants to the United States; and reform other immigration procedures. Passed 231-192: R 45-127; D 186-65 (ND 159-13, SD 27-52), Oct. 3, 1990. A "nay" was a vote supporting the president's position.

KEY

- Y Voted for (yea).
- # Paired for.
- + Announced for.
- N Voted against (nay).
- X Paired against.
- \- Announced against.
- P Voted "present."
- C Voted "present" to avoid possible conflict of interest.
- ? Did not vote or otherwise make a position known.

Democrats *Republicans*

	400	401	402	403	404	405	406
ALABAMA							
1 ***Callahan***	N	N	Y	N	Y	Y	N
2 ***Dickinson***	N	N	Y	N	N	Y	N
3 Browder	N	N	N	N	Y	Y	N
4 Bevill	N	N	N	N	?	Y	N
5 Flippo	Y	?	N	N	Y	Y	?
6 Erdreich	Y	N	N	N	Y	Y	N
7 Harris	N	N	N	N	Y	Y	N
ALASKA							
AL ***Young***	N	N	Y	?	Y	Y	Y
ARIZONA							
1 ***Rhodes***	N	N	Y	N	Y	Y	N
2 Udall	Y	N	N	N	N	N	Y
3 ***Stump***	N	N	Y	N	Y	Y	N
4 ***Kyl***	N	N	Y	N	Y	Y	N
5 ***Kolbe***	N	Y	Y	Y	N	Y	N
ARKANSAS							
1 Alexander	N	N	?	N	Y	Y	Y
2 ***Robinson***	N	N	Y	Y	Y	Y	N
3 ***Hammerschmidt***	N	N	Y	Y	Y	Y	N
4 Anthony	N	N	N	?	Y	N	Y
CALIFORNIA							
1 Bosco	N	N	N	N	N	N	Y
2 ***Herger***	N	Y	Y	Y	Y	Y	N
3 Matsui	Y	N	N	N	N	N	Y
4 Fazio	Y	N	N	N	N	N	Y
5 Pelosi	Y	N	N	N	N	N	Y
6 Boxer	Y	N	N	N	N	N	Y
7 Miller	Y	N	N	N	N	N	Y
8 Dellums	Y	N	N	N	N	N	Y
9 Stark	Y	N	N	N	N	N	Y
10 Edwards	Y	N	N	N	N	N	Y
11 Lantos	Y	N	N	N	N	N	Y
12 ***Campbell***	N	Y	N	?	?	?	?
13 Mineta	Y	N	N	N	N	N	Y
14 ***Shumway***	N	Y	Y	Y	Y	Y	N
15 Condit	N	N	N	Y	N	N	Y
16 Panetta	Y	N	N	N	N	N	Y
17 ***Pashayan***	N	N	N	N	N	Y	Y
18 Lehman	Y	N	N	Y	N	N	Y
19 ***Lagomarsino***	N	Y	Y	Y	Y	Y	N
20 ***Thomas***	N	N	Y	Y	Y	Y	Y
21 ***Gallegly***	N	Y	Y	Y	Y	Y	N
22 ***Moorhead***	N	Y	Y	Y	Y	Y	N
23 Beilenson	Y	N	Y	N	N	N	N
24 Waxman	Y	N	N	N	N	N	Y
25 Roybal	Y	N	N	N	N	N	Y
26 Berman	Y	N	N	N	N	N	Y
27 Levine	Y	N	N	N	N	N	Y
28 Dixon	Y	N	N	N	N	N	Y
29 Hawkins	?	?	?	N	N	N	Y
30 Martinez	N	N	N	N	?	N	Y
31 Dymally	Y	N	N	N	N	N	Y
32 Anderson	Y	N	N	Y	N	N	Y
33 ***Dreier***	N	N	Y	N	N	Y	N
34 Torres	Y	N	N	N	N	N	Y
35 ***Lewis***	N	N	Y	Y	Y	Y	N
36 Brown	Y	N	N	N	N	N	Y
37 ***McCandless***	N	N	Y	Y	Y	Y	N
38 ***Dornan***	N	N	Y	Y	N	Y	Y
39 ***Dannemeyer***	N	Y	Y	Y	Y	Y	N
40 ***Cox***	N	N	Y	Y	N	Y	N
41 ***Lowery***	N	Y	Y	Y	Y	Y	N
42 ***Rohrabacher***	N	N	N	Y	N	N	Y
43 ***Packard***	N	Y	Y	Y	Y	Y	N
44 Bates	Y	N	N	N	N	N	Y
45 ***Hunter***	N	Y	N	Y	Y	Y	Y
COLORADO							
1 Schroeder	Y	N	N	N	N	N	Y
2 Skaggs	Y	N	N	N	N	N	Y
3 Campbell	N	N	N	N	N	N	Y
4 ***Brown***	N	N	Y	N	Y	Y	N
5 ***Hefley***	N	N	N	N	Y	Y	N
6 ***Schaefer***	N	N	Y	Y	Y	Y	N
CONNECTICUT							
1 Kennelly	Y	N	N	N	N	N	Y
2 Gejdenson	Y	N	N	N	N	N	Y
3 Morrison	Y	N	N	N	N	N	Y
4 ***Shays***	N	N	N	N	N	N	Y
5 ***Rowland***	?	?	?	?	?	?	?
6 ***Johnson***	N	N	Y	N	N	N	Y
DELAWARE							
AL Carper	Y	N	N	N	N	N	Y
FLORIDA							
1 Hutto	Y	Y	Y	Y	Y	Y	N
2 ***Grant***	N	Y	N	Y	N	Y	N
3 Bennett	Y	Y	N	Y	Y	Y	N
4 ***James***	N	Y	Y	Y	Y	Y	N
5 ***McCollum***	N	Y	Y	Y	Y	Y	N
6 ***Stearns***	N	Y	Y	Y	Y	Y	N
7 Gibbons	N	N	N	N	N	N	Y
8 ***Young***	N	Y	Y	Y	Y	Y	N
9 ***Bilirakis***	N	N	Y	Y	Y	Y	N
10 ***Ireland***	N	N	Y	Y	Y	Y	N
11 Nelson	Y	Y	Y	Y	N	N	N
12 ***Lewis***	N	N	Y	Y	Y	Y	N
13 ***Goss***	N	Y	Y	Y	Y	Y	N
14 Johnston	Y	Y	Y	Y	Y	Y	N
15 ***Shaw***	N	Y	Y	Y	Y	Y	N
16 Smith	Y	Y	N	Y	N	?	Y
17 Lehman	Y	Y	N	Y	N	N	Y
18 ***Ros-Lehtinen***	N	Y	N	Y	N	N	Y
19 Fascell	Y	Y	N	Y	N	N	Y
GEORGIA							
1 Thomas	N	N	N	N	Y	N	N
2 Hatcher	N	N	N	N	Y	N	N
3 Ray	N	N	N	N	Y	Y	N
4 Jones	Y	N	N	N	N	N	?
5 Lewis	Y	N	N	N	N	N	Y
6 ***Gingrich***	N	N	Y	Y	Y	Y	Y
7 Darden	Y	N	N	N	N	N	Y
8 Rowland	N	N	N	N	Y	N	N
9 Jenkins	N	N	N	Y	Y	N	N
10 Barnard	N	N	Y	?	?	Y	N
HAWAII							
1 ***Saiki***	?	?	?	Y	N	N	Y
2 Mink	Y	N	N	N	N	N	Y
IDAHO							
1 ***Craig***	N	N	Y	Y	Y	Y	N
2 Stallings	N	N	N	N	N	Y	N
ILLINOIS							
1 Hayes	Y	N	N	N	N	N	Y
2 Savage	Y	N	N	N	N	Y	N
3 Russo	Y	N	N	N	N	N	Y
4 Sangmeister	Y	N	N	N	N	N	Y
5 Lipinski	Y	N	N	N	N	N	Y
6 ***Hyde***	N	Y	N	Y	N	N	Y
7 Collins	Y	N	N	N	N	N	Y
8 Rostenkowski	Y	N	N	N	N	N	Y
9 Yates	Y	N	N	N	N	N	Y
10 ***Porter***	N	N	Y	N	N	N	Y
11 Annunzio	Y	N	N	N	N	N	Y
12 ***Crane***	N	N	Y	N	Y	Y	N
13 ***Fawell***	N	N	Y	N	Y	Y	N
14 ***Hastert***	N	N	Y	Y	Y	Y	N
15 ***Madigan***	N	N	Y	Y	N	Y	Y
16 ***Martin***	?	?	?	N	N	N	Y
17 Evans	Y	N	N	N	N	N	Y
18 ***Michel***	N	N	Y	N	Y	Y	N
19 Bruce	Y	N	N	N	N	N	Y
20 Durbin	Y	N	N	N	N	N	Y
21 Costello	Y	N	N	N	N	N	Y
22 Poshard	Y	N	N	N	N	N	Y
INDIANA							
1 Visclosky	Y	N	N	N	N	N	Y
2 Sharp	Y	N	N	N	N	N	Y
3 ***Hiler***	N	N	Y	N	Y	Y	N

ND Northern Democrats SD Southern Democrats

	400	401	402	403	404	405	406
4 Long	Y	N	N	N	N	N	N
5 Jontz	Y	N	N	N	N	N	Y
6 ***Burton***	N	N	Y	N	Y	Y	N
7 ***Myers***	N	N	Y	N	Y	Y	N
8 McCloskey	Y	N	N	N	N	N	Y
9 Hamilton	N	N	N	N	N	N	Y
10 Jacobs	Y	N	N	N	N	N	Y
IOWA							
1 ***Leach***	Y	N	N	N	N	N	Y
2 ***Tauke***	N	N	Y	N	N	Y	Y
3 Nagle	N	N	N	N	N	N	Y
4 Smith	Y	N	N	N	N	N	Y
5 ***Lightfoot***	N	N	Y	N	Y	Y	N
6 ***Grandy***	N	N	Y	N	Y	Y	N
KANSAS							
1 ***Roberts***	N	N	Y	N	Y	Y	N
2 Slattery	N	N	N	N	N	N	Y
3 ***Meyers***	N	N	Y	N	N	Y	N
4 Glickman	Y	N	N	N	N	N	Y
5 ***Whittaker***	N	N	Y	N	Y	Y	N
KENTUCKY							
1 Hubbard	N	N	N	N	Y	Y	N
2 Natcher	Y	N	N	N	N	N	N
3 Mazzoli	N	N	N	N	N	N	N
4 ***Bunning***	N	N	Y	N	Y	Y	N
5 ***Rogers***	N	N	Y	N	Y	Y	N
6 ***Hopkins***	N	N	Y	Y	Y	Y	N
7 Perkins	Y	N	N	N	N	N	N
LOUISIANA							
1 ***Livingston***	N	N	Y	N	Y	Y	N
2 Boggs	?	?	?	?	?	?	?
3 Tauzin	N	N	N	N	Y	Y	N
4 ***McCrery***	N	N	Y	N	Y	Y	N
5 Huckaby	N	N	N	N	Y	Y	N
6 ***Baker***	N	N	Y	N	Y	Y	N
7 Hayes	N	N	N	N	Y	N	N
8 ***Holloway***	N	N	Y	N	Y	Y	N
MAINE							
1 Brennan	Y	N	N	N	N	N	Y
2 ***Snowe***	N	N	N	N	N	N	Y
MARYLAND							
1 Dyson	Y	N	N	N	N	N	N
2 ***Bentley***	N	Y	N	N	Y	Y	N
3 Cardin	N	N	N	N	N	N	Y
4 McMillen	N	N	N	N	N	N	Y
5 Hoyer	Y	N	N	N	N	N	Y
6 Byron	Y	N	N	N	Y	Y	N
7 Mfume	Y	N	N	?	N	N	Y
8 ***Morella***	N	N	N	Y	N	N	Y
MASSACHUSETTS							
1 ***Conte***	Y	N	N	N	N	N	Y
2 Neal	Y	N	N	N	N	N	Y
3 Early	Y	N	N	N	Y	Y	N
4 Frank	Y	N	N	N	N	N	Y
5 Atkins	Y	N	N	N	N	N	Y
6 Mavroules	Y	N	N	N	N	N	Y
7 Markey	Y	N	N	N	N	N	Y
8 Kennedy	Y	N	N	N	N	N	Y
9 Moakley	Y	N	N	N	N	N	Y
10 Studds	Y	N	N	N	N	N	Y
11 Donnelly	Y	N	N	N	N	N	Y
MICHIGAN							
1 Conyers	Y	N	N	N	N	N	Y
2 ***Pursell***	?	N	Y	N	Y	Y	N
3 Wolpe	Y	N	N	N	N	N	Y
4 ***Upton***	N	N	N	N	Y	Y	N
5 ***Henry***	N	N	N	N	Y	Y	N
6 Carr	N	N	N	N	N	N	Y
7 Kildee	Y	N	N	N	N	N	Y
8 Traxler	Y	N	N	N	Y	N	Y
9 ***Vander Jagt***	N	N	Y	N	Y	Y	N
10 ***Schuette***	?	?	?	N	Y	Y	N
11 ***Davis***	N	Y	?	N	N	Y	N
12 Bonior	Y	N	N	N	Y	N	Y
13 Crockett	Y	N	?	?	?	?	?
14 Hertel	Y	N	N	N	N	N	Y
15 Ford	Y	N	N	?	N	N	Y
16 Dingell	Y	N	N	N	N	N	Y
17 Levin	Y	N	N	N	N	N	Y
18 ***Broomfield***	N	N	Y	N	Y	Y	N
MINNESOTA							
1 Penny	N	N	N	N	N	Y	Y
2 ***Weber***	N	N	Y	N	N	N	Y
3 ***Frenzel***	N	?	Y	N	?	Y	N
4 Vento	Y	N	N	Y	N	N	Y
5 Sabo	Y	N	N	N	N	N	Y
6 Sikorski	Y	N	N	Y	N	N	Y
7 ***Stangeland***	N	N	Y	N	N	Y	Y
8 Oberstar	Y	N	N	N	N	N	Y
MISSISSIPPI							
1 Whitten	Y	N	N	N	N	?	?
2 Espy	Y	N	N	N	Y	N	Y
3 Montgomery	N	N	Y	N	Y	Y	N
4 Parker	N	N	Y	N	Y	Y	N
5 Taylor	Y	N	N	N	Y	Y	N
MISSOURI							
1 Clay	Y	N	N	N	N	N	Y
2 ***Buechner***	N	N	N	N	N	Y	N
3 Gephardt	Y	N	N	?	N	N	Y
4 Skelton	N	N	N	N	Y	N	N
5 Wheat	Y	N	N	N	N	N	Y
6 ***Coleman***	N	N	Y	N	Y	Y	N
7 ***Hancock***	N	Y	Y	N	Y	Y	N
8 ***Emerson***	N	N	N	N	Y	Y	N
9 Volkmer	N	N	N	N	Y	N	N
MONTANA							
1 Williams	N	N	N	N	N	N	Y
2 ***Marlenee***	N	N	Y	N	Y	Y	N
NEBRASKA							
1 ***Bereuter***	N	N	Y	N	N	Y	N
2 Hoagland	Y	N	N	N	N	Y	N
3 ***Smith***	N	N	Y	N	Y	Y	N
NEVADA							
1 Bilbray	Y	N	N	N	N	N	Y
2 ***Vucanovich***	N	N	Y	N	?	?	?
NEW HAMPSHIRE							
1 ***Smith***	N	N	Y	N	Y	Y	N
2 ***Douglas***	N	N	Y	N	Y	Y	N
NEW JERSEY							
1 Vacancy							
2 Hughes	N	N	N	N	N	Y	N
3 Pallone	Y	N	N	N	Y	N	Y
4 ***Smith***	N	N	N	Y	N	N	Y
5 ***Roukema***	N	N	Y	N	N	Y	N
6 Dwyer	Y	N	N	N	N	N	Y
7 ***Rinaldo***	N	N	N	Y	N	N	Y
8 Roe	N	N	N	N	N	N	Y
9 Torricelli	Y	N	N	N	N	N	Y
10 Payne	Y	N	N	N	N	N	Y
11 ***Gallo***	N	N	Y	N	Y	Y	N
12 ***Courter***	N	N	Y	Y	N	N	Y
13 ***Saxton***	N	N	N	Y	Y	Y	N
14 Guarini	N	N	N	N	N	N	Y
NEW MEXICO							
1 ***Schiff***	N	Y	N	Y	N	N	Y
2 ***Skeen***	N	Y	Y	Y	Y	Y	Y
3 Richardson	Y	N	N	N	N	N	Y
NEW YORK							
1 Hochbrueckner	Y	N	N	N	N	N	Y
2 Downey	Y	N	N	N	N	N	Y
3 Mrazek	Y	N	?	?	N	N	Y
4 ***Lent***	N	N	N	?	N	N	Y
5 ***McGrath***	Y	N	N	N	N	N	Y
6 Flake	Y	N	N	N	N	N	Y
7 Ackerman	Y	N	N	N	N	N	Y
8 Scheuer	Y	N	N	N	N	N	Y
9 Manton	Y	N	N	N	N	N	Y
10 Schumer	Y	N	N	N	N	N	Y
11 Towns	Y	N	N	N	N	N	Y
12 Owens	?	?	?	N	N	N	Y
13 Solarz	Y	N	N	N	N	N	Y
14 ***Molinari***	N	N	N	Y	N	N	Y
15 ***Green***	N	N	N	N	N	N	Y
16 Rangel	Y	N	N	N	N	N	Y
17 Weiss	Y	N	N	Y	N	N	Y
18 Serrano	Y	N	N	N	N	N	Y
19 Engel	+	-	-	-	-	-	+
20 Lowey	Y	N	N	N	N	N	Y
21 ***Fish***	N	N	N	N	N	N	Y
22 ***Gilman***	Y	N	N	N	N	N	Y
23 McNulty	Y	N	N	N	N	N	Y
24 ***Solomon***	N	N	Y	Y	Y	Y	N
25 ***Boehlert***	N	N	N	N	N	N	Y
26 ***Martin***	N	N	Y	Y	Y	Y	N
27 ***Walsh***	N	N	N	N	N	N	Y
28 McHugh	Y	N	N	N	N	N	Y
29 ***Horton***	N	N	N	N	N	N	Y
30 Slaughter	Y	N	N	N	N	N	Y
31 ***Paxon***	N	N	Y	N	Y	Y	N
32 LaFalce	Y	N	N	N	N	N	Y
33 Nowak	Y	N	N	N	N	N	Y
34 ***Houghton***	N	N	?	N	N	Y	N
NORTH CAROLINA							
1 Jones	Y	N	N	N	N	N	Y
2 Valentine	N	N	N	N	Y	Y	N
3 Lancaster	N	N	N	N	N	N	N
4 Price	N	N	N	N	N	N	Y
5 Neal	N	N	N	N	N	N	N
6 ***Coble***	N	N	Y	N	Y	Y	N
7 Rose	N	N	N	N	N	N	Y
8 Hefner	N	N	N	N	Y	N	N
9 ***McMillan***	N	N	N	N	Y	Y	N
10 ***Ballenger***	N	Y	Y	Y	Y	Y	N
11 Clarke	N	N	N	N	N	N	Y
NORTH DAKOTA							
AL Dorgan	Y	N	N	N	N	N	Y
OHIO							
1 Luken	Y	N	N	N	N	N	Y
2 ***Gradison***	N	Y	N	Y	N	N	Y
3 Hall	Y	N	N	N	N	N	Y
4 ***Oxley***	N	N	?	Y	N	Y	N
5 ***Gillmor***	N	N	Y	N	Y	Y	N
6 ***McEwen***	N	N	N	N	Y	Y	N
7 ***DeWine***	N	N	Y	N	N	N	Y
8 ***Lukens***	N	Y	Y	Y	Y	Y	N
9 Kaptur	Y	N	N	N	Y	N	Y
10 ***Miller***	N	N	Y	Y	Y	Y	N
11 Eckart	Y	N	N	N	N	N	Y
12 ***Kasich***	N	N	N	N	Y	Y	N
13 Pease	Y	N	N	N	N	N	Y
14 Sawyer	Y	N	N	N	N	N	Y
15 ***Wylie***	N	N	Y	N	Y	Y	N
16 ***Regula***	N	N	Y	N	N	Y	N
17 Traficant	Y	N	N	N	N	N	N
18 Applegate	Y	N	N	N	N	Y	N
19 Feighan	Y	N	N	N	N	N	Y
20 Oakar	Y	N	N	N	N	N	Y
21 Stokes	Y	N	N	N	N	N	Y
OKLAHOMA							
1 ***Inhofe***	N	N	Y	Y	Y	Y	N
2 Synar	Y	N	N	N	N	N	Y
3 Watkins	N	N	N	N	Y	Y	N
4 McCurdy	N	N	N	N	Y	Y	N
5 ***Edwards***	N	N	?	?	N	Y	N
6 English	N	N	N	N	Y	Y	N
OREGON							
1 AuCoin	Y	N	N	N	N	N	Y
2 ***Smith, B.***	N	N	Y	N	Y	Y	N
3 Wyden	Y	N	N	N	N	N	Y
4 DeFazio	Y	Y	N	Y	N	N	Y
5 ***Smith, D.***	N	Y	Y	Y	Y	Y	N
PENNSYLVANIA							
1 Foglietta	Y	N	N	N	N	N	Y
2 Gray	Y	N	N	N	N	N	Y
3 Borski	Y	N	N	N	N	N	Y
4 Kolter	Y	N	N	N	N	N	Y
5 ***Schulze***	N	N	Y	N	Y	Y	N
6 Yatron	Y	N	N	N	Y	N	Y
7 ***Weldon***	N	N	N	-	-	+	+
8 Kostmayer	Y	N	N	N	N	N	Y
9 ***Shuster***	N	N	Y	N	Y	Y	N
10 ***McDade***	Y	N	N	N	N	N	Y
11 Kanjorski	Y	N	N	N	N	N	Y
12 Murtha	Y	N	N	N	N	N	Y
13 ***Coughlin***	N	N	Y	N	N	Y	N
14 Coyne	Y	N	N	N	N	N	Y
15 ***Ritter***	N	N	Y	N	Y	Y	N
16 ***Walker***	N	N	Y	Y	Y	Y	N
17 ***Gekas***	N	Y	Y	Y	Y	Y	N
18 Walgren	Y	N	N	N	N	N	Y
19 ***Goodling***	?	Y	N	Y	Y	Y	N
20 Gaydos	Y	N	N	N	Y	N	Y
21 ***Ridge***	N	N	N	N	Y	Y	N
22 Murphy	Y	N	N	N	N	N	Y
23 ***Clinger***	N	N	Y	N	Y	Y	N
RHODE ISLAND							
1 ***Machtley***	N	N	N	N	N	N	Y
2 ***Schneider***	N	N	N	N	N	N	Y
SOUTH CAROLINA							
1 ***Ravenel***	N	N	N	N	Y	Y	N
2 ***Spence***	N	N	Y	N	Y	Y	N
3 Derrick	N	N	N	N	N	N	N
4 Patterson	N	N	N	N	Y	N	N
5 Spratt	N	N	N	N	Y	N	N
6 Tallon	N	N	N	N	Y	Y	N
SOUTH DAKOTA							
AL Johnson	Y	N	N	Y	N	N	Y
TENNESSEE							
1 ***Quillen***	N	Y	N	Y	Y	N	N
2 ***Duncan***	Y	N	Y	N	Y	Y	N
3 Lloyd	Y	N	N	N	Y	Y	N
4 Cooper	Y	N	N	N	N	N	N
5 Clement	Y	N	N	N	N	Y	N
6 Gordon	Y	N	N	N	N	N	N
7 ***Sundquist***	N	N	Y	Y	Y	Y	N
8 Tanner	N	N	N	N	Y	N	N
9 Ford	Y	?	N	N	N	N	Y
TEXAS							
1 Chapman	Y	N	Y	Y	Y	Y	N
2 Wilson	Y	N	N	N	N	N	Y
3 ***Bartlett***	N	Y	Y	Y	Y	Y	N
4 Hall	N	Y	Y	Y	Y	Y	N
5 Bryant	Y	Y	N	Y	Y	Y	N
6 ***Barton***	N	Y	Y	Y	Y	Y	N
7 ***Archer***	N	N	Y	Y	Y	Y	N
8 ***Fields***	N	Y	Y	Y	Y	Y	N
9 Brooks	Y	N	N	N	N	N	Y
10 Pickle	N	N	N	N	N	N	Y
11 Leath	N	Y	N	Y	Y	Y	N
12 Geren	N	N	Y	Y	N	N	N
13 Sarpalius	N	Y	N	Y	Y	Y	N
14 Laughlin	N	N	Y	N	N	N	N
15 de la Garza	Y	N	N	Y	N	N	Y
16 Coleman	Y	N	N	Y	N	N	Y
17 Stenholm	N	Y	Y	Y	Y	Y	N
18 Washington	Y	N	N	N	N	N	Y
19 ***Combest***	N	Y	Y	Y	Y	Y	N
20 Gonzalez	Y	N	N	N	N	N	Y
21 ***Smith***	N	Y	Y	Y	Y	Y	N
22 ***DeLay***	N	Y	Y	Y	Y	Y	N
23 Bustamante	Y	N	N	N	N	N	Y
24 Frost	Y	N	N	N	N	N	Y
25 Andrews	N	N	N	N	Y	Y	N
26 ***Armey***	N	N	Y	Y	N	Y	N
27 Ortiz	Y	N	Y	Y	N	N	Y
UTAH							
1 ***Hansen***	N	Y	?	Y	Y	Y	N
2 Owens	N	N	N	N	N	N	Y
3 ***Nielson***	N	N	Y	Y	N	Y	N
VERMONT							
AL ***Smith***	N	N	N	N	N	N	Y
VIRGINIA							
1 ***Bateman***	N	N	N	N	Y	Y	N
2 Pickett	Y	N	N	N	N	N	Y
3 ***Bliley***	N	N	Y	N	Y	Y	N
4 Sisisky	N	N	N	N	N	N	N
5 Payne	N	N	N	N	Y	N	N
6 Olin	N	N	N	N	Y	N	N
7 ***Slaughter***	N	N	Y	N	Y	Y	N
8 ***Parris***	N	-	Y	Y	Y	Y	N
9 Boucher	Y	N	N	N	N	N	Y
10 ***Wolf***	N	N	Y	Y	Y	Y	N
WASHINGTON							
1 ***Miller***	N	N	N	N	N	N	Y
2 Swift	Y	N	N	N	N	N	Y
3 Unsoeld	Y	N	N	N	N	N	Y
4 ***Morrison***	N	Y	N	Y	Y	Y	Y
5 Foley							
6 Dicks	Y	N	N	N	N	N	Y
7 McDermott	Y	N	N	N	N	N	Y
8 ***Chandler***	N	N	Y	N	Y	Y	N
WEST VIRGINIA							
1 Mollohan	Y	N	N	N	N	N	Y
2 Staggers	Y	N	N	N	Y	N	Y
3 Wise	Y	N	N	N	N	N	Y
4 Rahall	Y	N	N	N	N	N	Y
WISCONSIN							
1 Aspin	Y	N	?	N	N	N	Y
2 Kastenmeier	N	N	N	N	N	N	Y
3 ***Gunderson***	N	N	N	N	N	N	Y
4 Kleczka	Y	N	N	N	N	N	Y
5 Moody	Y	N	N	N	N	N	Y
6 ***Petri***	N	N	N	N	Y	Y	N
7 Obey	Y	N	N	N	N	N	Y
8 ***Roth***	N	N	Y	N	N	Y	N
9 ***Sensenbrenner***	N	N	Y	N	Y	Y	N
WYOMING							
AL ***Thomas***	N	N	Y	N	Y	Y	N

Southern states - Ala., Ark., Fla., Ga., Ky., La., Miss., N.C., Okla., S.C., Tenn., Texas, Va.
Omitted votes are quorum calls, which CQ does not include in its vote charts.

407. S 1511. Older Workers Benefit Protection Act/ Passage. Clay, D-Mo., motion to suspend the rules and pass the bill (thus clearing the measure for the president) to bar discrimination against older workers in employee benefits, effectively overturning a 1989 Supreme Court decision allowing age discrimination for certain benefits. The legislation would write into law regulations struck down by the court that banned age discrimination in employee benefits unless such bias is due to age-based cost differences. Motion agreed to 406-17: R 153-17; D 253-0 (ND 172-0, SD 81-0), Oct. 3, 1990. A two-thirds majority of those present and voting (282 in this case) is required for passage under suspension of the rules. A "nay" was a vote supporting the president's position.

408. HR 5269. Crime Bill/Antidrug Block Grants. Bustamante, D-Texas, amendment to strike provisions that would establish a direct pass-through of federal antidrug law enforcement block grant funds to local governments, based on a specific allocation formula for the funds that states already are required to share with local governments under the block grant. Adopted 236-189: R 130-39; D 106-150 (ND 47-126, SD 59-24), Oct. 3, 1990.

409. HR 5269. Crime Bill/Antidrug Block Grants. Martin, R-Ill., amendment to cut 10 percent from antidrug and law enforcement block grants for states that do not have a law requiring a defendant convicted of rape to be tested for the AIDS virus at the request of the victim. Adopted 415-3: R 163-0; D 252-3 (ND 172-1, SD 80-2), Oct. 3, 1990.

410. HR 5269. Crime Bill/Life Imprisonment. Staggers, D-W.Va., amendment to provide mandatory life imprisonment without the possibility of release for all cases for which the bill would impose the death penalty. The amendment also requires defendants convicted of these crimes to provide restitution of at least half of their earnings to the family or estate of the victim. Rejected 103-322: R 6-163; D 97-159 (ND 92-81, SD 5-78), Oct. 3, 1990. A "nay" was a vote supporting the president's position.

KEY

- Y Voted for (yea).
- # Paired for.
- + Announced for.
- N Voted against (nay).
- X Paired against.
- \- Announced against.
- P Voted "present."
- C Voted "present" to avoid possible conflict of interest.
- ? Did not vote or otherwise make a position known.

Democrats ***Republicans***

	407	408	409	410
ALABAMA				
1 ***Callahan***	Y	Y	Y	N
2 ***Dickinson***	Y	Y	Y	N
3 Browder	Y	Y	Y	N
4 Bevill	Y	Y	Y	N
5 Flippo	Y	Y	Y	N
6 Erdreich	Y	N	Y	N
7 Harris	Y	Y	Y	N
ALASKA				
AL ***Young***	Y	Y	Y	N
ARIZONA				
1 ***Rhodes***	N	Y	Y	N
2 Udall	Y	N	Y	Y
3 ***Stump***	N	Y	Y	N
4 ***Kyl***	N	Y	Y	N
5 ***Kolbe***	Y	Y	Y	N
ARKANSAS				
1 Alexander	Y	N	Y	N
2 ***Robinson***	Y	Y	Y	N
3 ***Hammerschmidt***	Y	Y	Y	N
4 Anthony	Y	N	Y	N
CALIFORNIA				
1 Bosco	Y	Y	Y	N
2 ***Herger***	Y	Y	Y	N
3 Matsui	Y	N	Y	Y
4 Fazio	Y	Y	Y	Y
5 Pelosi	Y	N	Y	Y
6 Boxer	Y	N	Y	N
7 Miller	Y	N	Y	Y
8 Dellums	Y	N	Y	Y
9 Stark	Y	N	Y	Y
10 Edwards	Y	N	Y	Y
11 Lantos	Y	N	Y	N
12 ***Campbell***	?	?	?	?
13 Mineta	Y	N	Y	Y
14 ***Shumway***	N	Y	Y	N
15 Condit	Y	N	Y	N
16 Panetta	Y	N	Y	N
17 ***Pashayan***	Y	Y	Y	N
18 Lehman	Y	Y	Y	N
19 ***Lagomarsino***	Y	Y	Y	N
20 ***Thomas***	Y	Y	Y	N
21 ***Gallegly***	Y	Y	Y	N
22 ***Moorhead***	Y	N	Y	N
23 Beilenson	Y	N	Y	N
24 Waxman	Y	N	Y	Y
25 Roybal	Y	N	Y	Y
26 Berman	Y	N	Y	Y
27 Levine	Y	N	Y	Y
28 Dixon	Y	Y	Y	Y
29 Hawkins	Y	N	Y	Y
30 Martinez	Y	N	Y	N
31 Dymally	Y	N	Y	Y
32 Anderson	Y	N	Y	Y
33 ***Dreier***	Y	Y	Y	N
34 Torres	Y	N	Y	N
35 ***Lewis***	Y	Y	Y	N
36 Brown	Y	N	Y	Y
37 ***McCandless***	Y	Y	+	N
38 ***Dornan***	Y	Y	Y	N
39 ***Dannemeyer***	N	Y	Y	N
40 ***Cox***	N	N	Y	N
41 ***Lowery***	Y	Y	Y	N
42 ***Rohrabacher***	Y	N	Y	N
43 ***Packard***	Y	Y	Y	N
44 Bates	Y	N	Y	Y
45 ***Hunter***	Y	Y	Y	N
COLORADO				
1 Schroeder	Y	N	Y	Y
2 Skaggs	Y	Y	Y	Y
3 Campbell	Y	Y	Y	N
4 ***Brown***	Y	N	Y	N
5 ***Hefley***	Y	N	Y	N
6 ***Schaefer***	Y	N	Y	N
CONNECTICUT				
1 Kennelly	Y	N	Y	N
2 Gejdenson	Y	N	Y	Y
3 Morrison	Y	N	Y	Y
4 ***Shays***	Y	N	Y	Y
5 ***Rowland***	?	?	?	?
6 ***Johnson***	Y	N	Y	N
DELAWARE				
AL Carper	Y	N	Y	N
FLORIDA				
1 Hutto	Y	Y	Y	N
2 ***Grant***	Y	Y	Y	N
3 Bennett	Y	N	Y	N
4 ***James***	Y	Y	Y	-
5 ***McCollum***	Y	Y	Y	N
6 ***Stearns***	Y	Y	Y	N
7 Gibbons	Y	N	Y	N
8 ***Young***	Y	Y	Y	N
9 ***Bilirakis***	Y	N	Y	N
10 ***Ireland***	Y	Y	Y	N
11 Nelson	Y	N	Y	N
12 ***Lewis***	Y	Y	Y	N
13 ***Goss***	Y	N	Y	N
14 Johnston	Y	N	Y	N
15 ***Shaw***	Y	Y	Y	N
16 Smith	Y	N	Y	N
17 Lehman	Y	N	Y	Y
18 ***Ros-Lehtinen***	Y	N	Y	N
19 Fascell	Y	N	Y	N
GEORGIA				
1 Thomas	Y	N	Y	N
2 Hatcher	Y	N	Y	N
3 Ray	Y	Y	Y	N
4 Jones	Y	N	Y	N
5 Lewis	Y	N	Y	Y
6 ***Gingrich***	Y	Y	Y	N
7 Darden	Y	Y	Y	N
8 Rowland	Y	N	Y	N
9 Jenkins	Y	Y	Y	N
10 Barnard	Y	N	Y	N
HAWAII				
1 ***Saiki***	Y	Y	Y	N
2 Mink	Y	Y	Y	Y
IDAHO				
1 ***Craig***	Y	Y	Y	N
2 Stallings	Y	Y	Y	N
ILLINOIS				
1 Hayes	Y	N	Y	Y
2 Savage	Y	N	Y	Y
3 Russo	Y	N	Y	N
4 Sangmeister	Y	N	Y	N
5 Lipinski	Y	N	Y	N
6 ***Hyde***	Y	Y	Y	N
7 Collins	Y	N	Y	Y
8 Rostenkowski	Y	N	Y	N
9 Yates	Y	N	Y	Y
10 ***Porter***	Y	Y	+	N
11 Annunzio	Y	N	Y	N
12 ***Crane***	N	Y	Y	N
13 ***Fawell***	Y	Y	?	N
14 ***Hastert***	Y	Y	Y	N
15 ***Madigan***	Y	Y	Y	N
16 ***Martin***	Y	Y	Y	N
17 Evans	Y	N	Y	Y
18 ***Michel***	Y	Y	?	?
19 Bruce	Y	N	Y	N
20 Durbin	Y	N	Y	N
21 Costello	Y	N	Y	N
22 Poshard	Y	N	Y	N
INDIANA				
1 Visclosky	Y	N	Y	Y
2 Sharp	Y	Y	Y	Y
3 ***Hiler***	Y	Y	Y	N

ND Northern Democrats SD Southern Democrats

	407	408	409	410
4 Long	Y	Y	Y	N
5 Jontz	Y	Y	Y	Y
6 ***Burton***	Y	Y	Y	N
7 ***Myers***	Y	Y	Y	N
8 McCloskey	Y	Y	Y	N
9 Hamilton	Y	Y	Y	Y
10 Jacobs	Y	N	Y	Y

IOWA

	407	408	409	410
1 ***Leach***	Y	Y	Y	N
2 ***Tauke***	Y	Y	Y	Y
3 Nagle	Y	N	Y	Y
4 Smith	Y	Y	Y	Y
5 ***Lightfoot***	Y	Y	Y	N
6 ***Grandy***	Y	Y	Y	N

KANSAS

	407	408	409	410
1 ***Roberts***	Y	Y	Y	N
2 Slattery	Y	Y	Y	N
3 ***Meyers***	Y	Y	Y	N
4 Glickman	Y	N	Y	N
5 ***Whittaker***	Y	Y	Y	N

KENTUCKY

	407	408	409	410
1 Hubbard	Y	Y	Y	N
2 Natcher	Y	Y	Y	N
3 Mazzoli	Y	N	Y	N
4 ***Bunning***	Y	Y	Y	N
5 ***Rogers***	Y	Y	Y	N
6 ***Hopkins***	Y	Y	Y	N
7 Perkins	Y	Y	Y	N

LOUISIANA

	407	408	409	410
1 ***Livingston***	Y	+	+	N
2 Boggs	?	N	Y	N
3 Tauzin	Y	Y	Y	N
4 ***McCrery***	Y	N	Y	N
5 Huckaby	Y	Y	Y	N
6 ***Baker***	Y	?	?	N
7 Hayes	Y	N	?	N
8 ***Holloway***	Y	Y	Y	N

MAINE

	407	408	409	410
1 Brennan	Y	Y	Y	Y
2 ***Snowe***	Y	Y	Y	N

MARYLAND

	407	408	409	410
1 Dyson	Y	Y	Y	N
2 ***Bentley***	Y	Y	Y	N
3 Cardin	Y	N	Y	N
4 McMillen	Y	Y	Y	N
5 Hoyer	Y	N	Y	Y
6 Byron	Y	Y	Y	N
7 Mfume	Y	N	Y	Y
8 ***Morella***	Y	N	Y	N

MASSACHUSETTS

	407	408	409	410
1 ***Conte***	Y	N	Y	N
2 Neal	Y	N	Y	Y
3 Early	Y	N	Y	N
4 Frank	Y	N	Y	Y
5 Atkins	Y	N	Y	N
6 Mavroules	Y	N	Y	N
7 Markey	Y	Y	Y	Y
8 Kennedy	Y	N	Y	N
9 Moakley	Y	N	Y	N
10 Studds	Y	N	Y	Y
11 Donnelly	Y	N	Y	N

MICHIGAN

	407	408	409	410
1 Conyers	Y	N	Y	Y
2 ***Pursell***	Y	Y	Y	N
3 Wolpe	Y	Y	Y	Y
4 ***Upton***	Y	Y	Y	N
5 ***Henry***	Y	Y	Y	N
6 Carr	Y	N	Y	N
7 Kildee	Y	N	Y	Y
8 Traxler	Y	Y	Y	N
9 ***Vander Jagt***	?	Y	Y	N
10 ***Schuette***	Y	Y	Y	N
11 ***Davis***	Y	Y	Y	N
12 Bonior	Y	N	Y	Y
13 Crockett	Y	N	Y	?
14 Hertel	Y	N	Y	Y
15 Ford	Y	Y	Y	Y
16 Dingell	Y	N	Y	N
17 Levin	Y	N	Y	Y
18 ***Broomfield***	Y	Y	Y	N

MINNESOTA

	407	408	409	410
1 Penny	Y	Y	Y	Y
2 ***Weber***	Y	Y	Y	Y
3 ***Frenzel***	Y	Y	Y	N
4 Vento	Y	?	?	Y
5 Sabo	?	N	Y	Y
6 Sikorski	Y	Y	Y	Y
7 ***Stangeland***	Y	Y	Y	Y
8 Oberstar	Y	N	Y	Y

MISSISSIPPI

	407	408	409	410
1 Whitten	?	Y	Y	N
2 Espy	Y	Y	Y	N
3 Montgomery	Y	Y	Y	N
4 Parker	Y	Y	Y	N
5 Taylor	Y	Y	Y	N

MISSOURI

	407	408	409	410
1 Clay	Y	N	Y	Y
2 ***Buechner***	Y	Y	Y	N
3 Gephardt	?	N	Y	N
4 Skelton	Y	Y	Y	N
5 Wheat	Y	N	Y	Y
6 ***Coleman***	Y	N	Y	N
7 ***Hancock***	N	Y	Y	N
8 ***Emerson***	Y	Y	Y	N
9 Volkmer	Y	Y	Y	N

MONTANA

	407	408	409	410
1 Williams	Y	N	Y	N
2 ***Marlenee***	Y	Y	Y	N

NEBRASKA

	407	408	409	410
1 ***Bereuter***	Y	Y	Y	N
2 Hoagland	Y	Y	Y	N
3 ***Smith***	Y	Y	Y	N

NEVADA

	407	408	409	410
1 Bilbray	Y	N	Y	N
2 ***Vucanovich***	?	Y	Y	N

NEW HAMPSHIRE

	407	408	409	410
1 ***Smith***	Y	Y	Y	N
2 ***Douglas***	?	Y	Y	N

NEW JERSEY

	407	408	409	410
1 Vacancy				
2 Hughes	Y	N	N	N
3 Pallone	Y	N	Y	N
4 ***Smith***	Y	N	Y	Y
5 ***Roukema***	Y	Y	Y	N
6 Dwyer	Y	N	Y	Y
7 ***Rinaldo***	Y	N	Y	N
8 Roe	Y	N	Y	N
9 Torricelli	Y	N	Y	N
10 Payne	Y	N	Y	N
11 ***Gallo***	Y	Y	Y	N
12 ***Courter***	Y	?	?	N
13 ***Saxton***	Y	Y	Y	N
14 Guarini	Y	N	Y	N

NEW MEXICO

	407	408	409	410
1 ***Schiff***	Y	N	Y	N
2 ***Skeen***	Y	Y	Y	N
3 Richardson	Y	Y	Y	N

NEW YORK

	407	408	409	410
1 Hochbrueckner	Y	N	Y	Y
2 Downey	Y	N	Y	Y
3 Mrazek	Y	N	Y	Y
4 ***Lent***	Y	Y	Y	N
5 ***McGrath***	Y	N	Y	N
6 Flake	Y	N	Y	Y
7 Ackerman	Y	N	Y	Y
8 Scheuer	Y	N	Y	N
9 Manton	Y	N	Y	N
10 Schumer	Y	N	Y	N
11 Towns	Y	N	Y	Y
12 Owens	Y	N	Y	Y
13 Solarz	Y	N	Y	Y
14 ***Molinari***	Y	?	?	N
15 ***Green***	Y	N	Y	N
16 Rangel	Y	N	Y	Y
17 Weiss	Y	N	Y	Y
18 Serrano	Y	N	Y	Y
19 Engel	Y	N	Y	Y
20 Lowey	Y	Y	Y	Y
21 ***Fish***	Y	Y	Y	N
22 ***Gilman***	Y	Y	Y	N
23 McNulty	Y	Y	Y	Y
24 ***Solomon***	Y	Y	Y	N
25 ***Boehlert***	Y	Y	?	N
26 ***Martin***	Y	Y	Y	N
27 ***Walsh***	Y	Y	Y	N
28 McHugh	Y	Y	Y	Y
29 ***Horton***	Y	Y	Y	N
30 Slaughter	Y	N	Y	Y
31 ***Paxon***	Y	N	Y	N
32 LaFalce	Y	Y	Y	Y
33 Nowak	Y	N	Y	N
34 ***Houghton***	Y	Y	Y	N

NORTH CAROLINA

	407	408	409	410
1 Jones	Y	Y	Y	N
2 Valentine	Y	Y	Y	N
3 Lancaster	Y	Y	Y	N
4 Price	Y	Y	Y	N
5 Neal	Y	Y	Y	N
6 ***Coble***	Y	Y	Y	N
7 Rose	Y	Y	Y	N
8 Hefner	Y	Y	Y	N
9 ***McMillan***	Y	N	Y	N
10 ***Ballenger***	N	Y	Y	N
11 Clarke	Y	Y	Y	N

NORTH DAKOTA

	407	408	409	410
AL Dorgan	Y	Y	Y	Y

OHIO

	407	408	409	410
1 Luken	Y	Y	Y	N
2 ***Gradison***	Y	Y	Y	N
3 Hall	Y	N	Y	N
4 ***Oxley***	Y	Y	Y	N
5 ***Gillmor***	Y	Y	Y	N
6 ***McEwen***	N	Y	Y	N
7 ***DeWine***	Y	Y	Y	N
8 ***Lukens***	Y	Y	Y	N
9 Kaptur	Y	Y	Y	N
10 ***Miller***	Y	Y	Y	N
11 Eckart	Y	Y	Y	N
12 ***Kasich***	Y	Y	Y	N
13 Pease	Y	N	Y	N
14 Sawyer	Y	N	Y	N
15 ***Wylie***	Y	Y	Y	N
16 ***Regula***	Y	N	Y	N
17 Traficant	Y	N	Y	N
18 Applegate	Y	Y	Y	N
19 Feighan	Y	N	Y	Y
20 Oakar	Y	N	Y	N
21 Stokes	Y	N	Y	Y

OKLAHOMA

	407	408	409	410
1 ***Inhofe***	Y	N	Y	N
2 Synar	Y	Y	Y	N
3 Watkins	Y	Y	Y	N
4 McCurdy	Y	Y	Y	N
5 ***Edwards***	Y	N	?	?
6 English	Y	Y	Y	N

OREGON

	407	408	409	410
1 AuCoin	Y	N	Y	Y
2 ***Smith, B.***	Y	Y	Y	N
3 Wyden	Y	N	Y	N
4 DeFazio	Y	N	Y	N
5 ***Smith, D.***	Y	Y	Y	N

PENNSYLVANIA

	407	408	409	410
1 Foglietta	Y	N	Y	N
2 Gray	Y	N	Y	Y
3 Borski	Y	N	Y	N
4 Kolter	Y	N	Y	N
5 ***Schulze***	Y	Y	Y	N
6 Yatron	Y	N	Y	N
7 ***Weldon***	+	N	Y	N
8 Kostmayer	Y	N	Y	Y
9 ***Shuster***	Y	Y	Y	N
10 ***McDade***	Y	N	Y	N
11 Kanjorski	Y	Y	Y	N
12 Murtha	Y	Y	Y	N
13 ***Coughlin***	Y	N	Y	N
14 Coyne	Y	N	Y	Y
15 ***Ritter***	Y	N	Y	N
16 ***Walker***	N	N	Y	N
17 ***Gekas***	Y	Y	Y	N
18 Walgren	Y	N	Y	N
19 ***Goodling***	Y	N	Y	Y
20 Gaydos	Y	N	Y	N
21 ***Ridge***	Y	N	Y	N
22 Murphy	Y	N	Y	N
23 ***Clinger***	Y	Y	Y	N

RHODE ISLAND

	407	408	409	410
1 ***Machtley***	Y	N	Y	N
2 ***Schneider***	Y	Y	Y	N

SOUTH CAROLINA

	407	408	409	410
1 ***Ravenel***	Y	N	Y	N
2 ***Spence***	Y	Y	Y	N
3 Derrick	Y	Y	Y	N
4 Patterson	Y	Y	Y	N
5 Spratt	Y	Y	Y	N
6 Tallon	Y	Y	Y	N

SOUTH DAKOTA

	407	408	409	410
AL Johnson	Y	Y	Y	N

TENNESSEE

	407	408	409	410
1 ***Quillen***	Y	Y	Y	N
2 ***Duncan***	Y	N	Y	N
3 Lloyd	Y	Y	Y	N
4 Cooper	Y	Y	Y	N
5 Clement	Y	Y	Y	N
6 Gordon	Y	Y	Y	N
7 ***Sundquist***	Y	Y	Y	N
8 Tanner	Y	Y	Y	N
9 Ford	Y	N	Y	Y

TEXAS

	407	408	409	410
1 Chapman	Y	Y	Y	N
2 Wilson	Y	Y	Y	N
3 ***Bartlett***	N	N	Y	N
4 Hall	Y	Y	Y	N
5 Bryant	Y	N	Y	N
6 ***Barton***	Y	Y	Y	N
7 ***Archer***	N	Y	Y	N
8 ***Fields***	Y	Y	Y	N
9 Brooks	Y	Y	Y	N
10 Pickle	Y	Y	Y	N
11 Leath	Y	Y	Y	N
12 Geren	Y	N	Y	N
13 Sarpalius	Y	Y	Y	N
14 Laughlin	Y	Y	Y	N
15 de la Garza	Y	Y	Y	N
16 Coleman	Y	Y	Y	N
17 Stenholm	Y	Y	Y	N
18 Washington	Y	N	N	Y
19 ***Combest***	N	Y	Y	N
20 Gonzalez	Y	Y	N	Y
21 ***Smith***	N	Y	Y	N
22 ***DeLay***	N	Y	Y	N
23 Bustamante	Y	Y	Y	N
24 Frost	Y	Y	Y	N
25 Andrews	Y	Y	Y	N
26 ***Armey***	N	Y	Y	N
27 Ortiz	Y	Y	Y	N

UTAH

	407	408	409	410
1 ***Hansen***	Y	Y	Y	N
2 Owens	Y	N	Y	N
3 ***Nielson***	Y	Y	Y	N

VERMONT

	407	408	409	410
AL ***Smith***	Y	Y	Y	?

VIRGINIA

	407	408	409	410
1 ***Bateman***	Y	Y	Y	N
2 Pickett	Y	Y	Y	N
3 ***Bliley***	Y	Y	Y	N
4 Sisisky	Y	Y	Y	N
5 Payne	Y	Y	Y	N
6 Olin	Y	Y	Y	N
7 ***Slaughter***	Y	Y	Y	N
8 ***Parris***	Y	+	+	-
9 Boucher	Y	N	Y	N
10 ***Wolf***	Y	N	Y	N

WASHINGTON

	407	408	409	410
1 ***Miller***	Y	N	Y	N
2 Swift	Y	Y	Y	Y
3 Unsoeld	Y	N	Y	N
4 ***Morrison***	Y	Y	Y	N
5 Foley				
6 Dicks	Y	N	Y	N
7 McDermott	Y	N	Y	Y
8 ***Chandler***	Y	N	Y	N

WEST VIRGINIA

	407	408	409	410
1 Mollohan	Y	Y	Y	Y
2 Staggers	Y	Y	Y	Y
3 Wise	Y	Y	Y	Y
4 Rahall	Y	Y	Y	Y

WISCONSIN

	407	408	409	410
1 Aspin	Y	N	Y	N
2 Kastenmeier	Y	N	Y	Y
3 ***Gunderson***	Y	Y	Y	N
4 Kleczka	Y	N	Y	Y
5 Moody	Y	N	Y	Y
6 ***Petri***	Y	Y	Y	N
7 Obey	Y	Y	Y	Y
8 ***Roth***	Y	Y	Y	N
9 ***Sensenbrenner***	Y	Y	Y	N

WYOMING

	407	408	409	410
AL ***Thomas***	Y	Y	Y	N

Southern states - Ala., Ark., Fla., Ga., Ky., La., Miss., N.C., Okla., S.C., Tenn., Texas, Va.
Omitted votes are quorum calls, which CQ does not include in its vote charts.

HOUSE VOTES 411, 412, 413, 414, 415, 416, 417, 418

411. Procedural Motion. Inhofe, R-Okla., motion to approve the House Journal of Wednesday, Oct. 3. Motion agreed to 293-121: R 54-115; D 239-6 (ND 159-6, SD 80-0), Oct. 4, 1990.

412. HR 5269. Crime Bill/Death Penalty. Hughes, D-N.J., amendment to authorize the death penalty for 10 additional federal offenses. The amendment also would require that only one aggravating factor be proved to impose the death penalty; heighten the burden of proof to establish a mitigating factor; revise the bill's standards for appellate review of death sentences; and strike provisions that allow death row prisoners to raise claims of racial bias in federal habeas corpus proceedings, even if the claims were not made in previous habeas corpus proceedings. Rejected 108-319: R 10-163; D 98-156 (ND 63-109, SD 35-47), Oct. 4, 1990. A "nay" was a vote supporting the president's position.

413. HR 5269. Crime Bill/Death Penalty. Gekas, R-Pa., amendment to authorize the death penalty for 10 additional federal offenses. The amendment also would require a judge or jury to impose the death penalty if the judge or jury found that one aggravating factor existed beyond a reasonable doubt and that it outweighed any mitigating factors or was sufficient alone to justify the death sentence; allow the prosecutor to ask the jury to consider any aggravating factor without notice to the judge and defendant; preclude death row inmates from challenging federal habeas corpus proceedings based on inadequate counsel at trial; and repeal free counsel for inmates challenging state death sentences through federal habeas corpus proceeding. Adopted 271-159: R 165-9; D 106-150 (ND 45-128, SD 61-22), Oct. 4, 1990. A "yea" was a vote supporting the president's position.

414. HR 5269. Crime Bill/Death Penalty. McCollum, R-Fla., amendment to authorize the death penalty for people found guilty of trafficking large amounts of drugs or a drug felony in which the defendant intended to cause death or acted with "reckless disregard" for life. The amendment also would establish death penalty procedures requiring a jury or judge to impose the death penalty if one aggravating factor existed beyond a reasonable doubt outweighed by any mitigating factors or if the crime alone were sufficient to justify the death penalty. Adopted 295-133: R 165-9; D 130-124 (ND 57-114, SD 73-10), Oct. 4, 1990.

415. HR 5269. Crime Bill/Forfeited Assets. Moorhead, R-Calif., amendment to strike provisions from the bill that prohibit the transfer of certain forfeited assets to state and local law enforcement agencies, if the transfer would circumvent state law. Adopted 309-120: R 162-13; D 147-107 (ND 85-87, SD 62-20), Oct. 4, 1990.

416. HR 5269. Crime Bill/Weapons Assembly. Unsoeld, D-Wash., amendment to modify provisions in the bill that make it illegal to assemble any semiautomatic weapon that is identical to weapons banned from importation. The modification would allow such weapons to be assembled from domestic parts. Adopted 257-172: R 141-34; D 116-138 (ND 52-120, SD 64-18), Oct. 4, 1990.

417. HR 5269. Crime Bill/Death Row Appeals. Hughes, D-N.J., amendment to reduce from one year to six months the time in which death row prisoners must file federal habeas corpus petitions after direct appeals have been exhausted; require qualified counsel; and limit circumstances in which federal courts would be required to hear successive habeas corpus petitions. Rejected 189-239: R 17-156; D 172-83 (ND 139-33, SD 33-50), Oct. 4, 1990. A "nay" was a vote supporting the president's position.

418. HR 5269. Crime Bill/Habeas Corpus Reform. Hyde, R-Ill., amendment to establish alternative habeas corpus reform, including provisions to establish an optional system under which states could limit the time within which prisoners must file habeas corpus petitions and limit filing of successive petitions. Adopted 285-146: R 167-7; D 118-139 (ND 50-124, SD 68-15), Oct. 4, 1990. A "yea" was a vote supporting the president's position.

KEY

- Y Voted for (yea).
- # Paired for.
- + Announced for.
- N Voted against (nay).
- X Paired against.
- \- Announced against.
- P Voted "present."
- C Voted "present" to avoid possible conflict of interest.
- ? Did not vote or otherwise make a position known.

Democrats ***Republicans***

	411	412	413	414	415	416	417	418
ALABAMA								
1 ***Callahan***	?	N	Y	Y	Y	Y	N	Y
2 ***Dickinson***	N	Y	Y	Y	Y	Y	N	Y
3 Browder	Y	N	Y	Y	Y	Y	N	Y
4 Bevill	Y	N	Y	Y	Y	Y	N	Y
5 Flippo	Y	N	Y	Y	Y	Y	N	Y
6 Erdreich	Y	N	Y	Y	Y	Y	N	Y
7 Harris	Y	N	Y	Y	Y	Y	N	Y
ALASKA								
AL ***Young***	N	N	Y	Y	Y	Y	?	Y
ARIZONA								
1 ***Rhodes***	N	N	Y	Y	Y	Y	N	Y
2 Udall	?	N	N	?	?	Y	Y	N
3 ***Stump***	N	N	Y	Y	Y	Y	N	Y
4 ***Kyl***	N	N	Y	Y	Y	Y	N	Y
5 ***Kolbe***	N	N	Y	Y	Y	Y	N	Y
ARKANSAS								
1 Alexander	Y	N	Y	Y	N	Y	N	Y
2 ***Robinson***	Y	N	Y	Y	Y	Y	N	Y
3 ***Hammerschmidt***	N	N	Y	Y	Y	Y	N	Y
4 Anthony	?	N	Y	Y	N	Y	N	Y
CALIFORNIA								
1 Bosco	Y	Y	N	Y	N	N	N	Y
2 ***Herger***	N	N	Y	Y	Y	Y	N	Y
3 Matsui	Y	Y	Y	Y	Y	N	Y	N
4 Fazio	Y	Y	N	N	Y	N	Y	N
5 Pelosi	Y	N	N	N	Y	N	Y	N
6 Boxer	Y	Y	N	N	Y	N	Y	N
7 Miller	N	N	N	N	N	N	Y	N
8 Dellums	?	N	N	N	N	N	Y	N
9 Stark	Y	N	N	N	Y	N	Y	N
10 Edwards	Y	N	N	N	Y	N	Y	N
11 Lantos	Y	N	N	N	Y	N	Y	Y
12 ***Campbell***	N	N	Y	N	Y	N	N	Y
13 Mineta	Y	Y	N	N	N	N	Y	N
14 ***Shumway***	Y	N	Y	Y	Y	Y	N	Y
15 Condit	Y	N	Y	Y	Y	Y	N	Y
16 Panetta	Y	Y	N	N	N	N	Y	N
17 ***Pashayan***	N	N	Y	Y	Y	Y	N	Y
18 Lehman	Y	N	Y	Y	Y	N	N	Y
19 ***Lagomarsino***	N	N	Y	Y	Y	Y	N	Y
20 ***Thomas***	N	N	Y	Y	Y	Y	N	Y
21 ***Gallegly***	N	N	Y	Y	Y	Y	N	Y
22 ***Moorhead***	N	N	Y	Y	Y	Y	N	Y
23 Beilenson	Y	Y	N	N	Y	N	Y	N
24 Waxman	Y	N	N	N	N	N	Y	N
25 Roybal	Y	N	N	N	Y	N	Y	N
26 Berman	Y	N	N	N	Y	N	Y	N
27 Levine	Y	N	N	N	Y	N	Y	N
28 Dixon	Y	N	N	N	Y	N	Y	N
29 Hawkins	Y	N	N	N	Y	X	?	N
30 Martinez	Y	Y	N	Y	Y	Y	Y	Y
31 Dymally	Y	Y	N	N	Y	N	Y	N
32 Anderson	Y	Y	N	N	Y	N	Y	N
33 ***Dreier***	Y	N	Y	Y	Y	Y	N	Y
34 Torres	Y	Y	Y	Y	Y	N	Y	N
35 ***Lewis***	N	N	Y	Y	Y	Y	N	Y
36 Brown	Y	Y	N	N	Y	N	Y	N
37 ***McCandless***	N	N	Y	Y	Y	Y	N	Y
38 ***Dornan***	?	N	Y	Y	Y	Y	N	Y
39 ***Dannemeyer***	N	N	Y	Y	Y	Y	N	Y
40 ***Cox***	Y	N	Y	Y	Y	Y	N	Y
41 ***Lowery***	N	N	Y	Y	Y	Y	N	Y
42 ***Rohrabacher***	N	N	Y	Y	Y	Y	N	Y
43 ***Packard***	N	N	Y	Y	Y	Y	N	Y
44 Bates	Y	Y	Y	N	Y	N	Y	N
45 ***Hunter***	N	N	Y	Y	Y	Y	N	Y
COLORADO								
1 Schroeder	N	N	N	N	N	N	Y	N
2 Skaggs	Y	N	N	N	Y	N	Y	N
3 Campbell	Y	Y	Y	Y	Y	Y	N	Y
4 ***Brown***	N	N	Y	Y	Y	Y	N	Y
5 ***Hefley***	N	N	Y	Y	Y	Y	Y	Y
6 ***Schaefer***	N	N	Y	Y	Y	Y	N	Y
CONNECTICUT								
1 Kennelly	Y	Y	N	N	N	N	Y	N
2 Gejdenson	Y	Y	N	N	N	N	Y	N
3 Morrison	?	N	N	N	Y	N	Y	N
4 ***Shays***	N	N	N	Y	Y	N	Y	Y
5 ***Rowland***	?	N	Y	Y	Y	Y	N	Y
6 ***Johnson***	Y	Y	Y	Y	Y	N	Y	Y
DELAWARE								
AL Carper	Y	Y	N	Y	Y	N	Y	N
FLORIDA								
1 Hutto	Y	N	Y	Y	Y	Y	N	Y
2 ***Grant***	Y	N	Y	Y	Y	Y	N	Y
3 Bennett	Y	N	Y	Y	Y	N	Y	Y
4 ***James***	N	N	Y	Y	Y	Y	N	Y
5 ***McCollum***	Y	N	Y	Y	N	Y	N	Y
6 ***Stearns***	N	N	Y	Y	Y	Y	N	Y
7 Gibbons	Y	Y	Y	Y	Y	N	N	Y
8 ***Young***	N	N	Y	Y	Y	Y	N	Y
9 ***Bilirakis***	N	N	Y	Y	Y	Y	N	Y
10 ***Ireland***	N	N	Y	Y	N	Y	N	Y
11 Nelson	Y	N	Y	Y	N	N	Y	Y
12 ***Lewis***	N	N	Y	Y	Y	Y	N	Y
13 ***Goss***	N	N	Y	Y	Y	N	N	Y
14 Johnston	Y	Y	N	Y	N	N	Y	N
15 ***Shaw***	Y	N	Y	Y	Y	Y	N	Y
16 Smith	Y	Y	N	N	N	N	Y	N
17 Lehman	Y	Y	N	Y	N	N	Y	N
18 ***Ros-Lehtinen***	N	N	Y	Y	Y	N	N	Y
19 Fascell	Y	N	N	Y	N	N	Y	Y
GEORGIA								
1 Thomas	Y	N	Y	Y	Y	Y	N	Y
2 Hatcher	Y	N	Y	Y	Y	Y	N	Y
3 Ray	Y	Y	Y	Y	Y	Y	N	Y
4 Jones	Y	N	Y	Y	Y	N	N	Y
5 Lewis	Y	N	N	N	N	N	Y	N
6 ***Gingrich***	N	N	Y	Y	Y	Y	N	Y
7 Darden	Y	N	Y	Y	Y	Y	N	Y
8 Rowland	Y	N	Y	Y	Y	Y	N	Y
9 Jenkins	Y	N	Y	Y	Y	Y	N	Y
10 Barnard	Y	N	Y	Y	Y	Y	N	Y
HAWAII								
1 ***Saiki***	Y	N	Y	Y	Y	N	N	Y
2 Mink	Y	N	N	N	Y	N	Y	N
IDAHO								
1 ***Craig***	N	N	Y	Y	Y	Y	N	Y
2 Stallings	Y	Y	Y	Y	Y	Y	Y	Y
ILLINOIS								
1 Hayes	Y	N	N	N	N	N	Y	N
2 Savage	Y	N	N	N	N	N	N	N
3 Russo	Y	N	Y	Y	Y	N	N	Y
4 Sangmeister	Y	Y	Y	Y	N	N	Y	Y
5 Lipinski	Y	Y	Y	Y	N	N	Y	Y
6 ***Hyde***	Y	N	Y	Y	Y	Y	N	Y
7 Collins	Y	N	N	N	N	N	Y	N
8 Rostenkowski	Y	N	Y	N	Y	N	N	Y
9 Yates	Y	N	N	N	N	N	Y	N
10 ***Porter***	Y	N	Y	Y	Y	N	N	Y
11 Annunzio	Y	N	Y	Y	Y	N	N	Y
12 ***Crane***	N	N	Y	Y	Y	Y	N	Y
13 ***Fawell***	N	N	Y	Y	Y	N	N	Y
14 ***Hastert***	N	N	Y	Y	Y	Y	N	Y
15 ***Madigan***	N	N	Y	Y	Y	Y	N	Y
16 ***Martin***	N	N	Y	Y	Y	Y	N	Y
17 Evans	Y	N	N	N	N	N	Y	N
18 ***Michel***	N	N	Y	Y	Y	Y	N	Y
19 Bruce	Y	Y	Y	Y	N	Y	Y	Y
20 Durbin	Y	N	N	Y	N	N	Y	N
21 Costello	Y	Y	Y	Y	N	Y	Y	Y
22 Poshard	Y	Y	Y	Y	N	Y	Y	Y
INDIANA								
1 Visclosky	Y	N	N	N	N	N	Y	N
2 Sharp	Y	N	N	N	Y	Y	Y	N
3 ***Hiler***	N	N	Y	Y	Y	Y	N	Y

ND Northern Democrats SD Southern Democrats

	411	412	413	414	415	416	417	418
4 Long	Y	Y	Y	Y	N	Y	Y	N
5 Jontz	Y	Y	N	Y	Y	Y	Y	N
6 ***Burton***	N	N	Y	Y	Y	Y	N	Y
7 ***Myers***	Y	N	Y	Y	Y	Y	N	Y
8 McCloskey	Y	N	N	N	Y	N	N	N
9 Hamilton	Y	Y	N	N	N	Y	Y	N
10 Jacobs	N	Y	N	N	Y	Y	Y	Y
IOWA								
1 ***Leach***	N	Y	N	Y	Y	N	Y	N
2 ***Tauke***	N	Y	N	N	Y	Y	Y	Y
3 Nagle	Y	N	N	N	N	N	Y	N
4 Smith	Y	N	N	N	Y	Y	Y	Y
5 ***Lightfoot***	N	N	Y	Y	Y	Y	N	Y
6 ***Grandy***	N	Y	Y	Y	Y	Y	N	Y
KANSAS								
1 ***Roberts***	N	N	Y	Y	Y	Y	N	Y
2 Slattery	Y	Y	Y	Y	Y	Y	Y	N
3 ***Meyers***	N	N	Y	Y	Y	N	N	Y
4 Glickman	Y	Y	Y	N	Y	N	Y	N
5 ***Whittaker***	N	N	Y	Y	Y	Y	N	Y
KENTUCKY								
1 Hubbard	Y	N	Y	Y	Y	N	Y	Y
2 Natcher	Y	N	Y	Y	Y	Y	N	Y
3 Mazzoli	Y	Y	N	N	Y	N	Y	Y
4 ***Bunning***	N	N	Y	Y	Y	Y	N	Y
5 ***Rogers***	N	N	Y	Y	Y	Y	N	Y
6 ***Hopkins***	N	N	Y	Y	Y	Y	N	Y
7 Perkins	Y	Y	N	Y	N	Y	N	Y
LOUISIANA								
1 ***Livingston***	Y	N	Y	Y	Y	Y	N	Y
2 Boggs	Y	Y	N	N	Y	Y	Y	N
3 Tauzin	Y	N	Y	Y	Y	Y	N	Y
4 ***McCrery***	N	N	Y	Y	Y	Y	N	?
5 Huckaby	Y	N	Y	Y	Y	Y	N	Y
6 ***Baker***	N	N	Y	Y	Y	Y	N	Y
7 Hayes	Y	N	Y	Y	Y	Y	N	Y
8 ***Holloway***	N	N	Y	Y	Y	Y	N	Y
MAINE								
1 Brennan	Y	N	N	N	N	N	N	N
2 ***Snowe***	Y	N	Y	Y	Y	Y	N	Y
MARYLAND								
1 Dyson	Y	N	Y	Y	Y	Y	N	Y
2 ***Bentley***	N	N	Y	Y	N	Y	N	Y
3 Cardin	Y	N	N	N	N	N	Y	N
4 McMillen	Y	N	Y	N	N	Y	Y	N
5 Hoyer	Y	N	N	N	N	N	Y	N
6 Byron	Y	N	Y	Y	Y	Y	N	Y
7 Mfume	Y	N	N	N	N	N	Y	N
8 ***Morella***	Y	Y	N	N	Y	N	Y	N
MASSACHUSETTS								
1 ***Conte***	Y	Y	N	N	Y	N	Y	N
2 Neal	Y	Y	N	N	Y	N	Y	Y
3 Early	Y	Y	Y	Y	N	N	N	Y
4 Frank	Y	N	N	N	N	N	Y	N
5 Atkins	?	Y	N	Y	Y	N	Y	Y
6 Mavroules	Y	N	N	Y	N	N	N	Y
7 Markey	Y	N	N	N	N	N	Y	N
8 Kennedy	Y	N	N	N	Y	N	N	N
9 Moakley	Y	Y	N	Y	N	N	Y	Y
10 Studds	Y	Y	N	N	N	N	Y	N
11 Donnelly	Y	N	Y	Y	N	N	N	Y
MICHIGAN								
1 Conyers	Y	Y	N	N	N	N	Y	N
2 ***Pursell***	Y	?	?	?	?	N	N	Y
3 Wolpe	Y	N	N	N	Y	N	Y	N
4 ***Upton***	N	N	Y	Y	Y	Y	Y	Y
5 ***Henry***	N	N	Y	N	Y	N	N	Y
6 Carr	Y	Y	N	Y	Y	Y	N	Y
7 Kildee	Y	N	N	N	N	N	Y	N
8 Traxler	Y	N	Y	Y	N	Y	N	Y
9 ***Vander Jagt***	Y	N	Y	Y	Y	Y	N	Y
10 ***Schuette***	N	N	Y	Y	Y	Y	N	Y
11 ***Davis***	Y	?	Y	Y	Y	Y	N	Y
12 Bonior	Y	N	N	N	N	N	Y	N
13 Crockett	?	N	N	?	?	?	?	N
14 Hertel	Y	N	N	N	N	N	Y	N
15 Ford	?	N	N	?	N	Y	N	N
16 Dingell	Y	N	Y	Y	N	Y	Y	Y
17 Levin	Y	N	N	N	Y	N	Y	N
18 ***Broomfield***	Y	N	Y	Y	Y	N	N	Y
MINNESOTA								
1 Penny	Y	N	N	N	Y	Y	Y	N
2 ***Weber***	N	N	N	N	Y	Y	N	Y
3 ***Frenzel***	?	N	Y	Y	Y	Y	N	Y
4 Vento	Y	N	N	N	N	N	Y	N

	411	412	413	414	415	416	417	418
5 Sabo	Y	N	N	N	N	N	Y	N
6 Sikorski	N	N	N	N	Y	N	Y	N
7 ***Stangeland***	N	N	Y	Y	Y	Y	N	Y
8 Oberstar	Y	N	N	N	N	Y	Y	N
MISSISSIPPI								
1 Whitten	Y	N	Y	Y	Y	Y	N	Y
2 Espy	Y	N	Y	Y	Y	Y	Y	Y
3 Montgomery	Y	N	Y	Y	Y	Y	N	Y
4 Parker	Y	N	Y	Y	Y	Y	N	Y
5 Taylor	Y	N	Y	Y	Y	Y	N	Y
MISSOURI								
1 Clay	N	Y	N	N	N	N	Y	N
2 ***Buechner***	N	N	Y	Y	Y	Y	N	Y
3 Gephardt	Y	Y	N	N	N	N	Y	N
4 Skelton	Y	N	Y	Y	Y	Y	N	Y
5 Wheat	Y	N	N	N	Y	N	Y	N
6 ***Coleman***	N	N	Y	Y	Y	N	N	Y
7 ***Hancock***	N	N	Y	Y	Y	Y	N	Y
8 ***Emerson***	Y	N	Y	Y	Y	Y	N	Y
9 Volkmer	Y	N	Y	Y	Y	Y	Y	Y
MONTANA								
1 Williams	Y	N	N	N	N	Y	Y	N
2 ***Marlenee***	N	N	Y	Y	N	Y	N	Y
NEBRASKA								
1 ***Bereuter***	N	N	Y	Y	Y	Y	N	Y
2 Hoagland	Y	Y	N	N	Y	N	Y	N
3 ***Smith***	Y	N	Y	Y	Y	Y	N	Y
NEVADA								
1 Bilbray	Y	N	Y	Y	Y	Y	N	Y
2 ***Vucanovich***	N	N	Y	Y	Y	Y	N	Y
NEW HAMPSHIRE								
1 ***Smith***	N	N	Y	Y	Y	Y	N	Y
2 ***Douglas***	N	N	Y	Y	Y	Y	N	Y
NEW JERSEY								
1 Vacancy								
2 Hughes	Y	Y	N	N	N	N	Y	N
3 Pallone	Y	Y	Y	Y	Y	N	Y	Y
4 ***Smith***	Y	N	N	N	Y	N	N	N
5 ***Roukema***	N	N	Y	Y	Y	N	N	Y
6 Dwyer	Y	Y	N	N	N	N	Y	Y
7 ***Rinaldo***	Y	N	Y	Y	Y	N	N	Y
8 Roe	Y	Y	Y	Y	N	N	Y	Y
9 Torricelli	Y	N	Y	Y	Y	N	N	Y
10 Payne	Y	N	N	N	Y	N	Y	N
11 ***Gallo***	N	N	Y	Y	Y	Y	N	Y
12 ***Courter***	N	N	Y	Y	Y	N	Y	Y
13 ***Saxton***	N	N	Y	Y	Y	N	Y	Y
14 Guarini	Y	N	Y	Y	Y	N	Y	Y
NEW MEXICO								
1 ***Schiff***	Y	N	Y	Y	Y	Y	N	Y
2 ***Skeen***	Y	N	Y	Y	Y	Y	N	Y
3 Richardson	Y	N	Y	Y	Y	Y	N	Y
NEW YORK								
1 Hochbrueckner	Y	N	N	N	N	N	Y	N
2 Downey	Y	N	N	N	N	N	Y	N
3 Mrazek	Y	Y	N	N	N	N	Y	N
4 ***Lent***	Y	N	Y	Y	Y	Y	N	Y
5 ***McGrath***	N	N	Y	Y	Y	N	N	Y
6 Flake	Y	N	N	N	N	N	Y	N
7 Ackerman	Y	N	N	N	N	N	Y	N
8 Scheuer	Y	N	N	N	N	Y	Y	N
9 Manton	Y	Y	Y	Y	Y	N	Y	Y
10 Schumer	Y	Y	N	Y	N	N	Y	N
11 Towns	Y	N	N	N	N	N	Y	N
12 Owens	Y	N	N	N	N	N	Y	N
13 Solarz	Y	N	N	N	N	N	Y	N
14 ***Molinari***	N	N	Y	Y	Y	Y	N	Y
15 ***Green***	Y	Y	Y	Y	Y	N	Y	N
16 Rangel	Y	Y	N	N	N	N	Y	N
17 Weiss	Y	N	N	N	N	N	Y	N
18 Serrano	Y	N	N	N	N	N	Y	N
19 Engel	Y	N	N	N	N	N	Y	N
20 Lowey	Y	N	N	N	N	N	Y	N
21 ***Fish***	Y	Y	Y	Y	Y	Y	Y	N
22 ***Gilman***	+	N	Y	Y	Y	Y	Y	Y
23 McNulty	Y	Y	N	N	Y	N	N	N
24 ***Solomon***	N	N	Y	Y	Y	Y	N	Y
25 ***Boehlert***	N	N	Y	Y	Y	Y	N	Y
26 ***Martin***	N	N	Y	Y	Y	Y	N	Y
27 ***Walsh***	N	N	Y	Y	Y	Y	N	Y
28 McHugh	Y	N	N	N	Y	N	Y	N
29 ***Horton***	Y	N	Y	Y	Y	Y	N	Y
30 Slaughter	Y	Y	N	N	Y	N	Y	N
31 ***Paxon***	N	N	Y	Y	Y	Y	N	Y

	411	412	413	414	415	416	417	418
32 LaFalce	Y	?	N	N	Y	N	Y	N
33 Nowak	Y	Y	N	Y	Y	N	Y	N
34 ***Houghton***	Y	N	Y	Y	Y	Y	N	Y
NORTH CAROLINA								
1 Jones	Y	Y	Y	Y	Y	Y	N	Y
2 Valentine	Y	N	Y	Y	Y	Y	N	Y
3 Lancaster	Y	Y	Y	Y	N	Y	Y	Y
4 Price	Y	Y	N	Y	Y	N	Y	N
5 Neal	Y	N	Y	Y	Y	Y	N	Y
6 ***Coble***	N	N	Y	Y	Y	Y	N	Y
7 Rose	Y	Y	N	Y	Y	Y	Y	N
8 Hefner	Y	N	Y	Y	Y	Y	N	Y
9 ***McMillan***	N	N	Y	Y	Y	Y	N	Y
10 ***Ballenger***	N	N	Y	Y	Y	Y	N	Y
11 Clarke	Y	Y	Y	Y	Y	Y	N	Y
NORTH DAKOTA								
AL Dorgan	Y	N	N	N	N	Y	Y	N
OHIO								
1 Luken	Y	N	N	N	Y	N	Y	N
2 ***Gradison***	Y	N	Y	Y	N	N	N	Y
3 Hall	?	Y	N	Y	Y	Y	Y	N
4 ***Oxley***	Y	N	Y	Y	Y	Y	N	Y
5 ***Gillmor***	Y	N	Y	Y	N	Y	N	Y
6 ***McEwen***	Y	N	Y	Y	Y	Y	N	Y
7 ***DeWine***	N	N	Y	Y	Y	N	N	Y
8 ***Lukens***	N	N	Y	Y	Y	Y	N	Y
9 Kaptur	Y	N	N	Y	N	N	Y	N
10 ***Miller***	N	N	Y	Y	Y	Y	N	Y
11 Eckart	Y	N	Y	Y	N	Y	Y	N
12 ***Kasich***	Y	N	Y	Y	Y	Y	N	Y
13 Pease	Y	N	N	N	N	N	Y	N
14 Sawyer	Y	N	N	N	N	N	Y	N
15 ***Wylie***	Y	N	Y	Y	Y	N	N	Y
16 ***Regula***	N	N	Y	Y	Y	Y	N	Y
17 Traficant	Y	Y	N	Y	N	N	Y	Y
18 Applegate	Y	N	Y	Y	N	Y	Y	Y
19 Feighan	Y	N	N	N	N	N	Y	N
20 Oakar	Y	N	N	N	N	N	Y	N
21 Stokes	Y	N	N	N	N	N	Y	N
OKLAHOMA								
1 ***Inhofe***	N	N	Y	Y	Y	Y	N	Y
2 Synar	Y	Y	N	N	N	N	Y	N
3 Watkins	Y	N	Y	Y	Y	Y	N	Y
4 McCurdy	Y	N	Y	Y	?	#	N	Y
5 ***Edwards***	N	N	Y	Y	Y	?	?	Y
6 English	Y	N	Y	Y	Y	Y	N	Y
OREGON								
1 AuCoin	Y	N	N	N	Y	N	N	N
2 ***Smith, B.***	N	N	Y	Y	Y	Y	N	Y
3 Wyden	Y	N	Y	Y	Y	Y	Y	Y
4 DeFazio	Y	N	N	N	Y	Y	Y	N
5 ***Smith, D.***	N	N	Y	Y	Y	Y	N	Y
PENNSYLVANIA								
1 Foglietta	Y	N	N	N	N	N	Y	N
2 Gray	Y	Y	N	N	Y	N	Y	N
3 Borski	Y	Y	Y	N	N	N	N	Y
4 Kolter	Y	?	Y	Y	Y	Y	Y	Y
5 ***Schulze***	Y	N	Y	Y	Y	Y	N	Y
6 Yatron	Y	N	Y	Y	Y	Y	N	Y
7 ***Weldon***	N	N	Y	Y	Y	Y	N	Y
8 Kostmayer	Y	N	N	N	N	Y	Y	N
9 ***Shuster***	Y	N	Y	Y	Y	Y	N	Y
10 ***McDade***	?	N	Y	Y	Y	Y	N	Y
11 Kanjorski	Y	N	?	Y	Y	Y	N	Y
12 Murtha	Y	N	Y	Y	Y	Y	N	Y
13 ***Coughlin***	N	N	Y	Y	Y	N	N	Y
14 Coyne	Y	N	N	N	N	N	Y	N
15 ***Ritter***	Y	N	Y	Y	Y	Y	N	Y
16 ***Walker***	N	N	Y	Y	Y	Y	N	Y
17 ***Gekas***	N	N	Y	Y	Y	Y	N	Y
18 Walgren	Y	Y	Y	N	Y	N	Y	N
19 ***Goodling***	?	P	P	P	Y	Y	P	P
20 Gaydos	?	N	Y	Y	Y	Y	N	Y
21 ***Ridge***	N	N	Y	Y	N	Y	N	Y
22 Murphy	N	N	Y	Y	Y	Y	Y	Y
23 ***Clinger***	Y	N	Y	Y	Y	Y	N	Y
RHODE ISLAND								
1 ***Machtley***	N	N	Y	Y	Y	N	N	Y
2 ***Schneider***	Y	Y	N	Y	N	N	Y	Y
SOUTH CAROLINA								
1 ***Ravenel***	Y	N	Y	Y	Y	Y	N	Y
2 ***Spence***	N	N	Y	Y	Y	Y	Y	Y
3 Derrick	Y	Y	Y	Y	Y	Y	Y	Y
4 Patterson	Y	Y	Y	Y	Y	Y	Y	Y
5 Spratt	Y	Y	Y	Y	Y	N	Y	Y
6 Tallon	Y	N	Y	Y	Y	Y	N	Y

	411	412	413	414	415	416	417	418
SOUTH DAKOTA								
AL Johnson	Y	N	Y	Y	Y	Y	N	Y
TENNESSEE								
1 ***Quillen***	Y	N	Y	Y	Y	Y	N	Y
2 ***Duncan***	N	N	Y	Y	Y	Y	N	Y
3 Lloyd	Y	N	Y	Y	Y	Y	N	Y
4 Cooper	Y	Y	Y	Y	Y	Y	Y	Y
5 Clement	Y	Y	Y	Y	Y	Y	Y	Y
6 Gordon	Y	Y	Y	Y	Y	Y	Y	Y
7 ***Sundquist***	N	N	Y	Y	Y	Y	N	Y
8 Tanner	Y	Y	Y	Y	Y	Y	N	Y
9 Ford	Y	?	N	N	N	N	Y	N
TEXAS								
1 Chapman	Y	Y	Y	Y	Y	Y	N	Y
2 Wilson	?	N	Y	Y	Y	Y	N	Y
3 ***Bartlett***	Y	N	Y	Y	Y	Y	N	Y
4 Hall	Y	N	Y	Y	Y	Y	N	Y
5 Bryant	Y	Y	N	Y	Y	N	Y	N
6 ***Barton***	N	N	Y	Y	N	Y	N	Y
7 ***Archer***	Y	N	Y	Y	Y	Y	N	Y
8 ***Fields***	N	N	Y	Y	Y	Y	N	Y
9 Brooks	Y	Y	N	N	N	Y	Y	N
10 Pickle	Y	Y	N	Y	N	Y	Y	Y
11 Leath	Y	Y	Y	Y	Y	Y	N	Y
12 Geren	Y	N	Y	Y	Y	Y	N	Y
13 Sarpalius	Y	N	Y	Y	Y	Y	N	Y
14 Laughlin	Y	N	Y	Y	Y	Y	N	Y
15 de la Garza	?	Y	N	Y	N	Y	Y	Y
16 Coleman	Y	Y	N	Y	Y	Y	Y	Y
17 Stenholm	Y	N	Y	Y	Y	Y	N	Y
18 Washington	Y	N	N	N	N	N	Y	N
19 ***Combest***	Y	N	Y	Y	Y	Y	N	Y
20 Gonzalez	Y	Y	N	N	Y	N	Y	N
21 ***Smith***	N	N	Y	Y	Y	Y	N	Y
22 ***DeLay***	N	N	Y	Y	Y	Y	N	Y
23 Bustamante	Y	Y	N	Y	N	Y	Y	Y
24 Frost	Y	Y	Y	Y	Y	Y	Y	N
25 Andrews	Y	Y	Y	Y	Y	Y	N	Y
26 ***Armey***	N	N	Y	Y	Y	Y	N	Y
27 Ortiz	Y	Y	Y	Y	N	Y	Y	Y
UTAH								
1 ***Hansen***	N	N	Y	Y	N	Y	N	Y
2 Owens	Y	Y	N	N	Y	Y	N	N
3 ***Nielson***	Y	N	Y	Y	Y	Y	N	Y
VERMONT								
AL ***Smith***	N	N	N	N	Y	N	N	Y
VIRGINIA								
1 ***Bateman***	Y	N	Y	Y	Y	N	N	Y
2 Pickett	Y	N	Y	Y	N	Y	N	Y
3 ***Bliley***	N	N	Y	Y	Y	Y	N	Y
4 Sisisky	Y	N	Y	Y	Y	Y	N	Y
5 Payne	Y	N	Y	Y	Y	Y	N	Y
6 Olin	Y	Y	N	N	Y	Y	N	N
7 ***Slaughter***	Y	N	Y	Y	Y	Y	N	Y
8 ***Parris***	N	N	Y	Y	Y	Y	N	Y
9 Boucher	Y	Y	N	Y	N	Y	Y	Y
10 ***Wolf***	N	N	Y	Y	Y	N	N	Y
WASHINGTON								
1 ***Miller***	N	N	Y	Y	Y	N	Y	N
2 Swift	Y	Y	N	N	N	Y	Y	N
3 Unsoeld	Y	Y	N	N	N	Y	Y	N
4 ***Morrison***	Y	N	Y	Y	Y	Y	N	Y
5 Foley								
6 Dicks	Y	N	N	Y	N	N	Y	Y
7 McDermott	Y	N	N	N	N	N	Y	N
8 ***Chandler***	N	N	Y	Y	N	N	N	Y
WEST VIRGINIA								
1 Mollohan	?	N	N	N	Y	Y	Y	N
2 Staggers	Y	N	N	N	N	Y	Y	N
3 Wise	Y	N	N	N	N	Y	Y	N
4 Rahall	Y	Y	N	N	N	Y	Y	N
WISCONSIN								
1 Aspin	Y	Y	N	Y	N	N	Y	N
2 Kastenmeier	Y	N	N	N	N	N	Y	N
3 ***Gunderson***	Y	N	Y	Y	Y	Y	Y	Y
4 Kleczka	Y	Y	N	N	N	N	Y	N
5 Moody	Y	Y	N	N	N	N	Y	N
6 ***Petri***	Y	N	Y	N	N	Y	N	Y
7 Obey	Y	Y	N	N	N	Y	Y	N
8 ***Roth***	Y	N	Y	Y	Y	Y	N	Y
9 ***Sensenbrenner***	N	N	Y	Y	Y	Y	N	Y
WYOMING								
AL ***Thomas***	N	N	Y	Y	N	Y	N	Y

Southern states - Ala., Ark., Fla., Ga., Ky., La., Miss., N.C., Okla., S.C., Tenn., Texas, Va.
Omitted votes are quorum calls, which CQ does not include in its vote charts.

419. HR 5269. Crime Bill/Industry Production. Frank, D-Mass., amendment to prohibit Federal Prison Industries from producing or expanding production of any item that is manufactured by the footwear, apparel, textile or furniture industries until after the market study required by the bill has been submitted. Adopted 226-204: R 61-113; D 165-91 (ND 126-47, SD 39-44), Oct. 4, 1990.

420. H Con Res 310. Fiscal 1991 Budget Resolution/Rule. Adoption of the rule (H Res 488) providing for House floor consideration of the conference report on the bill to set budget levels for fiscal 1991: budget authority, $1.49 trillion; outlays, $1.24 trillion; revenues, $1.73 trillion; deficit, $64 billion by incorporating the spending and revenue targets announced Sept. 30 by the budget summit. Adopted 339-94: R 125-51; D 214-43 (ND 135-39, SD 79-4), Oct. 4, 1990.

421. H Con Res 310. Fiscal 1991 Budget Resolution/Adoption. Adoption of the conference report on the bill to set binding budget levels for fiscal 1991: budget authority, $1.49 trillion; outlays, $1.24 trillion; revenues, $1.73 billion; deficit, $64 billion by incorporating the spending and revenue targets announced Sept. 30 by the budget summit. The agreement contains reconciliation instructions providing cost-saving changes in entitlement programs, increases in various user fees and taxes, and caps on annual appropriations for defense, international affairs, and domestic programs to reduce the deficit by $41 billion in fiscal 1991 and $500 billion in fiscal 1991 through 1995. Rejected 179-254: R 71-105; D 108-149 (ND 63-111, SD 45-38), Oct. 5, 1990 (in the session that began, and the Congressional Record dated, Oct. 4, 1990). A "yea" was a vote supporting the president's position.

KEY

- Y Voted for (yea).
- # Paired for.
- \+ Announced for.
- N Voted against (nay).
- X Paired against.
- \- Announced against.
- P Voted "present."
- C Voted "present" to avoid possible conflict of interest.
- ? Did not vote or otherwise make a position known.

Democrats ***Republicans***

	419	420	421
ALABAMA			
1 ***Callahan***	N	N	N
2 ***Dickinson***	N	Y	Y
3 Browder	N	Y	N
4 Bevill	N	Y	Y
5 Flippo	N	Y	Y
6 Erdreich	N	Y	Y
7 Harris	N	Y	N
ALASKA			
AL ***Young***	N	Y	Y
ARIZONA			
1 ***Rhodes***	N	Y	Y
2 Udall	Y	Y	Y
3 ***Stump***	Y	N	N
4 ***Kyl***	N	N	N
5 ***Kolbe***	N	Y	Y
ARKANSAS			
1 Alexander	Y	Y	N
2 ***Robinson***	N	Y	Y
3 ***Hammerschmidt***	Y	Y	Y
4 Anthony	N	Y	N
CALIFORNIA			
1 Bosco	Y	Y	Y
2 ***Herger***	N	N	N
3 Matsui	N	Y	Y
4 Fazio	N	Y	Y
5 Pelosi	Y	Y	N
6 Boxer	Y	N	N
7 Miller	Y	N	N
8 Dellums	Y	N	N
9 Stark	Y	N	N
10 Edwards	N	Y	N
11 Lantos	Y	Y	Y
12 ***Campbell***	N	N	N
13 Mineta	Y	Y	Y
14 ***Shumway***	N	Y	Y
15 Condit	N	Y	N
16 Panetta	N	Y	Y
17 ***Pashayan***	N	Y	N
18 Lehman	Y	Y	N
19 ***Lagomarsino***	N	Y	N
20 ***Thomas***	Y	Y	N
21 ***Gallegly***	N	Y	N
22 ***Moorhead***	N	Y	N
23 Beilenson	N	Y	Y
24 Waxman	Y	Y	N
25 Roybal	Y	Y	N
26 Berman	Y	Y	N
27 Levine	Y	Y	N
28 Dixon	Y	Y	N
29 Hawkins	Y	Y	N
30 Martinez	Y	N	N
31 Dymally	Y	N	N
32 Anderson	N	Y	Y
33 ***Dreier***	N	Y	N
34 Torres	Y	Y	Y
35 ***Lewis***	N	Y	Y
36 Brown	N	Y	N
37 ***McCandless***	N	N	N
38 ***Dornan***	N	Y	N
39 ***Dannemeyer***	Y	N	N
40 ***Cox***	N	Y	N
41 ***Lowery***	N	Y	Y
42 ***Rohrabacher***	N	N	N
43 ***Packard***	N	N	N
44 Bates	Y	Y	N
45 ***Hunter***	?	N	N
COLORADO			
1 Schroeder	N	Y	N
2 Skaggs	N	Y	Y
3 Campbell	Y	Y	N
4 ***Brown***	N	N	N
5 ***Hefley***	N	N	N
6 ***Schaefer***	Y	N	N
CONNECTICUT			
1 Kennelly	Y	Y	Y
2 Gejdenson	Y	N	Y
3 Morrison	Y	N	N
4 ***Shays***	N	Y	Y
5 ***Rowland***	Y	N	N
6 ***Johnson***	Y	Y	Y
DELAWARE			
AL Carper	N	Y	Y
FLORIDA			
1 Hutto	N	Y	N
2 ***Grant***	Y	Y	N
3 Bennett	N	Y	Y
4 ***James***	N	N	N
5 ***McCollum***	N	Y	N
6 ***Stearns***	N	Y	N
7 Gibbons	N	Y	Y
8 ***Young***	N	Y	Y
9 ***Bilirakis***	N	Y	N
10 ***Ireland***	Y	Y	Y
11 Nelson	N	Y	Y
12 ***Lewis***	N	Y	N
13 ***Goss***	N	Y	N
14 Johnston	N	Y	N
15 ***Shaw***	N	Y	Y
16 Smith	Y	Y	N
17 Lehman	N	Y	Y
18 ***Ros-Lehtinen***	N	Y	N
19 Fascell	N	Y	Y
GEORGIA			
1 Thomas	N	Y	Y
2 Hatcher	Y	Y	Y
3 Ray	N	Y	Y
4 Jones	Y	Y	N
5 Lewis	Y	Y	N
6 ***Gingrich***	N	Y	N
7 Darden	N	Y	Y
8 Rowland	Y	Y	Y
9 Jenkins	Y	Y	N
10 Barnard	N	Y	N
HAWAII			
1 ***Saiki***	N	Y	N
2 Mink	Y	Y	N
IDAHO			
1 ***Craig***	N	N	N
2 Stallings	N	Y	N
ILLINOIS			
1 Hayes	Y	N	N
2 Savage	Y	N	N
3 Russo	Y	N	N
4 Sangmeister	Y	N	N
5 Lipinski	Y	Y	N
6 ***Hyde***	Y	Y	N
7 Collins	Y	N	N
8 Rostenkowski	N	Y	Y
9 Yates	Y	Y	N
10 ***Porter***	Y	N	Y
11 Annunzio	Y	Y	N
12 ***Crane***	N	N	N
13 ***Fawell***	N	N	N
14 ***Hastert***	N	Y	Y
15 ***Madigan***	Y	Y	Y
16 ***Martin***	Y	N	N
17 Evans	Y	N	N
18 ***Michel***	N	Y	Y
19 Bruce	Y	Y	N
20 Durbin	N	Y	N
21 Costello	Y	N	N
22 Poshard	Y	N	N
INDIANA			
1 Visclosky	N	Y	Y
2 Sharp	Y	Y	N
3 ***Hiler***	N	Y	N

ND_ Northern Democrats SD Southern Democrats

	419	420	421
4 Long	Y	Y	N
5 Jontz	Y	Y	N
6 ***Burton***	N	N	N
7 ***Myers***	N	Y	N
8 McCloskey	?	N	N
9 Hamilton	N	Y	Y
10 Jacobs	N	N	N
IOWA			
1 ***Leach***	N	Y	Y
2 ***Tauke***	N	Y	N
3 Nagle	Y	Y	Y
4 Smith	N	Y	Y
5 ***Lightfoot***	N	N	N
6 ***Grandy***	Y	Y	Y
KANSAS			
1 ***Roberts***	N	N	Y
2 Slattery	N	Y	Y
3 ***Meyers***	N	Y	Y
4 Glickman	Y	N	Y
5 ***Whittaker***	Y	Y	Y
KENTUCKY			
1 Hubbard	N	Y	N
2 Natcher	N	Y	N
3 Mazzoli	N	Y	N
4 ***Bunning***	N	Y	N
5 ***Rogers***	Y	Y	N
6 ***Hopkins***	N	Y	N
7 Perkins	Y	Y	N
LOUISIANA			
1 ***Livingston***	N	Y	Y
2 Boggs	Y	Y	Y
3 Tauzin	N	Y	N
4 ***McCrery***	N	N	N
5 Huckaby	N	Y	N
6 ***Baker***	N	Y	Y
7 Hayes	N	Y	N
8 ***Holloway***	N	N	N
MAINE			
1 Brennan	Y	Y	N
2 ***Snowe***	Y	Y	N
MARYLAND			
1 Dyson	Y	N	N
2 ***Bentley***	Y	Y	N
3 Cardin	Y	Y	Y
4 McMillen	Y	Y	Y
5 Hoyer	N	Y	Y
6 Byron	N	Y	Y
7 Mfume	Y	Y	N
8 ***Morella***	Y	Y	Y
MASSACHUSETTS			
1 ***Conte***	Y	Y	Y
2 Neal	Y	Y	N
3 Early	N	N	N
4 Frank	Y	Y	N
5 Atkins	Y	N	N
6 Mavroules	N	Y	N
7 Markey	Y	Y	N
8 Kennedy	Y	N	N
9 Moakley	Y	Y	Y
10 Studds	Y	Y	N
11 Donnelly	Y	N	N
MICHIGAN			
1 Conyers	N	Y	Y
2 ***Pursell***	Y	Y	N
3 Wolpe	Y	Y	N
4 ***Upton***	Y	N	N
5 ***Henry***	Y	N	N
6 Carr	N	Y	N
7 Kildee	Y	Y	N
8 Traxler	Y	Y	Y
9 ***Vander Jagt***	Y	Y	Y
10 ***Schuette***	Y	N	N
11 ***Davis***	Y	Y	N
12 Bonior	Y	Y	N
13 Crockett	Y	Y	?
14 Hertel	Y	N	N
15 Ford	Y	Y	N
16 Dingell	Y	Y	Y
17 Levin	N	Y	Y
18 ***Broomfield***	Y	Y	N
MINNESOTA			
1 Penny	N	Y	Y
2 ***Weber***	N	Y	N
3 ***Frenzel***	N	Y	Y
4 Vento	N	Y	N

	419	420	421
5 Sabo	N	Y	Y
6 Sikorski	Y	Y	Y
7 ***Stangeland***	Y	N	N
8 Oberstar	N	Y	Y
MISSISSIPPI			
1 Whitten	N	Y	N
2 Espy	Y	Y	N
3 Montgomery	N	Y	Y
4 Parker	N	Y	Y
5 Taylor	N	Y	N
MISSOURI			
1 Clay	Y	N	N
2 ***Buechner***	N	Y	Y
3 Gephardt	Y	Y	Y
4 Skelton	Y	Y	Y
5 Wheat	Y	Y	N
6 ***Coleman***	N	Y	Y
7 ***Hancock***	Y	N	N
8 ***Emerson***	Y	Y	N
9 Volkmer	Y	Y	N
MONTANA			
1 Williams	Y	Y	N
2 ***Marlenee***	N	Y	N
NEBRASKA			
1 ***Bereuter***	N	Y	N
2 Hoagland	N	Y	N
3 ***Smith***	N	Y	Y
NEVADA			
1 Bilbray	N	Y	Y
2 ***Vucanovich***	Y	Y	Y
NEW HAMPSHIRE			
1 ***Smith***	Y	N	N
2 ***Douglas***	Y	N	N
NEW JERSEY			
1 Vacancy			
2 Hughes	N	Y	N
3 Pallone	Y	Y	N
4 ***Smith***	N	Y	N
5 ***Roukema***	N	Y	N
6 Dwyer	Y	Y	N
7 ***Rinaldo***	Y	Y	N
8 Roe	Y	Y	N
9 Torricelli	Y	Y	N
10 Payne	N	N	N
11 ***Gallo***	N	Y	Y
12 ***Courter***	N	Y	Y
13 ***Saxton***	N	Y	N
14 Guarini	N	Y	N
NEW MEXICO			
1 ***Schiff***	N	Y	Y
2 ***Skeen***	N	Y	Y
3 Richardson	Y	Y	Y
NEW YORK			
1 Hochbrueckner	Y	Y	N
2 Downey	Y	Y	N
3 Mrazek	Y	Y	N
4 ***Lent***	?	Y	Y
5 ***McGrath***	Y	Y	N
6 Flake	Y	N	N
7 Ackerman	Y	Y	Y
8 Scheuer	Y	Y	Y
9 Manton	Y	Y	Y
10 Schumer	Y	N	N
11 Towns	Y	N	N
12 Owens	Y	N	N
13 Solarz	Y	Y	Y
14 ***Molinari***	N	Y	Y
15 ***Green***	N	Y	Y
16 Rangel	N	N	N
17 Weiss	Y	N	N
18 Serrano	Y	Y	Y
19 Engel	Y	N	N
20 Lowey	Y	N	N
21 ***Fish***	Y	Y	Y
22 ***Gilman***	N	Y	N
23 McNulty	Y	Y	Y
24 ***Solomon***	Y	Y	N
25 ***Boehlert***	Y	Y	Y
26 ***Martin***	Y	Y	Y
27 ***Walsh***	N	Y	N
28 McHugh	N	Y	Y
29 ***Horton***	Y	Y	Y
30 Slaughter	Y	Y	N
31 ***Paxon***	N	Y	N

	419	420	421
32 LaFalce	Y	Y	Y
33 Nowak	N	Y	N
34 ***Houghton***	N	Y	Y
NORTH CAROLINA			
1 Jones	Y	Y	N
2 Valentine	Y	Y	Y
3 Lancaster	Y	Y	Y
4 Price	Y	Y	Y
5 Neal	Y	Y	N
6 ***Coble***	Y	Y	N
7 Rose	Y	Y	Y
8 Hefner	Y	Y	N
9 ***McMillan***	Y	Y	Y
10 ***Ballenger***	Y	N	N
11 Clarke	Y	Y	N
NORTH DAKOTA			
AL Dorgan	N	Y	N
OHIO			
1 Luken	Y	Y	Y
2 ***Gradison***	N	Y	Y
3 Hall	Y	Y	Y
4 ***Oxley***	N	Y	Y
5 ***Gillmor***	Y	Y	Y
6 ***McEwen***	N	N	N
7 ***DeWine***	N	Y	Y
8 ***Lukens***	Y	Y	Y
9 Kaptur	Y	Y	Y
10 ***Miller***	N	Y	Y
11 Eckart	Y	Y	N
12 ***Kasich***	Y	N	N
13 Pease	N	Y	Y
14 Sawyer	N	Y	Y
15 ***Wylie***	Y	Y	Y
16 ***Regula***	N	N	N
17 Traficant	Y	Y	N
18 Applegate	Y	Y	N
19 Feighan	Y	Y	N
20 Oakar	Y	N	N
21 Stokes	Y	N	N
OKLAHOMA			
1 ***Inhofe***	N	N	N
2 Synar	N	Y	N
3 Watkins	N	Y	Y
4 McCurdy	N	Y	Y
5 ***Edwards***	N	Y	N
6 English	N	Y	N
OREGON			
1 AuCoin	N	Y	Y
2 ***Smith, B.***	N	Y	N
3 Wyden	N	Y	N
4 DeFazio	Y	N	N
5 ***Smith, D.***	Y	N	N
PENNSYLVANIA			
1 Foglietta	Y	Y	Y
2 Gray	Y	Y	Y
3 Borski	Y	Y	N
4 Kolter	Y	Y	N
5 ***Schulze***	N	N	N
6 Yatron	N	Y	N
7 ***Weldon***	Y	N	N
8 Kostmayer	Y	Y	Y
9 ***Shuster***	Y	N	N
10 ***McDade***	N	Y	Y
11 Kanjorski	Y	Y	N
12 Murtha	Y	Y	Y
13 ***Coughlin***	N	Y	Y
14 Coyne	Y	N	N
15 ***Ritter***	Y	Y	N
16 ***Walker***	Y	N	N
17 ***Gekas***	N	Y	Y
18 Walgren	Y	Y	N
19 ***Goodling***	N	Y	Y
20 Gaydos	Y	Y	N
21 ***Ridge***	N	Y	Y
22 Murphy	Y	Y	N
23 ***Clinger***	N	Y	Y
RHODE ISLAND			
1 ***Machtley***	Y	Y	N
2 ***Schneider***	Y	Y	N
SOUTH CAROLINA			
1 ***Ravenel***	N	Y	N
2 ***Spence***	N	N	N
3 Derrick	Y	Y	Y
4 Patterson	Y	Y	N
5 Spratt	Y	Y	Y
6 Tallon	Y	Y	Y

	419	420	421
SOUTH DAKOTA			
AL Johnson	Y	Y	N
TENNESSEE			
1 ***Quillen***	Y	Y	Y
2 ***Duncan***	Y	Y	N
3 Lloyd	Y	Y	Y
4 Cooper	Y	Y	Y
5 Clement	N	Y	Y
6 Gordon	Y	Y	Y
7 ***Sundquist***	N	Y	Y
8 Tanner	Y	Y	Y
9 Ford	Y	N	N
TEXAS			
1 Chapman	N	Y	Y
2 Wilson	Y	Y	Y
3 ***Bartlett***	N	Y	Y
4 Hall	Y	N	Y
5 Bryant	Y	N	N
6 ***Barton***	N	Y	N
7 ***Archer***	N	Y	Y
8 ***Fields***	N	N	N
9 Brooks	N	Y	N
10 Pickle	N	Y	Y
11 Leath	Y	Y	Y
12 Geren	N	Y	N
13 Sarpalius	N	N	N
14 Laughlin	Y	Y	N
15 de la Garza	Y	Y	Y
16 Coleman	N	Y	Y
17 Stenholm	N	Y	Y
18 Washington	Y	Y	N
19 ***Combest***	N	Y	Y
20 Gonzalez	Y	Y	N
21 ***Smith***	N	N	N
22 ***DeLay***	Y	N	N
23 Bustamante	Y	Y	Y
24 Frost	Y	Y	Y
25 Andrews	N	Y	Y
26 ***Armey***	N	N	N
27 Ortiz	N	Y	Y
UTAH			
1 ***Hansen***	N	Y	Y
2 Owens	Y	Y	Y
3 ***Nielson***	N	Y	N
VERMONT			
AL ***Smith***	N	Y	Y
VIRGINIA			
1 ***Bateman***	N	Y	Y
2 Pickett	N	Y	N
3 ***Bliley***	Y	N	N
4 Sisisky	N	Y	Y
5 Payne	Y	Y	Y
6 Olin	Y	Y	Y
7 ***Slaughter***	Y	Y	N
8 ***Parris***	N	Y	N
9 Boucher	N	Y	N
10 ***Wolf***	N	Y	Y
WASHINGTON			
1 ***Miller***	N	Y	Y
2 Swift	Y	Y	Y
3 Unsoeld	Y	Y	N
4 ***Morrison***	N	Y	Y
5 Foley			Y
6 Dicks	Y	Y	Y
7 McDermott	Y	Y	Y
8 ***Chandler***	N	Y	Y
WEST VIRGINIA			
1 Mollohan	Y	Y	Y
2 Staggers	Y	Y	N
3 Wise	Y	Y	N
4 Rahall	Y	Y	N
WISCONSIN			
1 Aspin	N	Y	Y
2 Kastenmeier	N	Y	N
3 ***Gunderson***	Y	Y	N
4 Kleczka	Y	Y	N
5 Moody	Y	N	N
6 ***Petri***	N	N	N
7 Obey	N	Y	N
8 ***Roth***	N	N	N
9 ***Sensenbrenner***	Y	N	N
WYOMING			
AL ***Thomas***	N	Y	N

Southern states - Ala., Ark., Fla., Ga., Ky., La., Miss., N.C., Okla., S.C., Tenn., Texas, Va.
Omitted votes are quorum calls, which CQ does not include in its vote charts.

HOUSE VOTES 422, 423, 424, 425, 426, 427, 428, 429

422. HR 5269. Crime Bill/Racial Discrimination. Hughes, D-N.J., amendment to require courts to examine the validity of statistics in determining a pattern of racial discrimination in death-penalty cases, reduce the weight of statistics in proving discrimination, and lessen the burden of proof to rebut such cases from "clear and convincing evidence" to "a preponderance of evidence." Adopted 218-186: R 19-150; D 199-36 (ND 153-6, SD 46-30), Oct. 5, 1990. A "nay" was a vote supporting the president's position.

423. HR 5269. Crime Bill/Racial Discrimination. Sensenbrenner, R-Wis., amendment to strike the provisions of the bill that bar execution of prisoners who demonstrate that their death sentence was imposed because of racial discrimination. Rejected 204-216: R 153-17; D 51-199 (ND 14-158, SD 37-41), Oct. 5, 1990. A "yea" was a vote supporting the president's position.

424. HR 5269. Crime Bill/Exclusionary Rule. Douglas, R-N.H., amendment to establish a broad "good faith" exception to the exclusionary rule in federal cases with or without warrants. The amendment would permit the use of evidence gathered by police acting in good faith that their search or seizure was not unreasonable and was in compliance with the Fourth Amendment. Adopted 265-157: R 167-4; D 98-153 (ND 38-131, SD 60-22), Oct. 5, 1990. A "yea" was a vote supporting the president's position.

425. HR 5269. Crime Bill/Drug-Related Violence. Waxman, D-Calif., amendment to authorize $50 million in fiscal 1991 and such sums as necessary in fiscal 1992 and 1993 for grants to help to defray uncompensated costs incurred by trauma centers arising from drug-related violence. Adopted 262-160: R 49-121; D 213-39 (ND 160-10, SD 53-29), Oct. 5, 1990. A "nay" was a vote supporting the president's position.

426. HR 5269. Crime Bill/Drug Tests. Dingell, D-Mich., amendment to require the Health and Human Services Department to establish a certification program for laboratories that perform urine tests to detect drug use. The amendment also provides enforceable rights and remedies for individuals and drug testing programs harmed by inaccurate test results, breaches of confidentiality or improper laboratory procedures. Adopted 333-86: R 88-83; D 245-3 (ND 167-1, SD 78-2), Oct. 5, 1990. A "nay" was a vote supporting the president's position.

427. HR 5269. Crime Bill/Passage. Passage of the bill to increase the number of federal crimes subject to the death penalty; restrict federal habeas corpus appeals by state prisoners sentenced to death, increase funds for law enforcement at the state and local levels, enact into law judicially created exceptions to the exclusionary rule, and for other purposes. Passed 368-55: R 170-1; D 198-54 (ND 125-47, SD 73-7), Oct. 5, 1990.

428. HR 4739. Fiscal 1991 Defense Authorization/Closed Meetings. Aspin, D-Wis., motion to close to the public the conference committee meetings on the bill to authorize the appropriation of funds in fiscal 1991 for military programs of the Defense Department, when classified national security information is under consideration. Motion agreed to 410-2: R 168-0; D 242-2 (ND 164-2, SD 78-0), Oct. 5, 1990.

429. S 1430. National Service Act/Instruction of Conferees. Porter, R-Ill., motion to instruct the House conferees on the National Service Act to insist on House provisions, exempting unpaid volunteers from negligence. Motion agreed to 412-0: R 168-0; D 244-0 (ND 168-0, SD 76-0), Oct. 5, 1990.

KEY

Y Voted for (yea).
\# Paired for.
\+ Announced for.
N Voted against (nay).
X Paired against.
\- Announced against.
P Voted "present."
C Voted "present" to avoid possible conflict of interest.
? Did not vote or otherwise make a position known.

Democrats ***Republicans***

	422	423	424	425	426	427	428	429
ALABAMA								
1 ***Callahan***	N	Y	Y	N	N	Y	Y	Y
2 ***Dickinson***	N	Y	Y	N	Y	Y	Y	Y
3 Browder	N	Y	Y	N	Y	Y	Y	Y
4 Bevill	N	Y	Y	N	Y	Y	Y	Y
5 Flippo	N	Y	Y	Y	Y	Y	Y	Y
6 Erdreich	N	Y	Y	Y	Y	Y	Y	Y
7 Harris	N	Y	Y	N	Y	Y	Y	Y
ALASKA								
AL ***Young***	?	N	?	N	Y	Y	Y	Y
ARIZONA								
1 ***Rhodes***	N	Y	Y	N	N	Y	Y	Y
2 Udall	Y	N	Y	Y	Y	Y	?	?
3 ***Stump***	N	Y	Y	N	N	Y	Y	Y
4 ***Kyl***	N	Y	Y	N	N	Y	Y	Y
5 ***Kolbe***	N	Y	Y	N	N	Y	Y	Y
ARKANSAS								
1 Alexander	?	?	Y	Y	Y	Y	Y	Y
2 ***Robinson***	N	Y	?	?	?	?	?	?
3 ***Hammerschmidt***	N	Y	Y	N	Y	Y	Y	Y
4 Anthony	N	N	Y	Y	Y	Y	Y	Y
CALIFORNIA								
1 Bosco	N	Y	Y	Y	Y	Y	Y	Y
2 ***Herger***	N	Y	Y	N	N	Y	Y	Y
3 Matsui	Y	N	N	Y	Y	Y	Y	Y
4 Fazio	Y	N	N	Y	Y	Y	Y	Y
5 Pelosi	Y	N	N	Y	Y	N	Y	Y
6 Boxer	Y	N	N	Y	Y	Y	?	?
7 Miller	Y	N	N	Y	Y	Y	Y	Y
8 Dellums	Y	N	N	Y	Y	N	Y	Y
9 Stark	Y	N	N	Y	Y	Y	Y	Y
10 Edwards	Y	N	N	Y	Y	N	Y	Y
11 Lantos	Y	N	N	Y	Y	Y	Y	Y
12 ***Campbell***	Y	Y	N	Y	N	N	Y	Y
13 Mineta	Y	N	N	Y	Y	Y	Y	Y
14 ***Shumway***	N	Y	Y	N	N	Y	Y	Y
15 Condit	?	Y	Y	Y	Y	Y	Y	Y
16 Panetta	Y	N	N	Y	Y	Y	Y	Y
17 ***Pashayan***	N	Y	Y	N	Y	Y	Y	Y
18 Lehman	Y	N	N	Y	Y	Y	Y	Y
19 ***Lagomarsino***	N	Y	Y	Y	N	Y	Y	Y
20 ***Thomas***	N	Y	Y	N	N	Y	Y	Y
21 ***Gallegly***	N	Y	Y	N	N	Y	Y	Y
22 ***Moorhead***	N	Y	Y	N	N	Y	Y	Y
23 Beilenson	?	N	N	Y	Y	N	Y	Y
24 Waxman	?	N	N	Y	Y	Y	Y	Y
25 Roybal	Y	N	N	Y	Y	N	Y	Y
26 Berman	Y	N	N	Y	Y	N	Y	Y
27 Levine	Y	N	N	Y	Y	Y	?	Y
28 Dixon	?	N	N	Y	Y	Y	Y	Y
29 Hawkins	Y	N	N	Y	Y	N	Y	Y
30 Martinez	Y	N	Y	Y	Y	Y	Y	Y
31 Dymally	Y	N	N	Y	Y	N	Y	Y
32 Anderson	Y	N	N	Y	Y	Y	Y	Y
33 ***Dreier***	N	Y	Y	N	Y	Y	Y	Y
34 Torres	Y	N	N	Y	?	Y	Y	Y
35 ***Lewis***	N	Y	Y	N	N	Y	Y	Y
36 Brown	Y	N	N	Y	Y	Y	Y	?
37 ***McCandless***	N	Y	Y	N	Y	Y	Y	Y
38 ***Dornan***	N	Y	Y	N	Y	Y	Y	Y
39 ***Dannemeyer***	N	Y	Y	N	N	Y	Y	Y
40 ***Cox***	N	Y	Y	N	N	Y	Y	Y
41 ***Lowery***	-	+	+	+	+	+	?	?
42 ***Rohrabacher***	N	Y	Y	N	N	Y	Y	Y
43 ***Packard***	N	Y	Y	N	N	Y	Y	Y
44 Bates	Y	N	Y	Y	Y	Y	Y	Y
45 ***Hunter***	N	Y	Y	Y	N	Y	Y	Y
COLORADO								
1 Schroeder	Y	N	N	Y	Y	N	Y	Y
2 Skaggs	Y	N	N	Y	Y	Y	Y	Y
3 Campbell	Y	N	Y	Y	Y	Y	Y	Y
4 ***Brown***	N	Y	Y	N	N	Y	Y	Y
5 ***Hefley***	N	Y	Y	N	N	Y	Y	Y
6 ***Schaefer***	N	Y	Y	N	Y	Y	Y	Y
CONNECTICUT								
1 Kennelly	Y	N	N	Y	Y	Y	Y	Y
2 Gejdenson	Y	N	N	Y	Y	Y	Y	Y
3 Morrison	Y	N	N	Y	Y	Y	Y	Y
4 ***Shays***	Y	N	Y	Y	Y	Y	Y	Y
5 ***Rowland***	Y	N	Y	Y	Y	Y	Y	Y
6 ***Johnson***	Y	Y	Y	Y	Y	Y	Y	Y
DELAWARE								
AL Carper	Y	N	N	Y	Y	Y	Y	Y
FLORIDA								
1 Hutto	N	Y	Y	N	Y	Y	Y	Y
2 ***Grant***	N	Y	Y	N	Y	Y	Y	Y
3 Bennett	Y	Y	Y	Y	Y	N	Y	Y
4 ***James***	Y	Y	N	Y	Y	Y	Y	Y
5 ***McCollum***	N	Y	Y	Y	N	Y	Y	Y
6 ***Stearns***	N	Y	Y	Y	N	Y	Y	Y
7 Gibbons	Y	N	N	Y	Y	Y	Y	Y
8 ***Young***	N	Y	Y	Y	N	Y	Y	Y
9 ***Bilirakis***	N	Y	Y	Y	Y	Y	Y	Y
10 ***Ireland***	N	Y	Y	N	N	Y	Y	Y
11 Nelson	Y	N	Y	Y	Y	Y	Y	Y
12 ***Lewis***	N	Y	Y	Y	N	Y	Y	Y
13 ***Goss***	N	Y	Y	Y	N	Y	Y	Y
14 Johnston	Y	N	Y	Y	Y	Y	Y	Y
15 ***Shaw***	N	Y	Y	Y	N	Y	Y	Y
16 Smith	Y	N	Y	Y	Y	Y	Y	Y
17 Lehman	Y	N	N	Y	Y	N	Y	Y
18 ***Ros-Lehtinen***	?	?	?	Y	Y	Y	Y	Y
19 Fascell	Y	N	Y	Y	Y	Y	Y	Y
GEORGIA								
1 Thomas	N	Y	Y	N	Y	Y	Y	Y
2 Hatcher	N	Y	Y	Y	Y	Y	Y	Y
3 Ray	Y	Y	Y	Y	Y	Y	Y	Y
4 Jones	Y	N	Y	Y	Y	Y	Y	Y
5 Lewis	Y	N	N	Y	Y	N	Y	Y
6 ***Gingrich***	N	Y	Y	N	N	Y	Y	Y
7 Darden	N	Y	Y	Y	Y	Y	Y	Y
8 Rowland	N	Y	Y	Y	Y	Y	Y	Y
9 Jenkins	N	Y	Y	Y	Y	Y	Y	Y
10 Barnard	N	Y	Y	Y	Y	Y	Y	Y
HAWAII								
1 ***Saiki***	Y	N	Y	Y	Y	Y	Y	Y
2 Mink	Y	N	N	Y	Y	Y	Y	Y
IDAHO								
1 ***Craig***	N	Y	Y	N	N	Y	Y	Y
2 Stallings	Y	N	Y	N	Y	N	Y	Y
ILLINOIS								
1 Hayes	Y	N	N	Y	Y	Y	Y	Y
2 Savage	Y	N	N	Y	Y	N	Y	Y
3 Russo	N	Y	N	Y	Y	Y	Y	Y
4 Sangmeister	Y	N	N	Y	Y	Y	Y	Y
5 Lipinski	Y	N	N	N	Y	Y	Y	Y
6 ***Hyde***	N	Y	Y	Y	N	Y	Y	Y
7 Collins	Y	N	N	Y	Y	N	Y	Y
8 Rostenkowski	Y	N	N	Y	Y	Y	Y	Y
9 Yates	Y	N	N	Y	Y	Y	Y	Y
10 ***Porter***	N	Y	Y	N	N	Y	Y	Y
11 Annunzio	Y	N	N	Y	Y	Y	Y	Y
12 ***Crane***	?	?	Y	N	N	Y	Y	Y
13 ***Fawell***	N	Y	Y	N	Y	Y	Y	Y
14 ***Hastert***	N	Y	Y	N	N	Y	Y	Y
15 ***Madigan***	?	?	Y	N	?	?	?	?
16 ***Martin***	N	Y	Y	Y	Y	Y	Y	Y
17 Evans	Y	N	N	Y	Y	Y	Y	Y
18 ***Michel***	N	Y	Y	N	N	Y	Y	Y
19 Bruce	Y	N	N	Y	Y	Y	Y	Y
20 Durbin	Y	N	N	Y	Y	Y	Y	Y
21 Costello	Y	N	N	Y	?	Y	Y	Y
22 Poshard	Y	N	N	Y	Y	Y	Y	Y
INDIANA								
1 Visclosky	Y	N	N	Y	Y	N	Y	Y
2 Sharp	Y	N	Y	Y	Y	Y	Y	Y
3 ***Hiler***	N	Y	Y	N	N	Y	Y	Y

ND Northern Democrats SD Southern Democrats

	422	423	424	425	426	427	428	429
4 Long	Y	N	Y	Y	Y	Y	Y	Y
5 Jontz	Y	N	N	Y	Y	Y	Y	Y
6 ***Burton***	N	Y	Y	N	N	Y	Y	Y
7 ***Myers***	N	Y	Y	N	N	Y	Y	Y
8 McCloskey	Y	N	N	Y	Y	Y	Y	Y
9 Hamilton	Y	N	N	Y	Y	Y	Y	Y
10 Jacobs	Y	N	Y	Y	Y	Y	Y	Y
IOWA								
1 ***Leach***	Y	N	Y	N	Y	Y	Y	Y
2 ***Tauke***	N	Y	Y	N	Y	Y	Y	Y
3 Nagle	?	N	N	Y	Y	N	Y	Y
4 Smith	Y	N	N	Y	Y	Y	Y	Y
5 ***Lightfoot***	N	Y	Y	N	N	Y	Y	Y
6 ***Grandy***	N	Y	Y	N	N	Y	Y	Y
KANSAS								
1 ***Roberts***	N	Y	Y	N	Y	Y	Y	Y
2 Slattery	Y	N	N	Y	Y	Y	Y	Y
3 ***Meyers***	N	Y	Y	N	N	Y	Y	Y
4 Glickman	Y	N	N	N	Y	Y	Y	Y
5 ***Whittaker***	N	Y	Y	Y	Y	Y	Y	Y
KENTUCKY								
1 Hubbard	N	Y	Y	N	Y	Y	Y	Y
2 Natcher	Y	N	N	Y	Y	Y	Y	Y
3 Mazzoli	Y	N	N	Y	Y	Y	Y	Y
4 ***Bunning***	N	Y	Y	N	N	Y	Y	Y
5 ***Rogers***	N	Y	Y	N	Y	Y	Y	Y
6 ***Hopkins***	N	Y	Y	N	N	Y	Y	Y
7 Perkins	Y	N	N	Y	Y	Y	Y	Y
LOUISIANA								
1 ***Livingston***	N	Y	Y	N	N	Y	Y	Y
2 Boggs	Y	N	N	Y	Y	Y	Y	Y
3 Tauzin	N	Y	Y	N	Y	Y	Y	Y
4 ***McCrery***	N	Y	Y	Y	N	Y	Y	Y
5 Huckaby	N	Y	Y	N	?	?	?	?
6 ***Baker***	N	Y	Y	Y	N	Y	Y	Y
7 Hayes	N	?	?	?	?	?	?	?
8 ***Holloway***	N	Y	Y	N	N	Y	Y	Y
MAINE								
1 Brennan	Y	N	N	Y	Y	Y	Y	Y
2 ***Snowe***	N	Y	Y	Y	Y	Y	Y	Y
MARYLAND								
1 Dyson	Y	N	Y	Y	Y	N	Y	Y
2 ***Bentley***	N	Y	Y	N	N	Y	Y	Y
3 Cardin	Y	N	N	Y	Y	N	Y	Y
4 McMillen	Y	N	N	Y	Y	Y	Y	Y
5 Hoyer	Y	N	N	Y	Y	N	Y	Y
6 Byron	N	Y	Y	N	Y	N	Y	Y
7 Mfume	?	N	N	Y	Y	Y	Y	Y
8 ***Morella***	Y	N	N	Y	Y	Y	Y	Y
MASSACHUSETTS								
1 ***Conte***	Y	N	Y	Y	Y	Y	Y	Y
2 Neal	Y	N	N	Y	Y	Y	Y	Y
3 Early	Y	N	N	Y	Y	Y	Y	Y
4 Frank	Y	N	Y	Y	Y	Y	Y	Y
5 Atkins	Y	N	Y	Y	Y	Y	Y	Y
6 Mavroules	Y	N	N	Y	Y	Y	Y	Y
7 Markey	?	N	N	Y	Y	Y	Y	Y
8 Kennedy	Y	N	N	Y	Y	Y	Y	Y
9 Moakley	Y	N	N	Y	Y	Y	Y	Y
10 Studds	Y	N	N	Y	Y	Y	Y	Y
11 Donnelly	Y	N	N	Y	Y	Y	Y	Y
MICHIGAN								
1 Conyers	Y	N	N	Y	Y	N	Y	Y
2 ***Pursell***	N	Y	Y	N	Y	Y	Y	Y
3 Wolpe	Y	N	N	Y	Y	Y	Y	Y
4 ***Upton***	N	Y	Y	N	Y	Y	Y	Y
5 ***Henry***	N	Y	Y	N	N	Y	Y	Y
6 Carr	Y	N	N	Y	Y	Y	Y	Y
7 Kildee	Y	N	N	Y	Y	N	Y	Y
8 Traxler	Y	Y	N	Y	Y	Y	Y	Y
9 ***Vander Jagt***	N	Y	Y	N	Y	Y	Y	Y
10 ***Schuette***	N	Y	Y	Y	Y	Y	Y	Y
11 ***Davis***	N	Y	Y	N	Y	Y	?	Y
12 Bonior	Y	N	N	Y	Y	Y	Y	Y
13 Crockett	?	?	?	?	?	?	?	?
14 Hertel	Y	N	N	Y	Y	Y	Y	Y
15 Ford	?	?	?	?	?	Y	Y	Y
16 Dingell	Y	Y	N	Y	Y	Y	Y	Y
17 Levin	Y	N	N	Y	Y	N	Y	Y
18 ***Broomfield***	N	Y	Y	N	Y	Y	Y	Y
MINNESOTA								
1 Penny	Y	N	Y	N	N	N	Y	Y
2 ***Weber***	N	Y	Y	N	N	Y	Y	Y
3 ***Frenzel***	N	Y	Y	N	N	Y	Y	Y
4 Vento	Y	N	N	Y	Y	Y	Y	Y

	422	423	424	425	426	427	428	429
5 Sabo	Y	N	Y	Y	Y	N	Y	Y
6 Sikorski	Y	N	N	Y	Y	Y	Y	Y
7 ***Stangeland***	N	Y	Y	N	Y	Y	Y	Y
8 Oberstar	Y	N	N	Y	Y	N	Y	Y
MISSISSIPPI								
1 Whitten	N	Y	N	Y	Y	Y	Y	Y
2 Espy	Y	N	N	Y	Y	Y	Y	Y
3 Montgomery	N	Y	Y	N	Y	Y	Y	Y
4 Parker	N	Y	Y	N	Y	Y	Y	Y
5 Taylor	N	Y	Y	N	Y	Y	Y	Y
MISSOURI								
1 Clay	Y	N	N	Y	Y	N	Y	Y
2 ***Buechner***	N	Y	Y	N	N	Y	Y	Y
3 Gephardt	Y	N	N	Y	Y	Y	?	Y
4 Skelton	N	Y	Y	N	Y	Y	Y	Y
5 Wheat	Y	N	N	Y	Y	N	Y	Y
6 ***Coleman***	N	Y	Y	N	Y	Y	Y	Y
7 ***Hancock***	N	Y	Y	N	N	Y	Y	Y
8 ***Emerson***	N	Y	Y	N	Y	Y	Y	Y
9 Volkmer	Y	Y	Y	N	Y	Y	Y	Y
MONTANA								
1 Williams	Y	N	N	N	Y	N	Y	Y
2 ***Marlenee***	N	Y	Y	N	N	Y	Y	Y
NEBRASKA								
1 ***Bereuter***	N	Y	Y	Y	Y	Y	Y	Y
2 Hoagland	Y	N	N	Y	Y	Y	Y	Y
3 ***Smith***	N	Y	Y	?	?	?	?	?
NEVADA								
1 Bilbray	N	Y	Y	Y	Y	Y	Y	Y
2 ***Vucanovich***	N	Y	Y	N	N	Y	Y	Y
NEW HAMPSHIRE								
1 ***Smith***	N	Y	Y	N	N	Y	Y	Y
2 ***Douglas***	N	Y	Y	N	N	Y	Y	Y
NEW JERSEY								
1 Vacancy								
2 Hughes	Y	N	N	Y	Y	Y	Y	Y
3 Pallone	Y	N	Y	Y	Y	Y	Y	Y
4 ***Smith***	Y	N	Y	Y	Y	Y	Y	Y
5 ***Roukema***	N	Y	Y	N	Y	Y	Y	Y
6 Dwyer	?	N	N	Y	Y	Y	Y	Y
7 ***Rinaldo***	N	Y	Y	Y	Y	Y	Y	Y
8 Roe	Y	N	N	Y	Y	Y	Y	Y
9 Torricelli	Y	N	N	Y	Y	Y	Y	Y
10 Payne	Y	N	N	Y	Y	N	Y	Y
11 ***Gallo***	N	Y	Y	N	Y	Y	Y	Y
12 ***Courter***	N	Y	Y	Y	Y	Y	Y	Y
13 ***Saxton***	Y	N	Y	N	Y	Y	Y	Y
14 Guarini	Y	N	Y	Y	Y	Y	Y	Y
NEW MEXICO								
1 ***Schiff***	N	Y	Y	Y	Y	Y	Y	Y
2 ***Skeen***	N	Y	Y	N	Y	Y	Y	Y
3 Richardson	Y	N	Y	Y	Y	Y	Y	Y
NEW YORK								
1 Hochbrueckner	Y	N	N	Y	Y	Y	Y	Y
2 Downey	Y	N	N	Y	Y	Y	Y	Y
3 Mrazek	Y	N	N	Y	Y	Y	Y	Y
4 ***Lent***	N	Y	Y	N	Y	Y	Y	Y
5 ***McGrath***	N	Y	Y	N	Y	Y	Y	Y
6 Flake	Y	N	N	Y	Y	Y	Y	Y
7 Ackerman	Y	N	N	Y	Y	Y	Y	Y
8 Scheuer	Y	N	N	Y	Y	Y	Y	Y
9 Manton	Y	N	Y	Y	Y	Y	Y	Y
10 Schumer	Y	N	N	Y	Y	Y	Y	Y
11 Towns	?	N	N	Y	Y	N	Y	Y
12 Owens	Y	N	N	Y	Y	N	Y	Y
13 Solarz	Y	N	N	Y	Y	Y	Y	Y
14 ***Molinari***	N	Y	Y	Y	Y	Y	Y	Y
15 ***Green***	Y	N	Y	Y	Y	Y	Y	Y
16 Rangel	Y	N	N	Y	Y	Y	Y	Y
17 Weiss	Y	N	N	Y	Y	N	N	Y
18 Serrano	Y	N	N	Y	Y	N	Y	Y
19 Engel	+	N	N	Y	Y	Y	Y	Y
20 Lowey	Y	N	N	Y	Y	Y	Y	Y
21 ***Fish***	Y	N	Y	Y	Y	Y	Y	Y
22 ***Gilman***	Y	N	Y	Y	Y	Y	Y	Y
23 McNulty	Y	N	Y	Y	Y	Y	Y	Y
24 ***Solomon***	N	Y	Y	N	N	Y	Y	Y
25 ***Boehlert***	Y	N	Y	Y	Y	Y	Y	Y
26 ***Martin***	N	Y	Y	N	Y	Y	Y	Y
27 ***Walsh***	N	Y	Y	Y	Y	Y	Y	Y
28 McHugh	Y	N	N	Y	Y	N	Y	Y
29 ***Horton***	Y	N	N	Y	Y	Y	Y	Y
30 Slaughter	Y	N	N	Y	Y	Y	Y	Y
31 ***Paxon***	N	Y	Y	N	N	Y	Y	Y

	422	423	424	425	426	427	428	429
32 LaFalce	Y	N	?	Y	Y	Y	Y	Y
33 Nowak	Y	N	N	Y	Y	Y	Y	Y
34 ***Houghton***	N	Y	Y	N	N	Y	Y	Y
NORTH CAROLINA								
1 Jones	Y	Y	Y	Y	?	?	?	?
2 Valentine	N	Y	Y	N	N	Y	Y	?
3 Lancaster	Y	Y	Y	N	Y	Y	Y	Y
4 Price	Y	Y	Y	Y	Y	Y	Y	Y
5 Neal	?	?	Y	N	Y	Y	Y	Y
6 ***Coble***	N	Y	Y	N	N	Y	Y	Y
7 Rose	?	Y	N	Y	Y	Y	Y	?
8 Hefner	Y	Y	Y	Y	Y	Y	Y	Y
9 ***McMillan***	N	Y	Y	N	Y	Y	Y	Y
10 ***Ballenger***	N	Y	Y	N	N	Y	Y	Y
11 Clarke	Y	Y	Y	Y	Y	Y	Y	Y
NORTH DAKOTA								
AL Dorgan	Y	N	N	Y	Y	N	Y	Y
OHIO								
1 Luken	Y	N	?	?	?	?	?	?
2 ***Gradison***	N	Y	Y	N	Y	Y	Y	Y
3 Hall	Y	N	?	?	Y	Y	Y	Y
4 ***Oxley***	N	Y	Y	N	N	Y	Y	Y
5 ***Gillmor***	N	Y	Y	N	N	Y	Y	Y
6 ***McEwen***	N	Y	Y	N	N	Y	Y	Y
7 ***DeWine***	N	Y	Y	Y	N	Y	Y	Y
8 ***Lukens***	N	Y	Y	N	N	Y	Y	?
9 Kaptur	Y	N	N	Y	Y	Y	Y	Y
10 ***Miller***	N	Y	Y	N	Y	Y	Y	Y
11 Eckart	Y	N	N	Y	Y	Y	Y	Y
12 ***Kasich***	N	Y	Y	N	Y	Y	Y	Y
13 Pease	?	N	N	Y	Y	N	Y	Y
14 Sawyer	Y	N	N	Y	Y	Y	Y	Y
15 ***Wylie***	N	Y	Y	?	Y	Y	Y	Y
16 ***Regula***	N	Y	Y	N	Y	Y	Y	Y
17 Traficant	Y	N	Y	Y	Y	Y	Y	Y
18 Applegate	Y	N	Y	Y	Y	Y	Y	Y
19 Feighan	?	N	N	Y	Y	N	Y	Y
20 Oakar	Y	N	N	Y	?	Y	Y	Y
21 Stokes	?	N	N	Y	Y	N	Y	Y
OKLAHOMA								
1 ***Inhofe***	N	Y	Y	N	N	Y	Y	Y
2 Synar	Y	N	N	Y	Y	Y	Y	Y
3 Watkins	N	N	Y	Y	Y	Y	Y	Y
4 McCurdy	N	Y	Y	N	Y	Y	Y	Y
5 ***Edwards***	N	Y	Y	N	N	Y	Y	Y
6 English	N	N	Y	N	Y	Y	Y	Y
OREGON								
1 AuCoin	Y	N	N	Y	Y	N	Y	Y
2 ***Smith, B.***	N	Y	Y	N	N	Y	Y	Y
3 Wyden	Y	N	Y	Y	Y	Y	Y	Y
4 DeFazio	Y	N	N	Y	Y	N	N	Y
5 ***Smith, D.***	N	Y	Y	N	N	Y	Y	Y
PENNSYLVANIA								
1 Foglietta	Y	N	N	Y	Y	Y	Y	Y
2 Gray	Y	N	N	Y	Y	Y	Y	?
3 Borski	Y	N	Y	Y	Y	Y	Y	Y
4 Kolter	Y	Y	Y	Y	Y	Y	?	Y
5 ***Schulze***	N	Y	Y	Y	Y	Y	Y	Y
6 Yatron	N	Y	Y	Y	Y	Y	Y	Y
7 ***Weldon***	N	Y	Y	Y	Y	Y	Y	Y
8 Kostmayer	Y	N	N	Y	Y	N	Y	Y
9 ***Shuster***	N	Y	Y	N	Y	Y	Y	Y
10 ***McDade***	N	Y	Y	Y	Y	Y	Y	Y
11 Kanjorski	Y	Y	Y	Y	Y	Y	Y	Y
12 Murtha	Y	Y	Y	Y	Y	Y	Y	Y
13 ***Coughlin***	?	?	?	?	?	?	?	?
14 Coyne	Y	N	N	Y	Y	Y	Y	Y
15 ***Ritter***	N	Y	Y	N	N	Y	Y	Y
16 ***Walker***	N	Y	Y	N	N	Y	Y	Y
17 ***Gekas***	N	Y	Y	N	N	Y	Y	Y
18 Walgren	Y	N	Y	Y	Y	Y	Y	Y
19 ***Goodling***	P	P	Y	N	Y	Y	?	Y
20 Gaydos	Y	Y	Y	Y	Y	Y	Y	Y
21 ***Ridge***	N	Y	Y	Y	Y	Y	Y	Y
22 Murphy	Y	N	N	N	Y	Y	Y	Y
23 ***Clinger***	N	Y	Y	Y	Y	Y	Y	Y
RHODE ISLAND								
1 ***Machtley***	Y	N	Y	Y	Y	Y	Y	Y
2 ***Schneider***	Y	N	Y	Y	Y	Y	Y	Y
SOUTH CAROLINA								
1 ***Ravenel***	N	Y	Y	N	Y	Y	Y	?
2 ***Spence***	N	Y	Y	N	Y	Y	Y	Y
3 Derrick	Y	Y	N	Y	Y	Y	Y	Y
4 Patterson	Y	N	Y	N	Y	Y	Y	Y
5 Spratt	Y	N	Y	Y	Y	Y	Y	Y
6 Tallon	Y	N	Y	N	Y	Y	Y	Y

	422	423	424	425	426	427	428	429
SOUTH DAKOTA								
AL Johnson	Y	N	Y	Y	Y	Y	Y	Y
TENNESSEE								
1 ***Quillen***	N	Y	Y	N	N	Y	?	?
2 ***Duncan***	Y	Y	Y	N	N	Y	Y	Y
3 Lloyd	Y	N	Y	N	Y	Y	Y	Y
4 Cooper	Y	N	Y	Y	Y	Y	Y	Y
5 Clement	Y	Y	Y	N	Y	Y	Y	Y
6 Gordon	Y	N	N	Y	Y	Y	Y	Y
7 ***Sundquist***	N	Y	Y	N	Y	Y	Y	Y
8 Tanner	Y	N	Y	N	Y	Y	Y	Y
9 Ford	?	N	N	Y	Y	N	Y	?
TEXAS								
1 Chapman	?	?	Y	Y	Y	Y	Y	Y
2 Wilson	?	?	Y	Y	Y	Y	Y	Y
3 ***Bartlett***	N	Y	Y	Y	N	Y	Y	Y
4 Hall	N	Y	Y	Y	Y	Y	Y	Y
5 Bryant	Y	N	N	Y	Y	Y	Y	Y
6 ***Barton***	N	Y	Y	N	Y	Y	Y	Y
7 ***Archer***	N	Y	Y	N	N	Y	Y	Y
8 ***Fields***	N	Y	Y	N	Y	Y	Y	Y
9 Brooks	Y	N	N	Y	Y	Y	Y	Y
10 Pickle	Y	N	Y	Y	Y	Y	Y	Y
11 Leath	N	Y	Y	N	Y	Y	Y	?
12 Geren	Y	N	Y	N	Y	Y	Y	Y
13 Sarpalius	N	Y	Y	Y	Y	Y	Y	Y
14 Laughlin	N	Y	Y	N	Y	Y	Y	Y
15 de la Garza	Y	N	Y	Y	Y	Y	?	Y
16 Coleman	Y	N	N	Y	Y	Y	Y	Y
17 Stenholm	N	Y	Y	N	Y	Y	Y	Y
18 Washington	?	N	N	Y	Y	N	Y	Y
19 ***Combest***	N	Y	Y	N	N	Y	Y	Y
20 Gonzalez	Y	N	N	Y	Y	N	Y	Y
21 ***Smith***	N	Y	Y	N	N	Y	Y	Y
22 ***DeLay***	N	Y	Y	N	N	Y	Y	Y
23 Bustamante	Y	N	Y	Y	Y	Y	Y	Y
24 Frost	Y	N	N	Y	N	Y	Y	Y
25 Andrews	Y	N	Y	Y	Y	Y	Y	Y
26 ***Armey***	N	Y	Y	N	N	Y	Y	Y
27 Ortiz	Y	N	Y	Y	Y	Y	Y	Y
UTAH								
1 ***Hansen***	N	Y	Y	N	N	Y	Y	Y
2 Owens	Y	N	N	Y	Y	Y	Y	Y
3 ***Nielson***	N	Y	Y	-	Y	Y	Y	Y
VERMONT								
AL ***Smith***	N	N	Y	Y	Y	Y	Y	Y
VIRGINIA								
1 ***Bateman***	N	Y	Y	N	N	Y	Y	Y
2 Pickett	Y	N	N	N	Y	Y	?	Y
3 ***Bliley***	N	Y	Y	N	Y	Y	Y	Y
4 Sisisky	Y	N	Y	Y	Y	Y	Y	Y
5 Payne	Y	Y	Y	N	Y	Y	Y	Y
6 Olin	Y	N	N	N	Y	N	Y	Y
7 ***Slaughter***	N	Y	Y	N	Y	Y	Y	Y
8 ***Parris***	N	Y	Y	N	Y	Y	Y	Y
9 Boucher	Y	N	N	Y	Y	Y	Y	Y
10 ***Wolf***	N	Y	Y	N	Y	Y	Y	Y
WASHINGTON								
1 ***Miller***	N	Y	Y	N	Y	Y	Y	Y
2 Swift	Y	N	N	Y	Y	Y	Y	Y
3 Unsoeld	Y	N	N	Y	Y	Y	Y	Y
4 ***Morrison***	N	Y	Y	N	Y	Y	Y	Y
5 Foley								
6 Dicks	Y	N	Y	Y	Y	Y	Y	Y
7 McDermott	Y	N	N	Y	Y	Y	Y	Y
8 ***Chandler***	N	Y	Y	N	Y	Y	Y	Y
WEST VIRGINIA								
1 Mollohan	Y	N	N	Y	Y	N	Y	Y
2 Staggers	Y	N	N	Y	Y	N	Y	Y
3 Wise	Y	N	N	Y	Y	N	Y	Y
4 Rahall	Y	N	Y	Y	Y	N	Y	Y
WISCONSIN								
1 Aspin	Y	N	Y	Y	Y	Y	Y	Y
2 Kastenmeier	Y	N	N	Y	Y	N	Y	Y
3 ***Gunderson***	N	Y	Y	N	Y	Y	Y	Y
4 Kleczka	Y	N	N	N	Y	Y	?	Y
5 Moody	Y	N	N	Y	Y	N	Y	Y
6 ***Petri***	N	Y	Y	N	Y	Y	Y	Y
7 Obey	Y	N	N	Y	Y	N	Y	Y
8 ***Roth***	N	Y	Y	Y	Y	Y	Y	Y
9 ***Sensenbrenner***	N	Y	Y	N	Y	Y	Y	Y
WYOMING								
AL ***Thomas***	N	Y	Y	N	Y	Y	Y	Y

Southern states - Ala., Ark., Fla., Ga., Ky., La., Miss., N.C., Okla., S.C., Tenn., Texas, Va.
Omitted votes are quorum calls, which CQ does not include in its vote charts.

HOUSE VOTES 431, 432, 433, 434, 436, 437, 438, 439

431. H J Res 660. Fiscal 1991 Continuing Appropriations/Passage. Passage of the joint resolution to make continuing appropriations for fiscal 1991 from Oct. 5 to Oct. 12, 1990, for the departments, agencies and programs covered by the 13 regular appropriations bills; suspend until Oct. 12 sequestration (automatic budget cuts) required by the Gramm-Rudman antideficit law; and extend the debt limit until Oct. 12. Passed 300-113: R 66-101; D 234-12 (ND 160-6, SD 74-6), Oct. 5, 1990.

432. Procedural Motion. Brown, R-Colo., motion to approve the House Journal of Friday, Oct. 5. Motion agreed to 264-101: R 48-96; D 216-5 (ND 144-5, SD 72-0), Oct. 6, 1990.

433. H J Res 660. Fiscal 1991 Continuing Appropriations/Veto Override. Passage, over President Bush's Oct. 6 veto, of the bill to provide continuing appropriations from Oct. 5 to Oct. 12, 1990, for the departments, agencies and programs covered by the 13 regular appropriations bills; suspend sequestration (automatic budget cuts) required by the Gramm-Rudman antideficit law; and extend the federal debt limit until Oct. 12. Rejected 260-138: R 25-129; D 235-9 (ND 163-3, SD 72-6), Oct. 6, 1990. A two-thirds majority of those present and voting (266 in this case) of both houses is required to override a veto. A "nay" was a vote supporting the president's position.

434. H Con Res 310. Fiscal 1991 Budget Resolution/Rule. Adoption of the rule (H Res 496) to provide that the conference report on the budget be recommitted to conference. The rule also waives all points of order against any subsequent conference report on H Con Res 310 and provides for House floor consideration of any new conference report. Adopted 285-105: R 49-104; D 236-1 (ND 161-0, SD 75-1), Oct. 6, 1990.

436. H Con Res 310. Fiscal 1991 Budget Resolution/Conference Report. Adoption of the conference report on the bill to set binding budget levels for fiscal 1991: budget authority, $1.486 trillion; outlays, $1.237 trillion; revenues, $1.173 trillion; deficit, $64 billion. The resolution has the same overall spending targets as the budget summit agreement, but calls for smaller cuts in Medicare and leaves open the possibility for changes in the capital gains tax rate, the income tax rate on earnings above a certain level and in other taxes. Adopted 250-164: R 32-136; D 218-28 (ND 148-19, SD 70-9), Oct. 8, 1990 (in the session that began, and in the Congressional Record dated, Oct. 7, 1990).

437. H J Res 666. Fiscal 1991 Continuing Appropriations/Sequester. Michel, R-Ill., amendment to provide for a limited sequester (automatic budget cuts) of $40.1 billion on an annual basis, the amount of deficit reduction provided for in the budget summit agreement. Rejected 186-224: R 160-9; D 26-215 (ND 8-155, SD 18-60), Oct. 8, 1990 (in the session that began, and in the Congressional Record dated, Oct. 7, 1990).

438. H J Res 666. Fiscal 1991 Continuing Appropriations/Passage. Passage of the joint resolution to provide continuing appropriations for fiscal 1991 through Oct. 20; suspend sequestration (automatic budget cuts) through Oct. 20; and extend the debt limit through Oct. 20. Passed 305-105: R 67-102; D 238-3 (ND 160-3, SD 78-0), Oct. 8, 1990 (in the session that began, and in the Congressional Record dated, Oct. 7, 1990).

439. H J Res 666. Fiscal 1991 Continuing Appropriations/Concur in Senate Amendments. Whitten, D-Miss., motion to concur in Senate amendments to the resolution (thus clearing the measure for the president) to set the spending level for programs at the lowest of the House-passed bill, Senate-passed bill or fiscal 1990 spending level, as opposed to the lowest of the House- and Senate-passed bills; change the expiration date from Oct. 20 to Oct. 19 for the continuing resolution, sequester suspension and debt limit extension; and set a sense of the Congress timetable for legislation needed to carry out the budget resolution. Motion agreed to 362-3: R 156-2; D 206-1 (ND 137-1, SD 69-0), Oct. 9, 1990 (in the session that began, and in the Congressional Record dated, Oct. 8, 1990).

KEY

Y Voted for (yea).
\# Paired for.
\+ Announced for.
N Voted against (nay).
X Paired against.
\- Announced against.
P Voted "present."
C Voted "present" to avoid possible conflict of interest.
? Did not vote or otherwise make a position known.

Democrats *Republicans*

	431	432	433	434	436	437	438	439
ALABAMA								
1 *Callahan*	Y	?	?	?	N	Y	N	Y
2 *Dickinson*	N	N	Y	N	N	Y	N	?
3 Browder	Y	Y	Y	Y	Y	N	Y	Y
4 Bevill	Y	Y	Y	Y	Y	N	Y	Y
5 Flippo	Y	Y	Y	Y	Y	N	Y	Y
6 Erdreich	Y	Y	Y	Y	Y	N	Y	Y
7 Harris	Y	Y	Y	Y	Y	N	Y	Y
ALASKA								
AL *Young*	Y	N	Y	Y	N	N	Y	Y
ARIZONA								
1 *Rhodes*	N	N	N	N	N	Y	N	Y
2 Udall	Y	Y	Y	Y	?	?	?	?
3 *Stump*	N	?	?	?	?	?	?	?
4 *Kyl*	N	N	N	N	N	Y	N	Y
5 *Kolbe*	N	N	N	N	N	Y	N	Y
ARKANSAS								
1 Alexander	Y	Y	Y	Y	?	?	?	Y
2 *Robinson*	?	?	?	?	?	?	?	?
3 *Hammerschmidt*	Y	Y	Y	N	Y	Y	Y	Y
4 Anthony	Y	Y	Y	Y	Y	N	Y	Y
CALIFORNIA								
1 Bosco	Y	Y	Y	Y	Y	Y	Y	Y
2 *Herger*	N	?	N	N	N	Y	N	Y
3 Matsui	Y	Y	Y	Y	Y	N	Y	?
4 Fazio	Y	Y	Y	Y	Y	N	Y	Y
5 Pelosi	Y	Y	Y	Y	Y	N	Y	Y
6 Boxer	?	Y	Y	Y	Y	N	Y	Y
7 Miller	Y	Y	Y	?	Y	N	Y	Y
8 Dellums	Y	Y	Y	?	Y	N	Y	Y
9 Stark	Y	Y	Y	Y	Y	?	?	?
10 Edwards	Y	Y	Y	Y	Y	N	Y	Y
11 Lantos	Y	Y	Y	Y	Y	N	Y	Y
12 *Campbell*	Y	N	N	Y	N	Y	Y	Y
13 Mineta	Y	Y	Y	Y	Y	N	Y	Y
14 *Shumway*	N	Y	N	N	N	Y	N	Y
15 Condit	Y	Y	Y	Y	N	Y	Y	Y
16 Panetta	Y	?	Y	Y	Y	N	Y	+
17 *Pashayan*	Y	N	Y	N	N	Y	Y	Y
18 Lehman	Y	Y	Y	Y	Y	N	Y	Y
19 *Lagomarsino*	Y	Y	N	N	N	Y	N	Y
20 *Thomas*	N	N	N	N	N	Y	N	Y
21 *Gallegly*	Y	?	?	?	N	Y	N	Y
22 *Moorhead*	N	Y	N	N	N	Y	N	Y
23 Beilenson	Y	Y	Y	Y	Y	N	Y	?
24 Waxman	Y	?	Y	Y	Y	N	Y	?
25 Roybal	Y	Y	Y	?	Y	N	Y	Y
26 Berman	Y	?	?	?	Y	N	Y	?
27 Levine	Y	Y	Y	Y	Y	N	Y	Y
28 Dixon	Y	Y	Y	Y	Y	N	Y	Y
29 Hawkins	?	Y	Y	Y	Y	?	?	Y
30 Martinez	Y	Y	Y	Y	Y	N	Y	Y
31 Dymally	?	?	#	?	#	?	?	Y
32 Anderson	Y	Y	Y	Y	Y	N	Y	Y
33 *Dreier*	N	N	N	N	N	Y	N	Y
34 Torres	Y	Y	Y	Y	Y	N	Y	Y
35 *Lewis*	N	N	N	N	N	Y	N	Y
36 Brown	?	?	?	?	?	?	?	Y
37 *McCandless*	N	N	N	N	N	Y	N	Y
38 *Dornan*	N	N	N	N	N	Y	N	Y
39 *Dannemeyer*	N	?	?	?	N	Y	N	N
40 *Cox*	N	N	N	N	N	Y	N	Y
41 *Lowery*	?	?	N	N	N	Y	N	Y
42 *Rohrabacher*	Y	N	N	N	N	Y	N	Y
43 *Packard*	N	?	?	?	N	Y	N	Y
44 Bates	Y	?	?	?	Y	N	Y	Y
45 *Hunter*	N	N	N	N	N	Y	N	Y
COLORADO								
1 Schroeder	Y	N	Y	Y	Y	N	Y	Y
2 Skaggs	Y	Y	Y	Y	Y	Y	Y	Y
3 Campbell	Y	?	?	?	?	?	?	Y
4 *Brown*	N	N	N	N	N	Y	N	Y
5 *Hefley*	Y	N	N	Y	N	Y	Y	Y
6 *Schaefer*	Y	N	N	Y	N	Y	Y	Y
CONNECTICUT								
1 Kennelly	Y	Y	Y	Y	Y	N	Y	Y
2 Gejdenson	Y	Y	Y	Y	Y	N	Y	Y
3 Morrison	Y	?	Y	Y	N	N	Y	?
4 *Shays*	N	N	N	Y	Y	Y	N	Y
5 *Rowland*	Y	Y	Y	Y	N	Y	Y	?
6 *Johnson*	N	Y	N	Y	Y	Y	N	Y
DELAWARE								
AL Carper	N	Y	N	Y	Y	N	Y	?
FLORIDA								
1 Hutto	Y	Y	Y	Y	Y	N	Y	Y
2 *Grant*	Y	Y	Y	Y	N	Y	Y	Y
3 Bennett	Y	Y	Y	Y	Y	N	Y	Y
4 *James*	Y	N	N	N	N	Y	Y	Y
5 *McCollum*	N	Y	N	N	N	Y	N	Y
6 *Stearns*	N	N	N	N	N	Y	N	Y
7 Gibbons	Y	Y	Y	Y	Y	N	Y	Y
8 *Young*	N	N	N	N	N	Y	Y	Y
9 *Bilirakis*	Y	N	N	Y	N	N	Y	Y
10 *Ireland*	N	N	N	N	N	Y	N	Y
11 Nelson	Y	+	Y	Y	Y	N	Y	+
12 *Lewis*	N	N	N	N	N	Y	N	Y
13 *Goss*	N	N	N	N	N	Y	N	Y
14 Johnston	Y	Y	Y	Y	Y	N	Y	?
15 *Shaw*	N	Y	N	N	N	Y	N	Y
16 Smith	Y	Y	Y	Y	Y	N	Y	Y
17 Lehman	Y	Y	Y	Y	Y	N	Y	?
18 *Ros-Lehtinen*	Y	N	N	Y	N	Y	N	Y
19 Fascell	Y	Y	Y	Y	Y	N	Y	Y
GEORGIA								
1 Thomas	Y	Y	Y	Y	Y	N	Y	Y
2 Hatcher	Y	Y	Y	Y	Y	N	Y	Y
3 Ray	Y	?	N	Y	Y	N	Y	?
4 Jones	Y	Y	Y	Y	Y	N	Y	Y
5 Lewis	Y	Y	Y	Y	Y	N	Y	Y
6 *Gingrich*	N	N	N	N	N	Y	N	Y
7 Darden	Y	Y	Y	Y	Y	N	Y	Y
8 Rowland	Y	Y	Y	Y	Y	N	Y	Y
9 Jenkins	Y	Y	Y	Y	Y	N	Y	Y
10 Barnard	Y	Y	Y	Y	Y	N	Y	Y
HAWAII								
1 *Saiki*	Y	Y	Y	Y	N	Y	Y	Y
2 Mink	Y	Y	Y	Y	Y	N	Y	Y
IDAHO								
1 *Craig*	Y	N	N	Y	N	Y	N	Y
2 Stallings	Y	Y	Y	Y	Y	Y	Y	Y
ILLINOIS								
1 Hayes	Y	Y	Y	Y	Y	N	Y	Y
2 Savage	Y	?	Y	Y	N	N	Y	Y
3 Russo	Y	Y	Y	Y	N	N	Y	?
4 Sangmeister	N	Y	Y	Y	N	N	N	Y
5 Lipinski	Y	Y	Y	Y	Y	N	Y	?
6 *Hyde*	N	?	N	N	N	Y	N	Y
7 Collins	Y	Y	Y	Y	Y	N	Y	Y
8 Rostenkowski	Y	?	?	?	?	?	?	?
9 Yates	Y	Y	Y	Y	Y	?	?	?
10 *Porter*	N	Y	N	Y	N	Y	N	Y
11 Annunzio	Y	Y	Y	Y	N	N	Y	?
12 *Crane*	N	N	N	N	N	Y	N	N
13 *Fawell*	N	N	N	N	N	Y	N	Y
14 *Hastert*	N	N	N	N	N	Y	N	Y
15 *Madigan*	?	?	?	?	?	?	?	Y
16 *Martin*	N	?	?	?	N	Y	N	?
17 Evans	Y	Y	Y	Y	Y	N	Y	Y
18 *Michel*	N	?	N	Y	N	Y	N	Y
19 Bruce	Y	Y	Y	Y	Y	N	Y	Y
20 Durbin	Y	Y	Y	Y	Y	N	Y	Y
21 Costello	Y	Y	Y	Y	N	N	Y	Y
22 Poshard	Y	Y	Y	Y	N	N	Y	Y
INDIANA								
1 Visclosky	N	?	Y	Y	Y	N	Y	Y
2 Sharp	Y	Y	Y	Y	Y	N	Y	Y
3 *Hiler*	N	N	N	N	N	Y	N	Y

ND Northern Democrats SD Southern Democrats

	431	432	433	434	436	437	438	439
4 Long	Y	Y	Y	Y	N	N	Y	Y
5 Jontz	Y	Y	Y	Y	Y	N	Y	Y
6 ***Burton***	N	N	N	N	N	Y	N	Y
7 ***Myers***	Y	Y	Y	N	N	Y	N	Y
8 McCloskey	Y	Y	Y	Y	Y	N	Y	Y
9 Hamilton	Y	Y	Y	Y	Y	N	Y	Y
10 Jacobs	Y	N	Y	Y	?	?	?	Y
IOWA								
1 ***Leach***	N	N	N	N	Y	Y	Y	Y
2 ***Tauke***	N	N	N	N	N	Y	N	?
3 Nagle	Y	Y	Y	Y	Y	N	Y	Y
4 Smith	Y	Y	Y	Y	Y	N	Y	Y
5 ***Lightfoot***	N	N	N	N	N	Y	N	Y
6 ***Grandy***	N	N	N	N	Y	Y	N	Y
KANSAS								
1 ***Roberts***	Y	N	N	Y	Y	Y	Y	Y
2 Slattery	Y	Y	Y	Y	Y	Y	Y	Y
3 ***Meyers***	Y	N	Y	N	Y	Y	Y	Y
4 Glickman	Y	Y	Y	Y	Y	N	Y	Y
5 ***Whittaker***	Y	N	N	Y	Y	Y	Y	Y
KENTUCKY								
1 Hubbard	Y	Y	Y	Y	N	Y	Y	Y
2 Natcher	Y	Y	Y	Y	N	N	Y	Y
3 Mazzoli	Y	Y	Y	Y	Y	N	Y	Y
4 ***Bunning***	N	N	N	N	N	Y	N	?
5 ***Rogers***	Y	N	N	N	N	Y	N	Y
6 ***Hopkins***	Y	N	N	N	N	Y	N	Y
7 Perkins	Y	Y	Y	Y	N	N	Y	Y
LOUISIANA								
1 ***Livingston***	N	?	?	?	N	Y	N	Y
2 Boggs	Y	?	Y	Y	Y	N	Y	Y
3 Tauzin	Y	?	#	?	N	Y	Y	Y
4 ***McCrery***	#	?	?	?	N	Y	Y	Y
5 Huckaby	?	?	?	?	N	N	Y	Y
6 ***Baker***	N	?	?	?	N	Y	N	Y
7 Hayes	?	?	?	?	?	?	?	?
8 ***Holloway***	N	?	?	?	?	?	?	Y
MAINE								
1 Brennan	Y	?	Y	Y	N	N	Y	Y
2 ***Snowe***	Y	Y	Y	Y	N	Y	Y	Y
MARYLAND								
1 Dyson	Y	?	Y	Y	N	N	Y	Y
2 ***Bentley***	Y	N	Y	N	N	N	Y	Y
3 Cardin	Y	Y	Y	Y	Y	N	Y	Y
4 McMillen	Y	Y	Y	Y	Y	N	Y	Y
5 Hoyer	Y	Y	Y	Y	Y	N	Y	Y
6 Byron	N	Y	Y	Y	Y	N	Y	Y
7 Mfume	Y	Y	Y	Y	Y	N	Y	Y
8 ***Morella***	Y	Y	Y	Y	Y	N	Y	Y
MASSACHUSETTS								
1 ***Conte***	Y	Y	Y	Y	Y	Y	Y	Y
2 Neal	Y	Y	Y	Y	Y	N	Y	Y
3 Early	Y	Y	Y	Y	Y	N	Y	Y
4 Frank	?	Y	Y	Y	Y	N	Y	Y
5 Atkins	Y	Y	Y	Y	Y	N	Y	Y
6 Mavroules	Y	Y	Y	Y	Y	N	Y	Y
7 Markey	Y	Y	Y	Y	Y	N	Y	?
8 Kennedy	Y	Y	Y	Y	Y	N	Y	Y
9 Moakley	Y	Y	Y	Y	Y	N	Y	Y
10 Studds	Y	Y	Y	Y	Y	N	Y	Y
11 Donnelly	Y	Y	Y	Y	Y	N	Y	?
MICHIGAN								
1 Conyers	Y	?	Y	Y	Y	N	Y	Y
2 ***Pursell***	N	Y	N	N	N	Y	N	Y
3 Wolpe	Y	Y	Y	Y	Y	N	Y	Y
4 ***Upton***	N	N	N	N	N	Y	N	Y
5 ***Henry***	?	?	?	?	?	?	?	?
6 Carr	Y	Y	Y	Y	N	N	Y	Y
7 Kildee	Y	Y	Y	Y	Y	N	Y	Y
8 Traxler	Y	Y	Y	Y	Y	N	Y	?
9 ***Vander Jagt***	N	?	?	?	N	Y	N	?
10 ***Schuette***	Y	N	N	N	N	Y	N	Y
11 ***Davis***	Y	Y	N	N	N	Y	Y	Y
12 Bonior	Y	Y	Y	Y	Y	N	Y	Y
13 Crockett	?	?	?	?	?	?	?	?
14 Hertel	Y	Y	Y	Y	Y	N	Y	?
15 Ford	Y	?	Y	Y	Y	N	Y	?
16 Dingell	Y	Y	Y	Y	Y	N	Y	?
17 Levin	Y	Y	Y	Y	Y	N	Y	Y
18 ***Broomfield***	Y	Y	N	Y	N	Y	N	?
MINNESOTA								
1 Penny	N	Y	N	Y	Y	N	N	Y
2 ***Weber***	N	N	N	N	N	Y	N	?
3 ***Frenzel***	N	N	N	N	N	Y	N	Y
4 Vento	Y	Y	Y	Y	Y	N	Y	Y

	431	432	433	434	436	437	438	439
5 Sabo	Y	Y	Y	Y	Y	N	Y	Y
6 Sikorski	Y	N	Y	Y	Y	N	Y	Y
7 ***Stangeland***	Y	N	Y	N	N	Y	Y	Y
8 Oberstar	Y	Y	Y	Y	Y	N	Y	Y
MISSISSIPPI								
1 Whitten	Y	Y	Y	?	Y	N	Y	?
2 Espy	Y	?	Y	Y	Y	N	Y	?
3 Montgomery	N	?	?	?	Y	Y	Y	Y
4 Parker	Y	Y	N	Y	Y	Y	Y	Y
5 Taylor	Y	Y	Y	Y	Y	Y	Y	Y
MISSOURI								
1 Clay	Y	N	Y	?	Y	N	Y	Y
2 ***Buechner***	N	N	N	N	N	Y	N	Y
3 Gephardt	Y	?	Y	Y	Y	N	Y	Y
4 Skelton	Y	Y	Y	Y	Y	N	Y	?
5 Wheat	Y	Y	Y	Y	Y	N	Y	Y
6 ***Coleman***	N	N	N	N	Y	Y	Y	Y
7 ***Hancock***	N	N	N	N	N	Y	N	Y
8 ***Emerson***	Y	Y	N	Y	N	Y	Y	Y
9 Volkmer	Y	Y	Y	Y	Y	N	Y	Y
MONTANA								
1 Williams	Y	Y	Y	Y	N	N	Y	N
2 ***Marlenee***	N	N	N	N	N	Y	N	Y
NEBRASKA								
1 ***Bereuter***	Y	N	Y	Y	Y	Y	Y	Y
2 Hoagland	Y	Y	Y	Y	Y	N	Y	Y
3 ***Smith***	?	?	?	?	Y	Y	Y	?
NEVADA								
1 Bilbray	Y	Y	Y	Y	Y	N	Y	Y
2 ***Vucanovich***	N	N	N	N	N	Y	N	Y
NEW HAMPSHIRE								
1 ***Smith***	N	N	N	N	N	Y	N	Y
2 ***Douglas***	N	N	N	N	N	Y	N	Y
NEW JERSEY								
1 Vacancy								
2 Hughes	Y	Y	Y	Y	Y	N	Y	Y
3 Pallone	Y	Y	Y	Y	N	Y	Y	Y
4 ***Smith***	Y	Y	N	Y	N	Y	Y	Y
5 ***Roukema***	N	N	N	Y	N	Y	Y	Y
6 Dwyer	Y	?	Y	Y	Y	N	Y	Y
7 ***Rinaldo***	Y	Y	N	Y	N	Y	Y	Y
8 Roe	Y	Y	Y	Y	Y	N	Y	Y
9 Torricelli	Y	Y	Y	Y	Y	N	Y	?
10 Payne	Y	Y	Y	Y	Y	N	Y	Y
11 ***Gallo***	N	N	N	N	N	Y	N	Y
12 ***Courter***	N	?	?	?	?	?	?	Y
13 ***Saxton***	Y	N	N	N	N	Y	N	Y
14 Guarini	Y	Y	Y	Y	Y	N	Y	?
NEW MEXICO								
1 ***Schiff***	Y	Y	Y	Y	N	Y	Y	Y
2 ***Skeen***	Y	Y	Y	Y	N	Y	Y	Y
3 Richardson	Y	?	?	?	Y	N	Y	Y
NEW YORK								
1 Hochbrueckner	Y	Y	Y	Y	Y	N	Y	Y
2 Downey	Y	Y	Y	Y	Y	N	Y	Y
3 Mrazek	Y	Y	Y	Y	Y	N	Y	Y
4 ***Lent***	N	Y	N	Y	N	Y	N	Y
5 ***McGrath***	Y	N	Y	N	Y	Y	Y	Y
6 Flake	Y	?	Y	Y	Y	N	Y	Y
7 Ackerman	Y	Y	Y	Y	Y	N	Y	?
8 Scheuer	Y	Y	Y	Y	Y	N	Y	Y
9 Manton	Y	Y	Y	Y	Y	N	Y	Y
10 Schumer	Y	Y	Y	Y	Y	N	Y	?
11 Towns	Y	?	?	?	?	?	?	?
12 Owens	Y	?	Y	Y	Y	N	Y	?
13 Solarz	Y	Y	Y	Y	Y	N	Y	Y
14 ***Molinari***	Y	N	N	N	Y	Y	N	Y
15 ***Green***	Y	Y	N	Y	N	Y	N	Y
16 Rangel	Y	Y	Y	Y	Y	N	Y	Y
17 Weiss	Y	Y	Y	Y	Y	N	Y	Y
18 Serrano	Y	Y	Y	Y	Y	N	Y	Y
19 Engel	Y	Y	Y	Y	Y	N	Y	Y
20 Lowey	Y	Y	Y	Y	Y	N	Y	Y
21 ***Fish***	?	Y	N	Y	Y	Y	Y	Y
22 ***Gilman***	Y	+	Y	Y	Y	N	Y	Y
23 McNulty	Y	Y	Y	Y	Y	N	Y	Y
24 ***Solomon***	N	?	N	N	N	Y	N	Y
25 ***Boehlert***	Y	N	Y	Y	Y	Y	Y	Y
26 ***Martin***	Y	N	N	N	N	Y	Y	?
27 ***Walsh***	Y	N	N	N	Y	Y	Y	Y
28 McHugh	Y	Y	Y	Y	Y	N	Y	Y
29 ***Horton***	N	Y	N	Y	Y	N	Y	Y
30 Slaughter	Y	Y	Y	Y	Y	N	Y	Y
31 ***Paxon***	N	N	N	N	N	Y	N	Y

	431	432	433	434	436	437	438	439
32 LaFalce	Y	?	Y	Y	Y	N	Y	?
33 Nowak	Y	Y	Y	Y	Y	N	Y	?
34 ***Houghton***	N	Y	N	Y	Y	Y	Y	Y
NORTH CAROLINA								
1 Jones	?	?	?	?	?	?	?	?
2 Valentine	Y	Y	Y	Y	Y	Y	Y	Y
3 Lancaster	Y	Y	Y	Y	Y	Y	Y	Y
4 Price	Y	Y	Y	Y	Y	N	Y	Y
5 Neal	Y	Y	Y	Y	Y	N	Y	Y
6 ***Coble***	N	N	N	N	N	Y	N	Y
7 Rose	Y	Y	Y	Y	Y	N	Y	?
8 Hefner	Y	Y	Y	Y	Y	N	Y	?
9 ***McMillan***	N	N	N	N	Y	Y	Y	Y
10 ***Ballenger***	N	?	N	N	N	Y	N	Y
11 Clarke	Y	Y	Y	Y	Y	Y	Y	Y
NORTH DAKOTA								
AL Dorgan	Y	Y	Y	Y	Y	N	Y	Y
OHIO								
1 Luken	?	?	Y	Y	Y	N	Y	?
2 ***Gradison***	Y	Y	N	N	Y	Y	Y	?
3 Hall	Y	Y	Y	Y	Y	?	?	?
4 ***Oxley***	N	N	N	N	N	Y	N	Y
5 ***Gillmor***	N	Y	N	N	N	Y	N	Y
6 ***McEwen***	N	?	X	?	N	Y	N	Y
7 ***DeWine***	Y	N	N	N	N	Y	Y	Y
8 ***Lukens***	N	N	N	N	N	Y	N	Y
9 Kaptur	Y	Y	Y	Y	Y	N	Y	Y
10 ***Miller***	N	N	N	N	N	Y	N	Y
11 Eckart	Y	Y	Y	Y	Y	N	Y	Y
12 ***Kasich***	Y	Y	N	N	N	Y	N	Y
13 Pease	N	Y	N	Y	Y	N	N	?
14 Sawyer	Y	Y	Y	Y	Y	N	Y	Y
15 ***Wylie***	Y	Y	N	Y	Y	Y	Y	Y
16 ***Regula***	N	N	N	N	N	Y	Y	Y
17 Traficant	Y	Y	Y	Y	N	N	Y	Y
18 Applegate	Y	Y	Y	Y	N	N	Y	Y
19 Feighan	Y	Y	Y	Y	Y	N	Y	Y
20 Oakar	Y	Y	Y	Y	Y	N	Y	Y
21 Stokes	Y	Y	Y	Y	Y	N	Y	Y
OKLAHOMA								
1 ***Inhofe***	N	N	N	N	N	Y	N	Y
2 Synar	Y	Y	Y	Y	Y	N	Y	Y
3 Watkins	Y	Y	Y	Y	Y	N	Y	Y
4 McCurdy	Y	Y	Y	Y	Y	N	Y	Y
5 ***Edwards***	N	N	N	N	N	Y	N	Y
6 English	Y	Y	Y	Y	N	Y	Y	Y
OREGON								
1 AuCoin	Y	Y	Y	Y	Y	N	Y	Y
2 ***Smith, B.***	N	N	N	N	N	Y	N	?
3 Wyden	Y	Y	Y	Y	Y	N	Y	Y
4 DeFazio	Y	Y	Y	Y	Y	N	Y	Y
5 ***Smith, D.***	N	?	?	?	?	?	?	?
PENNSYLVANIA								
1 Foglietta	Y	Y	Y	Y	Y	N	Y	Y
2 Gray	Y	Y	Y	Y	Y	N	Y	Y
3 Borski	Y	Y	Y	Y	Y	N	Y	Y
4 Kolter	Y	Y	Y	Y	Y	N	Y	Y
5 ***Schulze***	N	Y	N	N	N	Y	N	Y
6 Yatron	Y	Y	Y	Y	N	N	Y	Y
7 ***Weldon***	N	?	N	N	N	Y	N	Y
8 Kostmayer	Y	Y	Y	Y	Y	N	Y	Y
9 ***Shuster***	Y	Y	Y	?	N	Y	Y	?
10 ***McDade***	Y	Y	N	Y	Y	Y	Y	?
11 Kanjorski	Y	Y	Y	Y	Y	N	Y	Y
12 Murtha	Y	Y	Y	Y	Y	N	Y	Y
13 ***Coughlin***	?	N	N	Y	N	Y	Y	Y
14 Coyne	Y	Y	Y	Y	Y	N	Y	Y
15 ***Ritter***	N	Y	N	N	N	Y	Y	Y
16 ***Walker***	N	N	N	N	N	Y	N	Y
17 ***Gekas***	N	N	N	N	N	Y	Y	Y
18 Walgren	Y	?	Y	Y	Y	N	Y	Y
19 ***Goodling***	N	N	N	N	Y	Y	Y	Y
20 Gaydos	Y	Y	Y	Y	N	N	Y	Y
21 ***Ridge***	N	?	N	Y	Y	Y	Y	Y
22 Murphy	Y	N	Y	Y	Y	Y	Y	?
23 ***Clinger***	N	Y	N	Y	Y	Y	Y	Y
RHODE ISLAND								
1 ***Machtley***	Y	N	N	Y	N	Y	Y	Y
2 ***Schneider***	Y	?	#	?	N	Y	Y	Y
SOUTH CAROLINA								
1 ***Ravenel***	Y	Y	Y	Y	N	Y	Y	Y
2 ***Spence***	Y	N	N	N	N	Y	Y	Y
3 Derrick	Y	Y	Y	Y	Y	Y	Y	Y
4 Patterson	Y	Y	Y	Y	N	Y	Y	Y
5 Spratt	Y	Y	Y	Y	Y	N	Y	Y
6 Tallon	Y	Y	Y	Y	Y	N	Y	Y

	431	432	433	434	436	437	438	439
SOUTH DAKOTA								
AL Johnson	Y	Y	Y	Y	Y	N	Y	Y
TENNESSEE								
1 ***Quillen***	X	?	X	?	Y	Y	N	Y
2 ***Duncan***	Y	Y	N	N	N	Y	N	Y
3 Lloyd	Y	Y	Y	Y	Y	N	Y	Y
4 Cooper	N	Y	Y	Y	Y	N	Y	Y
5 Clement	Y	Y	Y	Y	Y	N	Y	Y
6 Gordon	Y	Y	Y	Y	Y	N	Y	Y
7 ***Sundquist***	N	N	N	N	N	Y	N	Y
8 Tanner	Y	Y	Y	Y	Y	Y	Y	Y
9 Ford	Y	?	Y	Y	Y	N	Y	Y
TEXAS								
1 Chapman	Y	Y	Y	Y	Y	N	Y	Y
2 Wilson	Y	Y	Y	Y	?	?	?	?
3 ***Bartlett***	N	Y	N	N	N	Y	N	Y
4 Hall	N	Y	N	Y	Y	Y	Y	Y
5 Bryant	Y	Y	Y	Y	Y	N	Y	Y
6 ***Barton***	N	N	N	N	N	Y	N	Y
7 ***Archer***	N	Y	N	N	N	Y	N	Y
8 ***Fields***	N	N	N	N	N	Y	N	Y
9 Brooks	Y	Y	Y	Y	Y	N	Y	?
10 Pickle	Y	Y	Y	Y	Y	Y	Y	Y
11 Leath	Y	Y	Y	?	Y	?	?	?
12 Geren	Y	Y	Y	Y	Y	Y	Y	Y
13 Sarpalius	Y	Y	Y	Y	N	Y	Y	Y
14 Laughlin	N	Y	N	Y	N	Y	Y	Y
15 de la Garza	Y	Y	Y	Y	Y	N	Y	Y
16 Coleman	Y	Y	Y	Y	Y	N	Y	Y
17 Stenholm	N	Y	N	Y	Y	Y	Y	Y
18 Washington	Y	Y	Y	N	Y	N	Y	Y
19 ***Combest***	Y	Y	N	N	N	Y	Y	Y
20 Gonzalez	Y	Y	Y	Y	Y	N	Y	Y
21 ***Smith***	Y	N	N	?	N	Y	Y	Y
22 ***DeLay***	N	N	N	N	X	Y	N	Y
23 Bustamante	Y	Y	Y	Y	Y	N	Y	Y
24 Frost	Y	Y	Y	Y	Y	N	Y	Y
25 Andrews	Y	Y	Y	Y	Y	N	Y	?
26 ***Armey***	N	N	N	N	N	Y	N	Y
27 Ortiz	Y	Y	Y	Y	Y	N	Y	Y
UTAH								
1 ***Hansen***	N	?	?	?	N	Y	N	Y
2 Owens	Y	Y	Y	Y	Y	Y	Y	Y
3 ***Nielson***	N	Y	N	Y	N	Y	N	Y
VERMONT								
AL ***Smith***	Y	Y	N	Y	Y	Y	Y	Y
VIRGINIA								
1 ***Bateman***	Y	?	Y	Y	N	Y	Y	Y
2 Pickett	Y	Y	Y	Y	Y	N	Y	Y
3 ***Bliley***	N	N	N	Y	N	Y	N	Y
4 Sisisky	Y	Y	Y	Y	Y	N	Y	Y
5 Payne	N	Y	N	Y	Y	N	Y	Y
6 Olin	Y	Y	Y	Y	Y	N	Y	Y
7 ***Slaughter***	Y	Y	N	N	N	N	Y	Y
8 ***Parris***	Y	N	Y	Y	N	N	Y	Y
9 Boucher	Y	?	Y	Y	Y	N	Y	Y
10 ***Wolf***	Y	N	Y	Y	Y	N	Y	Y
WASHINGTON								
1 ***Miller***	N	N	N	N	N	Y	N	Y
2 Swift	Y	Y	Y	Y	Y	N	Y	Y
3 Unsoeld	Y	Y	Y	Y	Y	N	Y	Y
4 ***Morrison***	Y	Y	N	Y	Y	Y	Y	Y
5 Foley			Y		Y	N	Y	
6 Dicks	Y	Y	Y	Y	Y	N	Y	Y
7 McDermott	Y	Y	Y	Y	Y	N	Y	Y
8 ***Chandler***	N	N	N	N	N	Y	N	Y
WEST VIRGINIA								
1 Mollohan	Y	Y	Y	Y	Y	N	Y	Y
2 Staggers	Y	Y	Y	Y	Y	N	Y	Y
3 Wise	Y	Y	Y	Y	Y	N	Y	Y
4 Rahall	Y	Y	Y	Y	N	N	Y	Y
WISCONSIN								
1 Aspin	Y	Y	Y	Y	Y	N	Y	?
2 Kastenmeier	Y	Y	Y	Y	Y	N	Y	Y
3 ***Gunderson***	N	Y	N	N	N	Y	N	Y
4 Kleczka	Y	Y	Y	Y	Y	N	Y	Y
5 Moody	Y	Y	Y	Y	Y	N	Y	?
6 ***Petri***	N	Y	N	N	N	Y	N	Y
7 Obey	?	Y	Y	Y	Y	N	Y	Y
8 ***Roth***	Y	?	#	Y	N	Y	Y	Y
9 ***Sensenbrenner***	N	N	N	N	N	Y	N	Y
WYOMING								
AL ***Thomas***	Y	N	N	N	N	Y	Y	Y

Southern states - Ala., Ark., Fla., Ga., Ky., La., Miss., N.C., Okla., S.C., Tenn., Texas, Va.
Omitted votes are quorum calls, which CQ does not include in its vote charts.

440. HR 4328. Textile Trade Act/Veto Override. Passage, over President Bush's Oct. 5 veto, of the bill to limit the growth of imports of textiles and apparel to 1 percent annually, establish permanent quotas for most non-rubber footwear imports at 1989 levels, authorize the special allocation of textile quotas for countries increasing their purchases of U.S. agricultural goods, and for other purposes. Rejected 275-152: R 70-103; D 205-49 (ND 131-41, SD 74-8), Oct. 10, 1990. A two-thirds majority of those present and voting (285 in this case) of both houses is required to override a veto. A "nay" was a vote supporting the president's position.

441. HR 5053. Korean War Commemorative Coin/Passage. Lehman, D-Fla., motion to suspend the rules and pass the bill to authorize the Treasury Department to mint silver dollars to commemorate the 38th anniversary of the end of the Korean War, honor those who served in the Korean War, and create revenues to finance the completion of the Korean War Veterans memorial in Washington. Motion agreed to 421-0: R 172-0; D 249-0 (ND 169-0, SD 80-0), Oct. 10, 1990. A two-thirds majority of those present and voting (281 in this case) is required for passage under suspension of the rules.

442. S 1413. Aroostook Band of Micmacs Settlement Act/Passage. Gejdenson, D-Conn., motion to suspend the rules and pass the bill to provide federal recognition of the Aroostook Band of Micmacs as an Indian tribe, making all members of the band eligible to receive all of the federal benefits and services available to recognized Indian tribes. The bill also ratifies the Micmac Settlement Act and establishes a Land Acquisition Fund in the Treasury for the benefit of the Aroostook Band of Micmacs. The Congressional Budget Office estimates that if the full amount authorized is appropriated, outlays would be $900,000 in fiscal 1991, and the cost of providing federal benefits and services to the band would be $1 million annually. Motion rejected 248-172: R 46-125; D 202-47 (ND 153-16, SD 49-31), Oct. 10, 1990. A two-thirds majority of those present and voting (280 in this case) is required for passage under suspension of the rules.

443. HR 5311. Fiscal 1991 D.C. Appropriations/Previous Question. Gallo, R-N.J., motion to order the previous question (thus ending debate and the possibility of amendment) on the Gallo motion to instruct the House conferees to agree to the Senate amendment restoring $1.6 million for the University of the District of Columbia, the amount the university had planned to spend for displaying a controversial sculpture by Judy Chicago, the "Dinner Party." The House had eliminated the funds earlier this year. Dannemeyer, R-Calif., was seeking to defeat the previous question to offer a substitute motion to agree to Senate amendments restricting homosexual and bisexual persons from participating in juvenile programs. Motion agreed to 255-156: R 44-117; D 211-39 (ND 158-13, SD 53-26), Oct. 11, 1990. (The Gallo motion to instruct was subsequently adopted by voice vote.)

444. S 2104. Civil Rights Act of 1990/Rule. Adoption of the rule (H Res 477) to provide for House floor consideration and to waive all points of order against the conference report on the bill to reverse or modify six recent Supreme Court decisions that narrowed the reach and remedies of job discrimination laws and to authorize monetary damages under Title VII of the 1964 Civil Rights Act. Adopted 412-5: R 165-4; D 247-1 (ND 168-0, SD 79-1), Oct. 11, 1990.

445. S 2104. Civil Rights Act of 1990/Recommittal Motion. Michel, R-Ill., motion to recommit to the conference committee the conference report on the bill, with instructions to report it back with language making it clear that businesses would not have to adopt artificial hiring and promotion quotas and lessening the burden of proof required in defending a job-discrimination lawsuit. Motion agreed to 375-45: R 169-0; D 206-45 (ND 136-35, SD 70-10), Oct. 11, 1990.

KEY

Y Voted for (yea).
\# Paired for.
\+ Announced for.
N Voted against (nay).
X Paired against.
\- Announced against.
P Voted "present."
C Voted "present" to avoid possible conflict of interest.
? Did not vote or otherwise make a position known.

Democrats ***Republicans***

	440	441	442	443	444	445
ALABAMA						
1 ***Callahan***	Y	Y	N	N	Y	Y
2 ***Dickinson***	Y	Y	N	N	N	Y
3 Browder	Y	Y	N	Y	Y	Y
4 Bevill	Y	Y	N	Y	Y	Y
5 Flippo	Y	Y	N	Y	Y	Y
6 Erdreich	Y	Y	N	Y	Y	Y
7 Harris	Y	Y	N	?	?	?
ALASKA						
AL ***Young***	Y	Y	N	N	Y	Y
ARIZONA						
1 ***Rhodes***	N	Y	N	N	Y	Y
2 Udall	N	Y	Y	Y	?	Y
3 ***Stump***	N	Y	N	N	Y	Y
4 ***Kyl***	N	Y	N	N	Y	Y
5 ***Kolbe***	N	Y	Y	N	Y	Y
ARKANSAS						
1 Alexander	Y	Y	Y	N	Y	Y
2 ***Robinson***	N	Y	N	N	Y	Y
3 ***Hammerschmidt***	Y	Y	N	N	Y	Y
4 Anthony	Y	Y	Y	Y	Y	Y
CALIFORNIA						
1 Bosco	Y	Y	Y	Y	Y	Y
2 ***Herger***	N	Y	N	N	Y	Y
3 Matsui	N	Y	Y	Y	Y	Y
4 Fazio	Y	Y	Y	Y	Y	Y
5 Pelosi	N	Y	Y	Y	Y	Y
6 Boxer	N	Y	Y	Y	Y	Y
7 Miller	N	Y	Y	Y	Y	N
8 Dellums	Y	Y	Y	Y	Y	N
9 Stark	N	Y	Y	Y	?	N
10 Edwards	Y	Y	Y	Y	Y	Y
11 Lantos	Y	Y	Y	Y	Y	Y
12 ***Campbell***	N	Y	Y	Y	Y	Y
13 Mineta	Y	Y	Y	Y	Y	Y
14 ***Shumway***	N	Y	N	N	Y	Y
15 Condit	Y	Y	Y	N	Y	Y
16 Panetta	N	Y	Y	Y	Y	Y
17 ***Pashayan***	Y	Y	Y	N	Y	Y
18 Lehman	Y	Y	Y	Y	Y	Y
19 ***Lagomarsino***	N	Y	N	N	Y	Y
20 ***Thomas***	Y	Y	N	N	Y	Y
21 ***Gallegly***	N	Y	N	N	Y	Y
22 ***Moorhead***	N	Y	N	N	Y	Y
23 Beilenson	N	Y	Y	Y	Y	Y
24 Waxman	N	Y	Y	Y	Y	Y
25 Roybal	Y	Y	Y	Y	Y	N
26 Berman	N	Y	Y	Y	Y	Y
27 Levine	N	Y	Y	Y	Y	Y
28 Dixon	Y	Y	Y	Y	Y	Y
29 Hawkins	Y	Y	Y	Y	Y	Y
30 Martinez	Y	?	?	Y	?	N
31 Dymally	Y	Y	Y	Y	Y	N
32 Anderson	N	Y	Y	Y	Y	Y
33 ***Dreier***	N	Y	N	N	Y	Y
34 Torres	Y	Y	Y	Y	Y	Y
35 ***Lewis***	N	Y	N	Y	Y	Y
36 Brown	Y	Y	Y	Y	Y	Y
37 ***McCandless***	N	Y	N	N	Y	Y
38 ***Dornan***	Y	Y	N	?	Y	Y
39 ***Dannemeyer***	N	Y	N	N	Y	Y
40 ***Cox***	N	Y	N	N	Y	Y
41 ***Lowery***	N	Y	N	Y	Y	Y
42 ***Rohrabacher***	N	Y	N	N	Y	Y
43 ***Packard***	N	Y	N	N	Y	Y
44 Bates	Y	Y	Y	Y	Y	Y
45 ***Hunter***	Y	Y	N	Y	Y	Y
COLORADO						
1 Schroeder	N	Y	Y	Y	Y	N
2 Skaggs	N	Y	Y	Y	Y	Y
3 Campbell	Y	Y	Y	Y	Y	Y
4 ***Brown***	N	Y	N	N	Y	Y
5 ***Hefley***	N	Y	N	N	Y	Y
6 ***Schaefer***	Y	Y	Y	N	Y	Y
CONNECTICUT						
1 Kennelly	N	Y	Y	Y	Y	Y
2 Gejdenson	Y	Y	Y	Y	Y	N
3 Morrison	Y	Y	Y	Y	+	−
4 ***Shays***	Y	Y	Y	Y	Y	Y
5 ***Rowland***	X	?	?	?	?	?
6 ***Johnson***	N	Y	Y	Y	Y	Y
DELAWARE						
AL Carper	Y	Y	N	Y	Y	Y
FLORIDA						
1 Hutto	Y	Y	N	N	Y	Y
2 ***Grant***	Y	Y	N	N	Y	Y
3 Bennett	Y	Y	N	Y	Y	Y
4 ***James***	N	Y	Y	N	Y	Y
5 ***McCollum***	N	Y	N	N	Y	Y
6 ***Stearns***	N	Y	N	N	Y	Y
7 Gibbons	N	Y	Y	Y	Y	N
8 ***Young***	N	Y	N	N	Y	Y
9 ***Bilirakis***	N	Y	N	N	Y	Y
10 ***Ireland***	N	Y	N	N	Y	Y
11 Nelson	N	Y	Y	N	Y	Y
12 ***Lewis***	N	Y	N	N	Y	Y
13 ***Goss***	N	Y	N	N	Y	Y
14 Johnston	Y	Y	Y	Y	Y	Y
15 ***Shaw***	N	Y	N	Y	Y	Y
16 Smith	Y	Y	Y	Y	Y	Y
17 Lehman	Y	Y	Y	Y	Y	N
18 ***Ros-Lehtinen***	N	Y	Y	N	Y	Y
19 Fascell	Y	Y	Y	Y	Y	Y
GEORGIA						
1 Thomas	Y	Y	Y	Y	Y	Y
2 Hatcher	Y	Y	N	Y	Y	Y
3 Ray	Y	Y	Y	Y	Y	Y
4 Jones	Y	Y	Y	Y	Y	Y
5 Lewis	Y	Y	Y	Y	Y	N
6 ***Gingrich***	Y	Y	Y	N	Y	Y
7 Darden	Y	Y	Y	Y	Y	Y
8 Rowland	Y	Y	Y	N	Y	Y
9 Jenkins	Y	Y	N	N	Y	Y
10 Barnard	Y	Y	Y	N	Y	Y
HAWAII						
1 ***Saiki***	N	Y	Y	Y	Y	Y
2 Mink	Y	Y	Y	Y	Y	Y
IDAHO						
1 ***Craig***	N	Y	N	N	Y	Y
2 Stallings	N	Y	Y	Y	Y	Y
ILLINOIS						
1 Hayes	Y	Y	Y	Y	Y	N
2 Savage	Y	Y	Y	Y	Y	N
3 Russo	Y	Y	Y	Y	Y	Y
4 Sangmeister	N	Y	N	Y	Y	Y
5 Lipinski	Y	Y	Y	Y	Y	Y
6 ***Hyde***	N	Y	Y	N	Y	Y
7 Collins	Y	Y	Y	Y	Y	N
8 Rostenkowski	N	Y	Y	Y	Y	Y
9 Yates	Y	Y	Y	Y	Y	N
10 ***Porter***	N	Y	N	N	Y	Y
11 Annunzio	Y	Y	Y	Y	Y	Y
12 ***Crane***	N	Y	N	N	N	?
13 ***Fawell***	N	Y	Y	N	N	Y
14 ***Hastert***	N	Y	N	?	Y	Y
15 ***Madigan***	N	Y	N	N	Y	Y
16 ***Martin***	N	Y	Y	N	Y	Y
17 Evans	Y	Y	Y	Y	Y	Y
18 ***Michel***	N	Y	N	Y	Y	Y
19 Bruce	Y	Y	Y	Y	Y	Y
20 Durbin	Y	Y	Y	Y	Y	N
21 Costello	Y	Y	Y	Y	Y	Y
22 Poshard	Y	Y	N	N	Y	Y
INDIANA						
1 Visclosky	Y	Y	Y	Y	Y	Y
2 Sharp	Y	Y	Y	Y	Y	Y
3 ***Hiler***	N	Y	N	N	Y	Y

ND Northern Democrats SD Southern Democrats

	440	441	442	443	444	445
4 Long	Y	Y	Y	Y	Y	Y
5 Jontz	Y	Y	Y	Y	Y	Y
6 ***Burton***	Y	Y	N	N	Y	Y
7 ***Myers***	N	Y	N	N	Y	Y
8 McCloskey	Y	Y	Y	Y	Y	Y
9 Hamilton	N	Y	Y	Y	Y	Y
10 Jacobs	Y	Y	Y	N	Y	Y
IOWA						
1 ***Leach***	N	Y	Y	Y	Y	Y
2 ***Tauke***	N	Y	Y	N	Y	Y
3 Nagle	Y	Y	Y	Y	Y	Y
4 Smith	N	Y	Y	Y	Y	Y
5 ***Lightfoot***	N	Y	N	N	Y	Y
6 ***Grandy***	N	Y	N	N	Y	Y
KANSAS						
1 ***Roberts***	N	Y	N	N	Y	Y
2 Slattery	N	Y	Y	Y	Y	Y
3 ***Meyers***	N	Y	N	N	Y	Y
4 Glickman	N	Y	N	Y	Y	Y
5 ***Whittaker***	N	Y	N	N	Y	Y
KENTUCKY						
1 Hubbard	Y	Y	Y	Y	Y	Y
2 Natcher	Y	Y	Y	Y	Y	Y
3 Mazzoli	N	Y	Y	Y	Y	Y
4 ***Bunning***	N	Y	N	N	Y	Y
5 ***Rogers***	Y	Y	N	N	Y	Y
6 ***Hopkins***	Y	Y	N	N	Y	Y
7 Perkins	Y	Y	Y	Y	Y	N
LOUISIANA						
1 ***Livingston***	N	Y	Y	N	Y	Y
2 Boggs	?	?	?	?	?	?
3 Tauzin	Y	Y	Y	N	Y	Y
4 ***McCrery***	Y	Y	N	?	?	Y
5 Huckaby	Y	Y	Y	N	Y	Y
6 ***Baker***	Y	Y	N	N	Y	Y
7 Hayes	Y	Y	Y	N	Y	Y
8 ***Holloway***	Y	Y	N	N	Y	Y
MAINE						
1 Brennan	Y	Y	Y	Y	Y	Y
2 ***Snowe***	Y	Y	Y	Y	Y	Y
MARYLAND						
1 Dyson	Y	Y	N	Y	Y	Y
2 ***Bentley***	Y	Y	N	N	Y	Y
3 Cardin	Y	Y	Y	Y	Y	Y
4 McMillen	Y	Y	Y	Y	Y	Y
5 Hoyer	Y	Y	Y	Y	Y	Y
6 Byron	Y	Y	N	N	Y	Y
7 Mfume	Y	Y	Y	Y	Y	N
8 ***Morella***	N	Y	Y	Y	Y	Y
MASSACHUSETTS						
1 ***Conte***	Y	Y	Y	Y	Y	Y
2 Neal	#	Y	Y	Y	Y	Y
3 Early	Y	Y	Y	Y	Y	Y
4 Frank	Y	Y	Y	Y	Y	Y
5 Atkins	Y	Y	Y	Y	Y	Y
6 Mavroules	Y	Y	Y	Y	Y	Y
7 Markey	Y	Y	Y	?	?	Y
8 Kennedy	Y	Y	Y	Y	Y	N
9 Moakley	Y	Y	Y	Y	Y	Y
10 Studds	Y	Y	Y	Y	Y	Y
11 Donnelly	Y	Y	Y	Y	Y	Y
MICHIGAN						
1 Conyers	Y	?	?	Y	Y	N
2 ***Pursell***	N	Y	Y	Y	Y	Y
3 Wolpe	Y	Y	Y	Y	Y	Y
4 ***Upton***	N	Y	N	Y	Y	Y
5 ***Henry***	?	?	?	?	Y	Y
6 Carr	Y	Y	N	Y	Y	Y
7 Kildee	Y	Y	Y	Y	Y	N
8 Traxler	Y	Y	Y	Y	Y	Y
9 ***Vander Jagt***	N	Y	N	Y	Y	Y
10 ***Schuette***	?	?	?	?	?	?
11 ***Davis***	Y	Y	Y	N	Y	Y
12 Bonior	Y	Y	Y	Y	Y	Y
13 Crockett	N	?	?	Y	Y	N
14 Hertel	Y	Y	Y	Y	Y	Y
15 Ford	Y	?	?	Y	Y	Y
16 Dingell	Y	Y	N	Y	Y	N
17 Levin	Y	Y	Y	Y	Y	Y
18 ***Broomfield***	N	Y	N	N	Y	Y
MINNESOTA						
1 Penny	N	Y	N	N	Y	Y
2 ***Weber***	N	Y	N	N	Y	Y
3 ***Frenzel***	N	?	?	?	Y	?
4 Vento	Y	Y	Y	Y	Y	Y
5 Sabo	Y	Y	Y	Y	Y	Y
6 Sikorski	Y	Y	Y	Y	Y	Y
7 ***Stangeland***	N	Y	N	N	Y	Y
8 Oberstar	Y	Y	Y	Y	Y	Y
MISSISSIPPI						
1 Whitten	Y	Y	Y	Y	Y	Y
2 Espy	Y	Y	Y	Y	Y	N
3 Montgomery	Y	Y	N	N	Y	Y
4 Parker	Y	Y	N	N	Y	Y
5 Taylor	Y	Y	N	N	Y	Y
MISSOURI						
1 Clay	Y	Y	Y	Y	Y	N
2 ***Buechner***	N	Y	N	Y	Y	Y
3 Gephardt	Y	Y	Y	Y	Y	Y
4 Skelton	Y	Y	N	N	Y	?
5 Wheat	Y	Y	Y	Y	Y	N
6 ***Coleman***	Y	Y	N	Y	Y	Y
7 ***Hancock***	N	Y	N	N	Y	Y
8 ***Emerson***	Y	Y	N	N	Y	Y
9 Volkmer	Y	Y	N	N	Y	Y
MONTANA						
1 Williams	Y	Y	Y	Y	Y	Y
2 ***Marlenee***	N	Y	N	N	Y	Y
NEBRASKA						
1 ***Bereuter***	N	Y	Y	N	Y	Y
2 Hoagland	Y	Y	Y	Y	Y	Y
3 ***Smith***	N	Y	N	N	Y	Y
NEVADA						
1 Bilbray	Y	Y	Y	Y	Y	Y
2 ***Vucanovich***	Y	Y	N	N	Y	Y
NEW HAMPSHIRE						
1 ***Smith***	Y	Y	N	N	Y	Y
2 ***Douglas***	Y	Y	N	N	Y	Y
NEW JERSEY						
1 Vacancy						
2 Hughes	Y	Y	Y	Y	Y	Y
3 Pallone	Y	Y	Y	Y	Y	N
4 ***Smith***	Y	Y	N	N	Y	Y
5 ***Roukema***	Y	Y	N	?	Y	Y
6 Dwyer	Y	Y	Y	Y	Y	Y
7 ***Rinaldo***	Y	Y	N	N	Y	Y
8 Roe	Y	Y	Y	Y	Y	Y
9 Torricelli	Y	Y	Y	Y	Y	Y
10 Payne	Y	Y	Y	Y	Y	N
11 ***Gallo***	N	Y	N	Y	Y	Y
12 ***Courter***	N	Y	Y	Y	Y	Y
13 ***Saxton***	N	Y	Y	Y	Y	Y
14 Guarini	Y	Y	N	Y	Y	Y
NEW MEXICO						
1 ***Schiff***	Y	Y	Y	Y	Y	Y
2 ***Skeen***	Y	Y	Y	Y	Y	Y
3 Richardson	Y	Y	Y	Y	Y	Y
NEW YORK						
1 Hochbrueckner	Y	Y	Y	Y	Y	Y
2 Downey	N	Y	Y	Y	Y	Y
3 Mrazek	Y	Y	Y	Y	Y	Y
4 ***Lent***	N	Y	N	N	?	Y
5 ***McGrath***	Y	Y	Y	Y	Y	Y
6 Flake	Y	Y	Y	Y	Y	N
7 Ackerman	Y	Y	Y	Y	Y	Y
8 Scheuer	Y	Y	Y	Y	Y	Y
9 Manton	Y	Y	Y	Y	Y	Y
10 Schumer	N	Y	Y	Y	Y	Y
11 Towns	Y	Y	Y	Y	Y	N
12 Owens	#	?	?	Y	Y	Y
13 Solarz	N	Y	Y	Y	Y	Y
14 ***Molinari***	N	Y	Y	Y	Y	Y
15 ***Green***	N	Y	N	Y	?	Y
16 Rangel	Y	Y	Y	Y	Y	N
17 Weiss	Y	Y	Y	Y	Y	N
18 Serrano	Y	Y	Y	Y	Y	N
19 Engel	Y	Y	Y	?	Y	Y
20 Lowey	Y	Y	Y	Y	Y	Y
21 ***Fish***	Y	Y	Y	Y	Y	Y
22 ***Gilman***	Y	Y	Y	Y	Y	Y
23 McNulty	Y	Y	Y	Y	Y	Y
24 ***Solomon***	Y	Y	N	N	Y	Y
25 ***Boehlert***	Y	Y	Y	Y	Y	Y
26 ***Martin***	Y	Y	Y	Y	Y	Y
27 ***Walsh***	N	Y	Y	Y	Y	Y
28 McHugh	N	Y	Y	Y	Y	Y
29 ***Horton***	Y	Y	?	Y	Y	Y
30 Slaughter	Y	Y	Y	Y	Y	Y
31 ***Paxon***	N	Y	N	N	Y	Y
32 LaFalce	N	Y	Y	Y	Y	Y
33 Nowak	Y	Y	Y	Y	Y	Y
34 ***Houghton***	Y	Y	Y	?	Y	Y
NORTH CAROLINA						
1 Jones	Y	Y	Y	Y	Y	Y
2 Valentine	Y	Y	N	N	Y	Y
3 Lancaster	Y	Y	Y	N	Y	Y
4 Price	Y	Y	Y	Y	Y	Y
5 Neal	Y	Y	Y	?	Y	Y
6 ***Coble***	Y	Y	N	N	Y	Y
7 Rose	Y	Y	Y	Y	Y	Y
8 Hefner	Y	Y	Y	N	Y	Y
9 ***McMillan***	Y	Y	N	N	Y	Y
10 ***Ballenger***	Y	Y	N	N	Y	Y
11 Clarke	Y	Y	N	Y	Y	Y
NORTH DAKOTA						
AL Dorgan	N	Y	Y	Y	+	Y
OHIO						
1 Luken	Y	Y	Y	Y	Y	N
2 ***Gradison***	N	Y	N	Y	Y	Y
3 Hall	Y	Y	Y	N	Y	Y
4 ***Oxley***	N	Y	N	N	Y	Y
5 ***Gillmor***	N	Y	N	N	Y	Y
6 ***McEwen***	N	Y	Y	N	Y	Y
7 ***DeWine***	N	Y	N	N	Y	Y
8 ***Lukens***	Y	Y	Y	?	Y	?
9 Kaptur	Y	Y	Y	Y	Y	Y
10 ***Miller***	Y	Y	N	N	Y	Y
11 Eckart	Y	Y	Y	Y	Y	Y
12 ***Kasich***	N	Y	Y	N	Y	Y
13 Pease	N	Y	Y	Y	Y	Y
14 Sawyer	N	Y	Y	Y	Y	Y
15 ***Wylie***	N	Y	N	Y	Y	Y
16 ***Regula***	Y	Y	N	N	Y	Y
17 Traficant	Y	Y	Y	Y	Y	Y
18 Applegate	Y	Y	N	N	Y	Y
19 Feighan	Y	Y	Y	Y	Y	Y
20 Oakar	Y	Y	Y	Y	Y	Y
21 Stokes	Y	Y	Y	Y	Y	N
OKLAHOMA						
1 ***Inhofe***	N	Y	N	N	Y	Y
2 Synar	N	Y	Y	Y	Y	Y
3 Watkins	Y	Y	N	N	Y	Y
4 McCurdy	N	Y	N	Y	Y	Y
5 ***Edwards***	N	Y	N	N	Y	Y
6 English	N	Y	N	Y	Y	Y
OREGON						
1 AuCoin	N	Y	Y	Y	Y	N
2 ***Smith, B.***	N	Y	N	N	Y	Y
3 Wyden	N	Y	Y	Y	Y	Y
4 DeFazio	N	Y	Y	Y	Y	Y
5 ***Smith, D.***	Y	Y	N	N	Y	Y
PENNSYLVANIA						
1 Foglietta	Y	Y	Y	Y	Y	N
2 Gray	Y	Y	Y	Y	Y	Y
3 Borski	Y	Y	Y	Y	Y	Y
4 Kolter	Y	Y	Y	N	Y	Y
5 ***Schulze***	Y	Y	N	Y	Y	Y
6 Yatron	Y	Y	Y	N	Y	Y
7 ***Weldon***	Y	Y	N	N	Y	Y
8 Kostmayer	Y	Y	Y	Y	Y	Y
9 ***Shuster***	Y	Y	N	N	Y	Y
10 ***McDade***	Y	Y	N	Y	Y	Y
11 Kanjorski	Y	Y	Y	Y	Y	Y
12 Murtha	Y	Y	Y	Y	Y	Y
13 ***Coughlin***	N	Y	N	N	Y	Y
14 Coyne	Y	Y	Y	Y	Y	N
15 ***Ritter***	Y	Y	N	N	Y	Y
16 ***Walker***	N	Y	N	N	Y	Y
17 ***Gekas***	Y	Y	N	N	Y	Y
18 Walgren	Y	Y	Y	Y	Y	Y
19 ***Goodling***	Y	Y	Y	?	Y	Y
20 Gaydos	Y	Y	N	Y	Y	Y
21 ***Ridge***	Y	Y	Y	?	Y	Y
22 Murphy	Y	Y	Y	Y	Y	Y
23 ***Clinger***	Y	Y	Y	N	Y	Y
RHODE ISLAND						
1 ***Machtley***	Y	Y	Y	Y	Y	Y
2 ***Schneider***	Y	Y	Y	Y	Y	Y
SOUTH CAROLINA						
1 ***Ravenel***	Y	Y	Y	N	Y	Y
2 ***Spence***	Y	Y	N	N	Y	Y
3 Derrick	Y	Y	Y	N	Y	Y
4 Patterson	Y	Y	Y	N	Y	Y
5 Spratt	Y	Y	Y	Y	Y	Y
6 Tallon	Y	Y	Y	N	Y	Y
SOUTH DAKOTA						
AL Johnson	Y	Y	Y	N	Y	Y
TENNESSEE						
1 ***Quillen***	Y	Y	Y	N	N	Y
2 ***Duncan***	Y	Y	N	N	Y	Y
3 Lloyd	Y	Y	Y	N	Y	Y
4 Cooper	Y	Y	Y	Y	Y	Y
5 Clement	Y	Y	N	Y	Y	Y
6 Gordon	Y	Y	Y	Y	Y	Y
7 ***Sundquist***	N	Y	N	Y	Y	Y
8 Tanner	Y	Y	N	Y	Y	Y
9 Ford	Y	?	?	Y	Y	N
TEXAS						
1 Chapman	Y	Y	N	Y	Y	Y
2 Wilson	Y	Y	N	?	?	?
3 ***Bartlett***	N	Y	N	?	?	Y
4 Hall	Y	Y	N	N	Y	Y
5 Bryant	Y	Y	Y	Y	Y	N
6 ***Barton***	N	Y	N	N	Y	Y
7 ***Archer***	N	Y	N	?	Y	?
8 ***Fields***	N	Y	N	N	Y	Y
9 Brooks	Y	Y	Y	Y	Y	Y
10 Pickle	N	Y	N	Y	Y	Y
11 Leath	Y	Y	N	N	Y	Y
12 Geren	N	Y	N	Y	Y	Y
13 Sarpalius	Y	Y	Y	N	Y	Y
14 Laughlin	Y	Y	N	N	Y	Y
15 de la Garza	Y	Y	Y	N	Y	Y
16 Coleman	Y	Y	Y	Y	Y	N
17 Stenholm	Y	Y	N	N	Y	Y
18 Washington	Y	Y	Y	Y	N	N
19 ***Combest***	Y	Y	N	N	Y	Y
20 Gonzalez	Y	Y	Y	Y	Y	N
21 ***Smith***	Y	Y	N	N	Y	Y
22 ***DeLay***	N	Y	N	N	Y	Y
23 Bustamante	Y	Y	Y	Y	Y	Y
24 Frost	Y	?	?	Y	Y	Y
25 Andrews	Y	Y	N	Y	Y	Y
26 ***Armey***	N	Y	N	N	Y	Y
27 Ortiz	Y	Y	Y	Y	Y	Y
UTAH						
1 ***Hansen***	N	Y	N	N	Y	Y
2 Owens	N	Y	Y	Y	Y	Y
3 ***Nielson***	N	Y	N	N	Y	Y
VERMONT						
AL ***Smith***	Y	Y	Y	Y	Y	Y
VIRGINIA						
1 ***Bateman***	N	Y	N	N	Y	Y
2 Pickett	Y	Y	N	Y	Y	Y
3 ***Bliley***	Y	Y	N	Y	Y	Y
4 Sisisky	Y	Y	N	Y	Y	Y
5 Payne	Y	Y	N	Y	Y	Y
6 Olin	Y	Y	Y	Y	Y	Y
7 ***Slaughter***	Y	Y	N	N	Y	Y
8 ***Parris***	Y	Y	N	+	+	+
9 Boucher	Y	Y	Y	Y	Y	Y
10 ***Wolf***	N	Y	N	N	Y	Y
WASHINGTON						
1 ***Miller***	N	Y	N	Y	Y	Y
2 Swift	N	Y	Y	Y	Y	Y
3 Unsoeld	N	Y	Y	Y	Y	Y
4 ***Morrison***	N	Y	N	Y	Y	Y
5 Foley						
6 Dicks	N	Y	Y	Y	Y	Y
7 McDermott	N	Y	Y	Y	Y	N
8 ***Chandler***	N	Y	N	Y	Y	Y
WEST VIRGINIA						
1 Mollohan	Y	Y	N	Y	Y	?
2 Staggers	Y	Y	Y	Y	Y	Y
3 Wise	Y	Y	Y	Y	Y	Y
4 Rahall	Y	Y	N	N	Y	Y
WISCONSIN						
1 Aspin	Y	Y	Y	Y	Y	Y
2 Kastenmeier	Y	Y	Y	Y	Y	Y
3 ***Gunderson***	Y	Y	Y	N	Y	Y
4 Kleczka	N	Y	Y	?	Y	Y
5 Moody	Y	Y	Y	Y	Y	N
6 ***Petri***	N	Y	N	N	Y	Y
7 Obey	Y	Y	Y	Y	Y	Y
8 ***Roth***	Y	Y	N	N	Y	Y
9 ***Sensenbrenner***	N	Y	N	N	Y	Y
WYOMING						
AL ***Thomas***	N	Y	N	N	Y	Y

Southern states - Ala., Ark., Fla., Ga., Ky., La., Miss., N.C., Okla., S.C., Tenn., Texas, Va.
Omitted votes are quorum calls, which CQ does not include in its vote charts.

HOUSE VOTES 446, 447, 448, 449, 450, 451

446. HR 4825. Fiscal 1991-95 NEA Authorization/Abolishment. Crane, R-Ill., en bloc amendment to abolish the National Endowment for the Arts. Rejected 64-361: R 52-120; D 12-241 (ND 2-171, SD 10-70), Oct. 11, 1990.

447. HR 4825. Fiscal 1991-95 NEA Authorization/NEA Funding Standards. Rohrabacher, R-Calif., en bloc amendment to prohibit the National Endowment for the Arts (NEA) from funding child pornography; obscenity or material prohibited from broadcast under Federal Communications Commission definitions of indecency; works denigrating the beliefs or objects of a religion; works denigrating an individual on the basis of race, sex, handicap or national origin; works desecrating the U.S. flag; or works that contain any part of a human embryo or fetus. The amendment also includes changes in NEA procedures for applications, reports, meetings and other NEA activities. Rejected 175-249: R 114-58; D 61-191 (ND 18-154, SD 43-37), Oct. 11, 1990.

448. HR 4825. Fiscal 1991-95 NEA Authorization/NEA Funding Standards. Williams, D-Mont., substitute amendment to require the chairperson of the National Endowment for the Arts (NEA) in funding projects to take into account not only artistic excellence and merit but general standards of decency and respect for the diverse beliefs and values of Americans. The amendment also gives states a larger share of NEA funds, leaves the courts to decide what constitutes obscenity, requires artists convicted of obscenity to repay their grants and makes changes in the grant application process. Adopted 382-42: R 142-31; D 240-11 (ND 160-11, SD 80-0), Oct. 11, 1990.

449. HR 4825. Fiscal 1991-95 NEA Authorization/Passage. Passage of the bill to reauthorize the National Endowment for the Arts, the National Endowment for the Humanities and the Institute of Museum Services for fiscal 1991-95 at $364 million in fiscal 1991 and such sums as necessary in fiscal 1992-95. Passed 349-76: R 114-59; D 235-17 (ND 168-3, SD 67-14), Oct. 11, 1990.

450. S 2830. Farm Programs Reauthorization/Instruction of Conferees. Synar, D-Okla., motion to instruct the House conferees on the farm bill to insist on House provisions prohibiting the export of certain pesticides that have been banned from use in the United States and to agree to Senate provisions that require immediate revocation of "food tolerances" for banned pesticides. Motion rejected 162-248: R 41-130; D 121-118 (ND 106-54, SD 15-64), Oct. 11, 1990.

451. S 2830. Farm Programs Reauthorization/Instruction of Conferees. Durbin, D-Ill., motion to instruct the House conferees on the farm bill to insist on House provisions that authorize $10 million in each fiscal year 1991-95 for a public education program on the hazards of tobacco use. Motion agreed to 255-154: R 89-81; D 166-73 (ND 135-25, SD 31-48), Oct. 11, 1990.

KEY

- Y Voted for (yea).
- \# Paired for.
- \+ Announced for.
- N Voted against (nay).
- X Paired against.
- \- Announced against.
- P Voted "present."
- C Voted "present" to avoid possible conflict of interest.
- ? Did not vote or otherwise make a position known.

Democrats ***Republicans***

	446	447	448	449	450	451
ALABAMA						
1 ***Callahan***	Y	Y	Y	N	N	N
2 ***Dickinson***	Y	Y	Y	N	N	N
3 Browder	N	Y	Y	Y	N	N
4 Bevill	N	Y	Y	Y	N	N
5 Flippo	N	Y	Y	Y	N	N
6 Erdreich	N	Y	Y	Y	N	Y
7 Harris	N	Y	Y	Y	N	N
ALASKA						
AL ***Young***	N	Y	Y	N	N	N
ARIZONA						
1 ***Rhodes***	N	N	Y	Y	N	N
2 Udall	N	N	Y	Y	N	Y
3 ***Stump***	Y	Y	N	N	N	N
4 ***Kyl***	Y	Y	N	N	N	Y
5 ***Kolbe***	N	N	Y	Y	N	N
ARKANSAS						
1 Alexander	N	N	Y	Y	N	Y
2 ***Robinson***	Y	Y	N	N	N	N
3 ***Hammerschmidt***	N	Y	Y	N	N	Y
4 Anthony	N	N	Y	Y	N	N
CALIFORNIA						
1 Bosco	N	N	Y	Y	?	?
2 ***Herger***	Y	Y	N	N	N	N
3 Matsui	N	N	Y	Y	Y	Y
4 Fazio	N	N	Y	Y	N	Y
5 Pelosi	N	N	Y	Y	Y	Y
6 Boxer	N	N	N	Y	Y	Y
7 Miller	N	N	Y	Y	Y	Y
8 Dellums	N	N	N	Y	Y	Y
9 Stark	N	N	Y	Y	Y	Y
10 Edwards	N	N	Y	Y	Y	Y
11 Lantos	N	N	Y	Y	Y	Y
12 ***Campbell***	Y	N	N	N	N	Y
13 Mineta	N	N	Y	Y	Y	Y
14 ***Shumway***	Y	Y	N	N	N	Y
15 Condit	N	N	Y	N	N	Y
16 Panetta	N	N	Y	Y	Y	Y
17 ***Pashayan***	N	Y	Y	Y	N	N
18 Lehman	N	N	Y	Y	Y	Y
19 ***Lagomarsino***	N	Y	Y	Y	N	Y
20 ***Thomas***	N	Y	Y	Y	N	N
21 ***Gallegly***	N	Y	Y	Y	N	Y
22 ***Moorhead***	N	Y	Y	N	N	Y
23 Beilenson	N	N	Y	Y	Y	Y
24 Waxman	N	N	N	Y	Y	Y
25 Roybal	N	N	Y	Y	N	Y
26 Berman	N	N	N	Y	Y	Y
27 Levine	N	N	N	Y	Y	Y
28 Dixon	N	N	Y	Y	Y	N
29 Hawkins	N	N	Y	Y	?	?
30 Martinez	N	N	Y	Y	N	Y
31 Dymally	N	N	Y	Y	Y	Y
32 Anderson	N	N	Y	Y	N	Y
33 ***Dreier***	Y	N	N	N	N	N
34 Torres	N	N	Y	Y	Y	Y
35 ***Lewis***	N	N	Y	Y	N	N
36 Brown	N	N	Y	Y	N	N
37 ***McCandless***	Y	Y	Y	N	N	Y
38 ***Dornan***	Y	Y	N	N	N	N
39 ***Dannemeyer***	Y	Y	Y	N	N	N
40 ***Cox***	Y	N	N	N	N	N
41 ***Lowery***	N	N	Y	Y	N	N
42 ***Rohrabacher***	Y	Y	N	N	N	N
43 ***Packard***	N	Y	Y	Y	N	Y
44 Bates	N	N	Y	Y	Y	Y
45 ***Hunter***	Y	Y	N	N	N	N
COLORADO						
1 Schroeder	N	N	Y	Y	Y	Y
2 Skaggs	N	N	Y	Y	Y	Y
3 Campbell	N	N	Y	Y	N	Y
4 ***Brown***	N	Y	Y	Y	N	Y
5 ***Hefley***	N	Y	Y	Y	N	N
6 ***Schaefer***	N	Y	Y	Y	N	N
CONNECTICUT						
1 Kennelly	N	N	Y	Y	Y	Y
2 Gejdenson	N	N	Y	Y	Y	Y
3 Morrison	-	-	+	+	Y	Y
4 ***Shays***	N	N	Y	Y	Y	Y
5 ***Rowland***	?	?	?	?	?	?
6 ***Johnson***	N	N	Y	Y	N	Y
DELAWARE						
AL Carper	N	N	Y	Y	N	Y
FLORIDA						
1 Hutto	Y	Y	Y	N	N	Y
2 ***Grant***	Y	Y	Y	N	N	N
3 Bennett	Y	Y	Y	N	Y	Y
4 ***James***	N	Y	Y	Y	N	Y
5 ***McCollum***	N	Y	Y	Y	N	Y
6 ***Stearns***	Y	Y	Y	Y	Y	Y
7 Gibbons	Y	Y	Y	N	N	Y
8 ***Young***	N	Y	Y	Y	Y	Y
9 ***Bilirakis***	N	Y	Y	Y	N	N
10 ***Ireland***	N	Y	Y	Y	N	Y
11 Nelson	N	N	Y	Y	Y	Y
12 ***Lewis***	N	Y	Y	Y	N	N
13 ***Goss***	N	N	Y	Y	N	Y
14 Johnston	N	N	Y	Y	Y	Y
15 ***Shaw***	N	Y	Y	Y	N	N
16 Smith	N	N	Y	Y	Y	Y
17 Lehman	N	N	Y	Y	N	Y
18 ***Ros-Lehtinen***	N	Y	Y	Y	N	Y
19 Fascell	N	N	Y	Y	N	Y
GEORGIA						
1 Thomas	N	Y	Y	Y	N	N
2 Hatcher	N	N	Y	Y	N	N
3 Ray	N	Y	Y	Y	N	N
4 Jones	N	N	Y	Y	Y	N
5 Lewis	N	N	Y	Y	Y	Y
6 ***Gingrich***	?	Y	Y	N	N	Y
7 Darden	N	Y	Y	Y	N	N
8 Rowland	N	Y	Y	Y	N	N
9 Jenkins	N	Y	Y	Y	N	Y
10 Barnard	N	Y	Y	Y	N	Y
HAWAII						
1 ***Saiki***	N	N	Y	Y	Y	Y
2 Mink	N	N	Y	Y	Y	Y
IDAHO						
1 ***Craig***	N	Y	N	N	N	Y
2 Stallings	N	N	Y	Y	N	Y
ILLINOIS						
1 Hayes	N	N	?	?	?	?
2 Savage	N	N	Y	Y	Y	Y
3 Russo	N	N	Y	Y	Y	Y
4 Sangmeister	N	Y	Y	Y	Y	Y
5 Lipinski	N	Y	Y	Y	Y	Y
6 ***Hyde***	Y	Y	Y	N	N	Y
7 Collins	N	N	Y	Y	N	Y
8 Rostenkowski	N	N	Y	Y	Y	Y
9 Yates	N	N	Y	Y	?	?
10 ***Porter***	N	N	Y	Y	Y	Y
11 Annunzio	N	Y	Y	Y	N	N
12 ***Crane***	Y	Y	N	N	N	N
13 ***Fawell***	N	Y	Y	Y	Y	Y
14 ***Hastert***	Y	Y	Y	N	N	Y
15 ***Madigan***	N	Y	Y	Y	N	N
16 ***Martin***	N	Y	Y	Y	N	Y
17 Evans	N	N	Y	Y	Y	Y
18 ***Michel***	N	N	Y	Y	N	N
19 Bruce	N	N	Y	Y	N	N
20 Durbin	N	N	Y	Y	Y	Y
21 Costello	N	Y	Y	Y	Y	Y
22 Poshard	N	Y	Y	Y	Y	Y
INDIANA						
1 Visclosky	N	Y	Y	Y	Y	Y
2 Sharp	N	N	Y	Y	Y	Y
3 ***Hiler***	N	Y	Y	N	N	Y

ND Northern Democrats SD Southern Democrats

	446	447	448	449	450	451
4 Long	N	Y	Y	Y	N	Y
5 Jontz	N	N	Y	Y	Y	Y
6 ***Burton***	Y	Y	Y	N	N	Y
7 ***Myers***	N	Y	Y	Y	N	N
8 McCloskey	N	N	Y	Y	Y	Y
9 Hamilton	N	N	Y	Y	N	Y
10 Jacobs	N	N	Y	Y	Y	Y
IOWA						
1 ***Leach***	N	N	Y	Y	N	N
2 ***Tauke***	N	N	Y	Y	N	Y
3 Nagle	N	N	Y	Y	N	N
4 Smith	N	N	Y	Y	N	N
5 ***Lightfoot***	Y	Y	N	N	N	N
6 ***Grandy***	N	N	Y	Y	N	N
KANSAS						
1 ***Roberts***	N	N	Y	Y	N	N
2 Slattery	N	N	Y	Y	Y	Y
3 ***Meyers***	N	N	Y	Y	N	Y
4 Glickman	N	N	Y	Y	Y	Y
5 ***Whittaker***	N	N	Y	Y	N	Y
KENTUCKY						
1 Hubbard	N	Y	Y	N	N	N
2 Natcher	N	Y	Y	Y	N	N
3 Mazzoli	N	N	Y	Y	N	Y
4 ***Bunning***	Y	Y	Y	Y	N	N
5 ***Rogers***	N	Y	Y	Y	N	N
6 ***Hopkins***	N	Y	Y	Y	N	N
7 Perkins	N	N	Y	Y	N	N
LOUISIANA						
1 ***Livingston***	Y	Y	N	N	N	Y
2 Boggs	?	?	?	?	?	?
3 Tauzin	Y	Y	Y	N	N	Y
4 ***McCrery***	N	Y	Y	Y	N	Y
5 Huckaby	N	Y	Y	Y	N	Y
6 ***Baker***	N	Y	Y	N	Y	N
7 Hayes	N	Y	Y	Y	N	Y
8 ***Holloway***	Y	Y	N	N	N	N
MAINE						
1 Brennan	N	N	Y	Y	Y	Y
2 ***Snowe***	N	N	Y	Y	Y	Y
MARYLAND						
1 Dyson	N	Y	Y	Y	N	N
2 ***Bentley***	N	Y	Y	Y	N	Y
3 Cardin	N	N	Y	Y	Y	Y
4 McMillen	N	N	Y	Y	Y	Y
5 Hoyer	N	N	Y	Y	Y	Y
6 Byron	N	Y	Y	Y	N	N
7 Mfume	N	N	Y	Y	Y	Y
8 ***Morella***	N	N	Y	Y	Y	Y
MASSACHUSETTS						
1 ***Conte***	N	N	Y	Y	Y	Y
2 Neal	N	N	Y	Y	Y	Y
3 Early	N	N	Y	Y	Y	Y
4 Frank	N	N	Y	Y	Y	Y
5 Atkins	N	N	Y	Y	Y	Y
6 Mavroules	N	N	Y	Y	Y	Y
7 Markey	N	N	Y	Y	Y	Y
8 Kennedy	N	N	Y	Y	Y	Y
9 Moakley	N	N	Y	Y	Y	Y
10 Studds	N	N	N	Y	Y	Y
11 Donnelly	N	N	Y	Y	Y	Y
MICHIGAN						
1 Conyers	N	N	Y	Y	Y	Y
2 ***Pursell***	N	N	Y	Y	Y	Y
3 Wolpe	N	N	Y	Y	Y	Y
4 ***Upton***	N	Y	Y	Y	Y	Y
5 ***Henry***	N	N	Y	Y	Y	Y
6 Carr	N	N	Y	Y	?	?
7 Kildee	N	N	Y	Y	Y	Y
8 Traxler	N	N	Y	Y	N	Y
9 ***Vander Jagt***	Y	Y	N	N	Y	Y
10 ***Schuette***	?	?	?	?	?	?
11 ***Davis***	N	N	Y	Y	N	N
12 Bonior	N	N	Y	Y	Y	N
13 Crockett	N	N	Y	Y	?	?
14 Hertel	N	N	Y	Y	Y	Y
15 Ford	N	N	Y	Y	?	?
16 Dingell	N	N	Y	Y	N	N
17 Levin	N	N	Y	Y	Y	Y
18 ***Broomfield***	N	N	Y	Y	Y	Y
MINNESOTA						
1 Penny	N	Y	Y	Y	Y	Y
2 ***Weber***	N	Y	N	N	N	N
3 ***Frenzel***	N	N	Y	Y	N	N
4 Vento	N	N	Y	Y	Y	Y

	446	447	448	449	450	451
5 Sabo	N	N	Y	Y	Y	Y
6 Sikorski	N	N	Y	Y	Y	Y
7 ***Stangeland***	Y	Y	Y	Y	N	N
8 Oberstar	N	N	Y	Y	Y	Y
MISSISSIPPI						
1 Whitten	N	Y	Y	Y	N	N
2 Espy	N	N	Y	Y	Y	N
3 Montgomery	N	Y	Y	Y	N	N
4 Parker	Y	Y	Y	Y	N	N
5 Taylor	Y	Y	Y	N	N	Y
MISSOURI						
1 Clay	N	N	Y	Y	N	N
2 ***Buechner***	N	N	Y	Y	N	N
3 Gephardt	N	N	Y	Y	N	Y
4 Skelton	Y	Y	Y	N	N	N
5 Wheat	N	N	Y	Y	Y	Y
6 ***Coleman***	N	N	Y	Y	N	N
7 ***Hancock***	Y	Y	N	N	N	N
8 ***Emerson***	N	Y	Y	N	N	N
9 Volkmer	N	Y	Y	Y	N	N
MONTANA						
1 Williams	N	N	Y	Y	N	Y
2 ***Marlenee***	Y	Y	Y	N	N	N
NEBRASKA						
1 ***Bereuter***	N	N	Y	Y	N	Y
2 Hoagland	N	N	Y	Y	Y	Y
3 ***Smith***	N	?	Y	Y	N	Y
NEVADA						
1 Bilbray	N	N	Y	Y	N	Y
2 ***Vucanovich***	Y	Y	N	N	N	N
NEW HAMPSHIRE						
1 ***Smith***	Y	Y	N	N	Y	Y
2 ***Douglas***	Y	Y	Y	N	Y	Y
NEW JERSEY						
1 Vacancy						
2 Hughes	N	N	Y	Y	Y	Y
3 Pallone	N	Y	Y	Y	Y	Y
4 ***Smith***	N	Y	Y	Y	Y	Y
5 ***Roukema***	N	Y	Y	Y	Y	Y
6 Dwyer	N	N	Y	Y	?	?
7 ***Rinaldo***	N	Y	Y	Y	Y	Y
8 Roe	N	?	Y	Y	?	?
9 Torricelli	N	N	Y	Y	Y	Y
10 Payne	N	N	Y	Y	Y	Y
11 ***Gallo***	N	N	Y	Y	N	N
12 ***Courter***	N	Y	Y	Y	N	Y
13 ***Saxton***	N	N	Y	Y	Y	N
14 Guarini	N	N	Y	Y	N	Y
NEW MEXICO						
1 ***Schiff***	N	N	Y	Y	N	Y
2 ***Skeen***	N	N	Y	Y	N	N
3 Richardson	N	N	Y	Y	Y	Y
NEW YORK						
1 Hochbrueckner	N	N	Y	Y	Y	N
2 Downey	N	N	Y	Y	Y	Y
3 Mrazek	N	N	N	Y	Y	Y
4 ***Lent***	N	N	Y	Y	Y	Y
5 ***McGrath***	N	N	Y	Y	Y	N
6 Flake	N	N	Y	Y	N	Y
7 Ackerman	N	N	N	Y	Y	Y
8 Scheuer	N	N	Y	Y	Y	Y
9 Manton	N	N	Y	Y	Y	Y
10 Schumer	N	N	Y	Y	Y	Y
11 Towns	N	N	Y	Y	Y	N
12 Owens	N	N	Y	Y	Y	Y
13 Solarz	N	N	Y	Y	N	Y
14 ***Molinari***	N	N	Y	Y	N	Y
15 ***Green***	N	N	Y	Y	Y	Y
16 Rangel	N	N	Y	Y	?	?
17 Weiss	N	N	N	N	Y	Y
18 Serrano	N	N	Y	Y	Y	Y
19 Engel	N	N	Y	Y	Y	Y
20 Lowey	N	N	Y	Y	Y	Y
21 ***Fish***	N	N	Y	Y	Y	Y
22 ***Gilman***	N	N	Y	Y	Y	Y
23 McNulty	N	N	Y	Y	Y	Y
24 ***Solomon***	Y	Y	Y	N	Y	N
25 ***Boehlert***	N	N	Y	Y	Y	Y
26 ***Martin***	N	N	Y	Y	N	N
27 ***Walsh***	N	N	Y	Y	Y	N
28 McHugh	N	N	Y	Y	Y	Y
29 ***Horton***	N	N	Y	Y	?	?
30 Slaughter	N	N	Y	Y	Y	Y
31 ***Paxon***	N	Y	Y	Y	N	N

	446	447	448	449	450	451
32 LaFalce	N	N	Y	Y	N	Y
33 Nowak	N	N	Y	Y	Y	Y
34 ***Houghton***	N	N	Y	Y	N	N
NORTH CAROLINA						
1 Jones	N	Y	Y	Y	N	N
2 Valentine	N	Y	Y	Y	N	N
3 Lancaster	N	N	Y	Y	N	N
4 Price	N	N	Y	Y	N	N
5 Neal	N	N	Y	Y	N	N
6 ***Coble***	N	Y	Y	Y	N	N
7 Rose	N	N	?	Y	N	N
8 Hefner	N	Y	Y	Y	N	N
9 ***McMillan***	N	N	Y	Y	N	N
10 ***Ballenger***	N	Y	Y	Y	N	N
11 Clarke	N	N	Y	Y	N	N
NORTH DAKOTA						
AL Dorgan	N	N	Y	Y	N	Y
OHIO						
1 Luken	Y	N	Y	Y	N	Y
2 ***Gradison***	Y	Y	Y	Y	N	Y
3 Hall	N	N	?	?	?	?
4 ***Oxley***	N	Y	Y	Y	N	Y
5 ***Gillmor***	N	Y	Y	Y	N	Y
6 ***McEwen***	Y	Y	Y	Y	N	N
7 ***DeWine***	N	Y	Y	Y	Y	Y
8 ***Lukens***	Y	Y	Y	Y	N	Y
9 Kaptur	N	N	Y	Y	?	?
10 ***Miller***	Y	Y	Y	N	N	Y
11 Eckart	N	N	Y	Y	Y	Y
12 ***Kasich***	N	Y	Y	Y	N	Y
13 Pease	N	N	Y	Y	Y	Y
14 Sawyer	N	N	Y	Y	N	Y
15 ***Wylie***	?	?	?	?	?	?
16 ***Regula***	N	Y	Y	Y	N	Y
17 Traficant	N	N	Y	Y	N	Y
18 Applegate	N	Y	Y	Y	N	N
19 Feighan	N	N	Y	Y	Y	Y
20 Oakar	N	N	Y	Y	N	Y
21 Stokes	N	N	Y	Y	N	N
OKLAHOMA						
1 ***Inhofe***	Y	Y	Y	N	N	N
2 Synar	N	N	Y	Y	Y	Y
3 Watkins	N	Y	Y	Y	N	N
4 McCurdy	N	N	Y	N	?	?
5 ***Edwards***	Y	Y	Y	N	N	N
6 English	N	Y	Y	N	N	N
OREGON						
1 AuCoin	N	N	Y	Y	N	Y
2 ***Smith, B.***	N	Y	N	N	N	N
3 Wyden	N	N	Y	Y	Y	Y
4 DeFazio	N	N	Y	Y	N	Y
5 ***Smith, D.***	N	Y	Y	Y	N	Y
PENNSYLVANIA						
1 Foglietta	N	N	Y	Y	?	?
2 Gray	N	N	Y	Y	?	?
3 Borski	N	N	Y	Y	N	N
4 Kolter	N	Y	Y	Y	N	N
5 ***Schulze***	N	N	Y	Y	N	N
6 Yatron	N	Y	Y	Y	N	Y
7 ***Weldon***	N	Y	Y	Y	Y	Y
8 Kostmayer	N	N	N	Y	N	Y
9 ***Shuster***	Y	Y	Y	N	N	Y
10 ***McDade***	N	N	Y	Y	?	?
11 Kanjorski	N	N	Y	Y	Y	Y
12 Murtha	N	N	Y	Y	N	N
13 ***Coughlin***	N	Y	Y	Y	N	Y
14 Coyne	N	N	Y	Y	Y	Y
15 ***Ritter***	N	Y	Y	Y	N	Y
16 ***Walker***	Y	Y	N	N	N	N
17 ***Gekas***	Y	Y	Y	N	N	Y
18 Walgren	N	N	Y	Y	Y	Y
19 ***Goodling***	N	N	Y	Y	Y	Y
20 Gaydos	N	N	Y	Y	N	N
21 ***Ridge***	N	N	Y	Y	Y	Y
22 Murphy	N	Y	Y	Y	N	N
23 ***Clinger***	N	N	Y	Y	N	Y
RHODE ISLAND						
1 ***Machtley***	N	N	Y	Y	Y	Y
2 ***Schneider***	N	N	Y	Y	Y	Y
SOUTH CAROLINA						
1 ***Ravenel***	N	Y	Y	Y	Y	Y
2 ***Spence***	N	Y	Y	Y	N	N
3 Derrick	N	N	Y	Y	N	N
4 Patterson	N	Y	Y	Y	N	N
5 Spratt	N	Y	Y	Y	N	N
6 Tallon	N	Y	Y	Y	N	N

	446	447	448	449	450	451
SOUTH DAKOTA						
AL Johnson	N	N	Y	Y	Y	Y
TENNESSEE						
1 ***Quillen***	Y	Y	Y	Y	N	N
2 ***Duncan***	Y	Y	Y	N	N	N
3 Lloyd	N	Y	Y	Y	N	Y
4 Cooper	N	N	Y	Y	Y	Y
5 Clement	N	Y	Y	Y	N	N
6 Gordon	N	N	Y	Y	Y	Y
7 ***Sundquist***	Y	Y	Y	N	N	N
8 Tanner	N	Y	Y	Y	N	N
9 Ford	N	?	Y	Y	Y	Y
TEXAS						
1 Chapman	N	Y	Y	Y	?	?
2 Wilson	?	?	?	?	?	?
3 ***Bartlett***	N	Y	N	N	N	Y
4 Hall	Y	Y	Y	N	N	N
5 Bryant	N	N	Y	Y	Y	Y
6 ***Barton***	Y	Y	N	N	N	N
7 ***Archer***	Y	Y	Y	N	N	Y
8 ***Fields***	Y	Y	Y	N	N	N
9 Brooks	N	N	Y	Y	N	N
10 Pickle	N	N	Y	Y	N	Y
11 Leath	?	Y	Y	N	N	Y
12 Geren	N	N	Y	Y	N	Y
13 Sarpalius	Y	Y	Y	N	N	N
14 Laughlin	Y	Y	Y	N	N	N
15 de la Garza	N	Y	Y	Y	N	N
16 Coleman	N	N	Y	Y	N	Y
17 Stenholm	Y	Y	Y	N	N	N
18 Washington	N	N	Y	Y	Y	Y
19 ***Combest***	N	Y	N	N	N	N
20 Gonzalez	N	N	Y	Y	N	Y
21 ***Smith***	N	Y	Y	Y	N	Y
22 ***DeLay***	Y	Y	N	N	N	N
23 Bustamante	N	N	Y	Y	N	N
24 Frost	N	N	Y	Y	N	Y
25 Andrews	N	N	Y	Y	Y	Y
26 ***Armey***	Y	Y	N	N	N	N
27 Ortiz	N	N	Y	N	N	N
UTAH						
1 ***Hansen***	N	Y	N	N	N	Y
2 Owens	N	N	Y	Y	Y	Y
3 ***Nielson***	N	Y	Y	Y	N	Y
VERMONT						
AL ***Smith***	N	N	Y	Y	Y	Y
VIRGINIA						
1 ***Bateman***	N	Y	Y	Y	N	N
2 Pickett	N	Y	Y	Y	N	N
3 ***Bliley***	N	Y	Y	Y	N	N
4 Sisisky	N	Y	Y	Y	N	N
5 Payne	N	N	Y	Y	N	N
6 Olin	N	N	Y	Y	N	N
7 ***Slaughter***	Y	Y	Y	N	N	N
8 ***Parris***	N	Y	Y	Y	N	N
9 Boucher	N	N	Y	Y	Y	N
10 ***Wolf***	N	Y	Y	Y	N	Y
WASHINGTON						
1 ***Miller***	N	N	Y	Y	Y	?
2 Swift	N	N	Y	Y	N	N
3 Unsoeld	N	N	Y	Y	Y	Y
4 ***Morrison***	N	N	Y	Y	N	N
5 Foley						
6 Dicks	N	N	Y	Y	N	Y
7 McDermott	N	N	N	Y	Y	Y
8 ***Chandler***	N	N	Y	Y	Y	Y
WEST VIRGINIA						
1 Mollohan	N	N	Y	Y	N	N
2 Staggers	N	N	Y	Y	N	Y
3 Wise	N	N	Y	Y	N	Y
4 Rahall	N	Y	Y	Y	N	N
WISCONSIN						
1 Aspin	N	N	Y	Y	N	Y
2 Kastenmeier	N	N	Y	Y	Y	Y
3 ***Gunderson***	N	N	Y	Y	N	N
4 Kleczka	N	N	Y	Y	Y	Y
5 Moody	N	N	Y	Y	Y	Y
6 ***Petri***	Y	Y	N	N	Y	Y
7 Obey	N	N	Y	Y	Y	Y
8 ***Roth***	N	Y	Y	Y	N	Y
9 ***Sensenbrenner***	N	Y	N	N	Y	Y
WYOMING						
AL ***Thomas***	N	Y	Y	Y	N	N

Southern states - Ala., Ark., Fla., Ga., Ky., La., Miss., N.C., Okla., S.C., Tenn., Texas, Va.
Omitted votes are quorum calls, which CQ does not include in its vote charts.

HOUSE VOTES 453, 454, 455, 456, 458, 459, 460, 461

453. HR 5803. Fiscal 1991 Defense Appropriations/Across-the-Board Cut. Traficant, D-Ohio, amendment to cut defense spending in the bill by 5 percent across the board, resulting in a cut of about $14 billion. Rejected 97-319: R 11-158; D 86-161 (ND 77-91, SD 9-70), Oct. 12, 1990. A "nay" was a vote supporting the president's position.

454. HR 5803. Fiscal 1991 Defense Appropriations/Across-the-Board Cut. Penny, D-Minn., amendment to cut defense spending in the bill by 2 percent across the board, resulting in a cut of $5.4 billion. Rejected 201-215: R 58-112; D 143-103 (ND 120-49, SD 23-54), Oct. 12, 1990. A "nay" was a vote supporting the president's position.

455. HR 5803. Fiscal 1991 Defense Appropriations/Passage. Passage of the bill to appropriate $269,281,398 for the Department of Defense for military personnel, operations and maintenance, procurement, and research and development in fiscal 1991. The president requested $287,282,674,000. Passed 322-97: R 132-39; D 190-58 (ND 114-55, SD 76-3), Oct. 12, 1990.

456. HR 5769. Fiscal 1991 Interior Appropriations/Rule. Adoption of the rule (H Res 505) to waive certain points of order against the bill and to provide for House floor consideration of the bill to provide funding for the Interior Department and related agencies in fiscal 1991. Adopted 245-160: R 14-152; D 231-8 (ND 154-6, SD 77-2), Oct. 12, 1990.

458. HR 5769. Fiscal 1991 Interior Appropriations/Energy Conservation. Walker, R-Pa., amendment to reduce the account for carrying out energy conservation activities by $3.35 million to $494.334 million. Rejected 104-281: R 99-61; D 5-220 (ND 3-146, SD 2-74), Oct. 15, 1990.

459. HR 5769. Fiscal 1991 Interior Appropriations/Metal Casting Research Institute. Walker, R-Pa., amendment to strike from the bill $1.25 million to establish a National Metal Casting Research Institute at the University of Alabama. Rejected 106-295: R 99-66; D 7-229 (ND 5-154, SD 2-75), Oct. 15, 1990. A "yea" was a vote supporting the president's position.

460. HR 5769. Fiscal 1991 Interior Appropriations/Grazing Fees. Synar, D-Okla., amendment to gradually increase the fees charged for grazing livestock on federal lands administered by the Bureau of Land Management and Forest Service from $1.81 for one cow and calf per month to $8.70. Adopted 251-155: R 56-111; D 195-44 (ND 138-22, SD 57-22), Oct. 15, 1990.

461. HR 5769. Fiscal 1991 Interior Appropriations/NEA. Williams, D-Mont., substitute amendment to the Regula, R-Ohio, amendment, to insert into the bill the text of the National Endowment for the Arts (NEA) authorization bill (HR 4825) as passed by the House on Oct. 11, requiring the chairperson of the NEA to take into account, in funding projects, not only artistic excellence and merit but general standards of decency and respect for the diverse beliefs and values of the American people; changing the NEA grant process; giving states a larger share of NEA funds; and implementing other policy changes. Adopted 234-171: R 49-116; D 185-55 (ND 143-17, SD 42-38), Oct. 15, 1990.

KEY

Y Voted for (yea).
Paired for.
+ Announced for.
N Voted against (nay).
X Paired against.
- Announced against.
P Voted "present."
C Voted "present" to avoid possible conflict of interest.
? Did not vote or otherwise make a position known.

Democrats *Republicans*

	453	454	455	456	458	459	460	461
ALABAMA								
1 *Callahan*	N	N	Y	N	N	N	N	N
2 *Dickinson*	N	N	Y	N	Y	N	N	N
3 Browder	N	N	Y	Y	N	N	Y	N
4 Bevill	N	?	Y	Y	N	N	Y	N
5 Flippo	N	N	Y	Y	N	N	Y	N
6 Erdreich	N	N	Y	Y	N	N	Y	N
7 Harris	N	N	Y	Y	N	N	Y	N
ALASKA								
AL *Young*	N	N	Y	N	?	?	?	?
ARIZONA								
1 *Rhodes*	N	Y	N	N	Y	N	N	Y
2 Udall	N	Y	Y	Y	?	N	N	Y
3 *Stump*	N	N	N	N	Y	Y	N	N
4 *Kyl*	N	N	N	N	Y	Y	N	N
5 *Kolbe*	N	Y	Y	N	Y	N	N	N
ARKANSAS								
1 Alexander	N	N	Y	Y	N	N	Y	Y
2 *Robinson*	N	#	?	?	Y	Y	N	N
3 *Hammerschmidt*	N	N	Y	N	N	N	N	N
4 Anthony	N	Y	Y	Y	N	N	Y	Y
CALIFORNIA								
1 Bosco	Y	Y	Y	Y	?	?	N	Y
2 *Herger*	Y	Y	N	N	Y	Y	N	N
3 Matsui	N	Y	Y	Y	N	N	Y	Y
4 Fazio	N	N	Y	Y	X	?	?	?
5 Pelosi	Y	Y	N	Y	-	-	+	+
6 Boxer	Y	Y	N	Y	?	?	#	?
7 Miller	Y	Y	N	Y	N	N	Y	Y
8 Dellums	Y	Y	N	?	N	N	Y	Y
9 Stark	Y	Y	N	Y	N	N	Y	Y
10 Edwards	Y	Y	N	Y	N	N	Y	Y
11 Lantos	Y	Y	Y	Y	N	N	Y	Y
12 *Campbell*	Y	Y	N	N	N	Y	Y	N
13 Mineta	N	N	Y	Y	N	N	Y	Y
14 *Shumway*	N	N	N	N	Y	Y	N	N
15 Condit	?	Y	Y	Y	N	N	N	Y
16 Panetta	N	Y	N	Y	N	N	Y	Y
17 *Pashayan*	N	N	Y	Y	N	N	N	N
18 Lehman	N	Y	Y	?	?	?	N	Y
19 *Lagomarsino*	N	N	Y	N	N	N	N	N
20 *Thomas*	N	Y	Y	N	Y	Y	N	X
21 *Gallegly*	N	N	Y	N	N	Y	N	N
22 *Moorhead*	N	N	Y	N	N	Y	N	N
23 Beilenson	N	Y	N	Y	N	N	Y	Y
24 Waxman	N	Y	N	Y	N	N	Y	Y
25 Roybal	Y	Y	N	Y	N	N	Y	Y
26 Berman	Y	Y	N	Y	N	N	Y	Y
27 Levine	N	Y	Y	?	N	N	Y	Y
28 Dixon	N	N	Y	Y	N	N	Y	Y
29 Hawkins	Y	Y	Y	Y	N	N	?	?
30 Martinez	Y	Y	Y	Y	N	N	Y	?
31 Dymally	Y	Y	N	Y	N	N	Y	Y
32 Anderson	N	Y	Y	Y	N	N	Y	Y
33 *Dreier*	N	N	Y	N	N	Y	N	N
34 Torres	Y	?	Y	Y	N	N	Y	Y
35 *Lewis*	N	N	N	N	N	N	N	Y
36 Brown	N	N	Y	Y	?	?	?	?
37 *McCandless*	N	Y	N	N	Y	N	N	N
38 *Dornan*	N	X	N	N	Y	Y	N	N
39 *Dannemeyer*	N	N	Y	N	Y	Y	N	N
40 *Cox*	N	N	N	N	Y	Y	Y	N
41 *Lowery*	N	N	Y	N	N	N	N	Y
42 *Rohrabacher*	N	Y	Y	N	Y	Y	Y	N
43 *Packard*	N	N	Y	N	Y	Y	N	N
44 Bates	Y	Y	N	Y	N	Y	Y	Y
45 *Hunter*	N	N	Y	N	Y	Y	N	N
COLORADO								
1 Schroeder	Y	Y	N	Y	N	N	Y	Y
2 Skaggs	N	Y	Y	Y	N	N	Y	Y
3 Campbell	N	Y	Y	N	N	N	N	Y
4 *Brown*	N	Y	Y	N	Y	Y	N	N
5 *Hefley*	N	N	N	N	?	Y	N	N
6 *Schaefer*	N	N	N	N	Y	Y	N	N
CONNECTICUT								
1 Kennelly	N	N	Y	Y	N	N	Y	Y
2 Gejdenson	N	N	Y	Y	N	N	Y	Y
3 Morrison	+	+	+	#	−	−	+	+
4 *Shays*	Y	Y	N	Y	N	Y	Y	Y
5 *Rowland*	N	N	Y	Y	?	?	?	?
6 *Johnson*	N	N	Y	N	N	N	Y	Y
DELAWARE								
AL Carper	N	N	Y	Y	N	N	Y	Y
FLORIDA								
1 Hutto	N	N	Y	Y	N	N	Y	N
2 *Grant*	N	Y	Y	N	Y	N	N	N
3 Bennett	N	N	Y	Y	N	Y	Y	N
4 *James*	N	N	Y	N	Y	Y	Y	N
5 *McCollum*	N	N	Y	N	Y	Y	Y	N
6 *Stearns*	N	Y	Y	N	Y	Y	Y	N
7 Gibbons	N	N	Y	Y	N	N	Y	N
8 *Young*	N	N	Y	N	N	N	Y	N
9 *Bilirakis*	N	Y	Y	N	N	Y	N	N
10 *Ireland*	N	N	Y	N	?	?	?	?
11 Nelson	N	N	Y	Y	N	N	Y	Y
12 *Lewis*	N	N	Y	N	Y	Y	N	N
13 *Goss*	N	Y	Y	N	N	N	N	N
14 Johnston	N	Y	Y	Y	N	N	Y	Y
15 *Shaw*	N	Y	Y	?	Y	N	N	Y
16 Smith	N	?	Y	Y	N	N	Y	Y
17 Lehman	N	N	Y	Y	N	N	Y	Y
18 *Ros-Lehtinen*	N	Y	Y	N	N	Y	Y	Y
19 Fascell	N	N	Y	Y	N	N	Y	Y
GEORGIA								
1 Thomas	N	N	Y	Y	N	N	N	N
2 Hatcher	N	N	Y	Y	N	N	N	Y
3 Ray	N	N	Y	Y	?	?	?	?
4 Jones	N	N	Y	Y	N	N	Y	Y
5 Lewis	Y	Y	N	Y	N	N	Y	Y
6 *Gingrich*	N	N	Y	?	Y	Y	N	N
7 Darden	N	N	Y	Y	N	N	Y	N
8 Rowland	N	N	Y	Y	?	?	?	?
9 Jenkins	N	N	Y	Y	N	N	Y	N
10 Barnard	X	?	?	#	Y	N	Y	N
HAWAII								
1 *Saiki*	N	N	Y	Y	N	Y	N	Y
2 Mink	N	Y	Y	Y	?	?	?	?
IDAHO								
1 *Craig*	N	Y	Y	N	N	Y	N	N
2 Stallings	N	Y	Y	N	N	N	N	N
ILLINOIS								
1 Hayes	#	Y	N	Y	N	N	Y	Y
2 Savage	Y	Y	N	Y	?	?	Y	Y
3 Russo	Y	Y	N	Y	N	N	Y	Y
4 Sangmeister	N	N	Y	Y	N	N	Y	Y
5 Lipinski	N	N	?	Y	N	N	Y	N
6 *Hyde*	N	N	Y	N	Y	Y	N	N
7 Collins	Y	Y	N	Y	N	N	Y	Y
8 Rostenkowski	N	Y	Y	Y	N	N	Y	Y
9 Yates	N	Y	N	Y	N	N	Y	Y
10 *Porter*	Y	Y	Y	N	Y	Y	Y	N
11 Annunzio	N	N	Y	Y	N	N	Y	Y
12 *Crane*	N	N	N	N	Y	Y	N	N
13 *Fawell*	N	Y	Y	N	Y	Y	N	N
14 *Hastert*	N	Y	Y	N	Y	N	N	N
15 *Madigan*	N	N	Y	N	Y	Y	N	N
16 *Martin*	N	Y	N	N	?	?	?	?
17 Evans	N	Y	Y	Y	N	N	Y	Y
18 *Michel*	?	N	Y	N	Y	Y	N	N
19 Bruce	N	Y	Y	Y	N	N	Y	Y
20 Durbin	Y	Y	Y	Y	N	N	Y	Y
21 Costello	N	Y	Y	Y	N	N	Y	N
22 Poshard	Y	Y	Y	Y	N	N	Y	N
INDIANA								
1 Visclosky	N	N	Y	Y	N	N	Y	Y
2 Sharp	Y	Y	Y	Y	N	N	Y	Y
3 *Hiler*	N	N	Y	N	Y	N	N	N

ND Northern Democrats SD Southern Democrats

	453	454	455	456	458	459	460	461
4 Long	N	Y	Y	Y	N	N	N	N
5 Jontz	Y	Y	Y	Y	N	N	Y	N
6 ***Burton***	N	N	N	N	Y	Y	N	N
7 ***Myers***	N	N	Y	Y	N	N	N	N
8 McCloskey	N	Y	Y	Y	N	N	?	Y
9 Hamilton	Y	Y	Y	Y	N	N	Y	Y
10 Jacobs	Y	Y	Y	Y	Y	N	Y	Y
IOWA								
1 ***Leach***	N	Y	N	N	Y	Y	Y	Y
2 ***Tauke***	N	Y	N	N	Y	Y	Y	N
3 Nagle	N	Y	Y	Y	N	N	N	Y
4 Smith	N	N	Y	Y	N	N	N	Y
5 ***Lightfoot***	N	N	Y	N	Y	Y	N	N
6 ***Grandy***	Y	Y	N	N	Y	Y	N	Y
KANSAS								
1 ***Roberts***	N	Y	N	N	Y	N	N	Y
2 Slattery	N	Y	Y	Y	Y	N	N	Y
3 ***Meyers***	N	Y	Y	Y	Y	N	Y	Y
4 Glickman	N	N	Y	Y	N	N	Y	Y
5 ***Whittaker***	N	N	Y	N	N	N	N	Y
KENTUCKY								
1 Hubbard	Y	Y	Y	Y	N	Y	N	N
2 Natcher	N	N	Y	Y	N	N	N	N
3 Mazzoli	Y	Y	Y	Y	N	N	Y	Y
4 ***Bunning***	N	N	Y	?	Y	Y	N	N
5 ***Rogers***	N	N	Y	N	N	N	N	N
6 ***Hopkins***	N	N	Y	N	Y	Y	N	Y
7 Perkins	N	Y	Y	Y	N	N	N	Y
LOUISIANA								
1 ***Livingston***	N	N	Y	N	Y	N	N	N
2 Boggs	?	?	?	?	?	N	N	N
3 Tauzin	N	N	Y	Y	N	N	Y	N
4 ***McCrery***	N	N	Y	N	Y	Y	N	N
5 Huckaby	N	N	Y	Y	N	N	Y	N
6 ***Baker***	N	N	Y	N	?	N	N	N
7 Hayes	N	N	Y	Y	N	N	N	N
8 ***Holloway***	N	N	Y	N	?	?	N	N
MAINE								
1 Brennan	N	N	Y	?	?	?	?	?
2 ***Snowe***	N	Y	Y	Y	N	N	Y	Y
MARYLAND								
1 Dyson	N	N	Y	Y	N	N	N	N
2 ***Bentley***	N	N	Y	N	N	Y	N	N
3 Cardin	N	Y	N	Y	?	N	Y	Y
4 McMillen	N	N	Y	Y	N	N	Y	Y
5 Hoyer	N	N	Y	Y	N	N	Y	Y
6 Byron	N	N	Y	Y	N	N	Y	Y
7 Mfume	Y	Y	N	Y	N	Y	Y	Y
8 ***Morella***	N	Y	Y	Y	N	Y	Y	Y
MASSACHUSETTS								
1 ***Conte***	N	N	Y	Y	N	N	Y	Y
2 Neal	Y	Y	Y	Y	N	N	Y	Y
3 Early	N	N	N	Y	?	?	?	?
4 Frank	Y	Y	Y	Y	N	N	Y	Y
5 Atkins	N	N	Y	Y	N	N	Y	Y
6 Mavroules	N	N	Y	Y	N	N	Y	Y
7 Markey	Y	Y	Y	Y	N	N	Y	Y
8 Kennedy	?	?	?	?	N	N	Y	Y
9 Moakley	N	N	Y	Y	N	N	Y	Y
10 Studds	N	Y	N	Y	N	N	Y	Y
11 Donnelly	Y	Y	N	Y	N	N	Y	Y
MICHIGAN								
1 Conyers	Y	Y	N	Y	N	N	Y	Y
2 ***Pursell***	?	Y	N	N	Y	N	N	N
3 Wolpe	Y	Y	Y	Y	N	N	Y	Y
4 ***Upton***	Y	Y	Y	N	Y	Y	Y	N
5 ***Henry***	Y	Y	N	N	N	Y	Y	Y
6 Carr	N	N	Y	Y	?	N	Y	N
7 Kildee	N	Y	Y	Y	N	N	Y	Y
8 Traxler	Y	Y	Y	?	N	N	N	Y
9 ***Vander Jagt***	N	Y	Y	N	Y	Y	N	N
10 ***Schuette***	?	?	?	?	?	?	?	?
11 ***Davis***	N	N	Y	N	Y	N	N	Y
12 Bonior	N	N	Y	Y	N	N	Y	Y
13 Crockett	Y	Y	N	?	?	?	?	?
14 Hertel	N	Y	Y	Y	N	N	Y	Y
15 Ford	?	?	?	?	N	N	Y	?
16 Dingell	N	N	Y	Y	N	N	Y	Y
17 Levin	N	Y	Y	Y	N	N	Y	Y
18 ***Broomfield***	N	X	?	?	Y	Y	Y	N
MINNESOTA								
1 Penny	N	Y	Y	Y	Y	Y	Y	N
2 ***Weber***	?	Y	N	N	Y	Y	N	N
3 ***Frenzel***	N	Y	N	N	#	Y	N	Y
4 Vento	Y	Y	N	Y	N	N	Y	Y

	453	454	455	456	458	459	460	461
5 Sabo	N	N	Y	Y	N	N	Y	Y
6 Sikorski	Y	Y	N	Y	N	N	Y	Y
7 ***Stangeland***	N	Y	Y	N	Y	N	N	N
8 Oberstar	Y	Y	N	Y	N	N	Y	Y
MISSISSIPPI								
1 Whitten	N	N	Y	N	N	N	N	N
2 Espy	Y	Y	Y	Y	?	?	N	Y
3 Montgomery	N	N	Y	Y	N	N	N	N
4 Parker	N	N	Y	Y	N	N	N	N
5 Taylor	N	N	Y	Y	N	N	Y	N
MISSOURI								
1 Clay	Y	Y	N	Y	N	N	Y	Y
2 ***Buechner***	N	Y	Y	N	Y	Y	N	Y
3 Gephardt	N	N	Y	Y	N	N	Y	Y
4 Skelton	N	N	Y	Y	N	N	Y	N
5 Wheat	Y	Y	N	Y	?	N	Y	Y
6 ***Coleman***	N	N	Y	N	Y	N	N	Y
7 ***Hancock***	N	N	N	N	Y	Y	N	N
8 ***Emerson***	N	N	Y	N	Y	N	N	N
9 Volkmer	Y	Y	Y	Y	N	N	Y	N
MONTANA								
1 Williams	N	N	N	?	N	N	N	Y
2 ***Marlenee***	N	Y	Y	N	Y	Y	N	N
NEBRASKA								
1 ***Bereuter***	N	Y	N	N	N	N	Y	Y
2 Hoagland	N	N	Y	Y	N	N	Y	Y
3 ***Smith***	N	N	Y	N	N	N	N	Y
NEVADA								
1 Bilbray	N	N	Y	Y	N	N	N	Y
2 ***Vucanovich***	N	N	N	N	N	Y	N	N
NEW HAMPSHIRE								
1 ***Smith***	N	Y	N	N	Y	Y	Y	N
2 ***Douglas***	?	Y	N	N	?	?	?	N
NEW JERSEY								
1 Vacancy								
2 Hughes	N	Y	N	N	N	N	Y	Y
3 Pallone	N	N	Y	Y	N	N	Y	N
4 ***Smith***	N	Y	Y	N	N	Y	Y	N
5 ***Roukema***	N	#	?	X	N	N	Y	N
6 Dwyer	N	N	Y	Y	N	N	Y	Y
7 ***Rinaldo***	N	N	Y	N	N	Y	Y	N
8 Roe	N	N	Y	?	?	N	Y	Y
9 Torricelli	N	N	Y	Y	N	N	Y	Y
10 Payne	Y	Y	N	Y	N	N	Y	Y
11 ***Gallo***	N	N	Y	N	?	?	?	?
12 ***Courter***	?	N	Y	N	N	Y	N	Y
13 ***Saxton***	N	Y	Y	N	Y	Y	Y	Y
14 Guarini	N	N	Y	Y	N	N	Y	Y
NEW MEXICO								
1 ***Schiff***	N	N	Y	N	N	Y	N	Y
2 ***Skeen***	N	N	Y	N	N	N	N	N
3 Richardson	N	N	Y	Y	N	N	N	Y
NEW YORK								
1 Hochbrueckner	N	Y	Y	Y	N	N	Y	Y
2 Downey	N	Y	Y	Y	N	N	Y	Y
3 Mrazek	N	Y	Y	Y	N	N	Y	Y
4 ***Lent***	N	Y	?	N	N	N	Y	Y
5 ***McGrath***	N	Y	Y	N	N	N	Y	Y
6 Flake	Y	Y	N	Y	N	N	Y	Y
7 Ackerman	Y	Y	Y	Y	N	N	Y	Y
8 Scheuer	Y	Y	N	Y	N	N	Y	Y
9 Manton	N	N	Y	Y	N	N	Y	Y
10 Schumer	Y	Y	Y	Y	N	N	Y	Y
11 Towns	Y	Y	N	Y	N	N	Y	Y
12 Owens	Y	Y	N	Y	N	N	Y	Y
13 Solarz	N	Y	Y	Y	N	N	Y	Y
14 ***Molinari***	N	N	Y	N	N	N	N	Y
15 ***Green***	N	Y	Y	Y	N	N	Y	Y
16 Rangel	Y	Y	N	Y	?	N	Y	Y
17 Weiss	Y	Y	N	N	N	Y	Y	Y
18 Serrano	Y	Y	Y	Y	N	N	Y	Y
19 Engel	N	Y	Y	Y	?	?	?	?
20 Lowey	Y	Y	N	Y	N	N	Y	Y
21 ***Fish***	N	N	Y	N	N	Y	Y	Y
22 ***Gilman***	N	N	Y	N	N	N	Y	Y
23 McNulty	N	N	Y	Y	N	N	Y	Y
24 ***Solomon***	N	N	Y	N	Y	Y	Y	N
25 ***Boehlert***	N	N	Y	N	N	N	Y	Y
26 ***Martin***	N	N	Y	N	N	N	N	Y
27 ***Walsh***	N	Y	Y	N	N	N	N	Y
28 McHugh	N	Y	Y	Y	N	N	Y	Y
29 ***Horton***	N	N	Y	N	N	N	Y	Y
30 Slaughter	Y	Y	Y	Y	N	N	Y	Y
31 ***Paxon***	N	N	N	N	Y	Y	N	N

	453	454	455	456	458	459	460	461
32 LaFalce	Y	Y	Y	Y	N	N	Y	Y
33 Nowak	Y	Y	N	Y	N	N	Y	Y
34 ***Houghton***	N	Y	Y	N	N	N	N	?
NORTH CAROLINA								
1 Jones	Y	N	Y	Y	N	N	N	Y
2 Valentine	N	N	Y	Y	N	N	Y	N
3 Lancaster	N	N	Y	Y	N	N	Y	Y
4 Price	N	Y	Y	Y	N	N	Y	Y
5 Neal	N	Y	Y	Y	N	N	Y	Y
6 ***Coble***	N	N	Y	N	Y	Y	Y	N
7 Rose	N	N	Y	Y	N	N	N	Y
8 Hefner	N	N	Y	Y	N	N	Y	N
9 ***McMillan***	N	Y	Y	N	Y	Y	Y	Y
10 ***Ballenger***	N	N	Y	N	Y	Y	N	N
11 Clarke	N	N	Y	Y	N	N	Y	Y
NORTH DAKOTA								
AL Dorgan	Y	Y	N	Y	N	N	N	Y
OHIO								
1 Luken	N	Y	Y	Y	N	N	Y	N
2 ***Gradison***	N	N	Y	N	Y	Y	Y	N
3 Hall	?	?	?	?	N	N	Y	Y
4 ***Oxley***	N	N	Y	N	?	N	N	N
5 ***Gillmor***	N	N	Y	N	N	N	N	N
6 ***McEwen***	N	N	Y	N	Y	N	N	N
7 ***DeWine***	N	N	Y	N	N	Y	Y	N
8 ***Lukens***	N	N	Y	N	Y	Y	N	N
9 Kaptur	N	Y	Y	Y	N	N	Y	Y
10 ***Miller***	N	N	Y	N	Y	Y	Y	N
11 Eckart	Y	Y	Y	Y	N	N	Y	Y
12 ***Kasich***	N	N	Y	N	Y	N	N	N
13 Pease	N	Y	N	Y	N	Y	Y	Y
14 Sawyer	Y	Y	Y	Y	N	N	Y	Y
15 ***Wylie***	N	N	Y	N	Y	Y	N	N
16 ***Regula***	N	N	Y	N	N	N	Y	N
17 Traficant	Y	Y	N	Y	N	N	Y	Y
18 Applegate	Y	Y	Y	N	N	N	Y	N
19 Feighan	Y	Y	Y	Y	?	N	Y	Y
20 Oakar	Y	Y	Y	Y	N	N	Y	Y
21 Stokes	Y	Y	N	Y	?	?	Y	Y
OKLAHOMA								
1 ***Inhofe***	N	N	Y	N	Y	Y	N	N
2 Synar	Y	Y	Y	Y	N	N	Y	Y
3 Watkins	N	N	Y	Y	N	N	N	N
4 McCurdy	N	N	Y	Y	N	N	Y	Y
5 ***Edwards***	N	N	Y	N	Y	N	N	N
6 English	N	N	Y	Y	N	N	Y	N
OREGON								
1 AuCoin	N	Y	Y	Y	N	N	N	Y
2 ***Smith, B.***	N	N	Y	N	Y	Y	N	N
3 Wyden	Y	Y	N	Y	N	N	Y	Y
4 DeFazio	Y	Y	N	Y	?	N	N	Y
5 ***Smith, D.***	N	N	Y	N	?	?	X	?
PENNSYLVANIA								
1 Foglietta	N	N	Y	Y	N	N	Y	Y
2 Gray	N	N	Y	Y	N	N	Y	Y
3 Borski	N	N	Y	Y	N	N	Y	Y
4 Kolter	Y	N	Y	Y	N	N	Y	Y
5 ***Schulze***	N	Y	Y	N	Y	N	N	N
6 Yatron	Y	Y	Y	Y	N	N	Y	N
7 ***Weldon***	N	N	Y	N	Y	Y	Y	Y
8 Kostmayer	N	N	Y	Y	N	N	Y	Y
9 ***Shuster***	N	N	Y	N	Y	Y	N	N
10 ***McDade***	N	N	Y	N	N	N	Y	N
11 Kanjorski	N	N	Y	Y	N	N	Y	Y
12 Murtha	N	N	Y	Y	N	N	N	Y
13 ***Coughlin***	N	N	Y	N	Y	N	N	?
14 Coyne	Y	Y	Y	Y	N	N	Y	Y
15 ***Ritter***	N	Y	Y	N	Y	Y	Y	Y
16 ***Walker***	N	Y	N	N	Y	Y	Y	N
17 ***Gekas***	N	N	N	N	Y	Y	N	N
18 Walgren	Y	Y	Y	Y	N	N	Y	Y
19 ***Goodling***	N	N	Y	N	Y	N	N	Y
20 Gaydos	N	N	Y	?	N	N	Y	Y
21 ***Ridge***	N	N	Y	N	?	?	Y	Y
22 Murphy	Y	Y	Y	Y	N	N	Y	N
23 ***Clinger***	N	N	Y	Y	Y	N	Y	Y
RHODE ISLAND								
1 ***Machtley***	N	N	Y	N	N	N	Y	Y
2 ***Schneider***	N	N	Y	Y	N	N	Y	Y
SOUTH CAROLINA								
1 ***Ravenel***	N	N	Y	Y	Y	Y	Y	N
2 ***Spence***	N	N	Y	N	Y	N	Y	N
3 Derrick	N	Y	Y	Y	N	N	Y	Y
4 Patterson	N	N	Y	Y	Y	N	Y	N
5 Spratt	N	Y	Y	Y	N	N	Y	N
6 Tallon	N	Y	Y	Y	N	N	Y	N

	453	454	455	456	458	459	460	461
SOUTH DAKOTA								
AL Johnson	Y	Y	Y	N	?	N	N	Y
TENNESSEE								
1 ***Quillen***	N	N	N	X	N	N	N	N
2 ***Duncan***	N	N	Y	N	Y	Y	Y	N
3 Lloyd	N	N	Y	Y	N	N	Y	N
4 Cooper	N	Y	Y	Y	N	N	Y	Y
5 Clement	N	Y	Y	Y	N	N	Y	Y
6 Gordon	N	Y	Y	Y	N	N	Y	Y
7 ***Sundquist***	N	N	Y	N	Y	N	N	N
8 Tanner	N	N	Y	Y	N	N	Y	N
9 Ford	Y	Y	Y	Y	N	N	Y	Y
TEXAS								
1 Chapman	N	N	Y	Y	?	?	?	?
2 Wilson	?	?	?	?	N	N	N	N
3 ***Bartlett***	N	N	Y	N	Y	Y	Y	N
4 Hall	N	N	N	N	N	N	N	N
5 Bryant	Y	Y	Y	Y	N	N	Y	Y
6 ***Barton***	N	N	Y	N	Y	Y	N	N
7 ***Archer***	N	N	Y	N	Y	Y	N	N
8 ***Fields***	N	N	Y	?	Y	Y	N	N
9 Brooks	?	?	?	?	N	N	Y	Y
10 Pickle	N	N	Y	Y	N	N	Y	Y
11 Leath	N	N	Y	Y	N	N	N	N
12 Geren	N	N	Y	Y	N	N	Y	Y
13 Sarpalius	N	N	Y	Y	N	N	N	N
14 Laughlin	N	N	Y	Y	?	?	?	N
15 de la Garza	N	N	Y	Y	N	N	N	Y
16 Coleman	N	N	Y	Y	N	N	Y	Y
17 Stenholm	N	Y	Y	Y	N	N	N	N
18 Washington	Y	Y	N	Y	?	?	Y	Y
19 ***Combest***	N	N	N	N	?	Y	N	N
20 Gonzalez	N	N	Y	Y	N	N	Y	Y
21 ***Smith***	N	N	Y	N	Y	Y	N	N
22 ***DeLay***	?	N	Y	N	Y	N	N	N
23 Bustamante	N	N	Y	Y	N	N	Y	Y
24 Frost	N	N	Y	Y	N	N	N	Y
25 Andrews	N	Y	Y	Y	N	N	Y	Y
26 ***Armey***	N	N	N	N	Y	Y	N	N
27 Ortiz	N	N	Y	Y	N	N	Y	N
UTAH								
1 ***Hansen***	N	N	Y	N	Y	Y	N	N
2 Owens	Y	Y	Y	Y	N	N	C	Y
3 ***Nielson***	N	N	Y	N	Y	Y	N	N
VERMONT								
AL ***Smith***	Y	Y	N	?	N	Y	N	Y
VIRGINIA								
1 ***Bateman***	N	N	Y	N	N	N	N	N
2 Pickett	N	N	Y	Y	N	N	Y	Y
3 ***Bliley***	N	N	Y	N	?	?	?	?
4 Sisisky	N	N	Y	Y	N	N	Y	Y
5 Payne	N	Y	Y	Y	N	N	Y	Y
6 Olin	N	Y	Y	Y	N	N	N	Y
7 ***Slaughter***	N	N	Y	N	N	N	N	N
8 ***Parris***	N	-	Y	N	Y	Y	N	N
9 Boucher	N	N	Y	Y	N	N	Y	Y
10 ***Wolf***	N	N	Y	N	N	Y	N	N
WASHINGTON								
1 ***Miller***	N	Y	Y	N	N	Y	Y	Y
2 Swift	N	Y	Y	Y	N	N	Y	Y
3 Unsoeld	Y	Y	N	Y	N	N	Y	Y
4 ***Morrison***	N	N	Y	N	N	N	N	Y
5 Foley								
6 Dicks	N	N	Y	Y	N	N	Y	Y
7 McDermott	Y	Y	N	Y	N	N	Y	Y
8 ***Chandler***	N	Y	Y	N	N	Y	Y	Y
WEST VIRGINIA								
1 Mollohan	N	N	Y	Y	?	N	N	Y
2 Staggers	N	Y	Y	Y	N	N	N	Y
3 Wise	N	Y	Y	?	N	N	Y	Y
4 Rahall	Y	Y	N	Y	N	N	Y	N
WISCONSIN								
1 Aspin	N	Y	Y	Y	N	N	Y	Y
2 Kastenmeier	Y	Y	N	Y	N	N	Y	Y
3 ***Gunderson***	N	Y	Y	N	Y	N	Y	Y
4 Kleczka	Y	Y	Y	Y	N	N	Y	Y
5 Moody	Y	Y	N	Y	?	?	?	#
6 ***Petri***	Y	Y	N	N	Y	Y	Y	N
7 Obey	N	Y	N	Y	N	N	Y	Y
8 ***Roth***	Y	Y	N	N	Y	Y	N	N
9 ***Sensenbrenner***	Y	Y	N	N	Y	Y	N	N
WYOMING								
AL ***Thomas***	N	Y	Y	N	N	Y	N	N

Southern states - Ala., Ark., Fla., Ga., Ky., La., Miss., N.C., Okla., S.C., Tenn., Texas, Va.
Omitted votes are quorum calls, which CQ does not include in its vote charts.

HOUSE VOTES 462, 463, 464, 465, 466, 467, 468, 469

462. HR 5769. Fiscal 1991 Interior Appropriations/NEA Funding. Regula, R-Ohio, amendment to require the chairperson of the National Endowment for the Arts (NEA) to take into account, in funding projects, not only artistic excellence and merit but general standards of decency and respect for the diverse beliefs and values of the American people; changing the NEA grant process; giving states a larger share of NEA funds; and implementing other policy changes. Before being amended by the Williams, D-Mont., substitute, the Regula amendment would have established a new definition of artistic excellence to be used by the NEA and prohibited the NEA from funding obscene or indecent works. Adopted 342-58: R 149-13; D 193-45 (ND 122-37, SD 71-8), Oct. 15, 1990.

463. HR 5769. Fiscal 1991 Interior Appropriations/Discretionary Spending Cut. Frenzel, R-Minn., amendment to reduce all discretionary accounts in the bill by 4.6 percent. Rejected 167-234: R 129-34; D 38-200 (ND 17-144, SD 21-56), Oct. 15, 1990.

464. HR 5769. Fiscal 1991 Interior Appropriations/Passage. Passage of the bill to appropriate $11.9 billion for the Interior Department and related agencies in fiscal 1991. The president requested $9.9 billion. Passed 327-80: R 95-70; D 232-10 (ND 160-2, SD 72-8), Oct. 15, 1990.

465. HR 3960. Reclamation Water Projects/Technical Changes. Miller, D-Calif, en bloc amendment to make technical changes in the bill. Adopted 351-0: R 137-0; D 214-0 (ND 143-0, SD 71-0), Oct. 15, 1990.

466. HR 3960. Reclamation Water Projects/Utah Reclamation Mitigation and Conservation Account. Solomon, R-N.Y., amendment to require smaller payments into the Utah Reclamation Mitigation and Conservation Account from electric power revenues. The amendment would not count these payments toward fulfillment of the public utilities' Central Utah Project repayment obligations, and it would not allow deferral of the payments. Rejected 151-204: R 100-42; D 51-162 (ND 31-112, SD 20-50), Oct. 15, 1990.

467. HR 3960. Reclamation Water Projects/Passage. Passage of the bill to increase by about $680 million the authorization ceiling for the Colorado River Storage Project to provide for the completion of the Central Utah Project; establish procedures to mitigate adverse effects on the environment in Utah by projects in the bill; provide for the settlement of water rights claims of the Ute Indian Tribe; and include the text of HR 2567, the Reclamation Projects Authorization and Adjustment Act. Passed 211-143: R 43-99; D 168-44 (ND 117-26, SD 51-18), Oct. 16, 1990 (in the session that began, and the Congressional Record dated, Oct. 15, 1990).

468. Procedural Motion. Walker, R-Pa., motion to approve the House Journal of Monday, Oct. 15. Motion agreed to 245-110: R 41-105; D 204-5 (ND 139-5, SD 65-0), Oct. 16, 1990.

469. HR 5422. Fiscal 1991 Intelligence Authorization/Rule. Adoption of the rule (H Res 487) to provide for House floor consideration of the bill to authorize a classified level of funding for U.S. intelligence agencies and other government intelligence activities in fiscal 1991. Adopted 418-0: R 171-0; D 247-0 (ND 168-0, SD 79-0), Oct. 16, 1990.

KEY

- Y Voted for (yea).
- # Paired for.
- + Announced for.
- N Voted against (nay).
- X Paired against.
- \- Announced against.
- P Voted "present."
- C Voted "present" to avoid possible conflict of interest.
- ? Did not vote or otherwise make a position known.

Democrats ***Republicans***

	462	463	464	465	466	467	468	469
ALABAMA								
1 ***Callahan***	Y	Y	N	Y	N	Y	N	Y
2 ***Dickinson***	Y	Y	Y	Y	N	Y	?	Y
3 Browder	Y	N	Y	Y	N	Y	Y	Y
4 Bevill	Y	N	Y	Y	N	Y	Y	Y
5 Flippo	Y	N	Y	Y	N	Y	Y	Y
6 Erdreich	Y	N	Y	Y	Y	Y	Y	Y
7 Harris	Y	N	Y	Y	N	Y	Y	Y
ALASKA								
AL ***Young***	?	?	?	?	?	?	N	Y
ARIZONA								
1 ***Rhodes***	Y	Y	Y	Y	N	Y	N	Y
2 Udall	Y	N	Y	?	?	?	Y	Y
3 ***Stump***	Y	Y	N	Y	N	N	N	Y
4 ***Kyl***	N	Y	Y	Y	N	Y	N	Y
5 ***Kolbe***	Y	Y	Y	Y	N	Y	N	Y
ARKANSAS								
1 Alexander	Y	N	Y	?	?	?	Y	Y
2 ***Robinson***	N	Y	N	?	?	?	Y	Y
3 ***Hammerschmidt***	Y	Y	Y	Y	Y	N	N	Y
4 Anthony	Y	N	Y	Y	N	Y	Y	Y
CALIFORNIA								
1 Bosco	Y	N	Y	Y	Y	Y	Y	Y
2 ***Herger***	Y	Y	Y	Y	N	N	N	Y
3 Matsui	Y	N	Y	Y	?	?	Y	Y
4 Fazio	?	?	?	?	?	?	Y	Y
5 Pelosi	-	-	Y	Y	N	Y	?	Y
6 Boxer	?	X	?	?	?	?	Y	Y
7 Miller	Y	N	Y	Y	N	Y	Y	Y
8 Dellums	N	N	Y	Y	N	Y	Y	Y
9 Stark	N	N	Y	Y	?	?	Y	Y
10 Edwards	Y	N	Y	Y	N	Y	Y	Y
11 Lantos	Y	N	Y	?	?	?	Y	Y
12 ***Campbell***	N	Y	Y	Y	Y	N	N	Y
13 Mineta	Y	N	Y	Y	N	Y	Y	Y
14 ***Shumway***	N	Y	N	Y	N	N	Y	Y
15 Condit	N	Y	N	Y	N	N	?	Y
16 Panetta	Y	N	Y	Y	N	Y	Y	Y
17 ***Pashayan***	Y	N	Y	Y	Y	N	P	Y
18 Lehman	Y	N	Y	Y	N	N	Y	Y
19 ***Lagomarsino***	Y	Y	Y	Y	Y	Y	N	Y
20 ***Thomas***	?	#	X	?	?	?	?	?
21 ***Gallegly***	Y	Y	Y	Y	Y	Y	N	Y
22 ***Moorhead***	Y	Y	N	Y	N	N	N	Y
23 Beilenson	N	N	Y	Y	N	Y	Y	Y
24 Waxman	N	N	Y	Y	N	Y	Y	Y
25 Roybal	N	N	Y	Y	N	Y	Y	Y
26 Berman	N	N	Y	Y	N	Y	Y	Y
27 Levine	N	N	Y	Y	N	Y	Y	Y
28 Dixon	N	N	Y	Y	N	Y	?	Y
29 Hawkins	?	?	?	?	?	?	Y	?
30 Martinez	Y	N	Y	?	?	?	?	Y
31 Dymally	N	N	Y	Y	N	Y	?	Y
32 Anderson	Y	N	Y	Y	N	Y	Y	Y
33 ***Dreier***	N	Y	N	Y	Y	N	N	Y
34 Torres	Y	N	Y	Y	N	Y	Y	Y
35 ***Lewis***	Y	N	Y	Y	N	Y	N	Y
36 Brown	?	?	?	?	?	?	Y	Y
37 ***McCandless***	Y	Y	Y	Y	N	N	N	Y
38 ***Dornan***	Y	?	N	Y	Y	N	N	Y
39 ***Dannemeyer***	Y	Y	N	Y	Y	N	N	Y
40 ***Cox***	N	Y	N	Y	Y	N	N	Y
41 ***Lowery***	Y	N	Y	Y	N	Y	N	Y
42 ***Rohrabacher***	P	Y	N	Y	Y	N	N	Y
43 ***Packard***	Y	Y	N	Y	N	Y	Y	Y
44 Bates	Y	Y	Y	Y	N	Y	Y	Y
45 ***Hunter***	N	Y	N	Y	N	Y	?	Y
COLORADO								
1 Schroeder	Y	Y	Y	Y	?	?	N	Y
2 Skaggs	Y	N	Y	Y	N	Y	Y	Y
3 Campbell	Y	N	Y	Y	N	Y	Y	Y
4 ***Brown***	Y	Y	N	Y	N	Y	N	Y
5 ***Hefley***	Y	Y	N	?	?	?	N	Y
6 ***Schaefer***	Y	Y	N	Y	N	Y	N	Y
CONNECTICUT								
1 Kennelly	Y	N	Y	Y	N	Y	Y	Y
2 Gejdenson	Y	N	Y	Y	N	Y	Y	Y
3 Morrison	+	+	+	+	−	+	?	+
4 ***Shays***	Y	Y	Y	Y	Y	N	N	Y
5 ***Rowland***	?	?	?	?	?	?	?	?
6 ***Johnson***	Y	N	Y	Y	N	Y	Y	Y
DELAWARE								
AL Carper	Y	N	Y	Y	N	Y	?	Y
FLORIDA								
1 Hutto	Y	Y	Y	Y	Y	N	Y	Y
2 ***Grant***	Y	Y	N	Y	Y	N	Y	Y
3 Bennett	N	N	Y	Y	N	N	Y	Y
4 ***James***	Y	Y	Y	Y	Y	N	N	Y
5 ***McCollum***	Y	Y	N	Y	Y	N	?	Y
6 ***Stearns***	Y	Y	Y	Y	Y	N	N	Y
7 Gibbons	Y	N	Y	?	?	?	Y	Y
8 ***Young***	Y	N	Y	Y	Y	N	N	Y
9 ***Bilirakis***	Y	Y	Y	Y	Y	N	N	Y
10 ***Ireland***	?	?	?	?	?	?	?	Y
11 Nelson	Y	N	Y	Y	Y	Y	Y	Y
12 ***Lewis***	Y	Y	N	Y	Y	N	?	Y
13 ***Goss***	Y	N	Y	Y	Y	N	N	Y
14 Johnston	N	N	Y	Y	N	Y	?	Y
15 ***Shaw***	Y	Y	Y	?	?	?	Y	Y
16 Smith	Y	N	Y	Y	N	Y	Y	Y
17 Lehman	N	N	Y	?	?	?	Y	Y
18 ***Ros-Lehtinen***	Y	Y	Y	Y	Y	N	?	Y
19 Fascell	N	N	Y	Y	N	Y	Y	Y
GEORGIA								
1 Thomas	Y	N	Y	Y	N	Y	Y	Y
2 Hatcher	?	N	Y	Y	N	Y	?	Y
3 Ray	?	?	?	?	?	?	?	Y
4 Jones	Y	N	Y	Y	N	Y	Y	Y
5 Lewis	N	N	Y	Y	N	Y	Y	Y
6 ***Gingrich***	Y	Y	Y	Y	N	N	?	Y
7 Darden	Y	N	Y	Y	N	Y	Y	Y
8 Rowland	?	?	?	?	?	?	?	?
9 Jenkins	Y	N	Y	Y	N	Y	Y	Y
10 Barnard	Y	Y	N	Y	N	Y	Y	Y
HAWAII								
1 ***Saiki***	Y	N	Y	Y	Y	Y	Y	Y
2 Mink	?	?	?	?	?	?	?	Y
IDAHO								
1 ***Craig***	Y	Y	Y	Y	Y	N	N	Y
2 Stallings	Y	Y	Y	Y	N	N	Y	Y
ILLINOIS								
1 Hayes	N	N	Y	Y	N	Y	Y	Y
2 Savage	N	N	Y	Y	N	Y	Y	Y
3 Russo	Y	N	Y	Y	Y	N	Y	Y
4 Sangmeister	Y	Y	Y	Y	Y	N	Y	Y
5 Lipinski	Y	N	Y	Y	Y	N	Y	Y
6 ***Hyde***	Y	Y	?	?	?	?	Y	Y
7 Collins	N	N	Y	Y	N	Y	Y	Y
8 Rostenkowski	Y	N	Y	Y	Y	N	Y	Y
9 Yates	N	N	Y	?	?	?	Y	Y
10 ***Porter***	Y	Y	Y	Y	Y	N	N	Y
11 Annunzio	Y	Y	Y	?	?	?	Y	Y
12 ***Crane***	Y	Y	N	Y	Y	N	?	?
13 ***Fawell***	Y	Y	Y	Y	Y	N	N	Y
14 ***Hastert***	Y	Y	N	Y	Y	N	N	Y
15 ***Madigan***	Y	Y	Y	Y	N	N	?	Y
16 ***Martin***	?	?	?	?	?	?	N	Y
17 Evans	N	N	Y	Y	Y	Y	Y	Y
18 ***Michel***	Y	Y	N	Y	Y	N	N	Y
19 Bruce	Y	N	Y	Y	Y	Y	Y	Y
20 Durbin	Y	N	Y	Y	Y	N	Y	Y
21 Costello	Y	N	Y	Y	N	N	Y	Y
22 Poshard	Y	N	Y	Y	N	Y	Y	Y
INDIANA								
1 Visclosky	Y	N	Y	Y	N	N	Y	Y
2 Sharp	Y	N	?	?	?	?	Y	Y
3 ***Hiler***	Y	Y	N	Y	Y	N	N	Y

ND Northern Democrats SD Southern Democrats

	462	463	464	465	466	467	468	469
4 Long	Y	Y	Y	Y	N	Y	Y	Y
5 Jontz	N	N	Y	Y	Y	Y	Y	Y
6 ***Burton***	Y	Y	N	Y	Y	N	N	Y
7 ***Myers***	Y	N	Y	Y	Y	Y	?	Y
8 McCloskey	Y	N	Y	Y	N	Y	Y	Y
9 Hamilton	Y	Y	Y	Y	Y	Y	Y	Y
10 Jacobs	Y	Y	Y	Y	N	N	N	Y
IOWA								
1 ***Leach***	Y	Y	Y	?	?	?	N	Y
2 ***Tauke***	Y	Y	N	Y	Y	N	N	Y
3 Nagle	Y	N	Y	Y	N	Y	?	Y
4 Smith	Y	N	Y	Y	N	Y	Y	Y
5 ***Lightfoot***	Y	Y	Y	Y	N	N	N	Y
6 ***Grandy***	Y	Y	Y	Y	N	N	N	Y
KANSAS								
1 ***Roberts***	Y	Y	N	Y	N	N	N	Y
2 Slattery	Y	N	Y	Y	Y	N	Y	Y
3 ***Meyers***	Y	Y	N	Y	Y	N	N	Y
4 Glickman	Y	N	Y	Y	Y	N	Y	Y
5 ***Whittaker***	Y	Y	Y	Y	N	N	N	Y
KENTUCKY								
1 Hubbard	Y	Y	N	Y	N	N	Y	Y
2 Natcher	Y	N	Y	Y	N	Y	Y	Y
3 Mazzoli	Y	N	Y	Y	Y	Y	Y	Y
4 ***Bunning***	Y	Y	N	Y	Y	N	N	Y
5 ***Rogers***	Y	N	Y	?	Y	N	N	Y
6 ***Hopkins***	Y	Y	Y	Y	Y	N	N	Y
7 Perkins	Y	N	Y	Y	N	Y	Y	Y
LOUISIANA								
1 ***Livingston***	Y	N	Y	?	?	?	Y	Y
2 Boggs	Y	N	Y	?	?	?	Y	Y
3 Tauzin	Y	Y	N	Y	N	Y	Y	Y
4 ***McCrery***	Y	Y	N	Y	Y	N	?	Y
5 Huckaby	Y	?	Y	Y	N	N	Y	Y
6 ***Baker***	Y	Y	N	Y	Y	N	N	Y
7 Hayes	Y	N	Y	Y	?	?	Y	Y
8 ***Holloway***	P	Y	N	Y	Y	N	N	Y
MAINE								
1 Brennan	?	?	?	?	?	?	?	?
2 ***Snowe***	Y	N	Y	Y	Y	N	N	Y
MARYLAND								
1 Dyson	Y	N	Y	Y	N	N	?	Y
2 ***Bentley***	Y	Y	Y	Y	N	N	N	?
3 Cardin	N	N	Y	Y	Y	Y	Y	Y
4 McMillen	Y	N	Y	Y	N	Y	Y	Y
5 Hoyer	Y	N	Y	Y	N	Y	Y	Y
6 Byron	Y	N	Y	Y	Y	N	Y	Y
7 Mfume	N	N	Y	Y	?	?	?	Y
8 ***Morella***	Y	N	Y	?	?	?	Y	Y
MASSACHUSETTS								
1 ***Conte***	Y	N	Y	?	?	?	Y	Y
2 Neal	Y	N	Y	Y	N	Y	Y	Y
3 Early	?	?	Y	Y	N	Y	Y	Y
4 Frank	N	N	Y	Y	N	Y	Y	Y
5 Atkins	Y	N	Y	Y	Y	Y	Y	Y
6 Mavroules	Y	N	Y	?	?	?	Y	Y
7 Markey	Y	N	Y	Y	N	Y	Y	Y
8 Kennedy	Y	N	Y	Y	N	Y	Y	Y
9 Moakley	Y	N	Y	Y	N	Y	Y	Y
10 Studds	N	N	Y	Y	Y	Y	Y	Y
11 Donnelly	Y	N	Y	?	?	?	Y	Y
MICHIGAN								
1 Conyers	Y	N	Y	?	?	?	?	Y
2 ***Pursell***	Y	Y	N	Y	?	?	?	Y
3 Wolpe	Y	N	Y	Y	Y	Y	Y	Y
4 ***Upton***	Y	Y	N	Y	Y	N	N	Y
5 ***Henry***	Y	Y	N	Y	Y	N	N	Y
6 Carr	N	N	Y	Y	Y	N	Y	Y
7 Kildee	Y	N	Y	Y	N	N	Y	Y
8 Traxler	Y	N	Y	?	?	?	Y	Y
9 ***Vander Jagt***	Y	Y	Y	?	?	?	Y	Y
10 ***Schuette***	?	?	?	?	?	?	?	?
11 ***Davis***	Y	N	Y	?	?	Y	Y	Y
12 Bonior	N	N	Y	Y	N	Y	Y	Y
13 Crockett	?	?	?	?	?	?	Y	?
14 Hertel	Y	N	Y	Y	N	N	Y	Y
15 Ford	?	?	?	?	?	?	?	?
16 Dingell	Y	N	Y	Y	N	Y	?	Y
17 Levin	Y	N	Y	Y	N	Y	Y	Y
18 ***Broomfield***	Y	Y	Y	?	?	?	Y	Y
MINNESOTA								
1 Penny	Y	Y	Y	Y	N	Y	N	Y
2 ***Weber***	Y	Y	Y	?	?	?	N	Y
3 ***Frenzel***	Y	Y	N	Y	Y	N	N	Y
4 Vento	Y	N	Y	Y	Y	Y	Y	Y

	462	463	464	465	466	467	468	469
5 Sabo	Y	N	Y	Y	Y	Y	Y	Y
6 Sikorski	Y	N	Y	Y	N	Y	N	Y
7 ***Stangeland***	Y	Y	Y	Y	Y	N	?	Y
8 Oberstar	Y	N	Y	?	?	?	Y	Y
MISSISSIPPI								
1 Whitten	N	N	Y	Y	N	?	Y	Y
2 Espy	N	N	Y	Y	N	Y	Y	Y
3 Montgomery	Y	Y	Y	?	?	?	Y	Y
4 Parker	Y	Y	Y	Y	Y	N	Y	Y
5 Taylor	Y	Y	N	Y	Y	N	Y	Y
MISSOURI								
1 Clay	?	N	Y	?	?	?	?	Y
2 ***Buechner***	Y	Y	N	Y	Y	N	?	Y
3 Gephardt	Y	N	Y	Y	N	Y	Y	Y
4 Skelton	Y	Y	N	?	?	?	Y	Y
5 Wheat	Y	N	Y	Y	N	Y	Y	Y
6 ***Coleman***	Y	Y	Y	Y	Y	Y	?	Y
7 ***Hancock***	N	Y	N	?	Y	N	N	Y
8 ***Emerson***	Y	Y	N	Y	N	N	N	Y
9 Volkmer	Y	Y	Y	Y	N	N	Y	Y
MONTANA								
1 Williams	Y	N	Y	Y	N	Y	?	Y
2 ***Marlenee***	Y	Y	N	?	N	N	P	Y
NEBRASKA								
1 ***Bereuter***	Y	Y	Y	Y	Y	Y	?	Y
2 Hoagland	Y	N	Y	Y	Y	Y	Y	Y
3 ***Smith***	Y	N	Y	Y	N	Y	Y	Y
NEVADA								
1 Bilbray	Y	N	Y	Y	N	Y	?	Y
2 ***Vucanovich***	N	Y	N	Y	N	Y	N	Y
NEW HAMPSHIRE								
1 ***Smith***	Y	Y	N	Y	Y	N	N	Y
2 ***Douglas***	Y	Y	N	Y	Y	N	N	Y
NEW JERSEY								
1 Vacancy								
2 Hughes	Y	Y	Y	Y	Y	N	Y	Y
3 Pallone	Y	N	Y	Y	N	Y	Y	Y
4 ***Smith***	Y	Y	Y	Y	Y	Y	?	Y
5 ***Roukema***	Y	Y	N	Y	Y	N	N	Y
6 Dwyer	Y	N	Y	Y	Y	N	?	Y
7 ***Rinaldo***	Y	Y	Y	Y	Y	Y	Y	Y
8 Roe	Y	N	Y	Y	N	Y	?	Y
9 Torricelli	Y	N	Y	Y	N	Y	?	Y
10 Payne	Y	N	Y	Y	N	Y	Y	Y
11 ***Gallo***	?	?	?	?	?	?	N	Y
12 ***Courter***	Y	Y	Y	Y	?	?	N	Y
13 ***Saxton***	Y	Y	Y	Y	Y	N	N	Y
14 Guarini	Y	Y	Y	Y	N	N	?	Y
NEW MEXICO								
1 ***Schiff***	Y	N	Y	Y	N	Y	?	Y
2 ***Skeen***	Y	N	Y	Y	N	Y	N	Y
3 Richardson	Y	N	Y	Y	N	Y	Y	Y
NEW YORK								
1 Hochbrueckner	Y	N	Y	Y	N	Y	Y	Y
2 Downey	Y	N	Y	Y	N	N	Y	Y
3 Mrazek	Y	N	Y	Y	N	Y	Y	Y
4 ***Lent***	Y	Y	Y	Y	Y	Y	Y	Y
5 ***McGrath***	Y	Y	Y	Y	Y	N	N	Y
6 Flake	N	N	Y	Y	N	Y	Y	Y
7 Ackerman	N	N	Y	Y	N	Y	Y	Y
8 Scheuer	N	N	Y	Y	N	Y	Y	Y
9 Manton	Y	N	Y	Y	N	Y	Y	Y
10 Schumer	Y	N	Y	Y	N	Y	Y	Y
11 Towns	N	N	Y	Y	N	Y	N	Y
12 Owens	N	N	Y	Y	N	Y	?	Y
13 Solarz	Y	N	Y	Y	Y	Y	Y	Y
14 ***Molinari***	Y	N	Y	Y	Y	N	N	Y
15 ***Green***	Y	N	Y	Y	Y	Y	Y	Y
16 Rangel	N	N	Y	Y	N	Y	Y	Y
17 Weiss	N	N	Y	Y	N	Y	Y	Y
18 Serrano	Y	N	Y	Y	N	Y	Y	Y
19 Engel	?	?	?	?	?	?	?	?
20 Lowey	Y	N	Y	Y	N	Y	Y	Y
21 ***Fish***	Y	Y	Y	?	?	?	?	Y
22 ***Gilman***	Y	N	Y	Y	Y	N	Y	Y
23 McNulty	Y	N	Y	Y	Y	Y	+	Y
24 ***Solomon***	Y	Y	N	Y	Y	N	N	Y
25 ***Boehlert***	Y	?	?	?	Y	Y	N	Y
26 ***Martin***	Y	Y	Y	Y	Y	?	N	Y
27 ***Walsh***	Y	Y	N	Y	Y	N	Y	Y
28 McHugh	Y	N	Y	Y	N	Y	Y	Y
29 ***Horton***	Y	N	Y	?	?	?	Y	Y
30 Slaughter	Y	N	Y	+	N	Y	Y	Y
31 ***Paxon***	Y	Y	N	Y	Y	N	N	Y

	462	463	464	465	466	467	468	469
32 LaFalce	Y	Y	Y	Y	N	Y	Y	Y
33 Nowak	Y	N	Y	Y	N	Y	Y	Y
34 ***Houghton***	?	N	Y	Y	N	Y	Y	Y
NORTH CAROLINA								
1 Jones	Y	N	Y	?	?	?	?	Y
2 Valentine	Y	N	Y	Y	Y	N	?	Y
3 Lancaster	Y	N	Y	Y	Y	Y	Y	Y
4 Price	Y	N	Y	Y	Y	Y	Y	Y
5 Neal	Y	Y	Y	Y	Y	N	?	Y
6 ***Coble***	Y	Y	N	Y	Y	N	N	Y
7 Rose	Y	N	Y	Y	N	Y	Y	Y
8 Hefner	Y	N	Y	Y	Y	Y	Y	Y
9 ***McMillan***	Y	Y	N	Y	Y	N	N	Y
10 ***Ballenger***	Y	Y	N	Y	Y	N	N	Y
11 Clarke	Y	N	Y	Y	N	Y	Y	Y
NORTH DAKOTA								
AL Dorgan	Y	N	Y	?	N	Y	Y	Y
OHIO								
1 Luken	N	N	Y	Y	N	Y	Y	Y
2 ***Gradison***	Y	Y	N	?	?	?	N	Y
3 Hall	Y	Y	Y	Y	N	Y	Y	Y
4 ***Oxley***	Y	Y	N	?	?	?	N	Y
5 ***Gillmor***	Y	N	Y	?	Y	Y	?	Y
6 ***McEwen***	Y	Y	N	Y	Y	N	Y	Y
7 ***DeWine***	Y	Y	Y	Y	Y	N	N	Y
8 ***Lukens***	Y	Y	N	Y	Y	N	N	Y
9 Kaptur	Y	N	Y	Y	N	N	?	Y
10 ***Miller***	Y	Y	N	Y	Y	N	N	Y
11 Eckart	Y	N	Y	Y	Y	Y	Y	Y
12 ***Kasich***	Y	Y	Y	Y	Y	N	?	Y
13 Pease	N	N	Y	Y	N	Y	Y	Y
14 Sawyer	Y	N	Y	Y	N	Y	Y	Y
15 ***Wylie***	Y	Y	Y	Y	Y	N	Y	Y
16 ***Regula***	Y	N	Y	Y	Y	N	N	Y
17 Traficant	Y	N	Y	Y	N	Y	Y	Y
18 Applegate	Y	N	Y	Y	Y	Y	Y	Y
19 Feighan	N	N	Y	Y	N	Y	?	Y
20 Oakar	Y	N	Y	?	?	?	Y	Y
21 Stokes	?	N	Y	Y	N	Y	Y	Y
OKLAHOMA								
1 ***Inhofe***	Y	Y	N	Y	Y	N	N	Y
2 Synar	Y	N	Y	Y	N	Y	Y	Y
3 Watkins	Y	N	Y	Y	N	Y	Y	Y
4 McCurdy	Y	Y	Y	Y	Y	Y	Y	Y
5 ***Edwards***	?	?	Y	?	?	?	?	Y
6 English	Y	Y	Y	Y	N	Y	?	?
OREGON								
1 AuCoin	N	N	Y	?	N	Y	Y	Y
2 ***Smith, B.***	Y	Y	N	Y	N	N	N	Y
3 Wyden	Y	N	Y	Y	Y	Y	Y	Y
4 DeFazio	Y	N	Y	Y	N	Y	Y	Y
5 ***Smith, D.***	?	?	#	Y	N	N	N	Y
PENNSYLVANIA								
1 Foglietta	N	N	Y	Y	N	Y	Y	Y
2 Gray	Y	N	Y	Y	N	Y	?	Y
3 Borski	Y	N	Y	Y	N	Y	Y	Y
4 Kolter	Y	N	Y	Y	N	Y	Y	Y
5 ***Schulze***	Y	Y	Y	?	?	?	Y	Y
6 Yatron	Y	Y	Y	Y	N	Y	Y	Y
7 ***Weldon***	Y	N	Y	Y	Y	N	N	Y
8 Kostmayer	N	N	Y	Y	Y	Y	Y	Y
9 ***Shuster***	Y	Y	N	?	?	?	Y	Y
10 ***McDade***	Y	N	Y	Y	?	?	N	Y
11 Kanjorski	Y	N	Y	Y	N	N	Y	Y
12 Murtha	Y	N	Y	?	N	Y	Y	Y
13 ***Coughlin***	?	N	Y	Y	Y	N	N	Y
14 Coyne	N	N	Y	Y	N	Y	Y	Y
15 ***Ritter***	Y	Y	Y	Y	Y	N	Y	Y
16 ***Walker***	N	Y	N	Y	Y	N	N	Y
17 ***Gekas***	N	Y	N	Y	Y	N	N	Y
18 Walgren	Y	N	Y	Y	N	Y	Y	Y
19 ***Goodling***	Y	Y	Y	?	N	N	N	Y
20 Gaydos	Y	N	Y	Y	N	Y	Y	Y
21 ***Ridge***	Y	Y	Y	Y	Y	Y	N	Y
22 Murphy	Y	N	Y	?	?	?	?	Y
23 ***Clinger***	Y	N	Y	Y	N	N	N	Y
RHODE ISLAND								
1 ***Machtley***	Y	Y	Y	Y	Y	N	N	Y
2 ***Schneider***	Y	Y	Y	?	Y	Y	Y	Y
SOUTH CAROLINA								
1 ***Ravenel***	Y	Y	Y	?	?	?	Y	Y
2 ***Spence***	Y	N	Y	Y	Y	N	N	Y
3 Derrick	Y	N	Y	Y	N	Y	Y	Y
4 Patterson	Y	Y	Y	Y	Y	N	Y	Y
5 Spratt	Y	N	Y	Y	N	Y	Y	Y
6 Tallon	Y	N	Y	Y	N	N	Y	Y

	462	463	464	465	466	467	468	469
SOUTH DAKOTA								
AL Johnson	Y	N	Y	Y	N	Y	Y	Y
TENNESSEE								
1 ***Quillen***	Y	N	Y	Y	Y	Y	Y	Y
2 ***Duncan***	Y	Y	N	Y	Y	N	N	Y
3 Lloyd	Y	Y	Y	Y	N	N	Y	Y
4 Cooper	Y	Y	Y	Y	Y	N	Y	Y
5 Clement	Y	Y	Y	Y	N	Y	Y	Y
6 Gordon	Y	N	Y	Y	N	N	Y	Y
7 ***Sundquist***	Y	Y	N	Y	Y	N	N	Y
8 Tanner	Y	Y	Y	Y	N	Y	Y	Y
9 Ford	Y	?	Y	Y	N	Y	P	Y
TEXAS								
1 Chapman	?	?	?	?	?	?	?	?
2 Wilson	Y	N	Y	?	?	?	?	Y
3 ***Bartlett***	N	Y	N	Y	Y	N	Y	Y
4 Hall	Y	Y	N	Y	N	N	Y	Y
5 Bryant	Y	N	Y	Y	Y	Y	?	Y
6 ***Barton***	Y	Y	N	Y	Y	N	N	Y
7 ***Archer***	Y	Y	N	Y	Y	N	Y	Y
8 ***Fields***	Y	Y	N	?	?	?	N	Y
9 Brooks	Y	N	Y	Y	N	Y	Y	Y
10 Pickle	Y	N	Y	Y	N	Y	Y	Y
11 Leath	Y	N	Y	?	?	?	?	?
12 Geren	Y	Y	Y	Y	Y	N	Y	Y
13 Sarpalius	Y	Y	N	Y	Y	Y	?	Y
14 Laughlin	Y	Y	N	Y	Y	N	Y	Y
15 de la Garza	Y	N	Y	Y	N	Y	?	Y
16 Coleman	Y	N	Y	Y	N	Y	Y	Y
17 Stenholm	Y	Y	N	Y	N	N	Y	Y
18 Washington	N	?	Y	Y	N	Y	?	Y
19 ***Combest***	Y	Y	N	Y	Y	N	Y	Y
20 Gonzalez	Y	N	Y	Y	N	Y	Y	Y
21 ***Smith***	Y	Y	Y	?	?	?	N	Y
22 ***DeLay***	Y	?	N	Y	Y	N	N	Y
23 Bustamante	Y	N	Y	Y	N	Y	Y	Y
24 Frost	Y	N	Y	Y	N	Y	Y	Y
25 Andrews	Y	N	Y	Y	Y	Y	Y	Y
26 ***Armey***	N	Y	N	Y	Y	N	N	Y
27 Ortiz	Y	N	Y	Y	N	Y	Y	Y
UTAH								
1 ***Hansen***	Y	Y	Y	Y	N	Y	Y	Y
2 Owens	Y	N	Y	Y	N	Y	Y	Y
3 ***Nielson***	Y	Y	N	Y	N	Y	Y	Y
VERMONT								
AL ***Smith***	Y	Y	Y	?	?	?	?	Y
VIRGINIA								
1 ***Bateman***	Y	N	Y	?	N	Y	Y	Y
2 Pickett	Y	Y	Y	Y	Y	N	?	Y
3 ***Bliley***	?	?	?	Y	N	Y	N	Y
4 Sisisky	Y	N	Y	Y	N	Y	Y	Y
5 Payne	Y	N	Y	Y	N	Y	?	Y
6 Olin	Y	N	Y	Y	N	Y	Y	Y
7 ***Slaughter***	Y	Y	Y	Y	Y	Y	Y	Y
8 ***Parris***	Y	Y	Y	Y	Y	Y	?	Y
9 Boucher	Y	N	Y	?	?	?	?	Y
10 ***Wolf***	Y	Y	Y	Y	Y	N	?	Y
WASHINGTON								
1 ***Miller***	Y	Y	Y	Y	Y	N	N	Y
2 Swift	Y	N	Y	Y	N	Y	Y	Y
3 Unsoeld	Y	N	Y	Y	N	Y	Y	Y
4 ***Morrison***	Y	N	Y	Y	N	Y	Y	Y
5 Foley								
6 Dicks	Y	N	Y	Y	N	Y	Y	Y
7 McDermott	Y	N	Y	Y	N	Y	Y	Y
8 ***Chandler***	Y	Y	Y	Y	N	Y	N	Y
WEST VIRGINIA								
1 Mollohan	Y	N	Y	Y	N	Y	Y	Y
2 Staggers	Y	N	Y	Y	Y	Y	?	Y
3 Wise	Y	N	Y	Y	N	Y	Y	Y
4 Rahall	Y	N	Y	Y	N	Y	Y	Y
WISCONSIN								
1 Aspin	Y	N	Y	?	?	?	Y	Y
2 Kastenmeier	N	N	Y	Y	N	Y	Y	Y
3 ***Gunderson***	Y	N	Y	Y	Y	N	Y	Y
4 Kleczka	Y	N	Y	Y	N	Y	Y	Y
5 Moody	?	?	?	?	?	?	Y	Y
6 ***Petri***	Y	Y	N	?	?	?	Y	Y
7 Obey	Y	N	Y	Y	N	Y	Y	Y
8 ***Roth***	Y	N	Y	Y	Y	Y	Y	Y
9 ***Sensenbrenner***	Y	Y	N	Y	Y	N	N	Y
WYOMING								
AL ***Thomas***	Y	Y	Y	Y	N	Y	N	Y

Southern states - Ala., Ark., Fla., Ga., Ky., La., Miss., N.C., Okla., S.C., Tenn., Texas, Va.
Omitted votes are quorum calls, which CQ does not include in its vote charts.

HOUSE VOTES 470, 471, 472, 474, 475

470. HR 5835. Fiscal 1991 Omnibus Reconciliation Act/ Appeal of the Chair's Ruling. Derrick, D-S.C., motion to table (kill) the Walker, R-Pa., appeal of the chair's ruling, that the Michel, R-Ill., point of order was out of order. The Michel point of order said that the rule (H Res 509) to provide for House floor consideration of the reconciliation bill was in violation of House rules and precedent because it denied a motion to recommit with instructions. Motion agreed to 251-171: R 0-170; D 251-1 (ND 170-0, SD 81-1), Oct. 16, 1990.

471. HR 5835. Fiscal 1991 Omnibus Reconciliation Act/ Previous Question. Derrick, D-S.C., motion to order the previous question (thus ending debate and the possibility of amendment) on the rule (H Res 509) to waive points of order against the bill and provide for House floor consideration of the bill (containing provisions reported by House committees) to reduce spending and increase revenues as required by the reconciliation instructions contained in the budget resolution. The rule also incorporates HR 5835, making changes in budget procedures and enforcement. Motion agreed to 241-184: R 0-173; D 241-11 (ND 165-5, SD 76-6), Oct. 16, 1990.

472. HR 5835. Fiscal 1991 Omnibus Reconciliation Act/ Rule. Adoption of the rule (H Res 509) to waive points of order against the bill and provide for House floor consideration of the bill (containing provisions reported by House committees) to reduce spending and increase revenues as required by the reconciliation instructions contained in the budget resolution. The rule also incorporates into HR 5835 changes in budget procedures and enforcement. Adopted 231-195: R 0-173; D 231-22 (ND 161-9, SD 70-13), Oct. 16, 1990.

474. HR 5835. Fiscal 1991 Omnibus Reconciliation Act/ Democratic Alternative. Rostenkowski, D-Ill., en bloc amendment to provide smaller increases in the Medicare premium and deductible; delete revenue provisions, including the gas tax, the petroleum fuels tax, the extension of the Medicare tax to additional state and local employees, and the limit on itemized deductions; eliminate the "bubble" and lift the top marginal tax rate to 33 percent; create a 10 percent surtax on income above $1 million; increase the minimum tax rate; delay indexing for one year; provide a limited tax break for capital gains; and for other purposes. Adopted 238-192: R 10-164; D 228-28 (ND 157-16, SD 71-12), Oct. 16, 1990. A "nay" was a vote supporting the president's position.

475. HR 5835. Fiscal 1991 Omnibus Reconciliation Act/ Passage. Passage of the bill (containing provisions reported by House committees) to reduce spending and increase revenues as required by the reconciliation instructions contained in the budget resolution and making changes in budget procedures and enforcement. Passed 227-203: R 10-163; D 217-40 (ND 151-23, SD 66-17), Oct. 16, 1990. A "nay" was a vote supporting the president's position.

KEY

Y Voted for (yea).
\# Paired for.
\+ Announced for.
N Voted against (nay).
X Paired against.
\- Announced against.
P Voted "present."
C Voted "present" to avoid possible conflict of interest.
? Did not vote or otherwise make a position known.

Democrats ***Republicans***

	470	471	472	474	475
ALABAMA					
1 ***Callahan***	N	N	N	N	N
2 ***Dickinson***	N	N	N	N	N
3 Browder	Y	Y	Y	Y	Y
4 Bevill	Y	Y	Y	Y	N
5 Flippo	Y	Y	Y	Y	Y
6 Erdreich	Y	Y	Y	Y	N
7 Harris	Y	Y	Y	Y	Y
ALASKA					
AL ***Young***	N	N	N	N	N
ARIZONA					
1 ***Rhodes***	N	N	N	N	N
2 Udall	Y	Y	Y	Y	Y
3 ***Stump***	N	N	N	N	N
4 ***Kyl***	N	N	N	N	N
5 ***Kolbe***	N	N	N	N	N
ARKANSAS					
1 Alexander	Y	Y	Y	Y	Y
2 ***Robinson***	N	N	N	N	N
3 ***Hammerschmidt***	N	N	N	N	N
4 Anthony	Y	Y	Y	Y	Y
CALIFORNIA					
1 Bosco	Y	Y	Y	N	N
2 ***Herger***	N	N	N	N	N
3 Matsui	Y	Y	Y	Y	Y
4 Fazio	Y	Y	Y	Y	Y
5 Pelosi	Y	Y	Y	Y	Y
6 Boxer	Y	Y	Y	Y	Y
7 Miller	Y	Y	Y	Y	Y
8 Dellums	Y	Y	Y	Y	Y
9 Stark	Y	Y	Y	Y	Y
10 Edwards	Y	Y	Y	Y	Y
11 Lantos	Y	Y	Y	Y	Y
12 ***Campbell***	N	N	N	N	N
13 Mineta	Y	+	Y	Y	Y
14 ***Shumway***	N	N	N	N	N
15 Condit	Y	N	N	N	N
16 Panetta	Y	Y	Y	Y	Y
17 ***Pashayan***	N	N	N	N	N
18 Lehman	Y	Y	Y	Y	Y
19 ***Lagomarsino***	N	N	N	N	N
20 ***Thomas***	?	X	X	?	?
21 ***Gallegly***	N	N	N	N	N
22 ***Moorhead***	N	N	N	N	N
23 Beilenson	Y	Y	Y	Y	Y
24 Waxman	Y	Y	Y	Y	Y
25 Roybal	Y	Y	Y	Y	Y
26 Berman	Y	Y	?	Y	Y
27 Levine	Y	Y	Y	Y	Y
28 Dixon	Y	Y	Y	Y	Y
29 Hawkins	Y	Y	Y	Y	N
30 Martinez	Y	Y	Y	Y	Y
31 Dymally	Y	Y	Y	Y	Y
32 Anderson	Y	Y	Y	Y	Y
33 ***Dreier***	N	N	N	N	N
34 Torres	Y	Y	Y	Y	Y
35 ***Lewis***	N	N	N	N	N
36 Brown	Y	Y	Y	Y	Y
37 ***McCandless***	N	N	N	N	N
38 ***Dornan***	N	N	N	N	N
39 ***Dannemeyer***	N	N	N	N	N
40 ***Cox***	N	N	N	N	N
41 ***Lowery***	N	N	N	N	N
42 ***Rohrabacher***	N	N	N	N	N
43 ***Packard***	N	N	N	N	N
44 Bates	Y	Y	Y	Y	Y
45 ***Hunter***	N	N	N	N	N
COLORADO					
1 Schroeder	Y	Y	Y	Y	Y
2 Skaggs	Y	Y	Y	Y	Y
3 Campbell	Y	Y	Y	N	N
4 ***Brown***	N	N	N	N	N
5 ***Hefley***	N	N	N	N	N
6 ***Schaefer***	N	N	N	N	N
CONNECTICUT					
1 Kennelly	Y	Y	Y	Y	Y
2 Gejdenson	Y	Y	Y	Y	Y
3 Morrison	+	#	#	Y	Y
4 ***Shays***	N	N	N	N	N
5 ***Rowland***	?	?	?	?	?
6 ***Johnson***	N	N	N	N	N
DELAWARE					
AL Carper	Y	Y	Y	Y	Y
FLORIDA					
1 Hutto	Y	Y	Y	Y	Y
2 ***Grant***	N	N	N	N	N
3 Bennett	N	N	N	Y	Y
4 ***James***	N	N	N	N	N
5 ***McCollum***	N	N	N	N	N
6 ***Stearns***	N	N	N	N	N
7 Gibbons	Y	Y	Y	Y	Y
8 ***Young***	N	N	N	N	N
9 ***Bilirakis***	N	N	N	N	N
10 ***Ireland***	N	N	N	N	N
11 Nelson	Y	Y	Y	Y	Y
12 ***Lewis***	N	N	N	N	N
13 ***Goss***	N	N	N	N	N
14 Johnston	Y	Y	Y	Y	Y
15 ***Shaw***	N	N	N	N	N
16 Smith	Y	Y	Y	Y	Y
17 Lehman	Y	Y	Y	Y	Y
18 ***Ros-Lehtinen***	N	N	N	N	N
19 Fascell	Y	Y	Y	Y	Y
GEORGIA					
1 Thomas	Y	Y	Y	Y	Y
2 Hatcher	Y	Y	Y	Y	Y
3 Ray	Y	Y	Y	Y	Y
4 Jones	Y	N	N	N	N
5 Lewis	Y	Y	Y	Y	Y
6 ***Gingrich***	N	N	N	N	N
7 Darden	Y	Y	Y	Y	Y
8 Rowland	?	Y	Y	Y	Y
9 Jenkins	Y	Y	Y	Y	Y
10 Barnard	Y	Y	N	N	N
HAWAII					
1 ***Saiki***	N	N	N	N	N
2 Mink	Y	Y	Y	Y	Y
IDAHO					
1 ***Craig***	N	N	N	N	N
2 Stallings	Y	Y	Y	N	N
ILLINOIS					
1 Hayes	Y	Y	Y	Y	Y
2 Savage	?	Y	Y	N	N
3 Russo	Y	Y	Y	Y	Y
4 Sangmeister	Y	Y	Y	N	N
5 Lipinski	Y	Y	Y	Y	Y
6 ***Hyde***	N	N	N	N	N
7 Collins	Y	Y	Y	Y	Y
8 Rostenkowski	Y	Y	Y	Y	Y
9 Yates	Y	Y	Y	Y	Y
10 ***Porter***	N	N	N	N	N
11 Annunzio	Y	Y	Y	N	N
12 ***Crane***	N	N	N	N	N
13 ***Fawell***	N	N	N	N	N
14 ***Hastert***	N	N	N	N	N
15 ***Madigan***	N	N	N	N	N
16 ***Martin***	N	N	N	N	N
17 Evans	Y	Y	Y	Y	Y
18 ***Michel***	N	N	N	N	?
19 Bruce	Y	Y	Y	Y	Y
20 Durbin	Y	Y	Y	Y	Y
21 Costello	Y	Y	Y	Y	Y
22 Poshard	Y	Y	Y	Y	Y
INDIANA					
1 Visclosky	Y	Y	Y	Y	Y
2 Sharp	Y	Y	N	Y	Y
3 ***Hiler***	N	N	N	N	N

ND Northern Democrats SD Southern Democrats

	470	471	472	474	475
4 Long	Y	Y	Y	N	N
5 Jontz	Y	Y	Y	Y	N
6 ***Burton***	N	N	N	N	N
7 ***Myers***	N	N	N	N	N
8 McCloskey	Y	Y	Y	Y	Y
9 Hamilton	Y	Y	Y	Y	Y
10 Jacobs	Y	N	N	Y	Y
IOWA					
1 ***Leach***	N	N	N	Y	Y
2 ***Tauke***	N	N	N	N	N
3 Nagle	Y	Y	Y	Y	N
4 Smith	Y	Y	Y	Y	Y
5 ***Lightfoot***	N	N	N	N	N
6 ***Grandy***	N	N	N	N	N
KANSAS					
1 ***Roberts***	N	N	N	N	N
2 Slattery	Y	Y	Y	Y	Y
3 ***Meyers***	N	N	N	N	N
4 Glickman	Y	Y	N	Y	Y
5 ***Whittaker***	N	N	N	N	N
KENTUCKY					
1 Hubbard	Y	N	N	N	N
2 Natcher	Y	Y	Y	Y	Y
3 Mazzoli	Y	Y	Y	Y	Y
4 ***Bunning***	N	N	N	N	N
5 ***Rogers***	N	N	N	N	N
6 ***Hopkins***	N	N	N	N	N
7 Perkins	Y	Y	Y	Y	N
LOUISIANA					
1 ***Livingston***	N	N	N	N	N
2 Boggs	Y	Y	Y	Y	Y
3 Tauzin	Y	Y	N	N	N
4 ***McCrery***	N	N	N	N	N
5 Huckaby	Y	Y	Y	Y	Y
6 ***Baker***	N	N	N	N	N
7 Hayes	Y	Y	Y	N	N
8 ***Holloway***	N	N	N	N	N
MAINE					
1 Brennan	?	?	?	?	Y
2 ***Snowe***	N	N	N	N	N
MARYLAND					
1 Dyson	Y	Y	Y	N	N
2 ***Bentley***	N	N	N	N	N
3 Cardin	Y	Y	Y	Y	Y
4 McMillen	Y	Y	Y	Y	Y
5 Hoyer	Y	Y	Y	Y	Y
6 Byron	Y	Y	Y	Y	Y
7 Mfume	Y	Y	Y	Y	Y
8 ***Morella***	N	N	N	Y	Y
MASSACHUSETTS					
1 ***Conte***	N	N	N	Y	Y
2 Neal	Y	Y	Y	Y	Y
3 Early	Y	Y	Y	Y	Y
4 Frank	Y	Y	Y	Y	Y
5 Atkins	Y	Y	Y	Y	Y
6 Mavroules	Y	Y	Y	Y	Y
7 Markey	Y	Y	Y	Y	Y
8 Kennedy	Y	Y	Y	Y	Y
9 Moakley	Y	Y	Y	Y	Y
10 Studds	Y	Y	Y	Y	Y
11 Donnelly	Y	Y	Y	Y	Y
MICHIGAN					
1 Conyers	Y	Y	Y	Y	Y
2 ***Pursell***	N	N	N	N	N
3 Wolpe	Y	Y	Y	Y	Y
4 ***Upton***	N	N	N	N	N
5 ***Henry***	N	N	N	N	N
6 Carr	Y	Y	Y	Y	N
7 Kildee	Y	Y	Y	Y	Y
8 Traxler	Y	Y	Y	Y	Y
9 ***Vander Jagt***	N	N	N	N	N
10 ***Schuette***	?	?	?	N	N
11 ***Davis***	N	N	N	Y	Y
12 Bonior	Y	Y	Y	Y	Y
13 Crockett	Y	Y	Y	Y	Y
14 Hertel	Y	Y	N	Y	N
15 Ford	Y	Y	Y	Y	Y
16 Dingell	Y	Y	Y	Y	Y
17 Levin	Y	Y	Y	Y	Y
18 ***Broomfield***	N	N	N	N	N
MINNESOTA					
1 Penny	Y	Y	Y	Y	Y
2 ***Weber***	N	N	N	N	N
3 ***Frenzel***	N	N	N	N	N
4 Vento	Y	Y	Y	Y	Y

	470	471	472	474	475
5 Sabo	Y	Y	Y	Y	Y
6 Sikorski	Y	Y	Y	Y	Y
7 ***Stangeland***	N	N	N	N	N
8 Oberstar	Y	Y	Y	Y	Y
MISSISSIPPI					
1 Whitten	Y	Y	Y	Y	Y
2 Espy	Y	Y	Y	Y	Y
3 Montgomery	Y	Y	Y	Y	Y
4 Parker	Y	Y	N	Y	Y
5 Taylor	Y	N	N	N	Y
MISSOURI					
1 Clay	Y	Y	Y	Y	Y
2 ***Buechner***	N	N	N	N	N
3 Gephardt	Y	Y	Y	Y	Y
4 Skelton	Y	Y	Y	Y	Y
5 Wheat	Y	Y	Y	Y	Y
6 ***Coleman***	N	N	N	N	N
7 ***Hancock***	N	N	N	N	N
8 ***Emerson***	N	N	N	N	N
9 Volkmer	Y	Y	Y	Y	Y
MONTANA					
1 Williams	Y	Y	Y	Y	N
2 ***Marlenee***	?	N	N	N	N
NEBRASKA					
1 ***Bereuter***	N	N	N	N	N
2 Hoagland	Y	Y	Y	Y	Y
3 ***Smith***	N	N	N	N	N
NEVADA					
1 Bilbray	Y	Y	Y	N	N
2 ***Vucanovich***	N	N	N	N	N
NEW HAMPSHIRE					
1 ***Smith***	N	N	N	N	N
2 ***Douglas***	N	N	N	N	N
NEW JERSEY					
1 Vacancy					
2 Hughes	Y	Y	N	Y	Y
3 Pallone	Y	Y	Y	N	N
4 ***Smith***	N	N	N	N	N
5 ***Roukema***	N	N	N	N	N
6 Dwyer	Y	Y	Y	Y	Y
7 ***Rinaldo***	N	N	N	N	N
8 Roe	Y	Y	Y	Y	Y
9 Torricelli	Y	Y	Y	Y	Y
10 Payne	Y	Y	Y	Y	Y
11 ***Gallo***	N	N	N	N	N
12 ***Courter***	N	N	N	N	N
13 ***Saxton***	N	N	N	N	N
14 Guarini	Y	Y	Y	Y	Y
NEW MEXICO					
1 ***Schiff***	N	N	N	N	N
2 ***Skeen***	N	N	N	N	N
3 Richardson	Y	Y	Y	Y	Y
NEW YORK					
1 Hochbrueckner	Y	Y	Y	Y	Y
2 Downey	Y	Y	Y	Y	Y
3 Mrazek	Y	Y	Y	Y	Y
4 ***Lent***	N	N	N	N	N
5 ***McGrath***	N	N	N	N	Y
6 Flake	Y	Y	Y	Y	Y
7 Ackerman	Y	Y	Y	Y	Y
8 Scheuer	Y	Y	Y	Y	Y
9 Manton	Y	Y	Y	Y	Y
10 Schumer	Y	Y	Y	Y	Y
11 Towns	Y	Y	Y	Y	Y
12 Owens	Y	Y	Y	Y	Y
13 Solarz	Y	Y	Y	Y	Y
14 ***Molinari***	N	N	N	Y	Y
15 ***Green***	N	N	N	N	N
16 Rangel	Y	Y	Y	Y	Y
17 Weiss	Y	Y	Y	Y	Y
18 Serrano	Y	Y	Y	Y	Y
19 Engel	?	?	?	Y	Y
20 Lowey	Y	Y	Y	Y	Y
21 ***Fish***	N	N	N	Y	Y
22 ***Gilman***	N	N	N	N	N
23 McNulty	Y	Y	Y	Y	Y
24 ***Solomon***	N	N	N	N	N
25 ***Boehlert***	N	N	N	Y	Y
26 ***Martin***	N	N	N	N	N
27 ***Walsh***	N	N	N	N	N
28 McHugh	Y	Y	Y	Y	Y
29 ***Horton***	N	N	N	Y	Y
30 Slaughter	Y	Y	Y	Y	Y
31 ***Paxon***	N	N	N	N	N

	470	471	472	474	475
32 LaFalce	Y	Y	Y	Y	Y
33 Nowak	Y	Y	Y	Y	Y
34 ***Houghton***	N	N	N	N	N
NORTH CAROLINA					
1 Jones	Y	Y	Y	Y	N
2 Valentine	Y	N	N	Y	Y
3 Lancaster	Y	Y	Y	Y	Y
4 Price	Y	Y	Y	Y	Y
5 Neal	Y	Y	Y	Y	Y
6 ***Coble***	N	N	N	N	N
7 Rose	Y	Y	Y	Y	Y
8 Hefner	Y	Y	Y	Y	Y
9 ***McMillan***	N	N	N	N	N
10 ***Ballenger***	N	N	N	N	N
11 Clarke	Y	Y	Y	Y	Y
NORTH DAKOTA					
AL Dorgan	Y	Y	Y	Y	Y
OHIO					
1 Luken	Y	Y	Y	Y	Y
2 ***Gradison***	N	N	N	N	N
3 Hall	Y	Y	Y	Y	Y
4 ***Oxley***	N	N	N	N	N
5 ***Gillmor***	N	N	N	N	N
6 ***McEwen***	N	N	N	N	N
7 ***DeWine***	N	N	N	N	N
8 ***Lukens***	?	N	N	N	N
9 Kaptur	Y	Y	Y	Y	Y
10 ***Miller***	N	N	N	N	N
11 Eckart	Y	Y	Y	Y	Y
12 ***Kasich***	N	N	N	N	N
13 Pease	Y	Y	Y	Y	Y
14 Sawyer	Y	Y	Y	Y	Y
15 ***Wylie***	N	N	N	N	N
16 ***Regula***	N	N	N	N	N
17 Traficant	Y	N	N	N	N
18 Applegate	Y	N	N	N	N
19 Feighan	Y	Y	Y	Y	Y
20 Oakar	Y	Y	Y	Y	Y
21 Stokes	Y	Y	Y	Y	Y
OKLAHOMA					
1 ***Inhofe***	N	N	N	N	N
2 Synar	Y	Y	Y	Y	Y
3 Watkins	Y	Y	Y	Y	Y
4 McCurdy	Y	Y	Y	Y	Y
5 ***Edwards***	N	N	N	N	N
6 English	Y	Y	N	Y	N
OREGON					
1 AuCoin	Y	Y	Y	Y	Y
2 ***Smith, B.***	N	N	N	N	N
3 Wyden	Y	Y	Y	Y	Y
4 DeFazio	Y	Y	Y	Y	Y
5 ***Smith, D.***	N	N	N	N	N
PENNSYLVANIA					
1 Foglietta	Y	Y	Y	Y	Y
2 Gray	Y	Y	Y	Y	Y
3 Borski	Y	Y	Y	Y	Y
4 Kolter	Y	Y	Y	N	N
5 ***Schulze***	N	N	N	N	N
6 Yatron	Y	Y	Y	N	N
7 ***Weldon***	N	N	N	N	N
8 Kostmayer	Y	Y	Y	Y	Y
9 ***Shuster***	N	N	N	N	N
10 ***McDade***	N	N	N	N	N
11 Kanjorski	Y	Y	Y	Y	Y
12 Murtha	Y	Y	Y	Y	Y
13 ***Coughlin***	N	N	N	N	N
14 Coyne	Y	Y	Y	Y	Y
15 ***Ritter***	N	N	N	N	N
16 ***Walker***	N	N	N	N	N
17 ***Gekas***	N	N	N	N	N
18 Walgren	Y	Y	Y	Y	Y
19 ***Goodling***	N	N	N	N	N
20 Gaydos	Y	Y	Y	N	N
21 ***Ridge***	?	N	N	N	N
22 Murphy	Y	Y	Y	Y	N
23 ***Clinger***	N	N	N	N	N
RHODE ISLAND					
1 ***Machtley***	N	N	N	N	N
2 ***Schneider***	N	N	N	N	N
SOUTH CAROLINA					
1 ***Ravenel***	N	N	N	N	N
2 ***Spence***	N	N	N	N	N
3 Derrick	Y	Y	Y	Y	Y
4 Patterson	Y	Y	Y	N	N
5 Spratt	Y	Y	Y	Y	Y
6 Tallon	Y	Y	Y	Y	Y

	470	471	472	474	475
SOUTH DAKOTA					
AL Johnson	Y	Y	Y	Y	Y
TENNESSEE					
1 ***Quillen***	N	N	N	N	N
2 ***Duncan***	N	N	N	N	N
3 Lloyd	Y	Y	Y	Y	Y
4 Cooper	Y	Y	N	Y	Y
5 Clement	Y	Y	Y	Y	Y
6 Gordon	Y	Y	Y	Y	Y
7 ***Sundquist***	N	N	N	N	N
8 Tanner	Y	Y	Y	Y	Y
9 Ford	Y	Y	Y	Y	Y
TEXAS					
1 Chapman	Y	Y	Y	Y	Y
2 Wilson	Y	Y	Y	Y	Y
3 ***Bartlett***	N	N	N	N	N
4 Hall	Y	N	N	N	N
5 Bryant	Y	Y	Y	Y	Y
6 ***Barton***	N	N	N	N	N
7 ***Archer***	N	N	N	N	N
8 ***Fields***	N	N	N	N	N
9 Brooks	Y	Y	Y	Y	Y
10 Pickle	Y	Y	Y	Y	Y
11 Leath	Y	?	Y	N	N
12 Geren	Y	Y	Y	N	N
13 Sarpalius	Y	Y	N	N	N
14 Laughlin	Y	Y	N	N	N
15 de la Garza	Y	Y	Y	Y	Y
16 Coleman	Y	Y	Y	Y	Y
17 Stenholm	Y	Y	Y	Y	Y
18 Washington	Y	Y	Y	Y	Y
19 ***Combest***	N	N	N	N	N
20 Gonzalez	Y	Y	Y	Y	Y
21 ***Smith***	N	N	N	N	N
22 ***DeLay***	N	N	N	N	N
23 Bustamante	Y	Y	Y	Y	Y
24 Frost	Y	Y	Y	Y	Y
25 Andrews	Y	Y	Y	Y	Y
26 ***Armey***	N	N	N	N	N
27 Ortiz	Y	Y	Y	Y	Y
UTAH					
1 ***Hansen***	N	N	N	N	N
2 Owens	Y	Y	Y	Y	Y
3 ***Nielson***	N	N	N	N	N
VERMONT					
AL ***Smith***	N	N	N	Y	Y
VIRGINIA					
1 ***Bateman***	N	N	N	N	N
2 Pickett	Y	Y	Y	Y	N
3 ***Bliley***	N	N	N	N	N
4 Sisisky	Y	Y	Y	Y	Y
5 Payne	Y	Y	Y	Y	Y
6 Olin	Y	Y	Y	Y	Y
7 ***Slaughter***	N	N	N	N	N
8 ***Parris***	N	N	N	N	N
9 Boucher	Y	Y	Y	Y	Y
10 ***Wolf***	N	N	N	N	N
WASHINGTON					
1 ***Miller***	N	N	N	N	N
2 Swift	Y	Y	Y	Y	Y
3 Unsoeld	Y	Y	Y	Y	Y
4 ***Morrison***	N	N	N	N	N
5 Foley					
6 Dicks	Y	Y	Y	Y	Y
7 McDermott	Y	Y	Y	Y	Y
8 ***Chandler***	N	N	N	N	N
WEST VIRGINIA					
1 Mollohan	Y	Y	Y	Y	Y
2 Staggers	Y	Y	Y	Y	Y
3 Wise	Y	Y	Y	Y	Y
4 Rahall	Y	N	N	Y	Y
WISCONSIN					
1 Aspin	Y	Y	Y	Y	Y
2 Kastenmeier	Y	Y	Y	Y	Y
3 ***Gunderson***	N	N	N	N	N
4 Kleczka	Y	Y	Y	Y	Y
5 Moody	Y	Y	Y	Y	Y
6 ***Petri***	N	N	N	N	N
7 Obey	Y	Y	Y	Y	Y
8 ***Roth***	N	N	N	N	N
9 ***Sensenbrenner***	N	N	N	N	N
WYOMING					
AL ***Thomas***	N	N	N	N	N

Southern states - Ala., Ark., Fla., Ga., Ky., La., Miss., N.C., Okla., S.C., Tenn., Texas, Va.
Omitted votes are quorum calls, which CQ does not include in its vote charts.

476. Procedural Motion. Sensenbrenner, R-Wis., motion to approve the House Journal of Tuesday, Oct. 16. Motion agreed to 265-123: R 41-119; D 224-4 (ND 149-4, SD 75-0), Oct. 17, 1990.

477. HR 5803. Fiscal 1991 Defense Appropriations/Conference Meetings Closed to the Public. Murtha, D-Pa., motion to close to the public conference committee meetings on the bill to appropriate funds in fiscal 1991 for military programs of the Defense Department, when classified national security information is under consideration. Motion agreed to 401-4: R 163-0; D 238-4 (ND 161-4, SD 77-0), Oct. 17, 1990.

478. S 2104. Civil Rights Act of 1990/Conference Report. Adoption of the conference report on the bill to reverse or modify six recent Supreme Court decisions that narrowed the reach and remedies of job discrimination laws and to authorize monetary damages under Title VII of the 1964 Civil Rights Act. Adopted 273-154: R 34-139; D 239-15 (ND 169-3, SD 70-12), Oct. 17, 1990. A "nay" was a vote supporting the president's position.

479. HR 5422. Fiscal 1991 Intelligence Authorization/Aid to UNITA. Dellums, D-Calif., amendment to prohibit covert aid to the National Union for the Total Independence of Angola (UNITA), a rebel group fighting the Angolan government. Under the amendment, covert aid for military or paramilitary operations in Angola could only be provided if the president openly requested and the Congress enacted a joint resolution supporting military assistance as important to U.S. national security. Rejected 175-246: R 4-168; D 171-78 (ND 146-24, SD 25-54), Oct. 17, 1990. A "nay" was a vote supporting the president's position.

480. HR 5422. Fiscal 1991 Intelligence Appropriations/Aid to UNITA. Solarz, D-N.Y., amendment to suspend military aid to the National Union for the Total Independence of Angola (UNITA) — a rebel group fighting the Angolan government — if the government of Angola agrees to accept a cease-fire and a political settlement for the conflict in Angola and offers free and fair multiparty elections in which UNITA is free to participate. Before being adopted, the amendment was amended by Miller, R-Wash., to prohibit the Angolan government from receiving military aid from the Soviet Union. Adopted 213-200: R 20-150; D 193-50 (ND 156-10, SD 37-40), Oct. 17, 1990. A "nay" was a vote supporting the president's position.

481. HR 5422. Fiscal 1991 Intelligence Appropriations/Covert Action. Boxer, D-Calif., amendment to require approval by the House and Senate Intelligence committees before any type of covert action is performed by U.S. intelligence agencies, except in emergency situations. Rejected 70-341: R 0-168; D 70-173 (ND 62-104, SD 8-69), Oct. 17, 1990. A "nay" was a vote supporting the president's position.

482. HR 5422. Fiscal 1991 Intelligence Appropriations/Aid to UNITA. Separate vote at the request of Hyde, R-Ill., on the Solarz, D-N.Y., amendment to suspend military aid to the National Union for the Total Independence of Angola (UNITA) — a rebel group fighting the Angolan government — if the government of Angola agrees to accept a cease-fire and a political settlement for the conflict in Angola and offers free and fair multiparty elections in which UNITA is free to participate. Before being adopted, the amendment was amended by Miller, R-Wash., to prohibit the Angolan government from receiving military aid from the Soviet Union. (A separate vote on the Solarz amendment, adopted on vote 480, was demanded after the Committee of the Whole rose.) Adopted 207-206: R 12-156; D 195-50 (ND 158-10, SD 37-40), Oct. 17, 1990. A "nay" was a vote supporting the president's position.

KEY

- Y Voted for (yea).
- # Paired for.
- + Announced for.
- N Voted against (nay).
- X Paired against.
- \- Announced against.
- P Voted "present."
- C Voted "present" to avoid possible conflict of interest.
- ? Did not vote or otherwise make a position known.

Democrats ***Republicans***

	476	477	478	479	480	481	482
ALABAMA							
1 ***Callahan***	N	Y	N	N	N	N	N
2 ***Dickinson***	N	Y	N	N	N	N	N
3 Browder	Y	Y	Y	N	N	N	N
4 Bevill	Y	Y	Y	N	N	N	N
5 Flippo	Y	Y	Y	N	N	N	Y
6 Erdreich	Y	Y	Y	N	N	N	N
7 Harris	Y	Y	Y	N	N	N	N
ALASKA							
AL ***Young***	?	?	N	N	N	N	N
ARIZONA							
1 ***Rhodes***	N	Y	N	N	N	N	N
2 Udall	?	Y	Y	Y	Y	N	Y
3 ***Stump***	N	Y	N	N	N	N	N
4 ***Kyl***	N	Y	N	N	N	N	N
5 ***Kolbe***	N	Y	N	N	N	N	N
ARKANSAS							
1 Alexander	Y	Y	Y	Y	Y	N	Y
2 ***Robinson***	Y	Y	N	N	N	N	N
3 ***Hammerschmidt***	N	Y	N	N	N	N	N
4 Anthony	?	Y	Y	Y	Y	N	Y
CALIFORNIA							
1 Bosco	Y	Y	Y	Y	?	Y	Y
2 ***Herger***	?	?	N	N	N	N	N
3 Matsui	Y	Y	Y	Y	Y	N	Y
4 Fazio	Y	Y	Y	Y	Y	N	Y
5 Pelosi	Y	Y	Y	Y	Y	Y	Y
6 Boxer	Y	Y	Y	Y	Y	Y	Y
7 Miller	Y	Y	Y	Y	Y	Y	Y
8 Dellums	Y	Y	Y	Y	Y	Y	Y
9 Stark	Y	Y	Y	Y	?	Y	Y
10 Edwards	Y	Y	Y	Y	Y	Y	Y
11 Lantos	Y	Y	Y	N	N	N	N
12 ***Campbell***	N	Y	Y	N	N	N	N
13 Mineta	Y	Y	Y	Y	Y	Y	Y
14 ***Shumway***	Y	Y	N	N	N	N	N
15 Condit	?	Y	Y	Y	Y	N	Y
16 Panetta	Y	Y	Y	Y	Y	Y	Y
17 ***Pashayan***	N	Y	N	N	N	N	N
18 Lehman	Y	Y	Y	Y	Y	N	Y
19 ***Lagomarsino***	N	Y	N	N	N	N	N
20 ***Thomas***	N	Y	N	N	N	N	N
21 ***Gallegly***	N	Y	N	N	N	N	N
22 ***Moorhead***	N	Y	N	N	N	N	N
23 Beilenson	Y	Y	Y	Y	Y	N	Y
24 Waxman	?	?	Y	Y	Y	N	Y
25 Roybal	Y	Y	Y	Y	Y	Y	Y
26 Berman	?	Y	Y	Y	Y	N	Y
27 Levine	Y	Y	Y	Y	Y	N	Y
28 Dixon	Y	Y	Y	Y	Y	N	Y
29 Hawkins	Y	Y	Y	?	?	?	?
30 Martinez	Y	Y	Y	Y	Y	Y	Y
31 Dymally	Y	Y	Y	Y	Y	Y	Y
32 Anderson	Y	Y	Y	Y	Y	Y	Y
33 ***Dreier***	N	Y	N	N	N	N	N
34 Torres	?	?	Y	Y	Y	Y	Y
35 ***Lewis***	N	Y	N	N	N	N	N
36 Brown	Y	Y	Y	?	Y	N	Y
37 ***McCandless***	N	Y	N	N	N	N	N
38 ***Dornan***	N	Y	N	N	N	N	N
39 ***Dannemeyer***	N	Y	N	N	N	N	N
40 ***Cox***	N	Y	N	N	N	N	N
41 ***Lowery***	?	Y	N	N	N	N	N
42 ***Rohrabacher***	N	Y	N	N	N	N	N
43 ***Packard***	Y	Y	N	N	N	N	N
44 Bates	Y	Y	Y	Y	Y	Y	Y
45 ***Hunter***	?	?	N	N	N	N	N
COLORADO							
1 Schroeder	N	Y	Y	Y	Y	Y	Y
2 Skaggs	Y	Y	Y	Y	Y	N	Y
3 Campbell	?	?	Y	N	Y	N	N
4 ***Brown***	N	Y	N	N	N	N	N
5 ***Hefley***	N	Y	N	N	N	N	N
6 ***Schaefer***	N	Y	N	N	N	N	N
CONNECTICUT							
1 Kennelly	Y	Y	Y	Y	Y	N	Y
2 Gejdenson	Y	Y	Y	Y	Y	N	Y
3 Morrison	?	Y	+	+	+	+	+
4 ***Shays***	N	Y	Y	N	Y	N	Y
5 ***Rowland***	?	?	?	?	?	?	?
6 ***Johnson***	Y	Y	Y	N	N	N	N
DELAWARE							
AL Carper	Y	Y	Y	N	Y	N	Y
FLORIDA							
1 Hutto	Y	Y	N	N	N	N	N
2 ***Grant***	Y	Y	Y	N	N	N	N
3 Bennett	Y	Y	Y	Y	Y	Y	Y
4 ***James***	N	Y	Y	N	N	N	N
5 ***McCollum***	N	Y	N	N	N	N	N
6 ***Stearns***	N	Y	N	N	N	N	N
7 Gibbons	Y	Y	Y	Y	Y	Y	Y
8 ***Young***	?	?	N	N	N	N	N
9 ***Bilirakis***	N	Y	N	N	N	N	N
10 ***Ireland***	N	Y	N	N	N	N	N
11 Nelson	Y	Y	Y	N	N	N	N
12 ***Lewis***	N	Y	N	N	N	N	N
13 ***Goss***	N	Y	N	N	N	N	N
14 Johnston	Y	Y	Y	Y	Y	N	Y
15 ***Shaw***	Y	Y	N	N	N	N	N
16 Smith	Y	Y	Y	N	N	N	N
17 Lehman	Y	Y	Y	Y	Y	Y	Y
18 ***Ros-Lehtinen***	N	Y	Y	N	N	N	N
19 Fascell	?	Y	Y	N	N	N	N
GEORGIA							
1 Thomas	Y	Y	Y	N	N	N	N
2 Hatcher	?	?	Y	N	N	N	N
3 Ray	Y	Y	Y	N	N	N	N
4 Jones	Y	Y	Y	N	N	N	N
5 Lewis	Y	Y	Y	Y	Y	Y	Y
6 ***Gingrich***	?	?	N	N	N	N	N
7 Darden	Y	Y	N	N	N	N	N
8 Rowland	Y	Y	Y	N	N	N	N
9 Jenkins	Y	Y	N	N	N	N	N
10 Barnard	Y	Y	N	N	N	N	N
HAWAII							
1 ***Saiki***	Y	Y	Y	N	N	N	N
2 Mink	Y	Y	Y	Y	Y	Y	Y
IDAHO							
1 ***Craig***	N	Y	N	N	N	N	N
2 Stallings	Y	Y	Y	N	Y	N	N
ILLINOIS							
1 Hayes	Y	Y	Y	Y	Y	Y	Y
2 Savage	?	Y	Y	Y	N	Y	Y
3 Russo	Y	Y	N	Y	Y	N	Y
4 Sangmeister	Y	Y	Y	N	Y	N	Y
5 Lipinski	Y	Y	N	N	Y	N	Y
6 ***Hyde***	N	Y	N	N	N	N	N
7 Collins	Y	Y	Y	Y	Y	Y	Y
8 Rostenkowski	Y	Y	Y	Y	Y	N	Y
9 Yates	Y	Y	Y	Y	Y	Y	Y
10 ***Porter***	N	Y	N	N	N	N	N
11 Annunzio	Y	Y	N	Y	Y	N	Y
12 ***Crane***	?	?	N	N	N	N	N
13 ***Fawell***	N	Y	N	N	N	N	N
14 ***Hastert***	N	Y	N	N	N	N	N
15 ***Madigan***	N	Y	N	N	N	N	N
16 ***Martin***	?	?	?	?	?	?	?
17 Evans	Y	Y	Y	Y	Y	Y	Y
18 ***Michel***	N	Y	N	N	N	N	N
19 Bruce	Y	Y	Y	Y	Y	Y	Y
20 Durbin	Y	Y	Y	Y	Y	Y	Y
21 Costello	Y	Y	Y	Y	Y	N	Y
22 Poshard	Y	Y	Y	Y	Y	N	Y
INDIANA							
1 Visclosky	Y	Y	Y	Y	Y	N	Y
2 Sharp	Y	Y	Y	Y	Y	N	Y
3 ***Hiler***	N	Y	N	N	N	N	N

ND Northern Democrats SD Southern Democrats

	476	477	478	479	480	481	482
4 Long	Y	Y	Y	Y	Y	N	Y
5 Jontz	Y	Y	Y	Y	Y	Y	Y
6 **Burton**	N	Y	N	N	N	N	N
7 **Myers**	Y	Y	N	N	N	N	N
8 McCloskey	Y	Y	Y	Y	Y	Y	Y
9 Hamilton	Y	Y	Y	Y	Y	N	Y
10 Jacobs	N	Y	Y	Y	Y	Y	Y
IOWA							
1 **Leach**	N	Y	Y	Y	Y	N	Y
2 **Tauke**	N	Y	N	N	Y	N	Y
3 Nagle	Y	Y	Y	Y	Y	N	Y
4 Smith	Y	Y	Y	Y	Y	N	Y
5 **Lightfoot**	N	Y	N	N	N	N	N
6 **Grandy**	N	Y	N	N	Y	N	Y
KANSAS							
1 **Roberts**	N	Y	N	N	N	N	N
2 Slattery	Y	Y	Y	Y	Y	N	Y
3 **Meyers**	N	Y	Y	N	N	N	N
4 Glickman	Y	Y	Y	Y	Y	N	Y
5 **Whittaker**	N	Y	N	N	N	N	N
KENTUCKY							
1 Hubbard	Y	Y	Y	N	N	N	N
2 Natcher	Y	Y	Y	N	Y	N	Y
3 Mazzoli	Y	Y	Y	Y	Y	N	Y
4 **Bunning**	N	Y	N	N	N	N	N
5 **Rogers**	N	Y	N	N	N	N	N
6 **Hopkins**	N	Y	N	N	N	N	N
7 Perkins	Y	Y	Y	Y	Y	Y	Y
LOUISIANA							
1 **Livingston**	Y	Y	N	N	N	N	N
2 Boggs	Y	Y	Y	N	Y	?	Y
3 Tauzin	Y	Y	Y	N	N	N	N
4 **McCrery**	?	?	N	N	N	N	N
5 Huckaby	?	Y	N	N	N	N	N
6 **Baker**	N	Y	N	N	N	N	N
7 Hayes	Y	Y	Y	?	?	?	?
8 **Holloway**	N	Y	N	N	N	N	N
MAINE							
1 Brennan	?	?	?	?	?	?	?
2 **Snowe**	N	Y	Y	N	N	N	N
MARYLAND							
1 Dyson	Y	Y	Y	N	Y	N	Y
2 **Bentley**	?	Y	N	N	N	N	N
3 Cardin	Y	Y	Y	Y	Y	N	Y
4 McMillen	Y	Y	Y	N	Y	N	Y
5 Hoyer	Y	Y	Y	Y	Y	N	Y
6 Byron	Y	Y	Y	N	N	N	N
7 Mfume	Y	Y	Y	Y	Y	Y	Y
8 **Morella**	Y	Y	Y	N	Y	N	Y
MASSACHUSETTS							
1 **Conte**	Y	Y	Y	Y	N	N	N
2 Neal	Y	Y	Y	Y	Y	N	Y
3 Early	Y	Y	Y	Y	Y	N	Y
4 Frank	Y	Y	Y	Y	Y	N	Y
5 Atkins	Y	Y	Y	Y	Y	N	Y
6 Mavroules	Y	Y	Y	Y	Y	N	Y
7 Markey	Y	Y	Y	Y	Y	Y	Y
8 Kennedy	Y	Y	Y	Y	Y	N	Y
9 Moakley	Y	Y	Y	Y	Y	N	Y
10 Studds	Y	Y	Y	Y	Y	N	Y
11 Donnelly	Y	Y	Y	Y	Y	N	N
MICHIGAN							
1 Conyers	?	Y	Y	Y	Y	Y	Y
2 **Pursell**	Y	Y	Y	N	Y	N	N
3 Wolpe	Y	Y	Y	Y	Y	Y	Y
4 **Upton**	N	Y	N	N	N	N	N
5 **Henry**	N	Y	Y	N	Y	N	N
6 Carr	Y	Y	Y	Y	Y	N	Y
7 Kildee	Y	Y	Y	Y	Y	N	Y
8 Traxler	?	Y	Y	Y	Y	N	Y
9 **Vander Jagt**	Y	Y	N	N	N	N	N
10 **Schuette**	?	?	?	?	?	?	?
11 **Davis**	N	Y	Y	N	N	N	N
12 Bonior	Y	Y	Y	Y	Y	Y	Y
13 Crockett	Y	Y	Y	Y	?	?	?
14 Hertel	Y	Y	Y	Y	Y	Y	Y
15 Ford	?	?	Y	Y	?	?	?
16 Dingell	?	?	Y	Y	Y	N	Y
17 Levin	Y	Y	Y	Y	Y	N	Y
18 **Broomfield**	Y	Y	N	N	N	N	N
MINNESOTA							
1 Penny	Y	Y	Y	Y	Y	N	Y
2 **Weber**	N	Y	N	N	N	N	N
3 **Frenzel**	Y	Y	N	N	Y	N	?
4 Vento	Y	Y	Y	Y	Y	N	Y
5 Sabo	Y	Y	Y	Y	Y	N	Y
6 Sikorski	N	Y	Y	Y	Y	N	Y
7 **Stangeland**	N	Y	N	N	N	N	N
8 Oberstar	?	Y	Y	Y	Y	N	Y
MISSISSIPPI							
1 Whitten	Y	Y	Y	N	N	N	N
2 Espy	Y	Y	Y	Y	Y	N	Y
3 Montgomery	Y	Y	N	N	N	N	N
4 Parker	Y	Y	N	N	N	N	N
5 Taylor	Y	Y	N	N	N	N	N
MISSOURI							
1 Clay	?	Y	Y	Y	Y	Y	Y
2 **Buechner**	N	Y	N	N	Y	N	N
3 Gephardt	?	?	Y	Y	Y	N	Y
4 Skelton	Y	Y	Y	N	N	N	N
5 Wheat	Y	Y	Y	Y	Y	Y	Y
6 **Coleman**	N	Y	N	N	?	?	?
7 **Hancock**	N	Y	N	N	N	N	N
8 **Emerson**	N	Y	N	N	N	N	N
9 Volkmer	Y	Y	Y	N	Y	N	Y
MONTANA							
1 Williams	Y	Y	Y	Y	Y	?	?
2 **Marlenee**	N	Y	N	N	X	N	N
NEBRASKA							
1 **Bereuter**	N	Y	N	N	N	N	N
2 Hoagland	Y	Y	Y	Y	Y	N	Y
3 **Smith**	Y	Y	N	N	N	N	N
NEVADA							
1 Bilbray	Y	Y	Y	N	Y	N	Y
2 **Vucanovich**	N	Y	N	N	N	N	N
NEW HAMPSHIRE							
1 **Smith**	N	Y	N	N	N	N	N
2 **Douglas**	N	Y	N	N	N	N	N
NEW JERSEY							
1 Vacancy							
2 Hughes	Y	Y	Y	N	N	N	N
3 Pallone	Y	Y	Y	Y	Y	N	Y
4 **Smith**	Y	Y	N	N	N	N	N
5 **Roukema**	N	Y	Y	N	N	N	N
6 Dwyer	Y	Y	Y	Y	Y	N	Y
7 **Rinaldo**	Y	Y	Y	N	N	N	N
8 Roe	Y	Y	Y	N	N	N	N
9 Torricelli	Y	Y	Y	N	N	N	Y
10 Payne	Y	Y	Y	Y	Y	Y	Y
11 **Gallo**	N	Y	N	N	N	N	N
12 **Courter**	?	?	N	N	N	?	?
13 **Saxton**	N	Y	N	N	N	N	N
14 Guarini	Y	Y	Y	N	Y	N	Y
NEW MEXICO							
1 **Schiff**	Y	Y	Y	N	N	N	N
2 **Skeen**	Y	Y	N	N	N	N	N
3 Richardson	Y	Y	Y	Y	Y	N	Y
NEW YORK							
1 Hochbrueckner	Y	Y	Y	Y	Y	Y	Y
2 Downey	Y	Y	Y	Y	Y	Y	Y
3 Mrazek	Y	Y	Y	Y	Y	Y	Y
4 **Lent**	Y	Y	N	N	N	N	N
5 **McGrath**	N	Y	N	N	N	N	N
6 Flake	Y	Y	Y	Y	Y	Y	Y
7 Ackerman	Y	Y	Y	Y	#	?	?
8 Scheuer	Y	Y	Y	Y	Y	Y	Y
9 Manton	Y	Y	Y	Y	Y	N	Y
10 Schumer	Y	Y	Y	Y	Y	N	Y
11 Towns	Y	Y	Y	Y	Y	Y	Y
12 Owens	?	?	Y	Y	Y	Y	Y
13 Solarz	Y	Y	Y	Y	Y	N	Y
14 **Molinari**	N	Y	N	N	N	N	N
15 **Green**	Y	Y	Y	N	Y	N	Y
16 Rangel	Y	Y	Y	Y	Y	Y	Y
17 Weiss	Y	N	Y	Y	Y	Y	Y
18 Serrano	Y	Y	Y	Y	Y	Y	Y
19 Engel	Y	Y	Y	Y	Y	N	Y
20 Lowey	Y	Y	Y	Y	Y	Y	Y
21 **Fish**	Y	Y	Y	N	N	?	?
22 **Gilman**	Y	Y	Y	N	Y	N	Y
23 McNulty	Y	Y	Y	Y	Y	N	Y
24 **Solomon**	N	Y	N	N	N	N	N
25 **Boehlert**	N	Y	Y	N	Y	N	N
26 **Martin**	N	Y	N	N	N	N	N
27 **Walsh**	N	Y	Y	N	Y	N	N
28 McHugh	?	Y	Y	Y	Y	N	Y
29 **Horton**	Y	Y	Y	N	Y	N	N
30 Slaughter	Y	Y	Y	Y	Y	N	Y
31 **Paxon**	N	Y	N	N	N	N	N
32 LaFalce	Y	Y	Y	Y	Y	N	Y
33 Nowak	Y	Y	Y	Y	Y	N	Y
34 **Houghton**	Y	Y	Y	N	Y	?	Y
NORTH CAROLINA							
1 Jones	?	Y	Y	Y	N	N	N
2 Valentine	Y	Y	Y	Y	N	N	N
3 Lancaster	Y	Y	Y	N	N	N	N
4 Price	Y	Y	Y	Y	Y	N	Y
5 Neal	Y	Y	Y	Y	Y	N	?
6 **Coble**	N	Y	N	N	N	N	N
7 Rose	Y	Y	?	?	?	N	Y
8 Hefner	Y	Y	Y	Y	Y	N	Y
9 **McMillan**	N	Y	N	N	N	N	N
10 **Ballenger**	N	Y	N	N	N	N	N
11 Clarke	Y	Y	Y	Y	Y	N	Y
NORTH DAKOTA							
AL Dorgan	Y	N	Y	Y	Y	Y	Y
OHIO							
1 Luken	Y	Y	Y	Y	Y	N	Y
2 **Gradison**	Y	Y	N	N	N	N	N
3 Hall	Y	Y	Y	Y	Y	N	Y
4 **Oxley**	N	Y	N	N	N	N	N
5 **Gillmor**	Y	Y	N	N	N	N	N
6 **McEwen**	Y	Y	N	N	N	N	N
7 **DeWine**	N	Y	Y	N	N	N	N
8 **Lukens**	N	Y	N	?	?	N	N
9 Kaptur	Y	Y	Y	Y	Y	N	Y
10 **Miller**	N	Y	N	N	N	N	N
11 Eckart	Y	Y	Y	Y	Y	N	Y
12 **Kasich**	?	?	N	N	N	N	N
13 Pease	Y	Y	Y	Y	Y	N	Y
14 Sawyer	Y	Y	Y	Y	Y	N	Y
15 **Wylie**	Y	Y	N	N	N	N	N
16 **Regula**	N	Y	Y	N	N	N	N
17 Traficant	Y	Y	Y	Y	Y	Y	Y
18 Applegate	Y	Y	Y	Y	Y	N	Y
19 Feighan	Y	Y	Y	Y	Y	N	Y
20 Oakar	Y	Y	Y	Y	Y	Y	Y
21 Stokes	Y	Y	Y	Y	Y	Y	Y
OKLAHOMA							
1 **Inhofe**	N	Y	N	N	N	N	N
2 Synar	Y	Y	Y	Y	Y	N	Y
3 Watkins	Y	Y	Y	N	N	N	N
4 McCurdy	Y	Y	Y	N	N	N	N
5 **Edwards**	Y	Y	N	N	N	N	N
6 English	Y	Y	N	N	N	N	N
OREGON							
1 AuCoin	?	Y	Y	Y	Y	Y	Y
2 **Smith, B.**	N	Y	N	N	N	N	N
3 Wyden	Y	Y	Y	Y	Y	Y	Y
4 DeFazio	?	N	Y	Y	Y	Y	Y
5 **Smith, D.**	N	Y	N	N	N	N	N
PENNSYLVANIA							
1 Foglietta	Y	Y	Y	Y	Y	Y	Y
2 Gray	Y	Y	Y	Y	Y	?	Y
3 Borski	Y	Y	Y	Y	Y	N	Y
4 Kolter	Y	Y	Y	N	Y	N	Y
5 **Schulze**	Y	Y	Y	N	N	N	N
6 Yatron	Y	Y	Y	N	N	N	Y
7 **Weldon**	N	Y	N	N	N	N	N
8 Kostmayer	?	?	Y	Y	Y	N	Y
9 **Shuster**	Y	Y	N	N	N	N	N
10 **McDade**	N	Y	N	N	N	N	N
11 Kanjorski	Y	Y	Y	Y	Y	N	Y
12 Murtha	Y	Y	Y	N	N	N	N
13 **Coughlin**	N	Y	Y	N	N	N	N
14 Coyne	Y	Y	Y	Y	Y	N	Y
15 **Ritter**	Y	Y	N	N	N	N	N
16 **Walker**	N	Y	N	N	N	N	N
17 **Gekas**	N	Y	N	N	N	N	N
18 Walgren	Y	Y	Y	Y	Y	N	Y
19 **Goodling**	N	Y	N	N	N	N	N
20 Gaydos	Y	Y	Y	N	Y	N	Y
21 **Ridge**	N	Y	N	N	N	N	N
22 Murphy	N	Y	Y	Y	Y	Y	Y
23 **Clinger**	Y	Y	N	N	N	N	N
RHODE ISLAND							
1 **Machtley**	N	Y	Y	N	Y	N	Y
2 **Schneider**	N	Y	Y	Y	Y	N	Y
SOUTH CAROLINA							
1 **Ravenel**	Y	Y	N	N	N	N	N
2 **Spence**	N	Y	N	N	N	N	N
3 Derrick	Y	Y	Y	N	Y	N	Y
4 Patterson	Y	Y	Y	N	Y	N	Y
5 Spratt	Y	Y	Y	N	Y	N	Y
6 Tallon	Y	Y	Y	N	N	N	N
SOUTH DAKOTA							
AL Johnson	Y	Y	Y	Y	Y	Y	Y
TENNESSEE							
1 **Quillen**	N	Y	N	N	N	N	N
2 **Duncan**	N	Y	N	N	N	N	N
3 Lloyd	Y	Y	Y	N	N	N	N
4 Cooper	Y	Y	Y	N	N	N	N
5 Clement	Y	Y	Y	Y	Y	N	Y
6 Gordon	Y	Y	Y	N	Y	N	Y
7 **Sundquist**	N	Y	N	N	N	N	N
8 Tanner	Y	Y	Y	N	Y	N	N
9 Ford	Y	Y	Y	Y	?	?	?
TEXAS							
1 Chapman	?	?	Y	N	Y	N	Y
2 Wilson	?	?	Y	?	?	?	?
3 **Bartlett**	Y	Y	N	N	N	N	N
4 Hall	Y	Y	N	N	N	N	Y
5 Bryant	Y	Y	Y	Y	Y	Y	Y
6 **Barton**	N	Y	Y	N	N	N	N
7 **Archer**	Y	Y	N	N	N	N	N
8 **Fields**	?	Y	N	N	N	N	N
9 Brooks	Y	Y	Y	?	?	?	?
10 Pickle	Y	Y	Y	N	N	N	N
11 Leath	?	?	N	N	Y	N	Y
12 Geren	Y	Y	Y	N	N	N	N
13 Sarpalius	Y	Y	N	N	N	N	N
14 Laughlin	Y	Y	Y	N	N	N	N
15 de la Garza	Y	?	Y	Y	Y	?	?
16 Coleman	Y	Y	Y	Y	Y	N	Y
17 Stenholm	Y	Y	N	N	N	N	N
18 Washington	Y	Y	Y	Y	Y	Y	Y
19 **Combest**	N	Y	N	N	N	N	N
20 Gonzalez	Y	Y	Y	Y	Y	Y	Y
21 **Smith**	N	Y	N	N	N	N	N
22 **DeLay**	N	Y	N	N	N	N	N
23 Bustamante	Y	Y	Y	N	Y	N	Y
24 Frost	Y	?	Y	N	Y	N	Y
25 Andrews	Y	Y	Y	N	Y	N	Y
26 **Armey**	N	Y	N	N	N	N	N
27 Ortiz	Y	Y	Y	N	Y	N	Y
UTAH							
1 **Hansen**	N	Y	N	N	N	N	N
2 Owens	Y	Y	Y	Y	Y	N	Y
3 **Nielson**	N	Y	N	N	N	N	N
VERMONT							
AL **Smith**	N	Y	Y	N	Y	?	?
VIRGINIA							
1 **Bateman**	Y	Y	N	N	N	N	N
2 Pickett	Y	Y	Y	N	Y	N	Y
3 **Bliley**	N	Y	N	N	N	N	N
4 Sisisky	Y	Y	Y	N	N	N	N
5 Payne	Y	Y	Y	N	Y	N	Y
6 Olin	Y	Y	Y	Y	?	N	N
7 **Slaughter**	N	Y	N	N	N	N	N
8 **Parris**	N	Y	N	N	N	N	N
9 Boucher	Y	Y	Y	N	Y	N	Y
10 **Wolf**	N	Y	N	N	N	N	N
WASHINGTON							
1 **Miller**	N	Y	N	N	Y	N	Y
2 Swift	Y	Y	Y	Y	Y	Y	Y
3 Unsoeld	Y	Y	Y	Y	Y	Y	Y
4 **Morrison**	?	?	N	Y	Y	N	Y
5 Foley							Y
6 Dicks	Y	Y	Y	N	Y	N	Y
7 McDermott	Y	Y	Y	Y	Y	Y	Y
8 **Chandler**	N	Y	N	N	N	N	N
WEST VIRGINIA							
1 Mollohan	Y	Y	Y	N	N	N	N
2 Staggers	Y	Y	Y	Y	Y	N	Y
3 Wise	Y	Y	Y	N	Y	N	Y
4 Rahall	Y	Y	Y	Y	Y	N	Y
WISCONSIN							
1 Aspin	Y	Y	Y	N	Y	N	Y
2 Kastenmeier	Y	Y	Y	Y	Y	Y	Y
3 **Gunderson**	Y	Y	N	N	N	N	N
4 Kleczka	Y	Y	Y	Y	Y	N	Y
5 Moody	Y	Y	Y	Y	Y	Y	Y
6 **Petri**	Y	Y	N	N	N	N	N
7 Obey	Y	N	Y	Y	Y	N	Y
8 **Roth**	N	Y	N	N	N	N	N
9 **Sensenbrenner**	N	Y	N	N	N	N	N
WYOMING							
AL **Thomas**	N	Y	N	N	N	N	N

Southern states - Ala., Ark., Fla., Ga., Ky., La., Miss., N.C., Okla., S.C., Tenn., Texas, Va.
Omitted votes are quorum calls, which CQ does not include in its vote charts.

HOUSE VOTES 483, 484, 485, 486, 487

483. H J Res 467. China Trade Status/Passage. Passage of the joint resolution to disapprove the president's waiver of freedom of emigration requirements in 1990, thus denying most-favored-nation trade status to China. Current law prohibits granting most-favored-nation trade status to communist countries that have restrictive emigration policies. The president may waive these requirements if he determines that doing so would promote freedom of emigration. Passed 247-174: R 81-90; D 166-84 (ND 117-53, SD 49-31) Oct. 18, 1990. A "nay" was a vote supporting the president's position.

484. HR 4939. China Trade Status/Conditions for Favored Treatment. Pelosi, D-Calif., amendment, as amended by the Wolf, R-Va., amendment, to require the president to certify that the Chinese government has accounted for and released citizens detained following pro-democracy demonstrations in Tiananmen Square in May-June 1989, and that the Chinese government has made significant progress in meeting other human rights goals including granting freedom of travel, religion and of the press, before waiving freedom of emigration requirements and granting China most-favored-nation trade status in 1991. Adopted 347-74: R 128-44; D 219-30 (ND 149-20, SD 70-10), Oct. 18, 1990. A "nay" was a vote supporting the president's position.

485. HR 4939. China Trade Status/Conditions for Favored Treatment. Porter, R-Ill., amendment as amended by the Miller, R-Wash., amendment, to require the president to report to Congress that the Chinese government is adhering to the 1984 Joint Declaration on Hong Kong before granting China most-favored-nation trade status in 1991, and to require U.S. businesses engaged in joint ventures in China to adhere to principles chiefly regarding human rights. Adopted 409-7: R 169-2; D 240-5 (ND 164-2, SD 76-3), Oct. 18, 1990. A "nay" was a vote supporting the president's position.

486. HR 4939. China Trade Status/Passage. Passage of the bill to require the president to certify that the Chinese government is taking action to correct human rights violations before granting China most-favored-nation trade status in 1991. Passed 384-30: R 150-19; D 234-11 (ND 159-7, SD 75-4), Oct. 18, 1990. A "nay" was a vote supporting the president's position.

487. H J Res 677. Fiscal 1991 Continuing Appropriations/Passage. Passage of the joint resolution to provide continuing appropriations for fiscal 1991 through Oct. 24 at the lowest of the conference-agreed, House-passed, Senate passed or fiscal 1990 spending level; suspend sequestration through Oct. 24; and extend a temporary increase in the debt limit through Oct. 24. Passed 379-37: R 138-32; D 241-5 (ND 163-4, SD 78-1), Oct. 18, 1990.

KEY

- Y Voted for (yea).
- # Paired for.
- + Announced for.
- N Voted against (nay).
- X Paired against.
- \- Announced against.
- P Voted "present."
- C Voted "present" to avoid possible conflict of interest.
- ? Did not vote or otherwise make a position known.

Democrats ***Republicans***

	483	484	485	486	487
ALABAMA					
1 ***Callahan***	Y	N	Y	Y	Y
2 ***Dickinson***	Y	Y	Y	Y	Y
3 Browder	Y	Y	Y	Y	Y
4 Bevill	Y	Y	Y	Y	Y
5 Flippo	Y	Y	Y	Y	Y
6 Erdreich	Y	Y	Y	Y	Y
7 Harris	Y	Y	Y	Y	Y
ALASKA					
AL ***Young***	N	N	Y	Y	Y
ARIZONA					
1 ***Rhodes***	N	Y	Y	Y	Y
2 Udall	Y	Y	Y	+	Y
3 ***Stump***	N	N	Y	N	N
4 ***Kyl***	Y	Y	Y	Y	Y
5 ***Kolbe***	Y	N	Y	Y	Y
ARKANSAS					
1 Alexander	N	N	Y	Y	Y
2 ***Robinson***	N	N	Y	Y	N
3 ***Hammerschmidt***	N	N	Y	Y	N
4 Anthony	N	Y	Y	Y	Y
CALIFORNIA					
1 Bosco	N	Y	Y	Y	Y
2 ***Herger***	Y	Y	Y	Y	Y
3 Matsui	N	N	Y	Y	Y
4 Fazio	N	Y	Y	Y	Y
5 Pelosi	Y	Y	Y	Y	Y
6 Boxer	Y	Y	Y	Y	Y
7 Miller	Y	Y	Y	Y	Y
8 Dellums	Y	Y	Y	Y	Y
9 Stark	Y	Y	Y	Y	Y
10 Edwards	Y	Y	Y	Y	Y
11 Lantos	Y	Y	Y	Y	Y
12 ***Campbell***	N	N	N	N	Y
13 Mineta	Y	Y	Y	Y	Y
14 ***Shumway***	N	Y	Y	Y	N
15 Condit	Y	Y	Y	Y	Y
16 Panetta	N	Y	Y	Y	Y
17 ***Pashayan***	N	N	Y	N	Y
18 Lehman	Y	Y	Y	Y	Y
19 ***Lagomarsino***	Y	Y	Y	Y	Y
20 ***Thomas***	N	Y	Y	Y	N
21 ***Gallegly***	N	Y	Y	Y	Y
22 ***Moorhead***	N	Y	Y	Y	Y
23 Beilenson	Y	Y	Y	Y	Y
24 Waxman	Y	Y	Y	Y	Y
25 Roybal	N	Y	Y	Y	?
26 Berman	Y	Y	Y	Y	Y
27 Levine	Y	Y	Y	Y	Y
28 Dixon	N	Y	Y	Y	Y
29 Hawkins	?	Y	Y	Y	?
30 Martinez	N	Y	Y	Y	Y
31 Dymally	N	Y	Y	Y	Y
32 Anderson	N	Y	Y	Y	Y
33 ***Dreier***	N	N	Y	N	Y
34 Torres	N	N	Y	Y	Y
35 ***Lewis***	Y	N	Y	Y	Y
36 Brown	N	Y	Y	Y	Y
37 ***McCandless***	Y	Y	Y	Y	Y
38 ***Dornan***	Y	Y	Y	Y	Y
39 ***Dannemeyer***	Y	Y	Y	Y	N
40 ***Cox***	N	Y	Y	Y	Y
41 ***Lowery***	N	N	Y	Y	Y
42 ***Rohrabacher***	Y	Y	Y	Y	Y
43 ***Packard***	N	Y	Y	Y	Y
44 Bates	Y	Y	Y	Y	N
45 ***Hunter***	Y	Y	Y	Y	Y
COLORADO					
1 Schroeder	Y	Y	Y	Y	Y
2 Skaggs	Y	Y	Y	Y	Y
3 Campbell	N	Y	Y	Y	Y
4 ***Brown***	Y	Y	Y	Y	N
5 ***Hefley***	Y	Y	Y	Y	Y
6 ***Schaefer***	Y	Y	Y	Y	Y
CONNECTICUT					
1 Kennelly	Y	Y	Y	Y	Y
2 Gejdenson	Y	Y	Y	Y	Y
3 Morrison	?	+	+	+	+
4 ***Shays***	N	Y	Y	Y	N
5 ***Rowland***	?	?	?	?	?
6 ***Johnson***	N	N	Y	Y	Y
DELAWARE					
AL Carper	Y	Y	Y	Y	Y
FLORIDA					
1 Hutto	Y	Y	Y	Y	Y
2 ***Grant***	Y	Y	Y	Y	Y
3 Bennett	Y	Y	Y	Y	Y
4 ***James***	N	Y	Y	Y	Y
5 ***McCollum***	Y	Y	Y	Y	Y
6 ***Stearns***	Y	Y	Y	Y	N
7 Gibbons	N	N	N	N	Y
8 ***Young***	N	Y	Y	Y	Y
9 ***Bilirakis***	N	Y	Y	Y	Y
10 ***Ireland***	N	Y	Y	N	Y
11 Nelson	Y	Y	Y	Y	Y
12 ***Lewis***	Y	Y	Y	Y	Y
13 ***Goss***	N	N	Y	N	Y
14 Johnston	N	N	Y	Y	Y
15 ***Shaw***	N	Y	Y	Y	Y
16 Smith	Y	Y	Y	Y	Y
17 Lehman	N	N	Y	Y	Y
18 ***Ros-Lehtinen***	Y	Y	Y	Y	Y
19 Fascell	Y	Y	Y	Y	Y
GEORGIA					
1 Thomas	N	Y	Y	Y	Y
2 Hatcher	Y	Y	Y	Y	Y
3 Ray	N	Y	Y	Y	Y
4 Jones	Y	Y	Y	Y	Y
5 Lewis	Y	Y	Y	Y	Y
6 ***Gingrich***	N	Y	Y	Y	?
7 Darden	Y	Y	Y	Y	Y
8 Rowland	Y	Y	Y	Y	Y
9 Jenkins	Y	Y	Y	Y	Y
10 Barnard	Y	Y	Y	Y	Y
HAWAII					
1 ***Saiki***	N	Y	Y	Y	Y
2 Mink	Y	Y	Y	Y	Y
IDAHO					
1 ***Craig***	N	Y	Y	Y	Y
2 Stallings	N	Y	Y	Y	Y
ILLINOIS					
1 Hayes	Y	Y	Y	N	Y
2 Savage	Y	Y	Y	Y	Y
3 Russo	Y	Y	Y	Y	Y
4 Sangmeister	Y	Y	Y	Y	N
5 Lipinski	Y	Y	Y	Y	Y
6 ***Hyde***	Y	Y	Y	Y	Y
7 Collins	Y	Y	Y	Y	Y
8 Rostenkowski	N	N	N	N	Y
9 Yates	Y	Y	Y	Y	Y
10 ***Porter***	Y	Y	Y	Y	N
11 Annunzio	Y	Y	Y	Y	Y
12 ***Crane***	N	N	Y	N	N
13 ***Fawell***	N	Y	Y	Y	Y
14 ***Hastert***	N	N	Y	Y	Y
15 ***Madigan***	N	N	Y	Y	Y
16 ***Martin***	?	?	?	?	?
17 Evans	Y	Y	Y	Y	Y
18 ***Michel***	N	N	Y	N	Y
19 Bruce	Y	Y	Y	Y	Y
20 Durbin	Y	Y	Y	Y	Y
21 Costello	Y	Y	Y	Y	Y
22 Poshard	Y	Y	Y	Y	Y
INDIANA					
1 Visclosky	Y	N	Y	Y	Y
2 Sharp	N	Y	Y	Y	Y
3 ***Hiler***	Y	Y	Y	Y	Y

ND Northern Democrats SD Southern Democrats

	483	484	485	486	487
4 Long	N	Y	Y	Y	Y
5 Jontz	Y	Y	Y	Y	Y
6 ***Burton***	Y	Y	Y	Y	N
7 ***Myers***	N	N	Y	N	Y
8 McCloskey	Y	Y	Y	Y	Y
9 Hamilton	N	N	Y	N	Y
10 Jacobs	N	N	Y	Y	Y
IOWA					
1 ***Leach***	N	Y	Y	Y	Y
2 ***Tauke***	Y	Y	Y	Y	Y
3 Nagle	N	Y	Y	Y	Y
4 Smith	N	N	Y	N	Y
5 ***Lightfoot***	Y	Y	Y	Y	Y
6 ***Grandy***	N	N	Y	Y	Y
KANSAS					
1 ***Roberts***	N	Y	Y	Y	Y
2 Slattery	N	Y	Y	Y	Y
3 ***Meyers***	N	Y	Y	Y	Y
4 Glickman	N	Y	Y	Y	Y
5 ***Whittaker***	N	Y	Y	Y	Y
KENTUCKY					
1 Hubbard	Y	Y	Y	Y	Y
2 Natcher	N	Y	Y	Y	Y
3 Mazzoli	N	Y	Y	Y	Y
4 ***Bunning***	Y	Y	Y	Y	Y
5 ***Rogers***	Y	Y	Y	Y	Y
6 ***Hopkins***	Y	Y	Y	Y	Y
7 Perkins	Y	Y	Y	Y	Y
LOUISIANA					
1 ***Livingston***	N	N	Y	Y	Y
2 Boggs	N	Y	Y	Y	Y
3 Tauzin	Y	Y	Y	Y	Y
4 ***McCrery***	N	N	Y	N	Y
5 Huckaby	Y	Y	Y	Y	Y
6 ***Baker***	N	N	Y	Y	N
7 Hayes	Y	Y	Y	Y	Y
8 ***Holloway***	N	Y	Y	Y	N
MAINE					
1 Brennan	?	?	?	?	?
2 ***Snowe***	Y	Y	Y	Y	Y
MARYLAND					
1 Dyson	Y	Y	Y	Y	Y
2 ***Bentley***	Y	Y	Y	Y	Y
3 Cardin	Y	Y	Y	Y	Y
4 McMillen	Y	Y	Y	Y	Y
5 Hoyer	Y	Y	Y	Y	Y
6 Byron	N	Y	Y	Y	Y
7 Mfume	Y	Y	Y	Y	Y
8 ***Morella***	Y	Y	Y	Y	Y
MASSACHUSETTS					
1 ***Conte***	Y	Y	Y	Y	Y
2 Neal	Y	Y	Y	Y	Y
3 Early	Y	Y	Y	Y	Y
4 Frank	Y	Y	Y	Y	Y
5 Atkins	Y	Y	Y	Y	Y
6 Mavroules	Y	Y	Y	Y	Y
7 Markey	Y	Y	Y	Y	Y
8 Kennedy	Y	Y	Y	?	Y
9 Moakley	Y	Y	Y	Y	Y
10 Studds	Y	Y	Y	Y	Y
11 Donnelly	Y	Y	Y	Y	Y
MICHIGAN					
1 Conyers	Y	Y	Y	Y	Y
2 ***Pursell***	Y	N	Y	Y	N
3 Wolpe	Y	Y	Y	Y	Y
4 ***Upton***	Y	Y	Y	Y	N
5 ***Henry***	Y	Y	Y	Y	Y
6 Carr	Y	Y	Y	Y	Y
7 Kildee	Y	Y	Y	Y	Y
8 Traxler	Y	Y	Y	Y	Y
9 ***Vander Jagt***	N	N	Y	Y	Y
10 ***Schuette***	?	?	?	?	?
11 ***Davis***	Y	Y	Y	Y	Y
12 Bonior	Y	Y	Y	Y	Y
13 Crockett	N	N	?	?	?
14 Hertel	Y	Y	Y	Y	Y
15 Ford	N	Y	Y	Y	Y
16 Dingell	Y	Y	Y	Y	Y
17 Levin	Y	Y	Y	Y	Y
18 ***Broomfield***	N	N	Y	Y	Y
MINNESOTA					
1 Penny	N	Y	Y	Y	N
2 ***Weber***	N	Y	Y	?	Y
3 ***Frenzel***	N	N	N	N	N
4 Vento	Y	Y	Y	Y	Y

	483	484	485	486	487
5 Sabo	Y	Y	Y	Y	Y
6 Sikorski	Y	Y	Y	Y	Y
7 ***Stangeland***	N	Y	Y	Y	Y
8 Oberstar	Y	Y	Y	Y	Y
MISSISSIPPI					
1 Whitten	N	Y	Y	Y	Y
2 Espy	Y	Y	Y	Y	Y
3 Montgomery	N	Y	Y	Y	Y
4 Parker	N	Y	Y	Y	N
5 Taylor	Y	Y	Y	Y	Y
MISSOURI					
1 Clay	Y	Y	Y	N	Y
2 ***Buechner***	N	Y	Y	Y	Y
3 Gephardt	Y	?	Y	Y	Y
4 Skelton	N	Y	Y	Y	Y
5 Wheat	Y	Y	Y	Y	Y
6 ***Coleman***	Y	Y	Y	Y	Y
7 ***Hancock***	Y	Y	Y	N	N
8 ***Emerson***	Y	Y	Y	Y	Y
9 Volkmer	Y	Y	Y	Y	Y
MONTANA					
1 Williams	N	Y	Y	Y	Y
2 ***Marlenee***	N	N	Y	Y	N
NEBRASKA					
1 ***Bereuter***	N	Y	Y	Y	Y
2 Hoagland	N	Y	Y	Y	Y
3 ***Smith***	N	N	Y	N	Y
NEVADA					
1 Bilbray	Y	Y	Y	Y	Y
2 ***Vucanovich***	Y	Y	Y	Y	Y
NEW HAMPSHIRE					
1 ***Smith***	Y	Y	Y	Y	N
2 ***Douglas***	Y	Y	?	Y	N
NEW JERSEY					
1 Vacancy					
2 Hughes	N	Y	Y	Y	Y
3 Pallone	Y	Y	Y	Y	Y
4 ***Smith***	Y	Y	Y	Y	Y
5 ***Roukema***	N	Y	Y	Y	Y
6 Dwyer	Y	Y	Y	Y	Y
7 ***Rinaldo***	N	Y	Y	Y	Y
8 Roe	N	N	Y	N	Y
9 Torricelli	Y	?	?	?	?
10 Payne	Y	Y	Y	Y	Y
11 ***Gallo***	N	Y	Y	Y	Y
12 ***Courter***	Y	Y	Y	Y	Y
13 ***Saxton***	N	Y	Y	Y	Y
14 Guarini	N	Y	Y	Y	Y
NEW MEXICO					
1 ***Schiff***	Y	Y	Y	Y	Y
2 ***Skeen***	Y	Y	Y	Y	Y
3 Richardson	Y	Y	Y	Y	Y
NEW YORK					
1 Hochbrueckner	Y	Y	Y	Y	Y
2 Downey	Y	Y	Y	Y	Y
3 Mrazek	N	Y	Y	Y	Y
4 ***Lent***	Y	Y	Y	Y	Y
5 ***McGrath***	Y	Y	Y	Y	Y
6 Flake	Y	Y	Y	Y	Y
7 Ackerman	?	Y	Y	Y	Y
8 Scheuer	Y	Y	Y	Y	Y
9 Manton	Y	Y	Y	Y	Y
10 Schumer	Y	Y	Y	Y	Y
11 Towns	Y	Y	Y	Y	Y
12 Owens	Y	Y	Y	Y	Y
13 Solarz	N	N	Y	Y	Y
14 ***Molinari***	Y	Y	Y	Y	Y
15 ***Green***	N	Y	Y	Y	Y
16 Rangel	Y	Y	?	Y	Y
17 Weiss	Y	Y	Y	Y	Y
18 Serrano	Y	+	+	−	+
19 Engel	Y	Y	?	Y	Y
20 Lowey	Y	Y	Y	Y	Y
21 ***Fish***	Y	Y	Y	Y	Y
22 ***Gilman***	Y	Y	Y	Y	Y
23 McNulty	Y	Y	Y	Y	Y
24 ***Solomon***	Y	Y	Y	Y	Y
25 ***Boehlert***	Y	Y	Y	Y	Y
26 ***Martin***	N	Y	Y	Y	Y
27 ***Walsh***	Y	Y	Y	Y	Y
28 McHugh	Y	Y	Y	Y	Y
29 ***Horton***	Y	Y	Y	Y	Y
30 Slaughter	Y	Y	Y	Y	Y
31 ***Paxon***	Y	Y	Y	Y	Y

	483	484	485	486	487
32 LaFalce	Y	N	Y	N	Y
33 Nowak	N	Y	Y	Y	Y
34 ***Houghton***	N	N	Y	Y	Y
NORTH CAROLINA					
1 Jones	N	Y	Y	Y	Y
2 Valentine	Y	Y	Y	Y	Y
3 Lancaster	Y	Y	Y	Y	Y
4 Price	Y	Y	Y	Y	Y
5 Neal	Y	Y	Y	Y	?
6 ***Coble***	Y	Y	Y	Y	Y
7 Rose	Y	Y	Y	Y	Y
8 Hefner	Y	Y	Y	Y	Y
9 ***McMillan***	Y	Y	Y	Y	Y
10 ***Ballenger***	Y	Y	Y	Y	Y
11 Clarke	N	Y	Y	Y	Y
NORTH DAKOTA					
AL Dorgan	Y	Y	Y	Y	Y
OHIO					
1 Luken	N	N	Y	Y	Y
2 ***Gradison***	N	N	Y	N	Y
3 Hall	Y	Y	Y	Y	Y
4 ***Oxley***	N	N	Y	Y	Y
5 ***Gillmor***	N	N	Y	Y	Y
6 ***McEwen***	N	Y	Y	Y	N
7 ***DeWine***	?	Y	Y	Y	Y
8 ***Lukens***	N	N	Y	Y	Y
9 Kaptur	Y	Y	Y	Y	Y
10 ***Miller***	Y	Y	Y	Y	Y
11 Eckart	Y	Y	Y	Y	Y
12 ***Kasich***	Y	Y	Y	Y	Y
13 Pease	N	N	N	Y	N
14 Sawyer	Y	Y	Y	Y	Y
15 ***Wylie***	N	N	Y	Y	Y
16 ***Regula***	Y	Y	Y	Y	Y
17 Traficant	Y	Y	Y	Y	Y
18 Applegate	Y	Y	Y	Y	Y
19 Feighan	N	Y	Y	Y	Y
20 Oakar	Y	Y	Y	Y	Y
21 Stokes	Y	Y	Y	Y	Y
OKLAHOMA					
1 ***Inhofe***	Y	Y	Y	Y	N
2 Synar	Y	Y	Y	Y	Y
3 Watkins	N	Y	Y	Y	Y
4 McCurdy	Y	Y	Y	Y	Y
5 ***Edwards***	Y	Y	Y	Y	Y
6 English	N	Y	Y	Y	Y
OREGON					
1 AuCoin	N	N	Y	Y	Y
2 ***Smith, B.***	N	Y	Y	Y	N
3 Wyden	N	N	Y	Y	Y
4 DeFazio	N	N	Y	Y	Y
5 ***Smith, D.***	N	Y	Y	Y	N
PENNSYLVANIA					
1 Foglietta	Y	Y	Y	Y	Y
2 Gray	Y	Y	Y	Y	Y
3 Borski	Y	Y	Y	Y	Y
4 Kolter	Y	Y	Y	Y	Y
5 ***Schulze***	Y	Y	Y	Y	Y
6 Yatron	Y	Y	Y	Y	Y
7 ***Weldon***	Y	Y	Y	Y	Y
8 Kostmayer	Y	Y	Y	Y	Y
9 ***Shuster***	N	Y	Y	Y	Y
10 ***McDade***	N	Y	Y	Y	Y
11 Kanjorski	Y	Y	Y	Y	Y
12 Murtha	N	Y	Y	Y	Y
13 ***Coughlin***	N	Y	Y	Y	Y
14 Coyne	N	Y	Y	Y	Y
15 ***Ritter***	Y	Y	Y	Y	Y
16 ***Walker***	Y	Y	Y	Y	Y
17 ***Gekas***	N	N	Y	Y	Y
18 Walgren	Y	Y	Y	Y	Y
19 ***Goodling***	Y	Y	Y	Y	Y
20 Gaydos	N	Y	Y	Y	Y
21 ***Ridge***	Y	Y	Y	Y	Y
22 Murphy	N	N	Y	Y	Y
23 ***Clinger***	N	Y	Y	Y	Y
RHODE ISLAND					
1 ***Machtley***	Y	Y	Y	Y	Y
2 ***Schneider***	N	Y	Y	Y	Y
SOUTH CAROLINA					
1 ***Ravenel***	Y	Y	Y	Y	Y
2 ***Spence***	Y	Y	Y	Y	Y
3 Derrick	Y	Y	Y	Y	Y
4 Patterson	Y	Y	Y	Y	Y
5 Spratt	Y	Y	Y	Y	Y
6 Tallon	Y	Y	Y	Y	Y

	483	484	485	486	487
SOUTH DAKOTA					
AL Johnson	N	N	Y	Y	Y
TENNESSEE					
1 ***Quillen***	N	N	Y	Y	Y
2 ***Duncan***	Y	Y	Y	Y	Y
3 Lloyd	Y	Y	Y	Y	Y
4 Cooper	N	N	Y	Y	Y
5 Clement	N	N	Y	Y	Y
6 Gordon	Y	Y	Y	?	Y
7 ***Sundquist***	N	Y	Y	Y	Y
8 Tanner	N	Y	Y	Y	Y
9 Ford	Y	?	?	?	Y
TEXAS					
1 Chapman	N	Y	Y	Y	Y
2 Wilson	?	?	?	?	?
3 ***Bartlett***	Y	Y	Y	Y	N
4 Hall	N	N	Y	N	Y
5 Bryant	Y	Y	Y	Y	Y
6 ***Barton***	Y	Y	Y	Y	N
7 ***Archer***	N	N	Y	N	Y
8 ***Fields***	N	N	Y	N	N
9 Brooks	?	?	?	?	?
10 Pickle	N	Y	Y	Y	Y
11 Leath	?	Y	Y	Y	?
12 Geren	N	Y	Y	Y	Y
13 Sarpalius	N	Y	Y	Y	Y
14 Laughlin	N	Y	Y	Y	Y
15 de la Garza	Y	Y	Y	Y	Y
16 Coleman	Y	Y	Y	Y	Y
17 Stenholm	N	Y	Y	Y	Y
18 Washington	Y	Y	Y	Y	Y
19 ***Combest***	N	N	Y	Y	Y
20 Gonzalez	Y	Y	Y	Y	Y
21 ***Smith***	N	Y	Y	Y	Y
22 ***DeLay***	N	Y	Y	N	N
23 Bustamante	Y	Y	?	Y	Y
24 Frost	Y	Y	Y	Y	Y
25 Andrews	N	Y	Y	Y	Y
26 ***Armey***	N	Y	Y	N	N
27 Ortiz	Y	Y	Y	Y	Y
UTAH					
1 ***Hansen***	N	Y	Y	Y	Y
2 Owens	Y	Y	Y	Y	Y
3 ***Nielson***	N	N	Y	?	Y
VERMONT					
AL ***Smith***	?	?	?	?	?
VIRGINIA					
1 ***Bateman***	N	N	Y	Y	Y
2 Pickett	N	N	Y	Y	Y
3 ***Bliley***	N	Y	Y	Y	Y
4 Sisisky	Y	Y	Y	Y	Y
5 Payne	N	N	N	N	Y
6 Olin	N	N	N	N	Y
7 ***Slaughter***	N	Y	Y	?	Y
8 ***Parris***	N	Y	Y	Y	Y
9 Boucher	Y	Y	Y	Y	Y
10 ***Wolf***	Y	Y	Y	Y	Y
WASHINGTON					
1 ***Miller***	Y	Y	Y	Y	Y
2 Swift	N	Y	Y	Y	Y
3 Unsoeld	N	Y	Y	Y	Y
4 ***Morrison***	N	Y	Y	Y	Y
5 Foley					
6 Dicks	N	Y	Y	Y	Y
7 McDermott	N	Y	Y	Y	Y
8 ***Chandler***	N	Y	Y	Y	?
WEST VIRGINIA					
1 Mollohan	Y	Y	Y	Y	Y
2 Staggers	Y	Y	Y	Y	Y
3 Wise	Y	Y	Y	Y	Y
4 Rahall	Y	Y	Y	Y	Y
WISCONSIN					
1 Aspin	N	N	?	?	Y
2 Kastenmeier	N	N	Y	Y	Y
3 ***Gunderson***	Y	Y	Y	Y	Y
4 Kleczka	Y	Y	Y	Y	Y
5 Moody	N	Y	Y	Y	Y
6 ***Petri***	N	N	Y	N	N
7 Obey	Y	Y	Y	Y	Y
8 ***Roth***	N	Y	Y	Y	Y
9 ***Sensenbrenner***	Y	N	Y	Y	N
WYOMING					
AL ***Thomas***	N	N	Y	Y	Y

Southern states - Ala., Ark., Fla., Ga., Ky., La., Miss., N.C., Okla., S.C., Tenn., Texas, Va.
Omitted votes are quorum calls, which CQ does not include in its vote charts.

HOUSE VOTES 488, 489, 490, 491, 492, 493, 494, 495

488. H Res 512. Rule Expediting Budget and Appropriations Legislation/Rule. Adoption of the rule (H Res 512) to provide for expedited House floor consideration of the rules dealing with a continuing appropriations resolution, reconciliation bill or debt limit bill through Oct. 21 by waiving the two-thirds requirement for rules considered the same day that they are reported, thereby permitting their consideration after a simple majority vote. The rule also waives the three-day layover requirement for conference reports on appropriations through Oct. 21. Adopted 246-163: R 5-163; D 241-0 (ND 164-0, SD 77-0), Oct. 19, 1990.

489. HR 5019. Fiscal 1991 Energy and Water Appropriations/Conference Report. Adoption of the conference report on the bill to appropriate $20,164,632,000 in fiscal 1991 for the energy, water and nuclear weapons programs. The president requested $20,214,377,000. Adopted 362-51: R 129-38; D 233-13 (ND 155-11, SD 78-2), Oct. 19, 1990.

490. HR 5019. Fiscal 1991 Energy and Water Appropriations/Environmental Protection Reimbursement. Bevill, D-Ala., motion to recede and concur in the Senate amendment to authorize and direct the secretary of Interior to pay, without reimbursement, $1 million to the Fall River Rural Electric Cooperative as reimbursement for environmental protection requirements in connection with the development of hydroelectric power at the Island Park Dam and Reservoir in Idaho. Motion agreed to 246-172: R 70-100; D 176-72 (ND 112-57, SD 64-15), Oct. 19, 1990.

491. HR 5019. Fiscal 1991 Energy and Water Appropriations/Energy Activities. Bevill, D-Ala., motion to recede and concur in the Senate amendment, with an amendment to provide $90 million for energy research, supply and development activities. Motion agreed to 308-108: R 75-93; D 233-15 (ND 156-12, SD 77-3), Oct. 19, 1990.

492. HR 5229. Fiscal 1991 Transportation Appropriations/Conference Report. Adoption of the conference report on the bill to appropriate $12,987,662,569 in fiscal 1991 for the Department of Transportation and related agencies. The president requested $11,878,271,569. Adopted 394-17: R 150-15; D 244-2 (ND 165-2, SD 79-0), Oct. 19, 1990.

493. HR 5311. Fiscal 1991 D.C. Appropriations/Recommittal Motion. Dannemeyer, R-Calif., motion to recommit to the conference committee the conference report on the bill, with instructions to report it back to the House with Senate amendments restricting homosexuals and bisexuals from participating in juvenile programs in the District of Columbia. Motion rejected 186-210: R 134-26; D 52-184 (ND 17-141, SD 35-43), Oct. 20, 1990.

494. HR 5311. Fiscal 1991 D.C. Appropriations/Conference Report. Adoption of the conference report on the bill to appropriate $549,700,000 in federal funds in fiscal 1991 and to approve spending $3,862,574,000 in funds raised from local taxes for the District of Columbia. The bill would not limit the District in using local tax revenues for abortions. The president requested $519,278,000 and $3,818,652,000, respectively. Rejected 185-211: R 22-137; D 163-74 (ND 118-40, SD 45-34), Oct. 20, 1990. A "nay" was a vote supporting the president's position.

495. HR 5158. Fiscal 1991 VA and HUD Appropriations/Conference Report. Adoption of the conference report on the bill to appropriate $78,056,471,400 in fiscal 1991 for the Department of Housing and Urban Development (HUD), the Department of Veterans Affairs (VA), the Environmental Protection Agency, NASA, the National Science Foundation and various other agencies. The president requested $76,177,418,000. Adopted 366-32: R 134-26; D 232-6 (ND 152-6, SD 80-0), Oct. 20, 1990.

KEY

Y Voted for (yea).
\# Paired for.
\+ Announced for.
N Voted against (nay).
X Paired against.
\- Announced against.
P Voted "present."
C Voted "present" to avoid possible conflict of interest.
? Did not vote or otherwise make a position known.

Democrats ***Republicans***

	488	489	490	491	492	493	494	495
ALABAMA								
1 ***Callahan***	N	Y	Y	Y	Y	Y	N	Y
2 ***Dickinson***	N	Y	Y	Y	Y	Y	N	Y
3 Browder	Y	Y	Y	Y	Y	Y	Y	Y
4 Bevill	Y	Y	Y	Y	Y	Y	N	Y
5 Flippo	Y	Y	N	?	?	?	?	?
6 Erdreich	Y	Y	Y	Y	Y	Y	Y	Y
7 Harris	Y	Y	Y	Y	Y	Y	Y	Y
ALASKA								
AL ***Young***	?	Y	Y	Y	Y	Y	N	Y
ARIZONA								
1 ***Rhodes***	N	Y	Y	N	Y	Y	N	Y
2 Udall	Y	Y	?	#	Y	?	?	Y
3 ***Stump***	N	N	Y	N	N	Y	N	Y
4 ***Kyl***	N	Y	Y	N	N	Y	N	N
5 ***Kolbe***	N	Y	Y	Y	N	?	?	?
ARKANSAS								
1 Alexander	Y	Y	Y	Y	Y	Y	Y	Y
2 ***Robinson***	N	Y	Y	Y	?	?	?	?
3 ***Hammerschmidt***	N	Y	Y	N	Y	Y	N	Y
4 Anthony	Y	Y	N	Y	Y	N	Y	Y
CALIFORNIA								
1 Bosco	Y	Y	Y	Y	Y	N	N	Y
2 ***Herger***	N	Y	N	N	Y	Y	N	N
3 Matsui	Y	Y	N	Y	Y	N	Y	Y
4 Fazio	Y	Y	Y	Y	Y	N	Y	Y
5 Pelosi	Y	Y	N	Y	Y	N	Y	Y
6 Boxer	Y	Y	N	Y	Y	N	Y	Y
7 Miller	?	Y	N	Y	Y	N	Y	Y
8 Dellums	?	Y	N	Y	Y	N	Y	Y
9 Stark	Y	Y	N	Y	Y	N	Y	Y
10 Edwards	Y	Y	Y	Y	Y	N	Y	Y
11 Lantos	Y	Y	Y	Y	Y	N	Y	Y
12 ***Campbell***	N	N	N	N	Y	N	N	N
13 Mineta	Y	Y	Y	Y	Y	N	Y	Y
14 ***Shumway***	N	Y	Y	N	N	Y	N	N
15 Condit	Y	Y	Y	N	Y	?	?	?
16 Panetta	Y	Y	Y	Y	Y	–	+	Y
17 ***Pashayan***	N	Y	Y	Y	Y	Y	N	Y
18 Lehman	Y	Y	Y	Y	Y	N	Y	Y
19 ***Lagomarsino***	N	Y	Y	Y	Y	Y	N	Y
20 ***Thomas***	N	Y	Y	N	Y	Y	N	Y
21 ***Gallegly***	N	Y	Y	Y	Y	Y	N	Y
22 ***Moorhead***	N	Y	Y	?	Y	Y	N	Y
23 Beilenson	Y	Y	N	N	Y	N	Y	Y
24 Waxman	Y	Y	N	Y	Y	N	Y	Y
25 Roybal	Y	Y	Y	Y	Y	N	Y	Y
26 Berman	Y	Y	N	Y	Y	N	Y	Y
27 Levine	Y	Y	Y	Y	?	N	Y	Y
28 Dixon	Y	Y	Y	Y	Y	N	Y	Y
29 Hawkins	Y	?	N	Y	?	?	?	Y
30 Martinez	Y	?	Y	Y	Y	N	Y	Y
31 Dymally	#	?	?	#	?	N	Y	Y
32 Anderson	Y	Y	Y	Y	Y	N	Y	Y
33 ***Dreier***	N	N	N	N	Y	Y	N	N
34 Torres	Y	Y	Y	Y	Y	N	Y	Y
35 ***Lewis***	X	?	?	?	?	?	?	?
36 Brown	Y	Y	Y	Y	Y	N	Y	Y
37 ***McCandless***	N	Y	Y	Y	Y	Y	N	Y
38 ***Dornan***	N	Y	N	N	Y	Y	N	Y
39 ***Dannemeyer***	N	Y	N	N	N	Y	N	N
40 ***Cox***	N	Y	N	N	Y	Y	N	N
41 ***Lowery***	N	Y	Y	Y	Y	Y	N	Y
42 ***Rohrabacher***	N	Y	N	N	Y	Y	N	Y
43 ***Packard***	X	?	?	X	?	?	?	?
44 Bates	Y	N	N	N	N	N	Y	N
45 ***Hunter***	N	Y	Y	N	Y	Y	N	Y
COLORADO								
1 Schroeder	Y	Y	N	N	Y	N	Y	Y
2 Skaggs	Y	Y	Y	Y	Y	N	Y	Y
3 Campbell	Y	Y	Y	Y	Y	N	N	Y
4 ***Brown***	N	Y	N	N	Y	Y	N	Y
5 ***Hefley***	N	Y	N	N	Y	Y	N	Y
6 ***Schaefer***	N	Y	N	N	Y	Y	N	Y
CONNECTICUT								
1 Kennelly	Y	Y	?	Y	Y	N	Y	?
2 Gejdenson	Y	Y	N	Y	Y	N	Y	Y
3 Morrison	+	+	-	+	+	-	+	+
4 ***Shays***	N	N	N	N	Y	N	Y	Y
5 ***Rowland***	N	Y	N	Y	?	?	?	?
6 ***Johnson***	Y	N	N	N	Y	N	Y	Y
DELAWARE								
AL Carper	Y	Y	Y	Y	Y	N	Y	Y
FLORIDA								
1 Hutto	Y	Y	Y	Y	Y	Y	N	Y
2 ***Grant***	N	Y	Y	Y	Y	Y	N	Y
3 Bennett	Y	Y	Y	Y	Y	Y	Y	Y
4 ***James***	N	Y	N	N	Y	Y	N	Y
5 ***McCollum***	N	Y	N	N	Y	Y	N	Y
6 ***Stearns***	N	Y	N	N	Y	Y	N	Y
7 Gibbons	Y	Y	Y	Y	Y	N	Y	Y
8 ***Young***	N	Y	Y	Y	Y	Y	N	Y
9 ***Bilirakis***	N	Y	N	N	Y	Y	N	Y
10 ***Ireland***	N	Y	Y	Y	Y	Y	N	Y
11 Nelson	+	+	+	+	+	+	+	+
12 ***Lewis***	N	Y	Y	N	Y	Y	N	Y
13 ***Goss***	N	Y	N	Y	Y	Y	N	Y
14 Johnston	Y	N	Y	N	Y	N	Y	Y
15 ***Shaw***	N	Y	N	N	Y	Y	N	Y
16 Smith	Y	Y	N	Y	Y	N	Y	Y
17 Lehman	Y	Y	Y	Y	Y	N	Y	Y
18 ***Ros-Lehtinen***	N	Y	N	Y	Y	Y	N	Y
19 Fascell	Y	Y	N	Y	Y	N	Y	Y
GEORGIA								
1 Thomas	Y	Y	Y	Y	Y	N	Y	Y
2 Hatcher	Y	Y	Y	Y	Y	N	Y	Y
3 Ray	Y	Y	Y	Y	Y	Y	N	Y
4 Jones	Y	Y	N	Y	Y	N	Y	Y
5 Lewis	Y	Y	Y	Y	Y	N	Y	Y
6 ***Gingrich***	N	Y	N	N	Y	Y	N	Y
7 Darden	?	Y	Y	Y	Y	N	Y	Y
8 Rowland	Y	Y	Y	Y	Y	Y	Y	Y
9 Jenkins	Y	Y	N	Y	Y	Y	N	Y
10 Barnard	Y	Y	Y	Y	Y	Y	N	Y
HAWAII								
1 ***Saiki***	N	Y	N	N	Y	N	Y	Y
2 Mink	Y	Y	N	Y	Y	N	Y	Y
IDAHO								
1 ***Craig***	N	Y	Y	Y	Y	Y	N	Y
2 Stallings	Y	Y	Y	Y	Y	Y	N	Y
ILLINOIS								
1 Hayes	Y	Y	Y	Y	Y	N	Y	Y
2 Savage	Y	?	Y	?	Y	N	Y	Y
3 Russo	Y	N	N	N	Y	Y	N	N
4 Sangmeister	Y	Y	Y	Y	Y	N	N	Y
5 Lipinski	Y	Y	Y	Y	Y	Y	N	Y
6 ***Hyde***	N	Y	Y	N	Y	Y	N	Y
7 Collins	Y	Y	Y	Y	Y	N	Y	Y
8 Rostenkowski	Y	Y	Y	Y	Y	N	Y	Y
9 Yates	Y	Y	N	Y	Y	N	Y	Y
10 ***Porter***	N	Y	N	N	Y	Y	N	Y
11 Annunzio	Y	Y	Y	Y	Y	Y	N	Y
12 ***Crane***	N	N	N	N	N	Y	N	N
13 ***Fawell***	N	Y	N	N	Y	Y	Y	N
14 ***Hastert***	N	Y	Y	Y	?	Y	N	Y
15 ***Madigan***	N	Y	Y	Y	Y	Y	N	Y
16 ***Martin***	?	?	?	?	?	?	?	?
17 Evans	Y	Y	N	Y	Y	N	Y	Y
18 ***Michel***	N	N	Y	Y	Y	Y	N	Y
19 Bruce	Y	Y	Y	Y	Y	Y	N	Y
20 Durbin	Y	Y	Y	Y	Y	N	Y	Y
21 Costello	Y	Y	Y	Y	Y	Y	Y	Y
22 Poshard	Y	Y	Y	Y	Y	Y	N	Y
INDIANA								
1 Visclosky	Y	Y	Y	Y	Y	N	Y	Y
2 Sharp	Y	N	N	Y	Y	N	Y	Y
3 ***Hiler***	N	Y	N	Y	Y	Y	N	Y

ND Northern Democrats SD Southern Democrats

	488	489	490	491	492	493	494	495
4 Long	Y	Y	Y	Y	Y	N	Y	Y
5 Jontz	Y	N	N	Y	Y	N	Y	Y
6 ***Burton***	N	N	N	N	?	Y	N	Y
7 ***Myers***	N	Y	Y	Y	Y	Y	N	Y
8 McCloskey	Y	Y	Y	Y	Y	N	Y	Y
9 Hamilton	Y	Y	N	Y	Y	N	N	Y
10 Jacobs	Y	N	N	Y	Y	N	Y	Y
IOWA								
1 ***Leach***	N	Y	N	N	Y	N	N	Y
2 ***Tauke***	N	N	N	N	Y	Y	N	Y
3 Nagle	Y	Y	Y	Y	Y	N	Y	Y
4 Smith	Y	Y	Y	Y	Y	N	Y	Y
5 ***Lightfoot***	N	Y	Y	N	Y	Y	N	Y
6 ***Grandy***	N	N	Y	?	?	Y	N	Y
KANSAS								
1 ***Roberts***	N	N	Y	Y	Y	Y	N	Y
2 Slattery	Y	N	Y	Y	Y	N	N	Y
3 ***Meyers***	N	Y	N	Y	Y	Y	N	Y
4 Glickman	Y	N	Y	Y	Y	N	N	Y
5 ***Whittaker***	N	Y	Y	Y	Y	Y	N	Y
KENTUCKY								
1 Hubbard	Y	Y	Y	Y	Y	Y	N	Y
2 Natcher	Y	Y	Y	Y	Y	N	N	Y
3 Mazzoli	Y	Y	Y	Y	Y	N	N	Y
4 ***Bunning***	N	N	N	N	Y	Y	N	Y
5 ***Rogers***	N	Y	Y	Y	Y	Y	N	Y
6 ***Hopkins***	N	Y	N	Y	Y	Y	N	Y
7 Perkins	Y	Y	Y	Y	Y	N	N	Y
LOUISIANA								
1 ***Livingston***	N	Y	Y	Y	Y	Y	N	Y
2 Boggs	Y	Y	Y	Y	Y	N	N	Y
3 Tauzin	Y	Y	Y	Y	Y	Y	N	Y
4 ***McCrery***	N	Y	Y	Y	Y	N	N	Y
5 Huckaby	Y	Y	Y	Y	Y	Y	N	Y
6 ***Baker***	N	Y	Y	Y	Y	Y	N	Y
7 Hayes	Y	Y	Y	Y	Y	Y	N	Y
8 ***Holloway***	N	?	Y	Y	Y	Y	N	Y
MAINE								
1 Brennan	?	?	?	?	?	?	?	?
2 ***Snowe***	N	N	N	N	Y	Y	Y	Y
MARYLAND								
1 Dyson	Y	Y	Y	Y	Y	N	N	N
2 ***Bentley***	?	?	N	N	Y	Y	N	Y
3 Cardin	Y	Y	Y	Y	Y	N	Y	Y
4 McMillen	Y	Y	Y	Y	Y	N	Y	Y
5 Hoyer	Y	Y	Y	Y	Y	N	Y	Y
6 Byron	Y	Y	N	Y	Y	Y	N	N
7 Mfume	Y	Y	Y	Y	Y	N	Y	Y
8 ***Morella***	N	Y	N	N	Y	N	Y	Y
MASSACHUSETTS								
1 ***Conte***	N	Y	N	Y	Y	N	Y	Y
2 Neal	Y	Y	N	Y	Y	N	N	Y
3 Early	Y	Y	N	Y	Y	N	Y	Y
4 Frank	Y	Y	N	N	Y	N	Y	Y
5 Atkins	Y	Y	N	Y	Y	N	Y	Y
6 Mavroules	Y	Y	Y	Y	Y	N	N	Y
7 Markey	Y	Y	N	Y	Y	N	Y	Y
8 Kennedy	Y	Y	N	Y	Y	N	Y	Y
9 Moakley	Y	Y	Y	Y	Y	N	N	Y
10 Studds	Y	Y	N	Y	Y	N	Y	Y
11 Donnelly	Y	Y	Y	Y	Y	N	N	Y
MICHIGAN								
1 Conyers	Y	Y	Y	Y	Y	?	Y	Y
2 ***Pursell***	N	Y	N	N	Y	N	N	Y
3 Wolpe	Y	Y	N	N	Y	N	Y	Y
4 ***Upton***	N	N	N	N	Y	Y	N	N
5 ***Henry***	N	N	N	N	Y	Y	N	Y
6 Carr	Y	Y	Y	Y	Y	N	Y	Y
7 Kildee	Y	Y	Y	Y	Y	N	N	Y
8 Traxler	Y	Y	Y	Y	Y	N	N	Y
9 ***Vander Jagt***	N	Y	N	Y	Y	?	?	Y
10 ***Schuette***	?	?	?	?	?	?	?	?
11 ***Davis***	N	Y	Y	Y	Y	Y	N	?
12 Bonior	?	Y	Y	Y	Y	N	?	?
13 Crockett	Y	Y	Y	?	?	?	?	?
14 Hertel	Y	N	N	Y	N	N	N	Y
15 Ford	Y	Y	Y	Y	Y	?	?	?
16 Dingell	Y	Y	Y	Y	Y	N	Y	Y
17 Levin	Y	Y	Y	Y	Y	N	Y	Y
18 ***Broomfield***	N	N	N	N	Y	Y	N	Y
MINNESOTA								
1 Penny	Y	Y	Y	Y	Y	Y	N	N
2 ***Weber***	N	Y	N	Y	Y	Y	N	Y
3 ***Frenzel***	N	N	N	N	N	N	Y	N
4 Vento	Y	Y	N	Y	Y	N	Y	Y
5 Sabo	Y	Y	Y	Y	Y	N	Y	Y
6 Sikorski	Y	N	N	N	Y	N	Y	Y
7 ***Stangeland***	N	Y	Y	Y	Y	Y	N	Y
8 Oberstar	Y	Y	Y	Y	Y	N	N	Y
MISSISSIPPI								
1 Whitten	Y	Y	Y	Y	Y	N	N	Y
2 Espy	Y	Y	N	Y	Y	N	Y	Y
3 Montgomery	Y	Y	Y	Y	Y	Y	N	Y
4 Parker	Y	Y	N	Y	Y	Y	N	Y
5 Taylor	Y	Y	N	Y	Y	Y	N	Y
MISSOURI								
1 Clay	Y	Y	Y	Y	Y	N	Y	Y
2 ***Buechner***	N	Y	N	N	Y	Y	N	Y
3 Gephardt	Y	Y	Y	Y	?	N	Y	Y
4 Skelton	Y	Y	Y	Y	Y	Y	N	Y
5 Wheat	Y	Y	N	Y	Y	N	Y	Y
6 ***Coleman***	N	Y	Y	Y	Y	Y	N	Y
7 ***Hancock***	N	N	N	N	N	Y	N	N
8 ***Emerson***	N	Y	Y	N	Y	Y	N	Y
9 Volkmer	Y	Y	Y	Y	Y	Y	N	Y
MONTANA								
1 Williams	Y	Y	Y	Y	Y	N	Y	Y
2 ***Marlenee***	N	Y	Y	N	Y	Y	N	Y
NEBRASKA								
1 ***Bereuter***	N	Y	Y	Y	Y	Y	N	Y
2 Hoagland	Y	Y	Y	Y	Y	N	N	Y
3 ***Smith***	N	Y	Y	Y	Y	Y	N	Y
NEVADA								
1 Bilbray	Y	Y	Y	Y	Y	Y	Y	Y
2 ***Vucanovich***	N	Y	Y	Y	Y	Y	N	Y
NEW HAMPSHIRE								
1 ***Smith***	N	N	N	N	N	Y	N	N
2 ***Douglas***	N	N	N	N	N	Y	N	N
NEW JERSEY								
1 Vacancy								
2 Hughes	Y	Y	Y	Y	Y	N	N	Y
3 Pallone	Y	Y	Y	Y	Y	Y	Y	Y
4 ***Smith***	N	Y	N	Y	Y	Y	N	Y
5 ***Roukema***	N	Y	Y	Y	Y	?	?	?
6 Dwyer	Y	Y	Y	Y	Y	?	?	?
7 ***Rinaldo***	N	Y	N	Y	Y	Y	N	Y
8 Roe	Y	Y	Y	Y	Y	N	Y	Y
9 Torricelli	Y	Y	Y	Y	Y	N	Y	Y
10 Payne	Y	Y	Y	Y	Y	N	Y	Y
11 ***Gallo***	N	Y	Y	Y	Y	N	Y	Y
12 ***Courter***	N	Y	N	N	Y	Y	N	Y
13 ***Saxton***	N	Y	N	Y	Y	Y	N	Y
14 Guarini	Y	Y	Y	Y	Y	N	N	Y
NEW MEXICO								
1 ***Schiff***	N	Y	N	N	Y	N	Y	Y
2 ***Skeen***	N	Y	Y	Y	Y	Y	N	Y
3 Richardson	Y	Y	N	Y	Y	N	Y	Y
NEW YORK								
1 Hochbrueckner	Y	Y	Y	Y	Y	N	Y	Y
2 Downey	Y	Y	N	Y	Y	N	Y	Y
3 Mrazek	Y	Y	Y	Y	Y	N	Y	Y
4 ***Lent***	N	Y	Y	N	Y	Y	N	Y
5 ***McGrath***	?	Y	N	N	Y	Y	N	Y
6 Flake	Y	Y	N	Y	Y	N	Y	Y
7 Ackerman	Y	Y	Y	Y	Y	N	Y	+
8 Scheuer	Y	Y	N	Y	Y	N	Y	Y
9 Manton	Y	Y	Y	Y	Y	N	Y	Y
10 Schumer	?	Y	N	Y	Y	?	?	?
11 Towns	Y	Y	N	Y	Y	N	Y	Y
12 Owens	Y	Y	Y	Y	Y	N	Y	Y
13 Solarz	Y	Y	Y	Y	Y	N	Y	Y
14 ***Molinari***	N	Y	N	Y	Y	N	Y	Y
15 ***Green***	N	Y	N	Y	Y	N	Y	Y
16 Rangel	Y	Y	N	Y	Y	N	Y	Y
17 Weiss	Y	N	N	N	Y	N	Y	Y
18 Serrano	Y	Y	Y	Y	Y	N	Y	Y
19 Engel	Y	Y	Y	Y	Y	N	Y	Y
20 Lowey	Y	Y	N	Y	Y	N	Y	Y
21 ***Fish***	N	Y	N	Y	Y	N	N	Y
22 ***Gilman***	N	Y	N	Y	Y	N	Y	Y
23 McNulty	Y	Y	Y	Y	Y	N	Y	Y
24 ***Solomon***	N	N	N	N	Y	Y	N	Y
25 ***Boehlert***	N	Y	N	Y	Y	N	Y	Y
26 ***Martin***	N	Y	N	Y	Y	Y	N	?
27 ***Walsh***	N	Y	N	Y	Y	?	?	?
28 McHugh	Y	Y	Y	Y	Y	N	Y	Y
29 ***Horton***	Y	Y	Y	Y	Y	N	Y	Y
30 Slaughter	Y	Y	N	Y	Y	N	Y	Y
31 ***Paxon***	N	Y	N	N	Y	Y	N	Y
32 LaFalce	Y	Y	Y	Y	Y	N	N	Y
33 Nowak	Y	Y	Y	Y	Y	N	N	Y
34 ***Houghton***	N	Y	Y	Y	Y	?	?	Y
NORTH CAROLINA								
1 Jones	Y	Y	Y	Y	Y	N	Y	Y
2 Valentine	Y	Y	N	Y	Y	Y	Y	Y
3 Lancaster	Y	Y	Y	Y	Y	Y	Y	Y
4 Price	Y	Y	Y	Y	Y	N	Y	Y
5 Neal	Y	N	?	Y	Y	N	N	Y
6 ***Coble***	N	N	N	N	Y	Y	N	Y
7 Rose	Y	Y	Y	Y	Y	N	Y	Y
8 Hefner	Y	Y	Y	Y	Y	Y	Y	Y
9 ***McMillan***	N	Y	N	N	Y	Y	N	Y
10 ***Ballenger***	N	N	N	N	Y	Y	N	Y
11 Clarke	Y	Y	N	Y	Y	N	Y	Y
NORTH DAKOTA								
AL Dorgan	Y	Y	Y	Y	Y	N	Y	Y
OHIO								
1 Luken	Y	Y	Y	Y	Y	N	Y	Y
2 ***Gradison***	N	N	N	N	Y	N	Y	Y
3 Hall	?	?	N	Y	Y	Y	N	Y
4 ***Oxley***	N	N	Y	N	Y	Y	N	Y
5 ***Gillmor***	N	Y	N	Y	Y	Y	N	Y
6 ***McEwen***	N	N	Y	N	Y	Y	N	N
7 ***DeWine***	N	Y	N	Y	Y	Y	N	Y
8 ***Lukens***	N	N	N	Y	Y	Y	N	Y
9 Kaptur	Y	Y	Y	Y	Y	N	Y	Y
10 ***Miller***	N	Y	N	N	Y	Y	N	Y
11 Eckart	Y	Y	N	Y	Y	Y	Y	Y
12 ***Kasich***	N	N	N	N	Y	Y	N	Y
13 Pease	Y	Y	Y	N	Y	N	Y	N
14 Sawyer	Y	Y	Y	Y	Y	N	Y	Y
15 ***Wylie***	N	Y	N	Y	Y	?	?	?
16 ***Regula***	N	Y	Y	N	Y	Y	Y	Y
17 Traficant	Y	Y	Y	Y	Y	N	Y	Y
18 Applegate	Y	Y	Y	Y	Y	?	?	?
19 Feighan	Y	Y	Y	Y	Y	N	Y	Y
20 Oakar	?	Y	Y	Y	Y	N	Y	Y
21 Stokes	?	Y	Y	Y	Y	N	Y	Y
OKLAHOMA								
1 ***Inhofe***	N	Y	Y	N	Y	Y	N	Y
2 Synar	Y	Y	Y	Y	Y	N	Y	Y
3 Watkins	Y	Y	Y	Y	Y	Y	N	Y
4 McCurdy	Y	Y	N	Y	Y	N	N	Y
5 ***Edwards***	N	?	Y	Y	Y	Y	N	Y
6 English	Y	Y	Y	Y	Y	Y	N	Y
OREGON								
1 AuCoin	Y	?	Y	Y	Y	N	Y	Y
2 ***Smith, B.***	N	Y	Y	Y	Y	Y	N	Y
3 Wyden	Y	Y	N	Y	Y	N	Y	Y
4 DeFazio	Y	Y	Y	Y	Y	N	N	Y
5 ***Smith, D.***	N	Y	Y	Y	Y	Y	N	N
PENNSYLVANIA								
1 Foglietta	Y	Y	N	Y	Y	N	Y	Y
2 Gray	Y	Y	Y	Y	Y	N	Y	Y
3 Borski	Y	Y	Y	Y	Y	?	N	Y
4 Kolter	Y	Y	Y	Y	Y	?	#	?
5 ***Schulze***	N	Y	N	Y	Y	Y	N	Y
6 Yatron	Y	Y	Y	Y	Y	Y	N	Y
7 ***Weldon***	N	Y	N	N	Y	Y	N	Y
8 Kostmayer	Y	Y	N	Y	Y	N	Y	Y
9 ***Shuster***	N	Y	Y	N	Y	Y	N	N
10 ***McDade***	N	Y	Y	Y	Y	Y	N	Y
11 Kanjorski	Y	Y	Y	Y	Y	N	N	Y
12 Murtha	Y	Y	Y	Y	Y	N	N	Y
13 ***Coughlin***	N	Y	N	Y	Y	Y	Y	Y
14 Coyne	Y	Y	Y	Y	Y	N	?	?
15 ***Ritter***	N	Y	N	N	Y	Y	N	Y
16 ***Walker***	N	N	N	N	N	Y	N	N
17 ***Gekas***	N	N	Y	N	Y	Y	N	Y
18 Walgren	Y	Y	N	Y	Y	?	?	?
19 ***Goodling***	N	Y	?	Y	Y	N	N	Y
20 Gaydos	Y	Y	Y	Y	Y	?	?	?
21 ***Ridge***	N	Y	N	N	Y	N	Y	Y
22 Murphy	Y	Y	Y	Y	Y	N	N	Y
23 ***Clinger***	N	Y	N	Y	Y	Y	N	Y
RHODE ISLAND								
1 ***Machtley***	N	Y	N	N	Y	N	Y	Y
2 ***Schneider***	N	Y	N	N	Y	N	Y	Y
SOUTH CAROLINA								
1 ***Ravenel***	N	Y	N	N	Y	N	N	Y
2 ***Spence***	N	Y	N	Y	Y	Y	N	Y
3 Derrick	Y	Y	Y	Y	Y	Y	Y	Y
4 Patterson	Y	Y	N	Y	Y	Y	N	Y
5 Spratt	Y	Y	Y	Y	Y	Y	Y	Y
6 Tallon	Y	Y	Y	Y	Y	Y	N	Y
SOUTH DAKOTA								
AL Johnson	Y	Y	N	Y	Y	Y	N	Y
TENNESSEE								
1 ***Quillen***	Y	Y	Y	X	?	?	X	?
2 ***Duncan***	N	N	N	N	N	Y	N	N
3 Lloyd	Y	Y	Y	Y	Y	?	?	Y
4 Cooper	Y	Y	Y	N	Y	N	Y	Y
5 Clement	Y	Y	Y	Y	Y	N	Y	Y
6 Gordon	Y	Y	Y	Y	Y	N	Y	Y
7 ***Sundquist***	N	Y	N	N	Y	Y	N	Y
8 Tanner	Y	Y	Y	Y	Y	N	Y	Y
9 Ford	#	Y	N	Y	Y	N	Y	Y
TEXAS								
1 Chapman	Y	Y	Y	Y	Y	?	N	Y
2 Wilson	Y	Y	Y	Y	Y	Y	N	Y
3 ***Bartlett***	N	Y	N	N	Y	Y	N	N
4 Hall	Y	Y	Y	Y	Y	Y	N	Y
5 Bryant	Y	Y	Y	Y	Y	N	Y	Y
6 ***Barton***	N	Y	Y	Y	N	?	?	?
7 ***Archer***	N	N	N	N	Y	Y	N	N
8 ***Fields***	N	Y	N	N	Y	Y	N	N
9 Brooks	?	?	Y	Y	Y	Y	N	Y
10 Pickle	Y	Y	Y	Y	Y	N	Y	Y
11 Leath	Y	Y	?	?	Y	?	?	?
12 Geren	Y	Y	Y	Y	Y	N	N	Y
13 Sarpalius	Y	Y	Y	Y	Y	Y	N	Y
14 Laughlin	Y	Y	Y	Y	Y	Y	N	Y
15 de la Garza	?	?	?	Y	Y	N	N	Y
16 Coleman	Y	Y	Y	Y	Y	N	Y	Y
17 Stenholm	Y	Y	Y	Y	Y	Y	N	Y
18 Washington	?	Y	Y	Y	?	N	Y	Y
19 ***Combest***	N	N	N	N	Y	Y	N	N
20 Gonzalez	Y	Y	Y	Y	?	N	Y	Y
21 ***Smith***	N	Y	N	N	Y	?	?	?
22 ***DeLay***	N	Y	N	N	Y	Y	N	N
23 Bustamante	Y	Y	Y	Y	Y	N	Y	Y
24 Frost	Y	Y	Y	Y	Y	N	Y	Y
25 Andrews	Y	Y	N	Y	Y	Y	N	Y
26 ***Armey***	N	N	N	N	N	Y	?	N
27 Ortiz	Y	Y	Y	Y	Y	Y	Y	Y
UTAH								
1 ***Hansen***	N	Y	Y	Y	Y	Y	N	Y
2 Owens	Y	Y	N	Y	Y	N	Y	Y
3 ***Nielson***	N	Y	Y	N	Y	Y	N	Y
VERMONT								
AL ***Smith***	?	?	?	?	?	?	?	?
VIRGINIA								
1 ***Bateman***	Y	Y	Y	Y	Y	Y	N	Y
2 Pickett	Y	Y	Y	Y	Y	N	N	Y
3 ***Bliley***	N	N	N	N	Y	Y	N	Y
4 Sisisky	Y	Y	Y	Y	Y	N	Y	Y
5 Payne	Y	Y	Y	N	Y	N	Y	Y
6 Olin	Y	Y	Y	Y	Y	N	Y	Y
7 ***Slaughter***	N	N	N	N	Y	Y	N	Y
8 ***Parris***	Y	?	N	Y	Y	Y	N	Y
9 Boucher	Y	Y	Y	Y	Y	N	Y	Y
10 ***Wolf***	N	Y	N	Y	Y	Y	N	Y
WASHINGTON								
1 ***Miller***	N	Y	N	N	Y	N	N	Y
2 Swift	Y	Y	Y	Y	Y	N	Y	Y
3 Unsoeld	Y	Y	Y	Y	Y	N	Y	Y
4 ***Morrison***	N	Y	Y	Y	Y	Y	Y	Y
5 Foley								
6 Dicks	Y	Y	Y	Y	Y	N	Y	Y
7 McDermott	Y	Y	N	Y	Y	N	Y	Y
8 ***Chandler***	N	Y	Y	Y	Y	Y	N	Y
WEST VIRGINIA								
1 Mollohan	Y	Y	Y	Y	Y	N	N	Y
2 Staggers	Y	Y	Y	Y	Y	N	N	Y
3 Wise	Y	Y	Y	Y	Y	N	Y	Y
4 Rahall	Y	Y	Y	Y	Y	N	Y	Y
WISCONSIN								
1 Aspin	Y	Y	N	Y	Y	N	Y	?
2 Kastenmeier	Y	Y	N	N	Y	N	Y	Y
3 ***Gunderson***	N	Y	N	N	Y	N	N	Y
4 Kleczka	Y	Y	Y	Y	Y	N	Y	Y
5 Moody	Y	N	N	N	Y	N	Y	Y
6 ***Petri***	N	N	N	N	Y	Y	N	Y
7 Obey	Y	Y	N	Y	Y	N	Y	Y
8 ***Roth***	N	Y	N	N	Y	Y	N	Y
9 ***Sensenbrenner***	N	N	N	N	N	Y	N	N
WYOMING								
AL ***Thomas***	N	Y	Y	Y	Y	Y	N	Y

Southern states - Ala., Ark., Fla., Ga., Ky., La., Miss., N.C., Okla., S.C., Tenn., Texas, Va.
Omitted votes are quorum calls, which CQ does not include in its vote charts.

496. HR 5158. Fiscal 1991 VA and HUD Appropriations/Special Projects. Traxler, D-Mich., motion to recede and concur in a Senate amendment, with an amendment to provide $54 million for special purpose projects. Motion agreed to 232-167: R 39-120; D 193-47 (ND 136-25, SD 57-22), Oct. 20, 1990.

497. HR 5399. Fiscal 1991 Legislative Branch Appropriations/Budget Cuts. Synar, D-Okla., en bloc amendment to cut a total of $26.1 million from various accounts in the bill, in order to bring the bill into compliance with the new 302(b) allocations established in the revised fiscal 1991 budget resolution, H Con Res 310. Adopted 395-1: R 162-0; D 233-1 (ND 155-0, SD 78-1), Oct. 21, 1990.

498. HR 5399. Fiscal 1991 Legislative Branch Appropriations/Clerk Hires. Hefner, D-N.C., en bloc amendment to reduce the clerk hire appropriation by $16 million, eliminating the funds for the $50,000 increase in each member's clerk hire account. Adopted 275-139: R 139-30; D 136-109 (ND 70-93, SD 66-16), Oct. 21, 1990.

499. HR 5399. Fiscal 1991 Legislative Branch Appropriations/Across-the-Board Cut. Frenzel, R-Minn., amendment to provide an 8.9 percent across-the-board cut in all discretionary accounts, which would total approximately $150 million, making the bill roughly equal to the 1990 spending level. Rejected 191-223: R 147-22; D 44-201 (ND 18-146, SD 26-55), Oct. 21, 1990.

500. HR 5399. Fiscal 1991 Legislative Branch Appropriations/Two Percent Cut. Penny, D-Minn., amendment to provide a 2 percent cut, about $35 million, in the total amount to be appropriated in the bill. The allocation of the cuts would be determined by the committee of jurisdiction. Adopted 249-161: R 158-9; D 91-152 (ND 43-119, SD 48-33), Oct. 21, 1990.

501. HR 5399. Fiscal 1991 Legislative Branch Appropriations/Passage. Passage of the bill to appropriate $1,670,823,000 in fiscal 1991 for the legislative branch. The budget request was for $1,934,395,000. The amounts do not include the activities of the Senate that will be inserted later when the bill is considered by the Senate. Passed 292-117: R 64-102; D 228-15 (ND 156-7, SD 72-8), Oct. 21, 1990.

502. H Res 517. Rule Expediting Budget and Appropriations Legislation/Rule. Adoption of the rule (H Res 517) to provide for expedited House floor consideration of rules dealing with a continuing resolution, reconciliation bill, or debt limit bill through Oct. 24 by waiving the two-thirds requirement for rules considered the same day that they are reported, thereby permitting their consideration after a simple majority vote. The rule also waives the three-day layover requirement for conference reports on appropriations through Oct. 24, allowing their consideration after two hours of availability. Adopted 238-168: R 3-167; D 235-1 (ND 157-1, SD 78-0), Oct. 22, 1990.

503. HR 5400. Campaign Finance Reform/Instruction of Conferees. Thomas, R-Calif., motion to instruct the House conferees on the campaign finance reform bill to insist on the House position eliminating member controlled, "leadership" political action committees (PACs). Motion agreed to 403-6: R 168-0; D 235-6 (ND 157-4, SD 78-2), Oct. 22, 1990.

KEY

Y Voted for (yea).
\# Paired for.
\+ Announced for.
N Voted against (nay).
X Paired against.
\- Announced against.
P Voted "present."
C Voted "present" to avoid possible conflict of interest.
? Did not vote or otherwise make a position known.

Democrats *Republicans*

	496	497	498	499	500	501	502	503
ALABAMA								
1 *Callahan*	N	Y	Y	Y	Y	N	N	Y
2 *Dickinson*	N	Y	Y	Y	Y	Y	N	Y
3 Browder	Y	Y	Y	Y	Y	Y	Y	Y
4 Bevill	Y	Y	Y	N	N	Y	Y	Y
5 Flippo	?	Y	Y	N	N	Y	Y	Y
6 Erdreich	Y	Y	Y	Y	Y	N	Y	Y
7 Harris	Y	Y	Y	Y	Y	Y	Y	Y
ALASKA								
AL *Young*	Y	Y	N	N	N	Y	N	Y
ARIZONA								
1 *Rhodes*	N	Y	Y	Y	Y	N	N	Y
2 Udall	Y	Y	Y	N	N	Y	Y	Y
3 *Stump*	N	Y	Y	Y	Y	N	Y	Y
4 *Kyl*	N	Y	Y	Y	Y	N	N	Y
5 *Kolbe*	?	Y	Y	Y	Y	N	N	Y
ARKANSAS								
1 Alexander	Y	Y	N	N	N	Y	?	N
2 *Robinson*	?	Y	Y	Y	Y	N	N	Y
3 *Hammerschmidt*	N	Y	Y	Y	Y	?	N	Y
4 Anthony	Y	Y	Y	N	N	Y	Y	N
CALIFORNIA								
1 Bosco	Y	Y	N	N	N	Y	Y	Y
2 *Herger*	N	Y	Y	Y	Y	N	N	Y
3 Matsui	Y	Y	N	N	N	Y	Y	Y
4 Fazio	Y	Y	N	N	N	Y	Y	Y
5 Pelosi	Y	Y	N	N	N	Y	?	Y
6 Boxer	Y	Y	Y	N	N	Y	Y	Y
7 Miller	Y	Y	Y	N	N	Y	Y	Y
8 Dellums	Y	Y	N	N	N	Y	Y	Y
9 Stark	Y	Y	N	N	N	Y	Y	Y
10 Edwards	Y	Y	N	N	N	Y	Y	Y
11 Lantos	N	Y	N	N	N	Y	Y	Y
12 *Campbell*	N	Y	Y	Y	Y	N	N	Y
13 Mineta	N	Y	Y	N	N	Y	Y	Y
14 *Shumway*	N	Y	Y	Y	Y	N	N	Y
15 Condit	?	?	Y	Y	Y	Y	Y	Y
16 Panetta	Y	Y	Y	N	+	Y	Y	Y
17 *Pashayan*	Y	Y	Y	N	Y	Y	N	Y
18 Lehman	Y	Y	N	N	N	Y	Y	Y
19 *Lagomarsino*	N	Y	Y	Y	Y	N	N	Y
20 *Thomas*	N	Y	Y	Y	Y	Y	N	Y
21 *Gallegly*	N	Y	Y	Y	Y	N	N	Y
22 *Moorhead*	N	Y	Y	Y	Y	N	N	Y
23 Beilenson	N	Y	N	N	N	Y	Y	Y
24 Waxman	?	Y	N	N	N	Y	Y	?
25 Roybal	Y	Y	N	N	N	Y	Y	Y
26 Berman	Y	Y	N	N	N	Y	Y	N
27 Levine	Y	Y	N	N	N	Y	Y	N
28 Dixon	Y	Y	N	N	N	Y	Y	Y
29 Hawkins	Y	Y	N	?	?	?	?	?
30 Martinez	Y	Y	N	N	N	Y	Y	Y
31 Dymally	Y	Y	N	N	N	Y	Y	Y
32 Anderson	Y	Y	Y	N	N	Y	Y	Y
33 *Dreier*	N	Y	Y	Y	Y	N	N	Y
34 Torres	Y	Y	N	N	N	Y	Y	Y
35 *Lewis*	#	Y	Y	N	N	Y	N	Y
36 Brown	Y	Y	Y	N	Y	Y	Y	?
37 *McCandless*	Y	Y	Y	Y	Y	N	N	Y
38 *Dornan*	N	Y	Y	Y	Y	N	N	Y
39 *Dannemeyer*	N	Y	Y	Y	Y	N	N	Y
40 *Cox*	N	?	Y	Y	Y	N	N	Y
41 *Lowery*	Y	?	Y	Y	Y	Y	N	Y
42 *Rohrabacher*	N	Y	Y	Y	Y	N	N	Y
43 *Packard*	X	Y	Y	Y	Y	N	N	Y
44 Bates	N	Y	Y	Y	Y	N	Y	Y
45 *Hunter*	N	Y	Y	Y	Y	N	N	Y
COLORADO								
1 Schroeder	N	Y	Y	N	Y	Y	Y	Y
2 Skaggs	Y	Y	N	N	N	Y	Y	Y
3 Campbell	Y	Y	N	N	Y	Y	Y	Y
4 *Brown*	N	Y	Y	Y	Y	N	N	Y
5 *Hefley*	N	Y	Y	Y	Y	N	N	Y
6 *Schaefer*	N	Y	Y	Y	?	?	N	Y
CONNECTICUT								
1 Kennelly	Y	Y	Y	N	N	Y	Y	Y
2 Gejdenson	Y	Y	?	?	?	?	Y	Y
3 Morrison	+	+	#	+	+	+	#	+
4 *Shays*	N	Y	N	Y	Y	N	N	Y
5 *Rowland*	?	?	Y	Y	Y	N	?	?
6 *Johnson*	N	Y	N	Y	Y	Y	N	Y
DELAWARE								
AL Carper	Y	Y	Y	N	N	Y	Y	Y
FLORIDA								
1 Hutto	N	Y	Y	Y	Y	N	Y	Y
2 *Grant*	N	Y	Y	Y	Y	N	N	Y
3 Bennett	N	Y	Y	Y	Y	N	Y	Y
4 *James*	N	Y	Y	Y	Y	N	N	Y
5 *McCollum*	N	Y	N	Y	Y	Y	N	Y
6 *Stearns*	N	Y	Y	Y	Y	Y	N	Y
7 Gibbons	Y	Y	N	N	N	Y	Y	Y
8 *Young*	N	Y	Y	Y	Y	Y	N	Y
9 *Bilirakis*	Y	Y	Y	Y	Y	N	N	Y
10 *Ireland*	N	Y	Y	Y	Y	N	N	Y
11 Nelson	+	Y	Y	Y	Y	Y	Y	Y
12 *Lewis*	N	Y	N	Y	Y	N	N	Y
13 *Goss*	Y	Y	Y	Y	Y	N	N	Y
14 Johnston	N	Y	N	N	N	Y	Y	Y
15 *Shaw*	N	Y	Y	Y	Y	Y	N	Y
16 Smith	Y	Y	Y	N	N	Y	Y	Y
17 Lehman	Y	Y	N	N	N	Y	Y	Y
18 *Ros-Lehtinen*	Y	Y	Y	Y	Y	N	N	Y
19 Fascell	Y	Y	Y	N	N	Y	Y	Y
GEORGIA								
1 Thomas	Y	Y	Y	N	N	Y	Y	Y
2 Hatcher	Y	Y	Y	N	N	Y	Y	Y
3 Ray	N	Y	Y	N	Y	Y	Y	Y
4 Jones	Y	Y	Y	N	Y	Y	Y	Y
5 Lewis	Y	Y	N	N	N	Y	Y	Y
6 *Gingrich*	N	Y	Y	Y	Y	N	N	Y
7 Darden	N	Y	Y	N	N	Y	Y	Y
8 Rowland	N	Y	Y	N	Y	Y	Y	Y
9 Jenkins	N	Y	Y	Y	Y	Y	Y	Y
10 Barnard	?	Y	Y	Y	Y	Y	Y	Y
HAWAII								
1 *Saiki*	Y	Y	Y	Y	Y	Y	N	Y
2 Mink	Y	Y	Y	N	Y	Y	Y	Y
IDAHO								
1 *Craig*	N	Y	Y	Y	Y	Y	N	Y
2 Stallings	Y	Y	Y	Y	Y	Y	Y	Y
ILLINOIS								
1 Hayes	Y	Y	N	N	N	Y	Y	Y
2 Savage	Y	Y	N	N	N	Y	?	Y
3 Russo	N	Y	Y	N	N	Y	Y	Y
4 Sangmeister	Y	Y	Y	Y	Y	Y	Y	Y
5 Lipinski	Y	Y	Y	N	Y	Y	Y	Y
6 *Hyde*	N	Y	Y	Y	Y	Y	N	Y
7 Collins	Y	Y	N	N	N	Y	Y	Y
8 Rostenkowski	Y	Y	N	N	N	?	Y	Y
9 Yates	Y	Y	N	N	N	Y	Y	Y
10 *Porter*	N	Y	Y	Y	Y	Y	N	Y
11 Annunzio	Y	Y	Y	N	Y	Y	Y	Y
12 *Crane*	N	Y	Y	Y	Y	N	X	Y
13 *Fawell*	N	Y	Y	Y	Y	N	N	Y
14 *Hastert*	N	Y	Y	Y	Y	N	N	Y
15 *Madigan*	N	Y	N	Y	Y	Y	N	Y
16 *Martin*	?	?	?	?	?	X	X	?
17 Evans	Y	Y	N	N	N	Y	Y	Y
18 *Michel*	Y	Y	Y	Y	Y	Y	N	?
19 Bruce	Y	Y	Y	N	N	Y	Y	Y
20 Durbin	Y	Y	Y	N	N	Y	Y	Y
21 Costello	Y	Y	Y	N	Y	Y	Y	Y
22 Poshard	Y	Y	Y	Y	Y	Y	Y	Y
INDIANA								
1 Visclosky	Y	Y	N	N	N	Y	Y	Y
2 Sharp	Y	Y	Y	Y	Y	Y	Y	Y
3 *Hiler*	N	Y	Y	Y	Y	N	N	Y

ND Northern Democrats SD Southern Democrats

	496	497	498	499	500	501	502	503
4 Long	Y	Y	Y	Y	Y	Y	Y	Y
5 Jontz	Y	Y	Y	N	Y	Y	Y	Y
6 ***Burton***	N	Y	Y	Y	Y	N	N	Y
7 ***Myers***	Y	Y	N	N	Y	Y	N	Y
8 McCloskey	Y	Y	N	N	Y	Y	Y	Y
9 Hamilton	N	Y	N	N	Y	Y	Y	Y
10 Jacobs	N	Y	Y	Y	Y	N	Y	Y
IOWA								
1 ***Leach***	Y	Y	Y	Y	Y	N	N	Y
2 ***Tauke***	Y	Y	Y	Y	Y	N	N	Y
3 Nagle	Y	Y	N	N	N	Y	Y	Y
4 Smith	Y	Y	N	N	N	Y	Y	Y
5 ***Lightfoot***	Y	Y	Y	Y	Y	N	N	Y
6 ***Grandy***	Y	Y	Y	Y	Y	N	N	Y
KANSAS								
1 ***Roberts***	N	Y	Y	Y	Y	Y	N	Y
2 Slattery	N	Y	Y	N	Y	Y	Y	Y
3 ***Meyers***	Y	Y	Y	N	Y	Y	N	Y
4 Glickman	N	Y	Y	N	Y	Y	Y	Y
5 ***Whittaker***	N	Y	Y	Y	Y	Y	N	Y
KENTUCKY								
1 Hubbard	N	Y	Y	N	Y	Y	Y	Y
2 Natcher	Y	Y	Y	N	N	Y	Y	Y
3 Mazzoli	Y	Y	N	N	N	Y	Y	Y
4 ***Bunning***	N	Y	Y	Y	Y	N	N	Y
5 ***Rogers***	N	Y	Y	Y	Y	Y	N	Y
6 ***Hopkins***	N	Y	Y	Y	Y	N	N	Y
7 Perkins	Y	Y	N	N	N	Y	Y	Y
LOUISIANA								
1 ***Livingston***	Y	Y	N	N	Y	Y	N	?
2 Boggs	Y	?	?	?	?	?	Y	Y
3 Tauzin	Y	Y	Y	N	Y	Y	Y	Y
4 ***McCrery***	N	Y	Y	Y	Y	Y	N	Y
5 Huckaby	Y	Y	Y	Y	Y	Y	Y	Y
6 ***Baker***	Y	Y	N	Y	Y	Y	N	Y
7 Hayes	Y	Y	Y	N	N	Y	Y	Y
8 ***Holloway***	N	?	Y	Y	Y	N	N	Y
MAINE								
1 Brennan	?	?	?	?	?	?	?	?
2 ***Snowe***	N	Y	Y	Y	Y	N	N	Y
MARYLAND								
1 Dyson	N	?	Y	N	Y	Y	Y	Y
2 ***Bentley***	N	Y	N	N	Y	Y	N	Y
3 Cardin	N	Y	N	N	N	Y	Y	Y
4 McMillen	Y	Y	Y	N	N	Y	Y	Y
5 Hoyer	Y	?	N	N	N	Y	Y	N
6 Byron	N	Y	Y	N	Y	Y	Y	Y
7 Mfume	Y	Y	N	N	N	Y	Y	Y
8 ***Morella***	Y	Y	N	N	Y	Y	N	Y
MASSACHUSETTS								
1 ***Conte***	Y	Y	Y	Y	Y	Y	N	Y
2 Neal	Y	?	Y	N	N	Y	Y	Y
3 Early	Y	?	N	N	N	Y	Y	Y
4 Frank	Y	Y	N	N	Y	Y	Y	Y
5 Atkins	Y	Y	Y	N	N	Y	Y	Y
6 Mavroules	Y	Y	N	N	N	Y	Y	Y
7 Markey	Y	Y	?	?	?	?	Y	Y
8 Kennedy	?	?	?	?	?	?	?	Y
9 Moakley	Y	Y	Y	N	N	Y	Y	Y
10 Studds	Y	Y	N	N	N	Y	N	Y
11 Donnelly	Y	?	?	?	?	?	Y	Y
MICHIGAN								
1 Conyers	Y	?	?	N	N	Y	Y	Y
2 ***Pursell***	Y	Y	Y	Y	?	N	N	Y
3 Wolpe	N	Y	Y	N	Y	Y	Y	Y
4 ***Upton***	N	Y	Y	Y	Y	N	N	Y
5 ***Henry***	N	Y	Y	Y	Y	N	N	Y
6 Carr	Y	Y	N	N	N	Y	Y	Y
7 Kildee	Y	Y	N	N	N	Y	Y	Y
8 Traxler	Y	Y	N	N	N	N	Y	Y
9 ***Vander Jagt***	N	Y	Y	Y	Y	Y	N	Y
10 ***Schuette***	?	?	?	?	?	?	?	?
11 ***Davis***	Y	Y	N	N	N	Y	N	Y
12 Bonior	Y	Y	N	N	N	Y	Y	Y
13 Crockett	?	?	?	?	?	?	?	Y
14 Hertel	Y	Y	N	N	N	Y	Y	Y
15 Ford	?	Y	N	N	N	Y	?	?
16 Dingell	Y	Y	Y	N	N	Y	Y	N
17 Levin	Y	Y	Y	N	N	Y	Y	Y
18 ***Broomfield***	N	Y	Y	Y	Y	N	N	Y
MINNESOTA								
1 Penny	N	Y	Y	Y	Y	Y	Y	Y
2 ***Weber***	N	Y	Y	Y	Y	N	N	Y
3 ***Frenzel***	N	Y	Y	Y	Y	Y	N	Y
4 Vento	Y	Y	N	N	N	Y	Y	Y

	496	497	498	499	500	501	502	503
5 Sabo	Y	Y	N	N	N	Y	Y	Y
6 Sikorski	N	Y	Y	N	N	Y	Y	Y
7 ***Stangeland***	N	Y	N	Y	Y	N	N	Y
8 Oberstar	Y	Y	N	N	N	Y	Y	Y
MISSISSIPPI								
1 Whitten	Y	Y	N	N	N	Y	Y	Y
2 Espy	Y	Y	N	N	N	Y	Y	Y
3 Montgomery	Y	Y	Y	N	Y	Y	Y	Y
4 Parker	N	Y	Y	Y	Y	N	Y	Y
5 Taylor	N	Y	Y	Y	Y	N	Y	Y
MISSOURI								
1 Clay	?	Y	N	N	N	Y	Y	Y
2 ***Buechner***	N	?	Y	Y	Y	N	N	Y
3 Gephardt	Y	Y	N	N	?	Y	Y	Y
4 Skelton	N	Y	Y	N	N	Y	Y	Y
5 Wheat	Y	?	N	N	N	Y	Y	Y
6 ***Coleman***	N	Y	Y	Y	Y	Y	N	Y
7 ***Hancock***	N	Y	Y	Y	Y	N	N	Y
8 ***Emerson***	N	Y	Y	Y	Y	N	N	Y
9 Volkmer	Y	Y	Y	Y	Y	Y	Y	Y
MONTANA								
1 Williams	Y	Y	N	N	N	Y	Y	Y
2 ***Marlenee***	N	Y	N	N	N	Y	N	Y
NEBRASKA								
1 ***Bereuter***	Y	Y	Y	Y	Y	N	N	Y
2 Hoagland	Y	Y	Y	Y	Y	Y	Y	Y
3 ***Smith***	Y	Y	Y	Y	Y	Y	N	Y
NEVADA								
1 Bilbray	Y	Y	Y	N	N	Y	Y	Y
2 ***Vucanovich***	N	Y	Y	Y	Y	N	N	Y
NEW HAMPSHIRE								
1 ***Smith***	N	Y	Y	Y	Y	N	N	Y
2 ***Douglas***	N	Y	Y	Y	Y	N	N	Y
NEW JERSEY								
1 Vacancy								
2 Hughes	N	Y	Y	N	Y	Y	Y	Y
3 Pallone	N	Y	Y	Y	Y	N	Y	Y
4 ***Smith***	Y	Y	Y	Y	Y	Y	N	Y
5 ***Roukema***	?	Y	Y	N	N	Y	N	?
6 Dwyer	?	Y	N	N	N	Y	Y	Y
7 ***Rinaldo***	N	Y	N	Y	Y	Y	N	Y
8 Roe	Y	Y	N	N	N	Y	Y	Y
9 Torricelli	Y	Y	N	N	N	Y	?	Y
10 Payne	Y	Y	N	N	N	Y	Y	Y
11 ***Gallo***	Y	Y	Y	N	Y	Y	N	Y
12 ***Courter***	N	Y	Y	Y	Y	Y	N	Y
13 ***Saxton***	N	Y	Y	Y	Y	N	N	Y
14 Guarini	N	Y	N	N	Y	Y	Y	Y
NEW MEXICO								
1 ***Schiff***	N	Y	N	N	N	Y	N	Y
2 ***Skeen***	Y	Y	N	N	N	Y	N	Y
3 Richardson	Y	Y	N	N	N	Y	Y	Y
NEW YORK								
1 Hochbrueckner	Y	Y	Y	N	N	Y	Y	Y
2 Downey	Y	Y	N	N	N	Y	Y	Y
3 Mrazek	Y	Y	Y	N	N	Y	Y	Y
4 ***Lent***	N	Y	N	Y	Y	Y	N	Y
5 ***McGrath***	N	Y	N	Y	Y	Y	N	Y
6 Flake	Y	?	N	N	N	Y	Y	Y
7 Ackerman	Y	?	?	N	N	Y	Y	Y
8 Scheuer	Y	Y	N	N	N	Y	Y	Y
9 Manton	Y	Y	N	N	N	Y	Y	Y
10 Schumer	?	?	?	N	N	Y	Y	Y
11 Towns	Y	Y	N	N	N	Y	?	?
12 Owens	Y	Y	N	N	N	Y	Y	Y
13 Solarz	Y	Y	N	?	?	?	Y	Y
14 ***Molinari***	Y	Y	Y	Y	Y	Y	N	Y
15 ***Green***	Y	?	X	?	?	#	N	Y
16 Rangel	Y	Y	N	N	N	Y	Y	Y
17 Weiss	N	Y	N	N	N	Y	Y	Y
18 Serrano	Y	Y	N	N	N	Y	Y	Y
19 Engel	Y	+	N	N	N	Y	Y	Y
20 Lowey	Y	Y	Y	N	N	Y	Y	Y
21 ***Fish***	N	Y	N	N	Y	?	N	Y
22 ***Gilman***	N	Y	N	N	Y	Y	N	Y
23 McNulty	Y	Y	Y	N	N	Y	Y	Y
24 ***Solomon***	N	Y	Y	Y	Y	N	N	Y
25 ***Boehlert***	Y	Y	N	N	Y	Y	N	Y
26 ***Martin***	?	Y	Y	Y	Y	N	N	Y
27 ***Walsh***	?	Y	Y	N	Y	Y	N	Y
28 McHugh	Y	Y	Y	N	N	Y	Y	Y
29 ***Horton***	Y	Y	N	N	N	Y	Y	Y
30 Slaughter	Y	Y	Y	N	N	Y	Y	Y
31 ***Paxon***	N	Y	Y	Y	Y	N	N	Y

	496	497	498	499	500	501	502	503
32 LaFalce	Y	Y	Y	N	Y	Y	?	?
33 Nowak	Y	Y	Y	N	Y	Y	Y	Y
34 ***Houghton***	Y	Y	Y	Y	Y	Y	N	Y
NORTH CAROLINA								
1 Jones	Y	Y	Y	N	Y	Y	Y	Y
2 Valentine	N	Y	Y	N	Y	Y	Y	Y
3 Lancaster	Y	Y	Y	N	Y	Y	Y	Y
4 Price	Y	?	Y	N	Y	Y	Y	Y
5 Neal	N	Y	Y	Y	Y	Y	?	Y
6 ***Coble***	N	Y	Y	Y	Y	N	N	Y
7 Rose	Y	Y	Y	N	N	Y	Y	Y
8 Hefner	?	Y	Y	N	Y	Y	Y	Y
9 ***McMillan***	N	Y	Y	Y	Y	Y	N	Y
10 ***Ballenger***	N	Y	Y	Y	Y	N	N	Y
11 Clarke	Y	Y	Y	N	Y	Y	Y	Y
NORTH DAKOTA								
AL Dorgan	N	Y	Y	N	N	Y	Y	Y
OHIO								
1 Luken	Y	Y	N	N	N	Y	Y	Y
2 ***Gradison***	N	Y	Y	Y	Y	N	N	Y
3 Hall	Y	Y	N	N	N	Y	Y	Y
4 ***Oxley***	N	Y	Y	Y	Y	N	N	Y
5 ***Gillmor***	N	Y	Y	Y	Y	Y	N	Y
6 ***McEwen***	N	Y	Y	?	?	?	N	Y
7 ***DeWine***	N	Y	Y	Y	Y	N	N	Y
8 ***Lukens***	N	Y	Y	Y	Y	N	N	Y
9 Kaptur	Y	Y	Y	N	Y	Y	Y	?
10 ***Miller***	N	Y	Y	Y	Y	N	N	Y
11 Eckart	N	Y	Y	N	Y	Y	Y	Y
12 ***Kasich***	N	Y	Y	Y	Y	N	N	Y
13 Pease	N	?	Y	N	N	Y	#	?
14 Sawyer	Y	Y	N	N	N	Y	Y	Y
15 ***Wylie***	?	?	?	?	?	?	N	Y
16 ***Regula***	N	Y	Y	Y	Y	N	?	?
17 Traficant	Y	Y	Y	Y	Y	N	Y	Y
18 Applegate	Y	Y	N	N	Y	Y	Y	Y
19 Feighan	Y	Y	N	N	N	Y	Y	Y
20 Oakar	Y	Y	N	N	N	Y	Y	Y
21 Stokes	Y	Y	N	N	N	Y	?	Y
OKLAHOMA								
1 ***Inhofe***	N	Y	Y	Y	Y	N	N	Y
2 Synar	N	Y	Y	N	N	Y	Y	Y
3 Watkins	Y	Y	Y	N	Y	Y	?	Y
4 McCurdy	N	Y	Y	N	Y	Y	Y	Y
5 ***Edwards***	N	Y	Y	Y	Y	Y	N	Y
6 English	N	Y	Y	Y	Y	Y	Y	Y
OREGON								
1 AuCoin	Y	Y	N	N	N	Y	Y	Y
2 ***Smith, B.***	N	Y	Y	Y	Y	N	N	Y
3 Wyden	Y	Y	Y	N	N	Y	Y	Y
4 DeFazio	Y	Y	N	N	N	Y	Y	Y
5 ***Smith, D.***	N	Y	Y	Y	Y	N	N	Y
PENNSYLVANIA								
1 Foglietta	Y	Y	Y	N	N	Y	Y	Y
2 Gray	Y	?	N	N	N	Y	?	Y
3 Borski	Y	Y	Y	N	N	Y	Y	Y
4 Kolter	Y	Y	N	N	N	Y	Y	Y
5 ***Schulze***	?	Y	N	Y	Y	N	N	Y
6 Yatron	Y	Y	Y	Y	Y	Y	?	?
7 ***Weldon***	N	Y	Y	Y	Y	N	N	Y
8 Kostmayer	Y	Y	N	N	N	Y	Y	Y
9 ***Shuster***	N	?	?	Y	Y	N	N	Y
10 ***McDade***	Y	Y	Y	N	Y	Y	N	Y
11 Kanjorski	Y	Y	N	N	N	Y	Y	Y
12 Murtha	Y	Y	Y	N	N	Y	Y	Y
13 ***Coughlin***	Y	Y	N	Y	Y	Y	N	Y
14 Coyne	?	Y	N	N	N	Y	Y	Y
15 ***Ritter***	N	Y	Y	Y	Y	N	N	Y
16 ***Walker***	N	Y	Y	Y	Y	N	N	Y
17 ***Gekas***	N	Y	Y	Y	Y	N	N	Y
18 Walgren	?	Y	Y	Y	Y	Y	Y	Y
19 ***Goodling***	N	Y	Y	Y	Y	N	N	Y
20 Gaydos	Y	Y	N	N	N	Y	Y	Y
21 ***Ridge***	N	Y	N	Y	N	Y	?	?
22 Murphy	Y	Y	N	Y	N	Y	Y	Y
23 ***Clinger***	N	Y	Y	Y	Y	Y	N	Y
RHODE ISLAND								
1 ***Machtley***	N	Y	Y	Y	Y	Y	N	Y
2 ***Schneider***	X	?	N	Y	Y	Y	N	Y
SOUTH CAROLINA								
1 ***Ravenel***	Y	Y	Y	Y	Y	N	N	Y
2 ***Spence***	Y	Y	Y	Y	Y	N	N	Y
3 Derrick	Y	Y	Y	Y	Y	Y	Y	Y
4 Patterson	Y	Y	Y	Y	Y	Y	Y	Y
5 Spratt	Y	Y	Y	Y	Y	Y	Y	Y
6 Tallon	N	Y	Y	Y	Y	Y	Y	Y

	496	497	498	499	500	501	502	503
SOUTH DAKOTA								
AL Johnson	N	Y	Y	Y	Y	Y	Y	Y
TENNESSEE								
1 ***Quillen***	#	?	X	?	?	?	Y	Y
2 ***Duncan***	N	Y	Y	Y	Y	N	N	Y
3 Lloyd	Y	Y	Y	N	Y	Y	Y	Y
4 Cooper	N	Y	Y	N	Y	Y	Y	Y
5 Clement	Y	Y	Y	N	Y	Y	Y	Y
6 Gordon	Y	Y	Y	N	N	Y	Y	Y
7 ***Sundquist***	Y	Y	Y	Y	Y	Y	N	Y
8 Tanner	N	Y	Y	N	Y	Y	Y	Y
9 Ford	Y	?	Y	N	Y	Y	Y	Y
TEXAS								
1 Chapman	Y	Y	Y	N	N	Y	Y	Y
2 Wilson	Y	Y	Y	N	Y	?	Y	Y
3 ***Bartlett***	N	Y	Y	Y	Y	N	N	Y
4 Hall	Y	Y	Y	Y	Y	Y	Y	Y
5 Bryant	Y	Y	Y	N	N	Y	Y	Y
6 ***Barton***	?	Y	Y	Y	Y	N	N	Y
7 ***Archer***	N	Y	Y	Y	Y	N	N	Y
8 ***Fields***	N	Y	Y	Y	Y	N	N	Y
9 Brooks	Y	Y	Y	?	?	?	?	?
10 Pickle	Y	Y	Y	Y	Y	Y	Y	Y
11 Leath	Y	Y	Y	N	N	Y	?	?
12 Geren	Y	Y	Y	Y	Y	Y	Y	Y
13 Sarpalius	N	Y	Y	Y	Y	N	Y	Y
14 Laughlin	N	Y	Y	Y	Y	N	Y	Y
15 de la Garza	Y	Y	Y	N	N	Y	Y	Y
16 Coleman	Y	Y	Y	N	N	Y	Y	Y
17 Stenholm	N	Y	Y	Y	Y	Y	Y	Y
18 Washington	Y	N	N	N	N	Y	Y	Y
19 ***Combest***	N	Y	Y	Y	Y	N	N	Y
20 Gonzalez	Y	Y	N	N	N	Y	Y	Y
21 ***Smith***	?	Y	Y	Y	Y	N	N	Y
22 ***DeLay***	N	Y	Y	Y	Y	N	N	Y
23 Bustamante	Y	Y	N	N	N	Y	Y	Y
24 Frost	Y	Y	N	N	N	Y	Y	Y
25 Andrews	N	Y	Y	Y	Y	Y	Y	Y
26 ***Armey***	N	Y	Y	Y	Y	N	N	Y
27 Ortiz	Y	Y	N	N	N	Y	Y	Y
UTAH								
1 ***Hansen***	Y	Y	Y	Y	Y	N	N	Y
2 Owens	Y	Y	Y	N	Y	Y	Y	Y
3 ***Nielson***	N	?	Y	Y	Y	N	N	Y
VERMONT								
AL ***Smith***	?	?	#	?	?	?	N	Y
VIRGINIA								
1 ***Bateman***	Y	Y	Y	N	Y	Y	N	Y
2 Pickett	Y	Y	Y	N	Y	Y	Y	Y
3 ***Bliley***	N	Y	Y	Y	Y	N	N	Y
4 Sisisky	Y	Y	Y	N	Y	Y	Y	Y
5 Payne	Y	Y	Y	Y	Y	Y	Y	Y
6 Olin	Y	?	N	Y	Y	N	Y	Y
7 ***Slaughter***	N	Y	Y	Y	Y	N	N	Y
8 ***Parris***	N	Y	N	Y	Y	Y	N	Y
9 Boucher	Y	Y	N	N	N	Y	Y	?
10 ***Wolf***	N	Y	N	Y	Y	Y	N	Y
WASHINGTON								
1 ***Miller***	N	Y	Y	Y	Y	N	N	Y
2 Swift	Y	Y	Y	N	N	Y	Y	Y
3 Unsoeld	Y	Y	Y	N	Y	Y	Y	Y
4 ***Morrison***	Y	Y	N	N	Y	Y	N	Y
5 Foley								
6 Dicks	Y	Y	Y	N	Y	Y	Y	Y
7 McDermott	Y	Y	N	N	N	Y	Y	Y
8 ***Chandler***	N	Y	Y	Y	Y	Y	N	Y
WEST VIRGINIA								
1 Mollohan	Y	Y	N	N	N	Y	Y	Y
2 Staggers	Y	Y	N	N	N	N	Y	Y
3 Wise	Y	Y	N	N	N	Y	?	?
4 Rahall	Y	Y	N	Y	Y	N	Y	Y
WISCONSIN								
1 Aspin	?	?	?	?	?	?	Y	Y
2 Kastenmeier	Y	Y	N	N	N	Y	Y	Y
3 ***Gunderson***	N	Y	Y	Y	Y	N	N	Y
4 Kleczka	Y	Y	N	N	N	Y	Y	Y
5 Moody	Y	Y	N	N	N	Y	Y	Y
6 ***Petri***	N	Y	Y	Y	Y	N	N	Y
7 Obey	Y	Y	N	N	N	Y	Y	?
8 ***Roth***	N	Y	Y	Y	Y	N	N	Y
9 ***Sensenbrenner***	N	Y	N	Y	Y	N	N	Y
WYOMING								
AL ***Thomas***	N	Y	Y	Y	Y	N	N	Y

Southern states - Ala., Ark., Fla., Ga., Ky., La., Miss., N.C., Okla., S.C., Tenn., Texas, Va.
Omitted votes are quorum calls, which CQ does not include in its vote charts.

HOUSE VOTES 504, 505, 506, 507, 508, 509, 510, 511

504. 5257. Fiscal 1991 Labor-HHS Appropriations/Conference Report. Adoption of the conference report on the bill to appropriate $182,181,734,000 for the Departments of Labor, Health and Human Services and Education and related agencies, including advance appropriations of $21.1 billion in fiscal 1992 and $319 million in fiscal 1993. The president requested $174,845,772,000. The report includes the House provision prohibiting the use of funds to pay for an abortion, except if the life of the woman would be endangered. Adopted 335-74: R 92-74; D 243-0 (ND 162-0, SD 81-0), Oct. 22, 1990.

505. HR 5241. Fiscal 1991 Treasury Appropriations/-Conference Report. Adoption of the conference report on the bill to appropriate $20,906,325,000 in fiscal 1991 for the Treasury Department, Postal Service and other government agencies. The president requested $20,712,458,000. Adopted 343-67: R 104-63; D 239-4 (ND 159-3, SD 80-1), Oct. 22, 1990.

506. HR 5021. Fiscal 1991 Commerce, Justice, State Appropriations/Conference Report. Adoption of the conference report on the bill to appropriate $19,328,275,000 in fiscal 1991 for the Departments of Commerce, Justice and State, related agencies and the judiciary. President Bush requested $20,009,388,000. Adopted 377-40: R 141-26; D 236-14 (ND 160-10, SD 76-4), Oct. 23, 1990.

507. HR 5021. Fiscal 1991 Commerce, Justice, State Appropriations/Supercomputer Exports. Smith, D-Iowa, motion to concur in a Senate amendment with an amendment to prohibit funds from being used to approve export licenses for supercomputers to any country whose government the president determines is assisting Iraq to improve its ballistic missile technology or chemical, biological or nuclear weapons capability, or to a country the president determines has made inadequate efforts to restrict nationals from assisting Iraq in such endeavors. Motion agreed to 381-39: R 166-3; D 215-36 (ND 141-27, SD 74-9), Oct. 23, 1990.

508. S 2830. Farm Programs Reauthorization/Conference Report. Adoption of the conference report on the bill to revise and extend federal farm price- and income-support programs for major commodities as well as Agriculture Department nutrition programs. Adopted 318-102: R 119-51; D 199-51 (ND 124-43, SD 75-8), Oct. 23, 1990.

509. H Con Res 385. Yugoslavian Human Rights Violations/Adoption. Motion to suspend the rules and adopt the concurrent resolution to express the sense of Congress condemning the use of arbitrary, brutal and fatal force by any party in the Kosovo region in Southern Yugoslavia against the Albanian minority and urging a peaceful resolution of the ethnic crisis between the government of Serbia, the Albanian Democratic Alliance Movement and other parties. Motion rejected 55-362: R 21-148; D 34-214 (ND 28-137, SD 6-77), Oct. 23, 1990. A two-thirds majority of those present and voting (278 in this case) is required for passage under suspension of the rules.

510. HR 4333. Clean Coastal Beaches/Passage. Motion to suspend the rules and pass the bill to authorize $4 million in each of fiscal years 1991 and 1992 to establish uniform procedures for ensuring the quality of coastal recreational waters. The bill also authorizes $3 million annually for federal matching grants to states to assist in complying with new Environmental Protection Agency standards. Motion agreed to 326-89: R 94-75; D 232-14 (ND 160-4, SD 72-10), Oct. 23, 1990. A two-thirds majority of those present and voting (277 in this case) is required for passage under suspension of the rules.

511. H Con Res 382. Terms of Iraq and Kuwait Conflict Resolution/Adoption. Motion to suspend the rules and adopt the concurrent resolution to express the sense of Congress that the crisis created by Iraq's invasion and occupation of Kuwait must be addressed and resolved on its own terms separately from the other conflicts in the region. Motion agreed to 406-5: R 166-1; D 240-4 (ND 158-4, SD 82-0), Oct. 23, 1990. A two-thirds majority of those present and voting (275 in this case) is required for passage under suspension of the rules.

KEY

- Y Voted for (yea).
- # Paired for.
- + Announced for.
- N Voted against (nay).
- X Paired against.
- \- Announced against.
- P Voted "present."
- C Voted "present" to avoid possible conflict of interest.
- ? Did not vote or otherwise make a position known.

Democrats ***Republicans***

	504	505	506	507	508	509	510	511
ALABAMA								
1 ***Callahan***	N	Y	Y	Y	Y	N	Y	Y
2 ***Dickinson***	N	Y	?	?	?	?	?	?
3 Browder	Y	Y	Y	Y	Y	N	Y	Y
4 Bevill	Y	Y	Y	Y	Y	N	Y	Y
5 Flippo	Y	Y	Y	Y	Y	N	Y	Y
6 Erdreich	Y	Y	Y	Y	Y	N	Y	Y
7 Harris	Y	Y	Y	Y	Y	N	Y	Y
ALASKA								
AL ***Young***	Y	Y	Y	Y	Y	N	N	Y
ARIZONA								
1 ***Rhodes***	Y	Y	Y	Y	Y	N	N	Y
2 Udall	Y	Y	Y	Y	Y	N	Y	Y
3 ***Stump***	N	N	N	Y	N	N	N	Y
4 ***Kyl***	N	N	Y	Y	N	N	N	Y
5 ***Kolbe***	N	N	Y	Y	Y	N	N	Y
ARKANSAS								
1 Alexander	Y	Y	Y	Y	Y	N	Y	Y
2 ***Robinson***	N	N	Y	Y	Y	N	N	Y
3 ***Hammerschmidt***	Y	N	Y	Y	Y	N	Y	Y
4 Anthony	Y	Y	Y	Y	Y	N	Y	Y
CALIFORNIA								
1 Bosco	Y	Y	Y	Y	Y	N	Y	Y
2 ***Herger***	N	N	N	Y	Y	N	N	Y
3 Matsui	Y	Y	Y	Y	Y	N	Y	Y
4 Fazio	Y	Y	Y	Y	Y	N	Y	Y
5 Pelosi	Y	Y	Y	N	N	N	Y	Y
6 Boxer	Y	Y	Y	N	N	N	Y	Y
7 Miller	Y	Y	Y	Y	N	N	Y	Y
8 Dellums	Y	Y	Y	N	N	N	Y	Y
9 Stark	Y	Y	Y	Y	N	N	Y	Y
10 Edwards	Y	Y	Y	Y	Y	N	Y	Y
11 Lantos	?	?	Y	Y	Y	Y	Y	Y
12 ***Campbell***	N	N	N	Y	N	N	Y	Y
13 Mineta	Y	Y	Y	Y	Y	N	Y	Y
14 ***Shumway***	N	N	N	Y	N	N	N	Y
15 Condit	Y	Y	Y	Y	Y	N	Y	Y
16 Panetta	Y	Y	Y	Y	Y	N	Y	Y
17 ***Pashayan***	Y	Y	Y	Y	Y	N	N	?
18 Lehman	Y	Y	Y	N	Y	N	Y	?
19 ***Lagomarsino***	Y	Y	Y	Y	N	N	Y	Y
20 ***Thomas***	N	N	Y	Y	Y	N	N	Y
21 ***Gallegly***	Y	Y	Y	Y	N	N	Y	Y
22 ***Moorhead***	N	N	Y	Y	N	N	N	Y
23 Beilenson	Y	Y	Y	Y	N	N	Y	Y
24 Waxman	Y	Y	Y	Y	Y	Y	Y	Y
25 Roybal	Y	Y	Y	Y	Y	N	Y	Y
26 Berman	Y	Y	Y	Y	Y	Y	Y	Y
27 Levine	?	Y	Y	N	Y	Y	Y	Y
28 Dixon	Y	Y	Y	Y	Y	N	Y	Y
29 Hawkins	Y	Y	Y	Y	Y	N	?	?
30 Martinez	Y	Y	?	?	?	?	?	?
31 Dymally	Y	Y	Y	Y	N	N	Y	N
32 Anderson	Y	Y	Y	Y	Y	N	Y	Y
33 ***Dreier***	N	N	Y	Y	N	N	Y	Y
34 Torres	Y	Y	Y	N	Y	N	Y	Y
35 ***Lewis***	Y	Y	Y	Y	Y	Y	N	Y
36 Brown	Y	Y	Y	Y	Y	N	Y	Y
37 ***McCandless***	Y	Y	Y	Y	Y	N	Y	Y
38 ***Dornan***	N	N	Y	Y	N	N	N	Y
39 ***Dannemeyer***	N	N	N	Y	N	N	N	Y
40 ***Cox***	N	N	N	Y	N	N	Y	Y
41 ***Lowery***	Y	Y	Y	Y	N	N	N	Y
42 ***Rohrabacher***	N	N	Y	Y	N	Y	Y	Y
43 ***Packard***	N	N	Y	Y	N	N	N	Y
44 Bates	Y	Y	Y	Y	N	N	Y	Y
45 ***Hunter***	?	N	Y	Y	N	N	Y	Y
COLORADO								
1 Schroeder	Y	Y	N	N	N	N	Y	Y
2 Skaggs	Y	Y	Y	Y	N	N	Y	Y
3 Campbell	Y	Y	Y	Y	Y	N	Y	Y
4 ***Brown***	N	N	N	Y	N	Y	Y	Y
5 ***Hefley***	N	N	Y	Y	N	N	Y	Y
6 ***Schaefer***	N	N	Y	Y	Y	N	Y	Y
CONNECTICUT								
1 Kennelly	Y	?	Y	Y	Y	N	Y	Y
2 Gejdenson	Y	Y	Y	Y	Y	N	Y	Y
3 Morrison	+	?	?	?	?	?	?	?
4 ***Shays***	Y	N	Y	Y	N	N	Y	Y
5 ***Rowland***	?	?	?	?	?	?	?	?
6 ***Johnson***	N	N	Y	Y	Y	N	Y	Y
DELAWARE								
AL Carper	Y	Y	Y	Y	Y	N	Y	Y
FLORIDA								
1 Hutto	Y	Y	Y	Y	Y	N	N	Y
2 ***Grant***	Y	Y	Y	Y	Y	N	N	Y
3 Bennett	Y	Y	Y	Y	N	N	Y	Y
4 ***James***	Y	Y	Y	Y	Y	N	N	Y
5 ***McCollum***	N	Y	?	?	X	?	?	?
6 ***Stearns***	Y	Y	Y	Y	Y	N	N	Y
7 Gibbons	Y	Y	Y	Y	Y	N	Y	Y
8 ***Young***	Y	Y	Y	Y	Y	N	N	Y
9 ***Bilirakis***	Y	Y	Y	Y	Y	N	N	Y
10 ***Ireland***	Y	?	Y	Y	Y	N	N	Y
11 Nelson	Y	Y	Y	N	Y	Y	Y	Y
12 ***Lewis***	N	N	Y	Y	Y	N	N	Y
13 ***Goss***	+	N	N	Y	N	Y	N	Y
14 Johnston	?	Y	Y	Y	Y	Y	N	Y
15 ***Shaw***	Y	N	Y	Y	Y	N	N	Y
16 Smith	Y	Y	Y	N	Y	N	N	Y
17 Lehman	Y	Y	Y	N	Y	Y	Y	Y
18 ***Ros-Lehtinen***	Y	Y	Y	N	Y	N	N	Y
19 Fascell	Y	Y	Y	Y	Y	Y	N	Y
GEORGIA								
1 Thomas	Y	Y	Y	Y	Y	N	Y	Y
2 Hatcher	Y	Y	Y	Y	Y	N	Y	Y
3 Ray	Y	Y	Y	Y	Y	N	Y	Y
4 Jones	Y	Y	Y	N	Y	N	Y	Y
5 Lewis	Y	Y	Y	N	N	N	Y	Y
6 ***Gingrich***	N	?	Y	Y	Y	N	Y	Y
7 Darden	Y	Y	Y	Y	Y	N	Y	Y
8 Rowland	Y	Y	Y	Y	Y	N	Y	Y
9 Jenkins	Y	Y	Y	Y	Y	N	Y	Y
10 Barnard	Y	Y	Y	Y	Y	N	Y	Y
HAWAII								
1 ***Saiki***	Y	Y	Y	Y	Y	Y	Y	Y
2 Mink	Y	Y	Y	Y	Y	N	Y	Y
IDAHO								
1 ***Craig***	N	N	Y	Y	Y	N	N	Y
2 Stallings	Y	Y	Y	Y	Y	N	Y	Y
ILLINOIS								
1 Hayes	Y	Y	Y	Y	N	N	Y	Y
2 Savage	Y	Y	Y	N	Y	N	Y	N
3 Russo	Y	Y	Y	Y	N	N	Y	Y
4 Sangmeister	Y	Y	Y	Y	Y	N	Y	Y
5 Lipinski	Y	Y	Y	Y	Y	N	Y	Y
6 ***Hyde***	Y	Y	Y	Y	Y	Y	Y	Y
7 Collins	Y	Y	Y	Y	Y	N	Y	Y
8 Rostenkowski	Y	Y	Y	Y	N	N	Y	Y
9 Yates	Y	Y	Y	N	N	Y	Y	Y
10 ***Porter***	Y	N	Y	Y	N	Y	N	Y
11 Annunzio	Y	Y	Y	Y	Y	N	Y	Y
12 ***Crane***	N	N	?	Y	N	N	N	Y
13 ***Fawell***	N	N	N	N	N	N	Y	N
14 ***Hastert***	Y	Y	Y	Y	Y	Y	N	Y
15 ***Madigan***	Y	N	Y	Y	Y	N	N	Y
16 ***Martin***	?	?	?	?	#	?	?	?
17 Evans	Y	Y	Y	Y	Y	N	Y	Y
18 ***Michel***	?	?	Y	Y	Y	N	N	Y
19 Bruce	Y	Y	Y	Y	Y	N	Y	Y
20 Durbin	Y	Y	Y	Y	Y	Y	Y	Y
21 Costello	Y	Y	Y	Y	Y	N	Y	Y
22 Poshard	Y	Y	Y	Y	Y	N	Y	Y
INDIANA								
1 Visclosky	Y	Y	Y	Y	Y	N	Y	Y
2 Sharp	Y	Y	Y	Y	Y	N	Y	Y
3 ***Hiler***	N	N	Y	Y	Y	N	Y	Y

ND Northern Democrats SD Southern Democrats

Member	504	505	506	507	508	509	510	511
4 Long	Y	Y	Y	Y	Y	N	Y	Y
5 Jontz	Y	Y	Y	Y	Y	N	Y	Y
6 ***Burton***	N	Y	N	Y	Y	N	N	Y
7 ***Myers***	Y	Y	Y	Y	Y	N	N	Y
8 McCloskey	Y	Y	Y	Y	Y	N	Y	Y
9 Hamilton	Y	Y	Y	Y	Y	N	Y	Y
10 Jacobs	Y	N	N	Y	N	N	Y	Y
IOWA								
1 ***Leach***	N	Y	Y	Y	N	N	Y	Y
2 ***Tauke***	N	Y	Y	Y	N	Y	N	Y
3 Nagle	Y	Y	Y	Y	N	N	Y	Y
4 Smith	Y	Y	Y	Y	Y	N	Y	Y
5 ***Lightfoot***	N	N	Y	Y	N	Y	N	Y
6 ***Grandy***	Y	Y	Y	Y	Y	N	N	Y
KANSAS								
1 ***Roberts***	N	N	N	Y	Y	N	Y	Y
2 Slattery	Y	Y	N	Y	Y	N	Y	Y
3 ***Meyers***	Y	Y	Y	Y	Y	N	Y	Y
4 Glickman	Y	Y	N	Y	Y	N	Y	Y
5 ***Whittaker***	Y	Y	Y	Y	Y	N	Y	Y
KENTUCKY								
1 Hubbard	Y	Y	Y	Y	Y	N	Y	Y
2 Natcher	Y	Y	Y	Y	Y	N	Y	Y
3 Mazzoli	Y	Y	Y	Y	Y	N	Y	Y
4 ***Bunning***	N	N	Y	Y	Y	N	Y	Y
5 ***Rogers***	Y	Y	Y	Y	Y	N	Y	Y
6 ***Hopkins***	Y	Y	Y	Y	Y	N	N	Y
7 Perkins	Y	Y	Y	Y	Y	N	Y	Y
LOUISIANA								
1 ***Livingston***	Y	N	Y	Y	Y	N	Y	Y
2 Boggs	Y	Y	Y	Y	Y	N	Y	Y
3 Tauzin	Y	Y	Y	Y	Y	N	Y	Y
4 ***McCrery***	Y	Y	Y	?	Y	N	Y	Y
5 Huckaby	Y	Y	Y	Y	Y	N	Y	Y
6 ***Baker***	?	Y	Y	Y	Y	N	N	Y
7 Hayes	Y	Y	Y	Y	N	N	N	Y
8 ***Holloway***	Y	N	Y	Y	Y	N	N	Y
MAINE								
1 Brennan	?	?	?	?	?	?	?	?
2 ***Snowe***	Y	N	Y	Y	Y	Y	Y	Y
MARYLAND								
1 Dyson	Y	Y	Y	Y	Y	N	Y	Y
2 ***Bentley***	Y	Y	Y	Y	Y	N	N	Y
3 Cardin	Y	Y	Y	N	Y	Y	N	Y
4 McMillen	Y	Y	Y	Y	Y	N	Y	Y
5 Hoyer	Y	Y	Y	Y	Y	Y	Y	Y
6 Byron	Y	Y	Y	Y	Y	N	N	Y
7 Mfume	Y	Y	Y	N	N	N	N	Y
8 ***Morella***	Y	Y	Y	Y	N	N	Y	Y
MASSACHUSETTS								
1 ***Conte***	Y	Y	Y	Y	N	N	Y	Y
2 Neal	Y	Y	Y	Y	N	Y	Y	Y
3 Early	Y	Y	Y	Y	Y	Y	Y	Y
4 Frank	Y	?	Y	N	Y	Y	Y	Y
5 Atkins	Y	Y	Y	N	N	N	Y	Y
6 Mavroules	Y	Y	Y	Y	Y	N	Y	Y
7 Markey	Y	Y	Y	Y	Y	Y	Y	Y
8 Kennedy	Y	Y	Y	Y	Y	Y	Y	Y
9 Moakley	Y	Y	Y	Y	Y	Y	Y	Y
10 Studds	Y	Y	Y	Y	N	N	Y	Y
11 Donnelly	Y	Y	Y	Y	N	Y	Y	Y
MICHIGAN								
1 Conyers	Y	?	Y	N	Y	N	Y	Y
2 ***Pursell***	N	Y	Y	Y	Y	Y	Y	Y
3 Wolpe	Y	Y	Y	Y	Y	Y	Y	Y
4 ***Upton***	N	N	Y	Y	Y	Y	Y	Y
5 ***Henry***	N	N	N	Y	Y	Y	Y	Y
6 Carr	Y	Y	Y	Y	Y	?	?	?
7 Kildee	Y	Y	Y	Y	Y	Y	Y	Y
8 Traxler	Y	Y	Y	Y	Y	N	Y	Y
9 ***Vander Jagt***	N	Y	Y	Y	Y	N	Y	Y
10 ***Schuette***	?	?	Y	Y	Y	?	?	?
11 ***Davis***	Y	Y	Y	Y	Y	N	N	Y
12 Bonior	Y	Y	Y	Y	Y	Y	Y	Y
13 Crockett	Y	Y	Y	?	Y	?	?	?
14 Hertel	Y	Y	N	Y	N	Y	Y	Y
15 Ford	Y	Y	Y	Y	Y	N	Y	Y
16 Dingell	Y	?	N	Y	#	?	?	?
17 Levin	Y	Y	Y	Y	Y	N	Y	Y
18 ***Broomfield***	Y	N	Y	Y	Y	Y	Y	Y
MINNESOTA								
1 Penny	Y	N	N	Y	Y	N	Y	Y
2 ***Weber***	Y	?	Y	Y	N	N	Y	Y
3 ***Frenzel***	N	N	N	Y	N	N	Y	Y
4 Vento	Y	Y	Y	Y	Y	N	Y	Y
5 Sabo	Y	Y	Y	Y	N	N	Y	Y
6 Sikorski	Y	Y	Y	Y	Y	N	Y	Y
7 ***Stangeland***	Y	Y	Y	Y	Y	N	Y	Y
8 Oberstar	Y	Y	Y	Y	N	N	Y	Y
MISSISSIPPI								
1 Whitten	Y	Y	Y	Y	N	N	Y	Y
2 Espy	Y	Y	Y	Y	Y	N	Y	Y
3 Montgomery	Y	Y	Y	Y	Y	N	Y	Y
4 Parker	Y	N	N	Y	Y	N	Y	Y
5 Taylor	Y	Y	Y	Y	N	N	Y	Y
MISSOURI								
1 Clay	Y	Y	Y	Y	Y	N	Y	N
2 ***Buechner***	N	N	Y	Y	N	N	Y	Y
3 Gephardt	Y	Y	Y	Y	?	?	?	?
4 Skelton	Y	Y	?	Y	Y	N	N	Y
5 Wheat	Y	Y	Y	N	Y	N	Y	Y
6 ***Coleman***	Y	Y	Y	Y	Y	N	Y	Y
7 ***Hancock***	N	N	N	Y	N	N	N	Y
8 ***Emerson***	Y	Y	Y	Y	Y	N	Y	Y
9 Volkmer	Y	Y	Y	Y	Y	N	Y	Y
MONTANA								
1 Williams	Y	Y	Y	Y	N	N	Y	Y
2 ***Marlenee***	N	Y	Y	Y	N	N	N	Y
NEBRASKA								
1 ***Bereuter***	Y	Y	N	Y	N	N	Y	Y
2 Hoagland	Y	Y	Y	Y	Y	N	Y	Y
3 ***Smith***	Y	Y	Y	Y	Y	N	Y	Y
NEVADA								
1 Bilbray	Y	Y	Y	N	Y	N	Y	Y
2 ***Vucanovich***	Y	Y	Y	Y	Y	N	N	Y
NEW HAMPSHIRE								
1 ***Smith***	N	N	N	Y	N	N	Y	Y
2 ***Douglas***	N	N	N	Y	N	N	Y	Y
NEW JERSEY								
1 Vacancy								
2 Hughes	Y	Y	Y	Y	N	N	Y	Y
3 Pallone	Y	N	N	Y	N	N	Y	Y
4 ***Smith***	Y	Y	Y	Y	Y	N	Y	Y
5 ***Roukema***	-	X	?	Y	N	N	Y	Y
6 Dwyer	Y	Y	Y	Y	N	N	Y	Y
7 ***Rinaldo***	Y	Y	Y	Y	Y	N	Y	Y
8 Roe	Y	Y	Y	Y	Y	N	Y	Y
9 Torricelli	Y	Y	Y	N	?	?	?	?
10 Payne	Y	Y	Y	Y	Y	N	Y	Y
11 ***Gallo***	Y	Y	Y	Y	N	N	Y	Y
12 ***Courter***	Y	Y	Y	Y	Y	N	Y	Y
13 ***Saxton***	Y	Y	Y	Y	N	N	Y	Y
14 Guarini	Y	Y	Y	Y	Y	N	Y	Y
NEW MEXICO								
1 ***Schiff***	Y	Y	Y	Y	Y	N	N	Y
2 ***Skeen***	Y	Y	Y	Y	Y	N	N	Y
3 Richardson	Y	Y	Y	Y	Y	N	Y	Y
NEW YORK								
1 Hochbrueckner	Y	Y	Y	Y	Y	N	Y	Y
2 Downey	Y	Y	Y	Y	N	N	Y	Y
3 Mrazek	Y	Y	Y	Y	N	N	Y	Y
4 ***Lent***	Y	Y	Y	Y	Y	N	Y	?
5 ***McGrath***	Y	Y	Y	Y	Y	N	Y	Y
6 Flake	Y	Y	Y	Y	Y	N	Y	Y
7 Ackerman	Y	Y	Y	N	Y	Y	Y	Y
8 Scheuer	Y	Y	Y	?	N	N	Y	Y
9 Manton	Y	Y	Y	Y	Y	N	Y	Y
10 Schumer	Y	Y	Y	Y	Y	Y	Y	Y
11 Towns	?	?	Y	N	Y	N	Y	Y
12 Owens	Y	Y	Y	N	N	N	Y	Y
13 Solarz	Y	Y	Y	Y	Y	Y	Y	Y
14 ***Molinari***	Y	Y	Y	Y	Y	Y	Y	Y
15 ***Green***	Y	Y	Y	Y	N	Y	Y	Y
16 Rangel	Y	Y	Y	N	Y	N	Y	Y
17 Weiss	Y	Y	Y	N	N	Y	Y	Y
18 Serrano	Y	Y	Y	N	Y	Y	Y	Y
19 Engel	Y	Y	Y	?	Y	Y	Y	Y
20 Lowey	Y	Y	Y	Y	Y	N	Y	Y
21 ***Fish***	Y	Y	Y	Y	Y	N	Y	Y
22 ***Gilman***	Y	Y	Y	N	Y	Y	Y	Y
23 McNulty	Y	Y	Y	Y	Y	Y	Y	Y
24 ***Solomon***	N	Y	Y	Y	Y	N	Y	Y
25 ***Boehlert***	Y	Y	Y	Y	Y	N	Y	Y
26 ***Martin***	Y	Y	Y	Y	Y	N	Y	Y
27 ***Walsh***	Y	Y	Y	Y	Y	N	Y	Y
28 McHugh	Y	Y	Y	Y	Y	N	Y	Y
29 ***Horton***	Y	Y	Y	Y	Y	N	Y	Y
30 Slaughter	Y	Y	Y	Y	Y	N	Y	Y
31 ***Paxon***	N	N	Y	Y	Y	N	Y	Y
32 LaFalce	?	?	Y	Y	Y	N	Y	Y
33 Nowak	Y	Y	Y	Y	N	N	Y	Y
34 ***Houghton***	N	Y	Y	Y	Y	Y	N	Y
NORTH CAROLINA								
1 Jones	Y	Y	Y	Y	Y	N	Y	Y
2 Valentine	Y	Y	Y	Y	Y	N	Y	Y
3 Lancaster	Y	Y	?	Y	Y	N	Y	Y
4 Price	Y	Y	Y	Y	Y	N	Y	Y
5 Neal	Y	Y	Y	Y	Y	N	Y	Y
6 ***Coble***	Y	Y	Y	Y	Y	N	N	Y
7 Rose	Y	Y	Y	N	Y	N	Y	Y
8 Hefner	Y	Y	Y	Y	Y	N	Y	Y
9 ***McMillan***	N	Y	Y	Y	Y	N	Y	Y
10 ***Ballenger***	N	Y	Y	Y	Y	N	N	Y
11 Clarke	Y	Y	Y	Y	Y	N	Y	Y
NORTH DAKOTA								
AL Dorgan	Y	Y	Y	Y	N	N	Y	Y
OHIO								
1 Luken	Y	Y	Y	Y	Y	N	Y	Y
2 ***Gradison***	Y	Y	Y	Y	N	N	N	Y
3 Hall	Y	Y	Y	Y	Y	Y	Y	Y
4 ***Oxley***	N	Y	Y	Y	Y	N	N	Y
5 ***Gillmor***	N	Y	Y	Y	Y	N	N	Y
6 ***McEwen***	N	N	N	Y	Y	N	N	Y
7 ***DeWine***	Y	Y	Y	Y	Y	N	Y	Y
8 ***Lukens***	N	N	?	?	?	?	?	?
9 Kaptur	?	#	Y	Y	Y	N	Y	Y
10 ***Miller***	Y	Y	Y	Y	Y	Y	Y	Y
11 Eckart	Y	Y	Y	Y	Y	N	Y	Y
12 ***Kasich***	N	Y	Y	Y	Y	N	Y	Y
13 Pease	?	Y	Y	Y	Y	N	Y	Y
14 Sawyer	Y	Y	Y	Y	Y	N	Y	Y
15 ***Wylie***	Y	Y	Y	Y	Y	N	Y	Y
16 ***Regula***	Y	Y	Y	Y	Y	N	Y	Y
17 Traficant	Y	Y	Y	Y	N	N	Y	Y
18 Applegate	Y	Y	N	Y	Y	N	Y	Y
19 Feighan	Y	Y	Y	Y	Y	N	Y	Y
20 Oakar	Y	Y	Y	Y	Y	N	Y	P
21 Stokes	Y	Y	Y	Y	Y	N	Y	Y
OKLAHOMA								
1 ***Inhofe***	Y	Y	Y	Y	Y	N	N	Y
2 Synar	Y	Y	Y	Y	N	Y	Y	Y
3 Watkins	Y	Y	Y	Y	Y	N	Y	Y
4 McCurdy	Y	Y	Y	Y	Y	Y	Y	Y
5 ***Edwards***	Y	Y	Y	Y	Y	N	N	Y
6 English	Y	Y	Y	Y	Y	N	Y	Y
OREGON								
1 AuCoin	Y	Y	Y	Y	Y	N	Y	Y
2 ***Smith, B.***	N	Y	Y	Y	N	N	Y	Y
3 Wyden	Y	Y	Y	Y	Y	N	Y	Y
4 DeFazio	?	Y	Y	N	Y	N	Y	Y
5 ***Smith, D.***	N	N	Y	Y	Y	N	Y	Y
PENNSYLVANIA								
1 Foglietta	Y	Y	Y	Y	Y	N	Y	Y
2 Gray	?	Y	Y	Y	Y	N	Y	Y
3 Borski	Y	Y	Y	Y	Y	N	Y	Y
4 Kolter	Y	Y	Y	Y	N	N	Y	Y
5 ***Schulze***	Y	Y	Y	Y	Y	N	Y	Y
6 Yatron	?	?	Y	Y	Y	N	Y	Y
7 ***Weldon***	Y	Y	Y	Y	N	N	Y	Y
8 Kostmayer	Y	?	Y	N	Y	N	Y	Y
9 ***Shuster***	N	N	N	Y	Y	N	Y	Y
10 ***McDade***	Y	Y	Y	Y	N	N	Y	Y
11 Kanjorski	Y	Y	Y	Y	N	N	Y	Y
12 Murtha	Y	Y	Y	Y	?	?	?	?
13 ***Coughlin***	Y	Y	Y	Y	N	N	Y	Y
14 Coyne	Y	Y	Y	Y	Y	N	Y	Y
15 ***Ritter***	Y	Y	Y	Y	Y	N	Y	Y
16 ***Walker***	N	N	N	Y	Y	N	Y	Y
17 ***Gekas***	Y	Y	Y	Y	Y	N	Y	Y
18 Walgren	Y	Y	Y	Y	Y	N	Y	Y
19 ***Goodling***	Y	Y	Y	Y	Y	N	Y	Y
20 Gaydos	Y	Y	Y	Y	Y	N	Y	Y
21 ***Ridge***	?	?	Y	Y	Y	N	N	Y
22 Murphy	Y	Y	N	Y	Y	N	Y	Y
23 ***Clinger***	Y	Y	Y	Y	Y	N	Y	Y
RHODE ISLAND								
1 ***Machtley***	Y	Y	Y	Y	Y	N	Y	Y
2 ***Schneider***	Y	Y	Y	Y	Y	N	Y	Y
SOUTH CAROLINA								
1 ***Ravenel***	Y	Y	Y	Y	Y	N	Y	Y
2 ***Spence***	N	Y	Y	Y	Y	N	Y	Y
3 Derrick	Y	Y	Y	Y	Y	N	Y	Y
4 Patterson	Y	Y	Y	Y	Y	N	Y	Y
5 Spratt	Y	Y	Y	Y	Y	N	Y	Y
6 Tallon	Y	Y	Y	Y	Y	N	Y	Y
SOUTH DAKOTA								
AL Johnson	Y	Y	Y	Y	N	N	Y	Y
TENNESSEE								
1 ***Quillen***	Y	Y	Y	Y	Y	N	Y	Y
2 ***Duncan***	Y	Y	Y	Y	Y	N	N	Y
3 Lloyd	Y	Y	Y	Y	Y	N	Y	Y
4 Cooper	Y	Y	Y	Y	Y	N	Y	Y
5 Clement	Y	Y	Y	Y	Y	N	Y	Y
6 Gordon	Y	Y	Y	Y	Y	N	Y	Y
7 ***Sundquist***	N	Y	Y	Y	Y	N	N	Y
8 Tanner	Y	Y	Y	Y	Y	N	N	Y
9 Ford	Y	Y	Y	Y	Y	N	Y	Y
TEXAS								
1 Chapman	Y	Y	Y	Y	Y	N	Y	Y
2 Wilson	Y	Y	Y	Y	Y	N	Y	Y
3 ***Bartlett***	N	N	Y	Y	N	N	N	Y
4 Hall	Y	Y	N	Y	Y	N	Y	Y
5 Bryant	Y	?	Y	N	Y	N	Y	Y
6 ***Barton***	N	N	Y	Y	Y	N	N	Y
7 ***Archer***	N	N	N	Y	N	N	N	Y
8 ***Fields***	N	N	N	Y	N	N	Y	Y
9 Brooks	?	?	?	Y	Y	N	Y	Y
10 Pickle	Y	Y	Y	Y	Y	N	Y	Y
11 Leath	Y	Y	Y	Y	Y	N	Y	Y
12 Geren	Y	Y	Y	Y	Y	N	Y	Y
13 Sarpalius	Y	Y	Y	Y	N	N	N	Y
14 Laughlin	Y	Y	N	Y	Y	N	Y	Y
15 de la Garza	Y	Y	Y	Y	Y	N	Y	Y
16 Coleman	Y	Y	Y	Y	Y	N	Y	Y
17 Stenholm	Y	Y	Y	Y	Y	N	N	Y
18 Washington	Y	Y	?	N	N	N	?	?
19 ***Combest***	N	N	Y	Y	Y	N	N	Y
20 Gonzalez	Y	Y	Y	Y	Y	N	Y	Y
21 ***Smith***	N	Y	Y	Y	Y	N	N	Y
22 ***DeLay***	N	N	Y	Y	N	N	N	Y
23 Bustamante	Y	Y	Y	Y	Y	N	Y	Y
24 Frost	Y	Y	Y	Y	Y	N	Y	Y
25 Andrews	Y	Y	Y	Y	Y	N	Y	Y
26 ***Armey***	N	N	N	Y	N	N	N	Y
27 Ortiz	Y	Y	Y	Y	Y	N	Y	Y
UTAH								
1 ***Hansen***	N	Y	Y	Y	Y	N	N	Y
2 Owens	Y	Y	Y	N	Y	Y	Y	Y
3 ***Nielson***	N	N	N	Y	Y	N	N	Y
VERMONT								
AL ***Smith***	Y	Y	?	?	X	?	?	?
VIRGINIA								
1 ***Bateman***	Y	Y	Y	Y	Y	N	N	Y
2 Pickett	Y	Y	N	Y	Y	N	N	Y
3 ***Bliley***	Y	Y	Y	Y	Y	N	N	Y
4 Sisisky	Y	Y	Y	N	Y	N	N	Y
5 Payne	Y	Y	Y	Y	Y	N	Y	Y
6 Olin	Y	Y	Y	Y	Y	N	Y	Y
7 ***Slaughter***	N	N	Y	Y	Y	N	N	Y
8 ***Parris***	Y	Y	?	Y	Y	N	N	Y
9 Boucher	Y	Y	Y	Y	Y	N	Y	Y
10 ***Wolf***	Y	Y	Y	Y	Y	N	Y	Y
WASHINGTON								
1 ***Miller***	+	Y	Y	Y	Y	Y	Y	Y
2 Swift	Y	Y	Y	Y	Y	N	Y	Y
3 Unsoeld	Y	Y	Y	Y	Y	N	Y	Y
4 ***Morrison***	Y	Y	Y	Y	Y	N	Y	Y
5 Foley								
6 Dicks	Y	Y	Y	Y	Y	N	Y	Y
7 McDermott	Y	Y	Y	Y	Y	N	Y	Y
8 ***Chandler***	Y	Y	Y	Y	Y	N	Y	Y
WEST VIRGINIA								
1 Mollohan	Y	Y	Y	Y	Y	N	Y	Y
2 Staggers	Y	Y	Y	N	Y	N	Y	Y
3 Wise	?	Y	Y	Y	Y	N	Y	Y
4 Rahall	Y	Y	Y	Y	Y	N	Y	N
WISCONSIN								
1 Aspin	Y	Y	Y	Y	N	N	Y	Y
2 Kastenmeier	Y	Y	Y	Y	N	N	Y	Y
3 ***Gunderson***	Y	Y	Y	Y	Y	N	N	Y
4 Kleczka	Y	Y	Y	Y	Y	N	Y	Y
5 Moody	Y	Y	Y	Y	N	N	Y	Y
6 ***Petri***	N	N	N	Y	N	N	N	Y
7 Obey	Y	Y	Y	Y	N	N	Y	Y
8 ***Roth***	Y	Y	Y	Y	Y	N	N	Y
9 ***Sensenbrenner***	N	N	N	Y	N	N	N	Y
WYOMING								
AL ***Thomas***	N	N	Y	Y	Y	N	Y	Y

Southern states - Ala., Ark., Fla., Ga., Ky., La., Miss., N.C., Okla., S.C., Tenn., Texas, Va.
Omitted votes are quorum calls, which CQ does not include in its vote charts.

HOUSE VOTES 512, 513, 514, 515, 516, 517

512. S 1430. National and Community Service Act/Conference Report. Adoption of the conference report (thus clearing the measure for the president) on the bill to authorize grants to states and localities to encourage community service; create or expand Youth Service Corps; authorize demonstration national service programs offering post-service vouchers for education and housing; and authorize a Points of Light Foundation to coordinate and foster volunteerism. Adopted 235-186: R 22-145; D 213-41 (ND 159-14, SD 54-27), Oct. 24, 1990. A "nay" was a vote supporting the president's position.

513. S 2924. National Mandatory Fish Inspection/Rule. Adoption of the rule (H Res 511) to provide for House floor consideration of the bill to establish a national mandatory fish inspection program to be administered by the Food Safety and Inspection Service of the Agriculture Department. Adopted 300-119: R 62-106; D 238-13 (ND 161-7, SD 77-6), Oct. 24, 1990.

514. S 2924. National Mandatory Fish Inspection/Substitute. Studds, D-Mass., substitute amendment to establish a national shellfish inspection program, to be administered by the Food and Drug Administration; require the FDA to set health standards for fish and fish products; and require the president, within 18 months of the bill's enactment, to submit to Congress a proposal for a comprehensive mandatory fish inspection program for all fish and fish products. Adopted 277-153: R 96-78; D 181-75 (ND 140-34, SD 41-41), Oct. 24, 1990.

515. S 2924. National Mandatory Fish Inspection/Passage. Passage of the bill to establish a national shellfish inspection program, to be administered by the Food and Drug Administration; require the FDA to set health standards for fish and fish products; and require the president, within 18 months of the bill's enactment, to submit to Congress a proposal for a comprehensive mandatory fish inspection program for all fish and fish products. Passed 324-106: R 115-59; D 209-47 (ND 160-14, SD 49-33), Oct. 24, 1990.

516. HR 4739. Fiscal 1991 Defense Authorization/Rule. Adoption of the rule (H Res 521) to waive certain points of order against and to provide for House floor consideration of the conference report on the bill to authorize $210.3 billion for defense programs in fiscal 1991. Adopted 239-161: R 1-157; D 238-4 (ND 160-3, SD 78-1), Oct. 24, 1990.

517. HR 4739. Fiscal 1991 Defense Authorization/Conference Report. Adoption of the conference report on the bill to authorize $210,269,400,000 for defense programs in fiscal 1991. The president requested $229,326,000,000. Adopted 271-156: R 65-109; D 206-47 (ND 128-42, SD 78-5), Oct. 24, 1990.

** Rep. Donald E. "Buz" Lukens, R-Ohio, resigned Oct. 24, 1990. The last House vote for which he was eligible was vote 512.*

KEY

- Y Voted for (yea).
- # Paired for.
- + Announced for.
- N Voted against (nay).
- X Paired against.
- - Announced against.
- P Voted "present."
- C Voted "present" to avoid possible conflict of interest.
- ? Did not vote or otherwise make a position known.

Democrats ***Republicans***

	512	513	514	515	516	517
ALABAMA						
1 ***Callahan***	N	Y	Y	Y	N	Y
2 ***Dickinson***	N	N	Y	Y	N	N
3 Browder	Y	Y	N	N	Y	Y
4 Bevill	Y	Y	N	N	Y	Y
5 Flippo	N	Y	?	?	?	Y
6 Erdreich	Y	Y	Y	Y	Y	Y
7 Harris	Y	Y	N	N	Y	Y
ALASKA						
AL ***Young***	N	N	Y	Y	?	N
ARIZONA						
1 ***Rhodes***	N	N	Y	Y	N	N
2 Udall	Y	Y	Y	Y	Y	Y
3 ***Stump***	N	N	N	N	N	N
4 ***Kyl***	N	Y	N	Y	N	N
5 ***Kolbe***	N	N	Y	Y	N	Y
ARKANSAS						
1 Alexander	Y	Y	N	N	Y	Y
2 ***Robinson***	N	N	N	N	N	Y
3 ***Hammerschmidt***	N	N	N	N	?	N
4 Anthony	Y	Y	N	N	?	Y
CALIFORNIA						
1 Bosco	Y	Y	Y	Y	Y	Y
2 ***Herger***	N	N	N	N	N	N
3 Matsui	Y	Y	Y	Y	Y	Y
4 Fazio	Y	Y	Y	Y	Y	Y
5 Pelosi	Y	Y	Y	Y	Y	N
6 Boxer	Y	Y	N	Y	Y	N
7 Miller	N	Y	N	Y	?	N
8 Dellums	Y	Y	Y	Y	Y	N
9 Stark	Y	?	N	N	?	Y
10 Edwards	Y	Y	Y	Y	Y	N
11 Lantos	Y	Y	Y	Y	Y	Y
12 ***Campbell***	N	N	Y	Y	N	N
13 Mineta	Y	Y	N	Y	Y	Y
14 ***Shumway***	?	?	?	?	?	?
15 Condit	Y	Y	N	Y	Y	N
16 Panetta	Y	Y	N	Y	Y	Y
17 ***Pashayan***	N	N	N	N	N	N
18 Lehman	Y	Y	N	Y	Y	Y
19 ***Lagomarsino***	N	N	N	Y	N	N
20 ***Thomas***	N	N	N	N	N	N
21 ***Gallegly***	N	N	N	Y	N	N
22 ***Moorhead***	N	Y	Y	Y	N	N
23 Beilenson	Y	Y	Y	Y	Y	Y
24 Waxman	Y	Y	Y	Y	Y	N
25 Roybal	Y	Y	Y	Y	Y	N
26 Berman	Y	Y	Y	Y	Y	Y
27 Levine	Y	Y	Y	Y	Y	Y
28 Dixon	Y	Y	Y	Y	Y	Y
29 Hawkins	Y	?	Y	Y	?	?
30 Martinez	Y	Y	Y	Y	Y	Y
31 Dymally	Y	Y	Y	Y	Y	Y
32 Anderson	Y	Y	Y	Y	Y	Y
33 ***Dreier***	N	N	Y	Y	N	N
34 Torres	Y	Y	Y	Y	Y	Y
35 ***Lewis***	N	N	N	N	?	N
36 Brown	Y	Y	N	N	Y	Y
37 ***McCandless***	N	N	Y	Y	N	N
38 ***Dornan***	N	?	Y	N	N	N
39 ***Dannemeyer***	N	N	Y	Y	N	N
40 ***Cox***	N	N	N	Y	N	N
41 ***Lowery***	N	N	Y	Y	N	N
42 ***Rohrabacher***	N	N	Y	N	N	N
43 ***Packard***	N	N	Y	Y	N	N
44 Bates	Y	Y	Y	N	Y	Y
45 ***Hunter***	N	N	Y	Y	?	N
COLORADO						
1 Schroeder	Y	Y	Y	Y	Y	Y
2 Skaggs	Y	Y	Y	Y	Y	Y
3 Campbell	Y	Y	Y	Y	Y	Y
4 ***Brown***	N	N	N	N	N	N
5 ***Hefley***	N	N	N	N	N	N
6 ***Schaefer***	N	N	Y	Y	N	N
CONNECTICUT						
1 Kennelly	Y	Y	Y	Y	Y	Y
2 Gejdenson	Y	Y	Y	Y	Y	Y
3 Morrison	Y	Y	Y	Y	?	?
4 ***Shays***	Y	Y	Y	Y	N	N
5 ***Rowland***	?	?	Y	Y	N	Y
6 ***Johnson***	N	N	Y	Y	N	Y
DELAWARE						
AL Carper	Y	Y	Y	Y	Y	Y
FLORIDA						
1 Hutto	N	Y	Y	Y	Y	Y
2 ***Grant***	N	Y	N	Y	N	N
3 Bennett	N	N	Y	Y	Y	Y
4 ***James***	N	N	Y	Y	N	N
5 ***McCollum***	N	N	Y	Y	?	N
6 ***Stearns***	N	N	Y	Y	N	N
7 Gibbons	Y	Y	N	Y	Y	Y
8 ***Young***	N	N	Y	Y	N	N
9 ***Bilirakis***	N	N	Y	Y	N	N
10 ***Ireland***	N	N	N	N	N	Y
11 Nelson	Y	Y	Y	Y	Y	Y
12 ***Lewis***	N	Y	N	N	N	N
13 ***Goss***	N	N	Y	Y	N	N
14 Johnston	Y	Y	Y	Y	Y	N
15 ***Shaw***	N	N	Y	Y	N	N
16 Smith	Y	Y	Y	Y	Y	Y
17 Lehman	Y	Y	Y	Y	Y	Y
18 ***Ros-Lehtinen***	N	N	N	Y	N	N
19 Fascell	Y	Y	Y	Y	Y	Y
GEORGIA						
1 Thomas	Y	Y	N	N	Y	Y
2 Hatcher	N	Y	N	N	Y	Y
3 Ray	?	Y	N	N	Y	Y
4 Jones	N	Y	Y	Y	Y	Y
5 Lewis	Y	Y	Y	Y	Y	N
6 ***Gingrich***	N	N	Y	Y	?	N
7 Darden	Y	Y	N	N	Y	Y
8 Rowland	Y	Y	N	N	Y	Y
9 Jenkins	N	Y	N	N	Y	Y
10 Barnard	N	Y	Y	Y	Y	Y
HAWAII						
1 ***Saiki***	?	Y	Y	Y	N	Y
2 Mink	Y	Y	Y	Y	Y	Y
IDAHO						
1 ***Craig***	N	Y	N	N	N	Y
2 Stallings	N	Y	N	N	?	Y
ILLINOIS						
1 Hayes	Y	Y	Y	Y	Y	N
2 Savage	Y	Y	Y	Y	Y	N
3 Russo	Y	Y	N	Y	?	N
4 Sangmeister	Y	Y	Y	Y	Y	Y
5 Lipinski	Y	?	Y	Y	Y	Y
6 ***Hyde***	N	N	Y	Y	N	N
7 Collins	Y	Y	Y	Y	Y	N
8 Rostenkowski	Y	Y	N	Y	Y	Y
9 Yates	N	Y	N	Y	Y	N
10 ***Porter***	N	?	N	Y	N	N
11 Annunzio	Y	Y	Y	Y	Y	Y
12 ***Crane***	N	N	N	N	N	N
13 ***Fawell***	N	N	Y	Y	N	Y
14 ***Hastert***	N	Y	N	N	N	Y
15 ***Madigan***	N	Y	N	N	N	N
16 ***Martin***	?	?	Y	Y	N	N
17 Evans	Y	Y	Y	Y	Y	Y
18 ***Michel***	N	N	N	N	?	N
19 Bruce	Y	Y	Y	Y	Y	Y
20 Durbin	Y	Y	N	Y	Y	Y
21 Costello	Y	Y	Y	Y	Y	Y
22 Poshard	Y	Y	Y	Y	Y	Y
INDIANA						
1 Visclosky	Y	Y	Y	Y	Y	Y
2 Sharp	Y	Y	Y	Y	Y	Y
3 ***Hiler***	N	Y	N	N	N	Y

ND Northern Democrats SD Southern Democrats

	512	513	514	515	516	517
4 Long	Y	Y	N	N	Y	Y
5 Jontz	Y	Y	N	N	Y	Y
6 ***Burton***	N	N	Y	N	N	N
7 ***Myers***	N	Y	N	N	N	N
8 McCloskey	Y	Y	N	Y	Y	Y
9 Hamilton	Y	Y	N	Y	Y	Y
10 Jacobs	Y	N	Y	Y	N	Y
IOWA						
1 ***Leach***	Y	N	N	Y	N	N
2 ***Tauke***	N	Y	N	Y	N	N
3 Nagle	Y	Y	N	N	Y	Y
4 Smith	Y	Y	N	Y	Y	Y
5 ***Lightfoot***	N	N	N	N	N	N
6 ***Grandy***	N	Y	N	N	N	N
KANSAS						
1 ***Roberts***	N	Y	N	N	N	N
2 Slattery	N	Y	Y	Y	Y	Y
3 ***Meyers***	N	Y	N	Y	N	Y
4 Glickman	N	Y	N	Y	Y	Y
5 ***Whittaker***	N	Y	Y	Y	N	Y
KENTUCKY						
1 Hubbard	N	N	N	N	Y	Y
2 Natcher	Y	Y	N	Y	Y	Y
3 Mazzoli	Y	Y	Y	Y	Y	Y
4 ***Bunning***	N	N	N	Y	N	N
5 ***Rogers***	N	N	N	Y	N	N
6 ***Hopkins***	N	Y	N	Y	N	N
7 Perkins	Y	Y	Y	Y	Y	Y
LOUISIANA						
1 ***Livingston***	N	N	Y	Y	N	N
2 Boggs	Y	N	Y	Y	Y	Y
3 Tauzin	N	N	Y	Y	Y	Y
4 ***McCrery***	?	Y	N	Y	N	N
5 Huckaby	N	Y	N	Y	Y	Y
6 ***Baker***	N	N	Y	Y	N	N
7 Hayes	N	Y	Y	Y	Y	Y
8 ***Holloway***	N	N	Y	Y	N	N
MAINE						
1 Brennan	Y	Y	N	Y	Y	Y
2 ***Snowe***	N	Y	N	Y	N	Y
MARYLAND						
1 Dyson	Y	Y	N	N	Y	Y
2 ***Bentley***	N	N	N	N	N	Y
3 Cardin	Y	Y	Y	Y	Y	Y
4 McMillen	Y	Y	Y	Y	Y	Y
5 Hoyer	Y	Y	Y	Y	Y	Y
6 Byron	N	Y	N	N	Y	Y
7 Mfume	Y	Y	Y	Y	Y	N
8 ***Morella***	Y	Y	Y	Y	N	Y
MASSACHUSETTS						
1 ***Conte***	Y	Y	Y	Y	N	N
2 Neal	Y	Y	Y	Y	Y	Y
3 Early	Y	Y	Y	Y	Y	N
4 Frank	Y	Y	Y	Y	Y	Y
5 Atkins	Y	Y	Y	Y	Y	Y
6 Mavroules	Y	Y	Y	Y	Y	Y
7 Markey	Y	Y	Y	Y	Y	Y
8 Kennedy	Y	Y	Y	Y	Y	Y
9 Moakley	Y	Y	Y	Y	Y	Y
10 Studds	Y	Y	Y	Y	Y	Y
11 Donnelly	Y	Y	Y	Y	Y	Y
MICHIGAN						
1 Conyers	Y	Y	Y	Y	Y	Y
2 ***Pursell***	N	N	Y	Y	N	N
3 Wolpe	Y	Y	Y	Y	Y	Y
4 ***Upton***	N	N	Y	Y	N	N
5 ***Henry***	N	N	N	Y	N	N
6 Carr	Y	Y	Y	Y	Y	Y
7 Kildee	Y	Y	Y	Y	Y	Y
8 Traxler	Y	Y	Y	Y	Y	N
9 ***Vander Jagt***	N	N	Y	Y	?	N
10 ***Schuette***	N	N	Y	N	N	N
11 ***Davis***	Y	Y	Y	Y	N	N
12 Bonior	Y	Y	Y	Y	Y	Y
13 Crockett	Y	?	Y	Y	?	?
14 Hertel	Y	Y	Y	N	Y	Y
15 Ford	Y	Y	Y	Y	?	?
16 Dingell	Y	Y	Y	Y	Y	Y
17 Levin	Y	Y	Y	Y	Y	Y
18 ***Broomfield***	N	N	Y	Y	N	N
MINNESOTA						
1 Penny	N	Y	N	N	Y	Y
2 ***Weber***	N	Y	N	N	?	N
3 ***Frenzel***	N	N	N	N	N	N
4 Vento	Y	Y	Y	Y	Y	Y

	512	513	514	515	516	517
5 Sabo	Y	Y	Y	Y	Y	Y
6 Sikorski	Y	Y	Y	Y	Y	Y
7 ***Stangeland***	N	Y	N	N	N	N
8 Oberstar	Y	Y	Y	Y	Y	Y
MISSISSIPPI						
1 Whitten	Y	Y	N	Y	Y	Y
2 Espy	Y	Y	N	N	Y	Y
3 Montgomery	N	Y	N	N	Y	Y
4 Parker	N	Y	N	N	Y	Y
5 Taylor	N	N	Y	Y	Y	Y
MISSOURI						
1 Clay	Y	Y	Y	Y	?	Y
2 ***Buechner***	N	N	Y	Y	N	Y
3 Gephardt	Y	Y	Y	Y	Y	Y
4 Skelton	Y	Y	N	N	Y	Y
5 Wheat	Y	Y	Y	Y	Y	Y
6 ***Coleman***	N	Y	N	N	N	Y
7 ***Hancock***	N	N	N	N	N	N
8 ***Emerson***	N	Y	N	N	N	Y
9 Volkmer	N	Y	N	N	Y	Y
MONTANA						
1 Williams	Y	Y	N	Y	Y	N
2 ***Marlenee***	N	N	N	N	?	Y
NEBRASKA						
1 ***Bereuter***	Y	Y	N	Y	N	N
2 Hoagland	Y	Y	Y	Y	Y	Y
3 ***Smith***	N	Y	N	N	N	N
NEVADA						
1 Bilbray	Y	Y	Y	Y	Y	Y
2 ***Vucanovich***	N	N	N	N	N	Y
NEW HAMPSHIRE						
1 ***Smith***	N	N	Y	Y	N	N
2 ***Douglas***	N	N	Y	Y	N	N
NEW JERSEY						
1 Vacancy						
2 Hughes	N	N	Y	Y	N	N
3 Pallone	Y	Y	Y	Y	Y	N
4 ***Smith***	N	Y	Y	Y	N	Y
5 ***Roukema***	N	Y	Y	Y	N	Y
6 Dwyer	Y	Y	Y	Y	Y	Y
7 ***Rinaldo***	N	N	Y	Y	N	N
8 Roe	Y	Y	Y	Y	Y	Y
9 Torricelli	Y	Y	Y	Y	Y	Y
10 Payne	Y	Y	Y	Y	Y	N
11 ***Gallo***	N	Y	Y	Y	N	N
12 ***Courter***	N	Y	Y	N	N	Y
13 ***Saxton***	N	N	Y	Y	N	N
14 Guarini	N	Y	Y	Y	Y	Y
NEW MEXICO						
1 ***Schiff***	Y	N	N	N	N	Y
2 ***Skeen***	N	Y	N	N	N	Y
3 Richardson	Y	Y	Y	Y	Y	Y
NEW YORK						
1 Hochbrueckner	Y	Y	Y	Y	Y	Y
2 Downey	Y	Y	Y	Y	?	Y
3 Mrazek	Y	Y	Y	Y	Y	Y
4 ***Lent***	Y	N	Y	Y	N	Y
5 ***McGrath***	Y	N	Y	Y	N	Y
6 Flake	Y	Y	Y	Y	Y	Y
7 Ackerman	Y	Y	Y	Y	Y	Y
8 Scheuer	Y	Y	Y	Y	Y	N
9 Manton	Y	N	Y	Y	Y	Y
10 Schumer	Y	Y	Y	Y	Y	N
11 Towns	Y	Y	Y	Y	Y	N
12 Owens	Y	Y	Y	Y	Y	N
13 Solarz	Y	Y	Y	Y	Y	N
14 ***Molinari***	Y	N	Y	Y	?	Y
15 ***Green***	N	?	Y	Y	N	N
16 Rangel	Y	Y	Y	Y	Y	N
17 Weiss	Y	Y	Y	Y	Y	N
18 Serrano	Y	Y	Y	Y	Y	N
19 Engel	Y	Y	Y	Y	Y	Y
20 Lowey	Y	Y	Y	Y	Y	N
21 ***Fish***	Y	N	Y	Y	N	Y
22 ***Gilman***	Y	Y	Y	Y	N	Y
23 McNulty	Y	Y	Y	Y	Y	Y
24 ***Solomon***	N	N	Y	Y	N	Y
25 ***Boehlert***	Y	Y	Y	Y	N	Y
26 ***Martin***	N	N	Y	Y	N	N
27 ***Walsh***	N	Y	N	N	?	Y
28 McHugh	Y	Y	Y	Y	Y	Y
29 ***Horton***	Y	Y	Y	Y	N	Y
30 Slaughter	Y	Y	Y	Y	Y	Y
31 ***Paxon***	N	N	Y	Y	?	N

	512	513	514	515	516	517
32 LaFalce	Y	Y	Y	Y	Y	Y
33 Nowak	Y	Y	Y	Y	Y	Y
34 ***Houghton***	N	N	N	Y	?	Y
NORTH CAROLINA						
1 Jones	Y	Y	Y	Y	Y	Y
2 Valentine	N	Y	N	N	?	Y
3 Lancaster	Y	Y	N	N	Y	Y
4 Price	Y	Y	Y	Y	Y	Y
5 Neal	Y	Y	Y	Y	Y	Y
6 ***Coble***	N	Y	N	Y	N	N
7 Rose	Y	Y	N	N	Y	Y
8 Hefner	Y	Y	N	N	Y	Y
9 ***McMillan***	N	N	Y	Y	N	Y
10 ***Ballenger***	N	N	N	N	N	N
11 Clarke	Y	Y	N	N	Y	Y
NORTH DAKOTA						
AL Dorgan	N	?	N	N	Y	N
OHIO						
1 Luken	Y	N	Y	Y	Y	Y
2 ***Gradison***	N	Y	N	N	N	N
3 Hall	Y	Y	Y	Y	Y	Y
4 ***Oxley***	N	Y	Y	N	N	Y
5 ***Gillmor***	Y	Y	Y	Y	N	Y
6 ***McEwen***	N	N	N	N	N	N
7 ***DeWine***	N	N	N	Y	N	Y
8 ***Lukens***	?					
9 Kaptur	?	?	Y	Y	Y	Y
10 ***Miller***	N	Y	N	N	N	N
11 Eckart	Y	N	Y	Y	Y	N
12 ***Kasich***	N	N	Y	Y	N	Y
13 Pease	Y	Y	Y	Y	Y	N
14 Sawyer	Y	Y	Y	Y	Y	N
15 ***Wylie***	Y	N	Y	Y	N	Y
16 ***Regula***	Y	Y	Y	Y	N	N
17 Traficant	Y	Y	Y	Y	N	N
18 Applegate	Y	Y	Y	Y	Y	N
19 Feighan	Y	Y	Y	Y	Y	N
20 Oakar	Y	Y	N	Y	Y	Y
21 Stokes	Y	Y	Y	Y	?	N
OKLAHOMA						
1 ***Inhofe***	N	Y	N	N	N	N
2 Synar	Y	Y	Y	Y	Y	Y
3 Watkins	Y	Y	N	N	Y	Y
4 McCurdy	Y	Y	Y	Y	Y	Y
5 ***Edwards***	?	N	N	N	?	N
6 English	N	Y	N	N	Y	Y
OREGON						
1 AuCoin	Y	Y	Y	Y	Y	Y
2 ***Smith, B.***	N	Y	N	N	N	Y
3 Wyden	Y	Y	Y	Y	Y	Y
4 DeFazio	Y	Y	Y	Y	Y	N
5 ***Smith, D.***	N	N	N	N	N	N
PENNSYLVANIA						
1 Foglietta	Y	Y	Y	Y	Y	Y
2 Gray	Y	Y	N	Y	Y	Y
3 Borski	Y	Y	Y	Y	Y	Y
4 Kolter	Y	Y	Y	Y	Y	Y
5 ***Schulze***	?	Y	Y	Y	N	N
6 Yatron	N	Y	Y	Y	Y	Y
7 ***Weldon***	N	N	Y	Y	N	Y
8 Kostmayer	N	Y	Y	Y	Y	Y
9 ***Shuster***	N	Y	N	Y	N	N
10 ***McDade***	N	Y	Y	Y	N	Y
11 Kanjorski	N	Y	Y	Y	Y	Y
12 Murtha	Y	Y	Y	Y	Y	Y
13 ***Coughlin***	N	N	Y	Y	?	Y
14 Coyne	Y	Y	Y	Y	Y	Y
15 ***Ritter***	N	N	Y	Y	N	N
16 ***Walker***	N	N	Y	Y	N	N
17 ***Gekas***	N	N	Y	N	N	Y
18 Walgren	Y	Y	Y	Y	Y	Y
19 ***Goodling***	Y	N	Y	Y	N	N
20 Gaydos	Y	Y	Y	Y	Y	Y
21 ***Ridge***	N	Y	Y	Y	N	Y
22 Murphy	Y	N	Y	Y	Y	Y
23 ***Clinger***	N	N	Y	Y	N	N
RHODE ISLAND						
1 ***Machtley***	Y	Y	N	Y	N	Y
2 ***Schneider***	Y	N	N	Y	N	Y
SOUTH CAROLINA						
1 ***Ravenel***	N	N	Y	Y	N	Y
2 ***Spence***	N	N	Y	Y	N	N
3 Derrick	Y	Y	Y	Y	Y	Y
4 Patterson	N	Y	Y	Y	Y	Y
5 Spratt	Y	Y	Y	Y	Y	Y
6 Tallon	Y	Y	N	N	Y	Y

	512	513	514	515	516	517
SOUTH DAKOTA						
AL Johnson	Y	Y	N	Y	Y	N
TENNESSEE						
1 ***Quillen***	Y	Y	Y	Y	Y	Y
2 ***Duncan***	N	N	N	N	N	Y
3 Lloyd	Y	Y	N	Y	Y	Y
4 Cooper	Y	Y	Y	Y	Y	Y
5 Clement	N	Y	Y	Y	Y	Y
6 Gordon	Y	Y	Y	Y	Y	Y
7 ***Sundquist***	N	N	Y	Y	N	Y
8 Tanner	Y	Y	N	Y	Y	Y
9 Ford	?	Y	Y	Y	Y	Y
TEXAS						
1 Chapman	Y	Y	Y	Y	Y	Y
2 Wilson	N	Y	Y	Y	?	Y
3 ***Bartlett***	N	N	Y	Y	N	Y
4 Hall	N	N	N	N	Y	Y
5 Bryant	Y	Y	Y	Y	N	N
6 ***Barton***	N	Y	N	N	N	Y
7 ***Archer***	N	N	Y	Y	N	N
8 ***Fields***	N	N	Y	Y	N	N
9 Brooks	Y	Y	Y	Y	Y	Y
10 Pickle	Y	Y	N	Y	Y	Y
11 Leath	N	Y	N	N	Y	Y
12 Geren	N	Y	Y	Y	Y	Y
13 Sarpalius	N	Y	N	N	Y	Y
14 Laughlin	N	Y	N	N	Y	Y
15 de la Garza	Y	Y	N	N	Y	Y
16 Coleman	Y	Y	N	Y	Y	Y
17 Stenholm	N	Y	N	N	Y	Y
18 Washington	Y	Y	Y	Y	Y	N
19 ***Combest***	N	Y	N	N	N	N
20 Gonzalez	Y	Y	Y	Y	Y	N
21 ***Smith***	N	Y	Y	Y	N	N
22 ***DeLay***	N	N	Y	N	N	N
23 Bustamante	Y	Y	Y	Y	Y	Y
24 Frost	Y	Y	Y	Y	Y	Y
25 Andrews	Y	Y	Y	Y	Y	Y
26 ***Armey***	N	N	Y	N	N	Y
27 Ortiz	Y	Y	Y	Y	Y	Y
UTAH						
1 ***Hansen***	N	N	N	N	N	N
2 Owens	Y	Y	Y	Y	Y	N
3 ***Nielson***	N	Y	Y	N	N	N
VERMONT						
AL ***Smith***	?	?	Y	Y	N	N
VIRGINIA						
1 ***Bateman***	N	Y	N	Y	N	Y
2 Pickett	Y	Y	N	N	Y	Y
3 ***Bliley***	N	N	Y	Y	N	Y
4 Sisisky	Y	Y	N	N	Y	Y
5 Payne	N	Y	N	N	Y	Y
6 Olin	N	Y	N	N	Y	Y
7 ***Slaughter***	N	N	Y	Y	N	Y
8 ***Parris***	N	Y	N	Y	N	Y
9 Boucher	Y	Y	Y	Y	Y	Y
10 ***Wolf***	N	Y	N	Y	N	Y
WASHINGTON						
1 ***Miller***	N	N	Y	Y	N	Y
2 Swift	Y	N	Y	Y	Y	Y
3 Unsoeld	Y	Y	Y	Y	Y	N
4 ***Morrison***	Y	Y	N	N	N	N
5 Foley						
6 Dicks	Y	Y	Y	Y	Y	Y
7 McDermott	Y	Y	Y	Y	Y	N
8 ***Chandler***	N	N	Y	Y	N	N
WEST VIRGINIA						
1 Mollohan	Y	Y	Y	Y	Y	Y
2 Staggers	Y	Y	N	Y	Y	Y
3 Wise	Y	Y	Y	Y	Y	Y
4 Rahall	Y	Y	Y	Y	Y	Y
WISCONSIN						
1 Aspin	Y	Y	Y	Y	Y	Y
2 Kastenmeier	Y	Y	Y	Y	Y	N
3 ***Gunderson***	N	Y	N	N	N	Y
4 Kleczka	Y	Y	Y	Y	Y	Y
5 Moody	Y	Y	N	Y	Y	Y
6 ***Petri***	N	N	Y	Y	N	N
7 Obey	Y	Y	N	Y	Y	Y
8 ***Roth***	N	N	N	N	N	N
9 ***Sensenbrenner***	N	N	N	N	N	N
WYOMING						
AL ***Thomas***	N	N	N	Y	N	Y

Southern states - Ala., Ark., Fla., Ga., Ky., La., Miss., N.C., Okla., S.C., Tenn., Texas, Va.
Omitted votes are quorum calls, which CQ does not include in its vote charts.

518. H J Res 681. Fiscal 1991 Continuing Appropriations/Passage. Passage of the joint resolution to provide continuing appropriations for fiscal 1991 through Oct. 27; suspend sequestration through Oct. 27; and extend a temporary increase in the debt limit through Oct. 27. Passed 380-45: R 136-38; D 244-7 (ND 162-6, SD 82-1), Oct. 24, 1990.

519. H Res 527. Rule Expediting Budget and Appropriations Legislation/Rule. Adoption of the rule (H Res 527) to provide for expedited House floor consideration of rules dealing with a continuing resolution, reconciliation bill or debt-limit bill through Oct. 27 by waiving the two-thirds requirement for rules considered the same day that they are reported, thereby permitting their consideration after a simple majority vote. The rule also waives the three-day layover requirement for conference reports on appropriations through Oct. 27. Adopted 255-161: R 8-161; D 247-0 (ND 168-0, SD 79-0), Oct. 25, 1990.

520. S 605. CPSC Reauthorization/Conference Report. Walgren, D-Pa., motion to suspend the rules and adopt the conference report (thus clearing the measure for the president) on the bill to authorize $42 million in fiscal 1991 and $45 million in fiscal 1992 for the Consumer Product Safety Commission (CPSC) and make a number of changes in current law dealing with the commission and how it administers consumer product safety laws. Motion agreed to 375-41: R 137-34; D 238-7 (ND 163-2, SD 75-5), Oct. 25, 1990. A two-thirds majority of those present and voting (274 in this case) is required for passage under suspension of the rules.

521. HR 5112. Home Health Care/Concur in Senate Amendments. Waxman, D-Calif., motion to suspend the rules and concur in Senate amendments (thus clearing the measure for the president) on the bill to create and reauthorize programs aimed at reducing the need for costly long-term care for the elderly. The Senate amendments dealt with Alzheimer's disease centers, centers of geriatric research and training, and a task force on aging research. Motion agreed to 417-1: R 171-0; D 246-1 (ND 166-1, SD 80-0), Oct. 25, 1990. A two-thirds majority of those present and voting (279 in this case) is required for passage under suspension of the rules.

522. HR 5269. Crime Bill/Instruction of Conferees. McCollum, R-Fla., motion to instruct the House conferees on the bill to insist on House provisions dealing with the death penalty, habeas corpus and the exclusionary rule. Motion agreed to 291-123: R 162-6; D 129-117 (ND 62-104, SD 67-13), Oct. 25, 1990.

523. HR 5311. Fiscal 1991 D.C. Appropriations/Conference Report. Adoption of the conference report on the bill to appropriate $549,700,000 in federal funds and $3,862,574,000 in funds raised form local taxes for the District of Columbia in fiscal 1991. The president requested $519,278,000 in federal funds and $3,818,652,000 in local funds. (The bill was identical to the first conference report that the House rejected Oct. 20, including allowing the use of local tax revenues for abortions.) Rejected 195-211: R 31-138; D 164-73 (ND 115-44, SD 49-29), Oct. 25, 1990. A "nay" was a vote supporting the president's position.

KEY

- Y Voted for (yea).
- # Paired for.
- + Announced for.
- N Voted against (nay).
- X Paired against.
- - Announced against.
- P Voted "present."
- C Voted "present" to avoid possible conflict of interest.
- ? Did not vote or otherwise make a position known.

Democrats ***Republicans***

	518	519	520	521	522	523
ALABAMA						
1 ***Callahan***	Y	N	N	Y	Y	N
2 ***Dickinson***	Y	N	Y	Y	Y	N
3 Browder	Y	Y	Y	Y	Y	Y
4 Bevill	Y	Y	Y	Y	Y	N
5 Flippo	Y	Y	Y	Y	?	Y
6 Erdreich	Y	Y	Y	Y	Y	Y
7 Harris	Y	Y	Y	Y	Y	Y
ALASKA						
AL ***Young***	Y	?	Y	Y	Y	N
ARIZONA						
1 ***Rhodes***	Y	N	Y	Y	Y	N
2 Udall	Y	Y	Y	Y	N	Y
3 ***Stump***	N	N	N	Y	Y	N
4 ***Kyl***	Y	N	Y	Y	Y	N
5 ***Kolbe***	Y	N	Y	Y	Y	Y
ARKANSAS						
1 Alexander	Y	Y	Y	Y	?	Y
2 ***Robinson***	N	N	Y	Y	Y	N
3 ***Hammerschmidt***	N	N	N	Y	Y	N
4 Anthony	Y	Y	Y	Y	Y	Y
CALIFORNIA						
1 Bosco	Y	Y	Y	Y	Y	Y
2 ***Herger***	Y	N	Y	Y	Y	N
3 Matsui	Y	?	?	?	?	?
4 Fazio	Y	Y	Y	Y	N	Y
5 Pelosi	Y	Y	Y	Y	N	Y
6 Boxer	Y	Y	Y	Y	N	Y
7 Miller	Y	Y	Y	Y	N	Y
8 Dellums	Y	Y	Y	Y	N	Y
9 Stark	Y	Y	Y	Y	N	Y
10 Edwards	Y	Y	Y	Y	N	Y
11 Lantos	Y	Y	Y	Y	Y	Y
12 ***Campbell***	Y	N	Y	Y	N	Y
13 Mineta	Y	Y	Y	Y	N	Y
14 ***Shumway***	?	N	N	Y	Y	N
15 Condit	Y	Y	Y	Y	Y	Y
16 Panetta	Y	Y	Y	Y	N	Y
17 ***Pashayan***	Y	N	Y	Y	Y	?
18 Lehman	Y	Y	Y	Y	?	Y
19 ***Lagomarsino***	Y	N	Y	Y	Y	N
20 ***Thomas***	N	N	Y	Y	Y	N
21 ***Gallegly***	Y	N	Y	Y	Y	N
22 ***Moorhead***	Y	N	Y	Y	Y	N
23 Beilenson	Y	Y	Y	Y	N	Y
24 Waxman	?	Y	Y	Y	N	Y
25 Roybal	Y	Y	Y	Y	Y	Y
26 Berman	Y	Y	Y	Y	N	Y
27 Levine	Y	Y	Y	Y	N	Y
28 Dixon	Y	Y	Y	Y	N	Y
29 Hawkins	?	Y	?	Y	N	Y
30 Martinez	Y	Y	Y	Y	Y	Y
31 Dymally	Y	Y	?	?	N	Y
32 Anderson	Y	Y	Y	Y	N	Y
33 ***Dreier***	N	N	N	Y	Y	N
34 Torres	Y	Y	Y	Y	Y	Y
35 ***Lewis***	Y	N	Y	Y	Y	N
36 Brown	Y	Y	Y	Y	Y	Y
37 ***McCandless***	Y	N	Y	Y	Y	N
38 ***Dornan***	N	N	N	Y	Y	N
39 ***Dannemeyer***	N	N	N	Y	Y	N
40 ***Cox***	Y	N	N	Y	Y	N
41 ***Lowery***	Y	N	Y	Y	Y	N
42 ***Rohrabacher***	Y	N	Y	Y	Y	N
43 ***Packard***	N	N	Y	Y	Y	N
44 Bates	N	Y	Y	Y	Y	Y
45 ***Hunter***	Y	N	Y	Y	?	N
COLORADO						
1 Schroeder	Y	Y	Y	Y	N	Y
2 Skaggs	Y	Y	Y	Y	N	Y
3 Campbell	Y	Y	Y	Y	Y	Y
4 ***Brown***	N	N	Y	Y	Y	N
5 ***Hefley***	Y	N	Y	Y	Y	N
6 ***Schaefer***	Y	N	Y	Y	Y	N
CONNECTICUT						
1 Kennelly	Y	Y	?	Y	N	Y
2 Gejdenson	Y	Y	Y	Y	N	Y
3 Morrison	?	?	?	?	?	?
4 ***Shays***	N	N	Y	Y	Y	Y
5 ***Rowland***	Y	?	?	?	?	?
6 ***Johnson***	Y	Y	?	Y	Y	Y
DELAWARE						
AL Carper	N	Y	Y	Y	N	Y
FLORIDA						
1 Hutto	Y	Y	Y	Y	Y	N
2 ***Grant***	Y	N	Y	?	Y	N
3 Bennett	Y	Y	Y	Y	Y	Y
4 ***James***	Y	N	Y	Y	Y	N
5 ***McCollum***	Y	N	Y	Y	Y	N
6 ***Stearns***	Y	N	Y	Y	Y	N
7 Gibbons	Y	Y	Y	Y	Y	Y
8 ***Young***	Y	N	Y	Y	Y	N
9 ***Bilirakis***	Y	N	Y	Y	Y	N
10 ***Ireland***	Y	N	Y	Y	Y	N
11 Nelson	Y	#	+	Y	Y	Y
12 ***Lewis***	Y	N	Y	Y	Y	N
13 ***Goss***	Y	N	Y	Y	Y	N
14 Johnston	Y	Y	Y	Y	N	Y
15 ***Shaw***	Y	N	Y	Y	Y	N
16 Smith	Y	Y	Y	Y	Y	Y
17 Lehman	Y	Y	Y	Y	N	Y
18 ***Ros-Lehtinen***	Y	N	Y	Y	Y	N
19 Fascell	Y	Y	Y	Y	Y	Y
GEORGIA						
1 Thomas	Y	Y	Y	Y	Y	Y
2 Hatcher	Y	Y	Y	Y	Y	Y
3 Ray	Y	Y	Y	Y	Y	N
4 Jones	Y	Y	Y	Y	Y	Y
5 Lewis	Y	Y	Y	Y	N	Y
6 ***Gingrich***	Y	N	Y	Y	Y	N
7 Darden	Y	Y	Y	Y	Y	Y
8 Rowland	Y	Y	Y	Y	Y	N
9 Jenkins	Y	Y	Y	Y	Y	N
10 Barnard	Y	Y	Y	Y	Y	N
HAWAII						
1 ***Saiki***	Y	N	Y	Y	Y	Y
2 Mink	Y	Y	Y	Y	N	Y
IDAHO						
1 ***Craig***	Y	N	N	Y	Y	N
2 Stallings	Y	Y	Y	Y	Y	N
ILLINOIS						
1 Hayes	Y	Y	Y	Y	N	Y
2 Savage	Y	Y	Y	Y	N	Y
3 Russo	Y	Y	Y	Y	Y	N
4 Sangmeister	N	Y	Y	Y	Y	N
5 Lipinski	Y	Y	Y	Y	Y	N
6 ***Hyde***	Y	N	Y	Y	Y	N
7 Collins	Y	Y	Y	Y	N	Y
8 Rostenkowski	Y	Y	Y	Y	Y	N
9 Yates	?	Y	Y	Y	N	Y
10 ***Porter***	N	N	Y	Y	Y	N
11 Annunzio	Y	Y	Y	Y	Y	N
12 ***Crane***	N	X	Y	Y	Y	N
13 ***Fawell***	N	N	Y	Y	Y	Y
14 ***Hastert***	Y	N	Y	Y	Y	N
15 ***Madigan***	Y	N	Y	Y	Y	N
16 ***Martin***	N	N	Y	Y	Y	Y
17 Evans	Y	Y	Y	Y	N	Y
18 ***Michel***	Y	N	Y	Y	Y	N
19 Bruce	Y	Y	Y	Y	Y	N
20 Durbin	Y	Y	Y	Y	Y	Y
21 Costello	Y	Y	Y	Y	Y	N
22 Poshard	Y	Y	Y	Y	Y	N
INDIANA						
1 Visclosky	Y	Y	Y	Y	N	Y
2 Sharp	Y	Y	Y	Y	N	Y
3 ***Hiler***	Y	N	Y	Y	Y	N

ND Northern Democrats SD Southern Democrats

	518	519	520	521	522	523
4 Long	Y	Y	Y	Y	Y	Y
5 Jontz	Y	Y	Y	Y	Y	Y
6 ***Burton***	N	N	N	Y	Y	N
7 ***Myers***	Y	N	Y	Y	Y	N
8 McCloskey	Y	Y	Y	Y	N	Y
9 Hamilton	Y	Y	Y	Y	N	N
10 Jacobs	Y	Y	Y	Y	N	Y
IOWA						
1 ***Leach***	Y	N	Y	Y	Y	N
2 ***Tauke***	N	N	Y	Y	N	N
3 Nagle	Y	Y	Y	Y	N	Y
4 Smith	Y	Y	Y	Y	Y	Y
5 ***Lightfoot***	N	N	Y	Y	Y	N
6 ***Grandy***	Y	N	Y	Y	Y	N
KANSAS						
1 ***Roberts***	Y	N	N	Y	Y	N
2 Slattery	Y	Y	Y	Y	Y	N
3 ***Meyers***	Y	N	Y	Y	Y	Y
4 Glickman	Y	Y	Y	Y	N	Y
5 ***Whittaker***	Y	N	Y	Y	Y	N
KENTUCKY						
1 Hubbard	Y	Y	Y	Y	Y	Y
2 Natcher	Y	Y	Y	Y	Y	N
3 Mazzoli	Y	Y	Y	Y	Y	N
4 ***Bunning***	Y	N	Y	Y	Y	N
5 ***Rogers***	Y	N	Y	Y	Y	N
6 ***Hopkins***	Y	N	Y	Y	Y	N
7 Perkins	Y	Y	Y	Y	N	N
LOUISIANA						
1 ***Livingston***	N	N	N	Y	Y	N
2 Boggs	Y	Y	Y	Y	N	N
3 Tauzin	Y	Y	Y	Y	Y	?
4 ***McCrery***	Y	N	Y	Y	Y	N
5 Huckaby	Y	Y	Y	Y	Y	N
6 ***Baker***	N	N	N	Y	Y	N
7 Hayes	Y	Y	Y	Y	Y	N
8 ***Holloway***	N	N	N	Y	Y	N
MAINE						
1 Brennan	Y	?	?	?	?	?
2 ***Snowe***	Y	N	Y	Y	Y	Y
MARYLAND						
1 Dyson	Y	Y	Y	Y	Y	N
2 ***Bentley***	Y	N	Y	Y	Y	N
3 Cardin	Y	Y	Y	Y	N	Y
4 McMillen	Y	Y	Y	Y	N	Y
5 Hoyer	Y	Y	Y	Y	N	Y
6 Byron	N	Y	Y	Y	Y	N
7 Mfume	Y	?	Y	Y	N	Y
8 ***Morella***	Y	Y	Y	Y	N	Y
MASSACHUSETTS						
1 ***Conte***	Y	N	Y	Y	N	N
2 Neal	Y	Y	Y	Y	N	N
3 Early	Y	Y	Y	Y	Y	N
4 Frank	Y	?	?	?	?	?
5 Atkins	Y	Y	Y	Y	N	Y
6 Mavroules	Y	Y	Y	Y	Y	N
7 Markey	Y	Y	Y	Y	N	Y
8 Kennedy	Y	Y	Y	Y	N	Y
9 Moakley	Y	Y	Y	Y	Y	N
10 Studds	Y	Y	Y	Y	N	Y
11 Donnelly	Y	Y	Y	Y	Y	?
MICHIGAN						
1 Conyers	Y	Y	Y	Y	N	Y
2 ***Pursell***	N	N	Y	Y	Y	N
3 Wolpe	Y	Y	Y	Y	N	Y
4 ***Upton***	N	N	Y	Y	Y	N
5 ***Henry***	Y	N	N	Y	Y	N
6 Carr	Y	Y	Y	Y	Y	?
7 Kildee	Y	Y	Y	Y	N	N
8 Traxler	Y	Y	Y	Y	Y	N
9 ***Vander Jagt***	Y	N	N	Y	Y	N
10 ***Schuette***	N	N	Y	Y	Y	?
11 ***Davis***	Y	N	Y	Y	Y	N
12 Bonior	Y	Y	Y	Y	N	N
13 Crockett	?	Y	Y	Y	?	Y
14 Hertel	Y	Y	Y	Y	N	N
15 Ford	Y	?	Y	Y	?	?
16 Dingell	Y	Y	Y	Y	Y	Y
17 Levin	Y	Y	Y	Y	N	Y
18 ***Broomfield***	Y	N	N	Y	Y	N
MINNESOTA						
1 Penny	N	Y	N	N	N	N
2 ***Weber***	Y	N	N	Y	Y	N
3 ***Frenzel***	N	N	N	Y	Y	Y
4 Vento	Y	Y	Y	Y	N	Y

	518	519	520	521	522	523
5 Sabo	Y	Y	Y	Y	N	Y
6 Sikorski	Y	Y	Y	Y	N	Y
7 ***Stangeland***	Y	N	Y	Y	Y	N
8 Oberstar	Y	Y	Y	Y	N	N
MISSISSIPPI						
1 Whitten	Y	Y	Y	Y	Y	N
2 Espy	Y	Y	Y	Y	Y	Y
3 Montgomery	Y	Y	Y	Y	Y	N
4 Parker	N	Y	Y	Y	Y	N
5 Taylor	Y	Y	Y	Y	Y	N
MISSOURI						
1 Clay	Y	Y	Y	Y	N	Y
2 ***Buechner***	Y	N	Y	Y	Y	N
3 Gephardt	Y	Y	Y	Y	N	Y
4 Skelton	Y	Y	N	Y	Y	N
5 Wheat	Y	Y	Y	Y	N	Y
6 ***Coleman***	Y	N	Y	Y	Y	N
7 ***Hancock***	N	N	N	Y	Y	N
8 ***Emerson***	Y	N	Y	Y	Y	N
9 Volkmer	Y	Y	Y	Y	Y	N
MONTANA						
1 Williams	Y	Y	Y	Y	N	Y
2 ***Marlenee***	N	N	N	Y	?	N
NEBRASKA						
1 ***Bereuter***	Y	N	Y	Y	Y	N
2 Hoagland	Y	Y	Y	Y	N	N
3 ***Smith***	Y	N	Y	Y	Y	N
NEVADA						
1 Bilbray	Y	Y	Y	Y	Y	Y
2 ***Vucanovich***	Y	N	Y	Y	Y	N
NEW HAMPSHIRE						
1 ***Smith***	N	N	Y	Y	Y	N
2 ***Douglas***	Y	N	Y	Y	Y	N
NEW JERSEY						
1 Vacancy						
2 Hughes	Y	Y	Y	Y	N	Y
3 Pallone	Y	Y	Y	Y	Y	Y
4 ***Smith***	Y	N	Y	Y	N	N
5 ***Roukema***	Y	N	Y	Y	Y	Y
6 Dwyer	Y	Y	Y	Y	Y	Y
7 ***Rinaldo***	Y	N	Y	Y	Y	N
8 Roe	Y	Y	Y	Y	Y	N
9 Torricelli	Y	Y	Y	Y	Y	?
10 Payne	Y	Y	Y	Y	N	Y
11 ***Gallo***	Y	N	Y	Y	Y	Y
12 ***Courter***	Y	N	Y	Y	Y	Y
13 ***Saxton***	Y	N	Y	Y	Y	N
14 Guarini	Y	Y	Y	Y	Y	N
NEW MEXICO						
1 ***Schiff***	Y	N	Y	Y	Y	Y
2 ***Skeen***	Y	N	Y	Y	Y	N
3 Richardson	Y	Y	Y	Y	Y	Y
NEW YORK						
1 Hochbrueckner	Y	Y	Y	Y	Y	N
2 Downey	Y	Y	Y	Y	Y	Y
3 Mrazek	Y	Y	Y	Y	Y	Y
4 ***Lent***	Y	N	Y	Y	Y	N
5 ***McGrath***	Y	N	Y	Y	?	?
6 Flake	Y	Y	Y	Y	N	Y
7 Ackerman	Y	Y	Y	Y	N	Y
8 Scheuer	Y	Y	Y	Y	N	?
9 Manton	Y	Y	Y	Y	Y	?
10 Schumer	Y	Y	Y	Y	N	Y
11 Towns	Y	Y	Y	Y	N	Y
12 Owens	Y	Y	Y	Y	N	Y
13 Solarz	Y	Y	Y	Y	N	Y
14 ***Molinari***	Y	N	Y	Y	Y	Y
15 ***Green***	Y	N	Y	Y	N	Y
16 Rangel	Y	Y	Y	Y	N	Y
17 Weiss	Y	Y	Y	Y	N	Y
18 Serrano	Y	Y	?	Y	N	Y
19 Engel	Y	Y	Y	Y	N	Y
20 Lowey	Y	Y	Y	Y	N	Y
21 ***Fish***	Y	Y	Y	Y	Y	N
22 ***Gilman***	Y	N	Y	Y	Y	Y
23 McNulty	Y	Y	Y	Y	N	Y
24 ***Solomon***	Y	N	Y	Y	Y	N
25 ***Boehlert***	Y	N	Y	Y	Y	Y
26 ***Martin***	Y	N	Y	Y	Y	N
27 ***Walsh***	Y	N	Y	Y	Y	N
28 McHugh	Y	Y	Y	Y	N	N
29 ***Horton***	Y	N	Y	Y	Y	Y
30 Slaughter	Y	Y	Y	Y	N	Y
31 ***Paxon***	Y	N	Y	Y	Y	N

	518	519	520	521	522	523
32 LaFalce	Y	Y	Y	Y	N	N
33 Nowak	Y	Y	Y	Y	Y	N
34 ***Houghton***	Y	N	Y	Y	Y	Y
NORTH CAROLINA						
1 Jones	Y	Y	Y	Y	Y	Y
2 Valentine	Y	Y	Y	Y	Y	Y
3 Lancaster	Y	Y	Y	Y	Y	Y
4 Price	Y	Y	Y	Y	N	Y
5 Neal	Y	?	?	Y	Y	Y
6 ***Coble***	Y	N	Y	Y	Y	N
7 Rose	Y	Y	Y	Y	N	Y
8 Hefner	Y	Y	Y	Y	Y	N
9 ***McMillan***	Y	N	Y	Y	Y	N
10 ***Ballenger***	Y	N	N	Y	Y	N
11 Clarke	Y	Y	Y	Y	Y	Y
NORTH DAKOTA						
AL Dorgan	Y	Y	Y	Y	N	Y
OHIO						
1 Luken	Y	Y	Y	Y	N	Y
2 ***Gradison***	Y	N	Y	Y	Y	Y
3 Hall	Y	Y	Y	Y	Y	N
4 ***Oxley***	Y	N	Y	Y	Y	N
5 ***Gillmor***	Y	N	Y	Y	Y	N
6 ***McEwen***	Y	N	Y	Y	Y	N
7 ***DeWine***	Y	N	Y	Y	Y	N
8 Vacancy						
9 Kaptur	Y	Y	Y	Y	Y	N
10 ***Miller***	Y	N	Y	Y	Y	N
11 Eckart	Y	Y	Y	Y	Y	Y
12 ***Kasich***	Y	?	Y	Y	Y	N
13 Pease	N	Y	Y	Y	N	Y
14 Sawyer	Y	Y	Y	Y	N	Y
15 ***Wylie***	Y	N	Y	Y	Y	N
16 ***Regula***	Y	N	Y	Y	Y	Y
17 Traficant	Y	Y	Y	Y	Y	Y
18 Applegate	Y	Y	Y	Y	Y	N
19 Feighan	Y	Y	Y	Y	N	?
20 Oakar	Y	Y	Y	Y	Y	Y
21 Stokes	Y	Y	Y	Y	N	Y
OKLAHOMA						
1 ***Inhofe***	N	N	Y	Y	Y	N
2 Synar	Y	Y	Y	Y	N	Y
3 Watkins	Y	Y	Y	Y	Y	N
4 McCurdy	Y	Y	N	Y	Y	N
5 ***Edwards***	Y	N	Y	Y	Y	N
6 English	Y	Y	Y	Y	Y	N
OREGON						
1 AuCoin	Y	Y	Y	Y	N	Y
2 ***Smith, B.***	Y	N	Y	Y	Y	N
3 Wyden	Y	Y	Y	Y	Y	Y
4 DeFazio	Y	Y	?	?	?	Y
5 ***Smith, D.***	N	N	N	Y	Y	?
PENNSYLVANIA						
1 Foglietta	Y	Y	Y	Y	N	Y
2 Gray	Y	Y	Y	Y	N	Y
3 Borski	Y	Y	Y	Y	Y	N
4 Kolter	Y	Y	Y	Y	Y	N
5 ***Schulze***	Y	N	Y	Y	Y	N
6 Yatron	Y	Y	Y	Y	Y	N
7 ***Weldon***	Y	N	Y	Y	Y	N
8 Kostmayer	Y	Y	Y	Y	N	Y
9 ***Shuster***	Y	N	Y	Y	Y	N
10 ***McDade***	Y	N	Y	Y	Y	N
11 Kanjorski	Y	Y	Y	Y	Y	N
12 Murtha	Y	Y	Y	Y	Y	?
13 ***Coughlin***	N	N	Y	Y	Y	Y
14 Coyne	Y	Y	Y	Y	N	Y
15 ***Ritter***	Y	N	Y	Y	Y	N
16 ***Walker***	Y	N	Y	Y	Y	N
17 ***Gekas***	Y	N	Y	Y	Y	Y
18 Walgren	Y	Y	Y	Y	N	?
19 ***Goodling***	Y	?	?	?	Y	N
20 Gaydos	Y	Y	Y	Y	Y	N
21 ***Ridge***	Y	N	Y	Y	?	Y
22 Murphy	Y	Y	Y	Y	Y	N
23 ***Clinger***	Y	N	Y	Y	Y	N
RHODE ISLAND						
1 ***Machtley***	Y	Y	Y	Y	Y	Y
2 ***Schneider***	Y	N	Y	Y	Y	Y
SOUTH CAROLINA						
1 ***Ravenel***	Y	N	Y	Y	Y	N
2 ***Spence***	Y	N	Y	Y	Y	N
3 Derrick	Y	Y	Y	?	Y	Y
4 Patterson	Y	Y	Y	Y	Y	Y
5 Spratt	Y	Y	Y	Y	Y	Y
6 Tallon	Y	Y	Y	Y	Y	N

	518	519	520	521	522	523
SOUTH DAKOTA						
AL Johnson	Y	Y	Y	Y	Y	N
TENNESSEE						
1 ***Quillen***	N	Y	Y	Y	Y	N
2 ***Duncan***	Y	N	N	Y	Y	N
3 Lloyd	Y	Y	Y	Y	Y	N
4 Cooper	Y	Y	Y	Y	Y	Y
5 Clement	Y	Y	Y	Y	Y	Y
6 Gordon	Y	Y	Y	Y	Y	Y
7 ***Sundquist***	Y	N	Y	Y	Y	N
8 Tanner	Y	Y	Y	Y	Y	Y
9 Ford	Y	?	Y	Y	N	Y
TEXAS						
1 Chapman	Y	Y	Y	Y	Y	N
2 Wilson	Y	Y	Y	Y	Y	Y
3 ***Bartlett***	N	N	N	Y	Y	N
4 Hall	Y	Y	N	Y	Y	N
5 Bryant	Y	Y	Y	Y	Y	?
6 ***Barton***	N	N	N	Y	Y	N
7 ***Archer***	Y	N	N	Y	Y	N
8 ***Fields***	N	N	N	Y	Y	N
9 Brooks	Y	Y	Y	Y	Y	Y
10 Pickle	Y	Y	Y	Y	Y	Y
11 Leath	Y	Y	Y	Y	Y	Y
12 Geren	Y	Y	Y	Y	Y	Y
13 Sarpalius	Y	Y	N	Y	Y	Y
14 Laughlin	Y	Y	Y	Y	Y	N
15 de la Garza	Y	Y	Y	Y	Y	N
16 Coleman	Y	Y	Y	Y	N	Y
17 Stenholm	Y	Y	N	Y	Y	N
18 Washington	Y	Y	Y	Y	N	?
19 ***Combest***	Y	Y	N	Y	Y	N
20 Gonzalez	Y	Y	Y	Y	N	Y
21 ***Smith***	Y	N	N	Y	Y	N
22 ***DeLay***	N	N	N	Y	Y	N
23 Bustamante	Y	?	?	?	?	?
24 Frost	Y	Y	Y	?	Y	Y
25 Andrews	Y	Y	Y	Y	Y	Y
26 ***Armey***	N	N	N	Y	Y	N
27 Ortiz	Y	Y	Y	Y	Y	N
UTAH						
1 ***Hansen***	Y	N	N	Y	Y	N
2 Owens	Y	Y	Y	Y	N	Y
3 ***Nielson***	Y	N	N	Y	Y	N
VERMONT						
AL ***Smith***	Y	?	?	?	?	?
VIRGINIA						
1 ***Bateman***	Y	Y	Y	Y	Y	N
2 Pickett	Y	Y	N	Y	Y	?
3 ***Bliley***	Y	N	Y	Y	Y	N
4 Sisisky	Y	Y	Y	Y	Y	Y
5 Payne	Y	Y	Y	Y	Y	Y
6 Olin	Y	Y	Y	Y	Y	Y
7 ***Slaughter***	Y	N	Y	Y	Y	N
8 ***Parris***	Y	Y	Y	Y	Y	N
9 Boucher	Y	Y	Y	Y	N	Y
10 ***Wolf***	Y	N	Y	Y	?	N
WASHINGTON						
1 ***Miller***	Y	N	Y	Y	Y	Y
2 Swift	Y	Y	Y	Y	N	Y
3 Unsoeld	Y	Y	Y	Y	N	Y
4 ***Morrison***	Y	N	Y	Y	Y	Y
5 Foley						
6 Dicks	Y	Y	Y	Y	N	Y
7 McDermott	Y	Y	Y	Y	N	Y
8 ***Chandler***	Y	N	Y	Y	Y	Y
WEST VIRGINIA						
1 Mollohan	Y	Y	Y	?	N	N
2 Staggers	Y	Y	Y	Y	N	N
3 Wise	Y	Y	Y	Y	N	Y
4 Rahall	Y	Y	Y	Y	N	?
WISCONSIN						
1 Aspin	Y	Y	Y	Y	Y	Y
2 Kastenmeier	Y	Y	Y	Y	N	Y
3 ***Gunderson***	Y	N	Y	Y	Y	N
4 Kleczka	?	Y	Y	Y	N	Y
5 Moody	Y	Y	Y	Y	N	?
6 ***Petri***	N	N	Y	Y	Y	N
7 Obey	Y	Y	Y	Y	N	Y
8 ***Roth***	Y	N	Y	Y	Y	N
9 ***Sensenbrenner***	N	N	Y	Y	Y	N
WYOMING						
AL ***Thomas***	Y	N	Y	Y	Y	N

Southern states - Ala., Ark., Fla., Ga., Ky., La., Miss., N.C., Okla., S.C., Tenn., Texas, Va.
Omitted votes are quorum calls, which CQ does not include in its vote charts.

HOUSE VOTES 524, 525, 526, 527, 528, 529, 530

524. S 1630. Clean Air Act Reauthorization/Rule. Adoption of the rule (H Res 535) to waive certain points of order against and provide for House floor consideration of the conference report on the bill to amend the Clean Air Act to attain and maintain national ambient air quality standards, require reductions of emissions in motor vehicles, control toxic air pollutants, reduce acid rain, establish a system of federal permits and enforcement, and otherwise improve the quality of the nations's air. Adopted 390-26: R 148-23; D 242-3 (ND 163-2, SD 79-1), Oct. 26, 1990.

525. S 1630. Clean Air Act Reauthorization/Conference Report. Adoption of the conference report on the bill to amend the Clean Air Act to attain and maintain national ambient air quality standards, require reductions of emissions in motor vehicles, control toxic air pollutants, reduce acid rain, establish a system of federal permits and enforcement, and otherwise improve the quality of the nations's air. Adopted 401-25: R 153-20; D 248-5 (ND 166-4, SD 82-1), Oct. 26, 1990.

526. S 358. Legal Immigration Revision/Rule. Adoption of the rule (H Res 531) to waive certain points of order against and provide for House floor consideration of the conference report on the bill to increase the number of visas for those coming to the United States to work, establish a new category of diversity visas for immigrants from countries that have accounted for very few immigrants under the current system, impose an overall cap on immigration at 675,000 starting in fiscal 1996, suspend deportation of certain spouses and children of newly legalized aliens, and temporarily suspend deportation of Salvadorans. Rejected 186-235: R 58-112; D 128-123 (ND 98-71, SD 30-52), Oct. 26, 1990.

527. HR 5835. Fiscal 1991 Budget Reconciliation/Rule. Adoption of the rule (H Res 537) to provide for House floor consideration of the conference report on the bill to reduce spending and increase revenues as required by the reconciliation instructions contained in the budget resolution and to make changes in budget procedures and enforcement. Adopted 275-142: R 29-142; D 246-0 (ND 167-0, SD 79-0), Oct. 27, 1990 (in the session that began, and the Congressional Record dated, Oct. 26, 1990).

528. HR 5835. Fiscal 1991 Budget Reconciliation/Conference Report. Adoption of the conference report on the bill to reduce spending and increase revenues as required by the reconciliation instructions contained in the budget resolution and to make changes in budget procedures and enforcement. Adopted 228-200: R 47-126; D 181-74 (ND 120-54, SD 61-20), Oct. 27, 1990 (in the session that began, and the Congressional Record dated, Oct. 26, 1990). A "yea" was a vote supporting the president.

529. HR 5399. Fiscal 1991 Legislative Branch Appropriations/Conference Report. Adoption of the conference report on the bill to appropriate $2,161,366,500 in fiscal 1991 for the operations of Congress and legislative branch agencies. The president requested $2,411,881,000. Adopted 259-129: R 50-111; D 209-18 (ND 142-9, SD 67-9), Oct. 27, 1990.

530. S 358. Legal Immigration Revision/Conference Report. Adoption of the conference report (thus clearing the measure for the president) on the bill to increase the number of visas for those coming to the United States to work, establish a new category of diversity visas for immigrants from countries that have accounted for very few immigrants under the current system, impose an overall cap on immigration at 675,000 starting in fiscal 1996, suspend deportation of certain spouses and children of newly legalized aliens, and temporarily suspend deportation of Salvadorans. Adopted 264-118: R 93-64; D 171-54 (ND 137-15, SD 34-39), Oct. 27, 1990. A "yea" was a vote supporting the president's position.

KEY

- Y Voted for (yea).
- # Paired for.
- + Announced for.
- N Voted against (nay).
- X Paired against.
- - Announced against.
- P Voted "present."
- C Voted "present" to avoid possible conflict of interest.
- ? Did not vote or otherwise make a position known.

Democrats ***Republicans***

	524	525	526	527	528	529	530
ALABAMA							
1 ***Callahan***	Y	Y	N	N	N	N	?
2 ***Dickinson***	Y	Y	N	N	N	N	Y
3 Browder	Y	Y	N	Y	N	Y	N
4 Bevill	Y	Y	Y	Y	N	Y	N
5 Flippo	Y	Y	N	Y	Y	Y	?
6 Erdreich	Y	Y	N	Y	N	N	N
7 Harris	Y	Y	N	Y	Y	Y	N
ALASKA							
AL ***Young***	?	N	N	Y	N	Y	N
ARIZONA							
1 ***Rhodes***	Y	Y	N	N	Y	N	Y
2 Udall	?	Y	N	Y	Y	?	Y
3 ***Stump***	N	N	N	N	N	N	N
4 ***Kyl***	Y	Y	Y	N	N	N	Y
5 ***Kolbe***	Y	Y	N	N	N	N	Y
ARKANSAS							
1 Alexander	Y	Y	Y	Y	N	Y	Y
2 ***Robinson***	Y	N	N	N	N	N	?
3 ***Hammerschmidt***	N	N	N	N	N	N	N
4 Anthony	Y	Y	Y	Y	Y	Y	Y
CALIFORNIA							
1 Bosco	Y	Y	Y	Y	Y	Y	Y
2 ***Herger***	Y	Y	N	N	N	N	N
3 Matsui	Y	Y	Y	Y	Y	Y	Y
4 Fazio	Y	Y	Y	Y	Y	Y	Y
5 Pelosi	Y	Y	Y	?	Y	Y	Y
6 Boxer	Y	Y	N	Y	Y	#	?
7 Miller	Y	Y	N	?	Y	Y	Y
8 Dellums	?	Y	N	Y	N	Y	Y
9 Stark	Y	Y	Y	?	N	Y	Y
10 Edwards	Y	Y	N	Y	Y	Y	Y
11 Lantos	Y	Y	Y	Y	Y	Y	Y
12 ***Campbell***	Y	Y	N	N	N	N	N
13 Mineta	Y	Y	Y	Y	Y	Y	Y
14 ***Shumway***	N	N	N	N	N	N	Y
15 Condit	Y	Y	Y	Y	N	?	Y
16 Panetta	Y	Y	N	Y	Y	Y	Y
17 ***Pashayan***	Y	Y	Y	Y	N	Y	Y
18 Lehman	Y	Y	N	Y	Y	Y	Y
19 ***Lagomarsino***	Y	Y	N	N	N	N	N
20 ***Thomas***	Y	Y	N	N	N	Y	N
21 ***Gallegly***	Y	Y	N	N	N	N	N
22 ***Moorhead***	Y	Y	N	N	N	N	N
23 Beilenson	Y	Y	Y	Y	Y	Y	N
24 Waxman	Y	Y	Y	Y	Y	Y	Y
25 Roybal	Y	Y	N	Y	N	Y	Y
26 Berman	Y	Y	Y	Y	Y	Y	Y
27 Levine	?	Y	Y	Y	Y	Y	Y
28 Dixon	Y	Y	Y	Y	Y	Y	Y
29 Hawkins	?	?	?	?	Y	?	?
30 Martinez	Y	Y	N	Y	N	Y	Y
31 Dymally	Y	Y	N	Y	N	Y	Y
32 Anderson	Y	Y	N	Y	Y	Y	Y
33 ***Dreier***	Y	Y	N	N	N	N	N
34 Torres	Y	Y	N	Y	Y	Y	Y
35 ***Lewis***	N	Y	N	N	Y	Y	N
36 Brown	Y	Y	N	Y	Y	Y	Y
37 ***McCandless***	Y	Y	N	N	N	Y	N
38 ***Dornan***	Y	Y	N	N	N	N	N
39 ***Dannemeyer***	N	N	N	N	N	N	N
40 ***Cox***	Y	Y	N	N	N	N	N
41 ***Lowery***	Y	Y	N	N	Y	Y	N
42 ***Rohrabacher***	Y	Y	N	N	N	N	Y
43 ***Packard***	Y	Y	N	N	N	N	N
44 Bates	Y	Y	N	Y	N	?	?
45 ***Hunter***	N	?	Y	N	N	N	Y
COLORADO							
1 Schroeder	Y	Y	N	Y	Y	N	Y
2 Skaggs	Y	Y	N	Y	Y	Y	Y
3 Campbell	Y	Y	N	Y	N	Y	Y
4 ***Brown***	Y	Y	N	N	N	N	N
5 ***Hefley***	Y	Y	N	N	N	N	N
6 ***Schaefer***	Y	Y	N	N	N	N	N
CONNECTICUT							
1 Kennelly	Y	Y	Y	Y	Y	Y	Y
2 Gejdenson	Y	Y	Y	Y	Y	Y	Y
3 Morrison	Y	Y	Y	Y	Y	Y	Y
4 ***Shays***	Y	Y	Y	N	Y	N	Y
5 ***Rowland***	Y	Y	Y	Y	N	?	?
6 ***Johnson***	Y	Y	?	Y	Y	N	Y
DELAWARE							
AL Carper	Y	Y	Y	Y	Y	Y	Y
FLORIDA							
1 Hutto	Y	Y	Y	Y	Y	N	N
2 ***Grant***	Y	Y	N	N	N	N	Y
3 Bennett	Y	Y	N	Y	Y	N	N
4 ***James***	Y	Y	N	N	N	N	N
5 ***McCollum***	Y	Y	Y	N	N	Y	Y
6 ***Stearns***	Y	Y	N	N	N	Y	N
7 Gibbons	Y	Y	Y	Y	Y	Y	Y
8 ***Young***	Y	Y	N	Y	N	Y	N
9 ***Bilirakis***	Y	Y	N	N	N	N	N
10 ***Ireland***	Y	Y	N	N	Y	N	Y
11 Nelson	Y	Y	Y	Y	Y	?	?
12 ***Lewis***	Y	Y	N	N	N	N	N
13 ***Goss***	Y	Y	N	N	N	N	N
14 Johnston	Y	Y	Y	Y	Y	?	?
15 ***Shaw***	Y	Y	N	Y	Y	N	N
16 Smith	Y	Y	Y	Y	Y	Y	Y
17 Lehman	Y	Y	Y	Y	Y	Y	Y
18 ***Ros-Lehtinen***	Y	Y	N	N	N	N	Y
19 Fascell	Y	Y	Y	Y	Y	Y	Y
GEORGIA							
1 Thomas	Y	Y	N	Y	Y	Y	?
2 Hatcher	?	Y	N	Y	Y	Y	Y
3 Ray	Y	Y	N	Y	Y	Y	N
4 Jones	Y	Y	N	Y	Y	Y	Y
5 Lewis	Y	Y	N	Y	Y	Y	Y
6 ***Gingrich***	Y	Y	Y	N	N	?	?
7 Darden	Y	Y	Y	Y	Y	Y	Y
8 Rowland	Y	Y	Y	Y	Y	Y	N
9 Jenkins	Y	Y	N	Y	Y	?	?
10 Barnard	Y	Y	Y	Y	N	Y	N
HAWAII							
1 ***Saiki***	Y	Y	N	N	N	?	#
2 Mink	Y	Y	N	Y	Y	Y	Y
IDAHO							
1 ***Craig***	Y	Y	N	N	N	N	N
2 Stallings	Y	Y	N	Y	N	Y	N
ILLINOIS							
1 Hayes	Y	Y	N	Y	N	Y	Y
2 Savage	Y	Y	N	Y	N	Y	N
3 Russo	Y	Y	Y	Y	Y	?	?
4 Sangmeister	Y	Y	Y	Y	N	N	?
5 Lipinski	Y	Y	Y	Y	Y	Y	?
6 ***Hyde***	Y	Y	Y	N	N	Y	Y
7 Collins	Y	Y	N	Y	N	Y	Y
8 Rostenkowski	Y	Y	N	Y	Y	?	?
9 Yates	Y	Y	Y	?	?	Y	Y
10 ***Porter***	Y	Y	Y	N	N	Y	Y
11 Annunzio	Y	Y	Y	Y	N	Y	Y
12 ***Crane***	N	N	N	N	N	N	N
13 ***Fawell***	Y	Y	Y	N	N	N	Y
14 ***Hastert***	N	Y	Y	N	N	N	N
15 ***Madigan***	Y	Y	Y	Y	Y	Y	Y
16 ***Martin***	Y	Y	Y	N	N	?	?
17 Evans	Y	Y	N	Y	Y	Y	Y
18 ***Michel***	?	Y	Y	Y	Y	Y	Y
19 Bruce	Y	Y	N	Y	N	Y	Y
20 Durbin	Y	Y	N	Y	Y	Y	Y
21 Costello	Y	N	Y	Y	N	Y	Y
22 Poshard	Y	N	N	Y	Y	Y	Y
INDIANA							
1 Visclosky	Y	Y	N	Y	Y	Y	Y
2 Sharp	Y	Y	N	Y	N	?	?
3 ***Hiler***	Y	Y	N	N	N	N	Y

ND Northern Democrats SD Southern Democrats

	524	525	526	527	528	529	530
4 Long	Y	Y	N	Y	N	Y	N
5 Jontz	Y	Y	N	Y	N	Y	Y
6 **Burton**	N	N	N	N	N	?	?
7 **Myers**	N	N	Y	N	N	Y	N
8 McCloskey	Y	Y	Y	Y	Y	Y	Y
9 Hamilton	Y	Y	Y	Y	Y	Y	Y
10 Jacobs	Y	Y	N	Y	N	N	Y
IOWA							
1 **Leach**	Y	Y	N	N	Y	N	Y
2 **Tauke**	Y	Y	Y	N	N	N	Y
3 Nagle	Y	Y	Y	Y	Y	Y	Y
4 Smith	Y	Y	Y	Y	Y	Y	Y
5 **Lightfoot**	N	N	N	N	N	N	Y
6 **Grandy**	Y	Y	Y	N	Y	N	Y
KANSAS							
1 **Roberts**	Y	Y	N	N	Y	Y	N
2 Slattery	Y	Y	N	Y	Y	N	Y
3 **Meyers**	Y	Y	Y	N	Y	N	N
4 Glickman	Y	Y	Y	Y	Y	X	?
5 **Whittaker**	Y	Y	Y	N	Y	Y	Y
KENTUCKY							
1 Hubbard	N	N	N	Y	N	Y	N
2 Natcher	Y	Y	Y	Y	N	Y	N
3 Mazzoli	Y	Y	Y	Y	Y	Y	Y
4 **Bunning**	Y	Y	N	N	N	N	N
5 **Rogers**	Y	Y	N	N	N	N	N
6 **Hopkins**	Y	Y	N	N	N	N	N
7 Perkins	Y	Y	N	Y	N	Y	N
LOUISIANA							
1 **Livingston**	N	Y	N	N	Y	Y	Y
2 Boggs	Y	Y	N	Y	Y	Y	Y
3 Tauzin	?	Y	N	Y	N	Y	N
4 **McCrery**	Y	Y	N	N	Y	Y	Y
5 Huckaby	Y	Y	N	Y	N	Y	N
6 **Baker**	Y	Y	N	N	N	Y	Y
7 Hayes	Y	Y	N	?	?	Y	N
8 **Holloway**	N	Y	Y	N	N	N	?
MAINE							
1 Brennan	?	?	Y	Y	N	?	?
2 **Snowe**	Y	Y	N	N	N	N	Y
MARYLAND							
1 Dyson	Y	Y	N	Y	N	?	N
2 **Bentley**	Y	Y	N	N	N	Y	N
3 Cardin	Y	Y	Y	Y	Y	Y	Y
4 McMillen	Y	Y	Y	Y	Y	Y	Y
5 Hoyer	Y	Y	Y	Y	Y	Y	Y
6 Byron	Y	Y	N	Y	Y	Y	N
7 Mfume	Y	Y	N	Y	Y	Y	Y
8 **Morella**	Y	Y	Y	Y	Y	Y	Y
MASSACHUSETTS							
1 **Conte**	Y	Y	Y	Y	Y	Y	Y
2 Neal	Y	Y	Y	Y	Y	Y	Y
3 Early	Y	Y	Y	Y	N	Y	Y
4 Frank	Y	Y	Y	Y	Y	Y	Y
5 Atkins	Y	Y	Y	Y	Y	Y	Y
6 Mavroules	Y	Y	Y	Y	Y	Y	Y
7 Markey	Y	Y	Y	Y	Y	Y	Y
8 Kennedy	Y	Y	N	Y	Y	Y	Y
9 Moakley	Y	Y	Y	Y	Y	Y	Y
10 Studds	Y	Y	Y	Y	Y	Y	Y
11 Donnelly	Y	Y	Y	Y	Y	Y	Y
MICHIGAN							
1 Conyers	Y	Y	N	Y	Y	Y	Y
2 **Pursell**	Y	Y	N	N	N	?	?
3 Wolpe	Y	Y	N	Y	Y	Y	Y
4 **Upton**	N	Y	N	N	N	N	Y
5 **Henry**	Y	Y	Y	N	N	N	Y
6 Carr	Y	Y	N	Y	N	Y	Y
7 Kildee	Y	Y	N	Y	Y	Y	Y
8 Traxler	Y	Y	Y	Y	Y	?	?
9 **Vander Jagt**	Y	Y	Y	?	-	N	N
10 **Schuette**	Y	Y	N	N	N	?	?
11 **Davis**	Y	Y	N	Y	Y	Y	N
12 Bonior	Y	Y	Y	Y	Y	Y	Y
13 Crockett	Y	?	?	?	Y	?	?
14 Hertel	Y	Y	N	Y	N	Y	N
15 Ford	Y	Y	?	Y	Y	?	Y
16 Dingell	Y	Y	Y	Y	Y	?	?
17 Levin	Y	Y	Y	Y	Y	Y	Y
18 **Broomfield**	Y	Y	Y	N	N	N	Y
MINNESOTA							
1 Penny	Y	Y	Y	Y	Y	N	Y
2 **Weber**	Y	Y	Y	N	N	?	?
3 **Frenzel**	Y	Y	N	Y	Y	Y	Y
4 Vento	Y	Y	N	Y	Y	Y	Y
5 Sabo	Y	Y	Y	Y	Y	Y	Y
6 Sikorski	Y	Y	N	Y	Y	?	?
7 **Stangeland**	Y	Y	N	N	N	N	Y
8 Oberstar	Y	Y	Y	Y	Y	Y	Y
MISSISSIPPI							
1 Whitten	Y	Y	Y	Y	Y	Y	Y
2 Espy	Y	Y	N	Y	Y	Y	Y
3 Montgomery	Y	Y	Y	Y	Y	Y	N
4 Parker	Y	Y	Y	Y	Y	N	N
5 Taylor	Y	Y	N	Y	N	N	N
MISSOURI							
1 Clay	Y	Y	N	Y	N	Y	Y
2 **Buechner**	Y	Y	N	N	Y	N	Y
3 Gephardt	Y	Y	Y	Y	Y	Y	Y
4 Skelton	Y	Y	N	Y	Y	?	?
5 Wheat	Y	?	?	Y	Y	Y	Y
6 **Coleman**	Y	Y	N	N	Y	Y	Y
7 **Hancock**	N	N	N	N	N	N	N
8 **Emerson**	Y	Y	N	N	N	N	N
9 Volkmer	?	Y	N	Y	Y	Y	N
MONTANA							
1 Williams	Y	Y	?	Y	N	Y	Y
2 **Marlenee**	N	N	N	N	N	Y	N
NEBRASKA							
1 **Bereuter**	Y	Y	N	N	N	N	Y
2 Hoagland	Y	Y	Y	Y	N	Y	N
3 **Smith**	?	Y	N	N	Y	N	N
NEVADA							
1 Bilbray	Y	Y	Y	Y	N	Y	Y
2 **Vucanovich**	Y	Y	N	N	N	N	Y
NEW HAMPSHIRE							
1 **Smith**	Y	Y	N	N	N	N	N
2 **Douglas**	Y	Y	N	N	N	N	Y
NEW JERSEY							
1 Vacancy							
2 Hughes	Y	Y	Y	Y	N	Y	Y
3 Pallone	Y	Y	Y	Y	N	N	Y
4 **Smith**	Y	Y	Y	N	N	Y	Y
5 **Roukema**	Y	Y	Y	Y	N	Y	X
6 Dwyer	Y	Y	Y	Y	N	Y	Y
7 **Rinaldo**	Y	Y	Y	N	N	Y	Y
8 Roe	Y	Y	Y	Y	N	Y	Y
9 Torricelli	Y	Y	N	Y	N	Y	Y
10 Payne	Y	Y	N	Y	N	Y	Y
11 **Gallo**	Y	Y	N	N	N	Y	Y
12 **Courter**	Y	Y	Y	N	Y	N	Y
13 **Saxton**	Y	Y	N	N	N	Y	Y
14 Guarini	Y	Y	N	Y	N	Y	Y
NEW MEXICO							
1 **Schiff**	Y	Y	N	N	Y	Y	Y
2 **Skeen**	Y	Y	N	N	Y	Y	Y
3 Richardson	Y	Y	N	Y	Y	Y	Y
NEW YORK							
1 Hochbrueckner	Y	Y	Y	Y	Y	Y	Y
2 Downey	Y	Y	N	Y	Y	Y	Y
3 Mrazek	Y	Y	Y	Y	Y	Y	Y
4 **Lent**	Y	Y	N	N	Y	Y	Y
5 **McGrath**	?	?	?	?	?	#	?
6 Flake	Y	Y	N	?	N	Y	Y
7 Ackerman	Y	Y	Y	Y	Y	Y	Y
8 Scheuer	Y	Y	Y	Y	Y	Y	Y
9 Manton	Y	Y	Y	Y	Y	Y	Y
10 Schumer	Y	Y	Y	Y	Y	Y	Y
11 Towns	Y	Y	N	Y	N	Y	Y
12 Owens	Y	Y	N	Y	N	Y	Y
13 Solarz	Y	Y	Y	Y	Y	Y	Y
14 **Molinari**	Y	Y	Y	N	N	Y	Y
15 **Green**	Y	Y	Y	N	Y	Y	Y
16 Rangel	Y	Y	N	Y	N	Y	Y
17 Weiss	Y	Y	Y	Y	N	Y	Y
18 Serrano	Y	Y	N	Y	Y	Y	Y
19 Engel	Y	Y	Y	Y	Y	Y	Y
20 Lowey	Y	Y	Y	Y	Y	Y	Y
21 **Fish**	Y	Y	Y	Y	Y	Y	Y
22 **Gilman**	Y	Y	Y	Y	Y	Y	Y
23 McNulty	Y	Y	Y	Y	Y	Y	Y
24 **Solomon**	Y	Y	N	N	N	N	Y
25 **Boehlert**	Y	Y	Y	Y	Y	Y	Y
26 **Martin**	Y	Y	N	N	N	N	Y
27 **Walsh**	Y	Y	Y	N	N	?	?
28 McHugh	Y	Y	Y	Y	Y	Y	Y
29 **Horton**	Y	Y	?	Y	N	Y	Y
30 Slaughter	Y	Y	Y	Y	Y	Y	Y
31 **Paxon**	Y	Y	N	N	N	N	Y
32 LaFalce	Y	Y	Y	Y	Y	?	?
33 Nowak	Y	Y	Y	Y	N	Y	?
34 **Houghton**	Y	Y	Y	Y	Y	Y	Y
NORTH CAROLINA							
1 Jones	Y	Y	N	Y	Y	Y	Y
2 Valentine	Y	Y	N	Y	Y	Y	N
3 Lancaster	Y	Y	N	Y	Y	Y	N
4 Price	Y	Y	Y	Y	Y	Y	Y
5 Neal	Y	Y	N	Y	Y	Y	N
6 **Coble**	Y	Y	N	N	N	N	Y
7 Rose	Y	Y	Y	Y	Y	Y	?
8 Hefner	Y	Y	N	Y	Y	Y	Y
9 **McMillan**	Y	Y	N	Y	Y	Y	Y
10 **Ballenger**	Y	Y	N	N	N	N	Y
11 Clarke	Y	Y	N	Y	Y	Y	Y
NORTH DAKOTA							
AL Dorgan	Y	Y	Y	Y	N	Y	Y
OHIO							
1 Luken	Y	Y	Y	Y	Y	?	?
2 **Gradison**	Y	Y	Y	N	N	N	Y
3 Hall	?	Y	Y	Y	Y	Y	Y
4 **Oxley**	Y	Y	?	?	N	N	Y
5 **Gillmor**	Y	Y	N	?	N	Y	Y
6 **McEwen**	N	N	?	N	N	N	Y
7 **DeWine**	Y	N	Y	N	Y	N	Y
8 Vacancy							
9 Kaptur	Y	Y	N	Y	Y	Y	Y
10 **Miller**	N	N	Y	N	N	N	N
11 Eckart	Y	Y	N	Y	Y	Y	N
12 **Kasich**	Y	Y	N	N	N	N	Y
13 Pease	Y	Y	N	Y	Y	Y	Y
14 Sawyer	Y	Y	N	Y	Y	Y	Y
15 **Wylie**	Y	Y	Y	Y	Y	N	Y
16 **Regula**	Y	Y	N	N	N	N	N
17 Traficant	Y	Y	N	Y	N	N	N
18 Applegate	N	N	Y	Y	N	Y	N
19 Feighan	Y	Y	Y	Y	Y	Y	Y
20 Oakar	?	Y	Y	Y	Y	Y	Y
21 Stokes	Y	Y	N	Y	N	Y	Y
OKLAHOMA							
1 **Inhofe**	Y	Y	N	N	N	N	N
2 Synar	Y	Y	Y	Y	Y	Y	Y
3 Watkins	Y	Y	Y	Y	Y	?	?
4 McCurdy	Y	Y	N	Y	Y	Y	N
5 **Edwards**	Y	Y	N	N	N	N	N
6 English	Y	Y	N	Y	N	Y	N
OREGON							
1 AuCoin	Y	Y	Y	Y	Y	Y	Y
2 **Smith, B.**	Y	Y	N	N	N	N	N
3 Wyden	Y	Y	Y	Y	Y	Y	Y
4 DeFazio	Y	Y	Y	Y	Y	Y	Y
5 **Smith, D.**	N	Y	N	N	N	X	?
PENNSYLVANIA							
1 Foglietta	Y	Y	Y	Y	Y	Y	Y
2 Gray	Y	Y	Y	Y	Y	?	Y
3 Borski	Y	Y	Y	Y	Y	Y	Y
4 Kolter	Y	Y	Y	Y	N	Y	Y
5 **Schulze**	Y	Y	Y	N	N	N	Y
6 Yatron	?	Y	N	Y	N	Y	N
7 **Weldon**	Y	Y	Y	N	N	N	Y
8 Kostmayer	Y	Y	Y	Y	Y	Y	Y
9 **Shuster**	N	N	Y	N	N	N	N
10 **McDade**	Y	Y	Y	N	Y	Y	Y
11 Kanjorski	Y	Y	Y	Y	Y	Y	Y
12 Murtha	Y	Y	N	Y	Y	Y	Y
13 **Coughlin**	Y	Y	N	N	Y	Y	Y
14 Coyne	Y	Y	Y	Y	Y	Y	Y
15 **Ritter**	Y	Y	Y	N	Y	N	Y
16 **Walker**	Y	Y	N	N	N	N	Y
17 **Gekas**	Y	Y	N	N	N	N	Y
18 Walgren	Y	Y	Y	Y	Y	?	?
19 **Goodling**	Y	Y	N	Y	Y	N	N
20 Gaydos	Y	Y	Y	Y	N	Y	Y
21 **Ridge**	Y	Y	N	N	Y	N	N
22 Murphy	Y	Y	N	Y	N	?	?
23 **Clinger**	Y	Y	Y	Y	Y	Y	Y
RHODE ISLAND							
1 **Machtley**	Y	Y	Y	N	N	Y	Y
2 **Schneider**	Y	Y	Y	N	N	#	?
SOUTH CAROLINA							
1 **Ravenel**	Y	Y	N	N	N	N	Y
2 **Spence**	Y	Y	N	N	N	N	N
3 Derrick	Y	Y	Y	Y	Y	?	?
4 Patterson	Y	Y	Y	Y	N	Y	N
5 Spratt	Y	Y	Y	Y	Y	Y	Y
6 Tallon	Y	Y	N	Y	Y	Y	Y
SOUTH DAKOTA							
AL Johnson	Y	Y	Y	Y	Y	Y	Y
TENNESSEE							
1 **Quillen**	Y	Y	Y	N	N	X	?
2 **Duncan**	Y	Y	N	N	N	N	N
3 Lloyd	Y	Y	N	Y	Y	N	N
4 Cooper	Y	Y	Y	Y	Y	Y	N
5 Clement	Y	Y	Y	Y	Y	Y	N
6 Gordon	Y	Y	Y	Y	Y	Y	N
7 **Sundquist**	N	Y	N	N	N	N	N
8 Tanner	Y	Y	N	Y	Y	Y	N
9 Ford	Y	Y	N	?	Y	?	Y
TEXAS							
1 Chapman	Y	Y	N	Y	Y	Y	N
2 Wilson	Y	Y	N	Y	Y	Y	Y
3 **Bartlett**	Y	Y	N	N	N	N	Y
4 Hall	Y	Y	N	Y	N	Y	N
5 Bryant	Y	Y	N	Y	N	Y	N
6 **Barton**	Y	Y	N	N	N	N	Y
7 **Archer**	Y	Y	N	N	N	N	N
8 **Fields**	Y	Y	N	N	N	N	N
9 Brooks	Y	Y	Y	Y	Y	Y	Y
10 Pickle	Y	Y	N	Y	Y	Y	Y
11 Leath	Y	Y	N	Y	Y	?	?
12 Geren	Y	Y	N	Y	N	Y	N
13 Sarpalius	?	Y	N	Y	N	N	N
14 Laughlin	Y	Y	N	Y	N	N	N
15 de la Garza	Y	Y	N	Y	Y	Y	Y
16 Coleman	Y	Y	N	Y	?	Y	Y
17 Stenholm	Y	Y	N	Y	Y	Y	N
18 Washington	Y	Y	N	Y	N	Y	Y
19 **Combest**	Y	N	N	N	N	N	N
20 Gonzalez	Y	Y	N	Y	Y	Y	Y
21 **Smith**	Y	Y	Y	N	N	N	Y
22 **DeLay**	N	N	N	N	N	N	Y
23 Bustamante	Y	Y	N	?	Y	Y	Y
24 Frost	Y	Y	Y	Y	Y	Y	Y
25 Andrews	Y	Y	N	Y	Y	Y	N
26 **Armey**	N	N	N	N	N	N	Y
27 Ortiz	Y	Y	N	Y	Y	Y	Y
UTAH							
1 **Hansen**	Y	Y	N	Y	N	N	N
2 Owens	Y	Y	Y	Y	Y	Y	Y
3 **Nielson**	Y	Y	N	Y	N	N	Y
VERMONT							
AL **Smith**	Y	Y	N	Y	Y	?	?
VIRGINIA							
1 **Bateman**	Y	Y	N	Y	Y	Y	Y
2 Pickett	Y	Y	N	Y	N	Y	Y
3 **Bliley**	Y	Y	Y	N	N	N	Y
4 Sisisky	Y	Y	N	Y	Y	Y	Y
5 Payne	Y	Y	N	Y	Y	Y	N
6 Olin	Y	Y	N	Y	Y	N	N
7 **Slaughter**	Y	Y	Y	N	N	N	N
8 **Parris**	Y	Y	N	N	N	N	N
9 Boucher	Y	Y	?	?	Y	Y	?
10 **Wolf**	Y	Y	Y	Y	Y	N	Y
WASHINGTON							
1 **Miller**	Y	Y	Y	N	Y	N	Y
2 Swift	Y	Y	Y	Y	Y	Y	Y
3 Unsoeld	Y	Y	Y	Y	N	Y	Y
4 **Morrison**	Y	Y	Y	Y	Y	Y	Y
5 Foley					Y		
6 Dicks	Y	Y	N	Y	Y	Y	Y
7 McDermott	Y	Y	Y	Y	Y	Y	Y
8 **Chandler**	Y	Y	N	Y	Y	Y	Y
WEST VIRGINIA							
1 Mollohan	N	N	N	Y	Y	Y	Y
2 Staggers	Y	Y	N	Y	N	N	N
3 Wise	Y	Y	N	Y	Y	Y	N
4 Rahall	Y	Y	Y	Y	N	N	Y
WISCONSIN							
1 Aspin	Y	Y	Y	Y	Y	?	?
2 Kastenmeier	Y	Y	Y	Y	Y	Y	Y
3 **Gunderson**	Y	Y	Y	N	N	N	Y
4 Kleczka	Y	Y	N	Y	Y	Y	?
5 Moody	Y	Y	Y	Y	N	Y	Y
6 **Petri**	Y	Y	N	N	N	N	N
7 Obey	Y	Y	Y	Y	Y	Y	Y
8 **Roth**	Y	Y	N	N	N	N	N
9 **Sensenbrenner**	Y	Y	N	N	N	N	N
WYOMING							
AL **Thomas**	Y	Y	Y	N	N	N	Y

Southern states - Ala., Ark., Fla., Ga., Ky., La., Miss., N.C., Okla., S.C., Tenn., Texas, Va.
Omitted votes are quorum calls, which CQ does not include in its vote charts.

HOUSE VOTES 531, 532, 533, 534, 535, 536

531. HR 5114. Fiscal 1991 Foreign Operations Appropriations/Conference Report. Adoption of the conference report on the bill to appropriate $15,389,400,887 in fiscal 1991 for foreign military and economic assistance and export financing. The president requested $15,518,826,537. Adopted 188-162: R 63-82; D 125-80 (ND 92-46, SD 33-34), Oct. 27, 1990.

532. HR 5769. Fiscal 1991 Interior Appropriations/Conference Report. Adoption of the conference report on the bill to appropriate $11,735,825,000 for the Interior Department and related agencies in fiscal 1991. The president requested $9,856,902,000. Adopted 298-43: R 107-36; D 191-7 (ND 131-3, SD 60-4), Oct. 27, 1990.

533. H J Res 687. Fiscal 1991 Continuing Appropriations/Passage. Passage of the joint resolution to provide continuing appropriations for fiscal 1991 through Nov. 5, suspend sequestration through Nov. 5 and extend a temporary increase in the debt limit through Nov. 5. Passed 283-49: R 97-45; D 186-4 (ND 124-3, SD 62-1), Oct. 27, 1990.

534. S 3266. Crime Control/Passage. Brooks, D-Texas, motion to suspend the rules and pass (thus clearing for the president) the bill to crack down on drug and white-collar crime, including possible life imprisonment for savings and loan criminals. Motion agreed to 313-1: R 135-1; D 178-0 (ND 124-0, SD 54-0), Oct. 27, 1990. A two-thirds majority of those present and voting (210 in this case) is required for passage under suspension of the rules.

535. HR 4793. Small Business Authorization/Passage. Smith, D-Iowa, motion to suspend the rules and agree to a Senate amendment (thus clearing the measure for the president) to the bill to reauthorize the Small Business Act and the Small Business Investment Act of 1958. Motion agreed to 250-0: R 117-0; D 133-0 (ND 92-0, SD 41-0), Oct. 28, 1990 (in the session that began, and the Congressional Record dated, Oct. 27, 1990). A two-thirds majority of those present and voting (167 in this case) is required for passage under suspension of the rules.

536. S 280. Niobrara River Designation/Passage. Vento, D-Minn., motion to suspend the rules and concur in Senate amendments to House amendments to the bill to amend the Wild and Scenic Rivers Act by designating a segment of the Niobrara River in Nebraska as a component of the National Wild and Scenic Rivers System. Motion rejected 157-95: R 25-91; D 132-4 (ND 92-1, SD 40-3), Oct. 28, 1990 (in the session that began, and the Congressional Record dated, Oct. 27, 1990). A two-thirds majority of those present and voting (168 in this case) is required for passage under suspension of the rules.

KEY

- Y Voted for (yea).
- # Paired for.
- + Announced for.
- N Voted against (nay).
- X Paired against.
- - Announced against.
- P Voted "present."
- C Voted "present" to avoid possible conflict of interest.
- ? Did not vote or otherwise make a position known.

Democrats ***Republicans***

	531	532	533	534	535	536
ALABAMA						
1 ***Callahan***	?	?	?	?	?	?
2 ***Dickinson***	N	Y	Y	?	?	?
3 Browder	Y	Y	Y	Y	Y	Y
4 Bevill	N	Y	Y	?	?	?
5 Flippo	?	?	?	?	?	?
6 Erdreich	Y	Y	Y	Y	Y	Y
7 Harris	Y	Y	Y	Y	Y	Y
ALASKA						
AL ***Young***	Y	Y	Y	Y	Y	N
ARIZONA						
1 ***Rhodes***	N	Y	Y	Y	Y	N
2 Udall	Y	Y	Y	Y	?	?
3 ***Stump***	N	N	N	Y	Y	N
4 ***Kyl***	N	Y	N	Y	Y	N
5 ***Kolbe***	Y	Y	Y	Y	Y	N
ARKANSAS						
1 Alexander	N	Y	Y	Y	?	?
2 ***Robinson***	?	?	?	?	?	?
3 ***Hammerschmidt***	N	Y	N	Y	Y	N
4 Anthony	Y	Y	Y	Y	?	Y
CALIFORNIA						
1 Bosco	?	?	?	Y	Y	Y
2 ***Herger***	N	Y	Y	Y	Y	N
3 Matsui	Y	?	?	?	?	?
4 Fazio	Y	Y	Y	Y	Y	Y
5 Pelosi	Y	Y	Y	Y	?	?
6 Boxer	#	?	?	?	?	?
7 Miller	N	Y	Y	Y	Y	Y
8 Dellums	N	Y	Y	Y	Y	?
9 Stark	?	Y	Y	Y	?	?
10 Edwards	?	?	?	?	?	?
11 Lantos	Y	Y	?	?	?	?
12 ***Campbell***	Y	Y	Y	Y	Y	Y
13 Mineta	Y	Y	Y	Y	Y	Y
14 ***Shumway***	N	N	N	Y	Y	N
15 Condit	N	N	N	Y	Y	Y
16 Panetta	Y	Y	Y	+	Y	Y
17 ***Pashayan***	N	Y	Y	Y	Y	N
18 Lehman	N	Y	Y	Y	Y	Y
19 ***Lagomarsino***	Y	N	Y	Y	Y	N
20 ***Thomas***	N	Y	N	?	?	?
21 ***Gallegly***	N	Y	Y	Y	Y	N
22 ***Moorhead***	N	N	N	Y	Y	N
23 Beilenson	Y	Y	Y	Y	?	?
24 Waxman	Y	Y	Y	Y	?	?
25 Roybal	Y	Y	Y	Y	Y	Y
26 Berman	Y	Y	Y	Y	Y	Y
27 Levine	Y	Y	Y	Y	?	?
28 Dixon	Y	?	?	?	?	?
29 Hawkins	?	?	?	?	?	?
30 Martinez	Y	Y	Y	Y	?	?
31 Dymally	Y	Y	Y	Y	Y	Y
32 Anderson	N	Y	Y	Y	Y	Y
33 ***Dreier***	N	N	N	Y	Y	Y
34 Torres	Y	Y	Y	Y	Y	?
35 ***Lewis***	Y	Y	Y	Y	Y	N
36 Brown	Y	Y	Y	Y	?	?
37 ***McCandless***	N	Y	N	Y	Y	N
38 ***Dornan***	Y	N	N	Y	Y	N
39 ***Dannemeyer***	N	N	N	Y	Y	N
40 ***Cox***	Y	N	N	Y	Y	Y
41 ***Lowery***	Y	Y	Y	Y	Y	N
42 ***Rohrabacher***	Y	N	N	Y	Y	N
43 ***Packard***	N	Y	Y	Y	Y	N
44 Bates	?	?	?	?	?	?
45 ***Hunter***	Y	Y	Y	Y	Y	N
COLORADO						
1 Schroeder	N	Y	?	Y	?	?
2 Skaggs	Y	Y	Y	Y	Y	Y
3 Campbell	N	Y	Y	?	?	?
4 ***Brown***	N	N	N	Y	Y	N
5 ***Hefley***	N	Y	N	Y	Y	Y
6 ***Schaefer***	Y	Y	Y	?	?	?
CONNECTICUT						
1 Kennelly	Y	Y	Y	Y	Y	Y
2 Gejdenson	Y	Y	Y	Y	Y	Y
3 Morrison	?	?	?	?	?	?
4 ***Shays***	Y	Y	Y	Y	Y	Y
5 ***Rowland***	?	?	?	?	?	?
6 ***Johnson***	Y	Y	N	Y	Y	N
DELAWARE						
AL Carper	Y	Y	Y	Y	?	?
FLORIDA						
1 Hutto	N	Y	Y	?	?	?
2 ***Grant***	N	Y	Y	Y	?	?
3 Bennett	N	Y	Y	Y	Y	Y
4 ***James***	N	Y	Y	Y	Y	N
5 ***McCollum***	N	Y	Y	Y	Y	N
6 ***Stearns***	Y	Y	Y	Y	Y	N
7 Gibbons	N	?	?	?	?	?
8 ***Young***	N	Y	Y	Y	Y	N
9 ***Bilirakis***	N	Y	Y	Y	Y	N
10 ***Ireland***	N	Y	Y	Y	Y	N
11 Nelson	?	?	?	?	?	?
12 ***Lewis***	N	N	Y	Y	Y	N
13 ***Goss***	Y	Y	Y	Y	Y	Y
14 Johnston	?	?	?	?	?	?
15 ***Shaw***	?	?	?	?	?	?
16 Smith	Y	Y	Y	Y	Y	Y
17 Lehman	Y	Y	?	Y	?	?
18 ***Ros-Lehtinen***	Y	Y	Y	Y	Y	N
19 Fascell	Y	Y	Y	Y	Y	Y
GEORGIA						
1 Thomas	?	?	?	?	?	?
2 Hatcher	Y	Y	Y	Y	?	?
3 Ray	N	Y	Y	Y	Y	Y
4 Jones	N	Y	Y	Y	Y	Y
5 Lewis	N	Y	Y	Y	Y	Y
6 ***Gingrich***	?	?	?	?	?	?
7 Darden	N	Y	Y	Y	Y	Y
8 Rowland	N	?	?	?	?	?
9 Jenkins	?	?	?	?	?	?
10 Barnard	N	Y	Y	?	?	?
HAWAII						
1 ***Saiki***	?	?	?	?	?	?
2 Mink	?	?	?	?	?	?
IDAHO						
1 ***Craig***	N	Y	N	Y	?	?
2 Stallings	N	Y	Y	Y	Y	Y
ILLINOIS						
1 Hayes	N	Y	Y	Y	Y	Y
2 Savage	N	?	?	Y	?	?
3 Russo	?	?	?	?	?	?
4 Sangmeister	?	?	?	?	?	?
5 Lipinski	?	?	?	?	?	?
6 ***Hyde***	Y	Y	Y	Y	?	?
7 Collins	Y	Y	Y	Y	Y	Y
8 Rostenkowski	?	?	?	?	?	?
9 Yates	Y	Y	Y	Y	?	?
10 ***Porter***	Y	Y	N	Y	?	?
11 Annunzio	Y	Y	Y	Y	?	?
12 ***Crane***	?	?	?	?	?	?
13 ***Fawell***	N	Y	N	Y	Y	N
14 ***Hastert***	Y	Y	N	Y	Y	N
15 ***Madigan***	?	?	?	?	?	?
16 ***Martin***	?	?	?	?	?	?
17 Evans	N	Y	Y	Y	Y	Y
18 ***Michel***	Y	Y	Y	Y	Y	N
19 Bruce	N	Y	Y	Y	Y	Y
20 Durbin	N	Y	Y	Y	?	?
21 Costello	N	Y	Y	Y	Y	Y
22 Poshard	N	Y	Y	Y	Y	Y
INDIANA						
1 Visclosky	N	Y	Y	Y	Y	Y
2 Sharp	?	?	?	?	?	Y
3 ***Hiler***	N	Y	Y	Y	Y	N

ND Northern Democrats SD Southern Democrats

	531	532	533	534	535	536
4 Long	N	Y	Y	Y	Y	Y
5 Jontz	N	Y	Y	Y	Y	Y
6 ***Burton***	?	?	?	?	?	?
7 ***Myers***	N	Y	Y	Y	Y	N
8 McCloskey	N	Y	Y	Y	Y	Y
9 Hamilton	Y	Y	Y	Y	Y	Y
10 Jacobs	N	Y	Y	Y	Y	Y
IOWA						
1 ***Leach***	Y	Y	Y	Y	Y	Y
2 ***Tauke***	N	Y	Y	Y	Y	N
3 Nagle	Y	Y	Y	Y	Y	Y
4 Smith	Y	Y	Y	Y	Y	Y
5 ***Lightfoot***	Y	Y	N	Y	Y	N
6 ***Grandy***	Y	Y	Y	Y	Y	N
KANSAS						
1 ***Roberts***	N	Y	Y	Y	Y	N
2 Slattery	N	Y	Y	Y	Y	Y
3 ***Meyers***	Y	Y	Y	Y	Y	?
4 Glickman	?	?	?	?	?	?
5 ***Whittaker***	N	Y	Y	Y	Y	Y
KENTUCKY						
1 Hubbard	N	Y	Y	Y	Y	Y
2 Natcher	Y	Y	Y	Y	Y	Y
3 Mazzoli	N	Y	Y	Y	Y	Y
4 ***Bunning***	N	N	N	Y	?	?
5 ***Rogers***	N	Y	Y	Y	Y	N
6 ***Hopkins***	N	Y	Y	Y	Y	N
7 Perkins	N	Y	Y	Y	Y	N
LOUISIANA						
1 ***Livingston***	Y	Y	Y	Y	Y	N
2 Boggs	Y	Y	Y	Y	Y	Y
3 Tauzin	N	Y	Y	Y	Y	Y
4 ***McCrery***	Y	Y	Y	Y	Y	N
5 Huckaby	?	?	?	?	?	?
6 ***Baker***	N	N	?	?	?	?
7 Hayes	N	?	?	?	?	?
8 ***Holloway***	?	?	?	?	?	?
MAINE						
1 Brennan	?	?	?	?	?	?
2 ***Snowe***	N	Y	Y	Y	Y	N
MARYLAND						
1 Dyson	N	N	Y	Y	Y	Y
2 ***Bentley***	Y	Y	Y	Y	Y	N
3 Cardin	Y	Y	Y	Y	Y	Y
4 McMillen	Y	Y	Y	Y	Y	Y
5 Hoyer	Y	Y	Y	Y	Y	Y
6 Byron	N	Y	N	Y	Y	Y
7 Mfume	N	Y	Y	Y	Y	Y
8 ***Morella***	Y	Y	Y	Y	Y	Y
MASSACHUSETTS						
1 ***Conte***	?	?	?	?	?	?
2 Neal	?	?	?	?	?	?
3 Early	?	?	?	?	?	?
4 Frank	Y	Y	Y	Y	?	?
5 Atkins	Y	Y	Y	Y	?	?
6 Mavroules	Y	Y	?	?	?	?
7 Markey	Y	Y	Y	Y	Y	Y
8 Kennedy	Y	Y	Y	Y	?	Y
9 Moakley	Y	Y	Y	Y	Y	Y
10 Studds	Y	Y	Y	Y	?	?
11 Donnelly	N	Y	Y	Y	Y	Y
MICHIGAN						
1 Conyers	Y	Y	Y	Y	?	?
2 ***Pursell***	?	?	?	?	?	?
3 Wolpe	Y	Y	Y	Y	Y	Y
4 ***Upton***	N	Y	N	Y	Y	Y
5 ***Henry***	N	Y	N	Y	Y	Y
6 Carr	Y	Y	Y	Y	Y	Y
7 Kildee	Y	Y	Y	Y	Y	Y
8 Traxler	?	?	?	?	?	?
9 ***Vander Jagt***	Y	Y	Y	Y	Y	N
10 ***Schuette***	?	?	?	?	?	?
11 ***Davis***	Y	Y	Y	Y	Y	N
12 Bonior	Y	Y	Y	Y	Y	Y
13 Crockett	?	?	?	?	?	?
14 Hertel	Y	Y	Y	Y	Y	Y
15 Ford	Y	?	?	?	?	?
16 Dingell	?	?	?	?	?	?
17 Levin	Y	Y	Y	Y	Y	Y
18 ***Broomfield***	Y	?	?	?	?	?
MINNESOTA						
1 Penny	Y	N	N	Y	?	?
2 ***Weber***	?	?	?	?	?	?
3 ***Frenzel***	?	?	N	Y	?	?
4 Vento	Y	Y	Y	Y	Y	Y

	531	532	533	534	535	536
5 Sabo	Y	Y	Y	Y	Y	Y
6 Sikorski	?	?	?	?	?	?
7 ***Stangeland***	N	Y	Y	Y	Y	N
8 Oberstar	Y	Y	Y	Y	Y	Y
MISSISSIPPI						
1 Whitten	N	Y	Y	?	?	?
2 Espy	Y	Y	Y	Y	?	?
3 Montgomery	Y	Y	Y	Y	?	?
4 Parker	Y	Y	Y	Y	Y	Y
5 Taylor	N	N	Y	Y	Y	Y
MISSOURI						
1 Clay	?	?	?	?	?	?
2 ***Buechner***	Y	Y	Y	Y	?	N
3 Gephardt	Y	Y	Y	?	Y	Y
4 Skelton	?	?	?	?	?	?
5 Wheat	N	Y	Y	Y	Y	Y
6 ***Coleman***	N	Y	Y	Y	Y	N
7 ***Hancock***	N	N	N	Y	Y	N
8 ***Emerson***	N	Y	N	Y	Y	N
9 Volkmer	N	Y	Y	Y	?	?
MONTANA						
1 Williams	N	Y	Y	Y	Y	Y
2 ***Marlenee***	N	N	N	Y	?	?
NEBRASKA						
1 ***Bereuter***	N	Y	Y	Y	Y	Y
2 Hoagland	Y	Y	Y	Y	Y	Y
3 ***Smith***	N	Y	Y	Y	Y	N
NEVADA						
1 Bilbray	Y	Y	Y	Y	?	?
2 ***Vucanovich***	N	Y	Y	Y	Y	N
NEW HAMPSHIRE						
1 ***Smith***	N	N	N	Y	Y	N
2 ***Douglas***	N	Y	N	Y	Y	N
NEW JERSEY						
1 Vacancy						
2 Hughes	N	Y	Y	Y	Y	Y
3 Pallone	Y	Y	Y	Y	Y	Y
4 ***Smith***	Y	Y	Y	Y	Y	Y
5 ***Roukema***	X	?	?	?	?	?
6 Dwyer	Y	Y	Y	?	?	?
7 ***Rinaldo***	Y	Y	Y	Y	Y	Y
8 Roe	Y	Y	Y	Y	?	?
9 Torricelli	Y	Y	Y	Y	?	?
10 Payne	Y	Y	Y	Y	Y	Y
11 ***Gallo***	Y	Y	Y	Y	?	?
12 ***Courter***	Y	Y	Y	Y	?	?
13 ***Saxton***	Y	Y	Y	Y	Y	Y
14 Guarini	?	?	?	?	?	?
NEW MEXICO						
1 ***Schiff***	Y	Y	Y	Y	Y	Y
2 ***Skeen***	Y	Y	Y	Y	?	?
3 Richardson	Y	Y	Y	Y	Y	Y
NEW YORK						
1 Hochbrueckner	Y	Y	Y	Y	Y	Y
2 Downey	Y	Y	Y	Y	?	?
3 Mrazek	?	?	?	?	?	?
4 ***Lent***	Y	Y	Y	Y	Y	N
5 ***McGrath***	#	?	?	?	?	?
6 Flake	?	?	?	?	?	?
7 Ackerman	#	?	?	?	?	?
8 Scheuer	Y	Y	Y	Y	?	Y
9 Manton	Y	Y	Y	?	?	?
10 Schumer	Y	Y	Y	Y	Y	Y
11 Towns	?	?	?	?	?	?
12 Owens	Y	Y	?	?	?	?
13 Solarz	Y	Y	Y	Y	?	?
14 ***Molinari***	Y	Y	Y	Y	Y	N
15 ***Green***	Y	Y	Y	Y	Y	Y
16 Rangel	Y	Y	?	?	?	?
17 Weiss	Y	Y	Y	Y	Y	Y
18 Serrano	Y	Y	Y	Y	Y	Y
19 Engel	Y	Y	Y	Y	Y	Y
20 Lowey	Y	Y	Y	Y	Y	Y
21 ***Fish***	Y	Y	Y	Y	?	?
22 ***Gilman***	Y	Y	N	Y	Y	Y
23 McNulty	Y	Y	Y	Y	Y	Y
24 ***Solomon***	N	N	N	Y	Y	N
25 ***Boehlert***	Y	Y	Y	Y	Y	Y
26 ***Martin***	N	Y	Y	Y	Y	N
27 ***Walsh***	?	?	?	?	?	?
28 McHugh	Y	Y	Y	Y	Y	N
29 ***Horton***	?	?	?	?	?	?
30 Slaughter	Y	Y	Y	Y	Y	+
31 ***Paxon***	Y	N	N	Y	Y	N

	531	532	533	534	535	536
32 LaFalce	?	?	?	?	?	?
33 Nowak	?	?	?	?	?	?
34 ***Houghton***	Y	Y	Y	Y	Y	N
NORTH CAROLINA						
1 Jones	N	Y	Y	?	?	?
2 Valentine	N	?	Y	?	?	?
3 Lancaster	Y	Y	Y	Y	Y	Y
4 Price	Y	Y	Y	Y	Y	Y
5 Neal	N	Y	Y	Y	Y	Y
6 ***Coble***	N	N	Y	Y	Y	N
7 Rose	?	?	?	?	?	?
8 Hefner	N	Y	Y	Y	Y	Y
9 ***McMillan***	Y	Y	Y	Y	Y	Y
10 ***Ballenger***	Y	N	Y	?	?	?
11 Clarke	Y	Y	Y	?	?	?
NORTH DAKOTA						
AL Dorgan	N	Y	Y	Y	Y	?
OHIO						
1 Luken	?	?	?	?	?	?
2 ***Gradison***	?	?	?	?	?	?
3 Hall	?	?	?	?	?	?
4 ***Oxley***	N	Y	Y	Y	?	?
5 ***Gillmor***	Y	Y	?	Y	Y	N
6 ***McEwen***	N	?	?	?	?	?
7 ***DeWine***	N	Y	Y	Y	Y	Y
8 Vacancy						
9 Kaptur	N	Y	Y	Y	Y	Y
10 ***Miller***	N	N	Y	Y	Y	N
11 Eckart	N	Y	Y	Y	Y	Y
12 ***Kasich***	N	Y	Y	Y	Y	N
13 Pease	N	Y	Y	Y	Y	Y
14 Sawyer	Y	Y	Y	Y	Y	Y
15 ***Wylie***	N	Y	Y	Y	Y	N
16 ***Regula***	N	Y	Y	Y	Y	N
17 Traficant	N	Y	Y	Y	Y	Y
18 Applegate	N	Y	Y	Y	Y	Y
19 Feighan	Y	Y	Y	?	?	?
20 Oakar	Y	Y	Y	?	Y	Y
21 Stokes	Y	Y	Y	Y	Y	Y
OKLAHOMA						
1 ***Inhofe***	Y	N	N	Y	?	?
2 Synar	Y	Y	Y	Y	?	?
3 Watkins	?	?	?	?	?	?
4 McCurdy	N	Y	Y	Y	?	?
5 ***Edwards***	N	?	?	?	?	?
6 English	N	Y	Y	Y	?	Y
OREGON						
1 AuCoin	Y	Y	Y	Y	Y	Y
2 ***Smith, B.***	N	Y	Y	Y	Y	N
3 Wyden	Y	Y	Y	Y	Y	Y
4 DeFazio	N	Y	Y	Y	?	?
5 ***Smith, D.***	X	?	?	?	?	?
PENNSYLVANIA						
1 Foglietta	Y	Y	?	Y	Y	Y
2 Gray	Y	Y	?	?	Y	Y
3 Borski	Y	Y	Y	Y	Y	Y
4 Kolter	N	Y	Y	Y	?	?
5 ***Schulze***	?	?	?	?	?	?
6 Yatron	N	Y	Y	Y	?	?
7 ***Weldon***	N	Y	N	Y	Y	Y
8 Kostmayer	Y	Y	Y	Y	?	?
9 ***Shuster***	N	N	Y	?	?	?
10 ***McDade***	?	?	?	?	?	?
11 Kanjorski	N	Y	Y	Y	Y	Y
12 Murtha	Y	Y	Y	Y	Y	Y
13 ***Coughlin***	Y	Y	Y	Y	Y	Y
14 Coyne	Y	Y	Y	?	?	?
15 ***Ritter***	N	Y	Y	Y	Y	N
16 ***Walker***	N	N	N	Y	Y	N
17 ***Gekas***	Y	N	Y	N	Y	N
18 Walgren	?	?	?	?	?	?
19 ***Goodling***	N	N	N	?	?	N
20 Gaydos	N	Y	Y	Y	?	?
21 ***Ridge***	Y	Y	Y	Y	Y	N
22 Murphy	?	?	?	?	?	?
23 ***Clinger***	N	Y	Y	Y	?	?
RHODE ISLAND						
1 ***Machtley***	?	Y	Y	?	?	?
2 ***Schneider***	X	?	?	?	?	?
SOUTH CAROLINA						
1 ***Ravenel***	N	Y	Y	Y	?	?
2 ***Spence***	N	Y	Y	Y	Y	N
3 Derrick	?	?	?	?	?	?
4 Patterson	N	Y	Y	Y	Y	Y
5 Spratt	Y	Y	Y	Y	Y	Y
6 Tallon	?	?	?	?	?	?

	531	532	533	534	535	536
SOUTH DAKOTA						
AL Johnson	N	Y	Y	Y	Y	Y
TENNESSEE						
1 ***Quillen***	#	?	?	?	?	?
2 ***Duncan***	N	N	N	Y	Y	N
3 Lloyd	N	N	Y	Y	Y	Y
4 Cooper	Y	Y	Y	Y	Y	Y
5 Clement	N	Y	Y	Y	Y	Y
6 Gordon	?	?	?	?	?	?
7 ***Sundquist***	Y	Y	Y	Y	Y	Y
8 Tanner	N	Y	Y	Y	Y	Y
9 Ford	?	Y	Y	Y	Y	Y
TEXAS						
1 Chapman	N	Y	Y	?	?	?
2 Wilson	Y	Y	?	?	?	?
3 ***Bartlett***	Y	N	Y	Y	Y	N
4 Hall	N	Y	N	Y	Y	N
5 Bryant	N	Y	Y	Y	Y	Y
6 ***Barton***	?	?	?	?	?	?
7 ***Archer***	N	N	N	Y	Y	?
8 ***Fields***	N	N	N	Y	Y	N
9 Brooks	Y	Y	Y	Y	Y	Y
10 Pickle	Y	Y	Y	?	?	?
11 Leath	?	?	?	?	?	?
12 Geren	N	Y	Y	Y	Y	Y
13 Sarpalius	N	N	Y	Y	Y	Y
14 Laughlin	?	?	?	?	?	?
15 de la Garza	Y	Y	Y	Y	Y	Y
16 Coleman	Y	Y	Y	Y	Y	Y
17 Stenholm	Y	Y	Y	Y	?	?
18 Washington	Y	Y	Y	Y	?	?
19 ***Combest***	N	N	Y	Y	?	?
20 Gonzalez	Y	Y	Y	Y	Y	N
21 ***Smith***	N	Y	Y	Y	Y	N
22 ***DeLay***	N	N	N	Y	Y	N
23 Bustamante	Y	Y	Y	Y	Y	Y
24 Frost	Y	Y	Y	Y	Y	Y
25 Andrews	Y	Y	Y	Y	?	?
26 ***Armey***	N	N	N	Y	Y	N
27 Ortiz	Y	Y	Y	Y	Y	Y
UTAH						
1 ***Hansen***	N	Y	N	Y	Y	N
2 Owens	Y	Y	Y	Y	Y	Y
3 ***Nielson***	N	N	N	Y	Y	N
VERMONT						
AL ***Smith***	?	?	?	?	?	?
VIRGINIA						
1 ***Bateman***	Y	Y	Y	Y	Y	N
2 Pickett	N	N	Y	Y	Y	Y
3 ***Bliley***	Y	Y	Y	Y	Y	N
4 Sisisky	Y	Y	Y	?	?	?
5 Payne	Y	Y	Y	Y	Y	Y
6 Olin	?	?	?	?	?	?
7 ***Slaughter***	N	Y	Y	Y	Y	N
8 ***Parris***	Y	Y	Y	Y	?	?
9 Boucher	?	?	?	?	?	?
10 ***Wolf***	Y	Y	Y	Y	Y	N
WASHINGTON						
1 ***Miller***	Y	Y	Y	Y	Y	Y
2 Swift	Y	Y	Y	Y	?	?
3 Unsoeld	Y	Y	Y	Y	Y	Y
4 ***Morrison***	Y	Y	Y	Y	Y	?
5 Foley						Y
6 Dicks	Y	Y	?	Y	?	Y
7 McDermott	Y	Y	Y	Y	Y	Y
8 ***Chandler***	Y	Y	Y	Y	Y	N
WEST VIRGINIA						
1 Mollohan	N	Y	Y	Y	Y	Y
2 Staggers	N	Y	Y	Y	?	?
3 Wise	Y	Y	Y	Y	Y	Y
4 Rahall	N	Y	Y	Y	Y	Y
WISCONSIN						
1 Aspin	?	?	?	?	?	?
2 Kastenmeier	N	Y	Y	Y	?	?
3 ***Gunderson***	?	?	?	?	?	?
4 Kleczka	X	?	?	?	?	?
5 Moody	N	Y	Y	Y	Y	Y
6 ***Petri***	N	N	N	Y	?	?
7 Obey	Y	?	Y	Y	Y	Y
8 ***Roth***	N	Y	Y	Y	Y	N
9 ***Sensenbrenner***	N	N	N	Y	Y	N
WYOMING						
AL ***Thomas***	N	Y	Y	Y	Y	N

Southern states - Ala., Ark., Fla., Ga., Ky., La., Miss., N.C., Okla., S.C., Tenn., Texas, Va.
Omitted votes are quorum calls, which CQ does not include in its vote charts.

CQ

Appendix S

SENATE ROLL-CALL VOTES

	1
ALABAMA	
Heflin	Y
Shelby	Y
ALASKA	
Murkowski	N
Stevens	N
ARIZONA	
DeConcini	Y
McCain	N
ARKANSAS	
Bumpers	Y
Pryor	Y
CALIFORNIA	
Cranston	Y
Wilson	Y
COLORADO	
Wirth	Y
Armstrong	Y
CONNECTICUT	
Dodd	Y
Lieberman	Y
DELAWARE	
Biden	Y
Roth	N
FLORIDA	
Graham	Y
Mack	N
GEORGIA	
Fowler	Y
Nunn	Y
HAWAII	
Inouye	Y
Matsunaga	Y
IDAHO	
McClure	N
Symms	N
ILLINOIS	
Dixon	Y
Simon	Y
INDIANA	
Coats	N
Lugar	N

	1
IOWA	
Harkin	Y
Grassley	N
KANSAS	
Dole	N
Kassebaum	N
KENTUCKY	
Ford	Y
McConnell	N
LOUISIANA	
Breaux	?
Johnston	Y
MAINE	
Mitchell	Y
Cohen	Y
MARYLAND	
Mikulski	Y
Sarbanes	Y
MASSACHUSETTS	
Kennedy	Y
Kerry	Y
MICHIGAN	
Levin	Y
Riegle	Y
MINNESOTA	
Boschwitz	Y
Durenberger	N
MISSISSIPPI	
Cochran	N
Lott	N
MISSOURI	
Bond	N
Danforth	N
MONTANA	
Baucus	Y
Burns	N
NEBRASKA	
Exon	Y
Kerrey	Y
NEVADA	
Bryan	Y
Reid	Y

	1
NEW HAMPSHIRE	
Humphrey	N
Rudman	N
NEW JERSEY	
Bradley	Y
Lautenberg	Y
NEW MEXICO	
Bingaman	Y
Domenici	N
NEW YORK	
Moynihan	Y
D'Amato	N
NORTH CAROLINA	
Sanford	Y
Helms	Y
NORTH DAKOTA	
Burdick	Y
Conrad	Y
OHIO	
Glenn	Y
Metzenbaum	Y
OKLAHOMA	
Boren	Y
Nickles	N
OREGON	
Hatfield	N
Packwood	N
PENNSYLVANIA	
Heinz	N
Specter	N
RHODE ISLAND	
Pell	Y
Chafee	N
SOUTH CAROLINA	
Hollings	Y
Thurmond	N
SOUTH DAKOTA	
Daschle	Y
Pressler	Y
TENNESSEE	
Gore	Y
Sasser	Y

KEY

Y Voted for (yea).
\# Paired for.
+ Announced for.
N Voted against (nay).
X Paired against.
\- Announced against.
P Voted "present."
C Voted "present" to avoid possible conflict of interest.
? Did not vote or otherwise make a position known.

Democrats *Republicans*

	1
TEXAS	
Bentsen	Y
Gramm	N
UTAH	
Garn	N
Hatch	N
VERMONT	
Leahy	Y
Jeffords	N
VIRGINIA	
Robb	Y
Warner	N
WASHINGTON	
Adams	Y
Gorton	Y
WEST VIRGINIA	
Byrd	Y
Rockefeller	Y
WISCONSIN	
Kohl	Y
Kasten	Y
WYOMING	
Simpson	N
Wallop	N

ND Northern Democrats SD Southern Democrats Southern states - Ala., Ark., Fla., Ga., Ky., La., Miss., N.C., Okla., S.C., Tenn., Texas, Va.

1. HR 2712. Chinese Students/Veto Override. Passage, over President Bush's Nov. 30, 1989, veto, of the bill to defer indefinitely the deportation of Chinese students whose visas expire and to waive for students on "J" visas a requirement that they return to their home country for two years before applying for permanent residence in the United States. It would apply to Chinese nationals who were in the United States as of June 5, 1989. Rejected 62-37: R 8-37; D 54-0 (ND 38-0, SD 16-0), Jan. 25, 1990. A two-thirds majority of those present and voting (67 in this case) of both houses is required to override a veto. A "nay" was a vote supporting the president's position.

	2	3
ALABAMA		
Heflin	Y	Y
Shelby	Y	Y
ALASKA		
Murkowski	Y	Y
Stevens	Y	Y
ARIZONA		
DeConcini	Y	Y
McCain	Y	Y
ARKANSAS		
Bumpers	Y	Y
Pryor	Y	Y
CALIFORNIA		
Cranston	Y	Y
Wilson	Y	Y
COLORADO		
Wirth	Y	Y
Armstrong	Y	?
CONNECTICUT		
Dodd	Y	Y
Lieberman	Y	Y
DELAWARE		
Biden	Y	Y
Roth	Y	Y
FLORIDA		
Graham	Y	Y
Mack	Y	Y
GEORGIA		
Fowler	Y	Y
Nunn	Y	Y
HAWAII		
Inouye	?	?
Matsunaga	Y	Y
IDAHO		
McClure	Y	Y
Symms	Y	N
ILLINOIS		
Dixon	Y	Y
Simon	Y	Y
INDIANA		
Coats	Y	Y
Lugar	Y	Y
IOWA		
Harkin	Y	Y
Grassley	Y	Y
KANSAS		
Dole	Y	Y
Kassebaum	Y	Y
KENTUCKY		
Ford	Y	Y
McConnell	Y	Y
LOUISIANA		
Breaux	Y	Y
Johnston	Y	Y
MAINE		
Mitchell	Y	Y
Cohen	Y	Y
MARYLAND		
Mikulski	Y	Y
Sarbanes	Y	Y
MASSACHUSETTS		
Kennedy	Y	Y
Kerry	Y	Y
MICHIGAN		
Levin	Y	Y
Riegle	Y	Y
MINNESOTA		
Boschwitz	Y	Y
Durenberger	Y	Y
MISSISSIPPI		
Cochran	Y	Y
Lott	Y	Y
MISSOURI		
Bond	Y	Y
Danforth	Y	Y
MONTANA		
Baucus	Y	Y
Burns	Y	Y
NEBRASKA		
Exon	Y	Y
Kerrey	Y	Y
NEVADA		
Bryan	Y	Y
Reid	Y	Y
NEW HAMPSHIRE		
Humphrey	Y	Y
Rudman	Y	Y
NEW JERSEY		
Bradley	Y	Y
Lautenberg	Y	Y
NEW MEXICO		
Bingaman	Y	Y
Domenici	Y	Y
NEW YORK		
Moynihan	Y	Y
D'Amato	Y	Y
NORTH CAROLINA		
Sanford	Y	Y
Helms	Y	N
NORTH DAKOTA		
Burdick	Y	Y
Conrad	Y	Y
OHIO		
Glenn	Y	Y
Metzenbaum	Y	Y
OKLAHOMA		
Boren	Y	Y
Nickles	Y	Y
OREGON		
Hatfield	Y	Y
Packwood	Y	Y
PENNSYLVANIA		
Heinz	Y	Y
Specter	Y	Y
RHODE ISLAND		
Pell	Y	Y
Chafee	Y	Y
SOUTH CAROLINA		
Hollings	Y	Y
Thurmond	Y	Y
SOUTH DAKOTA		
Daschle	Y	Y
Pressler	Y	Y
TENNESSEE		
Gore	Y	Y
Sasser	Y	Y
TEXAS		
Bentsen	Y	Y
Gramm	Y	Y
UTAH		
Garn	Y	Y
Hatch	Y	Y
VERMONT		
Leahy	Y	Y
Jeffords	Y	Y
VIRGINIA		
Robb	Y	Y
Warner	Y	Y
WASHINGTON		
Adams	Y	Y
Gorton	Y	Y
WEST VIRGINIA		
Byrd	Y	Y
Rockefeller	Y	Y
WISCONSIN		
Kohl	Y	Y
Kasten	Y	Y
WYOMING		
Simpson	Y	Y
Wallop	?	?

KEY

Y Voted for (yea).
Paired for.
+ Announced for.
N Voted against (nay).
X Paired against.
- Announced against.
P Voted "present."
C Voted "present" to avoid possible conflict of interest.
? Did not vote or otherwise make a position known.

Democrats ***Republicans***

ND Northern Democrats SD Southern Democrats

Southern states - Ala., Ark., Fla., Ga., Ky., La., Miss., N.C., Okla., S.C., Tenn., Texas, Va.

2. HR 3792. Fiscal 1990-91 State Department Authorization/Passage. Passage of the bill (thus clearing the measure for the president) to authorize appropriations for fiscal years 1990 and 1991 for the State Department and related agencies. The bill also would mandate certain economic sanctions against China but give the president broad discretion to terminate them. Passed 98-0: R 44-0; D 54-0 (ND 37-0, SD 17-0), Jan. 30, 1990.

3. S 1630. Clean Air Act Amendments/CFCs. Chafee, R-R.I., amendment to add methyl chloroform to the list of chlorofluorocarbons (CFCs) and other substances whose production the bill would phase out by the year 2000. Adopted 95-2: R 41-2; D 54-0 (ND 37-0, SD 17-0), Jan. 31, 1990.

SENATE VOTES 4, 5, 6, 7, 8

	4	5	6	7	8
ALABAMA					
Heflin	Y	Y	N	Y	N
Shelby	Y	Y	N	Y	N
ALASKA					
Murkowski	Y	Y	Y	N	Y
Stevens	Y	Y	Y	N	Y
ARIZONA					
DeConcini	Y	Y	N	Y	N
McCain	Y	Y	Y	N	Y
ARKANSAS					
Bumpers	Y	Y	N	Y	N
Pryor	Y	Y	N	Y	N
CALIFORNIA					
Cranston	Y	Y	N	Y	N
Wilson	Y	Y	Y	N	Y
COLORADO					
Wirth	Y	Y	N	Y	N
Armstrong	Y	Y	Y	N	Y
CONNECTICUT					
Dodd	Y	Y	N	Y	N
Lieberman	Y	Y	N	Y	N
DELAWARE					
Biden	Y	Y	N	Y	N
Roth	Y	Y	N	Y	N
FLORIDA					
Graham	Y	Y	N	Y	N
Mack	Y	Y	Y	N	Y
GEORGIA					
Fowler	Y	Y	N	Y	N
Nunn	Y	Y	N	Y	N
HAWAII					
Inouye	Y	Y	N	Y	N
Matsunaga	Y	Y	N	?	?
IDAHO					
McClure	Y	Y	Y	N	Y
Symms	Y	Y	Y	N	Y
ILLINOIS					
Dixon	Y	Y	N	Y	N
Simon	Y	Y	N	Y	N
INDIANA					
Coats	Y	Y	Y	N	Y
Lugar	Y	Y	Y	N	Y
IOWA					
Harkin	Y	Y	N	Y	N
Grassley	Y	Y	Y	N	Y
KANSAS					
Dole	Y	Y	Y	N	Y
Kassebaum	Y	Y	Y	N	Y
KENTUCKY					
Ford	Y	Y	N	Y	N
McConnell	Y	Y	Y	N	Y
LOUISIANA					
Breaux	Y	Y	N	Y	N
Johnston	Y	Y	N	Y	N
MAINE					
Mitchell	Y	Y	N	Y	N
Cohen	Y	Y	N	Y	Y
MARYLAND					
Mikulski	Y	Y	N	Y	N
Sarbanes	Y	Y	N	Y	N
MASSACHUSETTS					
Kennedy	Y	Y	N	Y	N
Kerry	Y	Y	N	Y	N
MICHIGAN					
Levin	Y	Y	N	Y	N
Riegle	Y	Y	N	Y	N
MINNESOTA					
Boschwitz	Y	Y	Y	N	Y
Durenberger	Y	Y	N	N	Y
MISSISSIPPI					
Cochran	Y	Y	N	Y	Y
Lott	Y	Y	Y	N	Y
MISSOURI					
Bond	Y	Y	Y	N	Y
Danforth	Y	Y	Y	N	Y
MONTANA					
Baucus	Y	Y	N	Y	N
Burns	Y	Y	Y	N	Y
NEBRASKA					
Exon	Y	Y	N	Y	N
Kerrey	Y	Y	N	Y	N
NEVADA					
Bryan	Y	Y	N	Y	N
Reid	Y	Y	-	?	?
NEW HAMPSHIRE					
Humphrey	Y	Y	Y	N	Y
Rudman	Y	Y	Y	N	Y
NEW JERSEY					
Bradley	Y	Y	N	Y	N
Lautenberg	Y	Y	N	Y	N
NEW MEXICO					
Bingaman	Y	Y	N	Y	N
Domenici	Y	Y	Y	N	Y
NEW YORK					
Moynihan	Y	Y	N	Y	N
D'Amato	Y	Y	Y	N	Y
NORTH CAROLINA					
Sanford	Y	Y	N	Y	N
Helms	Y	Y	Y	N	Y
NORTH DAKOTA					
Burdick	Y	Y	N	Y	N
Conrad	Y	Y	N	Y	N
OHIO					
Glenn	Y	Y	N	Y	N
Metzenbaum	Y	Y	N	Y	N
OKLAHOMA					
Boren	Y	Y	N	Y	N
Nickles	Y	Y	Y	N	Y
OREGON					
Hatfield	Y	Y	N	Y	N
Packwood	Y	Y	Y	?	?
PENNSYLVANIA					
Heinz	Y	Y	N	Y	Y
Specter	Y	Y	N	Y	N
RHODE ISLAND					
Pell	Y	Y	N	Y	N
Chafee	Y	Y	N	N	Y
SOUTH CAROLINA					
Hollings	Y	Y	N	Y	N
Thurmond	Y	Y	Y	N	Y
SOUTH DAKOTA					
Daschle	Y	Y	N	Y	N
Pressler	Y	Y	Y	N	Y
TENNESSEE					
Gore	Y	Y	N	Y	N
Sasser	Y	Y	N	Y	N
TEXAS					
Bentsen	Y	Y	N	Y	N
Gramm	Y	Y	Y	N	Y
UTAH					
Garn	Y	Y	Y	N	Y
Hatch	Y	Y	N	N	Y
VERMONT					
Leahy	Y	Y	N	Y	N
Jeffords	Y	Y	N	Y	N
VIRGINIA					
Robb	Y	Y	N	Y	N
Warner	+	Y	Y	N	Y
WASHINGTON					
Adams	Y	Y	N	Y	N
Gorton	Y	Y	Y	N	Y
WEST VIRGINIA					
Byrd	Y	Y	N	Y	N
Rockefeller	Y	Y	N	Y	N
WISCONSIN					
Kohl	Y	Y	N	Y	N
Kasten	Y	Y	Y	N	Y
WYOMING					
Simpson	Y	Y	Y	N	Y
Wallop	Y	Y	Y	N	Y

KEY

- Y Voted for (yea).
- # Paired for.
- + Announced for.
- N Voted against (nay).
- X Paired against.
- \- Announced against.
- P Voted "present."
- C Voted "present" to avoid possible conflict of interest.
- ? Did not vote or otherwise make a position known.

Democrats *Republicans*

ND Northern Democrats SD Southern Democrats

Southern states - Ala., Ark., Fla., Ga., Ky., La., Miss., N.C., Okla., S.C., Tenn., Texas, Va.

4. S 1310. Literacy Training/Passage. Passage of the bill to authorize $229 million in fiscal 1991 and $1.1 billion over five years in new programs to combat illiteracy and to strengthen and coordinate current literacy programs. Passed 99-0: R 44-0; D 55-0 (ND 38-0, SD 17-0), Feb. 6, 1990.

5. S 169. Global-Change Research/Passage. Passage of the bill to amend the National Science and Technology Policy, Organization and Priorities Act of 1976 to improve coordination of national scientific research efforts and to provide for a national plan to improve scientific understanding of the Earth system and the effect of changes in that system on climate and human well-being. Passed 100-0: R 45-0; D 55-0; (ND 38-0, SD 17-0), Feb. 6, 1990.

6. S 695. Education Programs/National Standards. Helms, R-N.C., amendment to delete $25 million in federal matching funds for the National Board for Professional Teaching Standards, which is developing guidelines for voluntary certification of teachers. Rejected 35-64: R 35-10; D 0-54 (ND 0-37, SD 0-17), Feb. 6, 1990. A "yea" was a vote supporting the president's position.

7. S 695. Education Programs/Teacher Competency. Pell, D-R.I., motion to table (kill) the Helms, R-N.C., amendment to divert $15 million from Title X to the states for use in establishing minimum competency standards for teachers and $10 million to establish an alternative certification program for people who want to teach but lack teaching degrees. Motion agreed to 60-37: R 7-37; D 53-0 (ND 36-0, SD 17-0), Feb. 6, 1990.

8. S 695. Education Programs/Title X. Kassebaum, R-Kan., amendment to reduce the money for Title X from $25 million to $6 million and to require educational groups to compete for the funds. Rejected 40-57: R 40-4; D 0-53 (ND 0-36, SD 0-17), Feb. 6, 1990.

	9	10	11	12	13
ALABAMA					
Heflin	N	Y	Y	Y	Y
Shelby	N	Y	Y	Y	Y
ALASKA					
Murkowski	N	Y	Y	N	Y
Stevens	N	Y	Y	N	Y
ARIZONA					
DeConcini	Y	Y	Y	N	Y
McCain	N	Y	Y	N	Y
ARKANSAS					
Bumpers	Y	Y	Y	N	Y
Pryor	Y	Y	Y	N	Y
CALIFORNIA					
Cranston	Y	Y	Y	N	Y
Wilson	N	Y	Y	N	Y
COLORADO					
Wirth	Y	Y	Y	N	Y
Armstrong	N	N	Y	Y	N
CONNECTICUT					
Dodd	Y	Y	?	?	?
Lieberman	Y	Y	Y	N	Y
DELAWARE					
Biden	Y	Y	Y	N	Y
Roth	N	Y	Y	N	Y
FLORIDA					
Graham	Y	Y	Y	N	Y
Mack	N	Y	Y	Y	Y
GEORGIA					
Fowler	Y	Y	Y	N	Y
Nunn	Y	Y	Y	N	Y
HAWAII					
Inouye	Y	Y	Y	N	Y
Matsunaga	Y	Y	?	N	Y
IDAHO					
McClure	N	N	Y	Y	Y
Symms	N	N	Y	Y	Y
ILLINOIS					
Dixon	Y	Y	Y	N	Y
Simon	Y	Y	Y	N	Y
INDIANA					
Coats	Y	Y	Y	Y	Y
Lugar	N	Y	Y	N	Y
IOWA					
Harkin	Y	Y	Y	N	Y
Grassley	N	Y	Y	N	Y
KANSAS					
Dole	N	Y	Y	N	Y
Kassebaum	N	Y	Y	N	Y
KENTUCKY					
Ford	Y	Y	Y	N	Y
McConnell	N	Y	Y	N	Y
LOUISIANA					
Breaux	N	Y	Y	Y	Y
Johnston	Y	Y	Y	Y	Y
MAINE					
Mitchell	Y	Y	Y	N	Y
Cohen	N	Y	Y	N	Y
MARYLAND					
Mikulski	Y	Y	Y	N	Y
Sarbanes	Y	Y	Y	N	Y
MASSACHUSETTS					
Kennedy	Y	Y	Y	N	Y
Kerry	Y	Y	Y	N	Y
MICHIGAN					
Levin	Y	Y	Y	?	?
Riegle	Y	Y	Y	N	Y
MINNESOTA					
Boschwitz	N	Y	Y	N	Y
Durenberger	N	Y	Y	N	Y
MISSISSIPPI					
Cochran	N	Y	Y	N	Y
Lott	N	Y	Y	Y	N
MISSOURI					
Bond	N	Y	Y	N	Y
Danforth	N	Y	Y	N	Y
MONTANA					
Baucus	Y	Y	Y	N	Y
Burns	N	Y	Y	N	Y
NEBRASKA					
Exon	Y	Y	Y	N	Y
Kerrey	Y	Y	Y	N	Y
NEVADA					
Bryan	Y	Y	Y	Y	Y
Reid	Y	Y	Y	Y	Y
NEW HAMPSHIRE					
Humphrey	Y	N	Y	Y	N
Rudman	Y	Y	Y	N	Y
NEW JERSEY					
Bradley	N	Y	Y	N	Y
Lautenberg	N	Y	Y	N	Y
NEW MEXICO					
Bingaman	N	Y	Y	N	Y
Domenici	N	Y	Y	N	Y
NEW YORK					
Moynihan	Y	Y	Y	N	Y
D'Amato	N	Y	Y	N	Y
NORTH CAROLINA					
Sanford	Y	Y	Y	N	Y
Helms	N	N	Y	Y	N
NORTH DAKOTA					
Burdick	Y	Y	Y	N	Y
Conrad	Y	Y	Y	N	Y
OHIO					
Glenn	Y	Y	Y	N	Y
Metzenbaum	Y	Y	Y	N	Y
OKLAHOMA					
Boren	Y	Y	Y	N	Y
Nickles	N	Y	Y	Y	Y
OREGON					
Hatfield	N	Y	Y	N	Y
Packwood	N	Y	Y	N	Y
PENNSYLVANIA					
Heinz	N	Y	Y	N	Y
Specter	N	Y	Y	N	Y
RHODE ISLAND					
Pell	Y	Y	Y	N	Y
Chafee	N	Y	Y	N	Y
SOUTH CAROLINA					
Hollings	Y	Y	Y	N	Y
Thurmond	N	Y	Y	Y	Y
SOUTH DAKOTA					
Daschle	Y	Y	Y	N	Y
Pressler	N	Y	Y	N	Y
TENNESSEE					
Gore	Y	Y	Y	N	Y
Sasser	Y	Y	Y	N	Y
TEXAS					
Bentsen	N	Y	Y	N	Y
Gramm	N	N	Y	Y	Y
UTAH					
Garn	N	N	Y	N	Y
Hatch	N	Y	Y	N	Y
VERMONT					
Leahy	Y	Y	Y	N	Y
Jeffords	N	Y	Y	N	Y
VIRGINIA					
Robb	Y	Y	Y	N	Y
Warner	N	Y	Y	N	Y
WASHINGTON					
Adams	Y	Y	Y	N	Y
Gorton	N	Y	Y	N	Y
WEST VIRGINIA					
Byrd	Y	Y	Y	Y	Y
Rockefeller	Y	Y	Y	Y	Y
WISCONSIN					
Kohl	Y	Y	Y	N	Y
Kasten	N	Y	Y	N	Y
WYOMING					
Simpson	N	Y	?	?	?
Wallop	N	N	+	-	-

KEY

Y Voted for (yea).
Paired for.
+ Announced for.
N Voted against (nay).
X Paired against.
- Announced against.
P Voted "present."
C Voted "present" to avoid possible conflict of interest.
? Did not vote or otherwise make a position known.

Democrats ***Republicans***

ND Northern Democrats SD Southern Democrats

Southern states - Ala., Ark., Fla., Ga., Ky., La., Miss., N.C., Okla., S.C., Tenn., Texas, Va.

9. S 695. Education Programs/'Healthy Start.' Pell, D-R.I., motion to table (kill) the Wilson, R-Calif., amendment to authorize $10 million to establish a Healthy Start demonstration grant program that would allow local school districts to establish community councils to coordinate social services for public schoolchildren. Motion agreed to 51-49: R 3-42; D 48-7 (ND 35-3, SD 13-4), Feb. 7, 1990.

10. S 695. Education Programs/Passage. Passage of the bill to authorize funding of about $414 million in fiscal 1991 for programs to provide scholarships to outstanding science students, awards to excellent teachers, grants to schools that are working to overcome such problems as drug use and high dropout rates, $15 million to states to offer alternative certification programs for professionals who want to teach but lack teaching degrees, and a revision in the formula to determine college student aid needs. Passed 92-8: R 37-8; D 55-0 (ND 38-0, SD 17-0), Feb. 7, 1990. A "yea" was a vote supporting the president's position.

11. S 419. Hate-Crime Statistics/'Family Values.' Hatch, R-Utah, amendment to add language to the bill stating that American family life is the foundation of American society, that federal policy should encourage the well-being of the family and that no funds under the act should be used to promote or encourage homosexuality. Adopted 96-0: R 43-0; D 53-0 (ND 36-0, SD 17-0), Feb. 8, 1990.

12. S 419. Hate-Crime Statistics/Homosexuals. Helms, R-N.C., amendment to say that "the homosexual movement threatens the strength and survival of the American family" and that state sodomy laws should be enforced. Rejected 19-77: R 11-32; D 8-45 (ND 4-32, SD 4-13), Feb. 8, 1990.

13. S 419/HR 1048. Hate-Crime Statistics/Passage. Passage of the bill to require the Justice Department to compile and publish data for 1990-94 on crimes due to prejudice based on race, religion, sexual orientation or ethnicity. Before passing HR 1048, the Senate by voice vote substituted the text of S 419 as amended. Passed 92-4: R 39-4; D 53-0 (ND 36-0, SD 17-0), Feb. 8, 1990. A "yea" was a vote supporting the president's position.

	14	15	16
ALABAMA			
Heflin	Y	Y	Y
Shelby	Y	Y	N
ALASKA			
Murkowski	?	Y	Y
Stevens	Y	Y	Y
ARIZONA			
DeConcini	Y	Y	Y
McCain	Y	Y	N
ARKANSAS			
Bumpers	Y	Y	N
Pryor	Y	Y	N
CALIFORNIA			
Cranston	Y	Y	Y
Wilson	Y	Y	Y
COLORADO			
Wirth	Y	Y	N
Armstrong	Y	Y	Y
CONNECTICUT			
Dodd	Y	Y	?
Lieberman	Y	Y	N
DELAWARE			
Biden	?	Y	Y
Roth	Y	Y	N
FLORIDA			
Graham	Y	Y	N
Mack	Y	Y	N
GEORGIA			
Fowler	Y	Y	N
Nunn	Y	Y	N
HAWAII			
Inouye	Y	Y	N
Matsunaga	Y	?	N
IDAHO			
McClure	Y	Y	N
Symms	Y	Y	N
ILLINOIS			
Dixon	Y	Y	N
Simon	Y	Y	Y
INDIANA			
Coats	Y	+	?
Lugar	Y	Y	N
IOWA			
Harkin	Y	Y	Y
Grassley	Y	Y	Y
KANSAS			
Dole	Y	Y	Y
Kassebaum	Y	Y	Y
KENTUCKY			
Ford	Y	Y	N
McConnell	Y	Y	N
LOUISIANA			
Breaux	Y	Y	N
Johnston	Y	Y	N
MAINE			
Mitchell	Y	Y	Y
Cohen	Y	Y	Y
MARYLAND			
Mikulski	Y	Y	Y
Sarbanes	Y	Y	Y
MASSACHUSETTS			
Kennedy	Y	Y	Y
Kerry	+	+	Y
MICHIGAN			
Levin	Y	Y	Y
Riegle	Y	Y	Y
MINNESOTA			
Boschwitz	Y	Y	Y
Durenberger	Y	Y	Y
MISSISSIPPI			
Cochran	Y	Y	N
Lott	Y	Y	N
MISSOURI			
Bond	Y	Y	N
Danforth	Y	Y	N
MONTANA			
Baucus	Y	Y	N
Burns	Y	Y	Y
NEBRASKA			
Exon	Y	Y	N
Kerrey	Y	Y	N
NEVADA			
Bryan	Y	Y	N
Reid	Y	Y	N
NEW HAMPSHIRE			
Humphrey	Y	Y	Y
Rudman	Y	Y	Y
NEW JERSEY			
Bradley	Y	Y	Y
Lautenberg	Y	Y	Y
NEW MEXICO			
Bingaman	Y	Y	Y
Domenici	Y	+	Y
NEW YORK			
Moynihan	Y	Y	Y
D'Amato	Y	Y	Y
NORTH CAROLINA			
Sanford	Y	Y	N
Helms	Y	Y	Y
NORTH DAKOTA			
Burdick	Y	Y	Y
Conrad	Y	Y	N
OHIO			
Glenn	Y	Y	Y
Metzenbaum	Y	Y	N
OKLAHOMA			
Boren	?	Y	N
Nickles	Y	Y	N
OREGON			
Hatfield	Y	Y	N
Packwood	Y	Y	N
PENNSYLVANIA			
Heinz	Y	Y	Y
Specter	Y	Y	Y
RHODE ISLAND			
Pell	Y	Y	Y
Chafee	Y	Y	Y
SOUTH CAROLINA			
Hollings	Y	Y	N
Thurmond	Y	Y	Y
SOUTH DAKOTA			
Daschle	Y	Y	N
Pressler	Y	Y	Y
TENNESSEE			
Gore	Y	Y	Y
Sasser	Y	Y	N

KEY

- Y Voted for (yea).
- # Paired for.
- + Announced for.
- N Voted against (nay).
- X Paired against.
- \- Announced against.
- P Voted "present."
- C Voted "present" to avoid possible conflict of interest.
- ? Did not vote or otherwise make a position known.

Democrats *Republicans*

	14	15	16
TEXAS			
Bentsen	?	?	Y
Gramm	Y	Y	N
UTAH			
Garn	Y	Y	Y
Hatch	+	?	Y
VERMONT			
Leahy	Y	Y	N
Jeffords	Y	Y	Y
VIRGINIA			
Robb	Y	Y	N
Warner	Y	Y	Y
WASHINGTON			
Adams	Y	Y	N
Gorton	Y	Y	N
WEST VIRGINIA			
Byrd	Y	Y	N
Rockefeller	Y	Y	N
WISCONSIN			
Kohl	Y	Y	Y
Kasten	Y	Y	Y
WYOMING			
Simpson	Y	Y	N
Wallop	Y	Y	N

ND Northern Democrats SD Southern Democrats

Southern states - Ala., Ark., Fla., Ga., Ky., La., Miss., N.C., Okla., S.C., Tenn., Texas, Va.

14. Treaty Doc 101-2. ILO Convention/Adoption. Adoption of the resolution of ratification of the International Labor Organization's Convention No. 160, to call upon all participating countries to collect, compile and publish basic labor statistics in nine specified subject areas. Adopted 94-0: R 43-0; D 51-0 (ND 36-0, SD 15-0), Feb. 20, 1990. A two-thirds majority of those present and voting (63 in this case) is required for adoption of resolutions of ratification.

15. HR 2281. School Dropout-Prevention Programs/Passage. Passage of the bill to authorize $50 million annually for two years for projects demonstrating ways to reduce school-dropout rates. Passed 94-0: R 42-0; D 52-0 (ND 36-0, SD 16-0), Feb. 20, 1990.

16. S J Res. 212. Armenian Genocide Day of Remembrance/Cloture. Dole, R-Kan., motion to invoke cloture (thus limiting debate) on the Mitchell, D-Maine, motion to proceed to consideration of the resolution designating April 24, 1990, as a "National Day of Remembrance" for the approximately 1.5 million Armenians killed in 1915-23 under the Ottoman Empire. Motion rejected 49-49: R 26-18; D 23-31 (ND 20-17, SD 3-14), Feb. 22, 1990. A three-fifths majority vote (60) of the total Senate is required to invoke cloture.

	17	18	19	20	21	22
ALABAMA						
Heflin	Y	Y	Y	Y	Y	Y
Shelby	N	Y	Y	Y	Y	Y
ALASKA						
Murkowski	Y	Y	N	N	N	Y
Stevens	Y	Y	N	Y	N	Y
ARIZONA						
DeConcini	Y	Y	Y	Y	Y	N
McCain	N	Y	N	N	Y	Y
ARKANSAS						
Bumpers	N	Y	Y	Y	Y	N
Pryor	N	?	?	Y	Y	N
CALIFORNIA						
Cranston	Y	Y	Y	Y	Y	N
Wilson	Y	Y	N	?	?	?
COLORADO						
Wirth	N	Y	Y	Y	Y	N
Armstrong	Y	Y	N	N	Y	Y
CONNECTICUT						
Dodd	N	Y	Y	Y	Y	N
Lieberman	N	Y	Y	Y	Y	Y
DELAWARE						
Biden	Y	Y	Y	Y	Y	Y
Roth	N	Y	N	Y	N	Y
FLORIDA						
Graham	N	Y	Y	Y	Y	N
Mack	N	Y	N	N	Y	Y
GEORGIA						
Fowler	N	Y	Y	Y	Y	N
Nunn	N	Y	Y	Y	Y	N
HAWAII						
Inouye	N	Y	Y	Y	Y	N
Matsunaga	?	?	?	?	?	?
IDAHO						
McClure	N	Y	N	N	Y	Y
Symms	N	Y	N	N	Y	Y
ILLINOIS						
Dixon	N	Y	Y	Y	Y	Y
Simon	Y	?	?	Y	Y	N
INDIANA						
Coats	Y	Y	N	N	Y	Y
Lugar	N	Y	N	N	N	Y
IOWA						
Harkin	Y	Y	Y	Y	Y	Y
Grassley	Y	Y	N	N	N	Y
KANSAS						
Dole	Y	Y	N	N	N	Y
Kassebaum	Y	Y	N	N	N	N
KENTUCKY						
Ford	N	Y	Y	Y	Y	N
McConnell	N	Y	N	N	Y	Y
LOUISIANA						
Breaux	N	Y	Y	Y	Y	Y
Johnston	N	Y	Y	Y	Y	N
MAINE						
Mitchell	Y	Y	Y	Y	Y	N
Cohen	Y	Y	N	Y	Y	N
MARYLAND						
Mikulski	Y	Y	Y	Y	Y	N
Sarbanes	Y	Y	Y	Y	Y	N
MASSACHUSETTS						
Kennedy	Y	Y	Y	Y	Y	N
Kerry	Y	Y	Y	Y	Y	N
MICHIGAN						
Levin	Y	Y	Y	Y	Y	Y
Riegle	Y	Y	Y	Y	Y	N
MINNESOTA						
Boschwitz	Y	Y	N	N	Y	Y
Durenberger	Y	Y	Y	Y	Y	Y
MISSISSIPPI						
Cochran	N	Y	N	Y	Y	Y
Lott	N	Y	N	N	Y	Y
MISSOURI						
Bond	N	Y	N	N	N	N
Danforth	N	Y	N	N	N	N
MONTANA						
Baucus	N	Y	Y	Y	Y	Y
Burns	N	Y	N	N	Y	Y
NEBRASKA						
Exon	N	Y	Y	Y	Y	Y
Kerrey	N	Y	Y	Y	Y	N
NEVADA						
Bryan	N	Y	Y	Y	Y	N
Reid	N	Y	Y	Y	Y	Y
NEW HAMPSHIRE						
Humphrey	Y	Y	N	N	N	Y
Rudman	Y	Y	N	Y	N	Y
NEW JERSEY						
Bradley	Y	Y	Y	Y	Y	N
Lautenberg	Y	Y	Y	Y	Y	N
NEW MEXICO						
Bingaman	Y	Y	Y	Y	Y	N
Domenici	Y	Y	N	N	N	Y
NEW YORK						
Moynihan	Y	Y	Y	?	Y	N
D'Amato	Y	Y	N	N	Y	Y
NORTH CAROLINA						
Sanford	N	Y	Y	Y	Y	N
Helms	Y	Y	N	N	N	Y
NORTH DAKOTA						
Burdick	Y	Y	Y	Y	Y	N
Conrad	N	Y	Y	Y	Y	N
OHIO						
Glenn	Y	N	N	Y	Y	N
Metzenbaum	N	N	Y	Y	Y	N
OKLAHOMA						
Boren	N	Y	Y	N	Y	N
Nickles	N	Y	N	N	Y	Y
OREGON						
Hatfield	N	N	Y	N	Y	N
Packwood	N	Y	Y	Y	Y	Y
PENNSYLVANIA						
Heinz	Y	Y	Y	N	Y	Y
Specter	Y	Y	N	Y	Y	Y
RHODE ISLAND						
Pell	Y	?	Y	Y	Y	N
Chafee	Y	Y	N	Y	N	N
SOUTH CAROLINA						
Hollings	N	Y	N	Y	Y	N
Thurmond	Y	Y	N	Y	Y	Y
SOUTH DAKOTA						
Daschle	N	Y	Y	Y	Y	N
Pressler	Y	Y	N	N	Y	Y
TENNESSEE						
Gore	Y	Y	Y	Y	Y	N
Sasser	N	?	?	Y	Y	N
TEXAS						
Bentsen	Y	?	?	Y	Y	N
Gramm	N	Y	N	N	Y	Y
UTAH						
Garn	Y	Y	N	N	N	Y
Hatch	Y	Y	N	N	Y	Y
VERMONT						
Leahy	N	Y	Y	Y	Y	N
Jeffords	Y	Y	Y	Y	N	N
VIRGINIA						
Robb	N	Y	Y	Y	Y	N
Warner	N	Y	Y	Y	N	Y
WASHINGTON						
Adams	N	Y	Y	Y	Y	N
Gorton	N	Y	N	N	Y	Y
WEST VIRGINIA						
Byrd	N	Y	Y	Y	Y	N
Rockefeller	N	Y	Y	Y	Y	N
WISCONSIN						
Kohl	Y	Y	Y	Y	Y	N
Kasten	Y	Y	N	N	Y	Y
WYOMING						
Simpson	N	Y	N	Y	N	Y
Wallop	N	Y	N	N	N	Y

KEY

- Y Voted for (yea).
- # Paired for.
- \+ Announced for.
- N Voted against (nay).
- X Paired against.
- \- Announced against.
- P Voted "present."
- C Voted "present" to avoid possible conflict of interest.
- ? Did not vote or otherwise make a position known.

Democrats ***Republicans***

ND Northern Democrats SD Southern Democrats

Southern states - Ala., Ark., Fla., Ga., Ky., La., Miss., N.C., Okla., S.C., Tenn., Texas, Va.

17. S J Res 212. Anti-Genocide Commemoration/Cloture. Dole, R-Kan., motion to invoke cloture (thus limiting debate) on the joint resolution to designate April 24, 1990, as "National Day of Remembrance of the 75th Anniversary of the Armenian Genocide of 1915-1923." Motion rejected 48-51: R 25-20; D 23-31 (ND 20-17, SD 3-14), Feb. 27, 1990. A three-fifths majority vote (60) of the total Senate is required to invoke cloture.

18. S 1430. National and Community Service Act/Religious Organizations. Armstrong, R-Colo., amendment to make clear that religious organizations may participate in the service programs authorized under the bill provided that they do not use public funds for religious instruction, worship or proselytizing. Adopted 91-3: R 44-1; D 47-2 (ND 33-2, SD 14-0), Feb. 27, 1990.

19. S 1430. National and Community Service Act/Comparability of Benefits. Nunn, D-Ga., motion to table (kill) the McCain, R-Ariz., amendment to require that post-service benefits provided to participants in community and national service not exceed post-service education benefits provided to military veterans. Motion agreed to 54-41: R 6-39; D 48-2 (ND 35-1, SD 13-1), Feb. 27, 1990.

20. S 1430. National and Community Service Act/Liability Premiums. Heflin, D-Ala., motion to table (kill) the McConnell, R-Ky., amendment to abolish joint and several liability for non-profit organizations, create alternative dispute-resolution mechanisms for non-profits and provide limited immunity from liability to unpaid volunteers. Motion agreed to 65-32: R 13-31; D 52-1 (ND 36-0, SD 16-1), Feb. 28, 1990.

21. S 1430. National and Community Service Act/Peace Dividend. Sasser, D-Tenn., amendment to state the sense of the Senate that any reductions in military expenditures (the "peace dividend") shall be used for balancing the budget without relying on the Social Security trust fund surplus; for urgent national priorities, including anti-drug and anti-crime efforts, education, health care, the environment, rebuilding the infrastructure and assisting emerging democracies; and for tax reductions. Adopted 79-19: R 25-19; D 54-0 (ND 37-0, SD 17-0), Feb. 28, 1990.

22. S 1430. National and Community Service Act/Peace Dividend. Gramm, R-Texas, amendment to state the sense of the Senate that any savings from the "peace dividend" should be used to meet Gramm-Rudman deficit targets without relying on the Social Security trust fund surplus and should be returned to taxpayers in the form of a refundable child-care tax credit, repeal of the Social Security earnings test, an increase in the personal exemption, expansion of a permanent research and development tax deduction, a long-term capital gains tax cut, lowering of marginal tax rates, and other savings and investment incentives. Rejected 48-50: R 37-7; D 11-43 (ND 8-29, SD 3-14), Feb. 28, 1990.

	23	24	25	26	27	28
ALABAMA						
Heflin	Y	Y	Y	Y	Y	Y
Shelby	Y	Y	Y	Y	Y	Y
ALASKA						
Murkowski	Y	Y	N	Y	N	N
Stevens	Y	Y	N	N	Y	Y
ARIZONA						
DeConcini	N	Y	Y	Y	Y	Y
McCain	Y	Y	N	Y	N	Y
ARKANSAS						
Bumpers	N	Y	Y	Y	Y	N
Pryor	N	Y	Y	Y	Y	N
CALIFORNIA						
Cranston	N	Y	Y	Y	Y	Y
Wilson	N	Y	N	Y	Y	Y
COLORADO						
Wirth	N	Y	Y	Y	Y	Y
Armstrong	Y	Y	N	?	?	?
CONNECTICUT						
Dodd	N	Y	Y	Y	Y	Y
Lieberman	N	Y	Y	Y	Y	Y
DELAWARE						
Biden	N	Y	Y	Y	Y	Y
Roth	Y	Y	N	Y	N	Y
FLORIDA						
Graham	N	Y	Y	Y	Y	Y
Mack	Y	Y	N	Y	N	Y
GEORGIA						
Fowler	?	Y	Y	Y	Y	N
Nunn	?	Y	Y	Y	Y	N
HAWAII						
Inouye	N	Y	Y	Y	Y	Y
Matsunaga	?	?	?	?	?	?
IDAHO						
McClure	Y	N	N	N	N	N
Symms	Y	Y	N	Y	N	Y
ILLINOIS						
Dixon	N	Y	Y	Y	Y	Y
Simon	N	Y	Y	Y	Y	Y
INDIANA						
Coats	Y	Y	N	Y	Y	Y
Lugar	Y	Y	N	N	Y	Y

	23	24	25	26	27	28
IOWA						
Harkin	N	Y	Y	Y	Y	Y
Grassley	Y	Y	N	Y	Y	N
KANSAS						
Dole	Y	Y	N	N	Y	Y
Kassebaum	Y	Y	N	N	N	Y
KENTUCKY						
Ford	Y	Y	Y	Y	Y	Y
McConnell	Y	Y	N	Y	Y	Y
LOUISIANA						
Breaux	Y	Y	Y	Y	Y	Y
Johnston	Y	Y	Y	Y	Y	Y
MAINE						
Mitchell	N	Y	Y	Y	Y	Y
Cohen	N	Y	Y	Y	Y	Y
MARYLAND						
Mikulski	N	Y	Y	Y	Y	Y
Sarbanes	N	Y	Y	Y	Y	Y
MASSACHUSETTS						
Kennedy	N	Y	Y	Y	Y	Y
Kerry	N	Y	Y	Y	Y	Y
MICHIGAN						
Levin	Y	Y	Y	Y	Y	Y
Riegle	N	Y	Y	Y	Y	Y
MINNESOTA						
Boschwitz	Y	Y	N	N	N	Y
Durenberger	Y	Y	Y	N	Y	Y
MISSISSIPPI						
Cochran	Y	Y	N	N	Y	Y
Lott	Y	Y	N	Y	Y	Y
MISSOURI						
Bond	Y	Y	N	N	Y	Y
Danforth	Y	Y	Y	Y	Y	Y
MONTANA						
Baucus	Y	Y	N	Y	Y	Y
Burns	Y	Y	N	Y	N	Y
NEBRASKA						
Exon	Y	Y	Y	Y	Y	Y
Kerrey	N	Y	Y	Y	N	Y
NEVADA						
Bryan	N	Y	Y	Y	Y	Y
Reid	N	Y	Y	Y	Y	Y

	23	24	25	26	27	28
NEW HAMPSHIRE						
Humphrey	Y	Y	N	Y	N	N
Rudman	Y	Y	N	Y	N	N
NEW JERSEY						
Bradley	N	Y	Y	Y	Y	Y
Lautenberg	N	Y	Y	Y	Y	Y
NEW MEXICO						
Bingaman	N	Y	Y	N	Y	Y
Domenici	Y	Y	N	Y	Y	N
NEW YORK						
Moynihan	N	Y	Y	Y	Y	Y
D'Amato	Y	Y	N	Y	Y	Y
NORTH CAROLINA						
Sanford	N	Y	Y	Y	Y	Y
Helms	Y	Y	N	Y	N	N
NORTH DAKOTA						
Burdick	N	Y	Y	Y	Y	Y
Conrad	N	Y	Y	Y	Y	Y
OHIO						
Glenn	N	Y	Y	Y	Y	Y
Metzenbaum	N	Y	Y	Y	Y	Y
OKLAHOMA						
Boren	N	Y	Y	Y	Y	Y
Nickles	Y	Y	N	Y	N	Y
OREGON						
Hatfield	Y	Y	N	N	N	Y
Packwood	Y	?	?	?	?	?
PENNSYLVANIA						
Heinz	N	Y	N	Y	Y	Y
Specter	N	Y	N	Y	Y	Y
RHODE ISLAND						
Pell	N	Y	Y	Y	Y	Y
Chafee	N	Y	N	N	Y	Y
SOUTH CAROLINA						
Hollings	N	Y	Y	Y	Y	Y
Thurmond	Y	Y	N	N	N	Y
SOUTH DAKOTA						
Daschle	N	Y	Y	Y	Y	Y
Pressler	Y	Y	N	Y	Y	Y
TENNESSEE						
Gore	N	Y	Y	Y	Y	Y
Sasser	N	Y	Y	Y	Y	Y

KEY

- Y Voted for (yea).
- # Paired for.
- + Announced for.
- N Voted against (nay).
- X Paired against.
- \- Announced against.
- P Voted "present."
- C Voted "present" to avoid possible conflict of interest.
- ? Did not vote or otherwise make a position known.

Democrats *Republicans*

	23	24	25	26	27	28
TEXAS						
Bentsen	N	Y	Y	Y	Y	Y
Gramm	Y	Y	N	Y	N	Y
UTAH						
Garn	Y	Y	N	Y	N	N
Hatch	Y	Y	Y	N	Y	Y
VERMONT						
Leahy	N	Y	Y	Y	Y	N
Jeffords	N	Y	Y	Y	Y	Y
VIRGINIA						
Robb	N	Y	Y	Y	Y	Y
Warner	Y	Y	N	N	Y	Y
WASHINGTON						
Adams	N	Y	Y	Y	Y	Y
Gorton	Y	Y	N	Y	Y	Y
WEST VIRGINIA						
Byrd	N	Y	Y	N	Y	N
Rockefeller	N	Y	Y	Y	Y	Y
WISCONSIN						
Kohl	N	Y	Y	Y	Y	Y
Kasten	Y	Y	N	Y	Y	Y
WYOMING						
Simpson	Y	Y	N	N	Y	Y
Wallop	Y	Y	N	N	N	N

ND Northern Democrats SD Southern Democrats

Southern states - Ala., Ark., Fla., Ga., Ky., La., Miss., N.C., Okla., S.C., Tenn., Texas, Va.

23. S 1430. National and Community Service Act/Homosexuals. Armstrong, R-Colo., motion to table (kill) the Kennedy, D-Mass., amendment to modify the District of Columbia code to allow organizations to bar or restrict from coaching, teaching or serving as a role model to minors any homosexual, bisexual or heterosexual convicted of or charged with a sexual offense involving a minor. A volunteer could also be barred, based on his or her sexual orientation, from serving as coach, teacher or mentor to a minor if the parent or guardian of the minor objects to his or her participation. Motion rejected 47-50: R 39-6; D 8-44 (ND 3-34, SD 5-10), March 1, 1990.

24. S 1430. National and Community Service Act/Homosexuals. Kennedy, D-Mass., amendment *(see vote 23)* to the Armstrong, R-Colo., amendment to the District of Columbia Code to allow organizations to bar or restrict homosexual or bisexual adults from educating, coaching or training minors or serving as role models for minors. The Armstrong amendment, as modified by Kennedy, was subsequently adopted by voice vote. Adopted 97-1: R 43-1; D 54-0 (ND 37-0, SD 17-0), March 1, 1990.

25. S 1430. National and Community Service Act/Sunset. Mikulski, D-Md., motion to table (kill) the McCain, R-Ariz., amendment to terminate provisions of the bill as of Sept. 30, 1992. Motion agreed to 58-40: R 5-39; D 53-1 (ND 36-1, SD 17-0), March 1, 1990.

26. S 1430. National and Community Service Act/China. Humphrey, R-N.H., amendment to state the sense of the Senate condemning China for crushing student protests in Tiananmen Square in June 1989 and for continued human repression. Adopted 79-18: R 27-16; D 52-2 (ND 35-2, SD 17-0), March 1, 1990.

27. S 1430. National and Community Service Act/Passage. Passage of the bill to authorize $125 million for fiscal 1990-91 in grants to states and localities to encourage community service, create or expand youth service corps, authorize demonstration national service programs offering post-service vouchers for education and housing, and authorize a Points of Light Foundation to coordinate and foster volunteerism. Passed 78-19: R 25-18; D 53-1 (ND 36-1, SD 17-0), March 1, 1990.

28. S Res 255. Baseball Lockout/Adoption. Adoption of the resolution to call on baseball team owners, players and their negotiators to settle their differences promptly and to begin spring training and the regular season as soon as possible. Adopted 82-15; R 34-9; D 48-6 (ND 35-2, SD 13-4), March 1, 1990.

	29	30	31	32	33	34
ALABAMA						
Heflin	Y	Y	N	Y	N	Y
Shelby	Y	Y	Y	N	N	Y
ALASKA						
Murkowski	Y	Y	Y	N	N	Y
Stevens	Y	Y	Y	Y	Y	Y
ARIZONA						
DeConcini	Y	Y	Y	Y	Y	N
McCain	Y	Y	Y	Y	Y	Y
ARKANSAS						
Bumpers	Y	N	Y	Y	Y	Y
Pryor	Y	N	?	Y	Y	Y
CALIFORNIA						
Cranston	Y	N	N	Y	Y	N
Wilson	Y	N	N	Y	Y	N
COLORADO						
Wirth	Y	N	N	Y	Y	N
Armstrong	Y	Y	N	Y	N	Y
CONNECTICUT						
Dodd	Y	N	N	Y	Y	N
Lieberman	Y	N	N	Y	Y	N
DELAWARE						
Biden	Y	N	N	Y	N	Y
Roth	Y	N	N	Y	Y	N
FLORIDA						
Graham	Y	N	N	Y	Y	N
Mack	Y	N	N	Y	N	Y
GEORGIA						
Fowler	Y	N	Y	N	Y	Y
Nunn	Y	N	Y	Y	Y	Y
HAWAII						
Inouye	Y	Y	N	Y	Y	Y
Matsunaga	?	?	?	?	?	?
IDAHO						
McClure	Y	Y	Y	N	N	Y
Symms	Y	Y	N	N	N	Y
ILLINOIS						
Dixon	Y	N	Y	Y	Y	Y
Simon	Y	N	Y	Y	Y	N
INDIANA						
Coats	Y	N	Y	Y	Y	Y
Lugar	Y	Y	Y	Y	Y	Y
IOWA						
Harkin	Y	N	Y	Y	Y	N
Grassley	Y	Y	Y	N	Y	N
KANSAS						
Dole	Y	Y	Y	Y	N	Y
Kassebaum	Y	N	Y	Y	Y	Y
KENTUCKY						
Ford	Y	Y	Y	N	N	Y
McConnell	Y	Y	Y	Y	N	Y
LOUISIANA						
Breaux	Y	Y	N	Y	Y	Y
Johnston	Y	Y	N	Y	Y	Y
MAINE						
Mitchell	Y	N	N	Y	Y	Y
Cohen	Y	N	N	N	Y	N
MARYLAND						
Mikulski	Y	N	Y	Y	Y	Y
Sarbanes	Y	N	N	Y	Y	N
MASSACHUSETTS						
Kennedy	Y	N	N	Y	Y	N
Kerry	Y	N	N	Y	Y	N
MICHIGAN						
Levin	Y	N	Y	Y	Y	Y
Riegle	Y	N	?	?	?	Y
MINNESOTA						
Boschwitz	Y	N	Y	Y	Y	Y
Durenberger	Y	N	Y	Y	Y	Y
MISSISSIPPI						
Cochran	Y	Y	N	Y	Y	Y
Lott	Y	Y	N	N	Y	Y
MISSOURI						
Bond	Y	Y	Y	Y	Y	Y
Danforth	Y	Y	Y	Y	Y	Y
MONTANA						
Baucus	Y	Y	Y	Y	Y	Y
Burns	Y	Y	Y	Y	Y	Y
NEBRASKA						
Exon	Y	N	Y	Y	Y	Y
Kerrey	Y	N	Y	Y	Y	Y
NEVADA						
Bryan	Y	N	N	Y	Y	N
Reid	Y	N	Y	Y	Y	Y
NEW HAMPSHIRE						
Humphrey	Y	N	N	Y	Y	N
Rudman	Y	N	Y	Y	Y	Y
NEW JERSEY						
Bradley	Y	N	N	Y	Y	N
Lautenberg	Y	N	N	Y	Y	N
NEW MEXICO						
Bingaman	Y	Y	N	Y	Y	N
Domenici	Y	N	N	Y	Y	N
NEW YORK						
Moynihan	Y	N	N	Y	Y	N
D'Amato	Y	N	N	Y	Y	N
NORTH CAROLINA						
Sanford	Y	N	Y	Y	Y	Y
Helms	Y	Y	Y	N	N	Y
NORTH DAKOTA						
Burdick	Y	Y	Y	Y	Y	Y
Conrad	Y	N	Y	Y	Y	Y
OHIO						
Glenn	Y	N	Y	Y	Y	Y
Metzenbaum	Y	?	Y	Y	Y	N
OKLAHOMA						
Boren	Y	Y	N	Y	Y	Y
Nickles	?	Y	N	Y	N	Y
OREGON						
Hatfield	Y	N	Y	Y	Y	Y
Packwood	?	?	?	?	?	?
PENNSYLVANIA						
Heinz	Y	N	N	Y	Y	Y
Specter	Y	N	N	Y	Y	Y
RHODE ISLAND						
Pell	Y	N	Y	Y	Y	N
Chafee	Y	Y	Y	Y	Y	Y
SOUTH CAROLINA						
Hollings	Y	Y	Y	Y	Y	Y
Thurmond	Y	Y	Y	Y	N	Y
SOUTH DAKOTA						
Daschle	Y	N	Y	Y	Y	Y
Pressler	Y	N	Y	N	Y	N
TENNESSEE						
Gore	Y	N	Y	Y	Y	N
Sasser	Y	N	Y	Y	Y	Y
TEXAS						
Bentsen	Y	N	N	Y	Y	Y
Gramm	Y	N	N	Y	N	Y
UTAH						
Garn	Y	Y	N	N	Y	Y
Hatch	Y	Y	N	N	Y	Y
VERMONT						
Leahy	Y	N	Y	Y	Y	N
Jeffords	Y	N	Y	N	Y	Y
VIRGINIA						
Robb	Y	N	Y	Y	Y	Y
Warner	Y	Y	Y	Y	?	Y
WASHINGTON						
Adams	Y	N	N	Y	Y	N
Gorton	Y	N	Y	Y	Y	N
WEST VIRGINIA						
Byrd	Y	N	N	Y	Y	N
Rockefeller	Y	N	N	N	Y	N
WISCONSIN						
Kohl	Y	N	Y	Y	Y	N
Kasten	Y	N	Y	Y	Y	Y
WYOMING						
Simpson	Y	Y	N	Y	Y	Y
Wallop	Y	Y	N	N	N	Y

KEY

- Y Voted for (yea).
- # Paired for.
- + Announced for.
- N Voted against (nay).
- X Paired against.
- - Announced against.
- P Voted "present."
- C Voted "present" to avoid possible conflict of interest.
- ? Did not vote or otherwise make a position known.

Democrats *Republicans*

ND Northern Democrats SD Southern Democrats

Southern states - Ala., Ark., Fla., Ga., Ky., La., Miss., N.C., Okla., S.C., Tenn., Texas, Va.

29. S 1630. Clean Air Act Reauthorization/Emissions Standards. Baucus, D-Mont., amendment to establish emission standards for sources of ammonia to protect public health with an ample margin of safety. Adopted 97-0: R 43-0; D 54-0 (ND 37-0, SD 17-0), March 6, 1990.

30. S 1630. Clean Air Act Reauthorization/NRC Authority. Breaux, D-La., motion to table (kill) the Glenn, D-Ohio, amendment to strike a provision that would remove the authority of the Environmental Protection Agency and the states to regulate radioactive emissions at facilities regulated by the Nuclear Regulatory Commission (NRC), such as nuclear power plants, making the NRC the sole regulator under the Atomic Energy Act. Motion rejected 36-61: R 24-20; D 12-41 (ND 5-31, SD 7-10), March 7, 1990. A "yea" was a vote supporting the president's position. (The Glenn amendment was subsequently adopted by voice vote.)

31. S 1630. Clean Air Act Reauthorization/Fuel Standards. Baucus, D-Mont., motion to table (kill) the Lautenberg, D-N.J., amendment to reduce the average oxygen content requirement from 3.1 percent to 2.7 percent for fuels used in carbon monoxide non-attainment areas. Motion agreed to 53-43: R 25-19; D 28-24 (ND 18-18, SD 10-6), March 7, 1990.

32. S 1630. Clean Air Act Reauthorization/Air Toxics. Mitchell, D-Maine, motion to table (kill) the Symms, R-Idaho, amendment to prohibit importing any product whose production does not comply with the bill's air-toxics standards. Motion agreed to 81-16: R 32-12; D 49-4 (ND 35-1, SD 14-3), March 8, 1990. A "yea" was a vote supporting the president's position.

33. S 1630. Clean Air Act Reauthorization/CFCs. Gore, D-Tenn., amendment to phase out the use of hydrochlorofluorocarbons, to prohibit the export of chlorofluorocarbon equipment and technology, to strike provisions to pre-empt states' efforts to control ozone-depleting chemicals, and to modify federal procurement practices to ensure that chemicals known to harm health or the environment are not used as substitutes for chemicals that destroy the ozone layer. Adopted 80-16: R 31-12; D 49-4 (ND 35-1, SD 14-3), March 8, 1990.

34. S 1630. Clean Air Act Reauthorization/Air Toxics. Mitchell, D-Maine, motion to table (kill) the Lautenberg, D-N.J., amendment to require the regulation of mobile sources of air toxics. Motion agreed to 65-33: R 35-9; D 30-24 (ND 15-22, SD 15-2), March 8, 1990. A "yea" was a vote supporting the president's position.

KEY

- Y Voted for (yea).
- # Paired for.
- + Announced for.
- N Voted against (nay).
- X Paired against.
- \- Announced against.
- P Voted "present."
- C Voted "present" to avoid possible conflict of interest.
- ? Did not vote or otherwise make a position known.

Democrats ***Republicans***

	35	36	37	38
ALABAMA				
Heflin	Y	Y	Y	Y
Shelby	Y	Y	Y	Y
ALASKA				
Murkowski	Y	Y	Y	Y
Stevens	?	?	?	?
ARIZONA				
DeConcini	N	Y	N	Y
McCain	N	Y	N	Y
ARKANSAS				
Bumpers	Y	Y	Y	Y
Pryor	Y	Y	Y	Y
CALIFORNIA				
Cranston	N	Y	N	Y
Wilson	N	Y	N	Y
COLORADO				
Wirth	N	Y	N	Y
Armstrong	N	Y	Y	Y
CONNECTICUT				
Dodd	Y	Y	N	Y
Lieberman	N	Y	N	Y
DELAWARE				
Biden	Y	Y	N	Y
Roth	N	Y	Y	Y
FLORIDA				
Graham	N	Y	N	Y
Mack	Y	Y	N	Y
GEORGIA				
Fowler	N	Y	Y	Y
Nunn	N	Y	Y	Y
HAWAII				
Inouye	Y	Y	Y	Y
Matsunaga	?	?	N	Y
IDAHO				
McClure	N	Y	Y	N
Symms	N	Y	Y	N
ILLINOIS				
Dixon	Y	Y	N	Y
Simon	N	Y	N	Y
INDIANA				
Coats	Y	Y	N	Y
Lugar	Y	Y	Y	Y
IOWA				
Harkin	N	Y	N	Y
Grassley	Y	Y	Y	Y
KANSAS				
Dole	Y	Y	Y	Y
Kassebaum	N	Y	Y	N
KENTUCKY				
Ford	Y	Y	Y	Y
McConnell	Y	Y	Y	Y
LOUISIANA				
Breaux	Y	Y	Y	Y
Johnston	Y	Y	Y	Y
MAINE				
Mitchell	Y	Y	Y	Y
Cohen	N	Y	N	Y
MARYLAND				
Mikulski	N	Y	N	Y
Sarbanes	Y	Y	N	Y
MASSACHUSETTS				
Kennedy	N	Y	N	Y
Kerry	N	Y	N	Y
MICHIGAN				
Levin	Y	Y	Y	Y
Riegle	Y	Y	Y	Y
MINNESOTA				
Boschwitz	N	Y	Y	Y
Durenberger	Y	Y	Y	Y
MISSISSIPPI				
Cochran	Y	Y	Y	Y
Lott	Y	Y	Y	Y
MISSOURI				
Bond	Y	Y	Y	Y
Danforth	Y	Y	Y	Y
MONTANA				
Baucus	Y	Y	Y	Y
Burns	N	Y	Y	N
NEBRASKA				
Exon	Y	Y	N	Y
Kerrey	Y	Y	Y	Y
NEVADA				
Bryan	N	Y	N	Y
Reid	N	Y	N	Y
NEW HAMPSHIRE				
Humphrey	Y	Y	N	Y
Rudman	Y	Y	N	Y
NEW JERSEY				
Bradley	N	Y	N	Y
Lautenberg	N	Y	N	Y
NEW MEXICO				
Bingaman	N	Y	N	Y
Domenici	Y	Y	N	Y
NEW YORK				
Moynihan	N	Y	Y	Y
D'Amato	N	Y	N	Y
NORTH CAROLINA				
Sanford	Y	Y	Y	Y
Helms	N	Y	Y	N
NORTH DAKOTA				
Burdick	Y	Y	Y	Y
Conrad	N	Y	Y	N
OHIO				
Glenn	Y	Y	N	Y
Metzenbaum	Y	Y	N	Y
OKLAHOMA				
Boren	Y	Y	Y	Y
Nickles	Y	Y	Y	Y
OREGON				
Hatfield	N	Y	N	Y
Packwood	N	Y	N	Y
PENNSYLVANIA				
Heinz	Y	Y	N	Y
Specter	Y	Y	N	Y
RHODE ISLAND				
Pell	N	Y	N	Y
Chafee	Y	Y	Y	Y
SOUTH CAROLINA				
Hollings	Y	Y	N	Y
Thurmond	Y	Y	Y	Y
SOUTH DAKOTA				
Daschle	N	Y	Y	Y
Pressler	N	Y	Y	Y
TENNESSEE				
Gore	N	Y	N	Y
Sasser	Y	Y	Y	Y
TEXAS				
Bentsen	Y	Y	Y	Y
Gramm	Y	Y	Y	Y
UTAH				
Garn	N	Y	Y	Y
Hatch	N	Y	Y	Y
VERMONT				
Leahy	N	Y	N	Y
Jeffords	Y	Y	Y	Y
VIRGINIA				
Robb	Y	Y	N	Y
Warner	Y	Y	Y	Y
WASHINGTON				
Adams	N	Y	N	Y
Gorton	N	Y	N	Y
WEST VIRGINIA				
Byrd	N	Y	N	Y
Rockefeller	N	Y	Y	Y
WISCONSIN				
Kohl	N	Y	N	Y
Kasten	Y	Y	N	Y
WYOMING				
Simpson	Y	Y	Y	Y
Wallop	N	Y	Y	N

ND Northern Democrats SD Southern Democrats

Southern states - Ala., Ark., Fla., Ga., Ky., La., Miss., N.C., Okla., S.C., Tenn., Texas, Va.

35. S 1630. Clean Air Act Reauthorization/Motor Vehicles. Mitchell, D-Maine, motion to table (kill) the Wirth, D-Colo., amendment to provide for a second round of tailpipe emissions reductions in the year 2003; to require cleaner-burning reformulated gasoline in all ozone non-attainment areas; to require light-duty vehicles to meet new-car emission standards for 100,000 miles; and to provide for use of clean fuels and clean-fuel vehicles by the government and commercial and general passenger-car fleets in the nation's smoggiest cities. Motion agreed to 52-46: R 25-19; D 27-27 (ND 14-23, SD 13-4), March 20, 1990. A "yea" was a vote supporting the president's position.

36. S 1630. Clean Air Act Reauthorization/Small Business Assistance. Boschwitz, R-Minn., amendment to require states to adopt a small stationary-source technical and environmental compliance assistance program. Adopted 98-0: R 44-0; D 54-0 (ND 37-0, SD 17-0), March 21, 1990.

37. S 1630. Clean Air Act Reauthorization/Federal Implementation Plans. Mitchell, D-Maine, motion to table (kill) the Kerry, D-Mass., amendment to restore the current ability of the federal government to mandate Federal Implementation Plans when areas fail to meet the pollution targets, to strike the proposed cost and technology review, and to retain provisions in current law to control enough existing sources to achieve health standards. Motion agreed to 53-46: R 29-15; D 24-31 (ND 11-27, SD 13-4), March 21, 1990. A "yea" was a vote supporting the president's position.

38. S 1630. Clean Air Act Reauthorization/Parks and Wilderness. Adams, D-Wash., amendment to provide for research on visibility-impairing pollution in national parks and wilderness areas. Adopted 92-7: R 38-6; D 54-1 (ND 37-1, SD 17-0), March 21, 1990.

KEY

- Y Voted for (yea).
- # Paired for.
- + Announced for.
- N Voted against (nay).
- X Paired against.
- \- Announced against.
- P Voted "present."
- C Voted "present" to avoid possible conflict of interest.
- ? Did not vote or otherwise make a position known.

Democrats *Republicans*

	39	40	41	42
ALABAMA				
Heflin	N	N	Y	Y
Shelby	N	N	Y	Y
ALASKA				
Murkowski	Y	N	Y	Y
Stevens	?	Y	Y	Y
ARIZONA				
DeConcini	Y	N	Y	Y
McCain	Y	Y	Y	Y
ARKANSAS				
Bumpers	N	Y	Y	Y
Pryor	?	Y	Y	Y
CALIFORNIA				
Cranston	N	Y	Y	Y
Wilson	Y	N	Y	Y
COLORADO				
Wirth	N	Y	Y	Y
Armstrong	Y	N	Y	Y
CONNECTICUT				
Dodd	N	Y	Y	Y
Lieberman	Y	N	Y	Y
DELAWARE				
Biden	N	N	Y	Y
Roth	N	N	Y	Y
FLORIDA				
Graham	N	Y	Y	Y
Mack	Y	Y	Y	Y
GEORGIA				
Fowler	N	Y	Y	Y
Nunn	N	Y	Y	Y
HAWAII				
Inouye	N	Y	?	Y
Matsunaga	?	?	?	?
IDAHO				
McClure	Y	N	N	Y
Symms	Y	N	N	Y
ILLINOIS				
Dixon	N	N	Y	Y
Simon	N	N	Y	Y
INDIANA				
Coats	Y	Y	Y	Y
Lugar	N	Y	Y	Y
IOWA				
Harkin	Y	N	Y	Y
Grassley	Y	N	Y	Y
KANSAS				
Dole	N	N	Y	Y
Kassebaum	N	Y	Y	Y
KENTUCKY				
Ford	N	N	Y	Y
McConnell	N	N	Y	Y
LOUISIANA				
Breaux	N	N	Y	Y
Johnston	Y	Y	Y	Y
MAINE				
Mitchell	N	Y	Y	Y
Cohen	Y	N	Y	Y
MARYLAND				
Mikulski	Y	N	Y	Y
Sarbanes	N	Y	Y	Y
MASSACHUSETTS				
Kennedy	N	Y	Y	Y
Kerry	N	Y	Y	Y
MICHIGAN				
Levin	Y	N	Y	Y
Riegle	Y	Y	Y	Y
MINNESOTA				
Boschwitz	Y	N	Y	Y
Durenberger	N	Y	Y	Y
MISSISSIPPI				
Cochran	N	Y	Y	Y
Lott	Y	N	Y	Y
MISSOURI				
Bond	?	Y	Y	Y
Danforth	N	Y	Y	Y
MONTANA				
Baucus	N	Y	Y	Y
Burns	Y	N	Y	Y
NEBRASKA				
Exon	N	Y	Y	Y
Kerrey	N	Y	Y	Y
NEVADA				
Bryan	N	Y	?	Y
Reid	N	Y	Y	Y
NEW HAMPSHIRE				
Humphrey	Y	Y	?	+
Rudman	N	N	Y	?
NEW JERSEY				
Bradley	N	N	Y	Y
Lautenberg	N	N	Y	Y
NEW MEXICO				
Bingaman	N	Y	Y	?
Domenici	Y	N	Y	Y
NEW YORK				
Moynihan	N	Y	Y	Y
D'Amato	Y	N	Y	Y
NORTH CAROLINA				
Sanford	N	N	Y	?
Helms	Y	N	Y	Y
NORTH DAKOTA				
Burdick	N	Y	Y	Y
Conrad	N	N	Y	Y
OHIO				
Glenn	N	Y	Y	Y
Metzenbaum	N	N	Y	Y
OKLAHOMA				
Boren	N	Y	Y	Y
Nickles	Y	Y	Y	Y
OREGON				
Hatfield	N	Y	Y	Y
Packwood	N	Y	Y	Y
PENNSYLVANIA				
Heinz	Y	N	Y	?
Specter	Y	N	Y	Y
RHODE ISLAND				
Pell	N	N	Y	Y
Chafee	N	Y	Y	Y
SOUTH CAROLINA				
Hollings	N	Y	Y	Y
Thurmond	Y	N	Y	Y
SOUTH DAKOTA				
Daschle	N	Y	Y	Y
Pressler	Y	N	Y	Y
TENNESSEE				
Gore	N	Y	Y	Y
Sasser	N	Y	Y	Y
TEXAS				
Bentsen	N	Y	Y	Y
Gramm	Y	Y	Y	Y
UTAH				
Garn	Y	N	Y	Y
Hatch	Y	N	Y	Y
VERMONT				
Leahy	N	N	Y	Y
Jeffords	N	N	Y	?
VIRGINIA				
Robb	N	Y	Y	Y
Warner	N	N	Y	Y
WASHINGTON				
Adams	N	Y	Y	Y
Gorton	Y	N	Y	Y
WEST VIRGINIA				
Byrd	Y	Y	N	Y
Rockefeller	Y	N	N	Y
WISCONSIN				
Kohl	N	Y	Y	Y
Kasten	Y	N	Y	Y
WYOMING				
Simpson	N	Y	Y	Y
Wallop	?	Y	N	Y

ND Northern Democrats SD Southern Democrats

Southern states - Ala., Ark., Fla., Ga., Ky., La., Miss., N.C., Okla., S.C., Tenn., Texas, Va.

39. S 1630. Clean Air Act Reauthorization/Lithuania. Helms, R-N.C., amendment to commend President Bush for urging the Soviet Union to begin negotiations with the Lithuanian leaders, to urge the president to recognize and establish diplomatic representation at the ambassadorial level with the independent Republic of Lithuania and to urge the Soviet Union to stop military or economic threats to suppress democracy in Lithuania. Rejected 36-59: R 27-15; D 9-44 (ND 8-29, SD 1-15), March 21, 1990. A "nay" was a vote supporting the president's position.

40. S 1630. Clean Air Act Reauthorization/Import Fees. Chafee, R-R.I., motion to table (kill) the Gorton, R-Wash., amendment to ask the House to attach provisions to the bill that would impose import fees on foreign products made in ways that do not comply with the Clean Air Act. Motion agreed to 52-47: R 18-27; D 34-20 (ND 22-15, SD 12-5), March 22, 1990. A "yea" was a vote supporting the president's position.

41. S 1630. Clean Air Act Reauthorization/South Africa. Simpson, R-Wyo., motion to table (kill) the Symms, R-Idaho, amendment to require the Environmental Protection Agency to waive vehicle-emissions standards if they are found to increase U.S. dependence on strategic minerals from South Africa by more than 150 percent. Motion agreed to 91-5: R 41-3; D 50-2 (ND 33-2, SD 17-0), March 22, 1990. A "yea" was a vote supporting the president's position.

42. S Con Res 108. Lithuanian Self-Determination/Adoption. Adoption of the resolution to express the sense of the Senate that the U.S. government strongly supports Lithuania, that the Soviet Union should cease all intimidation of Lithuania and that the president should "consider the call of the elected Lithuanian government for recognition." Adopted 93-0: R 41-0; D 52-0 (ND 36-0, SD 16-0), March 22, 1990.

	43	44	45	46	47	48
ALABAMA						
Heflin	N	Y	N	N	Y	Y
Shelby	N	Y	N	Y	Y	Y
ALASKA						
Murkowski	N	Y	N	Y	N	Y
Stevens	N	Y	Y	N	Y	Y
ARIZONA						
DeConcini	N	#	Y	N	Y	N
McCain	N	Y	Y	N	N	N
ARKANSAS						
Bumpers	Y	N	Y	N	Y	N
Pryor	Y	N	Y	Y	N	N
CALIFORNIA						
Cranston	Y	N	Y	Y	Y	N
Wilson	Y	N	Y	N	N	N
COLORADO						
Wirth	Y	N	Y	Y	Y	N
Armstrong	N	Y	N	N	N	Y
CONNECTICUT						
Dodd	?	N	Y	Y	N	N
Lieberman	Y	N	Y	N	Y	N
DELAWARE						
Biden	Y	N	Y	N	N	Y
Roth	N	Y	Y	N	N	N
FLORIDA						
Graham	Y	N	Y	N	N	Y
Mack	N	Y	Y	N	N	Y
GEORGIA						
Fowler	Y	N	Y	N	N	N
Nunn	N	Y	Y	N	N	N
HAWAII						
Inouye	Y	N	Y	Y	Y	N
Matsunaga	?	?	?	?	Y	?
IDAHO						
McClure	N	Y	N	Y	Y	N
Symms	N	Y	N	N	N	N
ILLINOIS						
Dixon	N	Y	N	Y	Y	N
Simon	Y	N	N	Y	Y	N
INDIANA						
Coats	N	Y	N	N	Y	N
Lugar	N	Y	N	N	N	N

	43	44	45	46	47	48
IOWA						
Harkin	Y	N	Y	N	Y	N
Grassley	N	Y	Y	N	Y	N
KANSAS						
Dole	N	N	Y	N	N	N
Kassebaum	N	Y	Y	N	N	N
KENTUCKY						
Ford	N	Y	N	Y	Y	N
McConnell	N	Y	N	Y	Y	N
LOUISIANA						
Breaux	N	N	Y	Y	N	Y
Johnston	N	N	Y	Y	+	Y
MAINE						
Mitchell	Y	N	Y	Y	N	Y
Cohen	Y	N	Y	N	N	N
MARYLAND						
Mikulski	Y	N	Y	N	Y	N
Sarbanes	Y	N	Y	N	N	N
MASSACHUSETTS						
Kennedy	?	X	?	?	Y	N
Kerry	Y	N	Y	N	Y	N
MICHIGAN						
Levin	Y	N	Y	N	N	Y
Riegle	Y	N	Y	Y	N	Y
MINNESOTA						
Boschwitz	N	Y	Y	N	N	N
Durenberger	Y	N	Y	Y	N	N
MISSISSIPPI						
Cochran	N	Y	Y	Y	Y	Y
Lott	N	Y	N	N	N	Y
MISSOURI						
Bond	N	Y	N	N	Y	N
Danforth	N	Y	N	N	Y	N
MONTANA						
Baucus	N	N	Y	Y	N	Y
Burns	N	Y	Y	Y	N	N
NEBRASKA						
Exon	Y	N	Y	Y	Y	N
Kerrey	Y	N	Y	Y	Y	N
NEVADA						
Bryan	Y	N	Y	Y	Y	N
Reid	Y	N	Y	N	Y	N

	43	44	45	46	47	48
NEW HAMPSHIRE						
Humphrey	Y	N	Y	N	N	Y
Rudman	N	Y	Y	N	N	Y
NEW JERSEY						
Bradley	Y	N	Y	N	Y	N
Lautenberg	Y	N	Y	Y	Y	N
NEW MEXICO						
Bingaman	Y	N	Y	Y	Y	N
Domenici	N	Y	Y	Y	N	Y
NEW YORK						
Moynihan	Y	N	Y	Y	Y	Y
D'Amato	N	Y	N	N	N	N
NORTH CAROLINA						
Sanford	Y	N	Y	Y	Y	N
Helms	N	Y	N	N	N	N
NORTH DAKOTA						
Burdick	Y	N	Y	Y	Y	N
Conrad	N	Y	Y	Y	Y	N
OHIO						
Glenn	N	Y	N	N	Y	N
Metzenbaum	Y	N	N	N	Y	N
OKLAHOMA						
Boren	N	Y	?	?	N	Y
Nickles	N	Y	Y	Y	N	Y
OREGON						
Hatfield	Y	N	Y	N	Y	N
Packwood	Y	N	Y	N	N	N
PENNSYLVANIA						
Heinz	Y	Y	N	N	Y	N
Specter	Y	Y	N	N	Y	N
RHODE ISLAND						
Pell	Y	N	Y	N	Y	N
Chafee	Y	N	Y	N	N	Y
SOUTH CAROLINA						
Hollings	Y	N	Y	Y	Y	N
Thurmond	N	Y	N	N	N	N
SOUTH DAKOTA						
Daschle	Y	N	Y	N	N	N
Pressler	Y	N	Y	N	N	N
TENNESSEE						
Gore	Y	N	Y	Y	Y	N
Sasser	Y	N	Y	Y	Y	N

KEY

- Y Voted for (yea).
- # Paired for.
- + Announced for.
- N Voted against (nay).
- X Paired against.
- - Announced against.
- P Voted "present."
- C Voted "present" to avoid possible conflict of interest.
- ? Did not vote or otherwise make a position known.

Democrats *Republicans*

	43	44	45	46	47	48
TEXAS						
Bentsen	N	Y	Y	Y	Y	Y
Gramm	N	Y	Y	Y	N	Y
UTAH						
Garn	N	Y	N	N	N	Y
Hatch	N	Y	N	N	N	Y
VERMONT						
Leahy	Y	N	Y	N	N	N
Jeffords	Y	N	Y	N	N	N
VIRGINIA						
Robb	N	Y	Y	Y	N	N
Warner	N	Y	Y	N	N	Y
WASHINGTON						
Adams	Y	N	Y	N	Y	N
Gorton	N	Y	Y	N	N	Y
WEST VIRGINIA						
Byrd	N	Y	N	Y	Y	N
Rockefeller	N	Y	N	Y	Y	N
WISCONSIN						
Kohl	Y	N	Y	N	Y	N
Kasten	N	Y	Y	N	N	N
WYOMING						
Simpson	N	Y	Y	N	N	N
Wallop	N	Y	Y	Y	N	Y

ND Northern Democrats SD Southern Democrats

Southern states - Ala., Ark., Fla., Ga., Ky., La., Miss., N.C., Okla., S.C., Tenn., Texas, Va.

43. S 1630. Clean Air Act Reauthorization/Permits and Enforcement. Baucus, D-Mont., motion to table (kill) the Nickles, R-Okla., amendment to allow the states to issue operating permits to facilitate enforcement of the act without full review by the Environmental Protection Agency. Motion rejected 47-50: R 11-34; D 36-16 (ND 28-7, SD 8-9), March 27, 1990. A "nay" was a vote supporting the president's position. (The Nickles amendment was subsequently rejected on a separate roll call.)

44. S 1630. Clean Air Act Reauthorization/Permits and Enforcement. Nickles, R-Okla., amendment to allow the states to issue operating permits to facilitate enforcement of the act without full review by the Environmental Protection Agency. Rejected 47-50: R 35-10; D 12-40 (ND 5-30, SD 7-10), March 27, 1990. A "yea" was a vote supporting the president's position.

45. S 1630. Clean Air Act Reauthorization/Acid Rain Tax Credits. Bentsen, D-Texas, motion to table (kill) the Specter, R-Pa., amendment to provide a tax credit for equipment necessary to meet acid rain reduction standards. Motion agreed to 71-26: R 28-17; D 43-9 (ND 30-6, SD 13-3), March 28, 1990.

46. S 1630. Clean Air Act Reauthorization/Solar Energy Incentives. Baucus, D-Mont., motion to table (kill) the McCain, R-Ariz., amendment to provide regulatory incentives for solar and renewable energy. Motion rejected 40-57: R 10-35; D 30-22 (ND 19-17, SD 11-5), March 28, 1990. (The McCain amendment was subsequently adopted by voice vote.)

47. S 1630. Clean Air Act Reauthorization/Coal Miner Benefits. Byrd, D-W.Va., amendment to provide severance pay and retraining benefits to coal miners who lose their jobs as a result of provisions to control acid rain. Rejected 49-50: R 11-34; D 38-16 (ND 29-9, SD 9-7), March 29, 1990. A "nay" was a vote supporting the president's position.

48. S 1630. Clean Air Act Reauthorization/Reformulated Gasoline. Baucus, D-Mont., motion to table (kill) the Daschle, D-S.D., amendment to establish blending limits for alternative fuels and require that reformulated gasoline replace conventional gasoline in the nation's nine most smog-filled cities. Motion rejected 30-69: R 17-28; D 13-41 (ND 6-31, SD 7-10), March 29, 1990. (The Daschle amendment was subsequently adopted by voice vote.)

	49	50	51	52	53	54	55
ALABAMA							
Heflin	Y	N	Y	Y	Y	N	Y
Shelby	N	N	Y	Y	Y	N	Y
ALASKA							
Murkowski	N	N	N	N	Y	N	Y
Stevens	Y	N	N	Y	Y	N	Y
ARIZONA							
DeConcini	Y	N	Y	Y	Y	N	Y
McCain	Y	N	N	Y	Y	N	Y
ARKANSAS							
Bumpers	Y	Y	Y	Y	N	Y	Y
Pryor	Y	Y	Y	Y	N	N	Y
CALIFORNIA							
Cranston	Y	Y	Y	Y	N	N	Y
Wilson	Y	Y	?	Y	N	N	Y
COLORADO							
Wirth	Y	Y	Y	Y	N	Y	Y
Armstrong	N	N	N	N	Y	N	Y
CONNECTICUT							
Dodd	Y	Y	Y	Y	N	Y	Y
Lieberman	Y	Y	Y	Y	N	N	Y
DELAWARE							
Biden	Y	N	Y	Y	N	Y	Y
Roth	Y	N	Y	Y	Y	Y	Y
FLORIDA							
Graham	Y	Y	Y	Y	N	Y	Y
Mack	Y	Y	Y	Y	Y	N	Y
GEORGIA							
Fowler	Y	Y	Y	Y	N	N	Y
Nunn	Y	Y	Y	Y	Y	N	Y
HAWAII							
Inouye	Y	Y	Y	Y	N	N	Y
Matsunaga	?	?	?	?	N	N	Y
IDAHO							
McClure	N	N	N	N	Y	N	N
Symms	N	N	N	N	Y	N	N
ILLINOIS							
Dixon	Y	N	Y	Y	Y	Y	N
Simon	Y	N	Y	Y	N	N	N
INDIANA							
Coats	?	?	?	?	Y	N	Y
Lugar	?	?	?	?	Y	N	Y
IOWA							
Harkin	Y	Y	Y	Y	N	Y	Y
Grassley	N	Y	Y	Y	Y	N	Y
KANSAS							
Dole	N	Y	N	N	Y	N	Y
Kassebaum	Y	Y	Y	Y	Y	N	Y
KENTUCKY							
Ford	N	N	Y	Y	Y	N	Y
McConnell	N	N	Y	N	Y	N	Y
LOUISIANA							
Breaux	Y	N	Y	Y	N	N	Y
Johnston	N	N	Y	Y	N	N	Y
MAINE							
Mitchell	Y	Y	Y	Y	N	Y	Y
Cohen	Y	N	Y	Y	N	N	Y
MARYLAND							
Mikulski	Y	Y	Y	Y	N	Y	Y
Sarbanes	Y	Y	Y	Y	N	Y	Y
MASSACHUSETTS							
Kennedy	Y	Y	Y	Y	N	Y	Y
Kerry	Y	Y	Y	Y	N	Y	Y
MICHIGAN							
Levin	Y	Y	Y	Y	N	N	Y
Riegle	Y	Y	Y	Y	N	Y	Y
MINNESOTA							
Boschwitz	Y	N	N	Y	Y	N	Y
Durenberger	Y	Y	Y	Y	N	N	Y
MISSISSIPPI							
Cochran	N	Y	Y	Y	Y	N	Y
Lott	N	N	N	N	Y	N	Y
MISSOURI							
Bond	Y	N	Y	Y	Y	N	Y
Danforth	N	Y	Y	Y	Y	N	Y
MONTANA							
Baucus	Y	Y	Y	Y	N	N	Y
Burns	N	N	N	Y	Y	N	Y
NEBRASKA							
Exon	Y	Y	Y	Y	N	N	Y
Kerrey	Y	Y	Y	Y	N	Y	Y
NEVADA							
Bryan	Y	Y	Y	Y	N	Y	Y
Reid	Y	Y	Y	Y	N	Y	Y
NEW HAMPSHIRE							
Humphrey	Y	N	N	Y	Y	N	Y
Rudman	Y	N	Y	Y	Y	N	Y
NEW JERSEY							
Bradley	Y	Y	Y	Y	N	Y	Y
Lautenberg	Y	Y	Y	Y	N	Y	Y
NEW MEXICO							
Bingaman	N	Y	N	Y	N	N	Y
Domenici	N	Y	N	Y	Y	N	Y
NEW YORK							
Moynihan	Y	Y	Y	Y	N	Y	Y
D'Amato	Y	Y	N	Y	Y	N	Y
NORTH CAROLINA							
Sanford	Y	Y	Y	Y	N	N	Y
Helms	N	N	N	N	Y	N	N
NORTH DAKOTA							
Burdick	N	N	N	Y	N	N	Y
Conrad	N	N	N	Y	Y	Y	Y
OHIO							
Glenn	N	N	Y	Y	Y	Y	N
Metzenbaum	N	Y	Y	Y	N	Y	Y
OKLAHOMA							
Boren	N	Y	N	Y	Y	N	Y
Nickles	N	Y	N	N	Y	N	N
OREGON							
Hatfield	Y	Y	Y	Y	N	Y	Y
Packwood	Y	Y	Y	Y	N	Y	Y
PENNSYLVANIA							
Heinz	N	N	Y	Y	Y	N	Y
Specter	N	N	Y	Y	Y	N	Y
RHODE ISLAND							
Pell	Y	Y	Y	Y	N	Y	Y
Chafee	Y	Y	Y	Y	N	N	Y
SOUTH CAROLINA							
Hollings	Y	Y	N	Y	N	N	Y
Thurmond	N	N	N	N	Y	N	Y
SOUTH DAKOTA							
Daschle	Y	Y	Y	Y	N	N	Y
Pressler	Y	N	N	Y	N	N	Y
TENNESSEE							
Gore	Y	Y	Y	Y	N	Y	Y
Sasser	Y	Y	Y	Y	N	Y	Y
TEXAS							
Bentsen	Y	Y	Y	Y	N	Y	Y
Gramm	N	Y	N	N	Y	N	Y
UTAH							
Garn	N	N	N	N	Y	N	N
Hatch	N	N	N	N	Y	N	Y
VERMONT							
Leahy	Y	Y	Y	Y	N	Y	Y
Jeffords	Y	Y	Y	Y	N	N	Y
VIRGINIA							
Robb	Y	Y	N	Y	Y	N	Y
Warner	Y	Y	N	Y	Y	N	Y
WASHINGTON							
Adams	Y	Y	Y	Y	N	Y	Y
Gorton	Y	N	N	Y	Y	N	Y
WEST VIRGINIA							
Byrd	N	N	Y	Y	Y	Y	N
Rockefeller	N	N	Y	N	Y	Y	N
WISCONSIN							
Kohl	Y	Y	Y	Y	N	N	Y
Kasten	Y	N	N	Y	Y	N	Y
WYOMING							
Simpson	N	N	N	Y	Y	N	Y
Wallop	N	N	N	N	Y	N	N

KEY

- Y Voted for (yea).
- # Paired for.
- + Announced for.
- N Voted against (nay).
- X Paired against.
- - Announced against.
- P Voted "present."
- C Voted "present" to avoid possible conflict of interest.
- ? Did not vote or otherwise make a position known.

Democrats ***Republicans***

ND Northern Democrats SD Southern Democrats

Southern states - Ala., Ark., Fla., Ga., Ky., La., Miss., N.C., Okla., S.C., Tenn., Texas, Va.

49. S 1630. Clean Air Act Reauthorization/Clean Coal Utilities. Chafee, R-R.I., motion to table (kill) the McClure, R-Idaho, amendment to expand the definition of clean coal technology and to exempt refurbished and upgraded utility plants from new-source performance treatment if the modification does not result in an increase in the modified plant's maximum potential to emit. Motion agreed to 64-33: R 21-22; D 43-11 (ND 30-7, SD 13-4), April 3, 1990. A "yea" was a vote supporting the president's position.

50. S 1630. Clean Air Act Reauthorization/Canadian Electricity. Chafee, R-R.I., motion to table (kill) the McClure, R-Idaho, amendment to restrict the importation of electricity generated from Canadian fossil-fuel utilities. Motion agreed to 57-40: R 17-26; D 40-14 (ND 28-9, SD 12-5), April 3, 1990.

51. S 1630. Clean Air Act Reauthorization/Clean Coal Technology. Chafee, R-R.I., motion to table (kill) the Murkowski, R-Alaska, amendment to expand the definition of clean coal technology and modify the definition of "repowering" to allow precombustion technology, combined with the use of low-sulfur coal, to qualify for repowering benefits in Phase II of the acid rain control program. Motion agreed to 65-31: R 17-25; D 48-6 (ND 34-3, SD 14-3), April 3, 1990. A "yea" was a vote supporting the president's position.

52. S 1630. Clean Air Act Reauthorization/Community Referendums. Chafee, R-R.I., motion to table (kill) the Symms, R-Idaho, amendment to require a community referendum before any plant could be required to close because it exceeded health-risk standards for emissions from major sources of air toxics. Motion agreed to 82-15: R 29-14; D 53-1 (ND 36-1, SD 17-0), April 3, 1990. A "yea" was a vote supporting the president's position.

53. S 1630. Clean Air Act Reauthorization/Permits and Enforcement. Dole, R-Kan., amendment to allow states to issue operating permits to facilitate enforcement of the act without full review by the Environmental Protection Agency. Rejected 49-51: R 37-8; D 12-43 (ND 6-32, SD 6-11), April 3, 1990. A "yea" was a vote supporting the president's position.

54. S 1630. Clean Air Act Reauthorization/Radionuclides. Glenn, D-Ohio, motion to table (kill) the Simpson, R-Wyo., amendment to provide that nothing would prohibit states or localities from implementing more stringent standards for radionuclides. Motion rejected 33-67: R 3-42; D 30-25 (ND 25-13, SD 5-12), April 3, 1990. (The Simpson amendment was subsequently adopted by voice vote.)

55. S 1630. Clean Air Act Reauthorization/Passage. Passage of the bill to provide for attainment and maintenance of health ambient air quality standards, to limit the maximum allowable concentration of so-called criteria pollutants (ozone, lead, sulfur dioxide, particulates, nitrogen dioxide and carbon monoxide) and to require emissions reductions in motor vehicles; to limit emissions of airborne toxics; to require major utilities to reduce emissions of oxides of sulfur and nitrogen, precursors of acid rain; and to establish a system of federal permits and enforcement. Passed 89-11: R 39-6; D 50-5 (ND 33-5, SD 17-0), April 3, 1990. A "yea" was a vote supporting the president's position.

	56	57
ALABAMA		
Heflin	Y	Y
Shelby	Y	Y
ALASKA		
Murkowski	Y	Y
Stevens	Y	Y
ARIZONA		
DeConcini	N	Y
McCain	Y	Y
ARKANSAS		
Bumpers	N	Y
Pryor	N	Y
CALIFORNIA		
Cranston	N	Y
Wilson	Y	Y
COLORADO		
Wirth	N	Y
Armstrong	Y	Y
CONNECTICUT		
Dodd	N	Y
Lieberman	Y	Y
DELAWARE		
Biden	N	Y
Roth	Y	Y
FLORIDA		
Graham	N	Y
Mack	Y	+
GEORGIA		
Fowler	Y	Y
Nunn	Y	Y
HAWAII		
Inouye	Y	Y
Matsunaga	?	?
IDAHO		
McClure	Y	Y
Symms	Y	Y
ILLINOIS		
Dixon	N	Y
Simon	N	Y
INDIANA		
Coats	Y	Y
Lugar	Y	Y
IOWA		
Harkin	N	Y
Grassley	Y	+
KANSAS		
Dole	Y	Y
Kassebaum	Y	Y
KENTUCKY		
Ford	Y	Y
McConnell	Y	Y
LOUISIANA		
Breaux	Y	Y
Johnston	Y	Y
MAINE		
Mitchell	N	Y
Cohen	Y	Y
MARYLAND		
Mikulski	N	Y
Sarbanes	N	Y
MASSACHUSETTS		
Kennedy	N	Y
Kerry	N	Y
MICHIGAN		
Levin	N	Y
Riegle	N	Y
MINNESOTA		
Boschwitz	Y	Y
Durenberger	Y	Y
MISSISSIPPI		
Cochran	Y	Y
Lott	Y	Y
MISSOURI		
Bond	Y	Y
Danforth	Y	Y
MONTANA		
Baucus	Y	Y
Burns	Y	Y
NEBRASKA		
Exon	N	Y
Kerrey	N	Y
NEVADA		
Bryan	N	Y
Reid	Y	Y
NEW HAMPSHIRE		
Humphrey	Y	Y
Rudman	Y	Y
NEW JERSEY		
Bradley	N	Y
Lautenberg	N	Y
NEW MEXICO		
Bingaman	N	Y
Domenici	Y	Y
NEW YORK		
Moynihan	Y	Y
D'Amato	Y	+
NORTH CAROLINA		
Sanford	Y	Y
Helms	Y	Y
NORTH DAKOTA		
Burdick	N	Y
Conrad	N	Y
OHIO		
Glenn	N	Y
Metzenbaum	N	Y
OKLAHOMA		
Boren	Y	Y
Nickles	Y	Y
OREGON		
Hatfield	Y	Y
Packwood	Y	Y
PENNSYLVANIA		
Heinz	Y	Y
Specter	Y	Y
RHODE ISLAND		
Pell	N	Y
Chafee	Y	Y
SOUTH CAROLINA		
Hollings	Y	Y
Thurmond	Y	Y
SOUTH DAKOTA		
Daschle	N	Y
Pressler	Y	Y
TENNESSEE		
Gore	N	Y
Sasser	N	Y
TEXAS		
Bentsen	Y	Y
Gramm	Y	Y
UTAH		
Garn	Y	Y
Hatch	Y	Y
VERMONT		
Leahy	N	Y
Jeffords	Y	Y
VIRGINIA		
Robb	Y	Y
Warner	Y	Y
WASHINGTON		
Adams	N	Y
Gorton	Y	Y
WEST VIRGINIA		
Byrd	N	Y
Rockefeller	N	Y
WISCONSIN		
Kohl	N	Y
Kasten	Y	Y
WYOMING		
Simpson	Y	Y
Wallop	Y	Y

KEY

Y Voted for (yea).
\# Paired for.
\+ Announced for.
N Voted against (nay).
X Paired against.
\- Announced against.
P Voted "present."
C Voted "present" to avoid possible conflict of interest.
? Did not vote or otherwise make a position known.

Democrats ***Republicans***

ND Northern Democrats SD Southern Democrats

Southern states - Ala., Ark., Fla., Ga., Ky., La., Miss., N.C., Okla., S.C., Tenn., Texas, Va.

56. Ryan Nomination. Confirmation of President Bush's nomination of T. Timothy Ryan Jr. to be director of the Office of Thrift Supervision. Confirmed 62-37: R 45-0; D 17-37 (ND 5-32, SD 12-5), April 4, 1990. A "yea" was a vote supporting the president's position.

57. HR 7. Fiscal 1991-95 Vocational Education Reauthorization/Passage. Passage of the bill to authorize $1.5 billion in fiscal 1991, targeting 65 percent to 75 percent of all grants to secondary schools, and 25 percent to 35 percent to postsecondary schools, with an emphasis on funding programs for the disabled, the economically disadvantaged and those with limited proficiency in English. The bill would authorize 5 percent of the total appropriation for "Tech-Prep" programs, linking curricula between secondary and postsecondary schools. Passed 96-0: R 42-0; D 54-0 (ND 37-0, SD 17-0), April 5, 1990.

	58
ALABAMA	
Heflin	Y
Shelby	Y
ALASKA	
Murkowski	Y
Stevens	Y
ARIZONA	
DeConcini	?
McCain	Y
ARKANSAS	
Bumpers	Y
Pryor	Y
CALIFORNIA	
Cranston	Y
Wilson	Y
COLORADO	
Wirth	Y
Armstrong	Y
CONNECTICUT	
Dodd	Y
Lieberman	Y
DELAWARE	
Biden	Y
Roth	Y
FLORIDA	
Graham	Y
Mack	Y
GEORGIA	
Fowler	?
Nunn	Y
HAWAII	
Inouye	?
Vacancy*	
IDAHO	
McClure	Y
Symms	Y
ILLINOIS	
Dixon	Y
Simon	Y
INDIANA	
Coats	Y
Lugar	Y

	58
IOWA	
Harkin	Y
Grassley	Y
KANSAS	
Dole	Y
Kassebaum	Y
KENTUCKY	
Ford	Y
McConnell	Y
LOUISIANA	
Breaux	Y
Johnston	Y
MAINE	
Mitchell	Y
Cohen	Y
MARYLAND	
Mikulski	Y
Sarbanes	Y
MASSACHUSETTS	
Kennedy	Y
Kerry	Y
MICHIGAN	
Levin	Y
Riegle	Y
MINNESOTA	
Boschwitz	Y
Durenberger	N
MISSISSIPPI	
Cochran	Y
Lott	Y
MISSOURI	
Bond	Y
Danforth	N
MONTANA	
Baucus	Y
Burns	Y
NEBRASKA	
Exon	Y
Kerrey	Y
NEVADA	
Bryan	Y
Reid	Y

	58
NEW HAMPSHIRE	
Humphrey	?
Rudman	Y
NEW JERSEY	
Bradley	Y
Lautenberg	Y
NEW MEXICO	
Bingaman	Y
Domenici	Y
NEW YORK	
Moynihan	Y
D'Amato	Y
NORTH CAROLINA	
Sanford	Y
Helms	Y
NORTH DAKOTA	
Burdick	?
Conrad	Y
OHIO	
Glenn	Y
Metzenbaum	Y
OKLAHOMA	
Boren	?
Nickles	Y
OREGON	
Hatfield	Y
Packwood	Y
PENNSYLVANIA	
Heinz	N
Specter	Y
RHODE ISLAND	
Pell	Y
Chafee	Y
SOUTH CAROLINA	
Hollings	Y
Thurmond	Y
SOUTH DAKOTA	
Daschle	Y
Pressler	Y
TENNESSEE	
Gore	Y
Sasser	Y

KEY

Y Voted for (yea).
\# Paired for.
\+ Announced for.
N Voted against (nay).
X Paired against.
\- Announced against.
P Voted "present."
C Voted "present" to avoid possible conflict of interest.
? Did not vote or otherwise make a position known.

Democrats *Republicans*

	58
TEXAS	
Bentsen	Y
Gramm	Y
UTAH	
Garn	Y
Hatch	Y
VERMONT	
Leahy	Y
Jeffords	Y
VIRGINIA	
Robb	Y
Warner	Y
WASHINGTON	
Adams	Y
Gorton	Y
WEST VIRGINIA	
Byrd	Y
Rockefeller	Y
WISCONSIN	
Kohl	Y
Kasten	Y
WYOMING	
Simpson	Y
Wallop	Y

ND Northern Democrats SD Southern Democrats Southern states - Ala., Ark., Fla., Ga., Ky., La., Miss., N.C., Okla., S.C., Tenn., Texas, Va.

58. HR 1594. Miscellaneous Tariffs/Suspensions. Roth, R-Del., amendment to provide administrative procedures for non-controversial tariff suspensions. The underlying bill would permanently extend duty-free access to U.S. markets for exports from the Caribbean Basin. Adopted 90-3: R 41-3; D 49-0 (ND 34-0, SD 15-0), April 19, 1990.

** Sen. Spark M. Matsunaga, D-Hawaii, died April 15, 1990. The last vote for which he was eligible was vote 57.*

	59	60	61	62	63
ALABAMA					
Heflin	Y	N	Y	N	Y
Shelby	Y	Y	Y	Y	Y
ALASKA					
Murkowski	Y	Y	Y	Y	Y
Stevens	Y	Y	Y	N	Y
ARIZONA					
DeConcini	Y	Y	Y	N	Y
McCain	N	Y	N	N	Y
ARKANSAS					
Bumpers	Y	Y	Y	Y	Y
Pryor	Y	Y	Y	Y	Y
CALIFORNIA					
Cranston	Y	N	Y	N	Y
Wilson	Y	Y	Y	N	Y
COLORADO					
Wirth	Y	N	N	Y	Y
Armstrong	N	Y	N	?	?
CONNECTICUT					
Dodd	Y	Y	N	Y	Y
Lieberman	Y	N	Y	Y	Y
DELAWARE					
Biden	Y	N	Y	N	Y
Roth	Y	Y	N	Y	Y
FLORIDA					
Graham	Y	Y	N	Y	Y
Mack	N	N	N	Y	Y
GEORGIA					
Fowler	Y	N	Y	Y	Y
Nunn	Y	Y	Y	Y	Y
HAWAII					
Inouye	Y	Y	Y	N	Y
Vacancy					
IDAHO					
McClure	Y	Y	?	?	?
Symms	Y	Y	N	N	Y
ILLINOIS					
Dixon	Y	Y	Y	N	Y
Simon	Y	Y	Y	N	Y
INDIANA					
Coats	Y	Y	N	Y	Y
Lugar	Y	Y	N	Y	Y
IOWA					
Harkin	Y	Y	Y	Y	Y
Grassley	Y	Y	N	N	Y
KANSAS					
Dole	Y	Y	N	Y	Y
Kassebaum	N	Y	N	Y	Y
KENTUCKY					
Ford	Y	Y	Y	Y	Y
McConnell	Y	Y	Y	Y	Y
LOUISIANA					
Breaux	Y	N	Y	Y	+
Johnston	Y	N	Y	Y	Y
MAINE					
Mitchell	Y	Y	Y	Y	Y
Cohen	Y	N	Y	Y	Y
MARYLAND					
Mikulski	Y	Y	Y	Y	Y
Sarbanes	Y	Y	Y	N	Y
MASSACHUSETTS					
Kennedy	Y	Y	N	?	?
Kerry	Y	N	N	N	Y
MICHIGAN					
Levin	Y	Y	Y	Y	Y
Riegle	Y	Y	Y	Y	Y
MINNESOTA					
Boschwitz	Y	Y	?	?	?
Durenberger	Y	Y	N	Y	Y
MISSISSIPPI					
Cochran	N	Y	N	N	Y
Lott	N	Y	Y	Y	Y
MISSOURI					
Bond	N	Y	Y	Y	Y
Danforth	Y	N	Y	?	?
MONTANA					
Baucus	Y	Y	Y	Y	Y
Burns	Y	Y	N	Y	Y
NEBRASKA					
Exon	?	?	?	?	?
Kerrey	Y	Y	Y	Y	Y
NEVADA					
Bryan	Y	N	Y	Y	Y
Reid	Y	N	Y	Y	Y
NEW HAMPSHIRE					
Humphrey	N	N	N	Y	Y
Rudman	N	N	Y	Y	Y
NEW JERSEY					
Bradley	Y	N	N	Y	Y
Lautenberg	Y	N	Y	Y	Y
NEW MEXICO					
Bingaman	Y	Y	Y	N	Y
Domenici	Y	Y	Y	N	Y
NEW YORK					
Moynihan	Y	Y	Y	Y	Y
D'Amato	Y	Y	Y	N	Y
NORTH CAROLINA					
Sanford	Y	Y	Y	N	Y
Helms	N	Y	Y	N	Y
NORTH DAKOTA					
Burdick	Y	N	Y	Y	Y
Conrad	Y	Y	Y	N	Y
OHIO					
Glenn	Y	N	Y	Y	Y
Metzenbaum	Y	N	Y	Y	Y
OKLAHOMA					
Boren	Y	Y	N	Y	Y
Nickles	N	Y	N	Y	Y
OREGON					
Hatfield	Y	Y	Y	N	Y
Packwood	Y	N	N	Y	Y
PENNSYLVANIA					
Heinz	Y	N	Y	N	Y
Specter	Y	N	Y	N	Y
RHODE ISLAND					
Pell	Y	Y	Y	Y	Y
Chafee	N	Y	N	Y	Y
SOUTH CAROLINA					
Hollings	Y	Y	Y	N	Y
Thurmond	Y	Y	Y	N	Y
SOUTH DAKOTA					
Daschle	Y	Y	Y	Y	Y
Pressler	Y	N	N	N	Y
TENNESSEE					
Gore	Y	Y	Y	Y	Y
Sasser	Y	N	Y	Y	Y
TEXAS					
Bentsen	Y	N	Y	Y	Y
Gramm	N	Y	N	Y	Y
UTAH					
Garn	N	N	Y	N	Y
Hatch	N	Y	N	N	Y
VERMONT					
Leahy	Y	N	Y	Y	Y
Jeffords	Y	Y	N	Y	Y
VIRGINIA					
Robb	Y	Y	N	Y	Y
Warner	Y	Y	Y	N	Y
WASHINGTON					
Adams	Y	Y	N	Y	Y
Gorton	N	Y	N	Y	Y
WEST VIRGINIA					
Byrd	Y	Y	Y	Y	Y
Rockefeller	Y	Y	Y	Y	Y
WISCONSIN					
Kohl	Y	N	Y	Y	Y
Kasten	Y	Y	Y	N	Y
WYOMING					
Simpson	Y	Y	N	Y	Y
Wallop	N	Y	N	Y	Y

KEY

- Y Voted for (yea).
- # Paired for.
- + Announced for.
- N Voted against (nay).
- X Paired against.
- \- Announced against.
- P Voted "present."
- C Voted "present" to avoid possible conflict of interest.
- ? Did not vote or otherwise make a position known.

Democrats *Republicans*

ND Northern Democrats SD Southern Democrats

Southern states - Ala., Ark., Fla., Ga., Ky., La., Miss., N.C., Okla., S.C., Tenn., Texas, Va.

59. HR 1594. Miscellaneous Tariffs/Processed Timber. Packwood, R-Ore., amendment to prohibit the export of unprocessed timber from federally owned lands. Adopted 81-17: R 28-17; D 53-0 (ND 36-0, SD 17-0), April 24, 1990.

60. HR 1594. Miscellaneous Tariffs/Ranitidine Hydrochloride. Sanford, D-N.C., amendment to suspend the duty on ranitidine hydrochloride, an imported component in an ulcer-treating drug made in North Carolina. Adopted 68-30: R 35-10; D 33-20 (ND 22-14, SD 11-6), April 24, 1990.

61. HR 1594. Miscellaneous Tariffs/Footwear. Cohen, R-Maine, motion to table (kill) the Graham, D-Fla., amendment to reduce by 50 percent the duty on rubber-soled and fabric upper footwear imported from Caribbean Basin countries. Motion agreed to 63-33: R 19-24; D 44-9 (ND 30-6, SD 14-3), April 24, 1990. A "nay" was a vote supporting the president's position.

62. HR 1594. Miscellaneous Tariffs/Aircraft Transfer. Bentsen, D-Texas, motion to table (kill) the DeConcini, D-Ariz., amendment to require the secretary of the Treasury to transfer to the University Medical Center, in Tucson, Ariz., an airworthy turboprop aircraft that was forfeited under U.S. customs laws. Motion agreed to 62-31: R 23-18; D 39-13 (ND 25-10, SD 14-3), April 24, 1990.

63. HR 1594. Miscellaneous Tariffs/Passage. Passage of the bill to expand the Caribbean Basin Initiative, assure the constitutionality of the procedure for congressional approval of trade agreements with communist nations, authorize appropriations for U.S. trade agencies and make miscellaneous and technical changes to various trade laws. Passed 92-0: R 41-0; D 51-0 (ND 35-0, SD 16-0), April 24, 1990. A "yea" was a vote supporting the president's position.

KEY

- Y Voted for (yea).
- # Paired for.
- + Announced for.
- N Voted against (nay).
- X Paired against.
- - Announced against.
- P Voted "present."
- C Voted "present" to avoid possible conflict of interest.
- ? Did not vote or otherwise make a position known.

Democrats *Republicans*

	64	65	66	67
ALABAMA				
Heflin	N	N	Y	Y
Shelby	N	Y	Y	Y
ALASKA				
Murkowski	Y	Y	Y	Y
Stevens	Y	Y	Y	Y
ARIZONA				
DeConcini	Y	?	Y	Y
McCain	Y	?	Y	Y
ARKANSAS				
Bumpers	N	N	Y	Y
Pryor	N	N	Y	Y
CALIFORNIA				
Cranston	N	Y	Y	Y
Wilson	Y	Y	Y	Y
COLORADO				
Wirth	N	N	Y	Y
Armstrong	Y	Y	Y	Y
CONNECTICUT				
Dodd	Y	N	Y	Y
Lieberman	Y	Y	Y	Y
DELAWARE				
Biden	N	Y	Y	Y
Roth	Y	Y	Y	Y
FLORIDA				
Graham	Y	N	Y	Y
Mack	Y	Y	Y	Y
GEORGIA				
Fowler	N	N	Y	Y
Nunn	N	Y	Y	Y
HAWAII				
Inouye	N	?	?	?
Vacancy				
IDAHO				
McClure	Y	?	Y	Y
Symms	Y	Y	Y	Y
ILLINOIS				
Dixon	N	N	Y	Y
Simon	N	Y	Y	Y
INDIANA				
Coats	Y	Y	Y	Y
Lugar	Y	Y	Y	Y
IOWA				
Harkin	N	N	Y	Y
Grassley	Y	Y	Y	Y
KANSAS				
Dole	Y	Y	Y	Y
Kassebaum	Y	Y	Y	Y
KENTUCKY				
Ford	N	Y	Y	Y
McConnell	Y	Y	Y	Y
LOUISIANA				
Breaux	N	N	Y	Y
Johnston	N	N	Y	Y
MAINE				
Mitchell	N	N	Y	Y
Cohen	Y	Y	Y	Y
MARYLAND				
Mikulski	N	Y	Y	Y
Sarbanes	N	Y	Y	Y
MASSACHUSETTS				
Kennedy	N	?	Y	Y
Kerry	N	Y	Y	Y
MICHIGAN				
Levin	N	N	Y	Y
Riegle	N	N	?	?
MINNESOTA				
Boschwitz	Y	Y	Y	Y
Durenberger	Y	Y	Y	Y
MISSISSIPPI				
Cochran	Y	Y	Y	Y
Lott	Y	?	Y	Y
MISSOURI				
Bond	Y	Y	Y	Y
Danforth	Y	Y	Y	Y
MONTANA				
Baucus	N	N	Y	Y
Burns	Y	Y	Y	Y
NEBRASKA				
Exon	N	N	Y	Y
Kerrey	N	Y	Y	Y
NEVADA				
Bryan	N	Y	Y	Y
Reid	N	Y	Y	Y
NEW HAMPSHIRE				
Humphrey	Y	Y	Y	Y
Rudman	Y	Y	Y	Y
NEW JERSEY				
Bradley	N	Y	Y	Y
Lautenberg	N	N	Y	Y
NEW MEXICO				
Bingaman	N	N	Y	Y
Domenici	Y	Y	?	?
NEW YORK				
Moynihan	N	Y	Y	Y
D'Amato	Y	Y	Y	Y
NORTH CAROLINA				
Sanford	Y	Y	Y	Y
Helms	N	N	Y	Y
NORTH DAKOTA				
Burdick	N	N	Y	Y
Conrad	N	N	Y	Y
OHIO				
Glenn	N	Y	Y	Y
Metzenbaum	N	N	Y	Y
OKLAHOMA				
Boren	Y	Y	Y	Y
Nickles	Y	Y	Y	Y
OREGON				
Hatfield	Y	Y	Y	Y
Packwood	Y	?	Y	Y
PENNSYLVANIA				
Heinz	Y	Y	Y	Y
Specter	Y	Y	Y	Y
RHODE ISLAND				
Pell	N	Y	Y	Y
Chafee	Y	Y	Y	Y
SOUTH CAROLINA				
Hollings	Y	Y	Y	Y
Thurmond	Y	Y	Y	Y
SOUTH DAKOTA				
Daschle	N	N	Y	Y
Pressler	N	N	Y	Y
TENNESSEE				
Gore	N	N	Y	Y
Sasser	N	N	Y	Y
TEXAS				
Bentsen	N	N	Y	Y
Gramm	Y	Y	Y	Y
UTAH				
Garn	Y	Y	Y	Y
Hatch	Y	Y	Y	Y
VERMONT				
Leahy	N	N	Y	Y
Jeffords	Y	Y	Y	Y
VIRGINIA				
Robb	Y	Y	Y	Y
Warner	Y	Y	Y	Y
WASHINGTON				
Adams	N	Y	Y	Y
Gorton	Y	Y	Y	Y
WEST VIRGINIA				
Byrd	N	Y	Y	Y
Rockefeller	N	N	Y	Y
WISCONSIN				
Kohl	N	N	Y	Y
Kasten	Y	Y	Y	Y
WYOMING				
Simpson	Y	Y	Y	Y
Wallop	Y	Y	Y	Y

ND Northern Democrats SD Southern Democrats

Southern states - Ala., Ark., Fla., Ga., Ky., La., Miss., N.C., Okla., S.C., Tenn., Texas, Va.

64. HR 4404. Fiscal 1990 Supplemental Appropriations/Domestic Redistribution. Kasten, R-Wis., motion to table (kill) the Byrd, D-W.Va., amendment to reduce aid to Panama by $120 million and use the fund for American Indian health facilities, Energy Department environmental restoration and waste-management projects, agriculture disaster assistance programs, and food programs for women and infants. Motion agreed to 51-48: R 43-2; D 8-46 (ND 3-34, SD 5-12), April 26, 1990.

65. HR 4404. Fiscal 1990 Supplemental Appropriations/Gramm-Rudman Waiver. Hollings, D-S.C., motion to waive the spending-allocation limit in the Gramm-Rudman deficit-reduction law (PL 99-177) with respect to consideration of a Hollings amendment to repeal certain provisions of the fiscal 1990-91 State Department authorization, which holds the U.S. Information Agency (USIA) at fiscal 1989 spending levels. Repeal would result in $258 million more in outlays for the USIA. Motion agreed to 62-30: R 39-2; D 23-28 (ND 16-18, SD 7-10), April 26, 1990. A three-fifths majority (60) of the total Senate is required to waive the spending-allocation limit in Gramm-Rudman.

66. HR 4404. Fiscal 1990 Supplemental Appropriations/Foreign Aid. Byrd, D-W.Va., amendment to require a study and report on how U.S. foreign assistance programs may promote U.S. international economic competitiveness. Adopted 96-0: R 44-0; D 52-0 (ND 35-0, SD 17-0), April 27, 1990.

67. HR 4404. Fiscal 1990 Supplemental Appropriations/Nicaragua. Appropriations Committee amendment to provide $8 million for environmental activities in Nicaragua, including the preservation of rain forests, promotion of sustainable agriculture, control of pollution and restoration of the natural resource base. Adopted 96-0: R 44-0; D 52-0 (ND 35-0, SD 17-0), April 27, 1990.

	68	69	70	71	72	73	74	75
ALABAMA								
Heflin	Y	N	Y	N	N	N	Y	Y
Shelby	Y	N	Y	N	N	N	Y	Y
ALASKA								
Murkowski	Y	N	Y	N	Y	Y	N	Y
Stevens	Y	Y	Y	?	Y	Y	N	Y
ARIZONA								
DeConcini	Y	N	Y	N	N	N	Y	Y
McCain	Y	N	Y	?	Y	N	Y	Y
ARKANSAS								
Bumpers	N	Y	Y	N	N	N	Y	N
Pryor	N	Y	Y	N	N	N	Y	Y
CALIFORNIA								
Cranston	N	Y	Y	Y	N	N	Y	N
Wilson	N	Y	Y	N	Y	Y	N	Y
COLORADO								
Wirth	N	Y	Y	N	N	N	Y	Y
Armstrong	Y	N	Y	?	Y	Y	N	Y
CONNECTICUT								
Dodd	N	Y	Y	N	N	N	N	Y
Lieberman	N	Y	Y	N	N	N	Y	Y
DELAWARE								
Biden	N	Y	Y	N	Y	N	Y	Y
Roth	Y	Y	Y	N	Y	Y	N	Y
FLORIDA								
Graham	N	Y	Y	N	N	N	N	Y
Mack	Y	N	Y	N	Y	N	N	Y
GEORGIA								
Fowler	N	Y	Y	Y	N	N	Y	N
Nunn	N	Y	Y	N	Y	N	Y	N
HAWAII								
Inouye	?	?	?	?	N	Y	Y	N
Vacancy								
IDAHO								
McClure	Y	N	Y	N	Y	Y	N	Y
Symms	Y	N	Y	N	Y	Y	N	Y
ILLINOIS								
Dixon	N	Y	Y	N	Y	N	Y	Y
Simon	N	Y	Y	Y	Y	N	Y	Y
INDIANA								
Coats	Y	N	Y	N	Y	N	N	Y
Lugar	Y	N	Y	N	Y	N	N	Y
IOWA								
Harkin	N	Y	Y	Y	N	N	Y	N
Grassley	Y	N	Y	N	N	Y	Y	Y
KANSAS								
Dole	Y	N	Y	N	Y	Y	N	Y
Kassebaum	N	Y	Y	?	Y	Y	N	Y
KENTUCKY								
Ford	Y	N	Y	N	N	N	Y	Y
McConnell	Y	N	Y	N	Y	Y	N	Y
LOUISIANA								
Breaux	Y	N	Y	N	N	N	N	Y
Johnston	Y	N	Y	N	N	Y	Y	Y
MAINE								
Mitchell	N	Y	Y	Y	Y	N	Y	Y
Cohen	N	Y	Y	Y	Y	N	N	Y
MARYLAND								
Mikulski	N	Y	Y	Y	?	?	?	Y
Sarbanes	N	Y	Y	Y	N	N	Y	Y
MASSACHUSETTS								
Kennedy	N	Y	Y	Y	N	N	Y	N
Kerry	N	Y	Y	Y	N	N	Y	Y
MICHIGAN								
Levin	N	Y	Y	Y	Y	N	Y	Y
Riegle	?	?	?	?	N	N	Y	Y
MINNESOTA								
Boschwitz	Y	N	Y	N	N	Y	N	Y
Durenberger	Y	N	Y	Y	N	Y	N	Y
MISSISSIPPI								
Cochran	Y	N	Y	N	Y	Y	N	Y
Lott	Y	N	Y	N	Y	Y	N	Y
MISSOURI								
Bond	Y	N	Y	N	Y	Y	N	Y
Danforth	Y	N	Y	Y	Y	Y	N	Y
MONTANA								
Baucus	N	Y	Y	N	N	N	Y	N
Burns	Y	N	Y	N	N	Y	N	Y
NEBRASKA								
Exon	Y	N	Y	N	N	N	Y	N
Kerrey	N	Y	Y	N	N	N	Y	N
NEVADA								
Bryan	N	Y	Y	N	Y	N	Y	Y
Reid	Y	N	Y	N	Y	N	N	Y
NEW HAMPSHIRE								
Humphrey	Y	N	Y	N	Y	Y	N	Y
Rudman	N	Y	Y	?	Y	Y	N	Y
NEW JERSEY								
Bradley	N	Y	Y	N	Y	N	Y	Y
Lautenberg	N	Y	Y	Y	N	N	Y	Y
NEW MEXICO								
Bingaman	N	Y	Y	?	Y	N	Y	Y
Domenici	?	?	?	?	Y	Y	N	Y
NEW YORK								
Moynihan	N	Y	Y	Y	?	?	Y	Y
D'Amato	Y	N	Y	N	Y	Y	N	Y
NORTH CAROLINA								
Sanford	N	Y	Y	?	N	Y	N	N
Helms	Y	N	Y	?	Y	Y	N	Y
NORTH DAKOTA								
Burdick	N	Y	Y	Y	N	N	Y	N
Conrad	Y	N	Y	Y	N	N	Y	N
OHIO								
Glenn	N	Y	Y	Y	Y	N	Y	Y
Metzenbaum	N	Y	Y	Y	Y	N	Y	N
OKLAHOMA								
Boren	Y	N	Y	N	N	N	N	N
Nickles	Y	N	Y	N	Y	Y	N	Y
OREGON								
Hatfield	Y	N	Y	Y	Y	Y	N	Y
Packwood	N	Y	Y	Y	Y	Y	N	Y
PENNSYLVANIA								
Heinz	N	Y	Y	N	Y	Y	Y	Y
Specter	N	Y	Y	N	Y	Y	Y	Y
RHODE ISLAND								
Pell	N	Y	Y	Y	N	N	Y	N
Chafee	N	Y	Y	Y	Y	N	N	N
SOUTH CAROLINA								
Hollings	N	Y	Y	N	N	N	N	Y
Thurmond	Y	N	Y	N	Y	Y	N	Y
SOUTH DAKOTA								
Daschle	N	Y	Y	N	N	N	Y	N
Pressler	Y	N	Y	N	N	Y	Y	Y
TENNESSEE								
Gore	N	Y	Y	N	N	N	Y	?
Sasser	N	Y	Y	N	N	N	Y	N
TEXAS								
Bentsen	N	Y	Y	N	N	N	Y	?
Gramm	Y	N	Y	N	Y	Y	N	Y
UTAH								
Garn	Y	N	Y	?	Y	Y	N	Y
Hatch	Y	N	Y	N	Y	Y	N	Y
VERMONT								
Leahy	N	Y	Y	Y	N	N	N	N
Jeffords	N	Y	Y	Y	?	Y	N	Y
VIRGINIA								
Robb	N	Y	Y	N	Y	N	N	N
Warner	Y	N	Y	N	Y	N	N	N
WASHINGTON								
Adams	N	Y	Y	Y	N	N	Y	N
Gorton	N	Y	Y	N	N	N	N	Y
WEST VIRGINIA								
Byrd	Y	Y	Y	N	Y	N	Y	Y
Rockefeller	N	Y	Y	N	Y	N	Y	Y
WISCONSIN								
Kohl	N	Y	Y	Y	N	N	N	Y
Kasten	Y	N	Y	N	Y	Y	N	Y
WYOMING								
Simpson	Y	N	Y	N	Y	Y	N	N
Wallop	Y	N	Y	N	+	?	N	Y

KEY

- Y Voted for (yea).
- # Paired for.
- + Announced for.
- N Voted against (nay).
- X Paired against.
- - Announced against.
- P Voted "present."
- C Voted "present" to avoid possible conflict of interest.
- ? Did not vote or otherwise make a position known.

Democrats ***Republicans***

ND Northern Democrats SD Southern Democrats

Southern states - Ala., Ark., Fla., Ga., Ky., La., Miss., N.C., Okla., S.C., Tenn., Texas, Va.

68. HR 4404. Fiscal 1990 Supplemental Appropriations/ Appeal of the Chair's Ruling. Adams, D-Wash., appeal of the chair's ruling that the Appropriations Committee amendment to allow the District of Columbia to use local funds for abortions was out of order. Ruling of the chair rejected 45-51: R 34-10; D 11-41 (ND 5-30, SD 6-11), April 27, 1990.

69. HR 4404. Fiscal 1990 Supplemental Appropriations/ Abortion. Judgment of the Senate whether the Appropriations Committee amendment to allow D.C. to use local funds for abortions for the rest of the fiscal year was germane. Ruled germane 54-42: R 12-32; D 42-10 (ND 31-4, SD 11-6), April 27, 1990. A "nay" was a vote supporting the president's position. (The amendment was subsequently adopted by voice vote.)

70. HR 4404. Fiscal 1990 Supplemental Appropriations/ Preschool Programs. Adams, D-Wash., amendment to the Appropriations Committee amendment, to study the need for a District of Columbia early childhood educational development program for pre-school and school-age children, and working parents and parents on welfare seeking work. Adopted 96-0: R 44-0; D 52-0 (ND 35-0, SD 17-0), April 27, 1990.

71. HR 4404. Fiscal 1990 Supplemental Appropriations/ Death Penalty. Hatfield, R-Ore., motion to table (kill) the Gramm, R-Texas, amendment to the Appropriations Committee amendment on District of Columbia abortion funds to provide for the death penalty in the District of Columbia for drug-related murders. Motion rejected 27-60: R 7-30; D 20-30 (ND 19-15, SD 1-15), April 27, 1990.

72. HR 4404. Fiscal 1990 Supplemental Appropriations/ Disaster Relief. Hatfield, R-Ore., motion to table (kill) the Conrad, D-N.D., amendment to forgive producers who have been adversely affected by a major disaster or emergency in 1990 from having to repay certain advance deficiency payments. Motion agreed to 52-43: R 37-6; D 15-37 (ND 13-22, SD 2-15), April 30, 1990.

73. HR 4404. Fiscal 1990 Supplemental Appropriations/ Air Force. Stevens, R-Alaska, motion to table (kill) the Dixon, D-Ill., amendment to nullify language that would restrict spending $29 million appropriated in fiscal 1990 for the Air Force Operation and Maintenance Fund until the Air Force pays at least $7 million to settle a contract claim with a private construction company in Idaho, thereby leaving the claim to be settled in the courts. Motion rejected 39-57: R 36-8; D 3-49 (ND 1-34, SD 2-15), April 30, 1990. (The amendment was subsequently adopted by voice vote.)

74. HR 4404. Fiscal 1990 Supplemental Appropriations/ Gramm-Rudman Waiver. Wirth, D-Colo., motion to waive the allocation limit in the Gramm-Rudman antideficit law (PL 99-177) with respect to the Wirth amendment to transfer funds from Panama tourism programs to the Justice Department to prosecute savings and loan fraud. Motion rejected 48-50: R 5-40; D 43-10 (ND 32-4, SD 11-6), April 30, 1990. A three-fifths majority (60) of the total Senate is required to waive the spending-allocation limit in Gramm-Rudman. (The amendment subsequently fell when the Senate upheld a Kasten, R-Wis., point of order that the Wirth amendment would violate the Congressional Budget Act of 1974 by allowing the Commerce, Justice, and State budget account to exceed its budget authority.)

75. HR 4404. Fiscal 1990 Supplemental Appropriations/ Lithuania. D'Amato, R-N.Y., amendment to express the sense of the Senate that the president should submit no U.S.-Soviet trade agreement until the Soviet Union lifts its embargo against Lithuania and negotiates with the elected representatives of Lithuania to recognize an independent Republic of Lithuania. Adopted 73-24: R 42-3; D 31-21 (ND 23-14, SD 8-7), May 1, 1990.

	76	77	78	79
ALABAMA				
Heflin	Y	Y	Y	Y
Shelby	Y	Y	Y	Y
ALASKA				
Murkowski	Y	Y	Y	Y
Stevens	Y	Y	Y	Y
ARIZONA				
DeConcini	Y	Y	Y	Y
McCain	Y	Y	Y	Y
ARKANSAS				
Bumpers	Y	Y	Y	Y
Pryor	Y	Y	Y	Y
CALIFORNIA				
Cranston	Y	Y	Y	Y
Wilson	N	N	N	N
COLORADO				
Wirth	Y	Y	Y	Y
Armstrong	N	?	?	?
CONNECTICUT				
Dodd	Y	Y	Y	Y
Lieberman	Y	Y	Y	Y
DELAWARE				
Biden	Y	Y	Y	Y
Roth	N	N	N	N
FLORIDA				
Graham	Y	Y	Y	Y
Mack	N	N	N	N
GEORGIA				
Fowler	Y	Y	Y	Y
Nunn	Y	Y	Y	Y
HAWAII				
Inouye	Y	Y	Y	Y
Vacancy				
IDAHO				
McClure	N	N	N	N
Symms	N	N	N	N
ILLINOIS				
Dixon	Y	Y	Y	Y
Simon	Y	Y	Y	Y
INDIANA				
Coats	N	N	N	N
Lugar	N	N	N	N
IOWA				
Harkin	Y	Y	Y	Y
Grassley	N	N	N	N
KANSAS				
Dole	N	N	N	N
Kassebaum	N	N	N	Y
KENTUCKY				
Ford	Y	Y	Y	?
McConnell	N	N	N	N
LOUISIANA				
Breaux	Y	Y	Y	Y
Johnston	Y	Y	Y	Y
MAINE				
Mitchell	Y	Y	Y	Y
Cohen	Y	N	N	N
MARYLAND				
Mikulski	Y	Y	Y	Y
Sarbanes	Y	Y	Y	Y
MASSACHUSETTS				
Kennedy	Y	Y	Y	Y
Kerry	Y	Y	Y	Y
MICHIGAN				
Levin	Y	Y	Y	Y
Riegle	Y	Y	Y	Y
MINNESOTA				
Boschwitz	N	N	N	N
Durenberger	Y	Y	Y	N
MISSISSIPPI				
Cochran	N	N	N	N
Lott	Y	Y	Y	N
MISSOURI				
Bond	N	N	N	N
Danforth	N	N	N	N
MONTANA				
Baucus	Y	Y	Y	Y
Burns	Y	N	N	N
NEBRASKA				
Exon	Y	Y	Y	Y
Kerrey	Y	Y	Y	Y
NEVADA				
Bryan	Y	Y	Y	Y
Reid	Y	Y	Y	Y
NEW HAMPSHIRE				
Humphrey	N	N	N	N
Rudman	N	N	N	N
NEW JERSEY				
Bradley	Y	Y	Y	Y
Lautenberg	Y	Y	Y	Y
NEW MEXICO				
Bingaman	Y	Y	Y	Y
Domenici	Y	Y	?	?
NEW YORK				
Moynihan	Y	Y	Y	Y
D'Amato	Y	Y	Y	N
NORTH CAROLINA				
Sanford	Y	Y	Y	Y
Helms	N	N	N	N
NORTH DAKOTA				
Burdick	Y	Y	Y	Y
Conrad	Y	Y	Y	Y
OHIO				
Glenn	Y	Y	Y	Y
Metzenbaum	Y	Y	Y	Y
OKLAHOMA				
Boren	Y	Y	Y	Y
Nickles	N	N	N	?
OREGON				
Hatfield	Y	Y	Y	Y
Packwood	Y	Y	Y	Y
PENNSYLVANIA				
Heinz	Y	Y	Y	N
Specter	Y	Y	Y	N
RHODE ISLAND				
Pell	Y	Y	Y	Y
Chafee	Y	N	N	N
SOUTH CAROLINA				
Hollings	Y	Y	Y	Y
Thurmond	N	N		N
SOUTH DAKOTA				
Daschle	Y	Y	Y	Y
Pressler	N	N	N	N
TENNESSEE				
Gore	Y	Y	Y	Y
Sasser	Y	Y	Y	Y
TEXAS				
Bentsen	?	Y	Y	Y
Gramm	N	N	N	N
UTAH				
Garn	N	N	N	N
Hatch	N	N	N	N
VERMONT				
Leahy	Y	Y	Y	Y
Jeffords	Y	Y	Y	N
VIRGINIA				
Robb	Y	Y	Y	Y
Warner	Y	Y	Y	Y
WASHINGTON				
Adams	Y	Y	Y	Y
Gorton	N	N	N	N
WEST VIRGINIA				
Byrd	Y	Y	Y	Y
Rockefeller	Y	Y	Y	Y
WISCONSIN				
Kohl	Y	?	?	?
Kasten	Y	Y	Y	N
WYOMING				
Simpson	N	N	N	N
Wallop	N	N	N	N

KEY

- Y Voted for (yea).
- \# Paired for.
- \+ Announced for.
- N Voted against (nay).
- X Paired against.
- \- Announced against.
- P Voted "present."
- C Voted "present" to avoid possible conflict of interest.
- ? Did not vote or otherwise make a position known.

Democrats *Republicans*

ND Northern Democrats SD Southern Democrats

Southern states - Ala., Ark., Fla., Ga., Ky., La., Miss., N.C., Okla., S.C., Tenn., Texas, Va.

76. S 135. Hatch Act Reform/Cloture. Mitchell, D-Maine, motion to invoke cloture (thus limiting debate) on the motion to proceed to the bill to allow greater political activity by federal employees and to protect them from political pressure. Motion agreed to 70-28: R 17-28; D 53-0 (ND 37-0, SD 16-0), May 1, 1990. A three-fifths vote (60) of the total Senate is required to invoke cloture.

77. S 135. Hatch Act Reform/Politics. Glenn, D-Ohio, motion to table (kill) the Roth, R-Del., substitute amendment that the Office of Personnel Management clarify the prohibitions on political activity by federal and District of Columbia employees. Motion agreed to 67-30: R 14-30; D 53-0 (ND 36-0, SD 17-0), May 3, 1990.

78. S 135. Hatch Act Reform/Labor Organization Officials. Glenn, D-Ohio, motion to table (kill) the Roth, R-Del., substitute amendment to provide that the provisions of the U.S. Code shall not be applied to certain employees of the federal government serving as presidents of national labor organizations. Motion agreed to 66-29: R 13-29; D 53-0 (ND 36-0, SD 17-0), May 3, 1990.

79. S 135. Hatch Act Reform/GAO Report. Glenn, D-Ohio, motion to table (kill) the Wilson, R-Calif., amendment to require a report by the General Accounting Office concerning political activities of federal employees. Motion agreed to 59-35: R 7-35; D 52-0 (ND 36-0, SD 16-0), May 3, 1990.

	80	81	82	83	84	85	86
ALABAMA							
Heflin	Y	N	Y	Y	Y	Y	Y
Shelby	Y	N	Y	Y	Y	Y	Y
ALASKA							
Murkowski	N	N	N	N	N	N	N
Stevens	Y	Y	N	N	Y	Y	Y
ARIZONA							
DeConcini	Y	Y	Y	Y	Y	Y	Y
McCain	?	?	?	?	N	N	Y
ARKANSAS							
Bumpers	Y	Y	Y	Y	Y	Y	Y
Pryor	Y	Y	Y	Y	Y	Y	Y
CALIFORNIA							
Cranston	Y	Y	Y	Y	Y	Y	Y
Wilson	?	-	-	?	-	-	?
COLORADO							
Wirth	Y	Y	Y	Y	Y	Y	Y
Armstrong	N	N	N	Y	N	N	N
CONNECTICUT							
Dodd	Y	Y	Y	Y	Y	Y	Y
Lieberman	Y	Y	Y	Y	Y	Y	Y
DELAWARE							
Biden	Y	Y	Y	Y	Y	Y	Y
Roth	N	N	N	N	N	N	N
FLORIDA							
Graham	Y	N	Y	Y	Y	Y	Y
Mack	N	N	N	N	N	N	N
GEORGIA							
Fowler	Y	Y	Y	Y	Y	Y	Y
Nunn	Y	Y	Y	Y	Y	Y	Y
HAWAII							
Inouye	Y	Y	Y	Y	Y	Y	Y
Vacancy							
IDAHO							
McClure	N	N	N	N	N	N	N
Symms	N	N	N	N	N	N	N
ILLINOIS							
Dixon	Y	N	Y	Y	Y	Y	Y
Simon	Y	Y	Y	Y	Y	Y	Y
INDIANA							
Coats	N	N	N	Y	N	N	N
Lugar	N	N	N	N	N	N	N
IOWA							
Harkin	Y	Y	Y	Y	Y	Y	Y
Grassley	N	N	N	N	N	N	N
KANSAS							
Dole	N	N	N	N	N	N	N
Kassebaum	N	N	N	Y	Y	N	N
KENTUCKY							
Ford	Y	Y	Y	Y	Y	Y	Y
McConnell	N	N	N	Y	N	N	N
LOUISIANA							
Breaux	Y	Y	Y	Y	Y	Y	Y
Johnston	Y	Y	Y	Y	Y	Y	Y
MAINE							
Mitchell	Y	Y	Y	Y	Y	Y	Y
Cohen	N	N	N	N	Y	N	N
MARYLAND							
Mikulski	Y	Y	Y	Y	Y	Y	Y
Sarbanes	Y	Y	Y	Y	Y	Y	Y
MASSACHUSETTS							
Kennedy	Y	Y	Y	Y	Y	Y	Y
Kerry	Y	Y	Y	Y	Y	Y	Y
MICHIGAN							
Levin	Y	Y	Y	Y	Y	Y	Y
Riegle	Y	Y	Y	Y	Y	Y	Y
MINNESOTA							
Boschwitz	N	N	N	Y	N	N	N
Durenberger	Y	N	Y	Y	Y	Y	Y
MISSISSIPPI							
Cochran	N	N	N	N	N	N	N
Lott	N	N	N	N	N	Y	N
MISSOURI							
Bond	N	N	N	N	N	N	N
Danforth	N	N	N	Y	N	N	N
MONTANA							
Baucus	Y	Y	Y	Y	Y	Y	Y
Burns	N	N	N	N	N	N	N
NEBRASKA							
Exon	Y	Y	Y	Y	Y	Y	Y
Kerrey	Y	Y	Y	Y	Y	Y	Y
NEVADA							
Bryan	Y	Y	Y	Y	Y	Y	Y
Reid	Y	Y	Y	Y	Y	Y	Y
NEW HAMPSHIRE							
Humphrey	N	N	N	N	N	N	N
Rudman	N	N	N	N	N	N	N
NEW JERSEY							
Bradley	Y	Y	Y	Y	Y	Y	Y
Lautenberg	Y	Y	Y	Y	Y	Y	Y
NEW MEXICO							
Bingaman	Y	Y	Y	Y	Y	Y	Y
Domenici	Y	N	Y	Y	Y	Y	Y
NEW YORK							
Moynihan	Y	Y	Y	Y	Y	Y	Y
D'Amato	Y	N	Y	N	N	N	N
NORTH CAROLINA							
Sanford	Y	Y	Y	Y	Y	Y	Y
Helms	N	N	N	N	N	N	N
NORTH DAKOTA							
Burdick	Y	Y	Y	Y	Y	Y	Y
Conrad	?	Y	Y	Y	Y	Y	Y
OHIO							
Glenn	Y	Y	Y	Y	Y	Y	Y
Metzenbaum	Y	Y	Y	Y	Y	Y	Y
OKLAHOMA							
Boren	Y	N	Y	Y	Y	N	Y
Nickles	N	N	N	N	N	N	N
OREGON							
Hatfield	Y	Y	Y	Y	Y	Y	Y
Packwood	Y	Y	N	N	N	Y	N
PENNSYLVANIA							
Heinz	Y	N	N	Y	N	Y	Y
Specter	Y	N	N	N	N	N	N
RHODE ISLAND							
Pell	Y	Y	Y	Y	Y	Y	Y
Chafee	N	N	N	?	N	N	N
SOUTH CAROLINA							
Hollings	Y	N	Y	Y	Y	Y	Y
Thurmond	N	N	N	N	N	N	N
SOUTH DAKOTA							
Daschle	Y	Y	Y	Y	Y	Y	Y
Pressler	N	N	N	N	N	N	N
TENNESSEE							
Gore	Y	Y	Y	Y	Y	Y	Y
Sasser	Y	Y	Y	Y	Y	Y	Y
TEXAS							
Bentsen	Y	Y	Y	Y	Y	Y	Y
Gramm	N	N	N	N	N	N	N
UTAH							
Garn	N	N	N	N	N	N	N
Hatch	N	N	N	N	N	N	N
VERMONT							
Leahy	Y	Y	Y	Y	Y	Y	Y
Jeffords	Y	N	Y	Y	Y	Y	Y
VIRGINIA							
Robb	Y	Y	Y	Y	Y	Y	Y
Warner	Y	N	Y	Y	Y	N	Y
WASHINGTON							
Adams	Y	Y	Y	Y	Y	Y	Y
Gorton	N	N	N	N	N	N	N
WEST VIRGINIA							
Byrd	Y	Y	Y	Y	Y	Y	Y
Rockefeller	Y	Y	Y	Y	Y	Y	Y
WISCONSIN							
Kohl	Y	Y	Y	Y	Y	Y	Y
Kasten	Y	N	Y	N	Y	Y	Y
WYOMING							
Simpson	N	N	N	N	N	N	N
Wallop	N	N	N	N	N	N	N

KEY

- Y Voted for (yea).
- # Paired for.
- + Announced for.
- N Voted against (nay).
- X Paired against.
- \- Announced against.
- P Voted "present."
- C Voted "present" to avoid possible conflict of interest.
- ? Did not vote or otherwise make a position known.

Democrats *Republicans*

ND Northern Democrats SD Southern Democrats

Southern states - Ala., Ark., Fla., Ga., Ky., La., Miss., N.C., Okla., S.C., Tenn., Texas, Va.

80. S 135. Hatch Act Revisions/Political Parties. Glenn, D-Ohio, motion to table (kill) the Roth, R-Del., amendment to maintain the prohibition on federal employees from holding office in a political party or organization. Motion agreed to 64-32: R 11-32; D 53-0 (ND 36-0, SD 17-0), May 8, 1990.

81. S 135. Hatch Act Revisions/IRS, FEC, CIA, Justice Department. Glenn, D-Ohio, motion to table (kill) the Dole, R-Kan., amendment to prohibit employees of the Internal Revenue Service, the Federal Election Commission, the CIA and the Department of Justice from requesting, receiving or giving political contributions. Motion agreed to 51-46: R 3-40; D 48-6 (ND 36-1, SD 12-5), May 8, 1990.

82. S 135. Hatch Act Revisions/Effective Date. Glenn, D-Ohio, motion to table (kill) the Simpson, R-Wyo., amendment to delay the effective date of the act until bans on political action committee contributions and "soft money" (campaign funds that do not fall under federal reporting requirements) are enacted. Motion agreed to 61-36: R 7-36; D 54-0 (ND 37-0, SD 17-0), May 8, 1990.

83. S 135. Hatch Act Revisions/Military Personnel. Glenn, D-Ohio, motion to table (kill) the Gramm, R-Texas, amendment to provide military personnel the same political freedoms as federal civilian employees. Motion agreed to 66-30: R 12-30; D 54-0 (ND 37-0, SD 17-0), May 8, 1990.

84. S 135. Hatch Act Revisions/Union Activities. Glenn, D-Ohio, motion to table (kill) the McConnell, R-Ky., amendment to allow federal and Postal Service employees to object to a portion of their union dues' being used to support political causes without those employees losing their right to vote on collective bargaining issues. Motion agreed to 63-35: R 9-35; D 54-0 (ND 37-0, SD 17-0), May 9, 1990.

85. S 135. Hatch Act Revisions/Referendum. Glenn, D-Ohio, motion to table (kill) the Dole, R-Kan., amendment to require a referendum within agencies every five years through which employees could decide whether their agency will be covered by the Hatch Act now in existence or by the reforms that would be implemented under S 135. Motion agreed to 62-36: R 9-35; D 53-1 (ND 37-0, SD 16-1), May 9, 1990.

86. S 135. Hatch Act Revisions/Political Contributions. Glenn, D-Ohio, motion to table (kill) the Roth, R-Del., amendment to prohibit federal employees from soliciting, accepting or receiving political contributions from any person. Motion agreed to 63-35: R 9-35; D 54-0 (ND 37-0, SD 17-0), May 9, 1990.

	87	88	89	90
ALABAMA				
Heflin	Y	Y	Y	Y
Shelby	Y	Y	Y	Y
ALASKA				
Murkowski	N	Y	Y	N
Stevens	Y	Y	Y	Y
ARIZONA				
DeConcini	Y	Y	Y	Y
McCain	N	Y	Y	Y
ARKANSAS				
Bumpers	Y	Y	Y	Y
Pryor	Y	Y	Y	Y
CALIFORNIA				
Cranston	Y	Y	Y	Y
Wilson	-	+	+	-
COLORADO				
Wirth	Y	Y	Y	Y
Armstrong	N	Y	Y	N
CONNECTICUT				
Dodd	Y	Y	Y	Y
Lieberman	Y	Y	Y	Y
DELAWARE				
Biden	Y	Y	Y	Y
Roth	N	Y	Y	N
FLORIDA				
Graham	Y	Y	Y	Y
Mack	N	Y	Y	N
GEORGIA				
Fowler	Y	Y	Y	Y
Nunn	Y	Y	Y	Y
HAWAII				
Inouye	Y	Y	Y	Y
Vacancy				
IDAHO				
McClure	N	Y	Y	N
Symms	N	Y	Y	N
ILLINOIS				
Dixon	Y	Y	Y	Y
Simon	Y	Y	Y	Y
INDIANA				
Coats	N	Y	Y	N
Lugar	N	Y	Y	N

	87	88	89	90
IOWA				
Harkin	Y	Y	Y	Y
Grassley	N	Y	Y	N
KANSAS				
Dole	N	Y	Y	N
Kassebaum	N	Y	Y	N
KENTUCKY				
Ford	Y	Y	Y	Y
McConnell	N	Y	Y	N
LOUISIANA				
Breaux	Y	Y	Y	Y
Johnston	Y	Y	Y	Y
MAINE				
Mitchell	Y	Y	Y	Y
Cohen	N	Y	Y	N
MARYLAND				
Mikulski	Y	Y	Y	Y
Sarbanes	Y	Y	Y	Y
MASSACHUSETTS				
Kennedy	Y	Y	Y	Y
Kerry	Y	Y	Y	Y
MICHIGAN				
Levin	Y	Y	Y	Y
Riegle	Y	Y	Y	Y
MINNESOTA				
Boschwitz	N	Y	Y	N
Durenberger	N	Y	Y	Y
MISSISSIPPI				
Cochran	N	Y	Y	N
Lott	N	Y	Y	Y
MISSOURI				
Bond	?	?	?	?
Danforth	N	Y	Y	N
MONTANA				
Baucus	Y	Y	Y	Y
Burns	N	Y	Y	N
NEBRASKA				
Exon	Y	Y	Y	Y
Kerrey	Y	Y	Y	Y
NEVADA				
Bryan	Y	Y	Y	Y
Reid	Y	Y	Y	Y

	87	88	89	90
NEW HAMPSHIRE				
Humphrey	N	Y	Y	N
Rudman	N	Y	Y	N
NEW JERSEY				
Bradley	Y	Y	Y	Y
Lautenberg	Y	Y	Y	Y
NEW MEXICO				
Bingaman	Y	Y	Y	Y
Domenici	N	Y	Y	Y
NEW YORK				
Moynihan	Y	Y	Y	Y
D'Amato	N	Y	Y	Y
NORTH CAROLINA				
Sanford	Y	Y	Y	Y
Helms	N	Y	Y	N
NORTH DAKOTA				
Burdick	Y	Y	Y	Y
Conrad	Y	Y	Y	Y
OHIO				
Glenn	Y	Y	Y	Y
Metzenbaum	Y	Y	Y	Y
OKLAHOMA				
Boren	Y	Y	Y	Y
Nickles	N	Y	Y	N
OREGON				
Hatfield	Y	Y	Y	Y
Packwood	Y	Y	Y	Y
PENNSYLVANIA				
Heinz	N	Y	Y	Y
Specter	N	Y	Y	Y
RHODE ISLAND				
Pell	Y	Y	Y	Y
Chafee	N	Y	Y	N
SOUTH CAROLINA				
Hollings	Y	Y	Y	Y
Thurmond	N	Y	Y	N
SOUTH DAKOTA				
Daschle	Y	Y	Y	Y
Pressler	N	Y	Y	N
TENNESSEE				
Gore	Y	Y	Y	Y
Sasser	Y	Y	Y	Y

KEY

- Y Voted for (yea).
- # Paired for.
- + Announced for.
- N Voted against (nay).
- X Paired against.
- \- Announced against.
- P Voted "present."
- C Voted "present" to avoid possible conflict of interest.
- ? Did not vote or otherwise make a position known.

Democrats ***Republicans***

	87	88	89	90
TEXAS				
Bentsen	Y	Y	Y	Y
Gramm	N	Y	Y	N
UTAH				
Garn	N	Y	Y	N
Hatch	N	Y	Y	N
VERMONT				
Leahy	Y	Y	Y	Y
Jeffords	Y	Y	Y	Y
VIRGINIA				
Robb	Y	Y	Y	Y
Warner	N	Y	Y	Y
WASHINGTON				
Adams	Y	Y	Y	Y
Gorton	N	Y	Y	N
WEST VIRGINIA				
Byrd	Y	Y	Y	Y
Rockefeller	Y	Y	Y	Y
WISCONSIN				
Kohl	Y	Y	Y	Y
Kasten	N	Y	Y	Y
WYOMING				
Simpson	N	Y	Y	N
Wallop	N	Y	Y	N

ND Northern Democrats SD Southern Democrats

Southern states - Ala., Ark., Fla., Ga., Ky., La., Miss., N.C., Okla., S.C., Tenn., Texas, Va.

87. S 135. Hatch Act Revisions/Law Enforcement Employees. Glenn, D-Ohio, motion to table (kill) the Domenici, R-N.M., amendment to prohibit intelligence and law enforcement employees from requesting, receiving or giving political contributions. The amendment would also prohibit them from taking part in political management or campaigns. Motion agreed to 58-39: R 4-39; D 54-0 (ND 37-0, SD 17-0), May 10, 1990.

88. S 135. Hatch Act Revisions/FEC Employees. Dole, R-Kan., amendment to prohibit Federal Election Commission employees from requesting, receiving or giving political contributions. The amendment would also prohibit them from taking an active part in political management or political campaigns. Adopted 97-0: R 43-0; D 54-0 (ND 37-0, SD 17-0), May 10, 1990.

89. S 135. Hatch Act Revisions/Political Participation. Glenn, D-Ohio, amendment to prohibit federal employees from soliciting or discouraging the political participation of other federal employees. Adopted 97-0: R 43-0; D 54-0 (ND 37-0, SD 17-0), May 10, 1990.

90. HR 20. Hatch Act Revisions/Passage. Passage of the bill to allow greater political activity by federal employees and to protect them from political pressure. (Before passage, the text of S 135 was substituted for the text of HR 20, a similar bill passed by the House.) Passed 67-30: R 13-30; D 54-0 (ND 37-0, SD 17-0), May 10, 1990. A "nay" was a vote supporting the president's position.

KEY

- Y Voted for (yea).
- # Paired for.
- + Announced for.
- N Voted against (nay).
- X Paired against.
- - Announced against.
- P Voted "present."
- C Voted "present" to avoid possible conflict of interest.
- ? Did not vote or otherwise make a position known.

Democrats *Republicans*

	91	92	93	94	95	96	97
ALABAMA							
Heflin	Y	N	Y	Y	Y	Y	Y
Shelby	Y	Y	Y	Y	Y	Y	Y
ALASKA							
Murkowski	Y	Y	Y	Y	Y	Y	Y
Stevens	Y	Y	N	Y	Y	Y	Y
ARIZONA							
DeConcini	Y	N	Y	Y	N	Y	Y
McCain	Y	Y	N	Y	Y	Y	Y
ARKANSAS							
Bumpers	Y	N	N	Y	Y	Y	Y
Pryor	Y	N	N	Y	N	Y	Y
CALIFORNIA							
Cranston	Y	N	N	Y	N	Y	Y
Wilson	Y	N	N	Y	Y	Y	Y
COLORADO							
Wirth	?	N	N	Y	N	Y	Y
Armstrong	Y	Y	Y	Y	Y	Y	Y
CONNECTICUT							
Dodd	Y	N	N	Y	N	Y	Y
Lieberman	Y	N	N	Y	N	Y	Y
DELAWARE							
Biden	Y	N	N	Y	N	Y	Y
Roth	Y	Y	N	Y	Y	Y	N
FLORIDA							
Graham	Y	N	N	Y	N	Y	Y
Mack	Y	N	N	Y	N	Y	Y
GEORGIA							
Fowler	Y	N	N	Y	N	Y	Y
Nunn	Y	N	N	Y	N	Y	Y
HAWAII							
Inouye	Y	N	N	Y	N	Y	Y
Akaka *			N	Y	N	Y	Y
IDAHO							
McClure	Y	Y	Y	Y	Y	Y	Y
Symms	N	Y	Y	Y	Y	Y	Y
ILLINOIS							
Dixon	Y	N	N	Y	Y	Y	Y
Simon	Y	N	N	Y	N	Y	Y
INDIANA							
Coats	Y	Y	Y	Y	Y	Y	Y
Lugar	Y	Y	N	Y	Y	Y	Y
IOWA							
Harkin	Y	N	N	Y	N	Y	Y
Grassley	Y	Y	Y	Y	Y	Y	Y
KANSAS							
Dole	Y	Y	Y	Y	Y	Y	Y
Kassebaum	Y	N	N	Y	Y	Y	Y
KENTUCKY							
Ford	Y	N	?	?	Y	Y	Y
McConnell	Y	Y	Y	Y	Y	Y	Y
LOUISIANA							
Breaux	Y	N	N	Y	N	Y	Y
Johnston	Y	N	N	Y	Y	Y	Y
MAINE							
Mitchell	Y	N	N	Y	N	Y	Y
Cohen	Y	N	N	Y	N	Y	Y
MARYLAND							
Mikulski	Y	N	N	Y	N	Y	Y
Sarbanes	Y	N	N	Y	N	Y	Y
MASSACHUSETTS							
Kennedy	Y	N	N	Y	N	Y	Y
Kerry	Y	N	N	Y	N	Y	Y
MICHIGAN							
Levin	Y	N	N	Y	N	Y	Y
Riegle	Y	N	N	Y	N	Y	Y
MINNESOTA							
Boschwitz	Y	N	Y	Y	Y	Y	Y
Durenberger	Y	N	N	Y	N	Y	Y
MISSISSIPPI							
Cochran	Y	Y	Y	Y	Y	Y	Y
Lott	Y	Y	Y	Y	Y	Y	Y
MISSOURI							
Bond	Y	Y	Y	Y	Y	Y	Y
Danforth	Y	N	N	Y	Y	Y	Y
MONTANA							
Baucus	Y	Y	N	Y	Y	Y	Y
Burns	Y	Y	Y	Y	Y	Y	Y
NEBRASKA							
Exon	Y	N	N	Y	Y	Y	Y
Kerrey	Y	N	N	Y	N	Y	Y
NEVADA							
Bryan	Y	N	N	Y	N	Y	Y
Reid	Y	N	N	Y	N	Y	Y
NEW HAMPSHIRE							
Humphrey	N	Y	Y	Y	Y	Y	N
Rudman	Y	N	Y	Y	Y	Y	Y
NEW JERSEY							
Bradley	Y	N	N	Y	N	Y	Y
Lautenberg	Y	N	N	Y	N	Y	Y
NEW MEXICO							
Bingaman	Y	N	N	Y	N	Y	Y
Domenici	Y	Y	Y	Y	Y	Y	Y
NEW YORK							
Moynihan	Y	N	N	Y	N	Y	Y
D'Amato	Y	N	N	Y	N	Y	Y
NORTH CAROLINA							
Sanford	Y	N	N	Y	N	Y	Y
Helms	N	Y	Y	Y	Y	Y	N
NORTH DAKOTA							
Burdick	Y	N	N	Y	Y	Y	Y
Conrad	Y	Y	N	Y	N	Y	Y
OHIO							
Glenn	Y	N	N	Y	N	Y	Y
Metzenbaum	Y	N	N	Y	N	Y	Y
OKLAHOMA							
Boren	Y	Y	N	Y	Y	Y	Y
Nickles	Y	Y	Y	Y	Y	Y	Y
OREGON							
Hatfield	Y	N	N	Y	N	Y	Y
Packwood	Y	N	N	Y	N	Y	Y
PENNSYLVANIA							
Heinz	Y	N	N	Y	?	?	+
Specter	Y	N	N	Y	Y	Y	Y
RHODE ISLAND							
Pell	Y	N	N	Y	N	Y	Y
Chafee	Y	?	N	Y	N	Y	Y
SOUTH CAROLINA							
Hollings	Y	N	N	Y	N	Y	Y
Thurmond	Y	Y	Y	Y	Y	Y	Y
SOUTH DAKOTA							
Daschle	Y	Y	N	Y	N	Y	Y
Pressler	Y	Y	Y	Y	Y	Y	Y
TENNESSEE							
Gore	Y	N	N	Y	N	Y	Y
Sasser	Y	N	N	Y	N	Y	Y
TEXAS							
Bentsen	Y	N	N	Y	Y	Y	Y
Gramm	Y	Y	Y	Y	Y	Y	Y
UTAH							
Garn	Y	Y	Y	Y	Y	Y	Y
Hatch	Y	N	N	Y	N	Y	Y
VERMONT							
Leahy	Y	N	N	Y	N	Y	Y
Jeffords	Y	Y	?	?	N	Y	Y
VIRGINIA							
Robb	Y	N	N	Y	N	Y	Y
Warner	Y	Y	N	Y	Y	Y	Y
WASHINGTON							
Adams	Y	N	N	Y	N	Y	Y
Gorton	Y	N	N	Y	N	Y	Y
WEST VIRGINIA							
Byrd	Y	N	N	Y	Y	Y	Y
Rockefeller	Y	N	N	Y	Y	Y	Y
WISCONSIN							
Kohl	Y	N	N	Y	N	Y	Y
Kasten	Y	N	Y	Y	Y	Y	Y
WYOMING							
Simpson	Y	Y	Y	Y	Y	Y	Y
Wallop	Y	Y	Y	Y	Y	Y	N

ND Northern Democrats SD Southern Democrats

Southern states - Ala., Ark., Fla., Ga., Ky., La., Miss., N.C., Okla., S.C., Tenn., Texas, Va.

91. S 2240. AIDS Emergency Relief/Cloture. Mitchell, D-Maine, motion to invoke cloture (thus limiting debate) on the motion to proceed to the bill to authorize emergency grants to metropolitan areas reporting 2,000 or more cases of AIDS and grants to states to develop or improve comprehensive care for people infected with HIV, the infection that causes AIDS. Motion agreed to 95-3: R 42-3; D 53-0 (ND 36-0, SD 17-0), May 15, 1990. A three-fifths majority vote (60) of the total Senate is required to invoke cloture.

92. S 2240. AIDS Emergency Relief/Discretionary Funds. Wallop, R-Wyo., amendment to allow states with 100 or fewer AIDS cases reported in the past two years to use funds authorized under the bill to provide comprehensive care to people with other chronic diseases, including Alzheimer's and cancer. Rejected 33-65: R 28-16; D 5-49 (ND 3-34, SD 2-15), May 15, 1990.

93. S 2240. AIDS Emergency Relief/Needle Distribution. Helms, R-N.C., amendment to prohibit the use of funds authorized under the bill for the distribution of sterile needles or bleach for cleansing needles used for the injection of illegal drugs, unless the president certifies that such programs are effective against the spread of HIV, the infection that causes AIDS, and do not promote the use of illegal drugs. Rejected 28-70: R 25-19; D 3-51 (ND 1-37, SD 2-14), May 16, 1990.

94. S 2240. AIDS Emergency Relief/Needle Distribution. Kennedy, D-Mass., amendment to prohibit the use of funds authorized under this act to provide people with hypodermic needles or syringes for the use of illegal drugs. Adopted 98-0: R 44-0, D 54-0 (ND 38-0, SD 16-0), May 16, 1990.

95. S 2240. AIDS Emergency Relief/Blood Donations. Helms, R-N.C., amendment to make it a crime to donate or sell blood, semen or other bodily fluids or tissues if the individual knows he or she is infected with HIV, the infection that causes AIDS, or if the person has been an intravenous drug user or a prostitute at any time since Jan. 1, 1977. Rejected 47-52: R 34-10; D 13-42 (ND 6-32, SD 7-10), May 16, 1990.

96. S 2240. AIDS Emergency Relief/Enforcement. Kennedy, D-Mass., amendment to prohibit grants to states that do not have adequate criminal laws to prosecute someone who knowingly donates or sells bodily fluids or tissues after being diagnosed with HIV, the infection that causes AIDS, and informed of the risks of transmission to others. Adopted 99-0: R 44-0; D 55-0 (ND 38-0, SD 17-0), May 16, 1990.

97. S 2240. AIDS Emergency Relief/Passage. Passage of the bill to authorize $300 million annually in fiscal 1991 and 1992 and such sums as necessary for fiscal 1993-95 for emergency grants to metropolitan areas reporting more than 2,000 cases of AIDS and the same amounts in grants to states to develop or improve comprehensive care for people infected with HIV, the infection that causes AIDS. Passed 95-4: R 40-4; D 55-0 (ND 38-0, SD 17-0), May 16, 1990.

* *Sen. Daniel K. Akaka, D-Hawaii, was sworn in May 16. The first Senate vote for which he was eligible was vote 93.*

KEY

- Y Voted for (yea).
- # Paired for.
- + Announced for.
- N Voted against (nay).
- X Paired against.
- \- Announced against.
- P Voted "present."
- C Voted "present" to avoid possible conflict of interest.
- ? Did not vote or otherwise make a position known.

Democrats *Republicans*

	98	99	100	101
ALABAMA				
Heflin	Y	N	N	Y
Shelby	Y	N	N	Y
ALASKA				
Murkowski	Y	N	Y	Y
Stevens	Y	N	Y	Y
ARIZONA				
DeConcini	Y	N	Y	Y
McCain	Y	N	Y	Y
ARKANSAS				
Bumpers	Y	Y	Y	Y
Pryor	Y	Y	Y	Y
CALIFORNIA				
Cranston	Y	Y	Y	Y
Wilson	Y	N	Y	Y
COLORADO				
Wirth	Y	Y	Y	Y
Armstrong	?	?	?	?
CONNECTICUT				
Dodd	Y	Y	Y	Y
Lieberman	+	+	+	+
DELAWARE				
Biden	Y	Y	Y	Y
Roth	Y	N	Y	Y
FLORIDA				
Graham	Y	Y	Y	Y
Mack	Y	N	Y	Y
GEORGIA				
Fowler	Y	Y	Y	Y
Nunn	Y	Y	Y	Y
HAWAII				
Inouye	Y	Y	Y	Y
Akaka *	Y	Y	Y	Y
IDAHO				
McClure	Y	N	Y	Y
Symms	?	?	?	?
ILLINOIS				
Dixon	Y	N	Y	Y
Simon	Y	Y	Y	Y
INDIANA				
Coats	Y	N	Y	Y
Lugar	Y	Y	Y	Y
IOWA				
Harkin	Y	Y	Y	Y
Grassley	Y	N	Y	Y
KANSAS				
Dole	Y	N	Y	Y
Kassebaum	Y	Y	Y	Y
KENTUCKY				
Ford	Y	N	Y	Y
McConnell	Y	N	Y	Y
LOUISIANA				
Breaux	Y	Y	Y	Y
Johnston	Y	Y	Y	Y
MAINE				
Mitchell	Y	Y	Y	Y
Cohen	Y	Y	Y	Y
MARYLAND				
Mikulski	Y	Y	Y	Y
Sarbanes	Y	Y	Y	Y
MASSACHUSETTS				
Kennedy	Y	Y	Y	Y
Kerry	Y	Y	Y	Y
MICHIGAN				
Levin	Y	Y	Y	Y
Riegle	Y	Y	Y	Y
MINNESOTA				
Boschwitz	Y	N	Y	Y
Durenberger	Y	Y	Y	Y
MISSISSIPPI				
Cochran	Y	N	Y	Y
Lott	Y	N	Y	Y
MISSOURI				
Bond	Y	N	Y	Y
Danforth	Y	Y	Y	Y
MONTANA				
Baucus	Y	Y	Y	Y
Burns	Y	N	Y	Y
NEBRASKA				
Exon	Y	Y	Y	Y
Kerrey	Y	Y	Y	Y
NEVADA				
Bryan	Y	Y	Y	Y
Reid	Y	Y	N	Y
NEW HAMPSHIRE				
Humphrey	Y	N	?	?
Rudman	Y	Y	Y	Y
NEW JERSEY				
Bradley	Y	Y	Y	Y
Lautenberg	Y	Y	Y	Y
NEW MEXICO				
Bingaman	Y	Y	Y	Y
Domenici	Y	N	Y	Y
NEW YORK				
Moynihan	Y	Y	Y	Y
D'Amato	Y	N	Y	Y
NORTH CAROLINA				
Sanford	Y	Y	Y	Y
Helms	Y	N	N	Y
NORTH DAKOTA				
Burdick	Y	Y	Y	Y
Conrad	Y	Y	Y	Y
OHIO				
Glenn	Y	Y	Y	Y
Metzenbaum	Y	Y	Y	Y
OKLAHOMA				
Boren	Y	Y	Y	Y
Nickles	Y	?	?	?
OREGON				
Hatfield	Y	Y	Y	Y
Packwood	Y	Y	Y	Y
PENNSYLVANIA				
Heinz	Y	N	Y	Y
Specter	Y	N	Y	Y
RHODE ISLAND				
Pell	Y	Y	Y	Y
Chafee	Y	Y	Y	Y
SOUTH CAROLINA				
Hollings	Y	N	Y	Y
Thurmond	Y	N	Y	Y
SOUTH DAKOTA				
Daschle	Y	Y	Y	Y
Pressler	Y	N	Y	Y
TENNESSEE				
Gore	Y	Y	Y	Y
Sasser	Y	Y	Y	Y
TEXAS				
Bentsen	Y	Y	Y	Y
Gramm	Y	N	?	?
UTAH				
Garn	Y	N	Y	Y
Hatch	Y	N	Y	Y
VERMONT				
Leahy	Y	Y	Y	Y
Jeffords	?	?	?	?
VIRGINIA				
Robb	Y	Y	Y	Y
Warner	Y	Y	Y	Y
WASHINGTON				
Adams	Y	Y	?	Y
Gorton	Y	N	Y	Y
WEST VIRGINIA				
Byrd	Y	N	Y	Y
Rockefeller	Y	N	Y	Y
WISCONSIN				
Kohl	Y	Y	Y	Y
Kasten	Y	N	Y	Y
WYOMING				
Simpson	Y	N	Y	Y
Wallop	Y	N	?	?

ND Northern Democrats SD Southern Democrats

Southern states - Ala., Ark., Fla., Ga., Ky., La., Miss., N.C., Okla., S.C., Tenn., Texas, Va.

98. S 195. Chemical Weapons Sanctions/Multilateral Efforts. Heinz, R-Pa., amendment to call for stronger multilateral efforts to restrain trade in supplies and equipment needed to make chemical and biological weapons. Adopted 96-0: R 42-0; D 54-0 (ND 37-0, SD 17-0), May 17, 1990.

99. S 195. Chemical Weapons Sanctions/Verification. Pell, D-R.I., motion to table (kill) the McClure, R-Idaho, amendment to condemn violations the Soviet Union is alleged to have committed against the 1985 Intermediate Nuclear Forces (INF) treaty, under which the United States and the Soviet Union agreed to withdraw all medium-range nuclear missiles from Europe. Motion agreed to 56-39: R 10-31; D 46-8 (ND 33-4, SD 13-4), May 17, 1990.

100. S 195. Chemical Weapons Sanctions/Cloture. Mitchell, D-Maine, motion to invoke cloture (thus limiting debate) on the bill to penalize countries that use chemical weapons and foreign companies that help them obtain the weapons. Motion agreed to 87-4: R 37-1; D 50-3 (ND 35-1, SD 15-2), May 17, 1990. A three-fifths majority vote (60) of the total Senate is required to invoke cloture.

101. HR 3033. Chemical Weapons Sanctions/Passage. Passage of the bill to penalize countries that use chemical weapons and foreign companies that help them obtain them. (Before passage, the text of S 195 was substituted for the text of HR 3033, the House-passed bill, in which form it was voted on.) Passed 92-0: R 38-0; D 54-0 (ND 37-0, SD 17-0), May 17, 1990. A "nay" was a vote supporting the president's position.

	102	103	104	105
ALABAMA				
Heflin	Y	Y	Y	Y
Shelby	Y	Y	Y	Y
ALASKA				
Murkowski	Y	Y	Y	Y
Stevens	Y	Y	Y	Y
ARIZONA				
DeConcini	Y	N	N	N
McCain	Y	Y	Y	Y
ARKANSAS				
Bumpers	Y	N	N	N
Pryor	Y	N	N	N
CALIFORNIA				
Cranston	N	N	N	N
Wilson	N	N	N	Y
COLORADO				
Wirth	N	N	N	N
Armstrong	Y	Y	Y	Y
CONNECTICUT				
Dodd	N	N	N	N
Lieberman	Y	N	N	N
DELAWARE				
Biden	Y	N	N	N
Roth	Y	Y	Y	Y
FLORIDA				
Graham	Y	N	N	N
Mack	Y	Y	Y	Y
GEORGIA				
Fowler	Y	N	N	N
Nunn	Y	N	N	Y
HAWAII				
Inouye	Y	N	N	N
Akaka	Y	N	N	N
IDAHO				
McClure	Y	Y	Y	Y
Symms	+	Y	Y	Y
ILLINOIS				
Dixon	Y	N	N	Y
Simon	N	N	N	N
INDIANA				
Coats	Y	Y	Y	Y
Lugar	Y	Y	Y	Y

	102	103	104	105
IOWA				
Harkin	Y	N	N	N
Grassley	Y	Y	Y	Y
KANSAS				
Dole	Y	N	Y	Y
Kassebaum	Y	N	N	Y
KENTUCKY				
Ford	Y	Y	Y	N
McConnell	Y	Y	Y	Y
LOUISIANA				
Breaux	Y	Y	Y	?
Johnston	Y	Y	Y	?
MAINE				
Mitchell	Y	N	N	N
Cohen	Y	Y	Y	Y
MARYLAND				
Mikulski	N	N	N	N
Sarbanes	N	N	N	N
MASSACHUSETTS				
Kennedy	N	N	N	N
Kerry	N	N	N	N
MICHIGAN				
Levin	Y	N	N	N
Riegle	Y	N	N	N
MINNESOTA				
Boschwitz	Y	Y	Y	Y
Durenberger	Y	Y	Y	N
MISSISSIPPI				
Cochran	Y	Y	Y	Y
Lott	Y	Y	Y	Y
MISSOURI				
Bond	Y	Y	Y	Y
Danforth	Y	Y	Y	Y
MONTANA				
Baucus	Y	Y	Y	N
Burns	Y	Y	Y	Y
NEBRASKA				
Exon	Y	Y	Y	Y
Kerrey	Y	N	N	N
NEVADA				
Bryan	Y	Y	Y	N
Reid	Y	Y	Y	N

	102	103	104	105
NEW HAMPSHIRE				
Humphrey	Y	Y	Y	Y
Rudman	Y	Y	Y	Y
NEW JERSEY				
Bradley	N	N	N	N
Lautenberg	N	N	N	N
NEW MEXICO				
Bingaman	Y	Y	Y	N
Domenici	Y	Y	Y	Y
NEW YORK				
Moynihan	N	N	N	N
D'Amato	Y	N	N	Y
NORTH CAROLINA				
Sanford	Y	Y	Y	N
Helms	Y	Y	Y	Y
NORTH DAKOTA				
Burdick	Y	N	N	N
Conrad	Y	N	N	N
OHIO				
Glenn	N	N	N	N
Metzenbaum	N	N	N	N
OKLAHOMA				
Boren	Y	N	N	N
Nickles	Y	Y	Y	Y
OREGON				
Hatfield	Y	N	N	N
Packwood	Y	N	N	N
PENNSYLVANIA				
Heinz	Y	Y	Y	Y
Specter	Y	Y	Y	N
RHODE ISLAND				
Pell	N	N	N	N
Chafee	N	N	-	?
SOUTH CAROLINA				
Hollings	Y	Y	Y	Y
Thurmond	Y	Y	Y	Y
SOUTH DAKOTA				
Daschle	Y	N	N	N
Pressler	Y	Y	Y	Y
TENNESSEE				
Gore	Y	N	N	N
Sasser	Y	N	N	N

KEY

- Y Voted for (yea).
- # Paired for.
- \+ Announced for.
- N Voted against (nay).
- X Paired against.
- \- Announced against.
- P Voted "present."
- C Voted "present" to avoid possible conflict of interest.
- ? Did not vote or otherwise make a position known.

Democrats *Republicans*

	102	103	104	105
TEXAS				
Bentsen	Y	N	N	N
Gramm	Y	Y	Y	Y
UTAH				
Garn	Y	Y	Y	Y
Hatch	Y	Y	Y	Y
VERMONT				
Leahy	Y	N	N	N
Jeffords	Y	N	N	N
VIRGINIA				
Robb	Y	N	N	N
Warner	Y	N	N	Y
WASHINGTON				
Adams	N	N	N	N
Gorton	Y	Y	Y	Y
WEST VIRGINIA				
Byrd	Y	N	N	Y
Rockefeller	Y	N	N	Y
WISCONSIN				
Kohl	Y	N	N	N
Kasten	Y	Y	Y	Y
WYOMING				
Simpson	Y	Y	Y	Y
Wallop	Y	Y	Y	Y

ND Northern Democrats SD Southern Democrats

Southern states - Ala., Ark., Fla., Ga., Ky., La., Miss., N.C., Okla., S.C., Tenn., Texas, Va.

102. S 1970. Omnibus Crime Package/Assault-Style Weapons. McClure, R-Idaho, motion to table (kill) the Metzenbaum, D-Ohio, amendment to add 12 assault-style weapons, plus any nearly identical weapons, to the list of those banned by the bill, and to prohibit the sale of large-capacity magazines. Motion agreed to 82-17: R 42-2; D 40-15 (ND 23-15, SD 17-0), May 22, 1990.

103. S 1970. Omnibus Crime Package/Assault-Style Weapons. Hatch, R-Utah, amendment to strike provisions that would prohibit for three years making, selling and possessing nine types of semiautomatic assault-style weapons. Rejected 48-52: R 36-9; D 12-43 (ND 5-33, SD 7-10), May 23, 1990. A "yea" was a vote supporting the president's position.

104. S 1970. Omnibus Crime Package/Assault-Style Weapons. Dole, R-Kan., motion to reconsider the vote by which the Hatch, R-Utah, amendment was rejected. Rejected 49-50: R 37-7; D 12-43 (ND 5-33, SD 7-10), May 23, 1990.

105. S 1970. Omnibus Crime Package/Habeas Corpus. Thurmond, R-S.C., amendment to allow states to adopt expedited procedures for reviewing death penalty appeals if they provide competent counsel to inmates, and to require federal courts to complete review of habeas corpus petitions within a year of a state court death penalty order. Rejected 47-50: R 39-5; D 8-45 (ND 4-34, SD 4-11), May 23, 1990.

	106	107	108
ALABAMA			
Heflin	Y	Y	Y
Shelby	Y	Y	Y
ALASKA			
Murkowski	Y	Y	Y
Stevens	Y	N	Y
ARIZONA			
DeConcini	N	N	#
McCain	Y	Y	Y
ARKANSAS			
Bumpers	N	N	Y
Pryor	N	N	Y
CALIFORNIA			
Cranston	N	N	N
Wilson	Y	Y	Y
COLORADO			
Wirth	N	N	N
Armstrong	Y	Y	Y
CONNECTICUT			
Dodd	N	N	N
Lieberman	N	Y	Y
DELAWARE			
Biden	N	N	N
Roth	Y	Y	Y
FLORIDA			
Graham	N	N	Y
Mack	Y	Y	Y
GEORGIA			
Fowler	N	N	Y
Nunn	Y	N	Y
HAWAII			
Inouye	N	N	N
Akaka	?	X	X
IDAHO			
McClure	Y	Y	Y
Symms	Y	Y	Y
ILLINOIS			
Dixon	Y	Y	Y
Simon	N	N	N
INDIANA			
Coats	Y	Y	Y
Lugar	Y	Y	Y
IOWA			
Harkin	N	N	N
Grassley	Y	Y	Y
KANSAS			
Dole	Y	N	Y
Kassebaum	Y	N	Y
KENTUCKY			
Ford	N	N	Y
McConnell	Y	Y	Y
LOUISIANA			
Breaux	Y	N	Y
Johnston	Y	N	Y
MAINE			
Mitchell	N	N	N
Cohen	Y	N	N
MARYLAND			
Mikulski	N	N	N
Sarbanes	N	N	N
MASSACHUSETTS			
Kennedy	N	N	N
Kerry	N	N	N
MICHIGAN			
Levin	N	N	N
Riegle	N	N	N
MINNESOTA			
Boschwitz	Y	N	Y
Durenberger	Y	N	N
MISSISSIPPI			
Cochran	Y	Y	Y
Lott	Y	Y	Y
MISSOURI			
Bond	Y	Y	Y
Danforth	Y	N	N
MONTANA			
Baucus	N	N	Y
Burns	Y	Y	Y
NEBRASKA			
Exon	Y	Y	Y
Kerrey	N	N	N
NEVADA			
Bryan	N	N	Y
Reid	N	N	N
NEW HAMPSHIRE			
Humphrey	Y	Y	Y
Rudman	Y	Y	Y
NEW JERSEY			
Bradley	N	N	N
Lautenberg	N	N	N
NEW MEXICO			
Bingaman	N	N	Y
Domenici	Y	N	Y
NEW YORK			
Moynihan	N	N	N
D'Amato	Y	N	Y
NORTH CAROLINA			
Sanford	N	N	N
Helms	Y	Y	Y
NORTH DAKOTA			
Burdick	N	N	N
Conrad	N	N	N
OHIO			
Glenn	N	N	N
Metzenbaum	N	N	?
OKLAHOMA			
Boren	Y	#	N
Nickles	Y	Y	Y
OREGON			
Hatfield	N	N	N
Packwood	N	N	N
PENNSYLVANIA			
Heinz	Y	N	Y
Specter	Y	N	Y
RHODE ISLAND			
Pell	N	N	N
Chafee	?	-	?
SOUTH CAROLINA			
Hollings	Y	Y	Y
Thurmond	Y	Y	Y
SOUTH DAKOTA			
Daschle	N	N	N
Pressler	Y	Y	Y
TENNESSEE			
Gore	N	N	N
Sasser	N	N	N
TEXAS			
Bentsen	N	N	Y
Gramm	Y	Y	Y
UTAH			
Garn	Y	Y	Y
Hatch	Y	Y	Y
VERMONT			
Leahy	N	N	N
Jeffords	N	N	N
VIRGINIA			
Robb	N	Y	Y
Warner	Y	Y	Y
WASHINGTON			
Adams	N	N	N
Gorton	Y	Y	Y
WEST VIRGINIA			
Byrd	Y	Y	Y
Rockefeller	Y	N	N
WISCONSIN			
Kohl	N	N	N
Kasten	Y	Y	Y
WYOMING			
Simpson	Y	Y	Y
Wallop	Y	Y	Y

KEY

- Y Voted for (yea).
- # Paired for.
- \+ Announced for.
- N Voted against (nay).
- X Paired against.
- \- Announced against.
- P Voted "present."
- C Voted "present" to avoid possible conflict of interest.
- ? Did not vote or otherwise make a position known.

Democrats ***Republicans***

ND Northern Democrats SD Southern Democrats

Southern states - Ala., Ark., Fla., Ga., Ky., La., Miss., N.C., Okla., S.C., Tenn., Texas, Va.

106. S 1970. Omnibus Crime Package/Habeas Corpus. Specter, R-Pa., motion to reconsider the vote by which the Thurmond, R-S.C., amendment was rejected. Motion agreed to 52-46: R 41-3; D 11-43 (ND 4-33, SD 7-10), May 24, 1990. (The Thurmond amendment was subsequently adopted by voice vote.)

107. S 1970. Omnibus Crime Package/Mentally Retarded. Thurmond, R-S.C., amendment to prohibit executing a mentally retarded person only if he is wholly lacking in capacity to know right from wrong. Rejected 38-59: R 30-14; D 8-45 (ND 4-33, SD 4-12), May 24, 1990.

108. S 1970. Omnibus Crime Package/Racial Discrimination. Graham, D-Fla., amendment to strike provisions that would prohibit the death sentence in state and federal cases if a defendant could prove with statistical or other evidence that his race, or that of the victim, played a role in sentencing. Adopted 58-38: R 38-6; D 20-32 (ND 7-28, SD 13-4), May 24, 1990. A "yea" was a vote supporting the president's position.

	109	110	111	112
ALABAMA				
Heflin	?	N	Y	N
Shelby	N	N	N	N
ALASKA				
Murkowski	Y	N	Y	N
Stevens	Y	N	N	Y
ARIZONA				
DeConcini	Y	?	?	Y
McCain	N	N	Y	N
ARKANSAS				
Bumpers	Y	N	N	Y
Pryor	?	N	N	Y
CALIFORNIA				
Cranston	Y	Y	N	Y
Wilson	?	?	+	?
COLORADO				
Wirth	Y	Y	N	Y
Armstrong	N	N	Y	?
CONNECTICUT				
Dodd	?	?	?	?
Lieberman	Y	Y	N	Y
DELAWARE				
Biden	Y	Y	?	Y
Roth	N	N	Y	N
FLORIDA				
Graham	N	Y	?	?
Mack	N	N	Y	N
GEORGIA				
Fowler	Y	N	N	Y
Nunn	N	N	N	Y
HAWAII				
Inouye	Y	Y	N	Y
Akaka	Y	Y	N	Y
IDAHO				
McClure	N	N	Y	N
Symms	N	N	Y	N
ILLINOIS				
Dixon	Y	N	Y	Y
Simon	Y	Y	Y	Y
INDIANA				
Coats	N	N	Y	N
Lugar	N	N	Y	N
IOWA				
Harkin	Y	Y	N	Y
Grassley	N	N	Y	N
KANSAS				
Dole	Y	N	Y	Y
Kassebaum	Y	N	Y	Y
KENTUCKY				
Ford	Y	N	N	Y
McConnell	N	N	Y	N
LOUISIANA				
Breaux	Y	N	N	Y
Johnston	Y	N	N	Y
MAINE				
Mitchell	Y	Y	N	Y
Cohen	N	Y	N	N
MARYLAND				
Mikulski	Y	Y	N	Y
Sarbanes	Y	Y	N	Y
MASSACHUSETTS				
Kennedy	?	Y	N	N
Kerry	Y	+	N	Y
MICHIGAN				
Levin	Y	Y	N	Y
Riegle	Y	Y	N	Y
MINNESOTA				
Boschwitz	N	?	Y	N
Durenberger	?	Y	N	N
MISSISSIPPI				
Cochran	N	N	Y	N
Lott	N	N	Y	N
MISSOURI				
Bond	N	N	Y	N
Danforth	N	Y	Y	N
MONTANA				
Baucus	-	?	?	N
Burns	N	N	Y	N
NEBRASKA				
Exon	Y	N	Y	Y
Kerrey	Y	Y	N	Y
NEVADA				
Bryan	N	N	N	N
Reid	N	N	N	N
NEW HAMPSHIRE				
Humphrey	N	N	Y	N
Rudman	Y	N	N	Y
NEW JERSEY				
Bradley	Y	Y	N	Y
Lautenberg	Y	Y	N	Y
NEW MEXICO				
Bingaman	Y	Y	N	Y
Domenici	?	Y	Y	N
NEW YORK				
Moynihan	Y	Y	N	Y
D'Amato	N	N	Y	Y
NORTH CAROLINA				
Sanford	N	Y	N	N
Helms	N	N	Y	N
NORTH DAKOTA				
Burdick	Y	Y	N	Y
Conrad	Y	N	N	Y
OHIO				
Glenn	Y	Y	N	Y
Metzenbaum	Y	Y	N	Y
OKLAHOMA				
Boren	Y	N	Y	Y
Nickles	N	N	Y	N
OREGON				
Hatfield	N	Y	N	N
Packwood	Y	Y	Y	Y
PENNSYLVANIA				
Heinz	N	N	Y	N
Specter	N	N	Y	Y
RHODE ISLAND				
Pell	Y	Y	N	Y
Chafee	?	?	?	?
SOUTH CAROLINA				
Hollings	Y	Y	N	Y
Thurmond	Y	N	Y	Y
SOUTH DAKOTA				
Daschle	Y	Y	Y	Y
Pressler	N	N	Y	N
TENNESSEE				
Gore	Y	Y	N	Y
Sasser	Y	N	N	Y
TEXAS				
Bentsen	Y	N	N	Y
Gramm	N	N	Y	N
UTAH				
Garn	N	N	Y	?
Hatch	N	N	Y	N
VERMONT				
Leahy	Y	Y	N	Y
Jeffords	Y	Y	N	Y
VIRGINIA				
Robb	Y	Y	N	Y
Warner	Y	N	Y	Y
WASHINGTON				
Adams	Y	Y	N	Y
Gorton	N	N	Y	N
WEST VIRGINIA				
Byrd	Y	N	N	Y
Rockefeller	Y	Y	N	Y
WISCONSIN				
Kohl	Y	Y	N	Y
Kasten	N	N	Y	N
WYOMING				
Simpson	Y	N	Y	Y
Wallop	N	N	Y	N

KEY

- Y Voted for (yea).
- # Paired for.
- + Announced for.
- N Voted against (nay).
- X Paired against.
- - Announced against.
- P Voted "present."
- C Voted "present" to avoid possible conflict of interest.
- ? Did not vote or otherwise make a position known.

Democrats ***Republicans***

ND Northern Democrats SD Southern Democrats

Southern states - Ala., Ark., Fla., Ga., Ky., La., Miss., N.C., Okla., S.C., Tenn., Texas, Va.

109. S 1970. Omnibus Crime Package/Cloture. Mitchell, D-Maine, motion to invoke cloture (thus limiting debate) on the bill to ban nine types of assault-style weapons, broaden the federal death penalty to include 30 additional crimes, allow states to compel faster federal court reviews of death sentences if they provide competent counsel to inmates, and relax the exclusionary rule. Motion rejected 54-37: R 10-31; D 44-6 (ND 33-2, SD 11-4), June 5, 1990. A three-fifths majority vote (60) of the total Senate is required to invoke cloture.

110. S 933. Americans With Disabilities Act/Instruction of Conferees. Mitchell, D-Maine, motion to table (kill) the Helms, R-N.C., motion to instruct the Senate conferees to agree to the House amendment by Chapman, D-Texas, to allow employers to transfer a worker with a communicable disease out of a food-handling position, provided that the employer offers another position in which the employee would sustain no economic damage. Motion rjected 40-53: R 7-35; D 33-18 (ND 28-6, SD 5-12), June 6, 1990. (The Helms motion was subsequently adopted by voice vote).

111. S 341. Air Travel Rights for the Blind/Line-Item Veto. McCain, R-Ariz., motion to waive the Budget Act for consideration of the McCain amendment to grant the president the legislative line-item veto. Motion rejected 43-50: R 37-6; D 6-44 (ND 4-30, SD 2-14), June 6, 1990. A three-fifths majority (60) of the total Senate is required to waive the Budget Act. (A Hollings, D-S.C., point of order was subsequently sustained and the amendment thus fell.)

112. S 1970. Omnibus Crime Package/Cloture. Mitchell, D-Maine, motion to invoke cloture (thus limiting debate) on the bill to ban nine types of assault-style weapons, broaden the federal death penalty to 30 additional crimes, allow states to compel faster federal court reviews of death sentences if they provide competent counsel to inmates, and relax the exclusionary rule. Motion rejected 57-37: R 11-30; D 46-7 (ND 33-4, SD 13-3), June 7, 1990. A three-fifths majority vote (60) of the total Senate is required to invoke cloture.

	113	114	115	116
ALABAMA				
Heflin	Y	Y	Y	Y
Shelby	Y	Y	Y	Y
ALASKA				
Murkowski	Y	N	N	Y
Stevens	Y	N	N	Y
ARIZONA				
DeConcini	Y	Y	Y	Y
McCain	Y	N	N	Y
ARKANSAS				
Bumpers	Y	Y	Y	Y
Pryor	Y	Y	Y	Y
CALIFORNIA				
Cranston	Y	Y	Y	Y
Wilson	Y	N	N	Y
COLORADO				
Wirth	Y	N	Y	Y
Armstrong	Y	N	N	Y
CONNECTICUT				
Dodd	Y	Y	Y	Y
Lieberman	Y	Y	Y	Y
DELAWARE				
Biden	Y	Y	Y	Y
Roth	Y	Y	Y	Y
FLORIDA				
Graham	Y	Y	Y	Y
Mack	Y	N	N	Y
GEORGIA				
Fowler	Y	Y	Y	Y
Nunn	Y	N	Y	Y
HAWAII				
Inouye	Y	Y	Y	Y
Akaka	Y	Y	Y	Y
IDAHO				
McClure	Y	N	N	Y
Symms	Y	N	N	Y
ILLINOIS				
Dixon	Y	Y	Y	Y
Simon	Y	Y	Y	Y
INDIANA				
Coats	Y	N	N	Y
Lugar	Y	N	N	Y
IOWA				
Harkin	Y	Y	Y	Y
Grassley	Y	N	Y	Y
KANSAS				
Dole	Y	N	N	Y
Kassebaum	Y	N	Y	Y
KENTUCKY				
Ford	Y	N	Y	Y
McConnell	Y	N	N	Y
LOUISIANA				
Breaux	Y	Y	Y	Y
Johnston	Y	Y	Y	Y
MAINE				
Mitchell	Y	Y	N	Y
Cohen	Y	Y	Y	Y
MARYLAND				
Mikulski	Y	Y	Y	Y
Sarbanes	Y	Y	Y	Y
MASSACHUSETTS				
Kennedy	Y	Y	Y	Y
Kerry	Y	Y	Y	Y
MICHIGAN				
Levin	Y	Y	Y	Y
Riegle	Y	Y	Y	Y
MINNESOTA				
Boschwitz	Y	N	N	Y
Durenberger	Y	Y	Y	Y
MISSISSIPPI				
Cochran	Y	N	N	Y
Lott	Y	N	N	Y
MISSOURI				
Bond	Y	N	N	Y
Danforth	?	N	N	Y
MONTANA				
Baucus	Y	Y	Y	Y
Burns	Y	N	N	Y
NEBRASKA				
Exon	Y	Y	Y	Y
Kerrey	Y	Y	Y	Y
NEVADA				
Bryan	Y	Y	Y	Y
Reid	Y	Y	Y	Y
NEW HAMPSHIRE				
Humphrey	N	N	N	Y
Rudman	Y	N	N	Y
NEW JERSEY				
Bradley	Y	Y	Y	Y
Lautenberg	Y	N	Y	Y
NEW MEXICO				
Bingaman	Y	Y	Y	Y
Domenici	Y	N	N	Y
NEW YORK				
Moynihan	Y	Y	Y	Y
D'Amato	Y	N	Y	Y
NORTH CAROLINA				
Sanford	Y	Y	Y	Y
Helms	Y	N	N	Y
NORTH DAKOTA				
Burdick	Y	Y	Y	Y
Conrad	Y	N	Y	Y
OHIO				
Glenn	Y	Y	Y	Y
Metzenbaum	Y	Y	Y	Y
OKLAHOMA				
Boren	Y	Y	Y	Y
Nickles	Y	N	N	Y
OREGON				
Hatfield	Y	Y	Y	Y
Packwood	Y	N	N	Y
PENNSYLVANIA				
Heinz	Y	N	Y	Y
Specter	Y	N	Y	Y
RHODE ISLAND				
Pell	Y	Y	Y	Y
Chafee	?	N	N	Y
SOUTH CAROLINA				
Hollings	Y	Y	Y	Y
Thurmond	Y	N	N	Y
SOUTH DAKOTA				
Daschle	Y	Y	Y	Y
Pressler	Y	Y	N	Y
TENNESSEE				
Gore	Y	Y	Y	Y
Sasser	Y	Y	Y	Y
TEXAS				
Bentsen	Y	Y	Y	Y
Gramm	Y	N	N	Y
UTAH				
Garn	Y	N	N	Y
Hatch	Y	N	N	Y
VERMONT				
Leahy	Y	Y	Y	Y
Jeffords	Y	Y	N	Y
VIRGINIA				
Robb	Y	Y	Y	Y
Warner	Y	N	Y	Y
WASHINGTON				
Adams	Y	Y	Y	Y
Gorton	Y	N	N	Y
WEST VIRGINIA				
Byrd	Y	Y	Y	Y
Rockefeller	Y	Y	Y	Y
WISCONSIN				
Kohl	Y	Y	Y	Y
Kasten	Y	N	N	Y
WYOMING				
Simpson	Y	N	N	Y
Wallop	Y	N	N	+

KEY

- Y Voted for (yea).
- # Paired for.
- + Announced for.
- N Voted against (nay).
- X Paired against.
- - Announced against.
- P Voted "present."
- C Voted "present" to avoid possible conflict of interest.
- ? Did not vote or otherwise make a position known.

Democrats ***Republicans***

ND Northern Democrats SD Southern Democrats

Southern states - Ala., Ark., Fla., Ga., Ky., La., Miss., N.C., Okla., S.C., Tenn., Texas, Va.

113. S 1875. Calamus Dam and Reservoir/Passage. Passage of the bill to redesignate the Calamus Dam and Reservoir in Nebraska, authorized under the Reclamation Project Authorization Act of 1972 as the Virginia Smith Dam and Calamus Lake Recreation Area. Passed 97-1: R 42-1; D 55-0 (ND 38-0, SD 17-0), June 12, 1990.

114. S 341. Air Travel Rights for the Blind/Cloture. Mitchell, D-Maine, motion to invoke cloture (thus limiting debate) on the bill to amend the Federal Aviation Act of 1958 to prohibit discrimination against blind people in air travel. Rejected 56-44: R 6-39; D 50-5 (ND 35-3, SD 15-2), June 12, 1990. A three-fifths majority vote (60) of the total Senate is required to invoke cloture.

115. HR 2364. Amtrak Reauthorization/Veto Override. Passage, over President Bush's May 24 veto, of the bill to reauthorize the National Railroad Passenger Corporation (Amtrak) for fiscal years 1989-92. Rejected 64-36: R 10-35; D 54-1 (ND 37-1, SD 17-0), June 12, 1990. A two-thirds majority of those present and voting (67 in this case) of both houses is required to override a veto. A "nay" was a vote supporting the president's position.

116. HR 987. Tongass Forest Restrictions/Passage. Passage of the bill to amend the Alaska National Interest Lands Conservation Act and prohibit commercial logging on certain lands in the Tongass National Forest. Passed 99-0: R 44-0; D 55-0 (ND 38-0, SD 17-0), June 13, 1990.

	117	118	119	120
ALABAMA				
Heflin	Y	Y	Y	Y
Shelby	Y	Y	Y	Y
ALASKA				
Murkowski	Y	Y	Y	N
Stevens	Y	Y	Y	Y
ARIZONA				
DeConcini	Y	Y	Y	Y
McCain	Y	Y	Y	N
ARKANSAS				
Bumpers	Y	Y	Y	Y
Pryor	Y	Y	Y	Y
CALIFORNIA				
Cranston	Y	Y	Y	Y
Wilson	Y	Y	Y	N
COLORADO				
Wirth	Y	Y	Y	Y
Armstrong	N	Y	N	N
CONNECTICUT				
Dodd	Y	Y	Y	Y
Lieberman	Y	Y	Y	Y
DELAWARE				
Biden	Y	Y	Y	Y
Roth	?	Y	N	N
FLORIDA				
Graham	Y	Y	Y	Y
Mack	Y	Y	Y	N
GEORGIA				
Fowler	Y	Y	Y	Y
Nunn	Y	Y	Y	Y
HAWAII				
Inouye	Y	Y	Y	Y
Akaka	Y	Y	Y	Y
IDAHO				
McClure	Y	Y	N	N
Symms	Y	Y	N	N
ILLINOIS				
Dixon	Y	Y	Y	Y
Simon	Y	Y	Y	Y
INDIANA				
Coats	Y	Y	Y	N
Lugar	Y	Y	Y	N
IOWA				
Harkin	Y	Y	Y	Y
Grassley	Y	Y	Y	N
KANSAS				
Dole	Y	Y	N	N
Kassebaum	Y	Y	N	N
KENTUCKY				
Ford	Y	Y	Y	Y
McConnell	Y	Y	Y	N
LOUISIANA				
Breaux	Y	Y	Y	Y
Johnston	Y	Y	Y	Y
MAINE				
Mitchell	Y	Y	Y	Y
Cohen	Y	Y	Y	N
MARYLAND				
Mikulski	Y	Y	Y	Y
Sarbanes	Y	Y	Y	Y
MASSACHUSETTS				
Kennedy	Y	Y	Y	Y
Kerry	Y	Y	Y	Y
MICHIGAN				
Levin	Y	Y	Y	Y
Riegle	Y	Y	Y	Y
MINNESOTA				
Boschwitz	Y	Y	Y	N
Durenberger	Y	Y	Y	Y
MISSISSIPPI				
Cochran	Y	Y	Y	N
Lott	Y	Y	Y	N
MISSOURI				
Bond	Y	Y	Y	N
Danforth	Y	Y	Y	N
MONTANA				
Baucus	Y	Y	Y	Y
Burns	Y	Y	N	N
NEBRASKA				
Exon	Y	Y	Y	Y
Kerrey	Y	Y	Y	Y
NEVADA				
Bryan	Y	Y	Y	Y
Reid	Y	Y	Y	Y
NEW HAMPSHIRE				
Humphrey	?	Y	N	N
Rudman	Y	Y	N	N
NEW JERSEY				
Bradley	Y	Y	Y	Y
Lautenberg	Y	Y	Y	Y
NEW MEXICO				
Bingaman	Y	Y	Y	Y
Domenici	Y	Y	Y	N
NEW YORK				
Moynihan	Y	Y	Y	Y
D'Amato	Y	Y	Y	Y
NORTH CAROLINA				
Sanford	Y	Y	Y	Y
Helms	Y	Y	N	?
NORTH DAKOTA				
Burdick	Y	Y	Y	Y
Conrad	Y	Y	Y	Y
OHIO				
Glenn	Y	Y	Y	Y
Metzenbaum	Y	Y	Y	Y
OKLAHOMA				
Boren	Y	Y	Y	N
Nickles	Y	Y	Y	N
OREGON				
Hatfield	Y	Y	Y	Y
Packwood	Y	Y	Y	Y
PENNSYLVANIA				
Heinz	Y	Y	Y	Y
Specter	Y	Y	Y	Y
RHODE ISLAND				
Pell	Y	Y	Y	Y
Chafee	Y	Y	Y	N
SOUTH CAROLINA				
Hollings	Y	Y	Y	Y
Thurmond	Y	Y	Y	N
SOUTH DAKOTA				
Daschle	Y	Y	Y	Y
Pressler	Y	Y	Y	N
TENNESSEE				
Gore	Y	Y	Y	Y
Sasser	Y	Y	Y	Y
TEXAS				
Bentsen	Y	Y	Y	Y
Gramm	Y	Y	Y	N
UTAH				
Garn	Y	Y	Y	N
Hatch	Y	Y	Y	N
VERMONT				
Leahy	Y	Y	Y	Y
Jeffords	Y	Y	Y	Y
VIRGINIA				
Robb	Y	Y	Y	Y
Warner	Y	Y	Y	N
WASHINGTON				
Adams	Y	Y	Y	Y
Gorton	Y	Y	Y	N
WEST VIRGINIA				
Byrd	Y	Y	Y	Y
Rockefeller	Y	Y	Y	Y
WISCONSIN				
Kohl	Y	Y	Y	N
Kasten	Y	Y	Y	N
WYOMING				
Simpson	Y	Y	Y	N
Wallop	N	Y	N	N

KEY

- Y Voted for (yea).
- # Paired for.
- + Announced for.
- N Voted against (nay).
- X Paired against.
- - Announced against.
- P Voted "present."
- C Voted "present" to avoid possible conflict of interest.
- ? Did not vote or otherwise make a position known.

Democrats *Republicans*

ND Northern Democrats SD Southern Democrats

Southern states - Ala., Ark., Fla., Ga., Ky., La., Miss., N.C., Okla., S.C., Tenn., Texas, Va.

117. S 566. Housing Programs Reauthorization/Social Security. Heinz, R-Pa., substitute to the Heinz amendment, to prohibit the Senate from dealing with any bill, amendment or conference report relating to the public debt before Congress has acted to remove the Social Security Trust Fund from the calculation of the deficit for purposes of complying with the Gramm-Rudman Deficit Reduction Act. Adopted 96-2: R 41-2; D 55-0 (ND 38-0, SD 17-0), June 19, 1990. (The Heinz amendment was subsequently adopted by voice vote.)

118. S 566. Housing Programs Reauthorization/Video Equipment. Danforth, R-Mo., amendment to authorize the Transportation secretary to make grants to the states for video equipment to be used in detecting and prosecuting people driving under the influence of alcohol or a controlled substance. Adopted 100-0: R 45-0; D 55-0 (ND 38-0, SD 17-0), June 19, 1990.

119. S 566. Housing Programs Reauthorization/Homelessness. Kennedy, D-Mass., amendment to combat homelessness and dependency by establishing housing-based family support centers, housing-based services to frail elderly people and people with chronic and debilitating illnesses, residence-based outpatient mental health and substance-abuse services, and grants for the improvement of community development corporations. Adopted 89-11: R 34-11; D 55-0 (ND 38-0, SD 17-0), June 20, 1990.

120. S 566. Housing Programs Reauthorization/Resident Worker Program. Cranston, D-Calif., motion to table (kill) the Nickles, R-Okla., amendment to provide a resident worker program for tenants of public housing and tenants who receive rental assistance. Motion agreed to 61-38: R 8-36; D 53-2 (ND 37-1, SD 16-1), June 20, 1990.

	121	122	123
ALABAMA			
Heflin	Y	Y	Y
Shelby	Y	Y	Y
ALASKA			
Murkowski	N	Y	N
Stevens	Y	Y	N
ARIZONA			
DeConcini	Y	N	Y
McCain	Y	N	N
ARKANSAS			
Bumpers	Y	N	Y
Pryor	Y	Y	Y
CALIFORNIA			
Cranston	Y	Y	Y
Wilson	N	N	N
COLORADO			
Wirth	Y	Y	Y
Armstrong	N	N	N
CONNECTICUT			
Dodd	Y	Y	Y
Lieberman	Y	Y	Y
DELAWARE			
Biden	Y	Y	Y
Roth	N	N	N
FLORIDA			
Graham	Y	Y	N
Mack	N	N	N
GEORGIA			
Fowler	Y	N	Y
Nunn	Y	N	N
HAWAII			
Inouye	Y	Y	Y
Akaka	Y	Y	Y
IDAHO			
McClure	N	N	N
Symms	N	N	?
ILLINOIS			
Dixon	Y	Y	Y
Simon	Y	Y	Y
INDIANA			
Coats	N	N	N
Lugar	N	N	N
IOWA			
Harkin	Y	Y	Y
Grassley	N	N	N
KANSAS			
Dole	N	N	Y
Kassebaum	N	N	N
KENTUCKY			
Ford	Y	Y	Y
McConnell	N	N	N
LOUISIANA			
Breaux	Y	Y	Y
Johnston	Y	Y	Y
MAINE			
Mitchell	Y	Y	Y
Cohen	N	N	N
MARYLAND			
Mikulski	Y	+	+
Sarbanes	Y	Y	Y
MASSACHUSETTS			
Kennedy	Y	Y	Y
Kerry	Y	Y	Y
MICHIGAN			
Levin	Y	Y	Y
Riegle	Y	Y	Y
MINNESOTA			
Boschwitz	N	N	N
Durenberger	Y	Y	N
MISSISSIPPI			
Cochran	N	N	N
Lott	N	N	N
MISSOURI			
Bond	N	Y	N
Danforth	N	Y	N
MONTANA			
Baucus	Y	Y	Y
Burns	N	N	N
NEBRASKA			
Exon	Y	Y	Y
Kerrey	Y	Y	Y
NEVADA			
Bryan	Y	Y	Y
Reid	Y	Y	Y
NEW HAMPSHIRE			
Humphrey	N	N	N
Rudman	N	N	N
NEW JERSEY			
Bradley	Y	Y	Y
Lautenberg	Y	Y	Y
NEW MEXICO			
Bingaman	Y	Y	Y
Domenici	N	Y	N
NEW YORK			
Moynihan	Y	Y	Y
D'Amato	N	Y	N
NORTH CAROLINA			
Sanford	Y	Y	Y
Helms	N	N	N
NORTH DAKOTA			
Burdick	Y	Y	Y
Conrad	Y	Y	Y
OHIO			
Glenn	Y	Y	Y
Metzenbaum	Y	Y	Y
OKLAHOMA			
Boren	Y	?	?
Nickles	N	N	N
OREGON			
Hatfield	Y	Y	N
Packwood	Y	Y	N
PENNSYLVANIA			
Heinz	Y	Y	N
Specter	Y	Y	N
RHODE ISLAND			
Pell	Y	Y	Y
Chafee	N	N	N
SOUTH CAROLINA			
Hollings	Y	N	Y
Thurmond	N	N	N
SOUTH DAKOTA			
Daschle	Y	Y	Y
Pressler	N	N	N
TENNESSEE			
Gore	Y	Y	Y
Sasser	Y	Y	Y
TEXAS			
Bentsen	Y	Y	Y
Gramm	N	N	N
UTAH			
Garn	N	N	N
Hatch	N	N	N
VERMONT			
Leahy	Y	Y	Y
Jeffords	Y	Y	N
VIRGINIA			
Robb	Y	N	Y
Warner	Y	N	N
WASHINGTON			
Adams	Y	Y	Y
Gorton	N	N	N
WEST VIRGINIA			
Byrd	Y	Y	Y
Rockefeller	Y	Y	Y
WISCONSIN			
Kohl	Y	Y	Y
Kasten	Y	N	N
WYOMING			
Simpson	N	N	N
Wallop	N	N	N

KEY

- Y Voted for (yea).
- # Paired for.
- \+ Announced for.
- N Voted against (nay).
- X Paired against.
- \- Announced against.
- P Voted "present."
- C Voted "present" to avoid possible conflict of interest.
- ? Did not vote or otherwise make a position known.

Democrats ***Republicans***

ND Northern Democrats SD Southern Democrats

Southern states - Ala., Ark., Fla., Ga., Ky., La., Miss., N.C., Okla., S.C., Tenn., Texas, Va.

121. HR 20. Hatch Act Revisions/Veto Override. Passage, over President Bush's June 15 veto, of the bill to allow greater political activity by federal employees and to protect them from political pressure. Rejected 65-35: R 10-35; D 55-0 (ND 38-0, SD 17-0), June 21, 1990. A two-thirds majority of those present and voting of both houses (67 in this case) is required to override a veto. A "nay" was a vote supporting the president's position.

122. S 566. Housing Programs Reauthorization/Davis-Bacon. Cranston, D-Calif., motion to table (kill) the Chafee, R-R.I., amendment to exempt federal low-income housing construction and rehabilitation projects of less than $1 million from the Davis-Bacon Act. Motion agreed to 59-39: R 12-33; D 47-6 (ND 36-1, SD 11-5), June 21, 1990.

123. S 566. Housing Programs Reauthorization/National Affordable Housing Act. Cranston, D-Calif., motion to table (kill) the Mack, R-Fla., amendment to permit Housing Opportunity Partnership funds to be used for rental assistance. Motion agreed to 52-45: R 1-43; D 51-2 (ND 37-0, SD 14-2), June 21, 1990.

	124	125	126	127	128	129	130	131
ALABAMA								
Heflin	Y	Y	N	N	Y	Y	Y	N
Shelby	Y	Y	N	N	Y	Y	Y	N
ALASKA								
Murkowski	N	Y	N	N	Y	Y	Y	Y
Stevens	Y	Y	N	N	Y	N	N	Y
ARIZONA								
DeConcini	Y	N	N	N	Y	Y	N	N
McCain	N	Y	N	N	Y	N	Y	Y
ARKANSAS								
Bumpers	Y	N	N	N	N	Y	Y	N
Pryor	Y	N	N	N	N	Y	Y	N
CALIFORNIA								
Cranston	Y	N	N	N	N	Y	N	N
Wilson	N	Y	N	N	Y	N	N	Y
COLORADO								
Wirth	Y	N	N	N	N	Y	N	N
Armstrong	?	Y	Y	N	Y	?	?	?
CONNECTICUT								
Dodd	Y	N	N	N	N	Y	N	N
Lieberman	Y	N	N	N	N	Y	N	N
DELAWARE								
Biden	Y	N	N	Y	N	Y	N	N
Roth	Y	Y	N	N	Y	Y	Y	Y
FLORIDA								
Graham	Y	N	N	N	Y	N	Y	N
Mack	Y	Y	N	N	Y	N	Y	Y
GEORGIA								
Fowler	Y	N	N	Y	Y	Y	N	N
Nunn	Y	N	N	Y	Y	Y	N	N
HAWAII								
Inouye	N	N	N	N	N	Y	Y	N
Akaka	Y	Y	N	N	N	Y	Y	N
IDAHO								
McClure	?	Y	Y	N	Y	N	Y	Y
Symms	?	Y	Y	N	Y	N	Y	Y
ILLINOIS								
Dixon	Y	N	N	N	Y	Y	Y	N
Simon	Y	N	N	N	N	Y	N	?
INDIANA								
Coats	Y	Y	N	N	Y	N	N	Y
Lugar	Y	Y	N	N	Y	N	Y	Y
IOWA								
Harkin	Y	Y	N	N	N	Y	N	N
Grassley	Y	Y	N	N	Y	Y	Y	Y
KANSAS								
Dole	Y	Y	N	N	Y	Y	N	Y
Kassebaum	Y	Y	N	N	Y	Y	Y	Y
KENTUCKY								
Ford	Y	N	N	N	Y	Y	Y	N
McConnell	N	Y	Y	N	Y	Y	Y	Y
LOUISIANA								
Breaux	N	N	N	N	Y	Y	Y	N
Johnston	Y	Y	N	N	Y	Y	N	N
MAINE								
Mitchell	Y	N	N	N	N	Y	N	N
Cohen	Y	Y	N	Y	Y	Y	N	N
MARYLAND								
Mikulski	+	N	N	N	N	Y	N	N
Sarbanes	Y	N	N	N	N	Y	N	N
MASSACHUSETTS								
Kennedy	Y	N	N	N	N	Y	N	N
Kerry	Y	N	N	N	N	Y	N	N
MICHIGAN								
Levin	Y	N	N	Y	N	Y	N	N
Riegle	Y	N	N	N	N	Y	N	N
MINNESOTA								
Boschwitz	Y	Y	N	N	Y	Y	Y	Y
Durenberger	?	Y	N	N	N	Y	Y	Y
MISSISSIPPI								
Cochran	Y	Y	N	N	Y	Y	Y	Y
Lott	N	Y	Y	N	Y	Y	Y	Y
MISSOURI								
Bond	N	Y	N	N	Y	Y	Y	Y
Danforth	Y	Y	N	N	N	Y	Y	Y
MONTANA								
Baucus	?	N	N	N	Y	Y	N	N
Burns	Y	Y	N	N	Y	N	Y	Y
NEBRASKA								
Exon	Y	N	N	N	Y	N	Y	N
Kerrey	Y	N	N	N	N	N	Y	N
NEVADA								
Bryan	Y	Y	N	N	Y	N	Y	N
Reid	Y	Y	N	N	Y	N	Y	N
NEW HAMPSHIRE								
Humphrey	N	Y	N	N	N	N	N	Y
Rudman	Y	Y	N	N	N	Y	N	N
NEW JERSEY								
Bradley	Y	N	N	N	N	Y	N	N
Lautenberg	Y	N	N	N	N	Y	N	N
NEW MEXICO								
Bingaman	Y	Y	N	N	N	Y	Y	N
Domenici	Y	Y	N	N	Y	N	Y	Y
NEW YORK								
Moynihan	Y	N	N	N	N	Y	N	N
D'Amato	Y	Y	N	N	Y	Y	N	Y
NORTH CAROLINA								
Sanford	Y	N	N	N	N	N	Y	N
Helms	N	P	Y	N	Y	N	Y	Y
NORTH DAKOTA								
Burdick	Y	Y	N	Y	Y	N	N	N
Conrad	Y	N	N	N	Y	N	Y	N
OHIO								
Glenn	Y	N	N	N	N	Y	N	N
Metzenbaum	Y	Y	N	N	N	Y	N	N
OKLAHOMA								
Boren	?	N	N	N	N	N	Y	N
Nickles	N	Y	Y	N	Y	N	Y	Y
OREGON								
Hatfield	Y	N	N	N	Y	Y	N	Y
Packwood	Y	N	N	N	N	N	N	Y
PENNSYLVANIA								
Heinz	Y	Y	N	N	Y	Y	N	Y
Specter	N	Y	N	N	Y	Y	N	Y
RHODE ISLAND								
Pell	Y	N	N	N	N	+	+	-
Chafee	Y	Y	N	N	N	Y	N	Y
SOUTH CAROLINA								
Hollings	Y	N	N	Y	Y	Y	N	N
Thurmond	Y	Y	Y	N	Y	N	Y	Y
SOUTH DAKOTA								
Daschle	?	N	N	N	N	N	Y	N
Pressler	Y	Y	Y	N	Y	N	Y	Y
TENNESSEE								
Gore	Y	N	N	N	N	Y	N	N
Sasser	Y	N	N	N	N	Y	Y	N
TEXAS								
Bentsen	Y	N	N	N	Y	N	Y	?
Gramm	N	Y	N	N	Y	N	Y	Y
UTAH								
Garn	?	Y	Y	N	Y	Y	Y	Y
Hatch	Y	Y	N	N	Y	N	Y	Y
VERMONT								
Leahy	Y	N	N	N	N	Y	N	N
Jeffords	Y	N	N	N	N	Y	Y	Y
VIRGINIA								
Robb	Y	N	N	N	N	N	Y	N
Warner	Y	Y	N	N	Y	N	Y	Y
WASHINGTON								
Adams	Y	N	N	N	N	Y	N	N
Gorton	Y	Y	N	N	Y	N	Y	Y
WEST VIRGINIA								
Byrd	Y	N	N	N	Y	Y	Y	N
Rockefeller	Y	N	N	N	Y	Y	N	N
WISCONSIN								
Kohl	Y	N	N	N	N	Y	Y	N
Kasten	N	Y	N	N	Y	N	Y	Y
WYOMING								
Simpson	Y	Y	N	N	Y	N	Y	Y
Wallop	N	Y	N	N	Y	N	Y	Y

KEY

- Y Voted for (yea).
- # Paired for.
- + Announced for.
- N Voted against (nay).
- X Paired against.
- - Announced against.
- P Voted "present."
- C Voted "present" to avoid possible conflict of interest.
- ? Did not vote or otherwise make a position known.

Democrats ***Republicans***

ND Northern Democrats SD Southern Democrats

Southern states - Ala., Ark., Fla., Ga., Ky., La., Miss., N.C., Okla., S.C., Tenn., Texas, Va.

124. Procedural Motion. Mitchell, D-Maine, motion to instruct the sergeant-at-arms to request the attendance of absent senators. Motion agreed to 76-15: R 27-13; D 49-2 (ND 34-1, SD 15-1), June 22, 1990.

125. S J Res 332. Constitutional Amendment on the Flag/Point of Order. Wilson, R-Calif., point of order that the Bumpers, D-Ark., substitute amendment to make it a statutory offense for a person to purposely or knowingly deface, damage or physically mistreat the U.S. flag in a way that is likely to breach the peace would violate the Constitution if enacted into law. Point of order upheld 51-48: R 41-3; D 10-45 (ND 7-31, SD 3-14), June 26, 1990. (The Bumpers amendment was therefore ruled out of order)

126. S J Res 332. Constitutional Amendment on the Flag/Substitute. Helms, R-N.C., substitute amendment to make it a statutory offense to desecrate the U.S. flag, and remove from the federal courts jurisdiction to consider flag-desecration cases. Rejected 10-90: R 10-35; D 0-55 (ND 0-38, SD 0-17), June 26, 1990.

127. S J Res 332. Constitutional Amendment on the Flag/Substitute. Biden, D-Del., substitute amendment to propose an amendment to the Constitution to allow only Congress to enact a law making it unlawful to burn, mutilate or trample the U.S. flag. Rejected 7-93: R 1-44; D 6-49 (ND 3-35, SD 3-14), June 26, 1990.

128. S J Res 332. Constitutional Amendment on the Flag/Passage. Passage of the joint resolution to propose an amendment to the Constitution to prohibit the physical desecration of the U.S. flag. Rejected 58-42: R 38-7; D 20-35 (ND 10-28, SD 10-7), June 26, 1990. A two-thirds majority of those present and voting (67 in this case) of both houses is required for passage of a joint resolution proposing an amendment to the Constitution. A "yea" was a vote supporting the president's position.

129. S 566. Housing Programs Reauthorization/Community Development Block Grants. D'Amato, R-N.Y., motion to table (kill) the Gramm, R-Texas, amendment to allocate Community Development Block Grant funds proportionate to each state's population. Motion agreed to 63-35: R 21-23; D 42-12 (ND 30-7, SD 12-5), June 27, 1990.

130. S 566. Housing Programs Reauthorization/Check-Cashing Services. Bond, R-Mo., motion to table (kill) the Metzenbaum, D-Ohio, amendment to provide access to check-cashing services and basic banking services. Motion agreed to 55-43: R 31-13; D 24-30 (ND 12-25, SD 12-5), June 27, 1990.

131. S 566. Housing Programs Reauthorization/Housing Opportunity Zones. Boschwitz, R-Minn., amendment to create not more than 50 Housing Opportunity Zones in which federal incentives would be offered to spur construction of affordable housing. Rejected 42-54: R 42-2; D 0-52 (ND 0-36, SD 0-16), June 27, 1990.

	132	133	134	135	136	137	138
ALABAMA							
Heflin	Y	N	Y	Y	Y	Y	Y
Shelby	Y	N	Y	Y	Y	N	Y
ALASKA							
Murkowski	Y	N	Y	Y	Y	N	Y
Stevens	Y	N	Y	Y	Y	N	Y
ARIZONA							
DeConcini	Y	Y	Y	N	N	Y	Y
McCain	Y	N	Y	Y	Y	N	Y
ARKANSAS							
Bumpers	Y	Y	Y	Y	N	N	N
Pryor	Y	Y	Y	Y	N	Y	N
CALIFORNIA							
Cranston	Y	Y	N	Y	N	Y	N
Wilson	Y	Y	Y	Y	Y	N	Y
COLORADO							
Wirth	Y	Y	Y	Y	N	Y	N
Armstrong	?	X	?	?	?	?	?
CONNECTICUT							
Dodd	Y	Y	Y	Y	N	Y	N
Lieberman	Y	Y	Y	Y	N	Y	N
DELAWARE							
Biden	Y	Y	Y	N	N	Y	N
Roth	N	N	Y	N	Y	N	Y
FLORIDA							
Graham	Y	Y	Y	Y	Y	N	N
Mack	Y	N	Y	Y	Y	N	Y
GEORGIA							
Fowler	Y	Y	Y	N	N	Y	N
Nunn	Y	Y	Y	N	N	N	N
HAWAII							
Inouye	Y	Y	N	Y	N	Y	N
Akaka	Y	Y	N	Y	N	Y	N
IDAHO							
McClure	Y	N	Y	Y	Y	N	Y
Symms	Y	N	Y	Y	Y	N	Y
ILLINOIS							
Dixon	Y	Y	Y	Y	Y	N	N
Simon	Y	Y	Y	N	N	Y	N
INDIANA							
Coats	Y	N	Y	Y	Y	N	Y
Lugar	Y	N	Y	Y	Y	N	Y

	132	133	134	135	136	137	138
IOWA							
Harkin	Y	Y	Y	Y	N	Y	N
Grassley	Y	N	Y	Y	Y	N	Y
KANSAS							
Dole	Y	N	Y	Y	Y	N	Y
Kassebaum	Y	Y	Y	Y	N	N	Y
KENTUCKY							
Ford	Y	N	Y	N	N	Y	Y
McConnell	Y	N	Y	Y	Y	N	Y
LOUISIANA							
Breaux	Y	N	Y	Y	N	Y	N
Johnston	Y	N	Y	N	N	Y	N
MAINE							
Mitchell	Y	Y	Y	N	N	Y	N
Cohen	Y	N	Y	Y	N	Y	N
MARYLAND							
Mikulski	Y	Y	Y	N	N	Y	N
Sarbanes	Y	Y	Y	Y	N	Y	N
MASSACHUSETTS							
Kennedy	+	Y	N	N	N	Y	N
Kerry	Y	Y	Y	Y	N	Y	N
MICHIGAN							
Levin	Y	Y	Y	Y	N	Y	N
Riegle	Y	Y	Y	Y	N	Y	N
MINNESOTA							
Boschwitz	Y	N	Y	Y	Y	N	Y
Durenberger	Y	N	N	Y	N	Y	N
MISSISSIPPI							
Cochran	Y	N	Y	Y	N	N	Y
Lott	Y	N	Y	Y	Y	N	Y
MISSOURI							
Bond	Y	N	Y	Y	Y	N	Y
Danforth	Y	N	N	Y	N	Y	N
MONTANA							
Baucus	Y	N	Y	Y	Y	N	Y
Burns	Y	N	Y	Y	Y	N	Y
NEBRASKA							
Exon	Y	N	Y	Y	N	N	N
Kerrey	Y	Y	Y	Y	Y	N	N
NEVADA							
Bryan	Y	N	Y	Y	N	Y	N
Reid	Y	N	Y	Y	N	Y	N

	132	133	134	135	136	137	138
NEW HAMPSHIRE							
Humphrey	Y	N	Y	Y	Y	N	Y
Rudman	Y	N	Y	Y	Y	N	Y
NEW JERSEY							
Bradley	Y	Y	Y	N	N	Y	N
Lautenberg	Y	Y	Y	N	N	Y	N
NEW MEXICO							
Bingaman	Y	N	N	Y	N	Y	N
Domenici	Y	N	Y	Y	N	Y	Y
NEW YORK							
Moynihan	Y	Y	Y	N	N	Y	N
D'Amato	Y	Y	Y	Y	Y	N	Y
NORTH CAROLINA							
Sanford	Y	N	Y	N	N	?	N
Helms	Y	N	Y	Y	Y	N	Y
NORTH DAKOTA							
Burdick	Y	Y	Y	Y	N	Y	N
Conrad	Y	Y	Y	Y	N	Y	N
OHIO							
Glenn	Y	Y	Y	N	N	Y	N
Metzenbaum	Y	#	N	Y	N	Y	N
OKLAHOMA							
Boren	Y	Y	Y	Y	N	Y	N
Nickles	Y	N	Y	Y	Y	N	Y
OREGON							
Hatfield	Y	Y	N	Y	N	Y	N
Packwood	Y	Y	Y	Y	N	Y	N
PENNSYLVANIA							
Heinz	Y	N	Y	Y	Y	N	Y
Specter	Y	N	Y	Y	Y	N	Y
RHODE ISLAND							
Pell	+	Y	N	Y	N	Y	N
Chafee	Y	Y	N	Y	N	N	Y
SOUTH CAROLINA							
Hollings	Y	N	Y	Y	Y	N	N
Thurmond	Y	N	Y	Y	Y	N	Y
SOUTH DAKOTA							
Daschle	Y	Y	Y	N	N	Y	N
Pressler	Y	N	Y	Y	Y	N	Y
TENNESSEE							
Gore	Y	Y	Y	Y	N	Y	N
Sasser	Y	Y	Y	Y	N	Y	N

KEY

- Y Voted for (yea).
- # Paired for.
- + Announced for.
- N Voted against (nay).
- X Paired against.
- \- Announced against.
- P Voted "present."
- C Voted "present" to avoid possible conflict of interest.
- ? Did not vote or otherwise make a position known.

Democrats ***Republicans***

	132	133	134	135	136	137	138
TEXAS							
Bentsen	Y	Y	Y	Y	N	Y	N
Gramm	Y	N	Y	Y	Y	N	Y
UTAH							
Garn	Y	N	Y	Y	Y	N	Y
Hatch	Y	N	Y	Y	N	N	Y
VERMONT							
Leahy	Y	Y	N	Y	N	Y	N
Jeffords	Y	Y	Y	Y	N	N	N
VIRGINIA							
Robb	Y	Y	Y	Y	N	Y	N
Warner	Y	Y	Y	Y	Y	N	Y
WASHINGTON							
Adams	Y	Y	Y	Y	N	Y	N
Gorton	Y	N	Y	Y	Y	N	Y
WEST VIRGINIA							
Byrd	Y	Y	Y	N	N	Y	Y
Rockefeller	Y	Y	Y	N	N	Y	N
WISCONSIN							
Kohl	Y	Y	Y	N	N	Y	N
Kasten	Y	N	Y	Y	N	N	Y
WYOMING							
Simpson	Y	N	Y	Y	N	N	Y
Wallop	Y	N	Y	Y	N	N	Y

ND Northern Democrats SD Southern Democrats Southern states - Ala., Ark., Fla., Ga., Ky., La., Miss., N.C., Okla., S.C., Tenn., Texas, Va.

132. S 566. Housing Programs Reauthorization/Passage. Passage of the bill to reauthorize and expand federal housing programs and to create a $3 billion-per-year subsidy program to encourage development of low-income housing. Passed 96-1: R 43-1; D 53-0 (ND 36-0, SD 17-0), June 27, 1990. A "yea" was a vote supporting the president's position.

133. S 1970. Omnibus Crime Package/Semiautomatic Assault-Style Weapons. DeConcini, D-Ariz., amendment to the Gramm, R-Texas, amendment to prohibit for three years making, selling or possessing nine types of semiautomatic assault-style weapons. Adopted 50-48: R 8-36; D 42-12 (ND 32-5, SD 10-7), June 28, 1990. A "nay" was a vote supporting the president's position.

134. S 1970. Omnibus Crime Package/Use of Firearms in Crimes. Gramm, R-Texas, amendment to impose minimum mandatory prison sentences for using firearms in crimes of violence and drug trafficking. Adopted 87-12: R 40-4; D 47-8 (ND 30-8, SD 17-0), June 28, 1990. A "nay" was a vote supporting the president's position.

135. S 1970. Omnibus Crime Package/Drugs. Gorton, R-Wash., amendment to the Akaka, D-Hawaii, amendment, to expand the list of precursor chemicals used in making "ice," a pure, smokable form of methamphetamine, and to require licensing for people involved in transactions involving the chemicals. Adopted 79-20: R 43-1; D 36-19 (ND 24-14, SD 12-5), June 28, 1990. A "nay" was a vote supporting the president's position.

136. S 1970. Omnibus Crime Package/Death-Penalty Exemption. McClure, R-Idaho, motion to table (kill) the Inouye, D-Hawaii, amendment to exempt Indian country from coverage under the bill's death-penalty provisions unless a tribe elects to have capital punishment apply. Rejected 37-62: R 30-14; D 7-48 (ND 3-35, SD 4-13), June 28, 1990. A "yea" was a vote supporting the president's position.

137. S 1970. Omnibus Crime Package/Indian Lands. Inouye, D-Hawaii, motion to table (kill) the McClure, R-Idaho, amendment to the Inouye amendment, to change the definition of "Indian country" to lands or allotted lands that are owned by or under the control of a tribe or tribal member at the time of the offense. Motion agreed to 51-47: R 6-38; D 45-9 (ND 34-4, SD 11-5), June 28, 1990. A "nay" was a vote supporting the president's position.

138. S 1970. Omnibus Crime Package/Discrimination. Hatch, R-Utah, amendment to the Graham, D-Fla., amendment, to limit studies on the role of race in state criminal justice systems to review of whether the constitutional rights of criminal defendants have been violated. Rejected 44-55: R 38-6; D 6-49 (ND 3-35, SD 3-14), June 28, 1990.

	139	140	141	142	143
ALABAMA					
Heflin	Y	Y	Y	Y	N
Shelby	Y	Y	Y	Y	N
ALASKA					
Murkowski	N	Y	Y	Y	N
Stevens	N	Y	Y	Y	N
ARIZONA					
DeConcini	N	Y	N	Y	N
McCain	N	Y	Y	Y	N
ARKANSAS					
Bumpers	Y	Y	N	Y	N
Pryor	Y	Y	N	Y	N
CALIFORNIA					
Cranston	Y	N	N	Y	Y
Wilson	Y	Y	Y	Y	N
COLORADO					
Wirth	Y	N	Y	Y	N
Armstrong	?	?	?	?	?
CONNECTICUT					
Dodd	Y	N	N	Y	N
Lieberman	Y	Y	Y	Y	N
DELAWARE					
Biden	Y	N	Y	Y	N
Roth	N	Y	Y	N	N
FLORIDA					
Graham	Y	Y	Y	Y	N
Mack	N	Y	N	Y	N
GEORGIA					
Fowler	Y	Y	Y	Y	Y
Nunn	Y	Y	N	Y	N
HAWAII					
Inouye	Y	N	N	Y	Y
Akaka	Y	N	N	Y	Y
IDAHO					
McClure	N	Y	N	Y	N
Symms	N	Y	Y	N	N
ILLINOIS					
Dixon	N	Y	Y	Y	N
Simon	Y	N	N	Y	Y
INDIANA					
Coats	Y	Y	N	Y	N
Lugar	N	Y	N	Y	N
IOWA					
Harkin	Y	N	N	Y	Y
Grassley	N	Y	Y	Y	N
KANSAS					
Dole	Y	Y	Y	Y	N
Kassebaum	N	Y	N	Y	N
KENTUCKY					
Ford	Y	Y	N	Y	N
McConnell	Y	Y	Y	Y	N
LOUISIANA					
Breaux	Y	Y	N	Y	N
Johnston	Y	Y	N	Y	N
MAINE					
Mitchell	Y	N	N	Y	Y
Cohen	N	N	N	Y	Y
MARYLAND					
Mikulski	Y	N	N	Y	N
Sarbanes	Y	N	N	Y	N
MASSACHUSETTS					
Kennedy	Y	N	N	Y	Y
Kerry	Y	N	N	Y	Y
MICHIGAN					
Levin	Y	N	N	Y	Y
Riegle	Y	Y	Y	Y	N
MINNESOTA					
Boschwitz	Y	Y	Y	Y	N
Durenberger	N	N	N	Y	Y
MISSISSIPPI					
Cochran	N	Y	N	Y	N
Lott	Y	Y	N	Y	N
MISSOURI					
Bond	N	Y	Y	Y	N
Danforth	Y	N	N	Y	Y
MONTANA					
Baucus	Y	Y	Y	Y	N
Burns	N	Y	Y	Y	N
NEBRASKA					
Exon	Y	Y	Y	Y	N
Kerrey	Y	Y	N	Y	N
NEVADA					
Bryan	Y	Y	N	Y	N
Reid	Y	Y	N	Y	N
NEW HAMPSHIRE					
Humphrey	N	Y	N	Y	N
Rudman	N	Y	Y	Y	N
NEW JERSEY					
Bradley	Y	Y	Y	Y	N
Lautenberg	Y	N	N	Y	Y
NEW MEXICO					
Bingaman	Y	N	N	Y	N
Domenici	N	Y	Y	Y	N
NEW YORK					
Moynihan	Y	N	N	Y	Y
D'Amato	N	Y	Y	Y	N
NORTH CAROLINA					
Sanford	N	?	?	?	?
Helms	N	Y	Y	Y	N
NORTH DAKOTA					
Burdick	Y	N	N	Y	Y
Conrad	Y	N	N	Y	Y
OHIO					
Glenn	N	N	N	Y	Y
Metzenbaum	Y	N	N	Y	Y
OKLAHOMA					
Boren	Y	Y	N	Y	N
Nickles	N	Y	Y	Y	N
OREGON					
Hatfield	Y	N	N	Y	Y
Packwood	Y	Y	Y	Y	N
PENNSYLVANIA					
Heinz	Y	Y	Y	Y	N
Specter	Y	Y	Y	Y	N
RHODE ISLAND					
Pell	Y	N	N	Y	Y
Chafee	Y	N	N	Y	Y
SOUTH CAROLINA					
Hollings	N	Y	Y	Y	N
Thurmond	N	Y	Y	Y	N
SOUTH DAKOTA					
Daschle	Y	Y	N	Y	N
Pressler	N	Y	Y	Y	N
TENNESSEE					
Gore	Y	N	N	Y	N
Sasser	Y	N	N	Y	N
TEXAS					
Bentsen	Y	Y	N	Y	N
Gramm	Y	Y	Y	Y	N
UTAH					
Garn	N	Y	Y	Y	N
Hatch	N	Y	Y	Y	N
VERMONT					
Leahy	Y	N	N	Y	Y
Jeffords	N	N	N	Y	N
VIRGINIA					
Robb	Y	Y	Y	Y	N
Warner	Y	Y	Y	Y	N
WASHINGTON					
Adams	Y	Y	N	Y	N
Gorton	N	Y	N	Y	N
WEST VIRGINIA					
Byrd	N	Y	N	Y	N
Rockefeller	Y	Y	N	Y	Y
WISCONSIN					
Kohl	Y	N	N	Y	Y
Kasten	Y	Y	Y	Y	N
WYOMING					
Simpson	N	Y	Y	Y	N
Wallop	N	Y	Y	Y	N

KEY

- Y Voted for (yea).
- # Paired for.
- + Announced for.
- N Voted against (nay).
- X Paired against.
- \- Announced against.
- P Voted "present."
- C Voted "present" to avoid possible conflict of interest.
- ? Did not vote or otherwise make a position known.

Democrats *Republicans*

ND Northern Democrats SD Southern Democrats

Southern states - Ala., Ark., Fla., Ga., Ky., La., Miss., N.C., Okla., S.C., Tenn., Texas, Va.

139. S 1970. Omnibus Crime Package/Law Enforcement Scholarships. Specter, R-Pa., amendment to authorize $430 million in fiscal 1991 and such sums as necessary through fiscal 1995 for states to provide college scholarships to people who will become state or local law enforcement officers, and to provide scholarships to in-service law enforcement officers seeking further education. Adopted 64-35: R 15-29; D 49-6 (ND 34-4, SD 15-2), June 28, 1990. A "nay" was a vote supporting the president's position.

140. S 1970. Omnibus Crime Package/Death Penalty. D'Amato, R-N.Y., amendment to authorize the death penalty for a person convicted as a "drug kingpin," or head of a continuing criminal enterprise. Adopted 66-32: R 38-6; D 28-26 (ND 14-24, SD 14-2), June 28, 1990. A "yea" was a vote supporting the president's position.

141. S 1970. Omnibus Crime Package/Death Penalty. Wilson, R-Calif., amendment to authorize the death penalty in cases of death during an act violating the Civil Rights Act. Rejected 43-55: R 29-15; D 14-40 (ND 8-30, SD 6-10), June 28, 1990. A "yea" was a vote supporting the president's position.

142. S 1970. Omnibus Crime Package/Additional Provisions. Biden, D-Del., amendment to include several provisions of S 1972, to increase the number of FBI agents, Drug Enforcement Administration agents, border patrol officers and federal prosecutors; to provide for a "rural drug initiative"; to require the detention of certain offenders awaiting sentencing and appeal; and to require drug testing for all defendants released on probation, parole or supervised release. Adopted 96-2: R 42-2; D 54-0 (ND 38-0, SD 16-0), June 28, 1990.

143. S 1970. Omnibus Crime Package/Mandatory Life Imprisonment. Hatfield, R-Ore., amendment to provide for mandatory life imprisonment without the possibility of release for all cases in which the bill would impose the death penalty. Rejected 25-73: R 5-39; D 20-34 (ND 19-19, SD 1-15), June 29, 1990. A "nay" was a vote supporting the president's position.

	144	145	146	147	148	149
ALABAMA						
Heflin	N	Y	Y	Y	Y	Y
Shelby	N	Y	Y	Y	Y	Y
ALASKA						
Murkowski	N	Y	Y	Y	Y	Y
Stevens	?	?	Y	Y	Y	Y
ARIZONA						
DeConcini	?	?	Y	Y	N	Y
McCain	Y	N	Y	Y	N	Y
ARKANSAS						
Bumpers	N	Y	Y	Y	Y	Y
Pryor	?	?	Y	Y	Y	Y
CALIFORNIA						
Cranston	N	Y	Y	Y	N	Y
Wilson	Y	N	Y	Y	N	Y
COLORADO						
Wirth	N	Y	Y	Y	N	Y
Armstrong	N	N	N	N	Y	Y
CONNECTICUT						
Dodd	N	Y	Y	Y	N	Y
Lieberman	N	Y	Y	Y	N	Y
DELAWARE						
Biden	?	?	Y	Y	N	Y
Roth	N	Y	Y	N	Y	Y
FLORIDA						
Graham	N	Y	Y	Y	N	Y
Mack	N	N	Y	Y	Y	Y
GEORGIA						
Fowler	?	?	Y	Y	Y	Y
Nunn	N	Y	Y	Y	N	Y
HAWAII						
Inouye	N	Y	Y	Y	N	Y
Akaka	Y	N	Y	Y	N	Y
IDAHO						
McClure	N	Y	Y	Y	Y	Y
Symms	Y	N	Y	Y	Y	Y
ILLINOIS						
Dixon	N	Y	Y	Y	N	Y
Simon	Y	N	Y	Y	N	Y
INDIANA						
Coats	N	N	Y	Y	Y	Y
Lugar	N	Y	Y	Y	N	Y
IOWA						
Harkin	Y	N	Y	Y	N	Y
Grassley	Y	N	Y	Y	Y	Y
KANSAS						
Dole	N	N	Y	Y	N	Y
Kassebaum	N	Y	Y	Y	N	Y
KENTUCKY						
Ford	N	Y	Y	Y	Y	Y
McConnell	N	Y	Y	Y	Y	Y
LOUISIANA						
Breaux	N	Y	Y	Y	N	Y
Johnston	N	Y	Y	Y	Y	Y
MAINE						
Mitchell	N	Y	Y	Y	N	Y
Cohen	Y	N	Y	Y	N	Y
MARYLAND						
Mikulski	N	Y	Y	Y	N	Y
Sarbanes	N	Y	Y	Y	N	Y
MASSACHUSETTS						
Kennedy	N	Y	Y	N	N	Y
Kerry	N	Y	Y	Y	N	Y
MICHIGAN						
Levin	N	N	Y	Y	N	Y
Riegle	N	Y	Y	Y	N	Y
MINNESOTA						
Boschwitz	Y	N	Y	Y	Y	Y
Durenberger	Y	N	Y	N	N	Y
MISSISSIPPI						
Cochran	N	Y	Y	Y	Y	Y
Lott	N	Y	Y	Y	Y	Y
MISSOURI						
Bond	N	Y	Y	Y	Y	Y
Danforth	N	Y	Y	Y	N	Y
MONTANA						
Baucus	N	Y	Y	Y	Y	Y
Burns	N	Y	Y	Y	Y	Y
NEBRASKA						
Exon	N	Y	Y	Y	Y	Y
Kerrey	?	?	Y	Y	N	Y
NEVADA						
Bryan	N	Y	Y	Y	N	Y
Reid	N	Y	Y	Y	N	Y
NEW HAMPSHIRE						
Humphrey	Y	N	Y	Y	Y	Y
Rudman	N	Y	Y	Y	Y	Y
NEW JERSEY						
Bradley	N	Y	Y	Y	N	Y
Lautenberg	N	Y	Y	Y	N	Y
NEW MEXICO						
Bingaman	N	?	Y	Y	N	Y
Domenici	N	Y	Y	Y	N	Y
NEW YORK						
Moynihan	N	Y	Y	Y	N	Y
D'Amato	N	Y	Y	Y	Y	Y
NORTH CAROLINA						
Sanford	N	?	Y	Y	N	Y
Helms	Y	N	Y	Y	Y	N
NORTH DAKOTA						
Burdick	N	Y	Y	Y	N	Y
Conrad	N	Y	Y	Y	Y	Y
OHIO						
Glenn	N	Y	Y	Y	N	Y
Metzenbaum	N	N	Y	N	N	Y
OKLAHOMA						
Boren	N	Y	Y	Y	N	Y
Nickles	Y	N	Y	Y	Y	Y
OREGON						
Hatfield	N	Y	Y	N	N	Y
Packwood	N	?	Y	Y	N	Y
PENNSYLVANIA						
Heinz	N	Y	Y	Y	N	Y
Specter	Y	N	Y	Y	N	Y
RHODE ISLAND						
Pell	N	Y	Y	Y	N	Y
Chafee	N	Y	Y	Y	N	Y
SOUTH CAROLINA						
Hollings	N	Y	Y	Y	N	Y
Thurmond	N	N	Y	Y	Y	Y
SOUTH DAKOTA						
Daschle	N	Y	Y	Y	N	Y
Pressler	Y	N	Y	Y	Y	Y
TENNESSEE						
Gore	N	Y	Y	Y	N	Y
Sasser	Y	Y	Y	Y	Y	Y
TEXAS						
Bentsen	N	Y	Y	Y	N	Y
Gramm	N	Y	Y	Y	Y	Y
UTAH						
Garn	N	Y	Y	Y	Y	Y
Hatch	N	N	Y	Y	N	Y
VERMONT						
Leahy	N	N	Y	Y	N	Y
Jeffords	Y	N	Y	Y	N	Y
VIRGINIA						
Robb	N	Y	Y	Y	N	Y
Warner	N	Y	Y	Y	N	Y
WASHINGTON						
Adams	N	Y	Y	Y	N	Y
Gorton	N	Y	Y	Y	N	Y
WEST VIRGINIA						
Byrd	N	Y	Y	Y	Y	Y
Rockefeller	N	Y	Y	Y	N	Y
WISCONSIN						
Kohl	N	Y	Y	Y	N	Y
Kasten	Y	N	Y	Y	Y	Y
WYOMING						
Simpson	?	?	Y	Y	Y	Y
Wallop	-	-	Y	Y	Y	Y

KEY

Y Voted for (yea).
\# Paired for.
\+ Announced for.
N Voted against (nay).
X Paired against.
\- Announced against.
P Voted "present."
C Voted "present" to avoid possible conflict of interest.
? Did not vote or otherwise make a position known.

Democrats ***Republicans***

ND Northern Democrats SD Southern Democrats

Southern states - Ala., Ark., Fla., Ga., Ky., La., Miss., N.C., Okla., S.C., Tenn., Texas, Va.

144. S 2104. Civil Rights Act of 1990/Senate Employees. Grassley, R-Iowa, motion to table (kill) the Ford, D-Ky., amendment to the Ford amendment, to provide Senate employees the rights and protections provided for under the Civil Rights Acts of 1990 and 1964, the Age Discrimination in Employment Act of 1967, the Rehabilitation Act of 1973 and the Americans with Disabilities Act (S 933), and to provide that all claims raised by individuals with respect to violations under such acts shall be investigated and adjudicated by the Select Committee on Ethics. Motion rejected 18-74: R 14-28; D 4-46 (ND 3-32, SD 1-14), July 10, 1990. (The Ford amendment was subsequently adopted by voice vote.)

145. S 2104. Civil Rights Act of 1990/Senate Employees. Rudman, R-N.H., motion to table (kill) the Grassley, R-Iowa, amendment to allow Senate employees who are aggrieved by a violation of the Civil Rights Act of 1964 or the Americans with Disabilities Act (S 933) a private cause of action to be adjudicated in the appropriate district court. Motion agreed to 63-26: R 21-20; D 42-6 (ND 28-6, SD 14-0), July 10, 1990.

146. S 1970. Omnibus Crime Package/S&L Fraud. Wirth, D-Colo., amendment to increase the investigation and prosecution of savings and loan fraud through the establishment of special task forces and other means. Adopted 99-1: R 44-1; D 55-0 (ND 38-0, SD 17-0), July 11, 1990.

147. S 1970. Omnibus Crime Package/Passage. Passage of the bill to ban nine types of assault-style weapons, broaden the general death penalty to include more than 30 additional crimes, allow states to compel faster federal court reviews of death sentences if they provide competent counsel to inmates, and increase the investigation and prosecution of savings and loan fraud. Passed 94-6: R 41-4; D 53-2 (ND 36-2, SD 17-0), July 11, 1990.

148. S 933. Americans with Disabilities Act/Food Handlers. Helms, R-N.C., amendment to the Ford, D-Ky., motion, to instruct the Senate conferees to require the secretary of Health and Human Services to publish an annual list of infectious and communicable diseases — and to include the human immunodeficiency virus (HIV) — that may be transmitted through the food supply and to allow employers to refuse to assign an employee with such a disease to a food handling job. Rejected 39-61: R 27-18; D 12-43 (ND 4-34, SD 8-9), July 11, 1990.

149. S 933. Americans with Disabilities Act/Food Handlers. Hatch, R-Utah, amendment to the Ford, D-Ky., motion, to instruct the conferees to require the secretary of Health and Human Services to publish an annual list of infectious and communicable diseases that may be transmitted through the food supply and to allow employers to refuse to assign an employee with such a disease to a food handling job. Adopted 99-1: R 44-1; D 55-0 (ND 38-0, SD 17-0), July 11, 1990.

KEY

- Y Voted for (yea).
- # Paired for.
- + Announced for.
- N Voted against (nay).
- X Paired against.
- \- Announced against.
- P Voted "present."
- C Voted "present" to avoid possible conflict of interest.
- ? Did not vote or otherwise make a position known.

Democrats *Republicans*

	150	151	152
ALABAMA			
Heflin	Y	Y	Y
Shelby	Y	Y	Y
ALASKA			
Murkowski	N	N	Y
Stevens	N	Y	Y
ARIZONA			
DeConcini	Y	Y	Y
McCain	N	N	Y
ARKANSAS			
Bumpers	Y	Y	Y
Pryor	Y	Y	Y
CALIFORNIA			
Cranston	Y	N	Y
Wilson	N	N	Y
COLORADO			
Wirth	Y	N	Y
Armstrong	N	N	Y
CONNECTICUT			
Dodd	Y	Y	Y
Lieberman	Y	Y	Y
DELAWARE			
Biden	Y	Y	Y
Roth	N	Y	Y
FLORIDA			
Graham	Y	N	Y
Mack	N	N	Y
GEORGIA			
Fowler	Y	Y	Y
Nunn	Y	Y	Y
HAWAII			
Inouye	Y	Y	Y
Akaka	Y	Y	Y
IDAHO			
McClure	Y	?	?
Symms	N	N	N
ILLINOIS			
Dixon	Y	Y	Y
Simon	Y	Y	Y
INDIANA			
Coats	N	N	Y
Lugar	N	N	Y
IOWA			
Harkin	Y	Y	Y
Grassley	N	N	Y
KANSAS			
Dole	N	Y	Y
Kassebaum	N	N	Y
KENTUCKY			
Ford	Y	Y	Y
McConnell	Y	Y	Y
LOUISIANA			
Breaux	Y	Y	Y
Johnston	Y	Y	Y
MAINE			
Mitchell	Y	Y	Y
Cohen	Y	Y	Y
MARYLAND			
Mikulski	Y	Y	Y
Sarbanes	Y	Y	Y
MASSACHUSETTS			
Kennedy	Y	Y	Y
Kerry	Y	Y	Y
MICHIGAN			
Levin	Y	Y	Y
Riegle	Y	Y	Y
MINNESOTA			
Boschwitz	N	N	Y
Durenberger	N	N	Y
MISSISSIPPI			
Cochran	Y	Y	Y
Lott	Y	Y	Y
MISSOURI			
Bond	Y	N	N
Danforth	Y	N	Y
MONTANA			
Baucus	N	Y	Y
Burns	N	N	Y
NEBRASKA			
Exon	Y	Y	Y
Kerrey	N	N	Y
NEVADA			
Bryan	Y	Y	Y
Reid	Y	Y	Y
NEW HAMPSHIRE			
Humphrey	Y	Y	N
Rudman	Y	Y	Y
NEW JERSEY			
Bradley	N	N	Y
Lautenberg	Y	Y	Y
NEW MEXICO			
Bingaman	Y	N	Y
Domenici	Y	Y	Y
NEW YORK			
Moynihan	Y	Y	Y
D'Amato	Y	Y	Y
NORTH CAROLINA			
Sanford	Y	Y	Y
Helms	Y	Y	N
NORTH DAKOTA			
Burdick	Y	Y	Y
Conrad	Y	Y	Y
OHIO			
Glenn	Y	Y	Y
Metzenbaum	Y	Y	Y
OKLAHOMA			
Boren	Y	Y	Y
Nickles	N	N	Y
OREGON			
Hatfield	N	N	Y
Packwood	N	N	Y
PENNSYLVANIA			
Heinz	Y	Y	Y
Specter	Y	Y	Y
RHODE ISLAND			
Pell	Y	Y	Y
Chafee	N	N	Y
SOUTH CAROLINA			
Hollings	Y	Y	Y
Thurmond	Y	Y	Y
SOUTH DAKOTA			
Daschle	Y	Y	Y
Pressler	N	N	Y
TENNESSEE			
Gore	Y	Y	Y
Sasser	N	Y	Y
TEXAS			
Bentsen	Y	Y	Y
Gramm	N	N	Y
UTAH			
Garn	N	Y	N
Hatch	Y	Y	Y
VERMONT			
Leahy	Y	Y	Y
Jeffords	Y	Y	Y
VIRGINIA			
Robb	N	Y	Y
Warner	Y	Y	Y
WASHINGTON			
Adams	N	Y	Y
Gorton	N	N	Y
WEST VIRGINIA			
Byrd	Y	Y	Y
Rockefeller	Y	Y	?
WISCONSIN			
Kohl	Y	Y	Y
Kasten	Y	Y	Y
WYOMING			
Simpson	N	N	+
Wallop	N	N	N

ND Northern Democrats SD Southern Democrats

Southern states - Ala., Ark., Fla., Ga., Ky., La., Miss., N.C., Okla., S.C., Tenn., Texas, Va.

150. HR 4328. Textile Trade Act/Athletic Footwear. Cohen, R-Maine, motion to table (kill) the Packwood, R-Ore., amendment to exempt non-rubber athletic footwear from the bill's footwear quota. Motion agreed to 68-32: R 19-26; D 49-6 (ND 34-4, SD 15-2), July 12, 1990.

151. HR 4328. Textile Trade Act/International Obligations. Hollings, D-S.C., motion to table (kill) the Packwood, R-Ore., amendment to provide the president the discretion to have provisions of the act not apply, if he determines that they violate U.S. international obligations. Motion agreed to 69-30: R 20-24; D 49-6 (ND 33-5, SD 16-1), July 12, 1990.

152. S 933. Americans with Disabilities Act/Conference Report. Adoption of the conference report (thus clearing the measure for the president) on the bill to prohibit discrimination against the disabled in public facilities and employment and to guarantee them access to mass transit and telecommunications services. Adopted 91-6: R 37-6; D 54-0 (ND 37-0, SD 17-0), July 13, 1990. A "yea" was a vote supporting the president's position.

	153	154	155	156	157	158
ALABAMA						
Heflin	Y	Y	Y	Y	Y	Y
Shelby	Y	Y	Y	Y	Y	Y
ALASKA						
Murkowski	Y	Y	N	Y	Y	N
Stevens	Y	Y	Y	Y	Y	N
ARIZONA						
DeConcini	Y	Y	Y	Y	Y	Y
McCain	N	?	N	N	N	N
ARKANSAS						
Bumpers	Y	Y	Y	Y	Y	Y
Pryor	Y	Y	Y	Y	Y	Y
CALIFORNIA						
Cranston	N	Y	N	N	N	Y
Wilson	N	N	N	N	N	N
COLORADO						
Wirth	N	Y	N	N	N	Y
Armstrong	N	N	N	N	N	N
CONNECTICUT						
Dodd	Y	Y	Y	Y	Y	Y
Lieberman	Y	Y	Y	Y	Y	Y
DELAWARE						
Biden	Y	Y	Y	Y	Y	Y
Roth	Y	Y	Y	Y	Y	N
FLORIDA						
Graham	N	Y	Y	Y	N	Y
Mack	N	N	N	N	N	N
GEORGIA						
Fowler	Y	Y	Y	Y	Y	Y
Nunn	Y	Y	Y	Y	Y	Y
HAWAII						
Inouye	Y	Y	Y	Y	Y	Y
Akaka	N	Y	Y	Y	Y	Y
IDAHO						
McClure	?	?	Y	Y	Y	N
Symms	N	N	N	N	N	N
ILLINOIS						
Dixon	Y	Y	Y	Y	Y	Y
Simon	Y	Y	Y	Y	Y	Y
INDIANA						
Coats	N	N	N	N	N	N
Lugar	N	N	N	N	N	N

	153	154	155	156	157	158
IOWA						
Harkin	Y	Y	Y	N	Y	Y
Grassley	Y	N	N	N	N	N
KANSAS						
Dole	Y	Y	N	N	Y	N
Kassebaum	N	N	N	N	N	N
KENTUCKY						
Ford	Y	Y	Y	Y	Y	Y
McConnell	Y	Y	Y	Y	Y	N
LOUISIANA						
Breaux	Y	Y	Y	Y	Y	Y
Johnston	Y	Y	Y	Y	Y	Y
MAINE						
Mitchell	Y	Y	Y	Y	Y	Y
Cohen	Y	Y	Y	Y	Y	Y
MARYLAND						
Mikulski	Y	Y	Y	Y	Y	Y
Sarbanes	Y	Y	Y	Y	Y	Y
MASSACHUSETTS						
Kennedy	Y	Y	Y	Y	Y	Y
Kerry	Y	Y	Y	Y	Y	Y
MICHIGAN						
Levin	Y	Y	Y	Y	Y	Y
Riegle	Y	Y	Y	Y	Y	Y
MINNESOTA						
Boschwitz	N	N	?	N	N	N
Durenberger	N	N	N	N	N	Y
MISSISSIPPI						
Cochran	Y	Y	Y	Y	Y	N
Lott	Y	Y	Y	Y	Y	N
MISSOURI						
Bond	Y	N	Y	N	Y	N
Danforth	N	?	N	N	N	Y
MONTANA						
Baucus	N	N	N	N	N	Y
Burns	N	N	N	N	N	N
NEBRASKA						
Exon	Y	Y	Y	Y	Y	N
Kerrey	Y	Y	Y	Y	Y	Y
NEVADA						
Bryan	Y	Y	Y	Y	Y	Y
Reid	Y	Y	Y	Y	Y	Y

	153	154	155	156	157	158
NEW HAMPSHIRE						
Humphrey	Y	Y	Y	Y	N	N
Rudman	Y	Y	Y	Y	Y	N
NEW JERSEY						
Bradley	N	N	N	N	N	Y
Lautenberg	Y	Y	Y	Y	Y	Y
NEW MEXICO						
Bingaman	N	N	N	N	N	Y
Domenici	Y	Y	Y	N	Y	N
NEW YORK						
Moynihan	Y	Y	Y	Y	Y	Y
D'Amato	Y	Y	Y	Y	Y	N
NORTH CAROLINA						
Sanford	Y	+	Y	Y	Y	Y
Helms	Y	Y	Y	Y	Y	N
NORTH DAKOTA						
Burdick	Y	Y	Y	N	Y	Y
Conrad	Y	Y	Y	N	N	Y
OHIO						
Glenn	N	Y	Y	Y	N	Y
Metzenbaum	Y	Y	Y	Y	Y	Y
OKLAHOMA						
Boren	Y	?	Y	Y	Y	Y
Nickles	N	N	N	N	N	N
OREGON						
Hatfield	N	N	N	N	N	Y
Packwood	N	N	N	N	N	Y
PENNSYLVANIA						
Heinz	Y	Y	Y	Y	Y	Y
Specter	Y	Y	Y	Y	Y	Y
RHODE ISLAND						
Pell	Y	Y	Y	Y	Y	Y
Chafee	N	N	N	N	N	N
SOUTH CAROLINA						
Hollings	Y	Y	Y	Y	Y	Y
Thurmond	Y	Y	Y	Y	Y	N
SOUTH DAKOTA						
Daschle	Y	Y	Y	Y	Y	Y
Pressler	N	N	N	N	N	N
TENNESSEE						
Gore	Y	Y	Y	Y	Y	Y
Sasser	Y	Y	Y	Y	Y	Y

KEY

- Y Voted for (yea).
- # Paired for.
- \+ Announced for.
- N Voted against (nay).
- X Paired against.
- \- Announced against.
- P Voted "present."
- C Voted "present" to avoid possible conflict of interest.
- ? Did not vote or otherwise make a position known.

Democrats ***Republicans***

	153	154	155	156	157	158
TEXAS						
Bentsen	Y	Y	Y	Y	Y	Y
Gramm	N	N	N	N	N	N
UTAH						
Garn	Y	Y	Y	Y	Y	N
Hatch	Y	N	Y	N	Y	N
VERMONT						
Leahy	Y	Y	Y	Y	Y	Y
Jeffords	Y	Y	Y	Y	Y	Y
VIRGINIA						
Robb	Y	Y	Y	Y	Y	Y
Warner	Y	Y	Y	Y	Y	N
WASHINGTON						
Adams	N	N	N	N	N	Y
Gorton	N	N	N	N	N	N
WEST VIRGINIA						
Byrd	Y	Y	Y	Y	Y	Y
Rockefeller	Y	Y	Y	Y	Y	Y
WISCONSIN						
Kohl	Y	Y	Y	Y	Y	Y
Kasten	Y	Y	Y	Y	Y	N
WYOMING						
Simpson	?	?	N	N	N	N
Wallop	N	-	N	N	N	N

ND Northern Democrats SD Southern Democrats

Southern states - Ala., Ark., Fla., Ga., Ky., La., Miss., N.C., Okla., S.C., Tenn., Texas, Va.

153. HR 4328. Textile Trade Act/GATT. Thurmond, R-S.C., motion to table (kill) the Gorton, R-Wash., substitute amendment to express strong support for the negotiations at the Uruguay Round of the General Agreement on Tariffs and Trade (GATT) and recognize the undesirability of legislation that would jeopardize its successful conclusion. Motion agreed to 69-29: R 23-20; D 46-9 (ND 30-8, SD 16-1), July 13, 1990.

154. HR 4328. Textile Trade Act/Suspension. Thurmond, R-S.C., motion to table (kill) the Gramm, R-Texas, amendment to allow the president to suspend provisions of the act if the secretary of Labor determines that implementation will cause or has caused a 5 percent or greater increase in the cost of textiles and apparel for lower- and middle-income Americans. Motion agreed to 69-24: R 20-20; D 49-4 (ND 34-4, SD 15-0), July 13, 1990..

155. HR 4328. Textile Trade Act/Consumer Costs. Hollings, D-S.C., motion to table (kill) the Wilson, R-Calif., amendment to require the secretary of Commerce to submit a report to Congress on the increased cost to consumers of products affected by this act and to provide that the quotas in the act shall not apply if the president certifies that the increased cost to consumers for products affected under the act totals more than $1 billion a year. Motion agreed to 70-29: R 21-23; D 49-6 (ND 32-6, SD 17-0), July 17, 1990.

156. HR 4328. Textile Trade Act/Farm Products. Thurmond, R-S.C., motion to table (kill) the Gorton, R-Wash., amendment to eliminate the bill's 1 percent annual growth limit on textile, apparel and footwear imports for nations that increase their purchases of U.S. agricultural goods, granting these nations higher textile quotas equivalent to half their increased purchases of U.S. agricultural goods. Motion agreed to 65-35: R 19-26; D 46-9 (ND 29-9, SD 17-0), July 17, 1990.

157. HR 4328. Textile Trade Act/Passage. Passage of the bill to limit growth in imports of textiles, textile products and non-rubber footwear to 1 percent annually. Passed 68-32: R 22-23; D 46-9 (ND 30-8, SD 16-1), July 17, 1990. A "nay" was a vote supporting the president's position.

158. S 2104. Civil Rights Act of 1990/Cloture. Mitchell, D-Maine, motion to invoke cloture (thus limiting debate) on the Kennedy, D-Mass., substitute amendment to reverse or modify six 1989 Supreme Court decisions that narrowed the reach and remedies of job discrimination laws and to authorize monetary damages under Title VII of the 1964 Civil Rights Act. Motion agreed to 62-38: R 8-37; D 54-1 (ND 37-1, SD 17-0), July 17, 1990. A three-fifths majority vote (60) of the total Senate is required to invoke cloture.

	159	160	161	162
ALABAMA				
Heflin	Y	Y	Y	Y
Shelby	Y	Y	Y	Y
ALASKA				
Murkowski	N	N	N	N
Stevens	N	N	N	N
ARIZONA				
DeConcini	N	Y	Y	Y
McCain	N	N	N	Y
ARKANSAS				
Bumpers	Y	Y	Y	Y
Pryor	Y	Y	Y	Y
CALIFORNIA				
Cranston	Y	Y	Y	Y
Wilson	N	N	N	Y
COLORADO				
Wirth	Y	Y	Y	Y
Armstrong	N	?	?	?
CONNECTICUT				
Dodd	Y	Y	Y	N
Lieberman	Y	Y	Y	N
DELAWARE				
Biden	Y	Y	Y	Y
Roth	N	N	N	Y
FLORIDA				
Graham	Y	Y	Y	Y
Mack	N	N	N	Y
GEORGIA				
Fowler	Y	Y	Y	Y
Nunn	Y	Y	Y	Y
HAWAII				
Inouye	Y	Y	Y	Y
Akaka	Y	Y	Y	Y
IDAHO				
McClure	N	N	N	N
Symms	N	N	N	+
ILLINOIS				
Dixon	Y	Y	Y	Y
Simon	Y	Y	Y	Y
INDIANA				
Coats	N	N	N	Y
Lugar	N	N	N	Y
IOWA				
Harkin	Y	Y	Y	Y
Grassley	N	N	N	Y
KANSAS				
Dole	N	N	N	Y
Kassebaum	N	N	N	Y
KENTUCKY				
Ford	Y	Y	Y	Y
McConnell	N	N	N	Y
LOUISIANA				
Breaux	Y	Y	Y	Y
Johnston	Y	Y	Y	Y
MAINE				
Mitchell	Y	Y	Y	N
Cohen	Y	Y	Y	N
MARYLAND				
Mikulski	Y	Y	Y	N
Sarbanes	Y	Y	Y	N
MASSACHUSETTS				
Kennedy	Y	Y	Y	N
Kerry	Y	Y	Y	N
MICHIGAN				
Levin	Y	Y	Y	Y
Riegle	Y	Y	Y	Y
MINNESOTA				
Boschwitz	N	N	N	Y
Durenberger	Y	Y	Y	Y
MISSISSIPPI				
Cochran	N	N	N	Y
Lott	N	N	N	Y
MISSOURI				
Bond	N	N	N	Y
Danforth	Y	Y	Y	Y
MONTANA				
Baucus	Y	Y	Y	Y
Burns	N	N	N	?
NEBRASKA				
Exon	N	Y	Y	Y
Kerrey	Y	Y	Y	Y
NEVADA				
Bryan	N	Y	Y	N
Reid	Y	Y	Y	N
NEW HAMPSHIRE				
Humphrey	N	N	N	N
Rudman	N	N	N	N
NEW JERSEY				
Bradley	Y	Y	Y	N
Lautenberg	Y	Y	Y	N
NEW MEXICO				
Bingaman	Y	Y	Y	Y
Domenici	N	Y	Y	Y
NEW YORK				
Moynihan	Y	Y	Y	?
D'Amato	N	N	N	N
NORTH CAROLINA				
Sanford	Y	Y	Y	Y
Helms	N	N	N	Y
NORTH DAKOTA				
Burdick	Y	Y	Y	Y
Conrad	Y	Y	Y	Y
OHIO				
Glenn	Y	Y	Y	Y
Metzenbaum	Y	Y	Y	N
OKLAHOMA				
Boren	N	Y	Y	Y
Nickles	N	N	N	Y
OREGON				
Hatfield	Y	Y	Y	Y
Packwood	Y	Y	Y	Y
PENNSYLVANIA				
Heinz	Y	Y	Y	N
Specter	Y	Y	Y	N
RHODE ISLAND				
Pell	Y	Y	Y	N
Chafee	Y	Y	Y	N
SOUTH CAROLINA				
Hollings	Y	Y	Y	Y
Thurmond	N	N	N	Y
SOUTH DAKOTA				
Daschle	Y	Y	Y	Y
Pressler	N	N	N	Y
TENNESSEE				
Gore	Y	Y	Y	Y
Sasser	Y	Y	Y	Y
TEXAS				
Bentsen	Y	Y	Y	Y
Gramm	N	N	N	Y
UTAH				
Garn	N	N	N	N
Hatch	N	N	N	N
VERMONT				
Leahy	Y	Y	Y	N
Jeffords	Y	Y	Y	Y
VIRGINIA				
Robb	Y	Y	Y	Y
Warner	N	N	N	Y
WASHINGTON				
Adams	Y	Y	Y	Y
Gorton	N	N	N	Y
WEST VIRGINIA				
Byrd	Y	Y	Y	N
Rockefeller	Y	Y	Y	N
WISCONSIN				
Kohl	Y	Y	Y	Y
Kasten	N	N	N	N
WYOMING				
Simpson	N	N	N	N
Wallop	N	N	N	Y

KEY

- Y Voted for (yea).
- # Paired for.
- + Announced for.
- N Voted against (nay).
- X Paired against.
- - Announced against.
- P Voted "present."
- C Voted "present" to avoid possible conflict of interest.
- ? Did not vote or otherwise make a position known.

Democrats *Republicans*

ND Northern Democrats SD Southern Democrats

Southern states - Ala., Ark., Fla., Ga., Ky., La., Miss., N.C., Okla., S.C., Tenn., Texas, Va.

159. S 2104. Civil Rights Act of 1990/Due Process. Kennedy, D-Mass., amendment to the Hatch, R-Utah, amendment, to allow for challenges to the finality of court orders to resolve job discrimination claims. Adopted 60-40: R 9-36; D 51-4 (ND 35-3, SD 16-1), July 17, 1990.

160. S 2104. Civil Rights Act of 1990/Quotas. Kennedy, D-Mass., amendment to the Kennedy substitute amendment, to modify the burden for employers in "disparate impact" cases, to include language stating that the bill does not require quotas and to clarify that punitive and compensatory damages would not be allowed in disparate impact cases. Adopted 65-34: R 10-34; D 55-0 (ND 38-0, SD 17-0), July 18, 1990.

161. S 2104. Civil Rights Act of 1990/Passage. Passage of the bill to reverse or modify six recent Supreme Court decisions that narrowed the reach and remedies of job discrimination laws and to authorize monetary damages under Title VII of the 1964 Civil Rights Act. Passed 65-34: R 10-34; D 55-0 (ND 38-0, SD 17-0), July 18, 1990. A "nay" was a vote supporting the president's position.

162. S 2830. Farm Programs Reauthorization/Nutrition Programs. Pryor, D-Ark., motion to table (kill) the Reid, D-Nev., amendment to state that it is the sense of the Senate that federal nutrition programs are important elements of U.S. food and agriculture policy and should be authorized at levels that meet national needs. An underlying Reid amendment was killed as well when the Reid amendment was tabled. That amendment would have excluded people with gross sales of agricultural commodities of more than $500,000 a year from receiving payments for a commodity under programs established by the Agricultural Act of 1949. Motion agreed to 66-30: R 28-14; D 38-16 (ND 21-16, SD 17-0), July 19, 1990.

	163	164	165	166	167	168	169
ALABAMA							
Heflin	N	N	Y	Y	N	Y	Y
Shelby	N	N	Y	Y	N	Y	Y
ALASKA							
Murkowski	Y	Y	Y	N	Y	N	Y
Stevens	Y	Y	N	Y	Y	N	Y
ARIZONA							
DeConcini	N	N	N	Y	N	Y	Y
McCain	Y	Y	Y	N	Y	N	N
ARKANSAS							
Bumpers	N	N	Y	Y	N	Y	Y
Pryor	N	N	Y	Y	N	Y	Y
CALIFORNIA							
Cranston	N	?	?	Y	N	Y	Y
Wilson	?	?	?	Y	Y	N	Y
COLORADO							
Wirth	N	N	N	Y	N	N	Y
Armstrong	Y	Y	Y	N	Y	N	N
CONNECTICUT							
Dodd	N	N	N	Y	N	N	Y
Lieberman	N	N	N	N	N	Y	Y
DELAWARE							
Biden	Y	N	N	N	N	N	Y
Roth	Y	N	N	N	Y	N	N
FLORIDA							
Graham	N	N	N	Y	N	Y	Y
Mack	Y	Y	Y	Y	Y	Y	Y
GEORGIA							
Fowler	N	N	N	Y	N	Y	Y
Nunn	?	N	?	N	N	N	Y
HAWAII							
Inouye	N	N	N	Y	N	Y	Y
Akaka	N	N	N	Y	N	Y	Y
IDAHO							
McClure	Y	Y	Y	Y	Y	Y	N
Symms	?	Y	Y	Y	Y	Y	N
ILLINOIS							
Dixon	Y	N	Y	Y	N	N	Y
Simon	N	N	Y	Y	N	N	Y
INDIANA							
Coats	Y	Y	Y	N	N	N	N
Lugar	Y	Y	Y	N	N	N	N
IOWA							
Harkin	N	N	Y	Y	N	Y	N
Grassley	Y	Y	Y	N	N	Y	N
KANSAS							
Dole	Y	Y	Y	N	Y	N	N
Kassebaum	Y	N	Y	N	N	N	N
KENTUCKY							
Ford	N	N	Y	Y	N	Y	Y
McConnell	Y	Y	Y	N	N	N	N
LOUISIANA							
Breaux	N	N	Y	Y	N	Y	Y
Johnston	?	?	?	Y	N	Y	Y
MAINE							
Mitchell	N	N	N	N	N	N	Y
Cohen	Y	Y	N	N	Y	N	Y
MARYLAND							
Mikulski	?	?	?	Y	N	Y	Y
Sarbanes	N	N	N	N	N	N	Y
MASSACHUSETTS							
Kennedy	N	N	Y	N	N	N	+
Kerry	N	N	Y	N	N	N	Y
MICHIGAN							
Levin	N	N	N	Y	N	N	Y
Riegle	?	N	Y	Y	N	Y	Y
MINNESOTA							
Boschwitz	Y	Y	Y	Y	Y	Y	N
Durenberger	Y	Y	Y	Y	Y	Y	N
MISSISSIPPI							
Cochran	Y	Y	Y	Y	N	Y	Y
Lott	Y	Y	Y	Y	N	Y	Y
MISSOURI							
Bond	Y	Y	Y	N	Y	Y	N
Danforth	Y	Y	Y	N	Y	N	N
MONTANA							
Baucus	?	N	Y	Y	N	Y	N
Burns	?	Y	Y	Y	N	Y	N
NEBRASKA							
Exon	N	N	Y	Y	N	Y	N
Kerrey	N	N	Y	Y	N	Y	N
NEVADA							
Bryan	N	N	N	N	N	N	Y
Reid	N	N	N	N	N	N	Y
NEW HAMPSHIRE							
Humphrey	Y	N	N	N	Y	N	N
Rudman	N	N	Y	N	Y	N	N
NEW JERSEY							
Bradley	N	N	N	N	Y	N	Y
Lautenberg	N	N	N	N	Y	N	Y
NEW MEXICO							
Bingaman	N	N	N	N	N	N	Y
Domenici	Y	Y	Y	N	Y	Y	N
NEW YORK							
Moynihan	?	N	N	N	N	N	Y
D'Amato	Y	N	Y	Y	Y	N	?
NORTH CAROLINA							
Sanford	N	Y	Y	Y	N	Y	Y
Helms	Y	Y	Y	Y	Y	N	N
NORTH DAKOTA							
Burdick	N	N	Y	Y	N	Y	Y
Conrad	N	N	Y	Y	N	Y	N
OHIO							
Glenn	N	N	Y	N	N	N	Y
Metzenbaum	N	N	Y	N	N	N	Y
OKLAHOMA							
Boren	N	N	Y	Y	N	Y	N
Nickles	?	Y	Y	N	Y	N	N
OREGON							
Hatfield	Y	N	Y	N	N	N	Y
Packwood	Y	Y	Y	N	N	N	Y
PENNSYLVANIA							
Heinz	?	N	N	N	Y	N	Y
Specter	Y	Y	N	N	?	N	Y
RHODE ISLAND							
Pell	N	-	?	N	N	N	Y
Chafee	Y	N	Y	N	Y	N	N
SOUTH CAROLINA							
Hollings	N	N	Y	Y	N	Y	Y
Thurmond	Y	Y	Y	Y	N	N	N
SOUTH DAKOTA							
Daschle	N	N	Y	Y	N	Y	Y
Pressler	N	?	?	?	?	?	?
TENNESSEE							
Gore	N	N	Y	Y	N	Y	Y
Sasser	N	Y	N	Y	N	Y	Y
TEXAS							
Bentsen	N	N	Y	Y	N	N	Y
Gramm	Y	Y	Y	Y	Y	N	N
UTAH							
Garn	Y	?	?	?	?	?	?
Hatch	Y	Y	Y	Y	Y	N	N
VERMONT							
Leahy	N	N	Y	Y	N	Y	Y
Jeffords	Y	N	N	N	N	N	Y
VIRGINIA							
Robb	N	N	Y	N	N	N	Y
Warner	Y	N	Y	N	Y	N	Y
WASHINGTON							
Adams	N	N	N	Y	N	Y	Y
Gorton	N	Y	Y	N	Y	N	Y
WEST VIRGINIA							
Byrd	N	N	N	Y	N	Y	Y
Rockefeller	N	N	Y	Y	N	Y	Y
WISCONSIN							
Kohl	N	N	N	N	N	Y	Y
Kasten	Y	N	Y	N	Y	N	N
WYOMING							
Simpson	?	+	+	Y	Y	Y	N
Wallop	+	Y	Y	Y	Y	Y	N

KEY

- Y Voted for (yea).
- # Paired for.
- + Announced for.
- N Voted against (nay).
- X Paired against.
- - Announced against.
- P Voted "present."
- C Voted "present" to avoid possible conflict of interest.
- ? Did not vote or otherwise make a position known.

Democrats ***Republicans***

ND Northern Democrats SD Southern Democrats

Southern states - Ala., Ark., Fla., Ga., Ky., La., Miss., N.C., Okla., S.C., Tenn., Texas, Va.

163. S 2830. Farm Programs Reauthorization/Wheat and Feed Grains. Boschwitz, R-Minn., amendment to modify the acreage reduction requirements for wheat and feed grains that are triggered by carry-over stocks. Rejected 37-50: R 35-3; D 2-47 (ND 2-32, SD 0-15), July 20, 1990.

164. S 2830. Farm Programs Reauthorization/New Program. Grassley, R-Iowa, amendment to provide an alternative to the committee approach to establish a sustainable Agricultural Research and Education Program, emphasizing sustainability and de-emphasizing eliminating chemical use. Proponents argued that the amendment would do this by simplifying and removing unnecessary requirements in low-input research. Opponents argued that the amendment would weaken the bill by eliminating an emphasis on reduced chemical usage, a state/federal grant matching program, a requirement for the development of a technical guide, an Extension Service training program to advise farmers on low-input methods and a biotechnology authorization for risk assessment. Rejected 32-60: R 30-11; D 2-49 (ND 0-35, SD 2-14), July 23, 1990.

165. S 2830. Farm Programs Reauthorization/Toxic Substances in Feed. Lugar, R-Ind., motion to table (kill) the Reid, D-Nev., amendment to ban federal agencies from accepting the results of the LD-50 test, in which highly toxic substances were fed to a group of animals until 50 percent of the test group died, and the Draize eye irritancy tests, in which high concentrations of a toxic substance were squirted into the eyes of rabbits. Motion agreed to 62-29: R 34-7; D 28-22 (ND 16-19, SD 12-3), July 23, 1990.

166. S 2830. Farm Programs Reauthorization/Sugar Price Supports. Akaka, D-Hawaii, motion to table (kill) the Bradley, D-N.J., amendment to extend the current sugar program for five years and lower the sugar price-support program loan rate from 18 cents per pound to 16 cents per pound. Motion agreed to 54-44: R 17-26; D 37-18 (ND 22-16, SD 15-2), July 24, 1990.

167. S 2830. Farm Programs Reauthorization/Wheat Grains. Boschwitz, R-Minn., amendment to continue the formula of the 1985 farm bill for the loan and purchase authority for wheat and feed grains. The intent of the amendment is to keep the bill in a market-oriented direction by eliminating the floor on loan rates. Rejected 32-65: R 30-12; D 2-53 (ND 2-36, SD 0-17), July 24, 1990.

168. S 2830. Farm Programs Reauthorization/Honey Price Supports. Daschle, D-S.D., motion to table (kill) the Chafee, R-R.I., amendment to provide that the price of honey be supported through loans, purchases or other operations at levels determined appropriate by the secretary of Agriculture for fiscal 1991-94, but that beginning in 1995 the crop of honey shall not receive such supports. The amendment would also require the secretary to give priority attention to the funding of research regarding diseases affecting honeybees. Rejected 46-52: R 13-30; D 33-22 (ND 19-19, SD 14-3), July 24, 1990. (The Chafee amendment was subsequently adopted by voice vote.)

169. S 2830. Farm Programs Reauthorization/Cargo Preference. Breaux, D-La., motion to table (kill) the Symms, R-Idaho, amendment to allow cargo preference requirements to be lifted if it is determined that they would prevent completing an agricultural export sale from the United States. Motion agreed to 62-34: R 14-28; D 48-6 (ND 32-5, SD 16-1), July 24, 1990.

SENATE VOTES 170, 171, 172, 173, 174, 175

	170	171	172	173	174	175
ALABAMA						
Heflin	N	Y	Y	Y	Y	Y
Shelby	N	Y	Y	Y	Y	Y
ALASKA						
Murkowski	N	N	N	Y	Y	Y
Stevens	N	N	N	Y	Y	Y
ARIZONA						
DeConcini	N	Y	N	Y	Y	Y
McCain	N	N	N	N	Y	Y
ARKANSAS						
Bumpers	N	Y	Y	Y	Y	Y
Pryor	N	Y	Y	Y	Y	Y
CALIFORNIA						
Cranston	N	Y	N	Y	Y	Y
Wilson	N	Y	N	N	Y	Y
COLORADO						
Wirth	Y	Y	Y	N	Y	Y
Armstrong	N	N	N	N	Y	Y
CONNECTICUT						
Dodd	N	Y	N	N	Y	Y
Lieberman	Y	Y	N	N	Y	Y
DELAWARE						
Biden	Y	Y	N	N	Y	Y
Roth	N	Y	N	N	Y	Y
FLORIDA						
Graham	N	Y	N	Y	Y	Y
Mack	N	Y	N	Y	Y	Y
GEORGIA						
Fowler	Y	Y	Y	Y	Y	Y
Nunn	N	Y	N	Y	Y	Y
HAWAII						
Inouye	N	Y	N	Y	Y	Y
Akaka	Y	Y	N	Y	Y	Y
IDAHO						
McClure	N	Y	N	Y	Y	Y
Symms	N	Y	N	Y	Y	Y
ILLINOIS						
Dixon	N	N	N	N	Y	Y
Simon	Y	N	N	Y	Y	Y
INDIANA						
Coats	N	N	N	N	Y	Y
Lugar	N	N	N	N	Y	Y
IOWA						
Harkin	Y	Y	Y	Y	Y	Y
Grassley	N	N	Y	N	Y	Y
KANSAS						
Dole	N	N	N	Y	Y	Y
Kassebaum	N	N	N	N	Y	Y
KENTUCKY						
Ford	N	Y	Y	Y	Y	Y
McConnell	N	N	N	Y	Y	Y
LOUISIANA						
Breaux	N	Y	Y	Y	Y	Y
Johnston	N	Y	Y	Y	Y	Y
MAINE						
Mitchell	Y	Y	Y	N	Y	Y
Cohen	N	Y	N	N	Y	Y
MARYLAND						
Mikulski	N	?	N	Y	Y	Y
Sarbanes	N	Y	N	N	Y	Y
MASSACHUSETTS						
Kennedy	?	?	N	N	Y	Y
Kerry	Y	Y	N	N	Y	Y
MICHIGAN						
Levin	Y	Y	N	N	Y	Y
Riegle	Y	Y	N	N	Y	Y
MINNESOTA						
Boschwitz	N	N	N	Y	Y	P
Durenberger	N	N	N	N	Y	P
MISSISSIPPI						
Cochran	N	Y	N	Y	Y	Y
Lott	N	Y	N	Y	Y	Y
MISSOURI						
Bond	N	N	N	Y	Y	Y
Danforth	N	N	N	N	Y	Y
MONTANA						
Baucus	N	Y	Y	Y	Y	Y
Burns	N	Y	Y	Y	Y	Y
NEBRASKA						
Exon	N	Y	Y	Y	Y	Y
Kerrey	N	Y	Y	Y	Y	Y
NEVADA						
Bryan	Y	Y	N	Y	Y	Y
Reid	Y	Y	N	N	Y	Y
NEW HAMPSHIRE						
Humphrey	N	N	N	N	Y	Y
Rudman	N	N	N	N	Y	Y
NEW JERSEY						
Bradley	N	Y	N	N	Y	Y
Lautenberg	Y	Y	N	N	Y	Y
NEW MEXICO						
Bingaman	Y	Y	N	Y	Y	Y
Domenici	N	Y	N	Y	Y	Y
NEW YORK						
Moynihan	N	Y	N	N	Y	Y
D'Amato	?	N	N	N	Y	Y
NORTH CAROLINA						
Sanford	N	Y	Y	Y	Y	Y
Helms	N	Y	N	Y	Y	Y
NORTH DAKOTA						
Burdick	Y	Y	Y	Y	Y	Y
Conrad	Y	Y	Y	Y	Y	Y
OHIO						
Glenn	Y	Y	N	Y	Y	Y
Metzenbaum	Y	Y	N	N	Y	Y
OKLAHOMA						
Boren	N	Y	Y	Y	Y	Y
Nickles	N	N	N	Y	Y	Y
OREGON						
Hatfield	N	Y	N	N	Y	Y
Packwood	N	Y	N	N	Y	Y
PENNSYLVANIA						
Heinz	N	Y	N	N	Y	Y
Specter	N	N	N	N	Y	Y
RHODE ISLAND						
Pell	Y	Y	N	N	Y	Y
Chafee	N	N	N	N	Y	Y
SOUTH CAROLINA						
Hollings	Y	Y	N	Y	Y	Y
Thurmond	N	N	N	Y	Y	Y
SOUTH DAKOTA						
Daschle	Y	Y	Y	Y	Y	Y
Pressler	?	?	?	?	?	+
TENNESSEE						
Gore	N	Y	N	Y	Y	Y
Sasser	N	N	Y	Y	Y	Y
TEXAS						
Bentsen	N	Y	Y	Y	Y	Y
Gramm	N	Y	N	Y	N	Y
UTAH						
Garn	?	?	N	N	Y	Y
Hatch	N	N	N	Y	Y	Y
VERMONT						
Leahy	N	Y	N	Y	Y	Y
Jeffords	N	N	Y	Y	Y	Y
VIRGINIA						
Robb	N	Y	N	Y	Y	Y
Warner	N	Y	N	Y	Y	Y
WASHINGTON						
Adams	N	Y	N	N	Y	Y
Gorton	N	Y	N	N	Y	Y
WEST VIRGINIA						
Byrd	N	Y	N	Y	Y	Y
Rockefeller	Y	Y	N	Y	Y	Y
WISCONSIN						
Kohl	Y	N	Y	Y	Y	Y
Kasten	N	N	Y	N	Y	Y
WYOMING						
Simpson	N	N	N	N	Y	Y
Wallop	N	N	-	+	?	+

KEY

- Y Voted for (yea).
- # Paired for.
- + Announced for.
- N Voted against (nay).
- X Paired against.
- \- Announced against.
- P Voted "present."
- C Voted "present" to avoid possible conflict of interest.
- ? Did not vote or otherwise make a position known.

Democrats *Republicans*

ND Northern Democrats SD Southern Democrats

Southern states - Ala., Ark., Fla., Ga., Ky., La., Miss., N.C., Okla., S.C., Tenn., Texas, Va.

170. S 2830. Farm Programs Reauthorization/Limitation Requirements. Daschle, D-S.D., amendment to strengthen deficiency payments and acreage limitation requirements for wheat and feed grains. Rejected 24-72: R 0-42; D 24-30 (ND 22-15, SD 2-15), July 24, 1990.

171. S 2830. Farm Programs Reauthorization/Planting Program. Leahy, D-Vt., motion to table (kill) the Grassley, R-Iowa, amendment to provide for additional flexibility in the planting program of crops, oilseed or other crops on reduced acreage. Motion agreed to 66-30: R 17-26; D 49-4 (ND 33-3, SD 16-1), July 24, 1990.

172. S 2830. Farm Programs Reauthorization/Price Supports, Deficiency Payments. Baucus, D-Mont., amendment to modify the method of calculating the support price for milk and deficiency payments for wheat, feed grains, upland cotton and rice. Rejected 26-72: R 4-39; D 22-33 (ND 10-28, SD 12-5), July 25, 1990.

173. S 2830. Farm Programs Reauthorization/Peanut Price Supports. Warner, R-Va., motion to table (kill) the Roth, R-Del., amendment to eliminate the peanut price-support system. Motion agreed to 57-41: R 20-23; D 37-18 (ND 20-18, SD 17-0), July 25, 1990.

174. Procedural Motion. Mitchell, D-Maine, motion to instruct the sergeant-at-arms to request the attendance of absent senators. Motion agreed to 97-1: R 42-1; D 55-0 (ND 38-0, SD 17-0), July 25, 1990.

175. S Res 311. Denouncement of Sen. Durenberger/Adoption. Adoption of the resolution to denounce Sen. Dave Durenberger, R-Minn., for knowingly and willingly engaging in unethical conduct by setting up a book deal with Piranha Press that violated Senate limits on honoraria, receiving Senate reimbursement for stays in his Minneapolis condominium, converting campaign contributions to personal use and accepting prohibited gifts, actions that clearly and unequivocally violated statutes, rules and Senate standards. Adopted 96-0: R 41-0; D 55-0 (ND 38-0, SD 17-0), July 25, 1990.

	176	177
ALABAMA		
Heflin	N	Y
Shelby	N	Y
ALASKA		
Murkowski	Y	Y
Stevens	Y	X
ARIZONA		
DeConcini	N	N
McCain	Y	Y
ARKANSAS		
Bumpers	N	Y
Pryor	N	Y
CALIFORNIA		
Cranston	N	N
Wilson	Y	Y
COLORADO		
Wirth	N	N
Armstrong	?	?
CONNECTICUT		
Dodd	N	N
Lieberman	N	N
DELAWARE		
Biden	N	N
Roth	Y	Y
FLORIDA		
Graham	N	Y
Mack	Y	Y
GEORGIA		
Fowler	N	N
Nunn	N	Y
HAWAII		
Inouye	N	N
Akaka	N	N
IDAHO		
McClure	N	Y
Symms	Y	Y
ILLINOIS		
Dixon	N	N
Simon	N	N
INDIANA		
Coats	Y	N
Lugar	Y	N

	176	177
IOWA		
Harkin	N	N
Grassley	Y	N
KANSAS		
Dole	Y	N
Kassebaum	Y	Y
KENTUCKY		
Ford	N	N
McConnell	Y	Y
LOUISIANA		
Breaux	N	Y
Johnston	N	Y
MAINE		
Mitchell	N	N
Cohen	Y	Y
MARYLAND		
Mikulski	N	N
Sarbanes	N	N
MASSACHUSETTS		
Kennedy	N	N
Kerry	N	N
MICHIGAN		
Levin	N	N
Riegle	N	N
MINNESOTA		
Boschwitz	Y	N
Durenberger	?	-
MISSISSIPPI		
Cochran	Y	Y
Lott	N	Y
MISSOURI		
Bond	Y	Y
Danforth	Y	Y
MONTANA		
Baucus	N	N
Burns	N	Y
NEBRASKA		
Exon	N	N
Kerrey	N	N
NEVADA		
Bryan	N	N
Reid	N	N

	176	177
NEW HAMPSHIRE		
Humphrey	Y	Y
Rudman	Y	Y
NEW JERSEY		
Bradley	Y	N
Lautenberg	Y	Y
NEW MEXICO		
Bingaman	N	N
Domenici	Y	Y
NEW YORK		
Moynihan	Y	N
D'Amato	Y	N
NORTH CAROLINA		
Sanford	N	N
Helms	Y	Y
NORTH DAKOTA		
Burdick	N	Y
Conrad	N	N
OHIO		
Glenn	N	N
Metzenbaum	N	N
OKLAHOMA		
Boren	N	Y
Nickles	Y	Y
OREGON		
Hatfield	Y	Y
Packwood	Y	Y
PENNSYLVANIA		
Heinz	Y	N
Specter	Y	N
RHODE ISLAND		
Pell	N	N
Chafee	Y	Y
SOUTH CAROLINA		
Hollings	N	N
Thurmond	Y	Y
SOUTH DAKOTA		
Daschle	N	N
Pressler	N	N
TENNESSEE		
Gore	N	Y
Sasser	N	Y

KEY

- Y Voted for (yea).
- # Paired for.
- \+ Announced for.
- N Voted against (nay).
- X Paired against.
- \- Announced against.
- P Voted "present."
- C Voted "present" to avoid possible conflict of interest.
- ? Did not vote or otherwise make a position known.

Democrats ***Republicans***

	176	177
TEXAS		
Bentsen	N	Y
Gramm	Y	Y
UTAH		
Garn	Y	Y
Hatch	Y	Y
VERMONT		
Leahy	N	N
Jeffords	Y	Y
VIRGINIA		
Robb	Y	Y
Warner	Y	Y
WASHINGTON		
Adams	N	N
Gorton	Y	Y
WEST VIRGINIA		
Byrd	N	N
Rockefeller	N	N
WISCONSIN		
Kohl	N	N
Kasten	Y	N
WYOMING		
Simpson	Y	Y
Wallop	+	#

ND Northern Democrats SD Southern Democrats

Southern states - Ala., Ark., Fla., Ga., Ky., La., Miss., N.C., Okla., S.C., Tenn., Texas, Va.

176. S 2830. Farm Programs Reauthorization/Federal Crop Insurance. Bond, R-Mo., motion to table (kill) the Daschle, D-S.D., amendment to the Bond amendment to improve the operations of the federal crop insurance program. Motion rejected 42-55: R 38-4; D 4-51 (ND 3-35, SD 1-16), July 26, 1990. The Bond amendment was subsequently adopted by voice vote.

177. S 2830. Farm Programs Reauthorization/Cargo Preference. Cochran, R-Miss., motion to table (kill) the Glenn, D-Ohio, amendment to exempt certain U.S. Great Lakes vessels from the cargo preference requirements and provide for the phase-out of the Great Lakes set-aside. Motion rejected 46-50: R 31-10; D 15-40 (ND 2-36, SD 13-4), July 26, 1990.

	178	179	180	181	182	183	184	185
ALABAMA								
Heflin	Y	Y	N	Y	Y	Y	N	N
Shelby	Y	Y	Y	Y	Y	Y	N	N
ALASKA								
Murkowski	Y	Y	Y	Y	N	N	Y	Y
Stevens	Y	Y	Y	Y	N	Y	N	N
ARIZONA								
DeConcini	N	Y	Y	Y	N	Y	N	N
McCain	Y	Y	Y	Y	N	N	N	N
ARKANSAS								
Bumpers	Y	N	N	N	N	Y	N	N
Pryor	Y	N	N	N	N	Y	N	N
CALIFORNIA								
Cranston	N	Y	Y	Y	Y	Y	N	N
Wilson	Y	Y	Y	Y	Y	N	N	N
COLORADO								
Wirth	N	Y	Y	Y	Y	N	N	N
Armstrong	?	?	?	?	?	?	?	?
CONNECTICUT								
Dodd	N	Y	Y	Y	Y	N	Y	Y
Lieberman	Y	Y	Y	Y	Y	N	Y	Y
DELAWARE								
Biden	Y	Y	N	Y	Y	N	Y	Y
Roth	Y	Y	N	Y	N	N	Y	Y
FLORIDA								
Graham	Y	Y	Y	Y	Y	Y	N	N
Mack	Y	Y	Y	Y	N	Y	N	N
GEORGIA								
Fowler	N	Y	Y	Y	Y	Y	N	N
Nunn	N	Y	Y	Y	Y	N	N	N
HAWAII								
Inouye	Y	Y	Y	Y	Y	N	N	N
Akaka	Y	Y	Y	Y	Y	N	N	N
IDAHO								
McClure	Y	N	N	N	N	Y	N	Y
Symms	Y	Y	N	Y	N	Y	N	Y
ILLINOIS								
Dixon	Y	Y	N	Y	Y	N	Y	N
Simon	N	Y	N	Y	Y	N	N	N
INDIANA								
Coats	Y	N	N	Y	N	N	N	N
Lugar	Y	N	N	Y	N	N	Y	Y
IOWA								
Harkin	Y	Y	N	Y	N	Y	Y	N
Grassley	Y	Y	N	Y	N	Y	N	N
KANSAS								
Dole	Y	N	N	Y	N	Y	N	Y
Kassebaum	Y	Y	Y	Y	N	Y	N	N
KENTUCKY								
Ford	Y	Y	Y	Y	Y	N	N	N
McConnell	Y	Y	N	Y	N	N	N	N
LOUISIANA								
Breaux	N	N	N	N	N	N	N	N
Johnston	?	?	?	?	?	?	?	?
MAINE								
Mitchell	N	Y	Y	Y	Y	N	N	N
Cohen	Y	Y	Y	Y	Y	N	N	N
MARYLAND								
Mikulski	Y	Y	Y	Y	Y	N	Y	N
Sarbanes	N	Y	Y	Y	Y	N	Y	Y
MASSACHUSETTS								
Kennedy	N	Y	Y	Y	Y	N	N	N
Kerry	N	Y	Y	Y	Y	N	Y	Y
MICHIGAN								
Levin	N	Y	Y	Y	Y	N	N	N
Riegle	N	Y	Y	Y	Y	Y	N	N
MINNESOTA								
Boschwitz	Y	Y	Y	Y	N	Y	Y	Y
Durenberger	?	?	?	?	?	?	?	?
MISSISSIPPI								
Cochran	Y	N	N	Y	N	Y	N	N
Lott	Y	N	N	Y	N	Y	N	N
MISSOURI								
Bond	Y	Y	N	Y	N	Y	Y	Y
Danforth	N	N	N	N	Y	N	N	N
MONTANA								
Baucus	Y	N	N	N	N	Y	N	N
Burns	Y	Y	N	Y	N	Y	Y	N
NEBRASKA								
Exon	Y	Y	N	N	N	Y	N	N
Kerrey	Y	Y	N	N	Y	Y	N	N
NEVADA								
Bryan	N	Y	Y	Y	Y	N	N	N
Reid	Y	Y	Y	Y	Y	N	N	N
NEW HAMPSHIRE								
Humphrey	Y	Y	Y	Y	Y	N	Y	Y
Rudman	Y	Y	?	?	?	?	?	?
NEW JERSEY								
Bradley	Y	Y	Y	Y	Y	N	Y	Y
Lautenberg	N	Y	Y	Y	Y	N	Y	Y
NEW MEXICO								
Bingaman	N	Y	Y	Y	Y	N	N	N
Domenici	Y	Y	N	Y	N	Y	Y	Y
NEW YORK								
Moynihan	N	Y	Y	Y	Y	N	Y	N
D'Amato	Y	Y	Y	Y	N	N	Y	Y
NORTH CAROLINA								
Sanford	N	Y	Y	Y	Y	N	N	N
Helms	Y	Y	Y	Y	N	N	N	N
NORTH DAKOTA								
Burdick	Y	Y	N	Y	N	Y	N	N
Conrad	Y	N	N	N	N	Y	N	N
OHIO								
Glenn	N	Y	Y	Y	Y	N	Y	N
Metzenbaum	N	Y	Y	Y	Y	N	N	?
OKLAHOMA								
Boren	Y	N	N	N	N	Y	N	?
Nickles	Y	Y	Y	Y	N	Y	N	N
OREGON								
Hatfield	Y	N	N	Y	Y	N	N	N
Packwood	Y	Y	Y	Y	N	N	Y	Y
PENNSYLVANIA								
Heinz	Y	Y	Y	Y	Y	N	Y	Y
Specter	Y	Y	Y	Y	Y	N	Y	Y
RHODE ISLAND								
Pell	N	Y	Y	Y	Y	N	Y	Y
Chafee	Y	N	N	N	Y	N	Y	Y
SOUTH CAROLINA								
Hollings	Y	Y	Y	Y	Y	N	N	N
Thurmond	Y	Y	N	Y	N	Y	N	N
SOUTH DAKOTA								
Daschle	Y	Y	N	Y	N	Y	N	N
Pressler	Y	Y	N	Y	N	Y	Y	N
TENNESSEE								
Gore	N	Y	Y	Y	Y	N	N	N
Sasser	N	Y	Y	Y	Y	N	N	N
TEXAS								
Bentsen	Y	Y	N	Y	N	N	N	N
Gramm	Y	Y	N	Y	N	Y	N	N
UTAH								
Garn	Y	Y	Y	Y	N	N	N	N
Hatch	Y	Y	Y	Y	N	Y	N	N
VERMONT								
Leahy	N	Y	Y	Y	Y	N	N	N
Jeffords	N	N	N	N	Y	Y	Y	Y
VIRGINIA								
Robb	N	Y	Y	Y	Y	N	N	N
Warner	Y	Y	Y	Y	N	N	N	N
WASHINGTON								
Adams	N	Y	Y	Y	Y	N	N	N
Gorton	N	Y	N	Y	N	N	N	N
WEST VIRGINIA								
Byrd	N	Y	Y	Y	Y	N	Y	Y
Rockefeller	N	Y	Y	Y	Y	Y	N	N
WISCONSIN								
Kohl	Y	Y	Y	Y	Y	Y	N	N
Kasten	Y	Y	Y	Y	Y	Y	N	N
WYOMING								
Simpson	Y	Y	N	Y	N	Y	N	N
Wallop	+	-	-	-	-	+	-	-

KEY

- Y Voted for (yea).
- # Paired for.
- + Announced for.
- N Voted against (nay).
- X Paired against.
- \- Announced against.
- P Voted "present."
- C Voted "present" to avoid possible conflict of interest.
- ? Did not vote or otherwise make a position known.

Democrats *Republicans*

ND Northern Democrats SD Southern Democrats

Southern states - Ala., Ark., Fla., Ga., Ky., La., Miss., N.C., Okla., S.C., Tenn., Texas, Va.

178. S 2830. Farm Programs Reauthorization/Credit to Soviet Union. Helms, R-N.C., amendment to prohibit U.S. financial institutions, whose deposits are insured by the U.S. taxpayer, from extending credit to the Soviet Union at interest rates below those offered to U.S. farmers. Adopted 64-32: R 39-3; D 25-29 (ND 16-22, 9-7), July 27, 1990.

179. S 2830. Farm Programs Reauthorization/Iraq Sanctions. DeConcini, D-Ariz., amendment to the D'Amato, R-N.Y., amendment, to require a report by the president on U.S. oil purchases from Iraq, possible alternative sources of oil and the economic consequences of an embargo. Adopted 80-16: R 32-10; D 48-6 (ND 36-2, SD 12-4), July 27, 1990.

180. S 2830. Farm Programs Reauthorization/Iraq Sanctions. Cohen, R-Maine, motion to table (kill) the Gramm, R-Texas, amendment to ensure that restrictions on credit to Iraq are not imposed so as to hurt U.S. farmers and workers more than they hurt Iraq. Motion agreed to 57-38: R 19-22; D 38-16 (ND 28-10, SD 10-6), July 27, 1990.

181. S 2830. Farm Programs Reauthorization/Iraq Sanctions. D'Amato, R-N.Y., amendment to deny Iraq financial credits and benefits, including guarantees made by the Commodity Credit Corporation of loans, until the president certifies that Iraq is in substantial compliance with its obligations under international law. Adopted 83-12: R 37-4; D 46-8 (ND 34-4, SD 12-4), July 27, 1990.

182. S 2830. Farm Programs Reauthorization/Private Property. Leahy, D-Vt., motion to table (kill) the Symms, R-Idaho, amendment to require that the possibility of private property being taken for public purposes be assessed prior to the imposition of regulations on the use of that property. Motion agreed to 52-43: R 10-31; D 42-12 (ND 31-7, SD 11-5), July 27, 1990.

183. S 2830. Farm Programs Reauthorization/Honey Price Supports. Pressler, R-S.D., amendment to modify the honey price support program. Rejected 40-55: R 21-20; D 19-35 (ND 12-26, SD 7-9), July 27, 1990.

184. S 2830. Farm Programs Reauthorization/Chilean Fruits. Specter, R-Pa., amendment to establish a grading program for imports of Chilean fruits and vegetables. Rejected 29-66: R 15-26; D 14-40 (ND 14-24, SD 0-16), July 27, 1990.

185. S 2830. Farm Programs Reauthorization/Horticultural Crops. Heinz, R-Pa., amendment to authorize the president to enter into cooperative agreements with heads of state of foreign governments to establish grading programs to be applied to horticultural crops to be imported into the United States. Rejected 25-68: R 16-25; D 9-43 (ND 9-28, SD 0-15), July 27, 1990.

	186	187	188	189	190	191	192	193
ALABAMA								
Heflin	Y	Y	?	N	Y	Y	N	Y
Shelby	Y	Y	N	N	Y	Y	N	Y
ALASKA								
Murkowski	Y	Y	Y	Y	N	N	Y	Y
Stevens	Y	Y	Y	N	N	Y	N	Y
ARIZONA								
DeConcini	Y	Y	-	N	Y	Y	N	Y
McCain	N	Y	Y	Y	N	Y	Y	Y
ARKANSAS								
Bumpers	?	?	N	N	Y	Y	N	Y
Pryor	Y	Y	N	N	Y	Y	N	Y
CALIFORNIA								
Cranston	Y	Y	N	N	Y	Y	N	Y
Wilson	Y	Y	Y	Y	N	Y	Y	Y
COLORADO								
Wirth	Y	N	N	N	Y	Y	N	Y
Armstrong	?	?	?	Y	N	N	?	?
CONNECTICUT								
Dodd	Y	N	N	N	Y	Y	N	Y
Lieberman	Y	N	N	N	Y	Y	N	Y
DELAWARE								
Biden	Y	N	N	N	Y	Y	N	Y
Roth	N	N	Y	Y	N	N	Y	Y
FLORIDA								
Graham	Y	Y	N	N	Y	Y	N	Y
Mack	Y	Y	Y	Y	N	N	Y	Y
GEORGIA								
Fowler	Y	Y	N	N	Y	Y	N	Y
Nunn	Y	Y	N	N	Y	Y	N	Y
HAWAII								
Inouye	Y	Y	N	N	Y	Y	N	Y
Akaka	Y	Y	N	N	Y	Y	N	Y
IDAHO								
McClure	Y	Y	Y	Y	N	N	Y	N
Symms	N	Y	Y	Y	N	N	Y	Y
ILLINOIS								
Dixon	Y	Y	N	N	Y	Y	N	Y
Simon	Y	Y	N	N	Y	Y	N	Y
INDIANA								
Coats	N	Y	Y	Y	N	Y	Y	Y
Lugar	N	Y	Y	Y	N	N	Y	Y
IOWA								
Harkin	N	Y	N	N	Y	Y	N	Y
Grassley	N	N	Y	Y	N	Y	Y	Y
KANSAS								
Dole	N	Y	Y	Y	N	Y	Y	Y
Kassebaum	N	Y	Y	Y	N	Y	Y	Y
KENTUCKY								
Ford	Y	Y	N	N	Y	Y	N	Y
McConnell	N	Y	Y	Y	N	N	Y	Y
LOUISIANA								
Breaux	Y	Y	N	N	Y	N	N	Y
Johnston	?	?	N	N	Y	Y	N	Y
MAINE								
Mitchell	Y	Y	N	N	Y	Y	N	Y
Cohen	Y	N	Y	Y	N	Y	Y	Y
MARYLAND								
Mikulski	Y	Y	?	N	Y	Y	N	Y
Sarbanes	Y	Y	N	N	Y	Y	N	Y
MASSACHUSETTS								
Kennedy	Y	Y	N	N	Y	Y	N	Y
Kerry	Y	N	N	N	Y	Y	N	Y
MICHIGAN								
Levin	Y	Y	N	N	Y	Y	N	Y
Riegle	Y	Y	N	N	Y	Y	N	Y
MINNESOTA								
Boschwitz	N	Y	Y	Y	N	N	Y	Y
Durenberger	?	#	Y	Y	N	Y	Y	Y
MISSISSIPPI								
Cochran	Y	Y	Y	Y	N	N	Y	Y
Lott	Y	Y	Y	Y	N	N	Y	Y
MISSOURI								
Bond	N	Y	Y	Y	N	N	Y	Y
Danforth	N	Y	Y	Y	N	N	Y	Y
MONTANA								
Baucus	N	N	N	N	Y	Y	N	Y
Burns	N	Y	Y	Y	N	Y	Y	Y
NEBRASKA								
Exon	N	Y	Y	N	Y	Y	N	Y
Kerrey	Y	Y	N	N	Y	N	N	Y
NEVADA								
Bryan	Y	N	N	N	Y	Y	N	Y
Reid	Y	N	N	N	Y	Y	N	Y
NEW HAMPSHIRE								
Humphrey	N	N	Y	Y	N	N	N	Y
Rudman	?	?	Y	Y	N	Y	Y	Y
NEW JERSEY								
Bradley	Y	?	N	N	Y	N	N	Y
Lautenberg	Y	N	N	N	Y	N	N	Y
NEW MEXICO								
Bingaman	Y	Y	N	N	Y	Y	N	Y
Domenici	N	Y	Y	Y	N	Y	Y	Y
NEW YORK								
Moynihan	Y	N	N	N	Y	Y	N	Y
D'Amato	Y	Y	Y	N	N	Y	Y	Y
NORTH CAROLINA								
Sanford	Y	Y	N	N	Y	Y	N	Y
Helms	N	N	Y	Y	N	N	Y	Y
NORTH DAKOTA								
Burdick	Y	Y	N	N	Y	Y	N	Y
Conrad	N	Y	N	N	Y	Y	N	Y
OHIO								
Glenn	Y	Y	N	N	Y	Y	N	Y
Metzenbaum	?	?	N	N	Y	Y	N	Y
OKLAHOMA								
Boren	N	Y	N	N	Y	Y	N	Y
Nickles	N	Y	Y	Y	N	Y	Y	Y
OREGON								
Hatfield	Y	Y	Y	N	Y	N	N	Y
Packwood	Y	Y	Y	Y	N	N	Y	Y
PENNSYLVANIA								
Heinz	Y	Y	Y	Y	N	Y	Y	Y
Specter	Y	N	Y	Y	N	Y	Y	Y
RHODE ISLAND								
Pell	Y	N	-	N	Y	Y	N	Y
Chafee	N	Y	Y	Y	N	N	Y	Y
SOUTH CAROLINA								
Hollings	Y	Y	Y	N	Y	Y	N	Y
Thurmond	N	Y	Y	Y	N	N	Y	Y
SOUTH DAKOTA								
Daschle	Y	N	N	N	Y	Y	N	Y
Pressler	N	N	Y	Y	N	Y	Y	Y
TENNESSEE								
Gore	Y	Y	N	N	Y	Y	N	Y
Sasser	Y	Y	N	N	Y	Y	N	Y
TEXAS								
Bentsen	Y	Y	N	N	Y	Y	N	Y
Gramm	N	Y	Y	Y	N	N	Y	Y
UTAH								
Garn	N	N	Y	Y	N	Y	Y	Y
Hatch	?	?	Y	Y	N	N	Y	Y
VERMONT								
Leahy	Y	Y	N	N	Y	Y	N	Y
Jeffords	Y	Y	Y	N	Y	Y	Y	Y
VIRGINIA								
Robb	Y	Y	N	N	Y	Y	N	Y
Warner	N	Y	Y	Y	N	Y	Y	Y
WASHINGTON								
Adams	Y	Y	N	N	Y	Y	N	Y
Gorton	Y	Y	Y	Y	N	N	Y	Y
WEST VIRGINIA								
Byrd	Y	N	N	N	Y	Y	N	Y
Rockefeller	Y	Y	N	N	Y	Y	N	Y
WISCONSIN								
Kohl	Y	Y	N	N	Y	Y	N	Y
Kasten	N	Y	Y	Y	N	Y	Y	Y
WYOMING								
Simpson	N	Y	Y	Y	N	Y	Y	Y
Wallop	-	X	Y	Y	N	N	Y	Y

KEY

- Y Voted for (yea).
- # Paired for.
- + Announced for.
- N Voted against (nay).
- X Paired against.
- \- Announced against.
- P Voted "present."
- C Voted "present" to avoid possible conflict of interest.
- ? Did not vote or otherwise make a position known.

Democrats *Republicans*

ND Northern Democrats SD Southern Democrats

Southern states - Ala., Ark., Fla., Ga., Ky., La., Miss., N.C., Okla., S.C., Tenn., Texas, Va.

186. S 2830. Farm Programs Reauthorization/Cargo Preference Laws. Grassley, R-Iowa, motion to table (kill) the Grassley amendment to provide that in the administration of certain cargo preference laws, a U.S.-flag vessel may not charge a rate greater than 110 percent of the lowest bid by a foreign flag vessel. (Grassley moved to table his amendment after saying that because of second-degree amendments it was clear he could not get an up-or-down vote on his amendment.) Motion agreed to 62-30: R 15-25; D 47-5 (ND 33-4, SD 14-1), July 27, 1990.

187. S 2830. Farm Programs Reauthorization/Passage. Passage of the bill to revise and extend federal farm price- and income-support programs for major commodities as well as Agriculture Department nutrition programs. Passed 70-21: R 32-8; D 38-13 (ND 23-13, SD 15-0), July 27, 1990.

188. S 137. Campaign Finance Overhaul/Public Funding. McConnell, R-Ky., amendment to the Boren, D-Okla., substitute amendment, to eliminate all taxpayer funding of Senate campaigns. Rejected 46-49: R 44-0; D 2-49 (ND 1-34, SD 1-15), July 30, 1990.

189. S 137. Campaign Finance Overhaul/Union Dues. Hatch, R-Utah, amendment to the Boren, D-Okla., substitute amendment, to limit the fees non-union members must pay in closed-shop states to the cost of collective-bargaining activities and allow union members to request a refund for any dues spent on political activities. Rejected 41-59: R 41-4; D 0-55 (ND 0-38, SD 0-17), July 31, 1990.

190. S 137. Campaign Finance Overhaul/Union Dues. Boren, D-Okla., amendment to the Boren substitute amendment, to establish procedures to refund to non-union members in closed-shop states the portion of their dues or fees spent for political activities. Adopted 57-43: R 2-43; D 55-0 (ND 38-0, SD 17-0), July 31, 1990.

191. S 137. Campaign Finance Overhaul/PAC Prohibitions. Bentsen, D-Texas, amendment to the Boren, D-Okla., substitute amendment, to bar companies with majority foreign ownership from operating a political action committee. Adopted 73-27: R 22-23; D 51-4 (ND 35-3, SD 16-1), July 31, 1990.

192. S 137. Campaign Finance Overhaul/Tax-Exempt Organizations. McConnell, R-Ky., amendment to the Boren, D-Okla., substitute amendment, to remove the tax-exempt status of any organization that supports or opposes candidates for office. Rejected 41-58: R 41-3; D 0-55 (ND 0-38, SD 0-17), July 31, 1990.

193. S 137. Campaign Finance Overhaul/Mass Mailings. Nickles, R-Okla., amendment to the Boren, D-Okla., substitute amendment, to prohibit the use of mass mailings by members of Congress during an election year, bar senators from transferring their franking budget to one another, require full disclosure of franking by the House and the Senate, and otherwise restrict members' franking privileges. Adopted 98-1: R 43-1; D 55-0 (ND 38-0, SD 17-0), July 31, 1990.

	194	195	196	197	198	199	200	201
ALABAMA								
Heflin	N	Y	Y	N	N	Y	Y	N
Shelby	N	Y	Y	N	Y	Y	Y	N
ALASKA								
Murkowski	N	Y	Y	Y	Y	N	N	Y
Stevens	N	Y	Y	N	Y	N	N	Y
ARIZONA								
DeConcini	Y	N	Y	N	N	N	Y	N
McCain	N	Y	Y	Y	Y	N	N	Y
ARKANSAS								
Bumpers	Y	N	Y	N	N	Y	Y	N
Pryor	N	N	Y	N	N	Y	Y	N
CALIFORNIA								
Cranston	Y	N	Y	N	N	N	N	N
Wilson	N	Y	Y	N	Y	N	N	Y
COLORADO								
Wirth	Y	N	Y	N	N	Y	Y	N
Armstrong	?	?	N	N	Y	?	?	?
CONNECTICUT								
Dodd	Y	N	Y	N	N	Y	Y	N
Lieberman	Y	N	Y	N	N	N	Y	N
DELAWARE								
Biden	Y	Y	Y	Y	N	N	N	Y
Roth	N	N	N	N	Y	N	Y	Y
FLORIDA								
Graham	N	N	Y	N	N	N	Y	N
Mack	N	Y	N	N	Y	N	N	Y
GEORGIA								
Fowler	Y	N	Y	Y	N	Y	Y	N
Nunn	N	N	Y	N	N	Y	Y	N
HAWAII								
Inouye	Y	N	N	N	N	N	Y	N
Akaka	N	N	Y	Y	N	N	N	N
IDAHO								
McClure	N	N	N	Y	N	N	N	Y
Symms	N	Y	N	N	Y	N	N	Y
ILLINOIS								
Dixon	N	N	Y	N	N	Y	Y	N
Simon	Y	N	Y	N	Y	Y	Y	N
INDIANA								
Coats	N	N	Y	Y	Y	N	N	Y
Lugar	N	Y	N	Y	Y	N	N	Y
IOWA								
Harkin	Y	N	Y	Y	Y	N	N	N
Grassley	N	Y	Y	Y	Y	N	N	Y
KANSAS								
Dole	N	Y	N	N	Y	N	N	Y
Kassebaum	N	Y	Y	Y	Y	Y	Y	Y
KENTUCKY								
Ford	Y	N	Y	N	N	N	Y	N
McConnell	N	Y	N	Y	Y	N	N	Y
LOUISIANA								
Breaux	N	N	N	Y	N	Y	Y	N
Johnston	N	N	Y	Y	N	N	Y	N
MAINE								
Mitchell	Y	N	Y	Y	N	N	Y	N
Cohen	N	Y	Y	Y	Y	N	N	Y
MARYLAND								
Mikulski	Y	N	Y	Y	N	Y	Y	N
Sarbanes	Y	N	Y	Y	N	N	Y	N
MASSACHUSETTS								
Kennedy	Y	N	Y	N	N	N	Y	N
Kerry	Y	N	Y	Y	Y	N	N	N
MICHIGAN								
Levin	N	Y	Y	N	Y	Y	Y	N
Riegle	Y	N	Y	Y	Y	N	N	N
MINNESOTA								
Boschwitz	N	Y	N	Y	Y	N	N	Y
Durenberger	N	Y	Y	Y	Y	N	N	Y
MISSISSIPPI								
Cochran	N	Y	N	Y	Y	N	N	Y
Lott	?	?	N	Y	Y	N	N	Y
MISSOURI								
Bond	N	Y	Y	Y	Y	N	N	Y
Danforth	N	N	N	N	Y	N	Y	Y
MONTANA								
Baucus	Y	N	Y	Y	Y	Y	Y	N
Burns	N	Y	Y	Y	Y	N	N	Y
NEBRASKA								
Exon	N	Y	Y	Y	Y	Y	Y	N
Kerrey	N	Y	Y	Y	N	Y	Y	N
NEVADA								
Bryan	N	N	Y	N	N	Y	Y	N
Reid	Y	N	Y	N	N	Y	Y	N
NEW HAMPSHIRE								
Humphrey	N	Y	Y	N	Y	Y	Y	Y
Rudman	N	Y	Y	N	Y	N	N	Y
NEW JERSEY								
Bradley	Y	N	Y	N	Y	Y	Y	N
Lautenberg	Y	Y	Y	N	Y	Y	Y	N
NEW MEXICO								
Bingaman	Y	N	Y	N	N	Y	Y	N
Domenici	N	Y	N	Y	Y	N	N	Y
NEW YORK								
Moynihan	Y	N	Y	Y	N	Y	Y	N
D'Amato	N	Y	Y	Y	Y	Y	Y	N
NORTH CAROLINA								
Sanford	Y	N	Y	N	N	Y	Y	N
Helms	N	Y	Y	Y	Y	N	N	Y
NORTH DAKOTA								
Burdick	Y	N	Y	N	Y	Y	Y	N
Conrad	Y	N	Y	Y	N	N	Y	N
OHIO								
Glenn	Y	N	Y	N	N	N	N	N
Metzenbaum	Y	Y	Y	N	Y	N	Y	N
OKLAHOMA								
Boren	Y	N	Y	Y	Y	Y	Y	N
Nickles	N	Y	Y	Y	Y	N	N	Y
OREGON								
Hatfield	N	Y	N	Y	Y	N	N	Y
Packwood	N	Y	N	Y	Y	N	N	Y
PENNSYLVANIA								
Heinz	N	Y	Y	N	Y	N	N	Y
Specter	N	Y	Y	Y	Y	N	N	Y
RHODE ISLAND								
Pell	Y	Y	Y	N	N	N	Y	N
Chafee	N	Y	N	Y	Y	N	N	Y
SOUTH CAROLINA								
Hollings	N	Y	Y	N	N	Y	Y	N
Thurmond	N	Y	Y	Y	Y	N	N	Y
SOUTH DAKOTA								
Daschle	Y	N	Y	Y	N	N	Y	N
Pressler	N	Y	Y	Y	Y	N	Y	Y
TENNESSEE								
Gore	Y	N	Y	N	N	Y	Y	N
Sasser	Y	N	Y	Y	N	Y	Y	N
TEXAS								
Bentsen	Y	N	Y	N	N	Y	Y	N
Gramm	N	Y	N	N	Y	N	N	Y
UTAH								
Garn	N	Y	N	Y	Y	N	N	Y
Hatch	N	Y	N	Y	Y	N	N	Y
VERMONT								
Leahy	Y	N	Y	Y	Y	Y	Y	N
Jeffords	N	N	Y	Y	Y	Y	Y	Y
VIRGINIA								
Robb	N	N	Y	N	N	Y	Y	N
Warner	N	Y	Y	N	Y	N	N	Y
WASHINGTON								
Adams	Y	N	Y	N	N	Y	Y	N
Gorton	N	Y	N	Y	Y	N	N	Y
WEST VIRGINIA								
Byrd	Y	N	Y	N	N	Y	Y	N
Rockefeller	N	N	Y	N	N	Y	Y	N
WISCONSIN								
Kohl	N	Y	Y	N	Y	Y	Y	N
Kasten	N	Y	Y	Y	Y	N	N	Y
WYOMING								
Simpson	N	Y	Y	Y	Y	N	N	Y
Wallop	N	Y	N	N	Y	N	N	Y

KEY

Y Voted for (yea).
\# Paired for.
\+ Announced for.
N Voted against (nay).
X Paired against.
\- Announced against.
P Voted "present."
C Voted "present" to avoid possible conflict of interest.
? Did not vote or otherwise make a position known.

Democrats *Republicans*

ND Northern Democrats SD Southern Democrats

Southern states - Ala., Ark., Fla., Ga., Ky., La., Miss., N.C., Okla., S.C., Tenn., Texas, Va.

194. S 137. Campaign Finance Overhaul/Full Public Funding. Kerry, D-Mass., amendment to the Boren, D-Okla., substitute amendment, to give candidates meeting certain requirements public monies to finance 90 percent of the cost of their general election campaigns, with the funds coming from voluntary funds provided from taxpayers' returns. Rejected 38-60: R 0-43; D 38-17 (ND 30-8, SD 8-9), July 31, 1990.

195. S 137. Campaign Finance Overhaul/Campaign Funds. McCain, R-Ariz., amendment to the Boren, D-Okla., substitute amendment, to restrict the use of campaign money to bona fide election activities and to require all surplus funds at the end of a campaign to be turned over to the Treasury to reduce the deficit. Rejected 49-49: R 38-5; D 11-44 (ND 8-30, SD 3-14), July 31, 1990.

196. S 137. Campaign Finance Overhaul/Outside Income. Dodd, D-Conn., amendment to the Boren, D-Okla., substitute amendment, to bar senators from accepting honoraria, limit all outside earned income to 15 percent of a senator's salary, prohibit senators from maintaining a fiduciary relationship with a corporation or partnership, and restrict charitable contributions made in behalf of a senator. Adopted 77-23: R 24-21; D 53-2 (ND 37-1, SD 16-1), Aug. 1, 1990.

197. S 137. Campaign Finance Overhaul/Unearned Income. Moynihan, D-N.Y., amendment to the Boren, D-Okla., substitute amendment, to limit to 15 percent of each senator's salary, the amount a senator may receive in unearned income. The Dodd, D-Conn., amendment *(vote 196)* only limited earned income. Adopted 51-49: R 31-14; D 20-35 (ND 15-23, SD 5-12), Aug. 1, 1990.

198. S 137. Campaign Finance Overhaul/Public Financing. Wilson, R-Calif., amendment to the Boren, D-Okla., substitute amendment, to prohibit expenditures for public financing under the Federal Election Campaign Act unless $100 million is appropriated to carry out programs for pregnant and postpartum women and their infants, boarder babies. Adopted 59-41: R 44-1; D 15-40 (ND 13-25, SD 2-15), Aug. 1, 1990.

199. S 137. Campaign Finance Overhaul/Public Financing. Exon, D-Neb., amendment to the Boren, D-Okla., substitute amendment, to make certain that TV time provided free for candidates and other certain incentives to comply with spending limits are paid for with voluntary contributions to a government-run fund. Rejected 39-60: R 4-40; D 35-20 (ND 21-17, SD 14-3), Aug. 1, 1990.

200. S 137. Campaign Finance Overhaul/Public Financing. Boren, D-Okla., amendment to the Boren substitute amendment, to state that it is the sense of the Senate that TV time provided free for candidates and certain incentives to comply with spending limits are paid for with voluntary contributions collected from tax refunds. Adopted 55-44: R 7-37; D 48-7 (ND 31-7, SD 17-0), Aug. 1, 1990.

201. S 137. Campaign Finance Overhaul/Spending Limits. McCain, R-Ariz., amendment to the Boren, D-Okla., substitute amendment, to strike certain provisions allowing incumbent senators to exceed spending limits. Rejected 44-55: R 43-1; D 1-54 (ND 1-37, SD 0-17), Aug. 1, 1990.

	202	203	204	205	206	207	208	209
ALABAMA								
Heflin	N	N	Y	Y	Y	Y	N	N
Shelby	N	Y	Y	Y	Y	Y	N	N
ALASKA								
Murkowski	Y	Y	N	Y	Y	Y	N	N
Stevens	Y	N	N	Y	Y	Y	N	N
ARIZONA								
DeConcini	N	Y	Y	Y	Y	Y	Y	Y
McCain	Y	Y	Y	Y	Y	Y	N	Y
ARKANSAS								
Bumpers	N	Y	Y	Y	Y	Y	Y	Y
Pryor	N	Y	Y	Y	Y	Y	Y	Y
CALIFORNIA								
Cranston	N	Y	Y	N	Y	Y	Y	Y
Wilson	Y	Y	N	Y	Y	?	-	X
COLORADO								
Wirth	N	N	Y	Y	Y	Y	Y	Y
Armstrong	?	?	?	Y	Y	Y	N	N
CONNECTICUT								
Dodd	N	Y	Y	?	Y	Y	N	N
Lieberman	N	N	Y	Y	Y	Y	Y	Y
DELAWARE								
Biden	N	Y	Y	N	Y	Y	Y	Y
Roth	Y	Y	N	N	Y	Y	Y	N
FLORIDA								
Graham	N	N	Y	N	Y	Y	N	N
Mack	Y	Y	N	Y	Y	Y	N	N
GEORGIA								
Fowler	N	N	Y	Y	Y	Y	N	N
Nunn	N	N	Y	N	Y	Y	N	N
HAWAII								
Inouye	N	Y	Y	Y	Y	Y	N	N
Akaka	N	Y	Y	Y	Y	Y	Y	Y
IDAHO								
McClure	Y	Y	N	Y	Y	Y	N	N
Symms	Y	Y	N	Y	Y	Y	N	N
ILLINOIS								
Dixon	N	Y	Y	N	Y	Y	N	N
Simon	N	Y	Y	Y	Y	Y	Y	Y
INDIANA								
Coats	Y	Y	N	Y	Y	Y	N	N
Lugar	Y	Y	N	Y	Y	Y	N	N
IOWA								
Harkin	N	N	Y	Y	Y	Y	Y	Y
Grassley	Y	Y	N	Y	Y	Y	Y	N
KANSAS								
Dole	Y	Y	N	Y	Y	Y	N	N
Kassebaum	Y	Y	N	Y	Y	Y	Y	N
KENTUCKY								
Ford	N	Y	Y	Y	Y	Y	N	N
McConnell	Y	Y	N	Y	Y	Y	N	N
LOUISIANA								
Breaux	N	Y	Y	Y	Y	Y	N	N
Johnston	N	Y	Y	N	Y	Y	N	N
MAINE								
Mitchell	N	Y	Y	Y	Y	Y	Y	Y
Cohen	Y	Y	Y	Y	Y	Y	Y	Y
MARYLAND								
Mikulski	N	N	Y	Y	Y	Y	Y	Y
Sarbanes	N	N	Y	Y	Y	Y	Y	Y
MASSACHUSETTS								
Kennedy	N	Y	Y	N	Y	Y	Y	Y
Kerry	N	N	Y	N	Y	Y	Y	Y
MICHIGAN								
Levin	N	N	Y	Y	Y	Y	N	Y
Riegle	N	Y	Y	Y	Y	Y	Y	Y
MINNESOTA								
Boschwitz	Y	Y	N	Y	Y	Y	N	N
Durenberger	Y	Y	Y	Y	Y	Y	N	N
MISSISSIPPI								
Cochran	Y	Y	N	Y	Y	Y	N	N
Lott	Y	Y	N	Y	Y	Y	N	N
MISSOURI								
Bond	Y	Y	N	Y	Y	Y	N	N
Danforth	Y	Y	N	Y	Y	Y	N	N
MONTANA								
Baucus	N	Y	Y	Y	Y	Y	Y	Y
Burns	Y	Y	N	Y	Y	Y	N	N
NEBRASKA								
Exon	N	Y	Y	Y	Y	Y	N	N
Kerrey	N	Y	Y	Y	Y	Y	Y	N
NEVADA								
Bryan	N	N	Y	Y	Y	Y	N	N
Reid	N	Y	Y	Y	Y	Y	Y	Y
NEW HAMPSHIRE								
Humphrey	Y	Y	N	Y	Y	Y	Y	N
Rudman	Y	Y	N	Y	Y	Y	N	N
NEW JERSEY								
Bradley	N	N	Y	N	Y	Y	Y	Y
Lautenberg	N	N	Y	N	Y	Y	Y	Y
NEW MEXICO								
Bingaman	N	N	Y	N	Y	Y	N	Y
Domenici	Y	Y	N	Y	Y	Y	N	N
NEW YORK								
Moynihan	N	Y	Y	N	Y	N	Y	Y
D'Amato	Y	Y	N	Y	Y	Y	N	Y
NORTH CAROLINA								
Sanford	N	N	Y	Y	Y	Y	N	N
Helms	Y	Y	N	Y	Y	Y	N	N
NORTH DAKOTA								
Burdick	N	N	Y	Y	Y	Y	Y	Y
Conrad	N	Y	Y	Y	Y	Y	Y	Y
OHIO								
Glenn	N	Y	Y	N	Y	Y	Y	Y
Metzenbaum	N	Y	Y	N	Y	Y	Y	Y
OKLAHOMA								
Boren	N	Y	Y	Y	?	Y	N	N
Nickles	Y	Y	N	Y	Y	Y	N	N
OREGON								
Hatfield	Y	Y	N	Y	Y	Y	Y	Y
Packwood	Y	Y	N	Y	Y	Y	Y	Y
PENNSYLVANIA								
Heinz	Y	Y	N	Y	Y	Y	N	Y
Specter	Y	Y	N	Y	Y	Y	N	Y
RHODE ISLAND								
Pell	N	N	Y	Y	Y	Y	Y	Y
Chafee	Y	Y	N	Y	Y	Y	N	Y
SOUTH CAROLINA								
Hollings	N	Y	N	N	Y	Y	Y	Y
Thurmond	Y	Y	N	Y	Y	Y	N	N
SOUTH DAKOTA								
Daschle	N	Y	Y	N	Y	Y	Y	Y
Pressler	Y	N	Y	Y	Y	Y	Y	Y
TENNESSEE								
Gore	N	N	Y	Y	Y	Y	N	N
Sasser	N	Y	Y	N	Y	N	Y	Y
TEXAS								
Bentsen	N	N	Y	N	Y	Y	N	N
Gramm	Y	Y	N	Y	Y	Y	N	N
UTAH								
Garn	Y	Y	N	Y	Y	Y	N	N
Hatch	Y	Y	N	Y	Y	Y	N	N
VERMONT								
Leahy	N	N	Y	N	Y	Y	Y	Y
Jeffords	Y	Y	Y	Y	Y	Y	N	#
VIRGINIA								
Robb	N	N	Y	N	Y	Y	N	N
Warner	Y	Y	N	Y	Y	Y	N	N
WASHINGTON								
Adams	N	N	Y	Y	Y	Y	Y	Y
Gorton	Y	Y	N	Y	Y	Y	N	N
WEST VIRGINIA								
Byrd	N	Y	Y	N	Y	Y	Y	Y
Rockefeller	N	Y	Y	Y	Y	Y	Y	Y
WISCONSIN								
Kohl	N	N	Y	N	Y	Y	Y	Y
Kasten	Y	Y	N	Y	Y	Y	N	N
WYOMING								
Simpson	Y	Y	N	Y	Y	Y	N	N
Wallop	Y	Y	N	Y	Y	Y	N	N

KEY

- Y Voted for (yea).
- # Paired for.
- + Announced for.
- N Voted against (nay).
- X Paired against.
- - Announced against.
- P Voted "present."
- C Voted "present" to avoid possible conflict of interest.
- ? Did not vote or otherwise make a position known.

Democrats *Republicans*

ND Northern Democrats SD Southern Democrats

Southern states - Ala., Ark., Fla., Ga., Ky., La., Miss., N.C., Okla., S.C., Tenn., Texas, Va.

202. S 137. Campaign Finance Overhaul/Republican Substitute. Dole, R-Kan., substitute amendment to establish aggregate fundraising limits on personal funds and contributions from out-of-state individuals in excess of $250; eliminate political action committees (PACs); and cut the limit on out-of-state contributions by individuals to $500. Rejected 44-55: R 44-0; D 0-55 (ND 0-38, SD 0-17), Aug. 1, 1990.

203. S 137. Campaign Finance Overhaul/Debates. Boren, D-Okla., motion to table (kill) the Graham, D-Fla., amendment to the Boren substitute amendment, to require presidential candidates to participate in four general election debates and vice presidential candidates to participate in one debate in order to receive public campaign funding. Motion agreed to 73-26: R 42-2; D 31-24 (ND 22-16, SD 9-8), Aug. 1, 1990.

204. S 137. Campaign Finance Overhaul/Passage. Passage of the bill to revise federal laws governing the financing of federal campaigns by providing for a voluntary system of spending limits for general elections that gives candidates public subsidies as an incentive to participate; eliminating political action committees; limiting certain individual contributions; and making other changes. Passed 59-40: R 5-39; D 54-1 (ND 38-0, SD 16-1), Aug. 1, 1990. A "nay" was a vote supporting the president's position.

205. HR 5019. Fiscal 1991 Energy and Water Appropriations/Environmental Protection Reimbursements. McClure, R-Idaho, amendment to authorize the secretary of Interior to reimburse the Fall River Rural Electric Cooperative $1 million for environmental protection requirements that were met in connection with the development of hydroelectric power at the Island Park Dam and Reservoir in Idaho. Adopted 76-23: R 44-1; D 32-22 (ND 22-15, SD 10-7), Aug. 2, 1990. (The bill was subsequently passed by voice vote.)

206. HR 1465. Oil-Spill Liability and Compensation/Adoption. Adoption of the conference report on the bill to provide comprehensive oil-spill liability and compensation, cleanup and prevention measures. The bill would leave states free to maintain their own oil-spill cleanup funds and enforce their own liability laws. Adopted 99-0: R 45-0; D 54-0 (ND 38-0, SD 16-0), Aug. 2, 1990.

207. S 2884. Fiscal 1991 Defense Authorizations/B-2 Bomber. Nunn, D-Ga., amendment to the Warner, R-Va., amendment, to require that the B-2 stealth bomber meet certain testing requirements before the Defense Department can spend funds for production of two additional B-2s. Adopted 97-2: R 44-0; D 53-2 (ND 37-1, SD 16-1), Aug. 2, 1990. (The Warner amendment subsequently was adopted by voice vote.)

208. S 2884. Fiscal 1991 Defense Authorizations/B-2 Bomber. Leahy, D-Vt., amendment to the Cohen, R-Maine, amendment, to cancel $2.75 billion in procurement and advanced procurement funds for the B-2 stealth bomber in fiscal 1991; retain all $1.751 billion requested for research, development, testing and engineering of the B-2; complete construction only on the six B-2s that will be used for flight testing; and use $3 billion in unobligated funds for termination costs. Rejected 43-56: R 8-36; D 35-20 (ND 31-7, SD 4-13), Aug. 2, 1990. A "nay" was a vote supporting the president's position.

209. S 2884. Fiscal 1991 Defense Authorizations/B-2 Bomber. Cohen, R-Maine, amendment to eliminate $1.812 billion in procurement for two B-2 bombers in fiscal 1991; provide $942 million in procurement funds to allow for long-lead purchases and other activities to support the subcontractor base and avoid a break in production; and retain all $1.751 billion approved for research, development, testing and engineering of the B-2. Rejected 45-53: R 9-34; D 36-19 (ND 32-6, SD 4-13), Aug. 2, 1990. A "nay" was a vote supporting the president's position.

	210	211	212	213	214	215
ALABAMA						
Heflin	N	Y	N	Y	N	Y
Shelby	N	Y	Y	Y	Y	Y
ALASKA						
Murkowski	Y	Y	N	Y	Y	Y
Stevens	Y	Y	Y	Y	Y	Y
ARIZONA						
DeConcini	Y	Y	Y	N	Y	Y
McCain	Y	Y	N	Y	N	Y
ARKANSAS						
Bumpers	N	Y	Y	Y	N	N
Pryor	N	?	Y	N	N	N
CALIFORNIA						
Cranston	N	Y	Y	N	N	N
Wilson	+	+	Y	Y	N	Y
COLORADO						
Wirth	Y	Y	Y	N	Y	N
Armstrong	?	?	N	Y	Y	Y
CONNECTICUT						
Dodd	N	Y	Y	N	Y	Y
Lieberman	Y	Y	Y	Y	Y	Y
DELAWARE						
Biden	Y	Y	Y	N	N	N
Roth	Y	Y	N	Y	Y	N
FLORIDA						
Graham	Y	Y	Y	Y	Y	N
Mack	Y	Y	N	Y	Y	Y
GEORGIA						
Fowler	N	Y	Y	N	Y	N
Nunn	Y	Y	Y	Y	Y	N
HAWAII						
Inouye	N	Y	Y	Y	Y	Y
Akaka	N	Y	Y	Y	Y	Y
IDAHO						
McClure	Y	Y	N	Y	Y	Y
Symms	Y	Y	N	Y	Y	Y
ILLINOIS						
Dixon	N	Y	Y	N	Y	N
Simon	N	Y	Y	N	N	N
INDIANA						
Coats	Y	Y	N	Y	Y	Y
Lugar	Y	Y	N	Y	Y	Y

	210	211	212	213	214	215
IOWA						
Harkin	N	Y	Y	N	N	N
Grassley	N	Y	N	Y	Y	N
KANSAS						
Dole	Y	Y	N	Y	Y	Y
Kassebaum	Y	Y	Y	Y	Y	Y
KENTUCKY						
Ford	N	Y	N	Y	N	N
McConnell	Y	Y	N	Y	N	Y
LOUISIANA						
Breaux	N	Y	N	Y	N	N
Johnston	N	Y	N	Y	N	Y
MAINE						
Mitchell	N	Y	Y	N	Y	N
Cohen	Y	Y	Y	Y	Y	Y
MARYLAND						
Mikulski	N	Y	Y	N	Y	N
Sarbanes	N	Y	Y	N	N	N
MASSACHUSETTS						
Kennedy	N	Y	Y	N	N	N
Kerry	N	Y	Y	N	N	N
MICHIGAN						
Levin	N	Y	Y	N	Y	Y
Riegle	N	Y	Y	N	N	N
MINNESOTA						
Boschwitz	Y	Y	N	Y	Y	Y
Durenberger	Y	Y	N	Y	Y	Y
MISSISSIPPI						
Cochran	Y	Y	N	Y	Y	Y
Lott	Y	Y	N	Y	Y	Y
MISSOURI						
Bond	Y	Y	Y	Y	Y	Y
Danforth	Y	Y	N	Y	Y	Y
MONTANA						
Baucus	N	Y	Y	N	Y	N
Burns	Y	Y	N	Y	Y	Y
NEBRASKA						
Exon	N	Y	N	N	Y	N
Kerrey	N	Y	Y	Y	Y	N
NEVADA						
Bryan	N	Y	Y	N	Y	N
Reid	N	Y	N	N	Y	N

	210	211	212	213	214	215
NEW HAMPSHIRE						
Humphrey	N	Y	N	Y	Y	Y
Rudman	Y	Y	Y	Y	Y	Y
NEW JERSEY						
Bradley	Y	Y	Y	N	N	N
Lautenberg	Y	Y	Y	N	N	N
NEW MEXICO						
Bingaman	N	Y	?	?	?	?
Domenici	Y	Y	N	Y	Y	Y
NEW YORK						
Moynihan	N	Y	Y	N	N	N
D'Amato	Y	Y	N	Y	Y	Y
NORTH CAROLINA						
Sanford	Y	Y	Y	N	N	N
Helms	Y	Y	N	N	Y	Y
NORTH DAKOTA						
Burdick	N	Y	Y	N	Y	N
Conrad	N	Y	N	N	Y	N
OHIO						
Glenn	N	Y	Y	Y	N	Y
Metzenbaum	N	Y	Y	N	N	N
OKLAHOMA						
Boren	Y	Y	N	N	Y	Y
Nickles	Y	Y	N	N	Y	Y
OREGON						
Hatfield	N	Y	N	N	N	N
Packwood	Y	Y	Y	Y	Y	Y
PENNSYLVANIA						
Heinz	Y	Y	Y	Y	Y	Y
Specter	Y	Y	Y	Y	Y	Y
RHODE ISLAND						
Pell	N	Y	Y	N	N	N
Chafee	Y	Y	Y	Y	Y	N
SOUTH CAROLINA						
Hollings	N	Y	Y	Y	N	Y
Thurmond	Y	Y	N	Y	Y	Y
SOUTH DAKOTA						
Daschle	N	Y	Y	N	N	N
Pressler	N	Y	N	N	N	N
TENNESSEE						
Gore	N	Y	Y	Y	Y	N
Sasser	N	Y	Y	N	N	N

KEY

- Y Voted for (yea).
- # Paired for.
- + Announced for.
- N Voted against (nay).
- X Paired against.
- \- Announced against.
- P Voted "present."
- C Voted "present" to avoid possible conflict of interest.
- ? Did not vote or otherwise make a position known.

Democrats ***Republicans***

	210	211	212	213	214	215
TEXAS						
Bentsen	N	Y	Y	Y	Y	Y
Gramm	Y	Y	N	Y	Y	Y
UTAH						
Garn	Y	Y	N	Y	Y	Y
Hatch	Y	Y	N	Y	Y	Y
VERMONT						
Leahy	N	Y	Y	Y	N	N
Jeffords	Y	Y	Y	Y	N	Y
VIRGINIA						
Robb	Y	Y	Y	Y	Y	N
Warner	Y	Y	N	Y	Y	Y
WASHINGTON						
Adams	N	Y	Y	N	N	Y
Gorton	Y	Y	Y	Y	Y	Y
WEST VIRGINIA						
Byrd	Y	Y	Y	Y	Y	Y
Rockefeller	N	Y	Y	N	Y	N
WISCONSIN						
Kohl	N	Y	Y	N	Y	N
Kasten	Y	Y	N	N	Y	Y
WYOMING						
Simpson	Y	Y	N	Y	Y	Y
Wallop	Y	Y	N	Y	Y	Y

ND Northern Democrats SD Southern Democrats Southern states - Ala., Ark., Fla., Ga., Ky., La., Miss., N.C., Okla., S.C., Tenn., Texas, Va.

210. S 2884. Fiscal 1991 Defense Authorization/Base in Crotone, Italy. Warner, R-Va., motion to table (kill) the Dixon, D-Ill., amendment to prohibit the use by NATO of U.S. funds to construct an air base in Crotone, Italy. Motion agreed to 51-47: R 39-4; D 12-43 (ND 7-31, SD 5-12), Aug. 2, 1990. A "yea" was a vote supporting the president's position.

211. S Res 318. Condemnation of Iraq/Adoption. Adoption of the resolution to condemn Iraq's invasion of Kuwait, commend the president for his initial response and urge him to take additional unilateral and multilateral steps aimed at securing withdrawal of all Iraqi forces from Kuwait. Adopted 97-0: R 43-0; D 54-0 (ND 38-0, SD 16-0), Aug. 2, 1990. A "yea" was a vote supporting the president's position.

212. S 2884. Fiscal 1991 Defense Authorization/Cloture. Mitchell, D-Maine, motion to invoke cloture (thus limiting debate) on the Wirth, D-Colo., amendment to allow service members or their dependents stationed outside the United States to obtain abortions in U.S. military hospitals, provided the costs are privately paid for. Rejected 58-41: R 12-33; D 46-8 (ND 34-3, SD 12-5), Aug. 3, 1990. A three-fifths majority vote (60) of the total Senate is required to invoke cloture. In accordance with a previous unanimous consent agreement, the Wirth amendment was then withdrawn.

213. S 2884. Fiscal 1991 Defense Authorization/Forces in Europe. McCain, R-Ariz., motion to table (kill) the Conrad, D-N.D., amendment to reduce by 30,000 — to 231,855 — the number of U.S. military personnel stationed in Europe. Motion agreed to 59-40: R 40-5; D 19-35 (ND 7-30, SD 12-5), Aug. 3, 1990. A "yea" was a vote supporting the president's position.

214. S 2884. Fiscal 1991 Defense Authorization/Military Pay Raise. Nunn, D-Ga., motion to table (kill) the Glenn, D-Ohio, amendment to increase the amount of pay raise for military personnel from 3.5 percent to 4.1 percent. Motion agreed to 67-32: R 39-6; D 28-26 (ND 20-17, SD 8-9), Aug. 3, 1990. A "yea" was a vote supporting the president's position.

215. S 2884. Fiscal 1991 Defense Authorization/Iowa-Class Battleships. Warner, R-Va., motion to table (kill) the Bumpers, D-Ark., amendment to retire one *Iowa* -class battleship. Motion agreed to 55-44: R 40-5; D 15-39 (ND 9-28, SD 6-11), Aug. 3, 1990. A "yea" was a vote supporting the president's position.

	216	217	218	219	220	221
ALABAMA						
Heflin	Y	Y	N	Y	N	Y
Shelby	Y	Y	Y	Y	N	Y
ALASKA						
Murkowski	Y	Y	Y	Y	Y	N
Stevens	Y	Y	Y	Y	Y	N
ARIZONA						
DeConcini	N	Y	Y	N	N	Y
McCain	N	Y	Y	Y	N	N
ARKANSAS						
Bumpers	N	Y	Y	N	N	Y
Pryor	N	Y	Y	N	N	?
CALIFORNIA						
Cranston	N	Y	Y	N	N	Y
Wilson	N	Y	Y	Y	N	Y
COLORADO						
Wirth	N	Y	Y	N	N	N
Armstrong	Y	Y	N	Y	?	?
CONNECTICUT						
Dodd	N	Y	Y	N	N	Y
Lieberman	N	Y	Y	N	N	Y
DELAWARE						
Biden	N	N	N	N	N	Y
Roth	Y	N	N	Y	Y	N
FLORIDA						
Graham	Y	Y	Y	Y	N	N
Mack	Y	Y	Y	Y	Y	N
GEORGIA						
Fowler	N	Y	Y	Y	Y	N
Nunn	Y	Y	Y	Y	Y	N
HAWAII						
Inouye	N	Y	Y	Y	N	Y
Akaka	N	Y	Y	N	N	Y
IDAHO						
McClure	Y	Y	N	Y	Y	N
Symms	Y	Y	N	Y	Y	N
ILLINOIS						
Dixon	Y	Y	Y	Y	Y	N
Simon	N	Y	Y	N	N	Y
INDIANA						
Coats	Y	Y	N	Y	Y	N
Lugar	Y	Y	N	Y	Y	N
IOWA						
Harkin	N	Y	Y	N	Y	N
Grassley	N	Y	Y	Y	Y	N
KANSAS						
Dole	Y	Y	N	Y	N	N
Kassebaum	Y	Y	N	N	Y	N
KENTUCKY						
Ford	Y	Y	Y	N	N	Y
McConnell	N	Y	N	Y	N	Y
LOUISIANA						
Breaux	Y	Y	N	N	N	Y
Johnston	Y	Y	Y	N	N	Y
MAINE						
Mitchell	N	Y	Y	N	N	N
Cohen	N	Y	Y	Y	Y	N
MARYLAND						
Mikulski	N	Y	Y	N	N	Y
Sarbanes	N	Y	Y	N	N	Y
MASSACHUSETTS						
Kennedy	N	Y	Y	N	N	Y
Kerry	N	Y	Y	N	N	Y
MICHIGAN						
Levin	N	Y	Y	N	N	Y
Riegle	N	Y	Y	N	N	Y
MINNESOTA						
Boschwitz	Y	Y	Y	Y	Y	N
Durenberger	Y	Y	Y	N	Y	N
MISSISSIPPI						
Cochran	Y	Y	Y	Y	Y	N
Lott	Y	Y	Y	Y	Y	N
MISSOURI						
Bond	Y	Y	Y	Y	Y	N
Danforth	Y	Y	Y	Y	Y	N
MONTANA						
Baucus	N	Y	Y	N	Y	N
Burns	Y	Y	Y	Y	Y	N
NEBRASKA						
Exon	Y	Y	Y	Y	Y	N
Kerrey	Y	Y	Y	N	N	Y
NEVADA						
Bryan	Y	N	Y	Y	Y	N
Reid	N	N	Y	N	N	Y
NEW HAMPSHIRE						
Humphrey	Y	N	Y	Y	Y	N
Rudman	Y	Y	Y	Y	Y	N
NEW JERSEY						
Bradley	N	Y	Y	N	Y	N
Lautenberg	N	Y	Y	N	N	Y
NEW MEXICO						
Bingaman	?	?	?	?	?	?
Domenici	Y	Y	Y	Y	N	N
NEW YORK						
Moynihan	N	Y	Y	N	N	Y
D'Amato	N	Y	Y	Y	Y	N
NORTH CAROLINA						
Sanford	Y	Y	Y	N	N	Y
Helms	N	Y	N	Y	Y	N
NORTH DAKOTA						
Burdick	N	Y	Y	N	N	Y
Conrad	N	Y	Y	N	N	Y
OHIO						
Glenn	Y	Y	Y	N	N	Y
Metzenbaum	N	Y	Y	N	N	Y
OKLAHOMA						
Boren	N	Y	Y	?	?	N
Nickles	Y	Y	Y	Y	Y	N
OREGON						
Hatfield	N	Y	Y	N	Y	N
Packwood	N	Y	Y	Y	Y	N
PENNSYLVANIA						
Heinz	Y	Y	N	Y	N	Y
Specter	N	Y	N	Y	N	Y
RHODE ISLAND						
Pell	N	Y	Y	N	N	Y
Chafee	Y	N	Y	N	Y	N
SOUTH CAROLINA						
Hollings	Y	Y	Y	Y	N	Y
Thurmond	Y	Y	Y	Y	N	Y
SOUTH DAKOTA						
Daschle	N	Y	Y	N	N	Y
Pressler	N	Y	N	Y	Y	N
TENNESSEE						
Gore	Y	Y	Y	N	N	Y
Sasser	N	Y	Y	N	N	Y
TEXAS						
Bentsen	Y	Y	Y	Y	N	N
Gramm	Y	Y	Y	Y	N	N
UTAH						
Garn	Y	Y	N	Y	Y	N
Hatch	Y	Y	N	Y	Y	N
VERMONT						
Leahy	N	Y	Y	N	N	Y
Jeffords	Y	Y	Y	N	Y	N
VIRGINIA						
Robb	N	Y	Y	N	Y	N
Warner	Y	Y	Y	Y	Y	N
WASHINGTON						
Adams	N	Y	Y	?	N	N
Gorton	Y	Y	Y	Y	Y	N
WEST VIRGINIA						
Byrd	Y	Y	Y	Y	N	Y
Rockefeller	N	Y	Y	N	N	Y
WISCONSIN						
Kohl	N	Y	Y	N	N	Y
Kasten	Y	Y	Y	Y	Y	N
WYOMING						
Simpson	Y	Y	Y	Y	N	N
Wallop	Y	Y	Y	Y	Y	N

KEY

- Y Voted for (yea).
- # Paired for.
- \+ Announced for.
- N Voted against (nay).
- X Paired against.
- \- Announced against.
- P Voted "present."
- C Voted "present" to avoid possible conflict of interest.
- ? Did not vote or otherwise make a position known.

Democrats *Republicans*

ND Northern Democrats SD Southern Democrats

Southern states - Ala., Ark., Fla., Ga., Ky., La., Miss., N.C., Okla., S.C., Tenn., Texas, Va.

216. S 2884. Fiscal 1991 Defense Authorization/Drug-Abuse Treatment. Dixon, D-Ill., motion to table (kill) the DeConcini, D-Ariz., amendment to transfer $100 million from the Department of Defense to the Department of Health and Human Services to establish a program to allow drug-addicted mothers to reside in drug-abuse treatment facilities with their children. Motion agreed to 51-48: R 34-11; D 17-37 (ND 6-31, SD 11-6), Aug. 3, 1990. A "yea" was a vote supporting the president's position.

217. S 2884. Fiscal 1991 Defense Authorization/Land Purchase Limits. Dixon, D-Ill., motion to table (kill) the Roth, R-Del., amendment to prohibit the Department of Defense from acquiring during fiscal 1991 parcels of land larger than 25 acres apiece. Motion agreed to 93-6: R 42-3; D 51-3 (ND 34-3, SD 17-0), Aug. 3, 1990.

218. S 2884. Fiscal 1991 Defense Authorization/Base Closures. Dixon, D-Ill., motion to table (kill) the Roth, R-Del., amendment to change existing regulations dealing with the disposal of property resulting from the closure of military bases, to allow affected communities to voluntarily engage in a program to allow them to decide the best use of the property without federal interference. In return, the community would be responsible for funding displaced government employees' severance pay, training and retraining assistance, and a new category of adjustment allowance, one week's pay for each year's service up to 10 years.The community also would have to reimburse the U.S. government 25 percent of rents and revenues from the redeveloped property for 25 years. Motion agreed to 81-18: R 30-15; D 51-3 (ND 36-1, SD 15-2), Aug. 3, 1990.

219. S 2884. Fiscal 1991 Defense Authorization/ASAT. Nunn, D-Ga., motion to table (kill) the Kerry, D-Mass., amendment to reduce the Army's kinetic energy antisatellite (ASAT) program from $208 million to $77 million. Motion agreed to 52-45: R 40-5; D 12-40 (ND 5-31, SD 7-9), Aug. 3, 1990. A "yea" was a vote supporting the president's position.

220. S 2884. Fiscal 1991 Defense Authorization/Domestic Base Closure. Warner, R-Va., motion to table (kill) the Bumpers, D-Ark., amendment that would bar closure of any domestic military bases in fiscal 1991 and would require any future closures to be proposed as part of a long-term plan for the military's future shape. Motion rejected 43-54: R 34-10; D 9-44 (ND 6-31, SD 3-13), Aug. 3, 1990. A "yea" was a vote supporting the president's position.

221. S 2884. Fiscal 1991 Defense Authorization/Domestic Base Closures. Bumpers, D-Ark., amendment that would bar closure of any domestic military base in fiscal 1991 and would require any future closures to be proposed as part of a long-term plan for the future shape of the military. Rejected 43-54: R 5-39; D 38-15 (ND 28-9, SD 10-6), Aug. 3, 1990. A "nay" was a vote supporting the president's position.

	222	223	224	225	226	227
ALABAMA						
Heflin	N	Y	Y	Y	Y	Y
Shelby	N	Y	Y	Y	Y	Y
ALASKA						
Murkowski	?	?	?	?	?	+
Stevens	N	N	Y	Y	Y	Y
ARIZONA						
DeConcini	Y	Y	Y	N	N	Y
McCain	N	N	Y	Y	Y	Y
ARKANSAS						
Bumpers	Y	Y	Y	N	N	N
Pryor	?	Y	Y	N	N	N
CALIFORNIA						
Cranston	Y	Y	Y	N	N	N
Wilson	N	N	Y	Y	Y	Y
COLORADO						
Wirth	N	?	?	?	?	?
Armstrong	?	N	Y	Y	Y	N
CONNECTICUT						
Dodd	N	Y	Y	Y	N	Y
Lieberman	Y	Y	Y	N	N	Y
DELAWARE						
Biden	Y	Y	Y	N	N	Y
Roth	Y	N	Y	Y	Y	N
FLORIDA						
Graham	N	Y	Y	Y	Y	Y
Mack	N	N	Y	Y	Y	Y
GEORGIA						
Fowler	Y	Y	Y	N	N	Y
Nunn	N	Y	Y	Y	Y	Y
HAWAII						
Inouye	N	Y	Y	Y	Y	Y
Akaka	N	Y	Y	N	N	Y
IDAHO						
McClure	N	N	Y	Y	Y	Y
Symms	N	N	Y	Y	Y	Y
ILLINOIS						
Dixon	N	Y	Y	Y	Y	Y
Simon	Y	Y	Y	N	N	N
INDIANA						
Coats	N	N	Y	Y	Y	Y
Lugar	N	N	Y	Y	Y	Y
IOWA						
Harkin	Y	Y	Y	N	N	N
Grassley	Y	N	Y	Y	N	Y
KANSAS						
Dole	N	N	Y	Y	Y	Y
Kassebaum	N	N	Y	N	Y	Y
KENTUCKY						
Ford	N	Y	Y	Y	N	Y
McConnell	N	N	Y	Y	Y	Y
LOUISIANA						
Breaux	N	Y	Y	Y	N	Y
Johnston	N	Y	Y	N	N	Y
MAINE						
Mitchell	Y	Y	Y	N	N	Y
Cohen	Y	N	Y	Y	N	Y
MARYLAND						
Mikulski	N	Y	Y	N	N	Y
Sarbanes	Y	Y	Y	N	N	Y
MASSACHUSETTS						
Kennedy	N	Y	Y	N	N	Y
Kerry	N	Y	Y	N	N	Y
MICHIGAN						
Levin	Y	Y	Y	N	N	Y
Riegle	N	Y	Y	N	N	N
MINNESOTA						
Boschwitz	N	N	Y	Y	Y	Y
Durenberger	N	N	Y	Y	Y	Y
MISSISSIPPI						
Cochran	N	N	Y	Y	Y	Y
Lott	N	N	Y	Y	Y	?
MISSOURI						
Bond	N	N	Y	Y	Y	Y
Danforth	N	N	Y	Y	Y	Y
MONTANA						
Baucus	N	Y	Y	N	N	N
Burns	N	N	Y	Y	Y	Y
NEBRASKA						
Exon	N	Y	Y	Y	Y	Y
Kerrey	Y	Y	Y	N	N	Y
NEVADA						
Bryan	N	Y	Y	Y	Y	Y
Reid	Y	Y	Y	N	N	Y
NEW HAMPSHIRE						
Humphrey	N	N	Y	Y	Y	Y
Rudman	N	N	Y	Y	Y	Y
NEW JERSEY						
Bradley	N	Y	Y	N	N	N
Lautenberg	N	Y	Y	N	N	Y
NEW MEXICO						
Bingaman	?	Y	Y	Y	Y	Y
Domenici	N	Y	Y	?	?	?
NEW YORK						
Moynihan	Y	Y	Y	N	N	Y
D'Amato	N	N	Y	Y	Y	Y
NORTH CAROLINA						
Sanford	Y	Y	Y	Y	Y	Y
Helms	N	N	Y	Y	Y	Y
NORTH DAKOTA						
Burdick	Y	Y	Y	N	N	Y
Conrad	Y	Y	Y	N	N	N
OHIO						
Glenn	Y	Y	Y	N	Y	Y
Metzenbaum	Y	Y	Y	N	N	N
OKLAHOMA						
Boren	N	Y	Y	N	Y	Y
Nickles	N	N	Y	Y	Y	Y
OREGON						
Hatfield	Y	Y	N	N	N	N
Packwood	N	N	Y	Y	Y	Y
PENNSYLVANIA						
Heinz	Y	N	Y	Y	Y	Y
Specter	N	N	Y	Y	Y	Y
RHODE ISLAND						
Pell	N	N	Y	N	N	Y
Chafee	N	N	Y	N	N	Y
SOUTH CAROLINA						
Hollings	N	N	Y	Y	Y	Y
Thurmond	N	N	Y	Y	Y	Y
SOUTH DAKOTA						
Daschle	Y	Y	Y	N	N	Y
Pressler	Y	N	Y	Y	N	Y
TENNESSEE						
Gore	N	Y	Y	Y	Y	Y
Sasser	Y	Y	Y	N	N	N
TEXAS						
Bentsen	N	Y	Y	Y	Y	Y
Gramm	N	N	Y	Y	Y	Y
UTAH						
Garn	N	N	Y	Y	Y	Y
Hatch	N	N	Y	Y	Y	Y
VERMONT						
Leahy	Y	Y	Y	N	N	Y
Jeffords	N	N	Y	N	N	Y
VIRGINIA						
Robb	N	Y	Y	Y	Y	Y
Warner	N	N	Y	Y	Y	Y
WASHINGTON						
Adams	N	Y	Y	N	N	Y
Gorton	N	N	Y	Y	Y	Y
WEST VIRGINIA						
Byrd	N	Y	Y	N	Y	Y
Rockefeller	N	Y	Y	N	N	N
WISCONSIN						
Kohl	Y	Y	Y	N	N	Y
Kasten	N	N	Y	Y	Y	Y
WYOMING						
Simpson	N	N	N	Y	Y	+
Wallop	N	N	Y	Y	Y	N

KEY

- Y Voted for (yea).
- # Paired for.
- \+ Announced for.
- N Voted against (nay).
- X Paired against.
- \- Announced against.
- P Voted "present."
- C Voted "present" to avoid possible conflict of interest.
- ? Did not vote or otherwise make a position known.

Democrats *Republicans*

ND Northern Democrats SD Southern Democrats

Southern states - Ala., Ark., Fla., Ga., Ky., La., Miss., N.C., Okla., S.C., Tenn., Texas, Va.

222. S 2884. Fiscal 1991 Defense Authorization/Land Revenues. Glenn, D-Ohio, amendment to provide that funds from the sale or lease of Department of Defense land shall go to the U.S. Treasury instead of the Defense Department. Rejected 29-67: R 6-37; D 23-30 (ND 19-18, SD 4-12), Aug. 3, 1990.

223. S 2884. Fiscal 1991 Defense Authorization/SDI. Bingaman, D-N.M., amendment to change priorities within the strategic defense initiative (SDI), reducing funds for the so-called brilliant pebbles program of space-based interceptor missiles while increasing funds for research on ground-based antimissile systems and long-term technologies. Adopted 54-44: R 2-42; D 52-2 (ND 36-1, SD 16-1), Aug. 4, 1990. A "nay" was a vote supporting the president's position.

224. S 2884. Fiscal 1991 Defense Authorization/Missile Proliferation. Warner, R-Va., amendment to express the sense of Congress that development of a defense against short-range ballistic missiles should be speeded up. Adopted 96-2: R 42-2; D 54-0 (ND 37-0, SD 17-0), Aug. 4, 1990.

225. S 2884. Fiscal 1991 Defense Authorization/SDI. Nunn, D-Ga., motion to table (kill) the Bumpers, D-Ark., amendment to cut $594 million from the amount authorized for the strategic defense initiative (SDI). Motion agreed to 56-41: R 39-4; D 17-37 (ND 6-31, SD 11-6), Aug. 4, 1990. A "yea" was a vote supporting the president's position.

226. S 2884. Fiscal 1991 Defense Authorization/SDI. Nunn, D-Ga., motion to table (kill) the Kerry, D-Mass., amendment to transfer $400 million from the strategic defense initiative (SDI) to the war on drugs and veterans' health programs. Motion agreed to 54-43: R 37-6; D 17-37 (ND 7-30, SD 10-7), Aug. 4, 1990. A "yea" was a vote supporting the president's position.

227. S 2884. Fiscal 1991 Defense Authorization/Passage. Passage of the bill to authorize appropriations for the Department of Defense, military construction and the military activities of the Department of Energy. The bill would result in total defense-related budget authority of $289 billion and total outlays of $297 billion, $27 billion and $10 billion, respectively, below the fiscal 1990 baseline level. Passed 79-16: R 37-4; D 42-12 (ND 28-9, SD 14-3), Aug. 4, 1990.

	228	229	230	231	232	233	234
ALABAMA							
Heflin	N	N	Y	Y	N	Y	N
Shelby	N	Y	Y	Y	N	Y	N
ALASKA							
Murkowski	N	N	Y	Y	Y	Y	N
Stevens	N	Y	Y	Y	Y	Y	N
ARIZONA							
DeConcini	N	N	Y	Y	N	Y	N
McCain	N	N	Y	Y	Y	Y	N
ARKANSAS							
Bumpers	N	Y	Y	Y	N	Y	N
Pryor	Y	Y	Y	Y	N	Y	N
CALIFORNIA							
Cranston	Y	Y	Y	Y	N	Y	Y
Wilson	?	?	?	?	?	?	?
COLORADO							
Wirth	Y	Y	Y	Y	N	Y	Y
Armstrong	N	N	Y	Y	Y	Y	N
CONNECTICUT							
Dodd	N	Y	Y	Y	Y	Y	Y
Lieberman	Y	Y	Y	Y	N	Y	Y
DELAWARE							
Biden	Y	Y	Y	Y	Y	Y	Y
Roth	N	Y	Y	N	Y	Y	N
FLORIDA							
Graham	N	Y	Y	Y	N	Y	Y
Mack	N	N	Y	N	N	Y	N
GEORGIA							
Fowler	Y	Y	Y	Y	N	Y	Y
Nunn	Y	Y	Y	Y	N	Y	N
HAWAII							
Inouye	N	Y	Y	Y	Y	Y	Y
Akaka	Y	Y	Y	Y	Y	Y	Y
IDAHO							
McClure	N	N	Y	Y	N	Y	N
Symms	N	N	Y	Y	N	Y	N
ILLINOIS							
Dixon	N	Y	Y	N	N	Y	N
Simon	Y	Y	Y	Y	N	Y	Y
INDIANA							
Coats	N	N	Y	Y	N	Y	N
Lugar	N	N	Y	Y	N	Y	N
IOWA							
Harkin	Y	Y	Y	Y	N	Y	Y
Grassley	N	N	Y	Y	N	Y	N
KANSAS							
Dole	N	N	Y	Y	Y	Y	N
Kassebaum	N	Y	Y	Y	N	Y	N
KENTUCKY							
Ford	Y	N	Y	Y	Y	Y	N
McConnell	N	N	Y	Y	N	Y	N
LOUISIANA							
Breaux	N	N	Y	Y	Y	Y	N
Johnston	N	N	Y	Y	?	?	N
MAINE							
Mitchell	Y	Y	Y	Y	N	Y	Y
Cohen	Y	Y	Y	Y	N	Y	Y
MARYLAND							
Mikulski	N	Y	Y	Y	N	Y	Y
Sarbanes	Y	Y	Y	Y	N	Y	Y
MASSACHUSETTS							
Kennedy	N	Y	Y	Y	Y	Y	Y
Kerry	Y	Y	Y	Y	Y	Y	Y
MICHIGAN							
Levin	Y	Y	Y	Y	Y	Y	N
Riegle	Y	Y	Y	Y	N	Y	Y
MINNESOTA							
Boschwitz	N	N	Y	Y	N	Y	N
Durenberger	N	N	Y	Y	Y	Y	N
MISSISSIPPI							
Cochran	N	N	Y	Y	N	Y	N
Lott	N	N	Y	N	N	Y	N
MISSOURI							
Bond	N	Y	Y	Y	N	Y	N
Danforth	N	N	Y	Y	Y	Y	N
MONTANA							
Baucus	Y	Y	Y	Y	N	Y	N
Burns	N	N	Y	Y	N	Y	N
NEBRASKA							
Exon	Y	Y	Y	Y	N	Y	N
Kerrey	N	Y	N	Y	N	Y	Y
NEVADA							
Bryan	N	Y	Y	Y	Y	Y	Y
Reid	N	N	Y	Y	N	Y	Y
NEW HAMPSHIRE							
Humphrey	N	N	Y	N	Y	Y	N
Rudman	N	Y	Y	Y	N	Y	N
NEW JERSEY							
Bradley	Y	Y	Y	Y	N	Y	Y
Lautenberg	N	Y	Y	Y	N	Y	Y
NEW MEXICO							
Bingaman	N	Y	N	Y	N	Y	Y
Domenici	N	N	Y	Y	Y	Y	N
NEW YORK							
Moynihan	Y	Y	Y	Y	N	Y	Y
D'Amato	N	N	Y	Y	Y	Y	N
NORTH CAROLINA							
Sanford	Y	Y	Y	Y	N	Y	Y
Helms	N	N	Y	N	N	Y	N
NORTH DAKOTA							
Burdick	Y	Y	Y	Y	N	Y	Y
Conrad	Y	Y	Y	Y	N	Y	N
OHIO							
Glenn	Y	Y	Y	Y	N	Y	Y
Metzenbaum	Y	Y	Y	Y	Y	Y	Y
OKLAHOMA							
Boren	Y	Y	Y	Y	N	Y	N
Nickles	N	N	Y	Y	N	Y	N
OREGON							
Hatfield	N	Y	Y	Y	Y	Y	Y
Packwood	N	Y	Y	Y	Y	Y	Y
PENNSYLVANIA							
Heinz	N	Y	Y	Y	Y	Y	N
Specter	Y	Y	Y	Y	Y	Y	Y
RHODE ISLAND							
Pell	Y	Y	Y	Y	N	Y	Y
Chafee	N	Y	Y	Y	N	Y	Y
SOUTH CAROLINA							
Hollings	Y	Y	Y	Y	Y	Y	Y
Thurmond	N	N	Y	Y	Y	Y	N
SOUTH DAKOTA							
Daschle	Y	Y	Y	Y	N	Y	Y
Pressler	Y	N	Y	Y	N	Y	N
TENNESSEE							
Gore	Y	Y	Y	Y	Y	Y	Y
Sasser	N	Y	Y	Y	N	Y	Y
TEXAS							
Bentsen	N	Y	Y	Y	Y	Y	Y
Gramm	N	N	Y	Y	Y	Y	N
UTAH							
Garn	N	N	Y	Y	Y	Y	N
Hatch	N	N	Y	Y	Y	Y	N
VERMONT							
Leahy	N	Y	Y	Y	N	Y	Y
Jeffords	Y	Y	Y	Y	N	Y	Y
VIRGINIA							
Robb	N	Y	Y	Y	Y	Y	Y
Warner	N	Y	Y	Y	Y	Y	N
WASHINGTON							
Adams	Y	Y	Y	Y	Y	Y	Y
Gorton	N	Y	Y	Y	N	Y	N
WEST VIRGINIA							
Byrd	N	Y	Y	Y	Y	Y	N
Rockefeller	N	Y	Y	Y	Y	Y	Y
WISCONSIN							
Kohl	N	Y	Y	Y	N	Y	Y
Kasten	N	N	Y	Y	Y	Y	N
WYOMING							
Simpson	N	N	Y	Y	N	Y	N
Wallop	N	N	Y	Y	N	Y	N

KEY

- Y Voted for (yea).
- # Paired for.
- \+ Announced for.
- N Voted against (nay).
- X Paired against.
- \- Announced against.
- P Voted "present."
- C Voted "present" to avoid possible conflict of interest.
- ? Did not vote or otherwise make a position known.

Democrats ***Republicans***

ND Northern Democrats SD Southern Democrats

Southern states - Ala., Ark., Fla., Ga., Ky., La., Miss., N.C., Okla., S.C., Tenn., Texas, Va.

228. HR 5241. Fiscal 1991 Treasury-Postal Appropriations/Budget Act Waiver. Lieberman, D-Conn., motion to waive provisions of the Congressional Budget Act that would bar consideration of the Glenn, D-Ohio, amendment to provide $55.5 million to employ an additional 1,050 collection personnel in the Internal Revenue Service. Motion rejected 35-64: R 4-40; D 31-24 (ND 23-15, SD 8-9), Sept. 11, 1990. A three-fifths majority (60) of the total Senate is required to waive the Budget Act.

229. HR 5241. Fiscal 1991 Treasury-Postal Appropriations/Rights of Children. Bradley, D-N.J., motion to table (kill) the Helms, R-N.C., amendment to the Bradley amendment, to inform all parties to the Convention on the Rights of the Child that all children have a right to life and that the word "child" means all human beings under the age of 18, including the unborn at every stage of biological development. Motion agreed to 63-36: R 14-30; D 49-6 (ND 36-2, SD 13-4), Sept. 11, 1990.

230. HR 5241. Fiscal 1991 Treasury-Postal Appropriations/Iraqi War Crimes. Heinz, R-Pa., amendment to express the sense of the Senate that Iraqi President Saddam Hussein and other Iraqi leaders should be tried for war crimes in the event of hostilities between the United States and the government of Iraq. Adopted 97-2: R 44-0; D 53-2 (ND 36-2, SD 17-0), Sept. 11, 1990.

231. HR 5241. Fiscal 1991 Treasury-Postal Appropriations/Passage. Passage of the bill to appropriate $20.7 billion for fiscal 1991 for the Treasury Department, Postal Service, Executive Office of the President and independent agencies. The amount is $2.3 billion more than the fiscal 1990 appropriation, $2.5 million less than the president's request and $10.2 million less than the House-passed bill. Passed 93-6: R 39-5; D 54-1 (ND 37-1, SD 17-0), Sept. 11, 1990.

232. S 2924. National Mandatory Fish Inspection/Program Supervision. Hollings, D-S.C., substitute amendment to direct the secretaries of Health and Human Services and Commerce to establish a comprehensive seafood safety and quality assurance program for fish and fish products as opposed to establishing such a program under the purview of the Department of Agriculture. Rejected 39-59: R 21-23; D 18-36 (ND 12-26, SD 6-10), Sept. 12, 1990.

233. HR 5311. Fiscal 1991 D.C. Appropriations/Juvenile Programs. Adams, D-Wash., amendment to allow organizations in the District of Columbia to bar a person from participating in a juvenile program if the parent of a juvenile in the program objects to the person based on the person's sexual orientation or if the person has been convicted of or charged with a sexual offense with a juvenile or otherwise poses a threat of engaging in sex with a juvenile. Adopted 98-0: R 44-0; D 54-0 (ND 38-0, SD 16-0), Sept. 12, 1990.

234. HR 5311. Fiscal 1991 D.C. Appropriations/Juvenile Programs. Adams, D-Wash., motion to table (kill) the Armstrong, R-Colo., amendment to allow organizations in the District of Columbia to bar homosexual and bisexual persons from participating in programs involving juveniles under the age of 18. Motion rejected 45-54: R 6-38; D 39-16 (ND 31-7, SD 8-9), Sept. 12, 1990.

	235	236	237	238	239	240	241	242
ALABAMA								
Heflin	N	Y	Y	Y	Y	Y	Y	Y
Shelby	N	Y	Y	Y	Y	Y	Y	Y
ALASKA								
Murkowski	Y	Y	Y	Y	Y	Y	Y	Y
Stevens	Y	Y	Y	Y	Y	Y	Y	Y
ARIZONA								
DeConcini	Y	Y	Y	Y	Y	Y	Y	Y
McCain	Y	Y	Y	Y	Y	Y	Y	Y
ARKANSAS								
Bumpers	Y	Y	Y	Y	Y	Y	Y	Y
Pryor	Y	Y	Y	Y	Y	Y	Y	Y
CALIFORNIA								
Cranston	Y	Y	Y	Y	Y	Y	Y	Y
Wilson	?	?	?	?	?	?	?	?
COLORADO								
Wirth	Y	Y	Y	Y	Y	Y	Y	Y
Armstrong	N	Y	Y	Y	Y	Y	Y	Y
CONNECTICUT								
Dodd	Y	Y	Y	Y	Y	Y	Y	Y
Lieberman	Y	Y	Y	Y	Y	Y	Y	Y
DELAWARE								
Biden	Y	Y	Y	Y	Y	Y	Y	Y
Roth	Y	Y	Y	Y	Y	Y	Y	Y
FLORIDA								
Graham	Y	Y	Y	Y	Y	Y	Y	Y
Mack	N	Y	Y	Y	Y	Y	Y	Y
GEORGIA								
Fowler	Y	Y	Y	Y	Y	Y	Y	Y
Nunn	Y	Y	Y	Y	Y	Y	Y	Y
HAWAII								
Inouye	Y	Y	Y	Y	Y	Y	Y	Y
Akaka	Y	Y	Y	Y	Y	Y	Y	Y
IDAHO								
McClure	N	Y	Y	Y	Y	Y	Y	Y
Symms	N	Y	Y	Y	Y	Y	Y	Y
ILLINOIS								
Dixon	N	Y	Y	Y	Y	Y	Y	Y
Simon	Y	Y	Y	Y	Y	Y	Y	Y
INDIANA								
Coats	N	Y	Y	Y	Y	Y	Y	Y
Lugar	N	Y	Y	Y	Y	Y	Y	Y
IOWA								
Harkin	Y	Y	Y	Y	Y	Y	Y	Y
Grassley	Y	Y	Y	Y	Y	Y	Y	Y
KANSAS								
Dole	N	Y	Y	Y	Y	Y	Y	Y
Kassebaum	Y	Y	Y	Y	Y	Y	Y	Y
KENTUCKY								
Ford	N	Y	Y	Y	Y	Y	Y	Y
McConnell	N	Y	Y	Y	Y	Y	Y	Y
LOUISIANA								
Breaux	N	Y	Y	Y	Y	Y	Y	Y
Johnston	?	Y	Y	Y	Y	Y	Y	Y
MAINE								
Mitchell	Y	Y	Y	Y	Y	Y	Y	Y
Cohen	Y	Y	Y	Y	Y	Y	Y	Y
MARYLAND								
Mikulski	Y	Y	Y	Y	Y	Y	Y	Y
Sarbanes	Y	Y	Y	Y	Y	Y	Y	Y
MASSACHUSETTS								
Kennedy	Y	Y	Y	Y	Y	Y	Y	Y
Kerry	Y	Y	Y	Y	Y	Y	Y	Y
MICHIGAN								
Levin	N	Y	Y	Y	Y	Y	Y	Y
Riegle	N	Y	Y	Y	Y	Y	Y	Y
MINNESOTA								
Boschwitz	Y	Y	Y	Y	Y	Y	Y	Y
Durenberger	Y	Y	Y	Y	Y	Y	Y	Y
MISSISSIPPI								
Cochran	N	Y	Y	Y	Y	Y	Y	Y
Lott	N	Y	Y	Y	Y	Y	Y	Y
MISSOURI								
Bond	N	Y	Y	Y	Y	Y	Y	Y
Danforth	Y	Y	Y	Y	Y	Y	Y	Y
MONTANA								
Baucus	Y	Y	Y	Y	Y	Y	Y	Y
Burns	N	Y	Y	Y	Y	Y	Y	Y
NEBRASKA								
Exon	Y	Y	Y	Y	Y	Y	Y	Y
Kerrey	Y	Y	Y	Y	Y	Y	Y	Y
NEVADA								
Bryan	Y	Y	Y	Y	Y	Y	Y	Y
Reid	Y	Y	Y	Y	Y	Y	Y	Y
NEW HAMPSHIRE								
Humphrey	Y	Y	Y	Y	Y	Y	Y	Y
Rudman	Y	Y	Y	Y	Y	Y	Y	Y
NEW JERSEY								
Bradley	Y	Y	Y	Y	Y	Y	Y	Y
Lautenberg	Y	Y	Y	Y	Y	Y	Y	Y
NEW MEXICO								
Bingaman	Y	Y	Y	Y	Y	Y	Y	Y
Domenici	Y	Y	Y	Y	Y	Y	Y	Y
NEW YORK								
Moynihan	Y	Y	Y	Y	Y	Y	Y	Y
D'Amato	Y	Y	Y	Y	Y	Y	Y	Y
NORTH CAROLINA								
Sanford	Y	Y	Y	Y	Y	Y	Y	Y
Helms	N	Y	Y	Y	Y	Y	Y	Y
NORTH DAKOTA								
Burdick	Y	Y	Y	Y	Y	Y	Y	Y
Conrad	Y	Y	Y	Y	Y	Y	Y	Y
OHIO								
Glenn	Y	Y	Y	Y	Y	Y	Y	Y
Metzenbaum	Y	Y	Y	Y	Y	Y	Y	Y
OKLAHOMA								
Boren	N	Y	Y	Y	Y	Y	Y	Y
Nickles	N	Y	Y	Y	Y	Y	Y	Y
OREGON								
Hatfield	Y	Y	Y	Y	Y	Y	Y	Y
Packwood	Y	Y	Y	Y	Y	Y	Y	Y
PENNSYLVANIA								
Heinz	Y	Y	Y	Y	Y	Y	Y	Y
Specter	Y	Y	Y	Y	Y	Y	Y	Y
RHODE ISLAND								
Pell	Y	Y	Y	Y	Y	Y	Y	Y
Chafee	Y	Y	Y	Y	Y	Y	Y	Y
SOUTH CAROLINA								
Hollings	Y	Y	Y	Y	Y	Y	Y	Y
Thurmond	N	Y	Y	Y	Y	Y	Y	Y
SOUTH DAKOTA								
Daschle	Y	Y	Y	Y	Y	Y	Y	Y
Pressler	Y	Y	Y	Y	Y	Y	Y	Y
TENNESSEE								
Gore	Y	Y	Y	Y	Y	Y	Y	Y
Sasser	Y	Y	Y	Y	Y	Y	Y	Y
TEXAS								
Bentsen	Y	Y	Y	Y	Y	Y	Y	Y
Gramm	N	Y	Y	Y	Y	Y	Y	Y
UTAH								
Garn	?	Y	Y	Y	Y	Y	Y	Y
Hatch	N	Y	Y	Y	Y	Y	Y	Y
VERMONT								
Leahy	Y	Y	Y	Y	Y	Y	Y	Y
Jeffords	Y	Y	Y	Y	Y	Y	Y	Y
VIRGINIA								
Robb	Y	Y	Y	Y	Y	Y	Y	Y
Warner	Y	Y	Y	Y	Y	Y	Y	Y
WASHINGTON								
Adams	Y	Y	Y	Y	Y	Y	Y	Y
Gorton	Y	Y	Y	Y	Y	Y	Y	Y
WEST VIRGINIA								
Byrd	N	Y	Y	Y	Y	Y	Y	Y
Rockefeller	Y	Y	Y	Y	Y	Y	Y	Y
WISCONSIN								
Kohl	Y	Y	Y	Y	Y	Y	Y	Y
Kasten	N	Y	Y	Y	Y	Y	Y	Y
WYOMING								
Simpson	-	Y	Y	Y	Y	Y	Y	Y
Wallop	N	Y	Y	Y	Y	Y	Y	Y

KEY

- Y Voted for (yea).
- # Paired for.
- + Announced for.
- N Voted against (nay).
- X Paired against.
- - Announced against.
- P Voted "present."
- C Voted "present" to avoid possible conflict of interest.
- ? Did not vote or otherwise make a position known.

Democrats *Republicans*

ND Northern Democrats SD Southern Democrats

Southern states - Ala., Ark., Fla., Ga., Ky., La., Miss., N.C., Okla., S.C., Tenn., Texas, Va.

235. S 1224. Motor Vehicle Fuel Efficiency Act/Cloture. Mitchell, D-Maine, motion to invoke cloture (thus limiting debate) on the motion to proceed to the bill to require manufacturers of passenger vehicles and light trucks to increase their 1988 corporate average fuel economy (CAFE) standards by 20 percent by the 1995 model year and by 40 percent by the 2001 model year. Motion agreed to 68-28: R 23-19; D 45-9 (ND 34-4, SD 11-5), Sept. 14, 1990. A three-fifths majority vote (60) of the total Senate is required to invoke cloture.

236. Treaty Doc 99-13 and 101-9. Tax Convention With Tunisia, With Supplementary/Adoption. Adoption of the resolution of ratification of the treaty between the United States and Tunisia to prevent double taxation or evasion of taxes on income. The supplementary protocol incorporates changes in law from the Tax Reform Act of 1986. Adopted 99-0: R 44-0; D 55-0 (ND 38-0, SD 17-0), Sept. 18, 1990. A two-thirds majority of those present and voting (66 in this case) is required for adoption of resolutions of ratification.

237. Treaty Doc 100-22. Tax Convention With the Republic of Indonesia/Adoption. Adoption of the resolution of ratification of the treaty between the United States and Indonesia to prevent double taxation or evasion of taxes on income. Adopted 99-0: R 44-0; D 55-0 (ND 38-0, SD 17-0), Sept. 18, 1990. A two-thirds majority of those present and voting (66 in this case) is required for adoption of resolutions of ratification.

238. Treaty Doc 101-5. Tax Convention With the Republic of India/Adoption. Adoption of the resolution of ratification of the treaty between the United States and India to prevent double taxation or evasion of taxes on income. Adopted 99-0: R 44-0; D 55-0 (ND 38-0, SD 17-0), Sept. 18, 1990. A two-thirds majority of those present and voting (66 in this case) is required for adoption of resolutions of ratification.

239. Treaty Doc 101-6. Council of Europe — OECD Convention on Mutual Administrative Assistance in Tax Matters/Adoption. Adoption of the resolution of ratification of the treaty to provide for the exchange of information for the assessment, recovery, and enforcement of taxes and tax claims and to assist in the prosecution of taxpayers between the member states of the Council of Europe, the member countries of the Organization for Economic Cooperation and Development, and the United States. Adopted 99-0: R 44-0; D 55-0 (ND 38-0, SD 17-0), Sept. 18, 1990. A two-thirds majority of those present and voting (66 in this case) is required for adoption of resolutions of ratification.

240. Treaty Doc 101-10. Tax Convention With the Federal Republic of Germany/Adoption. Adoption of the resolution of ratification of the treaty between the United States and West Germany to prevent double taxation or evasion of income taxes or other levies. Adopted 99-0: R 44-0; D 55-0 (ND 38-0, SD 17-0), Sept. 18, 1990. A two-thirds majority of those present and voting (66 in this case) is required for adoption of resolutions of ratification.

241. Treaty Doc 101-11. Tax Convention With the Republic of Finland/Adoption. Adoption of the resolution of ratification of the treaty between the United States and Finland to prevent double taxation or evasion of taxes on income. Adopted 99-0: R 44-0; D 55-0 (ND 38-0, SD 17-0), Sept. 18, 1990. A two-thirds majority of those present and voting (66 in this case) is required for adoption of resolutions of ratification.

242. Treaty Doc 101-16. Tax Convention With Spain, With Protocol/Adoption. Adoption of the resolution of ratification of the treaty between the United States and Spain to prevent double taxation or evasion of taxes on income. Adopted 99-0: R 44-0; D 55-0 (ND 38-0, SD 17-0), Sept. 18, 1990. A two-thirds majority of those present and voting (66 in this case) is required for adoption of resolutions of ratification.

	243	244
ALABAMA		
Heflin	Y	Y
Shelby	Y	Y
ALASKA		
Murkowski	Y	Y
Stevens	Y	Y
ARIZONA		
DeConcini	Y	Y
McCain	Y	Y
ARKANSAS		
Bumpers	Y	Y
Pryor	Y	Y
CALIFORNIA		
Cranston	Y	N
Wilson	?	?
COLORADO		
Wirth	Y	N
Armstrong	Y	Y
CONNECTICUT		
Dodd	Y	N
Lieberman	Y	N
DELAWARE		
Biden	Y	N
Roth	Y	Y
FLORIDA		
Graham	Y	N
Mack	N	Y
GEORGIA		
Fowler	Y	N
Nunn	Y	N
HAWAII		
Inouye	Y	N
Akaka	Y	N
IDAHO		
McClure	N	Y
Symms	N	Y
ILLINOIS		
Dixon	Y	N
Simon	Y	N
INDIANA		
Coats	Y	Y
Lugar	N	Y

	243	244
IOWA		
Harkin	Y	N
Grassley	Y	Y
KANSAS		
Dole	N	Y
Kassebaum	Y	Y
KENTUCKY		
Ford	Y	Y
McConnell	Y	Y
LOUISIANA		
Breaux	Y	Y
Johnston	Y	Y
MAINE		
Mitchell	Y	Y
Cohen	Y	Y
MARYLAND		
Mikulski	Y	N
Sarbanes	Y	N
MASSACHUSETTS		
Kennedy	Y	N
Kerry	Y	N
MICHIGAN		
Levin	Y	Y
Riegle	Y	Y
MINNESOTA		
Boschwitz	Y	Y
Durenberger	Y	Y
MISSISSIPPI		
Cochran	N	Y
Lott	N	Y
MISSOURI		
Bond	N	Y
Danforth	N	N
MONTANA		
Baucus	Y	Y
Burns	N	Y
NEBRASKA		
Exon	Y	Y
Kerrey	Y	Y
NEVADA		
Bryan	Y	Y
Reid	Y	Y

	243	244
NEW HAMPSHIRE		
Humphrey	Y	Y
Rudman	N	Y
NEW JERSEY		
Bradley	Y	N
Lautenberg	Y	N
NEW MEXICO		
Bingaman	Y	Y
Domenici	Y	Y
NEW YORK		
Moynihan	Y	N
D'Amato	Y	N
NORTH CAROLINA		
Sanford	Y	N
Helms	N	Y
NORTH DAKOTA		
Burdick	Y	Y
Conrad	Y	Y
OHIO		
Glenn	Y	Y
Metzenbaum	Y	Y
OKLAHOMA		
Boren	Y	Y
Nickles	Y	Y
OREGON		
Hatfield	Y	Y
Packwood	Y	Y
PENNSYLVANIA		
Heinz	N	Y
Specter	Y	Y
RHODE ISLAND		
Pell	Y	Y
Chafee	N	Y
SOUTH CAROLINA		
Hollings	Y	Y
Thurmond	N	Y
SOUTH DAKOTA		
Daschle	Y	Y
Pressler	Y	Y
TENNESSEE		
Gore	Y	N
Sasser	Y	N

KEY

- Y Voted for (yea).
- # Paired for.
- + Announced for.
- N Voted against (nay).
- X Paired against.
- \- Announced against.
- P Voted "present."
- C Voted "present" to avoid possible conflict of interest.
- ? Did not vote or otherwise make a position known.

Democrats ***Republicans***

	243	244
TEXAS		
Bentsen	Y	N
Gramm	Y	Y
UTAH		
Garn	N	Y
Hatch	N	Y
VERMONT		
Leahy	Y	N
Jeffords	Y	N
VIRGINIA		
Robb	Y	N
Warner	Y	Y
WASHINGTON		
Adams	Y	N
Gorton	N	Y
WEST VIRGINIA		
Byrd	Y	Y
Rockefeller	Y	Y
WISCONSIN		
Kohl	Y	N
Kasten	Y	Y
WYOMING		
Simpson	N	Y
Wallop	Y	Y

ND Northern Democrats SD Southern Democrats

Southern states - Ala., Ark., Fla., Ga., Ky., La., Miss., N.C., Okla., S.C., Tenn., Texas, Va.

243. S 1511. Older Workers Benefit Protection Act/Implementation Delay. Pryor, D-Ark., amendment to the Hatch, R-Utah, amendment to the Metzenbaum, D-Ohio, substitute amendment, to delay for two years the application of the employee benefit practices provisions of the act to the federal sector and to require the director of the Office of Personnel Management to study and report on the compliance of federal agencies with Title I of the act. Adopted 80-19: R 25-19; D 55-0 (ND 38-0, SD 17-0), Sept. 18, 1990. (The underlying Hatch amendment was later adopted by voice vote).

244. HR 5311. Fiscal 1991 D.C. Appropriations/Interstate Garbage Dumping. Coats, R-Ind., amendment to the Nickles, R-Okla., amendment, to allow states to bar dumping of other states' garbage by private waste-disposal companies. Adopted 68-31: R 41-3; D 27-28 (ND 18-20, SD 9-8), Sept. 18, 1990. (The underlying Nickles amendment was later adopted by voice vote.)

	245	246	247	248	249	250	251	252
ALABAMA								
Heflin	Y	N	Y	N	Y	Y	Y	N
Shelby	Y	N	Y	N	Y	Y	Y	Y
ALASKA								
Murkowski	Y	Y	Y	N	Y	Y	N	Y
Stevens	Y	Y	Y	N	Y	Y	Y	Y
ARIZONA								
DeConcini	Y	N	Y	Y	Y	Y	Y	N
McCain	Y	Y	N	Y	Y	Y	Y	N
ARKANSAS								
Bumpers	Y	Y	Y	Y	Y	Y	Y	Y
Pryor	Y	Y	Y	Y	Y	Y	Y	Y
CALIFORNIA								
Cranston	Y	N	N	Y	Y	Y	Y	Y
Wilson	?	?	?	?	?	?	?	?
COLORADO								
Wirth	Y	Y	N	Y	Y	Y	N	Y
Armstrong	Y	Y	Y	N	Y	Y	N	N
CONNECTICUT								
Dodd	Y	N	N	Y	Y	Y	N	Y
Lieberman	Y	N	N	Y	Y	Y	N	Y
DELAWARE								
Biden	Y	N	Y	Y	Y	Y	N	Y
Roth	Y	Y	Y	Y	Y	Y	N	Y
FLORIDA								
Graham	Y	Y	N	Y	Y	Y	Y	Y
Mack	Y	Y	Y	N	Y	Y	N	N
GEORGIA								
Fowler	Y	Y	N	Y	Y	Y	Y	Y
Nunn	Y	Y	N	N	Y	Y	Y	Y
HAWAII								
Inouye	Y	N	N	Y	Y	Y	Y	Y
Akaka	Y	N	N	Y	Y	Y	Y	Y
IDAHO								
McClure	N	N	Y	N	Y	Y	Y	N
Symms	Y	Y	Y	N	Y	Y	Y	N
ILLINOIS								
Dixon	Y	Y	Y	N	Y	Y	Y	Y
Simon	Y	N	Y	Y	Y	Y	Y	Y
INDIANA								
Coats	Y	N	Y	N	Y	Y	Y	N
Lugar	Y	Y	Y	N	Y	Y	Y	N
IOWA								
Harkin	Y	N	Y	Y	Y	Y	Y	Y
Grassley	Y	N	Y	N	Y	Y	Y	N
KANSAS								
Dole	Y	Y	Y	N	Y	Y	Y	N
Kassebaum	Y	Y	N	N	Y	Y	Y	Y
KENTUCKY								
Ford	Y	N	Y	N	Y	Y	Y	N
McConnell	Y	N	Y	N	Y	Y	Y	N
LOUISIANA								
Breaux	Y	N	Y	N	Y	Y	Y	N
Johnston	Y	N	Y	N	Y	Y	Y	N
MAINE								
Mitchell	Y	Y	N	Y	Y	Y	Y	Y
Cohen	Y	Y	N	Y	Y	Y	Y	Y
MARYLAND								
Mikulski	Y	N	N	Y	Y	Y	Y	Y
Sarbanes	Y	N	N	Y	Y	Y	Y	Y
MASSACHUSETTS								
Kennedy	Y	N	N	Y	Y	Y	Y	Y
Kerry	Y	N	N	Y	Y	Y	N	Y
MICHIGAN								
Levin	Y	N	Y	N	Y	Y	Y	Y
Riegle	Y	N	Y	N	Y	Y	Y	Y
MINNESOTA								
Boschwitz	Y	Y	N	Y	Y	Y	Y	N
Durenberger	Y	Y	N	Y	Y	Y	Y	N
MISSISSIPPI								
Cochran	Y	Y	Y	N	Y	Y	Y	N
Lott	Y	Y	Y	N	Y	Y	Y	N
MISSOURI								
Bond	Y	N	Y	N	Y	Y	Y	Y
Danforth	Y	Y	Y	Y	Y	Y	Y	N
MONTANA								
Baucus	Y	Y	N	Y	Y	Y	Y	Y
Burns	Y	Y	Y	N	Y	Y	Y	N
NEBRASKA								
Exon	?	?	?	Y	Y	Y	Y	N
Kerrey	Y	Y	Y	Y	Y	Y	Y	Y
NEVADA								
Bryan	Y	Y	N	Y	Y	Y	N	Y
Reid	Y	N	N	Y	Y	Y	N	N
NEW HAMPSHIRE								
Humphrey	?	?	?	N	Y	Y	N	N
Rudman	Y	Y	N	Y	?	?	?	?
NEW JERSEY								
Bradley	Y	N	N	Y	Y	Y	N	Y
Lautenberg	Y	N	N	Y	Y	Y	N	Y
NEW MEXICO								
Bingaman	Y	Y	N	Y	Y	Y	Y	Y
Domenici	Y	Y	Y	N	Y	Y	Y	N
NEW YORK								
Moynihan	Y	N	N	Y	Y	Y	N	Y
D'Amato	Y	N	Y	Y	Y	Y	Y	N
NORTH CAROLINA								
Sanford	Y	Y	N	Y	Y	Y	Y	Y
Helms	Y	Y	Y	N	Y	Y	N	N
NORTH DAKOTA								
Burdick	Y	N	Y	Y	Y	Y	Y	Y
Conrad	Y	N	Y	Y	Y	Y	Y	N
OHIO								
Glenn	Y	Y	Y	N	Y	Y	Y	Y
Metzenbaum	Y	N	N	Y	Y	Y	N	Y
OKLAHOMA								
Boren	Y	N	Y	N	Y	Y	Y	N
Nickles	Y	Y	Y	N	Y	Y	Y	N
OREGON								
Hatfield	Y	N	N	Y	Y	Y	Y	Y
Packwood	Y	N	Y	Y	Y	Y	Y	Y
PENNSYLVANIA								
Heinz	Y	N	N	Y	Y	Y	Y	Y
Specter	Y	N	N	N	Y	Y	Y	Y
RHODE ISLAND								
Pell	+	?	-	Y	Y	Y	N	Y
Chafee	Y	Y	N	Y	Y	Y	Y	Y
SOUTH CAROLINA								
Hollings	Y	Y	N	Y	Y	Y	Y	Y
Thurmond	Y	Y	Y	N	Y	Y	Y	Y
SOUTH DAKOTA								
Daschle	Y	N	Y	Y	Y	Y	Y	Y
Pressler	Y	Y	Y	Y	Y	Y	Y	N
TENNESSEE								
Gore	Y	N	N	Y	Y	Y	Y	Y
Sasser	Y	N	N	N	Y	Y	Y	Y
TEXAS								
Bentsen	Y	N	Y	Y	Y	Y	Y	Y
Gramm	Y	Y	Y	N	Y	Y	Y	N
UTAH								
Garn	?	?	?	N	Y	Y	Y	N
Hatch	Y	Y	Y	N	Y	Y	Y	N
VERMONT								
Leahy	Y	Y	N	Y	Y	Y	Y	Y
Jeffords	Y	Y	Y	Y	Y	Y	Y	Y
VIRGINIA								
Robb	Y	Y	Y	Y	Y	Y	Y	Y
Warner	Y	Y	Y	N	Y	Y	Y	Y
WASHINGTON								
Adams	Y	N	N	Y	Y	Y	Y	Y
Gorton	Y	Y	N	Y	Y	Y	Y	Y
WEST VIRGINIA								
Byrd	Y	N	Y	N	Y	Y	Y	Y
Rockefeller	Y	N	Y	Y	Y	Y	Y	Y
WISCONSIN								
Kohl	Y	N	N	Y	Y	Y	Y	Y
Kasten	Y	Y	Y	N	Y	Y	Y	N
WYOMING								
Simpson	Y	Y	Y	N	Y	Y	Y	Y
Wallop	Y	Y	Y	N	Y	Y	N	N

KEY

- Y Voted for (yea).
- # Paired for.
- + Announced for.
- N Voted against (nay).
- X Paired against.
- - Announced against.
- P Voted "present."
- C Voted "present" to avoid possible conflict of interest.
- ? Did not vote or otherwise make a position known.

Democrats ***Republicans***

ND Northern Democrats SD Southern Democrats

Southern states - Ala., Ark., Fla., Ga., Ky., La., Miss., N.C., Okla., S.C., Tenn., Texas, Va.

245. S 1511. Older Workers Benefit Protection Act/Passage. Passage of the bill to bar discrimination against older workers in employee benefits, effectively overturning a 1989 Supreme Court decision allowing age discrimination for certain benefits. The legislation would write into law regulations struck down by the court that banned age discrimination in employee benefits unless such bias is due to age-based cost differences. Passed 94-1: R 41-1; D 53-0 (ND 36-0, SD 17-0), Sept. 24, 1990. A "nay" was a vote supporting the president's position.

246. S 1224. Motor Vehicle Fuel Efficiency Act/Job Loss Assistance. Bryan, D-Nev., motion to table (kill) the Simon, D-Ill., amendment to the committee substitute amendment, to direct the secretary of Labor to set up a program substantially similar to trade adjustment assistance for employees who lose their jobs as a result of the corporate average fuel economy bill. Motion agreed to 49-46: R 32-10; D 17-36 (ND 9-27, SD 8-9), Sept. 24, 1990.

247. S 1224. Motor Vehicle Fuel Efficiency Act/Credit Cap. Danforth, R-Mo., amendment to the committee substitute amendment, to remove the caps on the maximum fuel efficiency credit available to manufacturers for producing flexible fuel vehicles. Adopted 55-40: R 31-11; D 24-29 (ND 14-22, SD 10-7), Sept. 24, 1990.

248. S 1224. Motor Vehicle Fuel Efficiency Act/Cloture. Motion to invoke cloture (thus limiting debate) on the bill to require manufacturers of passenger vehicles and light trucks to increase their 1988 corporate average fuel economy standards by 20 percent by 1995 model year and by 40 percent by the 2001 model year. Motion rejected 57-42: R 15-29; D 42-13 (ND 33-5, SD 9-8), Sept. 25, 1990. A three-fifths majority vote (60) of the total Senate is required to invoke cloture.

249. Treaty Doc N(A), 94-2. Threshold Test Ban Treaty/Adoption. Adoption of the resolution of ratification of the treaty to limit underground nuclear weapons tests to 150 kilotons and to establish verification rights for tests over 50 kilotons. Adopted 98-0: R 43-0; D 55-0 (ND 38-0, SD 17-0), Sept. 25, 1990. A two-thirds majority of those present and voting (66 in this case) is required for adoption of resolutions of ratification.

250. Treaty Doc N(B), 94-2. Peaceful Nuclear Explosions Treaty/Adoption. Adoption of the resolution of ratification of the treaty to limit underground explosions for peaceful purposes (e.g. to excavate canals) to 150 kilotons and to establish verification rights for tests over 50 kilotons. Adopted 98-0: R 43-0; D 55-0 (ND 38-0, SD 17-0), Sept. 25, 1990. A two-thirds majority of those present and voting (66 in this case) is required for adoption of resolutions of ratification.

251. HR 5268. Fiscal 1991 Agriculture Appropriations/Passage. Passage of the bill to appropriate $52.3 billion in fiscal 1991 for the Agriculture Department's agriculture, rural development, domestic food assistance and international programs, and several other related agencies. The president requested $52,248,810,000. Passed 79-19: R 36-7; D 43-12 (ND 26-12, 17-0), Sept. 25, 1990.

252. S 110. Title X Family Planning Amendments/Counseling. Chafee, R-R.I., amendment to the Jeffords, R-Vt., amendment to the committee amendment, to specify that pregnant women receiving family planning services at federally funded facilities, upon request, be advised of all their legal and medical options, including abortion. Adopted 62-36: R 16-27; D 46-9 (ND 34-4, SD 12-5), Sept. 25, 1990.

	253	254	255	256	257
ALABAMA					
Heflin	Y	Y	N	N	N
Shelby	N	Y	N	Y	Y
ALASKA					
Murkowski	Y	Y	N	N	N
Stevens	N	Y	N	N	N
ARIZONA					
DeConcini	N	Y	N	#	Y
McCain	Y	Y	N	N	N
ARKANSAS					
Bumpers	N	Y	N	Y	Y
Pryor	N	Y	N	Y	Y
CALIFORNIA					
Cranston	N	Y	Y	Y	Y
Wilson	?	?	?	?	?
COLORADO					
Wirth	N	Y	Y	Y	Y
Armstrong	Y	Y	N	N	N
CONNECTICUT					
Dodd	N	Y	Y	Y	Y
Lieberman	N	Y	Y	Y	Y
DELAWARE					
Biden	N	Y	Y	Y	Y
Roth	Y	Y	N	N	N
FLORIDA					
Graham	N	Y	N	Y	Y
Mack	Y	Y	N	N	N
GEORGIA					
Fowler	?	Y	Y	Y	Y
Nunn	N	Y	N	Y	Y
HAWAII					
Inouye	N	Y	Y	Y	Y
Akaka	N	Y	Y	Y	Y
IDAHO					
McClure	Y	Y	N	N	N
Symms	+	Y	N	N	N
ILLINOIS					
Dixon	N	Y	Y	Y	Y
Simon	N	Y	Y	Y	Y
INDIANA					
Coats	Y	Y	N	N	N
Lugar	Y	N	N	N	N
IOWA					
Harkin	N	Y	Y	Y	Y
Grassley	Y	Y	N	N	N
KANSAS					
Dole	Y	Y	N	N	N
Kassebaum	N	Y	N	N	N
KENTUCKY					
Ford	N	Y	N	N	Y
McConnell	Y	?	?	?	?
LOUISIANA					
Breaux	Y	Y	N	N	Y
Johnston	?	Y	N	N	Y
MAINE					
Mitchell	N	Y	Y	Y	Y
Cohen	N	Y	Y	Y	N
MARYLAND					
Mikulski	N	Y	Y	Y	Y
Sarbanes	N	Y	Y	Y	Y
MASSACHUSETTS					
Kennedy	N	Y	Y	Y	Y
Kerry	N	Y	Y	Y	Y
MICHIGAN					
Levin	N	Y	Y	Y	Y
Riegle	N	Y	Y	Y	Y
MINNESOTA					
Boschwitz	Y	Y	N	N	N
Durenberger	N	Y	N	N	?
MISSISSIPPI					
Cochran	Y	Y	N	N	N
Lott	Y	Y	N	N	N
MISSOURI					
Bond	Y	Y	N	N	N
Danforth	Y	Y	N	N	N
MONTANA					
Baucus	N	Y	Y	Y	N
Burns	Y	Y	N	N	N
NEBRASKA					
Exon	Y	Y	N	N	Y
Kerrey	N	Y	Y	Y	Y
NEVADA					
Bryan	N	Y	N	Y	Y
Reid	Y	Y	N	N	Y
NEW HAMPSHIRE					
Humphrey	Y	Y	N	X	N
Rudman	?	?	?	N	N
NEW JERSEY					
Bradley	N	Y	Y	Y	Y
Lautenberg	N	Y	Y	Y	Y
NEW MEXICO					
Bingaman	?	Y	Y	Y	Y
Domenici	Y	Y	N	N	N
NEW YORK					
Moynihan	N	Y	Y	Y	Y
D'Amato	Y	Y	N	N	N
NORTH CAROLINA					
Sanford	N	Y	Y	Y	Y
Helms	Y	Y	N	N	N
NORTH DAKOTA					
Burdick	N	Y	Y	Y	Y
Conrad	N	Y	N	N	Y
OHIO					
Glenn	N	Y	Y	Y	Y
Metzenbaum	N	Y	Y	Y	Y
OKLAHOMA					
Boren	N	Y	N	N	Y
Nickles	Y	Y	N	N	N
OREGON					
Hatfield	N	Y	N	Y	Y
Packwood	N	Y	Y	Y	Y
PENNSYLVANIA					
Heinz	N	Y	Y	N	N
Specter	N	Y	Y	N	N
RHODE ISLAND					
Pell	-	Y	Y	Y	Y
Chafee	N	Y	N	N	N
SOUTH CAROLINA					
Hollings	N	Y	Y	Y	Y
Thurmond	Y	Y	N	N	N
SOUTH DAKOTA					
Daschle	N	Y	Y	Y	Y
Pressler	Y	Y	N	N	N
TENNESSEE					
Gore	N	Y	Y	Y	Y
Sasser	N	Y	Y	Y	Y
TEXAS					
Bentsen	?	Y	N	Y	Y
Gramm	Y	Y	N	N	N
UTAH					
Garn	Y	Y	N	N	N
Hatch	Y	Y	N	N	N
VERMONT					
Leahy	N	Y	Y	Y	Y
Jeffords	N	Y	Y	Y	N
VIRGINIA					
Robb	N	Y	Y	Y	Y
Warner	Y	Y	N	N	N
WASHINGTON					
Adams	N	Y	Y	Y	Y
Gorton	N	Y	N	N	N
WEST VIRGINIA					
Byrd	N	Y	N	Y	Y
Rockefeller	N	Y	Y	Y	Y
WISCONSIN					
Kohl	N	Y	Y	Y	Y
Kasten	Y	Y	N	N	N
WYOMING					
Simpson	N	Y	N	N	N
Wallop	Y	Y	N	N	N

KEY

- Y Voted for (yea).
- # Paired for.
- + Announced for.
- N Voted against (nay).
- X Paired against.
- \- Announced against.
- P Voted "present."
- C Voted "present" to avoid possible conflict of interest.
- ? Did not vote or otherwise make a position known.

Democrats *Republicans*

ND Northern Democrats SD Southern Democrats

Southern states - Ala., Ark., Fla., Ga., Ky., La., Miss., N.C., Okla., S.C., Tenn., Texas, Va.

253. S 110. Title X Family Planning Amendments/Exclusions. Hatch, R-Utah, substitute amendment to the committee substitute amendment, to make Title X of the Public Health Service Act of 1970 a state block grant program, excluding private nonprofit organizations such as Planned Parenthood from receiving direct federal funding under Title X. Rejected 34-58: R 30-12; D 4-46 (ND 2-34, SD 2-12), Sept. 25, 1990.

254. S 110. Title X Family Planning Amendments/Congressional Pay. Pressler, R-S.D., amendment to the committee substitute amendment, to cut pay for members of Congress and top White House officials and federal bureaucrats, if budget cuts are forced by the required sequestration of the Gramm-Rudman antideficit law. Adopted 96-1: R 41-1; D 55-0 (ND 38-0, SD 17-0), Sept. 26, 1990.

255. S 110. Title X Family Planning Amendments/Strategic Petroleum Reserve. Lieberman, D-Conn., motion to table the Lieberman amendment to express the sense of the Senate that the president should tap the Strategic Petroleum Reserve in response to rising oil prices brought on by the conflict in the Middle East. Rejected 43-54: R 5-37; D 38-17 (ND 32-6, SD 6-11), Sept. 26, 1990. (Subsequently, an underlying Armstrong, R-Colo., amendment was adopted by voice vote to require organizations that receive federal Title X funds and that also perform abortions using non-federal funds to provide a parent of a minor written notice 48 hours prior to the minor obtaining an abortion.)

256. S 110. Title X Family Planning Amendments/Cloture. Motion to invoke cloture (thus limiting debate) on the committee substitute amendment to authorize funds for fiscal 1991-95 for Title X of the Public Health Service Act, which helps fund programs that provide family planning (including infertility) services for low-income women and teenagers. The bill would also reauthorize Title XX of the Public Health Service Act, the Adolescent Family Life program, which provides services for pregnant and parenting adolescents, and funds services aimed at preventing or delaying sexual relations among adolescents. Motion rejected 50-46: R 4-38; D 46-8 (ND 34-3, SD 12-5), Sept. 26, 1990. A three-fifths majority vote (60) of the total Senate is required to invoke cloture.

257. S 874. National Motor-Voter Registration Act/Cloture. Motion to invoke cloture (thus limiting debate) on the motion to proceed to the bill to require states to permit registration simultaneously with applying for a driver's license. Motion rejected 55-42: R 2-40; D 53-2 (ND 37-1, SD 16-1), Sept. 26, 1990. A three-fifths majority vote (60) of the total Senate is required to invoke cloture.

	258	259	260
ALABAMA			
Heflin	Y	Y	Y
Shelby	Y	Y	Y
ALASKA			
Murkowski	Y	Y	Y
Stevens	Y	Y	Y
ARIZONA			
DeConcini	Y	Y	Y
McCain	Y	Y	Y
ARKANSAS			
Bumpers	Y	Y	Y
Pryor	Y	Y	Y
CALIFORNIA			
Cranston	Y	N	Y
Wilson	?	?	?
COLORADO			
Wirth	Y	Y	Y
Armstrong	Y	Y	N
CONNECTICUT			
Dodd	Y	Y	Y
Lieberman	Y	Y	Y
DELAWARE			
Biden	Y	Y	Y
Roth	Y	Y	N
FLORIDA			
Graham	Y	Y	Y
Mack	Y	Y	N
GEORGIA			
Fowler	Y	Y	Y
Nunn	Y	Y	Y
HAWAII			
Inouye	Y	Y	Y
Akaka	Y	N	Y
IDAHO			
McClure	Y	Y	Y
Symms	Y	Y	N
ILLINOIS			
Dixon	Y	Y	Y
Simon	Y	Y	Y
INDIANA			
Coats	Y	Y	Y
Lugar	Y	Y	Y

	258	259	260
IOWA			
Harkin	Y	Y	Y
Grassley	Y	Y	Y
KANSAS			
Dole	Y	Y	Y
Kassebaum	Y	Y	Y
KENTUCKY			
Ford	Y	Y	Y
McConnell	Y	Y	Y
LOUISIANA			
Breaux	Y	Y	Y
Johnston	Y	Y	?
MAINE			
Mitchell	Y	Y	Y
Cohen	Y	Y	Y
MARYLAND			
Mikulski	Y	N	Y
Sarbanes	Y	Y	Y
MASSACHUSETTS			
Kennedy	N	N	Y
Kerry	Y	N	Y
MICHIGAN			
Levin	Y	Y	Y
Riegle	Y	Y	Y
MINNESOTA			
Boschwitz	Y	Y	Y
Durenberger	Y	Y	Y
MISSISSIPPI			
Cochran	Y	Y	Y
Lott	Y	Y	Y
MISSOURI			
Bond	Y	Y	Y
Danforth	Y	Y	Y
MONTANA			
Baucus	Y	Y	Y
Burns	Y	Y	Y
NEBRASKA			
Exon	Y	Y	Y
Kerrey	N	Y	Y
NEVADA			
Bryan	Y	Y	Y
Reid	Y	Y	Y

	258	259	260
NEW HAMPSHIRE			
Humphrey	Y	Y	N
Rudman	Y	Y	Y
NEW JERSEY			
Bradley	Y	N	Y
Lautenberg	Y	N	Y
NEW MEXICO			
Bingaman	Y	Y	Y
Domenici	Y	Y	Y
NEW YORK			
Moynihan	Y	Y	Y
D'Amato	Y	Y	Y
NORTH CAROLINA			
Sanford	Y	Y	Y
Helms	Y	Y	N
NORTH DAKOTA			
Burdick	Y	N	Y
Conrad	Y	Y	Y
OHIO			
Glenn	Y	Y	Y
Metzenbaum	Y	Y	Y
OKLAHOMA			
Boren	Y	Y	Y
Nickles	Y	Y	Y
OREGON			
Hatfield	N	Y	Y
Packwood	Y	Y	Y
PENNSYLVANIA			
Heinz	Y	Y	Y
Specter	Y	Y	Y
RHODE ISLAND			
Pell	Y	Y	Y
Chafee	Y	Y	Y
SOUTH CAROLINA			
Hollings	Y	Y	Y
Thurmond	Y	Y	Y
SOUTH DAKOTA			
Daschle	Y	Y	Y
Pressler	Y	Y	Y
TENNESSEE			
Gore	Y	Y	Y
Sasser	Y	Y	Y

KEY

- Y Voted for (yea).
- # Paired for.
- + Announced for.
- N Voted against (nay).
- X Paired against.
- \- Announced against.
- P Voted "present."
- C Voted "present" to avoid possible conflict of interest.
- ? Did not vote or otherwise make a position known.

Democrats *Republicans*

	258	259	260
TEXAS			
Bentsen	Y	Y	Y
Gramm	Y	Y	Y
UTAH			
Garn	Y	Y	Y
Hatch	Y	Y	Y
VERMONT			
Leahy	Y	Y	Y
Jeffords	Y	Y	Y
VIRGINIA			
Robb	Y	Y	Y
Warner	Y	Y	Y
WASHINGTON			
Adams	Y	N	Y
Gorton	Y	Y	Y
WEST VIRGINIA			
Byrd	Y	Y	Y
Rockefeller	Y	Y	Y
WISCONSIN			
Kohl	Y	Y	Y
Kasten	Y	Y	N
WYOMING			
Simpson	Y	Y	Y
Wallop	Y	Y	N

ND Northern Democrats SD Southern Democrats

Southern states - Ala., Ark., Fla., Ga., Ky., La., Miss., N.C., Okla., S.C., Tenn., Texas, Va.

258. S Con Res 147. Persian Gulf Resolution/Adoption. Adoption of the concurrent resolution to express the sense of Congress supporting President Bush's pursuit of the passage of U.N. resolutions concerning Iraq's invasion of Kuwait and his actions consistent with those resolutions. The resolution only supports action in accordance with both the U.N. resolutions and U.S. constitutional and statutory processes. Adopted 96-3: R 43-1; D 53-2 (ND 36-2, SD 17-0), Oct. 2, 1990.

259. Souter Nomination. Confirmation of President Bush's nomination of David H. Souter of New Hampshire to be an associate justice of the U.S. Supreme Court. Confirmed 90-9: R 44-0; D 46-9 (ND 29-9, SD 17-0), Oct. 2, 1990. A "yea" was a vote supporting the president's position.

260. HR 5158. Fiscal 1991 VA and HUD Appropriations/Passage. Passage of the bill to appropriate $78,587,000,000 in fiscal 1991 for the Department of Housing and Urban Development (HUD), the Department of Veterans Affairs (VA), the Environmental Protection Agency, NASA, the National Science Foundation and various other agencies. The president requested $75,861,000,000. Passed 90-8: R 36-8; D 54-0 (ND 38-0, SD 16-0), Oct. 3, 1990.

	261	262	263	264	265
ALABAMA					
Heflin	N	Y	Y	Y	Y
Shelby	N	Y	Y	Y	Y
ALASKA					
Murkowski	Y	N	Y	Y	Y
Stevens	Y	N	Y	Y	Y
ARIZONA					
DeConcini	N	Y	Y	Y	Y
McCain	N	N	Y	Y	Y
ARKANSAS					
Bumpers	Y	Y	Y	Y	Y
Pryor	Y	Y	Y	Y	Y
CALIFORNIA					
Cranston	Y	Y	Y	Y	Y
Wilson	?	?	?	?	?
COLORADO					
Wirth	Y	N	Y	Y	Y
Armstrong	N	N	Y	Y	Y
CONNECTICUT					
Dodd	Y	Y	Y	Y	Y
Lieberman	Y	Y	Y	Y	Y
DELAWARE					
Biden	Y	Y	Y	Y	Y
Roth	N	N	Y	Y	N
FLORIDA					
Graham	Y	Y	Y	Y	Y
Mack	N	Y	Y	Y	Y
GEORGIA					
Fowler	Y	Y	Y	Y	Y
Nunn	Y	Y	Y	Y	Y
HAWAII					
Inouye	Y	Y	Y	Y	Y
Akaka	Y	Y	Y	Y	Y
IDAHO					
McClure	Y	N	Y	Y	Y
Symms	N	N	Y	Y	N
ILLINOIS					
Dixon	Y	Y	Y	Y	N
Simon	N	Y	Y	Y	Y
INDIANA					
Coats	N	N	Y	Y	N
Lugar	Y	N	Y	Y	Y

	261	262	263	264	265
IOWA					
Harkin	N	Y	Y	Y	Y
Grassley	N	Y	Y	Y	Y
KANSAS					
Dole	Y	N	Y	Y	Y
Kassebaum	Y	N	Y	Y	Y
KENTUCKY					
Ford	Y	Y	Y	Y	Y
McConnell	N	Y	Y	Y	Y
LOUISIANA					
Breaux	Y	Y	Y	Y	Y
Johnston	N	N	Y	Y	Y
MAINE					
Mitchell	Y	N	Y	Y	Y
Cohen	Y	Y	Y	Y	Y
MARYLAND					
Mikulski	Y	Y	Y	Y	Y
Sarbanes	Y	Y	Y	Y	Y
MASSACHUSETTS					
Kennedy	Y	N	Y	Y	Y
Kerry	N	Y	Y	Y	Y
MICHIGAN					
Levin	N	Y	Y	Y	Y
Riegle	Y	Y	Y	Y	Y
MINNESOTA					
Boschwitz	Y	N	Y	Y	Y
Durenberger	Y	N	Y	Y	Y
MISSISSIPPI					
Cochran	Y	N	Y	Y	Y
Lott	N	Y	Y	Y	Y
MISSOURI					
Bond	Y	N	Y	Y	Y
Danforth	Y	N	Y	Y	Y
MONTANA					
Baucus	N	Y	Y	Y	Y
Burns	N	N	Y	Y	Y
NEBRASKA					
Exon	N	Y	Y	Y	Y
Kerrey	Y	Y	Y	Y	Y
NEVADA					
Bryan	Y	Y	Y	Y	Y
Reid	Y	Y	Y	Y	Y

	261	262	263	264	265
NEW HAMPSHIRE					
Humphrey	N	N	Y	Y	N
Rudman	Y	N	Y	Y	Y
NEW JERSEY					
Bradley	Y	N	Y	Y	Y
Lautenberg	Y	Y	Y	Y	Y
NEW MEXICO					
Bingaman	Y	N	Y	Y	Y
Domenici	Y	N	Y	Y	Y
NEW YORK					
Moynihan	Y	Y	Y	Y	Y
D'Amato	N	Y	Y	Y	Y
NORTH CAROLINA					
Sanford	N	Y	Y	Y	Y
Helms	N	Y	Y	Y	N
NORTH DAKOTA					
Burdick	Y	Y	Y	Y	Y
Conrad	Y	Y	Y	Y	N
OHIO					
Glenn	Y	N	Y	Y	Y
Metzenbaum	Y	Y	Y	Y	Y
OKLAHOMA					
Boren	Y	Y	Y	Y	Y
Nickles	N	Y	Y	Y	Y
OREGON					
Hatfield	N	+	+	?	?
Packwood	Y	Y	Y	Y	Y
PENNSYLVANIA					
Heinz	Y	N	Y	Y	Y
Specter	Y	Y	Y	Y	Y
RHODE ISLAND					
Pell	N	Y	Y	Y	Y
Chafee	Y	N	Y	Y	Y
SOUTH CAROLINA					
Hollings	N	Y	Y	Y	Y
Thurmond	Y	N	Y	Y	Y
SOUTH DAKOTA					
Daschle	Y	Y	Y	Y	Y
Pressler	N	Y	Y	Y	Y
TENNESSEE					
Gore	Y	Y	Y	Y	Y
Sasser	Y	N	Y	Y	Y

KEY

- Y Voted for (yea).
- # Paired for.
- + Announced for.
- N Voted against (nay).
- X Paired against.
- - Announced against.
- P Voted "present."
- C Voted "present" to avoid possible conflict of interest.
- ? Did not vote or otherwise make a position known.

Democrats *Republicans*

	261	262	263	264	265
TEXAS					
Bentsen	Y	N	Y	Y	Y
Gramm	N	N	Y	Y	Y
UTAH					
Garn	Y	N	Y	Y	Y
Hatch	Y	N	Y	Y	Y
VERMONT					
Leahy	Y	Y	Y	Y	Y
Jeffords	Y	N	Y	Y	Y
VIRGINIA					
Robb	Y	N	Y	Y	Y
Warner	Y	N	Y	Y	Y
WASHINGTON					
Adams	Y	Y	Y	Y	Y
Gorton	N	N	Y	Y	Y
WEST VIRGINIA					
Byrd	Y	N	Y	Y	Y
Rockefeller	Y	N	Y	Y	Y
WISCONSIN					
Kohl	Y	N	Y	Y	Y
Kasten	N	Y	Y	Y	Y
WYOMING					
Simpson	Y	N	Y	Y	Y
Wallop	N	N	Y	Y	Y

ND Northern Democrats SD Southern Democrats Southern states - Ala., Ark., Fla., Ga., Ky., La., Miss., N.C., Okla., S.C., Tenn., Texas, Va.

261. H Con Res 310. Fiscal 1991 Budget Resolution/Conference Report. Adoption of the conference report on the bill to set binding budget levels for fiscal 1991: budget authority, $1.486 trillion; outlays, $1.237 trillion; revenues, $1.173 trillion; deficit, $64 billion. The resolution has the same overall spending targets as the budget summit agreement, but calls for smaller cuts in Medicare and leaves open the possibility for changes in the capital gains tax rate, the income tax rate on earnings above a certain level and other taxes. Adopted 66-33: R 24-20; D 42-13 (ND 30-8, SD 12-5), Oct. 9, 1990 (in the session that began, and the Congressional Record dated, Oct. 8, 1990).

262. S 3167. Social Security "Pay-As-You-Go" Plan/Budget Waiver. Moynihan, D-N.Y., motion to waive the Budget Act with respect to the Stevens, R-Alaska, point of order, which states that the bill to cut Social Security contribution rates and return the system to pay-as-you-go financing would violate section 311(a) of the Budget Act by increasing the deficit by $3.9 billion in fiscal 1991 and thus exceeding the maximum deficit amount. Motion rejected 54-44: R 12-31; D 42-13 (ND 29-9, SD 13-4), Oct. 10, 1990. A three-fifths majority (60) of the total Senate is required to waive the Budget Act. (The bill was subsequently placed back on the calendar for future consideration.)

263. Treaty Doc 101-20. Treaty on the Final Settlement with Respect to Germany/Adoption. Adoption of the resolution of ratification of the treaty to end the division of Germany into two states, make permanent the borders of the united Germany and bring to an end the special rights exercised in Germany and Berlin by the Four Allied Powers. Adopted 98-0: R 43-0; D 55-0 (ND 38-0, SD 17-0), Oct. 10, 1990. A two-thirds majority of those present and voting (66 in this case) is required for adoption of resolutions of ratification. A "yea" was a vote supporting the president's position.

264. HR 2061. Magnuson Fisheries Act/Passage. Passage of the bill to authorize appropriations for the Magnuson Fishery Conservation Act through fiscal 1992. Passed 98-0: R 43-0; D 55-0 (ND 38-0, SD 17-0), Oct. 11, 1990.

265. HR 5021. Fiscal 1991 Commerce, Justice, State and the Judiciary Appropriations/Passage. Passage of the bill to appropriate $19,307,228,000 for the Departments of Commerce, Justice and State, the federal judiciary and related agencies in fiscal 1991. The president requested $20,009,388,000. Passed 91-7: R 38-5; D 53-2 (ND 36-2, SD 17-0), Oct. 11, 1990.

	266	267	268	269	270	271	272
ALABAMA							
Heflin	N	N	N	Y	N	N	N
Shelby	N	Y	Y	Y	Y	Y	N
ALASKA							
Murkowski	N	Y	N	Y	N	N	N
Stevens	Y	+	Y	Y	Y	N	N
ARIZONA							
DeConcini	N	Y	Y	Y	Y	Y	Y
McCain	N	Y	Y	Y	?	N	Y
ARKANSAS							
Bumpers	Y	?	?	?	?	Y	Y
Pryor	Y	Y	Y	Y	Y	Y	Y
CALIFORNIA							
Cranston	Y	Y	Y	Y	Y	Y	Y
Wilson	?	?	?	?	?	?	?
COLORADO							
Wirth	Y	Y	Y	Y	Y	Y	Y
Armstrong	N	N	N	N	N	N	N
CONNECTICUT							
Dodd	Y	Y	Y	Y	Y	Y	N
Lieberman	Y	Y	Y	Y	Y	N	Y
DELAWARE							
Biden	Y	Y	Y	Y	N	Y	Y
Roth	N	N	N	N	N	N	Y
FLORIDA							
Graham	Y	Y	Y	Y	Y	N	Y
Mack	N	Y	Y	N	N	N	N
GEORGIA							
Fowler	Y	Y	Y	?	?	Y	N
Nunn	N	Y	Y	Y	Y	N	N
HAWAII							
Inouye	Y	Y	Y	Y	Y	N	N
Akaka	Y	Y	Y	Y	Y	N	Y
IDAHO							
McClure	N	N	N	Y	X	N	Y
Symms	N	N	N	N	N	N	N
ILLINOIS							
Dixon	N	Y	Y	Y	N	Y	N
Simon	Y	Y	Y	Y	Y	Y	Y
INDIANA							
Coats	N	Y	N	N	N	N	N
Lugar	N	Y	Y	Y	N	N	N
IOWA							
Harkin	Y	Y	Y	Y	Y	Y	Y
Grassley	N	N	N	N	N	N	Y
KANSAS							
Dole	N	Y	N	Y	N	N	N
Kassebaum	N	Y	?	?	?	?	?
KENTUCKY							
Ford	N	N	N	Y	N	N	N
McConnell	N	Y	N	Y	N	N	N
LOUISIANA							
Breaux	N	Y	Y	Y	N	N	N
Johnston	N	Y	Y	Y	N	N	N
MAINE							
Mitchell	Y	Y	Y	Y	Y	Y	Y
Cohen	Y	Y	Y	Y	Y	Y	Y
MARYLAND							
Mikulski	Y	Y	Y	Y	Y	Y	Y
Sarbanes	Y	Y	Y	Y	Y	Y	Y
MASSACHUSETTS							
Kennedy	Y	Y	Y	Y	Y	Y	Y
Kerry	Y	Y	Y	Y	Y	+	#
MICHIGAN							
Levin	Y	Y	Y	Y	Y	Y	N
Riegle	Y	Y	Y	Y	Y	Y	Y
MINNESOTA							
Boschwitz	N	N	Y	Y	N	N	N
Durenberger	N	Y	Y	N	N	N	N
MISSISSIPPI							
Cochran	N	N	N	Y	N	N	N
Lott	N	N	N	N	N	N	N
MISSOURI							
Bond	N	N	N	N	N	N	N
Danforth	N	Y	Y	Y	N	N	N
MONTANA							
Baucus	Y	N	Y	Y	Y	Y	Y
Burns	N	N	N	Y	N	N	N
NEBRASKA							
Exon	N	Y	Y	Y	N	Y	N
Kerrey	Y	Y	Y	Y	Y	Y	Y
NEVADA							
Bryan	Y	Y	Y	Y	Y	Y	N
Reid	N	Y	Y	Y	N	Y	Y
NEW HAMPSHIRE							
Humphrey	N	N	N	N	N	Y	Y
Rudman	Y	N	Y	Y	Y	N	N
NEW JERSEY							
Bradley	Y	Y	Y	Y	Y	Y	Y
Lautenberg	Y	Y	Y	Y	Y	Y	Y
NEW MEXICO							
Bingaman	Y	Y	Y	Y	Y	Y	N
Domenici	?	?	?	?	?	N	N
NEW YORK							
Moynihan	Y	Y	Y	Y	Y	Y	Y
D'Amato	N	Y	Y	Y	N	Y	N
NORTH CAROLINA							
Sanford	Y	Y	Y	Y	Y	Y	X
Helms	N	N	N	N	N	Y	N
NORTH DAKOTA							
Burdick	Y	Y	Y	Y	Y	Y	Y
Conrad	N	Y	Y	N	Y	Y	Y
OHIO							
Glenn	Y	Y	Y	Y	Y	N	Y
Metzenbaum	?	?	?	?	?	Y	Y
OKLAHOMA							
Boren	N	Y	Y	Y	N	Y	N
Nickles	N	N	N	N	N	Y	N
OREGON							
Hatfield	?	+	+	+	#	+	#
Packwood	Y	Y	Y	Y	Y	Y	Y
PENNSYLVANIA							
Heinz	Y	Y	Y	Y	Y	N	Y
Specter	Y	Y	Y	Y	Y	N	N
RHODE ISLAND							
Pell	Y	Y	Y	Y	Y	Y	Y
Chafee	Y	Y	Y	Y	Y	N	N
SOUTH CAROLINA							
Hollings	Y	Y	Y	Y	Y	N	Y
Thurmond	N	N	N	Y	N	N	N
SOUTH DAKOTA							
Daschle	Y	Y	Y	Y	Y	Y	Y
Pressler	N	N	N	Y	N	Y	Y
TENNESSEE							
Gore	Y	Y	Y	Y	Y	N	N
Sasser	Y	Y	Y	Y	Y	Y	Y
TEXAS							
Bentsen	N	Y	Y	Y	Y	N	N
Gramm	N	N	N	Y	N	N	N
UTAH							
Garn	N	N	?	?	?	N	N
Hatch	N	Y	Y	Y	N	N	N
VERMONT							
Leahy	Y	Y	Y	Y	Y	N	Y
Jeffords	Y	Y	Y	Y	Y	N	X
VIRGINIA							
Robb	Y	Y	Y	Y	Y	N	N
Warner	N	Y	Y	Y	N	N	N
WASHINGTON							
Adams	Y	Y	Y	Y	Y	Y	Y
Gorton	N	N	Y	Y	N	N	N
WEST VIRGINIA							
Byrd	N	Y	Y	Y	Y	N	Y
Rockefeller	Y	Y	Y	Y	Y	Y	Y
WISCONSIN							
Kohl	Y	Y	Y	Y	Y	Y	Y
Kasten	N	Y	N	N	N	Y	N
WYOMING							
Simpson	N	N	?	?	?	N	N
Wallop	N	N	N	N	N	N	N

KEY

- Y Voted for (yea).
- # Paired for.
- + Announced for.
- N Voted against (nay).
- X Paired against.
- - Announced against.
- P Voted "present."
- C Voted "present" to avoid possible conflict of interest.
- ? Did not vote or otherwise make a position known.

Democrats *Republicans*

ND Northern Democrats SD Southern Democrats

Southern states - Ala., Ark., Fla., Ga., Ky., La., Miss., N.C., Okla., S.C., Tenn., Texas, Va.

266. HR 5257. Fiscal 1991 Labor, HHS and Education Appropriations/Abortion. Harkin, D-Iowa, motion to table (kill) the Armstrong, R-Colo., amendment to the committee amendment, to permit federal funding of abortion in cases of rape or incest. The Armstrong amendment would require organizations receiving funds to notify the parent or legal guardian 48 hours before performing an abortion for a minor, unless there is a medical emergency. Motion rejected 48-48: R 8-34; D 40-14 (ND 31-6, SD 9-8), Oct. 12, 1990. (The Armstrong amendment was subsequently adopted by voice vote.)

267. HR 5257. Fiscal 1991 Labor, HHS and Education Appropriations/AIDS. Lautenberg, D-N.J., motion to table (kill) the Helms, R-N.C., amendment to cut $441 million in fiscal 1992 for treatment of AIDS. The money would be provided for fiscal 1992 in order to stay within spending limits set by the budget resolution for fiscal 1991 while at the same time making a future commitment for programs under an AIDS treatment bill passed by Congress in August. Motion agreed to 70-24: R 20-21; D 50-3 (ND 36-1, SD 14-2), Oct. 12, 1990.

268. HR 5257. Fiscal 1991 Labor, HHS and Education Appropriations/AIDS. Lautenberg, D-N.J., motion to table (kill) the Helms, R-N.C., amendment to shift $120 million from AIDS-related programs to programs relating to the prevention of infant mortality and sudden infant death syndrome, child-health research centers, mental retardation in children and Alzheimer's disease. Motion agreed to 69-23: R 18-21; D 51-2 (ND 37-0, SD 14-2), Oct. 12, 1990.

269. HR 5257. Fiscal 1991 Labor, HHS and Education Appropriations/Passage. Passage of the bill to appropriate $183,334,110,000 for the Departments of Labor, Health and Human Services, and Education and related agencies in fiscal 1991, and, in some cases, for subsequent years. The president requested $171,736,511,000. Passed 76-15: R 25-14; D 51-1 (ND 36-1, SD 15-0), Oct. 12, 1990.

270. HR 5114. Fiscal 1991 Foreign Operations Appropriations/Cloture. Mitchell, D-Maine, motion to invoke cloture (thus limiting debate) on the committee amendment to earmark $15 million for the United Nations population fund for voluntary family planning activities consistent with the Universal Declaration of Human Rights. The amendment prohibits funds from being used for abortion or from going to China, where programs of coercive abortion and sterilization are in effect. Motion rejected 51-38: R 8-29; D 43-9 (ND 33-4, SD 10-5), Oct. 12, 1990. A three-fifths majority vote (60) of the total Senate is required to invoke cloture. (After the Senate failed to invoke cloture, the amendment was deemed to have been stricken from the bill.) A "nay" was a vote supporting the president's position.

271. S 3189. Fiscal 1991 Defense Appropriations/Troop Cuts. Conrad, D-N.D., amendment to reduce U.S. forces in NATO by 30,000 troops below the Senate-passed authorization level and reduce the Department of Defense military personnel level by a corresponding 30,000 below the authorized level. Rejected 46-50: R 8-34; D 38-16 (ND 31-6, SD 7-10), Oct. 15, 1990. A "nay" was a vote supporting the president's position.

272. S 3189. Fiscal 1991 Defense Appropriations/B-2 Bomber. Leahy, D-Vt., amendment to cut funds for the two additional B-2 bombers in the bill, thereby terminating the expansion of the program with the 15 bombers being produced and tested. Rejected 44-50: R 9-32; D 35-18 (ND 30-7, SD 5-11), Oct. 15, 1990. A "nay" was a vote supporting the president's position.

	273	274	275	276	277	278
ALABAMA						
Heflin	Y	Y	N	Y	Y	Y
Shelby	Y	Y	N	Y	N	Y
ALASKA						
Murkowski	Y	Y	Y	N	N	N
Stevens	Y	?	?	?	N	N
ARIZONA						
DeConcini	Y	Y	N	Y	Y	N
McCain	Y	N	Y	N	N	Y
ARKANSAS						
Bumpers	Y	Y	N	Y	Y	N
Pryor	Y	Y	N	Y	N	N
CALIFORNIA						
Cranston	N	Y	N	Y	Y	N
Wilson	?	Y	Y	N	N	Y
COLORADO						
Wirth	N	Y	N	Y	N	N
Armstrong	Y	N	Y	N	N	Y
CONNECTICUT						
Dodd	Y	Y	N	Y	N	N
Lieberman	Y	Y	N	Y	N	Y
DELAWARE						
Biden	Y	Y	N	Y	Y	N
Roth	N	N	Y	N	N	Y
FLORIDA						
Graham	Y	Y	N	Y	Y	N
Mack	Y	N	Y	N	N	Y
GEORGIA						
Fowler	Y	Y	N	Y	N	N
Nunn	Y	Y	N	Y	N	N
HAWAII						
Inouye	Y	Y	N	Y	N	N
Akaka	Y	Y	N	Y	Y	N
IDAHO						
McClure	Y	N	Y	N	N	Y
Symms	Y	N	Y	N	N	Y
ILLINOIS						
Dixon	Y	Y	N	Y	N	Y
Simon	Y	Y	N	Y	Y	N
INDIANA						
Coats	Y	N	Y	N	N	Y
Lugar	Y	Y	Y	N	N	N
IOWA						
Harkin	N	Y	N	Y	Y	Y
Grassley	N	N	Y	N	Y	Y
KANSAS						
Dole	Y	Y	Y	N	N	N
Kassebaum	?	N	Y	N	N	N
KENTUCKY						
Ford	Y	Y	N	Y	N	N
McConnell	Y	Y	Y	N	N	Y
LOUISIANA						
Breaux	?	Y	N	Y	N	N
Johnston	Y	Y	N	Y	N	N
MAINE						
Mitchell	Y	Y	N	Y	N	N
Cohen	Y	Y	N	Y	Y	Y
MARYLAND						
Mikulski	Y	Y	N	Y	Y	N
Sarbanes	Y	Y	N	Y	N	N
MASSACHUSETTS						
Kennedy	?	Y	N	Y	Y	N
Kerry	N	+	-	+	N	Y
MICHIGAN						
Levin	Y	Y	N	Y	N	Y
Riegle	Y	Y	N	Y	N	Y
MINNESOTA						
Boschwitz	Y	N	Y	N	Y	N
Durenberger	Y	Y	N	Y	N	N
MISSISSIPPI						
Cochran	Y	Y	Y	N	N	Y
Lott	Y	N	Y	N	N	Y
MISSOURI						
Bond	Y	Y	Y	N	Y	Y
Danforth	Y	Y	N	Y	N	N
MONTANA						
Baucus	N	Y	N	Y	Y	Y
Burns	Y	Y	Y	N	N	Y
NEBRASKA						
Exon	Y	?	?	?	Y	Y
Kerrey	Y	N	N	Y	Y	Y
NEVADA						
Bryan	Y	Y	N	Y	N	N
Reid	Y	Y	N	Y	N	N
NEW HAMPSHIRE						
Humphrey	N	N	Y	N	N	Y
Rudman	Y	N	Y	N	N	N
NEW JERSEY						
Bradley	N	Y	N	Y	N	N
Lautenberg	Y	Y	N	Y	Y	N
NEW MEXICO						
Bingaman	Y	Y	N	Y	N	N
Domenici	Y	Y	Y	Y	N	N
NEW YORK						
Moynihan	Y	Y	N	Y	N	N
D'Amato	Y	Y	Y	N	N	Y
NORTH CAROLINA						
Sanford	Y	Y	N	Y	Y	Y
Helms	Y	N	Y	N	N	Y
NORTH DAKOTA						
Burdick	Y	Y	N	Y	Y	N
Conrad	N	Y	N	Y	Y	N
OHIO						
Glenn	Y	Y	N	Y	N	N
Metzenbaum	N	Y	N	Y	N	N
OKLAHOMA						
Boren	Y	Y	N	Y	Y	N
Nickles	Y	N	Y	N	N	Y
OREGON						
Hatfield	-	+	-	+	?	?
Packwood	Y	Y	N	Y	N	N
PENNSYLVANIA						
Heinz	Y	Y	N	Y	N	N
Specter	Y	Y	N	Y	Y	Y
RHODE ISLAND						
Pell	Y	Y	N	Y	Y	Y
Chafee	Y	Y	N	Y	N	N
SOUTH CAROLINA						
Hollings	Y	Y	N	Y	N	Y
Thurmond	Y	N	Y	N	N	N
SOUTH DAKOTA						
Daschle	N	Y	N	Y	Y	N
Pressler	N	Y	Y	N	Y	Y
TENNESSEE						
Gore	Y	Y	N	Y	Y	N
Sasser	Y	Y	N	Y	N	N
TEXAS						
Bentsen	Y	Y	N	Y	N	N
Gramm	Y	N	Y	N	N	N
UTAH						
Garn	Y	N	Y	N	N	Y
Hatch	Y	Y	Y	N	N	Y
VERMONT						
Leahy	Y	Y	N	Y	Y	N
Jeffords	Y	Y	N	Y	Y	N
VIRGINIA						
Robb	Y	Y	N	Y	N	N
Warner	Y	Y	Y	N	N	N
WASHINGTON						
Adams	Y	Y	N	Y	Y	N
Gorton	Y	N	Y	N	N	N
WEST VIRGINIA						
Byrd	Y	Y	N	Y	N	N
Rockefeller	N	Y	N	Y	N	N
WISCONSIN						
Kohl	N	Y	N	Y	Y	N
Kasten	Y	Y	Y	N	N	Y
WYOMING						
Simpson	Y	Y	Y	N	N	Y
Wallop	N	N	Y	N	N	Y

KEY

- Y Voted for (yea).
- # Paired for.
- + Announced for.
- N Voted against (nay).
- X Paired against.
- - Announced against.
- P Voted "present."
- C Voted "present" to avoid possible conflict of interest.
- ? Did not vote or otherwise make a position known.

Democrats ***Republicans***

ND Northern Democrats SD Southern Democrats

Southern states - Ala., Ark., Fla., Ga., Ky., La., Miss., N.C., Okla., S.C., Tenn., Texas, Va.

273. S 3189. Fiscal 1991 Defense Appropriations/Passage. Passage of the bill to appropriate $268,240,850,000 for the Department of Defense for military personnel, operations and maintenance, procurement, and research and development in fiscal 1991. The president requested $287,282,674,000. Passed 79-16: R 37-5; D 42-11 (ND 26-11, SD 16-0), Oct. 15, 1990. (The Senate on Oct. 16 vitiated passage of the bill and agreed to a Mitchell, D-Maine, motion that the vote on passage be considered as having occurred on final passage of the House companion, HR 5803, as amended by the Senate.)

274. S 1430. National and Community Service Act/Conference Report. Adoption of the conference report on the bill to authorize grants to states and localities to encourage community service, create or expand Youth Service Corps, authorize demonstration national service programs offering post-service vouchers for education and housing, and authorize a Points of Light Foundation to coordinate and foster volunteerism. Adopted 75-21: R 23-20; D 52-1 (ND 35-1, SD 17-0), Oct. 16, 1990. A "nay" was a vote supporting the president's position.

275. S 2104. Civil Rights Act of 1990/Recommittal Motion. Dole, R-Kan., motion to recommit to the conference committee the bill, with instructions to report it back to the Senate with provisions lessening the burden of proof for employers defending practices that are fair in form but have the effect of discriminating against women and minorities. Motion rejected 35-61: R 35-8; D 0-53 (ND 0-36, SD 0-17), Oct. 16, 1990. A "yea" was a vote supporting the president's position.

276. S 2104. Civil Rights Act of 1990/Conference Report. Adoption of the conference report on the bill to reverse or modify six recent Supreme Court decisions that narrowed the reach and remedies of job discrimination law and to authorize monetary damages under Title VII of the 1964 Civil Rights Act. Adopted 62-34: R 9-34; D 53-0 (ND 36-0, SD 17-0), Oct. 16, 1990. A "nay" was a vote supporting the president's position.

277. S 3209. Fiscal 1991 Budget Reconciliation/Budget Act Waiver. Conrad, D-N.D., motion to waive the Budget Act with respect to the Dole, R-Kan., point of order, which states the Conrad amendment to eliminate the income tax bubble, increase the minimum tax, surtax millionaires, scale back the gas tax, ease Medicare cuts, partially restore agriculture cuts, and eliminate the 5 percent deduction rule would violate Section 304(b) of the Budget Act by adding non-germane language (new substantive matter) to the bill. Motion rejected 32-67: R 7-37; D 25-30 (ND 19-19, SD 6-11), Oct. 17, 1990. A three-fifths majority (60) of the total Senate is required to waive the Budget Act. (The Conrad amendment subsequently fell to the Dole point of order.)

278. S 3209. Fiscal 1991 Budget Reconciliation/Highway-Related Taxes. Symms, R-Idaho, motion to table (kill) the Mitchell, D-Maine, amendment to modify the allocation formula for revenues from the increase and extension of gas taxes to require that 60 percent of the revenues go to the Highway Trust Fund and 40 percent to deficit reduction as opposed to a 50/50 split, sunset the provisions in 1995, and express the sense of the Senate that the conferees will try to modify the diesel fuel tax with regard to railroads in conference. Motion rejected 40-59: R 26-18; D 14-41 (ND 10-28, SD 4-13), Oct. 17, 1990. (A Symms amendment to strike the gas tax — the language that was modified by the Mitchell amendment — was subsequently rendered moot by Senate precedent because the language it was striking was changed.)

	279	280	281	282	283	284
ALABAMA						
Heflin	N	Y	Y	N	Y	N
Shelby	N	N	Y	N	Y	N
ALASKA						
Murkowski	N	N	N	N	Y	N
Stevens	N	N	N	N	Y	N
ARIZONA						
DeConcini	Y	Y	Y	N	Y	N
McCain	Y	N	Y	N	Y	N
ARKANSAS						
Bumpers	Y	Y	N	N	Y	N
Pryor	N	N	N	N	Y	N
CALIFORNIA						
Cranston	N	Y	Y	Y	Y	N
Wilson	N	N	Y	N	Y	N
COLORADO						
Wirth	Y	Y	Y	N	Y	N
Armstrong	N	N	N	N	N	N
CONNECTICUT						
Dodd	Y	N	Y	Y	Y	N
Lieberman	Y	Y	Y	Y	Y	N
DELAWARE						
Biden	Y	Y	N	N	Y	N
Roth	N	N	N	N	Y	N
FLORIDA						
Graham	Y	Y	Y	N	Y	N
Mack	Y	N	N	N	Y	N
GEORGIA						
Fowler	N	Y	Y	N	Y	N
Nunn	Y	N	Y	N	Y	N
HAWAII						
Inouye	N	N	Y	Y	Y	N
Akaka	Y	Y	N	Y	Y	N
IDAHO						
McClure	N	N	N	N	Y	N
Symms	N	N	N	N	Y	N
ILLINOIS						
Dixon	N	N	N	N	Y	N
Simon	Y	Y	Y	Y	Y	N
INDIANA						
Coats	N	N	Y	N	Y	N
Lugar	N	N	N	N	Y	N

	279	280	281	282	283	284
IOWA						
Harkin	Y	Y	Y	Y	Y	N
Grassley	Y	Y	N	N	Y	N
KANSAS						
Dole	N	N	N	N	Y	N
Kassebaum	Y	Y	N	N	Y	N
KENTUCKY						
Ford	N	Y	Y	N	Y	N
McConnell	N	N	Y	N	Y	N
LOUISIANA						
Breaux	N	N	Y	N	Y	N
Johnston	N	N	Y	N	Y	N
MAINE						
Mitchell	N	N	N	Y	Y	N
Cohen	Y	Y	N	N	Y	N
MARYLAND						
Mikulski	Y	Y	N	Y	Y	N
Sarbanes	N	Y	N	Y	Y	N
MASSACHUSETTS						
Kennedy	N	Y	N	Y	Y	N
Kerry	Y	Y	N	Y	Y	N
MICHIGAN						
Levin	Y	N	Y	N	Y	N
Riegle	N	Y	N	Y	Y	N
MINNESOTA						
Boschwitz	?	Y	N	N	Y	N
Durenberger	N	N	N	N	Y	N
MISSISSIPPI						
Cochran	N	N	N	N	Y	N
Lott	N	N	Y	N	Y	N
MISSOURI						
Bond	N	N	Y	N	Y	N
Danforth	N	N	N	N	Y	N
MONTANA						
Baucus	N	Y	Y	N	Y	N
Burns	N	N	N	N	Y	N
NEBRASKA						
Exon	Y	Y	Y	N	Y	N
Kerrey	Y	Y	N	N	Y	N
NEVADA						
Bryan	Y	Y	Y	N	Y	N
Reid	Y	Y	Y	N	Y	N

	279	280	281	282	283	284
NEW HAMPSHIRE						
Humphrey	N	N	N	N	Y	N
Rudman	N	N	N	N	Y	N
NEW JERSEY						
Bradley	Y	Y	N	Y	Y	N
Lautenberg	Y	Y	N	Y	Y	N
NEW MEXICO						
Bingaman	N	Y	N	N	Y	N
Domenici	N	N	N	N	Y	N
NEW YORK						
Moynihan	Y	Y	N	Y	Y	N
D'Amato	Y	N	Y	N	Y	N
NORTH CAROLINA						
Sanford	N	Y	N	N	Y	N
Helms	N	N	Y	N	Y	N
NORTH DAKOTA						
Burdick	Y	Y	Y	Y	Y	N
Conrad	Y	Y	N	N	Y	N
OHIO						
Glenn	N	Y	N	N	Y	N
Metzenbaum	Y	Y	N	Y	Y	N
OKLAHOMA						
Boren	N	N	Y	N	Y	N
Nickles	Y	N	Y	N	Y	N
OREGON						
Hatfield	Y	Y	Y	N	Y	N
Packwood	N	N	N	N	Y	N
PENNSYLVANIA						
Heinz	N	N	Y	N	Y	N
Specter	Y	Y	Y	N	Y	N
RHODE ISLAND						
Pell	N	Y	Y	Y	Y	N
Chafee	N	N	N	N	Y	N
SOUTH CAROLINA						
Hollings	Y	N	Y	N	Y	N
Thurmond	N	N	N	N	Y	N
SOUTH DAKOTA						
Daschle	N	N	Y	N	Y	N
Pressler	Y	Y	Y	N	Y	N
TENNESSEE						
Gore	Y	Y	N	Y	Y	N
Sasser	N	N	N	N	Y	N

KEY

- Y Voted for (yea).
- # Paired for.
- + Announced for.
- N Voted against (nay).
- X Paired against.
- \- Announced against.
- P Voted "present."
- C Voted "present" to avoid possible conflict of interest.
- ? Did not vote or otherwise make a position known.

Democrats ***Republicans***

	279	280	281	282	283	284
TEXAS						
Bentsen	N	N	Y	N	Y	N
Gramm	N	N	N	N	Y	N
UTAH						
Garn	N	N	N	N	Y	N
Hatch	N	N	N	N	Y	N
VERMONT						
Leahy	N	Y	N	N	Y	N
Jeffords	N	Y	Y	N	Y	N
VIRGINIA						
Robb	Y	N	N	N	Y	N
Warner	N	N	N	N	Y	N
WASHINGTON						
Adams	Y	Y	N	Y	Y	N
Gorton	N	N	Y	N	Y	N
WEST VIRGINIA						
Byrd	N	N	N	N	Y	N
Rockefeller	Y	N	N	N	Y	N
WISCONSIN						
Kohl	N	Y	Y	N	Y	N
Kasten	Y	N	Y	N	Y	N
WYOMING						
Simpson	N	N	N	N	Y	N
Wallop	Y	N	N	N	N	N

ND Northern Democrats SD Southern Democrats

Southern states - Ala., Ark., Fla., Ga., Ky., La., Miss., N.C., Okla., S.C., Tenn., Texas, Va.

279. S 3209. Fiscal 1991 Budget Reconciliation/Budget Act Waiver. Graham, D-Fla., motion to waive the Budget Act with respect to the Sasser, D-Tenn., point of order, which stated that the Graham amendment, to give the Federal Deposit Insurance Corporation (FDIC) the right to deny insurance to financial institutions that are too risky to the fund, would violate a Budget Act prohibition against non-germane amendments. Motion rejected 41-58: R 12-32; D 29-26 (ND 23-15, SD 6-11), Oct. 18, 1990. A three-fifths majority (60) of the total Senate is required to waive the Budget Act. (The Graham amendment subsequently fell on the Sasser point of order.)

280. S 3209. Fiscal 1991 Budget Reconciliation/Budget Act Waiver. Gore, D-Tenn., motion to waive the Budget Act with respect to the Domenici, R-N.M., point of order, which stated that the Gore amendment would violate a Budget Act prohibition against non-germane amendments. The Gore amendment would burst the "bubble" in the income tax rate structure; increase the alternative minimum tax from 21 percent to 25 percent; provide a surtax of 10 percent on taxable income above $1 million; delete all of the new burdens placed on Medicare recipients; reduce the increase in the gas tax from 9½ cents to 6 cents per gallon; and remove all the provisions that would disallow 5 percent of itemized deductions on the portion of income above $100,000. Motion rejected 45-55: R 8-37; D 37-18 (ND 30-8, SD 7-10), Oct. 18, 1990. A three-fifths majority (60) of the total Senate is required to waive the Budget Act. (The Gore amendment subsequently fell on the Domenici point of order.)

281. S 3209. Fiscal 1991 Budget Reconciliation/'Progressivity' Guarantee. Boren, D-Okla., amendment to express the sense of the Senate that any budget package should be progressive, dedicated to economic strength and competitiveness in world markets, and provide savings and investment incentives to middle-income people. The amendment also urged Senate conferees to work toward a final package that: increased the tax rate on incomes over $200,000 by a sufficient amount to allow family incomes below $100,000 to contribute $1,000 annually to an individual retirement account to be used for retirement, education, medical expenses and first-time home purchases; reduced the tax on capital gains; and reduced the proposed gas tax. Rejected 44-56: R 16-29; D 28-27 (ND 17-21, SD 11-6), Oct. 18, 1990.

282. S 3209. Fiscal 1991 Budget Reconciliation/OSHA Penalties. Metzenbaum, D-Ohio, motion to table (kill) the Hatch, R-Utah, amendment to eliminate the minimum civil penalties to be levied by Occupational Safety and Health Administration inspectors for violations of worker safety and health standards. Motion rejected 21-79: R 0-45; D 21-34 (ND 20-18, SD 1-16), Oct. 18, 1990. (The Hatch amendment was subsequently adopted by voice vote.) A "nay" was a vote supporting the president's position.

283. S 3209. Fiscal 1991 Budget Reconciliation/Social Security Trust Fund. Hollings, D-S.C., amendment to remove the Social Security Trust Fund from the calculation of the deficit for purposes of complying with the Gramm-Rudman antideficit law. Adopted 98-2: R 43-2; D 55-0 (ND 38-0, SD 17-0), Oct. 18, 1990.

284. S 3209. Fiscal 1991 Budget Reconciliation/Public Debt Limit. Sasser, D-Tenn., motion to table (kill) the Nickles, R-Okla., amendment to change the increase in the statutory limit on the public debt from $1.9 trillion, an amount estimated to be enough to carry the government through the next five years, to $321 billion, enough borrowing authority to last though fiscal 1991. Motion rejected 0-100: R 0-45; D 0-55 (ND 0-38, SD 0-17), Oct. 18, 1990. (The Nickles amendment was subsequently adopted by voice vote.)

	285	286	287	288	289	290
ALABAMA						
Heflin	Y	Y	N	N	Y	Y
Shelby	Y	Y	Y	N	Y	Y
ALASKA						
Murkowski	N	N	N	N	N	N
Stevens	N	Y	N	N	N	Y
ARIZONA						
DeConcini	Y	N	N	Y	Y	Y
McCain	Y	Y	Y	N	N	Y
ARKANSAS						
Bumpers	N	N	N	N	Y	Y
Pryor	N	N	N	N	Y	Y
CALIFORNIA						
Cranston	Y	N	N	Y	N	N
Wilson	Y	Y	Y	N	Y	N
COLORADO						
Wirth	N	Y	N	N	N	Y
Armstrong	N	Y	Y	N	N	N
CONNECTICUT						
Dodd	N	N	N	Y	Y	Y
Lieberman	Y	N	Y	Y	Y	N
DELAWARE						
Biden	Y	N	N	Y	Y	N
Roth	N	Y	Y	Y	N	N
FLORIDA						
Graham	Y	N	Y	N	Y	N
Mack	N	Y	Y	N	N	Y
GEORGIA						
Fowler	N	N	N	N	N	Y
Nunn	N	N	N	N	N	Y
HAWAII						
Inouye	N	Y	N	N	Y	Y
Akaka	Y	Y	N	Y	Y	Y
IDAHO						
McClure	N	N	Y	N	N	Y
Symms	N	Y	Y	N	N	Y
ILLINOIS						
Dixon	Y	N	Y	N	N	Y
Simon	Y	Y	N	Y	Y	Y
INDIANA						
Coats	N	Y	Y	N	N	N
Lugar	N	N	N	N	N	Y
IOWA						
Harkin	Y	N	Y	Y	Y	Y
Grassley	Y	Y	Y	N	N	Y
KANSAS						
Dole	N	N	N	N	N	Y
Kassebaum	N	Y	N	N	Y	Y
KENTUCKY						
Ford	N	N	Y	N	Y	Y
McConnell	Y	Y	Y	N	N	Y
LOUISIANA						
Breaux	N	N	N	N	N	Y
Johnston	Y	N	N	N	Y	Y
MAINE						
Mitchell	N	N	N	Y	Y	Y
Cohen	Y	N	Y	Y	Y	Y
MARYLAND						
Mikulski	Y	N	N	Y	Y	N
Sarbanes	Y	N	N	Y	Y	N
MASSACHUSETTS						
Kennedy	Y	N	N	Y	Y	Y
Kerry	Y	N	Y	Y	Y	N
MICHIGAN						
Levin	Y	N	Y	Y	Y	Y
Riegle	Y	N	N	Y	Y	Y
MINNESOTA						
Boschwitz	Y	N	N	N	N	N
Durenberger	N	N	N	N	N	N
MISSISSIPPI						
Cochran	N	Y	Y	N	N	Y
Lott	N	Y	Y	N	N	Y
MISSOURI						
Bond	N	Y	Y	N	N	Y
Danforth	N	N	N	N	N	Y
MONTANA						
Baucus	Y	N	Y	N	Y	N
Burns	N	Y	Y	N	N	Y
NEBRASKA						
Exon	Y	Y	Y	N	Y	Y
Kerrey	Y	N	Y	N	Y	Y
NEVADA						
Bryan	Y	N	Y	N	Y	Y
Reid	Y	N	Y	Y	Y	Y
NEW HAMPSHIRE						
Humphrey	N	Y	Y	N	N	Y
Rudman	N	N	N	N	N	N
NEW JERSEY						
Bradley	Y	N	N	Y	N	N
Lautenberg	Y	N	Y	Y	Y	N
NEW MEXICO						
Bingaman	Y	N	N	N	Y	Y
Domenici	N	N	N	N	N	N
NEW YORK						
Moynihan	N	N	Y	Y	N	N
D'Amato	Y	Y	Y	Y	N	N
NORTH CAROLINA						
Sanford	Y	Y	N	Y	Y	Y
Helms	N	Y	Y	N	N	Y
NORTH DAKOTA						
Burdick	Y	N	Y	N	N	Y
Conrad	Y	N	Y	N	N	Y
OHIO						
Glenn	N	N	N	N	N	Y
Metzenbaum	Y	Y	N	Y	Y	N
OKLAHOMA						
Boren	N	N	N	N	N	Y
Nickles	N	Y	Y	N	N	Y
OREGON						
Hatfield	Y	Y	Y	Y	Y	Y
Packwood	N	N	N	Y	N	Y
PENNSYLVANIA						
Heinz	N	N	N	N	N	Y
Specter	Y	Y	Y	N	N	Y
RHODE ISLAND						
Pell	Y	N	N	Y	Y	N
Chafee	N	N	N	N	N	N
SOUTH CAROLINA						
Hollings	Y	Y	Y	Y	Y	N
Thurmond	N	Y	N	N	N	Y
SOUTH DAKOTA						
Daschle	N	N	Y	N	Y	Y
Pressler	Y	Y	Y	N	Y	Y
TENNESSEE						
Gore	Y	N	N	N	Y	Y
Sasser	N	N	N	N	Y	N
TEXAS						
Bentsen	N	N	N	N	N	Y
Gramm	N	N	N	N	N	N
UTAH						
Garn	N	Y	Y	N	N	Y
Hatch	N	Y	Y	N	N	Y
VERMONT						
Leahy	Y	N	N	Y	Y	N
Jeffords	Y	Y	Y	Y	N	N
VIRGINIA						
Robb	N	N	N	N	N	Y
Warner	Y	N	Y	N	N	Y
WASHINGTON						
Adams	Y	N	N	Y	Y	Y
Gorton	N	Y	N	N	N	Y
WEST VIRGINIA						
Byrd	N	N	N	N	N	Y
Rockefeller	Y	N	N	N	N	Y
WISCONSIN						
Kohl	Y	N	N	Y	Y	Y
Kasten	N	Y	Y	Y	N	Y
WYOMING						
Simpson	N	N	Y	N	N	N
Wallop	N	Y	Y	N	N	N

KEY

Y Voted for (yea).
\# Paired for.
\+ Announced for.
N Voted against (nay).
X Paired against.
\- Announced against.
P Voted "present."
C Voted "present" to avoid possible conflict of interest.
? Did not vote or otherwise make a position known.

Democrats *Republicans*

ND Northern Democrats SD Southern Democrats

Southern states - Ala., Ark., Fla., Ga., Ky., La., Miss., N.C., Okla., S.C., Tenn., Texas, Va.

285. S 3209. Fiscal 1991 Budget Reconciliation/Budget Act Waiver. Harkin, D-Iowa, motion to waive the Budget Act with respect to the Sasser, D-Tenn., point of order, which stated that the Harkin amendment to impose a surtax on income over $1 million and eliminate the increase in the Medicare Part B deductible from $75 to $150 would violate a Budget Act prohibition against non-germane amendments. Motion rejected 49-51: R 12-33; D 37-18 (ND 30-8, SD 7-10), Oct. 18, 1990. A three-fifths majority (60) of the total Senate is required to waive the Budget Act. (The Harkin amendment subsequently fell on the Sasser point of order.)

286. S 3209. Fiscal 1991 Budget Reconciliation/Budget Act Waiver. Kasten, R-Wis., motion to waive the Budget Act with respect to the Sasser, D-Tenn., point of order, which stated that the Kasten amendment, to exclude charitable contributions from the overall limitation on itemized deductions, would violate a Budget Act prohibition against reconciliation bill amendments that are not deficit-neutral. Motion rejected 39-61: R 29-16; D 10-45 (ND 6-32, SD 4-13), Oct. 18, 1990. A three-fifths majority (60) of the total Senate is required to waive the Budget Act. (The Kasten amendment subsequently fell on the Sasser point of order.)

287. S 3209. Fiscal 1991 Budget Reconciliation Act/'Byrd Rule' Waiver. Symms, R-Idaho, motion to waive the "Byrd Rule" — an amendment to the Gramm-Rudman antideficit law — with respect to the Bentsen, D-Texas, point of order, which stated that the Symms amendment to deposit all new revenues from the motor fuels tax into the Highway Trust Fund except for taxes on railroads would violate a prohibition against amendments that do not produce changes in outlays or revenues. Motion rejected 48-52: R 29-16; D 19-36 (ND 15-23, SD 4-13), Oct. 18, 1990. A three-fifths majority (60) of the total Senate is required to waive the Byrd Rule. (The Symms amendment subsequently fell on the Bentsen point of order.)

288. S 3209. Fiscal 1991 Budget Reconciliation Act/Budget Act Waiver. Lieberman, D-Conn., motion to waive the Budget Act with respect to the Domenici, R-N.M., point of order, which stated that the Metzenbaum, D-Ohio, amendment to reinstate the windfall profit tax on domestic crude oil would violate a Budget Act prohibition against non-germane amendments. Motion rejected 33-67: R 7-38; D 26-29 (ND 24-14, SD 2-15), Oct. 18, 1990. A three-fifths majority (60) of the total Senate is required to waive the Budget Act. (The Metzenbaum amendment subsequently fell on the Domenici point of order.)

289. S 3209. Fiscal 1991 Budget Reconciliation Act/Indexing. Levin, D-Mich., amendment to express the sense of the Senate that Senate conferees should work for a package that would not delay indexing of the tax code; increase income tax only on income in excess of $200,000 at a rate of 35 percent; eliminate any increase in the gas tax; and eliminate changes in Medicare premiums and deductibles. Rejected 44-56: R 5-40; D 39-16 (ND 28-10, SD 11-6), Oct. 18, 1990.

290. S 3209. Fiscal 1991 Budget Reconciliation Act/'Byrd Rule' Waiver. Ford, D-Ky., motion to waive the "Byrd Rule" — an amendment to the Gramm-Rudman antideficit law — with respect to the D'Amato, R-N.Y., point of order, which stated that the Ford modifications of Title III, Subtitle B would violate a prohibition against amendments that do not produce changes in outlays or revenues. The Ford modifications would have established limitations on airport improvement program revenues, created a pool of air carrier special authorizations for Washington National Airport and established high-density traffic airport rules. Motion agreed to 69-31: R 30-15; D 39-16 (ND 25-13, SD 14-3), Oct. 18, 1990. A three-fifths majority (60) of the total Senate is required to waive the Byrd Rule. (The D'Amato point of order was subsequently overruled and the Ford modifications were ruled in order.)

	291	292	293	294	295
ALABAMA					
Heflin	Y	N	Y	Y	Y
Shelby	N	N	Y	Y	Y
ALASKA					
Murkowski	Y	Y	Y	Y	Y
Stevens	Y	Y	Y	Y	Y
ARIZONA					
DeConcini	N	N	Y	Y	N
McCain	Y	N	N	Y	Y
ARKANSAS					
Bumpers	Y	Y	Y	Y	N
Pryor	Y	Y	Y	N	N
CALIFORNIA					
Cranston	Y	Y	Y	Y	N
Wilson	Y	N	N	Y	Y
COLORADO					
Wirth	N	Y	Y	Y	N
Armstrong	Y	N	N	Y	Y
CONNECTICUT					
Dodd	Y	Y	Y	Y	N
Lieberman	Y	N	Y	Y	N
DELAWARE					
Biden	Y	N	Y	Y	N
Roth	N	N	Y	Y	Y
FLORIDA					
Graham	N	N	Y	Y	Y
Mack	Y	N	N	Y	Y
GEORGIA					
Fowler	Y	Y	Y	Y	N
Nunn	Y	Y	Y	Y	Y
HAWAII					
Inouye	Y	Y	Y	Y	N
Akaka	Y	N	Y	Y	N
IDAHO					
McClure	Y	Y	N	N	Y
Symms	Y	N	N	Y	Y
ILLINOIS					
Dixon	Y	Y	Y	Y	N
Simon	N	N	Y	Y	N
INDIANA					
Coats	Y	N	N	Y	Y
Lugar	Y	Y	N	Y	Y

	291	292	293	294	295
IOWA					
Harkin	Y	N	Y	Y	N
Grassley	Y	N	Y	Y	Y
KANSAS					
Dole	Y	Y	N	N	Y
Kassebaum	N	Y	Y	N	N
KENTUCKY					
Ford	Y	Y	Y	Y	N
McConnell	Y	N	N	Y	Y
LOUISIANA					
Breaux	Y	Y	Y	Y	Y
Johnston	Y	N	Y	Y	N
MAINE					
Mitchell	Y	Y	Y	Y	N
Cohen	Y	N	Y	Y	N
MARYLAND					
Mikulski	Y	Y	Y	Y	N
Sarbanes	N	Y	Y	Y	N
MASSACHUSETTS					
Kennedy	Y	Y	Y	Y	N
Kerry	N	N	Y	Y	N
MICHIGAN					
Levin	N	N	Y	Y	N
Riegle	N	N	Y	?	?
MINNESOTA					
Boschwitz	Y	Y	Y	Y	Y
Durenberger	Y	Y	Y	Y	N
MISSISSIPPI					
Cochran	Y	Y	N	Y	Y
Lott	Y	N	N	Y	Y
MISSOURI					
Bond	Y	Y	N	Y	Y
Danforth	Y	Y	Y	Y	N
MONTANA					
Baucus	Y	N	Y	Y	N
Burns	Y	N	N	Y	Y
NEBRASKA					
Exon	N	N	Y	Y	N
Kerrey	Y	N	Y	Y	N
NEVADA					
Bryan	Y	Y	Y	Y	Y
Reid	Y	Y	Y	Y	N

	291	292	293	294	295
NEW HAMPSHIRE					
Humphrey	N	N	N	Y	Y
Rudman	Y	Y	N	Y	Y
NEW JERSEY					
Bradley	N	N	Y	Y	N
Lautenberg	N	N	Y	Y	N
NEW MEXICO					
Bingaman	N	Y	Y	Y	N
Domenici	Y	Y	Y	Y	N
NEW YORK					
Moynihan	N	Y	Y	Y	N
D'Amato	Y	N	Y	Y	N
NORTH CAROLINA					
Sanford	N	N	Y	Y	N
Helms	Y	N	N	Y	Y
NORTH DAKOTA					
Burdick	Y	Y	Y	Y	N
Conrad	N	N	Y	Y	N
OHIO					
Glenn	Y	Y	Y	Y	N
Metzenbaum	N	N	Y	Y	N
OKLAHOMA					
Boren	Y	Y	Y	Y	N
Nickles	Y	N	N	Y	Y
OREGON					
Hatfield	Y	N	Y	Y	N
Packwood	Y	Y	Y	Y	N
PENNSYLVANIA					
Heinz	Y	Y	Y	Y	N
Specter	N	Y	Y	Y	N
RHODE ISLAND					
Pell	Y	N	Y	Y	N
Chafee	Y	Y	Y	Y	N
SOUTH CAROLINA					
Hollings	N	N	Y	Y	Y
Thurmond	Y	Y	N	Y	Y
SOUTH DAKOTA					
Daschle	Y	Y	Y	Y	—
Pressler	Y	N	Y	Y	N
TENNESSEE					
Gore	Y	Y	Y	Y	N
Sasser	Y	Y	Y	Y	N

KEY

- Y Voted for (yea).
- # Paired for.
- + Announced for.
- N Voted against (nay).
- X Paired against.
- \- Announced against.
- P Voted "present."
- C Voted "present" to avoid possible conflict of interest.
- ? Did not vote or otherwise make a position known.

Democrats *Republicans*

	291	292	293	294	295
TEXAS					
Bentsen	Y	Y	Y	Y	Y
Gramm	Y	N	?	?	?
UTAH					
Garn	Y	Y	N	N	Y
Hatch	N	Y	N	Y	Y
VERMONT					
Leahy	Y	Y	Y	Y	N
Jeffords	Y	Y	Y	N	N
VIRGINIA					
Robb	Y	Y	Y	Y	Y
Warner	Y	Y	Y	Y	N
WASHINGTON					
Adams	N	N	Y	Y	N
Gorton	Y	N	N	Y	Y
WEST VIRGINIA					
Byrd	Y	Y	Y	N	N
Rockefeller	Y	Y	Y	Y	N
WISCONSIN					
Kohl	N	Y	Y	Y	N
Kasten	Y	N	N	Y	Y
WYOMING					
Simpson	Y	Y	N	Y	Y
Wallop	Y	N	N	N	Y

ND Northern Democrats SD Southern Democrats

Southern states - Ala., Ark., Fla., Ga., Ky., La., Miss., N.C., Okla., S.C., Tenn., Texas, Va.

291. S 3209. Fiscal 1991 Budget Reconciliation Act/Budget Act Waiver. Sasser, D-Tenn., motion to waive the Budget Act with respect to the Hollings, D-S.C., point of order, which stated that the Mitchell, D-Maine, amendment would violate a Budget Act prohibition against non-germane amendments. The Mitchell amendment would revise the Gramm-Rudman antideficit law targets through 1995; set discretionary spending caps for 3 years; create a pay-as-you-go procedure for all new entitlement initiatives; remove Social Security from deficit calculations; and keep the cost of the savings and loan bailout on budget. Motion agreed to 75-25: R 40-5; D 35-20 (ND 22-16, SD 13-4), Oct. 19, 1990 (in the session that began, and the Congressional Record dated, Oct. 18, 1990). A three-fifths majority (60) of the Senate is required to waive the Budget Act. (The Hollings point of order was subsequently overruled, and the Mitchell amendment was adopted by voice vote.)

292. S 3209. Fiscal 1991 Budget Reconciliation Act/Passage. Passage of the bill to reduce spending and raise revenues as required by the reconciliation instructions in the budget resolution and make changes in the budget process. Passed 54-46: R 23-22; D 31-24 (ND 20-18, SD 11-6), Oct. 19, 1990 (in the session that began, and the Congressional Record dated, Oct. 18, 1990). (The Senate subsequently passed HR 5835 by voice vote after striking all after the enacting clause and inserting in lieu thereof the text of S 3209.)

293. HR 5114. Fiscal 1991 Foreign Operations Appropriations/El Salvador. Leahy, D-Vt., amendment to the committee amendment, to reduce military aid to the government of El Salvador by 50 percent and link future military aid to improvements in human rights and progress toward a negotiated peace settlement. Adopted 74-25: R 19-25; D 55-0 (ND 38-0, SD 17-0), Oct. 19, 1990. A "nay" was a vote supporting the president's position.

294. HR 5114. Fiscal 1991 Foreign Operations Appropriations/Israeli Settlements. Kasten, R-Wis., motion to table (kill) the Byrd, D-W.Va., amendment to the committee amendment, to reiterate U.S. support for U.N. Resolutions 242, 338 and 339 and state that Israeli government incentives for new settlements in the occupied territories are contrary to the intent or spirit of these resolutions; express congressional regret about the Oct. 14 decision to encourage and increase the settlement for Soviet Jewish refugees in East Jerusalem; and require the president to provide Congress periodic assessments of Israeli law, government policies and financial incentives for settlements in the occupied territories. Motion agreed to 90-8: R 38-6; D 52-2 (ND 36-1, SD 16-1), Oct. 19, 1990.

295. HR 5114. Fiscal 1991 Foreign Operations Appropriations/El Salvador. Graham, D-Fla., amendment to the committee amendment, to stop all U.S. military aid to El Salvador if the Salvadoran government has failed to request the United Nations to actively mediate negotiations with the Farabundo Marti National Liberation Front (FMLN), has rejected a good faith proposal for an internationally monitored cease-fire, or is not complying with the terms of a cease-fire. The amendment would restore the aid if the FMLN failed to cooperate on any of the conditions. Rejected 39-58: R 30-14; D 9-44 (ND 1-35, SD 8-9), Oct. 19, 1990. A "nay" was a vote supporting the president's position.

SENATE VOTES 296, 297, 298, 299, 300, 301

	296	297	298	299	300	301
ALABAMA						
Heflin	Y	Y	Y	Y	N	N
Shelby	Y	Y	N	Y	N	N
ALASKA						
Murkowski	Y	N	Y	Y	N	N
Stevens	Y	N	Y	Y	N	N
ARIZONA						
DeConcini	Y	N	Y	Y	N	N
McCain	Y	N	Y	Y	N	N
ARKANSAS						
Bumpers	Y	Y	N	Y	N	Y
Pryor	Y	Y	N	Y	N	Y
CALIFORNIA						
Cranston	Y	N	N	Y	N	Y
Wilson	Y	N	N	Y	N	Y
COLORADO						
Wirth	Y	N	N	Y	N	N
Armstrong	Y	N	Y	N	N	N
CONNECTICUT						
Dodd	Y	Y	N	Y	N	Y
Lieberman	Y	N	N	Y	N	Y
DELAWARE						
Biden	Y	Y	N	Y	N	Y
Roth	Y	N	N	Y	N	N
FLORIDA						
Graham	Y	Y	N	Y	N	Y
Mack	Y	N	Y	Y	N	N
GEORGIA						
Fowler	Y	N	N	Y	N	Y
Nunn	Y	Y	N	Y	N	Y
HAWAII						
Inouye	Y	N	N	Y	N	N
Akaka	Y	Y	N	Y	N	Y
IDAHO						
McClure	Y	N	Y	Y	N	N
Symms	Y	N	Y	Y	N	N
ILLINOIS						
Dixon	Y	Y	N	Y	N	Y
Simon	Y	Y	N	Y	N	Y
INDIANA						
Coats	Y	Y	Y	Y	N	N
Lugar	Y	N	Y	N	N	N
IOWA						
Harkin	Y	Y	N	Y	N	Y
Grassley	Y	Y	Y	Y	N	Y
KANSAS						
Dole	Y	N	Y	Y	N	N
Kassebaum	Y	Y	N	Y	N	N
KENTUCKY						
Ford	Y	Y	Y	Y	N	Y
McConnell	Y	N	Y	Y	N	N
LOUISIANA						
Breaux	N	Y	Y	Y	N	Y
Johnston	Y	Y	Y	Y	N	Y
MAINE						
Mitchell	Y	N	N	Y	N	Y
Cohen	Y	Y	N	Y	N	Y
MARYLAND						
Mikulski	Y	Y	N	Y	N	Y
Sarbanes	Y	N	N	Y	N	Y
MASSACHUSETTS						
Kennedy	Y	N	N	Y	N	Y
Kerry	Y	Y	N	+	-	+
MICHIGAN						
Levin	Y	Y	N	Y	N	Y
Riegle	?	?	?	Y	N	Y
MINNESOTA						
Boschwitz	Y	Y	Y	Y	N	N
Durenberger	Y	N	Y	Y	N	N
MISSISSIPPI						
Cochran	Y	N	Y	Y	N	N
Lott	Y	Y	Y	Y	N	N
MISSOURI						
Bond	Y	N	Y	Y	N	N
Danforth	Y	N	Y	Y	N	N
MONTANA						
Baucus	Y	Y	N	Y	N	N
Burns	Y	N	Y	Y	N	N
NEBRASKA						
Exon	Y	Y	Y	Y	N	Y
Kerrey	Y	Y	N	Y	N	Y
NEVADA						
Bryan	Y	Y	N	Y	N	N
Reid	Y	Y	Y	Y	N	N
NEW HAMPSHIRE						
Humphrey	Y	Y	Y	Y	N	N
Rudman	Y	N	Y	Y	N	N
NEW JERSEY						
Bradley	Y	N	N	Y	N	Y
Lautenberg	Y	N	N	Y	N	Y
NEW MEXICO						
Bingaman	?	N	N	Y	N	N
Domenici	Y	N	Y	Y	N	N
NEW YORK						
Moynihan	Y	N	N	N	N	N
D'Amato	Y	N	Y	Y	N	N
NORTH CAROLINA						
Sanford	Y	Y	N	Y	N	Y
Helms	N	Y	Y	Y	N	N
NORTH DAKOTA						
Burdick	Y	Y	N	Y	N	Y
Conrad	Y	Y	N	Y	N	N
OHIO						
Glenn	Y	N	N	Y	N	Y
Metzenbaum	Y	N	N	Y	N	Y
OKLAHOMA						
Boren	Y	N	Y	Y	N	Y
Nickles	Y	N	Y	Y	N	N
OREGON						
Hatfield	Y	Y	N	Y	N	N
Packwood	Y	N	N	Y	N	N
PENNSYLVANIA						
Heinz	Y	N	N	Y	N	N
Specter	Y	N	N	Y	N	Y
RHODE ISLAND						
Pell	Y	Y	N	Y	N	Y
Chafee	Y	N	N	Y	N	N
SOUTH CAROLINA						
Hollings	Y	Y	N	Y	N	Y
Thurmond	Y	N	Y	Y	N	N
SOUTH DAKOTA						
Daschle	+	+	N	Y	N	Y
Pressler	Y	Y	Y	Y	N	Y
TENNESSEE						
Gore	Y	N	N	Y	N	Y
Sasser	Y	Y	N	Y	N	Y
TEXAS						
Bentsen	Y	N	N	Y	N	Y
Gramm	?	?	?	?	?	?
UTAH						
Garn	Y	N	Y	Y	N	N
Hatch	Y	N	Y	Y	N	N
VERMONT						
Leahy	Y	N	N	Y	N	Y
Jeffords	Y	N	N	Y	N	Y
VIRGINIA						
Robb	Y	N	N	Y	N	Y
Warner	Y	N	Y	Y	N	N
WASHINGTON						
Adams	Y	N	N	Y	N	Y
Gorton	Y	N	Y	Y	N	N
WEST VIRGINIA						
Byrd	Y	Y	N	Y	Y	N
Rockefeller	Y	Y	N	Y	N	Y
WISCONSIN						
Kohl	Y	Y	N	Y	N	Y
Kasten	Y	N	Y	Y	N	N
WYOMING						
Simpson	Y	N	N	Y	N	N
Wallop	Y	N	Y	Y	N	N

KEY

- Y Voted for (yea).
- # Paired for.
- + Announced for.
- N Voted against (nay).
- X Paired against.
- \- Announced against.
- P Voted "present."
- C Voted "present" to avoid possible conflict of interest.
- ? Did not vote or otherwise make a position known.

Democrats ***Republicans***

ND Northern Democrats SD Southern Democrats

Southern states - Ala., Ark., Fla., Ga., Ky., La., Miss., N.C., Okla., S.C., Tenn., Texas, Va.

296. HR 5114. Fiscal 1991 Foreign Operations Appropriations/Egyptian Debt. Leahy, D-Vt., amendment to the committee amendment, to delay the forgiveness of Egyptian debt until Dec. 31, 1990, and require the president to convene an international conference on Egypt's international debt crisis for the purpose of securing a multilateral agreement by all donors for a comprehensive solution to Egypt's problem, and submit a report to Congress no later than Jan. 1, 1991, on the results of the conference. Adopted 94-2: R 43-1; D 51-1 (ND 35-0, SD 16-1), Oct. 19, 1990. A "nay" was a vote supporting the president's position.

297. HR 5114. Fiscal 1991 Foreign Operations Appropriations/Egyptian Debt. Harkin, D-Iowa, amendment to the committee amendment, to strike provisions canceling Egypt's debt to the United States and require the president to develop in cooperation with Congress a proposal to restructure Egypt's debt to the United States and convene an international conference to develop a comprehensive and multilateral solution to Egypt's international debt problem. Rejected 42-55: R 10-34; D 32-21 (ND 20-16, SD 12-5), Oct. 19, 1990. A "nay" was a vote supporting the president's position.

298. HR 5114. Fiscal 1991 Foreign Operations Appropriations/Family Planning. Dole, R-Kan., motion to table (kill) the Wirth, D-Colo., amendment to the committee amendment, to permit the Agency for International Development (AID) to provide funds to private organizations that engage in family planning and that use their own funds to provide information on abortion. AID adheres to the Mexico City policy, prohibiting non-governmental agencies from receiving U.S. assistance, if that agency provides information or services involving abortion. Motion rejected 41-57: R 33-11; D 8-46 (ND 3-34, SD 5-12), Oct. 19, 1990. A "yea" was a vote supporting the president's position.

299. HR 5114. Fiscal 1991 Foreign Operations Appropriations/Tied-Aid Credits. Byrd, D-W.Va., amendment to the committee amendment, to add $300 million for tied-aid credits. Adopted 95-3: R 42-2; D 53-1 (ND 36-1, SD 17-0), Oct. 22, 1990.

300. HR 5114. Fiscal 1991 Foreign Operations Appropriations/Defense Stock Drawdown. Byrd, D-W.Va., amendment to strike the Kasten, R-Wis., amendment, to authorize a defense stock drawdown of $700 million for the provision of military equipment to Israel. Rejected 1-97: R 0-44; D 1-53 (ND 1-36, SD 0-17), Oct. 22, 1990. (The Kasten amendment was previously adopted by voice vote.)

301. HR 5769. Fiscal 1991 Interior Appropriations/Germaneness. Judgment of the Senate whether the committee amendment to prevent the use of funds for one year for the issuance of 1872 Mining Law patents was germane. Ruled non-germane 48-50: R 6-38; D 42-12 (ND 27-10, SD 15-2), Oct. 22, 1990. (The committee amendment subsequently fell on the question of germaneness.)

	302	303	304	305	306	307	308	309
ALABAMA								
Heflin	N	N	Y	Y	N	Y	N	Y
Shelby	Y	Y	Y	Y	Y	Y	Y	Y
ALASKA								
Murkowski	Y	N	N	N	Y	Y	Y	Y
Stevens	Y	N	N	N	Y	N	Y	Y
ARIZONA								
DeConcini	Y	Y	Y	Y	Y	N	Y	Y
McCain	Y	Y	N	N	Y	Y	N	Y
ARKANSAS								
Bumpers	N	Y	Y	Y	Y	N	Y	Y
Pryor	Y	Y	Y	Y	N	N	Y	Y
CALIFORNIA								
Cranston	N	Y	Y	Y	Y	N	?	Y
Wilson	Y	Y	N	N	Y	N	N	Y
COLORADO								
Wirth	N	Y	Y	Y	Y	N	Y	Y
Armstrong	Y	N	N	N	N	Y	N	Y
CONNECTICUT								
Dodd	N	Y	Y	Y	Y	N	Y	Y
Lieberman	N	Y	Y	Y	Y	N	Y	Y
DELAWARE								
Biden	N	Y	Y	Y	N	N	Y	Y
Roth	N	Y	N	N	N	Y	Y	N
FLORIDA								
Graham	N	Y	Y	Y	Y	N	Y	Y
Mack	Y	N	N	N	Y	Y	N	Y
GEORGIA								
Fowler	N	Y	Y	N	Y	N	Y	Y
Nunn	N	Y	Y	N	Y	N	N	Y
HAWAII								
Inouye	Y	N	Y	Y	Y	N	N	Y
Akaka	N	Y	Y	Y	Y	N	Y	Y
IDAHO								
McClure	Y	N	N	N	N	Y	N	Y
Symms	Y	N	N	N	N	Y	N	Y
ILLINOIS								
Dixon	N	Y	Y	Y	Y	N	Y	N
Simon	N	Y	Y	Y	Y	N	Y	Y
INDIANA								
Coats	Y	N	N	N	Y	Y	N	Y
Lugar	Y	Y	N	N	Y	N	Y	Y
IOWA								
Harkin	N	Y	Y	Y	Y	N	Y	Y
Grassley	Y	N	N	Y	Y	Y	N	N
KANSAS								
Dole	Y	N	N	N	Y	Y	Y	Y
Kassebaum	Y	Y	N	N	Y	N	Y	Y
KENTUCKY								
Ford	N	N	Y	Y	Y	N	N	Y
McConnell	Y	N	N	N	Y	Y	N	Y
LOUISIANA								
Breaux	N	Y	Y	Y	N	N	Y	Y
Johnston	Y	X	Y	Y	N	N	Y	Y
MAINE								
Mitchell	N	Y	Y	Y	Y	N	Y	Y
Cohen	N	Y	Y	N	Y	N	Y	Y
MARYLAND								
Mikulski	N	Y	Y	Y	Y	N	Y	Y
Sarbanes	N	Y	Y	Y	Y	N	Y	Y
MASSACHUSETTS								
Kennedy	N	Y	Y	Y	Y	N	Y	Y
Kerry	X	#	Y	Y	Y	N	Y	Y
MICHIGAN								
Levin	Y	Y	Y	Y	Y	N	Y	Y
Riegle	Y	Y	Y	Y	Y	N	Y	Y
MINNESOTA								
Boschwitz	Y	N	Y	N	Y	N	?	?
Durenberger	Y	Y	Y	N	Y	N	Y	Y
MISSISSIPPI								
Cochran	Y	N	N	N	Y	Y	Y	Y
Lott	Y	N	N	N	Y	Y	N	Y
MISSOURI								
Bond	Y	N	N	N	Y	N	Y	N
Danforth	Y	N	Y	N	Y	N	Y	Y
MONTANA								
Baucus	Y	Y	Y	Y	N	N	Y	Y
Burns	Y	N	N	N	Y	Y	Y	Y
NEBRASKA								
Exon	N	Y	Y	Y	N	Y	Y	Y
Kerrey	N	Y	Y	Y	Y	N	Y	Y
NEVADA								
Bryan	N	Y	Y	Y	Y	N	N	Y
Reid	N	Y	Y	Y	Y	N	Y	Y
NEW HAMPSHIRE								
Humphrey	N	Y	N	N	N	Y	N	N
Rudman	Y	N	N	N	Y	N	N	Y
NEW JERSEY								
Bradley	–	+	Y	Y	Y	N	Y	Y
Lautenberg	N	Y	Y	Y	Y	N	Y	Y
NEW MEXICO								
Bingaman	N	Y	Y	Y	Y	N	Y	Y
Domenici	Y	N	Y	N	N	N	Y	Y
NEW YORK								
Moynihan	N	Y	Y	Y	Y	N	Y	Y
D'Amato	Y	Y	N	N	Y	N	Y	Y
NORTH CAROLINA								
Sanford	#	Y	Y	Y	Y	N	Y	Y
Helms	Y	N	N	N	N	Y	N	N
NORTH DAKOTA								
Burdick	Y	Y	Y	Y	N	N	Y	Y
Conrad	Y	Y	Y	Y	N	Y	Y	Y
OHIO								
Glenn	N	Y	Y	N	Y	N	Y	Y
Metzenbaum	N	Y	Y	Y	Y	N	Y	Y
OKLAHOMA								
Boren	N	N	Y	Y	N	N	Y	Y
Nickles	Y	N	N	N	Y	Y	N	Y
OREGON								
Hatfield	Y	N	Y	?	–	?	?	?
Packwood	Y	N	Y	N	Y	N	Y	Y
PENNSYLVANIA								
Heinz	N	Y	Y	N	Y	N	Y	Y
Specter	N	Y	Y	N	Y	N	Y	Y
RHODE ISLAND								
Pell	N	Y	Y	Y	Y	N	Y	Y
Chafee	Y	Y	Y	N	Y	N	Y	Y
SOUTH CAROLINA								
Hollings	Y	Y	Y	Y	N	Y	Y	Y
Thurmond	Y	N	N	N	Y	Y	N	Y
SOUTH DAKOTA								
Daschle	Y	Y	Y	Y	N	N	Y	Y
Pressler	Y	N	N	N	N	Y	Y	Y
TENNESSEE								
Gore	N	Y	Y	Y	Y	N	Y	Y
Sasser	N	Y	Y	Y	Y	N	Y	Y
TEXAS								
Bentsen	N	Y	Y	N	Y	N	Y	Y
Gramm	?	?	N	N	Y	Y	N	Y
UTAH								
Garn	Y	N	N	N	N	Y	Y	Y
Hatch	Y	N	N	N	Y	N	Y	Y
VERMONT								
Leahy	N	Y	Y	Y	Y	N	Y	Y
Jeffords	N	Y	Y	N	Y	N	Y	Y
VIRGINIA								
Robb	N	Y	Y	Y	Y	N	Y	Y
Warner	Y	Y	N	N	Y	N	Y	Y
WASHINGTON								
Adams	N	Y	Y	Y	Y	N	Y	Y
Gorton	Y	N	N	N	Y	N	N	Y
WEST VIRGINIA								
Byrd	Y	N	Y	Y	N	Y	N	Y
Rockefeller	N	Y	Y	Y	N	N	Y	Y
WISCONSIN								
Kohl	Y	Y	Y	Y	Y	N	Y	Y
Kasten	Y	Y	N	N	Y	Y	Y	Y
WYOMING								
Simpson	Y	N	N	N	Y	N	Y	Y
Wallop	Y	N	N	N	Y	Y	N	Y

KEY

- Y Voted for (yea).
- # Paired for.
- + Announced for.
- N Voted against (nay).
- X Paired against.
- - Announced against.
- P Voted "present."
- C Voted "present" to avoid possible conflict of interest.
- ? Did not vote or otherwise make a position known.

Democrats *Republicans*

ND Northern Democrats SD Southern Democrats

Southern states - Ala., Ark., Fla., Ga., Ky., La., Miss., N.C., Okla., S.C., Tenn., Texas, Va.

302. HR 5769. Fiscal 1991 Interior Appropriations/Timber Roads. McClure, R-Idaho, motion to table (kill) the Fowler, D-Ga., amendment to cut by $100 million the U.S. Forest Service's budget for building timber roads in national forests with $50 million to be returned to the Treasury for deficit reduction and $50 million to be transferred to underfunded programs in forestry research, fish and wildlife habitat protection, wetlands restoration, economic diversification, and historic preservation. Motion agreed to 52-44: R 38-6; D 14-38 (ND 10-26, SD 4-12), Oct. 23, 1990. A "nay" was a vote supporting the president's position.

303. HR 5769. Fiscal 1991 Interior Appropriations/Spotted Owl. Baucus, D-Mont., motion to table (kill) the Packwood, R-Ore., amendment to direct the U.S. Forest Service and Bureau of Land Management (BLM) to submit agency action plans for consultation as required by the Endangered Species Act and allow them to apply for a convening of the Endangered Species Committee, if the Interior secretary determines federal actions would jeopardize the spotted owl. Motion agreed to 62-34: R 15-29; D 47-5 (ND 34-2, SD 13-3), Oct. 23, 1990. A "nay" was a vote supporting the president's position.

304. S 2104. Civil Rights Act of 1990/Veto Override. Passage, over President Bush's Oct. 22 veto, of the bill to reverse or modify six recent Supreme Court decisions that narrowed the reach and remedies of job discrimination law and to authorize monetary damages under Title VII of the 1964 Civil Rights Act. Rejected 66-34: R 11-34; D 55-0 (ND 38-0, SD 17-0), Oct. 24, 1990. A two-thirds majority of those present and voting (67 in this case) of both houses is required to override a veto. A "nay" was a vote supporting the president's position.

305. HR 5021. Fiscal 1991 Commerce, Justice, State Appropriations/Foreign Trade Zone. Harkin, D-Iowa, motion to table (kill) the Heinz, R-Pa., motion to concur in the House amendment with an amendment to strike provisions directing the establishment of a foreign trade zone in Cedar Rapids, Iowa. Motion agreed to 52-47: R 1-43; D 51-4 (ND 37-1, SD 14-3), Oct. 24, 1990.

306. HR 5114. Fiscal 1991 Foreign Operations Appropriations/Passage. Passage of the bill to appropriate $15,533,040,543 for foreign military and economic assistance and export financing in fiscal 1991. The president requested $15,518,826,537. Passed 76-23: R 35-9; D 41-14 (ND 30-8, SD 11-6), Oct. 24, 1990.

307. HR 5769. Fiscal 1991 Interior Appropriations/NEA. Helms, R-N.C. amendment to the committee amendment, to prohibit the National Endowment for the Arts from using federal funds to promote, distribute, disseminate or produce materials that depict or describe, in a patently offensive way, sexual or excretory activities or organs. Rejected 29-70: R 23-21; D 6-49 (ND 3-35, SD 3-14), Oct. 24, 1990.

308. HR 5769. Fiscal 1991 Interior Appropriations/NEA. Hatch, R-Utah, amendment to the committee amendment, to require that funds be returned to the National Endowment for the Arts (NEA), if a court determines that the NEA-funded project is obscene or violates child pornography laws, thus leaving any restrictions on content to be determined by what state courts find violate local law. The amendment also requires the NEA to ensure broader representation and more access to procedures by the public. Adopted 73-24: R 25-18; D 48-6 (ND 34-3, SD 14-3), Oct. 24, 1990.

309. HR 5769. Fiscal 1991 Interior Appropriations/Passage. Passage of the bill to appropriate $11.70 billion for the Interior Department and related agencies in fiscal 1991. The president requested $9.86 billion. Passed 92-6: R 38-5; D 54-1 (ND 37-1, SD 17-0), Oct. 24, 1990.

KEY

- Y Voted for (yea).
- # Paired for.
- + Announced for.
- N Voted against (nay).
- X Paired against.
- - Announced against.
- P Voted "present."
- C Voted "present" to avoid possible conflict of interest.
- ? Did not vote or otherwise make a position known.

Democrats ***Republicans***

	310	311	312	313	314
ALABAMA					
Heflin	N	Y	Y	Y	Y
Shelby	N	Y	N	Y	Y
ALASKA					
Murkowski	N	Y	N	N	Y
Stevens	Y	Y	N	Y	N
ARIZONA					
DeConcini	?	Y	N	Y	Y
McCain	N	N	Y	Y	N
ARKANSAS					
Bumpers	N	Y	N	Y	Y
Pryor	Y	Y	N	Y	Y
CALIFORNIA					
Cranston	Y	?	?	Y	Y
Wilson	N	N	Y	Y	N
COLORADO					
Wirth	Y	Y	N	Y	Y
Armstrong	N	N	Y	N	N
CONNECTICUT					
Dodd	Y	Y	N	Y	Y
Lieberman	Y	Y	N	Y	Y
DELAWARE					
Biden	N	N	Y	Y	N
Roth	N	N	Y	N	N
FLORIDA					
Graham	N	N	Y	Y	Y
Mack	N	N	Y	N	N
GEORGIA					
Fowler	Y	Y	N	Y	N
Nunn	?	?	?	?	?
HAWAII					
Inouye	Y	Y	N	Y	Y
Akaka	N	Y	N	Y	Y
IDAHO					
McClure	Y	N	N	Y	Y
Symms	N	N	N	N	N
ILLINOIS					
Dixon	N	Y	N	Y	N
Simon	Y	Y	N	Y	Y
INDIANA					
Coats	N	N	Y	N	N
Lugar	N	N	Y	Y	Y
IOWA					
Harkin	N	N	Y	Y	Y
Grassley	N	N	Y	N	N
KANSAS					
Dole	N	N	Y	N	Y
Kassebaum	N	N	Y	Y	Y
KENTUCKY					
Ford	Y	Y	N	Y	Y
McConnell	N	N	Y	N	Y
LOUISIANA					
Breaux	N	Y	N	Y	Y
Johnston	Y	Y	N	Y	Y
MAINE					
Mitchell	Y	Y	N	Y	Y
Cohen	N	N	Y	Y	Y
MARYLAND					
Mikulski	Y	Y	N	Y	Y
Sarbanes	Y	Y	N	Y	Y
MASSACHUSETTS					
Kennedy	Y	Y	N	Y	Y
Kerry	N	N	Y	Y	Y
MICHIGAN					
Levin	N	N	Y	Y	N
Riegle	Y	Y	Y	Y	Y
MINNESOTA					
Boschwitz	?	?	?	?	?
Durenberger	N	N	Y	N	Y
MISSISSIPPI					
Cochran	N	?	?	?	Y
Lott	?	N	N	N	N
MISSOURI					
Bond	N	N	Y	N	Y
Danforth	N	N	Y	N	Y
MONTANA					
Baucus	N	N	N	Y	Y
Burns	N	Y	Y	Y	Y
NEBRASKA					
Exon	N	N	Y	Y	N
Kerrey	Y	N	Y	Y	Y
NEVADA					
Bryan	N	Y	N	Y	Y
Reid	Y	Y	N	Y	Y
NEW HAMPSHIRE					
Humphrey	N	N	Y	N	N
Rudman	?	N	Y	N	Y
NEW JERSEY					
Bradley	N	N	Y	Y	Y
Lautenberg	Y	N	Y	Y	Y
NEW MEXICO					
Bingaman	?	Y	N	Y	Y
Domenici	N	N	N	N	Y
NEW YORK					
Moynihan	Y	Y	N	Y	Y
D'Amato	N	N	Y	N	Y
NORTH CAROLINA					
Sanford	Y	Y	N	Y	Y
Helms	N	N	Y	N	N
NORTH DAKOTA					
Burdick	Y	Y	N	Y	Y
Conrad	N	Y	N	Y	Y
OHIO					
Glenn	N	N	Y	Y	Y
Metzenbaum	N	N	Y	Y	N
OKLAHOMA					
Boren	?	?	?	?	?
Nickles	N	N	Y	N	Y
OREGON					
Hatfield	?	+	?	+	+
Packwood	N	Y	Y	Y	Y
PENNSYLVANIA					
Heinz	N	N	Y	Y	Y
Specter	N	N	Y	Y	Y
RHODE ISLAND					
Pell	N	Y	N	Y	Y
Chafee	N	N	Y	Y	Y
SOUTH CAROLINA					
Hollings	Y	Y	Y	Y	Y
Thurmond	N	N	Y	N	Y
SOUTH DAKOTA					
Daschle	Y	Y	N	Y	Y
Pressler	N	N	Y	Y	N
TENNESSEE					
Gore	Y	Y	N	Y	Y
Sasser	Y	Y	N	Y	Y
TEXAS					
Bentsen	Y	Y	N	Y	Y
Gramm	N	N	Y	N	N
UTAH					
Garn	N	N	Y	Y	N
Hatch	N	N	N	Y	N
VERMONT					
Leahy	Y	Y	N	Y	Y
Jeffords	N	N	Y	Y	Y
VIRGINIA					
Robb	N	N	Y	Y	Y
Warner	N	N	Y	Y	Y
WASHINGTON					
Adams	Y	Y	N	Y	Y
Gorton	N	N	Y	Y	Y
WEST VIRGINIA					
Byrd	Y	Y	N	Y	Y
Rockefeller	Y	?	N	Y	Y
WISCONSIN					
Kohl	N	N	Y	Y	Y
Kasten	N	N	Y	Y	N
WYOMING					
Simpson	N	Y	Y	Y	Y
Wallop	N	N	N	N	N

ND Northern Democrats SD Southern Democrats

Southern states - Ala., Ark., Fla., Ga., Ky., La., Miss., N.C., Okla., S.C., Tenn., Texas, Va.

310. HR 5399. Fiscal 1991 Legislative Branch Appropriations/Five Percent Cut. Byrd, D-W.Va., motion to table (kill) the Nickles, R-Okla., amendment to reduce the total funds appropriated in the bill by 5 percent. Motion rejected 32-60: R 2-39; D 30-21 (ND 21-15, SD 9-6), Oct. 24, 1990. (The Nickles amendment was subsequently adopted by voice vote.)

311. HR 5399. Fiscal 1991 Legislative Branch Appropriations/Funds Transfers. Ford, D-Ky., substitute amendment to the Nickles, R-Okla., amendment, to prohibit senators from transferring funds from their franking accounts to other senators' accounts in an election year. Rejected 42-51: R 5-37; D 37-14 (ND 24-12, SD 13-2), Oct. 25, 1990.

312. HR 5399. Fiscal 1991 Legislative Branch Appropriations/Funds Transfers. Nickles, R-Okla., amendment to prohibit the transfer of funds between different senators' franking accounts. Adopted 50-44: R 34-8; D 16-36 (ND 12-25, SD 4-11), Oct. 25, 1990.

313. HR 5399. Fiscal 1991 Legislative Branch Appropriations/Library of Congress Exemption. Wirth, D-Colo., amendment to exempt the Library of Congress from the 5 percent cut in total funds appropriated in the bill. Adopted 73-22: R 20-22; D 53-0 (ND 38-0, SD 15-0), Oct. 25, 1990.

314. HR 5399. Fiscal 1991 Legislative Branch Appropriations/Passage. Passage of the bill to appropriate $2,072,426,425 for the operations of Congress and legislative branch agencies in fiscal 1991. The president requested $2,411,881,000. Passed 72-24: R 25-18; D 47-6 (ND 33-5, SD 14-1), Oct. 25, 1990.

	315	316	317	318	319	320
ALABAMA						
Heflin	Y	N	Y	Y	Y	Y
Shelby	Y	N	Y	Y	Y	Y
ALASKA						
Murkowski	Y	Y	Y	Y	Y	Y
Stevens	Y	Y	Y	Y	Y	Y
ARIZONA						
DeConcini	Y	N	Y	Y	Y	Y
McCain	Y	Y	Y	Y	Y	Y
ARKANSAS						
Bumpers	Y	N	N	Y	Y	Y
Pryor	Y	N	Y	Y	Y	Y
CALIFORNIA						
Cranston	Y	N	Y	Y	N	N
Wilson	Y	Y	Y	Y	Y	Y
COLORADO						
Wirth	Y	N	N	Y	N	Y
Armstrong	N	Y	Y	Y	N	N
CONNECTICUT						
Dodd	Y	N	N	Y	Y	Y
Lieberman	Y	N	N	Y	Y	Y
DELAWARE						
Biden	Y	N	N	?	Y	Y
Roth	N	Y	N	Y	N	N
FLORIDA						
Graham	Y	N	Y	Y	Y	Y
Mack	N	Y	Y	Y	Y	Y
GEORGIA						
Fowler	Y	N	Y	Y	Y	Y
Nunn	Y	N	Y	Y	Y	Y
HAWAII						
Inouye	Y	N	Y	Y	Y	Y
Akaka	Y	N	Y	Y	Y	Y
IDAHO						
McClure	Y	Y	X	Y	Y	Y
Symms	N	Y	N	Y	Y	Y
ILLINOIS						
Dixon	Y	N	N	Y	Y	Y
Simon	Y	N	N	Y	Y	Y
INDIANA						
Coats	N	Y	Y	Y	Y	Y
Lugar	Y	Y	Y	Y	Y	Y
IOWA						
Harken	Y	N	N	Y	N	N
Grassley	N	Y	N	Y	N	N
KANSAS						
Dole	Y	Y	Y	Y	Y	Y
Kassebaum	Y	Y	Y	Y	Y	Y
KENTUCKY						
Ford	Y	N	Y	Y	Y	Y
McConnell	Y	Y	Y	Y	Y	Y
LOUISIANA						
Breaux	Y	N	Y	Y	Y	Y
Johnston	Y	N	Y	Y	Y	Y
MAINE						
Mitchell	Y	N	Y	Y	Y	Y
Cohen	Y	N	N	Y	Y	Y
MARYLAND						
Mikulski	Y	N	Y	Y	Y	Y
Sarbanes	Y	N	Y	Y	Y	Y
MASSACHUSETTS						
Kennedy	Y	N	Y	Y	Y	Y
Kerry	Y	N	N	Y	N	N
MICHIGAN						
Levin	Y	N	Y	Y	Y	Y
Riegle	Y	N	Y	Y	Y	N
MINNESOTA						
Boschwitz	?	?	#	?	?	?
Durenberger	Y	Y	Y	Y	Y	Y
MISSISSIPPI						
Cochran	Y	Y	Y	Y	Y	Y
Lott	N	Y	Y	Y	Y	Y
MISSOURI						
Bond	N	Y	Y	Y	Y	Y
Danforth	Y	Y	Y	Y	Y	Y
MONTANA						
Baucus	Y	N	N	Y	Y	Y
Burns	Y	Y	N	Y	Y	Y
NEBRASKA						
Exon	Y	N	N	Y	Y	Y
Kerrey	Y	N	N	Y	Y	Y
NEVADA						
Bryan	Y	N	N	Y	Y	Y
Reid	Y	N	N	Y	Y	Y
NEW HAMPSHIRE						
Humphrey	N	Y	N	Y	N	N
Rudman	Y	Y	N	Y	Y	Y
NEW JERSEY						
Bradley	Y	N	N	Y	N	N
Lautenberg	Y	N	N	Y	Y	Y
NEW MEXICO						
Bingaman	Y	N	N	Y	Y	Y
Domenici	Y	N	Y	Y	Y	Y
NEW YORK						
Moynihan	Y	N	N	Y	N	N
D'Amato	Y	Y	Y	Y	Y	Y
NORTH CAROLINA						
Sanford	Y	N	Y	Y	Y	Y
Helms	N	Y	N	Y	Y	Y
NORTH DAKOTA						
Burdick	Y	N	Y	Y	Y	Y
Conrad	N	N	N	Y	N	N
OHIO						
Glenn	Y	N	Y	Y	Y	Y
Metzenbaum	Y	N	N	Y	N	N
OKLAHOMA						
Boren	?	?	-	?	?	+
Nickles	N	Y	N	Y	Y	Y
OREGON						
Hatfield	+	?	+	?	-	-
Packwood	Y	Y	Y	Y	Y	Y
PENNSYLVANIA						
Heinz	Y	Y	Y	Y	Y	Y
Specter	Y	Y	N	Y	Y	Y
RHODE ISLAND						
Pell	Y	N	Y	Y	Y	Y
Chafee	Y	Y	N	Y	Y	Y
SOUTH CAROLINA						
Hollings	Y	N	Y	Y	Y	Y
Thurmond	Y	Y	Y	Y	Y	Y
SOUTH DAKOTA						
Daschle	Y	N	N	Y	Y	Y
Pressler	Y	Y	N	Y	N	N
TENNESSEE						
Gore	Y	N	Y	Y	Y	Y
Sasser	Y	N	Y	Y	N	N
TEXAS						
Bentsen	Y	N	Y	Y	Y	Y
Gramm	Y	Y	Y	Y	Y	Y
UTAH						
Garn	N	Y	Y	Y	Y	Y
Hatch	Y	Y	Y	Y	Y	Y
VERMONT						
Leahy	Y	N	Y	Y	Y	Y
Jeffords	Y	Y	Y	Y	Y	Y
VIRGINIA						
Robb	Y	N	Y	Y	Y	Y
Warner	Y	Y	Y	Y	Y	Y
WASHINGTON						
Adams	Y	N	Y	Y	Y	Y
Gorton	Y	Y	Y	Y	Y	Y
WEST VIRGINIA						
Byrd	Y	Y	N	N	Y	Y
Rockefeller	Y	N	Y	Y	N	N
WISCONSIN						
Kohl	Y	N	N	Y	N	N
Kasten	N	Y	N	Y	Y	Y
WYOMING						
Simpson	Y	Y	Y	Y	Y	Y
Wallop	N	Y	Y	Y	N	N

KEY

- Y Voted for (yea).
- # Paired for.
- + Announced for.
- N Voted against (nay).
- X Paired against.
- \- Announced against.
- P Voted "present."
- C Voted "present" to avoid possible conflict of interest.
- ? Did not vote or otherwise make a position known.

Democrats ***Republicans***

ND Northern Democrats SD Southern Democrats

Southern states - Ala., Ark., Fla., Ga., Ky., La., Miss., N.C., Okla., S.C., Tenn., Texas, Va.

315. HR 5257. Fiscal 1991 Labor, HHS and Education Appropriations/Conference Report. Adoption of the conference report on the bill to appropriate $182,181,734,000 for the Departments of Labor, Health and Human Services, and Education and related agencies in fiscal 1991 and, in some cases, for subsequent years. The president requested $174,845,772,000. The agreement includes the House provision prohibiting the use of funds to pay for an abortion, except in cases in which the woman's life is in danger. Adopted 82-15: R 29-14; D 53-1 (ND 37-1, SD 16-0), Oct. 25, 1990.

316. HR 5257. Fiscal 1991 Labor, HHS and Education Appropriations/Education Goals. Cochran, R-Miss., motion to table (kill) the Bingaman, D-N.M., motion to concur in the House amendment to the Senate amendment with an amendment to earmark $2 million, if authorized by law, to remain available until expended for expenses for an independent National Council on Educational Goals or any similar entity whose function is to monitor progress toward the national education goals for the year 2000 or to publish a report that describes such progress. The amendment specifies that the entity would have a majority of voting members who were neither federal appointed officials, elected officials from the federal government or governors. Motion rejected 42-55: R 41-2; D 1-53 (ND 1-37, SD 0-16), Oct. 25, 1990.

317. S 2830. Farm Programs Reauthorization/Conference Report. Adoption of the conference report (thus clearing the measure for the president) on the bill to revise and extend federal farm price- and income-support programs for major commodities as well as the Agriculture Department's nutrition programs. Adopted 60-36: R 29-13; D 31-23 (ND 16-22, SD 15-1), Oct. 25, 1990.

318. HR 5257. Fiscal 1991 Labor, HHS and Education Appropriations/Job Training Partnership Act. Dole, R-Kan., amendment to the Bingaman, D-N.M., amendment, to strengthen the program of employment and training assistance under the Job Training Partnership Act. Adopted 95-1: R 43-0; D 52-1 (ND 36-1, SD 16-0), Oct. 25, 1990.

319. HR 5803. Fiscal 1991 Defense Appropriations/Conference Report. Adoption of the conference report (thus clearing the measure for the president) on the bill to appropriate $268,646,222,000 for the Department of Defense for military personnel, operations and maintenance, procurement, and research and development in fiscal 1991. The president requested $287,282,674,000. Adopted 80-17: R 37-6; D 43-11 (ND 28-10, SD 15-1), Oct. 26, 1990.

320. HR 4739. Fiscal 1991 Defense Authorization/Conference Report. Adoption of the conference report (thus clearing the measure for the president) on the bill to authorize appropriations of $288.3 billion for the Department of Defense, military construction, and the military activities of the Department of Energy. Adopted 80-17: R 37-6; D 43-11 (ND 28-10, SD 15-1), Oct. 26, 1990.

	321	322	323	324	325	326
ALABAMA						
Heflin	Y	Y	Y	Y	Y	N
Shelby	Y	Y	Y	Y	Y	N
ALASKA						
Murkowski	N	N	Y	Y	Y	N
Stevens	N	N	Y	Y	Y	Y
ARIZONA						
DeConcini	Y	Y	Y	Y	Y	N
McCain	N	N	Y	Y	Y	N
ARKANSAS						
Bumpers	Y	Y	N	Y	Y	Y
Pryor	Y	Y	?	Y	Y	Y
CALIFORNIA						
Cranston	Y	Y	Y	Y	Y	Y
Wilson	N	N	Y	Y	Y	N
COLORADO						
Wirth	Y	Y	Y	Y	Y	Y
Armstrong	N	N	N	Y	N	N
CONNECTICUT						
Dodd	Y	Y	Y	Y	Y	Y
Lieberman	Y	Y	Y	Y	Y	N
DELAWARE						
Biden	Y	Y	Y	Y	Y	N
Roth	N	N	N	Y	N	N
FLORIDA						
Graham	Y	Y	Y	Y	Y	Y
Mack	N	N	Y	Y	Y	N
GEORGIA						
Fowler	Y	Y	Y	Y	Y	Y
Nunn	Y	N	Y	Y	Y	Y
HAWAII						
Inouye	Y	Y	Y	Y	Y	Y
Akaka	Y	Y	Y	Y	Y	Y
IDAHO						
McClure	N	N	Y	N	Y	N
Symms	N	N	Y	N	N	N
ILLINOIS						
Dixon	Y	Y	Y	N	Y	N
Simon	Y	Y	Y	N	Y	N
INDIANA						
Coats	N	N	Y	Y	Y	N
Lugar	N	N	Y	Y	Y	Y
IOWA						
Harkin	Y	Y	Y	Y	Y	N
Grassley	N	N	Y	Y	Y	N
KANSAS						
Dole	N	N	Y	Y	Y	Y
Kassebaum	N	N	Y	Y	Y	Y
KENTUCKY						
Ford	Y	Y	Y	Y	Y	Y
McConnell	N	N	Y	Y	Y	N
LOUISIANA						
Breaux	Y	Y	Y	Y	Y	Y
Johnston	Y	Y	Y	Y	Y	N
MAINE						
Mitchell	Y	Y	Y	Y	Y	Y
Cohen	N	N	Y	Y	Y	N
MARYLAND						
Mikulski	Y	Y	Y	Y	Y	Y
Sarbanes	Y	Y	Y	Y	Y	Y
MASSACHUSETTS						
Kennedy	Y	Y	Y	Y	Y	Y
Kerry	Y	Y	Y	Y	Y	N
MICHIGAN						
Levin	Y	Y	Y	Y	Y	N
Riegle	Y	Y	Y	Y	Y	N
MINNESOTA						
Boschwitz	?	?	?	Y	Y	Y
Durenberger	N	N	Y	Y	Y	Y
MISSISSIPPI						
Cochran	N	N	Y	Y	Y	Y
Lott	N	N	N	Y	Y	N
MISSOURI						
Bond	N	N	Y	Y	Y	Y
Danforth	N	N	Y	Y	Y	Y
MONTANA						
Baucus	Y	Y	Y	Y	Y	N
Burns	N	N	Y	Y	Y	N
NEBRASKA						
Exon	Y	Y	N	Y	Y	N
Kerrey	Y	Y	Y	Y	Y	Y
NEVADA						
Bryan	Y	Y	Y	Y	Y	Y
Reid	Y	Y	Y	Y	Y	Y
NEW HAMPSHIRE						
Humphrey	N	N	Y	Y	N	N
Rudman	N	N	N	Y	Y	Y
NEW JERSEY						
Bradley	Y	Y	Y	Y	Y	N
Lautenberg	Y	Y	Y	Y	Y	N
NEW MEXICO						
Bingaman	?	Y	Y	Y	Y	Y
Domenici	N	N	Y	Y	Y	Y
NEW YORK						
Moynihan	Y	Y	Y	Y	Y	Y
D'Amato	N	N	Y	Y	Y	N
NORTH CAROLINA						
Sanford	Y	Y	Y	Y	Y	N
Helms	N	N	N	N	N	N
NORTH DAKOTA						
Burdick	Y	Y	Y	Y	Y	Y
Conrad	Y	Y	Y	Y	Y	N
OHIO						
Glenn	Y	N	Y	N	Y	Y
Metzenbaum	Y	Y	Y	Y	Y	Y
OKLAHOMA						
Boren	?	?	Y	Y	Y	Y
Nickles	N	N	Y	Y	Y	N
OREGON						
Hatfield	?	?	+	?	?	?
Packwood	N	N	Y	Y	Y	Y
PENNSYLVANIA						
Heinz	Y	N	Y	Y	Y	Y
Specter	N	N	Y	Y	Y	Y
RHODE ISLAND						
Pell	Y	Y	Y	Y	Y	N
Chafee	N	N	Y	Y	Y	Y
SOUTH CAROLINA						
Hollings	Y	Y	Y	Y	Y	N
Thurmond	N	N	Y	Y	Y	Y
SOUTH DAKOTA						
Daschle	Y	Y	Y	Y	Y	Y
Pressler	N	N	Y	Y	Y	N
TENNESSEE						
Gore	Y	Y	Y	Y	Y	Y
Sasser	Y	Y	Y	Y	Y	Y
TEXAS						
Bentsen	Y	Y	Y	Y	Y	Y
Gramm	N	N	Y	Y	Y	N
UTAH						
Garn	N	N	Y	N	Y	N
Hatch	N	N	Y	N	Y	N
VERMONT						
Leahy	Y	Y	Y	Y	Y	Y
Jeffords	N	?	Y	Y	Y	Y
VIRGINIA						
Robb	Y	Y	Y	Y	Y	Y
Warner	N	N	Y	Y	Y	Y
WASHINGTON						
Adams	Y	Y	Y	Y	Y	Y
Gorton	N	N	Y	Y	Y	N
WEST VIRGINIA						
Byrd	Y	Y	N	N	Y	Y
Rockefeller	Y	Y	Y	N	Y	Y
WISCONSIN						
Kohl	Y	Y	Y	Y	Y	Y
Kasten	N	N	Y	Y	Y	N
WYOMING						
Simpson	N	N	Y	Y	Y	Y
Wallop	N	N	Y	Y	N	N

KEY

- Y Voted for (yea).
- # Paired for.
- \+ Announced for.
- N Voted against (nay).
- X Paired against.
- \- Announced against.
- P Voted "present."
- C Voted "present" to avoid possible conflict of interest.
- ? Did not vote or otherwise make a position known.

Democrats *Republicans*

ND Northern Democrats SD Southern Democrats

Southern states - Ala., Ark., Fla., Ga., Ky., La., Miss., N.C., Okla., S.C., Tenn., Texas, Va.

321. HR 5229. Fiscal 1991 Transportation Appropriations/Pennsylvania Highways. Lautenberg, D-N.J., motion to table (kill) the Specter, R-Pa., motion to concur in a House amendment with an amendment to prohibit the secretary of Transportation from withholding any of the $142 million allocated to Pennsylvania for federal-aid highways and highway safety construction programs. Included in the bill is a provision that would require the secretary to withhold funds from Pennsylvania unless Pennsylvania established a dedicated transit tax for the improvement of mass transit. Motion agreed to 54-42: R 1-42; D 53-0 (ND 37-0, SD 16-0), Oct. 26, 1990.

322. HR 5229. Fiscal 1991 Transportation Appropriations/Pennsylvania Highways. Lautenberg, D-N.J., motion to table (kill) the Heinz, R-Pa., motion to reconsider the vote by which the Senate agreed to the Lautenberg motion to table (kill) the Specter, R-Pa., motion to concur in a House amendment with an amendment to prohibit the secretary of Transportation from withholding any of the $142 million allocated to Pennsylvania for federal-aid highways and highway safety construction programs. Included in the bill is a provision that would require the secretary to withhold funds from Pennsylvania unless Pennsylvania established a dedicated transit tax for the improvement of mass transit. Motion agreed to 52-44: R 0-42; D 52-2 (ND 37-1, SD 15-1), Oct. 26, 1990.

323. S 358. Legal Immigration Revision/Conference Report. Adoption of the conference report to increase the number of visas for those coming to the United States to work, establish a category of diversity visas for immigrants from countries that have accounted for very few immigrants under the current system, impose an overall cap on immigration at 675,000 starting in fiscal 1995, suspend deportation of certain spouses and children of newly legalized aliens, and temporarily suspend deportation of Salvadorans. Adopted 89-8: R 38-5; D 51-3 (ND 36-2, SD 15-1), Oct. 26, 1990.

324. S 1630. Clean Air Act Reauthorization/Conference Report. Adoption of the conference report (thus clearing the measure for the president) on the bill to amend the Clean Air Act to attain and maintain national ambient air quality standards, require reductions of emissions in motor vehicles, control toxic air pollutants, reduce acid rain, establish a system of federal permits and enforcement, and otherwise improve the quality of the nation's air. Adopted 89-10: R 39-5; D 50-5 (ND 33-5, SD 17-0), Oct. 27, 1990.

325. S 566. Housing Programs Reauthorization/Conference Report. Adoption of the conference report (thus clearing the measure for the president) on the bill to authorize and redirect federal housing programs, including creation of the HOME Investment Partnerships, a block grant program to provide seed money to communites for construction, renovation and rental assistance. Adopted 93-6: R 38-6; D 55-0 (ND 38-0, SD 17-0), Oct. 27, 1990.

326. HR 5835. Fiscal 1991 Budget Reconciliation Act/Conference Report. Adoption of the conference report (thus clearing the measure for the president) on the bill to reduce spending and raise revenues as required by the reconciliation instructions in the budget resolution, make changes in the budget process and expand programs in child care. Adopted 54-45: R 19-25; D 35-20 (ND 23-15, SD 12-5), Oct. 27, 1990. A "yea" was a vote supporting the president's position.

CQ

Appendix I

INDEXES

General Index 3-I
Roll Call Vote Index 58-I
Bill Number Index 62-I

General Index

A

A-6E aircraft - 818
A-12 attack plane
appropriations - 815 (chart), 818
authorization - 678, 685
AAAM missiles - 675, 685, 826
Aaron, Henry - 177
AARP. *See American Association of Retired Persons*
AAWS-M missiles - 674, 818, 824
Abandoned Mine Reclamation Fund - 154
ABC. *See Act for Better Child Care*
Abdnor, James - 324
Abercrombie, Neil - 916, 918 (chart), 922, 923, 925, 926
ABM. *See Antiballistic missile treaty*
Abortion. *See also Parental notification of abortion*
appropriations bills
District of Columbia - 528, 531, 846, 891-893
foreign aid - 531, 831, 837, 838-839 (box), 840
FY90 supplemental - 846
Labor/HHS - 811, 847, 850, 851-853
congressional action, 1990 - 528-531
congressional elections, 1990 - 901, 903, 911, 919, 934
counseling - 56, 605, 606
family planning authorization - 604-606
fetal tissue research - 531, 600-601
gubernatorial elections, 1990 - 927, 928-929
Legal Services Corporation - 533
military hospitals - 680, 683, 11-B
NIH authorization - 600-604
NIH director - 602 (box), 603
Panama aid - 779
RICO revision - 537
Souter confirmation - 508-515
summary - 7
Supreme Court rulings - 56, 510 (box), 528-529
U.N. population fund - 831, 837, 838-839 (box), 840
Abu Iyad - 800
Accidents
drunken driving - 52, 53
hazardous materials
release - 258
transport - 380, 381
missile launch defense - 692
pipeline safety inspection - 286 (box)
suit consolidation - 543
Accounting
federal financial centralization - 416
federal standards - 886, 889
Achille Lauro - 830
Acid-free paper - 429
Acid rain
Clean Air Act
action, 1990 - 229-230, 231, 232, 238-239, 242, 276-278
cleanup cost sharing - 230, 238-239, 242, 267, 276
highlights - 237 (box)
provisions - 259-267
summary - 4, 9
research - 274-275
Ackerman, Gary L. D-N.Y. (7)
drug-abuse treatment - 504
federal pay overhaul - 405, 407
Persian Gulf crisis - 753
Treasury, Postal appropriations - 890
ACORN (housing activist group) - 659
Acquired immune deficiency syndrome (AIDS)
AIDS Resources Emergency Act - 582-589
boxscore - 582
provisions - 584-587
Amtrak waste disposal - 392
blood supply safety - 586, 587
disabled civil rights - 447, 449, 450, 451, 460, 461
drug abuse - 586, 587
immigration exclusion - 480-481 (box)
intentional transmission - 586
mandated testing proposals
hospital patients - 587
marriage license applicants - 587
prisoners - 586, 587
rapists - 498, 507
universal testing - 588
notification of results, risk
blood recipients - 585
counseling - 586-587
emergency workers - 587, 588
public health officials - 586
sexual partners - 583, 585-586, 587, 588
patient care
AIDS bill - 582-589
hemophiliacs - 585, 586
housing aid - 640, 655, 656, 857
Labor/HHS appropriations - 847, 849, 850, 852, 853
Medicaid expansion - 569
minority health - 596
orphan drugs - 578
pediatric cases - 582, 585, 587, 588
TB prevention - 594
prevention and research
budget action - 125, 128, 148
foreign aid appropriations - 832 (chart), 843
orphan drug bill - 578
summary - 5
Act for Better Child Care (ABC) - 547-551
ACTION agency - 560, 849 (chart)
Action for Children's Television - 375
ACUS. *See Administrative Conference of the United States*
ADA. *See Americans with Disabilities Act*
Adams, Arlin M. - 589, 666, 667
Adams, Brock D-Wash.
D.C. appropriations - 891-893
defense authorization - 679
education proposals - 611
food-waste transport - 383
job training overhaul - 365
Labor/HHS appropriations - 851
Souter confirmation - 515
Adams, Paul A. - 668
ADATS missile launcher
appropriations - 815 (chart), 818, 823, 825
authorization - 674, 685
Adelman, Kenneth L. - 706
Adirondacks - 275
Adler, Marsha - 431
Administrative Conference of the United States (ACUS) - 414
Administrative law judges (ALJ)
corps plan - 523
Administrative Office of the U.S. Courts
appropriations - 883 (chart)
federal judgeships - 520, 521, 522
job bias cases - 468
RICO revision - 536
Administrative Procedures Act - 414, 523
Adolescent pregnancy. *See also Parental notification of abortion*
family planning authorization - 605-606
school dropout prevention - 618
Adolescents and youth. *See also Adolescent pregnancy; Colleges and universities; Dropout prevention; Elementary and secondary education; Juvenile delinquents; Parental notification of abortion; Student aid*
antismoking bills - 593, 594
community service programs - 559-562
disabled transition aid - 616, 617
employment
budget action - 123
conservation corps - 561
job training overhaul - 365-367
payroll taxes on student jobs - 159
summer jobs program - 365
targeted jobs tax credit - 160
family resource programs - 556
Foster Care Independent Living program - 150
literacy tutors - 616
middle-school teacher training - 613
sports at housing projects - 651
suicide prevention - 599
Adoption
abortion counseling - 605
family leave - 359-361
survivors' benefits - 150
Adoption assistance
AFDC eligibility - 150
sequestration procedures - 162
Adoption Assistance and Child Welfare Amendments - 556
Adult Basic Education program - 611
Adult day care - 147
Adult education. *See also Literacy*
appropriations - 848 (chart)
Head Start parent services - 555
teacher training - 611
vocational education authorization - 620
Adult Education Act - 620
Advanced Building Technology Council - 656
Advanced cruise missiles
appropriations - 815 (chart), 816-817, 822, 824
defense authorization - 674, 684
Advanced Launch System - 675
Advanced manufacturing - 440-441
Advanced Solid Rocket Motor - 859
Advanced Tactical Fighter (ATF) plane
appropriations - 812, 813, 815 (chart), 818, 823
authorization - 674, 677, 685
Advanced Technology Program - 440-441
Advertising
antismoking bills - 592-594
campaign finance reform - 58, 60-64, 66-67 (box)
children's television - 373-375
deceptive mail curbs - 417
Medigap plans - 574
military recruiting - 822
nutrition labels - 575
pornographic mail - 417
sports lotteries - 495
telemarketing curbs - 379
Advisory Council on Clean Air Compliance - 274
Advisory Council on Social Security - 609
Advisory panels
confliict of interest - 292
range of advice - 293
Aegis ship defenses
appropriations - 815 (chart), 818-819, 825, 826
authorization - 675, 686
naval home ports - 681 (box)
Aeroflot - 759
Aerosol products - 270
AFDC. *See Aid to Families with Dependent Children*
Affirmative action
broadcast license set-asides - 379 (box)
civil rights bill - 54, 462, 463, 468, 471
math, science scholarships - 612 (box)
Thomas confirmation - 519 (box)
Affordable Housing Preservation, Office of - 636
AFGE. *See American Federation of Government Employees*
Afghanistan
Pakistan-U.S. relations - 769
U.S. aid - 791, 792, 794-797
equitable share to women - 840
AFL-CIO. *See American Federation of Labor*
Africa. *See also specific countries*
development banks authorization - 206-207
elephant conservation - 837
Food for Peace - 803, 804
immigration law revision - 478
Panama aid - 776, 778
Persian Gulf crisis - 741
screwworm eradication - 355
strategic minerals - 443
Third World debt relief - 207
U.S. aid appropriations - 831-832, 832 (chart), 843, 845
African Development Bank and Fund - 206, 207, 832 (chart), 836, 843
African Development Foundation - 833 (chart)
African National Congress (ANC) - 787-789
Age discrimination
employee benefits - 54, 362-364
health care taxes - 608
Thomas confirmation - 518-519 (box)
Age Discrimination in Employment Act of 1967 - 54, 458, 362, 364
Aged persons. *See Elderly persons*
Agency for Health Care Policy and Research - 583, 587, 850
Agency for International Development (AID)
Caribbean scholarships - 214
Child Survival Fund - 832 (chart), 837, 843
environmental protection - 837
food aid - 21, 338, 345, 803, 804
foreign aid appropriations - 832 (chart), 835, 836, 837
Latin American debt - 218, 778
Panama aid - 778, 779
South Africa sanctions - 789

Agent Orange - 418-419
Aging research - 598, 599
Agreed Measures for the Conservation of Antarctic Flora and Fauna - 305
Agricultural Act of 1949 - 323, 344
Agricultural Act of 1970 - 324
Agricultural Adjustment Act of 1938 - 323
Agricultural Credit Insurance Fund - 869
Agricultural exports and imports
appropriations - 867, 868
cargo preference - 338-339 (box)
cotton quotas - 342
dairy exports - 343
export subsidies - 330-331, 337-338, 345
food with pesticide residue - 323, 333, 336, 349, 350
foreign food aid - 337-338, 344-345, 803-804
GATT talks - 209-210, 323, 325, 328, 344, 348, 351,
Iraqi loans - 718, 722, 723, 724, 830
Nicaragua aid - 771
peanuts - 330, 337, 343-344
screwworm eradication - 355
South Africa sanctions - 787
Soviet-U.S. trade - 204, 205, 758, 762
sugar - 328, 331-332
textile import quotas - 219, 220
value, world prices - 324, 325, 327
wheat - 350, 351
Carter Soviet embargo - 324
grain quality - 337
Yeutter RNC post - 910
Agricultural Extension Service - 336, 345, 353
Agricultural interest groups
farm bill - 323-339, 349
Food for Peace - 803
irrigation subsidies - 356
Legal Services Corporation - 532-533
pesticide residue in food - 358
Agricultural price and income supports
budget action - 122-123, 128, 129, 141
conservative coalition - 40
disaster relief - 326, 343, 346
farm bill - 323-351
boxscore - 323
key votes - 6-B, 7-B, 10-B, 11-B
provisions - 342-347
federal role history - 323-325
flexibility - 325-326, 327-328, 344, 351
food assistance programs - 354
irrigation subsidies - 356-357
GATT talks - 209-210
means testing - 332, 334, 339, 340
payments cap - 332, 344
payments in kind - 351
summary - 3, 4, 8
triple-base plan - 323, 344, 347-350
wetlands protection - 330, 332, 335, 345-346
Agricultural research
farm bill - 323, 331, 336-337, 345
Agricultural Resources Conservation Program - 346, 349
Agricultural Stabilization and Conservation Service - 346
Agricultural workers
housing aid - 654
immigration law revision - 476, 477
job training eligibility - 367
Legal Services Corporation - 532-533
Agricultural Workers Commission - 883 (chart)
Agriculture and Consumer Protection Act of 1973 - 324
Agriculture and farming. *See also Agricultural exports and imports; Agricultural interest groups; Agricultural price and income supports; Agricultural workers; Agriculture Department; Food and nutrition; Forests and wood products; Pests and pesticides; Rural development; Soil conservation; specific crops*
alcohol fuels - 241
animal rights activists - 441
crop rotation - 346
driver's license exemption - 383
environmental issues
alternative, sustainable agriculture - 331, 336-337, 345, 347
methane emissions - 236, 271
non-road vehicles - 233 (box)
water pollution - 289, 326, 330, 335-336, 346, 349, 869
wetlands protection - 330, 335-336, 345-346
farm credit
appropriations - 869
budget action - 123
farm bill - 326, 341, 347
small-issue bonds - 160, 173
student aid eligibility - 611
federal role history - 323-324
foreign aid - 835
narcotics crop alternatives - 836
Indian economic development - 621
irrigation subsidies - 300, 301, 356-357
organic farming - 323, 332-333, 347
pollination - 341
Agriculture Department, U.S. (USDA)
abandoned mines - 154
appropriations - 554 (box), 867-870
budget action - 122-123, 141
commodity loans, price supports - 325-326, 329, 333, 334, 340, 342-344, 349, 351
disaster relief - 346
export subsidies - 323, 330, 345
fish inspection - 396-399, 869
food assistance programs - 346, 354-355
food stamps - 346
foreign food aid - 21, 330, 338, 345, 803, 804
WIC program - 554 (box)
foreign ownership of U.S. business - 224
GATT talks - 209, 210
grain quality - 337
housing programs overhaul - 650, 654
Iraqi loans - 724, 830
irrigation subsidies - 357
methane assessment - 271
nutrition monitoring - 355
organic farming - 333, 347
pesticide recordkeeping - 346
research - 331, 345
rural development - 323, 346, 352-354
screwworm eradication - 355
soil, water conservation - 335-336, 349
conservation corps - 562
wetlands protection - 335, 346, 349
timber sales, exports
below-cost test - 358
Caribbean Basin Initiative - 214, 215
Interior appropriations - 875
Tongass forest - 295
tobacco programs - 593
tree-planting aid - 336, 346
Yeutter RNC post - 910
AHIP. *See Army Helicopter Improvement Program*
Aid to Families with Dependent Children (AFDC)
appropriations - 847
budget action - 150
child support enforcement - 149
job training overhaul - 365, 366
sequestration procedures - 162
AIDS. *See Acquired immune deficiency syndrome*
AIDS Action Council - 480, 850-851
Air-Carrier Access Act - 454
Air conditioning
energy conservation - 319
ozone-depleting chemicals - 270
Air defense initiative - 673
Air Force Reserve - 821
Air Force, U.S.
B-2 bomber - 688-691, 705
Crotone air base, 678, 826-830
defense appropriations - 812-826
defense authorization - 671-687
management efficiency - 673 (box)
military construction appropriations - 827, 828
Norton Air Force Base - 827-828
Persian Gulf crisis - 719
personnel
force structure changes - 672
limits - 672, 683
overseas deployment - 678
space shuttle - 846
Air National Guard - 821
Air pollution. *See also Acid rain*
alternative power regulation - 317
auto fuel efficiency - 279-281
Clean Air Act - 4, 229-279
indoor pollution - 395
international emissions - 274
research - 236, 274-275
smog standards - 235, 248-251
toxic air pollutants - 229, 230, 232, 234, 241-242, 247, 254-259, 276, 279
accidental release - 258
cleanup deadlines - 231 (box)
health effects research - 274
motor vehicles - 233, 242, 252
negligent releases - 272
visibility impairment - 244, 273, 274
Air safety
appropriations - 880
budget action - 126
child safety systems - 389
crash liability suits - 389
exit-row seat rules - 389 (box)
guidelines - 389-390
hijacking death penalty - 490
ozone-depleting chemicals - 270
security procedures - 389-390
Air-traffic control
appropriations - 880
aviation package - 384, 385
drug testing - 505
Air transportation. *See also Air safety; Federal Aviation Administration.*
airline takeover curbs - 388
alien workers - 483
budget reconciliation package - 384-388
disabled civil rights - 453-454
drug interdiction - 504
Eastern Airlines strike - 369
essential air service - 385, 386, 388, 877
Nicaragua-U.S. service - 771
noise guidelines - 384, 385, 388
slot allocation - 384-388
smoking ban - 592
South Africa sanctions - 787
Soviet-U.S. aviation agreement - 759
summary - 6
ticket taxes
passenger facility charges - 126, 159, 384-388
travel, tourist fees - 157, 386 (box)
whistleblower protection - 364
Aircraft. *See also Aircraft, military*
drug forfeiture donation - 216
fastener standards - 395
hydrogen fuel research - 318-319
inspection rules - 390
luxury taxes - 159, 172
noise guidelines - 156, 384, 385, 388
Aircraft carriers
Aegis defenses - 675
B-2 bomber - 689
defense authorization - 672
helicopter carrier - 675
SLEP reconstruction - 818, 825, 826
Aircraft, military. *See also Helicopters; specific planes*
aerospace plane - 675
CFE - 697 (chart), 700, 702-703
defense appropriations - 812-826
defense authorization - 671-687
military reserve equipment - 816, 821
overhauls - 821-822
Airport and Airways Trust Fund
appropriations - 877-880
aviation package - 384-388
budget action - 126, 156, 159, 172
Airports
aviation security - 389-390
Customs user fees - 157
facility improvements - 126, 156, 384-388, 877, 878
slot allocation - 156, 384-388
AK-47s. *See Firearms*
Akaka, Daniel K. D-Hawaii
characteristics of Congress - 902 (box), 923
minorities in Congress - 924 (chart)
congressional elections, 1990 - 14 (box), 913, 915
crime bill - 493
Hatch Act revision - 408
House successor - 934
Souter confirmation - 515
Alabama
acid rain - 262
corporate campaign limits - 59 (box)
federal judgeships - 522
gubernatorial election, 1990 - 919, 926
naval home ports - 681 (box)
SDI research - 692
water projects authorization - 299
Alabama, University of - 862, 863, 876
Alaska
abortion - 530
congressional election voter turnout - 901 (chart)
congressional mail - 75
gubernatorial election, 1990 - 902, 907, 927, 929
Hatch Act revision - 411
oil
Arctic refuge drilling - 313, 315 (box)
Exxon Valdez spill - 283, 284, 315 (box)
North Slope production - 270
offshore drilling - 230, 244, 313, 871, 872
Soviet air service - 759
Tongass forest preservation - 5-6, 294-295
water projects
appropriations - 866
authorization - 299
Alaska Land Conservation Act of 1980 - 294
Albemarle Sound - 299
Alcohol abuse and alcoholism
child welfare services - 556
disabled civil rights - 453, 459
drunken driving - 52, 53
education, treatment
antidrug measures - 502
community service programs - 561

Indian programs - 422, 423
Medicaid coverage - 148
minority health - 596
housing programs overhaul - 635, 651, 655, 665
veterans aid - 420
product liability suits - 400
veterans benefits ban - 156
workplace issues
civil rights/job bias - 471
ship operators - 284
transport worker tests - 453
Alcohol, Drug Abuse and Mental Health block grant program
antidrug measures - 503-504, 505
antismoking bills - 594
appropriations - 848 (chart)
Alcohol fuels. *See also Ethanol; Methanol*
budget action - 160, 172
energy issues, 1990 - 313
Alcohol, Tobacco and Firearms Bureau
appropriations - 887 (chart)
assault weapons - 488, 500 (box)
Alcoholic beverages
excise taxes - 114, 131, 158, 167, 169, 172
import duties - 213
taxes on Puerto Rican rum - 427
Alexander, Bill D-Ark. (1)
Commerce/Justice/State appropriations - 884
Energy, water appropriations - 863
Gingrich ethics case - 104-105
military construction appropriations - 828-829
Persian Gulf crisis - 724
rural development - 353
Alexander, Herbert E. - 59
Alexander, Lamar
Education appointment - 614 (box)
Algeria
Iran-Iraq War - 722
Aliens. *See also Chinese student visas; Deportation; Illegal aliens; Naturalization*
air, cruise travel fees - 157
grantor trusts - 160
temporary workers - 477-478, 479, 483
Alimony - 652, 653
ALJ. *See Administrative law judges*
All-terrain vehicles - 394, 395
Allard, Wayne - 905 (chart), 918 (chart), 926
Allen A.M.E. church and apartments - 106
Alliance for Acid Rain Control - 276
Alliance for Aging Research - 599
Alliance for Justice - 515
Alternative dispute resolution
civil rights/job bias - 470
disabled civil rights - 451, 459
federal judgeships - 521
regulatory negotiation - 413-414
Alternative fuels. *See also Hydrogen*
Clean Air Act - 229, 231, 232, 233 (box), 234-235, 240-241, 244, 246-247, 249, 273, 278, 279
energy tax incentives - 313 (box)
global warming - 307
main substitutes - 240 (box)
octane labeling - 282
research - 274
Alternative minimum tax
corporations - 160, 172, 313 (box)
individuals - 157, 164, 165, 171, 172
Alzheimer's disease
AIDS bill debate - 583
home, community-based care - 147, 598-599
Labor/HHS appropriations - 852
Medicare demonstration project - 145
America the Beautiful Foundation - 124, 346
American Airlines - 388
American Arts Alliance - 431
American Association of Letter Carriers - 410, 411
American Association of Retired Persons (AARP) - 572, 574
American Association of State Highway Transportation Officials - 384
American Bankers Association - 185
American Bar Association
judicial appointments - 516, 517
RICO revision - 536
Souter confirmation - 509
torture ban treaty - 806
vertical price fixing - 539, 540
American Battle Monuments Commission - 855 (chart)
American Cancer Society - 593
American Civil Liberties Union
child-care aid - 549
habeas corpus appeals - 488 (box)
Hatch Act revision - 408
immigration law revision - 485
RICO revision - 536
TV violence guidelines - 374 (box)
American Conservation Corps - 561, 562
American Continental Corp. - 78-97
American Council on Education - 627
American Enterprise Institute - 743
American Family Association - 431
American Farm Bureau Federation - 532-533
American Federation of Government Employees (AFGE) - 72 (box), 408, 411
American Federation of Labor-Congress of Industrial Organizations (AFL-CIO)
age discrimination - 362
displaced worker aid - 277 (box)
farm bill - 332
federal RCRA compliance - 308
Mexico-U.S. trade - 218
"motor voter" bill - 70
vertical price fixing - 539
American Federation of State, County and Municipal Employees - 548
American Federation of Teachers - 611
American Heart Association - 593
American Hospital Association - 567
American Hotel and Motel Association - 402
American Indian Higher Education Consortium - 888
American Institute of Certified Public Accountants - 536
American Institute of Merchant Shipping - 283, 285
American International Auto Dealers Association - 280
American Israel Public Affairs Committee - 734 (box)
American Labor Party - 922
American Legion - 418, 419
American Lung Association - 593
American Medical Association - 567
American Petroleum Institute - 243, 287
American Postal Workers Union - 408
American Samoa
child-care block grant - 152
community development - 655
American Schools and Hospitals Abroad - 832 (chart), 835
American Soybean Association - 335
American Taxpayers Union - 874
American Telephone and Telegraph Co. - 377-379
American Trader - 287
American West Airlines - 386
Americans to Limit Congressional Terms - 15
Americans with Disabilities Act (ADA)
AIDS bill - 583
civil rights/job bias - 467
congressional action, 1990 - 447-461
boxscore - 447
key votes - 6-B
provisions - 452-459
summary - 5
Amphibious ships - 675, 819, 826
AMRAAM missiles - 675, 685, 818, 826
Amtrak
appropriations - 877, 878, 879, 879 (chart)
authorization - 390-392
veto message (text) - 391
budget action - 126
Bush transportation policy - 384
disabled civil rights - 449, 453, 454
waste disposal - 392
Amusement park rides - 394
Anabolic steroids - 499
ANC. *See African National Congress*
Anchorage, Alaska - 759
Andean countries. *See also Bolivia; Colombia; Peru*
CBI benefits - 214
foreign aid appropriations - 844
military role in drug wars - 679
Andean Initiative - 805-806
Anderson, Glenn M. D-Calif. (32)
disabled civil rights - 449-450
highway trust fund - 385
leadership challenge - 11 (box), 12
oil pollution cleanup - 285, 287
Transportation appropriations - 877
water projects authorization - 297, 298
Anderson, Mark A. - 218
Andrews, Mark - 324
Andrews, Michael A. D-Texas (25)
civil rights/job bias - 470
Andrews, Robert E. D-N.J. (1)
characteristics - 902 (box)
congressional elections, 1990 - 14 (box), 922
House membership changes - 918 (chart)
marginal vote share - 905 (chart)
special elections, 1990 - 934
Andrews, Thomas H. - 918 (chart)
Andrus, Cecil D. - 530, 929
Anemia - 578, 597
Anesthesiologists - 144
Angola
South Africa-U.S. relations - 787
U.S. aid to rebels
intelligence authorization - 791-797
key votes - 13-B
Animal rights activists - 441, 603
Animals. *See also Livestock and ranching; Veterinary medicine; Wildlife*
agricultural research grants - 345
genetic engineering - 437
Annunzio, Frank D-Ill. (11)
coin redesign - 196
Commerce/Justice/State appropriations - 878
congressional elections, 1990 - 917
low winning percentage - 906 (chart)
marginal vote share - 905 (chart)
FDIC premiums - 186
money laundering - 187
leadership challenge - 11 (box), 12
savings and loan scandal - 84
thrift bailout - 179, 184
Anorexia drugs - 146
Antarctic Marine Living Resources Conservation Act of 1984 - 305
Antarctic Protection Act - 16-17, 305-307
Antarctic Treaty of 1959 - 305
Antarctica
environmental protection - 6, 16-17, 304-307
boxscore - 305
Anthony, Beryl Jr. D-Ark. (4)
China-U.S. relations - 766
congressional term limit - 15
taxes - 169
Antiballistic missile (ABM) treaty
Krasnoyarsk facility - 680
SDI - 691-693
Anti-Drug Abuse Act of 1988 - 487, 561
Antigua and Barbuda - 211
Antinuclear activists. *See Arms control groups*
Antisatellite (ASAT) missile
appropriations - 823, 824
defense authorization - 673, 680, 684
Antitactical missiles - 812
Antitrust law
Baby Bell restrictions - 378
civil suit damages - 541
electric power/acid rain - 260
insurance price-sharing - 401 (box)
interlocking directors - 540-541
Japanese practices - 208
joint production ventures - 541
technology programs - 440
TV violence guidelines - 374 (box), 523
vertical price fixing - 520, 539-540
boxscore - 539
Apache helicopters
appropriations - 823, 824
authorization - 674, 685
budget action - 122
CFE - 700
Persian Gulf crisis - 735 (box)
Apartheid. *See South Africa*
Apgar, William C. - 633
Appalachian Regional Commission - 862 (chart), 863
Appalachian states
abandoned mines - 154
acid rain - 230, 236, 237, 276
Appeals courts, U.S.
appropriations - 883 (chart)
Baby Bell restrictions - 377
drug testing - 505
federal RCRA compliance - 296, 308
Garcia conviction - 107
health, safety hazard notice - 412 (box)
HUD scandal investigation - 666
judges
Bush appointments - 516
new judgeships - 6, 520, 523
Supreme Court nominations - 508, 509, 518 (box)
Thomas confirmation - 516, 518-519 (box)
legislative intent - 54
North conviction overturn - 534-535
OMB review powers - 412 (box)
pocket veto power - 21
prisoner appeals limits - 6
radiation victims compensation - 590
student religious groups - 618
Applegate, Doug D-Ohio (18)
hazardous materials transport - 381
Applied Agricultural Research Commercialization Center - 345
Appointments. *See Nominations and appointments*
Apprenticeships
vocational education - 621, 622
Appropriations bills
boxscores
agriculture - 867
Commerce/Justice/State - 881
defense - 812
District of Columbia - 891

Energy, water - 861
foreign aid - 830
Interior - 870
Labor/HHS/Education - 847
legislative branch - 894
military construction - 827
supplemental FY90 - 845
Transportation - 877
Treasury, Postal - 886
VA/HUD - 854
funding totals (charts) - 811
agriculture - 869
Commerce/Justice/State - 882-883
defense - 813
District of Columbia - 892
Energy, water - 862
foreign aid - 832-833
Interior - 873
Labor/HHS/Education - 848-849
legislative branch - 895
military construction - 828
Transportation - 879
Treasury, Postal - 887
VA/HUD - 855
Appropriations Committee, Senate
jurisdiction - 800
leadership - 924
Appropriations process. *See also Earmarking*
authorization relationship
Commerce/Justice/State appropriations - 881, 884
defense appropriations - 812-813
El Salvador aid - 782
Energy, water appropriations - 866
Labor/HHS appropriations - 367, 851, 853
supplemental appropriations - 846
budget action - 111-112
Bush congressional relations - 16
deferrals - 20-21
discretionary spending caps - 162, 173
line-item veto - 177
president's authority when absent - 163
strategic materials - 203
supplemental, emergencies - 174-175
Aquatic Nuisance Species Task Force - 303-304
Aquatic Resources Trust Fund - 159
Arab countries. *See also specific countries*
Persian Gulf crisis - 726, 728, 729, 732, 743
questionable gulf allies - 740 (box)
Saudi arms sales - 734-735 (box)
Arab League - 719, 728, 741
Arafat, Yasir - 789
Arbitration
alternative dispute resolution - 414
civil rights/job bias - 470
Soviet-U.S. trade - 205
Archer, Bill R-Texas (7)
budget action - 130 (box)
presidential support in Congress - 31
unemployment compensation - 368
Archer, Dennis W. - 516-517
Architect of the Capitol
appropriations - 895 (chart)
disabled civil rights - 458
Architectural and Transportation Barriers Compliance Board - 458, 879 (chart)
Architecture and buildings. *See also Construction industry; Federal buildings; Housing*
copyright - 523, 541, 542
disabled access - 448, 449, 450, 454, 456
Arctic National Wildlife Refuge - 313, 315 (box)
Arctic Ocean
Soviet-U.S. island agreement - 760
ARENA. *See National Republican Alliance*
Arias Calderon, Ricardo - 775
Arias, Oscar - 772 (box)
Arizona
"colonias" housing aid - 654
congressional redistricting - 931, 933
Grand Canyon erosion - 300-301
gubernatorial election, 1990 - 902, 907-908, 926, 930
radiation victims compensation - 590
water projects authorization - 299
wilderness protection - 304
Arkansas
congressional elections, 1990 - 909, 916
Energy, water appropriations - 865
federal judgeships - 522
gubernatorial election, 1990 - 917, 919, 930
military base closings - 678
***Arleigh Burke*-class destroyers** - 686
Armed Forces Reserve Act of 1952 - 694 (box)
Armed Services Committee, House
leadership - 924
Armenia
genocide commemoration - 807-808
Armenian Assembly of America - 807
Armey, Dick D-Texas (26)
budget action - 136
election, 1990 - 908
farm bill - 327, 332
military base closings - 694
Arms control. *See also Antiballistic missile (ABM) treaty; Conventional forces in Europe (CFE) treaty; Nuclear test treaties; Strategic arms reduction treaty (START)*
biological weapons ban - 507
chemical weapons - 674, 709-711, 722-723
comprehensive test ban - 712-713
defense authorization - 672, 680
Energy, water appropriations - 866
export controls - 201
German unification - 762-763
nuclear material production cutoff - 680
SDI - 691, 692
Arms Control and Disarmament Agency
appropriations - 883 (chart)
CFE - 700
nuclear test treaties - 712
Arms Control Association - 700, 710
Arms control groups
B-2 bomber - 689
defense appropriations - 824
MX missile - 683
naval home ports - 681 (box)
nuclear tests damage suits - 679
Stello nomination - 309
uranium enrichment - 310
Washington summit - 702
Arms sales and transfers
aid to El Salvador rebels - 771, 783, 785
British Trident order - 684
China aid to Khmer Rouge - 837
China sanctions - 764, 799
Export-Import Bank financing - 200-201, 643, 656, 805
Iraq sanctions - 719
offsets - 203
Saudi Arabia - 674, 734-735 (box)
South Africa sanctions - 787
Soviet aid to Nicaragua - 770
Stinger sales to Qatar - 844
U.S. military aid
appropriations - 831, 835-841
drug control - 805-806, 836, 844
El Salvador - 779-786
foreign aid priorities - 831-833, 837
intelligence authorization - 791-799
Armstrong, William L. R-Colo.
abortion - 530
Clean Air Act - 235-236
community service programs - 561
crime bill - 490, 493-494
D.C. appropriations - 891, 892
defense authorization - 680
Durenberger ethics case - 103
family planning authorization - 606
financial institution fraud - 181, 182
"hate crime" statistics - 507
housing programs overhaul - 656
Labor/HHS appropriations - 852
oil-shale lands - 316
prepayment of subsidized mortgages - 664
roll call attendance - 48
Social Security earnings test - 558
successor - 913 (chart), 915
Army Corps of Engineers
environmental protection - 298
water projects
appropriations - 861-866
authorization - 297-300
Army Helicopter Improvement Program (AHIP) - 122, 674
Army, U.S.
budget action - 122
chemical weapons - 710
defense appropriations - 812-826
defense authorization - 671-687
military construction appropriations - 828
personnel
force structure changes - 672
limits - 672, 676
overseas deployment - 678
Aronson, Bernard W.
El Salvador aid - 785, 836
Nicaragua aid - 772
Panama aid - 776, 777, 778
sugar quotas - 213
Aroostook Band of Micmacs Settlement Act - 424
Arrow missiles - 822
Arson - 506, 507
Art
capital gains tax - 168 (box)
copyright, image integrity - 205, 520, 523, 541-542
donation tax deductions - 158, 171
immigration law revision - 482, 483
obscenity issues
"Dinner Party" exhibit - 47, 892
NEA appropriations - 870-875
NEA authorization - 430-433
Aruba - 211
Asarco - 304
ASAT. *See Antisatellite missiles*
Asbestos
Clean Air Act - 275
transport rules - 383
Ashley, Thomas Ludlow - 922 (box)
Asia. *See also Pacific area; specific countries*
textile import quotas - 219
U.S. immigration policy - 474, 475, 476
U.S. trade
auto fuel efficiency - 280
Food for Peace - 803
tobacco exports - 592
Tongass forest protection - 294
Asia Foundation - 883 (chart)
Asian Americans
characteristics of Congress - 923-924
minorities in Congress - 924 (chart)
Asian Development Fund - 832 (chart)
Aspin, Les D-Wis. (1)
B-2 bomber - 687-691
CFE - 701, 702
defense appropriations - 819
defense authorization - 671, 672, 677, 682, 683, 687
defense budget reprogramming - 676 (box)
defense management efficiency - 673 (box)
military base closings - 694
Panama aid - 775
Persian Gulf crisis - 726, 728, 737, 751
SDI - 692
START - 705
supplemental appropriations - 845, 846
ASPJ radar jammers - 680, 685
ASROC missiles - 686
Assad, Hafez al- - 740 (box)
Assassination
federal death penalty - 494, 497
Associated Financial Corp. - 667
Association of Biotechnology Companies - 579
Association of Data Users - 415
Association of Local Air Pollution Control Officers - 240
Association of South East Asian Nations - 837
Association of State Democratic Chairs - 59
Astoria, Ore. - 819
AT&T. *See American Telephone and Telegraph*
ATA attack aircraft - 674, 818
ATACMS missiles
appropriations - 815 (chart), 823, 824
authorization - 674, 685
ATF. *See Advanced Tactical Fighter plane*
Athletics. *See Sports*
Atkins, Chester G. D-Mass. (5)
antismoking bills - 593, 594
congressional elections, 1990
low winning percentage - 906 (chart)
marginal vote share - 905 (chart)
foreign aid appropriations - 837-839
Atlanta, Ga. - 582
Atlantic states
barrier island protection - 302-303
offshore drilling - 313, 871
Atlantic Striped Bass Conservation Act of 1988 - 300
Atlantis - 434
Atlas satellite launch vehicles - 675
ATP. *See Advanced Technology Program*
Attention deficit disorder - 617
Attorney general. *See Justice Department*
Attorneys. *See Law profession and practice*
Attorneys, U.S.
crime bill - 493, 503
drug enforcement - 502
federal caseload management - 522
financial institution fraud - 183
Atwater, Lee - 910
Atwood, Donald J. - 20
AuCoin, Les D-Ore. (1)
abortion - 531
defense appropriations - 817, 819
Interior appropriations - 871, 872
Labor/HHS appropriations - 850, 852-853
Aurora borealis - 866
Australia
Antarctica protection - 305
Persian Gulf crisis - 721
U.S. export controls - 198
U.S. immigration policy - 483
Auto Dealers and Drivers for Free Trade (AUTOPAC) - 280-281
Automobiles

clean-fueled cars - 229, 231 (box), 232, 233 (box), 240-241, 243, 244, 246-247, 249, 253-254, 278
displaced worker aid - 277 (box)
foreign ownership of U.S. business - 223
fuel efficiency
Clean Air Act - 233
standards - 7, 279-281, 313
tax - 159, 172
luxury taxes - 159, 172
small-car safety - 279-281
tailpipe emissions - 229, 232, 233 (box), 246-247, 251-252
cold weather - 229, 246, 252
control system warranty - 241, 244, 252
deadlines - 231 (box)
high altitudes - 236
inspection and maintenance - 249
transportation control plans - 249, 250-251
Avengers - 818
Avenson, Donald D. - 530, 929
Ayer, Donald B. - 463, 464
Ayres, Richard - 232, 233, 243, 245
Azerbaijan - 757
Aziz, Tariq - 721, 739, 741, 743, 748, 756
AZT - 588

B

B-1 bomber
appropriations - 822, 824
B-2 bomber - 688, 689, 690
START - 705
B-2 bomber
appropriations
defense - 812, 815 (chart), 816, 819-822
military construction - 829
supplemental FY90 - 846
budget action - 122
conservative coalition - 47
defense authorization - 671, 672, 674, 675-676, 677, 682, 684, 686-687, 687-691
defense budget reprogramming - 676 (box)
key votes - 8-B
START - 705, 708
B-52 bomber
B-2 bomber - 689, 690
deactivation plan - 672
Persian Gulf crisis - 721
START - 705
upgrades - 822, 824
Baath Socialist Party - 718
Babbit, Bruce - 78
Babies. *See Infants*
Bacchus, Jim - 905 (chart), 918 (chart)
Backfire bombers - 704, 706, 707
Badillo, Herman - 934
Baena Soares, Joao - 772
Bagert, Ben - 916
Bahamas
Caribbean Basin Initiative - 211
Bahr, Egon - 699
Baker, Bobby - 87
Baker, James A. III
Afghan rebel aid - 792
Cambodian rebel aid - 793, 794
CFE treaty - 696, 700-704, 758
chemical weapons pact - 709-710
El Salvador aid - 781, 782-783
intelligence authorization - 796
Kenya aid - 790
Nicaragua aid - 771, 773
Panama aid - 777
Persian Gulf crisis - 717-756
questionable gulf allies - 740 (box)
U.S. goals, rationales - 744 (box)
Soviet-U.S. relations - 758-762
START - 705-708
U.N. funding - 802
Balanced-budget amendment - 47, 173, 174-175 (box), 868
Ballenger, Cass R-N.C. (10)
age discrimination - 363
civil rights/job bias - 469
job training overhaul - 366-367
Ballistic Missile Organization - 827-828
Balog, James - 608
Baltic States. *See also Estonia; Latvia; Lithuania*
Soviet-U.S. relations - 757, 760-762
chemical weapons pact - 709
START - 704, 708
Bank Insurance Fund - 123, 141, 187
Bank Secrecy Act - 187
Banking Committee, House
leadership - 11, 935
Bankruptcy
Eastern Airlines strike - 369
financial institution fraud - 486, 498
pension plan guaranty - 368
student aid - 143
Banks and banking. *See also Deposit insurance; Federal Deposit Insurance Corporation; International development banks; Savings and loan associations; World Bank*
community development - 646
consumer issues
ATM deposit holds - 189
check-cashing companies - 188-189
interest computation - 187, 189
trust services - 191
failures - 123, 185
farm loans - 123, 649
Fed interest on reserves - 186
federal credit reform - 134, 163, 178 (box)
fraud - 6, 182
international banking
Eastern European trade - 836
foriegn-based banks - 202, 203
foreign markets - 189
Iraq loans - 722
money laundering
congressional action, 1990 - 187-189
crime bill provisions - 499
Panama secrecy laws - 776, 777, 779
government-sponsored enterprises - 163
RICO revision - 538
rural development - 353
student loan default - 626-627 (box)
Third World debt relief - 207, 217-218, 775-776, 834
Banks for Cooperatives - 163
Baptists - 549
Barbados
Caribbean Basin Initiative - 211
U.S. ambassador - 801 (box)
Barbiturates - 146
Barbour, Haley - 906
Barcelo, Carlos Romero - 427
Barco, Virgilio - 805
Barker, Robert B. - 713
Barletta, Nicolas - 775
Barley - 240 (box), 342
Barnard, Doug Jr. D-Ga. (10)
coin redesign - 197
congressional elections, 1990 - 903, 906, 917
low winning percentage - 906 (chart)
housing programs overhaul - 640
money laundering - 188
prepayment of subsidized mortgages - 663
Barrett, Bill - 905 (chart), 918 (chart)
Barry, Marion S. Jr. - 428, 531, 893
Bartholomew, Reginald - 735 (box)
Bartlett, Steve R-Texas (3)
civil rights/job bias - 468, 469
disabled civil rights - 447, 451, 460, 461
disabled education - 617
education proposals - 614
family leave - 359, 360
housing programs overhaul - 633-640
HUD scandal investigation - 668
job training overhaul - 367
money laundering - 188
prepayment of subsidized mortgages - 663, 664
VA/HUD appropriations - 860
Barton, Joe L. R-Texas (6)
balanced-budget amendment - 175
Clean Air Act - 241-242
CPSC authorization - 394
Energy, water appropriations - 864
family planning authorization - 605
Medicaid expansion - 571
SSC authorization - 439
Basilius, Bonifacio - 808
Bass, Gary - 412 (box)
Bateman, Herbert H. R-Va. (1)
congressional elections, 1990 - 919
low winning percentage - 906 (chart)
marginal vote share - 905 (chart)
vote-share falloff - 904 (chart)
Bates, Jim D-Calif. (44)
congressional elections, 1990
defeated House members - 917 (chart)
House membership changes - 918 (chart)
vote-share falloff - 904 (chart)
ethics case - 104
Battle, Fowler, Jaffin and Kheel - 666
Baucus amendment - 573, 575
Baucus, Max D-Mont.
Clean Air Act - 233, 235, 244-245, 276, 278
congressional elections, 1990 - 916
farm bill - 333-334, 338-341
flag desecration - 528
Japan-U.S. trade - 209
military construction appropriations - 830
"motor voter" bill - 70
Pepper Commission - 607
Bauerlein, Robert - 768-769
BEA. *See Economic Analysis, Bureau of*
Beaches. *See Coastal areas*
Beaver, Donald Jr. - 516
Becker, Bill - 240, 245-247, 279, 280
Becker, Gary S. - 15
Beekeepers - 337, 341
Beer. *See Alcoholic beverages*
Behavior disorders. *See also Alzheimer's disease*
disabled civil rights - 449, 452, 459
home, community-based elderly care - 147
immigration exclusion - 484
Beilenson, Anthony C. D-Calif. (23)
intelligence authorization - 791, 795-799
Belgium
CFE - 697, 700
Belize
Caribbean Basin Initiative - 211
Bell, Griffin B. - 515
Bell, Stephen - 132
Bell telephone companies - 377-379
Bell, Terrel H. - 506
Belle Glade, Fla. - 667
Bellmon, Henry - 928
Benavides, Guillermo Alfredo - 781
Bennett, Charles E. D-Fla. (3)
defense authorization - 682
naval home ports - 681 (box)
Persian Gulf crisis - 752
use-of-force debate - 753 (box)
SDI - 692
Bennett, Robert S.
Durenberger ethics case - 98-103
savings and loan scandal - 78-97
opening statement - 83-85
profile - 81 (box)
Bennett, William J.
"drug czar" resignation - 502, 503 (box)
drug treatment programs - 504
Education secretary - 614 (box)
Hatch Act revision - 411
Labor/HHS appropriations - 850
RNC post - 909-910
student loan defaults - 626-627 (box)
Benson, George - 83
Bentley, Helen Delich R-Md. (2)
congressional elections, 1990 - 908
Hatch Act revision - 410
minorities in Congress - 924 (chart)
Bentsen, Lloyd D-Texas
auto fuel efficiency - 281
budget action - 112, 130 (box)
campaign finance reform - 65
Caribbean Basin Initiative - 211-214
child-care aid - 551
China-U.S. relations - 768
Clean Air Act - 236
congressional pay, honoraria - 71
crime bill - 491
defense authorization - 678
energy tax incentives - 313 (box)
housing programs overhaul - 641
Japan-U.S. trade - 208
Medicaid expansion - 570
Medicare changes - 565
mammogram coverage - 564 (box)
Mexico-U.S. trade - 218
product liability - 401
Puerto Rico status - 427
Social Security
budget, deficit accounting - 170 (box)
earnings test - 558
Soviet-U.S. relations - 758
Benzene - 230, 240 (box), 252, 253, 275
Bereuter, Doug R-Neb. (1)
Food for Peace - 803
housing programs overhaul - 639, 640
Nicaragua elections - 770, 772 (box)
Persian Gulf crisis - 724, 746
Berger, Victor Luitpold - 922 (box)
Bergeson, Marian - 913 (box)
Berman, Howard L. D-Calif. (26)
campaign finance reform - 68
crime bill - 494
defense authorization - 676
immigration law revision - 475, 476, 478
Persian Gulf crisis - 730
RICO revision - 538
Berne Convention - 205
Berrocal, Jose - 427
Bessmernykh, Aleksandr - 762
Betti, John - 673 (box)
Bevill, Tom D-Ala. (4)
defense appropriations - 818
Energy, water appropriations - 861-866
Bexar County, Texas - 150
Bezuidenhout, Coenraad - 788
Bhutto, Benazir - 769
BIA. *See Indian Affairs, Bureau of*
Biaggi, Mario - 87
BIB. *See Board for International Broadcasting*
Biden, Joseph R. Jr. D-Del.
antidrug measures - 502, 503
"drug czar" post - 503 (box)

balanced-budget amendment - 175 (box)
CFE - 701
Clean Air Act - 237
congressional elections, 1990 - 916
congressional partisanship - 32
crime bill - 486-499
"dolphin-safe" tuna labels - 399
federal judgeships - 520-523
flag desecration - 524-528
judicial appointments - 516
juvenile justice nomination - 533
Persian Gulf crisis - 743
U.S. goals, rationales - 744 (box)
sex crime deterrence - 507
Souter confirmation - 509, 511, 512, 513, 515
Supreme Court term summary - 56
Thomas confirmation - 518-519 (box)
Bigeye bomb - 674
Bilbray, James D-Nev. (1)
radiation victims compensation - 590
Bilingual education - 848 (chart)
Bilirakis, Michael R-Fla. (9)
elderly health care - 599
Bill of Rights. *See Civil rights and liberties; specific amendments*
Binary weapons - 674
Bingaman, Jeff D-N.M.
conservative coalition - 47
defense appropriations - 820
defense authorization - 677, 679, 680
Energy, water appropriations - 866
EPA Cabinet status - 291
job training overhaul - 367
Labor/HHS appropriations - 847, 852, 853
OMB review powers - 413
SDI - 692
Bingham, Hiram - 99 (box), 100 (box)
Biodiversity - 837
Biofuels - 124, 317
Biological weapons
ban - 507
German unification - 763
Persian Gulf crisis - 721, 723, 732
protective clothing - 682
sanctions, aid ban - 197, 200, 201, 885
Biology. *See also Genetics; Medical research and technology*
Energy, water appropriations - 861, 866
Biomedical Ethics Board - 895 (chart)
Birds. *See also Northern spotted owl*
drift-net fishing - 399
wetlands preservation - 872
Birth control. *See also Abortion*
AIDS bill - 586
China policy condemnation - 561
contraception research - 600-604, 605
family planning (Title X)
appropriations - 852
Supreme Court - 56
authorization - 530, 531, 604-606
boxscore - 604
foreign programs - 530
U.N. population fund - 837, 838-839 (box), 840, 841, 843
population growth, global warming - 307
Birth defects
job bias/fetal protection case - 56, 465
toxic air pollutants - 247
Bisexuals
disabled civil rights - 452, 459
youth counselors - 561
Black, Charles - 60, 931
Black colleges
community development grants - 655
endowment awards - 611
EPA research - 275
HUD scandal investigation - 667
special education teacher training - 616-617
student loan programs - 143, 627 (box)
Black lung disability program - 848 (chart)
Black, Merle - 906
Black, William - 85, 88, 89, 93
Blackhawk helicopter - 675, 815 (chart)
Blackmun, Harry A.
abortion - 529
academic tenure - 623
Brennan career - 511 (box)
flag desecration - 525
habeas corpus appeals - 489 (box)
Medicaid pay suits - 571
OMB review powers - 412 (box)
patronage jobs - 933
right to die - 567 (box)
student religious groups - 618 (box)
Supreme Court term summary - 52
Blacks. *See also Black colleges; Discrimination; Discrimination in employment; Minorities; Minority business; Racial discrimination; South Africa*
Bush approval rating - 464
census count adjustment - 415, 932
characteristics of Congress - 923-924
minorities in Congress - 924 (chart)
civil rights/job bias - 462, 464
congressional elections, 1990 - 915, 916
Serrano election - 934
conservative coalition - 47
D.C. status - 428-429
death sentences - 490-491
defense authorization - 686
disabled education - 616
gubernatorial elections, 1990 - 928, 930
immigration law revision - 485
judicial appointments - 515, 516
Legal Services Corporation - 532
minority health - 596
"motor voter" bill - 70
radio, TV licenses - 510-511 (box)
SSC authorization - 439
Thomas confirmation - 518-519 (box)
Blackwell, J. Kenneth - 918 (chart)
Blanchard, James J. - 904 (chart), 926, 928, 929, 933
Blanton, Ted - 923
Blaz, Ben R-Guam
minorities in Congress - 924 (chart)
Bliley, Thomas J. Jr. R-Va. (3)
Hatch Act revision - 410
orphan drugs - 578-579
Blind persons
aircraft exit-row rules - 389 (box)
disabled civil rights - 452
SSI - 150
BLM. *See Land Management, Bureau of*
Block grants. *See also Alcohol, Drug Abuse and Mental Health; Community Development*
child-care aid - 152, 550
education - 123
housing - 631, 638
Palau autonomy - 808
Block III tanks - 823, 824
Blood
AIDS bill - 585, 586, 587
NIH authorization - 601
Blue Chip Economic Indicators - 127
Blue Cross and Blue Shield Association - 573, 574-575
Blue Ribbon Vocational Programs - 622
Blumstein, James F. - 413
BMY Corp. - 817
Board for International Broadcasting (BIB) - 799, 800, 883 (chart)
Boats and boating
Coast Guard fees - 136, 157, 386 (box)
fuel taxes - 158-159
luxury taxes - 159, 172
ramp user fees - 299
Boehlert, Sherwood R-N.Y. (25)
Clean Air Act - 278
disabled civil rights - 450
hotel fire safety - 402
SSC authorization - 438-439
Boehmer, John - 918 (chart), 922
Boggs, Lindy (Mrs. Hale) D-La. (2)
congressional elections, 1990 - 923
House membership changes - 918 (chart)
Energy, water appropriations - 862
Boggus, Eugenia - 553
Bolce, Don - 553
Bolick, Clint - 518
Bolivia
U.S. aid/drug control - 124, 502, 805-806, 836
Boll Weevils - 40
Bollaert, Barbara - 934
Bombers. *See also B-2 bomber; B-52 bomber*
air defense initiative - 673
long-range radar defense - 817
missiles - 674, 684
refueling tankers - 822
START - 704-708
strategic weapons triad - 688
Bond, Christopher S. R-Mo.
airline rights - 389 (box)
conservative coalition - 48
education proposals - 610
Ex-Im Bank arms loans - 200
farm bill - 326, 336, 337
FHA rules revision - 658
housing programs overhaul - 635-637
Persian Gulf crisis - 748
Senate leadership - 12
Bond, Dick - 918 (chart)
Bone marrow transplants - 596-597
Bonior, David E. D-Mich. (12)
congressional mail - 74
defense authorization - 682
El Salvador aid - 785
flag desecration - 526
Nicaragua aid - 771
Persian Gulf crisis - 730
Book conservation - 429, 617
Boren, David L. D-Okla.
Armenian genocide commemoration - 808
budget action - 165
campaign finance reform - 58-69
CFTC authorization - 195
civil rights/job bias - 467
Clean Air Act - 236
congressional elections, 1990 - 916
crime bill - 490, 491
farm bill - 333-334
intelligence authorization - 791, 792, 794, 795, 798
Medicaid pay suits - 571
nuclear test treaties - 712
Persian Gulf crisis - 725, 726, 750
U.S. Embassy in Moscow - 760 (box)
Bork, Robert H.
Brennan career - 510 (box)
civil rights/job bias - 464
flag desecration - 527
judicial appointments - 516, 519
Souter confirmation - 508, 509, 510, 515, 516
Thomas confirmation - 518 (box)
Boschwitz, Rudy R-Minn.
abortion - 530
budget action - 177
CFTC authorization - 195
civil rights/job bias - 462, 473
Clean Air Act - 236
congressional elections, 1990 - 911, 930
Senate membership changes - 913 (chart)
vote-share falloff - 904 (chart)
congressional partisanship - 32
crime bill - 493
Durenberger ethics case - 98
Energy, water appropriations - 865
farm bill - 334, 340
German unification - 763
immigration law revision - 480
Persian Gulf crisis - 724
Bosco, Douglas H. D-Calif. (1)
aviation package - 386, 387
congressional elections, 1990 - 903
defeated House members - 917 (chart)
House membership changes - 918 (chart)
vote-share falloff - 904 (chart)
defense authorization - 683
nuclear test treaties - 712
Boston College - 862
Boston, Mass.
AIDS relief - 582
airport slots - 387
Cambodian refugees - 837
housing issues - 662, 663
Irish immigrants - 477
Treasury, Postal appropriations - 888
Botanic Garden, U.S. - 458, 895 (chart)
Botha, P. W. - 787-788
Boucher, Rick D-Va. (9)
assault weapons ban - 501 (box)
cable TV regulation - 370-372
Clean Air Act - 246, 275
fire-safe cigarettes - 402
flag desecration - 527
handgun wait period - 501 (box)
House leadership - 11 (box)
RICO revision - 536-538
Bounpane, Peter A. - 416
Boxer, Barbara D-Calif. (6)
auto fuel efficiency - 281
defense authorization - 683
intelligence authorization - 796
minorities in Congress - 924 (chart)
Persian Gulf crisis
use-of-force debate - 752 (box)
Boy Scouts - 892
Brace, Kimball W. - 415
Bradley, Bill D-N.J.
Caribbean Basin Initiative - 213, 216
congressional elections, 1990 - 901, 911-912, 913, 926
vote-share falloff - 904 (chart)
D.C. appropriations - 893
education proposals - 613
Energy, water appropriations - 866
farm bill - 341
food-waste transport - 383
irrigation subsidies - 356-357
Japan-U.S. trade - 209
Labor/HHS appropriations - 852
Souter confirmation - 515
Soviet-U.S. trade - 759, 762
student right-to-know - 613, 624
Bradley troop carriers - 674, 685, 735 (box), 815 (chart)
Brady Handgun Violence Prevention Act - 500-501 (box)
Brady, James S. - 500-501 (box)
Brady, Nicholas F.
budget action - 130 (box), 131, 132
FDIC premiums - 185
Persian Gulf crisis - 732
stock market regulation - 190
Third World debt relief - 207, 218
thrift bailout - 179-181, 184
thrift supervision - 130 (box)
Brady Plan - 117, 207, 218

Brady, Sarah - 500-501 (box)
Brandeis University - 888
Branstad, Terry E. - 530, 903, 929
Brawley, Kevin - 934
Brazelton, T. Berry - 555
Brazil
U.S. trade - 208, 209
Breast cancer
mammography screening
grants to states - 606, 849
Medicare coverage - 145, 564 (box)
military dependents - 680
radiation victims compensation - 591
Breaux, John B. D-La.
antismoking bills - 593
aviation package - 387
campaign finance reform - 63
conservative coalition - 48
crime bill - 487, 490
"dolphin-safe" tuna labels - 399
Persian Gulf crisis - 751
pipeline safety inspection - 286 (box)
presidential support in Congress - 31
product liability - 401
Brennan, Joseph E. D-Maine (1)
gubernatorial election, 1990 - 919, 928, 930
House membership changes - 918 (chart)
Brennan, William J. Jr.
abortion - 529
flag desecration - 525
habeas corpus appeals - 489 (box)
legislative intent - 55 (box)
Medicaid pay suits - 571
minority broadcasters - 379 (box)
OMB review powers - 412 (box)
political patronage - 52, 933
retirement - 508, 510-511 (box)
right-to-die - 567 (box)
Souter confirmation - 514
student religious groups - 618 (box)
Supreme Court term summary - 52
Brewster, Bill - 918 (chart)
Brezhnev, Leonid I. - 707
Bribery
Garcia conviction - 107
HUD scandal investigation - 666, 667
Bridges
highway deficiencies - 384
Brilliant pebbles
appropriations - 820
authorization - 673, 677, 691, 692
budget action - 122
Bristol Bay - 313, 871, 872, 874
Britain. *See Great Britain*
British American Parliamentary Group - 883 (chart)
British Virgin Islands - 212
Broadcasting. *See Radio; Television*
Brodsky, William J. - 195
Bromley, D. Allan - 442
Brooke, Edward W. - 923
Brooke-Alexander amendment - 733, 777
Brookings Institution - 520
Brooks, Jack D-Texas (9)
assault weapons ban - 501 (box)
balanced-budget amendment - 175 (box)
civil rights/job bias - 470-471
congressional elections, 1990 - 904
low winning percentage - 906 (chart)
crime bill - 489, 494, 495, 498, 499
federal judgeships - 520-523
flag desecration - 524, 526
handgun wait period - 501 (box)
immigration law revision - 477
insurance price-sharing - 401
joint production ventures - 541
military construction appropriations - 830
North conviction overturn - 534
radiation victims compensation - 590
TV violence guidelines - 374 (box)
vertical price fixing - 539
Broomfield, William S. R-Mich. (18)
El Salvador aid - 782, 783, 784
Kenya aid - 790
Persian Gulf crisis - 738
Browder, Glen D-Ala. (3)
campaign finance reform - 68
defense authorization - 682
Brown, George E. Jr. D-Calif. (36)
animal rights activists - 441-442
congressional elections, 1990
marginal vote share - 905 (chart)
House leadership - 11 (box)
military construction appropriations - 828
nutrition monitoring - 355
Brown, Hank R-Colo. (4)
abortion - 530
characteristics of Congress - 925
congressional elections, 1990 - 915, 919
House membership changes - 918 (chart)
Senate membership changes - 913 (chart)
congressional pay, honoraria - 71
Social Security Administration independence - 558
Brown, Harold - 688
Brown, Ronald H. - 69-70, 473, 903, 910, 931
Brown, William H. - 105
Brownwood, Texas - 878
Bruce, Terry L. D-Ill. (19)
Clean Air Act - 238-239, 242
elderly health care - 598
nutrition labels - 576
Brunette, Mary S. - 636, 659, 859
Bryan, Jon L. - 922
Bryan, Richard H. D-Nev.
auto fuel efficiency - 279-281
Clean Air Act - 233
CPSC authorization - 394
defense authorization - 678
Interior appropriations - 876
Persian Gulf crisis - 751
telemarketing fraud - 402
Bryant, Barbara Everitt - 415-416, 930
Bryant, John D-Texas (5)
children's TV advertising - 373
Clean Air Act - 242
crime bill - 495
financial institution fraud - 183
flag desecration - 527
foreign ownership of U.S. business - 223-225
immigration law revision - 477-479
BSTS satellite system - 684, 817, 822-823, 824
Buck, Marilyn J. - 7
Buckland, Eric - 781
Budget, U.S. *See also Gramm-Rudman-Hollings law; Taxation; User fees*
accounting
credit reform - 134, 163, 178 (box)
SEC fees - 881
Social Security funds - 170 (box), 846
thrift bailout - 181, 846
administration proposal - 122-127
State of the Union address - 19
balanced-budget amendment - 47, 173, 174-175 (box), 868
budget process
changes, 1990 - 111-112, 161-163, 165, 173-178
discretionary spending caps (charts) - 161, 176
five-year resolutions - 163, 173
key dates - 177 (box)
budget reconciliation - 138-166
boxscore - 140
Bush message - 166 (box)
conservative coalition - 47
House, Senate instructions - 138-139 (chart)
key votes - 8-B, 13-B
provisions - 141-160
revenue raisers, losers (chart) - 171
Senate rules - 311
summary - 4, 112
tax provisions - 167-173
budget resolutions - 127-129, 136-138
boxscore - 136
House, Senate reconciliation instructions - 138-139 (chart)
key votes - 12-B
presidential support in Congress - 31
summary - 111
budget summit - 129-136
Bush statement - 131 (box)
congressional leadership - 8, 10
farm bill - 347-348
energy taxes - 313 (box)
players - 130 (box)
presidential support in Congress - 31
summary - 4, 111
congressional partisanship - 39
deficit, 1980-90 (graph) - 113
deficit reduction
airport, highway fund use - 385, 386
coin redesign - 197
community service programs - 561
discretionary spending limits - 161
farm bill - 324, 344, 349-351
foreign ownership of U.S. business - 223
pay-as-you-go limits - 161-162
savings, FY91, 91-95 (graph) - 112
sequestration reports, orders - 162
summary - 4, 111
surplus campaign funds - 66
targets - 162, 174
tax provisions of reconciliation - 167-173
federal debt
ceiling increase - 160, 161, 165 (box)
refinancing with gold-backed bonds - 128
FY91 budget
action outline - 111
authority, outlays by agency (chart) - 118
authority, outlays by function (chart) - 120-121
chronology - 114-115 (box)
economic assumptions (chart) - 119
spending allocations (chart) - 140
summary - 3-4
pie charts in IRS booklets - 160
revenue
FCC fee retention - 372
military land sales, leases - 678
NRC fees, 136, 311 (box)
uranium enrichment - 311
veterans health-plan receipts - 155
Buechner, Jack R-Mo. (2)
congressional elections, 1990 - 906, 917, 919
defeated House members - 917 (chart)
House membership changes - 918 (chart)
vote-share falloff - 904 (chart)
Buffalo, N.Y. - 650
Buildings. *See Architecture and buildings; Construction industry; Federal buildings; Housing*
Bulgaria
START - 707
Bumpers, Dale D-Ark.
Armenian genocide commemoration - 807
civil rights/job bias - 467
congressional leadership - 8
conservative coalition - 47
defense appropriations - 820, 821
defense authorization - 678
Ethics Committee special counsel - 81 (box), 103
flag desecration - 528
Interior appropriations - 875-876
military base closings - 695
SDI - 692
Bunning, Jim R-Ky. (4)
development bank loans - 207
Burdick, Quentin N. D-N.D.
agriculture appropriations - 811, 868
Souter confirmation - 515
water projects authorization - 298
Bureau. *See other part of name*
Burger, Warren E. - 508
Burials
Indian remains - 422
veterans benefits - 156
Burke, Sheila - 32
Burma. *See Myanmar*
Burns, Conrad R-Mont.
Armenian genocide commemoration - 808
cable TV regulation - 371
Burton, Dan R-Ind. (6)
AIDS bill - 588
budget action - 136-137
congressional elections, 1990
low winning percentage - 906 (chart)
Kenya aid - 790
South Africa sanctions - 788
Burton, Phillip - 933
Bus transportation
air pollution control - 231 (box), 241, 243, 254
disabled civil rights - 448-450, 453-454, 456, 460
radar detector ban - 880
safety rating information - 383
Bush, Barbara - 117, 610
Bush, George
abortion - 7, 528, 531, 838 (box), 840, 891, 893
agriculture - 323, 325, 327, 351
appointments. *See Nominations and appointments*
appropriations - 811
defense - 812, 814, 820
Energy, water - 866
foreign aid - 844
government shutdown - 8, 896-897
Interior - 876
military construction - 827
Treasury, Postal - 886, 890
VA-HUD - 860
arms control
CFE - 696-704
chemical weapons pact - 709, 710
START - 704-708
budget
balanced-budget amendment - 174-175 (box)
budget process changes - 173, 176
budget summit - 130-136
chronology - 114-115
congressional leadership - 8
continuing resolutions - 137, 896-897 (box)
messages
congressional address (text) - 133
economic report excerpts (text) - 116-117
reconciliation statement (text) - 166
TV address (text) - 135
proposed budget - 122-126

reconciliation - 164, 165
resolution - 136
summary - 3-4, 111-113, 116
business and labor
children's TV advertising - 373-375
displaced worker aid - 277 (box)
family leave - 6, 47, 359
veto (text) - 361
Indian preference - 421, 422
veto (text) - 423
product liability - 400
telemarketing curbs - 379
civil rights
disabled persons - 447, 448, 459
job discrimination - 6, 32, 54, 462-473
congressional relations - 9-10, 16-21
congressional term limit - 15
pocket veto power - 21-22
support in Congress (vote study) - 22-31
defense policy
B-2 bomber - 689, 820
defense authorization - 671, 672, 677, 680, 687
military base closings - 694
military construction - 827
SDI - 691-693
secret programs - 812
summary - 5
economic policy
financial institution fraud - 182
thrift bailout - 179, 181
education
proposals - 610-615
summary - 7
vocational education authorization - 619, 623
elections and politics
campaign finance reform - 57, 58, 60, 66, 69
congressional elections, 1990 - 901-902
RNC chair - 909-910
energy
energy issues, 1990 - 312
Strategic Petroleum Reserve - 312, 313-316
super collider - 438, 439, 863, 866
environment
Clean Air Act - 9, 229-245, 276-279
environmental education - 293
EPA Cabinet status - 291-293
federal RCRA compliance - 308
offshore drilling - 870, 876
wetlands protection - 335
federal government
secrecy agreements - 890
flag desecration - 525, 526
foreign aid
Andean Initiative - 805-806
Egyptian loans - 831
El Salvador - 779-780, 783-784, 786
intelligence authorization - 791, 792, 793, 798, 799
Latin America - 218
Nicaragua - 770-771, 772 (box), 773
Panama - 774-779
foreign policy
Armenian genocide commemoration - 807
China relations - 764, 765
Chinese student visas - 767 (box)
German unification - 762-763
Pakistan relations - 768
South Africa sanctions - 787-789
Soviet relations - 757-762
State Department authorization - 799, 800-802
U.N. funding - 802
U.S. Embassy in Moscow - 885
foreign trade
export controls - 198-202
Havel visit - 204 (box)
Japan - 208, 223
Mexico talks - 218
Poland - 206
Soviet Union - 204-205, 758-759
textile import quotas - 219-222
Hatch Act revision - 6, 408-411
veto message (text) - 410
health
AIDS bill - 582
Medicare changes - 566
orphan drugs - 577-579
radiation victims compensation - 590
housing
FHA rules revision - 658, 660
housing programs overhaul - 631-632, 634, 640, 642, 656
prepayment of subsidized mortgages - 665
immigration law revision - 474, 481 (box), 485
law enforcement and judiciary
crime bill - 486-499, 886
drug enforcement - 502-503
Persian Gulf crisis - 717-756
8/8 troop deployment announcement (text) - 726-727
8/28 Gulf policy remarks (text) - 729
9/11 address to Congress (text) - 731-732
11/30 news conference (text) - 741
1/8/91 use-of-force letter (text) - 747
1/16/91 war announcement (text) - 754-755
approval ratings - 745 (box)
call-up of reserves - 695 (box)
Saudi arms sales - 735 (box)
summary - 3
U.S. goals, rationales - 744-745 (box)
Puerto Rico status - 425, 426
space programs - 434-436
State of the Union address (text) - 18-20
taxation
budget action - 111-113, 117, 131, 131 (box), 167, 169
capital gains tax - 113, 168 (box)
energy incentives - 313 (box)
transportation
Amtrak authorization - 390-392
veto (text) - 391
aviation package - 6, 384
Eastern Airlines strike - 369
welfare and social services
child-care aid - 547-551
community service programs - 5, 559-562
Head Start authorization - 553, 554, 556
homeless aid - 665
Bush, Neil - 179, 180, 182, 183, 495
Bushnell, John - 801 (box)
Business and industry. *See also Antitrust law; Business interest groups; Business taxes; Competition and monopoly; Employment and working conditions; Federal contractors; Foreign trade and business; Labor unions; Minority business; Pensions and retirement; Regulation and deregulation; Small business; Stocks, bonds and securities; specific industries*
corporate takeovers
airline LBOs - 388
pension reversions - 367
railroad acquisitions - 390, 391
disabled civil rights - 447-448, 455
education proposals - 611, 614
environmental protection
Clean Air Act - 4, 229-279
coastal waters cleanup - 289-290
hazardous materials transport - 380
Head Start authorization - 552-553
product liability - 7, 400-401
Puerto Rico status - 425
racketeering suits - 7, 536-538
rural development - 347, 352
space industry - 434, 436
strategic materials - 202-203, 442-443
technology transfer - 345, 440
vocational education authorization - 620, 621, 622
Business Coalition for RICO Reform - 536
Business ethics
tobacco advertising - 594
Business interest groups
age discrimination - 362, 363
air safety guidelines - 389
antismoking bills - 592, 593
auto fuel efficiency - 279-281
cable TV regulation - 371
campaign finance reform - 52, 53, 57-69
corporate campaign limits - 59 (box)
civil rights/job bias - 462-473
Clean Air Act - 231-246, 275-279
CPSC authorization - 394, 395
disabled civil rights - 447, 448, 449
family leave - 359-361
FHA rules revision - 658-661
fish inspection - 397
fuel-efficiency standards - 7, 279-281
housing programs overhaul - 640, 644-646
immigration law revision - 479
logging/wildlife protection - 296, 870, 871, 872
Medicaid drug rebates - 570 (box)
nutrition labels - 576
oil pollution cleanup - 285, 287
orphan drugs - 577-579
pension reversions - 367
pipeline safety inspection - 286 (box)
product liability - 400-401
Puerto Rico status - 425
radio spectrum allocation - 377
RICO revision - 7, 536-538
space patent law - 437
vertical price fixing - 539
Business taxes
budget-reconciliation changes - 149, 159-160, 172-173
corporate transactions - 159
energy incentives - 160, 167, 173, 312-313, 866
gasohol blenders - 214, 216
enterprise zones - 167
environmental tax - 159
expiring provisions extensions - 160, 173
foreign ownership of U.S. business - 224
foreign workers - 475, 476, 478
incentives - 160, 164, 172
oil pollution cleanup - 287
Puerto Rico - 211, 214, 217, 425-427
research credit - 134, 160
small corporate investments - 57, 169
targeted job credit - 160
underpayment penalties - 159, 172
unemployment compensation - 368
Bustamante, Albert G. D-Texas (23)
civil rights/job bias - 470
congressional elections, 1990
low winning percentage - 906 (chart)
crime bill - 498
minorities in Congress - 924 (chart)
Butane - 240 (box)
Butter. *See Milk and dairy products*
Buy American provisions
FAA purchasing - 156
strategic materials - 202-203
water projects authorization - 298
Byrd, Robert C. D-W.Va.
appropriations
defense - 812, 819, 820
District of Columbia - 892
Commerce/Justice/State - 885
Energy, water - 865
foreign aid - 830, 840, 841-842
Interior - 874, 875, 876
Labor/HHS - 853
legislative branch - 894, 897
supplemental FY90 - 842
Transportation - 877, 879, 880
Treasury, Postal - 889
Armenian genocide commemoration - 807
aviation package - 388
budget action - 130 (box)
campaign finance reform - 58
Clean Air Act - 9, 230, 232-233, 236-238, 277 (box), 278
congressional leadership - 9 (box)
federal pay overhaul - 407
job training overhaul - 367
NEA authorization - 432-433
Panama aid - 778-779
Persian Gulf crisis - 737
use-of-force debate - 752 (box)
Soviet-U.S. relations - 761
Byron, Beverly B. D-Md. (6)
characteristics of Congress - 924
minorities in Congress - 924 (chart)
textile import quotas - 222

C

C-17 cargo plane
appropriations - 815 (chart), 819, 825, 826
authorization - 675, 686
Cabinet
"drug czar" post - 503 (box)
Education Department post - 614 (box)
EPA status - 291-293
Labor Department post - 369 (box)
Cable Communications Policy Act - 370
Cable News Network - 371, 721, 738
Cable television
copyright tribunal - 543
must-carry rules - 370-371, 372, 373
regulation - 7, 370-372
Cadmium - 276
CAFE. *See Corporate Average Fuel Economy levels*
Cairns Group - 210
California. *See also Los Angeles; San Francisco*
air pollution control
clean-fuel vehicles - 229, 231 (box), 233 (box), 240, 243, 246-247, 254, 278
non-road vehicles - 253
offshore drilling emissions - 230
alternative power regulation - 317, 318
Amtrak waste disposal - 392
"Big Green" pesticide initiative - 358, 927
campaign finance reform - 62
CDBG funding formula - 641
"colonias" housing aid - 654
congressional elections, 1990 - 903, 907, 909, 919
congressional leadership - 11 (box)
congressional redistricting - 931, 933
driver literacy - 611
earthquake research - 442
federal judgeships - 522
food aid cargo preference - 339 (box)

gubernatorial election, 1990 - 903, 927-928, 929
immigration law revision - 477
Indian land sale - 422
legislative term limits - 13-14, 902, 927
Medigap plans - 574
military base closing - 827-828
northern spotted owl protection - 296-297
nutrition labels - 576
octane labeling - 282
offshore oil drilling - 288, 872
oil spill - 283, 285
savings and loan scandal - 78, 79, 80
state, local tax deductibility - 165
water projects
appropriations - 865
authorization - 299
irrigation subsidies - 356-357
California Air Resources Board - 254
California State University - 888
Calio, Nick - 15
Cambodia
China-U.S. relations - 766
development bank loans - 207
Food for Peace - 803
U.S. aid to rebels
appropriations - 835, 837, 841, 843, 844
authorization - 791, 793-797
humanitarian aid to children - 837
Camp, David - 918 (chart)
Campaign finance. *See also Political action committees*
auto importers - 280-281
broadcasting rates - 66-67 (box)
bundling - 58, 62, 64
congressional ethics cases
D'Amato - 97
Durenberger - 98, 100
Dyson - 108
Gingrich - 104-105
savings and loan scandal - 78-97
congressional mail - 75
congressional partisanship - 32, 39
corporate limits - 59 (box)
election costs, 1990 - 766-767
Hatch Act revision - 408-411
legislative branch appropriations - 895
reform bill - 57-69
boxscore - 57
House, Senate bills compared - 62-63
key votes - 7-B
summary - 3, 6, 8
"soft money" - 58, 63
state reform efforts - 65 (box)
Supreme Court decisions - 52, 53, 58, 59 (box), 63
Campbell, Ben Nighthorse D-Colo. (3)
congressional term limit - 15
Indian legislation - 421
Interior appropriations - 874
Campbell, Carroll A. - 930
Campbell, John B. - 327, 328, 331, 335, 348, 350-351
Campbell, Tom R-Calif. (12)
assault weapons ban - 501 (box)
civil rights/job bias - 469-470
crime bill - 495
disabled civil rights - 450, 451
foreign ownership of U.S. business - 224
immigration law revision - 478
pocket veto power - 22
Campbell, W. Donald - 634, 636-637, 643
Canada
acid rain - 267
Great Lakes pollution - 290, 301
Persian Gulf crisis - 719
U.S. trade
Mexico talks - 218
strategic materials - 203
sugar quotas - 328
textile import quotas - 220
Cancer. *See also Breast cancer*
Agent Orange compensation - 418-419
AIDS bill debate - 583, 589
carcinogenic pesticides - 336, 358
"dread disease" medical insurance - 572, 574
minority health - 596
NIH authorization - 601
nutrition labels - 575, 576
radiation victims compensation - 590-591
toxic air pollutants - 230, 231 (box), 232, 233, 241-242, 246, 247, 256, 257, 259, 275-276, 279
Candy - 328, 330, 592, 593
Canola. *See Oilseeds*
Capital gains taxes
budget action - 112, 168 (box)
chronology - 114
deficit reduction - 167
proposal - 123
reconciliation - 157, 164, 165, 171
summit - 131-134
Bush economic report - 116-117
child-care aid - 550
community service programs - 561
supplemental appropriations - 846
Capital punishment
anticrime bill - 6, 40
aviation security - 390
Brennan career - 510 (box)
civil rights fatalities - 493
drug crimes - 40, 487, 493, 497, 502-503
abortion, D.C. appropriations link - 846, 852
federal death penalty - 486-487, 489-494, 496, 497, 499
gubernatorial elections, 1990 - 927
habeas corpus appeals - 486-490, 492-499, 886
Indian lands exemption - 493
Panama aid - 779
racial justice - 486, 487, 489, 490-491, 494, 496, 497-498
Souter confirmation - 514
South Africa - 788
Capitol, U.S.
bombing case sentences - 7
security - 12 (box)
Carbon dioxide
clean fuels - 231 (box), 233 (box)
fuel efficiency - 233, 280
global warming - 232, 274, 307
Carbon monoxide
clean-fuel vehicles - 229, 253-254
cold weather emissions - 229, 246, 252
international emissions - 274
motor vehicle emissions standards - 251-252
non-road vehicles - 253
urban smog reduction - 230, 235 (box), 248, 250-251
Carbon tetrachloride - 269
Carcinogens. *See Cancer*
Cardin, Benjamin L. D-Md. (3)
congressional elections, 1990
low winning percentage - 906 (chart)
Cargill Inc. - 331
Caribbean area. *See also Caribbean Basin Initiative; specific islands*
U.S. aid - 217-218
appropriations - 845
hurricane damage aid - 778
U.S. trade
sugar tariffs - 328, 331
textile import quotas - 220
Caribbean Basin Economic Recovery Act - 211, 213
Caribbean Basin Initiative (CBI)
congressional action - 211-217
boxscore - 211
provisions - 212-215
Hungary aid - 204
Nicaragua aid - 771
Panama aid - 777
textile import quotas - 220
Caribbean/Central American Action - 217
Carlson, Arne - 911, 930
Carnegie Corporation - 611
Carol, David J. - 392
Carper, Thomas R. D-Del. (AL)
housing programs overhaul - 638, 640
prepayment of subsidized mortgages - 663, 664
Carr, Bob D-Mich. (6)
aviation package - 387
Transportation appropriations - 880
Carr Square Village - 857, 859
Carrington, John - 923
Carter, Jimmy
Afghan rebel aid - 792
arms control - 711
B-2 bomber - 688
defense policy - 671
energy policy - 312
farm policy - 324
judicial appointments - 516, 517, 520, 535
Nicaragua elections - 770, 772 (box)
water projects authorization - 297
Case Western University - 862
Casey, Robert P. - 530, 929
Casey, William J. - 791
Cassity, James A. Jr. - 376
Castro, Fidel - 789, 884
Catastrophic health insurance. *See Medicare Catastrophic Coverage Act*
Catholic Church
characteristics of Congress - 926
El Salvador aid - 786, 842
Cavanaugh, Gordon - 636
Cavazos, Lauro F.
education proposals - 614
resignation - 614 (box)
CBO. *See Congressional Budget Office*
CBRA. *See Coastal Barrier Resources Act*
CDBGs. *See Community Development Block Grant program*
Ceauşescu, Nicolae - 838 (box), 840
Celebrezze, Anthony J. Jr. - 530, 929
Celeste, Richard F. - 106
Cellular telephones
radio spectrum allocation - 376
Censorship
TV violence guidelines - 374 (box)
Census Bureau, U.S.
appropriations - 415, 882 (chart), 884
census count adjustment - 415-416
congressional redistricting - 930, 932
employees - 213
foreign ownership of U.S. business - 222, 224, 225
OMB review powers - 412
Census, 1990
congressional redistricting - 930-933
count adjustment - 415-416
OMB review powers - 412
Center for Auto Safety - 281
Center for Devices and Radiological Health - 580
Center for Resource Economics - 335, 349
Center for Science in the Public Interest - 576
Center for Security Policy - 703, 705, 707, 711
Center for Tobacco Products - 592, 593
Center for Women's Health Research - 602
Center on Budget and Policy Priorities - 554 (box)
Centers for Disease Control
Agent Orange compensation - 418
AIDS - 460, 588
appropriations - 848 (chart)
disabilities - 589
injuries research - 598
TB prevention - 594
vaccine program authorization - 591-592
Central America. *See also specific countries*
Food for Peace - 803
National Guard training exercises - 52, 53, 694 (box)
Nicaragua peace proposals - 770, 772 (box)
screwworm eradication - 355
U.S. immigration policy - 478
U.S. sugar tariffs - 328
Central European Small Enterprise Development Commission - 886
Central Intelligence Agency (CIA)
diplomatic nominations - 801 (box)
Hatch Act revision - 409
intelligence authorization - 791, 792, 793, 799
Iran-contra cases - 535
Pakistan nuclear potential - 769
Central Utah Project - 357
Central Valley (Calif.) - 356
Ceramics - 440
Cerebral palsy - 609
Cervical cancer - 606, 680, 849
CFCs. *See Chlorofluorocarbons*
CFE. *See Conventional forces in Europe treaty*
CFTC. *See Commodity Futures Trading Commission*
CH-47, CH-53E helicopters - 675, 815 (chart), 819, 825
Chafee, John H. R-R.I.
barrier island protection - 302
China-U.S. relations - 765
Clean Air Act - 233-234, 244-245
congressional leadership - 9 (box), 12
family planning authorization - 605, 606
farm bill - 341
FDIC premiums - 186-187
federal RCRA compliance - 308-309
Medicaid expansion - 569
oil pollution cleanup - 285-286
Souter confirmation - 515
Chamber of Commerce, U.S.
age discrimination - 362, 363
family leave - 359-360
Hatch Act revision - 408
vertical price fixing - 539
Chambers, Julius - 464
Chamorro, Violeta - 5, 770-774, 777, 801 (box), 804, 844
CHAMPUS - 680, 816, 821
Chandler, Marguerite - 918 (chart), 923
Chandler, Rod R-Wash. (8)
congressional elections, 1990
low winning percentage - 906 (chart)
vote-share falloff - 904 (chart)
unemployment compensation - 368
Channel, Carl R. "Spitz" - 535
CHAP. *See Comprehensive Homeless Assistance Plan*
Chapman, Jim D-Texas (1)
disabled civil rights - 451, 460, 461
Energy, water appropriations - 861-866
Interior appropriations - 872-873
military construction appropriations - 828

Chapter 1. *See Compensatory education aid*
Charities and nonprofit organizations
AIDS bill - 582-587
campaign finance reform - 61, 65
community service programs - 559-562
deceptive mail curbs - 417
disabled civil rights - 453
education proposals - 611-612
environmental education grants - 293
foreign aid
food programs - 330, 803
Zaire - 790, 836, 843
Head Start authorization - 552, 555
housing programs overhaul - 631-647
veterans aid - 420
liability - 562
postal subsidies - 123
prepayment of subsidized mortgages - 663, 664
rural development - 346-347, 352
Taft Institute - 628
tax deduction for donations - 135, 158, 165
vocational education - 622
Charleston, W.Va. - 889
Charren, Peggy - 375
Charter of Paris for a New Europe - 703
Cheese. *See Milk and dairy products*
Chemical Safety and Hazard Investigation Board - 258
Chemical weapons
defense authorization - 674
German unification - 763
protective clothing - 682
Soviet-U.S. relations - 757, 758
pact - 709-711
Washington summit - 696, 702, 708
trade sanctions - 198-201
Iraq - 709, 718, 722-723, 724, 804, 885
Chemicals and chemical companies. *See also Agent Orange; Ozone-layer protection; Pests and pesticides*
accident prevention - 258-259
displaced worker aid - 237, 277 (box)
fish inspection - 396, 397
foreign ownership of U.S. business - 223
job bias/fetal protection case - 56
liquefied gas research - 274
pollution source reduction - 155
toxic air pollutants - 4, 231 (box), 232, 241-242, 275
transport safety - 380, 381
superfund tax - 159
urban smog reduction - 230
workplace safety - 258, 412
Cheney, Dick
appropriations
defense - 812, 818-822, 825, 826
military construction - 826-828
supplemental FY90 - 845, 846
B-2 bomber - 688, 691
budget action - 122
Bush congressional relations - 16
CFE - 701
defense authorization - 671-687
defense budget cuts - 673 (box)
defense budget reprogramming - 676 (box)
military base closings - 693-695
naval home ports - 681 (box)
Persian Gulf crisis - 719, 725, 728-730, 736-739, 742-743
Saudi arms sales - 734 (box)
U.S. goals, rationales - 745 (box)
SDI - 691, 693
strategic materials - 202
Chernobyl nuclear accident - 759
Chesapeake and Delaware Canal - 300
Chicago, Judy - 47
Chicago, Ill.
AIDS relief - 582
airport fees, slots - 386, 387
Clean Air Act - 239
housing issues - 651
Illinois gubernatorial election, 1990 - 928
Soviet air service - 759
stock-index futures trading - 190, 194-195
Chicago Mercantile Exchange - 195
Child abuse and neglect. *See also Child pornography*
child-care provider training - 153
child welfare services - 556
crime bill - 6, 486, 493, 498, 499
drug-related abuse - 493
homeless aid - 665
Indian programs - 422-423
kidnapping - 493
sexual abuse - 53, 422, 493
Child and Adolescent Service System Program - 599
Child care
budget action - 128, 139, 151-153
community service programs - 560, 562
congressional action, 1990 - 3, 4, 8, 547-551
family investment centers - 650
food stamp eligibility - 355
homeless aid - 655
information and referral services - 552, 555
Labor/HHS appropriations - 849, 851
library services for centers - 617
public housing supportive services - 651
Social Security earnings test - 557-558
vocational education authorization - 623
Child Care Block Grant - 550
Child Development Associate Scholarship Assistance program - 555, 556
Child development grants - 650
Child health and nutrition. *See also Immunizations; Women, Infants and Children (WIC) program*
AIDS bill - 582-588
budget action - 128, 147
child-care standards - 153, 547, 551
drug-abuse treatment for mothers - 679
emotional disorders - 599
family leave - 359-361
foreign aid - 832, 837, 838 (box), 840, 843
Head Start authorization - 552
Labor/HHS appropriations - 852
lead abatement - 858
Medicaid - 5, 569-571
minimum qualifications for physicians - 147
nutrition appropriations - 869 (chart)
safety
air travel - 389 (box)
child-resistant packaging - 417
garage doors - 394
toys - 394
school lunch program - 155, 354
SSI evaluations - 150
TB prevention - 594
Child labor law - 143
Child pornography
art, NEA debates - 431, 432, 874
congressional partisanship - 39
conservative coalition - 47
crime bill - 493, 499
Supreme Court decisions - 53, 55-56
Child support payments - 149-150, 652, 653
Child Survival Fund - 832 (chart), 837, 843
Child Victims Bill of Rights - 493
Childhood Immunization Program - 591
Children. *See also Adolescents and youth; Adoption; Aid to Families with Dependent Children; Child abuse and neglect; Child care; Child health and nutrition; Elementary and secondary education; Foster care; Infants; Juvenile delinquents; Preschool education; Schools*
family resources programs - 556
homosexual counselors - 561, 891, 892-893
immigration law revision - 474-485
television
advertising - 373-375
educational programming - 373-375
violence guidelines - 374 (box)
welfare services - 556
budget action - 150
homeless aid - 665
Children, Youth and Families Administration - 553
Children's Defense Fund - 547, 548
Children's Hospital (San Diego) - 888
Children's National Medical Center (Washington) - 888
Chiles, Lawton - 530, 928, 933
China
Cambodian arms aid - 766, 837
democracy demonstration suppression - 561
family planning - 561, 831, 838-839 (box), 841
human rights - 204, 207
ozone-layer protection - 271
Persian Gulf crisis - 717, 739, 740
U.S. relations - 764-768
Soviet-U.S. relations - 761-762
State Department authorization - 799-800
U.S. trade
export controls - 199
status - 204, 213, 764-765
textiles, shoes - 210, 214
World Bank loans - 207, 834, 835
Chinese student visas
immigration law revision - 483
key votes - 4-B
vetoes - 16, 22, 764, 767 (box)
Chloracne - 418
Chlorofluorocarbons (CFCs)
Clean Air Act - 4, 230, 234, 244-245, 269-271
foreign aid appropriations - 837
ozone-depleting chemicals tax - 158
Cholesterol - 575
Christopher Columbus Center on Marine Research and Exploration - 888
Christopher Columbus Quincentenary Jubilee Commission - 882 (chart)
Chronic fatigue syndrome - 603
Chrysler Corp. - 280-281
Church, Frank - 922
Church-state separation
child-care aid - 549, 551
student religious groups - 618 (box)
Churches and religious organizations
antismoking bills - 594
characteristics of Congress - 926
child-care aid - 152, 153-154, 549
civil rights/job bias - 462
community service programs - 559, 561
disabled civil rights - 453, 457
Head Start authorization - 552
living wills - 567 (box)
meetings in schools - 52, 53, 618 (box)
religious-worker visas - 482, 483
CIA. *See Central Intelligence Agency*
Cigarettes. *See Tobacco*
Cities. *See Urban areas*
Citizen participation. *See Public participation*
Citizens for a Free Kuwait - 744-745 (box)
Citizens for Congressional Reform - 15
Citizenship, U.S. *See also Naturalization*
family immigration limits - 475, 476, 477, 480, 482
Puerto Rico status - 425-427
repatriation aid - 150
voter registration - 69
Civil Rights Act of 1964
court impact study - 468
Senate coverage - 458
Title VII remedies
disabled persons - 447, 448, 450, 453, 459
job bias - 56, 462-473
Civil Rights Act of 1990
boxscore - 462
congressional action, 1990 - 462-473
congressional leadership - 10
congressional partisanship - 32
conservative coalition - 47
disabled civil rights - 458, 461
key votes - 9-B, 13-B
presidential support in Congress - 16, 31
summary - 6
Supreme Court term summary - 52, 54
veto message - 472
Civil rights and liberties. *See also Civil Rights Act of 1990; Civil rights interest groups; Discrimination; Fifth Amendment; First Amendment; Privacy; Voting rights*
coin redesign themes - 196-197
competent counsel - 488, 490, 494, 496, 497
death penalty for violations fatalities - 493
disabled persons - 447-461
double jeopardy - 107
11th Amendment rights - 616
exclusionary rule - 486, 492, 498, 499
Hatch Act revision - 411
immigration law revision - 485
job bias protection - 462-473
judicial appointments - 516
medical self-determination - 146
Souter confirmation - 509, 512, 514
Civil Rights Commission - 883 (chart)
Civil Rights Division (Justice) - 125, 465 (box)
Civil rights interest groups
age discrimination - 362
census count adjustment - 415, 932
civil rights/job bias - 462-473
disabled civil rights - 447
Dunne nomination - 465 (box)
environmental suits - 297
judicial appointments - 516
"motor voter" bill - 70
Souter confirmation - 510-511
South Africa sanctions - 788-789
Thomas confirmation - 514 (box)
Civil service. *See Federal employees*
Civil War sites - 304
Claims Court, U.S.
federal judgeships - 522
radiation victims compensation - 591
Clark, Dick - 793
Clark, Ramsey - 746
Clark, Richard W. - 892
Clarke, James McClure D-N.C. (11)
congressional elections, 1990 - 917
defeated House members - 917 (chart)
House membership changes - 918 (chart)

marginal vote share - 905 (chart)
Clay, William L. D-Mo. (1)
age discrimination - 363
civil rights/job bias - 468
congressional elections, 1990 - 904, 907
low winning percentage - 906 (chart)
congressional leadership - 11 (box)
family leave - 360
housing costs aid - 659 (box)
minorities in Congress - 924 (chart)
Clayton Antitrust Act of 1914 - 540
Claytor, Richard A. - 309
Clean Air Act
amendments, 1990 - 229-279
acid rain highlights - 237 (box)
alternative fuel highlights - 240 (box)
boxscore - 229
deadlines - 231 (box)
key votes - 5-B, 6-B, 9-B, 10-B
motor vehicle highlights - 233 (box)
provisions - 248-275
smog highlights - 235 (box)
summary - 3, 4, 8
Bush economic report - 117
congressional leadership - 9
conservative coalition - 40
EPA fees - 154
global warming - 307
job loss benefits - 277 (box)
presidential support in Congress - 31
Transportation appropriations - 879
Clean Air Working Group 233, 240, 242, 243, 245, 246, 279
Clean coal technology program - 238, 266, 267, 307, 873 (chart)
Clean Water Act - 283, 289, 301
Clement, Bob D-Tenn. (5)
foreign aid appropriations - 840
Cleveland, Ohio - 196
Climate. *See Global climate change; Weather*
Clines, Thomas G. - 535
Clinger, William F. Jr. R-Pa. (23)
food-waste transport - 383
Clinical nurse specialists - 145
Clinton, Bill - 930
Clothing
Caribbean Basin Initiative - 211, 212, 213
China-U.S. trade - 765
luxury tax on jewelry, furs - 159, 172
prison industries - 498
textile import quotas - 219-222
Coal
Abandoned Mine Reclamation Fund - 154
acid rain reduction - 9, 229-230, 232-233, 238, 242, 259-267, 276, 278
alternative power regulation - 317
displaced worker aid - 230, 236-238, 276, 277 (box)
methane assessment - 271
methanol - 240 (box)
non-fuel use research - 307
South Africa sanctions - 787
Coalition on Smoking OR Health - 593
Coalition to Stop U.S. Intervention in the Middle East - 746
Coast Guard, U.S.
appropriations - 384, 877, 879, 879 (chart)
aquatic nuisance species - 303
drug interdiction - 879
offshore drilling emissions - 273
oil pollution cleanup - 287, 879
pipeline safety inspection - 286 (box)
user fees - 126, 136, 157, 386 (box)
Coastal areas. *See also Wetlands*
barrier island protection - 302-303
beach erosion - 298, 863, 865
beach user fees - 299
development - 154, 288-289
Florida Keys protection - 303
water quality - 288-289, 290
Coastal Barrier Resources Act (CBRA) of 1982 - 302
Coastal Energy Impact Program - 154
Coastal Zone Enhancement Grants - 154, 289
Coastal Zone Management Act - 288-289, 312
Coastal Zone Management Fund - 154
Coats, Daniel R. R-Ind.
antismoking bills - 593
congressional elections, 1990 - 916
D.C. appropriations - 893
education proposals - 610, 613
family planning authorization - 605
food-waste transport - 382
NEA authorization - 431
NIH authorization - 601, 602
nutrition labels - 576
Persian Gulf crisis - 738
Coble, Howard R-N.C. (6)
congressional elections, 1990 - 908
Cobra helicopters - 700
Coca - 836
Cocaine - 502, 805
Cochran, Thad R-Miss.
congressional elections, 1990 - 916
congressional leadership - 9 (box), 10, 12
conservative coalition - 48
Energy, water appropriations - 865
farm bill - 338
fish inspection - 397
food aid cargo preference - 339 (box)
Labor/HHS appropriations - 853
library aid - 617
nutrition labels - 576
CoCom. *See Coordinating Committee on Multilateral Export Controls*
Coelho, Tony - 8, 10, 181, 448, 746, 923
Cogan, John - 607
Cohen, Herman J. - 789
Cohen, William S. R-Maine
B-2 bomber - 689, 690
campaign finance reform - 66
congressional elections, 1990 - 916
vote-share falloff - 904 (chart)
conservative coalition - 47
defense appropriations - 813, 821
farm bill - 351
flag desecration - 528
intelligence authorization - 791, 798, 799
Persian Gulf crisis - 724, 728, 735, 743
use-of-force debate - 753 (box)
textile import quotas - 220
VA/HUD appropriations - 859
Coins
Columbus commemorative - 197
redesign - 187, 189, 196-197
Coke ovens. *See Steel industry*
Coleman, E. Thomas R-Mo. (6)
congressional elections, 1990 - 906
low winning percentage - 906 (chart)
marginal vote share - 905 (chart)
NEA - 430-433, 873
rural development - 353-354
Taft Institute - 628
Coleman, William T. Jr. - 471
Collective bargaining agreements
housing costs aid - 659 (box)
Colleges and universities. *See also Black colleges; Student aid*
community service programs - 559, 561, 562
copyright infringement - 541, 542-543
developmental disabilities programs - 609
environmental education grants - 293
higher education appropriations - 849 (chart)
housing aid - 849 (chart)
immigration law revision - 481
Indian community colleges - 423
Japan-U.S. trade - 208
job discrimination - 623
literacy tutors in work-study - 611
middle-school teacher training - 613
peer review disclosure - 52
rape prevention - 507
research
acid rain - 267, 275
agricultural grants - 345
Alzheimer's disease - 599
defense fund earmarks - 812-813
Energy projects - 862-866
facilities - 126, 888
hydrogen-fuel vehicle - 273
injuries - 598
minerals - 442
NIH authorization - 601
tax credits - 160
toxic chemicals - 274
students' right-to-know - 613
tangible property donations - 158, 171
vocational education authorization - 621, 622
Collins, Barbara Rose - 916, 918 (chart), 923, 924 (chart), 926
Collins, Cardiss D-Ill. (7)
characteristics of Congress - 923, 924
minorities in Congress - 924 (chart)
Collins, John F. - 532, 533
Colombia
U.S. aid/drug control - 124, 502, 805-806, 836
Persian Gulf crisis - 740
Colon, Panama - 776
Colorado
community services block grants - 555
congressional term limit - 13-14, 902
Energy, water appropriations - 866
gubernatorial election, 1990 - 930
oil-shale lands - 316
radiation victims compensation - 590
wheat farming - 350
Colorado River - 300-301
Columbia - 434
Columbia Pictures - 223
Columbus, Christopher
commemorative coin - 197
quincentennial appropriations - 882 (chart)
Combest, Larry R-Texas (19)
conservative coalition - 47
Comets - 435
Commerce Department, U.S.
Antarctica protection - 305, 306
appropriations - 881-886
Caribbean tourism - 214
census count adjustment - 415, 930, 932
Clean Air Act economic impact - 274
clean coal technology - 267
coastal zone management - 154
disabled civil rights - 458
displaced defense workers - 683
economic growth reports - 162
export controls - 199-201
fish inspection - 396-399
Florida Keys protection - 303
foreign ownership of U.S. business - 222-225
Iraq-U.S. trade - 722, 724, 729
Nicaragua aid - 771
technology programs - 440
textile import quotas - 219
timber exports - 215
weather services user fees - 157
Commercial Motor Vehicle Safety Act of 1986 - 611
Commercial Space Launch Act - 157
Commercial State Bank (St.Paul) - 99
Commission for the Preservation of America's Heritage Abroad - 883 (chart)
Commission for the Study of International Migration and Cooperative Economic Development - 880 (chart)
Commission on Base Realignment and Closure - 693, 828
Commission on Immigration Reform - 483
Commission on National Service - 855 (chart)
Commission on Security and Cooperation in Europe - 800, 883 (chart)
Commission on the Bicentennial of the U.S. Constitution - 882 (chart)
Committee Against Torture - 806, 807
Committee for a Responsible Federal Budget - 134
Committee for Peace and Security in the Gulf - 746
Committee on Foreign Investment in the United States - 224, 225
Commodity Credit Corporation (CCC)
appropriations - 867, 868, 869 (chart)
budget action - 122
credit reform - 163, 178 (box)
crop insurance - 870
dairy price supports - 343
foreign food aid - 344, 345
Iraq trade sanctions - 722, 723, 724, 729
nutrition programs - 346
Commodity Futures Trading Commission (CFTC)
ALJ corps - 492
appropriations - 869 (chart)
authorization - 194-195
stock market regulation - 190-193
Commodity Supplemental Food Program - 346, 354
Common Cause
campaign finance reform - 57, 60, 64, 66-67 (box), 67
congressional pay, honoraria - 73
election costs - 909
Hatch Act revision - 408
savings and loan scandal - 80, 92
Communicable disease
child-care provider training - 153
disabled civil rights - 450, 451, 453, 461
immigration exclusion - 474, 480-481 (box), 484
notification of emergency workers - 587
TB prevention - 594
Communications. *See Radio; Telecommunications; Telephone communications; Television*
Communications Act of 1934 - 457, 376
Communist Party
U.S. immigration policy - 484
Community action agencies - 552, 555
Community-based health care. *See also Community health centers*
elderly, Alzheimer's authorization - 598
Medicaid coverage - 147, 569-571
mental health services - 599
Pepper Commission - 608
Community College Endowment Program - 423
Community colleges
student loans - 143
student right-to-know - 625
vocational education authorization - 619-623
Community development
appropriations - 855 (chart)

HUD pork-barrel spending - 857 (box)
displaced defense workers - 683
housing programs overhaul - 643, 647, 651
HUD scandal investigation - 667
rural health care - 595-596
Community Development Block Grant (CDBG) program
budget action - 123
census count adjustment - 415, 416
housing programs overhaul - 632, 639, 641, 655-656
Indian legislation - 423
Community education employment centers - 621, 623
Community Food and Nutrition Program - 552, 555, 556
Community health centers
AIDS bill - 583, 584, 586, 587
hospitals - 143
mental health centers - 145
minority health - 596
Community Housing Partnership program - 634, 638, 642, 646
Community service
national service demonstrations - 559-562
summary - 5
volunteer programs - 559-562
Community Services Block Grant (CSBG) program
authorization - 552-556
budget action - 123
Commuter rail
disabled civil rights - 453-455, 460
Conrail line use liability - 390
Compensated Work Therapy program - 420
Compensatory education aid
appropriations - 848 (chart), 849, 851, 853
budget action - 123
education proposals - 613, 615
nationwide assessment - 615
social support services - 613
Competition and monopoly. *See also Antitrust law; Competitiveness*
Air Force satellites - 684
airport slots - 386, 388
alternative power regulation - 317
Baby Bell restrictions - 377-379
cable TV regulation - 370-372
defense procurement - 816-817, 818, 823, 824
university research funds - 812, 813
federal contractors - 859
federal pay overhaul - 405
insurance price-sharing - 401 (box)
Medicaid drug discounts - 570 (box)
orphan drugs - 577-579
prison industries - 498
product liability - 400
strategic materials - 203
textiles - 210, 219, 221
vertical price fixing - 539
Competitive medical plans - 146
Competitiveness
agricultural trade - 210, 325
grain quality - 337
wheat exports - 350, 351
Bush economic report - 117
Caribbean Basin Initiative - 214
Clean Air Act impact - 234, 236, 274
coin redesign - 196
education
adult literacy - 610, 615
Head Start authorization - 552-553
math, science scholarships - 612 (box)
vocational education - 619, 622
emerging technologies - 440
export controls - 198
foreign military sales offsets - 203
foreign ownership of U.S. business - 223
immigration law revision - 474
intelligence authorization - 796
Japan-U.S. SII talks - 208
joint production ventures - 541
Mexico-U.S. trade - 218
product liability - 401
radio spectrum allocation - 376
SSC authorization - 439
tax policy - 167
telecommunications - 378
uranium enrichment - 310-311
Competitiveness Policy Council - 881 (chart)
Comprehensive Anti-Apartheid Act - 788
Comprehensive Child Development Centers - 552, 556
Comprehensive Homeless Assistance Plan (CHAP) - 655
Compressed natural gas - 240 (box)
Comptroller general. *See General Accounting Office*
Comptroller of the Currency
bank regulation - 186
Computers
congressional use - 11, 12 (box)
copyright - 205, 209
defense appropriations - 821
drug enforcement - 679
Energy, water appropriations - 866
export controls - 198, 201, 885
IRS tax compliance - 888, 889
Japan-U.S. trade - 208
rural development - 347, 352
software copyright - 523, 541, 542
South Africa sanctions - 787
supercomputer authorization - 441
telemarketing fraud - 402
training
employers of foreign workers - 478
math, science scholarships - 612 (box)
public housing support services - 650
Concurrent resolutions
Armenian genocide commemoration - 807
trade law procedures - 205, 211, 213
Condit, Gary D-Calif. (15)
job training overhaul - 367
Conference committees
addresses by non-members - 880
motions to instruct - 460
Conference of Mayors, U.S. - 371
Conference on Security and Cooperation in Europe (CSCE)
congressional observers - 800
permanent staff - 702, 703
Soviet participation - 702
Confidentiality. *See Information access and classification*
Conflict of interest. *See Congressional ethics; Ethics in government*
Congress, members of. *See also Congressional elections; Congressional ethics; Congressional mail; Congressional pay; House of Representatives; Incumbents; Senate*
changes, 101st Cong., 2nd sess. - 14 (chart)
characteristics, 101st Cong., 2nd sess. - 902 (chart)
characteristics, 102nd Cong. - 923-926
age - (chart) 923, 924-925
minorities - 923-924, (chart) 924
occupation - 925-926, (chart) 925
religion - (chart) 925, 926
women - 923, 924
constituent service - 83, 94
group ratings, 1990 - 22B-30B
list, 101st Cong., 2nd sess. - xiv-xv
party lineup, 101st, 102nd Cong. - 901 (chart)
revision of remarks - 105-106
roll call attendance - 48
Speech or Debate clause - 511 (box)
term limitation - 13-15
Congress, U.S. *See also Congress, members of; Congressional committees; Congressional districts; Congressional-executive relations; Congressional-judicial relations; Congressional staff and employees; Congressional votes; General Accounting Office; House of Representatives; Library of Congress; Senate*
leadership
101st Cong. - 8-10
102nd Cong. - 10, 12, 924
legislative branch appropriations - 894-897
public approval rating - 3, 5 (chart)
Congressional Black Caucus - 128, 788, 789
Congressional Biomedical Ethics Board - 601
Congressional Budget and Impoundment Act of 1974 - 175-176
Congressional Budget Office (CBO)
ALJ corps - 523
appropriations - 895 (chart)
barrier island protection - 303
budget process changes - 161, 166, 177, 178
budget summit - 130
campaign finance reform - 64
deficit projections - 114, 126, 127, 130
disabled civil rights - 458
Egypt debt relief - 732
FAA operations - 878
farm price supports - 340
FDIC premiums - 185, 186
federal credit reform - 163
federal pay overhaul - 406
federal retirement benefits - 407 (box)
government-sponsored enterprises - 163
housing programs overhaul - 633, 642
inflation rates - 328
Medicaid expansion - 571
Micmac tribal recognition - 424
pension reversions - 368
rural development - 353
Social Security earnings test - 557
thrift bailout - 184
veterans benefits - 156
Congressional Caucus for Women's Issues - 602
Congressional committees
chair re-elections - 901, 904
immunity - 534-535
jurisdiction conflicts
Antarctica protection - 306
campaign finance reform - 68-69
child-care aid - 548-551
clean air fees - 244
EPA Cabinet status - 291, 292
export controls - 198-200
fish inspection - 396, 398
job training overhaul - 365-366
State Department authorization - 800
leadership - 8, 11 (box)
legislative intent - 54
referral bypass - 591
Congressional districts
House members, 102nd Cong., by state (chart) - 920-921
redistricting - 930-933
Brennan career - 510 (box)
Civil Rights Division budget - 125
congressional elections, 1990 - 903
congressional mail - 74
gubernatorial elections, 1990 - 927
key states (chart) - 931
Legal Services Corporation - 533
teacher awards - 613
Congressional elections. *See also Campaign finance*
congressional partisanship - 32-40
costs, 1990 - 908-909, 923
D.C. "shadow" delegation - 428
franking privilege - 73, 75
incumbents' woes - 903-908
Indian voting - 421
issues, 1990
abortion - 528, 530, 852, 903, 919
auto fuel efficiency - 281
budget and taxes - 111, 130, 166, 901, 902-903, 911, 917
civil rights/job bias - 473
Clean Air Act - 245, 278
congressional pay, honoraria - 71
crime - 487, 488 (box), 494, 496, 497
deposit insurance - 185
drug enforcement - 502
ethics cases - 103, 104, 106, 107, 108
farm policy - 348
financial institution fraud - 182
flag desecration - 55, 524-528
Medicare changes - 566
NEA authorization - 431
Pepper Commission - 608
Persian Gulf crisis - 919
rural development - 352
savings and loan scandal - 80
thrift bailout - 181
open House seats - 919, 922
results, 1990 - 901-903
returns (chart) - 935-941
roll call attendance - 48
sophomore surge - 908
summary - 3
totals, 1990 (chart) - 907
Congressional ethics
D'Amato case - 97
disciplined senators, 20th c. - 99 (box)
Durenberger case - 98-103
Dyson case - 108
Fauntroy case - 107
financial institution fraud - 183, 495
Flake indictment - 106
Ford trial - 107
Frank case - 102-103
Garcia conviction - 107
Gingrich case - 104-105
House elections - 917
key votes - 11-B
Lukens resignation - 106
resignations, 101st Cong. - 106
Savage case - 105-106
savings and loan scandal - 78-97
appearance standard - 87 (box)
Senate leadership - 12
Sikorski case - 108
Stangeland case - 107
summary - 3, 4, 6
terms of opprobrium - 100 (box)
Congressional-executive relations. *See also Vetoes*
absent appropriations - 163
budget process - 137, 175-176
budget summit - 8
civil rights/job bias - 471
Clean Air Act - 229, 230-231, 278-279
congressional term limit - 13
defense authorization - 687
export controls - 198-199, 799
farm bill - 348
federal pay overhaul - 405-407, 886, 890
foreign aid flexibility - 773
foreign policy

Andean Initiative - 805
Antarctica protection - 305-307
chemical weapons pact - 709, 711
Chinese student visas - 767 (box)
covert actions - 791-792, 795, 796, 797-799
Food for Peace - 803-804
State Department authorization - 799
HUD project earmarking - 858-860
legislative intent - 52, 54, 55 (box)
oversight function
federal financial centralization - 416
HUD scandal investigation - 668
OMB review powers - 411-413, 889
savings and loan crisis - 86, 89-90
whistleblower protection - 683
Persian Gulf crisis - 719-756
summary - 3
war powers suit - 739 (box)
pocket vetoes - 21-22
presidential support in Congress - 16-31
secret defense programs - 812
thrift bailout - 179-184
water projects authorization - 297-298

Congressional-judicial relations
Brennan career - 510-511 (box)
environmental law compliance - 296
federal court caseload management - 520-523
judicial appointments - 516
Souter confirmation - 508, 509, 514

Congressional mail
franking privilege - 65, 68, 73-75
Gingrich ethics case - 105
legislative branch appropriations - 894-897

Congressional pay
outside income - 71, 72
Gingrich ethics case - 105
salary, honoraria - 71-73
Durenberger ethics case - 98-101

Congressional Record - 105-106

Congressional Research Service
alternative power regulation - 317
appropriations - 895 (chart)
congressional disciplinary terms - 100 (box)
Medigap plans - 572
vocational education - 619

Congressional staff and employees
civil rights/job bias - 467, 468, 469
disabled civil rights - 447, 451, 458-461
ethics cases
Dyson - 108
Fauntroy - 107
Sikorski - 108
family leave - 359
honoraria - 72 (box)
legislative branch appropriations - 894, 895

Congressional Textile Caucus - 212

Congressional votes
cloture votes, 1990 (chart) - 7
conservative coalition - 40-48
group ratings, 1990 - 22B-30B
House Journal approval - 39
House Speaker - 527, 795
key votes - 3B-13B
motions to instruct - 460
participation study - 49-51
party unity analysis - 32-40
Persian Gulf force authorization
House - 750-751 (box)
Senate - 749 (box)
presidential support, 1990 - 22-31
recorded votes
attendance - 48
totals, 1973-90 (table) - 4

Connally, John B. Jr. - 78

Connecticut
corporate campaign limits - 59 (box)
defense sales - 643
federal judgeships - 522
gubernatorial election, 1990 - 902, 907, 919, 928

Conover, David - 500

Conrad, Kent D-N.D.
budget process - 177
community service programs - 561
defense appropriations - 820-821
defense authorization - 678
farm bill - 324, 334-335
flag desecration - 528

Conrail
line use liability - 390, 391

Conservation. *See also Energy conservation; Forests and wood products; Soil conservation; Wetlands preservation; Wildlife refuges*
community service programs - 561, 562
debt-for-nature swaps - 778, 779

Conservation and Renewable Energy Reserve - 262

Conservation Reserve Program (CRP) - 326, 336, 346, 349, 867, 869 (chart)

Conservation Stewardship Program - 336

Conservative Caucus - 513

Conservative coalition
vote study - 40-48

Conservative Democratic Forum - 48

Conservative Party - 907, 934

Considine, Terry - 13, 15

Consistency provision - 154

Constituent service - 83, 94

Constitution, U.S. *See also Civil rights and liberties; Congressional-executive relations; Constitutional amendments; Separation of powers; specific amendments*
bicentennial commission appropriations - 882 (chart)
coin redesign themes - 196
congressional term limit - 13-15
D.C. status - 428
education about - 613
foreign policy, war powers - 736, 738, 739 (box), 800
militia clauses - 694 (box)
treaties - 807

Constitutional amendments. *See also specific amendments*
proposed amendments
balanced budget - 47, 173, 174-175 (box), 868
congressional term limit - 15
flag desecration ban - 6-7, 40, 524-528
line-item veto - 16, 173, 177
school prayer - 618 (box)

Construction industry
Davis-Bacon issues - 647, 656
foreign contract discrimination - 830, 866
vehicle emissions - 233 (box)

Consultants
HUD scandal investigation - 667-668

Consumer affairs. *See also Consumer interest groups; Consumer protection; Labeling and packaging*
air passenger facility fees - 386
auto fuel efficiency - 280-281
Baby Bell restrictions - 378
cable TV regulation - 370
Clean Air Act
costs - 278
non-polluting products - 239, 250
foreign banks - 189
insurance "tying" - 401
Medigap plans - 572-575
nutrition labels - 575-576
sugar price supports - 331
telemarketing fraud - 402
telephone operator services - 378
textile import quotas - 219-222
vertical price fixing - 539

Consumer Affairs, Office of - 855

Consumer Federation of America - 371, 398, 659

Consumer interest groups
Baby Bell restrictions - 378
congressional pay, honoraria - 71
CPSC authorization - 393-395
FHA rules revision - 659
fish inspection - 396, 397, 398
Medigap plans - 572
nutrition labels - 575-576
pesticide exports - 336
product liability - 400-401
RICO revision - 536-538

Consumer Price Index
projections - 328

Consumer Product Safety Commission (CPSC)
antismoking bills - 592
appropriations - 855, 855 (chart)
authorization - 393-395
fire-safe cigarettes - 402

Consumer protection
fastener standards - 395
fire-safe cigarettes - 402
fish inspection - 396-399
manufactured homes - 638
medical devices - 579-581
pesticide residue in food - 358
product liability - 400-401

Consumers Union - 401, 572, 574, 658, 659

Contact lenses - 580

Conte, Silvio O. R-Mass. (1)
appropriations
agriculture - 811
continuing resolutions - 897
Energy, water appropriations - 862, 863
Labor/HHS - 847, 850, 853
legislative branch - 894
Treasury, Postal - 887-888
Antarctica protection - 305
budget action - 130 (box)
drug treatment programs - 504
energy taxes - 313 (box)
farm bill - 332
NEA authorization - 432-433
NIH authorization - 603
session summary - 3

Continuing resolutions
budget action - 112, 137
congressional action, 1990 - 896-897 (box)
short-term appropriations - 811

Contraception. *See Birth control*

Contras (Nicaragua) - 770-774

Convention Against Torture and Other Cruel, Inhuman or Degrading Treatment or Punishment - 806-807

Convention on the Regulation of Antarctic Mineral Resource Activities - 305, 306

Conventional forces in Europe (CFE) treaty
action, 1990 - 696-704
weapons impact (chart) - 697
congressional observers - 800
German unification - 763
Soviet-U.S. relations - 757, 758
START - 705, 707

Conyers, John Jr. D-Mich. (1)
EPA Cabinet status - 292
federal financial centralization - 416
fish inspection - 398
flag desecration - 525
"hate crime" statistics - 507
minorities in Congress - 924 (chart)
"motor voter" bill - 70
OMB review powers - 412-413
RICO revision - 538
state grant funds transfers - 414
Treasury, Postal appropriations - 886, 888

Cook, Kenneth A. - 335, 348-349

Cooley, Claudia - 406

Cooper, Jim D-Tenn. (4)
cable TV regulation - 370, 372
Clean Air Act - 238, 244, 245
FHA rules revision - 660
flag desecration - 527
telephone operator services - 378 (box)

Coordinating Committee on Multilateral Export Controls (CoCom) - 198, 200, 201

Copyright
art - 520, 523, 541-542
computer software - 523, 541, 542
Czechoslovak-U.S. trade - 206
fees - 541, 543
GATT talks - 209
Soviet-U.S. trade - 205
tribunal commissioners - 541, 543
university infringement - 542-543

Copyright Office - 543

Copyright Royalty Tribunal - 541, 543, 895 (chart)

Coral reefs - 303

Corn
deficit reduction - 344
disposable diapers - 336
ethanol - 216, 234, 240 (box), 241
GATT talks - 210
grain quality - 337
price supports - 325-327, 333, 337, 340, 342, 348, 350

Corn sweeteners - 328

Cornell University - 400, 401

Corporal punishment - 617

Corporate Average Fuel Economy (CAFE) levels - 279-281

Corporation for Public Broadcasting - 849 (chart)

Corporations. *See Business and industry*

Corr, Bill - 579

Corrado, Ernest J. - 283, 285

Correctional institutions. *See Prisons and prisoners*

CORRTEX - 711-712, 713

Cosmetic surgery - 158

Costa Rica
Caribbean Basin Initiative - 212
U.S. ambassador - 801 (box)

Cotton
deficit reduction - 344
China-U.S. trade - 765
price supports - 325-327, 333-334, 337, 340, 342

Cough and cold remedies - 146

Coughlin, Lawrence R-Pa. (13)
HUD pork-barrel spending - 857 (box)

Council for a Livable World - 40, 710

Council of Economic Advisers - 887 (chart)

Council of Large Public Housing Authorities - 636

Council on Clean Air Compliance Analysis - 274

Council on Competitiveness - 579

Council on Environmental Quality - 855 (chart)

Counterfeiting - 189

Courter, Jim R-N.J. (12)
congressional elections, 1990 - 923
House membership changes - 918 (chart)
defense authorization - 682
naval home ports - 681 (box)

Courts. *See also Alternative dispute resolution; Appeals courts; District courts; Federal courts; Supreme Court*
obscenity in art - 430-433, 870-875
Cowper, Steve -927
Cox, Archibald - 534
Cox, Carol - 134
Cox, John W. Jr. - 905 (chart), 916, 918 (chart), 922
Coxe, Trudy - 918 (chart), 922
Coyne, Jim - 15
CPSC. *See Consumer Product Safety Commission*
Crack babies - 679
CRAFT-Cassini space probes - 436
Craig, Larry E. R-Idaho (1)
characteristics of Congress - 925
congressional elections, 1990 - 913, 922
House membership changes - 918 (chart)
Senate membership changes - 913 (chart)
Frank ethics case - 104
strategic minerals research - 442-443
Cramer, Bud - 918 (chart)
Crane, Philip M. R-Ill. (12)
China-U.S. relations - 766
Commerce/Justice/State appropriations - 884
NEA authorization - 433
Cranston, Alan D-Calif.
airline rights - 389 (box)
children's TV advertising - 374
coin redesign - 196, 197
congressional leadership - 9 (box), 12
defense authorization - 679
FHA rules revision - 657, 658, 660
housing programs overhaul - 632, 636, 640, 656
irrigation subsidies - 357
prepayment of subsidized mortgages - 662-664
Saudi arms sales - 735 (box)
savings and loan scandal - 6, 78-97
Souter confirmation - 515
veterans issues - 418, 420
Cranston-Gonzalez National Affordable Housing Act - 631-656, 657
Credit bureaus - 613
Credit cards
telemarketing fraud - 881
Credit unions
housing programs overhaul - 646
money laundering - 188
Crime and criminals. *See also Capital punishment; Courts; Drug-related crime; Drug-trafficking; Fraud; Juvenile delinquents; Money laundering; Police and law enforcement agencies; Prisons and prisoners; Sex crimes*
animal rights activists - 441-442
anticrime bill - 6, 486-499
appropriations - 884, 885, 886
boxscore - 486
congressional partisanship - 32
conservative coalition - 40
provisions - 499
asset forfeiture - 495, 498, 499
environmental disasters - 285 (box)
foreign aid
detection equipment export controls - 785
Salvadoran system failures - 781
handgun wait period - 501
"hate crime" statistics - 506-507
immigration law revision - 474, 477, 479, 484, 485
intentional HIV transmission - 586
mandatory sentences - 521
organized crime drug enforcement - 882 (chart)
public housing evictions - 639, 650
RICO revision - 7, 536-538
student right-to-know - 624-627
Supreme Court on evidence - 53
victims
compensation - 150, 495
information access - 493
rights - 498
Crime Control Act of 1990 - 486-499
Crime insurance - 143
Cristiani, Alfredo - 780, 781, 784-786, 839-840, 841
Crockett, George W. Jr. D-Mich. (13)
characteristics of Congress - 925
congressional elections, 1990
House membership changes - 918 (chart)
flag desecration - 525
Panama-Africa aid - 776
supplemental appropriations - 845
Cronin, John - 106
Crop insurance
agriculture appropriations - 867, 868, 870
budget action - 123
budget process changes - 163
farm bill - 326, 346
Crotone air base - 678, 682, 687, 826-827, 828-829
Crowe, William J. Jr. - 720, 742
Cruise missiles
B-2 bomber - 690
defense authorization - 675
long-range radar defense - 817
START - 704-708
Cruz, Arturo - 770
Cruzan, Nancy - 566-567 (box)
Cuba
Angola policies - 793
Persian Gulf crisis - 739, 740
TV Marti appropriations - 881, 884, 886
U.S. export controls - 201
U.S. sugar quotas - 328
Cunningham, Randy "Duke" - 905 (chart), 918 (chart)
Cuomo, Mario M. - 465 (box), 681 (box), 904 (chart), 907, 926, 931, 933
Currency. *See also Coins*
counterfeiting - 189
electronic scanning - 499
Currency exchange
Czechoslovak-U.S. trade - 206
Mexico-U.S. border businesses - 188-189
Soviet-U.S. trade - 205
Currency transaction reports - 187, 188
Curtis, Clifton E. - 283, 285
Customs and Trade Act of 1990 - 157, 205, 211-217
Customs duties
changes, 1990 - 212
Puerto Rico status - 427
Customs Forfeiture Fund - 157, 212
Customs Service, U.S.
appropriations - 887 (chart), 889
assault weapons ban - 495, 500
authorization - 211, 212
Caribbean tourism - 214
congressional intervention - 94
drug interdiction - 504
employee drug testing - 505
fees - 156-157, 212
small user-fee airports - 157
Cyclosporine - 597
Cyprus
U.S. aid - 831, 835
Czechoslovakia
CFE - 697, 698, 703
Havel visit - 204 (box)
Soviet-U.S. relations - 757
START - 707
U.S. aid - 204 (box), 836
U.S. trade - 204, 205-206
duty rates - 212
export controls - 199

D

Dairy. *See Milk and dairy products*
Daley, Richard M. - 387
Dallas, Texas - 582
D'Amato, Alfonse M. R-N.Y.
China-U.S. relations - 765
Chinese student visas - 767 (box)
Clean Air Act - 238
community service programs - 561
crime bill - 492-493
defense appropriations - 821
defense authorization - 679
diplomatic nominations - 801 (box)
drug testing - 505, 506
Dunne nomination - 465 (box)
El Salvador aid - 786
ethics case - 97
FHA rules revision - 657, 658
Hatch Act revision - 408
housing programs overhaul - 632, 635-637, 640-641, 656
Labor/HHS appropriations - 851
Panama aid - 777
Persian Gulf crisis - 724, 726
stock market regulation - 193
Transportation appropriations - 880
Dana, Howard H. Jr. - 532
Danforth, John C. R-Mo.
auto fuel efficiency - 281
cable TV regulation - 370-372
campaign finance reform - 60, 62, 67 (box)
civil rights/job bias - 467, 473
defense appropriations - 813
Japan-U.S. trade - 209
living wills - 566 (box)
NASA authorization - 435
Nicaragua policy debate - 772 (box)
NIH director - 602 (box)
Persian Gulf crisis
use-of-force debate - 752 (box)
product liability - 401
Thomas confirmation - 518-519 (box)
Danforth, William H. - 602 (box)
Dannemeyer, William E. R-Calif. (39)
AIDS bill - 582, 587-588
budget action - 128
Clean Air Act - 242
Commerce/Justice/State appropriations - 884
congressional elections, 1990 - 907
CPSC authorization - 394-395
disabled civil rights - 449, 450, 451, 461
Energy, water appropriations - 864
flag desecration - 525
Frank ethics case - 104
handgun wait period - 501
"hate crime" statistics - 533
housing programs overhaul - 642
Medicaid expansion - 571
radiation victims compensation - 591
South Africa sanctions - 789
VA/HUD appropriations - 855
vocational education authorization - 623
Darby, Michael R. - 224
Darden, George "Buddy" D-Ga. (7)
Frank ethics case - 104
DARE. *See Drug Abuse Resistance Education*
Darman, Richard G.
balanced-budget amendment - 175 (box)
budget action - 112-113
chronology - 114
proposal - 127
resolution - 127, 138
summit - 130-134
budget process changes - 176
child-care aid - 550
EPA Cabinet status - 292-293
farm bill - 331
federal credit reform - 178 (box)
FHA rules revision - 658
housing programs overhaul - 636, 640
OMB review powers - 412-413
Treasury, Postal appropriations - 888, 890
Daschle, Tom D-S.D.
campaign finance reform - 63
Clean Air Act - 238
congressional partisanship - 32
farm bill - 324, 326, 333-334, 337, 340, 341, 351
Indian legislation - 423
Daub, Hal - 913
Davidson, Roger H. - 48
Davis, Aaron C. - 107
Davis-Bacon Act issues - 656
Davis, James - 608
Davis, Michele - 926
Davis, Robert W. R-Mich. (11)
B-2 bomber - 688
oil pollution cleanup - 284
Dawson, Brennan - 593, 594
Day care. *See Adult day care; Child care*
Dayton, Wash. - 858
DCC. *See Development Coordination Committee*
DCCC. *See Democratic Congressional Campaign Committee*
Deaf. *See Hearing impaired*
Dean, Deborah Gore - 666, 667
Death
right to die - 52, 53, 55
Death penalty. *See Capital punishment*
Deaver, Michael K. - 533
DeConcini, Dennis D-Ariz.
balanced-budget amendment - 175 (box)
Caribbean Basin Initiative - 216
Clean Air Act - 236
copyright issues - 542, 543
crime bill - 491-493
defense authorization - 679
federal pay overhaul - 407
Grand Canyon erosion - 301
immigration law revision - 479
juvenile justice nomination - 506
RICO revision - 536-538
savings and loan scandal - 6, 78-97
Souter confirmation - 514
space patent law - 437
Treasury, Postal appropriations - 889-890
vertical price fixing - 540
DeFazio, Peter A. D-Ore. (4)
budget action - 136
Eastern Airlines strike - 369
farm bill - 332-333
Defense Advanced Research Projects Agency - 440
Defense Budget Project - 675
Defense Cooperation Fund - 733
Defense Department, U.S. (DOD)
administration
budget reprogramming - 676 (box), 845
federal retirement benefits - 407 (box)
non-appropriated fund employees - 155
overhead costs reductions - 673 (box)
RCRA compliance - 293, 308
research funds policy - 812, 813-814

scientist, engineer salaries - 679
appropriations
FY90 supplemental - 844-846
FY91 - 812-822
boxscore - 812
budget authority totals (chart) - 813
provisions - 824-825
weapons funding (chart) - 815
military construction - 826-830
arms control
CFE - 703, 707
chemical weapons - 709
nuclear test treaties - 713
authorization - 671-687
boxscore - 671
intelligence programs - 799
provisions - 684-686
budget action - 122, 127, 129, 135
bases
closings - 678, 682, 693-695
displaced workers - 683
environmental cleanup - 675, 679-680
land acquisitions, sales - 678
military construction appropriations - 826-830
naval home ports - 681 (box)
drug interdiction
Andean Initiative - 805
appropriations - 816
budget action - 122
crime bill - 504
defense authorization - 673, 675, 679
export controls - 199, 200, 201
foreign aid
excess weapons - 843
military personnel
Noriega ouster - 775
training - 288
VA medical research grants - 421
procurement policy - 678-679, 680, 682
contractor fraud - 683
strategic materials - 202-203
radio spectrum allocation - 376
weapons and aircraft
B-2 bomber - 688
SDI - 691-693
Defense Management Review project - 673 (box), 675
Defense policy. *See also Arms control; Defense Department; Military personnel; Military posts; specific armed services*
air toxics standards exemptions - 257
allied burden-sharing
defense appropriations - 820-821, 825
defense authorization - 682, 686
military construction appropriations - 827, 828, 830
appropriations deferrals - 20-21
authorization - 17
Bush State of the Union address - 20
conservative coalition - 40, 47
displaced worker aid - 277 (box)
energy issues, 1990 - 312
export controls - 198-201
foreign ownership of U.S. business - 224, 225
ozone-depleting chemicals - 270
presidential support in Congress - 30
radio spectrum allocation - 376-377
strategic materials - 202-203, 442-443
strategic weapons triad - 688
summary - 5
Defense Production Act - 189, 202-203
Defoliants. *See Agent Orange*
de Klerk, F. W. - 787, 788, 789
de la Garza, E. "Kika" D-Texas (15)
agriculture appropriations - 868
farm bill - 327, 331-333, 347-351
fish inspection - 398
minorities in Congress - 924 (chart)
DeLauro, Rosa - 905 (chart), 916, 918 (chart), 923, 924 (chart)
Delaware
congressional mail - 75
offshore drilling - 871
water projects authorization - 300
DeLay, Tom R-Texas (22)
budget action - 132
family leave - 359
Interior appropriations - 872
DelliBovi, Alfred A. - 633, 634, 660, 667-668
Dellums, Ronald V. D-Calif. (8)
B-2 bomber - 689-691
defense authorization - 677, 687
intelligence authorization - 792, 796
minorities in Congress - 924 (chart)
SDI - 693
South Africa sanctions - 788, 789
war powers suit - 739 (box)
de Lugo, Ron D-Virgin Islands
minorities in Congress - 924 (chart)
Palau autonomy - 808
Puerto Rico status - 424, 427
De Mars, Lewis - 918 (chart)
Dementias - 598
Demery, Thomas T. - 667
Democratic Caucus, House
budget action - 165-166
defense authorization - 676-677
independent members - 922 (box)
Intelligence Committee tenure - 799
leadership changes - 11 (box)
Persian Gulf crisis - 742-743
thrift bailout - 181
Democratic Caucus, Senate
campaign finance reform - 61
Democratic Congressional Campaign Committee (DCCC) - 904, 917
Democratic Governors' Association - 926
Democratic Leadership Council - 131
Democratic National Committee
congressional elections, 1990 - 902
congressional redistricting - 931
"motor voter" bill - 69-70
RNC chair - 910
Democratic Party
congressional leadership - 9-10
congressional partisanship - 32-40
congressional redistricting - 930-933
South African political training - 789
Democratic Policy Committee, Senate - 32
Democratic Senatorial Campaign Committee - 63, 93, 487, 911
Demonstration Partnership Agreement Addressing the Needs of the Poor - 556
Demonstrations. *See Protests, demonstrations etc.*
Dempsey, Charles L. - 668
Dennison, Joan Louise - 918 (chart)
Dental care and dentists
HIV demonstration project - 148
VA salaries - 126, 419-420
Department. *See other part of name*
Dependent-care tax credit - 152, 547-551
Deportation
criminal aliens - 479, 484
drugs, violent crime - 486
family unity of legalized aliens - 475-479, 483
farm worker families - 476
marriage fraud waivers - 484
procedures - 476, 484, 485
temporary protected status - 478, 483, 484
Salvadorans - 474, 478, 479, 484, 485
Deposit insurance
budget accounting - 162, 174
budget action - 123, 134, 141, 164
FDIC premiums - 184-187
federal credit reform - 163
money laundering - 187, 188
reform plan - 185
risk-based premiums - 186
De Priest, Oscar - 923
Deregulation. *See Regulation and deregulation*
Derrick, Butler D-S.C. (3)
pocket veto power - 22
Derwinski, Edward J.
Agent Orange compensation - 418
Developing countries. *See also Agency for International Development; International development banks; Third World debt*
child welfare - 832, 837
environmental protection - 218, 778
global warming - 307
ozone-layer depletion - 270, 271
tropical forest preservation - 773, 779, 837
Ex-Im Bank arms loans - 200, 656
food aid - 345, 803
GATT talks - 209, 210
missile-launch defense - 692
Persian Gulf crisis - 741
textile import quotas - 219
tobacco markets - 593
U.S. development aid
appropriations - 831, 836, 843
authorization - 771, 780, 790
Development Coordination Committee (DCC) - 804
Developmental disabilities - 609
DeWine, Mike R-Ohio (7)
assault weapons ban - 501 (box)
congressional elections, 1990
House membership changes - 918 (chart)
immigration law revision - 478
De Witt, Bill - 918 (chart)
Diabetes - 583, 596, 600
Diamond, Gary L. - 100-101
Dickinson, Bill R-Ala. (2)
B-2 bomber - 689, 691
congressional elections, 1990 - 917, 919
marginal vote share - 905 (chart)
defense authorization - 677, 683
export controls - 199
Dickman, Murray G. - 517, 519
Dicks, Norm D-Wash. (6)
defense appropriations - 814
Interior appropriations - 871
Persian Gulf crisis - 743
Transportation appropriations - 878
Diefenderfer, William M. III - 732
Diego Garcia - 814, 826
Diesel fuel - 252, 266
Dietary guidelines - 355
Dingell, John D. D-Mich. (16)
Amtrak authorization - 391
Amtrak waste disposal - 392
auto fuel efficiency - 281
campaign TV ad rates - 66-67 (box)
Clean Air Act - 229, 230, 231, 238-247, 275, 278
D.C. appropriations - 893
disabled civil rights - 449
fastener standards - 395
fish inspection - 398-399
food-waste transport - 383
NIH authorization - 604
nutrition labels - 576
Persian Gulf crisis - 752
radio spectrum allocation - 376-377
Dinkins, David N. - 415, 681
DiPrete, Edward D. - 569, 904 (chart), 922, 926, 928
Dire Emergency Supplemental Appropriations Act
congressional action - 844-846
boxscore - 845
Nicaragua aid - 770-774
Panama aid - 774, 777-779
Disability Rights Education and Defense Fund - 447
Disabled persons. *See also Blind persons; Disabled veterans; Hearing impaired; Mental retardation*
age discrimination - 364
barrier removal tax incentives - 160, 172
child support enforcement - 149
civil rights protection - 5, 447-461
boxscore - 447
key votes - 6-B
provisions - 452-459
Transportation appropriations - 879
community service programs - 561
definition - 452
developmental disabilities - 609
disability prevention - 589
education - 54-55, 615
appropriations - 848 (chart)
authorization - 616-617
funding - 562
Head Start - 552
math, science scholarships - 612 (box)
vocational education - 619-623
farmers - 869
home, community-based elderly care - 147, 608, 609
housing programs - 125, 631-656, 854, 857
Medicaid expansion - 570
Pepper Commission - 607
rehabilitation research - 604
SBA authorization - 395
Social Security
appeals - 557
definition - 150
trial work period - 151
widows' benefits - 558
SSI - 150
Supreme Court decisions - 54-55
Disabled veterans
Agent Orange compensation - 418
COLA raises - 155, 418, 419
education services - 421
federal hiring preference - 421
pensions - 421
vocational rehabilitation - 156
Disadvantaged. *See Poverty*
Disaster relief
appropriations
agriculture - 867, 868
foreign aid - 832, 835, 837
FY 1990 supplemental - 845, 846
VA/HUD - 856
farm aid - 123, 326, 328, 343, 346
Food for Peace - 803
housing aid authorization - 656
hurricane damage aid - 778, 845
job subsidies - 365-367
school impact aid - 852
tree-planting aid - 346
Discovery Channel - 371
Discrimination. *See also Age discrimination; Discrimination in employment; Racial discrimination; Religious discrimination; Sex discrimination*
AIDS bill - 583
air travel - 390 (box)
bank mortgage rules - 649
disabled persons - 5, 447-461
public accommodations - 455-457

public services - 453-454
transportation - 454-455
fair housing - 647, 656
library meeting space - 617
national service - 560
Discrimination in employment. *See also Affirmative action; Whistleblower protection*
academic tenure - 623
age bias
protection - 54, 362-364
Thomas confirmation - 518 (box)
civil rights bill - 6, 54, 462-473
boxscore - 462
veto message (text) - 472
congressional leadership - 8
congressional partisanship - 32
disabled civil rights - 447-461
Dunne nomination - 465 (box)
fetal protection - 56, 465
foreign workers - 479, 484, 485
hiring quotas - 462-464, 466, 467, 470, 472
political patronage - 52, 53, 54
religious preference - 453
sectarian child-care providers - 153-154, 549, 551
Souter confirmation - 514
Supreme Court decisions - 53, 463
Displaced homemakers
housing program overhaul - 647
job training authorization - 366 (box)
vocational education authorization - 619, 620
Distilled spirits. *See Alcoholic beverages*
District courts, U.S.
appropriations - 883 (chart)
decisions
census count adjustment - 415, 932
civil suits against terrorists - 830
executive branch honoraria - 72 (box)
federal RCRA compliance - 308
flag desecration - 524
obscenity ban compliance - 433
presidential war powers - 737, 738, 739 (box)
student religious groups - 618 (box)
thrift bailout - 180 (box)
judges
judicial appointments - 516, 517
new judgeships - 6, 520-523
jurisdiction
Clean Air Act enforcement - 273
disabled civil rights - 457
habeas corpus appeals - 487-488, 490
naturalization - 483-484
District of Columbia
abortion - 7, 528, 530-531, 811, 846
death penalty link - 846, 852
AIDS relief - 582
air travel
slot allocation - 384-388
Soviet air service - 759
appropriations - 891-893
boxscore - 891
budget authority totals (chart) - 892
community service programs - 561
federal government shutdown - 137
federal support for arts - 430
GWU emergency, trauma care - 598
housing projects - 647, 857, 859, 860
judicial appointments - 515
mayor, "shadow" delegation - 428-429, 891, 892
Metro aid - 429, 879 (chart)
Parris election defeat - 917
statehood issue - 107, 428-429, 893
District of Columbia, University of the - 47, 892
Divorce. *See Marriage and divorce*
Dixon, Alan J. D-Ill.
CFE - 699
CFTC authorization - 195
Clean Air Act - 236, 238, 278
congressional partisanship - 39-40
conservative coalition - 47
defense appropriations - 821
defense authorization - 678, 680
defense preparedness - 203
FDIC premiums - 186
food aid cargo preference - 339 (box)
Persian Gulf crisis - 743
Souter confirmation - 515
Dixon, Julian C. D-Calif. (28)
characteristics of Congress - 924
minorities in Congress - 924 (chart)
congressional elections, 1990
low winning percentage - 906 (chart)
D.C. appropriations - 891, 893
Frank ethics case - 103-104
Dixon, Sharon Pratt - 428
Dodd, Christopher J. D-Conn.
Caribbean Basin Initiative - 214
child-care aid - 550
Clean Air Act - 235
congressional pay, honoraria - 71-73
drug-abuse prevention - 504
education proposals - 611-613
El Salvador aid - 782, 785-786
Ex-Im Bank arms loans - 200
family leave - 361
foreign aid appropriations - 841, 842-843
foreign banks - 189
Head Start, human services authorization - 556
housing programs overhaul - 635, 643, 656
medical device safety - 581
Nicaragua aid - 770
policy debate - 772 (box)
Panama aid - 776, 777
Persian Gulf crisis - 725, 726, 730
stock market regulation - 191
Dodd, Thomas J. - 99 (box), 100 (box)
Doherty, James F. - 101
Dolan, Peter - 377
Dolbeare, Cushing N. - 634
Dole, Bob R-Kan.
defense, foreign policy and trade issues
Armenian genocide commemoration - 807-808
Caribbean Basin Initiative - 216
China-U.S. relations - 768
Chinese student visas - 767 (box)
defense authorization - 677
diplomatic nominations - 801 (box)
export controls - 200
foreign aid appropriations - 841-842
Nicaragua aid - 771, 773
Panama aid - 775
Persian Gulf crisis - 720, 737, 743, 747, 749-750, 754
use-of-force debate - 753 (box)
Soviet-U.S. relations - 758, 759, 760-761
textile import quotas - 219
domestic issues
Amtrak authorization - 391
assault weapons ban - 500 (box)
budget action - 113, 130, 132, 164, 165
capital gains tax - 168 (box)
civil rights/job bias - 466, 467
Clean Air Act - 232-238, 279
community service programs - 561
crime bill - 492
disabled civil rights - 460, 461
Energy, water appropriations - 865
farm bill - 324, 340
flag desecration - 524, 526-528
Hatch Act revision - 409, 411
judicial appointments - 516
money laundering - 189
pension plan guaranty - 368
student loan default - 626 (box)
Transportation appropriations - 880
Senate leadership - 9-12
campaign finance reform - 58-68
congressional partisanship - 32
congressional pay, honoraria - 72
Durenberger ethics case - 98
presidential support in Congress - 31
Dole, Elizabeth H.
Hatch Act revision - 411
job training overhaul - 366, 367
resignation - 369 (box)
Dolphins - 399
Domenici, Pete V. R-N.M.
alternative power regulation - 317
budget action - 113, 129, 130 (box), 132
campaign finance reform - 65
child-care aid - 549
community service programs - 561
congressional elections, 1990 - 916
congressional leadership - 12
defense authorization - 677
Hatch Act revision - 408-411
homeless aid - 665
SDI - 692
Treasury, Postal appropriations - 889, 890
Dominica - 212
Dominican Republic
Caribbean Basin Initiative - 212
Doniger, David - 242, 276
Donnelly, Brian D-Mass. (11)
living wills - 567 (box)
Dooley, Calvin - 905 (chart), 918 (chart)
Dooling, Jack - 39
Doolittle, John T. - 905 (chart), 918 (chart)
Dorgan, Byron L. D-N.D. (AL)
congressional leadership - 11 (box)
defense authorization - 682
unemployment compensation - 368
water projects authorization - 299
Dornan, Robert K. R-Calif. (38)
D.C. appropriations - 891-892
Persian Gulf crisis - 728
SDI - 693
Dos Santos, Jose Eduardo - 792, 793
Double jeopardy - 107
Douglas, Chuck R-N.H. (2)
civil rights/job bias - 469
congressional elections, 1990 - 917
defeated House members - 917 (chart)
House membership changes - 918 (chart)
crime bill - 495, 498, 499
disabled civil rights - 450
financial institution fraud - 183
handgun wait period - 501 (box)
immigration law revision - 478
Legal Services Corporation - 533
vertical price fixing - 540
Dowd, John M. - 87, 94, 96
Downey, Thomas J. D-N.Y. (2)
budget action - 132, 166
child-care aid - 548, 550
children's welfare services - 556
China-U.S. relations - 766
farm bill - 331-332
Social Security earnings test - 557-558
unemployment compensation - 368
Dreier, David R-Calif. (33)
congressional elections, 1990 - 907
Driesler, Stephen - 660, 661
Drinking water
zebra mussel control - 298, 303
Driver's licenses
drug offenders suspension - 506, 878, 880
farm exemptions - 383
immigration fraud - 485
literacy skills - 611
voter registration - 69-70
Dropout prevention
authorization - 618
community service programs - 561
education proposals - 613, 615
school awards - 611
Taft Institute authorization - 628
vocational education authorization - 619-623
Dropout Prevention and Re-entry Act of 1988 - 615
Drug abuse
children's welfare services - 556
disabled civil rights exclusions - 449, 452, 459
education, prevention and treatment
AIDS bill - 585, 586, 587
antidrug measures - 502, 503-505
appropriations - 850
budget action - 125, 148
community service programs - 561, 562
defense authorization debate - 679, 692
education proposals - 613
homeless aid - 665
Indian programs - 422, 423
library programs - 617
minority health - 596
public housing support services - 635, 651, 655
Waiting List Program - 504
ice (methamphetamine) - 493
immigration exclusions - 478, 484
incidental use by nominees - 180 (box)
prescription drugs - 146
product liability suits - 400
steroids - 499
testing
disabled civil rights - 452, 453, 459
high school student athletes - 505, 613
mass transit workers - 880
transportation workers - 502, 503, 505-506
TV depiction - 374 (box)
veterans benefits - 156, 420
Drug Abuse Resistance Education (DARE) - 505, 613
Drug "czar"
Bennett resignation, Martinez nomination - 502, 503 (box)
small office technology - 679
Drug Enforcement Administration (DEA)
antidrug measures - 502, 503
appropriations - 882 (chart), 884
budget action - 125
crime bill - 493, 499
steroids - 499
Drug-free schools
antibias in discipline - 459
crime bill - 499, 502
drug-abuse education - 499, 505
education proposals - 615
student aid cutoff - 614
Drug-Free Schools and Community Act - 505
Drug-Free Work Place Act of 1988 - 453
Drug-free workplaces
child-care aid - 153
civil rights/job bias - 465, 468
community service programs - 561
disabled civil rights - 453
health, safety jobs testing - 505
nuclear plant safety - 309

ship operators - 284
Drug-related crime
alien deportation - 487
child abuse - 493
death penalty - 846, 852
public housing
elimination grants - 652
evictions - 533, 637, 650, 651
rent adjustments - 651
youth sports programs - 651
weapons use penalties - 495
Drug trafficking
Andean military study - 679
anticrime bill - 6
death penalty - 40, 487, 493, 494, 497, 502-503
food stamp fraud - 346, 354
forfeited assets - 216
interdiction
Coast Guard appropriations - 879
defense appropriations - 816, 817
defense authorization - 673, 675, 677
defense budget - 122
military role - 504
international narcotics control
Andean nation aid - 214, 805-806
assault weapons ban - 501
budget action - 124
extradition expenses - 779
foreign aid appropriations - 833 (chart), 836, 844
foreign aid limits - 777
law enforcement
budget action - 125, 128
Commerce/Justice/State appropriations - 881, 885
crime bill - 487, 493, 496, 498, 502-503
immigration law revision - 474, 485
judicial workload - 520, 521
organized crime - 882 (chart)
rural areas - 499, 503
money laundering - 187
Panama aid - 776, 777, 779
legalization - 502
Noriega case - 774, 775, 777
truck stops, rest areas - 383, 502
Drugs and pharmaceuticals
abortion inducer - 531
AIDS bill - 582, 587, 588
Caribbean Basin Initiative - 211, 215, 217
child-resistant packaging - 417
contraceptives - 601, 602
FDA fees - 125
foreign medical aid - 205
hazardous materials transport - 381
HIV demonstration project - 148
Medicaid discounts - 146-147, 569, 570 (box)
Medicare coverage - 145, 569
organ transplant programs - 597
orphan drugs
marketing rights - 577-579
tax credit - 160, 173
osteoporosis therapy - 145
product liability - 401
Puerto Rico status - 425
space-based processing - 858
vaccine program authorization - 591-592
veterans copayments - 155
women, minorities in clinical trials - 602
DSP satellites - 684
Duarte, José Napoleón - 780
Due process
Brennan career - 511 (box)
civil rights/job bias - 466
obscenity in art - 432
right to die - 567 (box)
Souter confirmation - 513
Dugan, Michael J. - 719
Dukakis, Michael S. - 487, 665, 802, 913, 928, 930
Duke, David - 462, 916
Duncan, John J. "Jimmy" Jr. R-Tenn. (2)
roll call attendance - 48
Dunne, John R. - 465 (box)
Durable power of attorney - 567 (box)
Durbin, Richard J. D-Ill. (20)
Persian Gulf crisis - 742-743, 752-753
Durenberger, Dave R-Minn.
campaign finance reform - 60, 66
civil rights/job bias - 465, 466
Clean Air Act - 247
crime bill - 490
El Salvador aid - 786
ethics investigation - 6, 80, 81 (box), 87, 98-103
Medicare changes - 566
Pepper Commission - 609
vocational education authorization - 622
Durkin, John A. - 913 (chart), 915
Dwarfism - 578
Dwyer, Bernard D-N.J. (6)
congressional elections, 1990
low winning percentage - 906 (chart)
marginal vote share - 905 (chart)
Dymally, Mervyn M. D-Calif. (31)
congressional redistricting - 932
intelligence authorization - 796
minorities in Congress - 924 (chart)
Dyson, Roy D-Md. (1)
congressional elections, 1990
defeated House members - 917 (chart)
House membership changes - 918 (chart)
marginal vote share - 905 (box)
ethics case - 108
fish inspection - 397

E

Eagleburger, Lawrence S.
China-U.S. relations - 765, 766
Egyptian debt reliief - 730
Pakistan-U.S. relations - 768
Panama aid - 775, 778
Persian Gulf crisis - 754
PLO talks - 800
Eaker Air Force Base - 678
Early, Blake - 235
Earmarking. *See also Pork-barrel politics*
DOE research appropriations - 862, 866
public housing construction - 656
SDI - 693
Transportation appropriations - 878, 880
vocational education - 619, 622
Earned-income tax credit (EITC)
budget action - 151-152, 158, 164, 172
child-care aid - 547-551
Earth. *See Environmental protection; Geothermal energy; Global climate change; Ozone-layer protection*
Earth Observing System (EOS) - 434, 436
Earthquake Hazards Reduction Act of 1977 - 442
Earthquakes
research, preparedness - 442
San Francisco disaster aid - 845
East Germany. *See also Germany*
CFE - 697, 698, 703
claims of U.S. citizens - 763
German unification - 762-763
Soviet-U.S. relations - 757
START - 707
U.S. trade - 212
Eastern Airlines - 369, 901
Eastern Europe. *See also Warsaw Pact; specific countries*
B-2 bomber - 688
CFE - 696, 697, 698, 703
defense authorization - 671
development bank - 206-207
Persian Gulf crisis - 741
START - 706
U.S. aid
budget action - 124
development bank authorization - 207
election aid - 777
food aid - 337, 804
foreign aid appropriations - 811, 830, 831, 832, 833 (chart), 834, 836, 843
Havel visit - 204 (box)
Panama aid bill - 777
Soviet-U.S. relations - 759
U.S. immigration policy - 478
U.S. trade - 204-206
export controls - 199, 200, 201
Export-Import Bank - 207
foreign aid appropriations - 834, 836, 844
Eastern states. *See also Atlantic states; Northeastern states*
air-traffic plan - 156
food-waste transport - 382
EBRD. *See European Bank for Reconstruction and Development*
ECHO units - 655
Eckart, Dennis E. D-Ohio (11)
campaign finance reform - 67
Clean Air Act - 239, 275
Energy, water appropriations - 863
EPA Cabinet status - 293
federal RCRA compliance - 308
savings and loan investigations - 887-888
Economic Analysis, Bureau of (BEA) - 222-225
Economic conditions. *See also Budget, U.S.; Business and industry; Consumer affairs; Economic development; Employment and unemployment; Foreign trade and business*
budget assumptions - 127
budget process changes - 162, 178
Clean Air Act impact - 274
federal pay overhaul - 405-407
gubernatorial elections, 1990 - 928
industrial policy - 202
Panama aid - 775-776
Persian Gulf crisis - 744 (box)
State of the Union address - 18
stock market stabilization - 190-191
summary - 4
thrift bailout - 179
Economic development. *See also Community development; Developing countries; International development banks; Rural development*
Bush economic report - 116-117
enterprise zones - 167
environmental issues
Antarctica protection - 305-307
barrier island protection - 302-303
beach stabilization - 298
coastal zone management - 154, 288-289
Tongass forest protection - 294-295
Indian vocational education - 621
Latin America aid - 217-218
literacy - 610, 611
Puerto Rico status - 425
SBA authorization - 395
Third World population growth - 838-839 (box)
Economic Development Administration - 882 (chart), 884
Economic Dislocation and Worker Adjustment Assistance - 123
Economic Support Fund
foreign aid appropriations - 833 (chart), 835, 836, 841, 843
Pakistan-U.S. relations - 769
Economically Dislocated Workers Assistance Act - 277 (box)
Ecuador
U.S. aid/drug control - 836
Edelman, Marion Wright - 548
Edgar, Jim - 928, 933
Education. *See also Adult education; Colleges and universities; Dropout prevention; Education Department; Elementary and secondary education; Job training programs; Libraries; Literacy; Preschool education; Schools; Student aid; Teachers; Vocational education*
budget action - 128
characteristics of Congress - 926
children's TV programming - 373-375
close-captioned TV - 375
disabled students - 54-55
environmental education - 293
family investment centers - 650
foreign aid - 835
housing education - 646
immigration law revision - 474-485
key votes - 4-B, 5-B
State of the Union address - 18-19
summary - 7
veterans services - 421
Education and Labor Committee, House
leadership changes - 11 (box), 924
Education Department, U.S.
appropriations - 847-853
disabled education - 616
dropout prevention - 618
drug-abuse education - 505
education proposals - 615
library programs - 617
literacy programs - 611
math, science scholarships - 612 (box)
student loans - 143, 613, 626-627 (box)
student right-to-know - 624-627
Sweet nomination - 506
vocational education authorization - 620, 621, 622
Education of the Handicapped Act (EHA) - 54-55, 613, 616-617
Education Research and Improvement Office - 621
Educational Excellence and Equity Act - 610-615
Educational exchanges
Chinese student visas - 767 (box)
Soviet-U.S. relations - 760
Edwards, Carl R. Sr. - 918 (chart)
Edwards, Chet - 905 (box), 918 (chart)
Edwards, Don D-Calif. (10)
Brennan career - 511 (box)
child-care aid - 549
civil rights/job bias - 469, 473
congressional term limit - 15
crime bill - 494, 496
disabled civil rights - 450, 451
federal judgeships - 521
flag desecration - 525, 526
Panama aid - 776
RICO revision - 538
Supreme Court term summary - 54, 55
TV violence guidelines - 374 (box)
Edwards, Mickey R-Okla. (5)

congressional leadership - 9 (box)
El Salvador aid - 783, 786
foreign aid appropriations - 831, 832-833, 842-843
Persian Gulf crisis - 730
EEOC. *See Equal Employment Opportunity Commission*
EEP. *See Export Enhancement Program*
Egan, Paul S. - 419, 420
Egypt
debt relief
budget action - 161
continuing resolutions - 896 (box)
El Salvador aid - 786
foreign aid appropriations - 811, 830-831, 840, 841, 842, 844
key votes - 9-B
Persian Gulf crisis - 730, 733
Pakistan-U.S. relations - 769
Persian Gulf crisis - 729
tank sales - 674
U.S. aid - 831, 833, 837, 843
U.S. trade
textile import quotas - 221, 222
EHA. *See Education of the Handicapped Act*
Eighth Amendment
death penalty - 489 (box)
torture ban treaty - 807
Eisenhower, Dwight D. - 13
Eisenhower Mathematics and Science Education Act - 612 (box), 615
EITC. *See Earned-income tax credit*
El Salvador
arms aid from Nicaragua - 771
U.S. aid - 779-786
appropriations - 830, 831, 835, 839-841
key votes - 8-B, 9-B
Nicaragua aid - 773, 774
Panama aid - 777, 778
summary - 5
U.S. immigration policy - 474, 478, 479, 483, 484, 485
U.S. trade
Caribbean Basin Initiative - 212
Elderly cottage housing units - 655
Elderly persons. *See also Age discrimination; Alzheimer's disease; Medicare; Pensions and retirement; Social Security*
close-captioned TV - 375
community service programs - 559-562
deceptive mail curbs - 417
food stamps - 346, 354
health care
authorization - 598-599
budget action - 147
long-term care - 607
Medicaid expansion - 569-571
TB prevention - 594
House leadership challenges - 11 (box)
housing programs - 125, 631-656, 854, 857
Supreme Court workload - 56
Election Data Services - 415
Elections. *See Campaign finance; Congressional elections; Gubernatorial elections; Presidential elections; Voter registration*
Eastern Europe aid - 777
Hatch Act revision - 408-411
Nicaraguan presidency - 770
Puerto Rico status - 424
Electric power. *See also Hydroelectric power; Nuclear power plants*
acid rain reduction - 229-230, 231 (box), 232, 238, 242, 259-267, 276
tax break for scrubbers - 238
alternative sources - 317-318
clean-fuel cars - 240 (box), 247
Grand Canyon erosion - 300-301
railroad conversion - 877, 879
rural co-ops - 353
steam generator emissions - 258
utility capacity growth - 232, 238, 276
Electronic information services - 377-379
Elementary and secondary education. *See also Compensatory education aid; Dropout prevention; Drug-free schools; Literacy; Math education; Schools; Science education; Teachers*
block grants - 123
Bush economic report - 117
computer software copyright - 542
diploma requirement for student loans - 626-627 (box)
education proposals - 610-615
Follow Through programs - 552, 555
gifted, talented - 852
goals commission - 847, 853
homeless aid - 665
public housing support services - 651
school finance equity - 614
tuition ban on child-care aid - 153
vocational education authorization - 619-623
Elephants - 837
Elevators - 456
Eleventh Amendment
copyright infringement suits - 542
disabled civil rights - 458
disabled student education - 55, 616
Emergency Community Services program - 665
Emergency Food Assistance Program - 354
Emergency Low-Income Housing Preservation Act of 1989 - 142, 648-649
Emergency medical care
injuries research - 598
patient-dumping ban - 563
trauma care authorization - 597-598
Emergency services and personnel
aircraft donation - 216
autodialer curbs - 379
hazardous materials transport - 381-382
HIV protection - 587, 588
job-related medical exams - 453
911 service - 453
vessels in distress - 157
weather warnings - 157
Emergency shelter grants - 655
Emery, David F. - 918 (chart)
Emotional disorders - 599
Employment agencies - 277, 452, 453
Employment and unemployment. *See also Employment and working conditions; Job training programs; Unemployment compensation; Vocational education*
auto fuel efficiency - 280, 281
Bush economic report - 117
Caribbean Basin Initiative - 213, 214
dislocated workers
auto industry - 281
Clean Air Act - 230, 236, 238, 277 (box), 5-B, 6-B, 9-B, 10-B
compensation - 368
defense plants, closed bases - 678, 683
homemakers - 366 (box)
trade effects - 123
dropout prevention - 618
farm bill - 332, 349
foreign ownership of U.S. business - 223
forest logging - 296, 358, 871, 875, 876
immigration law revision - 474-485
job training funding formula - 365, 366
occupations of members of Congress - 925-926
public housing support services - 651
Persian Gulf crisis - 744 (box)
SSI - 150
targeted jobs tax credit - 160, 173
textile import quotas - 210, 219, 220, 222
Employment and Training Administration - 848 (chart)
Employment and working conditions. *See also Discrimination in employment; Drug-free workplaces; Federal employees; Health insurance; Income taxes; Occupational health and safety; Pensions and retirement; Unemployment compensation; Whistleblower protection*
child care - 548
failing thrifts - 183
family leave - 359-361
group legal services - 160, 173
housing costs aid - 659 (box)
immigration law revision
document fraud - 479, 485
employer sanctions - 477, 484
permits for legalized alien families - 476
public-private sector salaries - 405-407
severance pay - 53
tuition aid - 160, 173
workers' rights
Caribbean Basin Initiative - 213
Employment Retirement Income Security Act (ERISA) - 367-368
Employment Standards Administration - 848 (chart)
End stage renal disease - 145-146, 564
Endangered species
logging limits - 296, 871
toxic air pollutants - 254
Endangered Species Act of 1973 - 296, 297, 870, 875
Endara, Guillermo - 773, 774, 775-776, 777, 779, 846
Energy and Commerce Committee, House
membership - 924
Energy conservation
acid rain - 262
appropriations - 873 (chart)
auto fuel efficiency - 159, 172, 279-281
budget action - 123-124
energy issues, 1990 - 312
EPA Cabinet status - 291
global warming - 307
Persian Gulf crisis - 744
public housing standards - 644, 646, 651, 656
state programs - 313, 319
Energy Department, U.S. (DOE)
alternative power regulation - 317, 318
appropriations - 861-866
boxscore - 861
budget authority totals (chart) - 862
budget action - 126
Clean Air Act
acid rain - 260, 266, 267, 276
alternative fuels - 240 (box), 253, 273
coke oven technology - 258
liquefied gas research - 274
methane assessment - 271
defense programs
appropriations - 812
authorization - 679
budget action - 122
SDI - 122, 673, 692, 817
Stello nomination - 309-310
"superfund" reimbursement - 679-680
energy conservation - 313, 319
foreign ownership of U.S. business - 224
Interior appropriations - 873 (chart)
nuclear test treaties - 712
nuclear waste cleanup
appropriations - 861, 862
budget action - 122
Panama aid - 779
RCRA compliance - 293, 308
radiation victims compensation - 590
research
facilities earmarks - 862, 866, 876
gene mapping - 126, 865
global warming - 307
home energy efficiency - 656
hydrogen fuel - 313, 318-319
SSC - 438-439, 863
Strategic Petroleum Reserve - 314-315
uranium enrichment - 310-311, 864
user fees - 157
Energy Policy and Conservation Act of 1975 - 279, 319
Energy resources. *See also Coal; Electric power; Energy conservation; Energy Department; Natural gas; Nuclear energy; Oil; Solar energy*
aurora borealis - 866
national energy policy - 312-313, 872
research and development - 123-124, 865, 866, 873 (chart)
Engineers and engineering
air pollution research - 274
math, science scholarships - 612 (box)
drug ban - 505
Energy, water appropriations - 865
minerals research - 443
Pentagon salaries - 679
Engler, John - 928, 929, 933
English, Glenn D-Okla. (6)
farm bill - 330
rural development - 353-354
English language
closed-captioned TV - 375
immigration law revision - 475, 479
naturalization requirement - 476
student competency - 615
vocational education authorization - 619-623
Enhanced Structural Adjustment Facility - 832 (chart)
Enid, Okla. - 878
Enterprise for the Americas Initiative - 217-218
Entertainment and entertainers
antismoking bills - 592, 593, 594
visas - 479, 483
Entitlements
budget action - 111, 127
credit reform exemptions - 163, 178 (box)
pay-as-you-go increases - 174
Environmental Defense Fund - 306
Environmental disasters
Chernobyl nuclear accident - 759
Exxon Valdez oil spill - 283, 284, 285 (box), 315 (box)
Persian Gulf crisis - 721
Environmental Education Foundation - 293
Environmental Education Office - 293
Environmental Fund - 218
Environmental interest groups
alternative power regulation - 317
Arctic refuge drilling - 315 (box)
auto fuel efficiency - 280, 281
barrier islands protection - 302
Clean Air Act - 230-247, 276-279
coastal waters cleanup - 289
Energy, water appropriations - 861, 866
farm bill - 323, 326, 330, 332, 334-336, 348-349
federal RCRA compliance - 308
Grand Canyon erosion - 300
irrigation subsidies - 356-357

logging/wildlife protection - 296-297, 870-876
oil pollution cleanup - 283-287
pesticide residue in food - 358
exported banned chemicals - 323, 336, 349
Stello nomination - 309
Tongass forest protection - 294, 295
uranium enrichment - 310

Environmental protection. *See also Air pollution; Conservation; Environmental Protection Agency; Global climate change; Hazardous substances; Ozone-layer protection; Soil conservation; Water resources; Water pollution; Waste products; Wilderness areas; Wildlife*
Antarctica - 305-307
Army Engineers mission - 298
barrier islands - 302
budget action - 128
energy issues, 1990 - 312
Energy, water appropriations - 866
farm problems, solutions - 326, 331, 332, 335-336, 345
foreign aid - 836-837
Poland, Hungary - 834
Indian lands - 423
Nicaragua aid - 773
nuclear energy role - 307
State of the Union address - 19
summary - 5-6
Third World debt relief - 218, 778, 779

Environmental Protection Agency (EPA)
appropriations - 854, 855, 855 (chart), 858, 860
barrier island protection - 302
beach water quality - 290
budget action - 124, 154-155
Cabinet status - 291-293
Clean Air Act
acid rain - 260-267
alternative fuels, clean-fuel cars - 233 (box), 240 (box), 247, 252-254
cost estimate - 231, 243, 279
methane assessment - 271
municipal waste combustion - 259, 276
offshore drilling emissions - 244, 273
ozone-layer protection - 269-271
permits, enforcement - 236, 267-269, 271-273
radionuclide emissions - 234, 256, 258
smog standards - 235, 239, 246, 248, 250-251
tailpipe emissions - 229, 233 (box), 236, 246-247, 252
toxic air pollutants - 230, 254-259, 275
coastal water quality - 154, 289-290
criminal, civil investigations - 292 (box), 293
Environmental Education Office - 293
federal RCRA compliance - 308-309
food-waste transport - 383
Great Lakes cleanup - 301
military base cleanup - 679-680
octane labeling - 282
pesticide residue in food - 358
exported banned chemicals - 333, 336, 349
pollution source reduction - 155
radon measurement research - 157
user fees - 154

Environmental Statistics Bureau - 291, 292

EOS. *See Earth Observing System*

Epilepsy Foundation of America - 570 (box)

Episcopalians - 549

EPO - 578

Equal Access Act - 618 (box)

Equal Employment Opportunity Commission (EEOC)
academic tenure - 623
age discrimination in benefits - 362, 364
appropriations - 883 (chart)
civil rights/job bias - 464
disabled civil rights - 453, 458
immigrant job discrimination - 484
Thomas judicial confirmation - 518-519 (box)

Equitable Life Assurance Society - 101

Erdreich, Ben D-Ala. (6)
barrier islands protection - 302
housing programs overhaul - 640
prepayment of subsidized mortgages - 663

Erlenborn, John N. - 532, 533

Erosion. *See Soil conservation*

Erythropoietin - 145

Espionage
federal death penalty - 487, 490, 494
Soviet U.N. base - 802

ESPN - 370

Espy, Mike D-Miss. (2)
minorities in Congress - 924 (chart)
Transportation appropriations - 878

Establishment clause. *See Church-state separation*

Estate taxes - 160, 172

Estonia
CFE - 703
German unification - 763
Soviet-U.S. relations - 757, 761
U.S. aid - 844

Ethanol
Clean Air Act - 229, 232, 234, 238, 240 (box), 241, 244, 252
import duties - 211, 214, 216
tax incentives - 160, 167, 172, 313 (box)

Ethical issues. *See also Medical ethics*
export of banned pesticides - 336

Ethics Committee, Senate
disabled civil rights - 458
savings and loan scandal - 78-97

Ethics in government. *See also Congressional ethics; Fraud, waste and abuse in government programs*
ALJ corps - 523
Bennett RNC post - 909-910
disclosure by advisory panels - 292
financial institution fraud - 183, 495
Legal Services Corporation - 533
Stello nomination - 309
trade representative lobbying curbs - 881, 886
VA medical staff honoraria - 420

Ethics in Government Act - 668

Ethics Reform Act of 1989 - 73 (box)

Ethiopia
development loans/human rights - 207
Persian Gulf crisis - 740

Ethnic groups. *See also specific groups*
civil rights/job bias - 463
"hate crimes" statistics - 506
immigration diversity - 474-483
organ donor pool - 597

Etpison, Ngiratlal - 808

Europe. *See also Conventional forces in Europe treaty; Eastern Europe; North Atlantic Treaty Organization; specific countries*
Nicaragua policy debate - 772 (box)
technology competitiveness - 440
uranium enrichment - 310
U.S. immigration policy - 474, 475, 476, 481
U.S. troop deployment - 676, 677, 678, 686
weapons - 674, 684

European Bank for Reconstruction and Development (EBRD)
authorization - 206-207
foreign aid appropriations - 832 (chart), 834, 835, 836, 843, 844
Soviet-U.S. relations - 759

European Community
agricultural subsidies - 325, 332, 351, 910
GATT talks - 209-210
Persian Gulf crisis - 719

European Space Agency - 437

Evans, Lane D-Ill. (17)
Agent Orange compensation - 418, 419
congressional elections, 1990 - 908

Evans, Linda S. - 7

Even Start - 611, 615

Everett, Wash. - 681

Excise taxes. *See also Fuel and gasoline taxes*
airline tickets - 159, 172, 384-385
alcoholic beverages - 158, 164, 172
auto fuel economy - 159, 172
budget reconciliation - 158-159, 172
harbor maintenance - 159, 172
luxuries - 159, 167, 164, 172
ozone-depleting chemicals - 158, 172
pension reversions - 161, 172, 367-368
Puerto Rico status - 427
telephone service - 126, 172, 547, 550
tobacco - 158, 164, 172, 592, 594

Exclusionary rule
crime bill - 486, 492, 498, 499

Executive orders
Chinese student protections - 767 (box)
export controls - 198, 201
Iraq trade sanctions - 725-726
OIRA authority - 888

Exon, Jim D-Neb.
Armenian genocide commemoration - 807
B-2 bomber - 688-690
congressional elections, 1990 - 913
conservative coalition - 47
defense appropriations - 819
foreign ownership of U.S. business - 223, 224
product liability - 401
Souter confirmation - 515

Expedited Funds Availability Act - 656

Explosives - 380, 381

Export Administration Act
authorization - 198-201
boxscore - 198
veto message - 200-201
housing programs overhaul - 643, 656
intelligence authorization - 799

Export controls. *See also Export Administration Act*
missile technology - 680, 683
ozone-depleting chemicals - 271
sanctions
chemical weapons - 198-201, 709
China - 765, 768, 799-800
Iraq - 844, 885
South Africa - 787-789
supercomputer technology - 885
technology to China - 764
uranium - 864

Export Enhancement Program (EEP) - 330, 337-338, 345, 868

Export-Import Bank
arms sales - 200, 201, 643, 656
Andean Initiative - 805
China sanctions - 800
Eastern European trade - 207, 844
foreign aid appropriations - 833 (chart), 834
Iraqi loans - 722, 723, 724
Nicaragua aid - 771, 773
Panama aid - 777
Soviet trade - 205, 759

Exports. *See Foreign trade and business*

***Exxon Valdez* oil spill** - 283, 284, 285 (box), 315 (box)

Extradition - 779, 803

F

F-4 Wild Weasel - 846

F-14 fighter plane
appropriations - 818, 825, 826
authorization - 674
budget action - 122
modernization - 685

F-15 fighter plane
appropriations - 815 (chart), 818, 823, 825
authorization - 674, 685
budget action - 122
Saudi arms sales - 719, 734 (box)

F-16 fighter plane
alternative - 683
appropriations - 815 (chart), 818, 823, 825
authorization - 674, 685
NATO base in Italy - 678, 827
Pakistan nuclear potential - 769

F/A-18 fighter plane
appropriations - 815 (chart), 818, 825, 826
authorization - 674, 677, 682-683, 685

FAA. *See Federal Aviation Administration*

Fahd (King) - 719, 724, 731, 744 (box)

Fair Employment Practices Office, House - 458, 460

Fair housing
appropriations - 855 (chart)
authorization - 656

Fair Housing Act - 447

Fair Labor Standards Act - 143, 366

Faleomavaega, Eni F. H. D-Am. Samoa
minorities in Congress - 924 (chart)

Fall River Electric Cooperative - 866

Fallout. *See Radiation*

Families USA - 558

Family and Medical Leave Act - 359-361

Family Educational Rights and Privacy Act - 624, 625

Family investment centers - 650

Family issues. *See also Adoption; Aid to Families with Dependent Children; Children; Foster care; Home health care; Marriage and divorce; Parental notification of abortion; Parental rights*
AIDS bill - 583, 585
child-care aid - 547-551
estate freezes - 160
family leave - 6, 359-361
conservative coalition - 40, 47
key votes - 10-B
housing assistance
definition, for eligiblility - 652
evictions - 637, 639
large families - 641, 644
self-sufficiency programs - 635, 650, 651
immigration law revision - 474-485
intergenerational literacy programs - 611
mental health services - 599
separation prevention
deportation stays for aliens - 475-479, 483, 484
drug-abuse treatment - 679
housing aid - 642, 650, 651, 656, 665
welfare services - 556

Family learning centers - 617
Family Medical Leave Coalition - 360
Family planning. *See Birth control*
Family Support Act of 1988 - 150, 152, 569
Family Support Administration - 848 (chart)
Family violence prevention
battered women's shelter - 858
immigration law revision - 484
Indian programs - 423
services authorization - 599
violence against women deterrence - 507
Famine. *See Food assistance programs*
Farabundo Marti National Liberation Front (FMLN) - 779-780, 784-786, 836, 841
Farm Credit Administration
Farmer Mac oversight - 347
Farm Credit System
appropriations - 869 (chart)
budget process changes - 163
water, sewer loans - 347, 352
Farmer Mac. *See Federal Agricultural Mortgage Corporation*
Farmer-Owned Reserve - 344
Farmers Home Administration (FmHA)
appropriations - 811, 869 (chart)
authorization - 344
budget action - 123, 125, 141
housing programs overhaul - 633, 639, 653-654
inventory reduction - 347
loan caps, priorities, guarantees - 326, 347, 348
rural development - 347, 352, 353, 354
Farms. *See Agriculture and farming*
Farmworker Justice Fund - 533
Farmworkers. *See Agricultural workers*
Fascell, Dante B. D-Fla. (19)
chemical weapons pact - 710-711
Commerce/Justice/State appropriations - 884
environmental protection
Antarctica - 306
barrier island - 302
Florida Keys - 303
foreign aid
Andean Initiative - 805, 806
appropriations - 838
El Salvador - 782
Kenya - 790
Nicaragua - 773
Panama - 777
Persian Gulf crisis - 733-734, 736
Fauntroy, Walter E. D-D.C.
D.C. mayor, "shadow" delegation election - 428-429
ethics case - 107
Fawell, Harris W. R-Ill. (13)
civil rights/job bias - 467, 469
congressional elections, 1990
low winning percentage - 906 (chart)
legislative branch appropriations - 895
Treasury, Postal appropriations - 889
Fax machines - 379
Fay, Bill - 233, 240, 242, 243, 245, 246, 279
Fazio, Vic D-Calif. (4)
campaign finance reform - 68
congressional elections, 1990 - 904, 907, 917
low winning percentage - 906 (chart)
marginal vote share - 905 (chart)
congressional mail - 74, 75
defense authorization - 683
Energy, water appropriations - 863
Labor/HHS appropriations - 847
legislative branch appropriations - 894-896
FCC. *See Federal Communications Commission*
FDA. *See Food and Drug Administration*
FDIC. *See Federal Deposit Insurance Corporation*
FECA. *See Federal Election Campaign Act*
Federal Agricultural Mortgage Corporation (Farmer Mac) - 163, 347
Federal Aviation Act - 384
Federal Aviation Administration (FAA)
aging aircraft inspection - 390
airport slot allocation - 386-387
appropriations - 384, 385, 877, 878, 878 (chart), 879-880
budget action - 126, 156
exit-row seat rules - 389 (box)
safety guidelines - 389-390
trust fund spending - 385
Federal buildings
appropriations - 887 (chart), 888, 889
Federal Bureau of Investigation (FBI)
animal rights activists - 442
appropriations - 882 (chart), 884, 885
budget action - 125
college crime - 625
crime bill - 493, 499
drug enforcement - 502, 503
financial institution fraud - 182, 183
law enforcement on Indian lands - 424
Salvadoran Jesuit murder case - 781
supplemental appropriations - 846
Federal Communications Commission (FCC)
appropriations - 882 (chart), 884
authorization - 372
cable TV regulation - 7, 370-372
campaign TV ad rates - 66-67 (box)
children's TV advertising - 373-375
minority license set-asides - 52, 510-511 (box), 379 (box)
radio spectrum allocation - 376-377
TDD, relay services - 457-458
telemarketing curbs - 379
telephone operator service regulation - 378 (box)
Federal contractors
foreign construction companies - 866
inherently governmental functions - 293
nuclear damage suits - 679
payment suspension for fraud - 682
Pentagon procurement policy - 682, 816-817, 818, 822, 823
Israeli firm eligibility - 822
second source competition - 859
water quality standard - 289
Federal Corrupt Practices Act - 57
Federal courts. *See also Appeals courts; Claims Court; District courts; Supreme Court*
appropriations - 885
caseload management - 519-521
disabled civil rights - 461
disabled education - 616
financial institution fraud - 183
flag desecration - 528
job bias suits study - 468
judges
appropriations - 885
Bush appointments - 515-519
death penalth for murder of - 497
impeachment - 520, 522, 523
judicial activism - 509, 512
new judgeships - 520-523, 539, 540, 541
boxscore - 520
provisions - 522
presidential impact, 1933-90 (graph) - 517
salaries - 520
jurisdiction
disaster suit consolidation - 543
habeas corpus appeals - 487, 488 (box), 493, 494-495, 497
redistricting - 510, 514
RICO suits - 536-538
terrorism damage suits - 829, 830
juror, witness fees - 522
Supreme Court decisions - 52, 55, 56
thrift bailout - 180
water rights - 304
Federal Courts Study Committee - 521, 522
Federal credit reforms - 134, 163, 178 (box)
Federal Crop Insurance Corporation - 868, 869 (chart)
Federal debt. *See Budget, U.S.*
Federal Deposit Insurance Corporation (FDIC)
appropriations - 854, 855 (chart)
budget action - 123, 141 federal credit reforms - 163, 178 (box)
financial institution fraud - 182
asset recovery - 495
money laundering - 187, 188
premium increase - 184-187
thrift bailout - 179
thrift supervisor - 180 (box)
Federal Election Campaign Act (FECA) - 57-58
Federal Election Commission (FEC)
appropriations - 887 (chart)
auto importers - 280
campaign finance reform - 58, 65 (box)
Durenberger ethics case - 101, 102
election costs, 1990 - 908-909
savings and loan scandal - 80
Federal Emergency Management Agency - 122, 442, 855 (chart), 856
Federal employees. *See also Ethics in government; Federal contractors; Military personnel*
age discrimination - 363, 364
census workers - 213
death penalty for murder of - 494
disabled civil rights exclusion - 453
drug testing - 506
government shutdown - 137
Hatch Act revision - 6, 408-411
honoraria - 71, 72 (box)
immigration limits - 476
pay and benefits
copyright commissioners - 543
family leave - 359
health insurance - 155
housing bill - 664
NIH staff - 600
non-appropriated funds - 155
overhaul - 405-407
scientists, engineers - 600, 601, 603, 679
SEC lawyers - 193
Treasury, Postal appropriations - 886, 889, 890
procurement officers training - 682
retirement - 125, 155
double-dip waivers - 679
revolving door issues - 53, 881, 886
secrecy agreements - 890
student loans for critical skills - 682
travel
hotel fire safety - 402
veterans preference - 421
Federal Employees Health Benefits Program - 155
Federal Energy Regulatory Commission - 260, 273, 862 (chart)
Federal Financial Management, Office of - 416
Federal Financing Bank
FDIC borrowing - 141
Federal Food, Drug and Cosmetic Act of 1938 - 575, 580
Federal government (general)
accounting standards - 886, 889, 890
acid-free paper - 429
ALJ corps - 523
appropriations lapses - 163
centralized financial management - 416
Clean Air Act
alternative fuel use - 232
compliance - 248
ozone-layer protection - 271
deceptive mail curbs - 417
dislocated worker compensation - 368
OMB review powers - 411-413
radio frequency allocation - 376-377
RCRA compliance - 291, 292, 293, 308-309
regulatory agency control - 21
rulemaking procedures - 414
shutdown - 4, 8, 139, 896-897 (box)
sovereign immunity concept - 291, 292, 293
Federal Grain Inspection Service - 337
Federal Highway Administration - 384, 877, 879 (chart)
Federal Home Loan Bank Board
savings and loan scandal - 78-97
Federal Home Loan Bank System - 163
Federal Home Loan Mortgage Corporation - 123, 163
Federal Housing Administration (FHA)
appropriations - 855 (chart)
background - 632
budget action - 141-142
energy efficiency standards - 644
foreclosure-prevention counseling - 649, 652
mortgage insurance fund rules revision - 631, 635, 636, 640, 642-643, 647-649, 657-661
Federal Insecticide, Fungicide and Rodenticide Act - 336
Federal Judicial Center - 883 (chart)
Federal lands. *See also Indian lands and reservations; National forests; National parks; Wilderness areas*
barrier islands protection - 302-303
Defense Department acquisition - 678
grazing fees - 871, 873-874
Indian graves, remains - 422
mining patents - 871, 875-876
oil-shale claims - 316
timber exports - 211, 214-215, 216
Federal Maritime Commission - 882 (chart)
Federal Mediation and Conciliation Service - 849 (chart)
Federal Mine Safety and Health Review Commission - 849 (chart)
Federal National Mortgage Association (Fannie Mae) - 123, 163
Federal power marketing administrations - 267
Federal Prison Industries - 498
Federal Railroad Administration
appropriations - 879 (chart)
hazardous materials transport - 380
Federal Railroad Safety Act of 1970 - 157
Federal Reserve
CFTC authorization - 195
FDIC premiums - 186
money laundering - 188
stock market regulation - 190, 192, 193
Federal Rules of Civil Procedure - 543
Federal Savings and Loan Insurance Corporation - 88, 185
Federal Trade Commission (FTC)
ALJ corps - 523
antismoking bills - 594
appropriations - 882 (chart), 884
octane labeling - 282

telemarketing fraud - 379, 402
vertical price fixing - 540
Federalist Society - 17, 755
Federated States of Micronesia - 808
Federation of American Scientists - 702
Feed grains. *See Wheat and feed grains*
Feed Material Production Center - 308
Feighan, Edward F. D-Ohio (19)
insurance price-sharing - 401
Feinstein, Dianne - 40, 48, 927-928, 929, 933
Feinstein, Lee - 700, 710
Fenn, Peter H. - 902
Fernald, Ohio - 308
Fernandez, Joseph - 535
Fertilizer
farm alternatives - 326, 336
Fetal alcohol syndrome - 423
Fetal protection
job bias case - 56, 465
Fetal tissue
art funding ban - 47
research - 531, 600, 602 (box), 603, 604
transplants - 600, 601, 603
FHA. *See Federal Housing Administration*
Fiber Materials Inc. - 859
Fiber-optics - 199, 823
Fields, Jack R-Texas (8)
Clean Air Act - 240-242, 247
conservative coalition - 47
Eastern Airlines strike - 369
Fifth Amendment
immunity - 534-535
torture ban treaty - 807
Filibusters and cloture votes
cloture votes, 1990 (chart) - 7
congressional partisanship - 32
Financial Institutions Reform, Recovery and Enforcement Act - 179
Findley payments - 344
Fine Arts, U.S. Commission on - 196-197
Fingerprinting lab - 846
Finland
Persian Gulf crisis - 740
Finney, Joan - 928, 929, 930
Fire Administration, U.S. - 270
Firearms
assault weapons - 486, 488, 489, 491, 492, 495, 496, 497,498, 500-501 (box)
congressional partisanship - 32
conservative coalition - 40
food stamp fraud - 346, 354
handguns - 494, 495
wait period - 496, 500-501 (box)
INS agents - 485
key votes - 6-B
Panama police aid - 776
penalties for criminal use - 486, 494, 499
mandatory sentences - 492-493, 495
semiautomatic rifles and pistols - 491-492, 494, 495, 497
Fires and firefighters
BLM appropriations - 873 (chart)
federal pay overhaul - 406
fire-safe cigarettes - 402
forest fires - 346, 845, 846
halon ban - 270
hazardous materials transport - 381
HIV protection - 587
hotel safety - 402
First Amendment. *See also Church-state separation; Freedom of speech; Freedom of the press*
Brennan career - 510 (box)
campaign finance reform - 58, 59, 61, 64
children's TV advertising - 373-375
flag desecration - 52, 524-528

political patronage jobs - 52, 53, 933
Souter confirmation - 512
Fish and fishing
Antarctica - 306
"dolphin-safe" tuna labels - 399
drift net ban - 399
Energy, water appropriations - 861
fishermen's funds - 883 (chart)
hatchery transfer - 292
inspection - 396-399, 869
management plans - 399
nutrition labels - 575-576
pipeline safety inspection - 286 (box)
pollution contamination research - 301
salmon protection - 864
Tongass forest protection - 295
tonnage duty exemption - 157
water projects authorization - 299, 300
Fish and Wildlife Service, U.S.
acid rain - 267
appropriations - 871, 873 (chart), 875
endangered species - 296, 297
Texas wetlands - 872
wetlands protection - 335
Fish, Hamilton Jr. R-N.Y. (21)
balanced-budget amendment - 175 (box)
civil rights/job bias - 469
crime bill - 495
disabled civil rights - 450
Eastern Airlines strike - 369
federal judgeships - 521
financial institution fraud - 183
immigration law revision - 475, 476, 478
interlocking directors - 541
vertical price fixing - 540
Fisher, William F. - 436
Fitzwater, Marlin
civil rights/job bias - 464, 466
EPA Cabinet status - 293
export controls - 199
Hatch Act revision - 409
Nicaraguan elections - 771
Persian Gulf crisis - 746, 755-756
Soviet-U.S. relations - 204, 759, 762
thrift bailout - 181
Flag Protection Act - 53, 524, 525
Flag, U.S.
desecration ban
Brennan career - 510 (box)
congressional action, 1990 - 524-528
conservative coalition - 40, 47, 48
key votes - 6-B, 10-B
summary - 6-7
Supreme Court term summary - 52, 53, 55
Flake, Floyd H. D-N.Y. (6)
housing programs overhaul - 637-640
indictment - 106
minorities in Congress - 924 (chart)
Flake, Margarett - 106
Flemming, Arthur S. - 567
Flippo, Ronnie G. D-Ala. (5)
congressional elections, 1990
House membership changes - 918 (chart)
gubernatorial election, 1990 - 919
Flood control projects
Energy, water appropriations - 863, 865
water projects authorization - 297-299
Flood insurance
authorization - 143
barrier island protection - 302-303
budget process changes - 163
Floods
disaster relief - 845, 846
Florida
abortion - 529-530
acid rain - 264
Amtrak waste disposal - 392

barrier island protection - 302
CDBG funding formula - 641
congressional elections, 1990 - 905-906, 907 (box), 909
congressional redistricting - 931, 933
federal judgeships - 522
gubernatorial election, 1990 - 902, 903, 919, 928
Keys marine sanctuary - 302, 303
naval home ports - 681 (box)
offshore oil leases, drilling - 288, 313, 870, 871, 872, 874
Seminole land claim - 424
Transportation appropriations - 878
water projects authorization - 297, 299
Florio, James J.
Bradley election - 901, 926
gubernatorial election, 1989 - 529
resignation - 14 (box), 902, 911, 913
House membership changes - 918 (chart)
special elections - 934
Flowerlee, Charles - 710
Flynn, Norman D. - 659
FmHA. *See Farmers Home Administration*
FMLN. *See Farabundo Marti National Liberation Front*
Foglietta, Thomas M. D-Pa. (1)
congressional elections, 1990 - 908
independent House members - 922 (box)
money laundering - 188
FOG-M missile - 818
Foley, Thomas S. D-Wash. (5)
defense, foreign policy
defense authorization - 676
defense budget reprogramming - 676 (box)
El Salvador aid - 780, 782, 783-784
intelligence authorization - 795, 799
Nicaragua aid - 773, 774
Panama aid - 778
Persian Gulf crisis - 729-730, 736-738, 740, 751-753
use-of-force debate - 752 (box)
Soviet-U.S. relations - 762
Yeutter gulf remarks - 910
domestic issues
balanced-budget amendment - 175 (box)
budget resolution - 127, 128, 136, 136, 137
budget summit - 130, 131, 132
Bush budget proposal - 116-117
capital gains tax - 168 (box)
child-care aid - 549
Clean Air Act - 243, 244
crime bill - 495, 496
disabled civil rights - 451
farm bill - 341
federal judgeships - 523
flag desecration - 526, 527
handgun wait period - 500-501 (box)
Medicare changes - 566
Puerto Rico status - 424
supplemental appropriations - 845, 846
tax policy - 167
House leadership - 9 (box), 10, 12
campaign finance reform - 59, 66-69
congressional elections, 1990 - 906 (chart)
congressional mail - 74
congressional partisanship - 39
Follow Through - 552-556
Food, Agriculture, Conservation and Trade Act - 323-351
Food and Drug Administration (FDA)
AIDS bill - 586
appropriations - 869 (chart), 869-870
facilities consolidation - 581
fish inspection - 396-399

light butter - 868
medical device regulation - 579, 581
nutrition labels - 575-576
orphan drugs - 577-578
pesticide residue in food imports - 336
product liability - 401
user fees - 125
Food and nutrition. *See also Food assistance programs*
agricultural research, education grants - 345
communicable disease in food workers - 447, 451, 453, 460, 461
hazardous materials transport - 381
waste backhauling - 382-383
fish
"dolphin-safe" tuna labels - 399
inspection - 395-399
pollution contamination research - 301
GATT talks - 209, 210
Iraqi trade sanctions - 722-723, 724, 729
nutrition labels - 575-576, 868
nutrition monitoring - 355
"organically grown" labels - 323, 332-333, 347
pesticide residue - 336, 358
exported banned chemicals - 323, 333, 336, 349, 350
prescription vitamins, minerals - 146
Soviet distribution problems - 205
whistleblower protection - 364
Food assistance programs. *See also Food for Peace; Food stamps; Women, Infants and Children (WIC) program*
appropriations - 554 (box), 867, 869 (chart), 870
authorization - 323, 346, 354-355
budget action - 155
community planning - 552, 555
congregate housing services - 636, 656
donation liability standards - 562
Follow Through - 555
foreign aid
foreign aid appropriations - 837
Nicaragua aid - 773
Panama aid - 775, 777
Soviet Union - 759, 762
fraud controls - 326
homeless aid - 655, 665
supportive housing for the elderly - 654
surplus commodity donations - 346, 354
WIC funding - 554 (box)
Food banks - 562
Food for Freedom - 337, 804
Food for Peace
appropriations - 867, 869 (chart)
authorization - 21, 323, 330, 337-338, 344-345, 803-804
cargo preference - 338-339 (box)
Latin American debt - 218
Food Security Wheat Reserve - 344
Food stamps
appropriations - 554 (box)
agriculture - 867, 869 (chart), 870
FY90 supplemental - 844, 845, 846
authorization - 354-355
farm bill - 323, 326, 346, 348
Indian eligibility - 423
Puerto Rico status - 426
Ford, David A. - 871
Ford, Gerald R. - 57, 312, 408
Ford, Harold E. D-Tenn. (9)
fraud trial - 107
minorities in Congress - 924 (chart)
roll call attendance - 48
Ford Motor Co. - 280-281
Ford, Wendell H. D-Ky.
airline LBOs - 388
alternative power regulation - 317-318

aviation package - 384, 388
campaign finance reform - 61, 63
civil rights/job bias - 467, 469
Clean Air Act - 276
congressional leadership - 12
congressional mail - 75
congressional partisanship - 39
disabled civil rights - 461
Indian remains - 422
"motor voter" bill - 69
presidential support in Congress - 31
uranium enrichment - 310
Ford, William D. D-Mich. (15)
congressional leadership - 11 (box)
federal pay overhaul - 406
roll call attendance - 48
student right-to-know - 626
whistleblower protection - 364
Fordham University - 786
Foreign Affairs Committee, House
subcommittee joint aid hearing - 771-772
Foreign aid. *See also Food for Peace; International development banks; Third World debt; World Bank; specific countries*
appropriations
continuing resolutions - 896 (box)
FY90 supplemental - 844, 845
El Salvador - 782-784
Nicaragua - 770-774
Panama - 774, 777-779
FY91 - 830-844
boxscore - 830
budget authority totals (chart) - 832-833
authorization - 773, 777-778, 782
budget action - 124
environmental protection - 836-837
policy trends - 831, 843
reprogramming - 777-778
summary - 5
trade - 833 (chart)
enterprise funds - 834
export controls - 198
export promotion - 835
tied aid - 207, 830
Foreign currency. *See Currency exchange*
Foreign governments
murder of officials - 494, 497
Foreign languages. *See also English language*
census count adjustment - 416
federal pay overhaul - 407
health-care access - 596
Foreign Military Financing - 831, 833 (chart)
Foreign Military Sales
Andean Initiative - 805
foreign aid appropriations - 831
Foreign policy. *See also Arms control; Foreign aid; Foreign service and diplomacy; Foreign trade and business; Immigration and emigration; State Department; Treaties and international agreements; United Nations*
congressional-executive relations
Bush successes - 16, 17-20
presidential support in Congress - 30
Food for Peace - 803
Foreign Relations Committee, Senate
jurisdiction conflict - 800
Foreign service and diplomacy
appropriations - 832 (chart)
assassination death penalty - 494
Bush nominations - 801 (box)
congressional-executive relations - 800
intelligence authorization - 791
Persian Gulf crisis - 719, 720, 741
U.S. Embassy in Moscow - 760 (box), 881, 885
Foreign trade and business. *See also Agricultural exports and imports; Arms sales and transfers; Buy American provisions; Competitiveness; Customs Service; Export controls; Export-Import Bank; General Agreement on Tariffs and Trade; Import taxes; Oil; Ships and shipping; Tariffs; Trade agreements*
assault weapons - 488, 491, 496, 497, 500-501 (box)
auto fuel efficiency - 280
banking
foreign-based banks in U.S. - 202, 203
money laundering - 188
reciprocity - 189
Bush economic report - 117
China status - 764-768
drift-net fishing ban - 399
Eastern Europe - 206, 834, 836
export aid, promotion
appropriations - 882 (chart)
clean coal technology - 267
Food for Peace - 803
foreign aid appropriations - 835
tobacco promotion - 592, 593, 594
fish inspection - 397-398
foreign aid
appropriations - 833 (chart), 834, 835, 836
Kenya - 790
Latin American - 217-218
Nicaragua - 770, 771
Panama - 776, 777
tied aid - 207, 830
foreign ownership in U.S.
banks - 202
cable TV regulation - 372
foreign governments - 224
immigrant investors - 481, 482, 485
information analysis - 222-225
SSC - 438-439, 864, 865
Israeli defense contractors - 822
Japan-U.S. talks - 208-209
joint production ventures - 541
ozone-depleting chemicals - 270, 271
Persian Gulf crisis - 718, 723, 725, 726, 738
political action committees - 65
securities fraud - 193-194
South Africa sanctions - 787-789
Soviet Union - 204-205
space patent law - 437
strategic minerals - 442-443
textile import quotas - 219-222
timber exports - 214-215
Tongass forest protection - 294
unfair practices
construction contract discrimination - 830, 866
FAA contracts ban - 156
farm bill - 337
National Trade Estimate - 208
SSC contracts - 439
Super 301 process - 208-209
U.S. components - 213, 217
Forest Service, U.S.
appropriations - 873 (chart)
logging/wildlife protection - 296-297, 870, 871
supplemental appropriations - 845
timber sales - 358
Tongass forest protection - 294, 295
Forests and wood products. *See also National forests*
conservation, reforestation
budget action - 124
China - 834
farm bill - 336, 341, 346
rain forest preservation - 773, 779, 837, 861
displaced worker aid - 277 (box)
firefighting appropriations - 845, 846, 873 (chart)
global warming - 307
Indian forest management - 424
Japan-U.S. trade - 208-209, 294
logging limits/wildlife protection - 294-297, 870-876
methane assessment - 271
methanol - 240 (box)
SBA authorization - 395
timber exports - 211-217
Formaldehyde - 252, 383
Fornos, Werner H. - 838 (box)
Fort Hood, Texas - 122, 672
Fort Lauderdale, Fla. - 582
Fort Lewis, Wash. - 122, 672
Fortuna, Roger - 309-310
Foster care
abortion counseling - 605
administrative costs - 150
AFDC eligibility - 150
children's welfare services - 556
housing programs overhaul - 642, 650, 651, 652, 656
sequestration procedures - 162
vocational education authorization - 622
Foster Care Independent Living Program - 150
Fourteenth Amendment
disabled civil rights - 452
Souter confirmation - 514
torture ban treaty - 807
Fourth Amendment
crime bill - 498
Fowler, Mark - 373
Fowler, Wyche Jr. D-Ga.
budget action - 130 (box), 131
CFE - 701
defense appropriations - 820
farm bill - 324, 335
Interior appropriations - 876
NEA authorization - 431
Persian Gulf crisis
use-of-force debate - 752 (box)
thrift supervisor - 180 (box)
France
Antarctica protection - 305
CFE - 700
European development bank - 206
farm subsidies - 209, 210
Food for Peace - 803
German unification - 762, 763
Paris summit - 703
Persian Gulf crisis - 719, 740
Frank, Barney D-Mass. (4)
civil rights/job bias - 469
coin redesign - 197
crime bill - 498
defense authorization - 683
disabled civil rights - 451
ethics investigation - 6, 103-104
key votes - 11-B
executive branch honoraria - 72 (box)
housing programs overhaul - 642
immigration law revision - 476-478
Legal Services Corporation - 533
prepayment of subsidized mortgages - 663-664
radiation victims compensation - 591
Savage ethics case - 105
Franking privilege - 65, 68, 73-75, 894-896
Franks, Gary - 905 (chart), 916, 918 (chart), 919, 923, 924 (chart)
Fraud
deceptive mail curbs - 417
financial institutions
Commerce/Justice/State appropriations - 881, 884
crime bill - 486, 490, 493-494, 495, 498, 499
summary - 6
thrift bailout - 181, 182-183 (box)
Flake indictment - 106
Ford trial - 107
fraudulent made-in-America labels - 156
illegal aliens - 151, 479, 484, 485, 558
Medigap plans - 573, 574
nutrition labels - 575-576
octane labeling - 282
RICO revision - 537
securities violations - 5, 193-194
Social Security - 558
telemarketing fraud - 402, 881
voter registration - 69-70
Fraud, waste and abuse in government programs
centralized financial management - 416
defense procurement - 679, 682
farm subsidy limits - 122
food assistance programs - 326, 355
food stamps - 323, 346, 354-355
foreign aid - 338, 804
HUD scandal investigation - 636, 641, 666-668
Indian programs - 421
irrigation subsidies - 356
Free Congress Federation - 15
Free-market economies
defense preparedness - 202
Latin American aid - 217
Poland debt - 834
Freedom of Information Act
pesticide recordkeeping - 346
securities enforcement - 193-194
Freedom of religion
Souter confirmation - 512, 514
Freedom of speech
campaign finance reform - 61, 64
corporate campaign limits - 59 (box)
flag desecration - 524-528
student religious groups - 618 (box)
Freedom of the press
Brennan career - 510 (box)
China-U.S. relations - 765, 766
South Africa sanctions - 788
Freedom space station - 434, 436-437, 855
Frenzel, Bill R-Minn. (3)
appropriations
District of Columbia - 892
Energy, water - 864
Labor/HHS appropriations - 850
legislative branch - 896
military construction - 828
Treasury, Postal - 889
VA/HUD - 855
budget action - 112, 127, 130 (box), 133-134
campaign finance reform - 68
congressional mail - 74, 75
joint production ventures - 541
retirement - 918 (chart)
textile import quotas - 221, 222
Frieden, Lex - 448
Friends of the Earth - 283, 285
Fritts, Edward O. - 67 (box)
Frohnmayer, Dave - 530, 433, 907, 929,930
Fuel. *See also Alternative fuels; Fuel and gasoline taxes; Gasoline*
clean air summary - 4
efficiency standards - 7, 279-281
hydrogen - 273, 313, 318-319
Fuel and gasoline taxes
aviation fuel - 385
budget action - 126, 135, 140, 158-159, 164-165, 167, 172
Bush transportation policy - 384-385
congressional leadership - 10
energy issues, 1990 - 312, 313 (box)

gasohol - 214, 216
global warming - 307
home heating oil - 134, 139, 313 (box)
leaking tank fund - 159, 172
non-conventional fuel tax incentive - 160
Fujimori, Alberto - 805
Fulbright scholarship program -767 (box)
Furniture
chair safety - 394
prison industries - 498
Fuster, Jaime B. Pop. Dem.-Puerto Rico
minorities in Congress - 924 (chart)
Puerto Rico status - 426
Futures. *See Stocks, bonds and securities*

G

Gadsden, Ala. - 878
Gaffigan, Jim - 402
Gaffney, Frank J. - 696, 703, 704-705, 707, 711
Gaia, Pam - 107
Galbraith, Peter W. - 723
Gallegly, Elton R-Calif. (21)
congressional elections, 1990
low winning percentage - 906 (chart)
Gallo, Dean A. R-N.J. (11)
foreign aid appropriations - 834
oil pollution cleanup - 285
Galvin, John - 828
Gambling. *See also Lotteries*
disabled civil rights exclusion - 452, 459
Gantt, Harvey B. - 530, 915, 923
GAO. *See General Accounting Office*
Garage door openers - 394, 395
Garbage. *See Waste products*
Garcia, Alan - 805
Garcia, Robert
conviction appeal - 107
resignation - 6, 14 (box), 923, 934
Gardner, Bruce - 333
Garn, Jake R-Utah
Clean Air Act - 235, 238
foreign banks - 189
housing programs overhaul - 636
irrigation subsidies - 357
NASA authorization - 435
savings and loan scandal - 78, 85
thrift supervisor - 180 (box)
VA/HUD appropriations - 858-860
Gasohol
alternative fuel - 240 (box)
Caribbean Basin Initiative - 214, 216
octane labeling - 282
Gasoline. *See also Fuel and gasoline taxes*
emissions controls - 229, 251-252
evaporative emissions - 240 (box), 252
octane labeling - 282
reformulated gasoline - 229, 231 (box). 232, 233 (box), 240 (box), 241, 243, 244, 246-247, 250, 252-253, 278
summer volatility - 252
vapor recovery - 246, 249, 252
Gasoline taxes. *See Fuel and gasoline taxes*
GATT. *See General Agreement on Tariffs and Trade*
Gaydos, Joseph M. D-Pa. (20)
congressional leadership - 11 (box)
Transportation appropriations - 878
Gaza. *See West Bank and Gaza*
Gearan, Mark - 926
Gejdenson, Sam D-Conn. (2)
China-U.S. relations - 765
congressional pay, honoraria - 73
export controls - 199
irrigation subsidies - 356-357
Nicaragua aid - 772
Persian Gulf crisis
questionable gulf allies - 740 (box)
Gekas, George W. R-Pa. (17)
conservative coalition - 40
crime bill - 494, 495, 497, 499
disabled civil rights - 451
environmental disasters - 285 (box)
federal judgeships - 521
handgun wait period - 501 (box)
General Accounting Office (GAO)
agricultural export subsidies - 330
appropriations - 894, 895 (chart)
appropriations deferral - 20-21
budget process - 176
cable TV regulation - 370
census count adjustment - 415
Defense Department
antidrug funding - 679
naval home ports - 681 (box)
parts inventories - 821
procurement - 680
RAM missiles - 819
disabled civil rights - 458
DOE nuclear cleanup - 308
earned income tax credit - 152, 158
family leave - 360
FDIC premiums - 185-186
federal accounting standards - 890
federal judgeships - 522
foreign ownership of U.S. business - 223-225
Hatch Act revision - 409
hazardous materials transport - 380, 382-383
housing
affordable housing study - 647
HUD scandal investigation - 668
low-income rental aid - 651
immigration law revision - 481 (box), 485
irrigation subsidies - 356
medical device safety - 580
Medigap insurance - 148, 573-574
mining claims - 876
money laundering - 779
NIH authorization - 602
octane labeling - 282
Panama debt relief - 778, 779
product liability - 400
shipping industry - 338 (box)
SSC authorization - 439
student loan defaults - 626 (box)
student right-to-know - 624
veterans tax information access - 160
General Agreement on Tariffs and Trade (GATT)
agricultural subsidy talks - 209-210
auto fuel efficiency - 280
budget action - 141
Caribbean Basin Initiative - 212-213
China-U.S. relations - 766
Customs fees - 156-157, 212
Czechoslovak-U.S. trade - 206
East Europe trade - 204
farm bill - 323, 325, 328, 344, 348, 351
India-U.S. trade - 209
Japan-U.S. trade - 208, 209
Soviet participation - 205
textile import quotas - 219-222
timber exports - 215
General Motors Corp.- 280-281
General Services Administration
appropriations - 887 (chart), 888, 889
ozone-layer protection - 271
Generalized System of Preferences - 212, 771, 777
Generic drugs - 147, 570 (box)
Genetic engineering
patent law - 437
Genetics
human gene mapping - 126, 601, 861, 865
Genocide
Armenian genocide commemoration - 807-808
treaty - 806-807
Genscher, Hans Dietrich - 763, 699
Geography education - 615
Geological Survey, U.S.
appropriations - 873 (chart)
earthquake research - 442
Geology. *See also Global climate change*
earthquake research - 442
minerals research - 442-443
George Washington University Hospital - 598
Georgia
acid rain - 262
congressional elections, 1990 - 903, 906, 909
congressional redistricting - 931
federal judgeships - 522
gubernatorial election, 1990 - 930
peanut price supports - 329-330
Geothermal energy
alternative power regulation - 316
budget action - 160, 173
Energy, water appropriations - 861, 866
global warming - 307
tax credit - 313 (box)
Gephardt, Richard A. D-Mo. (3)
budget action - 130, 132, 137
congressional elections, 1990 - 904, 907, 917
low winning percentage - 906 (chart)
congressional leadership - 9 (box), 10, 12
defense authorization - 683
Energy, water appropriations - 863
family leave - 361
flag desecration - 526
Medicare coverage of mammograms - 564 (box)
"motor voter" bill - 70
Persian Gulf crisis - 730, 740, 747, 749, 752
Soviet aid - 759
Gerasimov, Gennadi I. - 698
Geren, Pete D-Texas (12)
congressional elections, 1990 - 908
Geriatric research - 599
Gerkin, David - 427
Germany. *See also East Germany; West Germany*
CFE - 700, 701, 702
defense burden-sharing - 682, 820
farm subsidies - 209, 210
Food for Peace - 803
Holocaust reparations - 148, 569
military construction appropriations - 827
Persian Gulf crisis - 717
RAM missiles - 819, 825
unification - 3, 762-763
CFE - 696, 698-699
customs fees - 212
Gerson, Stuart M. - 739 (box)
Gesell, Gerhard A. - 535
Ghana
U.S. aid - 836
Gibbons, Sam M. D-Fla. (7)
Caribbean Basin Initiative - 211, 212, 216, 217
China-U.S. relations - 765, 766
Persian Gulf crisis - 726
use-of-force debate - 753 (box)
textile import quotas - 221-222
Gigante, Robert - 934
Gilbert, Pamela - 538
Gilchrest, Wayne T. - 108, 918 (chart), 922
Gilliam, DuBois L. - 666, 667
Gillmor, Paul E. R-Ohio (5)
"motor voter" bill - 70
Gilman, Benjamin A. R-N.Y. (22)
defense authorization - 682
Gingrich, Marianne - 104
Gingrich, Newt R-Ga. (6)
budget action - 130 (box), 131, 137
congressional elections, 1990 - 901, 904, 906, 917, 922
low winning percentage - 906 (chart)
marginal vote share - 905 (chart)
congressional leadership - 8-12
congressional partisanship - 39
conservative coalition - 48
defense authorization - 683
Eastern Airlines strike - 369
education proposals - 614
El Salvador aid - 784
ethics case - 104-105
farm bill - 332
FHA rules revision - 660
flag desecration - 526
Frank ethics case - 103, 104
"motor voter" bill - 69
Persian Gulf crisis - 755
presidential support in Congress - 31
Social Security earnings test - 557
technology programs - 441
Ginnie Mae. *See Government National Mortgage Association*
Ginsburg, Douglas H. - 518 (box)
Giugni, Henry K. - 12 (box)
Glaspie, April C. - 725
Glauber, Robert R. - 181, 184, 192
Glaxo Inc. - 215-216
Glazier, Stephen - 14-15
Glen Canyon Dam - 300-301, 356
Glenn, John D-Ohio
B-2 bomber - 690
Clean Air Act - 234, 238, 278
defense authorization - 678, 679, 680
EPA Cabinet status - 291
executive branch honoraria - 72 (box)
federal financial centralization - 416
federal pay overhaul - 407
food aid cargo preference - 339 (box)
Hatch Act revision - 408, 409
savings and loan scandal - 6, 78-97
Stello nomination - 310
Treasury, Postal appropriations - 888, 889, 890
Glickman, Dan D-Kan. (4)
animal rights activists - 442
budget summit - 4, 8
campaign finance reform - 67
CFTC authorization - 195
civil rights/job bias - 470
crime bill - 495
disabled civil rights - 450-451
farm bill - 327, 341
federal judgeships - 521
financial institution fraud - 183
fish inspection - 397
food stamps - 355
insurance price-sharing - 401
intelligence authorization - 795, 796
Persian Gulf crisis - 724, 728
RICO revision - 538
stock market regulation - 190
Global Change, Office of - 307
Global climate change. *See also Ozone-layer protection*
alternative power regulation - 317
auto fuel efficiency - 280
budget action - 124, 126
Clean Air Act

auto emissions - 232, 233
greenhouse gas monitoring - 274
methane assessment - 271
Energy, water appropriations - 866
EPA Cabinet status - 291-292
NASA monitoring - 434, 436
research, energy policy - 307
tropical forest protection - 837
Global ecological commons - 306
Gobie, Steve - 103-104
Goddard Space Flight Center - 437
Goddard, Terry - 907-908, 926, 930, 933
Golar, Simeon - 934
Gold
federal bond security - 128
Golden, Colo. - 308
Goldman, Marshall - 762
Goldman, Sheldon - 515-516, 517, 519
Goldstein, Steve - 300
Goldston, David J. - 402
Goldthwait, Christopher E. - 21, 803
Gonzalez, Henry B. D-Texas (20)
barrier island protection - 302
coin redesign - 196, 197
congressional leadership - 11 (box)
FHA rules revision - 659-660
financial institution fraud - 183
housing programs overhaul - 631-644, 647, 656
HUD scandal investigation - 667
minorities in Congress - 924 (chart)
prepayment of subsidized mortgages - 663, 664
RICO revision - 538
savings and loan scandal - 80
thrift bailout - 184
Goodling, Bill R-Pa. (19)
age discrimination - 363
child-care aid - 550
civil rights/job bias - 468
community service programs - 562
displaced homemakers - 366 (box)
education proposals - 613-614, 615
Head Start authorization - 555
job training overhaul - 366
student right-to-know - 624-625, 627
Gorbachev, Mikhail S.
CFE - 696, 698, 700, 702
chemical weapons pact - 709, 710
defense authorization - 672
German unification - 763, 699
Nobel Peace Prize - 3
Paris summit - 703, 704
Persian Gulf crisis - 719, 720, 731-732, 740, 756
Soviet aid to Nicaragua - 770
Soviet-U.S. relations - 757, 758, 760, 761
Soviet-U.S. trade - 204-205
START - 705, 706, 707
Washington summit - 701, 707-708
nuclear test treaties - 711
Gordon, Bart D-Tenn. (6)
family leave - 360
Gore, Al D-Tenn.
budget action - 165
cable TV regulation - 370-372
Clean Air Act - 234
congressional elections, 1990 - 916
crime bill - 491
defense authorization - 679, 680
EPA cabinet status - 291
food-waste transport - 383
Interior appropriations - 875
Medicare changes - 568
NASA authorization - 435
Persian Gulf crisis - 751
U.S. goals, rationales - 745 (box)
space patent law - 437
Gorton, Slade R-Wash.
auto fuel efficiency - 279
Clean Air Act - 236
community service programs - 561
crime bill - 493
flag desecration - 528
food-waste transport - 383
nuclear test treaties - 713
textile import quotas - 220
Goss, Porter J. R-Fla. (13)
Nicaraguan policy debate - 772 (box)
Gough, Wayne - 286
Gould, George B. - 411
Government ethics. *See Congressional ethics; Ethics in government; Fraud, waste and abuse in government programs*
Government Ethics, Office of
executive branch honoraria - 72 (box)
HUD scandal investigation - 668
Government National Mortgage Association (Ginnie Mae)
appropriations - 855 (chart)
authorization - 649
fees - 123
Government Operations Committee, House
leadership - 924
Government Printing Office
appropriations - 895 (chart)
disabled civil rights - 458
Government securities
gold-backed bonds - 128
mine reclamation fund surpluses - 154
thrift bailout - 179
Treasury securities
Federal Reserve interest - 186
Social Security fund investment - 170 (box)
Government-sponsored enterprises
budget process changes - 163
uranium enrichment - 310-311
Governors. *See also Gubernatorial elections*
child-care aid - 549
education policy - 610, 613, 847, 853
list, 1991, by state - 927
Medicaid expansion - 569
National Guard training - 52, 53, 694 (box)
party lineup, 1990-91 - 926 (chart), 929 (map)
Gradison, Bill R-Ohio (2)
Bush congressional relations - 16
farm bill - 331
Pepper Commission - 607
taxes - 169
Graduate education
vocational education authorization - 622
Grady, Bob - 276
Graham, Bob D-Fla.
Amtrak waste disposal - 392
Armenian genocide commemoration - 808
budget action - 132
Caribbean Basin Initiative - 211, 212, 214
crime bill - 490, 491, 495
defense appropriations - 821
El Salvador aid - 786
FDIC premiums - 186
flag desecration - 528
Florida Keys protection - 303
foreign aid appropriations - 842
housing programs overhaul - 641
HUD scandal investigation - 668
Persian Gulf crisis - 755
Social Security in budget accounting - 170 (box)
textile import quotas - 220
veterans disability pay - 421
Graham, Elaine - 451
Grain. *See Wheat and feed grain*
Gramm, Phil R-Texas
abortion - 852
budget action - 130
budget process - 176
Clean Air Act - 237
community service programs - 561
congressional elections, 1990 - 909, 916
congressional leadership - 12
conservative coalition - 48
crime bill - 492-493
D.C. appropriations - 892, 893
D.C. status - 428
defense authorization - 678
defense preparedness - 203
foreign banks - 189
housing programs overhaul - 641
OMB review powers - 411
Persian Gulf crisis - 724
stock market regulation - 193
student loan default - 626 (box)
textile import quotas - 220
Gramm-Rudman-Hollings law
budget chronology - 115
budget process changes - 173-178
budget summit - 111, 132-133
Bush budget proposal - 117
Bush economic report - 136
continuing resolutions - 896-897 (box)
defense budget reprogramming - 676 (box)
Operation Desert Shield - 733
summary - 4
Social Security in budget accounting - 165, 846
VA programs - 420
Gramm, Wendy Lee - 412
Grand Canyon
erosion - 300-301, 356, 357
visibility impairment - 274
Grandy, Fred R-Iowa (6)
family leave - 360
NEA authorization - 433
Persian Gulf crisis - 724
Grant, Bill R-Fla. (2)
congressional elections, 1990 - 906, 917
defeated House members - 917 (chart)
House membership changes - 918 (chart)
Grant Foundation - 619
Grassley, Charles E. R-Iowa
ALJ corps - 523
budget action - 128
civil rights/job bias - 467
copyright infringement - 542-543
crime bill - 493
disabled civil rights - 460, 461
education proposals - 610
judicial appointments - 516
juvenile justice nomination - 506
military construction appropriations - 830
Persian Gulf crisis - 750
use-of-force debate - 752 (box)
Souter confirmation - 512
Thomas confirmation - 518 (box)
Graves. *See Burials*
Gray, C. Boyden - 17, 413, 799
Gray, Edwin J. - 79-96
Gray, William H. III D-Pa. (2)
budget action - 130 (box)
Bush congressional relations - 22
congressional leadership - 9 (box), 12
Kenya aid - 790
minorities in Congress - 924 (chart)
"motor voter" bill - 70
Savage ethics case - 106
South Africa sanctions - 789
Transportation appropriations - 876-877, 880
Treasury, Postal appropriations - 888
Great Britain
CFE - 698, 700, 701
European development bank - 206
export controls - 199
foreign ownership of U.S. business - 223
German unification - 762, 763
military construction appropriations - 827
Persian Gulf crisis - 719, 728, 740
Salvadoran Jesuit murder case - 781
Trident missile sales - 684
Great Lakes
acid rain - 258
barrier island protection - 302, 303
coastal zone management - 154, 288-289
food aid cargo preference - 338-339 (box), 804
pollution cleanup, control - 289-290, 301
water projects authorization - 299
zebra mussel control - 298, 303-304
Great Plains - 335, 873
Greece
U.S. aid - 831, 833, 835, 840
Green, Bill R-N.Y. (15)
AIDS bill - 588
D.C. appropriations - 893
space station - 436-437
VA/HUD appropriations - 856, 859
HUD pork-barrel spending - 857 (box)
Green, June L. - 524
Green, Mark - 97
Green, Thomas C. - 88
Greene, Harold H. - 378, 720, 738, 739 (box)
Greenhouse effect. *See Global climate change*
Greenspan, Alan
CFTC authorization - 195
foreign ownership of U.S. business - 223
Persian Gulf crisis - 741, 744 (box)
savings and loan scandal - 83, 89, 90
stock market regulation - 190
Greer, Frank - 487
Gregg, Judd - 530, 928, 929
Grenada
Caribbean Basin Initiative - 212
Grillo, Carl - 934
Grocery stores
food stamps - 346, 355
nutrition labels - 576
Grogan, James - 89, 94-95
Groundwater protection
farm bill - 327, 335
Group Health Association of America - 101
Grunseth, Jon - 907 (box), 911, 930
GSL. *See Guaranteed Student Loans*
Guam
child care block grant - 152
community development block grants - 655
food stamps - 346, 354
naval bases - 814, 826
Guaranteed Student Loans (GSLs) - 626-627 (box), 849 (chart)
Guarini, Frank J. D-N.J. (14)
China-U.S. relations - 766
Guatemala
Caribbean Basin Initiative - 212
Gubernatorial elections
abortion - 529
California - 357
incumbents' vote share - 904 (chart)
Puerto Rico status - 425
results, 1990 - 912, 926-930
returns, 1990 (chart) - 935-941

third-party candidates - 907
Guinot, Luis Jr. - 532
Gulf Cooperation Council - 719, 721
Gulf of Mexico
barrier island protection - 302-303
food aid cargo preference - 338-339 (box), 804
offshore drilling - 230, 313, 871, 872
pipeline safety inspection - 286 (box)
Gulf of Oman - 719
Gulf of Tonkin Resolution - 721, 733-734
Gun control. *See Firearms*
Gun Control Act of 1968 - 491, 500 (box)
Gunderson, Steve R-Wis. (3)
civil rights/job bias - 467
community service programs - 562
farm bill - 329
NEA authorization - 432
Gutting, Richard E. - 286 (box)
Guyana
Caribbean Basin Initiative - 212
U.S. ambassador - 801
Gynecology - 602

H

Haas, Ellen - 398
Habeas corpus appeals - 6, 486-499, 886
Hafer, Barbara - 929
Hager, Barry - 218
Haiti
Caribbean Basin Initiative - 212
Hakim, Albert A. - 535
Hall, J. Blakeley - 532
Hall, Ralph M. D-Texas (4)
Clean Air Act - 240-242, 247
Frank ethics case - 104
Interior appropriations - 872
Legal Services Corporation - 532
Hall, Robert - 695, 827
Hall, Tony P. D-Ohio (3)
WIC funding - 554 (box)
Hallock, John W. - 918 (chart), 922
Halons - 269, 270
Hamilton, James - 81 (box), 87, 96-97, 102
Hamilton, Lee H. D-Ind. (9)
foreign ownership of U.S. business - 224
intelligence authorization - 792, 796
Persian Gulf crisis - 725, 728, 742, 752, 756
Soviet-U.S. relations - 761
Transportation appropriations - 878
Hamm, Ron - 246
Hammerschmidt, John Paul R-Ark. (3)
disabled civil rights - 449
water projects authorization - 298, 299
Hampton University - 667
Hancock, Mel R-Mo. (7)
aviation security - 390
congressional elections, 1990 - 906
low winning percentage - 906 (chart)
marginal vote share - 905 (chart)
Handgun Control Inc. - 500
Handguns. *See Firearms*
Handicapped. *See Disabled persons*
Hanford, Wash. - 679
Hannemann, Mufi E. - 934
Hansen, James V. R-Utah (1)
congressional elections, 1990
marginal vote share - 905 (chart)
disabled civil rights - 459
Frank ethics case - 104
Harbor Maintenance Trust Fund - 159
Harkin, Frank - 461
Harkin, Tom D-Iowa
abortion - 530
congressional elections, 1990 - 903, 913
congressional partisanship - 40
D.C. status - 428
disabled civil rights - 447, 460, 461
disabled education - 616-617
Energy, water appropriations - 865
farm bill - 333, 337
foreign aid appropriations - 841
foreign ownership of U.S. business - 224
Interior appropriations - 876
Labor/HHS appropriations - 851, 852, 853
NIH authorization - 601-602, 603
public health planning - 609
HARM missiles - 818
Harpoon missiles - 675
Harrier aircraft - 674
Harrington, Toni - 280
Harris, Claude D-Ala. (7)
crime bill - 496
Harris, Elisa D. - 709-710
Harris, Leslie - 488 (box)
Hart, Stephen - 392
Hartigan, Neil F. - 928, 933
Hartnett, Thomas F. - 13
Harvard University - 633
Hastert, Dennis R-Ill. (14)
disabled civil rights - 450
EPA Cabinet status - 293
Social Security earnings test - 557
Hatch Act
Bush congressional relations - 16
revisions - 408-411
boxscore - 408
summary - 6
veto message (text) - 410
Hatch, Orrin G. R-Utah
age discrimination - 362-364
AIDS bill - 583
Amtrak waste disposal - 392
assault weapons ban - 500 (box)
balanced-budget amendment - 174 (box)
budget action - 130 (box), 165
campaign finance reform - 65
civil rights/job bias - 465, 467, 471
Clean Air Act - 235, 278
community service programs - 560, 561
copyright issues - 541, 542
crime bill - 490-493
defense authorization - 679
disabled civil rights - 460, 461
family planning authorization - 605
FDA facilities - 581
federal judgeships - 521, 523
immigration law revision - 480
Interior appropriations - 874, 875
job training overhaul - 367
juvenile justice nomination - 506
Labor/HHS appropriations - 853
NEA authorization - 430-433
North conviction overturn - 535
nutrition labels - 576
orphan drugs - 579
pesticide residue in food - 358
radiation victims compensation - 590-591
RICO revision - 537
sex crime deterrence - 507
Supreme Court term summary - 52, 56
Hatcher, Charles D-Ga. (2)
farm bill - 330
Hatfield, Mark O. R-Ore.
abortion - 530
U.N. population fund - 839 (box)
Clean Air Act - 278
congressional elections, 1990 - 903, 911, 915
vote-share falloff - 904 (chart)
crime bill - 490, 492, 493
defense authorization - 677, 680
Energy, water appropriations - 865
federal pay overhaul - 407
flag desecration - 528
Interior appropriations - 876
"motor voter" bill - 70
NIH authorization - 601
Persian Gulf crisis - 750-751
roll call attendance - 48
SDI - 692
Hathaway, Dale E. - 209
Havel, Vaclav - 204 (box)
Hawaii
congressional elections, 1990 - 909, 916
Energy, water appropriations - 861, 865, 866
federal judgeships - 522
gubernatorial election, 1990 - 930
native programs
library services - 617
vocational education authorization - 620
naval home ports - 678
Hawkins, Augustus F. D-Calif. (29)
characteristics of Congress - 924, 925
child care aid - 548, 550, 551
civil rights/job bias - 462, 468, 470-471, 473
community service programs - 562
congressional leadership - 11 (box)
disabled education - 617
education proposals - 613, 615
Head Start authorization - 555
job training overhaul - 366
retirement - 918 (chart)
vocational education authorization - 619
Hawkins, David - 239
Hayden, Mike - 926, 928
Hayes, Charles A. D-Ill. (1)
minorities in Congress - 924 (chart)
pornographic mail - 417
Hazardous Materials Transportation Act - 380
Hazardous Materials Transportation Uniform Safety Act - 380-382
Hazardous substances. *See also Acid rain; Air pollution; Alcohol abuse; Drug abuse; Hazardous waste cleanup; Lead; Nuclear waste; Ozone-layer protection; Pests and pesticides; Radiation; Superfund; Tobacco; Waste products; Water pollution*
Agent Orange compensation - 418-419
biological agents - 290, 301
child-resistant packaging - 417
fish inspection - 396-399
"negligible risk" standard - 358
poisoning prevention - 395
shipment tracking - 381
toxic torts - 543
transportation safety - 380-382
workplace notice - 412
Hazardous waste cleanup. *See also Nuclear waste; Superfund*
chemical weapons destruction - 709, 710
federal RCRA compliance - 291, 292, 293, 308-309
military posts - 122, 675, 679-680, 816, 827, 829
HBO - 371
Head Start
appropriations - 562, 846, 848, 851, 853
authorization - 552-556
budget action - 123, 128
Bush economic report - 117
census count adjustment - 415
child care aid - 548, 550, 551
education proposals - 613, 615
effects study - 555
summary - 5
Health and Human Services Department, U.S. (HHS). *See also National Institutes of Health; Public Health Service*
abortion counseling - 56
AIDS bill - 582-589
aging research - 598, 599
antismoking bills - 592-594
appropriations - 811, 847-853
child care standards - 153
communicable disease
disabled civil rights exclusions - 453, 460, 461
immigration exclusions - 480-481 (box), 484
emergency, trauma care - 597-598
federal health benefits - 155
fetal research - 600-601
food-waste transport - 383
Head Start authorization - 552, 554
Medicaid rebate - 146
medical device safety - 580
Medicare - 143-146
minority health - 596
nursing home regulation - 148, 589
nutrition labels - 575
nutrition monitoring - 355
organ transplants - 596, 597
orphan drugs - 578, 579
Pepper Commission - 609
perinatal services demonstration - 651
public health planning - 609
radiation victims compensation - 591
Social Security - 150-151
SSA independence - 558
vaccine program authorization - 591
vocational education - 620
Health and medical care. *See also Child health and nutrition; Community-base health care; Dental care and dentists; Drugs and pharmaceuticals; Emergency medical care; Food and nutrition; Hazardous substances; Health education; Health insurance; Health maintenance organizations (HMOs); Home health care; Hospices; Hospitals; Long-term health care; Medicaid; Medical devices; Medical ethics; Medical research and technology; Medicare; Mental health and illness; Nurses; Nursing homes; Occupational health and safety; Physicians; Preventive medical care; Primary health care; Public health; Rural health care; Veterans health care; specific health problems*
access for low-income families - 148
case management - 146, 148, 583, 584, 585
cost containment - 144
disabled civil rights - 459
family leave - 359-361
health promotion - 609
immigrant aid - 479
immigration exclusions - 480-481 (box), 484
Indian programs - 422-423
job-related medical exams - 452-453
low-income elderly - 598-599
military personnel - 686, 816
patient dumping - 144
perinatal services - 651
public housing support services - 640, 651, 654
SDI authorization debate - 692
state of the union address - 19
treatment effectiveness - 850
Health Care Financing Administration

- 589, 848 (chart)
Health Care for the Homeless program - 665
Health care workers. *See also Nurses; Physicians*
AIDS bill - 584
federal pay overhaul - 406
Health Service Corps authorization - 595
Medicare hospital payments - 143
minority opportunity - 596
VA staff honoraria - 420
Health education
cancer detection - 606
family planning - 605
HIV demonstration project - 148
public housing - 596
Health insurance. *See also Health maintenance organizations (HMOs); Medicaid; Medicare; Medicare Catastrophic Coverage Act*
AIDS bill - 583, 585, 587
child-care aid - 547, 548
"dread disease" policies - 572, 574
earned income tax credit - 152, 158, 172
family leave - 360
hostages - 844
Medicaid families - 569, 572-575
Medigap policies - 148-149, 563, 568, 572-575
military dependents - 680
pension fund assets - 161
Pepper Commission - 607-609
primary payers - 146
retirement benefits - 148, 363, 364, 368
self-employed persons - 160, 173
trauma care - 597
veterans benefits, fees - 126, 155, 420
Health Insurance Association of America - 573, 575
Health interest groups
antismoking bills - 592
disabled civil rights - 447
Labor/HHS appropriations - 847, 851
Medicaid drug discounts - 570 (box)
Medicare changes - 567
Health maintenance organizations (HMOs)
budget action - 125, 146
patient self-determination - 146
Health Resources and Services Administration - 584
Healthy Start - 613
Healy, Bernardine P. - 602 (box), 603
Hearing impaired
closed-captioned TV - 375
disabled civil rights - 447-453
small business access barrier removal - 160
TDD, relay services - 457-458
Heart disease
minority health - 596
NIH authorization - 601
Heath, Josie - 915 (chart)
Hecht, Chic - 281
Hefley, Joel R-Colo. (5)
congressional elections, 1990 - 905
low winning percentage - 906 (chart)
congressional term limit - 15
Heflin, Howell D-Ala.
ALJ corps - 523
animal rights activists - 441
balanced budget amendment - 175 (box)
Clean Air Act - 238
congressional elections, 1990 - 909, 916
conservative coalition - 48
D'Amato ethics case - 97
disabled civil rights - 461
Durenberger ethics case - 98, 102
farm bill - 334
federal judgeships - 520, 521
flag desecration - 528
juvenile justice nomination - 506
military construction appropriations - 830
"motor voter" bill - 70
Persian Gulf crisis - 750-751
savings and loan scandal - 80, 82, 92, 96
appearance standard - 87
Ethics Committee special counsel - 81 (box)
Tongass forest protection - 295
Hefner, W. G. "Bill" D-N.C. (8)
congressional elections, 1990 - 923
marginal vote share - 905 (chart)
military construction appropriations - 827, 828
Heftel, Cecil - 922
Heinz, John R-Pa.
budget action - 165
Caribbean Basin Initiative - 213, 215
civil rights/job bias - 467
Clean Air Act - 234
crime bill - 493
defense preparedness - 203
driver literacy - 611
export controls - 200
financial institution fraud - 182
housing programs overhaul - 635
Pepper Commission - 607
textile import quotas - 220
Transportation appropriations - 876-877, 880
Helicopters. *See also V-22 Osprey*
appropriations - 817-818, 824-825
carriers - 675, 819, 826
CFE - 697 (chart), 700, 702, 703
defense authorization - 675, 677-678, 685
Ex-Im Bank financing - 643
military reserve equipment - 816, 821
Hellfire missiles - 674, 817-818, 824
Helme, Ned - 276
Helms, Jesse R-N.C.
abortion - 530
AIDS bill - 582-583, 586
Caribbean Basin Initiative - 215, 217
Clean Air Act - 235, 236, 238
congressional elections, 1990 - 911, 915, 923
defense authorization - 680
diplomatic nominations - 801 (box)
disabled civil rights - 460, 461
education proposals - 610-615
export controls - 198
farm bill - 336-337, 351
flag desecration - 528
food stamps - 354
German unification - 763
hate crimes statistics - 507
housing programs overhaul - 656
immigration exclusions - 480 (box)
Interior appropriations - 870, 875
Labor/HHS appropriations - 852
Legal Services Corporation - 532
library programs - 617
NEA authorization - 430-433
Nicaragua aid - 773
nuclear test treaties - 713
Persian Gulf crisis - 723
savings and loan scandal - 80, 82, 97
South Africa sanctions - 789
Soviet-U.S. relations - 760-761
START - 706, 707
State Department authorization - 800
textile import quotas - 219
torture ban treaty - 806, 807
TV sex guidelines - 374 (box)
U.N. funding - 802
Helsinki process - 800
Hemophilia - 585, 586
Hempstone, Smith - 790
Henderson, James A. Jr. - 400, 401
Henkel, Lee H. Jr. - 84, 90
Henry, Paul B. R-Mich. (5)
civil rights/job bias - 469
congressional elections, 1990 - 908
NEA authorization - 432
student right-to-know - 624, 625-626
Henry's Fork - 861
Herbicides. *See also Agent Orange*
alternative farming research - 336
Hercules cargo planes - 821
Heritage Foundation - 515, 633, 792, 876
Hernandez Colon, Rafael - 425, 427
Hertel, Dennis M. D-Mich. (14)
Antarctica protection - 306
Hickel, Walter J. - 907, 927, 930
Hickman, Harrison - 902
High-definition television - 440
High Density Traffic Airport Rule - 386-387
High Energy Physics Advisory Panel - 438
High-fructose corn syrup - 328
Higher Education Act Amendments of 1980 - 628
Higher Education Act of 1965 - 611, 614
Highland, Calif. - 858
Highway Trust Fund - 159, 165, 172, 385, 877, 878, 880
Highways and roads
bridge deficiencies - 384
capital improvements - 385
drug enforcement - 502, 506
drunken driving - 52, 53
Clean Air Act compliance - 230, 239
conservation corps - 562
hazardous materials transport - 382
logging roads - 294, 295, 358, 871, 876
Transportation appropriations - 876, 877, 878, 880
Hiler, John R-Ind. (3)
coin redesign - 197
congressional elections, 1990 - 917
defeated House members - 917 (chart)
House membership changes - 918 (chart)
marginal vote share - 905 (box)
conservative coalition - 47
housing programs overhaul - 638
Hill, Baron P. - 916
Hills, Carla A.
Caribbean Basin Initiative - 212-213, 215
GATT talks - 209
India-U.S. trade - 209
Japan-U.S. trade - 208-209
Mexico-U.S. trade talks - 218
Yeutter RNC post - 910
Hinkle, Maureen - 330
Hispanics
characteristics of Congress - 923-924
minorities in Congress - 924 (chart)
defense authorization - 686
Education secretary - 614 (box)
EPA research grants - 275
health professions incentives - 596
immigration law revision - 485
judicial appointments - 516
Serrano election - 934
SSC authorization - 439
Thomas confirmation - 518 (box)
Historic buildings - 458
Historic sites - 304
Historic vehicles and rail cars - 454, 456
History education - 615
HIV. *See Human immunodeficiency virus*
HMOs. *See Health maintenance organizations*
Hoagland, Peter D-Neb. (2)
housing programs overhaul - 640
prepayment of subsidized mortgages - 663, 664
HoDAGs. *See Housing Development Action Grants*
Hofeller,Tom - 932
Hofman, Steve - 15
Holds
education proposals - 615
irrigation subsidies - 301, 357
Holiday Inn, Inc. - 402
Hollings Centers - 440, 441
Hollings, Ernest F. D-S.C.
airline rights - 389
auto fuel efficiency - 280
Baby Bell restrictions - 377-378
budget process - 176, 177
cable TV regulation - 371
campaign finance reform - 66
campaign TV ad rates - 67 (box)
Caribbean Basin Initiative - 216
Commerce/Justice/State appropriations - 884-885
Energy, water appropriations - 865
fish inspection - 398
GATT talkks - 210
global warming - 307
Legal Services Corporation - 532
NASA authorization - 434
Persian Gulf crisis
U.S. goals, rationales - 745 (box)
product liability - 400-401
savings and loan scandal - 94
Social Security in budget accounting - 165, 170 (box)
State Department authorization - 800
supplemental appropriations - 846
technology programs - 440-441
textile import quotas - 220
U.S. Embassy in Moscow - 760 (box)
Hollingsworth, E. Boyd Jr. - 16
Holmes, Peter - 425
Holocaust
German unification - 763
reparations payments - 148, 569
HOME. *See Home Ownership Made Easy Investment Partnerships*
HOME Corporation - 635, 636
Home health care
agency certification fees - 125
AIDS patients - 585, 640
congregate, supportive housing - 636, 654
elderly, Alzheimer's authorization - 598-599
family leave - 6, 359-361
kidney dialysis - 145
liability waivers - 146
Medicaid coverage - 145, 147, 569-571
Medicare changes - 563, 564
patient self-determination - 146
Pepper Commission - 607-609
prospective payment system - 146
respite care demonstration - 148
Home loans and mortgages
appraisals access - 187
bank disclosure, accountability rules - 649
barrier island protection - 302
community development guarantees - 655-656
energy efficiency incentives - 644, 656
federal role background - 632
FHA insurance
rules revision - 631, 635, 636, 640, 642-643, 647-649, 657-661

farm programs - 123, 347, 653-654
foreclosure-prevention counseling - 649, 652
insurance premiums - 141-142
low-income buyers aid - 856
mortgagor equity - 141
prepayment of subsidized mortgages - 631, 634, 635, 640, 643, 648-649, 652, 661-665, 856
public housing home ownership programs
appropriations - 857, 859, 860
authorization - 631, 635, 649-650, 662
savings and loan scandal - 83, 84-85
second mortgage aid - 646-647, 649
secondary market
farm loans - 347
fees - 123
Ginnie Mae authorization - 649
HUD auctions - 142, 648-649
mortgage revenue bonds - 160, 173
servicing transfer disclosure - 656
tax deductions for interest - 135
trust for first-time buyers - 631, 634, 638, 647, 656
veterans programs - 126, 420, 845
Home Ownership Counseling program - 636
Home schools - 613
Homeless persons
AIDS bill - 584, 585, 586
appropriations - 854, 855 (chart), 858
children's welfare services - 556
community services block grant - 555
food donation liability - 562
food stamps - 326, 346, 354
housing programs overhaul - 631-656
job training overhaul - 365
McKinney act authorization - 665
veterans housing aid - 420, 859-860
Homeownership and Opportunity for People Everywhere (HOPE) - 125, 631-656, 662, 860
Homeownership Made Easy (HOME) Investment Partnerships - 631, 644-647, 655
Homosexuals
AIDS bill - 582, 583, 587
disabled civil rights - 449-452, 459
Frank ethics case - 103-104
hate crime statistics - 506-507
immigration law revision - 478, 481 (box)
NEA controversies - 433, 870, 874
youth counselors - 561, 891, 892-893
Honda North America - 280
Honduras
Caribbean Basin Initiative - 212
Nicaragua aid - 772
U.S. National Guard training exercises - 694 (box)
Honecker, Erich - 698, 763
Honey
price supports - 141, 337, 339, 341, 343, 344
Hong Kong
China-U.S. relations - 765, 766, 768
U.S. immigration policy - 476, 481, 482
Honoraria
congressional pay - 71-73
Durenberger ethics case - 98-101
federal employees - 72 (box)
VA medical staff - 420
HOP. *See Housing Opportunity Partnerships*
HOPE. *See Homeownership and Opportunity for People Everywhere*
Hopkins, Larry J. - R-Ky. (6)
defense authorization - 683
Horn, Joan Kelly - 905 (chart), 906, 916, 918 (chart), 919, 923, 924 (chart)
Horn, Wade F. - 553
Horton, Frank R-N.Y. (29)
congressional elections, 1990
low winning percentage - 906 (chart)
OMB review powers - 412-413
state grant funds transfers - 414
Transportation appropriations - 878
Treasury, Postal appropriations - 888
Horton, Willie - 487
Hospices
AIDS bill - 584
budget action - 128, 144
Medicaid expansion - 570
Medicare changes - 564
patient self-determination - 146
Hospitals. *See also Nursing homes*
AIDS patients - 582-589, 640
antismoking bills - 594
community service programs - 560, 561
disabled civil rights - 448
disproportionate share of poor patients - 143, 144, 568
energy conservation - 319
Energy, water appropriations - 863
foreign aid appropriations - 835
Medicaid pay suits - 571
medical device safety - 580
Medicare payments - 125, 143-144, 563-568
Medigap plans - 572, 574
NIH research support - 601
parental notice of abortion - 847
patient dumping ban - 144, 563
patient self-determination - 146
rural development - 352
trauma care - 597
VA hospitals
construction appropriations - 855
salaries - 419-420
waste disposal - 259
Hostages
benefits - 833 (chart), 844
death penalty - 494, 497
Persian Gulf crisis - 719, 720, 728, 729, 732, 736, 737, 741, 743, 745 (box)
Hot Springs, Ark. - 878
Hotels
fire safety - 402
Houghton, Amo R-N.Y. (34)
NEA authorization - 433
House Administration Committee
chair challenge - 11 (box)
House Franking Commission - 73, 75, 894, 896
House Journal - 39
House of Representatives. *See also Congress, members of; Congressional committees; specific committees*
elections, 1990
changes (chart) - 918
defeats (chart) - 917
party gains, losses (chart) - 919
results - 901-903, 909, 916-923
returns (chart) - 935-941
special elections - 922, 934 (box)
summary - 3
leadership - 9, 10, 11 (box)
mail costs, curbs - 73-75
members
freshmen, 102nd Cong. - 925, 926
list, 102nd Cong. - 920-921
party lineup, 101st, 102nd Cong. (chart) - 916
Puerto Rico status - 426
partisanship - 32
Speaker's votes - 527, 471
House Office Building Commission - 458
Housing. *See also Low Income Home Energy Assistance Program; Home loans and mortgages; Housing and Urban Development Department; Housing assistance and public housing*
affordability - 633
colleges - 849 (chart)
energy efficiency - 644, 646, 656
foreign aid - 843 (chart), 834, 836
Soviet immigrants in Israel - 743, 841, 845
heating oil tax - 134, 139, 313
manufactured home safety - 638, 656
military facilities - 827, 828
national housing policy - 644
second homes - 649, 658
student aid eligibility - 611
vacancy rates - 633
weatherization aid - 319
Housing and Urban Development Department, U.S. (HUD)
appropriations - 854-860
pork-barrel spending - 857 (box)
budget action - 125
CDBG targets - 123
coin redesign - 196-197
D'Amato ethics case - 97
FHA rules revision - 647-649, 657
homeless veterans - 420
housing programs overhaul - 631-656
mortgage insurance premiums - 141-142
prepayment of subsidized mortgages - 652-653, 661-664
scandal investigation - 534, 535, 641, 666-668
Housing and Urban Development Reform Act of 1989 - 858, 865, 860
Housing assistance and public housing
block grants - 644-647
budget action - 125, 128
census count adjustment - 416
crime and security - 533, 637, 638, 639, 650, 651, 652
down payment vouchers for national service - 560, 561
federal policy - 631, 632, 644
health and social services - 631, 635
AIDS patients - 640, 655, 656, 857
congregate services - 636, 654
family self-sufficiency - 650, 651
foster care prevention - 642, 650, 651, 656
health-care access - 596
lead abatement - 857, 858
perinatal care - 651
supportive housing for special needs - 654-655
youth sports - 651
home repair grants - 646
homeownership trust - 647
housing programs overhaul - 631-656
coin redesign - 196-197
HUD appropriations - 854, 855, 856, 857, 860
management reforms - 650
mixed-income communities - 651
Panama aid - 775, 776
preference families - 638, 650
prepayment of subsidized mortgages - 631, 652-653, 661-665
rental assistance - 633-634, 651-653
rural areas - 633, 653-654, 867, 868, 869
sales to tenants (HOPE) - 631, 635, 649-650, 662
summary - 3, 4
sweat equity grants - 646
terminated programs - 636, 647
veterans programs - 420
Housing Development Action Grants (HoDAGs)
termination - 635, 636, 647, 656
Housing Opportunity Partnerships (HOP) - 635, 636, 638, 640-641
Housing opportunity zones - 635
Houston, Texas
AIDS relief - 582
air pollution - 239
census count adjustment - 415
drug enforcement - 503, 889
Howard Beach, N.J. - 507
Howard, William - 291
Howard University - 849 (chart)
Howell, Nathaniel - 743
Hoyer, Steny H. D-Md. (5)
campaign finance reform - 68
congressional leadership - 9 (box), 12
D.C. status - 429
disabled civil rights - 447, 448, 451, 461
federal pay overhaul - 407
Treasury, Postal appropriations - 890
Hubbard, Carroll Jr. D-Ky. (1)
housing programs overhaul - 640
prepayment of subsidized mortgages - 663
Hubbert, Paul - 926
Hubble Space Telescope - 434, 435
Huckaby, Jerry D-La. (5)
budget action - 128
farm bill - 328, 331-332
Hughes, Jim - 315 (box)
Hughes, William J. D-N.J. (2)
assault weapons ban - 500-501 (box)
beach water quality - 290
crime bill - 494-499
disabled civil rights - 451
flag desecration - 525
habeas corpus appeals - 488 (box)
immigration law revision - 478
RICO revision - 536-538
Human growth hormone - 578
Human immunodeficiency virus (HIV) carriers
AIDS bill - 582-589
disabled civil rights - 449, 450, 451, 461
immigration exclusion - 474, 480-481 (box)
Medicaid coverage - 148, 569
Human rights
Andean Initiative - 805
Burma-U.S. relations - 213, 801 (box)
Cambodian rebel aid - 793
China-U.S. relations - 204, 207, 764-768, 839 (box)
El Salvador aid - 779-786, 830, 839-840, 842
export controls bill - 199
farm export credit guarantees - 345
Helsinki commission - 800
Iraq - 718, 722, 724
Kenya aid - 790
Kuwait - 744-745 (box)
Panama aid - 776
Saudi Arabia - 744-745 (box)
Somalia - 836
Sudan - 836
torture ban treaty - 806
Yugoslavia - 843
Zaire aid - 790, 843
Human Services Reauthorization Act - 552-556
Humphrey, Gordon J. R-N.H.
AIDS bill - 583
Clean Air Act - 235
community service programs - 561
defense appropriations - 820
education proposals - 615
family planning authorization - 605
federal judgeships - 521
hate crime statistics - 507
housing programs overhaul - 656
juvenile justice nomination - 506
resignation, successor - 902 (box), 913, 913 (chart)

Souter confirmation - 513
Humphrey, Hubert H. - 803
Hun Sen - 837
Hungary
CFE - 697, 698, 703
U.S. aid - 207, 834
U.S. trade - 204, 214
export controls - 199
Hunger. *See Food assistance programs*
Hunt, Guy - 926
Hunt, James B. Jr. - 613, 915
Hunter, Duncan R-Calif. (45)
congressional leadership - 12
export controls - 199
naval home ports - 681 (box)
Huntsville, Ala. - 692
Hurricanes
Caribbean aid - 778, 845
Hutto, Earl D-Fla. (1)
congressional elections, 1990 - 906
low winning percentage - 906 (chart)
marginal vote share - 905 (chart)
vote-share falloff - 904 (chart)
Hyde amendment - 851
Hyde, Henry J. R-Ill. (6)
civil rights/job bias - 469
crime bill - 494, 496, 497, 499
El Salvador aid - 783
family leave - 360
flag desecration - 527
habeas corpus appeals - 488 (box)
intelligence authorization - 795, 797, 799
Soviet-U.S. relations - 758
Hydroelectric power
Clean Air Act - 267
Energy, water appropriations - 861, 866
salmon protection - 864
zebra mussel control - 298
Hydrogen
alternative fuel - 240 (box), 273
fuel research - 313, 318-319, 861, 864
Hydrogen sulfide - 258

I

ICBMs. *See Intercontinental ballistic missiles*
Ice. *See Methamphetamine*
IDA. *See International Development Association*
Idaho
Amtrak waste disposal - 392
congressional elections, 1990 - 916
defense appropriations - 821
Energy, water appropriations - 861, 865, 866
gubernatorial election, 1990 - 929
Idaho, University of - 443
Illegal aliens
census count adjustment - 416
conditional residency - 476
document fraud - 479, 485
Social Security amnesty - 151, 557, 558
employer sanctions - 477, 479, 485
interdiction - 474, 484
Irish immigrants - 477
Illinois. *See also Chicago*
acid rain - 237 (box), 238, 262, 278
aviation package - 387
CDBG funding formula - 641
congressional elections, 1990 - 916
congressional redistricting - 931, 933
federal judgeships - 521, 522
food aid cargo preference - 338-339 (box)
gubernatorial election, 1990 - 928
military base closings - 678
"motor voter" bill - 70
political patronage jobs - 933
Transportation appropriations - 878
wilderness protection - 304
Illinois Alliance for Better Child Care - 548
Immigration and emigration. *See also Aliens; Chinese student visas; Deportation; Illegal aliens; Immigration and Naturalization Service; Jackson-Vanik amendment; Naturalization; Refugees; Soviet emigration*
allotment totals - 474, 482
diversity visas - 475-476, 477, 478, 481, 482-483
education, health care - 479, 848 (chart)
exclusions - 474, 478, 480-481 (box), 484
family preference system - 482
foreign aid appropriations - 833 (chart)
job-based visas - 482
language
closed-captioned TV - 375
literacy programs - 610
law revision - 474-485
boxscore - 474
key votes - 11-B, 12-B
provisions - 482-484
summary - 5, 8
migration, development commission
appropriations - 883 (chart)
reform commission - 483
TB prevention - 594
wage tax for job training fund - 475, 476, 478
Immigration and Naturalization Service (INS)
AIDS visa guidelines - 481 (box)
appropriations - 882 (chart)
border patrol - 493, 504
criminal aliens - 484, 487
immigration law revision - 475
police authority - 485
Immigration Reform and Control Act of 1986 - 474, 482, 557
Immunity
North conviction overturn - 534-535
Immunizations
child care standards - 153
foreign aid appropriations - 837
Indian health care - 422
supplemental appropriations for measles - 846
vaccine program authorization - 591-592
Immunosuppressive drugs - 597
Impeachment
judicial commission - 520, 522, 523
Import taxes. *See also Customs duties; Tariffs*
Clean Air Act compliance - 236
ethanol - 211
hazardous chemicals - 159
Imports. *See Foreign trade and business*
Incest
abortion - 528, 531, 811, 847, 850, 851-852, 891, 893
Incinerators. *See Waste products*
Income taxes. *See also Business taxes; Capital gains tax; Earned income tax credit*
alternative minimum tax - 157, 164, 171, 165
budget action - 131
chronology - 114-115
reconciliation - 139, 156-158, 164-166, 167, 169-172
summit - 131-135
deductions
campaign finance reform - 57, 58, 62, 65
charitable contributions - 135, 158, 165
limits - 158, 164, 166, 167, 169, 171
mortgage interest - 135
state, local taxes - 114, 131, 132, 165
grantor trusts - 160
millionaire surtax - 139, 164, 165
personal exemptions - 139, 157-158, 165-166, 167, 169
Puerto Rico status - 427
rates - 113, 114, 115, 131, 132, 134-135, 139, 157, 164, 165-166, 167, 169, 568
refund interception for child support - 149
Social Security earnings test - 557-558
standard deduction - 551
unemployment compensation - 368
Incumbents
budget action - 166
campaign finance reform - 64, 66
congressional elections, 1990 - 903-908
average vote percentage 1956-90 (chart) - 908
costs - 909
defeated House members (chart) - 917
low winning percentages (chart) - 906
marginal vote share (chart) - 905
re-election rates, 1946-90 (chart) - 903
results - 901, 902, 911, 916, 917
summary - 3
vote-share falloff (chart) - 904
congressional leadership - 12
congressional term limit - 13-15
franking privilege - 73-75, 895-896
gubernatorial elections, 1990 - 926
roll call attendance - 48
Independent counsel. *See Special counsel and prosecutors*
Independent Offices Appropriation Act of 1952 - 311 (box)
Independent Service Co. - 102
India
displaced Tibetan nationals - 476
ozone-layer protection - 271
U.S. trade - 208, 209
Indian Affairs, Bureau of (BIA)
appropriations - 421, 873 (chart)
fraud, abuse investigation - 421, 422
Indian business preference - 422
law enforcement - 424
vocational education authorization - 620, 621
Indian Claims Commission - 424
Indian Health Service
community service programs - 562
Indian health care - 423
Indian lands and reservations
abandoned mines - 154
contract preference - 422
death penalty exemption - 493
environmental protection - 423
forest management - 424
irrigation subsidies - 357
law enforcement -423-424
Seminole claim award - 424
trust lands - 654
Indian Self-Determination Act of 1974 - 422
Indiana
acid rain - 237 (box), 238, 262, 278
congressional elections, 1990 - 909, 917, 933
job training overhaul - 365
Transportation appropriations - 878
water projects authorization - 299
Indiana State University - 862
Indians
business preference - 422
SSC authorization - 439
CDBGs - 423
child-care block grant - 152
community service programs - 561, 562
congressional action, 1990 - 421-424
disabled civil rights exclusions - 453
education
appropriations - - 873 (chart)
community colleges - 143, 423, 627 (box)
library services - 617
vocational education - 620, 621, 622
graves and remains - 422
health professionals incentives - 596
health programs - 422-423
AIDS bill - 585
appropriations - 873 (chart)
Health Service Corps authorization - 595
Panama aid debate - 779
housing programs
budget action - 125
overhaul - 632, 634, 635, 637, 649-652, 655
Micmac tribal recognition - 424
peyote ban - 514
Individual Retirement Accounts (IRAs) - 165
Individuals with Disabilities Act - 616-617
Infanticide - 839 (box)
Infants. *See also Women, infants and children (WIC) program*
abortion counseling - 605
AIDS bill - 585, 585
child-care aid - 547, 551
child development centers - 552
disabled education - 616
drug addiction - 504, 679
earned-income tax credit - 152, 158, 172
family leave - 359-361
Medicaid coverage - 147, 569
mortality reduction - 128
minority health - 596
perinatal services demonstration - 651
Inflation indexing
civil penalties - 393-394
discretionary spending caps - 173, 177, 178
health care taxes - 608
income tax deductions, exemptions - 158, 169
interlocking director antitrust - 540
Medicare hospital payments - 565
sugar price supports - 328
Information access and classification
Clean Air Act permits - 268
covert actions - 795, 796, 797
crime victims - 493
defense appropriations - 812
environmental statistics - 291, 292
foreign ownership of U.S. business - 222-225
health care primary payers - 146
home appraisals - 187
intelligence budget - 796, 797
international securities enforcement - 193-194
job-related medical exams - 453
pesticide recordkeeping - 346
savings and loan scandal press leaks - 80, 94
stock market regulation - 192
student right-to-know - 624-627
secrecy agreements - 21, 890
Information Agency, United States

(USIA) - 799, 883 (chart)
Information and Regulatory Affairs, Office of (OIRA) - 411-413, 886, 888
Information services
Baby Bell restrictions - 377-379
Ing, Charles E. - 280
Ingleside, Tex. - 678, 681
Inhofe, James M. R-Okla. (1)
aviation security - 390
Initiative and referendum
"Big Green" pesticide phase-out - 358
direct election of senators - 13
Inkatha - 789
Inouye, Daniel K. D-Hawaii
Baby Bell restrictions - 378
Bush congressional relations - 20
cable TV regulation - 371
campaign TV ad rates - 67 (box)
children's TV advertising - 375
crime bill - 493
defense appropriations - 813-814, 819-820
defense authorization - 678
Energy, water appropriations - 861, 865, 866
foreign aid appropriations - 841, 842, 843
minorities in Congress - 924 (chart)
Persian Gulf crisis
use-of-force debate - 753 (box)
product liability - 401
radio spectrum allocation - 376-377
savings and loan scandal - 94
Transportation appropriations - 879
INS. *See Immigration and Naturalization Service*
Inspectors general
HUD scandal investigation - 667, 668
NRC - 310
Institute for National Drug Abatement Research - 888
Institute of Peace, U.S. - 849 (chart), 850
Insurance. *See also Deposit insurance; Health insurance*
crop insurance subsidies - 870
disabled civil rights - 458
flood insurance - 143
India trade sanctions - 208, 209
price-sharing curbs - 401
product liability - 400
Intellectual property rights
Czechoslovak-U.S. trade - 206
GATT talks - 209, 210
Soviet-U.S. trade - 205
Intelligence agencies. *See also Central Intelligence Agency*
authorization - 791-799
boxscore - 791
veto message - 798
CFE - 704
covert operations rules - 791-792, 796, 797-798
economic information - 796
Intelligence Authorization Act - 791-799
Intelligence Committee, House
membership change - 791, 799
Intelligence Committee, Senate
membership change - 791, 799
Interagency Committee on Environmental Change - 291-292
Interagency Council on the Homeless - 855 (chart)
Inter-American Development Bank and Corporation
appropriations - 832 (chart)
Panama aid - 776, 777, 778
Inter-American Foundation - 833 (chart)
Intercontinental ballistic missiles (ICBMs). *See also Midgetman; MX missiles; SS-18 missiles*
SDI - 691
START - 704, 708
Interdepartmental Task Force on Vocational Education - 620
Interior Committtee, House
leadership - 924
Interior Department, U.S.
abandoned mines - 154
appropriations - 870-876
Arizona wilderness protection - 304
barrier island protection - 302, 303
budget action - 124
conservation corps - 562
Energy, water appropriations - 866
forests/wildlife protection - 875
Grand Canyon erosion - 300
Indian business preference - 422
irrigation subsidies - 356
offshore leases, drilling emissions - 244, 273, 288
oil-shale lands - 316
Palau autonomy - 808
Seminole land claim - 424
strategic minerals - 442
timber exports - 214, 215
zebra mussel control - 304
Intermediate-range nuclear forces (INF) treaty
compliance verification - 680
START - 707
Internal Revenue Service (IRS)
appropriations - 887 (chart), 888, 889
child support enforcement - 149
financial institution fraud - 183
foreign ownership of U.S. business - 224
Hatch Act revision - 409
management reforms - 126, 128
records access for Medicare - 146
SBA comments on regulations - 160
spending cap exemptions - 148
tax collection, compliance - 134, 159, 161, 172, 888, 889
taxpayer relations - 888-889
International Development Association (IDA)
appropriations - 832 (chart), 834, 835
authorization - 206, 207
budget action - 124
Soviet-U.S. relations - 759
International development banks. *See also World Bank*
authorization - 206-207
foreign aid appropriations - 834, 835
Panama aid - 777, 778, 779
International Emergency Economic Powers Act of 1976 - 198, 201
International Environmental Affairs Office - 292
International Finance Corporation - 832 (chart)
International Fund for Agricultural Development - 832 (chart), 840
International Fund for Ireland - 833 (chart), 844
International Institute for Strategic Studies - 730
International Mass Retail Association - 539
International Monetary Fund
Panama aid - 776, 777, 778
spending cap adjustments - 161
Third World debt relief - 207, 218, 834
U.S. appropriations - 832 (chart)
International organizations
appropriations - 883, 884, 885
immigration law revision - 476
U.S. dues - 802
International Planned Parenthood Federation - 831, 837, 838-839 (box), 840
International Trade Administration - 882 (chart)
International Trade Commission - 211, 212, 882 (chart)
International Trade, U.S. Court of - 883 (chart)
Interstate Child Support Commission - 149-150
Interstate Commerce Commission (ICC)
appropriations - 879 (chart)
railroad acquisitions - 390, 391, 392
Interstate highways - 384
Inventions
space patent law - 437
Iowa
abortion - 530
congressional elections, 1990 - 903
congressional redistricting - 931
corporate campaign limits - 59 (box)
Energy, water appropriations - 865
federal judgeships - 522
Iowa - 672, 678, 681, 846
Iran
Persian Gulf crisis - 717, 719
questionable gulf allies - 740 (box)
U.S. export controls - 201
Iran-contra affair
intelligence authorization - 791-792, 797, 798
North conviction overturn - 534-535
State Department authorization - 799
Iran-Iraq War - 718, 719, 722, 802
Iraq. *See also Persian Gulf crisis*
aid ban for sanctions violators - 840, 841, 843-844
chemical weapons
Food for Peace - 804
pact - 709
Persian Gulf war - 718, 722-723, 724
trade sanctions - 198, 201, 885
use - 718, 722-723
claims of U.S. citizens - 829, 830
food credits - 718, 722, 723-724, 729
human rights - 718, 722, 724
nuclear weapons
capability estimates - 722, 745
component smuggling - 723
export controls - 201, 729, 885
Iraq Sanctions Act of 1990 - 844
Ireland. *See also Northern Ireland*
U.S. aid - 833 (chart), 844
U.S. immigration policy - 475, 476, 477, 481
Ireland, Andy R-Fla. (10)
SBA authorization - 395
Irish Americans - 475, 477
Irrigation
subsidies - 300, 301, 356-357
Isaacs, John - 40, 47, 710
Isacson, Leon - 922 (box)
Isakson, Johnny - 930
Island Park Dam and Reservoir - 866
Israel
Pakistan-U.S. relations - 769
Palestinian policies, *intifada* - 720, 721, 743, 822, 837, 841
Persian Gulf crisis - 722, 723, 732, 743
Egyptian debt relief - 730
Iraqi missile attack - 721, 754, 755
Saudi arms sales - 734-735 (box)
U.S. goals, rationales - 744 (box)
Soviet immigrants - 778, 837, 841, 845
U.S. aid defense appropriations - 822, 825
foreign aid appropriations - 830, 831, 833, 837, 841, 843
U.S. trade
customs fees - 212
textile import quotas - 220
Italy
CFE - 698, 701
Crotone air base - 678, 682, 687, 826-827, 828-829
European development bank - 206
Food for Peace - 803
military construction appropriations - 827
Patriot missiles - 818
Ivory Coast
Persian Gulf crisis - 740
Izaak Walton League - 278

J

Jackson, Jesse - 70, 428-429, 462, 570 (box)
Jackson amendment - 707
Jackson-Vanik amendment
China-U.S. relations - 204, 766, 768
Czechoslovak-U.S. trade - 204 (box)
procedural change - 205, 211, 212-213, 215
Soviet-U.S. relations - 205, 759
Jacobs, Andrew Jr. D-Ind. (10)
congressional pay, honoraria - 71
Treasury, Postal appropriations - 889
Jacobson, Joy - 85, 86, 93, 94, 95
Jamaica
Caribbean Basin Initiative - 212
U.S. aid/drug control - 836
James, Craig T. R-Fla. (4)
congressional elections, 1990 - 919
flag desecration - 525
Japan
agricultural subsidies - 325
defense burden-sharing - 682, 687, 820-821, 828
defense preparedness - 202
drift-net fishing - 399
European development bank - 206
Ex-Im Bank financing of arms sales - 643
foreign ownership of U.S. business - 223
FS-X development - 16
Panama aid - 776, 778
Persian Gulf crisis - 717, 719, 730, 732
space patent law - 437
space station design - 437
technology programs - 440
Tokyo-Chicago air route - 387
U.S. trade
auto fuel efficiency - 280
banking - 189
construction contract discrimination - 830
export controls - 198, 201
Super 301, SII talks - 208-209
tobacco - 593
Tongass forest protection - 294-295
U.S. troop deployment - 686, 825, 827
Japan-U.S. Friendship Trust Fund - 883
Japanese American National Museum - 888
Jefferson, William J. - 905 (chart), 916, 918 (chart), 924 (chart)
Jeffords, James M. R-Vt.
age discrimination - 363, 363
campaign finance reform - 66
civil rights/job bias - 465
federal RCRA compliance - 309
nutrition labels - 576
pension reversions - 368
Jenckes, Linda - 575
Jenkins, Ed D-Ga. (9)
congressional elections, 1990 - 906

low winning percentage - 906 (chart)
family leave - 360
textile import quotas - 221, 222
Jersey City, N.J. - 582, 852
Jesuits
Salvadoran murder case - 779-786, 836, 842
Jews. *See also Soviet emigration*
characteristics of Congress - 926
child care aid - 549
Holocaust restitution claims - 763
Job Opportunities and Basic Skills (JOBS) pprogram
sequestration procedures - 162
Job Training Partnership Act (JTPA)
budget action - 123
Clean Air Act - 277 (box)
displaced homemakers - 366 (box)
Labor/HHS appropriations - 847, 853
overhaul - 365-366
vocational education authorization - 620, 621
Job training programs. *See also Vocational education*
budget action - 123, 128
census count adjustment - 415
child-care providers - 551
disabled civil rights - 452
dislocated workers - 621-622
Clean Air Act - 236-238, 242-243, 246, 275, 276, 277 (box)
displaced homemakers - 366 (box)
trade displacement - 123
foreign workers head tax - 473, 476, 478
Head Start - 552, 555
homeless aid - 665
JTPA overhaul - 365-366
Nicaragua aid - 771
public housing support services - 650, 651
veterans services - 421
John F. Kennedy - 818, 825, 826
John Paul II - 801 (box)
Johnson, Douglas - 530, 838 (box)
Johnson, Jeff - 410
Johnson, Michael S. - 31
Johnson, Nancy L. D-Conn. (6)
congressional elections, 1990 - 908
foreign ownership of U.S. business - 223
minorities in Congress - 924 (chart)
Johnson, Tim D-S.D. (AL)
farm bill - 329
Johnston, J. Bennett D-La.
alternative power regulation - 317-318
Arctic refuge drilling - 315 (box)
Clean Air Act - 237
congressional elections, 1990 - 916
crime bill - 490
disabled civil rights - 461
El Salvador aid - 786
Energy, water appropriations - 864-866
food aid cargo preference - 339 (box)
global warming - 307
irrigation subsidies - 357
Palau autonomy - 808
Persian Gulf crisis - 725, 751
Puerto Rico status - 424, 425, 427
Roemer election - 916
SSC authorization - 438-439
Strategic Petroleum Reserve - 314
Tongass forest protection - 295
uranium enrichment - 310
Johnston, Randall E. - 102
Joint Center for Housing Studies - 633
Joint Committee on Taxation
budget action - 169
capital gains tax - 168 (box)
Joint resolutions
chemical weapopns pact - 711
trade agreements - 204, 205, 211, 212-213
Joint sessions
Mandela address - 787, 789
Joint STARS - 674, 685, 818, 823, 824
Jolivette, Gregory V. - 918 (chart)
Jones, Ben D-Ga. (4)
congressional elections, 1990
low winning percentage - 906 (chart)
marginal vote share - 905 (chart)
Jones, David C. - 720, 738, 742
Jones, George Fleming - 801 (box)
Jones-Smith, Jacqueline - 393
Jones, Walter B. D-N.C. (1)
coastal zone management awards - 154
congressional elections, 1990
low winning percentage - 906 (chart)
Interior appropriations - 872
oil pollution cleanup - 287
Jonesboro, Ark. - 878
Jontz, Jim D-Ind. (5)
congressional elections, 1990
marginal vote share - 905 (chart)
farm bill - 327
Interior appropriations - 874
logging/wildlife protection - 297
Jordan
Persian Gulf crisis - 729
U.S. aid - 831, 837, 841, 843
Jordan, Carolyn - 93-94
JTPA. *See Job Training Partnership Act*
Judicial Conduct and Disability Act of 1980 - 522
Judicial Conference, U.S.
disaster liability suits - 543
new judgeships - 520-523
Judicial Improvements Act of 1990 - 520-523
Judicial review
environmental law compliance - 296
Jury trials
capital punishment - 488-489 (box)
job bias remedies - 463, 464
peremptory juror strikes - 489 (box)
Justice Assistance, Bureau of - 493
Justice Department, U.S. *See also Federal Bureau of Investigation; Immigration and Naturalization Service*
air safety violations - 389
animal rights activists - 442
appropriations - 881-886
budget action - 125
children's TV advertising - 373, 375
Chinese student protections - 767 (box)
Civil Rights Division head - 465 (box)
civil rights/job bias - 463
congressional-executive relations - 16
crime bill - 486, 493, 495, 498
disabled civil rights - 448, 453, 456, 457, 458
disaster liability suits - 543
drug control - 889
Durenberger ethics case - 102
Fauntroy ethics case - 107
financial institution fraud - 182-183, 486, 494, 495, 499
flag desecration - 524
hate crime statistics - 506-507
HUD scandal investigation - 666
immigration law revision - 476, 484
Iran-contra cases - 535
judicial appointments - 516
juvenile justice director - 506
legislative intent - 54
money laundering - 187, 499
nuclear plant investigations - 309
pornographic mail - 417
radiation victims compensation - 590-591
savings and loan scandal - 82, 89, 93, 97
secrecy agreements - 21
sex crime deterrence - 507
telemarketing fraud - 881
thrift bailout - 181
vertical price fixing - 539, 540
war powers suit - 739 (box)
Justice Statistics, Bureau of - 507
Juvenile delinquents
child-abuse victims - 493
federal death penalty - 491, 494
Sweet nomination - 506
Juvenile Justice and Delinquency Prevention, Office of - 506

K

Kaifu, Toshiki - 208
Kanawha River - 298
abortion - 530
congressional elections, 1990 - 919
congressional redistricting - 931, 933
Energy, water appropriations - 865
federal judgeships - 522
gubernatorial election, 1990 - 902, 928, 929, 930
Transportation appropriations - 880
wheat farming - 350
Kansas City, Kan. - 858
Kaptur, Marcy D-Ohio (9)
minorities in Congress - 924 (chart)
Kashmir - 769
Kasich, John R. R-Ohio (12)
B-2 bomber - 688, 689, 691
budget action - 128
defense authorization - 676, 677
Kassebaum, Nancy Landon R-Kan.
age discrimination - 363
airline rights - 389
Armenian genocide commemoration - 808
characteristics of Congress - 923
minorities in Congress - 924 (chart)
civil rights/job bias - 467
congressional elections, 1990 - 916
dropout prevention - 618
education proposals - 612-613
housing programs overhaul - 636
Medicare changes - 565
nutrition labels - 576
orphan drugs - 579
pension reversions - 368
Persian Gulf crisis - 738
South Africa sanctions - 788
U.N. population fund - 839 (box)
vocational education authorization - 622, 623
Kássouf, George - 515
Kasten, Bob R-Wis.
agriculture appropriations - 868
Amtrak authorization - 392
aviation package - 386-387
budget action - 165
Commerce/Justice/State appropriations - 885
congressional leadership - 12
El Salvador aid - 786
foreign aid appropriations - 841, 842-843
U.N. population fund - 839 (box)
Panama aid - 778
product liability - 400-401
technology programs - 440-441
Kastenmeier, Robert W. D-Wis. (2)
congressional elections, 1990 - 917
defeated House members - 917 (chart)
House membership changes - 918 (chart)
copyright issues - 542, 543
crime bill - 494, 496
disaster liability suits - 543
electoral defeat - 166
federal judgeships - 521, 523
flag desecration - 525
habeas corpus appeals - 488 (box)
space patent law - 437
Katz, Earl - 79, 85, 92
KC-135 aircraft - 674
Kean, Thomas H. - 559-560
Keating, Charles H. Jr. - 6, 12, 57, 78-97, 180, 537, 538
Keating Five scandal investigation
case overview - 83-85
effects on legislation
campaign finance reform - 57, 60
RICO revision - 537, 538
thrift bailout - 180
Ethics Committee hearings - 78-97
key players - 79 (box)
special counsel - 81 (box)
summary - 6
Keating, Kim - 79
Keefe, Joseph F. - 918 (chart)
Keet, Jim - 918 (chart)
Kelly, John H. - 722, 723, 725, 732, 743
Kemeny, Nicole - 660
Kemp, Geoffrey - 722
Kemp, Jack F.
FHA rules revision - 657-661
housing programs overhaul - 631-644, 656
HUD scandal investigation - 667, 668
prepayment of subsidized mortgages - 662, 664
U.N. population fund - 839 (box)
VA/HUD appropriations - 857-860
Kenilworth-Parkside - 857, 859, 860
Kennedy airport - 386
Kennedy, Anthony M.
abortion - 529
age discrimination - 362
civil rights/job bias - 462-467, 471, 473
corporate campaign limits - 59 (box)
flag desecration - 525
habeas corpus appeals - 489 (box)
legislative intent - 55 (box)
Medicaid pay suits - 571
OMB review powers - 412 (box)
political patronage jobs - 933
right to die - 567 (box)
Souter confirmation - 508, 510
student religious groups - 618 (box)
Supreme Court term summary - 52
Kennedy Center - 873 (chart)
Kennedy, Edward M. D-Mass.
AIDS bill - 582, 583, 586
antismoking bills - 593, 594
balanced budget amendment - 175 (box)
Chinese student visas - 767 (box)
Clean Air Act - 236
community service programs - 559-561
copyright issues - 541-542
crime bill - 487, 490-491, 492
D.C. status - 428-429
defense authorization - 675, 680
disabled civil rights - 460, 461
dropout prevention - 618
drug-abuse prevention - 504-505
education proposals - 615
elderly health care - 598
family planning authorization - 604, 606
federal judgeships - 523
fish inspection - 398
Head Start authorization - 553
Health Service Corps authorization -

595
immigration law revision - 474-475, 477, 479, 484-485
AIDS exclusion - 480 (box)
intelligence authorization - 796
job training overhaul - 365
juvenile justice nomination - 533
Legal Services Corporation - 532
medical device safety - 581
NIH authorization - 600, 603
nuclear test treaties - 712
Persian Gulf crisis - 734, 738, 754
use-of-force debate - 752 (box)
pesticide residue in food - 358
RICO revision - 537
sex crimes deterrence - 507
Souter confirmation - 509, 510-511, 514
South Africa sanctions - 788
TB prevention - 594
Thomas confirmation - 519 (box)
trauma care - 597
vaccine program authorization - 591
Kennedy, Edward M. Jr. 461
Kennedy, Joseph P. II D-Mass. (8)
development banks - 207
housing programs overhaul - 638
Persian Gulf crisis
use-of-force debate - 752 (box)
prepayment of subsidized mortgages - 662-664
VA medical salaries - 419
veterans housing aid - 420
Kennedy, Robert F. - 500 (box)
Kennedy, Rosemary - 461
Kennelly, Barbara D-Conn. (1)
congressional pay, honoraria - 73
minorities in Congress - 924 (chart)
Kentucky
acid rain - 262
aviation package - 388
congressional redistricting - 931
corporate campaign limits - 59 (box)
water projects authorization - 299
Kenya
U.S. aid - 790
Kerrey, Bob D-Neb.
Baby Bell restrictions - 378
crime bill - 492
defense appropriations - 821
farm bill - 333, 338, 340, 348
flag desecration - 527
Yeutter Gulf remarks - 910
Kerry, John D-Mass.
campaign finance reform - 63, 65
Clean Air Act - 234, 235
coastal zone management - 289
congressional elections, 1990 - 913
crime bill - 493
defense authorization - 680
housing programs overhaul - 637
juvenile justice nomination - 506
money laundering - 189
Persian Gulf crisis - 749
SDI - 692
Souter confirmation - 515
KGB - 759
Khmer Rouge - 766, 793, 794, 835, 837-839
Khomeini, Ruhollah - 722
Kidder, Ray E. - 712
Kidnapping
federal death penalty - 493, 494, 497
PLO talks - 800
Kidney disease - 145, 564, 578
Kiev
U.S. consulate - 802
Kildee, Dale E. D-Mich. (7)
child care aid - 548
congressional elections, 1990
low winning percentage - 906 (chart)
Transportation appropriations - 878
Kindergartens
Head Start authorization - 553, 554, 555
King, Bruce - 930
King, Coretta Scott - 462
King, Martin Luther Jr. - 500 (box)
Kirk, Mark S. - 839
Kirk, William Lee Jr. - 533
Kirkpatrick, Jeane J. - 746
Kissimmee River - 297, 298
Kissinger, Henry A. - 720, 742
Klatt, Victor F. - 615
Kleczka, Gerald D. D-Wis. (4)
FDIC premiums - 186
housing programs overhaul - 640
prepayment of subsidized mortgages - 663
Klepner, Jerry D. - 548
Kleptomania - 452, 459
Klinghoffer, Leon - 830
Klug, Scott L. - 166, 905 (chart), 917, 918 (chart)
Knowles, Tony - 927
Knutson, Harold - 174 (box)
Koeppel, William W. - 923
Kohl, Helmut - 698, 699, 701, 763
Kohl, Herb D-Wis.
balanced-budget amendment - 175 (box)
biological weapons ban - 507
crime bill - 493
food aid cargo preference - 339 (box)
juvenile justice nomination - 506
Medigap plans - 574
nutrition labels - 576
Souter confirmation - 513
vertical price fixing - 539, 540
Kohrs, Richard - 436, 437
Kolter, Joe D-Pa. (4)
congressional elections, 1990
low winning percentage - 906 (chart)
vote-share falloff - 904 (chart)
Transportation appropriations - 878
Koop, C. Everett - 593, 442
Kopetski, Mike - 905 (chart), 918 (chart), 922
Korn, David - 718, 722
Korologos, Tom - 9, 509
Kostmayer, Peter H. D-Pa. (8)
El Salvador aid - 782
Panama aid - 776, 777
Kozak, Michael - 772
Krasnoyarsk radar - 680
Kreiter, Nancy - 519 (box)
Kroese, Ron - 350
Kulp, David - 280, 281
Kunin, Madeleine M. - 928, 929, 930
Kunstler, William M. - 525
Kurds - 718, 722, 723, 724
Kuwait. *See also Persian Gulf crisis*
U.S. immigration policy - 478, 483, 484
Kyl, Jon R-Ariz. (4)
Arizona wilderness protection - 304
congressional elections, 1990
low winning percentage - 906 (chart)
SDI - 693

L

Labeling and packaging
chemical hazards at workplaces - 412 (box)
child-resistant packaging - 417
deceptive mail curbs - 417
disabled civil rights notices - 453
"dolphin-safe" tuna - 399
fish inspection - 397
fraudulent labels - 156
fuel octane - 282
nutrition information - 575, 868
"organically grown" food - 323, 332-333, 347
ozone-depleting chemicals - 270
tobacco products - 593, 594
Labor Department, U.S. *See also Occupational Safety and Health Administration*
appropriations - 847-853
Clean Air Act
economic impact - 274
job-loss benefits - 275
hazardous substance releases - 258, 259
construction industry wages - 647
foreign ownership of U.S. business - 224
immigration law revision - 475, 476, 478, 482, 484
Martin appointment - 369 (box)
pension reversions - 367
veterans rehabilitation - 421
vocational education authorization - 620, 622
whistleblower protection - 364
Labor interest groups
age discrimination - 362, 363
auto fuel efficiency - 280, 281
campaign finance reform - 57-69
Caribbean Basin Initiative - 211
child-care aid - 547, 548
family leave - 359, 361
farm bill - 332
federal RCRA compliance - 308
fish inspection - 398
Hatch Act revision - 408
immigration law revision - 479
pension reversions - 367
Labor Statistics, Bureau of
appropriations - 848 (chart)
federal pay overhaul - 406
foreign ownership of U.S. business - 223, 224
housing programs overhaul - 633
VA nurse salaries - 419
Labor unions
disabled civil rights - 452, 453
displaced worker aid - 275, 277 (box)
Eastern Airlines strike - 369
foreign aid appropriations - 834
foreign ownership of U.S. business - 223
Hatch Act revision - 408-411
teacher certification - 611
United Airlines buyout - 388
vocational education authorization - 620, 621, 622
Laboratories
animal rights activists - 441-442, 603
FDA facilities - 581
Medicare payments to clinical labs - 145
neutral buoyancy - 437
scientist, engineer salaries - 679
space station - 436
toxic air pollutants - 256
Lachance, Janice - 411
Laconia, N.H. - 878
LaFalce, John J. D-N.Y. (32)
civil rights/job bias - 470, 471
congressional elections, 1990 - 904
low winning percentage - 906 (chart)
marginal vote share - 905 (chart)
vote-share falloff - 904 (chart)
disabled civil rights - 459
LaGuardia Airport - 384, 386, 388
LaGuardia, Fiorello H. - 922 (box)
Lagomarsino, Robert J. R-Calif. (19)
congressional elections, 1990
marginal vote share - 905 (chart)
Puerto Rico status - 426
Lake Andes - 357
Lake Champlain - 258, 301
Lake Gaston - 297-300
Lake Onondaga - 301
Lakes. *See Great Lakes*
Lambda Legal Defense Fund - 481 (box)
Lamberth, Royce C. - 739 (box)
Lancaster, H. Martin D-N.C. (3)
congressional elections, 1990
low winning percentage - 906 (chart)
Lance missiles - 674, 863
Land Management, Bureau of (BLM)
appropriations - 873 (chart)
Arizona wilderness protection - 304
logging/wildlife protection - 296-297
supplemental appropriations - 845
Land Stewardship Project - 350
Landmark Legal Foundation Center for Civil Rights - 518
Lantos, Tom D-Calif. (11)
China-U.S. relations - 765
HUD scandal investigation - 666-668
Persian Gulf crisis - 723
Swett election - 916
Laos
development bank loans - 207
LaPierre, Wayne - 492
LaRocco, Larry - 905 (chart), 916, 919, 918 (chart), 922
Lasers
antisatellite weapons - 823, 824
missile guidance - 824
SDI - 692
Latin America. *See also specific countries*
debt relief - 207, 338
GATT talks - 209
U.S. aid - 217-218
food aid - 338
U.S. immigration policy - 474, 475
Latvia
CFE - 696, 703
German unification - 763
Soviet-U.S. relations - 757, 761
U.S. aid - 844
Laughlin, Greg D-Texas (14)
congressional elections, 1990
marginal vote share - 905 (chart)
Lautenberg, Frank R. D-N.J.
Amtrak authorization - 392
aviation security - 390
budget process - 177
Clean Air Act - 233-234
CPSC authorization - 393
D.C. appropriations - 893
food-waste transport - 383
foreign aid appropriations - 840, 841
Labor/HHS appropriations - 851, 852
Souter confirmation - 515
Transportation appropriations - 877, 879-880
VA/HUD appropriations - 858
vocational education authorization - 623
Law profession and practice. *See also Attorneys, U.S.; Legal Services Corporation*
attorneys' fees
copyright infringement - 542-543
disabled civil rights - 453, 458
job bias suits - 462, 463, 466, 468, 469-470
nuclear tests damage suits - 679
RICO revision - 536, 537
Social Security procedures - 151, 558
competency of counsel - 488, 490, 494, 496, 497
expert witness fees - 469
federal civil caseload management - 521
federal defenders - 522

group legal services - 160, 173
minority, women partners - 516
product liability - 400-401
SEC salaries - 193
Lawrence Livermore Laboratory - 712
LBOs. *See Leveraged buyouts*
LCAC barges - 675
Leach, Jim R-Iowa (1)
thrift bailout - 181
Lead
job bias/fetal protection case - 465
paint disposal, removal - 308, 857, 858
toxic air pollutants - 248, 251, 253, 254, 256
Leadership Conference on Civil Rights
civil rights/job bias - 463, 466, 473
Dunne nomination - 465 (box)
Souter confirmation - 510-511
League of Women Voters - 70
Leahy, Patrick J. D-Vt.
B-2 bomber - 689, 690
balanced-budget amendment - 175 (box)
CFTC authorization - 195
defense appropriations - 819-820, 821
El Salvador aid - 785-786
farm bill - 324-325, 333-341, 347-351
fish inspection - 396, 398
Food for Peace - 339 (box), 803
foreign aid appropriations - 840-843
U.N. population fund - 839 (box)
intelligence authorization - 794
judicial appointments - 517
juvenile justice nomination - 506
Kenya aid - 790
Nicaragua aid - 771
Pakistan-U.S. relations - 769
Panama aid - 777, 778
Persian Gulf crisis - 730, 746
rural development - 352
Leaking Underground Storage Tank Trust Fund - 159
Leath, Marvin D-Texas (11)
retirement - 918 (chart)
Leather goods
Caribbean Basin Initiative - 211-217
Lebanon
U.S. aid - 837, 840
U.S. hostages - 844
U.S. immigration policy - 478, 483, 484
Lebanon, Pa. - 857 (box)
Lederer, Raymond F. - 87
Legal Services Corporation
action, 1990 - 531-533
appropriations - 881, 883 (chart), 884, 886
Legal Services Reform Coalition - 532, 533
Legislative branch. *See Congress, U.S.*
Legislative process. *See also Appropriations process*
executive influence - 31
glossary - 7C-15C
how a bill becomes law - 4C
legislative intent - 54, 55 (box)
legislative process in brief - 3C-6C
Legislative veto
trade agreement procedures - 205, 211, 212-213
Lehigh University - 625
Lehman, Richard H. D-Calif. (18)
coin redesign - 196, 197
FDIC premiums - 186
irrigation subsidies - 356
Lehman, Ronald F. II - 700, 712, 713
Lehman, William D-Fla. (17)
Transportation appropriations - 877, 878, 880
Treasury, Postal appropriations - 888
U.N. population fund - 838 (box), 840
Leland, Mickey - 355
Lenoir, William - 436
Lent, Norman F. R-N.Y. (4)
AIDS bill - 588
Clean Air Act - 239, 241, 247, 275, 276
CPSC authorization - 394
disabled civil rights - 448
foreign ownership of U.S. business - 224, 225
radio spectrum allocation - 377
Strategic Petroleum Reserve - 315
Leonard, Daniel - 681
Leonesio, Michael V. - 557
Leprosy - 480 (box)
Lesher, William G. - 325, 349-350
Letterkenny Army Depot - 817
Leukemia - 597
Leveraged buyouts
airlines - 388
Levin, Carl D-Mich.
B-2 bomber - 688
congressional elections, 1990 - 913
defense authorization - 679, 680
federal pay overhaul - 406
Medicare changes - 565
regulatory negotiation guidelines - 414
Levin, Sander M. D-Mich. (17)
living wills - 566 (box)
Medicare coverage of mammograms - 564 (box)
Levine, Mel D-Calif. (27)
antismoking bills - 594
naval home ports - 681 (box)
Persian Gulf crisis - 732
Saudi arms sales - 734-735 (box)
RICO revision - 538
student right-to-know - 624, 625
Levy, David - 841
Lewis, Ann F. - 746
Lewis, Jerry R-Calif. (35)
congressional elections, 1990 - 904, 907
low winning percentage - 906 (chart)
congressional leadership - 9 (box), 12
foreign aid appropriations - 833, 834
military construction appropriations - 827-828
Lewis, John D-Ga. (5)
disabled civil rights - 451
minorities in Congress - 924 (chart)
"motor voter" bill - 70
Lewis, Tom R-Fla. (12)
immigration law revision - 479
Transportation appropriations - 878
Lewiston, Mont. - 878
LH helicopter
appropriations - 815 (chart), 823
authorization - 674, 677, 678, 685
budget action - 122
LHD helicopter carriers - 675, 815 (chart)
Liability and liability insurance. *See also Product liability*
air crash suits - 389
community service programs - 561, 562
Conrail line use - 390, 391
disaster suits consolidation - 543
home health agencies - 146
nuclear test damage suits - 679
oil spills - 5, 283-287
cleanup crews - 287
sovereign immunity concept - 590
Libel - 53 (box)
Liberal Party - 934
Liberia
U.S. aid/human rights - 836
U.S. immigration policy - 478, 483, 484
Libertarian Party - 907
Libraries
copyright issues - 542-543
federal aid - 617, 849 (chart)
HUD project appropriations - - 858
literacy programs - 611, 617
tangible property donations - 158, 171
Library of Congress
acid-free paper - 429
appropriations - 894, 895 (chart)
disabled civil rights - 458
Libya
chemical weapons - 723
U.S. aid to Kenya - 790
U.S. export controls - 201
Lieberman, Joseph I. D-Conn.
congressional pay, honoraria - 73
EPA Cabinet status - 291-292
EPA investigators - 292 (box)
Persian Gulf crisis - 746, 750-751
roll call attendance - 48
Strategic Petroleum Reserve/family planning - 606
Treasury, Postal appropriations - 889
Life insurance
taxes - 151, 159, 172
Light, Nancy - 291
Lightfoot, Jim Ross R-Iowa (5)
congressional elections, 1990 - 908
LIHEAP. *See Low Income Home Energy Assistance Program*
Lincoln Savings and Loan - 6, 60, 78-97, 180, 537
Line-item veto
Bush congressional relations - 16
congressional action, 1990 - 173, 177
Lipinski, William O. D-Ill. (5)
aviation package - 387
disabled civil rights - 460
Lipsen, Linda - 401
Liquefied Gaseous Fuels Spill Test Facility - 274
Liquefied natural gas - 240 (box)
Liquor. *See Alcoholic beverages*
LISA. *See Low-Input Sustainable Agriculture*
Literacy
Bush economic report - 117
closed-captioned TV - 375
commercial drivers - 611
community service programs - 561
education proposals - 610-611, 614, 615
family investment centers - 650
library aid - 617
prison programs - 614
Lithuania
CFE - 696, 703
German unification - 763
Persian Gulf crisis - 745
Soviet-U.S. relations - 204, 757-758, 760-762
U.S. aid - 844
U.S. recognition - 236, 758, 760
Little Sandy Hunting and Fishing Club - 872
Liu, Mike - 918 (chart), 922
Livestock and ranching
dairy herd buyouts - 334, 343
grazing fees - 871, 873-874
methane emissions - 236, 271
organic farming - 347
wool, mohair subsidies - 337
Living wills - 55, 146, 566-567 (box)
Livingston, Bob R-La. (1)
Interior appropriations - 872
Lloyd, Marilyn D-Tenn. (3)
characteristics of Congress - 924
minorities in Congress - 924 (chart)
congressional elections, 1990
marginal vote share - 905 (chart)
congressional leadership - 11 (box)
textile import quotas - 222
Lobbyists and lobbying. *See also Agricultural interest groups; Arms control groups; Business interest groups; Civil rights groups; Consumer interest groups; Environmental interest groups; Health interest groups; Labor interest groups; Political action committees*
contingency fee ban - 679
naval home ports - 681 (box)
Puerto Rico status - 424
trade representative limits - 881, 886
London, Meyer - 922 (box)
Long Island Sound - 301
Long, Jill D-Ind. (4)
characteristics of Congress - 923
minorities in Congress - 924 (chart)
congressional elections, 1990 - 908
Long-term health care
Durenberger ethics case - 101
elderly, Alzheimer's authorization - 599
Medicaid expansion - 569
Medicare changes - 563
Pepper Commission - 607-609
Longbow radar - 824
Longstreth, Thomas K. - 702
Lonsdale, Harry - 915
Lorenzo, Frank A. - 369
Los Alamos, N.M. - 861
Los Angeles, Calif.
AIDS relief - 582
air pollution - 231 (box), 239, 243
drug enforcement - 503, 889
federal pay overhaul - 406
trauma care - 597
water projects authorization - 297, 299
LOSAT missile launchers - 823
Lott, Trent R-Miss.
auto fuel efficiency - 281
coastal zone management - 289
crime bill - 493
Durenberger ethics case - 103
food aid cargo preference - 339 (box)
Hatch Act revision - 408
hate crime statistics - 507
Persian Gulf crisis - 738
savings and loan scandal - 80, 82, 88, 96, 97
Lotteries
D.C. appropriations - 891
sports events - 495
Louisiana
alternative power regulation - 317, 318
campaign finance reform - 62
congressional elections, 1990 - 907 (box), 916, 919
voter turnout - 901 (chart)
congressional redistricting - 931
disaster aid - 328
Energy, water projects
appropriations - 864, 865
authorization - 299
federal judgeships - 522
job training overhaul - 365
offshore drilling emissions - 230, 244
pipeline safety inspection - 286 (box)
SSC authorization - 439
Strategic Petroleum Reserve - 314
uranium enrichment - 310, 317
wetlands protection - 159
Louisiana Land and Exploration Co. - 314
Louisiana State University - 864
Louisiana Tech University - 864
Love, Jo Betts - 532
Low Income Home Energy Assistance Program (LIHEAP)
appropriations - 848, 853
authorization - 552-556
budget action - 125
Low Income Housing Information Service - 633, 634
Low-Income Housing Preservation and Resident Home Ownership Act of 1990 - 652-653
Low-input sustainable agriculture (LISA) - 331, 336-337

Lowery, Bill R-Calif. (41)
congressional elections, 1990 - 903, 907
low winning percentage - 906 (chart)
marginal vote share - 905 (chart)
vote-share falloff - 904 (chart)
Energy, water appropriations - 863
military construction appropriations - 827
savings and loan scandal - 80
Lowey, Nita M. D-N.Y. (20)
Medicare changes - 565
minorities in Congress - 924 (chart)
Loyola University (New Orleans) - 786
Loyola University (Marymount, Calif.) - 888
LSC. *See Legal Services Corporation*
LSD ships - 675, 815 (chart), 819
LTV Corp. - 368
Lucas, William - 465 (box), 518 (box)
Ludeman, Cal - 911
Lugar, Richard G. R-Ind.
Bush congressional relations - 16
CFE - 698
CFTC authorization - 195
defense authorization - 680
farm bill - 323, 333-341, 347-351
Food for Peace - 803
nuclear test treaties - 713
Persian Gulf crisis - 733, 736, 737, 747
South Africa sanctions - 787
START - 707
Lujan, Manuel Jr.
Grand Canyon erosion - 300
Luken, Charles - 905 (chart), 916, 918 (chart)
Luken, Thomas A. D-Ohio (1)
hazardous materials transport - 380-382
nutrition labels - 576
product liability - 400-401
retirement, successor - 916, 918 (chart)
Lukens, Donald E. "Buz"
ethics charges - 6
resignation - 14 (box), 106, 916, 917 (chart), 918 (chart)
Luxury taxes. *See Excise taxes*
Lynn, Mass. - 860

M

M-1 tank
appropriations - 815 (chart), 817, 823, 824
authorization - 674, 684-685
budget action - 122
CFE - 700
Saudi arms sales - 735 (box)
Machtley, Ronald K. R-R.I. (1)
congressional elections, 1990
low winning percentage - 906 (chart)
VA/HUD appropriations - 856
Mack, Connie R-Fla.
budget action - 130
FHA rules revision - 658
housing programs overhaul - 636, 641
Soviet-U.S. relations - 761-762
Mackinac Island, Mich. - 858
MacRae, James B. - 413
MacSharry, Raymond - 210
Madigan, Edward R-Ill. (15)
AIDS bill - 588-589
Clean Air Act - 242, 278
farm bill - 331, 348, 350
fish inspection - 396
Health Service Corps - 595
injuries research - 598
medical device safety - 581
NIH authorization - 604, 605-606
nutrition labels - 576
Magistrates - 522
Magnet schools - 611
Magnetic levitation - 880
Magnuson Fishery Conservation and Management Act of 1976 - 399
Mahe, Eddie - 15, 60-61
Mahoney, Michael C. - 101, 102
Maine
Caribbean Basin Initiative - 214
congressional elections, 1990
voter turnout - 901 (chart)
federal judgeships - 522
gubernatorial election, 1990 - 919, 928, 930
VA/HUD appropriations - 859
wilderness protection - 304
Malaysia
Persian Gulf crisis - 740
U.S. aid - 844
Malberg, Patricia - 918 (chart)
Maloney, Andrew - 106
Maloney, Paul - 442
Malta summit - 757
Mammograms - 145, 564 (box), 606, 680
Management and Budget, Office of (OMB)
appropriations - 887 (chart), 888, 890
aviation package - 384
budget, deficit projections - 111, 127
budget process changes - 161, 176-178
budget summit - 130
Bush congressional relations - 21
child-care aid - 550
civil rights/job bias - 470
Commerce/Justice/State appropriations - 884
community service programs - 559, 562
education proposals - 614
Egyptian debt relief - 732
EPA Cabinet status - 291, 293
family leave - 361
farm bill - 339, 347-348
federal accounting standards - 886, 889
federal credit reform - 163, 178 (box)
federal financial centralization - 416
federal pay overhaul - 407
federal retirement benefits - 407 (box)
FHA rules revision - 657, 658
Food for Peace - 804
foreign ownership of U.S. business - 224
Head Start authorization - 555
health and safety regulation - 53, 412
housing programs overhaul - 636, 640, 642, 643
Medicaid expansion - 571
OIRA review powers - 411-413
Pepper Commission - 607, 608
prepayment of subsidized mortgages - 664
radiation victims compensation - 590
radio spectrum allocation - 377
Treasury, Postal appropriations - 890
VA/HUD appropriations - 855, 856
VA pensions - 420
water projects authorization - 298, 299
Mandela, Nelson - 3, 787, 788, 789
Mangini, Daniel J. - 918 (chart), 922, 934
Mangusta helicopters - 700
Manion, Daniel - 90
Mann, Thomas E. - 30, 32
Manufactured housing - 638, 656
Maple products - 576
Mapplethorpe, Robert - 430
Marcantonio, Vito - 922 (box)
Marine Biomedical Institute for Advanced Studies - 888
Marine Corps, U.S.
defense appropriations - 812-826
defense authorization - 671-687
Persian Gulf War - 755
Marine Mammal Commission - 882 (chart)
Marine Protection Act of 1989 - 301
Maritime Administration
appropriations - 882 (chart)
ready reserve fleet - 814
Mark 48/50 torpedoes - 675
Market Facts Inc. - 572
Market Promotion Program - 345
Markey, Edward J. D-Mass. (7)
cable TV regulation - 371-372
campaign TV ad rates - 66 (box)
children's TV advertising - 373-374
closed-captioned TV - 375
radio spectrum allocation - 376
securities fraud - 194
stock market regulation - 190-192
Strategic Petroleum Reserve - 315
telemarketing curbs - 379
Marlenee, Ron R-Mont. (2)
farm bill - 327
Puerto Rico status - 426
Marriage and divorce
disabled civil rights - 452
immigration law revision - 474-485
fraud law waivers - 484
license applicants AIDS testing - 587
Social Security benefits - 151
veterans benefits - 155
Mars Inc. - 330
Mars space mission
appropriations - 854, 855, 856, 858, 860
authorization - 434, 435, 436
budget action - 126
Marsh, Ben - 217
Marshall Islands - 590, 808
Marshall, Thurgood
abortion - 529
Brennan career - 511 (box)
corporate campaign limits - 59 (box)
flag desecration - 525
habeas corpus appeals - 489 (box)
Medicaid pay suits - 571
political patronage jobs - 933
right to die - 567 (box)
Souter confirmation - 514
student religious groups - 618 (box)
Supreme Court term summary - 52
Thomas confirmation - 518 (box)
Marshals Service, U.S. - 779
Marshes. *See Wetlands protection*
Martin, David H. - 531-532, 533
Martin, David O'B. R-N.Y. (26)
defense authorization - 682
Martin Luther King Federal Holiday Commission - 882 (chart)
Martin, Lynn R-Ill. (16)
balanced-budget amendment - 175 (box)
characteristics of Congress - 923, 924
congressional elections, 1990 - 913, 915, 922
House membership changes - 918 (chart)
congressional partisanship - 40
crime bill - 498
EPA Cabinet status - 293
family leave - 360
Labor appointment - 369 (box)
OMB review powers - 412 (box)
Martinez, Bob - 502, 503 (box), 529-530, 904 (chart), 926, 928, 933
Martinez, Matthew G. D-Calif. (30)
age discrimination - 363
displaced homemakers - 366 (box)
job training overhaul - 366-367
minorities in Congress - 924 (chart)
Maryland
D.C. status - 428
food aid cargo preference - 339 (box)
gubernatorial election, 1990 - 930
Hatch Act revision - 410
offshore drilling - 871
space station design - 437
VA/HUD appropriations - 859
Maryland, University of - 888
Masanz, Tim - 636
Maskell, Jack - 100 (box)
Mason, James O. - 594, 601
Mass transit
budget action - 126
Bush transportation policy - 384
Clean Air Act - 241
commuter rail line - 390
disabled civil rights - 449-450, 453-455, 460
fuel taxes - 172
operator drug testing - 505, 880
Transportation appropriations - 876-879
Washington Metro aid - 429
Massachusetts. *See also Boston*
CDBG funding formula - 641
congressional elections, 1990 - 917
congressional redistricting - 931, 933
energy taxes - 313 (box)
federal judgeships - 522
gubernatorial election, 1990 - 902, 928, 930
living wills - 567 (box)
Medigap insurance - 148
water projects authorization - 299
Math education
employee training - 478
Energy, water appropriations - 865
scholarships - 7, 610, 612 (box)
drug ban - 505
student competency - 615
tech-prep education - 621
Matsui, Robert T. D-Calif. (3)
campaign finance reform - 68
congressional elections, 1990 - 907
minorities in Congress - 924 (chart)
Matsunaga, Spark M.
Clean Air Act - 237
death, successor - 14 (box), 934
hydrogen fuel research - 313, 318-319
successor - 913
Mattingly, Mack - 324
Mattox, William C. - 101
Mavroules, Nicholas D-Mass. (6)
defense authorization - 682, 683
naval home ports - 681 (box)
May, James C. - 377
Mayorga, Francisco - 771
Mazowiecki, Tadeusz - 206
McCain, John R-Ariz.
aviation package - 386-388
budget action - 132
campaign finance reform - 66
community service programs - 560-561
defense appropriations - 821
defense authorization - 678, 679
Grand Canyon erosion - 301
Indian legislation - 422, 423
Persian Gulf crisis - 728
savings and loan scandal - 6, 78-97
START - 705
VA/HUD appropriations - 859
McCandless, Al R-Calif. (37)
congressional elections, 1990 - 907
low winning percentage - 906 (chart)
marginal vote share - 905 (chart)
vote-share falloff - 904 (chart)
McCarran-Ferguson Act of 1945 - 401 (box)
McCarran-Walter Act of 1952 - 474, 480 (box), 799

McCarthy, Joseph R. - 99 (box), 100 (box)
McCarthy, Leo - 913 (box)
McCloskey, Frank D-Ind. (8)
  child-resistant packaging - 417
  congressional elections, 1990
    marginal vote share - 905 (chart)
  deceptive mail curbs - 417
  pornographic mail - 417
McClure, Fred - 509
McClure, James A. R-Idaho
  age discrimination - 364
  Clean Air Act - 235, 238
  CPSC authorization - 393-395
  crime bill - 493
  defense appropriations - 821
  Energy, water appropriations - 861, 865, 866
  global warning - 307
  irrigation subsidies - 357
  oil-shale lands - 316
  Puerto Rico status - 425
  successor - 913 (chart), 915
McCollum, Bill R-Fla. (5)
  assault weapons ban - 501 (box)
  conservative coalition - 40
  crime bill - 494, 495, 497, 498
  disabled civil rights - 450, 459
  federal judgeships - 521
  handgun wait period - 501 (box)
  immigration law revision - 478, 479
  Legal Services Corporation - 532-533
  money laundering - 188
  RICO revision - 537, 538
McConnell, Mitch R-Ky.
  campaign finance reform - 58, 60-65
  community service programs - 561
  congressional elections, 1990 - 911, 915-916
  congressional leadership - 12
  defense authorization - 679
  education proposals - 613
  Hatch Act revision - 409
  Soviet-U.S. relations - 762
McCurdy, Dave D-Okla. (4)
  civil rights/job bias - 470
  community service programs - 559, 560
  congressional leadership - 11 (box)
  defense authorization - 677, 686
  El Salvador aid - 780, 785
  flag desecration - 526
  intelligence authorization - 793, 799
McDade, Joseph M. R-Pa. (10)
  defense appropriations - 818, 825
McDermott, Jim D-Wash. (7)
  coin redesign - 197
  congressional elections, 1990
    low winning percentage - 906 (chart)
  housing programs overhaul - 640
McDonald, Albert - 918 (chart)
McFarlane, Robert C. - 535
McGrath, Raymond J. R-N.Y. (5)
  congressional elections, 1990
    low winning percentage - 906 (chart)
    marginal vote share - 905 (chart)
McGuire, Jean - 480 (box)
McHugh, Matthew F. D-N.Y. (28)
  defense appropriations - 816
  foreign aid appropriations - 830, 834
  intelligence authorization - 796, 797, 799
  Nicaragua aid - 772
  Savage ethics case - 105
McKernan, John R. - 928, 930
McKinney Homeless Assistance Act
  authorization - 665
  housing programs overhaul - 637, 655
McLaughlin, Joseph M. - 415, 932
McLaurin, John L. - 99 (box)
McMichael, Barbara - 553
McNichol, William J. - 336
McWherter, Ned - 930
Measles immunization - 591-592, 846
Meat
  Soviet export credits - 762
  USDA inspection - 396-399
Meacham, Ralph - 521
Mead, Mary - 929
Mecham, Evan - 930
Media Access Project - 375, 377
Mediation
  alternative dispute resolution - 414
Medicaid
  AIDS bill - 587
  appropriations - 847
  budget action - 125, 128, 144
  census count adjustment - 415
  child health - 147, 569-571
  drug discounts - 146-147, 570 (box)
  living wills - 55, 566 (box)
  Medigap policies - 149, 572-573
  nursing home regulation - 589
  outreach, benefits counseling - 149, 569, 571
  payment suits - 53, 571
  Pepper Commission - 607
  summary - 5
Medical aid
  Baltic States - 844
  development aid appropriations - 835
  Nicaragua - 773
  Palestinian *intifada* - 837
  Panama - 775
  Soviet Union - 205
Medical care. *See Health and medical care*
Medical devices and equipment
  contraception research - 601, 602
  Medicare changes - 145, 564, 568
  product liability - 401
  regulation overhaul - 579-581
    boxscore - 580
  Soviet aid - 205
Medical ethics
  fetal research - 600-601
  patient self-determination - 146
  right to die - 52, 53, 55, 566-567 (box)
Medical Recoveries Fund - 155
Medical research and technology
  aging - 598-599
  agricultural research grants - 345
  AIDS - 125
  air pollution - 236, 258, 274
  Alzheimer's disease - 598
  animal rights activists - 441
  drug companies in Puerto Rico - 425
  fetal tissue - 531, 600-601
  human gene-mapping - 126, 601
  infertility, contraception - 531, 601, 602, 604, 605
  injuries - 598
  long-term illness, disability - 608
  medical device safety - 581
  NIH authorization - 600-604
  pediatric AIDS - 587, 588
  rehabilitation - 604
  research facilities - 862, 864, 866
  trauma care - 598
  VA grants - 420-421
  vaccine program authorization - 591-592
  women's health initiatives - 602-603
Medical tests
  AIDS services - 585
  cancer screening - 606, 680, 849
  diagnostic tests - 144
  DRG payment window - 144
  drug tie-ins - 146
  Medicare changes - 564
Medical waste - 259, 290
Medicare
  benefits counseling - 149, 574
  budget action
    Bush proposal - 124-125, 126, 127
    reconciliation - 139, 143-146, 148-149, 159, 162, 165
    resolution - 128, 129
    summit - 132, 134, 135, 136
  federal health benefits - 155
  HMO participation - 125
  Labor/HHS appropriations - 847, 850
  living wills - 55, 566 (box)
  mammogram coverage - 564 (box)
  Medicaid expansion - 570-571
  Medigap policies - 148-149, 572-575
  nursing home regulation - 589
  orphan drugs - 578
  payroll taxes - 159, 164, 172, 564
  Pepper Commission - 607, 608
  program changes - 563-568
  sequestration procedures - 162
  state, local employees - 124, 126, 136, 159, 164
  summary - 5
Medicare Catastrophic Coverage Act of 1988
  case management provisions - 146
  hospice care provisions - 144
  mammogram coverage - 564 (box)
  Medicaid extension - 569
  Medigap policies - 572, 573
  Pepper Commission - 607, 608
  stop-loss coverage - 563
Medicine. *See Drugs and pharmaceuticals*
Meese, Edwin III - 533, 515, 519
Mega Borg - 284
Melton, Richard - 801
Mental health and illness
  AIDS bill - 584, 587
  community centers - 145
  emotionally disturbed children - 616
  home, community-based elderly care - 147
  homeless aid - 665
  housing programs
    budget action - 125
    overhaul - 635, 655
  immigration law revision - 478, 480 (box)
  Indian services - 422
  NIMH project authorization - 599
  nursing home regulation - 148, 589
  prison inmates - 53
  veterans housing aid - 420, 859-860
  whistleblower protection - 683
Mental impairment
  disabled civil rights - 447-461
Mental retardation
  budget action - 128
  community living - 147
  death penalty ban - 491, 494
  developmental disabilities programs - 609
  immigration law revision - 478, 480 (box)
  Medicaid expansion - 569-571
Merck and Co. - 570 (box)
Mercury - 258, 276
Mergens, Bridget - 618 (box)
Merritt, Wade - 731
Metals. *See Mines and mineral resources*
Methadone - 471
Methamphetamine - 493
Methane - 236, 271, 307
Methanol
  Clean Air Act - 229, 232, 240 (box), 247, 278
Methyl chloroform - 269
Metzenbaum, Howard M. D-Ohio
  age discrimination - 362-364
  auto fuel efficiency - 281
  balanced-budget amendment - 175 (box)
  children's TV advertising - 373
  Clean Air Act - 235, 238
  crime bill - 490, 491
  elderly health care - 599
  federal judgeships - 520
  joint production ventures - 541
  juvenile justice nomination - 506
  nutrition labels - 576
  orphan drugs - 577, 579
  RICO revision - 537
  Souter confirmation - 510-511, 513
  Thomas confirmation - 518-519 (box)
  vertical price fixing - 538, 540
  whistleblower protection - 364
Mexico
  drug interdiction - 679
  screwworm eradication - 355
  U.S. border area
    air pollution - 236, 273, 274
    "colonias" housing aid - 654
    drug enforcement - 503, 889
    money exchange businesses - 188-189
  U.S. trade
    free-trade talks - 218
    sugar quotas - 328
Meyers, Jan R-Kan. (3)
  congressional elections, 1990
    vote-share falloff - 904 (chart)
  minorities in Congress - 924 (chart)
MFA. *See Multi-Fiber Arrangement*
Mfume, Kweisi D-Md. (7)
  civil rights/job bias - 473
  congressional elections, 1990 - 905
    low winning percentage - 906 (chart)
  housing programs overhaul - 639
  minorities in Congress - 924 (chart)
Mi-24 helicopters - 700
Miami, Fla. - 503, 582, 759, 889
Miccousukee Tribe of Indians - 424
Michel, Robert H. R-Ill. (18)
  domestic issues
    Amtrak authorization - 391
    budget action - 130, 132, 136, 137, 165
    civil rights/job bias - 471
    continuing resolutions - 897 (box)
    Eastern Airlines strike - 369
    farm bill - 331-332
    federal judgeships - 523
    FHA rules revision - 660
    flag desecration - 524, 527
    Hatch Act revision - 410
    "motor voter" bill - 70
    Social Security earnings test - 557
  foreign issues
    China-U.S. relations - 765
    Persian Gulf crisis - 749, 751, 754
      use-of-force debate - 752 (box)
  House leadership - 9 (box), 10, 12
    campaign finance reform - 59
    congressional mail - 74
    congressional partisanship - 39
    conservative coalition - 48
    Frank ethics case - 104
    Lukens resignation - 106
    pocket veto power - 22
    presidential support in Congress - 31
Michelman, Kate - 514
Michigan
  abortion - 530
  acid rain - 264
  CDBG funding formula - 641
  congressional elections, 1990 - 919
  congressional redistricting - 931, 933
  corporate campaign limits - 59 (box)
  federal judgeships - 522
  gubernatorial election, 1990 - 902, 926, 928, 929
  HUD pork-barrel spending - 860
  job training overhaul - 365
  living wills - 567 (box)
  Transportation appropriations - 878, 880

water projects authorization - 299
Michigan Technological University - 888
Mickelson, George S. - 930
Micmac Indians - 424
Microwave transmissions - 370
Middle East. *See also Persian Gulf crisis; specific countries*
Food for Peace - 803
Pakistan-U.S. relations - 769
Midgetman missiles
appropriations - 815 (chart), 817, 822, 824
authorization - 673, 683, 684
budget action - 122
START - 707
Midwest Express Airlines - 386
Midwestern states
abandoned mines - 154
acid rain - 230, 232-233, 236, 238-239, 242, 262, 276-278
census count adjustment - 415
farm bill - 335, 341, 350
Migrant health centers
AIDS bill - 584, 586
minority health - 596
Migrant workers
housing aid - 654
job training eligibility - 367
Mikulski, Barbara A. D-Md.
budget action - 165
cancer screening - 606
characteristics of Congress - 923, 924
minorities in Congress - 924 (chart)
hate crime statistics - 507
Medicare changes - 568
NIH authorization - 601, 603
Souter confirmation - 515
space station - 437
U.N. population fund - 839 (box)
VA/HUD appropriations - 856, 858, 859, 860
Miles City, Mont. - 878
Military aid. *See Arms sales and transfers*
Military dependents
abortion - 683
military construction appropriations - 827, 829
Military pay and benefits
budget action - 122
community service comparison - 560-561
defense appropriations - 816, 821
defense authorization - 672, 680, 686
defense budget reprogramming - 676 (box)
Desert Shield bonus - 682
education benefits - 686
retirement benefits - 407 (box)
supplemental appropriations - 845
Military personnel. *See also Military dependents; Military pay and benefits; Military reserves; Operation Desert Shield; Persian Gulf crisis; Veterans*
budget action - 122
drug enforcement - 503 (box)
Andean Initiative advisers - 806
flag desecration - 528
management efficiency - 673 (box)
manpower levels
defense appropriations - 814, 816, 820, 821
force structure cuts - 671-687
medical programs - 816
overseas deployment
defense appropriations - 820, 822, 825
El Salvador deaths - 780, 786
Japan - 682, 686, 687
military construction appropriations - 827
National Guard training missions - 52, 53
Noriega ouster - 775-776
Europe
CFE - 697-698, 700-701, 703
defense authorization - 677, 678, 686
key votes - 7-B-8-B
Puerto Rico status - 426
recruiting - 822
reserve unit melding - 680
Salvadoran training - 781-782
vocational education - 621
Military posts
abortion in military hospitals - 530-531, 680, 683, 11-B
airport commercial conversion - 156
base closings
budget action - 122
defense authorization - 672-687, 693-695
military construction appropriations - 826-830
boxscore - 827
naval bases
home ports - 678, 681 (box)
Israel - 822, 825
overseas bases
foreign civilian salaries - 683, 686, 816, 822, 825
Palau autonomy - 808
toxic waste cleanup
budget action - 122
defense authorization - 675, 679-680
military construction appropriations - 816, 827, 829
Military reserves. *See also National Guard*
call-up period - 812-813
defense authorization - 672, 676, 680, 686
equipment - 816, 821, 824-825
military construction appropriations - 829, 830
Persian Gulf crisis - 719, 729
veterans home loan benefits - 420
Milk and dairy products
budget action - 141
deficit reduction - 344
herd buyouts - 334, 343
light butter - 868
nutrition labels - 576
price supports - 327-329, 333, 334, 343, 349-351
sequestration procedures - 162
surplus cheese donation - 346
Miller, Bob - 930
Miller, Clarence E. R-Ohio (10)
congressional elections, 1990 - 907
foreign aid appropriations - 830
Miller, George D-Calif. (7)
alternative power regulation - 318
campaign finance reform - 67-68
child-care aid - 548
community service programs - 562
congressional elections, 1990 - 907
Grand Canyon erosion - 300, 301
Interior Committee leadership - 924
irrigation subsidies - 356-357
Labor/HHS appropriations - 850
mental health projects - 599
oil pollution cleanup - 283, 287
Persian Gulf crisis - 747
Tongass forest protection - 294
uranium enrichment - 311
WIC funding - 554 (box)
Miller, John R-Wash. (1)
congressional elections, 1990
marginal vote share - 905 (chart)
intelligence authorization - 796
textile import quotas - 222
Miller, Richard R. - 535
Miller, Patrick K. - 918 (chart)
Miller, Zell - 930
Milstar communications satellites - 677
Milwaukee, Wis.
housing demonstration project - 647
Mine Safety and Health Act - 143
Mine Safety and Health Administration - 848 (chart)
Minerals Management Service - 873 (chart)
Mines and mineral resources. *See also Coal; Natural gas; Oil; Uranium*
Antarctica protection - 6, 305-307
Arizona wilderness protection - 304
cleanup - 154
federal land patents - 875-876
oil-shale lands - 316
research - 442-443
safety law penalties - 143
South Africa sanctions - 787
toxic air pollutants - 253, 257, 276
Mines, U.S. Bureau of - 443, 873 (chart)
Minesweepers - 675, 682, 819, 825, 826
Mineta, Norman Y. D-Calif. (13)
aviation package - 386
congressional leadership - 11 (box)
disabled civil rights - 449, 460
minorities in Congress - 924 (chart)
Minimum wage
Puerto Rico job training - 366
Mink, Patsy T. D-Hawaii (2)
characteristics of Congress - 902 (box), 923
minorities in Congress - 924 (chart)
congressional elections, 1990
special elections - 14 (box), 923, 934
Minnesota
abortion - 529
campaign finance reform
corporate campaign limits - 59 (box)
state efforts - 65 (box)
congressional elections, 1990 - 919
voter turnout - 901 (chart)
gubernatorial election, 1990 - 902, 930
Medicaid - 148
Medigap insurance - 148
National Guard training exercises - 694 (box)
vocational education - 622
Transportation appropriations - 880
water projects
appropriations - 865
authorization - 299
Minorities. *See also Minority business; specific groups*
broadcast license set-asides - 52, 53, 379 (box)
census count adjustment - 415, 932
characteristics of Congress - 923-924
minorities in Congress - 924 (chart)
civil rights/job bias - 32, 462-473
community development student aid - 655
conservative coalition - 47
disabled education - 616, 617
European separatism - 703
health care programs - 596
AIDS bill - 585
Alzheimer's disease - 598
clinical trials - 602, 603
organ donor pool - 597
TB prevention - 594
health professions opportunity - 596
housing programs overhaul - 644, 647
judicial appointments - 515-516
literacy programs - 610
math, science scholarships - 612 (box)
radio spectrum allocation - 377
textile import quotas - 220
Thomas confirmation - 518 (box)
vocational education - 621
Minority business
budget action - 123
EPA research grants - 275
housing programs overhaul - 647
Indian preference - 421, 422, 423
SBA authorization - 395
SSC authorization - 439
Minority Business Development Agency - 882 (chart)
Minority Health Office - 596
Mint, U.S. - 196, 197
Minuteman II missiles - 672
MIRACL weapons - 684
Missiles. *See also Arms control; Strategic defense initiative*
accidental launch defense - 692
defense appropriations - 817-819, 823, 824-825
early warning satellite defenses - 817, 823, 824
radar guidance systems - 824
strategic weapons triad - 688
technology export controls - 201, 680, 683
test launches - 706
Mission to Planet Earth - 126, 434, 436
Mississippi
congressional elections, 1990 - 906, 909
voter turnout - 901 (chart)
conservative coalition - 47
corporate campaign limits - 59 (box)
Energy, water appropriations - 863, 865
federal judgeships - 522
Hatch Act revision - 411
naval home ports - 681 (box)
offshore drilling emissions - 230, 244
Transportation appropriations - 878
Mississippi River
Lower Delta area housing - 654
Missouri
abortion - 528-529
acid rain - 262
B-2 bomber - 688, 689
congressional elections, 1990 - 903, 906-907
earthquake research - 442
federal judgeships - 522
right to die - 566 (box)
water projects authorization - 299
Missouri - 678
Missouri River
water projects authorization - 299
Mitchell, Cleta - 15
Mitchell, George J. D-Maine
defense, foreign and trade issues
Caribbean Basin Initiative - 214
CFE - 703
China-U.S. relations - 764, 765, 768
food aid cargo preference - 339 (box)
foreign aid appropriations - 843
intelligence authorization - 793, 794
Nicaragua aid - 773
oil-spill protocols - 284, 285
Panama aid - 778
Persian Gulf crisis - 720, 727, 734, 736-738, 747, 749-754
questionable gulf allies - 740 (box)
South Africa sanctions - 788
Soviet-U.S. relations - 758, 761
textile import quotas - 219
domestic issues
age discrimination - 363
AIDS bill - 583
airline rights - 389 (box)
Amtrak authorization - 391
budget action - 113-114, 117, 130-132, 164
cable TV regulation - 372
capital gains tax - 168 (box)

child-care aid - 548, 550
civil rights/job bias - 466, 467
Clean Air Act - 9-10, 230-238, 244
coastal water pollution - 290
community service programs - 559
crime bill - 491, 492
Eastern Airlines strike - 369
education proposals - 615
farm bill - 340
federal RCRA compliance - 308
fish inspection - 396-399
flag desecration - 527
Hatch Act revision - 409
Health Service Corps - 595
Interior appropriations - 875
Medicare changes - 568
Pepper Commission - 607
rural development - 352
Social Security - 170
Souter confirmation - 515
supplemental appropriations - 845-846
taxes - 167
thrift supervisor - 180 (box)
Transportation appropriations - 876-877, 880
VA/HUD appropriations - 859
Senate leadership - 8-12
campaign finance reform - 57, 60-63
congressional partisanship - 32, 39
conservative coalition - 40
presidential support in Congress - 30, 31
Mitchell, Theo - 930
MLRS artillery rockets - 674, 815 (chart)
Moakley, Joe D-Mass. (9)
Caribbean Basin Initiative - 212
coin redesign - 196, 197
congressional partisanship - 39
El Salvador aid - 779-781, 784, 785, 786
fire-safe cigarettes - 402
foreign aid appropriations - 842
immigration law revision - 478, 479, 484, 485
independent House members - 922 (box)
pocket veto power - 22
Treasury, Postal appropriations - 888
Mobil Oil Corp. - 287, 872
Mobile, Ala. - 681 (box), 302
Mobile homes - 638, 651, 656
Mobley, Al - 530, 929
Modrow, Hans - 699
Moe, Richard - 537, 538
Moffett, Toby - 918 (chart), 923
Mofford, Rose - 94, 929
Mohair - 141, 337, 343, 344
Moi, Daniel arap - 790
Molinari, Guy V.
Legal Services board - 532
naval home ports - 681 (box)
resignation, successor - 14 (box), 934
Molinari, Susan R-N.Y. (14)
AIDS bill - 589
characteristics of Congress - 902 (box)
minorities in Congress - 924 (chart)
election - 14 (box), 923, 934
naval home ports - 681 (box)
Mollohan, Alan B. D-W.Va. (1)
U.N. population fund - 840
Money. *See Coins; Currency*
Money laundering
congressional action, 1990 - 187-189
crime bill - 486, 499
Panama bank secrecy - 776, 777, 779
Monongahela River - 298
Monopoly. *See Competition and monopoly*
Montana
congressional elections, 1990
voter turnout - 901 (chart)
congressional redistricting - 931
corporate campaign limits - 59 (box)
Puerto Rico status - 426
Montgomery, G. V. "Sonny" D-Miss. (3)
call-up of reserves - 695 (box)
conservative coalition - 47
defense authorization - 677
flag desecration - 524
National Guard training exercises - 694 (box)
veterans programs - 418-420
Montreal Protocol on Substances that Deplete the Ozone Layer - 230, 269, 270, 271, 832 (chart), 837
Montserrat - 212
Moody, Jim D-Wis. (5)
U.N. population fund - 838-839 (box)
Moon space mission
appropriations - 854, 855, 856, 858, 860
authorization - 434, 435
budget action - 126
Mooney, James P. - 371
Moore, W. Henson - 314, 315, 438
Moorhead, Carlos J. R-Calif. (22)
civil rights/job bias - 469
congressional elections, 1990
vote-share falloff - 904 (chart)
crime bill - 498
federal judgeships - 521, 523
handgun wait period - 501 (box)
octane labeling - 282
pocket veto power - 22
Strategic Petroleum Reserve - 315
vertical price fixing - 540
Morals. *See ethical issues*
Moran, James P. Jr. - 530, 905 (chart), 917, 918 (chart)
Mordini, Kathleen - 280
Moreland, Charles - 428
Morella, Constance A. R-Md. (8)
Hatch Act revision - 410-411
minorities in Congress - 924 (chart)
South Africa sanctions - 789
thrift bailout - 181
Morgan, Robert - 94
Morial, Marc H. - 918 (chart)
Morocco
Persian Gulf crisis - 729
Morrison, Bruce A. D-Conn. (3)
gubernatorial election, 1990 - 919, 927
House membership changes - 918 (chart)
immigration law revision - 474-479, 485
insurance price-sharing - 401
Morrison, Sid R-Wash. (4)
logging limits/wildlife protection - 297
Mortgage Bankers Association of America - 658, 659
Mortgage revenue bonds - 160, 173
Mortgages. *See Home loans and mortgages*
Mosbacher, Robert A.
cable TV regulation - 372
Soviet-U.S. relations - 758
Moscow summit, 1991
Soviet-U.S. relations - 757, 762
Motion pictures - 541-542
Motley, John J. - 359
Motor Vehicle Fuel Efficiency Act - 279-281
Motor Vehicle Manufacturers Association - 246, 282
Motor vehicles. *See also Automobiles; Bus transportation; Fuel and gasoline taxes; Trucks and trucking*
armored military vehicles - 685, 817
ATV safety - 394, 395
emissions controls - 4, 229, 232, 234, 246-247, 251-254
deadlines - 231 (box)
highlights - 233 (box)
inspection and maintenance - 249, 250, 252
disabled access - 454
fastener standards - 395
ozone-depleting refrigerants - 270
toxic air pollutants - 233, 242, 252
wilderness ban - 304
Mount Sinai Medical Center (Miami) - 888
Mount St. Helens - 215
Mount Vernon, Ill. - 878
Movietime - 371
Moynihan, Daniel Patrick D-N.Y.
China-U.S. relations - 768
Clean Air Act - 247
congressional pay, honoraria - 72
Dunne nomination - 465 (box)
German unification - 763
Persian Gulf crisis - 733, 735
Social Security in budget accounting - 167, 170 (box)
torture ban treaty - 807
water projects authorization - 298
Mozambique
South Africa-U.S. relations - 787
U.S. aid - 845
Mrazek, Robert J. D-N.Y. (3)
congressional elections, 1990
marginal vote share - 905 (chart)
foreign aid appropriations - 839
Transportation appropriations - 880
Mubarak, Hosni - 719, 730, 831, 840
Muenster, Ted - 916
Mujahedeen. *See Afghanistan*
Mulford, David C. - 189, 203
Mulhall, James - 281
Multi-Fiber Arrangement (MFA) - 210, 219-222
Murder
D.C. drug crimes/abortion - 846, 852
federal death penalty - 487, 490, 494, 496, 497
hate crime statistics - 506, 507
Murkowski, Frank H. R-Alaska
Agent Orange compensation - 418, 419
Arctic refuge drilling - 315 (box)
congressional pay, honoraria - 72
Energy, water appropriations - 866
foreign ownership of U.S. business - 224
military construction appropriations - 830
Tongass forest protection - 295
U.S. Embassy in Moscow - 760 (box)
Murphy, Anne G. - 431
Murphy, Austin J. D-Pa. (22)
ethics case, 1987 - 103
octane labeling - 282
Murphy, Walter F. - 52
Murtha, John P. D-Pa. (12)
defense appropriations - 816, 818, 825
El Salvador aid - 780, 784
Persian Gulf crisis - 737, 748
supplemental appropriations - 845
Transportation appropriations - 878
Museums
artists' rights - 542
disabled civil rights - 448
Indian remains - 422
Lawrence Welk birthplace - 811
tangible property donations - 158, 171
Mutual funds
information disclosure - 194
Mutual Legal Assistance Agreement - 779
Mutual Mortgage Insurance Fund - 142, 640, 642, 648, 657-661
MX missiles
appropriations
FY90 supplemental - 846
FY91 - 815 (chart), 817, 822, 824
military construction - 829
authorization - 672, 673, 683, 684
B-2 bomber - 689
budget action - 122
START - 704, 707, 708
Myanmar (Burma)
U.S. ambassador - 801 (box)
U.S. trade/human rights - 211, 213
Myers, John T. R-Ind. (7)
Energy, water appropriations - 862, 863
Myers, Matthew - 593
Myers, Michael "Ozzie" - 922

N

NAACP. *See National Association for the Advancement of Colored People*
NAAQS. *See National Ambient Air Quality Standards*
Nader, Ralph - 15, 71, 537
Nagle, Dave D-Iowa (3)
farm bill - 327
NASA authorization - 434
NAIC. *See National Association of Insurance Commissioners*
Namibia
South Africa-U.S. relations - 787
U.S. aid - 845
NASA. *See National Aeronautics and Space Administration*
Natcher, William H. D-Ky. (2)
Labor/HHS appropriations - 847, 848, 850
roll call attendance - 48
Nathan, Richard P. - 416
National Abortion Rights Action League - 530, 514
National Academy of Sciences
Agent Orange-cancer link - 419
hazardous materials transport - 381
National Acid Lakes Registry - 267
National Acid Precipitation Assessment Program - 260
National Aeronautics and Space Administration (NASA)
appropriations - 846, 854-860
authorization - 434-436
boxscore - 434
budget action - 125-126
hydrogen fuel research - 273, 318-319
space station design overhaul - 436-437
National Aerospace Plane - 675
National Agricultural Chemicals Association - 336
National Airport *See Washington National Airport*
National Ambient Air Quality Standards (NAAQS) - 248, 252, 253
National and Community Service Act of 1990 - 559-562
National and Community Service Commission - 561
National Archives - 887 (chart)
National Assembly of National Voluntary Health and Social Welfare Organizations - 560
National Association for Biomedical Research - 441
National Association for the Advancement of Colored People (NAACP)
capital punishment - 490
civil rights/job bias - 464
Dunne nomination - 465 (box)
"motor voter" bill - 70
National Association of Attorneys General - 308, 539
National Association of Broadcasters
cable TV regulation - 371

campaign TV ad rates - 66-67 (box)
children's TV advertising - 373, 375
radio spectrum allocation - 377
National Association of Catalog Showroom Merchandisers - 539
National Association of Evangelicals - 549
National Association of Home Builders - 353, 658, 659
National Association of Housing and Redevelopment Officials - 632
National Association of Insurance Commissioners (NAIC) - 148, 573, 574, 575
National Association of Manufacturers - 536, 539
National Association of Realtors - 658-661
National Association of Wheat Growers - 335
National Association of Wholesaler-Distributors - 360
National Audubon Society - 308, 330, 332
National Black Caucus of State Legislators - 570 (box)
National Board for Professional Teacher Standards - 610, 611
National Bone Marrow Donor Registry - 596-597
National Cable Television Association - 370, 371
National Cancer Institute - 600, 601, 603
National Center for Complex Systems - 888
National Center for Human Genome Research - 601
National Center for Literacy - 611
National Center for Medical Rehabilitation Research - 600, 604
National Clean Air Coalition - 232, 233, 239, 243, 245
National Clearinghouse for Science, Mathematics and Technology Education - 612
National Coalition Against the Misuse of Pesticides - 336
National Coalition of Hispanic Health and Human Services Organizations - 570 (box)
National Collegiate Athletic Association - 625-626
National Commission for the Protection of Human Subjects of Biomedical and Behavioral Research - 600
National Commission on AIDS - 583, 849 (chart)
National Commission on Children - 150, 849 (chart)
National Commission on Financing Postsecondary Education - 849 (chart)
National Commission on Judicial Impeachment - 522
National Commission on Libraries - 849 (chart)
National Commission on the Public Service - 405
National Commission on Violent Crime Against Women - 507
National Commission to Prevent Infant Mortality - 849 (chart)
National Committee to Preserve Social Security and Medicare - 557, 417
National Conference of State Legislatures - 931
National Cooperative Research Act - 541
National Corn Growers Association - 335
National Council of La Raza - 474
National Council of Senior Citizens - 567
National Council of State Housing Agencies - 659
National Council on Aging - 519 (box)
National Council on Disability - 448, 458, 459, 849 (chart)
National Council on Educational Goals - 367, 852, 853
National Council on the Arts - 431
National Credit Union Administration - 163, 178 (box), 186, 855 (chart)
National debt. *See Budget, U.S.*
National Defense Authorization Act for Fiscal 1991 - 671-687
National Drug Control Policy, Office of - 502, 503 (box), 887 (chart), 889
National Drug Intelligence Center - 889
National Education Association - 549, 611
National Endowment for Children's Educational Television - 374
National Endowment for the Arts (NEA)
appropriations - 870-875
authorization - 430-433
boxscore - 430
congressional partisanship - 39
conservative coalition - 47
National Endowment for the Humanities
NEA authorization - 430
National Energy Strategy - 312
National Environmental Education Advisory Council - 293
National Environmental Policy Act of 1969 - 306-307
National Federation of Independent Business
disabled civil rights - 448, 451, 460
family leave - 359
National Federation of the Blind - 388
National Fisheries Institute - 286
National Food Policy Conference - 575
National Forest Products Association - 871
National forests
appropriations - 873 (chart)
below cost timber sales - 294, 358, 871, 874
logging roads - 294, 358, 871, 876
logging/wildlife protection
authorization - 296-297
Interior appropriations - 870, 871-872, 874-875
Tongass forest - 5-6, 294-295
recreational use - 358, 871
timber exports from public lands - 211, 214-215, 216
wilderness protection bills - 304
National Foundation for Biomedical Research - 600
National Foundation on the Arts and Humanities - 430
National Governors' Association
child-care aid - 549
housing programs overhaul - 636
Medicaid pay suits - 571
nursing home regulation - 589
National Guard
call-up period - 812-813
defense authorization - 676, 680, 686
drug interdiction - 122, 679
equipment - 816, 821, 824-825
military construction appropriations - 829, 830
overseas training exercises - 52, 53, 694 (box)
Persian Gulf crisis - 695 (box)
veterans home loan benefits - 420
war powers suit - 739 (box)
National Head Start Association - 553
National Health Service Corps - 147, 595-596
National Heart, Lung and Blood Institute - 597, 600, 601, 603
National Hemophilia Foundation - 570 (box)
National Highway Traffic Safety Administration - 879 (chart)
National Homeownership Trust - 647
National Housing Act - 632
National Housing Trust - 631, 634, 638, 647, 656
National Institute for Literacy - 615
National Institute of Building Sciences - 656, 855 (chart)
National Institute of Child Health and Human Development - 600, 603-604
National Institute of Environmental Health Sciences - 236
National Institute of Independent Colleges and Universities - 625
National Institute of Mental Health
mental health services authorization - 599
National Institute of Standards and Technology (NIST)
appropriations - 882 (chart)
authorization - 440
fastener standards - 395
National Institute on Drug Abuse - 504
National Institutes of Health (NIH)
animal rights activists - 441, 442
appropriations - 848 (chart), 849-850, 853
authorization - 531, 600-604
boxscore - 600
director - 602 (box), 603
gene-mapping project - 126, 861, 865
National Insurance Development Fund - 163
National Kidney Foundation - 417
National Labor Relations Board - 849 (chart)
National League of Cities
cable TV regulation 371
housing programs overhaul - 636
National Leased Housing Association - 663
National Legal Aid and Defender Association - 532-533
National Liberation Armed Forces (Cambodia) - 837-838
National Literacy 2000 Federal Interagency Council - 611
National Low Income Housing Coalition - 633, 634, 643, 663, 664
National Manufactured Housing Construction and Safety Standards Act of 1974 - 638, 656
National Mediation Board - 849 (chart)
National Nutrition Monitoring Advisory Council - 355
National Oceanic and Atmospheric Administration (NOAA)
appropriations - 882 (chart)
coastal water pollution - 289
fish inspection - 396-399
Florida Keys protection - 303
weather service user fees - 157, 386
National Opposition Union (UNO) (Nicaragua) - 770
National Organ Transplant Program - 597
National Park Act of 1960 - 301
National Park Service
appropriations - 873 (chart)
visibility impairment - 274
National parks. *See also Grand Canyon*
visibility impairment - 244, 246, 274, 276
National Rainbow Coalition - 570 (box)
National Republican Alliance (ARENA) (El Salvador) - 780
National Republican Congressional Committee - 12, 15, 59, 902, 917, 932
National Republican Senatorial Committee - 12, 63, 487, 911, 913
National Research Council - 803
National Restaurant Association - 451, 460
National Rifle Association - 491-492, 500 (box)
National Right to Life Committee - 530, 531, 602 (box), 838 (box)
National Science Foundation (NSF)
Antarctica protection - 305, 306
appropriations - 854, 855 (chart), 859, 860
budget action - 126
earthquake research - 442
math, science scholarships - 612 (box)
National Science Scholars - 612, 615
National Security Act of 1947 - 798, 799
National Security Council
appropriations - 887 (chart)
Food for Peace - 804
Hatch Act revision - 410
Iran-Iraq War - 722
National Service, Office of - 559
National service programs
authorization - 559-562
National Space Council - 434, 855 (chart), 856
National Steel Corp. - 276
National Taxpayers Union - 15, 73-74, 311
National Telecommunications and Information Administration - 376, 882 (chart)
National Trade Estimate - 208
National Traffic and Motor Vehicle Safety Act - 638
National Training and Information Center - 659-660
National Transportation Safety Board - 879 (chart)
National Treasury Employees Union - 72 (box)
National Union for the Total Independence of Angola (UNITA) - 791, 792-793, 795, 796, 797
National Urban League - 70
National Vaccine Program - 591-592
National Veterans Legal Services Project - 418
National Weather Service - 157
National Wilderness Preservation System - 459
National Wildlife Federation - 291, 298, 332, 335
National Wildlife Foundation - 874
National Women's Law Center - 464
National Wool Act - 162
Nationalist Party (South Africa) - 787
Native Americans. *See Indians; Hawaii, native programs*
NATO. *See North Atlantic Treaty Organization*
Natural disasters. *See also Disaster relief; Earthquakes; Floods*
coastal enhancement grants - 154
natural hazards management - 289
U.S. immigration policy - 483, 484
Natural gas
acid rain - 263, 264
alternative fuels - 240 (box), 247, 307
depletion allowances - 160, 172, 313 (box)
methane assessment - 271
offshore leases, drilling - 154, 870-871
coastal zone management - 288-289
emissions - 244, 273

ozone attainment - 246
pipeline safety inspection - 286 (box)
stripper wells - 274
tax incentives - 160, 169, 172, 313 (box)
Natural resources
Indian economic development - 621
Natural Resources Defense Council
Clean Air Act - 239, 242, 276
farm bill - 332, 335
START - 705
Naturalization
administrative procedures - 483-484
jurisdiction - 521
language requirement - 476
Navajo Community College - 143
Navajo Community College Act - 621
Navajo Indians
radiation victims compensation - 590
Navajo Trust Fund - 873 (chart)
Naval Petroleum Reserve - 873
Naval Reserve - 819
Naval ships. *See also Aircraft carriers; Submarines*
battleship retirement - 678
budget action - 122
cargo ships - 686, 814, 825, 826
defense appropriations - 818-819,825, 826
defense authorization - 675, 685-686
high-speed supply ships - 686
prepositioning ships - 814, 826
ready reserve fleet - 814, 885
Navy, U.S.
budget action - 122
defense appropriations - 812-826
defense authorization - 671-687
home ports - 681 (box)
management efficiency - 673 (box)
Persian Gulf crisis - 719, 726, 732, 814
personnel limits - 672
START - 706
NEA. *See National Endowment for the Arts*
Neal, Larry - 892
Neal, Stephen L. D-N.C. (5)
civil rights/job bias - 470
housing programs overhaul - 640
prepayment of subsidized mortgages - 663
Neas, Ralph G. - 463-464, 473
Nebraska
federal judgeships - 522
gubernatorial election, 1990 - 902, 928
living wills - 567 (box)
Nehemiah grants - 636, 647, 656
Neighborhood Reinvestment Corporation - 656, 855, 855 (chart)
Neighborhood revitalization - 641, 644
Nelson, Bill D-Fla. (11)
gubernatorial election, 1990 - 919, 928
House membership changes - 918 (chart)
NASA authorization - 435
roll call attendance - 48
Nelson, Richard Y. Jr. - 632
Nelson, Sheffield - 930
NEPA. *See National Environmental Policy Act*
Nepal
displaced Tibetan nationals - 476
Nerve gas - 674
Nestlen, Mark - 335
Netherlands
CFE - 697, 700
Netherlands Antilles - 212
Neurological disorders
toxic air pollutants - 230
Neutral buoyancy laboratory - 437
Nevada
abortion - 530
Amtrak waste disposal - 392
gubernatorial election, 1990 - 930
radiation victims compensation - 590
Senate election - 281
Nevada, University of - 274
New Columbia - 429
New England. *See Northeastern states*
New Hampshire
campaign finance reform
corporate campaign limits - 59 (box)
state efforts - 65 (box)
congressional redistricting - 932
federal judgeships - 522
gubernatorial election, 1990 - 928, 929
New Jersey
abortion - 529
AIDS funding - 852
beach water quality - 290
campaign finance reform - 62
congressional elections, 1990 - 901, 917
congressional redistricting - 931
federal judgeships - 522
food aid cargo preference - 339 (box)
interstate waste disposal - 383
living wills - 567 (box)
offshore drilling - 871, 872, 880
respite care demonstration project - 148
state, local tax deductibility - 165
water projects authorization - 297, 299
New Jersey - 672
New Mexico
"colonias" housing aid - 654
federal judgeships - 522
gubernatorial election, 1990 - 902
Hatch Act revision - 411
radiation victims compensation - 590
SDI research - 692
visibility impairment - 273
New Orleans, University of - 862
New Progressive Party (Puerto Rico) - 425
New York
acid rain - 275
CDBG funding formula - 641
congressional elections, 1990 - 907, 909, 917
congressional redistricting - 931, 933
corporate campaign limits - 59 (box)
federal judgeships - 522
gubernatorial election, 1990 - 926
living wills - 567 (box)
nuclear plant safety - 309
state, local tax deductibility - 132. 165
tailpipe emissions standards - 247
Transportation appropriations - 878, 880
waste disposal - 276, 383
water pollution - 301
water projects authorization - 297, 299
New York, N.Y.
AIDS relief - 582
air pollution - 239
airport slot allocation - 384-387
census count adjustment - 415-416, 932
drug-abuse treatment - 504
drug enforcement - 503, 889
federal pay overhaul - 406
Irish immigrants - 477
naval home ports - 681 (box)
octane labeling - 282
Soviet air service - 759
stock-index futures trading - 194-195
Newark, N.J. - 582, 852
Newman, Constance - 405
Newspapers
Baby Bell information services - 377, 378
cable TV regulation - 371
NFIB. *See National Federation of Independent Business*
NHSC. *See National Health Service Corps*
Nicaragua
Caribbean Basin Initiative - 213, 214
presidential election - 3, 770
U.S. aid - 770-774
appropriations - 834, 844
boxscore - 770
El Salvador aid - 782, 783, 784
Food for Peace - 804
Panama aid - 777, 778
summary - 5
U.S. ambassador - 801 (box)
U.S. immigration policy - 478, 479
Nichols, Dick - 918 (chart), 925, 933
Nickles, Don R-Okla.
AIDS bill - 586
auto fuel efficiency - 280, 281
budget action - 165
campaign finance reform - 63-64, 65
Clean Air Act - 238, 278
congressional leadership - 12
congressional mail - 74, 75
crime bill - 487
Ethics Committee special counsel - 81 (box)
foreign aid appropriations - 843
legislative branch appropriations - 897-898
Nielson, Howard C. R-Utah (3)
CPSC authorization - 394
NIH authorization - 603
retirement, successor - 918 (chart), 922
Night-viewing equipment - 679
NIH. *See National Institutes of Health*
NIST. *See National Institute of Standards and Technology*
Nitrogen oxides
acid rain - 229, 237 (box), 259-267, 278
alternative fuels - 240 (box), 253
motor vehicle emissions - 229, 231 (box), 233 (box), 246, 251-254
smog standards - 235 (box), 249, 250, 251
Nixon, Richard M.
budget process - 175
crime issues - 487
energy policy - 312
farm policy - 324
Watergate scandal - 57
NOAA. *See National Oceanic and Atmospheric Administration*
Noise abatement
budget action - 156
aviation package - 6, 384, 385, 388
Nominations and appointments
Civil Rights Division - 465 (box)
diplomatic posts - 801 (box)
"drug czar" - 502, 503 (box)
Education secretary - 614 (box)
Energy defense programs - 309-310
EPA Cabinet status - 291-293
judiciary - 6, 515-519, 521
Souter confirmation - 508-515
Thomas confirmation - 518-519 (box)
juvenile justice director - 506
Labor secretary - 369 (box)
Legal Services Corporation - 531-533, 886
NIH director - 600, 602 (box), 603
OIRA director - 413
thrift supervisor - 179, 180 (box)
Nonindigenous Aquatic Nuisance Act of 1990 - 303-304
Norfolk, Va. - 651
Noriega, Manuel Antonio
drug-trafficking charges - 777, 779
overthrow - 5, 212, 774, 776
Normandy - 681
Norris, Robert S. - 705
North Atlantic Treaty Organization (NATO)
Armenian genocide commemoration - 807-808
CFE treaty - 696-704, 758
Crotone air base - 678, 682, 687, 826-830
defense appropriations - 820
Ex-Im Bank arms sales financing - 643
foreign aid appropriations - 831
German unification - 699, 763
Persian Gulf crisis - 720, 729
U.S. bases for training - 678
U.S. export controls - 198, 201
North Carolina
Caribbean Basin Initiative - 215-216, 217
CDBG funding formula - 641
congressional redistricting - 931
corporate campaign limits - 59 (box)
federal judgeships - 522
offshore drilling - 283, 284, 287, 312, 872
water projects authorization - 297, 299
North Dakota
congressional mail - 75
corporate campaign limits - 59 (box)
voter registration - 69
Welk birthplace museum - 811
North Korea
Cambodian rebel aid - 837
North Miami Beach, Fla. - 860
North, Oliver L. - 534-535
Northeastern states
Amtrak authorization - 390
CDBG funding formula - 641
census count adjustment - 415
heating oil tax - 134, 139, 313 (box)
immigration law revision - 477
offshore oil drilling - 870, 872
textile import quotas - 219, 221, 222
Northern Iowa, University of - 876
Northern Ireland
U.S. aid - 844
U.S. immigration policy - 477, 482-483
Northern Mariana Islands
child-care block grants - 152
community development block grants - 655
Northern spotted owl - 296-297, 870, 874-875
Northrop Corp. - 690, 819
Northumberland - 286 (box)
Norton Air Force Base - 827-828
Norton, Eleanor Holmes - 428, 923, 924 (chart)
Nowak, Henry J. D-N.Y. (33)
water projects authorization - 298
NRA. *See National Rifle Association*
NRC. *See Nuclear Regulatory Commission*
NSF. *See National Science Foundation*
Nuclear energy
China-U.S. cooperation - 764, 799-800
global warming - 307
research appropriations - 861, 865, 866
South Africa sanctions - 787
Soviet-U.S. cooperation - 759
SSC authorization - 438
Nuclear facilities and power plants. *See also Nuclear waste*
fastener standards - 395
Hanford radiation exposure notice - 679
NRC fees - 136, 311 (box)
Stello nomination - 309-310
toxic air pollutants - 234
uranium enrichment - 310-311
Nuclear fusion 861
Nuclear non-proliferation treaty - 712
Nuclear Regulatory Commission (NRC)

appropriations - 862 (chart)
licensing fees - 124, 136, 155, 311 (box)
Stello nomination - 309
toxic air pollutants - 234, 256, 258
Nuclear test treaties
action, 1990 - 702, 711-713
defense authorization - 683
verification protocol - 758
Washington summit - 696, 707
Nuclear waste
Energy Department cleanup
appropriations - 861, 862, 863, 864, 866
budget action - 122
Panama aid - 779
federal RCRA compliance - 291, 293, 308-309
plutonium recovery - 684
uranium enrichment - 311
Nuclear weapons. *See also Arms control*
B-2 bomber - 689, 690
Iraq development
capability estimate - 722, 745
component smuggling - 723
export controls - 201, 729, 885
naval home ports - 681 (box)
Pakistan aid - 768-769, 835, 843
plutonium processing - 122, 684
radiation victims compensation - 590-591
contractor damage suits - 679
Soviet-U.S. trade - 205
uranium enrichment - 310
whistleblower protection - 364
Nunn, Sam D-Ga.
Armenian genocide commemoration - 808
B-2 bomber - 688, 690, 691
budget action - 129, 165
Bush congressional relations - 21
call-up of reserves - 695 (box)
CFE - 698, 700-701, 703
community service programs - 559, 560-561
congressional elections, 1990 - 909, 916
conservative coalition - 40, 47
crime bill - 491
defense appropriations - 813, 819, 821
defense authorization - 672, 675-676, 677, 678, 680, 686, 687
housing programs overhaul - 641
intelligence authorization - 792
military base closings - 695
military construction appropriations - 829
OMB review powers - 413
Persian Gulf crisis - 720, 727, 728, 735-736, 738, 742, 747, 750-751
U.S. goals, rationales - 745 (box)
use-of-force debate - 753 (box)
presidential support in Congress - 31
SDI - 692
Stello nomination - 310
Thomas confirmation - 519 (box)
Nurse anesthetists - 144, 145, 419
Nurse midwives - 144, 564, 595, 596
Nurse practitioners - 145, 595
Nurses
Health Service Corps - 596
home health care - 147
immigration law revision - 475
VA salaries - 126, 418, 419-420
Nurses' aides - 148, 589
Nursing homes
community service programs - 560, 561, 562
cost containment - 144
Medicaid expansion - 569
Medicaid pay suits - 571
Medicare certification fees - 125
Medicare changes - 563, 564
reform amendments - 148, 589
patient self-determination - 146
Pepper Commission - 607-609
veterans pensions - 155
Nussle, Jim - 905 (chart), 918 (chart), 925
Nutrition Labeling and Education Act - 575-576

O

Oakar, Mary Rose D-Ohio (20)
characteristics of Congress - 924
minorities in Congress - 924 (chart)
congressional elections, 1990 - 907
low winning percentage - 906 (chart)
defense preparedness - 203
foreign aid appropriations - 840
Medicare coverage of mammograms - 564 (box)
Oakley, Robert - 768
OAS. *See Organization of American States*
Oats - 342
Ober, Ron - 79
Oberstar, James L. D-Minn. (8)
air safety guidelines - 389
aviation package - 384-388
aviation security - 390
Transportation appropriations - 878
Obey, David R. D-Wis. (7)
agriculture appropriations - 868
budget action - 136
campaign finance reform - 67, 68
congressional leadership - 11 (box), 12
continuing resolutions - 896 (box)
El Salvador aid - 780, 783, 786
Energy, water appropriations - 863
foreign aid appropriations - 831-835, 840, 842-844
U.N. population fund - 838 (box)
Labor/HHS appropriations - 850
legislative branch appropriations - 895
Nicaragua aid - 771
Pakistan-U.S. relations - 769
Panama aid - 775, 778
Persian Gulf crisis - 730, 738
Soviet-U.S. relations - 759
Obscenity and pornography
crime bill - 493, 499
"Dinner Party" exhibit - 47, 892
NEA controversies
appropriations - 870-875
authorization - 430-433
congressional partisanship - 39
conservative coalition - 47
key votes - 13-B
sexually explicit mail - 417
Supreme Court decisions - 55-56
Occupational health and safety. *See also Drug-free workplaces; Worker's compensation*
chemical processes - 259
disabled civil rights exclusions - 452
fetal protection - 56, 465
OMB review powers - 412 (box)
radiation victims compensation - 590-591
Supreme Court decisions - 53, 56
violations penalties - 143, 165
whistleblower protection - 364
Occupational Safety and Health Act of 1970 - 143, 165, 257
Occupational Safety and Health Administration (OSHA)
appropriations - 848 (chart)
OMB review powers - 412 (box)
Occupational Safety and Health Review Commission - 849 (chart)
Occupational therapy - 145
Ocean thermal energy - 160, 173, 313
Oceans. *See also Coastal areas; Fish and fishing; Ships and shipping*
air pollutant deposit - 258
Soviet-U.S. research - 759-760
O'Connor, Sandra Day
abortion - 529
corporate campaign limits - 59 (box)
flag desecration - 525
habeas corpus appeals - 489 (box)
Medicaid pay suits - 571
minority broadcasters - 379 (box)
OMB review powers - 412 (box)
political patronage jobs - 933
right to die - 567 (box)
Souter confirmation - 508
student religious groups - 618 (box)
Supreme Court term summary - 52
Office. *See other part of name*
O'Hare airport - 384-387
O'Hare, William P. - 932
Ohio
abortion - 529, 530
acid rain - 237 (box), 238, 247, 262, 278
campaign finance reform - 62
corporate campaign limits - 59 (box)
congressional elections, 1990 - 907, 919
congressional redistricting - 931, 933
federal judgeships - 522
food aid cargo preference - 338-339 (box)
gubernatorial election, 1990 - 902, 928, 929
living wills - 567 (box)
Transportation appropriations - 878
Ohio River Valley
acid rain - 237
Oil. *See also Fuel; Fuel and gasoline taxes; Gasoline; Natural gas*
alternative power regulation - 317
auto fuel efficiency - 279-280
Caribbean Basin Initiative - 211
defense
military reserve in Israel - 822, 825
Pentagon supplies - 821, 846
Strategic Petroleum Reserve - 314-316
displaced worker aid - 237, 277 (box)
environmental protection
acid rain - 262, 263, 264
alternative fuel - 240 (box)
Arctic refuge drilling - 313, 315 (box)
Coast Guard cleanup appropriations - 879
criminal liability - 285 (box)
double-hulled tankers - 284-285
Florida Keys protection - 303
offshore drilling emissions - 230, 244, 273
pipeline safety inspection - 286 (box)
spill liability - 5, 283-287
stripper wells - 274
superfund tax - 159
toxic air pollutants - 231 (box), 232, 241-242, 275
home heating oil
public housing projects - 857
taxes - 134, 139
Nicaragua aid - 771
North Slope production - 270
offshore leases, drilling
budget action - 124, 154
coastal zone management - 288-289
energy issues, 1990 - 312, 313
Interior appropriations - 870-871, 872, 874
Persian Gulf crisis - 312, 718-732
U.S. goals, rationales - 744 (box)
South Africa sanctions - 787
taxation
depletion allowances - 160, 172, 313 (box)
enhanced recovery credits - 160, 172
incentives - 167, 169, 172, 313 (box)
Oil Pollution Prevention, Response, Liability and Compensation Act - 283-287
Oil shale
land claims - 313, 316
Oilseeds. *See also Soybeans*
budget action - 141
price supports - 325, 342, 343, 344
Soviet-U.S. trade - 762
OIRA. *See Information and Regulatory Affairs, Office of*
O'Keefe, Sean - 21
Oklahoma
congressional elections, 1990 - 919
corporate campaign limits - 59 (box)
federal judgeships - 522
gubernatorial election, 1990 - 902, 919,928
legislative term limits - 13-15, 902
Seminole land claim - 424
wheat farming - 350
Older Workers Benefit Protection Act - 362-364
Oleszek, Walter J. - 40, 47, 48
Olin, Jim D-Va. (6)
disabled civil rights - 459
farm bill - 329
Omaha, Neb. - 618 (box)
OMB. *See Management and Budget, Office of*
OMB Watch - 412
Omnibus Budget Reconciliation Act - 139-146
O'Neill, William A. - 926, 928
OPEC. *See Organization of Petroleum Exporting Countries*
"Open Skies" - 700
Operation Bootstrap - 635
Operation Desert Shield
budget process changes - 161
Commerce/Justice/State appropriations - 884
continuing resolutions - 896 (box)
costs - 135, 733
defense authorization - 682
export controls veto - 200
federal retirement benefits - 155, 407 (box)
foreign aid appropriations - 840-841, 842
foreign contributions - 813, 821
Persian Gulf crisis - 726-747
U.S. troop deployment announcement (text) - 726-727
summary - 3, 717
Operation Desert Storm
Persian Gulf crisis - 747-756
use-of-force resolution
debate - 752-753 (box)
House vote - 750-751 (box)
request letter (text) - 747
Senate vote - 749 (box)
text - 748 (box)
war announcement (text) - 754-755
Yeutter remarks - 910
Oppenheimer, Bruce I. - 48
Optometrists - 146
Oregon
abortion - 530
Amtrak waste disposal - 392
congressional elections, 1990 - 903, 922

congressional redistricting - 933
Energy, water appropriations - 865
federal judgeships - 522
gubernatorial election, 1990 - 907, 929, 930
logging/wildlife protection - 296-297, 870, 871, 876
offshore oil drilling - 872
peyote ban - 514
timber exports - 215
Organ Procurement and Transplantation Act - 597
Organ transplants
donation program authorization - 596-597
fetal tissue - 531, 600-601
Organization for Economic Cooperation and Development - 333, 349
Organization of American States (OAS)
contra resettlement - 773
Nicaraguan elections - 770
Panama-U.S. relations - 775
Organization of Petroleum Exporting Countries (OPEC) - 724, 744 (box)
Organized Crime Control Act of 1970 - 536
Organized Crime Drug Enforcement Task Force - 503
Ornstein, Norman J. - 9-10, 32
Orr, Kay A. - 926, 928, 929
Orphan Drug Act - 577-579
Orphan drugs
shared marketing rights - 577-579
boxscore - 577
veto message - 578
tax credit - 160, 173
Ortega, Daniel - 770-771, 801 (box)
Ortiz, Solomon P. D-Texas (27)
minorities in Congress - 924 (chart)
Orton, Bill - 918 (chart)
OSHA. *See Occupational Safety and Health Administration*
Oshkosh, Wis. - 252
Osprey. *See V-22 Osprey aircraft*
Osteoporosis - 145, 603
OTH-B radar - 673
OTS. *See Thrift Supervision, Office of*
Ottoman Empire - 807-808
Outer Banks - 312
Overgaard, Paul - 102
Overseas Private Investment Corporation
appropriations - 833 (chart)
China sanctions - 764, 799
Eastern Europe - 836, 844
Nicaragua aid - 771
Panama aid - 777
Soviet aid - 759
Owens, Jesse - 196
Owens, Major R. D-N.Y. (12)
disabled education - 617
education proposals - 613
minorities in Congress - 924 (chart)
Owens, Wayne D-Utah (2)
Antarctica protection - 306
congressional elections, 1990 - 908
Persian Gulf crisis - 746
radiation victims compensation - 590
Owls. *See Northern spotted owls*
Ozone
alternative fuels - 229, 240 (box)
research - 274
urban smog - 229, 230, 235 (box), 246, 248-250
Ozone-layer protection
appropriations - 832 (chart), 837
depleting chemicals phase-out - 4, 230, 234, 244, 269-271
methane assessment - 271
tax on depleting chemicals - 158, 172

P

P-3C patrol plane - 819
P-7 patrol plane - 675, 819
Pacific area
characteristics of Congress - 923-924
minorities in Congress - 924 (chart)
defense appropriations - 820
radiation victims compensation - 590
Pacific Islands Trust Territory
child care block grant - 152
community development block grants - 655
Palau autonomy - 808
Pacific Northwest states
barrier island protection - 303
logging/wildlife protection - 296-297, 870, 871, 874-875
textile import quotas - 220
timber exports - 211
Pacific Rim nations
U.S. trade
shoes - 214
textile import quotas - 219
Packaging. *See Labeling and packaging*
Packard, Ron R-Calif. (43)
congressional elections, 1990 - 907
Packwood, Bob R-Ore.
budget action - 130, 165
cable TV regulation - 370-372
campaign finance reform - 63, 64
capital gains tax - 168 (box)
Caribbean Basin Initiative - 213, 214-215
defense appropriations - 821
family planning authorization - 605
Interior appropriations - 875
Japan-U.S. trade - 209
"motor voter" bill - 70
NIH authorization - 601
product liability - 400
Saudi arms sales - 735 (box)
Social Security - 170
textile import quotas - 220
Paducah, Ky. - 310
Paint
federal RCRA compliance - 308
toxic air pollutants - 239
Pakistan
U.S. aid - 835, 843
U.S. relations - 768-769
Palau - 808
Palestine Liberation Organization (PLO)
Klinghoffer civil suit - 830
Mandela remarks - 789
U.S. talks - 800-801
Palestinians
Israeli policies, *intifada* - 822, 837, 841
Persian Gulf crisis - 719, 720, 721, 743
Pallone, Frank Jr. D-N.J. (3)
barrier islands protection - 302
congressional elections, 1990
low winning percentage - 906 (chart)
marginal vote share - 905 (chart)
Pan American Airlines - 387, 759
Panama
Caribbean Basin Initiative - 212, 213
U.S. aid - 774-779
boxscore - 774
El Salvador aid - 782, 783, 784
Nicaragua aid - 770, 771, 773, 774
summary - 5
supplemental appropriations - 844, 845, 846
Panama Canal
frozen fees - 775
Panama Canal Commission - 879 (chart)
Panama City, Panama - 776
Panamanian Defense Forces - 775, 776
Panetta, Leon E. D-Calif. (16)
balanced budget amendment - 175 (box)
budget action - 116, 127-128, 130 (box), 131
budget process changes - 176-177
coastal zone management - 288
food stamps - 355
Medicare changes - 565, 568
mammogram coverage - 564 (box)
thrift bailout - 181
Pap tests - 606, 680, 849
Paperwork Reduction Act - 21, 53, 411-413
Pappas, Tom - 108
Paratransit - 450, 454
Parent-Child Centers - 555
Parent education - 555, 651
Parental leave - 359-361
Parental notification of abortion
family planning authorization - 605-606
key votes - 7-B
Labor/HHS appropriations - 531, 811, 847, 851-852, 853
summary - 528
Supreme Court decisions - 52, 53, 54, 529
Parental rights
child-care choices, access - 152, 153, 154
family planning services notice - 605-606
Head Start participation - 552
homosexual youth counselors - human 17, 891, 893
student right-to-know - 624-627
Parents Against Drugs - 888
Paris Club - 207
Paris summit - 703
Parker, Mike D-Miss. (4)
conservative coalition - 47
Parkinson's disease - 600, 601
Parks. *See also National parks*
community service programs - 561, 562
Parole Commission, U.S. - 522, 543, 882 (chart)
Parris, Stan R-Va. (8)
abortion - 530
congressional elections, 1990 - 917, 919
defeated House members - 917 (chart)
House membership changes - 918 (chart)
vote-share falloff - 904 (chart)
conservative coalition - 47
D.C. status - 428-429
Hatch Act revision - 410
thrift bailout - 181
Washington Metro aid - 429
Pascagoula, Miss. - 681 (box)
Pashayan, Charles "Chip" Jr. R-Cailf. (17)
congressional elections, 1990 - 903, 917
defeated House members - 917 (chart)
House membership changes - 918 (chart)
vote-share falloff - 904 (chart)
irrigation subsidies - 356-357
savings and loan scandal - 80
Passaic River - 297, 298, 299
Patent and Trademark Office, U.S.
appropriations - 882 (chart)
salaries - 543
user fees - 157
Patents and trademarks
Czech-U.S. trade - 206
inventions in space - 437
orphan drugs - 577
Soviet-U.S. trade - 205
user fees - 157
Pathology Practice Association Federal PAC - 60
Pathology services - 144
Patriarca, Michael - 88, 93
Patrick, Dennis R. - 373
Patriot missiles
appropriations - 815 (chart), 818, 823
authorization - 674
Persian Gulf war - 754
Saudi arms sales - 735 (box)
Patronage
Hatch Act revision - 408
Supreme Court decisions - 52, 53, 54, 933
Patterson, Liz J. D-S.C. (4)
housing programs overhaul - 640
minorities in Congress - 924 (chart)
prepayment of subsidized mortgages - 663, 664
Payne, Donald M. D-N.J. (10)
minorities in Congress - 924 (chart)
Peace and Freedom Party - 907
Peace Corps
appropriations - 833 (chart), 835
Peace dividend
budget action - 117
community service programs - 561
defense authorization - 675-676
Nicaragua aid - 770
Peaceful Nuclear Explosions Treaty - 711
Peanuts
budget action - 141
price supports - 329-330, 337, 341, 343-344
Pearce, Trudy - 15
Pearl Harbor, Hawaii - 678
Pearson, Dave - 235
Pease, Don J. D-Ohio (13)
budget action - 165, 171
China-U.S. relations - 764, 765-766, 768
congressional elections, 1990 - 907
low winning percentage - 906 (chart)
regulatory negotiation guidelines - 413
Peer Review Organizations - 146
Pell, Claiborne D-R.I.
community service programs - 559
congressional elections, 1990 - 913
vote-share falloff - 904 (chart)
dropout prevention - 618
education proposals - 613
German unification - 762
Kenya aid - 790
NEA authorization - 432-433
nuclear test treaties - 712
Persian Gulf crisis - 723, 725, 727, 730, 733, 735
State Department authorization - 800
torture ban treaty - 807
vocational education authorization - 622
Pell grants - 611, 562, 851
Pelosi, Nancy D-Calif. (5)
China-U.S. relations - 765, 766, 768
minorities in Congress - 924 (chart)
prepayment of subsidized mortgages - 662
Pence, Mike - 923
Pendleton, Florence - 428
Penner, Rudolph G. - 177
Pennsylvania. *See also Philadelphia*
acid rain - 262
agriculture appropriations - 868
Caribbean Basin Initiative - 215-216
CDBG funding formula - 641
congressional elections, 1990 - 909, 917
congressional redistricting - 931, 933

corporate campaign limits - 59 (box)
defense appropriations - 817, 818, 825
federal judgeships - 522
gubernatorial election, 1990 - 929
living wills - 567 (box)
Transportation appropriations - 876, 877, 878, 880
V-22 Osprey support - 676
water projects authorization - 298
Penny, Timothy J. D-Minn. (1)
Agent Orange compensation - 419
appropriations
agriculture - 868
Commerce/Justice/State - 878
defense - 816
District of Columbia - 892
Energy, water - 864
Labor/HHS - 850
military construction - 828
Treasury, Postal Service - 889
VA/HUD - 856
congressional elections, 1990 - 908
family leave - 360
housing programs overhaul - 643
Pensacola, Fla. - 681 (box)
Pension Benefit Guaranty Corporation (PBGC) - 368
federal credit reform - 163
fees - 161, 172
fund responsibility - 53
Pensions and retirement. *See also Social Security*
age discrimination - 54, 362-364
alternative teacher certification - 612
budget action - 161
federal employees - 155, 405, 407 (box)
double-dip waivers - 679
fund guarantee fees - 161, 172
fund responsibility - 53
health insurance continuation - 148
pass-thru deposit insurance - 186
portable pensions - 368
reversions - 161, 172, 367-368
veterans eligibility - 155, 420, 421
Pentagon. *See Defense Department, U.S.*
Pentamidine - 578
People for the American Way - 431, 516, 517
People for the Ethical Treatment of Animals - 441
Pepper, Claude - 569, 598, 599, 607
Pepper Commission - 607-609
Pérez de Cuéllar, Javier - 729, 732, 782, 802
Perito, Paul L. - 666
Perkins, Carl C. D-Ky. (7)
congressional elections, 1990
low winning percentage - 906 (chart)
marginal vote share - 905 (chart)
student right-to-know - 625, 626-627
Perkins loans - 561, 562
Perkins Vocational and Applied Technology Education Act - 619-623
Perle, Richard N. - 701, 706, 742, 746
Perpich, Rudy - 694 (box), 926, 930
Persian Gulf crisis. *See also Operation Desert Shield; Operation Desert Storm*
background - 717-718, 722-723
budget process changes - 178
Bush leadership
9/11 address to Congress (text) - 731-732
10/30 news conference (text) -741
congressional relations - 17
call-up of reserves - 695 (box)
chronology - 719-721
congressional election issue - 917, 919, 922
economic sanctions - 725-726, 738, 742, 747
effects on legislation
Arab arms sales (box) - 734-735
B-2 bomber - 689, 690
budget summit - 132, 135
civil rights/job bias - 473
congressional mail - 74
defense appropriations - 812, 814, 816, 817, 820, 821, 822
defense authorization - 671, 677, 678, 680, 682, 684, 687
displaced worker aid - 277 (box)
El Salvador aid - 786
Food for Peace - 804
foreign aid appropriations - 831, 840, 842, 843-844
Kenya aid - 790
SDI - 692
Soviet-U.S. relations - 757, 761, 762
START - 704, 708
textile import quotas - 221, 222
U.N. funding - 802
veterans health package - 418
energy policy - 312
Arctic refuge drilling - 315 (box)
auto fuel efficiency - 279, 280
oil pollution cleanup - 287
Strategic Petroleum Reserve - 314-315
Kuwait invasion - 724-726
maps - 718, 725
questionable gulf allies - 740 (box)
rising tensions, 1989-90 - 723-724
summary - 3, 717
contents - 717 (box)
U.N. resolution 678 (text) - 737
U.S. goals, rationales - 744-745 (box)
war powers suit - 739 (box)
Personnel Management, Office of
age discrimination - 363
appropriations - 887 (chart)
federal health benefits - 155
federal pay overhaul - 405-407
Peru
U.S. aid/drug control - 124, 502, 836
Andean Initiative - 805-806
Pests and pesticides
alternatives, reductions in farming - 326, 330, 331, 333, 336, 345, 347
farm recordkeeping - 323, 330, 335-336, 346, 350
food residue - 336, 358
exported banned chemicals - 323, 333, 336, 349, 350
screwworm eradication - 355
zebra mussel control - 298, 303-304
Peterson, Collin C. - 107, 905 (chart), 918 (chart), 922
Peterson, Pete - 752 (box), 918 (chart)
Petit & Martin - 280
Petri, Thomas E. R-Wis. (6)
age discrimination - 363
civil rights/job bias - 469
disabled civil rights - 450
Energy, water appropriations - 864
FHA rules revision - 660
Frank ethics case - 104
Petroleum. *See Oil*
Petroleum Marketing Prac Philadelphia Navy Yard - 818, 825, 826
Philadelphia, Pa.
AIDS relief - 582
housing demonstration project - 647
mass transit - 876, 880
Philippines
environmental protection - 837
U.S. aid
appropriations - 833 (chart), 834-835, 837
budget action - 124
U.S. sugar quotas - 331
veterans U.S. naturalization - 484
Phillips, Howard - 513
Phoenix missiles - 674-675, 685, 826
Photographers - 541-542
Physical therapists - 564
Physician assistants - 595, 596
Physician Payment Review Commission - 850
Physicians
disabled civil rights - 448
Health Service Corps - 595-596
Medicare payments - 125, 144, 563, 565, 568
new practices - 144
patient dumping ban - 144
Peer Review Organizations - 146
minimum qualifications for Medicaid - 147-148
pollution-related conditions - 236
VA salaries - 126, 419-420
Physics
SSC authorization - 438
Pickett, Owen B. D-Va. (2)
water projects authorization - 298-299
Pickle, J. J. "Jake" D-Texas (10)
Caribbean Basin Initiative - 217
Pierce, Samuel R. Jr. - 534, 666-668
Piranha Press - 60, 98-101
PL 480. *See Food for Peace*
Plager, S. Jay - 413
Plants, industrial. *See Business and industry*
Platinum - 236, 443
PLO. *See Palestine Liberation Organization*
PLO Commitments Compliance Act - 802
Plotkin, Robert - 666-667
Plutonium - 122, 684, 861, 864
Pocket vetoes
Bush congressional relations - 16
proposed limits - 21-22
Podiatrists - 146
Poindexter, John M. - 534, 535
Points of Light Action Groups - 559
Points of Light Initiative Foundation - 559-562, 855 (chart)
Pol Pot - 837
Poland
CFE - 697, 698
debt relief - 161, 207, 730, 831, 833 (chart), 834, 844
Food for Peace - 803
German unification - 763
U.S. aid - 207, 834
U.S. trade - 204, 206
export controls - 199
Police and law enforcement agencies
assault weapons ban - 491
border patrol - 479, 484, 485
college crime - 625
Commerce/Justice/State appropriations - 885
community service programs - 561, 562
crime bill - 6, 486, 489, 493, 496, 498, 499
death penalty for murder - 494, 497
drug-abuse education - 505
drug interdiction
Andean Initiative - 805, 806
appropriations - 881
defense authorization - 675, 679
El Salvador aid - 783, 785
EPA investigators - 292 (box), 293
federal pay overhaul - 406
financial institution fraud - 881
handgun wait period - 501 (box)
hazardous materials transport - 381
HIV protection - 587
Indian reservations - 423-424
money laundering - 188
Panama aid - 776, 777
public housing
drug-elimination grants - 652
rent waivers - 638, 651
radar detector ban - 880
RICO revision - 537
scholarships - 493
Supreme Court decisions - 52, 53 (box)
Political action committees (PACs)
auto importers - 280-281
campaign finance reform - 57-69
foreign companies - 65
leadership PACs - 58
Hatch Act revision - 408-411
savings and loan scandal - 79, 80
summary - 6
Supreme Court decisions - 53 (box)
Political asylum
immigration law revision - 474, 482
Political beliefs
immigration law revision - 474, 480 (box), 484, 485, 799
Political parties and interest groups
campaign finance reform - 57
congressional leadership - 9
conservative coalition - 40-48
election results, 1990 - 901-933
foreign aid - 834
group ratings, 1990 - 22B-30B
Hatch Act revision - 408-411
independent House members - 922 (box)
judicial appointments - 516-517
lineup, 101st, 102nd Cong. (chart) - 901
party unity analysis - 32-40
patronage jobs
EPA Cabinet status - 292, 293
Supreme Court decision - 52, 53 (box), 54, 933
South Africa sanctions - 789
third-party candidates - 907, 926-927
Political prisoners
China-U.S. relations - 765, 766, 768
Kenya aid - 790
Myanmar (Burma) human rights - 213
South Africa sanctions - 787, 788, 790
Pollack, Ron - 558
Pollution. *See also Acid rain; Air pollution; Hazardous substances; Waste products; Water pollution*
source reduction - 155
Pollution Prevention Office - 292
Pollution Reduction Act of 1990 - 155
Polygamy - 478
Pomeroy, Earl R. - 574
Pope, Donna - 197
Pope, Martha S. - 12 (box)
Popular Democratic Party (Puerto Rico) - 425
Popular Movement for the Liberation of Angola - 793
Population. *See Birth control; Census, 1990*
Population Crisis Committee - 839 (box)
Population Institute - 838 (box)
Population Reference Bureau - 932
Pork-barrel politics. *See also Earmarking*
appropriations bills - 811
Energy, water - 861-866
Interior - 876
Treasury, Postal Service - 888, 889, 890
VA/HUD - 857 (box), 858, 860
B-2 bomber - 689
defense authorization - 677, 682-683
federal judgeships - 520, 521

House-Senate difference resolution - 890
SDI - 692
Pornography. *See Obscenity and pornography*
Porter, John R-Ill. (10)
foreign aid appropriations - 831, 834, 835, 840
U.N. population fund - 838 (box)
Porter, Roger B.
age bias - 363
Clean Air Act - 232, 245, 276, 277 (box)
community service programs - 559
education programs - 615
Portugal
U.S. aid - 831, 833, 835
Post Office and Civil Service Committee, House
leadership changes - 11 (box)
Postal Service, U.S.
appropriations - 886-890
campaign finance reform - 57, 60, 61, 62
child-resistant packaging - 417
Cleveland post office - 196
congressional mail - 73, 74
deceptive mail curbs - 417
health, retirement benefits - 155
mail subsidies - 888
pornography - 417
subsidies for nonprofit organizations - 123
Postsecondary schools. *See also Colleges and universities*
disabled education - 616
recruiter payment ban - 613
student loan default - 143
vocational education authorization - 619-623
Poverty. *See also Compensatory education aid; Developing countries; Food assistance programs; Housing assistance and public housing; Legal Services Corporation; Medicaid; Student aid; Welfare and social services*
child-care aid - 547-551
community service programs - 560
dropout prevention - 618
health care
access - 148
AIDS bill - 582-589
cancer screening - 606
disproportionate share hospitals - 143, 144
elderly - 598
emergency, trauma care - 598
health insurance - 607
TB prevention - 594
job training overhaul - 365-367
literacy programs - 611
South Africa aid - 789
targeted jobs tax credit - 160
vocational education authorization - 621, 622, 623
Powell, Gen. Colin L. Jr. - 729, 731
Powell, Lewis F. Jr. - 487-488, 488 (box)
Powell, William H. - 490
Power. *See Electric power*
Power, Jay - 277 (box)
Powerplant and Industrial Fuel Use Act of 1978 - 263
Practicing Physicians Advisory Council - 144
Prairie states
farm bill - 333-334
Preferred provider organizations - 125
Pregnancy. *See also Abortion; Adolescent pregnancy; Birth control; Infants; Women, Infants and Children (WIC) program*
AIDS bill - 587
drug-abuse treatment - 503-504
fertility drugs - 146
fetal alcohol syndrome - 423
in vitro fertilization - 601
infertility research - 531, 600, 601, 603, 604
labor patient dumping ban - 144, 563
Medicaid expansion - 147, 569
minimum qualifications for physicians - 147
perinatal services at public housing - 651
Puerto Rico status - 425
SDI authorization debate - 692
vitamins, fluoride - 146
vocational education authorization - 620
Presbyterians - 549
Preschool education. *See also Head Start*
child-care aid - 550, 551
disabled education - 616
early childhood development - 152, 153
education proposals - 611, 615
Preservation of Affordable Rental Housing - 652-653, 661-665
President, Executive Office of the
appropriations - 886
Presidential elections
campaign finance reform - 57-58, 63, 65
crime issues - 487
Puerto Rico status - 426
Presidential Merit Schools - 613
Presidential Task Force on Market Mechanisms - 190
President's Committee on Employment of People with Disabilities - 458
President's Council on Competitiveness - 400
President's Schools of Distinction - 613, 615
Presidents, U.S. *See also Congressional-executive relations; Nominations and appointments; Vetoes*
budget process changes - 161-163, 173
death penalty for assassination - 494, 497
former presidents' benefits - 889
nominating convention delegates - 408, 409
salary - 887 (chart)
Pressler, Larry R-S.D.
campaign finance reform - 66
congressional elections, 1990 - 916
vote-share falloff - 904 (chart)
housing programs overhaul - 637
Pakistan-U.S. relations - 768
prepayment of subsidized mortgages - 664
Preventive medical care
AIDS, HIV patients - 148, 586, 588
cancer screening - 606
disabilities prevention - 589
Indian health services - 422
injuries research - 598
Medicare changes - 563
mammogram coverage - 564 (box)
public health planning - 609
TB prevention - 594
Price, Bill - 928
Price, Charles R. - 436
Price, David E. D-N.C. (4)
children's welfare services - 549
congressional elections, 1990 - 903, 923
housing programs overhaul - 638, 640
prepayment of subsidized mortgages - 663, 664
Price, Melvin - 11
Price Waterhouse - 657, 658, 660-661
Primary medical care
AIDS bill - 587
family planning authorization - 605
Medicare - 143, 144
Primate Research Institute - 888
Prins, Curtis - 184, 196
Prison Testing Act of 1988 - 587
Prisoners of war
Persian Gulf crisis - 721, 754-755
Prisons and prisoners. *See also Capital punishment; Political prisoners*
AIDS bill - 585, 586, 587
alternatives - 6, 486, 494, 496
boot camp - 499
appropriations - 882 (chart), 884, 885
budget action - 125
competitive industries - 498
crime bill - 496, 498
death penalty for guard murder - 494, 497
literacy programs - 614
mental illness - 53
rehabilitation programs - 496
vocational education authorization - 620, 622
work requirement - 493
Prisons, Bureau of - 499, 779
Privacy. *See also Information access and classification*
driver's license/national ID - 485
drug testing - 505
Souter confirmation - 508, 511, 513, 515
student right-to-know - 624
Private clubs
disabled civil rights - 453, 457
Dunne nomination - 465 (box)
judicial appointments - 516, 517
Private schools
community service programs - 562
education proposals - 613
vocational education authorization - 621
Procter & Gamble Co. - 330
Product liability
congressional action, 1990 - 400-401
disaster suits - 543
suit disclosure - 393-395
summary - 7
technology programs - 440, 441
Product Liability Alliance - 401
ProPAC. *See Prospective Payment Assessment Commission*
Propane - 240 (box)
Prospective Payment Assessment Commission (ProPAC) - 143-144
Prostitution
Frank ethics case - 103-104
Protestants
characteristics of Congress - 926
Protests, demonstrations, etc.
Persian Gulf crisis - 720, 753 (box)
RICO revision - 537
Proxmire, William - 94, 95, 190, 511 (box)
Prudential Insurance Co. - 574
Pryor, David D-Ark.
age discrimination - 362
civil rights/job bias - 467
congressional elections, 1990 - 909, 916
congressional leadership - 9 (box), 12
deceptive mail curbs - 417
defense authorization - 680
executive branch honoraria - 72 (box)
farm bill - 333, 334, 340, 351
Hatch Act revision - 411
Medicaid drug discounts - 570
Medigap plans - 573
savings and loan scandal - 80, 82, 94, 97
Ethics Committee special counsel - 81 (box)
Thomas confirmation - 518 (box)
Psychiatry. *See Mental health and illness*
Psychologists - 564
Public accommodations
disabled civil rights - 455-457
Public Citizen's Congress Watch - 398, 537, 538
Public debt. *See Budget, U.S.*
Public Debt, Bureau of the - 887 (chart)
Public health
acid rain - 259
AIDS bill - 582-589
antismoking bills - 593
beach water quality - 290
Clean Air Act impact - 274
communicable disease in food handlers - 453
drug testing - 505
environmental statistics - 291, 292
ozone depletion - 270
planning grants - 609, 847
rural development - 347, 352
toxic air pollutants - 256-257, 275
Public Health Service Act - 56, 530, 604-606
Public Health Service, U.S. *See also National Institutes of Health*
AIDS immigration exclusion - 480 (box)
AIDS statistics - 582
minority health - 596
radiation victims compensation - 590
Public housing. *See Housing assistance and public housing*
Public Interest Research Group, U.S. - 401, 537
Public lands. *See Federal lands*
Public laws
list, 101st Cong., 2nd sess - 3A-22A
totals, 1981-90 (table) - 6
Public opinion polls
approval rating of Congress - 3, 5 (table)
campaign finance reform - 57
coin redesign - 197
congressional term limit - 13
disabled civil rights - 447
foreign ownership of U.S. business - 223
gun control - 500 (box)
immigration law revision - 478
Persian Gulf crisis - 726, 728, 736, 743, 745 (box), 746
Puerto Rico status - 426
savings and loan scandal - 80
Public participation
AIDS bill - 584, 585
Clean Air Act enforcement - 273
housing programs overhaul - 644
NEA grants panels - 431
schools - 614
water projects authorization - 298, 300
Public Rangelands Improvement Act of 1978 - 874
Public Utilities Regulatory Policies Act of 1978 - 317
Public Utility Holding Company Act of 1935 - 260
Public Voice for Food and Health Policy - 396, 398, 399
Public works
foreign construction firms - 866
Japan-U.S. trade - 208
Panama aid - 776, 777
Public Works Committee, House
chair challenge - 11 (box)
Publishers and publishing. *See also Freedom of the press*
copyright infringement - 541, 542-543
federal rulemaking procedures - 414
Puerto Rican Independence Party - 425

Puerto Rico
  AIDS relief - 582
  barrier island protection - 303
  business investment tax - 211, 214, 217
  Caribbean Basin Initiative - 213
  food aid - 346
  job training overhaul - 366
  U.S. relationship - 424-427
    boxscore - 425
    mainland voters - 426
  water projects authorization - 299
Puerto Rico U.S.A. Foundation - 425
Pullen, Penny L. - 532
Pulp mills - 294, 295
Pursell, Carl D. D-Mich. (2)
  congressional leadership - 12
  Energy, water appropriations - 863
Pyromania - 452, 459

Q

Qaddafi, Muammar el- - 789, 790
Qatar
  arms sales - 844
Qian Qichen - 740
Quandt, William - 734 (box)
Quayle, Dan
  congressional term limit - 15
  crime bill - 492
  job training overhaul - 365
  Nicaragua aid - 773
  Persian Gulf crisis
    use-of-force debate - 753 (box)
  product liability - 400
  VA/HUD appropriations - 856
Quayle, Marilyn - 606, 888

R

Racial discrimination
  broadcast license set-asides - 379 (box)
  civil rights/job bias - 462-473
  death penalty - 486, 487, 489, 489 (box), 490-491, 494, 496, 497-498
  hate crime statistics - 506-507
  judicial appointments - 516
  medical research - 600
  Souter confirmation - 511, 514
Racial Justice Act - 498
Racketeer Influenced and Corrupt Organizations (RICO) Act of 1970
  revision - 7, 536-538, 540
    boxscore - 536
Radar
  Aegis ship defenses - 675
  antiradar missiles - 818
  B-2 bomber - 674, 688, 689
  drug interdiction - 673, 817
  electronic warfare program consolidation - 685
  F-14 upgrades - 818, 825
  helicopter modernization - 674, 685
  jammers - 680, 685, 825
  Krasnoyarsk facility - 680
  missile guidance - 674, 685, 823, 824
  police radar detector ban - 880
  stealth cruise missiles - 684
  very long range systems - 673, 817
Radiation. *See also Nuclear waste*
  contaminated weapons plants - 684
  exposure notification - 679
  hazardous materials transport - 380, 381
  nuclear test victims compensation - 590-591
Radiation Exposure Trust Fund - 590
Radio Act of 1927 - 376
Radio communications
  campaign finance reform - 57, 61, 62, 63, 66-67 (box)
  malicious interference - 372
  minority set-aside licenses - 52, 53, 379 (box), 510-511 (box)
  public service rules - 377
  Senate administration - 12 (box)
  spectrum allocation - 376-377
  sports lottery ads - 495
  TDD, relay services - 457-458
Radio Free Europe - 800
Radio Liberty - 800
Radio Marti - 886
Radiology
  Medicare coverage - 144
Radionuclides - 234, 256, 258
Radon - 157
Rahall, Nick J. II D-W.Va. (4)
  congressional elections, 1990
    marginal vote share - 905 (chart)
  supplemental appropriations - 845
  transportation policy - 384
Railroad Retirement Board - 849 (chart)
Railroad retirement fund - 151, 162
Railroads. *See also Amtrak; Conrail; MX missiles*
  commuter line liability - 391, 392
  corporate takeovers - 390-392
  disabled civil rights - 448-450, 453-454, 456
  employee drug testing - 505
  food-waste transport - 382-383
  fuel tax - 159, 165, 172
  hazardous materials transport - 380
  inspection fees - 386 (box)
  Transportation appropriations - 877, 879
  user fees - 157
  Washington Metro aid - 429
RAM missiles - 675, 819, 825
Ramstad, Jim - 918 (chart)
Rangel, Charles B. D-N.Y. (16)
  antidrug measures - 502
    "drug czar" post - 503 (box)
  crime bill - 497
  minorities in Congress - 924 (chart)
  Savage ethics case - 106
Rantoul Air Force Base - 678
Rape
  abortion - 528, 531, 811, 847, 850-852, 891, 893
  AIDS test for defendents - 498, 507
  college crime - 507, 625
  "hate crime" statistics - 506, 507
  sex crime deterrence - 507
Rapeseed. *See Oilseeds*
Rappaport, Jim - 913
Rath, Tom - 533
Ray, Richard D-Ga. (3)
  congressional elections, 1990
    low winning percentage - 906 (chart)
RCRA. *See Resource Conservation and Recovery Act*
REA. *See Rural Electrification Administration*
Ready Reserve Force - 814, 885
Reagan, Ronald
  abortion - 529, 838 (box)
  arms control - 711, 712
  budget policy - 176
    balanced-budget amendment - 174-175 (box)
  children's TV - 373
  civil rights - 464
  Clean Air Act - 229, 230, 278
  CPSC background - 393
  defense policy - 671-672, 678
    B-2 bomber - 688
    SDI - 691, 692
  drug testing - 506
  Education secretary - 614 (box)
  energy policy - 312
  farm policy - 324
  food stamps - 354
  foreign policy
    Afghan rebel aid - 792
    Angola rebel aid - 793
    covert operations - 791
    El Salvador aid - 760
    Iran-contra affair - 534
    Nicaragua policy debate - 772 (box)
    Panama aid - 775, 777
    Persian Gulf crisis - 717, 722
    South Africa sanctions - 787
    torture treaty - 806
    U.N. funding - 802
  grazing fees - 874
  homeless aid - 665
  housing programs - 4, 632
  Indian legislation - 422
  judicial appointments - 515-520, 535
  Legal Services Corporation - 532
  nutrition monitoring - 355
  OMB review powers - 411
  pocket vetoes - 21
  radiation victims compensation - 590
  Souter confirmation - 508
  space station - 436
  textile import quotas - 219
  water projects authorization - 297
Real estate. *See also Home loans and mortgages; Housing*
  FHA rules revision - 631, 658, 659
  foreign government ownership - 126
  thrift bailout - 179
Real Estate Settlement Procedures Act of 1974 - 656
Reams, Henry Frazier - 922 (box)
Recess appointments - 531-533, 886
Reclamation Bureau
  appropriations - 862 (chart), 863, 866
  irrigation subsidies - 356-357
Reclamation Reform Act of 1982 - 356
Recordkeeping
  acid-free paper - 429
  farm chemicals use - 323, 330, 335-336, 346, 350
  medical device safety - 580
  money laundering - 188
  stock market regulation - 191, 192
Records access. *See Information access and classification*
Recreation. *See Boats and boating*
  Arizona wilderness protection - 304
  beach water quality - 290
  national forests - 358, 871
  sporting use of firearms - 501 (box)
  water projects authorization - 298, 299
Recycling
  EPA Cabinet status - 292
  strategic minerals - 443
Reed Act of 1954 - 150
Reed, John F. - 918 (chart), 922
Reformulated gasoline - 229, 231 (box), 232, 233 (box), 240 (box), 241, 243, 244, 246-247, 250, 252-253, 278
Refrigerants - 270
Refugees
  Americans trapped in Iraq, Kuwait - 844
  Cambodian civil war - 837
  education aid - 848 (chart)
  foreign aid appropriations - 832, 833 (chart), 837
  Nicaragua aid - 771
  Panama aid - 778
  Persian Gulf crisis - 732
  supplemental appropriations - 844, 845
  U.S. immigration policy
    displaced Tibetan nationals - 476, 483
    temporary protected status - 478, 483, 484
    visa allocation totals - 474, 476
Regan, Donald T. - 90
Regula, Ralph R-Ohio (16)
  congressional elections, 1990 - 907
    vote-share falloff - 904 (chart)
  D.C. status - 428
  Interior appropriations - 872
  oil pollution cleanup - 283
Regulation and deregulation
  ALJ corps - 523
  alternative power - 313, 317-318
  banking - 184-189
  Bush economic report - 117
  cable TV - 7, 370-372
  child-care providers - 153
  children's TV advertising - 373
  disabled civil rights enforcement - 453, 458-459
  displaced worker aid - 277 (box)
  fetal tissue research - 601
  financial institution fraud - 182
  Medigap insurance plans - 574-575
  negotiating guidelines - 413-414
  nursing homes - 148, 589
  nutrition labels - 575
  OIRA appropriations - 888
  OMB review powers - 21, 411-413
  radio spectrum allocation - 376-377
  savings and loan scandal - 86, 89-90
  stock market - 5, 190-193
  TDD, relay services - 457-458
  telephone operator services - 378 (box)
  thrift supervisor - 180 (box)
  vocational education - 622, 623
Rehabilitation Act of 1973
  disabled civil rights - 447, 449, 453, 459
  Senate coverage - 458
  vocational education - 620
Rehnquist, William H.
  abortion - 529
  federal judgeships - 520
  flag desecration - 525
  habeas corpus appeals - 489 (box), 490
  Medicaid pay suits - 571
  OMB review powers - 412 (box)
  political patronage jobs - 933
  right to die - 567 (box)
  Souter confirmation - 508
  student religious groups - 618 (box)
  Supreme Court term summary - 52
Reid, Harry D-Nev.
  crime bill - 493
  defense appropriations - 820
  defense authorization - 679
  Energy, water appropriations - 865
  farm bill - 339-340
  legislative appropriations - 897
  Persian Gulf crisis - 751
Reilly, William K.
  Clean Air Act - 234, 243, 279
Reischauer, Robert D. - 130, 185
Religion. *See also Church-state separation; Churches and religious organizations; Freedom of religion*
  sacrilegious art - 430-433, 870, 875
Religious discrimination
  child care - 153-154, 549, 551
  disabled civil rights - 453
  "hate crime" statistics - 506-507
  judicial appointments - 516
  meetings in schools - 618 (box)
Remedial education
  public housing support services - 651
Renewable energy

acid rain - 262
alternative power regulation - 317
budget action - 124, 160, 173
Energy, water appropriations - 863
EPA Cabinet status - 291
global warming - 307
incentives - 273
Renier, James J. - 553
Rensselaer Polytechnic Institute - 275
Republican Conference, House
budget summit - 131
campaign finance reform - 58
leadership - 12
Republican Conference, Senate
Durenberger ethics case - 98
leadership - 12
Republican Governors Association - 926
Republican Leadership Conference, House
housing programs overhaul - 642, 660
Republican National Committee
chair - 909-910
congressional redistricting - 931
Republican Party
congressional leadership - 9-10
congressional partisanship - 32-40
congressional redistricting - 930-933
congressional term limit - 13, 15
South Africa political training - 789
Republican Policy Committee, Senate - 12, 506
Resolution Trust Corporation (RTC)
appropriations - 855 (chart)
budget action - 123
federal credit reform - 163, 178 (box)
housing programs overhaul - 639, 650, 654-656
thrift bailout - 6, 179-184
Resource Conservation and Recovery Act (RCRA)
Clean Air Act - 276
federal compliance - 291, 293, 308-309
Respiratory disease
NIH authorization - 601
radiation victims compensation - 590
Respite care
AIDS bill - 585
HIV demonstration project - 148
home care for elderly - 147
New Jersey demonstration project - 148
Restaurants
disabled civil rights - 451, 460-461
food stamps - 346, 354
Revenue Act of 1971 - 57
Revenue Reconciliation Act of 1989 - 160
Reynolds, Mel - 105
Reynolds, William Bradford - 464, 465 (box)
Rhode Island
Energy, water appropriations - 865
gubernatorial election, 1990 - 902, 928
living wills - (box)
Rhodes, John J. III R-Ariz. (1)
Arizona wilderness protection - 304
executive branch honoraria - 72 (box)
Rice
Iraq sales - 722
price supports - 325-327, 333-334, 340, 342-344
Rice, Donald - 690, 700, 819
Rice, Thomas - 572-573
Richards, Ann W. - 530, 928-929, 933
Richards, Paul G. - 713
Richardson, Bill D-N.M. (3)
Clean Air Act - 241
congressional elections, 1990 - 908
Indian remains - 422
intelligence authorization - 796
minorities in Congress - 924 (chart)
rural health care - 595
State Department authorization - 800
RICO. *See Racketeer Influenced and Corrupt Organizations Act*
Ridge, Tom R-Pa. (21)
congressional mail - 75
defense authorization - 682
FHA rules revision - 659-661
housing programs overhaul - 637-642
pornographic mail - 417
SDI - 692
veterans housing aid - 420
Riegle, Donald W. Jr. D-Mich.
auto fuel efficiency - 280, 281
defense appropriations - 821
defense preparedness - 202
FDIC premiums - 186
FHA rules revision - 658
foreign banks - 189
Japan-U.S. trade - 209
savings and loan scandal - 6, 78-97
thrift bailout - 184
thrift supervisor - 180 (box)
Riggin, Philip - 419
Riggs, Frank - 905 (chart), 918 (chart)
Right to die - 566-567 (box)
Right-to-Life Party - 907, 934
Rill, James - 372
Rinaldo, Matthew J. R-N.J. (7)
cable TV regulation - 371
hazardous materials transport - 381
radio spectrum allocation - 377
Rinfret, Pierre A. - 926
Risk Assessment and Management Commission - 258-259
Ritter, Don R-Pa. (15)
congressional elections, 1990 - 908
technology programs - 441
Riviera Country Club - 516
Rivlin, Alice M. - 177
Roanoke River - 299
Robb, Charles S. D-Va.
Amtrak authorization - 391
aviation package - 388
community service programs - 560
flag desecration - 528
Hatch Act revision - 409
Persian Gulf crisis - 749, 750-751
presidential support in Congress - 31
product liability - 401
Thomas confirmation - 519 (box)
Robbins, Aldona and Gary - 557
Roberts, Barbara - 530, 929, 930
Roberts, Pat R-Kan. (1)
farm bill - 327, 349, 350
Persian Gulf crisis - 724
Robertson, Pat - 431, 549
Robinson, John D. - 701
Robinson, Tommy F. R-Ark. (2)
gubernatorial election, 1990 - 917, 919
House membership changes - 918 (chart)
Robotics
space station design - 437
Robson, John E. - 775, 776
Rochester Institute of Technology - 888
Rockefeller Center - 223
Rockefeller, John D. IV D-W.Va.
China-U.S. relations - 768
Clean Air Act - 238, 278
congressional elections, 1990 - 916
global warming - 307
Medicaid expansion - 569
Medicare changes - 566
Medigap plans - 572
Pepper Commission - 607, 608
product liability - 401
Puerto Rico status - 427
Rocky Flats Nuclear Weapons Plant - 308, 684, 861, 864
Rodino, Peter W. Jr. - 400
Roe, Robert A. D-N.J. (8)
Antarctica protection - 306
Bush congressional relations - 16
congressional leadership - 11 (box)
NASA authorization - 434, 436
nutrition monitoring - 355
space shuttle design - 436
SSC authorization - 438-439
Roemer, Buddy - 926, 931
Roemer, Tim - 905 (chart), 916, 918 (chart), 926
Rogers, Ed - 59
Rohrbacher, Dana R-Calif. (42)
congressional elections, 1990
low winning percentage - 906 (chart)
congressional partisanship - 39
conservative coalition - 47
NEA authorization - 430-433
Washington Metro aid - 429
Rolde, Neil - 916
Rollins, Edward J. - 526, 902
Romania
family planning aid - 837, 838 (box), 840
Persian Gulf crisis - 740
U.S. trade status - 765
Romer, Roy - 930
Roper, William L. - 460
Ros-Lehtinen, Ileana R-Fla. (18)
characteristics of Congress - 923
minorities in Congress - 924 (chart)
Rose, Charlie D-N.C. (7)
congressional leadership - 11 (box)
farm bill - 330, 353-354
Ross, Steven R. - 14-15, 21, 52, 511
Rostenkowski, Dan D-Ill. (8)
aviation package - 387
budget action - 113, 128, 130 (box)
campaign finance reform - 68
Caribbean Basin Initiative - 216
child-care aid - 548, 550
China-U.S. relations - 766
Clean Air Act - 244
congressional elections, 1990 - 917
defense authorization - 683
farm bill - 331
foreign ownership of U.S. business - 224
Medicare changes - 565, 568
mammogram coverage - 564 (box)
Persian Gulf crisis - 752
Social Security earnings test - 558
taxes - 165-167
textile import quotas - 221
Roth, Toby R-Wis. (8)
congressional elections, 1990
low winning percentage - 906 (chart)
marginal vote share - 905 (chart)
vote-share falloff - 904 (chart)
Roth, William V. Jr. R-Del.
crime bill - 490
defense authorization - 678, 679, 680
EPA Cabinet status - 291
executive branch honoraria - 72 (box)
farm bill - 341
federal pay overhaul - 406-407
Hatch Act revision - 409
housing programs overhaul - 636, 637, 640, 656
military base closings - 695
Treasury, Postal appropriations - 889, 890
Rothstein, Barbara J. - 524
Roukema, Marge R-N.J. (5)
age discrimination - 363
community service programs - 562
education proposals - 614
family leave - 359-360
FHA rules revision - 660
housing programs overhaul - 638, 640
minorities in Congress - 924 (chart)
Rowland, J. Roy D-Ga. (8)
AIDS bill - 588
AIDS visa guidelines - 481 (box)
cancer screening - 606
congressional elections, 1990
low winning percentage - 906 (chart)
Rowland, John G. R-Conn. (5)
gubernatorial election, 1990 - 919, 927
House membership changes - 918 (chart)
successor - 923
Roybal, Edward R. D-Calif. (25)
age discrimination - 362
elderly health care - 598-599
immigration law revision - 485
Medigap insurance plans - 574
minorities in Congress - 924 (chart)
Treasury, Postal appropriations - 887, 890
Rozet, A. Bruce - 667-668
RTC. *See Resolution Trust Corporation*
RU 486 - 531, 601, 602, 603, 605
Rudder, Catherine E. - 15
Ruder, David S. - 193
Rudman, Warren B. R-N.H.
budget action - 127
budget process - 176
campaign finance reform - 63
civil rights/job bias - 473
Commerce/Justice/State appropriations - 885
disabled civil rights - 461
Durenberger ethics case - 100
Legal Services Corporation - 532, 533
North conviction overturn - 534, 535
savings and loan scandal - 80, 82, 96
appearance standard - 87 (box)
Ethics Committee special counsel - 81 (box)
Souter confirmation - 508, 512
Ruff, Charles F. C. - 96
Rulemaking. *See Regulation and deregulation*
Rules and Administration Committee, Senate
disabled civil rights - 458
Rules Committee, House
characteristics of Congress - 924
congressional partisanship - 39
Rumsey Indian Rancheria - 422
Rural areas. *See also Agriculture and farming; Rural development; Rural health care; Rural housing*
abandoned mines - 154
cable TV regulation - 370-371
census count adjustment - 415
Clean Air Act - 239, 245
displaced worker aid - 237
congressional redistricting - 932
definition - 654
drug enforcement - 499, 503
federal rulemaking procedures - 414
SBA authorization - 395
teacher shortages - 615
Rural Business Incubator fund - 347, 352
Rural development
appropriations - 867, 869 (chart)
congressional action, 1990 - 352-354
enterprise zones - 167
essential air service - 388, 877, 878
farm bill - 323, 346-347
youth employment - 123
Rural Development Administration - 346, 352, 353
Rural Development Insurance Fund - 869
Rural Electrification Administration (REA)
appropriations - 869 (chart)
budget action - 123, 124
business incubators - 347, 352
loan guarantees - 348
water, sewer projects - 347, 352

Rural Electrification and Telephone Revolving Fund - 141, 344
Rural health care
AIDS bill - 582, 587
Alzheimer's programs - 598
drug-abuse prevention - 505
Health Service Corps - 595-596
Medicare hospital payments - 143, 144, 563, 568
nurse practitioners - 145
rural development - 346, 352
trauma care - 597-598
Rural housing
appropriations - 867, 868, 869
authorization - 633, 653-654
budget action - 125
Rural Housing Insurance Fund - 869 (chart)
Russo, Marty D-Ill. (3)
budget action - 128
campaign finance reform - 67-68
defense authorization - 676
Ruvolo, Jim - 59
Ryan, T. Timothy - 179, 180 (box)
Ryskamp, Kenneth L. - 516

S

Sabah, Jaber al Ahmed, al- - 724
Sabato, Larry J. - 909, 926, 927
Sabo, Martin Olav D-Minn. (5)
congressional elections, 1990 - 908
Saddam Hussein
Persian Gulf crisis - 717-756
Sadik, Nafis - 839 (box)
Sadomasochism - 870, 874
Safe haven. *See Refugees*
Safe Transportation of Food Act - 382-383
Saiki, Patricia R-Hawaii (1)
characteristics of Congress - 923
congressional elections, 1990 - 913, 915, 922
House membership changes - 918 (chart)
marginal vote share - 905 (box)
farm bill - 323
housing programs overhaul - 640
Salaverria, Miguel - 781
Salinas de Gortari, Carlos - 218
Sampol, William - 106
Samuel, William - 277 (box)
San Antonio, Texas - 150, 667
San Diego, Calif. - 582
San Francisco, Calif.
AIDS conference - 480 (box)
AIDS relief - 582
earthquake aid - 845
federal pay overhaul - 406
housing issues - 662
Soviet air service - 759
San Francisco Lesbian and Gay Film Festival - 433
San Juan, Puerto Rico - 582
Sand, Leonard - 107
Sanders, Bernard - 916, 918 (chart), 922, 922 (box)
Sandinistas - 770-771, 772 (box), 773, 804
Sanford, Terry D-N.C.
Caribbean Basin Initiative - 215, 217
savings and loan scandal - 80, 82, 83, 88
Social Security in budget accounting - 170 (box)
textile import quotas - 220
thrift supervisor - 180 (box)
U.S. Embassy in Moscow - 760 (box)
Sangmeister, George E. D-Ill. (4)
crime bill - 495
financial institution fraud - 183
Transportation appropriations - 878
Santorum, Rick - 905 (chart), 917, 918 (chart)
Saphos, Charles S. - 187
Sarbanes, Paul S. D-Md.
Clean Air Act - 235
diplomatic nominations - 801 (box)
FHA rules revision - 658
Persian Gulf crisis - 736, 742, 743
Sarpalius, Bill D-Texas (13)
food stamps - 355
Frank ethics case - 104
Sasser, Jim D-Tenn.
budget action - 128-129, 130 (box), 131
budget process - 176-177
community service programs - 561
defense authorization - 676
military construction appropriations - 829
Social Security in budget accounting - 170 (box)
Satellite Broadcasting and Communications Association - 370
Satellite communications. *See also Antisatellite (ASAT) missile; Strategic defense initiative*
antisatellite lasers - 823, 824
cable TV regulation - 370-371
copyright tribunal - 543
defense authorization - 677, 684
early warning missile defense - 677, 684, 817, 823, 824
Japan-U.S. trade - 208, 209
radio spectrum allocation - 376
Satellite launch vehicles
defense authorization - 675
NASA authorization - 434, 436
Saturn - 435
Saudi Arabia
arms sales - 674, 734-735 (box)
foreign aid appropriations - 843
Persian Gulf crisis - 717, 719, 720, 725-732, 737, 738, 740 (box)
U.S. goals, rationales - 744 (box)
Sautterfield, Steven - 358
Savage, Gus D-Ill. (2)
congressional elections, 1990
low winning percentage - 906 (chart)
ethics case - 104, 105-106
Fauntroy ethics case - 107
minorities in Congress - 924 (chart)
supplemental appropriations - 845
Savage, Thomas John - 107
Save Our Security - 567
Savimbi, Jonas - 792, 793
Savings and loan associations. *See also Keating Five scandal investigation*
deposit insurance - 123, 134-135, 141, 184, 854
direct investment - 82, 84-85
financial crisis
asset recovery - 486, 495
bailout action, 1990 - 179-184
budget accounting - 134, 135, 175, 181, 846
budget action - 123
Bush economic report - 117
effect on legislation
Clean Air Act - 238-239
crime bill - 495
federal credit reform - 134, 178 (box)
FHA rules revision - 657, 660
housing programs overhaul - 641
election issue, 1990 - 80, 903, 906, 903, 917
OTS director - 180 (box)
pocket veto - 22
study commission - 495
summary - 4, 6
thrift prosecutions
bailout action - 179
Commerce/Justice/State appropriations - 881, 884, 885
crime bill - 486, 490, 492, 493-494, 495, 498, 499
financial institution fraud - 182-183 (box)
RICO revision - 537, 538
Secret Service investigation - 886-888
money laundering - 188
Savings Association Insurance Fund - 141
Sawyer, Thomas C. D-Ohio (14)
community service programs - 562
congressional elections, 1990
vote-share falloff - 904 (chart)
education proposals - 615
Saxton, H. James R-N.J. (13)
barrier island protection - 302
congressional elections, 1990
low winning percentage - 906 (chart)
SBA. *See Small Business Administration*
Scalia, Antonin
abortion - 54, 529
corporate campaign limits - 59 (box)
flag desecration - 525
habeas corpus appeals - 489 (box)
judicial appointments - 516
legislative intent - 54, 55 (box)
Medicaid pay suits - 571
OMB review powers - 412 (box)
political patronage - 54, 933
right to die - 567 (box)
Souter confirmation - 508
student religious groups - 618 (box)
Supreme Court term summary - 52
Thomas confirmation - 518 (box)
Scanlon, John - 633
Scanlon, Terrence M. - 393
Schaefer, William Donald - 428, 904 (chart), 930
Scheppach, Raymond C. - 571
Scherer, Roger - 102
Scheuer, James H. D-N.Y. (8)
budget action - 166
Energy, water appropriations - 864
Schira, Jack - 918 (chart)
Schlaudeman, Harry M. - 771, 801 (box)
Schlesinger, James R. - 720, 742
Schneider, Claudine R-R.I. (2)
barrier island protection - 302
characteristics of Congress - 923
congressional elections, 1990 - 913, 922
House membership changes - 918 (chart)
Scholarships. *See Student aid*
School desegregation - 53
School lunch program - 155, 354
School prayer - 618 (box), 623
School Year Extension Study Commission - 852
Schools. *See also Colleges and universities; Drug-free schools; Elementary and secondary education; Teachers*
antismoking bills - 593, 594
child-care aid - 548-551
community service programs - 559-562
energy conservation - 319
environmental education grants - 293
family planning education - 605
Head Start authorization - 552
library hours - 617
religious group meetings - 52, 53, 618 (box)
revenue from timber sales - 215, 216
rural development - 346, 352
Schroeder, Jon - 101
Schroeder, Patricia D-Colo. (1)
CFE - 699
characteristics of Congress - 924
minorities in Congress - 924 (chart)
civil rights/job bias - 470, 473
congressional term limit - 15
defense authorization - 686
Energy, water appropriations - 864
family leave - 359-361
flag desecration - 525
military base closings - 694
military construction appropriations - 828
naval home ports - 681 (box)
NIH authorization - 602
Persian Gulf crisis - 730
Savage ethics case - 105
Schuelke, Henry F. III - 97
Schuette, Bill R-Mich. (10)
congressional elections, 1990 - 913, 922
House membership changes - 918 (chart)
farm bill - 331
Schulze, Richard T. R-Pa. (5)
China-U.S. relations - 766
congressional elections, 1990
low winning percentage - 906 (chart)
vote-share falloff - 904 (chart)
Schumer, Charles E. D-N.Y. (10)
campaign finance reform - 67-68
census count adjustment - 415-416
congressional redistricting - 932
crime bill - 495
criminal pollution liability - 285 (box)
defense appropriations - 816
farm bill - 327, 332
financial institution fraud - 183
hate crime statistics - 506
housing programs overhaul - 631-644, 646, 656
HUD scandal investigation - 666
immigration law revision - 475-476
money laundering - 188
octane labeling - 282
thrift bailout - 181, 184
VA/HUD appropriations - 856
Schwartz, Victor - 401
Schwartzman, Andrew J. - 375, 377
Schwarzkopf, Gen. H. Norman - 721, 731, 755
Science and technology. *See also Computers; Telecommunciations*
bilateral agreements - 883 (chart)
Commerce Department technology programs - 440-441
equipment
developmentally disabled - 609
disabled education - 616
drug traffic interdiction - 679
library aid - 617
export controls - 198-201
China sanctions - 800
missile technology - 683
immigration law revision - 482
NASA task force - 434
salaries
NIH - 600, 601, 603
Pentagon - 679
research
acid rain, air pollution - 236, 258, 274-275
animal rights activists - 441-442
budget action - 125-126, 128
defense projects at universities - 813-814
earthquake preparedness - 442
Energy, water appropriations - 861, 862, 865
global climate change - 124, 307
hydrogen fuel - 273, 313

Interior appropriations - 876
minerals mining - 442-443
NASA authorization - 436
NSF appropriations - 854
ozone-depleting chemicals - 271
Soviet-U.S. oceanography - 759-760
space patent law - 437
space station experiments - 437
Treasury, Postal appropriations - 888
strategic technologies - 202-203 (box)
technology transfer - 395, 440
Science and Technology Policy Office - 855 (chart)
Science education
budget action - 126
employee training - 478
Energy, water appropriations - 865
NSF appropriations - 854
scholarships - 7, 610, 612 (box)
drug ban - 505
student competency - 615
tech-prep education - 621
Science, Space and Technology Committee, House
jurisdiction conflicts - 306
leadership - 11 (box), 924
prestige - 434-435
Scofield, Sandra K. - 918 (chart)
Scotland Yard - 781
Scott, Thomas - 918 (chart)
Scout helicopters
appropriations - 817-818, 823, 824-825
authorization - 679, 685
Scowcroft, Brent
Armenian genocide commemoration - 807
CFE - 696, 699, 704
China-U.S. relations - 764, 767 (box)
Persian Gulf crisis - 745 (box)
START - 706
Screwworms - 355
Scud missiles - 721, 754
Scully, Thomas - 608
Sea Lance missiles - 686, 825, 826
Seafood. *See Fish and fishing*
SeaLand Corp. - 814
Search and seizure
asset forfeiture - 499
flawed warrants - 486, 498
***Seawolf*-class submarines**
appropriations - 815 (chart), 819, 825, 826, 846
authorization - 675, 678, 685
defense budget reprogramming - 676 (box)
SEC. *See Securities and Exchange Commission*
Secondary Schools Basic Skills program - 615
Secord, Richard V. - 535
Secrecy. *See Information access and classification*
Secret Service, U.S.
appropriations - 887 (chart), 889
crime bill - 499
financial institution fraud - 182
savings and loan investigation - 886-887
Securities. *See Stocks, bonds and securities*
Securities and Exchange Commission (SEC)
ALJ corps - 523
appropriations - 881, 882 (chart), 884
authorization - 193
budget action - 123
CFTC authorization - 194
Keating background - 78
market regulation - 190-193
securities fraud - 193-194
summary - 5
Securities Industry Association - 536
Securities Market Reform Act - 190-193
Security services
border patrol - 479, 484, 485
college crime - 625
public housing drug-elimination grants - 652
Senate sergeant-at-arms - 12 (box)
sex crime deterrence - 507
Sedlmayr, Laurie - 88
SEED. *See Support for Eastern European Democracies Act*
Seidman, Harold - 426
Seidman, L. William
FDIC premiums - 184, 186, 187
savings and loan scandal - 90
thrift bailout - 179-180, 181, 184
Selective Service System - 855 (chart)
Self-employed persons
health insurance, Medicare - 159, 160, 173
Semiautomatic weapons. *See Firearms*
Seminole Indians - 424
Senate Election Campaign Fund - 62
Senate, U.S. *See also Congress, members of; Congressional committees; specific committees*
confirmation power
military base commission - 687, 693
recess appointments - 531-533
congressional partisanship - 32
elections, 1990
changes (chart) - 913
costs - 909
party distribution, 102nd Cong., by state (map) - 915
results - 901-903, 911-916
leadership - 9-10
members
disciplined members, 20th c. - 99 (box)
freshmen, 102nd Cong. - 925, 926
honoraria - 6
list, 102nd Cong. - 912
party lineup 101st, 102nd Cong. (chart) - 911
Puerto Rico status - 426
shadow delegations - 428
term expiration year (chart) - 914
sergeant-at-arms - 12 (box)
treaty ratification power
chemical weapons pact - 709
nuclear test treaties - 712
oil-spill protocols - 284
process - 807
Senior Biomedical Research Service - 603
Senior citizens. *See Elderly persons*
Seniority
congressional elections, 1990 - 904
congressional leadership - 11 (box)
Seniority (job)
civil rights/job bias - 463, 466, 468
Sensenbrenner, F. James Jr. R-Wis. (9)
civil rights/job bias - 469, 470
crime bill - 497-498
disabled civil rights - 450, 459
flag desecration - 525
handgun wait period - 501 (box)
NASA authorization - 435
SSC authorization - 439
Sentelle, David B. - 535
Sentencing Commission, U.S. - 883 (chart)
Separation of powers. *See also Congressional-executive relations; Congressional-judicial relations*
budget process - 176
civil rights/job bias - 467
disabled civil rights - 459-461
Environmental Education Foundation - 293
regulatory agency control - 21
Sequestration
budget process changes - 161-162, 173
budget summit - 132-134
defense budget reprogramming - 676 (box), 845
1989 order - 176
reports, orders timetable - 162
Sergeant-at-arms, Senate - 12 (box)
Serrano, Andres - 430
Serrano, Jose E. D-N.Y.(18)
characteristics of Congress - 902 (box)
minorities in Congress - 924 (chart)
congressional elections, 1990
special elections - 14 (box), 923, 934
Puerto Rico status - 426
Sewer and sewage treatment systems
agriculture appropriations - 867
beach water quality - 290
budget action - 124
coastal, Great Lakes cleanup - 289-290
"colonias" housing aid - 654
rural development - 347, 352-354
toxic air pollutants - 256, 258
Sex crimes. *See also Prostitution; Rape*
child sexual abuse - 53, 422, 493
deterrence bill - 1507
offenders HIV testing - 586
rules of evidence - 53
youth counselors - 893
Sex discrimination
Dyson ethics case - 108
House facilities - 895
job bias
civil rights bill - 462-473
fetal protection case - 56, 465
medical research - 600, 601
Souter confirmation - 511
vocational education authorization - 619-623
Sexual harassment
civil rights/job bias - 469
Lukens resignation - 6, 106
Savage ethics case - 105
Sexual orientation and behavior. *See also Homosexuals*
disabled civil rights - 452, 459
"hate crime" statistics - 1506
immigration law revision - 474, 480 (box)
TV depiction guidelines - 374 (box)
Sexually transmitted diseases. *See also Acquired immune deficiency syndrome (AIDS)*
disabled civil rights - 449
immigration exclusion - 480 (box)
Seymour, John - 913 (box), 925
SH-60 helicopters - 675
Shamir, Yitzhak - 743, 754
Shane, Jeffrey N. - 387
Shapiro, David I. - 369
Sharp, Philip R. D-Ind. (2)
alternative power regulation - 317
Clean Air Act - 238-239, 242, 276, 278
congressional elections, 1990 - 923
foreign ownership of U.S. business - 224, 225
octane labeling - 282
Strategic Petroleum Reserve - 315
Transportation appropriations - 878
Shasta Dam - 864
Shatt-al-Arab - 722
Shaw, E. Clay Jr. R-Fla. (15)
child-care aid - 548-549
children's welfare services - 556
Transportation appropriations - 878
Shawnee National Forest - 304
Shea & Gardner - 464
Shearer, Gail - 572, 574
Shelby, Richard C. D-Ala.
conservative coalition - 47
defense appropriations - 820, 821
defense authorization - 677
Persian Gulf crisis - 750-751
SDI - 692
thrift supervisor - 180 (box)
Shellfish. *See Fish and fishing*
Shelter Plus Care - 631, 635, 640, 655
Shepard, William S. and Lois - 930
Sheridan, Tom - 850-851
Sherman Act - 541
Shevardnadze, Eduard A.
Afghan rebel aid - 792
CFE - 696, 700, 702
chemical weapons pact - 709-710
German unification - 699
Persian Gulf crisis - 740
Soviet-U.S. relations - 757-758, 759, 761
START - 706, 707, 708
Washington summit - 701
Shikles, Janet - 574
Shine, Hugh D. - 918 (chart)
Ships and shipping. *See also Boats and boating; Fish and fishing*
alien workers - 483
cruise ship tourism fees - 157
Florida Keys protection - 303
food aid cargo preference - 338-339 (box), 345, 804
food program abuse - 338, 804
harbor maintenance taxes - 159, 172
Nicaragua-U.S. trade - 771
oil pollution cleanup - 283
pipeline safety inspection - 286 (box)
ready reserve fleet - 814, 885
Soviet-U.S. maritime agreement - 760
tonnage taxes - 157, 386
Shoes
Caribbean Basin Initiative - 212, 213, 214-215
prison industries - 498
textile import quotas - 219, 220, 221
Showtime - 371
Shultz, George P. - 723
Shumway, Norman D. R-Calif. (14)
coastal zone management - 288
conservative coalition - 47
defense preparedness - 203
House membership changes - 918 (chart)
Shuster, Bud R-Pa. (9)
disabled civil rights - 449, 460
El Salvador aid - 780-781
Sidewinder missiles - 846
Sierra Club
auto fuel efficiency - 279, 280
Clean Air Act - 234, 235, 246, 276, 279
EPA Cabinet status - 291
federal RCRA compliance - 308
Sierra Research - 240 (box)
Sihanouk, Norodom - 793, 837-839
SII. *See Strategic Impediments Initiative*
Sikes, Robert L. F. - 87
Sikorski, Gerry D-Minn. (6)
Clean Air Act - 239, 244, 278
CPSC authorization - 394
ethics case - 108
hazardous materials transport - 381
Sikorsky helicopters - 643
Silber, John - 930
Silberman, Laurence H. - 535
Silkworms - 836
Silverado Savings and Loan Association - 179, 180, 182, 495
Silverglade, Bruce - 576
Silverman, Joy A. - 801 (box)
Simes, Dimitri K. - 702
Simon, Paul D-Ill.
ALJ corps - 523
auto fuel efficiency - 281

balanced-budget amendment - 174-175 (box)
Clean Air Act - 238, 278
congressional elections, 1990 - 913, 915
congressional partisanship - 40
D.C. status - 428-429
education proposals - 610
election - 369 (box)
federal judgeships - 523
"hate crime" statistics - 507
immigration law revision - 485
juvenile justice nomination - 506
Kenya aid - 790
library aid - 617
job training overhaul - 365
Panama, Africa aid - 776
Persian Gulf crisis - 749
Saudi arms sales - 735 (box)
savings and loan scandal - 94
Souter confirmation - 511
South Africa sanctions - 789
Soviet-U.S. relations - 761
Thomas confirmation - 518
TV violence guidelines - 374 (box)
Simpson, Alan K. R-Wyo.
Agent Orange compensation - 418, 419
China-U.S. relations - 765
civil rights/job bias - 473
Clean Air Act - 236-238, 276
congressional elections, 1990 - 916
vote-share falloff - 904 (chart)
congressional leadership - 9 (box), 10
congressional partisanship - 39
crime bill - 499
defense authorization - 679
federal judgeships - 521
immigration law revision - 474-475, 479-480, 484-485
juvenile justice nomination - 506
radiation victims compensation - 591
Soviet-U.S. relations - 759
Singapore
U.S. trade
ulcer drug ingredient - 215
Single parents
food stamps - 355
home loan aid - 647
vocational education authorization - 620
Sisisky, Norman D-Va. (4)
defense authorization - 680, 682
Sixth Fleet - 822
Skaggs, David E. D-Colo. (2)
Energy, water appropriations - 864
flag desecration - 526
Skeen, Joe R-N.M. (2)
Interior appropriations - 874
Treasury, Postal appropriations - 889
Skelton, Ike D-Mo. (4)
conservative coalition - 47
Skin cancer - 418
Skinner, Samuel K.
Amtrak authorization - 391
auto fuel efficiency - 279, 281
aviation package - 384-387
SL-7-class cargo ships - 814
Slattery, Jim D-Kan. (2)
child-care aid - 549
Medicaid expansion - 571
Slaughter, Louise M. D-N.Y. (30)
minorities in Congress - 924 (chart)
Transportation appropriations - 878
Sloan, John Jr. - 448
Sloane, Harvey - 915
Sloane, Morris - 387
Slobig, Frank J. - 560
SLS. *See Supplemental Loans for Students*
Small business. *See also Minority business; Small Business Administration*
civil rights/job bias - 473
Clean Air Act - 234, 235, 236, 246, 269, 279
community development block grants - 655
disabled persons
barrier removal tax incentive - 160
civil rights - 448, 450, 451, 457, 459
estate freezes - 160
health insurance - 607
OMB review powers - 411, 413
orphan drugs - 579
Panama aid - 776
rural development - 395
SBA authorization - 395
Soviet-U.S. trade - 205
tax incentives - 164, 167, 169, 172
technology transfer - 395
Small Business Administration (SBA)
appropriations - 882
authorization - 395
budget action - 123
disabled civil rights - 458
immigrant job discrimination - 484
IRS regulation comments - 160
Small Communities Coordinator - 274
Smedley, Lawrence T. - 567
Smith, Bob R-Ore. (2)
congressional elections, 1990 - 908
Interior appropriations - 874
Tongass forest protection - 294
Smith, Christopher H. R-N.J. (4)
U.N. population fund - 838-839 (box), 840
Smith, Denny R-Ore. (5)
congressional elections, 1990 - 903, 917, 919
defeated House members - 917 (chart)
House membership changes - 918 (chart)
marginal vote share - 905 (box)
defense authorization - 683
savings and loan scandal - 80
Smith Kline Beecham - 215
Smith, Lamar R-Texas (21)
handgun wait period - 501 (box)
immigration law revision - 475-477, 479, 485
Legal Services Corporation - 533
Smith, Lawrence J. D-Fla. (16)
Andean Initiative - 805
civil rights/job bias - 469
crime bill - 495
federal judgeships - 521
Persian Gulf crisis - 736
South Africa sanctions - 789
Smith, Neal D-Iowa (4)
Commerce/Justice/State appropriations - 881, 884
U.S. Embassy in Moscow - 801 (box)
Smith, Peter R-Vt. (AL)
civil rights/job bias - 467
congressional elections, 1990 - 916, 922 (box)
defeated House members - 917 (chart)
House membership changes - 918 (chart)
marginal vote share - 905 (chart)
congressional partisanship - 40
education proposals - 614
electoral defeat - 166
vocational education authorization - 623
Smith, Robert C. R-N.H. (1)
characteristics of Congress - 902 (box), 925
congressional elections, 1990 - 913, 922
House membership changes - 918 (chart)
Senate membership changes - 913 (chart)
veterans rehabilitation - 421
Smith, Virginia R-Neb. (3)
characteristics of Congress - 923
Energy, water appropriations - 863
House membership changes - 918 (chart)
Smithsonian Institution
appropriations - 873 (chart)
Indian remains - 422
Smoking. *See Tobacco*
Smuggling - 817
Smyser, C. A. "Skip" - 918 (chart), 922
Snake River - 861, 866
Snelling, Richard A. - 930
Snow, Karl - 918 (chart), 922
Snowe, Olympia J. R-Maine (2)
congressional elections, 1990
marginal vote share - 905 (chart)
vote-share falloff - 904 (chart)
minorities in Congress - 924 (chart)
NIH authorization - 602
Social Democratic Party (Germany) - 701
Social health maintenance organizations - 146
Social Security
advisory council - 609
budget action - 125, 134, 150-151
budget, deficit accounting - 162, 163, 165, 170 (box), 174-175, 177, 846
Bush economic report - 116
delayed retirement credit - 558
earnings, benefits statements - 151, 557
illegal aliens - 151, 485, 557, 558
minimum benefit - 151
payroll taxes - 167, 170 (box)
Puerto Rico status - 427
representative payees - 150, 557, 558
retirement earnings test - 550, 557
state, local employees coverage - 125, 136, 159, 164, 172, 558
State of the Union address - 19
veterans benefits claims - 156
Social Security Act
child-care aid - 547, 548, 551
Social Security Administration
agency independence - 558
ALJ corps - 523
appeals - 151
appropriations - 848 (chart)
earnings, benefits statements - 557
records access for Medicare - 146
SSI - 150
telephone service - 151, 557
Social Security Disability Amendments of 1980 - 573
Social services. *See Welfare and social services*
Social Services Block Grant
child-care aid - 548-551
Socialists
Sanders election - 922 (box)
Society for Research in Child Development - 553
Soil conservation
agriculture appropriations - 867
beach restoration - 863, 865
farm bill - 323, 326, 332, 336, 345-346, 348-349
FmHA inventory - 347
Grand Canyon erosion protection - 300-301, 356
Soil Conservation Service - 335, 869 (chart)
Solar energy
alternative power regulation - 317
budget action - 124, 160, 173
Energy, water appropriations - 861, 863, 865, 866
hydrogen-fuel research - 318
space station design - 437
tax incentives - 273, 313 (box)
Solarz, Stephen J. D-N.Y. (13)
China-U.S. relations - 765
defense authorization - 682
foreign aid appropriations - 835, 837-839
intelligence authorization - 794, 795, 797
Pakistan-U.S. relations - 769
Persian Gulf crisis - 733, 746, 747, 751-752
South Africa sanctions - 789
Soldiers' and Airmen's Home - 849 (chart)
Solicitor General, U.S. - 56
Solomon, Gerald B. H. R-N.Y. (24)
antidrug measures - 505, 506
China-U.S. relations - 768
congressional partisanship - 39
education proposals - 614
family leave - 360
flag desecration - 526
intelligence authorization - 798
Persian Gulf crisis
use-of-force debate - 752 (box)
Transportation appropriations - 878
Solomon, Richard H. - 765
Somalia
U.S. aid/human rights - 776, 836, 845
Son Sann - 793, 837
Sonobuoys - 819
Sorauf, Frank J. - 909
Sorghum - 342
Sosnick, Doug - 908
Sound recordings - 205
Souter, David H.
Legal Services Corporation - 533
Supreme Court confirmation - 508-515, 516, 523
Bush announcement (text) - 509
opening statement - 512-513
term summary - 52
South Africa
Angola rebel aid - 793
U.S. aid to promote democracy - 845
U.S. trade
sanctions - 787-789
strategic minerals - 236
South America. *See also specific countries*
drug extradition expenses - 779
screwworm eradication - 355
South Carolina
Energy, water appropriations - 865
federal judgeships - 522
fish hatchery - 292
gubernatorial election, 1990 - 930
water projects authorization - 299
South Dakota
congressional mail - 75
congressional redistricting - 932
corporate campaign limits - 59 (box)
gubernatorial election, 1990 - 930
living wills - 567 (box)
water projects - 357
South Korea
defense burden-sharing - 828
drift-net fishing - 399
military construction appropriations - 827
U.S. trade
F/A-18 planes - 821
Super 301 process - 208
tobacco exports - 593
South Yemen
development bank loans - 207
Southeastern Pennsylvania Transit Authority - 880
Southern states
civil rights/job bias - 467
conservative coalition - 40-48

disaster relief - 845, 846
farm bill - 328, 334, 341, 350, 351
textile import quotas - 219, 220, 222
Southland Corp. - 223
Soviet emigration
Jackson-Vanik rules - 205, 213
Soviet-U.S. trade accord - 204, 757, 758-759
U.S. refugee admissions - 474
U.S. aid
foreign aid appropriations - 837
housing in Israel - 743, 841, 845
supplemental appropriations - 778, 844, 845
Soviet Union. *See also Baltic States; Soviet emigration; Soviet-U.S. relations*
Afghan relations - 769, 792, 795
Angola policies - 792-793, 796, 797
European development bank - 206-207, 835
German unification - 762-763, 699
internal economic conditions - 205, 757
Nicaragua aid - 770, 772 (box)
Persian Gulf crisis - 717, 719, 721-722, 740, 747, 756
U.N. consulate - 802
uranium enrichment - 310
Soviet-U.S. relations. *See also Arms control; Conventional forces in Europe (CFE) treaty; Strategic arms reduction treaty (START)*
defense issues
B-2 bomber - 688, 689, 690
defense appropriations - 812, 813, 819-820, 822, 823
defense authorization - 671, 672, 682, 684
intelligence authorization - 791, 792
military construction appropriations - 827, 828, 829
SDI - 691, 692
diplomacy
U.N. espionage - 802
U.S. consulate in Kiev - 802
U.S. Embassy in Moscow - 124, 801 (box), 881, 884, 885
economic aid - 759
Havel visit - 204 (box)
trade - 758-760, 761
accord highlights - 205
aviation - 759
export controls - 198, 199, 201
MFN status - 204-205
shipping - 760
strategic minerals - 443
Washington summit - 204-205, 707
Sowell, David - 667
Soybeans
price supports - 325-328, 333, 340, 343, 350, 351
Space Exploration Initiative - 855
Space programs. *See also Space shuttle; Space station*
budget action - 125-126
commercial launch fees - 157
extraterrestrial life - 856
NASA authorization - 434-436
nuclear power pack research - 865
patent law extension - 437
Space shuttle
appropriations - 845
ASRM nozzle - 859
NASA authorization - 434, 435
space station design - 436
Space station
appropriations - 854, 855, 856, 858, 859, 860
Freedom design overhaul - 436-437
NASA authorization - 434-436
Spain
NATO base - 827
Speaker of the House
disabled civil rights - 458
votes - 527, 795
Special counsel and prosecutors
Durenberger ethics case - 103
financial institution fraud - 181, 182, 183, 486, 495
HUD scandal investigation - 666-667
Iran-contra affair - 534
savings and loan scandal - 81 (box)
Special education - 616-617
Special Isotope Separation project - 122
Special Supplemental Food Program. *See Women, Infants and Children (WIC) program*
Specter, Arlen R-Pa.
agriculture appropriations - 868
ALJ corps - 523
Caribbean Basin Initiative - 215
civil rights/job bias - 471, 473
Clean Air Act - 238
crime bill - 490, 493
federal judgeships - 521
flag desecration - 528
foreign aid appropriations - 842
Hatch Act revision - 408
immigration law revision - 480
juvenile justice nomination - 506
Labor/HHS appropriations - 852, 853
legislative intent - 54, 56
Saudi arms sales - 735 (box)
Souter confirmation - 514, 515
textile import quotas - 220
Transportation appropriations - 876-877, 880
vertical price fixing - 540
Spector, Leonard S. - 769
Speech or Debate Clause - 511 (box)
Speech disorders
disabled civil rights - 447, 457
911 service - 453
Speidel, J. Joseph - 839 (box)
Spielman, Alan P. - 573, 574-575
Spinal cord injury - 598
Sports
antismoking bills - 592, 593
disabled civil rights - 447
high-school athlete drug testing - 505, 613
immigration law revision - 479, 482
lottery ad ban - 495
student right-to-know - 613, 624
youth programs at public housing - 651
Sports Fish Restoration Account - 159
SPR. *See Strategic Petroleum Reserve*
Sprague, Lisa - 363
SRAM II missile - 674, 684, 822, 824
SRAM-T missile - 674, 684, 815 (chart), 816, 824
SS-18 missile - 704-705, 706, 707, 708
SS-23 missile - 680, 707
SS-24 missile - 704, 707
SS-25 missile - 707
SSC. *See Superconducting super collider*
SSI. *See Supplemental Security Income*
St. Christopher and Nevis - 212
St. Elizabeths Hospital - 892 (chart)
St. Lawrence Seaway - 338 (box), 879 (chart)
St. Louis, Mo.
public housing home ownership project - 857, 859
St. Lucia - 212
St. Vincent and the Grenadines - 212
Stafford loans - 561, 611
Staggers, Harley O. Jr. D-W.Va. (2)
assault weapons ban - 501 (box)
congressional elections, 1990
low winning percentage - 906 (chart)
crime bill - 494, 497
federal judgeships - 521
flag desecration - 525
food stamps - 355
handgun wait period - 501 (box)
immigration law revision - 478
Legal Services Corporation - 533
Stallings, Richard D-Idaho (2)
congressional elections, 1990 - 908
Standard missiles - 675, 819, 825
Standards of Official Conduct, Committee on, House
leadership - 924
Stangeland, Arlan R-Minn. (7)
congressional elections, 1990 - 922
defeated House members - 917 (chart)
House membership changes - 918 (chart)
marginal vote share - 905 (box)
ethics case - 107
farm bill - 328, 331
water projects authorization - 298
Stanley, Thomas P. - 376
Star wars. *See Strategic defense initiative*
Stark, Pete D-Calif. (9)
congressional elections, 1990
vote-share falloff - 904 (chart)
Medicare changes - 563, 568
mammogram coverage - 564 (box)
Medigap insurance - 572
Pepper Commission - 607, 608
Starr, Kenneth W. - 56, 525
START. *See Strategic arms reduction treaty*
State and local government. *See also Governors*
arts councils - 430, 431, 433
business and labor
bank regulation - 186-189
cable TV regulation - 370-372
family leave - 359
fish inspection - 397
job training overhaul - 365-367
octane labeling - 282
organic food labels - 332
product liability - 400-401
securities market regulation - 192, 193
telemarketing fraud - 402
timber exports - 215, 216
unemployment compensation - 150, 368
disabled civil rights - 453
economic policy
rural development - 336, 345, 346, 352-353
education
block grants - 123
disabled students - 54-55, 616-617
education, literacy proposals - 610-615
Head Start authorization - 552
teacher certification - 612
vocational education authorization - 619-623
employees
age discrimination - 363, 364
community service liability - 561
Medicare coverage - 124, 126, 136, 159, 164
political patronage - 52, 53
Social Security coverage - 125, 136, 159, 164, 172, 558
energy and environment
abandoned mine cleanup - 154
Clean Air Act - 229-279
coastal zone management - 154, 288
energy conservation - 124, 319
federal RCRA compliance - 291, 308-309
global warming - 307
offshore drilling - 312
oil pollution cleanup - 283-284, 287
pollution source reduction - 155
water pollution cleanup - 289
water projects authorization - 298-300
federal relations
census count adjustment - 415-416, 932
congressional campaign finance - 65 (box)
consistency provision - 154
environmental law compliance - 291, 308
funding risk-sharing - 439
grant funds transfers, pass-through - 414, 498
National Guard training exercises - 694 (box)
offshore activities - 288-289
pesticide residue laws - 358
Supreme Court term summary - 52
voter registration - 69
health
AIDS bill - 582-589
antismoking bills - 593, 594
cancer screening - 606
drug-abuse treatment - 503-505
elderly, Alzheimer's programs - 598-599
injuries research - 598
living wills - 566 (box)
Medicaid - 5, 146-147, 155, 569-571
Medigap insurance - 573, 574
mental health services - 599
nursing home reform - 148, 589
nutrition labels - 575-576
organ transplants - 597
patient self-determination - 146
Pepper Commission - 607-608
public health planning grants - 609, 845
trauma care - 597-598
housing
FHA rules revision - 659
housing programs overhaul - 631-656
law and judiciary
copyright - 541, 542-543
criminal aliens - 484
disaster liability suits - 543
drug enforcement - 493, 503, 521, 679
flag desecration - 528
habeas corpus appeals - 487-488, 489 (box), 490, 493, 494-495
Indian tribes - 422
juvenile delinquency - 506
Legal Services Corporation - 531-533
prison literacy - 614
RICO revision - 537
water rights - 304
legislatures
congressional redistricting - 931-933
term limits - 13-14
taxation
federal tax deductibility - 165
mortgage revenue bonds - 160, 173
securities - 170 (box)
transportation
airport noise abatement - 388
Amtrak waste disposal - 392
Bush transportation policy - 384
hazardous materials transport - 380-382
welfare and social services
child-care aid - 4, 152, 547-551
child-care referral services - 552, 555
children's welfare services - 150, 556
community, national service - 560, 561
home energy aid - 552
homeless aid - 346, 354, 655, 665

immigrant aid - 476, 479
WIC funding - 554 (box)
State and Territorial Air Pollution Program Administrators - 240
State Department, U.S.
appropriations - 881-886
authorization - 20, 799-802
aviation security - 390
budget action - 124
CFE - 704
diplomatic nominations - 801 (box)
environmental protection
air pollution - 273, 274
Antarctica - 305, 306
aquatic nuisance species - 304
EPA Cabinet status - 292
export controls - 199, 200
fisheries - 399
foreign aid
Afghan rebels - 795
Angola rebels - 793
appropriations - 842, 843
Cambodian rebels - 795
El Salvador - 785, 786
ESF spending - 769
Food for Peace - 804
Nicaragua - 771, 772, 773
Panama - 775
immigration law revision - 475, 476, 481 (box)
international narcotics control - 836, 844
money laundering - 499
Persian Gulf crisis - 720, 723, 725, 726, 728
questionable gulf allies - 740 (box)
Saudi arms sales - 734 (box)
South Africa sanctions - 789
U.N. funding - 802
U.S. Embassy in Moscow - 760 (box), 881, 885
State Dependent Care Development Grants - 552, 555, 556
State Energy Efficiency Programs Improvement Act - 319
State Justice Institute - 883 (chart)
State Legalization Impact Assistance Grants - 476
State of the Union address - 18-20
Statehood
District of Columbia - 428-429, 891, 892
Puerto Rico - 424-427
Staten Island, N.Y. - 681 (box)
Stayman, Allen - 808
Stealth bomber. *See B-2 bomber*
Stealth missiles - 674, 684
Steel industry
South Africa sanctions - 787
toxic air pollutants - 229, 232, 247, 256-258, 275-278
Steel Trade Liberalization Act - 214
Steelman, Deborah L. - 609
Stello, Victor Jr. - 309-310
Stenholm, Charles W. D-Texas (17)
animal rights activists - 441
balanced-budget amendment - 174-175 (box)
campaign finance reform - 67
child-care aid - 548-549
civil rights/job bias - 471
Commerce/Justice/State appropriations - 881
conservative coalition - 47, 48
family leave - 360
farm bill - 329, 332-333, 349, 350
fish inspection - 399
flag desecration - 526
Legal Services Corporation - 532-533
Sterilization. *See Birth control*
Steroids - 499
Stern, Leonard W. - 560
Steubenville, Ohio - 252
Stevens, David - 94
Stevens, John Paul
abortion - 529
Brennan career - 511 (box)
flag desecration - 525
habeas corpus appeals - 489 (box)
legislative intent - 55 (box)
Medicaid payment suits - 571
National Guard training exercises - 694 (box)
OMB review powers - 412 (box)
political patronage - 933
right to die - 567 (box)
student religious groups - 618 (box)
Supreme Court term summary - 52
Stevens, Ted R-Alaska
campaign finance reform - 60, 63
congressional elections, 1990 - 916
congressional mail - 75
defense appropriations - 813
defense authorization - 680
disabled civil rights - 461
Energy, water appropriations - 866
EPA Cabinet status - 291
fish inspection - 398
Hatch Act revision - 411
Interior appropriations - 875
Labor/HHS appropriations - 851
legislative branch appropriations - 897
regulatory negotiation guidelines - 414
Social Security in budget accounting - 170 (box)
Tongass forest protection - 295
Transportation appropriations - 879
Stewart, Rosemary - 95-96
Stinger missiles
Afghan rebel aid - 792
appropriations - 818, 825
authorization - 674
sales to Qatar - 844
Saudi arms sales - 734 (box)
Stinson, John M. - 276
Stocks, bonds and securities. *See also Government securities*
direct investment by S&Ls - 82, 83-84
dual trading - 194, 195
foreign banks - 189
index futures regulation - 190-193, 194-195
insider trading - 195, 537
market regulation - 190-193
boxscore - 190
provisions - 191
summary - 5
penny stocks - 193, 194
program trading - 191, 192
registration, transaction fees - 123
securities violations enforcement - 193-194
small corporations - 169
small-issue bonds - 160, 173
transactions oversight - 881
Stoddard, Tom - 481 (box)
Stokes, Louis D-Ohio (21)
Energy, water appropriations - 862
minorities in Congress - 924 (chart)
minority health - 596
SSC authorization - 439
Stoltenberg, Gerhard - 699
Strategic and Critical Minerals Act - 442-443
Strategic arms limitation treaty (SALT II) - 707
Strategic arms reduction treaty (START)
action, 1990 - 704-708
Bush, Gorbachev statement - 708
defense appropriations - 821
defense authorization - 672, 674, 680
Soviet-U.S. relations - 757, 758
Washington summit - 696, 701, 702
Strategic defense initiative (SDI)
appropriations - 812, 815 (chart), 816, 817, 820, 822-823, 846
budget action - 122
conservative coalition - 47
defense authorization - 671, 672-673, 676, 677, 682, 684, 686, 691-693
defense budget reprogramming - 676 (box)
key votes - 11-B
red team - 817
Strategic Petroleum Reserve
appropriations - 873 (chart)
congressional action, 1990 - 314-316
energy issues, 1990 - 312-313
family planning authorization - 606
Persian Gulf crisis - 732
Strauss, David A. - 509
Strikes
alien workers - 483
Eastern Airlines - 369
Stroke - 596
Structural Impediments Initiative (SII) talks - 208-209
Studds, Gerry E. D-Mass. (10)
Antarctica protection - 306
barrier island protection - 302
beach water quality - 290
congressional elections, 1990 - 922
marginal vote share - 905 (chart)
vote-share falloff - 904 (chart)
El Salvador aid - 782-783
fish inspection - 396-399
Nicaragua aid - 772
oil pollution cleanup - 284
Persian Gulf crisis
U.S. goals, rationales - 744 (box)
Student aid
appropriations - 849 (chart)
athletes right-to-know - 613
budget action - 123, 143
Caribbean Basin Initiative - 214
child-care providers - 153, 555
community development work-study - 655
community, national service - 559-562
drug penalties - 505, 614
eligibility - 610, 611
employer-paid aid - 160, 173
federal employees - 682
food stamps - 355
loan defaults - 614
federal court caseload - 520
ineligibility of high-rate schools - 143, 611, 613, 626-627 (box)
math, science scholarships - 612 (box)
medical scholarships, loans - 595
Poland, Hungary scholarships - 834
police scholarships - 493
sequestration procedures - 162
teacher training - 615
unaccredited schools ban - 613
veterans' benefits - 686
vocational education authorization - 619-623
Student Loan Default Act - 626-627 (box)
Student Loan Marketing Association - 163
Student Loan Reconciliation Amendments of 1989 - 627 (box)
Student Right-to-Know and Campus Security Act - 624-627
Stump, Bob R-Ariz. (3)
Agent Orange compensation - 419
Arizona wilderness protection - 304
congressional elections, 1990
vote-share falloff - 904 (chart)
Sturgulewski, Arliss - 927, 929
Sub-Saharan Africa
debt relief - 207
foreign aid appropriations - 831-832, 832 (chart), 836, 843
Submarine-launched ballistic missiles. *See also Trident II missiles*
START - 704, 708
Submarines
appropriations - 819
budget action - 122
deactivation plan - 672
defense authorization - 675, 685-686
strategic weapons triad - 688
Substance abuse. *See Alcohol abuse and alcoholism; Drug abuse*
Substance Abuse Prevention, Office for - 504
Suburban areas
Clean Air Act - 245
job training overhaul - 365
trauma care - 597
Sudan
U.S. aid/human rights - 776, 836, 845
Sugar
Caribbean Basin Initiative - 211, 212, 213, 216, 217
Nicaragua aid - 771, 773
price supports - 328, 331, 334, 341, 343, 349, 350
Suicide prevention
mental health services authorization - 599
Sulfur dioxide. *See Acid rain*
Sullivan, Joseph G. - 772
Sullivan, Louis W.
animal rights activists - 442
antismoking bills - 593
children's welfare services - 556
disabled civil rights - 451, 460
Head Start, human services authorization - 552, 556
immigration exclusions - 480-481 (box)
Medicaid - 125
Medicare changes - 565
minority health - 596
NIH authorization - 601, 604
nutrition labels - 576
orphan drugs - 578
public health planning - 609
Sullivan, Mike - 930
Sun Belt states
census count adjustment - 415
Sundlum, Bruce - 928
Sundquist, Don R-Tenn. (7)
children's welfare services - 556
congressional elections, 1990 - 917
vote-share falloff - 904 (chart)
congressional leadership - 12
Sunflowers. *See Oilseeds*
Sunset provisions
alternative power regulation - 318
student aid - 143
Sunstein, Cass - 52
Sununu, John H.
Armenian genocide commemoration - 807
budget action - 112, 113, 130-132, 137
campaign finance reform - 60
civil rights/job bias - 466, 467
Clean Air Act - 237, 243
community service programs - 559
currency joke - 197
Douglas election defeat - 917
Education secretary - 614 (box)
family leave - 360
Hatch Act revision - 408, 411
OMB review powers - 413
RNC chair - 910
Souter confirmation - 508, 509
Super Stallion helicopters - 675
Superconducting super collider (SSC)
appropriations - 861-866
authorization - 438-439

budget action - 126
Superconductivity
critical minerals - 443
technology transfer - 440
Superfund
appropriations - 858
budget action - 124, 155, 159
military base cleanup - 679-680
summary - 5
Supplemental appropriations - 174
Supplemental Assistance for Facilities to Assist the Homeless - 655
Supplemental Loans for Students (SLS) - 626-627 (box)
Supplemental Medical Insurance. *See Medicare*
Supplemental Security Income (SSI)
appropriations - 848 (chart)
budget action - 150
Indian eligibility - 423
representative payees - 557
Support for Eastern European Democracies Act of 1989 (SEED) - 207
Supportive Housing Demonstration Program - 655
Supreme Court, U.S. *See also Supreme Court cases; Supreme Court decisions*
appropriations - 883 (chart)
justices
Brennan career - 510-511 (box)
Reagan, Bush appointments - 516-519
Souter confirmation - 508-515, 523
term summary - 52-56
workload - 56
Supreme Court cases
Astroline Communications v. Shurberg Broadcasting - 379 (box)
Austin v. Michigan State Chamber of Commerce - 52, 53 (box), 59 (box)
Baker v. Carr - 510, 514
Beck v. Communications Workers of America - 63
Bellotti v. Baird - 529
Blanchard v. Bergeron - 54, 55 (box)
Board of Education of Westside Community Schools v. Mergens - 52, 53 (box), 618 (box)
Boeing Co. v. United States - 53 (box)
Brown v. Board of Education - 511 (box), 512
Buckley v. Valeo - 58, 64
Business Electronics Corp. v. Sharp Electronics - 539, 540
Butler v. McKellar - 489 (box), 496
Cooper v. Aaron - 510 (box)
Cruzan v. Director, Missouri Department of Health - 53 (box), 55, 566-567 (box)
Davis v. Passman - 511 (box)
Dellmuth v. Muth - 54, 616, 617
Dole v. United Steelworkers of America - 53 (box), 412 (box)
Dr. Miles Medical Co. v. John D. Parks and Sons - 539
Eastland v. United States Servicemen's Fund - 511 (box)
Employment Division, Department of Human Resources v. Smith - 514
Federal Election Commission v. Massachusetts Citizens for Life - 59 (box)
Goldberg v. Kelly - 510
Griggs v. Duke Power Co. - 463
Griswold v. Connecticut - 513
Hartigan v. Zbaraz - 529
H. J. Inc. v. Northwestern Bell Telephone Co. - 537
Hodgson v. Minnesota - 53 (box), 529
Hutchinson v. Proxmire - 511 (box)
Idaho v. Wright - 53 (box)
Immigration and Naturalization Service v. Chadha - 205, 212
Independent Federation of Flight Attendants v. Zipes - 463, 466
Kastigan v. United States - 535
Lorance v. AT&T Technologies - 463, 464, 466, 468
Martin v. Wilks - 463, 465, 466, 468, 469
Maryland v. Craig - 53 (box)
McClesky v. Kemp - 491
Metro Broadcasting v. Federal Communications Commission - 52, 53 (box), 379 (box), 510-511 (box)
Michigan v. Sitz - 52, 53 (box)
Milkovich v. Lorain Journal Co. - 53 (box)
Miranda v. Arizona - 514
Missouri v. Jenkins - 53 (box)
Monsanto v. Spray-Rite Service Corp. - 539
New York Times Co. v. Sullivan - 510
Ohio v. Akron Center for Reproductive Health - 53 (box), 529
Osborne v. Ohio - 53 (box)
Patterson v. McLean Credit Union - 463, 464, 466
Pennsylvania v. Union Gas Co. - 55 (box)
Pension Benefit Guaranty Corp. v. LTV - 53 (box), 368
Perpich v. Department of Defense - 52, 53 (box), 694 (box)
Price Waterhouse v. Hopkins - 463, 466, 468
Public Citizen v. Department of Justice - 55 (box)
Public Employees Retirement System of Ohio v. Betts - 362-364
Roe v. Wade - 54, 55, 528-529, 510 (box), 513-514, 515
Rutan v. Republican Party of Illinois - 52, 53 (box), 933
Saffle v. Parks - 489 (box), 496
Sawyer v. Smith - 489 (box)
Secretary of the Interior v. California - 154, 288
Sedima S.P.R.L. v. Imrex Co. - 536
Spallone v. United States - 52, 53 (box)
Sullivan v. Everhart - 55 (box)
Teague v. Lane - 489 (box), 496
Texas v. Johnson - 52, 524
United States v. Colgate & Co. - 540
United States v. Curtiss-Wright Export Corp. - 739 (box)
United States v. Eichman - 52, 53 (box), 55, 524
United States v. Haggerty - 524
University of Pennsylvania v. Equal Employment Opportunity Commission - 53 (box), 623
Wards Cove v. Atonio - 463, 465, 466, 467
Washington v. Harper - 53 (box)
Webster v. Reproductive Health Services - 528, 529
Wilder v. Virginia Hospital Association - 53 (box), 571
Supreme Court decisions
abortion - 55, 56, 528-529, 531, 604, 605
age discrimination in benefits - 362-364
budget process - 176
campaign finance - 58, 59 (box), 63
capital punishment - 486, 490, 491, 494, 496
habeas corpus appeals - 488-489 (box)
child pornography - 55
congressional elections - 14
disabled education - 616, 617
employee drug testing - 505
executive branch honoraria - 72 (box)
federal-state consistency provision - 154, 288
flag desecration - 55, 524-528
immunity - 535
job discrimination - 32, 462-473, 623
legislative veto - 205, 211, 212-213
major decisions, 1989-90 - 53 (box)
Medicaid pay suits - 571
minority broadcasting set-asides - 379 (box)
National Guard training exercises - 694 (box)
OMB review powers - 411, 412 (box)
outlawed religious practices - 514
pension guaranty - 368
pocket veto power - 21
political patronage jobs - 933
privacy - 513
religious groups in schools - 618
RICO revision - 536-538
right to die - 55, 566-567 (box)
school desegregation - 510-511 (box), 512
vertical price fixing - 539-540
war powers - 739 (box)
Surface Mining, Office of - 873 (chart)
Surgeon general
antismoking bills - 593, 594
radiation victims compensation - 591
toxic air pollutants - 256
Suzuki Motor Co. - 280
Swamps. *See Wetlands protection*
Swartz, Rick - 480
Sweden
U.S. immigration policy - 483
Sweet, Robert W. Jr. - 506
Swett, Dick - 905 (box), 916, 918 (chart)
Swift, Al D-Wash. (2)
campaign finance reform - 58-59, 66-68
TV ad rates - 66-67 (box)
congressional elections, 1990 - 909
low winning percentage - 906 (chart)
marginal vote share - 905 (chart)
"motor voter" bill - 70
toxic air pollutants - 239
Symington, Fife - 907-908, 926, 930, 933
Symms, Steve R-Idaho
AIDS bill - 583
budget action - 164, 165
Clean Air Act - 234-238, 245
CPSC authorization - 393-395
housing programs overhaul - 656
money laundering - 189
nuclear test treaties - 712
Synar, Mike D-Okla. (2)
antismoking bills - 594
campaign finance reform - 66-68
civil rights/job bias - 470
Clean Air Act - 244
EPA Cabinet status - 292, 293
farm bill - 349
flag desecration - 526
Interior appropriations - 873-874
Syria
questionable gulf allies - 740 (box)
U.S. export controls - 201

T

Tabor, Eric - 918 (chart)
Tacit Rainbow - 706, 707, 708, 818
Taft-Hartley Labor Management Relations Act of 1947 - 659 (box)
Taft Institute - 618, 628
Taiwan
China-U.S. relations - 766
drift-net fishing - 399
U.S. trade
tobacco exports - 593
Take Pride in America - 304
Talmadge, Herman E. - 98, 99 (box), 100 (box), 102
Tanker ships
double hulls - 284-285
Tanks, military
appropriations - 817-818, 823, 824
CFE treaty - 696, 697 (chart), 700, 702, 703, 757, 758
defense authorization - 674, 684-685
Tanks, storage
leaking underground tank fund - 159, 172
Targeted Export Assistance Program (TEAP) - 331, 338, 345, 868
Tariffs
China-U.S. trade - 765, 766
Czechoslovak-U.S. trade - 206
Latin American aid - 218
Mexico-U.S. trade - 218
MFN status - 204
textile import quotas - 219-220
Task Force on Campaign Reform - 58
Tate, Dan - 402
Tauke, Tom R-Iowa (2)
antismoking bills - 594
community service programs - 562
congressional elections, 1990 - 876, 913, 922
House membership changes - 918 (chart)
congressional partisanship - 40
energy conservation - 319
Head Start authorization - 554, 555
Pepper Commission - 608
Tauzin, W. J. "Billy" D-La. (3)
Clean Air Act - 241
conservative coalition - 47
family planning authorization - 605
hazardous materials transport - 381
offshore drilling - 312
oil pollution cleanup - 285, 287
Persian Gulf crisis - 743
pipeline safety inspection - 286 (box)
Strategic Petroleum Reserve - 315
Tavenner, Mary T. - 360
Tax Court, U.S. - 887 (chart)
Tax Reform Act of 1986 - 165, 214
Taxation. *See also Business taxes; Capital gains tax; Excise taxes; Fuel and gasoline taxes; Import taxes; Income taxes; Internal Revenue Service; User fees*
budget action - 111-113, 117, 128, 130-136
chronology - 114-115
key votes - 8-B, 13-B
revenue raisers, losers (chart) - 171
reconciliation provisions - 157-160, 167-173
Bush economic report - 116-117
Clean Air Act fees - 236, 244
compliance - 889
D.C. appropriations - 891
election issue, 1990 - 902-903
financial institution fraud - 183
Pepper Commission - 608
SEC fees - 881
Taxis - 229, 247
Taylor, Charles H. - 905 (chart), 917, 918 (chart)
Taylor, Gene D-Miss. (5)
conservative coalition - 47
roll call attendance - 48
Taylor, William W. III - 82, 87, 93, 96, 97
TB. *See Tuberculosis*
TDD. *See Telecommunications devices for the deaf*
Teachers
awards - 611

certification standards - 610-613
child-care aid - 551
disabled education - 616-617
drug-abuse education - 505
education proposals - 610-615
Head Start authorization - 552-556
math, science scholarships - 612 (box)
middle-schools - 613
minimum competency standards - 613
recruitment - 610, 615
student aid - 615
summary - 7
vocational education authorization - 620-623
TEAP. *See Targeted Export Assistance Program*
Teapot Dome scandal - 57
Tech-prep education - 621, 622-623
Technical and Miscellaneous Revenue Act of 1988 - 160
Technology Administration - 440-441, 882 (chart)
Technology Assessment, Office of
appropriations - 895 (chart)
disabled civil rights - 450, 456, 458
hazardous materials transport - 380
motor vehicle emissions standards - 252
Teenagers. *See Adolescents and youth*
TEFAP. *See Temporary Emergency Food Assistance Program*
Telecommunications
disabled civil rights - 447-449, 457-458
export controls - 199
Japan-U.S. trade - 209
rural development - 347, 352
vocational education authorization - 621
Telecommunications devices for the deaf (TDDs)
disabled civil rights - 457-458
Tele-Communications Inc. - 371
Telecommunications Research and Action Center - 378 (box)
Telephone Association, U.S. - 371
Telephone communications
Baby Bell restrictions - 377-379
cable TV regulation - 370-372
disabled civil rights - 448
911 service - 453
TDD, relay services - 457-458
emergency medical service - 597
equipment manufacture - 377-378
excise taxes
budget action - 126, 159, 172
child-care funding - 547, 550
operator services regulation - 378 (box)
radio spectrum allocation - 376
rural financing - 123, 353
Social Security centers - 151, 557
telemarketing curbs, fraud - 379, 402, 881
Television
campaign finance reform - 57, 60-65, 66-67 (box)
children's advertising, programming - 373-375
close-captioned broadcasts - 449, 458, 375
closed-circuit court testimony - 499
HDTV - 440
minority set-aside licenses - 52, 53, 379 (box), 510-511 (box)
must-carry rules - 370-372, 373
public service rules - 377
radio spectrum allocation - 376-377
Senate administration - 12 (box)
South Africa sanctions - 788
sports lottery ad ban - 495
violence guidelines - 374 (box), 520, 523
Teller, Edward - 691
Tellico Dam - 875
Temporary Emergency Food Assistance Program (TEFAP) - 346, 354-355
Tennessee
acid rain - 262
congressional elections, 1990
voter turnout - 901 (chart)
corporate campaign limits - 59 (box)
Energy, water appropriations - 865
federal judgeships - 522
gubernatorial election, 1990 - 930
wildlife protection - 875
Tennessee Valley Authority - 163, 862 (chart)
Territories, U.S.
duty-free allowances - 213
vocational education authorization - 620
Terrorism and counterterrorism
aviation security - 17, 389-390
biological weapons ban - 507
civil damages suits - 829, 830
death penalty - 487, 494
foreign aid appropriations - 833 (chart)
immigration law revision - 474
military role - 677
Persian Gulf crisis
Iraq-U.S. relations - 722, 724
questionable Gulf allies - 740 (box)
Saudi arms sales - 734 (box)
PLO talks - 800, 802
Texarkana, Texas - 828
Texas. *See also Houston*
abortion - 529, 530
barrier island protection - 302, 303
campaign finance reform - 62
corporate campaign limits - 59 (box)
CDBG funding formula - 641
child support enforcement - 150
Clean Air Act - 230, 237, 242
offshore drilling emissions - 230, 244
savings and loan bailout - 239
"colonias" housing aid - 654
congressional redistricting - 931, 933
energy taxes - 313 (box)
farm bill - 343
federal judgeships - 520, 522
gubernatorial election, 1990 - 902, 903, 928-929
immigration law revision - 477, 478
job training overhaul - 365
naval home ports - 678, 681 (box)
oil pollution cleanup - 283, 284
Strategic Petroleum Reserve - 314
super collider - 438-439, 861-862, 864, 866
V-22 Osprey support - 676
water projects authorization - 299
wetlands preservation - 872-873
Texas A&M University - 888
Texas Air Corp. - 369
Texas, University of (El Paso) - 888
Textile, Apparel and Footwear Trade Act - 219-222
Textiles
Caribbean Basin Initiative - 211, 212, 216
cotton import quota - 342
GATT talks - 209, 210
import quotas - 219-222
boxscore - 219
key votes - 12-B, 13-B
veto message - 221
prison industries - 498
Soviet-U.S. trade - 205 (box)
Textron, Inc. - 859
Thailand
Cambodian civil war - 838
U.S. tobacco exports - 593
Thatcher, Margaret - 725, 732
Third World debt
Andean Initiative - 806
Brooke-Alexander waivers - 777
budget process changes - 161, 178
commercial bank loans - 207, 834
debt-for-nature swaps - 778, 779
development bank authorization - 207
Egypt relief - 161, 730, 733, 786, 811, 830-831, 840, 841, 842
Food for Peace - 337-338, 804
Latin American aid - 217-218
Nicaragua aid - 771, 774
Panama aid - 775-779
Thomas, Bill R-Calif. (20)
campaign finance reform - 68
congressional elections, 1990 - 907
"motor voter" bill - 70
Thomas, Clarence - 516, 518-519 (box)
Thomas, Craig R-Wyo. (AL)
radiation victims compensation - 591
Thompson, James R. - 70, 933
Thompson, Robert L. - 324
Thompson, Tommy G. - 530, 929
Thornburgh, Dick
budget action - 125
civil rights/job bias - 464, 465-466
crime bill - 496
disabled civil rights - 448
financial institution fraud - 182, 495
Hatch Act revision - 408, 410
HUD scandal investigation - 666-667
judicial appointments - 517
Thornton, Ray - 916, 918 (chart), 919, 925
Threshold Test Ban Treaty - 711, 713
Thrift Supervision, Office of (OTS)
director - 179, 180 (box)
savings and loan scandal - 93, 95
thrift fraud prosecutions - 182
Thrifts. *See Savings and loan associations*
Thurmond, Strom R-S.C.
characteristics of Congress - 924-925
congressional elections, 1990 - 916
conservative coalition - 48
crime bill - 486-487, 489, 491-493, 498-499
defense authorization - 679
displaced homemakers - 366 (box)
flag desecration - 527
juvenile justice nomination - 506
NEA authorization - 431
nutrition labels - 576
savings and loan scandal - 94
Souter confirmation - 511-512, 514
textile import quotas - 220, 221
Thomas confirmation - 518 (box)
vertical price fixing - 539, 540
vocational education authorization - 623
Tibet
China-U.S. relations - 765, 766
displaced nationals - 476, 483
Tillman Act of 1907 - 59 (box)
Tillman, Benjamin R. - 99 (box)
Timber. *See Forests and wood products*
Timmons, Becky H. - 627
Titan IV satellite launch vehicles - 675
Tobacco
antismoking bills - 592-594
commodity loan fees - 141, 344
employee use in job bias suits - 471
excise taxes - 158, 167, 169, 172
fire-safe cigarettes - 402
lighter safety - 395
stop-smoking drugs - 146
Tobacco Institute - 593, 594
Tolley, Bill - 918 (chart)
Tomahawk missiles - 675, 706, 815 (chart), 818
Tongass National Forest
timber sales - 5-6, 294-295
boxscore - 294
Tongass Timber Reform Act - 294-295
Tongour, Michael - 39
Torres, Esteban E. D-Calif. (34)
immigration law revision - 485
money laundering - 188
Torricelli, Robert G. D-N.J. (9)
Antarctica protection - 306
congressional mail - 74
minorities in Congress - 924 (chart)
Torture - 806-807
TOW missiles - 674, 735 (box), 818, 823, 824
Towns, Edolphus D-N.Y. (1)
minorities in Congress - 924 (chart)
Toxic Substances Control Act - 154
Toxic substances. *See Hazardous substances*
Toyota - 280
Toys
children's TV advertising - 373-375
China-U.S. relations - 765
safety - 394
Trade Act of 1974 - 204, 208, 211
Trade Adjustment Assistance - 123
Trade agreements. *See also General Agreement on Tariffs and Trade*
approval procedures - 205, 211, 212-213
Canada-U.S. - 203
Czechoslovak-U.S. trade - 205-206
Japan-U.S. SII accords - 208
Mexico-U.S. talks - 218
Poland-U.S. trade - 206
MFN status - 204
Soviet U.S. accord - 205, 757, 758, 759, 761
textiles - 219
Trade Representative, U.S.
appropriations - 882 (chart), 884
authorization - 211, 212
foreign ownership of U.S. business - 224
GATT talks - 209
Japan-U.S. trade - 208-209
lobbying curbs - 881, 886
timber exports - 215
Trade schools
recruiter pay ban - 613
student loan defaults - 626-627 (box)
vocational education authorization - 619-623
Traficant, James A. Jr. D-Ohio (17)
appropriations
defense - 816
foreign aid - 840
supplemental FY90 - 845
Transportation - 878
Treasury, Postal Service - 888-889
congressional elections, 1990 - 908
crime bill - 497
defense authorization - 683
SSC authorization - 439
water projects authorization - 298
Trammell, William and Mary - 392
Tranquilizers - 146
Trans-Alaska Pipeline - 284
Trans-Alaska Pipeline Authorization Act - 283
Transportation. *See also Air transportation; Automobiles; Bus transportation; Fuel and gasoline taxes; Highways and roads; Mass transit; Motor vehicles; Railroads; Transportation Department; Trucks and trucking*
budget action - 128
disabled civil rights - 447-461
drug testing - 502, 503, 505
Transportation Department, U.S. (DOT)
appropriations - 876-880
aviation
airline LBOs - 388
airport fees, spending - 156, 385-386
noise abatement - 384, 388

security - 389-390
slot allocation - 385, 387
summary - 6
budget action - 126
disabled civil rights - 453-458
drug tests - 453, 505
motor vehicles
food-waste backhauling - 382-383
hazardous materials safety - 380-382
highway trust fund - 385
police radar detector ban - 880
railroads
Amtrak authorization - 390
user fees - 157
shipping
double hulls - 285
space launch fees - 157
transportation policy - 384
Trash. *See Waste products*
Travel agents - 386
Travel and Tourism Administration, U.S. - 386, 882 (chart)
Travel and tourist trade
Antarctica protection - 306
beach water quality - 290
Caribbean study - 214
China-U.S. relations - 766
congressional home visits - 102
federal government shutdown - 137
Florida Keys protection - 303
hotel fire safety - 402
Iraq trade sanctions - 725
Panama aid - 778
passenger fees - 157, 386
SBA authorization - 395
Soviet aviation agreement - 759
Traxler, Bob D-Mich. (8)
housing programs overhaul - 642
space station design - 436-437
Transportation appropriations - 878
VA/HUD appropriations - 856, 859, 860
HUD pork-barrel spending - 857 (box)
Treason
death penalty - 487, 490, 494
Treasury Department, U.S.
appropriations - 886-890
assault weapons ban - 495, 500-501 (box)
capital gains tax - 168 (box)
CFTC authorization - 195
Customs fees - 156
debt ceiling increase - 165 (box)
deposit insurance - 185
earned income tax credit - 152, 158
Food for Peace - 804
foreign banks - 189, 203
foreign ownership of U.S. business - 225
funds
coin sales - 197
EPA fees - 155
lost interest - 161
mine reclamation fund surplus - 154
patent user fees - 157
government-sponsored enterprises - 163
money laundering - 188, 189, 499
Panama aid - 775
state grant funds transfers - 414
stock market regulation - 191, 192, 193
textile import quotas - 220
Third World debt - 207, 730
thrift bailout - 179-184
World Bank China loans - 207
Treasury securities. *See Government securities*
Treaties and international agreements. *See also Arms control; Trade agreements*
Arctic islands - 760
congressional-executive relations - 800
environmental protection - 292
Antarctica - 305-307
Canada-U.S. water quality - 290, 301
global warming - 307
oil-spill protocols - 284
ozone-layer - 230, 269, 270, 271
German unification - 762-763
nuclear cooperation - 800
Panama bank secrecy - 779
torture ban - 806-807
Treatment Improvement, Office for - 504
Treverton, Gregory F. - 791
Tribes. *See Indians*
Trident II missiles
appropriations - 815 (chart), 817, 822, 824
authorization - 674, 684
Trident missile launching submarines
appropriations - 815 (chart), 817, 822, 824
authorization - 674
Trinidad and Tobago - 212
Trucks and trucking
clean-fuel vehicles - 253-254
emissions standards - 231 (box), 251-252
food-waste transport - 382-383
hazardous materials transport - 381
literacy of commercial drivers - 611
military vehicles - 685, 818
radar detector ban - 880
railroad fuel taxes - 172
rest area drug traffic - 383, 502
safety-rating information - 383
Trull, Frankie - 441
Trump, Donald J. - 388
Trump shuttle - 387
Trust Indenture Act - 194
Tuberculosis
immigration exclusion - 480-481 (box)
prevention services - 594
Tucker, Robert - 729
Tucson, Ariz. - 216
Tuna - 211, 399
Turkey
Armenian genocide commemoration - 807-808
CFE - 698, 701
helicopter sales - 643
Persian Gulf crisis - 729
textile import quotas - 221, 222
U.S. aid
defense appropriations - 822
foreign aid appropriations - 831, 833, 835, 840-841, 844
Turner, James P. - 448
Turner, Maurice T. Jr. - 428
Tutwiler, Margaret D. - 725
TV Marti - 881, 884, 886
Twenty-second Amendment - 14, 15
Twilegar, Ron J. - 913 (chart)

U

UDAG. *See Urban Development Action Grants*
Udall, Morris K. D-Ariz. (2)
Arizona wilderness protection - 304
Grand Canyon erosion - 301
Interior Committee leadership - 924
Udall, Stewart L. - 301, 590
Uddo, Basile J. - 533
Ukraine Famine Commission - 882 (chart)
Ulcer medication - 210-216
UMTA. *See Urban Mass Transit Administration*
Unanimous consent - 184
Unemployment compensation
appropriations - 853
census workers - 213
displaced workers
Clean Air Act - 236-238, 242-243, 275, 277 (box)
defense cutbacks - 683
increase proposal - 368
payroll taxes - 159, 172
surplus revenues - 150
Unemployment Trust Fund - 150
UNITA. *See National Union for the Total Independence of Angola*
United Airlines - 387, 388
United Arab Emirates - 724-725, 732
United Auto Workers - 280, 362
United Fisheries of Alaska - 295
United Jewish Appeal - 701
United Kingdom. *See Great Britain; Northern Ireland*
United Mine Workers of America - 277 (box)
United Nations (U.N.)
Cambodia seat - 793, 794
El Salvador talks - 782, 785, 841
Nicaragua aid - 772, 773
Palestinian issues - 743, 837
peacekeeping forces - 885
Persian Gulf crisis - 717-721, 728-733, 737-742
Resolution 678 (text) - 737
summary - 3
South Africa sanctions - 787
Soviet espionage - 802
torture ban treaty - 806-807
U.S. contributions - 802
budget action - 124
Commerce/Justice/State appropriations - 884, 885
State Department authorization - 799
United Nations Children's Fund (UNICEF) - 837
United Nations Fund for Population Activities - 831, 837, 838-839 (box), 840, 841
University. *See other part of name*
UNO. *See National Opposition Union*
Unsoeld, Jolene D-Wash. (3)
assault weapons ban - 501 (box)
congressional elections, 1990
marginal vote share - 905 (chart)
conservative coalition - 40
crime bill - 497
minorities in Congress - 924 (chart)
Upton, Fred R-Mich. (4)
congressional elections, 1990
low winning percentage - 906 (chart)
Uranium
Clean Air Act - 276
enrichment enterprise - 310, 317-318, 862 (chart)
Pakistan nuclear potential - 769
radiation victims compensation - 590
research - 864
Urban areas
census count adjustment - 415-416, 932
community service programs - 561
disabled civil rights - 449
dropout prevention - 618
drug-trafficking hot spots - 889
environmental issues
Clean Air Act - 229-259, 275-279
street water runoff - 289
waste disposal - 259
federal pay overhaul - 405-407
health care
AIDS - 582, 583, 584, 589, 852, 853
drug-abuse prevention, treatment - 504, 505
Health Service Corps - 595
Indian health care - 422-423
Medicare hospital payments - 563, 568
job training overhaul - 365
slum clearance - 632
teacher shortages - 615
youth employment - 123
Urban Development Action Grants (UDAG) program
HUD scandal investigation - 666-667
Urban homesteading - 636, 647, 656
Urban Mass Transit Administration
appropriations - 877, 879, 879 (chart)
budget action - 126
disabled civil rights - 449
Urgent Assistance for Democracy in Panama Act - 774, 776-777
Uruguay Round. *See General Agreement on Tariffs and Trade*
U.S.-Canada Great Lakes Water Quality Agreement - 290, 301
USDA. *See Agriculture Department, U.S.*
User fees
agricultural loan origination - 141
aviation package - 126, 156, 384, 385
budget action - 111, 117, 126, 128, 129, 134, 156-157
CFTC authorization - 194, 195
Coast Guard services - 126, 136, 157, 386 (box)
Copyright Office - 543
Customs processing - 156-157, 211
DOE study - 157
EPA services - 154-155, 157
FDA drug approvals - 125
fish inspection - 397
Medicaid, Medicare certification - 125, 146
NRC licenses - 124, 136, 155
patent registrations - 157
radio spectrum allocation - 377
railroad safety administration - 157
REA loan guarantees - 124
SEC filings - 881
securities transactions - 123
shipping, tonnage duties - 157
space launches - 157
travel, tourist fees - 157
VA services - 126, 155, 420
water projects authorization - 299
weather services - 157
USIA. *See Information Agency, U.S.*
USTR. *See Trade Representative, U.S.*
Utah
Amtrak waste disposal - 392
community services block grant - 555
congressional elections, 1990 - 916
congressional redistricting - 932
federal judgeships - 522
irrigation subsidies - 357
oil-shale lands - 316
radiation victims compensation - 590
water projects authorization - 299
Uzis. *See Firearms*

V

V-22 Osprey aircraft
appropriations - 812, 815 (chart), 819, 825
authorization - 671, 675, 676, 677, 680, 686
budget action - 122
VA. *See Veterans Affairs Department*
Valentine, Tim D-N.C. (2)

flag desecration - 526
Van Cleve, George W. - 285
Vandalism
"hate crime" statistics - 506
Van de Kamp, John - 15
Vander Jagt, Guy R-Mich. (9)
campaign finance reform - 58
congressional elections, 1990 - 904, 917
low winning percentage - 906 (chart)
marginal vote share - 905 (chart)
congressional leadership - 12
Van Hollen, Christopher Jr. - 723
Van Paasschen, Gwendolyn - 88
Vatour, Roland R. - 353
Vento, Bruce F. D-Minn. (4)
congressional leadership - 11 (box)
disabled civil rights - 459
FHA rules revision - 659-661
housing programs overhaul - 642
logging/wildlife protection - 296-297
Tongass forest protection - 295
Vermont
congressional elections, 1990 - 922 (box)
congressional mail - 75
gubernatorial election, 1990 - 902, 928, 930
Veterans. *See also Disabled veterans; Veterans Affairs Department; Veterans health care; Vietnam veterans*
appropriations - 846
benefit overpayment cases - 520
budget action - 155-156
community service programs - 561
education benefits - 421, 686
federal hiring preference - 421
Filipino naturalization - 484
housing aid - 126, 156, 420, 859-860
job training - 421
Persian Gulf War benefits - 755
rehabilitation, discharge upgrade - 421
SBA authorization - 395
Veterans Affairs Department, U.S. (VA)
Agent Orange compensation - 418-419
AIDS bill - 584
appropriations - 845, 854-860
budget action - 126, 155-156
homeless veterans - 420
housing programs - 420, 649, 650
jobs programs - 421
medical personnel retention - 419-420
medical research grants - 420-421
tax information access - 160
Veterans Appeals Court - 855 (chart)
Veterans' health care
Agent Orange compensation - 418-419
appropriations - 845, 854-855, 856, 858
budget action - 126, 155
nurses pay - 418, 419-420
personnel retention - 420
SDI authorization debate - 692
Veterans interest groups
Agent Orange compensation - 418, 419
flag desecration - 526
Veterans of Foreign Wars - 728, 729
Veterans Recruitment Authority - 421
Veterinary medicine
agricultural research - 345
screwworm eradication - 355
Vetoes
Bush congressional relations - 16
Bush vetoes, 1990 - 17 (box)
pocket veto limits - 21-22
Vice presidents, U.S.
death penalty for assassination - 494, 497
residence appropriations - 887 (chart), 888
Video
cable TV regulation - 370
Video games - 542
Vietnam
Cambodian policies - 793, 794, 837-838, 841, 844
development bank loans - 207
Vietnam veterans
Agent Orange compensation - 418-419
Vietnam Veterans of America - 418, 419, 420
Vietnam War
Persian Gulf crisis - 733, 739, 741, 746, 753 (box), 756
Violence
TV guidelines - 374 (box)
Virgin Islands
barrier island protection - 303
child-care block grants - 152
community development block grants - 655
food stamps - 346, 354
vocational education authorization - 620
Virginia
abortion - 529
airport slot allocation - 386
CDBG funding formula - 641
commuter rail line - 390-392
congressional elections, 1990 - 909, 916
congressional redistricting - 931
federal judgeships - 522
Hatch Act revision - 410
offshore oil drilling - 872
water projects authorization - 297-300
Virginia Beach, Va. - 297-300
Visas. *See Immigration and emigration*
Visclosky, Peter J. D-Ind. (1)
congressional elections, 1990
low winning percentage - 906 (chart)
VISTA Literacy Corps - 611
Vocational education
appropriations - 848 (chart)
budget action - 123
disabled education - 616
Perkins Act authorization - 619-623
boxscore - 619
provisions - 620-622
summary - 5
Vocational rehabilitation
program choice - 151
sequestration procedures - 162
SSI - 150
veterans - 156
Voight, Karsten - 699
Voinovich, George V. - 530, 929
Volcker, Paul A. - 405-406
Volkmer, Harold L. D-Mo. (9)
farm bill - 329
Interior appropriations - 871, 874
logging/wildlife protection - 297
timber sales - 358
Volunteers
community service programs - 5, 559-562
Volunteers in Service to America (VISTA) - 611, 560
Von Raab, William - 94
Voter participation
get-out-the-vote drives - 58, 62, 63
Indians - 421
"motor voter" bill - 70
Puerto Rico - 424
voter turnout, 1962-90 (chart) - 901
Voter registration
campaign finance reform - 58, 62, 63
driver's license tie-in - 69-70
savings and loan scandal - 85, 93
Voting rights
D.C. status - 428
Puerto Rico status - 426
Souter confirmation - 514
Voting Rights Act of 1965 - 69-70
Vreeland, Frederick - 801
Vroom, Jay J. - 336
Vucanovich, Barbara F. R-Nev. (2)
minorities in Congress - 924 (chart)
Persian Gulf crisis
use-of-force debate - 753 (box)

W

Wagner-Peyser Act - 620
Waihee, John III - 930, 934
Wald, Patricia M. - 54, 535
Walesa, Lech - 204, (box)
Walgren, Doug D-Pa. (18)
congressional elections, 1990 - 917
defeated House members - 917 (chart)
House membership changes - 918 (chart)
vote-share falloff - 904 (chart)
CPSC authorization - 394
Walker, Robert S. R-Pa. (16)
appropriations bills
agriculture - 868
Energy, water - 861, 864, 866
HUD pork-barrel spending - 857 (box)
Interior - 876
Labor/HHS - 850
community service programs - 562
crime bill - 488-489
education proposals - 614
Hatch Act revision - 410
presidential support in Congress - 31
revision of remarks - 105
SSC authorization - 439
technology programs - 441
Wall, M. Danny - 79, 84, 85, 89, 93, 180 (box)
Waller, Calvin A. H. - 721
Wallman, Katherine - 415
Wallop, Malcolm R-Wyo.
AIDS bill - 586
B-2 bomber - 689
cable TV regulation - 370, 372
Clean Air Act - 235, 238, 278
defense authorization - 672, 677, 679, 680
housing programs overhaul - 656
Nicaragua policy debate - 772 (box)
nuclear test treaties - 712
Persian Gulf crisis - 738
SDI - 692
Walsh, Lawrence E. - 534, 535
Walters, David - 928
War Powers Resolution of 1973
Persian Gulf crisis - 719, 727, 730, 733, 753
Warner, John W. R-Va.
Armenian genocide commemoration - 808
B-2 bomber - 690, 691
CFE - 701
congressional elections, 1990 - 916
defense authorization - 678, 679, 680
Hatch Act revision - 409
nuclear test treaties - 713
Persian Gulf crisis - 743
SDI - 693
Souter confirmation - 515
Stello nomination - 310
thrift supervisor - 180 (box)
Warren, Earl - 510 (box), 511 (box), 514
Warren, Jeffrey C. - 579
Wars *See also Persian Gulf crisis*
budget process - 162, 175
repatriation aid - 150
torture ban treaty - 806
U.S. immigration policy - 478, 483, 484
Warsaw Pact
B-2 bomber - 688
CFE - 697, 697 (chart), 700, 702, 703
defense appropriations - 824
defense authorization - 672, 685
INF treaty compliance - 680
military construction appropriations - 827
Soviet-U.S. relations - 757
Washington, Craig D-Texas (18)
civil rights/job bias - 469, 473
crime bill - 495
financial institution fraud - 183
flag desecration - 527
minorities in Congress - 924 (chart)
RICO revision - 538
Washington, D.C. *See District of Columbia*
Washington National Airport - 384-388
Washington (State)
congressional redistricting - 931
federal judgeships - 521, 522
food aid cargo preference - 339 (box)
job training overhaul - 365
logging/wildlife protection - 296-297, 870, 871
naval home ports - 681 (box)
offshore oil drilling - 872
timber exports - 215, 216
Transportation appropriations - 878
Washington summit
CFE treaty background - 696, 701-702
chemical weapons pact - 709
Soviet-U.S. trade - 204-205
START talks - 704, 707-708
Waste products. *See Hazardous waste cleanup; Nuclear waste; Sewer and sewage treatment systems*
alternative power regulation - 317
Amtrak disposal - 392
Antarctica protection - 306
beach water quality - 290
debris in outer space - 436
Energy Department cleanup - 779
federal RCRA compliance - 291, 292, 293, 308-309
food backhauling - 382-383
hazardous materials transport - 381
interstate transport - 382-383, 893
marine debris reduction - 154, 288
methane assessment - 271
methanol - 240 (box)
military base toxic waste cleanup - 816
mining wastes - 257
toxic air pollutants from combustion - 258, 259, 276
Water pollution
abandoned mines - 154
acid rain - 267
aquatic nuisance species - 303-304
beach water quality - 290
coastal, Great Lakes cleanup - 154, 289-290, 301
coastal zone management - 288-289
farm reduction - 327, 330, 335-336, 346, 349, 869
fish inspection - 396-399
oil-spill liability - 5, 283-287
sewer overflows - 289
Tongass forest protection - 295
toxic air pollutants - 254
Water Pollution Control Act - 154, 289
Water projects
appropriations - 861-866
boxscore - 861
budget authority totals (chart) - 862
authorization - 297-300
boxscore - 297
new projects - 300
irrigation subsidies - 356-357

Water Quality Incentives Program - 346
Water resources. *See also Oceans; Sewer and sewage treatment systems; Water pollution; Water projects; Water supply systems; Wetlands protection*
Grand Canyon erosion - 300
marine research - 292 (box)
zebra mussel control - 303-304
Water Resources Development Act - 297-300
Water rights - 304
Water supply systems
agriculture appropriations - 867
"colonias" housing aid - 654
irrigation subsidies - 300, 301, 356-357
mine reclamation fund - 154
rural development - 346-347, 352, 354
Watergate scandal - 57-59, 534
Waters, Maxine - 916, 918 (chart), 923, 924 (chart)
Watkins, James D.
auto fuel efficiency - 279
energy policy - 312
Energy, water appropriations - 865
plutonium plant - 122
Stello nomination - 309, 310
Watkins, Wes D-Okla. (3)
Energy, water appropriations - 863
gubernatorial election, 1990 - 919
House membership changes - 918 (chart)
Watson, Jay - 871
Watt, James B. - 302
Waxman, Henry A. D-Calif. (24)
AIDS bill - 582, 583, 589
animal rights activists - 441-442
antismoking bills - 592-594
budget action - 128, 132
cancer screening - 606
Clean Air Act - 230, 231, 238-247, 278
disabled civil rights - 449
drug-abuse prevention, treatment - 504-505
family planning authorization - 605
fish inspection - 396
Health Service Corps - 595
immigration exclusions - 481 (box)
Labor/HHS appropriations - 851
Medicaid expansion - 570-571
medical device safety - 581
NIH authorization - 603, 604
nutrition labels - 576
organ donation programs - 597
orphan drugs - 577-579
TB prevention - 594
vaccine program authorization - 591
Waxman, Margery - 96
Ways and Means Committee, House
Clean Air Act fees - 244
SEC fees - 881
Weapons. *See also Arms control; Arms sales and transfers; Chemical weapons; Firearms; Missiles; Nuclear weapons*
budget action - 122
defense authorization - 672-687
defense budget reprogramming - 676 (box)
management efficiency - 673 (box)
procurement policy - 678-679, 682
Wear, Terrance J. - 532
Weather. *See also Global climate change*
auto emissions
CO in cold starts - 229, 246, 252
summer volatility - 252
disaster relief
budget action - 123
farm bill, funding - 324, 328, 867
forests - 346
emergency warnings, watches - 157
energy conservation - 319
food price increases - 554 (box)
public housing utility subsidies - 650
weather service user fees - 157, 386 (box)
Weber, Vin R-Minn. (2)
congressional leadership - 12
Webster, William H.
Pakistan-U.S. relations - 769
Persian Gulf crisis - 738, 742
Soviet-U.S. relations - 757
Wedtech Corp. - 107
Weicher, John C. - 631, 661
Weicker, Lowell P. Jr. - 48, 73, 907, 926-927
Weight-loss drugs - 146
Weiss, Daniel - 234, 246, 276, 279
Weiss, Ted D-N.Y. (17)
Agent Orange compensation - 419
congressional elections, 1990 - 905, 923
low winning percentage - 906 (chart)
Persian Gulf crisis - 733
Welch, Larry D. - 700-701
Welch, Peter - 930
Weld, William F. - 930
Weldon, Curt R-Pa. (7)
family leave - 360
Welfare and social services. *See also Aid to Families with Dependent Children; Charities and nonprofit organizations; Food assistance programs; Food stamps; Foster care; Homeless persons; Housing assistance and public housing; Low Income Home Energy Assistance Program; Medicaid; Women, Infants and Children (WIC) program*
AIDS bill - 582, 584
Bush economic report - 117
child-care aid - 152
children's services - 556
families of legalized aliens - 476, 477
human services authorization - 552-556
Indian eligibility - 423
Puerto Rico status - 426
school support services - 613
vocational education - 623
Welk, Lawrence - 811
Welland Canal - 338 (box)
Wellington Convention - 305
Wellstone, Paul - 32, 530, 754, 902, 911, 913 (chart), 925
Wentworth, Marchant - 278
Wertheimer, Fred - 66 (box), 909
West Bank and Gaza - 719, 837
West Germany. *See also Germany*
CFE - 697, 698, 703
European development bank - 206
Persian Gulf crisis - 730
West Virginia
acid rain - 236-238, 262
congressional redistricting - 931
corporate campaign limits - 59 (box)
federal judgeships - 522
Transportation appropriations - 878
water projects
appropriations - 865
authorization - 298, 299
Westchester County, N.Y. - 652
Western Area Power Administration - 318
Western Europe
CFE - 700
U.S. export controls - 198
Western states
grazing fees - 873-874, 875-876
irrigation subsidies - 300, 301, 356
minerals research - 442-443
national park visibility - 276
textile import quotas - 220
timber exports - 211, 214-215
wilderness protection - 304
Wetlands
methane assessment - 271
Wetlands protection
barrier islands - 302-303
budget action - 124
coastal zone management - 154, 289
community service programs - 562
farm bill - 323, 326, 330, 332, 334-336, 345-347, 349
FmHA inventory - 347
fuel taxes - 159
Interior appropriations - 872-873
water projects authorization - 297, 298
Wetlands Reserve Program - 346
Wheat, Alan D-Mo. (5)
congressional elections, 1990 - 907
Energy, water appropriations - 863
minorities in Congress - 924 (chart)
Wheat and feed grains
acreage reduction - 344, 350
commodity reserves - 344
deficit reduction - 344
disposable diapers - 336
ethanol - 240 (box)
exports - 330, 350, 351
foreign food aid - 330, 803, 804
GATT talks - 210
grain quality - 337
Iraq - 722
Soviet trade - 204, 762
price supports - 325-327, 333, 337, 340, 341, 342, 348, 350
Wheelchairs - 454, 455, 456, 459, 460
Whistleblowers and whistleblower protection
animal rights activists - 441
defense authorization - 683
disabled civil rights - 458
fish inspection - 397-399
HUD scandal investigation - 667
money laundering - 188
private sector - 364
secrecy agreements - 890
White, Barney - 286
White, Byron R.
abortion - 529
flag desecration - 525
habeas corpus appeals - 489 (box)
Medicaid pay suits - 571
OMB review powers - 412 (box)
political patronage - 933
right to die - 567 (box)
Souter confirmation - 508
student religious groups - 618 (box)
Supreme Court term summary - 52, 56
White House Conference on Libraries - 617, 849 (chart)
White House Domestic Policy Office - 609
White Mountain National Forest - 304
White, Ryan - 586
Whitehorn, Laura J. - 7
Whiteman Air Force Base - 688, 689, 829
Whitley, Libby - 533
Whitman, Christine Todd - 911, 913
Whitmire, Kathy - 415
Whittaker, Bob R-Kan. (5)
antismoking bills - 594
House membership changes - 918 (chart)
Medicare changes - 565
Whitten, Jamie L. D-Miss. (1)
agriculture appropriations - 867, 868, 870
budget action - 130 (box)
Energy, water appropriations - 863
NEA controversies - 431-432, 872
rural development - 353
supplemental appropriations - 846
Treasury, Postal appropriations - 888, 890
WIC funding - 554 (box)
WIC. *See Women, Infants and Children program*
Wilder, L. Douglas - 529
Wilderness areas
Arizona - 304
disabled civil rights - 459
Tongass forest protection - 6, 294-295
visibility impairment - 244
Wilderness Society - 871, 874, 876
Wildlife. *See also Fish and fishing*
Antarctica protection - 305
barrier islands protection - 302
community service programs - 561
Grand Canyon erosion - 300
Interior appropriations - 870-876
international environmental protection - 837
logging - 296
toxic air pollutants - 254
wetlands protection - 335
zebra mussel control - 303-304
Wildlife refuges
Alaska oil drilling - 313, 315 (box)
Florida Keys marine sanctuary - 303
Texas wetlands - 872
Wildmon, Donald E. - 431
Wilkes-Barre, Pa. - 213, 214
Williams, Clayton - 530, 928-929
Williams, David C. - 309-310
Williams, Harrison A. - 98, 99 (box), 100 (box)
Williams, Pat D-Mont. (1)
community service programs - 562
congressional mail - 74
congressional partisanship - 39
education proposals - 614, 615
Interior appropriations - 873
job training overhaul - 366, 367
library aid - 617
NEA authorization - 430, 432, 433
students' right to know - 624-626
Taft Institute authorization - 628
Williams, Pete - 676, 687, 693, 695 (box), 735 (box)
Wilson, Charles D-Texas (2)
congressional elections, 1990
low winning percentage - 906 (chart)
foreign aid appropriations - 831, 833, 835, 842
intelligence authorization - 792
Pakistan-U.S. aid - 769
Wilson, Lance - 667
Wilson, Pete R-Calif.
Clean Air Act - 234-235
congressional partisanship - 40
congressional redistricting - 933
crime bill - 493
defense authorization - 679
drug-abuse education - 505
education proposals - 613
farm bill - 338
flag desecration - 528
Grand Canyon erosion - 301
gubernatorial election, 1990 - 927-928
Hatch Act revision - 409
irrigation subsidies - 356-357
roll call attendance - 48
savings and loan scandal - 78, 80
Souter confirmation - 515
successor - 913 (chart), 925
textile import quotas - 220
Wind energy - 124, 317
Wind River Reservation - 267
Windom, Robert E. - 601
Wine. *See Alcoholic beverages*
Wingert, George - 918 (chart)
Wireless Cable Association - 371
Wirth, Tim D-Colo.
cable TV regulation - 370, 372
CFE - 701
children's TV advertising - 373-375
Clean Air Act - 233, 234-236

conservative coalition - 40
crime bill - 493
defense appropriations - 821
defense authorization - 679
Energy, water appropriations - 866
family planning authorization - 606
financial institution fraud - 182
global warming - 307
oil-shale lands - 316
Persian Gulf crisis - 738
Stello nomination - 310
Tongass forest protection - 295
Wisconsin
congressional elections, 1990 - 917
corporate campaign limits - 59 (box)
food aid cargo preference - 338-339 (box)
gubernatorial election, 1990 - 929
Medigap insurance - 148
Wisconsin - 678
Wise, Bob D-W.Va. (3)
Clean Air Act - 243, 277 (box)
Witness Protection Program - 494
Wittgraf, George W. - 532
Wolbeck, Jeanine E. - 532
Wolf, Diane - 196-197
Wolfowitz, Paul - 735 (box)
Wolpe, Howard D-Mich. (3)
Energy, water appropriations - 863
Panama, Africa aid - 776
Kenya aid - 790
South Africa sanctions - 788-789
SSC authorization - 439
Women. *See also Displaced homemakers; Pregnancy; Women, Infants and Children (WIC) program*
Afghan aid - 840
characteristics of Congress - 923-924
minorities in Congress - 924 (chart)
employment
child-care aid - 547
discrimination - 32, 462-473
family leave - 359
fetal protection - 56, 465
textile import quotas - 220
vocational education - 619-623
gubernatorial elections, 1990 - 929-930
health
AIDS bill - 583, 585
cancer screening - 145, 564 (box), 606, 680, 849
drug-abuse treatment - 679
NIH authorization - 600-604
SDI authorization debate - 692
judicial appointments - 515-516
NIH director - 602 (box)
opportunity enhancement
housing programs overhaul - 647
math, science scholarships - 612 (box)
radio spectrum allocation - 377
radio, TV licenses - 510-511 (box)
SSC authorization - 439
Senate sergeant-at-arms - 12 (box)
welfare and social services
family violence shelter - 858
sex crimes deterrence - 507
widows' Social Security benefits - 558
Women Employed Institute - 519 (box)
Women, Infants and Children (WIC) program
appropriations - 554 (box), 867, 869 (chart), 870
authorization - 354
budget action - 125
education proposals - 613, 615
Panama aid debate - 779
Women's Health Equity Act - 602-603
Women's Health Research and Development Office - 602
Women's interest groups
family leave - 359
Medicare coverage of mammograms - 564 (box)
sex discrimination - 56
Souter confirmation - 515
Women's Legal Defense Fund - 359
Wood. *See Forests and wood products*
Wool - 141, 337, 343, 344
Woolsey, R. James - 696, 700
Worker's compensation
radiation victims compensation - 590
World Bank
authorization - 206-207
budget action - 124
China loans - 207, 764, 834
Third World debt relief - 207, 218, 834
Panama - 775-776, 777, 778
U.S. contributions - 832 (chart), 845
World War II
Filipino veterans naturalization - 484
Soviet lend-lease repayment - 205
Worley, David - 104, 922
Worm Gett'r - 393
Worthington, Minn. - 878
Wrangel Island - 760
Wright, Jim
campaign finance reform - 58
Gingrich ethics case - 104
public opinion of Congress - 4
resignation, effects - 8, 10, 30, 39, 80
savings and loan scandal - 96, 181
Wright, Pat - 447, 448, 449
Wyden, Ron D-Ore. (3)
Clean Air Act - 246, 276
energy conservation - 319
flag desecration - 527
Medicaid drug discounts - 570 (box)
Medigap insurance - 572, 573, 575
SBA authorization - 372
Wylie, Chalmers P. R-Ohio (15)
coin redesign - 197
congressional elections, 1990 - 907
low winning percentage - 906 (chart)
vote-share falloff - 904 (chart)
FHA rules revision - 660
housing programs overhaul - 638, 639, 642, 656
money laundering - 188
prepayment of subsidized mortgages - 664-665
Wyngaarden, James - 602 (box), 603
Wyoming
acid rain - 267
community services block grant - 555
congressional mail - 75
corporate campaign limits - 59 (box)
Energy, water appropriations - 865
federal judgeships - 522
gubernatorial election, 1990 - 930
oil-shale lands - 316
radiation victims compensation - 590, 591
Wyoming, University of - 267, 274

X

X-ray lithography - 440

Y

Yates, Sidney R. D-Ill. (9)
characteristics of Congress - 925
NEA controversies - 431-432, 871-872, 876
Yatron, Gus D-Pa. (6)
Kenya aid - 790
Yemen
Persian Gulf crisis - 739, 740
YES. *See Youth Engaged in Service to America*
Yeutter, Clayton
farm bill - 325-326, 339-340, 348-350
GATT talks - 209
Interior appropriations - 871
RNC chair - 909-910
tobacco advertising - 593
Young, Don R-Alaska (AL)
congressional elections, 1990
marginal vote share - 905 (chart)
"dolphin safe" tuna labels - 399
fish inspection - 397
oil pollution cleanup - 284
Youth. *See Adolescents and youth*
Youth, Children and Families Committee, House Select - 924
Youth Conservation Corps - 562
Youth Engaged in Service to America (YES) - 559
Youth Opportunities Unlimited (YOU) - 123
Youth Service America - 560
Youth Service Corps - 560, 561, 562
Yucca Mountain, Nev. - 865
Yugoslavia
election aid - 777
U.S. aid/human rights - 843
Yzaguirre, Raul - 474

Z

Zaire
Persian Gulf crisis - 740
U.S. aid/human rights - 790, 836, 843
U.S. aid to Angola rebels - 796
Zambia
U.S. aid - 845
Zamora, Jaime Paz - 805
Zamora, Ricardo - 781
Zapata Corp. - 286
Zebra mussels - 298, 299, 303-304
Zeliff, Bill - 918 (chart)
Zigas, Barry - 633, 643, 663
Zigler, Edward F. - 553
Zimmer, Dick - 918 (chart), 923
Zoellick, Robert B. - 763
Zoning
housing programs overhaul - 635

Roll Call Vote Index

A

Abortion
Agency for International Development and, 59-S
District of Columbia, in, 90-H, 156-H, 164-H, 18-S
federal funding of, 160-H, 54-S, 62-S
Mexico City policy, 59-S
military hospitals, in, 112-H, 44-S
parental notification of, 51-S, 54-S
Romania, contributions to, and, 68-H
Title X family planning and, 50-S, 51-S
United Nations, contributions to, and, 54-S
Acid rain, 166-H, 12-S, 13-S
Acquired immune deficiency syndrome (AIDS), 58-H, 132-H, 22-S, 33-S, 54-S. *See also* Communicable diseases
Act for Better Child Care, 36-H, 64-H
ADA. *See* Americans with Disabilities Act
Admiralty Island (Alaska), 74-H
Adolescent Family Life program, 51-S
Adult Education Act, 86-H
Afghanistan, 54-H
Age Discrimination in Employment Act of 1967, 33-S
Agency for International Development (AID), 68-H, 59-S
Agricultural Research and Education Program, 37-S
Agriculture Department. *See also* Farm programs
appropriations, 82-H, 50-S
credit guarantees, 92-H
credit restrictions, 92-H
dairy "make allowances," 86-H
Food Safety and Inspection Service, 162-H
food stamps, 96-H
income supports, 86-H, 96-H
nutrition programs, 86-H, 96-H, 36-S, 62-S
price supports, 86-H, 92-H, 96-H
water subsidies, 60-H
AID. *See* Agency for International Development
Aid, foreign. *See also* individual countries by name
1990 supplemental appropriations, 44-H, 48-H, 17-S
appropriations, 68-H, 70-H, 168-H, 60-S
authorization for, 48-H
Aid, military
Afghanistan, 54-H
Angola, 152-H
appropriations, 60-S
Cuba, 54-H
El Salvador, 44-H, 46-H, 58-S
Aid, non-military
Eastern Caribbean, 26-H
refugee assistance, 26-H
AIDS. *See* Acquired immune defiency syndrome
AIDS Prevention Act, 58-H
Airports, 57-S
Akaka, Daniel K., 40-Hn, 22-Sn
Alaska National Interest Lands Conservation Act, 27-S
Alaska Native Claims Settlement Act of 1971, 74-H
Albanian Democratic Alliance Movement, 160-H
Alzheimer's disease, 22-S, 54-S
Amendments. *See* Constitution, amendments to
American Indians, 108-H, 118-H, 142-H, 17-S, 31-S
Americans with Disabilities Act (ADA), 42-H, 44-H, 78-H, 26-S, 33-S, 34-S
Ammonia emissions, 9-S
Amtrak, 36-H, 56-H, 27-S
Angola, 152-H
Antarctica, Treaty to Protect, 128-H
Anticrime legislation. *See* Crime legislation; Gun control; Hate crimes
Anti-Flag Desecration Act, 18-H
Antisatellite Program (ASAT), 45-S
Antitrust legislation, 28-H
Appalachian Regional Commission, 26-H
Appropriate Technology for Rural Areas program, 50-H
Appropriations. *See also* individual departments and agencies by name
1990 supplemental, 26-H, 34-H, 44-H, 45-H, 46-H, 48-H, 49-H, 50-H, 17-S, 18-S
1991 continuing, 128-H, 140-H, 154-H 164-H, 168-H
AIDS, 58-H
customs and trade agencies, 20-H
defense, 26-H
energy and water, 62-H, 64-H
Head Start, 40-H
House committees, 18-H
job-loss benefits, 46-H
library grants, 10-H
nuclear weapons, 62-H, 64-H, 112-H
rules for, 156-H, 158-H
savings and loan investigation, 64-H
super collider, 34-H
Arizona, 8-H, 10-H
Arkansas, 48-H
Armenian Genocide Day of Remembrance, 6-S, 7-S
Aroostook Bank of Micmacs Settlement Act, 142-H
ASAT. *See* Antisatellite program
Atomic Energy Act, 9-S
Automobiles
catalytic converters, 46-H
clean-fuel vehicles, 48-H
emissions, 166-H, 10-S
fuel economy, 48-S

B

B-2 "stealth" bomber, 43-S, 54-S
Baha'is, Iranian, 10-H
Baseball lockout, 8-S
Bilingual Education Act, 86-H
Biological weapons, 36-H
Blind persons, 26-S, 27-S
Budget
1991 Reconciliation, 150-H, 166-H, 57-S, 58-S, 63-S
1991 Resolution, 30-H, 32-H, 136-H, 140-H, 53-S, 55-S
balanced, 80-H, 82-H, 84-H. *See also* United States, deficit of
rules, 158-H
Bureau of Export Administration, 52-H
Bureau of Land Management, 60-S
Bureau of Reclamation, 58-H
Business
small, 42-H

C

CAFE. *See* Corporate average fuel economy
Calamus Dam and Reservoir, 27-S
California National Historic Trail, 12-H
Cambodia, 6-H, 70-H
Campaign finance, 102-H, 104-H, 122-H, 158-H, 41-S, 42-S, 43-S
Camp W. G. Williams, 74-H
Cancer, 22-S
Capital gains tax. *See* Taxes, capital gains
Caribbean Basin, 14-S, 16-S
Cars. *See* Automobiles
CFCs. *See* Chlorofluorocarbons
CFE. *See* Conventional forces in Europe
Check-cashing business, 30-H
Chemical and biological weapons, 23-S
Chicago, Judy, 90-H, 142-H
Child-care legislation, 22-H, 24-H, 36-H, 64-H
Child pornography. *See* Obscenity
Chilean fruit, 40-S
China, 2-H, 52-H, 154-H, 2-S, 3-S, 8-S, 54-S
Chlorofluorocarbons (CFCs), 46-H, 3-S, 9-S, 10-S
Civil Rights Act of 1964, 44-H, 98-H, 142-H, 152-H, 33-S, 35-S, 55-S, 60-S
Civil Rights Act of 1990, 98-H, 100-H, 142-H, 152-H, 31-S, 33-S, 35-S, 36-S, 55-S
Clean Air Act, 46-H, 166-H, 3-S, 9-S, 10-S, 11-S, 12-S, 63-S
Clean Air Employment Transition Assistance program, 46-H *See also* Clean Air Act
Coal, 13-S. *See also* Miners
Coastal beaches, 160-H
Coastal Zone Management, 116-H, 118-H, 124-H
Coast Guard, 16-H
Colorado River Storage Project, 148-H
Commerce Department
Advanced Technology Program, 76-H
appropriations, 26-H, 68-H, 76-H, 160-H, 53-S
Commission on Reducing Capital Costs for Emerging Technology, 76-H
technical programs reauthorization, 76-H
Commodity Control List, 54-H
Communicable diseases, 42-H, 78-H. *See also* Acquired immune deficiency syndrome
Community Development Block Grants, 50-H, 30-S
Community Services Block Grant Act, 40-H
Congress. *See also* Franking; Partisanship; Party unity
appropriations and, 158-H, 164-H, 166-H, 61-S
Congressional Record, 6-H
pay, 51-S
rules, 158-H
Congressional Budget Act of 1974, 18-S, 47-S
Constitution, amendments to
balanced budget, 80-H, 82-H
flag desecration, 66-H, 30-S
Fourth, 138-H
Consumer Product Safety Commission (CPSC), 164-H
Convention on the Rights of the Child, 47-S
Coordinating Committee for Multilateral Export Controls, 54-H
Corporate average fuel economy (CAFE), 48-S
Council of Europe, 48-S
Covert actions, 152-H
CPSC. *See* Consumer Product Safety Commission
Crime legislation, 120-H, 132-H, 24-S, 25-S, 26-S, 31-S, 32-S. *See also* Death penalty; Gun control
Crotone, Italy air base, 44-S
Cuba, 40-H, 54-H, 66-H
Czechoslovakia, 52-H

D

Dairy price supports, 86-H
Davis-Bacon Act, 29-S
Death penalty, 120-H, 132-H, 134-H, 138-H, 164-H, 24-S, 26-S, 31-S, 32-S, 33-S
Defense. *See also* Military; Strategic defense initiative
biological weapons, 36-H
defense stock drawdown, 59-S
defense systems, acquisition force for, 106-H
spending for, 30-H
Defense Department
Air Force Operation and Maintenance Fund, 18-S
appropriations, 26-H, 48-H, 92-H, 94-H, 106-H, 112-H, 114-H, 146-H, 162-H, 46-S, 55-S, 62-S
closed meetings, 138-H, 152-H
land acquisition, 45-S
land sales, 46-S
Defense Economic Adjustment program, 112-H
Defense Production Act of 1950, 116-H, 120-H
Deficit. *See* United States, deficit
Disabled, 42-H, 44-H, 78-H, 14-S, 34-S
District of Columbia, 22-H, 90-H, 118-H, 156-H, 164-H, 8-S, 18-S, 47-S. *See also* University of the District of Columbia
Drug Abuse Resistance Education Act, 74-H
Drug-Free Schools and Community Act, 74-H
Drug war
appropriations, 132-H, 46-S
death penalty and, 132-H, 134-H
driving under the influence (DUI), 28-S
forfeited assets and, 134-H
guns and, 134-H. *See also* Gun control legislation, 168-H
methamphetamine, 31-S
sterile needles, 22-S
student loans and, 86-H
testing for, 22-H, 138-H, 32-S
trauma centers and, 138-H
treatment facilities, 45-S
Durenberger, Dave, 38-S

E

Earthquake Hazards Reduction Act, 116-H, 120-H
Eastern Airlines, 12-H
Economic Development Administration, 26-H
Education. *See also* Eisenhower Mathematics and Science Education Act
District of Columbia, 18-S
dropout prevention, 6-S
drugs and, 74-H
foreign workers and, 130-H
initiatives for, 78-H, 86-H
law enforcement scholarships, 32-S
literacy training, 4-S
math and science education, 80-H, 5-S
student aid/loans, 86-H
vocational education, 14-S
Education Department, appropriations, 74-H, 78-H, 80-H, 84-H, 86-H, 160-H, 54-S, 62-S
Egypt, debt relief for, 59-S
Eisenhower Mathematics and Science Education Act, 80-H
Electricity, Canadian, 13-S
El Salvador, 44-H, 130-H, 58-S
Emergency response information, 36-H
Employment. *See also* Disabled; Leave, family and medical
age discrimination, 132-H, 33-S, 49-S, 50-S
benefits, 49-S, 50-S
job discrimination, 44-H, 78-H, 98-H, 142-H, 152-H, 35-S, 36-S, 55-S, 60-S
job-loss benefits, 46-H, 12-S, 50-S
quotas, 100-H, 142-H
Endangered Species Act, 60-S
Energy conservation, 146-H
Energy Department appropriations, 120-H
Environmental Protection Agency (EPA), 22-H, 72-H, 156-H, 160-H, 9-S, 11-S, 12-S, 13-S, 52-S
Environmental Protection, Department of, 22-H
EPA. *See* Environmental Protection Agency
Ethics issues
Durenberger, Dave, 38-S
Frank, Barney, 90-H
Savage, Gus, 6-H
Exclusionary rule, 138-H, 164-H, 26-S
Export Administration Act, 52-H, 54-H
Exports, 52-H, 54-H, 37-S, 60-S

F

FAA. *See* Federal Aviation Administration
Fall River Rural Electric Cooperative, 156-H, 43-S
Family leave. *See* Leave, family and medical
Family trusts, 60-H
Farabundo Marti National Liberation Front (FMLN), 58-S
Farm programs. *See also* Agriculture Department
acreage reduction requirements, 37-S, 38-S
cargo preference, 39-S, 41-S
crop insurance, 39-S
deficiency payments, 88-H
dairy surpluses, 88-H
grading programs, 40-S
high-income farmers, 88-H
income supports, 86-H, 160-H, 41-S, 62-S
Iraqi oil and, 40-S
loan rates (grains), 88-H
nutrition programs, 86-H, 96-H, 36-S
organic foods, 96-H
payment limits, 96-H
pesticides, 144-H
price supports, 86-H, 160-H, 37-S, 38-S, 41-S, 62-S
water subsidies, 60-H
FDA. *See* Food and Drug Administration
FDIC. *See* Federal Deposit Insurance Corporation
Federal Aviation Act of 1958, 27-S
Federal Aviation Administration (FAA), 98-H
Federal Civil Penalties Adjustment Act, 118-H
Federal contracts. *See* Davis-Bacon Act
Federal Deposit Insurance Corporation (FDIC), 56-S
Federal Election Campaign Act, 42-S
Federal Energy Regulatory Commission (FERC), 20-H
Federal Housing Administration (FHA) mortgage insurance, 94-H
Federal Implementation Plans, 10-S
Federal Judgeship Act, 126-H
Federal-State Cash Management Improvement Act, 118-H
Federal workers, 58-H
FERC. *See* Federal Energy Regulatory Commission
FHA. *See* Federal Housing Administration
Finland, 48-S
Fire Administration, 36-H
Fish and Wildlife Conservation Act, 118-H
Fisheries, 6-H, 48-H, 128-H, 162-H, 47-S, 53-S
Flag desecration, 18-H, 66-H, 30-S
Flag Protection Act, 66-H
FMLN. *See* Farabundo Marti National Liberation Front
Follow Through Act, 40-H
Food and Drug Administration (FDA), 162-H
Food handlers, 33-S
Food Program for Women, Infants and Children, 82-H
Foreign aid. *See* Aid, foreign
Foreign relations, appropriations, 20-H. *See also* Aid, foreign
Foreign Trade Zones, 60-S
Forest Service, 60-S
Frank, Barney, 6-H, 90-H
Franking, 50-H, 110-H, 122-H, 41-S, 61-S
Fuels, 9-S, 12-S, 50-S. *See also* Gasoline taxes

G

Garbage
backhauling, 20-H
dumping, 49-S
Gasoline taxes, 9B, 150-H, 55-S, 57-S
GATT. *See* General Agreement on Tariffs and Trade
General Agreement on Tariffs and Trade, 35-S
Germany
tax convention and, 48-S
unification of, 53-S
Gobie, Stephen L., 90-H
Grains, 37-S, 38-S. *See also* Farm programs
Gramm-Rudman law, 94-H, 140-H, 7-S, 17-S, 18-S, 28-S, 51-S, 57-S, 58-S
Great Lakes Water Quality Improvement Act, 118-H
Gun control, 120-H, 134-H, 24-S, 26-S, 31-S. *See also* Semiautomatic weapons

H

Habeas corpus proceedings, 134-H, 164-H, 24-S, 25-S
Handicapped. *See* Americans with Disabilities Act; Disabled
Hatch Act, 58-H, 64-H, 19-S, 20-S, 21-S, 29-S. *See also* Federal workers
Hate crimes, 26-H
Head Start, 24-H, 40-H
Head Start Act, 40-H
Health and Human Services (HHS), Department of
appropriations, 84-H, 160-H, 54-S, 62-S
Healthy Start program, 5-S
Highway Trust Fund, 55-S, 57-S
Home health care, 164-H
HOME Investment Partnerships, 63-S
Homelessness, 28-S
Homosexuality, 142-H, 156-H, 5-S, 8-S, 47-S
Honey, 37-S, 40-S
Honoraria, 38-S, 42-S
House of Representatives, 6-H, 18-H. *See also* Congress
Housing and Urban Development (HUD), Department of
appropriations, 70-H, 72-H, 96-H, 156-H, 158-H, 52-S
Housing Opportunity Partnership, 29-S
Housing Opportunity Zones, 30-S
Housing programs, 92-H, 94-H, 28-S, 29-S, 30-S, 31-S
HUD. *See* Housing and Urban Development
Human rights
China, 154-H. *See also* China
Cuba, 40-H
credit guarantees and, 92-H
El Salvador, 44-H, 45-H, 46-H, 58-S
Liberia, 30-H
Universal Declaration of, 54-S
Yugoslavia, 160-H
Hungary, 52-H
Hussein, Saddam, 47-S. *See also* Iraq

I

Idaho, 156-H, 18-S, 43-S
Illinois, 32-H
Immigration, 128-H, 130-H, 166-H, 63-S. *See also* China
India, 48-S
Indian Environmental Regulatory Enhancement Act, 118-H
Indians. *See* American Indians
Indonesia, 48-S
Infant mortality, 54-S
INF treaty. *See* Intermediate Nuclear Forces (INF) treaty of 1985
Intelligence agencies
authorizations, 148-H
covert actions, 152-H
Interior Department
appropriations, 146-H, 148-H, 156-H, 168-H, 59-S, 60-S
grazing fees, 146-H
Intermediate Nuclear Forces (INF) treaty of 1985, 23-S
Internal Revenue Service
appropriations, 80-H
collection personnel, 47-S
International Labor Organization, 6-S
International Planned Parenthood Federation, 68-H
International Whaling Commission, 128-H
Iowa, 32-H, 48-H, 60-S
Iran, 10-H
Iraq, 98-H, 128-H, 160-H, 40-S, 44-S, 47-S, 52-S. *See also* Operation Desert Shield; Persian Gulf
Irrigation, federal subsidies for, 60-H
Israel, 30-H, 58-S, 59-S

J

Jemez River (N.M.), 28-H
Jerusalem, 30-H
Job discrimination. *See* Employment, discrimination
Job-loss benefits. *See* Employment, job-loss benefits
Job Training Partnership Act, 126-H, 62-S
Justice Department
appropriations, 64-H, 68-H, 160-H, 53-S
hate-crime statistics, 5-S
Juvenile programs, 8-S, 47-S

K

Khmer Rouge, 70-H
Korean War Commemorative Coin, 142-H
Kuwait, 130-H, 160-H, 44-S, 52-S. *See also* Iraq; Operation Desert Shield; Persian Gulf

L

Labor Department
appropriations, 84-H, 160-H, 54-S, 62-S
LD-50 test, 37-S
Leave, family and medical, 36-H, 38-H
Lebanon, 130-H
Liberia, 30-H, 130-H
Library of Congress, 61-S
Library Services and Construction Act, 10-H
Line-item veto, 26-S. *See also* Vetoes
Lithuania, 26-H, 52-H, 11-S, 18-S
Logging. *See* Timber
Louisiana Army Ammunition Plant, 48-H
Lukens, Donald E. "Buz," 162-Hn

M

Magnuson Fishery Conservation and Management Act, 6-H, 53-S
Matsunaga, Spark M., 15-Sn
McHugh, Matthew F., 6-H
Medals, striking of, 16-H
Medical leave. *See* Leave, family and medical
Medicare, 30-H, 140-H, 150-H, 53-S, 57-S. *See also* Budget
Mental retardation, 25-S
Metal casting competitiveness, 12-H, 116-H, 120-H
MetalCasting Research Institute, 146-H
Metrorails. *See* Subways

Michigan Wild and Scenic Rivers, 122-H
Military. *See also* Defense
base closings, 106-H, 45-S
battleships, 44-S
B-2 stealth bomber. *See* B-2 stealth bomber
dual basing, 106-H
F-16 fighter plane, 110-H
F/A-18 aircraft, 114-H
missiles, 112-H, 46-S
multilaunch rocket system, 110-H
pay raise for, 44-S
troops in Europe, 44-S, 54-S
troops in Japan, 106-H
troops in Korea, 106-H
unexploded munitions, Utah, 74-H
Miners, 12-S
Mining Law of 1872, 59-S
Mink, Pasty T., 126-Hn
Missiles. *See* Military, missiles
Molinari, Susan, 20-H
Money laundering, 30-H
Mortgages, 94-H, 96-H
Motor Vehicle Fuel Efficiency Act, 48-S
Munitions, 54-H

N

NASA. *See* National Aeronautics and Space Administration
National Aeronautics and Space Administration, 72-H, 156-H, 52-S
National and Community Service Act, 162-H, 7-S, 8-S, 55-S
National Board for Professional Teaching Standards, 4-S
National Council on Educational Goals, 62-S
National Endowment for the Arts (NEA), 144-H, 146-H, 148-H, 60-S
National Endowment for the Humanities, 144-H
National Fish and Wildlife Foundation, 118-H
National Institute of Standards and Technology, 76-H
National Motor-Voter Registration Act, 51-S
National Organic Standards Board, 96-H
National Park System, 44-H
National Railroad Passenger Corporation. *See* Amtrak
National Science and Technology Policy, Organization and Priorities Act of 1976, 4-S
National Science Foundation, 72-H, 156-H, 52-S
National Service Act, 108-H, 138-H
National Trails System Act, 12-H, 16-H
National Union for the Total Independence of Angola (UNITA), 152-H
National Wild and Scenic Rivers System, 28-H, 68-H, 122-H. *See also* Wild and Scenic Rivers Act
Native Americans. *See* American Indians
NATO. *See* troops in Europe
NEA. *See* National Endowment for the Arts
Nebraska, 68-H, 168-H, 27-S
Needles, sterile programs, 22-S
New Mexico, 28-H, 44-H
Nicaragua, 26-H, 44-H, 46-H, 48-H, 17-S
Niobrara River (Neb.), 68-H, 168-H
Nominations
Ryan, T. Timothy, Jr. to director of the Office of Thrift Supervision, 14-S
Souter, David H. to associate justice of the Supreme Court, 52-S
North American Van Lines, 112-H
North Atlantic Treaty Organization (NATO). *See* Military, troops in Europe
NRC. *See* Nuclear Regulatory Commission
Nuclear Regulatory Commission (NRC), 9-S
Nuclear test ban treaty, 50-S
Nuclear weapons, 62-H, 64-H, 112-H, 156-H

O

Obscenity, 90-H, 144-H, 148-H, 60-S
Occupational Safety and Health Administration, 56-S
OECD. *See* Organization for Economic Cooperation and Development
Oil. *See also* Gasoline; Natural gas
emissions, offshore, 48-H
Iraqi, 40-S
spills, liability for, 6-H, 104-H, 43-S
Strategic Petroleum Reserve, 16-H, 108-H, 51-S
windfall profits tax, 57-S
Oil tankers, 6-H
Older Workers Benefit Protection Act, 132-H
Operation Desert Shield, 110-H, 114-H. *See also* Persian Gulf
Operation Just Cause, 6-H
Organization for Economic Cooperation and Development (OECD), 48-S
OSHA. *See* Occupational Safety and Health Administration
Ozone layer, 46-H

P

PACs. *See* Political action committees
Panama, 6-H, 26-H, 44-H, 46-H, 48-H, 112-H, 17-S, 18-S
Peace Corps Memorial, 128-H
"Peace dividend," 7-S
Peanuts, 38-S
Pecos River (N.M.), 28-H
Pennsylvania, 63-S
Pensions, presidential, 80-H
Persian Gulf, 128-H. *See also* Operation Desert Shield
Petroglyph National Monument (N.M.), 44-H
Physician Payment Review Commission, 84-H
Plutonium Recovery Modification Project (Rocky Flats Plant, Colo.), 62-H
Points of Light Foundation, 162-H, 8-S, 55-S
Poland, 52-H
Political action committees (PACs), 104-H, 158-H, 19-S, 41-S, 43-S
Pony Express National Historic Trail (Calif.), 12-H
Postal Service
appropriations, 80-H, 160-H, 47-S
free mailing for troops in Persian Gulf, 110-H
Hatch Act and, 19-S
President, Executive Office of, 47-S
Presidential debates, 43-S
Price fixing, 28-H
Price supports. *See* Farm programs, price supports
Prison industries, 136-H
Public Health Service Act of 1970, 4-S, 50-S, 51-S

Q

Quad Cities Interstate Compact, 32-H
Quotas. *See also* Civil Rights Act of 1990
hiring, 100-H, 142-H, 36-S
textiles. *See* Textile quotas

R

Racial issues. *See also* Civil Rights Act of 1964, Civil Rights Act of 1990, Quotas
death penalty and, 134-H, 138-H, 25-S
defendants, rights of, 31-S
Radionuclides, 13-S
Railroads, 36-H, 44-H, 56-H. *See also* Subways
Ranitidine hydrochloride, 16-S
Reclamation projects, 58-H, 148-H
Reclamation Projects Authorization and Adjustment Act, 148-H, 27-S
Reclamation Reform Act (1982), 60-H
Red Rock Canyon Conservation Area, 122-H
Rehabilitation Act of 1973, 33-S
Romania, 68-H
Rulemaking, federal agency, 32-H
Rural Areas, Appropriate Technology for, 50-H
Rural Development Administration, 18-H
Rural Economic Development Act, 14-H, 18-H
Ryan, T. Timothy, Jr., 14-S

S

Salem Maritime Visitor Center, 74-H
Samoa, 48-H
San Juan Island, Wash., 16-H
Savage, Gus, 6-H
Savings and loan investigations, 64-H, 94-H, 168-H, 18-S, 33-S
Schroeder, Patricia, 6-H
SDI. *See* Strategic defense initiative
Search and seizure, 138-H
Semiautomatic weapons, 24-S, 31-S, 33-S. *See also* Gun control
Senate, 33-S, 42-S, 61-S. *See also* Congress
Serrano, Jose E., 20-Hn
Shasta Dam (Calif.), 62-H
Small Business Act, 168-H
Small Business Administration, 116-H, 122-H
Small business assistance, 10-S
Small Business Investment Act of 1958, 168-H
Smoking, 144-H
Social Security, 64-H, 94-H, 7-S, 28-S, 53-S, 56-S
Solar energy, 12-S
Souter, David H., 52-S
South Africa, 11-S
Soviet Union, 52-H, 54-H, 18-S, 23-S, 40-S
Soybean Promotion Act, 20-H
Spain, 48-S
Spotted owl, 60-S
State Department
appropriations, 20-H, 68-H, 160-H, 3-S, 17-S, 53-S
State Legalization Impact Assistance Grant program, 130-H
Staten Island home port, 106-H
Stealth bomber. *See* B-2 "stealth" bomber
Strategic defense initiative (SDI), 110-H, 46-S. *See also* Defense
Strategic Petroleum Reserve. *See* Oil, Strategic Petroleum Reserve
Subways, 22-H
Sugar, 86-H, 37-S
Super Collider, superconducting, 34-H

T

Tankers, oil, 6-H
Tariffs, 14-S, 15-S, 16-S. *See also* Textile quotas
Tax credits, 22-H, 24-H
1991 Budget resolution. *See* Budget, 1991 resolution
charitable deductions, 57-S
capital gains, 30-H, 140-H, 53-S
gas, 150-H, 55-S, 57-S
indexing, 57-S
treaties and, 48-S
Tax Reform Act of 1986, 48-S
Teaching, certification for, 4-S
Telecommunications technology, 54-H
Television
campaigns, during, 42-S
technology, 76-H
Texas, 34-H
Textile quotas, 110-H, 142-H, 34-S, 35-S
Textile Trade Act. *See* Textile quotas.
Timber, 16-S, 27-S, 60-S
Title VII. *See* Civil Rights Act of 1964
Title X. *See* Public Health Service Act of 1970
Tongass Forest (Alaska), 27-S
Toxic substances
airborne. *See* Clean Air Act
feed, in, 37-S
Trade. *See also* Caribbean Basin, Export Administration Act, Textile quotas
Soviet Union, with the, 18-S
tariffs, 15-S, 16-S
Transportation Department, appropriations, 78-H, 156-H, 63-S
Treasury Department
appropriations, 80-H, 160-H, 47-S
Federal-State Cash Management Improvement Act, 118-H
Treaties, 6-S, 48-S, 50-S, 53-S
Tree planting, 122-H
Tunisia, 48-S
TV Marti, 66-H

U

UDC. *See* University of the District of Columbia
Unemployment. *See* Employment, job-loss benefits
Unions, 19-S, 41-S
UNITA. *See* National Union for the Total Independence of Angola
United Nations
Fund for Population Activities, 68-H
Population Fund, 54-S
Resolutions, 52-S, 58-S
United States
budget of, *See also* Budget

debt limit, increase in, 94-H, 102-H, 56-S
debt of, refinancing, 30-H
deficit of, 30-H, 136-H, 140-H, 28-S, 42-S, 53-S
spending, 20-H
United States Capitol Preservation Commission, 50-H
United States Information Agency (USIA), 20-H, 66-H, 17-S
United States Institute of Peace, 84-H
University Medical Center (Tucson, Ariz.), 16-S
University of the District of Columbia (UDC), 90-H, 142-H
User fees, 30-H, 136-H, 146-H.
USIA. *See* United States Information Agency
Utah Reclamation Mitigation and Conservation Account, 148-H

V

Vance (Robert S.) Federal Building, 30-H
Vertical markets, 28-H
Veterans Affairs (VA), Department of
appropriations, 70-H, 72-H, 156-H, 158-H, 52-S
Vetoes
line-item, 26-S
override attempts, 2-H, 12-H, 56-H, 64-H, 88-H, 140-H, 142-H, 2-S, 27-S, 29-S, 60-S
Voter registration, 4-H, 6-H

W

Walker, Washington Center for Internships and Academic Seminars, 64-H
Washington, D.C. *See* District of Columbia; University of the District of Columbia
Washington National Airport, 57-S
Water Resources Development Act, 116-H, 124-H
Whaling, 128-H
Whistleblowers, 112-H
White House Office of Science and Technology, 76-H
Wild and Scenic Rivers Act, 68-H, 168-H. *See also* National Wild and Scenic Rivers System
Wilderness areas, 8-H, 10-H, 10-S
Woodrow Wilson International Center for Scholars, 16-H
Woodrow Wilson Memorial Act, 16-H

Y

Yosemite National Park, 16-H
Youth Service Corps, 162-H, 8-S, 55-S
Yugoslavia, 160-H

Bill Number Index

House, Senate Roll Call Votes

House Bills

HR 3, 22-H, 24-H, 36-H, 64-H
HR 7, 14-S
HR 20, 21-S, 29-S, 58-H, 64-H
HR 486, 116-H, 120-H
HR 644, 28-H
HR 743, 32-H
HR 770, 36-H, 38-H, 88-H
HR 908, 20-H
HR 987, 27-S
HR 988, 74-H
HR 1048, 26-H, 5-S
HR 1109, 12-H
HR 1180, 92-H, 94-H, 96-H
HR 1231, 12-H
HR 1236, 28-H
HR 1243, 12-H, 116-H, 120-H
HR 1463, 22-H
HR 1465, 6-H, 104-H, 43-S
HR 1594, 15-S, 16-S
HR 2015, 26-H
HR 2039, 126-H
HR 2061, 6-H, 53-S
HR 2190, 4-H, 6-H
HR 2209, 20-H
HR 2273, 42-H, 44-H
HR 2281, 6-S
HR 2364, 36-H, 56-H, 27-S
HR 2566, 16-H
HR 2567, 58-H, 60-H, 148-H
HR 2570, 8-H, 10-H
HR 2692, 16-H
HR 2712, 2-H, 2-S
HR 2742, 10-H
HR 3030, 46-H, 48-H
Hr 3033, 23-S
HR 3182, 16-H
HR 3386, 20-H
HR 3533, 116-H, 120-H
HR 3581, 14-H, 18-H
HR 3792, 3-S
HR 3834, 16-H
HR 3847, 22-H
HR 3848, 30-H
HR 3859, 64-H
HR 3950, 86-H, 88-H, 92-H, 96-H
HR 3954, 128-H
HR 3960, 148-H
HR 3961, 30-H
HR 4000, 98-H, 100-H
HR 4019, 122-H
HR 4151, 40-H
HR 4167, 16-H
HR 4279, 118-H
HR 4300, HR 4300, 128-H, 130-H
HR 4323, 118-H
HR 4328, 20-H, 110-H, 142-H, 34-S, 35-S
HR 4329, 76-H
HR 4330, 108-H
HR 4333, 160-H
HR 4380, 34-H
HR 4381, 24-H
HR 4404, 17-S
HR 4404, 26-H, 34-H, 48-H, 50-H, 18-S
HR 4450, 116-H, 118-H, 124-H
HR 4522, 36-H
HR 4559, 122-H
HR 4636, 44-H, 46-H
HR 4653, 52-H, 54-H
HR 4739, 106-H, 110-H, 112-H, 114-H, 138-H, 162-H, 62-S
HR 4785, 58-H
HR 4793, 116-H, 122-H, 168-H
HR 4825, 144-H, 146-H
HR 4834, 74-H
HR 4939, 154-H
HR 4982, 80-H
HR 5019, 43-S
HR 5019, 62-H, 64-H, 156-H
HR 5021, 64-H, 66-H, 68-H, 160-H, 53-S, 60-S
HR 5064, 74-H
HR 5112, 164-H
HR 5114, 68-H, 70-H, 168-H, 78-H, 86-H, 54-S, 58-S, 59-S, 60-S
HR 5115, 78-H, 86-H
HR 5158, 70-H, 72-H, 156-H, 158-H, 52-S
HR 5170, 98-H
HR 5229, 78-H, 156-H, 63-S
HR 5241, 80-H, 160-H, 47-S
HR 5254, 118-H
HR 5255, 118-H
HR 5257, 84-H, 160-H, 54-S, 62-S
HR 5258, 82-H, 84-H, 50-S
HR 5269, 120-H, 132-H, 134-H, 136-H, 138-H, 164-H
HR 5311, 90-H, 142-H, 156-H, 164-H, 47-S, 49-S
HR 5313, 92-H, 94-H
HR 5314, 116-H, 124-H
HR 5316, 126-H
HR 5350, 102-H
HR 5355, 94-H
HR 5399, 158-H, 166-H, 61-S
HR 5400, 102-H, 104-H, 122-H, 158-H
HR 5401, 94-H
HR 5422, 148-H, 152-H
HR 5431, 98-H
HR 5482, 118-H
HR 5611, 110-H
HR 5769, 146-H, 148-H, 168-H, 59-S, 60-S
HR 5803, 146-H, 152-H, 62-S
HR 5835, 150-H, 166-H, 63-S
HR 5932,

H Con Res 87, 10-H
H Con Res 254, 6-H
H Con Res 262, 6-H
H Con Res 289, 26-H
H Con Res 290, 30-H
H Con Res 310, 30-H, 32-H, 136-H, 140-H, 158-H, 53-S
H Con Res 329, 128-H
H Con Res 382, 160-H
H Con Res 385, 160-H

H J Res 268, 80-H, 82-H
H J Res 350, 66-H
H J Res 418, 128-H
H J Res 467
H J Res 471, 20-H
H J Res 655, 128-H
H J Res 658, 128-H
H J Res 660, 140-H
H J Res 666, 140-H
H J Res 677, 154-H
H J Res 687, 168-H

H Res 309, 4-H
H Res 330, 6-H
H Res 338, 8-H
H Res 346, 18-H
H Res 354, 30-H
H Res 355, 14-H
H Res 362, 18-H
H Res 368, 22-H
H Res 373, 28-H
H Res 379, 34-H
H Res 381, 40-H
H Res 388, 36-H
H Res 392, 40-H
H Res 394, 42-H
H Res 395, 44-H
H Res 399, 46-H
H Res 408, 58-H
H Res 409, 58-H
H Res 413, 62-H
H Res 417, 66-H
H Res 425, 68-H
H Res 426, 70-H
H Res 427, 78-H
H Res 430, 78-H
H Res 434, 80-H
H Res 435, 92-H
H Res 439, 86-H
H Res 440, 90-H
H Res 441, 92-H
H Res 442, 90-H
H Res 443, 94-H
H Res 448, 102-H
H Res 449, 98-H
H Res 452, 104-H
H Res 453, 102-H
H Res 464, 110-H
H Res 466, 116-H
H Res 468, 116-H, 118-H
H Res 469, 116-H
H Res 470, 120-H
H Res 473, 120-H
H Res 477, 142-H
H Res 484, 128-H
H Res 487, 148-H
H Res 488, 136-H
H Res 496, 140-H
H Res 505, 146-H
H Res 509, 150-H
H Res 511, 162-H
H Res 512, 156-H
H Res 517, 158-H
H Res 521, 162-H
H Res 527, 164-H
H Res 531, 166-H
H Res 535, 166-H
H Res 537, 166-H
H Res 681, 164-H

Senate Bills

S 110, 50-S, 51-S
S 135, 19-S, 20-S, 21-S
S 137, 41-S, 42-S, 43-S
S 169, 4-S
S 195, 23-S
S 280, 68-H, 168-H
S 286, 44-H
S 341, 26-S, 27-S
S 358, 166-H, 63-S
S 419, 5-S
S 535, 118-H
S 566, 96-H, 28-S, 29-S, 30-S, 31-S, 63-S
S 605, 164-H
S 666, 74-H
S 695, 4-S, 5-S
S 933, 44-H, 78-H, 26-S, 33-S, 34-S
S 1091, 16-H
S 1224, 48-S, 50-S
S 1310, 4-S
S 1413, 142-H
S 1430, 138-H, 162-H, 7-S, 8-S, 55-S
S 1485, 32-H
S 1511, 132-H, 49-S, 50-S
S 1630, 166-H, 3-S, 9-S, 10-S, 11-S, 12-S, 13-S, 63-S
S 1875, 27-S
S 1970, 24-S, 25-S, 26-S, 31-S, 32-S, 33-S,
S 2075, 118-H
S 2104, 142-H, 152-H, 33-S, 35-S, 36-S, 55-S,
S 2231, 16-H
S 2240, 58-H, 22-S
S 2830, 144-H, 160-H, 36-S, 37-S, 38-S, 39-S, 40-S, 41-S, 62-S
S 2884, 43-S, 44-S, 45-S, 46-S
S 2924, 162-H, 47-S
S 3033, 110-H
S 3167, 53-S
S 3189, 54-S, 55-S
S 3209, 55-S, 56-S, 57-S, 58-S
S 3266, 168-H

S Con Res 108, 11-S
S Con Res 147, 52-S

S J Res 212, 6-S, 7-S
S J Res 332, 30-S

S Res 255, 8-S
S Res 311, 38-S

Treaty Doc 99-13, 48-S
Treaty Doc 101-2, 6-S
Treaty Doc 101-5, 48-S
Treaty Doc 101-6, 48-S
Treaty Doc 101-9, 48-S
Treaty Doc 100-22, 48-S
Treaty Doc 101-10, 48-S
Treaty Doc 101-11, 48-S
Treaty Doc 101-16, 48-S
Treaty Doc 101-20, 53-S
Treaty Doc N(A), 94-2, 50-S
Treaty Doc N(B), 94-2, 50-S